Franz Joseph land
Novaya Zemlya
New Siberian Is
Alexandrovsk
Helsingfors (Helsinki)
St-Petersburg
Riga
Moscow
Novgorod
Warsaw
Kiev
Samara
Omsk
Semipalatinsk
Irkutsk
Jenissei
Yenissei
Ob
Lena
Amur
Amour
Wolga
Volga
Russian Empire
Romania
Bulgaria
Constantinople
Tiflis
Tashkent
Urumtsi
Chinese Empire
Vladivostok
Sakha
Port Arthur (Rus)
Korea
Empire of Japan
Peking
Tien-tsin
Seoul
Tokyo
Osaka
Kiao-chau (Ger)
Nanking
Shanghai
Yang tsé Kiang
Yangtze
Chung-king
Turkish Empire
Beirut
Baghdad
Teheran
Kabul
Persia
Afghanistan
Alexandria
Cairo
Egypt
Baluchistan
Delhi
Nepal
Bhutan
Er Riad
Muscat
Karachi
India (UK)
Calcutta
Canton
Macau (Port)
Hong Kong (UK)
Formosa (Jap.)
Ryukyu Islands
Pacific Ocean
Arabia
Oman
Diu (Port)
Bombay
Burma
Hanoi
Rangoon
Siam
Bangkok
Annam
Manila
Marianas Islands (Ger)
Philippines Is. (USA)
Guam (USA)
Nil
Nile
Khartoum
Eritrea
Aden (UK)
Socotra (UK)
Panjim (New Goa) (Port)
Madras
Laccadive Islands UK
Andaman Islands
Cambodia
Saigon
Addis Abeba
British Somaliland
Abyssinia
Ceylon
Colombo
Nicobar Island (UK)
Caroline Islands (Ger)
Somali (It)
Maldive Islands (UK)
Singapore
East Africa (UK)
Congo Free State
Mombasa
Sumatra
(British) Borneo (Dutch)
Celebes
Dutch East Indies
Bismarck Archipelago
German East Africa
Zanzibar (UK)
Seychelles Is. (UK)
Chagos Is. (UK)
Batavia
Java
(Dutch) New Guinea
Kaiser Wilhelm's Land (Germany)
(UK)
Amirante Islands (UK)
Comoro Island (Fr)
Timor (Port)
Solomon Island (UK)
Cocos Island
Indian Ocean
Darwin
Portuguese East Africa
Tamatave
Reunion Is (Fr)
Rodriguez (UK)
South Africa (UK)
Sofala
Madagascar
Mauritius (UK)
Pretoria
South African Republic
Free State
Australia (UK)
New Caledonia (Fr)
Cape Colony
Brisbane
Perth
Port Elizabeth
Norfolk Is (UK)
St-Paul (Fr.)
Adelaide
Sydney
Melbourne
Auckland
Prince Edward
Crozet (Fr)
New Zealand (UK)
Tasmania
Wellington
Kerguelen (Fr)
MacDonald Is.
Heard
Auckland Island (UK)
Antipodes (UK)
Macquarie (UK)
Antarctica
P9-BYT-184

Chronicle of the 20th Century, the history of our century, is truly an international publication already produced in 13 language editions and 15 countries enjoying multi-million copy sales.

No one edition is a reprint of another. In respect to editorial and photographic content, each has been individually designed for that nation's history and culture.

The American edition of **Chronicle of the 20th Century** was selected as the American and Canadian **Booksellers Association 1987** Book of the Year.

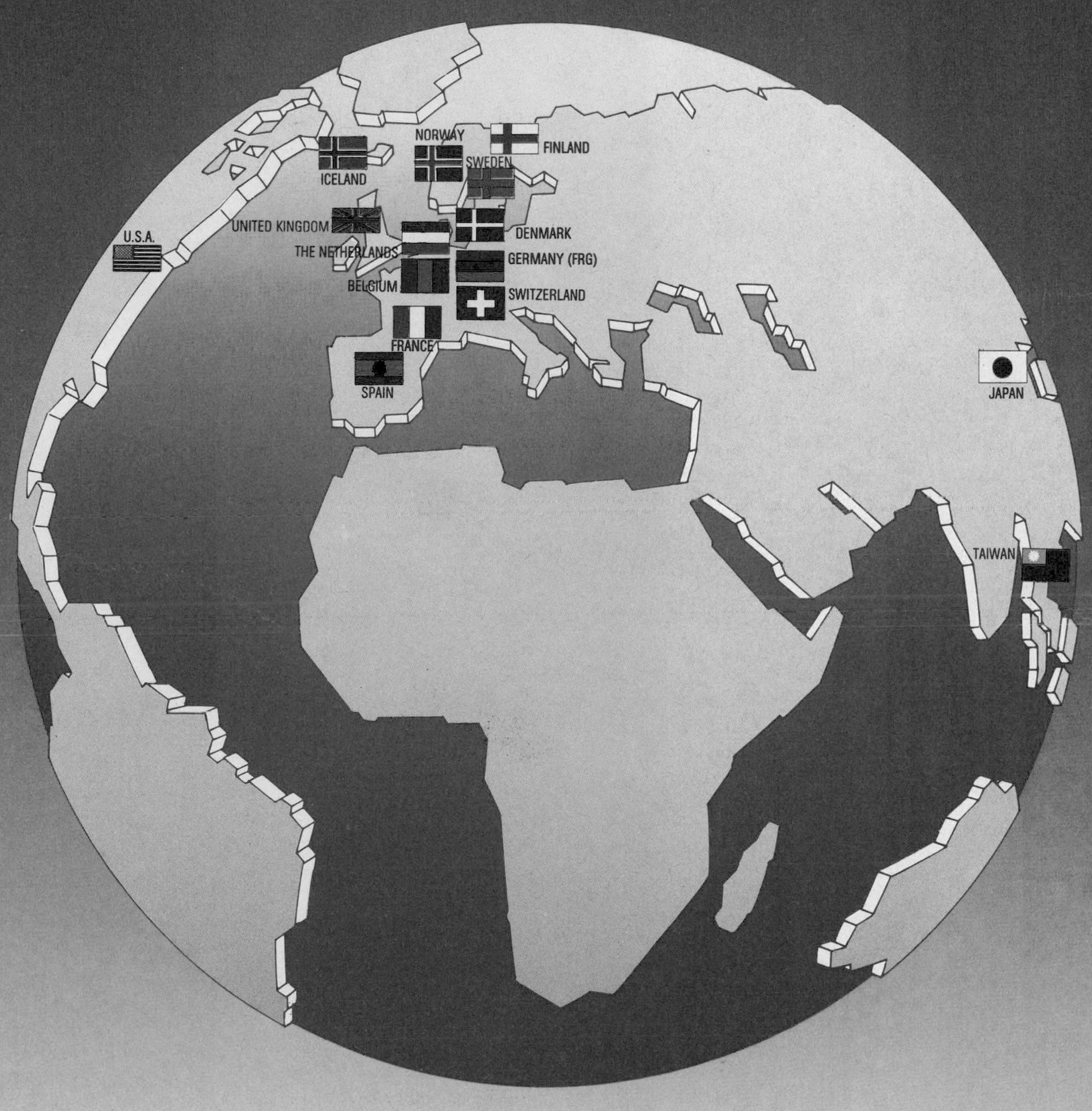

BELGIUM: Editions Chronique
DENMARK: Ladewmann Forlagsaktieslskab
FINLAND: Gummerus Kustannus OY
FRANCE: Librairie Larousse / Éditions Chronique
GERMANY (FRG): Harenberg Kommunikation
ICELAND: Svart a hvitu Bokaforlag
JAPAN: Kodansha Ltd.
THE NETHERLANDS: Elsevier Boeken B.V. / Agon
NORWAY: K.W. Cappelens Forlag A/S
SPAIN: Plaza & Janes
SWEDEN: Bonnier Fakta Bokforlag AB
SWITZERLAND: Ex. Libris
TAIWAN: Chin Show Cultural Enterprise
UNITED KINGDOM: Chronicle Communications/Longman
U.S.A.: Chronicle Publications, Inc.

Chronicle
of the 20th century

Chronicle
Publications
Mount Kisco, N.Y.

Chronicle Publications Inc. wishes to express its gratitude to the following institutions for their contributions to **Chronicle of the 20th Century:**

Advertising Council
After Six
Amana Inc.
American Advertising Museum
American Airlines
American Automobile Association
American Cancer Society
American Chemical Society
American Express
American Motors Corporation
American Petroleum Institute
American Telephone & Telegraph
Avon Products, Inc.
Aviation Hall of Fame
Ayer, N.W., Inc.
Batten, Barton, Durstine & Osborn,Inc.
Bethlehem Steel Corporation
Black & Decker Corporation
B'nai B'rith International
Boeing Company
Boy Scouts of America
Cadillac Motor Car Division
California Historical Society
Campbell Soup Company
Care
Caterpillar, Inc.
Chesebrough-Pond's, Inc.
Chrysler Corporation
Coca-Cola Company
Coleco Industries, Inc.
Colgate-Palmolive Company
Con Edison
Cunard Line Limited
Deere & Company
Delta Airlines
Dow Chemical Company
Dow Jones & Company, Inc.
Eastman Kodak Company
Firestone Tire and Rubber
Ford Foundation
Ford Motor Company
Geer-Dubois Inc.
General Mills, Inc.
General Motors Corporation
Gerber Products Company
Girl Scouts of the USA
Goodyear Tire & Rubber Company
Great Atlantic & Pacific Tea Company, Inc.
Greyhound Corporation
Hershey Foods Corporation
Hill & Knowlton, Inc.
Hughes Aircraft Company
International Business Machines Corporation
Indianapolis Motor Speedway Corporation
J. Walter Thompson Company
John F. Kennedy Center for the Performing Arts
Kaiser Aluminium & Chemical Corporation
Kellogg Company
Kimberly-Clark Corporation
Levi Strauss & Company
Lockheed Aircraft Corporation
Mack Trucks, Inc.
Martha Graham Dance Company
McCann-Erikson Worldwide
McDonnell Douglas Corporation
Metropolitan Museum of Art
Mercedes-Benz
Morton Thiokol, Inc.
Museum of City of New York
Museum of Modern Art
National Aeronautics & Space Adm.
Nabisco Brands, Inc.
National Education Association
New York Racing Association
New York Stock Exchange, Inc.
New York Times
Northwest Orient Airlines
Ogilvy & Mather
Pace University
Pan American World Airways, Inc.
Pepsico, Inc.
Philip Morris Companies Inc.
Pitney Bowes
Polaroid Corporation
Port Authority of NY & NJ
Procter & Gamble Company
Reader's Digest Association, Inc.
Rockwell International Corporation
Rolls Royce Motors
Ruder, Finn and Rotman
Safeway Stores, Inc.
Scott Paper Company
Sears, Roebuck
Singer Company
Smithsonian Institution
Sun Company, Inc.
Texaco, Inc.
Time-Life Inc.
Trans World Airlines, Inc.
United Parcel Service
West Point Military Academy
Whitney Museum
W.R. Grace & Company
Young & Rubicam
Zippo Corporation

ISBN 0-13-133703-3
Typesetting: Digital Prepress Center (DPC), Yonkers, N.Y.
Printing & Binding: Brepols, Turnhout (Belgium)
Reprint No. 2
Printed in Belgium

Distributed in the United States of America by:
Prentice Hall Trade.
A division of Simon & Schuster, Inc.
1 Gulf & Western Plaza
New York, NY 10023

Distributed in Canada by:
Raincoast Books Ltd.
112 East 3rd Avenue
Vancouver
British Columbia V5T 1C8

Original idea by Bodo Harenberg

Chronicle of the 20th century

Has been conceived and published by Jacques Legrand

Editor in Chief:	**Clifton Daniel**	
Executive Editor:	John W. Kirshon	
Correspondents:	Tom Anderson Edward Edelson John Finney	Marjorie Hunter Drew Middleton James Tuite
Staff Writers:	Susan Breen, Kevin Delaney, Phil Farber, James Forsht, John Goolrick, Catherine Hulbert, Tod Olson, Michael Quirk, Karen Rohan, Marianne Ruuth, Steven Taylor, Pascale Thumerelle	
Editorial Researchers:	Nicholas Lee Kristie Simco	
Editorial Associates:	Brigitte Bro, Marilyn Fishman, Laurine Garaude, Bob Gossiaux, Patricia Landry, Isabelle Mahe, Jiri Weiss	
Photo Researchers:	Merrie Terranova Peter Dervis (Bettmann Archive) Dominique Stephan (Sipa) Francoise Carminati (Sygma)	
Art:	Henry Marganne (Manager) Christian Baude Michael Colley	
EDP:	Catherine Balouet (Manager) Darin Hamilton (DPC) Carmen Siringo (DPC)	
Software Engineer:	Dominique Klutz	
Production:	Didier Camal (Manager) Deborah Bonardi Esther Gottfried	
Marketing:	Peter J. Clark (Director)	

1900-1909

Jules-Alexander Grun **"Salon Des Artistes Francais."** This painting, illustrating one of the pleasurable events of modern life, depicts a hundred turn-of-the-century Parisian celebrities basking in the luxury of an art exhibition. The pleasant ambiance reflects a carefree society, one devoid of burden and worry—an atmosphere marked by the splendor and innocence of the "fin de siecle" of the 19th century. Yet, paradoxically, grave problems lurk beneath the surface in that era, threatening the seemingly durable social structure.

1910-1919

Otto Dix. **"Flanders."** From deceptive comfort and ease comes anxiety and disaster. The world is tumbling down in the heavy crush of a war destined to devastate all of Europe, sowing ruin and desolation, plunging entire civilian populations into a miserable despair previously unknown in the annals of man. Injured in battle twice himself, Otto Dix represents here, in unbearably stark realism, the pain and suffering of soldiers huddled together in the mud of cold, burrowed trenches. The Great War will transform the shape of the world and the century.

1920-1929

Otto Dix. **Central part of the triptych of "The Nightbird."** Otto Dix knows better than perhaps any other artist how to express the fever that swept the world following the Great War—the thirst for ebullient life in the "Roaring Twenties." However, he does not neglect showing the darker aspects of that era in which everything seemed to be possible but never reached its lofty potential. Engineers, artists, writers, theater and movie directors displayed their creativity in this decade, and today their works still retain their relevance and strength.

1930-1939

Richard Oelze. **"Expectation."** This countryside, enigmatic but foreboding, was painted two years after the coming to power of the Nazis in Germany. Dream-like and haunting, it stages an expression of threat, of paralyzing horror. It can be interpreted as the veiled announcement of the gathering storm which again threatens the fragile peace of Europe. Germany has sold its soul to a maniacal dictator. Racism grows and, like the ominous skies in the painting, it extends itself as a destructive shadow, ushering in the most monstrous war.

1940-1949

Henry Moore. **Drawings from the series of the "Shelter Drawings."** This painting is part of the collection the artist created in 1940, when he was honored as "the artist of armies" by the British government. It shows two London residents, securely wrapped in blankets, fast asleep in one of the subway stations which acted as air raid shelters during the German bombardment. Thousands of Londoners were not so fortunate; they died in the merciless aerial blitz, which also damaged much of the city.

1950-1959

Fernand Leger. **"Country Party."** After years of suffering and deprivation, now comes freedom and prosperity. Fernand Leger knew how to reproduce splendidly the relaxation and pleasure enjoyed by the laboring classes, exemplified by a family excursion to the country in the luxury of the automobile—symbol of the emerging well-being of society at large. Grim wartime memories fade and the reconstruction of Europe is completed. People devoured the fruits of industry and commerce and relished their new leisure time.

1960-1969

"Moon Landing." The sixties mark the first peak on mankind's long journey into space. The race to the stars began with the launching of the Soviet Sputnik in October 1957. Quickly and with determination, the United States of America kept pace and eventually surpassed its rival in space technology and achievement. One of the oldest dreams of humanity came to fruition when Apollo XI touched down on the lunar surface in July 1969. Awestruck by the glory of extra-terrestrial soil, American astronaut Neil Armstrong became the first man on the moon.

1970-1986

Renato Guttuso. **"Newspaper Mural: May '68."** The Western world lives in affluence, but as depicted in this artwork, apprehension begins to arise. The younger generation rebels against a cold, materialistic world, caused by the fever of consumerism which has gripped their parents. The young dream of a society liberated from conformity. The rebellion is manifested in the work of Parisian art students; Renato Guttuso exhibits it in graphic detail. Nothing will ever be like it was before. A whole new world seems to beckon.

557
NAVY

Introduction

The 20th Century is glorious and damned—a century of triumph and tragedy, of grandeur and misery, of vision and disaster. This bountiful book, *Chronicle of the 20th Century*, presents our astonishing century in a vivid and original way, reproducing events as they happened, with the shock of immediacy and the unexpectedness of life itself. Combining the testimony of witnesses with the hindsight of scholars, *Chronicle* unrolls the images of our century before our eyes—not only politics and war, but also in social and intellectual currents, in science and technology, literature and arts, fashion and sports. Whether you turn to *Chronicle* for fun or for reference, for nostalgia or for enlightenment, you will rediscover your own lives.

As it draws to a close, we the living may be forgiven for wondering what this century of ours will turn out to mean in the long panorama of human history. The 20th has been a chaotic century, filled with anguish and blood and atrocity; filled too with heroism and hope and dream. How will historians of the future assess this bewildering and bewildered age?—assuming, that is, that the deadly weapons our century has devised will leave a posterity capable of remembering the past. What will the 20th Century's legacy be to the centuries still to come?

The illustration on the page opposite catches in a single brilliant frame the distinctive mark of the modern era—the acceleration in the pace of history: the sailing ship, for 20 centuries the great means of human communication, portrayed against the helicopters and mighty towers of the 20th Century megalopolis. This century has seen science and technology sweep humanity into the electronic epoch—the epoch unimagined even by Jules Verne and H.G. Wells, of the computer and the microchip. The onward rush is now carrying humanity even farther—beyond the planet Earth itself. If future historians recall anything about our century, it will surely be that this was the time when men and women burst their terrestrial bonds and began the adventure of space—the endless voyage into the illimitable dark. This will be remembered about the 20th Century when all else is forgotten.

All else except our most ambiguous technological triumph —the unlocking of the incredible force pent up within the atom. A generation ago, we hailed nuclear power as the solution to the world's energy dilemma. After Three Mile Island and Chernobyl, we look on nuclear power with increasing mistrust. Worse still: the development of nuclear weapons, with 50,000 warheads now scattered around the planet, offers humanity for the first time in history the means of its own extermination.

If the human race escapes suicide, historians of the future will record other legacies of the 20th Century. They will certainly note the end of the Eurocentric world. For five centuries, European ideas, values, technologies, weapons, dominated the far corners of the Earth. In the 20th Century, the Third World threw off the shackles of Western empire. East Asia even began to outcompete America and Europe in the West's own field of heavy industry and high technology. The age of the Atlantic wanes. The age of the Pacific is upon us. The European era is at end.

Technical leaps and geopolitical reversals have subjected inherited values and institutions to unprecedented strain. The 20th Century has been a time of fierce ideological conflict. The ideal of individual liberty became associated, especially during the years of the Great Depression, with economic insecurity and personal anxiety. One consequence was a revolt against free society. While fascism and communism differed in philosophy, the counterrevolutions had in common the goal of abolishing the torment of freedom by establishing totalitarian despotisms based on a single body of dogma as embodied in a single infallible party and expounded by a single infallible leader.

Ideological fanaticism has streaked the century with wars, both hot and cold. Nor can anyone dismiss the differences between democracy and despotism as insignificant. Still the angry ideological conflicts that obsess us today may not greatly interest our descendants. From the perspective of centuries to come, our Cold War may seem as obscure and incomprehensible as we ourselves find the Thirty Years War that devastated Europe a short three centuries ago. Looking back at the 20th Century, the future may be astonished at the disproportion between the causes of our global civil war, which may well seem trivial, and the consequences, which could include the destruction of the planet.

Yet, the 20th Century has still found time to affirm life and to pursue happiness. It has been a century of brilliant flowering in the arts—the century in painting of Picasso and Matisse; in sculpture of Henry Moore and Giacometti; in the novel, of Proust and James and Joyce, of Faulkner and Pasternak and Mann; in drama, of Pirandello and Shaw and O'Neill and Pinter; in poetry, of Yeats and Kipling, Frost and Eliot; in music, of Stravinsky and Sibelius and Richard Strauss; in the popular song, of Gershwin and Berlin, Rodgers and Ellington and the Beatles; in films, of Griffith and De Mille, of Ford and Welles and Fellini; in the human comedy, of Chaplin and W.C. Fields, of the Marx Brothers and Woody Allen. If it has been a century of sorrow, it has also been a century of joy.

And this very life-affirming passion may give us the will to master the dangers our century's scientific and technological virtuosity has bequeathed to humanity. Do we have the intelligence and the resolution to find means of saving the human race from extermination? The answer to this question, in the 4,000 or so days of the century that remain to us, will yield the ultimate meaning of the 20th Century.

Arthur M. Schlesinger jr.

Arthur M. Schlesinger, Jr.

1900 – 1909

1900

JANUARY

Su	Mo	Tu	We	Th	Fr	Sa
	1	2	3	4	5	6
7	8	9	10	11	12	13
14	15	16	17	18	19	20
21	22	23	24	25	26	27
28	29	30	31			

1. Washington: Hawaii asks for delegate at Republican national convention (→ 4/30).

1. Nigeria becomes British protectorate with Frederick Lugard as high commissioner.

2. Chicago Canal opens.

3. New York: Giuseppe Verdi's "Aida" performed.

5. Ireland: Nationalist leader John Edward Redmond calls for revolt against British rule (→ 9/2).

6. India: Millions reported to be dying of starvation (→ 5/7).

8. President McKinley places Alaska under military rule.→

8. South Africa: Boers attack Ladysmith; turned back by General White (→ 21).

13. Austria-Hungary: To combat Czech nationalism, Emperor Franz Joseph decrees German will be language of imperial army (→ 9/13).

14. Giacomo Puccini's "Tosca" opens in Rome (→ 2/4/01).

16. Washington: U.S. Senate consents to Anglo-German treaty of Nov. 1899, by which U.K. renounced rights to Samoan islands (→ 2/13).

17. U.S. takes Wake Island, important cable link between Hawaii and Manila.

17. Yaqui Indians in Texas proclaim independence from Mexico (→ 2/2/01).

17. Washington: Mormon Brigham Roberts denied seat in House for practicing polygamy.

21. Halifax: Canadian troops set sail to fight in S. Africa (→ 30).

22. South Africa: British release German steamer Herzog, seized Jan. 6.

27. China: Foreign diplomats in Peking fear revolt; demand imperial government discipline Boxer rebels (→ 5/17).

30. British demand larger army in South Africa (→ 2/1).

DEATH

20. John Ruskin, noted British cultural critic (*2/18/1819).

20th Century begins optimistically

St. James's Street, London. The city is the world's financial capital.

Jan 1. New York entered the 20th Century with a sense of euphoria and self-satisfaction. Wall Street was said to be undergoing a "prosperity panic." And banker James T. Woodward declared that America was "the envy of the world."

London reported that 1899 was a year of progress everywhere. Even the Boer War had a silver lining: the longer it lasted the more trade it would promote for America.

In Europe, only Emperor William of Germany sounded a belligerent note. He vowed his navy would become as strong as his army.

Socially, the beginning of the century was fairly dull in New York, but in Washington, 2,000 stood in line to shake hands with President and Mrs. McKinley at a reception at the White House.

Holiday dinners were served in prisons and other institutions to those who had no other reason to celebrate. In India, hundreds of thousands were dying of famine.

Amid California's bountiful farmlands, 50,000 turned out for Pasadena's 11th annual Tournament of Roses. Every train and electric car was jammed. Those seeking stimulation for the occasion could buy a bottle of Plantation Whiskey for 75 cents.

Havana staged a torchlight procession, in which almost the only tune heard was the "Cuban National Hymn." Cuba, formerly ruled by Spain, was agitating for freedom.

Wave of strikes spreads through Europe

Jan 4. Belgium and Germany have been severely shaken by a recent wave of strikes in their respective coal basins, and many factories, already running short of fuel, have been compelled to halt their output.

This month, labor revolts spread into other industries in Europe as well. In Vienna, steelworkers are on strike; in Brussels, it is glassworkers. And in western Bohemia, 5,000 workers in various fields are out on strike. These actions are reportedly spontaneous, not the result of an organized movement. But most of the laborers are making similar demands: an eight-hour day, a significant pay increase (up to 20 percent in some cases) and better working conditions. In spite of the disorders, company managers remain steadfast and do not appear to be making any concessions to their disgruntled employees (→ 3/3).

Gold! Klondike region still lures miners

Prospecting in the Klondike.

Canada's Klondike region east of the Alaskan border continues to draw folks with dreams of easy money, despite the fact that the more lucrative gold mines there have been staked out. Since news of the 1896 discovery of gold at Bonanza Creek reached the United States two and a half years ago, 60,000 prospectors have flocked to the Klondike, and about $50 million has already been mined. The population is booming. Dawson has burgeoned from a mining camp of a few shacks to a bustling town of 20,000 (→ 9/1).

Queensberry dies; made boxing rules

Jan 31. The eighth Marquess of Queensberry, creator of the rules of boxing under which all important ring contests are conducted, has died at the age of 66. The Queensberry boxing rules established a time period of three minutes for a round and set a ten-second count for knockouts. They also set up weight divisions and required boxing gloves "of the best quality and new." The code was written in 1867 by John Graham Chambers and published under the name of the marquess as patron and sponsor.

The Marquess of Queensberry.

1900

FEBRUARY

Su	Mo	Tu	We	Th	Fr	Sa
			1	2	3	4
5	6	7	8	9	10	11
12	13	14	15	16	17	18
19	20	21	22	23	24	25
26	27	28				

2. Six cities, Boston, Detroit, Milwaukee, Baltimore, Chicago and St. Louis, agree to form baseball's American League.

3. Kentucky: Dem. gubernatorial candidate William Goebels dies from assassin's bullet wounds as Republican rioters besiege city of Frankfort (→ 8/18).

5. U.S. and U.K. sign Hay-Pauncefote Treaty, giving U.S. right to build canal in Nicaragua, but not fortify it (→ 8/1).

6. N.Y.: Gov. Theodore Roosevelt declares, "Under no circumstances could I or would I accept the nomination for the vice presidency" (→ 6/19).

6. Holland: Senate ratifies 1899 peace conference decree; creates intl. arbitration court at The Hague (→ 5/22/02).

6. Pres. McKinley appoints W.H. Taft commissioner to report on Philippines (→ 6/21).

8. South Africa: Gen. Buller beaten at Ladysmith; British flee over Tugela River (→ 14).

13. Anglo-German accord of 1899 ratified by Reichstag; U.K. to renounce rights in Samoa in favor of U.S. and Germany (→ 6/15/01).

14. Russia: In response to intl. petition for Finland's freedom, czar orders tightening of imperial control (→ 6/26).

14. South Africa: Gen. Roberts invades Orange Free State with 20,000 British troops (→ 15).

15. British threaten to use natives in Boer War (→ 27).

18. San Francisco: Man claims X-rays have cured his cancer.

24. New York: Contract signed to begin work on rapid transit tunnel (→ 3/24).

27. South Africa: Lord Roberts receives unconditional surrender from Boer Gen. Piet Cronje at Paardeberg (→ 28).

28. South Africa: Gen. Buller's troops relieve Ladysmith, under siege since Nov. 2, 1899 (→ 3/11).

BIRTH

22. Luis Bunuel, film director (†7/29/1983).

Boer War: Lord Roberts in command

Feb 1. Great Britain, defeated by the Boers in key battles and bogged down in a frustrating war, has turned to one of its military heroes in an attempt to turn the tide in South Africa. Field Marshal Roberts, an aging veteran of the war in India, has been named commander of British forces in South Africa. He replaces Sir Redvers Buller.

Buller was put in charge in South Africa after the British suffered setbacks in the Cape Colony, at Mafeking and Kimberley. It was Buller's failure to end the siege of British forces at Ladysmith in Natal that brought about his downfall. General George White's troops have been bottled up by the Boers at Ladysmith since the beginning of November. The Boers have cut off supply routes to the community, and they have attacked Ladysmith several times. White's soldiers used their bayonets to turn back one of the latest assaults.

Buller might have succeeded in ending the siege if he had concentrated his attack. But he opted instead to attack the Boers in several places at once. Buller's soldiers reportedly mumble he is nearly incompetent. A letter from one of the soldiers ignited a large controversy after it found its way into print in Britain. The soldier accused Buller of dispatching troops indiscriminately, failing to gather adequate intelligence on enemy positions and leaving ambulances in the direct line of enemy fire.

British colonists welcome Lord Roberts to Kimberley.

British forces greatly outnumber the Boers in South Africa. But military superiority alone will not win this war. The Boers are more at home in the rough terrain of the country. Now, Lord Roberts, and his chief of staff, Lord Kitchener, must outsmart them (→ 8).

British trade unions create Labor Party

Feb 28. Working men in England decided to unite today. They are trying again to translate their muscle into political power. At a meeting of the Trade Unions Council, delegates voted to create the Labor Representation Committee, which has high hopes of electing candidates to Parliament. Ramsay MacDonald will serve as secretary.

Workers in England have had the right to vote for more than 30 years. But they have not done much with it. The last major workers' movement, called Chartism, died out in the infighting between socialists and communists. Local labor groups were able to elect some politicians to Parliament, but they were largely absorbed by the Liberal Party.

The new labor committee has the support of several British organizations. But to avoid the fate of Chartism, it must find a middle ground. On the far left are the Social Democrats, founded by Henry Hyndman. He has been more attracted to the ideas of Karl Marx than more reformist socialist principles.

The Fabian Society may hold the key to the success of this budding Labor Party. The society, composed of intellectuals such as George Bernard Shaw and H.G. Wells, opposed an association with trade unionists until recently. The Fabians reject the revolutionary ideas of Marx and argue that social reform and evolution will gradually bring about socialism.

World tennis cup

Feb 9. Dwight F. Davis, a very talented college player, has put up a new tennis trophy, a silver cup weighing 36 pounds, which will go to the winner of this year's matches against England, to be played at Newport, Rhode Island (→ 8/10).

The Davis Cup.

1900

MARCH

Su	Mo	Tu	We	Th	Fr	Sa
				1	2	3
4	5	6	7	8	9	10
11	12	13	14	15	16	17
18	19	20	21	22	23	24
25	26	27	28	29	30	31

2. Washington: Congress votes $2 million in aid to Puerto Rico (→ 19).

3. Germany: Striking miners return to work.

5. Two U.S. battleships leave for Nicaragua to halt revolutionary disturbances.

5. New York: Performances of the play "Sappho" curbed for immorality.

6. West Virginia: Explosion traps 50 coal miners underground (→ 5/1).

9. Germany: Women petition Reichstag for right to take university entrance exams.

11. London: British Prime Minister Lord Salisbury rejects peace overtures from Boer leader Paul Kruger (→ 13).

13. South Africa: Gen. Roberts takes Bloemfontein (→ 27).

14. Holland: Botanist Hugo de Vries rediscovers Mendel's laws of heredity.

15. Paris: Sarah Bernhardt stars in premiere of Edmond Rostand's "L'Aiglon."

19. Washington: McKinley asserts need for free trade with Puerto Rico (→ 4/12).

20. Washington: U.S. Sec. of State John Hay announces European powers have agreed to keep China's doors open to trade (→ 5/17).

24. New Jersey: Carnegie Steel Corp. formed; capitalization of $160 mil. is largest to date (→ 3/13/01).

27. Russian army mobilizes 250,000 troops for active duty (→ 5/21).

27. London: Parliament passes War Loan Act allocating 35 mil. pounds to Boer War (→ 4/9).

31. France: National Assembly passes law reducing work day for women and children to 11 hours (→ 7/30).

BIRTH

2. German composer Kurt Weill (†4/3/1950).

DEATH

6. Gottlieb Daimler, creator of Mercedes (*3/17/1834).

Gold backs the buck

March 14. It is now official: The United States of America is on the gold standard. Using a new, gold pen, President McKinley signed into law today a bill declaring that the gold dollar "shall be the standard unit of value and all forms of money issued or coined by the United States shall be maintained at a parity with this standard." The new law only makes legally definitive a gold standard system that had existed on a de facto basis (that is, in fact but not specifically spelled out in law) in the country since 1879. The president has long been a champion of the gold standard.

William McKinley, 25th President.

Debs for president

March 6. Hoping for broad labor support, Eugene V. Debs has announced he will run for president on a socialist ticket. The noted labor leader and onetime member of the Indiana Legislature will make his first run for the presidency on the ticket of the Social Democratic Party, which he helped to found in 1898, as well as the Socialist Labor Party. Debs, 45, gained national attention several years ago when jailed for six months for his part in the Pullman strike of 1894. While in jail, he announced he had become a socialist. A former railroad engineer, he was a founder of the American Railway Union (→ 5/10).

Mayor breaks ground for N.Y. subway

March 24. Wielding a sterling silver spade made by Tiffany & Company, New York Mayor Van Wyck turned over the first shovel of dirt in a ceremony inaugurating construction of the city's first rapid transit tunnel. When completed, the $36 million East River tunnel will link Manhattan with Brooklyn.

The tunnel marks the birth of a subway system promising to extend to Jersey City and even Staten Island. If Chief Engineer Parson is right, Harlem's 125th Street will be reached in only 13 minutes.

Subways are not a new means of transportation. London's system, which went into service in 1863, is the world's oldest. The first in the United States was Boston's, begun two years ago. And Paris is now building a subway of its own.

Dignitaries at subway ceremony.

Hailing it as "second only in importance to the Erie Canal," Van Wyck said "this rapid transit underground road is necessary" for "the accommodation and comfort" of residents (→ 10/27/04).

Relief of Ladysmith

March 1. After a siege that lasted more than four months, Ladysmith has been relieved. General Sir Redvers Buller announced today that a force of Natal Carabineers and a composite regiment entered the city yesterday and that the country around it was clear of Boers.

Ladysmith was a supply base for the British campaign in Natal. It was invested by the Boers on November 11. In the first days of the siege, Boer heavy artillery shelled the city from the surrounding hills.

Despite heavy shellings, the British under General White hung on. Buller, after two costly repulses, finally crossed the Tugela River and pushed on to the besieged city. Many Boer troops left to reinforce those facing Lord Roberts (→ 11).

Evans excavating Knossos Palace at Heraklion in Crete

March 19. The British archeologist Sir Arthur John Evans has begun excavating Knossos Palace, the center of Cretan civilization in the 16th century B.C. and the fabled capital of King Minos in Greek legend. This is an ambitious initiative which undoubtedly will cost Evans a lot of money. He possesses a personal fortune and plans to restore the ancient palace completely at his own expense. It is not known how long it will take to complete the project, but it should one day lead to the discovery of important, scientific information concerning Minoan civilization.

Ruins of the palace at Knossos, site of the fabled labyrinth.

1900

APRIL

Su	Mo	Tu	We	Th	Fr	Sa
1	2	3	4	5	6	7
8	9	10	11	12	13	14
15	16	17	18	19	20	21
22	23	24	25	26	27	28
29	30					

1. Greece: Prince George becomes absolute monarch of Crete.

2. New York: Automobile Club announces plans for transcontinental roadway (→ 1/10/01).

3. Vanderbilts take over 3 major Eastern railroads: Reading, Lehigh Valley and Erie lines.

4. Anarchist fires two shots at Prince of Wales, in Belgium for King Christian's birthday.

6. Gold Coast: Ashanti natives besiege Fort Coomassie after British demand they turn over their "Golden Stool," symbol of sovereignty (→ 6/26).

8. Texas: Colorado River engulfs 80 people in flood.

9. South Africa: British troops rout Boers at Kroonstadt (→ 10).

12. Washington: Foraker Act establishes civil government in Puerto Rico; U.S. president to appoint governor (→ 5/27/01).

16. Washington: First postage stamp booklet released.

17. London: British government publishes Lord Roberts' censure of Gens. Buller and Warren for retreating from Spion Kop (→ 23).

21. France: Thanks to Dugardin's innovation, color photography becomes more accessible.

21. Mississippi: Floods destroy $3 million in property.

23. South Africa: British, under Gen. Brabant, capture Leeuw Kop (→ 5/17).

25. New York: The Cuba Company formed by American financiers; $8 million to develop Cuban railways.

BIRTH

5. Film star Spencer Tracy (†6/10/1967).

DEATH

30. Railroad engineer Casey Jones, while trying to save passengers on a runaway train in Vaughan, Mississippi.

World Exposition opens in Paris

April 14. The Paris Exhibition of 1900, covering a vast site of 547 acres, larger than any previous European world's fair, has opened its gates to the public. Most of the nations represented have their own palaces on the Rue des Nations along the Quai d'Orsay. The most noteworthy attractions at the fair are the magnificent effects produced by electricity in the Chateau d'Eau and Hall of Illusions; the two palaces of the fine arts on the Champs Elysees; and the Alexander III Bridge over the Seine. The exotic exhibits about France's and England's colonies also promise to be popular.

This monumental gateway absorbed only part of a $23 million budget.

Hawaii is territory

April 30. Hawaii is now officially a territory of the United States. A chain of islands near the center of the northern Pacific Ocean, Hawaii had sought annexation by the United States for some years. In 1898, America agreed to annex the islands and grant territorial status. However, it was not until this spring that Congress enacted legislation spelling out terms for the new island government. President McKinley had pushed for territorial status, arguing that the islands are a natural gateway to trade in the Orient and are militarily strategic. Sanford B. Dole, the former President of the republic of Hawaii, will serve as the first Governor of the new territory.

Fire destroys two cities in Canada

April 26. A raging fire has reduced parts of Ottawa and Hull to ashes in less than 12 hours. Property loss is estimated at over $15 million, and some 12,000 people are without homes. Five square miles were leveled, and the lumber industry, the lifeline of this area, is in ruins. The blaze started in Hull, a town a few miles north of Ottawa. Winds fanned the flames across the Ottawa River, engulfing the west end of the city. Firemen had been summoned as far away as Montreal, but their numbers proved powerless. Only a shift of wind to the east prevented Ottawa's total destruction.

Boers strike British

April 10. A report from the battlefront in South Africa indicates that the British have suffered a sharp defeat by the Boers south of Brandfort. London's Daily News reports that "600 British troops were killed and wounded and 800 taken prisoner. Lord Roberts is declared to be finding great difficulty, owing to scarcity of water." The defeat appears to be the first major setback for Roberts in his ambitious effort to march all the way to Pretoria. Roberts has been trying to beat the Boer guerrillas at their own game, by using advance columns to make lightning attacks on their positions and then closing in with the rest of his army (→ 17).

As spring arrives, Yale is prepared to open the 1900 season. Baseball remains the national pastime, the National League drawing over 1.5 mil. fans last year. Ban Johnson's upstart American League, fighting for a spot in the majors since January, promises added excitement (→10/2/02).

William "Buffalo Bill" Cody performed with his Rough Riders at New York's Madison Square Garden on the 23rd of April.

1900

MAY

Su	Mo	Tu	We	Th	Fr	Sa
	1	2	3	4	5	6
7	8	9	10	11	12	13
14	15	16	17	18	19	20
21	22	23	24	25	26	27
28	29	30	31			

1. Utah: Explosion in coal mine takes 200 lives (→ 2/28/02).

3. Jockey Boland rides Lieutenant Gibson to victory in Kentucky Derby.

4. Berlin: Emperor Franz Joseph meets with Wilhelm II, reasserts Austria's friendship.

7. India: International fund created to fight mass hunger (→ 5/8/01).

10. South Dakota: Populists nominate William Jennings Bryan for president (→ 7/6).

14. Paris: Opening of World Amateur championships, also known as Olympic Games.

14. France: National Assembly rejects proposal to unionize civil servants.

17. South Africa: British troops relieve Maj. Gen. Robert Baden-Powell at Mafeking, besieged since Oct. 13, 1899 (→ 18).

17. China: Boxer rebels burn 3 villages near Peking, killing 60 Chinese Christians (→ 28).

18. Washington: Boer delegates seek aid from U.S. (→ 25).

19. Great Britain annexes Tonga Islands.

21. China: Taking advantage of chaos caused by Boxer unrest, Russia invades Manchuria (→ 24).

24. China: Russian army makes plans to defend Manchuria against possible Japanese attack (→ 7/7).

25. South Africa: Boer soldiers pass referendum to continue war with British (→ 30).

28. China: Boxers assail Belgian staff at Fengtai Railway Station (→ 29).

28. N.Y.: Frederick Church exhibit opens at Metropolitan Museum of Art (→ 9/30).

28. Solar eclipse darkens parts of Northern hemisphere.

29. China: Imperial govt. issues highly equivocal edict condemning Boxers (→ 31).

31. South Africa: As British troops seize Johannesburg, Boers withdraw to Pretoria (→ 6/5).

Boxer Rebellion breaks out in China

Chinese imperial troops oversee execution of Boxer rebels.

May 31. The Boxer Rebellion, an outgrowth of traditional anti-foreign sentiment combined with increasing animosity toward Christian missionaries, burst upon the Chinese Empire and foreigners living there earlier this month and shows no sign of letting up.

The Boxers (literally "Fists of Righteous Harmony") is the name given to a native patriotic society comprised of discontented Chinese who devote their spare time to boxing and swordsmanship. They came under the influence of Prince Tuan and other members of the imperial court, and their rebellion, although centered on Peking, has spread through the Southern provinces. Rioting has been reported in Nanking and Canton, and reports of massacres of American, French and German missionaries have poured into Peking. Heavy pressure for military intervention has been exerted on the McKinley administration by religious groups.

Yesterday, the Boxers occupied the city of Tientsin, the gateway to Peking, and they were brandishing spears surmounted with the heads of murdered missionaries. The imperial government announced an edict prohibiting Boxer activity. But reports indicate that imperial troops often mix with the Boxers.

Detachments of American, British, Russian, French, Italian and Japanese marines, 340 soldiers in all, arrived in Peking by train this evening. These troops were apparently scraped up hastily; the Americans wore winter uniforms and the Russians forgot their cannon. For the moment, all is calm (→ 6/1).

British take over Orange Free State

May 30. A triumphant British army entered Johannesburg in the Transvaal today after a whirlwind campaign. Led by Field Marshal Lord Roberts, universally known as "Bobs," 30,000 infantry, 20,000 cavalry and 150 guns crossed the Vaal River, occupied Johannesburg with insignificant casualties and prepared to conquer Pretoria, the capital. No serious opposition was reported, and the city is now quiet. Contrary to British fears, the gold mines have not been destroyed. Many of the outlying farms are deserted. British officers ask whether the recent Boer defeats will end the war or lead to a prolonged guerrilla war. But the bloody conflict is far from over in their view (→ 31).

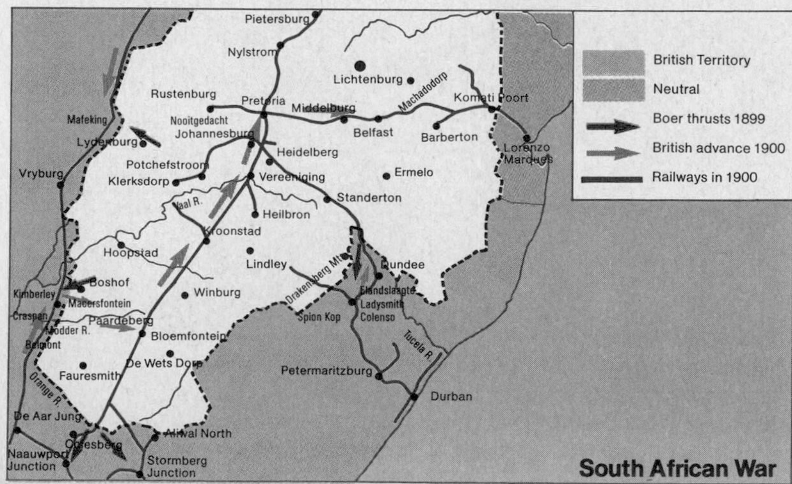

Jeffries is champ, defeating Corbett

Jim Jeffries, champ since last June.

May 11. After 23 rounds of brutal boxing, James Jeffries knocked out James J. Corbett and retained the world heavyweight championship. Corbett held off Jeffries for 22 rounds with his more skillful boxing, but then he tried to slug it out. That proved to be a mistake. Corbett went down from a right-hand smash to the jaw and the long battle in New York was over.

1900

JUNE

Su	Mo	Tu	We	Th	Fr	Sa
					1	2
3	4	5	6	7	8	9
10	11	12	13	14	15	16
17	18	19	20	21	22	23
24	25	26	27	28	29	30

1. China: Boxers conquer city of Tientsin (→ 7).

5. Atlantic Ocean: Liner Deutschland III sets new speed record of 23.61 knots (→ 8/13).

5. South Africa: Pretoria seized by British troops under Lord Roberts (→ 7/4).

7. China: Boxers cut off railway links between Peking and Tientsin (→ 9).

9. Peking: Foreign legations call for protection as Boxers ravage race course, symbol of Western privilege (→ 10).

10. England: British troops, under Admiral Seymour, embark for Peking (→ 13).

13. Peking: Dowager Empress expresses support for Boxers, calling them "people's soldiers" (→ 13).

13. Peking: Boxer rebels kill Sugiyama Akira, chancellor of Japanese legation (→ 19).

19. Philadelphia: Convention places McKinley and Theodore Roosevelt on Republican ticket (→ 7/6).

19. Peking: Imperial govt. orders foreign legations out of China within two days (→ 20).

20. Peking: German Ambassador Baron Klemens von Ketteler slain while on his way to imperial palace (→ 26).

23. Paris: Dome of Sacre-Coeur inaugurated.

23. Turkey: Dissident Young Turks demand that foreign powers expel Sultan Abdul Hamid and free Turkey from Ottoman Empire (→ 9/1).

26. Czar imposes Russian as official language of Finland (→ 1/21/02).

26. Gold Coast: 10,000 Ashanti natives attack British force of 400 at Cape Coast Castle (→ 10/4).

BIRTHS

25. Lord Mountbatten, British war hero and last viceroy of India (+8/27/1979).

29. French writer and aviator Antoine de Saint-Exupery (†7/31/1944).

Allied troops in China

June 26. The United States announced today it would send two regiments of infantry under Brigadier General Adna Chaffee, a veteran of both the American Civil War and the Spanish-American War, to join soldiers, marines and sailors from seven other nations fighting the Chinese Boxers. His orders are to proceed to Peking and establish a strong military presence at the center of the Chinese Empire.

British, French, German, Japanese, Austrian, Russian, Italian and some American troops already are on the scene. Russia has thus far sent the largest contingent. The allied force, under the command of Admiral Seymour of the British navy, is now concentrating around Tientsin, which was relieved three days ago after heavy fighting.

This month, the Boxer Rebellion spread far and wide. Reports indicate that the powers had underestimated the size of the Boxer armies and that not even an allied force of 50,000 can defeat them. Boxer soldiers in the Peking area alone are said to number 360,000.

Admiral Seymour's force reportedly marched into Peking on June 21, and dispatches indicated the legations were secured and the envoys were safe. But this was already too late to save German Ambassador Baron Klemens von Ketteler and the Chancellor of the Japanese legation, Sugiyama Akira. Both were killed by the Boxers (→ 7/5).

American novelist, Stephen Crane, dies

June 5. Tuberculosis has claimed Stephen Crane at 28 in Badenweiler, Germany. The restless, New Jersey-born writer thirsted to taste all the sensations of life. Renowned for his novel "The Red Badge of Courage: An Episode of the American Civil War" (1895), recounting a young man's experiences in battle, Crane earned his living as a freelance reporter. His first novel, "Maggie: A Girl of the Streets" (1893), displaying his knowledge of slum life, so appalled publishers with its characteristic impressionistic realism that the author paid to print it. In 1896, Crane was shipwrecked, spent four days adrift and thereafter suffered impaired health.

Hundreds die when ocean liners burn

June 30. A savage fire wrecked three steamships docked at a pier in Hoboken, New Jersey, today. Over 200 crew members and passengers were killed, and hundreds were injured. Property damage was estimated at more than $6 million. The fire ignited in cotton bales and turpentine stored on the pier. Flames immediately engulfed the ships, which were quickly towed to sea, preventing the spread of fire to land. Some passengers struggled vainly through portholes, where they died, trapped. The crowd onshore could only watch helplessly as the tragedy unfolded.

Germany is building more powerful navy

June 12. The Reichstag today approved new legislation continuing Germany's naval expansion program. This second naval law provides for construction of 38 battleships over a 20-year period. If the program is carried out, Germany's fleet will prove to be one of the largest in the world. Kaiser Wilhelm II's naval minister, Admiral Alfred von Tirpitz, who was instrumental in the passage of the first German naval law in 1898, has argued that Germany must have a larger and more powerful fleet in order to protect its colonies and trade routes.

MacArthur offers Filipinos amnesty

June 21. General Arthur MacArthur, the United States Military Governor of the Philippines, has offered an amnesty to the Filipino rebels in an effort to bring to an end an insurgency that began in opposition to Spanish rule. The amnesty grants full pardon to all those Filipinos who have taken part in the rebellion, on the condition that they take an oath of allegience and acknowledge the sovereignty of the American government. The Philippines came under American rule during the course of the Spanish-American War, when Admiral John Dewey sank the Spanish fleet in Manila Bay in 1898 (→ 10/26).

Ladies' play at Wimbledon. The Lawn Tennis Championships began in 1877, just four years after British Major Walter Wingfield invented the modern game to amuse the aristocratic revelers at lawn parties (→ 7/8).

1900

JULY

Su	Mo	Tu	We	Th	Fr	Sa
1	2	3	4	5	6	7
8	9	10	11	12	13	14
15	16	17	18	19	20	21
22	23	24	25	26	27	28
29	30	31				

3. Russia: Attempting to halt growth of popular discontent, Czar Nicholas promises to abolish Siberian exile as punishment for dissent (→ 2/27/01).

4. It is reported in New York that all foreigners in Peking are dead (→ 5).

4. South Africa: British under Roberts and Buller join at Vlakfontein; Boers dispersed (→ 30).

5. 100,000 Chinese surround 12,000 allied troops at Tientsin (→ 14).

6. Kansas City: Wm. Jennings Bryan takes Dem. presidential nomination with Adlai E. Stevenson as running mate (→ 9/17).

7. Russia announces it will condone Japanese military action in China (→ 3/15/01).

8. Wimbledon: Reginald Doherty over Sydney Smith 6-8, 6-3, 6-1, 6-2; Blanche Hillyard over Charlotte Cooper 4-6, 6-4, 6-4.

14. China: Allies win at Tientsin; U.S. Sec. of State John Hay reasserts open door policy (→ 22).

19. France: Paris subway opens.

22. Chinese Emperor Kwang-Su asks Pres. McKinley to extract him from perilous position between Boxers and Western powers (→ 27).

23. Pressed by expanding immigration, Canada closes its doors to paupers and criminals.

25. Angry mob terrorizes New Orleans; many blacks beaten and killed (→ 11/16).

29. Peking: Imperial edict declares envoys are hostages, will be killed if allies advance (→ 8/6).

30. British Parliament passes progressive legislation: mine act outlawing child labor, railway act to enhance safety, workmen's compensation act covering illness (→ 10/1).

30. South Africa: 5,000 Boer troops under Gen. Prinsloo give in to Lord Roberts (→ 8/27).

BIRTHS

4. Jazz great Louis Armstrong (†7/6/1971).

8. Avant-garde composer George Antheil (†2/13/1959).

100,000 Chinese slay foreigners

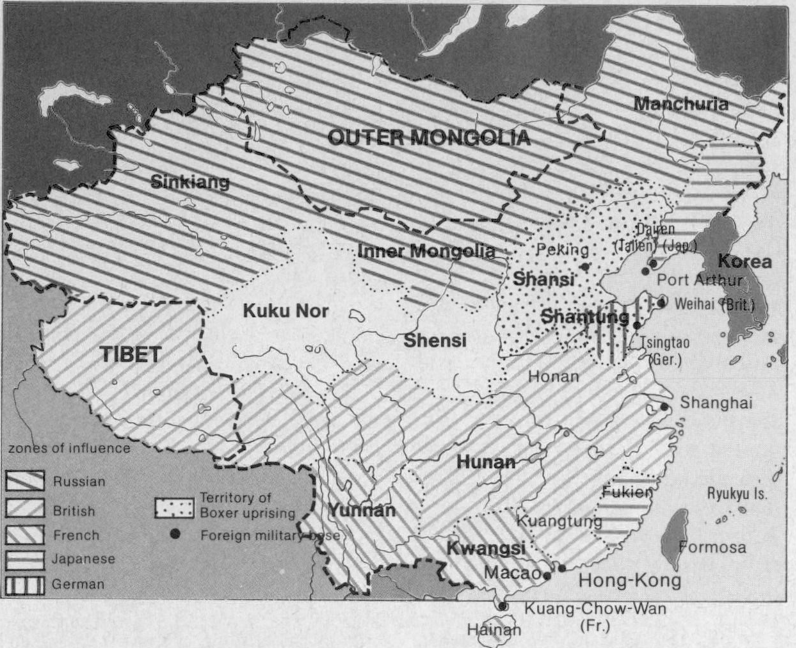

July 27. At least 100,000 Boxers unleashed a fierce attack in Tientsin earlier this month, and some 1,500 foreigners were brutally massacred, but the allies finally emerged victorious, and United States Secretary of State John Hay has reasserted the open door policy in China.

Despite their defeat, the rebels are not giving in. Reports from Peking say that at least 300,000 Boxers are massed in and around the city, although they are poorly trained and unfamiliar with modern weapons.

Great anxiety is still felt for missionary families. Hundreds have been reported slain. Chinese converts also are targets of the Boxers' wrath. Three familes were beheaded near Shanghai. And reports that the legations in Peking were secured are now said to be untrue. The Boxers are wrecking foreign buildings and churches (→ 29).

Italy's King shot and son succeeds

July 30. King Humbert I of Italy was shot to death late last night by an anarchist, Angelo Bresci. By this act, anarchists claimed to have won revenge for the "bloodbath" in Milan in 1898, in which the king had violently crushed a labor insurrection by calling out the artillery and killing workers. During his 22-year reign, Humbert strove to strengthen the monarchy and pursued increasingly conservative policies. His foreign policy led to the conclusion of the Triple Alliance. His son, Victor Emmanuel, 31 years old, succeeds to the throne (→ 5/23/01).

Australian colonies form confederation

July 9. The British Parliament has accepted the Commonwealth of Australia Act, uniting the Australian colonies of New South Wales, South Australia, Queensland, Tasmania, Victoria and Western Australia under a federal government. European and American expansion in the Pacific prompted the six colonies to settle their differences and form a common defense (→ 1/1/01).

Zeppelin airship makes first flight

July 20. An airship designed and constructed by Count Ferdinand von Zeppelin of Germany made its first flight today near Friedrichshafen. The airship, built in a floating hangar on Lake Constance, has a wire-braced aluminum hull covered with cotton cloth that contains 16 gas cells filled with hydrogen. Two 16-horsepower engines give it a speed of 14 miles an hour. Von Zeppelin made his first balloon ascent while serving with the Union Army during the American Civil War and has been working on airships since 1891 (→ 11/30/05).

Count Ferdinand von Zeppelin's historic flight in the dirigible LZ 1.

1900 Paris

France's Gustave Sandras, gymnastics champion of the world.

July 22. Fifty-five American athletes completed their domination of the second modern Olympic Games when J.W.B. Tewksbury won the only final-day event, the 200-meter run. With his second triumph, Tewksbury emerged as a star of the meet with his Penn teammate and four-time winner, A.C. Kraenzlein, and Ray Ewry, a former invalid who won thrice in the Paris Games.

Most of the collegians competed against 13 other nations without realizing that they were in the Olympics until medals were presented. The American athletes were privately financed and did not compete as a team. The Games were marred by controversy over Sunday participation and the behavior of the American "sauvages" but ended on a warm and friendly note.

Olympic athletes from the U.S. dominated sprints and field events this year in Paris. The Games reopened in 1896 after a lapse of 1,500 years.

Men Athletics

100 M Dash
1. Francis Jarvis USA 11,0
2. Walter B. Tewksbury USA 11,1
3. Stanley Rowley AUS 11,2

200 M Dash
1. Walter Tewksbury USA 22,2
2. Norman Pritchard IND 22,8
3. Stanley Rowley AUS 22,9

400 M Run
1. Maxey Long USA 49,4
2. William Holland USA 49,6
3. Ernst Schulz DEN

800 M Run
1. Alfred Tysoe GBR 2:01,2
2. John Cregan USA 2:03,0
3. David Hall USA

1500 M Run
1. Charles Bennett GBR 4:06,2
2. Henri Deloge FRA 4:06,6
3. John Bray USA 4:07,2

Marathon
1. Michel Theato FRA 2:59:45
2. Emile Champion FRA 3:04:17
3. Ernst Fast SWE 3:37:14

110 M Hurdles
1. Alvin Kraenzlein USA 15,4
2. John McLean USA 15,5
3. Fred Moloney USA

400 M Hurdles
1. Walter Tewksbury USA 57,6
2. Henri Tauzin FRA 58,3
3. George Orton CAN

300 M Steeplechase (2500 M)
1. George Orton CAN 7:34,4
2. Sidney Robinson GBR 7:38,0
3. Jacques Chastanié FRA

High Jump
1. Irving Baxter USA 1,90
2. Patrick Leahy GBR-IRL 1,78
3. Lajos Gönczy HUN 1,75

Pole Vault
1. Irving Baxter USA 3,30
2. M.B. Colkett USA 3,25
3. Carl-Albert Andersen NOR 3,20

Long Jump
1. Alvin Kraenzlein USA 7,185
2. Myer Prinstein USA 7,175
3. Patrick Leahy GBR-IRL 6,95

Triple Jump
1. Myer Prinstein USA 14,47
2. James Brendan Connolly USA 13,97
3. Lewis P. Sheldon USA 13,64

Shotput
1. Richard Sheldon USA 14,10
2. Josiah McCraken USA 12,85
3. Robert Garrett USA 12,37

Discus Throw
1. Rudolf Bauer HUN 36,04
2. Frantisek Janda-Suk BOH 35,25
3. Richard Sheldon USA 34,60

Hammer Throw
1. John Flanagan USA 49,73
2. Truxton Hare USA 49,13
3. Josiah McCraken USA 42,46

60 M (in 1900 and 1904 only)
1. Alvin Kraenzlein USA 7,0
2. Walter B. Tewksbury USA 7,1
3. Stanley Rowley AUS 7,2

200 M Hurdles (1900 and 1904 only)
1. Alvin Kraenzlein USA 15,4
2. Norman Pritchard IND 26,6
3. Walter B. Tewksbury USA

4000 M Steeplechase (1900 only)
1. John Rimmer GBR 12:58,4
2. Charles Bennett GBR 12:58,6
3. Sidney Robinson GBR 12:58,8

5000 Team
1. Great Britain
2. France

Standing High Jump (1900, 1904, 1906, 1908, 1912 only)
1. Ray Ewry USA 1,65
2. Irving Baxter USA 1,52
3. Lewis P. Sheldon FRA 1,50

Standing Long Jump (1900, 1904, 1906, 1908, 1912 only)
1. Ray Ewry USA 3,25
2. Irving Baxter USA 3,135
3. Emile Torcheboeuf FRA 3,03

Standing Triple Jump (1900 and 1904 only)
1. Ray Ewry USA 10,58
2. Irving Baxter USA 9,95
3. Robert Garrett USA 9,50

Tug-of-War (1900, 1904, 1906, 1908, 1912, 1920 only)
1. Sweden/Norway
2. USA
3. France

Men Fencing

Foil Individual
1. E. Coste FRA
2. Henri Masson FRA
3. Jacques Boulanger FRA

Epée Individual
1. Ramon Fonst CUB
2. Louis Perrée FRA
3. Léone Sée FRA

Sabre Individual
1. Georges de la Falaise FRA
2. Léon Thiébaut FRA
3. Siegried Flesh AUT

Foil for Fencing Masters (1896 and 1900 only)
1. Lucien Merignac FRA
2. Alphonse Kirchloffer FRA
3. Jean-Baptiste Mimiague FRA

Epée for Fencing Masters (1896 and 1900 only)
1. Albert Ayat FRA
2. Emile Bougnol FRA
3. Henri laurent

Epée for Amateurs and Fencing Masters (1900 only)
1. Albert Ayat FRA
2. Ramon Fonst CUB
3. Léon Sée FRA

Sabre for Fencing Masters (1900 and 1906 only)
1. Antonio Conte ITA
2. Italo Santelli ITA
3. Milan Neralic AUT

Men's Swimming

200 M Freestyle
1. Frederick C.V. Lane AUS 2:25,2
2. Zolan von Halmay HUN 2:31,4
3. Karl Ruberl AUT 2:32,0

See Table of Contents for abbreviations

1500 M Freestyle
1. John Jarvis GBR 13:40,2
2. Otto Wahle AUT 14:53,6
3. Zoltan von Halmay HUN 15:16,4

200 M Backstroke
1. Ernst Hoppenberg GER 2:47,0
2. Karl Ruberl AUT 2:56,0
3. Johannes Drost HOL 3:01,0

200 M Obstacle Event
1. Frederick Lane AUS 2:38,4
2. Otto Wahle AUT 2:40,0
3. Peter Kemp GBR 2:47,4

4000 M Freestyle (1900 only)
1. John Jarvis GBR 58:24,0
2. Zoltan von Halmay HUN 1:08:55,4
3. L. Martin FRA 1:13:08,4

60 M Underwater Swimming (1900 only)
1. Charles de Vandeville FRA
2. A. Six FRA
3. Peder Lykkeberg DAN

Distance, M	Time	Points
60	1:08,4	188,4
60	1:05,4	185,4
28,50	1:30,0	147,0

200 M Team (1900 only)
1. Germany
2. France
3. France

Water-polo
1. Great Britain
2. Belgium
3. France

Shooting

Pistol—Rapid-Fire Pistol
1. Maurice Larrouy FRA 58
2. Léon Moreaux FRA 57
3. Eugène Balme FRA 57

Free Pistol 50 M
1. Karl Röderer SUI 503
2. Achille Paroche FRA 466
3. Konrad Stäheli SUI 453

Live Pigeon Shooting (1900 only)
1. Léon de Lunden BEL 21
2. Maurice Faure FRA 20
3. D. MacIntosh AUS 18

Clay Pigeon Shooting
1. Roger de Barbarin FRA 17
2. René Guyot FRA 17
3. Justinien de Clary FRA 17

Running Wild Boar Shooting
1. Louis Debray FRA 20
2. P. Nivet FRA 20
3. de Lambert FRA 20

Military Rifle (1900, 1906, 1912, 1920 only) 3 positions
1. Emile Kellenberger SUI 930
2. Anders Peter Nielsen DEN 921
3. Ole Ostmo NOR 917

Military Rifle Standing Position
1. Lars Jörgen Madsen DAN 305
2. Ole Ostmo NOR 299
3. Charles Paumier du Verger BEL

Military Rifle Kneeling Position
1. Konrad Stahli SUI 324
2. Emil Kellenberger SUI 314
3. Anders Peter Nielsen DEN 314

Military Rifle Prone Position
1. Achille Paroche FRA 352
2. Andres Peter Nielsen DEN 330
3. Ole Ostmo NOR 329

Military Rifle Team 300 M (1900 and 1908 only)
1. Switzerland 4399
2. Norway 4290
3. France 4278

Military Revolver (1900, 1908, 1912, 1920 only)
1. Switzerland 2271
2. France 2203
3. Netherlands 1876

Archery

Au Cordon Doré 50 M
1. Henri Herouin FRA 31
2. Hubert van Innis BEL 29
3. Emile Fisseux FRA 28

Au Chapelet -50 M
1. Eugène Mougin FRA
2. Henri Helle FRA
3. Emile Mercier FRA

Au Cordon Dore -33 M
1. Hubert van Innis BEL
2. Victor Thibaud FRA
3. Charles Frédéric Petit FRA

Au Chapelet -33 m
1. Hubert van Innis BEL
2. Victor Thibaud FRA
3. Charles Frédéric Petit FRA

Sur la Perche a là Herse
1. Emmanuel Foulon FRA
2. Serrurier FRA
3. Duart jun BEL

Sur la Perche a là Pyramide
1. Emile Grumiaux FRA
2. Louis Glineux BEL

Men Gymnastics

Individual All-around Competition
1. Gustave Sandras FRA 302
2. Noël Bas FRA 295
3. Lucien Démaret FRA 293

Soccer

1. Great Britain
2. France
3. Belgium

Rowing

Single Sculls
1. Henri Barrelet FRA 7:35,6
2. André Gaudin FRA 7:41,6
3. Saint George Ashe GBR 8:15,6

Pairs with Coxswain
1. Netherlands 7:34,2
2. France 7:34,4
3. France 7:57,2

Fours with Coxswain—First Final
1. France 7:11,0
2. France 7:18,0
3. Germany 7:18,2

Fours with Coxswain—Second Final
1. Germany 5:59,0
2. Netherlands 6:33,0
3. Germany 6:35,0

Eight Oars
1. USA 6:09,8
2. Belgium 6:13,8
3. Netherlands 6:23,0

Tennis

Men's Singles (two bronze medals)
1. Hugh Doherty GBR
2. Harold Mahony GBR
3. Reginald Doherty GBR
A.B.Norris GBR

Women's Singles (two bronze medals)
1. Charlotte Cooper GBR
2. Helene Provost FRA
3. Marion Jones USA
Hedwiga Rosenbaumova BOH

Yachting

All Categories (1900 only)
1. Great Britain *Scotia*
2. Germany *Aschenbrödel*
3. France *Turquoise*

Class 0.5t (1900 only)
1. France *Quand-même*
2. France *Baby*
3. France *Sarcelle*

Class 0.5t-1.0t (1900 only)
1. Great Britain *Scotia*
2. France *Crabe II*
3. France *Scamasaxe*

Class 1-2t (1900 only)
1. Germany *Aschenbrödel*
2. Switzerland *Lerina*
3. France *Marthe*

Class 2-3t (1900 only)
1. Great Britain *Ollé*
2. France *Favorite*
3. France *Mignon*

Class 3-10t (1900 only)
1. USA *Bona Fide*
2. France *Gitana*
3. USA *Frimousse*

Class 10-20t (1900 only)
1. France *Estérel*
2. France *Quand-même*
3. Great Britain *Lauréa*

Cycling

1000 M sprint
1. Georges Taillandier FRA 2:52,0
2. Sanz FRA
3. Lake USA

Equestrian Sports

Individual Jumping Competition
1. Aimé Haegeman BEL 2:16,0
2. Georges van de Poele BEL 2:17,6
3. de Champsavin FRA 2:26,0

High jump (1900 only)
1. Dominique Maximien Gardères FRA 1,85
2. Gian Giorgio Trissino ITA 1,85
3. A. Moreau FRA 1,70

Long Jump (1900 only)
1. Constant van Long Jump (1900 only) BEL 6,10
2. Gian Giorgio Trissino ITA 5,70
3. de Prunelle FRA 5,30

1900

AUGUST

Su	Mo	Tu	We	Th	Fr	Sa
			1	2	3	4
5	6	7	8	9	10	11
12	13	14	15	16	17	18
19	20	21	22	23	24	25
26	27	28	29	30	31	

1. North Carolina: Riots break out as Red Shirts break up a meeting of populists.

1. Managua: Nicaragua cancels canal concession (→ 12/01).

2. Paris: Anarchist Francois Salsou attempts to assassinate Muzaffar ad-Din, shah of Persia.

5. Russia: Anti-Jewish riots break out in Odessa.

6. San Francisco: Chinese refugees arrive on the transport Logan (→ 12).

12. Washington: U.S. rejects Chinese request for an armistice (→ 14).

18. Kentucky: Ex-Sec. of State Caleb Powers found guilty of conspiracy to murder Gov. William Goebels (→ 4/23/09).

21. China: As allies overrun Peking's inner city, Empress Dowager flees with $70 mil. in treasure (→ 22).

22. Peking: Foreign troops and civilians loot city (→ 30).

25. Washington: Commission appointed to do preliminary work on great naval base at Guam.

27. Britain: Long-distance buses are brought into service.

27. South Africa: General Buller leads British forces at Bergendal; Louis Botha defeated (→ 9/3).

30. Germany: Cost of German expedition to China estimated at 100 mil. German marks (→ 30).

30. Britain to be arbiter on fate of China (→ 9/10).

BIRTH

6. Austro-American composer Ernst Krenek.

DEATHS

7. Leader of German Social Democrats Wilhelm Liebknecht (*3/29/1826).

14. Railroad tycoon Collis P. Huntington, of heart disease (*10/22/1821).

25. German philosopher Friedrich Nietzsche (*10/15/1844).

Allies enter Peking, free legations

Aug 14. The allies entered Peking today from the east, finally raising the 56-day siege of the foreign legations. The drive into the capital came after a long fighting advance from Tientsin. Chinese resistance to the allied column of 10,000 men was sometimes obstinate. The Boxers and renegades from the regular army had many modern field guns, but these were poorly used.

The personnel attached to the legations were found to be in a desperate position. All the women and children had gathered in the large British Embassy, which was under heavy but intermittent attack. Those inside estimated they had less than one week's food supply remaining when the troops arrived. The advance from Tientsin to Peking was slow because the Boxers had destroyed sections of the railroad. But when Ho Si Wu was taken August 9, the allies believed their enemy was demoralized. Tientsin was relieved earlier in the campaign.

U.S. troops raise the American flag at Peking.

There are reports that the Dowager Empress and part of the regular army have fled to Hsian Foo. Small pockets of Boxer resistance remain in the city and the surrounding countryside. Once the allies have consolidated their positions, rebel nests will be attacked. Allied losses are reportedly light (→ 21).

Davis and Ward win the first Davis Cup

Aug 10. The American team of Dwight F. Davis and Holcombe Ward defeated the visiting English pair of E.D. Black and H.R. Barrett and clinched the International Lawn Tennis Challenge Trophy, donated by Davis last February and named in his honor. The doubles victory, after two singles victories, gave the United States team an insurmountable 3-0 lead in the series. The fourth and last singles match was halted by rain after Davis won the first set 9-7.

Dwight Davis and teammates.

German thinker Nietzsche is dead

Portrait of Friedrich Nietzsche.

Aug 25. In Weimar today, death came to Friedrich Nietzsche after 11 years of madness. Foremost among German philosophers of the 19th century, he was the author of "The Birth of Tragedy," "Thus Spake Zarathustra" and "Beyond Good and Evil." A minister's son and classical scholar, he became a passionate moralist who renounced bourgeois Western civilization, reviled Christianity and envisaged a "superman" as the embodiment of a new heroic morality.

German liners set two speed records

Aug 13. The steamer Deutschland of the Hamburg American Line set a new record for the eastward passage when it docked in Plymouth, England, five days, 11 hours and 45 minutes after sailing from New York, breaking by three hours, six minutes the previous mark, also set by the Deutschland, during her maiden voyage in June.

Commanded by Captain Albers, the ship averaged 23.32 knots, with a top day's run of 552 knots. This record followed by one day another set by the steamer Kaiser Wilhelm der Grosse of the North German Lloyd Line for the run between New York and Cherbourg. With an average speed of 22.79 knots, the vessel covered the 3,184 knots in five days, 19 hours, 44 minutes. Her top daily run was 541 knots.

The arrival of the ships has generated a lot of interest, and that of the Deutschland, some concern. Her arrival in New York on August 5 was delayed by mechanical problems attributed to new machinery not fully broken in. This anxiety was allayed when she docked in Plymouth with time to spare (→ 9/9).

1900

SEPTEMBER

Su	Mo	Tu	We	Th	Fr	Sa
						1
2	3	4	5	6	7	8
9	10	11	12	13	14	15
16	17	18	19	20	21	22
23	24	25	26	27	28	29
30						

1. Epidemic rages among Alaskan Eskimos.→

1. Turkey: Twenty-fifth anniversary of Turkish Sultan Abdul Hamid; European statesmen attend spectacular celebration (→ 12/20).

2. Dublin: Nationalist demonstrators demand Ireland's freedom from British rule (→ 5/10/01).

3. China: Russians control Manchuria; drive 5,000 Chinese to their death in Amur River (→ 11/9).

3. South Africa: Great Britain annexes Transvaal as Boer leader Paul Kruger flees to Mozambique (→ 15).

5. Indiana: Donelson Caffery receives presidential nomination on 3rd party ticket (→ 11/6).

9. New York: The liner Deutschland beats the Kaiser Wilhelm der Grosse in race from Hamburg to New York (→ 7/17/01).

10. China: Li Hung-Chang receives authority to negotiate with Western powers (→ 30).

10. Germany: Empire's colonies become protectorates.

13. Austria-Hungary: Emperor Franz Joseph tells a Polish deputation they will lose even nominal autonomy if they continue to make demands.

15. The Hague: Boer delegation demands that major powers intervene on their behalf in S. Africa (→ 10/5).

17. Philippines: Taft commission begins to exercise legislative powers, appropriating sums for roads and harbors (→ 10/26).

19. France: President Loubet pardons Jewish army captain, Alfred Dreyfus, twice court-martialed and wrongfully convicted of spying for Germany (→ 12/19).

27. Paris: International Socialist Congress ends.

30. China: Allies begin withdrawal from Peking (→ 10/9).

BIRTH

23. American sculptor Louise Nevelson.

Storm sweeps Gulf coast

Sept 8. Cities near the Gulf of Mexico were ravaged by fierce hurricane winds and rain today.

In Galveston, Texas, telegraph and telephone wires were downed. Four bridges, the only connections from the island city to the mainland, were feared swept away. No reports left the city for hours, but there were rumors that flood waters had overpowered many homes.

In Houston, the only operating news line was that of the Associated Press. The electric light plant shut down after falling wires injured pedestrians. And strong winds blew roofs off several houses, but there were no casualties reported.

New Orleans experienced beachfront damage and winds of 48 miles per hour. One child was killed when winds hurled apart the balcony he stood upon. There were unconfirmed reports of worse conditions and loss of life on some of the Gulf islands.

Bryan accepts presidential nomination

William J. Bryan campaign poster.

Sept 17. William Jennings Bryan, the silver-tongued orator from the Plains, accepted the Democratic Party's nomination for president today, pledging he would seek but a single four-year term.

In his formal letter of acceptance, Bryan made only passing reference to the gold and silver monetary standard issue that had been the major theme of his presidential campaign four years ago. At that time, he had electrified his audience with the thundering words: "You shall not crucify mankind upon a cross of gold." This time, Bryan focused his attack on American "imperialism" abroad and corporate monopolies at home (→ 11/6).

Hard coal miners go out on strike

Sept 17. A massive strike of about 100,000 workers in the anthracite coal fields of Pennsylvania erupted today. These fields provide much of the entire hard coal output of the world.

According to United Mine Workers President John Mitchell, participation in the strike is very nearly complete with the holdout mines expected to join. "The number of men out on strike exceeds that of any other industrial contest in the history of our country," he said. Providers of auxiliary services in the area have also joined the strike, effectively closing down the mines. No progress has been made by the clergy attempting to arbitrate the dispute, which has not been marred by violence (→ 10/25).

Epidemic strikes Eskimos in Alaska

Sept 1. An epidemic of the grippe, accompanied by measles or pneumonia, or both, is raging among the Eskimos of Alaska, and in some places half the natives are dead, according to a dispatch sent by Governor Brady to Washington.

Brady's report states that in the town of Greyling the natives were sick in almost every tent near the shore and were "in a very deplorable condition. Some were lying on the ground, coughing and groaning. The pity of it was that nothing was being done for their relief." The governor has appealed for medical supplies to relieve the natives. If aid is not received soon, he warns, the Eskimos will continue "to become stupefied and utterly helpless, and lie down to die" (→ 10/16/03).

Frederick Church paintings shown

Frederick Church's "Mountain in Ecuador."

Sept 30. An exhibit currently at the Metropolitan Museum of Art in New York is focusing attention on the paintings of Frederick Church, who died April 7 at his home on the Hudson River. Church won riches and fame for his romantic landscapes. A member of the Hudson River school, he nevertheless roamed the world for subjects that ranged from Niagara Falls to tropical forests to icebergs.

Bostwick sets two auto speed records

Sept 18. Albert C. Bostwick set speed records today for five and ten miles on the Guttenberg, New Jersey, track with his new French automobile. His gasoline-run racer, which is quite different from any machine manufactured in the United States, sped five miles in 7:43.2 and ten miles in 15:09.2. His noisy motorcar was helped when the electric vehicle of A.L. Richter blew a battery fuse while leading. The pre-race parade of these new-fangled machines excited spectators, who appear to be thrilled by this dangerous but exciting sport.

1900

OCTOBER

Su	Mo	Tu	We	Th	Fr	Sa
	1	2	3	4	5	6
7	8	9	10	11	12	13
14	15	16	17	18	19	20
21	22	23	24	25	26	27
28	29	30	31			

1. Germany: Reichstag passes workmen's compensation act protecting laborers in case of accident or illness (→ 10/20/01).

4. Gold Coast: British defeat 4,000 rebels, dealing fatal blow to Ashanti revolt (→ 9/25/01).

4. Vladislav Zelensk's opera "Janek" opens in Austria.

5. Paris: Peace congress condemns British policy in S. Africa, asserts Boer Republic's right to self-determination (→ 11/6).

7. Boston: Helen Keller admitted to Radcliffe (→ 9/1/04).

8. Germany: Maximilian Harden given six-month sentence for publishing article critical of emperor.

9. China: Imperial government sentences guilty officials; Prince Tuan sent to Siberia (→ 16).

16. Russia decides to act alone in China (→ 20).

16. Joseph Chamberlain retains power in British elections.

18. Count Bernhard von Bulow becomes chancellor of Germany.

22. New York: Chartenus sets world record of 2.04 minutes in 1.25-mile horse race.

24. U.S. government announces plans to buy Danish West Indies for $7 million (→ 7/24/16).

25. Pennsylvania: Thirty-nine-day strike ends with 10% wage increase; union officials order coal miners back to work.

26. Philippines: 1400 rebels lay siege to small American force. (→ 28).

28. American deserter David Fag, acting as Filipino general, attacks cargo boat with 150 insurgents (→ 12/23).

29. Chinese to pay $200 mil. indemnity to West (→ 11/10).

BIRTHS

3. American novelist Thomas Wolfe (†9/15/1938).

7. Nazi leader Heinrich Himmler (†5/23/1945).

U.S. population reaches 76 million

Oct 30. The official population of the United States for 1900 stands at 76,295,220. Some 74,627,907 inhabit the 45 states. The remaining 1,667,313 include persons abroad in the service of the nation and residents of the seven territories: Alaska, Arizona, Dist. of Columbia, Hawaii, the Indian Territory, New Mexico and Oklahoma. Based on tax returns, the count does not include 145,282 Indians who live in the Indian Territory and pay no taxes.

The figure marks a gain of 13,225,464, or about 20%, over the 1890 census of 63,069,756. The 1900 count was computed with the latest tabulating machines. These eliminate the prior custom of the rough count and produce a more accurate, cheaper, quicker census.

New York led the states with 7,268,009; Nevada was last with 42,334. Oklahoma topped the territories with 398,245, followed by the Indian Territory with 391,960.

Germany and Britain arrive at an agreement on future of China

Expeditionary forces triumphantly parading captured Boxer flags.

Oct 20. Great Britain and Germany today announced that they have formed an alliance to maintain the territorial integrity of China and to keep that country's ports open to world trade. Agreement on the alliance was reached on October 16 by Prime Minister Lord Salisbury and Baron von Hatzfelt, the German Ambassador to Great Britain.

The new Anglo-German alliance echoes the American open door policy enunciated recently by Secretary of State John Hay. However, British diplomatic sources stress that, while assent to that policy was general, the determination of the two great powers announced publicly to defend China's integrity can be expected to have greater weight.

The two governments agreed on four principles which will guide future policy in China:

(1) The ports shall remain free and open to the trade of all countries.

(2) The two governments will not exploit the instability resulting from the Boxer Rebellion to obtain territorial advantages in China.

(3) Should a third party do so, Great Britain and Germany will agree on the steps to be taken to protect their interests in China.

(4) The two governments will communicate the agreement to other interested powers, especially Austria-Hungary, France, Italy, Japan and the United States, and invite them to accept its principles.

Russia, diplomats noted, was not named as one of the interested powers. This omission was seen as a reproof for Russian failures to cooperate in the recently completed and successful military campaign against the Boxers and as an indication of the British government's desire to strengthen its relations with the German government.

French and Russian diplomats in London said that the agreement did not add materially to declarations made in Paris and St. Petersburg on the same issue (→ 29).

Writer Mark Twain comes home again

Mark Twain, born Samuel Clemens.

Oct 15. Mark Twain, author of many fine books, including a travel manual called "A Tramp Abroad," ended an absence from the United States of some nine years today when he returned to New York aboard the Atlantic Transport Line steamship Minnehaha. Looking fit, and in high spirits, the writer, greeted at the pier by friends, associates and newspaper reporters, gave a chronology of his travels through Europe, India and Africa, delivered himself of a few political comments, made mention of his autobiography (to be published in 100 years) and said of his plans: "I am absolutely unable to speak of his plans, inasmuch as I have none, and I do not expect to lecture" (→ 4/21/10).

1900

NOVEMBER

Su	Mo	Tu	We	Th	Fr	Sa
				1	2	3
4	5	6	7	8	9	10
11	12	13	14	15	16	17
18	19	20	21	22	23	24
25	26	27	28	29	30	

5. Cuban constitutional convention opens in Havana (→ 2/21/01).

6. Washington: Republicans gain majority in Senate and House.

6. South Africa: Boer guerrilla raids on British outposts grow in Orange River Colony and Transvaal (→ 22).

7. New York: Business world optimistic about McKinley's re-election; prices soar on Stock Exchange.

9. Russia has completed occupation of Manchuria with 100,000 troops (→ 3/15/01).

10. Berlin: In speech at Reichstag, Social Democrat Auguste Bebel condemns German policy in China (→ 1/11/01).

12. New York: Musical "Florodora" premieres at the Casino Theatre.

13. British Somalia: Deputy Commissioner Jenner assassinated during nationalist uprising.

15. August Strindberg's "To Damascus" opens in Sweden.

16. Colorado: Negro youth, accused of murder, burned at stake (→ 3/7/01).

21. Tennessee: Tornado takes 50 lives.

22. France: Exiled Boer leader Paul Kruger warmly received in Marseilles (→ 30).

23. Paris: Claude Monet's paintings shown at Gallery Durand-Ruel (→ 12/5/26).

30. A German engineer patents front-wheel drive for autos.

30. Paris: French government denounces British, declaring sympathy for Boers (→ 12/1).

BIRTHS

8. American writer Margaret Mitchell (†8/16/1949).

14. American composer Aaron Copland.

DEATH

30. Controversial British playwright and poet Oscar Wilde (*10/16/1854).

McKinley and Roosevelt win election

Nov 6. President William McKinley has been re-elected, along with his vice-presidential running mate, Governor Theodore Roosevelt of New York, leader of the famed Rough Riders during the recent Spanish-American War. Republicans also swept the congressional elections, winning increased majorities in both the Senate and the House of Representatives.

The election marked the second defeat for presidential office for William Jennings Bryan of Nebraska, who lost to McKinley four years ago. His running mate on the Democratic ticket this year was Adlai Stevenson of Illinois. And nearly 100,000 votes were cast for Eugene Debs, the Socialist candidate.

As election returns poured in yesterday, the president's hometown of Canton, Ohio, reverberated with cheers. As midnight approached, supporters marched to the McKinley home while bands played and rockets sent streaks through the darkened sky. Appearing on the porch of his house, the president greeted the cheering throngs by saying: "Fellow citizens, I thank you for the great compliment of this call on this inclement night, and at this late hour."

News of the election returns was received by Governor Roosevelt at his home on Sagamore Hill in Oyster Bay, New York. Returns from the various states were relayed to him by messengers from the local telegraph office in the railroad station, three miles away. After reading early returns, the governor commented: "Isn't that fine. It shows what the American people are. It shows that they want the good times to continue." The office of vice president has been vacant since the death of Garret Hobart last year.

McKinley and Roosevelt: "Four more years of the full dinner pail."

Music's immortal Arthur Sullivan gone

Nov 22. Sir Arthur Sullivan, who wrote some of the world's most enchanting music, will write no more. He died today at 58.

A bandmaster's son and a musical prodigy, he launched a collaboration in 1871 with W.S. Gilbert that produced a very British and most enduring series of operettas. The most popular was "H.M.S. Pinafore." It ran for 700 nights when first presented. Others included "The Pirates of Penzance," "The Mikado" and "The Gondoliers." Gilbert and Sullivan, their names forever linked, symbolized melody and laughter in the musical theater. Their works are repeatedly being performed somewhere in the world.

Sir Arthur also composed a persistently popular song, "The Lost Chord," and the rousing hymn, "Onward Christian Soldiers," as well as one serious opera.

The divine Sarah arrives in America

Sarah Bernhardt.

Nov 20. Clad in a long-sleeved, lace-trimmed gown beneath a white satin cloak, the French actress Sarah Bernhardt received the press at the Savoy Hotel in New York at the outset of her first visit since 1896. Characteristically animated, her hair close-cropped, she chattered about her voyage, her impending tour with a troupe of more than 50 performers and her plans to play the title role in "Hamlet" —"a piece I fear very much the American public will not like owing to its seriousness, and, for that reason only, I doubt its success" (→ 3/26/23).

Dead: Oscar Wilde, naughty but witty

Nov 30. Oscar Wilde's wit made him famous; his indiscretions destroyed him. He died in exile in Paris today, 46 and poor.

Oscar Fingal O'Flahertie Wills Wilde, son of a noted Dublin surgeon, won literary honors at Oxford. He became an apostle of the English Aesthetic Movement: "Art for Art's Sake." A poseur, effeminate in manner, he wore his hair long and dressed exotically. He carried a huge lily or sunflower. In this guise, he began an American lecture tour in 1882. He was ridiculed, but drew big crowds. His greatest success was as a playwright; his most popular play, "The Importance of Being Earnest."

England imprisoned him for homosexuality.

Oscar Wilde at 26.

1900

DECEMBER

Su	Mo	Tu	We	Th	Fr	Sa
						1
2	3	4	5	6	7	8
9	10	11	12	13	14	15
16	17	18	19	20	21	22
23	24	25	26	27	28	29
30	31					

1. Nicaragua sells canal rights to U.S. for $5 million (→ 3/11/01).

1. Berlin: Kaiser Wilhelm II refuses to meet with Boer leader Paul Kruger (→ 9).

1. Philadelphia: Navy defeats Army 11-7 in annual football game (→ 11/30/01).

4. Paris: A stunned National Assembly rejects nationalist Gen. Mercier's proposal to plan invasion of England.

9. Russia: Czar rejects Kruger's pleas for aid to Boers (→ 30).

14. Berlin: Max Planck presents quantum theory at the Physics Society.

16. U.S.: National Civic Federation formed to mediate between capital and labor; Mark Hanna is president and Samuel Gompers vice president.

19. France: Parliament votes amnesty for all involved in army treason trial known as Dreyfus Affair (→ 4/6/03).

20. Italian Minister of Foreign Affairs Emilio Visconti-Venosta guarantees Turkish sultan's sovereignty (→ 2/9/01).

23. Philippines: Federal Party formed; recognizes American sovereignty (→ 1/14/01).

CULTURAL EVENTS, 1900

Literature: Collette's "Claudine a l'ecole" (1st Claudine novel); Joseph Conrad's "Lord Jim"; Edmond Rostand's "L'Aiglon"; Theodore Dreiser's "Sister Carrie"; Anton Chekhov's "Uncle Vanya"; Frank Baum's "The Wonderful World of Oz"; Beatrix Potter's "The Tale of Peter Rabbit."

Religion, Academia: Shintoism revived in Japan; Sigmund Freud's "The Interpretation of Dreams"; Wilhelm Wundt's "Comparative Psychology."

Music: Puccini's opera "Tosca"; Debussy's "Nocturnes"; the cakewalk dance.

The Arts: Picasso's "Le Moulin de la Galette"; Cezanne's "Still Life with Onions"; Renoir's "Nude in the Sun"; Toulouse-Lautrec's "La Modiste"; Georges Melies' film "Cinderella."

Moving pictures seen in viewing rooms

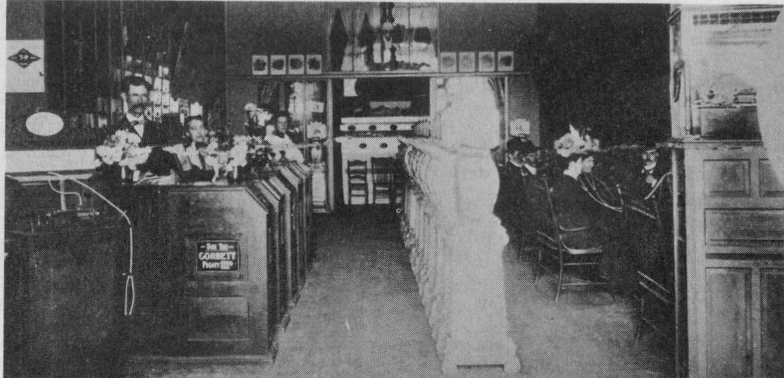

Phonograph and vitescope parlor, Spring Street, Los Angeles.

Moving pictures have been around since Thomas Edison and George Eastman designed their celluloid strips back in 1889, and over the last decade, millions of people have seen picture shows, but only individually and through some exertion. They have to turn the cranks on private viewing appliances to watch short films on small square screens. Projecting pictures on big screens in theaters is on the way.

$25,000 paid for kidnapped child

Dec 20. The 15-year-old son of Omaha millionaire Edward A. Cudahy, head of the Cudahy Packing Company, was released unharmed after Cudahy paid the $25,000 ransom in gold demanded by kidnappers. Thus ended two days of drama which saw Omaha's entire police and detective forces and private detective agencies scour the city to locate the young man, Edward. The kidnappers remain at large.

France and Italy share out Africa

Dec 16. Secret diplomacy today may have helped France tighten its grip on Morocco. In a secret exchange of letters, France agreed to respect Italy's sphere of influence in Libya, if Italy leaves France to its own devices in Morocco. Rome is very content with this agreement. But other European countries, aware of the strategic and commercial importance of Morocco, may not be quite so happy (→ 11/1/02).

This one-cyl. de Dion Bouton demonstrates how far motoring has come since N. Cugnot pumped the first steam-powered auto through the streets of Paris in 1769. Thanks to the de Dion high-speed engine, L. Renault and A. Peugeot are leading France to dominance in the auto industry.

Boer War still drags on wearily

Dec 30. Britain's Field Marshal Roberts has gone home from South Africa after a string of impressive victories against the Boers. He apparently thought the war was nearly over. It is not. Roberts' replacement, Lord Kitchener, has sent a series of confident cables home to London. They do not appear to tell the whole story of what is happening in South Africa.

This year, British forces have beaten the Boers at Kimberley, Ladysmith, Bloemfontein, Mafeking, Johannesburg and Pretoria. The British claimed they had swept the Boers from the Orange Free State, and they annexed the Transvaal. But the Boers have regrouped and they are stirring up new trouble.

British censors are restricting news about the war, but it appears the greatest threat from the Boers is in Cape Town. Dutch residents have been secretly hoarding ammunition and weapons, and they have joined insurgent Boers to fight against the British. There is concern in London that the Boers will be able to incite much of the Cape to rebel against Kitchener's forces.

The Boers are well-equipped, and the British troops are running low on supplies. The British War Office is trying to rush reinforcements and fresh horses to the Cape area. But heavy rains have knocked out key rail lines, and the poor weather has provided good cover for determined Boer guerrillas (→ 1/22/01).

Weary British troops cross a river in the Highveldt, central S. Africa.

1901

JANUARY

Su	Mo	Tu	We	Th	Fr	Sa
		1	2	3	4	5
6	7	8	9	10	11	12
13	14	15	16	17	18	19
20	21	22	23	24	25	26
27	28	29	30	31		

1. Sydney: Earl of Hopetoun sworn in as 1st governor general of Federated Australian Colonies (→ 5/9).

3. Washington: Census commissioner Robert Porter predicts U.S. population will be 300 mil. by 2001.

7. New York: Stock Exchange trading exceeds two mil. shares for first time in history.

10. Washington: Sen. Henry Cabot Lodge insists U.S. now dominates international trade.

10. New York: Automobile Club of America to install signs on major highways.

11. Russians and British agree on partition of China (→ 2/21).

14. Philippines: Leader of Iloilo province insurgents orders his men to lay down arms (→ 3/27).

16. Venezuelan troops demand surrender of American Asphalt Trust property; U.S. warship Scorpion sent to scene (→ 2/13).

18. Germany: Prussians celebrate bicentennial.

19. England: Queen Victoria stricken with paralysis (→ 22).

22. South Africa: Guerrilla raids drag on; Lord Kitchener begins burning Boer farms (→ 2/27).

23. Great fire ravages Montreal; $2.5 mil. in property lost.

23. France: First female intern accepted in Paris hospital.

30. Kansas: Twelve female Prohibitionists smash 12 saloons.

31. Anton Chekhov's "Three Sisters" premieres in Russia.

31. Pennsylvania: Pipeline links Penn. oil fields and Delaware Bay; first successful competition to Standard Oil.

31. France: Army and navy ban corporal punishment.

BIRTH

16. Cuban dictator Fulgencio Batista (†8/6/1973).

DEATH

6. Philip Armour, developed Chicago stockyards (*5/16/1832).

Queen Victoria dies; son is king

Jan 22. An era ended today when Queen Victoria died at Cowes on the Isle of Wight. She was 82. At her bedside were her son and successor, the Prince of Wales, who had decided to reign as Edward VII, and many other descendants, including her grandson William II, Emperor of Germany.

Queen Victoria's reign spanned more than half a century and saw the acquisition of many new lands overseas, resulting in a British Empire where "the sun never sets" and making her Empress of India. The stability and dignity of her reign also restored the popularity of the monarchy. Most of her subjects around the world had never known a Britain not ruled by Victoria.

Victoria was a young woman when she acceded to the throne in 1837. She became devoted to her husband, Prince Albert of Saxe-Coburg-Gotha, and relied on him for his advice. She was grief-stricken at his death in 1861, and spent the last 40 years in mourning.

Victoria, Queen of England and Ireland, Empress of India.

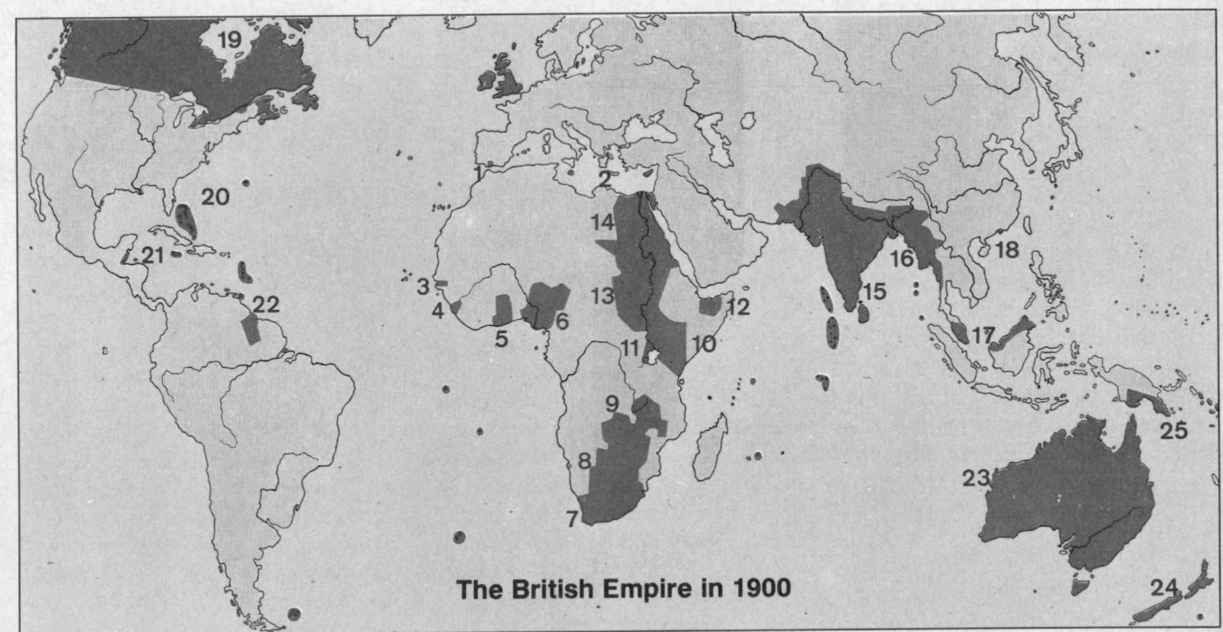

Europe
1 Gibraltar
2 Malta and Cyprus

Africa
3 Gambia
4 Sierra Leone
5 Gold Coast
6 Nigeria
7 Cape Colony
8 Bechuanaland
9 Rhodesia
10 Kenya
11 Uganda
12 British Somaliland
13 Anglo-Egyptian Sudan
14 Egypt

Asia
15 India, Ceylon
16 Burma
17 Malaysian States
18 Hong Kong

America
19 Canadian Confederation
20 Bahamas and Bermuda
21 Jamaica and Honduras
22 British Guyana

Australia
23 Australian Commonwealth
24 New Zealand
25 British New Guinea

Seas and Oceans
Many islands of the world

Spindletop gusher amazes oilmen

Jan 10. An oil strike greater than any the world has seen was reported today by a jubilant band of drillers. At 10:30 a.m., a well four miles south of the town of Beaumont, Texas, erupted with a roar, spewing a tower of oil 200 feet into the air. Estimates are that the well is producing at least 75,000 barrels a day, as much as the total pumped from the 37,000 wells in the eastern United States and about half of the nation's current oil consumption.

The Spindletop well, so called because it was drilled on Spindletown Heights, a barely visible rise on the Texas plain, is a tribute to the tenacity of Patillo Higgins, a Beaumont resident who became convinced years ago there was oil to be found in the area. In 1893, Higgins got financial support to start drilling a well, but it was abandoned at a depth of 418 feet when the money ran out. Two other efforts also were dry holes. Desperate for backing, Higgins placed an advertisement in a New York trade journal. It was answered by Captain Anthony Lucas, an Austrian mining engineer who had become a naturalized American citizen.

Lucas' studies led him to believe there was oil in the subterranean salt dome formation near Beaumont, a belief experts scoffed at. When Lucas asked Standard Oil, the world's largest oil firm, for money, one of its experts, Calvin Payne, looked at Spindletop and said, "You'll never find oil here." Another Standard Oil executive, John Archbold, offered to "drink every gallon of oil found west of the Mississippi." Lucas pressed on, even selling some of the family furniture at one time to pay for food. The well was brought in by the Hamill brothers of Texas, who invented a variety of techniques to overcome drilling problems.

The success at Spindletop not only confounds the experts but also could alter the global balance of petroleum power. Russia now is the world's leading oil producer, at 185,000 barrels a day. Two or three more wells like the "Lucas gusher," as it has been dubbed, would put the United States back in the lead it held until recently. As other oilmen hasten toward Beaumont, the Hillmans are considering how they can cap the gusher (→ 4/7/02).

The Lucas gusher at Spindletop.

Filipinos ask freedom from United States

Jan 14. Filipinos are rising up in protest against American annexation of their country, but a lack of coordination in their efforts makes their success uncertain. Today, a petition signed by 2,000 middle-class Manilans was presented to the United States Senate. It appeals for independence and even invokes the names of Washington and Jefferson.

Uncle Sam will guide the Philippines.

Meanwhile, radical insurgents, impatient with diplomacy, are murdering Americans and American sympathizers. General Arthur MacArthur, stationed in Manila, has ordered life imprisonment or hanging for convicted killers.

Despite differences in tactics, many guerrillas and moderates support Emilio Aguinaldo, who joined the United States in the ouster of Spain in 1898, and established the present republic in 1899. He maintains his hold on the presidency despite constant rumors of defeat.

A majority of Americans urge annexation, but a vocal few, including Mark Twain, Andrew Carnegie and several Senate Democrats, call the present policy a failure. No one can deny that more American lives have been lost in the last three years of insurgency than during the entire Spanish-American War. And whoever wins the Philippines will inherit the spoils: a tottering economy and rampant crime (→ 3/27).

Death takes Verdi from opera scene

Jan 27. Giuseppe Verdi, the foremost Italian composer of the 19th century, is dead in Milan. For nearly 60 years, Verdi dominated Italian opera, achieving success with his third effort, "Nabucco," the story of Nebuchadnezzar, in 1842. "Rigoletto," in 1851, followed rapidly by "Il Trovatore" and "La Traviata," in 1853, established his mastery. His admiration for Shakespearean drama was manifest in such operas as "Otello" and "Macbeth"; his most renowned works also included "Rigoletto" and "Aida."

It was an irony that Verdi, born in 1813, faced rejection early when he applied for admission to the Conservatory of Milan, where the musician in charge concluded that Verdi revealed no aptitude. Now the richness and inventiveness of his music have earned him a place in the pantheon inhabited by such composers as Mozart and Wagner.

1901

FEBRUARY

Su	Mo	Tu	We	Th	Fr	Sa
					1	2
3	4	5	6	7	8	9
10	11	12	13	14	15	16
17	18	19	20	21	22	23
24	25	26	27	28		

2. Mexico: Government troops badly beaten by Yaqui Indians; 100 killed.

4. New York: Puccini's "Tosca" makes U.S. debut at Metropolitan Opera.

7. Russia: Fires rage in Baku oil fields.

9. Austro-Hungarian foreign minister guarantees Turkish sovereignty (→ 4/5).

13. Asphalt trust yields to Venezuelan expropriation demands.

14. Spain: Martial law declared in Madrid to quell rioting in tax protest.

21. Allied powers agree on China; no more territorial concessions to be obtained without international consent (→ 3/15).

21. Cuban delegates adopt constitution; U.S. troops remain (→ 3/2).

21. Switzerland: Albert Einstein becomes citizen of Zurich.

22. San Francisco: Pacific mail steamer sinks in Golden Gate harbor; 128 passengers killed.

23. British and Germans agree on boundary between German East Africa and Nyasaland.

26. Peking: Boxer rebels Chi-Hsin and Hsu-Cheng-Yu publicly executed (→ 4/24).

27. England: Upon failure of Middleburg peace conference, Natl. Liberal Federation condemns British insistence on unconditional surrender of Boers (→ 5/31).

27. Russia: Angered at repression in schools, Socialist-Revolutionaries assassinate Minister of Education Bogolepov (→ 3/23).

BIRTHS

1. Clark Gable, American actor (†11/16/1960).

2. Russian Jascha Heifetz, violin virtuoso.

20. Ali Mohammed Naguib Egyptian general.

DEATH

11. Milan I, ex-king of Serbia (*8/22/1854).

Saloon smasher, Carrie Nation on warpath

Six-foot-tall crusader Carrie Nation.

Feb 15. Hatchet in hand, Mrs. Carrie Nation spent a busy day today thrashing vice in Topeka, Kansas, in her continued crusade against the evils of alcohol. Vowing never to rest until all saloons are closed, she and her army of 500 men and women laid siege to the town joints, leaving in their wake a flotsam of splintered kegs and fractured glass.

First to fall was Murphy's place, where Mrs. Nation hurled her hatchet through a window. After breaching the door, the group vented their wrath on beer kegs, bottles and mirrors, humbling in a matter of minutes the once proud saloon.

Between brief bouts in jail, Mrs. Nation addressed a mass meeting. "Women!" she implored. "We must be about the work of the Lord. There are yet some hell-holes here which have not been closed up in spite of promises to the contrary" (→ 9/1).

Morgan forms $1 billion steel company

Feb 5. J. Pierpont Morgan is the only man of steel today, having bought some of John D. Rockefeller's iron mines and Andrew Carnegie's entire steel business. The purchase is the most expensive act of consolidation in American business history. The mines, located in Mesabi, Minn., and the Pittsburgh steel works cost Morgan $1 billion.

Morgan bases his company, U.S. Steel Corporation, on methods used by the railroads to eliminate competition. Under his "community of interest" system, heads of giant corporations can privately cooperate while companies supposedly compete. "America is good enough for me," Morgan once said. To which William Jennings Bryan replied, "Whenever he doesn't like it, he can give it back" (→ 1/29/02).

Great Britain's King Edward VII and Queen Alexandra open the first session of Parliament since Queen Victoria's death last month.

1901

MARCH

Su	Mo	Tu	We	Th	Fr	Sa
					1	2
3	4	5	6	7	8	9
10	11	12	13	14	15	16
17	18	19	20	21	22	23
24	25	26	27	28	29	30
31						

2. Washington: Congress passes Platt amendment, limiting Cuban autonomy as a condition for withdrawal of U.S. troops (→ 25).

4. Wm. McKinley inaugurated president for second time; Theodore Roosevelt is vice president (→ 9/6).

5. Hoping to establish an alliance, Germany and Great Britain begin negotiations.

6. Bremen: Anarchist assassin tries to kill Wilhelm II.

7. Blacks found enslaved in parts of S. Carolina (→ 8/1).

11. Nicaraguan canal agreement fails; Great Britain rejects amended treaty (→ 8/7).

15. Berlin: Chancellor von Bulow declares that an agreement between China and Russia over Manchuria would violate Anglo-German accord of Oct. 1900 (→ 22).

17. Paris: Van Gogh's paintings shown at Bernheim Gallery.

22. Japan proclaims it is determined to prevent Russian encroachment near Korea (→ 4/3).

23. Shots fired at Privy Councilor Pobyedonostzev, Russia's most hated man (→ 31).

23. World learns with awe that Boers are starving in British concentration camps (→ 5/31).

24. French census estimates national population at 38,962,000.

25. It is reported in Washington that Cubans are beginning to fear annexation (→ 5/31).

31. Russia: Premiere of Anton Dvorak's opera "Rusalka."

31. Russia: Czar lashes out at Socialist-Revolutionaries; 72 arrested, two printing presses seized (→ 1/25/02).

BIRTH

18. Russo-German dancer Tatiana Gsovsky (†1/24/1982).

DEATH

13. U.S. politician Benjamin Harrison, 23rd president (*8/20/1833).

Retiring, Carnegie gives away fortune

March 13. Andrew Carnegie announced today that he is retiring from business and will spend the rest of his days giving away his fortune, which is now estimated to be greater than $300 million.

The steel baron made his announcement in a letter addressed to "the good people of Pittsburgh," the city where he made his money. He also announced a $4 million gift to establish a fund for old and disabled employees of the Carnegie Steel Company, the corporation that was the primary source of his wealth.

Carnegie began his philanthropic work several years ago, endowing libraries in cities throughout the United States. He continued this tradition today with a $1 million donation to establish libraries in the Pennsylvania cities of Braddock, Duquesne and Homestead.

Carnegie's retirement ends one of the most remarkable careers in American industry. Starting as a penniless immigrant, he became a millionaire in his mid-20's by shrewd and aggressive leadership in oil and railroads. Moving into the steel industry before the age of 30, Carnegie quickly became its dominant figure. When Carnegie Steel was sold to the newly formed United States Steel Corporation this year, his share of the proceeds was over $225 million. Carnegie sailed today for a summer-long stay at his estate in his native Scotland (→ 3/13/02).

Andrew Carnegie.

Americans capture Filipino rebel leader

Emilio Aguinaldo boards an American gunboat after his capture.

March 27. Emilio Aguinaldo, daring leader of the Filipino rebels, has been captured by the Americans. His arrest, less than two months after the surrender of the leader of the Iloilo province insurgents, has encouraged Washington to hope that the long rebellion in the Philippines may finally be at an end.

The capture of the elusive rebel leader was planned by General Frederick Funston, who tricked Aguinaldo into giving away the location of his headquarters by disguising himself as a prisoner of the rebels. Aguinaldo's fame as a nationalist leader precedes American control of the Philippines, which dates only from 1898. In 1896, Aguinaldo led a rebellion against Spanish rule, which had lasted 400 years (→ 4/19).

Effort to change Utah polygamy law fails

March 14. Utah Governor Heber M. Wells has vetoed a bill that would have eased restrictions on polygamy. The governor acted just days after the legislature passed the measure, which would have made it virtually impossible to prosecute those accused of plural marriages.

Polygamy, once widely practiced by members of the Church of Latter Day Saints (Mormons), early settlers in the state, was officially outlawed when Utah became a state of the union in 1894. But sponsors of the bill had argued that "agitators" have been crusading against Mormons by making widespread accusations of polygamy. Such attacks, they argued, were prompted by religious bias. The legislators argued that most persons in Utah with plural marriages are now dead and that the few remaining ones are quite old (→ 3/3/04).

Where did the Mercedes car get its name? From a pretty little Viennese girl named Mercedes Jellinek. Gottlieb Daimler's German firm made the car. It was named in honor of the daughter of Emil Jellinek, Austrian Consul General in Nice, in gratitude for his enthusiastic patronage. This month in Nice, Mercedes racers reached speeds of up to 53 mph.

1901

APRIL

Su	Mo	Tu	We	Th	Fr	Sa
	1	2	3	4	5	6
7	8	9	10	11	12	13
14	15	16	17	18	19	20
21	22	23	24	25	26	27
28	29	30				

1. Texas oil companies form billion dollar trust (→ 4/7/02).

1. According to census figures, British population has reached 37,093,436 plus 4.4 mil. Irish.

3. To avoid alienating Germany, England and Japan, China refuses to sign Manchurian treaty with Russia (→ 10).

5. Bulgaria: Under pressure from Ottoman Turkish govt., officials arrest Macedonians committed to Bulgarian independence from Turkey (→ 6/16).

8. Belgium: Congress of Social Democrats insists on enforcement of universal suffrage.

10. Japan accepts Russian declaration of good faith in Manchuria, averting Russo-Japanese rupture (→ 6/28).

11. American beef barred from British army.

14. New York: Actors arrested at Academy of Music for wearing costumes on Sunday.

15. Vatican: Pope Leo XIII condemns trend toward state regulation of Catholic Church throughout Europe (→ 7/1).

19. Manila: Aguinaldo issues proclamation acknowledging American sovereignty (→ 30).

22. New York: War play "Winchester" debuts at The American Theatre.

23. Venezuela ostracized; five allied powers refuse to recognize its supreme court's decisions on intl. debt (→ 12/9/02).

24. China: Allied troops rout Boxers to avenge killing of Major Browning (→ 5/29).

25. Spain: Catalonians demand separation of church and state as thousands demonstrate against Jesuits.

29. Budapest: Jewish students clash with anti-Semites at national university.

29. Jockey Winkfield rides His Eminence to victory in Kentucky Derby.

30. Manila: Gen. Tinio, prominent rebel leader, surrenders his entire command to U.S. Army (→ 7/4).

Sculpture by Rodin arouses passions

Auguste Rodin's "Hugo."

April 21. Auguste Rodin's sculpture of author Victor Hugo aroused some violent passions today during its display at the Grand Palais in Paris, and most of those emotions were not intended by the artist. His rendering of the renowned French novelist as a semi-nude figure shocked many art patrons.

It is not the first time that Rodin has elicited criticism. In 1897, his interpretation of another great writer, Honore de Balzac, won him scorn when he tried to fuse the image of the man with scenes of his multi-volume masterpiece "The Human Comedy." Detractors called that work clumsy and unfinished.

The 60-year-old sculptor may treasure all these denouncements the way he welcomed criticism of his first major work, "The Age of Bronze," in 1876. That statue, an unromanticized vision of a young man, was accused of being too lifelike not to have been cast directly from a model.

1901

MAY

Su	Mo	Tu	We	Th	Fr	Sa
			1	2	3	4
5	6	7	8	9	10	11
12	13	14	15	16	17	18
19	20	21	22	23	24	25
26	27	28	29	30	31	

1. Berlin: German authorities demand from China 65 mil. pounds sterling to cover allied losses in Boxer war (→ 29).

1. Belgium: Publication of Maurice Maeterlinck's "The Life of the Bee."

6. France: Miners end 3-month strike as negotiations fail.

8. India: British commission claims famine has taken 1.25 mil. lives since 1899; blames overpopulation.

9. First Australian Parliament meets in Melbourne (→ 7/17/02).

10. Dublin: Officials of the crown seize all copies of "The Irish People" for criticism of King Edward (→ 14).

18. San Francisco: President McKinley attends launching of battleship Ohio.

18. Albany: Striking railroad workers forced back to work by state militia.

21. West Point: Cadets convicted of hazing, insubordination; five dismissed, six suspended.

23. Italy: King Humbert's assassin, Gaetano Bresci, commits suicide while awaiting execution in prison.

27. Washington: Supreme Court outlaws customs duties on Cuban imports; non-continental territories appear to have U.S. citizenship rights (→ 7/25).

28. Tehran: William Knox D'Arcy granted concession to explore for oil in Persia.

29. Allied troops begin to pull out of China (→ 6/30).

30. London: World premiere of Charles Stanford's opera "Much Ado 'bout Nothing."

31. U.S. insists Cuba must accept Platt amendment or troops will not be withdrawn (→ 6/12).

31. South Africa: Guerrilla war rages; Boers kill 174 British at Vlakfontein (→ 6/21).

BIRTH

7. American film star Gary Cooper (†10/27/1964).

Panic sets in as market collapses

Traders rush to buy Northern Pacific as prices plunge.

May 9. In the largest single-day break on Wall Street since 1803, mayhem ruled today as previously rational men punched and kicked each other in the scramble to unload their plunging stocks.

Quotations started falling at about 1 p.m. By closing, some prices had crashed a full 20 points. The situation was so critical that bankers conferred late into the night to find a means to prevent total financial catastrophe. Although this plunge has been predicted by some, it caught many by surprise. All eyes had been on the phenomenal rise in Northern Pacific stock, which gained 70 points in three days. It remained unscathed, with a net gain of 16.5 at the end of an otherwise disastrous day.

British Prime Minister opposes freedom in any degree for the Irish people

May 14. Prime Minister Lord Salisbury reiterated his opposition to any degree of freedom for Ireland in a speech last night before the Nonconformist Unionist Association.

The prime minister, who helped defeat Gladstone's home-rule bill in 1893, speculated on the problem a free and hostile Ireland would have presented to Britain during the recent war in South Africa. "We know now that if we allowed those who are leading Irish politics unlimited power ... we should have to begin by conquering Ireland, if ever we had to fight any other power."

Prime Minister Lord Salisbury.

Heated debate over the Irish question has taken place recently in Parliament in the aftermath of the seizure of the weekly paper, The Irish People. Copies of the paper were ordered removed from newsdealers' shops May 10 because of an article viciously attacking King Edward. Nationalist members of Parliament have called the seizure "grossly illegal" since it was not carried out through the courts (→ 1/8/02).

10,000 homeless in Jacksonville fire

May 3. A defective wire at a factory in Jacksonville, Florida, is thought to have sparked the worst fire in the city's history. The fire caused about $15 million damage and left 10,000 to 15,000 homeless.

An area two miles long by a half-mile wide was razed and about 130 blocks were scorched, many in the heart of the business and residential sections of town. An estimated 1,300 houses were destroyed, along with hotels, theaters, shops and churches. Casualties could not be immediately determined. Fed by strong winds, the blaze spread so quickly that firefighters were unable to get it under control. After about ten hours, it finally burned itself out.

Speeders pay $10

May 11. Members of the Automobile Club of America were arrested today in Morristown, New Jersey, for breaking the speed limit. The drivers violated the posted eight-mile-an-hour ordinance during a cross-state race. Witnesses said the auto enthusiasts had reached speeds up to 30 miles per hour. When the gentlemen stopped for lunch at a local hostelry, the Morristown justice of the peace presented them with a lump fine of $10. The three drivers and one machinist promptly paid the ticket.

1901 Oldsmobile.

Shamrock wrecked with King aboard

May 22. A sudden squall has wrecked the yacht Shamrock II and dashed the hopes of the British challenger for this year's America's Cup races against the Americans.

The lives of King Edward and other distinguished persons on board were endangered when the wind rose and swept the mast and spars from the new yacht. All, including the owner, Sir Thomas Lipton, escaped without injury. "No one is more thankful than I am that the catastrophe ended without fatality," said Sir Thomas, "and I may say that throughout the trying moments, his Majesty was brave as a lion."

He said that he would ask the New York Yacht Club, host for the prestigious race, for extra time in which to repair the Shamrock II. "I have nothing but the hull left," he said sadly. "I was terribly cast down when I saw what a terrible wreck that beautiful boat was, but now I think things can be remodeled." The damage to the challenger, which was on a practice run, was estimated at $9,000 (→ 10/4).

1901

JUNE

Su	Mo	Tu	We	Th	Fr	Sa
						1
2	3	4	5	6	7	8
9	10	11	12	13	14	15
16	17	18	19	20	21	22
23	24	25	26	27	28	29
30						

2. New York: Police arrest Benjamin Adams of the Yonkers Board of Education for playing golf on Sunday.

10. Belgium: Parliament decides to postpone annexation date for Congo (→ 7/17).

13. New York: Collision sinks Staten Island Ferry.

15. Samoa's foreign governor imposes German as official language in schools.

16. Bulgaria: Macedonian demonstrators in Sofia demand independence from Turkey (→ 7/24/02).

18. Following 30% hike four months ago, Russia again raises tariffs on U.S. imports.

20. U.S. asks Russia to arbitrate dispute with U.K. over Alaskan boundary (→ 10/16/03).

21. London: A stormy pro-Boer meeting gathers; liberals remain divided on question of annexation (→ 7/3).

21. New Jersey: Mysterious explosion wrecks four-story building, killing 17.

22. New York: Genevieve Hecker retains Women's Metropolitan Golf Championship.

23. West Virginia: Cloudburst over mining towns kills 200.

24. West Virginia: Striking miners open fire on deputy marshals.

26. St. John's, Newfoundland: Lusitania wrecked off Cape Ballard; 350 rescued.

27. Connecticut: Yale defeats Harvard in annual crew competition.

28. Entire province of Manchuria in revolt against Russian occupation (→ 10/16).

30. China: Empress Dowager sets up future capital at Kai-fung-Foo in Ho-Nan province (→ 9/7).

BIRTHS

6. Akhmed Sukarno, Indonesian independence leader (†6/21/1970).

18. Anastasia, daughter of Russia's Czar Nicholas II (†7/16/1918).

Paris sees first Picassos

Detail of Pablo Picasso's self-portrait, "Yo Picasso."

June 24. The young Spanish artist named Pablo Picasso is exhibiting his work at Ambroise Vollard's fashionable gallery on the Rue Lafitte for the first time. And, in the words of a noted art critic, "Picasso is a painter definitely, he loves color for itself." Born in Malaga in 1881, Picasso came to Paris in October 1900. Though often near starvation, he became infatuated with the street life of Montmartre and has made many studies of the poor people of Paris.

Becquerel presents radium discoveries

Henri Becquerel at work.

June 12. The French physicist Antoine Becquerel has identified the source of the mysterious radiation he detected in a mineral sample as electrons from atoms of the element uranium. Becquerel's discovery is the first clear indication that atoms, the smallest units of matter, have an internal structure.

The initial discovery was made in 1896, when Becquerel placed a sample of potassium uranyl sulfate on a sheet of photographic film and found the film blackened a few hours later. Two years later, another physicist, Marie Curie, named this phenomenon "radioactivity." Becquerel now has discovered that the rays from the mineral have the same characteristics as the electrons (→ 12/10/03).

Cuba will become a U.S. protectorate

June 12. The Cuban constitutional convention has voted 16 to 11 to unconditionally adopt the Platt amendment. Under the provisions of the Platt amendment, Cuba may not enter into any treaty that would interfere with its independence; in the event that Cuban independence is threatened, the United States is empowered to intervene. The United States will also be allowed to purchase or lease sites on Cuba for naval bases and coaling stations.

McKinley administration officials were pleased by Cuban acceptance of the amendment and believe that withdrawal of American military forces will begin soon. However, officials note that American evacuation cannot take place until it is clear that a stable government is in place and that Cuba's police force is capable of maintaining order on the island, which was liberated from Spain in 1898.

Secretary of War Elihu Root, a strong proponent of the Platt amendment, characterized the constitutional convention's action as "the wisest and most patriotic thing possible for Cuba" (→ 5/20/02).

Henri Fournier wins Paris-Berlin race

June 15. Automobile enthusiasts throughout France are thrilled by the news that their countryman, Henri Fournier, has won the Paris-to-Berlin race for the Emperor William II prize. Second and third places also went to Frenchmen, Leonce Girardot and Henri-Charles Brasier, respectively. The race was divided into three legs totaling 750 miles, which Fournier covered in just 11 hours, 46 minutes and ten seconds.

Fournier approaches the finish line.

1901

JULY

Su	Mo	Tu	We	Th	Fr	Sa
	1	2	3	4	5	6
7	8	9	10	11	12	13
14	15	16	17	18	19	20
21	22	23	24	25	26	27
28	29	30	31			

1. France: Despite protest from Catholic Church, Association Law goes into effect, restricting public activities of religious groups (→ 9/19).

1. France: New electric railway inaugurated in Paris.

3. New Orleans: Boer delegation appeals to Americans to stop shipments of supplies to British (→ 27).

10. Wimbledon: Arthur Gore over Reginald Doherty 4-6, 7-5, 6-4, 6-4; Charlotte Sterry over Blanche Hill 6-2, 6-2.

12. Germany: Members of Reichstag unsuccessfully move to outlaw dueling.

13. France: Brazilian aviator Santos-Dumont crashes in Boulogne after circling Eiffel Tower in dirigible.

15. Pittsburgh: 74,000 steel workers go out on strike (→ 1/29/02).

16. Philippines: Miguel Malvas, Aguinaldo's successor as head of revolution, calls for insurgency to continue (→ 9/29).

17. Atlantic Ocean: Liner Deutschland sets east to west transatlantic record of 5 days, 11 hours and 5 minutes.

20. Franco-Moroccan accord fixes border between Morocco and Algieria, places trade and police functions under French control. (→ 1/13/03).

22. Serbia restores diplomatic relations with Montenegro.

22. Great Britain: House of Lords rules in Taff Vale Railway case; trade unions may be sued for actions of members.

25. Washington: President McKinley issues proclamation for free trade with Puerto Rico (→ 12/2).

27. South Africa: Boers invade Swaziland (→ 29).

29. Land lottery begins in Oklahoma (→ 8/9).

31. Revolt flares in Venezuela; 5,000 insurgents rise against President Castro (→ 7/7/02).

BIRTH

31. French artist Jean Dubuffet (†5/12/1985).

Taft installed as Governor of Philippines

A robust William Howard Taft greets dignitaries in the Philippines.

July 4. William Howard Taft, the Ohio-born judge, was inaugurated as Civil Governor of the Philippines this morning, bringing to an end military rule on most of the islands. At the same time, General Arthur MacArthur, the autocratic Military Governor of the islands since May 1900, turned over his powers to Major General Adna Chaffee, who will be subordinate to Taft. MacArthur then set sail with his family for Japan.

This day marked a victory for Taft in his year-long battle with MacArthur over the political control of the islands. Since the failure of the amnesty effort to end the rebellion of the Filipinos against American rule, MacArthur has been enforcing the law in Draconian fashion.

Taft, who has served as president of the U.S. Philippine Commission this last year, has indicated that he favors independence for the Filipinos and he has expressed sympathy for his "little brown brothers." A letter from President McKinley was read at the inauguration, congratulating Taft on his good works already accomplished (→ 16).

King Leopold will keep rights to exploit natural resources in Congo Free State

July 17. King Leopold of Belgium announced today that he will not formally annex the Congo. He will also not relinquish the control which has already made him an immense personal fortune. Under the agreement between Belgium and the Congo Free State, Leopold will have the primary rights to exploit the riches of the area.

It is likely he will also continue to exploit the natives. Leopold has outlawed the slave trade in the Congo, but reports from the area indicate he has turned many of the natives into his personal slaves. The profit from their work goes directly into Leopold's pockets.

Leopold became interested in the Congo as soon as he learned that the Congo River was navigable. Henry Stanley, the explorer, helped him set up the Congo Free State, whereupon Leopold set himself up as the monarch and chief stockholder. The wealth of the area is enormous. It is rich in diamonds, gold, copper and lead. And the climate is conducive to growing rubber, coffee and cotton (→ 5/20/03).

Oldsmobile cars to be made in quantity

Ransom E. Olds predicts he will produce and sell over 400 of his curved-dash Oldsmobiles before the year is out. The $650 vehicle, which resembles a horseless buggy, is affordable by many middle-class families. Still, Olds cannot assume the public will prefer his experimental internal-combustion engine to a steam-driven one. Among Olds' 20-odd competitors are the Stanley brothers, whose tough ten-horsepower Steamers are said to handle uphill climbs with superior ease.

Hills are no match for the Oldsmoblile curved dash.

Lorillard, patron of tuxedo, is dead

July 7. Pierre Lorillard IV made his money from tobacco; he spent it on pleasure and elegance. Unwittingly, he introduced to millions of Americans an unusual word: tuxedo. Today he died.

In 1886, he opened Tuxedo Park, a lavish walled refuge for his rich friends, near New York. That year Mr. and Mrs. James Porter Brown were invited to dine with the Prince of Wales, who is now King Edward VII. Surprisingly, the prince appeared in a short black coat instead of a tailcoat. Brown took the fashion back to Tuxedo; the young bucks chopped off their tailcoats, which became known as tuxedos. It is not recorded whether Pierre Lorillard ever wore a tuxedo or not.

This gentleman's jacket, a tailcoat without tails, debuted in 1886 at Lorillard's estate in Tuxedo, N.Y.

Kipling speaks out on the Boer War

July 29. Rudyard Kipling, the renowned author of stories and poems about colonial India and an unofficial spokesman for the British Empire, has joined the rising chorus of criticism in regard to Britain's conduct in the increasingly unpopular Boer War. He writes in the Times of London: "We have 40 million reasons for our failure, but not one excuse. Consequently, the more we work and the less we talk, the better it will be. If we learn this lesson of imperialism, we will keep our empire" (→ 10/23).

1901

AUGUST

Su	Mo	Tu	We	Th	Fr	Sa
				1	2	3
4	5	6	7	8	9	10
11	12	13	14	15	16	17
18	19	20	21	22	23	24
25	26	27	28	29	30	31

1. Great Britain: House of Commons votes additional 12.5 mil. pounds for navy and defense budget.

1. Carrollton, Mississippi: Black mother and 2 children lynched after white couple found dead. (→ 10/16).

7. Boston: Warship Machias sent to isthmus to help keep rail lines open during attacks by liberal revolutionaries in control of Panama (→ 11/20).

7. Francisco Alcantara, graduate of West Point, becomes president of Aragua, one of largest states in Venezuela.

14. Bridgeport, Conn.: It is claimed that G. Weisskopf has flown a motor-powered vehicle designed by Wright brothers.

15. Paintings of Wassily Kandinsky shown at Munich.

15. Brighton Beach, N.Y.: Cresceus takes trotting championship in record-breaking time.

17. England: Imperialist phrase, "and of the British Dominions beyond the Seas," added to King Edward VII's title.

20. France: President Emile Loubet invites Russia's Czar Nicholas II to attend French military maneuvers.

21. Turkey: French ambassador breaks off relations over Turkish refusal to settle indemnity claim for 1896 losses to French citizens (→ 11/7).

22. Detroit: Cadillac Co. founded, named after 18th c. French explorer Antoine de la Mothe Cadillac.

26. Austro-Hungarian press warns of Russian maneuvers in Balkans.

BIRTHS

3. Cardinal Stefan Wyszynski, Polish prelate (+4/28/1981).

29. Nuclear physicist Enrico Fermi (+11/24/1954).

DEATH

5. British Princess Victoria, wife of Emperor Frederick III (*12/21/1840).

Settlers given vast Indian lands

Aug 9. Oklahoma Territory has grown by 2,080,000 acres overnight, and a lucky 6,500 homesteaders have staked their claims. Federal agents acquired the fertile land south of the Cimarron River from the Comanche, Kiowa and Apache for $2 million. Ranchers and railway barons lobbied for the purchase, seeking grazing grounds and increased traffic, respectively. Miners know the area offers coal reserves, and farmers believe the soil is good for corn, wheat and cotton.

Previous expansion in Oklahoma had been a chaotic affair; in the 1889 land rush the mad scramble resulted in at least one death. This time, authorities submitted nearly 170,000 would-be claimants to an orderly lottery. The winners are required to remain on their allotments for five years before obtaining titles.

The land would have been available to the public sooner if the Indians living on the eastern half of the territory had not known their rights and exercised them so well. The tribes there have written constitutions and well-established systems of self-government. They demanded, in addition to the cash payment, a 160-acre allotment for each member of their tribes.

The lands opened to white settlers amount to 64,690 square miles.

Beginnings of a town; auction at Anadarko Townsite, Oklahoma Territory.

World bike record set for 1-mile run

Aug 26. Robert Walthour put on pressure for all 15 miles as he shattered numerous bicycle records in his match race against John Nelson at Madison Square Garden yesterday. He outsped the Chicagoan by a mile and a half and, on the way, lowered to 1:37.4 the mile mark set a week earlier by Jimmy Michaels of Wales. But where Michaels eased up after his record 1:52.4 mile, Walthour went on to shatter other records. Nelson, slowed by flat tires and burned-out motor pacers, was 50 yards behind Walthour after the second mile.

Wheelmen race to the finish line.

Slavery still found in a Southern state

Aug 1. The grand jury of Anderson County, Georgia, issued a report today containing shocking evidence that slavery is being practiced by three of the most prominent planters in the state.

A charge of false imprisonment was made against the planters, who reportedly had been confining in their stockades Negroes who had been sent there for some petty reason and never convicted of any legal offense. The Negroes were, in effect, undergoing a term of servitude under voluntary contracts they had signed in ignorance, according to the grand jury. The official report also included details of illegal arrests, whippings, kidnappings and other acts of cruelty. These revelations have demoralized the local work force just at the time when crops are being planted (→ 10/16).

1901

SEPTEMBER

Su	Mo	Tu	We	Th	Fr	Sa
1	2	3	4	5	6	7
8	9	10	11	12	13	14
15	16	17	18	19	20	21
22	23	24	25	26	27	28
29	30					

1. New York: Carrie Nation arrested on 8th Avenue after attracting dense crowds of unruly supporters.

2. Minnesota: Speaking at a state fair, V.P. Teddy Roosevelt quotes an African proverb, "Speak softly and carry a big stick, you will go far."

6. Buffalo, N.Y.: Anarchist Leon Czolgosz shoots President McKinley twice at close range (→ 7).

7. Buffalo: Czolgosz confesses to attempted assassination of McKinley (→ 10).

8. Russia: The battleship Borodino is launched.

9. Austria-Hungary re-establishes diplomatic relations with Mexico.

10. New York: Upon assassin's mention of her name, Emma Goldman is arrested on suspicion of conspiracy to kill the president (→ 14).

14. William McKinley, 25th U.S. president, dies of assassin's bullet wounds.→

16. Germany: Employers come out in favor of customs duties (→ 24).

19. Spain: Government decree requires that political and religious associations register at their prefectures (→ 10/3).

21. Louisiana's first oil well opens at Jenning's Field, Acadia Parish.

24. Germany: Lubeck congress of Social Democrats opposes reform of customs duties.

25. Britain annexes Ashanti kingdom to Gold Coast colony.

26. Buffalo: President's assassin Czolgosz sentenced to death (→ 10/29).

29. Philippines: Rebel attack kills 48 Americans (→ 5/4/02).

30. Paris: Max Decugis victorious in 1st European Lawn Tennis Championship.

30. France: Car registration now compulsory for vehicles driving over 18 mph.

DEATH

9. French painter Toulouse-Lautrec (*11/24/1864).

McKinley shot; Roosevelt President

Assassination of William McKinley.

Sept 14. Feebly mouthing the words of his favorite hymn, "Nearer My God to Thee," President William McKinley slipped into a coma and died early today in Buffalo, New York, the victim of an assassin's bullet eight days ago.

Hours later, after hurrying back by horseback and trains from a mountain-climbing trip in the remote Adirondacks, Vice President Theodore Roosevelt was sworn in as the 26th President of the United States.

Death came to the late president at the home of a Buffalo friend just before dawn today. He was the third president to have been assassinated in the nation's history. The others were Abraham Lincoln in 1865 and James A. Garfield in 1881.

President McKinley was shot on September 6, while holding a reception in the Temple of Music at the Pan-American Exposition in Buffalo. The assassin, Leon Czolgosz, a 28-year-old anarchist, was promptly arrested. He confessed to the crime the next day.

President Roosevelt, a 42-year-old former Governor of New York and Harvard graduate, took the oath of office in the library of the home of a close friend, Ansley Wilcox, who lives just a mile from the house in which McKinley had died about a dozen hours earlier.

Before the swearing-in ceremony, Roosevelt went to the house where the body of the late president still lay. Gazing upon his fallen leader, Roosevelt bowed his head for several minutes, then left the room, his body shaking and tears streaming from his eyes.

In taking the presidential oath, Roosevelt said solemnly: "I wish to say that it shall be my aim to continue absolutely unbroken the policy of President McKinley for the peace and prosperity and the honor of our beloved country" (→ 26)

Death comes to great painter of Paris

Sept 9. Henri de Toulouse-Lautrec is dead at the age of 36. An innovator in art, he is best known for his depictions of entertainers that captured the motion and energy of life in the bohemian haunts of the Montmartre section of Paris, entertainers such as Jan Avril and Louise Weber, better known as "La Goulue," or the Glutton.

Born into a wealthy, aristocratic family on November 24, 1864, Toulouse-Lautrec was the descendant of talented draftsmen, and when both his thighbones were broken within the span of a year during his adolescence, he devoted himself increasingly to art as he convalesced. His legs, however, atrophied, and he grew to adulthood with the body of a man on the legs of a dwarf.

He studied under various artists in Paris and in the mid-1880's began to gain recognition. His first poster, issued in 1891 and titled "Moulin Rouge — La Goulue," won him immense fame. During the final decade of his life, he turned to the lithograph to render his artistic insights. Heavy drinking and varied ailments led to mental illness and the artist's early death.

Toulouse-Lautrec's "La Clownesse" and "La Goulue."

Peking treaty ends the Boxer Rebellion

Sept 7. China officially ended the Boxer uprising today through a protocol signed with a dozen foreign powers. The rebellion, spearheaded by an anti-foreign secret society and backed up by thousands of peasants, was doomed by lack of arms and poor training. The Chinese must pay an indemnity of $739 million and allow the powers to station troops at Peking and major ports. Commercial agreements, always to the advantage of the Western nations, must be honored. The treaty weakens the control of Empress Dowager Tsu Hsi, who supported the rebellion as part of a nationwide conservative movement (→ 1/7/02).

The splendor of Buffalo, N.Y.'s Pan-American Exposition was darkened by McKinley's death.

1901

OCTOBER

Su	Mo	Tu	We	Th	Fr	Sa
		1	2	3	4	5
6	7	8	9	10	11	12
13	14	15	16	17	18	19
20	21	22	23	24	25	26
27	28	29	30	31		

3. France: Angered by restrictive Association Law, religious groups begin to leave the country (→ 6/27/02).

9. Italy: Minister of religion decrees churches shall not be used for non-religious purposes.

10. China: Imperial edict forbids the buying of positions in public service.

14. Steamer Hating wrecked off coast of Vancouver, B.C.; 200 persons, $250,000 in gold rescued.

16. London: Attempting to strengthen Japanese position vs. Russia, Baron Hayashi begins negotiations with Great Britain (→ 11/25).

16. Pres. Roosevelt incites controversy by inviting black leader Booker T. Washinton to White House (→ 28).

20. Belgian Parliament creates fund to compensate the unemployed (→ 2/5/02).

20. New York Times celebrates its 50th anniversary.

22. Mexico City: Second Pan-American Conference opens (→ 1/31/02).

23. Paris: Debut of Camille Saint-Saens' opera "The Barbarians".

23. London: Gen. Buller relieved of his command for "indiscretion" and "lack of military discipline" (→ 25).

23. New Haven, Conn.: Yale University commemorates her bicentennial.

25. Great Britain: Joseph Chamberlain defends British treatment of Boers in S. African concentration camps (→ 30).

28. New Orleans: Racial riots sparked by Booker T. Washington's visit to White House; 34 killed.

29. New York: Leon Czolgosz, McKinley's assassin, executed.

30. South Africa: Botha's forces attack British column at Brakenlaagte in one of bloodiest confrontations of guerrilla war (→ 11/18/01).

BIRTH

15. German writer Bernard von Brentano (†12/29/1964).

Once again, United States out-races British and retains America's Cup

The American yacht, Columbia.

Oct 4. With a thrilling victory in the third and final race of the series, the American yacht Columbia kept the coveted America's Cup from going to the British challenger Shamrock. The Columbia sailed home two seconds ahead of the Shamrock off the coast of New Jersey, but the Americans were awarded the victory on their adjusted time allowance. The conquest was attributed more to American seamanship than to the design of the yacht.

Those who could view the contest were treated to one of the most exciting yacht races in memory. If not for inexplicable tactical errors on the part of the Shamrock skipper, the challenger would have been the winner, expert observers said. The defeat was a crushing disappointment to Sir Thomas Lipton, who had seen his Shamrock rebuilt after being wrecked in a sudden squall last year. The Shamrock was also defeated by a 3-0 margin in the 1899 America's Cup series.

This year, the British yacht's larger sail spread provided her with greater speed, but her skipper's unexplained timidity in starboard tacks after bold port moves cost her the victory in the eyes of the experts. Throughout the race, the sea was as smooth as a pond but with sufficient breeze. The America's Cup began in 1851, when the United States' yacht America beat a British boat in a race around the Isle of Wight.

Santos-Dumont flies dirigible 30 minutes

Oct 19. The Brazilian-born aeronaut Alberto Santos-Dumont today won the $50,000 Deutsch de la Meurthe award for a successful flight from the Aero Club at Saint Cloud around the Eiffel Tower and back to the starting point in less than an hour. Santos-Dumont flew a lighter-than-air, cigar-shaped dirigible of his own design, 66-feet long with a 4.5-horsepower engine driving a five-foot propeller. The time of the flight was 29 minutes and 30 seconds, with the return leg made against a strong wind.

Santos-Dumont's first dirigible, built in 1898, crashed, but his later designs have been more successful, although he did suffer a crash just two months before his latest triumph. In 1899, he entertained Parisians by flying a dirigible around the Eiffel Tower several times. Next year, he plans to fly a new dirigible across the Mediterranean from Monte Carlo.

Eastman firm will manufacture Kodak

Kodak's big seller, The Brownie.

Oct 24. The Eastman Kodak Company has incorporated in Trenton, New Jersey, to manufacture and deal in Kodak cameras and photographic supplies. Of the authorized $35 million capital, $1 million is preferred stock.

Formed to consolidate the leading camera and supply companies of the United States and England, the new company marks the most recent step in the career of George Eastman. After an education in the public schools of Rochester, New York, Eastman worked in the banking and insurance fields before turning to the business of photography.

Much of his early work was conducted in a garage. After perfecting the process of making dry plates and inventing transparent film, he formed the Eastman Dry Plate and Film Company in 1884. In 1888, his Kodak camera hit the market. Photo enthusiasts now use the Kodak Brownie, which sells for one dollar.

Oct 24. Thousands of amazed spectators today watched Anna Edson Taylor, at 43, pass safely over Niagara Falls in a barrel. Suffering only from shock and minor cuts, she offered some sage advice: "Don't try it."

1901

NOVEMBER

Su	Mo	Tu	We	Th	Fr	Sa
					1	2
3	4	5	6	7	8	9
10	11	12	13	14	15	16
17	18	19	20	21	22	23
24	25	26	27	28	29	30

1. Chicago: Dr. J.E. Gillman announces an X-ray treatment for breast cancer.

7. Turkey: French navy, occupying island of Mytilene, forces Ottoman Turks to pay indemnity for 1896 losses.

16. New York: Frenchman Henri Fournier sets new auto speed record of 52 sec. in mile straightaway.

18. Britain publishes a white paper explaining policy in S. African concentration camps (→ 30).

19. France: It is reported that a general strike in the mines would endanger the republic (→ 3/5/02).

20. Colombia: As rebel forces capture Colon, American troops intervene to protect isthmus (→ 1/18/02).

22. Germany: Richard Strauss' opera "Feuersnot" premieres in Dresden.

23. Cambridge, Mass.: Harvard takes Ivy League football championship, beating Yale 22-0.

24. Kentucky: State troopers burn striking miners' camp, arrest 25 workers.

25. Japanese Prince Ito arrives in Russia to seek concessions in Korea (→ 1/30/02).

26. East Africa: Italy and Britain settle on border between Eritrea and Sudan.

26. The Hope diamond is brought to New York.

27. Michigan: Wrecked train catches fire, killing 100.

28. Alabama: New state constitution disenfranchises blacks by requiring literacy tests and proof that one's grandfather was eligible to vote.

30. Army defeats Navy 11-5 in annual football game.

BIRTHS

3. Leopold III, king of Belgium (†9/26/1983).

5. French novelist Andre Malraux (†11/23/1976).

18. George Horatio Gallup, American journalist and statistician (†7/27/1984).

Boer guerrillas keep resisting British despite many defeats

Nov 30. The Boer War has been dragging on for more than two years, and its end is still not in sight. The British are in control of the cities of South Africa. But Lord Kitchener cannot catch all the Boer guerrillas and he cannot destroy their determination.

The Boer generals, Botha, De Wet and Smuts, seem to move freely around the country, and their troops disappear into the veldt after sudden attacks on the British. Kitchener has tried and failed to protect his rail and communication lines by building a string of blockhouses. But the guerrillas have trickled through the leaky defense, attacked outlying settlements and knocked out British communication depots time and time again. The British find it nearly impossible to track the Boers after their assaults. British maps will never be as sophisticated as the Boers' familiarity with the countryside.

Earlier this year, Kitchener decided his only recourse was to sweep the country clean of the Boers. His troops moved into Boer settlements and herded all residents, including women and children, into concentration camps. Thousands of family members were locked up, and reports indicated large numbers of women and children died from starvation. Meanwhile, British Colonial Secretary Joseph Chamberlain claims the Boers have rejected favorable surrender terms. He warns that Kitchener may use even more severe measures to defeat them. It is hard to imagine what would be more severe than the concentration camps (→ 12/10).

British cavalry cross the Tugela under heavy fire from the Boers.

Britain agrees to U.S. canal rights

Nov 18. Through a second Hay-Pauncefote Treaty signed today, Britain has agreed to extensive rights for the United States in building and operating a canal through Central America. The agreement stipulates, however, that the canal must remain neutral and open to ships of both nations on equal terms.

The United States would have been granted most of these rights if the first Hay-Pauncefote Treaty had not been amended by the Senate. In 1899, Secretary of State John Hay and British Ambassador Lord Pauncefote designed an agreement based on the Suez Canal regulations. Foremost among that canal's ordinances is a provision for non-fortification of the region. The Senate insisted on fortifying the Central American canal, amending the treaty accordingly. Britain refused to ratify the amended pact. Today's treaty does not explicitly forbid military installations along the proposed canal, but both parties reportedly feel satisfied that such developments are discouraged (→ 20).

1901

DECEMBER

Su	Mo	Tu	We	Th	Fr	Sa
1	2	3	4	5	6	7
8	9	10	11	12	13	14
15	16	17	18	19	20	21
22	23	24	25	26	27	28
29	30	31				

2. U.S. Supreme Court decides Puerto Ricans do not qualify for U.S. citizenship.

2. King Camp Gillette to market razor with disposable blades.→

3. President Roosevelt addresses Congress; ambiguously asserts some trusts ought to be regulated "within reasonable limits" (→ 3/10/02).

4. Germany: Bavarian Landtag allows Jews access to judgeships in strict proportion to their share of Germany's population.

6. Germany: Polish organizations now required to use German at public meetings (→ 5/21/02).

10. Belgium: Government declares it will not intervene in Boer War (→ 1/10/02).

19. Anglo-German talks stalled over anti-German remarks in Chamberlain's Oct. 25th Edinburgh speech (→ 1/10/02).

21. Norway: Women vote for 1st time in communal elections.

26. Africa: Uganda railway completed from Mombasa to Lake Victoria.

BIRTHS

5. Cartoon producer Walt Disney (†12/15/1966).

16. U.S. anthropologist Margaret Mead (†11/15/1978).

27. German actress Magdalena von Losch, alias Marlene Dietrich.

CULTURAL EVENTS, 1901

Literature: Kipling's "Kim"; Maurice Maeterlinck's "The Life of the Bees"; Thomas Mann's "Buddenbrooks"; August Strindberg's "Dance of Death"; Booker T. Washington's "Up from Slavery"; Frank Norris' "The Octopus."

Religion, Academia: Rudolf Steiner breaks with Theosophists, founds anthroposophy.

Music: Richard Strauss' "Feuersnot"; Anton Dvorak's "Rusalka"; Scott Joplin's "The Easy Winners".

The Arts: Edvard Munch's "White Night"; Picasso's "The Old Woman."

Sweden awards first Nobel Prizes

Alfred Nobel.

Dec 10. The King of Sweden and the Norwegian Nobel Committee distributed the first Nobel Prizes today. These awards, according to Alfred Nobel's will, "should be annually made to those who, during the preceding year, shall have conferred the greatest benefit on mankind" in the specialized fields of physics, chemistry, medicine, literature and peace.

This year's Nobel laureates are: Wilhelm Roentgen of Germany (physics) for his discovery of X-rays; Jacobus Henricus van't Hoff of the Netherlands (chemistry) for his laws of chemical dynamics and osmotic pressure; Emil von Behring of Germany (medicine) for his work on serum therapy; and Sully Prudhomme of France (literature) for his poetry. The 1901 Nobel Peace Prize was awarded to both Jean Henri Dunant of Switzerland, who established the Red Cross in 1864, and the economist Frederic Passy, who founded the French Society of the Friends of Peace.

From this day forward, the prizes will be awarded by four institutions, three Swedish and one Norwegian, from a fund established under the will of Alfred Nobel. The ceremonial presentation of the prizes is to take place every year in Stockholm, Sweden, and Oslo, Norway, on December 10, the anniversary of Nobel's death.

In 1867, Nobel, a Swedish chemist, invented dynamite and later discovered many other explosive substances. As a result, he earned a fortune, which he left to a foundation when he died in 1886. The annual interest yielded by his wealth will finance the five Nobel Prizes. The Nobel Foundation is the legal owner and functional administrator of the funds, but it is not concerned with the prize deliberations, which rest exclusively with the Swedish and Norwegian institutions.

Wilhelm Conrad Roentgen, winner of the Nobel Prize in physics.

Sully Prudhomme, winner of the Nobel Prize in literature.

Guglielmo Marconi sends message from England to Newfoundland

Dec 12. The Italian physicist Guglielmo Marconi, who sent wireless telegraphic messages across the English Channel from Dover, England, to Boulogne, France, on March 29, 1899, repeated his experiment today over the Atlantic Ocean, a distance of 2,232 miles.

In order to carry out this experiment, Marconi set up a 164-foot-high antenna in Poldhu, Cornwall, England. Then, he erected a receiver in St. John's, Newfoundland, Canada. In spite of the earth's curvature, he received a Morse signal corresponding to the letter "S" from the Poldhu station across the ocean.

When Marconi realized the importance of his first discoveries in 1895, he asked the Italian Minister of Telecommunication to help him. But the minister found that Marconi's experiments were too extravagant. That's why Marconi went to England, where he won the support of Sir William Peace, the Postmaster General, who immediately understood the significance of the young Marconi's work. Thanks to Peace's perspicacity and the help of Professor Adolf Slaby, Marconi could hit his target today (→ 2/22/03).

Guglielmo Marconi and his first wireless.

Gillette to market a replaceable razor

Dec 2. An American businessman named King Camp Gillette, who in 1895 patented a new model of razor, is planning to market the gadget in the coming year. The razor is shaped like a hoe, and its double-edged blade is designed to be used just once or until dull, discarded and replaced with a new one. William Nickerson, the only employee of the Gillette Company, resolved the manufacturing problems.

The new Gillette model, with its double-edged, replaceable blades, is designed to be both a safety razor as well as more efficient. Yet it is very difficult to predict what kind of reception the male public, despite the decreasing popularity of beards, will give to this new type of razor, which has a very thin and sharp but dispensable blade (→ 7/10/32).

Scott Joplin, his popular ragtime tunes

With its syncopated rhythm, ragtime jazz is increasing in popularity, and among the best composers of the music is Scott Joplin, the 33-year-old pianist, bandleader and songwriter who came to wide notice in 1899 with the publication of his tune, the "Maple Leaf Rag."

Scott Joplin.

Nicknamed the "King of Ragtime," he is a native of Texarkana, Texas, where he was drawn toward music by his parents and received his early training. While still a youth, he left home, played piano in St. Louis and other Middle Western cities, and in 1893 organized his first band in Chicago, where the World Columbian Exposition was the attraction. It was there that the ragtime pianist Otis Saunders encouraged him to commit his ragtime compositions to writing.

In 1895, Joplin moved to Sedalia, Missouri, and began studying at the George R. Smith College for Negroes in an effort to gain technical knowledge in music. In that year and the next, publication of songs and piano works by Joplin began. The popularity of ragtime marks the first occasion that jazz, which is largely of Negro origin, has exerted a wide appeal, and sheet music and player pianos are playing an important role in the process.

Frank Norris novel attacks railroads

Having ushered in the 20th Century last year with bold new works, the established literary masters rested on their laurels in 1901. So much the better for newcomer Frank Norris, whose work is suddenly the center of attention. His novel "The Octopus" concerns the monopolistic stranglehold of American railroads. The book could only be written in this century; never before, it seems, has industry taken on enough greed and force to be the focus of a book, overshadowing the human drama we have always assumed so essential to a story. And Norris tells it in a style destined for future generations of readers.

California novelist Frank Norris.

Booker T. Washington's autobiography "Up from Slavery" was also published this year. Utterly unlike "The Octopus," its human drama is foremost. It was sheer determination that raised the Negro leader from an unlettered childhood on a Virginia plantation to the presidency of Tuskegee Institute in Alabama. His book's optimism, not the pessimism of "The Octopus," was warmly received by many this year.

Americans are still discussing the literary crop of 1900. Theodore Dreiser's "Sister Carrie," about a woman's immoral rise to power, continues to shock readers, even those who have never read it.

Two children's books published last year have also caught the public's fancy. Frank L. Baum's "The Wonderful Wizard of Oz" is the first American fairytale. Its heroes are a Kansas girl, a scarecrow, a tin man and a "cowardly lion." And from England comes "The Tale of Peter Rabbit," by Beatrix Potter. Miss Potter has written and illustrated the book herself, and her watercolors are painstakingly detailed. The entire effect is so convincing that a generation of children may grow up believing rabbits do indeed wear blue waistcoats.

1902

JANUARY

Su	Mo	Tu	We	Th	Fr	Sa
			1	2	3	4
5	6	7	8	9	10	11
12	13	14	15	16	17	18
19	20	21	22	23	24	25
26	27	28	29	30	31	

3. Miss Alice Roosevelt, the president's daughter, makes her debut at the White House.

4. Washington: Carnegie Institute founded to promote research in the humanities and sciences.

4. French offer to sell Nicaraguan canal rights to U.S. for $40 million (→ 18).

7. China: Imperial court returns to Peking; Empress Dowager rules again.

8. United Irish League convenes in Dublin.→

8. Italy: Catholic Church strongly opposes bill on divorce.

9. Paraguay: President Emilio Aceral dismissed; Hector Carvallo to succeed.

10. Germany: Provoked by Joseph Chamberlain's Edinburgh speech, Chancellor von Bulow leads attack on British conduct in S. Africa (→ 3/10).

15. Karlsruhe: Premiere of Emil Reznicek's "Till Eulenspiegel."

16. Germany granted right to build railway connecting Konia to Baghdad.

17. Mexico City: Earthquake takes 300 lives.

18. Washington: Isthmus Canal Commission shifts its support to Panama as canal site (→ 4/16).

21. Poland: Demonstrators in Lemberg commemorate 39th anniversary of Polish revolt against Russian rule (→ 3/13).

25. Russia abolishes death penalty (→ 3/25).

30. New York: Transatlantic carriers combine to raise rates 100 percent.

31. Mexico City: Pan-American Conference ends with all agreed to settle disputes in peace.

BIRTHS

8. American Carl Rogers, founder of client-centered psychotherapy.

8. Soviet leader Georgi Malenkov.

14. Polish-American mathematician Alfred Tarski

15. Ibn Saud, king of Saudi Arabia (†2/31/1969).

U.S. Steel makes $174 million profit

Wall Street titan J.P. Morgan.

Jan 29. In its first full statement to stockholders, the United States Steel Corporation has announced a profit of $174 million, all of which was earned in the brief 11 months since the trust's creation in February 1901. Of the vast capitalization of $1.4 billion, less than $1 million is outstanding. Some $676 million of the start-up costs represented cash and $726 million was "water" (promoter's profits, speculation and goodwill). Financier J.P. Morgan, who organized U.S. Steel and other major companies, and has kept control of them through voting trusts, was recently heard to growl, "I am not in Wall Street for my health."

Prado Museum shows El Greco paintings

Jan 1. Three centuries of neglect have not harmed the beauty of El Greco's paintings. The artist's works, maligned since his death in 1641, are given a late but thorough appreciation at the Prado in Madrid, Spain, this month.

El Greco, "the Greek," was born Domenikos Theotokopuli in 1541. Raised in Crete, he came to Rome when he was nearly 30 years old. There, he quickly made enemies when he suggested repainting Michelangelo's "Last Judgment" in the Sistine Chapel. He fled to Toledo, where he created several works depicting the life of Christ. For them he copied the sensuous colors of his Venetian instructor, Titian. Yet his singular style of distorting and elongating form alienated El Greco from the public for 300 years.

El Greco's "The Adoration of the Shepherds."

Michigan defeats Stanford 49-0 in California's first Rose Bowl game

Jan 1. The titanic struggle that was expected to develop between two intersectional football powers in the first Rose Bowl game failed to materialize. The national champions from the University of Michigan put the Stanford University team to rout, 49-0, with an amazing display of offensive might. The Midwestern array, coached by Fielding "Hurry Up" Yost, piled up 1,463 yards in 142 plays. The feat was achieved by the amazing speed with which Michigan was able to run off plays, and West Coast fans were quick to realize how Coach Yost achieved his unusual nickname.

United Irish League organizes in U.S.

Jan 8. The United Irish League opened its annual convention in Dublin today and decided to send two of its members, William H.K. Redmond and Joseph Devlin, to the United States to complete the work of organizing the league in America. Such a visit had been requested by the Irish League of America, which has arranged a national tour for the two representatives from Ireland.

The United Irish League, which has 1200 branches, is the leading force for unification of all Ireland and its independence from Britain. Its Chairman, John Edward Redmond, called for a renewed revolt against British rule in January 1900, and several nationalist demonstrations have taken place in Dublin. British Prime Minister Lord Salisbury has stated his firm opposition to freedom for Ireland, but this has not stopped the league from spreading like wildfire throughout the country, according to the Dublin Daily Express. The league is now planning a series of boycotts of those Irish who do not support its goals (→ 4/15).

Britain finds Pacific ally in Japanese

Jan 30. Japan and Great Britain signed a defensive alliance today. They agreed to respect each other's interests in China and Korea and to hold consultations before signing treaties with third countries.

The commercial and imperialistic designs of Japan and Britain have intersected in the Far East, and the new treaty seems to serve their mutual interests. After its war with China in 1894-1895, Japan learned the hard way that it needed a European ally. Russia, France and Germany forced Japan to return to China the piece of southern Manchuria she won in the war. After the Boxer Rebellion, Japan apparently felt even more threatened as Russia occupied southern Manchuria and moved closer to Korea.

Great Britain has been expanding her interests in China since the Opium War of 1839-42. And now she feels threatened by the advances of Russia, Germany and France. London also feels more secure with a new ally in the Far East.

Florodora musical plays 505 times

Jan 26. "Florodora" played its 505th performance last night, breaking the previous record for longest running show on Broadway. Belittled as a "musical comedy" when it originated in London, the show premiered in New York in November 1900 and proved so popular that soon local railroads were running "Florodora Expresses," their hours printed in red on timetables, for suburbanites.

The show, its story by Owen Hall, takes its title from a perfume made by an American on a mysterious Philippine island. The plot deals with engaging proper, young ladies to proper, young gentlemen. The show's hit is Leslie Stuart's "Tell Me Pretty Maiden," sung in the second act by six women dressed in full-length skirts with flounces, ruffled shirtwaists and ostrich-plumed hats. The song is addressed to six men wearing silk hats and gray morning coats, bearing walking sticks and responding on bended knee.

1902

FEBRUARY

Su	Mo	Tu	We	Th	Fr	Sa
						1
2	3	4	5	6	7	8
9	10	11	12	13	14	15
16	17	18	19	20	21	22
23	24	25	26	27	28	

1. U.S. Sec. of State John Hay protests Russian privileges in China as violation of open door policy (→ 3/20).

1. China: Imperial decree abolishes ban on marriages between Manchus and Chinese (→ 4/29).

5. France: Miners win victory in National Assembly; work day reduced to nine hours (→ 3/5).

9. Paris: Doctor Doyen performs successful operation on Siamese twins from Barnum and Bailey Circus.

9. New Jersey: Paterson fire destroys $8 mil. in property; martial law declared.

14. Italy: Martial law descends on Trieste as strikes for reduced working hours turn into bloody riots.

15. Germany: Felix Von Weingarten's opera "Oreste" premieres in Leipzig.

15. Berlin: Subway inaugurated.

18. Baku, Russia: Earthquake takes 2,000 lives.

19. France: Smallpox vaccination becomes obligatory.

20. Spain: Martial law fails to bring peace to Barcelona; 500 killed as strikers clash with police (→ 5/31).

22. Washington: Fist fight in the Senate; Sen. Benjamin Tillman suffers bloody nose for accusing Sen. John McLaurin of bias on Philippine tariff issue.

23. New York: Prince Henry of Prussia represents his brother the emperor in visit to U.S.

28. Colorado: 1000 miners buried in avalanche (→ 5/12).

BIRTHS

1. American poet Langston Hughes (+5/22/1967).

4. American pilot Charles Lindbergh, 1st to fly solo across Atlantic (+8/26/1974).

17. Opera star Marian Anderson, 1st black singer to appear in Metropolitan Opera.

20. American nature photographer Ansel Adams.

27. American novelist John Steinbeck (+12/20/1968).

Yellow fever is carried by mosquito

Feb 22. Major Walter Reed and Dr. James Carroll of the United States Army Yellow Fever Commission in Cuba published a scientific report today revealing that the dreaded disease endemic to the tropics is transmitted by a species of mosquito. Furthermore, based on the commission's advice, the city of Havana has instituted a mosquito eradication program that is helping to wipe out yellow fever in that populous locale.

Cuban physician Carlos J. Finlay had indicated to Reed, who is the President of the Yellow Fever Commission, that he believed the disease to be spread by a species of mosquito known as Aedes aegypti. The commission then proved Finlay's hypothesis, but not without the tragic loss of the heroic Dr. Jesse W. Lazear, who had been bitten by an infected mosquito in the midst of his work.

In today's publication, the commission goes on to report that the mysterious causative organism, which is introduced into the bloodstream of a human being by the mosquito, is able to pass through a fine porcelain filter and is smaller than any known bacteria. It may be a member of the class of ultramicroscopic organisms known to the scientific community as viruses.

Army surgeon Walter Reed.

Students showing unrest in Russia

Feb 4. More than 30,000 students are on strike throughout the Russian Empire. Supported by liberal professors, they are protesting the "temporary rules" decreed by the Minister of Education, General Vannovsky, on December 22, 1901, which empower the czarist administration to control student organizations. Student disorders are the most visible expression of the political opposition revived since the late 1890's. Russian authorities fear that the students are inclined not only to revolutionary doctrines but also to violence (→ 3/25).

Charles Tiffany dies

Feb 18. Charles Lewis Tiffany began his business career in a country store. He ended it as New York's most fashionable jeweler. Tiffany's had branches in London, Geneva and Paris and letters of appointment to serve a dozen monarchs.

Four days after his 90th birthday, Tiffany died today, laden with honors and wealth, socially prominent and generous with his money.

Five generations of the Tiffany family lived in Massachusetts. Tiffany's father lent him $1,000 to establish a stationery store in New York called Tiffany and Young, later transformed into Tiffany & Company, a treasure house full of silver, gold and gems.

Anglo-German relations are strained

Feb 8. The German Embassy in Great Britain has reported a conversation between the English Minister of Colonies, Joseph Chamberlain, and the Ambassador of France, Paul Cambon, concerning Anglo-German relations. According to the report, Chamberlain told Cambon that he had been humiliated by Chancellor von Bulow's recent speech in the Reichstag and that an alliance between Germany and Britain is now impossible.

As a matter of fact, the union between the two countries failed because Great Britain, which had reached a political agreement of neutrality with Germany, refused to conclude the same agreement with the two other allies of Germany, Austria-Hungary and Italy. A spokesman for the British Foreign Office suggested giving up the idea of alliance and replacing it by a project limited to "particular affairs." But the German answer was, "All or nothing." Negotiations stopped there.

This two-cyl. Stevens-Duryea evolved from one of the first gas-powered autos in the country. In Chicago, in 1895, the brothers Duryea, Frank and Charles, drove its prototype to victory in the first U.S. auto race.

1902

MARCH

Su	Mo	Tu	We	Th	Fr	Sa
						1
2	3	4	5	6	7	8
9	10	11	12	13	14	15
16	17	18	19	20	21	22
23	24	25	26	27	28	29
30	31					

5. France: National Congress of Miners decides to call general strike for 8-hour day (→ 5/22).

7. New York: J. Pierpont Morgan buys Garland collection of Oriental porcelains, keeping it in U.S.

10. South Africa: Boers score last victory, capturing British Gen. Methuen and 200 men (→ 4/10).

10. Turkey: Earthquake wipes out entire town of Tochangri.

10. Sherman Antitrust Act to be enforced; U.S. Attorney Gen. Philander Knox will bring suit against Morgan and Harriman's Northern Securities Co. (→ 3/14/04).

13. Poland: Schools shut down across the country as students refuse to sing Russian hymn "God Protect the Czar" (→ 9/22).

15. New Haven, Conn.: Yale beats Harvard 5-3 to capture college hockey championship.

15. Boston: 10,000 freight handlers back to work after week-long strike.

18. Turkey: Sultan grants a German syndicate 1st concession to access Baghdad by rail.

20. France and Russia acknowledge Anglo-Japanese alliance, but assert their right to protect interests in China and Korea (→ 4/8).

21. Romain Rolland's play "The 4th of July" premieres in Paris.

22. Great Britain and Persia agree to link Europe and India by telegraph.

23. Italy: Minimum legal working age raised from nine to 12 for boys, 11 to 15 for girls (→ 6/27).

25. Russia: 567 students found guilty of "political dissaffection"; 95 exiled to Siberia (→ 4/1).

31. Tennessee: Explosion kills 22 coal miners (→ 5/12).

DEATH

23. Austro-Hungarian statesman Kalman Tisza, prime minister from 1875 to 1890 (*12/10/1830).

Cecil Rhodes is dead

March 26. Cecil John Rhodes, one of the architects of the British Empire, died today in Cape Town, South Africa. He was 48 years old.

Rhodes was born in 1853 in Hertfordshire, England. Because of ill health, he was sent to live in South Africa. Rhodes staked out some diamond claims and soon became very wealthy. In 1880, he formed the DeBeers Mining Company, which reputedly has the most capital in the world. In 1881, he received a degree from Oxford, which he had been attending at intervals. By 1888, Rhodes had engineered the consolidation of all South African diamond mines, and a year later organized the British South Africa Company.

Rhodes became Prime Minister, and virtual dictator, of the Cape Colony in 1890. Five years later, his political career was shaken by the Jameson Raid. He denied authorizing the raid into the Transvaal, which was led by his close friend Dr. Jameson.

Rhodes had great financial interests in the Transvaal. Paul Kruger, leader of the Boers and of the Transvaal government, was violently opposed to any federation of South Africa under British rule, which was one of Rhodes' greatest dreams. Controversy over his part in the attempt to unseat Kruger's government led Rhodes to resign as premier in 1896. Rhodes' death leaves unfinished his final project, the Cape-to-Cairo railway (→ 2/1/03).

Cecil John Rhodes.

Carnegie donates to forty libraries

March 13. Steel magnate Andrew Carnegie, who recently retired to devote his time to philanthropy, spent the day today approving 40 applications for funds earmarked for library endowments.

In his 1890 essay "The Gospel of Wealth," Carnegie said that a rich man should spend the first half of his life acquiring wealth and the second half in philanthropic acts for the general welfare.

In a recent speech to 33 librarians at the seventh annual dinner of the New York Library Club, Carnegie said that Lord Acton once told him that a library of the world's best literature would require 4,000 volumes. Carnegie noted, "That is not more than one volume a year for all the years we have known man to have ever written at all." Observing that "thousands of books are written which bless their own generation, I would say that an author who helped his own generation deserved the gratitude of mankind." This sentiment was greeted by a wave of generous applause.

Tunnel collapses

March 21. Three Park Avenue mansions were destroyed and residents near 38th Street fled their homes today after a subway tunnel roof caved in, sending an avalanche of loose rock into a gaping pit. The contractor connected with the New York City subway has already been indicted once for a faulty dynamite explosion.

The perils of modern transportation: collapsed tunnel on Park Avenue.

American Automobile Association formed

March 4. Nine automobile clubs from around the nation united today in Chicago to create the American Automobile Association. Winthrop E. Scarritt is President. The group aims to improve the reliability of autos, push for better roads and lobby for uniform traffic laws. The 1,000 members hail from affluent and influential regions, from Princeton, New Jersey, to Grand Rapids, Michigan. They may prove powerful representatives of America's 23,000 automobile owners.

The little one-cylinder Baby Peugeot is one reason why French has replaced German as the "official" language of motoring.

1902

APRIL

Su	Mo	Tu	We	Th	Fr	Sa
		1	2	3	4	5
6	7	8	9	10	11	12
13	14	15	16	17	18	19
20	21	22	23	24	25	26
27	28	29	30			

1. Russia: Famine persists in countryside; starving peasants loot landowners' barns in Poltava and Kharkov (→ 15).

1. Pennsylvania: 10,000 miners go out on strike.

5. Two pieces by Maurice Ravel premiere in Paris: "Jeux d'eau" and "Pavane pour une infante defunte."

8. Russia and China sign Convention of Evacuation, binding Russia to withdraw from Manchuria within 18 months (→ 4/23/03).

9. German labor movement launches effort to unify all unions.

10. South Africa: Boers accept British terms of surrender (→ 5/31).

15. Russia: Socialist-Revolutionaries assassinate Sipyengin, head of secret police; he is succeeded by Vyacheslav Plehve (→ 27).

15. Ireland: To combat nationalist protest, Britain calls state of emergency in nine counties (→ 10/10).

16. Colombia: American troops arrive at Bocas del Toro to protect property at the isthmus during civil war (→ 6/28).

18. Belgium: Ten days of rioting end; government refuses to grant Socialist demands for universal male suffrage, right to strike (→ 6/7).

20. Paris: Thaddeus Robl becomes world's bicycling champion.

20. Illinois: Fire ravages the steamer City of Pittsburgh; 75 passengers die.

27. Russia: Rioting peasants destroy 80 estates (→ 7/2).

27. Pennsylvania: Eight girls killed in panic at Philadelphia factory.

28. Revolution breaks out in the Dominican Republic.

30. Debussy's opera "Pelleas and Mlisande" premieres in Paris.

BIRTH

4. French writer Louise de Vilmorin (†12/26/1969).

Chinese Exclusion Act passes Senate easily

Californians have not impressed the Chinese with their hospitality.

April 29. The Senate voted yesterday to extend the Chinese Exclusion Act for the second time. The law, barring all Chinese immigration to the United States for ten years, was first passed in 1882 and re-enacted a decade later. This time the bill will be in effect indefinitely. The arguments for restrictions remain unchanged: The livelihood of American workers would be threatened by cheap Asian labor. And few Americans see any kind of accommodation possible. As one senator said in the debates, "The Chinese do not harmonize with us. Upon their admission, they become an undigested and undigestible mass."

Major Texas oil company founded

April 7. The Texas Company, an oil firm that plans to challenge the near-monopoly of Standard Oil, was granted a corporate charter today. Its principals are Joseph S. Cullinan, an oilman who was named President, and Arnold Schlaet, who provides financial expertise. Cullinan and Schlaet plan to take advantage of the abundance of oil caused by discoveries at Spindletop and other fields. Instead of selling crude oil, as other companies do, the new firm hopes to expand the market by selling kerosene, gasoline and other refined products (→ 5/1/59)

... spawned competition for Standard Oil.

Art Nouveau style exhibited in Paris

Otto Wagner mosaic in Vienna.

April 20. At the Exhibition of La Societe Nationale des Beaux-Arts, Parisians are being exposed to the full flower of Art Nouveau, a trend that has been gathering force for a quarter of a century.

Taking its name from the Maison de l'Art Nouveau, Samuel Bing's Paris shop where fine and decorative arts are sold, and influenced by Japanese prints and the revival during the 19th century of rococo and Gothic styles, Art Nouveau is characterized by its energy, restless movement and curvilinear forms. Among its most influential practitioners are Hector Guimard, the French architect and furniture designer, whose most familiar works are the flowerlike, cast-metal gates at the entrances to Paris Metro stations; and Rene Lalique, whose glass and jewelry are creating much excitement at the exhibition.

Art Nouveau by Robert Engels.

1902

MAY

Su	Mo	Tu	We	Th	Fr	Sa
				1	2	3
4	5	6	7	8	9	10
11	12	13	14	15	16	17
18	19	20	21	22	23	24
25	26	27	28	29	30	31

1. India: Bengal swept by tornado; 416 killed.

3. Jockey Winkfield wins with Alan-a-Dale in Kentucky Derby.

4. Mindanao, Philippines: U.S. launches successful attack against sultan of Bayan, principle leader of Moro revolt (→ 7/1).

5. Germany: Prussian government denies women the right to political association.

10. Paris: $12 million stolen from Paris safe hiding inheritance of American millionaire Henry Crawford; called "biggest swindle of century."

10. Portugal: Parliament converts foreign debt as costly revolt in Angola brings country close to bankruptcy.

17. Maurice Maeterlinck's "Monna Vanna" premieres in Paris.

19. Tennessee: 200 killed as mine shafts crumble (→ 7/10).

20. Cuba: Tomas Estrada Palma becomes pres. of new republic upon long-awaited withdrawal of U.S. troops (→ 2/23/03).

21. Prussian Landtag offers bill to intensify Germanization of Polish territories (→ 6/5).

22. Intl. Miners Congress demands nationalization of mines, but vetoes strikes in France and Belgium (→ 10/9).

22. Roosevelt supports Intl. Court at The Hague; it will settle long-standing debt dispute with Mexico.

28. France: Waldeck-Rousseau steps down as head of Cabinet; Emile Combes new president.

31. Scotland: Glasgow doctor claims eucalyptus leaves will cure diabetes.

31. Spain: After suspending the Cortes (Parliament) yesterday, King Alfonso XIII imposes martial law to quell labor disturbances (→ 4/2/03).

DEATH

5. Writer Bret Harte, chronicler of the Wild West (*8/25/1836).

145,000 Pennsylvania coal miners strike

May 12. With more than 145,000 miners now on strike in the coal fields of Pennsylvania, the nation could face a frigid winter. The anthracite miners walked off the job this week when mine owners rejected their demands for increased pay, shorter hours and better working conditions. The strike could paralyze major industries dependent on coal for their operations, as well as result in a critical shortage of home fuel for the nation's consumers.

Officials of the United Mine Workers said that the anthracite miners will appeal to President Roosevelt to intervene in their behalf. Union officials blamed the breakdown of negotiations on four major railroads that have extensive holdings in the coal fields.

In rejecting the demands of the union, George F. Baer, President of Reading Iron & Coal and the Reading Railroad, explained: "Anthracite mining is a business and not a religious, sentimental or academic proposition." He also said the miners "don't suffer; why, they can't even speak English" (→ 19).

War ends; Boer Republic becomes colony

May 31. The bitterly fought Boer War came to an end today as the Treaty of Vereeniging was signed. The Boers lost their sovereignty to the British, but London promises they will not lose their political rights. Great Britain also agreed to pay the Boers $12 million to rebuild their farms and homes, and it promised not to levy any new taxes to pay for the war effort.

The war held Great Britain in a quagmire for nearly three years. Some British military commanders learned about guerrilla tactics the hard way, and they had to fend off mounted horsemen for the first time since the War of 1812. They finally won the war and the right to mine South African gold, but it remains to be seen how much ground the British have lost elsewhere in the world. While Britain was distracted in South Africa, Germany was busy building up its navy. Heinrich Friedjung, a German historian, has warned that Britain will pay for its war against the Boers (→ 8/16).

Melies mixes science and fantasy in film

May 1. In Paris, Georges Melies, a magician associated with the Theatre Robert Houdin, has brought his experiments with moving pictures to a startling new level with "A Trip to the Moon." His depiction of a space voyage brings fantasy to moving pictures and marks a departure from the use of these films merely to record. Audiences seem to be enchanted with this innovative use of these moving pictures.

Scene from Georges Melies' "A Trip to the Moon."

Volcano wipes out Martinique town

Saint-Pierre after eruption.

May 8. Saint-Pierre, the largest town in the French West Indies and the commercial capital of Martinique, has been entirely destroyed by a volcanic eruption from Mount Pelee, the highest of three mountains in the French colony. All ships in the harbor have been destroyed. And all of the inhabitants except one, a Mr. Cyparis who had been jailed for drunkenness, have been killed. According to the 1901 census, Saint-Pierre's population was 25,400. Martinique, which contains five or six extinct craters, is often subject to earthquakes.

Thomas A. Edison invents battery

May 28. Thomas A. Edison today announced the invention of a new storage battery which is lighter and longer-lived than lead-acid batteries. The prolific inventor says that the battery, composed of cells having nickel and iron in an alkaline solution, can keep the electric automobile competitive with gasoline models.

1902

JUNE

Su	Mo	Tu	We	Th	Fr	Sa
1	2	3	4	5	6	7
8	9	10	11	12	13	14
15	16	17	18	19	20	21
22	23	24	25	26	27	28
29	30					

2. Ballot reform in Oregon: General initiative and referendum adopted allowing voters to propose laws and veto legislative decisions (→ 5/23/03).

3. International Congress of Textile Workers at Zurich votes abolition of piecework.

5. Germany: Kaiser Wilhelm II counters growing nationalism by calling for "Germanization" of Slavs (→ 9/13).

7. Belgium: Strikers agitate for electoral reform (→ 9/15).

9. New Jersey: Francis Landley Patton resigns presidency of Princeton; Woodrow Wilson to take his place (→ 7/2/12).

14. Yale beats Princeton 5-4 to capture college baseball championship.

16. Train makes New York-to-Chicago trip in record 20 hours.

17. U.S. Congress passes Newlands Reclamation Act; irrigation in West to be funded by sale of public lands (→ 19).

21. Stuttgart, Germany: Govt. representatives attend a union congress for first time.

23. Switzerland: Albert Einstein becomes a state employee.

23. Germany, Austria-Hungary and Italy renew Triple Alliance for 12-year duration.

26. Yale out-rows Harvard in annual crew competition.

26. U.K.: Gordon-Bennett Auto Cup won by British Edge racer.

27. France: Minimum legal work day set at 10.5 hours.

27. France: Combes enforces Association Law of July 1, 1901;2,500 church schools close their doors.

BIRTH

28. Popular composer Richard Rodgers born in Hammels Station, N.Y. (†12/15/44).

DEATHS

10. Lord Acton, advocate of British liberalism (*1/10/1834).

18. British satirist Samuel Butler (*12/4/1835).

U.S. to pay $40 million for Panama canal

June 28. Prominent business and political interests in the United States have been arguing for years about where to build a canal in Central America. Today, Congress took a decisive step by passing Senator Spooner's bill. The new law stipulates that the canal should be built across the Panamanian isthmus. And it authorizes President Roosevelt to pay $40 million for the rights to the Panama concession.

The decision to dig the canal through Panama came after some very high-level political wheeling and dealing. During the last century, the United States and Great Britain were competing to build a waterway in Nicaragua. Only last year, Britain agreed in a treaty to give up its rights, and an American commission recommended that that the canal be built in Nicaragua.

At the same time, a French company that owned rights in Panama was lobbying hard for a canal there. Its representatives put pressure on the White House, and they finally convinced Roosevelt to buy them out and build in Panama (→ 9/17).

West Point celebrates 100th birthday

President Roosevelt at West Point's centennial exercises.

June 9. The Military Academy at West Point, New York, celebrated its centennial with three days of exercises at the end of the academic year. President Theodore Roosevelt was the guest of honor and distributed the diplomas.

Since its inception by an Act of Congress, the United States Military Academy has contributed many traditions which have become part of American life. The United States Military Academy Band, now the oldest military band in the country, was formed in 1812; the class ring custom originated in 1835; and, in 1890, West Point entered the field of collegiate sports with the first Army-Navy football game.

Cass Gilbert's U.S. Customs House opened in New York this year.

President signs bill to aid farms in West

Thomas Eakins' vision of the West.

June 19. President Roosevelt, in an effort to assist the agricultural development of the West, signed into law an irrigation bill yesterday. The Newlands Reclamation Act will allow the proceeds of Western public land sales to be used for the construction of dams, reservoirs, canals and other works necessary to irrigate arid tracts in the West.

The bill's sponsor, Rep. Francis G. Newlands of Nevada, applauded the signing of the measure. Under its provisions, $150 million of the proceeds of the sales of public lands will be available in the next 30 years without further appropriation.

However, not all political leaders support the legislation. Joseph G. Cannon, speaking for Eastern and Midwestern farmers, charged that the act will increase the amount of agricultural goods when they are already in oversupply. But the president, an ardent champion of conservation, refuted the charges, and with bipartisan support among Western legislators, the bill was enacted. Newlands believes the act will benefit the people of Nevada more than anything since the discovery of silver in the state.

1902

JULY

Su	Mo	Tu	We	Th	Fr	Sa
		1	2	3	4	5
6	7	8	9	10	11	12
13	14	15	16	17	18	19
20	21	22	23	24	25	26
27	28	29	30	31		

1. Philippine Government Act establishes Filipinos as citizens of their own country, governed by commission appointed by U.S. president (→ 11/22/03).

2. Rioting continues in Russia; workers rise in Rostov, peasants in South (→ 3).

7. Wimbledon: Hugh Doherty 6-3, 3-6, 6-0 over Arthur Gore; Muriel Robb 7-5, 6-1 over Charlotte Sterry.

7. Venezuela: Rebels rout 3,000 troops led by President Castro's brother (→ 8/12).

9. Hope for insomniacs: German scientist obtains patent for barbituric acid.

10. Pennsylvania: Explosion kills 125 miners (→ 17).

12. Britain: Aging Prime Minister Lord Salisbury retires; Arthur Balfour to succeed.

15. Duluth, Minn.: Minnesota Mining and Manufacturing Co. founded.

15. Paris: International Conference for the Repression of White Slave Trade convenes.

17. Australia: Lord Tennyson, son of the poet, named to succeed Lord Hopetoun as gov. general.

17. George Baer, pres. of Reading Iron & Coal, declares striking coal workers must defer to "the Christian men to whom God has given...the property interests of his country" (→ 8/29).

24. Turkey: Under pressure from Ottoman rulers, Sultan Abdul Hamid attempts to placate Macedonian revolutionaries with cosmetic reforms.

25. San Francisco: Heavyweight champ Jim Jefferies knocks out Robert Fitzsimmons in eight rounds.

30. Denver: Largest locomotive in world wrecked.

BIRTHS

1. American movie director Wylliam Wyler (/7/27/81).

25. American novelist Frank Waters, chronicler of the Southwest.

28. British-Austrian philosopher Karl Popper.

Riots rage through southern Russia following uprising of peasants

July 3. Violent riots are spreading in southern Russia. Recent days in Rostov-on-Don have seen rioters and troops clash, leaving countless protesters killed or wounded. Fanatical labor organizers, dressed in bizarre uniforms, confuse the public by destroying factories and machinery while claiming Czar Nicholas' approval. And they have convinced the peasants, who suffer from unemployment and starvation, that Finance Minister Count Sergei Witte's industrial drive is to blame for their misfortune.

In hopes of averting revolution, the czar decided today to confer with representatives of the people. He will hold private audiences with more than 200 Russians from all walks of life: professors, newspaper editors and political prisoners. His ministers, perhaps fearing for his safety, have advised the czar against such meetings. Observers agree, however, that something must be done to stem the bloody tide of rebellion; similar events in the central provinces last spring undermined the government (→ 3/12/03).

Seven Renaults triumph in Vienna race

Marcel Renault at the wheel of his victorious four-cylinder racer.

July 15. A great day arrived for the firm of Renault Freres today, when seven Renault cars triumphed in the Paris-Vienna race. This course introduced a new element in racing: mountain country. And the Renault brothers were right in believing that their light cars would better adapt to the rugged terrain.

The third day was the decisive one of the race, when the 148 competitors were confronted with the 5,912-foot Arlberg peak in western Austria. The descent was particularly dangerous; motorcar brakes had never before been put to such a test. Many incidents cost Louis Renault the race, and his brother, Marcel, won. Renault cars also took second and third places in the light car class.

The public is amazed at Marcel Renault's performance. People are saying, "He has beaten the Arlberg Express." Indeed, he has beaten the fastest train in all of Europe: Paris to Vienna in 26 hours, ten minutes and 47 seconds. The train's record is 33 hours, 43 minutes. Marcel Renault is the hero of the day.

20th Century sets rail speed record

The 20th Century Limited.

July 12. The Twentieth Century Limited established a new standard for railroad speed today by covering a 481-mile stretch of its New York-to-Chicago run on the Lake Shore and Michigan Southern Road at better than a mile a minute. A 16-hour schedule between New York and Chicago now is possible, railroad executives say.

The train was two hours and 28 minutes behind schedule 45 miles west of Buffalo, New York, when its engineers were told to open the throttle and make their best possible time. The results were impressive. The Twentieth Century Limited covered the 134 miles between Brockton and Cleveland in 131 minutes. Its time for the 113 miles between Cleveland and Toledo, Ohio, was 103 minutes, with top speeds up to 90 miles an hour. The final 244-mile stretch from Toledo to Chicago required only 228 minutes, including three stops, one to change engines.

Venice, July 14. The bell tower in St. Mark's Square toppled today, scattering tourists and ruining some of Italy's most treasured artwork.

1902

AUGUST

Su	Mo	Tu	We	Th	Fr	Sa
					1	2
3	4	5	6	7	8	9
10	11	12	13	14	15	16
17	18	19	20	21	22	23
24	25	26	27	28	29	30
31						

1. The Vatican agrees to U.S. demands to remove Spanish friars from the Philippines.

1. Australia: Explosion buries 100 workers in coal mines of Wollongong.

2. Switzerland: Social Democrats decide to participate in national elections (→ 10/26).

5. Germany: U.S. Ambassador White resigns post in Berlin.

9. London: King Edward VII and Queen Alexandra crowned at Westminster Abbey.

9. France: Lt. Col. de St. Remy arrested for refusing to close convent school (→ 10/20).

12. Venezuela: Rebels assail state of Barcelona and pillage consulates (→ 10/18).

12. New Jersey: International Harvester Co. incorporated with capital of $120 mil.

15. France: Minister of Defense Louis Andre pledges to revenge loss in Franco-Prussian War of 1870-71.

16. London: U.S., Britain, Japan and Germany sign the Chinese Tariff Protocol; Chinese ministers still hold out (→ 4/23/03).

16. London receives Boer Gens. Botha, Dewey and Delarney with cordial respect.

25. New York: Harry de Windt successfully completes his trek from Paris to New York via the Arctic. →

27. Newport: William Larned successfully defends the U.S. Lawn Tennis Championships, defeating R.F. Doherty 4-6, 6-2, 6-4, 8-6.

29. Pennsylvania: General Gobin orders militia to shoot if striking coal miners become hostile (→ 10/3).

BIRTHS

6. German opera singer Margarette Klose (†12/14/68).

8. British physicist Paul A.M. Dirac.

16. French fashion designer Lucien Lanvin.

22. German film director Leni Reifenstahl.

The French take their ease in August

French bathing beauties enjoy their end-of-summer leisure on the water.

Aug 1. More and more middle-class families in France are taking their vacations in August. And more and more often, they are going to the seaside resort of Deauville on the northern coast. Since the Duke of Morny created a resort there in 1860, and made it accessible by rail, Deauville has become a favorite watering hole. The town is a mecca for vacationers because of its luxurious villas, its wide terraces which border the sea, its casino and its racetrack, which opens in early August.

American buffalo saved from extinction

Buffalo, or American Bison, were a staple of Indian life on the Plains.

Aug 23. Federal efforts to prevent the buffalo from becoming entirely extinct are having an effect due to the policy of stricter game laws begun in 1889, when only 551 of the animals remained in the country.

The Indians always depended upon the buffalo for survival, using their flesh for food and their hides for clothing. In 1800, there were still vast herds of about 60 million roaming the Great Plains. With the arrival of European settlers, however, they were subjected to a slaughter that resulted in their near-extinction. In 1850, 20 million existed. Now, there are two herds of more than 1,000 head thriving in Yellowstone Park and Canada.

The American buffalo, or bison, when fully grown, measures 10-feet long and weighs about 2000 pounds.

Holmes appointed to U.S. Supreme Court

Aug 3. Oliver Wendell Holmes Jr., son of the physician, poet and essayist ("The Autocrat of the Breakfast Table"), was appointed to the United States Supreme Court by President Roosevelt today. Now Chief Justice of the Massachusetts Supreme Court, Holmes will succeed Associate Justice Horace Gray, who has been ill.

Oliver Wendell Holmes.

Holmes was born in Boston, graduated from Harvard University and was thrice wounded in the Civil War. He practiced law, edited the American Law Review, served as a professor of constitutional law and then took a seat on the Massachusetts high court, later becoming its leader.

Trans-Siberian trek

Aug 25. After a trip of 248 days from Paris, including a terrifying journey across Siberia by sled and dog team, Harry de Windt reached New York today. The intrepid traveler reported that it was the worst journey of his entire life; yet, he said he had lost only ten pounds.

The trek was meant to show that a railroad could span the Bering Strait between Siberia and Alaska. He also said the worst tales told about the horrors of Siberia are not exaggerated; temperature often drops to 70 degrees below zero. At the Imperial Hotel in New York City, de Windt was offered an iced drink. "Take it away," he said.

1902

SEPTEMBER

Su	Mo	Tu	We	Th	Fr	Sa
	1	2	3	4	5	6
7	8	9	10	11	12	13
14	15	16	17	18	19	20
21	22	23	24	25	26	27
28	29	30				

1. Martinique: Mount Pelee floods city with molten lava for second time in four months; 2,000 die.

3. Austria: Landslide kills 700 in Transcaucasia.

6. New York: World record set for speed on water, one nautical mile in 98 seconds.

7. Haiti: German gunboat Panther sinks Haitian warship Crete-a-Pierrot.

7. Australia: During national "day of humiliation," farmers pray for rain to end horrible drought.

9. Miners strike gold in Alaska.

13. Germany: Nationalists demand harsher measures against Polish culture and language.

15. Belgium: Workers Party breaks up; radical wing of socialists dominate new party.

17. U.S. troops sent to Panama to keep train lines open over isthmus as Panamanian nationalists struggle for independence from Colombia (→ 11/25).

17. U.S. government protests Rumanian persecution of Jews.

19. Birmingham, Ala.: Panic strikes as cry of "fight" is mistaken for "fire"; 78 Negroes killed.

19. Austria-Hungary: Anti-German demonstrators riot in Hungary upon the centenary of Lassos Kossuth, 19th-century liberal revolutionary.

22. Russia: Czar Nicholas II issues decree abolishing even nominal autonomy for Finland, installs Russian gov. general.

25. Sicily: Hundreds killed as tornado devastates region of Catane.

BIRTHS

12. Brazilian statesman Juscelino Kubitschek De Oliveira.

16. Norwegian statesman Halvard Lange (†5/19/1970).

DEATH

29. French novelist Emile Zola (*4/12/1840).

Greatest railroad merger in history planned by Gould and Rockefeller

Sept 20. Well-informed sources reported today that plans have been completed for the most massive railroad merger in the nation's history, leading to the creation of a new transcontinental line. The reported plan calls for the consolidation of such major railroads as the Missouri Pacific, Denver and Rio Grande, Texas and Pacific, Kansas and Texas, Wabash and Western Maryland, St. Louis and Southwestern, along with a number of other essential American lines.

According to these same sources, the merger is being organized by George J. Gould, the heir of Jay Gould, and various Rockefeller interests who are large holders of Gould securities. The new corporation reportedly would be named Trans-Continental Securities Company. It has been estimated by expert analysts in recent years that nearly two-thirds of the United States' railroad lines are, or are about to be, under the financial control of such giants as the Morgans, Goulds, Vanderbilts, Rockefellers and Harrimans (→ 3/14/04).

Army brought in as Croats, Serbs clash

Sept 1. For decades, the Austro-Hungarian monarchy has been trying to solve the Slavic problem. But it is only getting worse. Slavic nationalists are opposed to the influence of the dual monarchy. But there are also bitter rivalries among the different Slavic peoples.

In their capital of Agram today, Croats marched in the streets, ready to fight any Serbs who crossed their paths. The Croats threw rocks at stores owned by Serbs and then ransacked some of them. The Austro-Hungarian army was called in to restore the peace. Of all the Slavic peoples, the Serbs may very well be the most independent. They also consider themselves to be the real political leaders of the Pan-Slavic movement (→ 6/11/03).

Gusher in Alaska 200 feet high

Sept 17. Alaska has added oil to its growing list of potentially profitable natural resources. An Indiana-based company discovered a huge oil reserve in Cotella, a town on the southern Alaskan coast. The crude was struck only 200 feet below the surface and spurted another 200 feet into the air before it was capped.

The firm had drilled in the area for months without success. Only the discovery of coal in the vicinity had given the company encouragement. The Alaskan crude struck today was judged of fine quality, priced at $4 a barrel at the well. The syndicate plans to refine the oil at the source and transport it by waterway to Pacific coast ports. The transportation is expected to cost the company $3 a ton.

Zola, who defended Dreyfus, is dead

Emile Zola.

Sept 29. Emile Zola, controversial novelist, defender of the wrongfully accused Captain Alfred Dreyfus, was found dead of asphyxiation in his Paris home, the victim of a defective fireplace flue. At 62, he leaves a legacy of best-selling novels, including "L'Assommoir" (1877), "Nana" (1880) and "Germinal" (1885). All embody the idea that heredity determines destiny. In 1898, in a letter to the newspaper L'Aurore beginning with the words "J'accuse," he launched his fierce defense of Dreyfus, who had been accused of spying for Germany.

Sept 18. Fridtjof Nansen's ship, the Fram, returns to Stavanger, Norway, after an unsuccessful attempt to reach the North Pole.

St. Louis is already preparing to host the World's Fair in 1904. Buildings like this industrial tower will display the rapid growth of the U.S. steel industry.

1902

OCTOBER

Su	Mo	Tu	We	Th	Fr	Sa
			1	2	3	4
5	6	7	8	9	10	11
12	13	14	15	16	17	18
19	20	21	22	23	24	25
26	27	28	29	30	31	

2. Switzerland: Immigrant workers deported as strikes turn into riots (→ 26).

3. Washington: Pres. Roosevelt's coal conference stalled over question of union representation on committee of arbitration (→ 15).

4. Chicago: New Orpheon Theatre opens, with debut of the musical "Chow Chow."

9. France: Two-thirds of all mine workers go out on strike.

10. Ireland: English absentee landlords meet to discuss Irish nationalist no-rent campaign.

10. New York: Crown Prince of Siam arrives in U.S.

14. Rimsky-Korsakov's opera "Servilia" premieres in St. Petersburg.

15. Arthur Gardiner completes 488-mile New York-to-Boston-and-Return Reliability Run at an average speed of 14 mph.

17. Detroit: First Cadillac completed, sold and sent to Buffalo, NY.

18. Venezuela: President Castro's army overcomes rebels in seven-day battle (→ 12/7).

20. France: Responding to unrest over Association Act of July 1901, Chamber of Deputies appoints commission to study separation of church and state (→ 12/18).

24. French bicycle racer Henri Contenet hits new speed record of 47 mph.

26. Switzerland: Radical Democrats dominate elections of the National Council.

28. Colombia: Rebel Gen. Uribe-Uribe surrenders to Gen. Marjarres; revolt now confined to Panamanian isthmus (→ 11/3/03).

30. Guatemala: Volcanic eruption ravages coffee region.

BIRTH

2. Austrian statesman Leopold Figl (†5/9/1965).

DEATH

26. American suffragette leader Elizabeth Cady Stanton (*11/12/1815).

T.R. settles coal strike

Roosevelt and J.P. Morgan confer in attempt to resolve the strike.

Oct 15. Striking coal miners agreed today to return to work after President Roosevelt intervened by naming a panel of arbitrators. The five-month strike had threatened to paralyze the nation's big industries and held out the possibility that home heating fuel would be in short supply this winter.

After the president had consulted with top aides throughout much of the day and night, the White House issued a statement at 2:20 this morning, announcing plans to end the strike. The statement reported that the president had appointed a commission to "inquire into, consider, and pass upon all questions at issue between the operators and miners in the anthracite coal fields."

The day's dramatic events began shortly before noon yesterday when John Mitchell, the young head of the United Mine Workers, arrived at the White House to confer with the president. The two held still another meeting during the day. In late afternoon, the president went for a long drive before returning to the White House for additional meetings with top aides and several prominent businessmen.

Operators of the mines had proposed a five-member commission, but Mitchell had protested that this would fail to reflect the miners' interests. The final agreement provides for the addition of a sixth member acceptable to the United Mine Workers. A White House spokesman said that the miners will resume work soon.

Suffragette leader dies at age of 87

Oct 26. Elizabeth Cady Stanton, a pioneer in the fight for voting rights for women, died today at her home in New York City. She was nearly 87 years old. The daughter of a New York Supreme Court Justice, she first became aware of discrimination against women by reading cases in law books in her father's office. Several years later, while attending an anti-slavery conference in London with her husband, Henry Brewster Stanton, she met Lucretia Mott, a suffragette. In 1848, at Seneca Falls, New York, the two jointly sponsored the first women's rights convention, where the current struggle for the franchise officially began.

Elizabeth Cady Stanton.

Detroit, Oct 17. Cadillac Co. shipped a version of this sleek Runabout to Buffalo, N.Y., today. It is the first car sold by the new manufacturer, named after the French explorer who founded Detroit in 1701.

1902

NOVEMBER

Su	Mo	Tu	We	Th	Fr	Sa
						1
2	3	4	5	6	7	8
9	10	11	12	13	14	15
16	17	18	19	20	21	22
23	24	25	26	27	28	29
30						

1. France attempts to neutralize Triple Alliance, signing agreement with Italy to remain neutral in Africa.

3. Thousands of natives along Arctic coast reported to be dying of measles.

4. New York: Explosion at Madison Square Garden kills 15, injures 70.

8. England: Kaiser Wilhelm II arrives for 12-day visit in effort to improve Anglo-German relations.

11. New York: Roland Molineux acquitted in second trial, four years after murder of Margaret J. Adams.

14. Leo Tolstoy's novel "Resurrection" staged in Paris.

15. Brussels: Anarchist fires three shots at king of Belgium.

21. Canada: Government appoints a commission to overhaul obsolete public statutes passed over the years.

22. New Haven, Conn.: Yale defeats Harvard 23-0 to win college football championship.

23. Paris: Statue of Honore de Balzac inaugurated.

24. France: First congress of professional photographers convenes in Paris.

25. Colombia rejects U.S. canal offer, raising question of negotiations with Nicaragua or Costa Rica (→ 1/22/03).

26. Milan: Premiere of Francesco Cilea's opera "Adriana Lecouvreur."

29. Philadelphia: Army beats Navy 22-8 in annual football game.

29. Carl August Nielsen's opera "Saul and David" premieres in Copenhagen.

BIRTHS

9. British film director Anthony Asquith (/2/21/1968).

29. Italian writer Carlo Levi (/1/14/1975).

DEATH

22. Friedrich Krupp, industrialist, Germany's wealthiest man (*2/17/1854).

Span of the Williamsburg Bridge burns

The Williamsburg Bridge, decimated by fire.

Nov 22. The city of New York has survived many fires, but few were as dramatic as the blaze which ripped across part of the Williamsburg Bridge this afternoon. The bridge has not been completed yet, and workmen were just putting away their tools when flames jumped from one of their work stations, more than 100 yards above the surface of the East River.

Fireboats were rushed to the scene, but before they arrived, the fire spread to the wooden pedestrian walkway on the bridge. Sparks showered down to the river bank and houses in the area were evacuated as a precaution. Large crowds gathered to watch the fire, which caused considerable damage before it burned itself out. Officials are denying preliminary reports that four of the men who had been working on the bridge are missing.

Friedrich Krupp dies at age 48

Nov 22. Germany's greatest manufacturer, Friedrich Krupp, died suddenly from apoplexy this afternoon at his villa in Essen. After the death of his father, the original developer of the Krupp iron and steel works, Friedrich ensured the firm's growth, in spite of fierce competition. He devoted his attention to making weapons and armor plate.

Teddy says color no bar to office

Nov 27. President Roosevelt made it loud and clear today: A man's color or race is no bar to office. The president was responding to Southern critics of his recent appointment of a Negro to the post of Collector of the Port of Charleston. Roosevelt said he would appoint qualified men, whether white or colored (→ 1/2/03).

Victorious Army football team. Mgr. Douglas MacArthur at top right.

Barnum and Bailey back from Europe

Barnum & Bailey poster.

Nov 8. With lions, tigers, bears, horses, elephants and nearly every other creature aboard, the Barnum & Bailey Circus ship, resembling Noah's Ark, returned from Europe today. All of the animals and freaks, including the legless man, the armless man and the Siamese twins, are in good condition.

There were two deaths on board, though. At sea, 54 monkeys were put in the ship's hold. Jesse, the champion peanut eater, would not eat and died. And one of the zebras gave birth, but the baby only lived two days. Both animals were cast overboard with proper ceremony.

Also aboard were a buffalo, one hippopotamus, two giraffes, four zebras, four kangaroos, seven camels and Mandarin, the biggest of the circus' 23 elephants, who was in a bad mood during the entire voyage. If he fails to control his temper, the circus says it will have to destroy him.

Suitable dress for taking a stroll in the late autumn air. Patterns from McCall's, only 15 cents.

1902

DECEMBER

Su	Mo	Tu	We	Th	Fr	Sa
	1	2	3	4	5	6
7	8	9	10	11	12	13
14	15	16	17	18	19	20
21	22	23	24	25	26	27
28	29	30	31			

7. Britain, Germany demand compensation from Venezuelan Pres. Castro for losses suffered during his coup of 1899 (→ 9).

9. Venezuela: British and German warships seize Venezuelan navy (→ 20).

13. London: Committee of Imperial Defense holds first meeting.

18. Great Britain: Parliament passes Education Act, bringing church schools into state system (→ 3/18/03).

20. Roosevelt asked to arbitrate Venezuelan debt crisis (→ 31).

20. Spain: Swindler Therese Humbert and accomplices arrested in Madrid.

21. Newfoundland: Marconi sends messages across Atlantic by wireless.

25. Vatican: Pope Leo XIII endorses European Christian Democratic movement as alternative to socialism.

DEATHS

6. American politician Thomas B. Reed, ex-speaker of the House (*10/18/1839).

7. U.S. political cartoonist Thomas Nast (*9/27/1840).

CULTURAL EVENTS, 1902

Literature: A. Conan Doyle's "The Hound of the Baskervilles"; Kipling's "Just-so Stories"; Chekhov's "The Three Sisters"; Conrad's "Heart of Darkness"; Owen Wister's "The Virginian; Andre Gide's "L'Immoraliste."

Religion, Academia: William James' "The Varieties of Religious Experience"; Werner Sombart's "Modern Capitalism"; Benedetto Croce's "Philosophy of the Spirit"; J.A. Hobson's "Imperialism."

Music: Elgar's 1st "Pomp and Circumstance" march; Enrico Caruso's 1st phonograph recording; Frederick Delius' "Appalachia"; "In The Good Old Summertime" sells 1 mil.

The Arts: Gauguin's "Riders by the Sea"; Rodin's sculpture "Romeo and Juliet"; Oskar Messter's film "Solome."

Mile-long Aswan Dam blocks Nile and forms 200-mile artificial lake

The Aswan Dam has flooded the entrance to Egypt's Philae Temple.

Dec 10. The great dam at Aswan, 590 miles south of Cairo, Egypt, on the Nile River, was formally declared complete today after nearly four years of construction by a labor force of 11,000. A 200-mile lake holding more than 5.5 million cubic yards of water is beginning to form behind the new dam, which is expected not only to produce a revolution in the primitive and laborious methods of irrigation in Egypt but also to reclaim vast areas of arid land for agriculture.

The dam is a mile and a quarter long and 130-feet high. Its purpose is to impound water during the period when the Nile floods and to release it on a controlled schedule during the year. The dam has 180 sluices which can be opened to send water into a system of irrigation canals. It also has four locks, each 260-feet long and 32-feet wide.

Mommsen is one of Nobel laureates

Dec 10. Theodor Mommsen of Germany has won the Nobel Prize for literature. With the honor comes nearly $30,000 in Swedish currency. Mainly concerned with political history (he was a member of the Reichstag), Mommsen, 84, is the author of a "History of Rome," but he has also examined Roman society and culture.

He is joined by six other laureates: Ronald Ross, Emil Fischer, Hendrik Lorentz, Pieter Zeeman, Charles Gobat and Elie Ducommun. Ross earned the award in medicine. Fischer won the prize for chemistry with research on carbohydrates. Lorentz and Zeeman shared the prize for physics by contributing to the theory of electromagnetic radiation. Gobat, a Swiss statesman who founded a peace bureau this year, jointly won the Peace Prize with Ducommun.

Theodor Mommsen, historian.

Venezuela receives payment demands

Dec 31. Venezuelan President Cipriano Castro has agreed to abide by any ruling of the Hague Tribunal over a violent international dispute that has paralyzed his nation for nearly a month. Venezuela seeks removal of the German and British fleets from its harbors and dismissal of purported debts owed those nations. Germany and Great Britain will also appear before the tribunal, demanding payment of the arrears.

On December 7, the ambassadors from Germany and Great Britain had approached Venezuelan representatives, requesting that losses suffered in the Venezuelan coup of 1899 be repaid immediately. Some of those losses were incurred when Venezuela appropriated railroads previously owned by the European nations. Castro claims the proper congressional committee was never approached about the debts and that he was not aware of any liabilities. Two days later, the combined British and German fleets sailed into the harbor of La Guayvra and seized the entire Venezuelan navy, a fleet of four battleships.

Since December 9, both parties have engaged in brief sallies. When its fleet was taken, Venezuela arrested German and British subjects in Caracas. The foreign navies responded by bombarding a fortress at Puerto Cabello. Each government has expressed a desire for a mediating body. Castro invited President Roosevelt to arbitrate, but he declined (→ 1/21/03).

Show girls encourage "the new woman." Josie Hall, Carrie Coote and Kate Claxton offering "Between the Acts & Bravo" cigarettes.

1903

JANUARY

Su	Mo	Tu	We	Th	Fr	Sa
				1	2	3
4	5	6	7	8	9	10
11	12	13	14	15	16	17
18	19	20	21	22	23	24
25	26	27	28	29	30	31

2. President Roosevelt closes post office in Indianola, Miss., for refusing Minnie Cox, a colored postmistress

3. Bulgarian govt. renounces treaty of commerce tying it to Austro-Hungarian Empire.

3. Venezuela: 1400 revolutionaries defeated by 800 govt. troops at Guatire.

7. Vincent d'Indy's opera "L'Etranger" premieres in Brussels.

8. American Beet Sugar Assn. withdraws opposition to Cuban reciprocity treaty, but takes stand against agricultural supports to Philippines.

10. Argentina bars importation of American beef for sanitary reasons (→ 6/30/06).

13. South Sea Islands: Tidal wave kills upwards of 1,000 Tuamotu natives.

13. Morocco: Sultan flees Fez; imperial troops defeated by pretender's army (→ 5/8/04).

15. South Carolina: Lt. Gov. James Tillman critically wounds political foe N.G. Gonzales, who had denounced Tillman's nephew (→ 10/15).

19. France: Tour de France bicycle race to begin this year, the magazine "L'Auto" announces (→ 7/19).

19. China: Imperial government declares it cannot meet reparation payments for Boxer revolt.

21. Venezuela: 3 German warships shell the Fort of San Carlos (→ 26).

24. U.S. Sec. of State John Hay and British Ambassador Herbert create joint commission to establish Alaskan border (→ 10/16).

26. President Castro offers allies percentage of customs in Venezuelan ports (→ 2/13).

27. New York: It is reported that British policy in South Africa is leading toward forced labor for black natives.

DEATH

28. French composer Robert Planquette (*1848).

India acclaims Edward VII as Emperor

Procession in Delhi for the coronation of Edward VII.

Jan 1. A vast crowd thronged the great plain outside Delhi, India, today, waiting to hear the declaration that King Edward VII was Emperor of India. The crowd, clothed in brilliantly colored garments, was largely composed of common people who had come to the durbar to see India's princes pledge their fealty to the emperor.

The Duke of Connaught, representing King Edward, sat on the left of the Viceroy of India, Lord Curzon of Kedleston, who sat on a throne surrounded by giant silver footstools. Lord Curzon spoke briefly, then read a message from the king, who expressed regret at not being present at the durbar and his wishes for "the increasing prosperity of my Indian Empire." Among the dignitaries in the amphitheater were 600 veterans of the Sepoy Mutiny of 1857-58 (→ 7/20).

Ex-slaves demand to be paid pensions

Jan 14. Negro clergymen threatened today to lead a revolt against the Republican Party unless pensions are given to former slaves. Just last fall, the leaders of the revolt had promised to call off their movement after receiving promises from the Roosevelt administration that it would fight the "Lily Whites" in the South.

Arguing that the administration has not been forceful enough in smoothing race relations, Negro leaders have renewed their demands for pensions for ex-slaves, saying that if the President and Congress refuse, "we can change the color of things before the next election." A bill to grant pensions to former Negro slaves has been before Congress for a number of years, but it has never been passed into law (→ 6/30).

U.S. signs Colombia treaty for canal

Jan 22. The United States and Colombia have reached an agreement that will allow construction of the Panama canal. Secretary of State John Hay and Colombian Charge d'Affairs Tomas Herran signed the treaty today in Washington. It now must be ratified by the Senate.

Until the last minute, many interested observers feared that the Colombian government would never agree to all of the requests of the United States, requiring the President to begin talks with Nicaragua about the alternate canal route. At this time, details of the treaty are not known, especially the price and the annual rental the United States must pay. An earlier dispute over the length of the lease was settled when Colombia ceded the land in perpetuity (→ 3/14).

1903

FEBRUARY

Su	Mo	Tu	We	Th	Fr	Sa
1	2	3	4	5	6	7
8	9	10	11	12	13	14
15	16	17	18	19	20	21
22	23	24	25	26	27	28

1. Connecticut: Militia called out to prevent riots in Waterbury.

11. Washington: Congress passes the Expedition Act, giving antitrust cases priority in the courts (→ 18).

13. Venezuelan blockade lifted; envoys sign protocol granting Western allies settlement of claims (→ 2/22/04).

13. Balkans: Slaughters reported in Macedonia (→ 4/3).

14. Washington: Congress creates Dept. of Commerce and Labor to help foster long-term stability in U.S. economy.

17. Belgian government raises taxes on liquor (→ 3/10).

18. Illinois legislator David Underwood tries to bar football in his state.

18. U.S. Circuit Court judge rules against beef trust (→ 19).

18. Heirs of American businessman Henry Rudolff win $700,000 suit against Venezuelan govt. for annulment of an 1892 concession.

19. Washington: Congress passes Elkins Act, outlawing rail rebates on published freight rates, yet stopping short of rate regulation (→ 1/30/05).

19. Austria-Hungary: Government decrees mandatory two-year military service.

20. Germany: Kaiser Wilhelm declares his faith in Christian orthodoxy; German theologians reassured.

20. Vatican: Pope Leo XIII celebrates 25 years in papacy.

23. Turkey: Sultan agrees to Austro-Hungarian plan for reforms in Macedonia; Moslems, Christians to be represented proportionately on police force (→ 4/3).

26. J.P. Morgan receives letter from Socialist Party of Pennsylvania thanking him for advancing the cause of socialism in the U.S., and claiming 400,000 leftist voters.

DEATH

26. American Richard Jordan Gatling, invented machine gun.

Susan B. Anthony celebrates birthday

Feb 16. Susan B. Anthony, the seemingly tireless suffragette, celebrated her 83rd birthday today with a gift to the United States: her large collection of books on the fight for women's rights. The book collection, Miss Anthony announced at her home in Rochester, N.Y., will be housed in an alcove of the Library of Congress in Washington.

Already, she said, she has sent four boxes of books, and there are others now being packed. She said she is keeping only those that are "too dear to part with during my lifetime." Among the books to be given to the library is one written by a Lady Morgan 50 years ago, detailing early efforts in the struggle to win voting rights for women. Also in the collection are files of Miss Anthony's own suffrage newspaper, The Revolution, as well as files of the ex-slave Frederick Douglass' abolitionist newspaper, The Liberator.

Miss Anthony, born in Adams, Massachusetts, the daughter of a Quaker abolitionist, has been a leader of the fight for voting rights for women for nearly 50 years (→ 9/26).

Susan B. Anthony keeps images of noted U.S. women on view in her office.

First American gets Rhodes scholarship

Feb 1. A Rhodes scholarship has been awarded to an American for the first time. Eugene Heitler Lehman, a 22-year-old Yale graduate, was named recipient of the coveted Cecil Rhodes Scholarship at Oxford University in England.

The son of a wholesale tobacco dealer in Pueblo, Colorado, the young student of Zionism started at Colorado University but went in his sophomore year to Yale University, where he swept oratorical honors. During his first year in New Haven, he won the Griffen Gold Medal for oratory, the first time it was won by a sophomore. He also won several other oratory awards and managed the debating team. He won a Phi Beta Kappa key at Yale and said his goal was to study the conditions of the Jews in Russia and Eastern Europe with a view toward improving them.

Cuba forced to give U.S. naval bases

Feb 23. Left with little choice, Cuba's constitutional convention has ended with agreement to accept the Platt amendment urged on it by the United States. Had it not done so, the United States government would not have recognized any eventual Cuban constitution.

Under the amendment, Cuba accedes to American intervention if Cuban independence is threatened, or the Cuban government violates personal rights to life and property. In addition, Cuba consents to lease to the United States the naval bases of Guantanamo and Bahia Honda.

Cuba also agrees to incur no debts larger than it can repay, and to perpetuate sanitary improvements made during American military rule, which most notably stamped out yellow fever. The status of the Isle of Pines is to be determined later (→ 3/19).

Telegraphic news published at sea

Feb 22. The Cunard liner Etruria arrived in New York harbor today with a copy of the first newspaper ever published in the middle of the Atlantic Ocean. It features news accounts transmitted from Britain by wireless telegraphy.

One of the passengers on the Etruria was Guglielmo Marconi, who made the event possible by inventing the system of wireless telegraphy and demonstrating in 1901 that signals could be transmitted across the Atlantic Ocean. When Marconi and others aboard the Etruria awoke this morning, they were presented with a newspaper containing brief accounts of a coal shortage in New York, the dispatch of an American warship to Honduras and other events (→ 3/29).

Porcelain is used for filling teeth

Feb 16. Two new methods in the science of dentistry were revealed today at the 15th anniversary meeting of the Orthontographic Society of Chicago.

One was the restoration of teeth by the porcelain-inlay process. This means that porcelain can be used instead of gold, silver or amalgam in the filling of teeth. The second new procedure was the analysis of a patient's saliva to diagnose and prevent gum disease.

These important demonstrations were presented in clinics to some 2,000 professional dentists from all over the United States. Each state has sent five dentists to the meeting, and there are representatives from the larger cities. More than 200 clinics will be held.

Inventor of fast-firing weapon deceased

Feb 26. Dr. Richard J. Gatling, inventor of the gun which revolutionized modern warfare, died yesterday in New York City at 84.

As developed by Gatling early in the Civil War, the Gatling Gun fired 250 shots a minute as compared with its current 3,000 shots a minute. But the inventor was a mild, kind man whose aim was the contrary of violence or destruction. Because the gun could be fired by one man, he hoped it would spare an entire army from indiscriminate enemy fire. After perfecting the machine gun for 30 years, he sold his interest to Colt Firearms Company.

Nor did he invent only guns. Born on a farm, he helped his father design a device for thinning cotton. Later, while working as a merchant, he designed a screw propeller and then a machine for sowing rice, at which time he shifted exclusively to inventing. At his death, he headed the St. Louis Gatling Motor Power Company and planned to place his new motor plow on the market.

His friends speak of Gatling as a student and philosopher, having studied medicine to care for himself and his family. Though he made a considerable amount of money from his inventions, he lost a lot by investing in railroads in the West. He also had his share of setbacks, one being the recent explosion at Sandy Hook of his big gun, modeled after Krupp's, which he attributed to sabotage.

Richard Jordan Gatling's rapid-firing gun was used widely overseas.

1903

MARCH

Su	Mo	Tu	We	Th	Fr	Sa
1	2	3	4	5	6	7
8	9	10	11	12	13	14
15	16	17	18	19	20	21
22	23	24	25	26	27	28
29	30	31				

1. France: Republican liberals demonstrate against monarchy on the occasion of historian Edgar Quinet's centenary.

3. St. Louis: Barney Gilmore arrested for spitting.

10. N.Y.: Disease-stricken ship Karmania quarantined in port; six dead from cholera.

10. France: Academy of Medicine declares alcohol detrimental to health, proposes measures to fight it (→ 4/15).

12. Russia: Czar issues decree providing for nominal freedom of religion throughout his dominions (→ 7/29).

14. Washington: Senate ratifies Hay-Herran Treaty, guarantees U.S. right to build canal at Panama (→ 8/12).

15. British conquest of Northern Nigeria completed; 500,000 sq. miles controlled by U.K.

18. France dissolves Catholic religious orders (→ 8/5).

19. Washington: Senate ratifies Cuban treaty; U.S. gains naval bases at Guantanamo and Bahia Honda (→ 2/5/04).

20. Paris: Paintings of Henri Matisse shown at the "Salon des Independants."

22. Colombia: Volcanic eruption devastates region near Galera De Zamba.

22. New York: Niagara Falls goes dry.

23. U.S. troops sent to Honduras to protect American consulate during revolutionary activity.

28. Anatole France's "Crainquebille" premieres in Paris.

29. Regular news service begins between New York and London on Marconi's wireless.

30. Dominican Republic: Revolutionary outbreak brings U.S. troops to Santo Domingo to protect American interests (→ 1/2/04).

BIRTH

4. American painter Adolph Gottlieb (†3/4/1974).

Immigrants must pay a $2 head tax

March 3. A bill seeking to bar certain "undesirables" from the United States was passed today by the Congress. This latest move to curb growing immigration to what was once called the "Promised Land" will place a $2 head tax on all arriving aliens. The tax must be paid at the port of entry by the master or owner of the vessel on which the immigrant arrives.

The money would be placed in what is called the "Immigrant Fund" to defray the expenses of administering the new law. The tax would not be levied on those in transit through the United States nor on those who have previously paid it. The new law would also exclude from admission to the country certain persons, such as idiots, convicted felons, polygamists, anarchists, the insane, epileptics and women of bad repute.

Only in recent years has the United States sought to stem the flow of immigration. During the early to middle years of the last century, the country welcomed all comers. During that period, Ireland alone sent more than a million persons to the United States. By 1900, an estimated 35 million aliens had arrived in the United States from throughout much of the civilized world, principally from Europe.

The steady flow of new arrivals was prompted largely by such events as the potato famine in Ireland and lack of jobs in many of the other countries. Furthermore, many large steamship companies had engaged thousands of agents to drum up business by persuading foreigners to migrate to the United States in steerage. In recent years, though, organized labor has protested the importation of cheap labor, and social reformers have become concerned about crowded urban living conditions (→ 8/1/05).

Processing immigrants at Ellis Island.

Coal board rules for better labor terms

March 21. The Coal Strike Commission has come down on the side of increased wages and shorter hours for the anthracite coal workers. While forbidding strikes and lockouts, it also provides that labor-management disputes be settled by a board of conciliation.

In brief, the commission has established the following:

A ten percent increase in pay for all contract miners.

An eight-hour day for firemen and for engineers who hoist water, but at the current wage scale.

A five percent pay increase together with Sundays off for other engineers and pumpmen.

For all other employees, the work day will be reduced from ten hours to nine, at present wages.

Stating that miners must be represented on the board of conciliation by a worker's organization, the commission did not formally recognize the United Mine Workers.

Turkey-to-Baghdad rail line planned

March 5. A German syndicate has obtained a concession to build a railway through Turkey to Baghdad. The Baghdad Railway Company will have free right-of-way through Turkey and will have the right to exploit mineral resources within 12 miles on each side of the railway. Ownership of the railroad will revert to Turkey in 99 years.

This is the second Turkish rail project for the German group, which received a concession in 1888 to reconstruct and extend a rail line from Constantinople to Angora. The syndicate, made up of German bankers and headed by Georg von Siemens, had a difficult time negotiating this contract in spite of support for the project from both the Ottoman Sultan and Kaiser Wilhelm II, because of Russian opposition.

As a result of the Russian pressure, a southern route was finally chosen, beginning in Konia, which has rail links to Constantinople, and continuing to Baghdad, with a trunk line to Basra as well as Kuwait.

In spite of loans from the Turkish government, the Germans are expected to seek additional foreign financial assistance in building the railroad. So far, the French and British governments have expressed interest (→ 4/14).

1903

APRIL

Su	Mo	Tu	We	Th	Fr	Sa
			1	2	3	4
5	6	7	8	9	10	11
12	13	14	15	16	17	18
19	20	21	22	23	24	25
26	27	28	29	30		

1. Rome: International Congress of Historians opens, headed by Theodor Mommsen (→ 11/1).

2. Prussia: Mining accident in Silesia takes 30 lives.

2. Spain: Students riot in Saragoza, Madrid and Salamanca (→ 10/30).

3. Bulgaria: Turkish cavalry squadron attacks a band of Macedonian rebels (→ 5/6).

5. New Haven, Conn.: New ruling at Yale allows freshmen to choose their own course of study.

6. Holland: Rail workers go on strike (→ 11).

6. France: It is discovered that army nationalists had forged documents to guarantee conviction of Alfred Dreyfus, Jewish lieutenant accused of spying for Germany.

6. Albanians massacre Christians at Okhrida.

7. Carter Harrison re-elected mayor of Chicago.

11. Holland: Parliament adopts law punishing railway and civil service strikers.

14. Russians refuse to aid Baghdad railway.

15. Bremen: International Congress on Alcoholism opens.

22. Muldi Mohammed proclaimed sultan of Morocco.

23. Russia demands sovereignty in Manchuria (→ 5/8).

23. Great Britain: It is reported that military expenditures for Boer War and Chinese expedition total 1/3 of U.K. budget (→ 8/25).

23. Octave Mirbeau play "Business is Business" premieres

29. Vancouver, B.C.: Top of Turtle Mountain blows off, killing 95.

BIRTH

10. American journalist and politician Clare Boothe Luce.

DEATH

28. American naturalist Josiah W. Gibbs (*12/11/1839).

Violent pogrom occurs at Kishinev

Czarist policeman deals with a Jew.

April 16. Scores of Jews in Kishinev, Russia, were savagely murdered during the course of a pogrom that began Easter morning. Military officials were present, but did not try to stop the frenzied peasants as they raped and murdered. It is believed that the pogrom was incited by government officials.

Persecution of Jews has been a constant feature of the ten-year reign of Czar Nicholas II, but not since 1881 has such a massacre taken place. The czar is reportedly angered by the belief that Jews have been responsible for the 500 strikes against factories this year, as well as the organization of revolutionary groups.

Kishinev, a city of 100,000, almost half of them Jewish, was a likely spot for a pogrom. Its lower-class peasant population had been simmering with anger against the Jews since winter, when a Christian boy was murdered. Many peasants believed he was killed by Jews who needed his blood to prepare for the Passover feast.

The death of a Christian girl on the eve of Easter inflamed these superstitions. On Easter morning, handbills appeared throughout Kishinev announcing that the czar had granted permission to local Christians to wreak "bloody punishment" upon Jews. By noon, rioters had wrecked the city's Jewish section (→ 5/17).

France begins closing all monasteries

Monks quit La Grande Chartreuse.

April 29. The tense battle between church and state took a new turn in France today. Soldiers on horseback invaded the Chartreuse monastery in the Alps and ordered the evacuation of all residents. The monks tried to stop the government of President Combes from forcing them to leave by paying two million francs, but their offer was rejected. So were protests from the right.

The expulsion order is part of the anticlerical movement that has been growing steadily in France since the Dreyfus Affair nine years ago. Last year, the French government decreed that a school with even one religious teacher required special government authorization. And last month, the House of Deputies denied 21 separate groups of monks the riqht to teach at all. Conservative politicians have been critical of President Combes, and they question his motivation, because he was a seminarian before he became a politician (→ 5/21/04).

New York admires new Stock Exchange

April 24. Streams of ticker tape floated down on a crowd of 2,000 during the dedication of the New York Stock Exchange's new building at Broad and Wall Streets. Built for about $4 million on land valued at over $9 million, the exchange features a facade of white Georgian marble. Large Corinthian columns adorn the Wall Street entrance, with allegorical figures representing industry and commerce. Windows in the boardroom are 50-feet high and 96-feet long. In a speech today, J.P. Morgan observed that "the magnificence of our new home is only in keeping with the magnitude of our business."

Bulgarians massacre 165 in single village

April 14. The Balkan troubles may be worsening. In the latest incident, Bulgarians are reported to have destroyed a small Moslem village in the vilayet of Monastir, in Macedonia, killing in cold blood 165 men, women and children. This massacre is just an example of the murder, pillage and atrocities committed daily in this region by all sides: Turks, Albanians, Bulgarians as well as others.

In February, representatives of Austria-Hungary and Russia proposed reforms, such as including Christians in the security forces according to their proportion in the population, which were bitterly opposed by the Moslems. Then, in March, an Albanian assassinated the Russian Consul at Mitrovitza.

The Turkish government claims to have reached a settlement with the mostly Moslem Albanians. However, many question whether their shared religion can overcome the Albanian desire to achieve freedom from Turkish rule. The Turks still face major resistance from the Bulgarian guerrillas, who are also trying to liberate Macedonia from Turkish domination (→ 9/17).

Stately facade of the new exchange.

1903

MAY

Su	Mo	Tu	We	Th	Fr	Sa
					1	2
3	4	5	6	7	8	9
10	11	12	13	14	15	16
17	18	19	20	21	22	23
24	25	26	27	28	29	30
31						

1. British King Edward VII visits Paris in effort to improve Anglo-French relations (→ 7/6).

2. Jockey H. Booker rides Judge Himes to victory in Kentucky Derby.

3. Rome: Kaiser Wilhelm II meets with Pope Leo XIII.

5. Britain: Foreign Minister William Petty declares Persian Gulf a part of British dominion in India (→ 15).

6. Italian warships sent to Salonika help Turkish sultan quell rebellion in Macedonia (→ 8/6).

8. Manchuria: Russians re-occupy and fortify Niu-Chwang (→ 7/3).

10. Austria-Hungary: Upon announcement that Innsbruck Univ. will remain German, Italy asks for Italian univ. at Trieste.

15. Great Britain: Colonial Minister Joseph Chamberlain appeals for customs reform aimed at giving U.K. trade advantages over colonies and foreign powers (→ 6/22).

15. Britain: In implicit warning to Russia, For. Sec. Lansdowne declares a foreign naval base in Persian Gulf would be "a very grave menace" (→ 7/6).

17. Russia: Interior ministers found responsible for massacre of Jews at Kishinev (→ 6/4).

20. Belgium: House of Commons invites govt. to meet with Berlin treaty signers to monitor abuses in Congo (→ 8/19).

23. Paris and Rome linked by telephone for first time.

23. Wisconsin adopts direct primary; voters to choose presidential nominee.

27. Washington: Postmaster General August W. Machen arrested for accepting bribes.

28. Turkey: Earthquake ravages Constantinople; 2,000 dead.

BIRTHS

14. Iraqi statesman Mustafa Al-Barzani.

29. U.S. comedian Bob Hope.

Paul Gauguin is dead

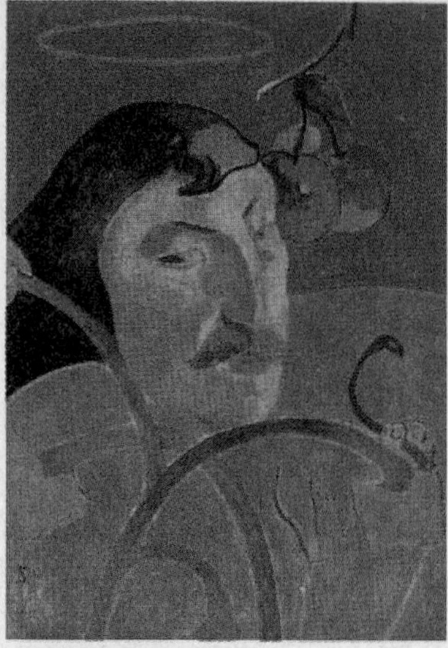

"Autoportrait."

"Contes barbares."

May 8. The French painter Paul Gauguin, 55 years old, has died in the Marquesas Islands in French Polynesia. Gauguin, who had once been a stockbroker, decided to devote himself to art after he met Camille Pissarro and Paul Cezanne. Gauguin also made friends with Vincent van Gogh in Paris. But his journey to Martinique in 1887 was the decisive experience. It enabled him to discover the brilliant colors of tropical landscapes and to appreciate the natural life of a primitive community.

Gauguin created a new style known as "cloisonnisme," in which the pictorial image consists of areas of pure color separated by black outlines, and he applied this technique in "Bonjour Monsieur Gauguin" in 1889. Gauguin had broken with his Impressionist past; he wanted his paintings, by their color and form, to be pleasing to the eye and to express ideas.

When Gauguin installed himself in Pont-Aven, Brittany, in 1889-90, a group of young followers gathered around him, including Charles Filiger and Maurice Denis, who transmitted Gauguin's ideas to Edward Vuillard and Pierre Bonnard. In 1891, Gauguin left his family to go to Tahiti, where he developed his primitivism and protested against social injustice in the South Sea Islands.

"Eh quoi! Serais-tu jalouse?"

Socialism growing in United States

Socialists demonstrate in New York.

May 1. A socialist tide seems to be rising in America. Some immigrants bring radical ideas, and a native movement, inspiring reformers, is growing. Eugene Debs polled nearly 100,000 votes in the 1900 presidential race and will run again. Years ago, Americans thought a socialist was a mysterious desperado from the dark places of Europe, who engaged in a monstrous conspiracy against civilization (→ 5/5/04).

Six die in auto race

May 1. The first stage of this year's Paris-Madrid popular automobile race was marked by new records. Unfortunately, this cost the lives of six persons (two chauffeurs, two soldiers, a child and a woman) in a series of shocking accidents unparalleled in the young history of the sport. Also in a very critical state are the automobilists Lorraine Barrows and Marcel Renault, the famous racer and maker of automobiles, who won the Paris-Vienna race last year.

Remains of Marcel Renault's racer.

1903

JUNE

Su	Mo	Tu	We	Th	Fr	Sa
	1	2	3	4	5	6
7	8	9	10	11	12	13
14	15	16	17	18	19	20
21	22	23	24	25	26	27
28	29	30				

1. Gainesville, Georgia destroyed by tornado; 100 killed.

3. Arizona: Several thousand miners go on strike (→ 30).

4. Russia: Czar decrees Jews allowed to have property only at their place of residence (→ 26).

7. Berlin: Professor Curie reveals discovery of new element, Polonium.

7. Marseilles: French steamship Liban sinks, killing 150.

8. St. Louis: Mississippi River floods several Missouri towns, killing 19.

12. Chicago: 3,000 hotel workers strike.

14. Belgrade: Prince Peter chosen king (→ 24).

15. Oregon: Floods follow sudden cloudburst; 500 dead.

16. A year after opening its doors, Pepsi-Cola Co. registers "Pepsi-Cola" with U.S. Patent Office.

19. Switzerland: Student Benito Mussolini put on police files for socialist affiliations.→

22. Great Britain: 100,000 workers demonstrate in Castleford against rise in customs duties (→ 9/8).

24. New Serbian King Peter I promises to abide by constitution.

26. Czar Nicholas II rejects petition from Pres. Roosevelt protesting Russian treatment of Jews (→ 9/4/04).

28. Jungfrau railway line inaugurated in Switzerland.

29. British government officially protests Belgian atrocities in Congo (→ 9/19).

30. Washington: Committee reports on racial conflict in South (→ 2/6/04).

30. Wyoming: 234 miners killed in explosion (→ 1/25/04).

BIRTH

25. British writer George Orwell, born Arthur Blair (†11/21/1950).

Negro killed; mob rules

The terror of the mob.

June 23. An angry crowd of about 5,000 persons forced the release today of a man accused of leading the mob that lynched a Negro a few days ago near Wilmington, Delaware. As the crowd milled around city hall, a coroner's jury cleared Arthur Corwell of any role in the lynching of George White, the confessed murderer of 17-year-old Helen Bishop, earlier this month. The jury held that White died at the hands of "persons unknown." He had been dragged from jail by the mob, burned at the stake and hanged. Before he died, White confessed to the murder (→ 30).

Serbian King and Queen assassinated

June 11. King Alexander and Queen Draga of Belgrade were murdered in their palace today. The assassinations were part of a revolutionary plot organized by the Serbian army and high-ranking government officials. Prince Peter Karageorgevitch has been proclaimed king by the army, and most observers believe the Serbian government will confirm the proclamation.

While many of the details are not known because of the extreme secrecy of the murder plot, it is believed the army, angered by the king's desire to oust the War School from Belgrade, began plotting the assassination after King Alexander suspended the constitution.

The conspirators, led by Colonel Maschin and Colonel Misches, burst into the palace in the middle of the night, shooting all who tried to stop them. Entering the royal bedroom, the assassins fired several shots which immediately killed the queen; the king clung to life for several hours until he finally died at 4:00 a.m.

The date of the coup was chosen to mark the 34th anniversary of the assassination of King Michael, Alexander's great-uncle, who was killed by agents of the Karageorgevitch family, which has continually opposed the ruling Obrenovitch house. Reports indicate that the Serbian people welcome the end of Obrenovitch rule and expect a brighter future (→ 14).

Mussolini watched

June 19. A young Italian teacher named Benito Mussolini was placed under investigation today by the police in Bern, Switzerland. He arrived almost a year ago and found work as a stonemason. Swiss police say that Mussolini, the son of a socialist blacksmith, has been spending time with revolutionary friends and studying the works of Karl Marx (→3/23/19).

Henry Ford forms an auto company

Ford's first certificate—255 shares.

June 16. Henry Ford, the engineer who has been tinkering for years with horseless carriages, formed his own automobile company in Detroit, Michigan, today. He will serve as Vice President and chief engineer, and his name will be on the front door of the Ford Motor Company. Ford owns a quarter of the stock, and his main job will be to design automobiles. His major partners are James Couzzens and the Dodge brothers. Ford has dreamed about building power-driven vehicles since he left his father's farm in Dearborn as a teenager and moved to Detroit to work in a machine shop (→ 7/23).

Edwin Porter's dramatic new film "The Great Train Robbery" is pleasing audiences across the country. George Barnes (above), as the bandit, heads a cast of 40. In the final scene (inset), Barnes caps a full 12 minutes of action with a gun shot fired directly at the audience.

1903

JULY

Su	Mo	Tu	We	Th	Fr	Sa
			1	2	3	4
5	6	7	8	9	10	11
12	13	14	15	16	17	18
19	20	21	22	23	24	25
26	27	28	29	30	31	

3. Japan and Britain demand Russian evacuation of Manchuria in compliance with 1902 treaty (→ 8/12).

4. France: Chamber of Deputies decides to fund Charcot's expedition to N. Pole.

6. Wimbledon: Hugh Doherty over Frank Riseley 7-5, 6-3, 6-0; Dorothea Douglass over Ethel Thomson 4-6, 6-4, 6-2.

6. French President Emile Loubet and For. Minister Theophile Delcasse visit London in effort to improve Anglo-French relations (→ 4/8/04).

7. Great Britain: Birth rate decline causing concern over long-term consequences.

16. Berlin: International Monetary Conference sets rate for trading gold-based with silver-based currencies.

17. Brussels: Social Democratic Workers Party convenes, its leaders exiled from Russia (→ 11/17).

17. Spain and France proclaim desire to maintain control in volatile Morocco (→ 5/18/04).

17. Russia: Imperial decree appears to abolish corporal punishment for convicts (→ 29).

20. London: International Telegraphic Conference decides technology must be simplified.

20. British to increase size of royal army in India.

20. Turkey: Macedonians rise against Ottoman Empire on St. Eloi's day (→ 8/6).

21. Venezuela: Rebel leader Bolivar seized by govt. troops.

27. Persia: Crowds massacre Babis religious dissenters with no interference from govt.

29. Russia: Discontent surfaces as strikes break out in Kiev, Odessa and Tiflis (→11/17).

BIRTH

2. Olaf V, king of Norway.

DEATHS

17. U.S. painter James Abbott McNeill Whistler (*7/10/1843).

22. U.S. abolitionist Cassius M. Clay (*10/19/1810).

Whistler, American artist, dies in London

"Whistler's Mother"

July 17. The picture was named "Arrangement in Grey and Black No. 1," but it is known by a vast public as "Whistler's Mother." James Abbott McNeill Whistler painted it in 1872. It is now in the Louvre in Paris. Its creator is dead in London at the age of 69.

Born in Lowell, Massachusetts, Whistler was taken as a child to Russia. His father, an engineer, helped build the Czar's great railway network. The young Whistler studied art in Paris, influenced by Courbet, Velazquez and the Japanese. Moving to London, he showed his work at the Royal Academy.

Despite his reputation, the French Salon refused to show his "White Girl." Accepted by the Salon des Refuses, it caused a sensation. Whistler was a master of "the gentle art of making enemies." When the English critic John Ruskin disparaged one of his works, he sued for slander. The cost of the suit bankrupted the artist.

Besides being a painter, Whistler was also a prolific and talented etcher. When he failed at West Point as a youth, he said, "If salicylate had been a gas, I should have been a soldier."

Pope Leo dies at 93 after active career

Pope Leo XIII.

July 20. The final moments of Pope Leo XIII, who died today, were marked by the same serenity and devotion which are associated with his 25-year pontificate.

Admitted to holy orders in 1837, Vincenzo Gioacchino Pecci was appointed Bishop of Perugia in 1846. Seven years later, Pope Pius IX conferred upon him the red hat of a Cardinal. In this period, he accomplished notable work in the field of education. After the death of Pius IX, Pecci, 68, was elected to the vacant papal chair in 1878 and became Pope Leo XIII.

To restore temporal power, to unite Christendom and to settle class strife were the three aims of Pope Leo XIII. And in his Encyclical on Christian Democracy of 1901, he gave Catholics "some injunctions so as to make their own action larger in scope and more benefical to the commonweal" (→ 8/4).

Ford company sells its first automobile

Henry Ford atop a new Model A.

July 23. The Ford Motor Company sold its first automobile in Detroit today. Its internal combustion engine, which is powered by two cylinders, was designed by the Vice President of the firm, Henry Ford. A native of Dearborn, Michigan, Ford has been experimenting with power-driven vehicles for more than 20 years. And he has come a long way since he built his first rather crude automobile 11 years ago while moonlighting from a job as a machinist. Ford hopes to mass-produce the new Model A's and keep their cost as low as possible so that many Americans will be able to afford one (→ 10/22/06).

Message circles earth in minutes

July 4. President Roosevelt celebrated Independence Day by sending the first official message over the new Pacific Cable. His message, from Oyster Bay, New York, to Governor Taft in the Philippines, circled the globe in 9.5 minutes. Previously, this would have taken hours. In his reply, Taft took the opportunity to lobby for a reduction in tariffs on Philippine goods.

July 19. Frenchman Maurice Garin emerged victorious today after 94 hours, 33 minutes on the road in the inaugural Tour de France. Some of the 60 racers are seen above leaving Villeneuve St.-Georges.

1903

AUGUST

Su	Mo	Tu	We	Th	Fr	Sa
						1
2	3	4	5	6	7	8
9	10	11	12	13	14	15
16	17	18	19	20	21	22
23	24	25	26	27	28	29
30	31					

4. Vatican: Highly orthodox Giuseppe Sarto elected Pope Pius X (→ 9).

5. Marseilles: Complying with government policy, teachers congress agrees to halt religious instruction (→ 5/21/04).

6. Ottoman Empire: Bulgarians occupy governor's palace at Krushevo, Macedonia (→ 18).

8. Russian troops sent to Constantinople to look into murder of Russian consul (→ 20).

9. Vatican: Pope Pius X crowned before 70,000 people.

12. Colombian Senate rejects Hay-Herran Treaty, signed in March (→ 10/18).

12. Responding to czar's desire for a Far East protectorate, Japan offers a free hand in Manchuria if Russia will stay out of Korea (→ 29).

17. Finland: First Social Democrat congress blasts constitution as unjust.

18. Macedonia: 210 Turks killed in fight with Bulgarians (→ 30).

19. Brighton Beach, N.Y.: Dan Patch brings record for mile horse race to 1:59 (→ 9/23).

19. Great Britain formally protests Belgian treatment of Congo natives (→ 9/4).

20. Constantinople: Turkey to compensate for loss of consul if Russia will remove squadron.

25. British commission reports Boer War casualties amounted to 100,000.

29. Russia: Finance Minister Count Witte dismissed; victory for expansionists (→ 10/3).

30. Bulgaria: 1,000 insurgents slain by Turks (→ 9/2).

BIRTHS

8. U.S psychologist Bruno Bettelheim.

31. French thinker Vladimir Jankelevitch (+6/6/1905).

DEATH

22. British statesman, former Prime Minister Lord Salisbury, born Robert Cecil (*2/3/1830).

Herzl defends his idea of Jewish state in Palestine at sixth Zionist Congress

Aug 19. Theodor Herzl, founder of the Zionist movement, declared Palestine to be the best site for a Jewish state in a speech before the sixth Zionist Congress in Basel, Switzerland. Controversy erupted at the congress in response to Britain's offer of land for a Jewish state in Uganda. Herzl had just received a message from the Protectorate Department of the Colonial Office approving the formation of a Zionist study commission to investigate the proposed site, located in East Africa.

In spite of his preference for Palestine, Herzl did not refuse the offer. The fact remains that attempts to obtain a colonization charter from the Ottoman Sultan have been fruitless. The East African site could be used as a haven for Jews fleeing pogroms. However, opposition voiced at the congress made it clear that many Jews refuse to consider Uganda. Delegates from Kishinev, Russia, recently the site of an extremely violent pogrom, said they would go only to Palestine, the site of ancient Israel, which many Jews believe was given to them by God (→ 7/3/04).

From ocean to ocean by auto in 51 days

Contestants in the first transcontinental auto race.

Aug 21. "Thank the Lord it's over," was the reaction of two exhausted men as they drove their Model F Packard into Columbus Circle in New York after two months and one day of grueling transcontinental driving from San Francisco, California.

The waiting crowd and the escort cars created a din as Tom Fetch of the Packard Company and M.C. Karrup, a journalist, arrived. Their actual running time was 51 days, covering an average of 80 miles daily. The automobile had been christened the Pacific by running its wheels in the ocean. The original plan of dousing the wheels of the car in the Atlantic off Coney Island had to be abandoned because of weather. As it was, the co-drivers arrived in New York covered with mud.

The Packard crossed the continental United States with only one incident. A front spring broke but was quickly replaced. It also used one extra tire but still carried two spares. Fetch said the interest of strangers who had never seen a motorcar was kindly if somewhat humorously critical. He said that a couple of Nebraska farmers threatened to chase them with a shotgun if they didn't leave.

Calamity Jane dead

Martha "Calamity Jane" Canary.

Aug 1. A life rich with adventure ended today as "Calamity Jane" Canary, so nicknamed because of her knack for aiding those in distress, died at age 51. An orphan at three, Jane roamed the frontier, quickly becoming a crack shot and rider. Dressed in buckskin, she served as scout for General Custer, mail carrier and friend to many, including the equally legendary "Wild Bill" Hickok, whom she will be buried beside in Deadwood, S.D.

Pulitzer gives $2m to journalism school

Aug 15. One of the pioneers of "yellow journalism" in America came forward today as an exponent of better education for the "ink-stained wretches" who write for the newspapers. Joseph Pulitzer, publisher of The World, the nation's biggest daily, gave Columbia University $2 million to found a school of journalism.

Son of a Hungarian grain merchant, Pulitzer was excluded from military service because of physical defects. Yet, he was recruited by an American agent to serve in the Union Army during the Civil War. He arrived in New York penniless. After the war, he rapidly made a fortune as owner of the St. Louis Post-Dispatch and later, the morning and afternoon editions of the New York World.

With his money, Columbia will build a journalism school and offer training similar to that for other professions. Previously, The World said, newspapermen, "the informers and teachers of the people" and "makers of public opinion" have had no such training.

1903

SEPTEMBER

Su	Mo	Tu	We	Th	Fr	Sa
		1	2	3	4	5
6	7	8	9	10	11	12
13	14	15	16	17	18	19
20	21	22	23	24	25	26
27	28	29	30			

2. Greek subjects freely enlist in Ottoman army to fight Bulgaria (→ 8).

3. New York: U.S. yacht Reliance beats Shamrock to capture America's Cup.

4. Belgium's Leopold III meets with Pres. Loubet of France to discuss his country's alleged mistreatment of Congo natives (→ 19).

7. China: Manchuria's ports opened to U.S. trade (→ 1/13/04).

7. U.S. troops sent to Beirut to protect consulate from possible Moslem uprising.

8. Sofia: Turks massacre 50,000 Bulgarians in the vilayet of Monastir.→

8. Great Britain: Trade union congress opposes Chamberlain's proposed customs reform (→ 17).

16. Austria-Hungary: Despite Magyar protests, Emperor Franz Joseph reaffirms need for united, German-speaking army (→ 8/27/04).

17. Bulgaria: Turks destroy town of Kastoria, killing 10,000 Bulgarians (→ 21).

19. Belgium: King Leopold rejects foreign interference in Congo, denying charges of Belgian cruelty (→ 2/10/04).

21. Bulgaria: 1,000 Turks killed in battle at Perin (→ 10/1).

23. Yonkers, N.Y.: Prince Alert, son of Crown Prince, bests Dan Patch's record in mile horse race with time of 1:57.

23. New York: Columbia University celebrates its 150th anniversary.

24. Australia: Liberal protectionist Alfred Deakin succeeds Edmund Barton to become 2nd prime minister.

26. Women get the vote in Connecticut (→ 12/9).

BIRTHS

11. German Marxist philosopher Theodor Adorno (†8/6/1969).

25. American artist Mark Rothko (†2/25/1970).

Turkish troops slay mass of Bulgarians

Macedonian revolutionaries prepare to fight Turkish troops.

Sept 8. Turkish troops are carrying out a policy of extermination in the vilayet of Monastir. Between 30,000 and 50,000 Bulgarian men, women and children were massacred and tens of thousands of refugees are slowly starving to death. In some areas, the Turks are burning the forests to flush out hiding refugees, and then killing them. No Bulgarian village is still standing in Monastir, according to dispatches.

The Macedonian Central Revolutionary Committee had called for a general uprising against Turkish domination, to take place August 31. The Turks, however, were well-prepared. Reliable estimates put the size of the Turkish force in Macedonia at 300,000, much larger than needed to put down the rebellion. This has led to fears that the Sultan is planning to attack Bulgaria. The Porte has ordered all European news correspondents to leave Macedonia, accusing them of issuing false reports. Leaders of the Macedonian uprising, meanwhile, have warned that they will retaliate against the Turks (→ 17).

Kit Carson subject of western picture

Sept 21. "Kit Carson," an 11-scene, 21-minute film, opens today. Since Edwin S. Porter's "Life of an American Fireman" opened in January, the public craves real-life, all-American excitement. Carson's history certainly fills the bill.

Christopher "Kit" Carson was born in 1809 in Kentucky. His parents, yeoman farmers, moved to Missouri when he was one year old. When he turned 15, Carson joined an expedition bound for Santa Fe. For the next 14 years, he guided traders and trappers over the Rockies. He battled hostile Indians, horse thieves and rival trappers. Carson married an Indian, and they had a daughter. He served in California during the Mexican War, and the Civil War found him scrapping with Apaches in the Southwest. Kit Carson died a Brigadier General in Colorado in 1868.

Son absconds with his father's legacy

Sept 2. A prominent Baltimore society member has caused shock and consternation by disappearing with more than $500,000 of his late father's savings. William T. Tucker, of the former firm Tucker, Smith & Company, is rumored to be living it up somewhere in Central America with his ill-gotten fortune.

It was well known that the younger Tucker's stocks had been failing. He had also been named in a suit brought by a Miss Sarah G. Morris when he failed to repay her a loan of $2,400. Tucker, 35, was authorized to open his father's safe deposit box on arrangement with his mother, Mrs. Wesley A. Tucker, who had turned a deaf ear to whispers of her son's profligate ways. When she recently returned from a European visit, however, she found only $93,000 of her husband's savings intact.

Chamberlain leaves British Cabinet

Joseph Chamberlain in Glasgow.

Sept 17. British Colonial Secretary Joseph Chamberlain has resigned from the Cabinet post that he has held for eight years. His departure from the government was not unexpected. Chamberlain would like Britain to set up a preferential tariff for goods from its colonies. In many cases, that would mean putting a tax on food imports, a plan unpopular with the public. Chamberlain decided he could better promote his cause from outside the government. His resignation has precipitated a government crisis and has split the Unionist Party. The Liberals look forward to the upcoming election, which they expect to win.

Sept 5. Walter Travis, winner of this year's national amateur title.

1903

OCTOBER

Su	Mo	Tu	We	Th	Fr	Sa
				1	2	3
4	5	6	7	8	9	10
11	12	13	14	15	16	17
18	19	20	21	22	23	24
25	26	27	28	29	30	31

1. Macedonia: Forty-thousand reported homeless as severe famine approaches (→ 5).

3. Colorado: Eight-week-old miners' strike has cost $2.5 mil. in mineral production.

3. Russia opens negotiations, responding to Japanese proposals of Aug. 12 (→ 8).

4. It is reported that 45% of Moscow's residents can neither read nor write.

5. Macedonia: Bulgarians reported ready for war with Turkey; 200,000 troops mobilized (→ 11/3).

8. Japanese troops embark for Manchuria as date set for Russian evacuation passes without action (→ 8)

8. Korea: Russian warships arrive at Masam-Pho (→ 13).

13. Northern France disrupted as 40,000 textile workers strike for shorter hours and wage hikes.

13. Large force of Russian troops leaves Kharkov for the Orient (→ 14).

13. Boston: Red Sox defeat Pittsburgh 3-0 to take 1st World Series 5 games to 3.→

15. South Carolina: Senator H. Tillman acquitted on charges of murdering N.G. Gonzales.

17. Belgium's King Leopold makes official visit to Vienna.

18. Colombia raises canal price to $25 million, demands that U.S. recognize full sovereignty of Colombian govt. (→ 11/2).

30. Spain: 40,000 miners strike in Balboa, demand to be paid weekly.

BIRTHS

17. American novelist Nathanael West (†12/21/1940).

22. American biologist George Beadle.

28. British satirist and novelist Evelyn Waugh.

DEATH

23. U.S. philosopher Francis Ellingwood Abbot (*11/6/1836).

First World Series played in Boston

Eager baseball fans mob the Huntington Ave. Ball Field in Boston.

Oct 13. The first inter-league series for the world baseball championship turned out to be something of an embarrassment for the established National League. The Bostons of the upstart American League upset Pittsburgh of the Nationals with a 3-0 victory in the eighth and final game of the series.

By winning five games to three, the Bostons cemented national acceptance from those cynics who saw the American as a refuge for players who had defected from the older circuit. Cy Young pitched two of Boston's victories and lost once. Honus Wagner got six hits for Pittsburgh. Dougherty's two homers in Boston's 3-0 victory in the second game proved a turning point.

U.S. favored in Alaskan border dispute

Oct 16. A conflict over the southeastern Alaskan boundary has been settled, with a tribunal ruling in favor of the United States, which will receive all waterways to Alaska, with the exception of the Portland Channel, which will go to Canada. The issue stems from an Anglo-Russian treaty of 1825, when the boundary of Russian America was defined as being ten leagues from the coast. The dispute worsened during the gold strikes in the Klondike.

John Bull: "Yes 'e's makin' a lot of noise Sam, but he'll get over it."

Langley plane fails

Oct 7. An attempt to fly a 60-foot airship, the climax of years of study by Professor Samuel Langley, Secretary of the Smithsonian Institute, ended in failure today when the ship plunged into the Potomac River in Washington, D.C. Langley's motorized flying machine sped along its 70-foot track and sailed for 100 yards before falling into the river, where it was completely wrecked. An official statement said the navigator was not injured (→ 2/27/06).

Korean issue stirs Russians to action

Oct 14. A Russian battle fleet of 90 ships has arrived at Masam-Pho, Korea, where a Japanese fleet is already anchored. As tension between the two powers rises, several brigades of infantry also have been moved by the Russian command to the borders of Korea, and still further troop movements have been reported throughout Siberia.

Alexander Savinsky, Secretary of the Russian Foreign Ministry, said yesterday, "Japan desires war and is prepared for it." In spite of these bellicose moves, diplomats in Paris and London see some hope of avoiding a war in the negotiations now going on between Russia and Japan in Tokyo over the future of Korea (→ 12/28).

Russia, Austria find accord on Balkans

Oct 3. Austria's Foreign Affairs Minister Count Goluchowsky issued a statement today announcing the continuation of the Balkan policy agreed upon last winter at a conference in Muerzsteg, Austria. The program provides for reforms in Macedonia and gives assurances that Turkey and Bulgaria will not engage in war.

Austrian Emperor Franz Joseph and the Czar, who were hunting today in a forest near Muerzsteg, sent word that the repatriation of Macedonians who have fled Bulgaria was also discussed at the conference and all signatories to the agreements reached at Muerzsteg will be notified by identical notes, which will be published simultaneously.

Autumn coats provide comfort and warmth as colder weather arrives, without hiding shapely figures. Patterns are available from McCall's for only 15 cents.

1903

NOVEMBER

Su	Mo	Tu	We	Th	Fr	Sa
1	2	3	4	5	6	7
8	9	10	11	12	13	14
15	16	17	18	19	20	21
22	23	24	25	26	27	28
29	30					

2. U.S. Pres. Teddy Roosevelt orders three warships to isthmus of Panama (→ 3).

3. Panama declares independence from Colombia (→ 6).

3. Holland: William Einthoven publicly describes his electrocardiograph, invented to monitor the heart.

3. Turkish govt. agrees to plans for reform in Bulgaria, but refuses to hire non-Turkish civil servants (→ 2/18/04).

3. Italy: Progressive Liberal Giovanni Giolitti becomes premier (→ 9/21/04).

6. U.S. officially recognizes new republic of Panama (→ 18).

7. Great Britain: Royal commission's criticism of army conduct in Boer War prompts creation of Lord Esher's committee to reform War Office.

8. Berlin: Operation removes polyp from Kaiser Wilhelm's larynx.

12. France: Lebaudy brothers set air-travel distance record of 34 miles in dirigible.

17. Bolivia cedes territory of Arce to Brazil in Treaty of Petropolis, gains rail, water access to east.

22. Philippines: Gen. Leonard Wood wins five-day battle with insurgents; 300 rebels killed (→ 12/16/04).

28. Philadelphia: Army routs Navy 40-5 in football.

29. Inquiry into U.S. Postal Service demonstrates govt. has lost millions to fraud.

30. Brooklyn Academy of Music destroyed by fire.

BIRTH

7. Austrian naturalist Konrad Lorenz.

DEATHS

1. German historian Theodor Mommsen (*11/3/1817).

12. French painter Camille Pissarro (*7/10/1830).

20. Ex-Governor of Iowa, Francis Marion Drake, founder of Drake University.

U.S. supports independent Panama

Roosevelt's crowning achievement.

Colombian troops ready for civil war.

Nov 18. The United States today concluded a treaty with the new republic of Panama which opens the way for the construction of a canal across the isthmus. The treaty follows the recent recognition of the new government of Panama, which seceded from Colombia earlier this month. Under the terms of the treaty, the United States will have territorial rights up to five miles on each side of the canal and will also have the right to station troops within the area.

Administration sources said that there could be no doubt about the new Panamanian government's right to sign the treaty. The new government now exercises power throughout the isthmus. All Colombian officials and military forces have reportedly left the country. After secession on November 6, the United States sent the Navy's U.S.S. Dixie to Panama with 400 Marines on board to maintain order. To support the Dixie, three other warships were ordered to the area.

Completion of the canal, official statements say, will increase the volume of trade between the American ports on the Gulf and Atlantic coasts and those of Latin America. And Navy sources point out that the completion of the canal will add to the Navy's flexibility because the ships of the Atlantic and Pacific fleets will be able to use it to reinforce each other in a crisis.

Government sources do not try to minimize the engineering task if construction of the canal begins. They point out that the job will require a large labor force and a number of excavating machines.

Tropical disease is also regarded as a very serious problem. The Army, as a result of its experiences in Cuba and the Philippines, is apprehensive about risking men in Panama until more is known in the service about fighting malaria and yellow fever and other diseases. France's attempt to build a canal, some sources said, failed as much because of disease as because of construction problems. There is general agreement that the isthmus of Panama's terrain is more suited to a canal than the area to the north chosen by France.

International reaction to the new treaty between the United States and the republic of Panama is generally favorable. The Times of London commented that the treaty is "a rational extension of American economic and strategic interests."

President Roosevelt is known to favor an early start on the canal. In 1902, when Colombia had rejected what he termed a generous offer of $10 million in cash and an annual rent of $250,000 for the isthmus territory, Roosevelt was said to be outraged. "We may have to give a lesson to those jack rabbits," he wrote to Secretary of State Hay (→ 12/8).

Russian socialists split by Lenin act

Nov 17. At a meeting in London, Vladimir Lenin's efforts to impose his own radical views on membership in the Russian Social Democratic Labor Party has split the socialists into two factions. Those who support Lenin are called Bolsheviks ("majority") although in fact they represent a minority view. They believe party membership should be restricted to an elite group of revolutionaries. The opposing Menshevik ("minority") faction is led by Yuly Martov, who favors a more open organization. Said Martov of Lenin's faction: It "is divided into those who sit and those who are sat upon" (7/4/04).

Nov 12. Camille Pissarro, dean of the Impressionists, died today in Paris. Above, his luminous "Enfants a la ferme" painted in 1887.

1903

DECEMBER

Su	Mo	Tu	We	Th	Fr	Sa
		1	2	3	4	5
6	7	8	9	10	11	12
13	14	15	16	17	18	19
20	21	22	23	24	25	26
27	28	29	30	31		

8. U.S. Marines land in Panama (→ 1/4/04).

9. Norway: Parliament strikes down attempt to give women the vote (→ 3/13/05).

15. Norway: Parliament places 15-year ban on whale fishing.

16. Under pressure from U.S.-supported civil government, Filipino friars agree to sell land for $7.25 million.

21. Holland: Senate passes workman's compensation act to protect accident victims (→ 3/22/05).

28. Korea: Japan takes control of Seoul-Fusan railway (→ 31).

28. French divide their part of Congo into Ubangi-Shari, Chad, Gabon and Middle Congo.

31. Japan: Parliament dissolved for publicly demanding Japan break diplomatic ties with Russia (→ 1/5/04).

BIRTH

17. U.S. novelist Erskine Caldwell (†4/12/87).

DEATH

8. British philosopher and pioneering social scientist Herbert Spencer (*4/27/1820).

CULTURAL EVENTS, 1903

Literature: Henry James' "The Ambassadors"; George Bernard Shaw's "Man and Superman"; Jack London's "The Call of the Wild"; Samuel Butler's "The Way of All Flesh"; W.E.B. DuBois' "The Souls of Black Folk"; Frank Norris' "The Pit"; Nobel Prize to Bjornsterne Bjornson.

Academia: Henri Poincare's "Science and Hypothesis"; Frederick Taylor's article "Shop Management," scientific principles of workplace organization known as Taylorism.

Music: 1st opera recording, Verdi's "Ernani"; 1st classical record to sell over one mil. copies, Caruso's "Vesti la giubba."

The Arts: Picasso's "The Old Guitarist"; Edwin Porter's "The Great Train Robbery," longest film to date at 12 min.

Wrights fly heavier-than-air plane

Dec 17. A claim by Orville and Wilbur Wright, self-taught inventors from Dayton, Ohio, that they have achieved heavier-than-air flight in an aircraft built by themselves, is being received with skepticism. Earlier this year, Simon Newcomb, a highly respected American scientist, published a proof that powered flight was impossible, and seven years ago, Otto Lilienthal, the celebrated German aeronautical engineer, died in a crash of his airplane. Nonetheless, the Wrights say they made four flights today on the beach at Kitty Hawk, North Carolina, the longest lasting almost a minute and covering 850 feet. Five other persons witnessed the flight.

The Wright brothers say they conquered the problems that have prevented heavier-than-air flight at their bicycle repair shop in Dayton. One important invention, they say, is the use of movable wingtips to control the aircraft, a problem that others had not been able to overcome. They also developed and built a lightweight 25-horsepower engine that provided more power with less weight than any previous engine. The brothers then tested a series of scale models in a wind tunnel that they designed and built. The work took more than seven years and cost over $1,000, the Wrights say. However, they say they will not publish a detailed description of their aircraft until they have filed a patent application (→ 9/20/04).

Friends of Orville and Wilbur watch first flight at Kitty Hawk, N.C.

Curies, man and wife, win Nobel Prize

Dec 10. Pierre and Marie Curie today were presented with the Nobel Prize in physics, sharing the award with Henri Becquerel. Madame Curie is the first woman to win a Nobel Prize. All three laureates were honored for their work with radioactivity, a phenomenon to which Marie Curie gave its name.

The field was born in 1895, when Wilhelm Roentgen of Germany discovered a strange sort of radiation that he called X-rays. Becquerel followed up that discovery the next year by showing that some mineral samples could emit the same sort of radiation. Using techniques developed by her husband, Marie Curie was able to show that the radiation detected by Becquerel was emitted by two elements, uranium and thorium. She also found that some mineral samples emitted much more radiation than their uranium content allowed, an indication that they contained a more powerful radioactive source.

In 1898, Pierre and Marie Curie isolated a new and highly radioactive element they named polonium, after her native Poland. Then, starting with several tons of uranium ore and working for four years, they isolated a tiny amount of an even more radioactive element, which they named radium. Eight tons of ore yielded just one gram of radium. The chemistry award this year went to Svante Arrhenius, and the medicine award to Niels Finsen.

Pierre and Marie Curie, at work.

Chicago theater fire kills 578 persons

Dec 31. Stunned by yesterday's fire in the Iroquois Theater which claimed 578 lives, the citizens of Chicago looked forward to a New Year ushered in by sorrow. The Mayor has asked that traditional festivities be suspended.

When the fire broke out, the audience of 2,000 was enjoying a double octette singing "Pearly Moonlight." In a mere ten minutes, the theater became an infernal tomb wherein those who weren't burned were trampled to death. Comedian Eddie Foy's appeal for an orderly exit only partly stemmed the panic as people inside jumped from the balcony to the main floor. Outside, others jumped from the fire escapes to their death.

Investigation has proven the theater, reputedly the safest in Chicago, in violation of numerous safety laws. Most important, when the asbestos stage curtain jammed, the uncontained backstage fire raced through the theater to become Chicago's worst since 1871.

1904

JANUARY

Su	Mo	Tu	We	Th	Fr	Sa
					1	2
3	4	5	6	7	8	9
10	11	12	13	14	15	16
17	18	19	20	21	22	23
24	25	26	27	28	29	30
31						

2. Dominican Republic: U.S. Marines sent to Santo Domingo to aid government against rebel forces (→ 2/21).

4. U.S. Supreme Court decides in Gonzales v. Williams that Puerto Ricans are not aliens and can enter U.S. freely, yet stops short of awarding full citizenship (→ 3/2/17).

4. Revolution erupts in Uruguay.

5. Korea: American Marines arrive in Seoul to guard U.S. legations (→ 6).

6. Korea: Japanese railway refuses to transport Russian troops (→ 7).

7. Russian fleet leaves Port Arthur to intercept Japanese squadron (→ 13).

7. Rome: Joan of Arc passes 2nd stage of canonization (→ 5/30/20).

11. Somaliland: British troops massacre 1,000 dervishes.

12. Michigan: Henry Ford sets world speed record, driving "999" 91.37 mph on frozen Lake St. Clair.

13. China: Treaty of Commerce with U.S. officially opens Manchu ports and Mukden to international trade.

13. Russian For. Minister Lambsdorff informs Japanese that Manchuria concerns only Russia and China (→ 15).

15. Japan stops all steamship service to U.S. (→31).

17. Russia: Anton Chekhov's "The Cherry Orchard" opens in Moscow.

18. Germany: Negotiations fail in Crimmitschau; textile labor leaders send strikers back to work.

25. Pennsylvania: Two hundred miners entombed by explosion (→ 2/7).

27. Florida: W.K. Vanderbilt shatters record for mile auto race, driving it in 39 seconds.

DEATHS

2.Frederick Pabst, brewer.

9. Confederate leader John Brown Gordon (*2/6/1832).

Roosevelt denies supporting Panama

Jan 4. In a message sent to Congress concerning the Panama Canal Treaty, President Roosevelt has sought to clarify his position prior to congressional consideration. Denying any sympathy for the military junta running the revolutionary Panama government, the president moved the issue from the political to the practical. In plain language, he said that his government has recognized the Panama government and that Panama will not be restored to Colombia even should Congress block the treaty. The only remaining question, he declared, "is whether or not we shall build an isthmian canal."

The president's definition of the issue is an attempt to allay Southern senators, who generally oppose the treaty even though many of their constituents want it. Typical is Alabama Senator Morgan who has accused the president of being in support of the Panama revolution and the junta. Senators from Nevada and Maryland, however, voiced their support for the administration's course of action (→ 2/3)

U.S. naval expedition, en route to the Isthmus of Panama.

Russia and Japan readying for fight

Jan 31. Several Russian warships left at midnight to reinforce the cruisers awaiting a Japanese squadron approaching Korea. A Russian battalion has been dispatched from Vladivostok to prevent a Japanese landing at Port Arthur. And a legation guard was landed at Chemui Po, but the Japanese railroad refused to transport the Russian marines to Seoul.

Japan's attitude remains undefined after the Japanese Premier and his Ministers of Foreign Affairs, War, Finance and Navy met in Tokyo yesterday. Russian officials assert that their government in St. Petersburg wants a peaceful resolution of the crisis with Japan. The population is reported to be apathetic (→ 2/1).

12,000 homeless as entire town burns

Jan 23. Fire rampaged through the small community of Aalesund, Norway, this morning, leaving two dead and 12,000 homeless.

Flames were first seen about 2:30 a.m.; rough winds quickly spread them throughout the town, igniting the church, schoolhouse, telegraph office, stores and homes. A steamer from Bergen laden with food, money and clothing is headed for the city. And two German steamship companies will aid in the relief, each sending a steamer tomorrow filled with medical supplies. A harbor town, Aalesund was a commercial center for cod fisheries. At the time of the fire, several boats were anchored there. One steamship was incinerated in the water. Other ships are still at risk.

Germans fighting African uprising

Proud Hottentot Chief Hendrik Wilbooi is a valuable ally to the Germans.

Jan 11. Herero tribesmen have massacred more than 120 German colonists in Southwest Africa. And German forces, to be led by Commander-in-Chief General Lothar von Trotha, have thus far failed to suppress the native revolt.

Two policies in particular seem responsible for the sudden rampage. The Germans never compensated the Hereros for land used for the construction of the Otave railroad. Also, a recent ordinance making African debt outstanding for more than a year invalid has resulted in mass seizures of Herero cattle as payment. The Germans were unaware of the unrest generated by these policies, and were taken by surprise by the uprising.

Major Theodor Leutwein, since becoming Governor General of Southwest Africa in 1894, has concluded alliances with many African chiefs. A pact with Hottentot Chief Hendrik Wilbooi ended one guerrilla war. But Herero leader Samuel Maherero is unwilling to negotiate, and his tribesmen are responsible for the massacre (→ 4/2).

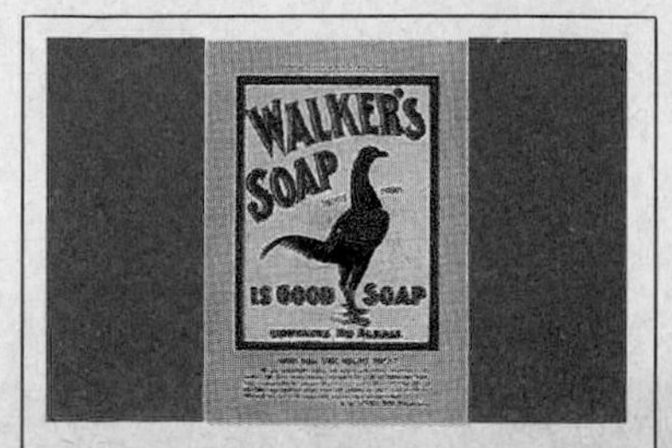

1904

FEBRUARY

Su	Mo	Tu	We	Th	Fr	Sa
	1	2	3	4	5	6
7	8	9	10	11	12	13
14	15	16	17	18	19	20
21	22	23	24	25	26	27
28	29					

1. Britain and France agree to stay neutral if Japan and Russia go to war (→ 4).

3. Colombian troops clash with U.S. Marines in Panama (→ 29).

4. St. Petersburg: Russia offers Korea to Japan, defends right to occupy Manchuria (→ 6).

6. Maryland joins Southern states, officially disenfranchising blacks (→ 3/7).

6. Japan's for. minister severs all ties with Russia, citing delaying tactics in negotiations over Manchuria (→ 8).

7. Coal Creek, Tennessee: Mine guards kill four, wound three in labor dispute (→ 3/26).

8. Korea: Surprise attack at Port Arthur; Japanese disable seven Russian warships (→ 9).

9. Korea: Japanese troops land near Seoul after disabling two Russian cruisers (→ 10).

10. Russia and Japan declare war.→

10. Belgium: British consul issues white paper detailing Belgian atrocities in Congo (→ 3/25).

11. Washington: Roosevelt proclaims strict neutrality in Russo-Japanese War (→ 23).

14. Kansas: "Missouri Kid," killer and desperado, caught.

18. Macedonia: Turks kill 800 Albanians in siege of Shemsi Pasha (→ 4/18).

21. Santo Domingo: U.S. Marines rout Dominican rebels.

22. Hague Tribunal decides official Venezuelan payment to Western powers following 1902 blockade.

23. Japan guarantees Korean sovereignty in exchange for military assistance (→ 3/4).

29. Washington: Seven-man commission created to expedite Panama canal construction (→ 5/4).

BIRTHS

16. U.S. diplomat George Kennan.

20. Soviet statesman Aleksei N. Kosygin (†12/18/1980).

Japanese attack surprises Russians

Feb 10. Japan and Russia are at war. The formal declaration follows the Japanese fleet's stunning victory in a surprise nighttime torpedo attack on the Russian fleet off Port Arthur. Shortly afterward, the Russian fleet sallied out, while the Japanese withdrew to the southeast.

Two Russian battleships, the Retvizan and the Czarevitch, and the cruiser Pallada were seriously damaged by Japanese torpedoes and sank at the entrance to Port Arthur channel, cutting off other Russian ships from the inner harbor. Two other cruisers, the Variag and Korietz, were trapped and then disabled by Japanese warships in the harbor of Chemui Po, situated on the west coast of Korea.

Admiralty sources in London see the Japanese victory as a crippling blow to Russian military plans in Korea and Manchuria. In addition to the earlier losses, a brief encounter between the two fleets resulted in serious damage to the battleship Poltava and the cruisers Novik, Askold and Diana. These Russian losses, admiralty sources said, will enable the Japanese to land troops wherever they wish in Korea and Manchuria.

Yesterday, about 8,000 Japanese infantry disembarked on Korean soil and began a march on Seoul, the capital of the Korean Empire. Other troops landed elsewhere in southern and western Korea, including 1,000 at Chemui Po under the guns of the two Russian cruisers. The only Russian warships that have not been engaged thus far are reported to be ice-bound at Vladivostok.

The Russian military reaction so far has been to accelerate the invasion of Korea. General Krastalinsky, at the head of three infantry brigades and one of artillery, is striking toward the Yalu River, which makes up Korea's northern frontier. Strong Russian reinforcements are also on their way from garrisons in Siberia. But the bulk of the imperial army is stationed in European Russia and the Caucasus. Military sources in London believe that it would take ten weeks to transport a sizable force by rail to the theater of war. And for naval reinforcements, Russia will have to reply with the eight battleships of the Baltic fleet and perhaps some ships of the Black Sea fleet.

The Korean and Russian governments have put forth contrasting views about the cause of the outbreak of hostilities. The Japanese government has issued a statement explaining that Moscow refused to recognize Japan's rights to give advice and assistance to Korea and that this was one of the primary causes. An official Russian communique, however, alleges that Japan, in negotiations with Russia, began to present greater and greater demands. At the same time, the Russians charged, the Japanese began extensive preparations for war (→ 11).

Port Arthur in flames after the Japanese bombardment.

Naval battle at close range, as seen by a Japanese artist.

Stealthy Japanese torpedo boat in night attack on Russian fleet.

Caruso makes first recording in America

Caruso as the Duke in "Rigoletto."

Feb 1. Tenor Enrico Caruso made his first recording in America today, singing "La donna e mobile" from "Rigoletto." The ten-inch Victor Company disk will bring his voice into thousands of homes, ending the exclusive pleasure New York Metropolitan Opera patrons have known the last two months.

In 1894, Caruso debuted in Naples in "L'Amico Francesco." The quality of his voice, fine in either verismo or bel canto repertory, was noted immediately. Conductor Arturo Toscanini said, "This Neapolitan will make the whole world talk about him." If the world talks, Caruso, who sings in seven languages, will not hesitate to talk back. The tenor is a feisty kind of man. He sketches biting caricatures (his rendering of Kaiser Wilhem II shows the emperor with his helmet falling over his eyes), smokes two packages of cigarettes a day and rigorously avoids exercise. He never discusses his two sons, born out of wedlock to an Italian soprano.

Thirty-year-old Caruso currently appears in "L'Elisir D'Amore" at the Metropolitan Opera. He is paid $960 for each performance. America has been denied his talents too long; he already recorded "I Pagliacci" and some Donizetti arias in England and Europe. While some of those recordings were pirated and shipped to American shores, he is finally seen as well as heard here.

Death comes to Ohio's Mark Hanna

Feb 15. Senator Mark Hanna, the master political strategist of the McKinley administration, died today in Washington at the age of 65.

Once regarded as the most influential political leader of his generation in this country, Hanna's influence in affairs of state waned after the assassination of President William McKinley in 1901. Of the slain president's successor, Theodore Roosevelt, Hanna once exclaimed to close friends: "Now look! That damned cowboy is president of the United States!"

An Ohio businessman and banker, Hanna served as Chairman of the Republican National Committee, mapping the winning strategy that led to McKinley's election in 1896 and re-election in 1900. He is credited with coining such campaign slogans as "The Full Dinner Pail" and "Keep On Letting Well Enough Alone." He was appointed to the United States Senate in 1897 to fill an unexpired term and later was elected to a full six-year term.

America quits Cuba

Feb 5. The American occupation of Cuba, which began January 1, 1899, ended this afternoon when the American flag was lowered from the Cabana barracks. The Cuban flag was then raised in its place and given a 21-gun salute, after which the last batallion of American soldiers boarded the transport ship Sumner. Tomas Palma, first President of the new republic, voiced his thanks for American friendship with Cuba.

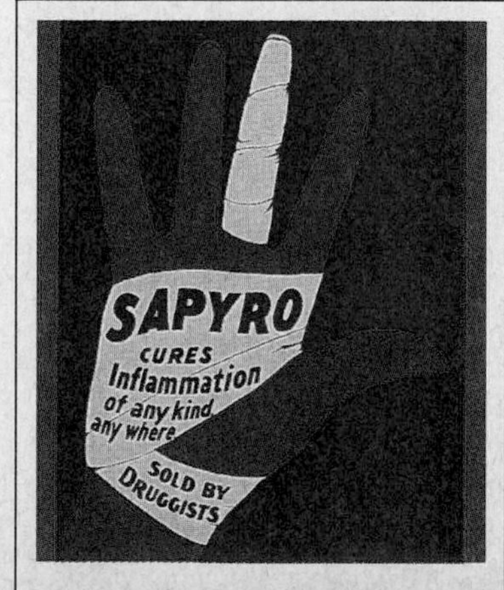

1904

MARCH

Su	Mo	Tu	We	Th	Fr	Sa
		1	2	3	4	5
6	7	8	9	10	11	12
13	14	15	16	17	18	19
20	21	22	23	24	25	26
29	28	29	30	31		

3. Washington: Inquiry to unseat Mormon Sen. Smoot; Joseph Smith, head of Church, testifies he too has divine revelations and practices polygamy.

3. Germany: Wilhelm II makes 1st recording of political document on Edison cylinder.

4. Korea: Russian troops retreat toward Manchurian border as 100,000 Japanese advance (→ 7).

7. Springfield, Ohio: Mob breaks into jail, shoots Negro accused of murder (→ 4/2).

7. Japanese bomb Vladivostok; Russian ships cut off from Pacific port (→ 15).

8. Germany: Bundestag lifts ban on Jesuit practice.

15. Korea: 300 Russians killed as Japanese shell Port Arthur (→ 24).

21. Great Britain: Parliament vetoes proposal to send Chinese workers to Transvaal.

22. First color photography published, in London Daily Illustrated Mirror.

24. Korea: Vice Adm. Togo sinks seven Russian ships; Japanese strengthen blockade of Port Arthur (→ 31).

25. Great Britain: E.D. Morel and Roger Casement form Congo Reform Assn. in Liverpool (→ 7/24).

26. Tennessee: Union and non-union workers battle at Dayton Coal & Iron Co (→ 27).

31. India: British slaughter hundreds of Tibetans (→ 8/3).

BIRTHS

1. Big Band leader Glenn Miller (†12/16/1944).

7. German SS leader Reinhard Heydrich, architect of the "final solution" (†6/4/1942).

20. U.S. psychologist B.F. Skinner, pioneer of Behaviorism.

DEATH

5. Prussian Marshall Count Alfred Von Waldersee (*4/8/1832).

N.Y. diggers finish tunnel under river

March 12. After 30 years of drilling, a tunnel under the Hudson River between Jersey City, N.J., and New York City was completed today. Officials of the Hudson and Manhattan Railroad say they expect rail service between the two states will begin little more than a year from now, so that travelers no longer will have to rely exclusively on the ferries that ply the Hudson.

The meeting between work crews digging from both sides of the river had not been expected for three more days, but the final few inches of soil separating the two ends of the tunnel were broken through just a few minutes before noon today. Workmen from both sides ran jubilantly through the opening to exchange greetings. Within a few hours, a party led by William Gibbs McAdoo, President of the Hudson and Manhattan Railroad, made an historic walk across the river beneath the surface.

Mother Jones must get out of Colorado

March 27. Mrs. Mary Harris "Mother" Jones, the fervent labor leader, has been ordered out of Colorado by state authorities who have accused her of stirring up striking coal miners. In asking for the deportation of "Mother" Jones and several other labor leaders, mine owners told state officials that two-thirds of the striking workers at Cripple Creek and other mines in Colorado would return to their jobs (→ 5/6).

Mary Harris "Mother" Jones.

Russian fleet destroyed near Vladivostok

Fighting at sea.

Russian Adm. Skrydlov

March 31. Russian naval power in the Far East has been virtually eliminated. Earlier this month, the Japanese bombed Vladivostok, cutting Russian ships off from the key port, and last week, Admiral Togo sank seven Russian ships, tightening the blockade of Port Arthur.

A report issued by the government in Tokyo and British reports also indicate the original estimates of Russian losses last month during the Japanese surprise nighttime attack at Port Arthur were low. Losses for the Russians, as now accepted, were one battleship sunk and one disabled, two battleships and one cruiser totally wrecked and extensive damage to smaller craft.

In addition, the Russian torpedo transport Yenisei hit a mine and blew up with the loss of 95 men, the entire crew. An official Japanese report claims only four killed and 54 wounded in the incident.

As a result of these events, the British government expects the Japanese to take possession of Port Arthur soon. The Russian military position in the Far East is nothing short of desperate. No other major warships are available. And the only reinforcements are in the Baltic and Black Sea. The Russians, belatedly, have put all troops in Siberia on a war footing and called out all their army and navy reserves in Kazan and Siberia. Most of these, however, are far from the present battlefields (→ 4/5).

Northern Securities loses in high court

March 14. In a five-four decision, the Supreme Court has upheld the government's claim that the Northern Securities Company represents an illegal merger between the Great Northern and Northern Pacific Railway companies.

The opinion, written by Justice Harlan, holds that Congress has a constitutional right to control interstate commerce. He finds that Northern Securities so restrained interstate commerce as to violate the Sherman Antitrust Act, and that the actual purpose of the merger was to prevent competition between its constituent companies.

Harlan notes that an act of Congress "is binding upon all as much as if it were included ... in the Constitution itself." He construes the antitrust act to apply not merely to unreasonable restraint on trade and commerce but to all restraint, reasonable or not, and holds that the court has the power to end unlawful combinations.

In a separate concurring opinion, Justice Brewer writes that while he thinks the antitrust act should apply only to unreasonable restraint, he nevertheless finds that the company in question constitutes such restraint (→ 4/4).

1904

APRIL

Su	Mo	Tu	We	Th	Fr	Sa
					1	2
3	4	5	6	7	8	9
10	11	12	13	14	15	16
17	18	19	20	21	22	23
24	25	26	27	28	29	30

1. Capt. R.F. Scott discovers Great Antarctic Plateau.

2. St. Charles, Arkansas: 14 Negroes lynched in race riots (→ 6/3).

2. Southwest Africa: Herero tribes defeated by German Maj. Von Glasenapp near Okaharui (→ 22).

3. Indonesia: Dutch kill 541 more Achinese in 30-year war in Sumatra (→ 10/4).

4. St. Paul, Minnesota: E.H. Harriman sues to recover holdings lost in Northwest rail merger (→ 1/30/05).

5. Korea: Japanese army reaches Yalu River; Russians in retreat (→ 5).

5. London: King Edward offers mediation in Russo-Japanese War; czar receptive (→ 13).

7. Spain: Anarchist attempts assassination of King Alfonso in Barcelona.

18. Salonika: Bulgarians and Turks clash (→ 11/22/05).

19. Toronto: Fire in wholesale business district causes $10 mil. damage.

21. Korea: Hundreds of Russian troops drown in Yalu River, fleeing from Japanese (→ 30).

21. New York: Polo Grounds opens.

22. Germany: Reichstag refuses to compensate German victims of Herero uprising (→ 8/11).

26. Australia: Workers Party founded.

30. Korea: Russian Gen. Zasulich routed at Yalu, losing 2,500 men (→ 5/14).

BIRTHS

6. German statesman Kurt Georg Kiesinger.

22. American physicist Robert J. Oppenheimer (†2/18/1967).

24. American painter Willem de Kooning.

DEATH

9. Isabella, former queen of Spain.

Britain, France in Entente Cordiale

"Damn! I thought it was paper."

April 8. England and France have formally signed a treaty amicably settling a number of simmering territorial disputes. One regards Morocco and Egypt. Great Britain recognizes the right of France to guard the peace of Morocco, while France will not impede in Egypt the actions of Great Britain, which adheres to the 1888 convention for neutrality of the Suez Canal.

Other articles of the treaty relate to Siam, the New Hebrides and boundary adjustments in West Africa. And in Newfoundland, France will maintain fishing rights but forgoes exclusive claims. The 1886 Bait Bill is modified so that locals may sell bait to French fishermen. The British and French regard their new "friendly understanding" as very important, but it is not an alliance (→ 7/12).

Spring fashion in Europe.

Russians lose ship, admiral and 600 men

Japanese fleet in formation at Port Arthur.

April 13. Russia has suffered another naval disaster at Port Arthur. The battleship Petropavlovsk today hit a mine in the roadstead outside Port Arthur and sank. She was flying the flag of Admiral Makarov, the naval Commander-in-Chief in the Far East. He went down with the ship, along with 600 others. Seven officers and 32 sailors were saved. Among them was the Grand Duke Cyril, the first officer, who was on the upper bridge at the time.

The Petropavlovsk, with other Russian ships, had sortied to meet the Japanese fleet. When it was seen that the enemy had been reinforced to a strength of 30 ships, the Russian squadron began to return to harbor.

Meanwhile, Japanese troops are advancing on the Korean front. They have reached the Yalu River, while the Russians are in retreat (→ 21).

St. Louis Exposition welcomes vast crowds

April 30. At 12:15 p.m. in Washington, President Roosevelt proudly touched a golden button, officially opening the St. Louis World's Fair. Known as the Louisiana Purchase Exposition, it celebrates the area's 100 years in the Union.

Secretary of War William H. Taft, representing the president, attended opening ceremonies. Officials from the states, territories and foreign governments were also present. John Philip Sousa's band thrilled visitors, while American gunboats volleyed salutes from the harbor.

Five years in the making, the fair's themes are education and American know-how. That wonder, the automobile, will be among featured exhibits. And a food purveyor promises an unlikely sounding treat called an ice-cream cone (→ 12/01).

Palatial grounds at St. Louis, open after four years of construction.

1904

MAY

Su	Mo	Tu	We	Th	Fr	Sa
1	2	3	4	5	6	7
8	9	10	11	12	13	14
15	16	17	18	19	20	21
22	23	24	25	26	27	28
29	30	31				

2. Elwood wins Kentucky Derby with jockey Prior aboard.

4. Work begins on Panama canal (→ 10).

5. British declare open war on Tibet (→ 8/3).

5. Cy Young, of Boston Americans, pitches major league's 1st perfect game.

5. Chicago: Socialist Party nominates Eugene Debs for president, Benjamin Hanford for v.p. (→ 6/23).

7. German steam locomotives reported to travel at 80-85 mph.

8. Morocco: U.S. Marines land at Tangier to protect Belgian legation (→ 27).

10. John Findley Wallace appointed chief engineer for Panama canal (→ 10/21).

14. Manchuria: Chinese reported to be rising against Russian occupation (→ 25).

15. Vienna: Emperor Franz Joseph amazes Austria-Hungary, asking for military budget of $51 million.

17. Maurice Ravel's "Scheherazade" premieres in Paris.

18. Morocco: Brigand Raizuli kidnaps American Ion H. Perdicaris (→ 22).

21. France recalls ambassador to Vatican, protesting Pope Pius X's attempt to discipline two French bishops (→ 7/29).

22. Chicago: Sec. of State Hay announces dispatch of cable to Morocco, "We want Perdicaris alive or Raizuli dead" (→ 6/8).

23. Haiti: Troops stone European ministers at Port-Au-Prince.

25. Korea: 4,500 Japanese, 3,000 Russians killed at Nanshan; Gen. Oku seals off Port Arthur by land and sea (→ 6/15).

27. Morocco: Thousands of Europeans reported at mercy of tribesmen; France takes no action (→ 6/3).

BIRTH

2. Bing Crosby, American singer (†10/14/1977).

Prague composer Anton Dvorak dead

Anton Dvorak.

May 1. A young Czech musician who hadn't enough money to buy music paper, son of a Bohemian village butcher. That was Anton Dvorak, who made his career in Prague, London and New York. He died today.

Dvorak wrote in nearly every form, but preferred orchestral music, influenced by Brahms and Wagner. His "Cello Concerto" of 1895 was a supreme example of that type. One of the Romantics, Dvorak was also distinguished by the way he wove Czech nationalist and folk music strains into his classical compositions. In 1892, he took that trait to New York City, where he ran the National Conservatory for two years. That visit produced the ever-popular Symphony No. 9, "From the New World," based on themes from American popular songs.

French 3-wheeled motorcycle.

Henry Stanley is dead

May 9. Sir Henry M. Stanley, the African explorer, adventurer and journalist, died in London today. He was 63. Stanley will perhaps be best remembered for his search for the missing David Livingstone in Central Africa 35 years ago. After an eight-month trek, Stanley found the sick and almost helpless explorer on Lake Tanganyika and greeted him casually, "Dr. Livingstone, I presume." Stanley was unable to convince Livingstone to return to Europe and decided to remain in Central Africa and join him in his explorations.

On a later expedition, Stanley survived the attacks of cannibals, discovered some sources of the Nile and traced the Congo River through most of Central Africa. Stanley also helped form the Congo Free State, under the rule of King Leopold II of Belgium. After his return to England, he was elected to Parliament in 1895, and he was knighted in 1899.

Sir Henry Morton Stanley.

Tanya sets a record

May 12. Tanya, a speedy filly racing in the colors of H.B. Duryea, set a world record today for four and one-half furlongs at Morris Park, New York. She covered the distance in 51.5 seconds, cutting a second off the old mark. However, some cynics pointed out that Tanya had the wind behind her and that she carried a light weight of 107 pounds. The well-dispositioned chestnut outran Blandy, a consistent winner at earlier meetings, and five others as the public choice. She was hardly breathing hard at the finish of her length-and-a-half victory. She raced from third place into the lead at the start of the race and was never threatened.

Tanya cools off in the shade.

Cripple Creek faces reign of terror

May 6. A reign of terror settled over Cripple Creek this week, bringing death to some striking coal miners as they battled with militia sent in by Colorado Governor James H. Peabody.

In the months since the strike began last autumn, violence has escalated sharply, with the miners firmly rejecting the owners' demands for a ten-hour work day. Mines have closed in Cripple Creek and nearby areas. Vigilantes have threatened to hang union sympathizers. Union leaders have been deported from the state. And there have been pitched battles in the streets and in the nearby valleys of the region.

Cripple Creek, ten miles south of Pike's Peak in mountainous central Colorado, is the major area of confrontation between the angry miners and the military troops sent in to quell sporadic uprisings. The Colorado Legislature had approved a bill calling for an eight-hour work day for the miners, but the law was later declared unconstitutional, and the strike was called (→ 6/6).

1904

JUNE

Su	Mo	Tu	We	Th	Fr	Sa
			1	2	3	4
5	6	7	8	9	10	11
12	13	14	15	16	17	18
19	20	21	22	23	24	25
26	27	28	29	30		

1. French authorities arrest three more officers indicted in Dreyfus scandal (→ 10/24).

1. Newport, R.I.: Submarine torpedo boat Fulton tested before naval inspection board.

2. Naples: Prof. Schron discovers microbe responsible for photosynthesis.

2. Paris: Matisse paintings shown at Gallerie Vollard.

2. China signs Geneva Convention.

3. Roosevelt names Negro to second his nomination in Chicago (→ 8/17).

3. Great Britain: Walter J. Travis wins U.S Amateur Golf Championship.

3. Germany: Foreign Minister Friedrich Von Holstein denounces French aim to annex Morocco (→ 8).

5. St. Louis: Bullfight stopped; mob of 7,000 burns arena, attempts to lynch manager.

6. Denver: Striking miners battle with state militia; 22 killed (→ 8/20).

8. Morocco: American Marines land at Tangier (→ 10/3).

15. Russian mines sink two Japanese battleships, yet fail to liberate Port Arthur (→7/18).

15. U.K., Brazilian envoys settle border dispute between Brazil and British Guyana.

17. Revolutionaries assassinate General Bobrikov, Russian gov. gen. of Finland (→ 7/5).

24. Japanese sink Russian battleship at Port Arthur (→ 7/16).

28. New York: Directors of Knickerbocker Steamboat Co. found guilty of negligence in Slocum fire.

29. Indianapolis: Prohibition Party nominates Silas C. Swallow for president, George W. Carroll for v.p. (→ 7/4).

BIRTHS

2. American actor and swimming champ Johnny Weissmuller, played Tarzan (†11/20/1984).

26. Hungarian actor Peter Lorre (†3/23/1964).

Roosevelt named for the presidency

Roosevelt and Fairbanks in '04.

June 23. Sweltering in the heat of a Chicago summer, Republicans today unanimously nominated President Theodore Roosevelt for another term in office. Waving flags and banners as they noisily paraded through the aisles of the vast coliseum, the throng of convention delegates cheered lustily when the popular president's name was placed in nomination. There were cheers, too, for Senator Charles Warren Fairbanks of Indiana, who was chosen to run for vice president (→ 29).

Eleanora Duse at 45 is at the summit of her fame as an actress. She has toured the world and introduced many of the plays of her fellow Italian and lover, soldier-poet Gabrielle d'Annunzio.

▷

Ship burns: 693 die, many children

June 15. A pleasure outing turned into an inferno today when fire consumed the excursion steamer General Slocum. Thus far, 693 bodies have been recovered, with estimates of up to 1,000 dead. Most of the victims were women and children on their annual excursion party from St. Mark's German Lutheran Church in New York City.

The pleasant spring day began happily enough with the band playing a lively air. An hour later, with the boat opposite 135th Street in the East River, the dread cry of "Fire!" began to spread as quickly as the sudden sheet of flame, its origin undetermined. Captain van Schaik then made a fatal error, heading for the more distant North Brother Island, with the New York shore a mere 300 feet away. As the blaze intensified, women roasted to death in sight of their families, and many frenzied mothers threw their babes into the river. Survivors tell how old, worthless life preservers rotted away at their touch. By the time the boat reached shore, it had burned to the water line, leaving hardly a home in the church parish spared by grief (→ 28).

The wrecked General Slocum in New York harbor.

Thery wins classic auto race for James Gordon Bennett Cup

June 17. Before an assemblage of European nobility, Leon Thery of France won the Gordon Bennett international racing trophy at Saalburg. Thêry dethroned the defending champion, Camille Jenatzy of Germany, after a magnificent driving performance over a difficult 350-mile course. Another German, De-Caters, was third after losing three minutes at the start because of a breakdown. Jenatzy escaped serious injury early in the race when he narrowly missed colliding with a locomotive on the course.

I. French Richard-Brasier; II. Italian Fiat; III. British Napier; IV. Swiss Dufaux; V. French Turcat-Mery; VI. French Mors; VII. German Opel-Darracq; VIII. British Wolseley; IX. Belgian Pipe; X. Mercedes.

The Kickapoo dance craze is sweeping the United States.

1904

JULY

Su	Mo	Tu	We	Th	Fr	Sa
					1	2
3	4	5	6	7	8	9
10	11	12	13	14	15	16
17	18	19	20	21	22	23
24	25	26	27	28	29	30
31						

3. New York: Tailors' strike puts 100,000 out of work.

3. Wimbledon: Hugh Doherty over Frank Riseley 6-1, 7-5, 8-6; Dorothea Douglass over Charlotte Sterry 6-0, 6-3.

4. Springfield, Illinois: Populists nominate Thomas E. Watson for pres.; Thomas H. Tibbles for vice president (→ 9).

4. Discontent reported rising in Russia; reformers fill prisons; peasant uprising feared (→ 28).

5. Czar Nicholas appoints conservative Ivan Obolensky gov. of Finland (→ 8/16).

9. St. Louis: Judge Alton B. Parker defeats Wm. J. Bryan for Dem. pres. nomination; Henry Davis for v.p. (→ 11/8).

12. Anglo-German treaty signed to resolve potential conflicts over next five years (→ 3/14/05).

16. Russians stop German liner in Red Sea; seize letters intended for Japan (→ 18).

18. London: British warships dispatched to protect merchant ships from harassment by Russian navy (→ 10/15).

20. Chicago: Meatpackers end 45-day strike.

24. France: Maurice Garin wins 2nd Tour de France.

24. Belgian committee designated to investigate Congolese civil service (→ 1/11/05).

25. Massachusetts: 25,000 textile workers strike at Fall River.

28. Russia: Socialist-Revolutionaries assassinate Interior Min. Vyacheslav Plehve, symbol of czarist oppression (→ 10/22).

28. Colombia: After losing Panama, Rafael Reyes assumes dictatorial powers in attempt to revitalize failing economy.

BIRTHS

2. French tennis champion Rene Lacoste.

12. Chilean poet Pablo Neruda (†9/23/1973).

14. U.S. writer Isaac Bashevis Singer.

DEATH

14. South African statesman Paul Kruger, leader in war against British (*10/10/1825).

Trans-Siberian finished

Peking to Siberia —wooden bridge at Lalinke.

July 31. Stretching over a distance of 4,607 miles from Chelyabinsk to Vladivostok, and linking the Ural Mountains to Russia's Pacific coast, the Trans-Siberian Railroad has been completed after 13 years of construction.

After numerous studies dating from the mid-19th century, the decision to build the railway was made in 1891. Construction began in May of that year northward from Vladivostok and in July 1892, eastward from Chelyabinsk. The Russians had to overcome enormous problems: wide rivers, steep grades around Lake Baikal, permafrost in eastern Siberia and extremes of temperature. Nevertheless, in 1898, the line stretched from Irkutsk to Khabarovsk.

In the meantime, the Russian government negotiated a treaty with China (1896) which enabled the Russians to build the Chinese Eastern Railroad, affording a shorter, more direct line between Vladivostok and Lake Baikal through Manchuria. The Russians built more than 1,000 railway stations. The distance established between stations depends on the nature of the land, but it is about 27 miles.

The Trans-Siberian is seen as the best way to populate Siberia and promote trade. From 1896 to 1900, the number of travelers to the Far East doubled to one million, and many of them helped in opening up the Chinese market (→ 1/1/05).

Chekhov, chronicler of Russian life, dies

July 15. Anton Chekhov, a serf's grandson who became one of Russia's most eminent dramatists and short story writers, is dead at 44 of tuberculosis at Badenweiler, a spa in Germany's Black Forest.

Chekhov began his career as a writer while studying medicine, and soon after obtaining his degree, learned that he had achieved a reputation. He then devoted himself wholeheartedly to literature and wrote hundreds of short stories and plays remarkable for their understanding of human nature. His most famous plays are "Uncle Vanya," "The Three Sisters" and "The Cherry Orchard."

Anton Chekhov.

Theodor Herzl, Zionist advocate, is dead

July 3. Theodor Herzl, founder of the Zionist movement to establish a Jewish state in Palestine, died today. He was 44 years old. Herzl was born in Budapest and attended law school in Vienna. Since 1891, he had been a correspondent for the Vienna-based Neue Freie Presse, a leading European newspaper. As a journalist, he reported on the Dreyfus Affair in France.

In 1896, Herzl published "Der Judenstaat," a pamphlet describing a separate Jewish state as a solution to anti-Semitism in Europe. Herzl also organized annual Zionist world congresses. Herzl met several times with the Ottoman Sultan in Constantinople in an effort to obtain a charter permitting colonization of Palestine, but to no avail.

Hungarian-born Theodor Herzl.

Japanese lose battle in war with Russia

July 18. Efforts to control Manchuria and the Korean Empire are resulting in devastating losses by both Japan and Russia. On July 12, Japanese land forces approaching Port Arthur experienced heavy casualties from land mines and gunfire. Russian correspondents put the number of dead and wounded as high as 30,000, but that figure could be exaggerated. Japanese reports made little mention of the attack, dwelling instead on maneuvers by Admiral Togo in Port Arthur harbor. Japanese boats torpedoed one of four Russian cruisers anchored in the bay. The extent of damage is not yet known.

Today, Russia lost 1,000 troops at Mo-Tien Ling, a pass 200 miles northeast of Port Arthur. Soldiers were told to retreat before using their arms. The Japanese eluded detection under a cover of fog.

Since Japan attacked Port Arthur without warning on February 8, it has surprised the Western world by its tactics and leadership. Japan knew Port Arthur was Russia's only year-round, ice-free Pacific harbor, and its subsequent blockade has effectively crippled Russia's transport of its 4.5 million armed men to the area. Japan's military includes a standing army of 283,000 and a navy brilliantly led by Togo, who studied naval science in England.

France breaks off links with Vatican

July 29. The increasing friction between church and state in France led today to the rupture of diplomatic relations between Paris and the Vatican. The French Foreign Ministry recalled its Ambassador to the Holy See. And the Pope's representative to Paris was summoned to the Quai d'Orsay and informed that his presence was no longer required in France. The anticlerical movement in France is being led by liberal politicians and President Emile Combes (→ 9/15).

Giacomo Puccini's opera "Madam Butterfly," is now playing in Milan, Italy.

1904

AUGUST

Su	Mo	Tu	We	Th	Fr	Sa
	1	2	3	4	5	6
7	8	9	10	11	12	13
14	15	16	17	18	19	20
21	22	23	24	25	26	27
28	29	30	31			

3. Tibet: British expedition reaches Tibet; Dalai Lama in flight (→ 9/7).

6. Korea: Japanese surround Gen. Kuropatkin's army, in retreat for Manchuria (→ 10).

7. Pueblo, Colorado: World's Fair Flyer wreck kills 76 in one of worst rail disasters in U.S. history. →

8. Austria-Hungary: Oil workers' uprising forces reduced hours and sanitary improvements.

9. Paris: International Congress of Miners demands minimum wage and eight-hour work day (→ 3/22/05).

10. Korea: Russian fleet in retreat at naval battle of Yellow Sea; Adm. Vilgelm Vitgeft lost (→ 16).

11. Southwest Africa: Gen. von Trotha defeats Hereros near Waterberg (→ 10/3).

13. Armenia: U.S. squadron demands compensation for destruction of U.S. legation.

16. Korea: Japan's Adm. Kaimura vanquishes Adm. Jessen at Ulsan, Japanese gain full control of seas at Port Arthur (→ 16).

16. Russians insist massacres in Poland are prompted by Jewish aggression (→ 9/4).

16. Korea: Japanese emperor demands Russian surrender of Port Arthur (→ 22).

20. Colorado: Miners seize town of Cripple Creek and deport officials (→ 2/20/05).

22. Russians refuse to surrender Port Arthur (→ 24).

24. Gen. Togi leads 2nd assault on Russian defenses at Port Arthur; loses 15,000 men to Russia's 3,000 (→ 26).

26. Manchuria: Great battle at Liao Yang begins as Japanese advance along Russian eastern front (→ 30).

27. Austro-Hungarian war minister orders all administrative correspondance written in German or Hungarian.

DEATH

10. French statesman Pierre Waldeck-Rousseau (*12/2/1846).

Russians failing fast

Russian Gen. Aleksey Kuropatkin.

Russians march in Manchuria.

Aug 30. Port Arthur's fall to the Japanese appears imminent. Japanese troops have captured all outlying forts and virtually severed the Trans-Siberian Railroad north of Liao-Yang, about 250 miles northeast of Port Arthur. Three Russian battleships are sinking in the harbor, torpedoed or shelled from the mainland. Over 22,000 Japanese reinforcements are expected at Port Arthur soon. The few Russian forces remaining in the city are expected to stage a brave but ultimately futile sortie. These losses, coupled with a defeat of General Kuropatkin's army earlier this month, have proved disastrous for Russia.

Strange new tactics may account for Japan's victories. Night attacks threw Russian troops into disorder. Searchlights were concentrated into Russian camps, blinding and terrifying soldiers. The Japanese chose to destroy strategic structures rather than allow them to fall into Russian hands; outside of Liao-Yang, they burned a bridge and shelled the railway station after Russians retreated. Japanese strategy seemed so elusive that Russian officers could not plan any manuevers. Even when Russians won a battle, there was little to show for it; Japanese prisoners denied them satisfaction by committing suicide (→ 9/3).

Aug 10. The Russian battleship Askold steams north to safety, leaving Port Arthur to its Japanese conquerors after six months of war.

Dozens die as rail bridge collapses

Aug 7. A gruesome railroad disaster outside Pueblo, Colorado, has left 76 people dead. The World's Fair Flyer, bound for St. Louis, was crossing a flood-damaged bridge on the Fountain River when the accident occurred. The engineer, sensing danger, applied the brakes to save the rear cars, which were still on firm ground. Yet he and passengers in the first three cars plunged 30 feet to the bottom of the arroyo. Torrential waters dragged bodies and wreckage eight miles downstream.

Two Negroes burned at stake in Georgia

Aug 17. Two Negroes were dragged from the courthouse in little Statesborough, Georgia, today and burned at the stake by an angry mob of white men. The action was the culmination of a series of violent incidents in this largely rural area, where white planters have vowed to rid their neighborhoods of those they call "obnoxious Negroes." In recent days, some Negroes have been flogged and others have been shot and wounded for their protests against white supremacy. In the wake of this escalating cycle of violence, a number of Negroes have fled the area to other parts of the state and nation (→ 9/7).

As railroads have opened the French coast to tourism, sunbathing has become all the rage, and fashions are changing.

1904 St. Louis

Aug 31. Twenty-one of the 22 track events in the third modern Olympics, held in St. Louis as an adjunct to the World's Fair, were won by athletes from the United States. The only "foreigner" to take a gold in track was a Montreal policeman, Etienne Desmarteau, winner of the weight throw.

There was little European competition at St. Louis, and four Americans won three events each. A sweep of the standing-jump events by Ray Ewry added three medals to the three he had won four years earlier at the Paris Games, making him the most productive Olympian to date.

Other three-time winners were Richie Hahn, who swept the 60-, 100- and 200-meter dashes; James D. Lightbody, who took the steeplechase, the 800-meters and the 1,500-meter run; and Harry Hillman, who won two hurdles events and the 400-meter flat race.

The marathon race was won by T.J. Hicks, who received small doses of strychnine during the race after his trainer's supply of brandy ran out. Fred Lorz, who was disabled during the marathon, rode in a chugging automobile most of the way and then jumped off at the stadium entrance and attempted to finish with the others, but his scam was detected. Almost all performances at Athens and Paris were surpassed.

For the first and last time, the barrel-jump race is included in the Olympics.

Men Athletics

100 M Dash
1. Archie Hahn USA 11,0
2. Nathaniel Cartnell USA 11,2
3. William Hogenson USA 11,2

200 M Dash
1. Archie Hahn USA 21,6
2. Nathaniel Cartnell USA 21,9
3. William Hogenson USA

400 M Run
1. Harry Hillman USA 49,2
2. Franck Waller USA 49,9
3. Herman Groman USA 50,0

800 M Run
1. James Kightbody USA 1:56,0
2. Howard Valentine USA 1:56,3
3. Emil Breitkreuz USA 1:56,4

1500 M Run
1. James Kightbody USA 4:05,4
2. W. Frak Verner USA 4:06,8
3. Lacey Hearn USA

Marathon
1. Thomas Hicks USA 3:28,53
2. Albert Corey USA 3:34,52
3. Arthur Newton USA 3:47,33

110 M Hurtles
1. Frederick Schule USA 16,0
2. Thaddeus Shideler USA 16,3
3. L. Ashburner USA 16,4

400 M Hurdles
1. Harry Hillman USA 53,0
2. Franck Waller USA 53,2
3. George Poage USA

300 M Steeplechase
1. James Lighbody USA 7:39,6
2. John Daly GBR/IRL 7:40,6
3. Arthur Newton USA 25 m

High Jump
1. Samuel Jones USA 1,803
2. Garret Serviss USA 1,778
3. Paul Weinstein GER 1,778

Pole Vault
1. Charles Dvorak USA 3,505
2. Leroy Samse USA 3,43
3. L. Wilkins USA 3,43

Long Jump
1. Myer Prinstein USA 7,34
2. Daniel Frank USA 6,89
3. Robert Stangland USA 6,88

Triple Jump
1. Myer Prinstein USA 14,325
2. Frederick Englehardt USA 13,90
3. Robert Stangland USA 13,365

Shotput
1. Ralph Rose USA 14,81
2. William Coe USA 14,40
3. Leon Feuerback USA 13,37

Discus Throw
1. Martin Sheridan USA 39,28
2. Ralph Rose USA 39,28
3. Nicolaos Georgantas GRE 37,68

Hammer Throw
1. John Flanagan USA 51,23
2. John Dewitt USA 50,265
3. Ralph Rose USA 45,73

Decathlon
1. Thomas Kiely GBR/IRL 6036
2. Adam Gunn USA 5907
3. Truxton Hare USA 5813

60 M (in 1900 and 1904 only)
1. Archie Hahn USA 7,0
2. William Hogenson USA 7,2
3. Fay Moulton USA 7,2

200 M Hurtles (1900 and 1904 only)
1. Harry Hillman USA 24,6
2. Franck Castleman USA 24,9
3. George Poage USA

Team Cross Country (1904, 1912, 1920 and 1924 only)
1. New York A.C. 21:17,8
2. Chicago A.A.

5000 Team
1. Great Britain
2. France

Standing High Jump (1900, 1904, 1906, 1908, 1912 only)
1. Ray Ewry USA 1,65
2. Irving Baxter USA 1,52
3. Lewis P. Sheldon FRA 1,50

Standing Long Jump (1900, 1904, 1906, 1908, 1912 only)
1. Ray Ewry USA 1,50
2. James Stadler USA 1,455
3. Lawson Robertson USA 1,45

56 lb. Weight Throw (1904 and 1920 only)
1. Ray Ewry USA 10,58
2. Irving Baxter USA 9,95
3. Robert Garrett USA 9,50

Tug-of-War (1900, 1904, 1906, 1908, 1912, 1920 only)
1. Sweden/Norway
2. USA
3. France

Men Swimming

100 m Freestyle
1. Zoltan von Halmay HUN 1:02,8
2. Charles Daniels USA
3. J. Scott Leary USA

200 m Freestyle
1. Charles Daniels USA 2:44,2
2. Francis Gailey USA 2:46,0
3. Emil Rausch GER 2:56,0

400 m Freestyle
1. Charles Daniels USA 6:16,2
2. Francis Gailey USA 6:22,0
3. Otto Wahle AUT 6:39,0

1500 m Freestyle
1. Emil Rausch GER 27:18,1
2. Géza Kiss HUN 28:28,2
3. Francis Gailey USA 28:54,0

100 m Backstroke
1. Walter Brack GER 1:16,8
2. Georg Hoffmann GER
3. Georg Zacharias GER

High Dive
1. Dr George Sheldon USA 12,66
2. Georg Hoffmann GER 11,66
3. Frank Kehoe USA 11,33

50 yards Freestyle (1904 only)
1. Zoltan von Halmay HUN 28,0
2. J. Scott Leary USA 28,6
3. Charles Daniels USA

400 m Breaststroke (1904, 1912, 1920 only)
1. George Zacharias GER 7:23,6
2. Walter Brack GER 20 m
3. H. Jamison Handy USA

880 yards Freestyle (1904 only)
1. Emil Rausch GER 13:11,4
2. Francis Gailey USA 13:23,4
3. Géza Kiss HUN

Plunge for Distance
1. W.E. Dickey USA 19,05
2. Edgar Adams USA 17,53
3. Leo "Budd" Goodwin USA 17,37

200 Yards Team Relay (1904 only)
1. New York A.C. 2:04,6
2. Chicago A.C.
3. Missouri A.C.

Waterpolo
1. New York A.C.
2. Chicago A.C.
3. Missouri A.C.

Boxing

Flyweight
1. George Finnegan USA
2. Miles Burke USA

Bantamweight
1. Olivier Kirk USA
2. George Finnegan USA

Featherweight
1. Olivier Kirk USA
2. Frank Haller USA

Lightweight
1. Harry Spanger USA
2. James Eagan USA
3. Russell Van Horn USA

Welterweight
1. Albert Young USA
2. Harry Spanger USA
3. Joseph Lydon USA

Middleweight
1. Charles Mayer USA
2. Benjamin Spradley USA

Heavyweight
1. Samuel Berger USA
2. Charles Mayer USA

Weightlifting

1 arm lifts (10 tractions)
1. Oscar Paul Osthoff USA 48 points
2. Frederick Winters USA 45 points
3. Franl Kungler USA 10 points

2 arm lifts
1. Perikles Kakousis GRE 111,58 kg
2. Oscar Paul Osthoff USA 84,26 kg
3. Frank Kingler USA 79,83 kg

Freestyle Wrestling

Light Flyweight
1. Robert Curry USA
2. John Keim USA
3. Gustav Thiefenthaler USA

Flyweight
1. George Mehnert USA
2. Gustave Bauers USA
3. William Nelson USA

Bantamweight
1. Isaac Niflot USA
2. August Wester USA
3. Z.B. Strebler USA

Featherweight
1. Benjamin Bradshaw USA
2. Theodore McLear USA
3. Charles Clapper USA

Lightweight
1. Otto Roehm USA
2. R. Tesing USA
3. Albert Zirkel USA

Welterweight
1. Charles Erickson USA
2. William Beckmann USA
3. Jerry Winholtz USA

Heavyweight
1. B. Hansen USA
2. Frank Kungler USA
3. F.C. Warmbold USA

Men Fencing

Foil Individual
1. Ramon Fonst CUB
2. Albertson Van Zo Post CUB
3. Charles Tatham CUB

Foil Team
1. Cuba
2. International Team

Epée Individual
1. Ramon Fonst CUB
2. Charles Tatham CUB
3. Albertson Van Zo Post CUB

Sabre Individual
1. Manuel Diaz CUB
2. William Grebe USA
3. Albertson Van Zo Post CUB

Single Sticks (1904 only)
1. Albertson Van Zo Post CUB
2. William Glebe USA
3. William Scott O'Connor USA

Men Rowing

Single Sculls
1. Frank Greer USA 10:08,5
2. James Juvenal USA 2 round trips
3. Constance Titus USA 1 round trip

Double Sculls
1. USA (Atlanta Boat Club, New York) 10:03,2
2. USA (Ravenswood Boat Club, Long Island)
3. USA (Independant Rowing Club, New Orleans)

Four Oars without Coxswin
1. USA (Century Boat Club, St Louis) 9:53,8
2. USA (Mound City Rowing Club, St Louis)

Eight Oars
1. USA (Vesper Boat Club) 7:50,0
2. Canada (Argonaut R.C. Toronto)

Men Archery

Double York Round (100 yards - 80 yards - 60 yards)
1. Phillip Bryant USA 820
2. Robert Williams USA 819
3. William H. Thompson USA 816

Double American Round (60 yards - 50 yards - 40 yards)
1. Phillip Bryant USA 1048
2. Robert Williams USA 991
3. William H. Thompson USA

Team Round (60 yards)
1. Potomac Archers, Washington, D.C. 1344
2. Cincinatti Archery Club 1341
3. Boston A.A. 1268

Women Archery

Double National Round (60 yards - 50 yards)
1. M.C. Howell USA 620
2. H.C. Pollock USA 419
3. E.C. Cooke USA 419

Double Columbia Round (50 yards - 40 yards - 30 yards)
1. M.C. Howell USA 867
2. E.C. Cooke USA 630
3. H.C. Pollock USA 630

Team Round
1. Cincinatti A.C. 506
2. Potomac Archers, Washington

Men Gymnastics

Individual All-around Competition
1. Julius Lehart AUT 69,80
2. Wilhelm Weber GER 69,10
3. Adolf Spinnler SUI 67,99

Team All-around Competition
1. Philadelphia 374,43
2. New York 356,37
3. Chicago 349,69

Individual Parallel Bars
1. George Eyser USA 44
2. Anton Heida USA 43
3. John Duha USA 40

Individual Vault Horse
1. Anton Heida USA 36
2. George Eyser USA 36
3. William Merz USA 31

Individual Sidehorse Vault
1. Anton Heida USA 42
2. George Eyser USA 33
3. William Merz USA 29

Individual Horizontal Bar
1. Anton Heida USA 40
2. Edward Henning USA 40
3. George Eyser USA 39

Individual Flying Rings
1. Hermann Glass USA 45
2. William Merz USA 35
3. Emil Voigt USA 32

Rope Climbing (1904, 1906, 1924, 1932 only)
1. George Eyser USA 7,0
2. Charles Krause USA 7,8
3. Emil Voigt USA 9,8

Club Swinging (1904 and 1932 only)
1. Edward Henning USA 13,0
2. Emil Voigt USA 9,0
3. Ralph Wilson USA 5,0

Triple Competition (Parallel Bars, Horizontal Bar, Vault Horse) (1904 only)
1. Adolf Spinnler SUI 43,49
2. Julius Lenahrt AUT 43,00
3. Wilhelm Weber GER 41,60

All-around 3 Exercise Competition (Long Jump, Shotput, 100m) (1904)
1. Max Emmerich USA 35,70
2. John Grieb USA 34,00
3. William Merz USA 33,90

Combined Competition (7 apparatus) (1904 only)
1. Anton Heida USA 161
2. George Eyser USA 152
3. William Merz USA 135

Basketball (demonstration)

1. USA 4 (Buffalo German (YMCA)
2. USA 3 (Chicago Central YMCA)
3. USA 0 (Xavier A.C. New York)

Soccer

1. Canada (Galt F.C. Ontario)
2. USA (Christian Brothers College)
3. USA (St Rose, St Louis)

See Table of Contents for abbreviations

1904

SEPTEMBER

Su	Mo	Tu	We	Th	Fr	Sa
				1	2	3
4	5	6	7	8	9	10
11	12	13	14	15	16	17
18	19	20	21	22	23	24
25	26	27	28	29	30	

1. St. Louis: M.J. Sheridan sets record of 132 ft. in discus throw.

3. San Francisco: L.L. Whitman sets record of 33 days in transcontinental auto run.

3. Korea: Gen. Kuropatkin abandons Liao-Yang; Russians in full retreat (→ 5).

3. London: U.S. cyclist Robert Walthour wins 100-km. Crystal Palace race.

4. Russia: Imperial decree defines civil rights of Jews (→ 5/7/05).

5. Korea: Japanese force Russians to give up Mukden (→ 20).

7. British gain control over Tibet, acquire trading posts and force Dalai Lama not to cede territory to foreign powers (→ 23).

7. Huntsville: Alabama mob of 2,000 burns jail, kills Negro accused of murder (→ 1/7/05).

11. New York: Battleship Connecticut launched, marking new era in naval construction.

15. Germany: Episcopal congress in Posen agrees to halt scrutiny of religion in schools (→ 7/3/05).

20. Russians purchase four cruisers from Argentina (→ 25).

21. Serbia: Coronation of King Peter I.

21. Italy: Socialist Party's nationwide general strike ends after weeks of violence (→ 3/12/05).

23. British military expedition leaves Tibet.

24. Tennessee: Head-on train crash kills 62, injures 120.

25. Russia: Czar orders reorganization of Manchurian forces; Gen. Kuropatkin loses command (→ 30).

28. New York: Woman arrested for smoking cigarette on Fifth Avenue.

30. Port Arthur: Heavy casualties end Gen. Nogi's 3rd assault on Russian defenses (→ 10/1).

BIRTH

17. Sir Frederick Ashton, founder British Royal Ballet.

King creates international commission to investigate Congo complaints

Congolese natives load bananas for export to Europe.

Sept 15. King Leopold II of Belgium has set up a three-man commission to investigate continuing reports of atrocities in the Congo. The British have been the most persistent critics. The question of treatment of natives in the Congo was raised in Parliament in 1897, and again last year. Lord Landsdowne, the Foreign Secretary, has complained to the other great powers, who expressed little interest.

Criticism of the system in the Congo began to appear in the 1890's. Although individual missionaries have reported atrocities, many missions are reluctant to criticize their host government. Humanitarian complaints revolve around the labor practices of the concessionary companies, eager to profit from the market for rubber, who compel Congolese natives to tap rubber trees in the jungle for extremely low wages under harsh conditions. Also, the Belgian government has been accused of abuses involving the Congolese natives who are forced to work on public projects, such as roads (→ 1/11/05).

Helen Keller wins Radcliffe degree

Sept 1. In a triumph of human will and education over adversity, Miss Helen Keller was graduated today with honors from Radcliffe College.

Miss Keller, who was born in Tuscumba, Alabama, in 1880, lost sight and hearing because of illness at the age of two. Her education was undertaken five years later by Miss Anne Sullivan, who taught her to read by braille, to converse by touch and to write on a special typewriter. Miss Keller prepared for college at the Cambridge School for Young Ladies, with Miss Sullivan repeating the lectures by touch.

In college, Miss Keller used special braille textbooks and once again was assisted by Anne Sullivan in comprehending the lectures. In addition to taking the full schedule of courses, she also led an active social life. Miss Keller's autobiography, "Story of My Life," was published last year.

Wrights show off control of plane

Sept 20. Orville and Wilbur Wright have silenced all skeptics with a convincing display of heavier-than-air flight in a craft of their own design. Flying at Huffman Prairie, near their hometown of Dayton, Ohio, the Wrights showed they could take off from level ground without assistance and remain aloft for many minutes. They flew a craft named Flyer II, an improved version of the ship in which they made their first flights at Kitty Hawk, North Carolina, last year.

Flyer II has a more powerful engine than the original Wright airplane, but it retains the system of movable wingtips that allows control of the airplane and the efficient propeller that the Wrights designed. Their application for a patent seems certain to be approved, but the Wrights reportedly are having difficulty convincing the Army that their machine has military uses.

1904

OCTOBER

Su	Mo	Tu	We	Th	Fr	Sa
						1
2	3	4	5	6	7	8
9	10	11	12	13	14	15
16	17	18	19	20	21	22
23	24	25	26	27	28	29
30	31					

1. Japanese siege artillery arrives at Port Arthur (→ 15).

3. Southwest Africa: To avoid being disarmed, chief of Hottentots declares war on Germany (→ 11/12).

3. Morocco: France and Spain agree on spheres of influence (→ 2/1/05).

4. Holland and Portugal sign treaty dividing up Indonesian island of Timor.

8. Germany and Rumania sign treaty of commerce to improve trade relations.

15. Russian Baltic fleet under Adm. Rojestvensky leaves Libau for the Orient with intent to relieve Port Arthur (→ 22).

15. Philadelphia: Georgiana Bishop takes U.S. women's golf championship.

18. Manchuria: Thirteen-day battle at Cha-Ho River ends in stalemate; Russians lose 40,000; Japanese 20,000 (→ 22).

21. Panamanians clash with U.S. Marines during brief uprising (→ 11/16).

22. North Sea: Russian Baltic fleet sinks British fishing boat, mistaking it for Japanese warship (→ 27).

22. Russia: Reserve troops leave St. Petersburg to shouts of "Down with the czar" and "Long live Japan" (→ 11/29).

24. France: Four officers, accused of lying in Dreyfus Affair, appear before Council of War (→ 7/12/06).

27. British warships surround Russia's Baltic fleet in North Sea (→ 12/22).

30. Korea: Japanese attempt another assault on Port Arthur; heavy casualties suffered under Russian machine-gun fire (→ 11/18).

BIRTHS

1. Russian pianist Vladimir Horowitz.

2. British novelist Graham Greene.

2. Indian statesman Lal Bahadur Shastri (†1/11/1966).

New York City subway formally opened as thousands of citizens ride first day

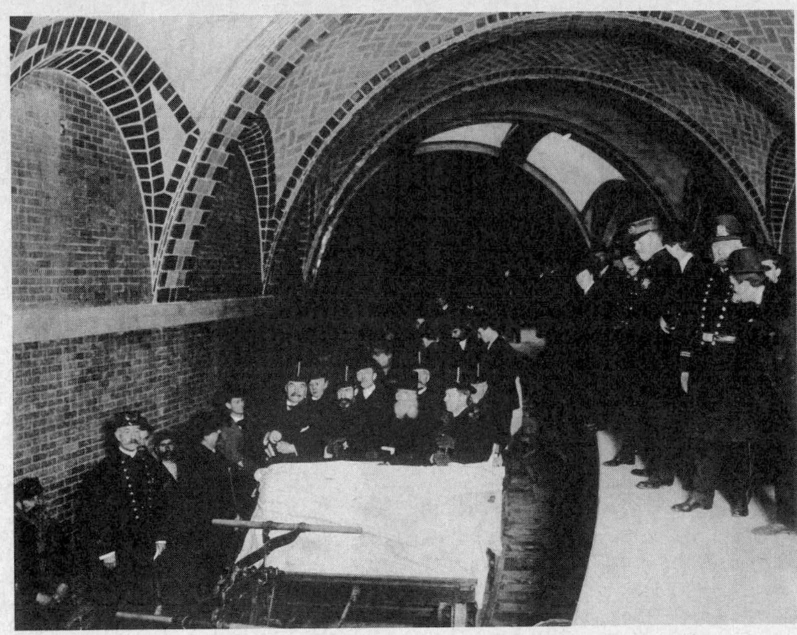
Mayor McClellan (white beard) takes first official ride on the subway.

Oct 27. New York City's underground railway opened this afternoon amid the blaring of tin whistles and the firing of salutes. Mayor McClellan, silver controller in hand, acted as motorman and drove the first train. The car completed its run, from Broadway to 145th Street, precisely on time. For the first rides, the mayor invited 15,000 guests, among them John B. McDonald, the contractor responsible for building the subway.

The general public was not admitted underground until 7 p.m., but they seized the opportunity to ride well past midnight. Passengers admired the handsome, white stations and virtually silent transport offered by the olive-green cars. Even the citizens above ground had something to marvel at, hovering near the little stations to watch the masses emerge from the tunnel.

Bartholdi, sculptor of Liberty Statue, dies

Oct 4. The French sculptor who lit up New York harbor died today in Paris. Frederic-Auguste Bartholdi called his massive symbol of freedom, "Liberty Enlightening the World." Americans call her simply Miss Liberty. The illuminated torch of Bartholdi's statue has welcomed immigrants to the United States since she was dedicated on Bedloe's Island in 1886.

Bartholdi constructed the steel and copper statue in Paris with the help of Gustave Eiffel. The 225-ton, 150-foot statue was then shipped by boat to New York, where it was erected on a large granite pedestal. Miss Liberty, one of the best-known statues in the world, holds the torch in her outstretched right hand and the Declaration of Independence in her left.

"Liberty Enlightening the World."

1904

NOVEMBER

Su	Mo	Tu	We	Th	Fr	Sa
		1	2	3	4	5
6	7	8	9	10	11	12
13	14	15	16	17	18	19
20	21	22	23	24	25	26
27	28	29	30			

2. St. Louis: Capt. Thomas S. Baldwin's unmanned airship disappears in clouds.

12. Troubled by revolt, the German gov. of S.W. Africa gives up post to Gen. Adolf von Trotha (→ 27).

12. Germany and Switzerland agree on advances in trade relations to begin Jan. 1906.

15. Washington: Marquis de Monstiers, founder of Catholic University, renounces Catholicism.

18. Korea: Gen. Stoessel announces Russians can hold Port Arthur if they receive fresh supplies (→ 26).

18. Austria: Opening of Italian law school at Innsbruck sparks student unrest; classes canceled.

19. New Haven: Yale blanks Harvard 12-0 in last big football game of season

21. Russia: Zemstvos representatives in St. Petersburg demand Russian parliament (→ 29).

21. Paris: Motorized omnibuses replace horse-drawn cars.

23. Russo-German talks break down over Russia's insistence on consulting France.

24. California: New "tracker" tractor tested, aiming at commercial use by 1906.

26. Korea: Twelve thousand Japanese troops die in 5th assault on Russian defenses at Port Arthur (→ 12/4).

26. Philadelphia: Army defeats Navy 11-0 in annual football game.

27. Southwest Africa: German colonial army defeats Hottentots at Warmbad (→ 10/12/06).

29. Russia: Students and workers organize nationwide demonstrations against Far East war (→ 12/10).

BIRTH

21. American jazz saxophonist Coleman Hawkins (†5/19/1965).

DEATH

4. French statesman Paul de Cassagnac (*1842).

Roosevelt elected to another 4 years

Nov 8. President Roosevelt won a full four-year lease on the White House today, carrying most of the Northern and Western states. With election returns showing a Republican sweep, the Democratic challenger, Alton B. Parker, sent the president a telegram, congratulating him on his overwhelming victory at the polls.

In a statement issued from the White House, President Roosevelt thanked the voters and assured the nation that "under no circumstances will I be a candidate for or accept another nomination." He is, of course, entitled to seek another full term in 1908. Roosevelt succeeded to the presidency in 1901 after the assassination of his fellow Republican, William McKinley (→ 3/4/05).

U.S. buys French Panama concession

Uncle Sam towers over Panama.

Nov 16. One of the last obstacles to the construction of a canal across the Panama isthmus was lifted today. The United States purchased the concession to build the waterway from a French company headed by Philippe Bunau-Varilla. The businessman helped convince President Theodore Roosevelt to build it across Panama instead of through Nicaragua. The United States has already bought control of the canal zone territory (→ 2/8/05).

1904

DECEMBER

Su	Mo	Tu	We	Th	Fr	Sa
				1	2	3
4	5	6	7	8	9	10
11	12	13	14	15	16	17
18	19	20	21	22	23	24
25	26	27	28	29	30	31

1. World's Fair at St. Louis closes.

4. Korea: Despite losses of 11,000 men, Japanese gain last hill at Port Arthur (→ 5).

5. Korea: Japanese destroy Russian fleet at Port Arthur; only torpedo boats left (→ 16).

10. Russian Grand Duke Sergius resigns after loss to Liberals (→ 11).

11. Russia: Mobs clash with police during demonstration against autocracy in St. Petersburg (→ 26).

16. Japanese warships quit Port Arthur to cut off Russian Baltic fleet's advance (→ 1/2/05).

16. Philippines: American troops suffer heavy losses to rebels at Samar (→ 5/14/05).

22. Intl. commission begins to investigate Baltic fleet's attack on British fishing vessel at Dogger Bank (→ 2/23/05).

28. Georgia: Farmers burn two million bales of cotton to prop up falling prices.

CULTURAL EVENTS, 1904

Literature: Anton Chekhov's "The Cherry Orchard"; J.M. Synge's "Riders to the Sea"; 1st volume of Romain Rolland's "Jean-Christophe"; Henry James' "The Golden Bowl"; O. Henry's "Cabbages and Kings," short stories; Jack London's "The Sea Wolf"; James Barrie's "Peter Pan."

Academia: Freud's "The Psychopathology of Everyday Life"; Weber's "The Protestant Ethic and the Spirit of Capitalism"; L.T. Hobhouse's "Democracy and Reaction."

Music: Puccini's "Madam Butterfly," in Milan; 1st concert of London Symphony Orchestra; 1st radio transmission of music at Graz, Austria; George M. Cohan's "Give My Regards to Broadway" and "The Yankee Doodle Boy," from musical "Little Johnny Jones."

The Arts: Picasso's "The Two Sisters"; Henri Rousseau's "The Wedding"; French films, "The Barber of Seville" and "The Damnation of Faust."

Monroe Doctrine extended to economics

Dec 6. President Theodore Roosevelt has indicated that the United States may force the debt-ridden Dominican Republic to repay its European financial creditors.

In his annual message to Congress, Roosevelt declared that adherence "to the Monroe Doctrine may force the United States, however reluctantly, to the exercise of an international police power." The sad state of economic affairs in the Dominican Republic has led to fears that foreign creditors, including Germany, in attempting to collect their debts, may establish a presence in the Caribbean Sea. This foreign presence would violate the Monroe Doctrine, according to the president, and would be especially unwelcome in light of the strategic importance of Panama, the site of the trans-isthmian canal (→ 2/13/05).

Roosevelt surveys the globe.

Dec 31. Fireworks will help New Yorkers open both the new Times Building and the New Year.

Czar offers reforms to end growing unrest

Dec 26. In an effort to stave off growing unrest, Czar Nicholas II has proposed a series of reforms, including liberty for the peasants, expansion of press rights and greater religious freedom. The reforms will be referred to the Council of Ministers, which will consider their feasibility. The czar did not agree to a constitutional assembly, the most important of the demands made by the Congress of Zemstvos Presidents in November. The zemstvos ("provisional assemblies") represent Russia's upper and middle classes. In announcing his reforms, the czar cautioned the Russians against any further acts of violence. About 500 strikes have taken place this year (→ 1/20/05).

Ivan Pavlov wins Nobel Prize for stimulus studies with dogs

Dec 10. Ivan Pavlov, the celebrated Russian physiologist, was presented with the Nobel Prize in physiology today for studies on the nature of the digestive process.

Pavlov showed that when a dog's gullet was severed so that food it swallowed never reached the stomach, digestive juices still flowed. The study indicated that nerves in the mouth stimulated when the dog was fed sent messages to the brain, which caused the flow of digestive juices. Pavlov then showed that by cutting other nerves, gastric juice secretion was stopped even though food reached the stomach.

In a later series of experiments, Pavlov showed that dogs who heard a bell ring when they were fed would salivate when a bell rang even if they got no food. Such "conditioned responses" are important in human learning, Pavlov says. Other winners of the Nobel Prize are Lord Rayleigh in physics and William Ramsey in chemistry.

In the course of his research on digestion, Dr. Pavlov seems to have stumbled upon findings with important implications for psychology. In order to obtain saliva for study, he gave meat powder to laboratory dogs. Soon they began salivating merely at the sight of the experimentor. On further investigation, Pavlov found the dogs would react to the sound of a bell if they associated it with food. If a dog's behavior can be conditioned by a bell, what of human beings?

Ivan Petrovich Pavlov.

1905

JANUARY

Su	Mo	Tu	We	Th	Fr	Sa
1	2	3	4	5	6	7
8	9	10	11	12	13	14
15	16	17	18	19	20	21
22	23	24	25	26	27	28
29	30	31				

1. Russia: Trans-Siberian Railway inaugurated; Vladivostok to Paris in 21 days.

1. British tennis team takes Davis Cup 5-0 over U.S.

9. George Bernard Shaw's play "You Never Can Tell" opens in New York to rave reviews.

11. Congo: Belgian colonists slain in native uprising (→ 3/9).

13. Philadelphia: Gessler Rousseau arrested on charges of sabotaging Cunard liner Umbria in 1903.

19. U.S. Sec. of State John Hay secures agreement with Britain, France, Italy to prevent partition of China following Russo-Japanese War (→ 27).

19. 215,000 German miners enter second month of strike asking shorter work day (→ 2/7).

20. Russia: Troops mobilized to protect St. Petersburg from brewing revolt (→ 21).

21. Russia: 140,000 workers and peasants begin march to czar's Winter Palace in St. Petersburg (→ 22).

22. Russia: "Bloody Sunday" strikes St. Petersburg (→ 23).

23. Russia: General strike called in Moscow (→ 24).

24. Russia's civil strife spreads to Finland, Poland (→ 26).

26. Russia: Thirty workmen shot by troops at Riga (→ 27).

27. Manchuria: Russian Gen. Kuropatkin takes offensive; Japanese under Gen. Oyama suffer heavy casualties (→ 2/21).

27. Russia: Students, professors protest imprisonment of Maxim Gorky (→ 29).

29. Poland: Warsaw in chaos as mobs, troops loot Polish capital (→ 2/1).

30. New York: Johann Hoch arrested for murdering 9 wives.

BIRTHS

21. French fashion designer Christian Dior (†10/24/1957).

31. American writer John O'Hara (†4/11/1970).

Bloody Sunday: Terror in Russia

Jan 22. A day that began with a peaceful march in St. Petersburg, Russia, by 100,000 workers and their families to petition Czar Nicho-Nicholas II for better working conditions has ended in unspeakable horror. Unwilling to listen to the marchers' requests, the czar instead ordered his troops to fire on the unarmed protesters. More than 500 are dead and many more marchers were wounded.

The events of this "Bloody Sunday" in Russia's capital have struck a death blow to the traditional affection the Russians feel for their czar, or "Little Father," and ended the workers' belief that the czar has been kept ignorant of their problems by his advisers.

Czarist troops fire on workers in front of the Winter Palace.

The march began at midday. At the head of the parade was its organizer, the radical priest Father Gopon, who has led many of this year's strikes. Dressed in his vestments, carrying a cross, Gopon led the workers toward the Winter Palace, where they planned to present a petition to the czar. Even when they saw the solid array of soldiers before them, the marchers continued, confident that the soldiers would not fire on fellow Russians and that the czar wanted to hear their requests and complaints.

But the czar was not at the Winter Palace and his troops had firm orders to disperse any crowds. When the marchers refused to retreat, the authorities became alarmed that this was the first sign of revolution and decided the mob's momentum could best be stopped by a show of force. Soldiers then fired and slashed at the panicked marchers from their horses. The result was a massacre that will not soon be forgotten (→ 23).

Russian army chief gives in to Japanese at Port Arthur

Jan 2. A savage half-year siege has led to General Anatoly Stoessel's surrender of Port Arthur. At 4:30 this afternoon, Stoessel's written capitulation was received in Tokyo by General Nogi Maresuke. The Japanese Emperor has offered assurances that all surrendering troops will be treated in a humane manner. According to Japanese custom, however, Stoessel will be condemned to death, unless Czar Nicholas intervenes on his behalf.

Stoessel and his forces waged an unbelievable effort. Of 45,000 Russians left in the city, 7,700 died in combat and 15,000 were wounded. Just prior to total capitulation, Stoessel surrendered 10,000 starving men. On the Japanese side, between November 27 and December 5, 11,000 soldiers lost their lives. Some were killed not by gunfire but by collapsing upon layers of barbed wire the Russians strung around the city. Survivors surged forward, balancing on the bodies of their comrades sunk deep within frozen snow.

Tokyo greeted victory with firecrackers and merrymaking. The Russian public was not informed of events. The czar, who expected victory for his side to quell internal unrest, can ill afford to alienate his people further. With Port Arthur gone, retaining central Manchuria may be impossible. English naval circles talk of Russia calling home its Pacific fleet. In the same circles are rumors President Roosevelt will be asked to mediate peace (→ 19).

Japanese troops overrun Russian defenses at Port Arthur.

Diamond big as fist insured for $2.5m

The Cullinan diamond.

Jan 30. The Premier Company in the Republic of Transvaal has reported the discovery of a large diamond, so far the biggest ever found on earth. It was insured in London today for the sum of $2.5 million against theft and marine risks.

Frederick Wells, the Mine Surface Manager, found it in the late afternoon on January 25th during a routine inspection. The stone was so large he was convinced he was being fooled by a piece of glass. William McHardy, General Manager, confirmed that the crystal was a true diamond of gem quality. The weight of the stone is 3,106 carats or 1.33 lbs. The same day it was named Cullinan in honor of the person who opened the mine in 1902.

Negro gets first high customs job

Jan 7. President Theodore Roosevelt is stubborn and has just proved it. Three times, he put a Negro, Mr. Gran, forward for a high customs post in South Carolina. Three times, the Senate rejected the appointment. But Roosevelt maintained his candidacy because he believed the senators' prejudice was ridiculous and unacceptable.

Roosevelt is convinced that racial discrimination is morally wrong. During his first term, he appointed a number of highly qualified Negroes to office in the South at the insistence of the educator Booker T. Washington. Roosevelt won a new victory today. The Senate gave in. Gran got the job (→ 1/1/06).

New York auto show proves great success

Jan 30. More than 250 foreign and American exhibitors displayed the latest automobile models and gadgets at the annual Madison Square Garden auto show.

More than 100 motorcars were shown, from the runabout type, which runs as low as $450, to the richly upholstered 20- to 40-horsepower limousines, which sell from $5,000 to $8,000. Also featured were car appliances such as lamps, tires and speedometers. The automobile industry has not witnessed a reduction in prices during the past year, but competition has produced better materials, simpler construction, more comfort and higher speed.

High court rules against beef trust

Jan 30. Granting an injunction against Swift & Company and other meatpacking companies, the Supreme Court upheld a Circuit Court decision in favor of the government's attempt to suppress unfair practices by the beef trust.

Written by Justice Oliver Wendell Holmes, the high court opinion charged the trust had acted in concert on a number of key points. These include not bidding against each other in the livestock markets, fixing their selling prices and getting "less than lawful rates from the railroads," all to the detriment of their competitors. The thrust of the decision prevents the trust from beating its competition through price-fixing (→ 2/16).

Uncle Sam and T.R. tame the trusts.

1905

FEBRUARY

Su	Mo	Tu	We	Th	Fr	Sa
			1	2	3	4
5	6	7	8	9	10	11
12	13	14	15	16	17	18
19	20	21	22	23	24	25
26	27	28				

1. Germany contests French rule in Morocco (→ 3/19).

2. Chicago: Railroad magnates Gould and Harriman fight for control over Gulf Line; Kansas City to Gulf of Mexico.

3. New York: Mary Arbogast, first person married in 1905, arrested for bigamy.

6. Soisalon Soininen, procurator general of Finland, assassinated.

7. Washington: Congress admits Oklahoma, to statehood; New Mexico, Arizona are only territories left (→ 1/6/12).

7. Argentine revolt crushed by government troops.

7. Germany: Ruhr miners go back to work.

8. Colombia asks U.S. to let Panama vote on independence (→ 10/5).

9. Poland: Russian troops slaughter 150 workers at Nifka mine (→ 12).

12. Russia: With support of Russian nobility, czar orders investigation into living conditions of working class (→ 17).

13. Washington: Senate attacks Roosevelt's control over Dominican economy (→ 3/28).

16. Washington: Roosevelt orders inquiry into Standard Oil business practices (→ 7/1).

20. Alabama: Explosion entombs 100 miners.

21. Manchuria: 300,000 Russian troops under Kuropatkin face Japanese as Battle of Mudken begins (→ 27).

23. Paris: Intl. commission vindicates Britain; Russia said to err in sinking British fishing boat at Dogger Bank.

24. Russian Min. of Agriculture Alexei Yermolov offers czar new constitution (→ 27).

27. Japanese push Russians back in Manchuria, cross Sha River (→ 3/5).

27. Russia: Maxim Gorky freed on bail, exiled to Riga (→ 3/3).

BIRTH

6. Polish statesman Wladyslaw Gomulka.

Czar has talk with workers' delegates

Protesters march in Moscow.

Feb 1. Czar Nicholas II has met with 34 handpicked workers in his Tsarskoye Selo palace to discuss the events of "Bloody Sunday." "I believe in the honest feelings of the working people and in their unshakable loyalty to me," said the czar. "Therefore I forgive them."

The czar's belated willingness to meet with the workers and his continued unwillingness to understand their complaints only stirred up the anger of those who had hoped to petition him for reform. Father Gopon, organizer of the march that lead to "Bloody Sunday," proclaimed: "There is no czar" (→ 12)

Lew Wallace, author of "Ben Hur," dead

Feb 15. Lew Wallace, the author of "Ben Hur," has died in Crawfordsville, Indiana, at age 71. Fully titled "Ben Hur: A Tale of the Christ," the book recounts the rise of Christianity during the Roman Empire. Written in 1880, it has proven to be one of the most popular historical novels of our time.

Wallace was also a lawyer, soldier and diplomat. During Civil War service in the Union Army he reached the rank of Major General. He served as Governor of the New Mexico Territory, 1878-1881, and Minister to Turkey, 1881-1885.

Wallace wrote three other novels: "The Fair God" (1873), "The Boyhood of Christ" (1888) and "The Prince of India" (1893); but none has rivaled the fame of "Ben Hur."

1905

MARCH

Su	Mo	Tu	We	Th	Fr	Sa
			1	2	3	4
5	6	7	8	9	10	11
12	13	14	15	16	17	18
19	20	21	22	23	24	25
26	27	28	29	30	31	

3. Russian Czar agrees to create elected assembly (→ 8).

5. Manchuria: Russians begin retreat from Mukden; 100,000 killed in 3 days fighting (→ 9).

8. Russia: Peasant revolt reported spreading to Georgia (→ 4/7).

9. Egypt: U.S. archeologist Davies unearths royal tombs of Yua and Tua.

9. Manchuria: Japanese surround 200,000 Russian troops in retreat from Mukden (→ 13).

9. Congo: Following investigation of colonial policy, Belgian Vice Gov. Costermans commits suicide (→ 9/28).

11. Parisian subway officially inaugurated.

12. Rome: Premier Giovanni Giolotti forced out of office by continuing civil strife.

13. Roosevelt calls on women to do their duty as mothers.

14. Paris: French bankers refuse to lend money to Russia until after war (→ 25).

14. U.K. House of Commons cites need to compete with German naval strength (→ 7/24).

18. New York: Franklin and Eleanor Roosevelt are married.

19. French explorer S. de Segonzac taken prisoner by Moroccans (→ 31).

22. U.K.: Child miners receive maximum 8-hour day (→ 7/2).

24. Crete: Group led by Eleutherios Venizelos claims independence from Turkey, union with Greece (→ 4/21).

25. Russia receives Japan's terms for peace (→ 30).

28. U.S. takes full control over Dominican revenues (→ 4/3).

30. Teddy Roosevelt chosen to mediate in Russo-Japanese peace talks (→ 4/19).

31. Morocco: Kaiser lands in Tangier, challenges France, proclaiming support for independent Morocco.→

DEATH

16. U.S. industrialist Meyer Guggenheim, "The Smelter King" (*2/1/1828).

Revolutionist kills Russian Grand Duke

Murder of Grand Duke.

Feb 17. As his carriage passed through the Kremlin gates in Moscow, Grand Duke Sergei Aleksandrovich, the uncle of Czar Nicholas II and one of his most influential advisers, was killed by an assassin who threw a bomb onto his lap.

The assassination did not come as a surprise. His name was at the top of a death list compiled by the Social Revolutionary Party, the group that killed Minister of the Interior V.K. Plehve last July. Few are mourning the grand duke's death. A haughty man with violently reactionary leanings, Sergei's tenure as Governor General of Moscow was marked by unusual brutality and incompetence. His wife, by contrast, is much loved by the people. The Grand Duchess Elizabeta Feodorovna received a warning not to ride in the grand duke's carriage. She decided not to ride with her husband, and her own carriage was not damaged (→ 24).

200,000 lost as Russians leave Mukden

Determined Japanese troops charge the Russians at Mukden.

March 13. Converging Japanese attacks have rolled up the Russian right flank, forcing General Kuropatkin to abandon Mukden and southern Manchuria. The Russian army is reported to have suffered some 200,000 casualties in the fighting, which was dominated by frenzied attacks by Japanese infantry. One regiment charged 13 times in a single action. Earlier attacks broke the Russian center on March 8. The defeated army left 13 heavy guns on the field.

A massive Japanese concentration northwest of Mukden, meanwhile, has forced the Russians to retreat toward the Tie pass, three days march to the north. The fleeing Russians have discarded weapons and other equipment. And as the Japanese armies close in on the Tie pass, the situation in the Russian capital of St. Petersburg is worsening. There have been anti-war demonstrations in the working quarters. Widespread unrest also is reported in the provinces, with landlords and government officials attacked by mobs (→ 14).

Kaiser visits Morocco; French provoked

March 31. The German Emperor's visit to Tangier was an immense political demonstration, even though Kaiser Wilhelm said to his subjects at the German legation that he had come to Morocco to protect German economic interests.

"I am happy," the emperor said, "to recognize that you are devoted pioneers of German industry and commerce, who are helping me in the task of always upholding in a free country the interests of the motherland. The sovereignty and integrity of Morocco will be maintained." The emperor's visit, however, is regarded as a provocation by the French, whose position in Morocco seemed to be put in doubt.

French Foreign Minister Delcasse was forced to restate his country's policy in the Senate: "France's Moroccan policy continues on the same conditions as it was begun. The Sultan's weakness and the anarchy resulting therefrom were prejudicial to everybody, and especially to France, in Algeria. France does not pretend to base her interests on disregard for the interests of others," but for establishing order "France possesses a special standing in Morocco" (→ 4/6).

Wilhelm: "Whom to call on next?"

Jules Verne, adored writer, deceased

Jules Verne.

March 24. In Amiens, death has come at age 77 to the popular French writer Jules Verne, who achieved wealth and renown in 1863 with his novel "Five Weeks in a Balloon" and followed it with such tales of adventure and scientific innovation as "Around the World in 80 Days," "20,000 Leagues Under the Sea" and "A Journey to the Center of the Earth."

Maurice Barrymore dies; famous actor

March 25. Alone and insane, the renowned actor and playwright Maurice Barrymore has died at the age of 58 in the Long Island Home, the sanitarium in Amityville, New York, where he has been confined for the past four years. With a range that extended from Shakespearean tragedy to light comedy, Barrymore was best known as a performer of captivating personality.

Born in Agra, India, and named Herbert Blythe, he was the son of a surveyor for the East India Company. Educated in England, he abandoned a career in law to become an actor, came to America in 1875 and appeared with leading troupes and performers. His marriage in 1876 to Georgina Drew, daughter of John Drew, related him to one of the most famous theatrical families in the United States. He is survived by a daughter, Ethel, and his sons, John and Lionel.

Roosevelt inaugurated for a full term

March 4. Joyous crowds paid homage today to President Roosevelt as he was inaugurated for a full term. Accompanied by a large military escort, the president rode in royal splendor from the White House to the Capitol to take his oath of office. Later, from a stand in front of the White House, the president reviewed the most gigantic parade ever staged in Washington. Tonight, he and members of his family attended an inaugural ball in the ornate Pension Building. "Great," said the president. "It touched me to the heart."

Roosevelt takes the oath of office for the first time in full ceremony.

1905

APRIL

Su	Mo	Tu	We	Th	Fr	Sa
						1
2	3	4	5	6	7	8
9	10	11	12	13	14	15
16	17	18	19	20	21	22
23	24	25	26	27	28	29
30						

1. Nova Scotia: The Victorian, 1st turbine steamer to cross Atlantic, arrives in Halifax.

1. Paris and Berlin linked by telephone.

3. Belgium, Santo Domingo's largest creditor, rejects U.S. intervention in debt settlement (→ 5/13).

5. India: Earthquake kills 1,000 at Khamarsia station.

6. Morocco: Sultan invites Germany to conference on Morocco; France angered (→ 5/5).

6. London: Edward VII meets with French Pres. Loubet.

7. Russia: Workers' soviet congress demands democratic constitution (→ 11).

11. Russia: Govt. commission on press lifts censorship on private telegrams (→ 30).

17. Supreme Court rules in Lochner v. N.Y. limitation of baker's working hours violates right to free contract (→ 6/27).

19. Japanese rebuke France for allowing Russians to use port at Kamranh Bay (→ 5/9).

19. Indiana: Anti-smoking law enforced; youth pays $35 for possession of rolling papers.

21. Crete: Assembly proclaims union with Greece (→ 11/11).

24. Texas: Dem. Congressman John Pickney killed by anti-Prohibitionist lawyer J.N. Brown; 3 wounded in struggle.

25. South Africa: Boers condemn new constitution awarded by British (→ 7/4).

25. French socialists unite into section of Socialist Intl.

30. St. Petersburg: Czar promises religious reform, frees peasants from penalties on late loan payments (→ 5/1).

BIRTH

24. American novelist Robert Penn Warren.

DEATH

4. Constantin Meunier, Belgian painter, sculptor (*4/12/1831).

21. Sen. Orville Platt, author of Platt amendment.

Pellagra caused by improper diet

April 19. Medical researcher Joseph Goldberger of the U.S. Public Health Service has completed a test proving the disease pellagra is caused by a nutritonal deficiency. By depriving inmates in a Mississippi jail of a proper diet, Goldberger determined that B vitamins can prevent the dreaded illness. Pellagra, in its early stages, shows the following symptoms: weakness, poor appetite, nervousness and depression. When mature, the disease causes dermatitis and inflammation of the mucuos membranes.

Naval hero's body discovered in France

April 14. The body of American naval hero John Paul Jones has finally been unearthed in a Protestant cemetery in Paris, thus ending a quest begun in 1889 by General Horace Porter, the American Ambassador to France.

Often called the "Father of the U.S. Navy," the famed sailor was buried in Paris in 1792. Because the old graveyard has since been covered by various buildings, the Captain's final resting place became a mystery. Last week, Porter's efforts struck pay dirt with a lead coffin suspected to contain the sailor's remains. The Paris Ecole de Medicine has proven beyond doubt that the corpse is indeed that of the misplaced American hero. Plans are underway to return the long-lost Jones to his native land (→ 6/23).

April 16. In Colorado, Roosevelt shot one bear yesterday and another today, setting a record.

1905

MAY

Su	Mo	Tu	We	Th	Fr	Sa
	1	2	3	4	5	6
7	8	9	10	11	12	13
14	15	16	17	18	19	20
21	22	23	24	25	26	27
28	29	30	31			

1. New York: Radium tested as cure for cancer.

1. Poland: Russian troops fire into innocent crowds in Warsaw, killing 100 (→ 8).

2. Chicago: Employers get injunction after worst day of rioting in month-old teamsters' strike; one killed, 150 hurt.

3. New York: Chorus at Met. Opera strikes.

5. France allows Germans to use Moroccan port in attempt to avoid conflict (→ 6/6).

7. Russia: Jews massacred in Ukraine (→ 11/8).

8. Russia: Liberal Union of Unions formed under Paul Miliukov demands Duma elected by universal suffrage (→ 24).

9. French evict Russian ships from Kamranh Bay (→ 28).

10. Jockey J. Martin rides Agile to victory in Kentucky Derby.

12. New York: Ten-foot boa constrictor loose on 5th Ave.

13. Dominican Republic: U.S. Marines defend Puerto Plata from attacks by rebels angered at U.S. intervention in Dominican economy (→ 6/10).

13. Mata-Hari acclaimed in Paris (→ 10/15/17).

14. Philippines: Moros attack U.S. troops under Leonard Wood; seven Americans, 300 rebels killed (→ 3/9/06).

22. Germany: 5th Union Congress, representing 2.5 mil. members, held in Cologne.

24. Russia: Prince Nadashidze, gov. of Baku, assassinated (→ 6/24).

28. American yacht Atlantic wins British Kaiser Cup.

31. Paris: Anarchist attempts assassination of Spanish King Alfonso, French Pres. Loubet.

BIRTH

16. American actor Henry Fonda (†8/12/1982).

DEATH

26. French banker and philanthropist Alphonse de Rothschild (*1827).

Disaster strikes Russia at Tsushima

Russian Admiral Rojestvensky.

Russian battleship Borodino, ravaged by Japanese torpedoes at Tsushima.

German cartoonist depicts the startling Japanese victory over Russia.

May 28. Admiral Rojestvensky's fleet, Russia's last hope in the naval war with Japan, has been destroyed in the Strait of Tsushima according to offical reports. The Japanese claim to have sunk 12 warships, including the battleships Orel and Borodino as well as two transports and two cruisers. The Japanese government has admitted to the loss of only one cruiser and one torpedo boat in the battle.

The Russian fleet had assembled in the Baltic Sea and then sailed halfway around the world to meet its fate. Admiral Togo of Japan pursued the enemy fleet through a dense fog. When it lifted, he attacked with torpedoes and shellfire. The Russians, apparently surprised, were very slow to reply and lost heavily in the battle's opening engagements. Japanese fire concentrated on the Russian battleships. The Russian ships which were not sunk are now in flight to neutral ports in China. The defeat practically eliminates all hopes of further Russian naval intervention in the Far East and raises doubts about Russia's future military capacity (→ 6/2).

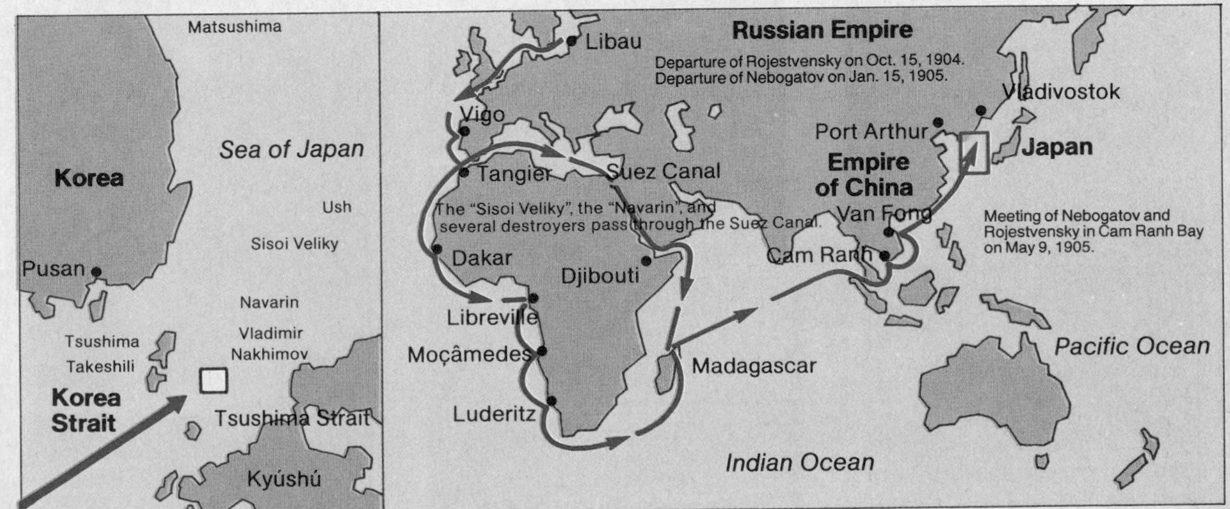

Positioning of the major Russian battleships on the eve of Tsushima.

Long journey of the Baltic fleet from Russia's western coast, around Cape Horn and into the waters of the Orient.

Beautiful Belmont race course opens

May 4. The newest, biggest race track in the world, Belmont Park, opened in suburban Long Island today with much hoopla and pageantry. A crowd of 40,000 enjoyed the start of the opening program in pleasant spring weather, but a sudden drop of the temperature and quickly developing winds spoiled the final hours. Belmont Park, built at a cost of $2.5 million, covers a little more than a square mile.

Revolutionists open office in Geneva

May 6. Seven Eastern European Socialist parties have united to counter the Czar's aggressions in Russia and Poland. The groups, which hail from Poland, Georgia, Finland, Armenia and other regions, developed a commission called the General Fighting Committee. Its headquarters will be located in Geneva, Switzerland.

The committee demands three constituent assemblies: one for Poland, one for Armenia and one for Russia proper. While the Polish Socialist Party is a member of the committee, it may be more interested in reconciliation than its brother parties. Following a Warsaw May Day strike, Polish Socialists urged laborers to return to their work, explaining time was not yet ripe for revolution (→ 8).

Ethel Barrymore displayed new skills this month in N.Y. as Nora in Ibsen's "A Doll's House."

1905

JUNE

Su	Mo	Tu	We	Th	Fr	Sa
				1	2	3
4	5	6	7	8	9	10
11	12	13	14	15	16	17
18	19	20	21	22	23	24
25	26	27	28	29	30	

2. Pres. Roosevelt officially agrees to mediate Russo-Japanese conflict (→ 5).

2. Oregon: Roosevelt opens Lewis and Clark Centennial Exposition in Portland.

5. Roosevelt bars fugitive warships from taking refuge at Manila.

5. New York: Clergymen declare Russians more pagan than Japanese (→ 10).

6. France: Foreign Minister Theophile Delcasse resigns over French refusal to ally with U.K. against German aims in Morocco (→ 7/8).

6. New York: Property at Broadway and Wall Street going for $4 per square inch.

7. France: Jean Charcot's expedition returns from South Pole.

7. Norway: Storting (Parliament) breaks off relations with Sweden (→ 8/13).

10. Japan and Russia agree to peace talks; proclaimed diplomatic triumph for Roosevelt (→ 7/8).

10. Santo Domingo rejects U.S. control over economic affairs (→ 1/5/06).

19. Vatican: Pope Pius X authorizes Italian Catholics to participate in public life.

22. 170 Christians massacred in Turkish Armenia.

23. John Paul Jones' body to be returned from France.

24. Poland: Chaos in Lodz; revolt leaves 2,000 dead or wounded (→ 26).

26. Poland: 20,000 Jews flee Lodz (→ 29).

27. Chicago: Industrial Workers of the World formed under "Big Bill" Haywood; "One big union for all" (→ 12/3/06).

29. Russia: Troops intervene as riots erupt in ports; ships looted; hundreds of victims reported (→ 7/20).

BIRTH

21. French existentialist writer Jean-Paul Sartre (†4/15/1980).

Mutiny on Potemkin

June 27. The red flag of revolution waves tonight over the Potemkin, the most powerful battleship of Russia's Black Sea fleet. The latest news dispatches indicate that the mutineers killed the captain and massacred most of the officers and then threw the bodies into Odessa harbor. A few other officers on board, as well as the crews of two Russian torpedo boats, also mutineed. The revolt on the battleship Potemkin is reported to have begun after the mess officer killed a sailor who had complained about the quality of his soup.

Meanwhile, the city of Odessa is in the grip of a general strike. Loyal troops have dispersed rioting workers. Shots have been exchanged in many districts and a bomb that exploded in Cathedral Place killed two. Dozens of buildings are on fire along the waterfront. The main squadron of the Black Sea fleet is expected to engage the Potemkin soon and a great naval battle is expected to follow. An army garrison is also now on patrol in the Russian city (→ 7/8).

The battleship Potemkin near Odessa.

May Sutton in action at Wimbledon. She took the title 6-3, 6-4 over Dorothea Douglass.

Steel rail makers divide up markets

June 30. The United States Steel Corporation and other American rail makers have finalized a pact with steel rail firms in England, France, Germany and Belgium to divide the markets of the world.

The cartel gives the American companies full control of all steel rail business from the Great Lakes to the Straits of Magellan at the tip of South America, while European firms will be safe from American competition in other parts of the globe. As a special extension of a European plan that had not included the United States, the new syndicate will mean larger profits for American firms, which will henceforth control all railroad development in the Western hemisphere.

1905

JULY

Su	Mo	Tu	We	Th	Fr	Sa
						1
2	3	4	5	6	7	8
9	10	11	12	13	14	15
16	17	18	19	20	21	22
23	24	25	26	27	28	29
30	31					

1. China reported taking steps to curb anti-American sentiment (→ 8/5).

1. Chicago: Seventeen leaders of meat industry indicted for violation of Sherman Antitrust Law (→ 9/6).

2. France enforces law limiting miners' work day to 9 hours.

4. South Africa: Boers protest against British privilege in new electoral law.

5. New York: World's record for mile in steam-powered car cut to 48.8 seconds.

5. France: Frenchman Thery takes Gordon Bennett Cup auto race; dismal showing by U.S.

5. Australia: Liberal Alfred Deakin returns as prime minister.

6. Washington: Elihu Root replaces late John Hay as sec. of state.

8. Paris: France consents to conference with Germany over Moroccan crisis (→ 9/28).

8. Mutinous crew of battleship Potemkin surrenders to Rumanian authorities (→ 8/25).

14. New York: Raid on women's poolroom led by female detective.

16. New York: Commander Peary's ship sails for North Pole.

18. West Africa: German railway inaugurated on coastline of Togoland.

20. Russian nobility vehemently opposes creation of Duma (→ 8/19).

26. Oyster Bay, N.Y.: Roosevelt meets with Japanese prior to formal opening of peace talks (→ 29).

29. Washington: Sec. of War W.H. Taft concludes secret agreement with Japanese Prime Minister Katsura; Japan to have free reign in Korea, U.S. in Philippines (→ 8/1).

30. Frenchman Louis Trousselier takes third Tour de France.

30. Washington: John D. Rockefeller establishes $10 mil. fund for higher education.

Emperors agree on pact

Kaiser Wilhelm II (far right) confers with Czar Nicholas II aboard a German battleship.

July 24. Kaiser Wilhelm II met Czar Nicholas II in Bjorkoe, northwest of St. Petersburg today. It was officially announced that the meeting was only "a visit of courtesy" by the German leader. It is said in diplomatic circles, however, that by this meeting the kaiser aims at bringing about an alliance between Germany and Russia, not only to break Great Britain's attempt to isolate Germany through her understanding with France, but also for the mutual protection of the European monarchical system.

As a matter of fact, Czar Nicholas, overwhelmed by his recent military defeat in Manchuria as well as revolutionary unrest in Russia, did agree to conclude a secret treaty with Kaiser Wilhelm in order to establish a defensive alliance between Germany and Russia. And it is reported that France will be invited to join in order to form a continental alliance. However, according to the Russian ministers who disapprove of an alliance with Germany, ratification of such a treaty is most unlikely.

John Hay dies after long diplomatic career

John Milton Hay, architect of American foreign policy.

July 1. Secretary of State John Hay, creator of the open door policy in China, died suddenly this morning at Sunapee, New Hampshire.

Hay was born October 8, 1838, at Salem, Indiana. He served as Lincoln's private secretary and penned a memoir of the experience. McKinley appointed him Ambassador to Britain, then named him secretary of state in 1898. Hay retained the office under Roosevelt. Hay negotiated peace with Spain after the 1898 war. In 1899, he advocated an open door policy toward China, entreating all nations to respect China's administrative and territorial integrity. His was virtually a lone voice during the fierce Boxer uprising (→ 6).

France separates church and state

July 3. The French Chamber of Deputies by a vote of 341 to 233, and the Senate by 179 to 103, today passed the bill for the separation of church and state, bringing to an end the Concordant signed in 1801 by Pope Pius VIII and Napoleon.

The principle of the measure is as follows: "The Republic assures liberty of conscience and guarantees the free exercise of religion, subject to the restrictions of public order. The Republic neither recognizes, pays stipends to nor subsidizes any sect, but provides funds for colleges, hospitals and asylum chaplains. Otherwise, the public worship budget is abolished and public establishments connected with religion are suppressed" (→ 2/21/06).

Japanese capture Sakhalin Island

July 8. General Liapounof of Russia has capitulated and the Japanese have taken Sakhalin Island, the southern part of which had been annexed by Russia in 1875. The loss of Mukden in March and the devastating defeat at Tsushima in May have aggravated unrest inside Russia. Exhausted financially and fearing a war of attrition far from their bases, the Japanese hope that this acute unrest will compel the Russian government to negotiate. Before entering into negotiations, however, Japan wanted to bolster its position by taking Sakhalin (→ 26).

The Automobile Gasoline Co. this year opened the world's first drive-in gas station in St. Louis.

1905

AUGUST

Su	Mo	Tu	We	Th	Fr	Sa
		1	2	3	4	5
6	7	8	9	10	11	12
13	14	15	16	17	18	19
20	21	22	23	24	25	26
27	28	29	30	31		

1. New York: Ellis Island reports 20% increase in Russian immigration this year.

1. St. Petersburg: Czar opposes settlement with Japan, refuses indemnity, cession of lands (→ 8).

4. U.S. government to support New Orleans in fight against yellow fever epidemic.

4. Russia: 30 strikers killed by cossack troops.

5. Nicaragua: U.S. syndicate granted exclusive rights to build railroads, exploit minerals in one-third of country.

5. Shanghai: Boycott on U.S. goods denounced as bane to China's economy (→ 9/25).

12. Chicago: H. Chandler Egan wins natl. golf championship.

12. Japan, England reach accord determining spheres of influence in Far East; India to remain British.

16. Germany: Wilhelm II and Britain's Edward VII meet in Bad Ischl.

20. Tokyo: Sun Yat-sen forms secret society T'ung Meng Hui to fight Manchu dynasty (→ 10/12/11).

20. Earl of Minto replaces George Curzon as viceroy of India.

22. Poland: Russian governor declares state of emergency to combat nationwide strike (→ 9/2).

24. Buffalo, N.Y.: French bicyclist Lucien Petit-Breton breaks record, covering 25 miles in one hour.

25. Russia: Eight sailors from Potemkin sentenced to death.

26. Japanese seize U.S. ship, claiming Russians aboard (→ 29).

29. Portsmouth, N.H.: Russian and Japanese envoys reach accord; Japan satisfied but fearful of 2nd war (→ 9/5).

31. Ohio: Dynamite explosion kills aviator John Baldwin in airship over Greenville.

BIRTH

2. Karl Amadeus Hartmann, German composer (†12/5/1963).

Czar establishes Duma

Aug 19. Czar Nicholas II took a half-hearted step toward constitutional monarchy today by establishing a representative assembly, which will be called the Duma. The new body is unlikely to infringe on the czar's powers, however, since it is to be a strictly consultative body, with no independent right to pass legislation.

To further ensure that the new Duma will not take on a revolutionary role, its election laws give disproportionate representation to the peasants, who are considered more conservative than urban residents and more likely to follow the czar. These reforms were pronounced unsatisfactory by the Union of Liberation, the liberal organization which has led the campaign for a national body with real legislative powers. The union is composed of politicians, students and others (→ 22).

T.R. brings Japanese, Russians together

Aug 8. President Theodore Roosevelt meets with Russian and Japanese representatives today in Portsmouth, New Hampshire, seeking a solution to the conflict in the Far East. Both sides want a settlement: Russia has lost vast numbers of men and arms, while Japan faces bankruptcy. Even if the parties agree on a mutual withdrawal of troops, many questions persist.

Sovereignty over Manchuria and Korea will still be in dispute, compounded by Chinese and Korean demands. Russia and Japan will need to discuss usage of the Southern Manchuria Railway (constructed by the Russians) and fishing rights in Russian waters. Both parties told the president the talks will not break over technicalities (→ 26).

Baron Komura and Sec. Sato in N. Y.

Belgians get free day on Sunday

Aug 15. Throughout Belgium today, the parks and the boulevards are full, and there is a sense of contentment in the air. Many Belgians say they finally feel free to do whatever they choose on this Sunday, and no one is looking over their shoulders. They are taking the day off from work, and it is all perfectly legal, thanks to a new law that took effect today.

The new law prohibits companies from forcing their employees to work more than six days a week. There are a few exceptions, however. Public markets are open, ferries are running and fishing boats are leaving port. And children can still be forced to do household chores.

Norway votes to cut its ties with Sweden

Aug 13. Norway yesterday voted to end its union with Sweden. In a national plebiscite, 368,208 elected to sever the union while only 184 expressed a desire to maintain it.

The union dates back to the 1814 Treaty of Kiel which gave Sweden sovereignty over Norway. Norway immediately repudiated the treaty, and relations between the two have been strained ever since. When the King recently refused to sanction a parliamentary bill which established a unilateral Norwegian consular service, the government isolated him by resigning. This paved the way for Parliament to dissolve the union, which it did in June. Yesterday's plebiscite confirmed that action (→ 9/23).

U.S. admits million immigrants in 1904

Aug 31. Despite efforts in recent years to curb immigration, a new report shows a sharp increase in the number of aliens arriving in the United States. The report states that 1,026,499 immigrants arrived in this country in 1904, up from 812,870 in the previous year. The principal ports of entry were on the East Coast.

The increase in immigration to the United States came despite a 1903 law placing a head tax on all arriving aliens and barring entry to such "undesirables" as anarchists, idiots, felons, women of bad repute, epileptics and insane persons.

For nearly 100 years, the United States kept the gates open to all comers, thus providing a ready work force for the nation's big businesses, farms and mines. But in recent years, labor leaders have been protesting importation of such cheap labor on the grounds that this threatens job security and demands for better pay and shorter hours.

The new report shows a sharp increase in immigrants from Italy and mid-European countries. It also shows a continuing decline in arrivals from Ireland, once the major source of newcomers to the United States.

Following are the principal countries from which the immigrants came last year:

Italy, 221,479.
Austria-Hungary, 111,990.
Great Britain, 64,709.
Ireland, 52,945.
Germany, 40,574.

Italian family arrives at Ellis Island.

1905

SEPTEMBER

Su	Mo	Tu	We	Th	Fr	Sa
					1	2
3	4	5	6	7	8	9
10	11	12	13	14	15	16
17	18	19	20	21	22	23
24	25	26	27	28	29	30

1. Canada: Alberta and Saskatchewan become provinces.

2. Russia: Famine reported to have reached worse proportions than in 1891 (→ 10).

5. Australia: Natl. Defense League founded to combat "yellow peril" by appealing for compulsory military training.

6. Roosevelt begins official investigation of corruption in insurance industry (→ 15).

7. Tokyo under martial law to quell revolt over peace treaty; 500 hurt in 3 days.

8. Solar eclipse sighted across globe.

8. Italy: Earthquake kills thousands; 25 villages razed.

8. British trade unions, 1.5-mil. strong, proclaim support for free trade, eight-hour day.

10. St. Petersburg: Tariffs removed on many American imports.

13. U.S. warship sent to Nicaragua on behalf of Wm. C. Albers, accused of evading tobacco tax.

14. New York: Plans made to connect Far East and U.S. by submarine telegraph lines.

15. New York: Commission reveals N.Y. Life Insurance Co.'s $50,000 contribution to T.R.'s campaign (→ 2/5/06).

22. Japan takes another U.S. ship.

23. Sweden, Norway settle terms of separation (→ 10/26).

25. Chinese govt. halts boycott of U.S. goods (→ 1/6/06).

28. Moroccan conference succeeds in bringing Franco-German accord (→ 1/7/06).

28. Congo: Reports circulate citing thousands of native deaths condoned by French governor (→ 10/31).

BIRTHS

5. Austro-Hungarian writer Arthur Koestler (†3/3/1983).

18. Swedish actress Greta Garbo.

28. German boxer Max Schmeling.

Treaty ends Russian-Japanese War

Sept 5. The Japanese and Russian empires signed the Treaty of Portsmouth today, ending the war in Korea and Manchuria. The text of the treaty shows that Japan has achieved virtually all of its original war aims, including Russian withdrawal from Manchuria.

As soon as the treaty was signed at 3:47 this afternoon in Portsmouth, New Hampshire, a 19-gun salute was fired from the United States Navy yard at Kittery Point, church bells rang and flags were hoisted. Foreign Minister Sergei Witte signed the treaty for Russia and Baron Komura, Minister of Foreign Affairs for Japan. Afterwards, the two shook hands.

Under the treaty, Russia recognizes Japan's preponderant political, military and economic interests in Korea. And Russia pledges not to interfere with Japanese actions in Korea. Both Russian and Japanese troops are to withdraw from Manchuria. But Russian rights to Port Arthur and to Dalny in Manchuria are turned over to Japan. Russia also cedes the southern part of Sakhalin Island to Japan, together with the dependent islands.

Japan also won fishing rights in Russian territorial waters in the Sea of Japan, the Sea of Okhotsk and the Bering Strait. The two nations will resume trade relations. President Roosevelt was warmly thanked by both delegations for his key role in arranging the peace (→ 7).

Japanese soldiers parade their colors.

Armenians, Tartars fight at Baku oil fields

Sept 7. More than 1,000 people have died in the oil fields of Baku as fighting continues between the Armenians and Tartars. The oil-rich area of the Caucasus has also suffered serious economic problems lately. There are 100,000 jobless, and a loss of about $100 million in state revenue has ensued.

The violence has struck fear into the residents of Baku. The fighting has yet to reach the center of the city, but many people, expecting outbursts, are fleeing. Most of the blood has been spilled at Balakhan.

Newspapers in St. Petersburg are condemning the Russian government for failing to take action to reconcile the Armenians and Tartars. The journals express concern that if decisions are not reached immediately to negotiate the end of the war, a vital industry, the oil business, will be completely destroyed by the raging infernos engulfing the oil fields.

Reports also indicate that Turkish factions are fueling the conflict by spreading inflammatory religious and racial propaganda about each side. Most officials agree it will take nearly a year to repair the damages incurred in the six days of fighting and looting.

Valuable Russian oil goes up in smoke at the Baku fields.

Elevated train falls to street, kills 12

Rescue efforts on Ninth Avenue.

Sept 11. Twelve persons were killed today when a New York elevated train plunged to the street below in the worst accident in the railway's history. The dramatic but tragic accident was the result of an improper setting of the switch at the dangerous curve at 53rd Street and Ninth Avenue. Police are blaming the motorman for the accident and have also arrested the towerman for manslaughter. The 7 a.m., rush-hour train was filled with passengers, nearly all of whom were injured.

1905

OCTOBER

Su	Mo	Tu	We	Th	Fr	Sa
1	2	3	4	5	6	7
8	9	10	11	12	13	14
15	16	17	18	19	20	21
22	23	24	25	26	27	28
29	30	31				

1. New York: Workmen stone 2,000 Jews (→ 11/26).

4. Washington: Roosevelt declares he will not run for president again (→ 8/5/12).

4. Daytona, Fla.: Orville Wright performs first 30-minute flight.

5. U.S. govt. issues $130 mil. in bonds to finance Panama canal (→ 3/24/06).

10. New York: George Bernard Shaw's "John Bull's Other Island" makes U.S. debut.

14. New York Giants capture World Series at Polo Grounds, 4 games to 1 over Philadelphia.

14. New York: Frenchman Hemery takes Vanderbilt Cup in Darracq auto.

20. Chicago: Storm over Lake Michigan sinks 11 boats; 21 die.

22. U.S. exports reported to suffer due to German tariff hikes.

24. German Social Democratic newspaper Vorwarts fires six editors, charged with radicalism by August Bebel.

25. Southern Russia in open revolt; communication with St. Petersburg cut off (→ 26).

26. Typographers create workers' council in St. Petersburg under leadership of Leon Trotsky (→ 28).

26. Norway, Sweden officially sign Treaty of Separation; Oscar II abdicates Swedish crown (→ 11/18).

28. Russia: General strike paralyzing, with over one million out; workers ask Duma to depose czar (→ 28).

28. Poland: Russian gov. gen. imposes 8 p.m. curfew in Warsaw (→ 30).

30. St. Petersburg: Czar issues October Manifesto granting constitution, legislative powers to Duma; general strike ends.→

31. Belgium: Committee established in Brussels to oversee reform in Congo (→ 11/5).

BIRTH

3. American actress Dolores del Rio (†4/11/1983).

Fauve artists show pictures at Paris salon

Oct 1. A startling display of brilliant color is on exhibition at the autumn festival in Paris, the latest sampling of the work of the painters Henri Matisse, Andre Derain and Maurice de Vlaminck.

Their vibrant, new style refuses to copy nature and expresses itself with strong, pure colors painted in well-defined spaces. The artists' work is popularly known as Fauvism, or the "wild beast" school, because a room full of their lively colors reminded an art critic of a cage of wild animals. Fauvism has replaced Impressionism as the most modern art movement in France. Other artists in the group are Georges Braque, Raoul Dufy and Georges Rouault.

Matisse's "Luxe, calme et volupte" (1904).

Henry Irving passes

Oct 13. Henry Irving, the first English actor ever to be knighted, has died at the age of 67 at his hotel in Bradford after a performance during a farewell tour of the provinces. Widely regarded as the foremost actor of his time, Sir Henry rose from humble origins to elevate the status of his profession and to achieve renown both in his own country and in the United States.

Actor Henry Irving.

Bernard Shaw play judged to be unfit

Oct 31. "Unfit" is the kindest epithet used to describe "Mrs. Warren's Profession," which opened in New York City tonight. George Bernard Shaw's play, making light of prostitution and incest, has been termed everything from "indecent" to "vicious" by critics. But some audience members were prepared to be shocked, having read "Mrs. Warren" in a published collection of Shaw's works called "Plays Pleasant and Unpleasant."

Shaw, a 49-year-old Irishman, delights in controversy. His previous plays, "The Devil's Disciple" (1897) and "Arms and the Man" (1896) also stirred things up. A founding member of the socialist Fabian Society, Shaw writes to educate as well as alarm. Judging by the laughter of the full house this evening, he also manages to entertain.

Workers' soviets spring up in Russia

Oct 13. Leon Trotsky, the 26-year-old leader of the St. Petersburg Soviet of Workers' Deputies, has begun urging other soviets, or workers' councils, to begin arming themselves in preparation for a revolution. The St. Petersburg soviet is the largest of the 50 soviets that workers in Russia have elected to organize strikes and present political demands to the government. Soviets are patterned on a council that was first established, spontaneously, on May 15, 1905, by striking workers at the Ivanovo-Voznesensk textile center. Its success in winning the strikers' demands earned it great loyalty among workers (→ 25).

Czar issues charter giving people rights

Oct 30. Europe's last major autocracy came to an end today when Czar Nicholas II granted his people the constitutional rights they have been demanding for the past year.

The czar's October Manifesto granted Russians such civil rights as freedom of speech, union and association; extended suffrage; and most importantly, established the rule that "no law shall be enforceable without the approval of the State Duma." The czar's reforms are in reaction to the open state of revolt that has existed throughout most of Russia for the past year. Strikers have completely interrupted railways and mail communication, and most industrial activity is at a halt. It remains to be seen what effect the reforms will have (→ 11/1).

Police charge St. Petersburg crowd.

1905

NOVEMBER

Su	Mo	Tu	We	Th	Fr	Sa
			1	2	3	4
5	6	7	8	9	10	11
12	13	14	15	16	17	18
19	20	21	22	23	24	25
26	27	28	29	30		

1. Russia: Czar promises amnesty to all political prisoners (→ 17).

4. Finland: Revolutionary govt. set up at Helingfors (→ 12/4).

5. Belgium: Investigatory commission admits faulty administration in Congo (→ 5/1/07).

7. George McClellan elected mayor of New York City.

8. Chicago and Northwestern rail becomes 1st to install electric lamps, on Overland Ltd., Chicago to California.

10. New York: British Rear Adm. Battenberg arrives; receives Navy salute in honor of King Edward's birthday.

11. Crete: Prince George offers amnesty to all involved in recent revolt (→ 10/7/08).

17. New York: U.S. and U.K. navy boxing champs battle; Briton E. Cocknaye triumphs over Jack Reine in 3rd round.

17. Russia: Agrarian riots continue; peasants demand land grants (→ 22).

19. One hundred drown in English Channel as steamer Hilda sinks.

22. St. Petersburg: Czar promises universal suffrage (→ 26).

22. Turkey: Great powers show naval strength at Mytiline to push Sultan Hamid into reforms in Macedonia (→ 12/12).

26. Russia: Sailors mutiny at Sevastopol, prepare for siege (→ 29).

27. Austria-Hungary: Czechs and Moravians sign compromise settling land dispute.

28. Ireland: Sinn Fein, Irish nationalist movement founded in 1899, declares itself a political party. (→ 5/26/07).

28. New York: Football abolished at Columbia University (→ 12/9).

29. Russia: Mutineers at Sevastopol captured (→ 12/1).

30. Switzerland: Count Ferdinand Zeppelin flies 2nd dirigible over Lake Constance.

Jews massacred; Americans raise aid

Nov 8. Only days after Czar Nicholas II attempted to end the year-long protests against his rule by issuing a manifesto granting his subjects greater political rights, a new round of violence has erupted, much of it directed against Jews. More than 1,000 Jews were killed in Odessa, Russia. The massacres were carried out by peasants who were incited by reactionary army officers and government officials who believe that Jews are behind the past year's protests. American Jewish leaders have issued an appeal for aid for the survivors. They have raised $70,000 (→12/12).

A few of the thousands of victims of Russian anti-Semitism.

Jews celebrate 250 years in America

Nov 26. Special synagogue services and prayers of thanksgiving yesterday commemorated the 250th anniversary of the settlement of Jews in America and their previous role in the discovery of the New World. Speakers noted that Columbus' expedition was funded by two Jewish merchants, as Queen Isabella had pawned or sold her jewels to pay for Spanish war expenses. And the first white man to set foot on American soil in 1492 was Louis de Torres, a Jewish interpreter.

In a service at New York's YMHA, the Rev. Dr. Joseph Krauskopf of Philadelphia, speaking on "The Jewish Pilgrim Fathers," said that "the more we study it, the stronger grows the belief that it was the hand of Providence that opened for Columbus and the Jews accompanying him the portals of the New World."

Temple Emmanuel, New York City.

Maude Adams stars in "Peter Pan"

Maude Adams is "Peter Pan."

Nov 6. At the Empire Theater, the elfin actress Maude Adams has opened to triumphal notices in the title role of Sir James Barrie's "Peter Pan." Once more, as she did in "The Little Minister" in 1897, when she first achieved stardom, the actress is enchanting New York.

Miss Adams, born in Salt Lake City, Utah, on November 11, 1872, as Maude Adams Kiskadden, made her debut at the age of six months when she was carried on stage on a platter. New York audiences first responded to her talent in 1892, when she appeared as John Drew's leading lady in Charles Frohman's production of "The Masked Ball."

Norwegians take Dane as new King

Nov 18. The guns of the fortress at Christiana, Norway, boomed a royal salute today, honoring the Norwegian Parliament's election of Prince Charles of Denmark as the next King of Norway. The prince is a grandson of Denmark's King Christian IX. Oscar II, the previous Norwegian king, relinquished the crown in October, following a rift with Parliament over its move to sever the union with Sweden.

A telegram announcing the election was read at a dinner in Copenhagen given by the Crown Prince and Crown Princess Frederick. The crown prince immediately toasted the new monarch, who was present. A return telegram from Prince Charles to Parliament announced that he would take the name of Haakon VII after a line of Norwegian kings and rulers dating back to the 10th century.

Siddeley convertible, with folding canvas roof.

1905

DECEMBER

Su	Mo	Tu	We	Th	Fr	Sa
					1	2
3	4	5	6	7	8	9
10	11	12	13	14	15	16
17	18	19	20	21	22	23
24	25	26	27	28	29	30
31						

1. St. Petersburg: Twenty officers, 230 guards arrested in revolt at Winter Palace (→ 16).

2. With Pres. Roosevelt looking on, Army-Navy annual football game ends in 6-6 tie.

4. New York: 125,000 march in mourning for persecuted Russian Jews (→ 12).

4. Finnish Senate renounces Russian as official administrative language.

5. U.K.: Liberal leader Henry Campbell-Bannerman becomes prime minister upon Arthur Balfour's resignation yesterday.

12. Turkey: Sultan yields to demands for reform; great powers to take financial control over Macedonia.

12. Russia: Elizabethgrad in flames as Jews are massacred (→ 1/4/06).

16. St. Petersburg: Workers' council dissolved; all members arrested (→ 22).

22. 125,000 strike in St. Petersburg as czar revokes promise of universal suffrage (→ 30).

30. Idaho: Gov. Frank Steunenberg killed by assassin's bomb (→ 12/3/06).

BIRTH

24. American industrialist Howard Hughes (†4/5/1976).

CULTURAL EVENTS, 1905

Literature: Baroness Orczy's "The Scarlet Pimpernel"; E.M. Forster's "Where Angels Fear to Tread"; Shaw's "Major Barbara"; Edith Wharton's "House of Mirth."

Academia: Lenin's "Two Tactics"; George Santayana's "The Life of Reason"; Binet-Simon IQ tests.

Music: Debussy's "La Mer"; Strauss' opera "Salome"; L.A. Coerne's "Zenobia," 1st U.S. opera produced in Europe.

The Arts: Picasso's "Pink Period," in Paris; Parisian artists Matisse, Derain, Rouault become known as "Les Fauves" ("The Wild Beasts") for their use of bright colors; Alfred Stieglitz opens photography gallery 291 in N.Y.

New football rules would cut roughness

Princeton and Cornell battle it out with abandon on the gridiron.

Dec 9. Public demand to erase the unnecessary brutality of football has brought some suggested reforms from the Intercollegiate Rules Committee. At a meeting in Philadelphia, the members of the committee acted to "render foul play unprofitable." And they urged the placing of officials under one governing body for consistent rules interpretation.

Walter Camp advanced his pet request to have the distance to be gained increased to ten yards. The Yale coach is Chairman of the panel, which is made up of notables in the sport. The ten-yard plan was supported by John C. Bell of Pennsylvania. He also suggested that the rules be relaxed to encourage forward passing. President Roosevelt met last week with college football leaders to discuss reforming the popular game. The president indicated that he favored modifying the rules (→ 2/25/07).

Czar's artillery puts down rebel rising

Dec 30. The Moscow uprising that began 23 days ago is over, and with it the year-long revolution of 1905. The most loyal and elite units of Czar Nicholas II's army bombarded the streets of Moscow with cannon fire earlier this month. By the time the last revolutionary post fell, in the Presnia section of Moscow, more than 1,000 were dead and the most serious threat to the czar's reign to date was over.

The uprising began December 7, when more than 150,000 workers took part in a general strike. By December 9, the workers had set up barricades throughout Moscow from which they fought a partisan-style campaign against the soldiers. But the protesters faced superior weapons and experience. General Fedor Dubasov made the Strastnoi Convent his command post. With cannon firing from its courtyard, and machine guns from its belfry, he dominated Moscow (→ 1/7/06).

Tuberculosis bacillus wins prize for Koch

Dec 10. Dr. Robert Koch of Germany was given the Nobel Prize in medicine and physiology today for his discovery of the bacillus that causes tuberculosis.

Koch made the discovery in 1882, using a set of techniques he developed years earlier. One important advance was the use of analine dyes to stain bacteria and make them more easily visible. A second development was the use of solid gelatin as a medium on which to grow bacteria outside the body. Koch first used a liquid medium but found that a solid substance allowed him to isolate and separate different varieties of bacteria more easily. He has since used his techniques to discover the cholera bacillus.

The Nobel Prize in physics went to Philip Lenard of Germany for cathode-ray research. The chemistry laureate is Adolph von Baeyer, also of Germany, for his work with organic dyes and hydrocarbons.

Explorer Amundsen finds magnetic pole

Dec 6. Roald Amundsen, the Norwegian explorer, has arrived at Fort Egbert, Alaska, after a perilous three-year voyage from the Atlantic to the Pacific Ocean along the Arctic Coast of North America, the famous Northwest Passage. Amundsen and his companions made the voyage in his 47-foot cutter, the Gjoa, which many thought too small for survival. They left Norway on June 1, 1903. The vessel was ice-bound for nearly two years of the journey. In the course of his explorations, Amundsen located the North Magnetic Pole on King William Island and found that it had moved somewhat since it was first located by John Ross, the British explorer, some 60 years ago.

Captain Roald Amundsen.

Tempestuous John Barrymore at 22. This year, he teamed with brother Lionel and sister Ethel in "Alice Sit by the Fire."

1906

JANUARY

Su	Mo	Tu	We	Th	Fr	Sa
	1	2	3	4	5	6
7	8	9	10	11	12	13
14	15	16	17	18	19	20
21	22	23	24	25	26	27
28	29	30	31			

1. Great Britain: Parliament curtails immigration for the insane, impoverished, criminal and diseased.

1. German Commander-in-Chief Alfred von Schlieffen retires, succeeded by Lt. Gen. von Moltke.

4. Berlin: Police forbid Isadora Duncan to dance in public.

4. Russian govt. reported hindering distribution of $3 mil. raised in U.S. for Jewish relief (→ 6/12).

5. British condemn U.S. action in Dominican Republic, demand payment of debt.

6. U.S. prepares for revolt in China, reinforces troops in Philippines (→ 2/26).

6. France denies Russia loan of $160 million.

7. German warships sent to Algeciras; British rendezvous in Cadiz Bay (→ 16).

7. France: Coalition govt. affirmed in senatorial elections; two socialists elected in South.

16. Morocco: Algeciras Conference opens; delegates hope to settle international claims in Morocco (→ 2/23).

19. Luke Wright becomes 1st U.S. ambassador to Japan.

19. 680,000 Japanese reported starving in northern provinces (→ 4/30).

21. Germany: Social Democrats demonstrate to protest electoral policy barring laborers from Reichstag.

23. Vancouver: Steamer Valencia runs aground; 119 passengers dead.

26. New York: M. Sheppard sets new indoor record for mile run at 4:25.2.

26. Florida: Stanley Steamer sets mile record in auto race at 28.2 seconds.

BIRTH

15. Greek industrialist Aristotle Onassis, married Jacqueline Kennedy (†3/15/1975).

DEATH

29. Christian IX, king of Denmark (*4/8/1818).

Balfour defeated as Liberals win election

Jan 13. The Liberal Party made an impressive showing in the first day of parliamentary elections, winning 22 seats, including those won by Laborites, out of 39 contested. This strong start, as well as the surprising defeat of Arthur J. Balfour, the former Unionist Prime Minister, are expected to have an enormous impact on the outcome of the elections, which continue for a fortnight.

Young Winston Churchill.

Balfour's defeat is all the more remarkable because his opponent, Liberal T.G. Horridge, although a successful barrister, was not well-known to the public. Although Horridge's aggressive campaign strategy was undoubtedly a factor in the election, his win is indicative of national support for the Liberals.

In order to retain a place on the opposition front bench, Balfour will have to find a safe seat before the elections conclude. Among the Liberal victors was Winston Churchill, who was elected to Parliament by the people of the northwest division of Manchester.

Wealthy merchant Marshall Field dies

Jan 16. The richest merchant in the world and the largest individual taxpayer in the United States died yesterday of exhaustion following a bad case of pneumonia.

Marshall Field, 70, a farm boy from Massachusetts, left home at 17 to become a dry goods clerk in Chicago, saving half his $400 yearly salary by sleeping in the shop. At age 30, he was a partner in the firm that became Marshall Field & Company in 1881. Last year, the public spent over $65 million in his Chicago store. He has stores in Paris and Manchester, England, as well. The twice-married Field (his second wedding was September 5 last year) also built a library, a natural history museum, and donated to the University of Chicago.

Negro celebration spoiled by violence

Jan 1. In a parade marked by sporadic violence, thousands of Negroes marched through the streets of Savannah, Georgia, today to mark the anniversary of the Emancipation Proclamation.

A former captain in the United States Army, who is now in the newspaper business, was badly beaten when he attempted to cross the line of marchers. A photographer who was trying to film the parade was chased away. There was further violence when a streetcar conductor, attempting to steer his car through the line of march, was painfully injured and forced to leave his vehicle.

President Lincoln issued his historic proclamation, seeking to free the slaves, in the fall of 1862. However, the proclamation was not to become effective until January 1, 1863, during the height of the Civil War. The slaves were finally freed after the Union forces defeated the Confederate Army in 1865.

Each year, Savannah Negroes have staged a parade through the city to mark the anniversary. However, this year, unlike in previous years, the marchers had no military escort. The last session of the Georgia Legislature voted to disarm the Negro military companies, and thus none were available to keep order along the line of march, which stretched for 12 blocks (→ 2/28).

Suffragettes urge violent campaign

Jan 31. In England today, a group of women said they are tired of waiting; they want the right to vote and they are willing to go to prison to win their battle. Emmeline Pankhurst, leader of the militant Women's Social and Political Union, declared that women may have to become violent and risk arrest in order to achieve their goals. In France, suffragettes are demanding a reduction in taxes so that deputies opposed to voting by women will not receive salaries from the state. Several American states have already given women citizens the right to vote (→ 2/15).

Revolt persists; Russians react harshly

Jan 7. Determined to restore order to his empire, Czar Nicholas II has authorized loyal and well-trained units of his army, called "punitive expeditions," to crush the surviving pockets of rebellion throughout Russia. Although weakened by the failure of a major uprising in Moscow in December, the rebellion against the czar, which had its origins in the protests of striking workers in St. Petersburg and Moscow, has spread to the countryside, where peasants are burning down manor houses and murdering nobles.

Punitive expeditions are concentrating on the Baltic provinces, where the rebellion is particularly critical. The army has relied on harsh measures to end dissent, arresting and shooting hundreds without trial and burning entire villages. Army forces have also been sent to Siberia, where workers on the Trans-Siberian Railway are reported to have grabbed control of Irkutsk and Chelyabinsk (→ 3/6).

Militancy in the streets.

1906

FEBRUARY

Su	Mo	Tu	We	Th	Fr	Sa
				1	2	3
4	5	6	7	8	9	10
11	12	13	14	15	16	17
18	19	20	21	22	23	24
25	26	27	28			

3. Japan: Navy tonnage to increase from 240,000 to 400,000 in two years.

4. New York: Police department decides to begin using fingerprint identification.

5. Andrew Hamilton, John McCall of Equitable Life Insurance sued for $1,074,744 (→ 22).

6. French writer Colette makes stage debut in Paris.

10. Switzerland: Social Democrats, at congress in Olten, disavow anarchist movement.

15. Washington: Three hundred suffragettes present demands for electoral reform to legislators (→ 3/7).

15. Austria-Hungary: Workers demonstrate at port of Fiume.

18. Denmark: King Christian IX buried in Copenhagen.

20. Russian troops seize large parts of Mongolia (→ 1/28/07).

21. New York: The Singer Co. files plans to build world's tallest office building (→ 8/24/07).

22. Washington: Armstrong report on mismanagement of insurance companies presented to Congress (→ 3/12).

23. Paris: Jean Jaures decouncees French position at Algeciras in speech at Chamber of Deputies (→ 3/18).

24. Cuba: Jose Gomez sponsors liberal revolt, calling newly elected Estrada Palma a tool of "Yankee imperialism" (→ 8/24).

24. Saint Saens opera "Forefather," makes debut in Monte Carlo.

26. China: Ten missionaries killed in riot at Nan Chang (→ 3/18).

28. Springfield, Ohio: One killed, many injured in racial rioting (→ 4/14).

BIRTHS

4. Astronomer Clyde Tombaugh, discovered Pluto.

4. German Dietrich Bonhoeffer, Protestant theologian.

World's biggest battleship launched

Feb 10. The British royal navy launched the world's largest battleship, the Dreadnought, today in Portsmouth, ushering in a new era of naval warfare. In a simple ceremony, the King pushed an electric button releasing the last block which enabled the behemoth vessel to take to the water.

Work on the ship began last October and when the finishing touches are completed she will cost $7.5 million. Even the British shipbuilders were surprised at the record-breaking construction time of four months. Carrying ten 12-inch guns, she is driven by turbines and is the fastest warship in the waters. The Dreadnought is also capable of sustaining serious torpedo attacks. One naval expert praised her, claiming: "The Dreadnought will make all other battleships obsolete." Another said in a few short years Britain will own a whole fleet like her.

Alice Roosevelt marries House Speaker

Feb 17. The East Room of the White House was the scene of the marriage today of Alice Lee Roosevelt, President Roosevelt's eldest daughter, and Representative Nicholas Longworth of Ohio, Speaker of the House. The Bishop of Washington, Henry Y. Saterlee, officiated.

Teddy poses proudly with newlyweds.

After the ceremony, the Marine Band entertained 800 guests.

The marriage follows a romance which has attracted the interest of the entire United States, and perhaps the world. Mrs. Longworth's princess-style gown was made of white satin trimmed with lace; the train was silver brocade satin. Her long veil was held in place by a crown of orange blossoms and she carried a bouquet of white and purple orchids.

After several hours of merrymaking, Mr. and Mrs. Longworth were ready to leave for John R. McLean's country estate, Friendship, in a rural part of the district, where the couple will spend a few days before beginning their honeymoon trip. They eluded crowds of well-wishers who were congregated outside the White House by using several decoy cars, finally exiting through a window in the Red Room. The honeymoon destination is rumored to be Cuba.

Storm sweeps over isles; 10,000 die

Feb 8. A fierce cyclone has humbled Tahiti and adjacent Society, Tuamotu and Cook islands. Winds of 120 miles an hour and 65-foot-high waves have wiped out whole villages and killed some 10,000 persons. Several islands have disappeared completely and damage is placed at $5 million. Tahiti's city of Papeete was inundated and about 75 buildings destroyed, including the American Consulate. People near the shore had to abandon their homes. Teffer Adams, the guardian of the arsenal as well as an expert swimmer, was in the water for many hours as he helped warn and rescue others who were in danger.

Perfume fit for royalty.

Pope Pius deplores church-state rift

Feb 21. Pope Pius X spoke out loudly and firmly today as he criticized the French government for its new law separating church and state in that country. The pope charged that the law shreds the Concordat which existed between Paris and the Vatican and tries to destroy religious sentiment in France. "We shall fight hate with love, fallacy with truth and intimidation and humiliation with forgiveness," the pope declared. "We pray to God that the enemies of religion will stop persecuting us."

The new French law imposes severe restrictions on church property and religious education. It guarantees freedom of religion, but it also prohibits the government from supporting any organization with a religious connection. Pope Pius and French church leaders have tried without success to fight the law. The pope has urged Catholics to take communion frequently. And he has said he would prefer to turn church property over to the state than see its religious mission compromised by the anticlerical movement (→ 8/9).

Langley, unlucky air pioneer, dead

Feb 27. Samuel Pierpont Langley died today in Aiken, South Carolina. Ironically, the eminent astronomer, physicist, author and inventor (the radiation-measuring bolometer) is most famous for a spectacular failure: two much-publicized attempts to fly a man-carrying aircraft in 1903. Massachusetts-born (1834) and largely self-educated, Langley held prominent positions at the Allegheny Observatory and the Smithsonian Institute.

Samuel Pierpont Langley.

1906

MARCH

Su	Mo	Tu	We	Th	Fr	Sa
				1	2	3
4	5	6	7	8	9	10
11	12	13	14	15	16	17
18	19	20	21	22	23	24
25	26	27	28	29	30	31

2. Missouri: Tornado kills 33, destroys $5 mil. in property.

3. Frenchman attempts 1st flight on plane with tires.

6. St. Petersburg: Czar grants Duma right to approve legislation, yet reserves absolute power of veto (→ 20).

7. Finland becomes first country to give women the vote, decreeing universal suffrage for citizens over 24, barring those supported by state (→ 31).

9. Philippines: Fifteen Americans, 600 Moros killed in two days of fighting (→ 10/16/07).

10. France: 1,200 miners buried in explosion at Courrieres.

12. Washington: Supreme Court rules corporations must yield incriminating evidence in antitrust suits (→ 4/14).

14. "Battling" Nelson defends lightweight crown in six-round bout with Terry McGovern.

14. Italy: 'Quake, volcano devastate island of Ustica.

18. Morocco: France and Germany reported in deadlock at Algeciras Conference (→ 31).

18. China: Shanghai press said to be agitating against foreigners (→ 9/30/07).

19. Reports from Berlin estimate cost of German war in S.W. Africa at $150 mil.

20. Russia: Army officers mutiny at Sevastopol (→ 24).

21. Ohio passes law banning hazing after two fatalities.

22. France loses 1st rugby game ever played against U.K.

24. Mexico: Tehuantepec Isthmian Railroad opens as rival to Panama canal (→ 6/21).

24. New York: N. Chaikovsky fsky arrives to solicit funding for Russian revolt (→ 4/8).

BIRTH

23. American screen star Joan Crawford (†5/11/1977).

DEATH

13. American Susan B. Anthony, women's suffrage pioneer (*2/15/1820).

Morocco parley ends

March 31. Tne Conference on Moroccan Reforms in Algeciras, Spain, successfully concluded today after more than two months of negotiations. France and Germany, whose dispute led to the meeting, appeared satisfied with the results. The agreement upheld the principles of Moroccan independence and the open door: equal commercial and economic rights for all nations trading with and doing business in Morocco. Thus, the Germans were reassured as to the safety of their investments.

The most divisive issue, which brought proceedings to a standstill when France and Germany could not agree, concerned French and Spanish policing of Morocco. The Germans had agreed to the police force, but inspection of the police remained a problem until the proposal of the American envoys saved the day. Their suggestion that a police inspector report both to the Sultan and the diplomatic corps at Tangier, which would have the authority to investigate any difficulties, was acceptable to all. Under the five-year agreement, France will police four ports, Spain two, and both will police Tangier and Casablanca (→ 6/3).

"Are you going to stay where you are?" the Frenchman asks of the German who insists on competing with French ambitions in Morocco.

Roosevelt, meeting Gompers, defends right of injunction; 500,000 strike

March 29. More than half a million coal miners walked off the job today, seeking higher wages. The strike, which had been in the offing for more than a week, began amidst signs that at least some mine operators are willing to come to terms on the wage issue. The strike involves miners in many states, including Pennsylvania, Iowa, Indiana and Illinois.

Labor demands have been much in the news recently. Last week, President Roosevelt met with Samuel Gompers and other officials of the American Federation of Labor. At the White House conference, the labor leaders asked for enforcement of an eight-hour day and for stricter exclusion of Chinese laborers from this country.

The president said he agreed on the immigration matter but differed with the demands of the labor leaders for an eight-hour day for those working on the Panama canal. He noted that the canal is being built primarily with laborers from the West Indies because American workers refuse to go to Panama.

During the meeting, the president defended a pending injunction bill, saying he would enjoin labor unions if necessary. However, he pointed out that he had never had to seek such a union injunction. "But understand me, gentlemen," the president continued. "If I ever thought it necessary, if I thought a combination of laborers were doing wrong, I would apply for an injunction against them just as quickly as against so many capitalists."

During the White House meeting, no mention was made directly of the threatened coal strike, which finally erupted today (→ 4/6).

Athletics endanger women, doctor says

March 31. In a speech last night, Dr. Dudley Sargent, Physical Director at Harvard University, cautioned women against playing any contact sports. "Let woman," he said, "rather confine herself to the lighter and more graceful forms of gymnastics and athletics, and make herself supreme along these lines as she has already done in aesthetic dancing. Let her know enough about the rougher sports to be the sympathetic admirer of men and boys in their efforts to be strong, vigorous and heroic."

While ladies have been playing tennis and competing in swimming, gymnastics and bicycling events for years now, some younger women have taken to playing such rougher sports as basketball.

Largest of empires

March 24. England rules one-fifth of the globe. This is the startling conclusion of the recently completed "Census of the British Empire," which enumerates 400 million persons living on 12 million square miles of land within Britain's colonies, dependencies and protectorates. These figures mark a 40 percent increase since 1861, when the last count was made.

According to the census, there are seven million persons living on four million square miles in the Americas, five million persons on three million square miles in Australasia, 43 million persons on two and a half million square miles in Africa and 300 million inhabit two million square miles in Asia. While only 41.5 million persons live in the United Kingdom itself, "the sun never sets on the British Empire."

Britain watches over the seas.

1906

APRIL

Su	Mo	Tu	We	Th	Fr	Sa
1	2	3	4	5	6	7
8	9	10	11	12	13	14
15	16	17	18	19	20	21
22	23	24	25	26	27	28
29	30					

6. Penn.: After fires and violence at Wilkes-Barre collieries, independent soft-coal owners grant wage hikes (→ 16).

6. Naples: Mt. Vesuvius sprays column of fire 1,000 feet high.

7. N.Y.: Jay Gould wins U.S. court tennis championship.

8. St. Petersburg: Progressives win seats in Duma due to peasant vote (→ 11).

11. Venezuela: Gen. Castro resigns as president.

11. Russia: Social Democrats kill Orthodox priest Father Gopon, organizer of "Bloody Sunday" revolt, on suspicion of betrayal (→ 30).

14. Washington: Roosevelt proposes inheritance tax on large fortunes.

14. Springfield, Ohio: Mob burns two Negroes to death before cheering crowd of 3,000 (→ 8/7).

16. Pennslyvania: Four strikers killed as 5,000 coal workers battle 100 deputy sheriffs in Johnstown (→ 30).

21. Washington: Justice Dept. begins investigation of Southern fertilizer combine for alleged price-fixing conspiracy (→ 5/4).

22. Athens: King George opens Intermediate Olympic Games (→ 5/1).

30. St. Petersburg: Czar accepts Premier Witte's resignation in triumph for conservatives; appoints Ivan Goremykin to succeed (→ 5/6).

30. Japan estimates losses in Russo-Japanese War at 457,035 men (→ 1/28/07).

30. Pennsylvania: Twenty striking miners shot by state troopers (→ 5/7).

BIRTH

13. Irish playwright Samuel Beckett, "Waiting for Godot."

DEATHS

5. American painter Jonathan Eastman Johnson (*7/29/1824).

11. James Bailey, of Barnum & Bailey Circus (*7/4/1847).

San Francisco 'quake kills thousand

April 19. Miles of flames are reducing most of San Francisco to ashes tonight, a day after a severe earthquake jolted the entire bay area. Military officials estimate that up to a thousand people may have been burned to death or crushed by falling debris. The city's business district has been destroyed, and the winds shifted today, allowing the flames to advance toward the fashionable Nob Hill residential area. Damage estimates range up to $200 million.

Martial law has been declared in San Francisco in an effort to keep the peace, and military units are helping police prevent looting. A number of thieves have reportedly been shot dead. Thousands of panicked citizens have streamed out of the city on ferries and rail lines, but many more are begging for transport. There are long lines on the docks. Half the city's population is spending the night in public squares, parks and open spaces. Many of them fled in a panic from their homes earlier today after new shock waves rattled through the city.

One reporter says that bodies are stacking up at the morgue. Two hundred and seventy inmates died in an insane asylum. And hundreds of seriously injured residents are being treated at hospitals throughout this devastated, terrified city.

Refugees from San Francisco helplessly watch their city burn.

President raps muckraking journalists

April 14. President Roosevelt took to task today those crusading journalists who persist in what he called too much "muckraking." He was alluding to those writers, such as Lincoln Steffens and Ida Tarbell, who have written exposes of business misconduct and lax government enforcement of laws. Steffens' "The Shame of the Cities" and Tarbell's "History of Standard Oil Company" were published in 1904.

Speaking at the dedication of a new House Office Building in Washington, the president noted that in Bunyan's "Pilgrim's Progress," there was a man who never looked up to the finer things, even when promised a celestial crown, but who constantly applied his muckrake to the filth of the floor. Roosevelt conceded that there is filth on the floor, and it must be scraped up from time to time. He also said politicians who betray the public trust must be exposed and corrupt businessmen must be prosecuted. "The men with the muckrakes," the president said, "are often indispensable but only if they know when to stop raking muck" (→ 21).

Yet Teddy wields the muckrake too.

Britain, China agree on Tibetan problem

April 27. China, as suzerain of Tibet, has agreed to the terms of a treaty proposed by Britain. According to the treaty, foreign powers may not send representatives to Tibet, receive transportation or mining concessions, or occupy, buy or lease any territory in Tibet without British permission. The British want to prevent the Russians from establishing a protectorate over Tibet, which lies on India's northern border. Lord Curzon, Viceroy of India, failed in attempts to communicate with Tibet's ruler, the Dalai Lama. A British military expedition fought its way to the capital at Lhasa and concluded the agreement.

1906

MAY

Su	Mo	Tu	We	Th	Fr	Sa
		1	2	3	4	5
6	7	8	9	10	11	12
13	14	15	16	17	18	19
20	21	22	23	24	25	26
29	28	29	30	31		

1. Athens: U.S. athletes dominate Intermediate Olympics.

1. Paris: Troops arrest 1,000 in May Day protest.

1. Germany: Six thousand workers fired after May Day strike.

2. Jockey R. Troxler rides Sir Huon to victory in Kentucky Derby.

4. Washington: Roosevelt warns Congress that Standard Oil is in violation of antitrust laws (→ 10).

6. South Africa: British kill 60 Zulus in punitive expedition.

6. Czar defines Duma's powers narrowly; imposes budgetary restrictions, retains right to legislate when Duma not in session (→ 10).

7. N.Y.: Coal strike settled; miners lose month's pay in 3-year peace with operators.

19. Portugal's King Carlos I appoints Joao Franco prime minister with dictatorial powers to purge political opposition (→ 31).

21. U.S. and Mexico agree on Rio Grande waters to be diverted to U.S. for irrigation.

22. Last British soldiers leave Canada after occupation of 1858.

23. Edward Payton Weston completes walk from Philadelphia to N.Y. in 23 hrs., 31 min.

24. Czar concedes only universal suffrage to Duma; amnesty for political prisoners considered farcical (→ 28).

26. New York: Lewis Nixon announces invention of sonar on submarine with "ears and eyes."

28. Salavadorans, Nicaraguans come to aid of Guatemalan rebels (→ 7/15).

28. Russia: Czar distributes 25 mil. acres to peasants (→ 6/13).

31. Germany: Industrialists begin producing fertilizer from lime.

BIRTH

8. Italian film director Roberto Rossellini (†6/3/1977).

Maxim Gorky here to raise revolt funds

April 11. The famous Russian novelist and revolutionary, Maxim Gorky, arrived in New York this morning to raise funds to buy arms for the Russian rebels. "If the Russian revolution goes through we will have a government framed along the lines of your own, with a federation of nations, such as Finland and Poland, instead of a federation of states," Gorky said.

A committee sympathetic to Gorky's cause, with American author Mark Twain as its spokesman, has been set up to help raise funds. "If we can build a Russian republic to give to the persecuted people of the Czar's domain the same measure of freedom that we enjoy, let us go ahead and do it," said Twain (→ 11).

Vesuvius erupts

April 10. The deadly flow of lava, red-hot stones, sand, cinders, flame and smoke from a raging Mount Vesuvius spewed forth again early today, headed toward Pompeii. Hundreds have been killed and injured. Ottajano is completely destroyed, and 50 corpses have been recovered so far there. In Naples, a 600-square-foot market collapsed, killing 12 outright and injuring 126, a fifth of those seriously or fatally. Heart-rendering cries of help continue to mingle with the sobs of rescue workers. Yesterday, 105 people were killed at the Church of San Giuseppe. Ashes make the air thick and hard to breathe.

The active cone of Mt. Vesuvius.

Czar opens Duma at brilliant affair

May 10. Russia's first democratic Parliament, the Duma, was inaugurated today by Czar Nicholas II in a ceremony of great splendor. The brilliance of the occasion, and indeed the significance of the new Parliament itself, was overshadowed by the presence of thousands of armed guards to protect the ceremony and the czar's half-hearted participation.

In his coolly received speech, the czar said that "not only freedom, but order founded upon justice are necessary." The czar did not grant amnesty to political prisoners, a move which had been expected. The Duma's first session began after the speech, and the delegates immediately called for an amnesty.

The Duma is the lower house of the Parliament. Its members were elected by universal male suffrage, though the election laws favor peasants, who are considered more conservative. Most of the delegates to the upper house, the Council of the Empire, are appointed (→ 24).

Czar opens Duma at Winter Palace.

Spain's King, Queen bombed; 18 killed

May 31. The wedding day of Spain's King Alfonso and his new bride was nearly their last. As they returned to Madrid's royal palace after their marriage today, a bouquet concealing a bomb was thrown at their carriage. Deflected by an electric wire, it struck to the right of the vehicle, killing a pair of horses and 18 persons but sparing the royal newlyweds. The bomb was thrown from the window of a room rented by a man from Barcelona who was seized by Madrid police while trying to flee.

The royal couple before the debacle.

Longest tunnel links Italy, Switzerland

Official opening on the Italian coast.

May 19. An ambitious project that was started by Napoleon 100 years ago was completed today on the border between Italy and Switzerland. Napoleon built the famous Simplon Road which slices through the Alps and connects the two countries. Today, a railway tunnel along the same route was put into service. It is an engineering marvel. The Simplon Tunnel is the longest in the world, beginning in Brig, Switzerland, and ending more than 12 miles later in Isella, Italy. King Victor Emmanuel of Italy officiated at the opening of the tunnel. ▷

Standard Oil under attack as monopoly

May 10. The Standard Oil Company was accused today of stifling competition through intrigue and trickery. The charges against the oil giant were made in Chicago at a hearing before the Interstate Commerce Commission.

Witnesses, including former employees of the oil company, recounted stories of alleged corruption of railroad workers, driving independent dealers out of business through price-cutting schemes, and of bribing the employees of the smaller, independent oil concerns to obtain vital information. One witness testified that Standard Oil at times even substituted inferior oil while guaranteeing it to be of superior quality. The findings of the ICC hearings will be reported to the United States Congress (→ 6/22).

Great dramatist Henrik Ibsen dead

May 23. The Norwegian poet and playwright, Henrik Ibsen, 78 years old, is dead in Christiana. He was the creator of the realistic prose drama and was acclaimed as the greatest playwright of our time. His plays, particularly "A Doll's House" (1879), "Ghosts" (1881) and "An Enemy of the People" (1882), demonstrated, perhaps for the first time in the history of drama, the power of the stage in motivating social conduct. Ibsen remains best known for describing precarious human relationships and exposing truths that society prefers to conceal.

Henrik Ibsen.

1906

JUNE

Su	Mo	Tu	We	Th	Fr	Sa
					1	2
3	4	5	6	7	8	9
10	11	12	13	14	15	16
17	18	19	20	21	22	23
24	25	26	27	28	29	30

2. Mexico: U.S. troops rush to intervene in Green Mine strike at Cananea.

3. Morocco: Pretender defeats sultan's troops in battle.

4. Howard Taylor Ricketts, pathologist at Univ. of Chicago, finds ticks cause Rocky Mountain spotted fever.

5. Russia: Peter Stolypin appointed prime minister.

5. Germany: Federation of Catholic school teachers opposes interdenominational schools.

6. Austria's Franz Joseph and Germany's Wilhelm II wire Italy's King Victor Emmanuel, reaffirming Triple Alliance.

9. Great Britain: 325 warships prepare for mock battle.

12. Russia: Hundreds of Jews killed in Bialystok (→ 17).

12. Norwegian royal couple crowned at Nidaros Cathedral in Trondheim.

13. Russian troops mutiny, come to aid of revolutionary Mujiks (→ 20).

14. Germany: Battleship Gneisenau launched.

17. St. Petersburg: Officials admit anti-Semitic pogrom at Bialystok had govt. sanction (→ 7/23).

18. France accepts loan of $50 mil. from Pennsylvania railroads.

20. Russia: Bokhovsky regiment rises up at Riazan, killing all officers (→ 7/2).

21. U.S. canal commission decides Panama canal will be equipped with locks (→ 11/26).

22. Washington: President opens antitrust suit against Standard Oil (→ 29).

29. Washington: Congress passes Hepburn Act, authorizing regulation of freight rates (→ 30).

BIRTHS

3. Josephine Baker, black-American dancer, singer (†4/12/1974).

22. Billy Wilder, U.S. film director.

Pure Food and Drug Act becomes the law

June 30. A bill to assure Americans a pure food and drug supply was signed into law by President Roosevelt today, the second stiff crackdown this year on adulterated products. The new law, to become effective next January 1, prohibits the misbranding or adulteration of all foods and drugs manufactured in or shipped within the United States. Just last month, under prodding by the president, Congress passed legislation requiring that all meat designed for human consumption must be inspected before leaving the packing houses.

President Roosevelt first became interested in the meat issue after reading Upton Sinclair's book, "The Jungle," an expose of filthy conditions in the Chicago packing houses. Sinclair told of slaughtering of diseased animals, of unclean workers and of scurrying rats. At first dubious about the writer's findings, the president later conferred with Sinclair and was finally convinced that they were true. He then urged a meat inspection law. Under the new Pure Food and Drug Act, a violator who is found guilty of misbranding or adulterating food or drugs will be subject to a fine of $500 or one year in prison, or both. The term food includes all food, drink or condiment used by humans and animals (→ 8/8).

Heroin for your cough?

Stanford White shot by angry husband

June 25. Harry Kendall Thaw was arrested late last night after the fatal shooting of Stanford White, the architect, on the roof of Madison Square Garden, a building designed by White. Thaw, member of a prominent, wealthy family, is married to Florence Evelyn Nesbit, former actress and artist's model. It was White who first put Miss Nesbit on the stage. The killing occurred near the end of a show, during the song, "I Could Love a Million Girls." After plugging his seated victim in the head three times, Thaw said to the arresting officer, "He ruined my wife and then deserted the girl" (→ 4/13/07)

Architect Stanford White.

Sysonby the Great will race no more

James R. Keene's Sysonby.

June 17. Sysonby, probably the greatest racehorse ever foaled in America, died today of septic poisoning at the Sheepshead Bay Race Course in Brooklyn, New York. An autopsy showed that the horse's ample lungs, nearly twice the size of an ordinary horse's and a reason for his great stamina, were badly infected. The great four-year-old, born in America of English breeding, had been ailing for two months. Veterinarians thought at first that he was suffering from eczema. Sysonby won $179,000 as a three-year-old and $88,000 as a two-year-old. His only defeat in 15 starts was in the Futurity.

1906

JULY

Su	Mo	Tu	We	Th	Fr	Sa
1	2	3	4	5	6	7
8	9	10	11	12	13	14
15	16	17	18	19	20	21
22	23	24	25	26	27	28
29	30	31				

1. King of Cambodia pays official visit to Paris.

2. Russia: Duma proposes abolition of capital punishment (→ 17).

3. Danish steamer Norge sinks in heavy weather off coast of Britain; 800 killed.

7. N.Y. court rules Shaw's play "Mrs. Warren's Profession" fit for performance.

8. Wimbledon: Hugh Doherty over Frank Risely 6-4, 4-6, 6-2, 6-3: Dorothea Douglass over May Sutton 6-3, 9-7.

8. Washington: Alexander Graham Bell reports one in 1,200 Americans are blind, one in 850 deaf.

15. Guatemala loses 2,000 in battle with Salvadoran army, reported ready for peace talks (→ 20).

15. Britain: House of Commons creates special ministry for Wales.

17. Russia: Mujiks renew assault on large estates, kill landlords, ruin property (→ 29).

18. British govt. reinforces troops in Egypt to halt protests over execution of British officer's murderers (→ 9/13/09).

23. Third Pan-American Conference convenes at Rio de Janeiro, Brazil.

23. Russia: Anti-Semitic pogroms continue in Odessa (→ 8/26).

27. New York: Two bombs dropped into meeting of plumbers union.

29. Rene Pothier wins fourth Tour de France.

29. New York: Pacific Express plunges into Hudson; 45 dead.

29. Ousted members of Russian Duma meet in Vyborg, Finland; urge Russians to revolt by withholding taxes (→ 31).

30. France: Gabriel Lippman presents new method of duplicating color photography at the Academy of Sciences.

BIRTH

18. American Clifford Odets, leftist dramatist of 1930's (†8/15/1963).

Dreyfus vindicated, gets Legion of Honor

July 21. Captain Alfred Dreyfus of the French army considered himself above all a man of honor. Yet, he was twice court-martialed and wrongly convicted of spying for Germany. He received the harshest penalty, life imprisonment on Devil's Island, a hellish penal colony off French Guiana in the South Atlantic, where he clung to life and sanity for four desperate years.

As Dreyfus is Jewish, anti-Semitism was a factor in the Affair, as it came to be called. It was one of the gravest crises of France's Third Republic. It split the nation into pro- and anti-Dreyfus factions, contending bitterly. The Affair is now ended, but not its effects, one of which was to strengthen the republic against the monarchists.

At the Ecole Militaire today, Dreyfus, now a Major, received the Legion of Honor. At that same place 12 years ago, he was stripped of his rank and insignia, and his sword was broken.

Captain Alfred Dreyfus.

Arrested in 1894, Dreyfus was accused of passing military secrets to the Germans. President Loubet pardoned him in 1900. Parliament granted an amnesty to all involved in the Affair, including those who had forged evidence against Dreyfus, lied about him and concealed their misdeeds. The highest military officers were involved. Finally, the Court of Appeals annuled the guilty verdict. Today, Dreyfus said, "My honor has been restored."

Treaty brings peace to Central America

July 20. A peace treaty sponsored by the United States was signed today, ending the Guatemalan war against El Salvador and Honduras. The government of Mexico also played a key role in the difficult negotiations, which culminated in the signing of the treaty aboard the American cruiser Marblehead off the coast of Central America.

The American role of moderator was accepted after a July 14th Salvadoran victory at Platanar, where Guatemala suffered the loss of 2,000 dead, wounded or captured. Honduras and El Salvador had allied themselves against Guatemala, which invaded both countries in the wake of a domestic revolt that erupted in May. Nicaragua claimed neutrality, denying reports that it aided in the war against Guatemala.

All countries involved issued a special thanks to the presidents of Mexico and the United States for their help in ending the conflict. President Roosevelt was gratified, but refused comment until news of the treaty's outcome reached him through official channels.

Russia still seethes as Duma dissolved

July 31. Angered by Czar Nicholas II's dissolution of Russia's first democratic institution, the Duma, the leaders of that assembly's moderate and radical parties have signed a revolutionary manifesto. The manifesto calls on Russians to refuse to pay taxes and to serve in the army. The document was drafted by the delegates in Vyborg, Finland, a city that is out of reach of the Russian police.

The czar announced the dissolution of the Duma on July 9, in an effort to cut off a proposed discussion of agrarian reform. But the tension between the czar and the Duma goes back to the first day the assembly convened in May. On that day, the delegates drafted a reply to the czar's inauguration address in which they called for political amnesty, a constitutional monarchy and the sale of all crown and church estates. The czar rejected all of the demands and the two sides have been deadlocked ever since then. The czar has announced that a second Duma will be convened on March 5, 1907 (→ 8/1).

Russell Sage dies leaving $80 million

July 22. Russell Sage, nearly 90 and leaving a fortune in excess of $80 million, died yesterday in his Long Island, New York, mansion.

Descended from New England pioneers (he was actually born in a covered wagon), Sage clerked at his brother's grocery store from age 12, began trading in his teens and bought the store at age 21. A former Whig member of Congress, he was a star figure in Wall Street finance, director of railroads, telegraph companies and more. He was often the object of press criticism and at least one attempt on his life. His widow, Margaret, plans to establish a foundation to support mainly education and the social sciences. Sage's death is not expected to affect the stock market.

Dancer St. Denis creates first work

July. A New Jersey-born woman is stirring up the European dance world with her exotic choreography. Ruth St. Denis, born Ruth Dennis, is touring in a work called "Radha." It is an Eastern-flavored, mystic dance to the tune of Leo Delibes's "Lakme." Miss Dennis insists that despite its innovation, the work is inspired by images in a mundane cigarette advertisement. The 29-year-old dancer never received formal training, and even those who fervently admire this first effort consider her actual dancing secondary to her artistic vision.

Ruth St. Denis.

1906

AUGUST

Su	Mo	Tu	We	Th	Fr	Sa
			1	2	3	4
5	6	7	8	9	10	11
12	13	14	15	16	17	18
19	20	21	22	23	24	25
26	27	28	29	30	31	

1. Russia: Mutinous crew of battleship Salva bombs town of Salva (→ 23).

4. Spain: Italian liner Sirio wrecked near Cape Palos; two hundred drown.

7. North Carolina: Mob defies courts, lynches five Negroes (→ 9/25).

8. Chicago: Standard Oil of Illinois indicted under Elkins Act for accepting freight rebates (→ 9/6).

9. Germany: Prussian teachers association appeals for non-denominational staff (→ 10).

10. Vatican: In encyclical "Gravissimi Officii," Pope Pius X exhorts French episcopacy to protest separation of church and state (→ 12/12).

11. France: First patent for talking film issued to Eugene Lauste.

12. New York: Brooklyn Rapid Transit Co. defies judge, raises fares to ten cents.

23. St. Petersburg: Czar declares intent to sell 20 mil. acres to Russian peasants (→ 25).

24. Two thousand rebels battle loyalist troops in Cuba (→ 31).

25. St. Petersburg: Assassin's bomb injures Premier Stolypin and 33 others, kills 28, including premier's daughter (→ 26).

26. New York: Thirty Russian-Jewish orphans ordered deported (→ 3/1/07).

26. Germany: Hamburg police uncover bomb factory run by Russian revolutionaries (→ 31).

28. Roosevelt proposes federal documents be written in simplified spelling (→ 10/30).

31. It is reported the Cuban uprising has spread to five provinces (→ 9/1).

31. Russia: Nineteen soldiers, three civilians executed for treason at Sveaborg Fortress (→ 9/10).

BIRTH

5. American film director John Huston, "The African Queen," "Moby Dick."

Edward VII talks politics with Kaiser

Aug 15. King Edward arrived in Kronberg, Germany, today and began discussions with Kaiser Wilhelm II. Although the precise subject of the talks is not known, it is believed they discussed the acquisition of a German port in the Persian Gulf which has been a menace to the British navy. The German construction of the Baghdad railway also probably came under review.

Arriving with a full staff, including Under Secretary of the Foreign Office Sir Charles Hardinge, the king was helped from the train by the kaiser himself. After the two had kissed each other on both cheeks and formal introductions were made, they proceeded via motorcar through cheering throngs to the Friedrichshof Castle. The two monarchs met alone for an hour this morning and for another hour after lunch before being joined by aides.

Kaiser Wilhelm and Edward VII.

Several hours of sightseeing were followed by dinner and a concert. The German press has praised the king, one paper calling him "a political artist" (→ 1/1/07).

Chile earthquake kills, maims thousands

Aug 18. An earthquake that hit Valparaiso, Chile, has reduced the city to smouldering wreckage and claimed the lives of some 5,000 people. Refugees are camped out on the hills while thousands have fled to the safety of harbor ships, each jammed to the limit.

Because telegraph and telephone lines have been cut, the precise extent of the disaster remains unknown, but at least half, and possibly most of the city has been destroyed, including the finest buildings in town. Those spared by the earthquake have been consumed by raging fires.

With the first shock, walls caved in, houses toppled and the electric lights went out. As the city's fire bells rang away, the streets became a haven for thousands of people wailing and praying. Looting has begun. Because laborers are fearful of undertaking rescue work, martial law has been declared to press them into service.

The outlying country has been hit even harder, with at least six towns partially or completely destroyed. From Santiago to the Andes, the rail lines are torn up, bridges are twisted and tunnels collapsed. Santiago has suffered severe damage, and the quake was felt as far away as Chile's northernmost province.

1906 Cadillacs come from the world's largest auto factory, in Detroit.

1906

SEPTEMBER

Su	Mo	Tu	We	Th	Fr	Sa
						1
2	3	4	5	6	7	8
9	10	11	12	13	14	15
16	17	18	19	20	21	22
23	24	25	26	27	28	29
30						

1. Boston: Philadelphia scores three runs in 24th inning to beat Boston 4-1 in longest baseball game (→ 5/1/20).

1. Cuba: Rebels capture Bahia Honda, site of U.S. naval base; Cuban govt. hopes for American intervention (→ 10).

3. Oyster Bay, Long Island: Atlantic fleet puts on prodigal display of U.S. naval strength.

6. Washington: Meatpackers agree to label all products (→ 10/4).

7. Morocco: Revolution in progress; rebel tribes attack Tangier (→ 3/27/07).

8. Norfolk, Va.: Robert Turner announces invention of automatic carriage return for typewriter.

9. New York: Clergy protests Bronx Zoo's display of pygmy in cage with apes.

10. Cuba's Pres. Palma kills peace talks with rebels, declares martial law (→ 14).

11. Spanish bishops publish pastoral letter denouncing civil marriage.

13. France: Santos-Dumont performs first flight with public audience.

14. Washington: Roosevelt threatens intervention in Cuba under Platt amendment; sends Sec. of War Taft and Sec. of State Root to investigate (→ 28).

16. Having failed to reach S. Pole, Roald Amundsen returns to Seattle, announces discovery of magnetic Pole.

17. Switzerland: Intl. conference on worker protection opens in Berne.

19. Germany: At 78th Medical and Scientific Assembly in Stuttgart, Max Planck reports Walter Kaufmann's refutation of Einstein's theory of relativity.

25. Atlanta: Three thousand state troopers move in as race riots spread to middle-class black suburb (→ 11/26).

BIRTH

25. Soviet composer Dimitry Shostakovich.

Taft takes over in Cuba; Palma leaves

Sept 28. U.S. Secretary of War William Howard Taft declared himself provisional Governor of Cuba today to fill the gap created in the wake of ex-President Palma's resignation last month and to bring an end to the hostilities between government and liberal forces. Taft said he only expects to be in Cuba a fortnight and that new elections will be held once peace is restored.

Palma is headed for New York and many Cubans seemed relieved at the news, believing American intervention will bring an end to the disturbances that have rocked their country. Palma and his moderate government are said to have abdicated to force the United States to intervene rather than to concede to any demands of the liberal insurgents. The liberals have called the abdication "treason," but many in Palma's government are satisfied that the liberals have lost, despite the downfall of their government (→ 10/6).

Peasants assault 142 Russian estates

Sept 10. Russian peasants, incited by revolutionaries, have burned down 142 estates in Veronezh province in southern Russia. And in retaliation, Cossacks, called in to crush the frenzied rampage, have brutally executed or sent to Siberia the ring leaders and filled the jails with everyone else.

The outburst began when the governor of the province canceled a meeting in which the local Duma representative was to have given a report to his constituents about the prospects of land reform. Peasants who had traveled many miles on foot to hear the speech were instead whipped by Cossacks and forced to return to their villages.

Agitators then urged the peasants to rise up in three days and take the land they claimed was rightfully theirs. When, three days hence, church bells across the province began to ring, the peasants began going from estate to estate, burning houses, destroying precious artwork and killing livestock. Most of the nobles escaped to the cities (→ 11/22).

1906

OCTOBER

Su	Mo	Tu	We	Th	Fr	Sa
	1	2	3	4	5	6
7	8	9	10	11	12	13
14	15	16	17	18	19	20
21	22	23	24	25	26	27
28	29	30	31			

1. Paris: American Frank P. Lahm wins first James Gordon Bennett Cup balloon race.

3. Berlin: First conference on wireless telegraphy adopts SOS as warning signal.

9. Roosevelt grants amnesty to Cuban rebels (→ 4/27/07).

11. San Francisco school board orders segregation of all Oriental school children (→ 25).

12. Southwest Africa: German troops crush Hottentot uprising (→ 11/28).

15. German Social Democratic Party creates school for political education of the working class.

16. British New Guinea becomes part of Australia.

18. Paris: Clemenceau named new French premier.

19. Florida: Tidal wave hits Elliot's Key; 2,500 drowned.

20. Britain and France agree to take joint control of New Hebrides islands in Pacific.

22. Henry Ford succeeds John S. Gray as pres. of Ford Motor Co., acquires 58.5% of stock.

23. Washington: Roosevelt appoints Oscar Strauss sec. of commerce and labor; first Jewish Cabinet member.

23. Paris: Santos-Dumont wins Deutsch-Archdeacon Prize for aviation.

25. Washington: Japanese ambassador declares Calif. school segregation law violates treaty of 1894 (→ 26).

26. Roosevelt sends sec. of comm. to S.F. to protest anti-Japanese legislation (→ 11/30).

30. U.S. Supreme Court bans "new spelling."

BIRTHS

14. German-American sociologist Hannah Arendt (†12/14/1975).

16. Cleanth Brooks, American literary critic.

DEATH

9. American Joseph Glidden, inventor of barbed wire (†1/18/1813).

Cezanne's hand is stilled

Paul Cezanne's "La Prison de Jourdain" (1906), one of his last achievements.

Oct 22. Just last month, the painter Paul Cezanne wrote to his son, "As an artist, I am developing a sharper appreciation for nature. But inside of myself, it is still very difficult to grasp my own feelings." Cezanne's efforts to be in touch with those feelings ended today. The great artist died in Aix-en-Provence, France. It is the town where he was born 67 years ago and the home where he returned in 1899. Cezanne spent his last years living alone and covering canvases with scenes from nature.

In his early years, Cezanne was influenced by Eugene Delacroix and the old Italian masters. But it was Camille Pissarro who affected him the most and introduced him to Edouard Manet and the other great Impressionists. Cezanne never fell completely into their camp. He started spending more time in Provence, where he developed his style, trying to capture nature in still-lifes and landscapes, many of them with nudes. The best of Cezanne's work is characterized by very bright colors, deep shadows and sharp outlines. He also painted many memorable portraits.

Cezanne was not well-known until 1895, when he had an exposition of his work organized in Paris. It brought him larger acclaim, but all the critics were not convinced of the value of his work. One of them brashly decried his paintings as "insanity, loud colors sprayed onto canvas." Cezanne's brilliance was not universally recognized until another exhibition just two years ago.

Baseball's best are all in Chicago: Nationals lose Series to White Sox.

▷

First American troops arrive in Cuba

Oct 6. More than 900 American troops arrived in Havana today, aboard the troop ship Sumner from New York. The troops, who will proceed by trolley car to Camp Columbia tomorrow, are here so that the surrender of arms by government and rebel forces can continue. The rebels have refused to give up more arms until government volunteers have disbanded, but the government has retained many volunteers to help protect the towns. Some 5,500 American troops are expected to arrive to garrison the towns.

While ex-President Palma has been denounced by the Cuban press for secretly asking the United States to intervene while publicly declaring his support for Cuba's sovereignty, Governor Taft has been warmly received for promising to keep Cuba a republic and giving amnesty to all insurgents (→ 9).

U.S. Marines settle in at Havana.

Combative President attacks plutocrats

"Having a bully time"—busting trusts in exchange for votes.

Oct 4. President Theodore Roosevelt called today for federal and state action to curb those seeking to rule the nation through wealth alone. While praising the nation's industrial growth, the president warned against letting the country become "the civilization of a mere plutocracy, a banking-house, Wall Street-syndicate civilization."

Speaking at the dedication of a new Capitol in Harrisburg, Pennsylvania, the president said that selfish commercialism, if unchecked, could lead to powers of destruction. He pledged to continue pressing for new laws to rein in "the forces of greed" and to curb "those ingenious legal advisers of the holders of vast corporate wealth" (→ 11/14).

German professor telegraphs pictures

Oct 17. Pictures transmitted almost instantaneously hundreds of miles around the globe. Not just the dream of a mad scientist. A German professor named Arthur Korn used a telegraph today to send such a photographic image more than a thousand miles. Korn calls his technique telephotography. For the past few years, he has been increasing the distance he sends his images, and today's transmission was his biggest success. To build his telephotographic machine, Korn perfected the invention of Italian physicist Luigi Cerebotani.

Autumn fashions for ladies.

1906

NOVEMBER

Su	Mo	Tu	We	Th	Fr	Sa
				1	2	3
4	5	6	7	8	9	10
11	12	13	14	15	16	17
18	19	20	21	22	23	24
25	26	27	28	29	30	

1. Philadelphia: Navy shuts out Army 10-0 in annual football game.

2. New York: Commander Robert Peary reported within 200 miles of North Pole.

2. Russia: Leon Trotsky exiled for life in Siberia (→ 22).

3. New York: Saint-Saens makes first U.S. appearance.

4. Shanghai: It is reported that ten million face starvation in central China.

6. U.S.: Republicans sweep every state but Rhode Island, win 84-seat majority in House.

6. Roosevelt orders dishonorable discharges for Negro Army battalion accused of murder in Brownsville, Texas (→ 1/7/07).

8. Germany: Max Reinhardt stages plays by Wedekind, Ibsen.

9. Roosevelt leaves for 17-day trip to Puerto Rico, Panama, becoming first president to make official visit outside U.S.

14. St. Louis: Standard Oil indicted under Sherman Anti-trust Act (→ 1/1/07).

18. Rome: Anarchists bomb St. Peter's Cathedral.

21. San Juan: Pres. Roosevelt pledges citizenship for Puerto Rican people (→ 3/2/17).

22. Peking: Imperial govt. redoubles efforts to rid China of opium abuse.

22. Russia: Prime Minister Peter Stolypin offers agrarian reforms allowing for private ownership of land (→ 2/15/07).

28. Germany: Center Party creates deadlock in Reichstag, joining Socialists to oppose funding of war in S.W. Africa (→ 12/13).

29. London: Pankhurst admits suffragettes don't mind being ridiculed for their violent methods (→ 1/20/07).

30. Roosevelt publicly denounces segregation of Japanese schoolchildren in San Francisco (→ 12/7).

BIRTH

2. Italian neo-realist film-maker Luchino Visconti (†3/17/1976).

Negro leader says race relations finer

Nov 27. The bitter riots in Atlanta that left more than a dozen Negroes dead have improved race relations, or so says Booker T. Washington. Speaking in New York City, the Negro leader repeated his view that those of his own race must work for advances in education and jobs instead of trying to win social equality with whites. In the weeks since the stormy clashes between Negroes and the militia earlier this fall, Washington said, Southern whites have praised the progress made by members of his own race, particularly at the Tuskegee Institute, the Negro school he heads in Alabama (→ 12/25).

Booker T. Washington.

Caruso fined $10 for zoo escapade

Nov 23. Enrico Caruso survived his day in court, vocal cords, if not honor, intact. The world-famous, operatic tenor was charged with annoying a Miss Hannah Graham in the Central Park Zoo monkey house in New York City. Caruso protested his innocence in low, soft tones, preserving his voice for an approaching production of "La Boheme." Some fellow admirers surrounded the singer and expressed their faith in him. A police officer present called them "curs and dogs," inviting hisses from the assembly. Miss Graham never appeared in court. The judge nevertheless found Caruso guilty, fining him $10 (→ 8/13/08).

Roosevelt surveys his great Panama feat

Teddy Roosevelt pilots a 95-ton steam shovel at the canal site.

Nov 26. President Theodore Roosevelt returned to Washington today after a history-making trip to Panama to view progress on the canal he pushed so hard to create.

Four years ago, the Roosevelt administration supported and quickly recognized a Panamanian junta which seceded from Colombia and then conceded the canal zone to the United States. And this month, Roosevelt broke a 117-year-old tradition by being the first president to leave United States territorial jurisdiction so he could "see how the ditch is getting on."

Roosevelt made the 12-day trip aboard the battleship Louisiana and was in touch with the White House the entire time by wireless telegraph. The president toured the isthmus by train and inspected the canal, Marine barracks, surrounding towns and labor conditions. Roosevelt plans to send a special report on the canal project to Congress. As he arrived home this evening, he remarked that he was deeply impressed with the construction (→ 2/26/07).

Mormon President fined for polygamy

Nov 23. President of the Mormon Church, Joseph F. Smith, has been charged with polygamy following the birth of his 43rd child. The baby was born to his fifth wife. Smith pleaded guilty and paid the maximum fine of $300.

Smith descends from the founder of the Church of Jesus Christ of Latter-day Saints (Mormons). The elder Smith started the faith in New York state in 1830. While plural marriage is a Mormon tenet, most members of the faith ceased to enter into such unions 16 years ago. Joseph Smith the younger told the Salt Lake City district judge he considered each of his marriages a solemn contract.

Liberia may become haven for Negroes

Nov 23. Addressing the congregation of New York's Bethel African Methodist Episcopal Church, Bishop C.S. Smith of Detroit spoke of his plan to resettle in Liberia those Negroes "who are praying for relief from the discrimination and injustice" they find in America.

Referring to Senator Tillman's speech in Atlanta, Georgia, that "there are not enough Yankees between Cape Cod and hell to prevent Southern people from doing as they please with the Negro," the bishop replied that "there are not enough Tillmanites between Cape Cod and hell to hurl the American Negro back into slavery or permanently impair his onward march."

1906

DECEMBER

Su	Mo	Tu	We	Th	Fr	Sa
						1
2	3	4	5	6	7	8
9	10	11	12	13	14	15
16	17	18	19	20	21	22
23	24	25	26	27	28	29
30	31					

3. U.S. Supreme Court orders I.W.W. leaders extradited to Idaho for trial in Steunenberg murder case (→ 5/4/07).

7. Roosevelt gains informal agreement from Japanese Ambassador Aoki to stop flood of immigration to U.S. (→ 23).

12. Paris: Pope's envoy driven from France; state halts funding for churches (→ 1/11/07).

13. Berlin: Chancellor von Bulow dissolves Reichstag for denying military funding to colonial struggle in Southwest Africa (→ 1/25/07).

13. Britain, France, Italy agree to maintain open door in Abyssinia.

14. Germany: First U1 submarine brought into service.

23. Mass meeting in S.F. passes resolution denouncing President Roosevelt's accord with Japan (→ 3/11/07).

25. Mississippi: Twelve Negroes, two whites killed in race riots (→ 2/17/07).

28. St. Paul, Minn.: James J. Hill announces retirement from railroad industry.

BIRTHS

5. American film director Otto Preminger (†4/23/86).

19. Soviet statesman Leonid Brezhnev (†11/10/1982).

CULTURAL EVENTS, 1906

Literature: John Galsworthy's "The Man of Property," 1st of "The Forsyte Saga"; O. Henry's "The Four Million"; Upton Sinclair's "The Jungle."

Academia: Albert Schweitzer's "The Search for the Historical Jesus"; Winston Churchill's "Life of Lord Randolph Churchill."

Music: Salzburg Mozart festival; Geraldine Farrar's American debut; George M. Cohan's musical "45 Minutes from Broadway"; Charles Ives' "The Unanswered Question."

The Arts: Picasso's "Portrait of Gertrude Stein"; Matisse's "The Joy of Life"; Rouault's "At the Mirror"; Ruth St. Denis introduces modern dance in U.S.

Nobel Peace Prize goes to Roosevelt

Dec 10. The Norwegian Nobel Committee conferred the Nobel Peace Prize upon President Roosevelt for his work in bringing about the end of the war between Russia and Japan. Roosevelt said he will use the prize money ($37,127) to establish a permanent Industrial Peace Committee in Washington. This committee will gather together representatives of capital and labor to discuss industrial problems and arrive at solutions.

A lively season on American stage

Foreign talent dominated the American stage in 1906. Alla Nazimova, the Russian actress who immigrated here last year, opened "Hedda Gabler" November 13. Five months prior, she spoke no English; yet her fine work honors the recent passing of Norwegian playwright Henrik Ibsen. Irishman George Bernard Shaw sent four works to our shores. The most controversial, "Man and Superman," retells Mozart's "Don Giovanni." But one American did make theatergoers proud. George M. Cohan, composer of "Little Johnny Jones" in 1904, opened "Forty-five Minutes From Broadway" last January 2. The first act has five fine tunes, the grandest being "Mary's a Grand Old Name."

Starring Victor Moore.

1907

JANUARY

Su	Mo	Tu	We	Th	Fr	Sa
		1	2	3	4	5
6	7	8	9	10	11	12
13	14	15	16	17	18	19
20	21	22	23	24	25	26
29	28	29	30	31		

1. British spokesman Sir Eyre Crowes accuses Germany of seeking hegemony in Europe (→ 8).

1. Pure Food and Drug Act becomes law in U.S. (→ 4).

4. Interstate Commerce Commission reports E.H. Harriman maintains dangerous control over railroad industry (→ 26).

7. Congress challenges Roosevelt's authority in Brownsville case, maintains he cannot give military discharges without congressional approval.

8. Germany: Committee on colonial policy, headed by Gustave von Schmoller, demands more territorial acquisitions (→ 25).

11. Pope insists French law aims to destroy church and de-Christianize France (→ 20).

20. Switzerland: Separation of church and state voted down by popular referendum (→ 27).

20. Paris: Workers clash with troops as Clemenceau closes Trade Union Center.

23. Harry K. Thaw, accused of murdering architect Stanford White, stands trial in New York (→ 4/13).

25. Berlin: Socialists defeated at polls; Chancellor von Bulow's colonial policy vindicated (→ 8/18).

26. Washington: Congress outlaws direct corporate campaign contributions (→ 2/22).

26. Austria: Vote granted to males over age of 24 (→ 4/14/08).

27. New York: 21,000 Catholics meet to denounce separation of church and state in France (→ 6/30).

28. Russian Czar Nicholas II informs China's emperor that troops will evacuate Manchuria by March 22 (→ 3/22).

BIRTHS

11. French statesman Pierre Mendes-France (†10/18/1982).

11. William J. Levitt, introduced low-cost suburban housing in U.S.

'Quake, fire in Jamaica

Crowds in Kingston survey the damage.

Jan 22. Officials in Kingston, Jamaica say many hundreds were killed in the earthquake and fire that struck the city on January 14. The death toll is not known yet; dozens of bodies still are being pulled from the wreckage every day by rescue workers. The earthquake began at 3:30 p.m. and leveled a substantial portion of the city within minutes.

A fire that broke out shortly afterward raged for hours before it was brought under control. Thousands of residents whose homes were destroyed are living in tents or in the open. Witnesses say that the destruction is as complete as that caused by the great earthquake which leveled San Francisco last April. The refusal of the British governor to accept an offer of food and medical aid from a visiting American fleet has aroused indignation in the United States.

Persian Shah dies and son succeeds

Jan 19. Soon after sunset this evening, the doors of the Tehran palace harem were closed, an official sign that death had taken 54-year-old Shah Muzaffar ad-Din. The Persian people are as yet uninformed. The enlightened leader had pushed the liberalization begun by his father, such as instituting the Parliament, framing a constitution and planning schools for female subjects. He is succeeded by his son, Muhammad Ali (→ 6/26/08).

Newly crowned Muhammad Ali.

Met Opera halts Salome production

Jan 26. The Richard Strauss-Oscar Wilde production of "Salome" has closed at the New York Metropolitan Opera House after one performance. A daughter of J.P. Morgan, member of the theater's board of directors, urged the cancellation. The opera includes a "dance of the seven veils" and a scene featuring a decapitated head.

"Salome" at the Met.

Licorice monopoly is ruled illegal

Jan 10. Two companies were convicted today of holding an illegal monopoly on licorice paste, widely used as flavoring in cigars, cigarettes and chewing tobacco. The verdict, returned by a United States Circuit Court in New York City, ended a three-week trial in which the federal government accused the defendants of violating the Sherman Antitrust Law.

The defendants in the case were the companies of MacAndrews and Forbes and J.S. Young. Individuals employed by the firms were acquitted of a conspiracy to control the licorice paste market. The attorneys for the defendants argued that the companies were merely trying to protect against any possible shortage of licorice paste, which comes from a raw root grown primarily in Asia as well as parts of southern Europe (→ 26).

Professor declares women are savages

Jan 20. "The savage and woman are not what we call intellectual because they are not taught to know and manipulate the materials of knowledge," declares Professor W. I. Thomas, sociologist at the University of Chicago. His new book, "Sex and Society," promises to create quite a sensation as it places modern woman on an intellectual par with savages.

Thomas writes, "The savage is outside the process" because of geography, while women do not participate because it is "neither necessary nor womenly." Acknowledging that "the American woman has made an approach toward the standards of professional scholarship" and that "a number of women of natural ability and character are realizing some definite aim," he nevertheless views these examples as "sporadic cases" (→2/13).

1907

FEBRUARY

Su	Mo	Tu	We	Th	Fr	Sa
					1	2
3	4	5	6	7	8	9
10	11	12	13	14	15	16
17	18	19	20	21	22	23
24	25	26	27	28		

8. Revolution breaks out in Argentina.

12. Rhode Island: Steamer Larchmont sinks off coast of Block Island; 150 drowned.

15. New York: Ex-member of Duma declares famine widespread in Russia (→ 18).

17. In a New York speech, W.E.B. DuBois claims that mixed blood aided white geniuses (→ 4/8/08).

18. New York: 600,000 tons of grain sent to relieve Russian famine (→ 20).

19. Japan denounces new U.S. bill restricting immigration of Japanese workers (→ 28).

19. Honduran troops defy U.S., invade Nicaragua to halt expansionist policy of Pres. Jose Zelaya (→ 3/21).

20. Russian reactionaries reported planning pogroms to end Duma and crush defiance of monarchy (→ 3/5).

22. New York: Company spokesman declares that Rockefeller has never controlled Standard Oil (→ 5/19).

25. Washington: Senate agrees to Roosevelt's arrangement for U.S. supervision of Dominican Republic's customs (→ 3/6).

25. Cambridge: Roosevelt advises Harvard students not to abolish football.

26. U.S. Congress raises pay for House and Senate members to $7,500; Cabinet members, v.p. to get $12,000.

26. President Roosevelt rejects private contractors' bids; Army to build Panama canal (→ 1/5/09).

28. California Legislature bars Orientals from holding land for more than five years (→ 3/11).

BIRTHS

3. American novelist James Michener.

28. British poet Wystan Hugh Auden (†9/28/1973).

DEATH

27. Wendell P. Garrison, editor of The Nation for 41 years (*6/4/1840).

Suffragettes storm Parliament; 60 arrested

Feb 13. A crowd of suffragettes stormed Parliament today, but their well-organized assaults were repelled by police. Some 60 women were arrested and many were hurt in fierce struggles with mounted police. The suffragettes' demonstrations began early this afternoon and continued until 10 o'clock tonight.

The women made further attempts to enter the legislative building in the evening, following a meeting. But the police, both mounted and on foot, successfully met each surge by the women. Several of the women involved now complain of alleged brutality on the part of the London police.

In order to draw attention to the cause of women's suffrage, more than 100 of the suffragettes have sworn to get themselves arrested.

Suffragettes flood streets of London.

Annie Kenny, one of the suffragette leaders, has promised to lead 1,000 women onto the floor of the House of Commons if British women are not granted the vote by the end of this session (→ 3/8).

Government costs double in ten years

Feb 23. The cost of running the federal government in Washington has more than doubled in the past ten years. That was the word today from congressional Democrats, members of the minority party. It is traditional for members of the minority party to accuse the opposition of spending too much money. On the basis of the Democratic Party's calculations, the current Congress will appropriate approximately $1 billion this year, with the largest increase going to the Navy. It is estimated that the appropriations for the full two-year period of this Congress will reach close to $2 billion. Some Americans are asking whether the growth of military and social programs is worth the cost.

Roosevelt inspired this creature, a 1903 creation of German Richard Steiff, by refusing to kill a bear cub on a hunting trip.

Japanese allowed in school by bill

Feb 18. President Roosevelt and San Francisco officials reached an agreement tonight to provide for the schooling of Japanese children who live in that city. Under the agreement, all alien children who are at least 16 years old and who speak English will be admitted to white schools. Special schools or classes will be set up for those who do not speak English.

The pact was reached after the president assured officials in San Francisco that he would sign an immigration bill excluding further immigration of Japanese laborers into the United States. The bill passed Congress today. And according to a statement issued by the White House, the president has assured the Californians that if the new bill fails to halt such immigration, he will seek a treaty with the Japanese government that would try to stem the flow of American workers to Japan and Japanese workers to the United States.

Californians, as well as other Americans, have long protested the heavy flow of what they term coolies, or unskilled Orientals, into the country. Such immigration, they have complained, has proved to be a threat to job security for American workers, as well as heavily taxing on a wide range of municipal services (→ 19).

How rich is rich? Less than you think

Feb 24. John D. Rockefeller is not as rich as some people think. His oil fortune is apparently no more than $300 million. But he's still the world's richest man. He is only one of half a dozen American individuals and family trusts controlling $100 million or more. The New York Times has counted them. On its list are:

Andrew Carnegie, who got $174 million when his company became the core of United States Steel. He already had a fortune.

The Astors, who've been buying Manhattan real estate for 100 years and never sell a foot. William Waldorf Astor, eldest son of John Jacob Astor, the founder, is alone worth $150 million.

The Goelet family, also property investors, probably has $100 million, as does Marshall Field of Chicago, the richest of American merchants.

Three women are on the list: Hetty Green, the frugal, eccentric financier; Mrs. Russell Sage, widow of the "Dean of Wall Street"; and Mrs. Anne Weightman Walker, who inherited her wealth, now grown to $120 million, from her father, who got into the lucrative quinine trade during the Civil War.

Some men like Edward Henry Harriman, master of 20,000 miles of coast-to-coast railroads, don't even know how rich they really are.

1907

MARCH

Su	Mo	Tu	We	Th	Fr	Sa
					1	2
3	4	5	6	7	8	9
10	11	12	13	14	15	16
17	18	19	20	21	22	23
24	25	26	27	28	29	30
31						

1. Russia: Only 15,000 Jews left in Odessa; attacks continue as more evacuate (→ 9/10).

1. Spain: Royal decree abolishes civil marriage.

1. New York: Salvation Army opens anti-suicide bureau.

2. Germany: Hamburg dockworkers strike to end night shift; shipowners bring in 2,000 British strikebreakers (→ 4/22).

5. St. Petersburg: New Duma opens; 40,000 demonstrators dispersed by troops (→ 4/1).

6. London: British creditors of Dominican Rep. claim U.S. failing to collect debts (→ 5/3).

8. London: House of Commons kills women's suffrage bill (→ 15).

11. Roosevelt induces California to revoke anti-Japanese legislation (→ 4/6).

11. Bulgaria: Anarchist kills Premier Nicolas Petkov; Joseph Gudev to succeed (→ 4/5).

14. Mexico: Earthquake ravages Acapulco.

15. Pittsburgh: Rivers reach highest point this century, cause $25 mil. in damages.

16. British cruiser Invincible, world's largest, completed at Glasgow shipyards.

21. U.S. Marines land in Honduras to protect American interests in war with Nicaragua (→ 25).

21. First Parliament of Transvaal meets in Pretoria (→ 7/1).

22. Russians complete evacuation of Manchuria (→ 4/8).

22. Paris: It is reported that male cab drivers masquerade as women to attract riders.

25. Nicaraguan troops take Tegucigalpa, capital of Honduras (→ 4/5).

27. Morocco: French troops occupy Oudja in punitive action for murder of French Dr. Muchamp (→ 8/4).

DEATH

18. French chemist Marcelin Berthelot, 1st to produce organic compounds synthetically (*10/25/1827).

Market has worst crash since 1901

March 14. The federal government moved today to ease this week's dramatic collapse in the stock market, the largest crash since the Panic of 1901. In Washington, officials of the Treasury Department made plans to pay off $25 million in government bonds and to seek other ways to relieve the situation on Wall Street. Despite the market collapse, there appeared to be little or no panic around the nation, primarily because the public has not invested heavily in stocks.

The big losers were such wealthy industrialists as E.H. Harriman. Such Harriman stock holdings as Union Pacific plunged 25 points, leading to speculation that he might have been forced to sell vast amounts of his holdings. "That is not true," Harriman said. "I have not been selling." While calling the stock collapse "nothing to gloat over," Harriman added that he was not at all worried about the outcome. In fact, he said, it might prove to be beneficial to the economy by making it possible "to get cheaper labor and cheaper money, for there will be less demand for both."

Worried investors crowd Wall Street.

In addition to the slump in Union Pacific, dozens of other securities sank dramatically during the past two days. The heavy losers were Great Northern, Reading and Union Pacific among railroad industry stocks, and Amalgamated Copper, American Smelting and National Lead in the metals industry. The overall declines, in fact, were described as even greater than those of the panic six years ago and the so-called Black Friday stock market collapse in the fall of 1869.

At the close of the market today, prominent bankers and heavy market investors met in uptown New York clubs to discuss what should be done. While there have been no failures, there were fears of what might happen (→ 8/7).

Gandhi new leader in Southern Africa

March 22. Perturbed by a new law restricting Asiatic immigrants, Mohandas Gandhi, a young Indian attorney now living in South Africa, has organized a campaign of civil disobedience to resist the statute. Passed by the new Boer government of the Transvaal Colony, the Asiatic Registration Bill is considered by Gandhi unjust and discriminatory to the large Chinese and Indian populations. However, the government expressed the belief that the ordinance is popular. "Over 90 percent of the white people thoroughly approve of it," said Sir Gilbert Parker, a Conservative member of Parliament.

Gandhi (center) in South Africa.

Women gain first seats in Parliament

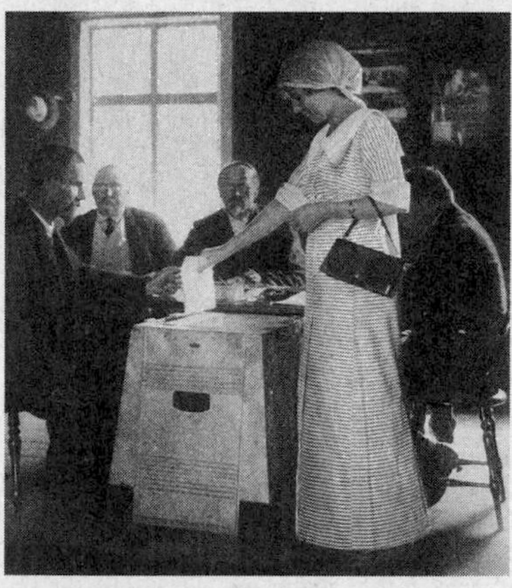

Finnish woman casts her first vote.

March 15. Women in the United States are still struggling for the right to vote, but women in Finland won much more than that today. They won their first seats in the Finnish Parliament. The deputies-elect come from all social classes, and most of them belong to the majority Social Democratic Party. They will be sworn in soon to their new seats. Finland is the first European country to give women the right to vote, doing so last year. The new elections will serve as a model to suffragists around the world. In America, women have the right to vote in only a handful of states (→ 5/25).

Making airplanes on industrial basis

March 30. The brothers Gabriel and Charles Voisin, who announced the opening of the first factory in France for the production of aircraft last November, report the successful test flight of their biplane, which is powered by an eight-cylinder engine that develops 50 horsepower. The flight proves the viability of the new industrial enterprise, according to the Voisin brothers.

The Voisin brothers' aircraft factory, located in Billaincourt, France, has a very small work force. There are exactly two employees. One is a former boat builder and the other is a cabinet maker. They are busy assisting the brothers in construction of the biplane. The Voisins are selling their aircraft to other manufacturers, who then modify them to meet their individual requirements.

1907

APRIL

Su	Mo	Tu	We	Th	Fr	Sa
	1	2	3	4	5	6
7	8	9	10	11	12	13
14	15	16	17	18	19	20
21	22	23	24	25	26	27
28	29	30				

1. Russian Duma agrees to maintain private property in hinterlands (→ 9).

1. European powers decide to install wireless network in Morocco.

5. Honduran and Salvadoran troops amass in Guatemala to resist Nicaraguan advance (→ 25).

5. New York: Andrew Carnegie hosts party for employers and workmen.

5. Bulgaria: Troops clash with 10,000 insurgents in worst conflict of peasant revolt.

6. Berlin: German Roentgen Society declares X-rays dangerous, urges restricted use only.

6. Washington: Sec. of Commerce Strauss bars five Japanese from U.S.; 1st act under new immigration law (→ 5/29).

8. Japanese troops evacuate Manchuria, leaving only minimal guard to protect railway (→ 15).

9. Swiss Federal Council lays guidelines for use of hydraulic resources in energy production.

12. Swiss government passes law requiring military training for all males.

14. Peace Congress opens in New York as preliminary to Hague Conference; Roosevelt urges intl. arbitration.

19. London: Lady Cooper inherits brother's fortune, becomes one of richest women in world.

22. Germany: Hamburg dock strike settled; British workers sent home.

25. Nicaragua, Salvador agree to hold Central American conference to establish permanent peace.

27. U.S. government sets date for withdrawal from Cuba at September 1908 (→ 10/5).

27. India: Fearing uprising in Punjab, British arm volunteers.

29. France: Clemenceau fires civil servants, crushing Paris strikes; army mobilized to quell May 1st disturbances.

Thaw murder case ends in mistrial

April 13. The two-month trial of millionaire Harry K. Thaw for the shooting murder of architect Stanford White ended in a mistrial when the jury could not agree on a verdict after 47 hours of deliberation. Their final vote was seven to five in favor of Thaw's conviction.

Thaw's defense was insanity, defined by the court as being "unable to know the nature and quality of the act," or "unable to know that it was wrong." Although Thaw was found sane during the course of the trial by the Insanity Commission, his court behavior was sufficiently odd as to plant doubts about his mental state.

Equally important was the "unwritten law" regarding Thaw's responsibility toward the honor of his wife, the former showgirl Evelyn Nesbit. White, who first put Miss Nesbit on the stage, was cast by the defense as a "tempest" and a dissolute "man about town." But Thaw was bitterly disappointed by the result. He now faces more months of confinement and the strain of another trial (→ 7/12/09).

Evelyn Nesbit Thaw.

Harry Kendall Thaw.

Tolstoy pamphlet banned in Russia

April 27. A revolutionary pamphlet by Count Leo Tolstoy has been banned in Russia. "The Way to Social Liberty" is forbidden for its inflammatory nature. It will be published in Germany in May.

The author of "War and Peace" has been a pacifist. He renounces wealth and lives a quiet, ascetic life. His passion for the poor is uppermost, however; he was driven to write "Social Liberty." In it he condemns the government's repression of the peasants, and he condones a change of government by temporary force. Tolstoy tells of two laborers whose personal ordeals, tales of torture and starvation, fired him to action. "They made it clear to me," Tolstoy writes, "that only through stopping every measure of force on the part of the government—not only the executions, but the arrests and banishments —could this fearful animal-like fight of a people be stopped" (→ 5/14).

Russians and Japanese quit Manchuria

April 15. Japanese troops completed their evacuation of Manchuria today, turning over administration of the last province to the Chinese. This completes one of the final provisions of the Treaty of Portsmouth, skillfully negotiated by President Theodore Roosevelt in Portsmouth, New Hampshire, four years ago to bring about an end to the Russo-Japanese War.

Russian troops on their way home.

Japanese fears about the duration and logistics of the war are said to have caused them to ask the United States to negotiate a peace, and Russian losses at Port Arthur, Mukden and Tsushima are said to have been the reasons why Russia agreed to it.

After the Japanese left Mukden today, the Chinese sent them a letter of thanks, explaining that they planned to post troops throughout Manchuria's three provinces to effect a rapid change of government. Hsu Shih-Chang is to oversee the administration of the territory and has been given special powers to help effect reforms. Chinese troops have already been dispatched to take over the administration of Kirin and Tsitsihar, the last two towns evacuated by the Russians.

The Russians completed the evacuation of their troops one month before the 18-month deadline was reached, but have left 8,000 railroad men. A statement issued by the Russian Foreign Office said the men are not connected with the War Ministry and their task is strictly limited to guarding the railroad, and that they are within the number allowed by the treaty (→ 11/23).

Executions, killings mounting in Russia

April 9. In an effort to halt the assassinations of those loyal to the Czar, Russian Prime Minister Peter Stolypin has announced that he will stop all military death sentences. The policy of the revolutionaries is that one loyalist should die for every revolutionary executed by military court. In the past seven months, 1,080 have been killed by military courts; and, 1,242 have been assassinated. An estimated 2,000 innocent bystanders have also been killed.

The prime minister himself has survived several attacks on his life, the most recent in 1906, when terrorists blew up his summer home. Fifty-four people were wounded or killed in that attempt.

Stolypin's action has drawn anger from some of the most important provincial governors, who favor a policy of fighting terror with terror. They have challenged his authority to overrule a court decision. Military courts are particularly feared by Russians because they usually pronounce and carry out sentences within 48 hours of arrest (→ 27).

1907

MAY

Su	Mo	Tu	We	Th	Fr	Sa
			1	2	3	4
5	6	7	8	9	10	11
12	13	14	15	16	17	18
19	20	21	22	23	24	25
26	27	28	29	30	31	

1. France rebukes Belgium's king, declares support for British interests in Congo.

3. Dominican Republic ratifies treaty with U.S., relinquishing control over customs.

4. N.Y.: Socialists lead 20,000 in parade proclaiming support for I.W.W. leaders accused of conspiracy to murder Governor Steunenburg (→ 9).

6. Jockey Minder, riding Pink Star, wins Kentucky Derby.

6. France, Japan reach accord, guaranteeing free trade and recognizing spheres of influence in Far East (→ 7/25).

9. India: 2,000 Dacoits riot in eastern Bengal.

14. Russia: Twenty-eight arrested under suspicion of conspiring to kill czar (→ 23).

15. New York: Gen. Kuroki arrives with Japanese fleet.

16. Pact of Cartagena signed, binding U.K., France, Spain to maintain status quo in Mediterranean and W. Africa.

19. Washington: Govt. report shows Standard monopolizes oil industry through extensive pipeline system (→ 7/6).

23. St. Petersburg: Premier Stolypin warns Duma members he will not allow expropriation of land (→ 6/16).

25. Finnish Diet opens, 1st national assembly in which women have seats (→ 6/14).

26. Ireland: Sinn Fein proposes boycott of British goods and businesses (→ 3/30/08).

29. San Francisco: Japanese ask police protection from continued assaults (→ 6/16).

31. New Jersey: Christian Scientists Edwin and Mary Watson get jail terms for allowing seven-year-old son to die without medical help.

BIRTHS

22. British actor Sir Laurence Olivier.

22. Herge, born Georges Remy, creator of "Tintin" (†3/3/1983).

Murder trial begins for Big Bill Haywood

May 9. Radical labor leader "Big Bill" Haywood, founder of the Industrial Workers of the World, went on trial today in Boise, Idaho.

Harry Orchard, a miner, has long since confessed to the December 1905 bombing murder of ex-Governor Frank Steunenberg, whose suppression of miners' strikes in Idaho cost him his political career in 1899. At issue today is Orchard's claim that in this and other acts of labor violence he acted as hit-man for Haywood, The Western Federation of Miners and activist George Pettibone (known as the "the Devil" for his interest in fireworks).

Clarence Darrow, the respected lawyer, has spent a year contesting the union leaders' extradition from Colorado. Meanwhile, the case has become a focus of class anger, and on the eve of the trial, the calm, shady streets of Boise stood in stark contrast to the rest of the nation. In Boston, 50,000 marched in support of the defendants. And in San Francisco, demonstrators paraded to the tune of the "Marseillaise." Such scenes support Darrow's assessment that the trial begins "a fight between capital and labor, of which this is but a manifestation up here in the woods" (→ 7/29).

Bill Haywood, head of the I.W.W.

Irish republicans ask real home rule

May 21. Three thousand Irish delegates tried to swarm into a convention hall in Dublin today. Their meetinq was orderly, but their message to London was firm. The proposal from Britain's new Liberal government for a limited Irish council is unacceptable, they said. And they unanimously passed a bill advocating nothing less than "a measure of self-government which will give the Irish people complete controI of their domestic affairs."

One of the few disruptions occurred after a priest took the podium. Father David Humphreys was shouted down when he said the British bill "would drive the priests out of the schools and let in the devil." Several American delegates attended the conference. One of them was cheered when he charged that Britain gave more home ruIe to the Boers, the South African farmers whom the British defeated in a war in 1902, than the Irish.

Immigrants keep on coming and coming

May 4. Steamers from all over Europe continue to unload new immigrants, with 5,335 passing through Ellis Island yesterday and as many due in the next two days. Those departing New York by railway for other parts of America include three-week-old Robert Ellis Natte, who was named for his birthplace. During the voyage, his Dutch parents lost three of their nine children to diphtheria, and a fourth right after their arrival.

Waiting for approval at Ellis Island.

Manufacturers plan to combat unions

May 20. The issue of labor relations dominated discussion today at the National Association of Manufacturer's annual convention in New York. J.W. Van Cleve, the group's leader, asked members gathered at the Waldorf Hotel to raise $500,000 for the fight against organized labor. "Industrial wars due to the arrogance and blindness of the labor unions," he claimed, "are a much greater menace to the United States today than foreign wars."

Van Cleve called upon employers to take an active interest in politics in order to combat efforts by labor leaders like "Big Bill" Haywood, head of the Industrial Workers of the World, "to terrorize President, Congress, Judge and juries." Industry might then be regulated with sanity and caution at a time "when hysteria and fanaticism are running amuck through the country." Foreign trade, he continued, might be aided by adding financial consuls to overseas embassies. He also denied "yellow" child labor stories, insisting that only 123,040 children under 14 actually work in factories.

Streetcar collision severely injures 40

May 21. A trolley and train collided in Brooklyn, New York, last night, injuring 40 people, perhaps five fatally. The fault may lie in a flagman's employment of an inexperienced young boy to signal the vehicles. At 9 p.m., the train and trolley approached a Coney Island crossing simultaneously. The signal boy raised his lantern, beckoning both. On impact, train passengers were hurled into the aisles and cut by flying glass. The trolley car plunged from its tracks. Lucky passengers were thrown clear. Most suffered severely, cruelly crushed by timber and iron wreckage.

N.Y. streetcar, often a menace.

1907

JUNE

Su	Mo	Tu	We	Th	Fr	Sa
						1
2	3	4	5	6	7	8
9	10	11	12	13	14	15
16	17	18	19	20	21	22
23	24	25	26	27	28	29
30						

2. Southern France: 200,000 wine growers, plagued by falling prices, protest competition from adulturated wines, threaten to withold taxes (→ 22).

6. Turkish: Arab tribes revolt against Turkish rule, defeat six Ottoman battalions.

6. Britain's State Secretary John Morley asserts U.K. will not withdraw from India under any circumstances (→ 10/5).

6. Guatemala now plagued by open revolt.

7. London: International Horse Show opens; U.S. wins three blue ribbons.

8. Flooding in Kentucky and Tennessee drowns 29.

13. San Francisco: Mayor Schmitz found guilty of graft.

14. Denmark's King Frederick VIII pays official visit to Paris.

15. Holland: Second Intl. Peace Conference opens at The Hague (→ 9/7).

16. St. Petersburg: Czar dissolves Duma (→ 26).

16. England, Spain, France establish an alliance.

16. Washington: Japanese immigration reported on the rise despite legal restrictions (→ 12/15).

18. George Bernard Shaw and Mark Twain meet in London.

21. Spain: Revolution reported brewing after dismissal of Cortes by Premier Franco in May.

22. France: Chamber of Deputies passes law to control fraud in wine industry.

26. Great Britain: Mark Twain receives honorary Doctorate of Letters from Oxford.

26. Russian nobility demands drastic measures be taken against revolutionaries (→ 8/8).

30. Geneva: Swiss government votes separation of church and state (→ 9/14).

BIRTH

30. American film director Anthony Mann (†4/29/1967).

Rough Peking-Paris auto race begins

The Itala is favored by many to reach Paris ahead of the field. Thousands of miles of rough terrain, however, promise an unpredictable finish.

June 10. It could be the most demanding race of all times. It certainly is an adventure fraught with peril. Five automobiles left Peking this morning. Their drivers have a dangerous 8,000-mile course ahead of them and they hope to arrive in Paris in about two months. Their route crosses the Great Wall of China, as well as the Gobi Desert, the Ural Mountains and Prussian Poland. The roads on most of the route are at best elementary, and the drivers will have to endure the extremes of bone-chilling cold and skin-burning heat. The race drivers have already turned down offers of protection from bandits who live along the route (→ 8/10).

Lumieres find three-color photo process

June 10. Auguste and Louis Lumiere, brothers who are film pioneers, say they have developed a practical method of color photography.

The method, devised at the family business in France, is based on the use of three separate images of a photographed scene. Each of the three images is used to make a negative in one of the basic colors, red, green and blue, with the use of appropriately colored filters. Screens consisting of microscopic dots then are placed over the three negatives. When the screens are superimposed and lights shined through them, the result is a full-color image.

Louis Jean and Auguste Lumiere.

Although color photographs were made as early as 1861, when James Maxwell demonstrated the first process at the Royal Institution in London, their use has been limited because the techniques used to produce full-color pictures have been expensive and cumbersome. The Lumieres say that their technique could make color photography a commonplace.

However, their experience with the exploitation of their photographic advances has not been promising. In 1895, the Lumieres began making motion pictures using a lightweight, portable camera that had notable advantages over the model developed by Thomas Edison. Over the next five years, the Lumieres made hundreds of motion pictures, most of them showing ordinary scenes of outdoor activity. They have lost their audience to producers who introduced the elements of comedy and drama into their motion pictures.

Norwegian women win right to vote

June 14. First Finland and now Norway. It has become the second country in Europe to grant women the right to vote. The Storting, the Norwegian Parliament, voted today to allow women to go to the polls. The vote was 95-26.

The new law allows a woman to vote as long as she or her husband has paid taxes regularly. Political observers in Norway estimate that there are about 300,000 women who are thus eligible to vote.

The major change in Norwegian election law comes at a turning point in the country's history. Two years ago, the Storting dissolved the government's union with Sweden that had existed since 1805. The Parliament also chased Oscar II back to his throne in Sweden and selected Haakon VII as the ruler of Norway. The government's decision on suffrage for women may inspire movements elsewhere, including the United States. In England, suffragists are becoming increasingly militant.

1907

JULY

Su	Mo	Tu	We	Th	Fr	Sa
	1	2	3	4	5	6
7	8	9	10	11	12	13
14	15	16	17	18	19	20
21	22	23	24	25	26	27
28	29	30	31			

1. U.S. Aeronautic Corps formed as division of Army Signal Corps.

1. South Africa: State of Orange gains independence from Britain (→ 9/17).

2. Italy: Nazarro takes Grand Prix at Dieppe at record pace of 70.5 mph (→ 6/8/08).

5. Guatemalan government purges dissent after attempt on president's life; hundreds of arrests made.

5. Italian Chamber of Deputies designates Sunday as day of rest for laborers (→ 8/3).

6. Chicago: Rockefeller takes the stand to defend Standard Oil in antitrust suit (→ 12).

7. Wimbledon: Australian Norman Brookes becomes first non-British winner, 6-4, 6-2, 6-2 over Arthur Gore; May Sutton over Dorothea Chamber 6-1, 6-4.

12. East Africa: German colonial office establishes regulations for physical punishment of natives.

12. Ohio: 23 brick and lumber trust men get jail terms for antitrust violations (→ 8/3).

19. Korea: Emperor abdicates as riots plague Seoul; crown prince reigns (→ 25).

22. California: Fifty dead in Columbia steamer wreck off coast of Eureka.

28. Russia, Japan sign treaty protecting sea-lions and seals in common waters (→ 30).

29. Idaho:"Big Bill" Haywood and two other labor leaders acquitted on charges of conspiracy to murder Idaho Gov. Steunenberg.

30. Filipinos elect first legislature (→ 10/16).

30. Russia, Japan sign accord guaranteeing equal access to Chinese trade (→ 10/8).

30. Italy, Germany, Austria renew Triple Alliance for six years.

BIRTHS

12. American comedian Milton Berle.

16. American actress Barbara Stanwyck, won three Emmies.

The birth of Cubist art

Picasso's first venture into Cubism: "Les Demoiselles d'Avignon."

A band of Parisian artists are venturing into unknown territory, stepping into a three-dimensional world on a two-dimensional canvas. Pablo Picasso, Juan Gris, Georges Braque and others are rendering still lifes and human figures in shattered, geometric planes. Sensual colors and textures are gone. The painters have abandoned traditional values (beautifying or flattering their subjects) by reaching beyond tradition to primitive African and Egyptian art. They are riveted by masks and murals that derive their power from distortion. The Parisians' paintings are likewise powerful, and vaguely upsetting.

July 25. An agreement has been signed today placing Korea under full Japanese control. It is unlikely that the action will halt riots that have raged here since the Japanese-sponsored abdication of Korea's Emperor. Reprisals have been fierce (above), but hatred runs deep, and it was inflamed by The Hague's rejection earlier this month of a delegation sent to protest Korea's exclusion from the Russo-Japanese treaty.

Scouting is started by Baden-Powell

July 29. Sir Robert Baden-Powell, the celebrated British General, has recruited 12 boys from the upper class and nine lower-class boys for a two-week sojourn into the woods of Brownsea Island in Poole Harbor. The general organized the trip as a field test for his essay, "Boy Scouts: A Suggestion." The plan is to develop in the boys a sense of community service, chivalry, general physical fitness and "to help in making the rising generation, of whatever class or creed, into good citizens at home or in the colonies."

The boys, under the guidance of Baden-Powell, will be given instruction in camp and fire skills, observation and tracking, lifesaving, first aid and woodcraft. Four patrols will also compete in games to test their knowledge of the acquired skills. The idea for the Boy Scouts came from a meeting between Baden-Powell and Ernest Thompson Seton, author of "The Birch Bark Roll," which inspired the British general to write his own paper about scouting (→ 2/8/10).

Pope Pius deplores modern theology

July 4. Pope Pius X, a humble but forceful leader, struck out today at the modernism that he believes is threatening the Roman Catholic Church. He outlined his views in a papal decree, "Lamentabili."

Since he succeeded Leo XIII, Pius has become known as an extremely devout man who is close to his congregation and the common people. He continues to hear confessions at the Vatican, and he has urged Catholics to take communion frequently. Pius wants the church to be loyal to its traditions. He has questioned and even removed bishops he considers negligent, and he has renewed emphasis on the Bible.

Today's decree against modernism seems to show that the pope is continuing his battle against secular influences, which he thinks are diluting the power of the Catholic Church. In France, Pope Pius preferred to abandon church property than see it gradually taken over by the government (→ 9/7).

1907

AUGUST

Su	Mo	Tu	We	Th	Fr	Sa
				1	2	3
4	5	6	7	8	9	10
11	12	13	14	15	16	17
18	19	20	21	22	23	24
25	26	27	28	29	30	31

3. Chicago: Standard Oil gets maximum fine of $29,240,000 for accepting rebates (→ 9/8).

3. Portugal: Royal decree establishes day of rest on Sunday.

3. Kaiser Wilhelm, Czar Nicholas meet to discuss Baghdad railway and Anglo-Russian relations (→ 31).

4. Morocco: France bombs Casablanca in retaliation for murder of French citizens.→

4. French racer Lucien Petit-Breton wins Tour de France.

4. New York: Race riot rages in Harlem.

7. N.Y.: Stock prices collapse to level of March panic.

8. Russia: Zemstvo demands obligatory schooling (→ 10/21).

12. U.S. telegraph operators strike nationwide.

14. Germany: Wilhelm II, Edward VII meet at Kassel.

16. Morocco: Sultan's brother, Mulai Hafid, proclaims himself head of Morocco in Marrakesh (→ 9/9).

17. British invade Venezuela from British Guiana, demand surrender of 4,000 lbs. balata gum.

18. Germany: Women's Intl. Socialist Congress in Stuttgart denounces German militarism, colonial policy (→ 10/12).

19. Ohio: Taft opens presidential campaign in Columbus, praising Roosevelt's policies (→ 2/9/08).

24. Philadelphia: Ben Franklin, largest balloon yet, makes maiden flight.

24. New York: Singer Building, still under construction, already highest in world.

29. Quebec: Bridge across St. Lawrence collapses, drowning 80.

31. Anglo-Russian entente allies Russia with Britain against Central Powers; treaty divides Persia, recognizes Chinese control in Tibet, British rights in Afghanistan.

BIRTH

8. U.S. jazz musician Benny Carter, born Benny Lester.

Borghese is winner of 8,000-mile race

Winner Prince Borghese in Russia.

Aug 10. The greatest automobile race in history has ended with Prince Borghese of Italy finishing ahead of five competitors in the race from Peking to Paris. His Itala car sped across 8,000 miles of rugged Asian and European terrain in 62 days. He narrowly avoided trouble several times, including getting stuck in a swamp, confronting a brush fire and being stopped by a Belgian policeman who, at first, refused to believe the speeding vehicle was in the contest.

Mary Baker Eddy mentally examined

Aug 14. Mary Baker Eddy, the 86-year-old leader of the Christian Science Church, convinced examiners today that she is mentally competent to run her business affairs.

Relatives of Mrs. Eddy had filed suit asking for an accounting of her property. They acted after widespread reports that she was feeble, decrepit and controlled by "designing persons" seeking large sums of her money. In response to the suit, Mrs. Eddy conveyed her entire estate last spring to three trustees. A spokesman said that the religious leader had planned to do this even before the suit was filed.

Mrs. Eddy greeted the mental examiners today at her home in Concord, New Hampshire, and freely answered their questions about her work habits and business dealings. She said her only infirmity is a "slight deafness." The examiners, representing both Mrs. Eddy and those who filed suit, said later that they were satisfied she is mentally competent. However, it is likely that further examinations will be made (→ 12/4/10).

Richard Mansfield lost to Broadway

Aug 30. Charismatic American actor Richard Mansfield died this morning of cancer. He was 53 years old. The son of an opera singer, German-born Mansfield made his New York debut in 1882.

Mansfield had a persuasive talent, encouraging playwright Clyde Fitch to write "Beau Brummel" expressly for him. That play, about a dandy who befriends the Prince of Wales, established his reputation as a romantic rogue. In fact, he was a private man whose only overblown passion was for the theater. He introduced Shaw's "Arms and the Man" (1894) and Ibsen's "Peer Gynt" (1906) to American audiences. Mansfield played nearly all Shakespeare's tragic and comic heroes, and he would rewrite any role to show him at his best advantage.

French troops to protect Casablanca

Aug 4. Another show of force was made by France today in troubled Morocco. A small French flotilla anchored off Casablanca and troops went ashore. France took the military action after an attack on European workers just last week by Moroccan Moslems. Several people were killed, most of them Frenchmen working on the construction of the Casablanca port. Only five months ago, French troops occupied Oujda after a French doctor was assassinated in Marrakesh.

France has made little secret of its desire to control Morocco since it signed a secret treaty with Spain in 1904 to partition the country. After the Algeciras Conference, both countries were given new and wider police powers inside Morocco's borders (→ 16).

Mary Cassatt: An American in Paris

Aug 24. New York galleries are featuring works by the American painter Mary Cassatt. Miss Cassatt is American only by chance; it is a happy accident she was born in Pittsburgh, daughter of railroad barons. She inherited a life of financial ease, comfortably pursuing the oft precarious career of painting. But France has a claim on Miss Cassatt. She has lived there for 30 years, and embraces and champions French Impressionism.

Miss Cassatt emulates Degas and Monet. Her pastels and oils use a similar high color key, but the exact attention to line is her own. In her early 20's, she studied Italian primitivists, who have influenced her subject matter for the past 40 years. They concentrated on adoration scenes, and she updates them, depicting the modern madonna and child. Her mothers peacefully sew or read while their children watch quietly. Connoisseurs are delighted with the paintings. The general public seems unmoved.

Degas' "Portrait of Mary Cassatt."

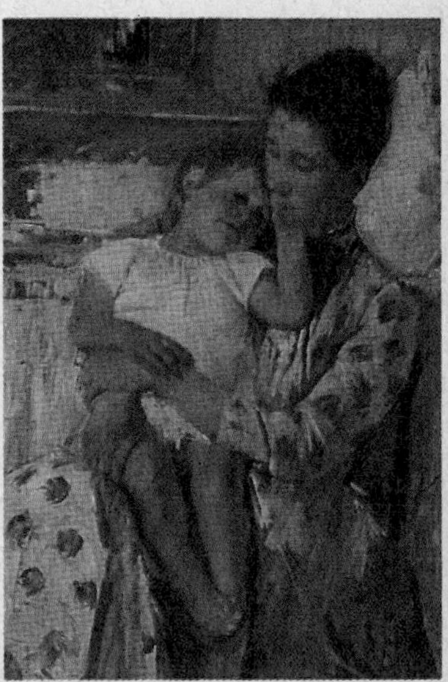

"Mother and Child" by Cassatt.

1907

SEPTEMBER

Su	Mo	Tu	We	Th	Fr	Sa
1	2	3	4	5	6	7
8	9	10	11	12	13	14
15	16	17	18	19	20	21
22	23	24	25	26	27	28
29	30					

6. Liner Lusitania leaves London on maiden voyage (→ 11).

7. Oscar Hammerstein announces plans for five opera houses in New York.

7. Russia: Cholera reports raise fear of epidemic.

7. Holland: Peace conference at The Hague rules powers must give advance declaration of war (→ 10/18).

7. Vatican: Pope Pius X recognizes validity of civil marriage.

8. New York: Investigation uncovers $100,000 Standard Oil contribution to 1904 Roosevelt campaign (→ 11/6).

9. Spain sends 7,000 troops to Morocco (→ 10/5).

10. Russia: Jews massacred at Kishinev (→ 2/13/08).

11. New York: Lusitania arrives from Queenstown, Ireland, setting new transatlantic record of five days, 54 minutes (→ 10/11).

11. Miss Lucy Gaston arrives in N.Y. to campaign against cigarette smoking (→ 1/20/07).

14. Vatican, Germany agree on religious instruction in German Poland; state will control non-religious teachings.

17. South Africa: Cape Parliament dissolved (→ 10/12/08).

17. Austria: Intl. miners congress at Salzburg split between Christian and Social Democratic unionists.

18. Belgium: Roman sarcophagus discovered in Liege.

25. New Zealand gains nominal autonomy as dominion within British Empire.

30. China: French priests killed by anti-foreign demonstrators; American lives spared.

DEATHS

4. Norwegian composer Edvard Grieg, drew on legacy of folk music (*6/15/1843).

7. French poet Sully Prudhomme (*3/16/1839).

22. American agricultural chemist W.C. Atwater (*5/3/1844).

Sun Yat-sen society attracting strength

Dr. Sun Yat-sen.

Sept 8. The Kuomintang, a secret society dedicated to overthrowing the Manchu rulers of China, is drawing many Chinese students away from more moderate political groups. The new nationalist group stems from the Tung Meng Hui, a revolutionary league founded two years ago in Japan by Sun Yat-sen, a Chinese doctor who has read the works of Karl Marx and other political theorists. The Kuomintang seeks to create a Chinese national state in the form of a republic, and advocates land redistribution (→ 12/28/11).

Riots drive 2,000 Chinese from homes

Sept 11. More than 2,000 Chinese were driven from their homes in Vancouver, British Columbia, last night during an anti-Oriental demonstration staged by some 10,000 laboring men. The attack was a continuation of recent demonstrations against Oriental laborers in San Francisco and elsewhere along the West Coast.

Police in Vancouver were unable to quell the riot for several hours, but they finally got the situation under control and made some arrests. In addition to driving the Chinese from their homes, the labor agitators caused about $5,000 worth of property damage. Laborers and others in British Columbia have repeatedly protested the government's encouragement of immigration of Orientals and other foreigners to that area.

1907

OCTOBER

Su	Mo	Tu	We	Th	Fr	Sa
		1	2	3	4	5
6	7	8	9	10	11	12
13	14	15	16	17	18	19
20	21	22	23	24	25	26
27	28	29	30	31		

1. German army buys Count Zeppelin's dirigible.

1. Unknown Chinese republic of Iman found on Russian soil near Vladivostok; strange laws include burial alive for stealing sables.

4. President Roosevelt makes public appeal for larger Navy.

5. Cuba: Rebels attack Americans in Havana (→ 8/1/08).

5. British agitator Keir Hardie reported fomenting rebellion in India (→ 11/6/13).

5. Morocco: Pretender Mulai Hafid seizes sultan's supplies; coup expected (→ 14).

8. U.S. Vice President Taft reasserts desire to keep China's doors open to free trade.

11. Lusitania breaks record again, returning to Europe in four days (→ 11/16).

12. Detroit: Chicago Nationals take World Series in 6th game 2-0 over Detroit.

12. Germany: Social Democrat Karl Liebknecht gets one and a half years in prison for publication of "Militarism and Antimilitarism."

14. Morocco: Mulai Hafid, sultan of South, reported gaining strength throughout country (→ 6/21/08).

16. Manila: Taft opens Filipino Assembly, declares independence must wait (→ 2/2/16).

16. N.Y.: Wall Street plunges into panic as Augustus Heringe and Charles Moore fail to corner United Copper (→ 11/4).

19. London: Queen Victoria's letters published.

20. New York Socialist William E. Walling arrested in Russia (→ 21).

21. Russia: Third Duma reported to be conservative, willing to cooperate with Stolypin (→ 11/11).

27. Germany: Maximilian Harden indicted for libeling Prince Philip Eulenberg.

29. Ottoman sultan complains to Western powers of Bulgarian, Greek agitation in Macedonia (→ 2/14/08).

Ringling Brothers buy Barnum Bailey

Oct 22. In London yesterday, the Ringling Brothers bought out Barnum & Bailey for $410,000. The move gives the Ringlings a virtual monopoly on the circus business throughout the United States.

The brothers, Alf, Al, Charles, Otto and John, who hail from Baraboo, Wisconsin, had competed with Barnum & Bailey for over a decade. On one occasion, both shows appeared simultaneously in neighboring towns, whereupon the rivals divided territories on mutual terms. Barnum & Bailey retains its name and management. Its famed property at Bridgeport, Connecticut, will be used by the Ringlings at their discretion. The companies have already pastured their 900 horses together for the winter.

Plaza, grand luxe hotel, has opened

Oct 1. New York's Plaza Hotel, described by one of the speakers as the "most beautiful in the world," opened last night with a gala celebration dinner attended by a flock of city notables. The festivities took place in the new hotel's main-floor, small banquet hall. Considered one of the prettiest in the city, the hall is decorated with mirrors hung with brocaded, old-rose satin and, last night, lighted by innumerable electric chandeliers.

Plaza Hotel from Fifth Avenue.

1907

NOVEMBER

Su	Mo	Tu	We	Th	Fr	Sa
					1	2
3	4	5	6	7	8	9
10	11	12	13	14	15	16
17	18	19	20	21	22	23
24	25	26	27	28	29	30

3. N.Y.: Annual auto show opens at Madison Sq. Garden.

4. New York: J.P. Morgan locks N.Y. bankers in his library, solicits $25 mil. to prop up stock market and failing banks; financial panic ends (→ 6).

4. U.S.: Govt. commission forecasts timber shortage in 20 years.

4. Floods in European vineyards promise increase in American wine exports.

6. U.S. Steel board of directors agrees to purchase Tennessee Coal, Iron and Railroad Co. (→ 4/11/08).

8. New discovery allows reproduction of photographs by cable.

9. American astronomer Prof. Lowell announces Saturn's rings are falling in.

11. St. Petersburg: Third Russian Duma opens (→ 26).

13. Washington: Conference of Central American States convenes to develop arbitration procedures for intl. conflict.

13. Vatican: Pope Pius X warns excessive liberty will corrupt American youth.

16. U.S.: Oklahoma becomes 46th state.

16. London: Mauretania sails on maiden voyage (→ 22).

18. New York: Caruso opens Metropolitan Opera season in "Adriana Lecouvreur."

20. Railway workers strike in India.

23. Russians reported bitter over reparation payments to Japan.

26. Stockholm: August Strindberg inaugurates theater with staging of his play "The Pelican."

26. Prussian government in Poland introduces bill to allow expropriation of land by state.

26. St. Petersburg: Duma lends support to czar, claims he has renounced autocracy (→ 12/31).

30. Philadelphia: Army football team shut out by Navy 6-0 at Franklin Field.

Rules of war are renewed at The Hague

Plenary session of the peace conference at The Hague.

Oct 18. An international peace conference at The Hague ended today without an armaments agreement, but the conventions of war were renewed with 11 new rules added. The new provisions concern the status of both neutral countries and merchant ships during war and call for a declaration of war at the onset of hostilities. The original conventions, or rules of war, were adopted at the 1899 conference at The Hague. Delegates from all 44 countries thanked President Roosevelt for initiating this current conference.

Nine balloons in race from St. Louis

Oct 24. The German balloon Pommern has been declared the winner of the James Gordon Bennett Cup. A $2,500 cash prize went, along with the cup, to the pilot, Oscar Erbslohan, and his assistant, H.H. Clayton. Second prize of $1,000 went to the French balloon, L'Ile de France. The contest committee for this second James Gordon Bennett international balloon race determined that the Germans covered 876,750 miles in an air line from St. Louis to the landing spot near Asbury Park. The Germans also won third place. The Dusseldorf finished 70.75 miles behind the French. And the American balloons, the St. Louis and the America, placed fourth and fifth.

Dirigibles vie for the Gordon Bennett Cup at St. Louis.

Treaty cedes Congo to Belgian state

Nov 28. Copies of the Transfer Treaty of the Congo were distributed to members of the Belgian Parliament last night, and after review, the treaty was signed by Prime Minister M. De Trooz, placing into law the conveyance of the Congo from King Leopold II's control to the Belgian government.

The action follows in the wake of international criticism of the king for tolerating brutal treatment of native Congolese. Allegations have circulated that the king, whose claims to the area in 1884 were recognized at the Berlin conference, disregarded the indigenous Africans, using them only as a source of cheap labor.

The official transfer of the African property will transpire on January 1, 1908, according to the provisions in the contract. A colonial commission of 17 was appointed to investigate the resources of the Congolese territory. Among those known are cobalt, gold, copper, iron ore, rubber and silver (→ 8/19/08).

William James, his view of Pragmatism

Nov 3. Pity Professor William James, whose philosophy of Pragmatism is not understood but appreciated. James released a paper today suggesting that he prefers a well-informed, unenthusiastic public to an ill-informed, enthusiastic one. His work published earlier this year, "Pragmatism: A New Name for Some Old Ways of Thinking," is embraced in ignorance at every strata of society. Doctors to dishwashers talk calmly of mastering the universe pragmatically.

James concedes his philosophy stresses empiricism, relating theory to facts and actions, but there is a bit more to it. How many people can understand much less accept that truth is "only the expedient in our way of thinking"? And how many would agree it is futile trying to understand God, should such a Being exist? Last spring, James resigned from Harvard's Chair of Philosophy to devote more time to explaining the subtler points of his philosophy. ▷

Sister ships contend for Atlantic record

Cunard liner Mauretania, named for the ancient Roman land in N. Africa.

Nov 22. The Cunard liner Mauretania set a new speed record for steamship travel yesterday, with a one-day run of 624 knots.

The Mauretania is expected to better that record today, since she is steaming toward New York at a speed that should enable her to do 635 knots in a day. The English ship thus has wrested the record from her sister ship, the Lusitania, which set the one-day mark of 618 knots just last month. If the Mauretania continues her pace, she bids to break the Lusitania's record of four days and 20 hours for a transatlantic voyage, also established last month. New speed records for ocean travel have become almost commonplace since the Lusitania's maiden voyage in September. That voyage won back for England the record held by Germany for the previous five years (→ 2/10/08).

World's first helicopter flight in France

Nov 13. Paul Cornu, a French inventor, today achieved the first flight of an aircraft that can lift vertically off the ground, but the flight fell far short of expectations.

The helicopter, which has a 24-horsepower engine driving horizontally mounted, twin propellers, lifted off several times, but only for a few seconds. Once airborne, the machine proved to be uncontrollable. Cornu's attempt was based on the performance of a model built on the design of an unmanned helicopter tested several years ago by Colonel Charles Renard. One inspiration for the effort is the fictional round-the-world helicopter flight made by Jules Verne's hero, Robur le Conquerant.

Paul Cornu's helicopter, ready for takeoff in France.

1907

DECEMBER

Su	Mo	Tu	We	Th	Fr	Sa
1	2	3	4	5	6	7
8	9	10	11	12	13	14
15	16	17	18	19	20	21
22	23	24	25	26	27	28
29	30	31				

2. Spain, France agree to enforce Moroccan measures adopted in Algeciras in 1906.

5. Germans announce unease over influx of U.S. immigrants.

6. Explosion kills 350 miners at Monongah, W.V. (→ 19).

8. Sweden's Oscar II dies; son Gustav V succeeds.

11. British reported to fear Japanese competition in trade.

15. Washington: Despite restrictions, it is reported that Japanese immigration doubled last year (→ 2/24/08).

15. Persia: Liberal Premier Nasir ul-Mulk imprisoned in shah's coup.

19. Penn.: Jacob's Creek mine blast kills 250 (→ 28).

20. N.Y.: Immigrants reported to bring infectious diseases.

28. Berlin: Germans indict U.S. for carelessness in mine.

BIRTH

29. Robert C. Weaver, 1st black American to serve in Cabinet, under F.D.R.

DEATH

17. British physicist William Thomson, Lord Kelvin (*6/26/1824).

Cultural events of 1907

Literature: Gorky's "Mother"; Strindberg's "The Ghost Sonata"; Conrad's "The Secret Agent"; J.M. Synge's "Playboy of the Western World."

Religion, Academia: Henri Bergson's "Creative Evolution"; William James' "Pragmatism"; United Methodist Church founded in Britain; Freud and Jung meet; Maria Montessori opens nursery schools in Italy.

Music: Mahler's "Symphony of a Thousand"; Franz Lehar's "The Merry Widow"; opening of N.Y.'s "Ziegfeld Follies."

The Arts: Marc Chagall's "Peasant Women"; Picasso's "Demoiselles d'Avignon"; Henri Rousseau's "The Snake Charmer"; 1st Cubist exhibition in Paris; slow-motion film invented by August Musger.

167 of 169 in Duma are sent to prison

Dec 31. A Russian court has found 167 delegates of the dissolved first Duma guilty of treason and has sentenced them to three months imprisonment. The defendants, most of whom are members of the Constitutional Democratic Party (also known as Kadets), signed the Vyborg Manifesto, a revolutionary document calling on Russians not to pay taxes or serve in the army. The sentence carries with it the loss of all political rights.

The first Duma was opened in May 1906 in the wake of the revolutionary turmoil of 1905. Czar Nicholas II dissolved the assembly in July 1906 in order to halt agrarian reform measures. The second Duma, even more hostile to the czar, was also dissolved. The third Duma, which is more moderate in composition, opened last month (→ 4/4/08).

Nobel Prize goes to Rudyard Kipling

Dec 10. The Nobel Prize for literature was awarded today to a writer whose nearest claim to a formal education is travel on three continents. The winner is Rudyard Kipling. His passport says he is British, but it was his life in colonial India that inspired most of his work. Kipling began his literary career by writing poems. One of the best known is "Gunga Din." Later, while living in the United States, he wrote his most famous stories, "The Jungle Book," "Captains Courageous" and "Kim." Kipling was born in Bombay, grew up in London and returned to India to work as a newspaper writer and editor.

Great White Fleet shows U.S. power

Dec 19. The Japanese today welcomed President Roosevelt's announcement that the Great White Fleet would tour the Pacific Ocean during a round-the-world voyage and said the ships would receive a warm reception if they visit Japan.

Though the voyage of the American fleet is intended to be of a friendly nature, it is also meant to be a demonstration of American strength and resolve in the face of increased Japanese naval power. The United States has shown an increasing interest in the Pacific since acquiring the Philippines, Hawaii, Guam and parts of Samoa over the last several years.

President Roosevelt has tried to balance Japanese and Russian naval power in the Far East since negotiating an end to the Russo-Japanese War three years ago, for which he received the Nobel Peace Prize.

The Great White Fleet will sail around the world.

Japanese Privy Councilor Viscount Kaneko said that he recently told ex-President Grover Cleveland that since America's Atlantic side had been fully explored and commercially developed, it was natural that America should turn toward the Pacific Ocean and that "commercial interests once developed, the natural consequence is that warships will follow the commercial carriers. Americans are largely interested in the Pacific; why, therefore, should not that include maintaining peace in the Pacific." Admiral Togo said that if the ships reach Japan, "We will greet the men as friends" (→ 8/20/08).

Determined suffragettes begin their American campaign

Dec 31. Playing to an audience of several hundred men and only a scattering of women, American suffragettes opened their campaign for the vote today with a rally in downtown New York City.

As frigid winds whipped through Madison Square, leaders of the movement addressed the outdoor gathering as they stood on an improvised bandstand, scarcely larger than a packing case, near a big red sign that read "Stop! Danger!"

"You don't know the importance of the ballot," Mrs. Boorman Wells, an English suffragette, told the crowd.

"Yes, we do," the men chorused.

Warming to the subject, Mrs. Wells remarked: "Do you think it would be possible for women to make a worse mess of politics than the men have?"

"No! No!" the men cried.

Leaders of the movement were pleased at the relatively large turnout of men.

"We have been wanting a long time to talk to the men, and that is why we are here," said Mrs. Christine Ross Barker.

"Goodbye, Sis," one man shouted.

"Goodbye, young man," Mrs. Barker said, good-naturedly. "Come again."

During the speeches today, several suffragettes moved through the crowd, asking for signatures on a petition urging the United States Congress to open the way to voting rights for women. Many of the men as well as a few women readily signed the petition (→ 4/06/08).

Women's Political Union members on 29th Street in New York.

Cultural life offers variety this year

Literature and drama were quiet and introspective in 1907. A nonfiction work set the tone. Henri Bergson's "L'Evolution Creatrice" ("Creative Evolution") examines Darwin's theories, concluding that the human experience is too complex for changes to be predicted mathematically. The French philosopher is well trained in mathematics, but he relied heavily on intuition to form his thesis. Russian Maxim Gorky is known for vociferous works: The drama "The Lower Depths" (1902) was a fierce attack on the upper class. This year, his novel "Mother" is more subdued. He describes the hopeless, silent lives of Russian laborers.

George Bernard Shaw examines hypocrisy in his stage production "Major Barbara," while Swedish writer August Strindberg examines the stage itself. His play "The Ghost Sonata" is an expressive, fantastic revolt against theater's current so-called realism.

Hungarian Franz Lehar's experimental opera, "The Merry Widow," came to New York this year. The work thumbs its nose at traditional opera, featuring waltz tunes and the Parisian can-can. Florenz Ziegfeld in turn thumbed his nose at sophistication, draping young women in extravagant garb and dubbing the event "Ziegfeld Follies." Finally, readers thumbing the San Francisco Chronicle are rebelling on Sundays. It is the only day of the week they cannot follow the foibles of a comic strip character named "Augustus Mutt."

Charles Dana Gibson's "Gibson Girl," a model of femininity.

1908

JANUARY

Su	Mo	Tu	We	Th	Fr	Sa
			1	2	3	4
5	6	7	8	9	10	11
12	13	14	15	16	17	18
19	20	21	22	23	24	25
26	27	28	29	30	31	

1. New York: Austrian composer Gustav Mahler makes U.S. conducting debut in "Tristan und Isolde" at Metropolitan Opera.

2. New York City births for 1907 total 125,126.

6. C. Arthur Pearson buys London Times from Walter family.

8. Subway linking Brooklyn and Manhattan opens.

9. Berlin: Count Zeppelin announces plans for airship to carry 100 passengers.

9. Somaliland: Italians report country under siege by Abyssinians.

11. New York: Coloratura soprano Mme. Tetrazzini arrives for U.S. debut (→ 3/30).

12. Paris: Wireless message sent long-distance for first time from Eiffel Tower.

14. Pennsylvania: Theater fire in Boyertown kills 150.

16. Haitian revolutionaries seize two towns.

17. New York: Times Tower picks up wireless message from Puerto Rico.

20. New York: Sullivan ordinance bars women from smoking in public facilities (→ 22).

22. Three submarines travel from Newport, R.I., to New York in record time of 17.5 hours.

25. Five San Francisco scientists photograph corona of sun.

27. New York Police Dept. deputizes dogs for duty.

27. Austrian government announces it will build railway to Salonika, European Turkey.

31. Portuguese King Carlos, alarmed by widespread revolt, plans severe measures to save monarchy (→ 2/1).

BIRTHS

9. French writer Simone de Beauvoir, author of "The Second Sex" (†4/14/86).

15. American physicist Edward Teller, developed hydrogen bomb.

Farman makes first long circular flight

Onlookers celebrate Henri Farman's landing near Paris.

Jan 13. Henri Farman, the French aeronaut, has won the $10,000 prize offered for the first heavier-than-air flight to cover a circular route of at least a kilometer. Flying a 300-pound aircraft powered by a 50-horsepower engine, he took off from a field at Issy, five miles southwest of Paris, today and easily fulfilled the requirement, flying well over a kilometer at a speed of 24 miles an hour and an altitude of 25 to 30 feet. The flight is being acclaimed as proof that heavier-than-air ships will replace steerable balloons for air travel (→ 3/21).

Georgia introduces Prohibition law

Jan 1. Georgia has surrendered. The white banner of Prohibition waves high, John Barleycorn stands banished and for the second time in its history, Georgia is dry. "Death watches" were kept last night in many Atlanta saloons. As the ominous hour of midnight rang out, glasses were lifted and emptied, and the crowds forlornly filed into the streets. Soon the lights were out and the saloons had passed into history. Thus is fulfilled the dream of the founders of the Georgia colony, who outlawed rum and slavery. But they proved unable to enforce either provision.

Surgery to replace diseased organs

Jan 1. Medical science will someday make it possible for surgeons to replace a diseased organ with a healthy one transplanted from another human being, Simon Flexner, head of the Rockefeller Institute for Medical Research, predicted today. In a paper written for the American Association for the Advancement of Science, Flexner said that his success in transplanting arteries between animals has pioneered surgical techniques that bring closer the day when hearts and other organs will be transplanted into humans. "No effort should be spared to reach this goal" he said.

Jan 27. Gladys Vanderbilt was married today in N.Y. to Hungarian Count Laszlo Szechenyi. An ostentatious brougham decoyed reporters while the happy couple slipped away in a small touring car.

No smoking: You've gone too far, lady

Jan 22. The Sullivan smoking act was invoked for the first time within a day of its passage when Katie Mulcahey was arrested early this morning after lighting up a cigarette in the Bowery in downtown New York City. When the arresting officer spied Miss Mulcahey strike a match on a house wall he shouted, "Madame, you musn't! What would Aiderman Sullivan say?"

"But I am, and I don't know," she replied. Later, in night court, she fumed, "I've got as much right to smoke as you have. I never heard of this new law and I don't want to hear about it. No man shall dictate to me." Magistrate Kernochan nonetheless did, sending the young lady to a cell when she was unable to pay the $5 fine. She took her cigarettes with her.

Actress Fanny Ward takes a puff.

It's possible there has been a misunderstanding, or neither the policeman nor the magistrate have had time to inhale the finer points of the ordinance, which does not make it an offense for women to smoke. Rather it enjoins restaurant and hotel managers to forbid such unladylike acts in such public places. How, then, was last night's scene beyond the pale?

At the meeting which debated the proposal, Alderman Doul said it was unconstitutional and warned of a feminine call-to-arms. Has Miss Mulcahey, in striking that match, also fired the first shot? (→ 2/28)

1908

FEBRUARY

Su	Mo	Tu	We	Th	Fr	Sa
						1
2	3	4	5	6	7	8
9	10	11	12	13	14	15
16	17	18	19	20	21	22
23	24	25	26	27	28	29

1. Lisbon: Portugal's King Carlos and crown prince assassinated (→ 2).

3. U.S. Supreme Court rules union-sponsored boycotts illegal, applies Sherman Antitrust Act to labor as well as capital (→ 10/15/14).

8. Miners Charles Russell and E.R. Monett navigate Grand Canyon in a rowboat.

8. Alarmed by Turkish penetration of Persia, Russia displays military might on Turko-Persian border.

9. Pres. Roosevelt denies he is supplying Taft with federal funds for campaign (→ 6/18).

10. London conference decision doubles transatlantic passenger rates (→ 6/3).

13. Berlin: Jewish Relief League reports Russian czar praises pogrom leaders as heroes.

14. Russia, Britain threaten action in Macedonia if peace does not come soon.

16. Japanese Ambassador Baron Kogoro Takahira arrives in U.S. (→ 24).

18. Washington: American merchants complain of Japan's advance in Manchuria.

18. American Thomas flyer reaches Toledo, Ohio, with 29-mile lead in N.Y.-to-Paris race (→ 3/1).

20. Upon receiving phonograph from Thomas Edison, Tolstoy announces he will send recording of his voice in return.

24. Japanese officially agree to restrict immigration to U.S.

24. French Parliament demands action in Morocco, protection for troops, or withdrawal.

24. New York: Henry Ludlowe opens in "Richard III."

27. Forty-sixth star added to U.S. flag, signifying Oklahoma's admission to statehood.

28. New York: Columbia Prof. Meyulan insists deleterious effects of tobacco are greatly exaggerated.

28. Tehran: Assassin attempts to murder shah of Persia.

Assassin strikes Portugal's King and heir

Feb 1. In Lisbon today, assassins succeeded in killing the King and Crown Prince of Portugal, but they failed if they were trying to start a revolution. King Carlos was shot twice in the back and Prince Luiz was shot at point-blank range with a rifle. Both were killed instantly as they were riding in a carriage near the Home Office. One of the gunmen also tried to assassinate the Queen, but he was stopped by a guard with a sword.

"After the assassination the crowd went absolutely crazy with fright," one eyewitness said. "Numbers of women and children were trampled under foot and some were seriously injured. The police fired at random." The ringleader of the assassins, who was shot dead, was later identified as a sergeant in the Portuguese cavalry.

After the shootings, Premier Franco, who is the dictator and real center of power in Portugal, vowed to preserve the monarchy and prevent any further violence. Franco as well as royalist splinter groups closed ranks behind their new King, 19-year-old Don Manuel, another son of the slain King Carlos.

Prince Manuel inherits the throne.

100,000 use tunnel to Jersey first day

Feb 25. The opening of railroad service under the Hudson River between New York and New Jersey is an enormous success, with 100,000 passengers having made the trip in the first day of operation, officials of the Hudson and Manhattan Railroad declare. Hundreds waited on line to board the first train, which left the 19th Street station in Manhattan at midnight and arrived in Hoboken 10.5 minutes later.

Service was started officially by President Theodore Roosevelt, who pressed a button in the White House to turn on electric power for the line. Among those making the trip on the first day were Edward Harriman and Cornelius Vanderbilt, who were unable to find seats because of the crowds. The new rail service is three times faster than the ferry trip across the Hudson.

Edison wins rights to film projector

Feb 11. Led by Thomas Edison, the major film-producing companies in the United States reached a patent rights agreement today that they say will keep competitors out of the business permanently. The agreement ends a long series of suits and countersuits arising from Edison's claims that other companies were infringing the patent for the motion picture camera, which he was awarded in 1891.

The Edison kinetoscope.

Thousands watch racers leave for Paris

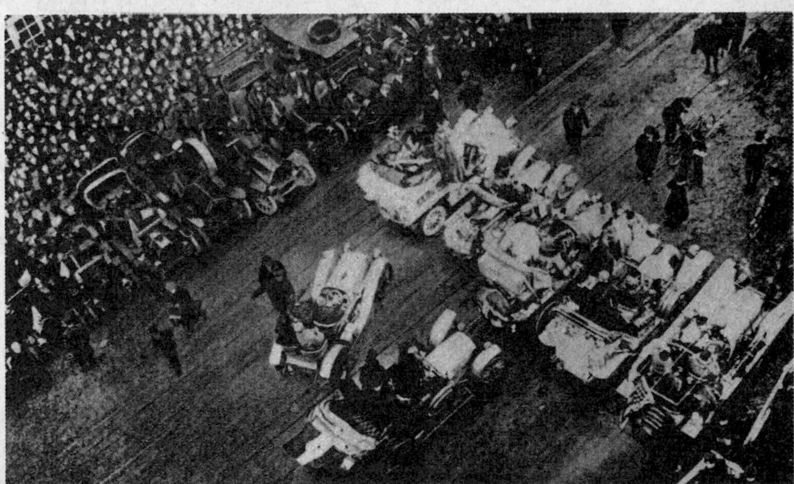

Six drivers rev up their engines at the starting line.

Feb 12. A carnival atmosphere prevailed in Times Square for the start of the New York-to-Paris automobile race. Before the day ended, nearly a quarter-million people saw the six cars, three French, one Italian, one German and one American, embark on the first leg of their grueling trip.

The American car, with Montague Roberts at the wheel, remained in fourth place heading out of the city but moved into the lead near Hudson, New York, where most of the cars had to be dug out of snow drifts. The Zust, the Italian car that set the early pace, gave way to Roberts as the roads became snow-slick. The De Dion of France sped into third place during the first 30 miles, but its crew stopped for luncheon and passing observers assumed it had broken down.

After nine hours of driving, Roberts' car reached Hudson, 116 miles on the road to Albany. But the drivers knew they were on a venture covering some 20,000 miles and were not overly concerned about the first-day standings. They were cheered on by thousands more who lined the route on the way (→ 18).

1908

MARCH

Su	Mo	Tu	We	Th	Fr	Sa
1	2	3	4	5	6	7
8	9	10	11	12	13	14
15	16	17	18	19	20	21
22	23	24	25	26	27	28
29	30	31				

1. New York-to-Paris racers mired in Iowa mud (→ 26).

2. New York: Committee of the Russian Republican Administration founded.

2. London: International conference on arms reduction opens (→ 6/9).

2. Paris: Gabriel Lippmann introduces new three-dimensional color photography at Academy of Sciences.

3. Washington: Government declares open war on U.S. anarchists (→ 5/23/09).

4. New York board of education bars whipping in schools.

4. France notifies signatories of Algeciras it will send troops to Chaouia, Morocco (→ 6/21).

9. New York Gov. Hughes insists overcrowding in N.Y.C. causes crime and wretchedness.

13. Jerusalem's inhabitants see first automobile, owned by Charles Glidden of Boston.

14. Soccer reported growing at rapid pace in U.S. colleges.

16. China releases Japanese steamship Tatsu Maru (→ 5/1).

19. Maryland bars Christian Scientists from practicing without medical diplomas.

20. New York: Beethoven's "Fidelio" opens at the Metropolitan Opera.

21. Frenchman Henri Farman carries passenger in biplane for first time ever.

25. Italy: Wilhelm II pays official visit to Italy's king in Venice.

26. American Thomas flyer sails for Alaska at head of pack in N.Y.-to-Paris race (→ 4/9).

30. Home rule for Ireland passes British House of Commons; House of Lords sure to veto (→ 1/30/12).

31. Indianapolis: 250,000 coal miners strike to await wage adjustment (→ 11/13/09).

BIRTH

23. American actress Joan Crawford (†5/10/1977).

Brava: New contract for Mme. Tetrazzini

March 30. Impresario Oscar Hammerstein played his ace today: He signed the great Italian coloratura soprana Luisa Tetrazzini to a five-year contract. Madame Tetrazzini made a triumphal tour of Europe before being enticed to New York. Hammerstein has challenged the Metropolitan Opera's supremacy with his newly built Manhattan Opera House, presenting such stars as Nelly Melba, Mary Garden and John MacCormack. Can the regal Metropolitan trump these aces?

Mme. Luisa Tetrazzini.

Autoists asking for licensing of vehicles

March 28. Automobilists from around the nation lobbied Congress today, supporting a bill calling for federal registration and licensing of vehicles. Passage of the bill does not seem likely, however.

The American Automobile Association and National Association of Automobile Manufacturers assigned a Columbia law professor to present their arguments. Charles Terry likened the country's federally controlled waterways to its dirt roads, citing both as sources of interstate transit. He argued that roads and their travelers should experience similar regulations. Auto enthusiasts would prefer federal control to the sometimes capricious laws of the many states. A few states tax autos for simply crossing their borders.

1908

APRIL

Su	Mo	Tu	We	Th	Fr	Sa
			1	2	3	4
5	6	7	8	9	10	11
12	13	14	15	16	17	18
19	20	21	22	23	24	25
26	27	28	29	30		

2. Populist Party offers Thomas Watson for president, Samuel Williams for v.p. (→ 5/10).

4. Russian czar dissolves recalcitrant Finnish Parliament (→ 9/9).

6. Carnegie Foundation announces teacher exchange between U.S. and Prussia.

6. Germany: Reichstag authorizes women to form political associations (→ 8/15).

8. Roosevelt announces injunction requiring equal railway accommodations for Negroes in South (→ 6/22).

8. Haitians ask U.S. help in quelling civil strife (→ 11/20).

11. U.S., Canada agree on fishing boundaries in Great Lakes.

11. Standard Oil found in restraint of trade under Sherman Act, ousted from Tennessee (→ 5/1).

13. De Dion and Zust racers leave for Japan, with American Thomas flyer trailing between Alaska and Seattle (→ 5/15).

14. Turkish sultan arrives in Washington bearing silk carpets for Pres. Roosevelt.

14. German Chancellor von Bulow and Italian Foreign Minister Tittoni agree to extend diplomatic relations.

14. Danish Parliament grants vote to men and women over 25, barring those supported by the state (→ 10/4).

20. T.P. Morrissey wins 12th Boston Marathon in 2:25:43.

23. Guatemala: President Cabrera executes 18 dissidents accused of plotting coup.

23. Germany: North Sea and Baltic Conventions signed, guaranteeing status quo on coastlines.

27. Austria: First Intl. Congress of Psychoanalysis opens.

29. U.S. Steel begins producing all-metal auto wheels.

30. Mass.: 267 towns vote in local Prohibition (→ 5/26).

BIRTH

5. American actress Bette Davis.

Doctor stitches up stabbed heart

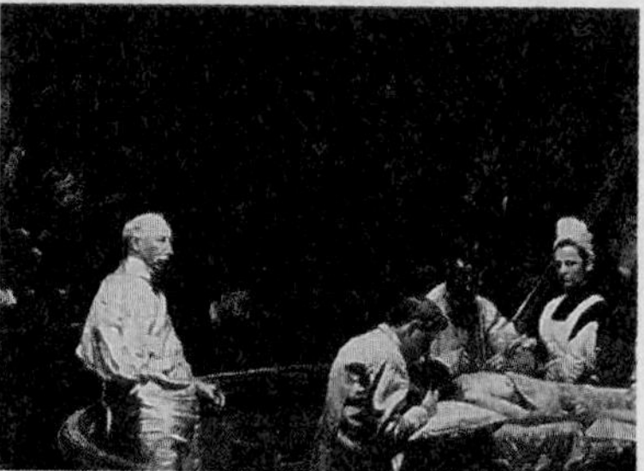

"The Agnew Clinic," by Eakins.

April 5. Surgeons at St. Joseph's Hospital in Yonkers, New York, saved the life of a young man early today by a daring operation during which they sewed up a stab wound in his heart. Robert Inglis, 23, of Yonkers was stabbed in an argument resulting from a street altercation at 1:30 a.m., as he was returning home with friends. He was taken to the hospital, where Drs. Edward Duffy and Philip McCormick removed two of his ribs and took three stitches in his heart and two in the layer of fat around it to repair the stab wound. Inglis awoke later in the day, asked for a drink of water and told his nurse that he was feeling strong. Such an operation succeeds only once every 14 years, the surgeons report.

Japanese learning how to grow taller

April 14. A program designed by the Japanese government to increase the height of its citizens is said to be showing remarkable success. K. Aishima, General Manager of an Osaka newspaper, described the prodigious feat to American reporters while visiting newspapers in New York City.

According to Aishima, about 15 years ago the government was disturbed by its people's lack of stature. It decided one cause was excessive sitting. Since then, schools have encouraged boys and girls to stand more often. The army too has made strides, building gymnasiums and starting a more rigorous course of physical culture. There is a feeling in Japan now, Aishima asserts, that the present generation is two inches taller than the last. The Japanese hope this trend will continue.

U.S. car in Paris race is leading in Alaska

April 9. Heavy snow and hail in a storm that raged for three days and powerful winds on the ocean slowed the progress of the American car in the international automobile race from New York to Paris.

The American Thomas vehicle arrived in Valdez, Alaska, on the steamer Santa Clara two days behind schedule. Still, on the 58th day of the grueling race, the Americans had traversed 6,036 miles, many more than any of their competitors.

The De Dion of France and the Zust of Italy were next with 4,090 miles each, followed by the Protos of Germany with 2,616. On the second day out from Seattle, homing pigeons, attempting to bring back news of the Americans' progress, were attacked and killed by gulls.

All 300 residents of Cordova, Alaska, were out in force to greet the American racers when they arrived there, and an additional 700 persons came to watch as their car continued. Huge snowbanks lined the streets in Valdez, presaging some difficult travel ahead for the leaders (→ 13).

The perils of the roadway.

Herbert Asquith is British Premier

April 8. Chancellor of the Exchecquer Herbert H. Asquith will succeed the ailing Sir Henry Campbell-Bannerman as Prime Minister. David Lloyd George, currently President of the Board of Trade, is rumored to be Asquith's choice as the new chancellor of the exchecquer. Most Liberals, with the exception of the Laborite and Irish Nationalist segments of the party, are pleased with the choice of Asquith.

Lord Asquith.

Yale consents to business courses

April 1. As business practices become increasingly complicated and students need more knowledge of the field than ever before, Yale University has announced that it will supply the current demand for business and commerce courses by offering 26 electives in the graduate school next year. These will be given by a new Department of Business Methods, and will include subjects such as banking, insurance, railroads and commerce.

Some of the courses already announced in the Yale curriculum are "Commerce and the Commercial Policy in the 19th Century," "Corporation Economies," "Morals in Modern Business," "Problems in Business Management," "Trade Statistics" and "Forest Management Abroad and in the U.S." Several courses on the commercial side of practical forestry will be given by Gifford Pinchot, the National Forester.

1908

MAY

Su	Mo	Tu	We	Th	Fr	Sa
					1	2
3	4	5	6	7	8	9
10	11	12	13	14	15	16
17	18	19	20	21	22	23
24	25	26	27	28	29	30
31						

1. U.S.: Hepburn Law activated, barring railways from handling products in which they hold an interest (→ 11/20).

1. Japan asks Britain's aid in resolving Chinese boycott following Tatsu Maru incident.

4. Colombia reinforces border guard, fearing invasion by Venezuela, Panama.

5. U.S. Circuit Court judge places moving pictures under copyright laws; royalties to be paid.

5. A. Pickens rides Stone Street to win in Kentucky Derby.

8. New York: Ellis Island cuts 100 employees due to falling immigration rates.

9. London: Winston Churchill elected to House of Commons.

10. Socialist Party picks Eugene Debs for pres., Benjamin Hanford for v.p. (→ 6/18).

12. N.Y.: Child Labor Assn. of Club Women formed (→ 28).

13. Roosevelt opens White House Conservation Conference in Washington (→ 6/8).

15. Paris: Claude Monet destroys "unsatisfactory" paintings valued at $100,000.

15. De Dion and Zust racers withdraw from N.Y.-to-Paris auto race (→ 20).

19. Paris: Feodor Chaliapin opens in "Boris Gudonov."

19. Ohio: Dr. John O. Brien discovers cause of paresis (partial paralysis), suggests cure.

20. French driver St. Chaffray corners all gas in Vladivostok, demands spot in Thomas flyer (→ 7/1).

22. Wright bros. register flying machine at U.S. Patent Office.

26. North Carolina becomes dry state (→ 7/15).

28. Congress passes law regulating child labor in D.C., hoping states will follow suit (→ 9/29/08).

BIRTHS

20. U.S. actor James Stewart.

28. British writer Ian Fleming, wrote "James Bond" books (†8/12/1964).

Franco-British expo launched in London

Queen's entourage enjoys the fair.

May 14. London's Franco-British exposition has opened with displays on an unparalleled scale of the products of the two nations.

Housed in 25 magnificent palaces and halls on over 200 acres, exhibits range from fine arts to metallurgy to shipbuilding to cuisine. The colonies are also represented, with the arts and products of India found in a white building of Saracen design, with graceful minarets.

A favorite attraction is Bally-Maclinton, a composite Irish hamlet. Its buildings include an exact replica of the "McKinley Cottage" in which was born the ancestor of the late American President.

The Olympic Games will also be held in a stadium specially built for more than 70,000 people. Revived by France in 1896 after 1,500 years, the Olympics should prove popular with the British, as generations may pass before they are again held in the British Isles.

1908

JUNE

Su	Mo	Tu	We	Th	Fr	Sa
	1	2	3	4	5	6
7	8	9	10	11	12	13
14	15	16	17	18	19	20
21	22	23	24	25	26	27
28	29	30				

3. U.S.: Booking on liners to Europe reported to be steadily increasing (→ 6/21/09).

4. Paris: Military journalist shoots, wounds Alfred Dreyfus at Emile Zola's bier (→ 7/28/11).

6. French Natl. Assembly legislates domestic life; divorce granted automatically after three years separation.

8. London: Italian racer Felice Nazzaro sets record auto speed at 120 mph for 2.75 miles.

8. Washington: Roosevelt names Gifford Pinchot to head National Conservation Commission.

10. Australian Parliament grants federal support to invalids and the aging.

13. Rome: Art work, believed to be Botticelli's, found on ceiling of Ellsworth Villa.

14. German Reichstag passes fourth navy bill, calling for sharp hikes in shipbuilding (→ 8/11).

16. James Barrie's "Peter Pan" opens in Paris.

18. Chicago: Republicans nominate Taft for pres., James Sherman for v.p. (→ 7/10).

21. Rome: Pope to be presented with Marconi wireless on jubilee.

21. Mulai Hafid again proclaims himself the true sultan of Morocco (→ 8/23).

22. Texas: Six Negroes lynched in Houston for alleged murder plot (→ 5/22/09).

22. Wimbledon: Charlotte Sterry, at 37, becomes oldest ladies' winner, 6-4, 6-4 over Agnes Morton; Arthur Gore beats Herbert Barrett in 5 sets.

23. U.S. breaks relations with Venezuela, citing failure to compensate for American losses in revolt of 1899 (→ 9/10/10).

27. Lord Northcliffe buys London Times from Walter family.

29. N.Y.: Plans submitted for 909-ft. Equitable Life building.

DEATH

24. Ex-U.S. President Grover Cleveland (*3/18/1837).

Republicans nominate Taft for president

June 18. Republicans nominated William Howard Taft for president today, but not before handing him a last-minute scare.

As the hand-picked candidate of outgoing President Roosevelt, it had appeared likely that Taft, the current Secretary of War, would have an easy time of it. But on the eve of his nomination yesterday, delegates at the Chicago convention had broken into a nearly 50-minute demonstration on behalf of the current president, chanting "four more years, four more years" as they paraded through the aisles.

The president, who had ruled out seeking another term, learned of the threatened stampede in his behalf while conferring with Taft at the White House. The two men appeared somewhat worried by the unexpected demonstration. But their worries eventually evaporated.

A formidable Taft on campaign trail.

The convention nominated Taft on the first ballot today, although giving him a more subdued round of cheers than they had given Roosevelt. James S. Sherman was chosen as his running mate (→ 11/3).

Historic visit to Russia by Edward VII

June 9. To signal improved British-Russian relations, and perhaps closer ties to come, King Edward VII of England exchanged visits today with Czar Nicholas II on the waters of the Bay of Reval. The historic encounter marked the first visit of a British monarch to Russian waters, and the first time in seven years that Edward has seen his nephew, the czar.

Relations between the two countries have been cool since the 1890s, when Britain, which had been allied with France, chose to remain aloof from the newly formed Russian-French alliance. Relations were further strained by disputes over control of Persia. These disputes have faded into insignificance of late because of the more pressing threat to both countries from Germany. Under the leadership of Kaiser Wilhelm, who is also a nephew of King Edward, Germany has launched an aggressive campaign to surpass Britain as the major naval power. Many observers hope that the two sovereigns will use this meeting to draw up an alliance which will formally unite Britain with Russia and France (→ 8/11).

L. to r. seated: Queen Alexandra, Czar Nicholas, King Edward, Czarina Alexandra.

Shah throws out Persia's basic law

June 26. The forces of the Shah of Persia have squelched the reformist elements in Parliament after several days of fighting. Although Shah Muhammad Ali claims to support both the principle of popular representation and the constitution, he has attacked Parliament, forcing deputies not killed to flee. In doing so, he is destroying the basic law, which established a parliamentary system of government in Persia with power concentrated in the legislature. The shah has also ordered the Parliament building to be completely demolished and has appointed as Governor of Tehran the Russian Colonel of Cossacks. The shah succeeded his father last year (→ 7/27).

Death ends career of music pioneer

June 21. Nicolai Rimsky-Korsakov, a great Russian musical leader and the first Russian ever to compose a symphony, died today outside St. Petersburg. He was 64. Rimsky-Korsakov will perhaps be best remembered for his operas, including "Sadko" and "Le Coq d'Or." He wrote "Scheherezade" for orchestra, but it was used by Diaghilev as ballet music. Rimsky-Korsakov was introduced to music by Balalirev, influenced by Liszt and Berlioz and later taught at the St. Petersburg Conservatory. One of his best known students was Stravinsky.

Shredded Wheat.

1908

JULY

Su	Mo	Tu	We	Th	Fr	Sa
			1	2	3	4
5	6	7	8	9	10	11
12	13	14	15	16	17	18
19	20	21	22	23	24	25
26	27	28	29	30	31	

1. American Thomas flyer sinks in Siberian swamp, needs major repairs (→ 26).

2. London: Lancet Medical Journal passes judgment on fashion: men who wear colored shirts are slovens.

5. Paris: French officer displays new powderless electric gun.

5. Turkey: Army officers, led by Nizai Bey, join growing revolt in Macedonia (→ 24).

7. Paris tribunal extends law guaranteeing copyright on moving pictures.

7. Mme. Anna Gould and Prince de Sagan are married in France.

8. Commander Peary leaves Cape Breton for Sydney to begin arctic voyage on the Roosevelt.

10. Denver: Democrats offer William J. Bryan for president, John Worth Kern for vice president (→ 13).

13. Samuel Gompers, head of American Federation of Labor, pledges support for W.J. Bryan (→ 15).

15. Ohio: Fast-growing Prohibition Party nominates Eugene Chafin for pres., Aaron Watkins for v.p. (→ 11/3).

22. Washington: Roosevelt appeals for strong Navy in War College speech.

22. Venezuela dismisses Dutch ambassador, charges Holland with harboring refugees in Curacao (→ 11/7).

27. Russia: Czar Nicholas II and French President Fallieres meet in Reval.

27. Tehran: Persian Shah Muhammad Ali dissolves Parliament, suspends constitution (→ 7/16/09).

30. France: Continuing labor strife in construction industry; several demonstrators killed by police.

31. New York-to-Europe freight rates for grain double.

BIRTH

26. Chilean leader Salvadore Allende Gossens (†9/11/1973).

Young Turk uprising forces Sultan to act

July 24. Panic created by the Young Turk movement has forced Sultan Abdul Hamid II to decree a constitution for the Turkish Empire. The rebellion in the Turkish army, led by European revolutionists, has been called unprecedented in the history of the empire.

Normally, the sultan could rely on the Albanians to quash any rebellion, however they have deserted him and sent a dramatic telegram calling for re-establishment of a constitution. This shocked Hamid into publicly announcing his decree in Salonika to a crowd cheering, "Long live liberty!"

Essentially, the constitution will be the one devised in 1876 when Abdul Hamid I succumbed to liberal demands. Among the chief provisions were then, and are now: freedom of all creeds, of the press and education; individual liberty; general elections every four years; equal and legal taxation; and, the establishment of a senate. Because of the popularity of the revolt, observers expect the transition to be successful (→ 8/16).

U.S. wins Paris race as German penalized

July 26. The German automobile Protos became the first to reach Paris in the grueling race from New York but there was little reason to break out the schnapps. The Germans were penalized days for infractions along the way, thus assuring the American Thomas car of carrying off the top honors.

The Protos motored into the French capital last night on a final run from Vladivostok and thereby won the Grand Duke Vladimir of Russia Trophy as the first machine to reach Paris. However, the Protos had been delayed in Idaho by repairs and thus was shipped by railroad from Pocatello to Seattle in order to sail with the Thomas car to Siberia. The Americans, meanwhile, had tried to go by way of Alaska but snow conditions forced a change in the route.

The automobile race committee decided not to disqualify the Germans for the railroad trip but rather penalized them 15 days on the final leg to Paris. And the Thomas car received a 15-day allowance for its fruitless journey to Alaska and back. The German driver, Lt. Koeppen, on leave from the Kaiser's army, concluded, "I wish the roads in America were as nice as the people. Altogether, the trip has been a great success."

8 West Point cadets may be expelled

July 23. Eight West Point cadets face possible dismissal by the Secretary of War on charges of hazing. The accusation follows a month-long investigation at the academy.

The cadets reportedly ordered 123 plebes to fall-in at the first beat of the drumroll instead of waiting the customary five minutes. If a plebe seemed too slow, he was told to step outside, locate 100 ants and place them in his hat. An upperclassman would check if the ants were all "present and accounted for." If not, the youth was made to fetch 50 more. The ants were then kept in his locker. One cadet is charged with striking several students. West Point officials said there was no question of that cadet being reinstated.

Author of Uncle Remus stories dies

July 3. Joel Chandler Harris, author of the "Uncle Remus" stories, succumbed today to cirrhosis of the liver. He bequeaths a rich legacy of American Negro songs and legends. Harris was to Georgia what Mark Twain is to Missouri, capturing local dialect and personality with tongue-in-cheek pride.

Harris was born December 9, 1848, in Putnam County, Georgia. At age six, he came across a novel that sparked his interest in literature and humor. "The Vicar of Wakefield," by Oliver Goldsmith, describes a county parson who endures fire, accident and other catastrophes with only shrugs and sighs. Harris imbued his own characters with the same wistfulness, whether they were doused liberally with tar or pitched into briar patches.

The first "Uncle Remus" tale appeared in the Atlanta Constitution in 1879. The elderly storyteller and his animal fables were soon a fixture of the paper. So was Chandler; he became its chief editorial writer. Several "Remus" books emerged over the next 20 years. The last was "The Tar Baby Story and Other Rhymes of Uncle Remus" in 1905. Harris also wrote nonfiction, including a history of Georgia, published in 1899.

French aviator Leon Delagrange shows Theresa Peltier the workings of a plane. Perhaps she will inspire women to seek the thrill of flying.

1908  London

John Flanagan's new style helped him throw the hammer a record 170' 4".

Ray Ewry in the standing high jump.

The controversies and bitterness that marred the resumption of the Olympics in 1896 after a lapse of centuries continued through the 1908 Games and two weeks of London rain did little to help. The Finns marched flagless because they refused to carry the Russian flag; the Irish were incensed that they would have to compete under the British flag; and charges of professionalism were widespread. On the track, Americans again excelled. Ray Ewry won three standing-jump events for a total of ten golds over the past three Olympics.

Men Athletics

100 M Dash
1. Reginald Edgar Walker SAF 10,8
2. James Rector USA 10,9
3. Robert Kerr CAN 11,0

200 M Dash
1. Robert Kerr CAN 22,6
2. Robert Cloughen USA 22,6
3. Nathaniel Cartmell USA 22,7

400 M Run
1. Wyndham Halswell GBR 50,0 (only 3 runners in Final)

800 M Run
1. Melvin Winfield Sheppard USA 1:52,8
2. Emilio Lunghi ITA 1:54,2
3. Hanns Braun GER 1:55,2

1500 M Run
1. Melvin Sheppard USA 4:03,4
2. Harold Wilson GBR 4:03,6
3. Norman Hallows GBR 4:04,0

Marathon (42.195 km)
1. John Joseph Hayes USA 2:55:18,4
2. Charles Heferon SAF 2:56:06,0
3. Joseph Forshaw USA 2:57:10,4

110 M Hurtles
1. Forrest Smithson USA 15,0
2. John Garrels USA 15,7
3. Arthur Shaw USA

400 M Hurdles
1. Charles Bacon USA 55,0
2. Harry Hillman USA 55,3
3. Leonard Tremeer GBR 57,0

3000 M Steeplechase
1. Arthur Russel GBR 10:47,8
2. Archie Robertson GBR 10:48,4
3. John Lincoln Eisele USA 20 m zurück

1600 M Relay
1. USA 3:29,4 (William Hamilton, Nathaniel Cartmell, John Taylor, Melvin Sheppard)
2. GER to 25 M (Arthur Hoffmann, Hans Eicke, Otto Trieloff, Hanns Brawn)
3. HUN one chest (Pal Simon, Frigyes Mezey-Wiesner, Jozsef Nagy, Odōn Bodor)

High Jump
1. Harry Portel USA 1,905
2. Con Leahy GBR-IRL 1,88
3. Istvan Somodi HUN 1,88
2. Géo André FRA 1,88

Pole Vault
1. Edward Cooke USA 3,71
1. Alfred Gilbert USA 3,71
3. Ed Archibald CAN 3,58
3. Charles Jacobs USA 3,58
3. Bruno Söderström SWE 3,58

Long Jump
1. Francis Irons USA 7,48
2. Daniel Kelly USA 7,09
3. Calvin Bricker CAN 7,085

Triple Jump
1. Timothy Ahearne GBR-IRL 14,915
2. J. Garfield MacDonald CAN 14,76
3. Edvard Larsen NOR 13,395

Shotput
1. Ralph Rose USA 14,21
2. Dennis Horgan GBR 13,62
3. John Garrels USA 13,18

Discus Throw
1. Martin Shendan USA 40,89
2. Merritt Giffin USA 40,70
3. Marquis Horr USA 39,445

Hammer Throw
1. John Managan USA 51,92
2. Matthew McGrath USA 51,18
3. Cornelius Walsh USA 48,50

Freestyle Javelin (1908 only)
1. Erik Lemming SWE 54,445
2. Michel Dorizas GRE 51,36
3. Arne Halse NOR 49,73

5 miles (8046 M) 1906 and 1908
1. Emil Voigt GBR 25:11,2
2. Edward Owen GBR 25:24,0
3. John Svanberg SWE 25:37,2

3 miles Team (1908)
1. Great Britain 6
2. USA 19
3. France 32

Standing High Jump (1900, 1904, 1906, 1908, 1912)
1. Ray Ewry USA 1,575
2. Konstantin Tsiklitiras GRE 1,55
3. John Biller USA 1,55

Standing Long Jump (1900, 1904, 1906, 1908, 1912)
1. Ray Ewry USA 3,335
2. Konstantin Tsiklitiras GRE 3,23
3. Martin Sheridan USA 3,225

Discus, Ancient Style (1906 and 1908)
1. Martin Sheridan USA 38,00
2. Marquis Horr USA 37,325
3. Werner Jarvinen FIN 36,48

Tug-of-War (1904, 1906, 1908, 1912, 1920 only)
1. Great Britain
2. Great Britain

3500 M Walk (1908)
1. George Larner GBR 14:55,0
2. Ernest Webb GBR 15:07,4
3. Harry Kerr NSE 15:43,4

10 mile walk (1908)
1. George Larner GBR 1:15:57,4
2. Ernest Webb GBR 1:17:31,0
3. Edward Spencer GBR 1:21:20,2

Swimming

100 M Freestyle
1. Charles Daniels USA 1:05,6
2. Zoltan von Halmay HUN 1:06,2
3. Harald Julin SWE 1:08,0

400 M Freestyle
1. Henry Taylor GBR 5:36,8
2. Frank Beaurepaire AUS 5:44,2
3. Otto Scheff AUT 5:46,0

1500 M Freestyle
1. Henry Taylor GBR 22:48,4
2. Thomas Battersby GBR 22:51,2
3. Frank Beaurepaire AUS 22:56,2

100 M Backstroke
1. Arno Bieberstein GER 1:24,6
2. Ludvig Dam DEN 1:26,6
3. Herbert Haresnape GBR 1:27,0

200 M Breaststroke
1. Frederick Holman GBR 3:09,2
2. William Robinson GBR 3:12,8
3. Pontus Hansson SWE 3:14,6

800 M Freestyle Relay
1. GBR 10:55,6 (John Henry Derbyshire, Paul Radmilovic, William Foster, Henry Taylor)
2. HUN 10:59,0 (Jozsef Munk, Imre Zachar, Bela von Las Torres, Zoltan von Halmay)
3. USA 11:02,8 (Harry Hebner, Leo "Bud" Goodwin, Charles Daniels, Leslie G. Rich)

Springboard Diving
1. Albert Zürner GER 85,5
2. Kurt Behrens GER 85,3
3. George Gaidzik USA 80,8

High Diving
1. Hjalmar Johansson SWE 83,75
2. Karl Malström SWE 78,73
3. Arvid Spangberg SWE 74,00

Water-Polo

1. Great Britain
2. Belgium
3. France

Boxing

Bantamweight
1. A.H. Thomas GBR
2. John Condon GBR
3. W.Webb GBR

Featherweight
1. Richard Gunn GBR
2. C.W. Morris GBR
3. Hugh Roddin GBR

Lightweight
1. Frederick Grace GBR
2. Frederick Spiller GBR
3. H.H. Johnson GBR

Middleweight
1. John Douglas GBR
2. Reginald Baker AUS
3. W. Philo GBR

Heavyweight
1. A.L. Oldham GBR
2. S.C.H. Evans GBR
3. Frederick Parks GBR

Greco-Roman Wrestling

Lightweight
1. Enrico Porro ITA
2. Nikolay Orlov RUS
3. Arvid Linden FIN

Middleweight
1. Frithiof Martensson SWE
2. Mauritz Andersson SWE
3. Anders Andersen DEN

Light Heavyweight
1. Verner Weckman FIN
2. Yrjo Saarela FIN
3. Carl Lenson DEN

Heavyweight
1. Richard Weisz HUN
2. Aleksandr Petrov RUS
3. Sören Marius Jensea DEN

Freestyle Wrestling

Bantamweight
1. George Mehnert USA
2. William Press GBR
3. Aubert Côté CAN

Featherweight
1. George Dole USA
2. James Slim GBR
3. William McKie GBR

Lightweight
1. George de Relwyskow GBR
2. William Wood GBR
3. Albert Gingell GBR

Middleweight
1. Stanley Bacon GBR
2. George de Relwyskow GBR
3. Frederick Beck GBR

Heavyweight
1. George Con O'Kelly GBR/IRL
2. Jacob Gundersen NOR
3. Edmond Barrett GBR/IRL

Men Fencing

Foil Individual (chow competition)

Epée Individual
1. Gaston Alibert FRA
2. Alexandre Lippmann FRA
3. Eugène Olivier FRA

Epée Team
1. France
2. Great Britain
3. Belgium

Sabre Individual
1. Dr. Jeno Fuchs HUN
2. Bela Zulvsky HUN
3. Vilem Goppold von Lobsdorf BOH

Sabre Team
1. Hungary
2. Italy
3. Bohemia

Rowing

Single Sculls
1. Harry Balckstaffe GBR
2. Alexander McCulloch GBR
3. Bernhard von Gaza GER

Pair Oars without Coxswain
1. Great Britain 9:41,0
2. Great Britain 2½ lengths

Four Oars without Coxswain
1. Great Britain 8:34,0
2. Great Britain 1½ lengths

Eight Oars
1. Great Britain 7:52,0
2. Belgium
3. Canada
4. Great Britain

Yachting

6 M (1908, 1912, 1920, 1924, 1928, 1932, 1936, 1952)
1. Great Britain
2. Belgium
3. France

7 M (1908 and 1920)
1. Great Britain

8 M (1908, 1912, 1920, 1924, 1928, 1932, 1936)
1. Great Britain
2. Sweden
3. Great Britain

12 M (1908 and 1912)
1. Great Britain
2. Great Britain

Cycling

1000 M Sprint (No winner, time limit exceeded)

2000 M Tandem
1. France 3:07,6
2. Great Britain
3. Great Britain

4000 M Team Pursuit
1. Great Britain 2:18,6
2. Germany 2:28,6
3. Canada 2:29,6

One Lap Race (660 yard 1909)
1. Victor L. Johnson GBR 51,2
2. Emile Demangel FRA (in the wheel)
3. Karl Neumer GER (one wheel)

5 km Track (1906 and 1908)
1. Benjamin Jones GBR 8:36,2
2. Maurice Schilles FRA (in the wheel)
3. André Auffray FRA

20 km Track (1906 and 1908)
1. Charles B. Kingsbury GBR 34:13,6
2. Benjamin Jones GBR (in the wheel)
3. Joseph Werbrouck BEL

100 km Track
1. Charles H. Bartlett GBR 2:41:48,6
2. Charles H. Denny GBR (one wheel)
3. Octave Lapize FRA

Shooting

Full-Bore Rifle 300 Meters, 3 Positions
1. Albert Helgerud NOR 909
2. Harry Simon USA 887
3. Ole Saether NOR 883

Free Rifle Individual (1896, 1906, 1908)
1. Jerry Millner GBR 98
2. Kellogg Kennon Casey USA 93
3. Maurice Blood GBR 92

Free Rifle Team (1906, 1908, 1912, 1920, 1924)
1. Norway 5055
2. Sweden 4711
3. France 4652

Small-Bore Rifle (freestyle position)
1. A.A. Camell GBR 387
2. Harry Robinson Humby GBR 386
3. G. Barnes GBR 385

Small-Bore Rifle Individual (25 yards, 1908 and 1912)

Moving Target
1. A.F. Fleming GBR 24
1. M.K. Matthews GBR 24
1. W.B. Marsden GBR 24

Disappearing Target
1. William Kensett Styles GBR 45
1. H.I. Hawkins GBR 45
1. E.J. Amoore GBR 45

Small-Bore Rifle Team (50 and 100 yards 1908, 1920, 1924)
1. Great Britain 771
2. Sweden 737
3. France 710

Pistol—Rapid Fire
1. Paul Van Asbroeck BEL 490
2. Reginald Storms BEL 487
3. James Edward Gorman USA 485

Clay Pidgeon Shooting Individual
1. Walter Henry Ewing CAN 72
2. George Beattie CAN 60
3. Alexander Maunder GBR 57

Clay Pigeon Shooting Team
1. Great Britain I 407
2. Canada 405
3. Great Britain II 372

Military Rifle Team (1900, 1908, 1912, 1920)
1. USA 2531
2. Great Britain 2497
3. Canada 2439

Running Deer Shooting (Single Shot) Individual (1900, 1908, 1912, 1920)
1. Oscar Swahn SWE 25
2. Ted Ranken GBR 24
2. A.E. Rogers GBR 24

Running Deer Shooting Team (1908, 1912, 1920, 1924)
1. Sweden 86
2. Great Britain 85

Running Deer Shooting (Double Shot) Individual (1908, 1912, 1920, 1924)
1. Walter Winans USA 46
1. Ted Ranken GBR 46
2. Oscar Swahn SWE 38

Military Revolver Team (1900, 1908, 1912, 1920)
1. USA 1914
2. Belgium 1863
3. Great Britain 1817

Men Archery

York Round (100 yards-80 yards-60 yards)
1. W. Dod GBR 815
2. R.B. Brooks King GBR 768
3. Henry B. Richardson USA 760

Continental Style (50 M)
1. E.G. Grisot FRA 263
2. Louis Vernet FRA 256
3. Gustave Cabaret FRA 255

Women Archery

National Round (60 yards-50 yards)
1. Q.F. Newall GBR 688
2. Lotti Dod GBR 642
3. Hill-Lowe GBR 618

Men Gymnastics

Individual All-around competition
1. Alberto Braglia ITA 317,0
2. S.W. Tysal GBR 312,0
3. Louis Segura FRA 297,0

Team All-around Competition
1. Sweden 438
2. Norway 425
3. Finland 405

Soccer

1. Great Britain
2. Denmark
3. Netherlands

1908

AUGUST

Su	Mo	Tu	We	Th	Fr	Sa
						1
2	3	4	5	6	7	8
9	10	11	12	13	14	15
16	17	18	19	20	21	22
23	24	25	26	27	28	29
30	31					

1. Havana: Cuba holds first election under American supervision (→ 11/14).

3. Philadelphia subway, "the tube," opens.

3. Huntington Bay, L.I.: Defending champion Dixie II wins British Intl. Motorboat Cup race for U.S.

3. France: Fossilized human skeleton found in Chapelle aux Saints.

6. International Congress of Historians opens in Berlin.

8. Washington: Father Doyle of Catholic University predicts Catholics will quadruple in several years, dominate religious life in U.S.

11. Germany: Britain's King Edward VII meets with Kaiser Wilhelm at Friedrichshof to protest growth of German navy.→

13. King Edward II visits Austria's Franz Joseph at Ischl to persuade him to oppose German aggression (→ 10/28).

13. London: Enrico Caruso's wife elopes; he comments, "It was the very thing I desired."

14. Illinois: Police intervene as racial riots erupt in Springfield.

15. Vatican: Pope to include Italian flag, banned by Catholic Church since fall of Rome, in papal jubilee.

15. Prussia: Women authorized to attend university (→ 10/13).

16. Young Turk dissidents declare support for rights of ethnic groups within Ottoman Empire (→ 12/14).

20. Australia: American Great White Fleet arrives in Sydney to a warm welcome (→ 9/18).

23. Morocco: Sultan Abd-el-Aziz deposed by rival Mulai Hafid at Marrakesh (→ 9/1).

BIRTHS

27. U.S. President Lyndon Baines Johnson (†1/22/1973).

31. American writer William Saroyan, "The Human Comedy" (†5/18/1981).

DEATH

25. French physicist Henri Becquerel (*12/15/1852).

Model T ready to roll

Aug 12. The first Model T rolled off the Ford Motor Company assembly line in Detroit today. The roadster, which seats two people, costs $850. It is not fancy to look at, but it is relatively easy to drive, and you do not have to be a mechanical genius to take the wheel. Ford says it is simple to maintain the automobile, which has been nicknamed the "Tin Lizzy."

Up until now, only the privileged classes have owned automobiles. Ford is hoping to keep the price tags on the Model T's relatively low so that millions of Americans can afford them. Henry Ford's company has direct control of raw materials and uses a conveyor belt on the assembly line. The Model T represents a milestone for Ford, but the company still has to make some changes to improve the vehicle's performance (→ 10/1).

The Detroit assembly line has cut work time on the Model T to 14 hours.

Orville Wright building first Army plane

Aug 21. Orville Wright says he is ready for a series of flights to prove that an aircraft he and his brother Wilbur have built can meet the demanding requirements set by the United States War Department.

The Army Signal Corps accepted the Wrights' bid of $25,000 for a military aircraft last February. To be accepted by the Army, the aircraft must demonstrate it can stay aloft for a full hour at a speed of 40 miles per hour. The Army also requires the airplane be transportable in a standard horse-drawn wagon.

Orville Wright says he will undertake the Army tests of the new machine next month at Fort Myer, Virginia. At the same time, Wilbur will be in France for a similar series of flights aimed at meeting the requirements of a French syndicate, which has offered $100,000 for exclusive use of the Wright patent (→ 9/17).

The Wright brothers display military uses of flight in Le Mans, France.

Edward VII pursues personal diplomacy

Aug 11. In an effort to extend diplomatic relations, King Edward arrived in Kronberg, Germany, this morning to meet with Kaiser Wilhelm. The two leaders, who are also related, greeted each other with embraces and kisses and were driven to the Friedrichshof Castle, where they had a long talk over lunch. Although the topics discussed remain unknown, it is believed they talked about the maintenance of proportional naval strength. Recently, there have been reports that Germany is attempting to upgrade her fleet. The meeting is important if only to keep communication lines open. The two agreed to meet again in 1909 (→ 13).

Belgium formally annexes the Congo

Aug 19. After years of abuse, torture and scandal in Central Africa, the Congo Free State was effectively abolished today. The area is no longer Belgian King Leopold's personal fiefdom to exploit. The Congo was formally annexed by the Belgian government. In Brussels, the national legislature agreed to cover the Congo's future debts, and it voted to pay King Leopold 120 million francs for the territory.

King Leopold became interested in equatorial Africa when Sir Henry Stanley reported some 30 years ago that the Congo River made its riches accessible to Europe. Stanley helped form the Congo Free State under the rule of the Belgian king. Subsequently, Leopold built up a huge personal fortune by exporting the mineral and agricultural wealth of the Congo and by exploiting the natives, often through forced labor. A treaty was passed last year paving the way for today's action.

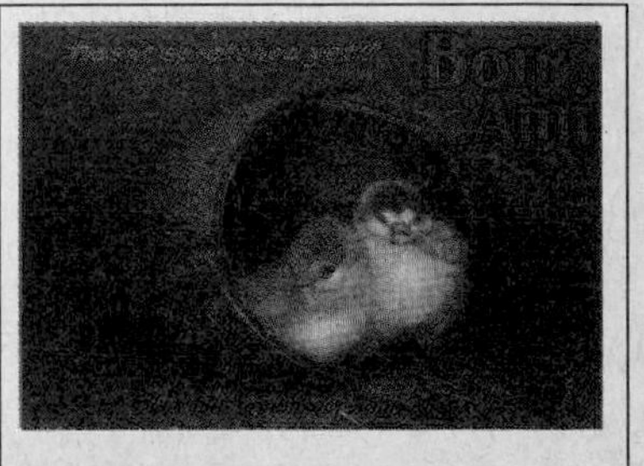

1908

SEPTEMBER

Su	Mo	Tu	We	Th	Fr	Sa
		1	2	3	4	5
6	7	8	9	10	11	12
13	14	15	16	17	18	19
20	21	22	23	24	25	26
29	28	29	30			

1. Despite French opposition, Germany recognizes new Moroccan sultan, asks Algeciras participants to follow (→ 14).

7. London: Botanist Harold Wager claims plants have eyes and can see.

9. Fort Myers: Orville Wright becomes first to stay airborne longer than one hour.

9. Russian Poland: Czar threatens to fire teachers who oppose unification of Polish and Russian school systems.

10. Russian newspapers celebrate Tolstoy's 80th birthday, calling him the Shakespeare of the 19th century.

12. Canadian govt. creates Civil Service Commission to monitor fairness in selection of civil servants.

14. France, Spain link recognition of new Moroccan sultan to his acceptance of Algeciras agreement (→ 9/2/09).

16. Austrian, Russian foreign ministers reach agreement sanctioning Bulgarian independence and Austria's annexation of Bosnia-Herzegovina (→ 10/2).

18. Australia: Great White Fleet leaves Albany for Manila (→ 10/10).

19. Berlin doctors announce inauguration of electric knife to be used for surgery.

20. Anti-German Slovenian demonstrators attack police in Vienna.

21. France: Mathematician Herman Minkowski gives address "Time and Space," defines time as the fourth dimension.

24. New York: Serum, reputed to cure tuberculosis, reaches U.S. from Russia.

25. Morocco: France arrests German deserters from French Foreign Legion in Casablanca (→ 11/10).

27. St. Petersburg: Cholera death toll reported at 7,102.

BIRTH

4. Afro-American writer Richard Wright, "Native Son" (†11/28/1960).

Plane crash kills man

Spectators at Ft. Myer rush to aid Orville Wright and Lt. Selfridge.

Sept 17. Lt. Thomas E. Selfridge of the United States Army Signal Corps died today in the crash of an airplane piloted by Orville Wright. Selfridge, who was 26 years old, is the first person to die in a crash since the Wright brothers opened the era of heavier-than-air flight. Orville Wright was injured severely but is expected to recover.

The crash occurred at Fort Myer, Virginia, where Orville Wright has been conducting a series of flights to demonstrate that the airplane meets the requirements set by the War Department. He and Selfridge took off at 5:14 p.m. today before 2,000 spectators, the largest crowd to witness the flights. The two-engine aircraft had flown three times around the parade ground from which it took off when a blade of the left propeller broke. The airplane plunged 75 feet to the ground.

Selfridge, who suffered a fractured skull, never regained consciouness. He died at 8:10 p.m. Luke Wright, the Secretary of War, says the accident will not stop the Army's experiments with aeronautics (→ 10/6).

Cholera devastates Russian population

Sept 23. Russia is in the grips of a devastating cholera epidemic that, at its current rate, will carry off thousands more than the record epidemic of 1892. More than 15,500 cases of Asiastic cholera have been reported in Russia this month and 7,102 are dead. In St. Petersburg, 4,931 cases have been reported with 1,875 dead. In two cases, death followed within 15 minutes of diagnosis. And one case of cholera has surfaced in the servants' quarters of the Winter Palace, the home of Czar Nicholas II.

Czar Nicholas and his wife, the Empress Alexandra, are not in Russia at present. They are on a cruise in Finnish waters.

Prime Minister Peter Stolypin has mounted an aggressive, though so far unsuccessful effort to fight the disease by ordering an improvement of St. Petersburg's unsanitary water. Russian workers and peasants, whether because of superstition or fear of the government, have been unwilling to get free innoculations. The high daily death rate has given St. Petersburg a nightmarish quality. Because of a shortage of gravediggers, hundreds of bodies, awaiting graves, have piled up.

Night work by young children opposed by protective body

Sept 29. An international conference on the protection of workers, meeting in Lucerne, Switzerland, today forbade nighttime employment in factories of children under age 14. The move will lend weight to the growing outcry against the excesses of child labor, but it will remain the responsibility of each nation to pass child labor laws.

In the United States, more than 1.75 million children under 16 years old work in factories. In Southern cotton mills, where there is little call for skill, about 25 percent of the "hands" are children, and 200,000 of them are under 12. Six-and seven-year-old girls work 13 hours a day spinning cotton. Despite legislation passed recently in some states, there is little evidence that conditions are improving nationwide,

The scant progress that has been made in curbing the evils of child labor has been mainly achieved by the National Child Labor Committee. Since 1904, the year it was founded by Dr. Edgar Gardner Murphy, an Alabama clergyman, the group has waged a tireless crusade in defense of the defenseless.

Perhaps the biggest impediment to reform is the surprising number of people who view child labor in a positive light. One cotton mill owner has been quoted as saying that children are hired "purely as a matter of charity" and they are much better off in the mill than on the loose, "learning the first lessons of a vagrant's life" (→ 12/9).

Young miners, faces blackened by coal, pose for Lewis Hine in W. Va.

Durant forming big auto-making firm

Buick owner Billy Durant.

Sept 16. William Crapo Durant organized an automobile corporation today called General Motors. Durant, who began as a carriage manufacturer, bought the Buick Motor Company in 1904. Lately, Buick has become the biggest auto producer in the nation. Earlier this year, Benjamin Briscoe, of the Maxwell-Briscoe Auto Company, proposed a merger. He suggested they could wield the kind of influence on the automobile business that the U.S. Steel Corporation has on the steel industry. In a questionable move, Durant circumvented Briscoe, acquiring 75 percent of Oldsmobile's stock. General Motors combines Buick and Olds, leaving Briscoe out in the cold.

Sept 12. An eager Winston Churchill arrives at the London Church where he is to wed Miss Clementine Hozier.

1908

OCTOBER

Su	Mo	Tu	We	Th	Fr	Sa
				1	2	3
4	5	6	7	8	9	10
11	12	13	14	15	16	17
18	19	20	21	22	23	24
25	26	27	28	29	30	31

1. Model T Ford hits U.S. market; first model with left-side steering (→ 8/16/13).

1. Seven European nations compete in first official international soccer contest.

2. Berlin receives reports of Turkish troops closing in on Bulgarian border (→ 5).

3. London: Wax figure of Winston Churchill installed at Madame Tussaud's.

4. Budapest: Police clash with demonstrators calling for universal suffrage.

5. Prince Ferdinand proclaims Bulgaria's independence from Ottoman Empire.

5. George M. Cohan's musical "The American Idea" opens in New York (→ 6).

6. Austria-Hungary annexes Bosnia and Herzegovina; Turkey, Serbia enraged (→ 8).

7. With Ottoman Empire in turmoil, Crete claims union with Greece (→ 7/13/09).

8. Serbia threatens war with Austria to gain freedom for Serbs in Boznia and Herzegovina (→ 12).

9. Severe drought in Indiana; water five cents a glass.

10. Great White Fleet leaves Manila for Japan (→ 19).

12. France: First intl. congress on roadways opens.

12. Russian Foreign Minister Isvolsky obtains Britain's support for intl. conference to avoid war in Balkans (→ 16).

12. South Africa: Constitutional convention meets at Durban (→ 9/20/09).

14. Chicago Cubs win World Series 2-0 in 5th game at Detroit.

16. Germany pledges support for Austria-Hungary's action in Balkans (→ 21).

21. Vienna: Austria bans export of guns, ammunition and horses to Serbia (→ 12/1).

28. Kaiser Wilhelm II cites German hostility to Britain in interview with London Daily Telegraph (→ 31).

Europe astonished by anti-British sentiments voiced in Kaiser interview

Oct 31. Kaiser Wilhelm's recent anti-British statements continued to send shock waves throughout Europe and resulted today in Chancellor von Bulow's offer to resign.

In an interview three days ago in the London Daily Telegraph, the kaiser said the prevailing sentiment among middle-and lower-class Germans was anti-British and he implied that it was only his and the military's efforts that held these feelings in check. The statement appears to contradict his remarks of last November that the good relations between Germany and England were the cornerstone of world peace. The kaiser's remarks were not limited to England, but seemed to jeopardize relations with Holland and Japan as well.

Kaiser Wilhelm II.

Emperor Wilhelm was said to have granted the interview in an effort to improve relations with England, but he has instead stirred up much anti-German feeling there. Many German officials believe it is the military, not the German public, that harbors such anti-British sentiments. Though Wilhelm has a reputation for abrasiveness, many Germans refused to believe he had uttered the remarks until they were printed in an official party newspaper. Chancellor von Bulow, who said that his job is to repair the windows the emperor breaks, will also have to patch up relations with the Japanese and the Dutch, toward whom the emperor made aggressive, militaristic remarks (→ 11/10).

Wilbur Wright sets record after record

Oct 6. Wilbur Wright climaxed a series of record-breaking flights today by staying aloft for more than an hour with a passenger. It was his second world-record flight in a week and won him the $100,000 offered by a French syndicate for patent rights in France. The syndicate already has placed an order for 50 planes of the Wright design.

Wilbur Wright, ready for flight.

Wright's flight was made at Le Mans, where he has been demonstrating his airplane for the syndicate since August. After some short hops to test the aircraft, Wright set one world record on September 21, when he made a flight of one hour and 32 minutes, covering a distance of 61 miles, thereby winning the $1,000 offered by the Aero Club of France for the longest flight over an enclosed ground. He set another record on October 3, when he stayed aloft for 55 minutes and 37 seconds, carrying a journalist as his passenger.

Today's flight lasted 64 minutes and 26 seconds, fulfilling the syndicate's requirement for two such flights within a week. Orville Wright, flying in the United States, had matched Wilbur's feats until his plane crashed September 17. ▷

Traffic stopped by a suffragette mob

Oct 13. A crowd of 100,000 stormed London's Parliament this evening, demanding voting rights for women. One woman reached the door to the House of Commons and was carried out by three men. Parliament immediately passed an order forbidding women access to the building. Twenty-four suffragettes and 12 people protesting unemployment were jailed (→ 4/26/09).

Suffragettes promote a new weekly.

Great White Fleet enters Tokyo Bay

Oct 19. Mists rose this morning to reveal something never seen before in Tokyo Bay, the ships of America's Great White Fleet. Rear Admiral Sperry, commander of the American fleet, said the purpose of the visit was peaceful and that he believed that nothing would ever happen to break the traditional friendship between Japan and the United States.

Japanese and American officials visited each other today amid the sounds of powerful salutes from the ships' guns and the voices of 2,000 Japanese schoolchildren singing the "Star Spangled Banner." Scores of boats clustered about the American ships as crowds jammed the waterfront through the day and into the night, when electric lights in huge letters spelled out a welcome to the visiting U.S. sailors (→ 2/22/09).

1908

NOVEMBER

Su	Mo	Tu	We	Th	Fr	Sa
1	2	3	4	5	6	7
8	9	10	11	12	13	14
15	16	17	18	19	20	21
22	23	24	25	26	27	28
29	30					

1. Postage between England and U.S. becomes two cents.

7. London: Prof. Ernest Rutherford announces he has isolated a single atom of matter.

7. Dutch navy blockades Venezuelan coast to protest expulsion of ambassador (→ 12/13).

7. Germany declares support for Taft's victory (→ 3/4/09).

10. France, Germany agree to settle two-month-old Casablanca affair by arbitration.

10. German Reichstag members express disapproval of kaiser's anti-British remarks to London Daily Telegraph.

12. Germany: 302 miners entombed in Hamm explosion.

12. Australia: Andrew Fisher becomes prime minister in 2nd Labor government since start of republic in 1901.

14. Einstein presents quantum theory of light.

14. Cuba: Liberal Jose Miguel Gomez wins presidency in U.S.-sponsored national elections (→ 2/1/09).

16. New York: Toscanini makes U.S. debut, "Aida" at the Metropolitan Opera.

20. Ohio: Federal court in Cleveland bars AT&T from interfering with business of Ohio's independent companies.

20. Port-au-Prince reports revolt in southern Haiti.

23. Belgium: Workers in Liege demonstrate for 8-hour day.

26. Washington: Census Bureau reports U.S. divorce rate higher than any other country (→ 7/18/09).

28. Philadelphia: Army football team defeats Navy 6-4 at Franklin Field.

30. U.S. Sec. of State Elihu Root and Japanese Ambassador Takahira exchange notes; U.S. recognizes Japan's annexation of Korea, reasserts demands for an independent China (→ 1/11/09).

BIRTH

28. French anthropologist Claude Levi-Strauss.

Dowager Empress dies, day after Emperor

Nov 14. The death of Tsu-Hsi, the Dowager Empress of China, followed closely that of her nephew, Emperor Kuang-Hsu. Rumors abound that foul play was involved in one or both of the deaths.

The long career of the dowager empress was marked by her ambition and cruelty. Tsu-Hsi, born Yehonala, at an early age became one of Emperor Hsien Feng's concubines. After his death in 1861, her young son was named emperor; she and the late emperor's widow became joint dowager empresses. When her son died in 1875, Tsu-Hsi arranged to place her infant nephew on the throne. In 1881, the older dowager empress died suddenly, possibly of poisoning.

The dowager empress opposed any attempt at reform. When her nephew began a radical modernization program in 1898, Tsu-Hsi forced him to renounce power, allowing her to rule in his place. The xenophobic dowager empress then supported the Boxer Rebellion in its futile attempt to drive foreigners from China (→ 12/2).

Dowager Empress Tsu-Hsi.

Taft easily elected President, 314-169

Nov 3. William Howard Taft dealt a crushing defeat to William Jennings Bryan today and was overwhelmingly elected as the 27th President of the United States. Taft won the Electoral College 314-169, and captured the popular vote with a majority of more than a million. It was Bryan's worst defeat in his three attempts to become president.

Taft will find strong support for his policies on Capitol Hill, where the Senate remains firmly in Republican hands. Taft's party also increased its majority in the House of Representatives to 65.

To secure his victory, Taft won handily in the Northeast and the West. He lost the South, but there was a surprising increase in the Republican vote there. Taft also won a majority in New York City. This is only the second time in history the city has voted Republican in a presidential election.

Taft was Theodore Roosevelt's choice to succeed him as president. After Taft served as Solicitor General and Civil Governor of the Philippines, it was Roosevelt who appointed him Secretary of War. As president, Taft is widely expected to follow Roosevelt's progressive policies (→ 7).

Mail carriers buy new autos for RFD

Nov 22. The U.S. Postal Service purchased automobiles today to aid delivery of Rural Free Delivery mail. Some congressional circles consider the expense exorbitant. Former Postmaster General William Bissell probably would have concurred; he thought any kind of RFD service would bankrupt the nation. However, the routes have proved extremely popular in farming states. West Virginia, site of the first route in 1896, is particularly dependent upon the service. RFD has meant improved roads (postal employees driving mail wagons insisted on them), diminished isolation of farm families and increased land values.

Mail delivery by auto.

1908

DECEMBER

Su	Mo	Tu	We	Th	Fr	Sa
		1	2	3	4	5
6	7	8	9	10	11	12
13	14	15	16	17	18	19
20	21	22	23	24	25	26
27	28	29	30	31		

1. Italian Parliament debates future of Triple Alliance, asks compensation for Austria's action in Bosnia-Herzegovina.

4. London: Great powers meet in attempt to regulate intl. naval policy (→ 1/3/09).

9. Child labor bill passes German Reichstag; no work for those under 13 (→ 2/12/13).

13. Dutch take two Venezuelan coast guard ships (→ 21).

14. First truly representative Turkish Parliament opens; Young Turks in majority (→ 2/24/09).

15. Paris: Earliest human remains found by priests at Chapelle-aux-Saints.

21. Venezuela: With Castro in Europe, V.P. Gomez dismisses Cabinet, names new govt.

21. Andrew Carnegie, appealing for tariff cuts, tells Congress, "Take back your protection; we are now men, and we can beat the world" (→ 4/9/09).

21. German Samoa: Natives threaten revolt to gain independence.

23. U.S. Federal Court sentences Gompers and all AFL officers for violating injunction.

CULTURAL EVENTS, 1908

Literature: E.M. Forster's "A Room with a View"; Kenneth Grahame's "The Wind in the Willows"; Anatole France's "Penguin Island."

Religion, Academia: Karl Liebknecht's "Militarism and Anti-militarism"; Georges Sorel's "Reflections on Violence"; first Bibles placed in hotel rooms by the Gideons.

Music: Ravel's "Spanish Rhapsody"; Oscar Strauss' operetta "The Chocolate Soldier," from Shaw's "Arms and the Man"; Isadora Duncan's first dancing successes in London and N.Y.

The Arts: Marc Chagall's "Nu Rouge"; Monet's "The Ducal Palace, Venice"; term "Cubism" coined by Matisse; "Ashcan School" (urban realism) founded in N.Y. by Wm. Glackens, George Bellows.

Baby Emperor to rule under regency

Dec 2. Pu Yi, the three-year-old nephew of the late Emperor of China Kuang-Hsu, ascended the Manchu dragon throne today under the name Hsuan-Tung. The infant's father, Prince Chun, the brother of the late ruler, will act as regent for the baby Emperor.

The passing of the emperor, and especially the Dowager Empress Tsu-Hsi, who had been the real power in China for more than three decades, could be the beginning of great change. The dowager empress resisted Westernization and any effort at reform. Now the reform elements, which the dowager empress never entirely destroyed, may have some influence.

However, opposition groups, including those pressing for a constitutional monarchy as well as the radical societies seeking to overthrow the Manchus and establish a republic, undoubtedly view the ascension of the baby emperor as an opportunity to act. Most of these groups are based outside of China and are led by reformists forced out by the dowager empress.

Prince Chun with Pu Yi (standing).

Jack Johnson wins title from Burns

Heavyweight champ Jack Johnson.

Dec 26. Jack Johnson from Galveston, Texas, became the first Negro to win the world heavyweight boxing championship today when he gained a technical knockout over Tommy Burns. Johnson, who had earned this chance at the title with an impressive record of knockouts, was beating Burns so badly that police in Sydney, Australia, where the match was held, had to step into the ring in the 14th round to stop the carnage. Burns had won the title on February 3, 1906, by beating Marvin Hart in a grueling 20-round battle.

100,000 or more die in Italian 'quake

Dec 28. The most devastating earthquake ever to hit Europe struck Italy today, killing up to 100,000 people and destroying an architectural heritage that may never be repaired. The earthquake struck on both sides of the Straits of Messina. The hardest hit area was the city of Messina, on the northeastern coast of Sicily. Some 84,000 people were reportedly killed, and 90 percent of Messina was reduced to rock and dust. Dozens of churches and palaces are in ruins, completely reduced to rubble.

Thousands of other victims died on the mainland, in and around Reggio di Calabria, at the toe of Italy's boot. Doctors and rescue workers are rushing to the earthquake zone from every corner of Europe. All over the world, money is being raised to help the unfortunate victims of the earthquake.

No one anticipated the devastation today, but the Straits of Messina have always played a foreboding role in classical mythology. The straits were home to the monster Scylla and the whirlpool of Charybdis. Odysseus escaped these dangers in his travels. Today, unfortunately, Messina was not so lucky (→ 1/2/09).

Big year in science: Helium and Bakelite

A highlight of science this year was the award of the Nobel Prize in chemistry to Ernest Rutherford for his work on radioactivity and his demonstration that most of the mass of the atom is concentrated in a dense nucleus. In medicine, the Nobel Prize went to Ilya Mechnikov and Paul Ehrlich for work on the body's immune defenses. The physics prize was won by Gabriel Lippmann for his research and experiments with color photography.

An outstanding achievement this year was the production of liquid helium by Heike Kammerlingh-Onnes, a Dutch physicist. An apparatus that lowered the temperature to four degrees above absolute zero was needed to liquify the gas.

Of more immediate practical importance was the invention by Leo Baekeland, a Belgian-born American chemist, of a plastic that can take the place of wood or metal in many applications. The plastic, which he has named Bakelite, is water-resistant, an electrical insulator and easily machined.

Also of practical importance was the invention by chemist Fritz Haber of Germany of a method of producing ammonia by combining nitrogen and hydrogen under pressure. The ammonia can be used to produce fertilizer or explosives, eliminating the need to use natural sources of nitrogen compounds.

Lovely young winner of one of America's new beauty pageants.

1909

JANUARY

Su	Mo	Tu	We	Th	Fr	Sa
					1	2
3	4	5	6	7	8	9
10	11	12	13	14	15	16
17	18	19	20	21	22	23
24	25	26	27	28	29	30
31						

1. London astronomers hint sightings of planet beyond Neptune.

3. Serbia's crown prince warns England of German militarism (→ 2/8).

5. U.S. Navy asks Congress to fund construction of new battleships capable of carrying eight 14-inch guns (→ 22).

5. Colombia recognizes Panama's autonomy (→ 7/15).

6. Pres. Roosevelt again asks Congress to empower Interstate Commerce Commission to fix rail freight rates (→ 12).

9. Tennessee: Six "night riders" sentenced to death for murder of Capt. Quentin Ranken.

11. First women's auto race leaves N.Y. for Philadelphia.

11. Tokyo: Japanese insist segregation of Orientals in Calif. will strain diplomatic ties (→ 19).

11. France: Four murderers guillotined in Bethune; first use of capital punishment in years.

12. Lists of largest rail stockholders publicized; Harriman leads with 116 million (→ 2/1).

16. New York: Reported that streetcars killed 444 in 1908.

19. Roosevelt tells Calif. Gov Gillett to kill anti-Japanese bills (→ 29).

19. Shackleton finds coal mines near S. Pole (→ 3/23).

21. Tennessee bans liquor production for 1910 (→ 2/21).

22. Washington: House rejects talk of war with Japan, yet votes funding hike for Navy.

28. Samuel Gompers defends boycott as inherent right.

29. California limits immigrants to five-year land titles (→ 2/4).

29. German Reichstag members admit workers are blacklisted for activism.

BIRTHS

1. Senator Barry Goldwater, conservative Republican.

15. Jazzman Gene Krupa (†10/16/1973).

16. Entertainer Ethel Merman.

Messina 'quake kills 200,000 Italians

Homeless Italians begin the exodus from Messina.

Jan 2. Early fears regarding the earthquake in Southern Italy last Monday were not unfounded. More than 200,000 are dead. Starvation and pneumonia may claim many more. Men and women, bereft of their entire families, have committed suicide. Bandits rob corpses of their jewelry. The financial damage, $1 billion, seems paltry next to the extent of human suffering.

The Pope is sheltering refugees in the Lazaretto. The Archbishop of Messina, buried alive for five days in his crumbled palace, is regaining his strength. The royal couple, now nursing the injured, narrowly escaped danger themselves. The King passed a wall moments before its collapse, and the Queen was nearly trampled by a mob panicking during an aftershock.

The French, Greek and Argentine governments donated generous relief funds. The United States Congress voted $800,000 in aid. And four American battleships, laden with food and medicine, are presently steaming through the Suez Canal, bound for Naples.

Metro Life gets largest office building

Jan 29. Metropolitan Life Insurance Company owns the largest office building in New York City — and the world. Completed today, the 50-story building is located at Madison Avenue and 24th Street. It boasts four clocks, one on each side, at the level of the 25th floor. Each numeral is four feet high, and each minute hand weighs half a ton.

Metropolitan Life Building, N.Y.

How can Metropolitan Life afford this monolith? Like other insurance companies, it attributes its success to extending policy offers to the working classes. Last year, Metropolitan sold nine million policies to wage-earner families. Company assets were over $236 million.

With giants like the Metro Tower and the Flatiron Building (built in 1902), New York now rivals Chicago in its number of skyscrapers. The technology for constructing such buildings has existed since 1890, when the Rand McNally Building was erected in Chicago. Its complete steel structure and efficient elevator system made it practical. Now a skyscraper can be attractive as well. The Metro Life Tower is modeled after the Campanile of St. Marks Church in Venice, Italy.

Moving pictures are now an industry

Jan 3. Moving pictures are a $40 million a year industry, according to statistics released today. Over 100,000 people are employed in making films, a business which has developed unique demands. Unlike in live theater, crowd scenes may call for hundreds of "supers," or extra actors. Employment opportunities continue after a film is a "wrap." A theater needs a piano player, a drummer, a lantern operator and his assistant and ushers.

There are now 10,000 picture theaters in the United States. One out of every two Americans attends one each week. Admission may cost as much as a dime.

Fashions fit figures

Jan 3. Recent Paris fashion shows suggest that women may soon resemble women again. Couturiers are emphasizing hips, delineating waistlines and generally allowing curves to assert themselves. The effect of these new fashions is to flatter plump and trim figures alike. Also this season, Parisian gowns are relying on high-busted corsets. American women, however, prefer the low-busted version, which accentuates a smaller bust while tempering a larger one.

Gibson Girl models the new look.

1909

FEBRUARY

Su	Mo	Tu	We	Th	Fr	Sa
	1	2	3	4	5	6
7	8	9	10	11	12	13
14	15	16	17	18	19	20
21	22	23	24	25	26	27
28						

1. U.S. troops quit Cuba after installing Jose Miguel Gomez as president (→ 3/16).

1. U.S. Supreme Court rules corporations violating Sherman Antitrust Act cannot legally collect on debts (→ 17).

4. Calif. law segregates Japanese schoolchildren (→ 6/12).

6. Virginia: Delaware launched at Newport News; largest U.S. warship, cost $4 mil. (→ 22).

6. James Crowley sets new marathon record at 2:38:48.

8. British Cabinet announces new navy plans include 6 Dreadnoughts (→ 3/12).

9. France agrees to recognize German economic interests in Morocco in exchange for political supremacy (→ 9/2).

13. Turkey: Kiamil Pasha steps down, rebuked by nationalist Parliament (→ 4/13).

14. Booker T. Washington asks U.S. aid for Liberia (→ 7/2).

17. Govt. commission reports six men control tobacco industry with 86 firms worth $450 million (→ 20).

17. Royal commission declares conditions in London produce "degenerate race, morally and physically enfeebled."

19. Roosevelt announces plans for 1910 world conference on conservation at The Hague.

20. U.S. Senate subcommittee finds Roosevelt let U.S. Steel violate antitrust law (→ 3/10).

22. Norfolk, Va.: Great White Fleet returns from around-the-world show of naval power (→ 4/11).

24. Austria considers declaring war on Serbia.→

28. Washington: Roosevelt becomes first U.S. pres. to visit Austrian Embassy; discusses Balkans crisis (→ 3/2).

BIRTH

3. French philosopher Simone Weil (†8/28/43).

DEATH

26. French artist Caran d'Ache. born Emmanuel Poire (*1859).

Turmoil besets Balkans

Feb 24. Tension, turmoil and territorial disputes are not new to the Balkans, and another movement of nationalist sentiment is threatening peace in the uneasy area again.

The alliance of officers and intellectuals known as the Young Turks proved in Bulgaria last year that it is possible to oust foreign powers. Jealous Serbia was watching as Bulgaria declared itself independent from the Turks. Now Serbia is arming itself and demanding that the Austro-Hungarians leave Bosnia and Herzegovina, an area they fully annexed just last year. Serbia has coveted the region since losing it 600 years ago.

The Western European powers are trying to prevent armed conflict in the Balkans by pressuring the Serbs to give up their territorial ambitions in return for economic compensation from Austria. But Serbia will have none of it. Prime Minister Stojan Novakovic's goal is a Pan-Slavic empire.

"It is not just the three million Serbs in Serbia and Montenegro that make up our nation," Novakovic declared. "We are only a third. The other two-thirds, seven million people, in Dalmatia, Croatia, Slavonia, Bosnia and Herzegovina, are all subjects of the Austrian monarchy and want to be free." Serbians say they want to gain freedom for the Balkans peacefully, but also feel the Russians will help again if necessary (→ 28).

Prohibition spreading rapidly in America

Feb 21. The battle between the temperance army and liquor interests reached a new peak during the past year, as saloons throughout much of the United States began closing their doors to the public.

With women in the forefront of the Prohibition movement, many states have outlawed all sales of liquor, while many others have adopted local option plans on a county-wide basis. For example, 315 townships in New York state have banned saloons in their areas.

The move to stem the flow of liquor has taken many forms. Tennessee has passed a law making it a misdemeanor to manufacture or sell liquor. Of Ohio's 66 counties, 57 have voted saloons out of business. And more than 48 towns in Colorado have closed saloon doors.

Anti-Prohibition forces have not been idle. They have bombarded Americans with pamphlets that challenge claims of dry leaders that liquor produces poverty. While conceding that heavy drinking might cause poverty in some cases, the wets say that statistics show that the average workman spent only $12.44 of his annual income of $768.54 on liquor, scarcely more than he spent on tobacco.

Liquor interests have also issued pamphlets detailing what they call the degenerative results of Prohibition, such as fraud, hypocrisy, drinking on the sly and the likely switch of former drinkers to use of cocaine and morphine. Furthermore, pro-liquor forces have argued that abolition of the saloon has not wiped out vice, crime or "grafting" politicians (→ 12/26).

Geronimo, famous Apache leader, dies

Geronimo, Apache leader.

Feb 17. He became a celebrity after appearing at the St. Louis World's Fair, but he will be best remembered as a symbol of the American Indian. Geronimo, leader of the Chiricahua Apaches, escaped from captivity four times before settling down to become a rancher. Before he died today at age 80, Geronimo said: "I was living peacefully with my family . . . perfectly contented. Now, there are very few of us left."

Feb 20. Filippo Tomaso Marinetti's "Futurist Manifesto," published in Le Figaro, calls for artistic revolt. Umberto Boccioni's "Riot in an Art Gallery" echoes Marinetti's words: "We want to glorify war, militarism, patriotism, the violence of anarchism, the beautiful ideas that kill . . . We want to demolish museums, libraries, fight moralism."

1909

MARCH

Su	Mo	Tu	We	Th	Fr	Sa
	1	2	3	4	5	6
7	8	9	10	11	12	13
14	15	16	17	18	19	20
21	22	23	24	25	26	27
28	29	30	31			

2. Lackawanna Co. cuts steel wages; general reductions likely to follow (→ 7/16).

2. Great powers advise Serbia to give up claim on Bosnia-Herzegovina (→ 15).

3. Aviators Herring, Curtiss and Bishop announce airplanes to be made commercially in U.S. (→ 9/24).

8. Pope Pius X lifts ban on inter-faith marriage in Hungary.

9. French Natl. Assembly passes income tax bill (→ 5/8).

10. Standard Oil wins suit in Chicago (→ 5/21).

10. U.K. extracts territorial concessions from Siam in Malaya.

12. British Parliament increases naval appropriations (→ 21).

12. Three U.S. warships ordered to Nicaragua to stem conflict with El Salvador (→ 11/27).

15. Italy proposes European conference on Balkans (→ 21).

16. Cuba: Six weeks after Gomez's inauguration, republic suffers first revolt.

17. France: Communications industry paralyzed by strikes (→ 5/6).

21. Under pressure from Germany, Russia withdraws support for Serbia, recognizes Austrian annexation of Bosnia-Herzegovina (→ 31).

23. British Lt. Shackleton finds Magnetic S. Pole (→ 1/6/10).

23. Roosevelt leaves for African safari sponsored by Smithsonian Institution and National Geographic (→ 5/1).

25. Russia: Revolutionary Mme. Popova arrested on 300 murder charges.

26. Russian troops invade Persia to support Muhammad Ali as shah in place of constitutional government (→ 6/26).

28. Census figures show surprising decrease in size of American family.

30. Oklahoma: Seminole Indians in revolt against meager pay for government jobs.

31. Serbia acquiesces, accepts Austrian control over Bosnia-Herzegovina (→ 4/27).

Naval race shocks U.K.

March 21. "I am forced to the conclusion that now, for the first time in modern history, we are face to face with a naval situation so dangerous that it is difficult to realize all its import." That's how Sir Arthur Balfour, leader of the opposition in Parliament, reacted to reports that Britain's navy has lost its supremacy. Earlier this week, Reginald McKenna, First Lord of the Admiralty, revealed that Germany has a capacity to rapidly build big battleships. The revelation shocked many Britons, with the notable exception of Sir John Fisher, the naval expert, who said, "There's no need for alarm. You can sleep easy."

According to new calculations, Germany will have 13 ships the size of England's own mammoth Dreadnought ready by late 1911, and 17 more vessels by 1912. These estimates are up from previous reports of nine and 13, respectively. McKenna pointed out that two years ago the idea of Germany building ships so large and so quickly would have been laughed at.

New proposals to allocate $15 million for construction of two more battleships received support in Parliament. McKenna, arguing for the allocations, said, "The safety of the country stands above all other considerations, and no matter what the cost, the safety of the country must be assured." (→ 6/12).

Submarines patrol Thames River.

Taft is inaugurated in big snowstorm

March 4. As thousands shivered outdoors in a blinding snowstorm, William Howard Taft was sworn in today as President in the warmth of the Senate chamber. Plans to hold the inaugural ceremony on the east front of the Capitol were hurriedly abandoned when the unexpected blizzard blanketed the city of Washington.

Taft and Roosevelt at White House.

Death claims Synge at early age of 38

March 24. Dramatist John Millington Synge died today. He is survived by a prolific band of writers creating an Irish Renaissance. W.B. Yeats, Lady Gregory and Sean O'Casey carry on, celebrating Irish lore and Irish peasantry. Yet Synge's acerbic wit stood alone.

Synge was born outside Dublin in April 1871. He studied at Trinity College and visited Europe. He met Yeats in Paris, who made him do an about-face to the Aran Islands off the west coast of Ireland. That wild place, littered with Celtic ruins, inspired Synge's love of the Irish. He was never blinded to their faults, however. His first comedy, "In the Shadow of the Glen," was unflattering and morose. In 1904, "Riders to the Sea" was greeted more kindly. "The Playboy of the Western World" (1907) enraged Irish audiences, who pelted the actors with vegetables. Synge leaves behind "Deirdre of the Sorrows," an unfinished drama.

1909

APRIL

Su	Mo	Tu	We	Th	Fr	Sa
				1	2	3
4	5	6	7	8	9	10
11	12	13	14	15	16	17
18	19	20	21	22	23	24
25	26	27	28	29	30	

4. French cut tariffs on U.S. goods to compel preferential rates to France (→ 9).

4. Switzerland: Proportional suffrage adopted by canton of Lucerne (→ 1/3/10).

9. Thousands of mill workers plan trip to Washington to demand higher tariffs (→ 5/8).

9. Caruso broadcasts from Met. to house of Lee de Forest, inventor of 3-element tube which made radio possible.

13. Turkey: Troops of conservative Albanian 1st Army Corps surround Parliament, deposing Hilmi Pasha (→ 19).

14. London: Anglo-Persian Oil Co. formed to operate D'Arcy concession in Persia.

19. Turkey: Macedonian troops invade Constantinople; sultan implicated in counterrevolution (→ 27).

19. Turkey recognizes Bulgarian autonomy (→ 27).

19. Ada, Oklahoma: Four prominent cattlemen taken from jail and lynched for killing marshal.

21. Vatican: Encyclical "Communium Rerum" lauds St. Anselm, symbolizing fight against modernism.

23. Kentucky: Ex-Gov. Taylor pardoned in 1900 murder of gubernatorial candidate William Goebels.

24. Thirty-thousand Armenians reported victimized by Turks in past month (→ 6/8).

25. Harvard Prof. Henry Pickering explains plan for signaling Mars by telescope.

27. Triple Alliance accepts Bulgarian autonomy.→

29. Lloyd George offers controversial budget to Parliament; includes heavy spending for social welfare (→ 12/1).

BIRTH

13. Author Eudora Welty.

DEATHS

10. Victorian literary critic and poet Algernon Charles Swinburne (*4/5/1837).

24. Peter Collier, publisher Collier's Wkly. (*12/12/1849).

Peary at the North Pole

Comm. Peary aboard the Roosevelt.

April 6. Commander Robert E. Peary of the United States Navy today planted the flag of the United States at the North Pole.

Accompanied by his Negro assistant Matthew Hensen, Peary reached the pole after a 36-day trek, achieving a goal that had occupied him for nearly a decade. He made his first attempt in 1902, after a number of expeditions, but was forced to turn back when he could not push his way across the frozen Arctic Sea. He returned in 1905, in a ship of his own design, built to force its way through the icebound ocean, that brought him closer to the Arctic continent, but his trip by dog sled fell short of the pole.

Peary's latest expedition began when his ship, the Roosevelt, sailed from the United States in July 1908. His party sailed to Greenland, went 90 miles overland from the ship and left Cape Columbia, Ellesmere Island, for the final dash to the pole on March 1. By Peary's plan, sections of the party turned back when they had done their share in trail-breaking. At the outset, the expedition included 17 Eskimos, 19 sledges and 133 dogs. Only 40 dogs and four Eskimos accompanied Peary and Hensen when they reached their ultimate goal.

Abdul Hamid ousted as Ottoman Sultan

April 27. The man who called himself "the Shadow of God" was dethroned as Sultan of Turkey today. Abdul Hamid, deposed by the unanimous vote of the two houses of Parliament, is replaced by his brother, Mohammed Rechad Effendi, who will be known as Sultan Mehmed V. Hamid was declared guilty on three counts by the Parliament. An official statement claimed the former leader of 200 million Moslems had squandered the wealth of the Ottoman Empire, broken the laws and burned the holy law books, and committed heinous bloody massacres.

The decision elicited grandiose celebrations as the streets of Constantinople filled with cheering throngs. However, the Young Turk military commander, Chefket Pasha, held tight reins on the city's inhabitants, keeping order by arresting 6,000 Moslem extremists who might stir up trouble while the government was in transition.

One report from the Turkish capital said Abdul Hamid had been executed, however that is believed to be a rumor. Most accounts say he has been placed under heavy guard at the Cheraghan Palace. Apparently, he did not handle his loss of power well, as he trembled and asked for mercy. "Let me live and I will do all you wish," he pleaded.

Abdul Hamid II.

His brother, on becoming sultan, articulated his support for parliamentary institutions and promised faithful service. "By the help of Allah, the most high," he said, "I shall follow unswervingly the path of duty, seeking to act justly and honorably to all men."

Three great powers recognize Bulgaria

April 27. Bulgaria made a big step toward world recognition this month as the Triple Alliance, comprised of Austria-Hungary, Italy and Germany, acknowledged her sovereign independence. Many international observers speculate that the crisis that erupted in February fortified the Black Sea country.

It was only last year that the Ottoman Empire principality proclaimed itself a legitimate independent kingdom under the leadership of Czar Ferdinand I and designated the central city of Sofia as its capital. Since that time, the Bulgarian government has made overtures to Serbia and Russia, apparently realizing the importance of having strong allies in this highly volatile Eastern European region.

U.S. Army raises strength to 77,000

April 11. Recruiters have been told to contain themselves as the U.S. Army ranks have grown to full strength for the first time since the Spanish war. Some 77,000 men are now in uniform. According to some reports, the hard economic times forced many to enlist. Yet one officer claims an article entitled "The Army as a Career," published in The New York Times, attracted many young men. The Army is now ridding itself of all undesirable soldiers to make way for the new recruits.

Sponsor of voting rights act dies

April 23. William M. Stewart, former United States Senator from Nevada and author of the 15th Amendment to the Constitution, died today at the Georgetown, Maryland, hospital. Passed in 1870, the amendment says that the right to vote shall not be denied because of race, color or previous condition of servitude. A familiar face in Congress, Stewart lost a fortune during the Civil War, but regained it when he took a 12-year break from politics to resume his mining interests.

Mrs. Catt presides at worldwide rally

Carrie Chapman Catt.

April 26. Carrie Chapman Catt, a leader of American suffragettes, refused today to take sides in a dispute over whether British women are being too militant in their fight for the vote.

Mrs. Catt is presiding at the convention being held in London by the International Woman's Suffrage Alliance. In rejecting all requests that she either condemn or approve tactics being used by militant suffragettes in Great Britain, Mrs. Catt explained that a neutral attitude was the proper one for those who are guests in a foreign country. During the opening session of the convention, the British militants drew applause by speaking out against the male leaders of that country.

Routine day for an ex-President: Teddy bags a rhino in Africa. The Smithsonian and Scribners are sponsoring Roosevelt in return for safari reports after the trip.

1909

MAY

Su	Mo	Tu	We	Th	Fr	Sa
						1
2	3	4	5	6	7	8
9	10	11	12	13	14	15
16	17	18	19	20	21	22
23	24	25	26	27	28	29
30	31					

1. Teddy bags three big lions in British East Africa.

2. U.S. baseball fans reported 3 mil. strong; support industry with annual $10 mil.

2. U.K. Parliament debates wisdom of excluding U.S. from calculation of 2-power standard for military might (→ 6/12).

3. Wintergreen wins Kentucky Derby with jockey V. Powers in the saddle.

3. First wireless press message sent from N.Y. to Chicago.

6. Pittsburgh: Press and pulpit denounce nude painting "Bridal Morning" at intl. show.

6. Paris postal and telegraph workers unionize (→ 14).

7. It is reported Turkish Sultan Abdul Hamid deposited over $10 mil. in U.S. and German banks (→ 6/8).

8. Philadelphian Joseph Fels revives Henry George's single tax movement, appeals for progressive land tax in U.S. and England (→ 7/12).

8. France warns U.S. increased duties on luxuries will bring trade war (→ 8/5).

14. Congressmen leave House restaurant when Negro official and guest are served (→ 22).

14. France: Natl. Assembly votes down civil servants' right to strike (→ 6/1).

14. New York mayor vetoes equal pay for female teachers (→ 9/18).

21. Standard Oil gains controlling interest in Austria; only Rumania remains as independent oil producer (→ 6/5).

22. Georgia rail workers strike against employment of Negroes (→ 6/1).

25. Tolstoy's publisher jailed for "Thou Shalt Not Kill"; govt. refuses to prosecute author.

30. Count Zeppelin flies 400 miles, aloft 22 hrs.

BIRTHS

15. James Mason, British actor (†7/27/1984).

30. Big band leader Benny Goodman (†6/13/1986).

Police break up Emma Goldman lecture

May 23. An indignant audience was left speechless yesterday when New York City policemen broke up a lecture by Emma Goldman, the professed anarchist. The police charged that Miss Goldman "wandered away" from her announced lecture topic, "Modern Drama, the Strongest Disseminator of Radical Thought," by talking about Joan of Arc and other martyrs.

As a police detective attending the lecture sought to halt the speech, chairs and tables were overturned, and the officer hurried from the hall to round up reinforcements from a nearby station. But an angry crowd had already gathered outside when a platoon of policemen arrived at the hall. One officer was assaulted and several persons were arrested. Miss Goldman, who was jailed in 1893 for inciting to riot, has denied that she advocates violence. The police often harass her, she says, because they are "very ignorant and don't understand what they hear."

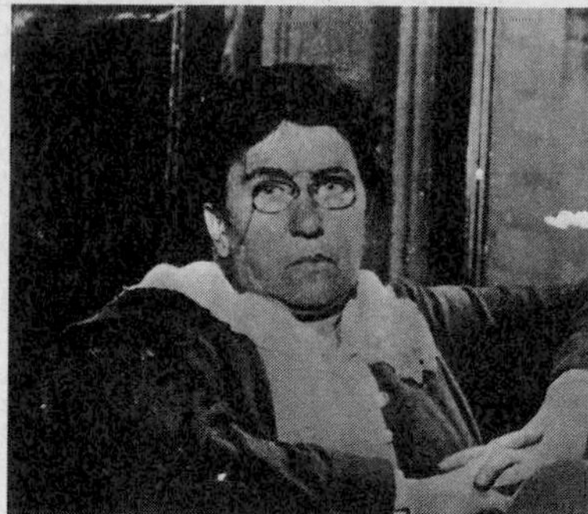

Emma Goldman.

Sargent dominates London art exhibit

May 1. The only bright spot in the Royal Academy art show is the dark paintings of John Singer Sargent. The 141st annual London exhibit features British, European and American artists, but only Sargent, an American with homes on both sides of the Atlantic, is drawing much attention. Eyes are riveted on his portraits, particularly one of an elderly man whose white face contrasts with a rich background. The art world may have some self-assessing to do. Sargent is not new; he is over 50 years old. And it is 25 years since he painted "Madame X," his portrait of a woman in a low-cut, black evening dress.

Sargent's "Mr. and Mrs. Stokes."

Mastermind of Standard Oil merger dies

May 19. Henry Huttleston Rogers, the financial wizard behind the phenomenal rise of the Standard Oil Company, died yesterday at his home in New York City after suffering an attack of apoplexy. He was 68 years old and a millionaire many times over.

The son of a country storekeeper in New England, Rogers began his working years as a newsboy, later drove a grocery wagon and also served as a railroad brakeman before beginning his rapid rise in the financial world. Wall Street analysts have estimated the Rogers fortune to be as large as $75 million. He had vast holdings in railroads, copper and gas, as well as Standard Oil. Rogers was to have met later in the day with his old friend, Samuel L. Clemens, better known as Mark Twain. "This is terrible, terrible, and I cannot talk about it," the author said when told of Rogers' death.

May 30. Count Ferdinand von Zeppelin has disappointed Kaiser Wilhelm and hundreds of spectators in Berlin's Tempelhof Field. Flying a record 22 hours from Friedrichshafen, he decided to turn around his Zeppelin II —the fifth of his self-designed dirigibles —and risk the journey back.

Life's work ends for George Meredith

May 18. The English novelist and poet George Meredith has died at his home in Surrey at age 81. He was born in Hampshire and orphaned early. His younger years were debt-ridden, and for a whole year, it is said, he lived on little but oatmeal. In 1859, his first successful novel, "The Ordeal of Richard Feverel," announced the arrival of a new master of English prose. Of numerous others which followed, the most famous is "The Egoist." Meredith's great ability lay in depicting the types of men and women commonly met in everyday life.

1909

JUNE

Su	Mo	Tu	We	Th	Fr	Sa
		1	2	3	4	5
6	7	8	9	10	11	12
13	14	15	16	17	18	19
20	21	22	23	24	25	26
27	28	29	30			

1. French high court rules postal union illegal (→ 15).

1. World's Fair opens in Seattle.

2. U.S. Signal Corps directed to plan for aerial defense of Atlantic Coast (→ 11/14).

4. Canada decides to build own navy.

4. Moroccan sultan bars Jews of Fez from viewing his palace (→ 5/25/10).

5. Chicago beef trust buys two Argentine packing plants, seeking monopoly (→ 10).

8. Turks execute ringleaders of Adna massacres; 100 more killed in protest (→ 1/31/13).

8. London publishers accuse Mark Twain of plagiarizing Shakespeare.

10. Taft orders inquiry into business practices of sugar trust (→ 8/24).

12. Hawaii: Japanese strikers on sugar plantations indicted for conspiring to incite disorder (→ 6/10/10).

12. As 144 British warships display naval might, Lord Roseberry asserts need to keep pace with Germany in arms race (→ 19).

12. Queensboro Bridge, linking Queens and Manhattan, officially opened.

15. France: Georges Clemenceau refuses amnesty to postal strikers.

17. Finland: Kaiser Wilhelm II and Czar Nicholas II meet in Pitpikas.

19. Andrew Carnegie proposes England host world conference to limit naval armaments (→ 9/7).

21. Liner Mauretania cuts 50 minutes off eastward voyage, New York to London in five days, eight hours (→ 8/30).

23. Britain: Darwin Museum opened to commemorate 100th anniversary of his birth.

26. Persia: Shah annuls electoral law, postpones promised constitution (→ 7/16).

BIRTH

6. Sir Isaiah Berlin, British philosopher and educator.

Du Bois forms Negro rights committee

W.E.B. Du Bois.

June 1. It has been four years since W.E.B. Du Bois and followers met at Niagara Falls to organize the Negro movement's left wing. The Niagara Movement opposes Booker T. Washington's call for vocational training and Protestant virtue as the road to advancement. Today, Du Bois (B.A., M.A., Ph.D., Harvard) founded with the aid of Jane Addams and John Dewey the National Negro Committee to agitate for suffrage and an end to racial prejudice. Du Bois' forecast? "The problem of the 20th Century is the problem of the color line" (→ 5/1/10).

Louis Chevrolet wins fast race in Buick

June 19. Louis Chevrolet, Swiss-born daredevil of auto racing, drove a 40-horsepower Buick to victory in the Cobe Cup race in Crown Point, Indiana. After 395.65 miles, he had out-raced Borque's Knox by one minute, five seconds. Borque closed the gap so quickly at the end of the race that spectators did not know who won. Chevrolet's car broke a cylinder valve on the 11th lap and he had to finish on three cylinders.

Louis Chevrolet is ready to race.

1909

JULY

Su	Mo	Tu	We	Th	Fr	Sa
				1	2	3
4	5	6	7	8	9	10
11	12	13	14	15	16	17
18	19	20	21	22	23	24
25	26	27	28	29	30	31

2. It is reported that British have seized 300 sq. miles in Liberia.

4. Since July 4, 1776, U.S. has acquired three million square miles of land worth $3 trillion.

4. Wimbledon: Arthur Gore becomes oldest men's winner at 41, beating Major Ritchie 6-8, 1-6, 6-2, 6-2, 6-2; Penelope Boothby takes women's title 6-4, 4-6, 8-6 over Agnes Morton.

5. Austria: Franz Joseph inaugurates Tauern railway in Spittal.

7. U.S. protests ratification of Russo-Chinese accord, claiming it violates open door policy.

8. Vatican denounces feminine fashions as immodest.

10. Detroit: 1,000 cars on display in Glidden Auto Parade; said to be biggest in history.

12. Harry Kendall Thaw begins appeal to prove sanity, gain release from asylum (→ 8/12).

12. U.S. Congress proposes 16th Amendment to Constitution; would allow income tax (→ 5/08/13).

13. Great powers announce plan to withdraw troops from Crete, yet warn Ottoman Empire they will protect interests (→ 8/5).

14. German Chancellor Bernhard von Bulow retires, State Secretary Theobald von Bethmann-Hollweg succeeds (→ 24).

14. Edward Payson Weston ends transcontinental walk in San Francisco 105 days, 3,805 miles after leaving N.Y.

15. Taft to raise Panama bond issue to $397 mil. due to budget deficit (→ 8/31/13).

16. Pittsburgh: Steel strikers clash with troops (→ 8/22).

16. Tehran: Persian shah deposed by nationalists; 12-year-old son Azad Mulk to succeed.

20. Orville Wright sets new U.S. record, staying in air 1:20:25; "Bully!" says Wilbur.

23. Ashes of Buddha reported found near Peshawar.

BIRTHS

18. Soviet statesman Andrei Gromyko.

28. British writer Malcolm Lowry (†6/27/1957).

America's Big Four of polo beats Britain

July 4. On the anniversary of the American Revolution, a band of American polo players invaded England to stage a little revolution of their own. They captured the American Polo Cup, which had been in British hands since it was first given in 1886, when a strong English team visited America.

The foursome of Lawrence Waterbury, J.M. Waterbury Jr., Harry Payne Whitney and Devereux Milburn scored an 8-2 victory in the second and deciding match in London. As captain, Whitney received the trophy from the Prince of Wales. All the experts admitted that Great Britain was beaten fairly and squarely by a superior team. And the referee, Walter Buckmaster, England's greatest player, said, "It was the best polo I have ever seen."

Little Gladys Smith, now Mary Pickford, has charmed D.W. Griffith out of $40/week for starring roles in Biograph films.

Channel flight succeeds

July 25. Louis Bleriot, the French aviator, successfully landed at Dover this morning after a flight in his airplane across the English Channel. He thus wins the $2,500 prize offered by the London Daily Mail for the first successful Channel flight.

Such a flight has been the goal this summer of three of Europe's best aviators, Bleriot, the Count de Lambert and Hubert Latham, all of whom have been encamped along the Pas-de-Calais preparing for the attempt. Lambert has not been able to make a flight because of damage to his aircraft. He tried six days ago, but it ended in failure.

Flying an Antoinette monoplane, Lambert took off from the top of a chalk cliff at Sangatte, near Calais, at 6:40 a.m. He appeared to be flying perfectly in ideal weather conditions at an altitude of about 1,000 feet (a new record for height, he says) when the engine of the aircraft quit about halfway across the Channel. Lambert glided gently down into the water and was rescued unharmed by a French torpedo boat which had been keeping abreast of his aircraft during the flight.

Bleriot arrived at the coast near Calais four days ago, flying a monoplane of a design similar to Lambert's but slightly smaller. It is powered by a three-cylinder engine that drives a two-bladed propeller. He wanted to make the Channel attempt immediately, but the flight was delayed by weather. Conditions were good today, and Bleriot took off at 5 a.m., making the 21-mile flight in 37 minutes. The only flaw was a slight injury that he suffered during the landing.

This successful flight is a climax to Bleriot's aviation career, which began with a flight of 600 feet in 1907. The following year, he made a flight of nearly half a mile, winning the French Aero Club Medal. Until today, his most notable achievement was a flight on July 3 of this year at Doue, in which he covered over 26 miles in a little more than 47 minutes. Last November, he narrowly escaped injury when his aircraft capsized during an attempted takeoff near Chartres. Bleriot was able to jump to safety. Yesterday, Bleriot was made a member of the Legion of Honor with two other aviators, Leon Delagrange and Ernest Archdeacon.

German and French premiers changed

July 24. Two governments in Europe were transformed this month as two noted leaders lost power.

In Germany, Prince von Bulow retired and Dr. Theobald von Bethmann-Hollweg follows him as the fifth Chancellor of the Empire. Most observers believe this change will allow Kaiser Wilhelm II more freedom to orchestrate political maneuvers. As the leader of the German government, von Bulow checked the kaiser's power. Bethmann-Hollweg, on the other hand, has been called "an absolute amateur in the subtle field of diplomacy and foreign politics." Furthermore, he and the kaiser are longtime friends, dating back to their days as students at Bonn University.

French Premier Georges Clemenceau left office in indignation after a violent debate in the Chamber. A political career spanning decades came tumbling down on Clemenceau as he erupted at former Foreign Minister Delcasse, who is currently investigating allegations of corruption in the French navy. Just as the Chamber was to vote confidence in the government, Clemenceau brought up Delcasse's eviction from a French ship at the hands of the Germans during the Moroccan crisis in 1905. The premier shouted, "You led us to the greatest humiliation France has experienced in 20 years." Clemenceau's majority abandoned him, forcing his resignation. Aristide Briand has succeeded as Premier and alteration of the political landscape is expected.

Ellis Island will use stricter new rules

July 18. Immigration Commissioner William Williams has submitted guidelines which he believes will reduce the number of so-called undesirables at Ellis Island.

His new policy follows concern over the change in immigration patterns. British and Northern Europeans of previous decades are being replaced by Southern Italians, Greeks, Poles and Russian Jews. The commissioner states that up to one-fourth of the newcomers "are not wanted and are of no benefit to the country." According to his revised restrictions, only those immigrants possessing $25 or more will be granted admission. Aliens must also guarantee lifelong independence from public and private charities.

Ellis Island doctor checks for typhus.

Reno of all places now divorce center

July 18. The 18,000 residents of Reno, Nevada, have marital misfortune to thank for the renewed financial vigor of their former mining town. Women nationwide are flocking there for divorces, granted after a shamefully brief waiting period of six months. The Reno Legislature relaxed the residency requirement in hopes of attracting unhappy, extravagant socialites. The plan succeeds; since the change in divorce laws a year ago, hotels, cottages, restaurants and small gambling establishments have flourished. And the town has increased its revenue by $1 million.

Sheet music cover for Percy Wenrich's "Hula Hula."

1909

AUGUST

Su	Mo	Tu	We	Th	Fr	Sa
1	2	3	4	5	6	7
8	9	10	11	12	13	14
15	16	17	18	19	20	21
22	23	24	25	26	27	28
29	30	31				

1. Belgian bicyclist Francois Faber wins Tour de France.

1. Spain: Catalonia in open revolt; 1,000 dead.

2. Great Britain: Workers demonstrate upon arrival of Czar Nicholas II's visit.

4. Sweden: Nationwide strikes begin.

5. Washington: Pres. Taft signs Payne-Aldrich Tariff Bill, effective today (→ 9/17).

5. Crete: As demonstrations for union with Greece continue, Ottoman Empire asks Greek govt. to repudiate Cretan rebels (→ 16).

7. French aviator Roger Sommer bests Wright's longest time in air, staying aloft 2:27:15 (→ 9/24).

7. Record harvest, increases in rail and factory construction signal general wave of prosperity in U.S.

12. Judge finds Harry K. Thaw still criminally insane, sends him back to asylum.

16. Under pressure from Ottoman Empire, Cretan unionists promise to lower Greek flag (→ 5/9/10).

19. Hungary: Imperial decree imposes Hungarian as official language for religious instruction in Rumanian schools.

19. Pres. Taft orders dismissal of seven West Point cadets for hazing.

21. Berlin reported taking the place of Paris as favorite spot for American tourists.

24. Chicago: Western railways win rate increases in fight with Interstate Commerce Commission (→ 9/20).

24. Revolt reported in northern Albania.

29. California: Flood takes over 1,200 lives in Monterey.

30. Liner Mauretania arrives in London 5 days, 9 hours, 22 minutes en route from N.Y.

BIRTH

27. Jazz musician Lester Young, in Woodville, Miss. (†3/15/1959).

Violence marks steel strike; troops and workers battle; 5 killed

Aug 22. At least five men were killed and scores injured in a pitched battle tonight between striking workers and law enforcement officials at the Pressed Steel Car Company plants near Pittsburgh. Among the dead are a deputy sheriff, a state trooper and several strikebreakers.

The bitter fighting climaxed a day of violence in which an attempt was made to blow up the mills and in which the company restaurants were wrecked by a mob of women throwing bombs. The day's rioting was the most violent in the more than week of fighting at the factories. Wives and mothers have also joined the strikers in recent days.

Tonight, as darkness fell, the strikers formed armed patrols to seek out the strikebreakers. Shots were fired, rocks were thrown at the state troopers, and other police officers rushed into the fray, herding scores of angry strikers and strikebreakers into box-car jails in the mill yards.

Immigrant steel workers in Pennsylvania want better working conditions.

Workers at the steel mills, known to many as the "slaughter house," have been on strike in order to achieve better working conditions. An ex-coroner has said that he believes at least one worker a day had been killed due to faulty machinery. Until the strike, the mills had been manufacturing cars for use in the Hudson and Manhattan tunnels in New York City (→ 12/14).

Glenn Curtiss wins aviation cup, cash

Aug 28. With a performance that awed spectators at Rheims, Glenn H. Curtiss of the United States captured the International Cup of Aviation and a $5,000 prize. The French were bitterly disappointed by the outcome, which they attributed to bad luck. Louis Bleriot made a desperate effort to keep the cup in France but fell 5.6 seconds short of Curtiss' mark. Curtiss flew 12.42 miles in 15 minutes, 50.6 seconds, leading Count de Lambert to note: "The day on which man in his primitive form crawled out of the water and found he could move and live on land was no more an epoch than this."

Glenn H. Curtiss.

In high-price era wife desertions rise

Aug 13. The number of cases of men deserting their wives rose 33 percent in Manhattan this year, and it is believed that many of the 3,000 men who abandoned their wives did so due to the high cost of living. Most of the men were poor, between the ages of 20 and 24, and left two or more children behind them. New York considers the crime a misdemeanor, sentencing offenders to a six-month prison term. Iowa, Oregon, Nevada, Tennessee and Texas inflict no penalty at all. And four states treat desertion as a felony.

Statistics from the New York Bureau of Charities cite drinking and meddlesome neighbors and relatives as major contributors to marital discord and desertion. Changes in marital roles may also be to blame. Necessities of life proving so dear, many young girls are driven to work in factories or stores to support their families. And when they wed, they sometimes demonstrate their lack of experience in domestic skills. Despairing husbands often choose desertion as a less expensive alternative to divorce, the price of which is also rising.

Oldfield sets world records at raceway

Aug 21. Barney Oldfield drove his German Benz racer to five world records today, but the luster of his accomplishment was diminished by a rash of death and injury at the Indianapolis Motor Speedway. The promoters had to prematurely end the final program of the three-day meet when three persons were killed and a fourth injured as a capacity crowd of 20,000 watched. The deaths occurred when the National car, driven by Merz, burst a tire and skidded off the track and into a cluster of onlookers. Oldfield drove his 120-horsepower machine to world records at five, ten, 15, 20 and 25 miles.

Barney Oldfield sets the pace.

1909

SEPTEMBER

Su	Mo	Tu	We	Th	Fr	Sa
			1	2	3	4
5	6	7	8	9	10	11
12	13	14	15	16	17	18
19	20	21	22	23	24	25
26	27	28	29	30		

2. Dr. Frederick A. Cook claims he reached N. Pole April 21, 1908 (→ 6).

2. European powers notify sultan that tortures in Morocco must end (→ 26).

6. Commander Robert E. Peary wires N.Y. Times from Atlantic Ocean he reached N. Pole on April 6, 1909, found no trace of Cook (→ 30).

7. Lord Northcliffe, owner of London Times, asserts Kaiser Wilhelm is rushing preparations for war with Britain (→ 11/1).

13. Geneva: Congress of Egyptian Youth demands British evacuation of Egypt (→ 11/19/19).

16. Spain: Editors meet in San Sebastian, demand guarantee of constitution, freedom of press (→ 6/11/10).

17. In Minnesota speech, Taft lauds Payne-Aldrich Tariff Bill as best ever in U.S. (→ 20).

17. New York: First trolley car crosses Queensboro Bridge, one of three great cantilever structures in world.

18. Great Britain: Two suffragettes sent to jail for throwing stones at Prime Minister Asquith (→ 10/19).

18. Paris: Over 1,000 women have applied for flying instruction.

20. British Parliament sanctions S. African constitution, establishes English, Dutch as official languages (→ 4/27/10).

20. Tariff bill reported to aid trusts; large manufacturers raise rates seven percent (→ 1/18/10).

24. Wilbur Wright announces desire to prevent foreign planes from entering U.S. (→ 25).

25. New York: First National Aeronautic Show opens at Madison Square Garden.

26. Spanish announce Moors beaten in Morocco (→ 10/7).

27. Taft reserves three mil. oil-rich acres in Midwest (including Teapot Dome) for future use by Navy (→ 5/31/21).

BIRTH

7. U.S. film director Elia Kazan.

Who discovered the North Pole, Peary or Cook? Experts ask for the evidence

Sept 30. A major controversy has erupted over the competing claims of Commander Robert E. Peary and Frederick A. Cook to have been the first to reach the North Pole.

Peary arrived in Labrador on September 6 to announce that he had reached the pole on April 6, 1909, only to learn of Cook's claim, made five days earlier, that he had reached the pole on April 21, 1908. Cook, an erstwhile associate of Peary's, says he made the trip accompanied by a few Eskimos, and that he buried an American flag in a metal tube at the top of the world.

Cook's claim came as a surprise, since he has received almost none of the public attention paid to Peary's three attempts to reach the North Pole. Until now, Cook has been known only as the first man to climb Mount McKinley. While Cook is now being acclaimed in Copenhagen, Peary has challenged his North Pole claim.

Peary says that when he arrived at the pole, he saw no signs that anyone had preceded him. He also says that he has interviewed two of the Eskimos who were in Cook's party and that both say that their expedition turned back far from the North Pole. It is significant that while the Royal Geographical Society of London has congratulated Peary and invited him to speak, it has sent no such message to cook (→ 10/13).

Conquest of the North Pole.

Millions celebrate Fulton's steamboat

Sept 9. Americans celebrated the 100th anniversary of the launch of Fulton's steamboat, the Clermont, yesterday with big parades and a display of the Atlantic fleet. Crowds at New York harbor hailed the ships by waving handkerchiefs and singing the national anthem.

The fleet's three armored cruisers, three scout cruisers, 16 battleships and squadron of auxiliaries constitute the greatest armada in the Western hemisphere and represent an outlay of 250,000 tons of steel and $75 million.

Many eyes were focused on the battleship New York, refitted after its exertions in the battle of Santiago. The graceful, three-funneled scout cruisers also awed onlookers, racing through the waves at nearly 30 miles per hour. Vessels from Mexico, Italy and France also participated in the exhibition.

Marching bands monopolize Fifth Avenue in New York.

Harriman, builder of rail empire, dies

Sept 9. Edward Henry Harriman, the prominent railroad tycoon, is dead. His wife and other members of the family were with the 61-year-old multimillionaire when he died at his estate, Arden, in Orange County, New York, today. Harriman was a giant in the field of railroads and once dreamed of owning a network embracing the entire nation. Indeed, at one point his holdings in such rail lines as Union Pacific, New York Central and many others covered 54,300 miles of tracks.

Edward Henry Harriman.

He was a principal organizer of the Northern Securities Company, a holding company designed to prevent railroad competition. In a far-reaching decision in 1904, the United States Supreme Court found the company in violation of the Sherman Antitrust Act and ordered it dissolved. That did not end Harriman's tilts with the federal authorities. Just two years ago, he was severely chided, though not disciplined, by the Interstate Commerce Commission for his tight grip on the railroad world. It was disclosed during the hearings, for instance, that he had spent $103 million for railroad holdings in just six months.

Harriman, the son of an Episcopal minister in Hempstead, New York, went to work at the age of 14 as an office boy in a Wall Street firm. Eight years later, he borrowed $3,000 from an uncle and bought a seat on the Stock Exchange. From then on, his rise in the financial world was a rapid one, particularly after he began delving into the lucrative railroad field.

1909

OCTOBER

Su	Mo	Tu	We	Th	Fr	Sa
					1	2
3	4	5	6	7	8	9
10	11	12	13	14	15	16
17	18	19	20	21	22	23
24	25	26	27	28	29	30
31						

2. Potsdam: Orville Wright soars to unprecedented height of over 1,600 feet.

2. China: Railway inaugurated between Peking and Kalgan; first built entirely by Chinese.

7. Spain: Gen. D'Amade placed on reserve for criticizing Spanish encroachment on French territory in Morocco (→ 10).

10. Morocco: Berber tribes in north submit to Spanish.

11. New York: George Cohan's musical "The Man Who Owns Broadway" premieres at the New York Theater.

13. Commander Peary discloses evidence indicating Cook's route was far from N. Pole (→ 14).

14. Cook's guide, Edward N. Barrill, swears Cook's claim is false (→ 12/21).

15. New York: One hundred steel manufacturers from U.S. and Canada gather to honor Elbert Gary of U.S. Steel.

16. Texas: Pres. Taft and Mexican Pres. Diaz meet in El Paso.

16. Pittsburgh Pirates trounce Detroit 8-0 to take World Series four games to three.

23. Holland: International court at The Hague determines boundaries off coasts of Sweden and Norway.

24. Racconigi Pact extablishes accord between Russia, Italy; recognizes spheres of influence in Balkans.

24. Germany: Social Democrat Auguste Bebel appeals for abolition of capital punishment.

31. New York: West Point cadet, injured in Harvard football game, dies; annual Army-Navy game canceled (→ 11/20).

BIRTHS

19. Pakistani statesman Mohammed Ali (†1/23/1963).

28. Francis Bacon, British figural painter.

DEATH

8. Jewish poet Napthall Herz Imber, author of Zionist natl. hymn.

Japan's Bismarck, Ito, killed by Korean

Prince Ito and Princess (seated) with their son and his children.

Oct 26. Prince Ito, 72, Japan's greatest statesman, has been assassinated by a Korean nationalist.

Ito has been compared in stature to Thomas Jefferson of the United States and Prussia's Prince Otto von Bismarck, the first because of his part in writing Japan's constitution, the latter because he built Japan into a world power. At the time of his death, the prince had just ended a tour of duty as Governor General of Korea. His harsh repression of an insurrection against Japan's control of the country is believed to be the cause of his assassination.

The son of a Samurai, one of Japan's feudal lords, Ito was sent to Britain to study weapons and learned instead that only by modernizing his country's government, through a constitution, would Japan be a great power. Ito was Prime Minister for two terms during the late 19th century. He earned his title of prince for his success in steering his country through a war with China. Prince Ito was also influential during the 1905 war with Russia.

Ferrer shot; Europeans protest violently

"Execution of Ferrer": painting by Constantin Flavio.

Oct 14. For the second night in a row, demonstrators are filling the streets of Paris to protest the execution in Barcelona of Professor Francisco Ferrer. The socialist educator was found guilty of taking part in the recent violent uprising against the Spanish government, even though he was in London at the time. Spain's King Alfonso was burned in effigy tonight. Last night, police fought back with swords as an angry mob tried to attack the Spanish Embassy. One officer was killed, 76 people were hurt and police say they arrested five notorious anarchists. There have also been protests in Austria, Italy and Spain over the execution (→ 11/8).

Harvard Law School excludes a woman

Oct 22. A young Vassar College graduate, denied admission to Harvard University Law School, sought help today from other suffragettes. Inez Milholland traveled from Boston to New York City to relate her plight to leaders of an upcoming gathering of women seeking the right to vote.

Miss Milholland said that the law school faculty favored admitting her as a student but that Harvard trustees opposed the move. She quoted one trustee as saying that they feared a drop in applications "because of the prejudice against men and women studying together." She also said that another trustee told her he was opposed to all change, including railroads and telephones. Miss Milholland is planning to apply to another law school.

Noted suffragette arrives for parley

Oct 19. Holding aloft a banner that read "Vote for Women," an excited crowd greeted the arrival in New York City tonight of Emmeline Pankhurst, the leader of the British suffragettes. Mrs. Pankhurst, whose gentle demeanor belies her militant actions in seeking the vote, arrived aboard the White Star steamer, the Oceanic. She will be a principal speaker next week at a Carnegie Hall convention of American suffragettes. At a press conference tonight, Mrs. Pankhurst predicted that women in Britain are on the verge of getting the right to vote.

Suffragette Emmeline Pankhurst.

1909

NOVEMBER

Su	Mo	Tu	We	Th	Fr	Sa
	1	2	3	4	5	6
7	8	9	10	11	12	13
14	15	16	17	18	19	20
21	22	23	24	25	26	27
28	29	30				

1. French deputies ask creation of native colonial army in case of European conflict.

2. U.S.: Party machines dominate big city elections; municipal reformers frustrated.

4. Mass.: Rachmaninoff makes U.S. debut at Smith College.

7. 24-hour train service opens between N.Y. and St. Louis.

8. Spain: Constitutional rights restored in Spain as protests over Ferrer's execution quiet.

9. Mrs. John Jacob Astor quietly obtains divorce; N.Y. lawyers condemn ease with which rich and prominent can annul marriages.

11. Hawaii: Work begins on naval base at Pearl Harbor.

13. Govt. investigator charges Roosevelt administration indifferent to obtaining evidence against sugar trust (→ 20).

13. Illinois: Explosion kills 400 miners at Cherry; mine deaths total 2,494 in last five years.

14. Brussels: Great powers meet to discuss regulation of arms market in Africa.

20. Minn.: Federal court rules Standard Oil in violation of Sherman Antitrust Act, orders cessation of trade; case to go to Supreme Court (→ 12/2).

20. Chicago Tribune reports 1909 saw 26 football deaths, 70 injuries.

23. Wright brothers form mil. dollar corporation for commercial manufacture of airplanes.

27. U.S. troops land in Bluefields, Nicaragua (→ 12/1).

28. French Natl. Assembly offers working women eight weeks vacation after childbirth (→ 12/19).

29. Russia: Maxim Gorki expelled from Revolutionary Party for bourgeois hedonism.

BIRTHS

8. American actress Katharine Hepburn.

14. American politician Joseph McCarthy (→ 5/2/1957).

26. French playwright Eugene Ionesco, theater of the absurd.

The best of times for American farmers

Bumper crop this year in the hinterlands has brought unprecedented profits.

Nov 30. Corn is the most valuable product in America today. Valued at $1.7 billion, it is worth more than all the gold and silver coin and bullion in the nation. This striking fact was revealed today in the Secretary of Agriculture's 13th annual report, which also proclaimed that 1909 is the most prosperous year in the history of American farming.

While corn earns $15 million a day for the American farmer, cotton and wheat are the second and third most valuable crops, according to the report. Cotton lint and seed were worth about $850 million to farmers this year, while wheat was worth about $725 million for the year. These sums vastly exceed all previous values.

The farm situation has changed markedly since the late 19th century when widespread discontent in rural areas found expression in the Populist revolt. In fact, today's report concludes that the current wave of agricultural prosperity "has established banks, made better homes and helped to make the farmer a citizen of the world."

Over 2 million Americans now own stocks

Nov 7. In the days of fully concentrated corporate ownership, sending out dividend checks wasn't much of a task. Now that some two million investors own the corporations, it's become a big job. Annual steel corporation checks alone would stretch for 50 miles.

Outdoor trading on Wall Street.

Things have certainly changed in recent years. Not too long ago a man who owned securities was considered snooty. Today, he's considered thrifty. The dividend check is no longer a mystery, and your fellow man, be he owner or worker, is likely to ask your opinion of some investment.

Stocks and bonds amount to about $40 billion, a third of the nation's wealth, with stock dividends about $1 billion a year and bond earnings only slightly less. Due to the industrial boom of the last ten years, railroad dividends are thrice what they were in the mid-90's. Carnegie Steel's 63 stockholders of nine years ago are now 100,000, and John D. Rockefeller now has 5,000 partners. Indeed, the boom would not have been possible without this modern method of raising huge amounts of capital.

Living costs at near record level in U.S.

Nov 12. The national cost of living, which fell after the panic of 1907, has not only bounced back but is close to the highest level ever recorded. Commodity prices reached their lowest level in 1896 during the depression preceding the Spanish-American War. Since then, prices have risen 56.7 percent. The Bradstreet index puts commodity prices at $8.9173. The figure represents a 7.9 percent rise in the cost of living since January 1, and a 10.5 percent rise during the past three years. Bradstreet says the rising price of raw materials has pushed up other prices and is prompting workers to demand higher wages.

Building naval base at Pearl Harbor

Nov 14. President Taft, resolving a controversy between the Navy and Army, has selected Pearl Harbor in the Hawaiian Islands as the principal naval base in the Pacific. The decision thwarts Navy plans for developing a major base at Subic Bay in the Philippines, an area the Army considered indefensible. President Taft was reported to have concluded that a naval base in the mid-Pacific would be more defensible against any potential threat from Japan. The decision also reflects the President's belief that the Panama canal holds the key to strategic supremacy in the Pacific.

Football deaths up

Nov 28. With the revelation that the death toll from football in 1909 had nearly doubled from the total for the previous year, the call was sounded anew for the reformation of the gridiron sport. Twenty-six players were killed and 70 seriously injured thus far this year, according to figures assembled by the Chicago Tribune. In 1907, there were 14 deaths and 13 in 1908. The rules committee is considering changes that would remove some of the perils of the sport, including one that would ban substitution of a player who has been ruled off the field for roughness.

1909

DECEMBER

Su	Mo	Tu	We	Th	Fr	Sa
			1	2	3	4
5	6	7	8	9	10	11
12	13	14	15	16	17	18
19	20	21	22	23	24	25
26	27	28	29	30	31	

1. London: House of Lords rejects Lloyd George's budget (→ 5/10/10).

1. Pres. Taft severs official relations with Nicaragua's Zelaya govt., declares support for revolutionaries (→ 16).

2. J.P. Morgan acquires majority holdings in Equitable Life Co.; called largest concentration of banking power (→ 17).

10. Nobel Prizes: G. Marconi, F. Braun for physics, Sweden's Selma Lagerlof for literature.

14. Pittsburgh: Labor conference ends in declaration of war on U.S. Steel (→ 1/6/10).

16. Nicaragua: Jose Zelaya yields to U.S. Marines, resigns as president (→ 17).

17. Standard Oil takes case to Supreme Court (→ 2/23/10).

17. Berlin attacks U.S. for inciting revolt in Nicaragua (→ 1/28/10).

19. U.S.: Socialist women denounce suffrage as movement of middle class (→ 3/8/10).

26. Germany: Ninth Zionist Congress opens in Hamburg.

26. U.S.: It is reported that dry counties in South consume more liquor than before passage of law (→ 11/6/11).

CULTURAL EVENTS, 1909

Literature: Filippo Marinetti's "Le Figaro," Futurist manifesto; Ezra Pound's first book of poetry, "Personnae."

Religion, Academia: Lenin's "Materialism and Empirico-Criticism"; Wm. Beveridge's "A Problem for Industry"; Jewish population at 5.2 mil. in Russia, 2 mil. in Austria-Hungary, 1.7 mil. in U.S., 600,000 in Germany, 400,000 in Turkey, 200,000 in Great Britain, 100,000 in France.

Music: Strauss' "Elektra" in Dresden; Mahler's "Symphony No. 9"; W.C. Handy's "Memphis Blues," first blues transcribed; Sergei Diaghilev takes Ballet Russe to Paris.

The Arts: Kandinsky's first abstract paintings; Frank Lloyd Wright's Robie House, Chicago; first newsreels.

Remington has depicted his last cowboy

Dec 26. Sculptor and painter Frederic Remington died this morning at age 48 when an acute case of appendicitis was not treated in time.

Remington once said, "I knew more about cowboys than I did about drawing." He was, in fact, an expert on both. Born in upper New York state, he studied art at Yale. Restless after college, he got work as a cow-herder out West. At six-feet tall with broad shoulders, he fared as well as any ranchhand.

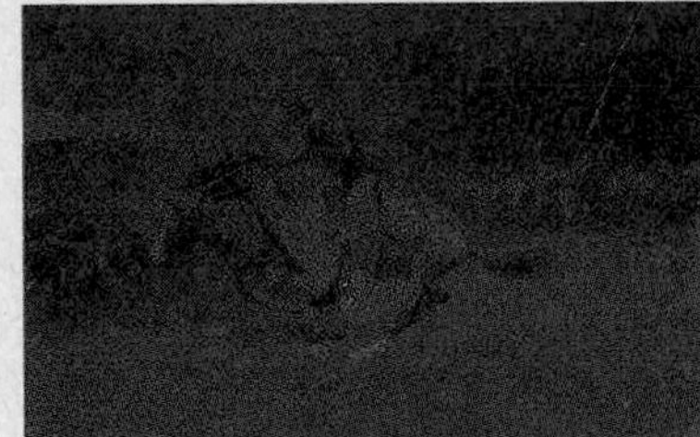

"Stampeded by Lightning."

Remington's first western-influenced painting was commissioned by Harper's Weekly in the early 1880's. It depicted a scene from Geronimo's campaign. Later, the artist illustrated Theodore Roosevelt's series of cowboy articles. Remington also worked deftly in bronze; "The Bucking Bronco" may be his finest sculpture.

Experts reject Cook and acclaim Peary

Dec 21. Experts have emphatically rejected the claim of Frederick A. Cook, and Commander Robert E. Peary is being hailed as the leader of the first expedition to reach the North Pole.

The decisive blow against Cook came today, when a committee appointed by the University of Copenhagen declared that documents submitted by Cook to support his claim "do not contain observations and information which can be regarded as proof that Dr. Cook reached the North Pole on his recent expedition." It is understood that some members of the committee say privately that Cook appears to have forged much of the information they examined.

Doubts about Cook's claim have been expressed from the start. While Peary readily supplied copious amounts of information about his expedition, Cook evaded requests for data submitted by several scientific bodies. Several Eskimos who were in Cook's expedition testified that his party came nowhere near the North Pole. An added blow to Cook's veracity came in October, when his claim to have been the first to climb Mount McKinley was challenged by the guide who accompanied him. Cook did not come within 20 miles of the peak, the guide testified.

While Cook now has been disgraced in the eyes of the public, Peary is being heaped with awards. Last week, he was presented with a gold medal by the National Geographic Society at a dinner attended by many dignitaries (→ 5/4/10).

Albert follows Leopold as Belgium's King

Dec 23. In a dazzling ceremony, Prince Albert pranced on his horse through the streets of Brussels today and took the oath to succeed his late uncle Leopold as King of Belgium.

Thousands of people started claiming places along the royal procession at dawn. Others waved from windows and stood on rooftops. A few socialists tried to disrupt the ceremonies, but they were drowned out by loud cries of "Long live the king." Albert's smile broke into an unabashed grin as flowers showered down on the coach of his wife, Queen Elizabeth.

In a speech, King Albert promised liberty for Belgians and fairness for the Congo. He defended his uncle's controversial policies in equatorial Africa. "The mission of colonization cannot be other than a mission of high civilization," the new king declared.

Through most of his reign, Leopold was criticized harshly for his ruthless exploitation and profiteering in the Congo. There was also much scandal about his personal life. When Leopold died nine days ago, reporters asked whether he was married to the Baroness Vaughan when she attended the intimate last-rights ritual.

Freud tours America expounding theory

Sigmund Freud, the controversial Austrian psychiatrist and founder of the movement known as psychoanalysis, has brought his theories to the United States.

Freud and his latest associate, the Swiss psychiatrist C.G. Jung, were invited this year to give a lecture series at Clark University in Worcester, Massachusetts. The lectures represent a major international recognition of Freudian theory. Earlier this year, a paper he co-authored, "On the Psychical Mechanism of Hysterical Phenomena," was translated into English.

Sigmund Freud.

In that paper, Freud outlined his theory that the symptoms of hysterical patients are related to psychic disturbances earlier in life. Freud uses hypnosis to make his patients recall and even act out those forgotten traumas. But he has been scorned by some members of the medical community because he says that many of those disturbances are sexual in nature.

Besides hypnosis, Freud tries to help his patients recognize their repressed thoughts and actions through a technique he calls "free association." Freud arrives at much of his psychoanalytic theory by interpreting dreams.

1909 eight-h.p. Humber.

1910 – 1919

1910

JANUARY

Su	Mo	Tu	We	Th	Fr	Sa
						1
2	3	4	5	6	7	8
9	10	11	12	13	14	15
16	17	18	19	20	21	22
23	24	25	26	27	28	29
30	31					

1. New York: Caruso sings in first radio broadcast from stage of Metropolitan Opera.

3. Germany: Social Democratic congress demands universal suffrage (→ 11).

3. British miners strike for eight-hour day.

3. John D. Rockefeller named to head grand jury on white slavery investigation (→ 12).

6. Union leaders ask Pres. Taft to investigate U.S. Steel trade practices.

6. German geographical society honors Ernest Shackleton, discoverer of Magnetic S. Pole (→ 6/1).

7. Taft dismisses Gifford Pinchot, head of Forest Service.

8. British elections raise German peril as major issue (→ 2/24/11).

10. Wilbur Wright appeals for tighter patent laws.

11. Berlin: Kaiser Wilhelm II promises suffrage reform (→ 3/6).

15. France reorganizes colonial territories into French Equatorial Africa.

16. U.S. annual defense budget reported at $2 billion.

18. German govt. warns U.S. it is ready for trade war.

19. Revolt breaks out in Uruguay.

21. Japan rejects U.S. proposal to neutralize ownership of Manchurian railway.

21. French press reveals Austro-Hungarian scheme to annex Serbia (→3/13/12).

23. Chicago grand jury to begin inquiry into high price of meat, as boycott has attracted over one million participants.

24. London: Lloyd George retains seat in Parliament; Liberals maintain bare majority.

25. Conn.: Electricity used as anesthetic to amputate man's toes.

26. Police rescue British Prime Minister Asquith from attack by suffragettes.

31. Russia, Britain announce intent to intervene as unrest grows in Persia (→ 8/8).

Paris flood imperils Louvre, costs millions

Paris' Saint-Lazare railway station, engulfed by water.

Jan 26. A cold, heartless rain has been falling on Paris for more than a week, flooding streets and homes and causing damage estimated at $200 million. The Seine has already reached record heights, and it is now threatening to overflow into the sculpture gallery of the Louvre. The Venus de Milo and countless other priceless pieces of art are reported to be in danger.

Thousands of residents have been evacuated from their homes, and Premier Briand is warning that the floods are approaching the most populous sections of the city. Most subway and rail lines have been shut down, and food is becoming scarce and expensive. There is enough water to drink but not enough to run factories in the city.

In the suburbs, at least seven soldiers have drowned while trying to perform rescue work. Food and drinking water are scarce, and hundreds of families are living in misery. Scarlet fever has broken out in one town, and police fear floods may start washing bodies out of cemeteries (→ 2/1).

Mann Act aimed at white slavery

Jan 12. A bill to curb "white slave" traffic in the United States passed the House of Representatives today. Sponsored by Rep. James Robert Mann of Illinois, the White Slave Traffic Bill, if passed by the Senate, would prohibit the interstate transportion of women for immoral purposes.

In addition to banning the actual transportation of women for such purposes, the bill also would make liable for prosecution anyone who merely buys a ticket for a woman who travels from state to state for an immoral purpose. Alien women arrested in these circumstances would be deported.

The bill is the outgrowth of an investigation made by the National Immigration Commission into the trafficking in aliens. Those who are found guilty of dealing in such trafficking would be subject to ten years in prison as well as a $5,000 fine.

Latham monoplane reaches 3,300 feet

Jan 8. Hubert Latham,the French aviator, set a new world's altitude record today when he flew his monoplane to a height of more than 3,300 feet. The achievement was all the more daring and unexpected because it came only four days after the death of one of Latham's chief rivals, Leon Delagrange, in a crash at Bordeaux.

Latham began his exploit at 2:30 p.m., when he taxied the monoplane Antoinette onto an airstrip at Bouy and then took to the air. Watched by an attentive crowd, he steadily gained altitude as he circled the field. As the onlookers cheered, Latham reached his maximum altitude, estimated at over 3,300 feet by appointed observers, at 3:15 p.m., after 45 minutes in the air. He then flew to a safe landing and was given an exultant greeting by the crowd that pressed around his aircraft. His exploit is new proof of the power of the airplane.

Nicaraguan rebels reported as winning

Jan 28. The rebel troops of General Chamorro defeated the Nicaraguan government troops led by General Vasquez in a bloody battle at La Libertad on January 25, according to dispatches received at Bluefields.

The rebel victory comes on the heels of President Madriz's announcement on the 20th to end peace negotiations and his subsequent order for government reinforcements to be sent to the front. General Estrada, the leader of the revolutionists, had agreed to an offer by Madriz to meet government representatives at Greytown, provided the president would recognize the rebels as constituting a provisional government. Madriz called the proposal preposterous, claiming acceptance of the insurgent terms would essentially delegitimize his own government. He then canceled all peace talks. Chamorro and Estrada have effectively demoralized Madriz's troops with the victory at La Libertad and an earlier win at Acoyapa, where the rebels surprised government forces.

Meanwhile, United States Rear Admiral Kimball issued a statement to Americans, insisting that all citizens keep out of the conflict: "(Americans should) absolutely abstain from any participation in political controversies and from any violation of the laws of neutrality (in) Nicaragua. No protection will be extended to any so-called American interests, which as a matter of fact have no existence in law or in right" (→ 2/24).

Aviation display in France.

1910

FEBRUARY

Su	Mo	Tu	We	Th	Fr	Sa
		1	2	3	4	5
6	7	8	9	10	11	12
13	14	15	16	17	18	19
20	21	22	23	24	25	26
27	28					

1. International Red Cross offers assistance to victims of Paris flood.

3. North African assembly gives German industrialist Krupp access to steel mines.

6. Vatican: Pope Pius X refuses audience to Methodist Charles Fairbanks, ex-vice pres. of U.S.

7. Belgium, Germany, Britain fix borders in Congo, Uganda, German E. Africa.

7. Paris audiences pleased by debut of Edmond Rostand's play "Chantecler."

11. Theodore Roosevelt Jr. and Eleanor Alexander announce wedding date (→ 6/20).

12. Liner General Chanzy sinks off coast of Minorca with 154 passengers aboard.

13. Rumanian Social Democratic Party formed.

13. China: 6,000 foreign-trained troops rebel, plunder Canton.

19. Jules Massenet's opera "Don Quixote" opens in Monte Carlo.

19. Germany, Switzerland and Italy agree to build railway through the Saint-Gothard pass in the Swiss Alps.

20. Egypt: Islamic revolt grows; British-supported Christian Copt Premier Butros Ghali assassinated by nationalist.

23. Germany attacks Standard Oil's foreign operations.

24. Nicaragua: American soldier killed in battle with govt. troops (→ 7/28).

25. Tibetan Dalai Lama flees from Chinese, takes refuge in India.

25. West Indies: Riots break out in Guadeloupe.

28. New York: Russian dancer Anna Pavlova makes U.S. debut at Metropolitan Opera.

BIRTH

13. American physicist William Shockley, invented transistor.

DEATH

25. American landscape artist Worthington Whittredge (*5/22/1820).

X-ray machine used to find and remove nail from boy's lung

Feb 27. Surgeons at Beth Israel Hospital in New York have used an X-ray machine to detect a nail in the lung of a 9-year-old boy and to guide its removal by forceps.

The boy, Jacob Miller, was brought to the hospital by his father, who was worried by his son's unexplained loss of weight. Several doctors who had been consulted earlier were baffled by the case. Young Jacob had not told his father that he had swallowed the inch-long nail, for fear of punishment.

The nail was discovered on an X-ray plate taken by Dr. Francis Huber, in charge of the children's ward. Huber then invited other doctors to witness an operation in which an incision was made in the boy's neck and the nail was removed by forceps inserted and guided by the images on a fluoroscope screen.

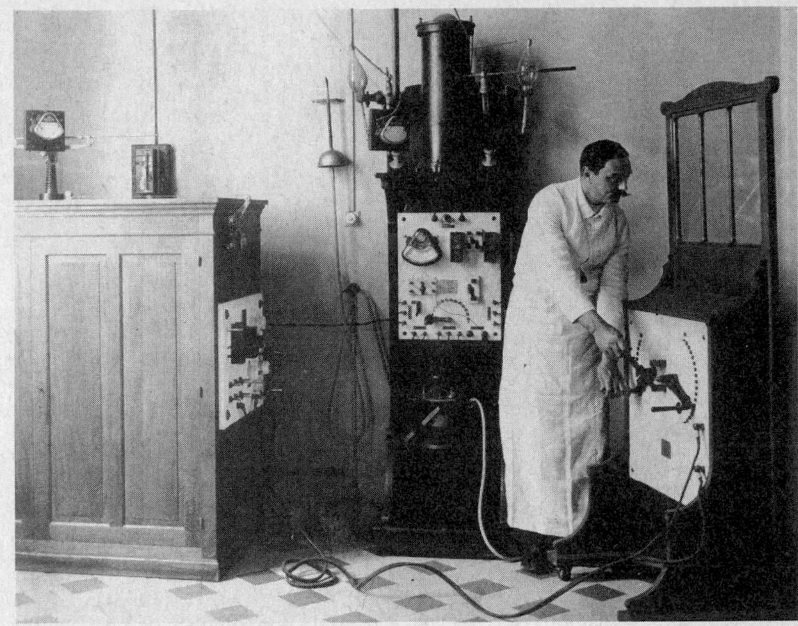

Technician uses the latest in X-ray technology.

Charcot pleased with Antarctic voyage

Jean Charcot's ship Pourquoi Pas? (Why Not?).

Feb 12. Why Not? is the ship's name, and it may have some of the answers scientists have been awaiting. The vessel of the French explorer Jean Charcot has arrived in Punta Arenas, on the Strait of Magellan in Chile, after a hard, wintry voyage into the depths of Antarctica. Word of the ship's return came in a message from Charcot to his wife.

Charcot said that he had completed most of the mission assigned to him by the Academy of Sciences. He said that his ship did run aground once, but he managed to reach a point close to the 69th latitude. "There were huge icebergs all around us," Charcot said. "We came back to the north and spent the winter on Petermann's Island. The winter was mild, but difficult. We made a number of interesting excursions, especially on the icebergs."

Neither Charcot nor any of the Antarctic explorers before him has succeeded in reaching the South Pole. But that was not Charcot's goal. He has reached Antarctic regions never visited before, and geographers are waiting anxiously to see his research.

British Boy Scout idea moves to U.S.

Feb 8. William D. Boyce, a Chicago publisher, has filed incorporation papers for the Boy Scouts of America in Washington, D.C.

Boyce learned of Robert Baden-Powell's British organization while on a business trip to London last year. He had lost his way in that city's proverbial fog when a boy with a lantern came to his aid. Boyce tried to tip the lad, who declared, "No, sir, I am a scout. Scouts do not accept tips for courtesies or good turns." Boyce was indelibly impressed.

Boyce and other scout leaders, such as Dan Beard, are recruiting American boys who want to learn "patriotism, courage, self-reliance and kindred virtues."

Dan Beard, E.T. Seton and scouts.

1910

MARCH

Su	Mo	Tu	We	Th	Fr	Sa
		1	2	3	4	5
6	7	8	9	10	11	12
13	14	15	16	17	18	19
20	21	22	23	24	25	26
29	28	29	30	31		

3. J.D. Rockefeller Jr. announces withdrawal from business to administer father's fortune for "uplift of humanity"; appeals to Congress for creation of Rockefeller Foundation.

3. Nicaraguan rebels admit defeat in open war, resort to guerrilla tactics in hope of U.S. intervention (→ 4/26).

3. New York: Robert Forest founds Natl. Housing Assn. to fight deteriorating urban living conditions.

5. Philadelphia: 60,000 leave jobs to show sympathy for striking transit workers; labor leaders promise "fight to a finish."

5. Moroccan envoy signs 1909 agreement with France.

6. Germany: Police shoot, saber socialists during suffrage demonstration (→ 4/27).

8. France: Baroness de Laroche becomes first woman to obtain pilot's license.

8. Spain: King authorizes women to attend university (→ 23).

9. Pennsylvania: Union men urge national sympathy strike for Pennsylvania miners.

10. Slavery abolished in China.

13. Labor leader John Mitchell joins clergy in appeal for holiday on Sunday, declares "We don't care what day it is, but we must have one day of rest."

19. Washington: Conservative Speaker of House "Uncle" Joe Cannon loses right to fill committees; members to be elected by House.

21. U.S. Senate grants ex-President Teddy Roosevelt yearly pension of $10,000.

22. Liberia: Telegraph cable links Tenerife and Monrovia.

23. Canary Islands: Women to offer candidates for legislative elections (→ 4/18).

26. U.S. Congress passes amendment to 1907 Immigration Act, barring criminals, paupers, anarchists and carriers of disease from settling in U.S.

28. France: Henri Fabre performs first seaplane flight in Martigues.

Otto Kahn gives $500,000 for Hals

March 15. J.P. Morgan was outbid this morning when his offer of $400,000 for a painting was topped by banker Otto Kahn's offer of $500,000. The work is a family portrait by Dutch artist Frans Hals. It was completed about 1640, when Hals' technique was at its peak. Kahn plans to lend the work to New York's Metropolitan Museum.

Lakeview gusher opens new oil field

March 18. Production of the greatest gusher yet to erupt, the Lakeview No. 1 well at Maricopa near Los Angeles, is being estimated at more than 50,000 barrels a day today. The well blew in three days ago, at a depth of 2,224 feet and has been out of control since. It makes California by far the nation's leading oil producer, the only state to produce more than it consumes.

Lakeview gusher, Midway Field, Ca.

1910

APRIL

Su	Mo	Tu	We	Th	Fr	Sa
					1	2
3	4	5	6	7	8	9
10	11	12	13	14	15	16
17	18	19	20	21	22	23
24	25	26	27	28	29	30

2. Berlin: Prof. Karl Harries perfects process for artificial synthesis of rubber.

2. Russia: 50,000 settlers sent to western Siberia to build railway line connecting Moscow and Irkutsk.

3. Roosevelt announces he will not visit pope because of limitations put on his behavior.

4. French minister of defense appeals for mandatory military training.

4. Washington: Climbers on Mt. McKinley reach 12,000 ft.

10. France: Revolutionaries demonstrate upon opening of Briand campaign.

13. New York: Pennsylvania Railroad begins running trains in Manhattan tunnels.

13. Australia: Labor Party under Andrew Fisher gains majority in House of Representatives.

14. U.S. baseball season opens in eight major cities.

15. Census reports 21% increase in U.S. population over last 20 years; figures now reach 91,972,266; 30 inhabitants per square mile.

16. Germany: 200,000 workers locked out as negotiators fail to agree on wage increases.

18. Suffragists present U.S. Congress with petition for vote signed by 500,000 (→ 3/17/11).

26. Opposing U.S.-supported revolutionaries, Germany recognizes Madriz as Nicaraguan leader.

27. South Africa: Louis Botha and James Herzog found nationalist South African Party, calling for independence and equality for Boers (→ 9/15).

27. France: National Assembly kills Socialist-sponsored universal suffrage bill.

28. Swedish govt. increases inheritance tax by 200%.

DEATHS

21. American author Mark Twain, born Samuel Langhorne Clemens (*11/30/1835).

26. Norwegian author Bjornsterne Bjornson (*12/8/1832).

Royals open World's Fair in Brussels

April 23. Albert and Elizabeth, the King and Queen of Belgium, opened the World's Fair in Brussels today. They were assisted by Prime Minister Franz Schollaert. Belgium is hoping to demonstrate through the fair the importance of its industries and its international ambitions in the industrial domain. Albert, who has become quite popular in only four months of rule, is trying to polish up Belgium's reputation. It was tarnished somewhat by the excesses of his uncle Leopold in the Congo.

Poster for the World's Fair.

Record arts sale takes place in N.Y.

April 6. A Joseph Turner painting, "Rockets and Blue Lights," fetched a record $129,000 at a New York auction today. Sales of several other expensive works made it the biggest single sale of paintings in the United States: 43 pictures changed hands for a total of $769,200. The art had been part of the estate of Charles Yerkes, Chicago financier.

Most of the pictures are landscapes by French masters. Eugene Delacroix, Jean Francois Millet, Constant Troyon and Jean-Antoine Watteau are represented. "The Fisherman" by Jean-Baptiste Corot (1796-1875) went for $80,500 to the same anonymous purchaser of the Turner canvas. "The Fisherman" depicts a broad stream lined by some of the majestic, sweeping trees Corot is known for.

1910

MAY

Su	Mo	Tu	We	Th	Fr	Sa
1	2	3	4	5	6	7
8	9	10	11	12	13	14
15	16	17	18	19	20	21
22	23	24	25	26	27	28
29	30	31				

1. Natl. Negro Committee, founded in June 1909 by W.E.B. Du Bois, becomes Natl. Assn. for the Advancement of Colored People (NAACP), continues fight for full equality.

1. Teddy Roosevelt pays unofficial visit to Amsterdam.

1. France: Labor federation C.G.T. cancels Paris demonstration as govt. mobilizes 20,000 troops.

3. Japanese troops mobilize, prepare to act in Korea (→ 6/24).

4. London: Commander Peary hailed by 30,000 as discoverer of North Pole.

5. Nicaragua: Cartago earthquake kills 500.

5. Alabama: Birmingham explosion kills 145 miners.

8. French electorate stabilizes; Socialists gain slightly in legislative elections; coalition govt. retains 370-227 majority.

9. Cretan Natl. Assembly asks union with Greece (→ 7/27).

10. Great Britain: House of Commons votes to abolish Lord's veto power over appropriations bills (→ 2/21/11).

10. Jockey Herbert rides Donau to victory in Kentucky Derby.

12. Paris: French fear Halley's comet will cause severe weather disturbances.

16. U.S. Bureau of Mines established within Dept. of Interior.

17. Russian govt. agrees to finance construction of Serbian port on Danube River.

18. Paris: First conference on air traffic opens (→ 19).

19. France: Henri Farman and Roger Sommer perform first night flight in Mourmelon.

20. Denmark: Socialists win majority in legislative elections.

25. French troops occupy southern Morocco (→ 12/3).

28. Russia: Thousands of Jews forced out of Kiev (→ 8/23/11).

DEATH

27. German bacteriologist Robert Koch, 1905 Nobel Prize (*12/11/1843).

Popular Mark Twain mourned in America

April 21. Several years ago, a newspaper erroneously ran an article announcing Mark Twain's demise. Twain saw the article and swiftly corrected the paper. "The reports of my death," he wrote, "are greatly exaggerated." Today, the passing is real. Samuel Langhorne Clemens, America's eminent author and humorist, is dead at 74.

Samuel Clemens, alias Mark Twain.

Clemens will always be associated with Hannibal, Missouri, his actual and "fictional" home. He was born on November 30, 1835, and grew up eavesdropping on other people's matters (his father was the town Justice of the Peace). When he was 12, his father died, and young Clemens helped support the family by working at a local print shop. A few years later, he was making a good living as a river pilot. He took his pen name, "Mark Twain," meaning two fathoms deep, from a shipman's common cry. Later, his experiences would flow into "Life on the Mississippi," published in 1883.

In March 1867, Clemens released his first book, a collection of short stories including "The Celebrated Jumping Frog of Calaveras County." Among his other popular works were "Tom Sawyer" (1876), "The Prince and the Pauper" (1882) and "Huckleberry Finn" (1884).

Clemens was ever restless, traversing the world, scribbling at every step. Now, in Danbury, Connecticut, writing and roaming are over. America will miss him.

King Edward VII is dead

May 6. Edward VII, King of Great Britain and Emperor of India, died suddenly of pneumonia at Buckingham Palace tonight. He ruled Britain for nine years. Power passed immediately to his son George, the Prince of Wales, who will rule as King George V.

King Edward VII, son of Queen Victoria.

The 68-year-old monarch's sudden death threw his country into a state of shock. Queen Alexandra rushed home from France when she learned her husband was sick. Few people, however, expected his death to come so quickly. Edward apparently caught cold during a visit this past weekend to the wet grounds of his estate at Sandringham. But he continued to conduct the affairs of state. And just this afternoon, the king was inquiring how his horse, Witch of the Air, had finished at Kempton Park. King Edward was pleased to hear the horse had won the race.

Crowds gathered around Buckingham Palace during the day, anxious to hear the latest news about the king. Their spirits rose when the sun came out from behind the clouds and shined more brilliantly than it had all year. Their spirits tumbled when the cold drizzle returned. Moments later, word came that the king was in critical condition. Five doctors rushed to his bedside, but to no avail. Just before midnight, the king was dead.

The Times of London called Edward "sagacious, popular, cautious, courageous and tactful." The king died, said the Times, "in the gravest domestic crisis of our time," a constitutional crisis over an effort to limit the veto power of the House of Lords. King Edward worked somewhat reluctantly with the Liberal government on the problem. But the crisis goes on. And it is hoped in London that King George will act even more forcefully to solve the problem once and for all.

Europe's royalty traveled from miles around to gather at Buckingham Palace for Edward VII's funeral. Standing (left to right): King Haakon VII of Norway, King Ferdinand I of Bulgaria, King Manuel II of Portugal, Kaiser Wilhelm II of Germany, King Gustav V of Sweden, King Albert I of Belgium. Seated: King Alfonso XIII of Spain, King George V (Edward's son), and King Frederick VII of Denmark.

1910

JUNE

Su	Mo	Tu	We	Th	Fr	Sa
			1	2	3	4
5	6	7	8	9	10	11
12	13	14	15	16	17	18
19	20	21	22	23	24	25
26	27	28	29	30		

1. Prussia: Breslau Social Democrats call for major protest against limited suffrage.

2. British explorers find Pygmies in Great Snow Mts. of Dutch New Guinea.

2. Britian's Charles Stewart Rolls becomes first to make round-trip flight across English Channel (→ 7/12).

2. Colombia: Anti-American demonstrations break out in Bogota.

3. Russian Duma comes out in favor of bill destroying legislative autonomy of Finnish Duchy.

3. China: Foreigners reported under attack in Nanking.

6. Paris: Jean Charcot acclaimed upon return from unsuccessful attempt to reach South Pole.

10. Japanese efforts are reported effective in restraining immigration to U.S. (→ 2/24/11).

11. Spanish King Alfonso XIII promises intellectual freedom for Spain (→ 8/4).

15. Devastating floods reach high point in Germany, Austria, Switzerland, Belgium, Serbia.

18. Washington: Congress passes Mann-Elkins Act, allowing Interstate Commerce Comm. to prosecute railways, regulate freight rates (→ 4/12/11).

20. Mexican President Diaz proclaims martial law, arrests hundreds for plotting revolt.

20. Theodore Roosevelt Jr. and Eleanor Alexander are married in New York.

22. Berlin: Zeppelin Deutschland becomes first airship to transport passengers (→ 28).

24. Japanese army invades Korea (→ 8/24).

28. Germany: Zeppelin Deutschland wrecked by gale in Teutoburgian forest.

29. Germany: At Munich art show, Russian ambassador forces removal of Fabianski painting depicting Kiev pogrom.

BIRTH

11. French oceanographer Jacques Cousteau.

Stravinsky ballet offered by Russians

Costume from "The Firebird."

June 25. It was just last year that the impresario Sergei Diaghilev brought his troupe of ballet dancers from Russia to Paris. And tonight, dancing a new composition by Igor Stravinsky, they enjoyed an enormous success. Called "The Firebird," the ballet represents the first collaboration between Diaghilev and Stravinsky, and it may become the chief attraction of the new season.

"The Firebird" is based on a Slavic fairy tale about a wandering prince who captures a fantastic bird of light in a mysterious forest. The prince lets the bird go free after it does a magical dance and leaves him a golden feather. The choreographer is Michel Fokine.

Brice sings Berlin

June 26. The new star named Fanny Brice is a standout at the Ziegfeld Follies this year. She is at her most inimitable in the dialect song "Good-Bye Becky Cohen," written by another Follies newcomer, Irving Berlin. Miss Brice has been on the stage since age 13, when she won an amateur night at Keeney's Theater in Brooklyn. In another show earlier this year, she was heard to sing Berlin's ragtime ditty, "Doin' the Grizzly Bear."

O. Henry, a master storyteller, is dead

June 5. Popular short-story writer William Sidney Porter, known by his pen name O. Henry, died this morning in New York. His passing was like the conclusion of a typical O. Henry tale: swift and unexpected. Death was attributed to a complication of diseases.

Porter was born in North Carolina in 1862. As a young man, he worked at The Houston Post. In 1896, he was arrested for embezzling funds at an Austin bank; he fled to Honduras but returned to face the consequences. Porter was sentenced to three years in prison. He made crime pay. While in the penitentiary, Porter wrote some of his best stories, strong in plot and ironic twists. Two collections, "Cabbages and Kings" (1904) and "The Four Million," (1906) display his best work.

Scott sets out to find South Pole

June 1. Captain Robert Falcon Scott and his party left England today on an expedition that hopes to be the first to reach the South Pole. Scott is vying with Roald Amundsen, the Norwegian explorer, who will lead a similar expedition later this summer. Scott plans to make the 1,800-mile overland trip to the pole using motorized transport and ponies, which his party will kill along the way for food. Scott is famous for an expedition in 1904 that reached the farthest point south yet penetrated (→ 12/14/11).

Robert Scott's ship Lena Nova.

1910

JULY

Su	Mo	Tu	We	Th	Fr	Sa
					1	2
3	4	5	6	7	8	9
10	11	12	13	14	15	16
17	18	19	20	21	22	23
24	25	26	27	28	29	30
31						

1. Baltimore: Black and Decker Co. founded by Duncan Black and Alonzo Decker.

2. Oscar T. Tamm of St. Louis becomes first man to cross Arctic Circle by automobile.

2. Paris shoemaker Liabeuf executed for killing two policemen.

4. Russia, Japan sign accord; Russia recognizes Japan's control over Korea, obtains freedom to act in Manchuria; U.S. attempt to neutralize Manchurian railway foiled.

5. British win twice at Wimbledon; Anthony Wilding 6-4, 7-5, 4-6, 6-2, over Arthur Gore; Dorothea Chambers 6-2, 6-2 over Penelope Boothby.

6. Spain: Govt. attacks Vatican's hold on Spanish Church.

9. Egypt: Archeologists find tablet chronicling fall of Jerusalem.

12. N.Y.: 10,000 cheer heavyweight champ Jack Johnson's arrival at Grand Central Station.

13. Prussia: German aviator Oscar Erbslok and four companions killed as dirigible falls 1,000 feet near Leichlingen.

13. Chinese Minister to Germany Gen. Yin Ch'ang asserts Russo-Japanese accord will "drive America and China into each other's arms" to prevent partitioning of Manchuria.

14. Newfoundlander William Brown wins $10,000 for traveling 25,000 miles (equal to circumference of earth) in a dog cart over seven years.

18. Interstate Commerce Commission reports 8,711 rail deaths in past year.

18. Pennsylvania Railroad and employees reach wage agreement, narrowly avert strike.

22. Russia: Tolstoy manuscripts destroyed in fire at residence, Yasnaia Poliana.

27. Ottoman Empire threatens war if Greek Parliament accepts Cretan deputies (→ 10/18).

28. Nicaragua: Pres. Jose Madriz denounces U.S. military intervention to European powers (→ 1/2/11).

31. Socialists gain seats in German legislative elections.

Riots break out as Johnson keeps title

July 4. No sooner had Jack Johnson knocked out Jim Jeffries in the 15th round in defense of his world heavyweight boxing title than fierce race riots erupted in all parts of the United States.

Negroes and whites traveling in mobs attacked each other when the battle in the Reno ring ended, and eight Negroes were reported killed.

Jack Johnson, champ.

Scores of others were injured. A colored man who had jeeringly proclaimed Johnson's victory on a trolley car in New Orleans was slashed to death by a white man and bled to death before he could be taken to a hospital.

Jeffries, overweight and out of shape, had agreed to come out of retirement. "I couldn't come back," said the beaten Jeffries. Johnson was so confident of victory that he had not trained diligently and this bravado was carried into the ring. From the fourth round, his confidence seemed to turn into cockiness. He was fighting for 60 percent of a $101,000 purse, but that seemed of little interest to him. "I thought this fellow could hit," Johnson was heard to say between rounds.

When Johnson opened a cut over Jeffries' eye in the sixth round, most in the crowd felt it signaled his eventual victory. And it made believers of those who had not really accepted Johnson as a champion after he won the title from Tommy Burns in Sydney in 1908. Feelings ran so high against the idea of a colored man holding the championship that in St. Joseph, Missouri, a mob attacked a white man who had taken the side of a Negro (→ 12).

British flier Rolls killed in his plane

July 12. Charles Stewart Rolls, 33, son of Lord and Lady Llangattock, was killed in a contest in Bournemouth today, England's first victim of the air. Rolls flew his French-built Wright biplane with skill when the rudders broke adrift and the plane fell sheer to the ground from over 80 feet. A stunned crowd witnessed the body being freed from the wreck, the pilot's neck broken. King George was said to be deeply moved when informed of the death of the celebrated young aviator, who had courted danger in automobiles and balloons before aviation became his passion.

Charles S. Rolls.

Poland celebrates victory over Teutons

July 15. Some 30,000 Poles celebrated their freedom from bondage in Krakow today, but were warned about new threats to their liberty. They observed the 500th anniversary of the Polish army victory over Teutonic horsemen at Tannenberg. The composer Jan Paderewski gave the country a statue of King Ladislaus II, who beat the Teutons. One speaker, though, a deputy from Germany, warned that a centuries-old enemy, Russia, had not been defeated. "Five centuries have passed, and our nemesis still tries to steal our land and destroy our spirit," he said. "The enthusiasm at this anniversary in Krakow shows he will never succeed."

Find ancient record of Jerusalem's fall

July 9. A unique archeological discovery in Upper Egypt amounts to a record of the siege of Jerusalem by Vespasian's army, under Titus. A wooden panel, bearing a 50-line Latin inscription, discharges one M. Valerius Quadratus after long service in the Roman army. Drawn up by the Emperor Domitian in 93 A.D., and copied on July 2, 94, it is the first authentic document emanating from a soldier actually engaged in the campaign against the Jews and the destruction of Jerusalem, thereby confirming statements by Josephus and the classical historians.

It takes two to tango, and they do

July 1. Twosomes at some New York ballrooms may currently be seen lending their terpsichorean energies to a new dance called the tango. It is a catchy step and, at least in the eyes of some, not without a provocative allure. The origins of this South American dance are rather unclear, though it seems to have gained prominence in Buenos Aires. Lately, it has been taken up by the more fashionable set in Europe, such as the Grand Duchess Anastasia of Russia and her friends, and is enjoying popularity in Paris, where it is played by genuine Argentine orchestras.

Tango, imported from Buenos Aires.

Homer, painter of American life, dies

Winslow Homer's "North Woods."

"Watching the Breakers."

July 31. A very American painter, Winslow Homer, died today at the age of 74. He spent his last years in seclusion, and his work reflects it. His final watercolors emphasize the immensity of the sea; when a human figure is present, it is scarcely visible. Homer may have withdrawn from the public only to concentrate on his greater love, nature.

Homer was born in Boston on February 24, 1836. He worked as a lithographer and magazine illustrator there. In 1861, Harper's Weekly sent him to the front line of the Civil War to record the action, and his sketches won accolades worldwide. Directly after the war, Homer traveled to France, but he was not impressed by Impressionism. He pursued objective reality with bold lines and vibrant color.

Up until the early 1880's, Homer depicted common American scenes. "Crack the Whip" (1872), a picture of barefooted children racing in a field, is a well-loved work from this period. In 1883, he moved to Prout's Neck, a town on the coast of Maine. In summer, he painted its rocky shores; in winter, he vacationed in the Caribbean and contemplated calmer sands. "Life Line," painted in 1884, brings out the drama in the sea. It shows treacherous waters threatening to engulf a shipwreck victim, whose tenuous tie to life is a thin rope. Homer's love of nature was tempered by his awe.

1910

AUGUST

Su	Mo	Tu	We	Th	Fr	Sa
	1	2	3	4	5	6
7	8	9	10	11	12	13
14	15	16	17	18	19	20
21	22	23	24	25	26	27
28	29	30	31			

4. Spain: Insurrectionary movement spreads to four provinces.

5. Germany: Hamburg employers fire 2,400 of 10,000 striking dockworkers (→ 9/19).

8. Persian troops capture rebel leaders Sattar Khan and Begir Khan, kill 300 followers (→ 10/27).

9. Hoboken, N.J.: Mayor William Gaynor shot by unemployed civil servant.

9. Belgium: Free trade congress opens in Antwerp.

14. Panama: Five-mile stretch of Panama canal opened, giving access to Atlantic Ocean (→ 10/15).

14. Brussels: World's Fair grounds decimated by fire; loss estimated at $100 million.

16. Sixty-one-year-old Chilean President Pedro Montt dies of heart attack while in Germany.

18. John B. Moissan becomes first American to cross English Channel by airplane.

19. New York: Col. Teddy Roosevelt urges Negroes to find jobs and stop asking govt. for privileges.

26. It is reported that X-rays are proving useful in detecting lung disease.

28. Russia declares Montenegro an independent kingdom under Nicholas II.

29. Poland: Kaiser Wilhelm II opens new palatial residence at Poznan.

31. Kansas: During 5,000-mile speaking tour, Roosevelt outlines progressive policy of New Nationalism, advocates "square deal"; "property shall be the servant and not the master of the commonwealth."

BIRTHS

4. American composer William Schuman.

20. Finnish architect Eero Saarinen (†7/1/1961).

DEATH

26. American William James, founder pragmatism (*1/11/1842).

Talking pictures: Edison's latest invention

Aug 27. Thomas Alva Edison tonight demonstrated his latest invention, talking motion pictures. A select audience was invited to Edison's laboratory in West Orange, New Jersey, to see the "kinetophone," which combines the sound of the phonograph with the images of the motion picture camera.

Others have tried to create talking motion pictures, but with limited success. Edison's achievement is to record both sound and picture at the same time, a process that others have not been able to duplicate. By using a machine that is part phonograph and part camera, Edison allows actors to move about freely, which has not been possible before.

Edison has been working to develop the talking picture machine for the past two years. He says that his goal is to have a complete talking picture presented in theaters within two years. It may be possible to have such a motion picture not only in sound but also in full color, if his present work succeeds, he says.

The self-educated Edison has had a remarkable career. He has invented automatic telegraphic transmitters and receivers (1874), the phonograph (1877), the carbon telephone transmitter (1877-8) and the first commercially successful incandescent lamp (1879). With hundreds of scientific patents in his name, Edison founded the Edison Electric Light Company, which became General Electric in 1892.

Thomas Alva Edison takes a moment's rest in his laboratory.

Death ends career of soldiers' angel

Florence Nightingale (left).

Aug 13. She was known as the "angel of the wounded" and the "lady of the lamp." Longfellow wrote a poem about her. Her name is synonymous with humanitarianism. Florence Nightingale died today in London. She was 90.

Miss Nightingale was interested from an early age in the nursing profession. But during the Crimean War she learned how unsanitary military hospitals could be. Her team of nurses organized and scrubbed down the hospitals at Scutari and Balaklava in Turkey. And she fought the military to provide clean supplies.

After she returned to her native England, she founded the Nightingale School and Home to train nurses. Later, Miss Nightingale proffered expert advice on health matters. She was the first woman to receive the British Order of Merit.

Japan announces annexation of Korea

Aug 24. News that Japan will formally annex Korea at the end of this month brought threats of riots in Seoul today. But Japan controls almost every aspect of life in Korea, and most diplomatic observers view the treaty as merely formalizing an already existing arrangement.

Korea has a long history of Japanese intervention, with the recent drive for total domination beginning in 1904. Then, the Russians from their base in southern Manchuria began extending their interests to Korea, enraging the Japanese who considered the country within their sphere of influence. The ensuing Russo-Japanese War, in which the Russians suffered heavy losses, was ended by the Treaty of Portsmouth, negotiated by President Roosevelt in 1905. The treaty not only ended the war, but endorsed Japanese domination over Korea.

Baron Uchida, the Japanese Ambassador to the United States, met with Secretary of State Philander C. Knox today and it is believed that he assured Knox that American business interests would be safeguarded by the Korean annexation treaty (→ 9/3).

Typhoon and flood overwhelm Japan

Aug 15. Japan has been ravaged by a violent typhoon and now is suffering severe flooding. Reports from Tokyo indicate that more than 800 people have perished from the monstrous Pacific storm as winds gusted over 100 miles per hour. The subsequent flooding has forced 400,000 people from their homes. Relief agencies are forming to help the victims of this terrible natural disaster. Witnesses say that the storm hit so fast it took most islanders by surprise.

1910

SEPTEMBER

Su	Mo	Tu	We	Th	Fr	Sa
				1	2	3
4	5	6	7	8	9	10
11	12	13	14	15	16	17
18	19	20	21	22	23	24
25	26	27	28	29	30	

1. Renovated Berlin Opera House reopened.

3. British govt. expresses fear of restricted trade with Orient due to high Korean tariff.

5. France: Marie Curie demonstrates transformation of radium ore to metal at the Academy of Sciences.

7. Intl. Court at The Hague settles fishing rights dispute between U.S. and Newfoundland.

8. Illinois: Miners go back to work after five-month strike.

8. Russia: Twelve arrested for suspected bomb plot.

10. Intl. Court at The Hague awards U.S. $54 mil. in reparations for losses suffered in 1899 Venezuelan revolt.

14. German Zeppelin VI engulfed in flames at Baden-Baden.

17. London: British doctor asserts that, at present rate, insane will outnumber sane in 40 years.

19. Paris: International conference on unemployment debates value of unemployment insurance.

19. To combat dockworkers' strike, employers import British mechanics to work in Bremen, Hamburg, Stetten.

23. Chavez, de Brigue and Domodossola perform first flight over Alps.

24. Two ex-presidents said to be preparing coup in Honduras.

25. New York: West Point cadets placed under arrest for giving silent treatment to captain.

27. New York: Anna Pavlova arrives with Russian dance troupe for U.S. tour.

27. Italy: 100,000 flee Naples to escape cholera epidemic (→ 9/6/11).

BIRTH

3. American composer Samuel Barber.

DEATH

7. British pre-Raphaelite painter Holman Hunt (*4/2/1827).

British dockers strike, 50,000 fired

Sept 3. The dockworkers' strike in Great Britain has seemingly backfired; employers have disregarded the work stoppage and fired all 50,000 of them. The dockers were upset over low wages and poor working conditions. Union organizers, seeing no quick, easy solutions, ordered the comprehensive strike.

However, the unemployed workers received a shot in the arm today as 10,000 mine workers in Wales, to show their allegiance and to firm up labor solidarity, have also walked off their jobs. It is not certain what action mine company management will take or what effect the Wales strike will have in England, but many feel it will bolster the dockworkers (→ 11/14).

Strikers flood the streets of London.

Hammerstein both contracts and expands

Oscar Hammerstein.

Sept 9. Oscar Hammerstein does not lack for nerve. An immigrant who set himself up as an impresario, he built the Manhattan Opera House to challenge the mighty Metropolitan. He failed, but nobly.

"The operatic war is suicide," he concluded last January 1; he was practically bankrupt. So, on April 26, a deal was closed at the home of Otto Kahn, the patron of the Metropolitan. For $1.2 million, Hammerstein agreed not to produce opera in New York, Boston, Chicago or Philadelphia for ten years. London was not on the list, and today Hammerstein announced he would build a $1.5 million opera house there to seat 3,500.

Douanier Rousseau will paint no more

Sept 2. Henri Rousseau, the self-taught French painter, died today in Paris. Rousseau was a very popular artist in the last 25 years of his life, but throughout his life remained nicknamed "Le Douanier," or customs official, because he worked for the government as a young man. In fact, he did not have his first exposition until he was 40. It was so successful he was able to quit his customs job and devote the rest of his life to painting. Many of his works seem romantically inspired, and his rich colors seem borrowed from both dreams and reality. His primitive, exotic jungle scenes are highly prized, and he was also fond of painting virgin forests. Among his best paintings are "Sleeping Gypsy" (1897) and "The Dream" (1910).

Detail of a Rousseau self-portrait.

Botha is Premier of South African Union

Sept 19. Despite his electoral defeat to Unionist candidate Sir Percy Fitzpatrick, Nationalist leader General Louis Botha will remain Prime Minister of South Africa. General Botha, representing the Dutch interests, lost his re-election bid in the federal Assembly two days ago to Fitzpatrick, who represents the British and mining interests under the leadership of Dr. Jameson, ex-Premier of the Cape Colony. The Nationalist Party, shocked at the initial loss of Botha, won the majority of seats in the Assembly, and they subseqently reinstalled their candidate (→ 12/17).

Botha as a General in the Boer War.

Citizen denounces ugly electric signs

"Keep the advertising atrocities away," pleads architect Arnold W. Brunner and others, wishing to protect the Times Square area from freak signs and shabby, cheap buildings. Hundreds of thousands of visitors to New York City come to see Broadway, the "Great White Way," lit up at its best, but the "billboard mentality" is threatening to make the brilliant electric display into a sloppy array of monstrosities. Brunner is calling on leading citizens to mobilize their sense of taste and aesthetics.

1910

OCTOBER

Su	Mo	Tu	We	Th	Fr	Sa
						1
2	3	4	5	6	7	8
9	10	11	12	13	14	15
16	17	18	19	20	21	22
23	24	25	26	27	28	29
30	31					

1. Paris: International conference on cancer opens.

2. Great Britain: 150,000 laid off as 700 Lancastershire mills shut down (→ 11/7).

12. France: Nationwide strike begins in transportation industry (→ 15).

15. N.J.: Aviator Wellman leaves Atlantic City for Europe in airship America (→ 18).

15. French govt. arrests several editors of leftist and union newspapers, accused of fomenting national unrest.

15. Cuba reported optimistic about effects of Panama canal on national economy (→ 11/16).

17. Portugal: Provisional govt. abolishes privileges of nobility, banishes royal family (→ 11/9).

18. First dirigible flown over English Channel by M. Baudry, La Motte-Breil to Wormwood Scrubbs.

18. Cretan Eleutherios Venizelos becomes Greek prime minister with backing from military (→ 12/12).

18. Royal Mail SS Trent rescues Wellman and crew 400 miles off Cape Hatteras.

23. Chicago: Philadelphia beats Chicago 7-2 to take World Series in five games.

23. G.P. Stokes, richest socialist in U.S., announces movement is making great gains (→ 11/8).

25. Italy: Storms, tidal waves devastate Gulf of Naples, kill 1,000.

25. Kaiser Wilhelm II and wife pay official visit to Belgian king.

27. British troops land in Persian Gulf to protect U.K. economic interests during revolutionary uprisings in Persia (→ 5/12/11).

BIRTHS

11. American journalist Joseph Alsop.

13. American jazz pianist Art Tatum (†11/4/1956).

DEATH

17. American suffragist Julia Ward Howe, wrote "Battle Hymn of the Republic" (*5/27/1819).

Portuguese King flees; republic planned

Oct 4. Cannon fire erupted in the pre-dawn quiet of Lisbon today. Revolutionary troops needed only a few hours to crush forces loyal to King Manuel II. But before the insurgents could set up their cannons in front of the royal palace, the king escaped to Gibraltar, apparently with a sizable fortune. Monarchy is dead in Portugal. The victorious troops want a republic.

A number of secret associations, like the Carbonari and the freemasons, allied themselves with the republican troops to topple the king. They want a professor of literature, Teofilo Braga, to head the new government, write a constitution and create new economic programs to restore prosperity (→ 17).

Soldiers of the Portuguese royal army in Lisbon.

Italians lead as immigrants flood in

Oct 16. An astounding total of 1,041,570 immigrants entered the United States last year. Many were unlettered and unaware of American values, but given time and opportunity, they will eventually find their place here, too.

Southern Italians lead all others with 192,673, followed by Poles, Jews and Slovaks. The Irish, the major alien group two decades ago, were outnumbered by Greeks. The newcomers seem to shun the countryside, often moving into the cities of California, Pennsylvania, Connecticut and New York.

Last year, some 24,000 immigrants were found guilty of polygamy, feeblemindedness and pauperism, and they were sent back home.

Immigrant women sit apprehensively in Ellis Island's assembly hall.

Red Cross founder dies; work goes on

Jean Henri Dunant.

Oct 30. Jean Henri Dunant, a Swiss philanthropist who was forever struck by the horror of war, died today. But his important legacy, the Red Cross, lives on.

Dunant was appalled when he saw wounded soldiers left writhing on the battlefield in the war between Napoleon III's French armies and Austria in 1859. So he recorded his impressions and put them in a book called "Memories of Solferino." The book was later retitled "The Origin of the Red Cross" because Dunant helped organize the international conference which formed the health group. Dunant shared the first Nobel Peace Prize in 1901.

Forest fires kill over 300 in Midwest

Oct 9. Merciless blazes are sweeping the forest areas of northern Minnesota. At least 5,000 people are homeless, and more than 300 have died. Lumber mills have burned, and huge property losses have been incurred by many businesses. The raging fire has reduced beautiful timberland to ashes and such towns as Beaudette, Spooner, Pitt and Graceton have been wiped from the map. About 3,000 persons were seen fleeing the flames, joined by cattle, moose, deer, bears, wildcats, caribou and timber wolves.

1910

NOVEMBER

Su	Mo	Tu	We	Th	Fr	Sa
		1	2	3	4	5
6	7	8	9	10	11	12
13	14	15	16	17	18	19
20	21	22	23	24	25	26
27	28	29	30			

3. Illinois: Chicago Grand Opera Company formed.

5. Germany: Kaiser Wilhelm and Czar Nicholas meet in Orianeburg; czar sanctions Baghdad railway in exchange for free hand in Persia (→ 1/6/11).

7. Great Britain: Miners' strike in Wales leads to clashes with police (→ 14).

8. U.S.: Democrats sweep congressional elections for first time since 1894.

8. Woodrow Wilson elected governor of N.J.; Franklin Delano Roosevelt elected to N.Y. State Senate.

8. Victor Berger of Wisconsin becomes first congressman elected on Socialist ticket.

9. France, Norway, Belgium, Germany, Spain, Russia, Great Britain establish diplomatic relations with new republic of Portugal (→ 1/11/11).

10. Japan: Twenty-six rebels executed for plotting assassination of emperor.

14. Great Britain: Welsh miners obtain wage hike, end strike.

16. Pres. Taft, in Panama, dispels rumors that U.S. is planning annexation (→ 2/4/11).

17. Leading U.S. Rabbi Stephen Wise announces support for woman suffrage, declares "we have no democracy here, only a manocracy" (→ 4/4/11).

17. Colorado: Aviator Ralph Johnstone, world record holder for altitude, dies in plane crash.

17. At meeting of Gen. Soc. of Mechanics and Tradesmen, A. Carnegie offers "pity" for "the son of a millionaire" who does not know value of family and hard work; "if I had my choice, I would be the poor boy."

19. New U.S. football rules appear successful; season's deaths reported at 14, down from last year's 24.

20. Moving picture industry booming in U.S.; 120,000 projectors sold so far.

26. Philadelphia: Navy wins annual football game, defeating Army 3-0 at Franklin Field.

Tolstoy's life has ended

Nov 20. Leo Tolstoy, the great Russian writer who was born a noble, died in a simple hut today. Scores of Russians are streaming through to pay their respect. They are not high government officials or members of the literary aristocracy. They are the peasants whom Tolstoy championed through most of his life.

The Russian Orthodox Church has forbidden a local requiem mass for Tolstoy because of his excommunication nine years ago. But there is such widespread popular admiration for the writer that the Church is being flouted in Moscow and St. Petersburg, and masses will be said in those cities.

In the West, Tolstoy will be remembered for his epic masterpieces "War and Peace" and "Anna Karenina." But the author rejected those great works in later life as he became more introspective and embraced the Christian doctrines of love and non-violence. The Russian government did not approve of his religious and political thinking, but it did not dare to interfere because of the cult that developed around the writer.

Tolstoy at home in Yasnaia Poliana.

In his last prayer, Tolstoy wrote, "Struggle on, relentless, true heart. Only the iniquitous will perish. He who suffered to the end will be saved."

Herbert triumphs in operetta again

Nov 7. Victor Herbert continues his winning ways as a master of operetta with his greatest hit to date, "Naughty Marietta." Set in 18th-century Louisiana, the show tells the spicy tale of a young, unhappily married lady of noble birth. Spectators are quickly captivated by a number of catchy tunes, including "Italian Street Song," "Tramp, Tramp, Tramp" and the evening's unforgettable finale, "Ah, Sweet Mystery of Life!"

This operetta, Herbert's sixth, fulfills the promise of "Babes in Toyland" (1903) and "The Red Mill" (1906.) Of Irish birth, Herbert received his training at the Stuttgart Conservatory in Germany as a cellist before arriving here to play in the Metropolitan Opera orchestra. He has distinguished himself as conductor of the Pittsburgh Symphony, and besides operettas, he has written choral, chamber and orchestral music.

Victor Herbert and daughter Ella.

Rebellion in Mexico

Nov 20. A revolution against President Porfirio Diaz, 81, who has dominated Mexico for 30 years, has been proclaimed by Francisco I. Madero Jr. The uprising was supposed to start yesterday, but the country was surprisingly calm except for a skirmish in one village.

Diaz, a general, seized power in 1876. He had amazing success in modernizing Mexico and winning international recognition. But his methods were harsh, he consorted with the rich and neglected the problems of poverty and land reform. Some 97 percent of rural families own no property.

Madero, presenting himself as a liberal and reformer, ran against Diaz for the presidency this year. At one point he was arrested for gathering a crowd, and was defeated by fraud. From San Antonio, Texas, on October 7, he declared himself provisional president. His call to arms was answered by Emiliano Zapata and Pancho Villa, among others (→ 1/24/11).

The longest laugh

Nov 8. A Lawrenceburg, Indiana, man alarmed friends, neighbors and the medical world today as a business deal tickled his fancy so much that he nearly died of laughter. S.H. Schrapp conned a local farmer into believing that a shaved-tail horse was actually a mule. The farmer bought the tale and the horse, much to the amusement of the tongue-in-cheek Schrapp, who began to smirk. The smirking turned to chuckles, the chuckles to giggles, until finally he was convulsed by laughter.

After an hour of uncontrollable laughter, a physician was summoned, but he could not help the guffawing Schrapp. When six hours of relentless laughing passed, he was proclaimed champion of ha-ha's, but still he rolled on the ground in hysterics. Finally, at the 12-hour mark, another doctor attended to the man with the bizarre condition. The second physician applied a heavy electrical shock to Schrapp and suddenly the laughter stopped.

Colonial Empires in 1910

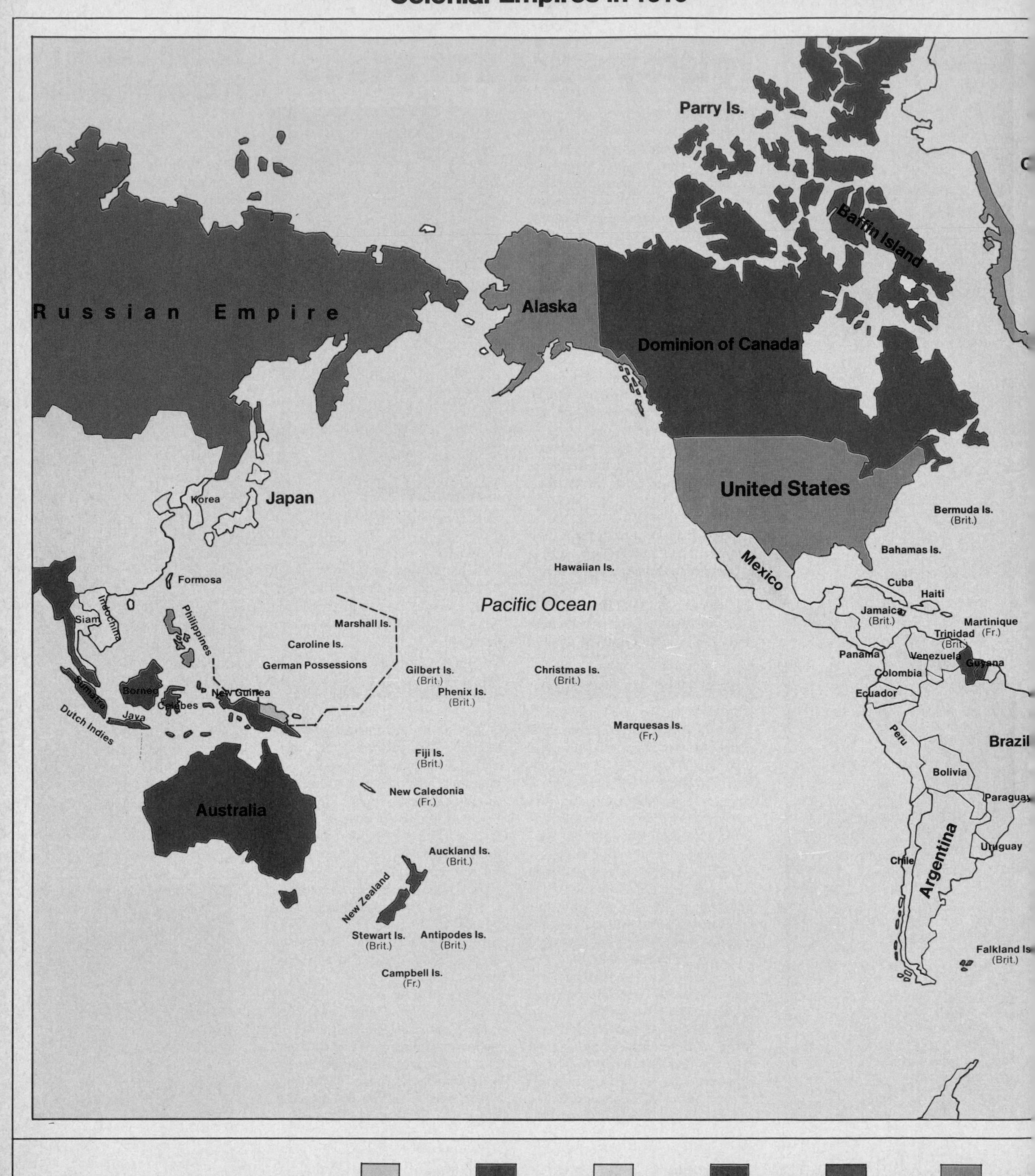

Iceland
Norway
Sweden
Finland
Russian Empire
Denmark
Great Britain
Netherlands
German Empire
France
Austria-Hungary
Italy
Spain
Portugal
Turkey
Malta (Brit.)
Algeria
Morocco
Tripoli
Egypt
Persia
Afghanistan
British Indian Empire
Arabia
Empire of China
Korea
Japan
Formosa
Burma
Siam
Indochina
Philippines
Rio de Oro
Senegal
Sudan
Fr. Guinea
Liberia
Togo-land
Cameroon
French Oubangui
French Congo
Congo Free State
British East Africa
German East Africa
Angola
Portuguese East Africa
Madagascar
Ger. S.W. Africa
British South Africa
Cape Colony
Seychelles (Brit.)
Amirante Is. (Brit.)
Mauritius (Brit.)
Reunion (Fr.)
Ceylon
Sumatra
Borneo
Java
Celebes
Dutch Indies
New Guinea
Marshall Is.
Caroline Is.
German Possessions
Australia
Fiji Is. (Brit.)
New Caledonia (Fr.)
New Zealand
Stewart Is. (Brit.)
Indian Ocean
c Ocean
nd
de Is.
n Georgia Is. (Brit.)
Portuguese
Italian
Spanish
Russian
Turkish
United States

1910

DECEMBER

Su	Mo	Tu	We	Th	Fr	Sa
				1	2	3
4	5	6	7	8	9	10
11	12	13	14	15	16	17
18	19	20	21	22	23	24
25	26	27	28	29	30	31

1. Census reports German population at 64,926,000, increase of over four mil. in last five years.

3. Morocco: French troops occupy Agadir, protect French interests during uprising.

9. Palestine: Arab uprising crushed by Ottoman troops.

10. N.Y.: Arturo Toscanini conducts Enrico Caruso in world premiere of Puccini's opera "Girl of the Golden West."

12. Greece: Supporters of Pres. Venizelos take legislative elections, hold 277-111 majority.

13. Russia: Students riot in Odessa and St. Petersburg to protest corporal punishment (→ 3/20).

17. South African Parliament opens.→

21. China: 2.5 mil. plague victims reported in An-Hul province.

28. British elections force coalition govt. as neither major party wins majority.

31. Moisant and Hoxsey, two of America's foremost aviators, die in separate plane crashes.

CULTURAL EVENTS, 1910

Literature: E.M. Forster's "Howard's End"; H.G. Wells' "The History of Mr. Polly"; John Galsworthy's "Justice."

Academia: Bertrand Russell and Alfred North Whitehead's "Principia Mathematica," seminal work in logic; Sir Norman Angell's "The Great Illusion," anti-war piece; Abraham Flexner's highly critical Carnegie Foundation report on medical education in Canada and U.S.

Music: R. Vaughan Williams' "Sea Symphony"; premiere of Stravinsky's "The Firebird" ballet, with Ballet Russe in Paris; Victor Herbert's operetta "Naughty Marietta"; tango becomes popular in U.S. and Europe.

The Arts: Picasso's "Nude Woman"; Roger Fry's Post-Impressionist exhibit in London (Cezanne, Matisse, van Gogh); Frank Lloyd Wright gains fame in Europe.

Kandinsky is the father of abstract art

Wassily Kandinsky's "Improvisation 10" (1910).

Dec 1. Is painting in the process of forsaking subject matter? Such is the astonishing gist of a new treatise, "Concerning the Spiritual in Art," penned by Wassily Kandinsky, a 44-year-old Russian painter.

Not only does he question the role played by traditional subject matter, but also he promotes the idea of a painting somehow purified by its rejection of figurative elements. Putting his radical theory into practice, Kandinsky has actually begun to paint "abstract" works, as they are called. Typical of these is his "Improvisation 10," a bedlam of color and line containing nothing we are accustomed to finding in normal painting.

But then, Kandinsky believes that colors possess their own reality. He thinks the way we ordinarily see is deceptive, and that the free use of color unlocks a deeper reality lodged in the artist's psyche. As he writes, "The harmony between form and color obeys but one principle, the close contact with the human soul." Which is all very well, but what is the good of a still life if we are unable to tell the pears from the plums?

South African Parliament in first session

Pastor offers prayers at Parliament.

Dec 17. The Union of South Africa held its first session of Parliament today. It is now the third nation with dominion status, after Canada and Australia, within the British Empire. The Boers, settlers of Dutch descent, have chosen their military leader Louis Botha to be Prime Minister. The country's population is six million; only 1.25 million are white. Indigenous Negroes constitute the majority, yet they have no voice in government. Statistics suggest that in 20 years the ratio of Negroes to whites will be ten to 1. Then the precarious scales of power will have to be reweighed.

Mary Baker Eddy passes from this life

Dec 4. Mary Baker Eddy, the controversial founder of the Christian Science Church, died yesterday at her home in Chestnut Hill, Massachusetts, at the age of 89.

A pioneer in the field of spiritual healing, Mrs. Eddy had been the center of controversy much of her adult life. The deaths of some of her followers had produced loud outcries against what many called "Eddyism." Seemingly unperturbed by her detractors, she continued to advocate spiritual healing, writing a number of books, including "Science and Health with Key to the Scriptures."

In 1879, her Church of Christ, Scientist, was chartered, and officially recognized in 1892. She founded her first Christian Science reading room in 1888, and the Christian Science Monitor began in 1908.

The daughter of a New Hampshire farmer, she had been in poor health during her early years and began a search for truth about God and bodily health. Her new church was based on the method Jesus had used for healing sins and sickness, she once explained.

Just three years ago, she was involved in further controversy when relatives filed suit, asking for an accounting of her property after widely published reports that she was feeble and controlled by persons seeking large sums of her money. However, the suit was withdrawn after examiners found her mentally competent.

British sheet music cover.

1911

JANUARY

Su	Mo	Tu	We	Th	Fr	Sa
1	2	3	4	5	6	7
8	9	10	11	12	13	14
15	16	17	18	19	20	21
22	23	24	25	26	27	28
29	30	31				

2. Pres. Taft recognizes Estrada's govt. in Nicaragua, removes U.S. troops (→ 5/31).

3. London police set fire to Sydney Street home of several Russian anarchists, killing all inhabitants.→

4. Russia: Hundreds die in Tashkent earthquake.

4. Belgium: Miners strike for eight-hour day.

6. Germany, Russia finalize agreement to build Baghdad railway from Persia to Berlin.

6. Brazilian Trade Corp. becomes first U.S. company to gain general trade concession in Brazil.

7. New York: State Supt. of Banks closes failing Carnegie Trust Company.

11. Chinese famine reported taking 1,000 lives daily.

11. Germany: Police arrest 23 alleged anarchists in Munich raid.

11. Portugal beset by strikes; Interior Minister Antonio Jose Almeida resigns as railway men, metal workers quit work.

14. Camden, N.J.: The Arkansas, largest U.S. battleship, launched from yards of N.Y. Shipbuilding Company.

14. National Republican Club urges uniform nationwide regulatory laws for business in order to avoid "state socialism."

17. France: Assassin attempts to kill Aristide Briand at Palais-Bourbon.

18. San Francisco: Aviator Ely performs first successful take-off and landing from a ship.

18. German Second Reich celebrates 40th anniversary.

23. French Academy of Sciences refuses to break barrier of sex, chooses Henri Becquerel over Marie Curie.

24. U.S. cavalry sent to preserve neutrality of Rio Grande during Mexican civil war (→ 3/6).

31. German Reichstag exempts royal families from tax obligations.

BIRTH

22. Bruno Kreisky, Austrian statesman.

Robert La Follette leads Progressives

Robert Marion La Follette.

Jan 21. Seeking to reform and liberalize their own party, a group headed by Senator Robert M. La Follette of Wisconsin has formed what they call the National Progressive Republican League.

The principal goal of the new league is to work for the nomination of a progressive at the next Republican convention in 1912. Senator La Follette has been at frequent odds with the head of his own party, President William Howard Taft. The league also favors direct election of United States senators, the election of delegates to party primaries and stiffer laws against corrupt business practices.

Fortune is paid for the Hope diamond

Jan 28. The famous Hope diamond, once worn by Marie Antoinette, was bought tonight for over $300,000 by Ned McLean, son of John McLean. Mrs. McLean will wear it as a head ornament, guarded by a former Secret Service man who in turn is guarded by two private detectives. Walnut-sized and exquisitely blue in color, the 44.5-carat stone stems from India. Its owners have included Louis XIV, Louis XVI and a London banker named Hope. A sinister history of ill luck, madness and violent death clings to the unique gem.

Der Rosenkavalier debuts in Dresden

Jan 26. Richard Strauss' new opera, "Der Rosenkavalier" or "The Knight of the Rose," has met with nearly universal praise following its initial presentation at the Dresden Opera House. It will be remembered that the operas "Elektra" and "Salome" by the same composer contained music and subject matter offensive to many, and that "Salome" was received with less than enthusiasm in New York and banned altogether in Boston.

The story of this new work, while not easily told, forsakes all that savagery in favor of a charming love story set in 18th-century Vienna, and the many disguises and assumed identities may remind one of Mozart's "The Marriage of Figaro." It also bears that musical complexity of which this composer appears to be so fond. One critic has counted no less than 101 motifs. And for all its charm, it frankly contains moments that closely skirt the lascivious. Yet the opera spins with graceful waltzes, the story is quite captivating, and finally, we are cheered by the German composer's renunciation of the frightful for the fanciful.

First cancer virus discovered by Rous

Jan 21. For the first time in the history of medicine, a cancerous tumor has been shown to be caused by a virus, according to a report published today by Dr. Francis Peyton Rous, a physician and virologist at the Rockefeller Institute in New York City.

Last year, a breeder provided Rous with a chicken which had a curious growth. Rous extracted the infectious agent from the cancerous chicken tumor. He then inoculated several healthy chickens from the same inbred stock with the agent, thereby transmitting the cancer to them. As the infectious agent is capable of slipping through a fine filter, it appears that it must be the smallest of all microorganisms, the virus.

Although Dr. Rous was educated at the Johns Hopkins University in Baltimore, Maryland, and has impeccable medical credentials, his results are considered highly controversial by the scientific establishment. So far, there is no evidence that cancer is infectious in human beings or any other mammals, and there is no cause for undue alarm.

Jan 3. Home Secretary Winston S. Churchill is out in front at the Siege of Sidney St. in London. Three alien, anarchist burglars killed six policemen, wounded two and holed up in a house. Churchill hurried to the scene. The house caught fire and Churchill let it burn. Two men died in the flames, but their leader "Peter the Painter" escaped.

1911

FEBRUARY

Su	Mo	Tu	We	Th	Fr	Sa
			1	2	3	4
5	6	7	8	9	10	11
12	13	14	15	16	17	18
19	20	21	22	23	24	25
26	27	28				

1. New Jersey: Cargo ship carrying dynamite explodes, killing 25, wounding 1,000.

2. Minnesota doctors announce tetanus can be cured by injecting epsom salts into spinal column.

2. St. Petersburg: Dr. Patchenko, "the poison doctor," confesses to murdering 40 for profit.

3. Haitian govt. issues call to arms to combat revolutionary disturbances.

4. Lt. Col. George Goethals, chief engineer of Panama canal, urges fortification of isthmus.

7. France: Prof. Gabriel Petit reports radium injections to have rejuvinating effects on horses; scientific community remains skeptical.

7. Swiss national council votes to begin importing U.S. meat.

14. U.S. House of Representatives passes bill calling for trade reciprocity with Canada, European nations.

21. France: Anti-Semitic demonstration at the Comedie Francaise.

22. Canadian Parliament votes to preserve union with British Empire.

24. German Reichstag decides to increase peace time army by 515,000 troops (→ 3/8).

24. U.S., Japan sign treaty, continuing restriction of Japanese immigration to U.S.

25. Victor Herbert's opera "Natoma" premieres in Philadelphia.

27. France: Briand Cabinet resigns in face of Republican opposition to policy of conciliation with Catholic Church.

28. Washington: Senate defeats proposed constitutional amendment for popular election of senators (→ 4/13).

BIRTH

6. American actor and 40th President Ronald Reagan.

DEATH

4. Piet Cronje, noted Boer general (*1835).

Parliament faces a new era of reform

House of Lords under siege.

Feb 21. The British Parliament is faced with potentially momumental reforms stemming from last year's general election which returned the country to a Liberal majority. Foremost on the House of Commons' Liberal agenda is the removal of the House of Lords' veto power.

The lords have acquiesced to movements to dilute their power over the past 80 years. The Reform Acts of the 19th century, including legislation in 1832 allowing middle-class Britons the right to vote and legislation in 1867 granting suffrage to urban laborers, reshaped British politics. If the House of Lords loses its veto power, a new era of political decision-making will ensue (→ 5/15).

Ramsay MacDonald heads Labor Party

Feb 6. The Labor Party's most effective speaker, James Ramsay MacDonald, today took over the party chairmanship from James Keir Hardie. MacDonald, a socialist who worked his way up through party ranks, was said to believe the chairmanship was just a figurehead position and was reluctant to give up his post as party secretary. MacDonald also had to overcome his personal grief over the deaths of his mother and son during the past year before being convinced by party officials that it was in the best interest of the British labor movement that he accept the position.

1911

MARCH

Su	Mo	Tu	We	Th	Fr	Sa
			1	2	3	4
5	6	7	8	9	10	11
12	13	14	15	16	17	18
19	20	21	22	23	24	25
26	27	28	29	30	31	

1. Jose Ordonez elected president of Uruguay.

2. Maurice Maeterlinck's "The Bluebird" opens in Paris.

2. France: Ernest Monis succeeds Aristide Briand as president of the council.

5. Census figures place French population at 39,601,509; increase of 350,000 in five years is Europe's lowest rate.

6. American soldier, fighting for Mexican rebels, killed by govt. troops at Casas Grandes.

8. British Minister of Foreign Affairs Edward Grey declares Britain will not support France in event of military conflict.

9. Funding for five new battleships added to British military budget (→ 5/15).

12. New York: Dr. Fletcher of Rockefeller Institute discovers cause of infantile paralysis.

13. Washington: Supreme Court approves corporate tax law (→ 4/12).

13. New York: Premiere of Ivan Caryll's operetta "My Pink Lady," featuring waltz "My Beautiful Lady."

17. Norway: School teacher Anna Rogstadt becomes first female member of Parliament (→ 4/4).

18. Arizona: Col. Teddy Roosevelt opens Roosevelt Reservoir Dam in Phoenix, largest in U.S.

20. St. Petersburg: Russian Premier Stolypin resigns (→ 9/18).

23. Population of Venice recorded at two million; Paris reaches 2,888,110.

24. Denmark: Penal code reform abolishes corporal punishment.

27. Scott and Amundsen meet in race for South Pole.

28. New York: Suffragists perform political play "Pageant of Protest."

BIRTH

26. American playwright Tennessee Williams, "Cat on a Hot Tin Roof" (†2/24/1983).

Triangle fire kills 146; most are girls

Fire at Triangle shirtwaist factory.

March 25. Fire swept through a shirtwaist factory in New York City yesterday, killing 146 workers, most of them young girls. The blaze at the Triangle Waist Company broke out just minutes before the workers were to go home. As flames spread rapidly through flimsy material, some employees were fatally burned while others leaped from the windows to their death on the pavement below, clutching their pay envelopes. The ten-story building had been classed as fireproof by the city inspectors and it had only one fire escape (→ 4/11).

Jane Addams issues book on Hull House

March 5. It was 20 years ago that Jane Addams founded Hull House in the slums of Chicago. Now, in a new book, Miss Addams tells of both the heartaches and the triumphs of those years in which she ran a settlement house for poor children of the city.

That she chose such a career comes as something of a surprise, for she was born to a prosperous family and had few encounters with the truly needy. But long bouts of ill health left her with a feeling of sympathy for the unfortunate. And so it was, at age 30, she left England and set up quarters in the worst of the Chicago slums. Hull House, and now the book about it, are testimony to Miss Addams' spirit of altruism and dedication.

1911

APRIL

Su	Mo	Tu	We	Th	Fr	Sa
						1
2	3	4	5	6	7	8
9	10	11	12	13	14	15
16	17	18	19	20	21	22
23	24	25	26	27	28	29
30						

1. Mexican Pres. Diaz promises sweeping reforms to National Assembly (→ 15).

3. British census counts population of 45,216,665; 9.1 percent increase since 1901.

3. Pres. Taft orders removal of Negro Ninth Cavalry unit from San Antonio for agitating against segregation on street cars.

4. Massachusetts Legislature refuses vote to women (→ 30).

6. Italian government establishes state life insurance.

6. Jacques Copeau stages Dostoyevsky's "The Brothers Karamazov" in Paris.

7. Chicago: Government wins first case against Italian Black Hand organization.

10. German navy orders two American Curtiss biplanes.

11. France: Jean Jaures announces scheme for reorganization of French socialism.

12. N.Y.: Carnegie trust placed in bankruptcy (→ 5/15).

12. Paris: Pierre Prier makes first non-stop flight from London to Paris.

13. U.S. House of Representatives votes in favor of direct senatorial elections (→ 6/12).

15. Mexico: American troops cross Rio Grande to aid Mexican rebels (→ 19).

19. Mexican President Diaz blasts U.S. for arming rebels, refuses to grant demands for reform (→ 20).

19. New Portuguese republic votes separation of church and state.

20. Mexican rebel leader Madero refuses armistice, gives Diaz one day to resign (→ 5/1).

23. Florida: Bob Burman covers Daytona Beach mile in record 25.4 seconds, driving 200-h.p. "Blitzen" Benz.

30. China: German warship Ilten arrives in Canton to guard Europeans from mounting hostility (→ 5/1).

30. Portuguese constitutional court authorizes women to vote (→ 5/7).

French march to aid of Moroccan Sultan

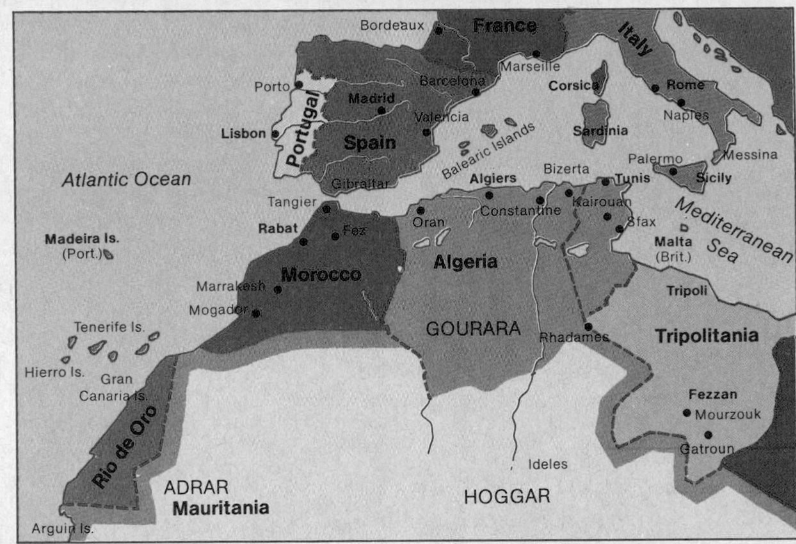

North Africa is increasingly becoming the scene of European intrigue.

April 20. A new crisis in Morocco has sent French troops rushing to Fez, and it is not clear what the international repercussions will be. France says a revolt was brewing against Sultan Moulai Hafid, who requested the troops to protect the royal palace and French citizens living in Morocco. The military action by France comes after five years of relative calm in the North African country.

The overt French intervention seems to violate the accords of the 1906 Algeciras Conference. France has been using its police powers to annex new territory in Morocco. However, it had stopped short of full military action. Germany has not yet announced an official protest against the new French move. But a German newspaper warns, "A permanent military occupation of the Moroccan capital would violate the Algeciras agreement and it could have consequences that are difficult to imagine." If the Algeciras accords are broken, Germany would be free to play its own hand in Morocco (→ 5/18).

Rembrandt's Mill: Who owns it now?

April 6. When the British National Gallery failed to buy "The Mill" by Rembrandt for $500,000 from Lord Lansdowne, The London Times reported that Peter Widener bought it. He denied it. Then the paper said Henry Frick was the purchaser. Now The Times' guess is that Benjamin Altman owns it.

Rembrandt's "The Mill."

Owners indicted for Triangle tragedy

April 11. Owners of New York City's Triangle Waist Company factory in which 146 persons perished in a fire last month were indicted yesterday on charges of first- and second-degree manslaughter.

The defendants, co-owners of the ten-story shirtwaist factory, pleaded not guilty, and they were freed on bail of $25,000 each. The penalty for conviction of first-degree manslaughter is up to 25 years in prison; for second-degree, the penalty is up to ten years.

The indictments were based on a grand jury finding that two girls employed at the factory had died because they had been trapped inside a locked door on the ninth floor. Labor laws forbid locking or bolting factory doors while employees are at work.

Gutenberg has a real best seller

April 25. Henry E. Huntington, prominent in railroads and other enterprises, may proudly claim to own the most expensive book in the world. Last night, he bought, through an agent, the famed Gutenberg Bible on vellum for $50,000, the highest price ever paid for a book, as bidders from all over the world competed for numerous literary rarities at the Robert Hoe Library Auction in New York. Huntington also purchased "The Boke of St. Albans," a fine folio copy on angling and hunting, for $12,000, adding both treasures to his San Marino estate in California.

Nijinsky dances new ballet in Paris

April 19. The Russian dancer Nijinsky has audiences on their feet in Paris as the hit of the season is "The Spectre of the Rose." It is a very romantic ballet, based on a poem by Theophile Gauthier. A young girl returns from a ball smelling a rose, which miraculously turns into a man who then dances through the window. Nijinsky dances with the dreaming girl and disappears again through the window. The production is another success for Diaghilev's Russian Ballet. Michel Fokine choreographed "The Spectre of the Rose." The music is by Carl Maria von Weber and Berlioz. And the ballerina Tamara Karsavina plays the young, dreaming girl.

Russian dancer Vaslav Nijinsky.

1911

MAY

Su	Mo	Tu	We	Th	Fr	Sa
	1	2	3	4	5	6
7	8	9	10	11	12	13
14	15	16	17	18	19	20
21	22	23	24	25	26	27
28	29	30	31			

1. New York: J.P. Morgan pays $42,800 for only perfect copy of "Le Morte d'Arthur," printed by Caxton in 1485.

1. Durango falls to Mexican rebels in worst government defeat of war (→ 25).

1. China beset by rebellion; looters in control of Kwangtung and Chansi provinces.

7. New York: Thousands parade down Fifth Ave., demanding vote for women (→ 8).

8. Danish colony Iceland gives vote to women (→ 11/21).

12. Despite Russian protests, U.S. economist W. Morgan Schuster takes control over Persia's finances (→ 11/11).

13. Meridian wins Kentucky Derby with G. Archibald riding.

15. Kaiser Wilhelm II pays official visit to King George in London; the two sovereigns tentatively reassert friendship.

15. London: House of Commons passes bill to limit power of House of Lords (→ 6/30).

16. London: English throat specialist declares Caruso's vocal chords normal.

16. German Zeppelin Deutschland crashes on inaugural flight.

16. N.Y.: First U.S. interview with Dalai Lama published.

18. Morocco: French Gen. Moinier enters Fez without resistance (→ 6/10).

21. Juarez: Madero signs peace accord, ending war in Mexico (→ 25).

22. French Min. of War Berteaux killed by crashing plane at start of Paris-Madrid race.

22. Biweekly passenger service by auto links N.Y. and Chicago.

24. Boston Pops premieres Henry Gilbert's "Americanesque," based on Negro minstrel tunes.

29. U.S. Supreme Court finds tobacco trust in violation of Sherman Act (→ 9/26).

31. Alsace-Lorraine gains constitution as autonomous state.

31. Managua: 18 killed as Nicaraguan rebels blow up presidential palace (→ 8/4/12).

Oil trust is held illegal

Standard boss John D. Rockefeller.

May 15. The Supreme Court of the United States, in a landmark decision today, found the Standard Oil Company guilty of restraint of trade and ordered its dissolution within six months.

However, in ordering that the oil trust be ended, the court made history in another field by holding that the Sherman Antitrust Law does not automatically forbid trade monopolies but only those found to be "unreasonable" in restraining trade. The highest court in the land thus wrote into the law a definition not heretofore spelled out by Congress.

The court interpretation, which could have far-reaching effect in future antitrust suits, was promptly criticized by Senator Robert M. La Follette of Wisconsin, a leader of the Progressive wing of the Republican Party, who said: "I fear that the court has done what the trusts wanted it to do and what Congress has steadily refused to do."

The Supreme Court opinion in the Standard Oil case upheld the order of the Eighth Circuit Court of Appeals, but the order modified the lower court judgment by giving the mammoth oil monopoly six months, instead of just 30 days, to dissolve itself.

Furthermore, the high court ruled that Standard Oil be permitted to engage in trade until the oil trust is dissolved, arguing that immediate cessation could seriously injure the public by bringing about a degree of uncertainty as to the adequacy and source of supplies of crude and refined oil (→ 29).

Indianapolis 500 run for first time

Poster for the new speedway.

May 30. The national driving champion, Ray Harroun, came out of retirement to help dedicate the new macadam track at Indianapolis Speedway. And then he zipped to victory in a locally built Marmon. Harroun used a rear-view mirror that he invented because his was the only car that did not have a mechanic along for the 500-mile grind.

President Diaz quits; Mexican rebels win

May 25. Mexico's latest uprising has come to an end after only six months of fighting as President Porfirio Diaz formally retired from his nation's top office today.

On May 21, a peace agreement was signed between the Diaz regime and the provisional president and rebel leader, Francisco I. Madero Jr. The signing took place at 10:35 p.m. in the glare of automobile headlights on the steps of the Juarez Custom House, which somebody had locked.

In April, as Madero's movement spread, Diaz called for volunteers, but too late. On May 1, Diaz suffered his greatest loss. The rebels took the city of Durango, the first state capital captured. Fifteen days later, Diaz signed his resignation.

While the fighting ebbed and flowed, 20,000 United States troops and two naval fleets kept watch. Officers were ordered not to cross the border. Some Americans and other foreigners, however, joined the rebels. One group took part in the battle of Casas Grandes. Some were killed, wounded or captured, but there was no official intervention.

One man who missed the final victory was Pancho Villa, a Madero ally. He was captured in 1910, escaped and fled to Texas (→ 6/21).

Porfirio Diaz as President of Mexico.

Gustav Mahler lost to world of music

May 18. Gustav Mahler, the Bohemian composer and conductor who has been justly praised as one of the towering musical figures of our day, or any day, is dead at the age of 50, the victim of a fatal pneumonic illness which had prostrated him for the last eight weeks.

After studying at the University of Vienna and the Vienna Conservatory, Mahler became the conductor of the Budapest Imperial Opera at age 28. He moved on to conduct in Hamburg and Vienna, and in 1907 sailed to America to become the conductor of the New York Philharmonic and the Metropolitan Opera.

The Czech musician composed nine complete symphonies, several songs and song cycles. Of the cycles, "Songs of a wayfarer," "Songs on the death of children" and "Song of the earth" are the most notable. Mahler died in his native land, as was his urgently expressed wish.

1911

JUNE

Su	Mo	Tu	We	Th	Fr	Sa
				1	2	3
4	5	6	7	8	9	10
11	12	13	14	15	16	17
18	19	20	21	22	23	24
25	26	27	28	29	30	

1. New York: Metropolitan Museum of Art buys Perugino's "Resurrection" for $25,000.

2. Guatemalan assembly grants U.S. syndicate access to all mineral wealth and franchises of republic.

4. Alaska: Gold found at Indian Creek.

8. Mexican earthquake, volcanic eruption kill 1,300.

9. New York: Americans defeat British challengers to keep polo trophy.

9. China asks $10 mil. indemnity of Mexican govt. for massacres of Chinese.

9. Italian foreign minister declares Italian interests in Africa limited to Tripoli and Cyrena (→ 8/3).

10. France protests landing of Spanish troops in Larrache, Morocco (→ 7/2).

10. Government estimates place Chinese population at 451 mil.

11. Greek Natl. Assembly under Venizelos adopts liberal constitution.

11. Japanese begin construction of military port on Bonin Island.

13. France: Opening performance of Igor Stravinsky's "Petrushka."

18. New York: Sarah Bernhardt ends 35-week tour of U.S. and Canada.

21. Porfirio Diaz, ex-president of Mexico, exiles himself to Paris (→ 10/2).

26. New York: Ziegfeld Follies feature Irving Berlin's "Everybody Does It" and "Woodman, Woodman Spare That Tune."

30. British govt. advises King George to replace Lords who favor weaker upper house (→ 7/20).

BIRTH

25. American biochemist Wm. Howard Stein, discovered structure of enzyme (†3/2/1980).

DEATHS

9. Carrie Nation, temperance crusader (*11/25/1846).

28. Abraham Abraham, founder of Abraham and Strauss.

King George crowned in unusual splendor

June 23. King George V was crowned today at Westminster Abbey in a ceremony evoking the continuity and tradition of the British monarchy. The clouds outside and the somber interior of the building contrasted with the magnificent gowns, jewels and uniforms of those assembled. By 8 o'clock in the morning, Westminster Abbey was full of people ready to spend the day. Thousands and thousands of spectators crowded the streets for hours, hoping to catch a glimpse of the royal procession. Perhaps the coronation ceremony seemed especially splendid because of the threatening political backdrop of socialism, strikes and recent attacks on the peerage.

Great Britain's royal family tree.

Senators choose direct election by voters

June 12. The Senate voted tonight to amend the Constitution so as to provide for election of senators by a direct popular vote. Currently, members of the United States Senate are chosen by state legislatures for four-year terms.

As approved by the Senate, and subject to passage by the House, the proposed amendment to the Constitution would clear the way for the voters of each state to elect their two senators for six-year terms.

The rationale for the proposed change is that the current way of choosing senators in almost all cases reflects solely the political bent of the individual state legislatures, rather than giving the voters a chance to elect their senators from whichever political party they choose.

Thousands march for women's votes

June 17. Between 40,000 and 60,000 supporters of women's suffrage marched in a five-mile procession through London today.

Many marchers were garbed in historical costumes, representing such eminent women as Boadicea, Catherine of Aragon and Queen Victoria. An impressive group of 700 women who had been jailed for the cause carried lances with banners in the suffragette colors of purple, green and white.

The parade brought together a wide range of suffragists, from sweatshop workers to collegians and titled women. The colossal procession, led by "General" Mrs. Drummond mounted on a charger, began at Victoria Embankment and ended with an enthusiastic meeting at Albert Hall, presided over by Mrs. Emmeline Pankhurst.

New York welcomes biggest ocean liner

June 20. A large crowd packed the piers in New York harbor this morning to watch the docking of the White Star steamship Olympic, the largest vessel in the world, equalled but not surpassed in size by her sister ship, Titanic. Both measure 882.5-feet long and 99.5 beam, representing an investment of $10 million each. The Olympic presently carries 1,316 passengers and 850 crew members. Every amenity is offered on board, from racket courts to Turkish baths. A fleet of tugboats prevented the gentle giant from inadvertently damaging the pier when she anchored.

White Star liner Olympic in N.Y.

1911

JULY

Su	Mo	Tu	We	Th	Fr	Sa
						1
2	3	4	5	6	7	8
9	10	11	12	13	14	15
16	17	18	19	20	21	22
23	24	25	26	27	28	29
30	31					

1. New York: Harry Atwood makes first airplane flight over Manhattan.

1. San Francisco rocked by severest shock since earthquake of 1906.

4. Great Britain sides with France in Morocco; Spain backs Germany (→ 10).

9. Anthony Wilding over Herbert Barret 6-4, 4-6, 2-6, 6-2 in 1st Wimbledon men's draw over 100; Dorothea Chambers blanks Penelope Boothby 6-0, 6-0.

10. Russia pledges support for France in Morocco (→ 29).

12. New York: 221 deaths from heat exhaustion reported since July 1.

14. Anglo-Japanese alliance renewed for four years, modified to include U.S.

16. Unprecedented heat wave sweeps Europe.

17. Brussels: Aviator Oliesiagers breaks record with uninterrupted flight of 388 miles.

20. British House of Lords attempts to protect power, passing watered-down version of House of Commons bill (→ 24).

23. Constantinople devastated by fire; 7,000 houses burn.

24. London: House of Commons adjourned following riots over Lords' attempt to maintain veto power (→ 8/10).

25. Bobby Leach becomes second person to survive trip down Niagara Falls in barrel.

28. French Commander-in-Chief Gen. Michel forced to resign over Dreyfus Affair; republican Joseph Joffre succeeds.

29. British reinforce Atlantic fleet, placed on alert over Moroccan crisis (→ 8/4)

30. French racer Victor Garrigou wins eighth Tour de France.

BIRTH

5. French statesman Georges Pompidou (†4/2/1974).

DEATH

5. Maria Pia, queen dowager of Portugal.

German threat at Agadir

July 2. Germany has sent the battleship Panther to Agadir, and a German military force landed there yesterday as the Kaiser's government appears to have staked a claim on southern Morocco. According to reports from Tangier, more German warships are on the alert and will be sent to the area if needed.

Germany, like Spain and France before her, covets the rich copper and mineral deposits, the agricultural possibilities and the pleasant climate Morocco possesses. As reported in the German press, the kaiser intends to take his share in the province of Sus, partitioning the country into another section unless the French and Spanish end their expeditions there and allow the nation to exercise its independence. In fact, Germany feels justified in intervening because of alleged violations by Spain and France of the Algeciras Act, which prohibits foreign occupation of Moroccan soil.

European reaction to the affair varies. In London, most feel the action is unnecessary but doesn't warrant serious concern. Paris diplomatic circles are naturally a bit more stirred. Premier Caillaux and German Ambassador Baron von Schoen conversed amicably for hours about the matter. However, French Foreign Minister de Selves expressed his remorse, disturbed that Germany sent warships to a place where no trouble was reported. Madrid considers Germany's move as complicating the Moroccan situation, but also views it as a confirmation of Spanish occupation. The Diario Universel reports that German aggression will force England into the affair, which worries the Spanish regime the most. Berliners predictably approve of the action. Many feel the kaiser should have moved sooner (→ 4).

The Panther watches over Agadir.

Indiana farm is center of U.S. population

July 30. The center of America's population inches westward, belying fears that the frontier is a hotel with no vacancies.

Every census, since the first taken in 1790, shows westward movement. In that year, the dividing line between East and West passed a few miles outside Baltimore. In 1870, the line leaped to 48 miles northeast of Cincinnati. Since 1890, however, the population center has been claimed by Indiana towns. Residents of Unionville, in Monroe County, have the present honor.

Monroe residents can scarcely believe their home is a symbol of settlement. Older residents can recall their parents breaking the ground in the fields, contending with timber wolves and battling rattlesnakes. They could just as easily believe that Jewell County, Kansas, the geographical center of the nation, is the population hub.

America's fertile heartland.

Self-starter made for automobiles

July 1. A device that eliminates the need for cranking in order to start an automobile engine has been developed by an American inventor, Charles F. Kettering. To start the engine, the automobile's battery supplies voltage to a small motor which turns the crankshaft and at the same time delivers an electrical spark to ignite the gasoline in the cylinders. The self-starter is expected to increase the popularity of the automobile, since brute force will no longer be required to get the engine into operation.

Pole gives name to chemical: vitamin

July 1. A Polish biochemist, in a newly published report, has suggested the name "vitamin" to describe those chemicals which are necessary in the diet of both animals and humans beings. The scientist, Casimir Funk, is a researcher at the Lister Institute in Germany.

The new scientific term is derived from the Latin words for life ("vita") and ammonia ("amine") derivatives. In his experiments, the Polish scientist noted that pigeons fed a diet of polished rice developed a nervous disorder unless they were also fed the rice polishings. From the rice polishings, he isolated a water-soluble crystalline material: a vitamin.

Irving Berlin, at 26, is already making a name for himself with show tune hits like this one.

1911

AUGUST

Su	Mo	Tu	We	Th	Fr	Sa
		1	2	3	4	5
6	7	8	9	10	11	12
13	14	15	16	17	18	19
20	21	22	23	24	25	26
27	28	29	30	31		

1. German government decides to fortify Heligoland in North Sea.

2. Haitian rebels score major victory, send head of state Simon into exile (→ 5).

3. French aviator Colliex pilots first amphibious plane, Le Canard, over the Seine.

3. First military use of aviation: Italian Commander Piazza flies reconnaissance missions over Tripoli (→ 9/30).

3. New York: Japanese naval hero Adm. Heihachiro Togo arrives for official U.S. visit (→ 4/19/13).

4. German Social Democrats call for nationwide protest against German aggression in Morocco (→ 21).

5. German cruiser Bremen sent to Haiti to protect German citizens threatened by civil unrest (→ 1/27/14).

10. British House of Commons fixes first salaries for members at 400 pounds sterling.

15. Great Britain: Two railway strikers killed by troops in Liverpool (→ 19).

17. Milwaukee: Russian naval mutineer Feodor Malkov gains asylum in U.S.

19. Great Britain: Union claims victory, as railway strike is settled.

21. Rumor spreads throughout Britain that France and Germany have declared war (→ 9/2).

23. Savage anti-Semitic rioting reported in Wales.

24. Lisbon: Portugal elects Arriaga first constitutional president of republic (→ 10/1).

26. Massachusetts: Enormous battleship Rivadavia launched at Quincy.

26. Pennsylvania: False fire alarm sparks stampede in Canonsburg; 25 killed, and 50 hurt.

27. German Southwest Africa: Railway line inaugurated, linking Windhoek and Karibib.

BIRTH

6. American TV comedienne Lucille Ball.

"Mona Lisa" is stolen

Where is the "Mona Lisa"?

Aug 22. In Paris, French police say it must be the work of a madman: Someone slipped into the Louvre, apparently during the night, and stole the "Mona Lisa," which may very well be the most famous painting in the entire world.

Curators at the Louvre are at a loss for words. Visitors to the museum are stopping to stare at the empty space on the wall in the Great Gallery, where the "Mona Lisa" has hung for more than a century. French investigators say that the theft cannot be the work of professional thieves, because the painting is too well-known to be sold. They suspect the "Mona Lisa" was stolen by a person who had lost all of his mental faculties.

The "Mona Lisa" has been a part of French art collections for 400 years, and it is considered a national treasure. Few pelople ever forget the sweet but enigmatic smile painted by Leonardo da Vinci → (9/7).

House of Lords yield, surrender veto power

Aug 10. The great constitutional struggle over the right of the British House of Lords to veto legislation is over. By a 131-114 vote, the lords surrendered to Prime Minister Herbert Asquith. Removing the threat of veto by the lords will enable the Liberals to pass reforms.

The Parliament Bill was passed last month by the House of Lords, but with amendments that Asquith opposed. He threatened to have King George create enough peers to pass the legislation. The idea of 400 or 500 "puppet" or "blackleg" peers, as the Unionists called them, was enough to change the votes of 20 to 30 Conservative peers.

The crisis began nearly two years ago when the House of Lords rejected Chancellor of the Exchequer David Lloyd George's budget, which included provisions for taxes on income and inheritances. Lloyd George charged the lords with breaching the constitution. The House of Lords strongly opposed the Liberal Party's attempts to introduce reform legislation in Britain. They had previously rejected two of the Liberal Party's education reform bills.

Reactions of members of Parliament were predictable. Elated Liberals believe the popular will has prevailed. The opposition considers the result an outrage. The Unionist Party, led by Arthur Balfour, has vowed to repeal the Parliament Act.

The issue has generated unprecedented heat. In July, when Asquith rose to speak in Parliament, he was met with such anger from the opposition that for an hour he stood speechless and had to take his seat without completing a full sentence.

Atwood flies from St. Louis to N.Y.

Aug 25. The longest flight in the history of American aviation has ended with the arrival of Harry N. Atwood in New York after a 1,365-mile trip from St. Louis.

Atwood beat the previous record by 101 miles. He probably covered another hundred miles in detours along the way. He was in the air for 28 hours and 31 minutes before landing on Governors Island.

Fog and rain had diminished hope that the young Bostonian would be able to complete his feat. He had contracted to end his long flight at Sheepshead Bay. A check for $1,000 was deposited by promoters there, but Atwood refused their request to put off his finish by one day to land at Sheepshead Bay. He forfeited the $1,000 prize but earned about $6,000 for his daring trip (→ 10/10).

First U.S. woman gets pilot's license

Harriet Quimby.

Aug 1. The first pilot's license ever issued to a woman by the Aero Club of America, and the second ever earned anywhere by a woman, has gone to Miss Harriet Quimby. Mme. Dutrie of France is the only other woman to hold such a license. Miss Quimby, a student at the Moisant Aviation School on Long Island, nearly matched the world record set by experienced fliers in her trial for the license; she landed her plane within seven feet, nine inches of a target. The official record is five feet, four inches. Miss Quimby had failed the same test a night earlier.

1911

SEPTEMBER

Su	Mo	Tu	We	Th	Fr	Sa
					1	2
3	4	5	6	7	8	9
10	11	12	13	14	15	16
17	18	19	20	21	22	23
24	25	26	27	28	29	30

2. Morocco: Spain obtains French sanction, occupies Ifni (→ 3).

2. William A. Larned takes National Singles tennis title at Newport, R.I.

3. Berlin: Social Democrats threaten strike if Germany goes to war over Morocco (→ 15).

4. Rhode Island: Bill Larned takes Newport tennis title for fifth straight time.

4. Chicago: American wrestler Frank Gotch defeats world champion Hackenschmidt.

6. Italy: Cholera victims number 30,000 for the year.

7. London: After 15 attempts, swimmer Burgess finally conquers English Channel in record 22.5 hours.

9. British open airmail route between Windsor and London.

15. Germany: French Ambassador Cambon reaches accord on Morocco with German Foreign Ministry (→ 11/4).

17. Vienna: Hungry rioters shot in streets; 200 injured.

18. Spain: Martial law proclaimed in Valencia as general strike breaks out.

21. Canada overwhelmingly defeats reciprocity agreement with U.S.

22. Russian military tribunal passes death sentence on Dimitri Bogroff, Stolypin's assassin.

23. Second International Aviation Meet opens in New York.

25. France: Battleship Liberty explodes, killing 350.

25. New York: George Cohan's musical "The Little Millionaire" opens at Cohan Theater.

26. New York: U.S. Steel Corp. resists dissolution, denies violating Sherman Law (→ 10/15).

30. Pennsylvania: Dam breaks in Austin; fire, flood kill 1,000.

BIRTHS

19. British author William Golding, "Lord of the Flies."

24. Soviet head of state Konstantin Chernenko (†3/10/1985).

Italians and Turks go to war over Tripoli

Sept 30. Italy declared war on Turkey yesterday, as each nation vies for the control of Tripoli. Italy wasted no time in attacking; hours after the declaration, she sunk a Turkish torpedo boat in the harbor of Prevesa. With her navy in place, Italy then blockaded Tripoli. This followed Turkey's defiance of an Italian ultimatum to surrender control of the Libyan city.

The conflict leads many Europeans to speculate that a vast Mediterranean war will break out and that the Ottoman Empire will fall. The chief concern is to localize the fighting, confining it to Tripoli. Italy's aggression has been widely condemned as hasty, as no specific hostile acts on Turkey's part were reported. One British newspaper described Italy as "pirate and brigand." However, the Italian people have taken to the streets to exhibit their support for the war (→ 10/20).

Casualty at Tripoli.

Apollinaire is held in Mona Lisa case

Sept 7. Last month, French police suspected their investigation into the theft of the Mona Lisa would lead them to a madman. Instead, it has led them to Guillaume Apollinaire. None of the gothic stories the poet has written is as strange as this case. Investigators are providing few details, but they say Apollinaire has been arrested and charged with the receipt of stolen property. The wall in the Great Gallery of the Louvre has been empty since the Mona Lisa was stolen. It is hoped that the painting will be found and returned as quickly as possible (→ 12/31/13).

Russian Premier Stolypin assassin's victim

Sept 18. Two shots disrupted a gala performance at the Kiev opera house four nights ago and when the noise died down, Premier Stolypin lay wounded. The shooting occurred in full view of Czar Nicholas II. Stolypin was not expected to survive the severe wounds to his liver and spine, and today he died. A socialist lawyer named Dimitri Bogroff fired the shots, and police grabbed him from a crowd that was ready to lynch him.

Known for his uncompromising and ruthless ways, Stolypin made many enemies since becoming premier five years ago. Though political parties, trade unions and the press enjoyed relative freedom during his tenure, the second Duma, Russia's legislative body, was disbanded when it refused to approve his proposal to allow serfs to be full property owners.

The trait which created the most resentment, however, was Stolypin's fervent Russian nationalism and his harsh policies toward minorities in Russia. He dissolved most Ukranian and Polish cultural organizations and his treatment of Finns was particularly brutal.

Stolypin had previously survived an attempt on his life at his country home outside St. Petersburg in 1906. Moments after he stepped into his study at the rear of his house, a bomb exploded, killing 23 persons including the premier's son and daughter (→ 22).

Crowds turn up in St. Petersburg for Stolypin's funeral.

Flood and famine devastate Chinese

Sept 10. The plague, famine and floods are exacting a heavy toll in China this year. Known deaths from the pneumonic plague this spring number well over 30,000. Deaths from famine, due to crop failure caused by heavy rains, cannot be estimated, but millions have tried to survive on roots and grass, with huge numbers dying a horrible death. The Yangtze River is now swelling to a width of 45 miles in places, with floods covering a territory over 700 miles long, drowning the crops before maturity. In and around the city of Nanking, an estimated 300 persons are dying daily.

Magazine cover.

1911

OCTOBER

Su	Mo	Tu	We	Th	Fr	Sa
1	2	3	4	5	6	7
8	9	10	11	12	13	14
15	16	17	18	19	20	21
22	23	24	25	26	27	28
29	30	31				

1. Portugal: Peasants revolt in north, demand return of monarchy (→ 13).

2. Francisco Madero elected president of Mexico (→ 24).

5. New York: Helen Hayes stars in premiere of musical "The Never Homes" at Broadway Theater.

7. London suffragette Ida Peploe announces Englishwomen plan to form army.

10. Revolution breaks out in China when government uncovers rebel headquarters in Hankow (→ 12).

10. C.P. Rodgers surpasses Atwood's cross-country flight record, reaching 1,398 miles.

11. Earthquake in Southern California kills 700.

12. Hankow: Provincial capitals of South in open revolt; republic proclaimed with Sun Yat-sen pres. of provisional assembly (→ 22).

13. Portugal: Monarchist revolt gains $2.5 mil. in Brazilian aid.

14. World aviation deaths number 100 to date.

15. U.S. investigators exonerate sugar trust, blame high prices on European monopoly (→ 12/1/12).

16. Chicago: First Natl. Conference of Progressive Republicans elects Robert La Follette president (→ 6/18/25).

22. Main Chinese army routed by 20,000 rebels (→ 30).

23. Cretan Parliament votes unification with Greece.

24. Mexico: Newly elected Madero plagued by Zapata raids in federal district (→ 3/29/12).

25. Georges Carpentier takes European boxing title.

26. Philadelphia: Athletics take World Series from N.Y. Giants 13-2 in sixth game.

31. Italian troops reported killing Arab women in Tripoli.

DEATHS

1. German philosopher Wilhelm Dilthey (*11/19/1833).

4. British Dr. Joseph Bell, model for Sherlock Holmes (*1837).

China dynasty tottering

Oct 30. Three centuries of Manchu domination over China were swept away today when the five-year-old boy Emperor, Pu Yi, guided by the regent, Prince Chun, granted a constitution and a Cabinet devoid of nobles to the Chinese people. It is not known, however, whether this late measure can appease a country seething with revolutionary discontent, and a strong contingent of troops guards the imperial palace in Peking tonight.

The rebellion which broke out in Wu-Ch'ang three weeks ago and has swept through the cities like wildfire has been smoldering since the turn of the century. Modernization of transportation and trade created a desire for more contact with the outside world and the throne was badly shaken by the Russo-Japanese War in 1905. The death of the Dowager Empress in 1908 postponed the parliamentary government promised in 1906, and the regent has never been able to consolidate his grasp on China. Revolutionary leaders such as Sun Yat-sen have fanned the desire for freedom and only a spark was needed to touch off open revolt.

Chinese republican army in the field.

In an extraordinary statement issued through the regent, the emperor took responsibility for conditions leading to the revolt and apologized, saying that administrators had deceived him in carrying out his policies. Most believe the reforms are too late and thousands of Manchus have fled the capital, believing that a bloodbath is inevitable (→ 11/10).

Death overtakes publisher Pulitzer

Oct 29. Joseph Pulitzer, publishing genius and staunch ally of democracy, died this afternoon of heart disease. His final moments were spent aboard his yacht in Charleston harbor with his wife and youngest son.

Pulitzer exemplified the self-made man. Born in Budapest in 1847, he arrived in America without a penny. He joined the Union Army, where his halting English proved no disadvantage. At war's close, he journeyed to St. Louis. There, despite a vision problem that would plague him all his life, he studied law. But Pulitzer sought greater challenges. He impulsively applied for a reporting position with a German-language newspaper. He swiftly advanced in the field, until at his death he was proprietor of the New York World and the St. Louis Post-Dispatch.

Pulitzer wrote editorials for the people, supporting their causes and defending them against injustice. It is the common man who mourns him today.

Italy's flag flies over Turkish Tripoli

Oct 20. Italian sailors planted Italy's flag on the shores of Tripoli earlier this month and now occupy several forts, declaring themselves "masters of Tripoli." The city of Benghazi has been bombarded by the Italian fleet, led by Rear Admiral Aubrey, and after a fierce but quick battle, Italians control most of the city. The Turks, despite heavy losses, refuse to surrender, saying national integrity is at stake. Italy's success seems to prove her claim that she is a military power (→ 31).

Occupying forces raise the Italian flag over Tripoli.

Churchill promoted to naval ministry

Oct 1. Winston S. Churchill was instructed today to put the British navy into a state of "instant and constant readiness" in case of a German attack. His instructions came from Prime Minister Herbert Asquith, who appointed him First Lord of the Admirality, civilian chief of the navy.

Still only 37 years old, Churchill had already held two government posts, President of the Board of Trade and Home Secretary. In the latter, he incurred criticism by rushing to the Sidney St. siege instead of leaving matters to the police.

From the very beginning of his public career, Churchill excited interest. As an army lieutenant, he took leave to be a war correspondent in the Boer War. He was captured and escaped, and a price was put on his head. It was too low, he said, only 25 pounds sterling. His adventures gave him material for his writing and lecturing. "I live from mouth to hand," he said.

1911

NOVEMBER

Su	Mo	Tu	We	Th	Fr	Sa
			1	2	3	4
5	6	7	8	9	10	11
12	13	14	15	16	17	18
19	20	21	22	23	24	25
26	27	28	29	30		

1. New York: President Taft reviews mobilization of U.S. Atlantic fleet.

1. Mary Garden sells kisses for charity at Chicago Opera's benefit production of Massenet's "Cendrillon."

1. Italy performs first aerial bombing on Tanguira oasis in Libya (→ 5).

5. Italy officially annexes Tripoli.

5. U.S.: Calbraith P. Rodgers ends first transcontinental flight; 49 days from N.Y. to Pasadena.

6. Maine becomes dry state.

6. New York: Metropolitan Museum of Art opens Egyptian Galleries.

10. Tennessee: President Taft ends 15,000-mile, 57-day speaking tour.

10. China: Imperial government retakes Nanking (→ 12/29).

11. Ignoring British protests, Russia invades northern Persia (→ 14).

13. Oscar Hammerstein opens London opera house.

14. American treasurer general of Persia blasts Britain and Russia for carving up Persia (→ 12/26).

16. Paris: King Peter I of Serbia pays official visit to France.

17. Italian census records 34,686,653 inhabitants, increase of 6.8% over ten years.

19. New York receives first Marconi wireless transmission from Italy.

19. Dominican Republic's President Ramon Caceres assassinated (→ 5/15/16).

20. France: Funeral of Paul and Laura Lafargue (daughter of Karl Marx); Lenin proclaims, "world bourgeois parliamentarism is drawing to a close."

21. London: Suffragettes arrested for storming Parliament all choose jail terms.

25. Philadelphia: Navy defeats Army 3-0 in football.

BIRTH

29. German atomic physicist Konrad Fuchs.

France gets Morocco in deal with Germany

Nov 4. A Franco-German treaty made public today disclosed that Germany has recognized the right of France to establish a protectorate in Morocco. In compensation, France ceded to Germany about 96,525 square miles in the northern French Congo. The ceded territory, with a population of about one million persons, borders in part on the German Cameroons and has an annual commerce of about $2.4 million. France retains a right to run railroad lines across new German territory so as to connect different parts of French Central Africa.

The treaty brings to an end a four-month diplomatic crisis that at times looked as if it might lead to a war between the two nations. The accord was hailed by the French press, which deplored the loss of much of the French Congo but noted with satisfaction that France had acquired an empire in North Africa consisting of Tunisia, Algeria and Morocco. One newspaper commented: "The historic work commenced by Charles X is thus crowned by the Third Republic."

In Berlin, the treaty provoked dissension within the government of Chancellor von Bethmann-Hollweig over whether Germany had been adequately compensated by France. The German Foreign Ministry issued a statement expressing hope that the treaty "will have a calming effect" on Franco-German relations (→ 12/20).

Auto firm formed by Louis Chevrolet

Louis Chevrolet in first Chevrolet.

Nov 1. The automotive team of William Durant and Louis Chevrolet have announced the incorporation of the Chevrolet Motor Company of Michigan. According to a public statement issued by the firm, they intend to establish a factory in Detroit for the manufacture of a new, high-priced car.

The chief distinctive feature of their new motorcar will be an engine perfected during the last winter by Chevrolet, assisted financially by Durant. In 1900, at age 22, Swiss-born Chevrolet left Europe for America. He has worked as an automobile mechanic and is known for his derring-do as a racing driver. Six years ago, he won New York's Morris Park race with a speed record of 68 mph at the wheel of a Fiat. Last year, he completed a new, six-cylinder touring car.

Synge's play causes rioting in New York

Nov 27. "The Playboy of the Western World" by Irish playwright John M. Synge opened dramatically at the Maxine Elliott Theatre last night. Synge's bitter humor awakened the audience's outrage, and the Irish Players were pelted with potatoes, other vegetables and asafoetida balls, spreading panic at first, then a foul odor. Disturbers were violently thrown out and the police finally appeared, after which the first act was repeated, still punctuated by cries of "Shame! Shame!" and a few more assorted vegetables. Nothing like this ever happened on a stage in this country before.

Society lady in an egret decorated hat.

1911

DECEMBER

Su	Mo	Tu	We	Th	Fr	Sa
					1	2
3	4	5	6	7	8	9
10	11	12	13	14	15	16
17	18	19	20	21	22	23
24	25	26	27	28	29	30
31						

7. China: Imperial decree authorizes Chinese to cut braids.

11. Britain, France, Russia restrict whale fishing to prevent extinction.

17. N.Y.: George Bonhag runs 3,000-meters in record 8:35.

18. New York: Katrina Geltzer, principal dancer of Moscow Imperial Opera, makes U.S. debut at Met. Opera House.

18. U.S. President Taft dissolves 1832 treaty with Russia.

20. French Natl. Assembly ratifies Franco-German accord on Morocco (→ 5/11/14).

26. Russians reportedly massacre 500 at Resht, Persia.

28. Russian government agrees to import 12 mil. rubles in grain to fight famine (→ 4/18/12).

29. Mongolia, Turkestan declare independence from China, pass under Russian influence.

31. Census places Luxembourg's population at 260,400.

31. France: Helene Dutrieu wins Femina aviation cup in Etampes, sets distance record for women at 158 miles.

CULTURAL EVENTS, 1911

Literature: Joseph Conrad's "Under Western Eyes"; Edith Wharton's "Ethan Frome"; Nobel Prize for Literature to Maurice Maeterlinck.

Academia: Swiss psychiatrist Herman Rorschach's ink blot tests; discovery of Inca capital Vilcabamba at Machu Picchu, Peru by American archeologist Hiram Bingham; anthropologist Franz Boas' "The Mind of Primitive Man;" Cambridge Medieval History.

Music: Richard Strauss' opera "Der Rosenkavalier," in Dresden; Charles Ives' "Symphony No. 3"; Arnold Schonberg's "Manual of Harmony."

The Arts: Braque's "Man with a Guitar"; "The Blue Rider" group forms in Munich under Kandinsky and Franz Marc, promotes abstract art; D.W. Griffith's film "Enoch Arden"; Italian films "Spartacus" and "Pinocchio"; Asta Nielsen's Danish film "The Abyss"; Russian film "Anna Karenina."

Amundsen at South Pole

Roald Amundsen and his dogs take a well-earned rest atop the S. Pole.

Dec 14. Norwegian explorer Roald Amundsen and four companions reached the South Pole today, winning a race with a British expedition led by Robert F. Scott. His achievement means that explorers have set foot at both ends of the earth within less than three years, since Commander Robert E. Peary reached the North Pole in 1909.

Amundsen's party arrived in the Bay of Whales last January 14, pitched a winter camp and began their arduous trip to the South Pole in October. Unlike Scott, who is using a combination of motorized transport and ponies, Amundsen relied on dog teams for his dash to the pole. Amundsen was aided by good weather and the meticulous planning for which he is known. No word has yet been received about the fate of the Scott expedition, which left McMurdo Sound in October and is pursuing its journey to the South Pole (→ 2/10/13).

Dec 12. British royalty on parade as Queen Alexandra takes refuge from the Indian sun under a native parasol. George V (left) was named Emperor today and transferred India's capital from Calcutta to Delhi.

Dr. Sun Yat-sen President of China

Dec 29. Dr. Sun Yat-sen, leader of the revolutionaries battling the Manchu dynasty, has been elected President of the provisional government of China by the Nanking conference. The peace talks in Shanghai between the imperial delegation, led by Tang Shao-Yu, and the rebel group, led by Wu Ting Fang, have ended and a ten-day armistice is in effect. During the truce, President Sun will establish the terms for Manchu abdication. Sun will negotiate with Yuan Shih-kai, who as Premier and head of the imperial military has been in charge of the country since the retirement of Prince Chun.

Sun was born near Macao, China, in 1866, was educated in Honolulu and attended medical school in Hong Kong, where he met other Chinese students who wanted to change the government in China. The Manchus tried unsuccessfully to put a stop to Sun's revolutionary activities.

Sun Yat-sen and his wife.

The Manchu princes have agreed to let a national convention decide what form the future Chinese government should take. Premier Yuan told the princes that with $10 million he could hold the region north of the Yangtze River. The princes would not provide the money, but rumors indicate that American bankers may be prepared to make a loan (→ 2/15/12).

Madame Curie wins second Nobel Prize

Dec 10. Madame Marie Curie was presented today with the Nobel Prize in chemistry. She thus became the first person to win two of the coveted awards. Madame Curie was awarded the Nobel Prize in physics in 1903, winning jointly with her husband, Pierre, and Henri Becquerel, for studies of radioactivity. Her award this year was given for her discovery of two new elements, radium, so called for the powerful radiation it emits, and polonium, named after her native country, Poland. Her husband doubtless would have shared the award, since he worked with her on both discoveries, but he was killed in a traffic accident five years ago and the Nobel is never presented posthumously.

Madame Curie has established a series of firsts in science. In 1903, she became the first woman to attend a meeting of the famed Royal Institution in London, at a gathering where her husband was a guest lecturer. In 1906, she became the first woman to teach at the Sorbonne when she took over the professorship made vacant by Pierre Curie's death. However, her nomination for membership in the august French Academy was defeated by one vote, reportedly because of objections to admitting a woman. Madame Curie's discoveries have stimulated others to similar achievements, such as the discovery of the radioactive gas argon by the German physicist Friedrich Dorn.

Wilhelm Wien of Germany was awarded the physics prize for his work on heat radiation. The medicine prize went to Allvar Gullstrand of Sweden for his studies of diseases of the eye.

Marie Curie.

1912

JANUARY

Su	Mo	Tu	We	Th	Fr	Sa
	1	2	3	4	5	6
7	8	9	10	11	12	13
14	15	16	17	18	19	20
21	22	23	24	25	26	27
28	29	30	31			

1. Washington: War Dept. claims it has pictures of AFL Pres. Gompers and John Kelly of Building and Trades Council trampling on American flag.

2. Belgian miners go out on strike in the Borinage mines.

3. New York: 423 driving deaths reported for 1911; city seeks new auto laws.

3. New York: Plans announced for new $150,000 Brooklyn stadium for Trolley Dodgers.

6. New Mexico becomes 47th U.S. state (→ 2/14).

9. N.Y.: Colonel T. Roosevelt announces he will run for presidency if forced (→ 2/5).

9. New York: $18 mil. Equitable Life Assurance building destroyed by fire.

9. U.S. lands troops in Honduras to protect American investments during revolt.

10. New York: World's first flying-boat airplane, designed by Glenn Curtiss, makes maiden flight at Hammondsport.

16. Chinese council pres. narrowly escapes assassin's bomb.

17. Robert Scott reaches South Pole only a month after Amundsen (→ 2/10/13).

22. Second Monte-Carlo auto race begins.

25. Germany: Social Democrats gain in legislative elections; now hold 25% of seats.

26. Chicago: Dixie Jazz Band of New Orleans opens at Reisenweber's Cabaret.

29. Paris: Marguerite Durand leads suffragist delegation to Palais-Bourbon to demand place for women in plans for electoral reform (→ 11/5).

30. British Lords oppose House of Commons, rejecting home rule for Ireland (→ 4/11).

BIRTH

28. American painter Jackson Pollock, abstract impressionist (†8/11/1956).

DEATH

4. American geologist Clarence E. Dutton, studied western frontier (*5/15/1841).

Chinese regime becomes a republic

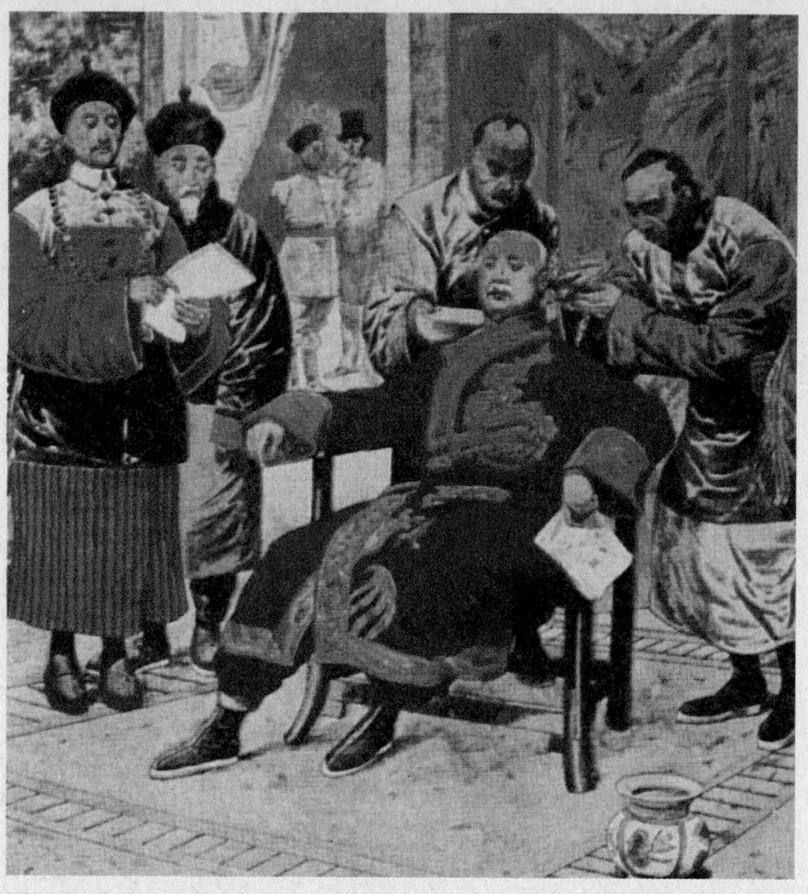

The symbolic end of dynasty in China. Gen. Yuan Shih-kai, President of the Council, breaks an ancient Chinese custom by having his queue cut.

Jan 1. The imperial Chinese government has been replaced by a new republic. Revolutionaries deposed Emperor Pu Yi last month and chose popular leader Sun Yat-sen to be their provisional president. Since that time, China has been burdened with two opposing governments, a republican one based at Nanking in the east central region of the country and the traditional Ching, or Manchu, dynasty located at Peking in Northern China.

The imperial government minister, General Yuan Shih-kai, fully realized that the royal family was fighting a lost cause. He is in a trusted position with them, having helped the former Empress Dowager fight the reform movement, for which he was rewarded with the highest imperial honor, the Viceregency of Chihli. Then, Yuan Shih-kai named himself Plenipotentiary. His power is formidable; the army and police are under his command.

Sun Yat-sen knows that any attempt to usurp Yuan's power would result in civil war. Therefore, he has said he will retire after a national Chinese election. He proposes that the people consider Yuan Shih-kai to govern in his place.

Lawrence workers strike for more money from textile mills

Jan 12. Protesting a cut in their pay, workers in the cotton and woolen mills in Lawrence, Massachusetts have gone on strike, leading to angry clashes between strikers and law enforcement officers.

Until recently, the average pay for the textile workers was 16 cents an hour for a 56-hour work week. The Massachusetts Legislature has now lowered the work week from 56 to 54 hours for women and children, who make up the bulk of the work force in the Lawrence mills.

After receiving paychecks reflecting the lowered hours, many women and children stopped their looms and went on strike, joined by a number of men workers. The mill workers, most of them foreign-born, make up nearly half the work force in the city, which has a population of about 85,000. With the active backing of the militant Industrial Workers of the World, the strikers are seeking a 15 percent pay increase for a 54-hour week with double pay for overtime.

The strikers, including children as young as 14 years old, have marched abreast through the city streets, forcing other pedestrians off the sidewalks. They have clashed repeatedly with law enforcement officials who were sent to the mills to protect the non-strikers.

Massachusetts militia holds strikers back from the Lawrence mills.

1912

FEBRUARY

Su	Mo	Tu	We	Th	Fr	Sa
				1	2	3
4	5	6	7	8	9	10
11	12	13	14	15	16	17
18	19	20	21	22	23	24
25	26	27	28	29		

1. Paris: Attempts to break two-month-old taxi drivers strike result in riots (→ 4/19).

2. Massachusetts: Four strike-breakers murdered in Lawrence.

3. N.Y.C. coroner reports 5,701 violent deaths last year, up 292 from 1910.

3. New U.S. football rules set: field shortened from 110 to 100 yds.; touchdown to count six pts. instead of five; four downs allowed instead of three; kick-off moved from midfield to 40-yd. line.

5. Robert La Follette withdraws from U.S. presidential race due to illness; Roosevelt men rejoice (→ 5/17).

5. British Arbitration League issues appeal against air war; signers include Sir Arthur Conan Doyle, Thomas Hardy, J.S. Sargent.

6. Turkey trot debuts in London; The Times reports, "Of course all of these dances are sensual in their aim ... abominably ugly."

8. British Defense Minister Lord Haldane visits Berlin, offers support for German colonial aspirations in Africa in exchange for limits on naval power (→ 1/12/13).

13. Chinese imperial government acknowledges new republic (→ 1/10/13).

14. U.S.: Arizona becomes 48th state in the union (→ 1/3/59).

21. Switzerland: Jungfrau tunnel completed at altitude of 9,000 feet.

24. Italians bomb Beirut in first act of war against Ottoman Empire (→ 3/5).

26. London coal miners strike begins (→ 3/1).

BIRTHS

19. American jazz pianist Stan Kenton (†1979).

27. British novelist and poet Lawrence Durell.

DEATH

10. British surgeon Joseph Lister, first to use antiseptics on infection (*4/5/1827).

Kitchener, British hero, ruling Sudan

Lord Kitchener.

Feb 27. Britain's Lord Kitchener took another step today in his master plan to maintain control over the Sudan by opening a railway linking Khartoum to El-Obeid, more than 200 miles to the southwest.

Kitchener started building a rail line along the Nile before the turn of the century. Britain recognized his brilliant military victories and administration by making him Governor General of the Sudan. Since then, he has been needed elsewhere in the empire. Kitchener has been in South Africa to help crush the Boers and in India to command British forces there. He returned to Egypt last year to serve as Consul General.

Feb 4. Austrian Franz Reichalt plunged like a stone to his death from the Eiffel Tower. Despite expert protests, the amateur parachute inventor had said: "I am confident of success."

1912

MARCH

Su	Mo	Tu	We	Th	Fr	Sa
					1	2
3	4	5	6	7	8	9
10	11	12	13	14	15	16
17	18	19	20	21	22	23
24	25	26	27	28	29	30
31						

1. St. Louis: Albert Berry completes first in-flight parachute jump, from Benoist plane piloted by Tony Janus over Kinlock Field.

1. One million British miners reported participating in five-day-old strike (→ 20).

4. French council of war unanimously votes mandatory three-year military service.

5. Italians become first to use dirigibles for military purposes—reconnaissance flights behind Turkish lines west of Tripoli (→ 4/18).

5. French army creates autonomous aeronautics corps.

6. Chile: Railway opened linking Arica on Pacific coast to La Paz, Bolivia; crosses Andes at 12,000 feet.

7. French aviator Henri Seimet flies non-stop London to Paris in three hours.

10. Germany: Ruhr miners go out on strike.

12. Paris: Sarah Bernhardt's second film "La Dame aux Camelias" is released.

12. Georgia: Inspired by Sir Robert Baden-Powell, Juliette Gordon Low organizes first American Girl Guide troops.→

13. Bulgaria and Serbia enter alliance against Austria, secretly providing for division of Turkish lands (→ 5/29).

14. Rome: Young anarchist Antonio Dalba fires unsuccessfully at Italy's King Victor Emmanuel III.

15. China: Yuan Shih-kai succeeds Sun Yat-sen as pres. of republic (→ 4/13).

16. Wireless record set: 55 minutes from London to N.Y.

20. British miners' unions ask members back to work (→ 27).

27. British House of Commons grants miners minimum wage.

29. U.S. sends rifles to ambassador in Mexico City; ships ready to transport troops to fight rebels (→ 7/31).

BIRTH

23. German engineer Werner von Braun (†6/16/1977).

France takes over Morocco in Fez pact

Mulai Hafid, Sultan of Morocco.

March 30. For years, France has been quietly spreading its tentacles around Morocco. Today, France's position was legitimized. Morocco is now a French protectorate. Under the terms of the Treaty of Fez, a French Resident General will reside in Morocco and will agree to respect the Sultan's religious prerogatives, Spain's interests and the special status of Tangier. Germany, which for years contested French predominance in the region, approved the pact last year (→ 4/17).

Amundsen tells tale

March 8. Roald Amundsen today gave the first complete account of his journey to the South Pole, which commenced in February 1911 and brought his party to a point 850 miles from the pole on December 14. Amundsen's group, using dog sleds, traveled an average of 15 miles a day, usually in sub-zero temperatures. Amundsen says he saw no sign of Capt. Robert F. Scott, the British explorer who is also attempting to reach the pole.

Amundsen (left) surveys the S. Pole.

1912

APRIL

Su	Mo	Tu	We	Th	Fr	Sa
	1	2	3	4	5	6
7	8	9	10	11	12	13
14	15	16	17	18	19	20
21	22	23	24	25	26	27
28	29	30				

1. Ohio: Anthracite coal miners strike in Cleveland (→ 10/28/13).

2. Paris: Miss Trehawke Davis, flying with Gustave Hamel, becomes first woman to cross English Channel in dirigible (→ 16).

3. Los Angeles: Calbraith Rodgers, first to fly across U.S., dies in plane crash.

10. London: First wireless message received on airplane.

10. England: Titanic leaves on maiden voyage, narrowly escapes collision with New York liner (→ 15).

11. London: Premier Asquith introduces third Irish home rule bill (→ 1/30/13).

13. China: Yuan Shih-kai lifts ban on mixed marriages (→ 12/6).

16. London: American aviator Harriet Quimby becomes first woman to pilot plane across English Channel.

17. Morocco: Rebels rise in Fez against French domination (→ 28).

17. Western Europeans witness total eclipse of sun.

18. Russian army intervenes to break gold miners' strike in Siberia (→ 5/5).

18. Italian bombing raids force Turks to close Dardanelles (→ 5/4).

19. Paris taxi drivers back to work after 144-day strike.

20. Washington: House of Representatives orders that campaign expenses of presidential and vice-presidential candidates be made public.

28. Morocco: France's Lyautey named Resident General to quell opposition to French rule (→ 7/1).

BIRTH

19. American chemist Glenn Seaborg, discovered transuranium elements for nuclear energy.

DEATH

12. Clara Barton, founder of American Red Cross (*12/25/1821).

Iceberg sinks Titanic, drowning 1,595

April 15. The unthinkable happened early this morning in the North Atlantic. The "unsinkable" Titanic, a gigantic hole ripped through its structure, sank with hundreds of people on board. The ship's much-praised water-tight compartments were useless after the ship slammed head-on into an iceberg before midnight. The Titanic was speeding, rather arrogantly some might say, at 21 knots through an ice field when the accident occurred. Several hours later, as the band played on stoically, the largest passenger vessel in the world disappeared beneath the surface.

Some 2,340 passengers and crew were on board the Titanic when the White Star liner left Southampton, England, for its maiden voyage to New York five days ago. And some 1,595 people perished in the accident. Only 745 were saved, many of them women and children. Many more could have been rescued, but there were enough lifeboats for only half the passengers and crew. Two boats full of people who had escaped from the ship were sucked beneath the ocean by the Titanic when it sank.

Most of the passengers were apparently not aware of the accident when it happened. A slight tremble, rather than a severe jolt, was felt at the time of the collision. At first, passengers were so unconcerned that they remained in their staterooms to dress for dinner.

Colonel Archibald Gracie may be the only passenger who stayed on the ship until the end and yet survived. "I managed to grasp the brass railing," he said, "and I hung on by might and main. When the ship plunged down, I was swirled around for what seemed an interminable time. Eventually, I came to the surface to find the sea a mass of tangled wreckage."

Colonel John Jacob Astor was not so lucky. One survivor watched as he gallantly helped his ailing new bride into a lifeboat, lit a cigarette and proceeded to help other women into lifeboats. Astor went down with the ship. So did the captain, most of his officers and a number of wives who refused to be rescued. They stayed on board to hold hands with their husbands as the Titanic sank beneth the sea (→ 5/28).

The Titanic's placid departure from Southampton.

Pleasure cruise turns to disaster off the Newfoundland coast.

Women and children had priority in getting seats on the lifeboats.

1912

MAY

Su	Mo	Tu	We	Th	Fr	Sa
			1	2	3	4
5	6	7	8	9	10	11
12	13	14	15	16	17	18
19	20	21	22	23	24	25
26	27	28	29	30	31	

2. Hungarian govt. monopolizes world's most importang natural gas reserves at Kissarmas, Transylvania.

3. Bob Fowler makes first West to East transcontinental flight, L.A. to Jacksonville in four months (→ 5/3/23).

4. Italy occupies Island of Rhodes (→ 18).

5. First issue of Bolshevik political organ Pravda published under editorship of Joseph Dzhugashvili (→ 1/12/13).

11. Worth wins Kentucky Derby with jockey G.H. Shilling.

14. Norway, Russia agree Spitzberg will remain neutral; Norway to administrate.

17. Indianapolis: Socialist Party nominates Eugene Debs for president, Wisconsin's Emil Seidel for v.p. (→ 6/22).

17. Annapolis: Battleship Texas launched (→ 2/26/13).

17. Pennsylvania: Liquefied petroleum gas first used for cooking and heating, on John W. Gahring's Waterford farm.

17. Rail line completed at Bionassay; highest in Alps at 7,800 feet.

18. Depths of Mt. Vesuvius' crater photographed for first time, by Prof. Mallada of London's Royal Observatory.

18. Turks reopen Dardanelles Straits (→ 6/12).

26. Havana: Cuban President Gomez cables Taft, warning against U.S. intervention in Cuban affairs (→ 31).

28. Washington: Senate rules operators were negligent in Titanic disaster (→ 4/15/13).

29. 100,000 British dockworkers strike for minimum wage.

29. Greek government forms allliance with Bulgaria against Turkey (→ 6/1).

31. American Marines land in Cuba to protect U.S. property (→ 6/6).

DEATHS

14. Frederick VIII, king of Denmark (*6/3/1843).

30. American aviator Wilbur Wright (*4/16/1867).

Tigers strike to protest Cobb action

Ty Cobb hit a record .420 last year.

May 17. Ty Cobb's teammates on the Detroit Tigers served notice on the American League President that they would not play again until the suspended star was reinstated.

Cobb recently climbed into the grandstand during a game in New York City and pummeled a man who had been taunting him. The American League President, Ban B. Johnson, was at the game, and he immediately suspended Cobb. In a telegram sent to Johnson, Cobb's teammates said, "We the undersigned refuse to play in another game after today until such action is adjudicated to our satisfaction. He was fully justified in his action and no one could stand such abuse from anyone."

May 1. The Beverly Hills Hotel opened today. Ringed by bean fields, its bar and fireplace at least provide a place to socialize.

Wilhelm II launches world's biggest ship

May 23. Germany regained one of the most coveted records of the sea today when the world's largest ship, Hamburg-American's 50,000-ton Imperator, was launched in Hamburg at a ceremony attended by Kaiser Wilhelm II.

The liner is 871-feet long with a beam of 97 feet and 11 separate decks. Its luxury provisions include several squash courts, a tennis court, a Ritz-Carlton restaurant and elevators to carry passengers between decks. It will be driven by four turbine engines of 70,000 total horsepower, capable of a cruising speed of more than 33 knots. A distinctive feature is the installation of special tanks to prevent rolling.

Of even greater significance is the inclusion of a number of safety features derived from the tragic loss of the White Star liner Titanic. The Imperator has a double bottom extending nearly half her length and a large number of watertight compartments. Unlike the Titanic, the Imperator will carry enough lifeboats and life rafts for her crew of 1,100 and 4,100 passengers. The ship will go into service next year, making the voyage between Hamburg and New York in eight and a half days (→ 7/22).

Nijinsky stars in an erotic new ballet

"The Afternoon of a Faun."

May. The ballet "The Afternoon of a Faun" is, according to critics, a show with "vile movements of erotic bestiality and gestures of heavy shamelessness." Created by Nijinsky, who plays the leading role of a faun, this ballet has divided Paris between passionate "faunists" and "anti-faunists." Claude Debussy composed the music of "The Afternoon of a Faun" and Bakst made the scenery and costumes.

May 30. America's fastest racing cars gathered today at Indianapolis for the second 500-mile Memorial Day race over the bricks. Joe Dawson topped the field, averaging 78.7 miles per hour in his four-cylinder National Racer.

1912

JUNE

Su	Mo	Tu	We	Th	Fr	Sa
						1
2	3	4	5	6	7	8
9	10	11	12	13	14	15
16	17	18	19	20	21	22
23	24	25	26	27	28	29
30						

1. Greece and Montenegro mobilize troops (→ 7/2).

4. Constantinople razed by fire; 1,000 houses destroyed.

4. Brussels: Belgians revolt in widespread protest over Catholic victory in recent elections.

6. Havana: President Gomez asserts he will take the field himself to prevent U.S. intervention (→ 9).

8. Los Angeles: Carl Laemmle founds Universal Studios.

8. Paris: Russian Ballet dances opening performance of Maurice Ravel's "Daphnis and Chloe."

9. French submarine Vendemiaire sinks, killing 24.

11. British transport workers' union calls for nationwide strike involving 200,000.

12. N.J.: 4,000 striking factory workers, mostly Slavs and Hungarians, drive police off streets of Perth Amboy after shooting of three laborers.

12. Tripoli: Second Aerial Company of Italian Aviation Corps makes night air raid on Turkish lines (→ 8/23).

16. U.S. sugar investments in Cuba reported highly profitable; investors fear $54 mil. jeopardized by Negro revolt.

17. German Zeppelin SZ III burns in hanger in Friedrichshafen.

19. Paris: Report of Dr. Alexis Carrel's work read at Academy of Medicine; animal tissue can live for 50 days separated from organism.

23. Niagara Falls bridge collapses; 47 fall to death.

26. Baltimore: Democratic convention abolishes unit rule in victory for Wilson; states to split vote (→ 7/2).

26. France: Two U.S. drivers disqualified in Dieppe Grand Prix for illegal refueling.

30. Belgian workers strike to demand universal suffrage.

DEATH

7. French aviator Hubert Latham, by a buffalo while hunting in Sudan (*1883).

Taft is nominated as Roosevelt loses

June 22. Republicans nominated William Howard Taft for another four-year term as President today during a turbulent session in the Chicago Coliseum marked by a walkout by supporters of former President Theodore Roosevelt. Within hours, meeting in nearby Orchestra Hall, the dissidents chose Roosevelt as their presidential candidate on an independent ticket. The new party's theme, Roosevelt told his supporters, will be "Thou shalt not steal" (→ 7/2).

William Howard Taft.

U.S. Navy rushing ships to Havana

June 9. Admiral Hugo Osterhaus, Commander-in-Chief of the Atlantic fleet, and two armored cruisers will leave Key West immediately for Havana. The Navy Department dispatched the ships after receiving alarming reports about escalating racial violence in the wake of an uprising by Negro laborers.

Frightened American plantation owners welcome the ships, but many Cubans think the United States has overreacted. Although many agree that the Platt amendment gives the United States the right to interfere in Cuba's domestic problems, they also hold that Cuba itself should first try to contain the uprising, or it will completely sacrifice its independence (→ 3/7/13).

1912

JULY

Su	Mo	Tu	We	Th	Fr	Sa
	1	2	3	4	5	6
7	8	9	10	11	12	13
14	15	16	17	18	19	20
21	22	23	24	25	26	27
28	29	30	31			

1. France declares Morocco a protectorate (→ 8/11).

2. Greece, Bulgaria and Serbia sign alliance against Ottoman Empire (→ 21).

4. Kaiser Wilhelm II and Czar Nicholas II meet to reassert ties between Germany and Russia.

6. Sweden: Fifth Olympic Games open in Stockholm, Americans dominate first day.

7. Wimbledon: Anthony Wilding over Arthur Gore 6-4, 6-4, 6-4; Ethel Larcombe over Charlotte Sterry 6-3, 6-1.

7. Victor L. Berger, first U.S. Socialist congressman predicts two mil. Socialist votes in upcoming election, foresees polarization of Am. politics into radicals and conservatives.

9. Britain: Explosion in Cadeby Colliery kills 80 miners.

11. Death toll reaches 21 in heat wave sweeping Eastern states.

12. Frederick Hoffman, Prudential Life statistician, reports 15,000 suicides in 1911; slight increase over 1910 rate.

13. Newport, R.I.: Mrs. Stuyvesant Fish begins new season of entertaining; guests rest at midnight, observing her ban on Sunday dancing.

15. British National Health Insurance Act goes into effect.

16. France and Russia sign naval convention (→ 22).

21. Albanian nationalists revolt against Ottoman rule (→ 8/3).

29. Copenhagen: Captain Ejnar Mikkelsen, widely thought dead, returns from Arctic after 2 years.

30. Tokyo: Japan's Emperor Meiji Tenno dies; son Yoshihito succeeds (→ 9/13).

31. Two Americans hanged by Mexican rebels (→ 10/23).

BIRTH

31. American economist Milton Friedman.

DEATHS

1. Harriet Quimby, first U.S. woman to get pilot's license, in plane crash.

17. French mathematician Henri Poincare (*4/29/1854).

British navy moves to counter Germans

July 22. Britain's Admiralty, in response to the German naval buildup, has recalled her battleships from the Mediterranean and dispatched them to the North Sea.

The action stemmed from recent naval negotiations between the two European powers. The newest German naval law sets high construction goals for the nation's shipyards. Britain, leery of the program, has met with German officials in what's been called the Haldane Mission, for the purpose of slowing German production. In return, Germany asked for a mutual declaration of neutrality in case either country becomes engaged in war. Britain refused, fearing this would endanger relations with France and Russia.

With the breakdown of the talks, an Anglo-French agreement to firm relations within the Triple Entente resulted in today's relocation of the British fleet (→ 9/16).

Wilson is chosen for top nomination

July 2. Democrats broke a long deadlock today by nominating Governor Woodrow Wilson of New Jersey for president on the 46th ballot. Tired delegates, meeting in Baltimore, made the nomination unanimous after Wilson had polled 900 votes to 84 for Champ Clark and 12 for Judson Harmon. The balloting began five days ago. The scholarly Wilson, a former President of Princeton University, received word of his nomination in a telephone call to his home in Sea Girt, New Jersey. He greeted the news solemnly (→ 8/5).

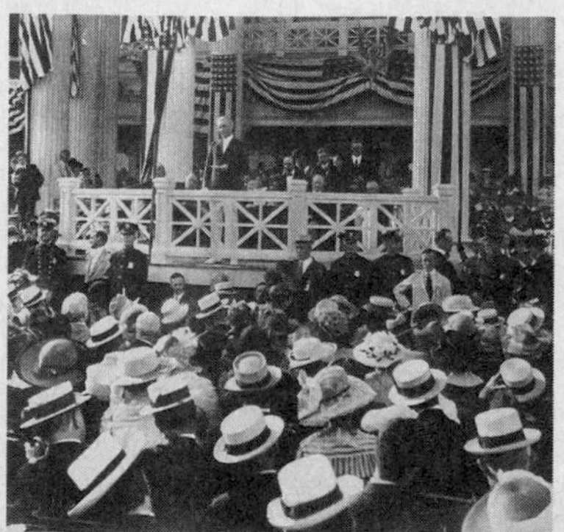

Wilson publicly accepts nomination.

1912 Stockholm

Men Athletics

100 M Dash
1. Ralph Cook Craig USA 10,8
2. Alvah Meyer USA 10,9
3. Donald Lippincott USA 10,9

200 M Dash
1. Ralph Cook Craig USA 21,7
2. Donald Lippincott USA 21,8
3. William Applegarth GBR 22,0

400 M Run
1. Charles Reidpath USA 48,2
2. Hanns Braun GER 48,3
3. Edward Lindberg USA 48,4

800 M Run
1. James Edwin Meredith USA 1:51,9
2. Melvin Sheppard USA 1:52,0
3. Ira Davenport USA 1:52,0

1500 M Run
1. Arnold Jackson GBR 3:56,8
2. Abel Kiviat USA 3:56,9
2. Norman Taber USA 3:56,9

5000 M Run
1. Hannes Kolehmainen FIN 14:36,6
2. Jean Bouin FRA 14:36,7
3. George Hutson GBR 15:07,6

10,000 M Run
1. Hannes Kolehmainen FIN 31:20,8
2. Louis Tewanima USA 32:06,6
3. Albin Stenroos FIN 32:21,8

Marathon (40.195 km)
1. Kenneth MacArthur SAF 2:36:54,8
2. Christian Gitsham SAF 2:37:52,0
3. Gaston Strobino USA 2:38:42,4

110 M Hurtles
1. Frederick Kelly USA 15,1
2. James Wendell USA 15,2
3. Martin Hawkins USA 15,3

400 M Relay
1. GBR 42,4 (David Jacobs, Harold Macintosh, Victor D'Arcy, William Applegarth)
2. SWE 42,6 (Ivan Möller, Charles Luther, Ture Persson, Knut Lindberg)

1600 M Relay
1. USA 3:16,6 (Melvin Sheppard, Edward Lindberg, James Meredith, Charles Reidpath)
2. FRA 3:20,7 (Charles Lelong, Robert Schurrer, Pierre Failliot, Charles Poulenard)
3. GBR 3:32,7 (George Nicol, Ernest Henley, James Tindal Souter, Cyril Seedhouse)

High Jump
1. Alma Richards USA 1,93
2. Hans Liersche GER 1,91
3. George Horine GER 1,89

Pole Vault
1. Harry Babcock USA 3,95
2. Frank Nelson USA 3,85
2. Marcus Wright USA 3,85
3. William Happenny CAN 3,80
3. Frank Murphy USA 3,80

Long Jump
1. Albert Gutterson USA 7,60
2. Calvin Bricker CAN 7,21
3. Georg Aberg SWE 7,18

Triple Jump
1. Gustal Landblorn SWE 14,76
2. Georg Aberg SWE 14,51
3. Erik Almlöf SWE 14,17

Shotput
1. Patrick McDonald USA 15,34
2. Ralph Rosee USA 15,25
3. Lawrence Whitney USA 13,93

Discus Throw
1. Annas Taipale FIN 45,21
2. Richard Byrd USA 42,32
3. James Duncan USA 42,28

Hammer Throw
1. Matthew McGrath USA 54,74
2. Duncan Gillis CAN 48,39
3. Clarence Childs USA 48,17

Javelin
1. Erik Lemming SWE 60,64
2. Juho Saaristo FIN 58,66
3. Mor Koczan HUN 55,50

Decathlon
1. Hugo Wieslander SWE 7724,495
2. Charles Lomberg SWE 7413,510
3. Gösta Holmer SWE 7327,855

3000 M Team (approx. 12 km; 1912, 1920, 1924 only)
1. USA
2. Sweden
3. Great Britain

Cross Country Individual (1912, 1920, 1924)
1. Hannes Kolehmainen FIN 45:11,6
2. Hjalmar Andersson SWE 45:44,8
3. John Eke SWE 46:37,6

Cross Country Team (approx. 12 km. 1904, 1912, 1920)
1. Sweden
2. Finland
3. Great Britain

Pentathlon (1906, 1912, 1920, 1924)
1. Ferdinand Bie NOR
2. James Donahue USA
3. Frank Lukeman CAN

Standing Long Jump (1900, 1904, 1906, 1908, 1912)
1. Konstantin Tsiklitiras GRE 3,37
2. Platt Adams USA 3,36
3. Benjamin Adams USA 3,28

Standing High Jump (1904, 1906, 1908, 1912)
1. Platt Adams USA 1,63
2. Benjamin Adams USA 1,60
3. Konstantin Tsiklitiras GRE 1,55

Shotput, Both Hands (addition 1912)
1. Ralph Rose USA 27,70 (15,23+12,47)
2. Patrick McDonald USA 27,53 (15,08+12,45)
3. Elmer Niklander FIN 27,14 (14,71+12,43)

Discus Throw, Both Hands (addition 1912)
1. Armas Taipale FIN 82,86 (44,68+38,18)
2. Elmer Niklander FIN 77,96 (40,28+37,68)
3. Emil Magnusson SWE 77,37 (40,58+36,79)

Javelin, Both Hands (addition 1912)
1. Julius Saaristo FIN 109,42 (61,00+48,42)
2. Vaino Siikaniemi FIN 101,13 (54,09+47,04)
3. Urho Peltonen FIN

Tug-of-War (1900, 1904, 1906, 1908, 1912, 1920)
1. Sweden
2. Great Britain

10 km Walk (1912 and 1920)
1. George Goulding CAN 46:28,4
2. Ernest Webb GBR 46:50,4
3. Fernando Altimani ITA 47:37,6

Men Swimming

100 M Freestyle
1. Duke Paoa Kahanamoku USA 1:03,4
2. Cecil Healy AUS 1:04,6
3. Kenneth Huszagh USA 1:05,6

400 M Freestyle
1. George Ritchie Hodgson CAN 5:24,4
2. John Gatenby Hatfield GBR 5:25,8
3. Harold Hardwick AUS 5:31,2

1500 M Freestyle
1. George Ritchie Hodgson CAN 22:00,0
2. John Gatenby Hatfield GBR 22:39,0
3. Harold Hardwick AUS 23:15,4

100 M Backstroke
1. Harry Hebner USA 1:21,2
2. Otto Fahr GER 1:22,4
3. Paul Keliner GER 1:24,0

200 M Breaststroke
1. Walter Bathe GER 3:01,8
2. Wilhelm Lutzow GER 3:05,0
3. Kurt Malisch GER 3:08,0

400 M Breaststroke (1904, 1912, 1920)
1. Walter Bathe GER 6:29,6
2. Thor Henning SWE 6:35,6
3. Percy Courtman GBR 6:36,4

800 M Relay
1. AUS 10:11,6 (Cecil Healy, Malcolm Champion, Leslie Boardman, Harold Hardwick)
2. USA 10:20,2 (Kenneth Huszagh, Harry Hebner, Perry McGillivray, Duke Paoa Kahanamoku)
3. GBR 10:28,2 (William Foster, Thomas Battersby, John Hatfield, Henry Taylor)

Springboard Diving
1. Paul Gunther GER 79,23
2. Hans Luber GER 76,78
3. Kurt Behrens GER 73,73

High Diving
1. Erik Adlerz 73.94
2. Albert Zurner 72,60
3. Gustaf Blomgren 69,56

Plain High Diving (1912, 1920, 1924)
1. Erik Adlerz SWE 40,0
2. Hjalmar Johansson SWE 39,3
3. John Jansson SWE 39,1

Water-Polo

1. Great Britain
2. Sweden
3. Belgium

Women Swimming

100 M Freestyle
1. Fanny Durack AUS 1:22,2
2. Wilhelmina Wylie AUS 1:25,4
3. Jennie Fletcher GBR 1:27,0

Ralph Rose of San Francisco, silver-medal winner in the shot put.

400 M Relay
1. GBR 5:52,8 (Bella Moore, Jennie Fletcher, Annie Spiers, Irene Steer)
2. GER 6:04,6 (Wally Dressel, Louise Otto, Hermine Stindt, Grete Rosenberg)
3. AUT 6:71,0 (Margarete Adler, Klara Mitch, Josephine Sucker Berta Zahourek)

High Diving
1. Greta Johansson SWE 39.9
2. Lisa Regneli SWE 36,0
3. Isabelle White GBR 34,0

Greco Roman Wrestling

Featherweight
1. Kaarlo Koskelo FIN
2. Georg Gerstacker GER
3. Otto Lasanen FIN

Lightweight
1. Eemil Vare FIN
2. Gustaf Malström SWE
3. Edvin Matiasson SWE

Middleweight
1. Claes Johansson SWE
2. Martin Klein RUS
3. Alfred Asikainen FIN

Light Heavyweight (no gold medalist)
1. Anders Ahlgren SWE
2. Ivar Bohling FIN
3. Bela Varga HUN

Heavyweight
1. Yrjo Saarela FIN
2. Johan Olin FIN
3. Soren Marius Jensen DEN

Men Fencing

Foil Individual
1. Nedo Nadi ITA 7
2. Pietro Speciale ITA 5
3. Richard Verderber AUT 4/10

Epée Individual
1. Paul Anspach BEL 6
2. Ivan Osiier DEN 5
3. Philippe le Harde de Beaulieu BEL 4

Epée Team
1. Belgium
2. Great Britain
3. Holland

Sabre Individual
1. Dr. Jeno Fuchs HUN 6
2. Bela Bekessy HUN 5/5
3. Ervin Meszaros HUN 5/6

Sabre Team
1. Hungary
2. Austria
3. Holland

Modern Pentathlon

1. Gustaf Lilliehook SWE
2. Gosta Asbrink SWE
3. Georg de Laval SWE

Rowing

Single Sculls
1. William Kinnear GBR 7:47,6
2. Polydore Veirman BEL (1 length)
3. Everard B. Butler CAN
4. Mikhait Kusik RUS

Fours with Coxswain
1. Germany 6:59,4
2. Great Britain (2 lengths)
3. Denmark

Eight Oars
1. Great Britain 6:15,0
2. Great Britain
3. Germany

Coxed Fours, Inriggers (1912)
1. Denmark 7:47,0
2. Sweden (1 length)
3. Norway

Yachting

6 M Class (1908, 1912, 1920, 1932, 1936, 1948, 1952)
1. France
2. Denmark
3. Sweden

8 M Class (1908, 1912, 1920, 1924, 1928, 1932, 1936)
1. Norway
2. Sweden
3. Finland

10 M Class (1912)
1. Sweden
2. Finland
3. Russia

12 M Class (1908 and 1912)
1. Norway
2. Sweden
3. Finland

Cycling

Individual Road Race
1. Rudolph Lewis SAF 10:42,39,0
2. Frederick Grubb GBR 10:51:24,2
3. Carl Schutte USA 10:52,38,8

Team Road Race (1912, 1920, 1924, 1928, 1932, 1936, 1948, 1952, 1956)
1. Sweden 44:35:33,6
2. Great Britain 44:44:39,2
3. USA 44:47:55,5

Equestrian Sports

Individual All-around Competition
1. Axel Nordlander SWE
2. Frederick von Rochow GER
3. Jean Cariou FRA

Team All-around Competition
1. Sweden 139,06
2. Germany 138,48
3. USA 137,33

Dressage Individual
1. Carle Bonde SWE 15
2. Gustaf Boltensternsen SWE 21
3. Hans von Blixen Finecke SWE 32

Grand Prix Jumping Individual
1. Jean Cariou FRA 186
2. Rabod von Krocher GER 186
3. Emanuel de Blommaert de Soye BEL 185

Grand Prix Jumping Team
1. Sweden 545
2. France 538
3. Germany 530

See table of contents for abbreviations

Shooting

Full-Bore Rifle, 300 Meters, 3 Positions
1. Paul Colas FRA 987
2. Lars Jorgen Madsen DEN 981
3. Niels Hansen Ditlev Larsen DEN 962

Free Rifle Team (1908, 1912, 1920, 1924)
1. Sweden 5655
2. Norway 5605
3. Denmark 5529

Small-Bore Rifle, Freestyle Position
1. Frederick Hird USA 194
2. William Milne GBR 193
3. Harry Burt GBR 192

Small-Bore Rifle, Individual (1908 and 1912) disappearing target
1. Wilhelm Carlbert SWE 242
2. Johan Hubner von Holst SWE 233
3. Gustaf Ericsson SWE 231

Small-Bore Rifle Team (1908, 1912, 1920) 25M
1. Sweden 925
2. Great Britain 917
3. USA 881

50 M
1. Great Britain 762
2. Sweden 748
3. USA 744

Rapid Fire Pistol
1. Alfred Lane USA 287
2. Paul Palen USA 286
3. Johan Hubner von Holst SWE 283

Free Pistol 50M
1. Alfred Lane USA 499
2. Peter Dolfen USA 474
3. Charles Edward Stewart GBR 470

30 M
1. Sweden 1145
2. Russia 1091-118
2. Great Britain 1107-117

Clay Pigeon Individual
1. James Granam USA 96
2. Alfred Goldel GER 94
3. Harry Blau RUS 91

Clay Pigeon Team (1912, 1920, 1924)
1. USA 532
2. Great Britain 511
3. Germany 510

Military Rifle Individual (1900, 1906, 1912, 1920) 3 Positions
1. Sandor Prokopp HUN 97
2. Carl Osburn USA 95
3. Embrest Skogen NOR 95

Rilitary Rifle Any Position
1. Paul Colas FRA 94
1. Carl Osburn USA 94
2. Joseph Jackson USA 93

Military Rifle Team (1900, 1908, 1912, 1920)
1. USA 1687
2. Great Britain 1602
3. Sweden 1570

Running Deer Shooting (Single Shot) Individual (1908, 1912, 1920, 1924)
1. Alfred Swann SWE 41
2. Ake Lundeberg SWE 41
3. Nestori Toivonen FIN 41

Running Deer Shooting (Single Shot) Team (1908, 1912, 1920, 1924)
1. Sweden 151
2. USA 132
3. Finland 123

Running Deer Shooting (Double Shot) Individual (1908, 1912, 1920, 1924)
1. Ake Lundeberg SWE 79
2. Edward Benedicks SWE 74
3. Oscar Swahn SWE 72

Military Revolver Team (1900, 1912, 1920)
1. USA 1916
2. Sweden 1849
3. Great Britain 1804

Men Gymnastics

Individual All-around Competition
1. Alberto Braglia ITA 135,0
2. Louis Segura FRA 132,5
3. Adolfo Tunesi ITA 131,5

Team All-around Competition
1. Italy 265,75
2. Hungary 227,25
3. Great Britain 184,50

Team Swedish System Gymnastics (1912 and 1920)
1. Sweden 937,46
2. Denmark 898,84
3. Norway 857,21

Free System Team
1. Norway 114,25
2. Finland 109,25
3. Denmark 106,25

Soccer

1. Great Britain
2. Denmark
3. Holland

1912

AUGUST

Su	Mo	Tu	We	Th	Fr	Sa
				1	2	3
4	5	6	7	8	9	10
11	12	13	14	15	16	17
18	19	20	21	22	23	24
25	26	27	28	29	30	31

1. L.I.: At Bull Moose Party convention, Roosevelt announces he is Negro's friend, but will bar them from party (→ 9/28/13).

1. Airmail service inaugurated between Paris and London.

2. Washington: Henry Cabot Lodge presents Congress with plan to regulate foreign companies operating in U.S.

3. Ottoman Empire grants limited autonomy to Albania; Albanian to be used in schools and government (→ 9).

7. Russia, Japan sign accord determining spheres of influence in Mongolia, Manchuria.

9. French Council President Raymond Poincare visits St. Petersburg, promises support for Russia in Balkans (→ 15).

11. Moroccan Sultan Mulai Hafid abdicates in face of internal dissent (→ 9/1).

14. New York: Startling new double-decked car appears on Broadway.

15. Austrian Foreign Minister Count Leopold Berchtold urges great powers conference to prevent war in Balkans (→ 9/4).

15. Boston: Helen Keller, born deaf and blind, announces she has learned to sing.

22. Swiss bicycle racer Oscar Eqq sets new record, traveling 26 miles in one hour.

23. Switzerland: Italy and Ottoman Empire begin peace talks at Caux (→ 10/18).

24. U.S. Congress authorizes Parcel Post system.

BIRTHS

13. American bacteriologist Salvador Edward Luria.

23. American entertainer Gene Kelly.

25. East German leader Erich Honecker.

30. American physicist Edward Purcell, radar technology.

DEATH

13. French composer Jules Massenet (*1842).

Marines in Nicaragua to guard property

Aug 4. About 100 U.S. Marines and bluejackets from the gunboat Annapolis have landed in Nicaragua to protect American property.

An American syndicate that operates rail and steamship lines in Nicaragua protested when some of its vessels were seized by General Luis Mena's rebel forces. The government of Adolfo Diaz requested the United States use its own forces to protect American citizens and their property in Nicaragua. If, as many fear, a larger force is needed, more Marines will be sent from Guantanamo, Cuba.

Marines clear out rebel barricades.

Secretary of State Philander C. Knox's "dollar diplomacy" policy, under which the United States loans money to small Central American republics to help their governments maintain stability, could benefit from this incident.

In order to protect American property and ensure order in Nicaragua, the Senate might finally be forced to ratify a pending Nicaraguan treaty and guarantee a $10 million loan. The long delay in deciding on the loan has already created severe problems for the Nicaraguan government. Its treasury is empty, and in some sections of the country people are starving. The military forces must deal with unrest and uprisings all over the country (→ 10/5).

Bull Moose Party nominates Roosevelt

Aug 5. The new Progressive Party chose Theodore Roosevelt today as its candidate for president. The move thus made official what dissident Republicans had done in June during a rump session protesting the GOP choice of President Taft for another four-year term in the White House.

This week's convention of the Progressives, also known as the Bull Moose Party, is being held in the same vast Chicago Coliseum where the Republicans met two months ago. Because of the almost religious overtones, it has been compared to a revival meeting. A former President, Roosevelt has been at odds in recent years with President Taft, his onetime Vice President, whom he had handpicked as his successor in the White House (→ 11/5).

Roosevelt's new party will be wooed by Democrats and Republicans alike.

Salvation Army's founder is dead

Aug 12. In poor health for several years, the Rev. William Booth has died at his home near London. The venerable founder and General of the Salvation Army was 83. One of the world's great religious leaders, Booth fought a lifelong battle against poverty by feeding the poor and clothing the naked. When told that his original Christian Mission Church seemed like a volunteer army, Booth renamed the group in 1878 and set about forming chapters all over the world.

Bramwell Booth will take over.

French doctor finds cancer microbe

Aug 13. Dr. Gaston Odin of Paris announced today that he has discovered, isolated and grown the microbe of cancer. This discovery could well lead to a vaccine for cancer, Odin says, adding that he already has an "active element" that allows him to kill the microbe when the disease is not too far advanced. Odin says that "the cancer amoeba is flat and gelatinous in composition, with irregular torn edges surrounding a central kernel." When it grows, Odin says, the microbe "spreads forth in all directions."

Odin says he began research to find the cancer microbe ten years ago, and his efforts were crowned with success six months ago. He says that renowned scientists and doctors at the Sorbonne have verified his claim. Physicians in the United States say they will reserve judgment until they see a full scientific account of his research.

1912

SEPTEMBER

Su	Mo	Tu	We	Th	Fr	Sa
1	2	3	4	5	6	7
8	9	10	11	12	13	14
15	16	17	18	19	20	21
22	23	24	25	26	27	28
29	30					

1. French crush Moroccan uprising (→ 11/27).

3. U.K. demands arbitration of British claim that Panama canal Toll Act violates Hay-Pauncefote Treaty.

4. Serbia promises support to Macedonian liberation organizations (→ 9).

7. French aviator Roland Garros reaches record altitude of 13,200 feet.

9. Seattle: Vilhjalmar Stefansson returns from four-year trip to Alaska, claims White Eskimos are descendants of Scandinavian colonists of Greenland.

9. Athens: Demonstrations break out, protesting persecution of Greeks in Ottoman Empire and demanding self-determination (→ 12).

9. Pilot J. Vedrines reaches 107 mph, becoming first to fly over 100 mph.

12. Bulgaria threatens mobilization if Ottomans fail to grant Macedonian independence (→ 15).

13. Tokyo: Following ancient custom, Gen. Nogi and wife commit suicide as last tribute to departed emperor.

14. Australia: Construction begins on 1,000-mile rail line linking Port-Augusta and Kalgoorlie.

15. Montenegro guerrillas clash with Turkish troops at border of Albania (→ 22).

16. Kaiser Wilhelm II attends German naval display at Heligoland (→ 1/12/13).

22. 350 Cretan partisans land in Samos, call for uprising against Ottoman Empire (→ 30).

23. Mack Sennet presents first Keystone Cops film.

30. Tension builds in Balkans: Serbia, Montenegro, Greece and Russia order mobilization.→

BIRTHS

5. American John Cage, avant-garde composer.

29. Italian film director Michaelangelo Antonioni.

Troubles in Balkans near boiling point

Sept 30. The situation in the Balkans is growing more volatile as Turkey and the Balkan allies have stepped up their military preparations in the area, according to the most recent reports from London.

In the latest development, Russia has mobilized seven army corps in Warsaw. The move is seen by Bulgaria, Serbia and Greece as threatening the stability of the region. Yet dispatches from a meeting between Russian and British officials indicate the Russian maneuvers are merely for peace-keeping purposes: "The Russian Embassy is seriously concerned and is using the utmost exertions to prevent the outbreak of war." Furthermore, Russian diplomats have urged their ally Turkey to "change its (Balkan) program and reassure the Bulgarians."

Bulgaria is decidely upset about the concentration of Turkish troops in Adrianople. Now, the Turkish government has decided to dismiss its Adrianople garrisons, but will relocate them to Macedonia. This action will also probably elicit strong responses from the Bulgarians, who "are so excited that it would require but little to provoke a declaration of war," according to reporters in Constantinople.

Some contend that the Balkan League is only looking for justification to start war in hopes that a Turkish defeat would allow them to grab additional territory. Turkey is presently vulnerable, as its military is quite weary from its exhausting war with Italy (→ 10/1).

Beyond control of the great powers.

1912

OCTOBER

Su	Mo	Tu	We	Th	Fr	Sa
		1	2	3	4	5
6	7	8	9	10	11	12
13	14	15	16	17	18	19
20	21	22	23	24	25	26
29	28	29	30	31		

1. German Minister of Foreign Affairs Alfred von Kiderlen Waechter announces great powers will not participate in a Balkan war (→ 3).

3. Serbia, Bulgaria, Montenegro and Greece insist Ottomans grant autonomy to Macedonia, Albania and Serbia within three days (→ 8).

5. Nicaragua: Four Americans killed in clash with revolutionaries (→ 7/22/13).

8. Montenegro declares war on Ottoman Empire (→ 15).

9. New York: Crowds swarm Times Square to see World Series score on N.Y. Times Electric Bulletin.

9. Cubist "gold" paintings of Picabia, Leger, Gleizes and others are shown in Paris.

11. Philadelphia: Leopold Stokowski, 30, leads opening concert of Philadelphia Orchestra's new season.

14. Milwaukee: Roosevelt saved when glasses case slows assassin's bullet; finishes speech before going to hospital.

15. Greek Parliament welcomes 62 Cretan deputies in challenge to Ottoman Turks (→ 17).

17. Bulgaria, Serbia declare war on Ottoman Empire (→ 18).

18. Bulgarian troops occupy Karkale, begin advance on Adrianople (→ 20).

20. King of Bulgaria promises aid to Macedonian Christians fighting for independence from Turkey (→ 26).

23. Mexico: General Diaz captured by federal troops at Vera Cruz (→ 2/9/13).

26. Serbian army occupies Urkub (→ 31).

27. Bienaime and Rumpelmayer win Gordon-Bennett Cup,for record 1,360-mile balloon flight from Stuttgart to Ribnoye, Russia.

29. Paris: Bernheim Gallery holds Douanier Rousseau retrospective.

31. 300,000 fighting in Balkans; Turks routed; Constantinople in peril.→

Error helps Boston win World Series

Sox pitchers (Ruth 4th from left).

Oct 20. Boston baseball fans who boycotted the final World Series game over their displeasure with management did themselves no favor. A scant 17,000 were on hand to see the Sox become world champions with a 3-2 victory over the New York Giants in ten innings.

The final game of the series (actually the eighth since the second was called at 6-6 by darkness) turned on an easy fly ball that Fred Snodgrass dropped in the 10th inning. All Snodgrass had to do was snag Engle's lazy hit, but the ball dribbled out of his glove. Engle took second on the play and tied the score when Merkle muffed Tris Speaker's foul pop. Speaker scored the winning run on a sacrifice fly.

Italy-Turkey pact concludes short war

Oct 18. Turkey and Italy have concluded a peace settlement after two months of negotiation at Ouchy, Switzerland. Under the terms of the agreement, Turkey cedes Libya to Italy, which in return agrees to remove its forces from the Aegean Sea.

Italy declared war on Turkey just over a year ago and quickly occupied the Libyan coast. The Turks put up little resistance, and after decisive Italian victories at Derna and Sidi Bilal asked to begin peace negotiations. During the last phase of the peace talks, the Turks were under pressure to reach a settlement quickly because a new war is now threatening to explode in the Balkans. Turkey wants to be prepared in the event it is attacked by Bulgaria, Greece, Montenegro and Serbia. ▷

War: Balkan powder keg explodes

Oct 31. After mounting tension in the Balkans, the fuse of war reached its end this month, as 2,000 Turks were killed by soldiers of the Balkan alliance in Kailer, Macedonia. The latest dispatches report the collapse of Turkish defenses at the Tchatalja line, the last barrier protecting Constantinople from advancing Bulgarian troops.

The Balkan allies —Serbia, Greece, Montenegro and Bulgaria —have unleashed fierce, strategic military actions, plunging the once invincible Turkish army into despair. And they have captured many Turkish prisoners and weapons in their multi-front battles.

War was officially declared at the beginning of the month after combined Balkan troops mobilized throughout the Ottoman Empire. Most observers claim the Balkan League provoked Turkey, with the intention of annexing Turk territories. Russia and other European powers attempted to prevent the war. Even Turkey submitted to certain Balkan demands and issued the following statement: "In view of the manifestly aggressive attitude of the Balkan states, Turkey reserves to itself full liberty of action, convinced that the civilized world will not fail to do justice to this moderate attitude." Regardless, war ensued and the determination of the Turk citizenry, who fully support the war effort, could not squelch the powerful and organized Balkan assaults.

Thrace refugees quit Adrianople to escape Serbo-Bulgarian invasion.

Reports from Sofia have emerged claiming that Nazim Pasha, Turkish Minister of War and Commander-in-Chief in Thrace, has been shot or taken prisoner. These are unconfirmed, but it is evident the Bulgarian Commander-in-Chief, General Ivanoff, has executed a near-perfect strategy in what may be the shortest, most remarkable war in history.

The possibility of intervention from the Triple Entente now looms heavily over the Balkans. Some speculate the powers will prevent the division of Turkish territories. It is assumed they will forge a "durable peace" before Bulgaria conquers Constantinople (→ 11/1).

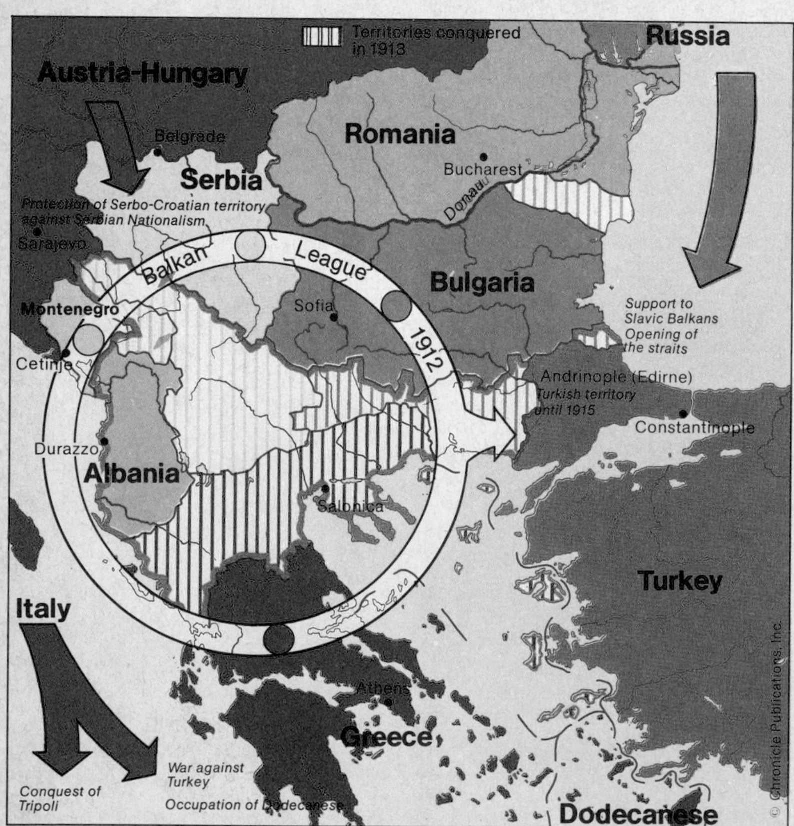

Balkan alliance against Turkey: Serbia, Bulgaria, Greece, Montenegro.

Serbian troops train for conflict in the Balkans.

1912

NOVEMBER

Su	Mo	Tu	We	Th	Fr	Sa
					1	2
3	4	5	6	7	8	9
10	11	12	13	14	15	16
17	18	19	20	21	22	23
24	25	26	27	28	29	30

1. Macedonia: Greece occupies Samothrace (→ 4).

3. France: First all-metal plane flown near Issy, piloted by Ponche and Prinard.

4. Ottoman Turks ask France, Austria-Hungary to mediate in Balkan War (→ 5).

5. Greek army, pressing toward Salonika, defeats Turks at Venije (→ 5).

5. 20,000 Turkish troops killed or captured by Serbian army at Monastir (→ 9).

5. Arizona, Wisconsin, Kansas grant vote to women (→ 1/28/13).

5. N.Y.: Sarah Bernhardt acclaimed for role in "L'Aiglon."

9. Fortress of Salonika surrenders to Greeks; Bulgars left out of conquest (→ 17).

9. Russia: Conservatives gain in Duma elections.

12. Madrid: Anarchist Manuel Pardinas assassinates Spain's Premier Jose Canalejas.

17. Bulgarian attack repelled at at Constantinople (→ 17).

17. Socialists lead anti-war demonstrations throughout Europe (→ 18).

18. Cholera breaks out in Constantinople (→ 19).

19. Balkan allies set conditions for peace talks, ask Ottoman withdrawal from Europe, except part of Bosphorus (→ 24).

24. Austria denounces Serbian gains in Balkans; Russia, France back Serbia; Italy, Germany back Austria (→ 28).

27. Spain, France sign treaty establishing spheres of interest in Morocco (→ 5/11/14).

28. Assembly at Valona proclaims Albanian independence from Turkey (→ 30).

30. N.Y.: Army blanks Navy 6-0 at Polo Grounds.

30. Samos declares unification with Greece.→

BIRTHS

3. Paraguayan dictator Alfredo Stroessner.

26. Eugene Ionesco, theater of the absurd.

Wilson wins presidency with minority vote

Nov 5. Woodrow Wilson, who has been called "the schoolmaster in politics," was elected President of the United States yesterday. While sweeping to victory in most states, the Democratic nominee was elected by a minority vote, that is, less than the total popular vote of his two chief opponents. The vote was: Wilson, 6,294,293; President Taft, a Republican seeking re-election, 3,486,000; Theodore Roosevelt, a former Republican President running on the Progressive, or Bull Moose, ticket, 4,117,000; and Eugene Debs, the Socialist Party candidate, 897,011 votes.

Wilson, who is now Governor of New Jersey, has called for a "New Freedom" for domestic reforms. His election ends more than 20 years of Republican control of the White House. A native of Staunton, Virginia, Wilson was graduated from Princeton University and practiced law before turning to college teaching. He became President of Princeton in 1902. Later, as governor, he initiated an extensive reform program. He is expected to do the same as president (→ 3/3/13).

Democratic campaign poster.

Czar's heir suffers from hemophilia

Nov 4. The court of Russia has been told that Czarevitch Alexis is suffering from hemophilia. After a boating accident in September, the Prince complained of an ache in the groin. Three weeks later, the bruise diminished so much that Alexis could get up again. But a new fall on October 11 caused a terrible hemorrhage which spread to the entire left groin region. Doctors have confirmed that this is due to hemophilia, a condition with which the prince has been afflicted since birth. It is said to be a potential cause of much anxiety in Russia.

Russian Czarevitch Alexis.

Ottomans are facing prospect of defeat

Nov 30. The Turkish armies lost their last Macedonian stronghold yesterday at Dibra as Serbian forces routed the dejected Turks. Meanwhile, 36,000 Montenegran troops concentrated at Scutari, creating a Turk surrender. These latest two battles will most likely bring the Ottomans to the bargaining table; Bulgaria and Turkey are expected to sign an armistice at Constantinople "in a day or two," according to correspondents in London.

Among the many conditions for a peaceful settlement is the recognition of Albanian autonomy. Ismail Kemal, an Albanian leader, has appealed to Austria, France and Italy to recognize the new state of Albania and to offer protection. Italy promises to be the biggest supporter of Albanian sovereignty, as ties between the two peoples date back centuries.

A key player in the peace negotiations is Russia. Russian leaders have pushed for the armistice and have proclaimed they have no desire to acquire Turkish territory; they only want the freedom of the Dardanelles for Black Sea grain exports. Most European powers are anxious for peace in the Balkans (→ 12/17).

1912

DECEMBER

Su	Mo	Tu	We	Th	Fr	Sa
1	2	3	4	5	6	7
8	9	10	11	12	13	14
15	16	17	18	19	20	21
22	23	24	25	26	27	28
29	30	31				

1. U.S. Supreme Court orders dissolution of Union Pacific and Southern Pacific railway merger (→ 6/9/13).

5. Italy, Austria, Germany renew Triple Alliance for six years.

6. Chinese obtain restricted suffrage, limited to males over 21 with college education and over $500 in property.

17. Balkan peace negotiations begin in London (→ 25).

18. Congress bars illiterate immigrants from entering U.S. (→ 3/31/13).

23. Egypt: Aswan Dam canal opened.

24. Japan: Explosion kills 245 miners on island of Hokkaido.

25. Italy lands troops in Albania to protect interests during revolt (→ 1/22/13).

BIRTH

12. American boxer Henry Armstrong, held three titles simultaneously.

CULTURAL EVENTS, 1912

Literature: Theodore Dreiser's "The Financier"; J.M. Synge's "Playboy of the Western World"; Anatole France's "The Gods are Thirsty"; Thomas Mann's "Death in Venice"; Shaw's "Pygmalion."

Academia: C.G. Jung's "The Theory of Psychoanalysis"; Alfred Adler's "The Neurotic Constitution"; Durkheim's "The Elementary Forms of Religious Life."

Music: Richard Strauss' opera "Ariadne auf Naxos"; Rudolf Friml's operetta "The Firefly," in New York; Al Jolson's popular hit "Ragging the Baby to Sleep."

The Arts: Modigliani's sculpture "Stone Head"; Duchamp's "Nude Descending a Staircase."

Film: Italian "Quo Vadis," Danish "Dance of Death," Russian "War and Peace," French "Queen Elizabeth" (with Sarah Bernhardt); 400 cinemas in London; five million U.S. film-goers daily.

Alexis Carrel wins Nobel for medicine

Dec 10. Dr. Alexis Carrel was presented with the Nobel Prize in medicine today for his achievements in surgery. Working at the Rockefeller Institute in New York, the French-born Carrel has developed methods for sewing blood vessels together and for keeping organs alive outside the body by perfusing them with a nutrient-rich solution. His goal is to transplant organs from one human to another. Victor Grignard and Paul Sabatier won the prize in chemistry and the physics laureate is Nils Dalen of Sweden.

Nefertiti's statue discovered in Egypt

Dec 7. Ludwig Borchardt, a German archeologist, has discovered the bust of Queen Nefertiti while excavating the ancient Egyptian city El-Amarna (Akhetaton). The bust is only a bit spoiled; some small fragments of the ears and left eye are missing. Nefertiti was the wife of King Akhenaton (Amenhotep IV) who ruled Egypt in the 14th century B.C. He moved with Nefertiti from Thebes to a new capital that he had founded and named Akhataton because of his devotion to Aton, the divine "Sun Disk." After the king's death, the city was abandoned.

Bust of Egyptian Queen Nefertiti.

1913

JANUARY

Su	Mo	Tu	We	Th	Fr	Sa
			1	2	3	4
5	6	7	8	9	10	11
12	13	14	15	16	17	18
19	20	21	22	23	24	25
26	27	28	29	30	31	

7. William M. Burton receives patent for first cracking process, designed to convert oil to gasoline.

10. Chinese Parliament is dissolved (→ 4/8).

12. Russian revolutionary Josef Dzhugashvili, co-editor of Pravda, signs Stalin ("man of steel") in a letter to the journal Social Democrat (→ 3/6).

12. Germany: Kiel and Wilhelmshaven become submarine bases (→ 2/7).

14. Annapolis: Turkey trot dancing barred; partners must keep three-inch space between them.

15. First telephone line inaugurated between Berlin and New York.

17. Paris: Raymond Poincare elected president of France.

22. London: Turkey consents to Balkan peace terms, gives up Adrianople (→ 23).

23. Young Turks revolt, angered by concessions at London peace talks (→ 27).

27. London: Balkan delegates, still dissatisfied, break negotiations with Turkey (→ 31).

28. London suffragists riot to protest Asquith's withdrawal of Franchise Bill; Pankhurst arrested (→ 2/6).

30. British House of Lords rejects home rule for Ireland (→ 7/12).

31. London: Balkan allies notify Turkey armistice has ended.→

31. New York: Venezuela's Gen. Cipriano Castro arrives, despite opposition from U.S. secretary of commerce.

BIRTHS

6. Edward Gierek, Polish statesman.

9. Richard Nixon, 37th U.S. president.

18. American comedian Danny Kaye. (†3/3/1987).

DEATH

4. Alfred von Schlieffen, Prussian marshal (*2/28/1833).

Jim Thorpe stripped of amateur honors

Jan 27. Jim Thorpe, considered by many the greatest athlete in the world after his victories in the 1912 Olympics, has confessed that he played professional baseball and is therefore ineligible to keep the medals he received as an amateur. Thorpe's admission stunned the American sports community, still glowing from the Stockholm feat. The athlete said he would give back the Pentathlon Trophy, presented by the King of Sweden, and the Decathlon Trophy, presented by the Czar. The athletes who finished second to Thorpe will get the awards.

The Carlisle, Pennsylvania, Indian School athlete admitted he had played professional baseball in 1909 and 1910 in responding to a letter sent to him by James E. Sullivan, Chairman of the Amateur Athletic Union registration committee. "I was not very wise to the ways of the world and did not realize this was wrong," Thorpe said.

Thorpe in the Olympic broad jump.

At the 1912 Games, Thorpe was first in the 200-meter dash, the 1,500-meter run, the broad jump and the discus in the pentathlon, and in the decathlon he placed first in the high jump, the 1,500-meter run and the shot put.

Young Turk nationalists seize government

Jan 31. A coup d'etat, orchestrated by the combined forces of Young Turks and Turkish military revolutionaries, has removed the Ottoman government, tossing peace negotiations into complete havoc in a tumultuous month in the Balkans.

The chaos began when Talaat Bey, a young militant of the Committee of Union and Progress (Young Turks), and Mahmud Shefket Pasha, a top military leader, overthrew the government of Kiamil Pasha a day after the National Assembly voted to accept the peace terms of the Balkan League. The revolutionaries are determined not to allow the surrender of Adrianople, despite the advice of the European powers to give in. To accomplish this and continue the war, the militants seized power with the declaration: "No compromise is possible. The change in the Cabinet means we are going to save the national honor or perish in the attempt." Most observers believe that they will indeed perish.

Bulgar troops besiege Adrianople.

The Young Turks uprooted the government quickly, as secrecy prevented the Kiamil Pasha Cabinet from adequately guarding against internal strife: After all, they had their hands full with the Balkan allies and pressure from the great European powers. The rebels rushed the steps of the Porte, shouting "Down with the government!" and killed all who tried to stop them, including ex-War Minister Nazim Pasha.

With these new developments, the Balkan peace delegates had difficult decisions to make. Two schools of thought dominated discussion at the London peace conference: one would immediately rupture peace negotiations and resume the war; the other would delay severing the talks for four days in hopes that the powers would apply pressure on the Young Turks. The latter was adopted, and now only time will tell if more blood will be shed (→ 2/7).

1913

FEBRUARY

Su	Mo	Tu	We	Th	Fr	Sa
						1
2	3	4	5	6	7	8
9	10	11	12	13	14	15
16	17	18	19	20	21	22
23	24	25	26	27	28	

3. New York: Grand Central Terminal opens.→

5. As a last resort, a Michigan surgeon implants dog's brain in man's skull.

6. Russian Duma rejects proposal to open legal profession to women (→ 8).

7. Gallipoli: Turks lose 5,000 in battle with Bulgarian army (→ 3/2).

7. Berlin: Germany accepts British limits on navy; fleet ratio set at 10 (Ger.) to 16 (G.B.) (→ 3/2).

8. British suffragettes destroy London-Glasgow telephone line (→ 24).

9. Mexico: Felix Diaz, nephew of ex-president, takes Mexico City, forces President Madero to flee (→ 18).

12. New York commission in Albany reports widespread violations of child labor laws.

15. New York: Kiviat sets new indoor mile record at 4:18.2.

18. Mexico: Victoriano Huerta proclaims himself president, imprisons Madero; Diaz will halt rebel violence (→ 23).

24. London: British suffragette Emmeline Pankhurst arrested upon admitting complicity in bombing of Lloyd George's country home (→ 3/10).

25. 16th Amendment to U.S. Constitution adopted; sets legal basis for income tax (→ 10/31).

26. U.S. Congress votes $33 mil. hike in naval budget; Navy men still dissatisfied (→ 3/16).

27. France: Four members of the Bonnot gang, accused of 22 murders, assorted armed robberies, are sentenced to death (→ 4/21).

28. U.S. Senate rejects presidential veto of Webb-Kenyon bill, outlawing transport of liquor into states which prohibit its sale (→ 3/28).

BIRTH

28. American film director Vincente Minnelli.

DEATH

19. Mexican President Gustavo Madero (*10/30/1973).

Madero killed as Huerta takes Mexico

Feb 23. Francisco I. Madero, deposed President of Mexico, was gunned down with his Vice President in the streets of the capital late tonight. Both Madero and his brother Gustavo, killed earlier, were victims of the "ley fugo" or "fugitive law," which allows the shooting of anyone said to be fleeing arrest.

In the dead of night, two cars with guards were taking Madero to the penitentiary, supposedly for his own safety. According to General Victoriano Huerta, earlier proclaimed provisional president, an armed group attacked the escort. Both prisoners tried to escape, he said. Huerta promised "a strict investigation."

Madero had led the revolution of 1910, which overthrew the dictatorship of Porfirio Diaz. He was called the "apostle of democracy," but proved to be an ineffectual one. Suddenly, on February 9, another revolution broke out. It was led by General Felix Diaz, a nephew of the ousted dictator. It was all over in nine days. Madero walked into the Hall of Ambassadors in the National Palace and found himself a prisoner of his own troops.

President Madero's brother Gustavo had already been killed in the arsenal, held by Diaz, who had made a deal with Huerta, commander of the troops who had been opposing him. Gustavo was known as the real power in his brother's administration and was widely accused of corruption. He left a fortune of $5 million. On the day he died, Gustavo made the mistake of lunching with Huerta and others in a restaurant. When the general learned of the president's arrest, he had Gustavo turned over to Diaz. The United States stayed out of this fight. But as a precaution, 4,000 troops went to the border (→ 3/2).

Mexican Pres. Victoriano Huerta.

New York's palatial new rail terminal

Feb 2. The New York Grand Central Terminal opened yesterday to the admiration and sometimes confusion of 150,000 visitors.

The throng, hailing mainly from the Bronx, Brooklyn and Manhattan, constantly asked attendants where and when trains departed or arrived. One attendant claimed he received 310 such queries in a little over 24 hours. Several travelers were curious about the architecture of the station, the system of electricity and the nature of the marble used in the building's construction. Countless heads tilted backward to examine the ceiling, which features the stars in the night sky.

William C. Brown, President of the New York Central, toured the place virtually incognito.

Grand Central at Park Avenue.

Scott found dead after polar effort

The Terra Nova, Scott's last ship.

Feb 10. The bodies of Captain Robert F. Scott and two members of his ill-fated expedition to the South Pole have been discovered on the Antarctic ice, ten miles from a depot where they would have found lifesaving shelter and supplies.

A diary left by Scott says that the party reached the pole on January 18, 1912, only to find that Roald Amundsen had become the first to achieve that goal more than a month earlier. Two members of the Scott party, Edgar Evans and L.E.G. Oates, died before the three survivors reached their final encampment, where they were overwhelmed by a blizzard on March 20. The bodies of Scott, Edward A. Wilson and H.R. Bowers were found by a relief expedition.

Abstract paintings shown at Armory; French nude causes scandal

Picabia's "Udnie," subtitled "Star Dancer on a Transatlantic-liner."

Feb 13. New York opened an "Armory Show" today. There are no weapons on display —simply 16,000 sculptures and paintings housed in an ordnance depot. The work is American and European, by pre-Impressionists, Impressionists, post-Impressionists, Expressionists, Cubists and Ash Can artists. There is something to delight and offend nearly everyone.

The Europeans are daring in technique and concept. Wassily Kandinsky, Fernand Leger and Francis Picabia have created bold, colorful abstractions. Rodin exhibits his sensuous sculpture. French innovator Marcel Duchamp has his "Nude Descending a Staircase" on display. The painting is the fractured image of a human in motion; features and details are indistinct. American art lovers are shocked. American painters are envious.

Though it would no doubt pass censors without a problem, Marcel Duchamp's "Nude Descending a Staircase" nonetheless scandalized crowds at the Armory Show.

Pujo inquiry finds money trust exists

Feb 28. A House committee, in a report released today, has proposed new laws to control what it calls the "menace" of the so-called money trust created by some of the nation's major financiers.

A principal target of the inquiry was J. Pierpont Morgan, head of a colossal financial and banking empire. He was questioned extensively by the committee, which is headed by Rep. Arsene Pujo, a Louisiana Democrat. The committee reported that it found large sectors of American business controlled by the House of Morgan and other large financial institutions, principally on Wall Street. The report calls for strict regulation of exchanges and for more stringent rules governing all of the nation's banks (→ 12/24/13).

1913

MARCH

Su	Mo	Tu	We	Th	Fr	Sa
						1
2	3	4	5	6	7	8
9	10	11	12	13	14	15
16	17	18	19	20	21	22
23	24	25	26	27	28	29
30	31					

1. French and German Socialist parties publish joint anti-war manifesto.

2. Reichstag votes $510m for German army (→ 29).

2. Arizona: Americans kill six Huerta soldiers at border (→ 5/7).

2. Balkan allies demand Turks hand over Adrianople, Gallipoli and Aegean Islands (→ 3).

3. Greeks take Yanina and 32,000 Turkish troops (→ 18).

6. Tercentenary of Romanov Dynasty celebrated throughout Russian Empire (→ 11/21).

7. Cuban President Gomez signs amnesty bill freeing political prisoners (→ 9).

9. Havana: Gomez, reversing himself, vetoes amnesty bill; considered victory for U.S. Sec. of State W.J. Bryan.

10. London: Several suffragettes arrested for offering petitions to King George (→ 4/3).

14. U.S.: Southern states hit by electrical storm; over 100 dead.

16. Virginia: 15,000-ton battleship Pennsylvania launched at Newport News (→ 4/2).

18. Salonika: Greek King George I killed by Greek assassin; Constantine I to succeed.

18. Balkan allies lose three big battleships in new attack on Dardanelles (→ 26).

19. New York: Metropolitan Opera features American premiere of "Boris Godunov."

24. Maryland: Victor Herbert's romantic operetta "Sweethearts" premieres in Baltimore.

25. U.S.: 250 die in tornado-swept states; Omaha worst victim.

26. Balkan allies take Adrianople (→ 4/22).

28. Washington reports Prohibition movement has shrunk tax revenues by $2m (→ 10/10/15).

29. German Reichstag passes tax hike to finance new military budget (→ 5/19).

31. N.Y.: Record immigration day; Ellis Island records 6,745 newcomers (→ 5/9).

Inaugural extra: Great suffrage parade

Suffragettes publicize their cause for inaugural crowds in Washington.

March 3. As masses of suffragettes paraded through the gaily bedecked streets of Washington, Woodrow Wilson slipped quietly into the city where he will be inaugurated tomorrow as President. Holding aloft banners inscribed with "Votes for Women" and "Tell Your Troubles to Woodrow," the suffragettes won cheers, and a few jeers, from the throngs lining the streets. A few disgruntled males waved banners of their own, bearing the words "Votes for Men."

Women's demand for the vote, which was once considered as little more than a joke, has become serious business in recent years. Already, some states allow voting by women, but the fight goes on. President-elect Wilson, avoiding the suffragette parade, rode along the back streets of the city after arriving at Union Station. On hand to greet him at the train was a small but enthusiastic group of friends. Tonight, he was given a rousing welcome at a "smoker" attended by 800 fellow Princetonians at the New Willard Hotel (→ 4/8).

J.P. Morgan, Wall Street wizard, is dead

March 31. J. Pierpont Morgan, the great financial wizard of Wall Street, died today at the Grand Hotel in Rome. He was 76 years old.

The multimillionaire banker had sailed from New York to Egypt in January, just a few weeks after testifying before a House committee inquiring into a money trust's control over American business. Morgan had appeared in good health during the hearings but became ill while in Cairo, before going on to Rome.

Financial titan J.P. Morgan.

Morgan's doctors attributed his death to an aggravated form of nervous prostration. News of his death brought condolences today from King Victor Emmanuel of Italy, Pope Pius X and hundreds of old friends, both in America and abroad. His body has already been cremated and the ashes will be shipped home to New York City.

A financial genius, Morgan had built a family fortune into a gigantic banking empire. His total wealth has been estimated to be close to $100 million. Morgan also was a philanthropist, having donated numerous Old Masters to various museums.

Death ends career of famous fugitive

March 10. Harriet Tubman, the brave but illiterate field hand who helped fellow Negro slaves escape to freedom on the Underground Railroad, died today at her home in Auburn, New York. She was 92 years old. Born on a plantation on the eastern shore of Maryland, she fled to the North in 1849, and then led 300 or more other slaves to safety. During the Civil War, she served as a cook, nurse, scout and spy with the Union Army in South Carolina. After the war, with the slaves freed, she was hailed as a true heroine by abolitionists and by members of her own race.

Abolitionist Harriet Tubman.

The Woolworth Building towers over New York City. Its completion this year makes it the tallest in the world at 60 stories.

1913

APRIL

Su	Mo	Tu	We	Th	Fr	Sa
		1	2	3	4	5
6	7	8	9	10	11	12
13	14	15	16	17	18	19
20	21	22	23	24	25	26
27	28	29	30			

2. Washington: U.S. Navy chief Adm. Fiske resigns, says Navy is unprepared (→ 11/3).

2. Three hundred Germans die of food poisoning.

5. Havana: Heavyweight Jack Johnson knocked out by Willard, announces retirement.

5. U.S. seeks trade with Germany through neutral ports.

8. Chinese Parliament convenes under President Yuan Shih-kai (→ 8/6).

9. German govt. sends official note to Washington, blasting U.S. for selling arms to Balkan allies while civilians starve.

10. Cold wave sweeping Europe reported causing extensive damage to crops.

13. Spanish King Alfonso XIII escapes assassination attempt.

14. Belgium: Workers begin general strike to demand universal suffrage (→ 24).

15. New York: Lighthouse inaugurated commemorating wreck of the Titanic.

16. Rockefeller War Commission reports typhus sweeping Serbia (→ 22).

18. German Professor Behring announces discovery of new diphtheria serum.

19. California passes Webb Bill, excluding Japanese from owning land (→ 7/15).

21. France: Four members of Bonnot gang executed.

22. Turks surrender Scutari to Montenegro (→ 5/5).

24. Belgian strike ends as govt. promises electoral reform.

24. French aviator Eugene Gilbert makes record non-stop 513-mile cross-country flight from Villacoublay, France, to Vitoria, Spain; 8 hrs., 23 min.

26. Holland: International Women's Peace Conference opens at The Hague.

27. Five powers sign $125 million loan to China (→ 6/5).

BIRTH

12. American jazz musician Lionel Hampton.

Wilson gives first State of Union message

President Woodrow Wilson addresses Congress.

April 8. Reviving a custom that was abandoned 112 years ago, President Wilson appeared before a joint session of Congress today to deliver his State of the Union message. Until today, no president since John Adams had delivered such a message in person. Instead, they had sent written reports.

In his nine-minute address, the president explained that he was seeking to verify for himself "the impression that the president of the United States is a person and not a mere department of the government." Both the House floor and galleries were packed and hundreds of other persons milled around the corridors outside the chamber as the president spoke. Wilson won loud applause when he called for new tariff legislation to stimulate foreign trade. Currently, he said, the United States has a system of special privileges for domestic industries (→ 5/8).

Triumph and tragedy for Isadora Duncan

April 20. Dancer Isadora Duncan has canceled all performances indefinitely, following news of her children's tragic deaths in Paris. Her young girl and boy, Deirdre and Patrick, were in a limousine with their nurse when the auto went out of control. It slipped off a bridge on the Seine and plunged into the river, drowning all three.

Isadora Duncan and children.

Miss Duncan meets this tragedy at the peak of success. Born in San Francisco in 1877, she rejected the little ballet training she received as a child. She developed a graceful, bold and unfettered style. She performed in England, Russia and France. In her own words, Miss Duncan "took Berlin by storm." In Hungary, she dedicated a dance to the memory of Hungarian revolutionists, moving to the mad tempo of Liszt's "Rakoczy March."

The dancer's loss is felt by millions who love her. When Claude Debussy heard the news, he went to her studio and stood in silence. Then he sat at a piano and played his "Danse Macabre."

Mrs. Pankhurst is jailed for arson

April 3. Emmeline Pankhurst, the passionate British suffragist who founded the Women's Social and Political Union in 1903 to promote enfranchisement of women, has been sentenced to three years in prison for inciting destruction of the home of the Chancellor of the Exchequer. Mrs. Pankhurst, who has attempted hunger strikes while incarcerated before, threatens to repeat the gesture. "I am probably going to my death," she asserts.

One militant leader declares that now "trouble of all sorts can be expected." In point of fact, a group of suffragettes immediately invaded

Pankhurst is carried off to court.

the Manchester Art Gallery, where they mutilated 18 paintings. Britons fear more attacks on national treasures will follow (→ 5/3).

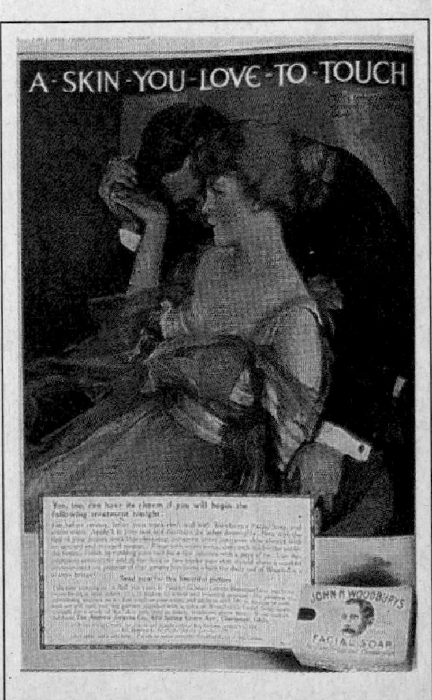

1913

MAY

Su	Mo	Tu	We	Th	Fr	Sa
				1	2	3
4	5	6	7	8	9	10
11	12	13	14	15	16	17
18	19	20	21	22	23	24
25	26	27	28	29	30	31

3. New York: 10,000 march in woman suffrage parade (→ 6).

3. New York: Henry Frick buys Holbein portrait of Oliver Cromwell for $235,000.

5. Italy, Austria declare they will not invade Albania (→ 19).

6. British House of Commons rejects woman suffrage bill 266-219 (→ 6/15).

7. Washington: Prudential Life statistician declares cancer a national menace.

7. Mexico: President Victoriano Huerta establishes mandatory military service (→ 6/2).

9. Washington reports 900,000 aliens have arrived in U.S. in last nine months (→ 2/5/17).

10. Jockey R. Goose wins Kentucky Derby riding Donerail.

13. Russian engineer Igor Sikorsky completes and flies first four-engine aircraft.

15. Nijinsky dances Claude Debussy's "Jeux" in Paris.

17. Havana: Aviator Rosillo becomes first to cross Florida Straits by air.

19. Turkish troops take offensive against Bulgaria (→ 31).

19. France: Demonstrators protest bill calling for three-year mandatory military service (→ 28).

22. E.G. Baker sets new coast-to-coast record in Stutz Bearcat, West Coast to N.Y. in 11 days, seven hrs., 15 min.

24. Berlin: Kaiser's daughter weds England's Prince Augustus; Czar Nicholas, driven in armored car, attends.

26. New Mexico: Grasshopper cloud reported, measuring five miles by 18 miles.

28. Military service becomes obligatory in Belgium (→ 6/30).

29. Stravinsky's "The Rites of Spring" opens in Paris.

30. Frenchman J. Goux wins Indianapolis 500, averaging 75.9 mph in Peugot racer.

31. Washington: 17th Amendment effective today; senators to be chosen by direct election.

Turkey signs treaty with Balkan states

Greek warship Georgios-Averof, the only modern vessel in the Balkans.

May 30. The Balkan War has officially ended with the signing of a peace treaty at St. James's Palace in London by Turkey and the Balkan League members. Sir Edward Grey, principle agent in the peace negotiations, presided over the signature ceremony. Additionally, Bulgarian and Turkish representatives signed a protocol providing for the withdrawal of their armies from the respective nations.

One outcome of the London conference is the establishment of a constitution for Albania. It also appears the Serbian and Bulgarian premiers will meet tomorrow to settle disputes regarding the administration of Macedonia, formerly ruled by Turkey. It is expected the two nations will share the territory.

The end of the eight-month war is welcomed by Europeans, who always watch the Balkans with trepidation. As Bulgarian delegate Dr. S. Daneff remarked, "I am rejoiced. This means not only peace for Bulgaria, but general peace, for Europe is saved from a most thorny problem of the Near East" (→ 6/1)

Income tax, lower tariff on the way

May 8. A bill to impose a graduated income tax and reduce tariffs passed the House of Representatives today by a wide margin. Congressional observers believe that the strong vote in the House will serve as a mandate for the Senate to enact the bill into law.

The way was cleared for imposing an income tax when a constitutional amendment was ratified earlier this year, after an earlier law for an income tax was held unconstitutional by the Supreme Court. The new legislation would levy up to six percent tax on those making above $500,000 a year. President Wilson had called for tariff reforms in his first address to Congress. Such legislation, he said, is essential in stimulating foreign trade as well as in curtailing special privileges for domestic industries (→ 10/31).

Wilson campaigned for lower tariffs.

Why do women love clothes? Ask a doctor

Stylish ladies enjoy the sun.

May 17. There are two distinct types of women who experience an "emotional accompaniment of elation following the putting on of attractive garments." So states Dr. C.T. Ewart, a distinguished London brain specialist, speaking to psychiatrists and attempting to analyze scientifically the motives that make women adore clothes.

Type one, according to the psychiatrist, loves pretty clothes for reasons of self-display. She is basically a slattern, careless of her appearance when no one is around. Unseen parts of her apparel are usually of a quite different order from that seen. Type two receives her impulses from an aesthetic sense, a love for the beautiful and delicate. She is more particular about her clothing, the more intimate its relationship to her body.

Browning letters sold for high price

May 2. What price these words of love? About 500 letters penned by poets Elizabeth Barrett Browning and Robert Browning at different times, including those written during their courtship which had to be secret because of her tyrannical father, brought no less than $32,750 at a London auction.

The buzz of excitement in the crowded room increased as the bidding went from $3,000 to the final price paid by a Mr. Sabin. Other letters, such as from Mrs. Browning to Mary Russell Mitford, as well as notebooks, works in progress and the original manuscript of Robert Browning's last volume of poems, published the day he died (December 12, 1889), were also sold at the auction.

1913

JUNE

Su	Mo	Tu	We	Th	Fr	Sa
1	2	3	4	5	6	7
8	9	10	11	12	13	14
15	16	17	18	19	20	21
22	23	24	25	26	27	28
29	30					

1. Serbia gains accord with Greece to pursue ambitions in Macedonia (→ 24).

2. Washington: Pres. Wilson threatens intervention in Mexico if peace is not achieved (→ 17).

3. Prussia: Conservative Party and Pan-Germanists hold majority in legislative elections.

5. China opens bank in New York.

9. U.S. Supreme Court upholds states' rights to fix rail freight rates (→ 9).

9. U.S. govt. announces intent to prosecute Eastman-Kodak Co. for violation of Sherman Antitrust Act (→ 9/26/14).

9. Zeppelin airship flies from Baden-Baden to Vienna in half time of fastest train.

14. South Africa passes Immigration Act, restricting entry and free movement of Asians.

15. Berlin: Germany celebrates kaiser's silver jubilee.

15. Carrie Chapman Catt of New York convenes Women's Suffrage Congress in Budapest (→ 8/28).

17. San Diego: U.S. Marines set sail for Mexico (→ 7/3).

18. German battleship Imperator, largest ship afloat, arrives in New York.

22. It is reported that U.S. faces "grave racial problem"; 14.7% foreign-born constitute "menace to our civilization."

24. Greece, Serbia annul alliance with Bulgaria following border disputes over Macedonia and Thrace (→ 30).

30. Germany: Despite Socialist opposition, Reichstag passes Army and Finance Bills, increasing armed forces by 135,000 (→ 7/9).

DEATH

2. Alfred Austin, Poet Laureate of England since 1906 (*5/30/1835).

8. Protestant theologian Charles Asa Briggs, popularized Darwin (*1841).

Balkan War no sooner off than on again

June 30. Just as it seemed the four nations of the Balkan League were about to submit their differences to Russian mediators, fighting erupted between Bulgaria and her ex-allies, Greece and Serbia. Some 36,000 Bulgarian troops captured Guevghali, apparently to disrupt Greek and Serbian cooperation. The assault spurred Greece to advance her army in Salonika, where an attack on Bulgar quarters forced a Bulgarian surrender.

It is expected that Montenegro and Rumania will join forces to combat Bulgaria. Announcement of the Bulgarian offensive reached Serbian Premier M. Pasitch as he was addressing the Serbian Parliament on the virtues of accepting the planks of Russian arbitration. Without officially declaring war, the Greek government has issued a stern protest to Bulgaria (→ 7/1).

Greek 5th Infantry regiment launches counterattack on Bulgarian lines.

Carpentier boxing champion of Europe

June 1. The coveted light-heavyweight boxing championship of Europe has been won by the talented Frenchman, Georges Carpentier. He outgunned the powerful British champion, Bombardier Wells, and won by a knockout in the fourth round. Carpentier cornered Wells against the ropes and battered him with rights and lefts.

Wells succumbs to Carpentier.

Archdeacon Stuck on Mt. McKinley

June 20. Archdeacon Hudson Stuck, Episcopal missionary for Alaska, and his three assistants have declared themselves the first to scale the supreme peak of Mount McKinley, the highest point on the North American continent.

Stuck and his party erected a six-foot cross and the American flag at the summit. Barometer readings indicated the mountain's height is 20,500 feet. The expedition, which left Fairbanks March 13, expected to reach the summit by early May but was delayed in cutting a passage through a three-mile glacier. The glacier was thrown across the ridge by an earthquake last year.

Many explorers in recent years have attempted to reach the top of Mount McKinley, and some have falsely claimed to do so. Stuck, a longtime missionary with the Alaskan Indians, has ascended nearly all the great peaks in the Canadian and Colorado Rockies and the Alps.

French President Poincare in London

Poincare reviews British troops.

June 24. The royal red carpet was rolled out from the English coast to Victoria Station in London today as President Poincare of France received a warm welcome in Britain.

Raymond Poincare, who has been president of France for only a few months, was greeted early in the morning at Portsmouth by the Prince of Wales and a flotilla of British warships. A royal train then sped Poincare to London, where he was welcomed by the King. This evening, King George and Queen Mary honored Poincare at a lavish state dinner, and the toasts seemed more intimate than usual. King George wished a "glorious future" for France. Poincare saluted the cooperation between his country and Great Britain and said they must work together to prevent conflicts between the world's great powers (→ 30).

1913

JULY

Su	Mo	Tu	We	Th	Fr	Sa
		1	2	3	4	5
6	7	8	9	10	11	12
13	14	15	16	17	18	19
20	21	22	23	24	25	26
29	28	29	30	31		

1. Greece and Serbia declare war on Bulgaria (→ 2).

2. Brindejonc des Moulinais completes longest air flight on record: 3,100 miles from Paris to St. Petersburg and back.

2. Serbian army routs Bulgars in bloodiest battle of campaign; at least 5,000 captured (→ 4).

3. Mexico: Gen. Figueroa, prominent Maderist, executed by Huerta's men (→ 8/25).

4. Rumania orders mobilization to join Balkan War (→ 17).

4. South Africa: Anarchy prevails in Johannesburg as troops fire on gold mine strikers, killing 40.

6. Wimbledon: Anthony Wilding 8-6, 6-3, 10-8 over Maurice McLoughlin; Dorothea Chambers 6-0, 6-4 over Slocock McNair.

12. Ireland: 150,000 Ulstermen prepare armed resistance to home rule proposed by British Liberals (→ 15).

15. Pres. Wilson signs Erdman Arbitration Act to avert strike.

15. Colorado: American workers attack Japanese railway laborers in Steamboat Springs.

15. British House of Commons votes home rule for Irish, but Lords reject bill for second time (→ 9/1).

16. French Natl. Assembly votes to draft 20-year-old males into three-year military service (→ 9/7).

21. Turks take Adrianople back from Bulgaria (→ 30).

22. Washington: U.S. proposes to make Nicaragua a protectorate; Costa Rica objects (→ 8/2).

27. Belgian racer Philippe Thys wins Tour de France.

28. Great Britain: U.S. regains Davis Cup after ten years.

30. Balkan states begin peace talks (→ 8/10).

BIRTH

14. Gerald Ford, 38th U.S. president.

DEATH

10. Engineer Burton Baker, invented X-ray machine.

Building hundreds of fighting ships for war

Naval force of the Great Powers (July 1913)

Country	Ships of the line		Armoured cruisers		Warships		Submarines	
	finished	under construction	finished	under construction	finished	under construction	finished	under construction
Great Britain	63	15	42	2	27	11	70	25
United States	33	6	15	–	8	6	30	20
Germany	33	8	13	3	15	11	23	?
France	27	10	22	–	8	10	60	15
Japan	16	4	14	3	5	7	13	2
Russia	12	7	6	4	–	11	30	25
Italy	14	8	10	–	1	8	20	4
Austria-Hungary	14	2	3	–	2	2	6	2

July 9. They are only numbers in a book, but they are disturbing figures that portend new dangers for peace in the world. "Nauticus," the German yearbook on naval forces, has published its latest research on shipbuilding by the great powers. There has been a sharp increase.

"Nauticus" reports that the powers have built 133 warships and 93 submarines. These figures do not include German submarines under construction because the German government refuses to release that information. The yearbook also claims that France is spending the most per capita to arm itself, followed by Germany, Great Britain and the United States. Germany, however, may leap to the top of the list soon, since the government has just decided to increase the size of its army from 120,000 to 660,000 men (→ 16).

Despite delays, Baghdad railway advances

The Baghdad railway is piercing the high plateaus of Asia Minor.

July 28. Germany and Great Britain have reached an agreement on the Baghdad railway that might relieve the intense rivalry and competitive pressures that have developed since Germany announced its plans for the rail line. After a difficult series of negotiations, Germany and Turkey have agreed not to build a spur that would connect Basra with the Persian Gulf.

Great Britain has been trying to prevent the Reich from gaining access to the rich Gulf region. The long railway, being built with German capital, is designed to connect Baghdad with Constantinople in Turkey. Under a 1903 agreement, a German society has the right to operate it for 99 years.

Atrocities reported; Rumania joins war

Dead Bulgarian soldiers.

July 17. Rumania invaded Bulgarian terrain last week amid stories of grave atrocities by Bulgarians against the Serbs and Greeks. Rumania issued a statement to Bulgaria, when the Bulgarian attacks on Greeks and Serbians were first publicized, that if the aggression continued, the Rumanian army would join Serbian, Greek and Montenegran forces. Bulgaria did not respond, and subsequent Rumanian attacks have nearly brought the Bulgar troops to their knees.

News reached New York from Greek King Constantine that since the first days of the Balkan War Bulgaria has slaughtered thousands of innocent people. The alleged massacres took place in several cities and villages, the worst of which occurred in Doxato, where all but 150 of its 3,500 inhabitants were reportedly annihilated. As the communique stated: "Everywhere Bulgarians have passed, one sees only blood, dishonor and ruin ... (It is) a refinement of cruelty which the imagination refuses to comprehend." Bulgarian King Ferdinand called the allegations of massacres and atrocities "infamous Greek calumnies" (→ 21).

Rumanian Gen. Prince Ferdinand.

1913

AUGUST

Su	Mo	Tu	We	Th	Fr	Sa
					1	2
3	4	5	6	7	8	9
10	11	12	13	14	15	16
17	18	19	20	21	22	23
24	25	26	27	28	29	30
31						

1. Heat wave sweeping U.S.; nearly 100 victims reported in last two weeks.

2. Senate commission kills plan to make Nicaragua a U.S. protectorate (→ 7/24/25).

2. Belgium: International conference on cancer research opens in Brussels.

5. Germany: Seven Krupp executives get light jail terms for bribing army men to secure defense contracts.

6. British Parliament considers building tunnel under English Channel.

6. Sun Yat-sen, ex-provisional president of republic, flees China due to conflict with President Yuan Shih-kai (→ 10/6).

7. Washington: U.S. signs non-intervention treaty with Salvador.

13. Orient-Express celebrates 25th anniversary.

16. Henry Ford predicts forthcoming assembly line will quadruple automobile production (→ 10/7).

20. Austria-Hungary: Council President Istvan Tisza and Margrave Georg Pallaviani wounded in duel.

21. Venezuelan troops crush Castro revolt.

25. Mexico City: President Huerta orders all Americans out of Mexico (→ 25).

25. President Wilson announces decision to boycott Mexico (→ 9/10).

26. U.S.: Keokuk Dam, world's largest, opened across Mississippi River.

28. British suffragettes assault Prime Minister Asquith in London (→ 10/15).

31. Panama: Last barrier blown up on Pacific end; water now reaches halfway mark (→ 9/26).

BIRTH

16. Israeli statesman Menachem Begin.

DEATH

13. German Socialist August Bebel (*2/22/1840).

Bulgarians obtain peace settlement

Aug 10. The Balkan peace treaty was signed this morning in Bucharest, Rumania, by Bulgaria and the Balkan states. Rumanian King Charles, Queen Elizabeth and representatives from all nations involved attended the peace conference as the king awarded decorations to all delegates. The Bulgarians, however, refused to accept.

The treaty provides that Rumania will pull her forces from Bulgaria in 15 days and Serbian and Greek armies will withdraw in three days. It also stipulates that Belgium, Holland and Switzerland will arbitrate if agreement is not reached over the delimitation of new frontiers. Bulgaria must disengage its troops.

Greek Premier Venizelos and King Constantine discuss peace treaty.

In a related matter, verification of some of the alleged Bulgarian atrocities reached New York as an American citizen working in Turkey witnessed massacres of innocent victims by Bulgar troops (→ 9/21).

Harry Thaw escapes from insane asylum

Aug 17. Harry Thaw has escaped from New York's Matteawan State Hospital for the Criminal Insane to which he was sentenced five years ago following his conviction for the murder of Stanford White. In a carefully arranged plot, Thaw darted through an open gate and into a waiting car. Police are scouring New England, and a man resembling Thaw boarded a launch at South Norwalk, Conn (→ 9/10).

1913

SEPTEMBER

Su	Mo	Tu	We	Th	Fr	Sa
	1	2	3	4	5	6
7	8	9	10	11	12	13
14	15	16	17	18	19	20
21	22	23	24	25	26	27
28	29	30				

1. France: Adolphe Pegoud flies upside down for a quarter-mile (→ 6).

1. Ireland: 500 hurt in Dublin streetcar strike riot; police charged with brutality (→ 3).

2. Connecticut: 21 killed, 50 hurt in New Haven train crash.

3. 50,000 attend Dublin funeral of worker killed by police two days ago (→ 21).

6. New York: Dr. Noguchi isolates rabies germ.

6. Frenchman Pegoud becomes first pilot to "loop the loop."

7. German aviator Friedrich performs Paris-to-Berlin flight with passengers aboard.

7. Tokyo: 15,000 Japanese storm Foreign Office to demand action against anti-Japanese policy in U.S. and China.

8. German Zeppelin LZ, largest yet at 520 feet, makes first flight (→ 9).

9. German naval airship LI goes down in hurricane off Heligoland; 15 missing.

10. 350 Americans reported captured in Mexico since start of U.S. arms embargo (→ 10/11).

10. Escapee Harry K. Thaw, deported from Canada, arrested in Colebrook, N.H. (→ 7/16/15).

11. Cholera spreading through Balkans; 700 dead in Rumania, 300 in Serbia since beginning of year.

20. Germany: Social Democratic Congress in Iena names Hugo Haase and Friedrich Ebert to succeed August Bebel.

21. In compliance with Balkan treaty, Bulgaria withdraws from Adrianople (→ 10/25).

26. Panama: First boat raised in canal locks (→ 10/10).

28. Mississippi: Race riot in Harriston; ten dead, 20 hurt (→ 7/21/15).

BIRTH

12. American athlete Jesse Owens (†3/31/1980).

DEATH

29. German engineer Rudolf Diesel (*3/18/1858).

Irish riot in South as North arms itself

Sept 21. Vicious street fights between striking streetcar workers and police flared again today in the streets of Dublin. The police clubbed milling strikers, and they retaliated by throwing bottles and other projectiles. One policeman was knocked from his horse by a bottle. More than 40 people, including a number of officers, were carried away to hospitals on stretchers. Some were seriously injured.

Police had to use all their muscle today to break up a mob of 10,000 strikers and supporters who swarmed through the streets and began to hold up and wreck streetcars. It was the worst flare-up of riots in three weeks, and the violence is the worst suffered by Dublin in 30 years. At the end of last month, one man was killed and more than 500 were injured. The strikers have shown little restraint in their attacks on police, but authorities have also been criticized for using excessive force.

In Northern Ireland, Unionists, who are opposed to home rule for Ireland, are forming a volunteer army. And they are doing it quickly. Reports from Belfast indicate that 100,000 men have already signed up, and that number may very well double. The army is expected to support a new provisional government, which will be formed if home rule passes. Sir Edward Carson, who is the leader of the Unionists and an outspoken opponent of home rule, has been in Belfast inspecting the army (→ 4/7/14).

Sir Edward Carson and Irish army. ▷

Powers consolidate Triple Alliance

Sept 7. Germany and Austria-Hungary have been uneasy for years about the depth of Italy's commitment to the Triple Alliance. Today, as international pressures grew to the east and west of the three countries, they agreed to consolidate their shaky alliance. The agreement was approved by William II of Germany, the Austrian Quartermaster-General, Count Franz Conrad von Hotzendorf, and Italy's General Alberto Pollio. Pollio declared, "The Triple Alliance must act as a single state in case of war."

The Triple Alliance is apparently concerned about several major international developments. The most pressing is Serbia's territorial expansion in the Balkans. The alliance is preparing to act against the Serbian presence in Albania. The alliance is also worried about the French government's decision to require men to serve three years in the military. And it views with alarm the agreement that Great Britain and Russia are about to sign. The two countries are reported to be close to a naval pact that would bind both of them to fight against the German navy in the Baltic Sea if war breaks out (→ 2/21/14).

Kaiser Wilhelm and German troops celebrate the Triple Alliance.

Incredible feat! Roland Garros flies across Mediterranean

Roland Garros made it from France to Tunisia in seven hrs., 53 min.

Sept 23. French aviator Roland Garros flew 558 miles (437 over sea) today from Frejus, near Cannes, to Bizerta, near Tunis. Garros had planned to cross the Mediterranean Sea for some time. Although his friends tried to dissuade him, Garros decided to make the attempt anyway. He even declined the offer made by French naval authorities to assist him with a chain of torpedo boats in case he should be forced to descend on the water.

This morning at 6 a.m., he flew south in a Morane-Saulnier monoplane fitted with a Gnome engine. The weather seemed fine; he had perfect visibility, but the south winds were against him. Between 7 and 8 a.m., a wireless message from Ajaccio, Corsica, announced the plane had passed there. He landed in Bizerta at 1:45 p.m. with only 1.3 gallons of gasoline left.

Garros' non-stop flight is the longest over sea ever accomplished, affirming his worldwide reputation as an aviator. He has won some of the most famous, long-distance races in Europe. He also has taken part in flying meets in many countries and set several altitude records. This feat adds to his long list of aerial achievements.

1913

OCTOBER

Su	Mo	Tu	We	Th	Fr	Sa
			1	2	3	4
5	6	7	8	9	10	11
12	13	14	15	16	17	18
19	20	21	22	23	24	25
26	27	28	29	30	31	

4. Washington: Wilson signs Underwood-Simmons Tariff Bill, activating first tariff cuts since Civil War.

5. New York: Strauss' "Der Rosenkavalier" opens at the Metropolitan Opera.

6. Peking: Yuan Shih-k'ai re-elected president of China (→ 1/10/14).

10. New York: 100 bombs reportedly traced to Italian Black Hand; 15 arrested.

11. New York Athletics take World Series 3-1 in fifth game against Giants.

11. Liner Volturno burns at sea; 136 lost; wireless SOS helps save 521.

11. Mexico City: President Huerta dissolves Congress (→ 28).

12. Alaska: Russian czar claims new land at 81 N. lat., 104 E. long., calls it Nicholas II Land.

14. Great Britain: Explosion at Cardiff mine; 418 miners dead.

15. New York suffragists hold "baby shows" to prove they are good mothers (→ 20).

17. Zeppelin L II explodes over Berlin, killing 28.

20. Pres. Wilson secures release of Emmeline Pankhurst, ordered deported two days ago on grounds of moral turpitude (→ 2/3/14).

25. Serbia succumbs to Austrian pressure, withdraws from Albania (→ 11/9).

28. Colorado governor sends troops to discipline coal miners during Berwind strike.

28. Gen. Felix Diaz flees Mexico to seek U.S. protection from Pres. Huerta (→ 11/3).

31. U.S. income tax law goes into effect.

BIRTH

22. Bao Dai, emperor of Annam.

DEATHS

7. Department store founder Benjamin Altman.

10. American brewer Adolphus Busch.

Henry Ford establishes first assembly line

Motorcars stream off of Henry Ford's new Highland Park assembly line.

Oct 7. Henry Ford has established a moving assembly line in his automobile manufacturing plant at Highland Park, Michigan, greatly increasing the efficiency of production. Instead of having workmen go to automobiles being built, as in other plants, Ford has the automobiles drawn along a 250-foot-long assembly line, with workmen adding parts along the way. The moving assembly line allows an automobile to be built in less than three hours. The innovation is needed to meet the steadily increasing demand for Ford's Model T. Nearly 250,000 are expected to be built in the next year alone.

Wilson gives signal; Panama Canal open

Oct 10. The waters of the Atlantic and Pacific Oceans joined today, as President Wilson pushed a button in Washington that ignited eight tons of dynamite, opening the last segment of the Panama Canal. Small vessels can travel through the canal already, and the path for larger ships from ocean to ocean is expected to be open within weeks. Work on the canal began a decade ago. Success was made possible by Dr. William Gorgas' conquest of malaria and yellow fever (→ 6/7).

Crowds watch first gallons of water penetrate the canal's western gate.

1913

NOVEMBER

Su	Mo	Tu	We	Th	Fr	Sa
						1
2	3	4	5	6	7	8
9	10	11	12	13	14	15
16	17	18	19	20	21	22
23	24	25	26	27	28	29
30						

3. Washington: For first time in history, War Dept. arranges for prompt mobilization of 500,000 troops (→ 8/5/14).

3. Democrats maintain control in U.S. national elections.

3. Pres. Wilson demands resignation of Mexican Pres. Huerta (→ 8).

5. German unemployment reported on the increase; 443,000 now jobless.

6. Paris: Camille Saint-Saens plays farewell concert at Salle Gaveau.

6. India: Gandhi, leader of Indian Passive Resistance Movement, arrested by British troops (→ 4/15/19).

7. German steelmakers, at Berlin conference, agree to push for British, U.S. markets in Far East.

8. Mexico: Pres. Huerta obtains vital British loan (→ 15).

9. Despite Italian and Austrian objections, Greece claims southern Albania (→ 12/6).

14. Paris: "Salon d'Automne" shows futurists Picabia, Gleizes and Kupka; Cubism barred.

15. Mexico: Huerta pressed; Villa takes Juarez (→ 30).

17. Louise is first vessel to transit Panama Canal (→ 6/7/14).

17. Berlin: Kaiser bans tango in German army and navy.

21. St. Petersburg: Imperial justice orders several Tolstoy manuscripts destroyed.

26. Imperial Russian Council bans Polish language in municipal councils of Russian Poland.

29. Army over Navy 22-0 at the Polo Grounds.

BIRTHS

2. American actor Burt Lancaster.

7. French existentialist writer Albert Camus (†1/4/1960).

22. British composer Benjamin Britten (†12/14/1976).

DEATH

7. Briton Alfred Russell Wallace, co-discoverer of natural selection.

On to Mexico! cries Villa, taking Juarez

Nov 30. General Francisco "Pancho" Villa says that northern Mexico will be under his control within two weeks. His campaign will then focus on storming the capital.

Villa, whose army recently took Juarez, is preparing his men for an attack on Chihuahua City, cut off from communications for more than two weeks. From there, Villa says, "We will move right on to Mexico City." At that time, his forces will be joined by those of General Carranza, head of the revolutionary movement whose constitutionalist rebels are pitted against the besieged federal troops of General Huerta, leader of the de facto government.

Pancho Villa rides in Mexico.

Accompanying Villa's army are 100 women carrying rifles and acting as cooks. Many of them fought at the battle of Tierra Blanca, and several were reported killed. The Red Cross has ordered its local branch to set up a hospital to aid the wounded of both sides (→ 1/10/14).

Charlie Chaplin made his film debut this month as a slick, monocled villain in Mack Sennett's "Making a Living."

Los Angeles to get aqueduct water

The Owens River Aqueduct.

Nov 5. "There it is, take it!" By this, possibly the shortest speech on record, Chief City Engineer William Mulholland declared the controversial Los Angeles Owens River Aqueduct open today. Then, thousands of citizens cheered as water from the Sierras came in a splashing torrent. The $25 million aqueduct, rated second only to the Panama Canal as an engineering feat, was built in five short years.

By pipeline and ditch, water is brought by gravity 234 miles across mountains, canyons and deserts. Options were bought as early as 1904 from willing Owens Valley farmers, who believed that a government irrigation project was to be undertaken. Much later, they realized that they had signed away their water rights. The operation was kept quiet, ostensibly to keep option prices from soaring. Voices have already been raised about "stolen water" and "the rape of a valley," but to those living in semi-desert Los Angeles, the guarantee of 260 million gallons of water every 24 hours is equivalent to life and prosperity.

Nov 29. Army team members after defeating Navy 22-9. Cadet D.W. Eisenhower 2nd from rt.

1913

DECEMBER

Su	Mo	Tu	We	Th	Fr	Sa
	1	2	3	4	5	6
7	8	9	10	11	12	13
14	15	16	17	18	19	20
21	22	23	24	25	26	27
28	29	30	31			

6. European powers recognize German Prince de Wied as king of Albania (→ 13).

10. Nobel Peace Prize to Belgian Henri La Fontaine; literature to Indian Rabindranath Tagore.

13. Britain proposes division of south Albania between Greece and Albania (→ 3/6/14).

14. Greek King Constantin I proclaims union of Crete with Greece.

19. Peking: Pres. Yuan Shih-kai closes China's Parliament (→ 1/10/14).

27. Chicago: Charles Moyer, pres. of Miners Union, shot in back and dragged through streets; accuses mine owners.

30. Britain, Germany agree to divide Portugal's African possessions.

BIRTH

18. German Socialist statesman Willy Brandt.

DEATH

7. Montgomery Ward, dept. store founder (*2/17/1844).

CULTURAL EVENTS, 1913

Literature: D.H. Lawrence's "Sons and Lovers"; Willa Cather's "O Pioneers"; Jack London's "John Barleycorn"; Marcel Proust's "Swann's Way," first part of "Remembrance of Things Past"; Robert Frost's poem "A Boy's Will."

Academia: Edmund Husserl's "Phenomenology"; Russell and Whitehead's "Principia Mathematica"; Freud's "Totem and Taboo"; John Watson introduces behaviorism; first crossword puzzle, in The New York World.

Music: Victor Herbert's musical "Sweethearts"; Rachmaninoff's "The Bells"; Stravinsky's "The Rites of Spring," Paris.

The Arts: J.S. Sargent's "Portrait of Henry Adams"; New York's Armory Show.

Film: Cecil B. De Mille's "The Squaw Man"; Thomas Ince's "The Battle of Gettysburg"; start of Charlie Chaplin's film career; first Paramount films.

Federal Reserve begins; 213 banks join

Dec 24. Some 213 of the nation's banks have applied for membership in the new Federal Reserve System that was created under a law signed just yesterday by President Wilson. The new federal banking system will provide a means whereby bank notes and credit will automatically expand in times of business prosperity and deflate as the volume of business declines.

By creating 12 Federal Reserve banks to serve as depositories for member banks, the United States will now have a central authority to serve banking interests without having a single large institution, such as the Bank of England. In signing the bill into law, President Wilson used several gold pens, and he said jokingly, "I'm drawing on the gold reserve."

213 banks have joined the Fed.

Nobel rewards Elihu Root's peace efforts

Dec 10. Because it was not awarded last year, two full Nobel Peace Prizes of $40,000 each have been granted this year to Senator Elihu Root of the United States and to Belgian Senator Henri la Fontaine.

The Nobel Prize Committee cites Root's eminent merits in the pacification of the Philippines and Cuba, and in the handling of the American-Japanese dispute. It also praises his lofty political and international ideals, his statesmanship and his constant efforts to promote pacifist ideas. The Nobel Prize for literature was awarded this year to Rabindranath Tagore, the Bengali poet from India.

Mona Lisa recovered; Italian arrested

Dec 13. The "Mona Lisa" is still smiling and there is joy at the Louvre in Paris this afternoon. The famous painting, stolen more than two years ago, has been found, apparently undamaged, in Florence. Leonardo da Vinci painted the portrait in Florence at the beginning of the 16th century, so it seems only appropriate that the "Mona Lisa" will be on view there for a week before it is returned to Paris.

The suspect in the theft is a painter, Vincenzo Perugia, who is now behind bars. Authorities in Italy say he stole the painting from the Louvre when he was in Paris in August 1911. Perugia was arrested after he allegedly tried to sell the painting to an antiques dealer. Experts say it would have been almost impossible to sell the "Mona Lisa" anywhere because the painting is so well-known.

"The Mona Lisa" was displayed in Florence under heavy guard before being returned to its home in The Louvre.

1914

JANUARY

Su	Mo	Tu	We	Th	Fr	Sa
				1	2	3
4	5	6	7	8	9	10
11	12	13	14	15	16	17
18	19	20	21	22	23	24
25	26	27	28	29	30	31

1. New Jersey sets minimum wage for women at $9/week.

1. Michigan: Detroit Symphony Orchestra founded.

1. Florida: Air passenger service inaugurated between Tampa and St. Petersburg.

1. Australia: Giants and Red Sox arrive in Brisbane for overseas baseball tour.

2. British aviator Trehawke Davis becomes first woman to perform "loop the loop."

8. Michigan: Doctors at Natl. Conference on Race Betterment call thin women imperfect, can't understand why they're favored by fashion.

9. South Africa: Militia called out in Johannesburg to battle 35,000 railway workers, on strike since yesterday (→ 12).

10. Peking: Yuan Shih-kai dissolves China's Parliament (→ 2/21).

10. Texas: Ojinaga attacked by Villa's rebels (→ 2/2).

12. South Africa on verge of general strike; 200,000 armed as miners vote to quit work.

14. France: Sarah Bernhardt awarded Legion of Honor.

14. Tokyo: Volcanic eruption kills 300; 25,000 in flight.

16. Maxim Gorky authorized to return to Russia after eight-year exile for political dissidence. (→ 5/3).

24. New York: Victor Herbert's lyric opera "Madeleine" premieres at Metropolitan Opera.

27. Haiti: Civil war in Port-au-Prince forces President Oreste out of office (→ 1/9/15).

28. Washington: Kaiser Wilhelm II sends first German wireless to Pres. Wilson.

28. California: Beverly Hills incorporated as city, extending boundaries to fill 500 population quota.

30. Va.: Battleship Monroe sunk in collision with the Nantucket; 41 lost, 99 rescued.

BIRTH

6. American actress Loretta Young.

Ford pays workers $5 day; output leaps

Jan 5. Henry Ford astounded the business world today by announcing that he will give his employees a minimum wage of $5 a day and will share with them $10 million in last year's profits.

The automobile magnate also disclosed that the Ford Motor Company will begin operating around the clock, with three shifts of eight hours each instead of the present two nine-hour shifts. This will provide employment for several thousand more workers.

Still another part of the new plan provides that no person be fired except for proven unfaithfulness or inefficiency. Anyone doing poor work in one department will be given the chance to make good in another part of the plant.

About ten percent of the workers, most of them women and boys, will not receive any profit-sharing. However, all employees will receive a wage of at least $5 a day, even the boys who sweep the floors.

The dramatic moves will affect about 26,000 employes, of whom about 15,000 are now at work in the Detroit factories, while others are in Ford branches throughout the world. The company's financial statement for 1914 showed assets of more than $35 million and a surplus of more than $28 million.

In announcing the new plan today, a Ford Motor Company representative said: "It is our belief that social justice begins at home. We want those who have helped us to produce this great institution and are helping to maintain it to share our prosperity."

Innovator Henry Ford.

Builder of Panama Canal to be Governor

Jan 23. George Washington Goethals, the United States Army engineer in charge of building the Panama Canal, has been appointed Governor of the Canal Zone. The zone is made up of a ten-mile-wide strip of land bordering the isthmian waterway. The Hay-Bunau-Varilla Treaty of 1903 granted the United States the use and control of the zone in perpetuity.

After graduating from West Point in 1880, Goethals worked on several inland water projects, including the Tennessee River dams and Muscle Shoals locks. President Theodore Roosevelt named him Chief Engineer of the Isthmian Canal Commission in 1907 after the resignation of John F. Stevens.

The canal excavations had been started in 1879 by Ferdinand de Lesseps, builder of the Suez Canal, but had to stop because the French company was not able to raise enough money to continue the project.

The monumental task of cutting a 50-mile path across the Continental Divide was complicated by several factors. Unanticipated problems arose in constructing the three giant locks, leading to delays. An unstable substrata created difficulties during the excavation of the Culebra Cut.

The climate and several outbreaks of yellow fever took their toll on the workers. The harsh working conditions contributed to labor difficulties, but Goethals managed to instill a spirit of cooperation in the men and the canal was completed earlier than expected. The canal cost over $300 million to build, and some 4,000 men died during construction (→ 4/10).

Col. Goethals, Gov. of Canal Zone.

Hollywood becomes world film center

Pianist accompanies a Keystone film.

Cecil B. De Mille, former state manager and playwright, has founded a film mecca in Hollywood, California. In 1913, De Mille was looking for a spot to shoot his first motion picture, a western. Flagstaff, Arizona, was De Mille's first choice, but the city had a few more snow-topped mountains than he bargained for. Hollywood, a peaceful, unpretentious town outside Los Angeles, offered the ideal landscape. Its countryside is varied enough to allow De Mille to film every kind of motion picture there.

De Mille is not alone. He is joined by producers fleeing New Jersey and New York, innovators who had nearly been strangled out of existence by an Eastern patents syndicate. Hollywood is their oasis.

Ideas and techniques are traded and stolen in the small community. Close-ups, cross-cutting, fade-outs and flashbacks are discussed. The upshot is some fine pictures.

Mary Pickford, everybody's favorite.

1914

FEBRUARY

Su	Mo	Tu	We	Th	Fr	Sa
1	2	3	4	5	6	7
8	9	10	11	12	13	14
15	16	17	18	19	20	21
22	23	24	25	26	27	28

1. New York: Aero Club of America announces plans to host race around the world.

1. Russia gains loan from France.

2.Tanganyika: 775-mile rail line inaugurated between Lake. Tanganyika and Dar-es-Salam.

2. Mexico: Pancho Villa shoots Diaz emissary Francisco Guzman (→ 3).

3. Washington: Wilson lifts arms embargo for Mexico, hopes for swift end to crisis (→ 24).

3. British suffragettes attempt to register to vote (→ 17).

9. London: William Marconi declares he can light a lamp six miles away by wireless.

12. Paris: Academie Francaise elects Henri Bergson.

13. N.Y.: American Society of Composers, Authors and Publishers (ASCAP) founded with Victor Herbert as director.

18. Long Island: Vanderbilt mansion in Jericho burns; $300,000 in damages.

21. China: Gangs plunder Lin-chuan, kill 1,000; govt. troops called out (→ 4/5).

21. St. Petersburg: Russian military leaders devise plan to seize Dardanelles (→ 24).

24. Mexico: Gen. Villa defies U.S. and Britain, refuses to return body of Briton William Benton (→ 3/10).

24. Great Britain: Granting Winston Churchill's request, Parliament votes additional funds for navy (→ 3/5).

26. St. Petersburg: Russian aviator Igor Sikorsky carries 17 passengers in twin-engine plane.

BIRTH

5. British neurologist Alan Hodgkin.

DEATHS

13. Criminologist Alphonse Bertillon, invented fingerprinting (*4/23/1853).

25. British artist Sir John Tenniel, illustrated "Alice in Wonderland" (*2/28/1820).

Suffragettes are violent in Britain

Veteran suffragette in Trafalgar Sq.

Feb 17. In their struggle for the right of women to vote, British suffragettes renounced non-violence some time ago. And this month, they continued their activities by breaking the window panes of the Home Secretary's London office and setting fire to the house of the exclusive Lawn Tennis Club.

Emmeline Pankhurst, the leader of the Women's Social and Political Union, an organization that she founded in 1903, has been released from a London jail after a hunger strike. Since 1912, Mrs. Pankhurst has been repeatedly arrested, imprisoned and then released. But Mary Richardson, one of her chief partners in the struggle for equality, who was sentenced to six months in prison for destroying paintings, did not fare so well. To gain release, Miss Richardson began a hunger strike too, but the prison doctor decided to subject her to forced feeding (→ 4/5).

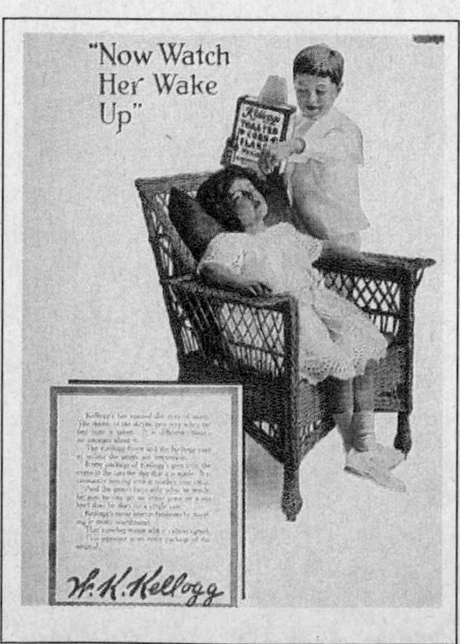

1914

MARCH

Su	Mo	Tu	We	Th	Fr	Sa
1	2	3	4	5	6	7
8	9	10	11	12	13	14
15	16	17	18	19	20	21
22	23	24	25	26	27	28
29	30	31				

4. Paris: Dr. Filliatre successfully separates siamese twins.

5. Great Britain: Military budget increased by 625,000 pounds to total of 29 mil. pounds (→ 17).

6. German Prince Wilhelm de Wied crowned King of Albania (→ 4/4).

7. Tris Speaker offered $37,000 in two-year contracts with Boston Red Sox, highest yet in baseball.

10. Washington demands justice for slain American found in Mexico two days ago by Texas Rangers (→ 28).

10. French newspaper Le Figaro publishes allegedly libelous report on Finance Minister Joseph Caillaux (→ 16).

11. New York: Jim Europe conducts Negro Symphony Orchestra with clarinets, trumpets, trombones, banjos, drums and ten pianos.

17. Russia increases active duty count in military from 460,000 to 1,700,000 (→ 25).

20. Japan: Akita earthquake takes 83 lives.

22. Brazil: Boat in Roosevelt expedition wrecked in rapids; Teddy reported safe.

23. London: Prime Minister Asquith renounces military option in Northern Ireland (→ 4/7).

25. Buffalo N.Y.: State troopers called out to monitor strike at Gould Coupler Company.

25. French Defense Minister Joseph Noulens demands 754 mil. francs for military.→

28. Mexico: Villa takes Gomez Palacio, boasts near-control of Torreon region (→ 4/5).

BIRTHS

1. American novelist Ralph Ellison, "Invisible Man."

26. William C. Westmoreland, U.S. general.

DEATHS

1. British Earl of Minto, former viceroy of India.

12. American engineer George Westinghouse, invented electrical appliances (*10/6/1846).

European arms race and war talk grow

March. All over Europe, countries are arming themselves. And war seems more and more likely.

In Britain, sharp debate greeted the government's decision to build more ships. Winston Churchill, the First Lord of the Admiralty, told the House of Commons, "It is our intention to put eight squadrons into service in the time it takes Germany to build five." A member of the Labor Party objected, saying "Churchill's attitude represents a danger for the security of the country and for world peace."

In Austria-Hungary, military expenditures are the largest part of the budget. Russia wants to quadruple the size of its army. In Berlin, a Frenchman told a group of pacifists, "There is no innate hostility between our countries. We all want to live in peace." To many in Europe, this message represents very wishful thinking (→ 4/7).

American fighter beats Europe's best

Joe Jeannette (rt.) faces Carpentier.

March 21. Georges Carpentier, the French boxing champion who has dominated the light-heavyweight scene in Europe, met his match against an underrated American, Joe Jeannette. Jeannette defeated many of the top heavyweights in the United States but did not get a chance at the championship, experts agree, because he is a Negro. He was able to make the most of his weight advantage against Carpentier, whose more skillful boxing could not offset it.

Cabinet minister's wife shoots editor

The assassination of Calmette.

March 16. The wife of the French Finance Minister is in jail tonight. Mrs. Joseph Caillaux is accused of shooting to death Gaston Calmette, the editor of the newspaper Figaro. Mrs. Caillaux says that she pulled the trigger "because there is no more justice in France. There is only the the revolver."

Minister Caillaux, a former Premier, a pacifist and a member of the Radical Party, has been harshly criticized by the conservative Figaro for advocating a progressive income tax. The paper also attacked his private life. Mrs. Caillaux allegedly walked into Calmette's office and shot him because he refused to return letters she had written to her husband several years ago.

Home appliances inventor is dead

March 12. George Westinghouse, inventor of over 400 mechanical and electrical appliances and head of the Westinghouse Electric Company, has died at the age of 68.

Westinghouse began his career by discovering an electrical system that would instantly brake an entire train. He went on to devise an electrical system of automatic signals to stop trains, using compressed air. One invention he could not sell was an automatic telephone system without a switchboard —which the telephone company adopted later. He also was a pioneer in developing the alternating current system for transmission of electricity.

1914

APRIL

Su	Mo	Tu	We	Th	Fr	Sa
			1	2	3	4
5	6	7	8	9	10	11
12	13	14	15	16	17	18
19	20	21	22	23	24	25
26	27	28	29	30		

1. Britain: Marconi conducts first wireless tests from a train.

2. Washington: New Federal Reserve Board announces plans to divide country into 12 districts.

4. Albania calls general mobilization, threatens war with Greece over territory in south (→ 6/13).

5. Minister from new Chinese republic arrives in U.S.

5. Mexico: Gen. Villa orders 600 Torreon Spaniards deported (→ 9).

5. British suffragettes bomb London church (→ 5/2).

7. British House of Commons carries Irish home rule bill by majority of 80 (→ 7/27).

7. Russian naval minister orders halt on shipbuilding imports from Germany (→ 5/3).

9. Violent thunderstorm strikes Newfoundland, kills 275.

9. Mexico: Huerta briefly seizes Americans in Tampico, apologizes yet refuses to salute U.S. flag; Wilson mobilizes 52 warships (→ 13).

10. U.S. Sec. of State W.J. Bryan opens Panama Canal to Colombian warships.

13. Washington: Wilson orders Atlantic fleet to Mexico (→ 16).

16. Mexican President Huerta agrees to salute U.S. flag (→ 21).

16. U.S. Secretary of the Navy claims Mexican crisis indicates urgent need for strong Navy.

23. Mexico: Carranza condemns American seizure of Vera Cruz, orders U.S. out of Mexico (→ 25).

25. Argentina, Brazil, Chile offer to mediate in U.S.-Mexican conflict (→ 26).

26. Pres. Huerta agrees to join peace talks (→ 5/4).

28. Wilson sends National Guard to Colorado to quell strike riots.

BIRTHS

2. British actor Alec Guiness.

26. American author Bernard Malamud, 1966 Pulitzer Prize for "The Fixer."

Thousands in Paris acclaim King George V

Parisians welcome Britain's King and Queen at the Arc de Triomphe.

April 21. The entente between France and Britain is more than cordial, from the look of things in the French capital today. The relationship has become downright friendly, and the French government has given Britain's King George and Queen Mary a very warm welcome.

The flags of both countries hung on all the major streets as the king and queen emerged from the Bois de Boulogne today and descended the Champs Elysees to the Foreign Office. More than 200,000 enthusiastic Parisians turned out to catch a glimpse of the royal couple. The king and queen are scheduled to attend a large military review tomorrow at Vincennes. In the evening, they will host President and Mrs. Poincare at a banquet at the British Embassy. On Thursday, the French will give a banquet for the royal couple.

U.S. Marines take Vera Cruz, kill 200

April 21. One thousand United States Marines have seized the Mexican seaport of Vera Cruz, with four killed and 20 wounded in the wake of an unopposed landing.

Heavy fighting continues for the Mexican federal army garrison, which has lost 200 men. Most of the federal officers have escaped, including Commandant General Maas, who fled with his family. Of several reasons given for the intervention one concerns an effort to thwart the imminent arrival of a German arms shipment to General Huerta's federal troops (→ 23).

American Marines and sailors fire at snipers in Vera Cruz.

1914

MAY

Su	Mo	Tu	We	Th	Fr	Sa
					1	2
3	4	5	6	7	8	9
10	11	12	13	14	15	16
17	18	19	20	21	22	23
24	25	26	27	28	29	30
31						

2. Suffrage Day declared in New York (→ 6).

3. Russia: Social Democratic members expelled following fights at Duma (→ 7/22).

3. Russian Duma votes 5% increase in military budget (→ 6/15).

4. Mexican rebels quit peace conference; new revolt threatens Huerta (→ 6).

6. Huerta offers to step down if U.S. will enter and pacify Mexico (→ 8).

6. British House of Lords rejects woman's suffrage bill (→ 1/12/15).

7. Washington: Pres. Wilson's youngest daughter Eleanor weds William McAdoo.

8. Mexico: Captured American soldier executed by federal troops at Vera Cruz (→ 14).

9. 182 killed in Sicilian earthquake.

9. Jockey J. McCabe rides Old Rosebud to victory in Kentucky Derby.

10. French Socialists score victory at legislative elections.

11. Morocco: French troops occupy Taza (→ 12/12/24).

14. Mexican rebels take Tampico after heavy fighting, fear Huerta naval blockade (→ 20).

19. Paris: Leontine Zanta becomes first French woman to present philosophy thesis.

20. British government acquires controling interest in Anglo-Persian Oil Co.

20. Niagara Falls: Mexican-American peace conference opens (→ 6/9).

25. Great Britain offers Ireland limited autonomy (→ 7/27).

29. Quebec: Canadian liner Empress of Ireland sinks in 14 minutes; 954 dead.

30. Rene Thomas wins 4th annual Indianapolis 500, averaging 82 mph in Delage racer.

BIRTHS

5. American actor Tyrone Power (†11/15/1958).

13. American boxer Joe Louis (†4/12/1981).

Jacob Riis, friend of poor, has died

Danish-American Jacob A. Riis.

May 26. Most immigrants come to America to make a fortune. In 1870, 21-year-old Jacob Riis emigrated from Denmark to seek his fortune. And ever since, through his innovative use of the camera, Riis has been an inspiration to the national crusade for social reform.

Riis began his career as a police reporter for New York newspapers. His penetrating articles and shocking photographs culminated in publication of "How the Other Half Lives" in 1890. The book, documenting "the foul core of New York's slums" —such wretched areas as Bandit's Roost and Thieves Alley —caused a sensation and earned him the friendship of Teddy Roosevelt and the respect of reformers everywhere. Riis' "The Battle with the Slum" a dozen years later reported on the progress of urban tenement reform efforts.

Riis was a pioneer in every sense of the word. He founded a settlement house, which was named for him in 1901. Relentlessly, he warned his countrymen: "You cannot let men live like pigs . . . We need not wait for the millenium to get rid of the slum. We can do it now." Today, Riis died. The slum lives on.

Riis photo: Bandit's Roost, N.Y.C.

1914

JUNE

Su	Mo	Tu	We	Th	Fr	Sa
	1	2	3	4	5	6
7	8	9	10	11	12	13
14	15	16	17	18	19	20
21	22	23	24	25	26	27
28	29	30				

4. British mine and railway unions join construction strike; two million workers out.

8. Italy: Riots follow as police suppress demonstration against military criminal code.

9. Wilson re-establishes embargo on arms export to Mexico (→ 17).

13. Greece formally announces intent to annex islands of Chios and Mitylene; Greco-Turkish war expected (→ 25).

13. St. Petersburg: Mystic monk Gregory Rasputin, "Richelieu of Russia," stabbed.

15. Holland, Switzerland, Denmark, Sweden form league for defense (→ 7/31).

17. New Haven: Yale Univ. awards honorary degree to Finnish composer Jean Sibelius.

17. Niagara Falls: Mexican delegates reject U.S. proposal at peace talks, offer sharp denunciation of U.S. aims (→ 24).

20. Germany launches Bismarck, largest liner yet built.

21. Collision between dirigible and plane kills nine in Vienna.

22. Hammondsport, N.Y.: Rodman Wanamaker conducts successful test flight of flying boat America.

24. Mexican rebels report capture of Zacatecas with loss of 2,000 men (→ 7/15).

24. New Portuguese Cabinet formed in Lisbon (→ 5/15/15).

25. Serbia's King Peter I transfers power to crown prince (→ 28).

27. Paris: Jack Johnson retains heavyweight title, defeating Frank Moran in 20 rounds.

30. Vienna: Anti-Serbian riots break out; students burn flag at Serbian legation (→ 7/5).

BIRTHS

15. Russian leader Yuri Andropov (†2/9/1984).

17. American author John Hersey, wrote "Hiroshima."

DEATH

21. Austrian writer, anti-war activist Bertha von Suttner, inspired Alfred Nobel to create Peace Prize (*6/9/1843).

First cargo vessel transits the canal

June 7. An enormous American steamer, the Alliance, today became the first of many vessels to pass from the Atlantic Ocean to the Pacific Ocean by way of the Panama Canal. The finished canal is 50 miles long and from 100 to more than 300 yards wide. Ships must pass through three locks to compensate for the changes in elevation.

Ferdinand de Lesseps of France, who built the Suez Canal in Egypt, began work on the Panama Canal in 1879. In 1903, the American government purchased the rights to the canal from a French firm (→ 8/15).

The canal is opening to traffic.

Pre-Biblical story of the Flood found

June 24. A professor at Jesus College, Oxford University, claims to have found a pre-Semitic account of Noah and the fall of man in early Babylonian tablets disinterred at Nippur. He described the account as "the original of that preserved in the book of Genesis."

The tablets came from a library at Nippur and are now in the University of Pennsylvania Museum. The professor copied inscriptions on about 50 of the tablets. One tablet relates the Babylonian version of the Flood which, like the Bible, names a gardener —"nuhu" —who saves the world from disaster during the Flood. The tablets also relate the story of the fall of man: because he ate of the tree of life, he lost eternal life. Contrary to the Biblical version, though, it is Noah, not Adam, who falls in this story.

Heir to Austrian throne assassinated in Sarajevo

The Archduke and his wife just before the assassination.

June 28. Shockwaves were felt all over Europe today as a Serbian nationalist assassinated Archduke Franz Ferdinand, heir to the throne of Austria-Hungary, and his wife, the Duchess of Hohenberg. They were both gunned down in cold blood as their motorcar was passing through the streets of Sarajevo, in Bosnia.

The assassin, identified as Gavrilo Princip, is a 19-year-old Bosnian student. He fired seven shots from his pistol. One bullet struck the duchess in the stomach. Another hit the archduke in the neck. He died almost immediately. The duchess died as she was being rushed to a hospital.

Reports from police indicate Princip has shown no remorse about the shootings. The killer told a judge that he wanted to avenge Serbs for the oppression they have been suffering. There are indications the assassinations are part of a political conspiracy organized in Serbia.

Earlier in the day, there was an unsuccessful attempt on the life of the archduke. He and the duchess were driving to a reception at the town hall in Sarajevo when a bomb was thrown at their car. One eyewitness said, "The bomb did not reach its goal, thanks to the quick reaction and composure of the archduke. He picked it up from the seat of his car and threw it into the street. I could not believe my eyes."

Eight people, including the archduke's aide-de-camp, were injured when the bomb exploded. Police arrested a young man named Gabrinovics. They say he is a Serbian nationalist who works as a typesetter in Herzegovina. He is also said to have shown no remorse.

After the first incident, the procession continued to the town hall, where the archduke declared angrily, "Herr Burgermeister, it is perfectly outrageous. We have come to Sarajevo on a visit and have had a bomb thrown at us." At first, the crowd in the hall did not understand what the archduke was talking about. Later, many of them cheered when they learned that a man had tried to kill him with a bomb.

Franz Ferdinand ignored a warning not to come to Bosnia. A Serbian minister said there was too much ill feeling in the Balkans toward Austria-Hungary. Ironically, the archduke was more inclined than others in the royal family to make compromises in the tense area. He had hoped to give the Slavic people more autonomy and possibly even create a third monarchy in the Balkans.

All over Europe, there seems to be an ominous reaction to the assassinations. A report from the Vatican says Pope Pius, who has been very sick, was praying when he heard the news. He fainted and had to be escorted back to his chambers. Kaiser Wilhelm interrupted a race in the Baltic and rushed back to Berlin. Emperor Franz Joseph and said, "Horrible, horrible. No sorrow is spared me." In London, the Daily Chronicle wrote, "The assassination comes like a clap of thunder to Europe." The Times of London said it shakes the conscience of the world (→ 30).

The Archduke had just visited the victims of a bomb that nearly took his life earlier in the day, when Gavrilo Princip stepped out of the crowd and fired two fatal shots at him and his wife Sophie von Hohenberg.

Princip is immediately apprehended by Serbian police.

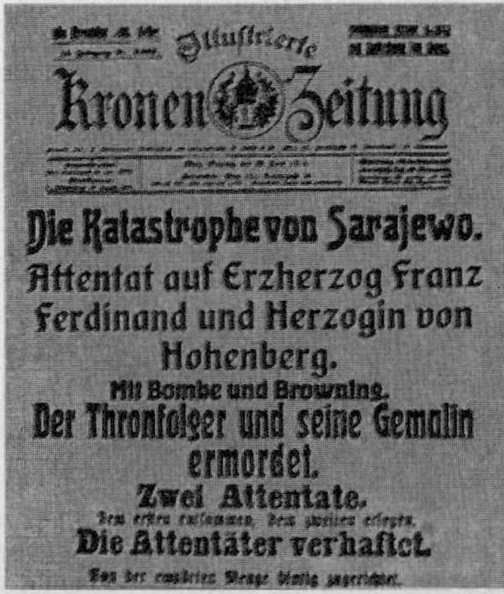

Illustrierte

Kronen Zeitung

Die Katastrophe von Sarajewo.

Attentat auf Erzherzog Franz Ferdinand und Herzogin von Hohenberg.

Mit Bombe und Browning.

Der Thronfolger und seine Gemalin ermordet.

Zwei Attentate.

Die Attentäter verhaftet.

The Vienna paper Kronen-Zeitung read "Castastrophe in Sarajevo."

1914

JULY

Su	Mo	Tu	We	Th	Fr	Sa
			1	2	3	4
5	6	7	8	9	10	11
12	13	14	15	16	17	18
19	20	21	22	23	24	25
26	27	28	29	30	31	

1. Minnesota: Swedish immigrant Carl Eric Wickman opens intercity motor transport, carrying miners from Hibbing to Alice for 15 cents.

3. U.S.: Telephone line installed between New York and San Francisco.

4. N.Y.: Bomb meant for J.D. Rockefeller explodes in assassins' apartment, killing many.

5. Germany: Wilhelm II reasserts alliance with Austria-Hungary (→ 10).

10. French dirigible Fleurus makes reconnaisance flight over German territory (→ 15).

15. Mexican Pres. Huerta quits under U.S. pressure; Francisco Carbajal succeeds (→ 22).

15. French President Raymond Poincare makes state visit to Russia to discuss crisis in Balkans (→ 23).

22. Mexico: Constitutionalists and Carbajal govt. sign accord to halt hostilities (→ 9/15).

22. Strikes severe in Russia; 160,000 out in St. Petersburg.

23. Austria prepares to invade Serbia, sends ultimatum demanding reparations for archduke's assassination (→ 25).

25. Serbia rejects Austrian demands; diplomatic relations broken (→ 25).

25. Russia declares it will act to protect Serbian sovereignty (→ 28).

26. Belgian racer Jean Thys wins Tour de France.

27. British troops invade streets of Dublin to disarm Irish rebels (→ 9/18).

28. Austria-Hungary declares war on Serbia (→ 29).

29. Russia mobilizes 1,200,000 troops (→ 29).

29. Austria bombs Belgrade (→ 31).

31. New York Stock Exchange closes, following lead of Paris, St. Petersburg and South American countries (→ 31).

31. Albert I announces general mobilization despite opposition from Belgian Cabinet.→

European powers spoiling for a fight

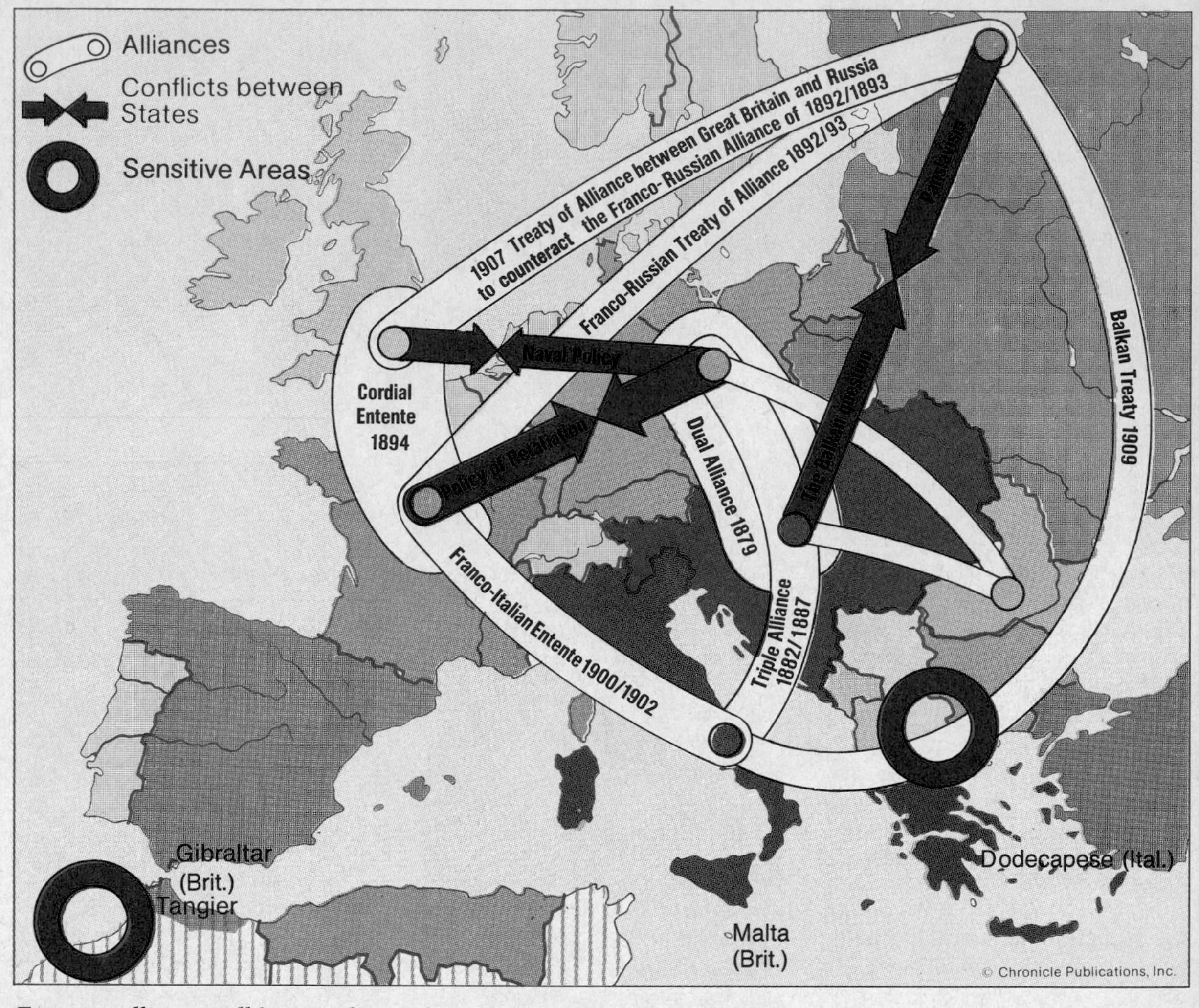

European alliances will be severely tested by the Austro-Serbian conflict.

July 31. When a young Serbian nationalist opened fire in Sarajevo a month ago, the bullets from his pistol may have been the first shots in a European war. The assassination of Archduke Franz Ferdinand and his wife has destroyed what little equilibrium remained in Europe. The continent is a powder keg. Countries are arming themselves with a speed that is ruining their treasuries and alarming the world.

Germany has vaulted to the top of the list of military expenditures. Once it decided to greatly enlarge the size of its army, Germany increased the size of its military budget by 50 percent. It spent 1.4 billion marks last year. This year, the budget jumped to 2.24 billion. And Germany is not alone. Russia is spending 1.8 billion rubles, and England and France are not far behind.

The friendship that used to exist between Russia and Germany has totally dissolved, and the competition between Austria and Russia in the Balkans is making things worse. Both countries want to expand their interests in the area. Russia is concerned that Austria will retaliate for the assassination of the archduke by attacking Serbia and strengthening its position in the Balkans. Czar Nicholas II apparently discussed his concern with French President Poincare last week. Several hours after the meeting, the czar announced his support for Serbia, even though there are indications the assassination of the archduke was planned in Serbia.

Germany is also putting pressure on Austria to demonstrate that it is intractable in the Balkans. Earlier this month, Wilhelm II received a letter from his ambassador to Vienna. The Kaiser wrote in the margin, "It is now or never. We must finish the Serbs off for good." Austria had been vacillating about the use of force in the Balkans, but the assassination and the pressure from Germany have tipped the balance. Last week, Vienna sent an ultimatum to Serbia. Austria demanded that it be allowed to assist Serbian police in their investigation of the murders. Serbia protested, but ultimately agreed.

Germany is apparently concerned that it will be attacked by the Russians in 1916, as soon as they have finished rearming themselves. For that reason, the kaiser and his government may be planning a preemptive attack against Russia. That would create problems for Germany on its western flank also. Russia and France have been allied for more than 20 years, and it is no secret that France would like to recover Alsace and Lorraine from Germany. It is not clear whether Britain would enter the war (→ 8/1).

1914

AUGUST

Su	Mo	Tu	We	Th	Fr	Sa
						1
2	3	4	5	6	7	8
9	10	11	12	13	14	15
16	17	18	19	20	21	22
23	24	25	26	27	28	29
30	31					

1. Germany declares war on Russia; first shots fired.

2. Russia invades Germany; Germany pushes into France, Luxembourg, Switzerland.

3. Germany declares war on France, invades Russia.

3. German cruiser Augsburg bombs Russian Baltic port of Libau in first naval battle.

3. Italy declares neutrality (→ 9).

4. Germany invades Belgium; England declares war on Germany, vows to protect Belgium, French coast (→ 19).

5. U.S. declares neutrality, offers mediation in Europe (→ 6).

6. N.Y.: Cruiser Tennessee sets sail for Europe with gold to aid Americans (→ 9/5).

6. Austria declares war on Russia, Serbia on Germany.

9. Germany, Austria threaten Italy with war if she remains neutral (→ 4/6/15).

9. French invade Alsace (→ 9/24).

12. France, Britain declare war on Austria-Hungary.

15. Panama Canal is formally opened to all traffic (→ 11/17).

16. Belgium: Liege falls to Germans (→ 20).

16. Czar offers autonomy to Poland.

19. British Expeditionary Force (BEF) lands in France (→ 9/10).

20. England issues Order of Council, expanding list of contraband goods to be confiscated at sea (→ 9/26).

20. Belgium: Germans take Brussels (→ 23).

23. Emperor of Japan declares war on Germany (→ 9/3).

23. Belgium: Germans occupy Namur (→ 9/3).

27. Africa: French and British troops occupy German Togo (→ 4/17/16).

DEATHS

6. Mrs. Helen Louise Axson Wilson, president's wife.

20. Giuseppe Sarto, Pope Pius X, fought Modernist trends in Catholicism (*6/2/1835).

War flares up on two European fronts

German infantry take the offensive on the Western Front.

August. War stormed across the European continent this month. The German Chief of General Staff, Count Alfred von Schlieffen, had worked on a military plan for years in the event his government would need sharp, effective tactics in a European war. It consisted of attacking his country's enemies on two fronts. And now, the Schlieffen Plan has been activated.

It was midnight July 31/August 1 when German Ambassador Count Pourtales presented an ultimatum from Kaiser Wilhelm II that if Russia did not cease troop mobilization in four areas near Austrian territory in 12 hours, Germany would order complete mobilization. National temper, already heated from a chaotic summer, reached feverish levels in Russia during those 12 hours. Czar Nicholas refused to budge, and instead, alerted four million men for a possible German attack, for "to do otherwise would be to court disaster." With the time limit expired, the kaiser declared war on Russia, and appealing to cheering German crowds, bellowed: "Let your hearts beat for God and your fists on the enemy." From that moment on, Europe has plummeted into a sea of blood.

Germany, while provoking the Russians, had asked France if it would remain neutral in the Russo-German conflict. France responded that "she would consult her own interests." To prepare for a surprise German offensive, Premier Rene Viviani ordered the mobilization of French forces and in a symbolic political shift, appointed Theophile Delcasse, a bitter adversary of Germany, Minister of War.

Russia, wasting no time after the kaiser's war proclamation, invaded Germany on August 2, seizing control of several rail stations and the town of Eydtkuhnen with little confrontation. Czar Nicholas, aghast at the German provocation, issued a fierce statement promising "the Russians will rise like one man and will repulse the insolent attack of the enemy."

While the first shots of the war occurred on the Eastern Front, when the advancing Russians fired on German troops in Prostken, East Prussia, the first big blow took place in France. Germany crossed French borders on two lines, one incursion in the southwest near Luxembourg and the other near Nancy in the southeast where 20,000 Germans surged across the frontier. The aggression came without formal proclamation of war. So, within hours, Schlieffen's Plan was implemented: two fronts, one in the East and one in the West.

German troops responded to the Russian penetration on the 3rd of August with an invasion of their own, occupying the cities of Czestochowa, Bendzin and Kaliez. Meanwhile, the kaiser's ships bombed the Russian naval port, Libau, in the Baltic, setting it ablaze. However, the first attacks of Germans on Russian soil were basically defensive. Nine German divisions were to hold off 22 Russian divisions in the northwest. The Germans realized from the war of 1870-71 that a 3-1 troop superiority was needed by Russian forces; railway facilities for shifting troops were excellent on the German side while they were poor on the Russian side. The plan was to divert as many Russian soldiers and weaponry away from the Austrian front as possible. Austria, with its hands full and completely engaged in fighting, officially declared war on Russia on the 6th.

At the close of August, 17 million men of eight nations are involved in what we know is a colossal European war, the magnitude of which has never before been witnessed.

Plan of operations in Europe

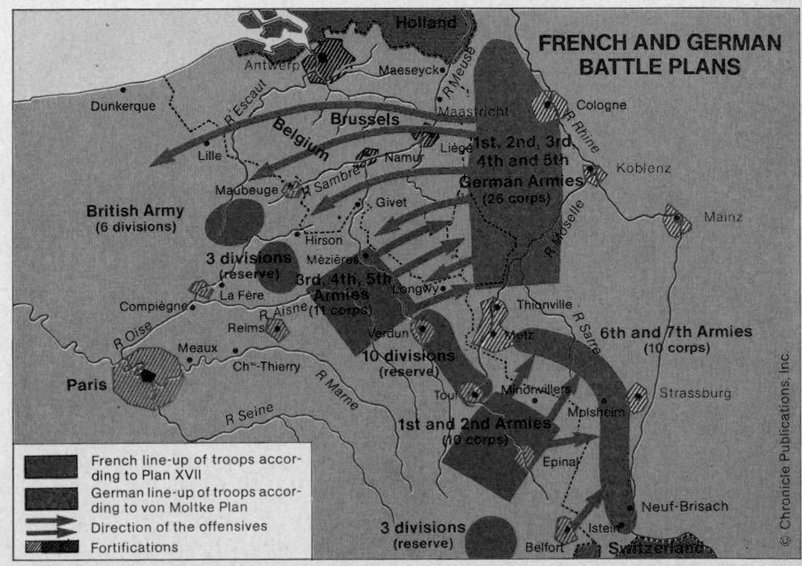

German war plans. Gen. von Moltke has activated the Schlieffen Plan to draw French troops into Alsace-Lorraine and encircle them by sending the bulk of German forces through Belgium around the French left flank. ▷

Germans drive into neutral Belgium and France

August. Western Europe became a battleground this month as Germany invaded Belgium and France, dragging the two nations and eventually Britain, Serbia and Montenegro into a Russo-German clash.

An international treaty of 1839 had established Belgium as a neutral state and the Chancellor, acknowledging that Germany was about to violate the agreement but contending that Belgium would cooperate with France, issued an ultimatum to Belgium: allow German forces access over Belgian soil or there will be war. Belgium refused to comply, and on August 2 Germany followed through with a proclamation of war on Belgium and a subsequent invasion.

Immediately, the Western Allies flew into action. King Albert of Belgium sent a telegram to Britain's King George requesting help. It read: "I make a supreme appeal to the diplomatic intervention of your Majesty's government to safeguard the integrity of Belgium."

Great Britain responded by offering an ultimatum to Germany: respect the neutrality of Belgium or Britain will fight. The Kaiser's government rejected it, doubting that Britain was ready to shed blood over "a scrap of paper," referring to the treaty of 1839. On the 4th, with the House of Commons' allocation of $525 million in war funds, Britain declared war on Germany. Sir Edward Grey addressed Parliament, invoking Belgian and French alliances, saying, "We cannot stand aside with our arms folded."

Meanwhile, France, apparently the victim of German propaganda that claimed French airplanes had bombed Germany, mobilized its troops, fearing a superior German army could run right over her land. On the 2nd, German soldiers did cross the French border without declaring war, some speculate to provoke France into its vaunted Schlieffen Plan, which includes a war on the French front. Little antagonism was needed and now battles rage between the nations.

Belgian forces, with help from Britain and France, fought remarkably well against the German invaders. At Amsterdam on the 6th, Belgian troops killed or wounded 3,500 Germans. Concurrently, intense fighting erupted at the Liege forts near Amsterdam. There, a reported 25,000 Germans of a force of 100,000 died at the hands of 30,000 Belgians. This battle proved once again how devastating war can be; in the aftermath of battle, innocent civilian corpses littered the streets. The German press denied the death toll reached such a total, saying instead that their cavalry engaged in "unique acts of heroism."

The kaiser's government rushed heavy artillery to the front to batter the forts, and after two weeks of warfare Germany forced Belgium's capitulation. The early success of Belgian resistance has waned as German troops are blistering along a 150-mile Belgian line (→ 9/3).

Russian cavalry in Poland.

Determined Belgian troops defend their homeland from the Germans.

German soldiers parade through Brussels, along the walls of Luna Park.

Situation at the end of August

GENERAL ADVANCE OF THE 1ST, 2ND AND THIRD GERMAN ARMIES AUGUST 17TH TO AUGUST 24TH 1914

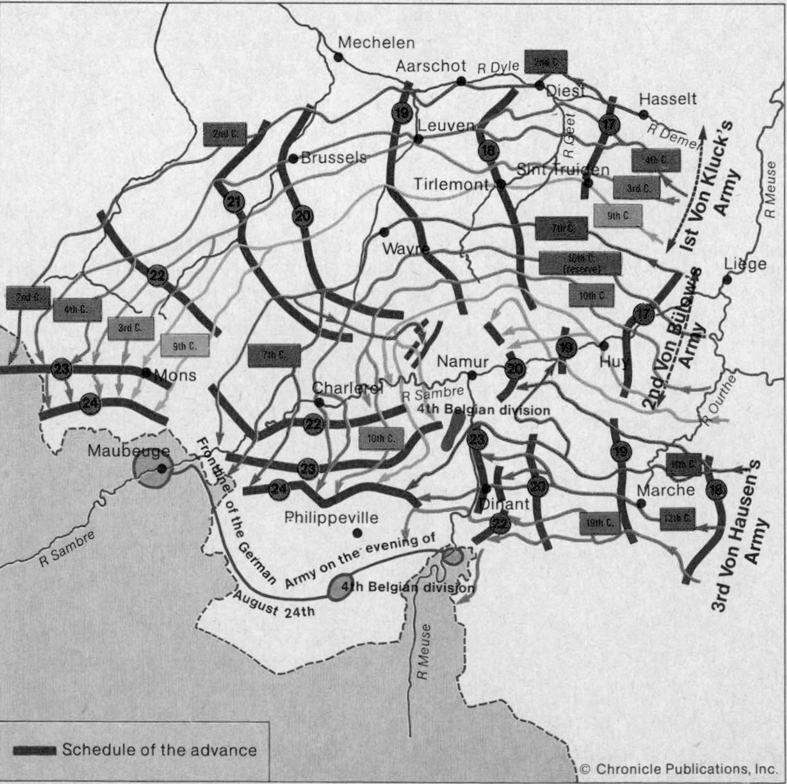

The Western Front at the end of August.

1914

SEPTEMBER

Su	Mo	Tu	We	Th	Fr	Sa
		1	2	3	4	5
6	7	8	9	10	11	12
13	14	15	16	17	18	19
20	21	22	23	24	25	26
27	28	29	30			

2. Ottoman Empire calls for general mobilization (→ 10/29).

3. French capital moves from Paris to Bordeaux (→ 10).

3. Vatican: Giacomo della Chiesa elected Pope Benedict XV.

3. China condemns Germany, Japan, England for violating her neutrality (→ 18).

4. Russians take Lemberg, capital of Galicia (→ 11).

5. Wilson orders Navy to open wireless stations for use by European powers, including Germany (→ 26).

9. Germans under von Francois launch counterattack on Russians in East Prussia (→ 15).

10. France: Six-day battle of the Marne ends; Allies, Germans lose 250,000 each (→ 14).

11. Russians control Galicia after week's fighting; captured 100,000, killed 250,000 (→ 28).

14. Gen. von Falkenhayn replaces von Moltke as German commander on W. Front.→

15. Wilson orders U.S. Army out of Mexico (→ 23).

17. Germany asks U.S. to elicit terms for peace from England, France, Russia.

18. Irish home rule bill becomes law, yet is effectively delayed until end of war (→ 4/28/16).

18. China: Japan begins siege of Tsingtao (→ 11/6).

22. German U-9 sub sinks three British cruisers off Dutch coast; 1,400 dead (→ 10/15).

23. Mexico: Villa declares war on Gen. Carranza (→ 11/2).

24. Alsace-Lorraine: Germans take St. Mihiel (→ 4/6/15).

26. Washington: Federal Trade Commission organized to oversee interstate commerce.

26. U.S. Sec. of State W.J. Bryan protests British naval blockade, upholds policy of supplying all powers (→ 10/22).

28. Hindenburg reinforces Austro-German armies in Poland (→ 10/12).

DEATH

26. August Macke, German Expressionist painter (*1/3/1887).

German advance halted at the Marne

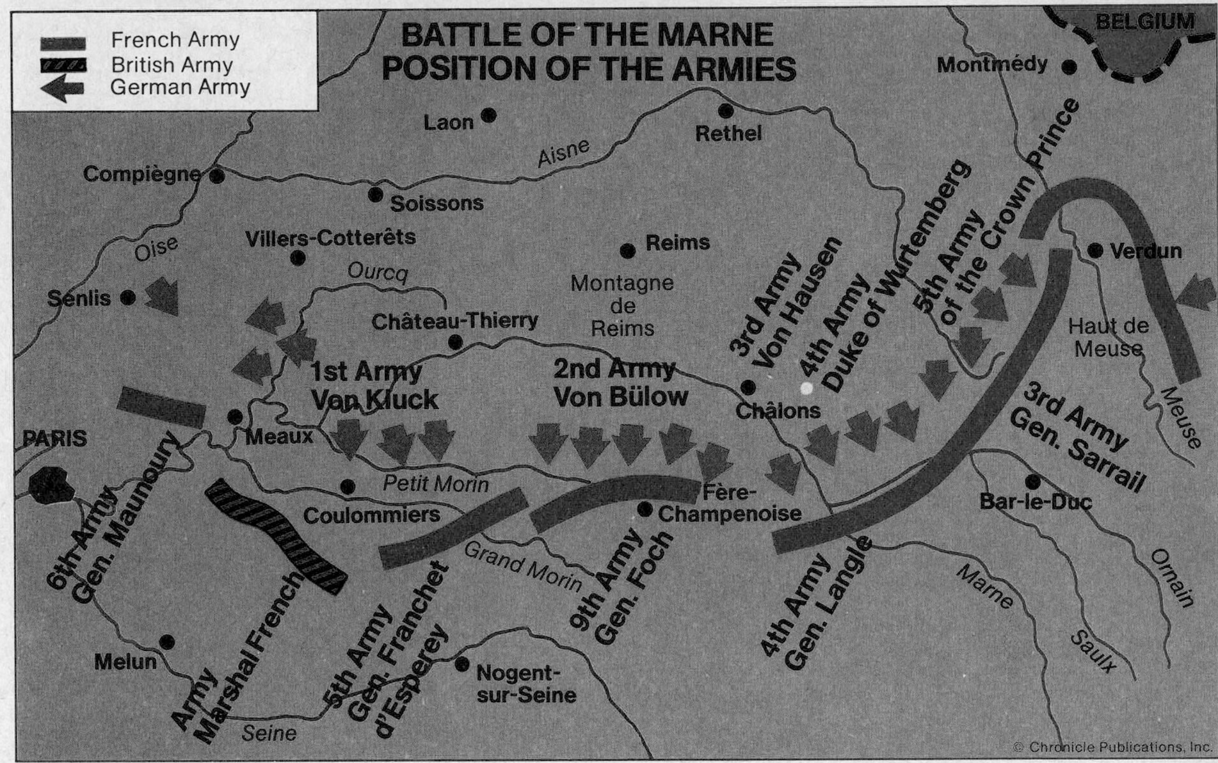

Sept 14. Paris is safe. The Allies can now claim a moral and strategic victory. German troops, who started retreating from the Marne Sept. 8, are fully behind the Noyon-Verdun line. And from Germany comes a report that General Helmuth von Moltke, chief of staff, has been stripped of his duties.

When Germany declared war on France last month, it knew there were a limited number of ways to reach French soil. Von Moltke decided against pressing through the flat open land of Holland; perhaps he thought that route too obvious. Instead, he instructed the armies of Alexander von Kluck and Karl von Bulow to invade Belgium and laboriously ford France's mighty rivers: the Meuse, the Somme, the Aisne and the Vesle. Finally, the two armies reached the Marne. A week ago, some German soldiers spotted the tip of the Eiffel Tower and hooted in triumph.

If any one man can take credit for the complete turn of events, it is General Joseph Joffre. In late August, he devised a plan to march north along the Ourcq River and on Sept. 6 attack the flank of the German right wing. It did not work out exactly as Joffre hoped. Some members of General Maunoury's army stumbled into the path of Kluck's corps Sept. 5, igniting the battle of the Marne then and there. Throughout six days of fighting, Joffre maintained close contact with the front lines. His counterpart, Moltke, did not.

Maunoury's troops were reinforced by the Sixth Army. They waged fierce combat with Kluck's men Sept. 7 and 8. The French faltered; then two regiments of infantry joined the Sixth, rushed to the battlefield in 700 Parisian taxicabs by General Joseph Gallieni. This was the first time troops have been mobilized by motor transport.

Kluck and Bulow failed to reinforce each other. Rumors say Kluck has an obstinate, independent nature and did not care to sacrifice his men for Bulow's. For whatever reason, a 30-mile gap appeared between their two wings. British forces and the French Fifth Army rushed in. Bulow, badly battered, withdrew half his numbers.

Sept. 8 was critical in the battle of the Marne. Ferdinand Foch's Ninth Army, a ragged band of Moroccans, Senegalese, boys and old men, settled east of the Fifth. Germans descended upon them. Foch sent Joffre this message: "Hard pressed on my right. My center is yielding. Impossible to maneuver. Situation is excellent. I attack!" That night, as if Bulow and Kluck had read the dispatch, they retreated behind the Aisne.

In the last three weeks, the Allies have had 250,000 casualties; the Germans only somewhat more. It is a Pyrrhic victory, but a victory nonetheless. One of Moltke's last acts while still at his post was to tell the Kaiser: "Your Majesty, we have lost the war!" (→ 10/9).

Von Bulow's 2nd German Army, pushing south from Belgium, wreaked havoc in Rheims, nearly destroying its famous cathedral.

▷

Hindenburg wins again over Russians

Beleaguered Russian infantry rests in a small Galician village.

Sept 15. Under the leadership of General Paul von Hindenburg and General Erich Wilhelm Ludendorff, German forces defeated the advancing Russian armies for the second time in less than a month at the battle of the Masurian Lakes. Russian losses have been placed at 125,000 men, 150 guns and about half of their transport. The Germans, however, did not escape the bloody battle unscathed as approximately 40,000 men were killed by forces commanded by Russian General Rennenkampf.

Despite a manpower advantage, the Russian troops could not contain the disciplined forces of Hindenburg. Observers on the scene have blamed poor leadership, a lack of effective reconnaissance, secrecy and faulty communications for the blundering Russian defeat.

The victory follows the convincing military success of the Germans at the battle of Tannenberg at the end of August. At this front in East Prussia near the Baltic Sea, the Hindenburg troops prevented the conquest of Konigsberg by trouncing the Second Russian Army led by General A.V. Samsonov. More than 100,000 Russians were killed and over 500 guns were confiscated. Furthermore, the dejected Samsonov, unable to cope with the embarrassing defeat, committed suicide. The German losses totaled between 10,000 and 15,000 men.

While the Tannenberg win strategically strengthened the German forces in this European war, it perhaps has done more to boost German morale. Additionally, Allied confidence in the ability of the Russian armed forces is reported to be dwindling.

It is clear that the leadership and experience of Hindenburg has greatly enhanced the German military. His illustrious career began during the Austro-Prussian War of 1866 and gained prominence in the Franco-Prussian War of 1870-71. He was appointed to the General Staff in 1878 and remained a powerful and influential officier until his retirement in 1911. Then, with the outbreak of war last month, Hindenburg was summoned to head the German troops in their defense of East Prussia, and he immediately appointed Ludendorff army chief of staff (→ 28).

Franz Joseph and the Kaiser; the Austro-German alliance.

1914

OCTOBER

Su	Mo	Tu	We	Th	Fr	Sa
				1	2	3
4	5	6	7	8	9	10
11	12	13	14	15	16	17
18	19	20	21	22	23	24
25	26	27	28	29	30	31

4. First German Zeppelin raids London (→ 12/25).

4. U.S.: Wilson appeals to nation to pray for peace (→ 22).

9. Belgium: Germans take Antwerp after 12-day siege.→

10. Rumanian King Charles I dies; Ferdinand II crowned.

12. Poland: Sixty Russian divisions check Austro-German advance (→ 17).

13. South Africa: Boers under Gen. Christian De Wet rise against martial law imposed by British yesterday (→ 3/12/22).

13. Boston: Boston Braves take World Series 3-1 over Philadelphia in fourth game.

14. Belgian government flees to France (→ 26).

17. Hindenburg withdraws in Poland, destroying countryside in retreat (→ 31).

18. German U-boats raid Scapa Flow; British fleet flees to Scottish coast (→ 27).

22. U.S. withdraws opposition to British naval blockade, placing economic support firmly behind Allies (→ 30).

23. British Indian army troops begin invasion of southern Mesopotamia (→ 11/22).

24. Britain: Westminster Abbey insured for 1.5 mil. pounds sterling.

26. German advance checked at Yser River; 7,000 Belgians facing starvation (→ 12/20).

27. British battleship Audacious hits German mine, sinks off Irish coast (→ 11/1).

30. U.S. announces $10 mil. war loan to France (→ 11/3).

31. Turks defy England, announce annexation of Egypt (→ 11/4).

31. Austro-German armies back to initial line in Poland; Russian advance checked, saving German industrial base in Silesia (→ 11/1).

BIRTHS

6. Norwegian explorer Thor Heyerdahl.

27. British poet Dylan Thomas (†11/9/1953).

Turks forced into war against Allies

Oct 29. The Turkish government, in dramatic fashion, declared war on the Allies by bombarding Odessa, Sevastopol and Theodosia on the Russian Black Sea coast. The pro-German sentiments of Turk Minister of War Enver Pasha and the presence of the German cruisers Goeben and Breslau in the Constantinople port provided impetus for the declaration. The Turkish alignment with the Central Powers will most probably close off the Dardanelles, the main line of communication between Russia and the Allies. German Admiral von Souchon is now commanding the Turkish fleet.

The entrance of Turkey into the war is destined to change the complexion of the Allies' strategy. British First Lord of the Admiralty Winston Churchill wasted no time in urging action against the Turks to restore access to the vital supply route to Russia (→ 31).

War at sea being fiercely fought

German sub surfaces.

Oct 15. The British cruiser Hawke has been torpedoed off the coast of Scotland. It is feared 500 of the crew are drowned. The U-9 submarine, which killed 1,400 when it sank three cruisers off the Holland shore last month, may be responsible for this latest tragedy.

The loss is particularly bitter for the British. Their initial clash with the enemy Aug. 28 was triumphant, sinking three light cruisers and a destroyer without losing a ship. The British are superior in numbers, with 24 dreadnoughts to the Kaiser's 13. They could blockade the North Sea, crippling Germany's overseas commerce. But undersea warfare evens the score (→ 18).

Belgians fight on as Antwerp collapses

Oct 9. Antwerp, a major Belgian port, has fallen after a German onslaught. King Albert is safe in an unrevealed location west of the city. The determined Belgian army is regrouping beyond the Ypres River.

When Germany thundered into the country on Aug. 4, no French forces met it. Belgians resisted fiercely at the Liege and Namur fortifications. King Albert commanded them to "hold to the end." When the last fort fell three weeks ago, British First Lord of the Admiralty Winston Churchill sent three brigades of marines. (Churchill himself was called home.) It was brave but doomed. Germans seized the coastal city after leaving thousands dead, including 5,000 civilians.

The Belgian army still has a card to play. If the Germans pursue, it can open locks on the sea embankments. Battlefields would flood, drowning the enemy (→ 14).

Belgian riflemen guard Antwerp.

Clayton Act gives labor new rights

Oct 15. A bill granting organized labor the right to strike and picket was enacted into law by the United States Congress today, reflecting the changing mood of the times. To be known as the Clayton Act, the new bill of rights for labor is aimed at exempting unions from antitrust prosecution. The new law also will restrict the powers of the courts to grant injunctions in labor disputes.

Samuel Gompers, President of the American Federation of Labor, hailed passage of the Clayton Act, saying it is the Magna Carta for the working man, recognizing that "the labor of a human being is not a commodity or article of commerce."

1914

NOVEMBER

Su	Mo	Tu	We	Th	Fr	Sa
1	2	3	4	5	6	7
8	9	10	11	12	13	14
15	16	17	18	19	20	21
22	23	24	25	26	27	28
29	30					

1. Hindenburg becomes Commander-in-Chief of Eastern Front (→ 11).

1. Chile: German Adm. Spee sinks two British cruisers in Battle of Colonel (→ 2).

2. Mexican Gen. Eulalie Gutierrez elected provisional president (→ 23).

2. Great Britain orders North Sea closed to traffic (→ 9).

3. Rockefeller Foundation launches liner Massapequa to carry food to Belgium (→ 1/28/15).

4. Turkey breaks diplomatic relations with England, Russia, France and Serbia (→ 5).

5. Britain, France, Russia declare war on Turkey; Britain annexes Cyprus (→ 12/18).

5. Austrians begin major offensive in Serbia (→ 20).

6. China: Tsingtao surrenders to Japanese (→ 5/9/15).

6. 433,241 prisoners reported in German war camps; British admit loss of morale (→ 12/24).

9. Australian cruiser Sydney sinks German cruiser Emden near Sumatra (→ 11).

11. Poland: German 9th strikes Russians at Lodz (→ 16).

13. German government asks citizens to exchange gold for paper money.

16. Poland: Germans win big battle near Lodz, take 23,000 Russian prisoners (→ 25).

17. President Wilson asserts Panama Canal's neutrality.

20. Bulgaria proclaims neutrality (→ 12/2).

22. Mesopotamia: Indian troops take Basra (→ 12/9).

23. Mexico: U.S. ends seven-month occupation of Vera Cruz (→ 1/9/15).

25. Poland: Hindenburg calls off Lodz offensive 40 miles from Warsaw; Russians lose 90,000 to Germans' 35,000 in 2 weeks' fighting (→ 30).

28. Philadelphia: Army shuts out Navy 20-0.

BIRTH

25. Baseball star Joe DiMaggio.

Hindenburg takes over on Eastern Front

Nov 30. General Paul von Hindenburg was appointed Commander-in-Chief of the Austro-German forces on the Eastern Front at the start of this month, which saw crucial developments in a long battle in Poland. The appointment honored the man who has dedicated his life to the German military and in early fall thwarted Russian advances in East Prussia.

Comm.-in-Chief von Hindenburg.

At the Battle of Lodz in Poland, Germany mounted an all-out attack on a Russian offensive in a battle array involving a combined total of seven million soldiers. The German Ninth Army, now commanded by General August von Mackensen, first hit between the First and Second Russian Armies, which were stationed on the northern frontier as part of the Grand Duke Nicholas' offensive strategy. With a gap wide open in the southeast, Mackensen surged through, pummelling the Russian First Army led by General Rennekampf. However, as the XXV Reserve Corps of Germany, orchestrated by General Reinhard von Scheffer-Boyadel, attempted to steer between the Russian forces and sandwich the enemy with Mackensen's men, the grand duke's fighters hardened. Scheffer's offensive backfired as his troops, not the Russians, were surrounded.

Just as it appeared the German Reserve Corps was to suffer annihilation, an unexpected reversal took place: Scheffer led his men out of trouble and even captured 16,000 prisoners and 64 valuable guns. Through nine bitterly cold November days, his men marched relentlessly. Yet they did suffer 1,500 killed and 2,800 wounded.

With the luxury of a week to analyze the Lodz battle, it can be said that while the Russians may have tactically won, the Germans forced the retirement of the Russian offensive. It was indeed bloody, as total German losses accumulated to 35,000, and 90,000 Russians died.

The virtual stalemate would have been impossible had October's Ninth Army drive, led by Hindenburg, not crossed the line, ravaging Russian troops before being pushed back. The advance and subsequent retreat delayed the projected Russian offensive (→ 1/31/15).

British soldiers, entrenched on the Western Front, search for German snipers. Deep gashes in the French countryside mark a new kind of war in which one-mile forays into enemy lines may be considered big gains.

1914

DECEMBER

Su	Mo	Tu	We	Th	Fr	Sa
		1	2	3	4	5
6	7	8	9	10	11	12
13	14	15	16	17	18	19
20	21	22	23	24	25	26
27	28	29	30	31		

2. Serbia: Austrian troops occupy Belgrade (→ 15).

8. New York: Irving Berlin's "Watch Your Step" opens at New Amsterdam Theater.

8. Adm. von Spee's fleet destroyed by British Adm. Sturdee at Falkland Islands; German naval hopes reduced to sub-warfare (→ 1/1/15).

9. N.J.: Edison manufacturing plant in West Orange burns.

9. Mesopotamia: Turks stop British offensive, occupy Akaba (→ 4/14/15).

15. Serbs retake Belgrade; Austrians have lost 227,000, Serbs 170,000 in five months of fighting (→ 2/14/15).

18. Britain declares Egypt a protectorate, moves to defend Suez Canal (→ 2/2/15).

20. French government returns to Paris (→ 24).

21. German Socialists issue manifesto justifying participation in govt., yet refuse to vote war funds (→ 3/28/15).

23. French elections postponed by National Assembly.

24. 577,875 Allied soldiers to spend Christmas as prisoners in Germany (→ 3/16/15).

29. Belgian newspapers halted to protest German censorship.

31. France: Allies end ten-day attack on German trenches; casualties number one mil., each side after five months of war.→

CULTURAL EVENTS, 1914

Literature: Conrad's "Chance"; James Joyce's "Dubliners"; Joyce Kilmer's "Trees"; Dreiser's "The Titan"; E.R. Burroughs' "Tarzan of the Apes"; Booth Tarkington's "Penrod"; Henry James' "The Golden Bowl."

Academia: Bertand Russell's "Our Knowledge of the External World."

Music: Prokofiev's "Scythian Suite"; Vaughan Williams' "London Symphony."

Film: Mack Sennet's "Making a Living," with Charlie Chaplin; British "The World, The Flesh and the Devil," first full-length color film.

Aussies hunt down and sink raider

The war at sea.

Nov 11. The Australian navy tasted what must be considered sweet revenge when its cruiser, the Sydney, shelled and sank Germany's light cruiser, the Emden, off the Cocos Islands 500 miles south of Sumatra. The Emden had been engaged in raiding commerce throughout the Indian Ocean; in its last raid, two months of supplies were seized from the Cocos' inhabitants, infuriating the Australians.

Two hundred German sailors perished and 30 more were wounded in the sea battle that lasted only few hours. The Sydney's crew captured the Emden's Captain von Muller and Prince Franz Joseph of Hohenzollern. No casualties were reported aboard the Sydney and she received little damage. The Emden was responsible for the bombing of Madras in late September and Penang a month later (→ 12/8).

Army caps season with win over Navy

Nov 28. With all of Europe transformed into a battlefield, America's armed forces are still in training on the playing fields. Army blanked Navy 20-0 today at Franklin Field in Philadelphia. Also this season, the cadets avenged last year's loss to little-known Notre Dame. Quarterback Gus Dorais and end Knute Rockne had baffled Army, scoring five touchdowns on unheard-of forward passes, but the schooled Army defense was ready this year, shutting the Irish down to seven points.

Also of note this year was Missouri Mines, led by running back John Imlay. Scoring a phenomenal 30 touchdowns, Imlay drove his team to outscore opponents 540-0 in eight games, bringing to mind the 1900 classic in which Dickinson smothered Haverford 227-0.

Aerial combat: A new form of warfare

A new form of warfare.

Dec 25. British residents of Southend-on-the-Sea settled down to their Christmas dinners when the sudden hum of airplanes brought them into the streets, gawking. Thousands looked skyward to see two German airplanes, which had flown up the Thames River, being chased by two British aircraft. Guns rattled, but no planes were downed. The British aviators were successful, though, in warding off the potentially dangerous German fliers in an air battle 9,000 feet above ground at the amazing speed of 70 miles per hour.

In response to the threat, Londoners were ordered to dim their lights this evening to hinder German aviators' visibilty in the event of a return visit (→ 1/19/15).

Casualties mount in ever-widening war

Dec 31. As we close the book on this blood-stained year, we take in the enormity of the death, destruction and horror of war. It all began in the dog days of August as a fairly regional conflict between Russia, Germany and Austria, but has escalated into a worldwide war, killing and terrorizing millions.

The death toll mounts, boggling the mind and emotions. The figures trickle in daily for each battle or each branch of a particular nation's armed services. For instance, at the end of last month, Great Britain released these casualty figures for her royal navy: 4,327 dead, 473 wounded, 968 missing and 1,573 captured. Serbia has estimated 170,000 of its citizens have perished in five months of war, while Austria reports 227,000 have died. The figures are hard to confirm, but most sources indicate each side has lost a staggering one million. It is also estimated that over 577,000 Allied soldiers are now held captive.

Germany initially thought her well-trained troops would quickly sweep aside enemy defenders, but the tenacity of the Allies has proven her wrong. With the war expanding to include the Far East, the Middle East, the South Pacific and Africa, we must ask: How much longer must we endure this madness?

The first full-length comedy feature. When Chaplin started with Keystone a year ago, he took second billing to Miss Normand; only three months later, he was writing and directing his own films.

1915

JANUARY

Su	Mo	Tu	We	Th	Fr	Sa
					1	2
3	4	5	6	7	8	9
10	11	12	13	14	15	16
17	18	19	20	21	22	23
24	25	26	27	28	29	30
31						

1. Pasadena: Washington State defeats Brown 14-0 in first Rose Bowl since 1902.

1. German sub U-24 sinks British liner Formidable off coast of Plymouth (→ 28).

3. Caucasus: Turk Enver's army decimated by Russians, desertion and extreme cold at Battle of Sarikamis (→ 4/20).

8. France: Germans counter French offensive at La Basse Canal (→ 14).

9. Mexico: Pancho Villa signs treaty with U.S. Gen. Scott, halting border conflict (→ 18).

9. Haiti: Rebellion forces Pres. Theodore out of office (→ 7/29).

12. Washington: House defeats woman suffrage amendment (→ 10/19).

12. U.S. Congress establishes Rocky Mountain Natl. Park.

13. Austro-Hungarian Minister of Foreign Affairs Leopold Berchtold resigns.

14. French abandon five miles of trenches to Germans near Soissons (→ 17).

18. Mexico: Gutierrez reported heading new revolt, denounces Villa as dictator (→ 3/12).

19. First German air raids on Great Britain inflict minor casualties.

25. A.G. Bell in N.Y., Thomas Watson in San Francisco make record telephone transmission.

28. U.S. Coast Guard founded to fight contraband trade and aid distressed at sea.

28. German navy attacks U.S. freighter William P. Frye, loaded with wheat for Britain (→ 31).

31. Eastern Front: German Ninth uses poison gas on Russians at Bolimov (→ 31).

31. German U-boats sink two British steamers in English Channel (→ 2/4).

31. Petrograd (formerly St. Petersburg): It is reported that Czar Nicholas II proposed arbitration at The Hague three days before kaiser declared war.

DEATH

23. American sculptor Anne Whitney (*9/2/1821).

British sink German battleship Blucher

The mammoth Blucher succumbs to British guns at Doggerbank.

Jan 24. British battle cruisers have sunk the German armored cruiser Blucher and seriously damaged two other German warships. The German squadron, attempting to repeat last year's bombardment of the coastal towns of Scarborough and Hartlepool, was sighted early this morning, and five British battle cruisers under the command of Vice Admiral Sir David Beatty opened fire at 9:30 a.m.

The Germans withdrew to the east. In a running fight, the Blucher came under the fire of the Lion's 13.5-inch guns. The German ship fell out of line, capsized and sank. The German Admiralty reports the Dorflinger, Seydlitz and Moltke, althouqh seriously damaged, continued their flight and reached the protection of German minefields and submarine squadrons.

British losses were light; there were 11 wounded in the Lion's crew. The British victory avenges the loss on January 1 of the battleship Formidable, sunk in the English Channel by torpedo or submarine. Only 150 of her crew of 750 were rescued.

Russian army of 800,000 heads for Prussia

Jan 31. The newly organized Russian army, 800,000 strong, is headed for Prussia to launch a new offensive. In August 1914, when the Russian forces lost their first battle with Germany, the Russians had outnumbered their opponents 2-1, but the offensive failed. It has since been disclosed that three days before war broke out, the Russian Czar had proposed arbitration at The Hague (→ 2/7).

Winter on the Eastern Front is taking its toll on the Russian army.

Cardinal Mercier detained in Belgium

Jan 4. Cardinal Mercier was detained by the Germans in his Malines Palace today because of the publication of his pastoral letter, entitled "Patriotism and Endurance." In this letter, Cardinal Mercier condemned the war in Europe and charged the Germans with breaking their oath because they disregarded Belgian neutrality.

An official report made to Pope Pius X states that the Germans destroyed 15,000 copies of the pastoral letter in Malines, subjected Cardinal Mercier to interrogations and demanded of him a retraction, which he refused to make. His arrest caused a protest by the pope and throughout the whole Roman Catholic world.

Earthquake kills thousands in Italy

Jan 13. An earthquake throughout central Italy has killed 29,500 people. The tremors were felt most severely in the province of Abruzzi, in the neighborhoods of Rome and around Naples. In Abruzzi, 17 villages were entirely destroyed. In Rome, there are no injuries reported yet, but after the earthquake, panic seized the inhabitants, who rushed into streets and sought refuge in the churches. The police ordered them out of the churches, which are in danger of collapsing. Many ancient buildings are already badly damaged. The shock, which lasted for several seconds, was one of the strongest ever felt.

German guns badly damage Soissons

January 17. The Germans, after driving back French troops, have now shelled Soissons, damaging the cathedral district and killing many people. Authorities in Soissons, who gave an order to evacuate the city, have settled in Chateau-Thierry. According to observers, the battles in the Soissons region have resulted in the greatest success for German troops, in France for three months now (→ 2/12).

1915

FEBRUARY

Su	Mo	Tu	We	Th	Fr	Sa
	1	2	3	4	5	6
7	8	9	10	11	12	13
14	15	16	17	18	19	20
21	22	23	24	25	26	27
28						

2. Egypt: Turk Djemal Pasha attacks British at Suez Canal, loses 2,000 but holds British reinforcements from Gallipoli (→ 19).

4. Germans decree British waters part of war zone; all ships to be sunk without warning (→ 10).

7. Eastern Front: Hindenburg moves on Russian 10th at Masurian Lakes (→ 10).

8. D.W. Griffith's "The Birth of a Nation" opens in L.A.'s Clune's Auditorium for exorbitant price of $2 (→ 3/3).

10. Wilson blasts British for using U.S. flag on merchant ships to deceive Germans, warns kaiser he will hold Germany "to a strict accountability" for U.S. lives and property endangered (→ 14).

10. Eastern Front: Germans encircle Russians near Nieman River, capture 100,000 (→ 21).

14. Berlin: Kaiser invites U.S. Ambassador Gerard to confer on war (→ 21).

14. Balkans: Serbian troops retreat under Albanian invasion (→ 6/11).

17. Poland: Austrian 10th takes 60,000 Russian prisoners in Galicia, yet fails to relieve Premysl (→ 3/22).

18. Luxembourg starving, appeals for Allied aid.

20. San Francisco: Wilson opens Panama-Pacific Expo., celebrating Panama Canal.

21. Eastern Front: 2nd Battle of Masurian Lakes ends; 200,000 Russians dead, 90,000 captured in 2 weeks (→ 3/9).

21. German mine destroys American steamer Evelyn; crew saved (→ 23).

23. France: Sarah Bernhardt has right leg amputated in Bordeaux.

26. Turkey: Allies renew naval bombardment of Dardanelles Straits (→ 3/4).

DEATH

15. American publisher Simon Brentano.

Germans order total sub warfare

Feb 23. The sinking of the American ships Carib and Evelyn off the German coast and the torpedoing of the Norwegian ship Regin have escalated the level of German attacks on neutral shipping in the waters around the British Isles.

This was foreshadowed by the German proclamation of February 2 declaring the waters around Great Britain and Ireland a war zone after February 18. Berlin announced that every enemy merchant ship in the zone will be destroyed and that it would be impossible to avert danger to crews and passengers. The Germans also said that attacks meant for enemy ships could endanger neutral vessels. The German government claimed that the order was necessary because the British Admiralty had ordered British merchantmen to fly the flags of neutral nations.

Earlier, Britain had ordered that cargoes of grain and flour seized by ships of the royal navy should be treated as contraband and held to prevent their reaching Germany. And in a diplomatic note, the United States had warned Germany against attacks on American vessels in the war zone.

The Germans disclaimed all responsibility for what might happen to neutral vessels and warned that

The key to German naval success.

mines would be laid in the waters around Britain and Ireland. Berlin called the step "solely a measure of self-defense" against the British naval blockade. Frederic C. Coudert, a New York lawyer, called it "a stroke of barbarism" (→ 3/1).

British fleet bombards Gallipoli forts

Feb 19. British and French battleships have opened a heavy bombardment of the Turkish forts on the Gallipoli Peninsula which guards entry to the Sea of Mamora and access to Constantinople.

The eventual seizure of the Turkish capital is the Allied objective. Winston Churchill, the First Lord of the Admiralty, and other Cabinet members believe that an offensive in this sector will force the Germans to ease pressure on Russian forces defending the Caucasus front.

The Russians, although they have twice asked for Allied intervention in this area, are suspicious of any Allied operations aimed at Constantinople. They regard that city as one of their military objectives.

Allied shelling was effective. Almost all the advanced forts on the peninsula were severely damaged and Turkish artillerymen withdrew. The Turkish guns, the royal navy reported, were outranged. The British ships' fire was directed by spotters in navy aircraft. The heavy guns of the Queen Elizabeth were said to have done great damage.

Royal navy trawlers report they have swept all the mines laid by the Turks under German direction. There are reports that a Turkish steamer has laid a new line of mines outside the original fields. British marines landed on the tip of the peninsula to destroy the guns remaining in the forts after the Turkish artillerymen withdrew (→ 26).

The H.M.S. Cornwallis answers Turkish guns at Gallipoli.

French launch Champagne attack

French defend against air attack.

Feb 12. A massive French offensive in Champagne has taken 20,000 unwounded Germans prisoners on its first day. At the same time, the British attacked on a five-mile front on both sides of the La Bassee canal to the north and pushed to within 12 miles of Lille.

The French attack was preceded by a very heavy artillery bombardment. The attacking infantry captured 20 miles of trenches and in some sectors penetrated to a depth of two and one-half miles.

This was the first heavy attack on the Germans in this sector since they fortified their positions after their defeat on the Marne last year.

French troops also retook the town of Souchez and miles of German trenches in the Arras sector. Meanwhile, the British on the French left captured 2,600 Germans and nine field guns. The official German communique tonight admitted reverses (→ 3/10).

1915

MARCH

Su	Mo	Tu	We	Th	Fr	Sa
	1	2	3	4	5	6
7	8	9	10	11	12	13
14	15	16	17	18	19	20
21	22	23	24	25	26	27
28	29	30	31			

1. Allies announce aim to cut off all German supplies, assure safety of neutrals (→ 10).

1. First British, all-woman battalion formed (→ 7/17).

4. Backed by France and Britain, Russia claims rights to Dardanelles, Istanbul (→ 18).

9. Eastern Front: Germans take Grodno (→ 22).

10. Rhode Island: German cruiser takes refuge at Newport News with 342 rescued from Allied ships (→ 30).

10. France: British attack at Neuve Chapelle (→ 13).

12. Mexico: Zapata troops kill American John McManus (→ 6/25).

13. France: Germans repel British Expeditionary Force, re-establish line (→ 20).

14. British navy sinks German battleship Dresden off Chilean coast (→ 12/31).

16. Germans reported forcing prisoners of war to work ten hours a day in mines (→ 9/23/16).

18. Six British battleships lost in Dardanelles minefields; naval assault halted (→ 4/25).

20. Western Front: French call off Champagne offensive (→ 4/6).

21. German Reichstag votes nine mil. marks for war effort.

22. German zeppelin makes night raid on Paris railway stations (→ 6/1).

22. Poland: Russians take Premysl after 194-day siege, resume advance through Carpathian Mountains (→ 4/25).

28. Switzerland: Intl. Socialist Women's Conference in Bern issues peace proposal (→ 5/28).

30. U.S. protests English blockade as interference with legitimate trade (→ 4/4).

BIRTH

17. American singer Nat King Cole (†2/15/1965).

DEATH

21. American engineer Frederick W. Taylor, scientific management (*3/20/1856).

"Birth of a Nation" shown in New York

March 3. D.W. Griffith's "Birth of a Nation" opened today amid controversy. The motion picture is a very long (three-hour) account of the Civil War and Reconstruction. It took a year to make and used countless costumed extras in elaborate battle scenes. Yet this epic is marred by an apparent condonation of racism. All Negroes in the film are foolish, evil or both.

Griffith uses all the current cinematic techniques to effectively tell the story of a white Southern family searching for dignity within turmoil. Lillian Gish plays a family member threatened by a Negro. Her honor is avenged by the Ku Klux Klan, who race to her rescue like knights in shining armor.

D.W. Griffith directs.

Negroes and white liberals plan to protest the film. A boycott is likely; but it could backfire. Even if the film proves to be popular, the ticket price, two dollars, is not.

Witte, progressive in Russia, is dead

March 13. Count Sergius Julievitch Witte is dead in Petrograd after an attack of influenza. After holding the post of Finance Minister, Count Witte became Russia's first constitutional Prime Minister. He promoted the industrialization of the country and reformed the fiscal system. He also succeeded in promoting the construction of the Trans-Siberian Railway, which was finally completed in 1904.

1915

APRIL

Su	Mo	Tu	We	Th	Fr	Sa
				1	2	3
4	5	6	7	8	9	10
11	12	13	14	15	16	17
18	19	20	21	22	23	24
25	26	27	28	29	30	

4. Germany protests British naval blockade, insists U.S. assert neutrality (→ 20).

6. Italy demands Tyrol, Trieste and Istria from Austria in exchange for neutrality (→ 26).

6. Alsace-Lorraine: French attack on Woevre in attempt to retake St. Mihiel (→ 15).

14. Mesopotamia: British troops under Gen. Sir John Nixon repulse Turkish attack at Qurna (→ 24).

15. Austria sets maximum age for military recruiting at 50.

15. Alsace-Lorraine: French conclude assault on St. Mihiel after heavy losses (→ 25).

20. New York: Wilson urges strict neutrality in speech at Waldorf Hotel (→ 5/2).

20. British Treasury Minister David Lloyd George demands austerity measures (→ 5/4).

20. Caucasus: Armenians, persecuted by Turks for allegedly aiding Russians, revolt, seizing fortress of Van (→ 7/16).

24. Mesopotamia: Turks fail in assault on British defenses at Ahwaz (→ 6/3).

25. Austro-German south army checks Russian advance in Carpathian Mts. (→ 5/2).

25. Dardanelles: Allies land at Gallipoli, move on Chunuk Bair heights and Achi Baba hills (→ 30).

26. London: In secret negotiations, Allies grant territory to Italy if she will go to war with Austria (→ 5/3).

30. German gun strikes British coast from Belgian front; Dunkirk in panic.

30. Wilson names 9,481 acres in Teapot Dome, Wy., for Naval Oil Reserves (→ 5/31/21).

BIRTH

7. Blues singer Billie Holiday (†7/17/1959).

DEATHS

16. American Nelson Aldrich, conservative politician (*11/5/1841).

27. Russian composer Aleksandr Scriabin (*11/6/1871).

Jess Willard takes title from Johnson

Johnson takes the count in Havana.

April 5. The search for the "Great White Hope" has ended in a Havana ring. Jack Johnson, the first Negro to hold the world heavyweight championship, was knocked out in the 26th round by Jess Willard, a 250-pound, white behemoth.

Thus also has ended a turbulent chapter of boxing history. The fight was held in Havana because of Johnson's problems with the law in America. While awaiting appeal of his jail sentence for transporting a woman across state lines for immoral purposes, Johnson jumped bail and left the country.

After fighting in exile in Paris, South America and Cuba, Johnson agreed to fight the so-called Pottawatomie Giant in Havana. It was felt that the moving-picture rights, worth a half-million dollars, would make up for any shortage of a live gate. Johnson won the title in 1908 with a 14-round knockout of Tommy Burns in Sydney, Australia. His victory touched off race riots throughout the United States in which at least a half-dozen Negroes died.

Chaplin's "The Tramp," his best film yet, opened this month.

British troops go ashore at Gallipoli

British imperial troops defend a hard-earned plateau.

April 30. Despite stubborn resistance from Turkish defenders, British troops have fought their way ashore at six positions on the Gallipoli Peninsula. And on the Asian side of the Dardanelles Strait, French troops have driven the Turkish troops from strategic positions on Cape Kum Kale.

Both landings were covered by the fire of the Allied fleet. The long-range guns of the British battleship Queen Elizabeth, aided by air spotting, sunk a Turkish troop ship off Maldos. By nightfall on the 28th, the British had halted at Krithia on the peninsula's main road, while troops from Australian and New Zealand were dug in on the peninsula's west (→ 7/6).

Germans use poison gas on Western Front

April 25. The German High Command has admitted that chlorine gas bombs and shells were used in the attack on the French front at Ypres three days ago.

The effect of the gas attack was to open a four-mile gap in the Allied line. The Canadian troops on one flank held against German attacks, and British and Indian forces filled the breach. Fortunately for the Allies, the Germans had no reserve forces available to push into the breach. No tactical advantage was won by this first use of the new weapon. The Germans promise, however, that "more effective substances can be expected." Meanwhile, they are condemned for the use of this novel weapon (→ 5/9).

John Singer Sargent's depiction of the victims of poison gas.

1915

MAY

Su	Mo	Tu	We	Th	Fr	Sa
						1
2	3	4	5	6	7	8
9	10	11	12	13	14	15
16	17	18	19	20	21	22
23	24	25	26	27	28	29
30	31					

1. Gen. Botha routs Germans in Southwest Africa (→ 13).

2. Eastern Front: Austro-German armies, reinforced by troops from W. Front, begin major assault on Russian 3rd Army in South (→ 8).

2. Germans sink U.S. merchant ship Gulflight in most serious affront yet (→ 7).

3. Italy quits Triple Alliance (→ 20).

4. Britain estimates cost of war's first eight months at $3.95 billion.

7. German U-20 sub torpedoes Cunard liner Lusitania; 1,198 dead, 124 Americans (→ 10).

8. Eastern Front: Austro-Germans take Libau (→ 6/3).

10. Wilson tells Philadelphia, "A nation may be so right that it does not need to fight" (→ 12).

13. U.S. Sec. of State Bryan demands German reparations in Lusitania incident (→ 29).

15. Portugese navy revolts, shells Lisbon (→ 16).

16. Portuguese Council Pres. Pinheiro Chagas killed (→ 29).

20. Italian Cabinet receives full war powers (→ 23).

23. British Cabinet reshuffled; Lloyd George is Minister of War, Balfour replaces Winston Churchill at Admiralty.

25. Western Front: British 2nd halts German advance along Ypres; in one month, Germans lose 35,000, British 60,000, French 10,000 (→ 6/21).

28. Berlin: Women demonstrate for peace (→ 6/26).

29. Portugal: Pres. Arriaga resigns, Teofilo Braga succeeds.

29. Germany replies to U.S. Lusitania note, makes no promise to curb subs (→ 6/6).

31. Ralph DePalma wins 5th annual Indianapolis 500 at 89.8 mph in a Mercedes.

BIRTHS

6. American film director Orson Welles (†10/10/1985).

20. Israeli military leader Moshe Dayan (†10/16/1981).

Japanese demand rights from China

May 9. China finds herself caught in a sticky web spun by the Japanese as leaders of Japan have threatened new aggression if the mainland does not agree to meet certain demands. Some 21 economic conditions set by the Japanese legation, including extensive mining and fishing rights, and other territorial privileges, have set the Orient into a panic as both nations prepare for the worst: war.

Western correspondents have learned that the Japanese have issued an ultimatum to Chinese leader Yuan Shih-kai that grants a delay of 48 hours for his acquiescence to the demands before Japan attacks Yuan's army. China has appealed to America to avert such Japanese aggression and "play the Good Samaritan," according to a Chinese communique. However, the United States has indicated that it intends to remain neutral in the conflict. Japan has reported that she desires to stay out of war, but if her "national integrity" is bruised she "must follow the path the situation justifies."

German colony lost to Allies in Africa

May 13. Union of South Africa troops led by General Louis Botha captured Windhoek, the capital of German Southwest Africa, yesterday. The city, populated by 3,000 Europeans and 12,000 natives, did not mount any resistance. Martial law is now in effect throughout German Southwest Africa. And the German women and children still in the capital will be put in the care of Botha's troops.

General Botha, in a victory address, characterized the capture of Windhoek as being of the "utmost importance to the Empire and the Union of South Africa, as it means practically complete possession of German Southwest Africa." The quick capture of Windhoek was not a surprise. Union of South Africa forces had occupied Keetsmanskop in mid-April, which allowed them to control rail lines leading to the capital. The retreating German troops poisoned wells, a violation of The Hague convention (→ 6/11).

Lusitania sunk; 124 Americans lost

May 12. President Wilson has protested vigorously to the German government over the sinking of the British liner Lusitania with the loss of at least 124 American lives.

Wilson's note will be delivered to the German Foreign Ministry by Ambassador Gerard tomorrow. It accuses Germany of acts indefensible under international law.

"In the name of humanity and international law," the note says, "the United States demands a guarantee that these rights (the rights of neutrals to travel on neutral or belligerent vessels) shall be respected and that there be no repetition of attacks on merchantmen carrying non-combatants."

The Lusitania, minutes after being crippled by German torpedoes.

The Cunard Line's Lusitania was sunk on May 8 by two torpedoes from a German submarine. She was nearing Liverpool, England, after a passage from New York and carried 1,251 passengers and 650 crew.

One torpedo struck forward, the other aft in the engine room. The Lusitania was then ten miles off the Old Head of Kinsale in Ireland at about two o'clock in the afternoon. The ship began to list almost immediately, so much so that many of her lifeboats could not be launched. All but two on the port side were jammed. Many survivors donned their life belts and jumped into the sea. Others crowded the lifeboats under the direction of the crew.

Despite these efforts, casualties are believed to have been very high. More than 1,000 of the total passenger list has not yet been accounted for, including the 124 Americans. Casualties were heavy among first-class passengers, most of whom were at lunch when the torpedoes struck. Many went below to their cabins and found the ship sinking when they returned to deck.

The sinking of the Lusitania and the heavy loss of American lives has aroused greater indignation than any incident of the submarine war. In response, Germany has pointed out that a newspaper advertisement warned neutrals against travel aboard ships of combatant powers. This appeared shortly before the Lusitania sailed. The German government also contends that the Lusitania was carrying munitions intended for Britain. This has been denied by the British government.

President Wilson's note to Germany is likely to appease some domestic political opponents irritated by a speech delivered recently in Philadelphia. In the address, the president said, "There is such a thing as a man being too proud to fight; there is such a thing as a nation being so right that it does not need to convince others by force that it is right."

Wilson's statement had been criticized by many of his opponents. One of these was former President Theodore Roosevelt who has condemned the sinking of the Lusitania as "an act of piracy" (→ 13).

Fierce fight rages at battle of Artois

May 9. The French have rushed into the "Labyrinth" and lost their souls there. Tonight, the series of winding German trenches in the countryside of Artois are a maze of blasted earth and bodies. A thousand Allies are dead following a French and British offensive begun this morning at six o'clock. It is the first full-scale attack since the successsful battle of the Marne.

The British, with fewer men and less ammunition than the French, went where they hoped fewer Germans were waiting. They stationed themselves at the northern part of the sector, near Festubert. In massed ranks they surged out of their trenches "over the top," racing for the German ditches. They were mowed down like toy soldiers. Lucky stragglers gained a yard before being impaled on barbed wire. Even if the British had reached the first line of trenches, the Germans could have retreated to a second.

Allies defend the village of Esparges from a German counterattack.

The French Tenth Army at Souchez congratulated itself on penetrating a few feet closer to their goal of Vimy Ridge. Hundreds of their heavy guns are bombarding German fortifications. General Henri Philippe Petain is on the front lines, demanding discipline from the men. He has nine divisions of fresh, untried soldiers. Nine more divisions are ready 20 miles away.

Immediate Allied victory is not expected. No immediate change is expected. As General Joffre, commander of the French forces, explained, "I am nibbling at them." The side with the most bodies standing at the end wins (→ 25).

Italy goes to war with Austria after leaving Triple Alliance

May 23. Austrian aircraft bombed seven cities along Italy's Adriatic coast on the first day of the war between Italy and Austria-Hungary.

Italy declared war on Austria on May 22 at 8:15 p.m. and ordered general mobilization. Both the declaration and mobilization were greeted with wild enthusiasm throughout the country. Earlier this month, Italy quit the Triple Alliance, and three days ago, the Cabinet received full war powers.

Germany, meanwhile, has recalled her ambassador from Rome and joined Austria in the war against Italy, which now joins Britain, France and Russia in an alliance against the Central Powers. Great indignation was registered in Italy because both Germany and Austria prevented more than 30,000 Italians from leaving those countries to return to their homeland to fight in the war.

Austria struck first. Aircraft bombed the arsenals at Venice, Porto Corsini, Ancona and four other targets along Italy's Adriatic coast. Italian anti-aircraft guns and aircraft reportedly drove off the attackers. Then, two Austrian warships joined in the attacks. According to the latest Italian reports, they were driven off by Italian torpedo boats.

Italy is prepared for war in two key areas. One is the Adriatic Sea, where the Austrian fleet is already deployed. Italy, however, believes it has the stronger fleet. Italy's northwest frontier with the Austro-Hungarian Empire is the other, more vulnerable front. There, King Victor Emmanuel's forces face a formidable Austrian army skilled in mountain fighting, plus the possibility of German reinforcement.

An Italian army is reported to be moving in the direction of Trieste tonight. The Austrian government has taken over that city as a military district. Allied military sources in Italy do not believe that at the moment the forces in France can offer assistance (→ 6/23).

1915

JUNE

Su	Mo	Tu	We	Th	Fr	Sa
		1	2	3	4	5
6	7	8	9	10	11	12
13	14	15	16	17	18	19
20	21	22	23	24	25	26
29	28	29	30			

1. German zeppelins bomb London, causing fires but few casualties.

2. Britain begins blockade of Asia Minor coastline.

3. Russian Eastern Front begins to collapse; Austro-Germans take Premysl (→ 22).

3. Mesopotamia: British troops under Maj. Gen. Townshend advance up Tigris River, take Amara (→ 7/24).

6. Kaiser declares passenger liners safe from sub attacks (→ 30).

7. Belgium: British Lt. Warneford downs zeppelin over Gand.

11. Africa: British troops take Cameroon.

11. Serbia invades Albania, occupies Tirana (→ 10/6).

17. Philadelphia: League to Enforce Peace founded at Independence Hall, with Wm. H. Taft as president.

19. San Francisco: Camille Saint-Saens conducts first performance of "Hail California" at Panama-Pacific Exposition.

22. Eastern Front: Austro-Germans occupy Lemberg; Russians in retreat (→ 7/20).

23. 200,000 Italian troops attack Austrian defenses in Isonzo salient (→ 7/18).

23. German industrial leaders meet with kaiser, agree on war aims: annexation of Poland, Baltic region and Ukraine (→ 7/8).

26. German govt. censors newspaper Vorwarts for publishing Social Democratic peace manifesto (→ 9/5).

27. Texas: Huerta arrested as he approaches border, accused of plotting against Mexico (→ 8/11).

30. Germans sink liner Armenian; 20 Americans lost (→ 7/9).

30. Western Front: 2nd battle of Artois ends as French fail to take Vimy Ridge (→ 9/8).

BIRTHS

10. American author Saul Bellow.

13. U.S. tennis player Don Budge, 1st Grand Slam winner.

Turks slaughter thousands of Armenians

Armenian families find refuge from Turks aboard a French cruiser.

June 17. "Those who are innocent today may be guilty tomorrow." With those words, Talaat Pacha, Turkish Minister of the Interior, sanctioned random "deportation" of Armenians. If the Armenians, a Christian minority in mostly Muslim Turkey, were truly faced with only the sorrow of deportation, they might be grateful. In fact, the Armenians are being led to a secluded location and summarily murdered.

Today, the German Ambassador at Constantinople sent a telegram home describing Turkey's tactics. The Ottoman Court, he wrote, "wants to profit from the war by putting an end to its interior enemies, the Christians, without any diplomatic interference." The army rounds up Armenian "traitors" and herds them onto caravans. They are driven north into the country, deep in the desert, where they are shot.

Armenians have been scapegoats for centuries. In the 1890's, 300,000 were massacred. Last January, hundreds of Armenians in the Turkish army were charged with spying, disarmed and executed.

Zapata overcomes Carranza in Mexico

June 25. In the continuing fight for control of Mexico, forces under General Carranza have failed in their bid to wrest Mexico City from the arms of General Zapata. Expecting an easy time, the Carranzistas were repulsed by heavy artillery fire and are expected to face stiff resistance when or if they defeat the Zapatistas, who apparently have obtained the ammunition they previously lacked. Foreign diplomats fear for the fate of some 25,000 foreigners living in Mexico City. The situation is seen as worse than on June 2 when President Wilson warned the warring factions to resolve their problems, and a sterner line of action may soon be announced.

Agrarian leader Emiliano Zapata.

Bryan resigns and Lansing appointed

June 9. William Jennings Bryan resigned yesterday as Secretary of State, the first of President Wilson's Cabinet members to depart.

Saying that prevention of war was "the cause nearest my heart," Bryan, a pacifist, indicated that he was leaving because he feared that the recent policies of the president might lead to America's entry into the war in Europe. President Wilson accepted the resignation "with a feeling of personal sorrow." To replace Bryan, the president has named Robert Lansing, an upstate New York Democrat who is now the Counsel of the Department of State.

Argonne battle won by German gassing

June 21. A heavy German barrage of gas shells preceding an infantry attack led to a limited German success in the Argonne today. The German infantry took several lines of French trenches over a front of one and one-half miles. The War Ministry in Paris, while admitting the initial German success, claims that the lost ground was regained. The Germans assert that the French counterattacks were repulsed and that 623 prisoners were taken in the battle (→ 30).

Georgia's Governor cuts Frank's term

June 21. Georgia Governor John M. Slaton commuted the death sentence of convicted murderer Leo Frank to a life term, and a mob of 10,000 Georgians responded today by attacking state troops guarding Slaton's home and burning the governor in effigy. Frank was tried for the strangulation of a Marietta, Georgia, woman. Slaton commuted the sentence in light of what he called "conflicting testimony." He had received 100,000 appeals for clemency nationwide, and several newspapers had labeled the proceedings anti-Semitic. Mobs have threatened Frank's life; Slaton has issued assurances that he is well-guarded.

1915

JULY

Su	Mo	Tu	We	Th	Fr	Sa
				1	2	3
4	5	6	7	8	9	10
11	12	13	14	15	16	17
18	19	20	21	22	23	24
25	26	27	28	29	30	31

2. Bomb explodes in reception room of U.S. Senate (→ 3).

3. New York: Frank Holt, angry over arms exports, fires on J.P. Morgan; admits to planting bomb in Capitol (→ 6).

3. British war costs estimated at 3 million pounds per day.

6. New York: Erich Muenter, alias Frank Holt, commits suicide in jail.

6. British gain ground against Turks in Gallipoli (→ 8/8).

8. 1,347 German intellectuals issue manifesto supporting annexation policy (→ 9).

9. Germany responds to 2nd Lusitania note from U.S.; sub war will continue (→ 20).

9. Hans Delbruck leads German dissenters to publish manifesto condemning annexation.

15. N.Y.: U.S. agent finds briefcase lost by German propaganda minister (→ 8/16).

16. Caucasus: Turks under Abdul Karim defeat Russians north of Van (→ 8/5).

17. London: 30,000 women march to demand war jobs.

18. Italian troops begin second Isonzo attack (→ 8/3).

20. Austro-German armies closing in on Warsaw; Russians in full retreat (→ 8/6).

20. Wilson sends 3rd warning to Germans; attacks on Americans to be viewed as "unfriendly acts" (→ 25).

21. U.S. Supreme Court finds "grandfather" clause unconstitutional; Negroes to vote even if grandfather did not (→ 7/26/18).

24. Steamer Eastland capsizes in Chicago River; 811 drown.

25. Two U.S. merchant ships sunk by Germans off Irish coast (→ 8/10).

27. First transatlantic radiotelephone communication between U.S. and Japan.

28. U.S. novelist Henry James becomes British citizen.

DEATH

2. Porfirio Diaz, ruler of Mexico for 30 years (*1830).

Marines land after Haitians kill leader

July 29. The armored cruiser Washington under the command of Rear Admiral Caperton landed 400 U.S. Marines at Port-au-Prince yesterday to protect the lives and property of Americans and other foreigners. The violence in Haiti's capital is directly related to the insurgency in the north, where supporters of Rosalvo Bobo are fighting President Vilbrun Guillaume's troops.

Fearing success of the northern revolutionists, General Oscar, Governor of Port-au-Prince, ordered the execution of 160 political prisoners, including the former President, General Orestes Zamor. An enraged mob executed Oscar, then stormed the French legation, seized Guillaume and killed and dismembered him (→ 9/4).

Harry K. Thaw free as sanity affirmed

July 16. Harry Thaw's battle for freedom ended victoriously today when New York State Justice Hendrick declared him sane. The killer of Stanford White was thus freed from the hospital for the insane where, except for a brief flight to Canada, he has spent the past nine years. Expressing disinterest in his wife, Evelyn, and their chiid, he disclaimed a possible divorce, but close friends say that one of his first acts as a sane man will be to cut his wife out of his will.

Harry K. Thaw at the tombs, N.Y.C.

1915

AUGUST

Su	Mo	Tu	We	Th	Fr	Sa
1	2	3	4	5	6	7
8	9	10	11	12	13	14
15	16	17	18	19	20	21
22	23	24	25	26	27	28
29	30	31				

3. Italians give up assault on Isonzo as artillery ammunition expended; lost 60,000 to Austrians' 45,000 in two attempts (→ 21).

5. Caucasus: Russians evacuate Van; Turks occupy (→ 9/24).

6. Austro-Hungarians demand Poland be reunited with Galicia and made part of Habsburg Empire.→

8. Dardanelles: 2nd Allied landing at Gallipoli fails after three days without adequate naval support (→ 10/15).

9. Germany proposes separate peace on Eastern Front; Russians reject (→ 25).

10. N.Y.: Gen. Leonard Wood opens military training camp in Plattsburg for volunteer civilians (→ 27).

11. U.S. and six Latin-Am. republics ask Mexico to agree to joint peace conference (→ 9/24).

16. Washington: Sec. of State Lansing informs Wilson of German espionage plans; spy inquiry underway (→ 24).

17. Atlanta: Alleged murderer Leo Frank taken from prison, lynched by anti-Semitic mob.

21. Italy declares war on Turkey (→ 10/18).

24. German spy arrested in Washington; general investigation ordered (→ 9/9).

25. Poland: Russians quit Brest Litovsk, retreat to east (→ 31).

27. Germany offers halt on sub-warfare if U.S. will pressure Allies to relax food embargo (→ 9/1).

29. N.Y.: $55 mil. in British gold arrives to pay for arms.

31. Poland divided into administrative districts; Warsaw to Germany, Kielce to Austria (→ 9/2).

BIRTH

29. Swedish actress Ingrid Bergman (†8/29/1982).

DEATH

20. German doctor Paul Erlich, discovered diptheria antitoxin (3/14/1854).

Germans in Warsaw as Russians retreat

Aug 6. German troops have smashed through the Russian defensive lines and taken the inner and outer fortresses, and Warsaw is tonight in German hands.

A Russian official bulletin reports that the troops covering the capital of Poland, the third largest city in the Russian Empire, were ordered to fall back across the Vistula River and were not attacked. In a defensive maneuver, all the bridges over the river have been blown up by the Russians. Previously, before the Russian withdrawal, military equipment and war materiel had been removed from Warsaw.

There was some fierce fighting during the attack on the capital. Bavarian troops, who formed the German vanguard, fought several sharp actions with the Russians.

The fall of Warsaw clearly weakens the Russian position on the central front in the East. There are four German and Austrian armies. The Russians have launched repeated counterattacks against all four armies and have delayed but not halted their advances. The Germans claim to have taken huge numbers of Russian prisoners. And neutral observers report some signs of disloyalty among the Russian prisoners of war.

Meanwhile, another potential strategic danger for Russia is developing in the northeast. German General von Bulow is moving on Dvinsk on the Vilna-Petrograd railway, endangering the capital (→ 9).

Will Pauline be saved again?

1915

SEPTEMBER

Su	Mo	Tu	We	Th	Fr	Sa
			1	2	3	4
5	6	7	8	9	10	11
12	13	14	15	16	17	18
19	20	21	22	23	24	25
26	27	28	29	30		

1. Germany offers written promise not to sink liners without warning (→ 18).

2. Poland: Austro-German armies take Grodno (→ 8).

4. U.S. Admiral places Haiti under martial law to quell rebellion in Port-au-Prince (→ 11/13).

5. Switzerland: European Socialists meet in Zimmerwald to discuss stance on war (→ 5/1/16).

8. Western Front: Germans begin new offensive in Argonne (→ 26).

9. U.S. asks Austria to recall Ambassador Dumba, accused of conspiring to prevent manufacture of munitions (→ 10/24).

9. German zeppelin bombs London, causing minor damage.

14. Triple Alliance offers part of Macedonia to Bulgaria as inducement to enter war (→ 24).

17. Stefansson discovers new Arctic land near Alaska.

18. N.Y.: Resta drives Peugot a record 108 mph at Sheepshead Bay Speedway.

18. Berlin: Kaiser approves new policy; neutral vessels and passenger ships exempt from attack (→ 11/7).

19. Poland: Austro-Germans occupy Vilna; Russians, in retreat, narrowly escape encirclement (→ 3/18/16).

19. New York syndicate agrees on loan to Allies: $500-800 million at five percent interest.

24. Texas: Mexican rebels raid Brownsville in one of most serious border incidents yet (→ 10/19).

24. Caucasus: Grand Duke Nicholas, relieved of command in north, arrives as Viceroy to prepare large scale offensive (→ 1/11/16).

24. Bulgaria mobilizes troops on Serbian border (→ 10/6).

28. Mesopotamia: British Gen. Townshend defeats Turkish Commander Nur-ud-Din Pasha at Kut on the Tigris; kills 5,300, loses 1,230 (→ 11/26).

Allies begin wide attack

French troops pour out of the trenches to advance on German positions.

Sept 26. An Allied offensive in France, launched yesterday to take some pressure off Russia's hard-pressed armies, is continuing to move forward on both the French and British fronts.

By nightfall, the Allies reported they had taken 20,000 unwounded German prisoners; 12,000 fell to the French. Twenty miles of German trenches were occupied and at some points in the French sector the penetration was as great as two and a half miles. The French army's most important gains were in Champagne, where after a very heavy artillery barrage, the infantry swept forward. The gains there are thought to weaken the German positions around Verdun.

The British attacked north of the La Bassee canal, penetrating to a depth of 4,000 yards and taking trenches on a five-mile front. They also cut one of the Germans' main roads. Heavy fighting on both sides of the canal forced the Germans to divert reserves to the area. Some 94 divisions, 1,800,000 Germans, are on this front (→ 10/14).

Czar takes command of Russian forces

Sept 8. In an effort to stop Germany's aggressive advance through Russia, Czar Nicholas II has taken over the leadership of the Russian army from his second cousin, Grand Duke Nicholas.

The grand duke has had little choice but to retreat since his poorly equipped troops have been overpowered by the well-trained German army. It is estimated that 30 percent of Russia's troops are without weapons and are therefore forced to take rifles from the dead.

The retreat has forced Russia to give up some 750,000 prisoners as well as large chunks of its southern territories, including parts of the Ukraine, Lithuania and Byelorussia. Although the czar has no experience of combat, it is hoped that his leadership will boost Russian morale. Since the war began, the peasants have hoped the czar would command (→ 19).

Czar Nicholas takes charge.

Spalding of sporting goods firm is dead

Sept 10. Albert Goodwill Spalding, founder of a sporting goods firm bearing bis name and called by some the "Father of Baseball," died today unexpectedly at his home near San Diego, California.

Spalding will be remembered as a man able to combine his executive ability with his experience as a major league player and manager to hold the divergent forces of baseball together then they threatened to destroy the game.

He was recruited for the Boston Red Stockings after news of his feats as an underhand pitcher trickled east from Rockford, Illinois. He switched to the Chicago White Stockings after leading Boston to four championships and remained on as Chicago Manager until 1895. At his death, he was the head of A.G. Spalding & Brothers and the American Sports Publishing Co.

Pilsudski seeking freedom for Poland

Pilsudski and his comrades.

Sept 30. This month saw a change of party leadership in Poland which, with the help of the popular statesman, General Joseph Pilsudski, will aim for political freedom. The Liberal-Progressive Party has replaced the Conservative majority in the Duma, and a dispatch from Petrograd reports it has agreed on a program seeking "autonomy for Poland, conciliation with Finland, amnesty for political prisoners and removal of restrictions on Jews."

1915

OCTOBER

Su	Mo	Tu	We	Th	Fr	Sa
					1	2
3	4	5	6	7	8	9
10	11	12	13	14	15	16
17	18	19	20	21	22	23
24	25	26	27	28	29	30
31						

6. Wilson announces engagement to Mrs. Norman Galt (→ 12/18).

6. Entente powers issue ultimatum to Bulgaria, warning against entrance in war (→ 6).

6. Austria, Germany, Bulgaria invade Serbia, force Putnik's army into retreat (→ 9).

9. Serbia: Austro-German troops seize Belgrade with aid from Bulgarians (→ 16).

13. Philadelphia: Boston beats Philly 5-4 to take World Series in five games.

14. Western Front: British stopped at Loos (→ 30).

15. Dardanelles: British Gen. Hamilton relieved of command; replaced by Gen. Sir Charles Monro (→ 11/23).

16. U.K. declares war on Bulgaria; Rumania neutral (→ 20).

18. Italians begin third assault on Isonzo (→ 11/4).

19. U.S. recognizes Carranza government in Mexico despite its refusal to negotiate with rebels (→ 12/20).

19. New Jersey defeats suffrage by referendum, despite Wilson's support, in first major test in East (→ 23).

23. 25,000 march in New York suffrage parade (→ 11/7/16).

24. New York: Several Germans arrested for alleged plot to blow up departing supply ships (→ 12/3).

28. Richard Strauss' "Alpine Symphony" opens in Berlin.

28. Mass.: 28 children die in Peabody school fire.

29. France: Viviani resigns; Aristide Briand forms Socialist Cabinet.

30. Western Front: French end assault on Vimy Ridge; French lose 100,000, British 60,000, Germans 65,000 in month-long battle of Artois (→ 11/3).

BIRTH

17. American playwright Arthur Miller.

DEATH

8. New York publisher John B. Putnam.

French, British troops land at Salonika

Allied troops unload heavy artillery at Salonika.

Oct 7. French and British troops have completed their landings at Salonika in Greece, and the Allied forces are now in the process of boarding trains for a journey across the country to Glevgell on the Serbian frontier.

The Bulgarians have evacuated all their positions along the coast. But they are arming the forts in the city of Dedeaghatch with long-range guns. Bulgarian forces also laid a double row of mines around the approaches to the port.

King Constantine of Greece did not raise any objections to the French and British operation in a conversation with the French minister today. Premier Eleutherios Venizelos, however, has resigned along with his Cabinet because of a disagreement with the king, who has German sympathies. The king is now forming a new Cabinet.

Crowds in the streets of Athens tonight demonstrated in favor of Venizelos. Shouts of "Hurrah for Venizelos" and "Hurrah for France" were heard, but otherwise the city is calm (→ 11/4).

Central Powers force Serbia into retreat

Oct 20. German, Austrian and Bulgarian armies are driving deep into Serbia and threatening to drive that country out of the war. Meanwhile, Russia is the latest member of the Quadruple Alliance, after England and Italy, to declare war on Bulgaria, which Russia once helped liberate from Turkey. Rumania has decided to remain neutral in the worsening conflict.

The gravity of Serbia's military position was emphasized by news that the Austrian army which had been checked on the Save River on Serbia's northwest frontier had broken through and occupied Obrenovatz. German and Austrian forces have also taken Belgrade and have now advanced 12 miles south of the city along the railroad.

The Bulgarian army, fresh to combat, also has taken Vranya and cut the railroad between Salonika, the Allied base, and Nish. Military sources doubt that any of the Allies will be able to send sufficient forces to Serbia to stem the invaders. Earlier this month, Allied troops landed at Salonika, bound for Serbia.

The railroads are far from adequate and the highways poor. Some help may be provided by sea power. An Italian naval sqadron has sailed to engage Bulgarian commerce and ports (→ 11/5).

Mayor orders dry Sunday in Chicago

Oct 10. Hymns of joy wafted up from Chicago's churches, as Mayor Thompson's restrictions on Sunday liquor sales went into effect, the first such measure in 43 years. Opponents of the law, meanwhile, managed to distract themselves at movie houses, poolrooms and parks. Chicago's chief of police reported few violations at hotels, clubs or saloons. Several pharmacists, however, have been approached by people with outdated prescriptions calling for alcohol. The pharmacists, suspecting the illnesses are the kind that will miraculously cure themselves on Monday, are honoring only legitimate requests (→ 11/7).

Germans execute nurse Edith Cavell

Oct 15. British nurse Edith Cavell was shot by German authorities two days ago, having been detained on charges of espionage. Miss Cavell, who had lived in Brussels since 1906, had run a successful school for nurses. Her students treated the wounded on both sides of the war, Allies as well as Germans, placing Miss Cavell seemingly above suspicion. Yet on August 5, the German command arrested her, insisting that she had harbored Belgians of military age. They also accused her of assisting French and English soldiers attempting to escape the country over the Dutch border.

1915

NOVEMBER

Su	Mo	Tu	We	Th	Fr	Sa
	1	2	3	4	5	6
7	8	9	10	11	12	13
14	15	16	17	18	19	20
21	22	23	24	25	26	27
28	29	30				

4. Italians break off third attack on Isonzo (→ 10).

4. Athens: Zaimis Cabinet hands resignation to King Constantine (→ 8/22/16).

5. Serbia: Bulgarians take Nish railway, connecting Vienna to Istanbul (→ 21).

6. Lord Kitchener and Aristide Briand meet in Paris.

7. Chicago: 40,000 parade to protest closing of saloons on Sunday (→ 3/3/18).

7. U.S. protests British naval blockade as violation of international law (→ 12/7).

13. U.S., Haiti sign treaty making Haiti a U.S. protectorate (→ 2/28/16).

19. Allies ask China to join Entente (→ 3/14/17).

21. Balkans: Austro-Germans reported in full control of Serbia (→ 24).

22. Mohandas Gandhi returns to India (→ 4/15/19).

23. Dardanelles: British approve Monro's plan for evacuation of Gallipoli (→ 1/8/16).

24. Balkans: Retreating Serbian troops reach Adriatic Sea through Albania and Montenegro (→ 12/11).

25. Atlanta: Col. William J. Simmons revives Ku Klux Klan (→ 7/2/17).

26. Mesopotamia: Townshend's advance on Baghdad halted by Turks at Ctesiphon; British retreat to Kut (→ 12/7).

27. New York: 40,000 watch Army defeat Navy 14-0 in annual football game.

28. Canada earmarks 20 mil. bushels of wheat for Britain.

30. Delaware: 31 die in explosion at Wilmington DuPont plant; sabotage suspected.

BIRTH

9. Robert Sargent Shriver, American lawyer, politician.

DEATH

19. Jewish theologian Solomon Schecter (*12/7/1847).

France's one aim: Regain Alsace-Lorraine

French troops bombard Alsace with cannons ironically named in German.

Nov 3. French officials state that despite last year's unsuccessful offensives in Alsace-Lorraine, the French General Staff remains confident of reclaiming the territory, lost to Bismarck's Germany during the Franco-Prussian War 45 years ago. That loss was a severe blow to the French people, and they regard it as a most important point of national honor to win back their province whatever the cost.

French offensives in Alsace-Lorraine last August had mixed results. When those in Alsace were clearly repelled, continued attempts were abandoned and the French forces were moved westward. The French offensive in Lorraine was less decisive. Following the strategy of the "offensive a outrance," the surging French soldiers discovered that German firepower held an answer for such heroics. A German counter-offensive soon thereafter caught the French by surprise and hurled them back at the Battle of Morhange-Sarrebourg, with the end result that the French were able to dig in at their previous line of defense, stiffen their resistance and thus check the German attack. Since then, the two opposing armies have remained at loggerheads (→ 12/15).

Masaryk calls for free Czechoslovakia

Nov 14. Determined to unite Slavs and Czechs in one independent nation, Tomas Masaryk, the exiled professor of philosophy, stands at the head of a liberation movement of this reluctant member of the Austro-Hungarian Empire. The wave of nationalism that surged across Europe in the last century has stirred passions for freedom for these people, desirous of it since 1620. As one countryman put it, "Austria cannot command the respect of the Slavs (and Czechs), because she did not keep the promises made to us. In the last 20 years, Vienna has been the servant of Berlin. Little good could be expected for us from such an arrangement."

Italians defeated again on Isonzo

Nov 10. The Italian army has again suffered defeat and heavy losses in their fourth attempt this year to gain a foothold on the Isonzo River, which flows through northeastern Italy before emptying into the Gulf of Trieste. Beyond the Isonzo lay the Austrian Alps and there are those who have questioned the purpose of an Italian offensive in terrain which would more logically dictate a defensive strategy. In what has proven to be a difficult campaign, the Italians have lost 250,000 dead and wounded in four battles despite a numerical advantage of two to one. It is believed that losses by the Austrian army have been nearly as high (→ 3/11/16).

Churchill to join troops in trenches

Nov 12. Winston Churchill announced today that he has resigned from the British Cabinet and said he was ready to join his regiment to fight in France. The resignation was a further manifestation of dissension within the coalition government formed by Prime Minister Asquith. Churchill, who resigned as First Lord of the Admiralty last spring, had been asked by Asquith to participate in a small War Council. However, in his letter of resignation, Churchill said that the role of the council had changed and he "could not accept a position without an effective share in its guidance and control."

Colonel Winston Churchill.

Journey ends for a famed Negro leader

Nov 14. Booker T. Washington, founder of the Tuskegee Institute and author of "Working with Hands," died today after a brief illness. A former slave, Washington believed he was born in April 1858, on a Virginia plantation. At the close of the Civil War, he traveled to West Virginia, where he worked in the kitchen of a woman who taught him to read and write. He entered the Hampton Institute for Negroes in 1871, and founded Tuskegee in Alabama ten years later.

As a Negro leader, Washington tackled the problems of his people pragmatically: occupational training was the solution to emotional and economic despair. He earned several honorary degrees, including one from Harvard, and generous endowments for his school.

1915

DECEMBER

Su	Mo	Tu	We	Th	Fr	Sa
			1	2	3	4
5	6	7	8	9	10	11
12	13	14	15	16	17	18
19	20	21	22	23	24	25
26	27	28	29	30	31	

3. U.S. expels German attaches Boy-ed and von Papen on spy charges (→ 1/14/16).

7. Pres. Wilson asks for standing army of 142,000, 400,000 reserves (→ 1/27/16).

7. Mesopotamia: Turks besiege British at Kut (→ 3/12/16).

10. Nobel Prize in Literature to Romain Rolland.

10. Ford produces one millionth car.

11. Balkans: Anglo-French forces pushed out of Serbia, retreat to Salonika (→ 29).

12. First all-metal plane completed by Hugo Junkers.

15. Sir Douglas Haig replaces Field Marshal French as commander of B.E.F. after failure at Loos.→

18. Washington: Pres. Wilson and Mrs. Galt are married.

20. U.S. gives refuge to Mexican rebel Villa (→ 1/10/16).

20. U.S.: Gas prices rise to 25 cents per gallon.

27. Ohio: Iron and steel workers strike for eight-hour day, higher wages (→ 1/8/16).

29. Peter I and Serbian army take refuge on Corfu Island (→ 1/13/16).

31. Germans torpedo British liner Persia without warning; 335 dead (→ 4/20/16).

BIRTHS

12. American singer Frank Sinatra.

19. French singer Edith Piaf (†10/11/1963).

CULTURAL EVENTS, 1915

Literature: Van Wyck Brooks' "America's Coming of Age"; Conrad's "Victory"; Somerset Maugham's "Of Human Bondage"; Edgar Lee Masters' "A Spoon River Anthology"; Kafka's "The Metamorphosis"; D.H. Lawrence's "The Rainbow."

The Arts: First Dadaist paintings, Marcel Duchamp.

Film: D.W. Griffith's "Birth of a Nation"; Cecil B. De Mille's "Carmen."

Einstein develops new theory of relativity

Professor Albert Einstein of the Kaiser Wilhelm Institute in Berlin has proposed a theory about the nature of time, space and gravity that will dramatically alter mankind's view of the universe if it is accepted. The new theory is an extension of Einstein's Special Theory of Relativity, which he published in 1905, and which gets its name from the thesis that there is no absolute time and absolute space. Instead, all motion is relative, and the rate at which time passes depends on the velocity of a body in motion.

The new General Theory of Relativity alters the view of gravity proposed by Sir Isaac Newton more than two centuries ago. Newton viewed gravity as a force exerted by one body on another. According to Einstein, gravity is a property of space that is induced by the presence of matter. Because the effects predicted by Einstein are subtle and occur only in intense gravitational fields, scientists will not be able to test relativity against Newtonian physics until the war in Europe has ended and peaceful research resumes.

Professor Einstein in Berlin.

Ford gives up peace mission to Europe

Dec 24. Henry Ford's peace mission to Europe has ended in disappointment. He and 120 other pacifists, including 54 reporters and four filmmakers documenting the event, set sail from Hoboken, New Jersey, on December 4. They had nearly reached Stockholm when Ford's physician recommended he go home. The illness is considered serious but not life-threatening.

The auto manufacturer had spent more than $60,000 on the endeavor, and left his companions with a $270,000 check. His slogan had been "out of the trenches by Christmas," and he calculated that if he could help shorten the war by one day he would have saved 30,000 lives. His strategy for achieving peace had never taken a concrete form, however, and the mission had been ridiculed in some circles.

Ford's party will continue without him under the leadership of the Women's International Peace Association. Members have telegraphed William J. Bryan in America and urged him to join them (→ 1/3/16).

Joffre takes command; Haig leads British

Dec 15. Field Marshal Sir Douglas Haig has been appointed Commander-in-Chief of the British forces in France and Belgium. He succeeds Field Marshal Sir John French who asked to be relieved after only 16 months in command. Sir John will become Commander-in-Chief of all forces in the United Kingdom.

These changes follow the appointment two weeks ago of General Joseph Joffre as Commander-in-Chief of the French army. He was previously the commander of troops in the northeast. Field Marshal Haig, who led the British First Army, now takes control of a force of over one million men holding 70 miles of front. His conduct of the retreat from Mons in Belgium won him high praise (→ 2/21/16).

General Joseph Joffre.

Field Marshal Sir Douglas Haig.

Somerset Maugham novel is published

This was a year when literature created imaginative characters. "Of Human Bondage," by Somerset Maugham, concerns a club-footed medical student who is destroyed by a love affair with a lower-class waitress. The novel "The Good Soldier" by Englishman Ford Madox Ford explores the dashed dreams of two married couples. Czech author Franz Kafka describes alienation and loneliness in "The Metamorphosis." It relates the literal and figurative transformation of a man into a hideous insect.

Kansas-born Edgar Lee Masters offered "Spoon River Anthology." This collection of free verse tells of people long buried in a cemetery. The ghosts recall their small-town lives, drenched in regret and despair. Japanese writer Akutagawa Ryunosuke also used ghosts in "Roshomon." In his story, a murder is explained many ways. The only honest witness is the dead man's soul.

1916

JANUARY

Su	Mo	Tu	We	Th	Fr	Sa
						1
2	3	4	5	6	7	8
9	10	11	12	13	14	15
16	17	18	19	20	21	22
23	24	25	26	27	28	29
30	31					

3. Henry Ford returns to U.S., denies deserting peace mission.

3. Tokyo: Three armored Japanese cruisers ordered to guard Suez Canal.

6. New York: German mark dropping dramatically; down 20 percent on the dollar in two months.

7. Germans assure U.S. they will abide by intl. rules in naval war (→ 31).

8. Ohio: Militia called to discipline Youngstown strikers; three killed, 19 shot.

10. U.S. Dept. of Justice rules baseball leagues do not violate Sherman Antitrust Act.

10. Mexican rebels execute 16 American engineers (→ 16).

11. Caucasus: Russian Gen. Yudenich launches winter offensive, advances west on Erzurum (→ 18).

13. Montenegro, overrun by Austrian army, sues for peace (→ 3/21).

14. British authorities seize German attache von Papen's financial records, confirming espionage activities in U.S.

15. New York: U.S. E-2 sub explodes, killing 4, injuring 10; Edison safety battery blamed.

18. Russians force Turkish 3rd Army back to Erzurum; Turks lose 25,000, many to frostbite (→ 2/13).

21. Holland: Zuiderzee bursts in violent thunderstorm.

23. Washington: Latin Am. republics frame Declaration of Rights of Nations.

24. U.S. Supreme Court finds income tax consitutional.

27. New York: Wilson opens preparedness program (→ 31).

31. Wilson refuses compromise on Lusitania reparations (→ 2/6).

BIRTH

12. South African leader Pieter Wilhelm Botha.

DEATH

13. Gen. Victoriano Huerta, ex-president of Mexico (*12/23/1854).

Dardanelles: Retreat from Gallipoli

British troops are ready to quit their failed task at Gallipoli.

Jan 8. Stripped of strategic advantage, the Allied forces of Great Britain and France have evacuated the Gallipoli Peninsula in the Dardanelles. Dispatches from London announced that the retreat, precarious because of powerful and aggressive Turkish troops, was successful. General Sir Charles Monro, commander of British forces, reported only one Allied casualty and the loss of 17 weapons, remarkable considering the tactical positioning of the Turks. Yet Turkish accounts of the retreat differ. They claim to have sunk a British battleship near Sedd-el-Bahr, resulting in "great enemy losses." One fact is certain: the Allied campaign in the Dardanelles was disastrous.

Feb 1915. The British navy, eluding mines and machine gun fire, silences Turkish guns on Gallipoli's shores.
March 18. Allied naval assault is halted as six ships are sunk in an undetected minefield.
April 25. Anzacs land at Ari Burnu, British at Helles.
Aug 6. Renewed assault after three months of intensive fighting.
Jan 8, 1916. Retreat; Allies have lost 252,000 to Turks 251,000.

Villa shoots 18 Americans to embroil U.S.

Jan 16. Eighteen Americans have been killed by Mexican soldiers of Pancho Villa's army after being taken off a train 50 miles west of Chihuahua City. The train was bound for mines owned by an American firm for whom most of the victims work. They were robbed, stripped naked, lined up against the cars and shot. One passenger, Thomas Holmes, managed to escape by hiding in a train lavatory. Troops under General Carranza have captured and condemned to death the soldiers responsible, and one general has already been shot (→ 3/9).

U.S. Marines watch Carranza troops set off in pursuit of Pancho Villa.

Cameroons capital seized by Allies

Jan 28. The Belgian Expeditionary Corps together with a strong French force successfully defeated German troops on the African front today, according to dispatches from Paris. A two-tiered attack enabled the Allies to take control of the capital of the Cameroons, Yaounde, which is located near the Sanaga River in West Africa.

French General Aymerich paid grand homage to the determined Belgian troops, extolling their "bravery under fire and tenacity." Since September of 1914, the Belgians have been protecting the main French fort with 500 men and heavy artillery against frequent German attacks. Germany proclaimed the Cameroons a protectorate in 1884 and subsequently made it a colony. While not a crucial front in this war, the region does possess fertile land with the potential for significant commercial development.

1916

FEBRUARY

Su	Mo	Tu	We	Th	Fr	Sa
		1	2	3	4	5
6	7	8	9	10	11	12
13	14	15	16	17	18	19
20	21	22	23	24	25	26
29	28	29				

2. U.S. Senate votes independence for Philippines, effective 1921 (→ 10).

2. Rep. McLemore asks Congress to vote on measure requiring Wilson to warn against travel on ships owned by war participants (→ 6).

3. German textile industry placed under govt. control.

3. Russia: Sturmer replaces Goryemkin as council pres.

4. Ottowa: Six die in Canadian Parliament fire; arson suspected.

6. Germany admits full liability for Lusitania incident, recognizes U.S. right to claim indemnity (→ 16).

8. Berlin: Demonstrators protest food shortage (→ 3/20).

10. U.S. Sec. of War Garrison resigns, citing Filipino independence and inadequate defense (→ 1/17/33).

11. Maryland: Baltimore Symphony Orchestra plays opening concert under Gustav Strube.

13. Caucasus: Gen. Yudenich attacks Turks at Erzurum; Russian navy supports on Black Sea coast (→ 3/8).

13. Census Bureau estimates U.S. population at 101,208,315.

13. British govt. recruits 400,000 women for agricultural work.

16. Germany again orders sinking of armed neutral ships; U.S. angered (→ 3/7).

21. Western Front: Germans begin major offensive at Verdun (→ 26).

26. Western Front: Gen. Henri Philippe Petain takes command of French forces at Verdun.→

28. U.S. Senate ratifies Haitian treaty; Haiti becomes U.S. protectorate.

BIRTH

19. American jockey Eddie Arcaro.

DEATHS

6. South American poet Ruben Dario (*11/18/1867).

19. Austrian physicist, philosopher Ernst Mach, (*2/18/1838).

Germans attack Verdun; battle rages

Casualties mount in the trenches.

French troops defend Allied positions at Verdun.

Feb 26. Seven German army corps —280,000 men —have launched an offensive against the series of French fortresses at Verdun. The attack is on a 25-mile front, the largest on the Western Front since the operations in Champagne last September.

The Verdun forts are of the greatest strategic importance to the defense of France. They guard one of the principal invasion routes into the country and their fall would imperil the entire Allied military position.

The French Ministry of War now concedes that several strategic positions were lost during the Germans' original onslaught. But the French also claim that their counterattacks have checked the German advances elsewhere and that they have inflicted heavy casualties on the attackers.

For their part, the Germans claim to have taken 3,000 French as prisoners of war. The German High Command also reports that several French trenches have been taken by mining operations. Once the mines under the trenches exploded, German infantry rushed the objectives. The French are presently moving reinforcements to the battle zone to make up for those soldiers already lost. Military circles in London and Paris expect that a long, fierce battle will ensue (→ 3/6).

American novelist Henry James dies

Feb 28. Henry James, who lived outside America to get a closer look at it, died today. He was 72. James spent most of his time in Europe (he spoke fluent French), and many of his 22 novels and 113 short stories dealt with bright-eyed Americans bullying Europeans into optimism. As his career progressed, James grew increasingly introspective. His work hinged on psychological investigation and what he called the "imagination of disaster."

James was born April 15, 1843, in New York City. His brother was philosopher William James. Their father was an eccentric millionaire who provided them an education in Europe. When Henry James was still a young man he suffered a back injury that kept him out of social circles. He became an observer.

In 1878 James published "Daisy Miller," about a plucky American girl destroyed by European mores. "The Portrait of a Lady" (1881) explores the same theme and more; it was hailed a masterpiece almost at once. "The Turn of the Screw" (1898) is a psychological horror tale. It, like many James works, contrasts innocence with the evil of experience.

Henry James, by John S. Sargent.

Joffre states war aims; names Petain

Feb 25. Determined to prevent further German gains at Verdun, French General Joseph Joffre has appointed General Henri Philippe Petain as chief of the French forces on that front. The move illustrates Joffre's new war strategy. Last December, he met with Allied military leaders in an effort to reorganize the fight against Germany; he maintained that the lack of tight control and leadership has plagued Allied attacks. Petain, a celebrated French commander, should help structure the defense of Verdun.

Germany, while making advances in its offensive, has also suffered serious losses. According to reports from Paris, over 150,000 Germans have died from heavy French fire. Conversely, while losing some ground, the French have lost fewer men in the battle.

1916

MARCH

Su	Mo	Tu	We	Th	Fr	Sa
			1	2	3	4
5	6	7	8	9	10	11
12	13	14	15	16	17	18
19	20	21	22	23	24	25
26	27	28	29	30	31	

6. France: Allies recapture Fort Douamont (→ 14).

7. Wilson wins majority in House, sustains tough stand on German sub war (→ 15).

7. French Defense Minister Joseph Gallieni resigns (→ 5/27).

8. Causcasus: Russians seize prot of Rizeh; 40,000 Armenians driven from Erzerum and killed (→ 4/18).

9. Germany declares war on Portugal.

9. Pancho Villa leads attack into New Mexico, kills 17 Americans (→ 10).

10. Gen. Funston and 5,000 U.S. troops enter Mexico to hunt for Villa (→ 15).

11. Italians, Austrians begin fifth battle of Isonzo (→ 29).

12. Persia: 20,000 Russian troops reach Karind intent on attacking Baghdad while Turks are occupied at Kut (→ 4/29).

14. Western Front: Germans drive on "Dead Man's Heights" near Verdun (→ 4/9).

14. British troops suppress Senussi rebellion in Egypt (→ 6/5).

15. Carranza troops join Pershing and 4,000 Americans, push into Mexico in search for Villa (→ 30).

15. U.S. House passes Army Reorganization Bill (→ 26).

18. Eastern Front: Russians counter Verdun assault with attack at Lake Naroch, lose 100,000 to Germans' 20,000 (→ 6/4).

20. Germans issue rationing cards to combat food shortage.

29. Italians call off fifth assault on Isonzo (→ 5/15).

30. Mexico: Villa kills 172 in Guerrero garrison (→ 31).

BIRTHS

11. British statesman Harold Wilson.

16. American author Irving Wallace.

DEATH

2. Mounet-Sully, dean of Comedie Francaise (*2/27/1841).

Pershing leads 4,000 men into Mexico

March 31. Two weeks after their arrival in Mexico, American troops under the command of Brigadier General John J. Pershing have routed Pancho Villa's army in their first military engagement.

The fighting took place in the early morning when a fiying detachment of United States Cavalry led by Colonel George Dodd launched a surprise attack on Villa's camp at Guerrero after riding 55 miles in 17 hours. Numbering 400, the cavalry engaged the Mexicans in a five-hour running battle, killing 30 of Villa's 500 troops and wounding numerous others. Four Americans were slightly wounded.

According to Pershing's communique, Villa himself was not present, but others report seeing him escape in a carriage. He is unable to ride due to a broken leg, possibly from falling off his horse. The punitive American expedition was ordered into Mexico following border raids by Villa into Arizona and New Mexico (→ 4/13).

Pershing and troops go after Villa.

Defeated Serbians regroup on Corfu

Austrians hang Serb civilians.

March 21. Based on Corfu since their tragic winter retreat across the Albanian mountains, the decimated Serbian army stands again ready to join the Allied forces. Early Serbian victories gave way last year to defeats as the Serbs, squeezed in a vise between the Austrian-Germans and Bulgarians, trekked south over the Montenegro mountains accompanied by thousands of refugees suffering from typhus, dysentery and starvation (→ 8/27).

Tirpitz resigns in protest on U-boats

March 15. Alfred von Tirpitz has resigned from control of the German navy and its strategy. As Naval Minister, he is known to have clashed sharply with Chancellor von Bethman Hollweg over submarine tactics.

Von Tirpitz sought a policy of submarine attacks on neutral shipping as well as on armed enemy merchantmen. The chancellor, apparently alarmed by hostile neutral opinion, sought moderation. The Foreign Ministry stressed there would be no modifications of current submarine policy.

Admiral von Tirpitz, who is known as the "Father of the German navy," was succeeded by Admiral von Capelle who was Director of Administration in the navy.

French and British divide up Mideast

March 9. An agreement is being worked out between Great Britain and France to divide the Middle East into spheres of influence.

Negotiations between the two powerful nations to shape the Allied partition of the Ottoman Empire are being conducted by Sir Mark Sykes for Great Britain and Georges Picot for France. As of now, they both agree to concede the Turkish city of Constantinople and the Turkish Straits with its adjacent area to Russia on the condition that Constantinople will be a free port and that the straits remain open to commercial shipping. Russia considers the arrangement vital to smooth postwar relations.

In return, Great Britain will be assigned control of Mesopotamia and Palestine while the French are to be designated to administrate Syria, Adana, Cilia and southern Kurdistan. Certain Arab areas will be left for administration by the Arabic peoples. However, it is safe to assume the Arabs will be suspicious of the Europeans' motives.

Underscoring the importance of such an arrangement, French diplomat Georges Leygues remarked, "We only have free hands in the Mediterranean if Syria comes under our influence." London's main concern is to eliminate any potential menace in Egypt.

French liner Sussex, sunk on the 24th, displays the gaping hole torn in her hull by a German torpedo. The death of several American passengers has reopened the possibility of war with Germany (→ 4/17).

1916

APRIL

Su	Mo	Tu	We	Th	Fr	Sa
						1
2	3	4	5	6	7	8
9	10	11	12	13	14	15
16	17	18	19	20	21	22
23	24	25	26	27	28	29
30						

4. Vatican: Pope Benoit XV meets with British Prime Minister Lord Asquith.

9. Western Front: Germans launch third offensive at Verdun (→ 5/2).

10. Paris: President of Interim Olympic Committee halts Games until war's end.

12. Four arrested in N.Y. for alleged plot to destroy supply ships leaving New Jersey.

13. Mexico: Rebel fire on U.S. troops, killing several (→ 20).

15. Military aviator drops false bombs over Washington in "preparedness lesson" (→ 17).

17. U.S. threatens to break diplomatic relations if Germany will not guarantee safety of merchant vessels (→ 5/5).

17. East Africa: Portugese and British troops begin advance on German colonies.

18. Caucasus: Russians capture Trebizond from Turks (→ 20).

20. Petrograd: Russia refuses armistice with Turkey (→ 7/2).

20. German and British navies clash off Flemish coast.

20. President Wilson decides to keep U.S. troops in Mexico indefinitely (→ 5/9).

23. New York: Socialist Labor Party nominates Arthur E. Reimer for pres., Caleb Harrison for v.p. (→ 6/7).

24. Switzerland: Intl. Socialist Conference at Kienthal dominated by pacifists (→ 8/1).

24. Yarmouth, Lowestoft, on British coast, bombed in German cruiser raids.

28. British declare martial law throughout Ireland (→ 30).

29. Mesopotamia: Starving British and Indian troops give in to Turks at Kut-el-Amara after four-month siege.→

29. New York: St. Thomas Cathedral dedicated.

30. Ireland: Irish rebel leaders surrender at Kingston, order followers to disarm (→ 5/3).

BIRTH

22. American Yehudi Menuhin, violin virtuoso.

Dublin Nationalists stage bloody uprising

Liberty Hall, Republican headquarters in Dublin, destroyed by the British.

April 24. Rebellion has erupted in Dublin as armed members of the nationalist Sinn Fein Society captured the Post Office, Stephen's Green and a number of adjacent private houses.

The attack was almost coincidental with Britain's capture of Sir Roger Casement and two aides. Sir Roger is a leader of the Irish separatists. He was attempting to land arms from Germany on the Irish coast. He is now in London in military custody awaiting trial. Casement's arms shipments were intended for the use of rebel groups elsewhere in Ireland.

The fighting in Dublin was short but fierce. Preliminary reports are that the British lost three officers, four or five soldiers, two volunteers and two policemen dead plus more than 20 wounded in skirmishes with the rebels.

According to the latest government reports, the uprising was entirely confined to the city of Dublin. There have been rumors for some weeks that an organized revolt against the British was imminent. The police and local army intelligence were aware of these (→ 28).

Best-known military correspondent is dead

April 11. Richard Harding Davis died today of a heart attack, minutes after completing an essay on America's role in the war, a role, he counsels, which may require the sacrifice of American soldiers.

Born in 1864 in Philadelphia, Davis covered the major wars of the last 30 years. He had recently returned from the Western Front, where he was often harassed by officials accusing him of spying. Davis was certainly no mere observer; he reported from the trenches as bombs exploded around him. But his motives were fine. "If women and children have cruelly and needlessly suffered," he wrote, "if without reason cities have been wrecked, the world should know that."

British task force surrenders to Turks

April 29. British troops under Major General Charles Townshend have laid down their arms at Kut-el-Amara in Mesopotamia. The force, which numbers 8,070, is one of the few fighting units in this war to surrender en masse. While London is discouraged at the news, it praises Townshend for holding his ground a remarkable 196 days.

Townshend first captured Kut-el-Amara in June 1915. At that time, he headed 40,000 Anglo-Indian soldiers. They moved north and west, attempting to circumnavigate Turk entrenchments and approach Baghdad 200 miles off. They made little headway. Townshend retreated with a few thousand men to Kut, where they have been since Dec. 3.

Kut-el-Amara is a small muddy town located on a peninsula on the Tigris River. It was besieged regularly after Townshend retrenched there. For months, a relief force was stationed only 20 miles away, but Turkish fire quashed all hopes of it joining Townshend's men.

Townshend's surrender is due less to the bombardment than to privation. The soldiers lacked food and fresh water. Efforts to bring in steamers with provisions failed following Turkish attack and the capricious flooding of the Tigris. The men thrived on morale, buoyed by a letter from King George.

Before surrendering, General Townshend destroyed his store of munitions. The enemy gains nothing but more mouths to feed (→ 6/1).

The Campbell's Soup Kids.

1916

MAY

Su	Mo	Tu	We	Th	Fr	Sa
	1	2	3	4	5	6
7	8	9	10	11	12	13
14	15	16	17	18	19	20
21	22	23	24	25	26	27
28	29	30	31			

1. German Socialist leader Karl Liebknecht arrested after anti-war protests (→ 8/2).

2. French Gen. Petain assumes central command; Nivelle takes over in Verdun (→ 24).

3. London: 4 Irish rebel leaders sentenced to death (→ 25).

5. Germany agrees to limit sub war if U.S. will oppose Allied blockade; diplomatic break averted (→ 10).

9. Wilson orders Texas, New Mexico and Arizona militias mobilized to serve on Mexican border (→ 31).

10. Germans issue Sussex pledge, offer payment for sunken liner Sussex, promise end of war on merchant ships (→ 13).

13. George Smith wins 42nd Kentucky Derby with jockey J. Loftus in the saddle.

13. Washington: A record 135,683 march in Citizens' Preparedness Parade (→ 26).

15. Austrian 3rd and 11th Armies surprise Italian Gen. Brusati at Trentino (→ 6/17).

15. Santo Domingo: U.S. Marines land to quell civil disorder (→ 10/24).

20. London: Britain agrees to supply France with coal, since most French collieries are under German occupation.

24. Western Front: Germans retake Fort Douamont in furious battle (→ 6/9).

25. Lloyd George sent to Ireland to seek peace (→ 7/1).

26. U.S. protests Allied seizure of mails at sea (→ 6/1).

30. Dario Resta takes Indy 500 in Peugot, averaging 84 mph.

30. Carranza demands immediate withdrawal of U.S. troops from Mexico (→ 6/18).

BIRTHS

10. Twelve-tone composer Milton Babbitt.

28. U.S. novelist Walker Percy.

DEATH

28. U.S. railroad magnate J.J. Hill (*9/16/1838).

Two big fleets clash in Jutland battle

May 31. The German High Seas Fleet retired tonight to the protection of the naval base at Wilhelmshaven after two days of battle with the British fleet in the North Sea.

British losses were heavy in this first encounter between the two most powerful fleets in the world. The royal navy is reported to have lost one battleship, one battlecruiser, four light cruisers and five destroyers. British battle casualties were 6,907 men. The Germans lost a battleship, a cruiser and a destroyer. Several of their major ships sustained heavy damage from British shells. German casualties were 2,545 dead.

The two battlecruiser squadrons opened action on May 30 at 2:45 p.m. and were in action for two hours. They fired salvos of four shells, each shell weighting half a ton. The British advantage in the number of ships, speed and weight of metal appears to have been wasted by Sir John Jellico, the Commander-in-Chief, who, because of poor communications, lost the German fleet at a critical point. Failing to advance in tactical formation, he lost 22 minutes realigning his ships. The question before the British Admiralty is whether the Germans, encouraged by the battle, will emerge again.

The Queen Mary, photographed from a British destroyer, goes up in flames.

Wilson urges peace league after war

May 27. President Wilson called tonight for creation of a league of nations to keep peace in the world once the war in Europe has ended. The president's proposal was made in a speech to the League to Enforce Peace, which is meeting in Washington. The league's President is William Howard Taft, the former President of the United States.

Saying that rule by force should end, President Wilson maintained that the United States would be willing to join in an organization that would ensure the freedom of the seas, protect all small countries from aggression and stop wars begun in violation of treaties. The world, Wilson said, has a right to live in peace.

Wilson, at center, in top hat.

Gallieni, savior of Paris, dies in France

Gallieni, architect of Marne victory.

May 27. General Joseph S. Gallieni, idolized throughout France as the "savior of Paris" during the critical days of August 1914, is dead at age 67. He will have a national funeral and his body will be interred at the Hotel des Invalides, which contains the tomb of Napoleon.

When the Germans in August 1914 were marching on Paris, Gallieni became Military Governor of the capital. On September 5, Gallieni collected every available motorcar in Paris, including the taxicabs, and rushed 80,000 reserve troops to counterattack. The French rolled the Germans back to the Marne, where the invaders were routed.

Well before this miracle, Gallieni had compiled a distinguished record. As a Lieutenant fresh from Saint-Cyr, he fought in the Franco-Prussian War (1870-71) and later commanded troops in the French Sudan, Indochina and Madagascar. As Governor General of Madagascar from 1890-1905, he put down several large native revolts, giving France a pacified colony of 228,000 square miles and a population of three million. Gallieni was the author of several books on colonial warfare and administration. Last year, he became Minister of War.

Norman Rockwell's first cover.

1916

JUNE

Su	Mo	Tu	We	Th	Fr	Sa
				1	2	3
4	5	6	7	8	9	10
11	12	13	14	15	16	17
18	19	20	21	22	23	24
25	26	27	28	29	30	

1. National Defense Act increases U.S. National Guard by 450,000 men (→ 7/21).

1. San Francisco: 4,000 waterfront workers quit in first unified W. Coast strike (→ 7/10).

1. Persia: Russian Gen. Baratov fails to take Khanikin, withdraws to Karind (→ 8/7).

4. Eastern Front: Russian Gen. Brusilov attacks in southwest to aid Italians, under heavy pressure from Austrians (→ 9).

5. French, British push Arabs into revolt in Hejaz; Hussein, grand sherif of Mecca, proclaims independence from Turks (→ 10).

7. Oyster Bay, L.I.: Roosevelt declines Progressive nomination (→ 10).

8. Montana: 162 killed in Butte mine disaster.

9. Eastern Front: Russians smash Austrian line, retake fortress of Lutsk (→ 26).

9. Verdun: French give in at Fort Vaux (→ 24).

10. Mecca falls to Arabs; Turks severely handicapped (→ 8/3).

10. Chicago: Charles Evans Hughes accepts Republican nomination (→ 15).

11. Italy: Salandra's Cabinet overthrown.

15. St. Louis: Democrats re-nominate Wilson and Marshall (→ 7/21).

17. Italy: Austrians retreat after loss of 81,000 to Italians' 147,000 (→ 8/6).

18. U.S. troops, warships head for Mexico again (→ 21).

21. Mexico: Carranza ambush kills 18 Americans at Carrizal (→ 7/20).

26. Brusilov renews offensive on Eastern Front (→ 30).

BIRTH

6. U.S. statesman Robert McNamara.

DEATH

6. Chinese President Yuan Shih-k'ai (*9/16/1859).

25. American realist painter Thomas Eakins (*7/25/1844).

Key offensive in Somme

French infantry on the move at the battle of the Somme.

June 30. The British Fourth Army under General Henry Ralinson is five days into an offensive made north of the Somme. Foch's army stays south of the river. They hope to lure Germans between their men, crushing them in a human vise.

The attack was planned months ago, but lack of progress at Verdun delayed it. Since Feb. 21, when 1,000 German cannons started bombarding the environs of the ancient city, casualties on both sides have been monstrous. Germans introduced a new kind of gas shell with diphosgene on June 20. Blind and paralyzed troops had to be replaced before there was any more chance of transferring forces to the Somme. Luckily, the Brusilov Offensive, an attack by the Russians on the Austro-German line that began June 2, has forced Germans to siphon some of their troops from Verdun.

How can the Somme avoid being a Verdun? Besides the northsouth attack strategy, the British are developing a new weapon. The machine-gun proof vehicle is codenamed "tank" (→ 7/1).

June 10. Charles Evans Hughes resigned from the Supreme Court today to run for president on the Republican ticket. His acceptance set the tone for the campaign, criticizing Wilson for weakness in foreign policy and pledging to recover American prestige by defending U.S. rights "on land and sea." Roosevelt is expected to quit the race to avoid a Hughes defeat.

Lord Kitchener is lost when ship hit

June 7. Lord Kitchener, the premier soldier of the British Empire, died tragically last night as the Hampshire, the cruiser on which he was traveling to Russia to boost sagging morale, struck a mine or was torpedoed off the Orkney Islands and sank, drowning all aboard. Life in London has come to a standstill while Paris and Washington are shocked by the news.

Lord Kitchener at Gallipoli.

In the last half-century, through tireless energy and devotion to imperial duty, Horatio Herbert Kitchener, 66, commanded in Palestine, Cyprus, Egypt, Sudan, South Africa and India. Two years ago, he became War Secretary (→ 7/7).

Russian offensive aimed at Austria

June 30. Proclaiming a great Russian victory, the Petrograd War Office has announced the capture of Kolomea in Galicia. To date, the offensive launched June 4th by General Aleksei Brusilov has the Austrian and German armies reeling, and Russia claims the capture of about 200,000 Austrian soldiers.

The Austrians, reported to be panic-stricken in their flight, have abandoned a large number of convoys, enabling the Russians to seize sizable stores of munitions. The offensive has also forced the Germans to divert troops from the Western and Italian fronts, where they are badly needed (→ 8/7).

1916

JULY

Su	Mo	Tu	We	Th	Fr	Sa
						1
2	3	4	5	6	7	8
9	10	11	12	13	14	15
16	17	18	19	20	21	22
23	24	25	26	27	28	29
30	31					

1. Irish nationalist leader Roger Casement sentenced to death by British court (→ 8/3).

2. Caucasus: Russians attack Turkish 3rd Army at Erzinjan (→ 25).

2. Race riots in East St. Louis leave 39 dead, hundreds hurt.

6. Russia, Japan sign treaty of alliance.

7. David Lloyd George replaces Lord Kitchener as minister of defense.

9. German U-boat Deutschland arrives in Baltimore with message for Wilson (→ 21).

10. San Francisco: Steel workers join striking longshoreman to demand eight-hour day; merchants fight back with Law and Order Committee.

13. Western Front: British cavalry dent German second line before being mowed down by machine gun fire (→ 16).

14. N.Y.: Federal health officials rush experts to fight infantile paralysis; 162 more ill.

15. William Edward Boeing founds Pacific Aero Products Co. with $100,000 capital.

16. Western Front: British cut German third line at Faureaux wood, reach Pozieres (→ 9/3).

17. Federal Farm Loan Act passes Congress, establishing land bank system and offering improvement loans.

20. Carranza agrees to arbitration in Mexican conflict (→ 8/12).

21. Congress passes $315 mil. Naval Appropriations Bill; largest in U.S. history (→ 8/13).

21. St. Paul: Prohibition Party nominates Frank Hanly and Ira Landrith (→ 11/11).

24. U.S., Denmark negotiate treaty for sale of Danish West Indies (→ 9/30).

25. U.S. Steel Corp. reports most brilliant quarter in history; $81,126,048 profit.

25. Caucasus: Russian Gen. Yudenich routs Turks at Erzinjan, killing 34,000 (→ 8/15).

30. N.Y.: Natl. Storage Munition Co. explodes; 26 dead.

Britain has biggest one-day war loss

July 1. The great Allied offensive launched this morning has been halted tonight with some French gains but only marginal British advances and very heavy casualties for the British.

After artillery preparation by 250 guns (half the French number), 11 divisions of the British Fourth Army attacked north of the Somme River. Closely packed waves of men, "systematically aligned" under army instruction, advanced into a hail of artillery, machine gun and mortar fire. Each man carried 66 pounds of equipment.

Unconcealed preparations behind the front and the prolonged artillery barrage robbed the British of any hope of surprise. The only successes were the taking of a few villages on the flanks. French attacks, although also lacking surprise, fared better, but penetrations were not deep.

The British, according to preliminary reports, suffered some 60,000 casualties today, the highest number yet reported in this costly war. French losses, although heavy, were not on that scale. Sir Douglas Haig, the British commmander, now must choose between continuing a battle of attrition or entrenching (→ 13).

Allies act on all fronts, capture thousands

Troops on the home front parade through Paris on Bastille Day.

July 11. On both the Western and Eastern Fronts, Allied forces are advancing, taking large numbers of German prisoners. In the battle of the Somme, British and French forces have captured 22,000 German prisoners. On the Eastern Front, a Russian communique said 271,620 prisoners have been taken in General Brusilov's drive toward Kovel.

Meanwhile, a British War Office communique today announced that the British army, after ten days of continuous day-and-night fighting, had finally captured the town of Contalmaison, occupied most of Mametz Wood and recaptured practically all of Trones Wood. The fierceness of the fighting was reflected in today's casualty list, which included the names of 73 officers, many from the Newfoundland contingent. And on the French front, there was heavy fighting reported on the right bank of the Meuse in the Verdun sector.

Hetty Green, world's richest woman, dies

July 3. Mrs. Hetty Green, believed to be the world's wealthiest woman, died yesterday in her 82nd year, leaving one son and one daughter. Born Henrietta Howland Robinson, she was the only child of a New Bedford, Massachusetts, merchant and shipowner, from whom she inherited about $9 million. Shortly after his death, an aunt died, leaving her $4 million, a bitterly contested legacy.

Concentrating on mortgages and money-lending rather than ships, Hetty Green kept increasing her fortune, now conjectured to be in the neighborhood of $100 million. Stories about her penurious habits are legendary. When those who had only a million or two would spend money for a cab to a party, she would put coarse stockings over her shoes and walk through the snow. In 1867, she married Edward H. Green, American Consul in Manila, but had a pre-nuptial agreement drawn up, so that her fortune remained entirely in her capable hands.

Miserly financier Hetty Green.

Six killed by bomb and scores injured

July 22. Six persons were killed and scores were injured today when a bomb exploded during an armed preparedness parade in downtown San Francisco. The bomb, believed to have been placed along the parade route by anarchists, went off just as the First California Regiment was marching by. Despite the explosion and ensuing commotion, the parade continued as planned.

Police arrested one man, Frank Josephs, a Finnish sailor, after he rushed to the site where bodies were strewn and bellowed: "This is nothing." The explosives had been stuffed into a suitcase and apparently set off by a timing device. The blast demolished one building and damaged others along the parade route (→ 1/7/39).

1916

AUGUST

Su	Mo	Tu	We	Th	Fr	Sa
		1	2	3	4	5
6	7	8	9	10	11	12
13	14	15	16	17	18	19
20	21	22	23	24	25	26
29	28	29	30	31		

2. Peace meetings held in 35 German cities (→ 24).

3. London: Roger Casement, leader of Irish uprising, hanged for high treason (→ 4/28/17).

3. Egypt: Germans under Gen. Kressenstein surprise British at Sinai, suffer 5,000 casualties to British 1,100 (→ 1/9/17).

5. American chewing gum introduced on French market.

6. Italians begin sixth attempt at Isonzo, take 9,000 prisoners (→ 27).

7. England, Russia form alliance with Persia (→ 12/13).

7. Eastern Front: Brusilov launches third offensive, advances toward Carpathian foothills (→ 11).

9. Congress creates Larsen Volcanic Natl. Park around only active volcano in U.S.

11. Poland: Czar's army takes Stanislau; Gen. Bothmer's Galician front broken (→ 9/20).

12. Washington: War Dept. orders 25,000 more troops to Mexican border (→ 11/4).

13. Naval tonnage destroyed since war's beginning totals 2,306,230; over half British; 218 neutral ships lost (→ 20).

15. Caucasus: Mustafa Kemal takes Mus, Bitlis (→ 8/17/18).

16. U.S., Canada sign accord to protect migratory birds.

19. Wilson demands railroads grant eight-hour day (→ 9/3).

20. London Times assails Am. neutrality, says will cost U.S. postwar rights (→ 9/29).

21. Federation of Catholic Societies reports on evils menacing U.S. —attacks on religion, immoral plays, easy divorce.

24. German Socialist Liebknecht given four-year sentence for peace protests (→ 10/23/18).

24. Eleutherios Venizelos calls Greeks to rise against King Constantine (→ 9/3).

27. Italy declares war on Germany (→ 9/14).

27. Balkans: Bulgarians, Germans push Allies back to Sturma River at battle of Florina (→ 9/10).

Hindenburg in top post; Rumania in war

Aug 27. The Kaiser has appointed Field Marshal von Hindenbûrg Chief of the German General Staff. The victor in the great battle of Tannenberg on the Eastern Front in 1914 replaces General Erich von Falkenhayn.

General von Ludendorff, who has been Hindenburg's chief of staff, assumes the post of First Quartermaster General or Army Chief of Staff. The two appointments were widely welcomed in the army and German political circles. Hindenburg and Ludendorff have proved to be a strong team in the past.

Meanwhile, the Allies have been encouraged by reports of progress by the Rumanian armies in the Balkans. Shortly after entering the war, Rumanian divisions joined the Russian army at Bukovina, where the Austrians were heavily engaged.

Military authorities in London hope that Rumanian reinforcements will help drive Austrian forces out of the present sector. Reports reaching the British capital say the Austrians are falling back. The King of England and the President of France have sent messages to Bucharest congratulating the Rumanian King and Cabinet (→ 9/1).

Hindenburg through French eyes.

Falkenhayn, relieved in the West.

Italians join Allies at Salonika

Aug 22. Allied soldiers cheered the arrival of Italian and Russian troops at Salonika as the regiments stormed ashore to bolster efforts on the Greek front. The French and British forces, stricken last month by widespread illness, have slowly recuperated and have recently been winning the battle against combined German-Bulgarian troops. The reinforcements are expected to speed up an Allied victory (→ 24).

Italian forces carry their colors into Salonika.

Ford plans ever cheaper car models

Aug 31. The horse and buggy days may be ending for many people when the new $250 touring automobiles roll off the Ford Motor Company's assembly lines.

The rollback in prices, in the works for several years, could increase dramatically the Ford share of the automobile market and open the way for perhaps one million new car owners who currently travel by horse-drawn vehicles. The effect of the cheaper models is expected to be felt primarily on the nation's farms and in small towns. Rural Americans, unlike most city dwellers, have enough space to store cars.

Said one motorcar dealer: "An automobile beats a horse and buggy in many ways, not only in speed and its range, but also in the cost of travel per mile." The dealer also said he believed that the lower cost of automobiles could reverse the recent exodus from the farms to the cities. "That's why they left such attractions as fresh milk and butter and new eggs and the old oaken bucket and then crowded into the city," he explained. "No way to get about and see anybody or anything. Now the automobile changes all this."

One feature of the cost-cutting plan is to do away with retail sales outlets and to appoint garage owners as salesmen of the automobiles. The Ford Motor Company is one of the most successful companies in the nation, reporting profits in the past year of nearly $60 million, of which many millions went into higher salaries and a profit-sharing plan for its employees. Ford automobile production topped 508,000 during the past year and plans are to double that output.

German sub Deutschland, bearing a note for Wilson, is greeted cautiously in Chesapeake Bay.

1916

SEPTEMBER

Su	Mo	Tu	We	Th	Fr	Sa
					1	2
3	4	5	6	7	8	9
10	11	12	13	14	15	16
17	18	19	20	21	22	23
24	25	26	27	28	29	30

1. U.S. Congress enacts Keating-Owens Act, barring items made by child labor from interstate trade.

1. Bulgaria declares war on Rumania (→ 10/23).

3. President Wilson signs bill requiring eight-hour day for railway workers.

3. Allies smash German Somme front in greatest victory of offensive (→ 15).

3. Greece grants Allies control over posts, telegraph (→ 27).

7. U.S. Congress activates Workmen's Compensation Act, encompassing 500,000 federal employees.

10. Balkans: Allies begin counteroffensive under Sarrail (→ 11/9).

14. Italians drive on Isonzo in seventh attempt (→ 10/10).

16. France and Britain recognize provisional Czech govt.

20. Eastern Front: Brusilov offensive collapses in exhaustion as German reinforcements save Austria from possible ejection from war (→ 11/23).

20. German Spartacus League publishes first copy of underground newspaper Die International.

23. Paris: It is reported that Germany deliberately spreads tuberculosis among prisoners.

24. Naturalist John Burroughs claims moving pictures deprive viewers of brain power.

25. New York Giants set new record, winning 21 in a row.

27. Greece: Constantine declares war on Bulgaria (→ 29).

28. British Defense Minister Lloyd George offers war aims; "We must fight until Germany's complete downfall."

29. Crete: Venizelos forms provisional government with authority to form army, join Allies (→ 10/11).

29. Germany asserts U.S. aviators violate American neutrality (→ 10/5).

30. Danish Parliament requires plebiscite on sale of West Indies to U.S. (→ 1/17/17).

Tanks aid Somme victory

Sept 15. A small force of British tanks has made important gains on one sector of the Somme front. Only 11 of the 49 new armored vehicles available were used in the attack. Delays in moving the iron monsters to the front and mechanical defects prevented the use of the entire force.

This first appearance of tanks on a battlefield was said by their supporters to prove that a strong tank force is the key to unlocking the trench barrier on the Western Front. For years now, Allied and German armies have been bogged down, forced to fight a seemingly fruitless form of trench warfare.

Soldiers and politicians, among them Winston Churchill, who advocate a greater role for the tank in European warfare, while pleased with today's success, fear that the chance for a major strategic surprise has been lost. They believe the tanks should not have been used until there was a sufficient number to force a major breakthrough of the German lines. They also fear the tanks will be used in driblets rather than in mass (→ 10/24).

The American-made Whippet tank.

New menace at the Somme.

Zeppelin is downed in raid on London

Sept 3. A squadron of German zeppelins staged a bombing raid tonight on England, with the eastern counties of England the apparent objective, the government announced. One of the airships was reported to have been brought down in flames while passing over the London district. The government statement said that "many bombs were dropped in widely separate locations," but there were no reports of casualties. It was the largest raid yet by German zeppelins (→ 10/3).

Zeppelin afloat in The Thames.

Wilson supports votes for women

Suffragists accept Wilson's backing.

Sept 8. President Wilson assured cheering suffragettes tonight that women will get the right to vote "in a little while." Speaking to a suffrage gathering in Atlantic City, New Jersey, the president said: "I have come here to fight with you." His pledge of support brought the 4,000 delegates to the convention to their feet. But a suffrage leader, Dr. Anna Howard Shaw, told the president that women are getting impatient. "We have waited long enough to get the vote," she said. "We want it now" (→ 11/7).

Rockefeller now worth $1 billion

Sept 29. The boom in Standard Oil stocks yesterday to over $2,000 a share makes John D. Rockefeller, founder and largest stockholder, almost certainly a billionaire.

In 1907, Rockefeller was shown to own 247,692 shares of Standard Oil, more than three times as much as anyone else and more than six times as much as the next individual shareholder. He also holds vast interests in various banks and railroads as well as enormous blocks of national, state and municipal bonds.

The Rockefellers, father and son, have donated many millions to education and medical research and about $10 million to various relief agencies since the war in Europe began (→ 10/10).

318 I.W.W. strikers jailed after raid

Sept 14. Striking members of the Industrial Workers of the World were arrested today on charges of rioting at the Jermyn and Company mines near Scranton, Pennsylvania. Police charge that for two weeks the I.W.W. members have been trying to tie up operations at the mines by assaulting other employees, members of the United Mine Workers, who are not on strike.

The arrests of the I.W.W. men took place at what was to have been a secret meeting in Old Forge. Upon learning of plans for the meeting, law enforcement officers issued orders that it not be held. When the I.W.W. members defied the order, state troopers and county deputies entered the hall and herded the strikers into ice and coal wagons, trucks and automobiles for the trip to the jail. Most of those arrested are foreign-born.

"One big union for all."

1916

OCTOBER

Su	Mo	Tu	We	Th	Fr	Sa
1	2	3	4	5	6	7
8	9	10	11	12	13	14
15	16	17	18	19	20	21
22	23	24	25	26	27	28
29	30	31				

2. Bank reports indicate New York is world's largest exporting city; $10.8 mil. daily, half in munitions (→ 10).

5. Wilson announces in Omaha speech, U.S. is ready to fight for a "just cause" (→ 31).

10. Italy, Austria clash in 8th battle at Isonzo (→ 5/12/17).

10. British insist to U.S. blacklist on "contraband" trade items does not violate international law (→ 11/7).

11. Athens: French take control of Greek navy (→ 17).

12. Boston: Red Sox beat Brooklyn 4-1 in fifth game to win third World Series in last four years.

16. Diaghilev's Ballet Russe opens at Manhattan Opera House.

16. U.S. Episcopalian Convention announces brides must still promise to obey husbands in marriage ceremony.

17. Entente recognizes Venizelos Cabinet in Greece (→ 12/1).

20. U.S. Congress awards Army $17,381,666 for 375 new planes (→ 27).

21. Austrian Premier Count Stuergkh assassinated.

24. Henry Ford awards equal pay to women, $5 per day.

24. Verdun: French break German line, recapture Fort Douamont (→ 11/2).

24. Dominican rebels kill two American officers (→ 11/30).

27. Germany announces all merchant ship captains will be regarded as prisoners (→ 31).

28. Nine Norwegian ships sunk in 24 hours.

31. Americans lost as U-boat sinks British liner Marina (→).

BIRTH

26. French Socialist Francois Mitterrand.

DEATHS

12. Mad King Otto of Bavaria (*4/27/1844).

25. American realist painter William Chase (*11/1/1849).

Costly undersea war; subs crowd U.S. coast

Deadly encounter with a U-boat.

Oct 31. German submarines are effectively operating in both the Mediterranean Sea and the Atlantic as two British ships and one Greek boat have been torpedoed and sunk in recent days. Six Americans aboard the British ship, the Marina, perished and 64 Britons died in the German sub attack off Ireland, while casualty figures of the English steamer, the Rowanmore, have not been released. It is believed few, if any, died in the second assault.

In Greek waters, a German U-boat struck the Angheliki, killing 200 Greeks and also hindering attempts of rescue ships by firing upon them. No warnings were issued before any of the attacks.

Earlier this month, the German sub, U-53, roared off the coast of Rhode Island. In a brazen raid, it sunk five merchant ships of British and Norwegian nationality, bringing a force of American destroyers to the scene. All crew members were saved, but President Wilson's anger was ignited. He has called for an investigation of the U-53 attacks and of the Marina and Rowenmore downings. And he's cabled Berlin demanding explanations. Some expect strong reactions from the White House. U.S. destroyers continue to patrol the New England coast in search of German subs (→ 11/1).

Mrs. Sanger offers birth control help

Oct 16. No social progress is possible, especially where poverty is a factor, unless we begin to limit the size of families. That, in a nutshell, is the argument of Margaret Sanger, the public health nurse, who has studied with Havelock Ellis and others in London. Mrs. Sanger was once jailed for 30 days for opening a birth control clinic, the first outside of Holland, in Brooklyn, New York. Last year, she was indicted for sending birth control information, printed in English, Italian and Yiddish, through the United States mails.

A Sanger worker informs the public.

Russellites' founder passes away at 64

Millenial prophet Charles Russell.

Oct 31. Charles Taze Russell, the founder of a religious sect that believes that the second coming of Christ has already occurred, died today at age 64. A Pennsylvania native, Russell was just 20 years old when he founded his religious group, which became known as the Russellites. The sect's teachings, based entirely on the Bible, are widely published through a paper known as the Watch Tower. The Russell sect believes that the second coming of Christ occurred in 1874, and that the world now exists in a state of social revolution that will end in chaos.

Hughes complains of Wilson's policy

Oct 31. With the election just a week away, Charles Evans Hughes has continued to step up his attacks on President Wilson. Hughes, the Republican candidate for president, has accused his Democratic opponent of mismanagement of the government and of failing to prepare the United States for the economic crisis that he maintains it will be sure to face after the war in Europe has ended.

In Brooklyn, Hughes ridiculed the president, accusing him of "weak timidity" by failing to build up an adequate military establishment to uphold the nation's honor. "American government," he told his enthusiastic Brooklyn audience, "has seemed to mean naught but impotence and unavailing words."

Addressing a large crowd in Rochester, New York, Hughes disputed the recent claim by the president that America is ready to meet any economic crisis that might arise after the fighting ends in Europe.

Continuing his campaign swing today in Indiana, Hughes told a crowd of 50,000 that he would oppose placing an embargo on war supplies to Europe and also combat legislation warning Americans off merchant ships owned by nations now at war. Hughes declared that he favors "maintenance of every right, including the right of travel and the right of shipment... We must consider our place as a great nation devoted to the interests of peace" (→ 11/9).

1916

NOVEMBER

Su	Mo	Tu	We	Th	Fr	Sa
			1	2	3	4
5	6	7	8	9	10	11
12	13	14	15	16	17	18
19	20	21	22	23	24	25
26	27	28	29	30		

1. Marina survivors testify liner had no warning (→ 8).

2. Verdun: French retake Fort Vaux (→ 13).

4. Pittsburgh steel mills report severe labor shortage, plan to import Southern Negroes.

4. Mexico: Villa rebels kill American physician in Chihuahua City (→ 2/19/17).

5. Germany proclaims Poland's autonomy (→ 1/14/17).

7. Projected U.S. foreign trade for 1916 to equal $8 bil., one fifth of intl. total (→ 12).

7. Woman suffrage defeated in S.D,, W.Va. (→ 6/19/17).

8. U-boat sinks U.S. liner Columbian; crew saved (→ 12/23).

9. Chancellor von Bethmann Hollweg declares Germany favors intl. league after war.

12. U.S. reports 100% increase in food prices over last year.

13. Western Front: Battle of Somme ends; eight-mile British advance in 4 months; 650,000 Germans die, 195,000 French, 420,000 British (→ 12/3).

14. Lansing officially protests German deportation of 300,000 Belgians (→ 30).

14. London reports 3.2m British women working outside homes.

19. Balkans: Italians help Allies take Monastir; year's losses total 50,000 Allies, 60,000 Bulgar-Germans (→ 6/12/17).

23. Eastern Front: Germans join Bulgarian Danube Army, push north across Danube to entrap Rumanians (→ 29).

24. Petrograd: Trepoff replaces Sturmer as premier in victory for progressives (→ 1/9/17).

25. Army over Navy 15-7 at the Polo Grounds in New York.

29. Rumanian Cabinet quits Bucharest for Jassy (→ 12/6).

30. U.S. troops place Santo Domingo under martial law.

30. Antwerp: 200 killed in riot over Belgian deportations.

DEATH

15. Polish novelist Henryk Sienkiewicz, "Quo Vadis" (*5/5/1846).

Franz Joseph dies after 68 years on throne

Franz Joseph's reign began in revolution (1848) and ended in war.

Nov 30. Austrian Emperor Franz Joseph, whose effort to hold his heterogeneous empire together by suppressing dissent led instead to European war, is dead. He reigned for more than two-thirds of a century.

The successor to the throne is Archduke Carl Francis Joseph, 29. The new Emperor was the younger brother of Archduke Francis Ferdinand, whose assassination by Serbian nationalists seeking independence for Bosnia caused war to break out between Austria and Serbia, and, because of alliances, through most of Europe. Franz Joseph annexed Bosnia in 1908.

Although personally popular with his people, Franz Joseph's long reign was characterized by continuing and ultimately unsuccessful efforts to hold together the 17 nationalities that made up his empire. Many lost wars in the last century cost Austria its Italian possessions, weakened its control of Hungary and also cost it authority over Germany.

Jeannette Rankin is first Congresswoman

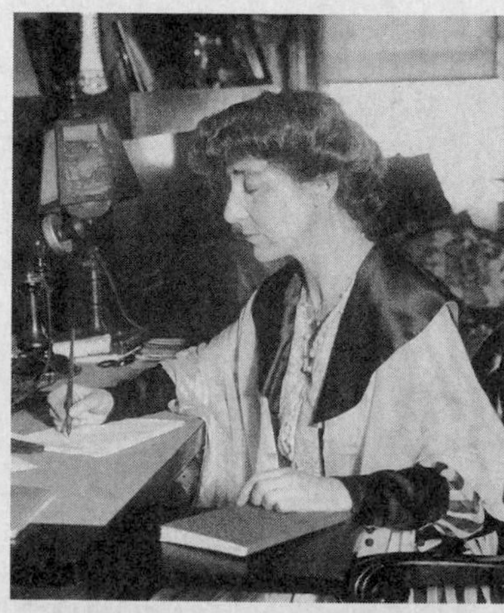

Jeannette Rankin of Montana.

Nov 7. Jeannette Rankin scored a major upset today by becoming the first woman ever elected to the United States Congress. A Montana Republican, now in her middle 30s, Miss Rankin became a familiar figure on the campaign trail this year, as she crisscrossed the state on horseback. While Montana gave its electoral votes to President Wilson, a Democrat, Miss Rankin bested her Democratic opponent by approximately 25,000 votes. She explained her victory by saying that women "got the vote in Montana because the spirit of pioneer days was still alive."

Wilson re-elected President 272-259

Nov 11. After days of uncertainty, final returns show that President Wilson eked out a narrow victory in his bid for re-election. A completed tally shows that the president won California's electoral votes, thus putting him over the top in his race against Republican Charles Evans Hughes, former Associate Justice of the United States Supreme Court.

The final vote shows 272 electoral votes for Wilson; 259 for Hughes. The popular vote was 9,129,000 for Wilson; 8,538,221 for Hughes. The president's re-election was all the more dramatic in that just the day after the November 7 voting, The New York Times and other papers had conceded the election to Hughes. Wilson's campaign slogan was: "He kept us out of war."

Maxim, inventor of fast-firing gun, dies

Nov 24. Sir Hiram Maxim, inventor of the first fully automatic machine gun, died at his home in London at the age of 76. Maxim was born in Maine, was apprenticed to a carriage builder at the age of 14 and began his career as an inventor in an uncle's engineering works in Massachusetts. He moved to England permanently in 1883.

The next year, he produced his machine gun, which used the recoil of a fired round to eject the cartridge and load the next bullet. The British government placed a large order for the Maxim gun after a demonstration at which it fired more than 600 rounds per minute. Maxim also had a major role in the invention of smokeless powder, which made his machine gun much more effective. It has been put to deadly use by both sides in the war.

Sir Hiram with his Maxim gun.

1916

DECEMBER

Su	Mo	Tu	We	Th	Fr	Sa
					1	2
3	4	5	6	7	8	9
10	11	12	13	14	15	16
17	18	19	20	21	22	23
24	25	26	27	28	29	30
31						

1. Athens: King Constantine refuses surrender to Allies (→ 6/12/17).

3. Western Front: Joffre dismissed after failure at Somme; Nivelle is new French commander-in-chief (→ 15).

5. David Lloyd George replaces Herbert Asquith as British prime minister.

12. Chancellor proposes peace talks in Reichstag, declares Central Powers inconquerable (→ 14).

13. Mesopotamia: British under Gen. Sir Frederick Maude renew advance up Tigris River (→ 2/23/17).

14. New York: Stock market responds to Germany's peace overture; leading issues drop four to ten points (→ 15).

15. Russian Czar, Duma reject German peace offers (→ 18).

18. Wilson asks peace terms of European powers (→ 26).

23. Sec. of State Lansing hints U.S. may have to abandon policy of avoiding "entangling foreign alliances" (→ 1/31/17).

24. Jules Verne's "20,000 Leagues Under the Sea" opens in New York.

26. Germany replies to Wilson, witholds terms, repeats call for conference (→ 30).

30. Allies call German proposal a "sham" and a "war maneuver" (→ 1/2/17).

CULTURAL EVENTS, 1916

Literature: James Joyce's "Portrait of an Artist as a Young Man"; Carl Sandburg's "Chicago Poems"; Dreiser's "The Genius," banned in New York.

Academia: Martin Buber's "The Spirit of Judaism"; Vilfredo Pareto's "Mind and Society"; John Dewey's "Democracy and Education."

The Arts: Dadaist movement founded in Zurich by Tristan Tzara, Hans Arp, Hugo Bak; Frank Lloyd Wright's Imperial Hotel, Tokyo.

Films: D.W. Griffith's "Intolerance"; Thomas Ince's "Civilization"; Charlie Chaplin's "The Pawn Shop."

Millions of women workers aid in war

Behind-the-scenes war effort.

Millions of women are being employed outside the home in jobs traditionally held by men. The Allied and Central Powers increasingly rely on women to produce munitions, and those not working directly in factories are tram drivers, porters and railway workers. German leaders, however, have expressed misgivings over women's assumption of these new roles.

Jack London, robust novelist, is dead

Nov 22. Jack London, author of Arctic and sea-faring tales, died tonight. He was 40 years old. London, who suffered from depression, had taken an excess of morphine.

London, born in San Francisco, left home early. He sailed on fishing boats in the Bering Sea and joined the Alaskan gold rush in 1897. His books reflect a personal fight for survival. "The Call of the Wild" (1903) and "The Sea Wolf" (1904) tell of two heroes, a dog and a man, overcoming the elements.

Jack London at 29.

Lloyd George takes office; Asquith out

New Prime Minister Lloyd George.

Dec 10. David Lloyd George has formed a government. The War Council will include only five members: Lloyd George; Lord Curzon, who will head the council; Chancellor of the Exchequer Andrew Bonar Law; Arthur Henderson; and Lord Milner. Arthur Balfour will be Foreign Secretary. Herbert H. Asquith resigned when his Cabinet could not reach agreement about the make-up and leadership of the council.

Germans capture Rumanian capital

Dec 6. Bucharest has fallen into German hands, and Rumanian soldiers are retreating in panic and disarray toward the Danube. Ploechti, a major railway junction in the Prahava Valley, has also been taken. Besides control of the trains, the Germans now have access to the oil produced there. The Rumanians still guard their harvests along the borders of the lower Danube.

The Germans are making a swift conquest. Defenders made brief sallies against them in the Carpathian woods, but they have only delayed the inevitable. The Transylvanian Mountains, a natural defense that guarded the area for ages, proved no barrier. The Arge River, a quarter-mile wide in parts, might have kept the Germans out, but the Rumanians neglected to burn their bridges behind them (→ 3/16/17).

Verdun's terrible toll: 700,000 dead

Dec 15. French troops today broke through the German lines in the Verdun sector north of Fort Douaumont on a front of six and one-half miles with some units penetrating up to two miles.

The French Ministry of War announced "success is complete" and that 7,500 prisoners have been taken, including 300 officers.

This tactical success may balance official concern over Verdun's drain on the French army. Unofficial estimates put German and French losses thus far at 700,000 men; the greater part French. Doubts are heard about France's role in the important upcoming battles of 1917 (→ 2/23/17).

Rasputin, Russia's evil genius, killed

Dec 30. The career of the hated Siberian monk Gregory Rasputin, who many believe has had such an unhealthy influence on the royal family, has come to a violent end. He has been assassinated by two members of the Russian nobility who apparently believed that Rasputin favored Germany in the war.

Although of a peasant background, Rasputin rose to be one of the most powerful men in Russia because of the Czarina's faith in his hypnotic powers. The Empress believed that this unordained religious teacher had used his powers to cure the heir apparent, Alexis, of hemophilia, and her trust in his judgment soon extended to political decisions as well as personal and family matters.

The hypnotic Rasputin.

1916

JANUARY

Su	Mo	Tu	We	Th	Fr	Sa
	1	2	3	4	5	6
7	8	9	10	11	12	13
14	15	16	17	18	19	20
21	22	23	24	25	26	27
28	29	30	31			

1. Pasadena, Ca.: Oregon shuts out Pennsylvania 14-0 in third Rose Bowl.

1. Simon Bamberger becomes first non-Mormon governor of Utah.

1. Ohio: Victor Herbert's romantic opera "Eileen" premieres in Cleveland.

2. U.S. instructs Ambassador Sharp in Paris to tell Entente America will reject German peace offer (→ 10).

5. Rumania: Bulgarian, German troops occupy port of Braila (→ 6/12/17).

9.Petrograd: Premier Trepov resigns; Prince Golitzin succeeds.→

9. Sinai: British push Turks from peninsula, capture 1,600, prepare to move on Palestine (→ 3/26).

10. Germany rebuked; Entente officially rejects proposal for peace talks, demands return of occupied territories (→ 6/6).

14. Provisional Parliament established in Poland (→ 5/1).

17. New York: Original Dixieland Jazz Band opens at Reisenweber's Restaurant.

17. Denmark concludes sale of Danish West Indies to U.S. for $25 million; considered important for protection of Panama Canal.

18. Petrograd: Duma President Rodzianko demands that czar form new govt. (→ 3/10).

20. London arms factory explodes, killing 80.

22. Wilson presents Senate with plan for peace league, calls for "peace without victory" (→ 26).

26. Russia endorses Wilson, arguing for independent Poland, free access to seas.

31. Germany resumes unlimited sub warfare; all neutral ships in war zone to be attacked (→ 2/3).

31. Russia: Allied representatives meet in Petrograd.

DEATH

16. U.S. Admiral George Dewey (*12/26/1837).

Prosperity unlimited

The shiny face of prosperity. Wartime growth continues to spur U.S. business.

Jan 1. While the war continues to rage on the other side of the Atlantic, the United States has just ended its most prosperous year in history. Prices are up, but so are wages. Unemployment is virtually nonexistent. Both labor and capital have shared in the year's record profits.

The past year saw the output of steel and iron soar to record levels. Foreign trade, too, set an all-time high, reaching near the $8 billion mark, while trade within the United States topped $45 billion. With more money to spend, more and more Americans are investing in an array of luxuries that were far beyond their reach only a few years ago. And the New World has become the creditor of the Old.

There are those who are concerned over the wartime prosperity, who fear that the bubble might burst and leave the nation saddled with debts once the war in Europe draws to an end. But Frank A. Vanderlip, President of the National City Bank of New York, says the business outlook for the new year is excellent.

Strikes in Russian cities protest war

Jan 9. Strikes called in munitions factories in Petrograd and neighboring cities face violent suppression from the Czar's troops as workers protest the country's involvement in the war. While Russian casualties grow at an alarming rate, people on the home front are starving. Officials seem indifferent to pleas for better transportation and distribution of food. Unfortunately, the strike may make a difference only to Russian soldiers in the trenches, defenseless without arms (→ 18).

Death on the front and austerity at home bring Russians into the streets.

Germany secretly approaches Mexico

Jan 16. In an amazing political move, Germany has proposed an alliance to Mexico to make war on the United States if this nation should not remain neutral in the European war. The Kaiser's government would reward Mexico with great financial support; the reacquisition of Texas, Arizona and New Mexico; and Mexico would share in Germany's victorious peace terms.

A correspondence between German Foreign Minister Alfred Zimmerman and German Minister in Mexico von Eckhardt was intercepted by British intelligence and forwarded to America. The proposition indicates to most that the Germans are desperate for help in their waning war effort (→ 2/24).

Symbol of America Buffalo Bill dead

Frontier showman "Buffalo Bill."

Jan 10. William F. Cody was so skilled with a rifle that in 1868 he managed to kill more than 4,000 buffalo. Ever since, he has been known as "Buffalo Bill." Born in Iowa, raised in Missouri and Kansas, Cody was also Army scout, Indian fighter, hotel owner and land speculator. But his greatest role was showman: his Wild West Show, featuring Sitting Bull and Annie Oakley, toured the world, earning Cody the friendship of European royalty. Buffalo Bill died today at 71.

1917

FEBRUARY

Su	Mo	Tu	We	Th	Fr	Sa
				1	2	3
4	5	6	7	8	9	10
11	12	13	14	15	16	17
18	19	20	21	22	23	24
25	26	27	28			

3. U.S. blasts sub warfare, severs diplomatic relations with Germany (→ 3).

3. German submarine sinks U.S. liner Housatonic off coast of Sicily (→ 7).

3. Berlin places restrictions on use of coal in order to combat severe shortages.

5. U.S. Congress nullifies Wilson's veto over Immigration Act; literacy tests required; Asian laborers excluded except for Japanese (→ 2/12/19).

7. British steamer California sunk off coast of Ireland by German U-boat (→ 7).

7. Germany announces it holds all American residents hostage (→ 14).

10. London: International Zionist leaders meet with British govt. to discuss Jewish settlement in Palestine.

14. Austria sinks American schooner Lyman M. Law (→ 21).

17. Australia: Nationalist Party under Laborite Wm. Hughes takes control of coalition govt.

19. American troops recalled from Mexican border (→ 12/15).

21. 134 non-belligerent Allied ships sunk in three weeks of unlimited sub warfare (→ 26).

23. U.S.: Smith Hughes Act establishes Federal Board for Vocational Education, offering funds to states for trade and agricultural schools.

23. Western Front: Germans begin secretly withdrawing 20 miles to tighter defensive lines (→ 4/5).

23. Mesopotamia: British forces under Gen. Maude retake Kut; Turks withdraw to Baghdad (→ 3/11).

24. Zimmerman telegram made public in U.S., revealing German attempt to bring Mexico into war against U.S.

26. Wilson publicly asks Congress for power to arm merchant ships.→

BIRTH

25. British writer Anthony Burgess.

Germany declares total submarine warfare; U.S. breaks relations

Feb 26. President Woodrow Wilson delivered a brief but important speech today, asking both houses of Congress to provide the means to maintain "an armed neutrality" to deal with unrestricted German submarine warfare.

After the president's speech, a bill was introduced in the House of Representatives providing for the arming of merchant and other shipping. This, in the president's words, would protect "our ships and our people in their legitimate pursuits on the sea."

The president read his brief speech in a tense atmosphere. While he was speaking, news of the sinking of the Cunard liner Lanconia passed by word of mouth among the legislators. A total of 207 survivors from the Lanconia have been landed in Ireland. At least 25 passengers are dead, including two American citizens.

Despite the news of the loss of the Lanconia, Republicans in both houses of Congress appeared reluctant to grant the president wide powers for the present.

Today's action by the president was seen as a natural sequel to the breaking of relations with Germany and Austria on February 3. This action followed Berlin's announcement that any vessel entering a proscribed area would be sunk without warning.

Count von Bernstorff that day received his passport from the State Department and departed. He had held the post of German Ambassador since 1908. United States Ambassador James W. Gerard was ordered home from Berlin on the same day.

Also this month, the Housatonic, a U.S. ship, and a British steamer, the California, were sunk by the Germans. A total of 134 non-belligerent ships have been sunk by Germany in the last three weeks.

Meanwhile, former President Theodore Roosevelt has offered Wilson his full support and has volunteered to raise a full division. And the New York State National Guard and the Navy Militia have been ordered into service.

The Navy has seized the interned German auxiliary cruisers, the Kronprinz Wilhelm and the Prinz Eitel. The North German Lloyd liner Kronprinzessen Cecelle also was taken over. She had been sabotaged (→ 3/9).

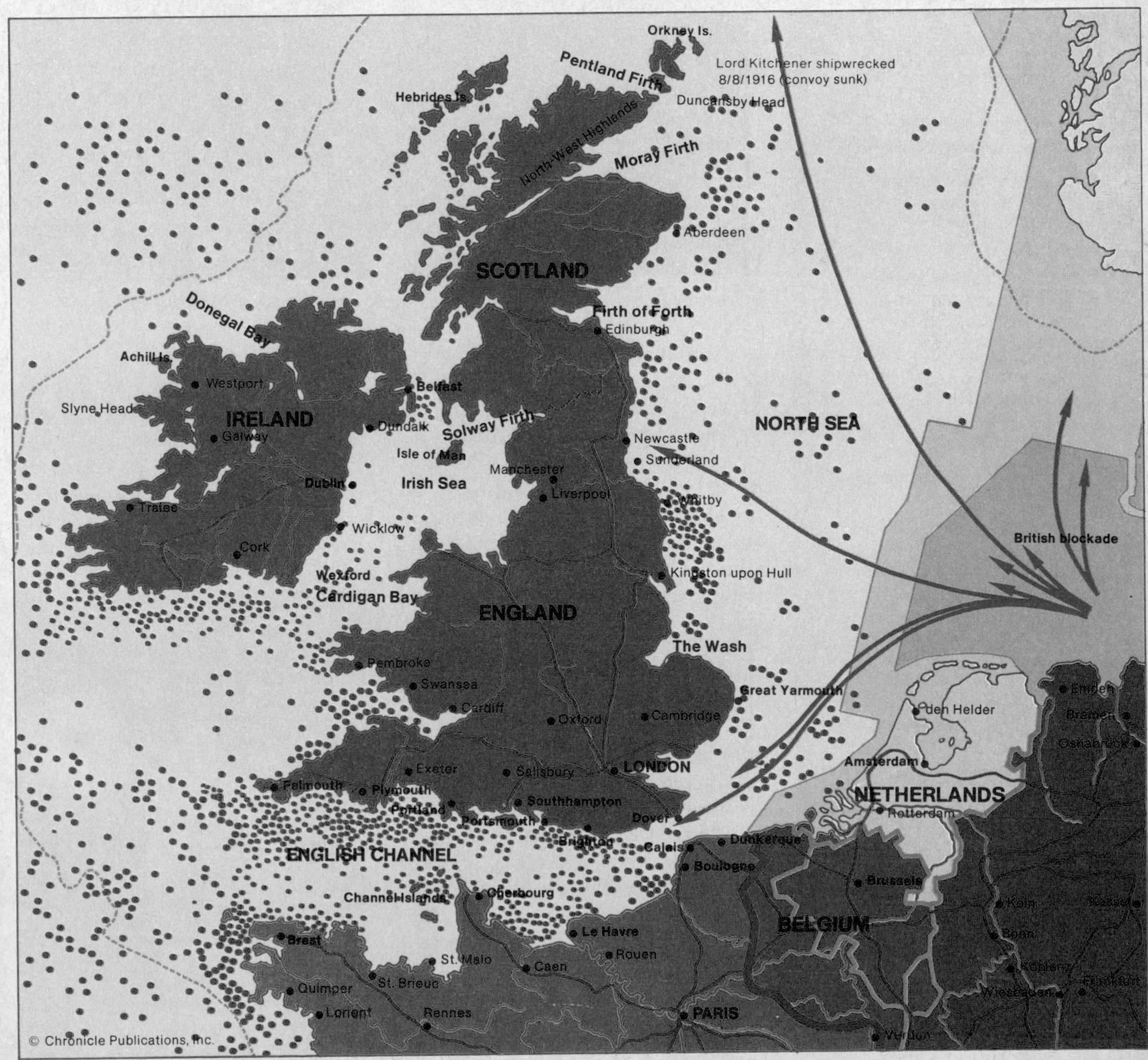

The war at sea. Red dots indicate sinkings of Allied ships by German submarines.

1917

MARCH

Su	Mo	Tu	We	Th	Fr	Sa
				1	2	3
4	5	6	7	8	9	10
11	12	13	14	15	16	17
18	19	20	21	22	23	24
25	26	27	28	29	30	31

2. Congress passes Jones Act; Puerto Rico becomes U.S. territory, its inhabitants U.S. citizens.

7. U.S.: Victor Co. issues first jazz recording featuring "Dixieland Jazz Band One-Step."

9. Wilson overrides Senate filibuster, exercises presidential power to arm merchant vessels (→ 12).

10. Petrograd: Workers demonstrate to protest war and famine (→ 16).

11. Mesopotamia: Baghdad falls to British (→ 9/28).

12. Germans torpedo American merchant ship Algonquin (→ 18).

14. French Defense Minister Lyautey and Briand Cabinet resign.

14. China breaks off diplomatic relations with Germany.

16. Petrograd Soviet issues Order one, abolishing disciplinary authority of army officers (→ 4/7).

17. German destroyers sink two British destroyers, one merchant ship in English Channel (→ 17).

18. Germans sink U.S. ships City of Memphis, Vigilante, Illinois without warning (→ 21).

21. Wilson calls special session of Congress for April 2 (→ 4/2).

22. Petrograd: U.S. becomes first to recognize Kerensky govt. in Russia (→ 4/6).

23. Austrian Emperor Charles I makes peace proposal to French President Poincare.

25. San Antonio: John McGraw gets record contract to manage Giants for $50,000 per year.

26. Palestine: British under Gen. Sir Charles Dobell fail at battle of Gaza (→ 4/19).

DEATH

8. German Count Ferdinand von Zeppelin, invented dirigible (*7/8/1838).

Facing revolt, Russian Czar abdicates

Citizens turn out by the thousands in Moscow to celebrate the end of czarist rule.

March 16. At 3 o'clock this afternoon, Russian Czar Nicholas II abdicated. He signed the document of relinquishment before officers at army headquarters in Pskov. "May God help Russia," he said.

The abdication caps months of turmoil. The Russian offensive on the German front has resulted in staggering casualties —two million in 1915 alone. The people's cries for peace go unheeded, the czar showing his approval of war by taking personal command of the army a few months ago. Starvation grips the nation; bureaucratic ineptitude and greed keep what little food there is from reaching the hungry. When workers struck this winter, demanding "Bread and Freedom," czarist troops gunned down hundreds of them.

On March 12, the czar ordered the Duma, the Russian Congress consisting of moderate liberals and supporters of the regime, to dissolve. It refused. A guard regiment was called on to enforce the decree, but it mutinied instead.

On that same day, two groups prepared to govern Russia: the progressive block, consisting of leftist Duma members, and the Petrograd Soviet of Workers' and Soldiers' Deputies. The latter includes factory workshop leaders, representatives of mutinying military units and heads of socialist groups.

The czar recommends his more liberal brother, the Grand Duke, assume the throne. He is unlikely to accept the honor. The former royal family must now either face the revolutionists or flee (→ 22).

The official photograph of the Czar and his family.

1917

APRIL

Su	Mo	Tu	We	Th	Fr	Sa
1	2	3	4	5	6	7
8	9	10	11	12	13	14
15	16	17	18	19	20	21
22	23	24	25	26	27	28
29	30					

2. Wilson asks Congress for war declaration vs. Germany; "The world must be made safe for democracy" (→ 4).

4. U.S. Senate votes 90-6 to enter war (→ 6).

5. Western Front: Germans complete withdrawal, establish Hindenburg line (→ 15).

6. House passes war declaration 373-50; Wilson signs; U.S. enters war.→

6. Petrograd: New Liberal govt. establishes 8-hour day, ends capital punishment (→ 16).

7. Russian Minister of Justice Kerensky calls on German people to oust kaiser (→ 5/10).

7. Panamanian Pres. Valdez promises to aid U.S. in defending Canal (→ 13).

13. Bolivia severs relations with Germany (→ 9/12).

14. House unanimously passes $7 billion war loan (→ 19).

15. Western Front: British, with Canadian help, gain victory at Arras, lose 84,000 to German 75,000 (→ 16).

16. Western Front: French begin Nivelle offensive, pierce 25-mile front (→ 20).

18. Pacific Aero Products Co. becomes Boeing Airplane Co.

19. Palestine: British beaten in 2nd battle of Gaza, lose 6,444 to Turks' 2,000 (→ 11/14).

19. Warship Mongolia fires first U.S. shot, sinks German submarine (→ 5/7).

22. British For. Sec. Arthur J. Balfour arrives in Washington to discuss war plans (→ 24).

24. U.S. awards Britain $200 million war loan (→ 25).

25. French leaders Viviani and Joffre welcomed in Washington.

28. U.S.: 200 members of Congress call on Lloyd George to free Ireland (→ 6/15).

30. France: Petain replaces Nivelle as chief of staff after failed offensive (→ 5/4).

DEATH

1. Ragtime pianist, composer Scott Joplin (*11/24/1868).

U.S. Congress votes to enter the war

April 6. America is at war.

The word was flashed around the world just minutes after President Woodrow Wilson signed into law the declaration of war approved this week by Congress. The United States' entry in the war against Germany came precisely at 1:18 this afternoon, the moment when the president, sitting in a tiny room just off the White House entrance lobby, signed the war document.

President Wilson, in an eloquent speech to a joint session of Congress on April 2, had called for America's entry into the war in Europe, proclaiming: "The world must be made safe for democracy."

In his speech, Wilson also said: "It is a fearful thing to lead this great peaceful people into war, the most terrible of all wars. But the right is more precious than the peace, and we shall fight for the things that we have always carried nearest our hearts, —for democracy, . . . for the rights and liberties of small nations, for a universal dominion of right by such a concert of free peoples as shall bring peace and safety to all nations and make the world itself at last free. To such a task we can dedicate our lives and our fortunes, everything that we are and everything that we have, with the pride of those who know that the day has come when America is privileged to spend her blood and her might for the principles that gave her birth . . . God helping her, she can do no other."

Boy Scouts mark entry into the war with a disorderly parade down 5th Ave.

It is said that upon his return to the White House, the president was heard to say, "My message was one of death for young men. How odd it seems to applaud that." And he put his head in his hands and wept.

The war resolution passed in the Senate, 90 to six, two days ago, after 13 hours of debate. House approval, by a vote of 373 to 50, came in the wee hours of this morning, climaxing an emotional 17-hour debate. In both houses, those crowding the galleries cheered lustily as the vote was announced.

Among those voting against entering the war was Jeannette Rankin, a Montana Republican, and the only woman ever elected to Congress. With tears streaming down her face, she rose slowly and said: "I want to stand by my country, but I cannot vote for war. I vote no."

The United States' move toward war had begun some weeks ago when the president had notified Congress that "the imperial German government" had announced it would sink every vessel that approached Great Britain, Ireland or various Mediterranean ports. This stand, the president said, was a reversal of an earlier promise made by Germany that passenger boats would not be sunk and that warning would be given to other vessels before any submarine warfare. The new policy, said the president, represented a "reckless lack of compassion" and constituted "a war against all nations."

In its first move of the war, the U.S. government seized 91 German-owned vessels, 27 of them in New York harbor. The government may use some of the vessels later as troop transports. Meeting this afternoon with his Cabinet, the president was told that about 65 persons suspected of being German spies had been ordered arrested and that the Navy would take over all radio stations.

America's entry into the war has been praised in London by Prime Minister David Lloyd George at a press conference. He said that "America has at one bound become a world power in a sense she never was before" (→ 14).

Marshal Joffre salutes Lafayette in Washington as America prepares to repay her debt to France.

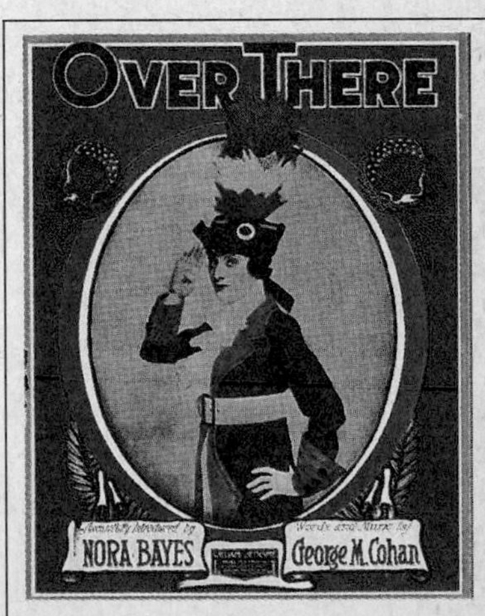

Cohan wrote "Over There" on the day war was declared.

Lenin, home from exile, in Petrograd

April 10. Vladimir Ilyich Lenin, vitriolic Marxist leader, has arrived in Petrograd. He has not stepped foot on Russian soil for 11 years. Germans arranged the journey home from Switzerland, sealing him in a railroad car and guiding it through the battlefields of Europe. The Germans think Lenin will further destabilize Russia, making the nation easier prey.

Lenin returns to a Russia in turmoil.

Lenin was born April 22, 1870, in Simbirsk. He was the son of a school administrator. Lenin joined the Russian Social Democratic Labor Party in 1893, but after ten years had enough of their tactics of delay and conciliation. He organized the more leftist members into the group known as the Bolsheviks, which had some power during the short-lived revolution of 1905. Lenin proceeded to Austria-Hungary, where he remained until the European war made itself felt. He then passed into Switzerland.

Lenin blames the current war on capitalism: Its ultimate aims are to procure enough raw materials and workers so as to keep the victorious engine (whatever nation that will be) blasting ahead at full steam. He would end the war at once, distribute land to the peasants and abolish the bureaucracy, army and the police. Lenin plans to publish these and other proposals in a few days.

The leader will find the number of Bolsheviks sadly diminished. They have done nothing politically for months. However, fellow exiles Leon Trotsky and Joseph Stalin are due to meet with Lenin soon to discuss their new tactics (→ 5/28).

French offensive is costly failure

April 20. General Nivelle's offensive, which had aroused the hopes of the wearied French nation, has ground to a halt. Although it is claimed that 28,000 Germans have been taken prisoner, French casualties are said to be just under 120,000 men. And there are rumors reaching Paris of disaffection among some of the combat troops.

General Nivelle launched his major attack on April 16 on a front of 25 miles between Soissons and Rheims. Before the attack, however, the Germans had pulled out of their salient and retired to a very strong line running along the base of the former salient. That area had been completely devastated and sown with mines and booby traps.

The initial French attack made at most 600 yards instead of the six miles promised by General Nivelle. One Senegalese regiment, caught in machine gun cross fire, broke and fled from the battlefield. Due to manpower shortages, France has recruited native soldiers from its colonial possessions to fight in the war in Europe.

All hope for tactical surprise was lost when the French unleashed a very heavy artillery bombardment prior to the infantry advance. The French took some ruined villages and a few thousand prisoners, but they failed to reach the main German defenses.

Reports from the front say that the French field divisions are exhausted. The basic question facing the Allied command is how and where the French can be deployed usefully in future campaigns (→ 30).

French at Chemin des Dames.

1917

MAY

Su	Mo	Tu	We	Th	Fr	Sa
		1	2	3	4	5
6	7	8	9	10	11	12
13	14	15	16	17	18	19
20	21	22	23	24	25	26
29	28	29	30	31		

1. Polish State Council demands Central Powers' sanction for creation of Polish state (→ 7/2).

4. Western Front: Mutinies begin in French army following Nivelle debacle (→ 6/7).

7. U.S. War Dept. announces 10,000 army engineers will be sent to France (→ 18).

10. Lloyd George gives order for beleagured British merchant vessels to travel in protected convoys.

10. Petrograd: Russian council moves for world peace conference (→ 18).

12. Italians begin 10th battle of the Isonzo (→ 6/8).

12. Omar Khayyam tops the field at Kentucky Derby with jockey C. Borel.

12. Bela Bartok's ballet "The Wooden Prince" opens in Budapest.

13. Virginia: German sub U-36 captured at Newport News (→ 15).

15. Austrians sink 14 Italian merchant vessels off coast of Albania.

15. First officers' training camp opens in Washington (→ 18).

18. U.S. troops under Gen. Pershing ordered to France (→ 6/27).

18. Petrograd: Provisional govt. reshuffled; Alexander Kerensky appointed minister of defense (→ 19).

18. Paris: Eric Satie's "Parade" opens with story by Jean Cocteau—danced by Russian Ballet.

19. Russian govt. makes peace proposal to Central Powers, bars annexation of Russian territory (→ 6/5).

21. Swedes ask separation of Grand Duchy of Finland from Russia.

28. Pan-Russian Peasant's Congress comes out in favor of a democratic federal republic for Russia (→ 6/2).

BIRTH

29. John F. Kennedy, 35th U.S. president (†11/22/1963).

Selective Service passes Congress

By James Montgomery Flagg.

May 18. President Wilson signed into law tonight a bill requiring all American men between the ages of 21 and 30 to register for possible service in the United States armed forces. Known as the Selective Draft Act, the new law is designed to mobilize an army of 500,000 men for service in the war against Germany. The draft bill passed Congress this month, but not without objections from a minority of members who argued that military recruiting should be done on a volunteer basis. It is estimated that approximately ten million men will be subject to registration. Their names will be placed in jury wheels from which the initial 500,000 recruits will be drawn (→ 6/1).

Recruits in training at Plattsburg.

1917

JUNE

Su	Mo	Tu	We	Th	Fr	Sa
					1	2
3	4	5	6	7	8	9
10	11	12	13	14	15	16
17	18	19	20	21	22	23
24	25	26	27	28	29	30

1. Wilson warns stiff punishment for draft resisters (→ 5).

2. Demonstrators march in Petrograd, demanding war on capitalists (→ 16).

4. Washington adopts prohibitive whiskey tax as part of War Revenue Bill (→ 12/18).

5. 10 mil. U.S. citizens reported registered for draft (→ 7/4).

5. Japan warns Russia against making peace with Central Powers (→ 17).

6. American warships anchor off French coast (→ 7/3).

6. French Chamber of Deputies resolves, "Peace will not be possible unless Alsace-Lorraine is returned to France" (→ 7/23).

7. Western Front: British take Messines Ridge after 17-day bombardment (→ 7/31).

8. 10th battle of Isonzo ends; Italians lose 157,000 to Austrians' 75,000 (→ 8/29).

15. U.K. pleges release of all Irish captured during Easter rebellion of 1916 (→ 4/9/18).

17. Petrograd: Duma, in secret session, votes for immediate Russian offensive (→ 7/1).

19. King George orders princes to drop German titles; British royal family becomes House of Windsor.

19. British give voting rights to women over 30 (→ 11/10).

19. Russia places first women volunteers in war service.

20. Washington: Trade Board urges govt. control of railroads and coal mines (→ 7/8).

23. Petrograd: Russian workmen vote to end Duma and state council (→ 7/17).

26. Athens: New King Alexander reappoints pro-Allied Venizelos as premier (→ 29).

29. Greece severs relations with Central Powers (→ 9/15/18).

29. Ukraine proclaims independence from Russia (→ 6/13/18).

BIRTHS

8. Byron R. White U.S. Supreme Court justice.

30. Lena Horne, black American blues singer.

Troops under Pershing land in France

"Black Jack" Pershing in France.

The first contingent of American troops in France assembles for review.

June 27. Major General John J. "Black Jack" Pershing's American troops arrived at a French seaport this morning. For security reasons, the precise location cannot yet be disclosed. The second contingent came ashore not far from a camp where Major General William L. Sibert and the first contingent are already established. Pershing himself arrived this evening.

The doughboys crossed the Atlantic swiftly. Despite mines and submarines in the waters, they did not lose a soul en route. A few of these men volunteered, and a few were drafted when conscription started in May. Others are army diehards, whose rugged tans suggest they served with Pershing when he routed Pancho Villa in Mexico. They are boys from small towns and farms. French villagers, rushing to the shore, call them heroes.

Pershing, 56 years old, earned the title Commander-in-Chief of the American Expeditionary Forces (A.E.F.) through his success in Mexico and the Philippines, where he defeated the Moros in 1913. He plans to keep his soldiers together, independent of other Allied leaders. Eventually, he hopes to command divisions of 28,000 men each.

French, British and other Allies on the Western Front realize that the Americans are still green. Therefore, they will be spared the front lines. For now (→ 7/4).

First Congress of Soviets is held

June 16. The Pan-Russian Congress of All Councils of Workmen's and Soldiers' Delegates has rejected Austria's proposal for a separate peace. Two speakers, Minister of War Alexander Kerensky and delegate V.I. Lenin, dominated the debate. Kerensky, just back from the front, advocates a continuing offensive. Lenin favored conciliation, describing involvement in the war "treason to the interests of international Socialism." Kerensky said Lenin misinterpreted Marxism, and agreeing to peace would be "fraternizing with the enemy" (→ 23)

Soldiers, workers and peasants meet to discuss Russia's uncertain future.

Greek king quits under war threat

June 12. Acceding to the demands of France, Great Britain and Russia, King Constantine I has abdicated in favor of his second son, Prince Alexander. If he had not done so, the Allies would have recognized the provisional war government based on Salonika.

The Allies charge that the king has curtailed the liberty of the Greek people. And they claim treaty rights to interfere in Greek affairs when such is the case. The king had dismissed the Liberal government and had also rigged elections.

A brother-in-law of the Kaiser, Constantine has violated Greek neutrality by pro-German acts. He has allowed German ships to use Greek bases and broken a 1913 Greek-Serbian treaty which pledged mutual support if either side was attacked by Bulgaria (→ 26).

1917

JULY

Su	Mo	Tu	We	Th	Fr	Sa
1	2	3	4	5	6	7
8	9	10	11	12	13	14
15	16	17	18	19	20	21
22	23	24	25	26	27	28
29	30	31				

1. Eastern Front: Under Kerensky's orders, Brusilov launches new offensive (→ 19).

2. East St. Louis: Many Negroes shot, hanged in vicious race rioting; 20-75 dead (→ 8/24).

2. Josef Pilsudski resigns from Polish State Council (→ 10/16/18).

3. U.S. Navy victorious in two battles with German subs off western coast of Europe (→ 15).

4. France: U.S. Col. Stanton, at Lafayette's tomb, announces, "Lafayette, we are here" (→ 9/19).

4. U.S. opens first military aviation training camp, at Rantoul (→ 20).

5. Chinese march on Peking to oust dictator (→ 8/14).

7. Germans kill 37 Londoners in biggest air raid yet (→ 9/7).

12. Spanish king pledges neutrality for duration of war.

14. Germany: Chancellor von Bethmann Hollweg ousted; Georg Michaelis appointed.

14. Finland proclaims full independence (→ 12/9).

15. British cut off German trade with Rotterdam, sinking two merchant ships, capturing four off Dutch coast (→ 10/2).

17. British Cabinet reshuffled; Churchill is munitions minister.

17. Russia: Lenin escapes arrest as Kerensky crushes Bolshevik demonstrations (→ 20).

19. Eastern Front: German counterattack halts on Galician border after dispersing demoralized Russian army (→ 9/1).

20. Washington: First numbers drawn for draft (→ 8/4).

23. Lloyd George claims, peace can "only be achieved with the German people but not with its authoritarian regime" (→ 8/1).

25. France: Dutch dancer Mata-Hari sentenced to death for espionage (→ 10/15).

31. Belgium: Allies attack in 3rd battle of Ypres (→ 8/17).

BIRTH

12. American painter Andrew Wyeth.

Kerensky becomes Premier of Russia

Kerensky will still lead war effort.

July 20. A lawyer and former head of a non-Marxist labor group succeeds Georgi Lvov as Prime Minister of Russia's provisional government. Alexander Kerensky has taken office while retaining the titles of Minister of War and the Navy. He inherits a country in chaos.

On July 1, Kerensky as war minister led an offensive against Austria in Galicia. Whille he was initially successful, yesterday a fierce German counter-offensive began. Russian troops are now deserting.

In the last two weeks, thousands of Ukrainians revolted, demanding autonomy. The Ukraine is the breadbasket of the nation; the provisional government cannot afford to lose it. Nor can it allow much rhetoric to reach the many other ethnic regions eager for freedom.

How has the provisional government responded to these crises? It introduced trial by jury, freedom of speech, press and assembly. Complete amnesty to political and religious prisoners is granted. Labor is given the right to organize and strike. While all these are rights the people have demanded, it results in angry masses flooding the streets, all with more insistent cries.

Kerensky received a telegram this afternoon from a radical socialist group in the Ukraine. It agrees to prevent civil war. Kerensky, fired at in an assassination attempt earlier today, is pleased (→ 8/15).

Wilson takes official control of necessities

July 8. President Wilson today declared absolute government control over exports of food, fuel and war supplies. His sweeping proclamation, to go into effect this week, came as somewhat of a surprise even to those who had urged that he implement such a measure.

In issuing the order, the president said that it is the duty of this nation to see to it that Germany receives no supplies from the United States so long as the war goes on. He also said a prime concern was to assure the United States of adequate supplies of needed commodities. Among the major items placed under export control are meats, flour and meal, fodder and feeds, coal, coke, fuel oils, iron and steel, fertilizers, arms, ammunition and explosives.

The order provides that none of these items are to be shipped out of the United States except under a special license. The export ban applies to 56 specific nations and their possessions, including enemy countries, American Allies and neutral nations. As spelled out in the president's order, violation of the export ban will carry a penalty of $10,000, two years in prison, or both. And the U.S. will confiscate all ships and cargo involved in any illegal export trade (→ 8/10).

Saving the world for democracy.

1917

AUGUST

Su	Mo	Tu	We	Th	Fr	Sa
			1	2	3	4
5	6	7	8	9	10	11
12	13	14	15	16	17	18
19	20	21	22	23	24	25
26	27	28	29	30	31	

1. Vatican: Pope Benedict XV issues plea for peace (→ 29).

2. German navy men mutiny on warship Prinzregent Luitpold (→ 25).

4. Washington announces draft resisters can be executed (→ 5).

5. U.S. National Guard drafted into federal service (→ 17).

9. Canadian Parliament passes Compulsory Military Act.

10. Herbert Hoover named to lead effort to raise food production, stabilize prices (→ 18).

14. Feng-Kua-Chang becomes president of China (→ 31).

14. Chinese Parliament declares war on Central Powers.

16. N.Y.: A.F.L. Pres. Samuel Gompers denounces workmen's council as pro-German.

17. President Wilson proposes drafting of aliens (→ 30).

17. Belgium: German troops occupy Langenmark (→ 9/18).

18. Food Administrator Hoover asks U.S. families to save a lb. of flour per week (→ 20).

20. Washington: Robert S. Lovett appointed head of coal board in move for govt. control of industry (→ 21).

20. Hungary frees prisoners with less than two-year terms to fight food shortage.

21. Wilson cuts base price of soft coal to $2 a ton (→ 30).

23. Berlin halts private bathing to save water and coal.

25. German war court sentences five Wilhelmshaven mutineers to death (→ 10/10).

27. South Dakota: 30 Germans jailed for opposing draft (→ 5/11/18).

30. Medical students exempted from U.S. draft (→ 10/1/18).

30. U.S. wheat prices fixed at $2.20 a bushel (→ 9/15).

31. China: Sun Yat-sen forms military govt. in Canton (→ 9/29).

BIRTHS

6. U.S. actor Robert Mitchum.

18. U.S. Sec. of Defense Caspar Willard Weinberger.

Peace talk spreads widely in Europe

Talks in the halls of diplomacy have yet had no effect in the Verdun trenches.

Aug 29. President Wilson's reply to Pope Benedict that the United States wanted no peace with Germany as long as its present rulers remained in power has won widespread support at home and abroad.

The peace movement in Britain, Germany and Austria has received a rebuff. In Britain, Socialist Ramsay MacDonald said Wilson's position means "a war of attriton," and he urged the German people to disown their government in order to end the war.

The German peace movement was recently mentioned by a speaker in the German Reichstag who also complained of army political censorship. And in Austria, many people are reported to be sick of the war and the mounting number of casualties.

The pope had proposed peace, cuts in armaments and the settlement of territorial questions by conciliation. The United States Senate, however, has passed a resolution aimed at preventing any move in Congress supporting peace moves toward Germany (→ 9/18).

Presence of Negro troops causes riot

Aug 24. The quartering of a Negro regiment in Houston led to a riot today that left 17 dead. And Texas now wants to try 34 Negroes in a state court rather than defer the matter to the military. The state has also requested that remaining Negro soldiers be ousted from its borders immediately. The troops were sent from Deming, New Mexico, to Houston three weeks ago. Their captain, who clearly has respect for his men, stated that they had all felt uneasy since their arrival.

This morning, a soldier who had been drinking witnessed a white policeman slapping a Negro woman. After the soldier objected to her treatment, the officer beat him and sent him to jail. A corporal, hearing of the arrest, approached the policeman for information. He too was beaten. When more troop members heard of this, they grabbed their weapons, ran into town and opened fire on white residents. Among the dead was a 15-year-old girl.

A few Southern senators and representatives had opposed stationing of any Negro regiments in their states months prior to today's incident. Some Southerners explained that they have no objections to Southern Negroes stationed in their area, but they are wary of Negroes from other parts of the United States who do not recognize the code of conduct followed by local Negroes (→ 10/9).

Italian troops take Austrian stronghold

Aug 29. Second Italian Army forces today captured the Bainsizza Plateau and entered the Chiapovano Valley. The Austrians have been routed, weakening the Tolmino defenses. Once in control of the Chiapovano Valley, the Italians will be able to cut Austria's communication lines, further fragmenting the retreating armies. During the past week, the Italian forces moving along the Isonzo front have decimated 11 Austrian army divisions. Some Italian brigades have fought continuously for three days and nights (→ 9/15).

U.S. needs $156.30 to outfit doughboy

Aug 19. The War Department revealed tonight that the startling sum of $156.30 is required to provide an infantryman with arms, clothes and eating utensils. Each soldier will receive 107 pieces of fighting equipment (including 100 rifle cartridges), 50 articles of clothing and 11 cooking implements. His weapons are priced as follows: trench tool, 50 cents; bayonet scabbard, $1.13; bayonet, $2.15; steel helmet, $3.00; cartridge belt, $4.08; cartridges, $5.00; gas mask, $12; rifle, $19.50. Included in the clothing costs are three wool blankets ($18.75) and a bedsack (98 cents).

Czar and family removed from palace

Czar under guard in the palace park.

Aug 15. Former Czar Nicholas II, his wife Alexandra and their children have been escorted under guard out of the Tsarskoye Selo palace in Petrograd. It is rumored they are being taken to Tobolsk in western Siberia. Bolshevik forces holding them captive feared that counterrevolutionary troops now encroaching on the city would liberate them. The royal couple, their four daughters and hemophiliac son, Alexis, have been held prisoner since March. A few servants and maids of honor see to their needs. The provisional government has not yet decided upon a plan for dealing with the former royal family on a permanent basis (→ 9/10).

Since the U.S. took Los Angeles in 1847, the city has grown rapidly. Population tripled between 1900 and 1910, and now rivals San Francisco.

1917

SEPTEMBER

Su	Mo	Tu	We	Th	Fr	Sa
						1
2	3	4	5	6	7	8
9	10	11	12	13	14	15
16	17	18	19	20	21	22
23	24	25	26	27	28	29
30						

1. German Gen. Hutier launches Riga offensive on northern Russian front (→ 17).

7. France: German air raid on hospitals kills Americans.

10. Petrograd: Premier Kerensky ousts army chief Kornilov for demanding supreme power (→ 11).

11. Kornilov moves on Petrograd with rebel troops; Kerensky halts attack, avoids civil war (→ 12).

12. Kerensky takes command of Russian army (→ 15).

12. Buenos Aires: Mobs burn German buildings, attack legation following expulsion of Count Luxburg (→ 19).

15. U.S. govt. takes control of sugar industry; Hoover to administrate (→ 25).

15. Italians call off 11th Isonzo attack, gain Bainsizza Plateau; Austrians weakened (→ 10/24).

15. Kerensky proclaims Russian republic (→ 10/21).

18. San Francisco shipping threatened as 3,500 strike; Gompers called to scene (→ 23).

18. Western Front: German attack fails in Champagne (→ 20).

18. France demands return of Alsace-Lorraine, reimbursement for war expenses (→ 26).

19. Argentine Senate votes for break with Germany (→ 24).

19. Americans receive war crosses for aiding French at Verdun; 101 captured so far (→ 10/27).

20. Belgium: Field Marshall Haig attacks Germans on 8-mile front at Ypres (→ 10/9).

24. Argentina orders mobilization of navy (→ 10/5).

25. U.S. Senate passes $8 bil. Urgent Deficiency Bill (→ 10/12).

26. Germany agrees to quit Belgium in return for trade, military guarantees (→ 1/5/18).

28. British Gen. Maude pushes Turks up Euphrates into Central Mesopotamia.

29. Chinese govt. issues warrants for arrest of Sun Yat-sen (→ 9/6/18).

Death takes Degas, French Impressionist

Edgar Degas' "Orchestra Musicians" depicts ballet dancers.

Sept 27. French painter Edgar Degas died today at the age of 83. Although considered one of the Impressionists, Degas shunned common subjects such as landscapes. He painted, in subtle colors, interiors of theaters, cafes and brothels. Degas often depicted ballet dancers bathed in bright stage light.

As a young man, Degas studied Renaissance artists in Italy. His palette suddenly burst with new color in 1862. In that year, he met a great influence: Edouard Manet.

Wilson's plea ends strike in shipyard

Sept 23. Thousands of American workers have demonstrated that love for country comes first, as they are returning to work after a paralyzing strike. The paramount issue is wages, and about 50,000 workers from 25 unions are involved.

This week, 25,000 workmen, mostly skilled mechanics, walked out of more than 100 factories, shipyards, and machine shops in the biggest strike in the history of the Pacific Coast. Today, however, 30,000 ironworkers at shipyards in San Francisco, Seattle and Portland have responded to a direct plea from President Wilson in Washington.

By telegram, appealing to their patriotism, the president urged the workers to accept a temporary wage settlement so as not to hinder the government's shipbuilding program, a vital factor in the successful prosecution of the war. His newly appointed Shipbuilding Labor Adjustment Board will work on more permanent solutions. In New York, meanwhile, 6,500 longshoremen also agreed to arbitration, realizing American soldiers in France are directly injured by the holding up of supplies and mail (2/17/18).

Germans capture Riga from Russians

Sept 17. German troops have captured the Russian port of Riga and the road to Petrograd is open.

A heavy artillery barrage preceded the attack, according to German general headquarters. The infantry, having taken Uxkull, then crossed the Dvina in two places and attacked. Troops of the 12th Russian Army counterattacked but were routed. The Russian War Ministry tonight announced that Riga had been abandoned.

The performance of the Russian troops at Riga, military experts point out, shows that they are far from recovering from the breakdown when the Czar was ousted. Petrograd, the Russian capital, is now only 350 miles from the German armies (→ 10/15).

Machine guns on the Russian front.

Sept 26. The charred remains of French aviator Georges Guynemer, shown above downing a German Luftwaffer, were identified today. He was a hero at 22.

1917

OCTOBER

Su	Mo	Tu	We	Th	Fr	Sa
	1	2	3	4	5	6
7	8	9	10	11	12	13
14	15	16	17	18	19	20
21	22	23	24	25	26	27
28	29	30	31			

1. Michigan: Fordson, world's first mass-produced tractor, made in Dearborn (→ 1/1/19).

2. Britain begins embargo on Sweden, Norway, Denmark, Holland to cut off supplies to Germans (→ 14).

5. Peru severs relations with Germany (→ 7).

7. Uruguay breaks diplomatic relations with Germany (→ 26).

8. U.S. destroyer mistakenly shells Italian sub; killing two.

9. U.S. Natl. Guard approves Negro division (→ 3/23/18).

9. Belgium: Allies smash German lines at Ypres (→ 23).

10. Five German naval crews mutiny in widespread plot.

12. U.S. shipping board requisitions all ships over 2,500 tons (→ 17).

14. Holland halts all Dutch shipping to England in reprisal for British embargo (→ 11/3).

15. Chicago: White Sox win World Series 4-2 over Giants in sixth game.

15. Baltic Sea: Seventh German Army takes Russian islands Oesel and Dago (→ 11/26).

17. U.S. Fuel Admin. finds one mil. tons soft coal hidden in Cleveland by private interests (→ 12/14).

20. France downs 5 zeppelins.

21. Russia: V.I. Lenin returns from exile in Finland (→ 23).

23. Western Front: French capture 7,500 Germans near Aisne (→ 27).

23. Russia: Bolshevik Central Committee votes armed uprising (→ 11/6).

26. Brazil declares war on Germany (→ 5/7/18).

27. New York: Violinist Jascha Heifetz makes first U.S. appearance at Carnegie Hall.

30. Italy gets $230 mil. loan from U.S. (→ 11/5).

BIRTHS

15. American historian Arthur Schlesinger jr.

21. Jazz trumpeter Dizzy Gillespie.

Americans move into front line trenches

Gas masks are standard equipment for the first U.S. troops on the front line.

Oct 27. American boys saw action only hours after they moved into the front lines. At 6 a.m., units of the 1st American Division arrived in the relatively quiet Toul sector of Lorraine, near Nancy. Almost at once they were fired upon by Germans in distant trenches. No casualties were reported.

Since June, doughboys have been arriving in France at the rate of 50,000 a month. They receive just three months of battle training from French veterans and then they are on their own. General Pershing, at his headquarters in Chaumont, keeps communication lines with the troops separate from those of the French and British. He will be sending men and material along an independent rail line east of congested Paris. American supply dumps and bases are already scattered throughout France (→ 11/3).

French execute Mata Hari for espionage

Oct 15. Mata Hari, 41, the Dutch dancer and adventuress, who, by a court martial two months ago was found guilty of espionage, was shot at dawn this morning by the French.

Mata Hari.

Known in Europe as an extremely attractive woman with a complicated romantic history, she was born as Margaretha Geertruida Zelle in Holland, though she at times claimed to stem from India. She was accused of having joined the German secret service in 1907 and of having betrayed important military secrets confided to her by the many high Allied officers who were on intimate terms with her. One such secret is said to be the construction of Allied tanks; this resulted in the Germans rushing work on a special gas to combat their operation.

The condemned woman was taken from St. Lazaire prison and brought by automobile to the parade ground at Vincennes, where the execution took place. Two Catholic nuns and a priest accompanied her.

Liberty Loan brings in over $3.5 billion

Oct 25. Liberty Loan sales passed the $3.5 billion mark today and headed for the $5 billion maximum. Parades to stimulate bond-buying flourished yesterday, and all over the nation Americans are responding to slogans such as "Bonds or bondage," "Build a monument to democracy," "Drive a nail in the Kaiser's coffin," and "Keep freedom's lights burning." Many banks have not set closing hours for the last two days of the campaign, but will remain open extra hours.

More than 20,000 persons, ranging in age from five to 70, marched in the Liberty Loan parade in New York. All of the adults owned bonds. Onlookers also saw an awesome display of the materials of modern war. A British tank, Italian airplanes, American armored motorcars, ambulances, transport wagons and a score of floats illustrating industrial activities essential to the success of armies reinforced the direct appeal of several thousand soldiers and sailors marching in the parade, cheered by crowds.

Italy suffers heavy losses at Caporetto

Oct 24. In a spectacular counteroffensive, the Austrian army, aided by equal numbers of German soldiers, have overrun the Italian army at Caporetto and handed the Allies one of their most humiliating defeats of the war.

Caporetto lies just to the north of recent fighting along the Isonzo River. After a brief but dense bombardment, the Germans poured across the plain through the rain and snow, taking about 12 miles and completely routing the surprised Italian 2nd Army.

Italian Commander-in-Chief Cadorna has withdrawn to the Piave River, about 15 miles east of Venice, and managed to establish a new defense line, but at a great toll. He is reported to have lost about 10,000 killed and 30,000 wounded. The Austrians have taken about 300,000 prisoners, and it is said that vast numbers of Italian soldiers, as many as 400,000, have deserted due to low morale (→ 30).

1917

NOVEMBER

Su	Mo	Tu	We	Th	Fr	Sa
				1	2	3
4	5	6	7	8	9	10
11	12	13	14	15	16	17
18	19	20	21	22	23	24
25	26	27	28	29	30	

3. British sink 11 German ships in the Cattegat (→ 6/4/18).

3. France: German patrols take 12 Americans on Rhine (→ 30).

5. Italy: Teuton forces cross Tagliamento River, pierce Cadorna's line (→ 12).

6. Western Front: Third battle of Ypres ends with British taking Passchendaele Ridge; five miles gained in three months at heavy cost (→ 21).

6. Petrograd: Trotsky's Red Guards take state buildings, dismiss Kerensky govt. (→ 7).

10. Forty-one U.S. suffragettes arrested outside White House (→ 1/10/18).

11. Kerensky, with troops from Eastern Front, moves on Petrograd (→ 15).

12. Italy: Cadorna stabilizes line at Mt. Pasubia after loss of 40,000, 275,000 captive (→ 16).

14. Palestine: Allenby strikes Turkish Eighth at Junction Station, prepares to move on Jerusalem (→ 12/9).

15. Russia: Kerensky in flight; Bolsheviks in command (→ 30).

16. Italians open floodgates of Piave and Sile to drown Austrians (→ 6/15/18).

26. Bolsheviks offer armistice to Central Powers (→ 29).

27. Germans threaten to seize Denmark if Norway awards base to Allies.

29. Allied Council meets in Paris, adopts Col. House plan.

29. Berlin: Chancellor von Hertling offers parley to Russia if Bolsheviks send envoys with full power (→ 12/1).

30. Bolshevik For. Min. Trotsky warns Allies not to interfere in Russia's affairs (→ 12/6).

30. Western Front: Germans recapture lost ground in Cambria (→ 12/3).

BIRTH

19. Indian leader Indira Gandhi (†10/30/1984).

DEATH

15. French sociologist Emile Durkheim (*10/15/1858).

Bolsheviks seize power in Russia

Nov 7. (Oct 25 on the Russian calendar) For the second time this year, the Russian government has been overthrown. But this time the revolution was organized by the radical Bolshevik Party.

In a coup d'etat that was virtually bloodless because the capital's troops offered little resistance, the Bolsheviks seized power from the provisional government of Premier Alexander Kerensky. The provisional government came to power in March in the wake of Czar Nicholas II's abdication.

The Bolsheviks believe that the October Revolution, (so called because the Russians use the older, Julian calendar), is a spark that will set off others. Said Bolshevik leader Vladimir Lenin, only recently returned from exile in Finland: "This is only a preliminary step toward a similar revolution everywhere."

The courtyard of Petrograd's Winter Palace, under siege.

Leon Trotsky is to be head of the new revolutionary government, but it is widely believed that Lenin will be in control. The new government immediately proclaimed its intention of negotiating peace, redistributing land to the peasants and calling the long-awaited elections for the constitutent assembly.

The Bolsheviks' actions were immediately endorsed by the All-Russia Congress of Workmen's Councils, an organization of workers' soviets. Lenin planned the revolution to coincide with that organization's second annual meeting in order to win that group's attention and support away from the larger revolutionary parties.

It remains to be seen whether the Bolsheviks will win the support of the rest of the country. So far, they are only in control of Petrograd and only 30,000 people are believed to have taken part in the revolution.

Kerensky fled to Moscow, where it is believed he will try to raise a loyal army. Some hope that the revolution will end in a constitutional monarchy under Grand Duke Michael, who was named successor at the time of the czar's abdication, but was later swept aside by the provisional government.

The causes of Kerensky's overthrow were established almost as soon as the provisional government came to power. Although the czar had been forced to abdicate because of Russia's failure in the war and widespread starvation, Kerensky could do no better.

The provisional government did not have the authority, as the czar did, to force its soldiers to fight and it did not have the military strength to win. But it was unwilling to take the step of ending the war on German terms. As a result, the war dragged on and public support for the government disintegrated.

The actual seizure of power by the Bolsheviks was quite easy, even though most of the details had been leaked by feuding revolutionaries to the newspapers.

A few weeks ago, the Bolsheviks formed a Military Revolutionary Committee to lead the insurrection. That committee began to organize the government's troops into revolutionary units. By the time the government decided to bring in loyal troops, the Bolsheviks were too strong and they were able to occupy government buildings and communications centers. Lenin has reportedly already decreed the redistribution of large estates (→ 11).

Chaos in the streets as Lenin's Bolsheviks take power.

Haig's army breaks Hindenburg's line

Nov 21. The Hindenburg line has been severed in two, and nearly 8,000 prisoners were seized during a daring British offensive at Cambrai this morning. Field Marshal Sir Douglas Haig had a smoke screen set up to hide 324 tanks as they smashed forward five miles.

No pre-bombardment gave away their plans. The tanks raced forward at four mph. Fascines, bundles of brushwood, were tied atop each vehicle, to be tossed into trenches when passing proved treacherous. General Julian Byng's Third Army took up the rear (→ 30).

Skillful sculptor Auguste Rodin dies

Nov 17. Sculptor of "The Kiss" (1886) and "The Thinker" (1881), Auguste Rodin died today. He was 77. Rodin's sculptures were timepieces; he clocked and captured the the greatest personages of his era. He built monuments to Honore de Balzac and Victor Hugo (1898 and 1909) and produced portraits of George Bernard Shaw (1906) and Pope Benedict XV (1915).

From his first piece "The Age of Bronze" to his unfinished interpretation of Dante's "Inferno," Rodin lived with controversy. His work was either too anatomically correct or too crude. Rodin was his best critic. Never satisfied, he constantly reworked everything.

"The Kiss," by Auguste Rodin.

MacArthur in France with Rainbow unit

Dashing Douglas MacArthur.

Nov 30. Yet another unit of the American Expeditionary Force has arrived in France, the 42nd Infantry or "Rainbow" Division commanded by Colonel Douglas MacArthur. They join the swelling numbers of the A.E.F., which began arriving in June and are mostiy billeted in small towns outside Paris.

Balfour promises homeland for Jews

Nov 2. The British government has announced its intention to officially support Zionist aspirations with regard to the establishment of a permanent national homeland for the Jewish people, to be located in Palestine.

Drafted by British Foreign Minister and former Prime Minister Arthur L. Balfour following consultation with Zionist leaders, the declaration was issued by Balfour in a special communication to the 2nd Baron Rothschild.

The basic intention of the Balfour Declaration may be judged from this most pertinent paragraph:

"His Majesty's Government views with favour the establishment in Palestine of a national home for the Jewish people and will use their best endeavors to facilitate the achievement of this object. It being clearly understood that nothing shall be done which may prejudice the civil and religious right of existing non-Jewish communities in Palestine, or the rights and political status enjoyed by Jews in any other country" (→ 12/17/18).

1917

DECEMBER

Su	Mo	Tu	We	Th	Fr	Sa
						1
2	3	4	5	6	7	8
9	10	11	12	13	14	15
16	17	18	19	20	21	22
23	24	25	26	27	28	29
30	31					

1. U.S. files protest against Russian armistice plan (→ 16).

3. Western Front: Haig orders withdrawal from Cambrai, ending first successful use of tanks (→ 3/21/18).

6. Former Czar Nicholas II and family made prisoners in Tobolsk (→ 1/19/18).

7. U.S. declares war on Austria-Hungary with only one dissenting vote in Congress.

9. New Finnish republic demands withdrawal of Russian troops (→ 1/6/18).

10. Nobel Peace Prize awarded to International Red Cross.

14. U.S. govt. takes control of commodities imports (→ 26).

15. U.S. offers non-interference in Mexican affairs (→ 3/5/19).

18. Prohibition passes Senate 47-8, House 282-128; amendment to go to states for ratification (→ 1/13/18).

24. Kaiser warns Russia he will use "iron fist" and "shining sword" if peace is spurned (→ 1/2/18).

26. Wilson places railroads under government control, with Sec. of War Wm. McAdoo as director general (→ 1/2/18).

BIRTH

9. U.S. actor Kirk Douglass.

DEATH

22. Frances X. Cabrini, first U.S. saint (*7/15/1850).

CUTURAL EVENTS, 1917

Literature: T.S. Eliot's "Prufrock and Other Observations"; first Pulitzer Prizes.

Academia: Freud's "Introductory Lectures on Psychoanalysis"; C.G. Jung's "Psychology of the Unconscious."

Music: Busoni's opera "Turandot," in Zurich; jazz flourishes in Chicago.

The Arts: Picasso's surrealist sets, costumes for Satie's ballet "Parade"; J.S. Sargent's "Portrait of John D. Rockefeller."

Films: "The Little Princess," with Mary Pickford; Chaplin gets yearly contract for $1 mil.

Jerusalem yielded to Allenby's forces

Gen. Allenby enters the sacred city.

Dec 9. Prime Minister Lloyd George wanted Jerusalem for his Christmas present, and General Sir Edmund "The Bull" Allenby delivered. He led seven infantry and three cavalry divisions (the latter on camels) into the city this morning. Palestine is British.

On Oct. 31, Allenby captured Bathsheeba. Turks who held the city neglected to destroy its wells. Refreshed, Allenby and his men proceeded north. General Falkenhayn, arriving in the region Nov. 1, offered weak defense with troops inefficiently stretched to the sea.

Allenby's forces were superior: He had 433 guns to the Turks' 258, and Falkenhayn's divisions were plagued by desertions. The Holy City was also won by some unholy strategy. Allenby sent an Arabic scholar named T.E. Lawrence to lead raids on the Turks. Lawrence dynamited railroads and bridges, confounding the enemy (→ 4/3/18).

The mysterious Theda Bara.

The Allied forces and their allies:
Great Britain, Italy, France and other allies
Colonies and states dependent on:
Great Britain
and other allies
France
Neutral States
Russia and its areas of influence
USA and its areas of influence
Central Powers
Germany
its allies
its colonies
Canada
Seattle
Minneapolis
Chicago
Detroit
Boston
New York
San Francisco
USA
Los Angeles
Washington,D.C.
Memphis
New Orleans
1917 1,98
1918 3,94
Bahamas Is.
Brit.
Mexico
Cuba
Dominican Republic
1861-1865 Spain
1905 U.S. port rights
British Honduras
Puerto Rico
1898 to U.S.
Guatemala
Honduras
San Salvador
Nicaragua
Costa Rica
Panama
1903 under U.S. prot.
Trinidad
Brit.
Venezuela
Brit.
Dutch
Fr.
Guiana
Colombia
Ecuador
Brazil
Peru
Bolivia
Paraguay
Chile
Uruguay
Argentina
1917 7,67
1918 4,75
1917 63
1918 69
Norway
Stockholm
Sweden
Denmark
Great Britain
German Empire
Russian Empire
London
Netherlands
Berlin
Brest Litovsk
Paris
Verdun
Austria-Hungary
Vienna
France
Switzerland
Romania
Sarajevo
Belgrade
Serbia
Bulgaria
Portugal
Madrid
Italy
Montenegro
Albania
Rome
Spain
Greece
Athens
Dodecanese
1911/12 Ital.
Gilbraltar
1704 Brit.
1848
French Algeria
Malta
1800 Brit.
Tunisia
Tripoli
Algeria
Libya
1912 Ital.
Egypt
1914 Brit.
Rio de Oro
French West Africa
Gambia
Port. Guinea
Sierra Leone
Liberia
Ivory Coast
Togo
1884 Ger. prot.
Nigeria
Cameroon
French Equatorial Africa
Belgian Congo
Angola
Port.
German South West Africa
Johannesburg
South Africa
Cape Town

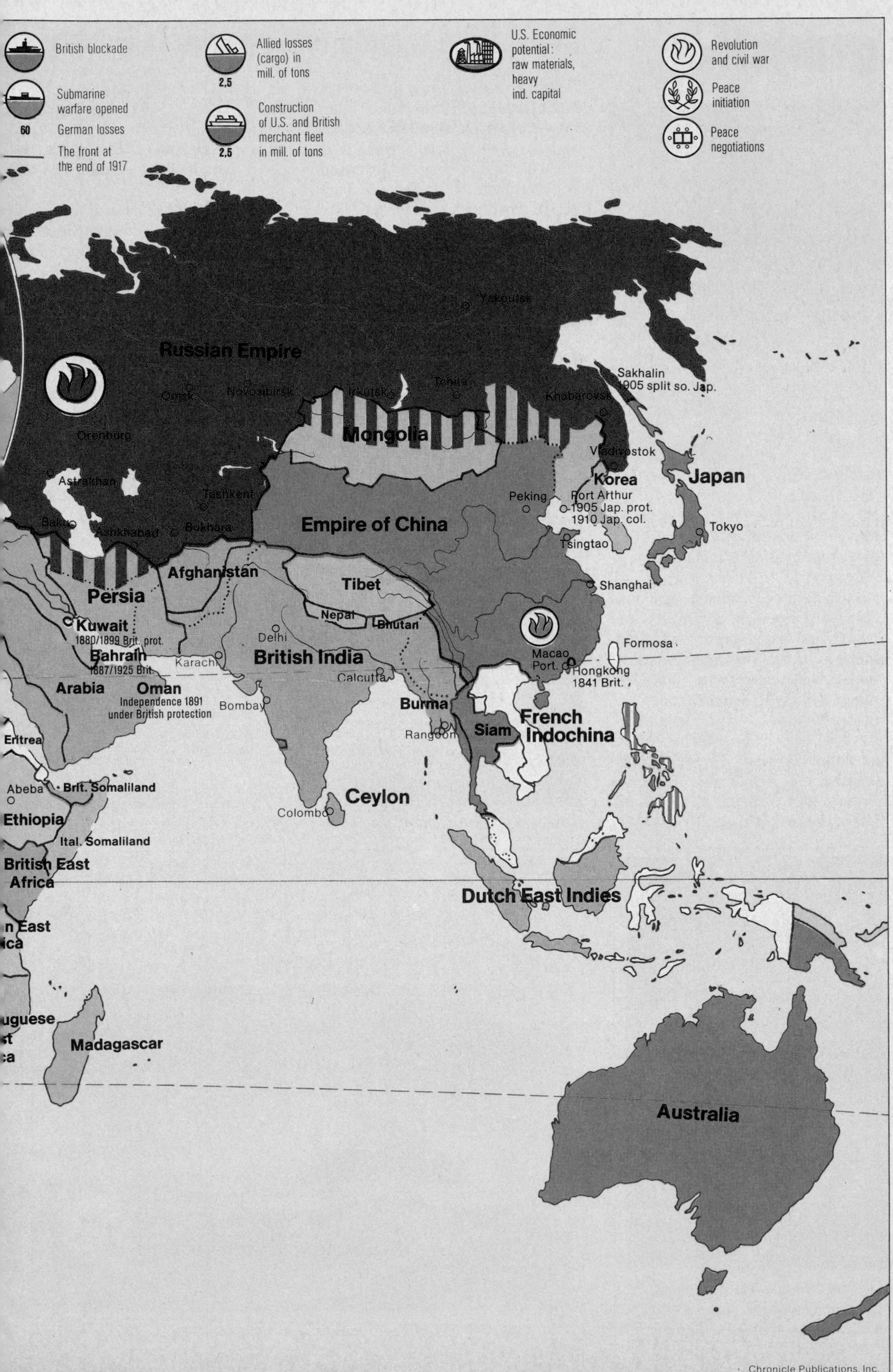

Chronicle Publications, Inc.

1917: turning point year in the war

The U.S. enters the war:
After the German Empire had declared total submarine warfare, also aimed at commercial ships of neutral nations, the United States declared war on Germany on April 6, 1917. The arrival of American troops in Europe in the summer of 1917 boosted the morale of the Allies while American industrial and financial aid definitely tipped the scales against Germany.

Allied offensive:
Expecting a vast French and British offensive in the West, the German High Command fortified its positions on the Siegfried line. Nevertheless, British tanks succeeded in crashing through the German front lines near Cambrai at the end of November. However, the British breakthrough, considered to be decisive too early, was soon repelled by a German counter-offensive, which managed to reconquer almost all the lost territory. Allied troops on one side and Central Powers troops on the other side were then respectively stationed in their own positions, and by the end of 1917 they were engaged in an exhausting face-to-face confrontation based on equipment and firepower.

Austria-Hungary:
Austria-Hungary was running out of resources. At the end of the year, it could repell the Italian military's continuing breakthroughs only with German help.

Russian Revolution:
The year 1917 was also a turning point year for Russia. In February, an uprising which took place in Petrograd (St. Petersburg) soon resulted in the Czar's abdication and the formation of a provisional government. This government was in favor of continuing to wage war against Germany while the Bolshevik Party, organized in workers' committees, advocated an end to the war. After a failed Bolshevik putsh in July, a second coup was more successful, and the Bolsheviks seized power with almost no resistance. The peace decree published November 8 was followed by a cease-fire with Germany and the Brest-Litovsk peace negotiations. The Eastern Front was therefore relieved, setting the stage for decisive battles in the West.

Russia signs armistice

The signing at Brest Litovsk halts the Russian death toll at 3.7 million.

Dec 16. Russia has broken away from the Triple Entente and signed a separate armistice with Germany and its allies, Austria-Hungary, Bulgaria and Turkey. Under the terms of the armistice, which was negotiated in the Byelorussian city of Brest Litovsk, Russia and Germany will immediately cease hostilities and begin negotiations for a peace treaty.

The armistice brings to an end a disastrous chapter in Russian history, which began with the country's entrance into a war for which it was woefully unprepared and ended in the abdication of Czar Nicholas II and the successful revolution of the radical Bolshevik Party in November.

Although the armistice is a success for the new Bolshevik regime, which had listed peace with Germany as its first priority, the cost to Russia is expected to be high. Germany is likely to demand control of those territories it has occupied during the war, among them Poland and the Ukraine. The remaining members of the Triple Entente, France and Britain, viewed with alarm the loss of their ally (→ 24).

Republican regime loses power in Portugal

Dec 9. An uprising in Portugal has forced the government to resign. President Bernardino Machado has been arrested. Former Premier Alfonso Costa has formed a provisional government. Gen. Sidonio Paes, former Portuguese minister to Germany, instigated the revolt and is expected to take over as President.

Paes is a member of a pro-German faction in the military. In January 1915, this faction, led by General Pimenta de Castro, set up a military dictatorship after the Portuguese National Asembly voted to ally itself with Great Britain and France and enter the war against Germany. Machado became president after the dictatorship was overthrown in a democratic revolt in May 1915. In March 1916, Germany declared war on Portugal.

The politically motivated revolt that toppled the government took place in Lisbon, but outbreaks of violence in Oporto were provoked by the high cost of food, particularly staples such as bread and potatoes. Many bakeries and grocery stores were pillaged. The Governor ordered a curfew in Oporto after two people were killed and 60 hospitalized during the rioting.

Ashes smolder in front of a newspaper office set aflame by republican rebels.

The Tuxedo Band. Back row (l. to r.): Jim Moore, William Ridgley, Papa Celestin, John Lindsley; Middle: Ernest Trepanier, Armand Piron, Tom Benton, John St. Cyr; Down front: Clarence Williams. The Dixieland sound is at home in New Orleans and spreading all over.

The Austrian government makes a propagandistic appeal to sustain morale among its citizenry: "Think of your European navy!"

1918

JANUARY

Su	Mo	Tu	We	Th	Fr	Sa
		1	2	3	4	5
6	7	8	9	10	11	12
13	14	15	16	17	18	19
20	21	22	23	24	25	26
29	28	29	30	31		

1. Pasadena: Mare Island Marines defeat Camp Lewis Army 19-7 in fourth Rose Bowl.

1. U.S. enters new year with debt of $5.6 million.

1. U.S.: First gasoline pipeline begins operation; 40 miles, three inches from Salt Creek to Casper, Wyoming.

2. 75 N.Y. schools close for lack of coal; Penn. Railroad drops 155 trains to conserve fuel (→ 12).

2. Petrograd: Bolsheviks talk of resuming war unless Germans quit Russian soil (→ 7).

6. Germany acknowledges Finland's independence (→ 27).

7. Germans move 75,000 troops from E. Front to West (→ 2/9).

7. German Socialists back Russians, denounce chancellor (→ 10).

10. Washington: House passes suffrage 274 to 136 (→ 5/24).

10. Bolshevik For. Min. Trotsky agrees to peace talks at Brest-Litovsk (→ 2/19).

12. U.S. to use state prisoners as farm laborers (→ 16).

15. Austria-Hungary: Strikes spread to Budapest, Prague.

16. Wilson orders all industries not involved in food production to close on Mondays (→ 19).

19. U.S.: Theaters, places of amusement allowed to open on "idle Mondays" (→ 2/1).

19. Petrograd: Soviets dissolve constituent assembly (→ 28).

25. Austria, Germany reject U.S. peace proposals (→ 26).

27. Communists attempt to seize power in Finland (→ 3/7).

28. Germany: Spartacists call for nationwide strike (→ 31).

29. France: Supreme Allied Council meets at Versailles.

31. Germany: Army called out to quell strikes (→ 2/3).

BIRTHS

15. Gamal Abdel Nasser, Egyptian nationalist leader (†9/28/1970).

26. Nicolae Ceaucescu, Rumanian statesman.

Wilson states 14 Points

Jan 8. President Woodrow Wilson presented today, in the form of Fourteen Points, his ideas for a post-war settlement. He addressed a hastily convened joint session of Congress and the world at large.

In summary, his 14 points are: 1. Open covenants of peace openly arrived at. 2. Freedom of the seas in peace and war. 3. Removal of economic barriers and equality in trade. 4. A reduction of armaments. 5. Impartial adjustment of all colonial claims, giving equal weight to the interests of colonial peoples. 6. Evacuation of all Russian territory and allowing Russia to choose her own institutions. 7. Evacuation of Belgium without any limits on her sovereignty. 8. All French territory to be freed, with Alsace-Lorraine restored to France. 9. Italy's frontiers to be readjusted along nationality lines. 10. The people of Austria-Hungary should have the right of autonomous development. 11. Rumania, Serbia and Montenegro should be evacuated and Serbia given access to the sea. 12. Turks in the Ottoman Empire should be given sovereignty, but the other nations should be allowed separate development. The Dardanelles should be open to all nations. 13. A Polish state should be created with access to the sea. 14. An association of nations must be formed to guarantee independence and territorial integrity to all. Wilson's points resembled those of British Prime Minister Lloyd George (→ 25).

President Woodrow Wilson.

Austrians seeking a separate peace

Jan 26. There are new indications that Austria is considering a separate peace treaty with Russia. A report from Petrograd says Austrian negotiators at Brest-Litovsk have actually proposed signing a treaty without Germany.

Russian propagandists say the pressure to sign the treaty comes from the Austrian proletariat, which wants to unite with the Russian masses and overthrow the Vienna government. And the Russians are playing up reports of dissension in Central Europe. One dispatch from Petrograd says, "Great demonstrations are taking place all over Austria-Hungary. Workmen's and soldiers' organizations have been formed at Vienna."

Reports from Vienna say striking workers and socialists are increasing pressure on the government to sign a peace treaty. Socialists claim that the Austrian people are being robbed of any influence in the negotiations, and they charge that the government has outlawed all criticism of foreign policy (→ 4/11).

Red army created; assembly dissolved

Trotsky examines Red army troops.

Jan 28. Leon Trotsky, the Russian revolutionary, has returned home from exile to form his own military unit. And Trotsky and Lenin plan to use this Red army to achieve their radical goals.

Lenin has already shown he will use force to win what he loses at the ballot box. Nine days ago, Bolshevik deputies allied with Lenin ordered the assembly dissolved after it rejected his motion to form a government of the soviets, or workers' councils. Red Guard units loyal to Lenin barred deputies from entering the chamber and fought with citizens who protested in the streets.

The Bolsheviks are still a minority party, but that makes little difference to Lenin. "Only idiots think that the proletariat will win a majority right away," Lenin said. "First we topple the bourgeoisie, then we seize power. That's the dictatorship of the proletariat" (→ 2/5).

Constituent assembly in Petrograd.

New Premier states Britain's war aims

Jan 5. In an attempt to heal a breach in national unity and allay doubts about the war's objectives, new British Prime Minister Lloyd George has deemed it necessary to restate his country's war aims.

They embody principles which the Labor Party considers essential, such as the freedom of Belgium, Serbia, Rumania and Montenegro, and the establishment of a league of nations for disarmament and the prevention of future wars.

He also emphasized his aim "to stand by the French democracy to the death" in their demand for the restoration of Alsace-Lorraine, "torn from the side of France" during the Franco-Prussian War.

He also said, "The adoption of a really democratic constitution by Germany would be the most convincing evidence that her old spirit of military dominance has died," but added that this was a matter that the Germans themselves must decide (→ 8).

1918

FEBRUARY

Su	Mo	Tu	We	Th	Fr	Sa
					1	2
3	4	5	6	7	8	9
10	11	12	13	14	15	16
17	18	19	20	21	22	23
24	25	26	27	28		

1. U.S. Senate limits govt. control over railroads to 18 months (→ 3/29).

3. N.Y. Times begins home delivery.

3. Germany: Gen. von Kessel, military commandant of Brandenburg province, tells strikers to work or be shot (→ 3/11).

4. Ottawa decrees three workless days for Canada as conservation measure.

5. Soviets proclaim separation of church and state (→ 3/5).

9. Ukraine makes separate peace with Central Powers (→ 14).

9. Western Front: Americans taken prisoner by Germans north of Xivry (→ 3/7).

11. Wilson tells Congress, Prussian autocracy makes lasting peace impossible (→ 26).

14. New York: Leon Forrest Douglass displays new method for producing motion pictures in color.

14. 19-year-old George Gershwin's "Swanee," his first popular hit, sung in revue "Sinbad."

14. Warsaw demonstrators protest transfer of Polish territory to Ukraine (→ 20).

17. U.S.: Ship carpenters' strike called off after rebuke from Wilson.

19. Day-old German invasion forces Russians to accept peace terms (→ 20).

20. Soviet Red army seizes Kiev, capital of Ukraine (→ 6/13).

20. First American-built battle planes leave for Western Front (→ 5/19).

23. New York: AFL Pres. Gompers pledges labor's support for war effort.

25. Wilson okays Muscle Shoals Dam over Tenn. River (→ 7/15/22).

26. Washington, London reject German peace proposals (→ 9/14).

DEATH

6. Gustav Klimt, Austrian painter, art nouveau (*7/14/1862).

German armies press Russians for peace

Feb 20. The armistice between the Central Powers and Russia ended at noon today, and German armies launched a ferocious attack on Russia. Germany's goal seems to be to bring Russia to its knees and force its negotiators to sign a peace treaty at Brest-Litovsk.

Troops under the command of Colonel General Count Kirchbach plowed through the towns and cities of Livonia and Estonia. They met little resistance and even received support from local residents opposed to the Bolshevik Revolution.

German forces quickly captured Riga and towns around the Gulf. A military bulletin announced that the army knocked out a key Russian supply line: "On both sides of the Riga-Petrograd railway, the Russian positions were crossed, and we advanced 20 kilometers beyond our front. Feeble resistance soon was broken." Nothing could stop the Germans, and they seem intent on pushing all the way to Petrograd.

The capture of the fortress of Dvinsk was another crushing setback for the Russians. A German military bulletin announced: "The majority of the enemy had fled. The Russians were not successful in blowing up the Dvina bridge, for which preparations had been made." The Russians also left behind a large supply of weapons and ammunition. The German military command, which had been unable to capture Dvinsk in the last offensive, was elated.

Another German army, under the command of General Alexander von Linsingen, has captured key positions in the Ukraine, with the approval of the Ukrainian government. The Germans seized Kiev and cut through a key rail line.

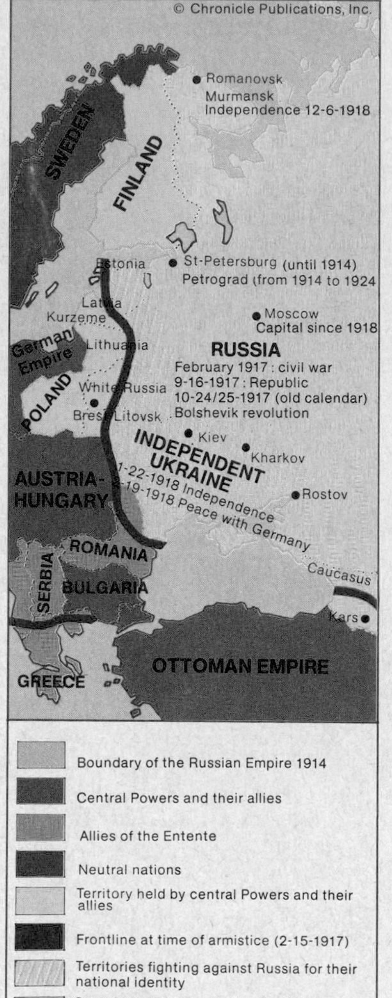

BREST-LITOVSK PEACE

In a very short time, the Germans have taken thousands of Russian officers and soldiers prisoner. They have also captured tens of thousands of guns, boxes of ammunition and armored vehicles.

Russian leaders have been terribly shocked by the accelerated German advance, and they have ordered retreating soldiers to destroy all military supplies. The Bolsheviks also made a major mistake in assuming that the German soldiers would refuse to attack revolutionary Russia. Leon Trotsky is trying to decide what to do next. At this point, a peace treaty looks tempting, and surrender would be less painful than agonizing defeat (→ 3/3).

Turks recoil under Middle East attack

Feb 22. The Ottoman Empire is contracting, and Turkish influence is shrinking, from the eastern Mediterranean to the Caspian Sea. The latest setback came today, as British forces under the command of Field Marshal Edmund Allenby entered Jericho in Palestine.

The Turks' fate in Palestine was sealed last November, when British Foreign Minister Balfour issued his declaration. He pledged Zionists the support of Britain in setting up a permanent homeland in Palestine.

The British have sought to undermine Turkish influence in the Middle East ever since they started to deal with Hussein Ibn Ali three years ago. The British promised Hussein, the Sheik of Hejaz, that they would assist in the creation of an Arab kingdom if he would organize a revolt against the Ottoman Empire.

With the help of T.E. Lawrence, the British adventurer and intelligence agent, Arab troops attacked Turkish rail lines, and they occupied Mecca and Jedda. The Germans tried and failed to stop Lawrence, but he overran the important port of Aqaba. Last December, British and Arab forces entered Jerusalem together. And last year, the Turks lost Baghdad to the British.

Over the past decade, the Turks have watched helplessly as Bulgaria declared its independence and nationalistic disorders erupted in the Balkans. The Turks lost Libya to Italy and their European territories to Albania, Bulgaria, Greece and Serbia. Osman I, the 13th-century founder of the Ottoman Empire, must be shuddering in his grave.

Prince Feisal led assault on Turks.

1918

MARCH

Su	Mo	Tu	We	Th	Fr	Sa
					1	2
3	4	5	6	7	8	9
10	11	12	13	14	15	16
17	18	19	20	21	22	23
24	25	26	27	28	29	30
31						

3. Soviets, Central Powers sign peace at Brest-Litovsk (→ 14).

3. U.S. Congress passes dry law for Puerto Rico (→ 1/13/19).

5. Soviets move Russian capital from Petrograd to Moscow (→ 7).

7. Finns sign alliance treaty with Germany (→ 6/3).

7. Bolsheviks change name to Russian Communist Party (→ 20).

7. Western Front: U.S. sentry attacks German patrol of 40, kills or wounds all (→ 21).

11. Germans alarmed by rising crime rate, reaching 300 cases daily (→ 8/25).

11. German planes bomb Paris; 106 dead, 79 wounded.

13. New York: Women to march in St. Patrick's Day parade due to shortage of men.

14. All-Russian Congress of Soviets ratifies peace treaty with Central Powers (→ 4/16).

20. Wilson orders Navy to take Dutch ships in U.S. waters.

20. Bolsheviks ask American aid to rebuild army (→ 4/6).

21. Western Front: Germans launch heavy attack on 50-mile front near Cambrai (→ 26).

23. New York: Union League awards colors to Negro 367th Infantry.

26. Western Front: Germans take French towns Noyon, Roye and Lihons (→ 27).

27. British Premier Lloyd George asks U.S. to rush aid to France (→ 31).

BIRTH

9. Mystery writer Mickey Spillane, "The Jury."

DEATHS

2. Hubert H. Bancroft, American historian (*5/5/1832).

8. Frank Wedekind, German expressionist playwright (*7/24/1864).

25. Claude Debussy, French composer (*8/22/1862).

27. Henry Adams, American historian (*2/16/1838).

Russian Reds sign peace

Official photograph at Brest-Litovsk. Leon Trotsky led talks for Russia, Richard von Kuhlmann for Germany, Count Czernin for Austria-Hungary.

March 14. A peace treaty was ratified today between the Central Powers and Russia, but several crucial matters were left unresolved. Under the terms of the Treaty of Brest-Litovsk, Russia agreed to dissolve its army and acknowledge the independence of Finland, Poland and the Ukraine. German troops will remain in the Ukraine and other regions, and that is the hitch. The Ukrainians want to be free of Russia and do not feel that German imperialism will rescue them from Russian domination.

The German leadership is trying to portray the peace treaty as a smashing victory. But it is no secret that German troops will have to remain on the Eastern Front because of the uncertainties in the Ukraine and elsewhere. And that will weaken the expected spring offensive in Western Europe. In the Reichstag, a conservative spokesman said German imperialism in the East will only increase the hate for Germany in the West and strengthen the resolve of enemy armies to fight to the death (→ 4/26).

Baruch to reform War Industries Board

March 29. Bernard N. Baruch, the wealthy financier, has been appointed by President Wilson to head the War Industries Board. As Chairman of the crucially important panel, Baruch will be the key man in seeing that supplies needed for the war effort are produced on time and that industrial production is coordinated. He succeeds Daniel Willard, President of the Baltimore and Ohio Railroad, who resigned.

The reorganization of the board under Baruch's leadership is in response to congressional demands for centralization of industrial production during the on-going war in Europe. Among the functions assigned to the board by the president are the creation of new sources of supply, conversion of existing facilities to new uses, advising the purchasing agencies of government on prices to be paid and making purchases of war materials for Allied governments.

In a recent letter to Baruch, President Wilson said that the new chairman of the War Industries Board should "act as the general eye of all supply departments in the field of industry" (→ 4/1).

L. to r.: Baruch, Herman Davis, Vance McCormick, Herbert Hoover.

Foch named to lead joint Allied armies

March 26. General Ferdinand Foch, chief of the French General Staff, has been made commander of the British and French forces on the Western Front. Yesterday, Foch, Prime Minister Georges Clemenceau and French and British military leaders conferred at Compiegne. They are faced with the recent attack by the German 7th Army on the Oise. Foch gave his assessment: "Faced with the danger of a rupture in Allied lines, we must cast into the fray all troops at our disposal." The others elected Foch as the best to coordinate this effort. Foch, 66, commanded at the Marne and the Somme.

General Foch.

Powerful new rifle successful in test

March 25. Who says generals can't shoot? With the new Browning automatic rifle they become veritable William Tells, as was demonstrated at Camp Dix today when one after another of those present riddled the paper targets with a neat, round circle. The new weapon is a perfected version of the .30 caliber rifle which appeared too late to be used in the war. The gas-operated, shoulder-fired gun weighs about 25 pounds with bipod support. Shooting from the prone position, a south Jersey corporal made a perfect score on a six-inch bull's-eye from 100 yards.

Bold German offensive strikes West

March 31. Germany mounted a massive offensive drive on the Western Front this month as Kaiser Wilhelm declared: "The prize of victory must not fail us; no soft peace, but one which corresponds with Germany's interests." Reinforced by divisions from the Eastern Front, German troops embarked on the most "decisive moment of the war," according to the kaiser.

On March 11, some 60 German planes bombed Paris in a night raid which killed 106 Parisians, wounded 79 more and destroyed many buildings. French artillery fought off many of the raiders, preventing extensive damage. One German aircraft was hit and plummeted down in a flaming wreck.

Intense fighting erupted against British lines in France on the 21st at Cambrai and simultaneously along the Fieurbaix-Armentieres sector. The Germans first launched a heavy artillery attack, creating a storm of gas shells mixed with dense ground fog. After five hours of hard shelling, German forces surged into the trenches where they fought with British troops who were prepared for the onslaught. "There was nothing in the nature of a surprise about the attack," remarked a British spokesman, adding that extra soldiers were planted on the line. The Germans gained some ground, but not without heavy losses.

By the 27th, the Germans had three million men on the Western Front. Supporting the claim that this could be the final German drive if Allied forces prevail, a Daily Mail correspondent wrote, "It is clear we have been struggling with the whole available strength of the German army, and the marvel is that our soldiers have held out so obstinately and steadily against such odds."

Despite the heroic spirit of Allied forces, the enormous German army seized many French towns, including Lihons and Noyon. Fresh British soldiers attempted a counter-drive from the direction of Albert, but after a bitter struggle, were pushed back. British losses in a week of defensive fighting on the 50-mile French line totaled 77,650.

Noting German victories, French and British military leaders met and appointed General Ferdinand Foch commander of Allied armies on the Western Front. Most military experts support the decision.

Germans advance across the battle-scarred terrain of the Western Front.

Despite German advances, enemy objectives have not been attained. The progress on the line was called "most unsatisfactory" by German General Crown Prince Rupprecht, who requested and was denied three extra divisions. German reinforcements are simply not available. The kaiser has only been able to offer encouraging words: "Everyone out here is staking everything; everyone knows and trusts we shall win everything. All of Germany fights for her future."

American troops are reportedly fighting "shoulder to shoulder" with the French and British south of the Somme as the German pounding continues. The spring may be destined to become a turning point in the West as many speculate the German offensive will run out of men, weapons and energy. Only time will tell (→ 4/9).

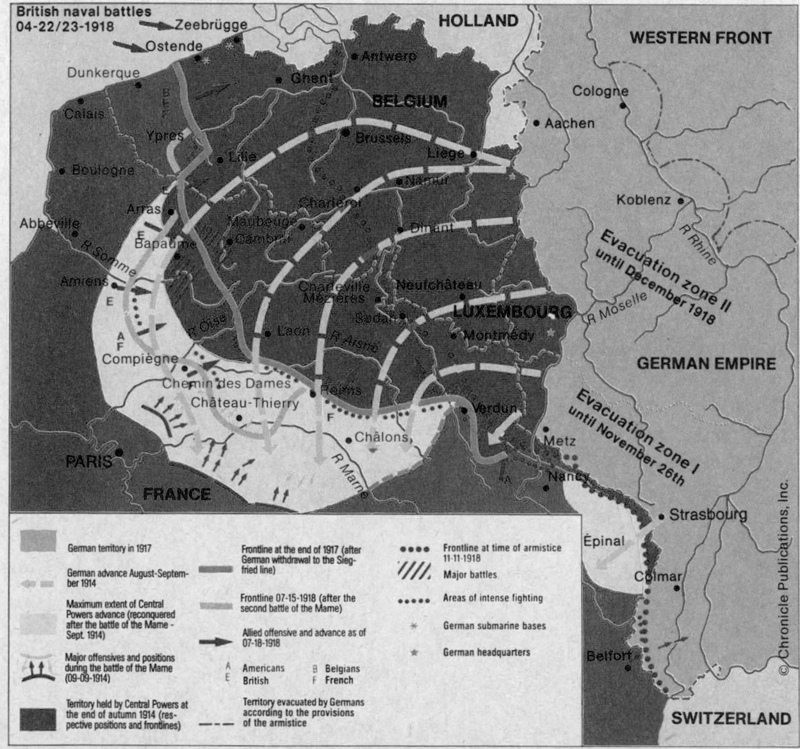

Four years of war on the Western Front.

1918

APRIL

Su	Mo	Tu	We	Th	Fr	Sa
	1	2	3	4	5	6
7	8	9	10	11	12	13
14	15	16	17	18	19	20
21	22	23	24	25	26	27
28	29	30				

1. First day of daylight savings reported as big success in conserving fuel for U.S. business concerns (→ 16).

1. Britain: Royal Air Force replaces Royal Flying Corps.

3. British troops cross River Jordan, enter Palestine (→ 9/22).

4. Belgium: Gen. Pershing receives Grand Cross of the Order of Leopold, highest honor bestowed by king.

6. British, Japanese troops land in Vladivostok, one day after U.S. Marines (→ 8).

8. Moscow: Lenin threatens war with Japanese for invasion of Vladivostok (→ 27).

9. Western Front: Germans force British to withdraw from Ypres to Armentieres (→ 30).

9. Lloyd George orders conscription for Ireland; sparking angry protests (→ 5/7).

11. Vienna: Emperor Charles, in peace offer to France, upholds "just claims on Alsace-Lorraine" (→ 9/14).

14. Charlie Chaplin's "A Dog's Life" released.

16. U.S.: Federal Food board begins prosecuting grocers who refuse to label food (→ 29).

16. Austria-Hungary: Baron Burian replaces Count Czernin as foreign minister.

21. French Minister of Provisions Boret encourages use of horse meat.

26. Germany opens diplomatic relations with Soviet govt.

27. Counterrevolution in Petrograd; Czarevitch Grand Duke Alexis named ruler (→ 30).

28. Austria-Hungary: Gavrilo Princip executed for June 1914 assassination of Austrian Archduke Franz Ferdinand.

29. U.S. Senate passes Overman Bill, giving pres. power to coordinate executive bureaus as war measure (→ 5/19).

30. Soviets re-establish mandatory military service (→ 5/31).

BIRTH

25. Ella Fitzgerald, American jazz singer.

Germans gas Americans; halted by French

A bare-faced American soldier succumbs to deadly German gas in France.

April 30. Americans were heavily gassed earlier this month, rallying later to help the French halt German inroads made on the Somme, Aivre and Oise. Gas is only one of many new hazards the Americans face as they move into the front lines. The French advise Americans to learn from their mistakes.

For security reasons, the site of the gassing could not be revealed; officials would only say it happened April 3 in a usually subdued sector not part of the Toul region. The attack erupted in the dead of night, when gas shells mingled with explosives were hurled into the Allied trenches. A list of casualties was not released to the press.

The front lines also offer booby traps. On April 21, when Americans recaptured the town of Seicheprey, some men tripped on wires slung low across the streets. Hidden caches of dynamite exploded. The traps were quickly dismantled.

On April 28, several of Pershing's troops moved to the tip of the Great Somme salient. They are still sheltered from the heavy fighting. The French, close by, are taking the brunt of it (→ 5/2).

Germany's Red Baron downed in plane

April 22. Germany's premier aviation ace, Manfred von Richthofen, known as the "Red Baron" because of the color of his Fokker triplane, was shot down and killed at the battle of the Somme yesterday.

During this war no pilot on either side had accumulated more aerial victories than the Red Baron. He destroyed 80 Allied aircraft in less than two years of fighting and his combat squadron, called Richthofen's Circus, had gained a reputation as fierce and accurate marksmen. It is believed the flying ace was so dedicated to the German war effort that he took great pleasure in annihilating the enemy. Yet, honoring the virtue of patience, he advised his men to wait for the enemy to advance before firing, or as he put it, "Let the customer come into the store." He was despised by many Allied fliers. Edward Mannock, the English fighter pilot, on hearing of the Red Baron's death said, "I hope he roasted all the way down."

Funeral services took place today at the site of his death where German dignitaries granted Richthofen high military honors.

Baron von Richthofen's squadron.

1918

MAY

Su	Mo	Tu	We	Th	Fr	Sa
			1	2	3	4
5	6	7	8	9	10	11
12	13	14	15	16	17	18
19	20	21	22	23	24	25
26	27	28	29	30	31	

2. Wilson asks Congress to abolish limits on military strength (→ 6).

5. German Socialists celebrate centenary of Karl Marx' birth.

6. Western Front: Germans drop 15,000 gas shells into American trenches (→ 27).

7. Nicaragua declares war on Central Powers (→ 24).

7. Rumania signs peace treaty with Central Powers.

7. Ulster Unionist leader Sir Edward Carson urges fight against home rule (→ 17).

9. Exterminator wins Kentucky Derby with jockey W. Knapp in the saddle.

11. N.Y.C. superintendent of schools asks Board of Education to ban teaching of German in high schools (→ 10/26).

17. Dublin Sinn Fein leaders arrested by police (→ 1/21/19).

17. Germany recommends marriage before age 20 to increase birth rate.

18. Traffic commissioner reports New York City has world's heaviest traffic.

19. U.S. railroads to get $1 bil. in government funds for upkeep (→ 6/9).

19. Western Front: Major Raoul Lufbery, foremost U.S. fighter pilot, killed in air battle north of Toul (→ 27).

24. 284,114 women register to vote in N.Y.C. (→ 11/5).

24. Costa Rica declares war on Central Powers (→ 8/24).

25. Bavarian Prince Leopold hangs two German battalions for refusing to go to Western Front.

26. Georgia, Armenia (Dashnak republic) proclaim independence from Russia (→ 8/17).

27. Western Front: Germans start new offensive between Soissons and Rheims, take Chemin des Dames (→ 31).

DEATHS

14. James Gordon Bennettt Jr., American publisher, sports patron (*5/10/1841).

30. Gheorgi Valentinovitch Plekhanov, Russian Socialist theorist (*11/29/1856).

Americans win fight on Amiens front

U.S. gunners defend scorched earth.

May 31. German attacks across the Aisne River, between the Oise and Marne, have been repulsed by French troops reinforced by Americans. The city of Amiens remains on the outskirts of destruction. Like a symbol of eternity, the cathedral at Amiens stands unscathed.

This third German offensive started May 27. General Erich Ludendorff ordered the First and Seventh armies to assault the French Sixth Army. Tanks led 17 divisions in the onrush. The French forces folded, and by 12 noon the Germans were crossing the Aisne.

At the same time, the battle of Cantigny was raging, 50 miles northwest of the Aisne attack. The First U.S. Division, commanded by Major General Robert Lee Bullard, launched a small offensive against the well-fortified German-held village. Heavy artillery was directed against the town while the weary infantry dug their trenches 300 meters away. French divisions joined in the artillery barrage. American machine gunners moved up.

The First Division had dug two lines of trenches. One was a "dummy," to draw off fire. From the real trench the men advanced in waves. Finally, they burst the village gates, taking 200 German soldiers prisoner. Cantigny was theirs. The small victory was the first American offensive of the war (→ 6/4).

German gunners near Rheims.

Civil war grips Russia

Cossacks from the Russian White army display their Bolshevik victims.

May 31. Russia may have signed a peace treaty with the Central Powers, but there is no peace in Russia. Foreign powers are making new inroads into the country, and Russian society has been torn apart in a blistering civil war.

Peter Krasnov, the new chief of the Don Cossacks, is organizing the chief resistance to the Bolsheviks. Allied with General Denikin, he is already in control of most of the territory from the German-occupied region to the Volga. The Cossacks have cut a key supply route to Moscow, and Bolshevik forces loyal to Joseph Stalin and General Voroshilov are trying to re-open it by capturing the city of Tsaritsyn.

Leon Trotsky's plan to break up the Czech volunteers has also backfired, and they are now a serious threat to the Red army. The ragtag band of deserters and prisoners of war was originally organized to fight the Germans. Now they are allied with an opposition government of Social Democrats and revolutionaries in Samara and they control the Trans-Siberian Railway in the Urals. In the city of Omsk, in Siberia, yet another government has been formed under the direction of former naval commander Alexander Kolchak. And all the gold bullion from the imperial bank of Russia has fallen into the hands of the anti-Bolshevik White army.

In addition to the civil warfare, German, British and Turkish forces are advancing in the north, west and southwest (→ 6/11).

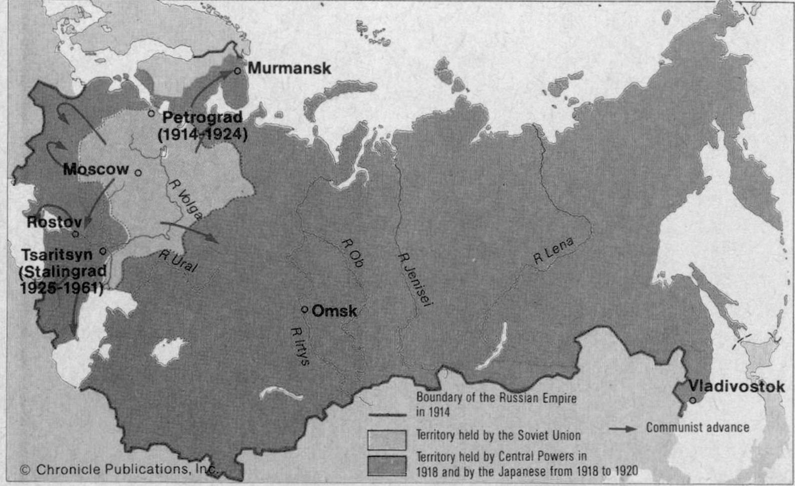

Communist expansion during the Russian civil war.

First U.S. warplanes fighting in France

May 25. The first American-built warplanes are sauntering in the skies of France. Most of the small squadron are "Jennys," Curtiss JN-4's developed by former bicycle mechanic Glenn Curtiss. While the aircraft are new to European skies, their American pilots are not.

The Lafayette Escadrille, a small group of American volunteer aviators, arrived in France in April 1916. Their work was very different then. Fliers were just observers; they did reconnaissance work, describing the placement of men and artillery, sometimes taking photographs of the enemy's placement. When an American sailed by a German flier, they would wave their gloved hands in greeting.

Camaraderie in the air ended when a German pilot mounted a machine gun on a Fokker. Now,

Lufberry, four days before he died.

American papers are filled with the exploits of aces like Eddie Rickenbacker, who has shot down four planes, and Major Raoul Lufberry, who last Sunday was shot down by a German biplane (→ 10/20).

German plane downed over France.

1918

JUNE

Su	Mo	Tu	We	Th	Fr	Sa
						1
2	3	4	5	6	7	8
9	10	11	12	13	14	15
16	17	18	19	20	21	22
23	24	25	26	27	28	29
30						

2. U.S. sets record for ship construction, launching destroyer Ward in 17.5 days.

3. Finnish Parliament ratifies treaty with Germany (→ 4/27/19).

4. New York ports close after yesterday's sinking of nine ships by German U-boats off Atlantic coast (→ 5).

4. Western Front: French and Americans halt German offensive at Chateau-Thierry on the Marne (→ 18).

5. German mines found off Delaware Bay (→ 10/21).

7. U.S. Marines win name of "Devil Hounds" for fierce fighting in France.

9. Wilson orders survey of all industries to help utilize those not producing for war (→ 7/1).

11. Soviets create peasants committee to oversee distribution of land (→ 28).

13. Henry Ford, at Wilson's urging, accepts Democratic nomination for senator from Michigan.

13. Fighting halted between Soviet Russia and Ukraine.

15. Italy: Austrian troops drive on Asiago Plateau (→ 24).

18. Western Front: Allies launch great counterattack (→ 30).

20. New York: X-ray expert Dr. Eugene Caldwell dies of X-ray burns.

24. Italy: Austrians fleeing across Piave River, have lost 45,000 prisoners to Italians.

26. Spanish influenza reported raging in German army.

27. German pilots Steinbrecher and Udet saved by parachutes for first time in history.

28. Soviets complete official nationalization of industry (→ 30).

29. U.S. war costs for fiscal year reported at $13.8 billion.

30. Russia: Red army defeats Cossacks in southwest (→ 7/7).

DEATH

4. Charles W. Fairbanks, ex-vice president (*11/5/1852).

Americans join in big counterattack

June 30. Germany launched its fourth greatest offensive of the war June 9, trying to sever the Noyon-Montdidier line. The Allies are waging a counterattack, thanks to our doughboys. The Americans are no mightier than the French or British, but they have the advantage of ignorance. They are too young to know victory is nowhere in sight.

Earlier in the month, Prime Ministers Georges Clemenceau, Lloyd George and Vittorio Orlando petitioned the U.S. for one hundred American divisions —about four million men. They are not interested in logistic support or technicians. They want infantry. At present, the Allies have 1.45 million riflemen to Germany's 1.64. America will do its best to bridge the gap.

Americans will boost Europe's morale. The British public has been demanding Parliament reduce Field Marshal Haig's forces; the people hear stories of soldiers on endless marches collapsing in the summer heat. In Paris, the mood is tenser. Marshal Foch only lately released a regiment quartered in the city to put down any possible revolution.

The Allies had some inkling of the latest offensive May 27, when 30 German divisions crossed the Aisne. They came in silence: the hooves of horses were padded with gunny sacks, harness buckles were greased to reduce clatter. Troops hid in the woods during the day, undetected by observation planes, and moved stealthily by night.

Troops from the 2nd U.S. Division watch for German planes at Montreuil.

On May 30, some Germans reached Chateau Thierry, a major communications center. Members of the U.S. 7th Infantry were already there. A few men with a machine gun at the main bridge to the city kept the German advance at bay. Scattered hand-to-hand combat followed. Lieutenant W.B. Flannery swam 50 yards along the Marne to rescue a wounded French soldier left to die on the shore.

The Germans veered east of Chateau Thierry and on June 3 they were once again upon the Marne. Paris stood a mere 56 miles away. Yet the German Crown Prince sensed his troops were spread too thinly east to west; they could not press on victoriously. The men were regrouped at the Matz, a tributary of the Oise. The Montdidier-Compiegne-Soisson railway was their goal. The June 9 assault began.

The Allies were not caught off guard; a German prisoner had divulged the time and date. But they could not match the German onslaught. Immediately, the Germans advanced a tremendous six miles. A French officer, rushing back from the front lines, breathlessly advised Wendell C. Neville, a Colonel of the U.S. 5th Marines, to retreat with his men. "Retreat, hell," said Neville, "we just got here."

On June 11, three French divisions and the First and Second American divisions seized the psychological advantage of a counterattack. The advantage is not always clear; both Allies and Germans are suffering terribly. Bombs leave the wheatfields plowed with bodies and abandoned arms. Some American soldiers who were gassed and sent to the hospital are returned to the front too soon. They froth at the mouth and bend in convulsions. Their comrades drag them back to safety. Some U.S. units experience casualties as high as 40 percent. As for the Germans, the Spanish influenza, a natural enemy, began decimating their ranks on the 26th.

As the month waned, most Germans retreated. No doubt they will try to forge the Marne again. The Allies, with a burgeoning American contingent, will be there (→ 7/11).

American Marines in combat at Belleau Wood, France.

Big Bertha resumes shelling of Paris

June 26. After a brief respite, Paris is again being barraged by "Big Bertha," the huge, unwieldy 420mm howitzer that has killed over 800 of the city's inhabitants.

The weapon first bombed the city on March 24, shortly after the start of the second battle of the Somme. It was soon located and identified by aerial photography. This was not easy; the cannon is mobile, kept on railway cars or hidden under sod on the side of hills. Once spotted, it is not indestructible. The Big Bertha now menacing Paris is the last of its kind; another three were demolished. One was wrecked by plane, one was silenced by ground fire and one seemingly exploded by itself on its second day of use.

The Allies have developed nothing to rival Big Bertha. The French rely on the 75mm field gun, developed in 1897, for defense against artillery. And the British Mark IV tank may easily wipe out a machine gun installation, but cannot withstand heavy cannon fire.

"Big Bertha" on the Somme.

Big Bertha was named after the wife of its manufacturer, Gustav Krupp von Bohlen und Halbach. The howitzer fires a shell weighing 1,764 pounds. While distance is assured (shells are ejected up to 65 miles away) direction is not. The cannon can be wildly inaccurate. If a measurement is one inch off the carriage, a target may be missed by miles. Some Parisians believe a particular church was shelled on Good Friday, not out of malice but ineptitude.

1918

JULY

Su	Mo	Tu	We	Th	Fr	Sa
	1	2	3	4	5	6
7	8	9	10	11	12	13
14	15	16	17	18	19	20
21	22	23	24	25	26	27
28	29	30	31			

1. Wilson asks power to control wire systems in order to prevent strikes; vetoes bill to raise working hours from seven to eight (→ 3).

2. U.S. recognizes Czech Natl. Council as provisional government (→ 8/13).

3. U.S. govt. calls for 25,000 women to study nursing to fill medical labor shortage (→ 11).

6. France reported in grip of Spanish flu epidemic (→ 10/31).

6. German ambassador assassinated in Moscow.

7. Entire Murmansk coast breaks with Russia, joins Entente (→ 15).

9. German Min. of For. Affairs von Kuehlmann resigns.

11. U.S.: Farmers in Northwest ask delay in draft to avoid labor shortage for wheat harvest (→ 12).

11. 37 U.S. Marines given war crosses for heroism at Chateau-Thierry (→ 28).

12. U.S.: Natl. Coal Assn. claims Prohibition is needed to maintain war effort (→ 19).

15. Russia: American, British forces reported in control of entire Murmansk coast (→ 16).

16. New York: Lexington Ave. Subway line opens.

19. U.S.: Sec. Baker rules baseball a non-essential occupation (→ 26).

19. U.S. armored cruiser San Diego sunk off Fire Island.

26. Wilson demands end to lynchings in U.S. (→ 7/30/19).

26. Sec. Baker allows organized baseball to continue until September 1 (→ 8/1).

28. Western Front: American troops cross Ourcq, enter Fere-en-Tardenois (→ 31).

29. Texas: "Fowler's Folly" well in Burkburnett comes in at 2,200 barrels per day.

29. Germany, Turkey sever relations.

BIRTH

14. Ingmar Bergman, Swedish film director.

Bolsheviks execute Czar and family

Czar Nicholas' son and daughters in Siberian exile before their execution.

July 16. The Bolsheviks have executed former Czar Nicholas II and his son and heir, Alexis, bringing to an end the Romanov dynasty that ruled Russia for three centuries.

Also executed were Nicholas' wife, the former Empress Alexandra, their four daughters, and several servants. All were shot to death in Siberia, where they had been imprisoned for most of the time since Nicholas' abdication in 1917.

The executions took place on the authority of local Soviet officials, who were concerned by the rapid advance of the White or pro-monarchist forces. Alive, Nicholas was the most serious threat to the legitimacy of the new Bolshevik regime.

As ruler from 1894 to 1917, Nicholas was a paternalistic autocrat, who was nevertheless not strong enough to repress his country's desire for reform and peace (→ 8/3).

President Wilson gives American war aims

July 4. "There can be no half-way peace," President Woodrow Wilson said in a stirring Independence Day speech delivered in the capital today. "The plot is written plain upon every scene and every act of the supreme tragedy." Before an emotional crowd of 10,000, including representatives from 30 nations, Wilson outlined America's goals for the conclusion of the European war.

Without theatrical gestures or show, the president enumerated four points for establishing a lasting peace. First, he called for the "destruction of every arbitrary power . . . that can disturb the peace of the world." Second, he would have all questions settled "whether of territory, or of sovereignty, of economic arrangement, or of political relationship . . . by the people immediately concerned, and not upon the basis of material interest or advantage of any other nation or people which may desire a different settlement for the sake of its own exterior influence or mastery." The third point seeks abolishment of secret pacts and observance of honorable covenants.

Wilson was most insistent on his fourth goal urging a league of nations, an international tribunal with executive powers for enforcing peaceful measures. Some listeners recognized this issue as the last of Wilson's Fourteen Points drawn up in January. If it is a radical proposal, his listeners did not seem to fear it. Wilson descended the podium to deafening cheers.

Wilson, a master orator.

War council agrees on Allied strategy

July 31. The military minds of France, Italy, Britain and the United States have formulated new tactics to employ against Germany, including more cohesive and combined attacks on the enemy. The war council, concerned by the relative success of the latest German drive, will order more counter offensives similar to the one initiated by General Foch on July 14. In that operation, at Champagne, Foch tripped advancing German troops with a coordinated Allied raid.

L. to r.: Gen. Petain, Field Marshal Haig, Gen. Foch, Gen. Pershing.

Paris celebrates the Fourth of July.

In August, observers expect an Allied assault on the forces of Germany's Eighteenth Army somewhere near Montdidier. Details of this plan have not been disclosed.

Conversely, General Pershing convinced a reluctant General Foch to allow a separate American force to work at the St. Mihiel front. But essentially, maneuvers will be coordinated from now on.

Allies halt drive, push Germans back

French machine gunners, now on the offensive in the West.

French War Decorations of Honor.

July 31. The collective mood of the German people is dismal, as they sense defeat and count the dead: nearly one million in the last three months. The grand offensive launched in March has been thwarted by coordinated and concentrated Allied resistance.

Defying an apparent last-ditch effort of a heavy barrage from German troops, combined American and French forces in the Fere-en-Tandnois thrust their lines forward in action yesterday. The Allied front between the Marne and the Vesle pushed German forces back two miles in what was called a "brillant operation" against the Prussian and Bavarian Guards.

Three days earlier, superior French strategy, orchestrated by General Petain, trounced German General Hindenburg's men at the Marne. Petain saw an opening for a counterattack, Commander-in-Chief Foch quickly approved it and Hindenburg's army was forced to retreat, narrowly averting disaster; the Germans rested and futilely tried to regain lost ground.

German officers captured at the Marne revealed a study in contrasts: The jubilant spirit of French soldiers against the despair and melancholy of the exhausted Germans.

On the 24th, American troops scored big victories in villages between Ourcq and the Marne. After see-saw battles for the villages of Epieds and Trughy-Epieds, American forces finally ousted the Germans and gained another mile. While in retreat, the Kaiser's men dodged a relentless shower of bombs, as Americans used heavy guns to disorganize the enemy's rearguard movements. Heavy rains forced the Germans to leave machine guns behind in the mud.

As German pride is humbled, France believes the end of the war is in sight. "If the Germans can be beaten to this extent before the Americans have more than barely entered the fight, what sort of licking shall we be able to give them in October when we shall have a million Americans in line with us," boasted the Paris press. Is it possible the German command will produce some miracle to prevent total defeat? (→ 8/6)

U.S. troops near Mezy, France.

1918

AUGUST

Su	Mo	Tu	We	Th	Fr	Sa
				1	2	3
4	5	6	7	8	9	10
11	12	13	14	15	16	17
18	19	20	21	22	23	24
25	26	27	28	29	30	31

3. Russia: Allied troops land at Archangel as Soviets flee (→ 8).

6. Gen. Pershing receives French Grand Cross (→ 8).

7. Washington: Ways and Means Committee decides to tax president's salary.

8. Trotsky's Red army takes Kazan from White Russians; Soviets claim England, Russia are in state of war (→ 11).

8. Kaiser at Spa, Belgium: "We have reached our limits"; Gen. Petain to Allied troops: "Tenacity, Audacity, Victory" (→ 10).

9. U.S. Food Admin. lifts restrictions on meat (→ 25).

10. Western Front: Allies take Montdidier on Somme, capture 30,000 Germans (→ 20).

11. Pope reported assisting ex-Empress Alexandra to flee Russia (→ 15).

13. Great Britain recognizes Czech nation (→ 9/3).

17. Turks reoccupy Armenia, begin new attack in Caucasus (→ 12/2).

17. Japanese govt. requisitions all rice stocks in attempt to end food riots.

20. France: French 4th smashes German lines between Oise and Aisne, capture 8,000 (→ 9/6).

24. Peruvian troops mutiny, demanding war with Germany (→ 9/25).

25. U.S.: War Industries Board declares moving pictures an "essential industry" (→ 27).

25. Berlin rioters trample poster of kaiser (→ 11/9).

27. Fuel Administration orders halt on Sunday driving east of Mississippi River (→ 9/6).

30. Lenin badly wounded by Socialist-Revolutionary Fanny Dora Kaplan (→ 31).

31. Soviets arrest British Consul Lockhart for counter-revolutionary activities (→ 9/5).

BIRTHS

8. Robert Aldrich, American film director.

25. Leonard Bernstein, American composer and conductor.

30. Ted Williams, baseball great.

Million U.S. women working in factories

Women aid the war effort at G.E.

Aug 1. Feminists are not altogether pleased with the record number of women in the workplace. Some suffragists, following the lead of pacifists Carrie Chapman Catt and Jane Addams, object to wartime efforts by either sex. Feminists who do approve argue that very few women are actually entering the work force for the first time.

The typical female worker is a young woman stepping up from a lower-paying position. And the nature of the work is not much more challenging than the old; only a handful of women are involved in any aspect of heavy industry.

Most labor unions refuse to admit women, and their health and pay go neglected. In New York, for example, 91 percent of female employees are paid less than men doing equivalent work. There is much speculation over what will happen to these women when the war is over. Several employers consider it women's patriotic duty to leave their pursuits as soon as the men return (→ 17).

The new American hero.

U.S., Russia break ties

7,000 U.S. Marines landed in Vladivostok this month to aid the Whites.

Aug 15. Days after President Woodrow Wilson's decision to join with France, Great Britain and Japan in sending troops to Russia, the American Ambassador has withdrawn from Moscow. Ambassador De Witt C. Poole's decision to leave Russia was provoked by the Bolsheviks' arrest of his British and French counterparts.

Allied intervention in Russia began in the spring of 1918 when British troops landed in northern Russia and Japanese in the Far East in order to protect military supplies from the German army.

Military goals soon turned into political ones, as the foreign troops began to encourage anti-Bolshevik forces, known as Whites. The Bolsheviks believe the Allies have a territorial as well as political interest in the outcome of the civil war. Japan, in particular, has had a long-standing interest in Siberia.

The United States was reluctant to send troops because Wilson feared that such an action would push the Russians into an alliance with Germany. Under Allied pressure, however, Wilson changed his mind and on August 3, announced the United States would send a small military force to Vladivostok. Wilson said the U.S. will also assist Czechoslovakian soldiers, once part of the Czar's army, who are fighting Germany from Russia (→ 30).

Kindergartens increase; 5 states pass laws

Aug 17. The U.S. Bureau of Education has seen its general guidelines for the development of kindergartens adopted by five states: Maine, Oregon, Tennessee, Texas and Washington. In Maine and Texas, school boards must now create kindergartens wherever parents petition for them. In Washington, petitions are unnecessary; kindergartens will be incorporated into the regular school system. Cities in Tennessee cannot rely on additional tax money to start preschool programs, but the state allows localities to redistribute present funds to support them. Oregon will permit kindergartens in Portland only.

Lobbying by various women's groups resulted in Washington's endorsement of preschool education. The Congress of Mothers specified five reasons for establishing kindergartens nationwide:

1) Early years are impressionable and should not be ignored.
2) Kindergartens prepare children not only for schoolwork but also for vital social interaction.
3) Few parents can afford private kindergartens.
4) Preschools are democratic arenas where children learn about each other on an equal basis before the less privileged go to work.
5) A dollar spent on assisting children now may prevent $100 in reformation later (→ 9/18).

1918

SEPTEMBER

Su	Mo	Tu	We	Th	Fr	Sa
1	2	3	4	5	6	7
8	9	10	11	12	13	14
15	16	17	18	19	20	21
22	23	24	25	26	27	28
29	30					

3. U.S. recognizes Czechoslovakia as a nation (→ 10/18).

5. Moscow: Capt. Cromie killed in raid on British consulate (→ 1/5/19).

6. U.S. Food Admin. orders all breweries closed on Dec. 1 (→ 10/23).

6. Hsu Shih Chang elected president of China.

6. Western Front: Germans in full retreat across Aisne, with British in pursuit (→ 12).

11. Boston: Red Sox take World Series from Chicago Cubs 2-1 in sixth game.

12. Western Front: German lines in total collapse as British take Havrincourt, Moeuvres, Trescault (→ 13).

13. Alsace-Lorraine: U.S. troops take St. Mihiel (→ 10/9).

14. Austria-Hungary proposes peace talks to Allies (→ 15).

15. Allied forces devastate Bulgarian army (→ 28).

18. New York: Ten-day drive begins in effort to enroll million women for farm labor.

22. Palestine: British army under Gen. Allenby wipes out Turks, takes Haifa, Nazareth (→ 4/25/20).

22. Two Goodyear trucks arrive in San Francisco after 22 days on road from Boston in first transcontinental trucking run.

23. New York: 114 new cases of influenza found (→ 10/31).

25. Brazil declares war on Austria.

27. Wilson opens fourth Liberty Loan campaign, declaring "War must achieve a peace based on equal justice for all peoples."

27. Count von Hertling resigns as German chancellor (→ 10/3).

28. N.Y.: Subway shuttle opens between Times Square and Grand Central terminal.

28. Germany sends troops to Bulgaria in effort to halt surrender (→ 30).

30. Bulgaria pulls out of war (→ 10/4).

Austria asks peace; Allies unresponsive

Sept 15. Flat rejection. That's the response of the Wilson administration to peace overtures issued by the Austro-Hungarian government to all belligerent powers yesterday. The note requested all warring nations to send delegates to some neutral meeting place for non-binding discussions of peace. In the communique, Austria stated: "An objective examination of all belligerent states no longer leaves doubt that all peoples, on whatever side they may be fighting, long for a speedy end to the bloody struggle."

American congressional leaders concur with the White House that a victorious end to the war should be pursued and that peace discussions at this time are not in the best interests of the Allies. The president has expressed the idea that this war is one of emanicipation and any acquiescence now will undermine the effective leadership of Marshal Foch, General Pershing and other key military strategists.

Britain will give "full consideration" to the plea for peace, but regards the Austrian statement as an "insincere" one from a foe. The "struggle is wearing them to a shadow," according to London cables. And it is expected that Britain will ask President Wilson to be the Allied spokesman in any preliminary negotiations. In England, it is agreed that an acceptance of Austria's peace offer would have but one of two results; either it would prolong the war with Germany or it would lead to an unsatisfactory peace (→ 10/5).

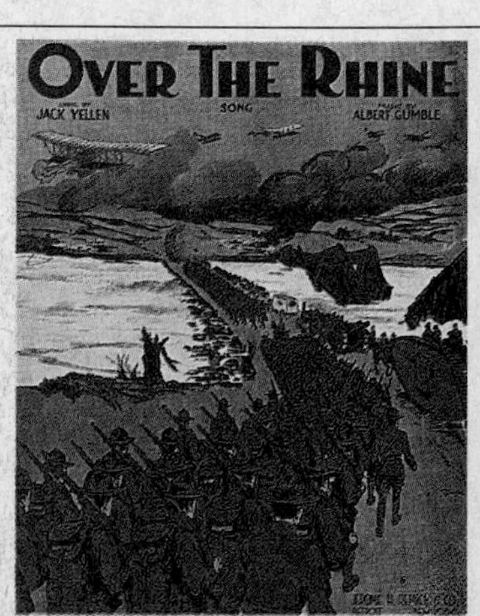

The latest marching song.

Allies hit German lines

British troops cross "no man's land" to advance on German lines.

Sept 30. The Allied armies have penetrated the German lines in France, scoring major victories, capturing thousands of prisoners and deflating enemy resilience. German manpower is dwindling with each Allied hit, worrying even the most optimistic Deutschlander. The stiff Allied push against the German lines has reduced the available German troop strength by 600,000 since March. "We cannot get a substitute for men," lamented a German college professor.

At St. Quentin on the 18th of this month, a combined French-British attack burst through the line held by German General Hindenburg. The advance occurred at two points, Villeret and Gouzeaucourt, with many German losses and 6,000 prisoners captured in a heavy, cold rain.

The next day, called the Britons' "finest day" of battle, Field Marshal Haig's experienced divisions pierced the enemy lines at every point. The Germans, still stinging from the previous day's defeat, launched a fierce attack with 40 batteries firing on the Allied forces. Yet Haig's forces averted the shelling, pushed forward and took another 8,000 prisoners.

Meanwhile, American troops blasted the German line at St. Mihiel. The penetration here is very significant; since 1914, the Kaiser's troops held the area, constantly posing a threat to Allied movements in Champagne. Now, with the sharp marksmanship of American soldiers, the Germans have been ousted from their stronghold. Over 15,000 prisoners were captured and 250 guns seized. Even the German press admits defeat, noting, "The attack at St. Mihiel was a carefully planned undertaking of considerable magnitude." With each Allied win, the war's end nears (→ 10/6).

Americans aid the Allies, more than making up for Russia's withdrawal.

1918

OCTOBER

Su	Mo	Tu	We	Th	Fr	Sa
		1	2	3	4	5
6	7	8	9	10	11	12
13	14	15	16	17	18	19
20	21	22	23	24	25	26
29	28	29	30	31		

1. British troops take Damascus, 7,000 Turkish prisoners.

1. Baltimore: First school of public health opens at Johns Hopkins Univ. under grant from Rockefeller Foundation.

3. Prince Max von Bade appointed chancellor of Germany.

4. Ferdinand I of Bulgaria abdicates in favor of son Boris I (→ 11/2).

5. Baron von Hussarek resigns as Austrian prime minister (→ 31).

6. Germans send appeal for peace to Pres. Wilson (→ 14).

7. Grain famine reported severe in Russia.

9. Western Front: Americans break through Kriemhilde line, taking Argonne forest (→ 13).

13. Germany loses Laon, last stronghold in France (→ 11/9).

16. British recognize Polish army as ally (→ 11/14).

17. Hungary declares independence from Austria (→ 2/20/19).

18. Czechs seize Prague, renounce Hapsburg rule (→ 28).

21. Germany suspends total submarine warfare.

23. Washington: Director McAdoo halts all new rail shipments except fuel, food, war necessities (→ 11/13).

23. Germany: Socialist Karl Liebknecht set free (→ 1/1/19).

23. Great Britain asks U.S. for 75 million bushels of wheat (→ 11/13).

25. Puerto Rico shocked by heavy earthquake.

26. New York: Butler Brothers refuses German-made toys bought before war.

28. N.Y.: Col. Roosevelt assails Wilson's conduct of war.

28. Prague: Czechoslovakia officially proclaims independence from Austria-Hungary (→ 11/14).

DEATH

7. Raymond Duchamp-Villon, French painter and sculptor (*11/5/1876).

Draft registration goes on in America

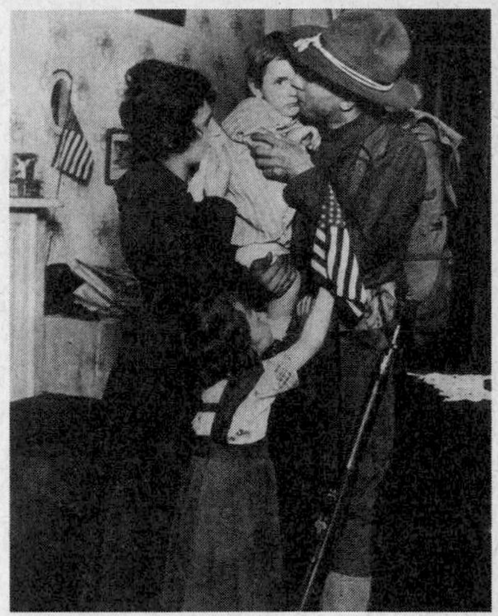

Will he come home?

Oct 1. The tide may have turned in Europe, but fledgling American doughboys keep pouring into training camps in unpredicted numbers. Thus far, about three million men have been drafted, with some one million volunteers, and their steady arrival in Europe has made the A.E.F a most powerful force.

There have been few draft dodgers. It is true that some farmers have been reluctant to leave their plows, and some "slackers" who would rather shoot pool have been rounded up by vigilante groups, but with some 14 million men now registered, the first Selective Service Act in our history has been a resounding success.

American prosperity finances Liberty Loans, which may pay for most of the war.

Germans seek peace; Wilson rejects plea

Oct 14. Germany's pleas for a "peace with honor" were rejected by President Wilson in a document published this afternoon. Germany sought a settlement based on Wilson's Fourteen Points, a charter seeking equitable treatment that Wilson drew up in January. Now however, America has more at stake overseas. Wilson seeks a guarantee of the safety of American soldiers.

On October 4, Prince Max von Baden was appointed German Chancellor. One of his first acts was to sue for peace according to the January guidelines. Wilson thought von Baden was not willing to bend enough. The United States has sent four million troops to Europe; since January, nearly 50,000 have died. Wilson seeks assurances that the fighting is truly over.

He demands an evacuation of all occupied territory. Germany must provide safeguards and guarantees of the Allies' military supremacy. Perhaps most important, he seeks some proof that Germany has "reformed," a veiled request for the abdication of the Kaiser (→ 11/11).

German prisoners on the Italian front await the outcome of peace talks.

Ace Rickenbacker downs 26th German

Rickenbacker, an ex-race car driver.

Oct 20. Captain Eddie Rickenbacker, the pride of the American Army Air Service, added to his stellar fighting record this month as he scored 14 victories, bringing his wartime destruction total to 22 aircraft and four observation balloons.

His love of automobiles, both as driver and mechanic, propelled Rickenbacker's interest in aviation, and at a late age, 26, he joined the air corps. (Most flyers start in their late teens.) Yet, he has more than made up for his slow beginnings. His appointment to the 94th Aero Squadron led to his first air victory, when he downed a German fighter on April 29th. His tenacity, bravery and passion for flying has made famous the "Hat in the Ring" insignia of the 94th Division.

Austrians declare republic; Emperor flees

Oct 31. Austria, co-instigator of this long and horrendous war, has burst into revolution. The people have proclaimed the empire a republic and the Emperor has been forced to abandon his capital city.

Demonstrating students and workers in Vienna and Budapest, crying "Down with the Hapsburgs!" have rejected the government. A correspondent reports: "No one pays any attention to the government or to the Lammasch Ministry." And in Czechoslovakia, the people have also renounced Hapsburg rule and seized Prague.

The insurrection has come on the heels of announcements that the Austrian war effort is all but exhausted; a total surrender is expected soon, as Italian troops have blasted the last Austrian stronghold at Ponte Nelle Alpi. This military loss is but one in a long line of defeats. Serbians, Russians and now the Italians have routed the Austrians. It is only when they have received help from their allies, the Germans, that the Austrians have even faintly tasted military success.

Emperor Charles has reportedly tucked himself away at the royal palace of Godolla, northeast of Budapest. Last month, he contacted German Emperor Wilhelm, announcing that Austria-Hungary was financially and militarily bankrupt, was obliged to accept a peace offer and that the war should come to an honorable end soon (→ 11/14).

Virulent flu is killing millions worldwide

Oct 31. Public health officials in the United States and abroad estimate that the influenza epidemic now raging across the globe may cause 20 million or more deaths.

The epidemic has raced around the world with unprecedented speed and virulence. The new strain of influenza germ seems to have appeared first in Spain. It spread rapidly through the ranks of the European and American armies and has created havoc among civilian populations weakened by the stress and poor nutrition caused by the war. From Europe, the epidemic moved quickly to Asia, where it is estimated to have caused millions of deaths in China alone.

In the United States, the federal Bureau of Public Health says that deaths among civilians far exceed those among troops abroad, and that more servicemen have died of influenza than of wounds suffered in battle. In the last two months, bureau reports from 46 cities, including a fifth of the nation's population, counted nearly 80,000 influenza deaths. The height of the epidemic thus far was the two weeks ending October 26, when 40,000 deaths were recorded, according to the bureau.

Attempts to develop anti-influenza vaccines have failed, and medical resources of most nations are strained to the breaking point, with no end of the epidemic in sight (→ 11/17).

Turks give up, sign armistice with Allies

Oct 30. Turkey surrendered at 12 noon. British and Turkish representatives signed the armistice aboard the battleship Agamemnon, anchored in Mudros Bay. Turkey will now disarm its forces, return prisoners and reopen the Dardanelles to Allied shipping.

Surrender follows a series of fine British offensives. Beirut, Tripoli and Damascus all fell earlier this month. The last battle, at Sharquat on Oct. 29, reaped 11,000 prisoners.

On that day, Sultan Mohammed VI dismissed all ministers who advocated a continuation of war. He cabled President Woodrow Wilson, asking him to mediate a settlement. Wilson did not reply. The sultan then released from prison General Charles Townshend, the hero of the battle of Kut el Amara. Released after two and a half years in confinement, he blinked in the sun and headed for the nearest British ship. There, as the sultan bid him, he sued for peace on behalf of Turkey.

Mesopotamia was freed of the Turks at the cost of 15,814 Allied lives. Of those, 12,807 died of disease. The Allies may not want to tarry in the region (→ 8/10/20).

1918

NOVEMBER

Su	Mo	Tu	We	Th	Fr	Sa
					1	2
3	4	5	6	7	8	9
10	11	12	13	14	15	16
17	18	19	20	21	22	23
24	25	26	27	28	29	30

2. Bulgaria: King Boris abdicates the throne (→ 11/27/19).

4. Austria signs armistice with Allies (→ 11).

5. Republicans win majority in U.S. Congress.

5. Louisiana defeats woman suffrage amendment (→ 1/10/19).

9. Germany proclaimed a republic as kaiser abdicates, flees to Netherlands.→

10. N.Y.: Louisa May Alcott's "Little Women," adapted for screen, shown at Strand.

10. Germany: Socialist Chancellor Friedrich Ebert takes command in Berlin (→ 12/7).

13. New York: Industrialist William Barr calls for postwar wages to drop (→ 12/22).

13. Wilson promises food aid to Germany (→ 1/3/19).

14. Poland: Joseph Pilsudski takes presidency with full dictatorial powers (→ 12/16).

14. Czechoslovakia: Tomas Masaryk elected president of republic (→ 30).

14. Britain: Lloyd George comes out in favor of keeping postwar wages high.

17. U.S.: Influenza deaths reported to have far exceeded war casualties (→ 1/28/20).

17. German troops evacuate Brussels (→ 21).

21. Belgium: King Albert I returns to capital, forms new goverment.

21. France: Last German troops quit Alsace-Lorraine (→ 27).

23. U.S. War Dept. reports 53,169 American war deaths.

24. N.Y.: Caruso appears in first film, "My Cousin."

25. Chile and Peru sever relations.

27. More than 1.5 million prisoners reported freed by Germans since peace (→ 12/1).

BIRTHS

9. Spiro Agnew, vice president under Nixon.

11. Alexander Solzhenitsyn, Soviet novelist.

Victory! Armistice signed by Germans

French Gen. Weygand (rt.) and Marshal Foch (standing) gain a long-awaited armistice from the Germans.

Nov 11. At 11:01 this morning, silence fell like a gentle mist on the battlefields of Europe. The Germans signed an armistice at 5 a.m., the cease-fire taking effect six hours later. The war is over.

Since Austria-Hungary surrendered November 3, the collapse of Germany was certain. It ran out of manpower: its latest recruits were 14-year-old boys and men in their 60's. It had no more food or supplies, due to the naval blockade. Internal unrest, fomented by Bolsheviks and liberals, shook the government. Yesterday, the Kaiser fled unceremoniously to Holland.

On November 8, Mattias Erzberger, head of the Catholic Centrists, led other German representatives to a spot outside Allied headquarters at Compiegne. They met with Marshal Foch, who took two days calculating the surrender demands. Germany was asked to give up its heavy guns and aircraft, 5,000 trucks, 5,000 train engines and 150,000 railroad cars. Large warships and most of the submarines will be docked at Allied ports. German troops in Austria-Hungary, Rumania, Turkey and Russia must retreat at once. Territory west of the Rhine must be evacuated. Erzberger and his compatriots agreed to the terms and signed the armistice in Foch's private railway car.

Western Europe and the outer theaters of the war face many years of rebuilding. Germany can count its blessings; no battles destroyed its fertile soil. Its economy, however, is in shreds. Yesterday, the Crown Prince chose Socialist Friedrich Ebert to be Chancellor. Europe will demand reparations of him.

More than ten million died in the four-year war. Six million were civilians. While today it is clear how the war ended, its beginnings are poorly comprehended. As long as its causes remain misunderstood, no one can be sure this was the first and last world war (→ 17).

Jubilant U.S. servicemen in France will leave the trenches for good.

▷

Hapsburg Empire comes to an end

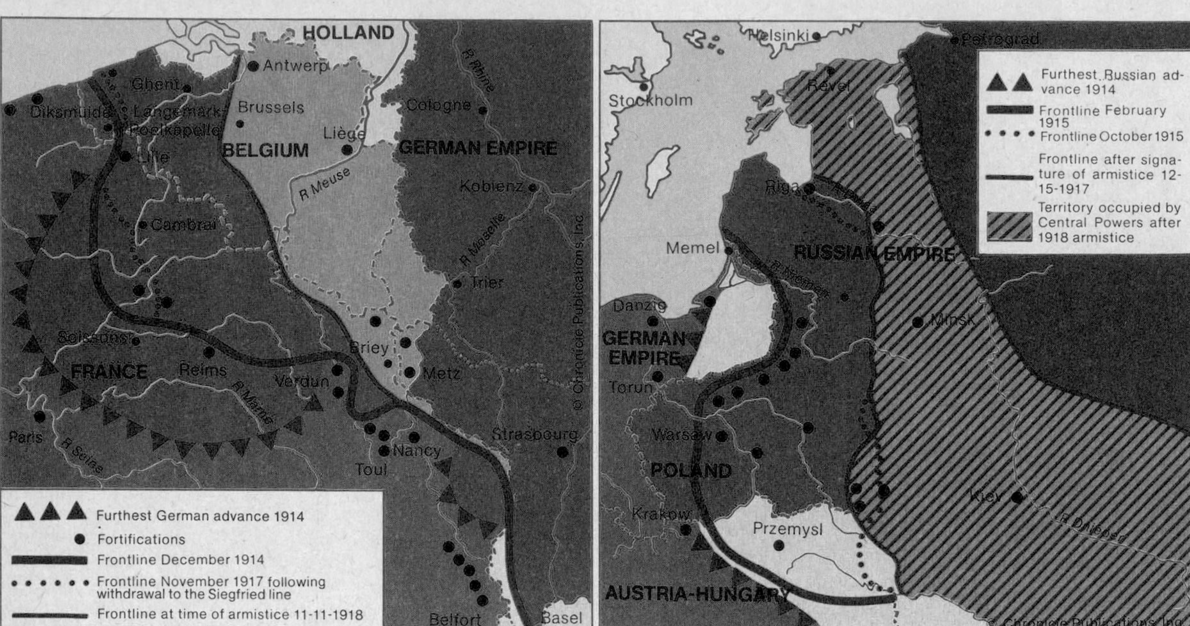

The Western Front, 1914 to 1918. *The Eastern Front, 1914-1918.*

Nov 30. The death of the Hapsburg Empire this month gave birth to four new nations: Austria, Hungary, Czechoslovakia and a Kingdom of Slovenes, Serbs and Croats. Their frontiers are drawn according to ethnicity, preserved despite centuries of Hapsburg domination.

The Hapsburg royal family, with beginnings dating to the 10th century, saw its lands grow and shift over time. Queen Maria Theresa, who ruled with an iron hand from 1740 to 1780, lost Silesia and fought most of Europe in a vain attempt to gain it back. In 1867, the Hapsburg lands were joined as the Dual Monarchy of Austria-Hungary. United only in name, its peoples were of divergent cultures: Czechs, Poles, Slavs, Slovaks, Italians and Rumanians. Germans were the majority in Austria, Magyars in Hungary.

Money divided the kingdom, too. The opulent Hapsburg life contrasted with the poverty of the peasantry. When Gavrilo Princip assassinated Archduke Francis Ferdinand in 1914, Serbs saw the act as a blow against an indifferent ruling class.

The last Hapsburg Emperor, Charles I, made Austria-Hungary a virtual military democracy during the war. This, with extreme inflation and the age-old ethnic grievances, could have led to a very bloody revolution. Yet nationalist groups had been meeting abroad for years and were willing to try peaceful solutions. In early November, Socialist and Pan-German parties petitioned Charles I to abandon the throne. He abdicated as emperor November 11 and abdicated as King of Hungary two days later. The nations immediately set about establishing their governments.

Czechoslovakia is in the hands of Tomas Mazaryk, a former representative of the Austrian Parliament married to an American. He is a liberal with lofty democratic ideals. His more practical notions may be realized by his pragmatic compatriot Eduard Benes.

Austria has made the transition to independence with few problems so far; a history of universal suffrage works on its behalf, and the old bureaucracy bows to change with little pressure. Hungary will not have it so easy. A liberal aristocrat named Michael Karolyi will have to accommodate resentful minorities and the Magyars, a virtual oligarchy. Civil war is a foregone conclusion.

The severest challenge may face the Serbs, Croats and Slovenes. The greatest common factor joining these mountain peoples is an independent nature (→ 9/10/19).

King Albert I returns to Brussels after heading the liberation of Belgium.

U.S. celebrates end of war twice

Nov 11. The war in Europe is over, and this time it is for real. Just days ago, Americans cheered lustily and marched through the streets all over the nation when a United Press bulletin announced that the armistice had been signed. The announcement turned out to be a bit premature, however, due to a series of misunderstandings. But today, appearing before Congress in Washington, President Wilson pronounced the official word: "The war thus comes to an end."

For a moment, the assembled lawmakers hesitated. Then there came a faint clapping of hands, a few cheers and finally a standing, cheering ovation from both the floor and the galleries.

The president had been awakened early this morning and told that the armistice had been signed at the headquarters of Marshal Foch. Wilson arose immediately and began making plans to address Congress later in the day. He also declared a government holiday.

Dancing in the streets.

America turns to welcome the boys.

Kaiser abdicates; German parties vie for power

Naval mutineers in front of their ships at Wilhelmshaven.

Nov 9. Socialist demonstrators filled the streets of Germany today. Sailors mutinied and army troops seized command posts. Revolutionary fervor has overwhelmed the German people, and Kaiser Wilhelm II, nowhere to be seen, has been forced to abdicate.

All over Germany, royalty has collapsed. King Louis III of Bavaria has fled. The Duke of Brunswick and five other kings, princes and grand dukes have all been chased from their castles.

Socialists have seized power, and different factions are vying for leadership positions. The Social Democrats seem to have the upper hand, but they are afraid of being abandoned by the masses, who are being wooed by the radical independent socialists. Events unfolded today with blinding speed:

11:30 a.m. A telegram from the commander of the German armies addressed to the chancellery announces the imminent departure of Wilhelm from the German throne.

Noon. The German Chancellor, Prince Maximilian of Baden, announces the official abdication of the kaiser.

12:30 p.m. Special editions of newspapers reporting the abdication are printed and distributed in Berlin.

12:30 p.m. The chancellor receives the leadership of the Social Democratic Party in his office and turns his powers over to the President of the S.D.P., Friedrich Ebert.

2:00 p.m. From a window in the chancellery, Philipp Scheidemann, the Social Democratic leader, announces to an enormous crowd the installation of the German republic.

3:00 p.m. A new telegram from the military command to the chancellery: "His Majesty Wilhelm II, in order to avoid a bloodbath, is ready to abandon the German crown, but in no event will he give up his title as King of Prussia."

3:30 p.m. The chancellery sends a telegram to military headquarters, saying it is not necessary to keep track of the location of Wilhelm II, since the news of his abdication was made public at noon.

4:00 p.m. Karl Liebknecht, leader of the Spartacus party declares the birth of the "free socialist republic of Germany."

During the day, Ebert consolidated his new power. He is a socialist, but not a revolutionary. It is likely that he will distance himself from the independent socialists.

The independents demand the formation of a soviet republic, patterned after the Russian model. Throughout the country today, workers and soldiers are forming committees, and they hope to translate their popular support into political power. They insist upon radical social improvements, including better working conditions, housing and food.

Wilhelm II virtually ignored social programs while he ruled. He was more interested in international affairs and military conquest. Occasionally, he advocated social reforms. But he was just as likely to respond to calls for social improvements with oppressive measures. Under Wilhelm, the radicals flourished. And they took their cues for new and even revolutionary experiments from the Bolsheviks in Russia.

Germany's setbacks on the field of battle this year seemed to seal Wilhelm's fate. There are a number of people in the country who feel that Wilhelm's imperialist machinations were partly responsible for the outbreak of the war. But he had little to do with military maneuvers on the field of battle. And President Wilson insisted on Wilhelm's abdication as a pre-condition of peace negotiations (→ 10).

Socialist demonstrations have erupted in Berlin in the struggle for power.

Kaiser Wilhelm II departs for exile from Germany.

Social Democrat Philipp Scheidemann proclaims the republic.

▷

The human consequences of the Great War

MEMO OF EVENTS RELATED TO WORLD WAR I

1879 : Secret agreements between the German Empire and Austria-Hungary.
1898 : Fleet's construction program is launched in Germany.
1904 : Signature of the Entente between France and Great Britain.
1905-06 : First Moroccan crisis.
1908 : First Balkan crisis.
1911 : Second Moroccan crisis.
1912-13 : Second Balkan crisis.

1914

6-28 : Assassination in Sarajevo.
7-28 : War declaration of Austria-Hungary on Serbia.
8-1 : War declaration of the German Empire on Russia.
8-3 : War declaration of the German Empire on France.
8-3/4 : The German Army invades Belgium.
8-26/30 : Battle of Tannenberg.
9-6/9 : Battle of the Marne.
11/2/5 : The Entente declares war on Turkey.

1915

5-23 : Italy declares war on the Central Powers.
7-1 : The Central Powers launch an offensive on the Eastern front.
10-14 : Bulgaria enters the war and sides with the Central Powers.

1916

2-21 to **7-21 :** Battle of Verdun.
5-31 to **6-1 :** Naval battle of the Skagerrak.
12-12 : The Central Powers make peace proposals.

1917

1-22 : Peace proclamation of President Wilson.
2-1 : Germany declares unrestricted submarine warfare.
3-10 : Revolution in Russia.
February-March : Withdrawal of the German Western frontline to the Siegfried line.
4-6 : The United States declares war on the German Empire.
7-19 : A peace resolution is voted at the Reichstag.
11-6/7 : October revolution in Petrograd; "peace decree".

1918

1-8 : President Wilson issues his 14 Points.
3-3 : Brest-Litovsk peace treaty.
3-21 : Beginning of the German offensive on the Western front.
5-7 : The Central Powers and Rumania sign the Bucharest peace treaty.
7-18 : Beginning of the German offensive.
9-30 : Armistice with Bulgaria.
10-3 : Prince Max of Baden is appointed Chancellor; message requesting armistice is sent to President Wilson.
10-30 : Allies sign an armistice with Turkey.
11-3 : Allies sign an armistice with Austria-Hungary.
11-11 : Allies sign an armistice with the German Empire.

1919

6-28 : Allies sign a peace treaty with the German Empire.
9-10 : Allies sign a peace treaty with Austria.
11-27 : Allies sign a peace treaty with Bulgaria.

1920

6-4 : Allies sign a peace treaty with Hungary.
8-10 : Allies sign a peace treaty with Turkey.

More than ten million men were killed in the war, a whole generation wiped out. In a single day, the British lost 60,000 in the battle of the Somme —19,000 of them killed. In the siege of Verdun, the two sides had 1.2 million killed. Worldwide, the Spanish influenza epidemic took more lives than even the war, an estimated 20 million. Genocide, such as the slaughter of the Armenians, while not directly connected to the war, took millions more.

Besides the dead, 21 million were wounded in the war; 7.5 million were taken prisoner or missing in action. Shipping losses totalled 15 million tons, of which 9 million were British.

All the belligerents mobilized 63 million. The total gross cost of the war was estimated by E.R.A. Seligman at more than $232 trillion during the fiscal years of combat. The daily expenditure by all belligerents was $164 million.

Metz and Lorraine return to France.

COST OF WORLD WAR I (in millions) IN HUMAN LIVES	
German Empire (without victims of starvation)	1,808
Austria-Hungary	1,200
Russia	1,700
France	1,385
Great Britain	0,947
Italy	0,460
Poland (civilians)	0,500
United States	0,115
Total	7,940
Wounded	19,536

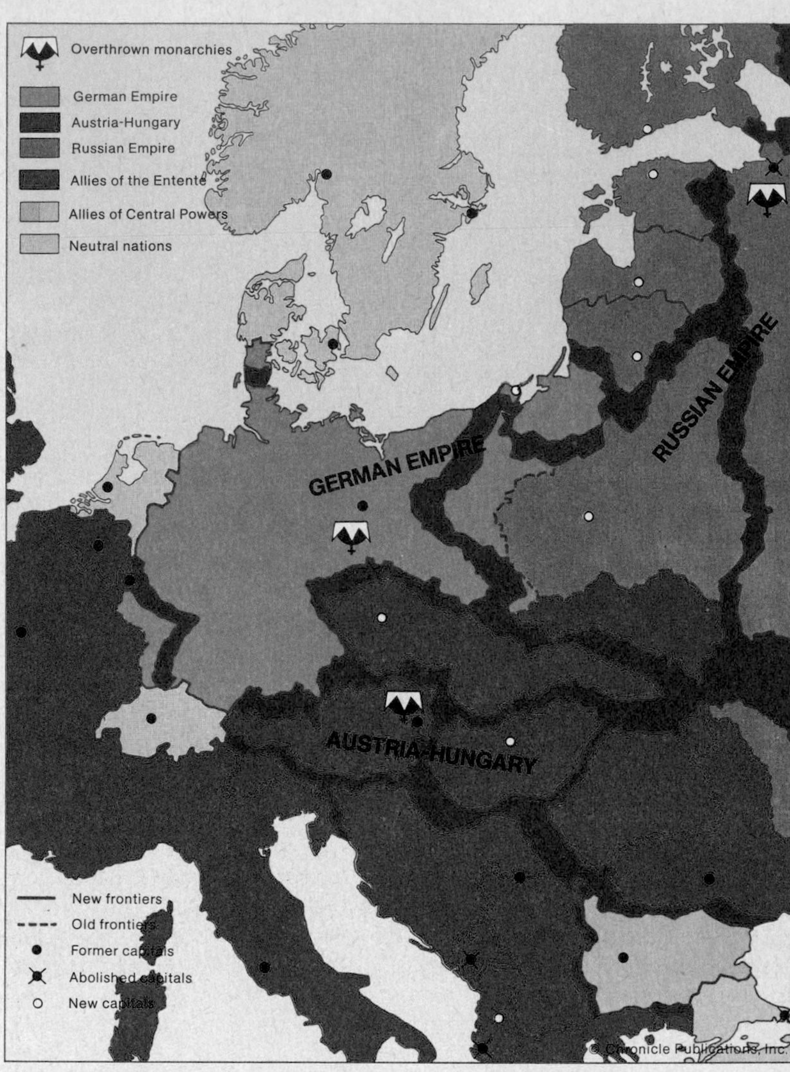

Central and Eastern Europe at the end of the war.

WORLD WAR I MILITARY BATTLE DEATHS	
Germany	† † † † † † † † † † † † † † † † † †
Austria-Hungary	† † † † † † † † † † † †
Russia	† † † † † † † † † † † † † † † † †
France	† † † † † † † † † † † † † +
Great Britain	† † † † † † † † †
Italy	† † † † † † +
Rumania	† † † +
Turkey	† † † +
United States	† +
† 100,000 deaths	+ 50,000 deaths

1918

DECEMBER

Su	Mo	Tu	We	Th	Fr	Sa
1	2	3	4	5	6	7
8	9	10	11	12	13	14
15	16	17	18	19	20	21
22	23	24	25	26	27	28
29	30	31				

1. Denmark: Union Act passed, providing for independence of Iceland (→ 6/17/44).

1. American Army of occupation enters Germany (→ 3).

2. Armenia proclaims independence from Turkey (→ 2/16/19).

3. London: Allied conference ends; Germany must pay to full limits (→ 1/21/19).

4. France cancels trade treaties to compete in postwar economic battle.

7. Berlin: Spartacists call for German revolution (→ 10).

10. U.S. troops called to guard Berlin as coup is feared (→ 25).

15. Portuguese Pres. Sidoni Paes killed by assassin.

16. Poland breaks relations with Germany.

22. Washington: Last food ban lifted (→ 6/5/19).

25. Revolt erupts in Berlin (→ 1/1/19).

BIRTHS

21. Austrian Kurt Waldheim, fourth Sec. Gen. of U.N.

25. Anwar Sadat, Egyptian statesman (†10/6/1981).

DEATH

2. Edmond Rostand, French playwright (*4/1/1868).

CULTURAL EVENTS, 1918

Literature: Willa Cather's "My Antonia"; Lytton Strachey's "Eminent Victorians"; "The Education of Henry Adams" wins Pulitzer Prize.

Academia, Religion: Oswald Spengler's "Decline of the West," 1st vol.; B. Russell's "Mysticism and Logic"; Harlow Shapley finds dimensions of Milky Way; United Lutheran Church founded in U.S.

Music: Bartok's opera "Bluebeard's Castle," Budapest; Stravinsky's "The Soldier's Story"; Irving Berlin's "Yip Yip Yaphank," N.Y.

The Arts: Joan Miro's first exhibit.

Film: Chaplin's "A Dog's Life," and "Shoulder Arms!"

Wilson warmly received in France and U.K.

Dec 31. President Wilson has been greeted as a conquering hero in key cities of Europe since arriving there December 13. He has been made an honorary citizen of Paris. He has been toasted by King George of England. And as his automobile crept through the streets of London, thousands of admirers sent up loud cheers: "Wilson, good old Wilson!"

The president and his party set sail aboard the George Washington in early December for key talks with European heads of state before the peace conference gets underway at Versailles, France, in the coming months. Looking fit, the president debarked at Brest, in France, as several thousand persons jostled for position on the dock and cheered his arrival. Later in the day, he received a gold medal from the city of Paris and visited key government leaders.

In London, the president and his wife were house guests at Buckingham Palace and were honored at a state banquet at the palace by King George. In a toast, the king noted that Wilson is the first president of the United States to be a guest in England, and he welcomed him as the "official head of a mighty commonwealth bound to us by the closest ties." While in London, Wilson also met for more than three hours with British Prime Minister David Lloyd George as well as other heads of state and diplomatic officials to discuss issues to come before the peace conference.

Wilson and Poincare in Paris.

After his visit to London, Wilson returned to France, where he spent a week at the American Army headquarters at Chaumont. However, the president ruled out visiting those areas left devastated by the war in Europe. A native of Virginia, he noted that he was reared in a region that was left in total ruin when General William T. Sherman marched through the South during Civil War. "I don't want to get mad," the president explained in an interview. "I think there should be one man at this peace table who hasn't lost his temper" (→ 1/25/19)

A hero's welcome: Wilson in Douvres is showered with flowers.

Planck is honored for quantum theory

Dec 10. Max Planck, the celebrated German physicist, was awarded the Nobel Prize in physics today for his revolutionary discovery about the nature of energy.

Working at the University of Berlin in the 1890s, Planck sought to explain why existing formulas could not account for the emission of heat radiation by hot bodies. In 1900, he worked out a new theory that described heat radiation accurately, but only by introducing a radical new concept, the idea that heat and all other forms of energy are not infinitely divisible. Instead, energy is emitted in small packets. Planck called such a packet a "quantum," from the Latin for "how much?"

The quantum theory was so revolutionary that it was not accepted in the world of physics for many years. Planck himself was suspicious of the idea and spent years unsuccessfully trying to find an alternative. Its acceptance was due to the work of physicists such as Albert Einstein, who used the quantum theory to explain a phenomenon called the photoelectric effect, and Nils Bohr, who in 1913 applied the quantum theory to develop a successful new description of the structure of atoms. Physicists now say that it may require decades to explore the full implications of the quantum theory and that it will drastically change the nature of physics.

The winner of the Nobel Prize in chemistry is Fritz Haber, for the synthesis of ammonia. No prizes were presented in the fields of medicine and literature or, oddly enough, peace (→ 12/10/20).

1919

JANUARY

Su	Mo	Tu	We	Th	Fr	Sa
			1	2	3	4
5	6	7	8	9	10	11
12	13	14	15	16	17	18
19	20	21	22	23	24	25
26	27	28	29	30	31	

1. Rosa Luxemburg and Karl Liebknecht found German Communist Party (→ 12).

1. Pasadena: Rose Bowl won by Great Lakes Navy, 17-0 over Mare Island Marines.

1. Edsel B. Ford succeeds father Henry as president of Ford Motor Co. (→ 4/12/21).

5. British ships shell Bolshevik headquarters in Riga (→ 15).

10. Chicago: Republican Natl. Committee urges woman suffrage (→ 23).

10. Luxembourg proclaimed a republic (→ 2/6).

13. California votes to ratify Prohibition amendment (→ 29).

15. Peasants in central Russia rise against Bolsheviks (→ 24).

19. Soft, blue-white, 388-carat diamond found in S. Africa.

21. 25 Sinn Fein members elected to British House of Commons decline seats in London, proclaim Irish Parliament in Dublin (→ 4/5).

21. German Krupp plant begins producing guns for U.S. under armistice terms (→ 2/7).

23. 34 women win seats in German elections (→ 2/6).

24. Washington: New director gen. of railroads asks $750 mil. for construction (→ 2/28/20).

24. Sergius Sazonov, ex-Russian minister in Paris exile, appeals for European volunteers to fight Bolsheviks (→ 2/4).

25. N.Y.: The 2,200-room Pennsylvania, world's biggest hotel, opens on Seventh Avenue.

25. U.S. Dept. of Labor announces serious increase in unemployment (→ 8/2).

25. Paris: League of Nations plan adopted by Allies (→ 27).

27. Paris: Despite reservations, 19 small nations lend approval to League plan (→ 2/14).

28. 200,000 now on strike in Britain, Ireland.

30. Allies float loan of 10 bil. Belgian francs to Belgium (→ 3/2).

BIRTH

1. J.D. Salinger, U.S. author.

Banner of revolution raised in Berlin

Jan 12. Troops loyal to the German government crushed a revolutionary cell of Spartacists in Berlin tonight. But a week-long battle in the streets of the city has taken its toll. One correspondent reports he saw the bodies of hundreds of dead and wounded piled on sidewalks.

The trouble started at the beginning of the month, when at a meeting of the radical Spartacus League, Karl Liebknecht and Rosa Luxemburg formed the German Communist Party. The new party demands a socialist republic. And it called for a boycott of the elections for the assembly on the 19th. At the same time, leftist socialists quit their government jobs all over the country. Only the Chief of the Berlin police, Erich Eichhorn, an independent socialist, stayed on the job.

German troops battle Spartacists in Berlin.

Ironically, it was the dismissal of Eichhorn by the Interior Ministry that sparked the rebellion. Liebknecht called on the workers of Berlin to revolt. One week ago tonight, leftist forces occupied newspaper offices and called on the working class to join their armed struggle.

But the call to arms was virtually ignored. Most of the army remained loyal to the government. The Spartacists had bullets, but not enough supporters to pull the triggers. The insurrection was crushed.

Liebknecht and Luxemburg went into hiding. And their political theory was denounced by Friedrich Ebert, the acting Chancellor. "Bolshshevism," he declared, "means the death of peace. And it means the death of liberty" (→ 16).

Berlin revolutionary leaders assassinated

Jan 16. Karl Liebknecht and Rosa Luxemburg, leaders of the German Communist Party, have been killed in Berlin while in government custody. An independent socialist newspaper declared, "Their blood is on the hands of the new government. The German proletariat will pass judgment upon them." The government promised a complete investigation, and later, the officers in charge of the two prisoners were taken into custody.

Luxemburg was beaten senseless by a mob as troops tried to remove her from the Hotel Eden, where she had been interrogated. Then she was shot in the head and her body was dumped in a canal. It has not been recovered. Liebknecht's guards managed to spirit him from the mob in a car. One report says they shot him down in cold blood a short while later. The guards say they fired when Liebknecht tried to escape (→ 5/14).

Karl Liebknecht and Rosa Luxemburg leaving a Spartacist meeting in Berlin.

Herbert Hoover will aid Europe's hungry

Jan 3. Herbert Clark Hoover of the United States has been named to coordinate efforts to feed an estimated 125 million people left nearly destitute after more than four years of total war in Europe. His appointment as Director General of an international organization for relief of the newly liberated countries was announced by President Wilson. Food supplies will be given to all nations in need, including Germany. According to Hoover, the United States has shipped about 150,000 tons of food to various ports in Europe (→ 30).

1919

Teddy takes his last rough ride

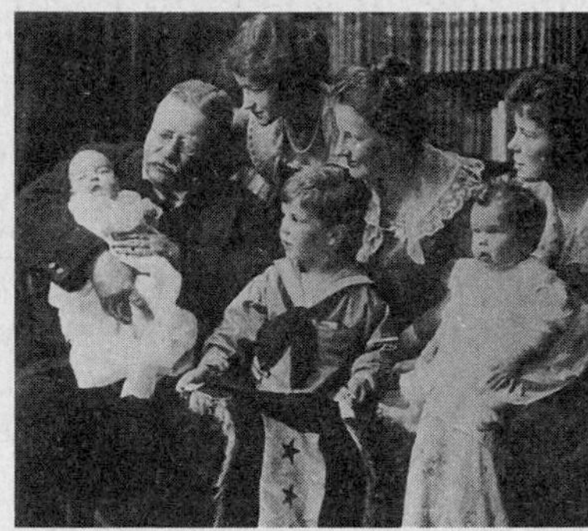

Teddy Roosevelt and family.

Jan 6. Theodore Roosevelt, the famed Rough Rider of both war and politics, is dead. The 60-year-old former President died unexpectedly in his sleep at his Sagamore Hill home in Oyster Bay, Long Island. Death was attributed to a blood clot in the lungs. His last words, to a colored servant, were prophetic: "Please put out that light, James."

A onetime Governor of New York and Rough Rider hero of the war with Spain in 1898, Roosevelt was elected Vice President in 1900, became president after the 1901 assassination of William McKinley and was elected in his own right in 1904. His presidency was noted for its progressive domestic reforms and "big stick" foreign policy. In 1912, disenchanted with the Republican Party, he sought a presidential comeback as a Progressive but failed.

Prohibition given final ratification

Jan 29. Americans will have just a little less than a year to drink their fill, at least legally. A dry amendment, adopted by the required number of states, was proclaimed today as part of the Constitution, effective next January 16.

Among those present as Frank L. Polk, acting Secretary of State, issued the historic proclamation, was William Jennings Bryan, the longtime presidential contender and Prohibitionist who served in the Wilson Cabinet as Secretary of State. Bryan's home state of Nebraska clinched the long drive to ban liquor when state lawmakers voted four days ago for the proposed amendment. Since then, other states, including New York and Vermont, have voted to ratify, thus giving the drys more than enough to assure Prohibition throughout the entire United States.

Meanwhile, officials of the Distillers Association of America, meeting at the Hotel St. Regis in New York, began mapping plans by which they hope to negate ratification of the Prohibition amendment in 14 of the 42 states that have given their approval. The distillers argue that constitutions in those states provide for allowing the voters to express their will before the legislatures can act on such issues (→ 2/20).

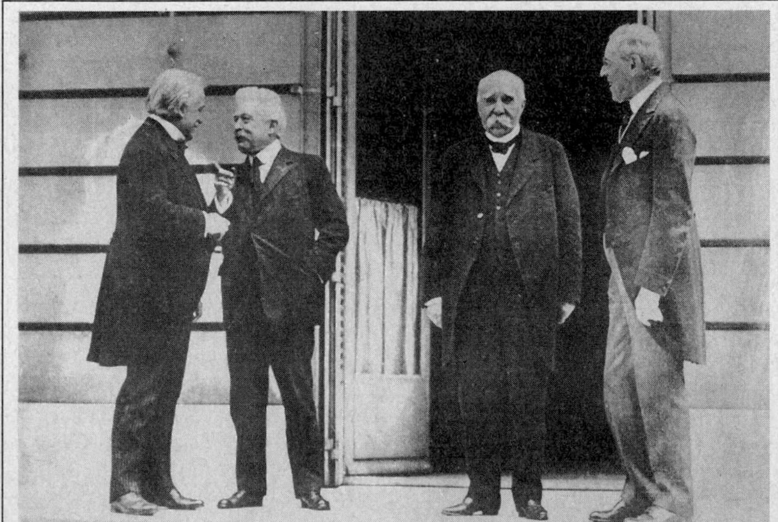

Jan 18. The "Big Four" (l. to r.: Lloyd George, Orlando, Chm. Clemenceau and Wilson) opened the peace conference at Versailles today with a profound sense of irony. It is the anniversary of the proclamation of the Kingdom of Prussia (1701) and of the German Empire (1871) (→ 25).

FEBRUARY

Su	Mo	Tu	We	Th	Fr	Sa
						1
2	3	4	5	6	7	8
9	10	11	12	13	14	15
16	17	18	19	20	21	22
23	24	25	26	27	28	

4. Russia: Americans inflict heavy losses on Bolsheviks at Archangel (→ 4/18).

6. Luxembourg gives women right to vote (→ 12).

7. Ebert, new German president, denounces terms of armistice (→ 17).

8. Chicago: James B. Herrick publishes first electrocardiogram of heart malfunction.

12. Washington: Commission of Naturalization reports ten percent of U.S. population is foreign-born (→ 3/25).

12. Insurrection strikes Rumania; King Ferdinand wounded trying to flee.

12. Intl. Woman's Suffrage Conference convenes in Paris (→ 4/7).

14. United Parcel Service incorporated in Oakland, Ca.

16. Armenian, Jewish, Greek representatives meet in N.Y., demand dismemberment of Turkey (→ 3/11/20).

17. Germany signs armistice, giving up territory to Poland (→ 25).

19. French Premier Georges Clemenceau wounded by anarchist Louis Cottin (→ 3/14).

20. Assassin kills Habibullah Khan, emir of Afghanistan.

20. Hungary: Communist revolt breaks out in Budapest (→ 3/21).

21. Germany: Independent Socialist Premier of Bavaria Kurt Eisner is assassinated (→ 22).

22. Munich: Soldiers and workers council declares Bavaria a soviet republic (→ 4/3).

25. Paris: French delegate Andre Tardieu proposes Franco-German border on the Rhine (→ 3/11).

25. Oregon introduces first state tax on gasoline; one cent per gallon, for use in road construction.

BIRTH

5. William S. Burroughs, American novelist.

First commercial Paris-London flight

The Berlin G-EACT, Paris-London.

Feb 9. Aviation history was made today in Europe, as a commercial plane completed its first round-trip between Paris and London. The aircraft, named the Goliath, took off from England at 12:20 p.m. Three hours and 30 minutes later, it arrived at a French airport near Versailles. The Goliath has two engines and a top speed of 97 miles an hour. The French pilot said he had a few problems on the Paris-London leg of the trip yesterday. He says there were very strong north winds. But the passengers did not seem to complain. They were very busy smoking and playing bridge.

Get it while it's cold and it's not too late

Feb 20. Beer drinkers, beware the Ides of March! Due to a shortage of raw materials, the popular beverage will be depleted nationally in March, with some northeastern taps drying up even earlier. Christian Feigenspan, President of the United Brewers Association, warns that for at least two months, May and June, "The country will be on a straight whiskey basis, and in these days of unrest it is dangerous to have steady beer drinkers switch to whiskey" (→ 12/1).

No more beer?

Versailles adopts League charter

Feb 14. President Wilson won a major victory today when delegates at Versailles agreed to create a League of Nations as part of the general peace treaty. Establishment of such a league was the president's main objective at the peace conference and it was he who led the 14-nation commission that drafted the document.

In a speech to the peace gathering, the president declared: "A living thing is born, and we must see to it what clothes we put on it." He described the league plan as "not a vehicle of power" but as both practical and humane. "I believe that the conscience of the world has long been prepared to express itself in some such way," he said.

President Wilson left Paris a short time later to return to the United States to sign bills sent him by an expiring Congress. He will return to the peace table to complete work on the treaty (→ 25).

Weimar Assembly holds first session

Feb 6. Germany turned to its history today in the hope of making a new beginning. The Assembly left the troubled city of Berlin and met in Weimar, its cultural capital and the home of Goethe and Schiller. The Assembly elected Friedrich Ebert President of the new republic. And it is expected to name Philipp Scheidemann Chancellor. The Assembly also exchanged messages with the Austrian Assembly. Both legislatures expressed the hope that German Austria will soon be reunited with Germany (→ 2/22).

The Weimar Assembly convenes.

1919

MARCH

Su	Mo	Tu	We	Th	Fr	Sa
						1
2	3	4	5	6	7	8
9	10	11	12	13	14	15
16	17	18	19	20	21	22
23	24	25	26	27	28	29
30	31					

1. Korean coalition proclaims independence from Japan (→ 8/15/48).

2. President Wilson announces support for Jewish commonwealth in Palestine (→ 6/21/22).

2. Washington: Herbert Hoover named director general of American Relief Administration (→ 3).

3. World's war bill estimated at $197 billion (→ 12).

3. Boeing flies first U.S. intl. airmail, from Vancouver, B.C. to Seattle, Washington.

5. Mexico: Morelos returns to govt. control after ten years under Zapata rule (→ 4/10).

8. Britain lifts restrictions on imports.

8. Paris reports indicate 6,000 Americans have married French women in past year.

11. Paris: Supreme Allied Council cuts German navy to 15,000 men (→ 13).

13. Britain announces German U-boats must be sold, profits distributed among Allies (→ 29).

14. Paris: Emile Cottin condemned to death for attempted murder of Clemenceau.

15. American Legion formed in Paris.

19. Typhoid reported raging in Petrograd, killing 200 daily.

21. Paris: Italian delegation announces it will withdraw from conference unless Fiume is given to Italy (→ 4/23).

25. Paris Peace Commission adopts plan to protect nations from influx of foreign labor.

26. Ex-Pres. of Hungary Count Michael Karolyi arrested; will be brought before revolutionary tribunal (→ 29).

29. Ex-Kaiser Wilhelm says he would rather kill himself than be tried before Allied tribunal (→ 4/8).

29. Allies demand resignation of Hungarian soviets, ask election under Allied control (→ 6/7).

31. Prussian schools ban kaiser's picture.

Lenin forms 3rd Communist International

March 4. An international Communist organization with the goal of fostering world revolution has been established in Moscow.

The Third International, or Comintern, is expected to play a key role in Soviet foreign policy. Bolshevik leader Vladimir Lenin has argued that the security of the Russian regime depends upon it sparking revolutionary, and therefore friendly, regimes throughout Europe.

The European people are ready for revolution, Lenin has argued, but they are being held back by the timidity and cowardice of the Second or Socialist International. This older organization lost all the solidarity it had at the outbreak of the war, when its members were consumed by nationalism.

The First International was established by Karl Marx in London in 1864, with the aim of coordinating working-class movements worldwide. It was dissolved in 1876.

Vladimir Ilyich Lenin.

The first meeting of the Third International drew 35 voting delegates, representing 19 groups. Only five came from outside Russia, as the war prevented attendance.

Bela Kun seizes control of Hungary

Bela Kun proclaims the revolution.

March 21. Not long ago, a revolutionary named Bela Kun was in jail in Russia. Today he heads a new government in Hungary. Kun leads a coalition of Communists and Social Democrats who seized control in Budapest after Count Michael Karolyi and his regime resigned to protest the Allies' decision to give Transylvania to Rumania.

In 1915, Kun was imprisoned in Russia. The Bolsheviks released him to be a commander in the Red army and sent him to Hungary to be a propagandist. The plan worked. Kun wants a dictatorship of the proletariat in Hungary (→ 26).

Allies make plans to supply Germany

Mar 12. The Allies have reached a compromise agreement to supply Germany with temporary food relief. For the first shipment, Germany will pay $200 million out of her own credits in neutral countries. Future payments will then be open to renegotiation.

The German food scene is grim. Pre-war German agriculture could feed 95 percent of its own people. That figure is now 45 percent. Crucial fertilizer plants lack coal, transport facilities and labor. German unemployment is about 1.5 million. Due to a milk shortage, infant mortality has soared. Some cities are on a potato ration of only two pounds per week.

The compromise included French insistence that Germany go to work immediately to pay for the food. The United States and Great Britain had felt that Germany has first to be fed before she could work. It was also felt that a hungry Germany might succumb to Bolshevism. Meanwhile, it is reported that German dance halls are crowded, and night life goes on (→ 5/6).

Benito Mussolini founds own party

Mussolini, head of Italian Fascists.

March 23. Troubled by Italy's postwar problems —strikes, social unrest and parliamentary disorganization —Benito Mussolini has organized a new movement. His Fasci di combattimento will attempt to fight liberal and communist influence through aggressive nationalism and rigid military discipline (→ 7/1).

Trip to the moon?

March 29. A trip to the moon by rocket may someday be possible, according to a monograph published by Robert A. Goddard, a professor of physics at Clark University in Massachusetts. Goddard has been experimenting with rockets since 1909 and demonstrated three models to the Army just before the armistice last year. Goddard's moon travel proposal is being ridiculed by newspapers, which have dubbed him the "moon man" (→ 7/16/69).

Goddard teaches physics in Mass.

1919

APRIL

Su	Mo	Tu	We	Th	Fr	Sa
		1	2	3	4	5
6	7	8	9	10	11	12
13	14	15	16	17	18	19
20	21	22	23	24	25	26
29	28	29	30			

3. Bavaria begins negotiating alliance with Russia (→ 5/3).

4. Italy opens public air service on dirigible, Rome to Naples.

7. Belgium: 160,000 women sign petition demanding universal suffrage (→ 10).

7. Service resumes on Baghdad Railway.

8. Geneva named as League of Nations headquarters (→ 10).

8. Paris: Allied Council rules out capital punishment for ex-Kaiser Wilhelm (→ 14).

10. Universal suffrage established in Belgium (→ 5/21).

10. Paris: Monroe Doctrine added to League draft (→ 5/30).

13. Gasoline hits 75 cents per gallon in Britain.

14. Paris: Allies ask $23 bil. in German reparations (→ 25).

15. India: British troops kill 400 Indians, demonstrating against British rule at Amritsar (→ 12/23).

17. French Natl. Assembly votes eight-hour day.

17. Rumanian army occupies Transylvania.

18. British and White Russians push Bolsheviks back, occupy Bolshie Ozerki (→ 20).

20. Bolshevik First Army surrenders to Ukranians (→ 5/23).

20. Montenegran King Nicholas abdicates throne.

21. Spanish flu reported to have taken 500,000 lives in Belgian Congo during war.

23. Paris: Italian delegation quits conference after Wilson refuses Fiume to Italy (→ 5/7).

25. Walter Gropius founds Bauhaus school in Weimar, Germany (→ 12/24/26).

25. Paris: First German delegates arrive at Versailles for peace conference (→ 5/7).

27. U.S.: Natl. Assn. of the Motion Picture Industry agrees to submit films to censorship.

27. Finnish Diet abolishes monarchy (→ 5/6).

30. Allied Council gives Shantung, China to Japan (→ 5/4).

Stars form own company, United Artists

L. to r. in foreground: Founders Griffith, Pickford, Chaplin and Fairbanks.

April 17. Four film pioneers have claimed their stake in celluloid. Charlie Chaplin, D.W. Griffith, Mary Pickford and Douglas Fairbanks have founded a film company in California called the United Artists Corporation. The firm will produce, release and distribute their new motion pictures.

While many people say business partners do not make good bedfellows, Pickford and Fairbanks, wed earlier this year, are good friends with Chaplin. Griffith is like a father to Pickford; he directed her in several pictures, including the mysterious "Broken Blossoms." This alliance, however, also stems from pure necessity: they were in danger of pricing themselves out of the market. Their huge salaries squeezed the margin of profit from their pictures; in time employers might have considered them a kind of liability. Now they can comfortably call their own shots.

Bela Kun's leftist regime under siege

April 22. The Hungarian revolution may become one of the shortest on record. Just one month after Bolshevik Bela Kun took power, he is being forced out of office in Budapest. Reports from Hungary indicate that both Czech and Rumanian troops are fighting the Kun government. The capital is in chaos.

Kun has failed to silence moderate elements in Budapest. Yesterday, the Associated Press reported his government tried to discipline the population by closing coffee houses and suspending telephone service because it is a bourgeois institution. But telephones are not the real problem. Kun is failing because he cannot convince peasants to become Bolsheviks (→ 6/7).

April 10. For nine years, Emiliano Zapata led Mexican rebels under the cry "land and liberty." Today, the agrarian hero was killed by govt. troops (→ 8/19).

New York native to head Irish party

De Valera as a young math professor.

April 5. Eamon de Valera is a fugitive from British police. But he is a hero and a major political force in his adopted country of Ireland. The New York-born de Valera is President of the nationalist Sinn Fein Society. He is also head of the Dail Eireann, the Gaelic name for the Irish Parliament, an association of the Irish politicians elected to the British House of Commons.

Half the members of the association are being held in British prisons. Some are charged with sedition. Others are simply being detained under the Defense of the Realm Act. De Valera himself broke out of the Lincoln jail in England in February.

De Valera was arrested a year ago during the police raids in Dublin. Earlier, he served time for taking part in the Easter Rebellion of 1916. De Valera has clashed constantly with British authorities over the future of Ireland because he advocates the use of force to achieve his nationalist political goals.

De Valera was born in New York City in 1882 and moved to Ireland as a child. His non-Irish last name came from a Spanish father; his mother was Irish (→ 12/19).

Growth of economy to depend on roads

April 27. The future economic growth of the United States depends on the development of road and highway construction, according to John S. Cravens, Chairman of the Highways Transport Committee.

Cravens told members of the National Association of Motor Truck Sales Managers at a recent convention that Americans are beginning to realize the importance of adequate and well-maintained roads.

"Good roads mean quicker and cheaper transportation, a saving of labor and the opening of new channels of employment, while being the avenues for wider and better social relations," Cravens said.

Auto in America's financial capital.

Statistics released last week by the American Automobile Association show that the main highways of the country total 203,523 miles. In a related area, urban road use continues to soar. New York City's Columbus Circle now holds the record for most traffic passing every hour during rush hours.

Cravens concluded, "The vehicle and the road must be demonstrated to be complements of each other and inseparable parts of a great agency of public service. Once people thoroughly realize this, they will demand to have good roads when and where they want them."

An innocent young patriot watches as returning war heroes flood N.Y.

1919

MAY

Su	Mo	Tu	We	Th	Fr	Sa
				1	2	3
4	5	6	7	8	9	10
11	12	13	14	15	16	17
18	19	20	21	22	23	24
25	26	27	28	29	30	31

3. Germany suppresses republic of Bavarian councils.

4. Demonstrations break out in Peking to protest transfer of Shantung to Japan, dominance of West over China (→ 8/5).

6. Britain recognizes Finnish independence (→ 3/20/20).

6. Belgium asks $500 mil. loan from U.S. (→ 6/7).

7. Paris: Peace terms presented to German delegation (→ 12).

7. Paris: Italy rejoins conference after council promises Fiume in four years (→ 9/12).

10. Sir Barton takes Kentucky Derby with J. Toftus in the saddle (→ 6/30).

10. Brig. Gen. Douglas MacArthur named to head West Point.

12. Berlin Natl. Assembly opposes Allied terms (→ 26).

14. Germany: Two charged with murder of Karl Liebknecht, six acquitted (→ 6/1).

20. Harry Hawker disappears during two-day attempt to cross Atlantic, U.S. to Ireland.

20. Volcanic eruption kills 16,000 in Central Java.

21. U.S. House passes suffrage amendment 304 to 89 (→ 6/4).

23. Bolsheviks reported to be evacuating Moscow (→ 26).

26. Allied Supreme Council recognizes White Russians, offers military support (→ 7/24).

26. Count von Brockdorff, head of German delegation, vows not to sign treaty until Allies lift blockade (→ 6/16).

28. Belgium annexes Moresnet, Eupen, Malmedy (→ 9/20/20).

30. Paris: Wilson speaks at Memorial Day ceremony, calls League of Nations a mandate of our dead (→ 7/5).

31. Howard Wilcox wins 7th annual Indianapolis 500 at 88.1 m.p.h. in Peugot racer.

BIRTH

3. Pete Seeger, folksinger.

DEATH

6. Author Frank Baum, "Land of Oz" books (*5/15/1856).

Navy's hydroplane crosses the Atlantic

May 27. The United States Navy seaplane NC-4 arrived in Lisbon today, completing the first transatlantic air flight. Starting from Rockaway, New York, on May 8, the NC-4 flew a total of 3,150 nautical miles in a little less than 44 hours of flying time. The NC-4 made an unscheduled stop on the first leg of the trip when it was forced down off Chatham, Massachusetts. After repairs, it continued on to Halifax, Nova Scotia, and then to Newfoundland.

The actual flight across the Atlantic was made in three stages: from Trepassay Bay in Newfoundland to the Azores, a distance of 1,200 nautical miles, on May 16-17; a short hop of 150 miles from one end of the Azores to the other on May 20; and the final 800-mile flight to Lisbon. A picket line of Navy destroyers was stationed between Newfoundland and Lisbon to keep track of the NC-4's progress and offer help if necessary.

Lt. Comm. Read and Lt. Stone.

The seaplane's arrival at Lisbon was greeted with cheers from a crowd that lined the waterfront and a five-minute salute from vessels in the harbor. The NC-4, piloted by Lt. Commander A.C. Read, now will proceed to Plymouth, England, where a jubilant reception is planned. Meanwhile, a British dirigible, the R-34, is preparing for a non-stop transatlantic flight.

1919

JUNE

Su	Mo	Tu	We	Th	Fr	Sa
1	2	3	4	5	6	7
8	9	10	11	12	13	14
15	16	17	18	19	20	21
22	23	24	25	26	27	28
29	30					

1. Germany: Body of Rosa Luxemburg found in Landwehr Canal (→ 9/12).

2 Bombs strike homes of U.S. officials (→ 5).

4. Woman's suffrage amendment passes U.S. Senate 56-25; sent to states for ratificlation (→ 9/3).

5. Postmaster Gen. Burleson orders return of wire operations to private control (→ 2/28/20).

7. N.Y. inaugurates written test for driver's license applicants.

7. U.S. firms obtain contracts to rebuild Rheims, Nancy, Soissons (→ 7/26).

7. It is reported that Bela Kun's Red army has shot or hanged 3,000 peasant rebels in Western Hungary (→ 26).

8. Britain completes largest plane in history; Triplane carries 50 people and four tons of explosives.

8. Baltimore: Scientists at Johns Hopkins find locusts an eating delicacy.

9. Fearing invasion from Costa Rica, Nicaragua asks U.S. to land troops (→ 7/24/25).

12. Wales demands local Parliament.

16. Allies hand revised peace treaty to Germans (→ 17).

16. Austria: Eight Viennese killed in riots during Communist demonstration.

17. Paris: German delegates stoned while leaving Versailles (→ 20).

19. Mustafa Kemal founds Turkish Nationalist Congress at Ankara, denounces partition of Turkey at Versailles (→ 8/5).

20. Weimar: Philipp Scheidemann, unwilling to sign peace with Allies, resigns as German chancellor (→ 23).

23. German government at Weimar announces intent to sign peace treaty (→ 28).

26. New York: Augustus D. Juilliard leaves $5 mil. in will for advancement of music.

26. Hungary: Bela Kun shot at by rebels in plot to overthrow Budapest soviets (→ 7/20).

Protesting Germans sign peace treaty

June 28. Five years to the day after gunshots in Sarajevo sparked a worldwide war, a peace treaty was signed in France today. The Treaty of Versailles formally ends the war, but it has created new resentment and friction in Germany.

As a matter of fact, the German representatives said they would not have come to Versailles if they had known in advance how they would be treated. The Germans were humiliated by being forced to use a separate entrance and exit to the Hall of Mirrors. And they refused to enter the hall until the Allies agreed to give them military honors at the conclusion of the ceremony.

The French hosts did all they could to surround the occasion with pomp and pageantry. Versailles, after all, is where they were humbled by the Germans in 1871. Most of the delegates to the conference drove down the splendid Avenue du Chateau and over the cobblestones of the Court of Honor. They were greeted by the impeccably groomed and uniformed officers of the Republican Guard.

Inside the hall, a very different mood prevailed. Spectators pressed forward for a better view and they surprised some of the delegates by cheering them. But the Allied leaders were restrained, and they wore austere civilian clothes. There were few resplendent uniforms that could create the mood of a bygone, monarchical era. The Allies wanted everyone to know that a new peace meant a new world era.

France is vindicated as Georges Clemenceau (center with white mustache) signs the treaty in Versailles' Hall of Mirrors, where the German Empire was proclaimed in 1871 following France's humiliating defeat.

French Premier Clemenceau was the first of the Allied leaders to arrive at Versailles, and he formally opened the session with a brief address that warned the Germans to respect the provisions of the treaty. But Clemenceau was not the first of the Allies to sign the treaty. That honor was given to President Woodrow Wilson.

After the ceremony, Wilson, Clemenceau and British Prime Minister Lloyd George thrilled thousands of spectators by descending from the Hall of Mirrors to a terrace at the rear of the Versailles Palace. The crowd pushed forward to see the statesmen and yelled, "Vive Clemenceau! Vive Wilson! Vive Lloyd George!" There was so much excitement and confusion that the other Allied delegates were trapped momentarily in the hall.

The German delegates left ignominiously, and reports from their hotel indicate they are fuming at the way they were treated. In Germany, critics of the Treaty of Versailles have done more than fume. Protesters spilled into the streets, and German students set fire to French military insignia. Off the coast of Scotland last week, the German Admiral, Ludwig von Reuter, scuttled his fleet rather than surrender.

The treaty includes a provision for President Wilson's plan to create a League of Nations. But it also imposes bruising punishment on Germany. It demands the payment of enormous reparations, and it calls for the trial of Wilhelm II and others as war criminals. In addition, Germany loses considerable territory and is prohibited from building new military weapons.

A British delegate to the treaty conference, economist John Maynard Keynes, warned that the treaty could create economic havoc in Germany. Other critics wonder if the Treaty of Versailles will really create a lasting peace (→ 7/5).

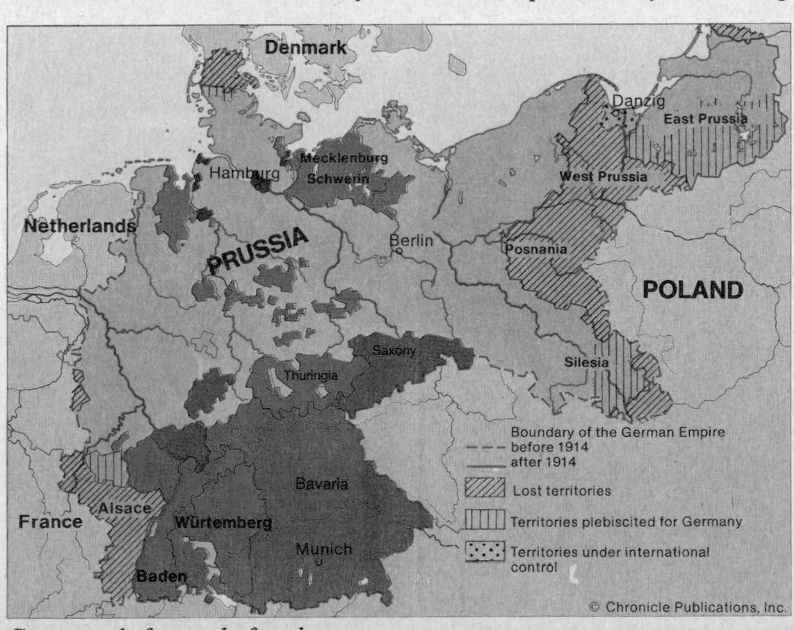

Germany, before and after the war.

Suzanne Lenglen wins at Wimbledon

Lenglen in action.

Miss Suzanne Lenglen, the fiery French player, completed a sweep of women's events with the resumption of tennis at Wimbledon. She teamed with Elisabeth Ryan in taking the doubles championship in straight sets today, following her triumph in the singles competition. The prestigious Wimbledon tournament in England was canceled from 1915 to 1918 during the Great War. Gerald Patterson was the winner of the men's singles.

Alcock and Brown make non-stop hop

June 15. A Vickers-Vimy biplane piloted by Captain John Alcock of England and navigated by Lt. Arthur W. Brown of the United States landed at Clifden on the Irish coast this morning, completing the first non-stop flight across the Atlantic Ocean. Alcock and Brown took off from Newfoundland at 4:28 p.m. yesterday and completed the 1,900-mile flight in 16 hours, 12 minutes, averaging 120 miles per hour. Experts say the feat opens the way to more daring long-distance flights and eventually to regular transatlantic air service.

The Vickers-Vimy biplane.

Interned Germans scuttle their ships

The cruiser Hindenburg sacrificed.

June 21. The hoisting of a red flag at noon today signaled to German officers and sailors aboard their interned ships at Scapa Flow to sink their vessels. All the big ships, battleships and battle cruisers, except the Baden, were scuttled quietly by pulling the seacocks. The British guardships fired on the Germans when they discovered what had happened. The German crews jumped overboard or took to lifeboats and went ashore, where they were captured by the Admiralty. Some Germans refused to give up and were killed by the angry and surprised Britons.

Bombs blast officials' homes; 67 arrested

June 5. Some 67 anarchists have been arrested and face deportation in the wake of a bomb explosion that shattered the homes of several top government officials three days ago in Washington. The blast, in which the bombers were blown to bits, damaged the home of Attorney General A. Mitchell Palmer and blew out the windows in the home of Assistant Navy Secretary Franklin D. Roosevelt. Five other homes along the street were also badly damaged (→ 11/25).

Bolshevik terror: Truth or propaganda?

Sir Barton claims first Triple Crown

June 29. Sir Barton today became the first Triple Crown winner in horse racing since the series was begun in 1875. With John Loftus riding him in the decisive Belmont Stakes, as he had in the Kentucky Derby and Preakness, Sir Barton has accomplished something never done before in thoroughbred history.

Sir Barton, 1st Triple Crown winner.

1919

JULY

Su	Mo	Tu	We	Th	Fr	Sa
		1	2	3	4	5
6	7	8	9	10	11	12
13	14	15	16	17	18	19
20	21	22	23	24	25	26
29	28	29	30	31		

1. Daily airmail service begins from New York to Chicago.

3. German Natl. Assembly adopts black, red and gold for Reich's flag, colors of 1848 revolution.

5. Ex-kaiser's sons offer to suffer in his place (→ 9).

8. Wilson returns home from Versailles on transport George Washington.

9. German Natl. Assembly ratifies peace treaty (→ 21).

11. Dutch Parliament adopts eight-hour work day.

14. U.S. resumes trade with Germany.

15. Gen. Pershing arrives in London to lead peace celebration parade.

16. Washington announces plans for a 440,000-man National Guard.

17. Britain restricts luxury imports to protect balance of trade.

20. Allies give Austrian peace terms to Vienna delegates (→ 9/10).

20. Budapest reported under siege by rebels (→ 8/4).

21. Dirigible Wing Fool, on display in Chicago, explodes; 11 dead, many hurt (→ 27).

21. British House of Lords ratifies Versailles treaty (→ 8/8).

24. White Russians on Archangel front mutiny, join Red army (→ 8/13).

26. Italy asks U.S. bankers for $1 billion loan (→ 8/12).

27. U.S. aviation engineers considering replacing hydrogen with less-flamable helium in dirigible construction.

28. Belgian racer Lambot wins Tour de France in 231 hours, seven minutes.

31. Washington: Cabinet opens campaign to cut cost of living (→ 8/28).

BIRTH

7. William Kunstler, radical U.S. lawyer, defended "Chicago Seven."

Mussolini publishes Fascist manifesto

July 1. Benito Mussolini, who has been a socialist newspaper editor in Switzerland and Austria, is back in his native Italy, still editing a newspaper. But he says he is no longer a socialist.

Mussolini broke with the Italian Socialist Party after the outbreak of the war and formed a new newspaper, the Popolo d'Italia. Many of the people who read the paper are nationalistic war veterans, and they call themselves the Fasci di combattimento. Now, Mussolini has published a manifesto for his followers.

The manifesto demands the following: universal suffrage, starting at 18 years; the right of women to vote; proportional representation; autonomy for local governments; popular referenda; the disbanding of the Senate and the political police force; an end to secret diplomacy; the creation of a purely defensive army; the confiscation of church property; a prohibition against speculation in the stock market; retirement at age 55; an eight-hour work day; a minimum wage; and a progressive tax on capital that would rise to 85 percent on war profits.

Mussolini says he is no longer a socialist, but some of his ideas are revolutionary. There also seems to be a little of something for almost everybody. It will be surprising if this son of a blacksmith and school teacher is content spending the rest of his life as a newspaper editor. Mussolini seems to have a much larger agenda (→ 2/26/21).

Jack Dempsey wins heavyweight crown

Dempsey, "The Manassa Mauler."

July 4. Jess Willard has been dethroned as world heavyweight champion by Jack Dempsey, a young challenger who pummeled him mercilessly for three rounds.

Willard was demolished in such thorough fashion that many of the 45,000 spectators in the Toledo Arena were screaming "Stop it! Stop it!" at the finish. Willard's trainer threw two towels into the ring 30 seconds after the third round ended, signifying surrender. Dempsey virtually punched Willard at will from the start of the fight, which drew a $1 million gate. Willard was not officially counted out, so the defeat is ruled a technical knockout.

Willard, who won the title by beating Jack Johnson, announced his retirement. His wife, who had never attended his fights, was at this one.

Joffre and Foch lead a victory parade through the Arc de Triomphe.

Troops called out to stop race riots

July 30. Military troops were called in today to help quell Chicago's race riots that have left at least 31 dead and more than 500 injured. Among the blunt orders to the militia: "Draw no color line. A white rioter is as dangerous as a Negro rioter."

The clashes between blacks and whites on Chicago's South Side have destroyed property and interrupted the flow of mail. Homes have been looted and stores have been razed. Both whites and Negroes have raced through the streets, hurling bricks and stones and firing pistols and shotguns. Police report that several Negroes have been tossed into Bubbly Creek, a stagnant stream that is polluted with sewage from the Chicago stockyards.

The Chicago race riots follow a pattern that has emerged in many of the nation's major cities in recent weeks. Earlier this month, several persons were killed and nearly 100 injured in fights between whites and Negroes in Washington. There, almost within sight of the White House and the Capitol, bands of Negroes roamed the streets, attacking whites, both men and women. Several children also were injured. The rioting in Washington was finally quelled by police and troops of cavalry and infantrymen, but not until several law-enforcement officers were killed.

Officials of the National Association for the Advancement of Colored People accused the militia of attacking "innocent and unoffending Negroes" in the nation's capital. There have been race riots, too, in Norfolk, Virginia, where six persons were shot after police tried to break up a fight in the Negro section of the city. Sailors and Marines from the nearby naval base were sent in to help patrol the streets until the disorders ended (→ 9/28).

Dirigible R-34 crosses Atlantic both ways

July 13. The British dirigible R-34 arrived at its station at Pulham early this morning, completing the first round-trip transatlantic air flight. Both legs of the flight were made non-stop, first from Edinburgh, Scotland, to Mineola, Long Island, and then back to England.

The R-34 left Edinburgh at 1:48 a.m. on July 2, and arrived at Mineola at 8:45 a.m. on July 6. Its flying time of four days and 12 hours was slightly longer than the steamship record made by the liner Mauretania in 1909, but the R-34 covered a much greater distance: 3,200 miles, which made its average speed just under 30 knots. Thousands of spectators gathered at Roosevelt Field in Mineola, New York, to see the airship arrive. They viewed the unusual arrival of the first crew member to set foot on American soil when Major John E. M. Pritchard, second officer of the R-34, parachuted to earth to help crews anchor the airship.

The R-34 remained at Mineola until July 10, when it began its return flight. The airship flew over New York City as it left, then proceeded to Newfoundland and across the Atlantic. The return flight was made in 75 hours, as the airship was able to take advantage of the prevailing westerly winds. Major G.H. Scott of the royal air force, commander of the R-34, says that a new airship now being built in England will be able to fly non-stop from Britain to Australia.

In addition to its crew of 30, the R-34 also carried an unscheduled passenger. William Ballantyne, a 23-year-old rigger who was dropped from the airship's crew at the last moment, hid away on board and thus became the world's first transatlantic air stowaway.

1919

AUGUST

Su	Mo	Tu	We	Th	Fr	Sa
					1	2
3	4	5	6	7	8	9
10	11	12	13	14	15	16
17	18	19	20	21	22	23
24	25	26	27	28	29	30
31						

2. Railway workers strike for higher wages, ask profit sharing, govt. ownership (→ 14).

4. Rumanian troops enter Budapest, crush Kun's 133-day Hungarian republic (→ 9).

5. Japan formally denies intent to hold China's Shantung province (2/4/22).

8. Belgian Parliament ratifies Treaty of Versailles (→ 19).

9. New Hungarian leader Archduke Joseph announces he will honor terms of armistice (→ 22).

12. U.S. War Dept. begins offering surplus supplies in Europe (→ 2/22/20).

13. U.S. govt. authorizes arms shipments to white Russians in Siberia (→ 1/1/20).

14. Court finds Chicago Tribune guilty of libel for calling Henry Ford an anarchist, awards trial costs and six cents in damages.

15. France reports 60 percent of air force were killed or wounded in war.

19. U.S. Cavalry crosses Mexican border seeking bandits who have seized two American aviators (→ 21).

19. Washington: Wilson meets with Senate Foreign Relations Committee, urges ratification of treaty without change (→ 9/4).

21. Mexico: U.S. Cavalry kills four bandits; Carranza demands immediate withdrawal (→ 9/2).

22. Archduke Joseph quits as Hungarian leader (→ 2/29/20).

23. Caruso returns to New York, offered $10,000 a night.

25. Wilson calls halt on railway wage hikes, predicts drop in prices (→ 28).

28. Samuel Gompers urges rail shopmen back to work to await result of war on living costs (→ 30).

31. Chicago: Am. Communist Party founded under slogan "Workers of the world unite!"

DEATH

9. Ruggero Leoncavallo, Italian opera composer (*3/8/1858).

Mustafa Kemal leads Turkish nationalists

Aug 5. A movement of national resistance to the peace terms agreed upon by the Allies has emerged in the Ottoman Empire. The peace conference intends to apply the principle of self-determination to the Arab and Armenian minorities and has sanctioned the partition of the empire by France, Italy and Greece. Although the Sultan has accepted the Allied terms, the landing of 20,000 Greek troops at Smyrna in May sparked resistance among Turks.

Mustafa Kemal Pasha, hero of the Dardanelles and Gallipoli, has been organizing both military and civilian nationalist forces. He has called for a nationalist congress to take place at Sivas. In the meantime, a preliminary congress of delegates from eastern provinces has been meeting at Erzurum. In his opening address to the congress, Kemal outlined his goal of forming a republican regime (→ 3/3/20).

Mustafa Kemal Pasha.

Man who gave away millions is gone

Aug 11. Andrew Carnegie, the steel baron who gave away millions of dollars, died this morning of bronchial pneumonia. Death came to the 83-year-old millionaire benefactor at his estate, Shadow Brook, in Lenox, Massachusetts.

Born in Scotland, the son of a poor weaver, Carnegie immigrated to America with his family, settling near Pittsburgh. He took a job as a bobbin boy in a cotton mill, became a telegraph messenger at age 14, and after a series of other jobs entered the steel business.

At the time of his death, his estate was estimated to exceed $500 million. During his lifetime, he poured about $350 million into various philanthropies, including a vast network of public libraries. He once said: "The man who dies thus rich dies disgraced."

Steel magnate Andrew Carnegie.

Fashions featuring femininity in Paris

Autumn stroll in Bois de Boulogne.

Aug 15. Soft contours and alluring curves was what about 800 American buyers found as they went to the first Paris fashion display since the war. Soft materials, flounces, often no corsets, panniers accentuating hips are in, and the tailor-made, mannish look is out. Skirts hang 7-8 inches from the ground. "Too short," sneer the Americans. Near-battle has ensued over the French backless evening gowns, which the Americans insist on filling in with lace.

Food costs soaring; Wilson takes action

Aug 14. The Wilson administration sought to crack down on profiteering by seizing food in warehouses in Chicago, St Louis and Birmingham. Attorney General A. Mitchell Palmer told the Senate Agriculture Committee the government would prosecute food dealers engaged in price gouging. The rampant inflation following the end of the war prompted President Wilson earlier in the month to urge Congress to extend the wartime Food Control Act and to license all corporations engaged in interstate commerce so as to control prices (→ 25).

AFL chief Gompers rejects radicalism

Aug 30. Samuel Gompers, President of the American Federation of Labor, has urged prompt Senate approval of the Treaty of Versailles and the League of Nations Covenant, which contains the first international charter for the rights of labor. In a statement issued through the League to Enforce Peace, Gompers criticized Republican members of the Senate Foreign Relations Committee for delaying action on the peace treaty and seeking to add amendments and reservations (→ 9/2).

Aug 8. Charles Godefroy flew under the Arc de Triomphe today, adding a postscript to last month's victory parade. "I wanted planes to be a part of the victory," he explained.

1919

SEPTEMBER

Su	Mo	Tu	We	Th	Fr	Sa
	1	2	3	4	5	6
7	8	9	10	11	12	13
14	15	16	17	18	19	20
21	22	23	24	25	26	27
28	29	30				

2. U.S. Congress passes bill barring railway strikes.

2. Texas: Capt. David McNabb shot by Mexican while on aerial patrol along boundary (→ 10/25).

3. Italy grants women right to vote (→ 11/30).

4. Washington: Senate Foreign Relations Committee adds 38 amendments to Versailles treaty (→ 5).

5. St. Louis: Wilson tells public "Peace partnership or armed isolation is our choice" (→ 26).

6. French commemorate U.S. effort during war, laying cornerstone of monument at Pointe de Grave, landing point for first U.S. troops.

9. Mobs ravage Boston as police go on strike (→ 15).

10. Treaty of Saint-Germain, signed by Austria, setting war reparations, forcing recognition of Czech, "Polish", Hungarian and Yugoslavian independence.

12. Munich: Adolf Hitler joins German Worker's Party (→ 2/24/20).

12. Gabriele d'Annunzio occupies Fiume with militant group of Italians (→ 22).

16. Assassin kills Peru's President Augusto B. Leguia.

21. Orient-Express resumes service from Constantinople to Paris.

21. Belgium, Holland break relations.

22. Pennsylvania: 279,100 steel workers go out on strike in Pittsburgh (→ 10/29).

22. Italy asks Allies to wrest Fiume from d'Annunzio (→ 23).

28. Nebraska: Mobs, enraged by alleged Negro attacks on women, burn courthouse and lynch one Negro (→ 2/9/20).

BIRTH

25. George Wallace, Alabama governor.

DEATH

9. John Mitchell, president of United Mine Workers of America (*4/2/1870).

Boston police strike; Coolidge breaks it

A non-striking policeman confers with a member of the National Guard.

Sept 15. Officials in Boston, Massachusetts, began hiring new policemen today to replace those who have been on strike in recent days. The backbone of the strike was broken four days ago when Governor Calvin Coolidge ordered the entire state militia to restore order in the city, where mobs had roamed the streets, smashed windows and looted stores.

In a telegram sent to labor leaders, the governor had declared firmly: "There is no right to strike against public safety by anyone, anywhere, any time."

More than 1,500 members of the Boston police force had walked off the job, complaining of inadequate pay and poor working conditions. They also were protesting the suspension of 19 of their fellow patrolmen found guilty by the police commissioner of violating department orders against union acticities. As officials began recruiting a new police force today, labor officials pleaded for reinstatement of the strikers. However, their demands were rejected (→ 11/5).

Soldier-poet holds Fiume in Adriatic

Sept 23. Italian poet-aviator Gabriele d'Annunzio and 2,600 soldiers have occupied the Adriatic city of Fiume in an attempt to return it to Italy.

D'Annunzio was provoked by the announcement of the Inter-Allied Military Commission that Italian troops in Fiume would be replaced by Maltese policeman and the National Council at Fiume would be dissolved. The peace conference recently decided that Fiume and Zara will become "free cities" under League of Nations supervision.

The Italian government of Francesco Nitti has condemned the occupation as mutinous. D'Annunzio's growing force is made up of soldiers who have deserted from the Italian army. The American commission has indicated that it will agree to any compromise as long as the Yugoslavs are satisfied (→ 9/1/20).

Crowd demands annexation to Italy.

Wilson breaks down on national tour

Sept 22. An exhausted President Wilson has been forced to abandon his national tour in which he has been crusading for Senate approval of the League of Nations. "I guess I'm all in," said the president after it was announced in Wichita, Kansas, that he would cut short the tour on the advice of his personal physician, Admiral Cary T. Grayson.

Since leaving Washington on September 3, aboard a special train, the president has traveled some 8,200 miles and delivered 40 speeches in 14 states in the West and Midwest. He had been scheduled to travel 1,714 more miles to speak in other states.

"The tour's off," Joseph P. Tumulty, the president's private secretary, told reporters waiting aboard the presidential train for the expected automobile trip into nearby Wichita, where Wilson was to have spoken this morning to an assembled crowd of 50,000. Admiral Grayson promptly issued a statement saying that President Wilson is suffering from "nervous exhaustion." While not serious, he said, the president needs to rest for "a considerable time."

Showing the strain.

The admiral attributed the president's condition to "overwork" during the tour and to the lasting effects of an attack of influenza suffered by the president during last April's conference on the Paris peace treaty. As the train began its trip back to Washington today, it was disclosed that the president had suffered a severe nervous attack during the night and that he had finally agreed to abandon the tour when he found it virtually impossible to dress himself this morning (→ 10/2).

1919

OCTOBER

Su	Mo	Tu	We	Th	Fr	Sa
			1	2	3	4
5	6	7	8	9	10	11
12	13	14	15	16	17	18
19	20	21	22	23	24	25
26	27	28	29	30	31	

2. French Chamber of Deputies ratifies Versailles treaty 372 to 53 (→ 11/13).

5. Norwegian referendum lifts ban on sale of alcohol.

7. U.S.: Theater producer George M. Cohan announces retirement.

8. First German enters U.S. since war declaration in April, 1917.

8. London: Dr. Voronov reports he has succeeded in making old goats young by grafting monkey glands.

9. Chicago: Cincinnati Reds are World Series champs; 10-5 over White Sox in eighth game (→ 9/28/20).

14. Federal authorities hint I.W.W. and Bolshevik groups are plotting overthrow of U.S. government (→ 29).

14. Paris: French President Poincare orders general demobilization.

15. Russia: Soviets ban giving Christian names to children.

16. German emigration colonies being planned in Paraguay and Argentina.

18. Spain: Subway opens in Madrid.

18. Roosevelt Field, L.I.: Lt. Belvin Maynard, preacher-aviator, wins 5,400-mile Army ocean-to-ocean air race.

24. Los Angeles Philharmonic gives first concert.

25. U.S. demands release of American consular agent William O. Jenkins, held hostage in Mexico (→ 12/4).

26. Tractors replacing U.S. farm labor; 9,000 reported in use in Iowa alone.

BIRTHS

8. Pierre Elliot Trudeau, Canadian prime minister.

22. Doris Lessing, British writer.

26. Mohammed Reza Pahlevi, shah of Iran (†7/27/1980).

DEATH

18. William Waldorf Astor, first Viscount Astor (*3/31/48).

Trotsky's army defeats White Russians

Red army, protector of revolution.

Oct 21. For months now, civil war has ripped Russia apart, but the Red army is beginning to get the upper hand. Earlier this month, Cossack forces under the control of General Anton Denikin were just outside Moscow, poised for a final assault on the city. Then the Red army counterattacked and forced Denikin to retreat. The Reds overran Orel, Voronezh and Kursk. It was a debacle for the White army, and it was only one of several serious defeats recently.

Until recently, an army of volunteers led by Generals Yudenich and Rodzianko was on the outskirts of Petrograd, threatening the city and supported by a British fleet in the Gulf of Finland. But then, Leon Trotsky, head of the Red army, defeated Yudenich and chased his troops as they scattered in Estonia. The British withdrew from the gulf and sailed toward Riga.

The Red army is also driving a wedge between the forces of General Alexander Kolchak and marching toward the Urals. Reports from that front indicate that Kolchak no longer has control of his troops, and it may not be long before the Reds reach the Urals (→ 12/24).

Troops on guard in bloody Gary strike

Oct 29. Federal troops took over control of Gary, Indiana, after rioting by striking steel workers swept the city. One of the first moves by Major General Leonard Wood was to issue a martial law order banning all public meetings in Gary.

More than 1,000 overseas veterans of the Fourth Division, armed with cannon, machine guns and rifles, patrolled the streets of the strike-torn city. The federal troops were called in after 2,000 strikers, led by former soldiers in uniform, held a parade and rally in defiance of orders of city officials. The rally was held to demand the release of strikers who had been arrested following serious rioting two days earlier that left some 50 persons injured. The rioting broke out after several thousand strikers, as they left a mass meeting, came upon a streetcar bearing 40 strikebreakers hired by the United States Steel Corporation.

The steel strike began on September 22 over the issue of unionizing workers in the steel industry. Elbert H. Gary, Chairman of the United States Steel Corporation who refused to negotiate with union leaders, told a Senate committee earlier in the month that he was fighting for the right of a man to work without dictation from a labor union. In Congress, there were charges that the I.W.W. and Bolshevik organizations were behind the steel and other strikes in an attempt to take over the labor movement and overthrow the government.

There has been a rash of strikes as the truce between labor and management broke down with the end of the war. The United Mine Workers, led by John L. Lewis, threatened a strike on November 1 for higher wages. In a statement issued from his sickbed, President Wilson said a coal strike would be unjustifiable and unlawful (→ 11/1).

Strikers on parade.

1919

NOVEMBER

Su	Mo	Tu	We	Th	Fr	Sa
						1
2	3	4	5	6	7	8
9	10	11	12	13	14	15
16	17	18	19	20	21	22
23	24	25	26	27	28	29
30						

1. U.S. opens Arizona Indian reservations to exploitation by prospectors.

1. U.S.: 425,000 coal miners go out on strike (→ 9).

1. Germany closes railways for ten days to save coal.

4. Berlin: Communist factory councils call strike; many workers resist.

5. Calvin Coolidge re-elected Republican governor of Massachusetts (→ 6/12/20).

8. Italian troops clash with D'Annunzio in Fiume; two reported dead (→ 9/1/20).

8. Scientists find gravity variation in results of May 29th solar eclipse.

9. Washington: A.F.L. denounces injunction against coal strike as "so autocratic as to stagger the human mind" (→ 12).

12. North Dakota places mines under rule of martial law (→ 27).

12. Washington: I.W.W. members arrested in Centralia, charged with four murders at Armistice Day parade (→ 25).

13. Senate adopts Article X reservations to League Covenant (→ 19).

19. Britain authorizes constitution of Egypt (→ 2/28/22).

22. U.S.: Labor conference committee urges eight-hour day, 48-hour week.

23. New outbreak of Turkish violence against Armenians is reported (→ 3/11/20).

25. Polo Grounds: Navy blanks Army 6-0.

26. Mexico refuses release of consular agent Jenkins (→ 12/4).

27. Washington: Coal conference ends in deadlock as miners refuse 14 percent wage hike (→ 12/10).

27. France: Bulgaria signs peace with Allies at Neuilly, fixing war reparations and recognizing Yugoslavian independence (→ 8/16/21).

30. Women vote for first time in French legislative elections (→ 1/5/20).

Lady Astor first woman in Parliament

Nov 28. Lord Astor himself today announced to his wife and successor in the House of Commons that she had beaten by 5,203 votes the Labor candidate and had a majority over the combined votes of her two rivals of 1,004. Next to congratulate Lady Astor was her 12-year-old son. "Well done, mum," he said to the first woman in the British Parliament.

Viscountess Astor ran for the Plymouth seat as a Conservative. She speaks of "Tory democracy," and has chosen for the House the kind of attire that the humblest woman who may be elected in the future can afford: black coat, skirt and hat and a simple white shirtwaist. Born in Virginia, Nancy Astor was one of the beautiful Langhorne sisters; another married Charles Dana Gibson and was the first model for his "Gibson girl" drawings.

The irreverent Lady Astor.

Lady Astor's sharp tongue in debate, her passionate espousal of temperance, women's rights and child welfare reform, together with a cheerful lack of reverence for any and all, have won her both attention and respect. "Obviously I can't say that the best man won," she quipped after the election. "But the best policy did" (→ 30).

Senate votes against Versailles treaty

Nov 19. The Republican-controlled Senate, after two months of debate, has refused to ratify the Versailles treaty ending the war and establishing a League of Nations.

The Senate action was a severe setback for President Wilson, who had prevailed upon the Paris peace conference to accept a League of Nations and then campaigned across the country on behalf of the treaty until he fell ill last month.

The controversy centered around reservations offered by Senator Henry Cabot Lodge of Massachusetts, Chairman of the Senate Foreign Relations Committee, to the Covenant in the treaty establishing the League. The reservations made clear the United States was under no obligation under Article X of the Covenant to come to the defense of League member states without the approval of Congress.

President Wilson urged senators to vote against the treaty with the Lodge reservations, which he said amounted to nullifcation of the treaty. The Senate voted 55 to 39 to reject the treaty containing the Lodge reservations, with 46 Republicans voting no (→ 1/10/20).

Samuel Halpert's oil painting depicts Daniel Hudson Burnham's Flatiron Building on Fifth Ave in New York. Built in 1902, its 20 stories made it the tallest in the world. The unique floor plan, demanded by its wedge-shaped site, indicates space was already at a premium two decades ago.

Raid on Russians finds bomb factory

Nov 25. In a raid today on the headquarters of the Union of Russian Workers in lower Manhattan, Department of Justice agents and New York City police discovered a large quantity of TNT, chemicals and acids that could be used to make explosives. The materials were found in a secret room behind the parlor that police discovered just as they were about to leave.

On a table in the center of the room was a large container marked TNT, the powerful explosive developed during the war, and some 60 bottles and vials containing materials that police said could be used to make explosives. Also found in a search of the room were three ledgers containing names believed by police to be the membership rolls of the Union of Russian Workers and several copies of a Russian newspaper, whose translated name is Bread and Freedom.

Police had gone to the building to serve warrants on several persons of radical sympathies wanted by authorities, but none of those sought was in the building. It was the sixth raid in less than a year on the headquarters of the Union of Russian Workers, regarded by police as a hotbed of radicalism (→ 12/15).

New law reduces child labor 40%

Nov 16. Child labor in the United States has decreased by more than 40 percent since a child labor provision of the tax code went into effect last April, the Internal Revenue Bureau reported today. The new law imposes a tax of ten percent on the earnings of companies employing children under 14 years old or between 14 and 16 years for more than eight hours a day producing commodities entering interstate commerce. The greatest decrease in the use of child labor was reported in the textile mills in the Southern states. A marked reduction also was reported in the coal mining and canning industries. The widespread compliance reflected a belief the Supreme Court would uphold the law.

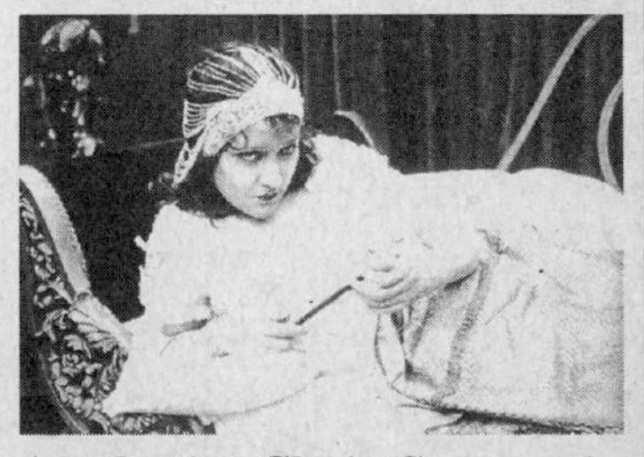

A seductive Gloria Swanson in Cecil B. De Mille's new film "Male and Female."

1919

DECEMBER

Su	Mo	Tu	We	Th	Fr	Sa
	1	2	3	4	5	6
7	8	9	10	11	12	13
14	15	16	17	18	19	20
21	22	23	24	25	26	27
28	29	30	31			

1. U.S. Prohibition Commissioner bans alcohol-based hair tonics, medicines (→ 1/16/20).

3. Northern Italy paralyzed by general strike.

4. Jenkins, consular agent, set free by Mexicans.

10. Nobel Prize in physics goes to German Johannes Stark.

10. Capt. Ross Smith becomes first to fly 11,500 miles from England to Australia.

15. U.S.: Travelers' Aid Society reports 68,000 runaway girls in past year.

15. U.S. asks S. America to join espionage plan to fight radicalism (→ 12/17).

18. Germany nationalizes electricity.

19. Dublin: Sinn Feiners make attempt on life of Lord French, British viceroy of Ireland (→ 3/10/20).

23. Britain publishes new constitution for India (→ 1/3/21).

30. Paris: Reports indicate French birth rates have doubled since start of year.

CULTURAL EVENTS, 1919

Literature: Sherwood Anderson's "Winesburg Ohio"; Hermann Hesse's "Demian"; first "Dr. Doolittle" stories, by Hugh Lofting; H.L. Mencken's "The American Language"; W.S. Maugham's "The Moon and Sixpence"; Pulitzer Prize to Carl Sandburg for "Corn Huskers."

Academia, Religion: Church and state separated in Germany; Henri Bergson's "Spiritual Energy"; Johan Huizinga's "The Waning of the Middle Ages."

Music: Jazz arrives in Europe; N.Y. Symphony Orchestra's first modern music concert, under Edgar Varese.

The Arts: Kathe Kollwitz's "Memorial to Karl Liebknecht"; Edvard Munch's "The Murder"; Picasso's "Pierrot and Harlequin."

Film: Stroheim's "The Devil's Passkey"; Abel Gance's "J'Accuse!"; Fritz Lang's "Half Caste."

Renoir, dazzling Impressionist, dies at 78

"Canoeists' Luncheon" by Pierre Auguste Renoir.

Dec 17. Pierre Auguste Renoir, Impressionist master, has died in the French seaside village of Cagnes. He captured beauty and light to the last day of his life. From 1907 to 1913, when arthritis made holding a paintbrush too painful, he kept one strapped to his hand. For the last six years, he created sculpture by having an assistant carry out designs as he described them.

Renoir was born in Limoges, France, on February 25, 1841. His first paid work was dabbing flowers on chinaware. In 1862, he met Claude Monet and Alfred Sisley; the trio began working outdoors. Renoir admired masters such as Delacroix, and his painting "Odalisk" (1870) reflects this. But by the mid-1870's he fully embraced the Impressionist emphasis on natural light and intense color. His exuberant "The Swing" (1876), a festive outdoor scene, typifies the period.

In the 1880's Renoir felt that Impressionism, once freeing, was now too confining. He went to Algiers and Italy, studied Renaissance masters, and concentrated on a new style. "Dance at Bougival" (1883) showed static figures closer to the picture plane. Some critics called this his "harsh" phase.

In the 1890's, Renoir returned to the gentle brushstroke. He focused on voluptuous female nudes, choosing warm flesh tones. His paintings knew no season but summer; even indoor portraits, such as "Young Girls at the Piano" (1892), were bathed in opulent shades. In his final decade, he sculpted in shapes as sensuous as his colors.

Rockefeller beats own record for giving

Dec 24. John D. Rockefeller, the industrial titan and Sunday school teacher, has given away $100 million, the largest recorded single philanthropic gift in the history of the world.

Half of the sum goes to the General Education Board, itself a Rockefeller creation, mainly to increase teaching salaries. The other half goes to the Rockefeller Foundation, established in 1913 to promote "the well-being of mankind throughout the world." And about $5 million, by request of the donor, is given to leading medical schools in Canada.

So far as it can be estimated, Rockefeller has handed out a total of nearly half a billion dollars to social, religious, welfare and educational institutions. Recently, he gave $20 million to medical schools in America. He aids medical research in Europe and China as well. The worldwide attack on disease includes control and eradication of malaria, hookworm and yellow fever. Rockefeller's aim is to promote higher standards of medicine and public health everywhere in the world.

Death ends career of financier Frick

Dec 3. Henry Clay Frick, a pioneer in the modern coke and steel industry and one of America's outstanding financiers, died yesterday, shortly before his 70th birthday.

Frick's name is intimately allied with the growth of big business in the nation. A millionaire before he was 30, a partner of the late Andrew Carnegie, and a man known for his anti-union policy, as in the bitter Homestead steelworkers' strike in 1892, he also truly cared about children and has left an undisclosed sum to needy little ones. Much of his estate, valued at between $75 and $100 million, including his art collection and New York mansion, goes to the cities of Pittsburgh and New York.

Controversial Henry Clay Frick.

Russian White army chief Kolchak quits

Kolchak, anti-Bolshevik in Siberia.

Dec 24. Admiral Kolchak, the head of the All-Russian government, has announced he is relinquishing command of the forces fighting the Bolsheviks in Siberia and will be succeeded as military commander by Gen. Semenoff, a Cossack chief (→ 1/1/20).

Coal miners end strike on Wilson's terms

Dec 10. The eight-week strike of 400,000 bituminous coal miners has officially ended with the leaders of the United Mine Workers agreeing to accept President Wilson's recent proposal, thus terminating one of the greatest labor union battles in American history.

The settlement calls for a pay increase of $14, with no increase in coal prices. The president will also appoint a commission of three composed of one miner, one operator and one public representative to recommend a new wage scale within 60 days and a readjustment of coal prices if necessary.

Acting U.M.W. President John L. Lewis was gratified by the union's decision to accept the proposal, stating that miners would return immediately to work and resume normal production. He said, "The action taken today should demonstrate . . . that the United Mine Workers are loyal to our country and believe in the perpetuity of our democratic institutions."

Because of the shortage of coal created by the strike, the National Fuel Administration in Washington has also put into effect regulations regarding the conservation of that fuel.

Keynes fears results of peace treaty

John Maynard Keynes' "The Economic Consequences of the Peace" is causing quite a stir. The 36-year-old, Cambridge-educated economist, who served as representative of the British Treasury to the peace talks at Versailles, resigned the position to write the book.

Keynes' main points are predictive: Germany will find it impossible to make reparations payments on the scale proposed at Versailles, and the treaty's financial provisions, in general, will have disastrous effects on the world economy.

Keynes also draws some severely critical portraits of the "Big Four." Clemenceau, he writes, "had one illusion —France; and one disillusion —mankind, including Frenchmen." Lloyd George emerges as a pompous know-it-all appealing to either vanity or weakness.

And President Wilson "could write Notes from Sinai or Olympus; he could remain unapproachable in the White House . . . and be safe. But if he once stepped down to the intimate quality of the Four, the game was evidently up" (→ 1/10/22).

Indians introduced popcorn to the early settlers of America. Little did they know it would one day be found in the aisles of movie theaters.

Eclipse test proves Einstein's theory

Complete verification of Albert Einstein's General Theory of Relativity was reported this year at a historical joint meeting in London of the Royal Society and the Royal Astronomical Society.

Teams of British astronomers who went on expeditions to northern Brazil and Principe Island off the coast of West Africa to observe a solar eclipse last March 29 indicated that the path of light as it passed close to the sun was bent by exactly the amount predicted by Einstein.

Joseph Thomson, President of the Royal Astronomical Society, said after hearing the report that Einstein's work is "one of the greatest, perhaps the greatest, of achievements in the history of human thought." The praise is especially meaningful because Einstein announced his theory in Berlin in 1915, during the war, and because bitterness between the two former enemy nations is still strong.

Verification of Einstein's theory means Sir Isaac Newton's picture of absolute time and space must be replaced by that of a universe in which time and space are relative. Einstein's theory of relativity is so complex that only a few people are said to understand it completely.

Plan to fight Reds with motion pictures

Dec 17. A nationwide campaign to combat the spread of Bolshevism and ultra-radical tendencies was initiated after meetings between administration officials, members of Congress and motion picture executives. They passed a resolution that the American motion picture industry "do all that is within its power to upbuild and strengthen the spirit of Americanism within our people."

The prime mover in the new campaign is Secretary of the Interior Franklin K. Lane, who expressed to the movie moguls his views about the seriousness of the present social situation in this country, and his belief that no other medium could so effectively disseminate propaganda or explain the true story of what Americanism really stands for (→ 1/2/20).

Carpentier defeats Beckett, takes title

Carpentier, in white trunks.

Dec 14. Georges Carpentier, the talented French light-heavyweight boxer, has captured the European championship by beating the English fighter, Joe Beckett. Carpentier's devastating right hook proved too vexing for Beckett. Said Carpentier after the bout: "I wanted to make him fall as if a ball had hit him in the heart." On the basis of this victory, boxing experts predicted a bright future for the French army aviator.

Boxing's light-heavyweight division was born around the turn of the century when a Chicago promoter, Lou Houseman, pointed out that there were many fighters who were too heavy for the middle-weight division's 158-pound limit. The top weight in the newer division is 175.

A lovely Parisian confounds city drivers. Fashions by Doeuillet.

1920 – 1929

1920

JANUARY

Su	Mo	Tu	We	Th	Fr	Sa
				1	2	3
4	5	6	7	8	9	10
11	12	13	14	15	16	17
18	19	20	21	22	23	24
25	26	27	28	29	30	31

1. Pasadena, Ca.: Harvard takes Rose Bowl, 7-6 over Oregon.

1. Estonia signs truce with Soviets, as Red army advances to Black Sea coast (→ 15).

2. U.S. Atty. Gen. Palmer conducts nationwide raids on suspected radicals; 2,700 arrested (→ 24).

3. Last U.S troops quit France.

5. Radio Corp. of Am. formed with capitalization of $20 mil. broadcasts to span globe.

5. Chicago: G.O.P. women demand equal representation at Republican natl. convention in June (→ 6/10).

6. Mexico: Earthquake kills 1,000 in Couztlan, more in surrounding area.

10. Treaty of Versailles goes into effect; U.S. tells Germany they are still at war (→ 16).

12. Wilson reports 29,000 Jews killed last year in Ukraine pogroms.

14. Berlin placed under martial law as 40,000 radicals rush Reichstag; 42 dead, 105 wounded in riots (→ 3/19).

15. U.S. approves $150 million loan to Poland, Austria, Armenia for war with Russian Communists (→ 16).

16. Paris: League of Nations holds first meeting (→ 2/11).

16. Paris: Allies demand extradition of kaiser (→ 23).

16. Paris: Allies lift blockade on trade with Russia (→ 24).

17. Paul Deschanel elected French pres. for seven years.

23. Dutch refuse to extradite Kaiser Wilhelm II (→ 2/3).

24. Soviets reject Allied trade, demand peace first (→ 2/7).

BIRTHS

2. Isaac Asimov, American bio-chemist, sci-fi writer.

20. Federico Fellini, Italian film director.

DEATH

24. Amadeo Modigliani, Italian painter, sculptor (*7/12/1884).

3,000 arrested in Red scare raids

Jan 24. Sweeping raids on alleged Communists in scores of American cities have captured the nation's attention this month while the Department of Justice has caustically condemned the Communist Party. In the latest development, Secretary of Labor William Wilson ordered the deportation of foreigners who are members of the Communist Party, citing as justification a law passed in 1918 which prohibits aliens' membership in groups desirous of overthrowing the U.S. government. Many of the more than 3,000 suspected Communists arrested so far may be subject to deportation.

Beginning January 2, Justice Dept. agents, on directions from Attorney General A. Mitchell Palmer and armed with thousands of warrants, stormed through 33 cities and arrested those individuals who "advocate the overthrow of the government by violence and force . . . and endeavor to establish a Soviet form of government in this country, similar to that which now obtains in Russia," according to a statement issued by the Justice Department.

The campaign, orchestrated by Palmer and Investigation Bureau Chief William Flynn, reached its climax with the mass arrests after investigation pointed to Communist infiltration and agitation in the recent coal and steel strikes. Among those arrested is Gregory Weinstein, co-editor with Leon Trotsky of some Communist publications.

While members of Congress push for severe penalties, including death sentences, for convicted Communists, American Socialists have fervently protested "against these activities on the part of the hot-headed and overzealous guardians of the safety" of the country. Hearings for the accused are now occurring in courts across America (→ 4/1).

Accused Communists solemnly board a ship for reprocessing at Ellis Island.

Palmer strong-arms the political left.

Pitcher Babe Ruth sold to Yankees

Jan 5. George Herman "Babe" Ruth, a pitcher who is the best home-run hitter in baseball, has been sold by the Red Sox to the New York Yankees for $125,000, the largest sum ever paid for a player. Ruth, who hit 29 home runs last season, had asked for a $10,000 salary increase to $20,000 a year.

Babe Ruth will shed his Sox uniform.

It's the law: Prohibition takes effect

Jan 16. As of today beer, wine and liquor have been officially banned by the 18th Amendment. It will be enforced by the National Prohibition or Volstead Act and is nothing new to those 25 states which have already passed their own Prohibition laws. By tomorrow persons who have stored liquor "for personal use only" in warehouses, safety deposit vaults and elsewhere must have it moved to their own residences. New York Mayor LaGuardia is skeptical about the law, saying that it will take 250,000 police to enforce it in that city alone, and nearly as many more to police the police (→ 3/2).

A somber toast on the last night of legal drinking.

Modigliani, creator of exotica, deceased

Jan 25. Amadeo Modigliani, the Italian painter and sculptor, is dead in Paris. He had contracted tuberculosis years ago and further damaged his health by an excess of alcohol and drugs.

Modigliani left school at age 14 after an attack of typhus, and, encouraged by his mother, studied at the academies of Venice, Florence and Rome. He became familiar with Italian Renaissance paintings and in 1906 moved to Paris. His paintings show the influence of Toulouse-Lautrec, Cezanne, the early Picasso, Gauguin, African sculpture and the Cubists. The characteristics of Modigliani's sculptured heads (long necks and noses, small mouths, simplified features, long oval faces) pervaded his paintings.

Modigliani's "Blue-eyed Woman."

Daily flu count continues to rise

Jan 28. The number of new influenza cases continues to rise, with 5,589 reported in New York City in the past 24 hours. This exceeds the largest daily total of 5,390 reported in the influenza epidemic of 1918. However, public health officials say influenza appears to be less virulent this year. There were 118 pneumonia deaths arising from influenza infections reported in New York in the past 24 hours.

1920

FEBRUARY

Su	Mo	Tu	We	Th	Fr	Sa
1	2	3	4	5	6	7
8	9	10	11	12	13	14
15	16	17	18	19	20	21
22	23	24	25	26	27	28
29						

2. Russian Soviets recognize Estonian independence.

3. Allies demand that 890 German military leaders stand trial for war crimes (→ 16).

7. Adm. Alexander Kolchak, ex-head of provisional Russian govt., killed by Reds (→ 26).

9. Kentucky: 5 killed attempting to lynch Lexington Negro accused of murder (→ 6/15).

9. Paris: League Council grants Spitzberg to Norway.

10. 75% of N. Silesia votes annexation to Denmark (→ 6/15).

13. U.S. Sec. of State Lansing resigns due to personal differences with president.

16. Allies accept Berlin's offer to try war criminals in Leipzig supreme court (→ 4/2).

17. Allies internationalize Dardanelles and Bosporus (→ 23).

18. Vuillemin, Chalus complete first flight over Sahara Desert.

19. U.S. Senate denies ratification of Versailles treaty for second time (→ 3/15).

19. U.S. reports thousands of Poles, Czechs, Yugoslavs now returning to home countries.

22. Berlin: 21 arrested for anti-Jewish violence (→ 24).

22. American Relief Administration appeals to people to pressure Congress into aiding starving European cities (→ 5/17).

23. Jerusalem: Famous olive tree "El Butini" blows down; seen as omen of Turkey's end (→ 3/3).

26. Soviets pledge democratic reform in return for peace, promise const. assembly, payment of 60% of debt (→ 27).

27. U.S. rejects Soviet peace offer as propaganda (→ 4/5).

29. Czechoslovakia adopts constitution in effort to keep independence from Germany, Soviet Russia (→ 5/27).

29. Budapest: Six months after leading counterrevolt, Miklos Horthy de Nagybanya becomes regent of Hungary (→ 3/28).

DEATH

20. Robert Peary, U.S. explorer, discovered N. Pole (*5/6/1856).

League Council meets for the first time

Feb 11. The first session of the Council of the League of Nations was held today in London, in the Picture Gallery of St. James's Palace. Spectators included members of the press and diplomats, but the public showed little interest. Arthur J. Balfour presided over the session and in his welcoming speech regretfully noted the absense of the American representatives. The United States has failed to join the League.

League of Nations meets.

Members of the Council represented eight countries: France, Great Britain, Italy, Japan, Belgium, Spain, Brazil and Greece. The agenda for the deliberations includes the appointment of the Sarre Basin Commission and the High Commissioner for Danzig. Leon Bourgeois of France will draw up plans for an international court of justice, as called for in the League Covenant (→ 19).

Famous explorer Robert Peary dead

Feb 20. Robert Edwin Peary, the man credited with discovering the North Pole, died today in Washington, D.C. He was 64 years old. The Navy recognized his achievement by making him a Rear Admiral in 1911, when he retired from service.

Pennsylvania-born Peary readied for his Arctic explorations by conquering first the more accessible land mass of Greenland. As a Navy civil engineer, he surveyed the interior of Greenland in 1886. He went back on several trips between 1891 and 1897, conducting scientists on meteorological and ethnological studies. On one of these journeys he picked up hefty meteorites, displaying them later in the United States.

The last few voyages to Greenland were actually his unpublicized attempts to reach the North Pole. While they were technical failures, he was developing survival skills. He learned which rations to pack and what kind of sled and sled dogs would prove the most durable.

In 1909, he left Ellesmere Island, this time with one assistant and four Eskimos. Peary reached the Pole April 6. To his intense disappointment, he was told upon his return of a claim by Dr. Frederick Cook, ship's surgeon on one of Peary's earlier voyages. Cook said he reached the Pole in 1908. Controversy raged, but Congress and world authorities recognized Peary as the first to stand at the top of the world.

Fanny dickers for Nicky's freedom

Feb 25. Miss Fanny Brice, the entertainer, must share the limelight today with her notorious husband "Nicky" Arnstein. He is wanted by the New York district attorney for conspiracy to steal $5 million worth of securities from a prominent brokerage house.

The attorney requested that Miss Brice surrender Nicky and answer questions about several bad checks they have attempted to pass. She agreed to deliver Arnstein on condition that he be immune from questioning and released on $50,000 bail. Although her terms were accepted, she and Arnstein failed to appear. A subpoena was issued, and detectives scoured the city.

Rumor had it Miss Brice was holed up in, of all places, Bronx Supreme Court. She was conferring there with her lawyer, who was handling another case. When detectives arrived on the scene, however, Miss Brice had already fled.

Comedienne Fanny Brice.

▷

1920

Hitler advocating anti-Semite policy

Feb. 24. The German Workers' Party announced its goals and program in Munich today. A small group of unhappy, alienated war veterans, the party attacks Jews and capitalists. Its propaganda chief is a man named Adolf Hitler.

Born in Austria, Hitler became a disciple of the anti-Semitic Mayor of Vienna when he was living there as a teenager. Hitler was poor and was rejected for admission at the art academy. He served in the Bavarian army during the war and was never promoted above the rank of corporal, but he was awarded the Iron Cross. He returned to Germany after the war, convinced that Germany had been "stabbed in the back" by Jews and Marxists (→4/1).

Wilson gives back railroads to owners

Feb 28. President Wilson tonight signed legislation returning the nation's railroads, operated by the government during the war, to private control. The transfer returning the railroads to their 230 corporate owners will take place tomorrow, ending a bitter labor-management dispute over peacetime ownership of the railroads.

President Wilson signed the legislation over the objections of the railway brotherhoods and the American Federation of Labor, which had advocated public ownership of the railroads. Government ownership of the railroads during the war had cost some $300 million, and Wilson had set a deadline of March 1 for their return to private control.

The legislation, the outgrowth of prolonged House-Senate negotiations, would increase the powers of the Interstate Commerce Commission to fix railroad rates, create a railroad labor board to settle labor disputes and establish a federal fund to help the railroads return to their pre-war status. The return to private control comes at a time when the railroad unions were requesting the president establish a special tribunal to act on their wage demands. In a letter to the railroad brotherhoods, President Wilson rejected the request (→ 4/9).

MARCH

Su	Mo	Tu	We	Th	Fr	Sa
	1	2	3	4	5	6
7	8	9	10	11	12	13
14	15	16	17	18	19	20
21	22	23	24	25	26	27
28	29	30	31			

1. Supreme Court finds U.S. Steel does not violate Sherman Antitrust Law.

2. New Jersey declares 3.5 beer legal (→ 11).

3. Constantinople: Turkish Cabinet resigns following Allied decree yesterday; Turkey to lose 24 million in population, retain only Asiatic province of Anatolia (→ 16).

7. Bolsheviks open major offensive on Polish front (→ 5/3).

8. Congress at Damascus proclaims Syrian independence (→ 11).

10. British Parliament passes Home Rule Bill dividing Ireland into two parts, both semi-independent; Ulster Unionist Council in North accepts provisions (→ 4/4).

11. Emir Feisal becomes king of Syria (→ 7/24).

11. Near East Relief Campaign asks U.S. aid for Armenians, claims 3.75 mil. out of 5 mil. killed since start of war (→ 11/1).

11. New York: Federal agent kills first dry law offender since start of Prohibition (→ 6/7).

13. German army officer von Kapp seizes power in Berlin coup (→ 17).

16. Allies occupy Constantinople, seize ministries (→ 4/11).

19. Germany beset by socialist unrest; Reds capture Essen; Saxony workers demand soviet congress (→ 27).

20. Bolsheviks attack Finland on 1,500-mile front (→ 10/14).

23. Britain denounces U.S. for delay in joining League of Nations (→ 5/16).

24. Communists control half of Berlin against Ebert; Americans to evacuate city (→ 27).

26. Senator Borah charges war profiteers are giving heavily to control U.S. party conventions.

27. Ebert orders all Russians in Berlin arrested (→ 3/24/21).

30. Copenhagen mobs demand Danish republic; palace under heavy guard.

U.S. Senate fails to approve peace treaty

March 15. By a seven-vote margin, the Senate for the second time refused to ratify the Treaty of Versailles, ending a long, bitter fight.

At the insistence of a majority of Democrats, the Senate made a renewed effort to approve the treaty after it was rejected by large margins last November. In an attempt to reverse the earlier votes, a compromise plan had been worked out by a group of Republican and Democratic senators.

Lodge, a formidable Wilson foe.

The Senate earlier this month, by a 56-to-26 vote, adopted a modified version of the reservation that Senator Henry Cabot Lodge has offered to Article X of the Covenant establishing the League of Nations. The Senate also adopted another Lodge reservation making clear the treaty did not supersede the Monroe Doctrine. President Wilson, who had not supported the renewed Senate effort to consider the treaty, continued to oppose the Lodge reservations.

On the crucial vote, a large group of Democrats broke with the president by voting for the treaty with reservations. By a majority of 57 to 39, the Senate approved the treaty, a margin just seven votes shy of the required two-thirds majority (→ 23).

Kapp leads brief army uprising in Berlin

Extremists of the right menace Berlin's Potsdamer Platz.

March 17. The monarchist coup in Germany has ended almost as soon as it began. Dr. Wolfgang von Kapp, the self-proclaimed Chancellor and dictator, fled from the city of Berlin yesterday. Troops commanded by his ally, General Baron von Luttwitz, are expected to pull back by tomorrow.

Kapp seized control last Friday. He seemed intent on restoring a Prussian-style monarchy, but he failed to secure the support of the entire army. And the Finance Ministry of President Ebert refused to pay his troops. Scores of people were wounded in Berlin and other cities as the troops supporting the putsch clashed with forces loyal to the government of Ebert.

Ebert also called on workers to strike in support of his government. Many of them did, despite threats from von Luttwitz that they would be executed. The strike, led by Socialists, inspired Communists to demonstrate in the streets. Their protest convinced Kapp to call it quits. The monarchist does not want to be remembered as the man who helped bring Communists to power in Germany (→ 4/17).

1920

APRIL

Su	Mo	Tu	We	Th	Fr	Sa
				1	2	3
4	5	6	7	8	9	10
11	12	13	14	15	16	17
18	19	20	21	22	23	24
25	26	27	28	29	30	

1. N.Y. State Assembly expels five Socialists, asks party to purge itself (→ 14).

1. German Worker's Party changes name to Nationalist Socialist German Worker's Party (→ 7/29/21).

3. William T. Tilden II wins first U.S. indoor tennis title.

4. Irish nationalists begin burning tax lists, symbol of British rule (→ 14).

5. Frederick Douglass becomes first Negro named to N.Y. University's Hall of Fame.

5. New Japanese force lands in Vladivostok (→ 7/7).

7. Chicago: 50,000 out in rail strike; 25 railroads affected (→ 14).

7. Germany: Colored French troops, jeered at in Frankfort, open fire on crowd, killing seven; Paris divided on occupation (→ 5/17).

9. U.S. Senate rejects compulsory military training in favor of voluntary service.

11. Americans besieged in two Turkish towns; French troops rushing to their relief (→ 5/24).

12. Guatemala: Estrada Cabrera driven out; Carlos Herrera is new president.

14. U.S. Atty. Gen. Palmer charges railroad strike is work of I.W.W., part of world Communist movement (→ 21).

14. Dublin prison releases 89 Sinn Fein hunger strikers (→ 5/14).

17. Wolfgang von Kapp, leader of German coup, arrested in Stockholm.

19. Italy: Allied powers meet in San Remo (→ 15).

21. Montana: 14 I.W.W. members shot by police in Butte riot (→ 29).

25. San Remo: Supreme Council offers Armenian mandate to U.S., Palestine to Britain (→ 26).

26. Palestine: Arabs attack British, fearing influx of Jews (→ 7/1).

28. Mexico: Carranza government pressed as rebels approach Mexico City (→ 5/9).

World War Admiral takes over Hungary

March 28. The Hungarian people have passionately rejected all traces of the Communist leadership of Bela Kun and of the Rumanian occupation, as Admiral Nicholas Horthy de Nagybanya has taken control of the new European nation.

Horthy was the last Commander-in-Chief of the Austro-Hungarian navy and is perhaps best known for the naval action off Valona in the Adriatic Sea on May 15, 1917, during the Great War. On that day, he led an Austrian squadron on a raid against Italian transports. He and his men sank 14 merchant ships and then in a brazen and high-speed sail, escaped British, French and Italian pursuit.

Following the disintegration of the Austro-Hungarian Empire and the Dual Monarchy at the end of the war and the subsequent rule of Kun's Marxist regime, Horthy and a group of anti-revolutionary officers led the opposition to the Communists. However, their battle could not have succeeded without the support of Rumanian troops, which defeated Kun last year.

Many observers fear that the military style of Horthy and his dictatorial character could lead to a reign of violence similar to that of the Red Terror employed by his Communist predecessor. Yet, others believe he will embody the necessary stabilizing influence that Hungary needs.

March 29. Screen stars Douglas Fairbanks and Mary Pickford were wed today in Los Angeles.

French occupy the Ruhr

Life goes on in Frankfurt despite the French tanks.

April 7. Angry mobs of German civilians are marching through the streets of Frankfurt tonight, taunting French soldiers. The troops, most of them colonial forces recruited from the native populations of the French Empire, are responding with gunfire. At least seven civilians were killed, including three women and a boy. The atmosphere in the city is tense, and French armored cars patrol the streets. The troops are under orders to fire again if the Germans become unruly.

The French forces moved into Frankfurt and nearby towns in the Ruhr Basin after German troops mobilized to fight a rebellion by a Communist army. France complained that the German military action violated the Versailles treaty, which outlaws German troops from a neutral zone extending 30 miles east of the Rhine.

The incidents in the Ruhr Basin have whipped France into an anti-German frenzy. The French did not give the Allies advance warning of the military action, and they are likely to oppose it (→ 5/17).

Palmer charges I.W.W. planned rail strike

April 29. Attorney General A. Mitchell Palmer told the Cabinet in mid-month that the illegal railroad strike had been fomented by the I.W.W. as part of an international Communist conspiracy. The strike, he said "is the largest and latest manifestation of the working out of the program of the International Communist Party, whose purpose is to capture the political and economic power, to overthrow the government and to establish a dictatorship on the part of what they call the proletariat, and transport to this country the exact chaotic condition that exists in Russia."

The attorney general singled out William Z. Foster, a Communist Party leader linked to the recent steel strike, as one of the instigators of the crippling railroad strike. The attorney general expressed hope that railroad workers would realize they had been "duped" and would return to work. Later in the month, the attorney general said federal agents had uncovered a nationwide plot by Reds to kill American officials on May Day (→ 5/5).

Atty. Gen. Palmer, anti-Red warrior. ▷

Short skirts, high prices are in fashion

April 11. Hemlines and clothing prices are rising throughout the nation. While the higher prices are decidedly unpopular, the new trend in women's fashions has been generally well-received, perhaps because less fabric means more savings.

Women's hemlines are escalating so much lately that they are astonishingly nearer the knee than the ankle. Short is indeed the watchword for feminine apparel. The new abbreviation applies not only to hemlines but to sleeves as well. Fashionable shops are giving little alternative but to wear short or indeed no sleeves at all.

Unlike the full-figured French ideal, women in this country aspire to a lean, lithe look. And it is for this pared-down silhouette that the leading designers love to ply their craft. The long-waisted dress lends an air of supple grace to the newly slender American female form. Callot, the eminent Parisian designer, does this new style to perfection; some of her imported modes feature skirts that are full or pleated.

But if prices don't come down soon, few women will be buying anything new. There are reports that due to rising clothing prices, calico frocks for women and blue denim for men will prove to be the most popular American fashions this spring.

With British and U.S. troops in Constantinople, and the Sultan weakened to Allied demands, Turkish nationalist Mustafa Kemal (above) has reportedly set up a rival govt. in Ankara (→ 5/24).

1920

MAY

Su	Mo	Tu	We	Th	Fr	Sa
						1
2	3	4	5	6	7	8
9	10	11	12	13	14	15
16	17	18	19	20	21	22
23	24	25	26	27	28	29
30	31					

3. Poles and Russians battle for control of Kiev (→ 7/11).

5. Massachusetts: Nicola Sacco and Bartolomeo Vanzetti arrested for murder, payroll robbery (→ 7/14/21).

5. U.S. Sec. of Labor Wilson announces membership in Communist Party is not grounds for deportation (→ 23).

8. Paul Jones wins Kentucky Derby with jockey T. Rice.

9. Rebels take Mexico City; four U.S. destroyers sail from Key West for Tampico (→ 21).

10. N.Y.: Socialist Labor Party picks W.W. Cox for pres., A. Gilhaus for v.p. (→ 6/12).

14. London reports 94 attacks on Irish police barracks in last few days (→ 6/24).

16. Switzerland joins League of Nations (→ 9/5).

17. Am. Red Cross announces Central Europe will perish without U.S. aid (→ 7/28).

17. Germany: Franco-Belgian troops quit Frankfort (→ 7/4).

19. 12 killed in W. Virginia pistol battle between detective agency and miners' union.

21. Mexico: Pres. Carranza killed by govt. troops (→ 26).

23. Gompers asks overthrow of Congress for legislative injustice to workers (→ 8/2).

24. Constantinople: Turkish leaders denounce Allied peace terms, demand revision based on Wilson's points (→ 6/25).

30. Coney Island beach censors ban socks for women, one-piece suits for men.

31. Gaston Chevrolet, wins Indy 500 at 88.6 mph (→ 11/25).

31. Vatican: Pope Benoit XV issues encyclical "Pax Dei."

BIRTHS

3. Sugar Ray Robinson, American boxer.

18. Karol Wojtyla, Pope Jean Paul II.

DEATH

11. William Dean Howells, American novelist, publisher (*3/1/1837).

Masaryk is elected Czech President

Tomas Masaryk in Prague.

May 27. The man who led Czechoslovakia in a liberation movement and eventually to its independence in 1918 after the Czech people had been dominated for over 1,000 years, has been elected President of the republic. By an overwhelming majority, Tomas Masaryk, who already held the respect of his countrymen, captured the vote. Most Westerners are delighted with the news as Masaryk has demonstrated strong support for civil liberties and democratic rule.

Carranza killed by own army in Mexico

May 26. Revolutionary turmoil continues in Mexico with the murder in Vera Cruz of General Venustiano Carranza, Mexican constitutional President since 1917.

Accused assassin General Rodolfo Herrera has surrendered and is en route to Mexico City, jointly governed by Generals Obregon and Gonzales since their recent ouster of Carranza, who fled the city after his wholesale slaughter of political prisoners, including 15 generals, at Santiago military prison.

Some witnesses claim that Carranza actually killed himself after being merely wounded by Herrera's shot, but the murderers may have been some of Herrera's own troops. Despite the recent turn of events, Obregon was reportedly deeply moved by the death of his former friend and colleague, who came to power largely thanks to Obregon's successful 1915 campaign against Pancho Villa (→ 6/1).

Debs is nominated while serving time

May 9. Some 6,000 members of the Socialist Party meeting in Madison Square Garden yesterday endorsed the nomination of Eugene V. Debs as the party's presidential candidate in the coming election. The formal nomination of Debs, who is serving a sentence in federal prison for violation of the Espionage Act, will be made later this week at the Socialist national convention. It will be the fifth time Debs has been selected as the Socialist Party's presidential candidate.

Morris Hillquit, a Socialist leader, predicted the Socialist Party would draw two million to three million votes in the presidential election. He said the Socialist Party "has the advantage of being the only conservative force in American politics. We are practically alone in upholding the somewhat antiquated American ideal of government of the people, by the people, for the people. The Democratic and Republican parties are revolutionary organizations trying to overthrow constituted American government by force and violence" (→ 11/2).

May 30. On this date in 1431, Joan of Arc, the Maid of Orleans, was burned at the stake for heresy at age 19. Today, only 489 years later, the Church canonized her, completing the vindication of France's national heroine.

1920

JUNE

Su	Mo	Tu	We	Th	Fr	Sa
		1	2	3	4	5
6	7	8	9	10	11	12
13	14	15	16	17	18	19
20	21	22	23	24	25	26
29	28	29	30			

1. Spanish Communist Party founded.

1. Adolfo de la Huerta becomes 10th president of Mexico (→ 7/28).

4. U.S. Congress passes Army Reorganization Act, establishing peacetime military force of 300,000.

4. France: Hungary signs Treaty of Trianon with Allies, shrinking country from 125,000 to 36,000 sq. miles, 22 mil. to eight mil. population.

5. Merchant Marine Act passes U.S. Congress, authorizing continuation of wartime shipping board.

7. U.S. Supreme Court unanimously upholds 18th Amendment, Volstead Law (→ 13).

9. U.S. census reports N.Y. is largest city at 5.6 mil., Chicago second, Philadelphia third; Los Angeles passes San Francisco with 575,480.

10. U.S. Congress creates Federal Power Commission to oversee energy production.

10. Chicago: Republican convention endorses woman suffrage (→ 8/26).

12. Chicago: Republicans nominate Warren G. Harding for president, Calvin Coolidge for vice president (→ 7/6).

13. U.S. Post Office Dept. rules children may not be sent by parcel post.

15. Minn.: Three Negroes lynched by Duluth mob 5,000 strong (→ 20).

15. Germany cedes North Silesia to Denmark.

16. Holland: Permanent Court of Justice opens at The Hague.

20. Chicago: Race riots leave two dead, many hurt (→ 6/1/21).

23. Shell opens new oil field in Long Beach, California.

24. Irish, British troops quell fierce riots in Londonderry (→ 8/3).

25. Greeks take 8,000 Turkish prisoners near Smyrna (→ 26).

26. British fleet at Ismid kills 1,000 Turks (→ 8/10).

Prohibition: It's a big headache

June 13. Prohibition may be reducing hangovers, but it's becoming a headache for law-enforcement officers. One problem is the way doctors use it for presumably medicinal purposes to treat everything from stomach cramps to insomnia.

Hubert Howard, Federal Prohibition Director for Illinois, estimated, for example, that since the dry law went into effect in mid-January, more than 300,000 spurious prescriptions for liquor have been written by Chicago physicians. In New York, Charles R. O'Connor, the Prohibition director for the state, said he did not have adequate manpower to check on fraudulent prescriptions. At the rate whiskey, at $15 a quart, is being prescribed, government stocks will be exhausted in 18 months. The Supreme Court meanwhile upheld the constitutionality of Prohibition (→ 9/1).

Dry agents bust a bootlegging operation, lucrative but untaxable.

Big Bill Tilden wins at Wimbledon

For the first time in history, an American man has won a Wimbledon tennis championship. William T. "Big Bill" Tilden, who has emerged as a world-class player at the age of 27, captured the men's singles title with a cannon ball serve and deceptive speed.

Tilden serves.

Max Weber's work in history is ended

June 14. Max Weber, German sociologist and historian, and perhaps the most influential social scientist of our century, is dead at 56.

Weber is best known for his work in the sociology of religion. "The Protestant Ethic and the Spirit of Capitalism," published in 1905, proposed an intimate link between Calvinist asceticism and the rise of modern capitalism. In "The Religion of China," "The Religion of India" and "Ancient Judaism," he showed that the vital link was missing.

In the field of methodology, Weber devised the concept of "ideal types," generalized historical models that can be used comparatively.

Weber's studies in political sociology evolved into new theories about social stratification and bureaucracy. He concluded that the rationalization of life was the most significant development in the modernization of Western civilization.

Dada, Dada, Dada Dada, da, da, da

Duchamp's Mr. "Mona Lisa."

June 1. If creation has been the motivation for most artistic movements, then negation seems to be the purpose of Dadaism. The first international exposition of Dadaist work opened at a gallery in Berlin. The work of Georg Grosz and other artists is represented, and it seems more designed to shock visitors than inspire them.

Dadaists do not like unifying themes, but if there is one in Berlin, it may be the industrial revolution and modern technology. Smoke billows from chimneys on canvases and photocollages, and stuffed puppets hang from the ceiling. Grosz and another of the artists posted themselves at the door with a sign reading, "Art is dead. This is the new machine art."

George Grosz's "Without Title."

1920

JULY

Su	Mo	Tu	We	Th	Fr	Sa
				1	2	3
4	5	6	7	8	9	10
11	12	13	14	15	16	17
18	19	20	21	22	23	24
25	26	27	28	29	30	31

1. Great Britain appoints Sir Herbert Samuel high commissioner of Palestine (→ 5/9/22).

4. Siberia's provisional govt. cedes Sakhalin Island, rich in coal and oil, to Japan (→ 28).

4. Spa, Belgium: Allied, German premiers meet for first time since Versailles (→ 9/20).

7. U.S. removes ban on trade with Soviet Russia; includes all non-military items (31).

11. East and West Prussia vote to remain part of Germany.

11. British For. Min. Lord Curzon offers proposal for fixing Russo-Polish border (→ 23).

12. Soviet Russia agrees to allow Lithuania to remain independent (→ 2/20/22).

18. Former German kaiser's youngest son Joachim commits suicide in Potsdam.

19. Second Intl. Communist Congress opens in Petrograd.

22. Lincoln, Nebraska: William Jennings Bryan declines Prohibition Party's presidential nomination; Aaron S. Watkins selected instead (→ 11/2).

23. Poles ask Soviets for peace, seek American support (→ 31).

24. New York: 150 women inmates at Bedford State Reformatory clubbed into submission during riot.

27. Resolute wins America's Cup, keeping trophy in U.S.

28. U.S. denounces Japanese occupation of Sakhalin Island.

28. London: Lloyd George appeals to America at Lincoln Statue, says "bleeding world" needs U.S. aid (→ 1/21/21).

31. Soviets postpone talks with Poles; Trotsky calls Red army to move on Warsaw (→ 8/10).

BIRTH

24. Bella Abzug, American lawyer and congresswoman.

DEATHS

4. Max Klinger, German painter (*2/18/1857).

10. Lord Fisher, British naval leader (*1/25/1841).

Democrats nominate Cox and Roosevelt

July 6. After 44 ballots, the Democratic national convention broke a deadlock early this morning by nominating Governor James M. Cox of Ohio as its presidential candidate. By acclamation, the convention then chose Franklin D. Roosevelt of New York, Assistant Secretary of Navy, as the party's vice-presidential candidate.

The break in the convention deadlock first came after the 38th ballot, when Attorney General A. Mitchell Palmer released his delegates. It then turned into a two-man race between Cox and William G. McAdoo, former Secretary of the Treasury. On the succeeding ballots, Cox steadily picked up strength until by the 44th ballot he had 699 votes and it was apparent that by the time the ballot was completed he would have more than the two-thirds majority of 729 votes necessary for nomination. At that point, McAdoo managers moved to interrupt the voting and make the nomination unanimous.

From the start, the convention had been marked by dissension. On the opening day, the New York delegation caused an uproar by refusing to join in a demonstration for President Wilson until Roosevelt seized the state's standard from Tammany supporters. There was also controversy over whether the party should endorse Irish independence (→ 21).

Cox, FDR to run on Wilson's legacy.

French take Syria under League terms

July 24. French troops under General Henri Gouraud occupied Damascus today after a fierce battle with the forces of Emir Feisal, the King of Syria. Feisal fled, and his war minister was killed in the fighting. Gouraud says he ordered his troops to advance after Feisal reneged on an agreement to reduce the size of his army and recognize the French mandate in Syria. The French were given the mandate at the League of Nations conference at San Remo. Ironically, the British helped put Feisal on the throne during the Arab revolt against the Ottoman Empire.

French General Henri Gouraud.

Pancho Villa submits to President Huerta

July 28. After years of raiding in northern Mexico, Pancho Villa has thrown in the towel. The Mexican government of President Huerta has accepted the bandit's unconditional surrender with the stipulation that his life will be spared.

Villa, who plans to retire and become a rancher, has also been granted full citizenship and a pension.

Villa has surrendered.

The government has agreed to pay his 600 soldiers their back pay for six months, too.

General Sarrano of the Mexican War Department said he thinks that "Villa is now acting from patriotic motives." He added that because of the many "outrages committed by Villa, he will be closely guarded against his enemies. Villa's final surrender means that the most famous bandit in Mexico is rendered helpless. No other known bandit remains in the field."

As revolutionary ardor in Mexico seems played out, the only trouble spot remaining is lower California. The local government has been slow to recognize the Huerta regime, and federal troops have been sent there to nip a possible revolt in the bud.

Villa could face extradition to the United States for murder committed during his 1916 raid on Columbus, New Mexico. But in view of the gallant treatment accorded him by the Mexican government, it doesn't seem likely they would consent to his extradition, and Villa probably made this one of his surrender terms.

Eugenie, noted for beauty, is deceased

July 11. Former Empress of France, Eugenie, known as one of the greatest beauties of her time, is dead at 94 in Spain. She had returned for a visit to her native land. Eugenie had a great influence over her husband, Napoleon III, the former Emperor of France. She acted three times as regent during his absence, in 1859, in 1865 and in 1870 during the Franco-Prussian War. On the collapse of empire in 1870, she fled to England, in exile with her husband and her son, the Prince Imperial, born in March 1856. After Louis Napoleon's death in 1873, her son, fighting with the British army, was killed in the Zulu War. In the war of 1914-1918, Eugenie worked for an Allied victory.

1920

AUGUST

Su	Mo	Tu	We	Th	Fr	Sa
1	2	3	4	5	6	7
8	9	10	11	12	13	14
15	16	17	18	19	20	21
22	23	24	25	26	27	28
29	30	31				

1. Red army 75 miles from Warsaw; Allies rush aid to Poland (→ 4).

1. British Communist Party founded.

1. London: Sir Robert Baden-Powell convenes second intl. Boy Scouts meeting.

2. Chicago: Millionaire radical William Lloyd and 19 others found guilty of conspiracy to overthrow U.S. government (→ 9/16).

3. Protestants reported expelling Catholic workmen from industry in Northern Ireland (→ 28).

4. French claim Bolsheviks plan to return Baltic Corridor to Germans (→ 10).

6. Denver: Police open fire on rioting streetcar strikers, killing three, injuring 13.

10. U.S. warns Soviets Polish political, territorial integrity must be preserved (→ 14).

10. Turkey signs peace with Allies in Sevres, cedes Smyrna, Adrianople, Gallipoli to Greece; Dardanelles and Bosphorus under intl. control (→ 2/21/21).

11. 1st ecumenical conference of European, American, Eastern churches held in Geneva.

14. Belgium: Antwerp opens VII Summer Olympic Games.

14. Polish officials claim Soviets plan to ally with Germans, overrun Europe (→ 16).

16. U.S. warships ordered to Danzig, Poland (→ 19).

19. Poles rout Red army, crushing three divisions (→ 23).

20. Detroit: Station 8MK opens first daily broadcasting, "Tonight's Dinner" (→ 11/2).

25. Navy sends gunboat to Honduras to watch over U.S. interests during civil strife.

25. Adrienne Bolland becomes first woman to cross English Channel aboard a plane.

BIRTHS

22. Ray Bradbury, American science-fiction writer.

29. Charlie "Bird" Parker, American jazz musician (†3/11/1955).

American women win right to vote

Aug 26. An 81-year struggle ended quietly this morning with the signing of a proclamation giving American women the right to vote. No women were present when Secretary of State Bainbridge Colby signed the papers certifying ratification of the 19th Amendment to the United States Constitution.

While hailing this final step in the long fight, leaders of the National Woman's Party protested their exclusion from the ceremony, held at Colby's home in Washington. "This was quite tragic," said Mrs. Abby Scott Baker, a leader in the suffrage drive. Many leaders of the movement had been on watch all night, awaiting arrival of a document certifying that Tennessee had ratified the amendment two days ago, thus meeting the required number of states needed for ratification.

Agitation for suffrage in America dates back to 1839 when Lucretia Mott was denied a seat with her husband at a slavery conference in London. However, it was not until many years later that Susan B. Anthony persuaded a member of Congress to introduce a proposed constitutional amendment for suffrage. Blocked for years, the amendment was approved by Congress and sent to the states. Some states have allowed women to vote within their borders for years. Wyoming, with its tradition of strong pioneer women, was the first state in the nation to do so, in 1869.

Today's victory puts American women ahead of their British sisters, who, despite years of militant struggle, have not yet established universal suffrage. After the world war broke out, British suffragettes devoted their time to the war effort. Recently, they won a limited franchise, and Lady Astor was elected to Parliament, but they are still working for full voting equality with men. The first countries to grant women suffrage were in Scandinavia. In 1906, women in Finland won the right to vote, and in 1913 the women of Norway (→ 9/25/21).

Victory at last!

Trotsksy's Red army halted at Warsaw

Pilsudski visiting troops in late July to prepare them for the Red army.

Aug 23. The heroic Polish army, which has been under attack for weeks, is beginning to turn the tide against the Russians. Warsaw has apparently been saved from the Bolshevik onslaught, and the Poles have made impressive gains in the north in the past few days.

Fighting has been raging near Miawa and Soldau, and the Polish army took 11,000 Russian prisoners. Russian soldiers are apparently trying to escape in the northwest, but two Polish armies have trapped them by a pincer movement.

The Russians severed peace talks with the Poles when they were in a much better strategic position three weeks ago. Britain urged the Polish government to succumb to the Russians' terms, but the French urged the Poles to keep fighting.

The Russian military setbacks have put a damper on their political goals. Bolshevik officials told an Associated Press correspondent earlier this month that they planned to create an alliance with Germany and attack successively France, England and America (→ 10/6).

Irish riot against British occupation

Aug 27. Irish nationalists, protesting British rule, set off serious fighting in the streets of Belfast Saturday night, leaving 13 dead and more than 40 wounded. It was the worst rioting in Ireland since the House of Commons earlier this month passed the Irish Coercion Bill extending martial law to Ireland.

Sinn Feiners, in strong force and apparently well-equipped with arms, led the fighting into Unionist sections of Belfast. The yells of the mob, the shrieks of women and children and the groans of the injured were audible throughout the fighting. In addition to gunfire, the fighting was marked by widespread incendiarism. Police charged crowds with their batons, but order was not restored until troops in armored cars were used against those protesting British rule (→ 9/2).

1920 Antwerp

Men Athletics

100 M Dash
1. Charles William Paddock USA 10,8
2. Morris Marshall Kirksey USA 10,8
3. Harry Edward GBR 11,0

200 M Dash
1. Allen Woodring USA 22,0
2. Charles Paddock USA 22,1
3. Harry Edward GBR 22,2

400 M Run
1. Bevjl Rudd SAF 49,6
2. Guy Butler GBR 49,9
3. Nils Engdahl SWE 50,0

800 M Run
1. Albert George Hill GBR 1:53,4
2. Earl Eby USA 1:53,6
3. Bevill Rudd SAF 1:54,0

1500 M Run
1. Albert George Hill GBR 4:01,8
2. Philip Baker GBR 4:02,4
3. Lawrence Shields USA 4:03,1

5000 M Run
1. Joseph Guillemot FRA 14:55,6
2. Paavo Nurmi FIN 15:00,0
3. Erik Backman SWE 15:13,0

10,000 M Run
1. Paavo Nurmi FIN 31:45,8
2. Joseph Guillemot FRA 31:47,2
3. James Wilson GBR 31:50,8

Marathon
1. Hannes Kolehmainen FIN 2:32,35,8
2. Juri Lossman EST 2:32,48,6
3. Valerio Arri ITA 2:36,32,8

110 M Hurtles
1. Earl Thomson CAN 14,8
2. Harold Barron USA 15,1
3. Frederick Murray USA 15,2

400 M Hurtles
1. Frank Loomis USA 54,0
2. John Norton USA 54,3
3. August Desch USA 54,5

3000 M Steeplechase
1. Percy Hodge GBR 10:00,4
2. Patrick Flynn USA
3. Ernesto Ambrosini ITA

400 M Relay
1. USA 42,2 (Charles Paddock, Jackson Scholz, Loren Murchison, Morris Kirksey)
2. FRA 42,6 (René Tirard René Lorain, René Mourlon, Emile Ali Khan)
3. SWE 42,9 (Agne Holmström, William Pettersson, Sven Malm, Nils Sandström)

1600 M Relay
1. GBR 3:22,2 (Cecil Griffith, Robert Ainsworth Lindsay, John Ainsworth-Davis, Guy Butler)
2. SAF 3:24,2 (Harry Davel, Clarence Oldfield, Jack Oosterlaak, Bevil Rudd)
3. FRA 3:24,8 (Geo André, Gaston Féry, Maurice Delvart, Jean Devaux)

High Jump
1. Richmond Landon USA 1,935
2. Harold Muller USA 1,90
3. Bo Ekelund SWE 1,90

Pole Vault
1. Frank Foss USA 4,09
2. Henry Petersen DEN 3,70
3. Edwin Myers USA 3,60

Long Jump
1. William Pettersson SWE 7,15
2. Carl Johnson USA 7,095
3. Erik Abrahamsson SWE 7,08

Triple Jump
1. Vilho Tuulos FIN 14,505
2. Folke Jansson SWE 14,48
3. Erik Almlöf SWE 14,27

Shotput
1. Ville Pörhölä FIN 14,81
2. Elmer Niklander FIN 14,155
3. Harry Liversedge USA 14,15

Discus Throw
1. Elmer Niklander FIN 44,685
2. Armas Taipale FIN 44,19
3. Augustus Pope USA 42,13

Hammer Throw
1. Patrick Ryan USA 52,875
2. Carl Johan Lind SWE 48,43
3. Basil Bennet USA 48,25

Javelin
1. Jonni Myyrä FIN 65,78
2. Urho Peltonen FIN 63,50
3. Pekka Johansson FIN 63,095

Decathlon
1. Helge Lövland NOR 6803,355
2. Brutus Hamilton USA 6771,085
3. Bertil Ohlson SWE 6580,030

300 M Team (1912, 1920, 1924 only)
1. Great Britain
2. Sweden
3. Sweden

Cross Country Individual approx. 8,000 M (1912, 1920, 1924 only)
1. Paavo Nurmi FIN 27:15,0
2. Erik Backman SWE 27:17,6
3. Heikki Limatainen FIN 27:37,4

Cross Country Team approx. 8000 M (1904, 1912, 1920, 1924 only)
1. Finland
2. Great Britain
3. Sweden

Pentathlon (1906, 1912, 1920, 1924 only)
1. Eero Lehtonen FIN
2. Everett Bradley USA
3. Hugo Lahtinen FIN

56 lb. Weight Throw (1904 and 1920 only)
1. Patrick MacDonald USA 11,265
2. Patrick Ryan USA 10,965
3. Carl Johan Lind SWE 10,25

Tug-of-War (1900, 1904, 1906, 1912, 1920 only
1. Great Britain
2. Netherlands
3. Belgium

3000 M Walk (1906 and 1920 only)
1. Ugo Frigerio ITA
2. George Parker AUS
3. Richard Frederick Remer USA

10,000 M Walk (1912 and 1920 only)
1. Ugo Frigerio ITA 48:06,2
2. Joseph Pearman USA
3. Charles Gunn GBR

Men Swimming

100 M Freestyle
1. Duke Paoa Kahanamoku USA 1:01,4
2. Pua Keloa Kealoha USA 1:02,2
3. William Harris USA 1:03,0

400 m Freestyle
1. Norman Ross USA 5:26,8
2. Ludy Langer USA 5:29,0
3. George Vernot CAN 5:29,6

1500 M Freestyle
1. Norman Ross USA 22:23,2
2. George Vernot CAN 22:36,4
3. Frank Beaurepaire AUS 23:04,4

100 M Backstroke
1. Warren Paoa Kealoha USA 1:15,2
2. Ray Kegeris USA 1:16,2
3. Gérard Blitz BEL 1:19,0

200 M Breastroke
1. Hakan Malmroth SWE 3:04,4
2. Thor Henning SWE 3:09,2
3. Arvo Aaltonen FIN 3:12,2

800 M Freestyle Relay
1. USA 10:04,4 (Perry MacGillivray, Pua Kela Kealoha, Norman Ross, Duke Paoa Kahanamoku)
2. AUS 10:25,4 (Henry Hay, William Herald, Ivan Stedman, Franck Beaurepaire)
3. GBR 10:37,2 (Leslie Savage, E. Percy Peter, Henry Taylor, Harold E. Annison)

Springboard Diving
1. Louis Kuehn USA 675,4
2. Clarence Pinkston USA 655,3
3. Louis Balbach USA 649,5

High Diving
1. Clarence Pinkston USA 100,67
2. Erik Adlerz SWE 99,08
3. Harry Prieste USA 93,73

Plain High Dive (1912, 1920, 1924 only)
1. Arvid Wallman SWE 183.5
2. Nils Skoglund SWE 183,0
3. John Jansson SWE 175,0

400 M Breaststroke (1904, 1912, 1920 only)

Water Polo
1. Great Britain
2. Belgium
3. Sweden

Women Swimming

100 M Freestyle
1. Ethelda Bleibtrey USA 1:13,5
2. Irene Guest USA 1:17,0
3. Frances Schroth USA 1:17,2

400 M Freestyle
1. Ethelda Bleibtrey USA 4:34,0
2. Margaret Woodbridge USA 4:42,8
3. Frances Schroth USA 4:52,0

M Freestyle Relay
1. USA 5:11,6 (Margaret Woodbridge, Frances Schroth, Irene Guest, Ethelda Bleibtrey)
2. GBR 5:40,8 (Hilda Janes, Constance Mabel Jeans, Charlotte Radeliffe, Grace McKensie)
3. SWE 5:43,6 (Aina Berg, Emy Machnow, Karin Nilsson, Jane Gylling)

Springboard Diving
1. Aileen Riggin USA 539,9
2. Helen Wainwright USA 534,8
3. Thelma Payne USA 534,1

High Diving
1. Stefani Fryland-Clausen DEN 34,6
2. Eileen Armstrong GBR 33,3
3. Eva Ollivier SWE 33,3

(tennis and shooting not listed)

Boxing

Flyweight
1. Frank Genaro USA
2. Anders Petersen DEN
3. William Cuthbertson GRB

Bantamweight
1. Clarence Walter SAF
2. Chris J. Graham CAN
3. James MacKenzie GBR

Featherweight
1. Paul Fritsch FRA
2. Jean Gachet FRA
3. Edouardo Garzena ITA

Lightweight
1. Samuel Mosberg USA
2. Gotfred Johansen DEN
3. Clarence "Chris" Newton CAN

Welterweight
1. Albert "Bert" Schneider CAN
2. Alexander Ireland GBR
3. Frederick Colberg USA

Middleweight
1. Harry Mallin GBR
2. Georges Arthur Prud'Homme CAN
3. Moe H. Herscovitch CAN

Light Heavyweight
1. Edward Eagan USA
2. Sverre Sörsdal NOR
3. H. Franks GBR

Heavyweight
1. Ronald Rawson GBR
2. Sören Patersen DEN
3. Xavier Eluére FRA

Greco Roman Wrestling

Featherweight
1. Oskari Friman FIN
2. Heikki Köhkönen FIN
3. Frithiof Svensson SWE

Lightweight
1. Eemil Väre FIN
2. Taavi Tamminen FIN
3. Frithjof Andersen NOR

Middleweight
1. Carl Westergren SWE
2. Artur Lindfors FIN
3. Matti Pertilä FIN

Light Heavyweight
1. Claes Johansson SWE
2. Edil Rosenqvist FIN
3. Johannes Eriksen DAN

Heavyweight
1. Adolf Lindfors FIN
2. Poul Hansen DEN
3. Marti Nieminen FIN

Freestyle Wrestling

Featherweight
1. Charles Edwin Ackerly USA
2. Samuel Gerson USA
3. P.W. Bernard GBR

Lighweight
1. Kalle Anttila FIN
2. Gottfrid Svensson SWE
3. Peter Wright GBR

Middleweight
1. Eino Leino FIN
2. Vainö Penttala FIN
3. Charles Johnson USA

Light-Heavyweight
1. Anders Larsson SWE
2. Charles Courant SUI
3. Walter Maurer USA

Heavyweight
1. Robert Roth SUI
2. Nathan Pendleton USA
3. Ernst Nilsson SWE

Men Fencing

Foil Individual
1. Nedo Nadi ITA 10
2. Philippe Cattiau FRA 9/14
3. Roger Ducret FRA 9/19

Foil Team
1. Italy
2. France
3. USA

Epée Individual
1. Armand Massard FRA 9
2. Alexandre Lippmann FRA 7
3. Gustave Buchard FRA 6

Epée Team
1. Italy
2. Belgium
3. France

Sabre Individual
1. Nedo Nadi ITA 11
2. Aldo Nadi ITA 9
3. Adrianus E. W. de Jong HOL 7

Sabre Team
1. Italy
2. France
3. Netherlands

CHART

Weightlifting

			Snatch, One Arm	Clean and Jerk, One Arm	Clean and Jerk, Two Arm	Total
	Featherweight					
1.	Frans de Haes	BEL	60,0	65,0	95,0	220,0
2.	Alfred Schmidt	EST	55,0	65,0	92,5	212,5
3.	Eugéne Ryther	SWE	55,0	65,0	90,0	210,0
	Lightweight					
1.	Alfred Neuland	EST	72,5	75,0	110,0	257,5
2.	Louis Williquet	BEL	60,0	75,0	105,0	240,0
3.	Florimond Rooms	BEL	55,0	70,0	105,0	230,0
	Middleweight					
1.	Henri Gance	FRA	65,0	75,0	105,0	245,0
2.	Pietro Bianchi	ITA	60,0	70,0	107,5	237,5
3.	Albert Pettersson	SWE	55,0	75,0	107,5	237,5
	Light Heavyweight					
1.	Ernest Cadine	FRA	70,0	85,0	135,0	290,0
2.	Fritz Hünenberger	SUI	75,0	85,0	115,0	275,0
3.	Erik Pettersson	SWE	62,5	92,5	117,5	272,5
	Heavyweight					
1,	Filippo Bottino	ITA	70,0	85,0	115,0	270,0
2.	Joseph Alzin	LUX	65,0	80,0	110,0	255,0
3.	Louis Bernot	FRA	65,0	75,0	110,0	250,0

Modern Pentathlon Individual

1. Gustav Dyrssen SWE
2. Erik de Laval SWE
3. Gösta Runö SWE

Rowing

Single Sculls
1. John Kelly sen. USA 7:35,0
2. Jack Beresford jun. GBR 7:36,0
3. D. Clarence Hadfield d'Acy NZE 7:48,8

Double Sculls
1. USA 7:09,0
2. Italy 7:19,0
3. France 7:21,0

Pairs with Coxswain
1. Italy 7:56,0
2. France 7:57,0
3. Suitzerland

Fours with Coxswain
1. Switzerland 6:54,0
2. USA 6:58,0
3. Norway 7:02,0

Eight Oars
1. USA 6:02,6
2. Great Britain 6:05,0
3. Norway 6:36,0

Yachting

Finn Monotype Class 12 ft
1. Netherlands *Beatrijs III*
2. Netherlands *Boreas*

Finn Monotype Class 18 ft.
1. Great Britain *Brat*

6 M Class (1908, 1912, 1920, 1924, 1928, 1932, 1936, 1948, 1952 only)
1. Norway *Jo*
2. Belgium *Tan-Fe-Pah*

6 M Class 1907 Rating (1920 only)
1. Belium *Edelweis*
2. Norway *Mami*
3. Norway *Stella*

6.5 M Class 1919 rating (1920 only)
1. Netherlands *Oranje*
2. France *Rose Pompon*

7 M Class (1908 and 1920 only)
1. Great Britain *Ancora*

8 M Class (1908, 1912, 1920, 1924, 1928, 1932, 1936 only)
1. Norway *Sildra*
2. Norway *Lyn*
3. Belgium *Antwerpia*

8 M Class rating 1907 (1920 only)
1. Norway *Ierne*
2. Norway *Fornebo*

10 M Class 1919 rating (1920 only)
1. Norway *Mosk II*

10 M Class 1907 rating (1920 only)
1. Norway *Eleda*

12 M Class rating 1919 (1920 only)
1. Norway *Atlanta*

12 M Class rating 1919 (1920 only)
1. Norway *Keira II*

30M² (1920 only)
1. Sweden *Kublan*

40M² (1920 only)
1. Sweden *Sif*
2. Sweden *Elsie*

Cycling

Individual Road Race
1. Harry Stenqvist SWE 4:40:01,8
2. Henry Justaves Kaltenbrun SAF 4:41:26,6
3. Fernand Canteloube FRA 4:42:54,4

Team Road Race (1912, 1920, 1924, 1928, 1936, 1948, 1952, 1956 only)
1. France 19:16:43,2
2. Sweden 19:23:10,0
3. Belgium 19:28:44,4

1000 M Sprint
1. Maurice Peeters HOL 1:38,3
2. Thomas Johnson GBR (one wheel)
3. Harry Ryan GBR

2000 M Tandem
1. Great Britain 2:49,4
2. South Africa
3. Netherlands

Team Pursuit Race 4000 M
1. Italy 5:20,0
2. Great Britain
3. South Africa

50 Km. Track Race (1920 and 1924)
1. Henri Goerge BEL 1:16,43,2
2. Cyril Albert Alden GBR
3. Piet Ikelaar HOL

Equestrian Sports

Individual All-around Competition
1. Helmer Mörner SWE 1775,00
2. Age Lundström SWE 1738,75
3. Ettore Caffaratti ITA 1733,75

Team All-round Competition
1. Sweden 5057,50
2. Italy 4735,00
3. Belgium 4560,00

Individual Dressage
1. Janne Lundblad SWE 27,937
2. Bertil Sandqtröm SWE 26,312
3. Hans von Rosen SWE 25,125

Individual Grand Prix Jumping
1. Tommaso Lequio ITA -2
2. Alessandro Valerio ITA -3
3. C. Gustaf Lewenhaupt SWE -4

Grand Prix Jumping
1. Sweden -14
2. Belgium -16,25
3. Italy -18,75

Individual Figure Riding
1. Bouckaert BEL 30,5
2. Fiel FRA 29,5
3. Finet BEL 29,0

Team Figure Riding
1. Belgium
2. France
3. Sweden

Gymnastics

Individual All-round Competition
1. Giorgio Zampori ITA 88,35
2. Marco Torrès FRA 87,62
3. Jean Gounot FRA 87,45

Team All-around Competotop,
1. Italy 359,855
2. Belgium 346,785
3. France 340,100

Free System Team (choice of apparatus and exercises) (by team only 1920)
1. Denmark
2. Norway

Soccer

1. Belgium
2. Spain
3. Netherlands

Field Hockey

1. Great Britain
2. Denmark
3. Belgium

(See Table of Contents for abbreviations)

1920

SEPTEMBER

Su	Mo	Tu	We	Th	Fr	Sa
			1	2	3	4
5	6	7	8	9	10	11
12	13	14	15	16	17	18
19	20	21	22	23	24	25
26	27	28	29	30		

1. Dry agents hit 50 saloons in first major N.Y.C. bust (→ 11/13).

1. France proclaims Lebanon an independent nation.

1. Gabriele d'Annunzio declares Fiume an independent state (→ 11/12).

2. New York: 3,000 Brooklyn longshoremen refuse to unload British ships until troops leave Ireland (→ 30).

5. Marion, Ohio: Harding promises, if elected, to seek revision of Versailles treaty so U.S. can join League (→ 11/4).

5. Comedian Roscoe "Fatty" Arbuckle accused of raping and murdering Virginia Rappe at Calif. party (→ 4/12/22).

6. Michigan: Jack Dempsey holds onto heavyweight crown, knocking out Billy Miske in third round at Benton Harbor.

6. New York: "Big Bill" Tilden wins National Tennis Championship at Forest Hills.

6. Italy: German, Italian envoys meet at Stresa.

9. Italian earthquakes leave 500 dead, 20,000 homeless.

11. Italy paralyzed by strikes; workers seizing industrial plants in Milan.

12. Peking reports 40 million Chinese now threatened by famine (→ 3/19/21).

15. Japanese Ambassador Shidehara begins formal negotiations with Sacramento on anti-Japanese California laws.

20. League of Nations Council authorizes Belgium's annexation of Eupen and Malmedy (→ 2/5/21).

23. Peking refuses recognition to czarist representatives; Russian residents in China imperiled.

29. U.S. Atty. Gen. Palmer orders inquiry into profiteering in construction materials.

30. French government takes mandate for Togo.

30. Irish President Eamonn de Valera rejects Grey's plan for full Irish independence, withdrawal of British troops (→ 10/17).

Scandal rocks baseball

Sept 28. Major league baseball has been shaken to its foundations by the indictment of eight Chicago White Sox players on charges that they had conspired with gamblers to fix the 1919 World Series.

Those indicted were "Shoeless" Joe Jackson, left fielder; Eddie Cicotte, star pitcher; Hap Felsch, center fielder; Swede Risberg, shortstop; Buck Weaver, third baseman; Arnold Gandil, former first baseman; Lefty Williams, pitcher; and Fred McMullin, utility player.

The indictments were based on evidence obtained for the Cook County grand jury by Charles A. Comiskey, owner of the White Sox, who immediately suspended the seven players still with the team. If convicted, they face up to five years in prison. Grand jury officials reveal that Cicotte and Jackson have confessed to their part in the fix. Cicotte admits receiving $10,000 for throwing two games and Jackson says he received $3,000 of $20,000 promised by the gamblers.

"Shoeless" Joe Jackson.

On his way out of court recently, Jackson met up with a young fan with tears in his eyes, who cried, "Say it ain't so, Joe." But it is (→ 10/29).

Bomb kills 30, injures 300 on Wall Street

Sept 16. An explosion, believed to have been caused by a time bomb, ripped through the Wall Street financial district today, killing 30 persons and injuring 300 others. The blast shattered windows for blocks around, threw the financial district into panic, and strewed the streets in the immediate vicinity with the bodies of the dead and injured.

Authorities believed the explosion was caused by a time bomb left on a one-horse wagon directly across the street from the J.P. Morgan Building. Law enforcement officials theorized the explosion was set off by Reds or anarchists. William J. Flynn, chief of the Justice Department's Bureau of Investigation, said that he believed the bombing was the work of a plot by Italian terrorists (→ 10/19).

Crowds mill about a dead horse, one of the bomb's inadvertent victims.

Notable life ends for Jacob Schiff

Sept 25. Heart disease ended 73 years of remarkable life, as Jacob H. Schiff died last night, leaving an estate of $50 million and mourners the world over. Schiff left his native Germany for America in 1865 at the age of 18 and began work as a bank clerk. Before the age of 50, he was hailed as one of the world's most constructive financiers as well as an idealist who hated suffering. His numerous and worldwide philanthropies include the endowment of the Jewish Theological Seminary, the Montefiore Home for Incurables, both in New York, and a museum at Harvard. However, much of his aid to institutions and individuals was made anonymously.

Jacob Schiff, banker.

Urban population exceeds rural in U.S.

Sept 30. How can you keep them down on the farm? A new census report shows the urban population exceeds the rural in the United States. And Chicago, New York and other cities are growing 7.5 times faster than rural areas.

The cities teem with young people dissatisfied with small-town life. Theater, motion picture houses and good-paying jobs are not found back home. New immigrants, Italians, Greeks and Poles, also prefer the intimacy of urban life.

Yet the unforeseen growth poses problems: housing shortages, lack of sewage treatment, the spread of disease. Crime festers in the cracks of the decaying tenements. And where can food for the urban millions come from? From the farmer still down home.

1920

OCTOBER

Su	Mo	Tu	We	Th	Fr	Sa
					1	2
3	4	5	6	7	8	9
10	11	12	13	14	15	16
17	18	19	20	21	22	23
24	25	26	27	28	29	30
31						

1. Peking revokes Soviet concessions in China.

2. U.S. Marines clash with Haitian rebels, killing leader.

5. Hamburg, Germany: Fire destroys Bismarck, world's largest liner.

9. Liner Aquitania arrives in U.S. with record bullion shipment, $18.5 million in loan payment.

10. Referendum makes Karntern a part of Austria.

12. Jersey City: Georges Carpentier takes world middleweight crown, knocking out Levinsky; 50 spectators hurt.

12. Cleveland: Indians defeat Brooklyn Robins to win World Series.

13. Evidence surfaces implicating U.S. Marines in unlawful killing of Haitians during five-year occupation.

14. Soviets acknowledge Finnish independence.

14. Italy: Fascists set fire to Socialist newspaper office in Trieste.

15. First contract intl. airmail route, linking Seattle and Victoria, B.C., awarded to Eddie Hubbard in Boeing B-1.

16. One million miners strike in Great Britain.

17. Cork, Ireland: Michael Fitzgerald, after 68-day fast, becomes first hunger striker to die in prison (→ 25).

19. N.Y. judge rules membership in Communist Party sufficient grounds for deportation (→ 12/28).

23. Pittsburgh: Andrew Carnegie's estate appraised at $23,247,161.

25. Lord Mayor of Cork Terence MacSwiney dies in London prison after 74-day fast.→

29. Chicago Grand jury indicts 13 more in baseball scandal.

31. New York: 40,000 demonstrate in tribute to late mayor of Cork (→ 11/21).

DEATH

25. Greek King Alexander I, from pet monkey bite (*7/20/1893).

Poles smash Russians, agree on armistice

Oct 6. An armistice between Warsaw and Moscow has been signed as part of the fundamental preliminaries of a peace package. The agreement comes on the heels of last Sunday's awesome victory by Polish troops over 16 Russian Bolshevist divisions. The Soviet collapse saw 42,000 men and thousands of weapons seized by Polish forces personally commanded by President Pilsudski.

Remaining Red divisions retreated—demoralized, suffering from hunger, cold and desertion. The Soviet government, sensing defeat, had forced contributions for its military men. "Let everyone who has two coats, two pairs of boots, two fur caps, give one and save the soldiers from perishing from cold," read the order.

The terms of peace include full recognition of Polish independence and sovereignty, a return of Polish national treasures and a halt to Bolshevik propaganda in Poland. Additionally, a boundary was drawn based on ethnographic lines cutting off Lithuania from Russia. It begins to the east of Dvinsk and runs south through Baranovitchi to the Rumanian border (→ 11/16).

Polish volunteers line up for review.

Million miners strike for 2-shilling raise

Oct 18. An otherwise peaceful London parade of some 5,000 unemployed turned into a riot just two days after one million coal miners laid down their tools. Heading the procession were the mayors of 15 London boroughs on their way to interview the Prime Minister. When the police let them pass but drew a cordon against the paraders, a struggle ensued resembling a football scrimmage in which 22 policemen were injured.

The striking miners demand a two-shilling raise and one million other miners may strike before the week's end. Coupled with dockers out of work due to no coal, a possible railroad strike by transport and railroad workers, and 200,000 demobilized, unemployed soldiers, Britain's postwar recovery faces one of the greatest industrial upheavals in the country's history.

Strikers and jobless are dispersed by charging British police.

Cork's Mayor dies after 74-day fast

Oct 25. Terence MacSwiney, Lord Mayor of Cork and a leader of the Republican Army in Ireland, died today in Brixton Prison following a 74-day hunger strike. MacSwiney began his hunger strike as a protest against a sentence by a British military court to a two-year imprisonment on charges of possessing seditious documents and speeches. His death, which had been expected for several days, prompted an outpouring of protests. Last week, Michael Fitzgerald became the first hunger striker to die in jail (→ 31).

Terence MacSwiney's funeral.

Young John Reed is dead; hero in Russia

Oct 20. John Reed, the poet-journalist best known for writing "Ten Days That Shook the World," died of typhus yesterday in Moscow. He would have been 33 tomorrow.

After graduating from Harvard in 1910, Reed went to work for American Magazine, where he developed a strong interest in social reform. A series of articles he wrote on Pancho Villa and the Mexican Revolution in 1914 earned him national fame as a reporter. In 1917, he married Louise Bryant and together they traveled to Russia to cover the Bolshevik Revolution.

After the revolution, Reed returned to the United States and published "Ten Days That Shook the World," his partisan, eyewitness account. He also helped found the Communist Labor Party, but in 1919, facing charges of sedition, he returned to Russia, where he had been lecturing when he died. His remains will rest in Red Square.

1920

NOVEMBER

Su	Mo	Tu	We	Th	Fr	Sa
	1	2	3	4	5	6
7	8	9	10	11	12	13
14	15	16	17	18	19	20
21	22	23	24	25	26	27
28	29	30				

1. Turks take town of Hadjin, massacre 10,000 Armenians (→ 14).

2. Pittsburgh: KDKA, first commercial radio station in U.S., begins weekly broadcasts.

3. Germans rejoice in Wilson's defeat (→ 4).

4. Marion, Ohio: Pres.-elect Harding pronounces League of Nations deceased (→ 11).

7. Atlanta: Socialist leader Eugene Debs, imprisoned for espionage, says he wouldn't want to be free under present chaotic conditions (→ 12/28).

7. Rabbis Silverman and Schulman denounce rise of anti-Semitism in U.S., accuse Henry Ford of libeling Jews.

9. Vatican: Pope Benedict bans film "The Holy Bible" for nude representations of Adam and Eve.

11. Texas: Harding, in Brownsville speech, declares U.S. fought war to protect American rights, not to make world safe for democracy (→ 15).

12. Mexican official presses U.S. to recognize Mexican govt. in order to stem growth of Bolshevism in Mexico.

12. Italy, Yugoslavia sign treaty; Fiume to be free state (→ 12/1).

14. Armenians evacuating own capital as Turks move in (→ 18).

15. 41 nations raise flags in Geneva as League of Nations opens first regular session (→ 12/8).

16. Stamford, Conn.: Metered mail born with setting of first Pitney Bowes postage meter.

18. Constantinople overrun with Armenian refugees as 140,000 arrive from Crimea (→ 12/9).

20. Polo Grounds: Navy defeats Army 7-0.

21. Ireland: British troops open fire on crowd at Crow Park (→ 12/14).

22. Du Pont and Morgan gain controlling interest in General Motors.

27. A.F.L. opens campaign for two-year ban on immigration, citing two million jobless.

Harding and Coolidge defeat Democrats

President-elect Harding (left) and his wife, with his V.P. and Mrs. Coolidge.

Nov 2. Warren G. Harding, an Ohio newspaper publisher, was elected President yesterday as Republicans swept to near-record victories throughout much of the nation. The big Republican triumph came on Harding's 55th birthday.

Senator Harding and his vice-presidential running mate, Governor Calvin Coolidge of Massachusetts, piled up victories even in the home precincts of their Democratic opponents, Governor James M. Cox of Ohio and Assistant Navy Secretary Franklin D. Roosevelt, as well as carrying such traditionally Democratic strongholds as Boston.

As president, Harding will be working with a Congress to his own liking, for Republicans also piled up heavy majorities yesterday in both the Senate and the House of Representatives. President Wilson heard only the early election returns. He retired at 9 p.m., which is his usual bedtime.

Counter-revolt ends with Wrangel debacle

Nov 16. The last vestige of protest against the Bolshevik regime has ended with the resounding defeat of the troops of counterrevolutionary leader Count Peter Wrangel. The battle at Crimea between the Reds and Whites was a desperate one. Wrangel's outnumbered troops survived 22 assaults, but ultimately collapsed after 30,000 were killed and 40,000 captured. The Bolsheviks have given Wrangel's forces eight days to evacuate. There is panic in the Crimea, which has been a base for the Whites (→ 2/9/21).

Gen. Wrangel, exiled to Turkey.

Medieval-like Red warrior.

Gaston Chevrolet drives his last race

Nov 25. A fiery crash on the Los Angeles Speedway has taken the life of Gaston Chevrolet, the noted auto racing driver, in competition for the title of "Speed King of the Year." Chevrolet, at 28 the youngest of three racing brothers, was born in France and came to America in 1901. Also killed was Lyall Jolls, mechanic for Eddie O'Donnell, whose car crashed with Chevrolet's near the finish of the 250-mile grind. O'Donnell was seriously hurt.

Chevrolet won the Indy 500 this year.

Dry agents invade while teams play

Nov 13. While Princeton and Yale were locked in gridiron combat, federal Prohibition agents quietly raided two nearby hotels and arrested seven persons. The Nassau Inn, a landmark known to all Princeton grads, and another hostelry, the Nassau House, were targets of the raids. No intoxicants were found at the Nassau Inn, but agents said they had been informed that liquor had been sold there. The proprietor and two waiters were promptly arrested. And a barrel of whiskey was found at Princeton House (→ 10/21/21).

Yale and Princeton battle it out.

1920

DECEMBER

Su	Mo	Tu	We	Th	Fr	Sa
			1	2	3	4
5	6	7	8	9	10	11
12	13	14	15	16	17	18
19	20	21	22	23	24	25
26	27	28	29	30	31	

1. D'Annunzio declares war on Italy from Fiume (→ 31).

7. Wilson gives last annual message to Congress, urging U.S. to set democratic example for world.

8. Wilson declines to send representative to League meeting in Geneva (→ 15).

9. Armenia greatly reduced in size by peace treaty with Turkey (→ 3/15/21).

14. N.Y.: Dempsey KOs Brennen in heavyweight title bout.

14. Geneva: League creates credit system to aid Europe; U.S. export trade threatened.

15. Geneva: China wins place on League Council; Austria admitted (→ 4/12/21).

18. Ty Cobb becomes manager of Detroit Tigers.

19. Athens: King Constantine returns on mandate of referendum.

28. "Uncle Joe" Cannon sets congressional record, celebrating 44 years in House.

28. U.S. resumes deportation of Communists (→ 4/4/21).

CULTURAL EVENTS, 1920

Literature: F. Scott Fitzerald's "This Side of Paradise"; Sinclair Lewis' "Main Street"; H.G. Wells' "Outline of History"; Edith Wharton's "The Age of Innocence"; Eugene O'Neill's "The Emperor Jones," "Beyond the Horizon," Pulitzer Prize for drama; Norwegian Knut Hamsen, Nobel Prize.

Academia: Adler's "The Practice and Theory of Individual Psychology"; Santayana's "Character and Opinion in the United States"; B. Russell's "The Theory and Practice of Bolshevism."

Music: Gustav Holst's "The Planets," in London; Camille Saint-Saens festival in Athens.

The Arts: Matisse's "L'Odalisque"; visitors allowed to smash paintings at Dada exhibit in Cologne.

Film: "The Cabinet of Dr. Caligari"; Chaplin's "The Kid"; Marcel Duchamps' first abstract films.

Ireland is partitioned

Troops controlling protesters in Dublin late last month.

Dec 14. The British House of Lords has approved a division of Ireland into two separate territories. Under the Government of Ireland Act, they will each have a parliament and an administration.

The Northern Parliament will represent Antrim, Armagh, Down, Fermanagh, Londonderry and Tyrone. The six counties have a Protestant majority. The Southern Parliament, representing a Catholic majority, will be located in Dublin. Communal interests will be handled by a new Council of Ireland, and both parts of the country will continue to be represented in the British Parliament. Politicians in the South have already said they oppose the new law (→ 1/23/21).

Man o' War retiring with only one loss

Dec 31. Man o' War, winner of 20 of his 21 career races, has been retired to stud. Though raced for only two seasons, Man o' War won a quarter of a million dollars, almost twice the sum won by any other horse. He won the Preakness and Belmont but did not compete in the Kentucky Derby. His only loss was to a horse appropriately named Upset, at Saratoga in 1919. Clarence Kummer was his jockey.

Man o' War winning the Dwyer Stakes at Aqueduct earlier this year.

Woodrow Wilson wins Peace Prize

Dec 10. Tonight Woodrow Wilson was awarded the Nobel Peace Prize in Christiana, Norway, for his work restoring a war-torn Europe to peace. It is a bittersweet moment for the president. He suffered a stroke in September 1919 that has left him partially paralyzed. American participation in the League of Nations, epitome of his peace-seeking ideals, was rejected by the Senate in March. In the recent election, a referendum on the League, his vision was badly defeated by Republican Warren G. Harding.

The small nations of the world are grateful to Wilson. The self-rule they enjoy now is due in large part to his personal lobbying at the peace conference at Versailles.

D'Annunzio cedes Fiume to Italy

Dec 31. Gabriele d'Annunzio has finally admitted defeat in his long occupation of Fiume. Italy's poet-soldier took over Fiume in September 1919 to keep the Adriatic port from becoming a "free city" as decided by the peace conference. At first the Italian government was reluctant to take action against the popular hero. However, Italy's desire to ratify the Rapallo Treaty with the Yugoslavs forced it to act against d'Annunzio (→ 1/27/24).

John Barrymore plays "Richard III" in New York.

1921

JANUARY

Su	Mo	Tu	We	Th	Fr	Sa
						1
2	3	4	5	6	7	8
9	10	11	12	13	14	15
16	17	18	19	20	21	22
23	24	25	26	27	28	29
30	31					

1. Pasadena: California trounces Ohio St. 28-0 in the Rose Bowl.

2. Spain: Liner Santa Isabel sinks off coast of Villa Garcia; 254 missing.

3. Italy halts issue of passports to those emigrating to U.S.

3. India's first Parliament convenes (→ 10/8).

4. Congress overrides Wilson's veto, reactivating War Finance Corp. to aid struggling farmers.

5. France: Wagner's "Die Walkyrie" opens, first German opera performed in Paris since war began.

6. Berlin: Out of 485,000 children, 29,000 reported ill with tuberculosis, 77,000 suffer from other disease, 12,000 underfed.

6. U.S. Navy orders sale of 125 flying boats to encourage commercial aviation.

13. Prima donna Mary Garden named director of Chicago Opera Association.

14. Great Britain reports 927,000 on jobless rolls.

15. U.S.: Bread prices return to five cents a loaf for first time since war.

17. Holland threatens to deport kaiser's family for suspected plot to invade Germany.

20. General strike begins in Austria.

21. New York: J.D. Rockefeller pledges $1 million for relief of Europe's destitute (→ 22).

22. U.S.: Midwest farmers give 15 million bushels of corn to Hoover for European relief.

23. Dublin: Eight killed in Sinn Fein revolt (→ 2/18).

24. Switzerland issues injunction barring import of foreign labor.

25. Washington: Employment Dept. reports 3.5 million unemployed in U.S. (→ 2/24).

28. Einstein startles Berlin, suggesting possibility of measuring universe (→ 4/2).

DEATH

1. Theobald von Bethmann Hollweg, German ex-chancellor (*11/29/1856).

Allies open talks on German war payments

Jan 24. In Paris, the Allies have decided how much Germany should pay in war reparations. The bottom line is nearly $56 billion, spread over 42 years. In addition, Germany would be forced to pay a 12.5 percent tax on her exports.

Germany was not represented at the meetings in Paris, but they were contentious nonetheless. There were sharp disagreements between French Premier Briand and British Prime Minister Lloyd George. At one point, Lloyd George was so upset about French demands for larger reparations that he refused to leave his suite at the Hotel Crillon.

Briand wanted more than reparations from Germany. He also demanded that Germany share profits from her new prosperity as she rebuilds from the war. The tax on exports was a concession to the French premier's demand.

German negotiators are likely to resist paying stiff reparations. If Germany fails to pay, the Allies threatened to seize German customs, keep troops in the Rhineland and reoccupy the Ruhr.

The Allies' financial experts have figured that Germany can cover half the cost of the reparations by reductions in the military budget and elimination of royal stipends. But the German mark is devaluating so quickly that one correspondent in Paris says that trying to collect the reparations is "like shooting at the moon" (→ 2/5).

French unknown soldier is buried

Jan 28. France honored its fallen war heroes today. At 8:00 a.m., as Parisians walked to work on the Champs Elysees, a solemn ceremony was taking place at the top of the avenue. Soldiers stood at attention in the cold morning light as a simple wooden casket was carried beneath the Arc de Triomphe. Inside was the body of a French soldier, his name unknown. "Vive la France," an official cried, and men tipped their hats. The body was lowered into the earth and a perpetual flame was lit. The Arc de Triomphe, built to commemorate Napoleon's glory, now honors the heroes of another war (→ 11/11).

Europe hit by hunger and unemployment

Jan 31. The war in Europe has been over for 18 months, but the list of victims is still growing day by day. Millions have lost their jobs, and women and children are hungry and starving. Americans are rushing to their aid.

John D. Rockefeller Jr. contributed a million dollars to the cause after Herbert Hoover, head of the American Relief Administration, made a dramatic appeal to the Young Men's Bible Class.

"Peace itself is not made by documents," Hoover said. "Peace is made by good will among men." Hoover is trying to raise $33 million for the hungry of Europe.

Midwest farmers are also responding to Hoover's call for help. They have agreed to donate 15 million bushels of corn. The farmers said, "We will market our surplus corn in relief and take our pay in good will." Hoover is also looking for donations of milk and cocoa.

Teachers are failing

Jan 16. Little dignity and low pay have resulted in too few and poorly trained teachers, falling below the standards of every other civilized country, claimed Joseph H. Defrees, President of the Chamber of Commerce of the United States, in a speech to the National Educational Association today. Some 450,000 children have no or, at best, overcrowded classrooms. And of the 600,000 teachers in the country, 100,000 are under 21 years of age, 30,000 have no education beyond eighth grade and 150,000 lack education beyond the third year of high school. This situation must change, Defrees said.

Fairbanks appears in "The Mark of Zorro"

January. "The Mark of Zorro," Douglas Fairbanks' 30th film, may prove his most popular, and maybe the most popular picture ever. On the day of its premiere last December 11, a record number of patrons, 19,547, paid a record sum, $11,708, to see it. And police even had to be summoned to calm the crowds.

Douglas Fairbanks (right), as popular in swashbuckling adventures as in his earlier farcical comedies.

"Zorro" stands out from Fairbanks' other works and from film's present trends. The actor has always played the American hero, as in "The Good Bad Man" and "His Picture in the Papers." But here, Fairbanks portrays a Spanish baron in colonial California, wielding a foil and branding his enemies with a "Z." Now it is hard to imagine him as anything but a foreigner.

"Zorro" is also the first successful costume picture made in years. All of a sudden, the public longs for capes, masks and swords. And the public wants to know everything about Fairbanks. The 37-year-old actor obliges, having already published his autobiography. Raised in Denver, Colorado, as Douglas Elton Ulman, Fairbanks now lives in Beverly Hills with his wife, Mary Pickford, at their home, "Pickfair."

1921

FEBRUARY

Su	Mo	Tu	We	Th	Fr	Sa
		1	2	3	4	5
6	7	8	9	10	11	12
13	14	15	16	17	18	19
20	21	22	23	24	25	26
	28	29				

1. The Cub, revolutionary new Napier aircraft engine undergoes successful tests in London.

2. Airmail service opens between N.Y. and San Francisco (→ 23).

8. Budapest denounces U.S. for deporting undesirable aliens to Hungary (→ 9).

9. Washington: House Immigration Committee charges Ellis Island has admitted 10,000 undesirable immigrants (→ 16).

9. Russo-Polish conflict ends with signing of Riga treaty; Poles give up Ukraine.

12. London: Winston Churchill appointed colonial secretary (→).

13. Polish ex-Premier Ignace Paderewski arrives in U.S., announces retirement as pianist.

16. U.S. suspends immigration from Central Europe due to typhus threat (→ 10/3).

17. U.S. reports nine mil. autos driven here in 1920 (→ 19).

19. U.S. Red Cross reports 20,000 children die yearly in auto accidents.

20. Persian Gen. Reza Khan occupies Tehran, ousts govt.

21. London: Allies open intl. conference on Near East; talks to center on Greco-Turkish border disputes (→ 6/19).

23. Airmail plane sets record, S.F. to N.Y. in 33 hrs., 20 min.

24. Herbert Hoover becomes U.S. Sec. of Commerce (→ 9/26).

25. Mongolia: Living Buddha Hutuktu crowned king, claims autonomy from China (→ 7/10).

26. Costa Rican troops invade Panama (→ 7/14).

26. Soviet Russia recognizes political and territorial integrity of Persia and Afghanistan.

26. Italian Fascists incite riots in Florence (→ 5/14).

28. Sailors start Kronstadt anti-Bolshevik movement (→ 3/18).

BIRTH

4. Betty Friedan, American feminist leader.

DEATH

8. Prince Kropotkin, Russian anarchist (*12/21/1842).

De Valera leads Irish revolt against British

Soldiers disperse protesting Dubliners with the help of armored trucks.

Feb 18. The leader of the Irish independence movement, Eamon de Valera, has instigated a violent rebellion against the British troops stationed in his country. And he has accused the British Parliament of allowing the troops occupying Dublin to torture prisoners, murder children and violate women. Ireland's nearest neighbors have so far completely ignored the fact that the Irish people live under a virtual reign of terror and that the country is in a state of full-scale war against British rule. After escaping from prison two years ago this month, de Valera was elected President of Ireland by the Dail Eireann, the revolutionary Parliament that declared the country independent (→ 4/24).

War debts cause outcry in all Germany

Feb 5. Germany is balking at paying the war reparations demanded by the European Allies. And a report from Washington says the German Foreign Office is asking to conclude a separate peace agreement with the United States. Germany apparently hopes that the Harding administration will pressure Great Britain and France to lower their economic demands.

In Germany, trade unions are protesting stiff reparations. In a manifesto, they said, "Slavery, which has been abolished in Africa, is to be introduced in Europe. The German people are ready to make good the damage done. But we are not prepared to perish for the benefit of international capitalists" (→ 3/1)

Churchill's new job

Feb 12. England's Winston Churchill, discredited by the failure of the Dardanelles campaign, which he had championed, has been appointed Colonial Secretary. He had previously been Secretary of State for War and Air, and before that job held a host of positions in successive governments, including Home Secretary and First Lord of the Admiralty. As a younger man, he also saw action in India and South Africa.

Anarchist Prince is dead in Moscow

Anarchist sage Prince Kropotkin.

Feb 8. Prince Kropotkin, the Russian revolutionary and theorist of anarchism, is dead in Moscow at 78. Kropotkin began to foster revolutionary propaganda among laborers in St. Petersburg and Moscow in 1872. Two years later, he was imprisoned. He escaped in 1876 and fled to Western Europe.

In his writings, Kropotkin proposed a society where all material goods are held in common: Individuals receive according to their needs; and education prepares members of this ideal society to do both mental and physical labor.

Kropotkin returned to Russia in June 1917 because he thought his country would become the first stateless society. Very disappointed by the Bolshevik seizure of power, the prince withdrew from public life.

Chaplin and Jackie Coogan are now starring in "The Kid"; a new sentimentality from the comic genius of Hollywood.

1921

MARCH

Su	Mo	Tu	We	Th	Fr	Sa
		1	2	3	4	5
6	7	8	9	10	11	12
13	14	15	16	17	18	19
20	21	22	23	24	25	26
27	28	29	30	31		

1. London: Allies reject $7.5 bil. reparations offer; German delegation quits talks (→ 8).

1. First Japanese census reports population of 77 million.

6. Natl. Assn. of Moving Picture Industry announces plan for censorship of U.S. movies.

6. U.S.: 1920 cancer deaths reported at 5,361, up six percent from 1919.

8. Madrid: Spanish Premier Eduardo Dato assassinated while leaving Parliament.

12. U.S.: Govt. announces new poison; 3 drops are lethal.

13. Australia: Mrs. Cowan is 1st woman elected to Parliament.

14. China: U.S. troops sent ashore to protect Am. lives during disturbances at Kiu-kiang.

15. Berlin: Armenian S. Tailirian assassinates former Turkish Vizier Talat Pasha (→ 4/23/24).

16. Britain signs bilateral trade agreement with Russia (→ 21).

16. Reparations Committee requests one billion marks in gold by March 23 (→ 22).

19. Harding asks U.S. citizens to fight Chinese famine by "picking a pal in China."

20. Upper Silesia votes to join Germany by 65 percent majority (→ 5/8).

21. U.S. Sec. of Commerce Herbert Hoover publicly opposes any trade with Russia.

22. Germany defaults on billion marks due today, requests new conference (→ 4/15).

23. Illinois: Arthur G. Hamilton sets new parachute record, safely jumping 24,400 feet.

24. Germany: 30 die in Hamburg riots; Moscow blamed.

28. Harding names William Howard Taft as chief justice of the United States.

31. Great Britain declares state of emergency with thousands of coal miners on strike (→ 4/15).

DEATHS

1. King Nicholas of Montenegro (*1841).

29. John Burroughs, American naturalist (*4/3/1837).

Allies occupy Germany to collect debts

Belgian troops march defiantly into Dusseldorf under Bismarck's statue.

March 8. The European Allies refused to blink when Germany rejected their reparation demands, and they have made good on a threat to occupy parts of Germany. French and Belgian troops moved into Dusseldorf, Mulheim and two other cities and disarmed their police forces. Last week, at the London Conference, Germany formally rejected the demand to pay $56 billion over 42 years. Germany offered to pay less than a quarter of the amount and finance the rest with a series of international loans. But the Allies said that they refuse to suffer greater financial hardship than Germany, and they quickly turned down the German counterproposal (→ 16).

New Economic Policy ordained for Russia

March 12. "We are forced to consider most seriously the internal situation of Soviet Russia," declared Soviet Premier V.I. Lenin at the opening of the Tenth All-Russian Congress of the Bolshevik Party. Lenin, at the conference in Moscow, went on to admit that the internal troubles are of an economic nature caused by Bolshevik maneuvers to restore industrial life too rapidly after the war.

Therefore, he announced, the Soviet Union will embark on a New Economic Policy, as it's called, which in effect curtails socialization and sanctions limited free enterprise. The policy is an attempt to win over the peasants, who comprise a large majority of the Russian population and who have been in dire straits since the war's end.

Foreign trade is expected to be left completely in the hands of the state in order to check foreign competition. The industrial base, which employs 85 percent of all workers, will also be primarily state-controlled. However, according to Lenin, agriculture will basically remain unrestricted by the government; this is to accommodate the desires of the peasants who cherish the private ownership of farms. The ultimate goal of the NEP is to push the Soviets out of their severe postwar depression, Lenin said (→ 4/3/22).

New Russian heroes.

Communists crush Kronstadt revolt

March 18. Over 60,000 members of the powerful Red army have crushed an anti-Soviet rebellion of sailors in a battle at Kronstadt on the Finnish frontier. Leaders of the revolt were inspired by the ideas of the Social Revolutionary Party, a Paris-based group dedicated to fighting the Communist regime, which to them represents "nothing but an indefinite sentence of hard labor without adequate food." The rebels persisted for several days, but the well-trained Soviet troops led by Field Marshal Trotsky defeated the remaining 16,000 Kronstadt defenders (→ 5/27).

Harding installed as 29th President

March 4. Promising no foreign entanglements, Warren G. Harding of Ohio was sworn in today as the nation's 29th President. The simple ceremony, held on the east front of the Capitol, came on a bright, sunny day. Accompanying the new president to the Capitol was his Democratic predecessor, Woodrow Wilson. Hours later, in a surprise move, the new Republican president ordered that the White House gates be opened to the public for the first time since the United States entered the war in Europe nearly four years ago. In his campaign, Harding had promised a return to "normalcy."

Police call a halt to rising skirts

March 6. The chief of police in Sunbury, Pa., has issued an edict requiring women to wear skirts at least four inches below the knee. The chief was driven to this decision following a dozen complaints from town residents. They expressed dismay over the sight of two women traversing the streets who had the lace on their skirts too distant from their ankles. The chief had sent some policemen in search of the offenders, but they returned empty-handed. Sunbury is one of several towns that object to exaggeratedly abbreviated fashions (→ 5/15).

1921

APRIL

Su	Mo	Tu	We	Th	Fr	Sa
					1	2
3	4	5	6	7	8	9
10	11	12	13	14	15	16
17	18	19	20	21	22	23
24	25	26	27	28	29	30

2. Albert Einstein arrives in New York to lecture on theory of relativity (→ 5/9).

4. A.F.L. head Samuel Gompers asks Harding to free all political prisoners (→ 12/23).

7. Massachusetts: Plymouth Rock moved to brick building for security.

7. China: Canton government proclaims independence in South with Sun Yat-sen as president (→ 6/16).

8. Titian's "The Man with the Falcon" arrives in N.Y. for sale to Duveen Bros. for $300,000.

9. U.S. troops intervene in Guatemala to protect legation from fighting between Unionists and government.

10. U.S. Reclamation Service announces plans to build world's highest dam in Boulder Canyon between Nevada and Arizona (→ 2/11/26).

11. Boxing match broadcast in U.S. marks first radio sports coverage.

12. Detroit: Ford Motor Co. returns to pre-war production rate of one mil. cars per year (→ 5/10).

15. France discloses plans to occupy entire industrial, mining region in the Ruhr (→ 27).

20. General John "Black Jack" Pershing selected as chief of staff of U.S. Army.

20. Budapest reports 1,200 famine deaths in March.

24. Plebiscite in Tyrol votes annexation to Germany.

26. Tennessee: George Smiley, Knoxville Pioneers center-fielder, makes history with unassisted triple play.

27. Havana: Cuba's Jose Capablanca defeats Dr. Emanuel Lasker to take World Chess Championship.

BIRTHS

16. Peter Ustinov, British actor.

25. Karel Appel, Dutch painter, Abstract Expressionism.

DEATH

11. Augusta Victoria, former German empress (†10/22/1858).

British strikes paralyze entire country

April 15. A two-week-old strike by more than a million miners has paralyzed industry in Britain. And railway and transport workers are threatening to join the walkout tonight. The strike deadline set by the rail and transport workers has already been extended at least once, and they are now threatening to walk off their jobs at 10:00 p.m.

The government of Lloyd George and the miners have both treated the strike as all-out war. The prime minister is outraged by the job action and by the miners' refusal to allow volunteers to pump the mines. They flood when they are not in use, and the mines are in danger of being destroyed for good.

Lloyd George accuses the miners' union of "intimidating the nation into surrender to their demands." The prime minister calls their attitude a desperate one "which will lead to whole villages which derive their support from mining interests becoming derelict." Lloyd George is threatening to use the military to pump the mines. And he has made contingency plans to use the Air Service to distribute food to the country if the rail and transport workers join the miners' strike.

The head of the miners' union charges that Lloyd George has declared war on his workers, and he promises to fight back. "This government must go," Frank Hodges said. "It is our duty to make sure that it does go" (→ 6/28).

Welsh miners assemble for a photograph before returning their lamps.

Harding turns down League of Nations

April 12. President Warren Harding told a joint session of Congress today that the United States "will have no part" in the League of Nations. The new president's rejection of the League, which his Democratic predecessor, Woodrow Wilson, had labored so hard to fashion, drew loud cheers, primarily from his fellow Republicans. While rejecting the League, the president promised that his administration will cooperate with foreign governments in forming what he termed a non-political association of nations and in rehabilitating war-torn European nations (→ 7/2).

First woman killed by Irish rebels

April 24. Sinn Feiners have executed their first woman in the Abstract Expressionism.

Kitty MacCarron, 45, was taken about midnight by masked men from her parent's home in Monaghan and shot on a river bank. A card found on her body read: "Spies and informers, beware. Tried, convicted and executed by the Irish Republican Army." Throughout Ireland, I.R.A. attacks on constabulary were reported. In County Galway, police fought for 12 hours with a Republican column entrenched near the home of Patrick O'Malley, member of Parliament (→ 5/25).

Allies give Germans $33 billion bill

April 27. Germany was formally presented with a bill tonight for war reparations. The bill is smaller than expected. It totals 132 billion marks. At current exchange rates, that is equal to almost $33 billion.

Announcement of the reparations bill follows bitter debate among the Allies and Germany. Last week, the Reparations Commission ordered Germany to place its entire gold reserve under the supervision of the Allies. And France warned it would carry out its threat to occupy the Ruhr on May 1st if the demand were not satisfied.

The United States government turned down a request from Germany to mediate the dispute. But some German newspapers acknowledge that President Harding acted behind the scenes to reduce the reparations amount (→ 5/4).

Paddock achieves world 100m record

April 23. Charley Paddock, striving to live up to his title as the "world's fastest human," sped to a world record of 10.4 seconds for the 100-meter dash. One of the few Americans to win gold medals in the 1920 Olympics at Antwerp, Paddock followed his customary practice of knocking on wood before he went on to the new record. He set a world record of 20.8 seconds for 200 meters in March of 1921.

The year's hit for Miss Normand, who Mack Sennett says is as "beautiful as a spring morning."

1921

MAY

Su	Mo	Tu	We	Th	Fr	Sa
1	2	3	4	5	6	7
8	9	10	11	12	13	14
15	16	17	18	19	20	21
22	23	24	25	26	27	28
29	30	31				

2. First Max Ernst exhibit opens in Paris.

4. French forces pour into Dusseldorf, ready to advance on the Ruhr in a week (→ 5).

5. Lloyd George hands ultimatum to German envoy in London; Germans must yield on reparations by May 12th (→ 11).

7. Jockey C. Thompson rides Behave Yourself to victory in Kentucky Derby.

8. Civil war reported raging in Silesia over question of annexation to Germany (→ 6/1).

8. Sweden abolishes capital punishment.

9. Princeton University awards honorary degree to Einstein.

10. Detroit: Ford sets record, turning out 4,072 cars in a day.

11. Germany offers unconditional acceptance of Allied reparations demands (→ 8/15).

14. Fascists gain 29 seats in Italian Parliament (→ 11/7).

15. Garden City, L.I.: Laura Bromwell breaks own aviation record, performing 199 loop-the-loops (→ 6/5).

19. University of Chicago announces male college graduates make average of $5,762 per year after ten years of work.

25. Sinn Feiners burn Dublin Customs House, clash with police (→ 7/8).

27. U.S. Congress passes Emergency Tariff Act under European protests; agricultural duties soar.

27. Kappel's anti-Bolshevik forces take Vladivostok (→ 8/30/22).

30. Tommy Wilson takes Indianapolis 500 at 89.6 mph in a Frontenac racer.

31. 341 German and Austrian immigrants given U.S. citizenship, first since war.

31. U.S. Sec. of Navy Edwin Denby transfers Teapot Dome naval oil reserve to Albert Fall's Dept. of Interior (→ 4/7/22).

BIRTH

21. Andrei Sakharov, Soviet scientist and dissident.

New immigrant act sets national quotas

Immigrants leaving Ellis Island.

May 19. Too many refugees from war-torn Europe have purportedly denied American-born workers their rightful employment. Heeding labor's complaints, Congress has instituted restrictions on immigration. The quota limits immigration to three percent of each nationality that lived in America in 1910. Northern and Western Europeans are favored; about 200,000 will now enter each year. Russians, Italians and Greeks will be admitted at one-fifth their previous number.

New dances, styles stir American youth

The shimmy was recently condemned by the Catholic Archbishop of Ohio.

May 15. The New York State Legislature has passed a law giving a state commissioner the right to censor dances. In Utah, a statute is pending providing for the imprisonment of women wearing skirts higher than three inches above the ankle. And in Virginia, it's the decolletage, front and back, that lawmakers are going to shrink.

Across the country, American youths are kicking up their heels and indulging themselves in what seems to be a frenzy of rebellion against the standards and values of their parents and grandparents. And according to a recent survey by the New York-based Literary Digest, a majority of college officials and reporters believe that the burgeoning youth revolt of our times is a sign of a serious moral crisis.

New styles of dress and dance have been singled out as the chief culprits. "There is a minimum of clothes and a maximum of cosmetics, head decorations, fans and jewelry," according to the New York University News. "It is, indeed, an alarming situation when our 20th Century debutante comes out arrayed like a South Sea Island savage."

The New Mexico College of Agriculture and Mechanic Arts newspaper writes that gliding smoothly over a dance floor while keeping in rhythm with music is pleasing to witness, "but to jig and hop around like a chicken on a red-hot stove, at the same time shaking the body until it quivers like a disturbed glass of jello, is not only tremendously suggestive, but it is an offense against common decency that would not be permitted in a semi-respectable road-house."

But the respected Nation offers a less alarmist view. "The rank and file of the virtues have not greatly changed," it reports reassuringly. "All that appears is a certain pendulum swing from one repression or indulgence to another, reaction setting in whenever the virtues or vices of an age begin to bore it."

Met presents big modern art exhibit

"Trees at Callioure," by Matisse.

May 2. Following the Brooklyn Museum's heralded display of Impressionist art, what does the New York Metropolitan do to top it? It gives its own lavish display of Impressionist art, with some post-Impressionism tossed in. The public cannot seem to view enough paintings and sculpture by Matisse, Manet, Degas, Jean-Francois Millet and Honore Daumier. New Yorkers and out-of-towners wander through the crowded, echoing chambers, wondering out loud how 19th-century viewers could have been displeased, much less shocked, by these works. Yet one artist is receiving exactly that 19th-century reaction: the post-Impressionist, analytical Cubist, Pablo Picasso.

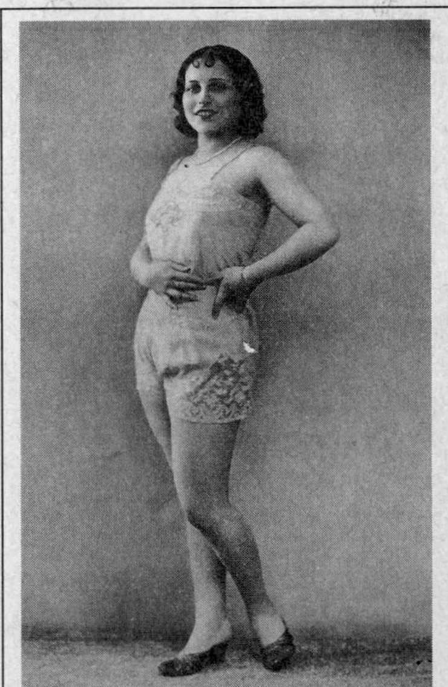

Today's young lady has jettisoned her corset for a new streamlined look. But as undergarments decrease in size, they seem to rise in importance. Working women spend half their clothes allowance on lingerie.

1921

JUNE

Su	Mo	Tu	We	Th	Fr	Sa
			1	2	3	4
5	6	7	8	9	10	11
12	13	14	15	16	17	18
19	20	21	22	23	24	25
26	27	28	29	30		

1. U.S. Senate passes $494 mil. Navy bill.

1. French repel German attack on garrison in Upper Silesia (→ 7/24).

3. Lord Byng appointed British governor general of Canada.

4. Floods sweep eastern Colorado; 500 dead.

7. Parliament opens in Belfast.

8. London: Lady Astor assures a gathering of mistresses and maids that "We are all someone's servant."

10. U.S. Congress passes Budget and Accounting Act, establishing Bureau of the Budget and General Accounting Office.

11. Penn State to graduate first woman engineer this year.

12. President Harding urges every young man to attend military training camp.

16. Sun Yat-sen asks Harding for official recognition of South China Republic (→ 12/1921).

19. Paris: Allies ask Greece to delay offensive against Kemal's Turkish government (→ 26).

20. Oklahoma's Alice Robertson becomes first woman to preside over House of Representatives (→ 9/25).

25. Samuel Gompers elected head of A.F.L. for 40th time (→ 10/12/21).

25. Stuttgart: German scientist Friedrich Bergius succeeds in liquefying coal into oil.

25. Los Angeles: Alamitos II well finds new oil reserve at Signal Hill.

26. Greece refuses mediation on Turkish issue, captures Ismid on Sea of Marmora (→ 7/16).

28. British coal strike finally settled after three months.

BIRTH

10. Philip Mountbatten, duke of Edinburgh, consort of Queen Elizabeth II.

DEATHS

5. Georges Feydeau, French playwright (*2/8/1862).

13. Jose Miguel Gomez, Cuban ex-president.

Race rioting in Tulsa causes 85 deaths

June 1. More than 85 persons were killed and hundreds injured in a raging race riot during the past 24 hours in Tulsa, Oklahoma. One of the most disastrous race wars ever staged in America, the fighting was brought under control late tonight by state guardsmen patrolling the streets with fixed bayonets.

In addition to the deaths and injuries, 30 densely populated blocks in the Negro section of the city were wiped out by fire, leaving thousands of residents homeless. Tonight, more than 6,000 Negroes were under heavy guard in hastily established detention camps at a local baseball park.

The rioting began yesterday after a Negro bootblack was arrested on a charge of attacking a white woman who operates the elevator in a downtown office building. As word of his arrest began circulating throughout the city, there were rumors that he was about to be lynched. Last night, some 500 heavily armed colored men gathered in front of the courthouse where the bootblack was being held. The police, after trying to disperse the mob, threw a cordon around the building and the Negroes began shooting.

Meanwhile, whites began breaking into every hardware and sporting goods store in the city to obtain weapons. By dawn, the whites began invading the Negro section of the city (→ 9/11).

Daredevil woman flier dies in crash

Daring Laura Bromwell.

June 5. Flying was her life, and flying took her life this afternoon on the outskirts of Garden City, Long Island. Laura Bromwell, the foremost American aviatrix, was killed instantly when she lost control of a single-seat Canadian airplane and fell from a height of more than 1,000 feet. As the airplane was upside down in a loop, she may have lost touch with the foot controls due to being strapped too loosely in her seat.

Only 23 years old, Laura Bromwell had held her pilot's license for two years. Last month, she set a double record for a woman when she looped the loop 199 times, a remarkable feat, and flew at a speed of 135 miles an hour. Miss Bromwell, whose home was in Cincinnati, had recently expressed to a reporter her belief that she would meet death in the air one day.

Flying Finn sets long-distance mark

June 22. Paavo Nurmi, whose speed has earned him the nickname of the "Flying Finn," has set a world record of 30 minutes, 40.2 seconds for the 10,000-meter run. He was also the star of the 1920 Olympics, winning the 1,500-, 5,000-and 10,000-meter events.

American mother of Churchill dies

Brooklyn-born Lady Churchill.

June 29. Lady Randolph Churchill, 67, formerly Jennie Jerome of Brooklyn, died yesterday of complications following the amputation of her leg. She had recently slipped and broken her ankle, which led to blood poisoning and then amputation. Her sons, Winston and John, were with her when her active life ended. The thrice-married beauty was not only a strong inspiration in the careers of her husband Lord Randolph and her son Winston; she was also a brilliant politician, writer, playwright, lecturer and organizer in her own right.

Tilden and Lenglen win Wimbledon again

The lanky American, William "Big Bill" Tilden, and the spirited French player, Suzanne Lenglen, have repeated their tennis victories at Wimbledon. Tilden and Miss Lenglen, respective champions in their homelands, won the 1920 Wimbledon championships when they were resumed after a four-year wartime lapse.

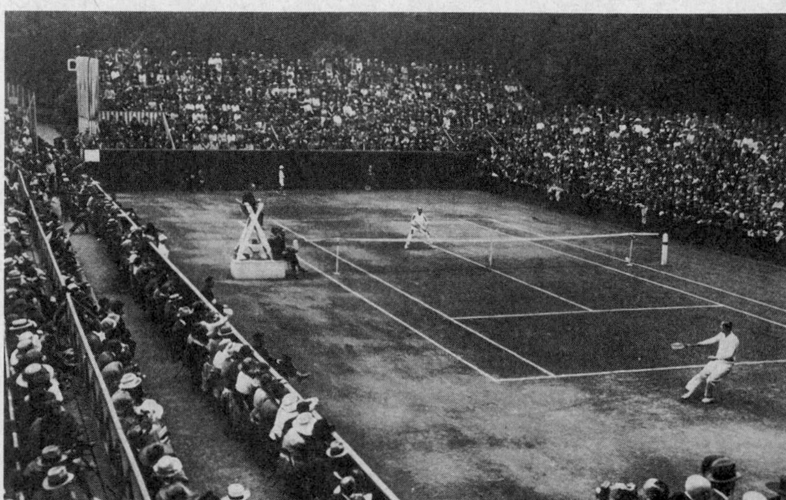

Nobody is better than Tilden (right).

1921

JULY

Su	Mo	Tu	We	Th	Fr	Sa
					1	2
3	4	5	6	7	8	9
10	11	12	13	14	15	16
17	18	19	20	21	22	23
24	25	26	27	28	29	30
31						

2. Raritan, N.J.: Harding signs peace decree ending war with Germany (→ 8/25).

4. Rome: Bonomi forms Italian Cabinet.

6. Slump in movie patronage reported puzzling Hollywood filmmakers.

8. Eamonn de Valera agrees to Irish truce, schedules meeting with Lloyd George (→ 12).

10. President Harding proposes disarmament conference (→ 11/12).

10. Outer Mongolia secedes from rest of country, forms provisional government (→ 11/5).

12. De Valera arrives in London for peace talks (→ 21).

12. London: Aviator Harry Hawker dies in explosion while testing plane for aerial derby.

14. Panama, Costa Rica begin boundary negotiations.

16. Greek troops take Kutaia from Kemal (→ 25).

18. France: Albert Calmette and Camille Guerin vaccinate first infant for tuberculosis.

23. Rebel leader Abd el Krim defeats colonial troops in Spanish Morocco (→ 3/31/22).

24. Tour de France won by Belgian racer Leon Scieur in 221 hours, 48 minutes.

24. Britain, France reach compromise on Silesia (→ 10/26).

25. Turks halt Greek advance at Altikeuk (→ 8/5).

26. Virginia: Monticello, Thomas Jefferson's old estate, offered for sale.

27. Germany: Minister of Education Matt proposes replacing French with English as compulsory language in German public schools.

27. Discovery of insulin reported by Canadian biochemists Frederick Banting and Charles Best.→

29. Germany: Adolf Hitler becomes President of Nationalist Socialist German Workers Party.

BIRTH

18. John Glenn, astronaut, first American to orbit earth.

Two Italian anarchists convicted of murder

Sacco, Vanzetti (center) in Dedham.

July 14. Sacco and Vanzetti have been found guilty of first-degree murder. The more than month-long trial of the two Italian anarchists, Nicola Sacco and Bartolomeo Vanzetti, had attracted national attention, with many American liberals as well as labor groups rallying to their defense. Sentencing has not yet been announced by presiding Judge Webster Thayer.

The jury in Dedham, Massachusetts, was closeted for nearly eight hours before finding the two men, both of whom are foreign-born, guilty of murdering the paymaster and guard of a shoe factory during a payroll holdup in South Braintree, Massachusetts, one year ago. Both Sacco, a skilled shoeworker, and Vanzetti, a fish peddler, had denied any involvement in the crime, and none of the $16,000 taken during the robbery was ever traced to either one of them (→ 10/29).

Eight million American women hold jobs

Teaching and secretarial work employ 87 percent of working women.

July 19. There are eight million gainfully employed women in the United States, Dr. Amelia Reinhardt, President of Mills College in Oakland, California, told the delegates of the third annual convention of the National Federation of Business and Professional Women's Clubs this afternoon. Of the eight million, 1.9 million are married.

Fifty percent of the women are teachers, Dr. Reinhardt said, while 37 percent occupy secretarial positions. Only 1,600 women have a graduate degree in law. The national president of the organization pleaded for better education, sane thinking, intelligent citizenship and a full acceptance of equal suffrage to improve the female job outlook.

Many professions still resist females, the medical one being outstanding in this respect. Some 92 percent of the nation's hospitals refuse to accept female interns, regardless of excellent performances in medical school, where about five percent of the students are women.

On the more positive side, a sharp and welcome decline has taken place in the area of child labor. Presently, only about 8.5 percent of children, ages ten to 14, are in the labor force. It was double that figure only ten years ago. It remains an indisputable fact that, on every level, women earn considerably less than men (→ 8/22).

De Valera in London to begin peace talks

July 21. Prime Minister David Lloyd George presented today to Eamon de Valera, the Irish Republican leader, the outlines of a British proposal for home rule in Ireland. Basically, the proposals envision a form of dominion home rule in Ireland, somewhat along the line granted to Canada and South Africa. Because of Ireland's propinquity to the center of the British Empire, however, Britain would maintain a military and naval presence in Ireland.

The British proposal for home rule was conditioned upon agreement first between Ulster and the Irish Republic. A communique issued after the meeting at 10 Downing Street said a basis for a formal conference had not yet been found but that de Valera, who is being treated as President of the Irish Republic, would talk further with Lloyd George after discussions with his collegues in Dublin. The communique was greeted with optimism in Parliament but some disappointment in Dublin (→ 8/14).

Dempsey floors French challenger

Carpentier floored in the fourth.

July 1. Jack Dempsey, who was set up to be the villain in a boxing drama designed to attract a million-dollar gate, easily knocked out Georges Carpentier of France in the fourth round before more than 100,000 at Boyle's Thirty Acres. The heavyweight champion made good use of his 20-pound advantage and power punching. Carpentier broke his thumb and sprained his right wrist on Dempsey's jaw in the second round. ▷

Mitchell shows air bombs can sink ship

Brigadier General Billy Mitchell.

July 21. Brigadier General William Mitchell and his fellow aviators gave a convincing display of the destructive power of the airplane today when, in a military test, they sank the former German battleship Ostfriesland with six 2,000-pound bombs in just 25 minutes.

Many Navy officers had scoffed at Mitchell's claim that aircraft could sink any ship, however well-armored. They said the Ostfriesland could be sunk only by big naval guns. But Mitchell and his men, flying from Langley Field, Va., did extensive damage this morning when they scored three direct hits with 1,000-pound bombs and delivered the coup de grace in the afternoon when a flight of six Martin bombers flew the 100 miles to where the Ostfriesland was anchored off the Virginia coast and dropped the 2,000-pounders close to the vessel, springing open her seams and sending her to the bottom. "A bomb was fired that will be heard around the world," one observer said.

Insulin isolated; can help diabetics

July 27. A substance that eliminates the often fatal symptoms of diabetes has been isolated from the pancreases of dogs by Frederick G. Banting, a Canadian doctor, and his collaborator, Charles Best. The extract has been named insulin by Dr. John MacLeod of the University of Toronto, who encouraged Banting and gave him lab space. Insulin is expected to save the lives of many diabetics, who now face slow deaths even if they follow a rigid diet. Its use to help diabetics is expected to begin quickly (→ 1/11/22).

1921

AUGUST

Su	Mo	Tu	We	Th	Fr	Sa
	1	2	3	4	5	6
7	8	9	10	11	12	13
14	15	16	17	18	19	20
21	22	23	24	25	26	27
28	29	30	31			

3. U.S.: Collier and Harper announce merger intent; to be one of largest in publishing history.

5. Dayton, Ohio: First driverless auto, radio-controlled, tested successfully.

7. New York: Organ music replacing customary orchestras in Broadway film theaters.

9. Musical comedy "Tangerine" opens in New York.

9. Washington reports food price increases in 11 out of 14 U.S. cities (→ 9/26).

12. Washington: House Ways and Means Committee lowers taxes, increasing exemption for married men (→ 12/6/23).

14. De Valera rejects dominion status for Ireland (→ 16).

15. German mark drops to 88 to the U.S. dollar (→ 29).

16. Yugoslav King Peter I dies; Alexander succeeds (→ 10/11).

16. Dublin: Dail proclaims allegiance to Irish Republic; de Valera demands total separation from England (→ 9/15).

17. Puerto Rican Gov. E. Mont Reilly refuses office to independence advocates.

22. Connecticut requires licensing of barbers who bob hair.

24. British dirigible ZR II explodes during trial flight, killing 44.

24. Four DeHaveland planes complete journey from New York to Nome, Alaska.

25. Germany signs peace treaty with U.S., officially ending state of war.

26. Germany: Ex-Minister of Finance Matthias Erzberger killed by ultra-nationalists.

27. Grass soup found to be staple of starving Russian peasants (→ 9/21).

29. Germany: State of emergency proclaimed to combat economic crisis (→ 9/30).

30. Holland: Human rights congress opens at The Hague.

BIRTH

11. Alex Haley, American author "Roots."

Lenin appeals for world aid against famine

Many Russian children, like these in Saratov, reportedly live on grass soup.

Aug 4. The Russian people are starving to death. More than 18 million are reported to be suffering from a lack of food, and 47,779 cases of cholera have been reported among the hungry. The conditions were acknowledged in an appeal for aid from V.I. Lenin, the Soviet leader. The Russian government asked all nations to send aid to help "their starving fellows in Russia."

Many countries are expected to do so. France has agreed to export food surpluses, citing the need to embark on a humanitarian project, but it also has indicated to the Allied Supreme Council that an effort should be made to replace the Soviet regime with a more representative government. The recent release of American prisoners held by the Soviets should result in assistance from the American Relief Administration (→ 27).

Golden voice of Enrico Caruso is silenced

Enrico Caruso: A golden voice.

Aug 2. Enrico Caruso, the most famous tenor of our time and one of the best-known and loved singers in the world, died today in his native Naples. But his voice was not stilled. Caruso recorded more than 160 records for the Victor Talking Machine Company. In the United States and in Italy, Caruso's voice was heard in many homes as grieving fans played the records.

Doctors say Caruso lapsed into a coma after suffering from pleurisy that he contracted on a visit to New York. His body lies in state in the Naples hotel room where he died. King Victor Emmanuel has ordered a special funeral service in the great tenor's honor.

Caruso will be remembered for his warm, technically perfect voice. He was able to sing more than 60 opera roles and 500 songs from memory. "Success," he once said, "requires a lot of breath and voice, 90 percent memory and ten percent intelligence, a lot of hard work and a little something in the heart."

Kemal gets powers to wage Greek war

Aug 5. The Grand National Assembly at Angora, the government of the Turkish nationalists, has appointed Mustafa Kemal Supreme Commander-in-Chief. He will not only control the armed forces, but will also have full power to act in the name of the assembly for a period of three months.

The Turkish nationalist forces have been fighting the Greeks since May 1919 when they landed at Smyrna. The Allies had approved Greek claims to the Aegean coast of Asia Minor. However, after the failure of the London Conference, where the Allies, Greeks and Turks attempted to negotiate modifications in the Treaty of Sevres, the Allies declared themselves neutral.

The Kemalist forces, in spite of their smaller numbers, had stopped Greek advances. However, a renewed Greek offensive in July resulted in the capture of Eskishehir. Further Greek successes prompted the assembly to grant full powers to Kemal (→ 9/9/22).

Women: The long and short of it

Aug 22. The State Barber's Commission of Connecticut has ruled that women who bob hair must procure a barber's license. The commission announced that the bobbing of hair is considered an act of haircutting, and so the perpetrators of the hair bob should be classed as barbers. Barbers, as a matter of course, are examined by the commission for competency, and they are expected to pay a yearly license of $5. And the bobbing barbers must also furnish their own subjects when they demonstrate their artistry before the panel.

Some young women may consider the ruling a rebuke, for hair bobbing is not popular in all circles. Neither is the practice of wearing skirts above the knees, smoking in public, drinking in private and sporting makeup. However, many decent girls prefer the bob, finding it not only stylish but safer to wear in modern offices and factories, where long hair can be damaged by contact with machinery (→ 10/16).

1921

SEPTEMBER

Su	Mo	Tu	We	Th	Fr	Sa
				1	2	3
4	5	6	7	8	9	10
11	12	13	14	15	16	17
18	19	20	21	22	23	24
25	26	27	28	29	30	

2. Russian Soviets declare state of war in Bessarabia, on Rumanian border.

3. W.Va.: 400 striking miners give up arms to federal troops.

5. Jimmy Doolittle flies San Diego to Jacksonville in 22.5 hours with only one stop.

7. New York: "Tarzan of the Apes" opens on Broadway, starring lions, apes and other jungle animals.

9. Tegucigalpa: Guatemala, Honduras, Salvador sign constitution creating Federation of Central American Republics.

11. Atlanta: Ku Klux Klan now in control of Lanier University, plans to teach "Americanism" (→ 12/20).

15. Lloyd George cancels talks as de Valera reiterates sovereignty claim for Ireland (→ 29).

19. Chicago railroad officials arrested for denying workers two hours to vote.

21. U.S. reportedly feeding 20,000 children in famine-plagued Petrograd (→ 10/4).

21. Germany: Over 500 perish in explosion at Badische dye plant near Ludwigshaffen.

22. Estonia, Latvia, Lithuania admitted to League of Nations (→ 9/18/22).

25. U.S.: Natl. Woman's Party publishes draft of non-discriminatory legal code (→ 11/22).

25. U.S.: Chaplin's "The Idle Class" gets first screening.

26. Washington: Sec. of Commerce Hoover presides over natl. conference on unemployment (→ 30).

29. Lloyd George invites Sinn Fein to talks scheduled for Oct. 11 (→ 10/21).

30. French evacuate Ruhr, lift economic sanctions on Germany (→ 11/4).

30. 20,000 U.S. businesses reported failed since start of year; 3.5 mil. unemployed.

DEATH

28. Engelbert Humperdinck, German composer "Hansel and Gretel" (*1/9/1854).

Moroccan Abd el Krim creates Rif republic

Sept 19. European interests in Morocco have been given a sudden jolt as a new republic was formed in the northern part of the country. Abd el Krim, the leader of the Riffian tribes, announced the formation of a Rif republic after a string of military victories against Spanish forces in the territory.

Abd el Krim's campaign against Spain is being widely praised in Northern Africa. "This is a brilliant military victory that makes Europe and the Christian world tremble," says the Algerian writer Messali Hadj. "It sets an example and encourages all the oppressed people in the Moslem world."

The Rif is a mountainous coastal area in northern Morocco. From the time Europeans arrived in the country, it has been the focal point of resistance to their imperialistic designs. Abd el Krim has crystallized that resistance by leading the three million people of the Rif against Spain. He is a member of the Beni Ouriaghel tribe and the son of a "cadi," a respected Moslem magistrate. Until 1915, Abd el Krim was a highly regarded government functionary (→ 3/31/22).

Rif leader Abd el Krim.

Hollywood's Big Three frolic in Paris

Charlie Chaplin, Douglas Fairbanks and Mary Pickford.

Sept 19. Three of the biggest stars in Hollywood arrived in Paris today after a stop in London. Charlie Chaplin, Douglas Fairbanks and Mary Pickford are taking Europe by storm as they set out on a two-month publicity tour.

The French are always attracted to a good love story, and they are captivated by the off-screen romance between Fairbanks and Pickford. They were married last year. Fairbanks recently completed making "The Three Musketeers," and he is getting ready to make another film called "The Sign of Zorro." Chaplin, who is adored in France and called "Charlot" by his fans, has made "The Kid" this year with Jackie Coogan, as well as a film called "The Idle Class."

All three actors are in Europe to promote their own films and United Artists, the independent film production and distribution company they founded two years ago.

1921

OCTOBER

Su	Mo	Tu	We	Th	Fr	Sa
						1
2	3	4	5	6	7	8
9	10	11	12	13	14	15
16	17	18	19	20	21	22
23	24	25	26	27	28	29
30	31					

2. New York: Babe Ruth of the Yankees hits 59th home run to end season.

3. Ellis Island to close on Sundays due to number of immigrants being detained (→ 3/29/22).

4. League of Nations refuses aid to Russia, blames famine on political failure (→ 11/24).

7. Italy: First international sociology congress convenes in Turin.

8. Indian nationalists call general strike on Prince of Wales' arrival in Bombay (→ 11/11).

11. Serbian Prince Alexander abandons Yugoslav crown.

13. N.Y. Giants take World Series in eight games, beating Yankees 1-0 at Polo Grounds.

18. Russian Soviets grant Crimean independence.

18. Germans have perfected electric triple-barreled gun, spreads 2,000 bullets per min.

20. Lisbon: Portuguese Premier Antonio Granjo assassinated in attempted military coup.

20. Ankara: France signs accord with Kemal govt. fixing Turko-Syrian border.

21. U.S. district court bars foreign liquor shipments from passing through U.S. (→ 11/23).

21. London: Irish-British peace talks begin (→ 12/5).

21. Ex-Emperor Charles I attempts second coup in Hungary (→ 25).

26. Poland, Germany accept Legue boundaries in Upper Silesia (→ 5/15/22).

29. U.S.: Sacco and Vanzetti begin appeal of death sentence (→ 8/27/27).

BIRTH

13. Yves Montand, French actor, singer.

DEATHS

18. Ludwig III, Bavarian ex-king (*1/7/1845).

25. Bat Masterson, American gunslinger, sports writer (*11/24/1853).

Ex-Emperor fails to regain throne

Charles celebrates mass in Budapest.

Oct 25. Ex-Emperor Charles and ex-Empress Zita, after a failed attempt to regain power in Hungary, are now held prisoners and await their sentencing from angry Allied judges. The former leader of Austria left Switzerland last week, enlisted 12,000 Hungarian troops and marched on Budapest determined to seize governmental reins.

At first, the renewed forces fought hard for Charles, winning the initial battle on the perimeter of Budapest. But the defending troops, with help from Allied armies, stopped the Carlists, killing 200, injuring 1,000 more and preventing a coup d'etat. Before the bloody battle, the Hungarian government offered Charles an armistice which would have deported him and his wife, disarmed but pardoned his troops and forced him to formally renounce power. Charles rejected the offer and subsequently his army was smashed. He and Zita will probably be exiled in disgrace to some remote land (→ 11/6).

Valentino as sheik makes fans swoon

Oct 31. Rudolph Valentino, who made women weak with longing in "The Four Horsemen of the Apocalypse," has done so again in "The Sheik." The film opened today at New York's Rivoli theater. Valentino plays the European adopted son of an Arab chieftain who falls in love with an English lass, played by Agnes Ayres, who was lately seen in Cecil B. De Mille's "Forbidden Fruit." The nation's male population cannot fathom the female's attraction to Valentino, a lithe and somewhat effeminate actor.

Rudolph Valentino is "The Sheik."

Can female freedom lead to divorce?

Oct 16. The St. Louis Court of Domestic Relations attributes the increase in local divorces to the growing economic independence of women. Nearly 700 divorce decrees were granted by the court during one of its last terms. Statewide, Missouri has experienced a 100% increase in divorces since 1896.

Statistics both confirm and refute the board's contention. A record eight million women are now employed nationwide, and the average number of children to support continues to decrease. However, their pay would not encourage women to divorce: they often receive half the salary of a man doing equivalent work. The income may be a helpful supplement to a husband's salary, but can hardly sustain a family.

1921

NOVEMBER

Su	Mo	Tu	We	Th	Fr	Sa
		1	2	3	4	5
6	7	8	9	10	11	12
13	14	15	16	17	18	19
20	21	22	23	24	25	26
29	28	29	30			

2. American Birth Control League formed by Margaret Sanger and Mary Ware Dennett.

3. New York: Striking milk drivers dump thousands of gallons of milk in city streets.

4. Tokyo: Japanese Premier Takashi Hara stabbed to death by Korean; Takahashi succeeds.

4. German mark continues collapse, reaches 225 to the dollar (→ 1/2/22).

5. Outer Mongolia signs accord with Russia to protect against Japanese, Chinese invasion (→ 3/7/25).

6. Hungary votes deposition of Hapsburgs following failed coup of Charles I (→ 4/1/22).

7. Henri Desire Landru, accused of killing and cooking eight women, comes to trial in Versailles (→ 12/1).

9. Rome hit by general strike as railway workers clash with Fascists (→ 3/14/22).

11. India: Gandhi urges Hindus to remove statue of ex-Viceroy Lord Lawrence (→ 2/7/22).

12. Disarmament Conference opens in Washington (→ 24).

14. Cherokee ask U.S. Supreme Court to review claim to one mil. acres in Texas.

18. N.Y. considering varied work hours to avoid traffic jams.

22. Iowa: Harding warns Des Moines audience of danger to nation if women voters unite as a class (→ 2/27/22).

24. Washington: Premier Briand claims French disarmament would invite war (→ 12/13).

24. First American women arrive in Moscow to aid famine victims (→ 2/11/22).

25. Hirohito becomes regent of Japan (→ 11/10/28).

BIRTH

19. Roy Campanella, baseball star.

DEATHS

5. Rev. Dr. Antoinette L. Brown Blackwell, first U.S. woman ordained pastor (*5/20/1825).

30. Abdul Baha Abbas, Syrian Bahai prophet (*5/23/1844).

Mussolini makes himself Duce of Fascists

Mussolini gives a typically vehement diatribe on the virtues of Fascism.

Nov 7. Benito Mussolini has declared the Fascist Party the Nationalist Fascist Party and named himself its "Duce" or leader. This Italian-based movement began in 1919 as a reaction to postwar revolutionary movements. It was, and still is, fiercely anti-Communist.

Mussolini rejected his socialist ties—he had been editor of the Milan Socialist Party newspaper Avanti prior to the war—to organize the Fasci di Combattimento with Italian industrialists, landowners and army officers shortly after the war. The party name is derived from the ancient Roman symbol of power, the Fasces.

The party has become known in political circles as an expression of "radicalism of the right," a movement which glorifies the state and subordinates individuals to state authority. Strict law and order and preservation of a rigid class structure are also party principles. According to observers in Italy, the goals of the party include battling Socialists, Communists, Catholics and Liberals, ideologically and militarily if necessary.

The party certainly identifies with the military as its black-shirted members use the ancient Roman warrior salute and adhere to stern army-like discipline (→ 9).

Psychiatric film: The Cabinet of Dr. Caligari

Nov 14. "The Cabinet of Dr. Caligari" premiered in Paris today. The story deals with an insane psychiatrist who uses hypnotism to commit murder. Directed by Robert Wiene, a German, the movie is a masterpiece of expressionist film.

It has many of the features of the movement: the confusion of identities, the inability to distinguish the real from the imaginary, the use of shadows for dramatic contrast, stylized and anti-naturalistic acting and unrealistic makeup that nonetheless expresses character. The screenwriters, the Czech Hans Janowitz and the Austrian Carl Meyer, aim to portray the absurdity of authority. The film shows a world characterized by horror and doubt, caused by the people in power.

Germany flooding America with drugs

Nov 18. Dr. Carleton Simon of the New York Police Narcotic Division has revealed that synthetic cocaine, heroine and other habit-forming drugs, manufactured in Germany, are being smuggled into this country. As a result, the United States government has put 150 more agents in his district.

Germany developed a synthetic method of producing drugs when it was cut off from its normal supply of raw materials during the war. Such drugs also include novocain, aminol, pyranadon, veronal, sulfonal and eucain. These are smuggled in frequently by way of South America. Simon advocates tougher congressional penalties for drug smuggling and said that it should be considered a form of treason. He also said that in his experience very little drug addiction was caused by doctors' prescriptions.

Beer goes the way of whiskey—out

Nov 23. Not only can you no longer abuse it, but doctors can no longer use it. Such is the impact of the Willis-Campbell Act, signed today by President Harding.

Better known as the anti-beer bill, the measure forbids doctors from prescribing beer for medicinal purposes. Actually, it is an official attempt to siphon off the market alleged medical cures being bought and sold as substitutes for alcoholic beverages, as very few doctors are guilty of prescribing liquor for people who don't absolutely need it.

The legislation also states that Prohibition officers may not search private dwellings without a warrant, but in other places they may act upon a reasonable suspicion. Meanwhile, the National Brewer's Association has declared that it will test the constitutionality of the new act (→ 6/15/22).

America's unknown soldier comes home

Nov 11. America's own hero, the unknown soldier, lies in state in the vast rotunda of the nation's Capitol, three years after the end of the war. For days now, they have come, the old and the young, the Negroes and the whites, even those who are badly crippled, to pay homage to the man, or perhaps he was little more than a boy, who died in France. The simple black coffin bearing his remains rests on the spot where only the nation's assassinated presidents, Lincoln, Garfield and McKinley, have slept in death.

As a cannon boomed down river, the body arrived at the Washington Navy Yard earlier this week aboard the great, gray cruiser Olympia and was taken to the Capitol. Since then, hundreds of thousands of Americans and foreign diplomats have filed by the flag-draped coffin. Among the wreaths are one sent by King George of England, bearing the words: "An unknown, and yet well known; as dying, and, behold, we live."

Harding solemnly places the War Cross on the casket of the unknown soldier.

1921

DECEMBER

Su	Mo	Tu	We	Th	Fr	Sa
				1	2	3
4	5	6	7	8	9	10
11	12	13	14	15	16	17
18	19	20	21	22	23	24
25	26	27	28	29	30	31

1. Washington reports 1,741 auto deaths to date in 1921.

1. Vienna: 300,000 demonstrate to protest high cost of living.

2. Virginia: C-7, first successful helium dirigible, makes test-flight in Portsmouth.

5. Chicago: Babe Ruth fined World Series prize, suspended until May for exhibition appearances following series.

5. Lloyd George reaches accord with Sinn Fein; Ireland to become free state within British Empire (→ 6).

6. Mackenzie King elected prime minister of Canada.

7. Chicago police clash with 100,000 stockyard strikers and sympathizers.

20. Washington: House Democrats filibuster to block anti-lynching bill (→ 3/15/22).

23. Pres. Harding frees Debs and 23 other political prisoners.

29. Chicago: Sears, Roebuck Pres. Julius Rosenwald pledges $20 mil. of personal fortune to help Sears through hard times.

DEATH

22. Colonel Henry Watterson, journalist (*2/16/1840).

CULUTRAL EVENTS, 1921

Literature: Sherwood Anderson's "The Triumph of the Egg"; Dos Passos' "Three Soldiers"; Huxley's "Chrome Yellow"; D.H. Lawrence's "Women in Love"; George Moore's "Heloise and Abelard"; Luigi Pirandello's "Six Characters in Search of an Author."

Academia: Hermann Rorschach's "Psychodiagnostic"; Ludwig Wittgenstein's "Logico-Philosophicus."

Music: Irving Berlin's first "Music Box Revue," N.Y.; Prokofiev's opera "Love for Three Oranges," Chicago.

The Arts: Georges Braque's "Still Life with Guitar"; Paul Klee's "The Fish"; Leger's "Three Women"; Picasso's "Three Musicians."

Film: D.W. Griffith's "Dream Street"; Fritz Lang's "The Weary Death."

Four powers sign naval pact in Washington

Dec 13. The Washington Conference has ended successfully, as the United States, Great Britain, France and Japan signed a treaty concerning the Pacific Ocean. The countries agreed to respect each other's possessions in the Pacific under League of Nations guidelines.

The four-power agreement gives the United States League of Nations privileges in the Pacific, even though it has refused to become part of the world organization. The United States will have trading access to Pacific territories held by the three other countries. And it will be able to use the important cable and telegraph center on the Yap Island group, which is administered by Japan (→ 1/5/22).

Europe looks again to America.

Southern Ireland becomes Free State

Dec 6. British and Irish representatives have signed a treaty creating the Irish Free State as a dominion of the British Empire.

Under the treaty, Southern Ireland would become self-governing, but Irish officials would swear loyalty to the British crown. In addition, there would be a British governor general, and Britain would be granted military base rights in Ireland in wartime. The treaty was hailed in Parliament as bringing an end to centuries of conflict between the two peoples, but it provoked political division within Ireland. Eamon de Valera, the President of Ireland, said he would oppose the treaty as being "in violent conflict" with Irish majority wishes (→ 1/7/22).

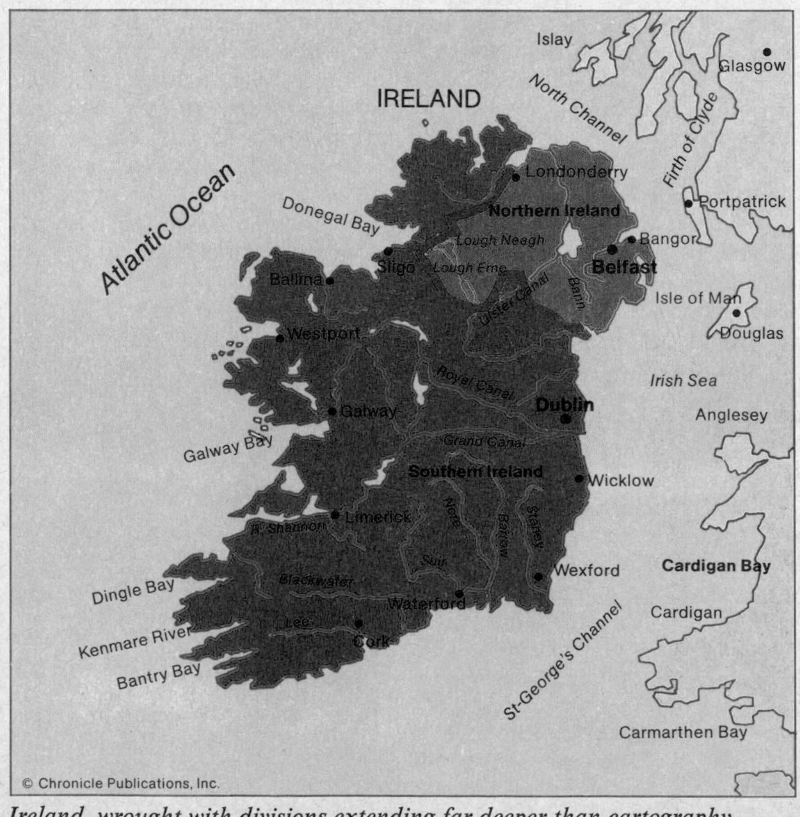

Ireland, wrought with divisions extending far deeper than cartography.

French Bluebeard sentenced to die

Dec 1. Henri Desire Landru, nicknamed "Bluebeard" in France, has been sentenced to death. He appears to be a gentleman, but prosecutors convincingly argued he is a killer who murdered a number of women. He was accused of enticing the women by promising to marry them. All but one disappeared, and she insists Landru is innocent. As each piece of evidence was introduced, Landru replied: "Show me the bodies." There are none. But railway officials testified that he often bought two tickets at the start of a trip, but only one for the return (→ 2/5/22).

Last chord struck for Camille Saint-Saens

Dec 16. French composer, organist and pianist Camille Saint-Saens, a disciple of Rameau and Bach and a leader in French musical life for almost 70 years, is dead at 86.

Saint-Saens began to compose at age six and appeared publicly as a pianist at ten. After his first symphony in Paris in 1853, he received a letter from Charles Gounod saying that the 18-year-old composer "had the obligation to become a great master." The opera "Samson and Dalila," the "Third Symphony," "Danse macabre" and "The Carnival of the Animals" are among his finest achievements.

Anatole France wins literature award

Dec 10. The French novelist, poet, literary critic and playwright Anatole France is this year's winner of the Nobel Prize in literature.

France is not only a famous writer, but he is also an enlightened, tolerant humanist who is committed to the ideal of social justice. Since the Dreyfus Affair, in which he supported Dreyfus, his writing has been slanted toward political satire. Among France's best works are "My Friend's Book" (1885); "Penguin Island" (1908); "The Gods are Athirst" (1913) and "The Revolt of the Angels" (1914).

1922

JANUARY

Su	Mo	Tu	We	Th	Fr	Sa
1	2	3	4	5	6	7
8	9	10	11	12	13	14
15	16	17	18	19	20	21
22	23	24	25	26	27	28
29	30	31				

1. Pasadena: Rose Bowl ends in 0-0 deadlock between Univ. of California and Washington and Jefferson College.

2. Portugal: Cunha Leal's Cabinet resigns.

2. German mark slides to 7,260 to the U.S. dollar (→ 6).

5. Washington: Five naval powers agree to ban use of subs to destroy merchant ships (→ 7).

6. Cannes: Allies defer German reparations payments (→ 31).

6. Cannes: Allies call all Europe to Genoa conference on economic restoration, scheduled for March (→ 4/10).

7. Washington: Committee passes American resolution outlawing use of poison gas (→ 2/6).

7. Dublin: Dail Eireann votes 64-57 to accept Irish Free State (→ 10).

10. Berlin shocked by German translation of Keynes' "Economic Consequences of the Peace."

11. Toronto diabetic reportedly aided by insulin treatment.

12. France: Briand Cabinet resigns; Poincare to form new Cabinet.

13. New York: Gene Tunney defeats Levinsky to capture light-heavyweight title.

17. U.S. Sec. of State Charles Evans Hughes proposes intl. board to maintain "open door" in China.

19. Geological survey indicates U.S. has oil supply for only 20 years.

19. Paris Independent Salon bars works of Dadaist painter Francis Picabia.

26. Egypt: 190 dead in Cairo riots protesting British mandate over Palestine (→ 5/9).

28. Washington: Knickerbocker Theater collapses under weight of snow; 100 dead.

31. German cost of living up 73.7 percent in past year (→ 3/15).

DEATH

5. Sir Ernest Shackleton, British Antarctic explorer (*2/15/1874).

Paul Poiret joins classic designers

Paul Poiret, the most fashionable designer of the pre-war period, has attained classic status. After serving as a designer in the house of Parisian fashion designer Charles Frederic Worth, Poiret opened his own small shop in Paris in 1903. Poiret became noted for the introduction of the hobble skirt, a vertical, tight-fitting style that compelled women to take mincing steps. His Oriental dresses and evening gowns, which appeared in brilliant shades of purple, red, blue, green and orange, were especially popular. Women around the world await his next creation.

The models of Paul Poiret.

Communist Party organized in China

The revolution in Russia, translation of Karl Marx's works and rise of a student movement led to the formation of a Communist Party in China this year. Meeting at a girl's school in Shanghai, the first party congress in June called for the "overthrow of the capitalist class." One of those attending was Mao Tse-tung, a library assistant and primary school teacher (→ 5/5/22).

Young revolutionary Mao Tse-tung.

Dail approves Free State; De Valera quits

Jan 10. By a seven-vote margin, the Irish Dail has ratified a treaty with Britain establishing the Irish Free State. Arthur Griffith, who led the delegation that negotiated the treaty, was elected President of the Dail and head of the provisional government that will preside until parliamentary elections are held.

While the treaty may end a centuries-old conflict with Britain, it caused serious new political divisions within Ireland. Eamon de Valera, his voice cracking with emotion, announced he would resign as president, insisting only the Irish people could disestablish the republic. De Valera had unsuccessfully advanced an alternative treaty, precluding allegiance to the British crown and excluding a British governor general. In repeated speeches, de Valera said Griffith was subverting the republic and was owed no allegiance by the army.

When the vote came on a new Cabinet headed by Michael Collins, de Valera and his republican supporters stalked out of the Dail. Collins in genial humor said the first responsibility of the new government was administration of a country which he said has been like a ship without a captain (→ 2/21).

Nellie Bly, globe girdler, is dead

World traveler Nellie Bly.

Jan 27. Elizabeth Cochrane Seamon, better known to newspaper readers as reporter Nellie Bly, died today of pneumonia. She was 54.

Raised in a small Pennsylvania town, Miss Bly started with the Pittsburgh Dispatch at age 17. She quickly advanced to Pulitzer's New York World. There, Bly became a famed traveler, documenting and conducting the swiftest solo trip around the world and completing it in less than the fictional Phineas Fogg's 80 days.

Her assignments were usually not so whimsical; she preferred crusades for social reform. In 1887, she feigned insanity to investigate conditions at a mental asylum and wrote about patients subjected to neglect and violence. Her expose resulted in nationwide reform.

Pope Benedict XV dies of pneumonia

Jan 22. Pope Benedict XV (Giacomo Della Chiesa) died of pneumonia early this morning. Orders were immediately given for the draping in purple and black of many church edifices, and special masses were held at the Vatican.

He was elected pope in September 1914 when the first major battles of the Great War started. In 1917, he offered himself as mediator. The failure of this initiative did not prevent him from working for peace during and after the war.

All Christians praise his work. Archbishop Patrick Hayes said: "His services during the war were of the highest order —services which he gave to all mankind, irrespective of race, nation or religion. His thought was to serve humanity, and this he did in a spirit of love and justice and conscientious neutrality. He was one of the Church's greatest Pontiffs" (→ 2/12).

Pope Benedict XV.

1922

FEBRUARY

Su	Mo	Tu	We	Th	Fr	Sa
			1	2	3	4
5	6	7	8	9	10	11
12	13	14	15	16	17	18
19	20	21	22	23	24	25
26	27	28				

4. Sino-Japanese accord restores Shantung province to China.

4. U.S.: Ford buys Lincoln Motor Co. for $8 million.

5. Brooklyn: William Larned's steel-framed tennis racquet gets first test.

6. Washington Disarmament Conference comes to end with signature of final treaty forbidding fortification of Aleutian Islands for 14 years (→ 3/24).

6. Cheka, Russian secret police, dissolved; replaced with GPU.

7. Cass Lake, Minn.: Chippewa Indian, allegedly oldest living human, dies at 137.

7. Paris: Marie Curie elected to Academy of Sciences.

7. Britain threatens crackdown in India to combat Gandhi's civil disobedience campaign (→ 3/10).

9. U.S. Congress establishes World War Foreign Debt Commission; Britain owes $4 bil., France $3 bil., Italy $1.6 bil.

11. Russian Soviets reported taking religious treasures to feed masses (→ 6/8).

15. Holland: World Court opens at The Hague (→ 3/3/23).

17. French reject baseball for 1924 Olympics.

18. U.S. Congress passes Capper-Volstead Act allowing farmers exemption from anti-trust laws.

20. Lithuania: Diet of Vilno votes annexation to Poland.

21. Virginia: 410-foot dirigible Roma explodes over Norfolk, killing 34 Americans.

21. De Valera pronounces Republicans only legitimate authority in Ireland (→ 3/22).

25. Mass-murderer Landru executed in France.

25. Boston: L.T. Brown sets high jump mark at 6 ft., 4.75 in.

26. British, French premiers agree to extend alliance for 20 years.

27. U.S. Supreme Court unanimously upholds woman suffrage amendment (→ 9/17).

28. Britain declares Egypt a sovereign state (→ 3/15).

Director victim of mysterious murder

Feb 2. Another murder mystery shocked Los Angeles today when William Desmond Taylor, the director of "Huckleberry Finn" and other films, was found with a bullet through his heart. Taylor lived alone, and a male servant found the body lying beside a writing desk.

Mabel Normand, Mack Sennett's leading comedienne and sometimes rumored to be engaged to Taylor, is said to be the last person seen with him. She states that she left his house about 9 o'clock last evening. Actress Mary Miles Minter hurried to Taylor's house in tears as soon as she heard the news. Robbery was not the motive, say the police, leaning toward the theory that a jealous woman either shot Taylor or had him shot. A man seen leaving the house and a secretary previously dismissed for theft also figure in the police investigation.

New Pope elected; takes name Pius XI

Feb 12. Cardinal Achille Ratti, Archbishop of Milan, has been elected Pope, and will reign under the name of Pius XI. He was born in Desio, a small town near Milan, of a middle-class family, all of whom were highly educated. The new pope, who is 65 years old, intends to follow the program of his immediate predecessor, Benedict XV, for the establishment of better relations between the Vatican and the Italian government and for world peace. He is the 257th pontiff.

Coronation of Pius XI in Rome.

A little magazine: The Reader's Digest

The first edition.

Feb 5. Young DeWitt Wallace, from St. Paul, Minnesota, has an unusual interest in magazine articles and a rare talent for condensing them. With Lila Acheson, his wife, he has decided to publish what they call The Reader's Digest, a pocket-sized magazine. With only $5,000 in capital, they opened an office beneath a speakeasy in Greenwich Village, New York, and began soliciting subscriptions. They sold 1,500, and today Vol. 1., No. 1 of the magazine was published. Its aim is to inform, entertain, inspire and guide people in their daily lives. The title of the first article is, "How to Keep Young Mentally." It is a page and a half long.

Dancing criticized in Paris, of all places

Feb 26. The dance craze is detracting the French from postwar reconstruction. America won't come to the aid of France because the French are dancing instead of working. The Germans are spreading yet another vice, namely drug use, in France. So claims La Revue Mondiale, a serious French periodical, which is launching a crusade against dancing to jazz music and tango bands. Couples gliding across polished floors to the strains of "Coal Black Mammy" are told that upon the merry movements of their feet may depend France's whole future and economy.

1922

MARCH

Su	Mo	Tu	We	Th	Fr	Sa
			1	2	3	4
5	6	7	8	9	10	11
12	13	14	15	16	17	18
19	20	21	22	23	24	25
26	27	28	29	30	31	

5. Murnau's film "Nosferatu" premieres in Germany.

8. Gen. Chang Tsao-lin, gov. of Manchuria, withdraws support from president, forms alliance to unite China (→ 4/29).

10. German minister of the interior bans all monarchical insignias from public buildings.

10. Bombay: Gandhi arrested on charges of sedition (→ 18).

12. South Africa: Strikers besiege the Rand; troops capture 1,500, bomb more (→ 5/19/30).

13. European Allies inform Washington they may withold German payments to U.S. pending recognition of Versailles treaty (→ 1/7/25).

14. Fascists and Socialists clash in Rome (→ 6/1).

15. Oklahoma anti-Ku Klux Klan society organized (→ 24).

15. France to accept raw materials instead of currency for German reparations (→ 24).

17. Mexico: Gen. Felix Diaz slain in Sonora (→ 11/2).

20. Harding orders U.S. troops back from Rhineland (→ 5/3).

22. Irish army moves for dictatorship to replace Dail (→ 30).

23. Emile Treville Holley becomes first Negro to enter Annapolis since Civil War.

24. KKK holds mass initiations in Tulsa, Ok. (→ 5/18).

24. U.S. Senate ratifies four-power naval treaty (→ 8/10).

24. German mark reaches new low of 329 to the dollar (→ 6/5).

29. Rail union asks Harding to abolish Labor Board (→ 7/1).

29. Census reports 11% of U.S. population speaks no English.

30. Dublin: Republicans demolish Freeman's Journal bldg. for advocating free state (→ 4/23).

31. 600,000 coal miners now on strike across U.S. (→ 4/3).

31. Morroco: 700 French killed or wounded by rebel ambush in Mouleuya Valley (→ 12/12/24).

BIRTH

1. Yitzhak Rabin, Israeli general and statesman.

Gandhi imprisoned for civil disobedience

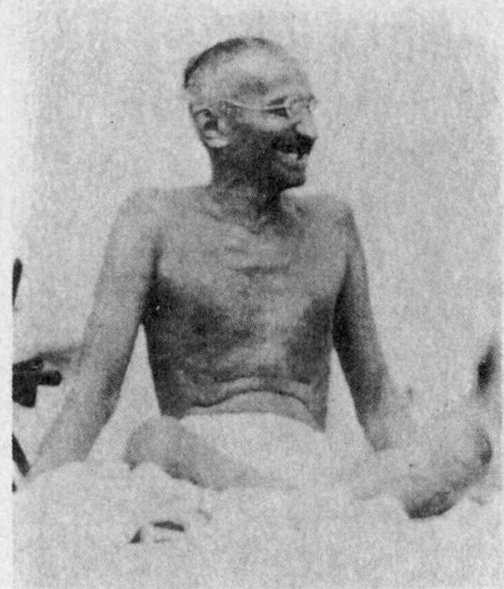

Mahatma Gandhi.

March 18. In India, the followers of Mohandas Gandhi call him "Mahatma," or the great spirit. Today, the great spirit is behind bars, sentenced by British authorities to six years in prison for sedition.

Gandhi was educated in India and London and trained as a lawyer. But he has given up his law office, and now he dresses in a loincloth and a shawl, preaching a life of abstinence and advocating civil disobedience to oppose the British colonial presence in India.

Gandhi was sentenced just eight days after he was arrested. The British acted hastily after government officials in London and India were criticized for not arresting him sooner. In London, the Secretary of State for India was forced to resign because of the controversy over Gandhi. In India, the arrests of Gandhi and other Indian nationalists have only increased sympathy for their cause.

Oakley's score: 98 out of 100 targets

March 5. Annie Oakley, the famous sharpshooter and for 17 years the star attraction in Buffalo Bill's Wild West Show, broke all existing records for women's trap shooting today at the Pinehurst Gun Club in North Carolina. Annie smashed 98 out of 100 clay targets thrown at 16 yards. She hit the first 50 and missed only the 51st and 67th pigeons, ending with a strong 32-straight finish. Phoebe Anne Oakley Mozee was born in a log cabin in Patterson Township, Ohio. She first picked up a gun at the age of nine and discovered to her great surprise that she was a "dead shot."

Dead-eye Annie Oakley.

Sultan appoints self King Fuad of Egypt

King Fuad I, schooled in Europe.

March 15. Sultan Ahmed Fuad Pasha has proclaimed himself King of Egypt "to insure the country's dignity and its international status." This announcement follows the recent British abandonment of the protectorate and recognition of Egypt as an independent sovereign state. The British government points out, however, that "special relations" exist between Great Britain and Egypt; it has reserved to its own discretion the following matters: security of British imperial communications in Egypt; defense of Egypt against all foreign aggression or interference; and protection of foreign interests and foreign communities in Egypt (→ 4/19/23).

1922

APRIL

Su	Mo	Tu	We	Th	Fr	Sa
						1
2	3	4	5	6	7	8
9	10	11	12	13	14	15
16	17	18	19	20	21	22
23	24	25	26	27	28	29
30						

2. New York: Charlie Chaplin's film "Pay Day" released.

3. John L. Lewis, pres. of United Mine Workers recommends nationalization of coal industry to House of Reps. (→ 5/10).

3. Soviet Russia: Lenin appoints Joseph Stalin general secretary of Communist Party, a post of little importance (→ 6/1).

4. Lacrosse revived at New York University after lapse of 30 years.

7. U.S. Sec. of Interior Fall leases Teapot Dome naval oil reserves in Wyoming to Harry Sinclair's Mammoth Oil Company (→ 15).

10. Italy: International economics conference opens in Genoa; French and Russians disagree on arms reductions (→ 16).

12. Russia: Council of Commissars restores right to private ownership of autos.

15. Wyoming Senator John Kendrick asks inquiry into Fall's lease of govt. oil reserves (→ 6/8).

16. Syria: Martial law proclaimed in Damascus to quell civil strife.

17. Honolulu orders Waikiki beach bathers to wear clothes.

21. N.Y.: Lee De Forest announces invention of motion picture device containing photoplay and voice on same film.

23. All Ireland joins in one-day strike to protest military (→ 5/23).

29. China: 100-mile battle rages near Peking between Generals Wu Pei-fu and Chang Tso-lin (→ 7/29).

BIRTHS

16. Kingsley Amis, British satirist.

22. Richard Diebenkorn, American painter.

DEATHS

1. Charles I, ex-emperor of Austria, king of Hungary (*8/17/1887).

8. Erich von Falkenhayn, German general (*11/11/1861).

28. Paul Deschanel, French statesman (*2/13/1855).

Fatty Arbuckle, a fallen star, freed

Baby-faced Fatty Arbuckle.

April 12. It took the San Francisco jury only one minute today to acquit comedian Roscoe C. "Fatty" Arbuckle of killing a starlet after a Labor Day drinking party at the Hotel St. Francis last year.

The actress, Virginia Rappe, had attended the party and complained of stomach pains to Arbuckle afterwards. She died a few days later of a ruptured bladder, but rumors circulated that Arbuckle had raped her with a champagne bottle and crushed her under his weight.

Tabloids across the country portrayed Arbuckle as a pervert and the public outcry over the affair has been so great that his films have been withdrawn by distributors and he has been fired by Paramount. With its mansions, parties and divorces, Hollywood is gaining a reputation as a new Babylon. "We are trying our present day morals," the judge announced at the trial.

Greek goddess, inspiration for Pierre Louis' "Songs of Bilitis."

Germany and Russia join in Rapallo pact

Delegates to the Genoa Conference. At center: Britain's P.M. David Lloyd George, and France's Louis Barthou, Pres. of the Reparations Commission.

April 16. Representatives of the Allies are sputtering and angry in Genoa. They have been meeting to discuss the financial reorganization of Europe, and they hope to force Soviet Russia to repay the debts of the Czar. With the meeting in Genoa barely underway, the Allies were shocked to learn that German and Soviet representatives were meeting separately in nearby Rapallo and had even signed a new treaty.

The agreement was reached by Walter Rathenau, the German Foreign Minister, and Georgi Chicherin, who has replaced Leon Trotsky as Soviet Russia's Foreign Commissar. Germany agreed to become the first country to recognize the Soviet government. And both countries agreed to cancel all debts contracted before the war and to renounce claims made during the war. Germany also received very favorable trading concessions.

The Rapallo meeting has already disrupted the larger Genoa Conference. And the Allies wonder if the new treaty will also undermine the Treaty of Versailles (→ 5/19).

Cellist Pablo Casals takes up the baton

Virtuoso cellist Pablo Casals.

April 7. Called by Fritz Kreisler "the best that draws a bow," cellist Pablo Casals last night took up the baton and demonstrated why he is earning a reputation as a conductor.

Leading an orchestra at Carnegie Hall, he quickly assured those present that this was no Quixotic tilt. With persuasive force, clear upbeat and colorful variety, he unfolded Beethoven's "Coriolan Overture," Beethoven's 6th, Brahms' 1st symphony and the "Prelude" and "Love Death" from Wagner's "Tristan und Isolde." Both at intermission and the end, the Spanish artist was repeatedly recalled by a most appreciative audience.

1922

MAY

Su	Mo	Tu	We	Th	Fr	Sa
	1	2	3	4	5	6
7	8	9	10	11	12	13
14	15	16	17	18	19	20
21	22	23	24	25	26	27
28	29	30	31			

3. Germany requests U.S. Army of occupation remain on the Rhine (→ 6/4).

5. New York: Shakespeare folio sold for $9,500.

7. Egyptians anger British, claiming sovereignty over Sudan.

9. Egypt issues decree making govt. sole legal trader in opium, cocaine, hashish, morphine.

9. Washington: U.S., Britain reach agreement on mandated territory of Palestine (→ 27).

10. Chicago: 200 labor leaders arrested for complicity in murder of two policemen, bombing of factories (→ 17).

13. Kentucky Derby won by Morvich with jockey A. Johnson.

14. Mexican govt. expropriates 1.9 million acres for land reform.

15. Germany officially cedes Upper Silesia to Poland.

17. Chicago buildings now under armed guard during riots (→ 18).

18. Illinois mine operators send open letter to U.M.W. Pres. John L. Lewis demanding end to nationwide strike (→ 6/22).

18. Georgia: Negro boy tortured and burned at stake for allegedly killing white woman (→ 11/19).

21. Communist revolt strikes Bulgaria; King Boris in flight.

22. Nicaraguan revolutionaries turn over govt. fort to U.S. Marines after eight-hour occupation.

23. Irish Free State declares Sinn Fein illegal in six counties (→ 6/16).

26. Babe Ruth loses captaincy for eruption during N.Y.-Washington game.

26. Pres. Harding signs bill creating Federal Narcotics Board.

27. Lucerne announces cheese industry suffering from import of U.S.-made Swiss cheese.

30. Washington: Harding dedicates Lincoln Memorial.

30. Jimmy Murphy takes 10th Indianapolis 500 at 94.5 mph.

BIRTH

25. Enrico Berlinguer, Italian statesman (*6/11/1984).

Russians told they must repay loans

May 19. The divisive and stormy Genoa Conference broke up today without a resolution of the touchy Soviet Russia financial problem. But the European countries are determined to make Russia pay its debts, and they plan to meet again next month at The Hague.

The Allies demand the Soviet government make good on the debts of the Czar, compensate foreigners for all the property that was seized during the revolution and agree to participate in an international tribunal that would resolve all future financial conflicts. The Allies refuse to recognize the new Russian government until the matters are settled. They are willing to be lenient about Soviet Russia's war debt.

The Western representatives failed to agree from the very beginning, partly because Belgium is insisting on the actual return of seized property. And Soviet Russia, which participated in the meeting, refuses to recognize the Czar's debts.

Most Eastern countries were excluded from the Genoa Conference. They issued a statement, saying, "The East does not hate Europe, for which it has done so much, but it does hate imperialism, the mixture of injustice and violence of certain conquering countries." The disgruntled Eastern nations have agreed to hold their own meeting next month in Moscow (→ 7/11).

Lillian Gish, "The First Lady of the Silent Screen," in the Griffith film "Orphans of the Storm," set during the French Revolution.

Britain to rule Palestine; Vatican objects

British troops guard the Jaffa Gate.

May 27. The United States and Great Britain have reached agreement on a treaty regarding Palestine. The British mandate for civilian rule of that territory, about to come up for confirmation before the League of Nations, guarantees equal treatment to the citizens of all members of the League of Nations.

As America has not joined the League, the British have agreed to a separate treaty guaranteeing the rights and interests of American citizens in Palestine, and giving them an equal footing in commerce, industry and use of natural resources.

The Vatican, in a note to the League of Nations, has objected to the proposed mandate on the grounds that it threatens religious equality. The creation of a Jewish national home in Palestine, it argues, gives the adherents of Zionism a privileged position (→ 6/21).

General Wu takes control in Peking

Sun Yat-sen foe Wu Pei-fu.

May 5. China's recent civil war has ended with the forces of General Wu Pei-fu driving those of General Chang Tso-lin out of the Peking region. The fighting, which claimed 7,000 casualties, left Wu in full control, as Chang's Manchurian army retreated in disorder.

Wu, recognized by the Peking government, says he will not interfere with President Hsu Shih-chang, expected to serve out his term. Wu also plans to call a constitutional convention with the intention of uniting the governments of North and South China.

The Kuomintang government of South China, in Canton, is led by Sun Yat-sen, nominal President of the Chinese republic (→ 7/29).

Skirts in Paris, once up, now down again

May 7. Jack Dempsey may have beaten Georges Carpentier in the ring, but in the fashion circle France is champ. And France has decreed that the long skirt is back. This afternoon at the elegant Longchamps racetrack, where couturiers traditionally see their designs vindicated, every Parisian woman sported a full-length skirt. The 10,000 Americans who attended the races, pugilist Dempsey among them, could not help but notice the more demure style. One American girl, wearing an abbreviated frock, declared she felt "quite naked" in it. Can we assume she and other fine American women will be donning long gowns this summer?

Below the knee in fashion in Paris.

1922

JUNE

Su	Mo	Tu	We	Th	Fr	Sa
				1	2	3
4	5	6	7	8	9	10
11	12	13	14	15	16	17
18	19	20	21	22	23	24
25	26	27	28	29	30	

1. Italy: Mussolini threatens full-scale rebellion at Bologna gathering of 50,000 Fascists; Prefect Mori forced out (→ 7/19).

1. Reports from Russia indicate Lenin has suffered stroke (→ 14).

4. War Dept. announces 1,000 U.S. troops to stay in Rhineland indefinitely (→ 1/10/23).

4. Budapest: First socialists win parliamentary seats.

5. Intl. bankers on Reparations Commission deny loan to Germany (→ 25).

5. London: Louis Brennen announces invention of helicopter that ascends at right angles to ground.

8. Washington: Harding approves Fall-Denby leasing of Navy oil lands (→ 12/11).

8. Russia: It is reported that Bolsheviks are robbing saints' tombs for riches.

11. Adm. Baron Kato accepts Japanese premiership.

14. Triumvirate to rule Russia while Lenin takes 6-month leave to improve health (→ 1/4/23).

15. Washington reports alcohol death rate cut 21 percent by Prohibition (→ 10/6).

16. De Valera's Republicans defeated in Irish elections; mandate leaves Irish Free State a British dominion (→ 29).

18. Baltimore: Dr. McCollum reports new vitamin D that will cure rickets.

21. U.K.: House of Lords rejects Palestine mandate (→ 7/24).

22. Illinois: 30 killed in rioting at Marion mine strike (→ 7/17).

25. German mark hits 348.5 to the U.S. dollar (→ 7/12).

29. Dublin: Free State forces storm Four Courts (→ 30).

30. London: Irish rebels assassinate Sir Henry Wilson, British deputy for N. Ireland.→

BIRTH

10. Judy Garland, American actress and singer (†6/22/1969).

DEATH

12. Wolfgang von Kapp, German politicain (*7/24/1858).

They loved her and she's gone forever

Flamboyant Lillian Russell.

June 6. Singer and actress Lillian Russell, born in Clinton, Iowa, as Helen Louise Leonard 61 years ago, died today. She began her career in light opera. In the early 1880s, Tony Pastor launched her as "The American Beauty" at his casino in New York City. After 1899, she appeared at Weber and Fields' Music Hall, with the McCaull Opera Company, and later with her own company. Miss Russell, who lectured across the country on "How to live a hundred years," was noted for her flamboyant personality and her love of jewelry. Her romance with "Diamond Jim" Brady, financier and philanthropist, famous for his elaborate meals, is legendary.

June 24. The British Open Golf Cup sailed for the U.S. with Walter Hagen, victor by one stroke.

▷

Irish assassinate former army chief

Wilson killed at his London home.

June 30. Field Marshal Sir Henry Wilson, chief of the Imperial General Staff during the war and a member of Parliament from Ulster, has been shot dead by two men outside his London home. After a chase through Eaton Square, police seized the two men and said papers on one of them identified him as an Irish Republican Army member.

Wilson, a native of Northern Ireland, recently developed plans for restoring order in Belfast. His murder marked the first time the factional strife in Ireland was exported to Britain and provoked statements of outrage in London. Meanwhile, factional fighting broke out in Ireland over the recent treaty establishing the Irish Free State. The fighting centered around the Four Courts Building, former seat of British justice in Dublin that was seized by a group of republican rebels in April, demanding preservation of the republic. Free State forces stormed the building, capturing Rory O'Connor, leader of the rebels, and 130 of his men (→ 7/3).

The Yale crew beat Harvard this year. Yale's first race, in 1844, was won by pranksters who tied a rock to their foe's stern.

Highest altitude reached: 26,800 ft.

June 7. According to reports reaching London, some members of a British mountain-climbing team have succeeded in reaching the highest altitude ever achieved by man. The Times revealed in its editorial columns that "three members of the Everest expedition, Mallory, Somerville and Norton, on May 20 reached an altitude of 26,800 feet, the highest ever reached by man." The Times noted that the new record, just 3,200 feet below the summit, exceeds by about the same margin the previous world record of 24,583 set in 1910.

Mallory-Bullock team on Everest.

German minister's policy brings death

June 24. Walter Rathenau, the German Foreign Minister, was assassinated today as he left his home in a suburb of Berlin. He was shot down in cold blood by at least two assailants who showered his automobile with automatic gunfire and grenades. Rathenau directed the distribution of raw materials in Germany during the war. More recently, he has been in charge of the reconstruction efforts. He has been sharply criticized in nationalist quarters for embracing war reparations and trying to make accommodations with France. Rathenau, who is Jewish, was also subjected to scurrilous attacks by anti-Semitic reactionaries (→ 7/17).

1922

JULY

Su	Mo	Tu	We	Th	Fr	Sa
						1
2	3	4	5	6	7	8
9	10	11	12	13	14	15
16	17	18	19	20	21	22
23	24	25	26	27	28	29
30	31					

3. Dublin: Free State troops begin intensive bombing of rebel strongholds (→ 8/7).

8. Illinois militia called to combat striking rail workers (→ 12).

8. Wimbledon: Gerald Patterson 6-3, 6-4, 6-2 over Randolph Lycett; Suzanne Lenglen 6-2, 6-0 over Molla Mallory.

12. Illinois: Rail heads refuse to meet with strikers until they return to work (→ 25).

12. Paris: German War Commissioner Fischer asks Reparations Commission to defer payments until 1924 (→ 8/15).

13. Ontario: Indians of six nations ask differences be submitted to International Court at The Hague.

15. U.S. Senate rejects Henry Ford's offer to build and operate Muscle Shoals Dam (→ 10/13/24).

17. Wellsburg, West Virginia: Seven killed in attack on nonunion mine (→ 25).

17. Germany: Police arrest two nationalists for last month's murder of Walter Rathenau.

19. Rome: Mussolini warns Italian Cabinet against repression of Fascists (→ 8/1).

20. League Council approves mandates; France gets Togoland, Britain gets Tanganyika; Cameroons divided (→ 26).

22. Barred from Olympics, Germany organizes alternative games in Leipzig.

24. Greece gives Macedonian oil rights to Anglo-Persian Oil Co.

24. League Council grants Palestine, Egypt to Britain (→ 9/11).

25. Harding orders federal rail and coal control to ensure distribution of food and fuel (→ 8/5).

26. Syria goes to France by League decree.

29. China: Sun Yat-sen attacks General Chen at Shiuchow (→ 5/6/23).

30. Greece proclaims protectorate over Smyrna (→ 9/9).

BIRTH

2. Pierre Cardin, French fashion designer.

U.S. struggling to settle two strikes

July 1. More than 400,000 railroad shopmen walked off the job today in the latest confrontation between organized labor and management in the United States. The railroad strike comes at a time when the Harding administration is already wrestling with the problem of how to end a coal strike that began three months ago. Wages are the key issues in both labor disputes, along with such other factors as working conditions, including the length of the work day.

Even as the railroad men were walking out, President Harding was meeting today in Washington with coal operators and union officials, urging them to come to an agreement. The president informed the group that his administration has no authority at this time to order the men back to work, despite the fact that the walkout has resulted in slowing coal production in the country to a mere trickle in recent months. The situation could become more crucial, however, if the strike continues into the winter months when coal consumption reaches a peak.

The railroad strike is a different matter, in the view of government officials. The president is said to feel that the federal government is in a better position to step into the railroad impasse since he views that strike as an outright defiance of the United States Railroad Labor Board's efforts to avoid a walkout. Meanwhile, railway executives issued a statement in which they said that "the trains will continue to run" (→ 8).

The Hollywood Bowl has opened in the world's film capital to help quench the region's fast-growing thirst for entertainment.

1922

AUGUST

Su	Mo	Tu	We	Th	Fr	Sa
		1	2	3	4	5
6	7	8	9	10	11	12
13	14	15	16	17	18	19
20	21	22	23	24	25	26
27	28	29	30	31		

1. Italian Fascists crush Socialist general strike, depose Milan govt., destroy headquarters in Genoa and Livorno (→ 5).

3. N.Y.: WGY, Schenectady, makes first radio sound effect, two wood blocks slammed together to imitate door slamming.

5. Rail union leaders meet with Harding, demand restoration of seniority, right to strike (→ 13).

5. Einstein flees Germany, fearing attempt on life by Rathenau killers.

7. IRA cuts cable link between U.S. and Europe at Waterville landing station (→ 22).

10. King George formally signs Washington arms treaties.

13. Unions reject Harding's plan to settle rail strike (→ 9/1).

15. German govt. offers one-fourth of total reparations payments (→ 24).

17. Cover Garden, largest dance hall in world, opens in N.Y.

19. German sailplane makes longest glider flight, two hours, ten seconds.

19. U.S. Senate passes Fordney-McCumber Tariff Bill.

20. Paris: Unofficial Women's Olympic Games organized by Intl. Fed. of Feminine Athletes.

22. U.S. Steel orders 20 percent wage increase.

22. Tong war erupts in San Francisco's Chinatown; police sweep area.

24. German mark falls to 2,000 to the U.S. dollar (→ 9/4).

26. Ford Motor Co. announces plans to shut doors in September due to coal shortage.

26. Japanese troops evacuate Siberia.

29. Paris: Mushroom fungus reported seriously threatening Palace of Versailles.

30. All of South Russia reported in revolt against Bolsheviks.

30. American dressmaker Nathaniel Gidding finds New York women best-dressed in U.S.

DEATH

12. Arthur Griffith, Dail Eireann president (*3/31/1872).

Irish government chief killed in ambush

Michael Collins.

Aug 22. Michael Collins, chief of the provisional government of the Irish Free State, and commander of the Irish National Army, was killed today in an ambush in his native county of Cork. Collins, 31, was in a cavalcade of cars proceeding up a hill near Bandon when fired upon by a small group of men, believed to be republicans.

Collins, who helped negotiate the Free State Treaty with Britain, had been the target of several recent attacks, and there is speculation that his death was in reprisal for the recent killing of Harry J. Boland, a close friend of Collins but an opponent of the treaty. Collins, a leader of the guerrilla war against the British, had been on a military inspection trip through southwestern Ireland.

Collins' death was the second grievous blow suffered by the Free State government this month. On August 12, Arthur Griffith, President of the Dail Eireann, died unexpectedly of a heart attack. Griffith was regarded as the brains and Collins as the military genius behind the new Irish Free State (→ 12/7).

Fascists fighting Communists in Italy

Aug 5. Hundreds have died and thousands more are wounded in a civil war between the two extreme political elements in Italy, the Fascists and Communists. Premier Facta, faced with militancy on both sides, has pleaded for an end to the violence, suggesting the two parties should negotiate in respect for the safety of all Italians.

Yet it seems the current lull in fighting will not last long as rumors circulate that the Fascists are mobilizing for an assault on Rome while the Communists continue making terrorist strikes. Their last attack occurred yesterday when a guerrilla group blew up a power transmission line near Naples. With such strife, government moderates will probably encounter strong resistance to peace efforts (→ 10/25).

Telephone inventor speaks for last time

Bell opens N.Y.-Chicago line, 1892.

Aug 2. Alexander Graham Bell, inventor of the telephone, died early today at his home in Nova Scotia. He was 76. Bell was born in Edinburgh in 1847 and came to Canada in 1870, working as a teacher of the deaf. He began working on the telephone in 1875 in Boston and achieved success on March 10, 1876, when his assistant, sitting in another room, heard Bell's voice say, "Mr. Watson, come here. I need you." Bell obtained a patent the same year and founded the American Bell Telephone Company, which has been enormously successful.

Feds now smelling out hip flasks

Aug 17. Declaring war on the clandestine hip flask, federal dry agents have served notice on some of the most fashionable and frequented Broadway establishments that patrons who "tote their own" do so at peril of the law. Managers of such places must force diners and dancers to obey the law, and patrol wagons will be backed up to the doors of the most famous establishments and flask users hauled out unceremoniously.

Beauty contests ban seductive aromas

Aug 28. Perfume, sweet-smelling face powder and flowers having a "burden of perfume" will be barred from Atlantic City's fall pageant at the suggestion of Hudson Maxim, who will portray "Father Neptune" during the carnival. The 19 shore beauties who will form Neptune's court consented at a "war council" today to form an anti-scent guard about Neptune. Miss America, Queen of Beauty, will have her looks accentuated solely by flowers which lack the olfactory powers of seducing the public and the judges.

Northcliffe, Fleet St. press lord, dies

Aug 14. Alfred Harmsworth, the first Lord Northcliffe, died today of heart disease. Born in Ireland in 1865, Northcliffe owned over 100 journals in Great Britain, including The London Times and the London Daily Mail. The newspapers' circulations rose dramatically when he gave people what they wanted: women's columns, society pages and gossip.

1922

SEPTEMBER

Su	Mo	Tu	We	Th	Fr	Sa
					1	2
3	4	5	6	7	8	9
10	11	12	13	14	15	16
17	18	19	20	21	22	23
24	25	26	27	28	29	30

1. Govt. gets sweeping injunction against rail workers (→ 4).

2. Pennsylvania: Operators yield to coal strikers; strike settled at Harding's urging (→ 13).

4. A.F.L. Pres. Gompers claims rail injunction violates U.S. Constitution (→ 13).

4. German industrialists agree to contribute to reparations (→ 15).

5. Jimmy Doolittle flies coast-to-coast with one stop in 22.5 hrs.

7. Brazil celebrates 100th anniversary of independence.

9. Greeks surrender Smyrna to Turks (→ 11).

11. Paris: Allies agree to keep Turks from controlling Dardanelles (→ 19).

11. Arabs declare national day of mourning as British mandate begins in Palestine (→ 4/1/25).

13. Russia challenges Allied occupation of Constantinople (→ 11/4).

15. German Chancellor Josef Wirth declares, "Bread first, then reparations" (→ 10/14).

17. Washington: Natl. Woman's Party discloses study on inequality in law (→ 7/21/23).

18. League of Nations admits Hungary (→ 9/28/23).

19. Harding vetoes cash bonus bill for veterans (→ 3/18/24).

19. Kemal notifies France he will respect Allied neutral zone if Turkey gets E. Thrace (→ 23).

22. Cable Bill passes U.S. Congress, equalizing citizenship rights of alien men and women.

23. U.S. Supreme Court upholds rail injunction (→ 8/31/23).

23. Brecht's play "Drums in the Night" opens in Munich.

23. Allies promise E. Thrace to Turks; straits to remain under international control (→ 27).

29. D.W. Griffith's "Two Orphans" gets first screening.

DEATHS

4. Georges Sorel, French syndicalist theoretician (*11/2/1847).

26. Thomas E. Watson, populist and KKK member (*9/5/1856).

Two major strikes ended in America

Sept 13. Striking railroad shopmen were given the green light today to return to their jobs. The end of the more than two-month-old walkout marks the second labor settlement reached this month. Coal miners agreed to end a five-month strike on September 2 after an appeal from President Harding. It is possible that some of the striking railroad workers will not return to work immediately because some of the rail lines have resisted the settlement plan.

The two major strikes in the key coal and railroad industries were marked by sporadic violence in some areas of the nation, prompting government officials to call out the militia to keep order. In late July, President Harding ordered emergency measures to assure delivery of food and other essential goods and services (→ 23).

Turks drive Greeks out of Asia Minor

Sept 27. Turkish nationalist troops, under the command of Mustafa Kemal Pasha, have soundly defeated Greek forces and driven them out of Asia Minor. One of the Turks' greatest victories was recapturing the city of Smyrna. Greek military commanders are now trying to arrange a cease-fire with the Turks. Their defeat has brought about the abdication of King Constantine. It is not clear yet what will happen when advancing Greek forces meet entrenched British troops still in the area (→ 10/1).

Haggard Greek soldiers march before Kemal's victorious troops.

1922

OCTOBER

Su	Mo	Tu	We	Th	Fr	Sa
1	2	3	4	5	6	7
8	9	10	11	12	13	14
15	16	17	18	19	20	21
22	23	24	25	26	27	28
29	30	31				

1. Mustafa Kemal orders troops to halt near British lines (→ 12).

4. New York recommends fingerprinting of all aliens.

4. Geneva: League Council grants rebuilding funds to Austria, reserves right to control foreign policy (→ 6/1/24).

6. Harding bans liquor from all ships entering U.S. ports (→ 24).

8. Polo Grounds: Giants over the Yankees 5-3 in fifth and final game of World Series.

9. British Laborites demand resignation of Lloyd George.

10. Harvard discovers new outpost of stellar system, widens universe two quintillion miles.

12. Turks invade neutral zones at Chanak and Ismid (→ 15).

14. German industrialist August Thyssen proposes longer work day as only road to economic recovery (→ 23).

15. Berlin: Several thousand armed Communists interrupt nationalist meeting of Union for Freedom and Order (→ 11/21).

15. Rumania's Ferdinand and Marie crowned rulers of Transylvania in Alba-Julia.

15. Greek troops begin evacuation of Thrace (→ 11/28).

21. New York woman Marjorie Howarth becomes first to cross third range of Andes.

24. N.Y.: British ship captains, caught carrying brandy, insist U.K. law requires five quarts in case of illness (→ 1/5/23).

25. Naples: Benito Mussolini warns he will seize Italy unless power is handed over peacefully (→ 30).

30. "Geometric art" reportedly the new movement in Paris.

31. Government spokesman claims U.S. will join World Court set up by League (→ 3/3/23).

BIRTH

19. Jack Anderson, U.S. columnist and investigative reporter.

DEATH

22. Lyman Abbott, Liberal Protestant theologian (*12/18/1835).

Liberals lose power in Downing Street

Oct 19. In a meeting with King George V at Buckingham Palace today, Prime Minister Lloyd George announced the resignation of his government and recommended that Andrew Bonar Law be invited to form a new government.

Although the Liberal premier has had his problems lately, few thought he would throw in the towel so quickly, and his fall came with unexpected speed. In recent years, the Liberal Party, weakened by the growing strength of the Labor Party, has relied on a coalition of Conservatives and Liberals to run the country. Growing distaste with this scheme by many Conservatives came to a head in the recent by-election in Newport, where the coalition candidate, expected to win easily, was defeated by the Tory candidate, expected to come in last. Tory MP's immediately voted 187-87 against the coalition, undermining Lloyd George's support and forcing his resignation. Andrew Bonar Law is a Conservative.

Other problems have recently plagued Lloyd George. Certain Tories felt betrayed last year by his treaty with Ireland. And critics have charged him with a reckless handling of foreign affairs that might even lead to a new war with Turkey (→ 11/15).

Station wagons are for play, not work

Oct 23. In a decision bound to interest many car owners, the New York State Appellate Court has ruled that the automobile known as a "suburban" or "station wagon" is not a commercial truck but a passenger car and thus entitled to lower license plate rates. Such owners will save, and the state will lose, thousands of dollars next year when the difference between the two will reach $6 a plate.

The case was brought by George Zabriskie, who argued that these large automobiles are not commercial vehicles but are used "for transporting people and for bringing packages from stores and carrying baggage to and from the railroad station."

Mussolini's Fascists march on Rome

Il Duce (center) leads 40,000 black-shirted Fascists into Rome.

Oct 30. Italy was given a choice in the past week. It could accept a bloodless revolution and a dictatorship, headed by Benito Mussolini. Or its army could fight Mussolini's forces, the Fascists, for the control of Rome and the destiny of the country. King Victor Emmanuel III looked around him, saw what was left of the government of Prime Minister Luigi Facta and made his choice. The king forced Facta and his Cabinet to resign and welcomed Mussolini with open arms.

Mussolini mobilized his Fascists last Tuesday and ordered them to march toward Rome. About 40,000 of his militia advanced north from Naples, wearing black shirts, carrying bayonets and awaiting the final order to attack Rome. They met some resistance from local authorities, but they were cheered wildly almost everywhere.

The order to attack never came. Facta's government was already preparing for the state of siege, but the king refused to sign Facta's decree or cooperate with him. Victor Emmanuel invited Mussolini to form a new government.

Mussolini, or "Duce," as he is called, traveled to Rome in a special train put at his disposal by the king. But he had to complete his journey in an open motorcar because government troops had blown up the rail tracks. Mussolini's black shirt was spattered with mud as he arrived, but he was quickly ushered in to meet the king at the Quirinal Palace. Three times, the king and the new Italian leader walked onto a balcony at the palace to wave at the huge crowd. And each time they appeared, the crowd's enthusiasm erupted into a wild frenzy.

Italians are trying desperately to restore their faith in the country, and they are afraid of the Communist menace. They have vowed to support Mussolini, and he has promised to give Italy "a strong government, such as she has needed for many years past, but never obtained." Mussolini has already named a new Cabinet, and his Fascists are in the majority. But the Duce has also invited enemies of his movement to join him.

It is beginning to look as if Mussolini hopes to govern Italy largely by the strength of his personality. Fascist leaders issued a manifesto today proclaiming: "From this moment, Mussolini is the government of Italy. He is now responsible for the safety of the state. Any act against government institutions would be rebellion against Mussolini" (→ 11/16).

First U.S. woman Senator, for a day

Oct 7. Rebecca Latimer Felton, an 87-year-old Georgia widow, received credentials today as the nation's first woman United States Senator. While her appointment to succeed the late Senator Thomas E. Watson of Georgia is a historic first, it is uncertain whether she will ever be sworn into office. By the time Congress convenes, an elected successor to Senator Watson will have been chosen. However, Helen Longstreet, the widow of General A.P. Longstreet, has appealed to President Harding to call Congress back into session for at least a day so that Mrs. Felton can take her oath of office.

Chocolate heir and philanthropist dies

Oct 24. By profession, George Cadbury, who died today in Birmingham, England, at 83 years of age, was a chocolate manufacturer. When not performing his duties as Chairman of Cadbury Brothers, Ltd., however, he was involved in social reform, and in support of such work, he bought four newspapers in the Birmingham district in 1891. Ten years later, he assumed financial responsibility for The Daily News. Along with his wife, Dame Elizabeth, he worked for improvement in education and housing. As a couple, they devoted themselves to activities which they hoped would lead to lasting world peace.

First flight by woman across U.S.

Oct 8. Lilian Gatlin became the first woman to cross the continent by airplane as she landed in a small mail plane equipped with a 400-horsepower Liberty motor at Curtiss Field, Long Island, at 5:45 this evening. The flight from San Francisco was completed in 27 hours and 11 minutes. Miss Gatlin undertook the 2,680-mile flight to draw attention to the National Association of Aviation Gold Mothers, which she founded, and initiate an annual government commemoration of the death of aviators, both male and female, who have given their lives "on the altar of patriotism and progress in pursuit of an ideal."

Liquor prohibited on all ships in port

Oct 6. To the dismay of those in New York shipping circles, the administration has issued orders banning the sale and transportation of liquor on all American ships, public and private. The controversial ban, announced by President Harding, also applies to all foreign ships that enter American ports or sail within the nation's three-mile continental limits. However, the liquor ban will not apply to foreign embassies within the country.

The United States officially became dry in 1920, a year after adoption of the 18th Amendment to the Constitution. The Harding administration order, however, is quite likely to prove a boon to Canadian ports, where no such liquor ban on domestic or foreign ships exists. The city of Quebec, for instance, can now handle vessels as large as those that now use New York City ports, but the Canadian city currently has only a modest amount of shipping traffic.

Collapse of mark imperils Germany

Oct 23. An impending financial crisis heightened today when Chancellor Karl Joseph Wirth proposed to his Cabinet that Germany declare bankruptcy. With the mark trading at 4,000 to the dollar, and the price of bread up 100 percent in a month, "Bread first, then reparation" is fast becoming the cry of the Germans. Agrarians and urbanites are violently split over policy on food prices. And Berlin's public baths will close next month to save on coal. It is no wonder the Allies, preparing for the Brussels financial conference, doubt whether reparations will come at all (→ 11/2).

The Coupe Docteur.

1922

NOVEMBER

Su	Mo	Tu	We	Th	Fr	Sa
			1	2	3	4
5	6	7	8	9	10	11
12	13	14	15	16	17	18
19	20	21	22	23	24	25
26	27	28	29	30		

2. With mark at 4,450 to the dollar, conference of German financial experts convenes in Berlin to discuss crisis (→ 1/4/23).

2. Mexican rebel Gen. Francisco Murguia executed (→ 7/20/23).

4. N.Y.: Postmaster General orders all homes to get mail boxes or relinquish delivery.

11. Canada: Vernon McKenzie urges fighting U.S. propaganda with taxes on U.S. magazines.

14. BBC begins first daily broadcasts, from Marconi House.

14. German strikes paralyze Dusseldorf; riots hit Cologne.

15. Labor takes 70 seats from Liberals in British elections; Conservatives hold strength.

16. Mussolini threatens Parliament with dissolution if Fascist policy is not followed (→ 25).

17. Mecca's King Hussein offers sanctuary to Turkish ex-Sultan Mohammed VI (→ 10/29/23).

19. U.S. Marines end 34-month guard in Vladivostok Bay.

19. Louisiana Gov. John Parker in Washington to discuss rise of KKK in South (→ 3/9/23).

21. Clemenceau speaks in N.Y., asks aid against rebirth of German militarism under Hitler (→ 30).

25. Italian Parliament grants Mussolini full power over finances until end of 1923 (→ 12/6).

27. Lausanne: Allied delegates bar Soviets from Near East peace conference (→ 3/21/23).

28. Athens: Six officials executed for high treason in Greek military disaster vs. Turks (→ 29).

29. King George held captive in palace by Gonatas govt. after trying to prevent execution of Cabinet members (→ 12/1).

30. Germany: 50,000 gather at Natl. Socialist demonstration to hear Hitler speak (→ 1/13/23).

BIRTH

8. Christiaan Barnard, South African surgeon, first heart transplant.

DEATH

7. Jacob Gimbel, department store founder (*9/26/1950).

King Tut's tomb found

Howard Carter carefully wraps one of the delicate treasures found at Luxor.

Nov 26. In Egypt today, archeologists Lord Carnarvon and Howard Carter opened underground doors that had not been opened for 3,300 years and found an extraordinary, priceless collection of antiquities in what's believed to be the tomb of King Tutankhamen. The Pharaoh was buried in 1337 B.C.

Two British Egyptologists, working in the Valley of the Kings near Luxor, discovered the riches in two rooms next to the crypt of Ramses VI. At the bottom of a flight of stairs was a door stamped with the seal of Tutankhamen. The men gasped when they opened it.

The first objects they saw were three gilt statues carrying beds carved from wood and inlaid with ivory and semi-precious stones. Inside a box they found embroidered robes, precious stones and sandals crafted from gold and painted with hunting scenes. The pharaoh's throne stood regally in one of the rooms. Nearby were two life-sized statues of Tutankhamen, four chariots and more furniture, most of it exquisitely carved and inlaid with stones. Word of the discovery spread quickly and guards had to restrain curious onlookers at the entrance to the tomb (→ 11/23/23).

Remembrances of Paris: Proust is dead

Reclusive Proust in Paris last year.

Nov 18. Marcel Proust, the French novelist who spent most of his adult life remembering and writing about things past, died today in Paris. He was 51. Proust passed his early years with the fashionable and intellectual aristocracy. After the death of his parents, he withdrew from society and wrote about it in a dark, sound-proof room.

Proust's major work is the cycle of novels titled "Remembrance of Things Past." He wrote majestic, long sentences and long novels about sensitivity and passion. But it was memory, surging forth at the least provocation, which fascinated Proust. The simple act of dipping a cookie in tea would transport characters, and presumably Proust himself, back to childhood.

Ottoman Sultan is out; empire finished

Nov 4. Six thousand years of Ottoman rule in Turkey have come to an end and Sultan Mohammed VI has been ousted by the Grand National Assembly at Angora.

By decree, the republican assembly declared the Sultanate had "through corrupt ignorance for several centuries provoked numerous ills for the country, (and now) has passed into the domain of history." The assembly will run the nation as its deputies voted unaminously to proclaim a "government of the people and peasants." They will elect the Caliph as religious leader.

It's expected the sultan will hand in his resignation, despite his vehement protestations that the Angora government acted illegally in removing him from the throne. The dramatic shake-up will undoubtedly receive much attention from Allied powers at the Near East peace conference later this month (→ 17).

Paderewski plays in New York again

Nov 22. Ignace Paderewski wore two of his many hats yesterday afternoon in his Carnegie Hall recital when the renowned pianist inevitably performed some works by the composer. The audience was clearly moved by his superb art, his feeling and enthusiasm. As a great patriot, Paderewski persuaded President Wilson to make Polish independence the 13th of his Fourteen Points, and the pianist served, however briefly, as the Premier of Poland in 1919.

Poland's Ignace Paderewski.

1922

DECEMBER

Su	Mo	Tu	We	Th	Fr	Sa
					1	2
3	4	5	6	7	8	9
10	11	12	13	14	15	16
17	18	19	20	21	22	23
24	25	26	27	28	29	30
31						

1. Joseph Pilsudski resigns as Polish president (→ 16).

1. Turkish leader Ismet Pasha issues banishment edict for one million Greeks (→ 2/4/23).

4. Second Central American Conference convenes in Washington (→ 2/8/23).

4. Dept. of Commerce claims U.S. women wear 1.6 million styles of shoes.

6. Mussolini threatens Italian newspapers with censorship if they keep reporting "false information" (→ 2/5/23).

7. Dublin: Dail Eireann deputy Sean Hales killed by rebels (→ 5/28/23).

11. Interior Sec. Albert Fall leases Elk Hills oil reserves to Edward Doheny's Pan-American Co. without competitive bidding (→ 10/25/23).

16. New Polish Pres. Gavriel Narutowicz assassinated after two days in office (→ 5/13/26).

30. Soviet Russia renamed Union of Soviet Socialist Republics (U.S.S.R.).

CULTURAL EVENTS, 1922

Literature: Willa Cather's "One of Ours"; T.S. Eliot's "The Waste Land"; F. Scott Fitzgerald's "Tales of the Jazz Age," "The Beautiful and the Damned"; Hesse's "Siddhartha"; Joyce's "Ulysses"; Sinclair Lewis' "Babbit"; O'Neill's "The Hairy Ape"; Pulitzer Prize to E.A. Robinson's "Collected Poems."

Academia: John Dewey's "Human Nature and Conduct"; Max Weber's "Methodology of the Social Sciences."

Music: Irving Berlin's "April Showers"; Intl. Society for Contemporary Music founded in Salzburg; Louis Armstrong joins Joe "King" Oliver's band in Chicago.

The Arts: Miro's "The Farm"; Kandinsky becomes professor at Bauhaus in Weimar; Marc Chagall leaves Russia for Paris.

Film: Murneau's "Nosferatu"; Lang's "Dr. Mabuse the Gambler"; Flaherty's "Nanook of the North"; Tourneur's "Last of the Mohicans."

Einstein and Bohr top Nobel winners

Atomic physicist Niels Bohr.

Dec 10. Niels Bohr of Denmark was given the Nobel Prize in physics today, sealing the triumph of the new quantum theory first enunciated by Max Planck. Albert Einstein was awarded the physics prize last year for successfully applying quantum theory to a phenomenon called the photoelectric effect, in which light causes the emission of electrons by a metal.

Bohr won the prize this year for using quantum theory to explain the internal structure of the atom. His model has a number of electrons circling the dense nucleus of the atom. Electrons jump to higher or lower orbits as they absorb or emit energy in packets called quanta. Bohr's model of the atom has been accepted because it successfully predicts the exact nature of the energy emitted by specific atoms.

The Nobel Prize in medicine was shared this year by Archibald Hill of England and Otto Meyerhoff of Germany. Francis William Aston of Britain won the chemistry prize.

German-born Albert Einstein.

"Ulysses" stands out in a big literary year

In the opinion of a reviewer in The New Republic, the novel "Ulysses," released in America this spring, is "a work of high genius." But James Joyce is only one of several writers receiving great praise this year. Poet T.S. Eliot gave us "The Waste Land," and Herman Hesse offered "Siddartha." John Galsworthy produced another volume in "The Forsyte Saga." Willa Cather and F. Scott Fitzgerald headed a list of prolific American short-story writers. Sinclair Lewis wrote his second novel, "Babbitt," the story of a self-deluded community leader. Dramatist Eugene O'Neill received the Pulitzer Prize for "Anna Christie" and notoriety for "The Hairy Ape."

This year's works frequently explore a new literary realm: the unconscious, an inner awareness often conveyed in shocking images and words. "Ulysses" is the worst offender. The U.S. Post Office burned 500 copies of the book when initial attempts were made to ship it here.

The cryptic James Joyce.

Great merchandiser makes his last sale

Dec 12. John Wanamaker, 84, died this morning at his Philadelphia home. All city schools will be closed for one session in honor of the merchant who was also a member of the Board of Education.

The report that Wanamaker died with a smile on his lips seems fitting for a man who made the world better for having lived. "Let acts follow your good wishes," was the motto of the owner of one of the first and best-known department stores, who began his working life as an errand boy at 14. For more than 50 years, he was in his store every day, treating his employees as family. This model of what a businessman could and should be included short inspirational "editorials" in the ads for the store.

Wanamaker was Postmaster General from 1889-93 and greatly improved the efficiency of the postal service. He was Secretary and then President of the Young Men's Christian Association and for many years Superintendent of the Bethany Presbyterian Sunday School. President Harding and leaders in public and private life joined to praise Wanamaker as a true lover of mankind, someone who "never met a man, woman, or child, in whom he did not see beauty."

"Satchmo" joins King Oliver's band

December. King Oliver and his seven-piece jazz band are shaking the walls of Chicago's Lincoln Gardens these days with some very bouncy sounds. Especially jazzy are the duets tossed back and forth between Oliver and his new second-trumpet player, Louis "Satchmo" Armstrong. Together, they make such foot-stomping music that the place has become a second home for white Chicago musicians who gather there to listen and learn. Armstrong was born in New Orleans, the birthplace of jazz music, and has played with various groups in that city. The day he received the telegram asking him to join Oliver, he was playing with a funeral band.

"Satchmo" (left) with his horn.

1923

JANUARY

Su	Mo	Tu	We	Th	Fr	Sa
	1	2	3	4	5	6
7	8	9	10	11	12	13
14	15	16	17	18	19	20
21	22	23	24	25	26	27
28	29	30	31			

1. Pasadena: Southern Cal. over Penn State 14-3 in Rose Bowl.

1. France: Sadi Lecointe sets new aviation speed record, flying average of 208 mph at Istres.

4. U.S.S.R.: Lenin asks Stalin's dismissal for repression of comrades (→ 1/21/24).

4. Paris conference on reparations hits deadlock as French insist on hard line, British on reconstruction (→ 7).

5. U.S. Senate debates benefits of peyote for American Indian.

5. N.Y.: Women bowlers fight four dry agents for right to keep beer in bowling alley (→ 4/22).

7. Paris: Reparations Commission decides to take Essen if Germany defaults on coal orders (→ 11).

10. U.S. withdraws last troops from Germany.

11. Germany: French enter Essen in the Ruhr unresisted (→ 25).

13. Washington: Senate Immigration Committee amends laws to admit 25,000 Armenian orphans (→ 4/23/24).

13. 5,000 stormtroopers demonstrate in Germany; Hitler denounces Republic (→ 27).

15. U.S.: National City Co. and Guaranty Co. join in $150 mil. copper merger.

16. Montreal: Heart of physician Sir William Osler to be placed in McGill University library.

19. French announce invention of new gun with range of 56 miles.

23. France: Monarchist Marius Plateau, sec. of Action Francaise, assassinated by anarchist.

27. Washington reports rising demand for postage stamps as indicator of prosperity.

28. Belgium: French crowds demonstrate against spread of Dutch in universities.

29. Twenty Germans killed in first fighting in Ruhr (→ 2/1).

BIRTH

31. Norman Mailer, American writer, "The Naked and the Dead."

French army occupies industrial Ruhr

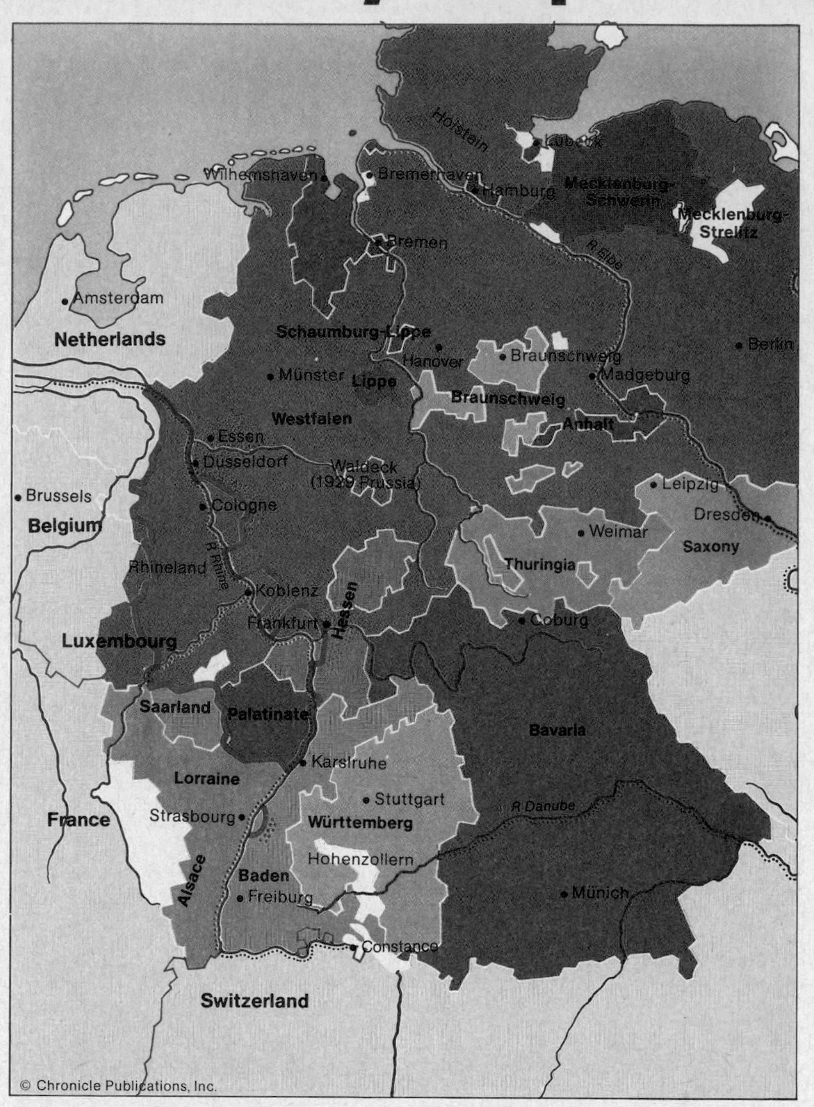

Postwar Germany. The solid red line delineates the portion of Rhineland and the Ruhr designated as occupied territory at Versailles; the dotted areas are zones occupied this month in reprisal for delayed reparations payments.

General Rampont leads occupying French troops into Essen.

Jan 25. The most violent demonstrations yet against the French and Belgian occupation of the Ruhr erupted tonight in Dusseldorf. Workers called a two-hour general strike, and French soldiers fired shots to disperse the protesters.

Large crowds gathered around the statues of Bismarck and other German heroes, singing "Deutschland Ueber Alles" and shouting insults against the French. Machine guns and tanks were pointed nervously at the protesters, and French cavalrymen finally advanced to make them disperse.

The French government released a statement vowing it would not be intimidated: "If Germany thinks her policy of resistance and sabotage will make France deviate one jot from her resolution to bring the German government to terms and collect reparations, she is sadly mistaken. France is here to stay until she gets complete satisfaction."

French and Belgian troops moved into the Ruhr district two weeks ago, after the Reparations Commission agreed that Germany had fallen behind in its deliveries of coal and timber. The action by the Allies was not unanimous, however. Britain voted against the majority, and President Harding announced he was removing American troops from the Rhineland.

Germany at once condemned the occupation as a violation of international law and put a halt to all reparations payments to France and Belgium. Chancellor Wilhelm Cuno urged a program of "passive resistance" to the occupation.

German workers heeded his call, and industrial production plummeted. A week ago, France took more severe measures. Troops occupied industrial installations, requisitioned coal, took control of the transportation system, confiscated salaries and abolished private ownership of certain businesses.

This is supposed to be a time of peace in Europe, but Germany is beginning to look like an armed camp. Nine French and Belgian infantry and cavalry divisions, 100,000 men in all, are trying to occupy an area filled with more than three million Germans. Most of the Germans are still armed from the last war (→ 29).

Nazi Party holds first congress in Munich

The swastika in Munich with the apparent support of local authorities.

Jan 27. In Munich, flags and banners emblazoned with a symbol known as the swastika are fluttering in the air. They are the insignia of Adolf Hitler's National Socialist Party, and his movement seems to be growing in numbers. Members applauded loudly when Hitler called for the repeal of the Treaty of Versailles, which they blame for many of Germany's present troubles. Up until now, Hitler's party has met only in private. This is the first public congress, and it is being held with the apparent support of police and military authorities (→ 5/1).

Every day in every way he helps U.S.A.

Jan 4. A beaming, rotund Frenchman arrived in New York City this morning, promising better things if only we can wish hard enough. Emile Coue, a 67-year-old pharmacist, is the founder of Coueism, a theory of mastering the will through auto-suggestion. Many Americans are already familiar with his chant, "Day by day, in every way, I'm getting better and better." Adherents credit Coue's positive thinking with curing everything from alcoholism to seasickness.

The "feel good" Dr. Coue.

Life of Katherine Mansfield ended

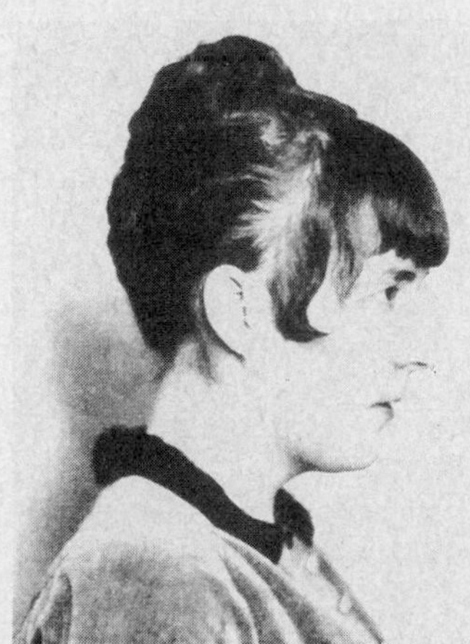

Mansfield, master of the short story.

Jan 9. Novelist Katherine Mansfield has died in France of a pulmonary disease. She left her native New Zealand for England at the age of 14 and became a subtle and brilliant critic before being recognized as a creative novelist. "The Garden Party" and "Bliss" revealed her capacity to depict reality, her power to analyze personality and her ability to capture individuality.

Aimee Semple McPherson opens temple

Jan 1. A large, rotating, illuminated cross, visible for 50 miles, marks the location of Angelus Temple, which the increasingly popular evangelist Aimee Semple McPherson has just opened in Los Angeles, having collected $1 million in offerings for that purpose.

This is the woman who arrived in the city in 1918, 28 years old, with $100, a tambourine, a touring car with the painted sign, "Jesus Is Coming Soon—Get Ready," and her mother, Minnie Kennedy, as her business manager. Canadian-born McPherson was converted to Pentacostalism as a young girl and married a preacher, Robert Semple. The couple went as missionaries to China. When he died a year later, she returned to the United States. She married Harold McPherson but left him soon to take up a life of itinerant preaching.

Sister Aimee's dramatic revival meetings have made her phenomenally successful. In her 5,000-seat temple, special effects produce thunder, lightning and wind, illustrating her "four-square gospel" with strong emphasis on faith-healing and adult baptism. A 50-piece band offers patriotic-religious music with a modern beat.

Sister Aimee looks heavenward.

French Sahara tour reaches Timbuktu

Jan 7. Andre Citroen and the members of his automobile crew, among them Lieutenant Dubreuil of the French Flying Corps and Paul Castelnau, a geographer, have reached Timbuktu after 20 days of motoring from Algiers. They traversed the desert at the rate of 112 miles per day. Five motors were used. But they have conquered the Sahara, the "dreariest and driest region of the world".

It takes the Arabs six months to get from northern Algeria to Timbuktu. The route of the Frenchmen was from the Mediterranean to Tuggurt, to Inifel, to Insalah, past the Hoggar Mountains (the Ahaggar plateau is equal to the Alps in area, with snow on its high peaks from December to March), then to Burem on the Niger and finally to Timbuktu. The Citroen mission made a success of its expedition only by good organization and by carefully mapping the sources of water.

Citroen and company are greeted in Ben Gardane, Tunisia.

1923

FEBRUARY

Su	Mo	Tu	We	Th	Fr	Sa
				1	2	3
4	5	6	7	8	9	10
11	12	13	14	15	16	17
18	19	20	21	22	23	24
25	26	27	28			

1. Vatican: Pope Pius XI calls for public prayers to avoid another war.

1. French cordon closed around Ruhr, cutting off coal supplies to unoccupied Germany, while exchange rate soars to 47,500 marks to the dollar (→ 4).

2. Italian troops clash with Turks again in Tripoli.

2. Ethylized, anti-knock gasoline sold for first time in Dayton, Oh.

3. Grandmother's shawls are new spring fashions in U.S.

4. Germany: French troops take Offenburg, Appenweier and Buhl in the Ruhr (→ 12).

4. Lausanne parley on Near East ends; Turks still defiant (→ 9).

5. Italy: Mussolini orders arrest of several hundred Socialists (→ 3/16).

8. Explosion entombs 122 in New Mexico mine.

8. Washington: Central American Conference reaches agreement reestablishing U.S. right of intervention.

9. Turks lift ban on Allied warships in Smyrna harbor (→ 3/6).

12. Germany: French troops requisition all German vehicles in Dortmund (→ 3/1).

15. Paris: French aviator Sadi Lecointe shatters speed record, reaching 234 mph.

18. John D. Rockefeller gives $1 million to Columbia University to aid foreign study at teachers college.

22. Freemen's League of Utah formed to fight anti-cigarette law.

23. Detroit: Democratic leaders succeed in preventing state convention from endorsing Henry Ford for president.

BIRTH

12. Franco Zefirelli, Italian film director.

DEATHS

10. Wilhelm Conrad Roentgen (*3/27/1845).

22. Theophile Delcasse, French statesman (*3/1/1852).

Roentgen, finder of X-rays, is dead

Feb 10. William Konrad Roentgen, the discoverer of X-rays, died in Munich today at the age of 77. Roentgen made his discovery in 1895 at the University of Wurzburg in Bavaria, when he detected the new radiation being emitted by cathode ray tubes. He designated the radiation X-rays because he did not know its nature and X is the mathematical symbol for an unknown.

The first X-ray picture, showing the bones of a human hand, was taken only a few weeks later, and Roentgen's discovery was quickly put to use in medicine, to diagnose disease and detect objects in the body. In 1901, Roentgen was awarded the first Nobel Prize given in physics for his achievement.

Bessie Smith makes first song recording

Bessie sings the blues.

February. A young Negro woman named Bessie Smith has come out of nowhere to capture the imagination of people who like that kind of jazz called "the blues." Possessed of a powerful yet eloquent voice, she made her first record this month and it promises to be a phenomenal success. The songs are "Tain't Nobody's Bizzness if I Do," and "Down-Hearted Blues." Miss Smith, a native of Chattanooga, Tennessee, has previously worked in honky tonks, carnivals and traveling tent shows (→ 9/26/37).

1923

MARCH

Su	Mo	Tu	We	Th	Fr	Sa
				1	2	3
4	5	6	7	8	9	10
11	12	13	14	15	16	17
18	19	20	21	22	23	24
25	26	27	28	29	30	31

1. Germany: Franco-Belgian officials threaten death for obstructing transportation in the Ruhr (→ 12).

2. U.S. Senate begins inquiry into corruption in Veterans Bureau headed by Charles Forbes (→ 15).

2. Rome: Mussolini admits women's right to vote, but insists time is not right (→ 6/3).

3. U.S. Senate rejects entry into World Court 49-24 (→ 6/21).

4. Washington: Congress passes Intl. Credit Act to aid in financing agricultural cooperatives.

5. Montana, Nevada pass nation's first old-age pension grants, $25 per month.

6. Ankara: Turkish Natl. Assembly rejects Lausanne Treaty (→ 4/23).

9. It is reported that 30 N.Y.C. policemen belong to Ku Klux Klan (→ 14).

14. Baton Rouge: Two judges barred from Louisiana appeals court for affiliation with Ku Klux Klan (→ 5/27).

14. Allies cede Vilna and East Galicia to Poland.

15. Charles F. Cramer, assistant to Forbes at Veterans Bureau, commits suicide (→ 1/30/25).

16. Rome police ban hissing and other signs of disapproval at theaters (→ 4/21).

20. Michigan: Wm. Z. Foster trial reveals Communist Party uses money order blanks for secret code.

21. Paris: Dr. Roger claims smoking beneficial to health.

21. U.S. Sec. of State Hughes denies recognition to U.S.S.R. until she acknowledges prerevolutionary debts and restores alien property.

27. Kansas City mayor orders one cent per gallon tax on gasoline.

BIRTHS

12. Walter Schirra, only astronaut to fly all three programs (Mercury, Gemini, Apollo).

22. Marcel Marceau, French mime.

The divine Sarah Bernhardt is dead

March 26. The great tragedienne Sarah Bernhardt passed away today at her home in Paris. The 78-year-old actress, who had recited passages from "Phedre" in the delirium of her illness, died in her son's arms.

Miss Bernhardt was born in 1844, the illegitimate child of an Amsterdam merchant. Years at a convent school inclined her toward life in a nunnery; her family distracted her by taking her to the theater. After successful acting lessons, she entered the Comedie Francaise in 1862. For the next 50 years she performed throughout Europe and America in all the most passionate roles, from Marguerite of "Camille" to the title role of "Hamlet."

The actress was famous for her lingering death scenes and murder scenes committed with daggers and hatpins. Bernhardt's art is preserved forever through a few films she made during her final years.

Agitators in Ruhr kill two French soldiers

French soldier guards a coal train requisitioned by occupying Allied troops.

March 12. Tensions created by the French occupation of Germany's Ruhr Valley exploded again today. Anti-French agitators assassinated two French soldiers. Earlier this month, a French officer fired into a crowd in Essen after disgruntled German workers walked off the job at the Krupp factory. Some 13 people were killed, and more than 30 were seriously wounded.

French authorities also accuse German transport workers of trying to sabotage the national rail system. Since French and Belgian officials started administering the railroads, mechanical failures and accidents are up sharply. The French and Belgians have punished the workers believed responsible by expelling them from the occupied zone, frequently with very little notice. So far, 150,000 Germans have been displaced (→ 5/3).

Health forces Lenin to quit; suffers stroke

March 9. A severe stroke, causing paralysis of his right side as well as a loss of speech, has forced Soviet leader Vladimir Lenin to retire from office. He retains his title of Chairman of the Soviet government.

Lenin has been plagued by ill health since May 1922, when he had his first stroke. He returned to work in November of that year, but one month later suffered a second stroke. He has not given a public address since November 20, 1922.

Lenin's prestige is such that, during the course of his illness, no one leader has emerged to take his place. Instead, three members of the highest rulng body in the Soviet Union, the Politburo, have created a "troika" or triumvirate, which serves as the collective leadership of the party and state. The troika includes General Secretary Joseph Stalin, Comintern leader Grigori Zinoviev, and head of the Communist organization in Moscow, Lev Kamenev.

In the months before his stroke, Lenin was preoccupied with assessing the character of his potential successors and with clearing up what he considers excessive bureaucratization of the government.

One of his last actions was to send a wire highly critical of Stalin to dissidents in Georgia, Stalin's home territory (→ 1/21/24).

1923

APRIL

Su	Mo	Tu	We	Th	Fr	Sa
1	2	3	4	5	6	7
8	9	10	11	12	13	14
15	16	17	18	19	20	21
22	23	24	25	26	27	28
29	30					

3. Moscow: Constantine Butchkavitch, Vicar Gen. of Roman Catholic Church, condemned to death for opposing Soviets (→ 4).

4. German unions call for intl. worker protest against French occupation of the Ruhr (→ 5/3).

8. Plague in India has killed 1,000 in past week.

9. Supreme Court rules unconstitutional D.C.'s minimum wage law for women and children.

14. Dance marathons now the rage in U.S. cities.

16. Ex-Mississippi Gov. Bilbo sent to jail for contempt of court.

18. Yucatan: Statue of Chac-Mool, tiger king of Mayas, discovered in ruins of Chichen Itza.

18. New York: 74,200 watch as Yankees open new stadium.

19. Egypt's King Fuad I promulgates new constitution (→ 3/15/24).

21. Mussolini declares national holiday on day Rome was founded, cancels May Day (→ 23).

22. Texas dry agents start air patrol to catch bootleggers (→ 5/1).

23. Lausanne conference on Near East reopens (→ 5/1).

23. Rome: Catholic Party quits Mussolini government (→ 7/10).

24. N.Y.: Gimbel Bros. merges with Saks & Co.

25. Chicago hosts meeting of 60 radio heads, called to fight for right to broadcast copyrighted music.

26. London: Albert, duke of York, weds Lady Elizabeth Bowes-Lyon.

27. Portuguese ship Mossamedes sinks off South African coast; 237 dead.

27. Mussolini decrees Italianization of names in South Tyrol (→ 10/1).

28. London: 1,000 hurt in riot at championship soccer match.

29. U.S. govt. to prosecute Kodak under antitrust laws.

DEATH

4. Julius Martov, Bolshevik theorist (*11/24/1873).

Harvard overseers ban discrimination

April 9. Harvard University's overseers have unanimously voted to maintain Harvard's "traditional policy of freedom from discrimination on grounds of race or religion." The vote represented approval of the report of a committee named last June to examine the university's admission policies.

The question of discrimination in the case of Jewish applicants came up last spring. The dispute lasted so long that President Lawrence Lowell appointed a faculty committee to study the issue. Discrimination against Negroes came to public attention when Lowell wrote to Roscoe Bruce, an alumnus, that his son could not be housed in a freshman dormitory because he was a Negro. This caused national criticism of Harvard.

Catholic prelate is executed by Soviets

April 3. Msgr. Konstantin Buchkavich, Vicar General of the Roman Catholic Church in Russia, was executed March 31 on charges of opposing the Soviet government. A Warsaw report said he was shot through the head from behind in the cellar of the Cheka (secret police) building in Moscow. This is a common form of Soviet execution.

Pravda said today that the priest was condemned "in the case of the Catholic counter-revolutionists." He and 18 others were tried under a law against organizations that engage in activities "detrimental to the proletarian revolution." Foreign protests did nothing to save Monsignor Buchkavich, a Russian citizen of Polish origin.

Harold Lloyd, daring in "Safety Last," despite losing two fingers in a 1920 film accident.

It's the rage: Dancing until you drop

Still "dancing" after 40 hours.

April 14. In Houston, they are worn out, staggering, pathetic, but still dancing after 45 hours. One couple, 20 and 19 years old, broke the world's record for continous dancing by a twosome, after which the young man collapsed and was rushed to a Turkish bath.

In Baltimore, a marathon involving eight couples was stopped by the police after 53 hours. In Cleveland, four couples are trying to shatter an earlier record of 52 hours and 11 minutes. The winning girl's ankles were swollen to twice their size afterwards, and she had worn out five male partners during the dancing which reduced her weight from 113 to 89 lbs.

Legal minds are wrestling with the question of whether dance marathons are legal or fall under the limitations of 12-hour participation during a 24-hour period, imposed on other endurance contests. The impressive purse received by winners has kept many poor parents of participants silent on this exhausting new craze.

Record dancer Alma Cummings.

War hero Weygand commands in Syria

April 19. Maxime Weygand, the French General, has left one troubled part of the world, only to arrive in another. Only a few weeks ago, Weygand was helping command the French occupation forces in Germany's Ruhr district. Today, he was named the French High Commissioner in Syria and Lebanon.

France has a mandate over the area, but its presence is fiercely opposed by Arab nationalists. France has divided the Levant states into districts, ostensibly to preserve the rights of minorities. But Arab leaders accuse the French of dividing just so they can rule.

General Weygand has little colonial experience, and this is a difficult mission. During the war in Europe, he was Chief of Staff to General Foch. Weygand directed the defense of Warsaw against the onslaught of the Russian Soviet forces, and he helped the Poles turn the tide in the war.

Carnarvon, sponsor of Tut dig, is dead

April 4. The Earl of Carnarvon, the gentleman archeologist who discovered the tomb of the Pharaoh Tutankhamen, died in Cairo at the age of 56 today of blood poisoning that resulted from an insect bite he received while working at the tomb.

Lord Carnarvon had pursued the hunt for the tomb in the Valley of the Kings for eight years, although many experts said that all the tombs of the Egyptian pharaohs had been looted over the millenia. His persistence was rewarded last November 24 when his associate, Howard Carter, pushed open a stone doorway and found the mummy of Tutankhamen and the riches that were entombed with him.

Lord Carnarvon fell ill three weeks ago and sank rapidly, despite his physicians' efforts. His death has revived superstitious talk of curses supposedly laid by ancient Egyptians on anyone who dared profane the tomb of a pharaoh.

1923

MAY

Su	Mo	Tu	We	Th	Fr	Sa
		1	2	3	4	5
6	7	8	9	10	11	12
13	14	15	16	17	18	19
20	21	22	23	24	25	26
29	28	29	30	31		

1. Nazi paramilitary forces seize military barracks, using May Day workers' demonstrations as excuse (→ 9/2).

1. New York Legislature votes to repeal enforcement of Prohibition (→ 7/6).

1. Turks reject all Allied proposals at Lausanne (→ 7/6).

2. British housewives start boycott on overpriced sugar, tea.

3. France refuses reparations offer of 30 billion marks (→ 26).

6. Chinese bandits kidnap 150 passengers on Tientsin-Pukow railway; Americans aboard (→ 6/14).

10. Lausanne: Soviet delegate M. Vorovsky killed by Swiss assassin claiming relatives were victimized by Bolsheviks.

15. Paris bread prices rise to highest mark since 1870.

17. Washington: Harding opens statue of Alexander Hamilton, echoes former president's attack on factionalism in politics.

19. Zev tops the field at Kentucky Derby with jockey E. Sande in the saddle.

20. Andrew Bonar Law resigns British premiership due to illness; Stanley Baldwin succeeds.

22. Indianapolis: Presbyterian General Assembly defeats Wm. Jennings Bryan's ban on creationism in church schools.

23. Sabena, Belgium's national airline, founded.

24. Socialist Youth International established in Hamburg.

26. French execute German officer Leo Schlageter for sabotage in the Ruhr (→ 6/13).

27. Ku Klux Klan openly defies law requiring publication of names of members (→ 10/24).

28. De Valera announces he will abandon war on Irish Free State (→ 11/7/24).

30. Tommy Milton crosses finish line first, averaging 90.9 mph in Indy 500.

BIRTHS

1. Joseph Heller, American novelist, "Catch-22."

27. Henry Kissinger, American statesman.

Non-stop across the country in 27 hours

May 3. Lts. Oakley Kelly and John Macready of the United States Army completed the first non-stop transcontinental flight today when they landed their T-2 monoplane in San Diego, California, at 12:26 p.m.

Kelly and Macready flew nearly 2,800 miles, by far the longest non-stop flight ever made, at an average speed of over 100 miles per hour. It was the second attempt at a non-stop flight across the United States by the two aviators.

The flight began yesterday when they took off from Hempstead, Long Island. Only a few minutes into the flight, they encountered a major problem when their aircraft's voltage regulator went out, but they were able to continue when Macready replaced the instrument as Kelly handled the controls.

The airplane first headed for Dayton, Ohio, arrived over Chicago at 10:15 p.m., and then turned south for St. Louis. It flew over Atchison, Kansas, at midnight and Santa Rosa, New Mexico, at 8:30 a.m. Its appearance over San Diego shortly after noon was greeted by whistles from all the factories in the city. Major Henry H. Arnold of the Army Air Force welcomed the fliers at San Diego's Rockwell Field, gleefully exclaiming, "The impossible has happened."

This record is in sharp contrast to the first west-to-east transcontinental flight, in 1912, when Bob Fowler took 151 days, with stops, to fly from Jacksonville to San Francisco. And a year earlier, Calbraith P. Rodgers took 49 days to make the trip from New York to Pasadena.

May 1. May Day in Leningrad. In 1899, the holiday was expropriated by radical labor.

1923

JUNE

Su	Mo	Tu	We	Th	Fr	Sa
					1	2
3	4	5	6	7	8	9
10	11	12	13	14	15	16
17	18	19	20	21	22	23
24	25	26	27	28	29	30

3. Mussolini approves bill giving women right to vote in Italian municipal elections.

8. British House of Commons passes equalizing legal terms of divorce for men and women.

13. French set trade barrier between occupied Ruhr and rest of Germany (→ 20).

14. Troops capture Chinese President Li Yuan-hung in flight from Peking (→ 1/9/24).

15. Earthquake buries five villages, killing thousands in northwest Persia.

15. Sofia: Bulgarian Premier Stambulisky slain by peasants.

16. Britain launches X-1 submarine, largest vessel of its kind.

17. Ten beach censors ban one-piece bathing suits in Atlantic City, New Jersey.

18. Italy: Mount Etna bursts in eruption; 30,000 flee villages.

19. Leviathan sails on trial trip from Boston harbor.

20. Harding begins tour of West and Alaska (→ 24).

20. France announces it will seize all Ruhr industries for reparations (→ 22).

21. Harding lauds World Court to St. Louis audience, but supports its separation from League (→ 1/27/26).

24. Two in Pres. Harding's party killed as auto leaps off cliff near Denver (→ 7/28).

27. British immigrants reported skirting Ellis Island, coming to U.S through Canada.

27. France, Belgium denounce pope's decree condemning Ruhr occupation and asking Christian settlement to reparations (→ 30).

27. Belgrade: Yugoslav Premier Nikola Pachitch wounded by Serb attackers.

28. At speech in Idaho Falls, Harding suggest consumers unite and cut living costs.

30. Dusseldorf: Ten Belgians killed by German bomb on Rhineland train (→ 7/6).

DEATH

10. Pierre Loti, French writer and academician (*1/14/1850).

Decline of mark called desperate

June 22. Germany's currency is fast becoming worthless, and German central bankers are throwing their hands up in despair. Rudolf Havenstein, the President of the Reichsbank, says the situation is becoming most desperate.

The value of the mark is dropping dangerously. In just three weeks, it has lost nearly half its value. At the beginning of the month, the dollar bought 74,500 marks. But today, its value is 136,000 marks.

The war damaged Germany's economy severely, but it is the French and Belgian occupation of the Ruhr which is destroying it. The occupation began after the Reparations Commission decreed that Germany was not exporting enough coal. Since the occupation, protesting miners have cut production dramatically. Today, they are not even producing enough to satisfy domestic consumption. Germany is forced to import, and that is costing dearly.

Germany also has enormous social welfare expenses, caused by the displacement of thousands of people from the Ruhr. Until April, the central bank had enough reserves to cover these costs. Today, those reserves are gone, and the mark is paying the price (→ 27).

At no time this month would 20,000 marks fetch even one U.S dollar.

Prices at Berlin market june 9th

500 g beef	8500 - 12000 marks	sugar	1400 - 1550 marks
500 g veal	6800 - 10000 marks	flour	1900 - 2600 marks
500 g mutton	7000 - 9000 marks	turbot	4000 - 5000 marks
500 g pork	9000 - 10500 marks	roach	5000 marks
500 g butter	13000 - 15000 marks	herring	2500 marks
500 g margarine	7600 - 9600 marks	tripe	4500 marks
500 g pork fat	12000 - 12400 marks	lard	13000 marks
500 g beef fat	9200 - 10000 marks	bard	10000 - 11000 marks
500 g vegetal fat	9000 - 9500 marks	new potatoes	2200 - 2500 marks
500 g potatoes	112 - 130 marks	sorrel	500 - 600 marks
500 g roasted coffee	26000 - 36000 marks	whortleberry	8000 marks
500 g tea	30000 - 48000 marks	1 bunch of kohlrabi	5000 - 6000 marks
500 g cocoa	7500 - 14000 marks	1 egg	800 - 810 marks

KKK Imperial Wizard opposes world court

Imperial Wizard Evans in full dress.

June 30. The leader of the the Ku Klux Klan says that his organization strongly opposes President Harding's proposal for a world court. Imperial Wizard H.W. Evans, speaking in Fort Worth, Texas, said that the Klan does not support any alliance with foreign nations.

Dr. Evans said that the Klan, a secret society with rabidly anti-Negro, anti-minority views, now has a membership of more than one million men and that there are more Klansmen in the Northern states than there are in the South, once the primary stronghold of the so-called "Invisible Empire." While adding that the Klan will not endorse anyone publicly for the presidency of the United States, Dr. Evans noted pointedly that President Harding's home state of Ohio now has more than 300,000 voters who are members of the the Klan (→ 9/15).

Coup overthrows Bulgarian regime

June 9. Without a drop of blood hitting Sofia streets, the army has overthrown the Bulgarian Cabinet and reorganized a new government comprised of representatives from all opposition parties except the Communists. The military surrounded the Parliament buildings and arrested all the ministers with well-planned precision.

The new regime proclaimed a state of siege and assailed former Premier Stamboulisky and his colleagues: "Bulgarian liberty dawns again. The regime of deceit, violence and murder has collapsed under the weight of its crimes, and a new era of law, harmony and peace has arrived." It is said King Boris helped instigate the coup by encouraging the Revolutionary Party, which was chiefly responsible (→ 15).

1923

JULY

Su	Mo	Tu	We	Th	Fr	Sa
1	2	3	4	5	6	7
8	9	10	11	12	13	14
15	16	17	18	19	20	21
22	23	24	25	26	27	28
29	30	31				

1. Philadelphian Edward Bok offers $100,000 prize for practical plan for keeping world peace.

1. Paris restaurants beginning to draw color lines to please American tourists.

1. Alfred P. Sloan Jr. takes over G.M. presidency from Pierre du Pont.

2. London: American Philip H. Rosenbach buys Gutenberg Bible at Sotheby's for $43,350.

4. Jack Dempsey takes 15-round decision over Tom Gibbons to retain heavyweight title.

5. Providence, R.I.: Ethel Barrymore wins divorce from R.G. Colt for neglect and brutality.

6. Federal judge rules Volstead Law unconstitutional where it restricts doctors' prescriptions (→ 8/16).

6. Greek, Turkish troops clash on Dardanelles (→ 24).

6. France, Belgium threaten to break relations with Germany if Chancellor Cuno fails to repudiate Ruhr crimes (→ 12).

10. Mussolini dissolves all non-Fascist parties in Italy (→ 16).

12. Lloyd George demands end to Ruhr occupation before new world war breaks out (→ 8/6).

15. Harding drives ceremonial spike to complete Alaskan interior rail line.

16. Mussolini bars gambling throughout Italy (→ 1/24/24).

21. Seneca Falls, N.Y.: National Woman's Party drafts equal rights amendment to federal Constitution (→ 6/27/24).

22. Tour de France won by French racer Henri Pelissier.

22. France: Belleau Wood dedicated in memory of American soldiers who died in combat.

23. Filipinos demand recall of new American Governor Wood.

28. Grants Pass, Oregon: Pres. Harding suffers attack of ptomaine poisoning (→ 8/2).

29. Albert Einstein takes part in Berlin pacifist demonstration.

BIRTH

6. General Wojciech Jaruzelski, Polish politician.

Turkish-Greek war ended by treaty

July 24. Seven powers signed the Near East Treaty today in Lausanne, Switzerland. Representatives from Great Britain, France, Italy, Japan, Greece, Rumania and Turkey took part in the simple ceremony concluding months of negotiations. The Yugoslavs, who refused to sign, objected to the treaty because it would apportion Ottoman debt among countries that acquired territory from the former Ottoman Empire. The treaty also establishes peace between Greece and Turkey. Under the pact, Greeks living in Turkey and Turks living in Greece will be repatriated. It did not create an Armenian state, obliging Armenians to turn to neighboring countries for refuge (→ 1/30/25).

Revenge taken on Villa; he's killed

July 20. The vengeance unleashed by the murderous past of Pancho Villa caught up with the former bandit-general this morning when he and three members of his bodyguard escort were killed by six gunmen as he was out motoring.

His death at 45 is attributed to the Herrera family, four members of whom Villa had executed during the Mexican Revolution. At 16, Villa killed a man for molesting his sister. Thereafter, he became a fugitive bandit who led his own revolutionary army. Recently, he had lived peacefully on his ranch, learned how to read and was learning how to type (→ 8/27).

Villa, the proud revolutionary.

1923

AUGUST

Su	Mo	Tu	We	Th	Fr	Sa
			1	2	3	4
5	6	7	8	9	10	11
12	13	14	15	16	17	18
19	20	21	22	23	24	25
26	27	28	29	30	31	

6. American Henry Sullivan swims English Channel in 28 hours.

6. Germany: Bread riots break out in Dresden (→ 7).

7. German mark reaches catastrophic level of 3.3 mil. to the dollar (→ 11).

10. German leftists, now seeking soviet republic, threatened with severe reprisals (→ 12).

11. British foreign minister declares Ruhr occupation violates Versailles treaty (→ 13).

12. German Chancellor Wilhelm Cuno replaced by Gustav Stresemann after Socialists in Reichstag vote no confidence in government (→ 9/27).

13. U.S. Steel, under pressure from unions and government, offers 8-hour day (→ 2/26/24).

13. Germany halts reparations; with Britain and France divided over response, Allies fear end of Entente (→ 22).

16. Georgia: 84 Savannah bootleggers arrested in biggest liquor bust yet (→ 12/5).

17. Pres. Coolidge warns Cuba U.S. will take necessary steps to defend American rights.

21. Michigan: Kalamazoo passes ordinance forbidding dancers to gaze into partners' eyes.

22. France replies to British reprisals; refuses to cut reparations claim or let World Court arbitrate on Ruhr (→ 9/30).

23. Indianapolis: Johnny Weissmuller wins AAU 50-and 100-yard swimming championships.

27. U.S. awards formal recognition to Mexico (→ 1/6/24).

29. Mussolini demands Greek apology for recent killing of Italian border commission (→ 31).

31. Penn.: Strike begins in hard coal mines as both sides reject Gov. Pinchot's terms (→ 9/7).

31. East Africa: Ruanda-Urundi becomes Belgian protectorate.

31. Italians invade Corfu to compel indemnity for border killings (→ 9/1).

BIRTH

16. Shimon Peres, Israeli prime minister.

President Harding dies; U.S. in shock

Warren Gamaliel Harding.

Aug 2. President Warren G. Harding died tonight in San Francisco. The death of the 57-year-old president came as a shock. He had been ill for a week, weakened by an exhausting tour to Alaska. But aides felt he was well on the road to recovery. The end came suddenly for the former newspaper publisher and Senator while his wife was reading to him in the presidential suite in the Palace Hotel.

"That's good! Go on, read some more," the president said. Then he shuddered and collapsed, dead of an apoplectic stroke. The body will be returned to Washington aboard a special train.

Great showing by Bauhaus in Weimar

Aug 15. The Bauhaus school of design in Germany is currently showing the work of many artists. Among them are the German architect Walter Gropius, who founded the Bauhaus in 1919; Paul Klee; Lyonel Feininger; Wassily Kandinsky; Laszlo Moholy-Nagy; and Gerhard Marcks. The Bauhaus philosophy maintains that all design — whether a chair, a building or a city —should be approached through a study of needs and problems, taking into account functional materials and modern construction techniques, without reference to previous forms or styles (→ 12/4/26).

1923

SEPTEMBER

Su	Mo	Tu	We	Th	Fr	Sa
						1
2	3	4	5	6	7	8
9	10	11	12	13	14	15
16	17	18	19	20	21	22
23	24	25	26	27	28	29
30						

1. Japan: Great earthquake ravages Tokyo and Yokohama; ensuing fire causes great damage (→ 9).

1. Italy seizes Greek islands of Paxos and Antipaxos (→ 8).

2. Hitler makes fierce attack on Weimar Repulic at German Congress in Nuremburg (→ 27).

4. New York: Dempsey floors Luis Angel Firpo in awesome second-round victory; 25,000 riot outside.

4. Canada: Spanking machine proposed in Winnipeg for first-time offenders.

7. Pennsylvania coal strike settled on Gov. Pinchot's plan; new contract talks begin.

8. Athens: Greece, Italy accept peace terms of Allied envoys (→ 27).

9. California: Seven destroyers wrecked on rocks off Santa Barbara; 23 sailors lost.

10. Mussolini mobilizes troops on Serb front in dispute with Yugoslavia.

10. U.S. Lt. Sanderson breaks all speed records, flying 238 mph in new Navy-Wright plane.

12. Britain annexes South Rhodesia.

12. Tidal wave wipes out San Jose de Cabo on southern California coast.

18. Earthquakes rock Sicily and Malta.

18. N.Y.: Intl. Pressman's Union launches unauthorized strike against daily newspapers.

19. Washington: Explosion at Bureau of Standards kills three, injures seven.

23. 100,000 peasants march on Sofia in Bulgar revolt.

27. Greece: Italian troops withdraw from Corfu under pressure from League.

28. Abyssinia admitted to League (→ 9/22/24).

29. Hugo Stinnes, major German industrialist, demands ban on strikes, end of eight-hour day (→ 11/3).

30. Dusseldorf: Scores killed, hundreds injured as separatists clash with foes in Ruhr (→ 10/3).

Tokyo and Yokohama destroyed by 'quake

A sea of refugees, estimated at 33,000, outside of devastated Tokyo.

Sept 9. In the desolate calm following last week's earthquake, Japan has begun the grim job of reconstruction. Some $265 million has been earmarked for reparation and foreign relief aid is pouring in.

The greatest earthquake in Japan's history leveled Tokyo, Yokohama and towns and cities for hundreds of miles around. Some 300,000 were killed, 500,000 injured and about 2.5 million left homeless. Thousands are reported insane. Half-starved survivors are trying to catch fish in ponds and lakes and waiting in two-mile-long lines for a daily ration or one rice ball each. An estimated 100,000 tons of rice alone is needed to feed them.

Cholera has reportedly broken out in Yokohama, where the people are said to have resorted to drinking muddy ditch water and eating contaminated food. And relief workers fear the possible spread of pestilence. Martial law has been declared in Tokyo, and no one can enter that city.

Oklahoma uses martial law against KKK

Sept 15. Declaring war on the Ku Klux Klan, Governor J.C. Walton placed Oklahoma under martial law tonight. In calling out more than 6,000 troops of the National Guard, the governor declared that a state of insurrection and rebellion against state authorities had been brought about by the notorious secret society. Furthermore, in his proclamation, Governor Walton said that any persons who aid the Klan in carrying out its nefarious program of white supremacy will be considered enemies of the state and will be dealt with by the military.

Ku Klux Klansmen.

The Oklahoma governor's action came at the end of a day of tension and reported threats against his life. Armed guards were stationed outside his office door throughout the day. Noting that a move is underway by some legislators to convene a special session in order to impeach him, Governor Walton has threatened to throw them in jail. Any move to impeach him, he said, would be solely because of his fight against the Klan (→ 10/25).

Germany declares major emergency

Sept 27. German President Ebert has declared a state of martial law following the appointment of Dr. von Kahr as dictator of Bavaria, lately wracked by labor unrest, a mutinous strike movement and agitation by communist and Bolshevist elements ever ready to create a revolt and, if possible, even foment a revolution.

President Ebert has also placed troops on the Bavarian border, but von Kahr says he has no quarrel with Berlin, his only aim being to quell those forces intent on exploiting the grave labor problems. These include the National Socialist Party of Adolf Hitler, headquartered in Bavaria. After a meeting with Hitler, von Kahr banned all 14 of Hitler's mass meetings in Munich's beer halls when Hitler refused to guarantee there would be no trouble (→ 29).

Primo de Rivera leads Spanish coup

Sept 13. The Cortes, the Spanish Parliament, was abolished today. The constitution was suspended, and so was the guarantee of civil liberties. The military is in charge of Spain, and Miguel Primo de Rivera is in charge of the military.

Rivera, Spain's brilliant wartime tactician, launched the coup d'etat and installed a new government with the approval of King Alphonso XIII. Many citizens are hoping Rivera can polish up the country's image. Spain has been foundering from one crisis to the next, and it has been tarnished by political stalemate and the military defeat in Morocco (→ 5/17/25).

Lon Chaney wears 70 pounds of costume as Quasimodo in "The Hunchback of Notre Dame."

1923

OCTOBER

Su	Mo	Tu	We	Th	Fr	Sa
	1	2	3	4	5	6
7	8	9	10	11	12	13
14	15	16	17	18	19	20
21	22	23	24	25	26	27
28	29	30	31			

1. Italian govt. bans teaching of German in South Tyrol schools.

3. Berlin Cabinet resigns; Stresemann asked to form new one (→ 8).

8. Portland, Oregon: A.F.L. ousts Communist leader Dunne from federation by vote of 27,838 to 130.

8. Reichstag rebukes nationalists, passes vote of confidence in Stresemann government (→ 13).

10. Paris sources report French women use average of two pounds of face powder per year.

12. Portland, Oregon: Samuel Gompers re-elected president of A.F.L. at 73 (→ 12/13/24).

13. Reichstag passes dictatorship bill 316-24, giving full powers to Stresemann govt. (→ 20).

15. Polo Grounds: Yankees over Giants in six games in all-New York World Series.

20. New York: Zev wins by five lengths in first international race at Belmont Park.

20. Germany: Bavaria breaks relations with Reich (→ 21).

21. Germany: Separatists proclaim republic in Rhineland (→ 24).

21. German exchange rate hits 12 bil. marks to the dollar (→ 22).

22. German mark slides dramatically to 40 billion to the U.S. dollar (→ 26).

24. Germany: 44 killed as troops put down Communist uprising in Hamburg (→ 27).

24. Texas: 20,000 Klansmen gather in Dallas (→ 25).

26. France accepts U.S. Sec. Hughes' proposal; Allies to form commission of experts to study German economy (→ 11/6).

BIRTHS

4. Charlton Heston, American actor.

15. Italo Calvino, Italian author.

27. Roy Lichtenstein, American pop artist.

DEATH

30. Andrew Bonar Law, British ex-prime minister (*9/16/58).

Startling Teapot Dome disclosures begin

Fall, suspected of wrongdoing.

Oct 25. A pattern of possible wrongdoing has begun to emerge in a Senate committee investigation into the leasing of the government's rich oil reserves at Teapot Dome and Elk Hills to private concerns. The two valuable naval oil reserves were transferred from the United States Navy to the Department of Interior in 1921 by President Harding. The fields had been set aside as Navy reserves in 1915 by President Wilson.

Last year, Interior Secretary Albert B. Fall leased, without competitive bidding, the Teapot Dome fields in Wyoming to Harry F. Sinclair, the President of Mammoth Oil Company, and the Elk Hills reserves in California to Edward L. Doheny, a friend.

As the first witness before the committee several days ago, Fall, who resigned his Cabinet post some months ago, defended the transfers of oil reserves as something of benefit to the federal government. Asked why he had failed to ask for competitive bids, he replied: "Business, purely. I knew I could get a better price without calling for bids."

Fall, a former United States Senator, was questioned closely by one of his former colleagues, Senator Thomas J. Walsh, a Montana Democrat who is chairman of the Senate Public Lands Committee, which has spent 18 months preparing for the inquiry. Despite repeated questioning, Fall denied accepting money from either Sinclair or Doheny, aside from expenses for a business trip to Europe on behalf of Sinclair after leaving the Cabinet. Other witnesses have suggested that Fall may have profited from the oil transfers (→ 1/26/24).

German against German: Unrest spreads

Oct 27. Germany threatens to be torn apart by continued internal turmoil, political in-fighting, separatist movements and purported coups against the Berlin regime. The situation is grave in the Rhineland, controlled by a Socialist-Communist government, and Hamburg was recently hit by a Communist uprising.

Bavaria, led by right-wing elements, continues to chart its own, independent course, and a kind of Mason-Dixon line has been drawn between Saxony and Bavaria, with forces on each side waiting for the other to start something.

Troops survey Hamburg barricades.

French troops have occupied Wiesbaden and Bonn in what is almost a state of war, albeit undeclared, between France and the Rhineland, where France has imposed an economic blockade because of alleged German failure to make good on timber shipments. This has further crippled Germany's already sick economy, stricken by runaway inflation.

Gustav Stresemann, appointed two weeks ago as the first constitutional dictator, has issued an ultimatum to the Communist government of Saxony, demanding that it step down, and government troops stand ready to occupy that region if the ultimatum is ignored. Stresemann has also demanded restoration of Reich military authority in Bavaria (→ 11/2).

Oklahoma Governor faces heavy threat

Oct 25. The Oklahoma Supreme Court has upheld a Senate vote suspending Governor J.C. Walton from office during his pending impeachment trial. The court action cleared the way for Lt. Governor M.E. Trapp to become the acting governor of the state.

The Oklahoma House began impeachment proceedings against Walton earlier this month. He has been the target of irate legislators opposing his efforts to rid the state of the Ku Klux Klan. Just last month, he placed the state under martial law in order to stem Klan activities. Upon learning today of the court action suspending him from office, Walton declared he intended to continue his fight to retain his office and to seek legislation curbing Klan domination of many of the crucial public offices in the state (→ 11/19).

Kemal is President of new republic

Oct 29. The Grand National Assembly at Angora has voted to establish a Turkish republic. And the deputies unanimously elected Mustafa Kemal President. The president's term will be four years; re-election is permitted. The capital of the new republic will be Angora, not Constantinople. Turkish is the official language, and Islam the religion. Kemal led the nationalist movement that brought an end to the Ottoman Empire. The Ottoman Sultan fled abroad in November 1922 (→ 1/7/24).

1923

NOVEMBER

Su	Mo	Tu	We	Th	Fr	Sa
				1	2	3
4	5	6	7	8	9	10
11	12	13	14	15	16	17
18	19	20	21	22	23	24
25	26	27	28	29	30	

1. Akron, Ohio: Goodyear Tire and Rubber Co. buys rights to manufacture Zeppelin dirigibles (→ 8/8/31).

2. Social Democratic ministers resign from German govt. (→ 5).

2. U.S. Navy aviator H.J. Brown sets new world speed record of 259 mph in Curtiss racer.

3. Sweden's heir Crown Prince Gustaf Adolf weds Lady Louise Mountbatten.

5. New York lifts height restrictions for new 5th Ave. buildings.

5. Allies insist crown prince not return to Germany (→ 8).

5. N.Y.: "David Copperfield" opens at the Cameo.

6. Berlin: One loaf of bread worth 140 billion marks (→ 15).

8. Pennsylvania: Candy maker Milton Hershey gives $60 mil. trust to start orphanage.

8. Hitler attempts German coup; proclaims self chancellor, Ludendorff dictator (→ 10).

8. London: British Empire conference ends, giving dominions right to set own foreign policy.

10. Ex-Crown Prince Frederick arrives in Germany (→ 12).

12. Albert Einstein flees Berlin after receiving anti-Semitic death threats.

16. French Council Pres. Raymond Poincare declares Ruhr occupation cost 691 bil. francs and brought in 520 mil.

19. Oklahoma Governor Walton ousted by state senate for anti-Klan measures (→ 7/12/24).

22. Samuel Gompers denounces Wm. Randolph Hearst for urging relations with Soviets.

23. Germany: Stresemann govt. resigns after Reichstag no-confidence vote (→ 2/26/24).

25. Transatlantic broadcasting, England to U.S., established for first time.

29. Intl. commission headed by American banker Charles Dawes set up to investigate German economy (→ 12/14).

BIRTH

18. Alan Shepard, first American astronaut in space.

Hitler is arrested after putsch fails

Ludendorff and Hitler.

Nov 12. Four nights ago in Munich, Adolf Hitler, the National Socialist leader, tried to whip up a coup against the German national government. He failed and today he is under arrest.

On September 26, Chancellor Gustav Stresemann of Germany announced the end of passive resistance to the French occupation of the Ruhr. In the outcry that followed, separatist movements sprang up in several German states. Bavaria, with its capital in Munich, declared a state of emergency; dictatorial powers were given to Gustav von Kahr, a nationalist former premier. President Friedrich Ebert of the German republic proclaimed a national emergency, giving full powers to Otto Gessler, Minister of Defense, and General Hans von Seekt, the army commander. The general warned Munich that any uprising would be met with force.

The fiery Hitler was dismayed. He did not have the strength to challenge the central government alone; he needed help from the Bavarians, who were showing caution. Indeed, their emergency measures seemed to be aimed at Hitler and his ally General Erich von Ludendorff, a hero of the Great War, rather than at the national government.

Hitler learned that Kahr would address a rally November 8 in the Buergerbraukeller, a vast beer hall, and that other Bavarian leaders would attend. He decided to kidnap them. While Kahr was speaking, several hundred storm troopers surrounded the hall, and Hitler entered, posting a machine gun crew to bar the door. Climbing up on a table, Hitler fired a shot from his pistol into the ceiling. He got instant attention, and he used it to proclaim, "The National Revolution has begun."

Hitler took Kahr's place as the speaker, and then forced the Bavarian leaders to join him in a private room. With gun in hand, he tried to persuade them to turn the Bavarian dictatorship into a national one, and to march on Berlin. Ludendorff appeared, and advised the Bavarians to go along with Hitler.

After hearing another Hitler harangue, the crowd dispersed. Kahr and his comrades also disappeared. No plans had been made, no action taken except that Ernst Roehm and some troopers had taken Munich army headquarters. Kahr moved the Bavarian government to Regensberg, leaving behind posters saying that the deal with Hitler had been "extorted" at gunpoint.

Next morning, after the fiasco of the Beer Hall Putsch, Hitler and Ludendorff led a column of storm troopers toward army headquarters to join Roehm. They approached through a narrow street blocked at the end by police. Somebody opened fire. Sixteen police and Nazis lay dead or dying, many more were hurt, and the crowd scattered, including Hitler. Ludendorff stood his ground, erect and unflinching. He was arrested.

Today, Hitler was found about 40 miles from Munich in a villa belonging to Ernest "Putzi" Hanfstaengl, a Harvard graduate, a former art dealer in New York and a supporter of Hitler's Nazi Party. Hitler was not injured except for a grazed shoulder, apparently hurt as he hit the ground when the shooting started in Munich (→ 23).

Storm troopers in Munich.

Ludendorff (2nd from left) watches as young Nazis brandish imperial flag.

One dollar now worth 4 trillion marks

Nov 15. In Germany today, children are making building blocks from bundles of worthless marks. The value of the currency drops so quickly and dramatically that machines no longer print the value of postage stamps. Postal workers do it by hand. At latest count, an American dollar will buy you four trillion marks.

Before the war, the dollar was worth about four marks. Today, a pound of sugar costs 250 billion marks; a pound of meat, more than three trillion. A construction worker in Berlin is paid nearly three trillion marks a day.

The fall of the currency has been a nightmare for everyone in Germany. Today, the central bank tried to wake the country up from its bad dream. It officially released a new mark, which will be worth a trillion of the devalued ones. The dollar will buy four of the new marks. All of this is bound to confuse everybody even more because there are now three different currencies in circulation in Germany: the new mark, the old one and the even older gold mark. Smart money has already left the country (→ 29).

German mark, nothing but a toy.

Exchange rates of dollars and marks

July	1914	4,2
January	1919	8,9
July	1919	14,0
January	1920	64,8
July	1920	39,5
January	1921	64,9
July	1921	76,7
January	1922	191,8
July	1922	493,2
January	1923	17 972,0
July	1923	353 412,0
August	1923	4 620 455,0
September	1923	98 860 000,0
October	1923	25 260 208 000,0
November	1923	4 200 000 000 000,0

American gowns comfortable and stylish

November. Fashion shows by American designers are featuring dresses that give ease of movement. Accent is on corduroy, flannel and knitted fabrics. The French circular skirt, in plaids and stripes, promises to be popular. Hemlines are found about ten inches from the floor.

New comfortable fashions for "the new woman."

More rare treasure found in Tut's tomb

Nov 23. More splendors have been uncovered in King Tutankhamen's tomb by Howard Carter and his excavation crew. It was believed nothing could be more exciting than the discovery last January of the pharaoh's personal effects within the outer shrine; yet a second shrine within the first was detected, and it houses even more precious goods.

The excavators found the door to the inner shrine with its clay seal intact. They carefully pried it open to reveal a room no eyes had seen for 3,370 years. Facing the men as they stepped inside was a huge alabaster urn laced with gold and silver. Mounted upon it were two god-like figures representing upper and lower Egypt. The neck of this vase is cracked, possibly due to an acidic reaction with its former contents. In two corners of the room are several staves, a scepter and a mace. These are gilded with gold.

Gold funeral mask, circa 1342 B.C.

As the excavators cast their lights about, they sighted religious scripture, also etched in gold, lining the walls. Carter identified among the writings the figure of the pharaoh worshipping the god Isis. The meaning of the other hieroglyphs will remain a mystery until the philologist Dr. Alan Gardiner arrives to decipher them. Less beautiful but just as intriguing is a giant linen coffin cloth, littered with golden flowers, bolted and tied down. More treasures are suspected to be hidden underneath (→ 1/4/24).

1923

DECEMBER

Su	Mo	Tu	We	Th	Fr	Sa
						1
2	3	4	5	6	7	8
9	10	11	12	13	14	15
16	17	18	19	20	21	22
23	24	25	26	27	28	29
30	31					

6. Pres. Coolidge presses for tax cut, World Court, opposes soldiers' bonus in first speech to Congress (→ 10).

10. Coolidge gives Congress natl. budget asking $300 mil. tax cut, $132 mil. drop in expenses (→ 5/21/24).

14. German work week set at 54 hours, 59 for heavy industry (→ 17).

16. N.Y. Rev. Dr. Parks flouts virgin birth doctrine, defies bishop to try him for heresy.

17. German civil servants to receive only half of December salaries (→ 20).

18. Athens: Military orders Greek rulers George II and Elizabeth into exile.

20. Germany: Krupp Co. fires workers who refuse to work ten hours a day (→ 1/14/24).

31. New York: Eddie Cantor opens in musical comedy "Kid Boots," with hit tune "Dinah."

31. Sahara crossed by automobile for first time in history (→ 2/5/24).

31. U.S. film industry on the rise; investments hit $750 million for 150 producers in 1923.

CULTURAL EVENTS, 1923

Literature: Felis Salten's "Bambi"; Dorothy L. Sayers' "Whose Body?"; e.e. cummings' "The Enormous Room"; Robert Frost's "New Hampshire."

Academia: Martin Buber's "I and Thou"; Freud's "The Ego and the Id"; Albert Schweitzer's "Philosophy of Civilization"; Sidney and Beatrice Webb's "The Decay of Capitalist Civilization"; Sir James Frazer's "The Golden Bough," in one volume.

Music: Gershwin's "Rhapsody in Blue"; Stravinsky's "Les Noces," Paris; jazz recordings by Joseph "King" Oliver and "Jelly Roll" Morton" "Yes We Have No Bananas."

The Arts: Chagall's "Love Idyll"; Raymond Hood's Chicago Tribune Building.

Film: "Robin Hood," with Douglas Fairbanks; Chaplin's "The Pilgrim"; L'Herbier's "Don Juan and Faust."

W. B. Yeats winner of a Nobel Prize

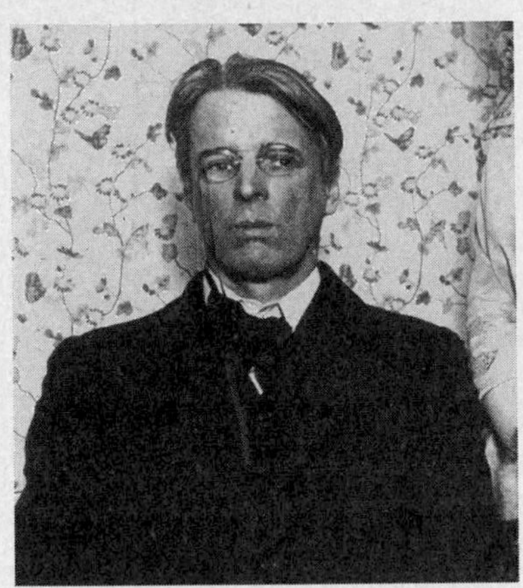

Ireland's William Butler Yeats.

Dec 10. The Nobel Prize for literature has been awarded to William Butler Yeats, the Irish poet and playwright. In his writings, Yeats advocates the fulfillment of Ireland's national aspirations; he believes all art should be national.

Yeats is, in fact, the leader of the new Irish nationalist school. He urges Irish writers to use Irish landscape, to take themes from Irish legends. On these principles, he wrote his first book, "The Wanderings of Oisin and Other Poems" (1889) and his first important play, "The Countess Kathleen" (1892).

Yeats' poetic development may be divided into two stages. The first, until 1900, is characterized by imaginary themes, for example "The Shadowy Waters" (1900). In the second, his writing is more combative and physical, for example "Responsibilities" (1914). In 1922, he was appointed a member of the new Irish Free State Senate.

The Nobel Prize in chemistry was won by Fritz Pregl of Austria and the physics prize went to Robert A. Millikan of the United States.

Cecil B. De Mille's new mammoth spectacle "The Ten Commandments" is now playing.

King of Bootleggers jailed, fined $10,000

Dec 5. Emanuel Kessler, the so-called King of the Bootleggers in the United States, was sentenced today in New York City to two years in prison and fined $10,000 for a series of liquor violations. Kessler and several of his associates were convicted yesterday of charges that they violated the Prohibition Act, defrauded the government out of revenue duties and removed liquor from a bonded warehouse.

Testimony during the trial revealed that Kessler and his companions used forged permits to withdraw from the warehouse some 4,900 cases of Auld Scottie whiskey and 1,295 cases of champagne.

After the trial, Major John Holley Clark Jr., who prosecuted the case for the government, told friends that he had been offered $100,000 by a "lawyer friend" to conduct the case in such a way that Kessler and his friends would be acquitted. And during the sentencing, the courtroom was filled to overflowing with men described by court attendants as the "cream of the bootlegging craft" (→ 4/22/24).

Dry agents pose with their booty, ironically set up to look like a bar.

Builder of Eiffel Tower deceased

Dec 28. Gustave Eiffel died this morning in Paris of a cerebral hemorrhage. He was 91 years old. Eiffel was renowned in Europe as one of the most brilliant engineers of the century who made major progress in metallic construction. His work includes the famous tower which bears his name, some of the biggest bridges and viaducts in France and the great railway bridge of Porto.

When, in 1886, Eiffel proposed the construction of the now famous tower for the Paris Exposition of 1889, his plan was not taken seriously. He persisted and finally obtained a large subsidy for the task. When the exposition opened in Paris three years later, Eiffel was able to hoist the French flag on the highest of all structures, now a symbol of France itself.

Dawes and Young to advise on debts

Dec 15. Charles G. Dawes and Owen D. Young have been chosen to serve as the American experts in the inquiry into Germany's financial situation. The appointments were announced in Paris by the Reparations Commission which, among other things, will seek to stabilize the German currency.

Dawes, a lawyer and banker, was General Purchasing Agent for the American Expeditionary Force in the recent war in Europe. He was also Comptroller of the Treasury during the McKinley administration and later served as the first Director of the United States Bureau of the Budget. Young, who practiced law in both New York City and Boston, is the Chairman of the Board of General Electric Company (→ 1/14/24).

F. Scott Fitzgerald: A jazz age saga

F. Scott Fitzerald.

Flappers, prep-school grads and the nouveau riche populate "Tales of the Jazz Age," a collection of short stories published last year. It remains a big seller. The author, a 27-year-old Princeton dropout, is making the rounds at all the smartest parties. Perhaps he is sniffing out material for his next work.

Fitzgerald has published two novels: "This Side of Paradise" (1920) and "The Beautiful and the Damned" (1922). He wrote "Damned" soon after marrying Zelda Sayre, a daughter of an Alabama judge. Reports are the book mirrors their marriage, a garrulous, drink-filled, passionate relationship. The couple recently had a baby girl; her presence has not calmed them down a wit.

Fitzgerald was educated at a Catholic prep school, and a kind of religious retribution often lurks behind the lives of his characters. They cavort today and grieve tomorrow. If this is the jazz age, it is also a time for singing the blues.

1924

JANUARY

Su	Mo	Tu	We	Th	Fr	Sa
		1	2	3	4	5
6	7	8	9	10	11	12
13	14	15	16	17	18	19
20	21	22	23	24	25	26
29	28	29	30	31		

1. Pasadena: Rose Bowl ends in 14-14 tie between Navy and Washington.

4. Luxor, Egypt: Tutankhamen's stone sarcophagus found intact inside fifth shrine (→ 25).

6. Coolidge opposes private arms to Mexican rebels (→ 19).

7. Athens: Latife Hanum, Mustafa Kemal's wife, wounded by bomb in attempt on life of Turkish premier.

9. Ford Motor Co. stock now valued at nearly $1 billion.

9. Sun Yat-sen appeals to U.S. to seek intl. pressure for peace in China (→ 3/1).

10. Weymouth, England: British sub L-24 sunk accidentally by battleship; all 43 feared dead.

13. "The Hummingbird," with Gloria Swanson, opens in N.Y.

13. N.Y.: Bantamweight boxer Frankie Jerome dies three days after being knocked out.

18. Albany: N.Y. state motion picture censorship board says Hollywood glorifies vice.

19. Washington: Seven warships sent to Mexico to confront rebels at Gulf ports (→ 2/6).

20. Railroad walkout ties up British trains.

24. Mussolini abolishes all non-Fascist trade unions (→ 4/7).

24. N.Y.: Famous Youssoupoff black pearl necklace sold to Mrs. Gerry for $400,000.

25. Luxor, Egypt: Clothes on mummy show Egyptian fashions have not changed in 2,642 years (→ 2/12).

25. France, Czechoslovakia sign accord supplementing Eastern European Little Entente.

26. Coolidge names counsel to handle prosecution of oil lease fraud (→ 2/18).

26. U.S.S.R.: Petrograd renamed Leningrad.

27. Italian-Yugoslav accord arranges annexation of Fiume to Italy (→ 3/9).

27. Moscow: Lenin's body laid in marble tomb near Kremlin (→ 2/2).

28. American economist to rule Hungarian finances for League.

Lenin, Soviet founder, dead at 54

Ailing Lenin, and Stalin at Gorky.

Jan 21. The man who masterminded Russia's revolution and then, as its first Communist head of state, achieved a degree of uncontested power that the Czar himself might have envied, is dead. Vladimir Ilyich Lenin was 54.

In a political "testament" that he left behind, Lenin advocated the removal of Joseph Stalin from the office of Secretary General of the party. It is believed that Lenin wanted Leon Trotsky to succeed him.

Lenin transformed the theories of the German Communist Karl Marx into a practical plan for revolution, and then applied them to Russia.

In adapting Marx's theories to Russia, an agrarian country that lacked the advanced workforce Marx thought was necessary for revolution, Lenin advocated the importance of a small, elite party which would guide the uneducated citizens. His Bolshevik Party, and then the Soviet government, were run in this elitist fashion.

As a man, Lenin was a paradoxical combination of an uncompromising ascetic, unwilling to consider reform instead of revolution, and a pragmatist, willing to negotiate with capitalist powers when it was in his interest. For example, in 1917 he allowed the capitalist German regime to help him return to Russia.

Lenin was born Vladimir Ulyanov into a middle-class family in Simbirsk. His father was a schoolmaster and his mother the daughter of a physician. His older brother, Aleksandr, was executed in 1887 for his attempt on the life of Czar Alexander III, father of the czar that Lenin overthrew.

Following his brother's death, Lenin became active in revolutionary circles. Not long after his graduation in 1891 from St. Petersburg University, with a degree in law, Lenin adopted the pen name Nikolai Lenin and began writing pamphlets. He was arrested in 1895 and sent to Siberia. Nadezhda Krupskaya joined him there and they were married in 1898. After his release, they went abroad to live.

In 1902, Lenin published his most influential tract, "What is to Be Done?" in which he advocated the formation of a centralized organization of professional revolutionaries, with the aid of which he could bring revolution to Russia. Disagreement over this policy led to a split in the Russian Social Democrats between the Bolsheviks, who supported Lenin, and the Mensheviks, who wanted a more democratic organization.

During the 1905 revolution, Lenin returned to Russia and played a key role. His unwillingness to allow his followers to support the Duma and to negotiate with the czar on reforms caused the nobility to crack down on the protesters even harder than they might have. The failure of the czar to establish meaningful reforms in 1905, even though he appeared to have quashed the revolution, paved the way for the Bolshevik success in 1917.

In the intervening years, Lenin lived in Finland and then Switzerland. He separated himself from the political infighting that took place among the various revolutionary groups by building up a small, but totally committed Bolshevik Party. In 1912, he began publishing a daily paper, Pravda.

Proclaiming the Soviet republic.

A restful moment in Gorky.

At the outbreak of the Great War, Lenin tried, unsuccessfully, to convince members of the Socialist Congress of the Second International to forget their nationality and join together in overthrowing their governments. The goal of world revolution remained a priority for him and after the success of the revolution he established the Third International, with that aim in mind.

Having spent years laying the foundation, Lenin's Bolshevik Party was able to seize control with relatively little effort, thereby confirming Lenin's theories. Lenin returned to Russia in the spring of 1917; on Nov. 9, he formed the first Soviet government and became its Chairman, a post he held until now.

Once in power, Lenin adopted a system of government similar to that which ran his party, small and elite. In his first five years in office, he was confronted with civil war, famine, epidemics and protests and he met these challenges with the unhesitating use of repression.

In 1921, in the wake of the Kronstadt revolt and spreading uprisings, Lenin decided that Russia's revolution would be endangered without greater support from the peasants. In March 1921, his last major policy initiative, he introduced the New Economic Policy, which gave peasants relatively free use of their land (→ 27).

MacDonald forms first Labor government

Jan 23. With the formation by Ramsay MacDonald of the first Labor government in England's history, the British Labor Party stands fully legitimized. Last November's election failed to give the Conservative Party the majority it had hoped for. With a new seat count of 258 Conservative, 191 Labor and 158 Liberal, the stage was set for the recent offer by the Liberals to support a minority Labor government.

MacDonald, 58, was born in Scotland. After his formal education ended at age 12, he became involved with various socialist organizations and busied himself with persuading the leading British trade unions and intellectuals to form their own, independent political party. The resultant Labor Representation Committee, formed in 1900 with MacDonald as the first secretary, has clearly vindicated MacDonald's early vision (→ 10/8).

MacDonald, a pacifist during war.

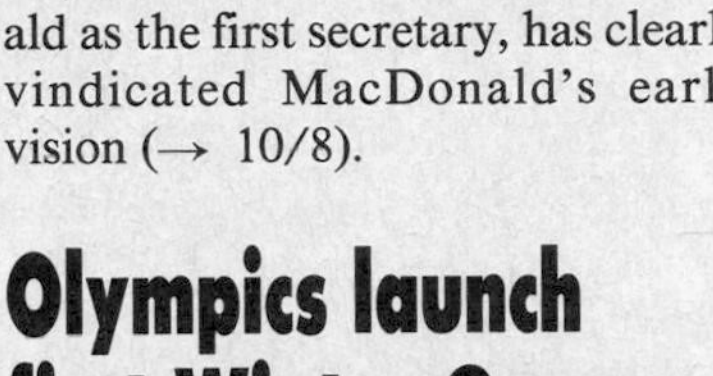

Olympics launch first Winter Games

Jan 31. A Norwegian, Thorleif Haug, winner of three gold medals, is the hero of the first Winter Olympics, held in Chamonix, France. And many other events were dominated by Scandanavians. But the United States did manage to take home a gold medal when Charlie Jetraw won the 1,500-meter speed-skating contest. Winter sports had been included in some earlier Olympics of the modern era, but this was the first time they were given their own showcase, as the annual winter festival in Chamonix received permission to designate the meet as the Winter Olympics (→ 2/4).

Olympics at Chamonix, France.

Dawes aims to help Germany get well

Dawes on the White House steps.

Jan 14. Charles G. Dawes has told the Reparations Commission that its main responsibility in the future is to find ways to cure Germany's economic ills. Dawes, an American expert on the commission, told the gathering in Paris the continent of Europe faces disaster unless "common sense is crowned king." And he warned against national pride on the part of those who fought against Germany in the most recent war. Dawes was also critical of those he called "foul and carrion-loving vultures who would exploit their pitiful personalities out of the common misfortune" (→ 3/24).

1924

FEBRUARY

Su	Mo	Tu	We	Th	Fr	Sa
					1	2
3	4	5	6	7	8	9
10	11	12	13	14	15	16
17	18	19	20	21	22	23
24	25	26	27	28	29	

1. British government recognizes U.S.S.R. (→ 3/15).

2. Moscow: Alexis Ivanovitch Rykoff appointed to succeed Lenin as pres. of Council of Commissars (→ 5/23).

4. France: Norway wins first-place title in Chamonix Winter Olympics.

4. Bombay: Mahatma Gandhi released from prison unconditionally (→ 9/28).

5. Renault vehicles open Sahara to automobile traffic.

5. Miami: Gertrude Ederle sets new 150-yd. freestyle swim mark of one minute, 44.2 seconds.

6. Mexico: Pres. Obregon's troops occupy Vera Cruz as Huerta flees (→ 10/21/26).

8. U.S.: Gas chamber used for first time to execute murderer.

9. Shandaken Aqueduct, longest in world, opened to supply New York City.

13. Boston retailers announce new slogan: "Dress well and you will succeed."

14. Thomas Watson founds Intl. Business Machines Corp.

19. N.Y. Court of Appeals upholds anti-scalping law, outlawing unauthorized sale of tickets.

22. N.Y.: Columbia University finds radio education a success.

22. Human heartbeat in St. Louis heard over radio 1,200 miles away in New Mexico.

24. Henry Ford proclaims high taxes on rich hurt the poor.

26. Pittsburgh: Steel industry finding eight-hour day increases efficiency, helps employee relations.

26. German authorities open trial of Hitler and Erich Ludendorff for Munich putsch (→ 3/13).

28. U.S. troops sent to Honduras to protect American interests during election conflict (→ 3/19).

DEATH

1. Maurice Prendergast, American post-Impressionist painter (*10/10/1859).

Gershwin's miracle: Rhapsody in Blue

Feb 12. From the first wail of the clarinet, George Gershwin's "Rhapsody in Blue" transfixed the audience gathered for its premiere last night at Aeolian Hall in New York City. Played by Paul Whiteman's orchestra, the "Rhapsody in Blue" is ingeniously metamorphosed by jazz-like instrumentation. Despite a certain immaturity, Gershwin expresses himself in a significant and, on the whole, highly original manner. The audience was stirred and many a hardened concert-goer was enraptured by this new musical talent.

Gershwin, trained in Tin Pan Alley.

Navy chief resigns

Feb 18. Secretary of the Navy Edwin Denby resigned today in the wake of growing evidence of scandal involving the so-called Teapot Dome oil leases. While Denby has not been accused of wrongdoing, he has defended the transfer of the rich oil reserves at Teapot Dome, Wyoming, and Elk Hills, California, from the Navy to the Interior Department in 1921.

A Senate committee currently is investigating the subsequent leasing of the rich Teapot Dome oil reserves by former Secretary of Interior Albert B. Fall to private interests without calling for competitive bids. President Coolidge said today that Denby's honesty in the affair has not been impugned (→ 3/28).

Wilson dies after dramatic political career

Thomas Woodrow Wilson.

Feb 3. Woodrow Wilson is dead, a shattered man with a shattered dream. The wartime President died in his sleep this morning at his home in Washington. Outside, hundreds of persons had kept a solemn vigil throughout much of the night.

Death came in a third floor bedroom where for years after leaving the White House he had sat quietly, looking out upon a city in which he had known joyous triumphs as well as bitter defeats. Just days ago, he told a friend: "I am a broken piece of machinery. When the machinery is broken . . ."

As the 28th president, he guided the nation through an impressive series of progressive domestic reforms and the war in Europe, and had later worked for his fondest dream, the creation of the League of Nations "to make the world safe for democracy." With Senate refusal to allow U.S. participation in the League, his health began declining. To some, he seemed as much a casualty of war as the men who died on the battlefields of Europe.

King Tut's coffin opened after 3,300 years

Feb 12. Today, a 3,300-year-old silence was shattered by gasps of wonderment as the golden mummy case of King Tutanhkamen was revealed. Howard Carter and his team of Egyptologists have labored months for this moment. Scientists and dignitaries, told that Tutankhamen's sarcophagus would now be uncovered, flocked immediately to Luxor, Egypt. Many stood in the stifling heat outside the pharaoh's tomb for the privilege of being among the first viewers.

The sarcophagus lid, carved of heavy granite, was hoisted with a tackle. Lights were aimed inside the casket. Carter rolled back a linen shroud to display a gold life-size figure clutching a scepter against its breast. A wilted wreath of olive leaves encircled its brow, a gilded serpent embraced its temples. The eyes, lifelike and lustrous, were chiseled crystal. For some scientists, the real beauty is yet to be seen: the mummified remains of the boy-king within (→ 11/13/25).

Carter and aide gently remove a protective substance from the gold figure.

1924

MARCH

Su	Mo	Tu	We	Th	Fr	Sa
						1
2	3	4	5	6	7	8
9	10	11	12	13	14	15
16	17	18	19	20	21	22
23	24	25	26	27	28	29
30	31					

1. China: Communists admitted to Kuomintang (→ 9/8).

8. Explosion entombs 173 miners in Utah.

9. Mussolini annexes all Adriatic lands to Fiume (→ 15).

10. U.S. Supreme Court upholds N.Y. state law forbidding late-night work for women.

11. U.S. Sec. of Commerce Hoover urges regulation of growing radio industry (→ 2/23/27).

13. Berlin: Reichstag dissolved for fifth time in German history (→ 4/1).

15. Rome: King Victor Emmanuel honors Gabriele d'Annunzio for Fiume heroism, naming him prince of Montenevoso.

15. Sweden recognizes U.S.S.R. (→ 5/31).

15. Egypt's King Fuad inaugurates first Nile Valley Parliament (→ 7/12).

17. Four Douglass Army aircraft leave Los Angeles for round-world flight (→ 5/11).

18. U.S. Congress passes Soldiers' Bonus Bill offering 20-year annuities for total of $2 billion (→ 4/23).

18. Douglas Fairbanks stars in premiere of "The Thief of Baghdad."

19. Berltolt Brecht's "The Life of Edward II of England" opens in Munich.

19. U.S. troops rushed to Tegucigalpa as Honduran capital is taken by rebel forces (→ 4/19/25).

24. Washington: House votes $10 million to aid German women and children (→ 4/9).

24. Rome: Pope Pius bestows rank of cardinal on U.S. Archbishops Hayes and Mundelein.

31. Washington: Harry Sinclair, accused in bribery scandal, indicted for contempt of Senate (→ 5/27/25).

DEATHS

1. Princess Louise of Belgium (*2/18/1858).

22. Robert Nivelle, French general (*10/15/1856).

Old-style Turkish customs abolished

March 3. Kemal Ataturk, also known as Mustafa Kemal, is moving quickly to bring Turkey into the twentieth century and align it more closely with Western Europe.

The new President of the Turkish republic has convinced his National Assembly to abolish many of the country's oldest religious and cultural traditions. Chief among them is the caliphate, the hereditary powers held by Moslem leaders.

Kemal is also planning to outlaw religious instruction, polygamy and clothing which dates back to the Ottoman Empire. Kemal abolished the sultanate last fall. Following his military victories against Greece, he seems to have carte blanche to institute even more reforms in Turkey (→ 1/15/26).

Radio broadcast spans 7,000 miles

Broadcasting in a tangle of wires.

March 7. A milestone in radio broadcasting was achieved tonight when speeches made at a dinner in New York City were transmitted over a six-station network spanning two continents and 7,000 miles. Signals from station WJZ in New York were relayed across the country to San Francisco and then to a British station in Manchester.

The landmark broadcast is being hailed as an example of the power of radio to link peoples around the globe. Latest figures indicate there are nearly 800 stations broadcasting in the United States and that as many as five million American homes now have radio receivers, with the number increasing rapidly.

Teapot Dome scandal: Daugherty ousted

Daugherty, felled by oil scandal.

March 28. Attorney General Harry M. Daugherty, the storm center of both the Harding and Coolidge administrations, was forced to resign today. His ouster, at the request of President Coolidge, is the latest episode in what has become known as the Teapot Dome scandal, involving the leasing of federal oil reserves to private interests.

While Daugherty has not been linked directly to the Teapot Dome affair at this time, he angered key senators who were unearthing details of the oil leases by ordering federal agents to spy on them. He also refused to testify before a Senate committee looking into the oil matter or to allow the panel to look at secret files.

Daugherty has been a controversial figure since first becoming attorney general in Warren G. Harding's administration. A member of the so-called Ohio Gang associated with the late president, he had run Harding's successful campaign for president. There have been allegations that Daugherty was directly involved in fraudulent dealings with the office of the alien property custodian and that he opened government liquor warehouses for use by friends.

In demanding Daugherty's resignation, President Coolidge, who has not been linked to any wrongdoing, said the attorney general's continuation in office was a source of "increasing embarrassment." Daugherty is the second Cabinet casualty resulting from the oil lease scandal. Edwin Denby resigned as Secretary of the Navy just a month ago (→ 31).

Athens Assembly makes Greece a republic

March 25. As of today, Greece is a republic. King George II has been deposed in favor of a non-royal government, and unless the upcoming popular referendum springs a surprise on the overconfident Greek republicans, the familiar title of King of the Hellenes will be relegated to the past.

The day found Athens in a holiday mood with people displaying small flags inscribed, "Republic and Reconciliation." In the Assembly chamber, filled to overflowing, a resolution was passed dethroning the king and his Glucksberg dynasty and barring them from succession. It "proclaims Greece to be a Republic on condition that such be confirmed by plebiscite," and it authorizes the "appropriation of property belonging to the deposed dynasty. Admiral Konduriotis continues to exercise his present powers until a republican constitution can be framed." The admiral now serves as regent. A plan to name him provisional governor was changed for diplomatic reasons.

Thus ends, the republicans hope, the torment ot recent Greek history, which saw the death of King Alexander, the restoration of King Constantine, a defeat in the war against their ancient rival, Turkey, an anti-royalist revolution and the subsequent abdication by Constantine in favor of Crown Prince George. With George's dethronement, the republic begins (→ 4/13).

Douglas Fairbanks is the daring "Thief of Baghdad," in Raoul Walsh's new adventure.

1924

APRIL

Su	Mo	Tu	We	Th	Fr	Sa
		1	2	3	4	5
6	7	8	9	10	11	12
13	14	15	16	17	18	19
20	21	22	23	24	25	26
29	28	29	30			

1. Al Capone's brother killed as Chicago gangsters steal ballots at gunpoint in Cicero village election.

2. N.Y.C. Transit Commissioner Harkness announces he will fight advertising in subways.

7. Newark radio station heard in Tokyo, 9,000 miles away.

8. Washington investigatory commission charges Du Pont family with war profiteering.

9. Paris: Dawes Committee issues report declaring Germany ready to pay reparations (→ 27).

11. Washington: House passes Johnson anti-Japanese immigration bill under heavy protests from Tokyo (→ 5/26).

13. Greek referendum demonstrates support for new republic (→ 8/22/26).

15. N.J.: Dr. Emmanuel Lasker wins intl. chess masters, defeating Austria's Dr. Tartakower.

21. Paris: Georges Rouault shown at Druet Gallery.

22. Washington report released indicating Volstead Act spurs crime (→ 8/21).

22. New York: Einstein-inspired play "Time is a Dream" opens on Broadway.

23. Allied premiers at San Remo Conference vote independence to Armenians (→ 7/25).

23. U.S. Senate passes Soldiers' Bonus Bill (→ 5/3).

28. West Virginia: 114 believed dead in Benwood mine explosion at Wheeling Steel.

29. Cuba: Open revolt breaks out in Santa Clara province (→ 5/2).

30. Indiana Governor Warren McCray sentenced to ten years in jail for mail fraud.

BIRTH

3. Marlon Brando, U.S. actor.

DEATHS

10. Hugo Stinnes, Germany's czar of finance (*2/12/1870).

21. Eleonora Duse, Italian actress (*10/3/1858).

25. Charles F. Murphy, Tammany Hall political boss.

Major film merger: Goldwyn and Mayer

MGM studios, Hollywood.

April 17. One of the largest mergers in the history of the motion picture industry was consummated yesterday by Marcus Loew, who heads the consolidated interests which will be operated under the name of the Metro-Goldwyn Corporation, involving Metro Pictures, Goldwyn Pictures and the Louis B. Mayer Company with a combined authorized capital stock of $65 million. It brings together the immense Loew chain of theaters and the Goldwyn-controlled houses.

Loew commented that the motion picture business is undergoing a "stabilizing process and is working itself out on sane economic principles." The production center will be the Goldwyn Studios at Culver City, California, covering 40 acres and representing a $14 million investment. The trademark, a roaring lion and the motto, "Ars Gratia Artis," was owned by Goldwyn.

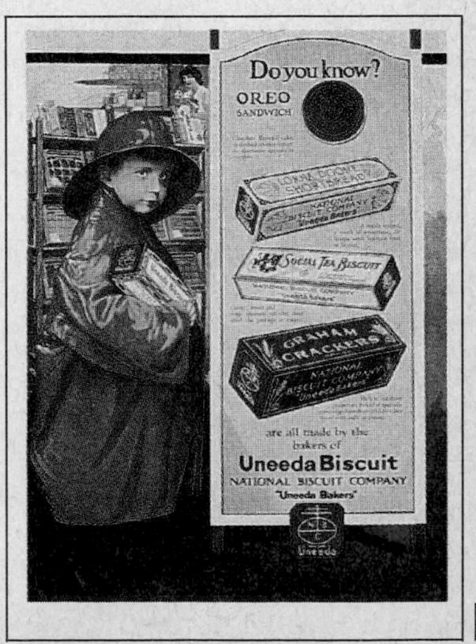

Hitler gets 5 years for Beer Hall Putsch

Principal collaborators in the failed Munich putsch of Nov. 1923 pose after the trial in front of the Bavarian Valksgericht. From left to right: Pernet, Weber, Frick, Kriebel, Ludendorff, Hitler, Bruckner, Rohm and Wagner.

April 1. Adolf Hitler, the Nazi leader in Germany, was sentenced today to five years in prison for his abortive putsch in a Munich beer hall last November. But the lenient judges also decreed that Hitler would be eligible for parole in six months. Most of the 60 journalists who covered the trial agreed that the sentence was a mere slap on the wrist. Their stories also transformed Hitler into a national hero and put his name on the front pages of papers all over the world.

Hitler was protected by the Bavarian Minister of Justice during the trial, and the judges allowed him to interrupt frequently and cross-examine witnesses at will. Hitler invoked the name of Wagner, he portrayed himself as the spirit of German nationalism and the enemy of Marxism and he vowed that prison would not destroy his will.

"You may pronounce us guilty a thousand times over," Hitler said, "but the goddess of the eternal court of history will tear to tatters the brief of the state prosecutor and the sentence of this court" (→ 5/4).

Dawes Plan given to war debts group

April 27. The German government signaled its support today of a plan, proposed by a committee headed by Charles G. Dawes of the United States, for settlement of the reparations issue. In its proposal, the Dawes panel calls for Germany to pay treaty charges "to the utmost limit of her capacity." It further proposes a $200 million foreign loan to help Germany meet these obligations.

In a letter made public in Paris, German officials said the proposal is a "practical basis for a rapid solution of the reparations problem." Earlier this month, both France and Great Britain indicated their support of the plan, which Dawes and his committee submitted to the International Reparations Commission (→ 6/4).

April 7. Benito Mussolini received a ringing endorsement at the Italian polls today, surprising even his Fascisti. Polling 64% of the popular vote in a record turnout of 62%, Il Duce is now free to govern through the Fascist-controlled Parliament. Lack of violence at the polls would seem to indicate that voters were not coerced (→ 5/30).

1924

MAY

Su	Mo	Tu	We	Th	Fr	Sa
				1	2	3
4	5	6	7	8	9	10
11	12	13	14	15	16	17
18	19	20	21	22	23	24
25	26	27	28	29	30	31

2. Pres. Coolidge bans sale of arms to Cuban rebels.

3. Coolidge sends first veto to Senate on veterans bonus bill (→ 19).

4. New York: Pola Negri opens in Dmitri Buchowetzki's first American film "Men."

4. German Socialists retain power despite heavy losses in legislative elections (→ 28).

7. American Soc. of Composers Authors and Publishers denounces movies, radio as "parasitic."

9. Mass.: Methodist Episcopal Church, at Springfield conference, grants women ordination.

11. Round-world Army aviator Martin arrives in Alaska after crashing into peak (→ 7/11).

11. Left wins in French elections; Radical Edouard Herriot, Socialist Leon Blum lead 328 into Natl. Assembly (→ 6/10).

12. World's largest steam generator inaugurated at Brooklyn Edison Company.

17. Black Gold and jockey J.D. Mooney are winners in Kentucky Derby.

20. California: Owens Valley farmers revolt over diversion of water to Los Angeles (→ 11/16).

21. Washington: Congress okays $472 mil. tax cut (→ 2/19/25).

21. Chicago: Nathan Leopold Jr. and Richard Loeb kidnap and murder 13-year-old boy (→ 31).

24. Karl Marx's grandson Jean Longuet refuses Soviet request to move Marx's body from London to Russia.

28. Germany: Nationalist Deputy Walraff elected pres. of Reichstag (→ 12/11).

30. Indy 500 won by Joe Boyer in five hours, five minutes.

30. Italy: Socialist Deputy Matteoti denounces electoral fraud of Fascists (→ 6/10).

31. China recognizes U.S.S.R. on own terms (→ 10/28).

DEATHS

4. Edith Nesbit, British novelist, children's stories (*8/15/1858).

26. Victor Herbert, U.S. composer, light opera (*2/1/1859).

Clothiers advise: Dress for success

May 31. The New England Association of Retail Clothiers and Furnishers met in Boston today. After much deliberation, the group issued this selfless resolution: "Whereas it has been abundantly proved that proper attire aids in success; therefore it is resolved that this association commends the efforts being made to stress the importance of pride in appearance." A motion for Congress to repeal all current excise taxes was also carried.

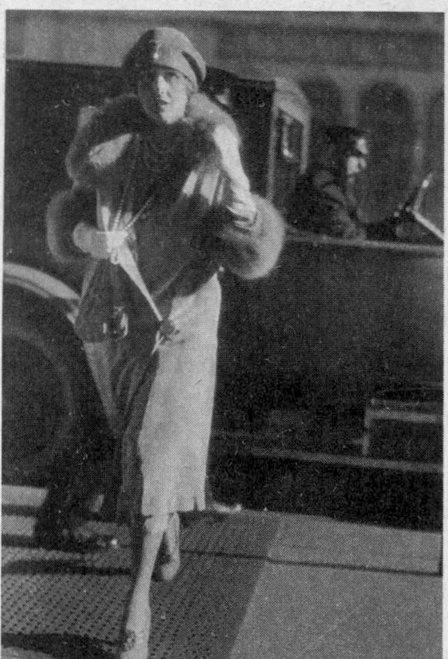

The worldly Claire Booth Luce.

Japanese barred by new entry rules

May 26. The Japanese government has protested the barring of immigrants to the United States, specified in legislation signed today.

The American Legion, AFL and other powerful groups outlined five reasons for Japan's exclusion:

1) The Japanese are unassimilable; their culture is too different.
2) Their birthrate, three times greater than whites' in California, may make whites a minority there.
3) They pose an economic threat.
4) Japanese laborers might set up foreign colonies within the U.S.
5) Japan excludes Chinese and Koreans from its own soil, so it has no right to protest this exclusion.

Japan recalled its ambassador, and "hate America" demonstrations are erupting in that nation.

Rich Chicago youths confess thrill murder

Loeb (left) and Leopold, in a Chicago prison, looking bored with the affair.

May 31. Nathan Leopold and Richard Loeb, brilliant students and sons of millionaires, have confessed to strangling a 14-year-old boy. Ten days ago, Leopold and Loeb gave Bobby Franks, a distant cousin of Loeb's, a ride in a rented car. Then, they beat him to death, dumped his body in a culvert on the Illinois border and sent Franks' parents a ransom note under assumed names. Detectives traced Leopold and Loeb to the crime from a pair of glasses Loeb had dropped near the body. The 19-year-olds related events of the murder impassively. Their lawyer, Clarence Darrow, plans to offer a unique defense: innocent on grounds of emotional illness.

Stalin survives censure by Lenin

May 25. Enemies of Joseph Stalin in the Soviet Communist Party missed a chance to get rid of him during the current party congress.

On January 21, death struck down Vladimir I. Lenin, the Bolshevik leader and founder of the Soviet state. In his last days, he dictated several letters to his comrades. One said Stalin was "too coarse" for the position of General Secretary, which he then held. Lenin recommended someone "more polite and more considerate."

After Lenin's death, his letters, usually called his "testament," were opened by his wife. She handed to the Central Committee the one about Stalin. It was not read to the whole congress or debated.

Stalin made a show of resigning, but he was "dissuaded" by Grigori Zinoviev and Lev Kamenev, who were allied with him against Leon Trotsky. The congress voted for Stalin.

Congress insists on soldiers' bonus

May 19. Brushing aside arguments that the government cannot afford it, Congress has overridden President Coolidge's veto of a $2.25 billion soldier bonus bill. Final action, assuring that the bill becomes law, came today when the Senate voted to override the veto. The bipartisan vote was 59 to 26. By a vote of 313 to 78, the House of Representatives, too, voted two days ago to override the president.

Under the new law, it is estimated that more than three million veterans will be entitled to insurance policies and more than 380,000 will be paid cash bonuses of $50 or less. All veterans up to and including those holding the rank of Captain in the Army and Marine Corps and Lieutenant in the Navy are eligible for the bonus. In vetoing the bill four days ago, the president stressed the need for economy in government and said that the bill was not morally justified.

1924

JUNE

Su	Mo	Tu	We	Th	Fr	Sa
1	2	3	4	5	6	7
8	9	10	11	12	13	14
15	16	17	18	19	20	21
22	23	24	25	26	27	28
29	30					

1. Vienna: Chancellor Ignaz Siepel wounded by Socialist would-be assassin.

2. U.S. Congress sends child labor amendment to states for ratification.

2. U.S. grants full citizenship to American Indians (→ 8).

4. Berlin: Chancellor Marx tells Reichstag Dawes Plan will save Germany (→ 6).

6. German Reichstag accepts Dawes report 247-183 (→ 19).

8. Oklahoma: 10,000 Indians gather in Sand Springs to discuss Native American future (→ 9/4).

9. Tokyo: Liberal Cabinet formed by Prime Minister Kato.

10. Paris: Pres. Millerand beaten by leftist majority in Parliament, announces resignation (→ 13).

12. Republican convention in Cleveland chooses Coolidge for president, William E. Borah as running mate (→ 7/4).

12. Explosions kill 48 on U.S.S. Mississippi off California coast.

13. Gaston Doumergue defeats Painlev for French presidency.

15. Sofia: Bulgarian agrarian leader M. Petkoff slain.

17. Italy: Fascist militia march into Rome singing war songs (→ 9/13).

19. German govt. announces it will accept Allied demand for renewed military control (→ 27).

20. A.C. Irvine and George Leigh Mallory reported dead in attempt to climb Mt. Everest.

23. Lt. R.L. Maugham arrives in San Francisco, completing 12 hr., 20 min. coast-to-coast flight.

27. Democrats to offer Mrs. Leroy Springs for vice presidential nomination—first woman considered for job (→ 8/13).

27. French open Ruhr to 210,000 German exiles (→ 7/16).

BIRTH

11. William Styron, American novelist, "The Confessions of Nat Turner."

DEATH

24. Terence Powderly, founder Knights of Labor (*1/22/1849).

Will Rogers always leaves 'em laughing

Will Rogers (left) with the Ziegfelds.

June 30. The new Follies opened last night, living up to expectations. The American girl was glorified again in the characteristic Ziegfeld way. The evening also marked the welcome return to the New York stage of Will Rogers after a self-willed year of exile in Hollywood. He was at his glorious best as he twirled old ropes and unleashed new jokes. ("I don't make jokes—I just watch the government and report the facts.")

Rogers, who first joined the Follies in 1915, did not spare salty comments worthy of our favorite "cowboy philosopher." There was also Lupino Lane, the English comedian and eccentric dancer who danced better than he joked. Favorites Ann Pennington and Edna Leedom sang and danced vigorously, and as for the rest of the girls . . . well, those who have never met a Follies beauty they didn't like will be pleased as punch with this shapely crop.

Anguished author Kafka dies young

A young, wide-eyed Kafka.

June 3. Franz Kafka, author of strange short stories exploring alienation and self-salvation, has died. He was 40 years old. At the time of his death, he was readying for publication a collection of stories to be called "A Hunger Artist."

Kafka was born in Prague in 1883. He both loved and hated his parents, a middle-class Jewish couple who demanded high standards from him. His works reflect his claustrophobia: "The Metamorphosis" (1915) concerns a son who is transformed into a repellent insect, while "The Country Doctor" (1919) is a tale of guilt and repression. Kafka leaves behind several unpublished novels.

Fascists murder Socialist leader

June 10. The Italian Socialist leader Giacomo Matteotti has been kidnapped and assassinated by Fascists in Rome. He was scheduled to speak in the Chamber of Deputies today and was expected to continue his attack on the government's financial policy. Indignant at this political murder, 127 deputies have refused to sit in Parliament and have asked the King of Italy, Victor Emmanuel, to fire Mussolini.

Matteotti was one of the most active members of the chamber. Frequently, he made sharply critical speeches against Mussolini's regime. He was elected as a Socialist Deputy in 1919, and he was reelected last April (→ 17).

1924

JULY

Su	Mo	Tu	We	Th	Fr	Sa
		1	2	3	4	5
6	7	8	9	10	11	12
13	14	15	16	17	18	19
20	21	22	23	24	25	26
29	28	29	30	31		

4. Cleveland: Conference for Progressive Political Action nominates Robert La Follette for president (→ 9).

5. Wimbledon: Jean Borotra over Rene Lacoste 6-1, 3-6, 6-1, 3-6, 6-4; Kathleen McKane over Helen Wills 4-6, 6-4, 6-4.

6. Brazilian rebels capture Sao Paulo; 250 dead (→ 14).

9. New York: Democrats pick John Wm. Davis for pres., Charles W. Bryan for v.p. (→ 10).

10. Chicago: Farmer-Laborites reject La Follette, endorse Communist Wm. Z. Foster for president (→ 11/4).

10. Denmark grants Norway fishing rights on eastern coast of Greenland.

11. American globe fliers arrive in Constantinople (→ 14).

12. Michigan: Pastor, missing since June, found in Battle Creek with "KKK" branded on back (→ 8/22).

12. Cairo: Egypt's Premier Zaghlul Pasha shot at by student (→ 8/19).

14. American round-world fliers hailed in Paris (→ 16).

14. Brazil: 3,000 slain as rebels clash with troops in Sao Paulo.

16. Crowds cheer globe fliers as they land in London (→ 9/6).

16. London conference on Dawes proposal opens (→ 8/2).

18. Italian racer Ottavio Bottechia wins Tour de France.

20. U.S. National Council of Catholic Women opens campaign for modesty in dress.

22. N.Y.C. taxi rates cut to ten cents per half-mile.

24. N.Y.: Gene Tunney scores TKO over Georges Carpentier in 15th round.

25. Greece announces deportation of 50,000 Armenians.

27. N.Y.: "Tess of the Dubervilles" opens at Capital Theater.

31. C.O. Johnson becomes first to broadcast from bottom of sea, on station WIP.

DEATH

27. Ferrucio Busoni, Italian composer (*4/1/1866).

Blood poisoning kills Coolidge boy

July 7. This evening Calvin Coolidge bid a final farewell to his son Calvin Jr. Not since Abraham Lincoln lost young William Wallace has a President seen his son die. Sixteen-year-old Calvin Jr. had contracted septicemia, for which, in its advanced stages, there is no cure.

A week ago, a healthy Calvin Jr. cut his foot playing tennis. After two days, he complained of severe pain in the lower abdomen. Suspecting appendicitis, doctors operated. Inflammation of the bone marrow was detected, and the truth was realized. Oxygen was administered, but there was no real hope of recovery.

The president, his wife and their older son, John, never experienced a tragedy of this kind. Public servants and private citizens have wired their condolences.

Paavo Nurmi wins four gold medals

July 30. The United States won the team championship, but Paavo Nurmi was the chief topic of conversation as the Summer Olympic Games ended today in Paris.

The "Flying Finn" won four gold medals at distances ranging from 1,500 to 10,000 meters. This was the greatest individual performance in the history of track and field. The stoic athlete, who lives on a diet of black bread and fish, finished first by two minutes in the 10,000-meter run. As others collapsed from heat or exhaustion, Nurmi won in a superhuman effort.

The United States captured 12 first places at Paris, a considerable improvement over its performance four years ago at Antwerp, when it was tied by Finland with nine first places.

1924 Paris

Men Athletics

100 M Dash
1. Harold Abrahams GBR 10,6
2. Jackson Scholz USA 10,7
3. Arthur Porntt NZL 10,8

200 M Dash
1. Jackson Scholz USA 21,6
2. Charles Paddock USA 21,7
3. Erie Liddell GBR 21,9

400 M Run
1. Erie Liddell GBR 47,6
2. Horatio Fitch USA 48,4
3. Guy Butler GBR 48,6

800 M Run
1. Douglas Lowe GBR 1:52,4
2. Paul Martin SU1 1:52,6
3. Schuyler Enck USA 1:53,0

1500 M Run
1. Paavo Nurmi FIN 3:53,6
2. Willy Schärer SUI 3:55,0
3. Henry Stallard GBR 3:55,6

5000 M Run
1. Paavo Nurmi FIN 14:31,2
2. Ville Ritola FIN 14:31,4
3. Edvin Wide SWE 15:01,8

10,000 M Run
1. Ville Ritola FIN 30:23,2
2. Edvin Wide SWE 30:55,2
3. Eero Berg FIN 31:43,0

Marathon
1. Albin Stenroos FIN 2:41:22,6
2. Romeo Bertini ITA 2:47:19,6
3. Clarence Demar US 2:48:14,0

110 M Hurtles
1. Daniel Kinsey USA 15,0
2. Sidney Atkinson SAF 15,0
3. Sten Pettersson SWE 15,4

400 M Hurtles
1. F. Morgan Taylor USA 52,6
2. Erik Vilén FIN 53,8
3. Ivan Riley USA 54,2

3000 M Steeplechase
1. Ville Ritola FIN 9:33,6
2. Elias Katz FIN 9:44,0
3. Paul Bontemps FRA 9:45,2

400 M Relay
1. USA 41,0 (Francis Hussey, Louis Clarke, Loren Murchison, Alfred Leconey
2. GBR 41,2 (Harold Abrahams, Walter Rangeley, Lancelot Royle, William Nichol)
3. HOL 41,8 (Jacob Boot, Henricus Broos, Jan de Vries, Marinus van den Berge)

1600 M Relay
1. USA 3:16,0 (Con Cochrane, Alan Helffrich, Olivier McDonald, William Stevenson)
2. SWE 3:17,0 (Arthur Svensson, Erik Byléhn, Gustaf Wejnarth, Nils Engdahl)
3. GBR 3:17,4 (Edward Toms, George Renwick, Richard Ripley, Guy Butler)

High Jump
1. Harold Osbom USA 1,98
2. Leroy Brown USA 1,95
3. Pierre Lewden FRA 1,92

Pole Vault
1. Lee Barnes USA 3,95
2. Glen Graham USA 3,95
3. James Brooker USA 3,90

Long Jump
1. William De Hart Hubbard USA 7,445
2. Edward Gourdin USA 7,275
3. Sverre Hansen NOR 7,26

Triple Jump
1. Anthony Winter AUS 15,525
2. Luis Bruneto ARG 15,425
3. Vilho Tuulos FIN 15,37

Shotput
1. Clarence Houser USA 14,995
2. Glenn Hartranft USA 14,895
3. Ralph Hills USA 14,64

Discus Throw
1. Clarence Houser USA 46,155
2. Vilho Nittymas FIN 44,95
3. Thomas Lieb USA 44,83

Hammer Throw
1. Frederick Tootell USA 53,295
2. Mathew McGrath USA 50,84
3. Malcolm Nokes GBR 48,875

Javelin
1. Jonni Myyrä FIN 62,96
2. Gunnar Lindström SWE 60,92
3. Eugène Oberst USA 58,35

Decathlon
1. Harold Osborn USA 7710,775
2. Emerson Norton USA 7350,895
3. Aleksander Klumberg EST 7329,360

300 M Team (1912, 1920, 1924 only)
1. Finland
2. Great Britain
3. USA

Cross Country Individual (1912, 1920, 1924)
1. Paavo Nurmi FIN 32:54,8
2. Ville Ritola FIN 34:19,4
3. Earl Johnson USA 35:21,0

Cross Country Team (1904, 1912, 1920, 1924 only)
1. Finland
2. USA
3. France

Pentathlon (1906, 1912, 1920, 1924 only)
1. Eero Lehtonen FIN
2. Elemér Somfay HUN
3. Robert Legendre USA

10,000 M Walk (1924, 1948, 1952 only)
1. Ugo Frigerio ITA 47:49,0
2. Gordon Goodwin GBR
3. Cecil Charles McMaster SAF

Men Swimming

100 M Freestyle
1. Johnny Weissmuller USA 59,0
2. Duke Paqa Kahanamoku USA 1:01,4
3. Samuel Kahanamoku USA 1:01,8

400 M Freestyle
1. Johnny Weissmuller USA 5:04,2
2. Arne Borg SWE 5:05,6
3. Andrew Charlton AUS 5:06,6

1500 M Freestyle
1. Andrew Charlton AUS 20:06,6
2. Arne Borg SWE 20:41,4
3. Frank Beaurepaire AUS 21:48,4

100 M Backstroke
1. Warren Paoa Keoloha USA 1:13,2
2. Paul Wyatt USA 1:15,4
3. Karoly Bartha HUN 1:17,8

200 M Breastroke
1. Robert Skelton USA 2:56,6
2. Joseph de Combe BEL 2:59,2
3. William Kirschbaum USA 3:01,0

800 M Relay Freestyle
1. USA 9:53,4 (Wallace O'Connor, Harry Glancy, Ralph Breyer, Johnny Weissmuller)
2. AUS 10:02,2 (Maurice Christie, Ernest Henry, Frank Beaurepaire, Andrew Charlton)
3. SWE 10:06,6 (Georg Werner, Orvar Trolle, Ake Borg, Arne Borg)

Springboard Diving
1. Albert White USA 696,4
2. Peter Desjardins USA 693,2
3. Clarence Pinkston USA 653,0

High Diving
1. Albert White USA 97,46
2. David Fall USA 97,30
3. Clarence Pinkston USA 94,60

Plain High Diving (1912, 1920, 1924 only)
1. Richmond Eve AUS 160,0
2. John Jansson SWE 157,0
3. Harold Clarke GBR 158,0

Water Polo

1. France
2. Belgium
3. USA

Women Swimming

100 M Freestyle
1. Ethel Lackie USA 1:12,4
2. Mariechen Wehselau USA 1:12,8
3. Gertrude Ederle USA 1:14,2

400 M Freestyle
1. Martha Norelius USA 6:02,2
2. Helen Wainwright USA 6:03,8
3. Gertrude Ederle USA 6:04,8

200 M Breaststroke
1. Lucy Morton GBR 3:32,2
2. Agnès Geraghty USA 3:34,0
3 Gladys Helens Carson GBR 3:35,4

100 M Backstroke
1. Sybil Bauer USA 1:23,2
2. Phyllis Harding GBR 1:27,4
3. Aileen Riggin USA 1:28,2

400 M Relay Freestyle
1. USA 4:58,8 (Gertrude Ederle, Euphrasia Donnelly, Ethel Lackie, Mariechen Wehsclau)
2. GBR 5:17,0 (Florence Barker, Grace McKenzie, Irène Vera Tanner, Constance Mabel Jeans)
3. SWE 5:35,0 (Aina Berg, Vivan Pettersson, Gulli Everlund, Hjördis Töpel)

Springboard Diving
1. Elizabeth Becker USA 474,5
2. Aileen Riggin USA 460,4
3. Caroline Fletcher USA 436,4

High Diving
1. Caroline Smith USA 33,2
2. Elisabeth Becker USA 33,4
3. Hjördis Töpel SWE 32,8

Boxing

Flyweight
1. Fidel Labarba USA
2. James McKenzie GBR
3. Raymond Fee USA

Bantamweight
1. William Smith SAF
2. Salvadore Tripoli USA
3. Jean Ces FRA

Featherweight
1. John *Jackie* Fields USA
2. Joseph Salas USA
3. Pedro Quartucci ARG

Lightweight
1. Hans Nielsen DEN
2. Alfredo Copello ARG
3. Frderick Boylstein USA

Welterweight
1. Jean Delage BEL
2. Hector Mendez ARG
3. Douglas Lewis CAN

Middleweight
1. Harry Mallin GBR
2. John Elliott GBR
3. Joseph Beecken BEL

Light Heavyweight
1. Harry Mitchell GBR
2. Thyge Petersen DEN
3. Sverre Sörsdal NOR

Heavyweight
1. Otto von Porat NOR
2. Sören Petersen DEN
3. Alfredo Porzio ARG

Greco Roman Wrestling

Bantamweight
1. Eduard Pütsed EST
2. Anselm Ahlfors FIN
3. Vänö Ikonen FIN

Featherweight
1. Kalle Anttila FIN
2. Aleksanteri Toivola FIN
3. Erik Malmberg SWE

Lightweight
1. Oskari Friman FIN
2. Lajos Kereszles HUN
3. Kalle Westerlund FIN

Middleweight
1. Edvard Vesterlund FIN
2. Artur Lindfors FIN
3. Roman Steinberg EST

Light Heavyweight
1. Carl Westerlgren SWE
2. Rudolf Svensson SWE
3. Onni Pellinen FIN

Heavyweight
1. Henri Deglane FRA
2. Edil Rosenqvist FIN
3. Raymond Bado HUN

Freestyle Wrestling

Bantamweight
1. Kustaa Pihlajama ki FIN
2. Kaarlo Måkinen FIN
3. Bryant Hines USA

Featherweight
1. Robin Reed USA
2. Chester Newton USA
3. Katsutoshi Naito JAP

Lightweight
1. Russel Vis USA
2. Volmari Vikström FIN
3. Arvo Haavisto FIN

Welterweight
1. Hermann Gehri SUI
2. Eino Leino FIN
3. Otto Mu ller SUI

Middleweight
1. Fritz Hagmann SUI
2. Pierre Ollivier BEL
3. Vilho Pekkals FIN

Light Heavyweight
1. John Spellman USA
2. Rudolf Svensson SWE
3. Charles Courant SUI

Heavyweight
1. Harry Steele USA
2. Henri Wemli SUI
3. Andrew McDonald GBR

Men Fencing

Foil Individual
1. Roger Ducret FRA 6
2. Philippe Cattiau FRA 5
3. Maurice van Damme BEL 4

Foil Team
1. France
2. Belgium
3. Hungary

Epée Individual
1. Charles Delporte BEL 8
2. Roger Ducret FRA 7
3. Nils Hellsten SWE 7

Epée Team
1. France
2. Beglium
3. Italy

Sabre Individual
1. Dr. Sandor Posta HUN 5
2. Roger Ducret FRA 5
3. Janos Garay HUN 5

Sabre Team
1. Italy
2. Hungary
3. Netherlands

Women Fencing

Foil Individual
1. Elken Osiier DEN 5
2. Gladys Muriel Davis GBR 4
3. Grete Hockscher DEN 3

FOR ABBREVIATIONS SEE TABLE OF CONTENTS

CHART

Weightlifting

			One Arm Snatch	Clean and Jerk, One Arm	2 Arm Press	2 Arm Snatch	Clean and Jerk, 2 Arm	Total
Featherweight								
1.	Pierino Gabetti	ITA	65,0	77,5	72,5	82,5	105,0	402,5
2.	Andreas Stadler	AUT	65,0	75,0	65,0	75,0	105,0	385,0
3.	Arthur Reimann	SUI	57,5	70,0	80,0	75,0	100,0	382,5
Lightweight								
1.	Edmond Deconttignies	FRA	70,0	92,5	77,5	85,0	115,0	440,0
2.	Anton Zwerina	AUT	75,0	80,0	77,5	82,5	112,5	427,5
3.	Bohumil Durids	TCH	70,0	82,5	72,5	90,0	110,0	425,0
Middleweight								
1.	Carlo Galimberti	ITA	77,5	95,0	97,5	95,0	127,5	492,5
2.	Alfred Neuland	EST	82,5	90,0	77,5	90,0	115,0	455,0
3.	Jean Kikas	EST	70,0	87,5	80,0	85,0	127,5	450,0
Light Heavyweight								
1.	Charles Rigoulot	FRA	87,5	92,5	85,0	102,5	135,0	502,5
2.	Fritz Hünenberger	SUI	80,0	107,5	80,0	97,5	125,0	490,0
3.	Leopold Friedrich	AUT	75,0	95,0	95,0	95,0	130,0	490,0
Heavyweight								
1,	Giuseppe Tonani	ITA	80,0	95,0	112,5	100,0	130,0	517,5
2.	Franz Aigner	AUT	80,0	97,5	112,5	95,0	130,0	515,0
3.	Harald Tammer	EST	75,0	95,0	90,0	97,5	140,0	497,5

Modern Pentathlon Individual

1. Bo Lindman SWE
2. Gustaf Dyrsen SWE
3. Bertil Uggla SWE

Canoeing

800 M Kayak-1 Demonstration
1. Charles Havens USA
2. Roy Nurse CAN
3. Harry Knight USA

800 M Kayak-2 demonstration
1. USA
2. Canada

800 M Kayak-4 demonstration
1. USA
2. Canada

800 M Canadian-1 demonstration
1. Roy Nurse CAN
2. Harry Greenshields CAN
3. A. H. Lindsay CAN

800 M Canadian-2 demonstration
1. Canada
2. Canada
3. USA

Rowing

Single Scull
1. Jack Bresford jun. GBR 7:49,2
2. William E. Garrett Gilmore USA 7:54,0
3. Josef Schneider SUI 8:01,1

Double Sculls
1. USA 6:34,0
2. France 6:38,0
3. Switzerland 3 lenghts

Pair Oars without Coxswain
1. Netherlands 8:19,4
2. France 8:21,6

Pair Oars with Coxswain
1. Switzerland 8:39,0
2. Italy 8:39,1
3. USA 3 lengths

Fours without Coxswain
1. Great Britain 7:08,6
2. Canada 1 length
3. Switzerland 2 lengths

Four Oars with Coxswain
1. Switzerland 7:18,4
2. France 7:21,6
3. USA 1 length

Eight Oars
1. USA 6:33,4
2. Canada 6:49,0
3. Italy

Yachting

Individual Monotype
1. Léon Huybrechts BEL 2
2. Henrik Robert NOR 7
3. Hans Dittmar FIN 8

6 M Class (1908, 1912, 1920, 1924, 1928, 1932, 1936 only)
1. Norway 2
2. Denmark 5
3. Netherlands 5

8 M Class (1908, 1912, 1920, 1924, 1928, 1932, 1936 only)
1. Norway 2
2. Great Britain 5
3. France 5

Cycling

Road Race Individual
1. Armand Blanchonnet FRA 6:20:48,0
2. Henri Hoevenaers BEL 6:30:27,0
3. René Hamel FRA 6:30:51,6

Road Race Team (1912, 1920, 1924, 1928, 1932, 1936, 1948, 1952, 1956 only)
1. France 19:30:14,0
2. Belgium 19:46:55,4
3. Sweden 19:59:41,6

1000 M Sprint
1. Lucien Michard FRA 12,8 (last 200 M)
2. Jacob Meijer HOL
3. Jean Cugnot FRA

2000 M Tandem
1. France 12,6 (last 200 M)
2. Denmark
3. Netherlands

Team Pursuit (4000 M)
1. Italy 5:15,0
2. Poland
3. Belgium

50 km track (1920 and 1924 only)
1. Jacobus Willems NET 1:18:24,0
2. Cyril Allert Alden GBR one wheel
3. Franc H. Wyld GBR one M

Equestrian Sports

All around Individual Competition
1. Adolf D.C. van der Voort van Zijp NET
2. Frode Kirkebjerb DEN
3. Sloan Doak USA

All around Team Competition
1. Netherlands
2. Sweden
3. Italy

Dressage Individual
1. Ernst Linder SWE
2. Bertil Sandström SWE
3. Xavier Lesage FRA

Grand Prix Jumping Individual
1. Alphonse Gemuseus SUI -6
2. Tommaso Lequio ITA -8,75
3. Adam Krolikiewicz POL -10

Grand Prix Jumping Team
1. Sweden -42,25
2. Switzerland -50,0
3. Portugal -53,0

Men Gymnastics

All around Individual Competition
1. Léon Stukelj YUG 110,340
2. Robert Prazak TCH 110,323
3. Bedrich Supcik TCH 106,930

All-around Team Competition
1. Italy 839,058
2. France 820,528
3. Switzerland 816,661

Parallel Bars Individual
1. August Güttinger SUI 21,63
2. Robert Prazak TCH 21,61
3. Giorgio Zampori ITA 21,45

Horse Vault
1. Frank Kriz USA 9,98
2. Jan Koutny TCH 9,97
3. Bohumil Markovsky TCH 9,93

Sidehorse
1. Josef Wilhem SUI 21,23
2. Jean Gütweniger SUI 21,13
3. Antoine Rebelez SUI 20,73

Sidehorse Vault (1924 only)
1. Albert Sequin FRA 10,00
2. Jean Gounot FRA 9,93
3. Francois Gangloff FRA 9,93

Horizontal Bar
1. Léon Stukelj YUG 19,730
2. Jean Gutweniger SUI 19,236
3. André Higelin FRA 19,163

Flying Rings
1. Franco Martino ITA 21,553
2. Robert Prazak TCH 21,483
3. Ladislav Vachs TCH 21,430

Rope Climbing (1896, 1904, 1908, 1924, 1932 only)
1. Bedrich Supeik TCH 7,2
2. Albert Seguin FRA 7,4
3. August Gu ttinger SUI 7,8
3. Ladislav Vacha TCH 7,8

Soccer

1. Uruguay
2. Switzerland
3. Sweden

1924

AUGUST

Su	Mo	Tu	We	Th	Fr	Sa
					1	2
3	4	5	6	7	8	9
10	11	12	13	14	15	16
17	18	19	20	21	22	23
24	25	26	27	28	29	30
31						

2. London: Allies agree on Dawes Plan, invite Germans to negotiations (→ 16).

8. Great Britain and U.S.S.R. sign trade agreement.

12. Albania renames port of San Giovanni di Medua Port Wilson, after American president.

13. Washington: Female federal employees now required to use husband's name, not maiden name (→ 9/15).

14. Coolidge announces he will base presidential campaign on "common sense" and his record (→ 11/4).

16. Report shows California has highest auto fatality rate in U.S.

16. London: Allies, Germans sign accord; French to quit Ruhr within a year (→ 17).

17. French troops evacuate German towns of Offenburg and Appenweier (→ 29).

19. Cairo: Civil disturbances put Port Sudan under martial law (→ 11/19).

21. Dutch, following Swedish accord of three days ago, agree to halt liquor trade to U.S. (→ 10/27).

22. Democratic nominee John Davis denounces Ku Klux Klan by name, challenges Coolidge to do same (→ 26).

23. Texas: "Ma" Ferguson nominated as Democratic candidate for governor (→ 11/4).

23. Paris crowds welcome French aviators Pelletier-Doisy and Besin on return from Tokyo-Paris flight.

24. "Lily of the Dust," with Pola Negri, opens in New York.

26. Montreal: Henry Ford defends KKK as group of patriots (→ 30).

28. U.S.: Premiere showing of John Ford's film "Iron Horse."

29. Berlin: Reichstag approves Dawes Plan, to go into effect Sept. 1 (→ 9/1).

30. Illinois: Six killed in KKK violence at Herrin (→ 11/1).

BIRTH

2. James Baldwin, American author and social critic.

Germany introduces currency reform

Aug 30. In a continued effort to stabilize the economy and instill new faith in the Berlin regime, the German Reichsbank has been made independent of the central government, and a new reichsmark currency introduced. This follows on the heels of the Dawes Plan for German reparations which featured a foreign loan of $8 million reichsmarks. A little more than one year ago, the mark's exchange rate was four trillion to the dollar, leaving many among the badly battered middle class to see in Adolf Hitler's controversial movement the hope for renewed economic stability and growth.

Tales of the sea: Joseph Conrad dies

Aug 3. Joseph Conrad died today at the age of 67. He mastered the English language and mastered sailing ships; he joined his loves in books about seafarers. "Heart of Darkness" (1902), about a voyage up the mysterious Congo River, may be his greatest work.

Josef Teodor Konrad Korzeniowski was born in Poland on December 3, 1857. After a childhood in a genteel family, he ran off to Marseilles, where he was hired to work on a succession of sailing vessels. Knowing only six words of English, he joined a British ship. Twenty years later, he was a world-renowned author of English works. "Lord Jim" (1900) and "The Secret Sharer" (1912) have typical Conrad heroes, men who wage their private wars in a world gone a bit mad.

Conrad, a year before his death.

1924

SEPTEMBER

Su	Mo	Tu	We	Th	Fr	Sa
	1	2	3	4	5	6
7	8	9	10	11	12	13
14	15	16	17	18	19	20
21	22	23	24	25	26	27
28	29	30				

1. Berlin makes first payment to Allies under Dawes Plan (→ 10/10).

3. Army flier makes Boston-to-New York trip in record time of 58 minutes.

4. Germany gains contract with U.S.S.R. for delivery of Russian petroleum.

4. Arizona: Indians vote for first time under new citizenship laws (→ 10/28/25).

6. Boston: American globe fliers get big ovation upon return to U.S. (→ 28).

6. Geneva: League votes unanimously for world parley on disarmament (→ 22).

8. China: Gen. Chang Tso-lin declares war on Peking (→ 9).

9. China: 1,100 U.S. Marines land to guard nationals in Shanghai area (→ 10/16).

10. U.S.S.R.: Red army under Ordjonikidz crushes Tiflis workers' uprising; several executed without trial.

13. Gen. John "Black Jack" Pershing retires from U.S. Army.

13. Italian Fascist Deputy Armando Casalini killed by Communists (→ 1/5/25).

14. France announces intent to close Devil's Island prison.

15. Washington: Natl. Woman's Party protests govt. payroll issue; asserts women have right to use maiden name (→ 11/4).

22. Geneva: Draft of protocol to end all wars presented to League of Nations (→ 10/2).

23. Germany asks admission to League of Nations (→ 9/15/25).

26. Teddy Roosevelt Jr. resigns as asst. sec. of Navy to run for governor of New York.

28. India: Gandhi, on hunger strike in Delhi, proclaims he will break fast only at death, in penance for riots (→ 8/31/28).

BIRTHS

16. Lauren Bacall, American actress.

28. Marcello Mastroanni, Italian actor.

30. Truman Capote, American novelist (*8/25/1984).

U.S. hails Army round-world fliers

Army fliers greeted in Labrador

Sept 28. Three Army airplanes arrived in Seattle, Washington, this afternoon, completing an historic round-the-world flight that began five months and 22 days ago. The American fliers succeeded in making the first air circuit of the globe after aviators of three other countries had failed earlier this year.

Starting from Sand Point Field on April 6, the six aviators who piloted the aircraft went around the world in a total of 57 hops that averaged 483 miles, touching 21 foreign countries and 25 states. They were greeted in Seattle by a crowd of 50,000 and a congratulatory telegram from President Calvin Coolidge.

Sept 29. Ten-year-old Jackie Coogan met the Pope today. His thoughts on Rome? "The best place in the world for shooting pictures, after Hollywood."

Big Bill Tilden wins for fifth time

Sept 2. "Big Bill" Tilden continues to dominate men's tennis. The lanky Philadelphian won the national championship for the fifth year in a row today by defeating William Johnston of San Francisco 6-1, 9-7, 6-2. Tilden breezed through the match at Forest Hills, New York, in 58 minutes, keeping his rival on the defensive throughout. With this victory, he tied the record of consecutive national triumphs set by William A. Larned from 1907-11. Expert observers said that Tilden's tennis in the opening set was the greatest ever seen. He abandoned his usual relaxed style and went straight for the kill.

Tilden warms up for Johnston.

Arrest coke king loaded with drugs

Sept 5. Three years of investigation paid off today when federal agents seized Albert Marino, dubbed "the coke king." An agent masquerading as a drug user had met Marino in Boston and trailed him to a Brooklyn tenement. Detectives surrounded the building, and a few agents, revolvers in hand, broke down the door to Marino's apartment. He leaped for the fire escape. The detectives grabbed him, and there was a hand-to-hand struggle before he was subdued. Marino, 26 years old, allegedly sold heroin, cocaine and other drugs in the United States, Germany and Britain. He was found with $50,000 worth of narcotics when he was arrested.

1924

OCTOBER

Su	Mo	Tu	We	Th	Fr	Sa
			1	2	3	4
5	6	7	8	9	10	11
12	13	14	15	16	17	18
19	20	21	22	23	24	25
26	27	28	29	30	31	

1. Viborg, England: Paavo Nurmi sets world five-mile mark at 24 minutes, 6.1 seconds.

2. Geneva: 47 nations sign protocol calling for compulsory arbitration.

5. Washington: Aluminum Co. of America declared a monopoly in federal report.

6. King Hussein of Hejaz resigns following Ibn Saud's declaration of holy war (→ 12/5).

8. N.Y.: Natl. Lutheran Council bans jazz in church music.

10. Washington Senators take World Series 4-3 in seventh game against Giants.

10. London: 800 mil. gold mark loan signed over to Germany under Dawes Plan (→ 11/30).

13. Washington: Henry Ford withdraws bid for Muscle Shoals Dam, claiming politics is destroying project (→ 3/13/25).

14. Buster Keaton's new film "Navigator's Cruise" released.

14. Russian dancer Anna Pavlova begins farewell tour in N.Y.

16. China: 1,000 die as tradesmen rise against Sun Yat-sen in Canton (→ 25).

16. Alicante elects Spain's first woman mayor —Senora Maria Perez y Mora.

20. Chicago court orders auto speeders to visit home for destitute and crippled children.

23. U.S.: Tax returns made public under new law; J.D. Rockefeller paid $7.4 million, Ford and Co. $19 million.

25. Chang Tso-lin's revolt in Peking forces resignation of Pres. Tsao Kun (→ 1/15/25).

27. U.S. Atty. Gen. Stone ousts 10 federal attys. for lax enforcement of dry law (→ 5/21/25).

28. France acknowledges U.S.S.R. (→ 12/18).

29. British Conservatives win big in legislative elections, take 400 seats to Labor's 151 (→ 11/6).

BIRTHS

1. Jimmy Carter, 39th U.S. pres.

29. Frances Hodgson Burnett, British writer, "Little Lord Fauntleroy" († 11/24/1849).

ZR-3 flies 5,000 miles to New York

Oct 15. The German dirigible ZR-3 completed the longest flight ever made by an airship today when she arrived at Lakehurst, N.J., after a 5,060-mile voyage from Friedrichshafen. The ZR-3, which is being turned over to the United States as part of Germany's war reparations, made the trip in 81 hours.

The dirigible's route brought it to the Azores, then to Newfoundland and over New York City on the last leg of its trip. The first action of the ZR-3's commander on arrival was to strike the German flag and turn the airship over to Navy officers. The ZR-3 thus becomes part of a growing Navy airship fleet that is expected to play a major role in American military activities.

Anna Pavlova on farewell U.S. tour

Oct 14. Miss Anna Pavlova, a dancer who often imitates the flight and grace of birds, is giving her swan song. Her current American tour, with her 42-member company, will be her last. The 43-year-old Russian ballerina says she wants to retire while still in her prime. She plans to live outside London and establish a dancing school there.

Miss Pavlova had an unpromising childhood. Her parents were poor, and she was a sickly, frail child. In 1899, she joined the Imperial Ballet in Petrograd (now Leningrad) and soon earned wide attention for her solos and pas de deux. She frequently toured the world, occasionally with Diaghilev's Russian Ballet. Her beautiful signature solo piece, which she first performed in 1907, is "The Dying Swan."

Anna Matveyevna Pavlova.

Revered Anatole France dies at 80

Satirical sage Anatole France.

Oct 12. The French writer, Jacques Anatole Thibault, who adopted the name of Anatole France, is dead at 80. He was a great stylist and humanist.

In the Dreyfus Affair, he responded to Emile Zola's appeal to support the accused officer. When Zola died, France was one of the most illustrious remaining Dreyfusard intellectuals. He was an officer of the Legion of Honor and a member of the French Academy. In 1921, he was awarded the Nobel Prize.

France was hailed as the greatest living man of letters in France, pursuing the line that was established successively by Chateaubriand, Victor Hugo and Renan in the 19th century. His better known works are "The Crime of Sylvestre Bonnard" and "The Gods are Athirst."

Valentino's big box office hit.

1924

NOVEMBER

Su	Mo	Tu	We	Th	Fr	Sa
						1
2	3	4	5	6	7	8
9	10	11	12	13	14	15
16	17	18	19	20	21	22
23	24	25	26	27	28	29
30						

1. Ohio: Federal troops enter Niles as 12 are wounded in KKK riots (→ 3/9/25).

4. Strauss' opera "Intermezzo" opens in Dresden.

6. N.Y.: "Boris Gudenoff" opens to wide acclaim at the Met.

7. Ireland proclaims amnesty for all offenders in 1923 civil war.

8. Austrian rail strike forces resignation of Chancellor Seipel; R. Ramek forms new Pan-Germanist, Social Democrat coalition government.

10. Chicago's florist bootlegger Dion O'Banion shot dead by gunman in own flower shop.

16. Lone Pine, Ca.: Local farmers continue protest against water diversion, blow up section of aqueduct.

16. Constantinople: Zora Agrah, "oldest man in world," celebrates 150th birthday.

19. Sir Lee Stack, gov. gen. of Sudan, killed by Egyptians in Cairo (→ 23).

20. Swedish Ballet premieres Darius Milhaud's "La Creation du Monde" in Paris.

23. Responding to British ultimatum, Egypt offers indemnity and apology for Stack's murder, but denies blame (→ 24).

24. Egypt: British seize customs at Alexandria, force Zaghlul Pasha to resign (→ 7/19/28).

25. Mexico City: Charlie Chaplin weds 16-year-old Lita Grey (→ 12/1/26).

29. New York: Army blanks Navy 12-0 at Polo Grounds.

30. Germany: Last Franco-British troops withdraw from Ruhr (→ 1/10/25).

BIRTHS

5. Greek painter Byzantios.

30. Shirley Chisholm, first black congresswoman in U.S.

DEATHS

4. Gabriel Faure, French composer (*5/12/1845).

9. Henry Cabot Lodge, U.S. senator (*5/12/1850).

19. George Plunkitt, ex-head of Tammany Hall (*1842).

Coolidge and Dawes elected 379 to 139

Nov 4. President Calvin Coolidge swept aside all opponents today to win a new four-year lease on the White House. The taciturn Republican scored a major victory despite the growing Teapot Dome oil scandal, a legacy of the previous Harding administration.

To fill the now vacant office of Vice President, which Coolidge once held, the nation chose Coolidge's running mate, Charles G. Dawes, who has served in several Republican administrations, most recently as an American expert on the Reparations Commission dealing with the German economy.

The Coolidge-Dawes ticket carried much of the nation, with Democrat John W. Davis winning only the South, losing even his own state of West Virginia. An even poorer showing was made by Senator Robert M. La Follette of Wisconsin, the candidate on the Progressive Party ticket. President Coolidge is the second man to win a full term after having served an unexpired term. The only other was Theodore Roosevelt (→ 11).

Official photo of the 30th President.

Ma Ferguson first woman Governor

Nov 4. Miriam "Ma" Ferguson was elected Governor of Texas today. She is the first woman in the United States ever elected to such office. Once the first lady of that state, Mrs. Ferguson, a Democrat, ran for office to vindicate her husband, James F. Ferguson, who was impeached as Governor of Texas in 1917 on charges of diverting state funds to personal uses. Mrs. Ferguson, an outspoken foe of the Ku Klux Klan, won her nickname when she campaigned across the state this year on the slogan of "Me for Ma" (→ 1/5/25).

Texas Gov. Miriam "Ma" Ferguson.

Puccini, prolific composer, is dead

Puccini, master of Italian opera.

Nov 29. Giacomo Puccini, composer of "La Boheme" and many other operas strong in sentimentality, has died in Brussels. He was 65. He leaves one unfinished opera, an ambitious work called "Turandot."

Puccini was born in Lucca, Italy, to a long line of musicians. A scholarship from Queen Margherita of Italy enabled him to study composition at a conservatory in Milan. His third opera, "Manon Lescaut" (1893), won critical acclaim, but "Tosca" (1900) and "The Girl of the Golden West" (1910) were sometimes condemned as overwrought and weepy. The public, however, prefers them that way.

Wall Street boom sets new record

Nov 11. Wall Street remains bullish on President Coolidge. For the fifth consecutive business day following his national landslide victory, the market has surged to ever higher records. Yesterday's trading saw an aggregate turnover of 2,226,220 shares in a total of 526 issues, the largest number ever handled, and the average price of 50 representative shares topped the previous record set in 1919. Caught unprepared, most of the larger brokerage houses worked their clerks far into the night.

Rapid action on the Curb Exchange.

Conservatives win; Baldwin in office

Nov 6. The British are keeping their fingers crossed tonight. A brand new, Conservative Cabinet was appointed by Prime Minister Stanley Baldwin. It replaces the Labor government, which was defeated after serving just 11 months. It is hoped that the new Cabinet can bring an end to the turmoil created by three years of paralyzing strikes.

There are two Chamberlains in the new Cabinet. Sir Austen Chamberlain, the former Secretary of State for India, will serve as Foreign Secretary. His half-brother Neville is Secretary of Health. For the Chancellor of the Exchequer, Prime Minister Baldwin turned to a man who switched from the Conservative Party to the Liberals in 1904 and then back again. His name is Winston Churchill.

1924

DECEMBER

Su	Mo	Tu	We	Th	Fr	Sa
	1	2	3	4	5	6
7	8	9	10	11	12	13
14	15	16	17	18	19	20
21	22	23	24	25	26	27
28	29	30	31			

1. Gershwin's "Lady Be Good" makes debut in New York.

5. Ibn Saud occupies Medina, site of prophet Mohammed's grave (→ 1/8/26).

8. Charlotte, N.C.: J.B. Duke offers $40 mil. to found Duke Univ.

9. Discovery of 5,000-year-old art in Indus Valley raises challenge to theory that Mesopotamia is cradle of civilization.

11. Marx Cabinet quits in Berlin (→ 20).

12. Abd el Krim pushes Spanish troops out of Morocco (→ 4/23/25).

12. Bernard Shaw's "Candida" opens in New York.

15. Soviets warn U.S. against repeated entry of ships into territorial waters of U.S.S.R.

18. Rome: Pope Pius denounces Bolshevik regime (→ 1/20/25).

20. Germany: Adolf Hitler released from prison (→ 2/1/25).

26. Germany: Weimar Bauhaus closed permanently.

27. Albania made dictatorship under Ahmed Bey Zogu (→ 9/1/28).

CULTURAL EVENTS, 1924

Literature: E.M. Forster's "A Passage to India"; Paul Robeson in O'Neill's "All God's Chillun Got Wings"; Mark Twain's "Autobiography"; "The American Mercury" magazine founded by George Jean Nathan and H.L. Mencken.

Academia: Irving Babbitt's "Democracy and Leadership"; Andre Breton's "Manifesto of Surrealism."

Music: George Gershwin's "Rhapsody in Blue."

The Arts: Picasso's "Still Life with Biscuits and Green Tablecloth"; Miro's "Catalan Landscape"; Lewis Mumford's social history of architecture, "Sticks and Stones."

Film: D.W. Griffith's "America"; Cecil B. De Mille's "The Ten Commandments"; Douglas Fairbanks in "The Thief of Baghdad"; Fernand Leger's "Mechanical Ballet."

A.F.L. leader Samuel Gompers deceased

Gompers, A.F.L. President.

Dec 13. Americans mourned the death today of Samuel Gompers, the grand old man of organized labor. Gompers, who was President of the American Federation of Labor for more than 40 years, died in San Antonio at age 74. He had been taken there after becoming ill while attending a labor conference in Mexico City.

Aware that death was near, Gompers spoke his final words to a nurse, saying, "This is the end. God bless our American institutions. May they grow better day by day." Tonight, the body of the labor leader, resting in a bronze casket, was placed aboard a special train for the trip to Washington to lie in state in the nation's Capitol. The funeral will be held at the Elks Club in New York City and burial in the Sleepy Hollow Cemetery in Tarrytown, New York.

Adolf Hitler freed after eight months

Dec 20. Adolf Hitler, the German Nazi leader who tried to topple the government in a beer hall coup, was paroled today after serving just eight months in prison. The original sentence was five years, and even that was considered lenient.

Hitler was convicted last April of high treason, but he was treated royally by the guards at the fortress in Landsberg. He was given his own room with a magnificent view over the River Lech, and vistors were allowed to come with gifts. Hitler spent much of his time dictating a book to an old friend and colleague named Rudolf Hess (→ 7/18/25).

Opera and racing lose great patron

Dec 11. August Belmont, financier and sportsman, died last evening in his Park Avenue apartment of blood poisoning after a sudden inflammation of his arm 36 hours earlier. Belmont, 71, organized and financed the original New York subway company, was Chairman of the Interborough Rapid Transit Company and head of the banking firm, August Belmont & Company. One of the principal sponsors of horse racing and dog breeding in America, he was also a patron of opera.

Financier August Belmont.

Electrocardiogram wins for developer

Dec 10. Dutch physiologist Willem Einthoven has won the Nobel Prize in medicine for his discovery of the electrocardiogram.

In the early 1900's, Einthoven constructed an electrocardiograph that was sufficiently sensitive and reliable to detect and record accurately the variations in electrical impulses associated with the human heartbeat. Then he used the recording, or electrocardiogram, for diagnosing various types of heart disease. Einthoven's electrocardiograph, which weighed more than 600 pounds, was simplified. Then it was manufactured in quantity and sent to different parts of the world.

The Nobel Committee did not distribute the Peace Prize nor the prize in chemistry. The Polish writer Vladislav Stanislas Reymond was awarded the Nobel Prize in literature.

Rockne undefeated with Four Horsemen

Dec 31. Notre Dame, which rose from nowhere to national football supremacy in just over a decade, ended its season this year with a perfect record of nine straight triumphs and faces its severest test tomorrow in the Rose Bowl.

Norwegian-born Knute Rockne.

The innovative "Fighting Irish" team, coached by Knute Rockne, will face Stanford, its hopes resting on the small but mighty "Four Horsemen" in its backfield. Notre Dame's Elmer Layden, Harry Stuldreher, Jim Crowley and Don Miller have been nicknamed the "Four Horsemen" because of their devastating speed. They work well out of the Notre Dame box, an adaptation of the Harper formation that was popular when Rockne played for Notre Dame. Rockne followed the pattern set by his coach, Jesse Harper, which emphasizes speed more than power (→ 1/1/25).

The Duchess of York yields to the charm of John Barrymore as "Beau Brummel."

1925

JANUARY

Su	Mo	Tu	We	Th	Fr	Sa
				1	2	3
4	5	6	7	8	9	10
11	12	13	14	15	16	17
18	19	20	21	22	23	24
25	26	27	28	29	30	31

1. Pasadena: Notre Dame over Stanford 27-10 in Rose Bowl.

1. N.Y.: John McCormack and Lucrezia Bori broadcast from Met to six million listeners (→ 9/20).

1. Crossword puzzle stockings are latest novelty of Paris hosiery makers.

5. Nellie Taylor Ross becomes first woman governor to take office in U.S. (→ 20).

7. New York: Al Jolson returns to stage in musical "Big Boy."

7. London: Allied financial talks open; U.S., U.K. strike tentative accord on debts (→ 8/18/25).

8. California ratifies child labor amendment (→ 6/25/38).

10. Charles Evans Hughes resigns as U.S. sec. of state.

10. Allies delay Rhine evacuation, accuse Germans of violating disarmament accord (→ 6/4).

15. China: U.S. forces land in Shanghai to protect nationals during factional stife (→ 3/12).

20. Miriam "Ma" Ferguson takes oath as governor in Texas.

20. Japanese acknowledge U.S.S.R., return northern part of Sakhalin Island.

21. U.K. dreadnought Monarch sunk to meet quota of Washington disarmament treaty.

27. Alaska reports diphtheria epidemic in Nome (→ 2/2).

28. London Dr. W.R. Baker finds crossword puzzles cause headaches, eye strain (→ 3/8).

30. Chicago: Charles Forbes, ex-head of Veterans' Bureau found guilty of taking bribes for hospital construction contracts.

30. Turkish government expels Greek patriarch Constantin II from Constantinople.

BIRTHS

14. Yukio Mishima, Japanese writer (*11/25/1970).

24. Maria Tallchief, star dancer of N.Y.C. Ballet.

26. U.S. actor Paul Newman.

DEATH

31. George Washington Cable, U.S. author (*10/12/1844).

Trotsky, Stalin's rival, ousted from post

Jan 16. The competition for power succeeding Bolshevik leader Vladimir Lenin's death appears to have claimed its first major victim. Leon Trotsky has been dismissed from the Soviet War Council.

Trotsky is better respected abroad than at home, where he is distrusted because of his recent conversion to Bolshevism. Up until 1917, Trotsky belonged to the Menshevik faction and opposed Lenin.

Trotsky remains a member of the ruling Politburo, but his ouster as War Commissar represents a victory for Joseph Stalin, Grigori Zinoviev and Lev Kamenev, who have sought control of the party.

They have accused Trotsky of fostering Trotskyism, which means placing undue emphasis on international revolution. Trotsky's theory of "permanent revolution" implies that without international revolution, the Bolsheviks must make concessions on socialism to appease the peasants (→ 5/13).

Trotsky, shunned in post-Lenin era.

Stravinsky appears in U.S. first time

Stravinsky at the piano with German composer Wilhelm Furtwangler.

Jan 8. Igor Stravinsky, whose 1913 masterpiece "Le Sacre du Printemps" galvanized the world of music, made his long-awaited American debut a night to remember. Leading the New York Philarmonic in a program devoted to his own genius, the composer proved he can beat tricky rhythms as well as he can write them. Stravinsky put in his first full day in America rehearsing, gazing at skyscrapers, discussing his plans with reporters and dining out to hear the dance music the Old World has called American jazz. When a box of flowers was bought to his door, he exclaimed, "I hope not my immortal crown."

Coolidge wouldn't be seen dead in 'em

Jan 24. President Coolidge was not "Silent Cal" today; he spoke up to protest a foolish college fad. While at Princeton University, where he was invited to address the American Whig Society, he noticed some students sporting wide-bottom trousers. The president politely asked the young men if they did not prefer the traditional cut of trousers. He admitted that his own son, John, had once come home from college wearing such pants, and it had hardly pleased him. The president procured a pair of suspenders and forced his son to use them. Following his lecture to the students, Coolidge consented to pose with them for a photograph.

Oxford Bags, 70 inches at the cuffs.

Mussolini moves against opposition

Jan 5. Italy's Premier, Benito Mussolini, has taken action against opponents of Fascism both within and outside of the government. His Cabinet ministers have turned in their portfolios, but in all likelihood only the Liberal ministers Sarrocchi and Casati will be excluded from the new Cabinet. About two dozen Liberal deputies still vote with the government.

Mussolini: The air of command.

Police searched the homes of members of the opposition and seized documents, closed meeting halls and disbanded political clubs, including the Republican Italia Libera, a group of former soldiers led by General Peppino Garibaldi. Newspapers accused of printing "false news" were seized and journalists were arrested (→ 3/26).

The Wills Sainte Claire (above) vies with Duesenberg for the loyalty of rich U.S. auto enthusiasts.

1925

FEBRUARY

Su	Mo	Tu	We	Th	Fr	Sa
1	2	3	4	5	6	7
8	9	10	11	12	13	14
15	16	17	18	19	20	21
22	23	24	25	26	27	28

1. Berlin: Communist association KPD founded to organize workers against Fascism (→ 14).

2. Nation applauds Gunnar Kasson as he arrives in Nome with frozen diphtheria serum after five-day dog sled trip.

3. South Africa: Australian anthropologist finds fossilized skull of early man believed to be "missing link" (→ 12/1925).

5. Luxembourg govt. dissolved following dispute with Belgium over railway convention rejected in January.

7. San Diego: Jack Dempsey weds actress Ida Estelle Taylor.

11. Germany: Explosion in Ruhr mine smothers 136 workers.

12. Sabena establishes first air connection between Belgium and Belgian Congo.

14. German govt. lifts state of emergency in Bavaria, restores Hitler's NSDAP to legal status (→ 27).

15. London announces it will install lights to cheer up fogged-in animals residing at London zoo.

17. AT&T completes arrangement for cross-country broadcasting with N.Y. radio station WEAF.

19. Pres. Coolidge proposes phasing out of inheritance tax (→ 2/26/26).

21. First issue of New Yorker magazine hits the newsstands.

24. Revolt against Ankara govt. breaks out in Turkish Kurdistan.

26. New York Zoological Soc. expedition begins exploration of Sargasso Sea in the ship Arcturus.

27. Alaska: Glacier Bay National Monument dedicated.

BIRTH

20. American film director Robert Altman, "M*A*S*H."

DEATHS

5. Julius Fleischmann, head of yeast firm (*6/8/1872).

28. Friedrich Ebert, first pres. of Weimar Republic (*2/4/1871).

Hitler reorganizes his banned party

Feb 27. In Germany, Adolf Hitler has been out of prison for only two months. But he wasted little time in reorganizing the political party which was banned after the failed putsch at the Burgerbrau Keller, a beer hall in Munich.

Hitler chose another beer hall today, the Hofbrau, to announce the resurgence of his German National Socialist Workers Party. His military ally, General Ludendorff, was noticeably absent. But Hitler was surrounded by other colleagues who believe in the Nazi cause, including Julius Schaub, Julius Streicher, Gottfried Feder and Herman Esser.

In his party newspaper, Hitler is promising "a new beginning." He renounces the use of force, and he pledges to gain power only through legal means.

It is not clear yet how the German people will react to Hitler's party. Right-wing parties have declined in favor since the abortive putsch in 1923. Hitler impressed many people with his impassioned, nationalistic statements at his trial. But most of the country forgot him while he was in prison.

Fervent followers, however, expect Hitler to make good on the promises he made at the trial. "The army we have formed is growing from day to day," Hitler said. "I nourish the proud hope that one day the hour will come when these rough companies will grow to battalions, the battalions to regiments, the regiments to divisions, and that the old flags will fly again" (→ 4/25).

An Italian commission reports the leaning tower of Pisa is in danger. It leans more each year.

1925

MARCH

Su	Mo	Tu	We	Th	Fr	Sa
1	2	3	4	5	6	7
8	9	10	11	12	13	14
15	16	17	18	19	20	21
22	23	24	25	26	27	28
29	30	31				

1. American Telephone and Telegraph Co. sends photo by wire to three cities simultaneously.

2. Japan abolishes property restrictions on suffrage.

2. Austria issues shilling as new currency.

3. Ottawa House of Commons approves treaty with U.S., calling for enforcement of laws against border smuggling.

6. New York: Babe Ruth sued for $7,700 in unpaid racing bets.

7. Red army occupies Outer Mongolia.

8. Chicago Dept. of Health insists "crosswordities" improves health.

9. In attack on KKK, Texas Governor "Ma" Ferguson bans wearing of masks in public (→ 8/8).

9. Egyptian Ministry of Public Works announces discovery of 5,000-year-old tomb of King Sneferu.

10. U.S. Circuit Court of Appeals in Philadelphia gives autos right of way over pedestrians on certain streets.

12. 279 reported dead in Chicago grippe epidemic.

13. Coolidge appoints commission to study Muscle Shoals project (→ 8/28).

16. Direct cable line opened between New York and Rome, covering 5,422 miles.

17. Midwest tornado kills 950 in Illinois, Indiana and Missouri.

18. Florida: Fire destroys famous Breakers Hotel in Palm Beach, said to be largest wooden structure in world.

26. Germany: Mine explosion in the Sarre takes 51 lives.

26. Rome: Fascists and Communists clash in Italian Chamber of Deputies (→ 11/5).

DEATHS

20. Lord Curzon, British statesman (*1/11/1859).

30. Rudolf Steiner, Austrian anthroposophist and philosopher (*2/27/1861).

Tennessee bans teaching evolution

Darwin, rebuked in Tennessee.

March 23. A bill banning the teaching of evolution in schools was signed into law today by Tennessee Governor Austin Peay, who said "the very integrity of the Bible in its statement of man's divine creation is denied by any theory that man descended or has ascended from any lower order of animals."

The bill makes it a crime for a teacher in any state-supported public school or college to teach any theory that contradicts the Bible's account of man's creation. Peay called the bill "a distinct protest against an irreligious tendency to exalt so-called science and deny the Bible." Plans to challenge the bill are being made by opponents, who have denounced it as a violation of the constitutional principle of separation of church and state (→ 5/25).

Lord Curzon dies after an operation

March 20. The Marquess Curzon of Kedleston died this morning at 66 from complications following an operation. Long a kingpin of the Conservative Party, Lord Curzon spent 40 years in public life, serving as Viceroy and Governor General of India and, at the end of his career, as Secretary of State for Foreign Affairs. Though he came close to becoming prime minister in 1923, his aristocratic past militated against him in an era which nominated leaders from the House of Commons. He twice wed American women and enjoyed fame as an author of books about politics and his own travels.

Chiang succeeds Sun as Chinese leader

Sun Yat-sen (insert), founder of the Chinese republic, entombed in Nanking.

March 12. Sun Yat-sen, the revolutionary Chinese leader who was known as "Father of the Republic," died in Peking this morning after a long battle with cancer. Sun, whose followers chased the Manchu emperors from power, will apparently be succeeded as leader of the Kuomintang, or people's party, by Chiang Kai-shek.

General Chiang was trained in Japan in military affairs, and he is a banker by profession. He was an aide to Sun in the 1911 revolution, and he was at Sun's side in his long struggle for political and military supremacy. Sun and Chiang appealed to the Soviet Union for help in building a modern army, and Chiang spent several months with the Soviets two years ago. He organized the Kuomintang's army, which is presently estimated to have some 40,000 soldiers (→ 5/10).

Jazz age night life in Paris, now a mecca for American expatriates.

1925

APRIL

Su	Mo	Tu	We	Th	Fr	Sa
			1	2	3	4
5	6	7	8	9	10	11
12	13	14	15	16	17	18
19	20	21	22	23	24	25
26	27	28	29	30		

1. Geneva: Jurisprudence experts under M. Hammarskjold meet to establish basis for international law.

1. Arabs demonstrate to protest opening of Hebrew University of Jerusalem (→ 2/20/28).

5. Belgian Labor Party gains its first majority in legislative elections.

5. 250,000 German steel workers go on strike.

10. France: Herriot Cabinet resigns in Paris.

11. New York: U.S. industrial leaders meet to discuss fight to eliminate industrial waste.

13. U.S. gastronomic survey reveals Americans are primarily steak eaters.

14. 150 killed by bomb at Sofia funeral, as Bolshevik agrarians attempt assassination of Bulgaria's King Boris (→ 20).

15. Ohio's Lucille Atcherson to go to legation at Berne, Switzerland, as first U.S. woman to fill diplomatic post.

19. Camara military revolt suppressed in Portugal.

19. U.S. troops sent to Honduras to protect foreigners during La Ceiba revolt.

20. Bulgaria: Captain Ninkoff, suspected architect of funeral bombing, slain in Sofia.

23. St. Louis: Rogers Hornsby suffers concussion after being hit on head by fastball.

23. Abd el Krim's rebel troops enter French Morocco (→ 6/22).

28. U.K. restores gold standard.

30. Ohio: Orville Wright to give first airplane invention to science museum at South Kensington.

BIRTH

14. Rod Steiger, American character actor, "In the Heat of the Night."

DEATHS

13. Elwood Haynes, inventor of America's first automobile (*10/14/1857).

18. Charles H. Ebbets, dean of organized baseball's leaders (*10/29/1958).

In memorium: Artist John Singer Sargent

April 15. American painter John Singer Sargent died of a stroke in his sleep tonight. He was 69. Singer was the darling of the upper class, which paid and posed for his flattering portraits. He ruffled a few feathers in 1884 when he painted "Madame X." It featured a woman whose dress strap had inched precariously over her shoulder.

Sargent's "Mrs. George Swinton."

Hindenburg elected German President

April 25. Field Marshal Paul von Hindenburg is the victor in the extremely close German presidential elections. He becomes Germany's first popularly elected President. Although Hindenburg supports a return to the monarchy, he has promised to uphold the republican constitution. His principal opponent, Dr. Wilhelm Marx, was the candidate of the republican coalition made up of those who support the Weimar constitution, including the Centrists, Socialists and Democrats.

The outcome of the close race could not be determined until returns from 33 out of 35 districts were tabulated. Hindenburg's win is partly attributed to strong support among women voters (→ 5/6).

Major decorative arts showing opens in Paris

"The Mirror," evening wear designed by Paul Poiret.

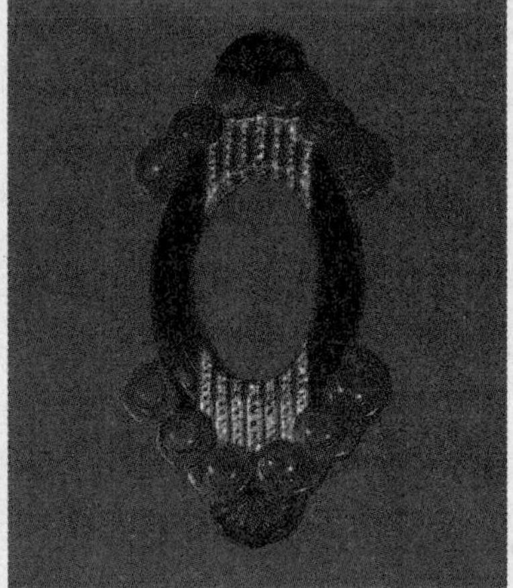
Jewelry by Boucheron.

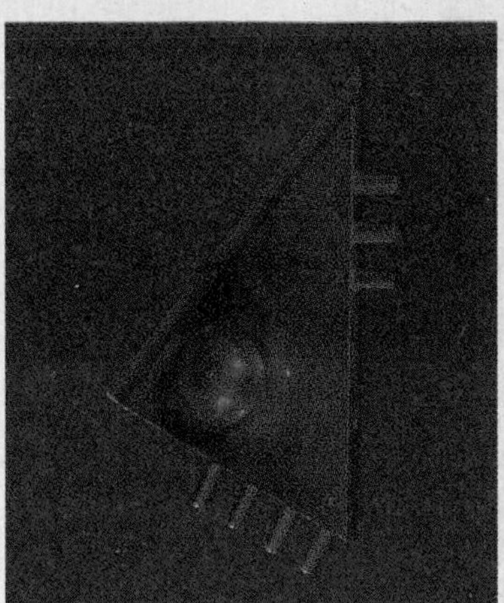
Gold jewelry by Fouquet.

Poiret models in outdoor wear. Painting by Raoul Dufy (1925).

May 31. The "Arts decoratifs" show in Paris, from which derives the term "art deco," appears to be the most important artistic event of the postwar period. The art deco style combines good design with new materials. Opposed to the fine arts, which are intended first for aesthetic enjoyment, the decorative arts have some utilitarian purpose. The most important decorative arts include furniture, ceramics, glass, silver, woodwork, textiles and architecture, which is considered to be one of the fine arts too.

Art deco is influenced by art nouveau, Egyptian and Aztec styles and the sleekness of modern technology. The trend is toward the simplification of lines and the use of solid, rectilinear forms. The furniture designer Emile-Jacques Ruhlam, the dress designer Paul Poiret and the architect and furniture designer Le Corbusier are among the most famous art deco artists.

Art Deco perfume bottles in glass, by Marinot.

The abrupt geometric shapes of an Art Deco dining room, on display in Paris.

1925

MAY

Su	Mo	Tu	We	Th	Fr	Sa
					1	2
3	4	5	6	7	8	9
10	11	12	13	14	15	16
17	18	19	20	21	22	23
24	25	26	27	28	29	30
31						

1. Cyprus becomes British colony (→ 2/19/59).

4. Geneva conference debates outlawing poison gas.

6. Germany: Reich republicans, fearing restoration of monarchy, protest Hindenburg's election (→ 7/18).

10. China: British troops fire on anti-foreign demonstrators in Shanghai (→ 30).

13. Moscow: Leon Trotsky elected member of Soviet Cabinet (→ 8/20).

16. E. Sande rides Flying Ebony to victory in Kentucky Derby.

17. Spanish King Alfonso lifts state of siege in force since Primo de Rivera's 1923 coup (→ 9/11/26).

20. New York City's homicide rate reported at 387 per year.

20. Gerardo Machado sworn in as Cuba's fifth president.

21. Norwegian explorer Roald Amundsen leaves for North Pole (→ 6/18).

21. Americans pour into Canada for beer, being dispensed for first time since war (→ 24).

22. Doctors now blaming auto exhaust, bad liquor for increase in throat disease (→ 7/9).

24. New York Governor Al Smith signs law legalizing 2.75 beer (→ 9/13).

25. Niagara Falls illuminated by 1.3 bil. candle power of electric light generated by own power.

27. Fall, Doheny, Sinclair reindicted for fraudulent lease of govt. oil lands (→ 3/16/27).

30. Peter DePaolo takes 13th annual Indy 500, at 101.1 mph in Duesenberg Special.

30. China: Nationalists revolt at Shanghai international concessions (→ 6/6).

BIRTHS

19. Malcolm X, black militant, born Malcolm Little, (†2/21/1965).

31. Otto Frei, German architect.

DEATH

22. Field Marshal French, British war hero (*9/28/1852).

Teacher indicted under anti-evolution law

May 25. John T. Scopes, a young high school teacher in Tennessee, was indicted tonight on a charge of having taught Darwin's theory of evolution to students in his science class. The trial is expected to attract national attention to the little mountain town of Dayton.

William Jennings Bryan, the spellbinding orator and perennial Democratic candidate for president, will serve as a prosecutor for the state. Clarence Darrow, the noted Chicago lawyer, and Dudley Field Malone of New York City will serve as the defense team for the Tennessee teacher.

Scopes is accused of violating a new law, passed earlier this year by the Tennessee Legislature, banning the teaching of theories denying the divine creation of man as told in the Bible. The indictment charges that Scopes "did teach thereof that man has descended from a lower order of animals."

Young biology teacher John Scopes.

Judge John T. Raulston, in his charge to the grand jury, said that the schoolroom is the place to develop the power of thought, discipline, restraint and character, not to violate the laws. The judge also read from Genesis, the first book of the Bible in which the story of creation is written (→ 6/10).

Silk stockings said to thicken ankles

May 22. A report in the British Medical Journal cautions women against wearing silk stockings in cold weather. The practice results in erythema, a chafing and puffiness of the skin. One doctor states that the "scanty" covering of the legs, from dress hem to the tops of boots or shoes, accounted for this modern illness. The condition was rarely reported before short dresses and silk stockings came into vogue.

"But they look so good."

Amy Lowell, skilled poetic Imagist, dies

Amy Lowell, at home in Brookline.

May 12. Amy Lowell, an Imagist poet who was also a critic, died today. She was born February 9, 1874, to a literary New England family. In 1913, she traveled to England, where she met Ezra Pound. She championed his work, and openly envied it. "Lilacs" and "Patterns," poems of vivid clarity, are among her most popular works. Miss Lowell described herself and her poetry with some verse: "Hung all over with mousetraps of metres, and cages/Of bright-plumed rhythms, with pages and pages/Of colors slit up into streaming confetti."

1925

JUNE

Su	Mo	Tu	We	Th	Fr	Sa
	1	2	3	4	5	6
7	8	9	10	11	12	13
14	15	16	17	18	19	20
21	22	23	24	25	26	27
28	29	30				

1. Belgium signs treaty of commerce with Japan.

4. Allies hand Germans conditions for evacuation of Rhineland (→ 12/1).

5. Willie MacFarlane beats Bobby Jones on 36th hole to take U.S. natl. golf championship.

6. China: Gen. Yang Hsi-min takes Canton, establishes government (→ 12/26).

6. Munich and Berlin hold official celebrations for Thomas Mann's 50th birthday.

10. Tennessee adopts new biology textbook denying theory of evolution (→ 7/2).

10. United Church of Canada established.

11. Britain: Gem dealer thrown out of plane in first recorded murder in skies.

12. New York: Metropolitan Museum of Art buys George Barnard's The Cloisters with $600,000 gift from Rockefellers.

14. Germany: Neue Sachlichkeit (New Realist) exhibition opens in Mannheim.

14. Long Island: Gertrude Ederle sets world swim mark at 1:41.6 for 150-yard free style.

15. New York taxi drivers begin wearing white collars under new city requirements.

15. N.J.: Natl. Assn. of Taxicab Owners reports one in three women drive; brunettes more careful than blondes (→ 7/18).

16. New Jersey: Lackawanna train wreck kills 39, injures 48.

16. France accepts German proposal for security pact.

18. Capt. Roald Amundsen arrives in Spitzbergen after four-week attempt to reach N. Pole.

20. Berlin: Wireless phone for autos demonstrated by Herr Schaetzle.

22. France and Spain agree to join forces against Abd el Krim in Morocco (→ 7/4).

25. Athens: General Pangalos leads military coup, ousting current Greek govt. (→ 1/3/26).

29. Earthquake ravages Santa Barbara, causing millions in property damage.

1925

JULY

Su	Mo	Tu	We	Th	Fr	Sa
			1	2	3	4
5	6	7	8	9	10	11
12	13	14	15	16	17	18
19	20	21	22	23	24	25
26	27	28	29	30	31	

2. Loren H. Wittner asks for judicial order to ban teaching of evolution in District of Columbia (→ 17).

4. Moroccan Sultan Mulay Yussef orders supporters to organize against Abd el Krim's propaganda in French zone (→ 17).

5. Swedish actress Greta Garbo arrives in New York en route to Hollywood.

9. Reports that auto exhaust injures health prompt testing of N.Y.C. air for carbon monoxide (→ 7/7/26).

13. Standard Oil adopts eight-hour day in oil fields.

14. Intl. Match Co. of N.Y. gets contract to manufacture all Polish matches.

16. First Iraqi Parliament opened in Baghdad by King Feisal (→ 12/14/27).

17. Dayton, Tenn.: Judge Raulston kills Scopes'defense, barring testimony of scientists (→ 21).

17. French Marshal Petain begins Moroccan mission against Abd el Krim (→ 10/2).

18. American Automobile Assn. declares women drivers as competent as men.

19. Tour de France won by Italian Ottavio Bottechia in 219 hours, 10 minutes.

20. Syria: Druze religious sect launch uprising against French rule (→ 8/7).

21. Dayton, Tenn.: John Scopes found guilty for teaching Darwin, fined $100 (→ 26).

21. U.K. prime minister grants special bonus to miners, narrowly averting nationwide strike.

23. Vienna: Sigmund Freud accepts chair of Intl. Psychoanalytical Foundation.

24. U.S. missions in Nicaragua reported under attack (→ 12/25).

29. U.S. rejects invitations to participate in League security parley at Locarno (→ 9/15).

31. Great Britain passes Unemployment Insurance Act.

DEATH

7. Clarence H. White, American photographer (*4/8/1871).

Walter P. Chrysler founds auto firm

Chrysler, rivaled only by Ford.

June 6. Walter Chrysler has formed Chrysler Motor Company. This was inevitable; he has made money for nearly every major manufacturer in America. The Kansas-born mechanic was President of Buick Motor Company, a division of General Motors, in 1916. He joined the Maxwell Motor Company in 1921, and after he made it profitable, he bought it and named the new firm after himself. He introduced his first car today. The automobile sports an innovative high-compression engine and four-wheel brakes. It doesn't come cheap; the asking price is $1,500.

La Follette, clarion of liberalism, dies

June 18. Senator Robert Marion La Follette, the picturesque leader of Republican insurgents, died quietly today at his home in Washington. "Fighting Bob," as he was widely known, had observed his 70th birthday just a few days before his fatal heart attack.

Despite his declining health, the Wisconsin senator had run for president last year on the Progressive ticket, tallying less than four million votes in the race won by President Coolidge. From his earliest days as a poor farm boy, LaFollette was something of a radical, tilting against special interests. After earning a law degree, he was elected Governor of Wisconsin, where he instituted many progressive reforms, and served four terms in the United States Senate.

Scopes guilty in Monkey Trial; Bryan dies

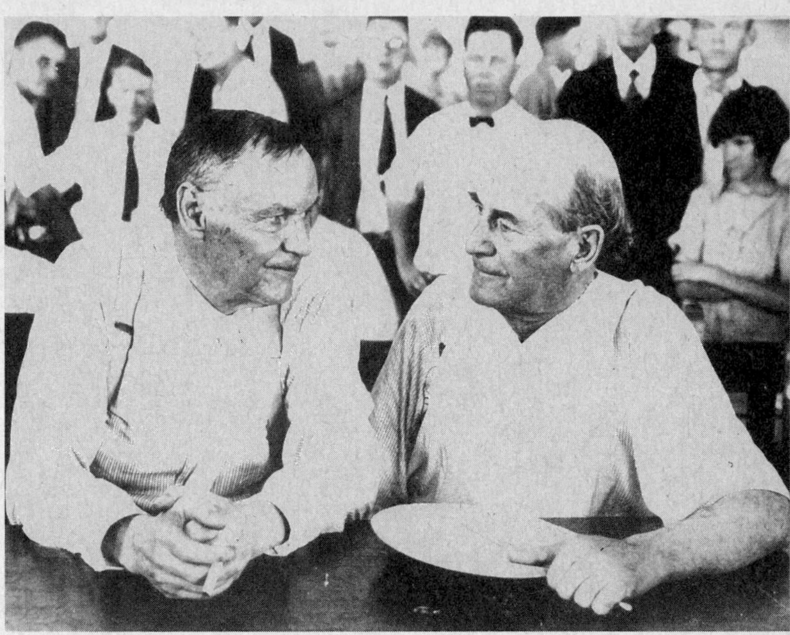

Chicago lawyer Darrow (left) and Bryan, defender of fundamentalism.

July 26. William Jennings Bryan died today in Dayton, Tennessee, just days after scoring a final victory with the conviction of John T. Scopes for teaching evolution. The noted lawyer, orator and three-time Democratic nominee for president had been resting at the home of a friend in the little mountain town since the end of the emotionally draining Scopes trial five days ago. Doctors attributed his death to a cerebral hemorrhage.

Bryan, 65 years old, appeared to have come through the trial in good shape, aside from losing a bit of weight. Friends had urged him to take a vacation but he refused, saying he planned a speaking tour of the nation to urge laws to protect the Bible against the teaching of evolution in schools. "We must strike while the iron is hot," he said.

It was just such a law, passed earlier this year by the Tennessee Legislature, that Scopes, a high school science teacher, was accused of breaking. At one point during the trial, Bryan took the witness stand and espoused the Biblical account of man's creation. Scopes was found guilty and fined $100. The trial was characterized by Clarence Darrow, defense attorney, as "the first case of its kind since we stopped trying people for witchcraft" (→ 1/21/27).

Mein Kampf tells Hitler's policies

July 18. Adolf Hitler has published a book that he dictated to Rudolf Hess during his imprisonment last year in the jail at Landsberg. The book appears to have many objectives. It is a demagogic appeal to the German people, a manual for Hitler's growing National Socialist Party, and a personal testament. The title is "Mein Kampf," or "My Struggle." Hitler calls for a national revival and a battle against communism and Jews. And he expresses his faith in German solidarity. Hitler dedicates the book to his followers who died in the streets of Munich after his abortive putsch (→ 11/9).

First edition of "Mein Kampf."

Ash Can artist Bellows is dead

"The Bridge," by George Bellows.

July 8. George Bellows, a leader of the Ash Can School of artists, is dead. He was 42. Bellows taught at the Arts Student League in New York, after having studied under Robert Henri. He helped develop the values of the Ash Can School, a realistic yet celebratory examination of lower-class life.

Henri tried to describe the common factors of Ash Can artists by denying there were any; they had come together because they were so unlike. In fact, Bellows' work was typical of the movement. He never went to Europe and scorned European trends. He worked with dark, moody colors. He painted athletes, children from the tenements, and the down-and-out.

Born in Columbus, Oh., Bellows is best known for "Forty-two Kids" (1907), a painting of city children diving into the unsavory waters of Manhattan's East River. "Dempsey and Firpo" is one of many studies of boxers (→ 10/12).

July 6. Jan Hus, 15th-century instigator of Protestant Reformation, was celebrated in Prague on the anniversary of his birth.

1925

AUGUST

Su	Mo	Tu	We	Th	Fr	Sa
						1
2	3	4	5	6	7	8
9	10	11	12	13	14	15
16	17	18	19	20	21	22
23	24	25	26	27	28	29
30	31					

3. Indianapolis driver, convicted of manslaughter, sentenced to spend hour alone with deceased.

6. Former Italian Premier Orlando goes into voluntary exile.

6. N.Y.C. residents receiving "I am vaccinated" buttons in campaign against smallpox.

7. Druze tribesmen clash with French, kill 200, wound 600 (→ 10/18).

8. French aviators Landry and Drouhin set new non-stop record, covering 2,732 miles.

13. Norwegian decree places Spitzberg and Bears' Island under single administrative body.

14. French and Germans sign customs treaty.

16. Chaplin film "Gold Rush" opens for U.S. audiences.

17. Rioting disrupts Zionist conference in Vienna.

18. At Coolidge's urging, Congress agrees to modify Belgian war-debt terms, spreading payments over 62 years (→ 9/23).

19. American expedition ordered out of Mongolia on suspicion of espionage.

19. Ecumenical conference of Protestant churches convenes in Stockholm.

20. Trotsky becomes head of Soviet Economic Council (→ 12/18).

22. U.S. women announce plan for nationwide appeal to promote World Court.

26. Paris: Professor Charles Henri of Sorbonne reports radiation findings have confirmed existence of a soul.

28. Muscle Shoals plant to begin operation in effort to remedy power shortage caused by low water levels (→ 5/25/28).

28. German racer Auguste Momber wins first intl. auto race held in Germany since war.

29. St. Louis: Babe Ruth fined $5,000 for general misconduct.

31. Philadelphia: 150,000 miners walk out as major coal strike begins (→ 11/30).

31. Snakeskin dresses are latest in London fashions.

40,000 Klansmen march

Bare-faced "Ghouls" parade in military-like order before the Capitol.

Aug 8. White-robed Klansmen, more than 40,000 strong, paraded through the streets of the nation's capital today. It was the largest display of Ku Klux Klan power in history, witnessed by over 200,000 spectators, many of them astonished at the size of parade line.

While robed, the members of the Klan were not wearing the hooded masks behind which they so often hide their identities. As the last of the marchers reached the Sylvan Theatre at the foot of the Washington Monument, darkness had set in and a heavy rain was falling, resulting in cancellation of plans to hold a massive ceremony. The inclement weather also caused the Klansmen to postpone their plans for burning an 80-foot cross in the state of Virginia (→ 11/14).

Wide search is made for human forbearers

Aug 19. Where is the cradle of humanity? Since the mid-19th century, most anthropologists believed Europe was the site of human origins. Yet in the last two decades, there have been older findings in India and Africa. And today an expedition sponsored by the New York Museum of Natural History suggested the earliest humans lived in Outer Mongolia hundreds of thousands of years ago.

An anthropological expedition led by scientist and explorer Roy Champman Andrews has left Mongolia after finding traces of an early human type. Andrews feels these forbearers may have migrated to Asia from Europe. They settled in an area of lakes and sand dunes now covered by the Gobi Desert.

The "dune dwellers" made tools of flint and jasper and left vestiges of fireplaces. While no complete skeletons were seen, ornaments were discovered in good condition. Some were made from petrified dinosaur eggs, which the dune dwellers must have found preserved in the sand. Our yen for excavation seems an inherited trait (→ 8/27).

Chaplin makes a meal out of a shoe in "The Gold Rush," his most accomplished work yet. The shoelace is made of licorice.

1925

SEPTEMBER

Su	Mo	Tu	We	Th	Fr	Sa
		1	2	3	4	5
6	7	8	9	10	11	12
13	14	15	16	17	18	19
20	21	22	23	24	25	26
29	28	29	30			

1. Philadelphia: "Big Bill" Tilden leads U.S. team to Davis Cup title for sixth year in row.

1. Ernst Thelmann named head of German Communist Party.

3. Navy dirigible Shenandoah crashes in Ohio storm, killing 14 crew members.

4. AAA car arrives in Washington after record-setting transcontinental trip of four days, 21.5 hours.

5. U.S.: Water being sold by gallon as prolonged drought grips West and South (→ 30).

11. Royal tomb of Indian Mound Builders unearthed in Chillicothe, Ohio.

12. New York: Seven Lackawanna workers arrested in Buffalo for $2 mil. mail robbery.

13. Federal Council of Churches finds increase in U.S. drinking since Prohibition (→ 12/3).

15. Germany invited to Locarno conference on security pact (→ 10/16).

15. Rumanian troops put down Soviet-inspired revolt; 50 dead.

15. San Francisco celebrates diamond jubilee.

16. New York: Musical comedy "No No Nanette" opens on Broadway.

18. Bolivia struggling with rebellion, declares state of siege in La Paz, Oruro, Cochabamba.

20. U.S.: 25 of world's leading opera singers and musical stars sign contract for Sunday night radio concerts.

22. J. Kern's musical "Sunny" opens in N.Y.C., featuring season's pop hit "Who."

23. French Finance Minister Caillaux arrives in U.S. for debt negotiations with Sec. Mellon (→ 10/1).

25. Rhode Island: U.S. sub S-51 sunk in collision with steamship off Block Island; 37 dead.

30. Illinois Gov. Lowden tells Am. Bankers Assn. they must help American farmers or crops will fail (→ 4/29/26).

BIRTH

16. B.B. King, American blues guitarist.

American dirigible explodes in storm

Sept 3. The U.S. Navy dirigible Shenandoah, whose silver beauty has been sighted over many American cities, fell broken and shattered on the fields below when it was ripped apart during a thunder storm this morning near Cadwell, Ohio. With 70-mile-an-hour winds, the storm broke the great ship in two, tearing loose the control cabin which fell to earth like a stone. Its 14 crew members were killed, including Captain Zachary Lansdowne. Twenty-seven men survived the disaster.

The Charleston is newest dance craze

"Up on your heels, down on your toes . . ." So begin instructions for accomplishing the Charleston, a fad fast becoming an institution. Developed in Charleston, South Carolina, the steps were first noted at an all-Negro review that opened in New York in 1923. With turned-in toes, syncopated arms and flying legs, dancers move more frantically than film clown Charlie Chaplin. The dance is cutting across age lines; the middle-aged ballroom set are doing it in 4/4 time. And people who usually loathe exertion enjoy standing perfectly still while criss-crossing the hands back and forth across the knees.

Doing the Charleston.

1925

OCTOBER

Su	Mo	Tu	We	Th	Fr	Sa
				1	2	3
4	5	6	7	8	9	10
11	12	13	14	15	16	17
18	19	20	21	22	23	24
25	26	27	28	29	30	31

1. Washington: Conferees fail to settle French debt; five-year plan tentatively arranged for $40 mil. per year (→ 4/1/26).

2. Morocco: Spanish take Riffian base at Agadir (→ 4/18/26).

3. New York: Metropolitan Opera raises ground floor ticket prices from $7.70 to $8.25.

4. Russia abolishes 11-year-old partial Prohibition laws, allowing free flow of liquor.

8. Record $125,000 paid for seat on N.Y. Stock Exchange.

12. Panama: Strikes, rent riots provoke landing of U.S. troops to protect American interests.

12. Moscow and Berlin sign treaty of commerce.

15. Pittsburgh: Pirates beat Washington Senators 9-7 in seventh game of World Series.

16. U.S. Census Bureau reports 75,000 fewer farms than 1920.

18. Syria: French fleet bombs Damascus to put down Druze uprising (→ 3/18/26).

19. Italy completes occupation of Italian Somaliland under terms of 1889 protectorate.

19. U.S. Sec. of Treasury Mellon recommends income tax reduction to maximum of 25 percent.

22. Greek troops invade Bulgaria (→ 26).

26. Chicago Art Institute finds American art standards higher than Europe's; Cubism and post-Impressionism fading.

26. Greeks submit to League demand for withdrawal from Bulgaria (→ 12/3).

28. Census shows U.S. Indian population at 349,595.

30. Scotsman John L. Baird performs first TV broadcast of moving objects (→ 1/26/26).

31. Reza Khan becomes shah of Persia, deposing Qadjar dynasty (→ 2/18/26).

BIRTH

22. Robert Rauschenberg, American painter.

DEATH

7. Christy Mathewson, star baseball pitcher.

Josephine Baker is new star in Paris

The exotic Josephine Baker.

Oct 7. "The Negro Review," produced in the Paris Theatre des Champs-Elysees, is causing excitement. The audience seems to be in ecstasy before Josephine Baker's stupefying wiggles. Miss Baker is always smiling and sings with a warm voice. Appearing on stage almost naked, she is also a splendid dancer. Some critics say this show is decadent, crazy, lustful; others maintain it is brilliant. The show is already very successful. With "The Negro Review," Miss Baker accepted her first prominent dancing part. The American singer began in a traveling theatrical company and in 1923 joined the chorus of the Broadway musical "Shuffle Along." Now she is the toast of Paris.

Duke has become richest university

Oct 27. James Buchanan Duke, tobacco king and philanthropist, died last night of pneumonia. Duke, 68, rose from extreme poverty. He began working in an old log barn, hauling tobacco by driving "a pair of blind mules and a tumble-down wagon." Last year, he established Duke University by a trust fund of $40 million to give North Carolina "preachers, teachers, lawyers, chemists, engineers, and doctors." This gift doubles under the provisions of his will, making Duke the wealthiest university. ▷

Peace pact reached at Locarno meeting

Oct 16. It was seven years ago that Germany and France stopped fighting. But it was not until today that the two former enemies made peace. Joined by other European countries, they initialed a treaty at Locarno, Switzerland.

Germany and France agreed never to fight each other again and to respect a demilitarized zone along the Rhine. In the event of an attack by either country, Britain and Italy both agreed to defend the victim of aggression.

The agreement is a major victory for French Premier Briand, who has demanded greater protection from Germany. British Foreign Secretary Austen Chamberlain said if this treaty does not bring peace to Europe, nothing will. Others note that the agreement treats Germany as an equal partner in Europe (→ 11/26).

France's proconsul Lyautey goes home

Oct 7. After nearly a lifetime overseas as a career soldier in the colonies, Marshal Louis Hubert Lyautey is going home to France. After serving in Indochina, Madagascar and Algeria, Lyautey was named Resident General of Morocco in 1912, with the establishment of the French protectorate. Except for a two-year period during the Great War in which he served as War Minister, he spent the last 13 years extending control over Morocco through the use of traditional forces. Recently, he had been fighting the war against Abd el Krim.

Lyautey in Morocco.

1925

NOVEMBER

Su	Mo	Tu	We	Th	Fr	Sa
1	2	3	4	5	6	7
8	9	10	11	12	13	14
15	16	17	18	19	20	21
22	23	24	25	26	27	28
29	30					

1. Billy Mitchell court martialed by Army after accusing superiors of treason for supporting inadequate air defense (→ 12/17).

2. Berlin bars skyscrapers as health hazards.

3. Jimmy Walker chosen mayor of New York.

5. Italian Fascists ban leftist parties after uncovering plot on Mussolini's life (→ 7).

6. U.S. Steel jumps to record high of $138 per share.

7. Italy: Liberals join Mussolini's Fascists (→ 12/14).

9. Germany: NSDAP protection squads (SS) formed (→ 7/4/26).

12. Washington: Debt negotiators settle; Italy to pay $2.4 bil. to U.S. in 62 years (→ 4/1/26).

14. Noblesville, Ind.: D.C. Stephenson, grand dragon of KKK, sentenced to 20 years for murder (→ 2/24/27).

14. Paris holds its first Surrealist exhibition.

17. Dr. W. Blair Bell gives London lecture advocating treatment of cancer with lead injections.

23. U.S. audiences enjoy release of Buster Keaton's "Go West."

26. French leftist block dissolves as Socialists break ranks with Radicals.

26. Reichstag passes Locarno accord 271-159, opening door for entrance into League (→ 12/1).

28. Grand Ole Opry begins Saturday night "Barn Dance" broadcasts on WSM, Nashville.

28. New York: Army tops Navy 10-3 in annual football game.

30. Philadelphia: Coal operators reject peace plan in three-month-old strike, refuse negotiations (→ 1/12/26).

BIRTHS

20. Robert F.Kennedy, U.S. atty. general († 6/6/1968).

24. William F. Buckley Jr., journalist, conservative spokesman.

DEATH

21. England's Queen Mother Alexandra (*5/6/1844).

The flapper dress is the in thing

The new flapper dresses.

This year saw the birth of the popular flapper dress, distinguished not so much by its brevity, but more by its shape. Skimming a barely discernible bosom, it features a drop waist or no waist at all, creating an abbreviated columnar look.

Egyptian Pharaoh was youth of 15

Nov 13. Egyptologists believe King Tutankhamen was no more than 15 years old when he died. Clothing fragments found in the king's tomb and the manner of bone calcification in his body lend credence to the claim. The young Pharaoh had been married since age five.

Gold treasure from Tut's tomb.

Surrealists display dreams at Paris show

Nov 14. The hitherto distinct barriers between dreams and reality faded a bit today in Paris. A major art show opened at the Pierre Loeb Gallery. It is the first collective exposition of the Surrealists. The artists represented include Max Ernst, Man Ray, Joan Miro, Pablo Picasso and Giorgio De Chirico.

Andre Breton, the Surrealist poet, believes in what he calls automatic writing, guided by pure thought and devoid of logic or moral preoccupations. The painters on display today are trying their own kind of new, imaginary language. Their images are often contradictory and even irrational. And they hope their new images will even create a social revolution.

"Carnival of the Harlequin," by Joan Miro (1925).

1925

DECEMBER

Su	Mo	Tu	We	Th	Fr	Sa
		1	2	3	4	5
6	7	8	9	10	11	12
13	14	15	16	17	18	19
20	21	22	23	24	25	26
29	28	29	30	31		

1. Germany: 7,000 British troops evacuate Cologne after seven-year occupation (→ 1/31/27).

1. Seven nations plegde peace as movies record historic signing of Locarno pact (→ 3/7/26).

3. Geneva: League orders Greece to pay indemnity for October invasion of Bulgaria.

4. 600,000 living in tents in Florida as migration outstrips housing construction.

14. Russia grants Japan coal and oil leases on Sakhalin Island.

14. N.Y. Rep. Hamilton Fish asks Congress to warn Italy against using Fascist propaganda in U.S. (→ 1/20/26).

17. Army finds Billy Mitchell guilty of insubordination for accusing superiors of weakening air defense (→ 2/23/26).

18. U.S.S.R.: Lev Kamenev and Grigori Zinoviev break with Stalin (→ 10/17/26).

25. Motor Magazine reveals 20 mil. autos are registered in U.S.

25. U.S. Adm. Latimer disarms Nicaraguan insurgents, in support of Diaz regime (→ 5/7/26).

26. Six U.S. destroyers ordered from Manila to China to protect interests in civil war (→ 4/10/26).

CULTURAL EVENTS, 1925

Literature: Theodore Dreiser's "An American Tragedy"; John Dos Passos' "Manhattan Transfer"; F. Scott Fitzgerald's "The Great Gatsby"; Sinclair Lewis' "Arrowsmith"; Franz Kafka's "The Trial"; Ford Madox Ford's "No More Parades"; Virginia Woolf's "Mrs. Dalloway"; Pulitzer Prize for poetry to E.A. Robinson's "The Man Who Died Twice."

Academia: Harold Laski's "The Grammar of Politics"; Australian anthropologist Raymond Dart finds Australopithecus fossils in South Africa.

Music: "Show Me the Way to Go Home"; James Weldon Johnson's "The Book of American Negro Spirituals."

Film: Chaplin's "The Gold Rush"; Rene Clair's "The Ghost of Moulin Rouge"; King Vidor's "The Big Parade."

Eisenstein's Potemkin leads movie parade

Eisenstein's "The Battleship Potemkin" opens a new era for Russian cinema.

The premiere of "Potemkin" by Sergei Eisenstein, 27, was met with praise and condemnation this year. It is Eisenstein's second film; the first, "Strike," released earlier this year, had only half the emotional impact of "Potemkin." Its Communist message is well-served; the work is a technical masterpiece.

The Potemkin was a Russian battleship that mutinied in the short-lived revolution of 1905. At first, Eisenstein was going to make the event just one scene in a longer political film. But he felt the mutiny and the accompanying rebellion in Odessa, violently suppressed by the Czar's troops, was worth a film of its own. With tight shots, pans and other innovations (he makes the soldiers seem less human by keeping the camera on their striding boots) he brings the turmoil of the era into vivid focus.

Among the American movies that were very well-received this year were "The Phantom of the Opera," starring Lon Chaney, and "Go West," with the comedian Buster Keaton.

Buster Keaton in "Go West."

"The Phantom of the Opera."

Dawes shares Peace Prize; Shaw wins too

Dec 10. In Oslo, the Nobel Peace Prize has been awarded to British Foreign Secretary Austen Chamberlain, and to American Vice President Charles Gates Dawes for his work on reparations. Dawes headed the committee which worked out the Dawes Plan. The plan is designed to reorganize the German financial system and establish a new feasible reparations payment schedule. The Dawes Plan, published in April 1924, was fully accepted by the European leaders in the summer of the same year.

In Stockholm, the Nobel Committee conferred the prize in literature upon the British playwright George Bernard Shaw. Shaw is one of the most influential figures in modern literature. His attitude toward drama and the stage is unconventional. Most of his plays deal with social problems.

Biggest booze ring busted by feds

Dec 3. Calling it the "greatest roundup in the history of Prohibition," federal agents armed with 43 warrants swooped down on an international rum ring controlling millions in money, ships and liquor. Those arrested included William Dwyer, widely known race track owner and head of the ring. Also arrested were five members of the United States Coast Guard, bribed by the group with "money, wine, women and song" (→ 2/3/26).

Gleeful keg-smashing in Philly.

Socialism in one nation is Stalin aim

Dec 18. At the 14th Soviet Communist Party Congress, Joseph Stalin has won approval of a new policy called "socialism in one country." The U.S.S.R. will no longer pursue world revolution as its first priority, but will concentrate on developing socialism in the Soviet Union itself.

Fitzgerald's latest

This year saw the publication of "The Great Gatsby," a glamorous novel of today by F. Scott Fitzgerald. The "philosopher of the flapper" has turned to the lives of the jazz age set now grown up. But marriage has not changed them, only the locale of their parties. The story of Jay Gatsby of West Egg is narrated by Nick Carraway, who tells of Gatsby's wealth, power and love for Daisy Buchanan.

1926

JANUARY

Su	Mo	Tu	We	Th	Fr	Sa
					1	2
3	4	5	6	7	8	9
10	11	12	13	14	15	16
17	18	19	20	21	22	23
24	25	26	27	28	29	30
31						

1. N.Y. and London celebrate New Year together over radio.

1. Pasadena: Alabama edges Washington 20-19 in Rose Bowl; 235 injured as grandstand collapses during parade.

3. Greek Premier Pangalos declares self dictator; opposition leaders exiled (→ 8/22).

6. Lufthansa airline founded in Germany.

7. Archduke Albert quits as Hungarian Fascist pres., as v.p. arrested for counterfeiting.

8. Ibn Saud proclaimed king of Hejaz, renames it Saudi Arabia (→ 5/20/27).

9. Berlin: Six more murders laid to Black Reichswehr; killings by German secret army now at 25.

10. Fritz Lang's film "Metropolis" opens in Berlin.

11. Mexican bandits kill 50 on train, many burned alive.

12. U.S. coal talks end, leaving both sides bitter as strike drags on into fifth month (→ 13).

13. Pennsylvania Gov. Pinchot demands laws making coal a public utility (→ 2/12).

13. Oklahoma: 65 dead in Wilburton mine explosion.

14. Germany: Rhine and Ruhr steel industries merged into United Steel with capitalization of $150 million.

15. Kemal's Turkey adopts entire Swiss civil code (→ 4/29/28).

20. France: Banned Italian Communists hold third congress in Lyons (→ 3/24).

21. Leningrad: Bolsheviks open Romanov tombs, finding $1m in jewels to be placed in museums.

27. U.S. Senate votes to join World Court with five reservations (→ 9/2).

29. Russian Soviets order compulsory military training in colleges.

31. New York: Lon Chaney opens in "The Black Bird."

BIRTH

5. W.D. Snodgrass, American poet, "Heart's Needle."

Scot shows something called television

Scottish inventor John L. Baird, at work in the laboratory.

Jan 27. A new machine capable of the wireless transmission of moving pictures was demonstrated to members of the Royal Institution in London today by John L. Baird, a Scottish inventor. Baird calls his invention "television."

The device does not use a conventional motion picture projector but instead shows its images electronically on what is called a cathode ray tube, which was developed in England for scientific purposes. Observers who saw the demonstration say the quality of the images is not as good as that achieved by films, but they noted that the invention is still in its early stages. It could someday turn every home into a motion picture theater, Baird says (→ 4/7/27).

Irving Berlin weds heiress Ellin Mackay

Jan 4. Composer Irving Berlin and society girl Ellin Mackay quickly and quietly married today. The bride's father, who had not been told of the couple's plans, expressed disapproval of the match. The public speculated over the propriety of the union, for Berlin is Jewish and Miss Mackay is Roman Catholic.

Berlin, born Isadore Baline, is the son of a Russian rabbi. He has never learned to read or write music, and he plays the piano in only one key. Yet he is the most popular songwriter of our time. He is composer and lyricist of "Oh! How I Hate to Get Up in the Morning" and "Alexander's Ragtime Band." The latter song has sold more than two million copies. Berlin recently wrote the score for "Cocoanuts," the Marx brothers stage show.

Miss Mackay, who at 22 is 11 years younger than her husband, is the daughter of Clarence H. Mackay, President of the Postal Telegraph Company. Mackay issued a statement that the wedding had been performed without his "knowledge or approval."

Cartoonist John Held Jr. has hit that peak of success at which the artist becomes not just a mirror for his culture, but a source of styles and manners for an era.

1926

FEBRUARY

Su	Mo	Tu	We	Th	Fr	Sa
	1	2	3	4	5	6
7	8	9	10	11	12	13
14	15	16	17	18	19	20
21	22	23	24	25	26	27
28						

2. Baseball's National League to celebrate 50th year this season.

3. Prague: Official decree establishes Czech as natl. language.

3. U.S.: Episcopal Society asks for modification of Volstead Act (→ 4/24).

4. New York: 12 die as record winds and snow sweep city.

6. Mussolini warns Germany to stop agitation in Tyrol.

6. Moscow: Princess Obolensky found murdered in street.

9. Botanical Gardens reports autos are driving birds out of New York City.

9. Baseball's American League bans use of resin by pitchers.

11. Arizona Governor Hunt warns U.S. Senate he will fight Boulder Dam (→ 12/21/28).

11. Mexican government nationalizes all church property.

12. Philadelphia: Anthracite coal strike settled in compromise after 165 days.

14. John D. Rockefeller offers $10 million to King Fuad for museum in Egypt.

15. New York: Dr. A.S.W. Rosenbach buys Gutenberg Bible for $106,000.

17. 28 dead, 29 missing as Utah avalanche buries mine hamlet.

18. Treaty extends British mandate over Persia for 25 years (→ 4/25).

19. New Jersey: Dr. Lane of Princeton places earth's age at one billion years.

21. Nice: Suzanne Lenglen retires from amateur singles play (→ 8/2).

22. Pope Pius rejects Mussolini's offer of aid to Vatican.

23. Coolidge opposes large air force as menace to world peace (→ 7/2).

25. Poland demands permanent seat on League Council.

26. Washington: Pres. Coolidge signs $388 million tax cut.

BIRTH

2. Valery Giscard d'Estaing, French ex-president.

Garbo's beauty captivates Hollywood

February. America adores an actress it hardly knows, a Swede named Greta Garbo. She has made only one film here, a slight romance in which she plays a naive Spanish peasant girl. Yet that single picture, "The Torrent," has opened a flood of admiration. With one of the most beautiful faces on the screen, Garbo is cool, reserved and mysterious. She has qualities Lillian Gish and Mary Pickford have never sought to offer, and probably never knew were desirable. But now the public has discovered a longing only this distant, crystal-eyed woman can fulfill.

Garbo was born September 18, 1905, as Greta Gustafsson. She studied at the Royal Dramatic Theater of Stockholm before being noticed by her mentor, Mauritz Stiller. Louis B. Mayer of MGM offered Stiller a contract, but he refused to come to America unless Garbo was signed up. Mayer accepted her with reluctance; she had made merely a handful of Swedish films. The pair arrived in New York last July. The actress is currently at work on "The Temptress," with Stiller directing. There are rumors he will be fired for being too attentive on and off the set. He is probably no more loving than the camera.

The classic beauty of Greta Garbo.

Lenglen beats Wills in their only match

Feb 16. Suzanne Lenglen, the dynamic French tennis star, scored a two-set victory in a close match against America's reigning woman player, Helen Wills, in a special match at Cannes, France. This was the first meeting of the pair, who for years have dominated tennis on both sides of the Atlantic. Miss Wills has been the United States singles champion for the past three years. And the coveted Wimbledon title has been won six times by Miss Lenglen, starting in 1919, and missing only in 1924 (→ 21).

Wills (left) congratulates Lenglen.

Buried Mayan city found in Yucatan

Mayan pyramid in Yucatan.

Feb 8. An American archeological expedition that has been exploring the jungle of Yucatan today reported the discovery of a buried Mayan city near the Caribbean coast. The city, whose name is believed to be Muyil, once was part of an important trade route between Mayan cities in north Yucatan and Central America. The explorers say they found a dozen buildings and six temples in fair condition. The discovery verifies persistent rumors of a lost Mayan city in the jungle.

1926

MARCH

Su	Mo	Tu	We	Th	Fr	Sa
	1	2	3	4	5	6
7	8	9	10	11	12	13
14	15	16	17	18	19	20
21	22	23	24	25	26	27
28	29	30	31			

4. China, claiming one-fourth of world's population, asks representative on League Council.

6. Paris: Chamber of Deputies overthrows Briand Cabinet 274-221 (→ 9).

7. William H. "Big Bill" Edwards accepts presidency of American Professional Football League.

7. As League plenary session opens, powers fail to agree on admission of Germany (→ 10).

9. France: Briand stays as premier, forms new Cabinet to combat monetary crisis (→ 27).

10. Geneva: Brazil registers vote against Germany's admission to League (→ 17).

16. Auburn, Mass.: First liquid-fuel rocket launched by physicist Robert H. Goddard.

16. Costa Rican railway disaster kills 178 in San Jose.

17. "The Girl Friend," music by Richard Rogers, opens in N.Y.

17. Geneva: League adjourns, deferring Germany's entry until September with Brazil as only obstacle (→ 6/12).

18. Syria: 42 French soldiers slain in Druze ambush (→ 5/19).

24. Psychoanalytic film "The Secrets of the Soul" opens in Berlin.

24. Maryland: After 11 years selling goods for cash to Idaho wheat farmers, M.B. Skaggs incorporates Safeway Stores.

26. American oil companies buy 190,000 tons of kerosene from Russia for $3.2 million.

27. French exchange rate slides to 29.1 francs to the U.S. dollar (→ 6/15).

BIRTH

11. Rev. Ralph Abernathy, civil rights leader, organized 1955 bus boycott.

DEATHS

13. Edward W. Scripps, newspaper publisher (*6/13/1854).

17. Alexei A. Brusiloff, Russian general.

26. Constantin Fehrenbach, German ex-president (*1/11/1852).

Rail stocks break in heaviest trading

March 24. Stock prices collapsed today, the second severe break in prices in less than a month. The new wave of selling affected a broad range of securities, not just rail stocks which tumbled sharply on March 3 in the greatest day of trading on Wall Street on record. That earlier stock decline was in response to the refusal of the Interstate Commerce Commission to ratify the Nickel Plate merger. Factors affecting today's break in prices included a planned investigation of the oil industry by the government, a decline in commodity prices and a possible cutback in iron and steel production.

Fascists held guilty of killing Socialist

March 24. The courtroom crowd applauded today's decision in the trial of the five Fascists accused of kidnapping and murdering Giacomo Matteotti, a Socialist Deputy. Two of the accused men were acquitted. The other three were found guilty of "unintentional murder" and received six-year sentences, which will be reduced to 75 days because of the recent political amnesty in Italy and the prison time they have already served. The jury found that Matteotti was not attacked because of his anti-Fascist parliamentary activity, but because he was head of the Italian Socialist Party. Crimes against members of Parliament require a heavier sentence (→ 4/7).

1926

APRIL

Su	Mo	Tu	We	Th	Fr	Sa
				1	2	3
4	5	6	7	8	9	10
11	12	13	14	15	16	17
18	19	20	21	22	23	24
25	26	27	28	29	30	

1. Washington: Sen. Borah attacks Italy and Britain, demanding payment of war debts (→ 27).

3. India: Moslem-Hindu riots destroy temples, killing 12, wounding 100 in Calcutta.

6. Byrd party leaves on first leg of trip to explore Arctic (→ 5/9).

7. Rome: Mussolini's nose wounded by bullet fired by Irish woman Violet Gibson (→ 11).

10. Germany announces Hohenzollerns owe Reich seven million marks in unpaid taxes.

10. China: President Tuan deposed in Peking (→ 9/6).

11. Mussolini greeted with royal honors on African soil (→ 5/19).

12. Riot police with clubs rout 5,000 strikers in Passaic, N.J.

16. German jobless granted unemployment benefits for 39 wks.

18. Morocco: French, Spanish meet Rif envoys in Taourirt, yet fail to reach armistice (→ 5/23).

20. Check from London crosses ocean by radio to be cashed in New York—first in history.

24. Washington dry law hearings end; wets make final plea for modication (→ 7/2).

24. Germans sign accord with Russians, extending Rapallo pact of April 1922.

25. American Assn. of Univ. Professors assails college football as moral menace.

25. Milan: Toscanini directs opening performance of Puccini's opera "Turandot."

27. London: World bankers draft scheme to pay off intl. war debts by private sale of Dawes Plan bonds (→ 29).

29. Washington: 11 farm-belt senators start revolt against Coolidge's opposition to agricultural relief bill (→ 2/25/27).

29. French debt agreement signed in Washington, calling for $6.85 billion in 62 years.

30. Picture service via radio opened between London and N.Y. Times.

BIRTH

21. Elizabeth II, queen of England.

Reza Khan crowns self Shah of Persia

Reza Shah Pahlevi.

April 25. Reza Khan, a former trooper in the Persian army, crowned himself Shah today in the Palace of the Shahs in Tehran. Reza became Premier in 1923, and in 1925 had the Majlis, or Parliament, depose Shah Ahmad, the last ruler of the Qahar dynasty. Although Reza reportedly considered transforming his country into a republic, the opposition of the clergy changed his mind. In December, the Majlis proclaimed him shah, and he chose the name Pahlevi for the new dynasty (→ 8/20).

Professors brand football immoral

April 25. College football promotes drinking, dishonesty and neglect of academic work, according to a report issued by a committee of the American Association of University Professors. The panel proposes a limitation of one year's participation for college football players, among other reforms.

Character-building or degeneracy?

1926

MAY

Su	Mo	Tu	We	Th	Fr	Sa
						1
2	3	4	5	6	7	8
9	10	11	12	13	14	15
16	17	18	19	20	21	22
23	24	25	26	27	28	29
30	31					

2. India: Hindu women gain right to seek elected office.

3. Revival of Wilde's "The Importance of Being Earnest" opens in New York.

3. Trade Unions begin general strike in Britain; Baldwin worried civil war will ensue (→ 12).

5. Eisenstein's film "Battleship Potemkin" shown in Germany for first time.

5. Sinclair Lewis refuses 1925 Pulitzer for "Arrowsmith."

7. U.S. report demonstrates motors now comprise one-third of nation's exports.

7. Revolutionary activity following Chamorro coup brings U.S. troops to Nicaragua (→ 8/28).

9. Spitzbergen: Comm. Byrd flies to N. Pole and back (→ 31).

13. Warsaw: Pilsudski arrests Pres. Wojciechowski (→ 6/1).

15. Amundsen and Ellsworth forced down in Alaska after four-day flight over icecap as ice forms on dirigible Norge.

15. Bubbling Over takes Kentucky Derby with jockey A. Johnson in the saddle.

17. Argentina: Bombs ascribed to Sacco and Vanzetti sympathizers damage U.S. Embassy in Buenos Aires (→ 10/26).

18. Disarmament talks open in Geneva; U.S.S.R. not present.

19. Rome: Mussolini pronounces democracy deceased, replaced by Fascism (→ 6/29).

19. Syria: French shells kill 600 in Damascus (→ 7/25).

20. U.S. Congress passes Air Commerce Act, giving Dept. of Commerce right to license pilots and planes.

23. Moroccan Rif capital captured by French (→ 26).

28. Gen. da Costa takes power in Portuguese coup (→ 7/9).

31. Frank Lockhart win 14th Indy 500 averaging 95.9 mph.

BIRTH

25. Miles Davis, jazz trumpeter.

DEATH

16. Mohammed VI, Turkish ex-sultan.

Abd el Krim gives up, ends Rif war

May 26. In Morocco, rebel leader Abd el Krim has surrendered. He was a hero to the Riffian tribes when he defeated Spanish troops in the north. But he bit off more than he could chew when he invaded French Morocco. France and Spain joined forces against Abd el Krim, and his troops were no match for their superior firepower.

Since last Saturday, the rebels have been surrounded in Targuist, which Abd el Krim had previously boasted was impregnable. At most, however, he had only 30,000 men under his command. Opposing him

Scene from the battle of Wazzan.

was the French Marshal, Henri Philippe Petain, and 160,000 soldiers backed by powerful artillery. The rebels were trapped, and they have been forced to beg for mercy.

Abd el Krim was a thorn in the side of the European powers in Morocco. The French now plan to resume the policy they call a pacification program. They have been in control in Morocco since 1912, when a French protectorate was established and recognized by the other European powers. Both French and Spanish forces were given police powers in the area.

Byrd and Bennett circle North Pole by air

May 31. Two daring teams of fliers made history this month by completing the first flights over the North Pole. First to overfly the pole were two Americans, Floyd Bennett and Navy Commander Richard E. Byrd. Flying a Fokker tri-motor aircraft, they took off from the Spitzbergen Islands north of Norway on the morning of May 9 and arrived over the pole a little more than seven hours later despite trouble with one engine, returning to Spitzbergen after a flight of nearly 16 hours.

Comm. Byrd and Floyd Bennett.

Amundsen and the Norge at landing.

Just two days later, the dirigible Norge with an international crew including Roald Amundsen of Norway, Lincoln Ellsworth of the United States and Umberto Nobile of Italy took off from Spitzbergen. The fliers reached the North Pole early the next day, dropping flags of their three nations. The Norge then continued its flight across the Arctic and over Alaska, arriving safely at Nome on May 13 (→ 8/25/28).

Utter defeat for unions in Britain

May 12. With shouts of joy and thanksgiving, the British people heard the report that the great general strike was over. Thus ended the shutdown of the coal mines, transportation, press, and iron and steel works which paralyzed the country for 12 days as four million workers walked off the job.

It is emphasized that the coal miners' strike, which precipitated the crisis, is still on. The miners struck when postwar subsidies were withdrawn by the government, thus reducing their pay. Backed by a coalition of other unions, the miners seemed certain of success, but public opinion saw the strike as coercive, and as the government dug in its heels, volunteer workers filled vacant jobs in a mood of virtual war.

When the miners refused a compromise offered by the Trade Union Committee, the latter called an end to the strike on the grounds that no settlement was possible without compromise. Thus some one million miners remain on strike, dangling with no support.

U.S.-bred males are tall and vigorous

May. The public is fascinated by a study released this spring showing the American man growing taller and stronger. Dr. Alex Hrdlicka, an anthropologist with the Smithsonian, compared Americans who have been here for three generations with more recent arrivals. He found the average "Old American" is 68.6 inches tall, has a high forehead and an excellent brain capacity. Former President Theodore Roosevelt had offered to volunteer for the study.

New man confronts the new woman.

1926

JUNE

Su	Mo	Tu	We	Th	Fr	Sa
		1	2	3	4	5
6	7	8	9	10	11	12
13	14	15	16	17	18	19
20	21	22	23	24	25	26
29	28	29	30			

1. Joseph Pilsudski declines Polish presidency in favor of Ignacy Moscicki, yet retains dictatorial powers (→ 10).

1. World's Fair opens in Philadelphia.

5. Paris Prof. Charles Henry announces invention of catalysis process to run autos on water.

9. N.Y. Telephone offers home phones for $4 per month.

10. Polish troops suppress industrial strike, firing into Warsaw crowds (→ 13).

12. Brazil quits League in protest over plans to admit Germany (→ 17).

14. Ten killed, 40 hurt as plant explodes at Gary Indiana Steel Co.

15. Paris cheers premiere of Jean Cocteau's film "Orphee."

15. France: Briand Cabinet out again as franc continues slide (→ 23).

17. Spain threatens to quit League of Nations if Germany allowed to join (→ 9/8).

18. London: American women take Wightman Tennis Cup.

19. Montana: 20,000 Indians trek to Little Big Horn to commemorate Custer battle.

19. London women, 100,000-strong, march for peace.

22. Canada gains further autonomy from Britain, requiring military, economic action to be ratified by Canadian Parliament.

23. France: New Briand Cabinet formed with Joseph Caillaux as finance minister (→ 7/8).

26. Memorial to first U.S. troops in France unveiled at St. Nazaire.

29. Rome: Fascists add hour to work day in economic efficiency measure (→ 7/23).

BIRTHS

1. Marilyn Monroe, American screen star († 8/5/1962).

3. Allen Ginsburg, American poet, beat generation.

DEATH

7. Antonio Gaudi, Catalan architect (*6/26/1852).

Bobby Jones wins British Open title

June 25. Americans have swept the first four places in the British Open golf championship, and the winner, for the first time in 29 years, was an amateur. When Bobby Jones, the ex-lawyer from Atlanta, dropped his final putt for a score of 291, a burst of applause broke from the 5,000 spectators on hand at the St. Anne's course. Most of them obviously wanted to see Jones win. Al Waltrous finished second, just two strokes behind Jones, who in 1923 won the playoff for the United States Open title.

Jones, a former lawyer.

Mackenzie King out because of scandal

June 28. There is cheering and jubilation in Ottawa tonight, most of it by Conservatives. Liberal Premier Mackenzie King was forced to resign earlier today after scandal rocked his administration. Ottawa is dry, and much of the scandal relates to drinking.

Charges have been made that the Minister of Customs allowed the release of denatured alcohol without the payment of excise tax. Most of it was distributed in the United States. It has also been revealed that the government had wild parties on one of the ships owned by customs.

At any other time, the government might have survived such scandals. But the Liberals, a minority party in Parliament, were forced to form a shaky coalition with the Progressives. The next government will be Conservative. ▷

Pilsudski sets up Polish dictatorship

Warsaw passers-by rushed to safety as Pilsudski's troops took over last month.

June 13. Marshal Joseph Pilsudski now holds dictatorial power in Poland. The President and Cabinet have accepted Pilsudski's conditions, agreeing to name him permanent Commander-in-Chief of the armies. His position will not be affected by changes of government and cannot be restricted by the Cabinet or acts of Parliament.

Pilsudski's grab for power began just one month ago when he led the armed revolt that ousted Premier Wincenty Witos, leader of the Peasant Party. In a series of interviews with Radical Party newspapers, Pilsudski accused the new Witos government of corruption, including bribery and misuse of government funds. Witos ordered the papers containing the interviews be confiscated, enraging the Radicals. When armed men attacked Pilsudski's house, troops loyal to him mutineed and marched on Warsaw. Witos resigned May 14.

Many Poles believe Pilsudski's successful coup d'etat heralds a period of agressive military action. The army supports him, and although it now numbers only 300,000, its potential strength is four million. Given Pilsudski's hatred of Soviet Russia, an attack on the Bolsheviks is apparently not out of the question (→ 10/1).

Artist Mary Cassatt was one of the best

June 14. Mary Cassatt, the only American given the privilege of exhibiting with the European Impressionists, has died in a Paris suburb. She was 81 years old. She always considered France her country, but most of her works hang proudly in American homes and museums.

Miss Cassatt was born in Pennsylvania and trained at the Pennsylvania Academy of Fine Arts. She settled permanently in Paris in 1874. Edgar Degas became her mentor; they had similar tastes and ideas. Yet Miss Cassatt painted her subjects, mothers and their children, with a unique and intimate detail. One of her best portraits is "Lady at the Tea-table."

Cassatt's "Young Woman Reading."

1926

JULY

Su	Mo	Tu	We	Th	Fr	Sa
				1	2	3
4	5	6	7	8	9	10
11	12	13	14	15	16	17
18	19	20	21	22	23	24
25	26	27	28	29	30	31

1. First U.S. mail flown by private carrier —Colonial Air Transport.

2. Army Air Corps created by U.S. Congress (→ 4/13/27).

3. Wimbledon: Jean Borotra over Howard Kinsey 8-6, 6-1, 6-3; Kathleen Godfree over Lili De Alvarez 6-2, 4-6, 6-3.

4. Hitler's Nazis hold first congress since Feb. 1925 reorganization in Weimar (→ 11/1).

5. Washington reports one in six Americans owns a car.

7. Paris: French test neutralizer of auto exhaust, hoping to purify city air poisoned by fumes.

8. French franc continues collapse, reaching 49 to the U.S. dollar (→ 17).

9. Portugal: Gen. Antonio Carmona replaces da Costa as prime minister (→ 2/9/27).

10. New Jersey: Blinding blast, seen for 30 miles, blows up Navy munitions plant at Dover; 19 dead, nine still missing.

16. Reich bans Soviet film "Battleship Potemkin" throughout Germany.

16. Valentino film "The Son of the Sheik" opens for U.S. audiences (→ 8/23).

17. France: Briand govt. overthrown for third time; Herriot to form new Cabinet (→ 23).

18. Belgian bicycle racer Lucien Buysse wins Tour de France.

22. Garden City, L.I.: Babe Ruth catches baseball dropped from plane.

23. Rome: Mussolini asserts Italy must expand or explode (→ 9/11).

25. Syria: French crush Druze uprising (→ 5/22/30).

26. U.S. governor vetoes Filipino Legislature's call for plebiscite on independence.

28. U.S., Panama reach accord protecting canal in event of war.

28. Mexican Catholics begin trade boycott in protest against religious restrictions (→ 8/7).

DEATH

2. Emile Coue, French popular psychologist (*2/26/1857).

Collapse of franc undermines regime

July 23. Politicians who have spent most of their careers battling each other in France are trying to unite this morning. They are part of a new coalition government formed to save France from bankruptcy. To succeed, they must find a way to prop up the ailing franc and keep down the price of bread.

It is the fourth time Raymond Poincare has formed a government. He will also serve as Finance Minister. Five of his ministers are former premiers, some from the left, some from the right. One of them, Radical leader Edouard Herriot, almost single-handedly toppled the last government.

Somehow, the politicians must find a way to work together, because France is in disastrous financial shape. The franc has fallen daily in recent weeks. Almost all of the state reserves in the Bank of France have been depleted. The Treasury would have closed its doors long ago without the Morgan credits from the United States. And French citizens are angry because the price of bread seems to rise a few centimes every day.

The French people are very suspicious of politicians in this financial crisis. The last government fell after it demanded the power to decree economic adjustments, without the approval of the Parliament. The new government is treading more lightly. It will apparently ask, but not require, that citizens pay part of their taxes early so that it can meet domestic expenses and make payments on its foreign debt.

One in six U.S. citizens owns a car. We top the list, and Hejaz is last with 4 cars; 1 in 225,000.

Murder: A minister and a choir singer

July 28. The case of the minister and the choir singer, a double murder nearly four years old, took a dramatic turn tonight. The minister's widow, Mrs. Frances Stevens Hall, was arrested near midnight at her home in New Brunswick, New Jersey, and charged with the crime.

The victims were the Rev. Edward W. Hall, pastor of a fashionable Episcopal church, and Mrs. Eleanor Mills, wife of the sexton. Their bodies were found in 1922 under a crabapple tree on a deserted farm, with some love letters. Police said the case was reopened on new evidence. Bribery of a witness was alleged (→ 12/3).

Prohibition causing crime and insanity

July 2. Testifying before the House Judiciary Committee today, several witnesses, including a Congregational minister and former federal judge, claimed that the Volstead or Prohibition Law is responsible for an increase in crime and insanity in the United States.

Makeshift comfort in a speakeasy.

Officials at state asylums said the number of demented persons due to alcoholism had increased by 1000 percent since 1920, when the law took effect. During the hearing, a truck delivered petitions from seven million persons who want relief from Prohibition and what they consider its evil effects (→ 10/8/28).

1926

AUGUST

Su	Mo	Tu	We	Th	Fr	Sa
1	2	3	4	5	6	7
8	9	10	11	12	13	14
15	16	17	18	19	20	21
22	23	24	25	26	27	28
29	30	31				

1. Soviet land owners to pay taxes in securities; no longer legal to pay in kind.

2. Suzanne Lenglen announces plan to tour U.S. for $200,000 as professional.

5. Paris: France and Germany sign trade accord.

6. Vitaphone shows first talkie, featuring music by Henry Hadley, head of N.Y. Philharmonic.

7. Coolidge pledges non-intervention in Mexico, as Mexican Pres. Calles rules out foreign mediation in church conflict.

10. Berlin: Inexpensive chemicals now replacing silver salts in movie film.

10. Northwest Airways incorporated in Michigan.

12. Hungary's only munitions works destroyed, killing 24, injuring 300.

14. Twenty-eight Rumanians arrive in N.Y. to study education.

15. Copenhagen: Intl. Congress of Astronomers holds first meeting in 13 years.

18. British miners resume negotiations with govt. in attempt to settle three-month strike (→ 24).

20. Persia: Uprising against Shah Reza Pahlevi breaks out in Southeast.

22. South Africa: 50,000 begin crowding Johannesburg as British announce discovery of largest diamond mines yet.

22. Greece: Military coup led by George Condylis ousts Pangalos regime (→ 5/31/28).

24. Coal strike riots break out in Britain (→ 11/9).

25. "Messiah" Jeddu Krishnamurti arrives in N.Y. to spread world happiness.

26. Pennsylvania: 30 miners die from poisonous gases after mine explosion in Clymer.

28. U.S. Marines land in Nicaragua to protect nationals and fight Sandino rebels (→ 11/12).

29. Nepalese slavery abolished; 55,000 freed from bondage.

30. German swimmer Ernst Vierkoetter sets new Channel record at 12 hours, 43 minutes.

Rudolph Valentino dies; fans desolate

Valentino fans line up in New York to pay final homage to their idol.

Aug 23. Thousands of women are sobbing next to their radios today, overcome by news that Rudolph Valentino is dead. The actor, thrilling them for the last five years with films like "Blood and Sand," "The Young Rajah" and "Cobra," was only 31 years old. A ruptured appendix and gastric ulcer hastened him to a Manhattan hospital. There, he spoke his final words, a sad, delirious babble of French and Italian. Women can't agree on how to honor his memory: Pola Negri has ordered 4,000 roses for his bier, and one fan has chosen to shoot herself.

"Son of the Sheik," Valentino's last.

Ederle 1st woman to swim Channel

New York's hardy swimmer Gertrude Ederle.

Aug 6. Gertrude Ederle became the first woman to swim the English Channel today, and she accomplished the feat faster than any of the men who have done it over the previous 51 years. The gritty New Yorker crossed the Channel in 14 hours, 31 minutes. The best previous time was 16 hours, 23 minutes by an Italian swimmer, Sebastian Tirabocchi, in 1923.

Miss Ederle walked, instead of diving, into the surf at 7:09 a.m. at Cape Gris-Nez, France, barely acknowledging the cheers of a few spectators. She was slowed somewhat after five hours in the water when the wind increased. However, her biggest delay occurred at the finish. There, the 19-year-old swimmer was held up again when customs officials insisted on interrogating her before permitting her on shore.

1926

SEPTEMBER

Su	Mo	Tu	We	Th	Fr	Sa
			1	2	3	4
5	6	7	8	9	10	11
12	13	14	15	16	17	18
19	20	21	22	23	24	25
26	27	28	29	30		

2. Geneva: Canada bars American entry into World Court, saying fifth reservation gives U.S. virtual veto (→ 2/9/27).

6. Chiang Kai-shek reaches Hankow in northern campaign in Chinese civil war (→ 10/7).

10. Frenchman Georges Michel swims English Channel in record time of 11 hrs., five min.

11. Rome: Eight passers-by wounded in failed attempt on Mussolini's life (→ 10/7).

11. Spanish referendum demonstrates public support for Primo de Rivera dictatorship (→ 4/14/29).

11. Spain quits League over Germany's admittance.

13. N.Y.: San Carlo Grand Opera Co. performs "Carmen" at Metropolitan Opera House.

13. London: World's longest tube completed, serving 2.5 million people.

15. Chicago: Jelly Roll Morton and Red Hot Peppers hold first recording session for RCA.

17. Mexican officials execute seven in retaliation for yesterday's murder of New Yorker Jacob Rosenthal (→ 10/21).

18. New York Times celebrates 75th anniversary.

19. New York: Rene Lacoste over Jean Borotra 6-4, 6-0, 6-4 in U.S. open, ending Bill Tilden's six-year reign at Forest Hills.

21. Philadelphia audiences acclaim new opera "Deep River."

25. Bertolt Brecht's "Man for Man" opens in Dusseldorf.

28. N.Y.: "Gentlemen Prefer Blondes" opens on Broadway.

28. Batavia, Java: Dutch scientist finds skull of prehistoric man believed to be "missing link".

30. European Steel Cartel formed.

30. U.S.: 7,000-mile trip planned in Byrd polar plane to show safety of commericial aviation.

BIRTHS

23. John Coltrane, jazz saxophonist († 7/17/1967).

30. Edmond de Rothschild, French financier.

Tunney beats Dempsey as 130,000 watch

Sept 23. Gene Tunney, the fighting Marine, pummeled Jack Dempsey through ten rounds under rainy skies in Philadelphia today and walked off with the world heavyweight boxing championship.

This was the first time in the history of the division that the championship changed hands on a decision. A crowd of about 130,000 was clearly on the side of the ex-Marine, who was in charge throughout.

Tunney pounded away at Dempsey's jaw with his right and his whip-like left caught Dempsey's nose time and again. Dempsey's nose was made fragile by the rebuilding it took to get him ready for the moving picture shows. A long layoff from boxing and three years of living in luxury did little to prepare Dempsey for the fight. "I have no alibis to offer," said the ex-champ afterwards. "I lost to a good man, an American, a man who speaks the English language."

"I never fought a harder socker," said Tunney.

Tunney and Dempsey, all business, before the fight.

Germany admitted to League of Nations

Sept 8. Germany took another step today in changing its role from international villain to respected member of the world community. This afternoon, German delegates left Berlin for Geneva. They are on their way to claim a permanent seat in the League of Nations. The League's Assembly had unanimously approved Germany's admission at noon.

The enthusiasm in Geneva was dampened somewhat by disagreements within the League. Brazil resigned and Spain is also threatening to leave the League because they were not accorded permanent seats. And some diplomats wonder whether the League will ever have much power or authority as long as the United States and Russia are not members of the league (→ 11).

Machine guns hit Capone's headquarters

Sept 20. Gangster Al Capone barely escaped injury at noon when rival gunmen sprayed his Cicero, Illinois, headquarters with bullets.

"Scarface" Al Capone.

The men opened fire with machine guns, shotguns and pistols as they drove by in 11 cars, shattering windows, ripping plaster from the walls, destroying furniture and damaging 35 cars parked nearby. The bullets hit one of Capone's men in the shoulder and injured a woman sitting in one of the cars, but Capone, who was having lunch at a restaurant next door, ducked when he heard the bullets.

The gunmen were retaliating for the murder of Al Capone's rival gang leader Dion O'Banion, a onetime florist who was murdered a couple of years ago after a dispute with Capone over gambling profits. Cicero, an industrial suburb of Chicago famous for its gambling and bordellos, proved once more it is America's toughest little town.

Wind kills 1,000; 38,000 lose homes

Sept 19. Florida's thriving east coast was dealt a crushing blow yesterday when a tropical hurricane swept in at 130 mph. Miami, whose population has soared from 1,681 to 69,754 in the last 25 years, was reduced to a mass of broken glass and wrecked buildings. More than a dozen ships, including ex-Kaiser Wilhelm's, now line the street in front of the McAllister Hotel, leaving fewer than six in their rightful places on the waterfront.

Flattened car in Miami Beach.

Miami, Fort Lauderdale and Hollywood are now under martial law, and three looters have been shot by police. Though the Red Cross is rushing supplies to the needy, famine and disease still threaten to kill more than the storm. The death toll has reached more than 1,000; there are 38,000 homeless.

A German gastronomic survey has recently found the U.S. to be a "great nation of steakeaters."

1926

OCTOBER

Su	Mo	Tu	We	Th	Fr	Sa
					1	2
3	4	5	6	7	8	9
10	11	12	13	14	15	16
17	18	19	20	21	22	23
24	25	26	27	28	29	30
31						

1. Warsaw: Marshal Pilsudski heads new Polish Cabinet.

7. A.F.L. announces plan to unionize men in auto industry.

7. Mussolini abolishes all political opposition in Italy; Fascist Party is assimilated into the state (→ 31).

7. 500,000 Chinese reportedly facing death as Communists beseige Hankow (→ 11/30).

13. New York: August Heckscher offers $500 million for plan to end city slums.

13. Pie and cake head list as favorite foods in U.S.

14. London: Lord Asquith steps down as leader of Liberals.

16. Baltimore: Dr. Dunlap of Johns Hopkins asserts smoking makes men more dependable.

17. Moscow: Trotsky admits defeat, bows to Stalin group as leaders of U.S.S.R. (→ 11/19).

18. New York extends warm welcome to Rumania's Queen Marie.

20. Cuba: Havana ravaged by 130-mph hurricane; 30 dead, 300 injured.

21. Mexican deputies, fearing revolt, pass bill allowing Obregon (ousted in 1924) to return to presidency (→ 1/13/27).

23. Italy bars women from civic offices.

23. Florence: Operatic soprano Luisa Tetrazzini weds Pietro Vernati, 20 years her junior.

26. Belgian franc stabilized by creation of new currency, the Belga, worth five paper francs.

29. British writer MacKenzie warns U.S. birth control may allow rapidly multiplying Chinese to overrun Western Civilization.

31. Rome: Mussolini escapes bullet; mob kills boy assailant (→ 11/2).

BIRTHS

15. Evan Hunter, American novelist, "The Blackboard Jungle."

18. Klaus Kinski, German actor.

18. Chuck Berry, rock and roll pioneer.

Escape artist Houdini entrapped by death

Oct 31. Harry Houdini, the master of magic, died today in Detroit. Renowned as a defier of locks and sealed chests, even prisons, he lost his final battle against death from peritonitis. He was 52 years old.

His final weeks were marked by bouts of pain, starting early this month in Albany, New York, when a piece of apparatus used in his famous water-torture cell trick overturned and struck him on the foot. After finishing his show, he went to a hospital and found that he had a fractured bone. Advised to rest for a few days, he refused to cancel his planned tour.

Several days later, speaking to a class of students in Montreal, he claimed that his stomach muscles could withstand hard blows. A student, without warning, jumped up and hit him twice in the stomach, just above the appendix. Later, upon arriving in Detroit, Houdini began suffering great pain, but he performed there that night. The next day, doctors removed his appendix, but it was too late. His system had been poisoned.

Houdini in a familiar predicament.

Struggle ends for Socialist pioneer

Debs ran for president five times.

Oct 20. An era in American politics ended today, when Eugene V. Debs, perennial candidate for president on the Socialist Party ticket, died at age 71. Debs' passing comes at a time when the Socialist Party casts but a shadow of its former influence in the United States.

In 1900, 1904, 1908, 1912 and 1920, Debs ran for president. In 1912, touring the nation in his "Red Special" train, he told the people, "Every capitalist is your enemy. Every working man is your friend." In 1920, campaigning from jail after having been convicted for wartime sedition, he got 919,799 votes, his highest total. Released in 1920, his health broken, Debs' dream of a socialist America was still a dream.

First Paneuropean Congress meets

Oct 1. An idea created by Count Richard Nicholas Condenhove-Klergi, to bring the nations of Europe together as one body has come to fruition as representatives of 28 nations gathered in Vienna, Austria. Called the Paneuropean Congress, the assembly of countries intends to establish a line of communication to abolish economic and strategic barriers between European states. The congress will be presided over by Paul Lobe, leader of Germany's Reichstag.

Protesters threaten U.S. Paris Embassy

Oct 26. Anarchists and Communists threatened the American Embassy in Paris on learning Sacco and Vanzetti will not receive a retrial. Nicola Sacco and Bartolomeo Vanzetti, admitted anarchists, were tried for murder in Massachusetts five years ago. The world rallied to their defense, arguing American xenophobia led to a mistrial. Bowing to global pressures, the Governor has stayed their execution several times. Retrial was proposed when a condemned criminal said they were innocent (→ 4/9/27).

Hornsby is boss as Cards win series

Oct 10. Grover Cleveland Alexander took the mound for the Cardinals in the seventh with a 3-2 lead and three Yankees on base in the seventh game of the World Series. He struck out the next batter, Tony Lazzeri, retiring the side, and ended a 38-year series wait by St. Louis, now managed by Rogers Hornsby.

The stage had been set by three unearned runs in the fourth inning after a Babe Ruth solo homer in the third and a run-scoring St. Louis double in the sixth. When the Yanks filled the bases against Jesse Haines in the seventh, Hornsby, a player-manager, called his infield to a pitcher's-mound conference and Haines was sent to the showers.

Hornsby, who won six straight batting titles from 1920 to 1925 and hit a record .424 in 1924, was a star of the series with a double, four runs batted in and two runs scored. For Ruth, his seventh-inning homer was his fourth of this match with the Cardinals, setting a record for a single series.

Cards Manager "Rajah" Hornsby.

Garbo and Antonio Moreno in MGM's "The Temptress."

1926

NOVEMBER

Su	Mo	Tu	We	Th	Fr	Sa
	1	2	3	4	5	6
7	8	9	10	11	12	13
14	15	16	17	18	19	20
21	22	23	24	25	26	27
28	29	30				

1. Germany: Joseph Goebbels appointed head of Berlin NSDAP (→ 3/10/27).

2. Alfred Smith elected governor of New York State.

4. Prince Leopold and Princess Astrid wed in Stockholm.

9. British to import 15.4 million tons of coal to cover losses from strike, now totaling 300 million pounds sterling (→ 19).

12. Nationalists rise against Dutch in Java.

12. Nicaraguan Pres. Diaz asks U.S. aid in crushing Liberal Party's revolt (→ 1/5/27).

12. Rome: Duke of Marlborough and Consuelo Vanderbilt get marriage annuled by Catholic court.

14. Seven-car Chief starts daily train service between Los Angeles and Chicago.

15. New York: Shaw's "Pygmalion" hits Broadway.

18. "The Battleship Potemkin" opens at Paris theater.

18. London: George Bernard Shaw accepts Nobel Prize for literature, but turns down cash award.

19. New York: Adolph Zukor opens new Paramount Theater in Times Square.

19. British miners end strike without gaining settlement.

19. U.S.S.R.: Trotsky, Zinoviev expelled from Politburo (→ 6/10/27).

25. Italy: Mussolini reinstates capital punishment (→ 4/21/27).

27. Chicago: Army-Navy game at Soldiers Field ends in 21-21 tie.

30. U.S. warships sent to Hankow where Communists are said to threaten attack on foreigners (→ 1/1/27).

30. S. Romberg's operetta "The Desert Song" opens in New York

DEATHS

3. Annie Oakley, sharpshooter (*8/13/1860).

26. John Moses Browning, inventor of automatic rifle (*1/21/1855).

Queen heads home after dazzling U.S.

Marie, a Red Cross nurse in the war.

Nov 14. Queen Marie of Rumania must abandon her American tour. She has been warmly welcomed in the Midwest: the Sioux gave her an eagle headdress, cowboys lent her a horse at a rodeo and farmers offered their advice on growing corn in Rumania. The queen cuts her trip short at King Ferdinand's behest. He claims their country wants her home in time for Christmas, but it is also known that his majesty is growing very ill.

British Empire is changing character

Nov 20. In London today, King George V lost part of his title. Ireland and other members of the British Empire gained a little respect and authority.

George will still preside over the empire. But the Imperial Conference agreed that the term "United Kingdom" should be dropped from his title as Southern Ireland has left the kingdom.

The changes are more than cosmetic. The Irish Free State demanded, and received, equal status in the empire. And all members, or dominions, will now have greater authority to manage domestic affairs and international relations.

This is the third time that the monarch's title has been changed in the past 50 years, but George still has plenty to be proud of. His official title now reads, "George V, by the Grace of God, of Great Britain, Ireland, and the British Dominions Beyond the Seas King, Defender of the Faith, Emperor of India."

U.S. has highest living level ever

Nov 28. Americans are enjoying the highest standard of living in the nation's history, says Secretary of Commerce Herbert Hoover. His economic picture was drawn in a government report stating that wages are up and unemployment virtually nonexistent except in some textile mills in New England and some of the nation's coal mines.

With both production and consumption at an all-time high, he said, the nation has never enjoyed so much prosperity. Hoover also said that the economic situation represented a remarkable recovery from the nation's losses after the war in Europe. And he added that economic conditions abroad have improved, too.

Fascists impose rule with guns and blood

Nov 2. Following an attempt on Benito Mussolini's life by an 18-year-old boy, parades of angry Fascists throughout Italy have sworn a vendetta against all enemies. Secretary General Turati, addressing 50,000 of his black-shirted cohorts in Rome's Colonna Square, shouted, "Nothing short of death will satisfy us!" To which the huge throng responded, "Death! Hand over all of them!" The Duce, praised for his cool behavior following the attack, received thousands of sympathetic telegrams. And Pope Pius lauded his fortunate escape by saying: "This is a new sign that Mussolini has God's full protection" (→ 25).

Il Duce: "Believe, Obey, Fight!"

1926

DECEMBER

Su	Mo	Tu	We	Th	Fr	Sa
			1	2	3	4
5	6	7	8	9	10	11
12	13	14	15	16	17	18
19	20	21	22	23	24	25
26	27	28	29	30	31	

1. Canada: Ontario wets win, overturning Prohibition after 10-year fight.

1. Lita Grey leaves Charlie Chaplin, taking their two children.

3. British reports claim German soldiers being trained in U.S.S.R.

8. Chicago suffers 67 holdups in two days.

9. Wilson peace prize won by Elihu Root.

10. Chamberlain, Briand and Stresemann share Nobel Peace Prize.

12. W.V. Lawrence gives $1.25 mil. for founding of Sarah Lawrence College in Bronxville.

17. Dictatorship set up in Lithuania as revolution ousts government.

19. Washington: Court rules women authors must copyright under husband's name.

23. Twenty killed, 65 hurt as Florida trains crash head-on in Georgia.

29. Germany, Italy sign arbitration treaty.

DEATH

29. Raier Maria Rilke, Austrian poet (*12/4/1875).

CULTURAL EVENTS, 1926

Literature: Faulkner's "Soldier's Pay"; Hemingway's "The Sun Also Rises"; Kafka's "The Castle"; D.H. Lawrence's "The Plumed Serpent"; A.A. Milne's "Winnie the Pooh"; Book of the Month Club founded.

Academia: J.M. Keynes' "The End of Laissez Faire"; R.H. Tawney's "Religion and the Rise of Capitalism."

Music: Puccini's "Turandot," Milan; "When Day is Done"; "I Found a Million-Dollar Baby in the Five-and Ten-Cent Store"; "Bye, Bye Blackbird"; Duke Ellington's first recordings.

The Arts: Chagall's "Lover's Bouquet"; Henry Moore's "Draped Reclining Figure."

Films: Fritz Lang's "Metropolis"; Murmau's "Faust"; Niblo's "Ben Hur"; John Barrymore in "Don Juan."

Claude Monet is dead

Monet's "La Gare Saint-Lazare a Paris."

Dec 5. Claude Monet has died in his prime at the age of 86. His work of the last ten years, scenes of the garden and lily pond on his Giverny estate, may be his best. In them, with nearly sightless eyes, Monet seized the lush colors and ephemeral light he pursued all his life.

Monet was born in Le Havre, on the north coast of France, on Nov. 14, 1840. The sea was part of his childhood; he spent many adult years trying to paint the play of light on its surface. When he met Auguste Renoir and Alfred Sisley in the 1870's, he urged them to examine an object at different times of day, noting the colors dawn and dusk bring. His studies of the Rouen Cathedral, bathed in morning and evening light, typify those aims.

The artist's first 70 years were burdened with poverty. By 1883, however, he could afford the small estate in Northern France. "Giverny is a splendid country for me," he wrote in a letter last May. Joyous words from an artist in his prime.

The Hall-Mills trial ends in acquittal

Dec 3. New Jersey's longest, costliest and most sensational trial, the Hall-Mills murder case, has ended in acquittal. Mrs. Frances Stevens Hall was found not guilty of killing Mrs. Eleanor R. Mills. Her two brothers were also absolved.

More than four years ago, the bodies of Mrs. Mills and Mrs. Hall's husband, Edward, an Episcopal pastor, were found side by side with some love letters. Only one eyewitness testified and no juror believed her.

Jealousy was cited as the motive for the murder. Mrs. Hall was described as a woman who saw a younger one taking her husband away. Charges of murdering him will be dropped.

A mystery: Agatha Christie vanishes

Dec 14. She couldn't have written it better herself: Missing for nine days, Agatha Christie has been found alive and well and suffering from amnesia. On December 5, the mystery writer left her home in Berkshire, saying she would not return that day. The next morning her car was found at the edge of a precipice. Searchers fanned out for miles, but no trace of her was discovered. Her husband, Col. Archibald Christie, feared that she experienced a nervous breakdown. Today, Mrs. Christie was found under an assumed name at a Yorkshire health spa. Guests had noted nothing amiss in her behavior. Her husband prays for the swift restoration of her memory.

Bauhaus now in Dessau

Chairs by Mies Van der Rohe.

Desk lamp by Christian Dell.

Dec 4. Germany's famous Bauhaus school of art, architecture and design has influenced artists around the world. But it has had trouble finding a home in Germany. Forced to leave Weimar, the school opened its doors today in Dessau.

The Bauhaus philosophy is represented by the school's rectangular complex of shimmering steel and glass. Architect Walter Gropius, the Bauhaus leader, believes art is inseparable from function and craftsmanship. He also thinks artists should be well-versed in industrial production.

Wassily Kandinsky and Paul Klee are among the Bauhaus disciples. But many of the artists in the school have gone underground since right-wing politicians attacked Bauhaus as being too radical.

The vibrant colors of Bauhaus: Tapestry by Gunta Stolzl.

1927

JANUARY

Su	Mo	Tu	We	Th	Fr	Sa
						1
2	3	4	5	6	7	8
9	10	11	12	13	14	15
16	17	18	19	20	21	22
23	24	25	26	27	28	29
30	31					

1. Massachusetts becomes first state to require auto insurance.

1. China: Nationalist govt. established at Hankow (→ 5).

5. Coolidge lifts ban on arms to Nicaragua in to clear aid for Pres. Diaz (→ 12).

5. N.Y.: Fox Studios exhibits Movietone —new invention synchronizing sound and motion pictures (→ 10/6).

5. National Geographic publishes world's first underwater color pictures.

5. China: Rioters battle in streets of Hankow concessions, haul down British flag (→ 24).

9. Panic, fire kill 77 children in ten minutes in Montreal theater.

12. U.S. Sec. of State Kellogg claims Mexican rebel Plutarco Calles is aiding communist plot in Nicaragua (→ 2/6).

13. Woman takes seat on N.Y. Stock Exchange, breaking all-male tradition.

13. U.S. mobilizes Marines on Mexican border to back up claims on oil lands (→ 20).

15. Dumbarton bridge opens in San Francisco, carrying first auto traffic across bay.

17. Mexico: 100 killed as archbishop heads Catholic revolt (→ 3/18).

20. Mexico accepts arbitration on dispute with U.S. over oil-land ownership laws (→ 9/20).

20. France suspends naturalization laws in face of labor protests against foreign workers.

21. U.S. Supreme Court denies retrial in Scopes evolution case.

24. British expeditionary force of 12,000 sent to China to protect concessions at Shanghai (→ 31).

31. Inter-Allied military control ends in Germany according to Dawes Plan schedule (→ 9/12/28).

BIRTH

30. Olof Palme, Swedish statesman († 2/28/1986).

DEATH

9. Houston Stewart Chamberlain, German anti-Semitic theorist (*9/9/1855).

British troops go to China; Peking protests

Troops laden with supplies cross Westminster Bridge to debark for China.

Jan 31. Britain has ordered an army division of 12,000 men to proceed immediately to China to defend Shanghai and protect British nationals in the international city.

The British move came in the wake of rioting in the streets of Shanghai and seizure by Chinese coolies of the British concession in Hankow. Admidst this surge of nationalist protest against foreigners, Shanghai was threatened by the factional fighting wracking China. Cantonese or Nationalist forces headed by General Chiang Kai-shek were reported massing for an attack on Shanghai, where 40,000 foreigners reside. The Chinese government in Peking, controlled by the Northern faction, protested against the British military move as unnecessary and provocative, as did the government in Canton.

As the crisis mounted, the United States and Britain signaled their willingness to accede to Chinese demands by renegotiating treaties giving foreigners extra-territorial rights and limiting China's authority to establish tariffs (→ 2/3).

America is the land of the automobile

January. According to recently released statistics, there are nine million cars registered in the United States, a whopping 39 percent of the world's total. That global number has increased by eight million since 1924. There is one car for every six Americans. In England the ratio is one for every 57 people, and in Germany it is one for every 289.

Franklin Sport Coupe. Franklin was one of the first to offer six-cyl. engines.

Films better made but plots childish

January. The National Board of Review has finished screening a work called "Thirty Years of Motion Pictures." It showed film's technological advances: high-speed photography, depicting movement of microscopic organisms; special effects, making the parting of the Red Sea in "The Ten Commandments" so realistic; and close-up photography helping surgeons to teach interns. But what of intellectual progress? Film today, one board member said, is designed for the mentality of a 12 year old.

Garbo in "Flesh and the Devil," which premiered January 10.

Girl Scouts founder dies in Savannah

Mrs. Low and two of her proteges.

Jan 17. The founder of the Girl Scouts, Mrs. Juliette Low, died today in Savannah, Georgia. She was 67. In 1911, Mrs. Low consulted with Lady Baden Powell, founder of the British Girl Guides. The next year, Mrs. Low gathered 18 American girls to form the Girl Scouts. Today their number is 167,925 strong. Mrs. Low, whose life was marked by marital misfortune (her husband flaunted his mistress), encouraged girls to be resourceful. She designed all kinds of merit badges, from camping "Pioneer" to sky-high "Flyer."

1927

FEBRUARY

Su	Mo	Tu	We	Th	Fr	Sa
		1	2	3	4	5
6	7	8	9	10	11	12
13	14	15	16	17	18	19
20	21	22	23	24	25	26
27	28					

3. U.S. warships sent to China to protect nationals during uprising (→ 18).

6. Nicaraguan rebels seize and burn Chinandega (→ 21).

9. U.S. Senate drops World Court hopes as British reject terms of admission (→ 12/11).

9. France, Spain begin talks on spheres of influence in Morocco.

14. Earthquake engulfs southern Yugoslavia; 600 dead as lanslide hits Sarajevo.

16. Worst storm in California history kills 24 in San Francisco.

18. U.S., Canada establish diplomatic relations independently of Great Britain (→ 8/7).

18. China: Shanghai workers strike to aid approaching rebel army, demand removal of British troops (→ 19).

19. Chinese Nationalists gain reduction of British concessions at Hankow, Kiukiang (→ 22).

21. Pres. Diaz, plagued by rebel threat, asks U.S. to take virtual control over Nicaraguan affairs (→ 25).

24. U.S. Supreme Court upholds right of states to control KKK activities (→ 3/7).

25. Coolidge lends approval to British cruiser sent to Nicaragua yesterday (→ 5/4).

25. Coolidge vetoes McNary-Haugen farm bill; government would have bought agricultural surplus at inflated prices to sell on world market (→ 7/31).

25. Warsaw agreement allows free circulation of intl. traffic between Poland and autonomous city of Danzig.

26. Babe Ruth asks $200,000 over two years with Yankees.

BIRTHS

10. Leontyne Price, American operatic soprano.

19. Ernest Trova, widely exhibited American sculptor.

20. Hubert Taffin de Givenchy, French fashion designer.

DEATH

13. Brooks Adams, American historian (*6/24/1848).

Boy violinist in Paris after debut at 7

Feb 6. A new sensation had hundreds of music lovers on their feet applauding in Paris today. He is a violinist who seems to play his instrument almost as easily as a bird sings. His name is Yehudi Menuhin. And his fans are captivated and astounded because the virtuoso is only ten years old.

The young Menuhin selected a piece by a French composer, Edouard Lalo. And he played "Symphonie espagnole" for violin and orchestra flawlessly.

This was Menuhin's Paris debut, but not his first professional appearance. Three years ago, he played with the San Francisco Symphony Orchestra. Menuhin was born in the United States of Russian parents. He started listening to music before he was two years old. At age three, he asked to learn to play the violin. Now, he is paid $5,000 for a concert.

Young prodigy Yehudi Menuhin.

Portugal crushes short civil war

Feb 9. The new Portuguese government of General Antonio Carmona has survived its first revolution by crushing the various factions united in their determination to topple his dictatorship. These include disaffected military enemies and staunch democrats, neither being able to rule very long nor very effectively in a republic wracked since its founding in 1910 by an apparently endless chain of revolutions, military coups and counter-coups. Carmona himself came to power through an army coup last May. He has been Premier since July, and Executive Director since November.

Rebels in city trenches.

Chinese factions fight for Shanghai

Feb 22. Chinese Nationalist forces, headed by General Chiang Kai-shek, advanced on Shanghai after routing a Northern army holding Hangchow, a key rail and water center 113 miles northwest of Shanghai. The army of Marshal Sun Chuan-fang, one of the Northern war lords and provincial Governor of Shanghai, was reported beating a disorderly retreat toward the city, as the battle for Shanghai is shaping up as a crucial test in the civil war between the Nationalist and Peking governments for future control of China.

Chiang Kai-Shek, who over the past year has led his forces on a steady march northward from Southeastern China, was believed anxious to make a thrust at Shanghai before British troops arrived in force. Meanwhile, in the city, there was growing disorder. Prompted by the Nationalists, 65,000 workers staged a general strike that paralyzed tramway service. After rioting broke out, the police beheaded 20 strikers. The United States ordered more Navy ships and Marines to proceed to the city. Some 21 foreign warships are offshore in the Whangpoo River (→ 3/15).

Washington creates federal radio board

Feb 23. President Coolidge signed into law today a bill to regulate the nation's rapidly expanding network of radio stations. As provided in the bill, the president will appoint a Federal Radio Commission to classify all stations, assign wave lengths and to make such regulations necessary to assure that there will be no interference between stations.

The commission will be composed of five members, one from each of five zones into which the country will be divided. Not more than three members may be of the same party. The legislation prohibits the appointment of any one who has a financial interest in the manufacturing or sale of radio equipment or in the operation of "radio telegraphy, radio telephony or radio broadcasting" (→ 6/19/34).

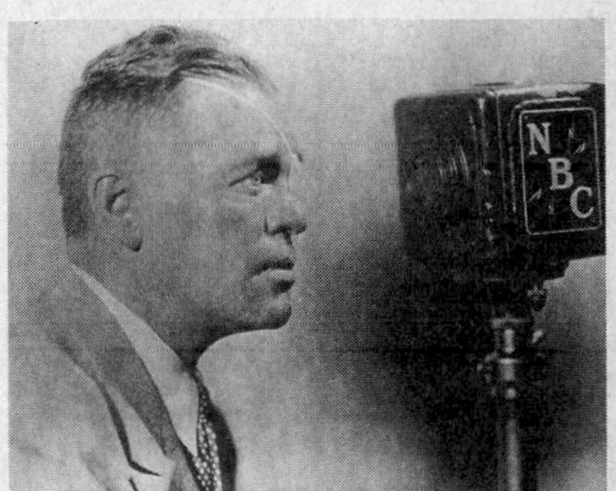

Floyd Gibbons, radio news pioneer.

London talks to Frisco by telephone

Feb 26. A new record for long-distance telephone service was set today when a line between San Francisco and London went into operation. The first call, at 9:05 a.m. San Francisco time (5:05 in the afternoon in London), was between H.D. Pillsbury, President of Pacific Telephone, and H. E. Shreeve, who represents American Telephone and Telegraph in London. Although they were 7,287 miles apart, both said they heard each other's words clearly. The number of calls between London and East Coast cities has been increasing rapidly, and a conference will be held soon on plans to extend service so that Americans will be able to call several major cities in Europe.

1927

MARCH

Su	Mo	Tu	We	Th	Fr	Sa
		1	2	3	4	5
6	7	8	9	10	11	12
13	14	15	16	17	18	19
20	21	22	23	24	25	26
27	28	29	30	31		

2. Alexander Kerensky, ex-head of provisional Russian govt., arrives in U.S. predicting overthrow of Soviets.

4. Cable line inaugurated, linking N.Y. and Emden, Germany.

5. Madagascar hurricane wrecks Tamatave, killing 600.

7. Texas law banning vote for Negroes held unconstitutional by Supreme Court (→ 2/12/28).

8. Japanese earthquake kills 1,700.

8. Pan American Airlines incorporated in New York (→ 10/28).

10. Germany: Prussia lifts Nazi ban; Hitler allowed to speak in public (→ 5/1).

10. Albania mobilizes against Yugoslav border threat (→ 6/4).

11. Roxy Theater holds gala opening in New York.

15. China: American warship fires on rebels near Shanghai (→ 21).

16. Elsie Eaves becomes first woman elected to American Society of Civil Engineers.

16. Washington: N.Y. oil man Harry Sinclair found guilty of contempt of Senate (→ 17).

17. U.S. Supreme Court returns disputed Teapot Dome and Elk Hills naval oil reserves to control of U.S. Navy (→ 10/10).

18. Mexico on verge of revolution with millions alienated by anti-clerical and anti-Red laws (→ 4/20).

21. China: British guard concession as Chiang's Cantonese troops take Shanghai.→

23. Washington: Capt. Hawthorne Gray sets U.S. balloon record, soaring to 28,510 feet.

24. Chinese Communists seize Nanking, break with Chiang over Nationalist goals (→ 4/11).

31. Philadelphia: Miners quit pits as strike begins in soft coal fields (→ 11/21).

BIRTHS

27. Mistislav Rostropovich, Russian-American cellist.

31. Cesar Chavez, migrant labor organizer.

Chiang takes Shanghai; Allies patrol city

U.S. naval forces in sparkling white return to Nanking after quelling riots.

March 21. Chiang Kai-shek's Nationalists entered Shanghai today in their victorious march north from Canton. They barely fired a shot as the Shantung forces scurried away in retreat. It was a major step forward for Chiang as he tries to unify both halves of the country.

For the past few days, agitators, apparently Communists, have been disrupting life in Shanghai as Chiang advanced. Today, a general strike was declared in the city, China's center of commerce.

There have been few disruptions in the international sector of Shanghai. An international naval fleet is anchored offshore, and 20,000 armed foreign troops are on patrol in Shanghai. Most are British, but there are also 4,000 American Marines and bluejackets and smaller Japanese and French forces.

The situation in China is becoming more confusing. Chiang's earlier seizure of Hankow has been compromised by a widening split between his supporters and Communists in the Kuomintang. New reports indicate the Communists have engineered a coup in Hankow (→ 24).

Clara Bow, the "It" girl, has that something extra, that unself-conscious energy that makes the modern young woman stand out in a crowd.

Vienna celebrates life of Beethoven

March 26. Vienna today honored the anniversary of the death of Ludwig van Beethoven with a general celebration and concerts featuring the great man's works. One hundred years ago, in a less happy mood, a Viennese funeral procession of 20,000 paid tribute to perhaps the greatest composer of all time, who reputedly died at the height of a thunderstorm after shaking his fist at heaven.

Ludwig van Beethoven.

Major Segrave sets record of 203 mph

Segrave tests the Golden Arrow.

March 29. Major H.O.D. Segrave came to America determined to drive his Sunbeam racer over the Daytona Beach course at more than 200 miles an hour. He surpassed his goal by setting a world record of 203.79 mph. And he eclipsed the old record, also held by a Briton, by 30 mph, reaching a top speed of 211. Segrave beat by 47 mph the best American time for the distance.

1927

APRIL

Su	Mo	Tu	We	Th	Fr	Sa
					1	2
3	4	5	6	7	8	9
10	11	12	13	14	15	16
17	18	19	20	21	22	23
24	25	26	27	28	29	30

5. Chicago Mayor Wm. Hale Thompson re-elected for third time.

6. Washington: Coolidge vetoes Filipino plebiscite calling for independence (→ 1/17/33).

7. Abel Gance's film "Napoleon" opens in Paris (→ 1/23/81).

7. Television broadcasts get successful tests in New York (→ 2/8/28).

9. Massachusetts: Death sentences for Nicolas Sacco and Bartolomeo Vanzetti are upheld (→ 8/6).

11. U.S., England, Japan, France and Italy demand reparations from Cantonese for abuses in Nanking (→ 12).

12. China: Chiang Kai-shek sets up Shanghai government, battles strikers as Reds and Nationalists split in Kuomintang (→ 15).

12. British Cabinet comes out in favor of voting rights for women 21 and over (→ 5/7/28).

13. U.S. rejects control of national defense policy by League of Nations.

15. China: New government in Nanking denounces Hankow; Chiang orders Michael Borodin and other Communist leaders seized (→ 19).

18. Baron Tanaka named premier of Japan.

19. China: Hankow Communists declare war on Chiang Kai-shek (→ 28).

20. One hundred slain or burned alive in Mexican train hold-up (→ 10/4).

21. Mussolini promulgates Fascist "work chart," turning Italy into corporative state (→ 3/30/28).

22. Tennessee flood kills 150, leaves 75,000 homeless (→ 30).

26. Virginia: Lieutenants Davis and Wooster killed in crash during test for non-stop N.Y. to Paris flight (→ 5/9).

DEATHS

15. Gaston Leroux, French writer, dectective stories (*5/6/1868).

27. Albert J. Beveridge, U.S. ex-senator.

Reds call strike in Shanghai as Chiang seizes city and sets up government

April 28. The decision by Chinese Communist labor leaders in Shanghai to call the second general strike in less than a month has sparked a violent confrontation with Chiang Kai-shek, who is setting up a new government in the city. His soldiers raided union strongholds early today. Both sides traded fire, and 16 people died.

The Shanghai strike has become a symbol of the increasing friction between Chiang's moderate supporters and Communists within the Nationalist Party. Foreign diplomats say there are added tensions in Shanghai because the more radical soldiers in Chiang Kai-shek's army support the strikers.

Chiang Kai-shek is trying to patch up the differences by inviting Communist leaders to a conference in Nanking. So far, they have not replied to his invitation (→ 5/27).

General Chiang Kai-shek (center) poses with two of his Nationalist comrades.

One man sets three swim marks in day

April 5. Johnny Weismuller, the swimming star from Windber, Pa., set three world records today and became the holder of every freestyle mark from 100 yards to a half-mile. In the 1924 Olympics, he won the 100-meter swim, in 59 seconds, and the 400-meter event, in 5:04.

Johnny Weismuller at 17.

Mississippi flood covers vast areas

April 30. New Orleans is fairly optimistic that floodwaters ravaging the Midwest will not reach its doors. The Mississippi River was breached 13 miles outside city limits when dynamite, set off at the Poydras levee, created an outlet. For the past three weeks, the river and its tributaries have destroyed countless communities in Missouri, Illinois, Kentucky, Tennessee, Iowa, Arkansas, Mississippi and northern Louisiana. Approximately 30 million acres are submerged. Over 200,000 people lost their homes.

Americans have donated $4 million to the Red Cross, but it is feared three times that total is needed for flood victims to start their lives anew. President Coolidge vetoed plans for Congress to raise funds, faulting congressional procedures for being too slow (→ 5/15/28).

De Mille spectacle: The King of Kings

De Mille directs from on high.

April. Cecil B. De Mille, director of a lavish "Ten Commandments," has followed it up with "The King of Kings." De Mille, son of playwrights, has been grinding out film epics since his 1914 six-reeler "The Squaw Man." He is often aided by his brother William, who advised actors in "King" to mind their morals on and offstage. "It would never do," he said, "to have the Virgin Mary getting a divorce or St. John cutting up in a nightclub."

Mae West guilty of sexy acting

April 19. Miss Mae West, author and leading player of "Sex," her Broadway production, has been found guilty of indecency. She was given a ten-day sentence and fined $500. The diminutive Miss West, who also produced "The Virgin Man," claimed police viewed the opening of "Sex" and could not fault it. But after a year's run, it was subject to Miss West's lewd improvisations. The court ordered it closed February 5 (→ 10/1/28).

Would you arrest this woman?

1927

MAY

Su	Mo	Tu	We	Th	Fr	Sa
1	2	3	4	5	6	7
8	9	10	11	12	13	14
15	16	17	18	19	20	21
22	23	24	25	26	27	28
29	30	31				

1. Adolf Hitler holds first NSDAP meeting in Berlin (→ 9/16).

4. U.S. supervises elections in Nicaragua, bringing civil war to a temporary halt (→ 6/14).

9. Captain Charles Nungesser lost over Atlantic during attempted France-New York flight (→ 21).

9. Canberra chosen as new Australian capital.

12. London: 150 British police raid Soviet Agency, seizing all documents (→ 24).

13. Germany suffers "Black Friday" economic collapse.

14. Paris: Actress Pola Negri weds Prince Serge Mdivani.

18. Louisiana: 15,000 Acadians reported fleeing from water avalanche over 30 feet high (→ 5/15/28).

18. Man known to have protested high taxes blows up school in Bath, Michigan, killing 42.

20. Britain acknowledges Saudi Arabian independence by dictates of Djeddah Treaty.

23. Paris awards Charles Lindbergh with Legion of Honor (→ 28).

24. U.K. breaks relations with U.S.S.R., charging Soviet plot to foster Communist revolt in Britain (→ 10/3/29).

26. U.S. Treasury Dept. to cut size of paper money by one-third.

27. China: Japanese intervene in Shantung, blocking Nationalist advance on Peking (→ 6/6).

27. Tomas Masaryk re-elected as Czech president.

28. Belgian King Albert decorates Charles Lindbergh (→ 31).

30. Igor Stravinsky's oratorio "Oedipus Rex" makes world debut.

30. Averaging 97.5 mph, George Souders wins 15th annual Indy 500 in Duesenberg racer.

31. King George receives Lindbergh in London (→ 6/13).

DEATHS

11. Juan Gris, Spanish painter, Cubism (*3/13/1887).

Charles Lindbergh flies Atlantic alone

Lindbergh soars over Paris in The Spirit of St. Louis, unaware of the hero's welcome waiting at Le Bourget.

May 21. Nearly 100,000 Parisians rushed onto the tarmac of Le Bourget Airport tonight to cheer a new international hero. Charles Lindbergh has touched ground safely, completing the first solo non-stop flight from New York to Paris.

Others have flown the Atlantic, but none have captured the public imagination as has this lanky, soft-spoken, 25-year-old aviator. When his Ryan NYP monoplane, the Spirit of St. Louis, landed after a 3,600-mile flight of more than 33 hours, not even two companies of French soldiers could keep the crowd from engulfing Lindbergh and his plane. Born in Detroit and raised in Minnesota, Lindbergh is the quintessential Midwesterner. He doesn't understand what all the fuss is about, and he's not sure he likes it.

Until a few weeks ago, Lindbergh was a dark horse in the hot race to win the $25,000 prize offered for the first non-stop flight from New York to Paris. Only his backers, St. Louis businessmen, believed in him. But he made a daring one-stop flight from California to New York to gain the lead over his rivals. Lindbergh took off from Roosevelt Field on Long Island at dawn yesterday, a departure making front-page news on both continents. Overloaded with gasoline, his plane sailed like a drunken seagull, barely clearing the trees at the end of the runway.

Alerted by newspaper and radio stories, thousands of spectators watched for Lindbergh's airplane as he flew north along the coast, turning westward over the Atlantic at St. John's, Newfoundland, at 7:15 p.m. New York time. From then on, Lindbergh flew by dead reckoning, sometimes dipping to within ten feet of the sea, sometimes climbing as high as 10,000 feet. The aviator stayed alert munching on a stash of five homemade sandwiches.

Lindbergh saw the lights of Paris at 10 p.m. and touched down at Le Bourget at exactly 10:24, setting off a celebration as non-stop as his flight. While a few may see his feat as a money-making stunt, to others it has greater implications: The future of aviation and air travel is prepared to soar (→ 23).

Man and machine: Lindbergh continually refers to his plane as a companion.

1927

JUNE

Su	Mo	Tu	We	Th	Fr	Sa
			1	2	3	4
5	6	7	8	9	10	11
12	13	14	15	16	17	18
19	20	21	22	23	24	25
26	27	28	29	30		

4. Jakarta: Indonesian Nationalist Party founded under Akhmed Sukarno (→ 11/13/45).

4. Belgrade: Yugoslavia severs diplomatic relations with Albania.

5. Bucharest: King Ferdinand of Rumania ousts Averescu Cabinet (→ 7/20).

6. Relations broken between U.S.S.R. and Chiang Kai-shek's Nanking government (→ 17).

7. Clarence Chamberlain and Charles Levine end transatlantic flight, landing Bellanca Columbia plane in Berlin 43 hrs. in air from N.Y.

10. Bolsheviks execute 20 in Moscow for alleged counter-revolutionary activities (→ 8/19).

12. Guglielmo Marconi, 57-year-old inventor of wireless, weds Countess Maria Cristina Bezzi-Scali in Rome.

13. French authorities arrest Leon Daudet, royalist leader of Action Francaise.

14. President Diaz signs treaty with U.S. to allow American intervention in Nicaragua (→ 7/25).

15. Belgrade: Yugoslav King Alexander dissolves Parliament, orders elections (→ 1/6/29).

16. U.S.: Charles Lindbergh presented with $25,000 Orteig prize for first non-stop, transatlantic flight (→ 1/6/28).

20. U.S. urges 5-5-3 naval ratio at Geneva arms parley (→ 7/9).

23. Dublin: Dail (Irish Parliament) re-elects William T. Cosgrave as its chief.

27. U.S. Marines take on English bulldog as new mascot.

27. Tokyo conference opens in attempt to settle Sino-Japanese dispute.

29. Britons in northern England witness total eclipse of the sun.

30. Commander Byrd, from plane over Atlantic, radios Washington in longest message yet (→ 7/1).

DEATH

14. Jerome K. Jerome, British humorist, "Three Men in a Boat" (*5/2/1859).

15 millionth "Tin Lizzie" is produced

May 26. The 15 millionth Model T made by the Ford Motor Company rolled off the assembly line today at the River Rouge plant near Detroit. Although the "Tin Lizzie" is the most successful automobile ever made, sales have been declining because of competition from more modern autos. There are rumors that Henry Ford plans to replace the Model T with a new and better car in the near future (→ 12/1).

End of the line for Model T?

Paris is featuring boyish fashions

New fashions for women.

May. The new woman is becoming one of the boys. Paris fashions are reducing bustlines and emphasizing slim hips. The narrowness is accented by big belts that look tempted to slip down to the ankles. This stylish simplicity agrees with the new woman: whether skier, aviator or homemaker, she demands freedom of movement.

Chang Tso-lin acts to block revolution

Chang Tso-lin.

June 17. China's Northern warlords, under siege on two fronts, have united to approve a plan to give Chang Tso-lin dictatorial powers in Peking. Chang Tso-lin was already considered the most powerful of the Northern generals. Now, he will have command of all Northern armies, the Shantung, Chihli and Manchurian forces.

Chang Tso-lin's official new title will be "Generalissimo of the forces for the suppression of Communism." He hopes to tighten the noose around radical forces under the control of Chinese and Russian generals holed up in Hankow.

Chang Tso-lin also has to contend with the more moderate forces from the South which are under the control of Chiang Kai-shek. Negotiations between the two sides collapsed after the Northerners charged that the Southerners "did not show the necessary sincerity." Chiang Kai-shek is intent upon invading Shantung (→ 8/14).

Gehrig hits three homers in one day

June 23. Lou Gehrig jogged the calm of a balmy summer afternoon in Boston by blasting three home runs in one game in leading the New York Yankees to an 11-4 triumph over the Red Sox.

Gehrig became the second Yankee to perform the feat this season but only the 20th major leaguer ever to turn the trick. He is only three homers behind the mighty Babe Ruth, who has smacked 24 round-trippers for the season.

The Babe has said that Gehrig is the only player capable of reaching Ruth's record total of 59 in a season. And Columbia Lou's homers carried all of the authority of the second Ruthian smash in yesterday's second game, which was literally out of sight.

Gehrig at batting practice.

One homer cleared the fence in left center. Another was a line drive that exploded into the right center field seats. The third was an arching gem that soared high into the stands in left center. Gehrig's heroics helped the Yanks to win the 20th of their last 24 games. His output was part of a 15-hit attack against two Boston hurlers.

Miss Florida wins at this month's intl. contest in Galveston, Texas.

"Lucky Lindy" given a hero's welcome

Lindbergh is showered with ticker tape on the streets of New York.

June 13. Charles A. Lindbergh was given a hero's welcome when he came home after his historic transatlantic solo flight. As the "Lone Eagle" sailed through the Virginia Capes aboard the cruiser Memphis, he was met by four destroyers, more than 40 airplanes and cheering crowds along the banks of Chesapeake Bay. "I am glad to be home again," he said simply. Captain Lindbergh also met with President Coolidge in Washington, where he was decorated with the Flying Cross. And today, there was a big parade in New York City, where "Lindy" was showered with ticker tape (→ 16).

Lizzie Borden dies a peaceful death

June 2. "Lizzie Borden took an ax
And gave her mother forty whacks.
When she saw what she had done,
She gave her father forty-one!"

That was a popular rhyme in the 1890's after Lizzie (Miss Lisbeth A. Borden) was acquitted of murdering her father and step-mother in Fall River, Massachusetts. Their mutilated bodies were found August 4, 1892, after Lizzie had rushed into the house of a neighbor and reported her father dead. Lizzie was subsequently arrested, and her trial was one of the most celebrated in New England. Famous lawyers appeared on both sides of the case.

Andrew J. Borden was rich. The prosecution argued that Lizzie believed her stepmother might get a large share of the fortune, and killed her parents to ensure that she and her sister would inherit it all. Lizzie denied everything, and the ax was never found. Today, a virtual recluse, she died at 68.

Army fliers cross Pacific to Hawaii

June 29. Two Army fliers, Lts. Lester Maitland and Albert Hegenberger, completed the longest ocean flight on record today when they set down in Hawaii after a 2,400-mile trip from California. It was also the first flight from the continental United States to Hawaii.

The aviators took off from Oakland at 7:09 a.m. yesterday and landed at Wheeler Field on the island of Oahu at 8:59 Pacific time this morning, a total flying time of just under 26 hours. They said the only trouble they encountered was when one engine of their Fokker trimotor airplane ran irregularly for a time in the early hours of the morning. Although plans had been made to guide the flight by radio beacons from San Francisco and Hawaii, the aviators had to make the trip by dead reckoning because their radio malfunctioned several times. Maitland and Hegenberger have declined a newspaper offer of $10,000 for exclusive rights to their story.

1927

JULY

Su	Mo	Tu	We	Th	Fr	Sa
					1	2
3	4	5	6	7	8	9
10	11	12	13	14	15	16
17	18	19	20	21	22	23
24	25	26	27	28	29	30
31						

1. Commander Byrd picked up 120 miles from Paris after plane downed in ocean.

4. Wimbledon: Henri Cochet over Jean Borotra 4-6, 4-6, 6-3, 6-4, 7-5 in all-French men's final; Helen Wills over Lili De Alvarez 6-2, 6-4 in women's final.

9. Washington: Trade Commission finds producers Lasky and Zukor guilty of film trust conspiracy.

9. Germany: Saxony devastated by hurricane; 150 dead, 359 injured.

9. Geneva parley stalled as U.S. angers U.K., proposing boost in large cruiser limit to 25 (→ 8/4).

10. N.Y.: Giant army bomber carrying six machine guns tested successfully at Mitchell Field.

10. Irish Free State V.P. Kevin O'Higgins killed on way to church by I.R.A. assassins.

12. One thousand now dead in Palestine earthquake.

16. Aaron Sapiro gains out-of-court settlement in libel suit against Henry Ford.

17. Luxembourg bicycle racer Nicolas Frantz tops the field in Tour de France.

20. Five-year-old Michael I assumes Rumanian throne as King Ferdinand I dies after long illness (→ 21).

21. Ex-Crown Prince Carol, from Paris exile, proclaims himself king of Rumania (→ 30).

21. N.Y.: Jack Dempsey, in a bout before 80,000 in Yankee Stadium, floors Jack Sharkey in seventh round (→ 2/1/28).

27. Reports indicate malaria, tuberculosis and trachoma are ravaging wide areas in U.S.S.R.

30. Paris: Crown Prince Carol, rebuked in Rumania, asserts right to throne (→ 10/25).

31. Coolidge tells South Dakota audience he favors $300 million fund to aid farmers (→ 5/23/28).

BIRTHS

4. Gina Lollobrigida, Italian actress.

4. Neil Simon, American playwright.

Sandino lays trap for U.S. Marines

Sandino, rebel leader in Nicaragua.

July 25. For the second time in a week, United States Marines and Nicaraguan regular troops have been ambushed by General Augusto Sandino's rebel forces. But U.S. Major Floyd's troops routed the attackers and even succeeded in killing and wounding a few.

Today's skirmish occurred near San Fernando, 20 miles from Ocotal, the village where five few days ago a group of Marines, aided by bombing aircraft, fought a 17-hour defense and killed 300 of Sandino's men. More raids with aircraft are expected to be launched soon.

Sandino recently issued a defiant proclamation, denouncing President Coolidge and warning of future rebel conquests in Nicaragua (→ 9/19).

Dempsey over Sharkey in seven.

Nationwide revolt breaks out in Austria

Christian Socialist poster depicts the burning of the Palace of Justice.

July 15. In Austria tonight, the city of Vienna is a tinder box. Fire has already destroyed the Palace of Justice. Gunshots are echoing throughout the city, bodies are piling up in the streets and leftists are calling for the resignation of Chancellor Ignaz Seipel's government.

The trouble started when three members of the Veterans' Movement were acquitted of charges resulting from a confrontation with the Republican Defense League. The veterans were accused of striking a worker and a child. As soon as the verdict was announced, workers went on strike and poured into the streets. Some of them occupied the University of Vienna, considered a center for Nazi activity. Others seized the Palace of Justice and set it on fire.

Police acted swiftly to control the riots. They opened fire on the strikers. At least 89 people were killed. More than 600 were injured.

Leaders of the Social Democratic Party are capitalizing on the extremely tense situation by calling for the resignation of Austrian Chancellor Seipel. The Social Democrats accuse him of tolerating the illegal activities of the veterans. Monsignor Seipel, a fervent anti-socialist who survived an attack on his life three years ago, shows no signs of capitulating.

Vienna newspapers are accusing Moscow of inciting the riots. An editorial in Frankfurt says Austria should be annexed to Germany if the troubles continue (→ 12/5/28).

1927

AUGUST

Su	Mo	Tu	We	Th	Fr	Sa
	1	2	3	4	5	6
7	8	9	10	11	12	13
14	15	16	17	18	19	20
21	22	23	24	25	26	27
28	29	30	31			

2. Pres. Coolidge announces he will not run in 1928 (→ 5/27/28).

3. Berlin and Buenos Aires linked by wireless for first time.

4. Geneva naval parley ends in stalemate (→ 7).

6. Massachusetts high court hears final plea from Sacco and Vanzetti; protest bombs hit homes of Baltimore mayor, Boston juror (→ 9).

7. Dawes opens "peace bridge" over Niagara Falls, linking Canada and U.S.; criticizes failure of Geneva talks (→ 11/30).

9. Rome: Father of Nicolas Sacco appeals to Duce to save son from execution (→ 21).

10. Pres. Coolidge dedicates unfinished Mt. Rushmore to Washington, Jefferson, Lincoln and Roosevelt (→ 1/1942).

12. Aviators A. Goebel and Wm. Davis win $25,000 Dole Derby, reaching Hawaii from mainland; 12 have died in competition.

14. China: Chiang resigns Nanking command (→ 12/1).

19. U.S.S.R.: Orthodox Church recognizes legitimacy of Soviet state.

21. U.S. Supreme Court Justice Brandeis refuses to hear request for stay of execution in Sacco and Vanzetti case (→ 23).

22. Los Angeles: Lita Grey wins $825,000 in divorce from Charlie Chaplin.

24. Moscow censors opera star Feodor Chaliapin for collaboration with exiles (→ 10/23).

25. 129 dead in Japanese military disaster, as four warships crash during night maneuvers.

27. Bill Brock, piloting Pride of Detroit in round-world flight, sighted over London (→ 9/4).

27. Thousands turn out in Paris for violent protests over death of Sacco and Vanzetti (→ 9/4).

BIRTH

13. Fidel Castro, Cuban revolutionary leader.

DEATH

7. General Leonard Wood, American gov. of Philippines (*10/9/1860).

Edison marks 50th year of phonograph

Aug 12. Thomas Alva Edison today celebrated the 50th anniversary of the invention of the phonograph by reciting "Mary Had a Little Lamb," the nursery rhyme he recorded on his first talking machine, in a broadcast from his laboratory at West Orange, New Jersey. Edison recalled that the idea of the phonograph came to him when he used a disk to record telegraph transmissions. "All I had to do was substitute a diaphragm with a point to record the voice," he said.

1903 model, after the 18th patent.

Elbert Gary, boss of U.S. Steel, dies

Aug 15. Judge Elbert H. Gary, the powerful head of the United States Steel Corporation, died yesterday at his home on Fifth Avenue in New York City. The 80-year-old steel baron had been in poor health for some time. He died of what his doctors described as "chronic myocarditis." A former county judge in his native Wheaton, Illinois, Gary became a leader in building up the steel empire over which he presided. The town of Gary, Indiana, site of large steel plants, was named for him.

While opposed to labor unions, Gary led successful moves to assure better pay for workers and to reduce work hazards. Just recently, he wrote an editorial, to appear in the next issue of Coal Age, saying that safety equipment had resulted in cutting serious accidents in the workplace by more than 60 percent. While his salary was reported to be only about $100,000 a year, his wealth was said to be more than $25 million.

Sacco and Vanzetti die

Innocent or guilty, Sacco and Vanzetti have polarized the country.

Aug 23. Their long fight for freedom over, Nicola Sacco and Bartolomeo Vanzetti walked calmly to death in the electric chair early this morning in Massachusetts. The two Italian-born anarchists were convicted six years ago of murdering a paymaster and a guard of a shoe factory during a payroll holdup in South Braintree, Massachusetts.

In the years since then, theirs has been a cause celebre throughout much of the world, with thousands of persons, loudly proclaiming their innocence, holding demonstrations.

As he seated himself in the electric chair shortly after midnight, Sacco cried out: "Long live anarchy." He was dead a few minutes later. Mere seconds later, Vanzetti was led from his cell to the chair. He made a statement, declaring that he was innocent, and then spoke his final words: "I wish to forgive some people for what they are now doing to me" (→ 27).

Calvin Coolidge will not run in 1928

Aug 2. With 12 words, taciturn Calvin Coolidge put an end to speculation over his future political career. In Rapid City, South Dakota, at 9:32 this morning, he handed reporters a slip of paper that read: "I do not choose to run for President in nineteen twenty-eight."

The President has never been one to mince words. At a baseball game once, his only utterance through nine innings was directed at his wife: "What time is it?" he asked.

"Four twenty-four," she replied.

Coolidge is scheduled to be made an honorary Sioux chief at a ceremony later this week. It just might leave him speechless (→ 5/27/28).

Java man may be the missing link

Consensus is growing that "Java man," pithecanthropus erectus, is the earliest human forbear. The first fossils were found in 1891, and a complete skull was unearthed in September last year. The ensuing analysis took months. Java man lived 500,000 years ago in what is today Central Java. It had a brain capacity slightly superior to that of an ape, which suggests it is the link sought in the evolutionary chain.

The main human types are the Neanderthal, found near Dusseldorf, Germany, and the more advanced Cro-Magnon, found in Southern France. No one is sure which is the most direct human ancestor.

1927

SEPTEMBER

Su	Mo	Tu	We	Th	Fr	Sa
				1	2	3
4	5	6	7	8	9	10
11	12	13	14	15	16	17
18	19	20	21	22	23	24
25	26	27	28	29	30	

4. World fliers reach Karachi, India (→ 9).

4. Germany: U.S. consular attache Steger shot in Dresden; police suspect Sacco sympathizer.

6. U.S. movie houses close across country to mourn death of film mogul Marcus Loew.

8. U.K.: Television inventor John Baird sends own image, Leeds to London (→ 1/13/28).

9. World fliers reach Hong Kong, leave for Shanghai (→ 14).

9. Italy: New York Mayor Jimmy Walker visits Pope and Mussolini (→ 3/18/31).

10. French team of Jean Borotra, Henri Cochet, Jacques Brugnon and Rene Lacoste take Davis Cup for first time (→ 7/31/32).

12. U.S. Sec. of State Kellogg states League has no authority in Panama Canal zone affairs.

13. Tidal waves hit Japanese coast, killing 700.

14. Storms force world fliers to drop Pacific hop and return to U.S. by steamer.

15. Geneva: Belgium loses post in League of Nations Council.

16. Berlin: Pres. Hindenburg repudiates Germany's responsibility for Great War (→ 3/5/28).

19. Las Flores: Sandino rebel forces make first big attack on Nicaraguan regime (→ 1/1/28).

19. Paris: Crowds turn out by the thousands for American Legion parade.

20. Coolidge names Dwight Morrow as envoy to Mexico to negotiate settlement on oil lands (→ 11/17).

21. Ground broken at Ft. Lee for George Washington bridge across Hudson River (→ 10/24/31).

23. Chicago: Am. Assn. for Medico-Physical Research says cigarette smoking by mothers kills 60% of babies in infancy.

23. Ago von Maltzann, German ambassador to U.S., killed in Berlin plane crash.

26. "Loves of Carmen," with Dolores del Rio, opens in N.Y.

26. Cuba declares San Juan Hill a national park.

Tunney battered but keeps title

Sept 22. Jack Dempsey failed in his effort to dethrone Gene Tunney and regain the world heavyweight title because he ignored a simple rule of boxing. He failed to return to a neutral corner after flooring Tunney and lost five or six seconds of the knockout count.

From the verge of being knocked out, Tunney fought back and won a unanimous decision at Soldiers Field in Chicago. Dempsey said he would appeal the verdict to the Illinois Boxing Commission. "I was robbed of the championship," he said after the fight, whose outcome will undoubedly be debated by boxing enthusiasts for decades.

A long count.

Tunney won seven of the ten rounds, losing only the third, sixth and seventh. It was in the seventh that Dempsey committed his faux pas. In a last-ditch thrust, the heavier Dempsey sent Tunney sprawling to the canvas. The timekeeper delayed his count until Dempsey returned to a neutral corner and the usual ten-second count spanned 15 or more seconds (→ 7/25/28).

Isadora Duncan is strangled by scarf

Sept 14. Isadora Duncan, who modernized dance by evoking ancient Greece, died tonight in Nice. The 47-year-old dancer was strangled when her scarf caught in a spinning automobile wheel. Her life was one long tragedy, from the drownings of her two illegitimate children to the suicide of her husband, poet Sergei Essenin. Despite the traumas, Duncan still danced, unshod and barely clad.

The Babe hits his 60th

Sept 30. George Herman "Babe" Ruth, holder of the World Series record for consecutive scoreless innings pitched, added to his legend by smashing his 60th home run of the season, a plateau never before achieved in baseball history.

As a forlorn Boston southpaw pitcher watched, the ball soared into the bleacher seats of Yankee Stadium, and the Babe jogged around the bases, carefully stomping each one so as not to invalidate his feat. The pitcher knew that his name of Thomas Jonathan Walton Zachary would live in baseball infamy.

Let the record show that Ruth's three hits accounted for all four of the Yankee runs on this autumn day. The wildly cheering fans were more concerned with the fact they were sitting in on history. The home run surpassed by one the record set by the Babe in 1921. Homer 60 hats were tossed in the air, torn papers were cast on the field and handkerchiefs waved in celebration. The Babe acknowledged it all after the inning with a snappy salute from the outfield.

The Babe at bat.

In 5 minutes wind kills 69, injures 600

Sept 30. A ninety-mile-per-hour tornado devastated the affluent west side of St. Louis today. Winds left 600 injured and 69 dead. The death count may rise as high as 100 when all debris has been cleared. On the six square miles affected, 5,000 homes were destroyed. Many of the toppled houses and factories were supposedly stormproof. Damages may total $75 million.

A violent rainstorm accompanied the twister. Strange sheets of flame were seen swirling within its currents. Uprooted, huge trees were hurled like missiles. Telephone poles snapped in half. Children poured into the streets, screaming for their mothers. As soon as the storm subsided, the St. Louis chief of police issued an order for all looters to be shot on sight.

St. Louis traffic inches through debris-crowded streets in the aftermath.

1927

OCTOBER

Su	Mo	Tu	We	Th	Fr	Sa
						1
2	3	4	5	6	7	8
9	10	11	12	13	14	15
16	17	18	19	20	21	22
23	24	25	26	27	28	29
30	31					

1. U.S.S.R. signs non-aggression pact with Persia.

3. Los Angeles: W.C. Fields breaks vertebrae in bicycle crash during comedy scene.

4. Gen. Francisco Serrano and 13 aides executed for attempting to seize Mexican presidency (→ 10).

6. New York Stock Exchange inaugurates world stock mart.

8. New York: Yankees take World Series in four straight games over Pirates.

10. Washington: Teapot Dome Naval Oil Reserve restored to govt. ownership (→ 2/21/28).

10. Mexico: Gomez rebel army routed in six-hour battle; 50 slain (→ 22).

15. Iraqis discover oil in Kirkuk.

16. London: Dorothy Cochrane Logan admits fabricating time for last week's English Channel swim; Gertrude Ederle still holds record.

17. Norway's first Labor government takes over in Oslo.

22. Mexican rebel leader Gen. Gomez reportedly escapes into Guatemala (→ 11/23).

25. Rumanians uncover plot to restore Crown Prince Carol as king; martial law declared on boy-king's birthday (→ 5/6/28).

27. Fox Movie-tone News, world's first sound news film, released in N.Y. (→ 3/10/28).

28. Pan Am Airways launches world's first scheduled intl. flight—Key West to Havana in one hr., 10 min. (→ 1/16/28).

29. Russian archaeologist Peter Kozloff uncovers tomb of Genghis Khan in Gobi Desert.

30. France bolsters Little Entente, completing defense treaty with Yugoslavia.

BIRTHS

7. R.D. Laing, British theorist, existential psychiatry.

16. Gunther Grass, German writer, "The Tin Drum."

DEATH

5. Sam L. Warner, American movie pioneer (*8/10/1887).

Stalin rids party of Trotsky, Zinoviev

Zinoviev, out with Trotsky.

Oct 23. In the Soviet Union, Joseph Stalin tightened his control on the Communist Party leadership today by expelling Leon Trotsky and Grigori Zinoviev from the Central Committee. After the death of Lenin, Zinoviev and Stalin were two members of the triumvirate that ruled the Soviet Union. More recently, however, Zinoviev has joined Trotsky in criticizing Stalin's economic programs as being counterrevolutionary (→ 12/2).

Ruth Elder fails in transatlantic flight

Oct 13. Ruth Elder, a 23-year-old pilot, failed to cross the Atlantic today but set a long-distance oversea record. She and her co-pilot flew 2,623 miles from Roosevelt Field, L.I., to an ocean location 520 miles west of Portugal. Their plane, The American Girl, dove into the Atlantic when its oil line broke. The craft caught fire and sank in seconds. The fliers, who escaped harm, were rescued by a tanker.

Elder failed but was rescued.

Al Jolson in first talkie

Oct 6. Al Jolson stars in "The Jazz Singer," a talking film that opens today. The rendering is slightly mechanical, with less clarity than a telephone transmission. Movement of the actors is not faithfully reflected in their voices; sound never fades in or out as on radio. Still, it is a first.

The plot of "Jazz Singer" partially reflects Jolson's real life. Like his character, Jolson comes from a Jewish family that frowned on a jazz-singing career. Estrangement from his parents and ensuing success are the tensions that move this motion picture. Jolson gives a feeling rendition of the hymn "Kol Nidre" and sings "Mammy" passionately in blackface. Warner Oland and Eugenie Besserer play the parents (→ 27).

The Warners' marquee in New York.

Russian-born Jolson in blackface.

Italian liner sinks; 1170 of 1238 saved

Oct 26. Carrying more than 800 Italian immigrants bound for the promised land of South America, the Italian liner Principessa Mafalda now lies at the bottom of the Atlantic Ocean off the Brazilian coast. Rescue vessels have saved all but 68 of the 1,238 passengers and crew members. Anticipating their arrival in Rio de Janeiro, the immigrants aboard the Mafalda began to celebrate after last night's supper. When the ship ground to a halt following an explosion in the boiler room, the high spirits turned to tears and trembling as the passengers hit the main deck in frantic quest of lifeboats and life preservers.

The team of Browning and Chaney have produced Hollywood's scariest.

1927

NOVEMBER

Su	Mo	Tu	We	Th	Fr	Sa
		1	2	3	4	5
6	7	8	9	10	11	12
13	14	15	16	17	18	19
20	21	22	23	24	25	26
27	28	29	30			

3. New York: "A Connecticut Yankee," music by Richard Rodgers, opens on Broadway.

5. Tennessee: Balloonist Capt. Gray found dead in treetops, killed by lack of oxygen or cold at 44,000 feet.

7. Cold wave hits as New England flood waters begin to recede after killing 150; Army called in to aid victims.

12. New York: Holland Tunnel officially opened to traffic.

12. China: Gen. Tang Shen-tse, in retreat from Chiang troops, sets fire to Hankow (→ 12/1).

15. Canada admitted to League of Nations.

16. Washington: White House and grounds valued at $22m.

17. Under pressure from U.S., Mexican Supreme Court rules Petroleum Law unconstitutional; oil lands to revert to corporate ownership (→ 12/25).

18. Bogota: Colombia nationalizes oil industry.

21. Police turn machine guns on Colorado mine strikers, killing five and wounding 20.

21. New York metropolitan area widened to include population of 9.5 million.

22. N.Y. enjoys premiere of Gershwin musical "Funny Face."

23. N.Y.: 11-year-old violinist Yehudi Menuhin makes debut.

24. Troops battle 1,200 inmates after Folsom Prison revolt kills nine.

26. Polo Grounds: Army over Navy 14-9 in football.

26. Berlin eases tension in Europe, disavowing aid for Soviet ambitions in Lithuania.

29. Soviets suppress Ukraine revolt; 5,000 dead in three months of fighting.

29. Buenos Aires: Jose Capablanca loses world chess title to Russian Alexander Alekhine.

30. Geneva: Soviet Commissar Litvinov proposes immediate and total disarmament; plan rejected as Communist trick (→ 12/17).

30. Price for new Ford auto jumps from $385 to $570.

G.M.'s dividend is biggest in history

Chevy, a big seller for G.M.

Nov 10. Wall Street let out a collective cheer today as General Motors declared the largest dividend in the nation's history. The total disbursement to those holding the 17.4 million shares of stock was $65,250,000. The action reflects what corporation officials termed the automobile company's strong cash position (→ 2/18).

Marcus Garvey has sentence commuted

Nov 23. President Coolidge has commuted the prison sentence of Marcus Garvey, the self-styled "Provisional President of Africa."

Garvey, a controversial Negro colonizer, has been imprisoned in Atlanta Penitentiary since 1925 after his conviction on a charge of using the mails to defraud. He will be deported to Jamaica as an undesirable alien.

As leader of what he called a "Back to Africa" movement, Garvey was accused of collecting more than a million dollars to finance ships in which to transport Negroes out of the United States. Government prosecutors charged that investors in the scheme received only "an old steamer or two."

Garvey, still seeking Negro republic.

Helen Hayes leads theater hit parade

Vibrant young Helen Hayes.

Nov 30. Broadway is booming. Miss Helen Hayes, who played the ultimate flirt, Cleopatra, in Shaw's "Caesar and Cleopatra" two years ago, returns as another ill-fated lover in "Coquette." Three weeks ago, it opened to a packed house.

"A Connecticut Yankee," adapted faithfully and irreverently from Mark Twain's book about a New Englander at King Arthur's Court, looks as successful as "Coquette." The Rodgers and Hart musical opened November 2. At one point during the show, a peasant wears a sandwich board advertising a popular play: "Ye Hiberian Rose of Abie." The jibe is directed at "Abie's Irish Rose," which closed a month before "Yankee" started. The comedy romance between an Irish girl and a Jewish boy ran for five years and five months, setting a new Broadway record.

Teenage Moroccan ruler shows his muscle

White-robed Sultan of Morocco.

Nov 20. Morocco has a new Sultan. Moulay Hamada is only a teenager, but he is already calling himself Moulay Mohammed. He lays claim to great wisdom. The Moslem leaders who selected Moulay Hamada to succeed his father, Moulay Youssef, realize that he is too young to provide his country with all the spiritual guidance it needs. So they have asked the Grand Vizier, El Mokri, to head a regency council. Like his late father, Moulay Hamada will hold only religious powers in the North African country. The French, of course, control the politics.

Nov 23. Luis Vilchis, a priest and two others, implicated in the Nov. 13 failed bomb attack on Pres. Obregon, die before a Mexican firing squad.

1927

DECEMBER

Su	Mo	Tu	We	Th	Fr	Sa
				1	2	3
4	5	6	7	8	9	10
11	12	13	14	15	16	17
18	19	20	21	22	23	24
25	26	27	28	29	30	31

1. Sec. of Commerce Herbert Hoover pronounces U.S. wages highest in world at $1,280/year.

2. U.S.S.R.: XVth Communist Party Congress opens, confirming exclusion of Stalin's opponents (→ 1/10/28).

2. New Ford Model A introduced to American public.

10. Nobel Prize for Literature to Henri Bergson.

11. 395 world leaders sign letter to Coolidge asking U.S. to join World Court (→ 12/9/29).

12. Coolidge approves five-year, bil. dollar Navy bill (→ 9/28/28).

12. China: Communists seize Canton (→ 19).

14. Great Britain recognizes Iraq's independence.

17. U.S. Sec. of State Kellogg suggests worldwide pact renouncing war (→ 1/4/28).

25. Mexican Congress opens land to foreign investors, reversing 1917 ban enacted to preserve domestic economy (→ 3/27/28).

27. Ziegfeld's "Show Boat" opens on Broadway with music by Jerome Kern.

CULTURAL EVENTS, 1927

Literature: Virginia Woolf's "To the Lighthouse"; Sinclair Lewis' "Elmer Gantry"; Thornton Wilder's "The Bridge of San Luis Rey"; Herman Hesse's "Steppenwolf"; Upton Sinclair's "Oil."

Academia: John Dewey's "The Public and its Problems"; Heidegger's "Being and Time"; Heisenberg proposes "uncertainty principle"; Hermann J. Muller finds X-rays create mutations; Belgian Georges Lemaitre publishes "big bang" theory.

Music: Stravinsky's "Oedipus Rex"; "Ol' Man River" from "Show Boat"; "My Blue Heaven"; "Blue Skies."

The Arts: Edward Hopper's "Manhattan Bridge"; Matisse's "Figures with Ornamental Background."

Film: "Flesh and the Devil," Garbo; "The Jazz Singer," Jolson; De Mille's "King of Kings"; Academy of Motion Picture Arts and Sciences founded.

Chiang married to Sun's sister-in-law

Madame Chiang Kai-shek.

Dec 1. General Chiang Kai-shek, once chief of the Chinese Nationalist armies, married Miss Meling Soong today. There were two ceremonies, a religious one held at a Methodist Episcopal church and a civil one at a major Shanghai hotel. The bride is a sister-in-law of Dr. Sun Yat-sen, former President of the republic. Miss Soong was educated at Wellesley College.

From 1926 to 1927, Chiang suppressed labor movements and rid China of Communists and Russian advisers. He is now considering abandoning military life and pursuing a political career (→ 12).

Ford offers Model A; gets 50,000 orders

Dec 1. Henry Ford's new Model A went on display in New York's Waldorf Hotel this morning, with an instant back order of 50,000. The auto boasts non-shatterable glass for the windshield and a gearshift raised for easy manipulation. The Model A reaches speeds up to 71 mph, having twice the horsepower of the old Ford. Prices run only $10 to $35 higher than previous models, but Americans are not feeling tight-fisted anyway.

As President Herbert Hoover asserted in his yearly fiscal report today, American workers' wages remain "higher than anywhere else in the world or than at any other time in world history." Hoover cited coal and textile as among the few businesses not prospering now. ▷

"Duke" Ellington's band at the Cotton Club

"Duke" Ellington (standing, center) leads his band in Harlem.

Dec 4. Those who haven't yet visited Harlem's renowned Cotton Club now have a particularly compelling reason to do so, for the band of Edward Kennedy Ellington, better known as "the Duke," has just begun what promises to be a long and exciting run.

The club, located at 142nd Street and Lenox Avenue, is a big place, seating about 500, and the floor show spotlights a number of beautiful girls who nightly put their best foot forward. Yet it is the Ellington band which most commands attention as it mesmerizes the crowd with many of the Duke's own inimitable compositions. Ranging from the naughty to the nostalgic, these include "Hophead," "Black Cat Blues," "Bouncing Bouyancy" and "Washington Wabble." The Duke, 28, was born in Washington, has been playing professionally since he was 17, and just ended a long run at New York's Kentucky Club.

On Sunday nights you can expect to see many of Broadway's biggest stars in the audience, and if you find yourself rubbing elbows with some of Chicago's more notorious mobsters, that too is part of the club's special attraction. Visitors should be advised that the Cotton Club is not a "dive," and impeccable behavior is the rule. Those who talk too loudly during the show will be politely admonished. If the chatter continues, they'll be asked to leave or be thrown out.

Chiang smashes Red uprising in Canton

Dec 19. With military force and mass executions, General Chiang Kai-shek has crushed a Communist uprising in the city of Canton.

The uprising broke out on December 11, when Red revolutionaries, aided by armed peasants and laborers, protesting against the military regime, seized control of the city after what was described by refugees as a reign of terror.

Tens of thousands of refugees poured into Hong Kong, carrying tales of wholesale executions. At least 600 Chinese were reported executed in one group, and eight or nine Russians, including a vice consul, were summarily executed.

One result is a rupture of the cooperative relations between the Nationalist movement and Moscow. The Nationalist government in Nanking accused Russian agents of fomenting the uprising and demanded the withdrawal of all Soviet officials in China. A Soviet official is threatening China on account of the murders (→ 3/6/28).

Laurel and Hardy and fans double up

Film audiences have gotten their bellyful this year—a bellyful of laughs, that is. Harold Lloyd, Buster Keaton and Charlie Chaplin are partly responsible. Now the Hal Roach studio offers a pair known informally as "the fat one and the skinny one." Englishman Stan Laurel is the skinny one. He scratches his head with his fingers outstretched and cries unmanfully. Georgia-born Oliver "Babe" Hardy is the fat one. He flutters his tie and tips his bowler hat obsessively. Both men tend to drop, spill, or otherwise destroy things. Hardy blames Laurel, who whimpers. The owner of the destroyed items usually plots a violent revenge, but the duo hightails it off screen just in the nick of time.

Ollie and Stan.

Laurel and Hardy teamed up in 1926 and made ten pictures this year. One of their most recent films is titled "Call of the Cuckoos." Their humor hinges on a formula shared with Lloyd et al: the ordinary, simple person undone by grandiose dreams, And clumsiness.

Lloyd in his trademark glasses.

1928

JANUARY

Su	Mo	Tu	We	Th	Fr	Sa
1	2	3	4	5	6	7
8	9	10	11	12	13	14
15	16	17	18	19	20	21
22	23	24	25	26	27	28
29	30	31				

1. Five U.S. Marines killed, 23 wounded in battle with Nicaraguan rebels (→ 3).

3. U.S. orders 1,000 additional Marines to Nicaragua (→ 26).

3. Pope Pius XI issues encyclical "Mortabum Animos," denouncing ecumenical conferences.

4. French Foreign Minister Aristide Briand sends note to Sec. Kellogg praising plan to outlaw war (→ 4/13).

6. Charles Lindbergh hailed by Diaz Congress in Managua as envoy of peace (→ 7).

7. Forty-thousand Costa Ricans turn out to welcome Lindbergh in San Jose (→ 16).

8. Fifteen die in London as Thames overflows banks.

9. Central Committee of French Communist Party disavows alliances with non-revolutionary parties (→ 11/4).

13. Schenectady, N.Y.: General Electric demonstrates TV broadcasts to home receivers (→ 2/8).

16. Coolidge opens 21-nation Pan-American Conference in Havana (→ 28).

23. Coolidge welcomes Irish Free State Pres. Cosgrave, in Washington for state visit.

23. Presidential hopeful Herbert Hoover comes out against repeal of dry law.

24. Twenty-one inmates dig way out of Detroit prison; 19 escape to Canada.

24. New York City's social center moving uptown to East 70th Street.

24. William Fox buys controlling interest in 250 theaters in West, seating 350,000 and valued at $100 million.

28. Latin American states at Pan-American Conference rebuke Chm. Hughes, upholding right to revolution (→ 2/20).

DEATHS

28. Blasco Ibanez, Spanish poet and novelist, in French exile (*1/29/1867).

30. Douglas Haig, British field marshal, WWI Western Front commander-in-chief (*6/19/1861).

1,000 more Marines sent to Nicaragua

Pack mules are the mode of transportation for U.S. Marines in Nicaragua.

Jan 26. The Coolidge administration ordered 1,000 more Marines to Nicaragua this month to fight the troublesome guerrilla leader, General Sandino. The order to nearly double the American military presence in the Central American country comes two days after five Marines were killed in a bloody ambush by Sandino. Despite the losses, the Marines were able to capture Sandino's capital of Quilali.

Sandino, known popularly as the "Pancho Villa of Nicaragua," is the self-proclaimed fighter for liberty in his country. He rejects the Stimson settlement and all efforts by the United States to increase its influence in Nicaragua. American commanders in Nicaragua are convinced Sandino is receiving outside assistance. His men are suddenly better trained, they are wearing new uniforms and they seem equipped with new weapons. Officially, the United States calls Sandino a bandit. And he does little to dispel the image. His flag is red and black, adorned by crossed knives and a skull (→ 3/16).

Lindy joins Pan Am, now serving Havana

Jan 16. Pan American Airways has initiated passenger service between Key West, Florida, and Havana, Cuba. The flight, a round-trip journey of 220 nautical miles, costs $100. Stewards have been hired to see to passengers' needs.

Naval aviator Juan Terry Trippe founded PAA August 16, 1927, using two Fokker F-7 trimotors to deliver U.S. mail between Cuba and the States. Trippe apparently has big dreams; two weeks ago, he hired "The Lone Eagle," Charles Lindbergh, as a technical adviser. The move may indicate Trippe's intention to expand service southward. Lindbergh will prove particularly familiar with Central and South America. Last month, he flew to Mexico at the invitation of that nation's President.

Passengers debark in Havana.

Greeted by joyous crowds, Lindbergh was entertained through the holidays by U.S. Ambassador Dwight Morrow and his daughters. Lindbergh is continuing his South American goodwill tour. While greeting dignitaries, he is also charting air routes and scouting accessible landing sites. Lindbergh is encountering some storms on these hops, a hazard future passengers do not care to contemplate (→ 2/8).

Millions hear Will Rogers radio broadcast

Jan 4. Will Rogers and stars across the nation enthralled an audience of millions tonight.

National Broadcasting Company hooked up all 48 states to a giant "studio" where entertainers hundreds of miles apart sang, laughed and bantered. Cowboy humorist Rogers broadcast from his home in Beverly Hills. He delivered a pithy monologue, part of it in Spanish for Mexican listeners. He then introduced Al Jolson in New Orleans, who sang "California, Here I Come" and other hits. Next, Paul Whiteman and his orchestra in New York performed Gershwin's "Rhapsody in Blue." Finally, the spotlight fell on Chicago, where Fred and Dorothy Stone sang duets.

The program's sponsor, Dodge Brothers, took the opportunity to introduce its Victory Six. The company president described the automobile in a brief broadcast from Detroit. Dodge Brothers should thank Mother Nature for delivering clear skies and crisp transmissions nationwide.

Rogers, "the cowboy philosopher."

The British novelist Thomas Hardy dies

Thomas Hardy at 73.

Jan 11. Thomas Hardy died at his home in Dorchester tonight, three miles from the thatched cottage where he was born 87 years ago. The impoverished son of a stonemason was apprenticed to an architect at 16, studied the Greek and Latin classics and began (and ended) his literary career as a poet. From the age of 27, novels such as "Far From the Madding Crowd," "The Mayor of Casterbridge," "Jude the Obscure" and "Tess of d'Ubervilles" flowed from his gifted pen. His ashes will be interred at Westminster Abbey, but his heart will be buried separately near the Egdon Heath made famous by his novels.

Trotsky exiled to remote Alma-Ata

Jan 10. In one dramatic move, Joseph Stalin has banished all of the major opposition leaders from Moscow. Leon Trotsky has been exiled to Alma-Ata, in distant Kazakstan. Grigori Zinoviev and 28 other anti-Stalin Bolsheviks have been sent to Siberia or equally remote places. Reports from the Soviet Union say the 30 dissidents were seized in the middle of the night and placed in guarded train compartments by secret police. The luckier ones were given minor party jobs in small villages. The others will have to fend for themselves (→ 1/23/29).

Flappers: Beth & Betty Dodge.

1928

FEBRUARY

Su	Mo	Tu	We	Th	Fr	Sa
			1	2	3	4
5	6	7	8	9	10	11
12	13	14	15	16	17	18
19	20	21	22	23	24	25
26	27	28	29			

1. Miami, Florida: Jack Dempsey announces retirement from boxing.

4. Austrian National Socialists protest presence of Negro singer Josephine Baker on Vienna stage (→ 2/14/29).

7. New York: Miss Grace Moore makes debut as Mimi in Puccini's "La Boheme."

7. U.S. signs arbitration treaty with France.

8. J.L. Baird makes first overseas television broadcast—London to New York (→ 25).

8. Havana: Charles Lindbergh greeted by 100,000 Cubans (→ 3/21).

10. Ontario: 47 miners trapped in shafts by severe explosion.

11. St. Moritz hosts 25 countries for second Winter Olympics.

12. Ku Klux Klan announces plans to establish natl. headquarters near Catholic church in Washington D.C. (→ 12/28).

15. London: Scholars complete new Oxford English Dictionary after 70 years; 300,000 pounds sterling worth of labor.

18. Wall Street shocked by record stock turnover of 1.8 million in two hours (→ 3/3).

20. Transjordan, buffer state between Palestine and desert Arabs, given nominal autonomy by Great Britain (→ 8/11/29).

20. Tokyo holds Japan's first universal suffrage elections.

20. Havana: U.S. envoy Charles Evans Hughes blocks resolution barring intervention in internal affairs of Latin American states as Pan-Am. Conference closes (→ 12/17/28).

21. Washington: Harry Sinclair, William Burns and Henry Day get jail terms for jury shadowing in govt. oil scandal (→ 4/8/29).

21. Film "Dawn" released in Britain, detailing life of Belgian nurse Edith Cavell, shot by Germans during war.

24. N.Y.: New Gallery exhibits Archibald Motley in first show to feature Negro artist.

25. Bell Labs displays new device to end fluttering of television image (→ 9/11).

Asquith, longtime Premier, deceased

Asquith, pillar of British liberalism.

Feb 15. Herbert Henry Asquith, the Liberal Party leader who served as British Prime Minister for eight years, died today at the age of 75. Asquith, one of the most outstanding figures in the Liberal Party since Gladstone, presided over the British Empire in the turbulent period leading up to the Great War and for the first two years of the war. He then became the first Earl of Oxford and Asquith. Ramsay MacDonald called him "a great parliamentarian."

Woman claiming to be Czar's daughter

Feb 6. Today a woman purporting to be the youngest daughter of Czar Nicholas II arrives in the United States. Mme. Anastasia Chaikovsky may be suffering from mental delusions or perpetrating a fraud. As the mystery woman tells it, when her family was assassinated a soldier named Chaikovsky ran away with her. The pair were later married in Rumania. A German duke and a Russian prince believe she is genuine and have entertained her at their palaces.

Anastasia in 1915. Still alive today?

Racing driver Lockhart thrown into sea

Feb 22. In one of the most spectacular accidents ever seen on the Daytona course, an auto racing driver was hurtled into the ocean. Frank Lockhart's small, streamlined car swerved from the course during his effort to set a world record and plunged into the surf. Lockhart was pinned within the partly crushed machine, which was completely submerged 100 yards from shore. He suffered cut tendons in his hand and minor bruises, as well as severe shock. Lockhart was traveling at about 225 miles per hour when the accident occurred. He said that the mist off the ocean had impaired his view.

A rescue team drags the Black Hawk and its unconscious driver back to shore.

1928

MARCH

Su	Mo	Tu	We	Th	Fr	Sa
				1	2	3
4	5	6	7	8	9	10
11	12	13	14	15	16	17
18	19	20	21	22	23	24
25	26	27	28	29	30	31

3. N.Y.: General Motors stock up $89 mil. in one day; rise of 5.2 per share in two hours is largest in Stock Exchange history.

5. Germany: Hitler's National Socialists win majority in Bavaria (→ 6/28).

6. British colonial troops mobilize to protect Iraqi-Transjordanian border against Ibn Saud.

6. China: Communist attack kills 3,000 in Peking; 50,000 flee to Swatow (→ 4/1).

10. N.Y.: Radio Corp. issue soars in huge turnover due to disclosure of big talking movie plans after acquisition of Victor Talking Machine Co. (→ 5/15).

10. N.Y.: American premiere of Puccini's "La Rondine" hailed as great success.

12. Island of Malta becomes British dominion (→ 9/20/64).

14. N.Y. Stock Exchange page buys seat on floor for $315,000, highest price ever (→ 28).

15. Norway celebrates centenary of great playwright, as Ibsen Exposition opens.

16. U.S. to send 1,000 more Marines to Nicaragua (→ 4/23).

21. Coolidge gives Congressional Medal of Honor to Charles Lindbergh (→ 2/12/29).

22. Peasants in Soviet Union protest food shortages.

25. Pope Pius XI condemns French royalist group Action Francaise.

27. U.S. accepts new Mexican oil-land laws, ending long-standing dispute (→ 7/1).

30. Italy: All non-Fascist youth movements ordered dissolved within 30 days (→ 5/12).

BIRTHS

4. Alan Sillitoe, British writer, working class themes.

12. Edward Albee, American playwright, "Who's Afraid of Virginia Woolf."

DEATHS

3. Loie Fuller, American dancer (*1/22/1862).

20. James W. Packard, American auto pioneer.

Prices swing madly in record trading

March 28. Fortunes were both made and lost in yesterday's record trading on the New York Stock Exchange.

The biggest day in Wall Street history found 4,790,270 shares changing hands as the tickers stuttered fitfully in trying to keep up with the day of frantic trading. At one point, the stock tickers fell 33 minutes behind the actual trading on the floor, thus adding to the general confusion.

It was a day of spectacular changes, a feverish battle for the dollar. Even within the space of just ten minutes, price swings made the difference of millions of dollars in the open market value of the leading securities.

General Motors, whose stock had soared to record highs earlier this month, proved to be the center of attack yesterday, retreating down the ladder in breathtaking jumps. By day's end, its stock had declined more than eight points from a high of 198. Other big losers during the day included Chrysler Corporation, Hudson Motors, Hupp Motors, United States Steel, Vanadium Corporation, Atlas Powder and Du Pont.

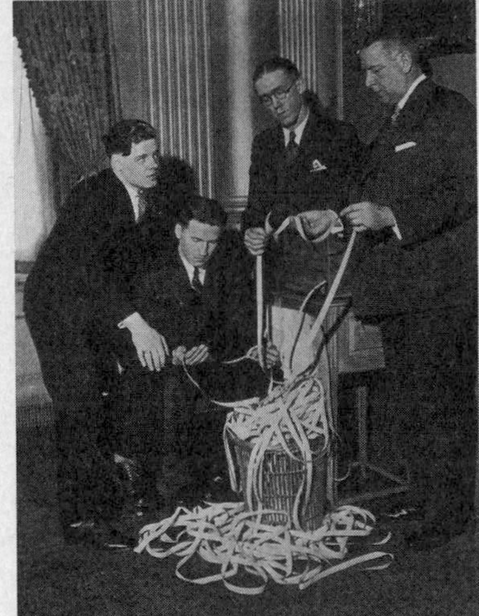

Biggest day on the market.

Radio Corporation of America led in the day's gains, its stock advancing more than 12 points to a new high of 169. Other stocks recording big gains included American Can, General Electric, International Harvester, Montgomery Ward, New York Central and Sinclair Oil (→ 5/16).

Dam breaks, killing 400 in California

March 13. A water wall, 78 feet high, swept away homes, ranches, roads, bridges, livestock, and, tragically, human beings, as the great St. Francis Dam of the Los Angeles water supply collapsed and 12 billion gallons of water flooded the San Francisquito Canyon and Santa Clara River Valley early this morning. At least 700 residents of the area are missing, and the death toll is expected to exceed 400.

There was hardly any warning. Hundreds of houses were crushed like egg shells, their inhabitants in most cases swept to their doom in an area sometimes 60 miles wide. The monetary damage is between $15 million and $30 million. Beds of quicksand hamper the heroic rescue work carried out by an army of men. Inoculations against typhoid fever have begun. A thorough investigation has been ordered into this, yet another in a series of disasters which have hit the Los Angeles water system since 1924 (→ 5/15).

Gary Cooper stars in adventure film

March 10. "Legion of the Condemned," starring Gary Cooper, opens today. It is the ninth feature film by this tall, laconic actor. The public craves to see more of him, even if former love Clara Bow does not. Cooper acts as if he never wanted to act. And he never did. Son of a Montana judge, he trained to be a political cartoonist.

"The Legion of the Condemned."

1928

APRIL

Su	Mo	Tu	We	Th	Fr	Sa
1	2	3	4	5	6	7
8	9	10	11	12	13	14
15	16	17	18	19	20	21
22	23	24	25	26	27	28
29	30					

1. China: Chiang crosses Blue River, launching campaign in North (→ 6/2).

3. Lewis Carroll's original "Alice in Wonderland" manuscript bought in U.S. for $75,260.

9. Turkish Natl. Assembly at Angora denies Islam recognition as state religion (→ 29).

12. Aviators Koehl, Hunefeld and Fitzmau pilot Junkers from Ireland to N.Y. in first East-West flight over North Atlantic.

12. Milan: 16 killed, 40 wounded by bomb meant for King Victor Emmanuel III.

13. Washington: Negotiations begun on multilateral anti-war treaty proposed by U.S. Sec. of State Frank Kellogg (→ 19).

13. N.Y.: Norman Thomas and James H. Maurer to fill Socialist Party ticket this year (→ 5/27).

14. French pilots Costes and Le Brix land at le Bourget, ending 45,000 mile round-world flight.

19. Clarence de Mar finishes Boston Marathon in record time of 2:37:07.8.

19. China: 5,000 Japanese troops occupy Shantung in defiance of Chiang Kai-shek (→ 7/10).

19. Arbitration treaty signed between U.S and Italy (→ 5/19).

20. Carl Dreyer's film "The Passion of Joan of Arc" released.

23. Nicaraguan rebel Sandino captures American mines, taking five prisoners (→ 11/27).

25. American auto racer Lockhart killed at Daytona Beach after reaching speed of 232 mph.

27. Hungarian Communist leader Bela Kun seized by Vienna police.

BIRTHS

6. James D. Watson, American biologist, structure of DNA.

23. Shirley Temple, child actress, later diplomat.

DEATHS

16. Ellsworth Statler, American hotel pioneer (*10/26/1863).

25. General Pieter Wrangel, Russian anti-Bolshevik leader (*8/27/1878).

Turks drop Islam, change alphabet

April 29. Thanks to recent legislation, Turkish schoolboys will soon be reciting the A's to Z's of the English alphabet instead of the traditional Alif-Yen of the Arabic. The reason given is that Turkish illiteracy stems mainly from the difficulty of Arabic.

The nation of 14 million will have a 15-year transition period before the new letters become obligatory. Newspapers will be printed in both Arabic and Latin and a new dictionary is being prepared to teach the English alphabet in schools.

Kemal teaches the Latin alphabet.

This reform continues Premier Mustafa Kemal's Westernization program and follows closely the passage of a bill divorcing the nation from the Islamic religion. Four years ago, Kemal, who regards Islam as a conservative influence, abolished the Caliphate, thereby beginning the disestablishment of the state religion (→ 1/11/29).

1928

MAY

Su	Mo	Tu	We	Th	Fr	Sa
		1	2	3	4	5
6	7	8	9	10	11	12
13	14	15	16	17	18	19
20	21	22	23	24	25	26
29	28	29	30	31		

6. 200,000 Rumanians meet at Alba Julia, demand overthrow of Bratianu govt. (→ 11/9).

7. Herbert Hoover announces, if chosen to run for president, he will campaign with radio and movies (→ 6/15).

7. Age for women voters in Britain reduced from 30 to 21.

12. Mussolini reduces Italian electorate from 12 million to three million (→ 23).

13. New York City commission forecasts nine million commuters by 1965.

13. Trans-African auto expedition leaves Brussels for Capetown, South Africa (→ 9/20).

15. Coolidge signs Jones-Reid bill allotting $340 mil. for flood control in West and Midwest.

15. MGM, Paramount, U.A. get licenses from Electrical Research Products to use Movietone for sound films (→ 8/21).

17. N.Y.: Shakespeare's "The Tempest," starring John Barrymore, opens on Broadway.

19. Britain comes out in favor of Kellogg anti-war plan (→ 8/27).

19. Jockey C. Lang and Reigh Count victorious in Kentucky Derby.

23. Washington: Coolidge vetoes subsidy farm-relief bill, calling it price-fixing plan (→ 10/27).

23. Argentinian anti-Fascists bomb Italian Embassy, killing 22, wounding 41 (→ 2/11/29).

25. Washington: Both houses pass Muscle Shoals Bill, calling for govt. ownership at Tennessee hydroelectric plant (→ 3/3/31).

27. U.S. Congress passes $4.5 billion budget, setting peacetime record.

27. Gen. Umberto Nobile's dirigible Italia crashes on ice after dropping Italian and Milanese flags at N. Pole (→ 6/20).

27. New York: Workers Party nominates Wm. Z. Foster and Benjamin Gitlow (→ 6/15).

30. Louis Meyer drives Miller Special to victory in Indy 500.

31. Eleutherios Venizelos returns as premier to head Liberal government in Greece (→ 8/19).

Heavy Chinese-Japanese fighting ceases

May 11. After three days of heavy fighting between Japanese and Chinese Nationalist troops, quiet descended today on Tsinan-Fu, the capital of Shantung province. The Japanese were in control of the city after inflicting heavy casualties on the Chinese. More than 1,000 were reported to have been killed and an undetermined number wounded as the Chinese Nationalist troops in successive human waves were mowed down by Japanese machine guns. Japan had 41 soldiers and 16 civilians killed and 189 wounded.

The fighting broke out after Chinese Nationalist forces, pushing toward Peking, occupied part of Tsinan-Fu, where Japanese troops had been sent following the retreat of Northern forces. Each side accused the others of committing atrocities. General Fukada of the Japanese forces delivered an ultimatum demanding the punishment of Chinese troops responsible for atrocities against civilians. General Chiang-Kai-shek of the Nationalist army rejected the ultimatum and ordered an attack on Japanese forces barricaded in the city (→ 7/10).

Chinese troops on the march.

Stock market trading hits record high

May 16. Stocks tumbled without warning yesterday in the largest trading volume ever to hit Wall Street. By day's end, sales had totaled 4,820,840 shares, more than half of these changing hands in the final two hours, with many of the most active stocks breaking from five to more than 40 points before the selling wave could be checked.

The dramatic break in the market began with a rush to unload such airplane stocks as Curtiss Aero and Wright Aeronautical. From there, the selling panic spread to other issues, including Montgomery Ward, U.S. Steel, General Motors, General Electric, Allied Chemical, and American Can.

Wall Street financial analysts were at a loss to explain why the market had cracked, since nothing had taken place to undermine confidence (→ 6/12).

Aero-wheels, London's latest traffic hazard, were made in Germany to train pilots for looping-the-loop. England has found them just plain fun.

Chrysler and Dodge in biggest merger

May 28. Automotive history was made today with the announcement of a merger of Dodge Brothers, Inc., and the Chrysler Corporation. The merger, the largest ever in the automobile industry, will place the newly consolidated firm third in line in production and yearly sales, exceeded only by General Motors and Ford Motor Company.

The deal was worked out by Walter P. Chrysler, who grew up as a poor boy in Kansas, and Clarence Dillon, whose banking firm purchased the Dodge Motor Car Company for $148 million in cash several years ago from the widows of the two company founders.

Walter P. Chrysler, rags to riches.

Big Bill Haywood dies in Soviet exile

May 18. William Dudley "Big Bill" Haywood, founder of the International Workers of the World, dead of a stroke, is to be eulogized in Red Square as a proletarian hero.

The tall, broad-shouldered son of a Pony Express rider, once called "as American as Mark Twain," defied suspicions that the American left had been imported from Russia. His tenure in the labor movement ended when he jumped bail in 1921, leaving nearly 100 fellow "wobblies" back in the U.S. facing charges of opposing the Great War.

From a Chicago jail, the Russian Revolution seemed miraculous. In Moscow, he learned that, "We aren't so long on this ideological stuff as the Russians." At death, his belief that "the man who makes the wagon will ride in it himself" must have seemed but a dream.

1928

JUNE

Su	Mo	Tu	We	Th	Fr	Sa
					1	2
3	4	5	6	7	8	9
10	11	12	13	14	15	16
17	18	19	20	21	22	23
24	25	26	27	28	29	30

2. Peking: Chang Tso-lin abandons Peking in face of Nationalist advance (→ 7).

3. Aviatrix Amelia Earhart leaves Boston to begin transatlantic flight (→ 18).

4. New Jersey: Five radium victims win $50,000 and pensions in suit against U.S. Radium Corp.

5. Kingsford Smith lands Southern Cross in Fiji six days after leaving Pacific coast of U.S. for longest sea flight ever.

7. China: Gen. Chang Tso-lin killed by Nationalist foes (→ 8).

9. France convenes Natl. Assembly with Nationalist majority.

12. New York: Stocks drop in day of furious trading; five mil. shares change hands (→ 7/11).

15. Kansas City: Republicans name Herbert Hoover for president with Charles Curtis as running mate (→ 29).

18. London: Keel laid for biggest ship yet —1,000-foot, 60,000-ton Oceanic to cost $30 million.

24. Detroit: Johnny Weissmuller selected to head U.S. Olympic swim team (→ 7/28).

24. French Parliament devalues franc to 25.5 to the dollar.

25. N.Y. audiences hear George Bernard Shaw in new Movietone produced by Fox (→ 8/21).

28. Louis Armstrong and Hot Five record "West End Blues."

28. Socialist Hermann Muller appointed German chancellor (→ 9/24).

29. Houston: N.Y. Gov. Al Smith wins Democratic nomination with Joseph T. Robinson for vice president (→ 8/11).

BIRTHS

10. Maurice Sendak, American illustrator, children's books.

14. Ernesto "Che" Guevara, Cuban revolutionary leader (†10/9/1967).

DEATH

14. Emmeline Pankhurst, British suffrage leader, founder of Women's Social and Political Union (*7/4/1858).

Chiang's Nationalist flag rises over Peking

Many of Chiang's troops fell prisoner to the Japanese en route to Peking.

June 8. No shots were fired as the city of Peking peacefully changed hands. Republican flags disappeared from the streets, and they were soon replaced by the Nationalist and Kuomintang banners. Chiang Kai-shek is master of Peking.

Hundreds of students welcomed the Shansi troops as they entered the city from the south. Their uniforms were tattered, and their guns were old and outdated, but the soldiers swaggered through the streets with pride. The Peking elders were so relieved at the orderly change in command that they raised cups of tea in celebration.

Peking's capture is an important step for Chiang Kai-shek in his march to unify China. The country has been divided since the death of Sun Yat-sen. Chiang Kaishek, however, has managed to defeat the Northern warlords. And he has forced the Communists, his chief rivals for control of the Kuomintang, to go underground (→ 7/19).

Jobless figure disputed: 2 million or 4?

U.S. Employment Service poster encourages the hiring of veterans.

June 25. The United States government cannot agree on the exact figures, but the country has an unemployment problem. That may shock the rest of the world, which still views America as the land of bounty. The Commerce Department says two million Americans are out of work. The Labor Department says it is closer to four million. That means up to ten per cent of American workers do not have jobs. They also do not have any government benefits to tide them over until they find work.

The unemployment problem began in the textile industry and then spread to other areas of the economy, including agriculture. Many workers are being squeezed out by high salaries and mechanization. American investors are starting to put their money overseas.

Earhart first woman to fly over Atlantic

June 18. Miss Amelia Earhart of Atchison, Kansas, is the first woman to successfully cross the Atlantic. The 29-year-old flew in a multi-engine Fokker accompanied by two male pilots. They took off from Boston 22 hours ago and landed today in Carthmenshire, South Wales. Their craft averaged slightly over 120 mph. Miss Earhart, Director of three aeronautical companies, flew because she wanted to show that "this type of travel is comparatively safe and ought to be developed." She downplays her role in the crossing, denying she was ever at the controls of Friendship, even though she logged 500 hours' solo experience prior to the flight (→ 7/6).

Daring aviatrix Amelia Earhart.

Amundsen killed in rescue attempt

June 20. Roald Amundsen, the Norwegian polar explorer, died today when his seaplane crashed near Spitzbergen in an attempt to rescue the crew of a downed Italian dirigible. Ironically, General Umberto Nobile, captain of the dirigible, and five of his men already had been located by another rescue plane when Amundsen's aircraft crashed. Amundsen and a companion, Rene Guilband, took off from Tromsoe, Norway, on the rescue flight two days ago. Their radio signals ceased hours later, and a search confirmed fears about their fate (→ 7/12).

1928

JULY

Su	Mo	Tu	We	Th	Fr	Sa
1	2	3	4	5	6	7
8	9	10	11	12	13	14
15	16	17	18	19	20	21
22	23	24	25	26	27	28
29	30	31				

1. India: 15 killed in Calcutta as Hindus attack Moslems.

1. Gen. Alvaro Obregon elected Mexican president (→ 17).

4. Jean A. Lussier, age 36, becomes third to conquer Niagara Falls in barrel.

6. New York welcomes Amelia Earhart on return to U.S. (→ 5/21/32).

7. Wimbledon: Rene Lacoste over Henri Cochet 6-1, 4-6, 6-4, 6-2; Helen Wills over Lili De Alvarez 6-2, 6-3.

9. Chilean warship Angomoa sinks in Arauco Gulf, 290 dead.

10. Japan recalls 7,000 troops from Shantung; will ask reparations for Japanese killed during Tsinan siege (→ 5/20/29).

11. New York: Stock market hits worst break since war; leading issues drop avg. of 4.41 (→ 10/10).

12. Soviet icebreaker Krassine rescues crew of the Italia at North Pole (→ 3/13/29).

15. Tour de France won by Luxembourg racer Nicolas Frantz.

17. President-elect Obregon assassinated during official luncheon at Mexico City (→ 9/1).

19. King Fuad orchestrates coup in Egypt, dissolving Parliament.

19. China: Chiang annuls all unequal treaties made prior to Nationalist takeover (→ 25).

25. China: U.S. signs treaty in Peking, giving China tariff autonomy (→ 10/6).

25. Gene Tunney defends title in N.Y., flooring New Zealander Tom Heeney in 11th (→ 29).

28. VIIIth Olympic Games open in Amsterdam (→ 8/12).

29. Gene Tunney announces he will quit ring to study philosophy at Sorbonne in Paris.

29. France inaugurates Roland Garros Stadium with Davis Cup victory over U.S.

BIRTH

26. Stanley Kubrick, American film director.

DEATH

21. Dame Ellen Terry, British stage actress (*2/27/1847).

Ellen Terry, queen of theater, is dead

Dame Ellen Terry.

July 21. Few tears were shed this day at the passing of Dame Ellen Terry. Smiles and joyful music were the last request of this great actress, who demanded "no funeral gloom" when she was gone. Two generations of admirers are left only with exquisite memories: her portrayals of Shakespearean ingenues such as Portia, Olivia and Beatrice live on.

Dame Ellen Alicia Terry was born to a prominent English theatrical family February 27, 1847. Her stage debut came at age eight, playing a boy in "The Winter's Tale." When she was 16, Terry married painter George Frederick Watts, who was twice her age. Their marriage was unhappy and brief. For the next 30 years, she dominated the London stage and frequently toured the United States. George Bernard Shaw wrote a play, "Captain Brassbound's Conversion," expressly for her. In 1902, she became the manager of the Imperial Theatre. Her son, Edward Gordon Craig, was set designer. Miss Terry was made a Dame of the British Empire in 1925.

Can you believe it? A TV set for $75

July 3. The magazine Television announced that the Daven Corporation of Newark, New Jersey, has put on the market the first television receiving set to be manufactured in the United States. The television is quite inexpensive, only $75. A more advanced model will be presented at an exhibition in Berlin on July 31, according to the magazine.

1928

AUGUST

Su	Mo	Tu	We	Th	Fr	Sa
			1	2	3	4
5	6	7	8	9	10	11
12	13	14	15	16	17	18
19	20	21	22	23	24	25
26	27	28	29	30	31	

1. Yugoslavia: Croat deputies form separatist Parliament in Agram.

2. Los Angeles: Cecil B. De Mille quits as film producer, joins MGM as director.

3. "Lilac Time" (Coleen Moore and Gary Cooper) opens in N.Y.

5. Polish fliers Idzikowski and Kubals, en route Paris to N.Y., saved by German ship Samos 60 miles off Spanish coast.

5. Belgium: Intl. Socialist Congress opens in Brussels.

6. Wyoming: New geyser sprays 75-ft. high at Yellowstone Park.

9. Volcanic eruption kills 1,000 in Dutch East Indies.

9. Italian diver finds 400,000 pounds sterling in diamonds in wreck of Belgian steamship Elizabethville, sunk during war.

16. Military service becomes obligatory in U.S.S.R.

17. Peking: Canadian anthropologist Davidson Black finds ancient tools in Gobi Desert believed to be 150,000 years old.

18. Haitian storm kills 200, leaves 10,000 homeless.

19. Liberals under Premier Venizelos gain majority in Greece.

21. N.Y.: Joseph M. Schenck, pres. of United Artists claims talkies are just a fad.→

23. Irving Berlin to write music and lyrics for new talkie "Say it With Music" (→ 9/19).

24. U.K.: Hilda Sharp, at 18, is 2nd woman to swim Channel.

25. Commander Byrd sails with 32 adventurers on first lap of Antarctic voyage (→ 9/30).

31. Nehru report published in India; demands dominion status in British Empire (→ 12/6/29).

31. U.S.S.R. accepts Kellogg-Briand Pact (→ 2/6/29).

BIRTH

6. Andy Warhol, American counter-culture artist (†2/22/87).

DEATH

12. Leos Janaceck, Czech composer (*7/3/1854).

Kellogg-Briand Treaty outlaws war

Aug 27. The United States, France, Great Britain, Germany and 11 other countries signed a treaty in Paris today renouncing war. The signing ceremony for the Kellogg-Briand Treaty was extremely simple. Speeches were outlawed at the French Foreign Ministry, and most of the diplomats were very upset. For the first time ever, the pictures and sounds of the treaty ceremony were recorded on film. More than one diplomat felt that the world would be unfairly deprived of his oratory.

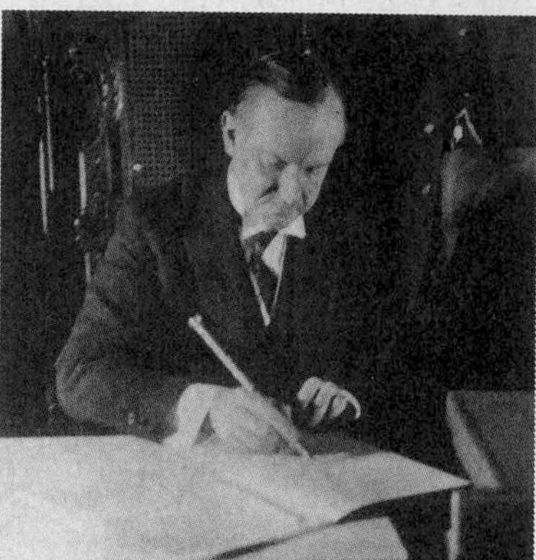

Coolidge signs Kellogg-Briand Pact.

The treaty grew out of an idea from French Foreign Minister Briand for a French-American nonaggression pact. Frank Kellogg, President Coolidge's Secretary of State, suggested that other world powers also sign it. Americans will be able to see the film of the treaty ceremony in about a week. The negative is being rushed back to New York on the liner Ile de France (→ 31).

Movie mogul says talkies just a fad

Aug 21. Joseph Schenk, President of United Artists, says that "people will not want talking pictures long." He says he makes such films only to satisfy the passing interest. Schenk admits that certain sound effects, such as a rapping when an actor knocks on a door, are agreeable. However, his faith in silence is noted in his recent hiring of Sergei Eisenstein, director of the heated, hushed "Potemkin" (→ 23).

1928  Amsterdam

Men Athletics

100 M Dash
1. Percy Williams CAN 10,8
2. Jack London GBR 10.8
3. Georg Lammers GER 10,9

200 M Dash
1. Percy Williams CAN 21,8
2. Walter Rangely GBR 21,9
3. Helmut Konig GER 21,9

400 M Run
1. Raymond Barbutti USA 47,8
2. James Ball CAN 48,0
3. Joachim Bichner GER 48,2

800 M Run
1. Douglas Lowe GBR 1:51,8
2. Enk Bylehn SWE 1:52,8
3. Hermann Engelhard GER 1:53,2

1500 M Run
1. Harri Larva FIN 3:53,2
2. Jules Ladoumègue FRA 3:55,8
3. Eino Purje FIN 3:56,4

5000 M Run
1. Ville Ritola FIN 14:14,0
2. Paavo Nurmi FIN 14:38,0
3. Edvin Wide SWE 14:41,2

10,000 M Run
1. Paavo Nurmi FIN 30:18,8
2. Ville Ritola FIN 30:19,4
3. Edvin Wide SWE 31:00,8

Marathon
1. Mohamed El Ouafi FRA 2:32:57,0
2. Miguel Plaza CHI 2:33:23,0
3. Marti Marttelin FIN 2:35:02,0

110 M Hurtles
1. Sidney Atkinson SAF 14,8
2. Stephen Anderson USA 14,8
3. John Collier USA 14,9

400 M Hurtles
1. David Burghley GBR 53,4
2. Frank Cuhel USA 53,6
3. F. Morgan Taylor USA 53,6

3000 M Steeplechase
1. Toivo Loukola FIN 9:21,8
2. Paavo Nurmi FIN 9:31,2
3. Ove Andersen FIN 9:35,6

400 M Relay
1. USA 41,0 (Frank Wykoff, James Quinn, Charles Borak, Henry Russell)
2. GER 41,2 (Georg Lammers, Richard Corts, Hubert Houben, Helmut Koning)
3. GBR 41,8 (Cyril Gill, Ellis Smouha, Walter Rangeley, Jack London)

1600 M Relay
1. USA 3:14,2 (George Baird, Emerson Spencer, Fred Alderman, Raymond Barbutti)
2. GER 3:14,8 (Otto Neumann, Richard Krebs, Harry Storz, Hermann Engelhard)
3. CAN 3:15,8 (Alexander Winson, Philipp Edwards, Stanley Glover, James Ball)

High Jump
1. Robert King USA 1,94
2. Benjamin Hedges USA 1,91
3. Claude Mènard FRA 1,91

Pole Vault
1. Sabin Carr USA 4,20
2. William Drogemuller USA 4,10
3. Charles McGinnis USA 3,91

Long Jump
1. Edward Hamm USA 7,73
2. Silvio Cator HAI 7,58
3. Alfred Bates USA 7,40

Triple Jump
1. Miko Oda JAP 15,21
2. Levi Casey USA 15,17
3. Vilho Tuulos FIN 15,11

Shotput
1. John Kuck USA 15,87
2. Hermann Brix USA 15,75
3. Emil Hirschield GER 15,72

Discus Throw
1. Clarence Houser USA 47,32
2. Antero Kivi FIN 47,23
3. James Corson USA 47,10

Hammer Throw
1. Patrick O'Callaghan IRL 51,39
2. Ossian Skiold SWE 51,29
3. Edmund Black USA 49,03

Javelin
1. Enk Lundkust SWE 66,60
2. Bèla Szepes HUN 65,26
3. Olav Sunde NOR 63,97

Decathlon
1. Paavo Yrjölä FIN 8053
2. Akilles Järvinen FIN 7931
3. John Kenneth Doherty USA 7706

Women Athletics

100 M Dash
1. Elisabeth Robinson USA 12,2
2. Fanny Rosenfeld CAN 12,3
3. Ethel Smith CAN 12,3

800 M Run
1. Lina Radke GER 2:16,8
2. Kinuye Hitomi JAP 2:17,6
3. Inga Gentzel SWE 2:17,8

400 M Relay
1. CAN 48,4 (Fanny Rosenfeld, Ethel Smith, Florence Bell, Myrtle Cook)
2. USA 48,8 (May Washburm, Jessie Gross, Lorata McNeil, Elisabeth Robinson)
3. GER 49,0 (Rosa Kellner, Leni Schmidt, Ami Holdmann, Leni Junker)

High Jump
1. Ethel Catherwood CAN 1,59
2. Carolin Gisolf HOL 1,56
3. Mildred Wiley USA 1,56

Discus Throw
1. Halina Konopacka POL 39,62
2. Lillian Copeland USA 37,08
3. Ruth Svedberg SWE 35,92

Men Swimming

100 M Freestyle
1. John Weissmuller USA 58,6
2. Istvan Barany HUN 59,8
3. Katsuo Takaishi JAP 1:00,0

400 M Freestyle
1. Alberto Zorilla ARG 5:01,6
2. Andrew Charlton AUS 5:03,6
3. Arne Borg SWE 5:04,6

1500 M Freestyle
1. Arne Borg SWE 19:51,8
2. Andrew Charlton AUS 20:02,6
3. Clarence Crabbe USA 20:28,8

100 M Backstroke
1. George Kojac USA 1:08,2
2. Walter Laufer USA 1:10,0
3. Paul Wyatt USA 1:12,0

200 M Breaststroke
1. Yoshiyuki Tsurtna JAP 2:48,8
2. Erich Rademacher GER 2:50,6
3. Teofilo Yldefonzo PHI 2:56,4

800 M Freestyle Relay
1. USA 9:36,2 (Austin Clapp, Walter Laufer, George Kojac, John Weissmuller)
2. JAP 9:41,4 (Hiroshi Yoneyama, Nabuo Arai, Tokuhei Sada, Katsuo Takaishi)
3. CAN 9:47,8 (F. Murno Burne, James Thompson, Garnet Ault, Walter Spence)

Springboard Diving
1. Peter Desjardins USA 185,04
2. Michael Galitzen USA 174,06
3. Farid Simaika EGY 172,46

High Diving
1. Peter Desjardins USA 99,58
2. Michael Galitzen USA 98,40
3. Farid Simaika EGY 92,34

Water Polo

1. Germany
2. Hungary
3. France

Women Swimming

100 M Freestyle
1. Albina Osipowich USA 1:10,0
2. Eleonor Garatti USA 1:11,4
3. Margaret Joyce Cooper GBR 1:13,6

400 M Freestyle
1. Martha Norelius USA 5:42,8
2. Maria Johanna Braun HOL 5:57,8
3. Josephine McKim USA 6:00,2

200 M Breaststroke
1. Hilde Schrader GER 3:12,6
2. Mietje Baron HOL 3:15,2
3. Lotte Mühe GER 3:17,6

100 M Backstroke
1. Maria Johanna Braun HOL 1:22,0
2. Ellen Elisabeth King GBR 1:22,2
3. Margaret Joyce Cooper GBR 1:22,8

400 M Freestyle Relay
1. USA 4:47,6 (Adelaide Lamberg, Eleonora Garatti, Albina Osipowich, Martha Norelius)
2. GBR 5:02,8 (Margaret Joyce Cooper, Sarah Stewart, Irène Vera Tanner, Ellen E. King)
3. SAF 5:13,4 (Kathleen Russel, Rhoda Rennie, Maria Bedford, Frederica J. van der Goes)

Springboard Diving
1. Helen Meany USA 78,62
2. Dorothy Poynton USA 75,62
3. Georgia Caloman USA 73,38

High Diving
1. Elisabeth Pinkston-Becker USA 31,60
2. Georgia Colement USA 30,60
3. Lala Sjöqvist SWE 29,20

Boxing

Flyweight
1. Antal Kocsis HUN
2. Armand Appel FRA
3. Carlo Cavagnoli ITA

Bantamweight
1. Vittorio Tamagnini ITA
2. John Daley USA
3. Harry Isaacs SAF

Featherweight
1. Lambertus *Bep* van Klaveren HOL
2. Victor Peratta ARG
3. Harold Devine USA

Lightweight
1. Carlo Orlandi ITA
2. Stephen Michael Halaiko USA
3. Gunnar Berggren SWE

Welterweight
1. Edward Morgan NZL
2. Raùl Landini ARG
3. Raymond Smillie CAN

Middleweight
1. Piero Toscani ITA
2. Jan Hermanek TCH
3. Lénard Steyaert BEL

Light Heavyweight
1. Victor Avendano ARG
2. Ernst Pistulla GER
3. Karl Leendest Miljon HOL

Heavyweight
1. Arturo Rodriguez Jurado ARG
2. Nils Ramm SWE
3. M. Jacob Michaelsen DEN

Greco Roman Wrestling

Bantamweight
1. Kurt Leucht GER
2. Jindrich Maudr TCH
3. Giovanni Gozzi ITA

Featherweight
1. Voldemar Vali EST
2. Erik Mamberg SWE
3. Giacomo Quaglis ITA

Lightweight
1. Lajos Kereszetes HUN
2. Eduard Sperling GER
3. Edvard Esterlund FIN

Middleweight
1. Vàino Kokkinen FIN
2. Làzzlo Papp HUN
3. Albert Kusnets EST

Light Heavyweight
1. Ibrahim Moistafa EGY
2. Adolf Rieger GER
3. Omni Pellinen FIN

Heavyweight
1. Rudolf Svensson SWE
2. Hjalmar Eemil Nystrom FIN
3. Georg Gehring GER

Freestyle Wrestling

Bantamweight
1. Kaarlo Màkinen FIN
2. Edmond Spapen BEL
3. James Trifunor CAN

Featherweight
1. Allie Morrison USA
2. Kustaa Pihlajamàki FIN
3. Hans Minder SUI

Lightweight
1. Osvald Kàpp EST
2. Charles Pacome FRA
3. Eino Leino FIN

Welterweight
1. Arvo Haavisto FIN
2. Lloyd Appleton USA
3. Maurice Letchford CAN

Middleweight
1. Ernst Kyburz SUI
2. Donald Parker Stockton CAN
3. Samuel Rabin GBR

Light Heavyweight
1. Thure Sjöstedt SWE
2. Arnold Bögli SUI
3. Henri Lefevre FRA

Heavyweight
1. Johan Richthoff SWE
2. Aukusti Sihvola FIN
3. Edmond Dame FRA

Men Fencing

Foil Individual
1. Lucien Goudien FRA
2. Erwin Casmir GER
3. Giulio Gandini ITA

Foil Team
1. Italy
2. France
3. Argentina

Epée Individual
1. Lucien Goudien FRA
2. Georges Buchard FRA
3. George Calnan USA
   Léon Tom BEL

Epée Team
1. Italy
2. France
3. Portugal

Sabre Individual
1. Odön Tersztyanszky HUN
2. Attila Pertschauer HUN
3. Bino Bini ITA

Sabre Team
1. Hungary
2. Italy
3. Poland

Women Fencing

Foil Individual
1. Hélène Mayer GER
2. Muriel B. Freemann GBR
3. Olga Oelkers GER

Modern Pentathlon

1. Sven Thofelt SWE
2. Bo Lindman ARG
3. Helmuth Kahl GER

Rowing

Single Scull
1. Henry Pearce AUS 7:11,0
2. Theodore David Collet GBR 7:19,8
   (2nd and 3rd determined as result of a special contest in which Collet made better time than Myers).
3. Kenneth Myers USA 7:20,8

Double Sculls
1. USA 6:41,4
2. Canada 6:51,0
3. Australia

Pairs Oars without Coxswain
1. Germany 7:06,4
2. Great Britain 7:08,8
3. USA 7:20,4

Pair Oars With Coxswain
1. Switzerland 7:42,6
2. France 7:48,4
3. Belgium 7:59,4

Four Oars Without Coxswain
1. Great Britain 6:36,0
2. USA 6:37,0
3. Italy

Four Oars with Coxswain
1. Italy 6:47,8
2. Switzerland 7:03,4
3. Poland

Eight Oars
1. USA 6:03,2
2. Great Britain 6:05,6
3. Canada 6:03,8

Yachting

Monotype Individual
1. Sven Thorell SWE
2. Hendrik Robert NOR
3. Bertil Bromann FIN

6 M Class
1. Norway
2. Denmark
3. Estonia

8 M Class
1. France
2. Netherlands
3. Sweden

Cycling

Road Race Individual (168 km)
1. Henry Hansen DEN 4:47:18
2. Franc W. Southall GBR 4:55:06
3. Gösta Carlsson SWE 5:00:17

Road Race Team
1. Denmark
2. Great Britain
3. Sweden

1,000 M Time Trial
1. Willy Falck Hansen DEN 1:14,4
2. Gérald D.H. bosch van Drakestein HOL 1:52,2
3. Edgar Gray AUS 1:15,6

Sprint (1000 M)
1. René Beaufrand FRA 13,2
2. Antoine Mazairae HOL
3. Willy Falck Hansen DEN

Tandem 2000 M
1. Holland 11,8
2. Great Britain
3. Germany

Pursuit Race Team (4,000 M)
1. Italy 5:01,8
2. Netherlands 5:06,2
3. Great Britain

Equestrian Sports

All around Individual Competition
1. Charles F. Pahud de Mortanges HOL 1969,82
2. Gérard Pieter C. de Kruijff HOL 1967,26
3. Bruno Neumann GER 1944,42

All Around Team Competition
1. Netherlands 5865,68
2. Norway 5395,68
3. Poland 5067,92

Dressage Individual
1. Carl Friedrich Frhr. V. Langen GER 237,42
2. Charles Marion FRA 231,00
3. Ragnar Olson SWE 229,78

Dressage Team
1. Germany 669,72
2. Sweden 650,86
3. Netherlands 642,96

Grand Prix Jumping Individual
1. Frantisek Ventura TCH 0/0/0
2. Pierre Bertan de Balanda FRA 0/0/2
3. Charley Kuhn SUI 0/0/4

Grand Prix Jumping Team
1. Spain 0/2/1:33,0
2. Poland 0/2/1:36,0
3. Sweden 0/2/1:39,0

Men Gymnastics

All Around Individual Competition
1. Georges Miez SUI 247,500
2. Hermann Hánggi SUI 246,625
3. Léon Stukelj YUG 244,875

All Around Team Competition
1. Switzerland 1718,625
2. Czechoslovakia 1712,250
3. Yugoslavia 1648,750

Parallel Bars
1. Ladislav Vacha TCH 18,83
2. Josip Primozic YUG 18,50
3. Hermann Hànggi SUI 18,08

Horse Vault
1. Engen Mack SUI 9,58
2. Emanuel Löffler TCH 9,50
3. Stane Dergane YUG 9,46

Sidehorse
1. Hermann Hànggi SUI 19,75
2. Georges Miez SUI 19,25
3. Heikki Savdainen FIN 18,83

Horizontal Bar
1. Georges Miez SUI 19,17
2. Romeo Neri ITA 19,00
3. Eugen Mack SUI 18,92

Flying Rings
1. Léon Stukelj YUG 19,25
2. Ladislav Vacha TCH 19,17
3. Emanuel Loffler TCH 18,83

Women Gymnastics

All Around Team Competition
1. Netherlands 316,75
2. Italy 289,00
3. Great Britain 258,25

Soccer

1. Uruguay
2. Argentina
3. Italy

Field Hockey

1. India
2. Netherlands
3. Germany

CHART

Weightlifting

			2 Arm Press	Snatch 2 Arm	Clean & Jerk 2 Arm	Total
Featherweight						
1.	Franz Audrysek	AUT	77,5	90,0	120,0	287,5
2.	Pierino Gabetti	ITA	80,0	90,0	112,5	282,5
3.	Hans Wolpert	GER	92,5	82,5	107,5	282,5
Lightweight						
1.	Kurt Helbig	GER	90,0	102,5	135,0	322,5
2.	Hans Haas	AUT	85,0	97,5	135,0	317,5
3.	Fernand Arnour	FRA	85,0	97,5	120,0	302,5
Middleweight						
1.	Roger Francois	FRA	105,0	105,0	130,0	340,0
2.	Carlo Gamlimberti	ITA	102,5	102,5	130,0	330,0
3.	August Scheffer	HOL	97,5	97,5	125,0	320,0
Light Heavyweight						
1.	Sayed Nosseir	EGY	100,0	112,5	142,5	355,0
2.	Louis Hostin	FRA	100,0	110,0	142,5	352,5
3.	Johannes Verheijen	HOL	95,0	105,0	137,5	337,5
Heavyweight						
1,	Josef Strabberger	GER	122,5	110,0	150,0	382,5
2.	Arnold Luhaär	EST	100,0	107,5	142,5	357,5
3.	Jaroslav Skobla	TCH	100,0	107,5	142,5	350,0

See table of contents for abbreviations

U.S. wins Olympics with 437 points

Olympic gymnasts on the rings.

Aug 12. The United States carried off the unofficial point championship of the 1928 Olympics but only because of the prowess of its field event heroes. Ray Barbuti, in the 400-meter run, won the only individual gold medal in track for the Americans, but they still were able to roll up 437 points.

Of the 22 events on the Amsterdam program, Finland won four in track and captured one of the field contests. The Americans were helped considerably by taking both relay events, but were hurt by Percy Williams' double victory for Canada in the sprints. Williams, a 19-year-old high school student who had hitchiked across Canada to take part in the trials, was a virtual unknown when he arrived at the Amsterdam Olympics.

The second shock to the United States came when Lord Burghley of England won the 400-meter hurdles. The prestigious marathon was won by El Ouafi, an auto mechanic from Paris, as the American Joie Ray failed to finish in the money.

Miss Del Rio: from a Mexican convent school to Hollywood.

Hoover says U.S. near end of poverty

Aug 11. Predicting an end to poverty in America, Herbert Clark Hoover accepted the Republican Party's nomination for president today, running on a platform slogan, "A chicken in every pot, a car in every garage."

Facing a crowd of 70,000 cheering partisans gathered in the Stanford University stadium, Hoover said confidently: "We in America today are nearer the final triumph over poverty than ever before in the history of the land." The Republican nominee also declared firmly that he was opposed to repeal of the 18th Amendment, which outlawed liquor in America, and called for rigid enforcement of the Prohibition law (→ 11/7).

Hoover (center) on campaign trail.

Three-Penny Opera opens in Berlin

Aug 31. "Three-Penny Opera," now playing at the Theater am Schiffbauerdamm in Berlin, is, according to one critic, "The fashionable show, always sold-out. One simply has to have seen it."

Based on John Gay's "Beggar's Opera," "Three-Penny Opera" is the seventh dramatic effort by 30-year-old German playwright Bertolt Brecht, who wrote it with German composer Kurt Weill.

Born in 1898, Brecht studied medicine in Munich from 1917 to 1921 and served in an army hospital in 1918. From this period date his first plays. Brecht worked with Max Reinhardt, the greatest of German directors, and went on to develop new theatrical theories.

1928

SEPTEMBER

Su	Mo	Tu	We	Th	Fr	Sa
						1
2	3	4	5	6	7	8
9	10	11	12	13	14	15
16	17	18	19	20	21	22
23	24	25	26	27	28	29
30						

1. Ahmed Bey Zogu crowned king of Albania.

1. Mexico: Plutarco Calles renounces office of president for all time (→ 25).

8. Geneva: Despite official U.S. non-participation, American Charles Evans Hughes is elected World Court judge by League.

11. General Electric makes history in Schenectady, N.Y., broadcasting play over radio and TV at same time (→ 6/27/29).

12. Geneva: Germany, angry at Briand, cancels French concessions in Rhine (→ 21).

15. Tornado levels Rockford, Illinois, killing 100.

17. Florida hurricane kills 800, more threatened by disease.

18. Pilot Juan de la Clerva flies English Channel in new Autogiro plane.

19. N.Y.: "Singing Fool," with Al Jolson, opens in Vitaphone (→ 3/24/29).

20. Trans-African auto expedition returns to Belgium.

21. Germans propose inviting Owen D. Young to redraft Dawes Plan (→ 1/1/29).

23. Madrid's Novadades Theater struck by fire, leaving 45 dead and 200 injured.

24. Berlin: Reich Nationalists ask for referendum on ending republic (→ 28).

25. Emilio Portes Gil elected provisional president of Mexico (→ 11/30).

28. Washington: Franco-British accord on naval limitation rejected by U.S. (→ 10/6).

28. Germany: Prussia lifts public speaking ban on Adolf Hitler (→ 5/1/29).

30. Commander Byrd's expedition reaches equator (→ 1/16/29).

BIRTH

13. Maurice Jarre, French composer.

DEATH

25. Richard Outcault, illustrator, creator of Buster Brown (*1/14/1863).

Fleming discovers germ-killer by luck

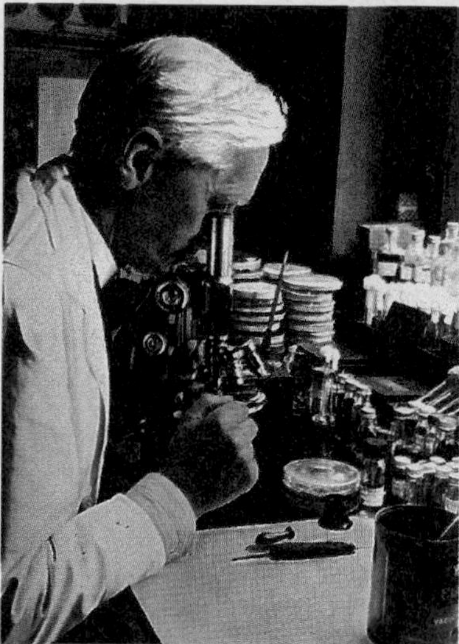

Fleming in his London laboratory.

Sept 15. Alexander Fleming, a bacteriologist working at the University of London School of Medicine, has reported the discovery of a bacteria-killing compound that he believes could be of major importance in the field of medicine.

The discovery was made when he left a plate containing a culture of staphylococcus bacteria uncovered in his laboratory for several days and then noticed that the bacteria had died in areas where an airborne mold had fallen on the culture. Fleming has identified the mold as Penicillium notatum, a variety that is closely related to the mold that grows on stale bread.

Tests have shown that the compound does not harm white blood cells and so might be useful in treating common infections. Fleming is attempting to isolate and purify the compound for medical use but says he is handicapped by a lack of equipment and chemical expertise.

Mortimer has a squeaky voice and a new name, "Mickey," for his 2nd film "Steamboat Willie."

Air mail delivered from ship to shore

Sept 3. The first ship-to-shore delivery of transatlantic mail was accomplished today when a seaplane launched from the westbound French Line steamer Ile de France arrived in Boston bearing sacks of registered mail and films of the signing of the world war peace treaty.

The plane, with a crew of three, was catapulted from the deck of the Ile de France shortly after 2 a.m. when the liner was 900 miles from New York, its destination on this trip. The seaplane, flying through heavy rain and fog, arrived six hours later at Halifax, Nova Scotia, where it refueled and took on more mail, and landed at Boston at 3:15 p.m.

The mail arrived in New York at 10:10 p.m., well in advance of the Ile de France, which is scheduled to dock at 3 p.m. tomorrow. The delivery is the latest demonstration of the value of air mail, which has come into common use in the past few years for the delivery of urgent messages.

A long way from the Pony Express.

Al Jolson, last year's "Jazz Singer," has another hit with "The Singing Fool."

1928

OCTOBER

Su	Mo	Tu	We	Th	Fr	Sa
	1	2	3	4	5	6
7	8	9	10	11	12	13
14	15	16	17	18	19	20
21	22	23	24	25	26	27
28	29	30	31			

1. Louis Bunuel and Salvador Dali's disturbing film "Un Chien Andalou" opens in Paris.

1. Mae West and cast of "Pleasure Man" arrested and held for indecency.

3. Argentina takes World Polo Championship, defeating U.S. team 10-7.

3. Forty-three killed as French sub Ondine sinks after colliding with Greek steamship off Spanish coast.

6. Canada denounces U.S. and Britain for blocking arms control efforts (→ 2/13/29).

9. St. Louis: Yankees capture second World Series in row, defeating Cardinals in four straight games.

9. Maurice Chevalier leaves Paris for Hollywood.

10. Stock prices soar on Wall Street; exchange seat sold for record $450,000 (→ 11/12).

12. First commercial iron lung used —on girl with infantile paralysis, at Chidren's Hospital in Boston.

15. Graf Zeppelin arrives in Lakehurst, N.J., after 111-hour flight from Germany (→ 30).

16. Chrysler Corp. announces plans for 68-story building in Manhattan.

20. Nanking govt. invites Henry Ford and four other Americans to become economic advisers to China (→ 2/23/29).

23. Dr. Mansfield Robinson, who sent wireless to Mars, says he has received reply but needs time to decode it.

25. U.S.: New coast-to-coast air record set by Harry Tucker in monoplane Yankee Doodle in 24 hours, 51 minutes.

25. Rumania: 31 killed, 50 injured in train wreck on Paris-Bucharest line.

27. Hoover promises, if elected, to call Congress to special session on farm aid (→ 3/7/29).

28. Los Angeles: Calif. Inst. of Technology completes immense 200-inch telescope.

29. Honduras chooses coalition liberal president in first peaceful election in years.

Soviet Union's first 5-year plan begins

Oct 1. Joseph Stalin's first five-year plan went into effect today in the Soviet Union. It sets a timetable to expand industrial production, take farms out of private hands and create schools that will turn out enough Communist bureaucrats to administer the system. The plan also represents a political turnabout for Stalin. The Communist leader is abandoning the more capitalistic New Economic Policy, begun by Lenin, that has been so harshly criticized by Leon Trotsky. Stalin is also turning the Soviet Union away from its role as leader of world revolution to concentrate on its internal problems.

Communist development: Hydroelectric power on the Dnieper.

Zeppelin makes its first New York trip

Oct 30. The dirigible Graf Zeppelin became the first commercial aircraft to span the Atlantic Ocean when she arrived in Friedrichshafen, Germany, after a round trip to Lakehurst, New Jersey. The trip begins what promises to be regular passenger service between America and Europe (→ 11/1).

The monstrous Graf Zeppelin.

Chiang is Chairman of Chinese republic

Oct 6. In China, Chiang Kai-shek has two new titles to match his string of military victories against the warlords and the Communists. Under the new constitution, Chiang is both Chairman of the Nationalist government and Commander-in-Chief of all Chinese forces.

For his capital, Chiang has chosen Nanking, which was also the capital of Sun Yat-sen. Chiang rose to power as a principal aide to Sun, and he originally shared his philosophy of collaborating with Chinese Communists and appealing to the Soviet Union for military help. Chiang ultimately changed course and battled the Communists after they challenged him for control of the Kuomintang. Many of the Communists are still waiting for Chiang to falter. But he seems to have a fairly steady alliance with another group of former enemies, the Northern warlords (→ 20).

Agents raid 20 speakeasies in New York

Oct 8. New York police raided 20 speakeasies yesterday as the toll of deaths from poison liquor continued to mount. In recent days, 33 persons in that city have died of liquor poisoning, 21 of them just yesterday.

The speakeasy raid, ordered by Mayor Jimmy Walker, resulted in the arrest of 21 bartenders and owners. Liquor samples taken from the bars were sent to the New York toxicologist for analysis. If any poison is found in any sample, the owner of that speakeasy will be charged with homicide.

Deaths from consumption of undiluted alcohol have risen sharply since the 18th Amendment outlawing liquor went into effect in 1920. In that year, just 84 deaths in New York City were attributed to poison alcohol, while the total last year was 719. Alcohol deaths in that city have reportedly reached 518 already this year (→ 5/20/29).

Renowned dry agents "Izzy" Einstein and "Moe" Smith in disguise.

Ethiopian King crowned amid splendor

Oct 7. British, French and Italian officials watched the crowning of Ras Tafari as "King of Kings of Ethiopia, the Conquering Lion of Judah and the Elect of God" in ceremonies at the Ethiopian capital of Addis Ababa today. While honored with the illustrious titles, Ras Tafari must still share his power with his aunt, Empress Zauditu, daughter of Menelik II, who was crowned empress in 1917.

Ethiopian King Ras Tafari.

Recently, the new king reconciled his differences with the mighty tribal forces which have waged civil war in the African nation, and this smoothed the way for his coronation. The coronation legalizes the rule that Ras Tafari has jointly held with Zauditu for ten years. Ras Tafari is said to be a descendant of King Solomon and the Queen of Sheba.

The coronation will be followed by a seven-day feast for the Ethiopian army, which includes almost every able-bodied male in the country. The week of joyous festivities is traditional in this ancient Biblical civilization (→ 11/2/30).

1928

NOVEMBER

Su	Mo	Tu	We	Th	Fr	Sa
				1	2	3
4	5	6	7	8	9	10
11	12	13	14	15	16	17
18	19	20	21	22	23	24
25	26	27	28	29	30	

4. Charlie Chaplin's "The Kid," with 12-year-old Jackie Coogan, opens in Paris.

4. British flier Grieg hits 319.57 mph in seaplane.

4. French Radicals break with Poincare govt. (→ 11).

9. Maniu sets up Cabinet in Rumania; power now reported to rest with peasants (→ 6/8/30).

11. Catania: 200-foot lava wave from Mt. Etna rushes over Sicilian villages, causing horrible damage.

11. France: Poincare forms own Cabinet, excluding Radicals.

12. New York: Stock trading wave sweeps to new peak of 5.7 million shares (→ 16).

12. Liner Vestris sinks off Virginia Cape with over 300 aboard.→

16. New York: 6.6 million share day shatters all records for New York Stock Exchange (→ 23).

19. President-elect Herbert Hoover gets 21-gun salute as he sails for goodwill tour of Latin America (→ 27).

20. Mrs. Glen Hyde becomes first woman to dare Grand Canyon rapids in a scow.

22. Financier Payne Whitney's estate settled at $179 million, an American record.

22. Washington report indicates cigarette output rising at 1.4 billion per month.

22. British King George confined to bed with congested lung; queen to take over duties.

23. New York: Young Max Schmeling defeats Joe Monte in first professional fight.

23. Bulgaria sends troops to hunt down Ivan Michailoff, Macedonian revolutionary leader.

27. Nicaragua: Hoover meets with President Moncada in Managua to discuss tactics against Sandino rebels (→ 1/1/31).

30. London reports 872 deaths in auto accidents over last nine months.

30. Emilio Portes Gil sworn in as Mexican president (→ 12/25).

Hirohito is crowned Emperor of Japan

Hirohito in ceremonial dress.

Nov 10. Japanese Emperor Hirohito, who ascended the throne in December 1926 upon the death of his father, has been crowned at a ceremony in Kyoto. In a confident voice, the 27-year-old emperor declared that the spiritual union between the sovereign and the people is the essence of Japanese nationality, and he pledged to improve the moral and material condition of his "beloved subjects." He also vowed to work for world peace (→ 11/14/30).

Heaviest trading shuts stock market

Nov 23. Trading on the New York Stock Exchange has been suspended after the most turbulent buying demonstration ever known on Wall Street. The governing committee of the exchange ordered the suspension after the trading volume reached 6,954,020 shares, setting a new record, topping that set just seven days ago.

Today's closing, coming before the weekend, will give the swamped employees of commission houses several days in which to post their books and restore their records to some semblance of order.

Meanwhile, competitive bidding for seats on the Stock Exchange has set a new record, too, with the price of a seat rising to $550,000, topping the previous high of $530,000 per seat (→ 12/8).

Hoover is President; Roosevelt Governor

Nov 7. Herbert Clark Hoover won a landslide victory for President in yesterday's elections. The president-elect, a Republican, soundly defeated the Democratic candidate, Governor Alfred E. Smith of New York, by carrying most of the states.

But while returns from throughout the nation showed strong support for Republicans, the governorship of New York state was won by a Democrat, Franklin D. Roosevelt, a former Assistant Secretary of the Navy in the Wilson administration.

In a statement issued in his home state of California, Hoover pledged that he would carry out "the ideals of the American people."

Governor Smith, who had been dubbed "the happy warrior" during the campaign, was disappointed by his poor showing. That was attributed, in part, to his New York accent and image, with brown derby and cigar; his promise to repeal Prohibition; and his Roman Catholic religion. Smith says he does not intend to seek public office again. "I have had all I can stand of it," he remarked (→ 3/4/29).

Hoover and Curtis in 1928.

Liner Vestris is lost; death toll is 111

Nov 12. The American cruise ship Vestris, buffeted by high seas and 45-mile-an-hour winds, sank today 240 miles off the Virginia coast. There were 328 passengers and crew members aboard the liner, which was bound from New York to Barbados and South America. Some 111 people are known dead or missing. None of the 20 children on board the Vestris was rescued.

Three ships rushed to the Vestris after she flashed an SOS call at 10:45 a.m. The three vessels, the American Shipper, the French tanker Myriam and the German steamer Berlin, are all bringing survivors back to New York.

Captain William Carey is believed to have gone down with the ship. Authorities in New York will almost certainly convene a special board of inquiry to investigate the disaster. Already, questions are being raised about the seaworthiness of the Vestris. One surviving passenger says the ship had problems as soon as it left port.

A lifeboat escapes the Vestris only minutes before she was engulfed by the sea.

1928

DECEMBER

Su	Mo	Tu	We	Th	Fr	Sa
						1
2	3	4	5	6	7	8
9	10	11	12	13	14	15
16	17	18	19	20	21	22
23	24	25	26	27	28	29
30	31					

2. Sofia: King Boris of Bulgaria, lowest paid monarch, has salary raised 50% to $43,000.

5. Vienna: Wilhelm Miklas chosen second president of Austrian republic (→ 2/24/29).

8. Bolivia severs relations with Paraguay (→ 1/3/29).

10. N.Y.: John Heydler reelected Natl. League pres., recommends ten-man baseball team.

11. U.S. Senate votes compromise on Boulder Dam, leaving Ca. and Ariz. short on water demands (→ 21).

17. U.S. official J. Reuben Clark claims Roosevelt Corollary, allowing intervention in internal affairs of foreign nations, does not apply to Latin America.

20. 47th Street Playhouse, built for Ethel Barrymore, opens in New York City.

21. Coolidge signs Boulder Dam bill (→ 7/7/30).

25. Mexican Pres. Emilio Portes Gil orders abolition of summary executions (→ 3/3/29).

28. NAACP claims nine Negroes lynched in 1928, lowest figure in 40 years (→ 9/21/29).

30. N.Y.C. police, in record round-ups, arrest 454 crime suspects.

CULTURAL EVENTS, 1928

Literature: Evelyn Waugh's "Decline and Fall"; Virginia Woolf's "Orlando"; D.H. Lawrence's "Lady Chatterley's Lover"; Carl Sandburg's "Good Morning America"; Aldous Huxley's "Point Counterpoint."

Academia: Margaret Mead's "The Coming of Age in Samoa"; George Bernard Shaw's "The Intelligent Woman's Guide to Socialism and Capitalism."

Music: Gershwin's "An American in Paris"; Ravel's "Bolero"; "Am I Blue?"; "You're the Cream in My Coffee."

The Arts: Chagall's "Wedding"; Georgia O'Keefe's "Nightwave"; Elisabeth Scott's Shakespeare Memorial Theatre, Stratford-upon-Avon.

Film: Chaplin's "The Circus"; first Mickey Mouse films; Lang's "The Woman on the Moon."

Wilder's Bridge of San Luis Rey et al

Bibliophiles had trouble keeping their libraries orderly this year; non-fiction seemed to fall into fiction, and vice versa.

Thornton Wilder's "The Bridge of San Luis Rey," given the Pulitzer Prize this year, serves as example. The novel begins relating a fact: a suspension bridge in colonial Peru collapsed, killing the people upon it. But then the work explores the mystical loves that led the travelers to their fate. What is a reader to think? Non-fiction seems just as fantastic; psychologist Carl Jung's "Relationship between the Ego and the Unconscious" is incredible.

Authors questioned women's roles this year. D.H. Lawrence wrote "Lady Chatterly's Lover," about a married upper-class woman taking a lower-class lover. The book was banned in America. Virginia Woolf offered a fantasy called "Orlando," in which the heroine is alternately a hero. Eugene O'Neill's play "Strange Interlude" had characters addressing dialogue to each other and their thoughts to the audience.

To undo the confusion, readers sought books that clarified things. "Main Currents in American Thought" by Vernon L. Parrington offered economic explanations. "The Logical Structure of the World," a neo-positivist work by Rudolf Carnap, was enlightening. And both sexes read G.B. Shaw's "The Intelligent Woman's Guide to Socialism and Capitalism."

Lilian Gish and Lars Hanson star in Victor Seastrom's MGM film "The Wind."

Major break occurs in market values

Dec 8. Stocks continued their downward tumble yesterday, led by a 72-point decline that clipped more than $83 million from the open market value of shares in Radio Corporation of America.

It was a day of the heaviest selling ever to take place in just a two-hour period on the New York Stock Exchange. Stocks were dumped on the market for whatever they would bring and the ticker machines ran more than an hour behind.

Suffering from a bloated economy?

Aside from the Radio Corporation slump, the net declines in the main body of stocks ranged up to more than 61 points. Among the heavy losers were International Harvester, Case Thrashing Machine, Wright Aero, Montgomery Ward, National Tea, Federal Mining and Smelt, and Kolster Radio (→ 2/15/29).

Gershwin's new hit: American in Paris

Dec 13. George Gershwin conducted "An American in Paris," a tone poem incorporating elements of jazz and sound effects at Carnegie Hall last night. The performance was sold out. The American composer and pianist, born in Brooklyn, New York, in 1898, became famous in 1923 with "Rhapsody in Blue," a symphonic jazz composition for piano and orchestra. He also wrote the popular song "Swanee."

1929

JANUARY

Su	Mo	Tu	We	Th	Fr	Sa
		1	2	3	4	5
6	7	8	9	10	11	12
13	14	15	16	17	18	19
20	21	22	23	24	25	26
29	28	29	30	31		

1. Paris: S. Parker Gilbert, reparations official, reports German economy stabilized (→ 2/11).

3. Bolivia, Paraguay turn to Pan-American Union for arbitration of border dispute.

4. George Antheil's music premieres in Berlin.

7. N.Y.: Sheffield Farms begins using wax paper cartons instead of glass bottles for milk delivery.

10. Cartoonist Herge introduces "Tintin" in Belgian newspaper The 20th Century.

11. Turkey adopts European metric system (→ 12/7/29).

11. U.S.S.R.: Bolsheviks reduce work day to seven hours.

14. Gershwin musical "Strike Up the Band" opens in N.Y., featuring hit song "I've Got a Crush on You."

15. U.S. Senate ratifies Kellogg-Briand anti-war pact.

15. Afghani King Amanullah abdicates, succeeded by Inayatullah.

16. Commander Byrd explores 1,200 miles of Antarctic by plane (→ 2/20).

19. N.Y.: Jazz opera "Jonny Spielt Auf" a big hit at Metropolitan Opera.

20. Twelve-year-old musical prodigy Yehudi Mehuhin given violin by Henry Goldman of Goldman Sachs & Co.

23. Soviet police arrest 150 followers of Leon Trotsky for alleged civil war plot (→ 30).

25. Members of N.Y. Stock Exchange asked to authorize 275 additional seats (→ 2/15).

BIRTHS

15. Rev. Martin Luther King Jr., U.S. civil rights leader, Nobel Peace Prize, 1964 (†4/4/1986).

28. Claes Oldenburg, American pop artist.

DEATHS

6. Russia's Grand Duke Nicholas.

25. Oscar W. Underwood, prominent U.S. congressman (*5/6/1862).

Alexander becomes Yugoslav dictator

Alexander led Serb forces in WWI.

Jan 6. In Yugoslavia, King Alexander has dissolved Parliament and made himself the supreme ruler of the badly divided country. Alexander has no designs to be dictator for life, but felt he had no other choice but to seize power. The Allies ignored the nationalistic ambitions of the Serbs, Croats and Slovenes when they created Yugoslavia at the Paris peace conference. Last August, the Croats established their own Parliament, and the National Assembly has been useless ever since. Alexander must somehow unify his country and protect it from all its external enemies.

Trotsky expelled; followers jailed

Jan 30. Joseph Stalin has succeeded in banishing his most persistent critic, Leon Trotsky, from Russia. In a split vote, the Politburo approved Stalin's decision to eject Trotsky. Some of his followers have reportedly been arrested, but his family will be allowed to leave with him. A number of countries have refused to admit Trotsky, and he will apparently settle in Turkey.

This is not the first time Trotsky has been forced into exile. Before the revolution succeeded, he was banished to Siberia. Later, he was Lenin's Commissar for Foreign Affairs. After Stalin took power, he exiled Trotsky to Alma-Ata. But that was not far enough, because Trotsky has continued to criticize Stalin as being counterrevolutionary (→ 2/18).

Dickinson poems hidden forty years

Jan 24. Publisher Little, Brown & Company announces that 150 unknown poems by Emily Dickinson have been uncovered. A niece of the poet explained that Miss Dickinson's sister suppressed the works for 40 years. A Harvard University English professor has examined the poems and avows that the poet had written them "at the height of power." Emily Dickinson was raised in Amherst, Massachusetts, where she died in 1886. She was a master of metaphor and a keen observer of nature.

Reclusive poet Emily Dickinson.

Army plane stays aloft for 150 hours

Jan 7. The Army aircraft Question Mark landed at Metropolitan Airport in Los Angeles today after a flight of 150 hours and 40 minutes that shattered all records for endurance flying. The Question Mark had flown more than 11,000 miles on a closed course between its takeoff, at 7:46 a.m. New Year's Day, and its landing after 2 p.m. today.

During the flight, it took on fuel from a sister ship several times. The flight would have been even longer, but the Fokker trimotor airplane was forced to land when one of its engines failed and attempts at midair repairs were unsuccessful. Army Air Force officials say the demonstration that aircraft can be refueled while they remain aloft has enormous significance for military and commercial aviation.

Wyatt Earp always quick on the trigger

Wyatt Earp, lawman.

Jan 13. For decades, the name Wyatt Earp was legendary across the American frontier. Wherever he went, his reputation as "incorruptible lawman" and "gunfigher without equal" followed him. When he became Marshall of Dodge City in 1876, Earp said, "I was hired to stop the killing," and with his Buntline Special, that's exactly what he did. At age 80, Earp died peacefully in his sleep last night.

Einstein reduces physics to one law

Jan 24. A new theory by Albert Einstein that unites gravity and electromagnetism in one set of formulas is arousing great interest in the world of physics. Einstein has been working on the new theory without interruption for the past ten years. Four years ago, he reported success, but then said he had discovered a flaw in his reasoning.

The theory consists of a set of equations demonstrating that gravity, electricity and magnetism are just different manifestations of the same basic force. If it is confirmed, it will be a major step toward Einstein's goal of uniting all the basic forces of nature in one unified field theory. Physicists who have seen preliminary versions of the theory say it will require long and careful study to verify. But it could be of even greater importance than Einstein's theory of relativity, they say.

1929

FEBRUARY

Su	Mo	Tu	We	Th	Fr	Sa
					1	2
3	4	5	6	7	8	9
10	11	12	13	14	15	16
17	18	19	20	21	22	23
24	25	26	27	28		

3. Henry L. Stimson, accepts post as Hoover's sec. of state.

3. New York City reports avg. business girl earns $33.50 for 50-hour work week.

5. Belfast: Irish Republican leader Eamon De Valera arrested for entering Ulster.

6. Germany accepts Kellogg-Briand Pact (→ 7/24).

9. U.S.S.R. Poland, Estonia, Rumania, Latvia renounce war, sign Litvinov Protocol (→ 4/3).

11. Paris: Owen D. Young convenes first conference of Young Commission on German reparations (→ 4/13).

12. Charles Lindbergh announces engagement to Anne Morrow (→ 21).

13. U.S. Congress authorizes building of 16 naval cruisers, one aircraft carrier (→ 4/22).

14. Negro singer Josephine Baker banned from Munich stage for "indecent public behavior."

15. U.S. Federal Reserve council comes out in favor of curb on stock speculation (→ 3/26).

15. Germany reports 3.2 million unemployed.

18. Leon Trotsky, to be expelled from Turkey, asks political asylum in France, Germany (→ 21).

20. Comm. Byrd names vast new Antarctic area Marie Byrd Land, after wife (→ 1/22/30).

21. Trotsky denied political asylum in France (→ 4/11).

21. Lindbergh named aviation adviser to aeronautics branch of Dept. of Commerce (→ 27).

21. Largest bank in U.S. formed by $2 bil. merger; Natl. Bank of Commerce and Guaranty Trust.

23. Chinese rebels defy Nanking, seize Hunan (→ 10/14).

24. Austria: Conflict heats up as 6,000 Fascists, 18,000 Socialists parade through Vienna.

BIRTH

6. Keith Waterhouse, British satirist, "Billy Liar," "Jubb."

DEATH

24. Andre Messager, French composer (*12/30/1853).

Gangsters stage Valentine's Day massacre

Feb 14. In what has been called a Valentine's Day massacre, seven Chicago gangsters have been slain by a firing squad of rivals, some of the killers wearing police uniforms.

The killings took place in a beer warehouse located just a block from a wealthy residential area. The victims were lined up and mowed down by machine gun fire.

The dead men were said by police to be the remnants of a mob under the command of George "Bugs" Moran. Among those under investigation is "Scarface" Al Capone.

Angered that some slayers were impersonating officers, Police Commissioner William F. Russell said: "It's a war to the finish. I've never known a challenge like this."

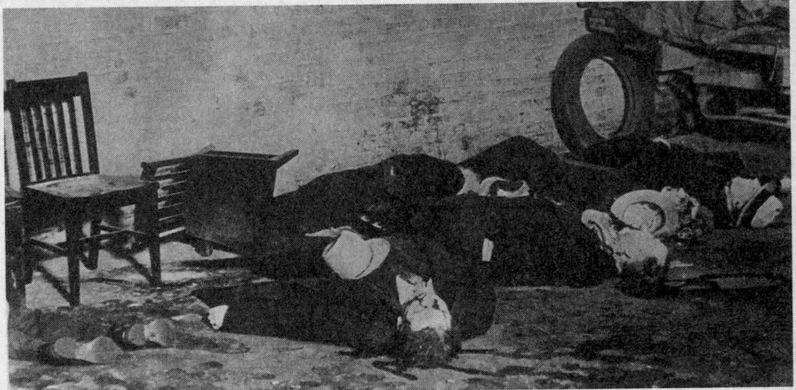

Members of Moran's gang lay dead outside an illicit Chicago beer warehouse.

Lindbergh and fiancee escape plane crash

Feb 27. Charles A. Lindbergh and his fiancee, Anne Spencer Morrow, narrowly escaped serious injury when their airplane crashed at Valbuena Flying Field near Mexico. The monoplane lost its right wheel, and Lindy piloted it down to a soft landing, but it overturned when the bare axle and then a wingtip hit the ground. Lindbergh dismissed the accident as "a mere mishap that could happen to anyone" (→ 5/27).

Lily Langtry takes final curtain call

"The Jersey Lily."

Feb 12. Famed actress and society beauty Lily Langtry passed away today at her home on the Riviera. She was 74 years old. Daughter of a wealthy ship merchant, "The Jersey Lily" was raised on the Isle of Jersey until she was 18. Then an infatuated Irish yachtsman spirited her away. Miss Langtry became Lady de Bathe when her third husband, 19 years her junior, inherited a title. Her acting skill was negligible, but her pale violet eyes and flawless complexion were outstanding. One fan likened her to Helen of Troy. That fan was Oscar Wilde.

Hollywood makes 1st musical comedy

February. Harry Beaumont has been paid off. Last year, he directed Joan Crawford in the film "Our Dancing Daughters," with Crawford doing a vigorous Charleston in silence. Now MGM gives Beaumont the honor of directing "The Broadway Melody," Hollywood's first musical comedy. The film, released this month, also boasts a Technicolor sequence.

Beaumont's "Broadway Melody."

Papacy gets state in pact with Italy

Feb 11. Six decades of ill feeling and tension between the government of Italy and the Papacy have ended with the signing of the Lateran Treaty. The agreement re-establishes the sovereignty of the Pope.

The treaty was signed in the Lateran Palace by Benito Mussolini and Cardinal Gaspari, the Vatican Secretary of State. Pope Pius XI, who did not attend, did supply the gold pen used for the signing.

Under the pact, Italy recognizes the sovereignty of the Vatican and guarantees it the use of public services. The government also agrees that Roman Catholicism is the state religion. Catholic education will be obligatory in primary and secondary school. Matrimony is viewed as a sacrament, and the state does not have the power to grant divorces. Italy also agrees to pay the Vatican $87.5 million (→ 7/27).

Gaspari signs as Mussolini looks on.

Passengers watch movie on airplane

Feb 17. Universal Air Line reports it showed a film during a scheduled flight, possibly the first commercial airline to do so. A screen was lowered behind the pilot's cabin, and a technician monitored the projector. The dozen passengers, traveling from Minneapolis and St. Paul to Chicago, had not anticipated this pleasure. They reclined in comfortable seats while watching the ten-reel motion picture. The title of the film, which might have been a talkie, was not released.

1929

MARCH

Su	Mo	Tu	We	Th	Fr	Sa
					1	2
3	4	5	6	7	8	9
10	11	12	13	14	15	16
17	18	19	20	21	22	23
24	25	26	27	28	29	30
31						

3. Army in revolt in eight Mexican states; rebels seize Vera Cruz and Nogales (→ 8).

5. Sound film "Broadway Melody" released in U.S.

7. Pres. Hoover calls special session of Congress for April 15 to settle tariff and farm aid questions (→ 4/15).

8. Mexico: Two Americans killed as rebels take Juarez; Hoover agrees to sell arms to Gil government (→ 18).

11. Jules S. Bache, in New York, buys "Giuliano de Medici" — only privately owned Raphael — for $600,000.

11. Daytona Beach: Maj. Seagrave shatters auto speed record, reaching avg. of 223.2 mph in a 450 h.p. Golden Arrow.

12. Gov. Franklin D. Roosevelt proposes state-built dams for New York.

13. Italy: Committee forces Umberto Nobile to quit army for June 1928 dirigible accident.

16. Massive floods threaten 20,000 in Alabama.

17. U.S.: 13 killed when Ford air transport crashes with sightseers aboard.

17. Spain: Student protests force closing of Madrid University.

18. Mexico: Rebel peace plea denied; Gen. Calles takes Torreon (→ 4/2).

21. Twenty-one killed, ten missing in Pittsburgh mine blast.

21. Oslo: Norwegian Prince Olaf weds Princess Martha, niece of Sweden's King Gustav.

22. N.Y.: Baritone Titta Ruffo quits Metropolitan Opera for $350,000 contract with talkies.

24. Fox Film Corp. announces it will produce exclusively musical films (→ 5/9).

26. N.Y.: Stocks hit big downturn in 8.2 mil.-share day, then rally as bankers come to aid of market (→ 4/1).

DEATHS

6. David D. Buick, auto pioneer (*9/17/1854).

20. Ferdinand Foch, French marshal (*4/6/1851).

Hoover takes oath of office in the rain

Hoover gives his inaugural address.

March 4. His face spattered by a cold, driving rain, Herbert Hoover was sworn in as President of the United States today. The ceremony, held on the east front of the Capitol, was witnessed by a huge throng that included outgoing President Calvin Coolidge.

Coca-Cola founder Asa Candler dead

March 12. Asa G. Candler, 77, died today. A poor Georgia farm boy, he started his Coca-Cola business in a small shed in 1888. In 1919, he sold it to the Coca-Cola Company of Delaware for $25 million. He has frequently aided worthy causes in the South.

Coca-Cola outlives its creator.

Harlem: A decade of cultural efflorescence

The barbershop, hub of Harlem's thriving social life.

The 1920's may come to be remembered as the time when Harlem became the capital of Negro social and cultural life. Thousands of Negroes from the rural South have emigrated to the New York area.

In Harlem, still owned by whites but increasingly inhabited by Negroes, Bessie Smith, Duke Ellington and Bill "Bojangles" Robinson entertain audiences at The Cotton Club, Barron's and Leroy's while Langston Hughes, Claude McKay, James Weldon Johnson and others work to make names for themselves in the annals of literature.

In Hughes' words: "We younger Negro artists . . . intend to express our individual dark-skinned selves without fear or shame. If white people are pleased we are glad. If they are not, it doesn't matter."

General Motors buys back German firm

March 17. Opel AG, the largest auto company in Germany, has been bought by the General Motors Corporation of the United States for 120 million marks. The Opel family will remain in charge of operations for the time being. The sale is another sign of growth for General Motors, which is rapidly overtaking Ford in the American auto industry. The sale comes only a few days after the death in Detroit of David D. Buick, the inventor whose auto company is now part of General Motors. Buick, who sold his company early, died in poverty.

A lime green Opel Reinette, one of the most popular cars of the twenties.

1929

APRIL

Su	Mo	Tu	We	Th	Fr	Sa
	1	2	3	4	5	6
7	8	9	10	11	12	13
14	15	16	17	18	19	20
21	22	23	24	25	26	27
28	29	30				

1. N.Y.: Stocks drop heavily with interest rate at 15 percent; traders fear credit curb by board (→ 9/3).

2. Mexico: Federals take Jimenez after fierce two-day fight; revolt in collapse (→ 6/21).

3. Persia signs Litvinov Protocol, calling for abolition of war.

5. "Coquette," with Mary Pickford, opens in New York.

8. U.S. Supreme Court upholds oil boss Harry Sinclair's three-month sentence for contempt of Senate (→ 5/6).

11. Germany denies political asylum to Leon Trotsky (→ 6/8).

13. Paris: Germany rejects new debt total; envoy Schacht says Dawes Plan is better (→ 18).

14. Racer Williams wins first Grand Prix auto race at Monaco in Bugatti special.

14. Madrid: 70,000 demonstrate to show loyalty to de Rivera regime (→ 12/29).

15. Washington: As Congress meets in special session, Hoover tells congressmen he favors experimental farm board (→ 6/15).

16. Am. Engineering Council announces plans for uniform traffic signals across nation.

18. Paris: Dr. Hjalmar Schacht forces deadlock in debt parley; wants lower payments, return of Sarre and Silesia (→ 5/4).

19. Italy: Mussolini's fasces incorporated into national coat of arms.

21. Berlin: Erich Muhsam stages new play "Sacco and Vanzetti."

22. Geneva: Hugh Gibson, head of U.S. delegation, proposes naval cuts based on equivalent values (→ 6/28).

24. Ruth Chatterton in "Madame X" opens in N.Y.

26. British fliers make record non-stop, 4,130-mile trip from London to India.

29. Prokofiev's "The Player" debuts in Brussels.

BIRTHS

1. Milan Kundera, Czech writer.

8. Jacques Brel, Belgian singer and composer († 10/9/1978).

Carl F. Benz dies; was auto pioneer

April 4. Carl F. Benz, the German engineer who designed and built the first practical automobile powered by an internal combustion engine, died today at his home in Ladenburg at the age of 84.

Carl Friedrich Benz.

The original Benz auto, a three-wheeler using a gasoline engine developed by Otto Daimler, ran early in 1885, and Benz obtained a patent on the design in 1886. His company, originally founded to build engines for use in factories, began producing passenger cars in 1893 and turned out a series of racing cars starting in 1893. Benz left the company in 1906, starting another firm with his sons. In 1926, the first Benz company merged with the Daimler Motor Company to form Daimler-Benz, which manufactures Mercedes-Benz cars.

"Shipwreck" Kelly, flagpole-sitting champ, deserves his title, "Luckiest Fool Alive."

▷

Mexicans on rampage; U.S. planes sent

Rebel cavalry poses in the arid underbrush near the Texas border.

April 6. With the army revolt in Mexico near collapse, President Hoover has asked the War Department to protect American lives and property at Naco, Arizona. Accordingly, 18 U.S. Army planes armed with machine guns and equipped for bombing are now flying to the scene. Naco, on the Mexican border, is menaced by gunfire from the battle at Naco, Mexico, where rebel armies unsuccessfully stormed the federal fort. Stray bullets wounded four Americans, and a U.S. patrol has clashed with the rebels.

The trouble began last year when General Antonio Obregon was re-elected President. When Obregon was assassinated, Congress made Emilio Gil acting President. The rebellion in eight Mexican states is an attempt to topple Gil and install their own man, presidential candidate Gilberto Valenzuela (→ 6/21).

Billy Sunday packs 'em in for Jesus

April. Ever since William Ashley "Billy" Sunday, a former baseball player who descended the pitching mound to ascend the pulpit as a flamboyant Presbyterian minister, began touring the United States in 1896, warning sinners of the Lord's retribution, his popularity has reached a frantic, feverish pitch.

Sunday, pro baseball star in 1880's.

Double-decker bus far from Picadilly

Cross-country by double-decker bus.

Greyhound Lines bus company has bought a fleet of double-decker buses to be used throughout the country. Buses with transcontinental routes will have sleeping accomodations on the upper level. The double-deckers confirm the company's prosperity, for Greyhound sold $2.5 million in notes last year.

Buses emulate trains. They are rivals for speed: A San Francisco-New York trip takes only five days and 14 hours. Drivers dress like conductors in jaunty caps and boots. And the heaviest investors in bus firms are railroads. They figure if you can't beat 'em, join em.

1929

MAY

Su	Mo	Tu	We	Th	Fr	Sa
			1	2	3	4
5	6	7	8	9	10	11
12	13	14	15	16	17	18
19	20	21	22	23	24	25
26	27	28	29	30	31	

1. Berlin: Eight killed, 140 wounded as Communists clash with police (→ 9/22).

2. Southern states ravaged by tornadoes; 25 killed in eight states.

4. Paris: Owen D. Young's new debt plan wins over Germans and British (→ 29).

6. Frenchman Alain Gerbault completes one-man round-world trip on sailboat.

9. U.S. Army announces plan to use talkies in training (→ 11/3).

10. Scotland: Walter Hagen wins British Open Golf Championship.

11. French Min. of Commerce E. Bonnefous welcomes 33 nations to Paris Fair.

12. Metropolitan Museum of Art acquires "Descent from the Cross," rare 16th-century relief by Jean Goujon.

15. Poison gas kills 124 in Cleveland hospital as explosions spread fumes and fire.

18. L. McAtee rides Clyde Dusen to win Kentucky Derby.

19. Spain: World's Fair opened in Barcelona.

20. Hoover appoints commission to study dry law's effect on U.S. crime problem (→ 1/12/30).

20. China: Under international pressure, Japan begins evacuation of Shantung (→ 9/18/31).

24. N.Y. begins construction on elevated West Side highway.

29. Paris: Germans agree to total reparations of $27 bil., as proposed in Young Plan (→ 6/8).

30. Indy 500 won by Ray Keech at 97.6 mph in Simplex Special.

31. Labor wins plurality in British elections, but lacks majority (→ 6/5).

BIRTHS

4. Audrey Hepburn, British actress.

25. Beverly Sills, American coloratura soprano.

DEATH

18. Adolf Braun, Austrian politician, founder of Social Democratic Party (*3/20/1862).

Lindbergh-Morrow: A hero's wedding

Newlyweds Anne and Charles.

May 27. Col. Charles A. Linbergh and Miss Anne Spencer Morrow were married quietly yesterday at her parents' home in Englewood, New Jersey. The world-famous aviator himself picked his bride's bouquet in the garden. After the wedding ceremony, the couple, who met in Mexico City in December 1927 during his tour with his plane The Spirit of St. Louis, eluded the cordon of reporters and disappeared as utterly as did he alone that dawn two years ago when he soared over the Atlantic on his path to glory. Mrs. Lindbergh's father is Dwight Morrow, a Morgan partner who was Ambassador to Mexico when the newlyweds met (→ 1/20/30).

Lord Roseberry got his three wishes

May 21. Archibald Philip Primrose, 5th Earl of Roseberry, had three ambitions:

1. To win the English Derby.
2. To marry the richest heiress in England.
3. To become Prime Minister.

He satisfied them all: He won the Derby not once but thrice. In 1878, he married Hannah, the only child of Baron Amschel de Rothschild. And in 1884, when British Prime Minister Gladstone died, Queen Victoria called on him to form a government. A celebrated orator and wit, who wrote as well as he spoke, Lord Roseberry died today at 82.

First Academy Awards

Janet Gaynor, winner in three films.

May 16. An evening of long speeches at the Hollywood Roosevelt Hotel ended by Al Jolson saying, "They didn't give me one. I could use one; they look heavy and I need another paper weight. For the life of me, I can't see what Jack Warner can do with one of them. It can't say yes." He was referring to the statuette, designed by Cedric Gibbons and sculpted by George Stanley, presented for excellence in various areas of motion pictures by Douglas Fairbanks, President of the newly formed Academy of Motion Picture Arts and/or Sciences.

Janet Gaynor, a 22-year-old newcomer, won for three films, Emil Jannings for two (Charles Chaplin was a runner-up). The movie "Wings" was voted best picture, while writer Ben Hecht and directors Frank Borzage and Lewis Milestone were among other winners of the statuette (13.5 inches tall, 6.75 lbs.), a gold-plated naked man plunging a sword into a reel of film, the five holes in the reel representing the academy's five branches: actors, directors, writers, technicians and producers.

The idea of the academy was born when Louis B. Mayer, one of filmdom's giants, invited 36 Hollywood bigwigs to a banquet on January 11, 1927, to find ways to give films a more dignified image. The awards will be an annual event.

Al Capone jailed for carrying a gat

May 17. "Scarface" Al Capone, who in his own words has "not had peace of mind in years," is behind prison bars for the first time in his notorious career, with a quiet year to think things over. Such was the sentence handed the Chicago gang leader and bodyguard Frank Cline for carrying concealed weapons. They were arrested in Philadelphia as they left a movie.

Ford will help Soviets build cars

May 31. Henry Ford signed an agreement today with Soviet trade officials to build an automobile factory at Nizhni Novgorod capable of producing 100,000 cars a year. As part of the agreement, Soviet Russia will purchase $30 million worth of Ford products over four years. "No matter where industry prospers, whether in India or China or Russia, all the world is bound to catch some good from it," Ford said.

Sinclair jailed for contempt of Senate

May 6. Harry F. Sinclair, the oil tycoon, began serving a 90-day jail sentence in the District of Columbia tonight for contempt of the Senate for refusing to answer questions about his involvement in the Teapot Dome oil scandal. He declined five years ago to explain what role he had played in the leasing of government oil reserves to private interests (→ 11/1).

The Marx Brothers started as a vaudeville musical team called "The Four Nightingales." They have spent the last few months on Broadway at night and in the studio by day, shooting their zany screen debut "The Cocoanuts."

1929

JUNE

Su	Mo	Tu	We	Th	Fr	Sa
						1
2	3	4	5	6	7	8
9	10	11	12	13	14	15
16	17	18	19	20	21	22
23	24	25	26	27	28	29
30						

3. Bolivia, Peru settle 46-year border dispute with Hoover's mediation; Tacna to Peru, Arica to Chile.

3. N.Y.: Douglas Fairbanks Jr., at 19, weds Joan Crawford.

5. London: Ramsay MacDonald accepts second premiership, one day after resignation of Stanley Baldwin (→ 10).

8. Constantinople: Trotsky asks P.M. MacDonald to admit him to England for medical treatment and literary work (→ 7/11).

9. Swedish aviators attempting Atlantic flight go down on Iceland with broken fuel pipe.

13. Florenz Ziegfeld signs agreement with Goldwyn to produce movie musicals.

15. Pres. Hoover signs farm relief bill, creating Federal Farm Board to stabilize prices, fund farm cooperatives (→ 8/11).

16. French fliers Assolant, Lotti and Lefevre reach Paris after N. Atlantic flight from Maine.

17. Seven killed when British Imperial Airways plane falls into English Channel.

17. International conference on working women opens in Berlin.

21. Mexican govt. signs peace with Catholic Church, modifying anti-religious laws (→ 6/16/35).

28. Fifty years after Planck's graduation, German Inst. for Physics awards Max Planck Medal to Planck and Einstein.

28. At newly opened London arms talks, U.S. urges Britain to show good faith by scrapping W. Indian naval bases (→ 7/24).

29. R.H. Macy & Co. announces purchase of L. Bamberger & Co. of Newark.

BIRTHS

12. Anne Frank, young Jewish refugee from Nazis (†3/12/1945).

18. Jurgen Habermas, German sociologist.

23. Ted Lapidus, French fashion designer.

DEATH

16. Gen. Bramwell Booth, head of Salvation Army.

Dawes takes stand against silk pants

June 26. Ever since 1776, Americans have been asserting their independence of the British crown in various ways. Charles G. Dawes, Ambassador to the Court of St. James's and former Vice President, chose his way tonight: he declined to wear silk knee breeches, prescribed for court dress, to a reception in Buckingham Palace. Being the only man without them, he attracted some attention amid the splendor of the court. He wore 100 percent American, he-man long pants with his tailcoat.

Color television is shown by Bell Labs

June 27. A system for transmitting television pictures in full color was demonstrated today by scientists at Bell Laboratories in New York. Viewers said the images, which included the American flag, the Union Jack and a bouquet of roses, were impressively true to life.

The system uses three separate tubes, one for each primary color, with a set of mirrors to create the full-color picture. In the demonstration, the images were transmitted by wire and the picture was only the size of a postage stamp, but its developers say it will not be difficult to make a much bigger screen and transmit pictures through the air. Color could provide a boost to the new industry. At present, three television stations in New York are limited to broadcasting animated silhouette movies (→ 2/12/31).

British Labor in power; woman in Cabinet

A massive crowd awaits election results in London's Trafalgar Square.

June 10. The new British Prime Minister, Ramsay MacDonald, made history twice today as he introduced his new Labor Cabinet on the lawn outside 10 Downing Street. For the first time, one member of the Cabinet is a woman. And for the first time, a microphone and klieg lights were turned on as the prime minister used the talkies to make the names of his Cabinet public.

The woman is Margaret Bondfield, whom MacDonald called "our old friend." The trade union leader will serve as Minister of Labor. MacDonald played to the cameras like a veteran actor, saving the introduction of Miss Bondfield until last. The prime minister is making improved relations with the United States one of his major goals. MacDonald also plans to resume diplomatic relations with Russia and to pursue a policy of disarmament. On the domestic level, his top priority is reducing unemployment.

Young Plan cuts German payments

June 8. After spirited debate, the Allies have managed in Paris to readjust the total sum of reparations due from Germany. The Young Plan, named after the American banker, Owen Young, reduces the penalties and establishes an orderly framework for their payment.

Between now and 1966, Germany is scheduled to pay a total of $7.8 billion. The yearly payment averages about $488 million. Additional payments would be made until 1988, but the new plan saves Germany millions of dollars. It is designed to cover the Allies' war debts, but not the total cost of reconstruction. Under the Young Plan, Allied controls over the German economy will be terminated, and Germany will make the payments to an international bank. Despite the concessions, many Germans refuse to accept the plan (→ 8/2).

Coco Chanel is the queen of fashion

Gabrielle "Coco" Chanel of France is the epitome of the new woman of the 1920's. Surmounting humble beginnings as both an illegitimate and orphaned child, she has reached dizzying heights of success in the world of fashion. Originator of the jersey dress, the twin sweater set and the understated knitted suit, her byword is simplicity.

"Coco," queen of fashion.

1929

JULY

Su	Mo	Tu	We	Th	Fr	Sa
	1	2	3	4	5	6
7	8	9	10	11	12	13
14	15	16	17	18	19	20
21	22	23	24	25	26	27
28	29	30	31			

1. U.S.: 1924 Immigration Act goes into effect; quotas to be based on 1920 population.

1. British sign accord at Nanking, pledging to aid China in building up navy.

3. N.Y. Telephone reports N.Y. City makes 100 calls/second.

3. Hoover announces he will stop handshaking until Sept. due to hot weather and sore hand.

6. Wimbledon: Henri Cochet over Jean Borotra; Helen Wills over Helen Jacobs 6-2, 6-2.

9. Thirty-eight nations present protest to U.S. on high tariffs (→ 6/17/30).

10. Chinese seize Eastern Railway from Russia in Manchuria (→ 17).

11. Ten U.S. citizens on study trip arrested in Moscow on espionage charges.

11. British Cabinet bars Trotsky from England (→ 11/17).

12. Clarke brothers bankers jailed in U.S. for transferring millions in bank funds to wives.

17. Washington: Women's bureau of Labor Dept. demands housewives be included in federal census on employment.

17. U.S.S.R. breaks diplomatic relations with China over seizure of Manchurian Railway (→ 19).

19. U.S. Sec. of State Stimson warns China and Russia, under Kellogg-Briand Pact, they must settle dispute peacefully (→ 22).

23. N.Y.: Colleen Moore opens in "Smiling Irish Eyes."

24. Kellogg-Briand Pact now in effect; Britain, U.S. suspend building of cruisers (→ 9/15).

27. Italy: Anti-Fascist leaders Rosselli, Lussu and Fausto escape from penal colony on Lipari Islands (→ 7/11/30).

28. N.Y.: 1,700 convicts riot, putting torch to Auburn Prison; four escape over wall (→ 12/11).

28. Tour de France won by Belgian racer Maurice de Waele.

28. French "Four Musketeers" win Davis Cup for third time.

28. Forty-eight nations sign Geneva Convention governing treatment of war prisoners.

1st Pope in 59 years leaves the Vatican

July 25. Pope Pius XI made his first appearance outside the Vatican today in a brilliant procession blending mysticism and medieval splendor. Setting his final seal on the Italo-Vatican concordat, he abandoned the custom of the last 59 years which had made him and his predecessors prisoners in the Vatican. He then issued forth to take possession of the territory ceded him by the Lateran treaties.

This was the first ceremony organized in common by both Vatican and Italian authorities. As 400 church bells rang, a multitude of about 300,000 thronged St. Peter's Square in heat hovering near 100 degrees, and roared their welcome when the pontiff, borne aloft on a richly decorated platform, moved through the piazza in a creamy silk cloak.

First air service coast to coast

July 7. Transcontinental Air Transport inaugurates cross-country service today. TAT claims to be the first airline formed expressly for carrying passengers rather than mail. Two days and two nights of nearly continuous travel take customers from New York's Penn Station to Glendale Airport outside Los Angeles. The hardy passengers journey by plane during the day and sleep on trains at night. Meals on the planes will not rival railway repasts; lunchboxes and thermoses must suffice. Stops are made at Port Columbus, Ohio, Indianapolis, St. Louis, Kansas City, Wichita, Waynoka, Oklahoma, and Clovis, N.M. Total one-way fare is $351.94.

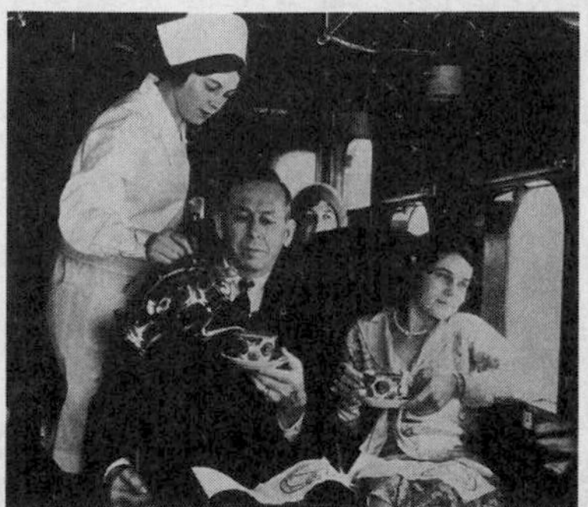

Crowded, but treated like royalty.

Russia and China may fight over border

Protesters in Moscow carry signs attacking the Chinese as "reactionaries."

July 22. Washington has received assurances that the Russian and Chinese governments have no intention of going to war regarding their dispute over the jointly operated Chinese Eastern Railway in Manchuria. Both, however, threaten war if the other crosses the Siberian-Manchurian border. Chinese and Russian troops are massed along the Amur River, and Chinese President Chiang Kai-shek has called on his country's armies to "stand united against the menace of Soviet Russia."

The Russian government accuses China of having provoked ths border crisis by arresting Soviet citizens who worked on the railway and thus effectively taking charge of the eastern end of the line. And China charges Russia with the persecution of Chinese citizens who live in neighboring Soviet territory. Following Russia's ultimatum to the Nanking government, giving them three days to rescind their seizure of the line, Russia broke off diplomatic relations with China, which then followed suit.

Both sides in the escalating conflict have assured Secretary of State Stimson that they do not intend to start a war, and negotiations are continuing, but tensions are continuing to mount as well (→ 8/15).

Poincare resigns; Briand gets job

July 27. The French received a surprise when Raymond Poincare announced he is resigning as Premier. He is suffering from medical problems, and doctors say he needs rest and possibly an operation.

Poincare admits he is exhausted. He has been in and out of French Cabinets for more than 35 years. And for the past three years, he has almost single-handedly stabilized the franc and negotiated repayment of the French war debt. Recently, he was distressed by concessions he had to make on the debt and also by the prospect that the French will evacuate the Rhineland. Aristide Briand is forming a new government (→ 10/22).

Hitchcock has given Britain its first fully synchronized sound film. "Blackmail's" impressive array of special effects climax in a thrilling chase scene across the roof of the British Museum.

1929

AUGUST

Su	Mo	Tu	We	Th	Fr	Sa
				1	2	3
4	5	6	7	8	9	10
11	12	13	14	15	16	17
18	19	20	21	22	23	24
25	26	27	28	29	30	31

1. Kansas: One killed, many hurt at Leavenworth prison riot.

2. Holland: Intl. Conference on Young Plan for German reparations opens at The Hague (→ 6).

6. The Hague: Britain attacks Young Plan for denying U.K. due payment (→ 31).

7. Lakehurst, N.J.: Graf Zeppelin takes off on round-world flight (→ 19).

8. RKO Radio's Keith Orpheum buys 26 new theaters.

11. U.S.: Natl. and local farmers form $50 mil. cooperative marketing association (→ 8/7/30).

11. Cleveland: Babe Ruth hits 500th major league home run.

11. Chaim Weizmann founds Jewish Agency for Palestine in Zurich (→ 24).

15. Russia, China on verge of war as Russian warships raid Manchuria (→ 21).

18. Austria bans "All Quiet on the Western Front" —a best-seller in Germany —from army libraries.

19. Graf Zeppelin reaches Tokyo in four days, two hours (→ 29).

23. Hicksville, L.I.: Anne Morrow Lindbergh makes first solo flight.

24. Jews and Arabs battle in Jerusalem, killing 47 (→ 25).

25. Arabs kill 12 Americans in Hebron; British troops reach Jerusalem (→ 29).

29. British troops seize Transjordanian Arab leader at gates of Jerusalem (→ 31).

30. Steamship San Juan sinks in three minutes after colliding with Standard Oil tanker off coast of San Francisco; 70 dead.

31. Young Plan adopted at The Hague (→ 10/26).

BIRTH

5. Alfred Alvarez, British poet and critic, "The Savage God."

DEATHS

3. Emil Berliner, German inventor of gramophone (*5/20/1851).

19. Serge Diaghilev, founder of Russian Ballet (*3/31/1872).

Zeppelin completes trip around world

Inside the Graf Zeppelin.

Aug 29. The dirigible Graf Zeppelin completed a historic trip around the world today when she arrived at Lakehurst, New Jersey. The Graf Zeppelin's travel time of 21 days, seven hours and 26 minutes is a new record for round-the-world travel. Carrying 16 passengers and a crew of 37, the airship left Lakehurst in the early morning hours of August 8. She made only three stops on her 19,500-mile trip. Her first destination was her home base of Friedrichshafen in Germany. From there, she flew over Siberia to Japan, where she stopped at Tokyo, then westward over the Pacific to Los Angeles and on to Lakehurst, landing at 8:47 a.m.

Thorstein Veblen, social critic, dies

Aug 3. Thorstein Veblen, who introduced the famous phrase "conspicuous consumption" to readers throughout the civilized world, died today at the age of 71. His "Theory of the Leisure Class" (1899) held that the wealthy are engaged in a wasteful display of materialism.

After receiving a Ph.D. from Yale in 1884, the Wisconsin-born Veblen taught at the University of Chicago, Stanford University and the New School for Social Research.

In 1904, he published "The Theory of Business Enterprise." Veblen maintained that a fundamental conflict exists between the making of money and the making of products. He viewed the entrepreneur as a reactionary predator who manipulates prices for his own benefit while the engineer or industrialist, who actually produces goods and services, strives for efficiency.

▷

Arabs revolt as result of dispute with Jews

Jews gather for prayer at Jerusalem's Wailing Wall.

Aug 31. British machine guns are now silent in the strife-torn city of Jerusalem and Friday and Saturday, the days most feared here, have passed without incident thanks to British military efforts in putting down Arab riots.

Yet the crisis is far from over. The Moslem revolt has spread to Damascus, Syria, and reports claim that Syrian Arabs have crossed the border to march on Jerusalem. A squadron of 13 British planes circled the Mosque of Omar, thus informing the Arab mob gathered there for weekend devotions that General Dobbie and his men meant business. But desperate Arab mobs are ready to attack unguarded spots.

Three British officers have been killed, along with 12 Americans. Counts thus far estimate some 100 Jews killed and 300 wounded. The British, who have done a good job in quelling the murderous revolt, claim over 100 Arabs killed.

The reason for the uprising is unclear, but apparently stems from Arab hostility regarding Jewish access to the Wailing Wall. Meanwhile, British plans announced earlier this month for immigration of non-Zionist Jewish sympathizers go forward. Jewish immigration has slowed recently to but ten arrivals last year, and the new proposal should help swell the non-Arab population (→ 9/2).

Chinese-Soviet border fighting breaks out

Aug 21. As the Manchurian crisis develops toward formal war, fighting has broken out between Russian and Chinese troops following the invasion of Manchuria by a Soviet regiment. Russian tanks, cavalry and artillery penetrated about 20 miles before withdrawing, leaving 90 Chinese dead. Constant skirmishes are reported along the Siberian frontier and Soviet gunboats are said to have steamed up the Sungari River.

While Soviet officials do not disguise the gravity of the situation, they emphasize that raids and skirmishes are not the same as war, which they hope may still be averted. Meanwhile, the tone of the Soviet press has toughened. The army newspaper Red Star trumpets, "Bestial Outrages Upon Soviet Citizens," while the Moscow Daily Worker insists that "Chinese Bandits Must Be Stopped."

In a note to Washington, the Chinese government accuses the Soviets of plotting to overthrow the Chinese government, using the Chinese Eastern Railway and other Soviet-controlled institutions to further "the nefarious schemes" of the Bolsheviki. China also charges Russia with a policy of wholesale assassination meant partly to foment a worldwide revolution (→ 9/9).

1929

SEPTEMBER

Su	Mo	Tu	We	Th	Fr	Sa
1	2	3	4	5	6	7
8	9	10	11	12	13	14
15	16	17	18	19	20	21
22	23	24	25	26	27	28
29	30					

2. Radio service opens between N.Y. and Costa Rica.

3. New York: Market reaches all-time high of 381.17 (→ 24).

4. Eight killed as Transcontinental Air Transport downed by lightning over New Mexico.

8. Typhoon strikes Manila, leaving 200 Filipinos dead, thousands homeless.

9. Heavy fighting reported on Manchurian border with Soviets on offensive against Chinese (→ 9/18/31).

14. Amanullah, ex-king of Afghanistan, and his queen converted to Catholicism in Italian exile.

15. Britain begins to scrap cruisers under terms of disarmament treaty (→ 10/4).

17. Coup overthrows Voldermaras, dictator of Lithuania.

18. Charles Lindbergh starts 10,000-mile air tour of South America.

19. British recommend admission of Iraq to League of Nations.

20. Fire and panic kill 18, injure 47 in Detroit cabaret.

21. New York Vestry of St. Matthew's upholds barring Negroes from Episcopalian parish.

22. Germany: Communists and Nazis clash amid gunfire in Berlin (→ 10/26).

24. New York: Stock leaders sag in wave of liquidation (→ 10/19).

24. American Army pilot James Doolittle makes first flight using only instruments for guidance.

24. U.S.S.R.: Soviets issue new work regulations, calling for five-day week.

24. Washington: Hoover insists on tariff flexibility; Senate divided over issue (→ 6/17/30).

26. U.S.: Calvin Coolidge signs 1,000 copies of autobiography in 3.5 hours.

30. First rocket plane, invented by Fritz von Opel, makes successful test flight.

BIRTH

10. Arnold Palmer, American golfer.

Briand proposes European union

Briand: Dream of a united Europe.

Sept 5. French Premier Aristide Briand made a radical proposal in Geneva today. He called for the creation of a United States of Europe. Briand received polite applause at the League of Nations but a rather cool reaction from Germany and Britain. One diplomat said the idea received "a first class burial" at a lunch after the speech.

Arabs continuing Palestine revolt

Sept 2. With one million Arabs reported near revolt, British troops rushed to the Syrian border have captured 1,000 Arab tribesmen massed for an attack on the Palestinian town of Hibbon. The British High Commissioner in Palestine, condemning the Moslem attacks, promises stern punishments and upholds the Jewish right of access to the Wailing Wall. (→ 10/20/30).

Daily life on the streets of Jerusalem.

1929

OCTOBER

Su	Mo	Tu	We	Th	Fr	Sa
		1	2	3	4	5
6	7	8	9	10	11	12
13	14	15	16	17	18	19
20	21	22	23	24	25	26
29	28	29	30	31		

3. Diplomatic relations restored between U.S.S.R. and U.K.

3. Official name of Kingdom of Serbs, Croats and Slovenes changed to Yugoslavia.

4. Colorado prison riot ends as leader kills comrades, then self; ten guards killed in day-long tragedy.

4. British P.M. Ramsay MacDonald arrives in Washington to discuss naval parity, bolster Kellogg-Briand Pact (→ 9).

9. Hoover and MacDonald join in proclaiming war between U.S. and Britain "unthinkable" (→ 12/26).

14. Philadelphia Athletics win World Series at home, 3-2 over Cubs in fifth game.

14. Chiang's Nationalists threatened as revolt spreads through all China (→ 18).

15. Commander Byrd begins spring expedition in Little America, Antarctica (→ 11/29).

17. Nadir Khan elected emir of Afghanistan.

18. China: Foreigners flee to Japanese, British gunboats as Chinese mutiny in Shanghai (→ 11/3).

19. New York: Stocks driven way down as wave of selling engulfs market (→ 23).

21. Washington: Edison, Ford, Hoover celebrate 50th anniversary of electric light.

22. Eleventh Briand Cabinet overthrown in France.

22. N.Y. Natl. City Bank's Pres. insists, "I know of nothing fundamentally wrong with the stock market or with the underlying . . . credit structure" (→ 23).

23. N.Y.: Stocks crash in massive liquidations; total drop equals billions (→ 24).

23. First transcontinental all-air service begins, N.Y. to L.A. in 36 hours with overnight stop.

26. Germany: Hitler and Nationalist leader Hugenberg head large demonstration against Young Plan (→ 11/30).

DEATH

3. Gustav Stresemann, ex-chancellor of Weimar Republic (*5/10/1878).

Black Thursday: Stock market crash

Oct 24. From one end of the United States to the other, financial uncertainty and fear fed on rumor and cascaded into panic today. Frightened investors ordered their brokers to sell at whatever the price, and the stock market crashed. Dazed brokers on the floor of the Wall Street exchange waded in paper and tried to add up their losses. This is a day that will be known for years as "Black Thursday."

It is hard to quantify the losses, but they are believed to rise into the billions of dollars. Thousands of accounts were wiped out as a record number of shares were traded. It would not be a large exaggeration to say that some stocks were almost given away. Nearly 13 million shares traded hands.

There were spectacular declines in individual stocks in the middle of the day. The most precipitous declines occurred between 11:15 a.m. and 12:15 p.m. General Electric dropped 17 points after tumbling 20 yesterday. Johns-Manville stock lost almost 25% of its value. Montgomery Ward fell from 84 to 50. The companies recovered later in the afternoon, but still posted significant losses for the day.

Brokers on the floor of the exchange have never seen a day like this, and they hope it will never happen again. They could not keep up with the excesses of the market, and neither could their machines. The ticker fought a losing battle all day; by the time the final bell sounded at 3:00, it was four hours behind.

The shocks on Wall Street spread to other exchanges and markets. There was near-panic on the Chicago commodities exchange.

One of the primary villains was rumor, on and off the exchange. One report said at least 11 speculators had committed suicide.

The market stabilized in the afternoon. That was too late for many smaller investors, but prices did start to rise as soon as word spread that a meeting was being held at J.P. Morgan & Co. Bankers emerged from the meeting to assure investors that the market, despite the unprecedented losses, was essentially sound. They also indicated they would prop up the exchange to prevent it from dropping further.

"I am still of the opinion that this reaction has badly overrun itself," said Charles Mitchell, Chairman of the National City Bank.

A banker who did not attend the meeting agreed. "Severe disturbances in the stock market are nothing new in American experience," said Lewis Pierson, Chairman of the Board of Irving Trust. "The pendulum always swings widely, and it would seem as though the long-expected break should bring about an equilibrium."

The market dropped dramatically in the last hour of trading yesterday as 2.6 million shares were traded. But the fears of a decline started building several weeks ago, when reports spread that managers of large trusts were liquidating many of their securities.

There are a few theories to explain what happened today. Several analysts have been warning that the euphoric buying spree had to stop at some point. They said that prices had been pushed too high, and some stocks were selling at 15 to 150 times their earnings.

Thousands of foreign investors have sold their portfolios recently and are reinvesting at home as their countries recover from the war. Domestic speculators have also been probing the market for profits.

Psychology also played a large role. Investors were hoping for some life in the market yesterday. When it remained in the doldrums, they started calling their brokers with sell orders. No theory is implausible, and some analysts say weather may even have played a part. Many Western cities were blanketed by snow and sleet, which made communication with New York more difficult. With all the uncertainties, the Westerners did not want to be left out in the cold. They also decided to sell (→ 11/9).

Washington watches over anxious crowds in front of The Stock Exchange.

STAGE BROADWAY SCREEN

VARIETY

PRICE 25¢

VOL. XCVII. No. 3 NEW YORK, WEDNESDAY, OCTOBER 30, 1929 88 PAGES

WALL ST. LAYS AN EGG

The entertainment industry awakes to the abrupt end of the Coolidge Boom.

1929

NOVEMBER

Su	Mo	Tu	We	Th	Fr	Sa
					1	2
3	4	5	6	7	8	9
10	11	12	13	14	15	16
17	18	19	20	21	22	23
24	25	26	27	28	29	30

1. Ex-Sec. of Interior Albert B. Fall given one-year sentence, fined $100,000 for taking bribe for lease of govt. oil lands (→ 3/22/30).

3. Fox Film Corp. sells first natl. holdings to Warners, says talkies have made silent films obsolete.

3. Chinese rebels score decisive victory at Hankow; Nationalists in flight (→ 24).

8. Bank for Intl. Settlements picks Switzerland as site of world bank.

9. N.Y.: James J. Riordan, pres. of County Trust Co., commits suicide with pistol (→ 11).

11. N.Y.: Stocks break again in new selling rush; U.S. Steel at year's low (→ 18).

13. Baghdad: Iraqi Premier Sir Abdul Muhsin commits suicide.

16. N.Y.: WEAF broadcasts "Madame Butterfly," first Puccini opera heard over air.

17. Stalin expels Bukharin and other leaders from Russian Communist Party (→ 9/24/30).

18. Sec. of Commerce urges $423 mil. building plan on eve of Hoover's trade parleys (→ 23).

20. Paris: Surrealist writer Andre Breton presents first Salvador Dali exhibit.

21. Henry Ford, in attempt to bolster confidence in economy, announces he will raise wages in all plants.

24. Revolt in China halted to save Manchuria from Soviets (→ 4/23/30).

26. Belgian Prime Minister Henri Jaspar overthrown due to conflict between French and Dutch speakers.

27. Cole Porter's "Fifty Million Frenchmen" opens in N.Y.

30. Germany: Allies evacuate second occupation zone in Rhineland (→ 12/22).

BIRTH

12. Grace Patricia Kelly, U.S. actress and princess of Monaco (†9/14/1982).

DEATH

6. Max de Bade, German ex-chancellor (*7/10/1867).

Byrd ends vast Antarctic air survey

Nov 29. Commander Richard E. Byrd and three companions returned to their home base at Little America in the Antarctic today after completing the first flight over the South Pole. The polar flight is part of a systematic effort by Byrd and his team to explore the uncharted five million square miles of the Antarctic continent. The achievement was made possible by a flight on November 18, during which Byrd established a supply base 440 miles south of Little America.

Flying a Ford trimotor, the Byrd party took off from Little America at 10:29 p.m. yesterday. The aircraft stopped for an hour to refuel at the supply base and arrived over the South Pole at 8:55 this morning, after a hazardous, wind-buffeted flight. Byrd circled the pole for an hour, then headed the airplane for his home base. It landed at Little America at 10:10 a.m. Among other discoveries, Byrd and the dog team party he sent out have found two previously uncharted Antarctic mountain ranges, which they hope to explore more thoroughly in a series of expeditions.

Commander Byrd.

New York's dapper Mayor wins again

Nov 5. New York City voters gave Tammany Hall a rousing victory yesterday, re-electing dapper James J. "Jimmy" Walker to another four-year term as Mayor.

Mayor Walker, a Democrat, piled up a plurality of 497,165 votes in defeating the Republican candidate, Fiorello LaGuardia, and the Socialist Party's Norman Thomas. In a statement issued after his reelection, Walker criticized what he called the malicious and slanderous comments made against him by his opponents, adding: "I hope this will be the last of the time-worn, motheaten imaginary slogan, Anti-Tammany" (→ 3/18/31).

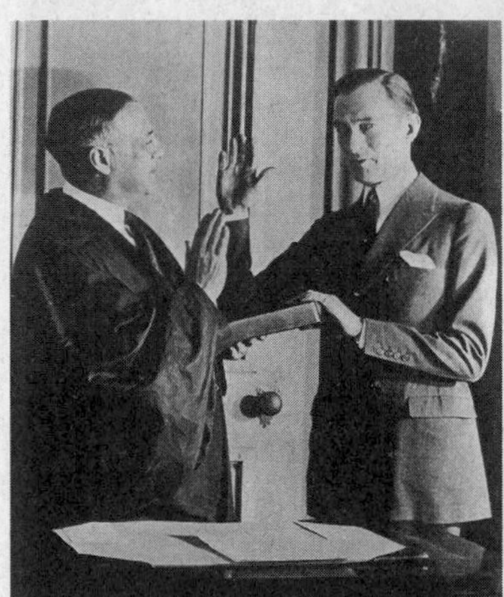

Walker sworn in by Judge Wagner.

France's grand old man gone forever

Nov 23. George Clemenceau, nicknamed the "Tiger" and known as the "Father of Victory," is dead at 88. He began his political career in 1870 with the Paris Commune when he became the Mayor of the 18th arrondissement. Then as Deputy, Senator, Home Secretary and Premier, Clemenceau earned the reputation of statesman. After negotiating the Versailles treaty, he lost the 1920 presidential elections.

Clemenceau, "The Tiger."

Hoover seeking to bolster economy

Nov 23. President Herbert Hoover is trying to use the power of his office to catalyze the economy and prevent it from crashing as the stock market did one month ago.

Hoover is planning to expand federal construction to create new jobs. He will ask Congress for an additional $175 million for new buildings, most of them to be erected outside Washington. The president is also appealing to the 48 governors to speed up their own public works programs.

Hoover has formed a high-powered council of business and banking leaders to advise and assist him. Their chief job, said the president, will be to "keep the country's business on an even keel." Hoover is also asking the businessmen to increase production, and he wants labor to unite with business to keep wages level.

Henry Ford met with Hoover at the White House this week. Afterwards, Ford surprised other business leaders by announcing from his car that he would give his workers a raise. He also warned that business would have to make itself more attractive to executives who have gone off to make bigger profits as Wall Street speculators (→ 12/4).

"Le Choix d'un Coeur," by Erte. The popular French artist's vibrant colors have captured the glamor of the twenties.

1929

DECEMBER

Su	Mo	Tu	We	Th	Fr	Sa
1	2	3	4	5	6	7
8	9	10	11	12	13	14
15	16	17	18	19	20	21
22	23	24	25	26	27	28
29	30	31				

4. Hoover forecasts big surplus in message to Congress; asks 1931 budget of $3.8 mil. (→ 5).

5. 400 U.S. business leaders set up council to foster trade under Hoover's plan (→ 1/2/30).

6. British viceroy meets with Indian leaders to discuss dominion status for India (→ 21).

6. Hoover rushes Marines to Haiti, under martial law due to widespread revolt (→ 2/6/30).

7. Turkey grants vote to women (→ 3/28/30).

9. U.S. envoy in Geneva signs "Root formula" calling for U.S. to join World Court (→ 9/4/30).

11. N.Y.: Auburn warden saved, eight convicts killed as prison suffers second revolt in year.

15. Peking: Canadian archeologist Davidson Black discovers cave with fossilized bones believed to be 400,000 years old.

19. Britain gives 7.5-hour day to coal miners.

21. Indian National Congress convenes in Lahore (→ 3/12/30).

22. Plebiscite set up by German rightists upholds Young Plan on reparations (→ 1/3/30).

23. Operetta "Babes in Toyland" a big hit at New York opening.

26. Paris note demands navy to protect "wide empire," calls Kellogg Pact weak (→ 1/15/30).

29. Spanish dictator Primo de Rivera announces retirement from political life (→ 1/28/30).

CULTURAL EVENTS, 1929

Literature: Jean Cocteau's "Les Enfants Terribles"; Hemingway's "A Farewell To Arms"; Faulkner's "The Sound and the Fury"; Erich Marie Remarque's "All Quiet on the Western Front"; Thomas Wolfe's "Look Homeward Angel."

Academia: Walter Lippman's "A Preface to Morals"; Jose Ortega y Gasset's "The Revolt of the Masses"; Richard and Harriet Lynd's "Middletown."

Music: "Tiptoe Through the Tulips"; "Singin' in the Rain"; "I've Got A Crush on you."

Film: Hitchcock's "Blackmail"; silent films overrun by talkies.

Big year in books; Mann wins Nobel

Dec 10. Thomas Mann, eminent German author, has been awarded the 1929 Nobel Prize for literature. Although he has produced little this year, he is recognized for his first novel "Buddenbrooks," published in 1901; his novella "Death in Venice," published in 1912; and "The Magic Mountain," published in 1924. Mann, who is 52, has been fascinated by youth and age, health and illness. Through his heroes and anti-heroes, he explores the clash of Dionysian impulses and the constraints of civilization.

Other authors found 1929 a great year to recall the Great War. Erich Maria Remarque's "All Quiet on the Western Front" is a riveting account of battle as seen through German eyes. Robert Graves' "Goodbye to All That" has a particularly pessimistic view of combat. Former newspaperman Ernest Hemingway has written "A Farewell to Arms." The semi-autobiographical novel takes place in an Italian hospital during the war, but some readers consider it more of a love story. The most belligerent thing about the book may be its style: tough, terse and arrestingly honest.

Mann's 1901 first edition.

Hemingway: "A Farewell to Arms."

Hemingway was joined by several other American authors: Thomas Wolfe published "Look Homeward, Angel," William Faulkner wrote "The Sound and the Fury" and Sinclair Lewis offered "Dodsworth." Experimental French works garnered much attention this year; Jean Cocteau's "Les Enfants Terrible," Andre Gide's "L'Ecole des Femmes" and Jean Giraudoux's "Amphitryon 38" were among them.

New York's Museum of Modern Art opens

December. The Museum of Modern Art, which opened to the public November 8, is already planning its second exhibit. Its first, featuring Impressionist art, was extremely successful. Yet there were patriotic grumblings over the choice; not a single American painter was showcased. The next exhibit will include Americans Charles Demuth, Max Weber, Georgia O'Keefe, Walt Kuhn and Edward Hopper.

On the last day of the Impressionist exhibit early this month, 5,300 people crowded the galleries at 731 Fifth Avenue in New York City. The works of Vincent van Gogh, Paul Gauguin, Georges Seurat and Paul Cezanne were welcomed warmly.

A modern masterpiece by van Gogh.

Soviet troops leave Manchuria after truce

Dec 22. Sino-Soviet negotiations on the Chinese Eastern Railway dispute were concluded today with a truce that restores the status quo ante on the railway and diplomatic relations.

The treaty includes the following points:

1. Both sides agree to "call off" their troops.
2. Soviet and Chinese railroad executives who lost their jobs because of the dispute will have them restored.
3. All arrested citizens will be released.
4. The Chinese agree to dissolve the White Guard Corps, consisting of White Russians, and expel the leaders and organizers from Manchuria.
5. Sino-Soviet economic organizations will be re-established.

The trouble began when the Chinese, in raids on Russian consulates in Manchuria, allegedly found evidence that Soviet railway officials were using their offices to dispense Communist propaganda. They thereupon detained many Russians, expelled others and seized the Eastern Railway. The Chinese were defeated in the border skirmishes and the Russians occupied a considerable section of western Manchuria. The Soviets said this was necessary to protect Siberian villages from border raids by irresponsible White Russians and Chinese.

Flapper fad fades with the onset of hard times.

1930–1939

1930

JANUARY

Su	Mo	Tu	We	Th	Fr	Sa
			1	2	3	4
5	6	7	8	9	10	11
12	13	14	15	16	17	18
19	20	21	22	23	24	25
26	27	28	29	30	31	

1. Pasadena: S. Cal. trounces Pittsburgh 47-14 in Rose Bowl.

2. Hoover calls congressional leaders to discuss public works program (→ 2/3).

3. The Hague: Second conference on war reparations begins (→ 23).

10. New York: Plane fare to West Coast cut to $159.92.

11. Vatican: Pope condemns naturalism taught in schools.

12. Hoover urges Congress to rebuild dry law enforcement machinery (→ 28).

14. Mr. and Mrs. Albert Einstein dine with Charlie Chaplin at his Hollywood home.

15. Amelia Earhart sets aviation record for women at 171 mph in Lockheed Vega (→ 5/21/32).

15. British P.M. MacDonald urges abolition of battleship by all world powers (→ 21).

17. U.S.S.R. violates Lausanne Convention, sending battleships through Dardanelles straits.

20. Lindbergh arrives in N.Y., setting cross-country flying record of 14.75 hours (→ 6/22).

20. Lt. James Doolittle resigns from U.S. Army.

21. London: International arms parley opens (→ 31).

22. Adm. Richard Byrd charts vast new 15,000-mile area of Antarctica (→ 2/19).

23. Wilhelm Frick becomes Min. of Interior for Thuringia, first Nazi to take office in Germany (→ 3/30).

24. New York: Primo Carnera scores first-round knockout over "Big Boy" Peterson.

25. N.Y. police rout Communist rally at Town Hall (→ 3/6).

28. Madrid: Spanish dictator Miguel Primo de Rivera resigns (→ 3/16).

BIRTHS

20. Edwin E. "Buzz" Aldrin, U.S. astronaut.

23. Derek A. Walcott, Caribbean poet and playwright.

24. Kjell Laugerud Garcia, president of Guatemala.

Stalin starts collectivizing agriculture

"Red Rye" train departs from collective farms in the Central Black Soil Belt.

Jan 5. Joseph Stalin, the Soviet leader, gave Russian farmers another lesson today on what Communism is all about. He formally collectivized Russian farms and created agricultural cooperatives.

Under the system, land, livestock and all farm equipment become the property of the state cooperative. Farmers are granted free use of the state property, which is managed by a government bureaucrat. Income from the farms is divided among the farmers, based on the quality and quantity of their work. Each peasant family is allowed to own a house, garden, stable and one cow. And they are allowed to keep any income from the sale of their garden vegetables.

Stalin has conceded that the Communist experiment requires sacrifice and discipline if it is to succeed. The sorry state of the Western economies has given him a little time to maneuver (→ 3/1).

Major naval powers seek to cut fleets

Jan 31. The world's five major naval powers —Britain, the United States, France, Japan and Italy — met in London to discuss limitations on naval armaments. The London Naval Arms Conference was opened by King George V, himself a naval officer, who told the delegates the world was looking to them to find ways to reduce fleets and eliminate the threat of war.

The conference, a sequel to the Washington Conference of 1921 that led to limitations in the construction of capital ships, was convened at the suggestion of Britain and the United States. From the outset, there were suspicions on the French and Japanese sides that the two English-speaking powers had entered into an arrangement to protect their fleets at the expense of other powers. As head of the American delegation, Secretary of State Henry L. Stimson sought to reassure the other nations that there was no such understanding except a tentative agreement on Anglo-American parity in warship tonnage.

As the conference proceeded, France proposed a compromise between the British approach of limiting warships by categories and the French proposal to set a total naval tonnage for each nation (→ 2/6).

Dry law 10 years old; alcoholism soars

Jan 28. The friends of temperance celebrated and its enemies tolled bells as America observed the 10th anniversary of Prohibition this month. The ban on alcohol, as provided under the 18th Amendment, has been the center of nationwide controversy since it took effect at the stroke of midnight, January 15, 1920.

Thriving business at a speakeasy.

Prohibitionists have called it a blessing, with money once spent on liquor now being used by working families to feed and clothe their children. Opponents, in turn, claim that the law has spawned graft and murder, enriching bootleggers and causing countless deaths from impure alcohol. Because of Prohibition, say the officials of the Moderation League, "a spirit of revolt" is abroad in the nation.

Meanwhile, the Metropolitan Life Insurance Company has reported that deaths from alcoholism among its policyholders last year was six times the rate of ten years ago (→ 2/10).

The drive for a secular society: Soviet troops transfer icons from Moscow's Simonov Convent to the coffers of the Politburo.

1930

FEBRUARY

Su	Mo	Tu	We	Th	Fr	Sa
						1
2	3	4	5	6	7	8
9	10	11	12	13	14	15
16	17	18	19	20	21	22
23	24	25	26	27	28	

3. Washington: William Howard Taft resigns as chief justice of Supreme Court (→ 13).

3. Report indicates U.S. incomes over $1 million increased 40 percent in 1928 (→ 24).

3. New Zealand struck by earthquake, leaving 800 dead, 66,000 homeless.

6. U.S. commission recommends reforms for Haiti, urges Stenio Vincent for president.

6. London: U.S. Sec. of State Stimson demands naval parity with Britain at 15 battleships (→ 3/21).

8. French Natl. Assembly passes social security bill.

8. Vactican: Pope Pius XI condemns U.S.S.R. for persecution of Christians (→ 3/15).

9. Andres Segovia plays New York's Town Hall.

9. Bavaria: World's first auto race on ice won by German Hans Stuck in Daimler.

10. Cardinal Eugenio Pacelli appointed head of Vatican diplomatic corps (→ 3/2/39).

10. Chicago: 186 indicted in huge rum-running plot (→ 20).

14. Rome: Vatican orders ban on indecent dress.

15. St. Louis: Bill Tilden voted world's best tennis player.

17. Paris: Tardieu Cabinet overthrown by five votes.

19. Antarctica: Adm. Byrd leaves for U.S. (→ 6/19).

20. Washington: Fredrick Courdet predicts civil war if dry law is enforced (→ 27).

20. Poland: 14 Jews facing trial in Warsaw for religious views.

24. Washington: Hoover tells Congress to economize or face 40 percent tax hike (→ 3/7).

27. Miami: Jack Sharkey KOs Phil Scott in third round (→ 6/20/32).

27. Washington: Pierre DuPont comes out in favor of Prohibition repeal (→ 3/10).

DEATH

23. Mabel Normand, American silent film star (*11/10/1897).

Hughes is Chief Justice as Taft resigns

Feb 13. After days of intense debate, the Senate voted tonight to confirm Charles Evans Hughes as the Chief Justice of the Supreme Court. Hughes will succeed William Howard Taft, who resigned the high court's top post earlier this month because of ill health.

Conservative Republican Hughes.

Hughes served as an Associate Justice of the Supreme Court from 1910 until 1916, resigning that year to run for president on the Republican ticket. He was narrowly defeated by President Woodrow Wilson in one of the closest elections ever held in the United States. A former Governor of New York, Hughes served as Secretary of State under Presidents Harding and Coolidge.

Senate confirmation of Hughes came on a vote of 52 to 26, after a fight in which opponents argued that Hughes would only deepen the Supreme Court's already conservative hue (→ 3/8).

Red lights will protect pedestrians

Feb 26. New York City is installing traffic lights. The decision follows complaints from drivers who say pedestrians stray into the path of vehicles. The signals, placed at Manhattan intersections, will be used citywide if successful.

New York studied traffic plans in other cities and rejected the common use of amber lights. Amber or yellow lights mean to slow autos for the complete stop signaled by red. The New York Board ruled amber lights ineffective.

Traffic lights were developed in 1923 by Garrett A. Morgan, a Negro businessman. Morgan is also the inventor of the gas mask.

Norway's Sonja Henie keeps skating title

Feb 5. Sonja Henie, the dimpled Norwegian sprite who has captured the affection of figure-skating fans everywhere, has been crowned the world's amateur singles champion for the fourth consecutive time. She charmed and excited a crowd of 13,000 at Madison Square Garden with a brilliant performance. The 17-year-old surpassed her previous efforts of Oslo, London and Budapest in her three previous wins.

Karl Schafer of Vienna, last year's runner-up, won the men's singles title. Schafer was nearly as graceful as the diminutive Norwegian, but he also was bold and daring. The 19-year-old skater performed his figures and leaping spins with an abandon for which he has striven for years. Roger F. Turner, the national champion, was runner-up to Schafer. Miss Cecil Smith of Canada was the second-place finisher in the women's division.

Miss Henie nearly fell when she started a jump spin but quickly recovered and, smiling at the crowd, went into a series of back glides with unexpected pivots and swirls.

Graceful Sonja Henie started skating at the tender age of eight.

Garbo talks: Asks for shot of whiskey

Lovely Garbo in "Anna Christie."

February. The public's fears are allayed: Garbo talks. Her first talkie, "Anna Christie," has just been released. In her first scene in the film, she strides into a bar and says, "Gif me a visky, ginger ale on the side. And don't be stingy, baby."

Some of Garbo's fans wondered if she could make the transition to sound. She is Swedish, after all, and no one knew how impenetrable her accent might be. Her frequent costar in silent pictures, John Gilbert, looks like a casualty; his first talkie reveals a "white voice"—flat, tinny, and anything but seductive.

"Anna Christie" seems made for Garbo. Adapted from a play by Eugene O'Neill, the film centers on the tragic, driven life of a Swedish-American woman. Garbo's husky, alluring accent is ideal for the role, and the plot calls forth the tears her fans yearn to shed.

1930

MARCH

Su	Mo	Tu	We	Th	Fr	Sa
						1
2	3	4	5	6	7	8
9	10	11	12	13	14	15
16	17	18	19	20	21	22
23	24	25	26	27	28	29
30	31					

1. Thousands of Russians reported fleeing to Poland to escape collective work (→ 12/22).

2. "Love Parade" released, starring Maurice Chevalier and Jeannette MacDonald.

3. Southwest France plagued by floods; at least 200 dead.

7. Washington: Hoover reportedly proclaims, "Prosperity is just around the corner" (→ 24).

10. Washington: Republican Club votes for dry law repeal (→ 26).

10. N.Y. Police Commissioner Whalen gives employers blacklist of Communists (→ 7/5).

10. 104 killed in Japanese theater fire.

13. Arizona: Scientists report discovery of ninth planet (→ 5/24).

15. Moscow reportedly bars coercion of churches (→ 19).

17. Philadelphia: Al Capone released from jail (→ 6/13).

19. Rome: Pope Pius XI gives special mass for Russian churches (→ 3/11/31).

21. London: French walk out of naval parley (→ 4/21).

22. Doheny acquitted on charges of bribing ex-Sec. of Int. Albert Fall for oil lease in Elk Hills.

24. U.S. Senate passes bill increasing tariffs (→ 31).

26. Washington: Ex-Premier of Ontario calls Prohibition failure in U.S. (→ 4/13).

28. Turkish Nationalists change Greek name of Constantinople to Istanbul (→ 4/20/31).

30. Berlin: Socialist Cabinet replaced by Heinrich Bruning's coalition of the Right (→ 5/9).

31. Congress adopts Public Buildings Act; appropriates $230 mil. for program (→ 4/4).

BIRTHS

22. Stephen Sondheim, Broadway composer.

26. Sandra Day O'Connor, first woman appointed to U.S. Supreme Court.

26. Gregory Corso, American poet, beat generation.

Gandhi leads Salt March

Gandhi speaks on role of non-violence in India's fight against colonialism.

March 12. Accompanied by a small group of followers, Mahatma Gandhi began a "march to the sea" in symbolic defiance of British rule over the Indian subcontinent.

It was the boldest act of civil disobedience thus far by the nationalist leader who has been campaigning for an end to British rule. His objective is to march to the Gulf of Gambay and there manufacture salt in defiance of a British law establishing a government monopoly for production of salt. At the first stop in Asiali in the long journey, Gandhi told a large gathering that his followers must be prepared "for the worst, even death, for defiance of the salt tax." He also defied the British authorities to arrest him.

Throughout Upper India, there were reports of demonstrations, largely orderly, in sympathy for the Gandhi protest. Among British authorities, there was a belief that a campaign of civil disobedience inevitably would lead to violence, and British troops were placed on alert. It was expected Gandhi would be arrested shortly (→ 4/5).

Communists battle police; two killed

The perils of leftist politics in N.Y.

March 6. Two persons were killed and scores of others injured in clashes yesterday between police and demonstrators in America and much of Europe. The demonstrations were staged, apparently by Communists, to protest unemployment on the two continents.

In New York City, onlookers were swept into the battle between police and protesters, resulting in what some observers called the worst riot in that city's recent history. Police also routed demonstrators in front of the White House in Washington. In Germany, two persons were killed in the town of Halle, and there was violence, too, in Spain and elsewhere in Europe (→ 10).

Noted novelist is dead in France

March 2. David Herbert Lawrence, author, died in France today at 45. His last novel, "Lady Chatterley's Lover," published two years ago, is best known for the fact that it is banned in the United States and England because of its explicit treatment of an affair between an English noblewoman and her husband's gamekeeper. And "Sons and Lovers" (1913) and "Women in Love" (1921) are both concerned with the consequences of trying to deny man's union with nature.

Lawrence was born September 11, 1885, to a coal miner. He became a teacher and scandously married a divorcee. Because of the Lawrences' opposition to the war, they were accused of espionage. In 1919, they left England to live a nomadic life.

D.H. Lawrence in Taos, N.M.

Balfour, writer of famed letter, dead

March 19. Arthur Balfour, former British Prime Minister, statesman and staunch spokesman for the Conservative Party, has died at his home at Fisher's Hill, at 81. Outside England, Balfour is perhaps best known as author of the Balfour Declaration, actually a letter to Lord Rothschild stating his government's commitment to a Jewish national home in Palestine, and influenced by a desire to sway Jewish opinion to the Allied cause during the Great War.

1930

APRIL

Su	Mo	Tu	We	Th	Fr	Sa
		1	2	3	4	5
6	7	8	9	10	11	12
13	14	15	16	17	18	19
20	21	22	23	24	25	26
29	28	29	30			

1. Josef von Sternberg film "Blue Angel," starring Marlene Dietrich, released in Germany.

4. U.S. Congress votes $300 mil. for road construction (→ 5/4).

5. India: Mahatma Gandhi makes salt, defying British law (→ 16).

11. New York scientist predicts man will reach moon by 2050 (→ 7/16/69).

13. New York: Women stage mass protest against dry law (→ 5/24).

14. Washington: Herbert Hoover throws first ball in to start baseball season.

16. Rioting continues in India, as British police fire on mob of 10,000 (→ 23).

16. Chinese rebels launch offensive in North against Chiang Kai-shek's Nanking government (→ 23).

18. Rumania: Church fire kills 144.

19. Los Angeles: 16 die in plane crash.

21. Ohio: Horrible fire kills 355 out of 4,300 convicts held in prison designed to hold 1,500 (→ 28).

23. India: Riots break out in Peshawar; 20 Indians shot down after killing of three British (→ 5/4).

26. Belgium: King Albert I inaugurates international exhibition at Antwerp.

27. Buster Keaton's latest film "The Cameraman" released in U.S.

28. Ohio: Troops drop bombs as prisoners revolt a week after fatal fire.

28. California witnesses total eclipse of the sun.

BIRTH

3. Helmut Kohl, German statesman.

DEATHS

19. Charles Scribner, American publisher.

21. Seymour Bridges, poet laureate of England (*10/25/1844).

Taft, who occupied many offices, dies

March 8. Former President William Howard Taft died today at his home in Washington at age 72. In recent years, Taft had been Chief Justice of the Supreme Court. He resigned just a month ago because of ill health. During his long career of public service, Taft, a Republican, held many offices, including Secretary of War during the administration of President Theodore Roosevelt. With Roosevelt's backing, he was elected president in 1908 and served one term before losing to Democrat Woodrow Wilson in 1912.

Rivera, who quit as dictator, dead

Rivera, victim of diabetes.

March 16. General Primo de Rivera, who until six weeks ago was dictator of Spain, died in his Paris hotel this morning. He was 60. Rivera's ascent to power was due largely to his settlement of the uprising, in French Morocco, directed against Spanish-held interests, where Moorish tribesmen cut to pieces a modern Spanish army of 20,000. He went to Africa, took personal charge, and his success made him a national hero.

Vowing that his dictatorship would last but three months, Rivera launched economic reforms at home which reduced unemployment, introduced public works and helped modernize the country. As his popularity increased, so did his rule, stretching from three months to six years. And as Spain began to grow restive with his regime, Rivera lost the King's support and resigned in February.

Chiang routs rebel attackers in China

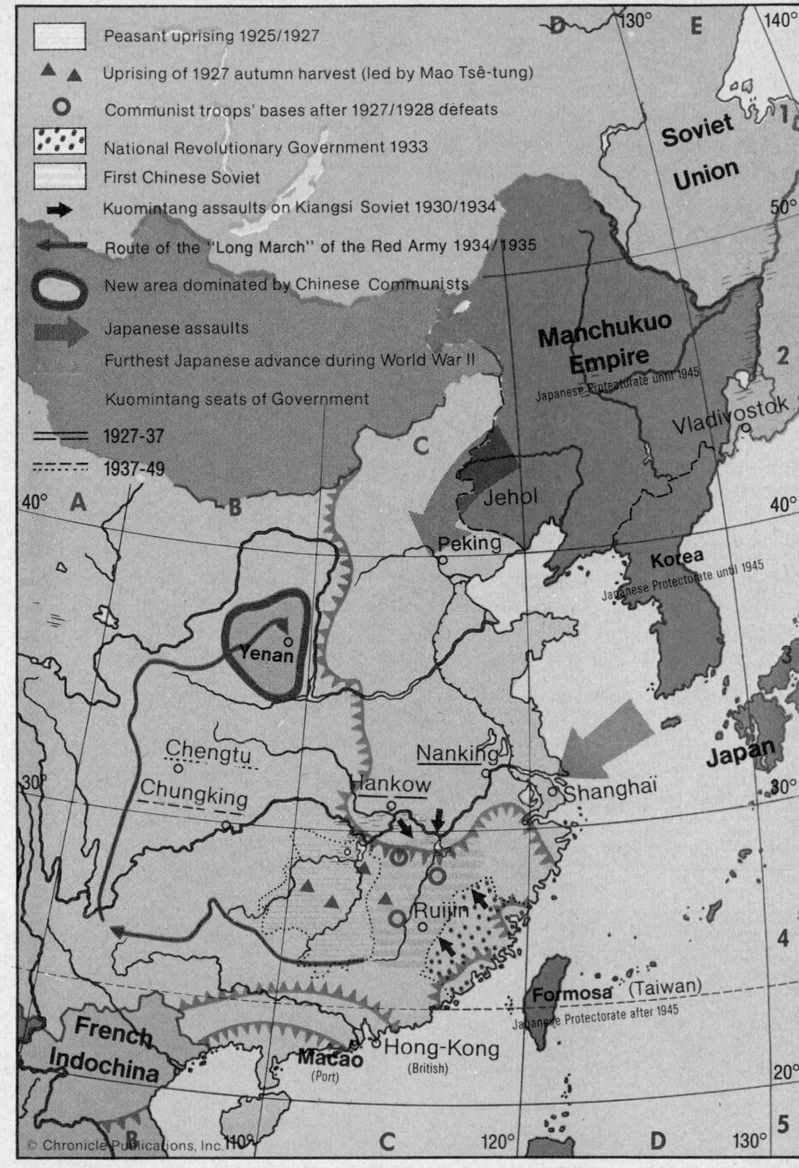

Military operations and civil war in China between 1925 and 1949.

April 23. Internal rivalries have exploded again in China and tested the will and the power of Chiang Kai-shek. The latest challenge comes from the belligerent commander of the Northern forces, General Yen Hsi-chan.

Chiang, Chairman of the Nationalist government based in Nanking, was also named Commander-in-Chief of all Chinese forces in 1928. Earlier this year, however, tensions grew in Nanking. In January, Chiang was able to consolidate his political power, but he was forced to share his military responsibilities with General Yen Hsi-chan. The general quickly became a political rival. He also revived anti-Chiang sentiment in the North.

At the beginning of the month, General Yen declared war on Chiang's government. He led his army on what was called a "punitive expedition" against Chiang. At first, the general's offensive succeeded. Just last week, he forced troops loyal to Chiang to retreat to the southern banks of the Yellow River. Chiang recovered quickly to defeat the general's forces, and he is now preparing a counter-offensive against the Northern provinces.

During the latest developments, forces hostile to Chiang have been waiting and watching for a sign of weakness. The Communists have been hiding south of Nanking since they were defeated, but not destroyed. Japan, the victor in the war with China before the turn of the century, is also watching (→ 7/10). ▷

Five great powers sign naval treaty

April 21. The London Naval Treaty seeking to control a naval arms race was signed today at a ceremony in St. James's Palace. The treaty is the product of a 14-week-long conference by the five major naval powers—Britain, the United States, Japan, France and Italy.

France and Italy refused to agree to the specific terms of the treaty, and the naval limitations will apply only to the United States, Britain and Japan. The treaty imposes tonnage limitations on various types of warships and reduces their number of battleships.

In a speech broadcast by radio from London to New York, Secretary of State Henry L. Stimson said the conference had "given me more confidence in my belief that the peaceful methods of diplomacy can eventually take the place of war" (→ 7/22).

Dietrich discovered in The Blue Angel

Dietrich stars in "The Blue Angel."

April. American director Josef von Sternberg has brought the German Garbo to the United States. Marlene Dietrich stars in "The Blue Angel." The film is darkly erotic; Dietrich plays an indifferent chorus girl named Lola Lola who brings a disciplined schoolteacher to his knees. Sternberg fills this picture with disturbing images, peopling the Blue Angel nightclub with misfits and freaks. In one of the final scenes, the professor, played by Emil Jannings, wears a clown costume onstage while Lola Lola cuckolds him behind the curtains. His laughs are horrible cries.

1930

MAY

Su	Mo	Tu	We	Th	Fr	Sa
				1	2	3
4	5	6	7	8	9	10
11	12	13	14	15	16	17
18	19	20	21	22	23	24
25	26	27	28	29	30	31

3. Washington: John D. Rockefeller congratulates Mother Jones on her 100th birthday (→ 11/30).

4. 1028 U.S. economists sign petition warning that Smoot-Hawley protectionist bill will cripple intl. trade (→ 11).

4. India: Gandhi arrested by British (→ 8).

6. Earthquake kills 6,000 in Burma; wipes out city of Pegu.

6. Japan acknowledges China's customs autonomy.

7. U.S. Senate rejects John Parker for Supreme Court.

8. Gandhi followers mob Bombay to protest his arrest (→ 27).

9. Britain, Italy, Belgium and France ratify Young Plan (→ 17).

11. New Canadian tariffs to cost U.S. $225 million (→ 6/17).

13. French aviator Jean Mermoz establishes airmail link between Paris and Brazil.

17. Jockey E. Sande becomes three-time Kentucky Derby winner on Gallant Fox.

17. Young Plan for war reparations goes into effect (→ 6/30).

19. White women enfranchised in South Africa.

22. France grants constitution to Syria.

24. Arizona: New planet given name Pluto.

24. Amy Johnson finishes solo flight from London to Australia in 19.5 days.

24. Readers Digest poll shows majority of Americans favor repeal of dry law (→ 6/9).

30. Billy Arnold takes 18th annual Indy 500 at 100.4 mph in Miller Hartz Special racer.

BIRTHS

5. Douglas Turner Ward, stage director, playwright, co-founder of Negro Ensemble Company.

15. Jasper Johns, U.S. painter.

31. Clint Eastwood, U.S. actor.

DEATH

13. Fridtjof Nansen, Norwegian explorer (*10/10/1861).

India seethes as Gandhi is arrested

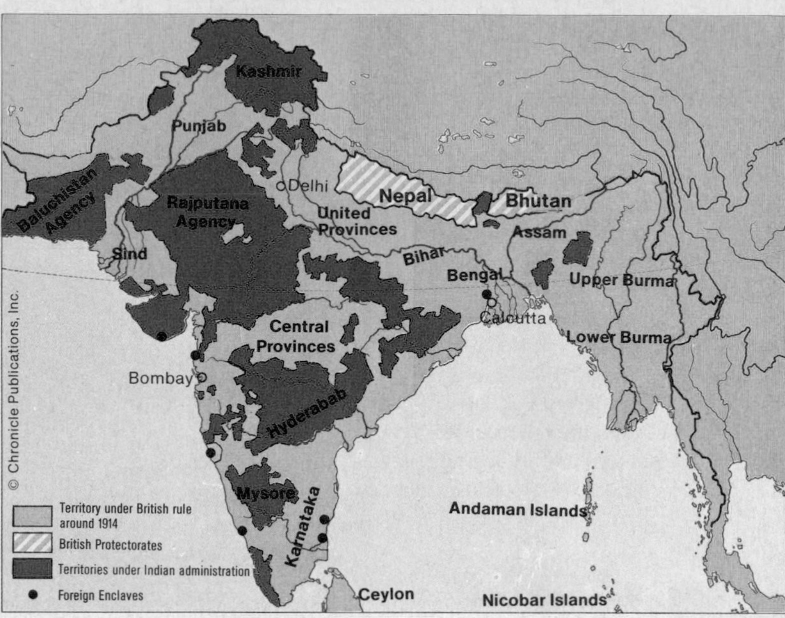

Zones of influence in India. As Gandhi's struggle for independence gathers momentum, Britain finds her authority diminishing throughout the country.

May 27. India's major cities seethed with unrest following the arrest of Mahatma Gandhi and thousands of his followers in the campaign of civil disobedience against British rule.

In Bombay, at least six were killed and 60 injured when rioters clashed with Indian police and British army units. Significantly, Moslems, who until now have refrained from any support of the civil disobedience campaign, joined Hindus in the Bombay riots.

In an interview in his cell in a jail near Poona, Gandhi said he was alarmed at the violence but said he was convinced it had not come from his disciples in civil disobedience.

Asked if he had calculated the perils of his campaign of civil disobedience, he replied, "I have taken what has been called a mad risk, but it is a justifiable risk. No great end has been achieved without incurring danger."

Gandhi's philosophy of non-violence is said to have begun when in 1919 a mob of Indians was massacred by the British at Amritsar. This led him to believe that freedom could not be won by force. Gandhi also worked as a lawyer in South Africa and used his knowledge and position to try to end the oppression of Indians there (→ 6/21).

British soldiers struggle to keep order in the tumultuous streets of India.

1930

JUNE

Su	Mo	Tu	We	Th	Fr	Sa
1	2	3	4	5	6	7
8	9	10	11	12	13	14
15	16	17	18	19	20	21
22	23	24	25	26	27	28
29	30					

1. Gangsters raid Chicago hotel, killing three.

2. 100,000 new drivers reported in U.S. over last year.

3. New York City population reported at 6.4 million.

6. Massachusetts: Frozen Food (processed by Clarence Birdseye) hits commercial market for first time (→ 2/1/54).

8. Prince Carol, back from Munich exile, ascends throne of Rumania.

9. George Wickersham condemns harshness of dry law after yesterday's shooting of 16-year-old by N.Y. detective in Speakeasy (→ 8/28).

13. Miami: Al Capone arrested on perjury charge (→ 10/24/31).

15. New York: Plans submitted for Rockefeller Center.

19. British Parliament rejects Conservatives' proposal to reduce unemployment payments.

19. New York: Adm. Byrd cheered in Broadway parade.

20. Six climb Jonsong peak in Himalayas, highest yet scaled by man.

20. U.S. golfer Bobby Jones wins British Open (→ 7/12).

21. India: 500 hurt as police charge Bombay mob (→ 7/17).

22. New Jersey: Son born to Charles and Ann Morrow Lindbergh (→ 7/28/31).

26. Charles Kingford Smith arrives in New York after non-stop flight from Ireland.

27. New England struck by electrical storms; 51 dead.

28. London: 1,000 Communists routed in assault on British consulate.

30. British promise independence to Iraq (→ 10/3/32).

BIRTH

26. Colonel Juan Melgar Castro, president of Honduras.

DEATHS

1. Jules Pascin, French painter, suicide in Paris (*3/31/1885).

13. Henry Segrave, American speed boat racer.

French troops evacuate Rhineland early

June 30. France may have given more than it received today as it pulled its last troops out of Germany's Rhineland. The withdrawal comes five years earlier than the date set by the Versailles treaty. Much of the credit for the early pull-out must be given to German Foreign Minister Gustav Stresemann, who negotiated expertly.

It remains to be seen what benefit France will receive. Her troops were in the Rhineland as insurance that Germany would respect the Versailles treaty and not re-arm itself. The Germans have always opposed the occupation forces. But they seem so preoccupied now with mounting unemployment and political instability that they are not likely to thank France for leaving early.

Now that the French troops are gone, Germany is not allowed to send any forces to the left bank of the Rhine. Germany must also respect a demilitarized zone that extends about 30 miles east of the Rhine. Those were the original terms of the Versailles treaty, reaffirmed by Germany at Locarno. Paul Tirard, the French High Commissioner who supervised the occupation, was congratulated by the Foreign Ministry for "handling a difficult and particularly delicate responsibility" (→ 7/16).

The French leave the Rhine behind.

Sharkey's foul makes Schmeling champ

Jack Sharkey waits patiently in his corner after dropping Schmeling to the canvas in the fourth round with a conspicuous low blow.

June 12. The fight to determine a successor to the world heavyweight title vacated by Gene Tunney in 1928 turned out to be something of a farce. Max Schmeling was declared the winner and new champion on a foul, something that never happened in boxing before.

Sharkey had been outfighting the German through the first three rounds when the fight went to pieces. Sharkey threw a hard, but low, left in the fourth. Schmeling went down. Joe Jacobs, Schmeling's manager, rushed into the ring with his seconds and carried his warrior off. Jacobs exchanged harsh words with the referee, who, after waffling indecisively, stopped the fight and declared Schmeling champion.

Gangster gunmen on a big rampage

June 1. With the nation in the grip of a crime wave, a new Chicago gang war was launched this morning when machine guns served up death at a dinner party at the Fox Lake Hotel, a resort 50 miles from Chicago favored by the remnants of the "Bugs" Moran gang.

The killers appeared at a dining room window and began showering the guests with a leaden entree, killing three and wounding two. Those who will never lift another spoon are Sam Pellar, late of the Al Capone gang; Michael Quirk of the Klondike O'Connell gang, twice charged with murder; and Joseph Bertsche of the Druggan Valley gang, killer, mail robber and a crook of 30 years' standing.

Attributed to internecine warfare, the massacre would appear to terminate the recent gang truce.

Art mirrors life: Edward G. Robinson portrays a ruthless gangster in Le Roy's film "Little Caesar."

Stiff new U.S. tariff is signed into law

June 17. President Hoover has signed the Smoot-Hawley Tariff Bill, ushering in a new era of protectionism. The Republican-sponsored bill will place the highest tariffs ever on American exports. Especially affected will be minerals, chemicals, textiles and farm goods.

The bill incenses Democrats, who have strong political ties with farmers, who could be economically damaged by the legislation. Many economists believe the bill will bring retaliatory tariffs. But Hoover and the bill's authors celebrated the signing and are certain it will stimulate the economy (→ 9/9).

Stalin speech seeks to justify purges

Stalin, the face of dictatorship.

June 26. Joseph Stalin, head of the Soviet Communist Party, is defending his severe treatment of his opponents. He spoke this morning in Moscow as the party opened its 16th congress. Since the last congress convened three years ago, 6,500 party members have been exiled, banished or imprisoned for supporting the views of Leon Trotsky, Stalin's most vociferous critic. Stalin claims that another 5,800 party members have willingly abandoned Trotskyism. And 34,000 people considered too "right-wing" for the party have lost their memberships (→ 9/24).

Fats Waller makes a hit on Broadway

June. Fats Waller's Broadway show of last year, "Hot Chocolates," is gone but not forgotten as the hit tune, "Ain't Misbehavin," promises to become a classic. Waller is 26. Beneath his comic facade there lurks the lean soul of a unique pianist-composer.

Fats Waller at the organ.

1930

JULY

Su	Mo	Tu	We	Th	Fr	Sa
		1	2	3	4	5
6	7	8	9	10	11	12
13	14	15	16	17	18	19
20	21	22	23	24	25	26
29	28	29	30	31		

1. Northland Transportation Co. extends bus service across nation, changes name to Greyhound Company.

3. Auto plants reopen in Detroit, sending 150,000 back to work.

3. U.S. Congress creates Veterans Administration, consolidating all federal programs for vets.

5. Moscow: Pravda urges American Communists to revolution (→ 13).

7. Construction begins on Boulder Dam (→ 5/1/35).

10. China: Communist armies unite to attack Hankow (→ 9/2).

11. Chicago: Heat wave kills 72.

11. Milan: Catholic Giovanni Bassanesi and Republican Gioacchino Dolci drop anti-Fascist tracts from plane (→ 10/27).

12. Minneapolis: Bobby Jones wins U.S. Open golf title (→ 11/17).

13. Washington: Elihu Root urges new federal police to curb Communist intrigue (→ 27).

13. Turkish troops crush uprising in Kurdistan (→ 8/12).

16. Germany: Hindenburg shows strong-arm tactics, overruling Reichstag to pass budget (→ 9/14).

17. British Viceroy Lord Irwin allows Indian moderates to visit Gandhi in prison (→ 8/12).

20. U.S.S.R.: Maxime Litvinov appointed People's Commissar of Foreign Affairs.

22. Washington: Hoover signs naval treaty (→ 10/8).

23. Italy: Earthquake devastates Naples and Pouilles; 2,500 dead, 4,250 wounded.

27. U.S. labor leaders move to ban all Soviet products (→ 29).

27. Andre Leducq wins Tour de France.

29. Hoover opposes barring Soviet trade (→ 8/1).

30. Portuguese National Union Party formed by fascists (→ 7/5/32).

DEATH

23. Glenn H. Curtiss, U.S. aviation pioneer (*5/21/1878).

Doyle dies: created Sherlock Holmes

Doyle, a spiritualist in later years.

July 7. Sir Arthur Conan Doyle, creator of sleuth Sherlock Holmes, died today. He was 71. Holmes solved his first case in "A Study in Scarlet," published in 1887. Four novels and 55 stories followed, some penned reluctantly by Doyle. He tired of his detective long before the public did. An attempt to kill him off in 1893 failed, so he resurrected the man in 1904 with "The Return of Sherlock Holmes."

Doyle was born in Edinburgh and attended medical college there. His knowledge of poisons and their effects served him well later in several of his mysteries. After his son died in the Great War, Doyle abandoned his analytical style and leaned toward spiritualism. Doyle was knighted in 1902.

Cigarette smoking soars by a billion

July 20. The Department of Internal Revenue reports the sale of cigarettes in the United States topped last year's total by one billion. Consumption rose from ten to 11 billion nationwide. Sales of other tobacco products, however, including the larger-size cigarettes, snuff and cigars, declined steadily.

Cigarettes have proved the most popular form of smoking tobacco since the invention of the rolling machine in 1881. In the last decade, the number of female smokers climbed rapidly with public acceptance. Men and women find it an inexpensive pleasure in these hard economic times.

Gallant Fox second Triple Crown champ

With Earl Sande in the saddle, Gallant Fox romped home the winner of the Belmont Stakes this year and became the second throughbred in history to achieve the Triple Crown. Not since Sir Barton performed the feat in 1919 had any three-year-old been able to win the Kentucky Derby, Preakness and Belmont. But William Woodward's racer completed the difficult triple with style and class.

Gallant Fox.

Gallant Fox outran Whichone and Questionnaire, who finished third, in taking the winner's share of $66,040. He negotiated the Belmont course in 2:31.4. Sande, one of the nation's leading jockeys, rode Gallant Fox in all three races.

Grant Wood's sister and his dentist served as models for "American Gothic," his satiric depiction of puritanical life in the Midwest.

1930

AUGUST

Su	Mo	Tu	We	Th	Fr	Sa
					1	2
3	4	5	6	7	8	9
10	11	12	13	14	15	16
17	18	19	20	21	22	23
24	25	26	27	28	29	30
31						

1. New York: Police battle Communists in Union Square riot (→ 12/1).

4. Odessa: Soviet troops kill 200 strikers.

5. Douglas MacArthur named U.S. Army chief of staff.

5. Census reports U.S. population at 122.7 million.

7. Washington: Hoover mobilizes credit facilities for drought relief (→ 11).

7. Conservatives under R.B. Bennet take over in Canada.

11. Drought has cut U.S. corn output 690 mil. bushels (→ 16).

12. Persian troops, in collaboration with Turks, launch offensive against Kurdish rebels.

12. British bombers destroy several Indian villages to punish Afrid rebels (→ 11/12).

15. Washington: Pres. Hoover gives Lindbergh Congressional Medal of Honor (→ 7/28/31).

16. U.S. allocates $121.9 million for drought relief (→ 1/3/31).

17. Endurance fliers land in St. Louis after 647 hours aloft.

21. Pan American merger gives U.S. world's largest airline.

23. Four Long Island clubs raided; 19 arrested for gambling.

24. Two killed in Indochina riots on third anniversary of Sacco and Vanzetti's execution.

25. Slawek Cabinet resigns in Poland; Marshal Pilsudski appointed president of council and minister of defense.

25. Peru: Pres. Augusto Leguia forced out by military coup.

27. New York Mayor Jimmy Walker admits to widespread petty graft (→ 3/10/31).

28. N.Y. labor leaders demand legal beer to create jobs (→ 9/10).

BIRTHS

5. Neil Armstrong, American astronaut, first to walk on moon.

25. British actor Sean Connery, "James Bond."

DEATH

26. Lon Chaney, American actor (*4/1/1883).

Barrymore stars in Moby Dick film

"Moby Dick," Barrymore (center).

Aug 14. The film "Moby Dick" opened today, and it is not the first time its star, John Barrymore, has gone in search of a great white whale. Barrymore also appeared in "The Sea Beast" in 1926, an earlier adaptation of Herman Melville's classic American novel.

Melville's work is finally getting the attention it deserves. When "Moby Dick" was published in 1851, it sold poorly. Critics either ignored the book or reviled its lofty, rhetorical style. In this century, "Moby Dick, or The Great White Whale" is admired as many books in one. It is a natural history study of the whale; it is a psychological study into the mind of a sea captain obsessed with a whale; and it is a heavily symbolic study of fate.

"Moby Dick" of the large screen was directed by Lloyd Bacon, known for directing Mack Sennett comedies. Barrymore lends the proper weight, creating a Captain Ahab as tragic as Hamlet.

Babe Ruth making more than Hoover

Babe Ruth earlier this year accepted a two-year contract worth $160,000 to play for the New York Yankees and said he would try to hit a homer for every thousand dollars "the club put on the line" to get him. In agreeing to $80,000 a year, more than President Hoover earns, the Babe explained that he had a better year than the president did. Now, it is estimated that with his potential World Series shares this year and next, plus his salary, Ruth's income could reach the staggering sum of $750,000.

1930

SEPTEMBER

Su	Mo	Tu	We	Th	Fr	Sa
	1	2	3	4	5	6
7	8	9	10	11	12	13
14	15	16	17	18	19	20
21	22	23	24	25	26	27
28	29	30				

1. Budapest: Communists lead jobless march; two killed, 275 hurt in clash with police.

1. Edison tests first U.S. electric passenger train between Hoboken and Montclair, New Jersey.

2. French aviators Costes and Bellonte complete first Paris-to-N.Y. hop in 37 hrs., 18 min.

2. China: Rebels form Peking government under Gen. Yen Hsi-Chan (→ 10/22).

3. Hurricane hits Dominican capital at 160 mph; death toll reaches 1,200.

4. Geneva: Frank Kellogg accepts election to World Court, despite official U.S. non-participation (→ 1/29/35).

6. Argentinian president arrested as General Uriburu seizes power in military coup.

9. U.S. State Dept. restricts immigration of foreign laborers to combat unemployment (→ 10/17).

10. Albany: Franklin Roosevelt takes stand for dry law repeal (→ 19).

10. German Graf Zeppelin arrives in Moscow.

10. New York: U.S. beats Britain to retain Polo Cup.

13. New York: John Doeg wins Natl. Tennis Championship at Forest Hills.

19. New Jersey: Gangsters raid dry agents in seized brewery; one killed in retaliation (→ 1/19/31).

21. Ecuador: Archeologists discover $15 mil. in Incan treasure.

22. Chilean govt. foils attempted coup; revolt still feared.

24. Russia: Soviet authorities execute 48 for plotting revolt (→ 11/30).

25. Hitler, in testimony at trial of three German officers, claims he would scrap Versailles treaty (→ 30).

30. German President Hindenburg asks dictatorial powers to push fiscal reform (→ 10/6).

BIRTHS

7. King Baudouin I of Belgium.

17. Thomas P. Stafford, American astronaut.

Nazis 2nd largest party in Germany

National Socialist poster.

Sept 14. The German government has suffered a stunning setback in legislative elections, and the party that expressed nothing but contempt for the Parliament has registered spectacular gains. Adolf Hitler's National Socialists have gone from 12 seats in the old Reichstag to 107 in the new. The Nazis are now more powerful than the Communists, and they are the second biggest party in Germany.

The rest of Western Europe is greatly alarmed by Hitler's success. He is viewed as a warmonger who says Germany must rise from her ashes and get even for the last war. Hitler's younger followers are fascinated by his fiery oratory. Older Germans are attracted to his vitriolic hatred of Jews, war reparations and the parliamentary form of government (→ 25).

Americans take yachting cup again

Sept 18. Sir Thomas Lipton's 31-year quest for the America's Cup ended off Newport, Rhode Island, when he saw his valiant Shamrock defeated again by the United States yacht Enterprise. The American defender defeated the Shamrock for the fourth straight time and thus kept the trophy in this country, where it has been for 79 years. Sir Thomas said that he would try no more.

1930

OCTOBER

Su	Mo	Tu	We	Th	Fr	Sa
			1	2	3	4
5	6	7	8	9	10	11
12	13	14	15	16	17	18
19	20	21	22	23	24	25
26	27	28	29	30	31	

1. London parley on Ireland opens; Irish delegates ask freedom from Britain (→ 3/9/32).

3. "Dad" Joiner's well strikes oil, opening East Texas Field.

6. Germany: Hitler meets with Chancellor Bruening (→ 13).

8. U.S. Navy scraps 49 ships, 4,800 men under naval treaty (→ 10/11/31).

8. Philadelphia: Athletics take World Series at home, beating St. Louis 7-1 in sixth game.

10. Transcontinental & Western Air Inc. (TWA) formed through merger of three airlines.

12. Jack "Legs" Diamond shot five times in New York hotel (→ 12/18/31).

13. Nazi deputies scandalize Reichstag, attending in uniform, as Hitlerites stone Jewish shops in Berlin (→ 11/30).

14. Gershwin musical "Girl Crazy" opens in N.Y. featuring hit song "I Got Rhythm."

14. Fascist coup fails in Finland (→ 11/11).

17. Hoover establishes Committee for Unemployment Relief (→ 23).

20. British publish Passfield White Paper on Palestine, asking halt in Jewish immigration to curb Arab unemployment (→ 2/25/33).

22. China: 8,000 killed by rebels in Shanghai (→ 23).

23. Chinese President Chiang Kai-shek converts to Christianity (→ 4/30/31).

27. Mussolini demands revisions in Versailles treaty (→ 2/8/31).

30. Greece and Turkey sign treaty of friendship at Ankara.

BIRTHS

10. Harold Pinter, British playwright.

17. Jimmy Breslin, American journalist.

31. Michael Collins, U.S. astronaut.

DEATH

15. Herbert Dow, founder Dow Chemical Co. (*2/26/1866).

Vargas takes power in Brazil after revolt

Vargas and Brazil's new leaders.

Oct 26. Revolutionary forces of the Liberal Party of Brazil have toppled the Luis government and inserted Dr. Gertulio Vargas into the office of provisional President.

Disenchanted with "the power clique that has dominated Brazil for forty years," opposition forces ignited a popular revolution that swept the country in three tumultuous weeks. The goal of the rebels, to uproot President-elect Dr. Julio Prestes, who was seen as a puppet of former President Luis, was achieved when Luis was captured and Prestes was forced into hiding.

Order has been restored in the torn nation and now Vargas is expected to implement a new governmental program devoid of "savagery and armed despotism." Vargas declared: "I am now at the frontier with 30,000 men, well-armed and supplied, not to dispose of Luis but to realize the program of the revolution." The success of the uprising astounded the U.S. State Department, which had supported the unpopular Luis regime. It is uncertain what effect the revolt will have on United States-Brazil relations (→ 11/8).

Hoover seeks aid to combat depression

Oct 23. Saying that the nation must "prevent hunger and cold" for those in real trouble, President Hoover has announced he has named a committee to draw plans for combatting unemployment. The president's action came amidst definite signs of a deepening depression in the United States.

In naming the Cabinet-level panel to devise ways to create jobs, the president called on state governors and private industry to cooperate in solving the growing problem. It would appear that the president is leaning toward creation of an organization patterned after that which he, as head of President Harding's unemployment conference in 1921, had set up. That earlier program was a joint venture of public and private agencies working to spur industry and accelerate public works. It was credited with starting the business curve upward toward prosperity (→ 12/11).

Doling out bread and coffee to the jobless at St. Peter's Mission in N.Y.

1930

NOVEMBER

Su	Mo	Tu	We	Th	Fr	Sa
						1
2	3	4	5	6	7	8
9	10	11	12	13	14	15
16	17	18	19	20	21	22
23	24	25	26	27	28	29
30						

2. Haile Selassie—formerly Ras Tafari—crowned Emperor of Ethiopia, following April death of Empress Zauditu (→ 7/16/31).

4. U.S.: Democrats win control of House in mid-term elections, gain eight seats in Senate.

5. Prominent Italians seized for alleged plot to overthrow Mussolini (→ 2/8/31).

5. Ohio: Explosion entraps 160 miners.

8. Washington recognizes Vargas govt. in Brazil.

9. Austria: Social Democrats win elections; no seats for Nazis or Communists (→ 6/21/31).

9. London: Elephant stampede injures 50.

11. Finnish government passes legislation designed to suppress Communists (→ 2/29/32).

12. Indians ask immediate dominion status as talks open in London (→ 20).

13. Yale physicist sets earth's age at 1.825 billion years.

14. Right-wing militarists attempt assassination of Japanese Premier Hamagushi (→ 5/15/32).

15. Spain: Madrid paralyzed by general strike, riots (→ 12/12).

16. London negotiates billion-dollar loan from France.

19. Oklahoma tornado kills 19, injures 124.

20. Washington: $5 mil. federal fund created to fight racketeers.

22. New Haven: Harvard blanks Yale 13-0 in annual football game.

25. Japan: Earthquake kills 187 in Shizouka.

28. Geneva Economic Conference, called to discuss spreading depression, ends (→ 1/20/31).

28. Rain of mud falls on Paris from African sandstorm.

30. Germany: National Socialists win victory at Bremen municipal elections (→ 12/12).

BIRTH

16. Chinua Achebe, Nigerian novelist, "Things Fall Apart."

Bobby Jones retires with a Grand Slam

Jones: Golf's first Grand Slam.

Nov 17. Bobby Jones, winner of the Grand Slam of golf, has announced his retirement from the sport after capturing 13 major championships in 14 years. With the sweep of the 1930 United States and British Opens and United States and British Amateurs, there are no new worlds for the dedicated amateur to conquer.

Hampered by a fiery temper, Jones took five years to win his first championship. After winning the Open in 1923, he conceived the idea of playing against par instead of his opponent and swept to victory after victory. It was estimated that between 1922 and 1927, his victories cost the professionals at least $200,000 in lost purses. Yet the pros recognized that they were being repaid in other ways by the attention that Jones has brought to golf.

British open talks on Empire issues

Nov 20. With all the pageantry of the British Empire, a conference of Indian and British leaders has been convened in London to discuss dominion status for India. Surrounded by Maharajahs in turbans, King George V convened the roundtable conference in the Royal Gallery of the House of Lords. Notably absent was Mahatma Gandhi, a leader of the nationalist movement. The conference saw a breakdown of the Indian caste system as Brahmans dealt with spokesmen for "untouchables" (→ 12/8).

Defendants plead guilty in Moscow

Nov 30. Defendants in a Soviet treason case have testified so convincingly against themselves that a Soviet reporter whispered, "Why have a prosecutor at all?"

Professor L.K. Ramsin and two fellow conspirators pleaded guilty in a Moscow courtroom to charges of attempting to subvert the Soviet government. According to his own testimony, Ramsin planned "to produce a crisis in the Soviet land and to plunge the country into a bloody war" by supplying France and England with military secrets. Both European governments intend to investigate the charges (→ 12/21).

Mother Jones, labor leader, dies at 100

Nov 30. Labor organizer Mary Harris "Mother" Jones died today in Silver Spring, Maryland. She spent 60 of her 100 years defending the rights of coal miners and other workers. In 1871, Mrs. Jones, a widow who lost all she had in the Chicago Fire, received kind assistance from the Knights of Labor. Ten years later, she was beating the drum on their behalf, her slogan being "Join the Union, boys." She was a co-founder of the Social Democratic Party in 1898 and the International Workers of the World in 1905. She had opposed John D. Rockefeller during a coal strike in Colorado in 1914. On her 100th birthday, he sent her his best wishes.

"Mother" Jones at 98.

1930

DECEMBER

Su	Mo	Tu	We	Th	Fr	Sa
	1	2	3	4	5	6
7	8	9	10	11	12	13
14	15	16	17	18	19	20
21	22	23	24	25	26	27
28	29	30	31			

1. Washington: 500 Communist protesters dispersed from Capitol with teargas (→ 1/17/31).

8. India: British Gen. Norman Simpson shot at desk by Indian nationalists (→ 1/27/31).

10. Frank Kellogg gets Nobel Peace Prize; medicine prize to Karl Landsteiner for work on blood groups.

11. Washington: Bank of U.S. closes its doors (→ 31).

11. Germany bans film "All Quiet on the Western Front."

12. Revolution begins in Spain; rebels take border town (→ 16).

12. Germany: Last Allied troops leave the Saar (→ 2/2/31).

13. New York: Army over Navy 6-0 in football.

16. Spain: General strike called in support of revolution (→ 20).

19. Stravinsky's "Symphony of Psalms" debuts in Boston.

20. Thousands, including publicly known Spaniards, sign revolutionary manifesto (→ 2/16/31).

21. Politburo ousts Soviet ex-Premier Rykoff (→ 1/30/31).

31. Brewery heir Adolphus Busch kidnapped.

BIRTHS

3. Jean-Luc Godard, French film director.

11. Jean-Louis Trintingant, French movie actor.

CULTURAL EVENTS, 1930

Literature: Faulkner's "As I Lay Dying"; Dashiell Hammett's "The Maltese Falcon"; Oliver La Farge's "Laughing Boy," Pulitzer Prize; Edna Ferber's "Cimarron."

Academia: Freud's "Civilization and Its Discontents"; Leon Trotsky's "Autobiography."

Music: "Georgia on My Mind"; "I Got Rhythm"; "Body and Soul."

The Arts: Grant Wood's "American Gothic."

Film: "Blue Angel," Marlene Dietrich; Hitchcock's "Murder"; "All Quiet on the Western Front," Academy Award (picture, director).

Sinclair Lewis wins Nobel literary prize

Dec 12. Sinclair Lewis, enemy of middle-class complacency, received the Nobel Prize for literature today. In his acceptance speech, he cited other Americans worthy of the award. Among those he named were Ernest Hemingway, Sherwood Anderson and Willa Cather.

The peace prize went to Swedish theologian Nathan Soderblom. Soderblom, a Lutheran, seeks to influence politics and society with Christian teachings. Physician Karl

Lewis with coveted Nobel Prize.

Landsteiner won the award in medicine. The American has identified major blood groups A, B, AB and O. German scientist Hans Fischer received the prize for chemistry, having synthesized chlorophyll and hemoglobin. Chandrasekhara Raman, Indian physicist, was awarded the prize in physics for studies on light wavelengths.

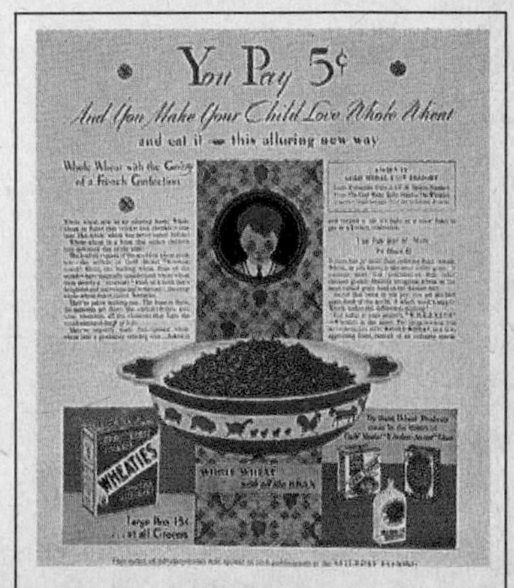

Jobless reach over four million; aid sought

As unemployment climbs, hungry protesters flood the streets of N.Y.

Dec 31. With unemployment continuing to soar, President Hoover has urged Congress to provide up to $150 million for public works to create jobs. The president's message had no sooner reached the Capitol than an avalanche of bills to help the jobless began pouring into both Senate and House hoppers. Among them was one to increase funds for the construction of public roads to $500 million.

William Green, President of the American Federation of Labor, has estimated that about 4.8 million Americans are now unemployed, an increase of 360,000 in just the past month. In his message to Congress, however, the president put the nation's jobless rate much lower, at about 2.5 million. While voicing concern, he said that the United States is much better off than the rest of the world (→ 1/3/31/).

Soviets take control of all food supplies

Dec 22. Russia's food cooperatives and distribution system are not working as Joseph Stalin intended. And the Central Committee of the Communist Party has a solution: clear out the bureaucracy and give food only to hard workers who are dedicated Communists.

State farm as big as R.I.

The Central Committee is especially critical of the Commissariat of Internal Supply. It charges "the meat and vegetable trusts are clogged with anti-Soviet agents, 48 of whom were shot recently."

The Central Committee decree admits Russia has a labor problem, and it orders that food be used as a weapon to bring workers into line. "Distribution must help to increase the productivity of the worker and to combat desertion from the labor front," the decree says.

Communist leaders are also trying to outlaw the sale of food by privately owned stores and the preparation of food by individual households. Workers should make and serve food at the lowest prices possible. In order to eat, a Russian would have to prove that he is a worker at a factory or business sanctioned by the government (→ 1/10/31).

1931

JANUARY

Su	Mo	Tu	We	Th	Fr	Sa
				1	2	3
4	5	6	7	8	9	10
11	12	13	14	15	16	17
18	19	20	21	22	23	24
25	26	27	28	29	30	31

1. Pasadena: Alabama trounces Wash. St. 24-0 in Rose Bowl.

1. Nicaragua: Eight U.S. Marines killed in ambush (→ 4/14).

1. Jorge Ubico comes to power in Guatemala.

2. Revolt in Panama overturns government.

3. 500 Arkansas farmers storm small town demanding food (→ 2/14).

4. Burmese rebel chief "King Golden Crow" killed defending his palace.

6. Brazil: Ten Italian fliers complete transatlantic flight from North Africa.

10. U.S.S.R.: Vyacheslav Molotov tells Communist Party Central Committee half of Russian agriculture will be collectivized by end of year.

13. Bridge connecting N.Y. and N.J. named George Washington Memorial Bridge (→ 7/9).

17. Hamilton Fish report calls for deportation of American Communists (→ 8/25/35).

19. Washington: Wickersham Committee issues report asking for revisions in dry law, but not repeal (→ 2/24).

23. Los Angeles: Daisy De Boe found guilty of embezzling from film star Clara Bow.

24. League of Nations rebukes Poland for mistreatment of German minority in Upper Silesia.

28. Thirty-one killed in Indiana mine explosion.

29. Washington: Bank of U.S. heads go to trial (→ 2/14).

29. London: Winston Churchill resigns as aide to Stanley Baldwin.

30. Helsinki: Report claims Russian Soviets hold 662,200 in penal camps (→ 2/21/32).

30. U.S. awards civil government to Virgin Islands.

BIRTH

5. Alvin Ailey, American modern dance choreographer.

DEATH

23. Anna Pavlova, Russian ballerina (*1/31/1881).

Unemployment in Europe sets record

Jan 20. As the worldwide economic depression deepened last year, European unemployment figures for winter 1930 reached historic levels. Germany and England were hit particularly hard; over 2.5 million were without jobs in England and nearly 5 million Germans were out of work.

Coupled with prices which did not fall as much as normal, unemployment created the worst economic situation in Europe since statistics have been kept, according to R.M. Stephenson, chief of the European section of the Department of Commerce. And this winter looks even bleaker. "It is generally expected that European unemployment in the coming winter will surpass even last year's winter figures," Stephenson said (→ 3/21/31).

Joseph Joffre, hero of Great War, dies

Marshal Joffre.

Jan 3. One of France's most popular military leaders died today. Marshal Joseph Joffre was 78. Joffre began his career as a military engineer in the colonies and served in Indochina, the Sudan and Madagascar. In 1911, he was appointed Commander-in-Chief of French forces. In September 1914, he led his troops against the Germans in the battle of the Marne and was largely responsible for the Allied victory. Joffre was elevated to marshal, but two years later, he nearly lost a key battle to the Germans at Verdun. He was replaced by General Nivelle and made Chairman of the Allied War Council.

1931

FEBRUARY

Su	Mo	Tu	We	Th	Fr	Sa
1	2	3	4	5	6	7
8	9	10	11	12	13	14
15	16	17	18	19	20	21
22	23	24	25	26	27	28

1. India: Gandhi chiefs order civil disobedience to continue (→ 16).

2. Nazis demand Germany quit League of Nations; Foreign Ministry denounces aim (→ 3/17).

3. New Zealand: Earthquake and typhoon kill hundreds in Napier.

5. Florida: Malcolm Campbell sets 245 mph land speed record at Daytona Beach.

6. Chaplin film "City Lights" released in U.S.

7. Amelia Earhart weds George Putnam in Connecticut.

10. Washington: Sec. of Commerce Mellon orders embargo on Soviet pulp and lumber.

12. Japan's first television broadcast is a baseball game (→ 5/8).

14. Washington: $20 million drought aid bill made law (→ 24).

16. Spanish King Alfonso promises reform and Labor Cabinet in effort to quell mounting revolt (→ 18).

16. India: Viceroy Lord Irwin receives Mahatma Gandhi for first time (→ 3/3).

18. Madrid: Admiral Aznar forms royalist Cabinet (→ 4/12).

18. Bill Tilden makes tennis debut as professional at Madison Sq. Garden before 13,600 fans.

20. Peruvian troops quell riots; 61 killed in Callao with navy supporting rebels (→ 3/1).

21. London: Charlie Chaplin visits Prime Minister Ramsay MacDonald.

24. U.S. Supreme Court rules dry law constitutional (→ 6/12).

26. New York: World newspapers sold to Scripps-Howard.

27. U.S. Senate overrides president's veto of bonus bill, opening federal loans to vets.

BIRTHS

8. James Dean, American film star (†9/30/1955).

23. Tom Wesselmann, painter, pop art.

27. Joanne Woodward, American actress.

Gandhi free but insists on demands

Jan 27. Mahatma Gandhi has been released from jail, ending eight months of imprisonment for his campaign of civil disobedience against British rule. To avoid demonstrations, Gandhi was released late in the evening from the Yerovda jail and put on a night train to Bombay. There was hope in British circles that the release of Gandhi would end the strife and lead to discussions of dominion status. Gandhi made clear, however, that he would persist in his campaign of civil disobedience (→ 2/1).

Pope is against sexual freedoms

Jan 8. Pope Pius XI has issued an encyclical denouncing trial marriage, all forms of birth control and divorce. The 16,000-word document comprises three parts. The first section affirms the sanctity of matrimony. Media such as novels, newspapers and films are accused of trivializing the institution. The next section deals with the evils of birth control, focusing on the legalization of "killing of innocent creatures ... before they are born." Finally, the paper urges Catholics to rededicate themselves. The pope entreats public officials to join the Church in defending morality, citing a recent concordat between the Vatican and the Italian government.

Skiers at Mont Blanc.

U.S. Bank officers said to misuse funds

Feb 24. All defendants in the Bank of United States trial are seeking to have their indictments dismissed. They claim three grand jurors involved in the case own stock in the bank and could not, therefore, objectively hear testimony. Bank President Bernard K. Marcus and five bank officers are charged with willfully misusing over $27 million from the bank. It is doubtful the court will even consider dismissing the charges.

The credibility of banks has suffered since the stock market crash in 1929 and the current allegations do little to restore public trust. However, a plan has been offered to reorganize the Bank of the United States. It is based on the successful restructuring of the Knickerbocker Trust Company by J.P. Morgan in 1907. And a group of financiers may be willing to assume the Bank of U.S. assets and liabilities while assuring full payment to depositors (→ 3/22).

American General vs Benito Mussolini

Feb 8. The court martial of General Smedley D. Butler, for his remarks that Benito Mussolini was a hit-and-run driver, has been canceled. Butler, a celebrated Marine Corps officer, recently recounted an incident where the Italian Premier and American dignitary Cornelius Vanderbilt were touring Italy by car. The vehicle driven by Mussolini allegedly struck and killed a small child. According to the story, the premier refused to stop.

Secretary Stimson and the U.S. State Department, embarrassed by Butler's remarks, sent an official apology to the Italian government. Rather than proceed with the court martial, U.S. officials accepted a letter of regret from Butler and issued him a public reprimand.

Some observers claim the Italian Embassy asked to cancel the court martial, fearing evidence would be produced proving Butler's story. The embassy denied this allegation (→ 5/31).

Bela Lugosi in "Dracula," vampire film

Feb 1. A film titled "Dracula," a retelling of Bram Stoker's bloodcurdling novel, is in production. The vampire was to be portrayed by Lon Chaney, who died suddenly last year. His replacement is a virtual unknown named Bela Lugosi. In some ways, Lugosi may be better suited for the role. He played the part in a stage production in 1927 and hails from Hungary, a stone's throw from Transylvania. Tod Browning, an expert at special effects, directs.

Browning chose Lugosi as his vampire only after Lon Chaney died.

1931

MARCH

Su	Mo	Tu	We	Th	Fr	Sa
1	2	3	4	5	6	7
8	9	10	11	12	13	14
15	16	17	18	19	20	21
22	23	24	25	26	27	28
29	30	31				

1. Peru: Navy rebels oust govt.; Ricardo Elias takes over.

3. Hoover vetoes bill proposing govt. control of hydroelectric power at Muscle Shoals Dam (→ 1/21/33).,

3. Hoover signs bill making Francis Scott Key's "Star Spangled Banner"—sung to old English drinking tune—the National Anthem.

3. India: Gandhi and Viceroy Irwin sign Delhi Pact, giving Indians right to make salt if civil disobedience stops (→ 25).

8. Turkey, U.S.S.R. sign naval accord limiting Black Sea fleets.

10. N.Y.: Society for Prevention of Crime forms charges against Mayor Jimmy Walker (→ 18).

10. British Labor Party ousts Sir Oswald Mosley after his proposal of fascist-influenced platform (→ 6/8/34).

11. U.S.S.R. bans sale or importation of Bibles (→ 8/2).

16. F.W. Murnau and Robert Flaherty release "Tabu," exotic film set in South Seas.

17. Germany: Paderhorn bishop condemns Catholics who join Nazi Party (→ 7/9).

20. U.S. Federal Council of Churches approves limited birth control.

21. Germany, Austria propose full customs union (→ 25).

22. U.S. reports per capita wealth at $2,977 (→ 5/2).

25. Paris: Britain demands review of Austro-German customs union by League (→ 4/5).

25. Fifty killed in riots in India; Gandhi assaulted (→ 6/13).

31. Nicaragua: Managua destroyed by quake; 1,100 dead.

BIRTHS

2. Mikhail Gorbachev, U.S.S.R. leader.

11. Rupert Murdoch, media magnate.

DEATHS

27. Arnold Bennett, British novelist (*5/27/1867).

28. Ban Johnson, World Series organizer (*1/6/1864).

Alabama charges Negro youths with rape

March 31. They have come to be called the Scottsboro Boys—nine Negro youths, all teenagers but one. They were arrested in Scottsboro, Alabama, on the complaint of some young white men, who said that the Negroes had driven them off a freight train in Chattanooga, Tennessee, six days ago. All the boys, white and colored, were drifters, a common enough situation in America today.

When the Negroes were arrested in Scottsboro, two young white women, Ruby Bates and Victoria Price, were also found on the train. They were cotton mill workers from Huntsville, Alabama, going to Memphis to look for work, they said. One had recently been jailed for adultery. Both claimed to have been raped by the Negroes. They were sent to doctors, neither of whom found any evidence of rape.

Still, local newspapers were outraged. One headline called the Negroes "Black Fiends." A mob soon formed outside the jail, demanding that the Negroes be lynched. A trial was quickly arranged. Heywood Patterson, 19, was tried first. It took the jury all of 25 minutes to find him guilty. The sentence was death. Trials are planned for the others, the youngest being 13 (→ 12/29).

The "Scottsboro Boys" in Alabama.

Jimmy Walker faces serious accusations

March 18. New York City Mayor James J. "Jimmy" Walker was accused today of inefficiency, neglect and incompetency. The charges, leveled by the City Affairs Committee, were disclosed by New York Governor Franklin D. Roosevelt, who refused to say whether he would seek a full-scale investigation into the fitness of Mayor Walker to continue in office.

The accusations are but the latest in a series of charges leveled against Tammany Hall politicians in the Walker regime by assorted civic and church groups. Mayor Walker has been away from his office for some weeks because of ill health. The dapper, fun-loving, popular mayor received word of the charges against him by telephone as he rested in the wealthy resort town of Palm Springs, California. The mayor, wearing pajamas, met members of the press there today and declined to comment on the charges. Aides had advised him to keep silent, saying that the time for wisecracking was past (→ 4/28).

Plane crash kills great Knute Rockne

March 31. Knute Rockne, who coached Notre Dame from football obscurity to national fame, was among eight persons killed in the crash today of a mail plane in the cattle country of southwestern Kansas. The trimotored Fokker was delayed by rain on its flight to Wichita. Rockne was on his way to Los Angeles, where he was to make a talking picture in Hollywood.

Notre Dame was little known in the football world in the early 1900's, but Rockne changed that as both player and coach. He helped popularize the forward pass, which the "Irish" used extensively to make up for their lack of bulk. As coach, Rockne developed a backfield that was nicknamed the "Four Horsemen" because of their great speed. They led Notre Dame to 29 victories in 31 games, including a 27-10 upset of Stanford in the 1925 Rose Bowl. In 13 seasons, Rockne produced five unbeaten teams. It took Rockne six years to get to Notre Dame. He had to work as a railroad brakeman to earn tuition money.

1931

APRIL

Su	Mo	Tu	We	Th	Fr	Sa
			1	2	3	4
5	6	7	8	9	10	11
12	13	14	15	16	17	18
19	20	21	22	23	24	25
26	27	28	29	30		

2. New York: $1 million in opium seized by police.

5. Berlin declares it will proceed with customs union despite international opinion (→ 5/11).

6. Portugal: State of emergency declared in Madeira and Azores after attempted military coup (→ 7/5/32).

10. Fiftieth anniversary of French protectorate in Tunisia.

11. Alleged Communist industrial spy network uncovered in Germany.

12. Spain: Republicans sweep polls in most cities (→ 14).

13. Ruth Nichols sets women's air speed record at 210.5 mph.

14. Nicaragua: Four Americans killed in Sandino advance on Puerto Cabezas (→ 17).

17. Washington: U.S. withdraws protection of citizens in central Nicaragua (→ 4/29/32).

19. French auto racer Louis Chiron wins Monaco Grand Prix in Bugatti.

20. Turkey: Kemal's Republican People's Party—though only choice at polls—wins huge vote of confidence in Natl. Assembly elections (→ 5/4).

22. Egypt signs treaty of friendship with Iraq, first between Egypt and Arab state.

25. Spain: Gen. Berenguer jailed for embezzlement (→ 5/1).

25. London rejects Franco-Italian navy pact.

27. Albany: After shooting of "Legs" Diamond yesterday, Gov. Roosevelt orders crack down on organized crime.

28. Albany: FDR dismisses charges against Jimmy Walker (→ 8/21).

29. King and Queen of Siam visit White House, claim suffrage planned in their country to test democracy.

30. Washington: FDR says Hoover regime is reactionary (→ 9/9).

DEATH

26. George Herbert Mead, U.S. philospher and sociologist (*2/27/1863).

King Alfonso flees; Spain now a republic

April 14. The wave of political turbulence sweeping Europe claimed another victim today. King Alfonso XIII was forced to flee from Spain, and the country became a republic after 15 centuries of nearly uninterrupted monarchy.

Under cover of darkness, Alfonso and a small contingent slipped out of the palace in Madrid through a garden gate. He is headed for Paris by a southern route that will take him to Cartagena and then by ship to Marseilles. Hostile elements in northern Spain and Portugal posed too many risks for the king.

Some analysts foresaw the downfall of the king when the military dictatorship of Primo de Rivera collapsed last year. Alfonso had supported the Rivera regime.

Two days ago, Alfonso's departure became inevitable as the Republicans won an enormous victory in the elections for the Cortes. Flags flew in Republican-controlled cities all over the country. Niceto Alcala Zamora was installed as the first President, without bloodshed.

The Republican flag flies in Madrid.

Alfonso has not abdicated, and he hopes to return. For the time being, however, Spain wants nothing more than a republic (→ 25).

Chiang fighting rebels on two fronts

General Chiang Kai-shek.

April 30. Through all the challenges to his authority in China, Chiang Kai-shek always appeared to retain his stronghold in the South. Today, there was a rebellion in Canton. Forces under General Chan Chai-tong announced their split with the Nanking government and seized most of Kwangtung province. They revolted after Chiang refused to step down from the government. The rebellion poses a new threat to Chiang, who is still battling the Communists on another front. Today, officials loyal to Chiang tried to downplay the rebellion as they prepared for the opening of the People's Convention in Nanking (→ 5/5).

David Belasco, dean of Broadway, is dead

April 14. Lights on the Great White Way are dimmed, honoring the passing today of producer David Belasco. Belasco, called "the dean" after his education in a monastery and his austere attire, produced plays with extravagantly accurate scenery. He "discovered" countless actors and playwrights, penning several plays of his own. "Madame Butterfly" (1900) was later adapted by Puccini for the opera.

Belasco was born in San Francisco in 1853. As a child actor, he toured with Charles Kean in "Richard III." By 1890, he was producing in New York, having outwitted the monopoly of a local syndicate. In 1906, he acquired a theater and named it after himself.

1931

MAY

Su	Mo	Tu	We	Th	Fr	Sa
					1	2
3	4	5	6	7	8	9
10	11	12	13	14	15	16
17	18	19	20	21	22	23
24	25	26	27	28	29	30
31						

1. Several thousand Socialists demonstrate in Madrid (→ 11).

2. U.S. Treasury Dept. predicts billion-dollar deficit (→ 30).

2. Nevada: Divorce suit filed in Reno every two minutes.

4. Turkey: Natl. Assembly re-elects Mustafa Kemal president (→ 2/5/33).

5. China: People's Natl. Convention in Nanking adopts provisional constitution providing for civil rights, education (→ 7/17).

8. London sends first overseas TV broadcast.

8. Farmers Party comes to power in Norway.

11. Fritz Lang's "M," with Peter Lorre, gets premiere screening.

11. Austria: Credit Anstalt folds, partly due to French credit withdrawals in reprisal for Austro-German customs union (→ 14).

11. Martial law declared in seven Spanish cities to quell serious revolutionary fighting (→ 6/8).

11. New Haven: Yale ends classics requirement.

14. Paris: Aristide Briand proposes European customs union (→ 6/6).

15. Vatican: Pope delivers radio message asking justice for labor, yet abhoring Communism.

16. Jockey C. Kurtsinger rides Twenty Grand to victory in Kentucky Derby.

19. Moscow: U.S.S.R. announces second five-year plan.

30. Hoover asks country to remain steadfast in this "Valley Forge" of depression (→ 31).

30. Lou Schneider averages 96.6 mph in a Bowes Seal Fast Special racer to win Indy 500.

31. Deficit forces Treasury to sell $800 mil. in bonds (→ 6/19).

BIRTHS

6. Willie Mays, baseball great, Hall of Fame in 1979.

DEATH

9. American A.A. Michelson, Nobel Prize for physics, 1907, helped to verify Theory of Relativity (*12/19/1852).

Pius XI denounces Mussolini's Fascists

Pius XI: Fascists can't be Catholics.

May 31. The recent split between the Italian government and the Vatican has compelled Pope Pius XI to issue a statement calling the Fascists violent and hateful.

The papal proclamation described recent attacks on clerics and church property and the closings of hundreds of Catholic organizations by the state as "the first manifestation of proof of an education that is the antithesis of Christian and civil education, and entirely given to hate, to irreverence and to violence." The denunciation came two weeks after His Holiness delivered a papal address condemning communism as being irreconcilable with the doctrine of the Catholic Church (→ 6/3).

James Cagney as a remorseless, rum-running gangster in his second film "The Public Enemy."

▷

Empire State Building is world's tallest

The Empire State Building.

May 1. The Empire State Building, the world's tallest structure, was formally opened today in ceremonies that included President Hoover and former Governor Alfred E. Smith of New York, head of the firm that erected the building. The Empire State, with 86 floors of office space topped by a mooring mast for passenger dirigibles, towers 1,245 feet above Fifth Avenue and 34th Street in New York.

The president, in Washington, pushed a button turning on the building's lights at 11:30 a.m., just minutes after a ribbon was cut to open the doors. Completion of the structure is being hailed as a gesture of confidence in the midst of depression. The Empire State is expected to boost air transport by enabling dirigible passengers to debark in the center of the city.

France inaugurates Colonial Exposition

May 6. The French Colonial Exposition has opened, and Paris is suddenly teeming with people from every corner of the globe. They have come to see the temple of Angkor Wat, Tunisian souks, an African village, and more, all specially rebuilt for the occasion.

Greater France numbers about 100 million inhabitants, second only to the British Empire in size and population. Since the conquest of Algeria began in 1830, France has extended its sway over French West Africa, French Equatorial Africa, Indochina, Madagascar, Tunisia, Morocco, French Congo, Syria, French Polynesia, New Caledonia and such islands as the Comoros in the Indian Ocean.

The guiding spirit of French colonization is the "civilizing mission." "We help backward peoples raise themselves up the ladder of humanity," is the way Marshal Lyautey, the greatest of French colonial officers, has explained it.

France has benefitted enormously from its mission. Some 600,000 colonial troops helped the French defeat the Germans in the Great War. And about a third of French exports go to the colonies, which produce a quarter of France's imports. "The colonies are a reservoir," says Lyautey, "where we can always find whatever we need."

Poster by Demeures.

On the spot in Africa.

Piccard's balloon reaches 52,462 feet

May 28. A stratospheric balloon flight that reached an unprecedented altitude of 52,462 feet has been concluded successfully by Prof. Auguste Piccard of Switzerland and a fellow scientist, Charles Kipfer. The balloon, with an airtight aluminum gondola designed by Piccard, landed safely last night on the Gurgl glacier in the Austrian Alps after an 18-hour flight that began at Augsburg, Germany. Piccard and Kipfer walked down the glacier to safety this morning. They planned the flight to study cosmic rays, mysterious radiation from outer space. The balloonists say they experienced bitter cold and thirst, but the flight was a success (→ 8/18/32).

Will Rogers refuses all degrees but A.D.

May 19. The most learned man born in Oolagah has refused an honorary degree. Will Rogers, down-home humorist, declined a Doctorate of Humanity and Letters from Oklahoma City University. Rogers, raised in Oklahoma Indian Territory, defends his decision. "What are you trying to do," he reasons, "make a joke out of college degrees? They are in bad enough repute as it is, without handing 'em around to comedians." However, Rogers said he might possibly accept an A.D. (Doctor of Applesauce).

Will Rogers, Dr. of Applesauce.

1931

JUNE

Su	Mo	Tu	We	Th	Fr	Sa
	1	2	3	4	5	6
7	8	9	10	11	12	13
14	15	16	17	18	19	20
21	22	23	24	25	26	27
28	29	30				

1. U.S. contracts to build 90 Soviet steel plants.

3. Rome: Mussolini begins purge of opposition; several Catholic leaders jailed (→ 4).

6. London: Germany pressing for debt cuts in Britain (→ 16).

8. Spain: Madrid's royalist mayor lynched by revolutionaries (→ 28).

12. Chicago: Al Capone and 68 henchmen indicted for violating Prohibition laws (→ 23).

13. Denmark files complaint with League Council against Norwegian occupation of eastern Greenland (→ 4/5/33).

13. Gandhi to live in garret with London poor (→ 8/29).

13. Venezuela: Juan Bautista Perez quits presidency.

14. France: 350 drown when excursion boat sinks on Loire.

16. Bank of England offers 150 mil. shillings aid to Credit Anstalt, Austrian natl. bank (→ 22).

17. Indochinese Communist leader Nguyen Ai Quoc (Ho Chi Minh) arrested by British authorities in China.

17. Rome: Mussolini calls religion indispensable, but says state takes priority and "That's me" (→ 9/2).

19. Canadian Lissant Beardmore crosses English Channel in glider.

21. Austria: Agrarians, Christian Socialists form coalition govt. under Karl Buresch in attempt to halt economic collapse (→ 9/13).

22. Rome: 124 Mafia members get life sentences.

23. Newfoundland: Wiley Post and Harold Gatty leave for round-world flight (→ 7/2).

24. U.S.S.R. and Afghanistan sign treaty of neutrality.

26. U.S. rejects France's reply on war debt proposal (→ 7/6).

28. Socialists make gains in Spanish elections (→ 10/1).

BIRTH

26. Colin Wilson, British writer, "The Outsider."

1931

Toscanini refuses to play Fascist hymn

Toscanini, an impulsive genius.

June 10. Maestro Arturo Toscanini was today given permission to leave his homeland after nearly a month of virtual house arrest which saw his passport taken and his life and property threatened.

Because Toscanini had stated his refusal to play the Fascist anthem "Giovinezza," Bologna marked the May 14th concert as a Fascist festival for high officials, thereby hoping to pressure the maestro into playing the hymn. When he refused to recant, Fascist thugs outside the theater beat him and his wife with canes. They were not seriously hurt, but Toscanini's passport was confiscated.

Though the Italian press was silent, many Italians were outraged. Days later, a student demonstration was broken up by police amid shouts of "Evviva Toscanini!" and "Abbasso il Fascismo!" (→ 17).

Three Bank of U.S. heads found guilty

June 19. Three officials of the Bank of the United States have been found guilty of misappropriation of funds. The men are Bernard K. Marcus, President of the bank; Saul Singer, Executive Vice President; and his son, Herbert Singer. They face up to seven years in prison. The bank, which had 400,000 depositors, was closed six months ago after it was alleged that up to $27 million in bank funds had been misused. The three-month trial was the longest held in the New York Court of General Sessions in the past 30 years (→ 8/19).

Authorities seize two bootleg kings

June 23. Two public enemies, "Scarface" Al Capone and Arthur "Dutch Schultz" Flegenheimer, are in custody today. Beer runner Flegenheimer is free on $75,000 bail, soon to face charges of tax evasion. This morning, federal agents found a dummy bank account in which he deposited $856,000 over the last half year. Agents estimated the Bronx gang leader's daily undeclared income at $5,500.

Capone and 68 members of an alleged beer syndicate were indicted June 12 on 5,000 offenses against the Prohibition law. The racketeer is accused of conspiracy dating back to 1922, the year he reportedly bought his first truck brimming with illegal brew (→ 7/28).

Dutch Schultz at court in New York.

Hoover proposes to delay reparations

June 22. President Hoover has proposed a one-year delay in war debt payments, including German reparations. The move is said to have been prompted by American concern over the financial situation in Germany. German officials welcomed the proposed moratorium, but France has indicated that it is not ready to make such a sacrifice. Owen D. Young, author of the war debt and reparations plan now in effect, said that the moratorium was "not only the action of a wise creditor but the helpful word of a great democracy" (→ 26).

JULY

Su	Mo	Tu	We	Th	Fr	Sa
			1	2	3	4
5	6	7	8	9	10	11
12	13	14	15	16	17	18
19	20	21	22	23	24	25
26	27	28	29	30	31	

1. Opening of Benguella-Katanga line completes first trans-African railway.

3. Cleveland: Max Schmeling KOs W. Stribling in 15th round.

6. Hoover's moratorium on war debts signed in Paris (→ 13).

6. TWA begins first air-freight service with shipment of livestock from St. Louis to Newark.

9. Germany: Pres. Hindenburg and Hitler meet in Berlin (→ 10/11).

9. New York: 50-cent toll set on G.W. Bridge (→ 10/25).

13. German Danatbank declares bankruptcy (→ 14).

16. Ethiopia: Hailie Selassie sets up constitution (→ 4/17/32).

17. China: Rebels start drive to take Tientsin in North (→ 31).

19. Cordiality marks second day of Paris talks on Reich; France agrees on importance of keeping Germany solvent (→ 8/1).

22. Washington: First U.S. helicopter given to Smithsonian.

24. Pittsburgh: Tragic fire in home for aged kills 30; 20 still missing.

25. Leningrad: 100,000 greet Graf Zeppelin, on way to Arctic.

26. France wins tennis' Davis Cup for fifth time running.

26. French racer Antonin Magne wins Tour de France.

26. Chilean rebels win as Pres. Carlos Ibanez resigns (→ 9/7).

28. Washington: Lindbergh and wife leave to survey air route, Alaska to Orient (→ 11/17).

28. New York: Five children hit in beer war shootout; one dead (→ 8/12).

29. Moscow: George Bernard Shaw received by Stalin.

30. Turkey: Polando and Boardman land in Istanbul (formerly Constantinople), setting flying distance record of 5,011 miles in 49 hours from New York.

31. China: Chiang Kai-shek scores victory over Communist insurgency in North (→ 12/12).

BIRTH

1. Leslie Caron, French actress.

Post and Gatty end round-world flight

Post and Gatty at Roosevelt Field.

July 2. Wiley Post and Paul Gatty were given a traditional ticker-tape parade in New York today after completing a round-the-world flight in a record time of eight days, 15 hours and 51 minutes. The aviators took off from Roosevelt Field on Long Island on June 23 and landed there yesterday after a 15,474-mile flight that took them from Newfoundland to England, over Siberia and then through Alaska and Canada to New York.

Lang's new thriller "M" captures the mood of a city terrorized by a compulsive child murderer.

1931

AUGUST

Su	Mo	Tu	We	Th	Fr	Sa
						1
2	3	4	5	6	7	8
9	10	11	12	13	14	15
16	17	18	19	20	21	22
23	24	25	26	27	28	29
30	31					

1. Britain gets 50 mil. pound loan from France and U.S. to help cover estimated 100 mil. pound deficit (→ 5).

2. Moscow: Communists burn Russia's greatest church, Cathedral of Christ the Redeemer.

3. China: 200,000 killed in massive floods along Yangtze River.

5. German banks reopen after three-week moratorium (→ 18).

12. Germans find Greenland ice shelf is 8,850 feet deep.

12. New York: "Legs" Diamond sentenced to four years, $11,000 fine on two liquor charges (→ 6/6/32).

18. Switzerland: Six-month extension on reparations urged by Basle commission (→ 29).

19. Hoover names Walter Gifford to head new commission to get relief to jobless (→ 23).

20. Cuba: Havana hit by revolt; Danish steamer bombed.

23. Brooklyn: Three shot against wall in gangland execution.

23. Michigan: Ford orders employees to grow vegetables or give up jobs (→ 28).

24. U.S.S.R., France sign pact of non-aggression.

24. Ecuador: Army ousts Pres. Isidro Ayora and Cabinet.

28. Albany: F.D.R. proposes 50 percent income tax hike to raise $20 mil. for unemployed (→ 30).

29. Gandhi arrives in London for second Round Table Conference on India (→ 9/7).

29. Vienna: Austrians proclaim they will drop customs union plan (→ 9/5).

30. New York: Report shows book industry thriving despite depression (→ 10/2).

30. Statue of Roman Emperor Hadrian discovered in Athens.

BIRTH

8. Andy Warhol, American pop artist († 2/22/1987).

DEATH

7. Bix Beiderbecke, American jazz musician (*3/10/1903).

All German banks close as one fails

July 14. An acute financial crisis has closed all banks in Germany. Capital is fleeing the country, the value of the mark is declining and Germany cannot pay its bills.

The Federal Reserve Bank of New York has extended some help by announcing it is renewing its part of a $100 million credit that had come due. Other banks say it is time for an international political solution to the crisis. One suggestion is that German banks not pay out any marks unless they are traded for foreign exchange. That would force Germans who have accounts abroad to use them, but it would not be very popular with many German workers (→ 19).

Britons produce an atom-smasher

July 1. Two British physicists, John Cockcroft and Ernest Walton, report they have smashed lithium atoms apart by accelerating protons to high speeds and energies. Working at Cambridge University, Cockcroft and Walton developed a device called an electrostatic accelerator, which imparts great energy to protons by building up high voltages. They succeeded in breaking apart the nucleus of lithium atoms using protons with an energy of several hundred thousand electron volts.

The electrostatic accelerator is the first of a family of atom smashers that are expected to give scientists invaluable information about the nature of matter. An even more powerful device, called the cyclotron, has been built by Ernest O. Lawrence of the University of California (→ 5/1/32).

Lawrence invented the cyclotron.

Labor Party's chief makes deal with right

MacDonald, caught in the middle.

Aug 24. In a series of surprise moves, Ramsey Macdonald's second Prime Ministry quickly became his third after he handed his own and his Cabinet's resignations to King George. The king accepted them, then immediately asked MacDonald to resume his briefly interrupted duties and form a new government to handle the country's financial crisis.

To solve this crisis MacDonald, to the dismay of his own Labor Party, had sided with Conservatives in cutbacks which included unemployment pay. Labor's subsequent revolt left the premier without a party and Labor now stands on the verge of naming Arthur Henderson party leader (→ 11/1).

Goodyear produces first rigid aircraft

Aug 8. A crowd of 150,000 assembled in Akron, Ohio, to watch Mrs. Herbert Hoover christen the U.S.S. Akron, the first of two giant dirigibles being built for the Navy by the Goodyear Corporation. The 785-foot-long airship was designed by Karl Arnstein, who was responsible for most of Germany's wartime Zeppelins. It will be delivered to the Naval Air Station in Lakehurst, New Jersey, this fall, after it makes several test flights in Ohio. The Akron and its sister ship Macon, now under construction, are expected to form the backbone of the Navy's air fleet. The dirigibles will be able to launch and recover airplanes in flight (→ 4/3/33).

Christening of the U.S.S. Akron.

Do-X makes first Atlantic crossing

Aug 27. The Dornier Do-X, the largest passenger airliner in the world, completed its first transatlantic flight today when it landed in New York. With its 12,558-horsepower engines, the Do-X can carry 100 passengers at a maximum speed of 150 miles per hour. The 150-foot craft made the trip from Germany via Amsterdam, Lisbon, Rio de Janeiro and Miami. The high spot of the trip was the flight across the south Atlantic, during which the Do-X averaged 110 miles per hour.

Mayor seeks refuge from his troubles

Aug 21. New York City Mayor James J. "Jimmy" Walker sought today to drown his troubles in a stein of Pilsener beer.

Faced with charges of inefficiency, neglect and incompetency, Mayor Walker came to Europe earlier this month for a rest cure. Today, he motored to the town of Pilsen, Czechoslovakia, to spend the afternoon "where the Pilsener flows." There, he joined the town's mayor in inbibing some of the brew. Describing the beer as a work of art, Mayor Walker said that he hoped to see it on sale someday in his own city, which, of course, still is under Prohibition laws (→ 9/21).

1931

SEPTEMBER

Su	Mo	Tu	We	Th	Fr	Sa
		1	2	3	4	5
6	7	8	9	10	11	12
13	14	15	16	17	18	19
20	21	22	23	24	25	26
29	28	29	30			

2. Belgrade: King puts end to dictatorship in Yugoslavia.

2. Italy: Mussolini and Vatican reach accord bringing halt to tension in Rome (→ 2/11/32).

3. Buffalo: Chemists find growth hormone in pituitary gland.

5. Holland: Intl. Court of Justice at The Hague disallows Austro-German customs union (→ 10).

7. London: Second Conference on India opens with Gandhi as only Indian delegate (→ 26).

7. Chile: Last mutinous ship gives in, ending Communist revolt (→ 6/4/32).

8. Finland: Judges find dry law has hiked drinking 50%, created vast crime problem (→ 1/30/32).

9. New York: F.D.R., Hoover differ widely on aid to idle at Red Cross talks (→ 1/23/32).

10. London hit by street riots as Parliament raises taxes, cuts wages to cover deficit (→ 15).

12. New York: Ellsworth Vines takes tennis title at Forest Hills.

13. Austria: Coup led by fascist Gen. Walter Pfrimer fails (→ 3/4/33).

15. British sailors strike to protest pay cuts; navy paralyzed (→ 21).

18. Japanese seize Manchurian railroad, posing challenge to Kellogg-Briand Pact (→ 10/16).

21. N.Y.: Jimmy Walker arrives home to face inquiry (→ 11/30).

21. Britain abandons gold standard, closes stock market; pound falls from $4.86 to $3.49 (→ 27).

22. London: Gandhi meets with Charlie Chaplin.

26. Lancashire: Gandhi sees textile workers hurt by Indian boycott but says home spinning must go on (→ 11/4).

27. Sweden, Norway, Egypt suspend gold standard (→ 30).

29. Eleven-year-old Jackie Chapman, youngest pilot yet, solos biplane at Westhampton Airport, N.Y.; federal govt. considering age-curbs for flying.

BIRTH

25. Barbara Walters, broadcast journalist.

London unemployed riot

Bankers crowd London's exchange.

Sept 30. Police in London clashed with demonstrators through the day and night as opposition grew to the government's new austerity program. Some of the protesters were believed to be Communists. But most of them were unemployed workers who are opposed to the recent reduction in benefits.

Near the Battersea Town Hall tonight, there was a riot as 5,000 out-of-work protesters demanded the restoration of the full dole and an increase in maternity and child benefits. And in the West End, traffic was disrupted for an hour as postal workers held an orderly demonstration opposing pay cuts.

Earlier in the day, shoppers fled for cover on Oxford Street as mounted police charged demonstrators carrying a red flag. Near the Bow Street Court, several protesters were trampled by police.

Some of the demonstrators expressed their solidarity with the young woman who was arrested in the protest outside the House of Commons last night. Irene Porteus is accused of hitting an officer in the face with a blackjack.

The cut in unemployment benefits is not the only step taken by the government. It devalued sterling by 20 percent. And to stop the run on the banks, it abandoned the gold standard and increased interest rates (→ 10/11).

Submarine attempts to reach North Pole

The sleek Nautilus cruises near Brooklyn, the site of its baptism.

Sept 20. The submarine Nautilus arrived at Bergen, Norway, today after a voyage in which Australian explorer George Hubert Wilkins tested the feasibility of reaching the North Pole by sailing under the polar ice cap. Although its periscope was put out of action near Spitzbergen on September 7, the Nautilus pressed northward, reaching the edge of the polar ice cap on September 11. The submarine made a successful test dive beneath the ice before returning to its home base.

Doolittle crosses country in 11 hours

Sept 4. Major James H. Doolittle today set a record for coast-to-coast travel when he flew from California to Newark in 11 hours, 16 minutes and 10 seconds. Flying a specially built biplane, Doolittle clipped 68 minutes and 53 seconds from his previous record, set less than a year ago. His average speed was just under 240 miles per hour, including three fuel stops.

Air daredevil Jimmy Doolittle.

Civil war threatens in Kentucky area

Sept 27. Coal fields in Harlan County, Kentucky, have turned into an armed camp, as miners and operators continue one of the bloodiest industrial wars of recent years. Since May, a dozen or so men have been killed, including three deputy sheriffs who had been serving as mine guards. In addition, dozens of other persons have been injured and hundreds of miners arrested.

Machinery has been wrecked and houses destroyed. A soup kitchen, set up for hungry mine families by Communists, has been blown to bits.

Even before the bitter fighting began, many miners were out of work, while those on the job were earning only about $9 to $12 a week and deeply in debt to mine company stores. Children of unemployed miners go to school hungry or, in come cases, roam around the area, begging money from strangers.

Operators, in turn, claim they are selling coal below the cost of production, due to higher freight rates and stiff competition, and were forced to reduce wages.

1931

OCTOBER

Su	Mo	Tu	We	Th	Fr	Sa
				1	2	3
4	5	6	7	8	9	10
11	12	13	14	15	16	17
18	19	20	21	22	23	24
25	26	27	28	29	30	31

1. New Spanish republic grants women the vote (→ 13).

2. U.S. living costs reported down 15% from 1925 (→ 8).

5. Clyde Pangborn, Hugh Herndon make first non-stop hop over Pacific, 4,400 miles from Tokyo to Seattle in 41 hours.

8. Hoover and advisers draw up plans for $500 mil. credit pool to aid business (→ 11/30).

10. St. Louis: Cardinals take Series in seven games, avenging last year's loss to Athletics.

11. U.S. Navy retires 17 ships to meet budget cuts (→ 31).

11. 100,000 protest pay cuts in streets of London (→ 25).

11. Germany: Hitler gains commercial alliance with Nationalist leader and publisher Alfred Hugenberg (→ 18).

12. Brooklyn: Heavyweight Jack Sharkey beats Primo Carnera.

13. Madrid: Spain separates church and state (→ 16).

16. Geneva: American Prentiss Gilbert sits with League to apply Kellogg Pact to Japanese seizure of Manchurian railroad (→ 27).

16. Madrid: Spain legalizes divorce (→ 11/20).

18. Hitler promises he can maintain order as fascists and foes clash in Germany (→ 11/15).

19. New York reported to have passed London in population.

25. Washington: Hoover and French Premier Laval agree gold standard must be kept in interest of economic stability (→ 12/22).

26. Eugene O'Neill's "Mourning Becomes Electra" opens in N.Y.

31. Geneva: 21 nations accept one-year arms truce (→ 2/2/32).

BIRTH

20. Mickey Mantle, American baseball great.

DEATHS

2. Sir Thomas Lipton, British tea magnate (*5/10/1850).

5. Dwight Morrow, American banker, diplomat (*1/11/1873).

21. Arthur Schnitzler, German playwright (*5/15/1862).

Capone goes to prison

Capone in Chicago after sentencing.

Oct 24. "Scarface" Al Capone, the dapper lord of crime, was sentenced today to 11 years in prison for tax evasion. The heavy sentence, imposed in a federal court in Chicago, stunned the city's most notorious gangland chieftain. It was the stiffest sentence ever imposed in the nation's history for evading income taxes. In addition to the long term in prison, Capone was fined $50,000 and ordered to pay prosecution costs as well as $137,328 in back taxes.

It was perhaps poetic justice that taxes, not his other alleged crimes such as murder or racketeering, proved to be Capone's downfall. Since moving to Chicago from Brooklyn, New York, 11 years ago, he had worked his way up in the rackets from a poorly paid liquor hustler to the wealthy chief of the city's gangsters, a man who fancied silk shirts, expensive flashy suits and diamond belt buckles.

It is widely believed, but never proven, that he instigated such gang-war killings as the St. Valentine's Day massacre in which members of the rival "Bugs" Moran gang were mowed down by machine guns last year (→ 5/3/32).

The end of a genius: Thomas A. Edison

Oct 18. Thomas Alva Edison, the greatest inventor of our time, died early today at the age of 84. The man who gave the world the electric light, the phonograph, the motion picture and hundreds of other inventions passed away quietly in his sleep at his home in West Orange, New Jersey at 3:24 a.m.

Edison was born in Milan, Ohio, on February 11, 1847. At age 12, he set up a chemistry laboratory in his house and took a job as a newsboy on a train to buy supplies and equipment. Soon he purchased a second-hand printing press and began to publish a newspaper—the first ever printed on a train. When he was 15, Edison rescued a small boy on the train tracks. The grateful father taught Edison telegraphy, and he soon earned a reputation as the fastest telegrapher in the country.

Edison patented his first invention, an automatic vote-recording device, in 1868, when he moved to Boston. He was unable to sell it because politicians preferred to do their own vote-counting. Edison made his first sale the following year, after he moved to New York. It was a stock ticker, for which he was paid $40,000. He used the money to set up as a consulting engineer. He did well enough to open up his own industrial laboratory in Menlo Park, New Jersey, in 1876. Some 1,300 inventions came out of the laboratory, including the phonograph, developed in 1877.

Thomas Alva Edison.

Edison's reputation was so great that when he announced in 1878 he was working on electric lighting, the price of illuminating gas stocks plunged. After thousands of experiments, Edison demonstrated the electric light for the first time at the end of 1879. He produced the first practical motion picture in 1889. In his later years, the "Wizard of Menlo Park," as he was known, enjoyed unequalled public admiration.

Manchurian peace efforts beginning

Sec. of State Stimson seeks peace.

Oct 27. American Secretary of State Henry L. Stimson has brought about a temporary peace accord in Manchuria and the League of Nations is now studying the situation after weeks of sustained battle.

Last month, Japanese troops took the Manchurian city of Mukden following a four-hour battle with Chinese forces. The Japanese said the attack was in retaliation for an alleged attempt by the Chinese to destroy a nearby bridge on the Southern Manchurian Railway, owned by the Japanese. The Chinese denied the charge.

Manchuria is an uneasy mix of competing interests. Japanese have invested heavily in the area and because of the railway control much of southern Manchuria (→ 11/7).

Oct 24. Cass Gilbert's George Washington Bridge opens, spanning 3,500 ft. over the Hudson.

1931

NOVEMBER

Su	Mo	Tu	We	Th	Fr	Sa
1	2	3	4	5	6	7
8	9	10	11	12	13	14
15	16	17	18	19	20	21
22	23	24	25	26	27	28
29	30					

1. France: Divers find $5 million in gold bullion intact on sunken liner Egypt.

2. Ohio: Du Pont announces it will market synthetic rubber.

2. Airship Akron flies over N.Y. with record 207 aboard.

3. Tammany Hall sweeps N.Y. elections with record pluralities.

7. Japanese, fearing clash with Russia, halt pursuit of Chinese after three days fighting (→ 20).

7. U.S.S.R. celebrates Bolshevik anniversary with great military display.

8. American chemist Frederick Allison reports disovery of halogen, 85th element.

8. Panama: Landslide closes canal to all traffic.

9. New York: Seabury inquiry reveals George Olvanys pulled in $2 million while he was Tammany leader (→ 30).

10. Chicago: Experiments reveal nature of atom's nucleus (→ 5/1/32).

15. Germany: Nazis win regional elections in Hesse (→ 12/1).

17. Lindbergh inaugurates Pan Am service from Cuba to South America in Sikorsky flying boat American Clipper (→ 3/2/32).

19. N.J.: Christian Gauss, dean of Princeton, claims nearly every college subsidizes athletes.

19. Germany: Vitamin D-1 crystals produced in Gottingen.

20. Spain: Parliament charges King Alfonso XIII with high treason, violation of constitution (→ 29).

20. Geneva: Japan and China reject League Council terms for settlement in Manchuria (→ 28).

25. Labor govt. defeated in Australia; pundits see reaction against socialism.

29. Spain seizes large estates for land redistribution (→ 12/10).

30. Report claims U.S. had 19,700 millionaires in 1930 (→ 12/7).

DEATH

4. Charles "Buddy" Bolden, American jazz musician (*1868).

Japanese halt their offensive in Manchuria

Nov 28. After having thrashed the Chinese in southern Manchuria, captured most of the key cities and bombed others into submission, the Japanese have apparently called an abrupt halt to their offensive against the city of Chinchow, and the two-month Manchurian conquest is currently at a standstill.

Thus have Secretary of State Henry L. Stimson's peace efforts paid off. Stimson, who continues to work with the League of Nations in an attempt to moderate the Japanese, announced yesterday he had the pledge of the Japanese government that the city of Chinchow would be spared. Hopes are now high that peaceful elements in Tokyo have gained ascendancy of the military clique ruled by General Honjo.

Yet these hopes seem inconsistent with a recent report that General Honjo has the Emperor's approval for the complete occupation of Manchuria. Neither do they tally with statements by high Japanese officials that Japan will drop out of the League of Nations if the League orders any withdrawal of Japanese troops (→ 1/2/32).

Japanese troops in Manchuria.

MacDonald wins seat, forms Cabinet

Nov 1. British politics took a new turn last week as the Conservatives won the largest proportion of seats in Parliament in the history of the institution, and Ramsay MacDonald surprisingly won re-election. MacDonald, through sheer tenacity, won a seat in Parliament and is forming a bipartisan Cabinet. The Conservatives soundly defeated the Laborites and Liberals, capturing 551 seats in the House of Commons, against a mere 58 for the opposition.

Election tally declared in London.

MacDonald won in Seaham, one of the toughest constituencies in England, without the backing of an organized party. His opponent, Labor Party candidate William Coxon, seemed to have the advantage because of Seaham's working-class electorate. But MacDonald's charisma and reputation as a Labor Party founder won the hearts and votes of the region's miners.

Gandhi goes formal to palace affair

Nov 4. Clad in his loin cloth and homespun shawl, Mahatma Gandhi paid a visit to Buckingham Palace and met India's Emperor today. Gandhi's sandals pattered on the floor as he crossed the drawing room to greet King George V and Queen Mary, who were holding a party for 500 guests. Gandhi bowed low to the king, who was dressed in a frock coat, and then to the queen, dressed in a silvery gown. They then shook hands warmly.

The king and the leader of the nationalist movement in India held a friendly, five-minute talk. The king appeared to do most of the talking, as the Mahatma listened, with his eyes twinkling behind his steel-framed spectacles. Gandhi declined to discuss his conversation with the king, saying, "It would not be dignified." But he suggested the conversation consisted mostly of pleasantries about the English weather and how it affected one who had recently come from India.

Asked if the king had given any encouragement for Indian independence, he closed his palms and said "only God gives encouragement, not Kings" (→ 12/12).

Tammany boss piles up millions

Nov 30. George W. Olvany had an income of more than $2 million during the four and one-half years he served as Tammany Hall leader. The financial status of the former Tammany boss was disclosed by a legislative committee that is probing possible diversion of New York's unemployment relief funds to campaign uses by the Democratic machine once headed by Olvany, a Madison Ave. lawyer (→ 7/27/32).

Loretta Young, Robert Williams and Jean Harlow star in Frank Capra's "Platinum Blonde."

1931

DECEMBER

Su	Mo	Tu	We	Th	Fr	Sa
		1	2	3	4	5
6	7	8	9	10	11	12
13	14	15	16	17	18	19
20	21	22	23	24	25	26
29	28	29	30	31		

1. Defying Moscow, German Communist leader Ernst Thaelmann proposes alliance with Social Democrats (→ 7).

7. Report indicates German Nazis would ensure "Nordic dominance" by sterilizing certain races (→ 12).

7. Hundreds of Communist-led hunger marchers turned away from White House (→ 8).

8. Washington: Hoover acknowledges need for public works program (→ 1/14/32).

11. British Parliament passes Statute of Westminster, giving dominions virtual sovereignty.

11. Japan gives up gold standard.

12. New York: Army over Navy 17-7 in annual football game.

12. China: Under pressure from Canton, Chiang resigns as pres. of Nanking govt. (→ 7/17/32).

12. Hitler tells U.S. journalists, "I am a democrat" (→ 1/7/32).

12. Gandhi barred from meeting with pope for refusing to don Western clothes (→ 28).

22. U.S. Senate ratifies foreign debt moratorium (→ 2/29/32).

29. Clarence Darrow, angered at Communist exploitation of case, drops fight to save Scottsboro Negroes accused of killing two white girls (→ 11/7/32).

DEATH

26. Melvil Dewey, Dewey Decimal System (*12/26/1831).

CULTURAL EVENTS, 1931

Literature: Pearl S. Buck's "The Good Earth," best seller; Dreiser's "Tragic America."

Academia, Religion: John Dewey's "Philosophy and Civilization"; Harold Urey discovers Deuterium at Columbia Univ.; Jehovah's Witnesses formed; Elijah Muhammed founds Black Muslims in Detroit.

Music: William Grant Still's "Afro-American Symphony"; "Minnie the Moocher"; "Mood Indigo."

The Arts: Salvador Dali's "Persistence of Memory."

Film: Chaplin's "City Lights"; Karloff's "Frankenstein."

Zamora is President of Spanish republic

A modern Betsy Ross waves the Republican flag at Puerta del Sol in Madrid.

Dec 10. Niceto Alacara Zamora was elected the first constitutional President of Spain today by the National Assembly. Often called "the father of the Spanish republic," the president-elect supported the monarchy until it became a dictatorship in 1923. Zamora led the successful revolutionary movement to victory under the Republican banner.

Zamora's landslide victory was not the only news in the assembly today as Minister of Communications Martinez Barrios declared the Compania Telefonica National illegal. Stating that the contract establishing a monopoly in the telephone system was an illegal arrangement, Barrios called for the entire system to be seized. The new president is expected to act on the matter following his inauguration (→ 1/22/32).

British India talks end unsuccessfully

Dec 28. The second round of a British-Indian conference on the political future of India collapsed in disagreement over demands by Indian nationalists for complete independence. The British government had seemed willing to grant a limited dominion status, with Indians controlling all aspects of government finance. But Mahatma Gandhi, who had come to the conference to present the demands of the all-India Nationalist Congress, refused to accept anything less than complete independence.

The breakdown of the talks set off a new round of disorders in India and renewed steps by authorities to crack down on the independence movement. Gandhi was greeted by rioting in the streets of Bombay between upper-caste Hindu members of the Congress Party and "untouchable" caste members who had turned against Gandhi (→ 1/4/32).

Jane Addams gets Nobel Peace Prize

Dec 10. The Nobel Peace Prize was awarded tonight to two Americans: Miss Jane Addams and Dr. Nicholas Murray Butler.

Miss Addams, 71 years old and in frail health, leads the Women's League for Peace and Freedom. Her organization and the League of Nations have nominated her for the prize each year for several years. Twenty years ago, she established Chicago's Hull House, a shining model for social services.

Butler is President of Columbia University. While a pacifist, he is no isolationist. He advocates worldwide cooperation, having founded the Carnegie Endowment for International Peace in 1910.

Butler may follow Miss Addams' example for handling the prize money. According to her secretary, Miss Addams will do as she has done in previous instances. She will give it away.

Legs Diamond shot dead in Albany

Dec 18. Fourteen is Jack "Legs" Diamond's unlucky number. The "beer baron of the Catskills" died in Albany this morning from a bullet wound to the head, the 14th time in his life he had been shot. Diamond may have been killed by friends of one of his henchmen, who took the rap for a murder he committed.

Since 1914, Philadelphia-born Diamond allegedly committed robbery, assault and homicide a dozen times, yet no court found him guilty He laughed at rivals' attempts to rub him out, but when his brother died he deemed it wise to attend the funeral incognito. He came disguised as a priest.

"Legs" (center) with his lawyers.

Despite a pronounced lisp, Boris Karloff has turned in a superb performance as the monster in "Frankenstein."

Abstraction-Creation

Piet Mondrian's "Composition in Red, Yellow and Blue" (1928).

Wassily Kandinsky's "Watercolor without title" (1923).

New concepts in abstract painting during the decade led to the formation this year of a new group called "Abstraction-Creation." Its members are Hans Arp, Willi Baumeister, Fernand Leger, Piet Mondrian, Carl Buchheister, Kurt Schwitters and Wassily Kandinsky. They are displaying their works at galleries in France and Germany.

Some of these painters and sculptors, Dutch artist Mondrian in particular, argue that their art does not derive from a process of abstraction but from mathematical rules. His paintings, accordingly, rely on right angles and purified primary colors. Others say their inspiration is the environment, suggesting space, color, surfaces and volume. All agree the elements of their work are not in any way symbolic.

Fernand Leger said, "Eighty percent of the elements and objects that help us to live are noticed by us in our everyday lives, while only 20 percent are seen." The artists of "Abstraction-Creation" try to make the public 100 percent aware.

Fernand Leger, a member of the group Abstraction-Creation, painted "Dead Nature" in 1928. Initially trained in architecture, Leger studied painting at Paris' Beaux Arts School and became known for his Cubist work in 1910.

1932

JANUARY

Su	Mo	Tu	We	Th	Fr	Sa
					1	2
3	4	5	6	7	8	9
10	11	12	13	14	15	16
17	18	19	20	21	22	23
24	25	26	27	28	29	30
31						

1. Pasadena: Southern Cal. takes Rose Bowl 21-12 over Tulane.

2. Five U.S. cities hit by bombing attacks linked to anti-fascists.

2. China: Japanese occupying forces in Manchuria set up puppet govt. of Manchukuo (→ 7).

2. Missouri: Gunman Harry Young and brother, besieged in farmhouse, kill six officers (→ 5).

5. Missouri: Harry and Jennings Young shoot each other to avoid capture.

7. Sec. of State Stimson demands rights for Manchurian people, insists U.S. will not recognize gains made by force (→ 28).

7. Chancellor Bruning declares Germany will not resume reparations; asks Hitler to help extend Hindenburg's term (→ 2/22).

9. French For. Min. Aristide Briand resigns due to ill health (→ 3/7).

9. Col. Teddy Roosevelt Jr. named to replace Dwight Davis as head of Philippines.

12. Hattie Carraway of Arkansas replaces deceased husband in U.S. Senate.

12. Oliver Wendell Holmes quits Supreme Court at age 90.

14. A.F.L. estimates U.S. jobless at 8.2 million (→ 22).

20. New York bankers to lend City $350 million.

22. Government troops crush Communist uprising in northern Spain (→ 3/28).

23. Albany: F.D.R. enters presidential race (→ 4/7).

25. U.S.S.R. signs non-aggression pact with Poland.

25. Salvador: 600 killed in attempted revolt.

26. Fifty die as British sub M-2 goes down in English Channel.

28. China: Japanese attack Shanghai; martial law declared in foreign district (→ 31).

30. Finland lifts Prohibition on alcohol (→ 3/17).

DEATH

6. Andre Maginot, French min. of war, architect of Maginot Line on German border (*2/17/1877).

Japan pounds Shanghai; takes Manchuria

Jan 31. Japanese occupation forces are spreading out in Shanghai, and fierce fighting is also reported in Manchuria. The effort by the League of Nations and the United States to mediate this second war between Japan and China has failed miserably. The United States even threatens to become an active participant. President Hoover is sending more military reinforcements to Shanghai to protect American interests.

In Manchuria, Chinese forces ambushed a Japanese supply train and attacked an enemy encampment south of Harbin. But the element of surprise did not help the Chinese. They lost hundreds of men in fierce hand-to-hand combat.

President Hoover has dispatched the 31st Infantry to Shanghai. He also ordered the commander of the Asiatic Fleet, Admiral Montgomery Taylor, to proceed from Manila to Shanghai with his flagship, the cruiser Houston, together with 600 Marines on seven destroyers.

Japanese troops attack at Shanghai.

Great Britian and France both announced they will send men and ships to Shanghai, and Italy has already landed marines (→ 2/10).

$2 billion provided for business loans

Jan 22. President Hoover has signed into law a bill to establish a $2 billion agency to help prop up industry and create jobs.

The Reconstruction Finance Corporation, said the president, has been designed to "stop deflation in agriculture and industry and thus to increase employment by the restoration of men to their normal jobs."

With the United States now in the midst of a severe depression, the bill creating the new agency won speedy approval in Congress. It is the first of a series of economic relief bills to become law.

Beginning next week, the agency will begin making loans to various private industries, banks and farm organizations. In response to some critics, the president said the Reconstruction Finance Corporation "is not created for the aid of big industries or big banks" but to aid in the nation's recovery (→ 2/27).

Congress Party outlawed; Gandhi jailed

Jan 4. Mahatma Gandhi and other members of his All-India National Congress are back in jail again. After the collapse of the London conference, British authorities have cracked down even harder on Gandhi and his followers, and the Mahatma urged Indians to increase their acts of civil disobedience.

"Wake up from sleep," Gandhi said as he ordered a boycott of British goods. "Discard foreign cloth. Discard narcotics. Discard violence. Defy all orders calculated to crush the national spirit."

The government has declared Gandhi's Congress an illegal organization. Under new laws, even peaceful picketing is illegal. The Congress Party responded to the crackdown by recruiting more followers and striking more plants (→ 3/22).

Indian militant Kamaladevi Chattopadhy leads protest against Union Jack.

Four on probation for Hawaii killing

Jan 29. Four Americans held under arrest for the slaying of a Hawaiian native will be free on bail immediately, having given a $7,500 bond. The defendants now on probation are Mrs. Granville Fortescue, wife of Major Granville Fortescue; Lieutenant Thomas H. Massie, her son-in-law, and two Navy enlisted men, Albert O. Jones and E.J. Lord. They are accused of the second-degree murder of Joseph Kahahawai, who allegedly raped Mrs. Massie a few days ago.

The defendants were indicted at 9 o'clock this morning in a Honolulu courtroom. The room was filled with local spectators and reporters from the mainland. Mrs. Fortescue and Massie seemed ill at ease, while the enlisted men smiled and joked with reporters. Within an hour, they were escorted to police headquarters under heavy guard.

Probation makes an overnight stay in jail unnecessary for the defendants. They are undoubtedly relieved: While no jail is pleasant, this one houses three friends of Kahahawai, accomplices in the alleged attack on Massie's wife (→ 4/16).

1932

FEBRUARY

Su	Mo	Tu	We	Th	Fr	Sa
	1	2	3	4	5	6
7	8	9	10	11	12	13
14	15	16	17	18	19	20
21	22	23	24	25	26	27
28	29					

2. Cuba: Earthquake in Santiago kills 1,500.

2. Geneva: Arms talks open with delegates from 60 countries (→ 6/22).

4. Andrew Mellon accepts post as envoy to England; Ogden Mills to succeed as head of U.S. Treasury.

4. F.D.R. inaugurates Winter Olympics at Lake Placid (→ 15).

7. Oslo convention establishes economic cooperation between Belgium, Netherlands and Scandinavian countries.

8. Bulgaria renounces reparations payments.

10. China: Japan lands 20,000 for drive on Shanghai (→ 18).

15. Benjamin N. Cardozo named to U.S. Supreme Court.

18. Manchurian independence formally declared (→ 3/9).

18. South Africa: De Beers diamond mines closing down.

21. Soviets strip Trotsky of Russian citizenship (→ 10/9).

22. Germany: Adolf Hitler chosen NSDAP candidate for presidential elections (→ 3/13).

27. U.S.: Glass-Steagall Act passed, giving Federal Reserve right to expand credit to increase money circulation (→ 3/25).

27. London: James Chadwick announces discovery of neutron (→ 12/10/35).

29. 202 U.S. Navy warships meet in Pacific for war maneuvers.

29. Protective Tariff Act passed in Britain despite considerable dissent in Parliament (→ 4/1).

29. Finnish army guards Helsinki as 4,000 attack, led by fascist Gen. Kurt Wallenius.

BIRTHS

6. Francois Truffaut, French film director († 10/21/1984).

7. Gay Talese, American journalist.

18. Milos Forman, Czech film director.

22. Edward Kennedy, U.S. senator.

27. Elizabeth Taylor, American actress.

Mussolini meets Pope for the first time

Mussolini and Pope Pius XI meet for the first time.

Feb 11. Premier Benito Mussolini and Pope Pius XI met for the first time today. The meeting at the Vatican was to honor Lateran Treaty Day, a holiday created three years ago to mark the celebration of the pact which freed popes from their "imprisonment" in the Vatican, and to celebrate the tenth anniversary of the pope's coronation. It was monumental considering the strained relations between Italy and the Catholic Church.

The premier and the pontiff stood silently face to face upon meeting. Mussolini then threw himself to his knees and kissed the pope's hand. The pope invited the head of state through the doors to his private library where the two talked for an hour. The meeting was taken as a clear indication that the split between Fascists and Catholics has been mended (→ 10/20/33).

Games at Lake Placid: Henie wins twice

Feb 15. The charm and radiance of Sonja Henie, so wildly acclaimed at San Moritz last year, continued to excite the crowd at the 1932 Olympics at Lake Placid, New York, where she won her second gold medal in figure skating today. In the 1924 Games, at age 11, as the youngest Olympian ever, she finished in last place.

Jack Shea sings the Olympic hymn to open the Games at Lake Placid.

Rockefeller Center underway in N.Y.

A project of hope in the midst of despair is rising in the heart of Manhattan. Begun last year, Rockefeller Center will one day include 14 steel-framed office buildings arranged in a rectilinear pinwheel form. The complex is being constructed under the financial sponsorship of John D. Rockefeller Jr., son of the renowned oil baron.

The anchor of the plan is the 70-story RCA Building, to be surrounded by smaller skyscrapers built parallel or at right angles to the anchor. The center will house not only offices and broadcasting facilities, but also shops, restaurants, two theaters, an ice-skating rink, a maze of underground streets and walkways, and murals (→ 12/39).

RCA Building will reach 70 stories.

1932

MARCH

Su	Mo	Tu	We	Th	Fr	Sa
		1	2	3	4	5
6	7	8	9	10	11	12
13	14	15	16	17	18	19
20	21	22	23	24	25	26
27	28	29	30	31		

2. Twenty-month-old son of Charles Lindbergh kidnapped in New Jersey.→

3. Congress sends 20th Amendment to states, asking inauguration of pres. on Jan. 20 to shorten "lame duck" period (→ 2/6/33).

7. Detroit: Four killed, 100 wounded in riot at Ford plant as police fire on crowd.

7. German liner Bremen wins Blue Riband.

9. Eamon De Valera elected president of Irish Free State, pledges to abolish loyalty to British crown (→ 23).

9. China: Emperor Pu Yi, who abdicated in 1912, installed as president of Manchukuo (→ 21).

13. Berlin: Hindenburg, with 18 mil. votes to Hitler's 11 mil. to Communists' five mil., fails to gain majority (→ 4/10).

17. Finland orders 875,000 bottles of liquor as official end of Prohibition nears.

20. German dirigible Graf Zeppelin makes first flight to South America on regular schedule.

20. Minneapolis: Robin Lee, 12-year-old figure skater, wins national title.

21. China: Shanghai foes sign truce agreement (→ 4/27).

22. Indian Moslems break with Great Britain (→ 4/24).

23. Norris-La Guardia Act passes Congress, restricting use of injunction to end strikes.

23. Britain warns Ireland loyalty oath is mandatory (→ 5/11).

25. Washington: Hoover insists balanced budget is key to business recovery (→ 30).

28. Madrid: Spanish Communists burn monastery (→ 8/10).

30. U.S. farm prices rise for first time in nine months (→ 4/13).

BIRTH

12. Andrew Young, U.S. ambassador to U.N., mayor of Atlanta.

DEATHS

7. Aristide Briand, French statesman (*3/28/1862).

14. George Eastman, Kodak founder, a suicide (*7/12/1854).

Lindy's baby kidnapped

The Lindbergh baby, happy at home.

March 2. The most intensive manhunt in American history has been mounted in search of the infant son of Charles A. Lindberg, who has been kidnapped.

The 20-month-old boy, Charles A. Lindbergh Jr., was snatched from his crib in the family's home at Hopewell, near Princeton, New Jersey, last night while his father, the famous transatlantic aviator, and Mrs. Lindbergh were at dinner.

Police have no clues, aside from muddy footprints in the nursery, a homemade ladder down which the infant was carried, and a note, pinned to the windowsill, demanding $50,000 for the child's safe return. Colonel Lindbergh said he would willingly pay the ransom. However, the note made no mention of where or how to pay the money.

News of the kidnapping shocked the nation. President Hoover has ordered all federal law enforcement agencies to assist in the search. More than 100,000 officers, aided by civilian volunteers, have joined the search along the entire eastern seaboard, stopping cars, quizzing passengers and assisting Colonel Lindbergh in combing the wooded areas around the home (→ 5/12).

John Philip Sousa was "March King"

"The March King."

March 5. John Philip Sousa has succumbed to a heart attack. The musician was 77. Born in Washington, Sousa was the son of a Marine Band member. At age nine, he himself was apprenticed to the band, and at 26 was its leader. His musicians performed for five presidents, the first being Benjamin Harrison. Sousa was a composer; not surprisingly, his work was patriotic. "Semper Fidelis" and "Stars and Stripes Forever" will be played for generations, as will his namesake instrument, the sousaphone.

Swedish "Match King" is a suicide

March 12. Ivar Kreuger, a Swedish financier called the "Match King," shot and killed himself in Paris today. He went to the United States in 1893 and built up an international construction business. In 1913, he established two match firms and acquired a near-monopoly of the world's match trade. The 1929 Crash brought down his empire, causing heavy losses to stockholders and banks in many nations.

Ex-Olympic swimmer Johnny Weissmuller plays "Tarzan."

1932

APRIL

Su	Mo	Tu	We	Th	Fr	Sa
					1	2
3	4	5	6	7	8	9
10	11	12	13	14	15	16
17	18	19	20	21	22	23
24	25	26	27	28	29	30

1. League economic committee holds debts and tariffs bar world recovery (→ 8).

4. Pittsburgh: Chemist C.C. King isolates vitamin C.

7. FDR declares campaign will be geared to "the forgotten man at the bottom of the economic pyramid" (→ 5/22).

8. Italy asks end to all war reparations and debts (→ 19).

10. Berlin: Hindenburg gets full majority on second ballot.→

12. Russian Ballet split in two after Diaghilev's death.

13. U.S. deficit passes $2 billion, highest peacetime mark (→ 21).

13. Germany: Statutory order on "Safety and State Authority" bans Nazi military units SA and SS (→ 5/25).

16. Honolulu: Thomas Massie pleads insanity in murder trial, says can't remember killing wife (→ 30).

17. Ethiopia: Haile Selassie abolishes slavery (→ 9/29/34).

19. British budget published with no reference to $171.5 mil. owed to U.S. (→ 21).

21. Washington: Daughters of American Revolution ask deportation of jobless aliens (→ 7/21).

21. Britain increases tariff to 20 percent, 33.3 percent on steel products (→ 6/16).

24. India: 450 seized by British for defying ban on Indian National Congress (→ 5/16).

27. Japanese fail to take Shanghai after 13-hour air raid (→ 10/2).

28. Arturo Toscanini returns to New York to perform at Carnegie Hall.

28. First yellow fever vaccine announced; developed by Wilbur Sawyer, Wray Lloyd and Stuart Kitchen.

29. Nicaragua: Ten slain in raid on Sandino camp (→ 9/26).

30. Honolulu: Troops guard city divided over Massie verdict (→ 5/13).

DEATH

27. Hart Crane, American poet, a suicide (*7/21/1899).

Hindenburg gains in vote; so does Hitler

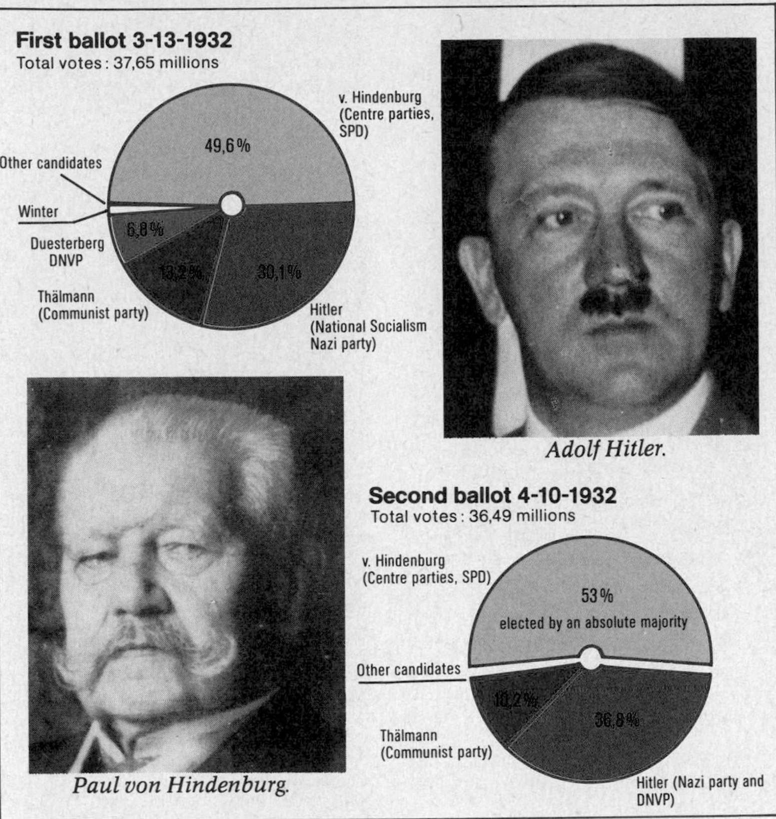

Adolf Hitler.

Paul von Hindenburg.

April 10. In the run-off election for the presidency of Germany, the incumbent, Paul von Hindenburg, beat Adolf Hitler by six million votes. Hindenburg improved upon his showing in the last election, but Hitler did even better, gaining an additional two million votes.

Hindenburg received 53% of the vote. Hitler had nearly 37%. Traditionalists in Germany hope the result will catalyze liberal forces, but Hitler calls the race a victory for National Socialism.

"Victory obliges me to thank all who worked to create the basis of the victory, but it carries a heavy obligation to continue," Hitler said. "The National Socialists know not what rest is and must not tarry until the goal of German liberation has been reached" (→ 5/25).

April 23. Stratford came alive today to celebrate Shakespeare's birthday and, with help from the Prince of Wales, open his Memorial Theatre.

1932

MAY

Su	Mo	Tu	We	Th	Fr	Sa
1	2	3	4	5	6	7
8	9	10	11	12	13	14
15	16	17	18	19	20	21
22	23	24	25	26	27	28
29	30	31				

1. Atom split in London; yields 60 percent more energy than used. →

1. One million march through Moscow in May Day parade.

2. Gershwin's "Of Thee I Sing" is first musical to win Pulitzer.

3. Al Capone, appeal denied by Supreme Court, sent to prison in Atlanta (→ 8/22/34).

7. Burgoo King wins Kentucky Derby with jockey E. James up.

7. Paris: Pres. Paul Doumer killed by assassin (→ 10).

8. Communists in Peruvian navy seize two cruisers.

11. Britain warns Ireland will lose tariff preferences if Oath of Loyalty is abrogated (→ 19).

15. Marseilles: French liner George Phillippe burns; 50 dead.

15. Tokyo: Japanese Premier Ki Inukai killed by military extremists; party government ended (→ 12/27/33).

16. Bombay: Hundreds die in fighting between Moslems and Hindus (→ 8/16).

19. Dublin: Irish Dail (Parliament) passes ban on Oath of Loyalty to Britain (→ 1/2/33).

21. Eleutherios Venizelos quits as Greek premier (→ 3/11/35).

21. Amelia Earhart is first woman to solo across Atlantic, flying Newfoundland to Ireland on Lindbergh day in record time of 15 hours.→

25. Germany: Prussian Diet hall wrecked in fight between Communists and Nazis (→ 30).

28. Chicago: Communist Party nominates William Z. Foster for presidency (→ 6/16).

30. Fred Fame drives Miller Hartz Special racer to victory in Indy 500, averaging 104.1 mph.

30. German Chancellor Bruening resigns over Hindenburg's refusal to allow small farmers use of bankrupt estates (→ 31).

31. Berlin: Franz von Papen forms new Cabinet excluding National Socialists (→ 6/14).

BIRTH

24. Arnold Wesker, British playwright, working-class themes.

Atom is split by two British scientists

May 1. The atom has been split. This is the claim of Dr. J.D. Cockroft and Dr. E.T.S. Walton, working in a Cambridge University laboratory of which Lord Rutherford is the director. In the experiment, hydrogen atoms were transmuted into helium atoms, and the energy of part of an atom was released in a quantity 60 percent greater than the amount used. On January 3, 1919, Lord Rutherford became the first to split an atom, but of this new experiment, he says, "For the first time in history we have got more energy out of something than we put in it" (→ 1/8/33).

With Doumer slain, Lebrun is President

May 10. By an overwhelming majority, the French Parliament has elected a moderate, Albert Lebrun, to replace assassinated Paul Doumer as President of France. Lebrun received 643 votes, while Socialist and Communist candidates got 122. France is still recovering from the shock of the assassination. Last week, Doumer was shot to death by a man who later identified himself as Paul Brede, but whose real name is Gorguloff. He is a Russian emigre who claims to fight communists. Doctors say he is insane (→ 1/22/34).

Amelia Earhart flies solo across Atlantic

May 21. Amelia Earhart landed her airplane in a pasture in Northern Ireland today, becoming the first woman to fly solo across the Atlantic Ocean. Her 14-hour, 16-minute flight from Newfoundland was one hour and 16 minutes faster than the record of Alcock and Brown on the pioneer flight to Ireland in 1919. It also comes five years to the day after Lindbergh's historic flight and four years after she became the first woman to fly the Atlantic as an airplane passenger. Ever since then, said the author of "The Fun of It," "I have wanted to do it alone (→ 7/18/37).

Bonus claimants march on capital

Bonus marchers arrive in D.C.

May 29. Calling themselves the "Bonus Expeditionary Force," about 11,000 veterans marched on Washington this week, demanding a bonus for serving in the Great War. Congress had voted for a bonus for such veterans, but delayed any payment at this time. The bonus army, as it has been dubbed, has settled in makeshift flats along the marshy banks of the Anacostia River and in some of the abandoned buildings along Pennsylvania Avenue. Each day, the men stage a quiet, orderly vigil at the Capitol (→ 6/7).

Engelbert Dollfuss is Austria's Premier

May 20. Austria also has a new, moderate leader, but he is on much more shaky ground than Albert Lebrun, the new President of France. It took two tries before Engelbert Dollfuss was able to create a majority, and he has but one vote to spare in the Austrian Parliament.

The core of Chancellor Dollfuss' strength is in his minority Christian Socialist Party. He formed a coalition with the so-called patriotic bloc. The first effort by Dollfuss to form a government failed when he tried to ignore the other parties, and the "national economic bloc" of delegates deserted him.

Dollfuss was formerly Minister of Agriculture. He was called upon to create a new government after former Chancellor Karl Buresch, who lost support in the last election, could not form a majority.

Body of Lindbergh baby found in wood

May 12. The decomposed body of the Lindbergh baby has been found in a wooded patch in the Sourland Mountains, less than five miles from the family's home.

The discovery ended an intensive 72-day search that began the night the 20-month-old infant, Charles A. Lindbergh Jr., was snatched from his crib in the nursery of the Lindbergh home near Princeton, New Jersey. More than 100,000 officers and civilians had joined the infant's father, Colonel Charles A. Lindbergh, the famous transatlantic aviator, in combing much of the East Coast during that time.

The body was found by a Negro truck driver who notified police. A doctor who conducted an autopsy said that the infant apparently had been brutally murdered soon after the kidnapping (→ 6/10).

Norman Thomas to run for president

May 22. Norman Thomas was nominated as the Socialist Party's candidate for president of the United States at the party's convention in Milwaukee today.

Citing the election campaign as the most promising opportunity for Socialists to promulgate their ideas, Thomas said, "The choice now confronting the world is between socialism and catastrophe." Distinguishing himself from the Soviet Communists, Thomas expressed the hope that the U.S. could solve its problems without employing Soviet methods. "We are not Communists preaching a ruthless doctrine of inevitable bloodshed and dictatorship," he said (→ 28).

Thomas only recently left ministry.

Art imitates life: Scarface is a film

Paul Muni (center) in "Scarface."

May. "Scarface" Al Capone, bootlegger and extortionist now held in a penitentiary, is the subject of a new film. "Scarface: The Shame of a Nation," directed by Howard Hawks, is now in theaters. Its title would suggest no glorification of hoods like Capone, but audiences often look back on the picture with a strange respect for the man's violent exploits. Paul Muni portrays Capone convincingly.

America cannot get its fill of molls, gats and spats. "The Public Enemy" and "Little Caesar" were hits last year. Their respective stars, James Cagney and Edward G. Robinson, face typecasting.

Massie defendants out after hour in jail

May 13. Defendants in the Massie case are free, having served only one hour of a ten-year prison term. The four defendants, Lieutenant Thomas Massie, his mother-in-law and two Navy enlisted men, are understandably overjoyed. Their lawyer, Clarence Darrow, also expressed his deep gratification.

Massie and his co-defendants had been charged with the second-degree murder of a Hawaiian named Kahahawai. Kahahawai had been accused of raping Massie's wife. The man allegedly committed the assault with four accomplices who are now awaiting trial.

Hawaiians resent the turn of events. As Princess Kawanakoa asked, "Are we to infer . . . that there are two sets of law in Hawaii—one for the favored few and another for the people generally?"

1932

JUNE

Su	Mo	Tu	We	Th	Fr	Sa
			1	2	3	4
5	6	7	8	9	10	11
12	13	14	15	16	17	18
19	20	21	22	23	24	25
26	27	28	29	30		

3. Philadelphia: Lou Gherig ties record with four straight home runs.

4. Earthquake kills 300 in Mexico.

4. Chile: Revolt upsets Montero regime; Marmaduke Grove declares Socialist Republic (→ 17).

6. New York: John D. Rockefeller denounces dry law (→ 29).

7. 7,000 veterans march in Washington, demanding bonuses (→ 14).

10. N.J.: Violet Sharpe, suspect in Lindbergh kidnapping, commits suicide (→ 15).

14. Washington: Rep. Edward Eslick dies on floor of House while pleading for passage of bonus bill (→ 17).

14. Germany: Hitler pledges cooperation with von Papen government (→ 16).

15. Washington: Gaston Means sentenced to 15 years for fraud in Lindbergh baby kidnapping (→ 9/20/34).

16. Chicago: Hoover and Charles Curtis renominated as Republican candidates (→ 7/2).

16. Switzerland: Conference on war reparations opens in Lausanne (→ 24).

16. Germany: Ban on Nazi storm troopers lifted by von Papen government (→ 7/20).

17. U.S. Senate defeats bonus bill as 10,000 veterans mass around Capitol (→ 7/28).

17. Chile: Marmaduke Grove and Eduardo Matte exiled to Easter Island, ending Socialist Republic (→ 7/10).

21. Federal gasoline tax of one cent per gallon goes into effect.

22. Washington: Hoover asks world arms cut of one-third to save $10 bil.; Italy accepts (→ 9/14).

24. Lausanne: German delegates tell France reparations will not be paid (→ 7/9).

29. Chicago: Democrats pledge to repeal dry law (→ 8/11).

BIRTH

15. Mario Cuomo, governor of New York.

Siam's army ends absolute monarchy

The coup's military leaders are planning constitutional government for Siam.

June 29. Sixty years of absolute monarchy have ended in Siam as the armed forces in Bangkok seized control of the government, embarking on a "peaceful revolution."

Sweeping through the city, revolutionary leaders captured members of the royal family, occupied law courts and reportedly killed one resister, the King's chief of staff. King Prajadhipok was not in Bangkok when the coup occurred.

One of the few remaining absolute monarchies, weakened by an economic crisis and subsequent public sector layoffs, Siam has encountered open protest and general discontent in recent months. The king, in his attempts to quell the masses, only aggravated them to the breaking point. The leaders of the rebellion intend to restrict the king's absolute power by instituting constitutional rule, eliminating the princes entirely from the government and forcing the resignation of the Cabinet. While there was much excitement among the people, the takeover was relatively peaceful and orderly (→ 10/12/33).

June 25. At 32, a dapper Gene Sarazen, who began his golf career in Rye N.Y., has taken his second U.S. Open title. With a British Open victory in hand, he is shooting for a Grand Slam.

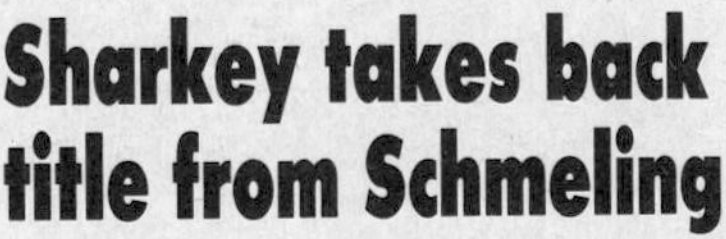

Sharkey takes back title from Schmeling

June 21. Jack Sharkey brought the world heavyweight boxing championship back to America with a 15-round split decision over the German Max Schmeling at Madison Square Garden Bowl in New York. Sharkey was declared the winner by a 2-1 vote. However, many of the ringside fans booed the verdict. A survey of newspaper writers seated at ringside also favored a victory for Schmeling.

Schmeling himself thought he had won. "I was never so surprised in all my life," he said afterward. Schmeling got off to a slow start, apparently trying to figure Sharkey's style. He pressed in tirelessly in the third and fourth rounds. Sharkey's best fighting came in the fifth, sixth and seventh. Sharkey paid tribute to the German's ability and promised him a return bout.

1932

JULY

Su	Mo	Tu	We	Th	Fr	Sa
					1	2
3	4	5	6	7	8	9
10	11	12	13	14	15	16
17	18	19	20	21	22	23
24	25	26	27	28	29	30
31						

1. Wimbledon: Ellsworth Vines 6-4, 6-4, 6-0 over "Bunny" Austin; Helen Wills Moody 6-3, 6-1 over Helen Jacobs for fifth career title.

5. Portugal: Antonio de Oliveira Salazar becomes virtual dictator of fascist regime.

9. Hoover opposes canceling war debts owed to U.S. (→ 21).

10. Chile: Ex-Pres. Carlos Ibanez fails in attempted army coup.

13. Britain, France form new entente to make joint decision on war debts to U.S. (→ 14).

14. Washington: Hoover denies U.S. was consulted on debt accord at Lausanne; Britain says pact will not affect U.S. (→ 21).

17. China: 10,000 die in battle as Chiang opens campaign against Communists (→ 8/9/34).

18. Turkey becomes 56th member of League of Nations.

18. Culturally divided Belgium makes French official language in Walloon provinces, Flemish in Flanders.

20. Germany: Von Papen removes Socialist premier of Prussia, declares martial law (→ 31).

21. Ottawa: British Empire nations open trade parley (→ 8/20).

21. Hoover signs Relief and Reconstruction Act, raising credit capacity of RFC to $3 billion (→ 22).

22. Federal Home Loan Act passed by U.S. Congress, allowing regional banks to provide cheap homeowners' loans (→ 27).

25. U.S.S.R. signs non-aggression pact with Poland, Japan.

26. Tour de France won by French racer Andre Leducq.

27. N.Y.: Govt. drops tax inquiry on Jimmy Walker (→ 9/1).

27. RFC loans Illinois $3 mil. in first relief act (→ 8/22).

30. Summer Olympics open in Los Angeles (→ 8/14).

31. Chaco War opens in struggle over border between Paraguay and Bolivia (→ 10/1).

DEATH

24. Alberto Santos-Dumont, Brazilian aviator (*7/20/1873).

FDR is nominated, promises new deal

FDR greets supporters from train.

July 2. Franklin Delano Roosevelt promised a "new deal" for America as he accepted the Democratic nomination for president of the United States today.

Standing before the convention delegates who had nominated him for president the night before in Chicago, the New York Governor shouted: "I pledge you, I pledge myself to a new deal for the American people."

Governor Roosevelt won the nomination on the fourth ballot after California and Texas delegates, who had been pledged to House Speaker John Nance Garner, broke the long deadlock by casting their votes for Roosevelt. Speaker Garner later was given the Democratic Party's nomination for vice president. While polling far more than enough votes for the nomination, Roosevelt failed to carry his home state of New York, which stayed with his nearest rival, Alfred E. Smith (→ 10/22).

Bonus army driven out

Washington police fight it out with a hostile army of bonus marchers.

July 28. Acting on orders from President Hoover, federal troops, armed with machine guns and tear gas, evicted the bonus army from Washington tonight, setting fire to their makeshift shanties and tents near the Capitol and along the Anacostia River. By midnight, only a few veterans were still in the city.

In calling out the troops, which were commanded by General Douglas MacArthur and Major Dwight Eisenhower, Hoover said the ranks of the bonus seekers had been infiltrated by Communists and persons with criminal records, a fact perhaps unknown to those veterans who had been camped here since May in their drive for a bonus for service in the Great War. Before federal troops moved in, city police fought with the squatters, resulting in the death of one veteran and several injuries on both sides.

Ziegfeld is gone, but the show goes on

July 22. Florenz Ziegfeld, the "glorifier of the American girl," died this night in Hollywood. The 63-year-old impresario never recovered from a bout with pneumonia. His wife, actress Billie Burke, was near his side at his passing.

Ziegfeld was born in Chicago. He was the son of a classical musician, but he was never known for his highbrow pursuits. At the Chicago World's Fair, he managed bodybuilder Eugene Sandow, billed as "the perfect man," and pocketed 90 percent of the act's gross. He then produced several successful Broadway shows starring Anna Held. After a string of flops, Ziegfeld visited Europe, where he was intrigued by the Parisian Folies Bergeres. He returned to New York in 1907 and staged his first "Follies." Sophie Tucker and Mae Murray were two of the girls he "glorified." Ziegfeld produced a "Follies" show every year for 20 years.

The Ziegfeld legacy: "Glorifying the American girl."

Nazis double seats in Berlin Reichstag

July 31. Adolf Hitler's National Socialists have doubled their strength in the legislative elections and are now the biggest party in the Reichstag. The Nazis increased their seats from 107 two years ago to 229 today. But the German legislature is badly divided.

The National Socialists received about 37% of the votes. The Social Democrats tallied about 22%. The Center Party of former Chancellor Bruening came in fourth behind the Communists, but it is key to the formation of a working majority, since the Communists do not like to cooperate with anyone.

The election ended as it began, with a fierce battle at Altona, Hamburg's port. "Bloody Sunday" erupted as Communists attacked Nazis with guns. It did not take long for Socialists to join the battle and turn it into a bloodbath (→ 8/4).

Four Musketeers win 6th Davis Cup

July 31. France's "Four Musketeers" worked tennis magic today at Roland Garros Stadium, winning their sixth straight Davis Cup 3-2 over the favored Americans Wilmer Allison and Ellsworth Vines.

On Friday, Jean Borotra stole the cup and the hearts of all France. The 34-year-old Basque, only on the court because an ill Rene Lacoste had pleaded with him, played inspired tennis to defeat Vines, 13 years his junior. Fighting for every point as if his life depended on it, he came back from 3-1 in the fourth, then collapsed and had to be revived before greeting President Lebrun.

The feat climaxed a glorious career for the veteran and his compatriots. Between them, Borotra, Lacoste, Henri Cochet and Jacques Brugnon have won no less than 23 major singles titles and numerous doubles titles since 1924.

Late King Gillette made shaving easy

July 10. King Camp Gillette, millionaire inventor of the safety razor, died today in Los Angeles. He was 77. Despite his enviable success in the business world, Gillette loathed the inherent evils of competition. In 1894, long before his success, he wrote books advocating the construction of a utopian society near Niagara Falls. Gillette envisioned a community of trust and cooperation, living on the clean power produced by the falls.

Gillette was born in Fond du Lac, Wisconsin. His father was a part-time inventor and his mother wrote a best-selling cookbook. Young Gillette held various low-paying jobs throughout the Midwest. In 1903, he founded the Gillette Safety Razor Company. That year he sold 168 safety razors. The next year, he sold 15 million. The present annual output is one billion.

Reparations ended by Lausanne deal

July 9. Europe in general, and France in particular, extended Germany an olive branch today. After three weeks of negotiations in Lausanne, Switzerland, German reparation payments were suspended.

The last hurdle was crossed late last night, when the European Allies agreed not to criticize or blame Germany in the treaty. That judgment was left for history.

France fought the suspension of payments until the end of the conference. But it was French Premier Herriott who was perhaps the most eloquent about the final agreement. "To passion we have shut the door," he said. "To violence we have preferred reason. We have proclaimed a new message of good will." German Chancellor von Papen could have responded in kind. Instead, he gave a long speech about German suffering (→ 13).

1932

AUGUST

Su	Mo	Tu	We	Th	Fr	Sa
	1	2	3	4	5	6
7	8	9	10	11	12	13
14	15	16	17	18	19	20
21	22	23	24	25	26	27
28	29	30	31			

4. Rioting between Communists, Nazis plaguing Berlin; Reich threatens death penalty (→ 7).

7. Berlin: For. Min. Schleicher warns Germany will not wait for reductions to create arms equality (→ 24).

9. Briton R.S. Willows de Glossop claims invention of fabric that doesn't wrinkle.

10. Spain: Gen. Jose Sanjurjo seizes Seville before Zamora govt. crushes uprising (→ 9/6).

11. Hoover admits failure of Prohibition, favors state liquor laws (→ 10/29).

13. Rome: Marconi successfully tests first short wave radio.

13. Germany: Unmanned balloon reaches height of 17 miles, disproves theory that cosmic rays increasingly gain intensity.

16. Britain institutes new electoral plan for India, allowing untouchables limited and separate representation (→ 9/20).

18. Swiss balloonist Auguste Piccard reaches altitude of 10 miles in second trip.

19. John Mollison arrives in Canada after first westward solo flight across North Atlantic.

20. Ottawa conference ends, establishing system of imperial preference for British trade (→ 9/28).

21. Brazil places Sao Paulo under martial law.

24. Berlin: Nazi newspaper banned for inciting riots (→ 29).

26. Washington: Natl. conference adopts Hoover's recovery program; moratorium called on mortgage foreclosures (→ 9/29).

30. Germany: Nazi leader Hermann Goering elected president of Reichstag (→ 9/1).

30. Ecuadorian rebels yield after long battle; failed military coup kills 500.

31. Millions in Maine watch solar eclipse.

BIRTH

17. V.S. Naipaul, Indian writer.

DEATH

14. Canine actor Rintintin.

95,000 at closing of Los Angeles Olympics

Olympic teams parade before a gigantic crowd in Los Angeles.

Aug 14. While a crowd of 95,000 persons watched in the Los Angeles Coliseum, the 1932 Olympic torch flickered out on the most numerous medal collection of any American team. On the basis of unofficial scoring, the United States rolled up 740.5 points to 262.5 for the runner-up, Italy. No other nation was even close. Record weather, record crowds, record performances and record receipts marked the West Coast Games, which many had thought were doomed to failure.

Eddie Tolan led the parade, winning both dashes, and his teammate, W.A. Carr, took the 400-meter run. Europeans, as usual, dominated the distance events but the Americans balanced that by winning most field events. Juan Carlos Zabala of Argentina won the marathon.

Eleven million jobless; RFC lends $49m

Aug 22. With 11 million still out of work, President Hoover, optimistic that the "major financial crisis" has been overcome, called on the nation's leaders to attack what remains of the depression. Meanwhile, the Reconstruction Finance Corporation announced loans of over $49 million in the last weeks of July to 450 applicants. Some $32.9 million of that amount went to banks (→ 26).

Kids wait in a "Hooverville" for fathers to return from the bonus march.

Papen bars Hitler from government

Aug 29. Talks between the German government and Adolf Hitler, who recently got 13.5 million votes, have broken off with Chancellor von Papen's refusal to give the Nazi leader a Cabinet seat. Earlier, President Hindenburg had denied Hitler's demand to be made dictator. Addressing the 230 Nazi Reichstag members, by far the strongest bloc, Hitler said he could no longer tolerate the present government and that the Nazi Party's total victory was only a matter of time (→ 30).

Von Papen, trying to stave off Hitler.

Alien departures exceeding arrivals

Aug 17. For the first time in U.S. history, emigration exceeds immigration. According to statistics released in Washington today, 35,576 people were admitted in fiscal year 1932 while 103,295 left the country. About one-third of the latter were formally or informally deported. Most of the deported were penniless within three years of their arrival in America. It is estimated a majority of the immigrants leaving on their own initiative did so anticipating a collapse in their fortunes.

Where are the aliens bound? A few head for Canada and Australia; rumors persist that times are better there. But most are going to the "old country." Five years ago, when the American economy was good, there were still great numbers of Greeks and Italians who returned to their native lands after a few years in America earning money. Home, however destitute, is still home.

1932 Los Angeles

Men Athletics

100 M Dash
1. Eddie Tolan USA 10,3
2. Ralph Metcalfe USA 10,3
3. Arthur Johath GER 10,4

200 M Dash
1. Eddie Tolan USA 21,2
2. George Simpson USA 21,4
3. Ralph Metcalfe USA 21,5

400 M Run
1. William Carr USA 46,2
2. Benjamin Eastman USA 46,4
3. Alexander Wilson CAN 47,4

800 M Run
1. Thomas Hampson GBR 1:49,7
2. Alexander Wilson CAN 1:49,9
3. Philip Edwards CAN 1:51,5

1,500 M Run
1. Luigi Beccali ITA 3:51,2
2. John Comes GBR 3:52,6
3. Philip Edwards CAN 3:52,8

5,000 M Run
1. Lauri Lethinen FIN 14:30,4
2. Ralph Hill USA 14:30,0
3. Lauri Virtanen FIN 14:44,0

10,000 M Run
1. Janusz Kusocinski POL 30:11,4
2. Volmari Isohollo FIN 30:12,6
3. Lauri Virtanen FIN 30:35,0

Marathon
1. Juan Carlos Zabala ARG 2:31:36,0
2. Samuel Ferris GBR 2:31:55,0
3. Armas Toivonen FIN 2:32:12,0

110 M Hurdles
1. George Saling USA 14,6
2. Percy Beard USA 14,7
3. Donald Finlay GBR 14,8

400 M Hurdles
1. Robert Tisdall IRL 51,7
2. Glenn Hardin USA 51,9
3. F. Morgan Taylor USA 52,0

3000 M Steeplechase
1. Volman Isohollo FIN 10:33,4
2. Thomas Evenson GBR 10:46,0
3. Joseph McCluskey USA 10:46,2

400 M Relay
1. USA 40,0 (Robert Kiesel, Emmet Toppirro, Hector Dyer, Frank Wykoff)
2. GER 40,9 (Helmut Köning, Friedrich Hendrix, Erich Borchmeyer, Arthur Jonath)
3. ITA 41,2 (Giuseppe Castelli, Ruggero Maregatti, Gabrielle Salviati, Edgardo Toetti)

1600 M Relay
1. USA 3:08,2 (Ivan Fuqua, Edgar Ablowich, Carl Warner, William Carr)
2. GBR 3:11,2 (Crew Stoneley, Thomas Hampson, David Burghley, Godfrey Rampling)
3. CAN 3:12,8 (Raymond Lewis, James Ball, Philip Edwards, Alexander Wilson)

50 km Walk
1. Thomas Green GBR 4:50,10
2. Janis Dalinsch LIT 4:57,20
3. Ugo Frigerio ITA 4:59,06

High Jump
1. Duncan McNaughton CAN 1,97
2. Robert Van Osdel USA 1,97
3. Simeon Toribio PHI 1.97

Pole Vault
1. William Miller USA 4,315
2. Shuhei Nishida JAP 4,30
3. George Jefferson USA 4,20

Long Jump
1. Edward Gordon USA 7,64
2. Charles Lambert Redd USA 7,60
3. Chuhei Nambu JAP 7,45

Triple Jump
1. Chuhei Nambu JAP 15,72
2. Erik Svensson SWE 15,32
3. Kenkichi Oshima JAP 15,12

Shotput
1. Leo Sexton USA 16,005
2. Harlow Rothert USA 15,675
3. Frantisek Douda TCH 15,61

Discus Throw
1. John Anderson USA 49,49
2. Henri Jean Laborde USA 48,47
3. Paul Winter FRA 47,85

Hammer Throw
1. Patrick O'Callaghan IRL 53,92
2. Ville Porhola FIN 52,27
3. Peter Zaremba USA 50,33

Javelin
1. Matti Järvinen FIN 72,71
2. Matti Sippala FIN 69,80
3. Eino Penttila FIN 68,70

Decathlon
1. James Aloysius Bausch USA 8462,23
2. Akilles Järvinen FIN 8292,48
3. Wolrad Eberle GER 8030,80

For abbreviations see Table of Contents

Women Athletics

100 M Dash
1. Stabislawa Walasiewicz POL 11,9
2. Hilda Strike CAN 11,9
3. Wilhemina von Bremen USA 12,0

80 M Hurdles
1. Mildred Didrikson USA 11,7
2. Evelyne Hall USA 11,7
3. Marjorie Clark SAF 11,8

400 M Relay
1. USA 47,0 (Mary Carew, Evelyn Furtsch, Annette Rogers, Wilhemina von Bremen)
2. CAN 47,0 (Mildred Frizzel, Lilian Palmer, Mary Frizzel, Hilda Strike)
3. GBR 47,6 (Eileen Hiscock, Gwendoline Porter, Violet Webb, Nellie Halstead)

High Jump
1. Jean Shiley USA 1,657
2. Mildred Didrikson USA 1,657
3. Eva Dawes CAN 1,60

Discus Throw
1. Lillian Copeland USA 40,58
2. Ruth Osborn USA 40,12
3. Jadgiwa Wajsowna POL 38,74

Javelin
1. Mildred Didrikson USA 43,68
2. Ellen Braumuler GER 43,49
3. Tilly Fleischer GER 43,00

Men Swimming

100 M Freestyle
1. Yasuji Miyazaki JAP 58,2
2. Tatsugo Kawaishi JAP 58,6
3. Albert Schwartz USA 58,8

400 M Freestyle
1. Clarence Crabbe USA 4:48,4
2. Jean Taris FRA 4:48,5
3. Tsutomu Oyokota JAP 4:52,3

1,500 M Freestyle
1. Kusuo Kitamura JAP 19:12,4
2. Shozo Makino JAP 19:14,1
3. James Cristy USA 19:39,5

100 M Backstroke
1. Masaji Kiyokawa JAP 1:08,6
2. Toshio Irie JAP 1:09,8
3. James Cristy USA 1:10,0

200 M Breaststroke
1. Yoshiyuki Tsuruta JAP 2:45,4
2. Reizo Koike JAP 2:46,6
3. Teofilo Ydefonzo PHI 2:47,1

800 M Relay
1. JAP 8:58,4 (Yasuji Miyazaki, Masanori Yusasa, Takashi Yokoyama, Hisakichi Toyoda)
2. USA 9:10,5 (Frank Booth, George Fissler, Marola Kalili, Manuella Kalili)
3. HUN 9:31,4 (Andras Wannie, Laszlo Szabados, Andras Székely, Istvan Barany)

Springboard Diving
1. Michael Galitzen USA 161,38
2. Harold Smith USA 158,54
3. Richard Degener USA 151,82

High Diving
1. Harold Smith USA 124,80
2. Michael Galitzen USA 124,28
3. Frank Kurtz USA 121,98

Water Polo

1. Hungary
2. Germany
3. USA

Women Swimming

100 M Freestyle
1. Heléne Madison USA 1:06,8
2. Willemintje den Ouden HOL 1:07,8
3. Eleonor Saville Garatti USA 1:08,2

400 M Freestyle
1. Heléne Madison USA 5:28,5
2. Lenore Kight USA 5:28,6
3. Jennie Makaal SAF 5:47,3

200 M Breaststroke
1. Claire Dennis AUS 3:06,3
2. Hideko Machata JAP 3:06,4
3. Else Jacobsen DEN 3:07,1

100 M Backstroke
1. Eleanor Holm USA 1:19,4
2. Philomena Mealing AUS 1:21,3
3. Elisabeth Valerie Davies GBR 1:22,5

400 M Relay Freestyle
1. USA 4:38,0 (Josephine McKin, Helen Johns, Eleanor Saville Garetti, Heléne Madison)
2. HOL 4:47,5 (Marie Vierdag, Maria Oversloot, Cornelia Laddé, Willemejnte den Ouden)
3. GBR 4:52,4 (Elisabeth Valerie Davies, Helen Varcoe, Margaret Joyce Cooper, Edna Hughes)

Springboard Diving
1. Georgia Coleman USA 87,52
2. Katherine Rawls USA 82,56
3. Jane Fauntz USA 82,12

High Diving
1. Dorothy Poynton USA 40,26
2. Georgia Coleman USA 35,56
3. Marion Roper USA 35,22

Men Gymnastics

All-Around Individual Competition
1. Romeo Neri ITA 140,625
2. Istvan Pelle HUN 134,925
3. Heikki Savolainen FIN 134,575

All-Around Team Competition
1. Italy 541,850
2. USA 522,275
3. Finland 509,995

Parallel Bars
1. Romeo Neri ITA 18,97
2. Istvan Pelle HUN 18,60
3. Heikki Savolainen FIN 18,27

Floor Exercise
1. Istvan Pelle HUN 9,60
2. Georges Miez SUI 9.47
3. Mario Lertora ITA 9.23

Horse Vault
1. Savino Guglielmetti ITA 18.03
2. Alfred Jochim USA 17,77
3. Edward Carmichael USA 17,53

Sidehorse
1. Istvan Pelle HUN 19,07
2. Omero Bonoli ITA 18,87
3. Frank Haubold USA 18,57

Horizontal Bar
1. Dallas Bixler USA 18,33
2. Heikki Savolainen FIN 18,07
3. Einari Terasvirta FIN 18,07

Flying Rings
1. Georges Gulack USA 18,97
2. William Denton USA 18,60
3. Giovanni Lattuada ITA 18,50

Rope Climbing (1896, 1904, 1908, 1924, 1932)
1. Raymond Bass USA 6,7
2. William Gilbraith USA 6,8
3. Thomas Connelly USA 7,0

Club Swinging (1904 and 1932 only)
1. Georg Roth USA 8,97
2. Philip Erenberg USA 8,90
3. William Hermann USA 18,37

Tumbling
1. Rowland Wolfe USA 18,90
2. Edward Gross USA 18,67
3. William Hermann USA 18,37

Field Hockey

1. India
2. Japan
3. USA

Boxing

Flyweight
1. Istvan Enekes HUN
2. Francisco Chabanás MEX
3. Louis Salica USA

Bantamweight
1. Horace Gwynne CAN
2. Hans Ziglarski GER
3. José Villanueva PHI

Featherweight
1. Carmelo Robledo ARG
2. Josef Scheinkofer GER
3. Carl Carlsson SWE

Lightweight
1. Lawrence Stevens SWE
2. Thure Ahlqvist SWE
3. Nathan Bor USA

Welterweight
1. Edward Flynn USA
2. Erich Campe GER
3. Bruno Ahlberg FIN

Middleweight
1. Carmen Barth USA
2. Amado Azar ARG
3. Ernest Pierce SAF

Light Heavyweight
1. David Castens SAF
2. Gino Rossi ITA
3. Peter Jörgensen DEN

Heavyweight
1. Santiago Lovell ARG
2. Luigi Rovati ITA
3. Frederick Feary USA

Greco Roman Wrestling

Bantamweight
1. Jakob Brendel GER
2. Marcello Nizzola ITA
3. Louis Francois FRA

Featherweight
1. Giovanni Gozzi ITA
2. Wolfgang Ehrl GER
3. Lauri Koskella FIN

Lightweight
1. Erik Malmberg SWE
2. Abraham Kurland DEN
3. Eduard Sperling GER

Welterweight
1. Ivar Johansson SWE
2. Väinö Kajander FIN
3. Ercole Gallegati ITA

Middleweight
1. Väinö Kokkinen FIN
2. Jean Fodeak GER
3. Axel Cadier SWE

Light Heavyweight
1. Rudolf Svensson SWE
2. Onni Pellinen FIN
3. Mario Gruppioni ITA

Heavyweight
1. Carl Westergen SWE
2. Josef Urban TCH
3. Nikolaus Hirschl AUT

Freestyle Wrestling

Bantamweight
1. Robert Pearce USA
2. Odön Zombori HUN
3. Aatos Jaskari FIN

Featherweight
1. Hermanni Pihlajamaki FIN
2. Edgar Nemir USA
3. Einar Karlsson SWE

Lightweight
1. Charles Pacôme FRA
2. Karoly Karpati HUN
3. Gustaf Klaren SWE

Welterweight
1. Jack Van Bebber USA
2. Daniel MacDonald CAN
3. Eino Leino FIN

Middleweight
1. Ivar Johansson SWE
2. Kyosty Luukko FIN
3. Jozsef Tunyogi HUN

Light Heavyweight
1. Peter Mehringer USA
2. Thure Sjöstedt SWE
3. Eddie Scarf AUS

Heavyweight
1. Johan Richthoff SWE
2. John Riley USA
3. Nikolaus Hirschl AUT

Men Fencing

Foil Individual
1. Gustavo Marzi ITA
2. Joseph Lewis USA
3. Giulio Gaudini ITA

Foil Team
1. France
2. Italy
3. USA

Epée Individual
1. Giancarlo Comaggia Modici ITA
2. Georges Buchard FRA
3. Carlo Agostini ITA

Epée Team
1. France
2. Italy
3. USA

Sabre Individual
1. Gyorgy Piller HUN
2. Giulio Gaudini ITA
3. André Kabos HUN

Sabre Team
1. Hungary
2. Italy
3. Poland

CHART

Weightlifting

			2 Arm Press	2 Arm Snatch	2 Arm Clean and Jerk	Total
Featherweight						
1.	Raymond Suvigny	FRA	82,5	87,5	117,5	287,5
2.	Hans Wolpert	GER	85,0	87,5	110,0	282,5
3.	Anthony Terlazzo	USA	82,5	85,0	112,5	280,0
Lightweight						
1.	René Duverger	FRA	97,5	102,5	125,0	325,0
2.	Hans Haas	AUT	82,5	100,0	125,0	307,5
3.	Gastone Pierini	ITA	92,5	90,0	120,0	302,5
Middleweight						
1.	Rudolf Isnayr	GER	102,5	110,0	132,5	345,0
2.	Carlo Galimberti	ITA	102,5	105,0	132,5	340,0
3.	Karl Hiplinger	AUT	90,0	107,5	140,0	337,5
Light Heavyweight						
1.	Louis Hostin	FRA	102,5	112,5	150,0	365,0
2.	Svend Olsen	DEN	102,5	107,5	150,0	360,0
3.	Henry Duey	USA	92,5	105,0	132,5	330,0
Heavyweight						
1,	Jaroslav Skobla	TCH	112,5	115,0	152,5	380,0
2.	Vaclav Psenicka	TCH	112,5	117,5	147,5	377,5
3.	Josef Stramberger	GER	125,0	110,0	142,5	337,5

Women Fencing

Foil Individual
1. Ellen Preis AUT
2. Judy Heather Guinness GBR
3. Ema Bogen HUN

Modern Pentathlon

1. Johan Oxenstierna SWE
2. Bo Lindoman SWE
3. Richard Mayo USA

Rowing

Single Scull
1. Henry Pearce AUS 7:44,4
2. William Miller USA 7:45,2
3. Guillermo Douglas URU 8:13,6

Double Sculls
1. USA 7:17,4
2. Germany 7:22,8
3. Canada 7:27,6

Pairs without Coxswain
1. Great Britain 8:00,0
2. New Zealand 8:02,4
3. Poland 8:08,2

Pairs with Coxswain
1. USA 8:25,8
2. Poland 8:31,2
3. France 8:41,2

Fours without Coxswain
1. Great Britain 6:58,2
2. Germany 7:03,0
3. Italy 7:04,0

Fours with Coxswain
1. Germany 7:19,0
2. Italy 7:19,2
3. Poland 7:26,8

Eight Oars
1. USA 6:37,6
2. Italy 6:37,8
3. Canada 6:40,4

Yachting

Finn Monotype Class
1. Jacques Lebrun FRA
2. Adrian Lambertus Maas HOL
3. Santiang Amat Cansino ESP

Star Class
1. USA
2. Great Britain
3. Sweden

6 M Class
1. Sweden
2. USA
3. Canada

8 M Class
1. USA
2. Canada

Cycling

Road Racing Individual (100 km)
1. Attilio Pavesi ITA 2:28:05,6
2. Guglielmo Segato ITA 2:29:21,4
3. Bernhard Britz SWE 2:29:45,2

Road Racing Team
1. Italy 7:27:15,2
2. Denmark 7:38:50,2
3. Sweden 7:39:12,6

1,000 Meter Time Trial
1. Edgar Gray AUS 1:13,0
2. Jacobus Van Egmond HOL 1:13,3
3. Charles Rampelberg FRA 1:13,4

Sprint 1,000 M
1. Jacobus Van Egmond HOL 12,6
2. Louis Challiot FRA
3. Bruno Pellizzari ITA

2,000 M Tandem
1. France 12,0
2. Great Britain
3. Denmark

Team Pursuit (4,000 M)
1. Italy 4:53,0
2. France 4:55,7
3. Great Britain 4:56,0

Equestrian Sports

All-Around Individual Competition
1. Charles F. Pahud de Mortanges HOL 1813,83
2. Earl Thomson USA 1811,00
3. Clarence von Rosen jr. SWE 1809,43

All-Around Team Competition
1. USA 5038,083
2. Netherlands 4689,083

Dressage Individual
1. Xavier Lesage FRA 343,75
2. Charles Marion FRA 305,42
3. Hiram Tuttle USA 300,50

Dressage Team
1. France 2818,75
2. Sweden 2678,00
3. USA 2576,75

Grand Prix Jumping Individual
1. Takeichi Nishi JAP - 8
2. Harry Chamberlin USA - 12
3. Clarence von Rosen jr. SWE - 16

Grand Jumping Team
(No winner, all of the participating nations disqualified.)

1932

SEPTEMBER

Su	Mo	Tu	We	Th	Fr	Sa
				1	2	3
4	5	6	7	8	9	10
11	12	13	14	15	16	17
18	19	20	21	22	23	24
25	26	27	28	29	30	

1. Germany: Five Nazis, convicted of killing a Communist, get death sentences commuted to life imprisonment (→ 12).

1. Cleveland: Jimmy Doolittle is first to fly over 300 mph.

4. World Peace Conference convenes in Vienna, attended by 80 delegates from 14 countries.

5. Little Entente opens Stresa Conference in Italy.

6. Spanish republic abolishes death penalty (→ 25).

9. New York: Excursion liner Observation sinks in East River, killing 37, injuring 60.

10. N.Y.: Ellsworth Vines retains tennis title at Forest Hills.

12. Berlin: Von Papen dissolves Reichstag after vote of no confidence (→28).

14. Algerian rail crash kills 120; 150 wounded.

14. Poland, Latvia, Estonia ask two-year delay on debt payments to U.S.

14. Geneva: Germany quits disarmament conference (→ 12/11).

20. India: Gandhi begins hunger strike in Poona prison to protest separate electorate for untouchables (→ 24).

24. India: Hindus and untouchables sign Poona Pact, allowing increased representation for untouchables; Gandhi ends fast (→ 11/17).

25. Spain: Catalonia gains self-rule from Zamora government (→ 1/10/33).

26. Nicaragua: Govt. troops and rebels caught in heavy fighting at Lindo Lugar and Jinotega (→ 1/2/33).

28. Germany reports 155 victims of political violence in Prussia since January (→ 10/16).

28. Three Liberal ministers and seven others resign from British govt. in protest over protectionist trade policy (→ 10/30).

29. Detroit: 15,000 begin five-day work week at G.M. (→ 12/23).

30. Rome: Pope decries religious persecutions in Mexico, yet orders Catholics to obey laws (→ 10/6).

Jimmy Walker quits as scandal exposed

Walker to leave his mayoral desk.

Sept 1. Jimmy Walker resigned this evening, the first New York Mayor to leave office under fire. Walker described his resignation as a protest against Governor Franklin Roosevelt's removal hearing. In a written statement released today, Walker called the proceedings in Albany "un-American," "unfair" and "a travesty." He plans vindication, if not revenge, by simply running for re-election.

Walker was charged with legal improprieties during his first and second terms in office. The accusations include acceptance of $246,000 from newspaper publisher Paul Block. Block denies seeking any favors in return for the donation. He applauds the ex-mayor's denunciation of the hearing and predicts the public will re-elect him in November. Another publisher, William Randolph Hearst, pledged support in a recent editorial.

Walker objected to his hearing on three counts. First, he was forbidden to confront or cross-examine witnesses. Second, two-thirds of the charges relate to Walker's first term ("a thing of the past") and decisions by earlier mayors. According to the Constitution, says Walker, he cannot be held accountable for these acts. Finally, some of the charges have nothing to do with public affairs, bearing only on what Walker considers private matters.

Walker's lawyer supported the resignation, explaining Walker would have been vindicated but only after a long, exhausting process. Alderman Joseph V. McKee replaces Walker as the Mayor of New York.

1932

OCTOBER

Su	Mo	Tu	We	Th	Fr	Sa
						1
2	3	4	5	6	7	8
9	10	11	12	13	14	15
16	17	18	19	20	21	22
23	24	25	26	27	28	29
30	31					

1. Bolivia: 16,000 clash in border war between Bolivia and Paraguay (→ 11/13).

2. Geneva: League finds Japan violated Pact of Paris in Manchuria; recommends independent govt. in Manchukuo (→ 9).

3. Iraq joins League of Nations upon end of British mandate.

4. Hungary: Julius Gombos forms anti-Semitic nationalist ministry (→ 3/5/37).

6. Mexico: State of Vera Cruz bans priests as citizens (→ 6/16/35).

9. U.S.S.R.: Soviets open world's largest hydroelectric plant on Dnieper River.

9. Rebels reported in control of most of Manchuria (→ 11/21).

12. Illinois: 1,200 striking miners jailed for one day (→ 7/5/35).

13. Washington: Hoover lays cornerstone for Supreme Court building.

15. San Francisco Opera House dedicated with performance of "La Tosca."

15. Rome: Gugliemo Marconi praises work of Italian Fascists.

16. Berlin: Einstein places age of earth at ten billion years.

16. Papen says Reich can only pay debts with goods (→ 11/6).

17. Ontario: Troops quell prison uprising; 900 convicts threaten to burn themselves to death.

19. Kangaroo bones found in South Africa, reviving question of lost continent.

22. Detroit: Hoover lists ten signs of economic recovery (→ 31).

28. Bulgaria expels all Communist deputies from Parliament.

29. N.Y.: Ex-Atty. Gen. Palmer claims dry law repeal would save U.S. $2 bil. (→ 3/22/33).

29. French liner Normandie sails from Saint Nazaire (→ 6/3/35).

31. Boston: FDR urges five-day week, federal aid for unemployed (→ 11/8).

BIRTH

12. Dick Gregory, writer, comedian, civil rights activist.

Yankees win Series in four straight

Ruth and Gehrig cross the plate.

Oct 2. The Yankees did more than just prove their might in the 1932 World Series. They not only won the world championship but they did it in the minimum four games. They crushed the Chicago Cubs by 13-6 in the final contest and thereby restored the title to the American League. This marked the third time with Babe Ruth and Lou Gehrig in the cast that they recorded a World Series sweep.

The victory was especially sweet for Yankee Manager Joe McCarthy. Three years earlier, he tried to win a series with the Cubs. The Yanks were a little concerned when their starter, Johnny Allen, was shelled from the mound in Chicago's four-run first. But Tony Lazzeri and Earle Combs of the Yankees hit two homers each. The Yanks seem invincible.

John Wayne fights for his life in the fifth episode of Nat Levine's "The Hurricane Express."

Jobless fight London cops, menace palace

Mounted police try to keep order at Marble Arch in Hyde Park.

Oct 30. A fourth day of rioting rocked the streets of London today as over 15,000 unemployed youths smashed windows, overturned cars and clashed with police. The violence broke out in Trafalgar Square after 2,000 hunger marchers demonstrated against the lack of adequate employment promised by the Labor Party in last year's election.

Mounted and foot police fought back the crowds trying to attack the King's palace amid chants of "Smash the palace windows!" Today's casualty list numbered 12, down from 70 injured in Thursday's rioting at Hyde Park. Protesters are hoping the proximity of the riot to the palace will prompt greater attention to their needs (→ 11/1).

Onetime allies are expelled by Stalin

Oct 9. Joseph Stalin proved today that there are no limits to his purges of the Communist Party. He ejected two men who formed a power-sharing triumvirate with him after the death of Lenin.

This was actually the second time Stalin threw Grigori Zinoviev and Lev Kamenev out of the party. They were first dismissed in 1927 for siding with Leon Trotsky. Kamenev was later readmitted and given minor party jobs. Zinoviev was also allowed back in the party after he disavowed Trotsky. The two former members of the triumvirate were not the only party members purged today. Stalin also evicted about 18 other dignitaries. Some of them were caught reading a 200-page text that Stalin considered seditious. It was a severe criticism of his policies by a Bolshevik, M.N. Riutin (→ 12/26).

Machinist designs new Zippo lighter

George G. Blaisdell realized this year that Americans lacked something essential: a wind-proof and easy-to-use cigarette lighter. So, using his experience as a machinist, he designed the Zippo lighter. Initial sales seem promising, and Blaisdell hopes his invention will soon catch on like wildfire.

Zippo lighter.

1932

NOVEMBER

Su	Mo	Tu	We	Th	Fr	Sa
		1	2	3	4	5
6	7	8	9	10	11	12
13	14	15	16	17	18	19
20	21	22	23	24	25	26
27	28	29	30			

1. London police repel jobless raid on Parliament after three-hour riot (→ 10).

4. Germany: Three killed in transit strike paralyzing Berlin.

6. Germany: Communists gain in Reich election; Nazis lose 35 seats (→ 21).

7. Washington: Supreme Court demands new trial in Scottsboro case (→ 3/27/33).

7. U.S.: "Buck Rogers" aired on CBS radio.

10. Hurricane kills 1,000 in Cuba.

10. Washington: Britain, France ask for debt relief; Greece defaults; Hungary can't pay (→ 16).

11. Washington: Tomb of the unknown soldier dedicated.

13. Paraguay claims 500 Bolivian victims in one battle (→ 12/2).

16. Washington: Hoover refuses to ask Congress to suspend war debt payments (→ 22).

17. London: Third Round Table Conference on India opens (→ 5/8/33).

21. Berlin: Hitler refuses limited chancellorship offered by Hindenburg (→ 12/2).

21. Geneva: League holds hearings on Manchuria (→ 12/8).

22. London: King George opens Parliament with speech deliberately ignoring war debts (→ 12/22).

27. U.S. National Labor Committee begins drive to end child labor.

28. Tehran: Persia cancels concession to Anglo-Persian Oil Co.

29. Washington: Committee on Cost of Medical Care urges socialized medicine in U.S.

29. U.S.S.R. signs non-aggression pact with France.

29. Cole Porter's "The Gay Divorce" opens in N.Y., featuring hit song "Night and Day."→

30. Russia to allow emigration for large fee in foreign currency.

BIRTH

29. Jacques Chirac, conservative French politician.

Cole Porter show plays on Broadway

Nov 29. Cole Porter's latest Broadway effort, "Gay Divorce," is at best a mixed success. Gaiety, there is. Jo Mielziner's sets are a visual feast and comic moments are not wanting, as when Eric Blore, that quintessential English butler, wonders "What Will Become of Our England?" And the show surely contains one of Porter's most inspired songs, "Night and Day," which nearly, but not quite, redeems the evening.

The problem is the divorce. Most of the numbers, themselves amusing, have little to do with the central yarn, itself weak. But the main divorce concerns the ever elegant Fred Astaire, now dancing without his main partner, and sister, Adele. That takes getting used to. Still, he acquits himself well with the help of a cast including Clare Luce, Luella Gear, Erik Rhodes, and the indomitable Blore.

With "Night and Day," Porter continues to distance himself from his days at Yale, where his youthful tunes "Eli" and "Bull Dog" may still be heard on football afternoons.

Stalin's wife dead; suicide suspected

Nov 9. Joseph Stalin's wife, Nadya Aliluieva, died last night under questionable circumstances. She was 30 years old. Initial reports attributed her death to an auto accident; later, natural causes were mentioned. However, no reports of ill health preceeded her death, and some Westerners suspect she died at her own hand.

Stalin met Miss Aliluieva's father in the early 1900's. Stalin and Aliluiev, who was an unschooled locksmith, together planned subversive Bolshevik activities. Stalin knew Miss Aliluieva as a child. They married when he was 40 and she was barely 17. Mrs. Stalin qualified for a high administrative post, having recently studied textile production at the All-Union Industrial Academy. She had not been seen by Westerners since a Red Square rally in September. The Soviet leader's wife leaves two children, a son and a daughter.

Roosevelt wins 472-59

President-elect Roosevelt with his wife, Eleanor, and his mother, Sara.

Nov 8. Franklin D. Roosevelt won a landslide victory for President of the United States today, carrying all but six states by promising "to restore this country to prosperity." His stunning defeat of President Herbert Hoover comes at a time when the nation is in a deep depression, a time of growing bread lines and soup kitchens, of bank failures and farm foreclosures and soaring unemployment.

Roosevelt, now Governor of New York, carried his Democratic campaign across the nation. Despite the fact he is badly crippled from polio, he was buoyant, joyous and confident as he spoke of what he called a "new deal" for Americans.

"The country needs, the country demands, bold, persistent experimentation," he said early in the campaign. "It is common sense to take a method and try it. If it fails, admit it frankly and try another. But above all, try something."

He vowed to revive prosperity on the farms, to rehabilitate the railroads, to regulate the banks and security exchanges. He called for public development of electric power, for public works, for unemployment insurance. And he promised that, if elected, he would see to it that no American would starve.

"I am waging a war in this campaign," he said, "a frontal attack, an onset, against the Four Horsemen of the present Republican leadership: The Horsemen of Destruction, Delay, Deceit and Despair" (→ 2/15/33).

"The Roosevelt Special" at campaign stop in Syracuse, New York.

1932

DECEMBER

Su	Mo	Tu	We	Th	Fr	Sa
				1	2	3
4	5	6	7	8	9	10
11	12	13	14	15	16	17
18	19	20	21	22	23	24
25	26	27	28	29	30	31

2. Kurt von Shleicher named German chancellor (→ 1/25/33).

2. Bolivians accept Paraguayan terms for truce in Chaco War (→ 5/10/33).

3. Philadelphia: Army scores 20-0 shut out over Navy.

8. Geneva: Japan tells League it has no control over her designs in China (→ 1/3/33).

11. Reich returns to arms talks after powers sign Geneva Protocol recognizing Germany's intl. rights (→ 3/16/33).

16. Lithuanian National Union adopts fascist program.

23. Telephone service inaugurated between U.S. and Hawaii.

23. U.S.: 185 tons of food given out to needy in Christmas welfare gesture (→ 1/31/33).

26. China: 70,000 killed in massive earthquake.

26. Report from Moscow says one mil. Communists face party expulsion in efficiency drive (→ 2/4/33).

27. S. Africa quits gold standard.

29. U.S.S.R. bars food handouts for housewives under 36; must work to eat.

CULTURAL EVENTS, 1932

Literature: Erskine Caldwell's "Tobacco Road"; Hemingway's "Death in the Afternoon"; Huxley's "Brave New World"; Faulkner's "Light in August."

Academia: "Story of Civilization" begun by Will Durant.

Music: Ferde Grofe's "Grand Canyon Suite"; "Brother Can You Spare a Dime"; "I'm Getting Sentimental Over You"; "Night and Day."

The Arts: Grant Wood's "Daughters of the American Revolution"; Ben Shahn's "Sacco and Vanzetti"; Alexander Calder's first "mobiles," movable hanging sculptures.

Film: "A Farewell to Arms," with Gary Cooper; first "Tarzan," with Johnny Weissmuller; "Red-Haired Alibi," Shirley Temple's first; Frederick March wins Best Actor for "Dr. Jekyll and Mr. Hyde"; Best Picture to "Grand Hotel," with Garbo.

Brave New World, by Aldous Huxley

Aldous Huxley, a British writer who is nearly blind, opened the eyes of readers this year to a "Brave New World." His science-fiction novel depicts a 25th century where art and personal relations are controlled by technology. His characters rely on a drug named "soma" and attend the "feelies," picture shows where the audience feels the onscreen action. Huxley obviously holds a dim view of progress.

Also this year, Georgia-born author Erskine Caldwell deplored the lives of the Southern poor in "Tobacco Road." And Mississippi-born William Faulkner published

Huxley, a gloomy prophet.

the neatly woven novel "Light in August." Ohioan Sherwood Anderson has the same interest in simple, rural folks. His book "Beyond Desire" examines the large drama hidden in small-town lives.

Picasso, at 51 the father of Cubism, created "Girl before a Mirror" this year.

Debts plague Allies; FDR stuck with them

Dec 22. President Hoover's efforts to enlist President-elect Roosevelt in the creation of a commission to handle the war-debt question has been rejected by Roosevelt, who thus takes upon his own shoulders a solution to the problem.

The crisis has been triggered by the worldwide depression and unstable foreign exchange rates. Last week, Hoover said the best approach to currency stabilization was to re-examine the debts of those nations that had "sought to maintain their obligations."

This month, six nations paid: Great Britain, Italy, Czechoslovakia, Finland, Lithuania and Latvia. Four defaulted: France, Belgium, Poland and Hungary.

Though Britain has asked for a revision of its debt, and hopes that this will be its last, it met the payment of over $95 million from its gold reserves—the biggest gold operation ever performed by the Bank of England in a single day. Some 11,000 gold bars were tagged "Federal Reserve Bank" and will be shipped to the United States in small lots in the coming weeks.

Both the Belgian and French governments resigned, the latter when Premier Herriot's proposal to make the $19.5 million payment was rejected by the Chamber of Deputies (→ 1/24/33).

The Forsyte Saga wins for Galsworthy

Galsworthy, creator of the Forsytes.

Dec 10. John Galsworthy, the British playwright and novelist, was awarded the Nobel Prize in literature in Stockholm today. The writer, who is recuperating at home from an illness, received the prestigious honor in absentia.

Galsworthy is known for "The Forsyte Saga," a series of novels about upper-middle-class families in the late Victorian and Edwardian eras. He wrote them over 27 years.

The Nobel Prize in medicine was shared by two British doctors, Sir Charles Sherrington of Oxford and Professor E.D. Adrian of Cambridge. They were honored for their research into nerve cells.

An American, Dr. Irving Langmuir of the General Electric Company, received the chemistry prize.

Caught in the throes of depression, Americans still seem willing to buy alcohol and entertainment. Radio City Music Hall, largest of its kind with 6,000 seats, has opened in N.Y. to satisfy the legal half of these cravings.

1933

JANUARY

Su	Mo	Tu	We	Th	Fr	Sa
1	2	3	4	5	6	7
8	9	10	11	12	13	14
15	16	17	18	19	20	21
22	23	24	25	26	27	28
29	30	31				

2. U.S. task temporarily ended in Nicaragua, as Juan Sacasa becomes president (→ 2/2).

2. Dublin: Dail dissolved; De Valera orders elections for January 24 (→ 28).

3. China: Japanese take Shuangyashan, killing 500 (→ 21).

8. American physicist Dr. Irving Langmuir measures force of single atom (→ 10/4/34).

12. Washington: Douglas MacArthur, appealing for increased war budget, ranks U.S. 17th in military strength.

13. Balloonist Auguste Piccard predicts cosmic rays will someday power motors, light cities.

16. Finland: 78 put on trial as Communists.

21. Alabama: F.D.R. pledges government operation of Muscle Shoals power plant.

21. Geneva: League rejects Japanese terms for settlement with China (→ 2/17).

21. U.S.: Police hunt Dutch Schultz for tax evasion.

24. U.S. Sec. of State Stimson invites debtor nations to negotiate in Washington (→ 4/21).

25. Germany: Police kill nine Communists at political meeting in Dresden (→ 30).

27. Peru, under pressure from U.S., yields Leticia to Colombia.

28. De Valera faction wins electoral victory in Ireland (→ 11/3/36).

31. U.S. jobless figure reaches 15 million; in Detroit, Henry Ford says times are good, insists we are in ox cart stage of machine age (→ 2/14).

BIRTH

16. Susan Sontag, American cultural critic.

DEATHS

5. Calvin Coolidge, 30th U.S. president (*7/4/1872).

21. George Moore, Irish novelist, pioneer in naturalism (*2/24/1852).

31. John Galsworthy, British writer, "Forsyte Saga," 1932 Nobel Prize (*8/14/1867).

Congress promises Philippines freedom

Jan 17. The Philippine independence bill became law today when the Senate voted 66 to 26 to override President Hoover's veto. It calls for conditional independence in about ten years, but the Filipinos have two chances to nullify it. It becomes operative when ratified by the island legislature, and irrevocable when a popular vote ratifies a constitution for the new island government.

The bill sets quotas for Filipino immigration to the United States, stops free entry of island imports into this country, sets tariff rates on imported sugar and permits the United States to maintain island military bases.

Manuel Quezon, President of the Philippine Senate, denounced the act as "shameful and unfriendly" and "not an independence bill at all," describing it rather as a tariff and immigration bill aimed at Philippine products and labor with "the element of independence being merely a sugar coating."

Stating that if it were to be submitted to the legislature at the present time "the bill would be overwhelmingly rejected," Quezon suggested that "the least Congress can do is repass the present bill over our objections" (→ 3/24/34).

Xerxes and Darius palaces discovered

Jan 22. The magnificent palaces of Kings Darius and Xerxes have been uncovered after 2,500 years. Excavators from the University of Chicago made the find in Persepolis, the ancient capital of Persia. According to legend, in 330 B.C. Alexander the Great torched the city while in a drunken rage. The excavators are thankful; it is the burned debris that hid and preserved the fine carvings and murals found throughout the palaces.

While many treasures are yet to be disclosed, panel sculptures on the palace walls have been thoroughly examined. They depict scenes of ambassadors paying tribute to the kings. Slaves and servants offer jars of perfume, gold and silver. The figures are still outlined in the original flaming scarlet paint.

Hitler is named German Chancellor

Hitler is received by President von Hindenburg.

Postcard commemorating "the historic day."

Jan 30. After a month of secret negotiations, Nazi leader Adolf Hitler became Chancellor of Germany today. The flamboyant, tempestuous and power-hungry Hitler takes over the job at a very volatile moment in German history. The country seems poised on the brink of civil war. Almost daily, bloody street battles erupt between Hitler's National Socialist followers and their hated adversaries, the Communists.

Hitler is feared by some of his opponents, but some hope he will be less dangerous in office than in the street commanding his storm troopers. Others believe Hitler's thirst for power will be checked by the coalition Cabinet that was largely assembled by the deft political skills of former Chancellor Franz von Papen. But Hitler showed little restraint in his first proclamation.

"The National Socialist Party knows that the new government is no National Socialist Government," the chancellor declared in the proclamation, "but it is conscious that it bears the name of its leader, Adolf Hitler. He has advanced with his shock troops and has placed himself at the head of the government to lead the German people to liberty."

Communist agitators started milling in the streets of Berlin as soon as news of Hitler's title was no longer a secret. They plastered walls with handbills calling for a nationwide general strike.

Violence erupted when 100 Nazis were walking home after a pro-Hitler demonstration. A police officer accompanying them was shot to death. One of the Nazis was also killed.

Hitler will surely not forget the incident. He is likely to make elimination of the Communists one of his key goals. The new government press chief, Walther Funk, has already made an oblique attack on the Communists, stating the Cabinet will not tolerate any "experiments of a financial or economic nature."

Scenes of jubilation in Berlin greatly outnumbered the Communist demonstrations. Large crowds greeted columns of Hitler's storm troopers as they marched in a torchlight parade through the Brandenburg Gate. The crowds raised their hands in the fascist salute to President von Hindenburg, who stood in one lighted window of the Chancellery. In another stood Hitler, next to his new Aviation Minister, Hermann Goering.

Hitler, Goering and Dr. Wilhelm Frick are the only Nazis in the Cabinet for the time being. It was put together by former Chancellor von Papen after President Hindenburg gave Hitler and National Party leader Alfred Hugenberg an ultimatum and ordered the two adversaries to form a coalition. At that moment, von Papen acted quickly and drew up the Cabinet, with Hitler as Chancellor, himself as Vice Chancellor and Hugenberg as Minister of Economy and Food.

Two Hitler allies played key roles in the month-long secret meetings that brought the Nazi leader to power. They are Cologne banker Kurt von Schroeder, who has been impressed by Hitler's anti-Communist rhetoric, and Nazi bureaucrat Joachim von Ribbentrop (→ 2/1).

Revolt in Spain spreads to south

Jan 10. Rioting, bombing and gunfighting continue throughout Spain as the revolution has spread to the southern cities of Seville, Granada and Jerez de la Frontera. Fanning the fire are Communists who have joined anarchist rebels. The combined forces have threatened to instigate a general strike tomorrow. These developments have prompted the Spanish government to authorize Premier Manuel Azana to declare martial law if necessary. As of yet, no declaration has been made. With tensions rising, however, armed guards in many areas have cast the nation into a virtual state of martial law.

In Seville, and across the river in the Triana district, seven anarchists and a member of the Civil Guard were wounded by various batteries of gunfire. People in the streets are being searched for firearms and bombs after several explosions rocked the city, including a blast at the door of the famous Medicini Palace, which was slightly damaged. Because the government fears disturbances in the work force, which would cripple all of Andalusa, the Governor of Seville has ordered troops to guard workers.

A joint Syndicalist-Anarchist manifesto was issued from Barcelona, where some of the bloodiest violence has occurred, including a rash of bombings that killed five on Sunday. The manifesto urges rebels to disrupt telephone, telegraph and railway lines and "to burn all old-fashioned archives".

The government has stated that most Spaniards oppose the revolution (→ 5/17).

Communists in Madrid.

1933

FEBRUARY

Su	Mo	Tu	We	Th	Fr	Sa
			1	2	3	4
5	6	7	8	9	10	11
12	13	14	15	16	17	18
19	20	21	22	23	24	25
26	27	28				

1. Berlin: Hitler wins dissolution of Reichstag (→ 2).

1. Bucharest: Rumanians destroy Standard Oil office.

2. Augusto Sandino, rebel leader for six years, meets with Nicaraguan pres. in Managua (→ 8/2).

2. Berlin: Hitler places curbs on leftist opposition (→ 6).

4. U.S.S.R.: Thousands forced out of Leningrad under new passport system (→ 12/29/34).

5. Java: Native mutineers seize Dutch battleship.

5. Istanbul: Moslem Turks rebel at Arabic prayer ban (→ 1/9/34).

6. Berlin: Reich begins press censorship (→ 27).

6. U.S. adopts 20th Amendment, shortening "lame duck" period.

11. Hoover reserves 1.6 million acres in Ingo County, Calif., for Death Valley Natl. Monument.

14. Detroit defaults on $400 million debt (→ 3/5).

14. Boxer Ernie Schaff, KO'd by Primo Carnera, dies in N.Y.

16. Czechoslovakia, Rumania, Yugoslavia extend Little Entente.

17. League censures Japan in worldwide broadcast (→ 25).

20. Washington: House passes dry law repeal, sends to states for ratification (→ 3/22).

21. Cordell Hull named to FDR Cabinet (→ 3/4).

25. Sir Arthur Wauchope, British high comm. in Palestine, rejects Arab demand for outlawing sale of Arab lands (→ 10/27).

25. The Ranger, first U.S. aircraft carrier, launched at Newport News, Virginia.

26. California: Ground broken for Golden Gate Bridge (→ 4/1937).

28. Playwright Bertolt Brecht leaves Germany (→ 3/1).

BIRTH

13. Henri Costa Gavras, Greek-born film director.

DEATH

25. Pat O'Sullivan, American cartoonist, "Felix the Cat."

Mysterious fire destroys Reichstag

Feb 27-28. A quickly moving fire gutted the German Reichstag in Berlin last night. The chamber where the legislature meets has been reduced to rubble and ashes. Police arrested a young man near the scene of the fire and charged him with setting it. The suspect is identified as a Communist, and the government of Adolf Hitler wasted no time in linking the fire to a Communist conspiracy. "Now you can see what Germany and Europe have to look for from Communism," Hitler is quoted as saying today.

The Associated Press reported early this morning that Minister Hermann Goering used the fire as a pretext to place all 100 Communist members of the Reichstag under arrest. Politicians under arrest will not be able to campaign in the legislative elections, which are less than one week away.

Smoke was first noticed by a police officer on patrol in the Reichstag at 9:00 last night. Before sending an alarm, the officer fired several shots at men seen running from the scene. The officer says he seized one of them, the young suspect said to be a Communist and identified as Marinus Van der Lubbe.

By the time the firefighters arrived, the blaze had already spread in many directions. Whoever started the fire apparently set a match to furniture piled on rugs. The wood paneling, chairs and desks in the Reichstag chamber were all very dry, and they burned easily. The flames crawled to the very top of the elegant, Italian Renaissance chamber and caused the ornate glass ceiling to crash to the floor.

Ten thousand Berliners heard the fire alarm and rushed to police barricades around the burning Reichstag. In the crowd were Hitler, Goering and Vice Chancellor Franz von Papen. The brave firefighters stopped the fire before it burned through the cupola in the Reichstag. They also saved the library and reading room, where countless, priceless documents are stored.

Chancellor Hitler placed Goering in charge of the investigation into the fire. Before dawn, police were rounding up Communists and locking them up until the investigation has been completed. Tonight, President von Hindenburg signed an emergency decree which suspended constitutional guarantees of individual freedom, freedom of the press, private property and the secrecy of postal communications. Communist newspapers were shut down until the election, and suspected Communist meeting places were closed. Parts of Berlin have begun to look more and more like a police state. The regular police, backed up by Nazi auxiliaries armed with rifles, patrolled through many neighborhoods in armored cars.

Hitler's opponents are questioning his accusation that Communists are responsible for the Reichstag fire. They wonder what the Communists could have hoped to gain. They also ask why the 24-year-old Dutchman accused of the arson would have allowed himself to be captured with all his identification and his Communist Party card.

The new crackdown on the Communists is an outgrowth of the government repression which has been on the rise since Hitler became chancellor one month ago. Three days after he took power, he ordered homes of Communists searched without warrants. All their meetings have been either banned or strictly controlled. Before the fire last night, scores of Communists disappeared underground because of the increasing harassment.

Communists were not the only targets. Catholics have been attacked by Nazis. And two dozen provincial governors and police chiefs were dismissed by Goering and replaced by National Socialists. Much of the German population is in a state of panic as the elections approach. Hitler apparently hopes they will turn to his Nazi Party and the program of National Socialism as their only possible hope of salvation (→ 28).

The Reichstag in flames: Communist terror or simply a pretext for repression?

Roosevelt is target of assassination

Feb 15. President-elect Franklin D. Roosevelt narrowly escaped assassination tonight just after he ended a speech in the Bay Front Park in Miami. As he sat in his car near the bandstand, five shots rang out, wounding Chicago's Mayor Anton Cermak, who was standing on the running board of the car, and four other persons. Mayor Cermak is not expected to live.

The would-be assassin, Giuseppe Zingara of Hackensack, New Jersey, was knocked to the ground by a policeman and taken to prison. Police quoted the gunman as saying, "I'd kill every president." Found in his clothing was a clipping telling of the assassination of President McKinley by an anarchist in 1901.

The president-elect, who won a landslide victory just three months ago and who will be inaugurated in a few weeks, had spent the day on a fishing cruise aboard Vincent Astor's yacht before going to the park for a brief speech to a crowd numbering more than 10,000. Microphone in hand, he spoke while standing in the car. He had just ended the speech by saying "Many thanks" and was posing for photographers when the first shot came, followed by four more blasts. Mayor Cermak slumped to his knees and rolled to the pavement, a bullet in his chest. A woman standing nearby grabbed the gunman's wrist and the final shot was deflected before a policeman knocked the gunman to the ground (→ 21).

Mae West and admirers in the entertaining new film "She Done Him Wrong."

Japan walks out of League over China

Japanese sentries guard a captured railway station in Manchuria.

Feb 25. The Japanese delegation has withdrawn from the Assembly of the League of Nations following a censure against Japan passed unanimously yesterday morning by that body. Though the move does not constitute withdrawal from the League itself, this now seems likely.

The censure confirms the report of the Lytton Commission on Manchuria—or Manchukuo, as renamed by the Japanese. Proclaiming that "sovereignty over Manchuria belongs to China," the report dismisses Manchukuo as a Japanese puppet regime and declares that Japanese troops in this Chinese territory are incompatible with the League Covenant since Japan was not acting in self-defense.

The report recommends that Japan withdraw her troops and that China establish an autonomous Manchuria, taking into account special Japanese interests. It further advocated a League advisory committee, with the special participation of the United States and Russia.

Meanwhile, Japan has launched its main offensive in the Manchurian province of Jehol by capturing four cities. The drive aims at the capture of Chengteh, just north of the Great Wall and about 110 miles from Peking. Yosuke Matsuoka, Japanese delegate to the League, said that peace lay in a Chinese withdrawal from Jehol. Scoffing at the 150,000 Chinese troops there, he said that "one Japanese soldier is worth ten Chinese" (→ 3/3).

1933

MARCH

Su	Mo	Tu	We	Th	Fr	Sa
			1	2	3	4
5	6	7	8	9	10	11
12	13	14	15	16	17	18
19	20	21	22	23	24	25
26	27	28	29	30	31	

1. German police arrest hundreds as Hitler intensifies drive on left (→ 5).

3. Japan: Earthquake and tidal wave kill 3000 near Yokohama.

3. China: Japanese take Chengteh, capital of Jehol (→ 27).

4. Austria: Dollfuss dissolves Parliament, bans public meetings to quell Nazi riots (→ 5/28).

4. FDR inaugurated in Washington.→

5. Washington: FDR orders four-day bank holiday to halt massive withdrawals (→ 12).

5. Hitler and Nationalist allies win Reichstag majority (→ 12).

12. FDR holds first radio "fireside chat" (→ 4/19).

12. Hindenburg drops flag of German republic, orders swastika and empire banner flown side-by-side (→ 20).

16. Geneva: Ramsay MacDonald offers military equality to France, Germany (→ 6/21/34).

20. N.Y.: American Jewish Committee demands Washington act on Hitler (→ 27).

20. FDR signs Economy Act, reducing federal salaries and benefits to veterans (→ 31).

22. FDR signs bill legalizing beer and wine (→ 4/7).

23. Reichstag gives Hitler power to rule by decree.→

25. San Fransisco: New trial granted for Thomas Mooney, accused of Preparedness Day bombing (→ 8/29/34).

27. New York: 55,000 stage anti-Hitler protest (→ 10/13).

27. Alabama: Retrial in Scottsboro case begins (→ 4/10).

27. Japan announces she will quit League in 1935 (→ 5/3).

28. Berlin: Nazis order ban against Jews in business, professions and schools (→ 29).

29. Film director Fritz Lang quits Germany, refusing collaboration with Nazis (→ 4/1).

31. Congress passes Reforestation Relief Act, creating Civilian Conservation Corps (CCC) to relieve rampant unemployment (→ 1/31/34).

Earthquake kills 123 in California

March 10. A violent earthquake spread death, injury and destruction over a path 200 miles long and 30 miles wide in Southern California, beginning at 5:55 p.m. yesterday, and 16 aftershocks threw people into panic over the next seven hours. Some 123 were listed as dead and more than 4,150 as injured in still incomplete reports. Fires by the dozens raged. The brunt of the terrifying convulsions was borne by Long Beach, but all over Los Angeles and Orange Counties terror stalked inhabitants as buildings crumbled and recurring tremors hampered rescue work.

Cross-section of a Long Beach home.

Nazis open first concentration camp

March 20. Nazi authorities in Germany have arrested so many political opponents that the jails are bursting. This month alone, 15,000 people were arrested in Prussia. There was nowhere to send them until Heinrich Himmler, the Nazi Police Commissioner in Munich, came up with a solution. It is called a concentration camp. The first one has been built at an old powder factory near the town of Dachau, ten miles outside of Munich. Three more camps are ready to open near Berlin. It is believed that mostly Communists will be sent to the camps. But they will not be alone. Nazi forces are also arresting Social Democrats and members of a Social Democratic military unit (→ 23). ▷

FDR: Only thing to fear is fear itself

Roosevelt at the inauguration: An inspirational voice amid financial chaos.

March 4. Under dark clouds that mirrored the despair of the country, Franklin D. Roosevelt was sworn in as President of the United States today, assuring the troubled nation that "the only thing we have to fear is fear itself."

Pale and tense, yet speaking in ringing tones, the 51-year-old Democrat seemed to breathe new hope into his audience of more than 100,000 gathered on the east plaza of the Capitol as well as to the millions of others listening by radio throughout the United States.

Despite the grave economic crisis in the nation, the city was festooned with flags and lively with the music of marching bands as the new president, smiling and waving, rode from the Capitol to the White House after the oath-taking, his limousine moving slowly along the streets lined with an estimated half million persons.

In his inaugural address, the new president denounced the nation's financial leaders, saying that these "money changers" should be driven from the temple and never again be allowed to misuse other people's money. His biggest applause of the day came when he said that if necessary, he was prepared to ask Congress for power "as great as the power that would be given to me if we were in fact invaded by a foreign foe."

As he spoke, 13 million Americans were jobless, one out of every four heads of households. In the final years of the administration of President Herbert Hoover, scores of banks failed, factories closed and farmers were evicted from their lands. In many cities, entire families are now living in tarpaper shacks and scavenging for food in city dumps.

Sensing the despair of the people, President Roosevelt said: "This nation asks for action, and action now. Our greatest primary task is to put people to work."

Scarcely hours after his inaugural speech, President Roosevelt acted, meeting with key advisers and legislative leaders to work out plans for banking relief and for putting the millions of jobless Americans back to work. He also announced that he was calling Congress into emergency session, in the middle of next week, to enact legislation to deal with the economic crisis (→ 12).

"King Kong" brings to the screen the latest in special-effects technology. Even better is Fay Wray, the prolific young actress whose terrified scream is quickly becoming the most celebrated vocal performance of the year.

Many banks FDR shut will reopen

March 12. Many of the nation's banks will reopen tomorrow after a seven-day bank holiday ordered by President Roosevelt to shore up the nation's economy. All banks were closed on March 6, two days after the new president took office, to allow time for passage of emergency legislation by Congress.

The bank holiday was to have lasted just four days. But even after Congress, now in special session, had speedily passed the emergency bank bill sought by the president, the holiday had to be extended until the Treasury Department could make new regulations. Now that that has been done, major banks found by federal and state authorities to be sound will reopen (→ 20).

Dictatorial power granted to Hitler

Hitler, absolute master of the Reich.

March 23. Adolf Hitler won today what observers suspected he wanted from the very beginning. He was granted virtually dictatorial powers, and the German Parliament adjourned, perhaps for good.

The last action by the Reichstag actually gives the supreme powers to Hitler's Cabinet, rather than the Nazi leader himself. And the President of Germany retains the right to dismiss the Chancellor. But almost everyone concedes that President Hindenburg is an aging figurehead who has virtually retired from politics. And no one would dare to say out loud that the Cabinet is more powerful than Hitler himself.

As things stand now, Hitler and his Cabinet can make laws by decree, without submitting them to the Reichstag. And they have the power to override the constitution.

In a speech to the Parliament before it adjourned, Hitler said the Cabinet is not ready to discuss a return to monarchy. It is agreed, however, that Hitler is the most powerful chancellor in history.

Hitler wore his Nazi uniform at the podium, but his address was restrained. He did use a curious expression at one point. "Treason toward the nation and the people," he warned, "shall in future be stamped out with ruthless barbarity."

Later in the day, Minister Goering reproved the Western press for accusing the government of barbarity. He denied reports that scores of bodies are floating in a Berlin canal and that Nazis have cut off the ears of Communists (→ 28).

1933

APRIL

Su	Mo	Tu	We	Th	Fr	Sa
						1
2	3	4	5	6	7	8
9	10	11	12	13	14	15
16	17	18	19	20	21	22
23	24	25	26	27	28	29
30						

1. Berlin: Nazis seize Einstein funds in German bank (→ 4).

3. First flight over Mt. Everest performed by British pilots Clydesdale and MacIntyre.

4. Berlin: Foreigners barred from leaving Germany without police permit (→ 9).

5. Intl. Court at The Hague condemns Norwegian occupation of eastern Greenland.

7. U.S. suffering severe shortage as one million barrels of beer are consumed legally for first time in 14 years (→ 9/11).

8. West Australia votes to secede from British Commonwealth.

9. German ex-Chancellor von Papen arrives in Rome to seek Vatican's support in rebuilding German Centrist Party (→ 22).

10. New York: Blacks riot on Broadway to protest yesterday's conviction of Scottsboro defendant in Alabama (→ 11/19).

11. New York: George Bernard Shaw says U.S. must lead way to saving Western Civilization by scrapping Constitution.

13. Washington: Louisianans ask removal of Huey Long for tax evasion (→ 8/16/34).

14. Tokyo: Anti-Jewish drive staged on Nazi example.

19. Britain orders ban on Soviet imports after U.S.S.R. convicts three Britons of espionage.

21. Ramsay MacDonald meets with FDR in Washington to discuss world economic recovery (→ 25).

21. Ohio: Dirigible Macon, Akron's sister ship, makes maiden flight (→ 6/23).

22. Berlin: Nazis seize church of German state (→ 5/2).

25. British balance budget, but omit payment to U.S. (→ 7/27).

28. U.S. astronomers find Milky Way stars receding, supporting theory of expanding universe.

29. Cuban troops sent to counter rebel attack near Santiago (→ 5/18).

BIRTH

9. Jean-Paul Belmondo, French movie actor.

FDR takes the dollar off gold standard

April 19. The United States went off the gold standard today, a move ordered by President Roosevelt to put the nation on an equal monetary footing with most countries in the world by placing an embargo on all exports of gold except that earmarked for foreign countries.

Federal officials said that the move was only "for the time being" but declined to say how long that might be, depending on domestic and world conditions.

Abandonment of the gold standard sent stock prices up on Wall Street, which had its most active trading day in more than six months, with a total volume of five million shares traded.

But the move came under heavy attack abroad, particularly in France. There, fluctuations in the American dollar were described by one economist as "scarcely dignified for a money that pretends to be based on gold." The American move was seen in London as a possible opening of a great trade war between the United States and Great Britain (→ 5/12).

Nazis enforce ban on Jewish merchants

Boycott posters and an SA guard, a forbidding barrier outside a Jewish shop.

April 1. The billboards have been up in Germany for 24 hours, and the boycott is in effect today. "Jews the world over are trying to crush the new Germany," the signs read. "German people, defend yourselves! Do not buy from Jews!"

Until yesterday, Adolf Hitler's government tried to distance itself from this boycott of Jewish businesses. The official explanation was that the action was the idea of Nazi citizens. That deception vanished last night when one of Hitler's ministers, Dr. Paul Joseph Goebbels, gave a fiercely anti-Semitic speech and explained to an excited audience how the boycott would work.

Goebbels claimed that the boycott is temporary. But the Minister of Popular Enlightenment and Propaganda also threatened to continue it unless Jews around the world stop their boycott of German goods and stop accusing the German government of atrocities (→ 4).

Farm relief bill is passed in the Senate

April 28. A bill to aid America's struggling farmers passed the Senate today and now awaits action by the House. The measure provides for alternative ways to raise farm values, such as guaranteeing the cost of production, refinancing farm mortgages at interest rates of just four and one-half percent, withdrawing from production sufficient acreage so as to cut production of agricultural commodities to actual domestic needs and stabilizing farm prices generally equal to those of 1909-1914, a more prosperous era.

The Senate also included in the farm relief bill a provision, sought by President Roosevelt, to help fight inflation in a variety of ways. The president could increase Federal Reserve credits by up to $3 billion, issue Treasury notes to buy back government securities and devalue the gold content of the dollar by up to 50 percent.

Although the bill is one of the most important passed during the new Roosevelt administration, much of the Senate debate focused on a proposal, opposed by the president and finally defeated, to add to the measure a bonus for war veterans. Watching intently from the galleries were many of the veterans who had marched on Washington last year to demand a war bonus.

Airship Akron down at sea; 73 drowned

April 4. The dirigible Akron, pride of the Navy air fleet, crashed near the Barnegat Lightship off the New Jersey coast early this morning. First reports said that only four of the 77 officers and men aboard the airship were saved. Navy reports gave no hint of the cause of the disaster, but it is believed that the Akron was struck by lightning. The Akron, 785 feet long and built at a cost of $8 million, returned from a successful flight to the Canal Zone only ten days ago. She took off a[illegible] sundown last night from the Nava[illegible] Air Station at Lakehurst, New Je[illegible]sey, on her ill-fated flight. The d[illegible]aster is not expected to delay [illegible] maiden flight of the Akron's s[illegible]ship, the Macon, later this mo[illegible]

1933

MAY

Su	Mo	Tu	We	Th	Fr	Sa
	1	2	3	4	5	6
7	8	9	10	11	12	13
14	15	16	17	18	19	20
21	22	23	24	25	26	27
28	29	30	31			

3. Japanese pledge to continue open door policy in Manchukuo (→ 31).

4. FDR asks pay raise for U.S. workers under theory that demand must be maintained for economy to recover (→ 7).

6. Brokers Tip and jockey D. Meade come out on top in Kentucky Derby.

7. Washington: FDR promises partnership with business, farmers and workers (→ 12).

8. India: Gandhi starts hunger strike to protest British repression of untouchables (→ 7/4).

10. Paraguay formally declares war on Bolivia (→ 12/11).

12. Agricultural Adjustment Act and Federal Emergency Act adopted in U.S., the latter authorizing grants to replace loans to states (→ 18).

16. FDR asks peace through arms cuts at opening of 66-nation London parley (→ 8/3).

16. Moscow lifts ban on jazz (→ 3/18/34).

17. Associations Law in Spain bans church schools, nationalizes church property (→ 7/24).

18. FDR names Hugh Johnson as "dictator of industry" (→ 27).

18. U.S. creates Tennessee Valley Authority (TVA), landmark federal program for rural development (→ 27).

18. Troops mass in Havana as Cuban revolt grows (→ 6/15).

24. New York's Brooklyn Bridge celebrates 50th anniversary.

27. Federal Securities Act requires registration of securities with Federal Trade Commission (FTC) (→ 31).

27. World's Fair opens in Chicago (→ 11/12).

28. Nazis confiscate all property of Communist Party (→ 6/11).

28. Vienna: Chancellor Dollfuss insists Austria will fight Nazis to e finish (→ 6/14).

ouis Meyer wins Indy 500 d by deaths of three racers.

, Japan sign truce g large part of North- 2/28/34).

Nazis make bonfires of banned books

Nazis oversee a bonfire of books in the homeland of Hegel, Marx and Mann.

May 10. A large bonfire lit a square in front of Berlin University tonight. The flames were not fed by logs or kerosene. Books were burned. Books that Nazis have decided are "un-German."

In Munich yesterday, thousands of school children watched as books described as Marxist were burned. "As you watch the fire burn these un-German books," the children were told, "let it also burn into your hearts love of the Fatherland."

The book burnings are only part of the new Nazi crackdown on intellectuals, scientists and cultural leaders in Germany. Among the individuals dismissed from universities or cultural organizations are writer Thomas Mann, philosopher Paul Tillich and Nobel Prize winners Gustav Hertz and James Franck.

School curricula are also being revised to teach "race science." "The schools must constantly emphasize," said Nazi Interior Minister Wilhelm Frick, "that the infiltration of the German people with alien blood, especially Jewish and Negro, must be prevented" (→ 28).

Mexican artist admits work is Communist

May 13. Mexican mural painter Diego Rivera explained in a speech at New York City's Town Hall last night that his work means to further the cause of the proletariat. Last Tuesday night, Rivera was asked to abandon a work commissioned by Rockefeller Center because the mural included a portrait of Lenin. Rivera foresaw their objections, quoting a Russian friend who said the subject matter "goes well in a peasant country but would not . . . in an industrialized country."

Rivera mural: Trotsky and workers.

Artistically, the 46-year-old painter has been influenced by Paul Cezanne, Auguste Renoir and Pablo Picasso. Politically, his mentors have been Trotsky and other revolutionaries whom he met in Paris before 1917. He toured Russia six years ago. Rivera's frescoes are found throughout Mexico City and the U.S., including one at the San Francisco Stock Exchange (1931) and the Detroit Institute of Art (1932). Bold and immense, the works usually depict the struggle between the classes.

Morgan paid no 1931 or 1932 taxes

May 23. J.P. Morgan, one of the nation's richest men, paid no income tax in 1931 and 1932 and just $48,000 in 1930, according to information provided to the Senate Banking and Currency Committee. Morgan, head of the international banking firm that bears his name, has said that his company suffered a loss of $21 million during the depression years of 1931 and 1932 and thus had no tax liability. But the committee counsel contends that the loss was a contrived one, by revaluation of securities.

Hitler breaks up all trade unions

May 2. Nazi storm troopers swept through German union offices today, arresting labor leaders and confiscating union property. Nazi leaders say the unions themselves will not be outlawed, but reorganized under new Nazi management. The raids were carried out under the supervision of Dr. Robert Ley, the new Prussian State Council President. "Marxism today is playing dead," Ley explained, "but it is not altogether abolished." But the real targets of the raids are not Marxists, but the Socialists, who derive most of their strength to fight the Nazis from the unions (→ 9).

Three billion voted for works program

May 31. F oman and child s of a public w e National In- Bill, as more than been allocated for yet old initiative to boost the eleaguered American economy.

The enormous allocation will be used to fund federal, state, county and municipal projects, employing thousands and enhancing both the face and infrastructure of the nation. The works program will be paid for in one of two ways which has yet to be determined: A manufacturers' sales tax, or a "breakfast table" tax on sugar, coffee, tea, and other such items (→ 6/6).

1933

JUNE

Su	Mo	Tu	We	Th	Fr	Sa
				1	2	3
4	5	6	7	8	9	10
11	12	13	14	15	16	17
18	19	20	21	22	23	24
25	26	27	28	29	30	

1. Charlie Chaplin secretly wedded to Paulette Goddard.

2. Frank Hawks sets West-East flying record, L.A. to N.Y. in 13 hours, 26 minutes, 15 seconds.

5. Italy: Arturo Toscanini boycotts participation in German music festival to protest Nazi repression of artists (→ 9/1).

6. U.S. Employment Service created to match state funds for jobs programs (→ 13).

6. First drive-in movie theater opens in Camden, N.J.

7. Germany, Italy, France, U.K. sign peace pact in Rome.

8. New York: Max Baer KOs Max Schmelling in tenth round.

11. Munich: Nazis bar cardinal from mass, halt Catholic rally (→ 18).

12. FDR repeals protectionist tariffs of Hoover administration (→ 13).

12. London trade parley opens (→ 7/27).

13. Home Owner Loan Corp. set up to offer low-cost mortgages to U.S. home owners (→ 16).

14. Austria expels Theodor Habricht, Hitler's inspector for Austria (→ 19).

15. Cuban rebels accept mediation of U.S. envoy (→ 8/9).

18. Hitler threatens to take children from parents who fail to follow Nazi program (→ 22).

19. Vienna: Dollfuss govt. bans Austrian Nazi party (→ 9/6).

19. France grants Leon Trotsky political asylum (→ 7/25).

22. Illinois waterway opens, linking Great Lakes with Gulf of Mexico.

23. U.S. Navy commissions $2.25 million dirigible Macon at Lakehurst, N.J. (→ 2/12/35).

BIRTHS

10. F. Lee Bailey, U.S. criminal lawyer, defended Patty Hearst.

14. Jerzy Kosinski, Polish novelist, "The Painted Bird."

DEATH

20. Clara Zetkin, German feminist, socialist (*7/5/1857).

NRA: Recovery program

June 16. Calling it the most important bill ever passed by Congress, President Roosevelt signed into law today the National Industrial Recovery Act, giving the government control over industry in an effort to bring the nation out of the current depression.

Under the new law, which will be administered by the National Recovery Administration, also known as NRA, the federal government will seek labor and management cooperation in fixing minimum wages, shorter working hours and regulation of production. The law further provides federal funds for public works programs.

The NRA, the president said in a statement, is "to put people back to work, to let them buy more of the products of the farms and factories and start our business at a living rate again." He said he hoped that many hundreds of thousands of those now unemployed would be "back on the payroll by snowfall."

FDR, architect of our New Deal.

Meanwhile, Roosevelt said, the public works provisions of the new law "will start tomorrow," with the $400 million he has just made available for state roads and $200 million for building Navy ships (→ 7/15).

Carnera is champ; Sharkey is kayoed

June 29. Primo Carnera, the Italian giant, became the first Italian to win the world heavyweight boxing championship when he dethroned Jack Sharkey in the sixth round of what was to have been a 15-round fight.

Carnera's right caught Sharkey's chin in a devastating uppercut that sent the champion to the canvas of Long Island City Bowl. Most of the 40,000 spectators watched in stunned silence. The end came at two minutes, 27 seconds of the sixth, until which time Sharkey showed no sign of weakening. Of the five completed rounds, Sharkey won four of them. He had won the title in June 1932.

Carnera in training in New York.

Nazis now Germany's only political party

June 22. Acting with the efficiency of a guillotine, Adolf Hitler's government outlawed the Social Democratic Party today. The move banishes from the Cabinet the last major opposition to Hitler. It also dissolves the results of the March election, when the Socialists were second in power only to the Nazis.

Shortly after that election, Hitler outlawed the Communist Party. Yesterday, the German Nationalist Party was dissolved and party leader Alfred Hugenberg resigned from the Cabinet.

Hitler's ruthless communique on the Socialists accused them of treason and called the party "subversive and inimical." Actually, it has held little power in the Hitler Cabinet, and its main source of support was destroyed with the recent crackdown on the labor unions.

The goal of many of the government's actions, according to Propaganda Minister Goebbels, is the creation of "German democracy, in which people do not themselves engage in politics but entrust this to men having their confidence.

"It is a democratic fallacy to believe that people want to govern themselves," Goebbels explained in Frankfurt. "People only ask to be governed decently."

Goebbels' "paternal benevolence" is tempered by Hitler's iron fist. In a speech four days ago, Hitler threatened to take children away from parents who oppose him. "We shall rear them as needful for the Fatherland," he said during a review of storm troopers (→ 7/2).

...ducing idols of the Fuhrer.

Big spending makes millions of jobs

June 23. More Americans are back to work. According to American Federation of Labor statistics, over 1.6 million new jobs have been created since the end of March. The Roosevelt administration, which has allocated millions of dollars for jobs, is credited with the improvement. The rate of unemployment dropped from 13.4 million in March to 12.7 million in April.

Clothing, shoes and food producers have seen large increases in employment. And reforestation services, due to the creation of the Civilian Conservation Corps, have also employed many more people (→ 7/15).

1933

JULY

Su	Mo	Tu	We	Th	Fr	Sa
						1
2	3	4	5	6	7	8
9	10	11	12	13	14	15
16	17	18	19	20	21	22
23	24	25	26	27	28	29
30	31					

1. Roscoe Turner sets N.Y. to L.A. flying record at 11 hours, 30 minutes.

1. Amelia Earhart flies L.A. to Newark in 17 hours, 17 minutes.

2. Washington: Reconstruction Finance Corp. (RFC) lends U.S.S.R. $4 mil. to buy cotton.

2. Berlin: 94 Nazis married in mass service (→ 3).

3. German Nazis begin evicting Jews from civil service (→ 14).

4. India: Mahatma Gandhi sentenced to one year in prison (→ 8/23).

8. Wimbledon: Jack Crawford over Ellsworth Vines 4-6, 11-9, 6-2, 2-6, 6-4; Helen Wills Moody takes sixth title 6-4, 6-8, 6-3 over Dorothy Round.

14. Hitler decrees NSDAP sole legal party in Germany (→ 20).

15. Washington: Steel code gives 15 percent pay raise to skilled labor (→ 17).

15. Germany: Protestant churches merge into German Evangelical Church.

17. One million U.S. laborers get shorter hours or higher wages as NRA goes into effect (→ 8/5).

19. World Petroleum Congress meets for first time at London's Imperial College of Science and Technology.

20. Japanese scientist demonstrates machine gun capable of firing 1,000 shots per minute.

20. German Nazis round up 300 Jews in Nuremburg, while 50,000 Londoners march against anti-Semitism in Hyde Park (→ 26).

22. Wiley Post returns to N.Y., setting record for round-world flight at seven days, 19 hours.

23. France's Georges Speicher wins 27th Tour de France.

24. Madrid: 500 seized for alleged revolutionary plot (→ 9/8).

25. Trotsky and wife arrive in Marseilles (→ 4/17/34).

30. Paris: Britain takes Davis Cup from France.

31. German govt. reports 26,789 are held as political prisoners (→ 8/29).

Aviation now seen as safe and practical

Globe flier Wiley Post has brought both publicity and credibility to air travel.

The all-metal Boeing 247, first flown in February, will carry 10 passengers.

July 22. This afternoon, a plane was flying over the Rockies when one of its engines failed. The pilot was serene. This was a test on the maiden flight of the DC-1, a plane made of aluminum alloy designed for TWA by the Donald Douglas Corporation. The DC-1 can remain safely airborne even when one of its two engines has died. The innovation is one of many that is convincing the public of the safety and practicality of commercial aviation.

Earlier in the decade, flying was for the rich: swift, chic and expensive. And dangerous. In 1931, a plane carrying Notre Dame football coach Knute Rockne crashed in Kansas. One wing, constructed of wood, rotted and gave way. The government immediately ordered all-metal construction for planes.

United Airlines bought the tri-motor, all-metal Boeing 247 earlier in 1933. The ten-seater is fine aside from a few problems: the fuselage shakes, heating is spasmodic, the engine produces a noticeable odor and it is noisy enough to drive a person deaf. But it is progress.

On August 2, 1932, Jack Frye, Vice President of TWA, wrote a letter to Donald Douglas asking his engineers to design an all-metal plane for his company. Adviser Charles Lindbergh wanted it to meet the dead-engine criteria. Frye wanted it as quiet and stable as possible. The DC-1 reportedly passes every test with flying colors.

Nazis pass law to purify German race

July 26. For months now, Germans have been hearing from the Nazis about the "perfection of the Aryan race." Today, Adolf Hitler's government announced a new program to weed out Germans who are less than perfect. Doctors will sterilize them for the glory of the Reich.

Under the new law, men and women will be sterilized if they are idiots or schizophrenics, if they suffer from depression, epilepsy or chorea, or if they have physical weaknesses, like deafness or blindness, that are serious or hereditary.

The law does not specify whether certain races will be sterilized.

It says Germans should consent to sterilization voluntarily. But it also says that minors can be sterilized involuntarily with the consent of their guardians.

"Aryan" Hitler at Nuremburg.

The new law shows that Hitler's government is committed to its racial ideology and is willing to interfere with nature if necessary (→ 31).

Economic parley ends in failure

July 27. An international trade summit murmured into uselessness today. Representatives from Japan, the U.S., Europe and South America had met in London to discuss trade barriers, most-favored nation status and the gold standard. No consensus on any issue was reached, including the question of whether to reconvene in Geneva in the fall. The only optimistic note was struck by U.S. Secretary of State Cordell Hull, who reasoned, "To impute failure is to impute the bankruptcy of world statesmanship in the face of unparalleled universal economic distress and suffering" (→ 8/25).

1933

AUGUST

Su	Mo	Tu	We	Th	Fr	Sa
		1	2	3	4	5
6	7	8	9	10	11	12
13	14	15	16	17	18	19
20	21	22	23	24	25	26
29	28	29	30	31		

1. Britain's royal couple inaugurate world's largest dry dock in Southampton.

1. Hungary: 20,000 Boy Scouts gather near Budapest for fourth Jamboree.

2. Managua: Martial law declared for all of Nicaragua (→ 2/22/34).

3. U.S. Navy places record order of 37 ships (→ 11/1/33).

5. FDR names Robert Wagner to head National Labor Board, charged with task of enforcing collective bargaining (→ 18).

5. Poland signs treaty with Nazi government of Danzig.

8. New dance craze sweeps N.Y., called Nira, in honor of NRA.

9. Washington: FDR calls on Cuba to end political strife as martial law begins (→ 13).

12. Hollywood: New narrative style used in "The Power and the Glory," with Spencer Tracy.

12. Rome: Italo Balbo's air armada, ends world flight amid wild acclaim.

13. Wisconsin: Gene Sarazen wins his third PGA golf title.

17. Washington: Federal govt. allots $37 million for building of New York's Triboro Bridge.

18. FDR approves steel agreement; NRA code to set eight-hour day (→ 31).

18. 600 killed in border conflict between Iraq and Syria.

19. Italy: Mussolini meets with Austrian Chancellor Dollfuss.

25. London: 21 nations sign wheat agreement to combat worldwide glut (→ 4/13/34).

25. Italy and U.S.S.R. agree on non-aggression treaty.

30. Air France incorporated.

31. New York grand jury asks flogging for three thugs, wants public whipping post restored.

BIRTHS

15. Stanley Milgram, American psychologist, obedience studies.

18. Roman Polanski, Polish film director.

21. Janet Baker, British opera singer.

Violent revolt ousts Machado in Cuba

The people of Havana join in a funeral procession for Machado's many victims.

Aug 13. Stressing "no possible question of intervention," President Roosevelt tonight ordered three U.S. warships to Cuban waters to protect American citizens. The move followed by one day Cuban President Machado's hasty departure to Nassau and the sudden elevation to the presidency of Dr. Carlos Manuel de Cespedes. Both events result from recent Cuban violence triggered by Machado's declaration of a state of war.

Machado was first elected president in 1925 and re-elected in 1928. The reforms he initially proposed quickly gave way to a dictatorship and terror tactics. As Cuba's economy eroded, growing opposition to his rule led to a general strike which he couldn't end, and his declaration of war five days ago merely inflamed the situation. Privately, it is known that the backbone of the Cuban government is the army, led by Sgt. Fulgencio Batista, which stood ready to abandon Machado if the United States showed its displeasure with his strong-arm tactics (→ 9/5).

NRA goes into action on all fronts

Aug 31. The blue eagle, emblem of the National Recovery Administration, now adorns thousands of American business establishments, signifying acceptance of a code designed to bring peace between labor and management and to boost the nation's economy.

The NRA Eagle, symbol of duty.

One of the major keystones of the Roosevelt administration's New Deal, the NRA was authorized by Congress two months ago. It called for "a great cooperative movement throughout all industry" to obtain more emloyment, pay decent wages, shorten the work week and prevent unfair competition and disastrous overproduction.

Since then, truces have been reached in several major labor disputes, including the coal and steel industries. But the NRA has been criticized, too, by some who fear it closely parallels the pattern of the Fascist corporate state (→ 9/13).

Gandhi out of jail weighing 90 pounds

Aug 23. Mahatma Gandhi has been released from government detention in the Poona Civil Hospital after doctors warned that his fast was endangering his life. Gandhi, who undertook the fast eight days ago in protest over being arrested again by British authorities, weighed 90 pounds at the time of his release. Two doctors who examined Gandhi on his release from the hospital said there was no cause for alarm over his condition. There was considerable speculation over what the nationalist leader would do upon regaining his strength, but the common assumption was that he would be arrested again by British authorities if he resumes his civil disobedience (→ 9/14).

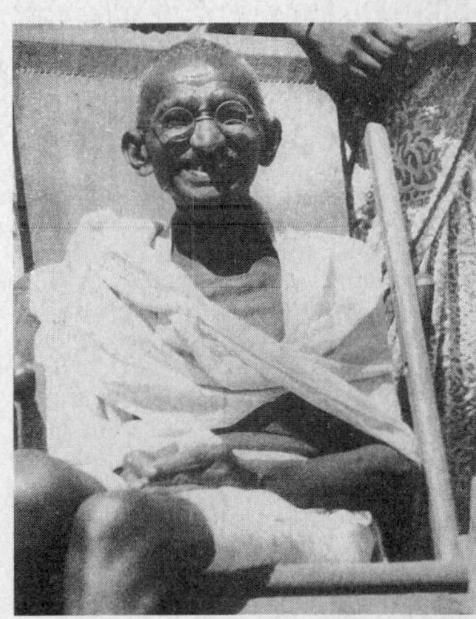

A free Gandhi smiles in the sunlight.

Nazis sending Jews to prison camps

Aug 29. From Germany this month came official confirmation that Nazis are arresting large numbers of Jews and sending them to concentration camps. Some have been imprisoned for fighting storm troops, others for insulting the state, some for merely "consorting with German girls" and one for imitating the Nazi salute. The outlawed Socialist Party has reported that 45,000 prisoners are being held in 65 camps, the largest at Dachau. The London Times reports that many prisoners are being held for their political views, are poorly fed and are beaten by Nazi guards (→ 9/1).

SEPTEMBER

Su	Mo	Tu	We	Th	Fr	Sa
					1	2
3	4	5	6	7	8	9
10	11	12	13	14	15	16
17	18	19	20	21	22	23
24	25	26	27	28	29	30

1. Nuremberg: Hitler says he will keep art on strictly Nordic basis (→ 20).

5. Havana: Radical junta rules Cuba as army ousts President Cespedes (→ 7).

5. New York: 14 killed, 30 hurt in wreck of New York flier.

5. Hurricane sweeps Texas, killing 32 and injuring 1,500.

6. Austria deploys troops on German border (→ 23).

7. Washington: 29 U.S. warships placed on Cuban duty (→ 10).

8. Madrid: Spanish Premier Manuel Azana resigns (→ 11/19).

10. Havana: Grau San Martin sworn in as president (→ 29).

10. Louisiana: 12 convicts kill two guards in prison break.

11. Maine, first dry state, votes for Prohibition repeal (→ 11/7).

14. Pennsylvania: 15 striking miners shot.

14. Gandhi declares one year moratorium on civil disobedience in India (→ 10/24/34).

18. Ghazi I crowned Iraqi king on Feisal's death.

20. Communists go on trial in Germany for February Reichstag fire (→ 11/1).

21. Washington: FDR orders outlay of $75 million to clothe and feed the jobless (→ 30).

23. Austria to set up prison camps to intern Nazis (→ 10/3).

25. Geneva: League of Nations session opens (→ 10/14).

25. Mexico: Port of Tampico destroyed by gale; hundreds killed.

27. Philadelphia: Jack Sharkey outpointed by Tommy Loughran in heavyweight bout.

29. Havana: Six slain as police rout Communist parade (→ 10/3).

DEATHS

2. Georges Leygues, French statesman (*10/26/1857).

7. Edward Grey, British statesman (*4/25/1862).

8. King Feisal of Iraq (*1855).

FDR orders millions in aid to most needy

The bony faces of the depression fill up on rations of free bread and soup.

Sept 30. Promising to cut the red tape, President Roosevelt unveiled a new program today to feed and clothe the nation's needy during the coming winter. Federal officials say that an estimated $700 million in federal, state and local funds will be available for this purpose in the coming months.

Heretofore, federal relief grants have been made only if matched by state funds. While state and local governments will be urged to continue such aid, the requirement for matching funds will be relaxed in cases of those who are in desperate straits. An estimated 3.5 million American families are currently on the nation's relief rolls.

The expanded program of aid to the needy will not mean a diet of just "salt pork and beans," according to Harry L. Hopkins, administrator of federal relief. "We will give them a balanced diet," he said. Much of the food will come from surpluses now held in storage by the U.S. Department of Agriculture.

The growing plight of the needy is perhaps best pointed up by the fact that the announcement of the new program comes just nine days after the president authorized the distribution of $75 million of surplus food and clothing to those in desperate need (→ 10/1).

Promoter who ate own salve dead at 96

Sept 9. On his death bed today, Robert A. Chesebrough attributed his longevity to ingesting one spoonful of Vaseline every day of his life. The 96-year-old chemist invented the petroleum product in 1870. He considered it a virtual cure-all. Millions of customers would agree.

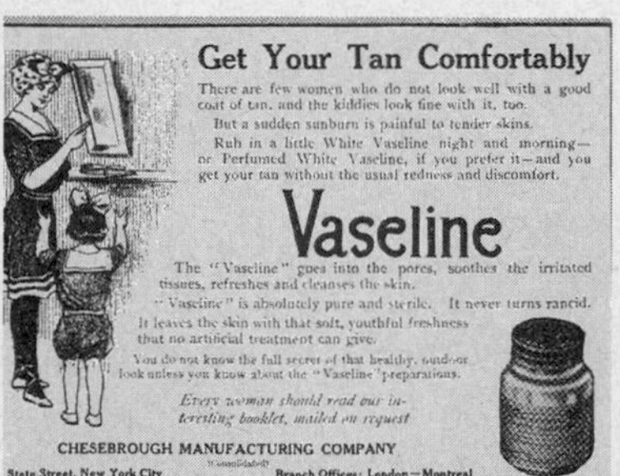

For bronzed skin and a long life.

Chesebrough developed the clear, odorless salve in a Brooklyn laboratory. In 1876, he formed the Chesebrough Company, which was sold to Standard Oil in 1881. Chesebrough was a civic-minded man; in the 1890's he ran for Congress on the Republican ticket against a Tammany Hall candidate. Chesebrough lost the election.

Vaseline lubricates hinges and doorknobs, protects leather from mildew, heals cuts and burns, rustproofs firearms, conditions hair and substitutes for shaving cream. Blind Braille readers use it to keep their fingertips supple.

The common man's chronicler is gone

Sept 25. Humorous short-story writer Ring (Ringgold) Lardner died today of a longtime heart ailment. As a youth, he had treasured three ambitions (or so he claimed in a tongue-in-cheek autobiography): to author a play, write stories for magazines and watch a heap of baseball. He did them all.

Lardner was born in Niles, Michigan, in 1885. In the early 1900's, he was sports editor for the South Bend Times in Indiana. He had to keep his eye firmly on the baseball: he was also the local team's official scorer. Lardner went on to cover sports in Chicago, Boston and St. Louis. He noted each city's particular dialect and slang, and in 1913 he put his notes to use. He invented a Giants pitcher who reported on the World Series in a colorful, gutsy style. The public loved it. Lardner was soon being published in The Saturday Evening Post.

Ring Lardner touched all bases. Besides ball players he wrote about secretaries, salesmen, bartenders and barbers. His style was sharp and quick. "You Know Me, Al" (1916) was his first collection of short stories. "Gullible's Travels" (1917) and "Treat 'em Rough" (1918) swiftly followed. In 1929, Lardner saw his characters speak. That year he co-wrote the comedy play "June Moon" with dramatist George S. Kaufman.

Sept 13. The Blue Eagle hovers over N.Y.'s 5th Ave. as 250,000 march in an NRA parade.

1933

OCTOBER

Su	Mo	Tu	We	Th	Fr	Sa
1	2	3	4	5	6	7
8	9	10	11	12	13	14
15	16	17	18	19	20	21
22	23	24	25	26	27	28
29	30	31				

1. German Post Office establishes first telex communication, between Hamburg and Berlin.

2. Eugene O'Neill's "Ah Wilderness!" debuts in New York.

3. Vienna: Dollfuss shot at by Austrian Nazi (→ 11/10).

4. Czechoslovakia: Sudeten Natl. Socialist Party disbands on day before government ban (→ 5/24/34).

7. Washington: N.Y. Giants win World Series 4-3 in fifth game over Senators.

9. Geneva: World disarmament conference reconvenes (→ 14).

10. Rio de Janeiro: Treaty of Non-Agression and Conciliation signed by nations of Western hemisphere.

11. Swiss and Belgians hike defense spending after report of German invasion plot.

12. California: Alcatraz Island made a federal maximum security prison.

12. Hollywood: Charles Laughton stars in premiere of "The Private Life of Henry VIII."

12. Siam: Royal prince leading military uprising as country hit by army mutinies.

13. A.F.L. votes U.S. boycott on German products (→ 17).

17. Einstein, a self-exile from Germany, arrives in U.S. to settle in Princeton, New Jersey.

17. FDR orders fines and jail terms for NRA violators (→ 25).

17. Berlin: Hitler assures Ambassador William Dodd, Nazi attacks on American nationals will cease (→ 30).

18. Maryland: Mob of 2,000 lynches Negro accused of attacking white woman (→ 11/29).

20. Rome: Mussolini calls FDR a dictator.

22. Primo Carnera defends heavyweight title, defeating Spaniard Paolino Uzcudun.

25. Washington: RFC begins buying gold to devalue dollar (→ 11/8).

30. New York: Natl. Conference of Christians and Jews links Hitlerism to lynch justice in U.S. (→ 11/14).

Hitler leaves League, demanding equality

Oct 14. Adolf Hitler lashed out at the Versailles treaty today, complained publicly that the world community treats Germany like a "second-class citizen," and withdrew from both the League of Nations and the disarmament conference.

Hitler's declaration seems designed to rally Germany behind his National Socialist Party. He simultaneously announced the dissolution of the Reichstag. But there is international concern because Hitler also committed himself publicly for the first time to rearm Germany.

The policy was couched in criticism of the disarmament movement. Hitler said he favors total disarmament, but he also said that Germany was singled out unfairly when it was forced to disarm. Hitler stated Germany needs defensive weapons and knows how to handle them because "the men who today lead Germany have nothing in common with the traitors of 1918."

Hitler decides to go it alone.

German voters will be given a chance, but not a choice, to approve Hitler's actions in a referendum next month. Only the name of the Nazi Party will be on the ballot, since all other parties have been outlawed by Hitler (→ 6/14/34).

Cuban army besieges hotel, killing 119

Oct 3. Blood flowed in the streets of Havana today as government forces battled with rebel officers trying to engineer a coup from the National Hotel. The government won, but 119 people were killed. And a vacillating United States policy toward Cuba was thrown into even greater disarray.

Sumner Welles, the Roosevelt confidante and troubleshooter who was named Ambassador to Havana this year, supported the insurgents in their coup attempt. It was an act of desperation. The rebels were loyal to Gerardo Machado, the Cuban President ousted this year after Welles supported his opponents.

Welles apparently decided to support the new coup attempt because the new government of Cuba has turned out to be even more anti-American than Machado. President Grau San Martin and Army Chief of Staff Fulgencio Batista dissolved the constitution this year and refused to recognize the Platt amendment. The amendment, an act of Congress which was also inserted into the Cuban constitution, has been the basis of American intervention into Cuban affairs for more than 30 years.

Government troops outside the hotel.

Machado was also troublesome to the United States. When he first took power after the 1924 election, he promised American companies easy access to Cuban labor. Machado pledged that "no labor strike would last more than 15 minutes." As the years passed, however, Machado tried to free his country from United States domination by taxing American investment and expanding Cuba's own industry and tourist trade. Welles turned against Machado after his own mediation failed and the army demanded his ouster. Machado fled in August (→ 11/9).

Arab rioters oppose Jewish immigration

Oct 27. More than 20 persons were killed and 130 wounded in Jaffa as police clashed with Arabs protesting Jewish immigration to Palestine. After a police order failed to disperse the group of 9,000, the police charged them with clubs. When members of the crowd opened fire, the police returned it and the main square was converted into a violent battleground.

Clashes also occurred in Haifa and Nablus, where Arabs attacked police stations. A state of emergency has been declared in Jaffa and the neighboring towns near Tel Aviv, and a curfew has been imposed (→ 4/21/36).

Helped by NRA, AFL recruits 1.3m

Oct 1. Since the National Recovery Act became law, more than 1.3 million workers have joined the American Federation of Labor, pushing its membership to about four million, according to A.F.L. President William Green.

The figures emerged in the union's Executive Council Report, made public yesterday, which also contained a 12-point plan of the union's goals. Among the policy goals are: a 30-hour work week; an increase in the minimum wage; and a boycott on German goods until the persecution of Jewish people in that country stops.

The report credited the NRA with ushering in a "new industrial era" in the United States (→ 17).

1933

NOVEMBER

Su	Mo	Tu	We	Th	Fr	Sa
			1	2	3	4
5	6	7	8	9	10	11
12	13	14	15	16	17	18
19	20	21	22	23	24	25
26	27	28	29	30		

1. New York: 200 Columbia students pledge non-cooperation in event of war (→ 12/28).

1. Nazis take over Ullstein press, largest in German Reich (→ 12).

7. Utah votes dry, assuring repeal of Prohibition (→ 12/5).

8. FDR creates Civil Works Administration (CWA) under Harry Hopkins to create jobs through federal spending (→ 16).

9. Cuban rebels lose fort in Havana battle; 100 killed (→ 23).

10. Austria: Martial law decreed to block plans of both Nazis and Socialists (→ 2/12/34).

12. Nazis, only party in Germany, get 92% of vote at Reichstag elections; 93% approve leaving League; 3 mil. cast invalid protest ballots (→ 23).

14. Washington begins investigations into Nazi propaganda in U.S. (→ 4/8/34).

14. Stockholm: Nobel committee decides not to award peace prize for 1933.

16. First NRA violator indicted; Brooklyn filling station charged with 66-hour week (→ 24).

17. Claude Rains makes film debut in "The Invisible Man."

18. Trotskyites and Stalinists clash during N.Y. parade of 8,000 Communists (→ 2/16/34).

19. F.D.R. asked to intervene to protect defendants in Scottsboro case (→ 12/1).

19. First official elections for Spanish Cortes fail to produce majority; right wins 44%, left wins 22% (→ 12/9).

23. Berlin: Nazis supress two monarchist leagues, fearing plot to return ex-kaiser (→ 12/1).

23. FDR recalls Ambassador Welles from Havana, urges stability in Cuba (→ 1/18/34).

24. FDR refuses return to gold standard, despite advice of Federal Reserve (→ 28).

25. Philadelphia: Army over Navy 12-7 at Franklin Field.

28. U.S. Army bans consumption of foreign-produced food, even bananas (→ 1/5/34).

29. Maryland: Court frees four held as lynchers (→ 12/15).

U.S. recognizes U.S.S.R.

Nov 17. An historic international event occurred today as President Roosevelt announced that the United States now officially recognizes the Communist government of the Soviet Union. The opening of relations resulted from extensive correspondence between the president and Soviet Commissar for Foreign Affairs Maxim Litvinoff. Roosevelt, to a crowd of 200 reporters, read from the letter addressed to Litvinoff: "I trust that the relations between our peoples may forever remain normal and friendly, and that our nations may cooperate for their mutual benefit and for the preservation of the peace of the world."

Russia conceded certain points intrinsic to the signing of the pact, including: promises not to disseminate Communist propaganda in America; freedom of religion and full legal rights to U.S. residents in the Soviet Union; rejection of all claims to damages arising from the American military expedition to Siberia in 1918. The agreements are said to be the most conciliatory the Soviets have ever negotiated.

Russians from all walks of life are reportedly elated about the new diplomatic relations (→ 1/7/34).

First Ambassador Wm. C. Bullitt.

Richard III guilty after 450 years

Richard III of England.

Nov 30. Examination of royal bones proves King Richard III guilty of murders he committed at the Tower of London in 1483. The remains of Edward V and the Duke of York were discovered hidden in an urn last June and were promptly exhumed. Forensic studies reveal that the boys met their deaths at the time Richard III was on the throne. Anatomists put their ages at 12 and 14. Blood stains on one boy's skull point to a violent demise.

LaGuardia is Mayor of New York City

Nov 7. Fiorello H. LaGuardia, a former member of Congress, was elected Mayor of New York City today, wresting political control from Tammany Hall. Running on a fusion ticket, LaGuardia rolled up a stunning victory over Mayor John P. O'Brien, a Democrat, in the largest voter turnout in the city's history. News of Tammany's defeat was greeted silently by a crowd of thousands in Times Square, watching election bulletins flashed on the electric ribbon around The New York Times building (→ 1/5/34).

LaGuardia, "The Little Flower."

Chicago Fair had 22 million visitors

Nov 12. The Chicago Fair has closed for the winter. In a quiet ceremony, light from the heavenly star Arcturus activated switches in the Court of the Hall of Science, flooding the fairgrounds in brilliant color for the last time this year. The lights will brighten again June 1, when the exposition reopens.

Over 22 million visitors have seen the "Century of Progress" thus far. Exhibits from 18 nations, most of them concentrating on science and technology, enlightened the crowds. Displays from Hollywood studios and a "Treasure Island" park kept one and all enthralled.

A ray of hope in the midst of crisis.

Italo Balbo made Governor of Libya

Nov 6. Marshal Italo Balbo, known worldwide for piloting long-distance flights, has been appointed Governor of Libya. Premier Benito Mussolini assigned him the post in an apparent attempt to squelch rumors of his disapproval of the flier. Balbo led a squadron of demonstration planes over Chicago and Rio de Janeiro earlier this year, earning widespread popularity.

Balbo is reportedly unhappy over leaving the Aviation Ministry. Mussolini now holds the Cabinet post for Aviation, as well as the Navy, War, Foreign Affairs, Home Affairs, Corporations, and of course, the premiership. The Duce does it all.

1933

DECEMBER

Su	Mo	Tu	We	Th	Fr	Sa
					1	2
3	4	5	6	7	8	9
10	11	12	13	14	15	16
17	18	19	20	21	22	23
24	25	26	27	28	29	30
31						

1. Nazi storm troops become official organ of Reich (→ 20).

1. Alabama: Jury gives death penalty to Heywood Patterson in Scottsboro case (→ 3/17/34).

9. Spain crushes anarchist rebel uprising; 42 killed, hundreds wounded (→ 1/14/34).

11. Reports say Paraguay has captured 11,000 Bolivians in war over Chaco (→ 1/6/34).

15. Tenn.: Mob lynches Negro freed by court (→ 9/8/34).

16. Lindberghs land in Miami after 30,000-mile survey, N.Y.-Europe-Africa-South America.

20. Berlin: 400,000 Germans to be sterilized for hereditary defects (→ 22).

21. First dried human blood serum prepared by Earl W. Flosdorf and Stuard Mudd of University of Pennsylvania.

22. Germany: Marrinus van der Lubbe gets death penalty for burning Reichstag (→ 23).

23. Pope condemns Nazi sterilization program (→ 1/7/34).

27. Moscow: Stalin calls Japan a "grave danger" (→ 1/2/34).

28. FDR states, "The definite policy of the U.S. from now on is one opposed to armed intervention." (→ 5/31/34).

29. Rumania: Liberal Premier Ion Duca killed by outlawed Iron Guard (→ 11/27/34).

30. Mass.: Scientist reports senators' brains average two ounces heavier than representatives'.

CULTURAL EVENTS, 1933

Literature: Andre Malraux's "Man's Fate"; Gertrude Stein's "The Autobiography of Alice B. Toklas"; H.G. Wells' "The Shape of Things to Come"; Nathanael West's "Miss Lonelyhearts"; James Hilton's best-seller "Lost Horizon"; ban on "Ulysses" lifted in U.S.

Academia: C.G. Jung's "Modern Man in Search of a Soul"; Trotsky's "History of the Russian Revolution."

Music: Prokofiev returns to U.S.S.R. after 15-year exile; Ballanchine founds School of American Ballet.

Prohibition comes to a jubilant end

Dec 5. Imbibers jubilantly toasted the end of Prohibition in America today. It had been a long time between legal drinks, nearly 14 years, to be exact. The repeal of the 18th Amendment that had prohibited all alcoholic beverages in the United States ended precisely at 5:32.5 this afternoon when Utah became the last of 36 states to ratify the 21st Amendment to end the nation's long dry spell.

President Roosevelt called on the nation to practice moderation and thus prevent recurrence of what he termed the "repugnant conditions" that had brought about Prohibition in 1920. He also asked states not to allow the return of the saloon.

Jubilant young ladies on their first night at a public bar.

A great year for films: From Three Little Pigs to Henry VIII

Hepburn (left) in "Little Women."

No one was afraid to see the Big Bad Wolf in Walt Disney's "Three Little Pigs" this year. The all-animated short tickled everyone with its brilliant color and tuneful soundtrack. "The Invisible Man" with Claude Rains was a must-see. Special effects rendered the mad scientist faceless and handless, a set of clothes that committed murders. "King Kong," about a big ape that dies for the love of a maiden, also relied on special effects. Kong had real personality, quite a feat considering he was made of clay.

Viewers preferring human affairs enjoyed "Little Women." The Alcott classic starred Katharine Hepburn. And audiences willingly sat with Charles Laughton as he wed and wed and wed in "Henry VIII."

"The Private Life of Henry VIII."

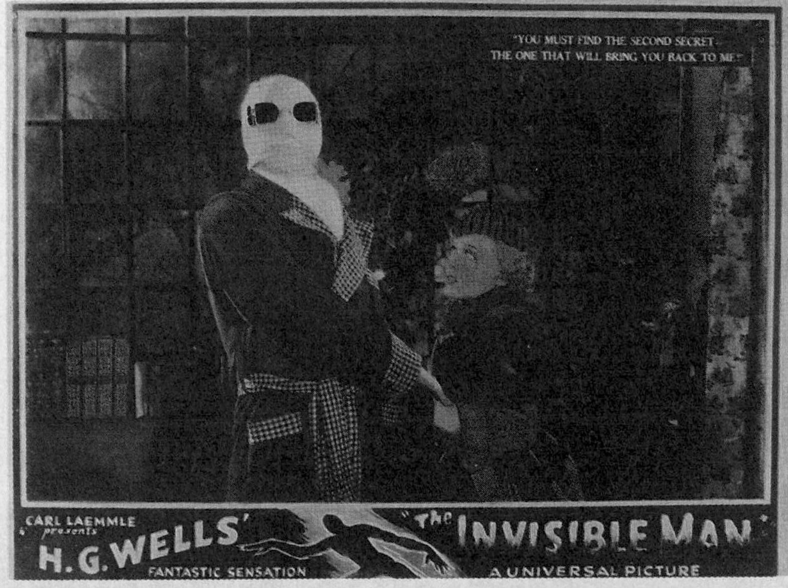

Claude Rains was rendered "invisible" with a white sheet.

Stormy Weather, other lovely tunes

This was a year to sing the blues. With no hope of making money somewhere down the road, it was just a "Boulevard of Broken Dreams." Men who couldn't find work left their wives to sing about "Stormy Weather" since they "ain't" together. For some people, it felt a "lovely flame" had died, when "Smoke Gets in Your Eyes."

Once the blues were blown away, loneliness, money troubles and politics be damned. It was time to sing Irving Berlin's joyous tune "Easter Parade" and demand like Walt Disney's piglet trio, "Who's Afraid of the Big Bad Wolf?"

1934

JANUARY

Su	Mo	Tu	We	Th	Fr	Sa
	1	2	3	4	5	6
7	8	9	10	11	12	13
14	15	16	17	18	19	20
21	22	23	24	25	26	27
28	29	30	31			

1. Pasadena: Columbia blanks Stanford in Rose Bowl 7-0.

2. Rome: Italy calls Japan's naval policies a menace (→ 11/19).

5. New York: Gov. Herbert Lehman says new Mayor LaGuardia is asking dictatorship.

5. Geneva: League committee reports U.S. is leading world in job recovery (→ 21).

6. War resumes in Chaco as League mediation fails to prolong truce (→ 4/15).

7. Berlin: 6,000 pastors defy Nazis, insisting they will not be muzzled (→ 10).

7. U.S.S.R.'s first ambassador to U.S. arrives in N.Y. (→ 4/29).

9. Istanbul: Turkey issues five-year industrial plan based on research of American experts (→ 11/25).

11. Berlin: Police raid homes of dissident clergy (→ 2/2).

14. Spain: Luis Companys becomes Catalonian president in electoral victory for left (→ 4/7).

18. Havana: Carlos Mendeita sworn in as Cuban pres. (→ 23).

21. F.D.R. extends life of RFC, adds $850 mil. to budget (→ 31).

22. Paris police arrest 750 as Communists and Royalists battle (→ 27).

23. FDR grants recognition to Cuban government (→ 5/29).

26. 17th Party Congress—"Victors Congress"—convenes in Moscow.

26. Germany signs 10-year non-aggression pact with Poland, breaking French alliance system (→ 9/1/39).

27. Paris: Chautemps Cabinet resigns over bank scandal riots (→ 2/6).

27. Moscow: Stalin says he fears capitalists will choose war to get out of depression.

31. Washington: Federal Farm Mortgage Corp. set up to provide low-interest loans backed by govt. bonds.→

BIRTH

9. Bart Starr, Green Bay Packers quarterback, coach.

Embezzler kills himself as police arrive

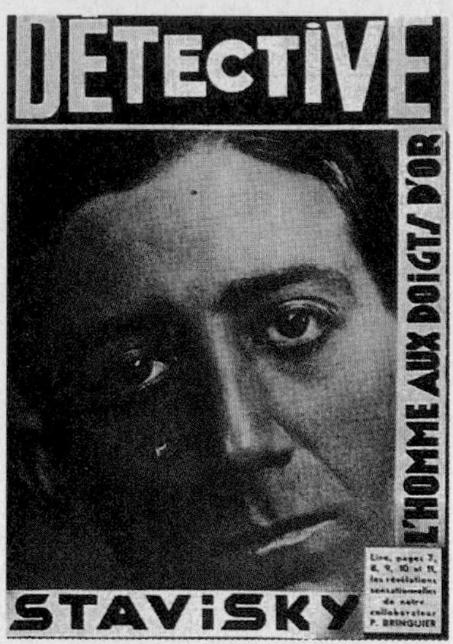

Detective magazine covers the story.

Jan 8. More questions are being asked about a notorious swindler named Alexander Stavisky after police in Chamonix, France, say he committed suicide in a ski chalet.

Authorities say Stavisky, who called himself Mr. Alexander, shot himself in the head after police from Chamonix and Paris jumped through an open window in the chalet. He died a short while later.

Already, rumors are spreading about who will benefit from Stavisky's suicide. To be sure, many people lost money to the swindler. And 240 million francs are missing from a bank in Bayonne. Who protected this thief who is a sensation in France? Was he going to talk? It's too late for answers (→ 22).

Jobless join Civilian Conservation Corps

CCC boys line up at Fort Dix, New Jersey, to be measured for new shoes.

Jan 31. Earlier this month, President Roosevelt spoke to the nation in his State of the Union address, in which he declared that the New Deal is here to stay. While not everyone is completely enthralled with that notion, it would be difficult to find many who wish for the demise of one New Deal program: The Civilian Conservation Corps.

Since its inception last March 31, the CCC has employed thousands of young people in jobs that enhance and rebuild the nation's great outdoors. Within the first five months, 300,000 youths were put to work. They are fed, sheltered and paid a monthly rate of $30 to build roads, construct flood control systems, engage in reforestation, check forest fires and protect in other ways America's natural resources.

Roosevelt intended to provide emergency relief for the jobless and at the same time preserve natural resources. The plan continues the Rooseveltian committment to conservation, begun by FDR's cousin, President Theodore Roosevelt. As FDR has said: "No one will ever be able to estimate in dollars and cents the (program's) value to the men themselves and to the nation in morale, in occupational training, in health and in adaptability to later competitive life" (→ 2/2).

Roosevelt devalues dollar to 60 cents

Jan 31. President Roosevelt issued a proclamation today, devaluing the dollar to 59.6 cents and setting the price the government will pay for gold at $35 an ounce. Acting under authority given him by recent action of Congress, the president said the moves were needed to protect the nation's foreign trade from the effects of the depreciated currencies in other countries.

The proclamation took title for the government to all gold now held by Federal Reserve banks, in exchange for new gold certificates, creating a dollar profit of about $2.8 billion for the Treasury. Of this sum, $2 billion will be used to stabilize the dollar on the international exchange and support the government bond market, if necessary (→ 2/2).

Dutchman executed for Reichstag fire

Jan 10. Marinus Van der Lubbe, the young Dutchman convicted of arson in the German Reichstag fire last year, was executed in Leipzig. Anywhere else in Nazi Germany, his head would have been lopped off with an ax. But Leipzig is in Saxony, and Saxons use the guillotine.

The execution was unannounced, unlike the publicity surrounding the arrest of the young Communist. Dutch authorities, who had pleaded with Germany to spare Van der Lubbe, were shocked by the news. Witnesses say the Dutchman died unemotionally (→ 11).

Dillinger, bank robber, is caught

Jan 28. Bank robber John Dillinger and six accomplices are being held in a Tucson, Arizona, jail, awaiting extradition to Indiana. Dillinger is wanted for the murder of a policeman two weeks ago during a bank holdup in East Chicago, Indiana. Dillinger and the officer exchanged fire. Dillinger strode off unscathed, having worn a bulletproof vest. He will not beat this rap; he was positively identified by an Indiana police chief (→ 2/17).

1934

FEBRUARY

Su	Mo	Tu	We	Th	Fr	Sa
				1	2	3
4	5	6	7	8	9	10
11	12	13	14	15	16	17
18	19	20	21	22	23	24
25	26	27	28			

2. FDR establishes Export-Import Bank to expand foreign trade (→ 15).

2. Berlin: Alfred Rosenberg made philosophical chief of Nazi party (→ 3).

3. Berlin: Psalms rewritten by Nazis with modified references to Jews (→ 3/21).

3. Spanish Supreme Court pardons four Americans court martialed in Majorca for espionage.

9. Greece, Rumania, Turkey, Yugoslavia sign Balkan Pact; Bulgaria declines (→ 7/31/38).

11. New York: Vladimir Horowitz solos with Philharmonic.

12. Austria: 129 die as Dollfuss govt. purges Socialists (→ 17).

15. U.S. Congress passes Civil Works Emergency Relief Act, allotting new funds for Federal Emergency Relief Administration (FERA) (→ 3/15).

16. N.Y.: 5,000 Socialists battle Communists at rally in Madison Square Garden (→ 8/25/35).

17. King Albert of Belgium dies in mountaineering accident; Leopold III to succeed.

17. Indiana: John Dillinger gets 20-year jail term (→ 3/3).

19. N.Y.: Ellsworth Vines beats Cochet in pro tennis debut.

20. The Utopian Society incorporated in L.A.; uses chain mail to tell U.S. that profit is root of all evil (→ 6/23).

21. Paris: Albert Prince, witness in Stavisky scandal, killed (→ 3/11).

28. Hsingking: Head of state Pu Yi crowned Emperor of Manchukuo (→ 1/31/35).

BIRTHS

5. Hank Aaron, U.S. baseball great, most career home runs.

27. Ralph Nader, American consumer advocate.

DEATHS

13. August Busch, American beer magnate, a suicide.

23. Sir Edward Elgar, British composer (*6/2/1857).

25. John McGraw, baseball's "Little Napolean" (*5/7/1873).

Bloody riots threaten public order in Paris

Barricades in Paris, a French revolutionary tradition dating back to 1789.

Feb 6. Angry mobs who were fed up with French politicians fought with police throughout Paris tonight. They tore up pavement and set buses on fire. Reports from Paris say 17 people were killed and more than 700 injured.

One of the fiercest battles was fought in the Place de la Concorde. Police opened fire as part of the crowd tried to cross the Seine to the Chamber of Deputies. An innocent chambermaid at the elegant Crillon Hotel caught a bullet between the eyes and died a short while later.

Other protesters left a path of destruction on the Champs Elysees and wrecked street lights near the Hotel de Ville. The mobs became more violent when they heard that war veterans who were parading near the Elysee Palace were cut down by a volley of gunfire from the Republican Horse Guard.

Authorities say the protesters did not have a single motive. Some were upset by the arbitrary reassignment of a police commissioner. Others accused the government of complicity in the Stavisky Affair (→ 21).

Georgia O'Keeffe retrospective opens

Feb 1. A retrospective on the art of Georgia O'Keeffe has opened at a New York gallery. The painter's earliest canvases, sensuous treatments of flowers and still lifes, are highlighted. Samples of her more recent work, inspired by the harsh landscape of New Mexico, are few. The present exhibit is one of several the 46-year-old artist has held in New York since 1917.

"Lake George by Early Moonrise."

Austrian regime imposes martial law

Feb 17. The revolt by the Social Democrats in Austria has collapsed, and the government has declared a state of emergency. Fighting in Vienna was particularly violent, as the army attacked workers with machine guns and howitzers. Hundreds were killed or wounded.

The Socialist Mayor of Vienna, Karl Seitz, and many other party leaders are under arrest. The government is expected to outlaw the party altogether. Some foreign newspapers have been confiscated, and the government handling of the crisis has reminded observers of Nazi Germany. Many Jews have already left Austria.

Reports are circulating that Adolf Hitler may move to annex Austria. Britain, France and Italy issued a joint statement calling for an independent Austria (→ 3/28).

Sandino is seized and slain by guards

Feb 22. In a machine gun bloodbath, General Augusto Sandino, his brother and two aides were slain last night by National Guardsmen at the Managua, Nicaragua Airfield.

The assailants seized Sandino and his entourage shortly after they had dined with President Juan B. Sacasa. The guardsmen, on hostile terms with Sandino because of his denunciation of their leader, General Anastasio Somoza, ordered the rebel, his brother and the aides into a truck and sped off to the airfield.

Sandino, a future martyr?

The attack shocked and saddened many, as Sandino has been working peacefully with the Sacasa government for a year since the withdrawal of the United States Marines, who were aligned with former President Moncada and the feared National Guard. Dr. Pedro Jose Zepeda, a friend of President Sacasa, expressed the nation's grief: "The standing of Sandino before the world was as one of the greatest patriots of the present generation." He said the stability of the government was jeopardized as Somoza is likely to take power (→ 4/24/35).

Fresh new stars Clark Gable and Claudette Colbert in Capra's "It Happened One Night."

1934

MARCH

Su	Mo	Tu	We	Th	Fr	Sa
				1	2	3
4	5	6	7	8	9	10
11	12	13	14	15	16	17
18	19	20	21	22	23	24
25	26	27	28	29	30	31

1. Miami: Primo Carnera defends world heavyweight title against Tommy Loughran.

2. Tunisia: Habib Bourguiba forms Neo-Destour Party (→ 9/3).

3. Indiana: John Dillinger breaks jail using wooden pistol (→ 31).

5. Paris: French intellectuals sign anti-fascist manifesto (→ 11).

10. Arizona Governor Moeur orders National Guard to prevent construction of Parker Dam (→ 11/14).

11. French veterans reported turning to fascism (→ 4/20).

12. Estonia: Pres. of Assembly K. Prats takes dictatorial power.

14. Salvador: Train explodes, killing 250, wounding 1,000.

15. Henry Ford restores $5 per day wage (→ 26).

17. New York: 5,000 Negroes battle police in protest over Scottsboro trial (→ 4/1/35).

17. Rome: Austria, Hungary and Italy sign Rome Protocols, pledging economic and poltical cooperation.

18. Moscow: Jazz and baseball reported gaining great popularity in U.S.S.R.

20. Dr. Rudolph Kuehnald tests radar apparatus for German navy.

26. Switzerland bans slanderous criticism of state institutions in press; threatens suspension of publications.

26. Pittsburgh: Steel industry raising wages 10 percent (→ 4/6).

27. Two killed in Kansas City elections; thugs roaming streets with guns.

28. Vienna: Chancellor Dollfuss orders end to jokes about his size (→ 4/12).

BIRTHS

9. Yuri Gargarin, Soviet cosmonaut (†3/27/1968).

25. Gloria Steinem, American feminist, editor of Ms. magazine.

DEATH

29. Otto Kahn, American philanthropist.

Dillinger shoots his way out of trouble

March 31. John Dillinger has blasted his way out of a police trap, firing a machine gun into a ring of officers, leaping into a green sedan and speeding off for parts unknown. Police in St. Paul, Minn., were sure they had the hood this time, having got a tip to his whereabouts from the wife of Dillinger's landlord. They were wrong. At most they wounded Dillinger or one of his accomplices (an unidentified man and woman fled with him). Blood was found on the ground near the shootout, suggesting one of them was hit.

Dillinger is wanted in several Midwestern states on charges of bank robbery and murder. He was seized and escaped imprisonment twice before. Dillinger usually leads a gang of five or more thugs and a retinue of female companions. He claims he drinks and smokes very little, his only bad habit being that of robbing banks.

The U.S. Department of Justice seeks any information on Dillinger. He stands 5'7" and weighs about 153 pounds. He has a scar on the back of his left hand and a mole between the eyebrows (→ 4/23).

Dillinger, armed to the teeth.

U.S. promises Philippines future freedom

March 24. Congress has passed a new Philippine independence bill only slightly different from the one passed last year, which failed ratification by the island legislature largely because of Manuel Quezon's objections. Since the new bill was worked out with Quezon's advice, its ratification seems likely. Calling for independence by 1946, it set graduated duties on island imports and does not grant the United States absolute rights to military bases. It also maintains quotas on Filipino immigration to the United States (→ 9/17/35).

Filipino army will be instructed by the U.S. Army.

Hitler plans vast highway system

March 21. It's springtime in Germany, and Adolf Hitler has a new project to keep thousands of people busy. He is going to put them to work on the roads. Hitler's goal is to create a new highway system that will link all parts of the Reich. The Chancellor wants to greatly enlarge the present 900-mile-long network of four-lane highways, called autobahns. Hitler also plans better roads around major ports. The Nazi leader calls the project a "spring work battle." He wants it done for the glory of the Reich. He also hopes to reduce unemployment in the country (→ 5/1).

Sam Insull found on ship to Persia

March 31. Rogue and financier Samuel Insull sleeps snug on a Greek steamer tonight, closing his eyes to an international dispute he has engendered. Insull is wanted in the United States on charges of mail fraud, embezzlement and violation of bankruptcy laws. When it was learned Insull was aboard a ship bound for Persia, the United States asked Turkey to intercept the ship and deliver him. However, Greek officials refuse to hand him over, and relations among the three countries are suddenly strained.

Insull was born in England and came to America in 1881. His company, Chicago Edison, reputedly monopolized the Midwestern electrical industry for years (→ 4/12).

1934

APRIL

Su	Mo	Tu	We	Th	Fr	Sa
1	2	3	4	5	6	7
8	9	10	11	12	13	14
15	16	17	18	19	20	21
22	23	24	25	26	27	28
29	30					

4. Moscow: Latvia, Estonia and Lithuania renew Soviet friendship pacts until 1945 (→ 6/12/40).

6. New Jersey silk plant becomes first to be fined for violation of NRA codes (→ 21).

7. Spain: Police suppress Socialist-led strike in Barcelona (→ 25).

10. Washington: William Wirt claims several of FDR's "brain trusters" plan to overthrow govt.

12. Istanbul: Turkey sends Sam Insull back to U.S. (→ 5/11).

12. Austria: 12 Natl. Socialists and five Social Democrats, charged with high treason, are expelled from country (→ 30).

12. Washington: Nye Commission begins investigation into munitions profiteering from the war.

13. U.S. Congress forbids loans to countries in default (→ 5/13).

15. Chaco: Bolivia reports 1,000 Paraguayan casualties in big battle (→ 5/24).

16. Italian bombing kills 10 Greeks on island of Rhodes.

18. Washeteria, one of first laundromats, opens in Fort Worth, Texas.

20. San Francisco: Astronomers record sun spot 16,000 miles in diameter.

20. Paris: 6,000 riot for jobs; 1,000 arrested (→ 7/27).

21. Cotton Control Act passed in U.S., requiring tax on production exceeding quotas (→ 5/9).

23. Berlin's police chief bans fortune telling and horoscopes.

23. Minnesota: Dillinger escapes two posses near St. Paul; two left dead, five wounded (→ 7/22).

25. Martial law declared in Spain as Cabinet quits (→ 10/7).

29. Moscow: U.S. Ambassador William Bullitt delivers first speech in Russian.

29. China: Panchen Lama, exiled spiritual leader of Tibet, announces plans to return.

BIRTH

3. Jane Goodall, British animal behaviorist.

Dollfuss is made Austria's legal dictator

Dollfuss addresses an Austrian gathering at the Prater Racetrack.

April 30. The Austrian Parliament went to work today, but half the seats were empty. They belong to Social Democrats, and most of them are in prison or concentration camps. The Parliament met for only three hours, but it managed to rubber-stamp 471 government decrees. When the chamber was dismissed, Chancellor Engelbert Dollfuss had dictatorial powers.

One measure approved by the Parliament allows Dollfuss to send anyone suspected of working for an outlawed political party to a concentration camp without trial.

Two members of the Pan-German Party dared to protest what one of them called "12 months of unconstitutional rule of this government which has no majority behind it but that of bayonets.

"We protest against the destruction of liberty," he said, "the persecution of innocent women and children, concentration camps and the systems of spies and informers."

As the two Pan-German protesters walked out, they were jeered by Dollfuss supporters (→ 7/25).

France cancels Trotsky's political asylum

Trotsky and wife, homeless again.

April 17. Leon Trotsky has been secretly living in a cottage on the edge of the French forest, Fontainbleau. Secretly, that is, until Friday evening when suspicious police gained entry through the barbed wire fence surrounding the exiled Russian Communist's home near Barbison. Once inside the villa, the police, on orders from the Barbison Mayor whose curiosity was piqued by the voluminous amounts of mail being received, found Trotsky working diligently in his study.

The police had no search warrant, but they inspected the revolutionist's mail and notes, finding plans for an organization Trotsky was building called the Fourth International, a movement to upset all existing governments. Trotsky, living as "M. Sodoroff," had obtained permission from France to live in the forest. Today, in Paris, Minister of the Interior Albert Sarraut canceled the political asylum granted Trotsky in June 1933 (→ 8/26/36).

40,000 attend first Soviet fashion show

April 21. Russian women workers saw red today, as well as brown, navy and olive green at the first public fashion show in the U.S.S.R. About 40,000 factory and farm workers attended the extravaganza, held in a Moscow theater lobby in response to charges of monotony and monochrome in the garments issued by the Dress and Lingerie Trust. The trust tried to ease complaints by emulating Parisian couture. Most of the clothes were everyday wear, but a few evening dresses were modeled.

Rioting occurs at New York Nazi rally

April 8. Shouting "Heil Hitler," Nazi sympathizers clashed with opponents during and after a New York City rally held last night by supporters of Germany's Adolf Hitler. The pro-Nazi rally, in a Queens stadium, attracted a crowd of more than 9,000 persons, most of whom were there to protest the United States boycott of German goods.

Police estimated that there were 18 clashes in and around the stadium between the Nazis and those who oppose the German regime, including about 200 Communists. A dozen or so persons were arrested. Even after the police had left the scene, fighting broke out again when 50 pro-Nazi storm troopers, armed with small rubber clubs, moved through the crowd gathered outside the stadium.

Inside, a resolution was passed, asking President Roosevelt to end the boycott of German goods. Then, the rally over, the audience marched out singing the Nazi anthem, "Horst Wessel," and shouting "Heil Roosevelt" (→ 5/17).

1934

MAY

Su	Mo	Tu	We	Th	Fr	Sa
		1	2	3	4	5
6	7	8	9	10	11	12
13	14	15	16	17	18	19
20	21	22	23	24	25	26
29	28	29	30	31		

1. Berlin: Hitler tells crowd of two million that Germany is enobling labor (→ 3).

3. New York: H.G. Wells stands by his prediction of war by 1940.

3. Hitler creates People's Court to try treason cases (→ 30).

3. Saudi Arabian King Ibn Saud invandes Yemen (→ 6/27).

5. Cavalcade wins Kentucky Derby with jockey M. Garner.

5. U.S.S.R., Poland extend pact of non-aggression to 1945.

9. U.S. Congress passes authorizes controls on sugar (→ 20).

11. Chicago court lets Sam Insull out on $250,000 bail, largest ever paid (→ 11/24).

11. Dust dims N.Y.C. for five hours as West and South hit by vicious dust storm (→ 4/11/35).

13. Berlin debt talks deadlocked by Anglo-U.S. rift (→ 6/13).

15. Latvia: Agrarian Party coup ends parliamentary government.

16. Sen. Erickson falls asleep while presiding over U.S. Senate.

17. N.Y.: Nazi rally at Madison Sq. Garden draws 20,000 (→ 21).

18. FDR signs six bills — including death penalty for kidnapping —opening federal war on crime.

18. TWA begins commercial service on DC-2.

19. Sofia: Fascists take over in Bulgarian coup aided by king (→ 12/16).

20. Washington: Clarence Darrow issues report claiming NRA encourages monopoly (→ 6/4).

21. New Jersey: Mob of 1,000 raid Nazi rally (→ 7/11).

24. Tomas Masaryk elected president of Czechoslovakia for fourth time (→ 5/19/35).

28. Dionne quintuplets born.

28. FDR bars arms sales to Bolivia and Paraguay (→ 6/21).

30. Bill Cummings outraces the field at 104.9 mph in Indy 500.

30. Berlin: Nazis open trial of 111 alleged Comunists (→ 7/9).

31. New York: FDR reviews spectacular naval pageant; 81 ships, 185 planes (→ 8/31/35).

Bonnie and Clyde killed in police ambush

May 23. Fifty bullets have riddled the bodies of Clyde Barrow and Bonnie Parker, ending the careers of the two bank robbers. A posse of Texas Rangers ambushed the pair this afternoon on a little-traveled road outside Shreveport, Louisiana. The man and his moll were in a gray automobile speeding along at 85 miles per hour when the officers opened fire from the roadside. After the volley, Barrow and Parker were found crumpled up, their guns clutched in lifeless hands.

Bonnie and Clyde menaced the Southwest for the past four years, holding up banks, gas stations and luncheonettes. The desperadoes, both from Texas and in their mid-20's, collaborated on the murders of 12 people in the last two years. Parker was reputed to be as good a shot as Barrow, if not better.

When the final shootout was over, Barrow and Parker were found with a sawed-off shotgun and a revolver, respectively. A half-eaten sandwich and a saxophone were in the car. One of the Rangers said, "I hate to bust a cap on a woman, especially when she was sitting down. However, if it hadn't been her, it would have been us."

Bonnie and Clyde show off their art.

60,000 men in biggest battle of Chaco War

May 24. The recent Paraguayan offensive in the Chaco War with Bolivia was at least momentarily checked this afternoon by a fierce Bolivian counterattack. The war is now in its third year.

With both armies at full field strength, the Bolivians invited an attack about 125 miles northwest of the Paraguayan objective, Fort Ballivian, and the veteran Paraguayan regiments accepted. Advancing across seemingly innocuous open fields, they were relentlessly cut down by entrenched Bolivian machine gunners. As Bolivian aviators completed the rout, the ground counterattack forced the stunned remnants to fall into disorder, leaving behind large stores of arms and ammunition, some 6,000 dead and 12,000 wounded, and more than 1,000 prisoners.

As church bells pealed in the jubilant capital of La Paz, President Salamanca sent word to Commanding General Peneranda lauding the "great victory of Bolivian arms."

Ownership of the Chaco, an ill-defined border region shared by the two warring nations, had long been claimed by both. While Paraguay seeks its possible petroleum wealth, Bolivia is no less determined to claim an area offering it a river outlet to the Atlantic. Both maintain regional military posts. While raids and skirmishes between the two may be dated to 1928, the recent battle, fought by 60,000 men, is the deadliest in the last three years of full-scale war (→ 28).

United States gives up rights in Cuba

May 29. A new period of political relations between the United States and Cuba is expected as President Roosevelt signed a treaty annulling the Platt amendment of 1903, which has allowed United States intervention in Cuban affairs.

The agreement, awaiting Senate approval, assures Cuba of her complete independence. President Roosevelt, in a message urging ratification, stated, "By the consummation of this treaty, this government will make it clear that it not only opposes the policy of intervention, but that it renounces those rights of intervention and interference in Cuba which had been bestowed upon it by treaty." However, the United States will retain the rights to the Guantanamo Naval Base.

The streets of Havana erupted in celebration upon hearing of FDR's initiative. Churchbells, sirens and marching bands trumpeted the news and President Carlos Mendieta issued a cable of gratitude to Roosevelt and called the signing of the treaty "an event that will go down in history among the true and memorable events of our national existence." Secretary of State Hull congratulated Cuba, assuring it that the United States "will watch with great interest the progress of the Cuban people"(→ 6/29).

TWA cut rail connections out of their coast-to-coast trips in Oct. 1930. In less than four years, flight time has been cut from 36 to 18 hours.

1934

JUNE

Su	Mo	Tu	We	Th	Fr	Sa
					1	2
3	4	5	6	7	8	9
10	11	12	13	14	15	16
17	18	19	20	21	22	23
24	25	26	27	28	29	30

4. FDR asks $525 million for drought relief (→ 6).

5. Jan Smuts' South African Party and P.M. Hertzog's nationalists merge to form United South African Party.

6. Congress creates Securities Exchange Commission.→

8. FDR sets New Deal objectives as security for homes, jobs and old age (→ 12).

8. Geneva: Poland, Rumania and Russia sign pact guaranteeing present borders.

10. Mussolini watches Italy defeat Czechoslovakia to capture soccer's World Cup.

11. Geneva: Disarmament conference ends in failure (→ 21).

12. Farm Mortgage Foreclosure Act allows farmers to buy back foreclosed property (→ 19).

12. Reciprocal Trade Agreements Act allows president to make trade agreement without congressional consent (→ 19).

13. Washington: George Peek shows U.S. has lost $22 billion in foreign accounts (→ 14).

13. Berlin: Germany rejects Russian mutual aid pact.

19. Communications Act establishes Federal Communications Commission (FCC) (→ 28).

21. London: Britain seeks big naval increase in talks with U.S. (→ 11/28).

21. Chaco: 80,000 in battle between Bolivians and Paraguayans (→ 9/24).

23. Albanian resistance crumbles as Italian fleet arrives in Durazzo; Italy gains right to colonize Albania (→ 7/26).

23. L.A.: Utopian Society gathers 20,000 at Hollywood Bowl.

27. Ibn Saud, Imam of Yemen sign peace ending Desert War.

28. Congress creates Federal Housing Administration (FHA) to insure construction loans (→ 8/9).

29. Washington: FDR embargoes arms to Cuba (→ 8/24).

DEATH

10. Frederick Delius, British composer (*1/29/1862).

Night of the Long Knives: Gestapo murders

June 30. Some are calling it a "blood purge." Others call it the "night of the long knives." In Germany and Prussia, Adolf Hitler moved quickly and mercilessly to stamp out what he called a revolt ready to happen by the leadership of the storm troopers.

Hitler himself flew from Bonn to Munich early this morning to deal with Captain Ernst Rohm, Chief of Staff of the storm troopers. Rohm, who was reportedly caught in a compromising position with a top aide in the bedroom of his country house, was given a chance to commit suicide. When he refused, he was executed in a Munich prison.

Karl Ernst, leader of the Berlin storm troopers, was found in a house near Bremen. He was either shot while trying to escape or flown to Berlin and executed.

The Gestapo, under the command of Prussian Premier Hermann Goering, say they tried to arrest former Chancellor Kurt von Schleicher at his house near Potsdam. The police say he and his wife were both killed when they tried to resist. Other officials and storm trooper leaders were also executed or committed suicide.

Hitler says the rebels were threatening to take action against him with the help of an unnamed third power, possibly Russia. Whatever the threat, Hitler has once again consolidated his power (→ 7/3).

In Venice, two weeks prior to the bloody purges, Hitler and Mussolini met for the first time.

Max Baer takes world title from Carnera

June 13. Primo Carnera, the "Ambling Alp" of Italy, was leveled in short order by the amiable Max Baer, who stopped clowning long enough to win the world heavyweight boxing championship at Madison Square Garden in N.Y.

Baer virtually decimated the 6-foot, 6-inch Carnera over 11 rounds before finishing him off. The big Italian was knocked down 12 times until the referee finally stopped the fight. Baer thus became the fourth champion in four years in the fluid heavyweight picture. This was Carnera's third defense of the crown since he dethroned Jack Sharkey a year ago.

Carnera, nose displaying the rigors of his profession, takes a left from Baer.

Oswald Mosley at Fascist meeting

Mosley (rt.) leads parade in London.

June 8. Trying to convince 15,000 Londoners that he should be dictator of England proved explosive for Sir Oswald Mosley. As he shouted his speech at a Fascist demonstration in the Olympia Auditorium, fistfights erupted throughout the arena and hecklers interrupted his address several times. His guards, the Black Shirts, subdued a number of disorders on Mosley's cry of "Black Shirts aloft, attention! I want no fighting under this roof!"

The anti-Fascist protesters shouted from the rafters, literally that is, as several had scaled to the ceiling girders to yell, "Mosley, public enemy number one!" More than 100 people were injured, some seriously and dozens more were arrested. The hostile reaction surprised Mosley and his supporters because at a recent speech in Albert Hall over 10,000 persons listened without a trace of violence (→ 9/9).

WANTED

JOHN HERBERT DILLINGER

$10,000.00

SEC is formed to police Wall Street

June 6. In an effort to curb abuses within the Stock Exchange, President Roosevelt has created the Securities Exchange Commission and has announced that Joseph Kennedy will head the organization. Despite cries of outrage from the financial world, the commission will license stock exchanges and require all securities to be registered; makes pooling illegal; and empowers the Federal Reserve Board to set credit extensions for speculative and marginal loans.

Kennedy was chosen as SEC Commissioner because of his broad experience on Wall Street and his close political and personal ties with the president. He is to serve a five-year term (→ 8).

Hitler stops paying all foreign debts

June 14. Adolf Hitler shocked the international banking community today by announcing he would no longer pay off any of Germany's foreign debt. The Fuhrer did not ask for any extensions. He said simply he does not have the money.

Reaction from the Allies was extremely restrained. The United States, Germany's principal creditor, made a general threat to block international credits for all its debtor nations.

Germany is not the only country that will fail to make the payment on the war debt that is due tomorrow. Out of 15 countries, only one, Finland, will pay. That means the United States will receive only $166,000 of the half-billion dollars that is due (→ 9/6).

Leslie Howard, and Bette Davis as Mildred, the nasty waitress in "Of Human Bondage."

1934

JULY

Su	Mo	Tu	We	Th	Fr	Sa
1	2	3	4	5	6	7
8	9	10	11	12	13	14
15	16	17	18	19	20	21
22	23	24	25	26	27	28
29	30	31				

3. Franz von Papen resigns as German vice chancellor (→ 9).

3. Tokyo: Keisuke Okada chosen Japanese premier.

5. San Francisco: Two killed, 115 hurt as police clash with dockyard strikers (→ 16).

7. Wimbledon: Fred Perry over Jack Crawford 6-3, 6-0, 7-5; Dorothy Round over Helen Jacobs 6-2, 5-7, 6-3.

8. Pennsylvania: Joseph Harriman begins four and a half year jail term.

9. Germany: SS Commander-in-Chief Heinrich Himmler placed in charge of concentration camps (→ 13).

9. American Airlines opens sleeper plane service between Chicago and New York.

11. Washington: Ivy Lee, U.S. public relations expert, admits accepting $25,000 to work for Nazis (→ 7/26/35).

16. San Francisco dockyard strike turns into general strike (→ 19).

19. Tibet: England's Maurice Wilson dies attempting a solo climb of Mt. Everest.

20. Minneapolis: Fifty shot as police open fire on striking truckers.

21. U.S.: Midwest heat wave kills 206 in last three days.

26. Moscow: U.S.S.R. witnesses first polo game.

26. Italy: Mussolini masses 48,000 troops on Austrian border (→ 8/24).

27. Paris: French Socialist and Communist Parties join in Popular Front alliance against fascism (→ 7/14/35).

29. French racer Antonin Magne wins Tour de France.

29. Kurt Schuschnigg named Austrian chancellor (→ 31).

31. Vienna: Two rebels hanged for Dollfuss killing (→ 8/21).

DEATHS

4. French physicist Marie Curie, radiation studies (*11/7/1867).

21. Marshal Louis Hubert Lyautey, French resident general of Morocco (*11/17/1854).

Himmler takes over camps; SA disarmed

Berliner Ausgabe / Ausgabe A

Ausgabe A / Berliner Ausgabe

Berlin, Sonnabend, 14. Juli 1934

VÖLKIS HER BEOBACHTER

Kampfblatt der national-sozialistischen Bewegung Großdeutschlands

Adolf Hitler über den 30. Juni:

„Es soll jeder wissen, daß wenn er die Hand zum Schlage gegen den Staat erhebt, der sichere Tod sein Los ist"

Der Wortlaut der Führerrede vor dem Reichstag

Der Führer spricht zum deutschen Volk

Rechenschaft und Abrechnung

Am 30. Januar 1933 ist nicht zum soundsovielten Male eine neue Regierung gebildet worden, sondern ein neues Regiment hat ein altes und krankes Zeitalter beseitigt

The People's Observer, the Nazi Party newspaper, underlines the following sentence: "Let everybody know that whoever dares to raise his hand against the state is sure to die." Hitler explained the circumstances of the purge of the SA in a speech delivered at the Reichstag. SA prisoners have been summarily executed. Himmler's SS, constantly gaining in importance, has taken over nearly all the duties of policing the Reich.

July 13. Heinrich Himmler, chief of the SS, has taken command of Germany's concentration camps. The SS will assume responsibilities once held by the SA. The change reflects Adolf Hitler's increasing faith in Himmler and increasing distrust of the SA. Last month's "night of the long knives," involving the SA, carved a deep and lasting impression on the Fuhrer.

On June 30, Hitler personally foiled an alleged attempted coup by SA chief Ernst Rohm and several other SA members. All were executed. The SA, "Sturmabteilung" (storm troopers), had been the indispensible Nazi militia. Hitler saw it evolve into Rohm's personal army. Reducing duties such as camp administration may weaken the SA and keep it obedient.

Himmler has been Hitler's trusted aide since the Beer Hall Putsch of 1923. He has controlled the SS since 1929. Now 33 years old, he is a nearsighted and seemingly frail bureaucrat. He is proud to be a racist. Himmler considers himself a personal friend of Hitler, but so did Rohm until a month ago.

The SS under Himmler is well suited for its new responsibility. The black-shirted "Schutzstaffeln" (defense echelon) is an elite corps of unwavering allegiance to the Nazi Party. The SS has often rounded up people shipped to the camps; now it will simply see things through.

The SS keeps secrets well. Practices at the half-dozen concentration camps, found outside Munich and Berlin, will remain elusive. Jews, Communists and other enemies of the state have been sent there by the Nazi regime since March 1933 (→ 8/2).

Himmler, replacing Rohm.

Dillinger killed leaving Chicago theater

July 22. Desperado John Dillinger was gunned down tonight in front of a Chicago movie theater. The U.S. Attorney General considered the news "exceedingly gratifying as well as reassuring." Dillinger was Public Enemy #1, wanted for daring bank hold-ups, spectacular prison breaks and 16 murders.

Dillinger had been in custody in Midwestern jails several times. Last March, while in an Indiana prison, he whittled a piece of wood to fit in his hand, smeared it with shoe polish and waved the instant revolver at guards and other inmates. Later, they were very embarrassed.

Dillinger eluded capture through disguise. He grew a mustache and a physician gave him a facelift. He poured acid on his fingertips to eradicate fingerprints. Rumors that he had dyed his hair, however, were disproved at the autopsy.

Tonight, Dillinger chose to see a Clark Gable gangster film. He watched it with a woman who was wearing a red dress. Federal agents surrounded the theater. When he walked out, the show was over.

Austrian Nazis kill Chancellor Dollfuss

July 25. Austrian Chancellor Engelbert Dollfuss was assassinated tonight by Nazi insurgents in Vienna. They shot him in his office, where he lay bleeding to death for four hours, crumpled on the floor.

Doctors were not allowed to treat the chancellor while the rebels, who held members of the Cabinet hostage, tried to negotiate their freedom. At 9:00 tonight, officials relented and promised the insurgents free passage to Germany in exchange for the release of the Cabinet members. The rebels left the building and were arrested when it was revealed that Dollfuss was dead. The Austrian government declared martial law after citizens tried to lynch the assassins. Kurt Schuschnigg is the new Chancellor (→ 29).

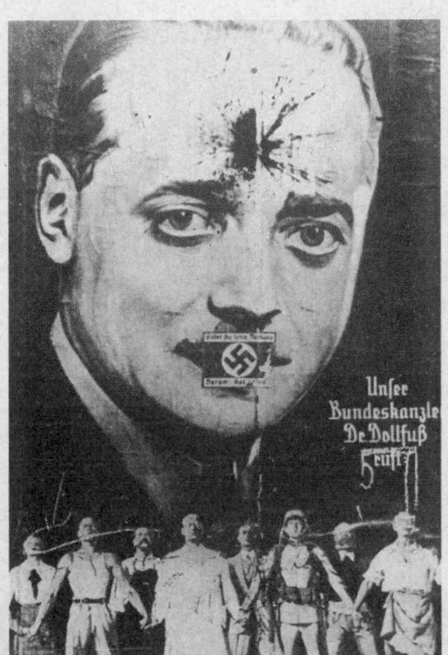

Dollfuss poster, vandalized by Nazis.

General strike ends in San Francisco

July 19. A general strike that has nearly paralyzed the San Francisco Bay area was called off today by labor union leaders. By late afternoon, the streets of San Francisco were clogged with trucks hauling food, beer, gas and oil. For the first time in days, taxicabs were back in business, as well as streetcars and buses. And hotels, bars, restaurants and movie houses that had closed during the strike threw open their doors once again to happy throngs of customers.

The strike, centering on working conditions, had its origins in a walkout last May by longshoremen, who were seeking more collective bargaining and union recognition. The labor unrest then spread a few days ago to other unions. An estimated 100,000 workers in the city joined the general strike. Concerned officials had termed the walkout a "civil war."

1934

AUGUST

Su	Mo	Tu	We	Th	Fr	Sa
			1	2	3	4
5	6	7	8	9	10	11
12	13	14	15	16	17	18
19	20	21	22	23	24	25
26	27	28	29	30	31	

2. Berlin: Pres. Hindenburg dies; German army swears fealty to Hitler upon his succession (→ 6).

4. Soviet Union opens diplomatic relations with Bulgaria.

6. Germany: 65 miles of torches light route to Hindenburg's tomb (→ 19).

8. Los Angeles Police captain claims movie stars contribute heavily to Communist Party.

9. FDR nationalizes silver at 50.01 cents per ounce (→ 20).

9. China: Chiang takes command of govt. troops to crush Communist uprisings (→ 10/16).

11. London: Germany wins fourth Intl. Women's Games.

13. 15,000 tons of stone fall from edge of Niagara Falls.

14. Riga: Andrew Mellon buys a Raphael for $1.5 million.

15. Last U.S. Marines leave Haiti, there since 1915.

16. Louisiana: Gov. Huey Long pushes 27 bills through Legislature (→ 9/7).

16. American William Beebe descends record 3,000 feet in bathysphere.

20. FDR drops tariffs on livestock feed to aid Midwest farmers (→ 9/30).

20. Geneva: U.S. becomes member of Inernational Labor Organization (ILO).

21. Austrian Chancellor Schuschnigg meets with Benito Mussolini (→ 4/3/35).

22. San Francisco: Al Capone locked up at Alcatraz.

24. Washington: U.S., Cuba sign reciprocal tariff treaty (→ 10/1).

24. Bologna: Mussolini warns Italy to prepare for war (→ 11/13).

29. California: Upton Sinclair says, if elected governor, he will pardon Mooney for Preparedness Day bombing (→ 1/7/39).

31. Textile strike sweeping U.S. now extended to wool; 650,000 out (→ 9/1).

BIRTH

3. Leon Uris, American screenwriter, historical novelist.

Hindenburg dead; Hitler is President

Aug 19. Not too long ago, Germany had a Kaiser, a President and a Parliament. Today, 17 days after the death of President Paul von Hindenburg, Germany has one man filling all functions. Adolf Hitler has more power than Stalin or Mussolini. And a correspondent for The New York Times says he is more powerful than Genghis Khan.

In a plebiscite today, almost 90% of German voters approved Hitler's ascending to the presidency while retaining his title as Chancellor. Hitler's critics do point out that 10% of the voters dared to vote no, and one million of them expressed their dissatisfaction by tampering with the ballots.

Hitler eulogizes Hindenburg at the Tannenberg Monument in Berlin.

With his new powers, Hitler can make war and peace, create new laws, abolish old ones, execute suspects and pardon convicts. He is both legislator and executive.

True conservatives wish Hindenburg's old and wasted body had held out a little longer. They acknowledge that in his waning years he was the man who made Hitler chancellor. But they also remember that he rebuffed the Fuhrer in two earlier attempts, and he retained the power to check Hitler's extremism. Hindenburg also controlled the army, and that too now passes to Hitler, along with his storm troopers and his secret police (→ 9/5).

1934

SEPTEMBER

Su	Mo	Tu	We	Th	Fr	Sa
						1
2	3	4	5	6	7	8
9	10	11	12	13	14	15
16	17	18	19	20	21	22
23	24	25	26	27	28	29
30						

1. Washington: Textile talks fail; silk workers ordered out (→ 11).

3. Tunisia: Habib Bourguiba and Neo-Destour leaders placed under house arrest (→ 4/10/38).

4. New York: John Smiuske gets six months in jail for burning satirical painting of FDR.

5. Hilter predicts Reich will survive for 1,000 years (→ 16).

6. Washington reports Reich is building U-boats in foreign factories (→ 10/30).

8. N.Y.: Revived Westchester Ku Klux Klan places support behind Nazis (→ 3/20/35).

9. London: Fascists and anti-Fascists stage huge demonstrations in Hyde Park.

10. Cleveland: Aristid van Grosse isolates Proactinium, element 91.

11. R.I. Eight shot as 3,000 textile strikers battle troops (→ 22).

12. Latvia, Lithuania, Estonia sign Baltic Entente.

16. Lutherans in Munich march to anti-Nazi songs (→ 11/2).

18. Geneva: U.S.S.R. admitted to League of Nations.

20. Bronx: Bruno Hauptmann, believed to have received Lindbergh ransom, is arrested (→ 28).

24. Chaco: Bolivians kill 1,400 Paraguayans at Algodonal (→ 11/17).

25. Washington: Hugh Johnson quits NRA post (→ 30).

25. Rhode Island: Rainbow takes America's Cup for U.S.

26. Geneva: Afghanistan becomes 60th member of League.

26. Scotland: 200,000 attend launching of Queen Mary.

29. Rome: Italy, Ethiopia issue statement of friendship (→ 12/5).

30. FDR pleads for truce between capital and labor to give NRA a chance (→ 10/1).

BIRTHS

14. Kate Millet, American feminist author.

20. Sophia Loren, Italian actress.

28. Brigitte Bardot, French actress.

Thousands watch as liner burns; 130 dead

Thousands gather on Asbury Beach to see the charred hull of the Morro Castle.

Sept 8. Over 125,000 people today helplessly witnessed the deaths of 130 people aboard a burning ship. The Morro Castle, a luxury liner anchored off the Jersey shore, erupted in flames in the midst of a storm early this morning. The cause of the fire has not yet been determined.

Some passengers suffocated in their cabins. Some clung to the decks and prayed aloud. Others defied reality, banded together and sang "Hail, Hail, the Gang's All Here." Most abandoned ship when the searing red plates became too unbearably hot to stand upon.

For some, the leap into the sea was a leap to life. A 20-year-old Cuban mess boy swam the two miles to shore, exhausted but alive. Some people floated in the frigid waters six or seven hours before rescue vessels arrived. The rest drowned.

Rumors are circulating about the cause of the fire. The ship's captain died the previous night of a heart attack; his last words were a warning to the acting captain to keep an eye on one of the telegraph operators. The boat received a sabotage threat while anchored at Havana. The radio man is Cuban (→ 10/16).

Hauptmann is held in Lindbergh crime

Sept 28. Bruno Hauptmann, an illegal German immigrant, is being held for the murder of the Lindbergh baby last March. Hauptmann was found in possession of some of the ransom money Colonel Charles A. Lindbergh paid for the return of the infant. The suspect has an arrest record and escaped from a German prison years ago.

Hauptmann is currently in the Bronx County jail. Today, a spoon bent into a knife-like implement was discovered hidden in his cell. Prison authorities do not know if he intended to use it for an escape attempt or to commit suicide (→ 10/8).

Hauptmann, finally a captive.

Huey Long becomes Louisiana dictator

Sept 7. Two thousand troops have moved into New Orleans on orders of Senator Huey P. Long, who last month became the dictator of Louisiana by virtue of laws passed by the Legislature.

The troops were stationed in anticipation of next week's primary election, as the political feud between Long and New Orleans Mayor T. Semmes Walmsley has heated.

Determined not to give up "without a fight," Walmsley alerted the 1,400-member New Orleans police force. Reports indicate the mayor is preparing for a proclamation of martial law nullifying the elections as the Governor has been empowered to declare martial law as he sees fit. But most are confident the elections will proceed as usual (→ 11/6).

Turner flies across country in 10 hours

Sept 1. Colonel Roscoe Turner flew from New York to Los Angeles today in ten hours, two minutes and 51 seconds, beating the old record (his own) by two minutes and 39 seconds. His Wedell-Williams Racer averaged 250 mph. He made the trip in only four stops.

Turner and pet after the flight.

Big textile strike ended by FDR action

Sept 22. Franklin D. Roosevelt has asked a halt to the crippling, 20-day strike called by 421,000 textile workers, and union leaders appear to be willing to cooperate.

The cotton, woolen and silk industries have been devastated by the strike, the largest the nation has ever known. The United Textile Workers of America, affiliated with the A.F.L., held protest marches in Washington, destroyed machinery and defied federal troops. Thirteen strikers have been killed.

The President's request that the strikers return to work was exactly that: a request, not an executive order. Most labor officials seem confident that the president's independent Textile Inquiry Board will mediate a fair settlement (→ 30).

1934

OCTOBER

Su	Mo	Tu	We	Th	Fr	Sa
	1	2	3	4	5	6
7	8	9	10	11	12	13
14	15	16	17	18	19	20
21	22	23	24	25	26	27
28	29	30	31			

1. Havana: Cuba suspends constitution to fight Communists (→ 3/10/35).

1. New York Stock Exchange registers with SEC (→ 15).

4. Britain: Enrico Fermi measures speed of neutron (→ 1/28/39).

8. Spain: Revolt strikes Madrid; 52 soldiers killed (→ 2/16/36).

8. Bronx: Col. Lindbergh identifies Bruno Hauptmann by sound of his voice (→ 2/13/35).

9. Detroit: St. Louis Cardinals take World Series, blanking Tigers 11-0 in seventh game.

11. Munich police use sabers in attack on Protestants (→ 11/2).

12. Riga: Archbishop of Latvia Johan Pommer slain.

13. New York: 1,155 slot machines sunk in Long Island Sound by police.

14. Hungary: 1,200 miners refuse to leave mine, threaten mass suicide unless demands are met.

14. China places export tax on silver to stop drain to U.S.

15. U.S. reports 10.8 million unemployed (→ 19).

16. China: Mao abandons Communist base in Kiangsi, begins long march north (→ 11/6).

16. New York: Five officers found guilty of negligence in Morro Castle fire.

19. FDR bars veterans' bonus, placing jobless aid first (→ 28).

20. New York: Gloria Vanderbilt, age 10, receives threat on her life.

24. Mahatma Gandhi quits Indian Natl. Congress in struggle over tactics (→ 3/19/35).

26. FDR declares opposition to Upton Sinclair's campaign for governorship of California.

28. Washington: FERA to buy surplus Long Island potatoes to feed needy (→ 11/6).

30. Paris: Henri Petain warns French to prepare to defend Saar Basin from Nazis (→ 11/13).

DEATH

15. Raymond Poincare, French statesman (*8/20/1860).

Catalonian secession from Spain crushed

Spanish troops in Barcelona pose in front of the Palace of Gemerarite.

Oct 7. The newly elected government of Premier Alejandro Leroux succeeded in crushing an insurrection in Catalonia after fierce fighting in the streets of Barcelona. The insurrection coincided with a general strike called by Socialist and Syndicalist labor unions to protest the inclusion of three Catholic Popular Actionist ministers in the Cabinet of the new, right-leaning government.

Martial law was imposed after fighting broke out between the strikers and government forces in several Spanish cities, including Madrid. Unofficial estimates were that 500 persons on both sides, including 200 in Barcelona alone, were killed in the fighting. President Luis Companys of the Catalan Generalidad, who had proclaimed Catalonia to be an independent state, surrendered after army troops, supported by naval reinforcements, shelled buildings seized by the insurrectionists. The Leroux government, which was squelching the general strike, proclaimed it had saved the Spanish republic (→ 8).

Yugoslav King killed on visit to France

Oct 9. King Alexander of Yugoslavia has been assassinated, apparently by a Crotian gunman, shortly after he had arrived in Marseilles for a visit to France. French Foreign Minister Louis Barthou, who was in the car with the king, also was shot and died a few hours later. King Alexander, who joined Yugoslavia under a Serbian crown after the world war, decreed in his will that the country be ruled by a regency council until his 11-year-old son Peter came of age.

French police rush to smother the King's assassin, Petrus Kalemen.

Little Gloria says she prefers aunt

Oct 24. Gloria Vanderbilt, the ten-year-old girl who has a $2.8 million trust fund, says she does not want to live with her mother. She prefers to stay with her aunt, Mrs. Harry Payne Whitney, with whom she has lived for years. The girl's mother, Mrs. Gloria Morgan Vanderbilt, seeks charge of Gloria and the generous trust fund.

In court, Mrs. Vanderbilt heard the most damning evidence from, of all people, her mother. Mrs. Laura Kilpatrick Morgan testified that Mrs. Vanderbilt lived in Europe soon after giving birth to Gloria and "never wrote or inquired as to the baby's condition" (→ 11/21).

Little Gloria Vanderbilt.

G-men wipe out Pretty Boy Floyd

Oct 22. Bankers in the Midwest may breathe a lot easier tonight, as Charles "Pretty Boy" Floyd, the notorious outlaw who was called the most dangerous man alive, was shot and killed on a farm in Ohio while fleeing from federal agents and East Liverpool police. Melvin Purvis, Chicago Department of Justice chief and nemesis of John Dillinger, led the sensational manhunt.

Purvis shouted "halt!" but the bandit sprinted toward a wooden structure. Machine guns and pistols fired, and Floyd fell, mortally wounded. He died 15 minutes later. Floyd had a .45-calibre automatic in his hand, a second automatic in a shoulder holster and $120 in cash. So ended a "career" that began with auto theft and graduated to robbery and murder.

1934

NOVEMBER

Su	Mo	Tu	We	Th	Fr	Sa
				1	2	3
4	5	6	7	8	9	10
11	12	13	14	15	16	17
18	19	20	21	22	23	24
25	26	27	28	29	30	

1. Union Pacific's new streamlined diesel train cuts 14 hours, 32 minutes from L.A.-N.Y. run.

2. Berlin: Nazis order new music to replace Jewish composer Mendelssohn's score for "Midsummer Night's Dream" (→ 26).

4. New York: Metropolitan opens exhibit of industrial art.

6. New Orleans: Huey Long asks Louisiana to secede (→ 1/1/35).

7. Baltimore: Philadelphia Symphony Orchestra premieres Rachmaninoff's "Rhapsody on a Theme by Paginini."

13. Rome: Mussolini orders all teachers to wear Fascist uniforms at school (→ 6/12/35).

13. Joachim von Ribbentrop admits Reich is rearming (→ 1/13/35).

14. Sec. of Int. Ickes orders Parker Dam halted until states rights questions are settled.

17. Chaco: Paraguay captures 10,000 at Bolivian fort (→ 28).

19. London: Japan asks 5-4-4 naval ratio favoring Britain (→ 23).

21. New York: Court rules Gloria Vanderbilt unfit for custody of her daughter.

23. London: U.S. and Britain agree on 5-5-3 naval ratio; Japan to denounce treaty (→ 12/6).

24. Chicago: Jury acquits Sam Insull in mail fraud case.

25. Istanbul: Premier Kemal gets name Ataturk (→ 12/14).

26. Bonn: Karl Barth suspended from professorship for balking at Hitler loyalty oath (→ 1/8/35).

27. Rumanian army bans all communist groups (→ 4/17/38).

28. London: Winston Churchill warns House of Commons of German air threat (→ 5/22/35).

28. Bolivia: Pres. Daniel Salamanaca ousted, as army retreats in Chaco (→ 2/23/35).

30. Egypt: Royal decree annuls constitution, dissolves Parliament (→ 12/12/35).

BIRTH

9. Carl Sagan, American scientist, studied extraterrestrial life, nuclear winter.

Mao Tse-tung marches north to save army

Nov 6. Chiang Kai-shek, the Chinese General and leader of the Nationalist government, has built himself a solid reputation as a survivor in his country's wars and equally bloody political struggles. But in a country where legend and myth are as important as reality, Chiang has a new rival in the battle to capture the imagination of the Chinese people. He is the Communist leader, Mao Tse-tung.

Until recently, Mao was hiding underground. He disappeared after his ruthless defeat at the hands of Chiang's Nanking troops. But now, Mao is re-emerging and hoping to create a new legend.

Mao is trying to unite the Communist troops who were badly scattered after the defeat of General Chu-Teh. And he is challenging them to march with him a total of 6,000 miles from Kiangsi province all the way to Yenan.

It seems like an impossibly long journey through hostile territory. But it gives Mao a chance to spread his Communist message into the northwest part of China. It would prove that his establishment of the Soviet republic of China is more than a whim. And it would give Mao more visibility and power as he aims to displace Chiang as the true leader of China (→ 10/20/35).

Mao, from Hunan peasant stock.

Baby Face Nelson found dead in ditch

Nov 28. George "Baby Face" Nelson, the nation's number one outlaw, avenged the slaying of his partners in crime, John Dillinger and "Pretty Boy" Floyd, as he and a companion engaged two federal agents in a gun battle in Illinois, and, using machine guns, killed one agent and fatally wounded the other. Himself wounded, Nelson fled with his pal and a woman, possibly his wife, but today his body, pierced by 17 bullets, was found in a roadside ditch outside of Chicago.

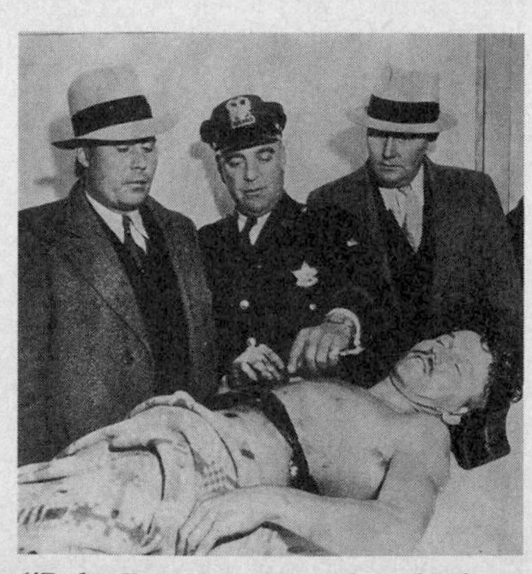

"Baby Face" at the undertaker's.

Salvador Dali shows tantalizing works

Dali's "Persistence of Memory."

Nov 22. Erotic or neurotic is how viewers choose to judge Salvador Dali's paintings now on display at a New York gallery. His works have titles such as "Commode Used as a Diurnal Fly" and the less obscure "Myself at the Age of Ten When I Was a Grasshopper Child." Dali has been creating surrealist works since "The Persistence of Memory" (1931), but praise for the art form is belated. It is hard for viewers to accept work that is antiaesthetic by nature, and the art's attack on common forms of communication leaves critics speechless.

Cole Porter: He's the top composer

Nov 21. Everything goes swell in "Anything Goes," the Cole Porter musical that opened tonight. "I Get a Kick Out of You" and "You're the Top" are two of its best tunes. For a Yale graduate who did additional study at Harvard, Porter is not particularly lofty in his subject matter. "Let's Do It" and "Love for Sale" are among his most popular songs. (The latter is generally banned from the radio.) Porter rose above himself in 1932 when he wrote "Night and Day." Anyone can like that melody without blushing.

Ivy Leaguer Cole Porter.

New Deal wins big test at the polls

Nov 6. The Democrats scored big gains in Tuesday's election, underlining the public's support for President Roosevelt and his New Deal.

Capturing additional seats in both houses of Congress, the Democrats now control more than two-thirds of the Senate and the House. Winning but three governorships, in New Jersey, Maryland and Michigan, and few congressional seats, the Republicans have hit bottom.

Republican National Committee Chairman Henry P. Fletcher says that the party must rebuild on more liberal lines but will continue to repudiate the New Deal philosophy. He feels the pendulum will swing back to old-time economic principles, that Americans will reject the New Deal programs based on "taking money from the thrifty to keep the improvident." But for now, the pendulum has stopped in the Democratic camp (→ 1/4/35).

1934

DECEMBER

Su	Mo	Tu	We	Th	Fr	Sa
						1
2	3	4	5	6	7	8
9	10	11	12	13	14	15
16	17	18	19	20	21	22
23	24	25	26	27	28	29
30	31					

1. Stalin aide Sergei Kirov assassinated in Moscow (→ 29).

1. Philadelphia: Navy triumphs over Army 3-0 for first time in ten years.

2. Washington: New 60-mph army tank developed.

5. Italian and Ethiopian troops clash at Ualual on disputed Somali-Ethiopian border (→ 16).

6. London: Ambassador Davis says Japan is grave security threat in Pacific (→ 29).

10. Geneva: League asks Hungary to punish plotters against Yugoslav government.

14. Turkey grants vote to women (→ 2/6/35).

16. Rome: Mussolini rejects mediation by League in clash with Ethiopia (→ 1/3/35).

16. Bulgaria: 540 arrested for alleged Communist plot (→ 4/21/35).

18. Switzerland: Delegates from 16 countries attend Fascist Congress at Montreux.

29. Japan formally denounces Washington Naval Treaty of 1922 (→ 1/27/35).

CULTURAL EVENTS, 1934

Literature: Fitzgerald's "Tender is the Night"; Robert Graves' "I, Claudius"; James Hilton's best-seller "Good-Bye Mr. Chips"; William Saroyan's "The Daring Young Man on the Flying Trapeze"; Henry Miller's "Tropic of Cancer"; first Soviet Writers' Congress under Maxim Gorky.

Academia: Reinhold Niebuhr's "Moral Man and Immoral Society"; Bertrand Russell's "Freedom and Organization"; Arnold Toynbee's "A Study of History," first volume; Lewis Mumford's "Technics and Civilization."

Music: Shostakovich's opera "A Lady Macbeth of Mzensk"; Cole Porter's "Anything Goes"; "Blue Moon"; "All Through the Night."

The Arts: Dali's "William Tell."

Film: Capra's "It Happened One Night," Academy Award; Leslie Howard's "Of Human Bondage"; Clair's "The Last Millionaire."

Stalin uses Kirov murder to purge rivals

Stalin at a funeral last year.

Dec 29. The Stalin government summarily tried and executed more than 100 persons following the assassination of Sergei M. Kirov, a member of the Politburo and one of the principal aides of Joseph Stalin. Kirov, a member of the Bolshevik Party since 1904 and Secretary of the Leningrad Regional Party Committee for the past eight years, was shot and killed by a gunman on December 1 in the headquarters of the Communist Party in Leningrad.

In a statement extolling Kirov as a "fiery and fearless revolutionary," the Central Committee of the Communist Party said he had been "killed at the treacherous hand of an enemy of the working class." The government announced that Leonid Nikolaev, who was not otherwise identified, had been arrested and would be tried.

Meanwhile, it appeared that Stalin was using the assassination as a reason for a purge of Communist Party rivals who were accused of "terrorist" plots against the government. Within a week after the assassination, 66 persons in Moscow and Leningrad, described by the Soviet press as "White Guard terrorists," were convicted in secret trials and immediately executed. Ten days later, another 27 persons were found guilty and shot in Kiev. Subsequently, Grigori Zinoviev, former President of the Communist International, and Lev Kamenev, former editor of Pravda, were arrested for the Kirov murder (→ 1/17).

Luigi Pirandello wins Nobel Prize

Dec 10. The only person at the Nobel awards ceremony tonight who may have doubted the veracity of the proceedings was Luigi Pirandello. The dramatist, who received the prize in literature, is known for doubting and delving into appearances. His hallmark is "Six Characters in Search of an Author" (1921), an existentialist play questioning the boundaries of reality. That work and others were collected in a book titled "Naked Masks," published last year in Italy.

Pirandello is intimately familiar with sanity and the unreal. When he was financially ruined in 1903, his wife went into shock. The trauma became a kind of paranoid condition, and she was permanently institutionalized in 1919.

The prize in chemistry went to Indiana-born chemist Harold Claton Urey, who discovered and isolated heavy hydrogen (deuterium). American scientists George Minot, William Murphy and George Whipple earned the prize in medicine for discovering that the ingestion of beef liver is a successful treatment for pernicious anemia.

A night out with Claudette, Marlene, Greta, Ginger and Fred

Romantic couples loved, danced and sleuthed on the screen in 1934. Claudette Colbert and Henry Wilcoxon starred as star-crossed lovers Cleopatra and Marc Antony in "Cleopatra." The Cecil B. De Mille picture was typically opulent. When the queen of Egypt drifted on her barge, surrounded by countless slaves waving peacock feather fans, Antony naturally swooned.

Women conquered in two other sumptuous films: Marlene Dietrich in "The Scarlet Empress" and Greta Garbo in "The Painted Veil." Dietrich played Catherine the Great, while John Lodge was an ardent admirer. Garbo played an unfaithful wife opposite George Brent.

Wilcoxon and Colbert, "Cleopatra."

"Treasure Island."

The Cole Porter musical "The Gay Divorce" added an "e" when it came to the screen. Fred Astaire and Ginger Rogers starred in "The Gay Divorcee," about a couple who who choose to wrestle rather than nestle. "The Thin Man," a comedy-mystery, featured another lively pair. William Powell and Myrna Loy were Nick and Nora Charles, a detective duo invented by author Dashiell Hammett.

Finally, Wallace Beery portrayed pirate Long John Silver in "Treasure Island." His partner was a parrot. If you had a treasure waiting for you, you might think twice about a mate too.

"Gay Divorcee," Fred and Ginger.

1935

JANUARY

Su	Mo	Tu	We	Th	Fr	Sa
		1	2	3	4	5
6	7	8	9	10	11	12
13	14	15	16	17	18	19
20	21	22	23	24	25	26
27	28	29	30	31		

1. Pasadena: Alabama downs Stanford 29-13 in Rose Bowl.

1. FDR warns Louisiana to repeal laws pushed by Huey Long, or lose federal loans (→ 9).

1. Cyrenaica, Tripoli and Fezzan, Italian colonies in Africa, are merged under name of Libya.

3. Geneva: Ethiopia asks League to assure peace with Italy (→ 7).

4. FDR, in State of Union talk, says govt. will provide jobs for 3.5 mil. on welfare (→ 2/27).

8. Germany: Reich's steel production up 104% in year since Hitler's ascendancy (→ 2/14).

9. Huey Long radio address opens "Every man a king" drive (→ 26).

10. Los Angeles: Mary Pickford obtains divorce from Douglas Fairbanks.

13. Saar plebiscite shows 90.8% favor return to Germany (→ 17).

17. Geneva: League votes to award Germany the Saar Basin on March 1 (→ 3/1).

19. China: Red army captures Zunyi; Mao back in command (→10/20).

19. Mao, back in command, leads Red army out of Zunyi (→ 10/20).

20. Brussels: Belgium arrests Nazi agitators urging return to Reich.

21. Somalia: Ethiopians kill 107 on border of French colony (→ 2/11).

24. Ward liner Mohawk sinks in crash with freighter off New Jersey coast; 33 dead, 13 lost.

25. Istanbul turns St. Sophia's Mosque into museum after Byzantine frescoes found by archeologist Thomas Wittemore.

27. Geneva: League majority favors depriving Japan of mandates (→ 4/1).

29. U.S. Senate again votes down entry to Intl. Court of Justice.

30. Moscow: U.S.S.R. doubles army to 940,000.

31. Soviet premier tells Japan to get out of Manchuria (→ 3/22).

BIRTH

8. Elvis Presley, American rock and roll pioneer (†8/16/77).

Huey: Every man a king

Jan 26. Poised for warfare, 500 Louisiana National Guardsmen have forced the surrender of 100 armed citizens of the Square Deal Association in the streets of Baton Rouge. The Square Dealers oppose the dictatorship of Senator Huey P. Long and the state of martial law that was imposed yesterday by Long's ally, Governor O.K. Allen.

While civil war was narrowly averted, 40 leaders of the Square Deal Association were arrested, adding fuel to the political inferno in the volatile Southern state.

The showdown culminated as rumors circulated that the Standard Oil Company was instigating the revolt and has plotted to assassinate Long, which in part prompted the declaration of martial law.

All of this came two weeks after Long, in a radio address, asked for support of his "Share Our Wealth" and "Every Man is a King" programs. In that speech, he condemned the policies of the Roosevelt administration, saying the President had failed to live up to his promises of "breaking down the big fortunes (of the Rockefellers and Astors) to give enough to the masses to end poverty" (→ 7/25).

Every man's "Kingfish."

Laval, Mussolini agree on African policy

Laval signs at the Palace of Venice, while a stern Mussolini (rt.) looks on.

Jan 7. French Foreign Minister Pierre Laval and Italian Premier Benito Mussolini have signed the Italo-French agreements they arrived at over the past two days.

According to unofficial sources, the pact includes a protocol in which the two governments consider the rearming of Germany illegal. The focus of the treaty, however, is on competing claims in Africa.

The agreement reportedly includes a harmonization of the two governments' views on Africa, specifically in regard to the status of Italian residents in Tunis and territorial concessions to be made by France in Libya and Somaliland.

According to some observers, it appears that with this agreement Mussolini has been given a freer hand to pursue a more active policy in Africa, which could mean an Italian takeover of Ethiopia (→ 21).

FBI guns down Ma Barker and Fred

Jan 16. Federal agents trailed Kate "Ma" Barker, 55, and her 32-year-old son Fred, long-sought members of the Karpis gang, to their Florida hiding place and killed them both after a fierce gun battle. "Ma" Barker has been called the brains of the gang, which had been robbing banks and was reported to have been behind the kidnapping of the St. Paul banker, Edward Bremer. The dozen or more federal agents escaped injury, but weapons blazed for six hours. The $200,000 ransom money was not found.

"Ma" and friend Arthur Dunlop.

Kirov accused get total of 137 years

Jan 17. Soviet courts have sentenced Grigori Zinoviev, the former President of the Communist International, Lev Kamenev, former editor of Pravda, and 17 other defendants to a total of 137 years of imprisonment on charges of "moral responsiblity" for the murder of Sergei Kirov. Kirov, a longtime member of the Communist Party and a close aide to Joseph Stalin, was assassinated last month. The killing has prompted mass convictions of Communist rivals, leading some Soviet observers to speculate that Stalin ordered the murder so he could "clean house" (→ 8/25/36).

1935

FEBRUARY

Su	Mo	Tu	We	Th	Fr	Sa
					1	2
3	4	5	6	7	8	9
10	11	12	13	14	15	16
17	18	19	20	21	22	23
24	25	26	27	28		

2. Washington: U.S. and Brazil sign trade accord.

5. New York: 15 rounds set as standard for title bouts.

6. Women vote in Turkish elections for first time (→ 11/11/38).

7. Argentinian troops put down short-lived rebellion at La Plata.

9. Belgium brings govt., labor and capital together in tripartite commission to study economy.

11. New York: Mary Cassatt exhibit opens.

11. While League debates Italo-Ethiopian conflict in Geneva, Mussolini mobilizes 35,000 troops for African duty (→ 18).

12. The Macon, last U.S. Navy dirigible crashes off California coast, killing two.

14. Adolf Hitler opens world's biggest auto show in Berlin (→ 17).

17. Eight-hour work day established in Germany (→ 18).

17. Thirty-one escape Oklahoma prison after murdering guard.

18. Berlin: Nazis behead two women for revealing military secrets (→ 3/15).

18. Rome reports sending troops to Italian Somalia (→ 28).

19. Tennessee votes to retain anti-evolution law.

22. Plane flights barred over White House for disturbing President Roosevelt's sleep.

23. Saxophonist Coleman Hawkins and guitarist Django Reinhardt gig in Paris to celebrate founding of journal "Jazz Hot."

23. Paraguay resigns from League of Nations (→ 6/12).

24. Swiss referendum votes extension of military training.

26. Boston: Babe Ruth, just back from world tour, signs three-year contract as v.p./manager/player for Boston Braves.

27. Kentucky: Judge rules NRA is unconstitutional bar to free enterprise (→ 5/1).

DEATH

8. Max Liebermann, German painter (*7/20/1847).

Hauptmann found guilty

Feb 13. Bells pealed from the belfry of the Flemington, N.J., court house today, as they always do when a verdict is reached within the jury room. This time the bells were also sounding a death knell. Bruno Hauptmann, accused of kidnapping and killing the Lindbergh baby in March 1933, has been found guilty of murder in the first degree. The judge passed sentence immediately: execution is slated for March 18.

Circumstantial evidence pointed to Hauptmann's guilt. The ladder found outside the Lindbergh home, used in the kidnapping, belonged to Hauptmann. The ransom note contained spelling errors that Hauptmann had frequently been known to make. Most damning was the ransom money found on Hauptmann's property. Yet no one witnessed the murder, and Mrs. Hauptmann has protested his innocence.

A few of the jurors walked away from the jury box with tears in their eyes. Hauptmann, manacled in irons to two guards, was impassive as he was escorted from the room. As soon as doors were closed behind him, he slumped, seemingly lifeless, to the floor (→ 10/14).

Hauptmann in N.J. after conviction.

Italians mobilize in dispute with Ethiopia

Feb 28. As some 10,000 Italian soldiers steam toward Africa and the scene of the Italo-Ethiopian dispute, volunteers continue to swell the ranks of the recently mobilized army of 35,000 following Mussolini's threat of possible retaliation for border attacks made by Ethiopians against neighboring Italian Somaliland. Reports reaching Rome claim that 90,000 armed Ethiopians are massing near the colony's frontier.

Border incidents have lately erupted between Ethiopians and Italian colonial troops, each charging the other as responsible. In the most serious skirmish, at Ualual, several were killed on both sides, whereupon both countries protested to the League of Nations, and Italy demanded a $70,000 indemnity (→ 4/3).

Mussolini, far left, addresses an Italian division mobilized for African duty.

Archeologists find oldest known city

Feb 10. The ruins of the oldest known city, a site nearly 5,700 years old, have been found by archeologists digging into the great mound of Tepe Gawra in northern Mesopotamia, the University of Pennsylvania Museum announced today. The city is the 11th found in a systematic exploration of the site, halfway between Baghdad and the Persian Gulf, by an expedition headed by Charles Bache.

The ruins excavated by the archeologists include the walls of a temple and private dwellings, household pottery, knives and scrapers and receptacles for the kohl that women used as a cosmetic. Spindles, loom-weights and other household utensils have also been uncovered. And a number of tombs containing bodies that had been placed in wooden coffins have been found, with the valuables left untouched.

The newly found city, dated at 3750 B.C., is at least older than the earliest known Chaldean culture. The archeologists say they expect to find even older ruins as they continue digging into the mound, which was last inhabited in 1500 B.C.

Kreisler confesses to a musical hoax

Feb 7. For many years now, the great violinist Fritz Kreisler has programmed rare but enchanting old classics by Baroque composers. It now develops that these "originals" are actually his own —much to the chagrin of certain "authorities." Kreisler explains that he wrote them to enrich his own programs, but that "tact and modesty" prevented the use of his own name. As a "real" composer, his lovely violin pieces are staple items, and his 1919 hit operetta "Apple Blossoms" ran for a year on Broadway.

1935

MARCH

Su	Mo	Tu	We	Th	Fr	Sa
					1	2
3	4	5	6	7	8	9
10	11	12	13	14	15	16
17	18	19	20	21	22	23
24	25	26	27	28	29	30
31						

1. Germany celebrates return of Saar Basin to Reich (→ 11).

7. Florida: Malcolm Campbell sets auto speed record of 276.8 mph.

9. U.S.S.R.: Nikita Khrushchev elected party secretary (→ 3/5/53).

10. Cuba: Army rule set up as strike spreads (→ 7/3).

11. Greece crushes military revolt led by ex-Premier Venizelos (→ 5/5).

11. German air force becomes official organ of Reich (→ 16).

12. Paris: Natl. Assembly calls for big warships rivaling Italy and Germany.

13. Jerusalem: 3,000-year-old archives found, confirming biblical history.

15. U.S.: 2,000 arrested in surprise raid on organized crime.

15. German Minister of Propaganda Joseph Goebbels bans four Berlin newspapers (→ 17).

16. Germany: Hitler renounces Treaty of Versailles, reinstates military conscription (→ 17).

17. Berlin: 500,000 watch Hitler review military parade (→ 20).

17. German Reich arrests 700 pastors (→ 4/12).

19. India: British fire on 20,000 Moslems, killing 23 (→ 8/2).

20. N.Y.: Police end two-day Harlem riot; one dead (→ 11/12).

20. France asks League for action on Germany (→ 23).

22. Manchuria: Russia sells Chinese Eastern Railway to Japan (→ 6/10).

22. Persia renamed Iran.

23. Moscow: Unmanned balloon sets altitude record of 24.6 miles.

23. Paris: France, Italy, Britain agree to present united front in response to Germany (→ 25).

25. Hitler says Soviet imperils peace in Europe (→ 30).

29. Brussels: Belgium devalues franc as stock exchange closes.

30. Britain, Russia agree on treaties to curb Reich (→ 31).

31. India: 374 infants wed at mass ceremony.

Storm clouds gathering over Europe

March 31. A meeting yesterday between Russian and British officials capped a turbulent month, as the situation in Europe became more complex and volatile.

On the 1st, Chancellor Adolf Hitler received his most enthusiastic ovation in the Saar on the day the territory was transferred from French to German control. Hope was expressed at the ceremonies that the transfer would help pacify rising tensions in Europe. However, nothing was pacific in Saarbruck that day as ecstatic celebrants rejoiced when the Fuhrer addressed them as "my Saarlanders."

German troops march through Saarbruck for the first time since the war.

Three days later, England announced a new, beefed-up defense policy. A White Paper report, signed by Prime Minister Ramsay MacDonald, stated British defense needs bolstering because of Germany's "aggressive spirit" and because "all over the world . . . armaments are being increased."

British concern about Germany heightened when the Third Reich announced on the 16th that it was reinstituting military conscription. The action breached the Versailles treaty's military clauses and the German press exalted the move with headlines like: "End of Versailles, Germany Free Again!" The text of the legislation stated that the German people will be protected from an "arms-bristling Europe only through the rebirth of the German army." Responses were predictably mixed with most the great powers upset—France, discouraged but not surprised; England, angered but willing to send Foreign Minister John Simon to Berlin for negotiations; and Japan, outwardly silent, appeared to be happy with the renewal of German militarism.

Britain sent Anthony Eden to Moscow to confer with Stalin and Molotov.

A week later, Mussolini followed suit by expanding Italy's conscription laws to include the class of 1911. By this time next month, Italy will have one million men armed and ready to fight. While many Europeans are uncertain what Mussolini's motives are, it is clear the increase in military clout is for the European situation and not for the Italian operations in Ethiopia, which don't require such strength. The dictator told crowds at a Fascist celebration: "I wish the whole Italian people to know that no event will catch us unprepared."

The meeting between England's Simon and Hitler did take place, but little good was gained. Hitler condemned the Soviet Union as an instigator of war and disclaimed any intent to attack Lithuania.

Finally yesterday, Russia and Britain agreed that to maintain peace, collective security measures in the League of Nations must be created. Author J.L. Garvin wrote in support of such measures: "There will be peace if Britain is strong and known to be; there will be war if she is weak and thought to be" (→ 4/7).

Upon renouncing the Versailles treaty, Hilter staged a great display in Berlin.

1935

APRIL

Su	Mo	Tu	We	Th	Fr	Sa
	1	2	3	4	5	6
7	8	9	10	11	12	13
14	15	16	17	18	19	20
21	22	23	24	25	26	27
28	29	30				

1. U.S. Supreme Court orders new trial in Scottsboro case (→ 12/9).

1. Japan rejects alliance with Reich (→ 1/15/36).

2. Thomas Hart Benton exhibit opens in New York.

3. Austria to increase army, plans two-year service (→ 7/4).

3. Ethiopian troops massing on border of Italian Somalia (→ 6/3).

7. Danzig voters reject dominance by German Nazis (→ 11).

8. Emergency Relief Appropriations Act allots $5 bil. for relief and jobs programs (→ 5/1).

11. Italy: Stresa Conference opens to discuss German threat (→ 17).

12. Germany: Reich Chamber of Writers excludes all non-Aryan members (→ 26).

13. Experimental Cinema Center founded in Italy.

17. Geneva: League Council unanimously condemns German rearmament (→ 20).

19. 500,000 watch Johnny Kelley win Boston marathon.

19. German army pays Hitler a birthday tribute.

20. Berlin: Reich rejects League verdict on rearmament (→ 5/11).

21. Bulgarian King Boris arrests several high officers, forestalling army revolt.

21. Earthquake off coast of Formosa kills 2,000, leaves 13,000 homeless.

22. Poland: Parliament dissolved by new constitution (→ 3/1/37).

24. Nicaragua thwarts attempted army coup (→ 5/31/36).

25. New York limits autos to three people in front seat.

26. Berlin: 15,000 turn out for rally against religion (→ 30).

30. Berlin: Court upholds Hitler's plea for non-belief in Naziism as grounds for divorce (→ 7/30).

DEATH

6. Edwin Robinson, American poet.

U.S. hit by dust storm

April 11. Increasingly severe dust storms are hanging like a black scourge over about half of the United States, destroying millions of dollars worth of wheat crops, forcing untold numbers of people to flee from their farm homes as from a plague, and completely paralyzing all activity in some districts.

The brunt of today's storm fell on western Kansas, eastern Colorado, Wyoming, western Oklahoma, nearly all of Texas and parts of New Mexico. Breathing was not only difficult but dangerous. While human beings could protect themselves with masks of every sort, all livestock suffered miserably. Dust pneumonia is rapidly increasing among children. And the crop damage is staggering in this, the "nation's breadbasket."

Little relief is in sight, as dust piles up inside houses, schools and businesses are closed, traffic is stopped and bereaved families are unable to bury their dead. In Texas, even the birds are afraid to fly.

Great clouds of dust cover the arid land of the Texas Panhandle.

Publisher Ochs of N.Y. Times is dead

April 8. In 1896, Adolph Ochs, owner of the Chattanooga Times, arrived in New York aiming to become a big-city publisher. He had been told by a reporter that The New York Times was for sale. Its circulation had fallen to 9,000 and it was losing $1,000 a day. With only $75,000, mostly borrowed, Ochs gained control of The Times. One of his backers was J.P. Morgan. Ochs proclaimed he would print the news "without fear or favor." By the time of his death today at 77, the paper's circulation had risen to nearly 500,000 daily and over 700,000 Sunday.

Adolph Ochs.

Montreal Maroons win Stanley Cup

April 9. Hockey-mad Montreal was in a frenzy following the return of the Stanley Cup to the Quebec city. Their Maroons upset the Toronto Maple Leafs with their third victory in a row, 4-1, over their Canadian rivals.

Professional hockey was born in Montreal and it was there in 1893 that Lord Stanley presented a trophy in his name with the directions that it was to be a challenge trophy. The Montreal Canadians and Toronto Arenas were among the charter members when the National Hockey League was formed in 1917. Expansion came in 1926 with the addition of the New York Rangers, Chicago Black Hawks and Detroit Cougars. That year, the season schedule of 44 games for each of the ten teams was also inaugurated.

Pan Am launches Orient air service

April 16. A giant Pan American Clipper seaplane took off from San Francisco this afternoon in the first step toward air service that eventually will span the Pacific.

The Sikorsky S-24 flying boat, powered by four 700-horsepower engines and carrying a crew of six, is expected to arrive in Hawaii in 16 hours. It will later fly on to Wake Island, Guam and the Orient. Advance parties of technicians are working on the operating bases needed to establish regular passenger, cargo and mail service over the 8,500-mile route to China. The only cargo on this trip is a 102-pound package of 8,000 air mail letters, many sent by stamp collectors. Some 5,000 spectators turned out to watch the plane fly over the Golden Gate to start its historic flight.

Soviets inaugurate first subway section

April 23. The first section of the Moscow subway has been opened to the public, and 150,000 Muscovites are crowding in each day to take advantage of the free rides being offered until service begins officially next month. The subway is a Soviet showpiece, with broad staircases, marble pillars, the first escalators to be installed in the Soviet Union and ornamental lighting fixtures. No two stations are alike in design.

The first seven and a half mile section of the subway, which eventually will run through all of Moscow, was built in record time. Plans were drawn in 1931 and construction began in 1933. Almost every Moscow resident has done some work on the subway. Soviet dictator Joseph Stalin took a ride last night, waving to surprised workers.

1935

MAY

Su	Mo	Tu	We	Th	Fr	Sa
			1	2	3	4
5	6	7	8	9	10	11
12	13	14	15	16	17	18
19	20	21	22	23	24	25
26	27	28	29	30	31	

1. Resettlement Administration set up by executive order under Rexford Tugwell to help impoverished farmers relocate (→ 6).

1. Boulder Dam completed after four years, 354 days (→ 7/21).

2. Paris: France, U.S.S.R. sign pact of mutual assistance.

4. Omaha wins Kentucky Derby with jockey Saunders (→ 6/8).

5. Athens military tribunal sentences Venizelos, in Paris exile, to death for attempted anti-monarchist coup (→ 10/10).

6. Works Progress Administration (WPA) created by executive order (→ 11).

6. Britain celebrates royal Silver Jubilee.

7. John Ford film "The Informer" released.

11. FDR creates Rural Electrification Administration to provide energy loans (→ 23).

11. Germans fortify Schleswig defying treaty ban (→ 6/18).

16. U.S.S.R. agrees to protect Czechoslovakia from invasion.

18. Moscow: World's largest plane Maxim Gorky crashes, killing 49.

19. Czech Nazis strengthen position with Sudeten Party victory in elections (→ 11/2).

22. London: Britain to triple air force by 1938 (→ 6/27).

23. U.S. Senate upholds presidential veto over Patman Bill; vets not allowed to cash in on bonus until 1945 (→ 27).

25. Michigan: Jesse Owens sets long jump record of 26.5 feet.

29. French launch liner Normandie on maiden voyage (→ 6/3).

30. Kelly Petillo wins 23rd Indy 500 at 106.2 mph in Gilmore Special racer.

30. Pakistan: Earthquake devastates Quetta, killing 26,000.

DEATHS

12. Marshal Joseph Pilsudski, Polish leader (*12/5/1867).

21. Jane Addams, American feminist, social reformer, founded Hull House (*9/6/1860).

NRA closing down as WPA begins work

May 27. The NRA, one of the chief recovery weapons of the New Deal, has been ruled unconstitutional today by the United States Supreme Court. In a unanimous decision, the court held that the National Industrial Recovery Act, under which the NRA has operated since mid-1933, exceeded constitutional limits by allowing government intervention in the setting of wages and hours in private industry.

The court decision was a severe blow to President Roosevelt and his advisers. But it brought rejoicing on Wall Street, where bankers and top industrialists termed the court action the "best thing in years." And many key Republicans in the Congress called the controversial decision a vindication of recent attacks on the New Deal by former President Herbert Hoover.

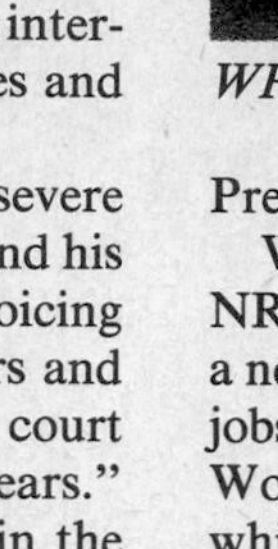

WPA will put the jobless to work.

While unhappy over scuttling NRA, the administration now has a new weapon in its fight to provide jobs for needy Americans. It is the Works Progress Administration, which is now providing jobs for thousands of construction workers, teachers, musicians, artists, actors and workers of all kinds (→ 6/4).

Lawrence of Arabia meets mundane end

May 19. Col. T.E. Lawrence, known to all as "Lawrence of Arabia," died this morning as a result of the severe injuries he suffered six days ago in a motorcycle accident in Dorset, England. The legendary leader of the Arab revolt against the Turks during the world war was killed as as he swerved to avoid hitting a boy on a peaceful country road. Regarded as a genius, Lawrence remarked in his book "Seven Pillars of Wisdom" that he "wrote (his) will across the sky in stars."

The mysterious Lawrence of Arabia.

Sequel: The Bride of Frankenstein

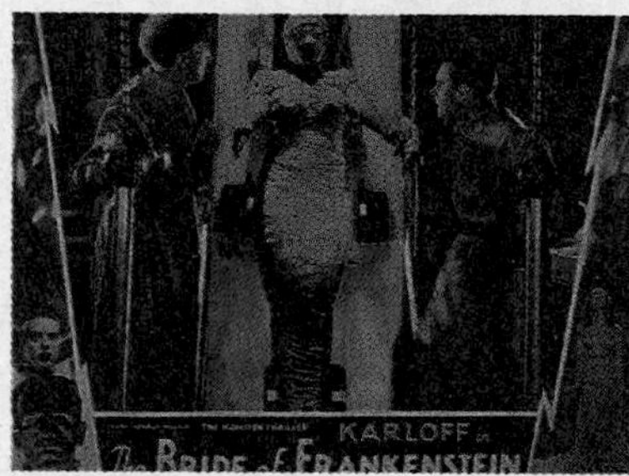

"The Bride of Frankenstein."

May. In 1818, English feminist Mary Wollstonecraft Shelley wrote a philosophical novel about isolation, prejudice and blasphemous ambitions. She would have been horrified to learn it became the horror film "Frankenstein," released in 1932. But she may have been pleased by its sequel, "The Bride of Frankenstein." This picture, now in release, has a prologue about Mary Shelley, while the film touches on her themes of loneliness and ostracism. It's plenty scary too.

"Frankenstein" and its sequel were both directed by James Whale. Whale lends them an expressionistic gloom and black humor. Boris Karloff simultaneously elicits sympathy and terror as the man-made monster. And Elsa Lanchester's performance as both Mary Shelley and the creature's bride can make one's hair stand on end.

1935

JUNE

Su	Mo	Tu	We	Th	Fr	Sa
						1
2	3	4	5	6	7	8
9	10	11	12	13	14	15
16	17	18	19	20	21	22
23	24	25	26	27	28	29
30						

1. Tornado and floods kill 250 in Nebraska.

2. Babe Ruth quits the Boston Braves.

3. Somalia: Ethiopians attack two Italian outposts; 30 natives killed (→ 7/13).

4. Herbert Hoover charges FDR with setting up European form of rule (→ 19).

7. Paris: Pierre Laval gets emergency powers to save franc.

7. London: Stanley Baldwin replaces Ramsay MacDonald as British prime minister.

10. Alcoholics Anonymous organized in New York City.

11. Washington grants Liberia recognition.

12. Buenos Aires: Bolivia and Paraguay agree to 12-day truce in Chaco War (→ 1/21/36).

12. Mussolini bars N.Y. Times for editorial criticism of Italian Fascists (→ 3/23/36).

13. New York: James Braddock outpoints Max Baer to take world heavyweight title (→ 6/22/37).

13. Explosion in German munitions plant kills 52.

14. Cardeas Cabinet resigns in Mexico.

15. Omaha: Martial law declared in wake of strike rioting.

16. Mexico City: 15,000 Catholics demonstrate for greater religious freedom (→ 7/10/37).

18. London: Britain offers Reich 35% naval ratio, 45% on U-boats (→ 7/8).

19. FDR asks inheritance tax, big levies on fortunes (→ 7/14).

25. N.Y.: Joe Louis KOs Primo Carnera in sixth round (→ 8/7).

27. British "Peace Ballot" results published; public opinion lends support to League, arms reductions (→ 7/16).

28. Alfred Perry wins British Open golf title.

DEATH

6. Oliver Wendell Holmes Jr., U.S. Supreme Court justice, legal theorist, legal realism (*3/8/1841).

Japanese forces squeezing Northern China

Japanese marines march through the seaport of Tsing-tao.

June 10. The Chinese Nationalist government in Nanking has acquiesced to Japanese demands that it remove one of its armies from Northern China. Japan, which had laid down an ultimatum to the Nanking government, also had demanded the right to approve all Chinese administrators in the Peking and Tientsin areas.

The Japanese moves were similar to those in Manchuria four years ago before the establishment of the Japanese-sponsored empire of Manchukuo. In complying with the Japanese demands, the Nationalist government of Chiang Kai-shek lost all political and military influence in Northern China.

There were reports that the next move by Japan would be to establish a self-governing zone in the Peking and Tientsin areas run by Chinese acceptable to the Japanese. The effect would be turn North China into a buffer zone between Manchuria and Central China, still held by the Nationalists (→ 10/13).

Lumber heir freed; calls Karpis captor

June 1. George Weyerhaeuser, kidnapped nine-year-old heir to a lumber fortune, was released unharmed at dawn for a $200,000 ransom. Immediately, federal agents and local officers swung into action. The hunt centers around Seattle, and repeated clues given by the boy point to the Alvin Karpis gang of kidnappers and killers.

The boy trudged six miles from where they let him out with a blanket and a $1 bill near Issaquah, 25 miles from Tacoma, Washington. He arrived at a chicken farm and announced, "I'm the little boy who was kidnapped."

He had been allowed to read newspaper stories about himself during his eight days of captivity. He said that he had been kept blindfolded much of the time. When his blindfold was removed, the men wore face masks.

Lindy helps invent an artificial heart

June 20. The creation of a "chamber of artificial life" that can keep vital organs alive outside the body for prolonged periods was announced today by Charles A. Lindbergh and Alex Carrel, the Nobel Prize-winning scientist. Writing in the journal Science, they said they had used their device to maintain thyroid glands, ovaries, adrenal glands, hearts and other organs from animals for periods ranging from days to weeks in their laboratory at the Rockefeller Institute for Medical Research in New York.

They said their chamber includes an artificial heart and a synthetic bloodstream that together supply the organs with the nutrients needed for survival. The chamber will help scientists isolate and study the factors essential to the growth and development of vital organs, Carrel and Lindbergh said.

Stylish Normandie awarded Blue Riband

June 3. France regained the transatlantic speed record for ships after 42 years today when the luxury liner Normandie arrived in New York after a crossing from Southampton at an average speed of 29.7 knots.

Carrying a crew of 1,250 and 1,070 passengers, the Normandie easily broke the 28.92-knot record set by the German liner Bremen on a trip from Cherbourg to New York. Even greater feats are expected from the Normandie, which averaged 31.5 knots during the last leg of the crossing. The last French vessel to hold the record was the Touraine, which set its mark in 1893. Cheering crowds lined the Manhattan waterfront today to greet the Normandie, which was escorted through the harbor to her berth by thousands of small boats.

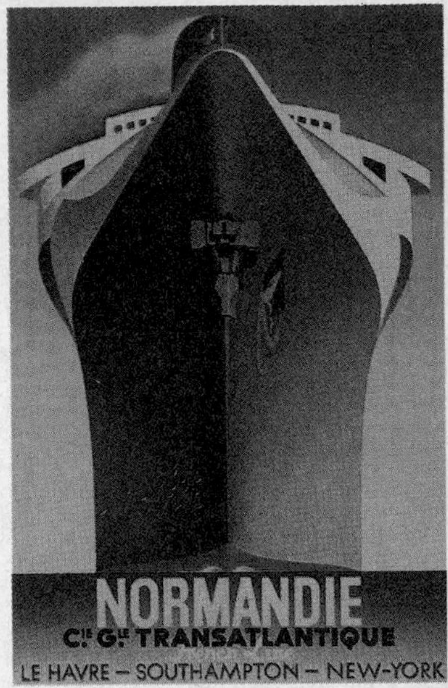

Poster for a great ship.

Omaha becomes third Triple Crown winner

June 8. Omaha waded through mud and rain to win the historic Belmont Stakes and become the third thoroughbred in horse-racing history to win the coveted Triple Crown. And to his owner, William Woodward, went the honor of being the one man to have bred and owned two Triple Crown winners. Omaha won by a length and a half, but there was no chance that runner-up Firethorn could catch him. He gallantly charged at Omaha at the head of the stretch, but then he had nothing left.

Omaha and jockey at Belmont.

June 30. Some 100,000 disciplined Soviet youths demonstrate their readiness to reinforce the Red army. In Moscow's Red Square, they form a hammer and sickle inside a five-pointed star.

1935

JULY

Su	Mo	Tu	We	Th	Fr	Sa
	1	2	3	4	5	6
7	8	9	10	11	12	13
14	15	16	17	18	19	20
21	22	23	24	25	26	27
28	29	30	31			

3. Japan: 104 die as Japanese cruiser sinks.

3. Cuba deports 15 American liberals, seized yesterday (→ 5/20/36).

4. Austria repeals anti-monarchy laws (→ 4/1/36).

5. Wimbledon: Fred Perry wins second 6-2, 6-4, 6-4 over Gottfried von Cramm; Helen Wills Moody 6-3, 3-6, 7-5 over Helen Jacobs for seventh title.

8. Germany announces it is building two battleships, 28 U-boats (→ 11/28).

12. Belgium opens diplomatic relations with U.S.S.R. (→ 8/26).

13. Haile Selassie rejects Italian sphere of influence in Ethiopia (→ 18).

14. 100,000 New York welfare recipients to get jobs under PWA (→ 8/3).

14. Paris: Hundreds of thousands watch military parade on Champs Elysees.

16. Britain's King George reviews huge naval fleet (→ 22).

18. Haile Selassie urges Ethiopians to fight to last man (→ 8/5).

21. Colorado: Boulder Dam reservoir now largest man-made lake (→ 4/30/47).

22. London: British end naval quotas, propose parley in 1942 (→ 2/24/36).

25. Communist Third Intl. convenes in U.S.S.R. (→ 8/30).

26. FDR frees 151 aliens from prison for deportation.

26. China: Devastating floods on Blue River kill 200,000.

26. New York: Communists raid liner Bremen, rip swastika off, throw it in Hudson (→ 8/28).

28. Belgian cyclist Romain Maes wins Tour de France.

29. New York: Racket inquiry begins; Thomas Dewey sworn in as special prosecutor.

DEATHS

3. Andre Citroen, French auto engineer (*2/5/1878).

12. Alfred Dreyfus, Jewish officer in French army, victim of national scandal (*10/19/1859).

New law protects American labor's rights

July 5. President Roosevelt has signed the National Labor Relations Act, which supports the rights of employees to join labor organizations and authorizes the National Labor Relations Board to investigate unfair employment practices.

Also called the Wagner Act, after its chief sponsor, Senator Robert F. Wagner of New York, it is seen as a landmark piece of legislation for workers. It requires management to recognize unions, bargain collectively with them and prohibits employers from interfering with a worker's right to join a union.

The bill was initiated after years of complaints that employers discriminated against those employees who enrolled in union membership. The Norris-LaGuardia Act of 1932, which outlawed two anti-labor weapons, the injunction and the "yellow dog contract," paved the way for the passage of this bill.

Naturally, the bill has been criticized by employers, who claim the government is unnecessarily interfering with their right to conduct business. Some voiced opinions that the act is in violation of the Constitution. Advocates of the legislation, however, seem certain it would pass a Supreme Court review (→ 14).

Paris, July 14. France's Popular Front, as the coalition of Communists, Socialists, Radical Socialists and other left-wing groups is called, displayed its strength today, Bastille Day, in huge demonstrations protesting the views of fascist leagues like the Croix de Feu.

Kingfish says FDR policy is mishmash

July 25. In another verbal assault on President Roosevelt, Senator Huey Long of Louisiana announced he would desert the Democratic Party in 1936 if FDR refused to drop his New Deal program. "I won't hesitate to bolt the Roosevelt New Deal convention," the Kingfish said yesterday, "unless he stops deliberately perverting the course he promised the people to follow."

Long called the president a "faker" without a "sincere bone in his body." He continued to advocate his "Share the Wealth Plan" as he mixed drinks for members of the press behind the bar of the Hotel New Yorker. (The senator assumed bartending responsibilities, claiming no one in the city knew how to mix a gin fizz.) Predicting revolution if conditions did not change, Long characterized the New Deal as "a combination of Stalinism and Hitlerism with a dash of Italian Fascism." The Louisiana dictator repudiated notions that his own program reeked of fascism (→ 9/10).

Nazi repression of Jews is intensified

July 30. Recent Berlin dispatches that the Nazis would abate their campaign against Jews, Catholics and "reactionaries" have not been borne out by the facts.

Not long ago, terror gripped Berlin's fashionable Kurfurstendamm as Jews, blood pouring down their faces, fled from a gang of 200 Nazi bullies who chased after them howling, "Destruction to Jews!"

Any cooperation of Germans with Jews brings punishment. Towns in the Cologne district forbid Jews to settle in them, and one has declared purchases from Jews "treason to the people." Jewish mail-order houses are mostly out of business as patrons fear to receive their parcels. Under Julius Streicher's orders, boycotts have even reached minor services, such as barbers, and arrests of "race defilers" are not uncommon. In Breslau, 24 Jews and "Aryan" girls, so charged, were taken away to concentration camps, the men to Lichtenberg, the girls to Moringen (→ 9/10).

1935

AUGUST

Su	Mo	Tu	We	Th	Fr	Sa
				1	2	3
4	5	6	7	8	9	10
11	12	13	14	15	16	17
18	19	20	21	22	23	24
25	26	27	28	29	30	31

2. British pass Government of India Act, separating Burma, Aden from India (→ 2/8/36).

3. Washington: 18,000 musicians to get jobs in federal arts relief program (→ 14).

5. Haile Selassie likens Ethiopia-Italy conflict to David and Goliath (→ 6).

6. Italy: Mussolini calls up three divisions, 300,000 men (→ 15).

7. Chicago: Joe Louis KOs King Levinsky in first round (→ 9/24).

13. Italy: 1,000 die in flood as dam collapses near Turin.

15. London ready to let Italy take land in Ethiopia (→ 18).

18. Paris talks fail as Italy rejects economic concessions, demands control of all Ethiopia (→ 26).

21. St. Louis: Lou Gehrig sets record with 17 grand slams.

21. Benny Goodman opens at Palomar Ballroom (→ 3/3/37).

26. Public utilities placed under jurisdiction of SEC (→ 30).

26. Ethiopia: Evacuation of Addis Ababa begins as war threat grows (→ 9/3).

26. U.K., Latvia insist Moscow stop exporting revolution (→ 31).

28. Berlin: Clarence Campbell, American eugenist, hails Nazi racial policies (→ 9/6).

30. U.S.S.R.: Third Intl. ends, advocating alliance of left and liberals against fascism.

30. Revenue Act passes U.S. Congress, raising inheritance taxes (→ 10/26).

31. FDR signs first Neutrality Act, forbidding arms shipments to countries at war (→ 2/29/36).

31. Cordell Hull charges Soviets aim to overthrow U.S. political and social structure (→ 9/2).

BIRTHS

31. Eldridge Cleaver, writer, black activist, "Soul on Ice."

31. Frank Robinson, first black to manage U.S. baseball team.

DEATH

17. Charlotte Perkins Gilman, American feminist theoretician (*7/3/1860).

Social Security enacted

SOCIAL SECURITY ACT
ACCOUNT NUMBER
002-03-3122
HAS BEEN ESTABLISHED FOR
RICHARD LANCASTER KRAYBILL
WORKER'S SIGNATURE Richard L. Kraybill
FOR SOCIAL SECURITY PURPOSES • NOT FOR IDENTIFICATION

A major accomplishment, but only for those in commercial and industrial jobs.

Aug 14. President Roosevelt signed into law the Social Security Act today, fulfilling a 1932 campaign promise. In that year, the Democrats pledged: "We advocate unemployment and old-age insurance under state laws." Now, America joins many other industrial nations in providing comprehensive care for its elderly, handicapped and unemployed. Payroll taxes will fund the legislation which has taken over 14 months to enact; conservatives have fought the bill since FDR proposed it last June. One congressman believes the bill will "threaten the integrity of our institutions." But the majority of congressmen feel it will relieve the burden of many Americans (→ 26).

U.S. warns Soviets: Stay out of America

Aug 25. The State Department issued a "most emphatic protest" to the Soviet government to cease its interference in "the internal affairs of the United States." A note presented by Ambassador William C. Bullitt to the U.S.S.R. stated that the U.S. "anticipates the most serious consequences" if the infiltration of Communist groups into American organizations is not halted.

Earlier this month, the Communist International announced it intended to infiltrate American labor unions. This prompted leaders of the American Federation of Labor to plan strategies to fight Communist tactics of "boring from within." It is expected the A.F.L. will deal with Communist propagandists' attempts to influence union decisions at its annual convention in October.

Such interference hinders "the maintenance of friendly relations" between the two nations, according to the text of today's warning. The Soviets have yet to respond, but some say they will refuse to discuss the matter (→ 8/5/36).

Scientists discover Vitamin E crystals

Aug 20. Successful isolation of pure crystals of vitamin E, the most elusive of the vitamins, was announced today by Herbert McLean Evans, head of the Institute for Experimental Biology of the University of California. Reporting at the annual meeting of the American Chemical Society, Evans said the vitamin was isolated from wheat germ by a chemical process using cyanic acid. Evans, who discovered vitamin E in 1922 and later showed that it plays an essential role in animal reproduction, said the feat will soon make possible commercial production of the vitamin and its use to treat human sterility.

The isolation of vitamin E caps a remarkable decade of research. Vitamin B-1 was isolated in 1926, vitamin D in 1930, vitamin A in 1931, vitamin C in 1932 and vitamin B-2 in 1933. All of these vitamins now can be synthesized in the laboratory and mass-produced, making possible their use to prevent such vitamin deficiency diseases as pellagra, rickets and beri-beri.

Rogers and Post die in Alaska air crash

Aug 16. America was shocked to learn today that its most popular humorist, Will Rogers, and famed aviator Wiley Post have died in a plane crash. Rogers and Post were touring Alaska, just starting a ten-minute hop from an Eskimo village to Point Barrow, when their plane engine died. The craft plummeted into a frozen riverbank, killing both men instantly. An Eskimo ran three hours to Barrow to bring the news.

Earlier in the day, fog had forced Rogers and Post to lay low in a town outside Anchorage. Some construction workers there spotted them and struck up a conversation. One of the workers gave Rogers a fresh batch of cookies. "They're good," said Rogers, reboarding the plane, "but I'll toss them out if we can't get off the ground."

Will and Wiley just before takeoff.

Aug 17. American painter Childe Hassam died today at 85. "Winter in Union Square" (above) displays his love of Impressionism.

1935

SEPTEMBER

Su	Mo	Tu	We	Th	Fr	Sa
1	2	3	4	5	6	7
8	9	10	11	12	13	14
15	16	17	18	19	20	21
22	23	24	25	26	27	28
29	30					

2. Japan protests to Moscow over propaganda spread by Comintern.

3. Hurricane sweeps Florida, killing over 200.

3. League of Nations arbitration tribunal rules neither side at fault in Ethiopia-Italy conflict (→ 13).

6. New York: Louis Brodsky releases six men charged in riot on liner Bremen (→ 14).

9. Geneva: Czech Edvard Benes elected President of League Council.

10. Germany: Seventh NSDAP Congress opens in Nuremburg (→ 15).

12. N.Y.: Wilmer Allison takes U.S. tennis title at Forest Hills.

13. Geneva: Pierre Laval places France behind League, isolating Italy (→ 26).

14. Washington: Cordell Hull apologizes to Reich for Louis Brodsky's talk against Nazi rule (→ 3/5/37).

15. Berlin: Reich adopts swastika as national flag.→

17. Philippines: Manuel Luis Quezon wins presidency in first elections under own constitution (→ 18).

18. Douglas MacArthur named to supervise organization of Filipino army (→ 11/14).

23. Berlin: Nazis planning to buy out all Jewish firms (→ 10/1).

24. New York: Joe Louis KOs ex-title holder Max Baer in fourth round (→ 8/18/36).

26. Washington: $90 million pay raise settles four-day coal strike; 40,000 back to work.

26. Geneva: League decides to invoke sanctions if Italy resorts to war (→ 30).

30. Italy: 30,000 Italian troops sent to Africa (→ 10/2).

30. Gershwin's "Porgy and Bess" opens for dry run in Boston before going to New York (→ 10/10).

BIRTH

17. Ken Kesey, American writer, "One Flew Over the Cuckoo's Nest."

Huey Long assassinated in Baton Rouge

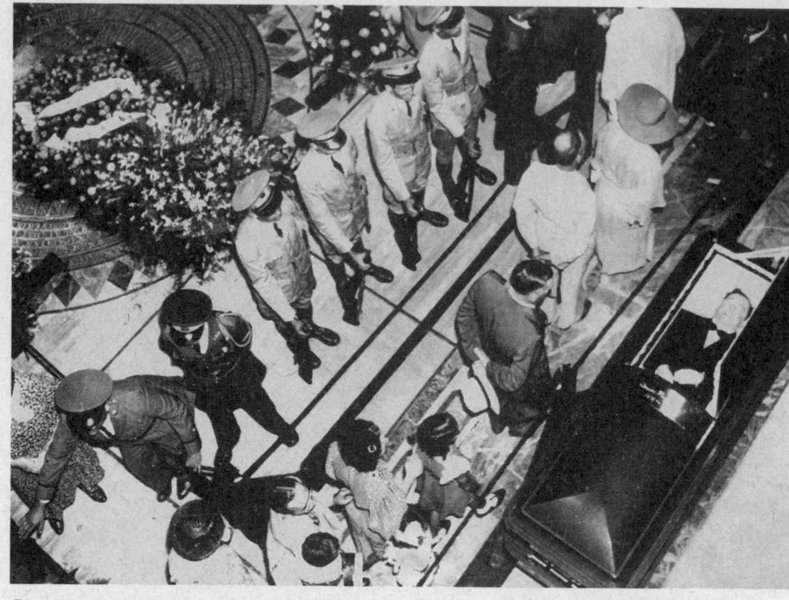

Louisiana mourners file slowly by the coffin of their benevolent dictator.

Sept 10. Senator Huey Long died today after doctors conducted a third blood transfusion in a last-ditch effort to prolong his life.

The Louisiana dictator was gunned down Sunday night by Dr. Carl Weiss, a leader of an anti-Long faction and son-in-law of Judge B.H. Pavy, also an opponent of the senator. Weiss shot Long in the stomach just outside the chambers of the Louisiana House of Representatives, where among the legislation being enacted was a gerrymandering of Judge Pavy's judicial district which would have virtually prevented his re-election. Weiss was then killed by the senator's bodyguards.

Many Louisiana residents are grief-stricken over the loss of their leader and recalled that a month ago Long predicted there would be an assassination attempt on his life.

Senator Thomas of Utah, one of Long's political colleagues, on hearing of the attack, remarked, "Shooting always invites more shooting. It cannot bring better conditions. The American system of recall is to use ballots not bullets."

Nazis' new laws ban Jews from politics

Sept 15. In Nuremberg today, Adolf Hitler unveiled new laws that state categorically Jews are not German citizens and therefore can never vote or participate in German politics. The laws on German "citizenship, blood and honor" prohibit Jews from: marrying German citizens; having extra-marital relationships with German citizens; employing German women less than 45 years old; raising the German flag. The new law says violators will be sentenced to prison terms (→ 23).

The Reich has put the swastika on its new official flag.

Malcolm Campbell exceeds 300 mph

Sept 3. Sir Malcolm Campbell, the British land speed ace, set a world record today when his racing car Bluebird made two runs over a measured one-mile course on the Bonneville Salt Flats in Utah at an average speed of 301.337 miles per hour. Campbell broke his own record of 276.816 miles per hour, set last March at Daytona Beach.

Born in 1885, Campbell has been a racing enthusiast since boyhood, and over the years he has set numerous speed records for motorcycles, airplanes, automobiles and motorboats. He was knighted for these accomplishments in 1931. But today's feat is surely his greatest.

At Daytona in March, Campbell hit 276 mph in his monstrous Bluebird.

Hughes plane hits 351 miles per hour

Sept 15. Howard Hughes sped his airplane four times over a closed course at an average speed of 351 miles per hour today to set a new aviation speed record. The old record, 328 miles per hour, was set by Hughes only yesterday.

Crowds gather to watch Hughes fly.

1935

OCTOBER

Su	Mo	Tu	We	Th	Fr	Sa
		1	2	3	4	5
6	7	8	9	10	11	12
13	14	15	16	17	18	19
20	21	22	23	24	25	26
29	28	29	30	31		

1. Sports made compulsory in German schools (→ 12).

2. Large Italian force invades Ethiopia (→ 3).

2. Hayden Planetarium opens in New York.

3. Ethiopia: Italian planes bomb Adowa, Adigrat; 1,700 die (→ 5).

5. FDR embargoes arms to Italy and Ethiopia (→ 7).

7. Detroit: Tigers win World Series in six games over Chicago.

7. Geneva: League Council finds Italy at fault for war in Ethiopia, moves for sanctions (→ 11).

10. "Porgy and Bess" opens in New York.

10. Greece: Natl. Assembly restores monarchy; George Condylis named regent until King George's return (→ 11/3).

11. Geneva: League places arms embargo on Italy, lifts ban for Ethiopia (→ 13).

12. Jazz banned from German radio broadcasts (→ 11/17).

13. Ethiopia: Mussolini annexes Adowa (→ 16).

13. Moscow protests Japanese raids on Soviet-Manchurian border (→ 11/9).

14. New York: Lindbergh baby-killer Bruno Hauptmann given 30-day stay of execution for appeal to Supreme Court (→ 12/9).

16. American oil companies to sell to Italy despite British plea for embargo (→ 19).

16. New Jersey: A.F.L. urges Olympic boycott (→ 11/6).

19. Geneva: 50 nations vote to boycott Italian exports (→ 28).

23. Gangster Dutch Schultz gunned down in New Jersey.

26. Referenda in 16 farm states support continuation of Agricultural Adjustment Admin. by 6-1 vote (→ 1/6/36).

28. Hungary institutes eight-hour work day.

31. China: Premier Wang Ching-wei assassinated (→ 12/1).

DEATHS

20. Arthur Henderson, founder British Labor Party (*9/13/1863).

Mussolini's armies invade Ethiopia

Oct 28. Italian troops advanced up to 50 miles along their southern front in Ethiopia today. The Fascists control a 400-mile stretch of land from British Somaliland all the way to the British colony of Kenya.

The northern front was relatively quiet today. Italian planes remained grounded. And there were no new charges from Ethiopia that Italy bombed civilian hospitals.

Italy is consolidating its gains in the north following its recent annexation of Adowa. The city is festooned with flowers and flags as Italy savors the fruits of victory that were denied her at Adowa in the last war in 1896.

Emperor Haile Selassie has vowed to fight back the Italian invasion by mobilizing up to ten million men. But his military commanders have taken little action in the last few days. They are hoping that rain will slow down the Italian tanks and trucks while they rely on mules and horses. Privately, a top aide to the emperor has conceded that the war could be over in six weeks.

The war has sharply increased friction between Italy and Britain because Sir Anthony Eden pushed hard for sanctions to punish Benito Mussolini. The League of Nations called for the sanctions after a decisive vote condemning the Italian government for its invasion.

British warships are on patrol in the Mediterranean, and Italy has warned it will treat a blockade as an act of war. France has told Britain it will assist the fleet only if Britain pledges to help France in a time of need. France is apparently worried about the German threat (→ 11/18).

Selassie, seated at center, is a powerful symbol of Ethiopian nationalism.

Communists reach Yenan after long march

Oct 20. Mao Tse-tung's dream has become a reality and his inspiration a legend. His long march is over. Mao's exhausted Communist army has arrived in Yenan, in the North of China, less than a year after it left Kiangsi province in the South. The army marched 6,000 miles.

The trek was not without cost. The army was attacked by Chiang Kai-shek's Nationalist forces. Some 30,000 men arrived in Yenan, and 100,000 died along the way.

But the long march has also turned Mao into a legendary hero and made him the top leader among Communists. Other party leaders have already approved Mao's plan for a united, Communist China. Mao also converted more Chinese to communism along the route of the march. And he has a new power base in Yenan, where he will create a Communist government that he hopes will be supported throughout Chensi province (→ 31).

Yenan headquarters. From left: Mao, UP's Earl Leaf, Chu Teh, Madame Mao.

Painter Charles Demuth dead at 52

"I Saw the Figure 5 in Gold."

Oct 23. Charles Demuth, an artist born and educated in Pennsylvania, died today. He progressed from gentle watercolors to Cubist-Realist works inspired by the geometric shapes of modern technology. "I Saw the Figure 5 in Gold" (1928) may be his best-known painting.

1935

NOVEMBER

Su	Mo	Tu	We	Th	Fr	Sa
					1	2
3	4	5	6	7	8	9
10	11	12	13	14	15	16
17	18	19	20	21	22	23
24	25	26	27	28	29	30

2. Prague: Czechs arrest 28 alleged German spies (→ 12/14).

3. Greece: Plebiscite turns out 95% majority in favor of return of King George (→ 25).

6. Berlin: Hitler promises to remove anti-Jewish signs during 1936 Olympics (→ 21).

9. China: Japanese troops invade Shanghai (→ 27).

11. South Dakota: Albert Stevens and Orvil Anderson set altitude record, floating to 74,000 feet in balloon.

12. Texas: Mob of 700 lynches two Negroes accused of murder (→ 5/10/37).

13. Cairo: Two dead, 88 hurt in anti-British riots (→ 12/12).

14. Conservatives win majority in British elections.

14. Manuel Luis Quezon sworn in as first Filipino president, as Commonwealth of the Philippines is inaugurated (→ 7/4/46).

15. Washington: U.S. signs trade treaty with Canada.

17. Berlin: Rudolph Hess calls on Reich peasants to foil "Jewish Bolshevization" (→ 30).

18. League nations begin economic sanctions against Italy, yet reject crucial oil embargo (→ 19).

19. Ethiopia: 2,000 killed in Italian air raid (→ 12/6).

21. U.S. Protestants ask for Olympic boycott (→ 7/11/36).

21. New Jersey: 16-year-old Jacob Ciemiengo gets death sentence for murder.

22. Pan Am inaugurates first transpacific airmail service, San Francisco to Manila.

25. Brazil: President Vargas declares martial law to fight rebels holding Natal.

27. China: Japanese troops move into Peking and Tientsin provinces (→ 30).

28. Berlin: Reich declares all men 18 to 45 army reservists (→ 1/17/36).

30. Philadelphia: Army tops Navy 28-6 in football.

30. Berlin: Reich makes non-belief in Naziism grounds for divorce (→ 12/21).

Lewis heads industrial union committee

Nov 9. President of the United Mine Workers John L. Lewis will preside over the newly formed Committee of Industrial Organizations. The C.I.O. will attempt to unionize skilled, unskilled and white-collar workers in the steel, auto and textile industries who have traditionally resisted efforts to enlist them into the ranks of the American Federation of Labor and other groups.

The creation of the new organization comes in response to workers' dissatisfaction with the cautiousness of the A.F.L. The C.I.O. is expected to run into conflict with the A.F.L., particularly under the leadership of the dynamic and sometimes volatile Lewis. One of his biggest gripes with the federation has been its refusal to enlarge its executive council so that "new blood" might be "injected into the old guard." Lewis will now have the opportunity to work with new union members, as the C.I.O. is expected to generate a high enrollment.

A.F.L. Pres. William Green, Sec. of Labor Frances Perkins, first female Cabinet member, and Lewis.

Pro-Japanese coup takes over North China

Nov 30. A pro-Japanese coup was staged in Northern China with the creation of an autonomous state in Hopei province. Yin Ju-keng, who was named Commissioner of the demilitarized zone in North China created following the withdrawal of Chinese troops, announced that the zone could be turned into an autonomous state known as the Autonomous Federation for Joint Defense against Communism. The capital will be in Tungchow, only 12 miles from Peking.

Yin said the new state would recognize Chinese sovereignty, but that he would "work closely" with Japan "for the rescue of China." General Sung Cheh-yuan, commander of the Peking-Tientsin garrison, sent a telegram to the Nationalist government stating the autonomy move was beyond the control of local authorities (→ 3/19/36).

Greeks vote for King; George II returns

Nov 25. King George II of Greece became the first of those monarchs deposed during the Great War to experience restoration when he set foot on his native land after a 12-year exile. His friendly if not exuberant welcome indicates less than total enthusiasm from the Greeks, despite last month's referendum favoring his return.

The restoration caps recent infighting between the Populist and Liberal Parties. It also seemingly ends the distinguished career of Eleutherios Venizelos, statesman, former President and Liberal leader whose objection to the Populist-backed restoration led him to stage a coup this past March. It was put down by another power broker in Greek politics, General Georgios Kondylis, who in June was named Deputy Premier in the new rightist government headed by Populist leader Tsaldaris (→ 8/4/36).

President Zaimis is forced out.

1935

DECEMBER

Su	Mo	Tu	We	Th	Fr	Sa
1	2	3	4	5	6	7
8	9	10	11	12	13	14
15	16	17	18	19	20	21
22	23	24	25	26	27	28
29	30	31				

1. Chiang Kai-shek named Chinese president (→ 12/25/36).

1. Iran, Iraq, Turkey, Afghanistan sign pact of non-aggression.

6. Ethiopia: Italian air raid destroys Dessye palace; 32 dead, 200 wounded (→ 18).

6. TWA "air hostesses" begin flying on 14-passenger DC-2.

9. U.S. Supreme Court denies Hauptmann appeal (→ 23).

9. London: U.S. asks for 20% naval cut as arms talks open (→ 1/15/36).

10. Nobel Prize for chemistry awarded to Irene and Frederick Joliot-Curie.

11. Frick Gallery opens in New York.

12. Egyptian nationalists restore constitution (→ 4/28/36).

14. Prague: Tomas Masaryk resigns Czech presidency; Benes to succeed (→ 10/16/37).

15. Detroit Lions win professional football title.

18. Anthony Eden becomes British for. sec. upon resignation of Samuel Hoare over rejection of plan to cede parts of Ethiopia to Italy (→ 1/5/36).

21. Germany: Jewish doctors forced to resign from private hospitals under Nuremburg Laws (→ 1/2/36).

27. Cold kills 212 across U.S.

29. Moscow says consumption of vodka down 50% since 1913.

BIRTHS

1. Woody Allen, American comedian, film director.

31. Sandy Koufax, American baseball pitcher.

CULTURAL EVENTS, 1935

Literature: John Steinbeck's "Tortilla Flat"; Clifford Odets' "Waiting for Lefty"; Thomas Wolfe's "Of Time and the River"; James T. Farrell's "Studs Lonigan."

Academia: Sidney and Beatrice Webb's "Soviet Communism: A New Civilization?"

Music: Prokofiev's ballet "Romeo and Juliet"; swing popularized by Benny Goodman.

DC-3, carrying 21, makes initial flight

American Airlines hopes the DC-3's 21 seats will turn them a profit.

Dec 21. The Douglas DC-3, a new airliner capable of carrying 21 passengers at nearly 160 miles an hour, made its first flight today. Designed by Donald Douglas, the new aircraft is an improved version of the DC-2, which has broken most airline speed and cargo records. The DC-3 has an enlarged fuselage for greater capacity and two 900-horsepower Curtiss-Wright engines, more powerful than those of the DC-2. The original version of the DC-3, ordered by American Airlines, had 14 beds to compete with railroad Pullman sleeper service, but other airlines demanded the 21-seat version.

Lindbergh family leaves the U.S.

Dec 23. Charles A. Lindbergh has given up residence in America and is on his way to establish a new home in England. With him, as passengers on a ship at sea, are his wife Anne and their son Jon, born in August 1932. After the kidnapping and death of their first-born three years ago, the couple has been plagued by threats promising the same fate for Jon (→ 1/30/36).

The Chicago Bears, pictured here showing a strong defense, have been at the peak of pro football since the NFL's inception in 1921. The third annual championship game this year, won by the Detroit Lions, was the first not to include the Bears.

Basic plastic and home color film

Introduction of the first color film for home photography and development of a tough new plastic with a wide range of uses are technological highlights of 1935. The new film, Kodachrome, makes color negatives or transparencies with the snap of a shutter. The plastic, polyethylene, can be used for water-resistant packaging and many other applications.

It Can't Happen Here, can it?

Socialism and Fascism were praised and excoriated in drama and literature this year. "It Can't Happen Here," by Sinclair Lewis, warned against Fascists spreading their doctrine across the Atlantic to the United States. "Soviet Communism: A New Civilization" tried to outline the advantages of Russia's present government. The authors, Beatrice and Sidney Webb, have been active in the English Labor Party. "Waiting for Lefty," a play by Clifford Odets, was a vehement cry for full employment and fair labor practices, two things democracy cannot always guarantee.

Movies offer an escape from hard times

Motion pictures offered several avenues of escape in 1935. Filmgoers, burdened with daily woes, gladly fled down those streets. Adventure, romance, classics and comedy waited there.

"Mutiny on the Bounty" offered all of the above. Clark Gable played Fletcher Christian, the 18th-century mutineer who pitted himself against the tyrannical Captain Bligh (Charles Laughton). Love was found upon the island Pitcairn with an exotic actress named Movita. "Captain Blood" was another swashbuckler starring Errol Flynn, a Tasmanian who made his first American film this year. "Lives of a Bengal Dancer," with Gary Cooper, was an action-packed tale of comrades in a British regiment.

"Anna Karenina," starring Greta Garbo, was the ultimate love story. Garbo played Tolstoy's tragic heroine beautifully. And why not? She played her before in "Love" (1927) with John Gilbert. Director Josef von Sternberg cast Marlene Dietrich as a heartbreaker once again in "The Devil Is a Woman." The picture is set against a lavish backdrop of 19th-century Spanish war. "Dangerous" is a tale of a woman reformed by the love of a man. Bette Davis delivers Oscar-level acting.

Two classics came to the screen: "David Copperfield" retells Dickens' tale faithfully; and Shakespeare's "A Midsummer Night's Dream" had music and special effects. James Cagney, as the man named Bottom, wore an ass's head on top. Perhaps the best time was spent at "A Night at the Opera." The Marx Brothers (Harpo et al) wreaked havoc. As usual.

Erroll Flynn is "Captain Blood."

The Marx Brothers go to the opera.

Laughton and Gable on the Bounty.

Hitchcock's latest is a delightful mix of comedy, romance and suspense.

1936

JANUARY

Su	Mo	Tu	We	Th	Fr	Sa
			1	2	3	4
5	6	7	8	9	10	11
12	13	14	15	16	17	18
19	20	21	22	23	24	25
26	27	28	29	30	31	

1. Pasadena: Stanford wins Rose Bowl 7-0 over SMU.

2. South Africa: 19 killed by giant hailstones.

2. Berlin: German officials say Nazi treatment of Jews is not League's business (→ 2/11).

3. Poland gives amnesty to 27,000 political prisoners.

4. N.Y.: Billboard magazine publishes first music hit parade.

5. Ethiopia: Daggha Bur razed by Italian bombs (→ 24).

6. U.S. Supreme Court finds Agricultural Adjustment Act unconstitutional (→ 24).

15. London: Denied parity, Japan quits naval talks (→ 2/29).

17. Chicago: Joe Louis KOs Charley Retzlaff in first round.

17. Paris: Nine Stavisky aides get jail terms for January 1934 embezzlement scandal.

21. Buenos Aires: Paraguay and Bolivia sign peace treaty ending Chaco War (→ 2/4).

21. King Edward VIII proclaimed in London (→ 28).

22. Paris: Premier Pierre Laval resigns over diplomatic failure in Ethiopian crisis.

23. Alabama: Heywood Patterson gets 75 years in Scottsboro case (→ 24).

24. Washington: House overrides FDR's bonus veto, allowing veterans immediate redemption of bonus certificates (→ 26).

24. Alabama: Scottsboro defendant Ozie Powell shot in escape attempt (→ 7/24/37).

26. Washington reports U.S. industrial output at five-year peak (→ 2/13).

28. Illinois: Infamous kidnapper Richard Loeb slashed to death by fellow inmate in prison.

29. New Jersey: Mabel Eaton loses custody of children for Communist affiliation.

30. N.J.: Gov. Harold Hoffman orders new inquiry into Lindbergh kidnapping (→ 2/6).

DEATH

27. Ivan Pavlov, Russian physiologist (*9/26/1849).

George V dies, succeeded by Edward VIII

Jan 28. As massed bagpipes of his Highland regiments wailed laments of his Northland and the pipes of his own navy shrilled him home, King George V of England was laid to rest today in St. George's Chapel in Windsor amid the tombs of his ancestors and a general mourning such as England has never before seen. He was 70 years old.

Neither has Britain ever equalled the magnificence of the royal procession. Behind the gun carriage bearing his body walked the President of France, ambassadors, ministers and military leaders from all over the world, a score of princes and five Kings —Haakon of Norway, Carol of Rumania, Leopold of Belgium, Christian of Denmark and Boris of Bulgaria.

In London, the cortege was delayed by three million mourners, with 7,000 fainting cases reported, as his loyal subjects paid their last respects to their "good" king. His own ideal, expressed in a public speech and exemplified in private life, was the family, fidelity, brotherhood and peace.

His eldest son, who now reigns as King Edward VIII, has declared his determination to follow his father's example and work for the welfare of all classes (→ 12/11).

George V lies in state in London.

Edward VIII succeeds.

First big battle fought in Ethiopia

Jan 24. Italy is claiming its first major victory since its invasion of Ethiopia. After three days of fierce fighting on the northern front, Italy says its troops killed 8,000 Ethiopian forces and took another 4,000 prisoner. Ethiopia has not conceded defeat in the fighting at Makale, however. Its military leaders estimate they have killed or imprisoned about 3,000 enemy troops.

An Italian communique says that its forces struck after learning that Ethiopia was massing troops in the south for a major assault. The attack apparently took the Ethiopians by complete surprise. The Italian assault with tanks and artillery was impeded at first by heavy rainfall, but Marshal Badoglio's men overcame the obstacle.

The reported Italian victory follows a rout of Ethiopian troops in the south. Those forces are under the command of Ras Desta Demtu, the son-in-law of Haile Selassie.

The Italian victory evened the score after Demtu, helped by heavy rains, repulsed the Italians in the south at the beginning of the month. Then, 60,000 Ethiopians forced 40,000 enemy forces to retreat (→ 2/28).

Goebbels seeks colonies for raw materials

Jan 17. In a fiery speech before 18,000 Nazis, German Minister of Propaganda Dr. Joseph Goebbels declared that Germany must soon have colonies. "The German people," he said, "are a truly poor nation. We have no colonies and no raw materials."

Goebbels, a hypnotic orator.

Referring to the army's increasing need of copper, wool and other products either not or insufficiently produced in Germany to equip the new military establishment, he said, "We can get along with butter, but never without cannon."

Meanwhile, in the wake of the recent Nuremberg laws denying citizenship to German Jews, agents of good faith have relayed to Jewish citizens prominent in Great Britain a Nazi plan calling for the mass deportation of German Jews to Palestine, or British territories, if British and American Jews reimburse Germany for the subsequent removal of Jewish capital. Since such compensation may be made only in the form of German goods, the plan would really subsidize German industries and exports. The alternative would be a further tightening of the screws of Jewish persecution in Germany (→ 3/7).

Kipling, famed for tales of India, dies

Jan 18. Rudyard Kipling, one of Great Britain's foremost authors, died at the age of 70 early this morning at the Middlesex Hospital in London. Perhaps best known for his masterpieces about India, Kipling wrote volumes of prose and poetry. Among his most celebrated works are "The Man Who Would Be King" and "Kim," which portray his various styles —from army barracks dialect to sophisticated British parlance. Denied the Poet Laureateship for his references to Queen Victoria, Kipling was the first Englishman to win the Nobel Prize for literature in 1907.

His work was so voluminous that the English language is left with scores of Kiplingesque phrases, from "the white man's burden" to "East is East and West is West and never the twain shall meet."

1936

FEBRUARY

Su	Mo	Tu	We	Th	Fr	Sa
						1
2	3	4	5	6	7	8
9	10	11	12	13	14	15
16	17	18	19	20	21	22
23	24	25	26	27	28	29

4. Switzerland: German Nazi leader Wilhelm Gustloff slain by Jewish youth (→ 20).

4. Paraguay ousts war hero Rafael Franco for communist sympathies (→ 18).

5. New York: U.S. indicts Teamsters in trucking racket.

6. Washington: Atty. Gen. Cummings refuses to reopen Lindbergh kidnapping case (→ 4/3).

6. Germany: Hitler opens IVth Winter Olympics in Garmisch-Partenkirchen (→ 28).

8. India: Jawaharlal Nehru elected president of Indian Natl. Congress (→ 4/12).

11. Construction begins on Treasure Island in San Francisco Bay.

11. Chaplin's "Modern Times" opens in London.

11. Berlin: Reich arrests 150 Catholic youth leaders (→ 3/9).

13. Washington: First social security checks put in mail (→ 6/10).

13. France: To counter rightist violence, government bans Action Francaise (→ 5/3).

15. Chicago: "Machine Gun Jack" McGurn slain.

16. Spain: Manuel Azana takes premiership at head of new popular front government (→ 21).

18. Paraguay: President Eusebio Ayala resigns as army rebels seize capital (→ 3/11).

20. Switzerland bars Nazis from entering country.

21. Spain: Amnesty declared for 30,000 political prisoners as leftist riots hit Madrid (→ 3/15).

23. Russia: Unmanned balloon rises to record height of 25 miles.

24. London: For. Sec. Eden says Britain must be strong to prevent war in Europe (→ 3/9).

28. Ethiopia: Italians take Mt. Alaji, avenging massacre of 1895 (→ 3/2).

29. Washington: FDR signs second Neutrality Act, banning loans to belligerents (→ 3/23).

DEATH

8. Charles Curtis, vice president under Hoover (*1/25/1860).

German Volkswagen makes its debut

German manufacturers have made the compact VW 30 entirely from steel.

Feb 26. Built by Ferdinand Porsche, the Volkswagen, which means "people's car" in German, has been born. The first factory to manufacture the vehicle has just been inaugurated by Adolf Hitler at Fallersleben, Saxony. The Germans are admirers of the American automaker Henry Ford. With the Volkswagen, Hitler seeks to emulate Ford by undertaking mass production of a low-priced car.

Adolf Hitler opens Winter Olympics

The U.S. hockey team loses to Italy.

Feb 28. Chancellor Adolf Hitler declared open the Winter Olympics at Garmisch-Partenkirchen earlier this month and there followed the most successful Games to date. Sonja Henie of Norway won the figure-skating title for her third straight Olympics and helped to attract many of the 500,000 spectators who attended. The program was expanded to include Alpine events, with women competing for the first time, as well as cross-country relay races. Norwegians swept all of the major titles.

Pitcher matches Washington's feat

Feb 22. Johnson winds up. He delivers. It's a strike! Right across the river! Walter Johnson, pitching ace, stood on the bank of the Rappahannock River for this pitch. As part of a ceremony for George Washington's Birthday, the baseball hero threw a silver dollar from one bank to another, duplicating the first President's legendary feat.

Japanese military coup is thwarted

Feb 29. An attempted coup by a group of young military officers was suppressed by the Japanese army, but only after causing considerable uncertainty about the future direction of the Japanese government.

The militarist insurgents, numbering about 1,000, seized several government buildings and assassinated several government officials, including Korekiyo Takahashi, the aged Finance Minister. Initially, it was reported that Premier Keisuko Okada had been killed in his home, but after the coup was put down, Okada emerged from hiding. His miraculous escape resulted from the fact that the assassins did not know him by sight and mistakenly killed his brother-in-law. Prince Kimmochi Saionji, one of the elder statesmen advising Emperor Hirohito, also narrowly escaped assassination.

For three days, there was a bloodless standoff in the center of Tokyo. The Imperial Guard surrounded the rebels, who defied repeated orders to return to their barracks. Finally, under a threat to use force, the insurgents capitulated, and Captain Teruzo Ando, the leader of the mutiny, shot himself. The insurgents were said to have been dissatisfied over government financing of the military and upset over the influence of big business in the government. The speculation in Washington was that the upheaval would lead to a Japanese government dominated by the army (→ 3/9).

In "Modern Times," Chaplin's first in five years, the master sticks to pantomime and proves a film doesn't need to talk to be popular or artistic.

1936

MARCH

Su	Mo	Tu	We	Th	Fr	Sa
1	2	3	4	5	6	7
8	9	10	11	12	13	14
15	16	17	18	19	20	21
22	23	24	25	26	27	28
29	30	31				

2. Geneva: League sends ultimatum to Italy; peace in Africa or oil sanctions (→ 23).

4. Washington: FDR turns gold key, opening Norris Dam in Tennessee.

7. Germany: Hitler sends troops into Rhineland, violating Locarno Pact.→

9. London: For. Sec. Eden says Britain will not give France military aid to force Reich out of Rhineland (→ 25).

9. Tokyo: Koki Hirota forms Cabinet empowering military (→ 7/6).

9. German press warns Jews who vote will be arrested (→ 4/5).

11. Paraguay sets up first fascist regime in Americas.

12. London: Four Locarno powers condemn Reich action in Rhineland (→ 14).

14. Munich: Hitler tells crowd of 300,000 Germany's only judge is God and itself (→ 29).

15. Madrid: Army threatens to act if Premier Azana cannot curb civil strife (→ 4/7).

19. U.S.: Floods sweep 12 Midwest states; 134 dead, 200,000 homeless.

19. U.S.S.R. signs pact of assistance with Mongolia against Japan (→ 6/2).

23. Washington: School Superintendant Harold Campbell bars teaching of pacifism (→ 5/1/37).

23. Mussolini nationalizes key defense industries (→ 29).

25. London: Britain, U.S. and France sign naval accord (→ 30).

29. Berlin: Plebiscite gives Hitler 99% vote of confidence (→ 9/7).

29. Ethiopia: Italians firebomb Harar; city of 40,000 destroyed (→ 4/9).

30. Britain announces naval construction program of 38 warships, largest in 15 years (→ 4/14).

BIRTH

3. Ursula Andress, Swiss actress.

DEATH

18. Eleutherios Venizelos, Greek ex-premier (*8/23/1864).

Nazis enter Rhineland

The first detachment of German infantry goose-steps into Cologne.

March 7. It has been almost a year to the day since Adolf Hitler re-established obligatory military service in Germany. Today, he put his troops to use. They crossed into the Rhineland, which is supposed to be a demilitarized area.

The military action violates the treaties of Versailles and Locarno. But Hitler, in a speech to the Reichstag, called it "the close of the struggle for German equality." The Fuhrer explained that Germany is no longer bound by the treaties because of the mutual assistance pact between France and the Soviet Union. Hitler said he moved his troops because of the Communist threat and what he called France's "iron ring around the Reich."

Hitler was also concerned by overtures made by France toward Great Britain for a defense treaty. Tonight, British Foreign Secretary Anthony Eden harshly condemned the German move into the Rhineland, but Britain shows no signs of taking any military action (→ 12).

At the movies: Muni; Grant and Hepburn

March. Two films getting plenty of publicity this month are "Sylvia Scarlett," starring Katharine Hepburn and Cary Grant, and "The Story of Louis Pasteur" with Paul Muni. Hepburn won an Oscar in 1933 for "Morning Glory"; Muni may have his turn with his strong performance in "Louis Pasteur."

Grant and Hepburn team up.

"The Story of Louis Pasteur."

17,000 Ky. Colonels

March 27. State Attorney General B.M. Vincent demoted 17,000 Kentucky Colonels, saying their terms had expired when the Governor who issued them retired. "No person has the right now to be designated as a Kentucky Colonel," the attorney general said (→ 4/27).

1936

APRIL

Su	Mo	Tu	We	Th	Fr	Sa
			1	2	3	4
5	6	7	8	9	10	11
12	13	14	15	16	17	18
19	20	21	22	23	24	25
26	27	28	29	30		

1. Austria violates 1919 Treaty of St. Germaine, reinstating military draft (→ 5/15).

2. Austro-Czech trade treaty signed.

3. New Jersey: Lindbergh baby killer Bruno Hauptmann executed (→ 12/5/37).

5. Berlin: Germans who failed to vote losing jobs (→ 5/26).

6. U.S.: Tornadoes sweep South, killing 421.

7. Madrid: Socialists in Parliament oust President Zamora (→ 5/10).

7. South Africa passes Representation of Natives Act, allowing Negroes to register to vote, but not to run for office (→ 4/2/37).

8. Paris: French propose plan for intl. commission to rule Europe.

9. Italy admits plan to set up puppet state in Ethiopia (→ 30).

11. Turkey requests revision of 1923 Lausanne Convention to regain control of Dardanelles (→ 7/20).

12. Nehru urges socialism for India (→ 10/16).

14. London: French ask Britain to guard Belgium (→ 5/8).

18. New York: Racketeer "Lucky" Luciano jailed; bail set at $350,000 (→ 6/18).

20. Germany parades military power on Hitler's birthday.

22. Public enemy number two John Torrio arrested in New York City.

24. Akron, Ohio: Five-week Goodyear strike ends; company union retains recognition.

25. Monte Carlo: Opening performance of Tchaikovsky's "Nutcracker Suite."

26. New York: Socialist Labor Party nominates John Aiken for president (→ 5/25).

27. Rank restored to 17,000 Kentucky Colonels.

29. New York: Admirers storm Carnegie Hall for Arturo Toscanini's farewell performance.

DEATH

30. A.E. Housman, American poet and scholar (*3/26/1859).

1936

Ethiopia seen yielding capital to Italians

April 30. Ethiopia's defenses against Italy have crumbled, and Italian forces are poised to take the capital. The streets of Addis Ababa are jammed with refugees seeking a way out, and there are few army troops to be seen. The defense of the Ethiopian capital has been left to the small police force.

Benito Mussolini has been ruthless in his determination to crush the forces of Haile Selassie. "Security will be achieved in the full," he told his Cabinet, "with the total annihilation of Ethiopian military formations, and this annihilation cannot fail and is not distant."

Mussolini's ground troops have been backed by the air force, which is still dropping cannisters of mustard gas on civilians as well as the enemy. The poisonous gas has disabled, asphyxiated and burned Ethiopian soldiers and created large gaps in their lines.

Red Cross units have also been decimated by the gas. There are few doctors or nurses to treat wounded Ethiopian soldiers.

Most observers do not believe the emperor's men can hold out much longer. They are on the run, and they are no match for the advancing Italian armor (→ 5/3).

A proud chieftain, fighting for Italy.

Arabs resist Jewish entry; 11 more dead

April 21. The Tel Aviv-Jaffa district of Palestine has been wracked by violence again as clashes between Arabs and Jews resulted in 11 killed and 50 wounded. With British troops standing guard, the curfew law has been invoked.

Elsewhere, Arabs at a huge demonstration in Nablus decided to go on strike indefinitely until Britain stopped both Jewish immigration to Palestine and the sale of land to Jews. They declared that Britain alone was responsible for the trouble here because she was pursuing the wrong policy (→ 7/3).

The flag of Islam waves in Jaffa.

Farouk succeeds to Egypt's throne at 16

Young Farouk, ready to take over.

April 28. Prince Farouk is King of Egypt tonight, following the death of his father, King Fuad. Farouk, studying at a London military academy, will reach Egypt later this week. The 16-year-old will be assisted by a regent (→ 5/2).

MAY

Su	Mo	Tu	We	Th	Fr	Sa
					1	2
3	4	5	6	7	8	9
10	11	12	13	14	15	16
17	18	19	20	21	22	23
24	25	26	27	28	29	30
31						

2. Egypt: Nationalists gain in first elections under King Farouk (→ 11/14).

2. Jockey I. Hanford rides Bold Venture to victory in Kentucky Derby.

3. France: Popular Front gains electoral victory (→ 6/8).

3. Rome: Mussolini says 400,000 Italians will stay in Ethiopia as settlers (→ 9).

4. New Jersey: Atomic power used to cure cancer in mice.

8. Britain sends questionnaire to Hitler to clear up questions about his ambitions (→ 14).

9. Mussolini annexes Ethiopia, proclaims self emperor.→

9. Dirigible Hindenburg arrives in Lakehurst, N.J., completing first scheduled transatlantic flight (→ 5/6/37).

10. Madrid: Cortes appoints ex-President Manuel Azana head of Spanish government (→ 6/16).

10. Census reports U.S. population at 127.5 million.

14. Missouri: Doctors assail use of drugs for painless childbirth.

14. London: Stanley Baldwin seeks to bring Germany, Japan and U.S. into League (→ 7/14).

16. New York: Samuel Reshevsky becomes U.S. chess champ.

18. Mexico: 50,000 rail workers on strike; communist flags raised over train stations.

20. Havana: Miguel Gomez sworn in as president (→ 12/24).

24. Philadelphia: Tony Lazzeri hits two grand slams in one game.

25. Cleveland: Socialists nominate Norman Thomas for president (→ 6/12).

25. Britain accuses Italy of stirring up nationalism in Palestine, India through radio broadcasts.

26. Berlin: 276 monks on trial for immorality (→ 6/17).

27. England: Queen Mary sets out on maiden voyage.

30. Louis Meyer takes 24th Indy 500, averaging 109.1 mph.

31. Nicaragua: National Guard fails in attempt to seize palace (→ 12/8).

Schuschnigg heads only Austrian party

Schuschnigg before the Vienna Diet.

May 15. Chancellor Kurt Schuschnigg has consolidated his control over Austria by assuming command of the Fatherland Front, the country's only authorized political party. At an assembly of party leaders in Vienna, Prince Ernst von Starhemberg, the former Vice Chancellor, was stripped of his leadership of the Fatherland Front.

Instead, amidst smiles among party officials, Prince Starhemberg was named patron of the Fatherland Front's Mothers' Help Section. The prince was en route to Rome to attend an Austrian-Italian soccer match and was not in a position to object to his humiliation. The effect of the move was to give Schuschnigg full control over Austria's military forces, including the militia which had been commanded by Prince Starhemberg. Schuschnigg said he had assumed leadership of the Fatherland Front because the grave problems facing Austria forced him to unite leadership of the nation. Dual control, he said, had brought difficulties to Austria (→ 6/1).

Italy conquers Ethiopia

An Italian column sets up camp in unfamiliar terrain near Gondar, Ethiopia.

May 9. Benito Mussolini's Palazzo Venezia was bathed in bright light tonight and crowds packed into the square as the Duce proclaimed victory in Ethiopia and the rebirth of an empire.

"Italy at last has her empire," Mussolini boasted as the people cheered. "It is a Fascist empire because it bears the indestructible sign of the will and power of Rome."

Ethiopia has been formally annexed to Italy, Mussolini said. Victor Emmanuel, the King of Italy, will also assume the title of Emperor. Marshal Pietro Badoglio, the victorious general, has been named Viceroy. He will administer the new colonial territory in Africa.

Badoglio entered Addis Ababa four days ago. Part of the capital city had been pillaged and burned after the quick departure of Haile Selassie. But Badoglio was saluted by long lines of Italian soldiers and Ethiopian civilians as he took possession of the city.

In Geneva, the League of Nations shows no signs of lifting its sanctions against Italy, despite the end of the war. For his part, Mussolini is trying to patch up relations with Britain. "Believe me," the Premier told the Daily Mail, "this victory in East Africa puts Italy into the group of satisfied powers" (→ 6/6).

May 30. Driver Lou Meyer and his mechanic, after speeding to an unprecedented third victory in the Indy 500. Meyer also won in 1928 and 1933.

Spengler, prophet of decline, is dead

May 8. Oswald Spengler, the German historian and philosopher who won worldwide fame as the author of "The Decline of the West" (1918-22), is dead at age 55.

Trained in mathematics and the natural sciences, Spengler argued in his famous work that history follows organic laws of growth, and that every culture is destined to decay. Western culture is now in its twilight, according to Spengler, and will fall prey to mass manipulation and materialism. His rejection of Nazi racial theories led to his ostracism after Hitler came to power.

Gloomy Spengler, shunned by Hitler.

FBI captures two long-sought men

May 13. The FBI nabbed two kidnappers, Thomas Robinson Jr. and Alvin Karpis. Robinson was tried and convicted this afternoon; Karpis, captured today, goes on trial within a week. FBI chief J. Edgar Hoover claims neither man had a chance to "get away with it."

On Oct. 10, 1935, Robinson hit socialite Mrs. Alice Stoll over the head with a lead pipe and abducted her from her New York home. He led FBI officials on an unmerry chase. He received a life sentence.

Karpis kidnapped brewery king William A. Hamm in 1933 for a $100,000 ransom, and a St. Paul banker in 1934 for $200,000. The Department of Justice offered a $5,000 bounty for him. Karpis was cornered in New Orleans (→ 7/27).

1936

JUNE

Su	Mo	Tu	We	Th	Fr	Sa
	1	2	3	4	5	6
7	8	9	10	11	12	13
14	15	16	17	18	19	20
21	22	23	24	25	26	27
28	29	30				

1. Austrian Chancellor Schuschnigg makes state visit to Rome (→ 7/11).

2. China: Canton demands war on Japan, seeks to rally all of China (→ 7/17).

6. Haile Selassie arrives in England (→ 15).

9. Rome: Mussolini names son-in-law Count Ciano foreign minister (→ 10/25).

10. Cleveland: Herbert Hoover calls New Deal fascism (→ 20).

14. Puerto Rico names model city Eleanor Roosevelt.

15. London: Britain abandons sanctions against Italy (→ 20).

16. Madrid: 36 churches burned in 48 hours (→ 7/13).

17. Berlin: Heinrich Himmler named head of Reich police (→ 9/7).

19. New York: Max Schmeling KOs Joe Louis in 12th round (→ 8/18).

19. William Lemke announces intent to split from Republican Party, run on Union ticket with populist support (→ 27).

20. FDR lifts arms embargo on Ethiopian war (→ 30).

20. Robinson-Patman Act passes U.S. Congress, barring price-lowering to drive out competition (→ 7/22).

22. U.S. Congress grants Virgin Islands right to elect own legislature.

25. American Airlines conducts first commercial DC-3 flight.

27. Philadelphia: FDR and John Garner nominated on Democratic ticket (→ 28).

28. N.Y.: Communist Party picks Earl Browder for president (→ 9/30).

29. Queens: Work officially begins on New York World's Fair (→ 4/26/38).

30. Geneva: Fascists in uproar as Haile Selassie appears at League meeting (→ 7/25).

DEATHS

14. Gilbert K. Chesterton, British essayist (*5/29/1874).

14. Maxim Gorky, Soviet writer (*3/16/1868).

Leon Blum forms leftist government

Blum (center) and first Cabinet.

June 8. Just five days after taking office, French Premier Leon Blum, backed by his new coalition government of Socialists and Communists, has negotiated a sweeping, national labor agreement. The pact should end the strikes which paralyzed France and swept Premier Albert Sarraut out of office.

The agreement, approved by labor and management leaders, provides pay raises that average 12 percent, a 40-hour work week, two weeks of paid vacation, collective bargaining and binding arbitration.

"For the first time in history," one labor leader said, "an entire class will see its living conditions improved immediately."

Spontaneous strikes and occupations of factories have disrupted production, but they have been orderly for the most part. There has been little violence, and workers even organized factory parties (→ 7/5).

Republicans choose Landon and Knox

June 12. Governor Alfred M. Landon of Kansas has been nominated as the Republican candidate for president. His running mate for the vice-presidential spot will be Colonel Frank Knox, the publisher of the Chicago Daily News.

The Landon nomination climaxed a day in which the Republicans, meeting in Cleveland, adopted a platform critical of President Roosevelt and his New Deal programs, saying that the Democratic administration has usurped the powers of Congress, flouted the Supreme Court and violated the rights and liberties of the people. But at the same time, the GOP platform embraces some social welfare programs of the New Deal (→ 19).

Landon faces a tough task.

Luciano, big mobster, guilty on 62 counts

"Lucky" on his way up the river.

June 18. Charles "Lucky" Luciano has been found guilty on 62 counts of compulsory prostitution. His eight co-defendants face a maximum 25 years in prison. Luciano himself may receive life. He ran a $12 million-a-year prostitution ring in New York City since 1933.

Luciano monopolized the business in New York, employing 1,000 women in a total of 200 "houses." He lived in luxury at the Waldorf-Astoria Hotel, dipping into the narcotics racket and loan sharking. Nearly 120 women, former employees, testified against Luciano. The state will pay them $36,000 for their helpful deposition (→ 1/26/62).

1936

JULY

Su	Mo	Tu	We	Th	Fr	Sa
			1	2	3	4
5	6	7	8	9	10	11
12	13	14	15	16	17	18
19	20	21	22	23	24	25
26	27	28	29	30	31	

2. Rome: Pope orders world drive to raise film standards.

4. Geneva: League abandons Ethiopia, discontinuing sanctions on Italy (→ 9/18).

5. Paris: Many injured as police battle rightists (→ 3/16/37).

6. Japan: 17 officers sentenced to death for Tokyo mutiny (→ 8/24).

11. N.Y.: Jesse Owens wins two spots on Olympic team (→ 8/1).

11. Berlin: Hitler signs pact with Schuschnigg, conceding Austrian freedom (→ 10/10).

11. New York: 200,000 cross Triboro Bridge on opening day.

11. L.A.: Police disperse 2,500 striking Mexican citrus growers with tear gas.

13. Madrid: Monarchist chief Jose Sotelo murdered (→ 19).

14. U.S.: Heat-wave death toll reaches 3,000.

14. London: Britain begins mass production of gas masks, one for each citizen (→ 10/22).

16. London: King Edward escapes attempt on life.

17. China: Cantonese leader Chen Chi Tang flees China as uprising collapses (→ 19).

19. Spanish army uprising in Morocco spreads to south Spain; Franco lands in Cadiz with foreign legion troops (→ 20).

19. China: Chiang takes Kwantung, provoking Japan (→ 10/1).

20. Switzerland: Montreux Conference authorizes Turkey to fortify Dardanelles.

20. Madrid revolt crushed; 25,000 estimated dead (→ 21).

21. Two U.S. warships head for Spain to protect nationals (→ 24).

22. Virginia: Sec. of Int. Ickes flips power switch, starting first fully automated farm (→ 9/1).

24. Spain: Mola forms junta of national defense as provisional government in Burgos (→ 28).

25. Berlin recognizes Italian conquest of Ethiopia (→ 9/18).

27. St. Paul: Mobster Alvin Karpis gets life sentence.

28. Spain orders churches confiscated, decrees government control of industry (→ 31).

Perry, Jacobs win Wimbledon singles

Perry lunges for a forehand volley.

July 8. Fred Perry breezed past Baron Gottfried von Cramm so easily in taking his third straight Wimbledon title that fans wondered what was wrong with the German star. It turned out that von Cramm strained a thigh muscle on his opening service and played the rest of the match in pain. Helen Jacobs won her final against Mrs. Hilda Krahwinkel Sperling by 6-2, 4-6, 7-5. It was her first British title.

Jew kills himself at League session

July 3. A Czechoslovakian shot himself today during a session of the League of Nations to protest the treatment of Jews in Germany. Stefan Lux, a 48-year-old Jewish journalist associated with a Prague newspaper, killed himself during a sparsely attended conference. Letters in his briefcase explained his act meant to draw attention to the plight of German Jews (→ 1/12/37).

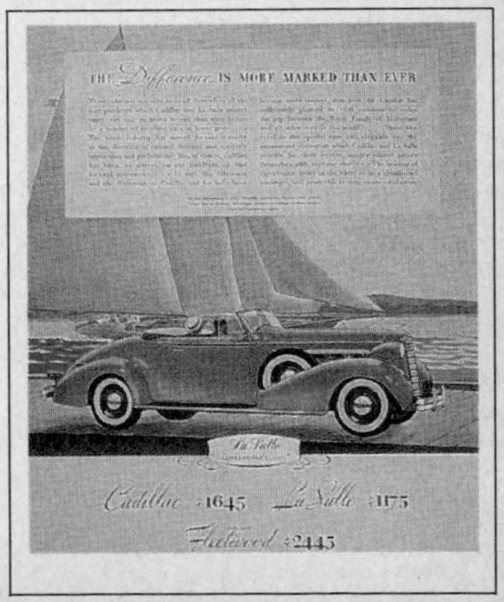

Rightist forces start war against Republican Spain

July 31. The civil war that erupted in Spain earlier this month has spread quickly around the entire country. General Francisco Franco, leader of the Fascist troops, vows to press on until he has installed himself in Madrid. Loyalist forces are under orders to fight the rebels to the death and turn the Guadarrama Mountains north of Madrid into the "tomb of Fascism."

The outbreak of war unleashed tensions throughout Europe. New reports that Italy dispatched planes to Spanish Morocco to assist Franco have only heightened the alarm.

France has sent an urgent appeal to Britain and Italy, calling for a joint conference that would emphasize the need for neutrality in the war. The British Foreign Office reacted coolly to France's appeal.

The United States acted quickly to remove Americans trapped by the war. About 150 Americans ran for shelter in the Madrid Embassy. Many of them are sleeping on floors and in bathtubs.

The Coast Guard cutter Cayuga snatched up American refugees in San Sebastian, and other Americans took refuge in Saint Jean de Luz. Ambassador Claude Bowers fled to his summer residence at Fuenterrabia, close to the French border. The Cayuga will hover near his residence for the next few days.

The American liner Exeter made an unscheduled stop in Barcelona to evacuate more than 160 Americans. A great number of them are women and children.

Chilling stories of nighttime terror in Barcelona have residents there paralyzed with fear. The Loyalist military committee openly condones house searches by leftists. Individuals and whole families have been known to disappear during the night, and there have been reports of assassinations, even of priests and nuns, in isolated areas near the city.

In Madrid, the Interior Minister has ordered an end to house searches for rebels and arms. One report says hundreds of rebel officers have been arrested, and the capital is very tense. Officials have tried to ease concerns by announcing there is no shortage of food, but they have also warned citizens they will be prosecuted if they hoard food. Five thousand Loyalist troops are guarding the capital's water supply.

General Franco, who launched the civil war by landing at Cadiz with troops from Morocco, has since moved to Algeciras. He is trying to move up the coast to Malaga, which is considered a rebel stronghold. "No earthly power," Franco declared, "can check our triumphant movement. Spain is saved!" Franco demanded the resignation of the Republican regime.

Elsewhere on the southern front, leftists are marching on Seville. Off the coast, government planes bombed rebel positions in Palma on the island of Majorca. A number of insurgents tried to escape in small motorboats, but they were picked up by government submarines.

The rebels' march from the north toward Madrid has been slowed down by a vicious Republican counterattack. The government claims it has killed thousands of rebels.

In the north, rebels control the countryside around San Sebastian. Loyalist troops supported by Communists and Socialists have not been able to stop their steady advances. The rebels have reportedly been joined by thousands of Basques, and their aircraft have strafed the streets of San Sebastian.

The government's recent display of military might near Madrid has not been matched by its political strength. Franco's threat created so much instability earlier this month that Spain had three governments within 24 hours (→ 8/1).

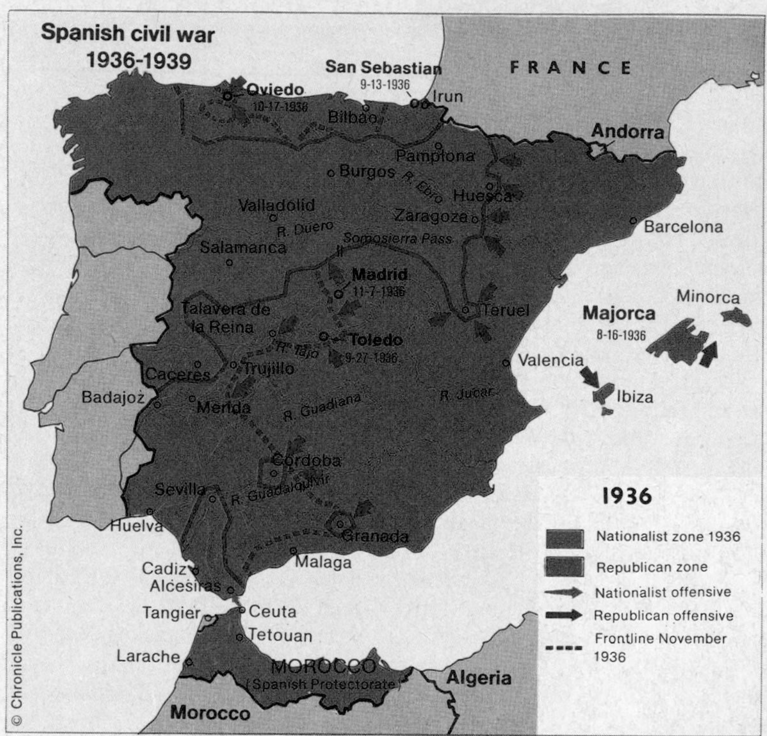

Republican Spain, ringed by northern rebels and Franco's Moroccan army.

Nationalists shell Loyalist positions. Franco's 30,000 troops in the south and Gen. Mola's 15,000 in the north seek to converge on Madrid by year's end.

Republican troops man a barricade in Madrid. The Spanish conflict is certain to divide further an already torn Europe.

1936

AUGUST

Su	Mo	Tu	We	Th	Fr	Sa
						1
2	3	4	5	6	7	8
9	10	11	12	13	14	15
16	17	18	19	20	21	22
23	24	25	26	27	28	29
30	31					

1. Berlin: 100,000 hail Hitler at Olympic opening ceremony (→ 16).

1. France: Leon Blum declares non-intervention in Spanish Civil War; asks European powers to follow (→ 7).

2. Tour de France won by Belgian racer Sylvere Maes.

4. Greece placed under military rule by Council President Ionnis Metaxas.

5. Washington: A.F.L. to suspend 10 unions unless they quit C.I.O. (→ 12/31).

7. U.S. proclaims non-intervention in Spain (→ 8).

8. Spain: General Francisco Franco promises liberal regime should revolt succeed (→ 15).

11. Berlin: Joachim Ribbentrop named Reich envoy to Britain.

15. Madrid: Leftists execute 733 priests (→ 16).

16. Spain: Rebels execute 1,200 Badajoz leftists (→ 17).

17. Spain: Rebels, with 80% of army on their side, begin shelling Irun and San Sebastian (→ 18).

18. New York: Joe Louis KOs Jack Sharkey in third round (→ 9/22).

18. Rome: Italy offers air help to Spanish rebels if France continues to aid Madrid (→ 21).

21. Berlin: Reich charges Soviet with libel for anti-Nazi radio broadcasts in Spain (→ 24).

24. Germany, Russia ban arms exports to Spain (→ 29).

24. Tokyo: Japan executes nine as Russian spies (→ 10/1).

26. Oslo: Trotsky signs pledge to avoid revolutionary activity while in Norway (→ 12/6).

29. Rumanian rightists depose Foreign Minister Titulescu for ties with Little Entente.

BIRTHS

1. Yves Saint-Laurent, French fashion designer.

21. Wilt Chamberlain, American basketball star.

DEATH

19. Federico Garcia Lorca, Spanish poet and playwright (*6/15/1899).

Soviets execute 16 alleged Trotskyites

Aug 25. There are no limits to the power of Joseph Stalin in Soviet Russia. Sixteen of his political opponents, all said to be Trotskyites, were executed today. Two of them were former Stalin allies, Grigori Zinoviev and Lev Kamenev.

All the defendants were tried for high treason. They were not allowed defense attorneys, but 200 spectators, including foreign diplomats, were permitted to watch the proceeding. Zinoviev and Kamenev had already been in custody for the assassination of Sergei Kirov, the Leningrad boss and Stalin confidante. During the trial, both confessed to plotting with the exiled Leon Trotsky to overthrow Stalin's government (→ 1/29/37).

Franco takes Badajoz, uniting rebel front

Left to rt.: Rebel Generals Calvalcanti, Franco and Mola visit Burgos.

Aug 29. There have been no trials in Badajoz, Spain. And the jails are empty. Rebel troops in this vicious civil war did not bother to take prisoners when they stormed into this town on the border with Portugal. They lined Loyalists up against the wall and fired. The streets of Badajoz are running with blood.

"In each street there was a barricade," a Portuguese journalist said, "and each was heaped with corpses. Women were searching among the corpses for their menfolk."

Moroccan troops under the command of Colonel Juan Yague were backed up by Legionnaires and Fascist militia when they surrounded the town Thursday night. They opened fire with artillery on Friday before their final assault.

Most of their victims were young and did not plead for mercy. Many did ask for a priest. Priests who had been fighting as Fascists heard their last confessions.

The Fascist victory in Badajoz was the biggest in the rebels' move north and west from Seville. Spain is now divided in half. Franco's troops hold the southwest and the north, and they are trying to open a line to connect the divided forces. The government is in control of Madrid, the northeast and part of the northwest. Both sides are trying to expand their control by appealing to civilians for support (→ 9/3).

British to control Suez for 20 years

Aug 26. Under the terms of the Anglo-Egyptian treaty signed today, Britain grants Egypt virtual independence but reserves for 20 years special rights regarding the ownership of the Suez Canal.

Technically, the canal remains under the aegis of the Suez Canal Company, of which Britain has long held controlling interest. Though the Canal Zone is theoretically neutral in time of war and open to all ships, Britain effectively blocked enemy shipping during the world war by its military presence in Egypt and the refusal by the Allies to grant enemy ships the right of asylum.

Dancers learn all you do is swing

Aug 5. Swing is in, and tonight dance instructors from around the nation met in New York to determine what exactly swing is. The dance, they agreed, is done in 4/4 time. Music depends on the drums, accented instead of syncopated. And there is the swing itself, men and women relaxing the hip and letting the gam fly. Teachers noted the popularity of the "conversation" dance, where a couple face each other, linked by one hand. The most popular bands playing swing music are Duke Ellington's, Count Basie's and Benny Goodman's.

Aug 31. The Queen Mary has recaptured the treasured Blue Riband for Great Britain, crossing the Atlantic at an average speed of 30.7 knots.

Jesse Owens star performer in Berlin

Aug 16. The Berlin Olympics ended with record crowds, record receipts and record performances, a smashing success for the German organizers, the 53 competing nations and 5,000 athletes.

Sixteen records were set and one equalled in the 23 events on the track and field program. The United States took 12 first places, more than all the other nations put together. However, the Olympic quest for peace and harmony among nations was again strained, this time by Chancellor Adolf Hitler.

Jews not only contributed to the United States Olympic coffers but were also among the visiting American athletes, much to the dismay of Hitler and his anti-Jewish National Socialist regime.

In addition, ten Negroes showed up on the talent-laden American team. Hitler has called Negroes an "inferior race." But they more than showed up; they made a shambles of the sprints and hurdles and dominated the field events as well.

The undisputed star of the show was a modest Negro athlete from Ohio State, Jesse Owens. He won the 100-and 200-meter dashes, the running broad jump and was on the winning 400-meter relay team. He also was in a drama with Hitler.

When Hans Woellke won the shotput on opening day, Hitler had the first German champion of any Olympics paraded before him. But when Owens and his "black auxiliaries," as Hitler called them, exploded on the scene, it was a far different matter.

Owens ran the 100 meters in a record 10.2 seconds but it was disallowed because of a following wind. Other Negroes also dominated their events. This put the Fuhrer on the spot. Hitler, who had congratulated other Olympic victors publicly, was faced with a dilemma: recognize the Negroes or flout world opinion by ignoring them.

His solution was to leave the stadium hastily, ostensibly because of threatening rain and the lateness of the hour. Hitler congratulated no other Olympic champions publicly. When Germans finished one-two in the hammer throw, he received them under the stands. Even when Lutz Long finished second to Owens in the broad jump, Hitler congratulated him privately and ignored Owens completely.

But when Owens completed his triumphal performance at the Olympics by winning the 200-meter race in a record 20.7 seconds, the spectators rose as one to pay tribute to the American Negro athlete from Ohio State, and the applause was thunderous. Of course, by that time Hitler again had left the stadium.

Americans Archie Williams and John Woodruff won the 400-and 800-meter races, respectively. Another American, Glenn Morris, won the decathlon.

Owens (left) in the 400-meter relay.

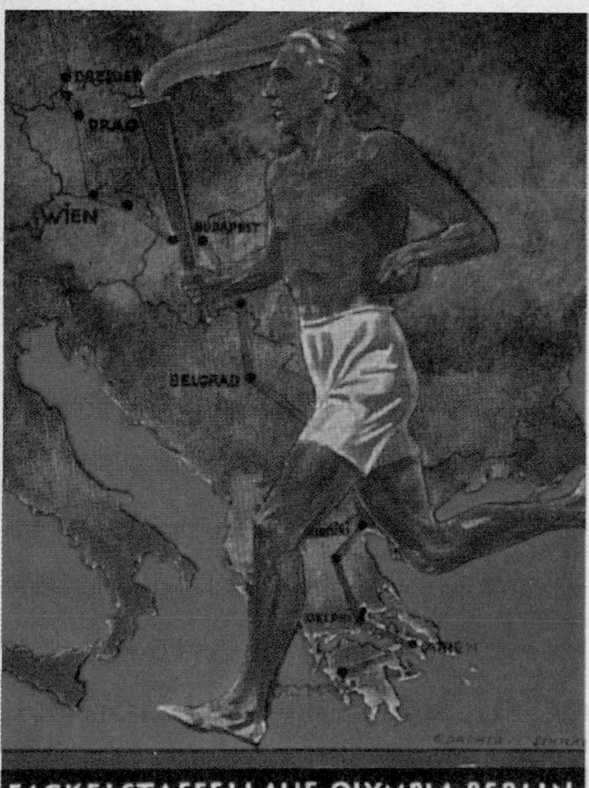

The Aryan images hanging over Berlin didn't stop Owens from winning four gold medals in track and field.

Men Athletics

100 M Dash		
1. Jesse Owens	USA	10,3
2. Ralph Metcalfe	USA	10,4
3. Martinus Osendarp	HOL	10,5
200 M Dash		
1. Jesse Owens	USA	20,7
2. Matthew Robinson	USA	21,1
3. Martinus Osendarp	HOL	21,3
400 M Run		
1. Archie Williams	USA	46,5
2. Arthur Godfrey Brown	GBR	46,7
3. James Lu Valle	USA	46,8
800 M Run		
1. John Woodruff	USA	1:52,9
2. Mario Lanzi	ITA	1:53,3
3. Philip Edwards	CAN	1:53,6
1500 M Run		
1. John Lovelock	NZL	3:47,8
2. Glenn Cunningham	USA	3:48,4
3. Luigi Beccali	ITA	3:49,2
5000 M Run		
1. Gunnar Höckert	FIN	14:22,2
2. Lauri Lethinen	FIN	14:25,8
3. Henry Jonsson	SWE	14:29,0
10,000 M Run		
1. Ilmari Salminen	FIN	30:15,4
2. Arvo Askola	FIN	30:15,6
3. Volmari Isohollo	FIN	30:20,2
Marathon		
1. Kitei Son	JAP	2:29:19,2
2. Ernest Harper	GBR	2:31:23,2
3. Shoryu Nan	JAP	2:31:42,0
110 M Hurdles		
1. Forrest Towns	USA	14,2
2. Donald Finlay	GBR	14,4
3. Frederick Pollard	USA	14,4
400 M Hurtles		
1. Glenn Hardin	USA	52,4
2. John Loaring	CAN	52,7
3. Miguel White	PHI	52,8
3000 M Steeplechase		
1. Volmari Isohollo	FIN	9:03,8
2. Kaarlo Tuominen	FIN	9:06,8
3. Alfred Dompert	GER	9:01,2
400 M Relay		
1. USA (Jesse Owens, Ralph Metcalfe, Foy Draper, Frank Wykoff)		39,8
2. ITA (Orazio Mariani, Gianni Caldana, Elio Ragni, Tullio Gonelli)		41,1
3. GER (Wilhem Leichum, Erich Borchmeyer, Erwin Gillmeister, Gerd Homberger)		41,2
1600 M Relay		
1. GBR (Frederick Wolff, Godfrey Rampling, William Roberts, Arthur Godfrey Brown)		3:09,0
2. USA (Arold Cagle, Robert Young Edward O'Brien, Alfred Fitch)		3:11,0
3. GER (Helmut Hamann, Friedrich von Stulpnagel, Harry Voigt, Rudolf Harbig)		3:11,8
50 Km Walk		
1. Harold Whitlock	GBR	4:30:41,4
2. Arthur T. Schwab	SUI	4:32:09,2
3. Adalbert Bukenko	LIT	4:32:42,2
High Jump		
1. Cornelius Johnson	USA	2:03
2. David Albritton	USA	2,00
3. Delos Thurber	USA	2,00
Pole Vault		
1. Earle Meadows	USA	4,35
2. Shuhei Nishida	JAP	4,25
3. Sueo Oe	JAP	4,25
Long Jump		
1. Jesse Owens	USA	8,06
2. Luz Long	GER	7,87
3. Naoto Tajima	JAP	7,74
Triple Jump		
1. Naoto Tajima	JAP	16,00
2. Masao Harada	JAP	15,66
3 John Patrick Metcalfe	AUS	15,50
Shotput		
1. Hans Woellke	GER	16,20
2. Sulo Bàrlund	FIN	16,12
3. Gerhard Stöck	GER	15,66
Discus Throw		
1. Kenneth Carpenter	USA	50,48
2. Gordon Dunn	USA	49,36
3. Giorgio Oberwegger	ITA	49,23
Hammer Throw		
1. Karl Hein	GER	56,49
2. Erwin Blask	GER	55,04
3. Fred Warngard	SWE	54,83
Javelin		
1. Gerhard Stoöck	GER	71,84
2. Yrjo Nikkanen	FIN	70,77
3. Kalervo Toivonen	FIN	70,72
Decathlon		
1. Glenn Morris	USA	7900
2. Robert Clark	USA	7601
3. Jack Parker	USA	7275

1936 Berlin

Women Athletics

100 M Dash
1. Helen Stephens USA 11,5
2. Stanislawa Walasiewicz POL 11,7
3. Kathe Krauss GER 11,9

80 M Hurtles
1. Trebisonda Valla ITA 11,7
2. Anny Steuer GER 11,7
3. Elisabeth Taylor CAN 11,7

400 M Relay
1. USA 46,9 (Harriet Bland, Annette Rogers, Elisabeth Robinson, Helen Stephens)
2. GBR 47,6 (Eileen Hiscock, Violet Olney, Audrey Brown, Barbara Burke)
3. CAN 47,8 (Dorothy Brookshaw, Mildred Dolson, Hilda Cameron, Aileen Meagher)

High Jump
1. Ibolya Csak HUN 1,60
2. Dorothy Odam GBR 1,60
3. Efriede Kaun GER 1,60

Discus Throw
1. Gisela Mauemayer GER 47,63
2. Jadwiga Wajsowna POL 46,22
3. Paula Mollenhauer GER 39,80

Javelin
1. Tilly Fleischer GER 45,18
2. Luise Kruger GER 43,29
3. Maria Kwasniewska POL 41,80

Men Swimming

100 M Freestyle
1. Ferenc Csik HUN 57,6
2. Masanori Yusa JAP 57,9
3. Shigeo Arai JAP 58,0

400 M Freestyle
1. Jack Medica USA 4:44,5
2. Shumpei Uto JAP 4:45,6
3. Shozo Makino JAP 4:48,1

1500 M Freestyle
1. Noboru Terada JAP 19:13,7
2. Jack Medica USA 19:34,0
3. Shumpei Uto JAP 19:34,5

100 M Backstroke
1. Adolf Kiefer USA 1:05,9
2. Albert Van de Weghe USA 1:07,7
3. Masaji Kiyokawa JAP 1:08,4

200 M Backstroke
1. Tetsuo Hamuro JAP 2:41,5
2. Erwin Sietas GER 2:42,9
3. Reizo Koike JAP 2:44,2

800 M Freestyle Relay
1. JAP 8:51,5 (Masanori Yusa, Shigeo Sugiura, Masaharu Taguchi, Shigeo Arai)
2. USA 9:03,0 (Ralph Flanagan, John Macionis, Paul Wolf, Jack Medica)
3. HUN 9:12,3 (Arpad Lengyel, Oszkar Abay-Nemes, Odön Grof, Ferrene Csik)

Springboard Diving
1. Richard Degener USA 163,57
2. Marshall Wagne USA 159,56
3. Al Greene USA 146,29

High Diving
1. Marshall Wagne USA 113,58
2. Elbert Root USA 110,60
3. Hermann Stork GER 110,31

Water Polo

1. Hungary
2. Germany
3. Belgium

Women Swimming

100 M Freestyle
1. Hendrika Mastenbrock HOL 1:05,9
2. Jeanette Campbell ARG 1:06,4
3. Gisela Arendt GBR 1:06,6

400 M Freestyle
1. Hendrika Mastenbrock HOL 5:26,4
2. Ragnhild Hveger DEN 5:27,5
3. Lenore Wingard Kight USA 5:29,0

200 M Breaststroke
1. Hideko Maenata JAP 3:03,6
2. Martha Genenger GER 3:04,2
3. Inge Sörensen DAN 3:07,8

100 M Backstroke
1. Dina Whilhelmina Senff HOL 1:18,9
2. Hendrika Mastenbrock HOL 1:19,2
3. Alice Bridges USA 1:19,4

400 M Freestyle Relay
1. HOL 4:36,0 (Johanna Selbach, Catherina Wagner, Willemijntje den Ouden, Hendrika Mastenbrock)
2. GER 4:36,8 (Ruth Halbsguth, Leni Lohmar, Ingeborg Schmitz, Gisela Arendt)
3. USA 4:40,2 (Katherine Rawis, Bernice Lapp, Warvis Freeman, Olive Mckean)

Springboard Diving
1. Marjorie Gestring USA 89,27
2. Katherine Rawis USA 88,35
3. Dorothy Hill-Poynton USA 82,36

High Diving
1. Dorothy Hill-Poynton USA 33,93
2. Velma Dunn USA 33,63
3. Käthe Köhler GER 33,43

Boxing

Flyweight
1. Willy Kaiser GER
2. Gavino Matta ITA
3. Louis Daniel Lauria USA

Bantamweight
1. Ulderico Sergo ITA
2. Jack Wilson USA
3. Fidel Ortiz MEX

Featherweight
1. Oscar Casanovas ARG
2. Charles Catterall SAF
3. Josef Miner GER

Lightweight
1. Imre Harangi HUN
2. Nikolai Stepulov EST
3. Erik Agren SWE

Welterweight
1. Sten Suvio EIN
2. Michael Murach GER
3. Gerhard Petersen DEN

Middleweight
1. Jean Despeaux FRA
2. Henry Tiller NOR
3. Raul Villareal ARG

Light Heavyweight
1. Roger Michelot FRA
2. Richard Vogt GER
3. Francisco Risiglione ARG

Heavyweight
1. Herbert Runge GER
2. Guillermo Lovell ARG
3. Erling Nilsen NOR

Greco Roman Wrestling

Bantamweight
1. Marton Lorincz HUN
2. Egon Svensson SWE
3. Jakob Brendel GER

Featherweight
1. Yasar Erkan TUR
2. Aarne Reini FIN
3. Einar Karlson SWE

Lightweight
1. Laun Koskela FIN
2. Josef Herda TCH
3. Voldemar Väll EST

Welterweight
1. Rudolf Svedberg SWE
2. Fritz Schäfer GER
3. Elno Virtanen FIN

Middleweight
1. Ivar Johansson SWE
2. Ludwig Schweickert GER
3. Jozsef Palotas HUN

Light Heavyweight
1. Axel Cadier SWE
2. Edwins Bietags LIT
3. August Neo EST

Heavyweight
1. Kristjan Palusalu EST
2. John Nyman SWE
3. Kurt Hornfischer ALL

Freestyle Wrestling

Bantamweight
1. Odön Zombori HUN
2. Ross Flood USA
3. Johannes Herbert GER

Featherweight
1. Kustaa Philajamäki FIN
2. Francis Millard USA
3. Gösta Jönsson SWE

Lightweight
1. Karoly Karpati HUN
2. Wolfgang Ehrl GER
3. Hermanni Pihlajamäki FIN

Welterweight
1. Frank Lewis USA
2. Ture Andersson SWE
3. Joseph Schleimer CAN

Middleweight
1. Emile Polivé FRA
2. Richard Voliva USA
3. Ahmet Kirecci TUR

Light Heavyweight
1. Knut Fridell SWE
2. August Neo EST
3. Erich Siebert GER

Heavyweight
1. Kristian Palusalu EST
2. Josef Klapuch TCH
3. Hjalmar Nyström FIN

Men Fencing

Foil Individual
1. Giulio Gaudini ITA
2. Edward Gardère FRA
3. Giorgio Bocchino ITA

Foil Team
1. Italy
2. France
3. Germany

Epée Individual
1. Franco Ricardi ITA
2. Saverio Ragno ITA
3. Giancardo Cornaggia Medici ITA

Epée Team
1. Italy
2. Sweden
3. France

Sabre Individual
1. Endre Kabos HUN
2. Gustavo Marzi ITA
3. Aladar Gerevich HUN

Sabre Team
1. Hungary
2. Italy
3. Germany

Women Fencing

Foil Individual
1. Ilona Elek HUN
2. Helene Mayer GER
3. Ellen Preis AUT

Owens, with four gold medals in track and field events, presented at Berlin an implicit challenge to Nazi theories of racial superiority.

CHART

Weightlifting

			2 Arm Press	2 Arm Snatch	2 Arm Clean & Jerk	Total
Featherweight						
1.	Anthony Terlazzo	USA	92,5	97,5	122,5	312,5
2.	Saleh Mohammed Soliman	EGY	85,0	95,0	125,0	305,0
3.	Ibrahim Hassan Shams	EGY	80,0	95,0	125,0	300,0
Lightweight						
1.	Anwar Mohammed Soliman	EGY	92,5	105,0	145,0	342,5
2.	Robert Fein	AUT	105,0	100,0	137,5	342,5
3.	Karl Jansen	GER	95,0	100,0	132,5	327,5
Middleweight						
1.	Khadr Sayed el Toumi	EGY	117,5	120,0	150,0	387,5
2.	Rudolf Ismayr	GER	107,5	102,5	142,5	352,5
3.	Adolf Wagner	GER	97,5	112,5	142,5	352,5
Light Heavyweight						
1.	Louis Hostin	FRA	110,0	117,5	145,0	372,5
2.	Eugen Deutsch	GER	105,0	110,0	150,0	365,0
3.	Ibrahim Wasif	EGY	100,0	110,0	150,0	360,0
Heavyweight						
1.	Josef Manger	GER	132,5	122,5	155,0	410,0
2.	Vaclav Psennicka	TCH	122,5	125,0	155,0	402,5
3.	Arnold Luhaaär	EST	115,0	120,0	165,0	400,0

Modern Pentathlon

1. Gotthard Handrick GER
2. Charles Leonard USA
3. Silvano Abba ITA

Men Canoeing

Kayak-1 1000 M
1. Gregor Hradetzky AUT 4:22,9
2. Helmut Càmmerer GER 4:25,5
3. Jacob Kraaier HOL 4:35,1

Kayak-2 1000 M
1. Austria 4:03,8
2. Germany 4:08,9
3. Netherlands 4:12,2

Canadian-1 1000 M
1. Francis Amyot CAN 5:32,1
2. Bohuslav Karlik TCH 5:36,9
3. Erich Koschik GER 5:39,0

Canadian-2 1000 M
1. Czechoslovakia 4:50,1
2. Canada 4:53,8
3. Austria 4:56,7

Kayak—1 10000 M (1936,1948, 1952, 1956)
1. Ernst Krebs GER 46:01,6
2. Fritz Landertinger AUT 46:14,7
3. Ernest Riedel USA 47:23,9

Kayak—2 10000 M (1936, 1948, 1952, 1956)
1. Germany 41:45,0
2. Austria 42:05,4
3. Sweden 43:06,1

Canadian—2 10,000 M (1936, 1948, 1952, 1956)
1. Czechoslovakia 50:33,5
2. Canada 51:15,8
3. Austria 51:28,0

Folding Kayak—1 10,000 M (1936 only)
1. Gregor Hradetzly AUT 50:01,2
2. Henri Eberrhardt FRA 50:04,2
3. Xavier Hörmann GER 50:06,5

Folding Kayak—2 10,000 M (1936 only)
1. Sweden 45:48,9
2. Germany 45:49,2
3. Netherlands 46:12,4

Rowing

Single Scull
1. Gustav Schäfer GER 8:21,5
2. Josef Hasenöhrl AUT 8:25,8
3. Daniel Barrow USA 8:28,0

Double Sculls
1. Great Britain 7:20,8
2. Germany 7:26,2
3. Poland 7:36,2

Pairs without Coxswain
1. Germany 8:16,1
2. Denmark 8:19,2
3. Argentina 8:23,0

Pairs wih Coxswain
1. Germany 8:36,9
2. Italy 8:49,7
3. France 8:54,0

Fours without Coxswain
1. Germany 7:01,8
2. Great Britain 7:06,5
3. Switzerland 7:10,6

Fours with Coxswain
1. Germany 7:16,2
2. Switzerland 7:24,3
3. France 7:33,3

Eight Oars
1. U.S.A. 6:25,4
2. Italy 6:26,0
3. Germany 6:26,4

Yachting

Finn Monotype Class
1. Daniel Marinus J. Kagchelland HOL 163
2. Werner Krogmann GER 150
3. Peter M. Scott GBR 131

Star Class
1. Germany 80
2. Sweden 64
3. Netherlands 63

6 M Class
1. Great Britain 67
2. Norway 66
3. Sweden 62

8 M Class
1. Italy 55
2. Norway 53
3. Germany 53

Cycling (100 km)

Individual Road Race
1. Robert Charpentier FRA 2:33:05,0
2. Guy Lapébie FRA 2:33:05,2
3. Ernst Nievergelt SUI 2:33:05,8

Road Race Team
1. France 7:39:16,2
2. Switzerland 7:39:20,4
3. Belgium 7:39:21,0

1000 M Time Trial
1. Arie van Vliet HOL 1:12,0
2. Pierre Georget FRA 1:12,8
3. Rudolf Karsch GER 1:13,2

1000 M Sprint
1. Toni Merkens GER 11,8
2. Arie van Vliet HOL
3. Louis Chaillot FRA

Tandem 2000 M
1. Germany 11,8
2. Netherlands
3. France

Team Pursuit (4000 M)
1. France 4:45,0
2. Italy 4:51,0
3. Great Britain 4:53,6

Equestrian Sports

All-around Individual Competition
1. Ludwig Stubbendorf GER 37,70
2. Earl Thomson USA 99,90
3. Hans Mathiesen-Lundling DEN 102,20

All-around Team Competition
1. Germany -676,65
2. Poland -911,70
3. Great Britain -995,5

Dressage Individual
1. Heinz Pollay GER 1760,0
2. Friedrich Gerhard GER 1745,5
3. Alois Podhajsky AUT 1721,5

Dressage Team
1. Germany 5074,0
2. France 4846,0
3. Sweden 4660,5

Grand Prix Jumping Individual
1. Kurt Hasse GER -4/4/59,2
2. Henri Rang RON -4/41:12,8
3. Jozsef von Platthy HUN -8/0/1:02,6

Grand Prix Jumping Team
1. Germany -44,00
2. Netherlands -51,50
3. Portugal -56,00

Shooting

Small-Bore Rifle (prone)
1. Willy Rogeberg NOR 300
2. Ralf Berzsenyi HUN 296
3. Wladyslaw Karas POL 296

Rapid-Fire Pistol (25 M)
1. Cornelius van Oyen GER 36
2. Heinz Hax GER 35
3. Torsten Ullman SWE 34

Free Pistol (50 M)
1. Torsten Ullamn SWE 559
2. Erich Krempel GER 544
3. Charles de Jammonières FRA 540

Gymnastics

All-around Individual Competition
1. Alfred Schwarzmann GER 113,100
2. Eugen Mack SUI 112,334
3. Konrad Frey GER 111,532

All-around Team Competition
1. Germany 657,430
2. Switzerland 654,802
3. Finland 638,468

Parallel Bars
1. Konrad Frey GER 19,067
2. Michael Reusch SUI 19,034
3. Alfred Schwarzmann GER 18,967

Floor Exercise
1. Georges Miez SUI 18,666
2. Josef Walter SUI 18,500
3. Eugen Mack SUI 18,466

Horse Vault
1. Alfred Schwarzmann GER 19,200
2. Eugen Mack SUI 18,967
3. Matthias Volz GER 18,467

Sidehorse
1. Konrad Freu GER 19,333
2. Eugen Mack SUI 19,167
3. Albert Bachmann SUI 19,167

Horizontal Bar
1. Aleksenteri Saarvala FIN 19,367
2. Konrad Frey GER 19,267
3. Alfred Schwarzmann GER 19,233

Flying Rings
1. Alois Hudee TCH 19,433
2. Léon Stukelj YUG 18,867
3. Matthias Volz GER 16,667

Women Gymnastics

All-around Team Competition
1. Germany 506,50
2. Czechoslovakia 503,60
3. Hungary 499,00

Basketball

1. U.S.A.
2. Canada
3. Mexico

Soccer

1. Italy
2. Austria
3. Norway

Handball

1. Germany
2. Austria
3. Switzerland

Field Hockey

1. India
2. Germany
3. Netherlands

1936

SEPTEMBER

Su	Mo	Tu	We	Th	Fr	Sa
		1	2	3	4	5
6	7	8	9	10	11	12
13	14	15	16	17	18	19
20	21	22	23	24	25	26
29	28	29	30			

1. Washington: $1 billion rise in federal deficit forecast for 1937 (→ 10/4).

3. Rome: Italy sends more warships to Spain after murder of Italian citizen in Barcelona (→ 4).

4. Spain: Popular front representing Basques and Catalonians replaces Giral Cabinet (→ 12).

7. Paris: France plans big arms increase in reply to Hitler (→ 9).

7. Berlin: Reich orders confiscation of 25% of Jewish fortunes (→ 10).

9. Paris: France signs treaties with Syria and Lebanon, promising independence in three years.

9. Nuremburg: Hitler denies war aims; asserts right to colonies (→ 21).

10. Nuremburg: 50,000 youths with spades march for Hitler (→ 10/19).

10. Berlin: Goebbels accuses Czechs of buying Soviet aircraft.

12. New York: Fred Perry and Alice Marble win U.S. tennis titles at Forest Hills.

12. Spain: Rebels win port of San Sebastian (→ 21).

16. Iceland: French explorer Jean Charcot and crew of 32 die in wreck of ship Pourquoi Pas?

18. Geneva: Italy asks League to bar Ethiopians (→ 23).

21. Spain: Insurgents occupy Maqueda, prepare to move on Toledo (→ 27).

21. German army holds largest manuevers since 1914 (→ 10/14).

22. Philadelphia: Joe Louis KOs Al Ettore in fifth (→ 10/9).

23. Geneva: Ethiopia seated by League, as Britain gives up opposition (→ 10/24).

27. Spain: Rebels take Toledo; Franco named chief of insurgent forces (→ 30).

27. France, Switzerland, Holland give up gold standard.

29. Detroit: 11 members of "Black Legion" secret organization found guilty of murder.

30. Terra Haute: Officials jail Communist presidential candidate Earl Browder for appearing in public (→ 11/3).

Franco's army takes Alcazar in Toledo

Sept 30. When the bitterly contested civil war in Spain is over, the country will still be talking about the heroics of determined rebel soldiers in the Alcazar in Toledo.

The insurgents seized control of the palace fortress two months ago, when the war broke out. The 1,200 cadets and officers, together with hundreds of women and children, have been holding out ever since. The troops of the popular front attacked incessantly and finally blew up part of the tower, but the defenders refused to surrender. They pulled back into the ruins of the palace and continued to fight.

General Franco made the rescue of the soldiers a chief objective. And in the past few days, help finally arrived. Today, troops under the command of Generals Varela and Moscardo had complete command of the streets of Toledo. They plastered walls with warnings to civilians to lay down their arms.

The defense of the Alcazar and the seizure of Toledo are more than psychological victories for Franco's troops. They now have another base for a new assault on Madrid.

In the north also, the rebels are poised to attack the capital. Their capture of Irun and San Sebastian has tightened their grip on the strategically important Bay of Biscay. The victories there have also freed more of the insurgents for the march south on Madrid.

Southwest of Madrid, German flyers are giving the rebels air support for their attack on the capital. Franco claims the Germans are simply training his aviators, but it is clear the Germans are at the controls during the raids (→ 10/1).

Toledo smolders in the wake of the crucial battle for control of the Alcazar.

Battle-weary insurgents walk into Irun unmolested after heavy bombing.

Right-wing priest rebuked by Rome

Father Coughlin, "the radio priest."

Sept 2. The political activities of Father Charles E. Coughlin, a radio priest from Detroit, have been severely criticized by Osservatore Romano, which usually reflects the opinion of the Vatican. The newspaper said that Father Coughlin had violated proprieties in his harsh attacks on President Roosevelt's efforts to aid the poor and bring America out of the depression.

Father Coughlin, a self-styled champion of the poor, had been an ardent Roosevelt supporter in 1932. But in recent months, the Catholic priest's sermons, broadcast from the Shrine of the Little Flower, have been highly critical of the president, saying that his programs have done far too little for the poor (→ 11/7).

First woman flies Atlantic alone

Sept 5. Mrs. Beryl Markham, an English flier, is the first woman to cross the Atlantic alone from east to west. She left Abingdon, England, yesterday at 1:50 p.m. and crash-landed near a swamp in Cape Breton, Nova Scotia, this afternoon at 1:05 p.m. She was not badly hurt.

Bad weather forced Mrs. Markham to fly "blind," relying on her instrument panel. She was virtually out of gas when she landed nose first. The plane is now a wreck.

Only two men have managed non-stop east-west flights. Twenty-nine others have done it with short stopovers at Greenland or elsewhere. Of the three women who have tried to go non-stop, one gave up the attempt in the Azores. The other two drowned at sea.

1936

OCTOBER

Su	Mo	Tu	We	Th	Fr	Sa
				1	2	3
4	5	6	7	8	9	10
11	12	13	14	15	16	17
18	19	20	21	22	23	24
25	26	27	28	29	30	31

1. Japanese make seven demands on China, including autonomy for Northern provinces, Japanese advisers in govt. (→ 11/22).

1. Spain: Rebels name Franco dictator in Burgos regime (→ 3).

3. Spain: Anarchists brought into Madrid government (→ 8).

4. U.S. imports exceed exports for first time in ten years (→ 16).

6. N.Y.: Yankees win World Series in fifth game over Giants.

6. British Labor Party rejects alliance with Communists.

8. Spain: Popular front offers independence to Basques (→ 10).

9. New York: Joe Louis floors Jorge Brescia in third (→ 12/14).

10. Berlin: Reich threatens to counter any Russian aid to Spain (→ 23).

10. Vienna: Schuschnigg dissolves fascist bodies, becomes dictator (→ 2/14/37).

12. Oswald Mosley leads anti-Semitic march in London (→ 10/3/37).

14. Brussels: Belgium returns to old neutrality, fearing Germans in Rhineland (→ 11/1).

15. Albany: Einstein calls Social Darwinism pseudo-scientific.

16. Philadelphia: Hoover charges false accounts conceal huge government expenses (→ 31).

16. Bombay: 35 killed in Hindu-Moslem riots (→ 12/27).

19. Berlin: Hermann Goering appointed to manage Reich four-year economic plan (→ 11/8).

22. Britain orders 300 planes from Boeing in U.S. (→ 11/27).

23. Germany sends Condor military unit to fight with Nationalist rebels in Spain (→ 29).

24. Berlin: Reich becomes first to recognize Italian conquest of Ethiopia (→ 11/28).

25. Berlin: Hitler and Italian For. Min. Count Ciano draft treaty of alliance (→ 11/1).

26. Moscow: Stalin says reports of his death are true and asks to be left in peace.

31. Albany: Alfred Smith accuses FDR of paving way for Communism (→ 11/8).

Rebel drive on Madrid repulsed

Oct 29. Spanish government forces struck decisively at rebel positions south of Madrid today and slowed down their relentless attack on the capital. The Loyalists battered the insurgents with artillery attacks and bombed their positions with new planes that just arrived from the United States.

Joan Miro is only one of many artists mobilizing talents for Loyalist Spain.

The government also plans new air assaults on air bases controlled by rebels in Seville and Grenada.

"The enemy has exhausted its forces," Premier Francisco Caballero exhorted his troops, "and the time has come for us to give them the coup de grace."

General Franco insists the defeats are minor setbacks. His forces are moving heavy guns closer to Madrid for a new attack (→ 11/6).

Burlington Zephyr sets speed record

Oct 23. The Burlington Railroad's Denver Zephyr set a world's long-distance speed record for trains today when it made its run from Chicago to Denver in just over 12 hours, 12 minutes at an average speed of 83.3 miles per hour. The stainless steel Zephyr broke its own record of 77.6 miles per hour, set two years ago. The eight-car train hit its top speed of 116 miles an hour just after it crossed the Colorado state line. Its passengers included 120 Chicago executives who made the trip in anticipation of a record.

1936

NOVEMBER

Su	Mo	Tu	We	Th	Fr	Sa
1	2	3	4	5	6	7
8	9	10	11	12	13	14
15	16	17	18	19	20	21
22	23	24	25	26	27	28
29	30					

1. Milan: Mussolini announces pact with Reich, urges France, Britain to join (→ 25).

3. Ireland: Dail revives Senate in new constitution; ignores Anglo-Irish relations (→ 7/21/37).

4. New York: Communists fail to get 50,000 votes required to maintain party status.

6. Spain: Republican govt. moves to Valencia as Franco's troops reach Madrid (→ 18).

8. Washington: Report shows U.S. business at highest level since 1930 (→ 1/20/37).

8. Berlin: Nazis dropping thousands of alien words from German vocabulary (→ 4/20/37).

12. Vienna: Hungary, Austria recognize Italian Empire; Italy backs Hungary's right to rearm.

12. California: Oakland Bay Bridge opens.

14. Reich defies Versailles treaty, claiming national control over German rivers (→ 25).

14. Cairo ratifies treaty ending British occupation of Egypt (→ 9/25/37).

18. Rome and Berlin recognize Franco govt. in Burgos (→ 20).

18. San Francisco: Main span of Golden Gate Bridge joined (→ 2/17/37).

20. Spain: Republicans execute rebel leader Antonio Prima de Rivera in Alicante (→ 23).

20. Joseph Davies named U.S. ambassador to Russia.

22. China: 1,200 shot in battle between Japanese and Mongolians (→ 7/13/37).

23. Spain: U.S. abandons embassy in Madrid (→ 12/16).

27. London: Eden warns Hitler Britain will fight to protect Belgium (→ 1/2/37).

28. New York: 100,000 watch Navy beat Army 7-0 in last three minutes.

28. Japan recognizes Victor-Emmanuel II as emperor of Ethiopia (→ 2/19/37).

29. Moscow: Russia claims world's greatest air force with 7,000 planes.

30. England: Crystal Palace destroyed by fire.

Roosevelt elected President 2nd time

Nov 3. President Roosevelt won re-election today by a landslide, defeating Alfred M. Landon in the greatest outpouring of voters in the nation's history. Returns showed the president with 523 electoral votes, while his Republican opponent captured just eight.

The election proved to be an overwhelming endorsement of the New Deal, the president's innovative program that seeks to bring the nation out of the depression. Vast numbers of workers, as well as the unemployed, went to the polls, many of them for the first time. Governor Landon, a Kansan, had stepped up his attacks in recent weeks, accusing the president of trying to be a dictator (→ 1/20/37).

FDR, a valiant triumph over polio. ▷

Fascist states form Axis

Japan's Kursu, Italy's Ciano, and Hitler, in Berlin for the signing.

Nov 25. Germany and Japan signed an anti-Communist pact today pledging cooperation in defending against the spread of Soviet influence. The treaty, which was described as a "measure for defense of European culture and civilization and world peace," complements a similar pact reached last month between Germany and Italy.

In effect, an anti-Communist Axis has now been forged between the three authoritarian states, and the result is to bring to reality German Chancellor Adolf Hitler's dream of a worldwide anti-Communist bloc.

The text of the German-Japanese treaty does not mention the Soviet Union; rather, it states the objective is a police pact for mutual cooperation directed against the international activities of the Moscow Comintern or Communist International. Despite denials from Berlin and Tokyo, suspicion was voiced in Europe that the anti-Communist front was a cover for a traditional military alliance and creation of spheres of influence in the western Pacific and East Indies (→ 1/9/37).

Father Coughlin suspends his show

Nov 7. Saying that his National Union for Social Justice had been "thoroughly discredited" by the recent election, Father Charles E. Coughlin said goodbye today to his radio audience. In his farewell radio speech, the controversial Catholic priest said that his union "is not dead; it merely sleeps." But from now on, he said, the union will adopt a "policy of silence" toward the Roosevelt New Deal.

A self-styled champion of the poor, Father Coughlin said his decision to suspend his radio talks was based on the landslide victory of President Roosevelt, whom he had accused of doing too little to help the underprivileged (→ 11/27/38).

A gallant Errol Flynn rides into disaster in "The Charge of the Light Brigade." Ironically, our film hero was classified 4F for malaria, TB and a heart defect.

1936

DECEMBER

Su	Mo	Tu	We	Th	Fr	Sa
		1	2	3	4	5
6	7	8	9	10	11	12
13	14	15	16	17	18	19
20	21	22	23	24	25	26
29	28	29	30	31		

1. Buenos Aires: FDR opens Pan-American Conference.

5. U.S.S.R.: New constitution promises universal suffrage; Communists remain only legal party (→ 10).

6. Mexico grants Trotsky political asylum (→ 1/9/37).

8. Anastasio Somoza elected pres. of Nicaragua (→ 5/5/39).

9. New York: Alfred Barr sets up exhibit entitled "Fantastic Art, Dada and Surrealism."

10. Moscow: 11 seized for making arrests without warrants; first under new constitution.

14. Cleveland: Joe Louis KOs Eddie Simms in 26 seconds (→ 1/29/37).

16. Spain: Rebels bomb Catalonia for first time (→ 28).

24. Havana: Federico Laredo Bru replaces impeached Pres. Gomez (→ 11/26/37).

27. Nehru urges India to strike at British imperialism (→ 11/18/37).

28. Neutrality law loophole allows $2.8 mil. U.S. planes to go to loyalists in Spain (→ 1/6/37).

DEATHS

10. Luigi Pirandello, Italian playwright (*6/28/1867).

31. Miguel de Unamuno, Spanish philosopher, fiction writer (*9/29/1864).

CULTURAL EVENTS, 1936

Literature: Faulkner's "Absalom Absalom!"; Robert Sherwood's "Idiot's Delight," Pulitzer for drama; Dale Carnegie's "How to Win Friends and Influence People."

Academia: A.J. Ayer's "Language, Truth and Logic"; Freud's "Autobiography."

Music: Prokofiev's "Peter and the Wolf"; Constant Lambert's "Summer's Last Will and Testament"; "Pennies from Heaven."

The Arts: Mondrian's "Composition in Red and Blue"; Nazi exhibition of "Degenerate Art."

Film: Lang's "Fury"; Chaplin's "Modern Times"; Bergman's "Intermezzo"; "The Great Ziegfeld," Academy Award.

O'Neill is winner of Nobel drama award

New Yorker Eugene O'Neill.

Dec 10. The prolific playwright Eugene O'Neill has received the Nobel Prize for literature. O'Neill is the recipient of three Pulitzer Prizes —thus far —and the writer of two dozen works —thus far. He is an insatiable dramatist.

O'Neill sailed to South America when he was a young man, and his first plays, produced in the early 1920's, often dealt with seafaring. They were simple one-acts; two actors on a rocking crate would serve as castaways upon a raft. He now favors longer works, such as the trilogy "Mourning Becomes Electra" (1931), and remains restless in style: He borrows liberally from ancient Greek drama and modern existential French philosophy. O'Neill, 50 years old, suffers from a rare, slow-acting degenerative disease.

O'Neill is not the only American at the podium claiming an award. The Dutch-born American scientist P.J.W. Debye won the prize in chemistry for determining the distribution of an electrical charge within a molecule. Cosmic rays were investigated by Carl David Anderson and Victor Hess, jointly given the prize in physics.

Edward VIII abdicates to marry divorcee

Dec 11. King Edward VIII gave up the throne of Great Britain and the British Empire tonight to marry a twice-divorced American from Baltimore, Wallis Warfield Simpson. In a radio broadcast to Britain and the world, the king, who has now been created Duke of Windsor, told his audience that he had "found it impossible to carry the heavy burden of responsibility and to discharge my duties as King as I would wish to do without the help and support of the woman I love."

Yesterday, the king informed the Cabinet of his decision to abdicate, and his message was read to the House of Commons, which had no alternative but to accept it. Edward VIII was automatically succeeded by his next younger brother, the Duke of York, who will reign as George VI, supported by his popular Scottish wife and two daughters. The Duke of Windsor is leaving England. The most profound constitutional crisis in modern English history is over (→ 5/12/37).

Seven G.M. plants shut by sit-down strikes

Luxury accommodations for sit-down strikers in Flint, Michigan.

Dec 30. Sit-down strikers have forced the closing of seven General Motors plants in Flint, Michigan, in a dispute over collective bargaining. The closings have idled 33,400 of the company's more than 200,000 employees and could eventually lead to work stoppages in such industries as those that manufacture steel, glass and batteries.

At issue is whether workers will be allowed to engage in collective bargaining on a plant-by-plant basis, as proposed by the United Automobile Workers of America. Officials of General Motors insist that such bargaining must be on a company-wide basis. The company manufactures Chevrolets, Buicks and Fisher automobile bodies in 35 towns and cities in 14 states.

In a statement tonight, William S. Knudson, Executive Vice President of General Motors, said that the work stoppage came at a time when the company was setting an all-time record for production and sales and when wages were the highest ever paid. The strike could lead to a loss of more than a million dollars a day in wages for workers, he said. He insisted that bargaining on the basis of individual plants would fail to take into consideration certain local conditions as well as individual grievances.

Tonight, several hundred strikers remained in two of the plants, even taking over the company cafeterias to prepare their own meals. Outside the plant gates, manned by strikers, several fights have occurred during the day, resulting in injury to at least one striker (→ 1/3).

Chiang held, forced to change policy

Chiang, under attack from two sides.

Dec 25. General Chiang Kai-shek was dramatically released on Christmas Day after being held captive for 13 days in Sian by General Chang Hsueh-liang, the former "young Marshal" of Manchuria.

Chiang had gone to Sian to spur Chang into greater action against the Chinese Communist forces in Yenan. Instead, he found himself seized by Chang's bodyguard and held in captivity. The incident, which at one point threatened civil war between Nationalist forces, was finally resolved after negotiations that involved Madame Chiang Kai-shek and Communist delegates.

As a condition for his release, Chiang, who had been emphasizing civil war against the Communists, agreed to give priority to warring against the Japanese. Chang surrendered and was jailed (→ 1/2/37).

Townsend, old age planner, indicted

Dec 3. Dr. Francis E. Townsend, an advocate of old-age pensions, was indicted today by a federal grand jury for contempt of the House of Representatives. Also indicted were two aides of the California physician. Dr. Townsend had stormed out of a House committee room earlier this year, calling the panel both unfair and unfriendly in its inquiry into his pension organization. Since then, he and his aides had ignored repeated committee subpoenas to testify about the Townsend Plan, which would provide $200 monthly old-age pensions.

Keynes publishes new economic plan

This year, John Maynard Keynes published "The General Theory of Employment, Interest, and Money," his answer to the riddle of our times: how can people who are willing to work find jobs?

Keynes writes that a depression results when the total demand of consumers and investors is insufficient to purchase all the goods society produces. His solution is to increase the money supply, thus lowering interest rates and stimulating investment. He also favors an active government fiscal policy of deficit spending on public works and an unbalanced budget to increase aggregate demand for goods.

Frank Lloyd Wright, at 68, has influenced architectural styles the world over. The "Falling Water" home in Bear Run, Pa., finished this year, displays his genius for reducing man's intrusion on nature to a minimum.

1937

JANUARY

Su	Mo	Tu	We	Th	Fr	Sa
					1	2
3	4	5	6	7	8	9
10	11	12	13	14	15	16
17	18	19	20	21	22	23
24	25	26	27	28	29	30
31						

1. Pasadena: Pittsburgh 21-0 over Washington in Rose Bowl.

2. Rome: Britain and Italy sign Mediterranean peace pact (→ 7).

3. Michigan: United Auto Workers call general strike at all GM plants (→ 11).

6. U.S. Congress bars shipment of arms to Spain (→ 13).

6. New York: Fred Perry makes debut in professional tennis.

7. Holland: Princess Juliana weds Prince Bernhard de Lippe-Biesterfeld.

7. Berlin: Reich agrees to support British non-intervention pact if other powers follow (→ 5/28).

9. Italy bans racial mixed marriages in North African colonies.

9. Trotsky arrives in Mexico, asks impartial retrial for alleged crimes against Stalin (→ 4/18).

9. Berlin: Reich admits extracting promise from Portugal for return of colonies acquired under Versailles treaty (→ 30).

11. Michigan: 24 hurt in auto strike riots (→ 21).

12. Jerusalem mufti tells British commission Jewish immigration to Palestine must cease (→ 6/9).

13. U.S. bars Americans from serving in Spanish war (→ 2/8).

17. China: 17 die in train fire.

18. Michigan: 25 millionth Ford driven off assembly line.

19. Howard Hughes flies L.A. to N.Y. in seven hours, 22 minutes.

19. U.S.S.R.: People's Commissars Council formed under Molotov.

21. Washington: GM President Alfred Sloan quits strike talks (→ 2/1).

22. California: Half of citrus crop destroyed by freeze.

26. France: Popular Front govt. bans Algerian nationalist group North African Star (ENA).

28. Canada: Privy Council declares Socialist legislation of Bennett govt. unconstitutional.

29. New York: Joe Louis defeats Bob Pastor (→ 2/17).

30. Hitler guarantees neutrality of Belgium and Holland (→ 2/2).

FDR says third of nation underprivileged

FDR is sworn in, becoming the first President to be inaugurated in January.

Jan 20. President Franklin Roosevelt was sworn in for a second term today, heralding the nation's steady climb out of the depression but sounding a somber note by saying: "I see one-third of a nation ill-housed, ill-clad, ill-nourished."

Facing an audience standing in the rain at the Capitol, President Roosevelt said he was not speaking out of despair but out of hope. "If I know aught of the spirit and purpose of our nation," he said, "we will not listen to comfort, opportunism and timidity. We will carry on."

The inauguration marked the first held on a date other than March 4, a change adopted by constitutional amendment in 1933. Despite the rain, the president rode in an open limousine to the Capitol, saying of the crowds lining the streets: "If they can take it, I can" (→ 2/5).

Floods make nearly one million homeless

Jan 27. Nearly a million persons have been made homeless and hundreds killed by one of the worst floods in the history of the Ohio and Mississippi rivers, and it is feared the toll will rise. Louisville, Cincinnati and other cities are still underwater and Army engineers have drawn up plans to evacuate as many as half a million people living along the Mississippi from Cairo, Illinois, to the Gulf of Mexico. Property damage is estimated to be over $400 million in what Cary Grayson, National Chairman of the Red Cross, calls "the greatest emergency the nation and the Red Cross have faced since the world war."

The quiet town of Portsmouth drowns in the runaway waters of the Ohio.

Second Soviet trial dooms seventeen

Jan 29. Joseph Stalin managed to eliminate 17 more of his political opponents today. Like others before them, they were given a trial, but no defense. Thirteen of them, including Georgi Piatakov, were ordered executed. The four others, including Karl Radek, the editorial writer for Izvestia, were sentenced to hard labor.

All the defendants were accused of high treason, collusion with foreign powers and conspiracy with Leon Trotsky to overthrow Stalin. Authorities claimed that the defendants confessed, but no evidence was introduced at the trial to support the charges.

Trotsky, the alleged ringleader of the conspiracy, is charged with communicating with supporters from his exile in Norway. He has vehemently denied conspiring with the defendants, officials in Nazi Germany or anyone else in a plot to remove Stalin from office. Trotsky may continue to protest, but Stalin continues the purges (→ 2/1).

Mellon gives huge art gift to U.S.

Jan 2. Andrew W. Mellon does not seem to be a man who holds a grudge. In the midst of an investigation of his income taxes, it was announced in Washington today he was giving his $19 million art collection to the people of the United States, along with a $9 million National Gallery to house it and a staff to maintain it.

Mellon's gift was disclosed in letters between him and President Roosevelt, who described the gift as "wonderful." Mellon's plans were indicated two years ago during hearings on a complaint that he had been overcharged on his taxes. The case is still pending.

A Pittsburgh banker and investor, Mellon served as Secretary of the Treasury from 1921 to 1932. He got Congress to cut taxes on the rich and reduced the national debt. His art, some of which was bought from Russia, is one of the finest private collections in existence. It will make Washington a world-class art center.

1937

FEBRUARY

Su	Mo	Tu	We	Th	Fr	Sa
	1	2	3	4	5	6
7	8	9	10	11	12	13
14	15	16	17	18	19	20
21	22	23	24	25	26	27
28						

1. Michigan: Troops surround G.M. plants following strike riots (→ 11).

1. Moscow: 13 alleged Trotskyites executed (→ 5/16).

2. Paris: Deputies vote 19 billion francs for defense to match Reich's budget (→ 10/13).

4. San Francisco dock strike ended; 40,000 back to work.

4. London: German envoy Joachim Ribbentrop gives Nazi salute to King George.

5. Georgia O'Keeffe art exhibit opens in New York.

8. Spain: Malaga falls to rebels aided by 15,000 Italian troops; 5,000 leftists arrested (→ 19).

10. Mexico: Vera Cruz ends ban on Catholicism (→ 5/5).

14. Austrian leader Schuschnigg threatens restoration of Hapsburg monarchy (→ 4/22).

14. Rome: Pope, recovering from paralyzed leg, walks for first time in two months.

17. Missouri: Joe Louis KOs Natie Brown in fourth round (→ 6/22).

17. San Francisco: Ten workers die as scaffolding on Golden Gate Bridge collapses.

19. Ethiopian rebels make attempt on life of Italian Viceroy Gen. Rudolfo Graziani (→ 21).

19. Spain: Foes deadlocked in biggest battle of Madrid siege (→ 3/29).

20. Chicago: Hoover calls FDR's court reforms a "road to suicide" (→ 3/1).

21. Ethiopia: 2,000 seized for questioning in Graziani assassination attempt (→ 23).

23. Ethiopia: Italians annihilate 3,000 rebels planning attack on Addis Ababa, (→ 11/20).

24. Hollywood: Lou Gehrig takes screen test for "Tarzan."

BIRTH

26. Eduardo Arroyo, Spanish painter.

DEATH

6. Elihu Root, sec. of state under Teddy Roosevelt, 1912 Nobel Peace Prize (*2/15/1845).

Strikers win wage hike, end G.M. sit-down

Police patrol a crowd of strikers in front of a besieged factory in Flint.

Feb 11. The 44-day strike of automobile workers ended at noon today after officials of General Motors Corporation promised a $25 million wage increase. The first major labor dispute in the automobile industry had badly crippled production.

The settlement will put 105,000 of the firm's idle employees back to work and 120,000 others, now on part-time duty, back to work on a full-time basis. The strike had meant a loss of more than a million dollars a day to the workers and untold losses to the company.

The streets of Flint, Michigan, site of the seven plant closings, were filled with joyous workers, hailing the end of the strike by marching through the city. Hundreds of sit-down strikers evacuated plants which they had held hostage for weeks. Although the strike has ended, talks between management and the Automobile Workers of America will continue on such issues as collective bargaining, abolition of piecework, shortening the work week, speeding up production and extra pay for overtime (→ 3/2).

FDR has Supreme Court reform plans

Feb 5. President Roosevelt sought today to pump new blood into the Supreme Court by submitting a plan allowing him to name up to six additional justices if those 70 or older refuse to retire. Too often, he said, judges stay beyond their "physical and mental capacity."

His proposal, in a surprise message to Congress, was promptly criticized as "court packing" by former President Herbert Hoover and other leading Republicans. They said it was merely designed to assure Supreme Court approval of questionable New Deal programs. The Supreme Court has ruled one of the president's key measures, the National Recovery Act, unconstitutional, as well as the Agricultural Adjustment Act.

One administration critic of such decisions has written: "In striking at New Deal laws, the Court allowed its language to run riot. In overthrowing the A.A.A., the Court cast doubt upon all federal aid to agriculture; in laying low the NRA, the Court struck at all national efforts to maintain fair labor standards. The Court not merely challenged the policies of the New Deal but erected judicial barriers to the reasonable exercise of legislative powers, both state and national, to meet the needs of a 20th Century community" (→ 20).

Du Pont patents a new thread, nylon

Feb 16. A patent on a versatile new plastic called nylon was obtained today by E.I. du Pont de Nemours and Company. Nylon can replace silk in a number of consumer products such as hosiery at a substantial reduction in cost, Du Pont says. The military is interested in nylon for parachutes, and the material can also be used to make bristles for toothbrushes and hairbrushes. Nylon moldings are also being made for industrial mechanical parts such as cams, bearings and fastenings. Du Pont already has begun plans to build factories for large-scale production of nylon, which is expected to reach the market in two or three years (→ 3/39).

Chiang and Mao disagree on war policy

Feb 23. Mao Tse-tung, the Chinese Communist leader, impressed many people with his long march through China two years ago. But China's ruling party, under the direction of Chiang Kai-shek, is not impressed with his politics.

The Communist leader sent a message to the Kuomintang last week, suggesting they join forces to battle the Japanese invaders. Mao said his troops would have a separate identity and be called "the national revolutionary guard," but they would fight with Chiang. The Kuomintang, which has been holding a conference in Nanking, firmly rejected the proposal and, for that matter, any association with Mao.

Chiang is still smarting from a political defeat by Mao. Earlier this month, Northern war lords turned Sianfu, which had been occupied by government troops, over to Mao.

Mao Tse-tung and Chou En-lai.

Chiang told the Chinese people they will have a chance later this year to judge his policy toward Mao. An assembly will be convened to write a new constitution.

1937

MARCH

Su	Mo	Tu	We	Th	Fr	Sa
	1	2	3	4	5	6
7	8	9	10	11	12	13
14	15	16	17	18	19	20
21	22	23	24	25	26	27
28	29	30	31			

1. Congress offers compromise to FDR, giving Supreme Court justices retirement with full pay at age 70 (→ 4/12).

1. Polish right unites under Col. Adam Koc in Camp of National Unity (→ 5/24).

2. Pittsburgh: C.I.O gains recognition, pay raise and 40-hour week from Carnegie Steel (→ 6).

3. Rome: Italy to adjust pay to family size in effort to promote births (→ 5/25).

5. U.S. Sec. of State Hull apologizes to Reich for insults by N.Y. Mayor LaGuardia (→ 8).

5. Budapest reveals coup plot by Ferenc Szalasi's Agrarian Party (→ 10/11).

6. Ohio: Firestone plants in Akron closed by union (→ 10).

8. Berlin: Nazis say Ben Franklin urged ban on Jews (→ 14).

10. Detroit: Chrysler sues John L. Lewis and local unions for property seizure (→ 15).

10. Washington: President Manuel Quezon asks full independence for Philippines.

14. New York: Swastikas found painted on Temple Rodeph Shalom (→ 5/19).

15. New York: Remington Rand Co. defies NLRB, refusing to rehire 4,000 strikers (→ 24).

15. Chicago: Bernard Fantus opens first blood bank at Cook County Hospital.

16. Paris: Communists, fascists riot; four dead, 310 hurt (→ 6/9).

16. Bolivia: La Paz govt. seizes Standard Oil holdings.

18. Texas: 500 killed in horrible gas explosion at school.→

21. Puerto Rico: Police fire on nationalists; seven dead, 50 hurt (→ 1/10/38).

28. A.F.L. calls sit-in strikes illegal property seizure (→ 4/2).

DEATHS

13. H.P. Lovecraft, U.S. writer, supernatural (*8/20/1890).

16. Joseph Chamberlain, British statesman (*10/16/1863).

26. Frederick Louis Maytag, American inventor, electric washing machine (*7/14/1857).

Goodman swings as teenagers scream

"The King of Swing" blows his horn.

March 3. The Benny Goodman Band is taking the country by storm. If you were at the Paramount Theater in New York today, you would know why. The crowned "King of Swing" not only had them tapping their feet and snapping their fingers, but dancing with wild abandon in the aisles.

It promised to be something special as early as 7 a.m., when the line outside stretched halfway around the block. As the day wore on, and extra cops were called to contain the frenzied crowd, some 21,000 plunked down their 35 cents to hear one of the five shows.

The morning show began calmly enough with Goodman's theme song, "Let's Dance." By the time several more tunes were heard, pandemomium had broken loose with the kids stompin' in the aisles. And no wonder, with the likes of Gene Krupa banging away on his drums, and Ziggy Elman and Harry James pushing their trumpets sky high. If anybody cares, there's also a movie at the Paramount: "Maid of Salem," with Claudette Colbert and Fred MacMurray.

Sit-down strikers yield at Chrysler plants

March 24. A tentative pact has been reached, ending a strike affecting 60,000 workers at Chrysler plants in Michigan. John L. Lewis, the head of the Committee for Industrial Organization, will seek evacuation of 6,000 sit-down strikers from eight plants occupied for 17 days. The United Automobile Workers, a C.I.O. affiliate, has been demanding sole bargaining rights for all Chrysler workers (→ 28).

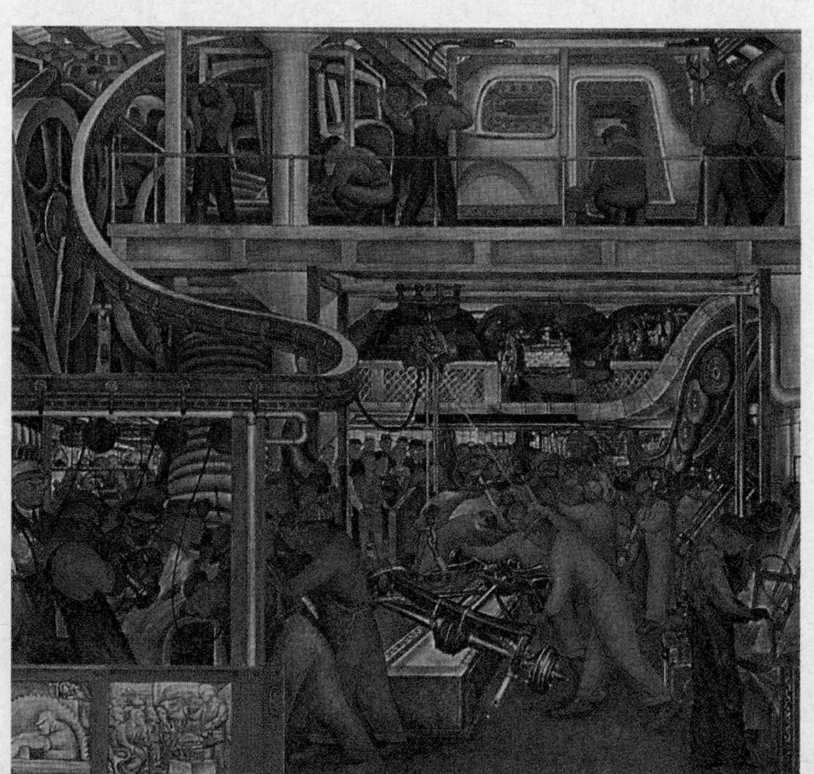

Mexican artist Diego Rivera depicts the rigors of a Detroit assembly line.

Hemingway reports decisive battle

March 29. Ernest Hemingway, author of "The Sun Also Rises," now serving as a war correspondent in Spain, reported on a decisive battle at Brihuega yesterday. Loyalists, in a well-planned attack, killed hundreds of fascist troops and their Italian allies. Hemingway writes, ". . . the Italians were forced to build rocky parapets rather than attempt to dig the soil where a spade would not cut, and the horrible effect of shells—from the guns of the 60 tanks that fought with the infantry in the Brihuega battle—bursting in and against these rock piles made a nightmare of corpses" (→ 4/4).

Hemingway in Madrid.

Texas school fire kills 500 children

March 18. A devastating explosion and fire at a school has left the residents of New London, Texas, numb with grief, as about 500 people, mostly children, burned to death today. The cause of the blast has yet to be determined, but the school's superintendent, W.C. Shaw, suspects that a gas leak in an unused heating system ignited the deadly inferno.

Bodies and fragments of bodies litter the funeral parlor and makeshift morgues as families line up to try to identify their loved ones. A dismal torrential rain has slowed the search for bodies and cleanup efforts, while the weather symbolizes the emotions of everyone in the area. Manpower and supplies from all across the nation have been donated to help ease the suffering from this terrible tragedy.

1937

APRIL

Su	Mo	Tu	We	Th	Fr	Sa
				1	2	3
4	5	6	7	8	9	10
11	12	13	14	15	16	17
18	19	20	21	22	23	24
25	26	27	28	29	30	

1. Washington: Mrs. J.B. Harriman named minister to Norway.

2. South Africa outlaws political activity by foreigners.

2. Michigan: C.I.O. promises to strengthen purge of Communists (→ 6).

4. France: 29 Americans held at border for violating law against volunteering in Spain (→ 5).

5. Spain: Reports indicate Loyalists are using 140 Russian planes (→ 19).

6. Michigan: Chrysler strike ends; 65,000 back to work (→ 7).

7. Georgia: Henry Ford says company will never recognize U.A.W. (→ 14).

11. Belgium: Leon Degrelle's Rexist movement defeated at general elections.

12. U.S. Supreme Court upholds Wagner Act (→ 5/24).

14. Detroit: Tear gas routs 150 sit-down strikers (→ 23).

14. New York: Rogers and Hart musical "Babes in Arms" opens, featuring songs "My Funny Valentine," "The Lady is a Tramp."

15. Art dating from 4,500 B.C. found in Egyptian tomb.

16. Washington: New U.S. warplane Flying Fortress seen for first time.

19. Spain: 27 nations start patrols to enforce neutrality agreements (→ 20).

20. Spain: Rebels gain in Bilbao sector; Franco proclaims Phalange only legal party (→ 27).

21. British inaugurate Ark Royal, their first naval aircraft carrier.

22. Mussolini denies support for monarchy in Vienna; refuses to protect Austria from possible German coup (→ 2/12/38).

23. New York: Andrew Mellon company sued as aluminum monopoly.

23. California: 50 hurt in strike battle at cannery (→ 5/30).

28. Pan Am Clipper arrives in Hong Kong, completing first commercial flight across Pacific.

29. Berlin: Nazis to try 1,000 monks in war on Catholics (→ 7/1).

The horrors of war: German bombers devastate Guernica

The horrible devastation of the Basque capital by German bombers moved Pablo Picasso to paint "Guernica," a disturbing depiction of the horrors of war and the destructiveness of fascism in Europe.

April 27. Hundreds of people, mostly civilians, are dead in the town of Guernica, Spain, near Bilbao. They were killed by German warplanes which swept out of the skies yesterday to strafe a marketplace and farm houses. The small town is still burning tonight.

Junkers and Heikel bombers dropped half-ton bombs, grenades and firebombs and fired mercilessly at peasants working in fields. Those who were lucky enough to escape arc still streaming out of Guernica, their possessions loaded into crude farm wagons pulled by oxen.

The Fascists, who have denied all along that German pilots are even involved in this war, rejected any responsibility for the raid. But Guernica is the capital of the Basques, and this raid seemed designed to teach them a lesson: join us, or this will be your fate (→ 5/5).

Trotsky calls for overthrow of Stalin

April 18. Leon Trotsky, exiled Soviet leader now living in Mexico, said today that a new revolution is necessary to overthrow Joseph Stalin and his Soviet bureaucracy.

Trotsky spoke before the subcommittee convened in Mexico, and headed by Professor John Dewey, investigating Moscow charges that Trotsky is conspiring with Germany and Japan to form "an anti-Soviet alliance." Declaring that Stalin should be "eliminated" but not killed, Trotsky railed against the current Soviet bureaucracy and its privileges, asserting that it must be toppled by a new revolution.

Trotsky added that if war came and Russia found itself allied with Britain and France, it might emerge capitalist because it now teeters between socialism and capitalism, and the Allies would bring political pressure to bear. "If the Soviet Union resists this pressure, her allies will go after her after the war," he added (→ 8/21/40).

Mann pleads for saving German culture

April 20. Nobel Prize winner Thomas Mann addressed the American Guild for German Cultural Freedom in New York tonight, calling for an end to Nazi repression of artistic freedom. Mann has been living in Switzerland in exile since authorities objected to his criticism of Nazism. He charges the German government with erasing previous culture and suppressing new forms.

Mann finds one advantage to the repression. It reawakens us to "fundamental truths," among which is "the fact that the spirit must be free to be at all interesting" (→ 29).

The Golden Gate Bridge, perched tenuously in the heart of California's earthquake belt, is now the world's longest at 4,200 feet (→ 5/27).

1937

MAY

Su	Mo	Tu	We	Th	Fr	Sa
						1
2	3	4	5	6	7	8
9	10	11	12	13	14	15
16	17	18	19	20	21	22
23	24	25	26	27	28	29
30	31					

1. FDR signs third Neutrality Act embodying "cash and carry law" (→ 12/28).

3. Margaret Mitchell wins Pulitzer for "Gone With the Wind."

4. Massachusetts: German ex-Chancellor Heinrich Bruning named to Harvard faculty.

5. Spain: Barcelona quells revolt by Catalonian anarchists (→ 17).

5. Mexico: Court eases church law, abolishing arbitrary quotas for priests.

8. Jockey C. Kurtsinger, on War Admiral, becomes two-time winner of Kentucky Derby.

10. Washington: Negro Congressman Mitchell sues for $50,000, charging he was barred from a Pullman (→ 7/20).

11. Berlin: Hitler orders ban on hydrogen zeppelin flights.

15. Denmark acclaims King Christian X on his silver jubilee.

16. Moscow: Trade union chiefs arrested for Trotskyism (→ 20).

17. Spain: Socialist Juan Negrin replaces Largo Caballero's popular front in Valencia (→ 29).

18. New York: 14 arrested as big insurance racket is uncovered.

19. Hitler asks Vatican to rebuke Chicago Cardinal Mundelein for criticism of Nazis (→ 7/1).

20. Moscow: 44 Russians shot as Japanese spies (→ 6/12).

24. U.S. Supreme Court upholds Social Security Act (→ 7/22).

24. Poland: Three million Jews leave jobs for two hours to protest anti-Semitism (→ 9/1/39).

25. Mussolini tells Italian Jews back Fascists or leave (→ 6/18).

27. San Francisco: 200,000 pedestrians cross the Golden Gate Bridge on its opening day.

28. London: Neville Chamberlain takes premiership, promises peace in Europe (→ 7/29).

29. Spain: Reich battleship set afire in the Mediterranean by Loyalist bombs (→ 6/19).

30. Chicago: Four killed, 84 hurt as police battle strikers (→ 6/7).

31. Wilbur Shaw takes Indy 500 at 113.6 mph.

Hindenburg blows up

The hydrogen-filled Hindenburg, a tragic fireworks display over Lakehurst.

May 6. The dirigible Hindenburg was destroyed by fire tonight in a disaster that killed at least 33 of its 97 passengers and crew. The giant airship was consumed in minutes as it came in for a landing at the Naval Air Station at Lakehurst, New Jersey. The cause of the fire is unknown, but it is believed to have started when either static electricity or sparks from the engines ignited hydrogen gas that was being released preparatory to landing. Until tonight's disaster, the Hindenburg had a perfect safety record in the ten round-trips it made across the Atlantic with 1,002 passengers.

The Hindenburg was 12 hours late on its last flight because of headwinds encountered over the Atlantic. It had cruised slowly down the East coast so it would arrive at dusk, the best time for a landing. The airship dropped its two landing lines at 7:20 p.m. and was settling toward earth when its hydrogen caught fire. At 7:23, witnesses heard a boom and saw a flash from the ship's rear gondola. The flames enveloped the airship in moments, and the Hindenburg collapsed in clouds of smoke. Heroic efforts by Navy personnel and crew members saved many lives (→ 11).

May 12. One million enthusiasts crowded London for the coronation of King George VI. Above, on the Buckingham Palace balcony are Queen Elizabeth, Queen Mary, King George and the two royal princesses.

No more free dimes: Rockefeller is gone

May 23. He wanted to be a hundred, but John D. Rockefeller died this morning, missing the century mark by a little more than two years. The richest man in the world was also the greatest giver of all. More than $530 million has been handed out to educational, scientific and religious institutions.

For years, Rockefeller crossed the Hudson River by ferry, passing out dimes, and many Nyack inhabitants possess such "Rockefeller dimes." The founder of the Standard Oil Company, the son of a country doctor, started his business life with little formal education and no capital. From boyhood, he kept account of every cent he earned, having been taught to work, to save and to give. He wished for his wealth to educate people to help themselves.

4,000 screen actors win in Hollywood

May 9. Threat of a general strike by the Screen Actors Guild, which would have paralyzed the motion picture industry, was averted tonight. Wild cheers went up from 4,000 guild members, including Joan Crawford and Franchot Tone, when President Robert Montgomery announced that most of the studios had agreed to demands for a closed shop as well as benefits for extra and bit players. Minimums for extras doing "mob stuff" went from $3.20 to $5.50 a day.

The tallest dinosaur

May 30. Some hundred million years ago, the tallest creature ever known, standing 35 feet high, walked with 16-foot strides along the primeval ooze. Dr. Barnum Brown of the American Museum of Natural History has been following the elusive foot prints of the giant for years and has now found the first actual bones of the Iguanodont dinosaur, a kangaroo-shaped herb-eater almost twice as large as the Tyrannosaurus, near Rock Springs in Wyoming. Excavation, complete with steam shovels, is under way.

1937

JUNE

Su	Mo	Tu	We	Th	Fr	Sa
		1	2	3	4	5
6	7	8	9	10	11	12
13	14	15	16	17	18	19
20	21	22	23	24	25	26
27	28	29	30			

7. Michigan: C.I.O. seizes Lansing to protest arrest of pickets (→ 10).

8. New Jersey: American Medical Association officially accepts birth control.

9. France: Nello and Carlo Rosselli, leaders of anti-fascist Justice and Freedom League, killed by rightist group Hood (→ 21).

9. Jerusalem: Royal commission considers partition of Palestine between Jews and Arabs (→ 7/7).

10. Michigan: Monroe police smash picket lines; 500 return to jobs (→ 13).

11. Chicago: 50 seized in window-breaking racket, including head of large glass firm.

13. Washington: John L. Lewis calls mine strikes to halt coal to steel mills (→ 21).

13. Moscow: Leaders given ten days to reorganize tractor and auto industry or face trial (→ 14).

14. U.S.S.R.: Soviet executes 28 alleged spies in Siberia (→ 16).

16. Moscow announces suicide of A.G. Cherviakov, pres. of White Russians (→ 7/2).

18. Rome: Mussolini decrees all Fascists must subscribe to party organ Popo d'Italia (→ 7/1/38).

19. Spain: Bilbao falls to Nationalists (→ 23).

20. Russian fliers land in Vancouver, completing first transpolar flight.

21. Philadelphia: Court rules sit-down strikes illegal (→ 25).

21. Paris: Leon Blum's Popular Front Cabinet resigns (→ 3/13/38).

23. London: Reich and Italy pull out of four-power patrols in Spain (→ 8/7).

25. Ohio: Steel mills in Youngstown reopen; 18,556 resume work (→ 7/8).

27. Berlin: 150,000 German war veterans cheer King George VI.

DEATHS

18. Gaston Doumergue, French statesman (*8/1/1863).

19. Sir James Barrie, Scottish writer, "Peter Pan" (*5/9/1860).

Hollywood favorite Jean Harlow dies

Hollywood's first sex goddess.

June 7. "The Platinum Blonde," Jean Harlow, has died in a Hollywood hospital. The 26-year-old actress succumbed to uremic poisoning after a year of poor health. Frequent co-star William Powell kept vigil at her bedside.

Harlow was born Harlean Carpenter in Kansas City, Mo. When she was only 16 she eloped with a businessman and moved with him to Hollywood. Restless, she sought bit parts in films. Harlow separated from her husband and finagled her way into an early talkie, the aerial war saga "Hell's Angels" (1930). She developed a tough-girl image, as in "The Public Enemy" and "Redheaded Woman." Lately, she played screwballs in comedies like "Riffraff" and "Wife vs Secretary."

June 3. The Duke (England's ex-King) and Duchess of Windsor married today in France, ending the scandal of the century.

8 Soviet generals shot

June 12. Joseph Stalin's purges reached into the highest levels of the Russian military. At a secret trial, eight generals were sentenced to death for treason, and were executed today. Officials say they all pleaded guilty to charges of trying to overthrow the Stalin regime.

"Down with traitors!" Pravda, the official Communist Party newspaper declared. "No mercy to spies and betrayers."

One of the generals executed was Marshal Mikhail Tukhachevsky, who until recently was the Vice Commissar of Defense. Secret police arrested him in the middle of the night and wounded him when he allegedly tried to escape.

The generals were all accused of conspiring against the Soviet Union with an unnamed foreign power, presumably Germany. Pravda criticized what it called "the foul boot of German and Japanese Fascism."

"The reptile of Fascist espionage has many heads," Pravda said, "but we will cut off every head, paralyze and sever every tentacle and extract the snake's venom" (→ 13).

Joe Louis champ at last; beats Braddock

Braddock and Louis pose after signing the contract to fight.

June 22. Joe Louis battered James J. Braddock for seven rounds before finishing him off in the eighth to become the new world heavyweight boxing champion.

With a head-jarring right to the jaw, the "Brown Bomber" from Detroit ended Braddock's two-year reign and emerged as the first Negro heavyweight champion in 22 years. There were those who said Louis had been denied a title chance until now because of his color.

Just over a minute of the eighth round had passed when Louis connected. Battered, bruised and bleeding, Braddock slumped to the canvas. The jarring smash caused a hemorrhage and blood stained the floor where Braddock's head had rested after he was carried off.

Braddock managed to knock his 23-year-old rival to the canvas briefly in the first round, but thereafter the 31-year-old Irishman from New York's West Side was at the mercy of Louis. Two years of inactivity and luxurious living had taken their toll on Braddock, although he did enter the ring in the best shape possible for him (→ 8/30).

June 5. War Admiral, third winner of racing's Triple Crown.

1937

JULY

Su	Mo	Tu	We	Th	Fr	Sa
				1	2	3
4	5	6	7	8	9	10
11	12	13	14	15	16	17
18	19	20	21	22	23	24
25	26	27	28	29	30	31

1. Berlin: IBM President Thomas Watson decorated by Hitler (→ 10/30).

2. Moscow: Soviet reveals execution of 120 as spies (→ 8/1).

2. Amelia Earhart disappears during flight over Pacific (→ 18).

3. Wimbledon: Don Budge becomes first to win singles, doubles and mixed; Dorothy Round over Jadwiga Jedrzejowska 6-2, 2-6, 7-5.

7. London: Peel Commission report suggests ending Palestine mandate and dividing area between Arabs and Jews (→ 8/2).

8. Detroit: Press witness calls Ford men, charged with assault in strike riots, "typical hoodlums" (→ 9/3).

9. U.S.: 109 dead in heat wave.

9. Tehran: Iran, Iraq, Turkey and Afghanistan sign nonaggression pact.

13. Japanese battle Chinese at gates of Peking (→ 30).

17. India: Train wreck kills 95.

20. Florida: Two Negro youths lynched (→ 9/12).

21. Ireland: Eamon de Valera re-elected Free State president (→ 28).

22. U.S. Senate kills FDR's court reform bill 70-20 (→ 10/3).

22. Tour de France won by French racer Roger Lapebie.

23. Yale professors announce isolation of pituitary hormone.

23. London: Divorce reform enacted, ending era of "holy deadlock."

27. U.S. defeats Britain to capture Davis Cup.

28. Belfast: King George VI escapes I.R.A. bombs (→ 12/29).

29. London: Neville Chamberlain sends note to Mussolini as peace gesture (→ 8/6).

BIRTH

9. David Hockney, British artist.

DEATHS

11. George Gershwin, American composer (*9/26/1898).

19. Guglielmo Marconi, Italian inventor, wireless (*4/25/1874).

Earhart lost at sea on round-world trip

July 18. At sunset tonight, the search for Amelia Earhart will be called off. The famed flier went down in the Pacific about 100 miles from Howland Island two weeks ago. She vanished without a trace.

Miss Earhart and her navigator, Fred Noonan, were attempting to circle the globe. They started May 21 at Oakland, Calif., heading east. The trip was more than halfway completed when they landed at Lae, New Guinea, on June 28. They rested and prayed for good weather. July 2nd dawned with perfect visibility. After the hop to Howland, it would have been straight to Honolulu, San Francisco and home.

That evening, two radio amateurs in Los Angeles picked up a faint signal on the wave frequency assigned to the plane. Low on fuel, it said. Other details were garbled. A Coast Guard cutter combed the general area at once, joined over the next days by a dozen ships and aircraft.

The sea was calm; the plane floats; Miss Earhart kept extra rations. The public remains unconvinced that it is time to grieve.

Earhart in Africa, six months ago.

Japanese rout Chinese on a wide front

July 30. In a major offensive led by tanks and supported by bombers, the Japanese army routed Chinese troops and established control over the whole area from Tientsin to Peking. The undeclared war broke out after an incident earlier this month at the Marco Polo Bridge near Peking in which Japan said its troops were fired upon by Chinese soldiers. Japanese troops, marching down from Manchuria, routed Chinese defenders in Tientsin and occupied the city. The bodies of Chinese soldiers were dumped by the hundreds into the Pei River.

Meanwhile, after several days of skirmishing around Peking, a Japanese mechanized army defeated the Nationalist 37th Division, seized the Marco Polo Bridge and occupied a strategic rail center southwest of Peking, thus blocking any Nationalist counterattack (→ 8/8).

Four of Scottsboro boys free; five held

July 24. Four of the "Scottsboro boys" were set free today after years in prison awaiting new trials. Three of them had earlier been sentenced to death, and the fourth sent to prison, after sensational trials in Scottsboro, Alabama. Their convictions were reversed by the Supreme Court and new trials were ordered. The Negro youths were among the nine accused of attacking two white women on a Southern freight train on March 25, 1931. Four of the nine have been sentenced to serve prison terms ranging from 20 to 99 years and the fifth has been sentenced to death.

Niemoeller jailed for resisting Nazis

July 1. The Rev. Martin Niemoeller, a leading Protestant critic of the Nazi regime in Germany, has been arrested and jailed. The Hitler government said he had been arrested for his "agitatory" speeches, his slander of leading government officials and his urging of opposition to government laws. His arrest, which presumably was made with Hitler's personal approval, had been expected for some time. Rev. Niemoeller was the last member of the Prussian Council of the Confessional Church, which has defied the Nazi government, to be at liberty (→ 8/4).

1937

AUGUST

Su	Mo	Tu	We	Th	Fr	Sa
1	2	3	4	5	6	7
8	9	10	11	12	13	14
15	16	17	18	19	20	21
22	23	24	25	26	27	28
29	30	31				

1. Moscow: Thirty churchmen on trial for fascist plot (→ 10/21).

2. World Zionist Congress endorses Peel plan for Palestinian independence (→ 23).

4. Berlin: Teachers manual issued, stressing need for preaching anti-Semitism (→ 8).

5. Rhode Island: Yacht Ranger keeps America's Cup in U.S.

5. Tokyo: Japan demands China enter Tokyo-Berlin pact against Communism (→ 21).

6. London: Three German journalists expelled from Britain (→ 11/17).

7. Madrid: Senor Nin, leader of United Marxist Workers Party, is assassinated (→ 26).

8. China: Japan occupies Peking, sets up army rule (→ 11).

8. Berlin: 115 seized in rally protesting Niemueller's internment; first mass anti-Nazi gathering.→

11. China: 32 Japanese warships collect at Shanghai (→ 15).

13. U.S. Senate approves Hugo Black's nomination to Supreme Court (→ 9/12).

15. China: U.S. women and children evacuate Shanghai as Japanese launch attack (→ 20).

20. China: U.S. cruiser Augusta hit by Japanese shell at Shanghai; one dead, 18 hurt (→ 22).

21. Nanking: China signs nonaggression pact with U.S.S.R.

23. Palestine: Jews ask direct negotiations with Arabs before partition of Palestine (→ 9/8).

25. Japan blockades Chinese coast (→ 9/9).

26. Spain: Santander taken by Nationalist rebels (→ 9/10).

30. N.Y.: Joe Louis beats Tom Farr in first title defense (→ 1/25/39).

BIRTHS

3. Diane Wakoski, prolific American poet.

8. Dustin Hoffman, U.S. actor.

DEATH

26. Andrew Mellon, American industrialist, philanthropist (*3/24/1855).

Bombs shatter Shanghai in heavy fighting

Aug 22. Japanese bombers and warships spread fire and terror throughout Shanghai as Japanese forces stood poised to occupy the famous port city. Great billows of smoke hung over the city, which was turned into a seething inferno after several days of bombing by Japanese warplanes. The apparent Japanese strategy was to use airpower to eliminate all Chinese resistance before moving in ground troops to occupy the city.

In pursuit of this strategy, Japanese planes dropped incendiary bombs to set buildings afire and drive out the defenders and then drop high explosive bombs upon the exposed troops. The fires extended into the city's International Settlement, to which Chinese refugees had flocked. The Japanese attack on the city began after an incident earlier this month in which a Japanese naval officer and enlisted man were killed at a nearby airfield.

Meanwhile, Japanese troops took possession of Peking. Japanese planes dropped leaflets saying: "Japanese troops have driven out your wicked rulers and their wicked armies and will keep them out." Southwest of Peking, the first major battle of the undeclared war broke out as Chinese Nationalist troops counterattacked (→ 25).

Surveying the damage at Shanghai.

Buchenwald: Fourth concentration camp

August. This month, Heinrich Himmler's SS (defense echelons) gave Adolf Hitler an account of the results of the reorganization of the concentration camps. With Dachau, Sachsenhausen and Lichtenburg (a women's camp), Buchenwald is the fourth such camp in Germany. Nazi concentration camps are under the administration of the SS, Hitler's elite guard.

Each camp is exclusively guarded by 1,500 SS. The SS Colonel Karl Koch is the commander of the very large camp at Buchenwald. Most of the inmates are German political prisoners and homosexuals. They have primitive shelter and minimal food. Those who are sick and starved are forced to work. It is not unusual for a prisoner to lose 50 percent of his weight. This camp was built according to the criteria of "functional unity and capacity." The Nazi regime has been sending Communists, Jews and other enemies of the state to concentration camps since March 1933 (→ 9/5).

A vehicle dignified enough for the world's most heroic firefighters.

1937

SEPTEMBER

Su	Mo	Tu	We	Th	Fr	Sa
			1	2	3	4
5	6	7	8	9	10	11
12	13	14	15	16	17	18
19	20	21	22	23	24	25
26	27	28	29	30		

3. Washington: John L. Lewis warns FDR to back C.I.O. or lose labor support (→ 10/3).

3. Hong Kong: Typhoon kills 300.

6. Moscow: Soviets accuse Italy of torpedoing two Russian ships in Mediterranean (→ 10).

8. Syria: Pan-Arab conference rejects Peel plan, insists on Arab state in Palestine (→ 26).

9. China: Japanese air raid kills 300 refugees in train; Tokyo warns all transportation routes between Nanking, Shanghai and Hangkow will be bombed (→ 14).

10. Switzerland: Nine powers agree to halt piracy by patroling Mediterranean in zones (→ 17).

11. New York: Don Budge wins U.S. national tennis title.

12. Pittsburgh: It is reported that Justice Black is still member of Ku Klux Klan (→ 29).

14. Washington: U.S. ships forbidden to take arms to Far East (→ 22).

17. Mediterranean: Rebel submarines convoyed by German and Italian submarines (→ 30).

21. American aviatrix Jacqueline Cochran sets women's airspeed record at 292 mph.

22. U.S. sends note to Tokyo protesting yesterday's Nanking air raid (→ 29).

25. Germany: Mussolini and Hitler meet in Munich.

25. Egypt: 22 killed in mob of 80,000 showing loyalty to new King Farouk (→ 10/23).

26. Palestine: British chief Lewis Andrews killed by Arabs in Galilee (→ 10/1).

27. China: Japanese subs sink fishing junks; hundreds die.

28. Geneva: Belgium granted seat in League Council.

30. Geneva: League threatens to end non-intervention if Italy keeps troops in Spain (→ 10/5).

DEATH

2. Baron Pierre de Coubertin, founder of modern Olympic Games (*1/1/1863).

13. Tomas Masaryk, first Czech president (*3/7/1850).

The Blues Empress will reign no more

Sept 26. Bessie Smith, who sang the blues nobly, has died in an automobile accident in Mississippi. There are rumors she would have lived, but she was denied treatment because she was a Negro.

Miss Smith was born in Chatanooga, Tennessee, in 1894 or 1898. In her late teens, she became the protege of Gertrude "Ma" Rainey. Miss Smith soon developed a rich, dark voice and a hearty stage presence. In 1923, she recorded her first songs (among them "Downhearted Blues") which sold millions. Miss Smith was a victim of alcoholism and changing musical tastes; of late she played in the small honky-tonks where she began.

Chiang, Mao unite to oppose Japanese

Sept 29. Politics can make strange bedfellows, and that was proved again today in China. Just seven months after rejecting any cooperation with Communist leader Mao Tse-tung, Chiang Kai-shek reversed himself. Chiang decided he has an even greater enemy, the invaders from Japan. Chiang and Mao agreed at Nanking that their armies will fight together. Mao agreed to dissolve his Red army, reorganize his militia and place his soldiers under the direction of a committee of military operations. The united Chinese forces may be a formidable foe (→ 10/2).

Autumn fashions for women.

Biggest Nazi rally held in Nuremberg

A foreboding sea of Nazis turn out in Nuremberg to listen to their Fuhrer.

Sept 5. The streets of Nuremberg were lined with storm troopers today and all the church bells rang at once as Adolf Hitler arrived for the opening of the National Socialist Congress. The event is designed to be the largest display of Nazi power in Germany's history.

The size of the congress is staggering. Hitler will review a parade of 600,000 men. Hundreds of trains are transporting army and paramilitary units to Nuremberg. The men are being housed in 13 tent cities.

An anti-Bolshevik exhibit that links communism with Judaism was opened today. The local Nazi leader, Julius Streicher, made the astounding charge that the Talmud gives Jews the right to murder people who are not Jewish.

The diplomatic corps, including the American charge d'affaires, is due in a few days. Benito Mussolini is also coming. Hitler and Mussolini are expected to exchange high military honors, and Hitler is likely to greet the Duce, the founder of Fascism, as one of Europe's leading anti-Communists (→ 1/1/38).

Black, appointee to Court, joined KKK

Sept 29. Hugo L. Black, who was recently appointed to the Supreme Court, refused today to confirm or deny reports that he is now or ever was a member of the Ku Klux Klan.

The allegation was made recently by the Pittsburgh Post-Gazette, which reported that the former Alabama Senator joined the Klan in 1923 at the time he was a county prosecutor. Returning today from a vacation in Europe, the newly appointed Supreme Court Justice made it plain that he does not intend to resign. President Roosevelt, who appointed Black to the judicial position, has declined to comment on the allegations, saying, "I know only what I have read in the papers" (→ 10/4).

Japan labels some goods USA-made

Sept 19. The newest trick in Japanese competition with the United States for Latin American markets involves labeling Japanese goods "Made in USA" and shipping them to several countries in violation of quotas limiting Japanese imports to the value of the country's exports to Japan. In Colombia, Japanese machinery with false USA trademarks has been sold by a German agent.

The Japanese goods flooding the Latin market the past few years have been generally cheap and shoddy, which, with low labor costs, makes possible the underselling of American goods, and at the same time makes American manufacturers appear to be exporting inferior products to those nations.

1937

OCTOBER

Su	Mo	Tu	We	Th	Fr	Sa
					1	2
3	4	5	6	7	8	9
10	11	12	13	14	15	16
17	18	19	20	21	22	23
24	25	26	27	28	29	30
31						

1. Palestine: Britain deports several Arab leaders (→ 15).

2. China: Japanese invade Shantung, drive on Nanking (→ 6).

3. Chicago: Rail unions win pay raise of 44 cents/day (→ 11/21).

3. Washington: Report indicates federal govt. paid 14 percent of U.S. income in 1936 (→ 11/15).

3. London: Mob raids Fascist meeting; 111 arrested (→ 10).

5. Spain: Mussolini's son flies in combat for rebel air force (→ 21).

5. London: British Laborites bar link with Communists (→ 11/1).

6. Washington: U.S. drops neutral stand on China, condemns Japan as invader (→ 11/3).

10. New York: Yankees beat Giants in five games to take World Series second year in row.

11. Hungarian opposition parties, Agrarian and Legitimist, join forces, support return of monarchy to oppose fascists (→ 2/22/38).

12. Maine: G-Men kill public enemy #1 Al Brady and half his gang as they plan bank robbery.

13. Berlin: Reich pledges to defend Belgium if Brussels will renounce military action against Germany (→ 28).

15. Palestine: Two British constables killed (→ 20).

16. Czechs crush Sudeten German Party meeting (→ 3/4/38).

21. Spain: Franco's army takes Gijon, giving Nationalists control of northern Spain (→ 11/28).

21. U.S.S.R.: 62 more executed in Soviet purge (→ 11/3).

23. Egypt: 60 hurt in Cairo in anti-government riots.

28. Rome: Mussolini pledges support for Hitler's colonial claims (→ 31).

30. New Jersey: Dr. Joachim Prinz predicts extinction of German Jewry in ten years (→ 1/16/38).

31. Italy, Germany vow mutual aid if attacked (→ 11/6).

DEATH

19. Lord Rutherford, British physicist, 1908 Nobel Prize (*8/30/1871).

Fascist stoned at rally in London

Oct 10. Sir Oswald Mosley, British Fascist leader, suffered a concussion and scalp wounds today when stoned by a crowd of 10,000 Liverpool demonstrators prior to his delivery of a speech.

As Mosley climbed on the loudspeaker wagon, a number of men began hurling stones, one of which struck him on the left temple. Twelve mounted policemen immediately came to the aid of 100 patrolmen, quickly dispersing the mob but not before it had wrecked the speaker wagon.

Fights also broke out between Fascists and Communists. The meeting ended with the singing of "God Save the King." Both Communists and Fascists sang lustily as they gave their respective salutes of upraised palms and clenched fists.

Mosley lacks none of Hitler's zeal.

Earlier this year, two mobs attacked Mosley as he marched under police protection (→ 11/1).

Black admits KKK link, joins Court

Oct 4. While having admitted that he was once a member of the Ku Klux Klan, Hugo L. Black took his seat on the United States Supreme Court today. The new Justice, his face inscrutable, sat quietly as the court heard, but took no action on, motions to deny him a seat. Black did not repeat the oath of office. He had been sworn in nearly two months ago, not long after his appointment (→ 4/28/41).

British restrict Jewish access to Palestine

Polish and Rumanian Jews greet an uncertain future at the port of Jaffa.

Oct 20. Rejecting a previous principle of economic absorptive capacity, the Palestine government has issued an ordinance restricting Jewish immigration. Now, the limits of Jewish immigration will depend not on economic circumstances but on national political conditions.

The Hebrew press vehemently attacked the new ordinance. It claims Britain's wording of the law—"persons of the Jewish faith"—clearly violates the mandate, which states all religions in Palestine shall stand on an equal basis. Newspapers in Bethlehem and Jerusalem also point to the Council of the League of Nations, which demands that England adhere to the economic absorptive principle.

Since July 7, when Britain, as the mandatory power, proposed a partition of Palestine into Arab and Jewish states, 39 people have died from terrorist attacks. Yesterday, snipers fired on a police station near a Bethlehem church. No one was hurt in the attack (→ 12/23).

This new television set will soon be available for home use.

1937

NOVEMBER

Su	Mo	Tu	We	Th	Fr	Sa
	1	2	3	4	5	6
7	8	9	10	11	12	13
14	15	16	17	18	19	20
21	22	23	24	25	26	27
28	29	30				

1. London: Labor wins 17 of 28 borroughs, Fascists crushed.

2. New York: Fiorella LaGuardia re-elected mayor.

3. Belgium: Parley opens in Brussels in move to align democracies against dictators.

3. China: U.S. troops halt invasion of American sector in Shanghai (→ 8).

3. France: Soviet diplomat Alexandre Barmine resigns and denounces Stalin, says will die if forced to return (→ 1/16/38).

6. Rome joins Berlin, Tokyo in anti-Soviet pact (→ 2/4/38).

7. Moscow: One million parade on 20th anniversary of Bolshevik revolution.

8. Chinese quit Shanghai burning buildings in retreat (→ 14).

12. Mexico grants concessions to Shell Oil Company (→ 12/26).

14. Japan balks at Brussels conference on China (→ 24).

15. Tennessee: 18 suits brought against TVA, calling for dissolution (→ 29).

17. British official Lord Halifax visits Germany, seeking ways to appease Nazis (→ 4/16/38).

18. India: 1,100 prisoners freed after appeal by Gandhi, his first political act in year (→ 1/29/39).

20. Rome: Mussolini takes over Ministry for Italian Africa (→ 11/30/38).

21. Michigan: Gov. Murphy threatens to end GM strike with state troops (→ 12/23).

23. Steinbeck's "Of Mice and Men" staged in New York.

26. New York: Cuban ex-Pres. Machado arrested in hospital; Havana to press for extradition (→ 11/11/38).

27. Philadelphia: Army blanks Navy 6-0 in football.

28. Franco blockades Spanish coast (→ 12/1).

29. F.D.R. asks U.S. Congress to allot $16 billion for federal housing program (→ 1/1/38).

DEATH

8. James Ramsay MacDonald, British ex-prime minister, head of Labor Party (*10/12/1866).

Nazis take parents away from children

Nov 29. In Waldenberg, Germany, a court has taken parents away from their children because they refused to teach them Nazi ideology. The parents are pacifists, members of a Christian sect called International Bible Researchers. The court accused them of creating an environment where the children would grow up "enemies of the state." The children were delivered into the state's care.

The judge delivered a lengthy statement reading in part, "The law as a racial and national instrument entrusts German parents with the education of their children only under certain conditions, namely, that they educate them in the fashion that the nation and state expect" (→ 1/1/38).

Germany's future. And Europe?

Nov 23. Redskins, aiming for the title, score upset over Chicago.

Father Divine's Heaven burns to ground

Nov 7. "Super-super Heaven," an 80-room mansion owned by the self-styled Reverend Father Divine, burned to cinders this afternoon. The home, located in Ulster County, New York, had housed 50 of Father Divine's "angels," fanatic cult followers. They all escaped unharmed; Father Divine himself was out of town at the time.

Father Divine's following consists mostly of middle-aged female Harlem residents. They credit Divine with improved financial and spiritual fortunes. They call him, almost casually, "God." This "God" was arrested and released on charges relating to a stabbing last spring. The vast majority of Harlemites find Divine's cult an embarrassment or an outrage.

The fire broke out just as the "angels" were sitting down to their noon meal in the banquet hall. Someone cried, "Heaven's on fire!" In seconds everyone was safe, but the mansion was destroyed. At least one "angel" was not perturbed. "Let 'er burn," she said. "Father will build one more beautiful."

Last Easter, a throng of Father Divine supporters marched in New York City.

Japan responds to quarantine speech

Nov 24. With the capture of Soochow, the Japanese now envision smooth sailing into Nanking and Shanghai. The Chinese have already retreated from the latter, burning buildings as they fled.

Meanwhile, the Japanese refused to join the Brussels conference, which has ended after failing to resolve the war in China, and Koki Hirota, Japanese Foreign Minister, has accused the U.S. of fomenting an anti-Japanese league, specifically referring to President Roosevelt's October 5th speech declaring that "when an epidemic starts to spread," patients must be quarantined "in order to protect the health of the community" (→ 12/13).

Mexico takes over at Standard Oil

Nov 4. Abrogating an international treaty, Mexican President Lazaro Cardenas has nationalized 350,000 acres of oil lands leased to the Standard Oil Company of California as part of the nationalization of two million acres.

This is the first time in its recent nationalization of all potential oil lands that Mexico has seized land under lease. The move is considered a step toward the gradual elimination of American and British oil companies, capitalized at $400 million, in Mexico. It is also seen to endanger all U.S. and British concessions, which are mostly organized, under Mexico law, as Mexican corporations (→ 12).

1937

DECEMBER

Su	Mo	Tu	We	Th	Fr	Sa
			1	2	3	4
5	6	7	8	9	10	11
12	13	14	15	16	17	18
19	20	21	22	23	24	25
26	27	28	29	30	31	

1. Japan recognizes Franco's Nationalists as official government of Spain (→ 1/12/38).

5. N.Y.: Lindberghs arrive on holiday visit after two-year voluntary exile (→ 10/10/38).

11. Rome: Fascist High Council votes immediate withdrawal from League of Nations.

13. China: Japanese army occupies Nanking (→ 22).

21. New York: Lincoln Tunnel opens.

23. NLRB convicts Ford of violating labor laws (→ 5/26/38).

23. London warns Rome to stop anti-British propaganda in Palestine (→ 1/4/38).

26. U.S. asks Mexico to slow industrialization (→ 1/19/38).

28. F.D.R. to ask for larger Navy, voices "growing concern" for world events (→ 1/28/38).

29. Irish Free State promulgates new constitution, refusing to acknowledge British king's sovereignty, yet remaining member of Commonwealth (→ 4/25/38).

BIRTH

21. Jane Fonda, U.S. actress.

DEATHS

20. Erich Ludendorff, German general (*4/9/1865).

21. Frank Kellogg, American ex-sec. of state (*12/22/1856).

27. Maurice Ravel, French composer (*3/7/1875).

CULTURAL EVENTS, 1937

Literature: Malraux's "Man's Hope"; Steinbeck's "Of Mice and Men"; Van Wyck Brooks' "The Flowering of New England," Pulitzer Prize history; Clifford Odets' "Golden Boy."

Academia: Karen Horney's "The Neurotic Personality of Our Time."

Music: Harold Rome's revue "Pins and Needles"; Israel Philharmonic founded; "The Lady Is a Tramp"; "Whistle While You Work"; "A Foggy Day in London Town."

The Arts: Picasso's "Guernica"; Mellon endows Natl. Gallery in Washington D.C.

Japanese sink U.S. ships; five are dead

Dec 22. As the Japanese press their invasion of China, the Tokyo Foreign Office reports that the sinking of the United States gunboat Panay ten days ago in the Yangtze River, 25 miles above Nanking, was a mistake. Two Standard Oil ships were also sunk at the same time by the combination of aerial bombardment and ground machine-gunning. The statement claims that the American ships were mistaken for Chinese vessels. When the local Japanese army commander discovered his error, the U.S. wounded were immediately cared for.

The report seems plausible as Japanese front-line soldiers are well disposed toward foreigners, especially Americans, witness the quick treatment of the wounded. In all, five Americans were killed.

The occupation of the Shanghai-Nanking area complete, Japanese troops are knocking on the gates of Hanchow, south of Shanghai, and expect to mark New Year's with a triumphal entry into that city. Japan is expected to place all of the conquered Chinese provinces under the recently established Peking provisional government. The city has been officially renamed Peking, meaning "northern capital."

Japan is plainly intoxicated by her military victories and all hopes for an armistice, which seemed possible a fortnight ago, have been abandoned as China and Japan now appear engaged in a fight to the bitter end (→ 1/10/38).

Dec 8. President Roosevelt has chosen Joseph Kennedy (left) to be Ambassador to England.

Song has ended for romantic Ravel

Impressionistic composer Ravel.

Dec 28. Maurice Ravel has died in Paris at the age of 62. The French composer suffered from aphasia. Early this month, he underwent brain surgery, which was unsuccessful. Ravel was a major figure of 20th Century French music. He always strived for perfection of form and style.

Ravel began to study piano at seven and harmony at 11. At 14, he entered the Paris Conservatory, where he remained until 1905. During this period, he composed some of his most famous works, including "Miroirs" and "Sonatine."

With these works, Ravel became well-known to the public. Of his purely orchestral works, the "Rapsodie espagnole" (1907) and "Bolero" (1928) are the most famous and reveal his mastery of the art of instrumentation. "L'enfant et les Sortileges" is his best-known opera.

Lord Cecil receives Nobel Peace Prize

Dec 10. Not passive pacifism but aggressive peace-keeping is what the brand-new Nobel Peace Prize winner, Viscount Cecil of Chelwood, preaches. Lord Cecil is a founder of the League of Nations and an advocate of disarmament. Recently, he was in America to receive an honorary Doctor of Laws degree from Columbia University, his first visit since receiving the Woodrow Wilson peace prize 12 years ago. France's Roger Martin du Gard won the literature prize.

Dos Passos finishes his trilogy: U.S.A.

Gritty pessimism marked American literature this year. John Dos Passos, the son of a Portuguese immigrant, completed his trilogy "U.S.A." The first two volumes, published earlier, are "The 42nd Parallel" and "1919"; the final is "The Big Money." "U.S.A." is a lonely country, according to Dos Passos. He describes a dozen lives in short, cinematic clips, reducing human existence to a few swift impersonal bulletins.

Ernest Hemingway, like Dos Passos a student of journalistic style, offered "To Have and Have Not." Hemingway gives a variation on his typical hero; this time the man is a shiftless mercenary at sea near the West Indies. John Steinbeck came out with a short novel called "Of Mice and Men." The book tells of two itinerant Southern fieldhands fleeing a past marred by murder. The novel is read quickly, a swift assessment of fleeting lives.

Missing link search turns up Java man

Dec 10. Humankind is about one million years old, judging from the age of a skull recently discovered on the island of Java. The Carnegie Institution of Washington released its findings this morning on "Java man," the oldest link between homo sapiens and the apes. Previously, the oldest specimen had been Pithecanthropus Erectus, bones of which had also been found on Java. This latest discovery predates Pithecanthropus by 500,000 years.

The Java man skull includes an intact lower jaw and a few teeth. The teeth are typical of primitive humans, as is the lower jaw socket. The lack of a fully developed mastoid process near the ear, however, was termed "ape-like." The skullcap had been badly cracked, and it was difficult to reassemble. Scientists surmised that a head-hunting enemy of this particular Java man may have chosen to feast on the brain, a head-hunting delicacy.

Something for everybody in 1937 movies

Walt Disney's "Snow White and the Seven Dwarfs."

The world of film subjects grew wider this year with a new entry: animation. Walt Disney's first full-length picture "Snow White and the Seven Dwarfs" was screened privately this month, and the public can see it in February. It has a memorable score, including the tune "Whistle While You Work."

For adventure, nothing could beat "Lost Horizon" or "Captains Courageous." Ronald Colman was the intrepid wanderer who stumbles upon Shangri-La. Frank Capra directed. Victor Fleming took the helm of "Captains Courageous." He had Spencer Tracy wear dark makeup and a curly wig to look halfway Portuguese as a Portuguese fisherman. Freddie Bartholomew played the boy who learns about life upon the high seas.

Marx Bros.: "A Day at the Races."

Romance? Greta Garbo suffered beautifully as Marguerite in the film "Camille," based on the Alexandre Dumas novel. George Cukor, who brings out the best in women actors, directed. The work of a 19th-century French writer was brought to the screen in "The Life of Emile Zola." Paul Muni starred in the title role. Muni is good at stepping into other people's shoes; he received an Oscar for the title role last year in "The Story of Louis Pasteur".

"A Day at the Races" and the Sonja Henie vehicle "Thin Ice" were pleasantly foolish. Groucho Marx was veterinarian Dr. Hackenbush, who takes a stab at general practice with Margaret Dumont at the other end of the hypodermic needle. In "Thin Ice," Henie was a mere peasant girl who skates her way into the arms of a prince.

Spencer Tracy (left).

Frank Capra's "Lost Horizon."

1938

JANUARY

Su	Mo	Tu	We	Th	Fr	Sa
						1
2	3	4	5	6	7	8
9	10	11	12	13	14	15
16	17	18	19	20	21	22
23	24	25	26	27	28	29
30	31					

1. Pasadena: California over Alabama 13-0 in Rose Bowl.

1. Germany: Jewish doctors lose insurance under Nuremburg Laws (→ 6/3).

2. U.S.: 36 million now on Social Security (→ 3).

2. China: Chaing Kai-shek gives up premiership to H.H. Kung (→ 12/23/40).

3. Washington: FDR asks capital and labor to cooperate in recovery effort (→ 21).

4. Britain postpones partition of Palestine, names new commission under Sir John Woodhead (→ 7/8).

8. Berlin: 30,000 Italian farm workers reported emigrating to Germany to aid labor shortage.

10. Washington: House narrowly defeats measure asking right for Congress to declare war.

10. China: Tsing-tao occupied by Japanese army (→ 2/12).

10. Puerto Rico: Eight nationalists convicted in attempt on life of U.S. Justice Robert Cooper.

12. Hungary, Austria recognize Franco govt. in Spain (→ 19).

12. Vatican: Pope praises Mussolini, rebukes Hitler.

16. Forty-eight U.S. publishers reject invitation to International Congress in Germany (→ 3/8).

17. First international Surrealist exhibit opens in Pairs.

19. Detroit: GM begins mass production of diesel engines.

19. Barcelona: Rebel air raid kills 200 (→ 30).

19. Mexico raises tariffs on U.S. products 100-200 percent (→ 3/18).

21. Tennessee: Court upholds validity of TVA (→ 2/6).

28. FDR asks Congress for increased military spending (→ 3/31).

28. Athens: Premier Ionnis Metaxas jails 100 critics.

30. Sixty in U.S. Congress send sympathy note to Loyalist Parliament at Barcelona (→ 31).

31. British steamer Endymion sunk by torpedo in Mediterranean; 11 dead (→ 2/1).

U.S. census shows nearly 8 million jobless

Jan 1. At least 7.8 million Americans are jobless, according to the government's first national unemployment census, and the total could be over ten million. The census indicates that up to a fifth of all American workers are unemployed.

The jobless estimates are based on replies from 72 percent of American households. In delivering the report to President Roosevelt, officials noted that the job situation has worsened since late November, when the census was carried out.

Total employment is estimated at 44 million by the American Federation of Labor. The numbers include more than two million Americans on government emergency payrolls such as the Works Progress Administration and the Civilian Conservation Corps. Another report, from the Social Security Board, shows that more than 36 million wage earners now have Social Security accounts and that 21 million workers are now covered by unemployment compensation programs run by the states. The first regular Social Security payments will be made in 1942 (→ 2).

Tenant farm family in California.

NBC rebuked for Mae West's show

Jan 14. The Federal Communications Commission reprimanded the National Broadcasting Company for airing a lewd program last month starring Mae West. Miss West, Don Ameche and Edgar Bergen's ventriloquist dummy Charlie McCarthy were part of Miss West's feature "Adam and Eve." The FCC told NBC it has a responsibility to curb material "offensive to the great mass of right-thinking, clean-minded American citizens."

Lousy plot costs movie chief his job

Jan 16. A Russian film producer has been ousted from his post, following a slew of poor quality films that relied on anti-Marxist themes. Boris Shumiatsky is responsible for a version of "Treasure Island" pulled from theaters last week. The picture featured a female Jim Hawkins (rumored to be Shumiatsky's girlfriend) digging for gold against the unlikely background of the Irish Rebellion. The film was shot at four times the planned budget (→ 3/2).

Benny Goodman's music saves Busby Berkeley's latest film, marred by a paper-thin plot. Ronald Reagan (center) appears as a radio announcer.

1938

FEBRUARY

Su	Mo	Tu	We	Th	Fr	Sa
		1	2	3	4	5
6	7	8	9	10	11	12
13	14	15	16	17	18	19
20	21	22	23	24	25	26
27	28					

1. Britain sends eight warships to Mediterranean to seek "pirate" submarine (→ 4).

3. California: 11 killed as two bombers collide during night war games.

4. Spain: British freighter Alcira sunk in Mediterranean (→ 15).

6. New York: Andres Segovia plays Town Hall.

6. FDR backs $8 million transcontinental highway system (→ 18).

12. Germany: Schuschnigg meets Hitler, agrees to amnesty for Austrian Nazis (→ 15).

12. Japan refuses to reveal naval data requested by U.S. and Great Britain (→ 23).

15. Vienna: Nazis get key posts in Austrian Cabinet (→ 16).

15. Spain: Franco launches drive to Mediterranean (→ 3/17).

16. Toscanini withdraws from Salzburg music festival over Nazi victory in Austria (→ 20).

18. FDR signs second Agricultural Adjustment Act; appoints Emory Land to head Maritime Commission (→ 5/27).

20. Berlin: Hitler demands self-determination for Germans in Austria, Czechoslovakia (→ 24).

20. Argentina: President Roberto Ortiz inaugurated.

22. London: Neville Chamberlain says League is incapable of enforcing collective security.

22. Hungary: Nazi chief and 72 aides seized for alleged coup plot (→ 8/22).

23. New York: Joe Louis defends title, knocking out Nathan Mann in third round (→ 4/1).

23. Twelve Chinese fighters drop bombs on Japan (→ 4/14).

24. Tooth brushes —first nylon-based products —marketed in New Jersey.

24. Vienna: Schuschnigg pledges to defend Austria's independence, offers protection to German minority in Austria (→ 3/9).

DEATH

7. Harvey Firestone, American tire and rubber magnate (*12/20/1868).

Hitler promotes himself to military chief

Feb 4. Adolf Hitler resolved the escalating tension between his Cabinet and the army today by giving himself unprecedented power. The Fuhrer named himself Supreme Commander of the German armed forces, and he seized direct control of foreign policy.

Hitler forced two generals to take early retirement. A scandal surrounding one of them, Field Marshal and War Minister Werner von Blomberg, helped precipitate the crisis. Blomberg was married just last month, and Hitler himself was a witness. Since the wedding, charges have been flying that his wife is a former prostitute.

General Werner von Fritsch, Commander-in-Chief of the army, was also forced to retire. He has been accused of being a homosexual. Two generals, Wilhelm Keitel and Walther von Brauchitsch, were both promoted to top positions.

Hitler now commands Reich troops.

Hitler established a secret Cabinet council to advise him on foreign policy, and he named several old cronies to the group, including Rudolf Hess, Hermann Goering and Joachim von Ribbentrop (→ 20).

King puts army in control of Rumania

Feb 12. After breaking a seven-week marriage of convenience with Octavian Goga's National Christian Party, proclaiming himself dictator and putting the army in charge, Rumania's King Carol today promised a new constitution.

The king's break with the Transylvanian poet followed Goga's refusal to curb his virulent Jew-baiting. Though Carol has anti-Semitic sympathies, Goga's tactics had spread panic among Rumanian Jews and endangered the country's economy. With Goga gone, business has improved as the Jews return to a regular economic life.

Since foreigners who have settled in Rumania without official permits must leave the country, most Jews will be seeking homes elsewhere. They yet noted with relief that today's Porunca Vremel, newspaper of the Goga faction, appeared without of its customary anti-Jewish cartoon and diatribe (→ 4/17).

Carol II, plumed head of Rumania.

Eden quits British Cabinet over policy

Feb 20. Anthony Eden, the British Foreign Secretary, has resigned, citing as his reason his disapproval of Prime Minister Neville Chamberlain's methods to seek settlements with Italy and Germany. Despite pleas from fellow Cabinet members to change his mind or to claim ill-health as his reason for leaving, Eden openly declared his distaste for Chamberlain's policy. He pointed to a "difference of outlook between us in respect to international problems." The French government fears this will affect the battle against fascism (→ 5/2).

1938

MARCH

Su	Mo	Tu	We	Th	Fr	Sa
		1	2	3	4	5
6	7	8	9	10	11	12
13	14	15	16	17	18	19
20	21	22	23	24	25	26
29	28	29	30	31		

2. Washington acts to claim small islands in Pacific.

2. U.S.S.R.: Third major purge trial begins in Moscow (→ 15).

3. California: Pacific floods leave 144 dead, 20,000 homeless.

4. Prague: Premier Milan Hodza warns Reich Czechoslovakia will defend itself (→ 4/24).

8. Berlin: Herbert Hoover tells Hitler his doctrine would be intolerable in U.S. (→ 5/5).

9. Vienna: Kurt Schuschnigg defies Nazis, calls for plebiscite on independence (→ 11).

11. Vienna: With Hitler massing troops on border, Schuschnigg resigns, succeeded by Nazi leader Arthur Seyss-Inquart (→ 12).

12. German troops enter Austria (→ 14).

13. Paris: Leon Blum forms second Cabinet after Chautemps' resignation over split with Socialists (→ 4/10).

15. Aramco makes first commercial oil find in Saudi Arabia.

17. Spain: Rebel air raid kills 1,000 in Barcelona (→ 4/3).

19. Polish troops force Lithuania to sign peace agreement.

23. N.Y.: Jimmy Caras regains world pocket billiard title.

24. U.S. asks powers to help refugees flee from Nazis (→ 7/6)

26. Vienna: Hermann Goering warns Jews to leave Austria (→ 4/2).

27. U.S. stops buying Mexican silver in reprisal for seizure of oil companies (→ 5/13).

31. New York: Hoover warns U.S. of fascist trend, yet opposes alliances with Europe (→ 5/17).

31. Spain: 6,000 Loyalist troops seek haven in France (→ 4/3).

BIRTH

17. Rudolf Nureyev, celebrated Russian dancer.

DEATHS

1. Gabriele d'Annunzio, Italian poet, soldier (*3/12/1863).

13. Clarence Darrow, American criminal defense lawyer (*4/18/1857).

Bukharin, 17 others executed for treason

March 15. The most sensational of the Soviet treason cases ended two days ago with execution of 18 confessed conspirators, including Nikolai Bukharin, chronicler of the Russian Revolution, and Alexis I. Rykoff, former Premier of Russia.

In an official announcement, the Soviet government said the executions had already been carried out shortly after the Supreme Soviet rejected a plea for clemency.

Rykoff, Bukharin and colleagues were charged and convicted earlier this month with belonging to a "conspirative group organized on the instruction of foreign intelligence services to rupture Soviet military power . . . for the ruin of the U.S.S.R . . . for the overthrow of the Socialist regime and the reestablishment of capitalism and the power of the bourgeoisie." The defendants were also tried for assassination attempts on Stalin and Lenin (→ 5/6/41).

Mexico takes all oil

March 18. Mexico has seized 17 American and British oil companies representing a $450 million investment after they were unable to comply with a new decree requiring them to pay $40 million in wages and compensation. President Cardena's Six-Year Plan calls for "Mexicanization of Industry." This is the first major move in that direction, though the government drive on foreign industry is nothing new. Recent high tariff rates, for example, may all but cancel American business there (→ 27).

Adolf Hitler hailed as Nazis take Austria

March 14. This has been a day of unparalleled glory for Adolf Hitler. The German leader, who left Austria in his youth as a penniless artist, was cheered by thousands as he returned to Vienna today to pronounce the "Anschluss," or union, of the country with Germany.

Hitler was driven to the Austrian capital from Linz, where he had set up his temporary headquarters. Forty tanks led the way, and police cars filled with officers brought up the rear. Along the route, Nazis from all over Austria cheered the man who once pledged that Austria's borders were inviolable.

Hitler stood in the open car for most of the drive wearing his brown storm trooper uniform and returning the nearly hysterical salutes of his ardent supporters. Many of them waved banners emblazoned with swastikas. Some of the Nazis had stitched the symbol into the middle of the Austrian flag.

"What we are experiencing at this moment," Hitler proclaimed in Vienna, "is being experienced also by all other German people. Whatever happens, the German Reich as it stands today shall never be broken by anyone again and shall never be torn apart."

Hitler has already signed a decree making himself the Commander-in-Chief of the armed forces of Germany and Austria. All soldiers in Austria must swear allegiance to the Nazi leader, who is now the Fuhrer of more than 70 million people.

Adolf Hitler is hailed in Vienna as the new master of Austria.

Hitler's victory is Kurt Schuschnigg's defeat. Since 1934, the Austrian Chancellor has tried to prevent the National Socialists from coming to power, but the ground was cut out from under him when his benefactor, Benito Mussolini, allied himself with Hitler in 1936.

Schuschnigg tried to save his government last Tuesday by calling for a referendum so that Austrians could choose between the Nazis and him. The vote was never held. Hitler contacted Austria's Nazi Interior Minister, Arthur Seyss-Inquart, and ordered him to have the referendum canceled. Schuschnigg tried to resist but capitulated when he heard that German troops were massing on his border.

Tonight, Schuschnigg and thousands of his supporters are learning the hard way what happens to opponents of Adolf Hitler. They are all under arrest (→ 26).

Lunt and Fontanne in Chekhov play

March 29. Alfred Lunt and Lynn Fontanne opened tonight in Anton Chekhov's "The Sea Gull" in New York. The couple excel at romantic comedy, as when they starred in Noel Coward's "Design for Living" five years ago. While "Sea Gull" is largely an introspective work, Lunt and Fontanne infuse its rare lighter moments with spirit and zest.

Lunt and Fontanne were already well-established actors when they wed in 1922. She, born in England, is 50ish; he, born in Milwaukee, Wisconsin, is 40ish. They appeared in New York in 1935 in Shakespeare's "The Taming of the Shrew" and last made a splash in "Idiot's Delight" on Broadway in 1936.

Edward Hopper's "New York Movie" sets a characteristically lonely tone.

1938

APRIL

Su	Mo	Tu	We	Th	Fr	Sa
					1	2
3	4	5	6	7	8	9
10	11	12	13	14	15	16
17	18	19	20	21	22	23
24	25	26	27	28	29	30

1. Chicago: Joe Louis KOs Harry Thomas in five rounds (→ 6/22).

2. London recognizes German seizure of Austria; 34,000 arrests reported in Vienna (→ 6).

3. Spain: Nationalists seize Lerida, one of Catalonia's four capitals (→ 4).

4. Spain: Sources report the Lincoln-Washington battalion—comprised of Americans—has been devastated (→ 19).

5. Scandinavian countries fail to agree on common defense against German threat, as Denmark balks at tough stand.

6. U.S. recognizes German conquest of Austria (→ 10).

10. Paris: Daladier forms anti-Communist Cabinet upon Leon Blum's resignation.

10. Tunisia: Nationalist Neo-Destour leaders arrested following riots in Tunis (→ 8/25/46).

12. New York: George Ballanchine quits as ballet leader at Metropolitan Opera House.

12. Chicago: Black Hawks beat Maple Leafs to win Stanley Cup.

13. France: 157,000 auto workers strike, occupy 213 factories.

14. China: Japan suffers major defeat, losing 40,000 soldiers near Taierchwang (→ 6/8).

16. Rome: Anglo-Italian pact signed; Italy to quit Spain after war, U.K. to recognize Italian sovereignty in Ethiopia (→ 5/2).

17. Rumania arrests 100 Iron Guard members in move to halt terrorism (→ 9/22/39).

22. Eddie Rickenbacker buys Eastern Airlines for $3.5 million.

24. Sudeten chief Heinlen demands concessions for Germans in Czechoslovakia (→ 5/21).

25. U.K., Ireland sign three-year miltary, trade treaty (→ 6/25).

26. Reich withdraws from 1939 N.Y. World's Fair (→ 4/30/39).

DEATHS

8. Joe "King" Oliver, American jazz pioneer (*5/11/1885).

26. Edmund Husserl, German philosopher, phenomenology (*4/8/1859).

Franco, dividing Loyalists, says war won; American volunteer battalions devastated

American volunteers in Spain before their tragic defeat.

April 19. General Francisco Franco says the Spanish Civil War is over, and he is urging Loyalist troops to surrender. Franco addressed the nation by radio after a key military victory against government troops and foreign supporters.

Franco says he has beaten "the Reds," but he bears "no hostile sentiments toward other nations. We are fighting purely for our civilization. We do not believe in a democratic liberal regime, for the damage it has done to Spain is very great."

Franco spoke after his troops won a brilliant victory on the Mediterranean coast. They abandoned their assault on Tortosa and shifted slightly to the south, driving all the way to the beaches of Vinaroz. The victory effectively split the country in half and separated the Loyalists' power base in Barcelona from the rest of the country.

An American contingent known as the Lincoln-Washington Battalion was chewed up badly in the attack by the insurgents. They were no match for Franco's armor. Most of the battalion was killed in the assault on Tortosa, and the few soldiers who survived mounted guerrilla attacks behind enemy lines. Six of them drowned when they heroically tried to swim the Ebro River rather than surrender (→ 5/25).

Germans, Austrians approve Anschluss

April 10. Adolf Hitler crushed all resistance when his opponents tried to hold a referendum in Austria a month ago. Today, Hitler held his own referendum on the union of Germany and Austria, and he won handily. More than 99% of the voters in the two countries reportedly approved the Anschluss.

One prominent Austrian campaigned against Hitler. Otto de Hapsburg, a descendant of the Austrian rulers, also called on the rest of the world to react against what he called the German aggression in his country. Hapsburg did his campaigning outside Germany, in French newspapers. A warrant has been issued for his arrest in his native Austria (→ 24).

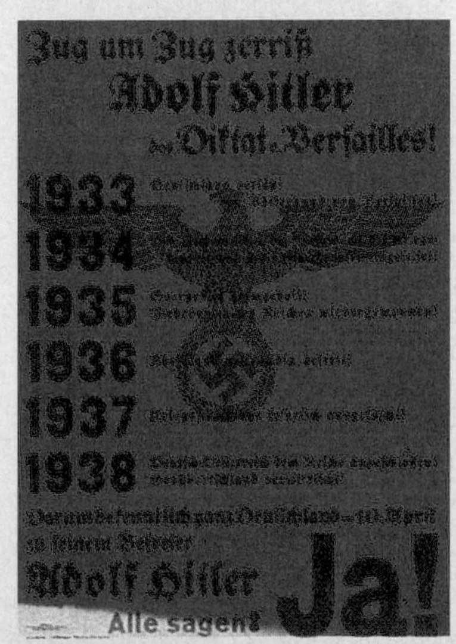

Nazi propaganda in Austria.

Bette Davis turns down role; censured

April 1. Warner Brothers studios suspended Bette Davis tonight when she refused to rehearse the latest film called for in her contract. Miss Davis, who has been keeping to her bed for an undisclosed illness, said, "Had it been 'The Life of Sarah Bernhardt' or 'Maximilian and Carlotta,' which have both been scheduled for me, I would have attempted to go to the studio, but I did not feel justified in jeopardizing my health in behalf of such an atrocious script." Miss Davis's last picture was the Oscar-caliber "Jezebel."

The compelling eyes of Bette Davis.

Dizzy Dean traded to Chicago Cubs

Dizzy lets one fly.

April 15. The baseball world, and especially his St. Louis teammates, were stunned when the Cardinals traded Dizzy Dean to the Chicago Cubs for three players and cash. Just as Dean was about to start his "comeback," the righthander was traded for pitchers Curt Davis and Clyde Shoun and outfielder George Stainback. It seemed clear that the Cards were trying to unload their "problem child" rather than strengthen their pitching staff. Dean (133-75 won-lost record for his career) was voted most valuable player in the National League in 1934.

Russian basso Chaliapin to sing no more

April 12. Feodor Chaliapin, the Russian basso considered by many the greatest singer of all time, died in Paris today at 65. Only Enrico Caruso, a tenor, loomed larger. Chaliapin's reputation was special, as no basso had achieved such worldwide acclaim.

In 1936, Pan Am, seeking efficiency in air travel, ordered a 75-seat plane. The Clipper 314 flying boat, ready for testing, is Boeing's answer.

1938

MAY

Su	Mo	Tu	We	Th	Fr	Sa
1	2	3	4	5	6	7
8	9	10	11	12	13	14
15	16	17	18	19	20	21
22	23	24	25	26	27	28
29	30	31				

2. London: Commons ratifies Anglo-Italian pact; Chamberlain extols Mussolini (→ 6/9).

5. New York: Six leaders of Nazi summer camp arrested (→ 6/20).

6. Rome: Hitler attends review of Italy's land forces (→ 14).

7. Lawrin wins Kentucky Derby with Eddie Arcaro in the saddle.

10. England: 79 dead, 40 injured in mine explosions.

13. Belgium: Leopold III names Socialist Paul-Henri Spaak prime minister.

13. Mexico breaks relations with Britain in oil dispute (→ 7/11).

14. Rome: Mussolini says fascists will fight together if democracies make war (→ 21).

17. U.S. Congress passes Naval Expansion Act, financing plan to build two-ocean Navy (→ 9/9).

21. Czechs place 400,000 troops on border of Germany (→ 24).

24. Prague: Konrad Henlein, leader of Sudeten Germans, breaks off talks with Czech Premier Milan Hodza (→ 30).

25. Spain: Rebel air raid kills 250 in Alicante; British ship sunk (→ 7/10).

26. Washington: House forms committee to purge "un-Americanism" (→ 6/29).

27. Despite FDR's opposition, Revenue Act becomes law, reducing corporate taxes to stimulate economy (→ 6/21).

28. Wisconsin: Bob and Phil La Follette start National Progressive Party.

30. Floyd Roberts wins 26th Indy 500, averaging 117.2 mph in Burd Piston Ring Special.

30. Prague: All Czechs between six and 60 ordered to train for defense work (→ 7/23).

31. London: BBC broadcasts "Spelling Bee," first game show on television.

BIRTH

28. Jerry West, basketball star with L.A. Lakers.

DEATH

22. William Glackens, U.S. realist painter (*3/13/1870).

Sentiment wins: Wilder's Our Town

Wilder, chronicler of the ordinary.

May 2. Tonight a radical yet reassuring play opened in New York. "Our Town," by Thornton Wilder, is performed without a stick of scenery. The narrator, ironically called the "Stage Manager," requests members of the audience to imagine it for themselves. "Our Town" is a typical village—but is it found in New Hampshire or the Garden of Eden? Thornton embraces the human experience by framing it in an ambiguous, timeless, but familiar place.

Thornton wrote the Pulitzer Prize-winning book "The Bridge of San Luis Rey" (1927). He masters many styles. His latest novel is "Heaven's My Destination."

Police break Goodyear strike; 100 hurt

May 29. Years of labor trouble at the Goodyear plants in Akron, Ohio, came to a climax three days ago when police ordered striking workers to disperse from the gates of Plant I. A brawl erupted and after tear gas and clubs found their way into the melee, 100 men were hurt.

Today, Goodyear and the United Rubber Workers struck an agreement which both sides feel may improve conditions in the plants.

For the past two years, more than 150 unauthorized work stoppages have plagued the Goodyear Company. Last August, the situation seemed as though it would improve when, at the company's request, the National Labor Relations Board intervened to conduct an election on whether to replace the company union with representation by the United Rubber Workers of America. Of the 13,000 workers eligible to vote, about 8,500 voted yes.

Despite the change, sit-down strikes, which one newspaper called "guerrilla warfare—undeclared, ruthless and uncontrollable," continued. Many are hoping today's agreement will lead to a more lasting peace.

Goodyear strikers persist, despite the demise of the company union last year.

May 22. Ash Can artist William Glackens is dead. Despite his Impressionist work (above), his legacy is the harsh depiction of city life.

Lord Bute sells half a Welsh city

May 17. The Marquess of Bute sold half the City of Cardiff in Wales today for 20 million pounds. It appeared to be the biggest real estate deal in British history. The sale included 20,000 houses, 1,000 stores, 250 saloons, theaters, farmland and villages. Lord Bute kept his two castles. Holder of 13 titles of nobility, the Marquess is descended from one of the 19 sons of Robert III, a 14th-century Scottish King. His main title derives from the Island of Bute. He used his family name, Crichton-Stuart, when he joined the army as a private for two shillings nine pence a day in the world war.

1938

JUNE

Su	Mo	Tu	We	Th	Fr	Sa
			1	2	3	4
5	6	7	8	9	10	11
12	13	14	15	16	17	18
19	20	21	22	23	24	25
26	27	28	29	30		

3. Berlin: Reich votes to confiscate "degenerate art" (→ 15).

4. Vienna: Sigmund Freud leaves Austria for refuge in London.

9. Britain contracts for purchase of 400 planes in U.S. (→ 8/27).

12. China: Yellow River dikes burst; catastrophic flood kills 150,000.

15. New York: Johnny Vander Meer pitches second no-hitter in row.

15. Berlin: Reich beheads husband and wife Georg and Anna Schwitzer as spies (→ 22).

17. Washington demands Reich pay Austria's debt.

18. U.S.S.R.: Soviet Film Festival features Mark Donskoi's "Gorki's Childhood."

19. Italy wins soccer's second World Cup.

19. Montana: 30 dead, ten missing, 65 hurt in train wreck.

19. Uruguay: Alfredo Baldomir inaugurated president.

20. Washington: U.S. jury indicts 18 as Reich spies (→ 26).

21. Washington: FDR signs $3.75 billion Emergency Relief Appropriation Act (→ 22).

22. U.S.: Chandler Act establishes bankruptcy laws (→ 25).

22. Berlin: Reich institutes mandatory national service to combat labor shortage (→ 7/22).

23. U.S.: Civil Aeronautics Authority established to regulate air traffic.

25. Dublin: Douglas Hyde inaugurated as first Irish president under new constitution (→ 7/26/39).

26. New York: Columbia University survey calls American Legion fascist (→ 7/12).

28. China: 10,000 Chinese killed in one-week battle below Hankow (→ 7/11).

DEATHS

15. Ernst Ludwig Kirchner, German Expressionist painter, graphic artist (*5/6/1880).

23. Countess of Strathmore, mother-in-law of King George V (*1862).

Johnson, Negro reformer, deceased

James Weldon Johnson.

June 26. "If the Negro is made to fail, America fails with him." So said James Weldon Johnson, who died today, 67 years old. Born in Florida, educated at Atlanta University (B.A. 1894) and at Columbia University, he was the first Negro admitted to the Florida bar. Johnson was posted as Consul in Venezuela and later in Nicaragua. A prolific writer of novels, essays, poetry, songs and operas, he also helped found and was for 14 years the secretary of the National Association for the Advancement of Colored People.

China, Spain air raids are deplored

June 8. The Roosevelt administration called in reporters and movie cameras to denounce the "barbarous" bombing of civilians in the Spanish Civil War and the war between China and Japan.

Acting Secretary of State Sumner Welles spoke as Japanese bombers refused to let up in their savage attack on Canton. The once attractive city has been decimated by exploding bombs and raging fire. Thousands of Chinese civilians have been killed or wounded, fires are burning out of control and much of Canton does not have electrical power. Welles charged that the bombings in China and Spain violate "the most elementary principles of humane conduct" (→ 28).

Browder admits his ties to Moscow

June 29. The Communist Party in the United States exists as part of a worldwide organization to propagate the teachings of Marx, Lenin and Stalin, according to the testimony of Earl Browder, the head of the U.S. Communist Party. Browder, questioned today by Senator John McNaboe as part of the investigative committee looking into links between Moscow and American Communists, admitted to the connection but also stated that the Communists are not opposed to the present U.S. government and in fact support "any or all institutions of American democracy whereby the American people have obtained power to determine their own destiny to any degree" (→ 7/13).

Browder opposed the draft in 1917.

Joe Louis floors Max in first round

June 22. With a fury that welled from deep within him, Joe Louis flattened Max Schmeling in the first round and avenged the only knockout defeat of his illustrious career.

The "Brown Bomber" from Detroit rendered the German challenger helpless with an opening barrage keyed to his right hook. Schmeling went down three times before his trainer threw in the towel at two minutes, four seconds.

Louis, in his fourth defense of his title, floored the German for a count of 3 and then for 1. The count had reached 5 at the end of the fight. The German later asserted he had been fouled by a kidney punch. Schmeling had knocked out Louis in the 12th round in 1936.

Minimum wage set at 40 cents an hour

June 25. President Roosevelt has signed the Fair Labor Standards Act, which establishes a mimimum wage of 40 cents an hour and a maximum work week of 44 hours. The new regulations will apply only to those American businesses engaged in interstate commerce.

Five days ago, the president signed the Recovery-Spending Act, allocating over $3.7 billion for the employable jobless and to stimulate industrial and business activity.

In an upbeat mood, Roosevelt punctuated that signing ceremony at his Hyde Park, New York, home with a prediction: the national income will increase to $60 billion, up from previous estimates of $50 billion. He declined to say when this upswing will begin but offered the following metaphor: "A few drops of rain have been coming from the heavens and probably will be followed by a much needed shower."

The legislation adheres to a principle prevalent in most New Deal initiatives: economic and social welfare go hand in hand and federal agencies must work in concert with state agencies. The president also emphasized that for every man or woman employed in a public works project about two and a half other workers are employed in the private sector. Thus the New Deal "primes the pump" of private industry. (→ 7/5).

June 15. German painter Ernst Ludwig Kirchner is dead. Above: "Self-portrait with Model."

1938

JULY

Su	Mo	Tu	We	Th	Fr	Sa
					1	2
3	4	5	6	7	8	9
10	11	12	13	14	15	16
17	18	19	20	21	22	23
24	25	26	27	28	29	30
31						

1. Rome: Italy places curbs on books written by Jews (→ 8/3).

1. N.Y.: Morris and William Goldis confess murdering Teamster leader William Snyder.

5. FDR calls South most depressed region in U.S. (→ 8/10).

6. U.S. hosts first intl. parley on Jewish refugees in Europe (→ 11/21).

8. Palestine: Arabs begin wide strike as violence grows (→ 12).

10. Spain: Journalist allowed to see 80 American prisoners held in rebel camp (→ 9/21).

11. Mexico: Five U.S. mines seized by local unions (→ 8/4).

11. Soviet and Japanese forces clash along Manchukuo-Korean frontier (→ 8/2).

12. N.Y.: Six Nazi summer-camp heads convicted of violating civil rights laws (→ 10/10).

12. Jerusalem: Sheik Abd Nour Khativ, Imam of Omar Mosque, assassinated (→ 8/26).

13. California: Town of Westwood ousts C.I.O. workers; 30 beaten, one shot (→ 8/13).

21. Bolivia, Paraguay sign treaty, drawing permanent boundary in Chaco region.

22. Berlin: Reich issues special identity card for Jews (→ 8/2).

23. London: Britain asks Czechs to make concessions to Sudetens to appease Nazis (→ 8/12).

29. Denmark: Jenny Kammersgaad becomes first to swim Baltic Sea —37 miles in 40 hours.

31. Italian racer Gino Bartali wins Tour de France.

31. Balkan Pact signatories agree to allow Bulgaria's rearmament.

31. New York: Father Divine and 1,500 followers parade to celebrate buying of Hudson River estate facing FDR's.

DEATHS

4. Otto Bauer, Austrian Socialist (*9/5/1881).

9. Benjamin Cardozo, U.S. Supreme Court justice (*5/24/1870).

16. Samuel Insull, controversial Chicago utilities financier (*11/11/1859).

8th Wimbledon for Helen Wills Moody

Graceful Helen Wills Moody.

July 4. Helen Wills Moody swept to her eighth Wimbledon singles title today by defeating her archrival, Helen Jacobs.

Mrs. Moody, who dominated women's tennis for nearly two decades by winning seven United States titles as well as her Wimbledons, once again proved her mastery over the woman who upset her in the 1933 Wimbledon. That match was close, but Mrs. Moody was hampered by a leg injury.

In 1935, Miss Jacobs seemed to have Wimbledon won, but Mrs. Moody took five games in a row to take the title. Again, in winning her eighth Wimbledon, "Little Poker Face," as Mrs. Moody is called, flashed her usual tireless style.

Corrigan goes west, ends up in Ireland

July 18. Douglas G. Corrigan, the daredevil American aviator who had been forbidden to make a solo transatlantic flight, landed in Dublin today, explaining with a straight face that his compass misled him into believing that he was flying from New York to California. Corrigan says he flew in clouds when he took off from Roosevelt Field, Long Island, and his compass said he was heading west. He adds that he realized his mistake only when he sighted land at the end of the 28-hour flight. U.S. and Irish officials say he will get little or no punishment although he broke the rules of both countries, earning the nickname of "Wrong-Way Corrigan" (→ 8/5).

Hughes sets new round-world mark

July 15. Millionaire aviator Howard Hughes was welcomed with a traditional New York ticker-tape parade today after setting a new record for round-the-world flight.

Hughes and his four-man crew landed at Floyd Bennett Field in Brooklyn yesterday just three days, 19 hours and 17 minutes after their departure on the trip, whose aim was to publicize the World's Fair of 1939. Their twin-engined Lockheed aircraft averaged 208 mph.

Young Hughes, ready to fly.

The 14,824-mile trip included stops at Paris; Moscow; Omsk and Yakutsk in Siberia; Fairbanks, Alaska; and Minneapolis. Hughes halved the previous record for a flight around the world of seven days and 18 hours, set by Wiley Post five years ago. More than two million New Yorkers cheered Hughes along the parade route.

"Two Men Standing," by Willem de Kooning, oil on canvas.

1938

AUGUST

Su	Mo	Tu	We	Th	Fr	Sa
	1	2	3	4	5	6
7	8	9	10	11	12	13
14	15	16	17	18	19	20
21	22	23	24	25	26	27
28	29	30	31			

2. Hitler opens Wagner research center in Germany (→ 10/16).

2. U.S.S.R.: Six Soviet divisions, 30 tanks sent into border battle with Japan (→ 10).

3. Italy: Schooling, intermarriage forbidden to Jews (→ 9/1).

4. Mexico seizes more American-owned land (→ 9/1).

5. Brooklyn: Douglas Corrigan given error-proof compass.

10. Japan, U.S.S.R. sign truce halting border conflict in Manchukuo (→ 18).

10. U.S. Dept. of Agriculture reports grass now thriving in dust bowl region (→ 9/10).

12. Europe alarmed as Hitler calls up one mil. reserves (→ 15).

13. Washington: A.F.L. Vice Pres. John Frey says C.I.O. is run by Communists (→ 20).

15. British liner Queen Mary wins Blue Riband, crossing Atlantic in three days, 21 hours.

15. German army begins war maneuvers (→ 28).

17. New York: Henry Armstrong takes lightweight title, becoming first to hold three boxing titles at once.

18. Tokyo: Japan summons one million recruits (→ 24).

20. Washington: J.B. Matthews testifies American Peace League linked to Moscow (→ 9/4).

22. Germany: Hungarian chief Miklos Horthy views naval parade on official visit (→ 23).

23. Little Entente to allow Hungarian rearmament (→ 10/23).

24. China: Japanese shoot down U.S.-Chinese airliner, machine gun 19 trying to flee (→ 9/14).

26. Palestine: Bomb kills 21, wounds 37 at Arab market (→ 10/6).

27. Utah: George Eyston sets auto speed record at 345 mph.

27. London warns Hitler attack on Czechs may mean world war (→ 9/15).

28. Sudeten Nazis and Czech Pres. Benes begin talks (→ 9/8).

DEATH

30. Max Factor, make-up expert.

Stanislavsky, the method man, dies

Aug 7. Constantin Stanislavsky of the Moscow Art Theatre has died at the age of 75, but his remarkable training of actors, the "Stanislavsky method," lives on, not the least through Lee Strasberg's classes at the Group Theater in New York.

Stanislavsky proposed to eliminate artificial and mechanical acting techniques, stressing the importance of inner identification with the character. As a director, he emphasized ensemble acting and the emotional truth of characters before exterior truth, such as of historical period.

In 1897, Stanislavky founded the Moscow Art Theatre, which was dedicated to bringing art to the masses and to a more realistic production of new plays. After a historically accurate production of Tolstoy's play about Ivan the Terrible, the new group won its first success with Chekhov's "The Seagull." It went on to present "Uncle Vanya," "The Three Sisters" and "The Cherry Orchard," also by Chekhov. The absence of purposeful plot and dramatic gesture in Chekhov's works demanded the new acting techniques which Stanislavsky went on to develop.

Other dramatic works directed by Stanislavsky include Ibsen's "An Enemy of the People" and Gorky's "The Lower Depths."

Don Budge has already won the Australian, Wimbledon and the French. His play at Forest Hills next month could net him an unparalleled Grand Slam (→ 9/24).

1938

SEPTEMBER

Su	Mo	Tu	We	Th	Fr	Sa
				1	2	3
4	5	6	7	8	9	10
11	12	13	14	15	16	17
18	19	20	21	22	23	24
25	26	27	28	29	30	

1. Mexico: Pres. Cardenas rejects U.S. demand for land payment (→ 11/12).

1. Italy expels all Jews entering since 1919 (→ 11/30).

3. Fourth International (Trotskyite) founded in France.

4. Oregon: Communist leader Earl Browder asks followers to support FDR (→ 10/27).

5. Philadelphia: U.S. retains Davis Cup.

8. Czechoslovakia: Sudeten Germans hold mass demonstrations for union with Reich (→ 15).

9. New York: FDR denies U.S. is allied with Europe against Hitler (→ 25).

10. Pittsburgh: 55,000 hungry overwhelm Republican feast, trample tons of food (→ 11/8).

14. Tokyo: Japan says it will back Reich and Italy with arms if necessary (→ 22).

15. Neville Chamberlain flies to Berlin to meet Hitler (→ 16).

16. 23,000 Sudetens reported fleeing to Germany (→ 18).

18. France, Britain give in to Hitler, will ask Czechs to surrender German areas (→ 22).

21. Spanish Loyalists announce immediate withdrawal of foreign fighters (→ 10/8).

22. Munich: Chamberlain meets Hitler for second time (→ 26).

22. Japanese in Peking form United Council for China, aiming to oust Chiang (→ 10/21).

24. New York: Don Budge wins U.S. tennis title at Forest Hills to capture Grand Slam.

25. FDR appeals to Hitler to negotiate with Czech Pres. Benes, as 20,000 demonstrate solidarity with Czechs in Madison Square Garden (→ 11/14).

26. France, Britain call partial mobilization (→ 30).

27. Britain: Queen Elizabeth launched on maiden voyage.

30. Munich: Four powers sign accord, allowing Germans to take Sudetenland.→

BIRTH

23. Romy Schneider, French actress (†5/29/1982).

Powers agree in Munich

Sept 30. In Munich yesterday, at a four power conference, British Prime Minister Neville Chamberlain and Premier Edouard Daladier of France reached a peaceful agreement concerning the future of Czechoslovakia with German Chancellor Adolf Hitler and Italian Premier Benito Mussolini.

No Czech representative was present at the conference, which took place under a German threat of war. In the face of criticism, Chamberlain believes that the agreement will bring "peace in our time."

The pact transfers to Germany the Sudeten region of Czechoslovakia, which is inhabited by a German-speaking minority. At the same time, it guarantees that the remainder of the country will be protected against unprovoked aggression.

Czechoslovakia's President Eduard Benes had tried to resist Adolf Hitler's plans to "liberate" Germans from Sudetenland. But he did not receive much support from the other European nations.

Just last week, Chamberlain met with Hitler in Bad Godesberg. And he capitulated to the major demands of the Fuhrer by following a policy of appeasement.

Hitler greets Neville Chamberlain.

Yesterday's agreement provides that Britain and Germany will settle their differences by consultation rather than war. Earlier in the month, Germany was warning that it has more warplanes than Britain, France and Czechoslovakia combined, and in London officials were handing out air raid gas masks (→ 10/1).

Thomas Wolfe, volcanic novelist, is dead

Wolfe, one of America's greatest.

Sept 15. The author of "Look Homeward, Angel" has left this world. Thomas Wolfe, one of America's greatest novelists, died today after an operation for tuberculosis of the brain.

Wolfe was born in Asheville, N.C., to parents with little interest in his literary career. He studied at the University of North Carolina and wrote about the local mountain people. Wolfe earned a Master's at Harvard in 1922 and wrote two more plays. One was another study of mountain folk, while the other, "Welcome to Our City," centered on an urban race riot. Wolfe failed to convince a producer to stage it.

Wolfe taught English at New York University from 1924 to 1930. He grew disillusioned with playwriting, despite the love and support of a scenic designer 19 years his senior named Aline Bernstein. His first novel, "Look Homeward, Angel" (1929), was a critical triumph. "Of Time and the River" (1935) was also well-received.

Wolfe's work is always autobiographical. He was a hard-drinking, tempestuous, quarrelsome man. Yet, he was also prolific, leaving hundreds of pages of unfinished manuscripts. His editors, who eased him through serious cases of writers' block, vow to bring these works to print.

1938

OCTOBER

Su	Mo	Tu	We	Th	Fr	Sa
						1
2	3	4	5	6	7	8
9	10	11	12	13	14	15
16	17	18	19	20	21	22
23	24	25	26	27	28	29
30	31					

1. Czecholovakia: Poland annexes Silesia and Teschen (→ 3).

3. Czechoslovakia: Hitler and army march into Sudetenland (→ 5).

6. Palestine: Government troops kill 60 Arabs (→ 10).

8. Spain: Rebels to send 10,000 Italian volunteers home (→ 12/16).

9. Altimeter, new device for airplane safety, demonstrated in New York.

10. Palestine: British troops occupy Bethlehem (→ 18).

10. Moscow: Soviet fliers denounce Lindbergh as "hired liar" for Nazis (→ 19).

16. Vienna: Catholic holdings assailed by Nazis as depriving poor (→ 28).

17. Chicago: Ex-Czech Pres. Benes accepts post at University of Chicago.

18. Palestine: Martial law rules as Arab siege of Jerusalem continues (→ 11/9).

19. Berlin: Hitler decorates Lindbergh with Service Cross (→ 11/27).

20. Communist Party outlawed in Czechoslovakia (→ 29).

21. China: Japanese troops occupy Canton, find buildings razed (→ 25).

23. Budapest: Hungary rejects Czech proposals for territory (→ 11/2).

25. China: Japanese troops occupy government's temporary base at Hankow (→ 12/15).

27. N.J.: Court writ bars further deportation of C.I.O. speakers and organizers (→ 11/18).

28. Germany deporting Jews to Poland; thousands seized (→ 11/7).

29. Berlin: Germany demands all lost colonies (→ 12/6).

BIRTH

3. Eddie Cochran, American rock and roll singer (†4/17/1960).

DEATH

17. Karl Kautsky, Socialist theoretician (*10/16/1854).

Hitler's army takes over Sudetenland

Swastikas and Sudetens greet the Nazis as they enter a Czech city unhindered.

Oct 5. Adolf Hitler's troops are fanning out through Sudetenland, occupying the hotly disputed border area of Czechoslovakia. And Hitler himself was treated as a hero today as he arrived in Eger.

It looked like Austria all over again. Large crowds waved Nazi banners and threw flowers into the street as they greeted the Fuhrer.

Konrad Henlein, the local Nazi official who helped Hitler destabilize the government of Eduard Benes, welcomed the German leader. "We are happy because no longer do we have to accept a regime strange and hostile to us but one that is part of ourselves," Henlein said. "It is now a section of your own homeland that greets you."

The road to Eger was paved last week when British and French resistance to Hitler's designs on Czechoslovakia collapsed in Munich. President Roosevelt and Benito Mussolini both urged Neville Chamberlain and Edouard Daladier to do whatever they could to avoid a new war in Europe.

Czech officials were not even invited to Munich, France decided to overlook its treaty with Prague and Hitler received everything he wanted. He agreed to hold a plebiscite after his troops occupied Sudetenland, but it is unlikely that it will ever be held. German troops have arrived, and they will never agree to leave. Poland and Hungary have already acted to reclaim their parts of Czechoslovakia (→ 20).

Americans panic over scary radio show

Oct 30. Aliens from Mars and other figments of the imagination caused havoc throughout the nation tonight during a radio broadcast of H.G. Wells' "The War of the Worlds." Orson Welles, known to the listening public as the voice of "The Shadow," directed the radio play. It aired over the Columbia Broadcasting System at 8 p.m.

Welles panics the populace.

Welles gave fair warning. At the opening, he told the audience they were hearing H.G. Wells' classic science-fiction story. Three more announcements in the hour followed, and newspaper program guides spelled it out in black and white.

Why, then, did a Dayton, Ohio, man call a newspaper to ask, "What time will it be the end of the world?" Why did hundreds of New Yorkers rush out of their doors with handkerchiefs over their mouths to guard against Martian gas? Why the traffic jams, clogged phone lines and patients checking into hospitals reporting shock? And why did one woman phone a bus company and interrupt the drawling dispatcher with the impatient statement, "The world is coming to an end and I have a lot to do"?

The hoax was set up as a music program interrupted by "bulletins" about Martians landing near Princeton, N.J. In one hour, the aliens were pretty nearly everywhere.

Yanks beat Cubs for third Series in row

Oct 9. The Yankees have become the first major league club to win three successive World Series, beating the Chicago Cubs, 8-3, in the final game for a four-game sweep.

Ten-year-old Shirley Temple, Oscar winner at four, is now Hollywood's top box office attraction.

1938

NOVEMBER

Su	Mo	Tu	We	Th	Fr	Sa
		1	2	3	4	5
6	7	8	9	10	11	12
13	14	15	16	17	18	19
20	21	22	23	24	25	26
29	28	29	30			

1. Britain concedes Reich dominates Central Europe (→ 1/17/39).

1. Hitler's firm stand on Czechoslovakia reported to have been guided by astrologer.

2. Berlin: Axis arbiters give Hungary Slovakia and Ruthenia in Czechoslovakia (→ 2/2/39).

5. New York: Benny Goodman plays Mozart with Budapest String Quartet.

7. Paris: Reich embassy aide Ernst von Rath shot at to avenge expulsions of Jews (→ 9).

8. Republicans make first gains in ten years in U.S. congressional elections (→ 1/16/39).

9. British commission declares partition of Palestine unfeasable; London proposes talks (→ 13).

11. Istanbul: Ismet Onu becomes Turkish president upon Mustafa Kemal's death.

11. Cuban leader Batista, in Washington for Armistice Day, visits White House (→ 7/14/40).

12. Mexico agrees to compensate U.S. for land seizures (→ 24).

13. Vatican: Mother Cabrini beatified in Rome, becoming first American saint.

13. Palestine: British capture Jericho (→ 2/7/39).

14. Washington: U.S. recalls envoys in Berlin (→ 18).

18. Berlin: Reich recalls ambassador in Washington (→ 12/9).

18. Officially independent C.I.O. elects John L. Lewis first president (→ 1/10/39).

21. Britain offers German Jews land in Africa (→ 6/6/39).

24. Mexico seizes oil land adjacent to Texas (→ 12/4).

26. Poland renews non-aggression pact with U.S.S.R. to protect against German invasion.

26. Philadelphia: Army defeats Navy 14-7 on gridiron.

30. Italy appeals for sovereignty over French-controlled Corsica and Tunisia (→ 12/14).

DEATH

10. Mustafa Kemal Ataturk, Turkish president, independence leader (*3/12/1881).

Crystal Night horror

Victimized Jewish merchants sweep up broken glass in the aftermath.

Nov 9. Throughout Berlin tonight, anti-Semitism exploded. Young Nazis went on a rampage, killing Jews at random, destroying stores owned by Jews and setting fire to the largest synagogue.

More than 90 people were killed, most of them Jewish merchants. Thousands of store windows were smashed in what is being called "Crystal Night." Hundreds of homes and Jewish places of worship were set on fire or ransacked.

The violence was unleashed after the assassination of Ernst von Rath, Third Secretary of the German Embassy in Paris. The killer was a teenaged Polish Jew, Herschel Grynspan. He said that he was avenging the treatment of his parents in Germany.

"Being a Jew is not a crime," Grynspan told police in Paris. "I am not a dog. I have a right to live and the Jewish people have a right to exist on this earth. Wherever I have been, I have been chased like an animal."

The men who looted and killed in Berlin were all dressed in civilian clothes. But many of them wore boots normally worn with Nazi uniforms; and they drove party cars.

Before the night of horror, Jewish leaders in Berlin tried in vain to publicize their opposition to the assassination in Paris. They were stymied. The Propaganda Ministry had already issued a decree banning all Jewish publications (→ 1/17/39).

Coughlin says Jews paid for Soviet revolt

Nov 27. Father Coughlin, the radio priest of the radical right and self-styled apostle of the poor, is defending a broadcast he delivered in Newark, New Jersey, claiming that the Russian Revolution of 1917 was financed by Jewish groups. Such allegations seem to be common fodder among right-wing political thinkers who equate both communism and Jews with "the devil."

Coughlin, who has both rabid supporters and vehement opponents, has also attacked President Roosevelt. He claims the president has done too little to help the poor. These notions have earned Coughlin the censure of Rome (→ 12/2).

Coughlin supporters in Philadelphia.

Kate Smith sings God Bless America

Nov 12. The ever-popular Kate Smith surely lifted that popularity a notch higher last night when she introduced an Irving Berlin song, "God Bless America," on her Armistice Eve radio show. Berlin wrote the tune originally for his 1918 musical, "Yip, Yip, Yaphank," but it was withdrawn and never before publicly performed.

With its simple sentiment and solid, four-square rhythm, the song seems tailor-made for the homespun Miss Smith, whose new radio program, "Kate Smith Speaks," is becoming as popular as her evening musical shows. Though one critic has dismissed the daytime talk show as "sentimental, with a thick fudge frosting that the housewives love," those wives are tuning their dials to hear her discuss subjects of interest to women. Miss Smith is, after all, special, a symbol of America ever since her 1931 radio debut enshrined her theme song, "When the Moon Comes Over the Mountain."

Kate Smith sings.

1938

DECEMBER

Su	Mo	Tu	We	Th	Fr	Sa
				1	2	3
4	5	6	7	8	9	10
11	12	13	14	15	16	17
18	19	20	21	22	23	24
25	26	27	28	29	30	31

1. British plan national register, stating what each citizen will do in case of war (→ 3/17/39).

2. Washington: Hofmann, Voss, Glaser receive jail terms as German spies (→ 2/22/39).

4. Peru: Latin American nations seek ban on U.S. military action after property seizures (→ 7/30/40).

6. Paris: Germany, France sign treaty of friendship (→ 1/17/39).

9. N.Y.: 4,000 cheer as Anthony Eden calls on democracies to face fascist challenge (→ 15).

14. London warns Italy pact bars attack on Tunisia (→ 17).

15. Washington sends fourth note to Berlin demanding amnesty for U.S. Jews (→ 1/5/39).

15. U.S. loans China $50 mil. in reprisal for Japan's move to close China's doors to trade (→ 1/4/39).

16. Spain: Franco restores citizenship to ex-King Alfonso XIII (→ 1/26/39).

17. Italy disavows 1935 pact with France (→ 28).

28. France orders doubling of forces in Somaliland; two warships sent (→ 1/1/39).

CULTURAL EVENTS, 1938

Literature: J.R.R. Tolkien's "The Hobbit"; John Dos Passos' "U.S.A."; Faulkner's "The Unvanquished"; Marjorie Kinnan Rawlings' "The Yearling"; Robert Sherwood's "Abe Lincoln in Illinois."

Academia: Lewis Mumford's "The Culture of Cities"; Johan Huizinga's "Homo Ludens"; John Dewey's "Experience and Education."

Music: Marian Anderson gets honorary degree from Harvard; "Flat Foot Floogie with a Floy Floy"; "September Song"; "A Tisket, A Tasket"; "Jeepers Creepers."

The Arts: Raoul Dufy's "Regatta"; The Cloisters built in upper Manhattan.

Film: Howard's "Pygmalion"; Eisentein's "Alexander Nevski"; Hitchcock's "The Lady Vanishes"; "You Can't Take it with You," Academy Award.

The line-up: Bogey, Hank, Jimmy, Spence

Errol Flynn as "Robin Hood."

It was a big year for the Big Boys. Humphrey Bogart, Spencer Tracy and Errol Flynn dueled and scuffled on the screen. The only woman getting her due was Bette Davis, who acts as though she could take them all on with one arm tied behind her back.

Jimmy Cagney and Bogey star in "Angels With Dirty Faces." They cornered the market on gangster pictures; this is their first one together. Pat O'Brien plays a priest. Spencer Tracy also takes the vows in "Boys Town." His Father Flanagan tames

"Jezebel," with Fonda and Davis.

Jean Renoir's "Grand Illusion."

Bogart and Cagney in "Angels . . ."

a feisty teen (Mickey Rooney). Errol Flynn leads a band of Merry Men through the woods in "Robin Hood." Flynn does his own stunts, as Douglas Fairbanks did in his 1922 version.

"Grand Illusion," directed by Jean Renoir, concerns men in less buoyant times. His explores the dynamics between a German camp commandant (Erich von Stroheim) and French prisoners of war. "Jezebel," directed by William Wyler, has an equally good script. Bette Davis is a Southern belle who flouts every convention to make her man (Henry Fonda) jealous.

Tracy and Rooney in "Boys Town."

Exposed swindler commits suicide

Dec 17. F. Donald Coster, President of the $86 million drug concern McKesson & Robbins, shot and killed himself today in his Connecticut home after his mask of respectability was ripped away, revealing him as Philip Musica, ex-convict and swindler. His associates have turned out to be his brothers, all under assumed names. As the shot rang out, federal agents were outside, ready to arrest him in connection with $18 million missing from the firm's assets. The government also has proof of his involvement in extensive arms traffic disguised as regular foreign trade.

Pearl S. Buck wins Nobel for literature

King Gustav gives the Nobel to Buck.

Dec 10. Pearl Sydenstricker Buck, author of "The Good Earth," has won the Nobel Prize for literature. She published twin biographies of her parents, "The Exile" and "Fighting Angel: Portrait of a Soul," in 1936. These with "The Good Earth," a Pulitzer Prize-winning novel, earned her the award.

Mrs. Buck was raised in China by American missionaries and lived there until she was 32. She understood first-hand Chinese culture and customs, and deals sympathetically with them in her books. "The Good Earth," published in 1929, tells of a peasant who survives famine, betrayal and dishonor to rise to the status of wealthy landowner.

Another notable Nobel winner is Enrico Fermi. Fermi received the prize in physics for work in radioactivity. Formerly a professor in Fascist Rome, he escaped to the United States this year.

New hero "Superman," created by Jerry Siegel and Joe Shuster.

1939

JANUARY

Su	Mo	Tu	We	Th	Fr	Sa
1	2	3	4	5	6	7
8	9	10	11	12	13	14
15	16	17	18	19	20	21
22	23	24	25	26	27	28
29	30	31				

1. French Premier Daladier goes to North Africa to investigate Italian demands for cession of territory (→ 11).

2. Pasadena: S. California takes Rose Bowl 7-3 over Duke.

3. N.Y.: Don Budge upsets Ellsworth Vines in pro tennis debut.

4. Tokyo: Fascist Baron Hiranuma becomes Japanese premier (→ 2/10).

5. Washington: FDR offers $9 mil. budget, including record $1.3 bil. for defense (→ 27).

5. FDR names Felix Frankfurter associate justice of Supreme Court (→ 8/29/62).

10. Washington: FDR assigns Harry Hopkings to reconcile A.F.L. and C.I.O. (→ 19).

11. Rome: Neville Chamberlain meets with Mussolini (→ 3/29).

16. FDR asks extension of Social Security Act to more women and children (→ 30).

17. Denmark, Estonia, Latvia sign non-aggression pact with Germany; Norway, Sweden, Finland refuse (→ 30).

17. Reich issues order forbidding Jews to practice as dentists, veterinarians, chemists (→ 22).

19. New York: C.I.O. suspends two teachers unions, ousts five delegates for Communist activities (→ 2/25).

22. Berlin: Nazi order erases old officer caste, tying army directly to party (→ 2/3).

25. N.Y.: Joe Louis KOs John Henry Lewis in first (→ 4/17).

25. Chile: Quakes ruin 20 towns, leaving thousands dead.

27. FDR approves sale of U.S. warplanes to France (→ 3/18).

29. Radical Subhas Chandra Rose beats Gandhi's candidate to become Indian pres. (→ 3/3).

30. U.S. Supreme Court upholds validity of TVA (→ 4/3).

30. Berlin: Hitler demands return of colonies for Japan, Italy; warns U.S. not to meddle (→ 3/16).

BIRTH

21. Germaine Greer, Australian feminist writer.

Franco in Barcelona; government leaves

Barcelona residents, hoisting a poster of Franco, greet rebel troops.

Jan 26. Wildly cheering throngs welcomed General Franco's victorious troops into Barcelona today. Loyalist forces had been evacuating the city over the past three days and put up only sporadic resistance as Franco's Nationalist forces swept into the city.

The capture of the city came in a two-pronged attack this morning. Flag-waving Nationalist troops overwhelmed several machine gun nests while advancing from the north, while Moroccan troops swept in from the west firing only few shots. Throngs of people, many giving the Franco salute and waving red and white bunting, surrounded the troops as they entered the city.

Large numbers of refugees and Barcelonians emerged from the underground stations, where they had been living, and fleets of trucks began distributing food to the near-starved city. The celebration was tempered by scenes of crying soldiers, who made their way to their homes only to discover that members of their family had died in the struggle (→ 2/6).

W.B. Yeats, famed Irish poet, dead

Jan 28. W.B. Yeats, the great lyric poet, has died in his 74th year. Yeats was thoroughly Irish, born in Dublin in June 1865. His deep pride in his native culture is reflected in his poetry, drama, and his politics (he was a Senator in the Irish Free State for six years).

Yeats urged John Millington Synge and Ezra Pound to explore Irish myths. His own passion is seen in his first collection of poems "The Rose" (1893), which includes his famed "The Lake Isle of Innisfree." Yeats wrote poems right up to his death. In his words, "An aged man is but a paltry thing/A tattered coat upon a stick, unless/Soul clap its hands and sing."

William Butler Yeats.

Atomic explosion releases 200m volts

Jan 28. News that atoms have been split to release 200 million volts of energy was reported at a meeting of theoretical physicists in Washington today by Enrico Fermi of the University of Rome. Fermi said the enormous amount of energy was released in an experiment by Otto Hahn, a German physicist, who bombarded atoms of a synthetic element called ekauranium with neutrons. Physicists at the Washington meeting said Hahn's achievement was as important as the original discovery of radioactivity, but that it would take at least 20 years to put it to practical use. Efforts to duplicate Hahn's experiment have begun at Columbia University and the Carnegie Institution (→ 8/2).

Basketball is too rough for inventor

Jan 30. The man who invented the game of basketball doesn't like the way it is being played. Dr. James Naismith says that the use of the zone defense is a violation of the sport's fundamental principles. In fact, says Naismith, "I feel, at times, I'd rather not see basketball."

The mild-mannered educator, now 77 years old, was bitter in his denunciation of the "modernized" style of basketball. His grievances went beyond the zone defense, which he described as a stalling tactic conducive to roughness.

Dr. Naismith also said that the dribbling rule was misused, that officiating was often improper and elimination of the center jump slowed the game.

Mooney pardoned after doing 22 years

Jan 7. Thomas J. Mooney has been pardoned by California Governor Culbert L. Olson. Mooney, often revered by labor groups as a representative of "class persecution," was absolved of all guilt in the 1916 San Francisco Preparedness Day Parade bombing after spending 22 years in prison. Mooney vowed to spend the rest of his life building "a new and better social order."

Governor Olson, professing his belief that Mooney was innocent of the bombing charges, freed the former radical labor leader at a ceremony in Sacremento. He pardoned Mooney unconditionally but asked him to refrain from urging people into "a futile and inhumane chaos of bloodshed and revolution."

1939

FEBRUARY

Su	Mo	Tu	We	Th	Fr	Sa
			1	2	3	4
5	6	7	8	9	10	11
12	13	14	15	16	17	18
19	20	21	22	23	24	25
26	27	28				

1. Czechs order expulsion of all foreign Jews within six months.

2. Hungary breaks relations with U.S.S.R. (→ 4).

3. Berlin: Joseph Goebbels ends careers of five actors for "misrepresenting" Naziism (→ 25).

3. Mexico City: Great crowds greet Cuban leader Batista as he urges Latin solidarity.

4. Hungary: Martial law declared in wake of Budapest synagogue bombing (→ 24).

6. France: 130,000 refugees cross border from Spain (→ 9).

7. London parley on Palestine opens (→ 3/17).

9. Spain: Rebels reach border of Catalonia (→ 11).

10. Japanese occupy island of Hainan in French Indochina (→ 3/31).

11. Spain: Negrin government returns to Madrid (→ 27).

13. Louis Brandeis, first Jewish justice, retires from U.S. Supreme Court.

13. Mexico seizes American firm United Sugar Co. (→ 7/21).

14. German Reich launches battleship Bismarck.

16. Rome: German envoy asks cardinals to elect a pope who favors fascism (→ 3/2).

18. San Francisco: Golden Gate International Exposition opens.

19. Peru: Gen. Rodriguez killed in failed coup attempt.

23. Massachusetts: American Assn. for the Advancement of Science closes labs to visitors from totalitarian states (→ 28).

24. Budapest: Hungary signs anti-Communist pact with Italy, Reich and Japan (→ 3/16).

25. Miami: FDR calls on C.I.O. and A.F.L. to end breach (→ 27).

25. Berlin issues order requiring 100 Jews to leave Reich each day (→ 6/9).

27. Washington: Supreme Court outlaws sit-down strikes (→ 6/5).

28. Contractor pleads guilty to erasing "Made in Germany" from machines sold to New York City (→ 3/25).

22,000 Nazis hold rally in New York

American Nazis gather in the Garden under the image of George Washington.

Feb 22. The German-American Bund staged what it considered an "Americanism" rally tonight at New York City's Madison Square Garden, denouncing the nation's Jews for their hatred of German Nazis and National Socialism.

In a speech, Fritz Kuhn, the national leader of the Bund and one of Adolf Hitler's original followers, told the crowd of 22,000: "We do not say all Jews are communists but we do say that the Jew is the driving force of communism." Bernard M. Baruch, an adviser to President Roosevelt, was among those Jews denounced during the rally.

The hall was decorated with anti-Jewish and pro-Nazi banners but the program had a patina of pro-Americanism, with the assembled crowd singing "The Star Spangled Banner" and reciting the pledge of allegiance. There was also a George Washington poster on display. The crowd jeered and booed, however, when one speaker mentioned the name of President Roosevelt.

With 1,700 policemen on duty, there was only scattered fighting outside the arena and just 13 persons were arrested on minor charges. Inside the hall, there was one incident, when a young Jewish man mounted the platform, only to be tackled and forced to leave (→ 23).

Marian Anderson denied DAR hall

Feb 27. The Daughters of the American Revolution have refused to allow Marian Anderson to sing at Constitution Hall in Washington, D.C. Miss Anderson is a Negro contralto who has sung for audiences worldwide. First Lady Eleanor Roosevelt reportedly resigned from the D.A.R. when she heard about the organization's action.

Miss Anderson excels at operatic arias and spirituals. Conductor Arturo Toscanini judged her voice "one that comes once in a hundred years." Mrs. Roosevelt and Miss Anderson's manager are arranging an outdoor concert for the singer.

Beautiful Marian Anderson.

Franco recognized as Spain's leader

Feb 27. Amid cries of impeachment and shame in the British House of Commons, Prime Minister Chamberlain announced recognition of Franco's regime in Spain today. France's President Lebrun took similar steps but with the unanimous backing of the French Cabinet. President Azana of the collapsing Spanish republic, who has refrained from political action while in Paris, left the Spanish Embassy there, but refused resignation.

Recognition was deemed inevitable, but many, particularly in Britain's vocal opposition party, do not trust Franco's vague guarantees of a free Spain and are concerned about the remaining Italian and German forces in Spain (→ 3/6).

Democratic boss took bribes; jailed

Feb 25. A Tammany Hall district leader, James J. Hines, was convicted last night in New York City of taking bribes to cover up the Dutch Schultz policy racket. He faces up to 25 years in prison.

The conviction of the Tammany leader was a victory for New York District Attorney Thomas E. Dewey, who has spent nearly four years investigating the policy rackets. On the basis of his findings, Dewey claimed that Hines was the Schultz court fixer and intimidator of police. The trial in New York City lasted 29 days. The 63-year-old Hines appeared impassive as the verdict was announced. Later, Hines called it "a kick in the belly."

Pius XI, advocate of concord, dies

Feb 10. Pope Pius XI, 261st head of the Roman Catholic Church, died early this morning. His heart, weakened by two years of illness, stopped beating. The "Pope of Peace" was 81 years old and had ruled for 17 years.

Pius XI's reign was marked by his will to create a new relationship between church and state. He signed many contracts, with Latvia in 1922, Bavaria in 1924, Poland in 1925, Rumania, Lithuania, Italy and Prussia in 1929, Austria and then Hitler's Reich in 1933. He solved the Roman question by concluding the Lateran Pact with Mussolini. In his March 1937 Encyclical, Pius XI warned against the evils of Nazism (→ 16).

1939

MARCH

Su	Mo	Tu	We	Th	Fr	Sa
			1	2	3	4
5	6	7	8	9	10	11
12	13	14	15	16	17	18
19	20	21	22	23	24	25
26	27	28	29	30	31	

2. Rome: Cardinal Pacelli elected Pope Pius XII (→ 12).

3. Bombay: Gandhi begins fast unto death to protest state's autocratic rule (→ 1/16/42).

4. Laurence Steinhardt named U.S. ambassador to U.S.S.R.

6. Spain: Republican Jose Miaja takes over Madrid govt. after military coup, vows to seek "peace with honor" (→ 17).

9. Czech Pres. Emil Hacha ousts pro-German Joseph Tiso as Premier of Slovakia in effort to preserve Czech unity (→ 15).

10. Moscow: Stalin claims West seeks Reich-Soviet war.

12. Vatican: Coronation of Pope Pius XII (→ 5/8).

16. Slovakia joins Moravia and Bohemia as German protectorate (→ 22).

16. Hungary annexes Carpatho-Ukraine (→ 4/11).

17. London talks on Palestine end in failure (→ 5/23).

17. France: Marshal Philippe Petain appointed French ambassador to Spain (→ 28).

17. London: Chamberlain recalls envoy to Berlin (→ 31).

18. U.S. raises duties on German imports by 25 percent (→ 4/15).

20. FDR names William Douglas to U.S. Supreme Court.

21. Gandhi calls on world to disarm, thinks Hitler would follow.

22. Lithuania: Hitler annexes port of Memel (→ 4/1).

29. Arizona: Clark Gable marries Carol Lombard.

29. Paris: Premier Daladier calls on Italy to clarify colonial demands (→ 4/8).

30. N.Y.: FDR meets with George Washington Carver.

30. Spain: 100,000 arrested so far by Franco regime (→ 4/1).

30. New York: Nephew William Hitler calls Uncle Adolph "a menace."

31. London: Chamberlain reasserts British aid offer to Poland in case of Reich attack (→ 4/1).

31. Spratly Islands: Seven French islands annexed by Japan (→ 6/14).

Czechs collapse; Nazis in Prague

Czech police restrain crowds gathered in Prague to see their conquerors.

German expansion in central Europe.

March 15. With startling efficiency, Adolf Hitler arrived triumphantly in Prague this afternoon just eight hours after the first of his German troops entered the capital of what used to be the Czechoslovak republic. The country is now divided into several regions, all of them obedient to Hitler's Reich.

The swastika was raised above the castle of the Bohemian kings, and Germans cheered as they greeted the Fuhrer. But Hitler's arrival was not so majestic as his conquests of Austria and Sudetenland. Many Czechs who do not claim a German heritage jeered at the soldiers of the Reich. Others hid in side streets and wept openly.

Just hours before Hitler arrived, radio broadcasts announced that all of Moravia and Bohemia would be occupied by German troops by the end of the day.

To the east, Slovakia is also dominated by Germany. The Prime Minister of the area, Monsignor Josef Tiso, struck a deal with Hitler two days ago after Czech President Emil Hacha tried to arrest him.

Hacha's effort earlier this month to dissolve the autonomous government of Carpatho-Ukraine also failed. The area has been invaded by Hungarian troops, reportedly with the full blessing of Hitler.

Throughout Prague tonight, a curfew is in effect. Public buildings and banks have been taken over by Germans. And the Gestapo are fanning out through the city with lists in their hands (→ 16).

Nylon, though lacking the prestige or romance of silk, promises to bring hosiery to the masses.

Ford's Stagecoach triumphs with Wayne

March 3. "Stagecoach," a riveting film western, opened tonight. John Ford, director of the electrifying "The Informer" (1935), is responsible. Ford has been making films for nearly 20 years, and he seems to be hitting his stride now.

"Stagecoach" follows a coach and cavalry crossing the desert. The Ringo Kid, a tough hombre, is the hero. A six-foot-four, slow-talking actor named John Wayne is Ringo. Wayne has made about 80 films, but either the pictures were forgettable or his role was negligible.

Ford uses the camera well, pulling back to take in breathtaking vistas. Subtlety is not his forte, so unsubtle Wayne suits his work. The men have been friends since 1928, and will probably team up more.

John Ford's "Stagecoach."

Franco in Madrid; Spanish War ended

March 28. Hitler and Mussolini both sent congratulations as Franco's troops marched past barricades to seize control of Madrid. The surrender of 40,000 Republican or Loyalist forces in Toledo, Cordoba and Madrid marks an end to the bitter 32-month-old Spanish Civil War. Franco's Nationalist troops took the city without firing a shot this morning as war-weary Republicans hoisted the white flag. The Nationalists immediately began the release of over 18,000 political prisoners and Nationalist sympathizers (→ 30).

Franco, victorious in Spain.

20,000 in New York anti-Nazi march

March 25. A half-million persons lined the streets of New York City yesterday as more than 20,000 marchers staged a "stop Hitler" parade in protest of Germany's invasion of Czechoslovakia. In a speech at Columbus Circle, New York Mayor Fiorello LaGuardia condemned the Nazi invasion, saying: "My only purpose in being here is to take part with my fellow New Yorkers in this public protest against the latest outrage in international affairs." He called it a black mark in history.

Three days ago, Hitler's troops also occupied the Lithuanian city of Memel. The Fuhrer himself entered the port aboard the battleship Deutschland (→ 4/2).

1939

APRIL

Su	Mo	Tu	We	Th	Fr	Sa
						1
2	3	4	5	6	7	8
9	10	11	12	13	14	15
16	17	18	19	20	21	22
23	24	25	26	27	28	29
30						

1. Berlin: Hitler rejects Anglo-German naval treaty (→ 5).

1. U.S. recognizes Franco in Spain, lifts embargo (→ 5/7).

2. Japan, U.S.S.R. reach accord on fishing rights.

2. American Civil Liberties Union defends Nazi right to distribute propaganda in U.S. (→ 7/16).

3. Administrative Reorganization Act signed by FDR, consolidating executive bureaus (→ 5/16).

5. Paris: Albert Lebrun re-elected French president.

5. Berlin: Hitler conscripts all German youth, 10-18 (→ 28).

10. British Mediterranean fleet sails to protect Greece and Turkey from possible Italian aggression (→ 7/13).

10. Holland places troops on German border (→ 5/10/40).

11. Hungary quits League of Nations (→ 5/3).

13. Rome conducts air-raid drills.

15. FDR asks dictators for ten-year peace, orders U.S. fleet to return to Pacific (→ 26).

16. Boston Bruins take hockey's Stanley Cup.

17. Los Angeles: Joe Louis KOs Jack Roper in first round (→ 6/28).

18. Atlantic: Dutch liner Simon Bolivar sunk by mine; 140 killed.

19. Ellison Brown wins Boston Marathon in record time of two hours, 28 minutes, 51.8 seconds.

23. Hollywood: Tyrone Power marries Annabella.

23. Britain unexpectedly sends envoy back to Berlin (→ 6/29).

26. Washington: 571 planes ordered as FDR signs military appropriations bill (→ 5/27).

28. Hitler turns down FDR proposal to meet at sea (→ 5/22).

29. New York: Mayor LaGuardia opens Whitestone Bridge to traffic.

30. U.S.S.R. proposes military alliance with France, Great Britain (→ 5/25).

N.Y. World's Fair open

April 30. "The World of Tomorrow" was a reality today as the New York World's Fair opened. President Franklin Roosevelt formally dedicated the exposition in a speech delivered to 600,000 listeners huddled in a chilly spring breeze.

The president's speech was the climax of a parade through the 1,216-acre grounds. Nearly 20,000 armed servicemen marched, joined by people from Europe, Asia and the Americas clad in native costumes. Those who truly made the fair possible, the workmen, also marched past the crystal ball Perisphere and gold Trylon, the two main structures of the fair.

A gigantic statue of George Washington stands on Constitution Mall. The Hall of Nations features the Soviet pavilion, with a statue of a laborer lofting a red star. The Italian pavilion sports a water-power generator. Many other displays remain uncompleted. There is a faint air of self-consciousness about the proceedings. The official theme is progress and peace, but everyone knows Europe is on the brink of war. The knowledge, like the clouds hanging over the fairgrounds, looms uncomfortably (→ 5/4).

Perisphere and Trylon.

Albania invaded by Italy; Zog flees

April 8. Italian forces have invaded the tiny Balkan kingdom of Albania. There was little resistance, and King Zog was chased from the throne. He is expected to seek asylum in Greece, which is only one of the countries nervous about the intentions of Benito Mussolini.

The invasion was carried out swiftly and without any warning from Rome. A spokesman for Mussolini says he ordered the troop movement to protect Italian residents of Albania who have been threatened by roving armed bands.

Italy and Albania had been conducting peace negotiations, but King Zog was resisting Mussolini's military demands. The Duce insisted that his navy be given permanent access to Albanian harbors and that army garrisons be established along Albania's borders with Greece and Yugoslavia.

Count Ciano, the Italian Foreign Minister, met with Yugoslav Ambassador Bosko Hristic and assured him that Mussolini has no designs on his country. Yugoslavian diplomats said privately they were satisfied with the assurances (→ 10).

Britain, Poland sign mutual aid treaty

April 1. Prime Minister Neville Chamberlain has pledged to support Poland militarily against threats to her sovereignty. The official statement issued from London declared: "Should the Polish government feel that its independence would be threatened to such an extent that it had to resist by force, Poland would find Britain and France on her side."

Realizing the British statement referred to German aggression, Chancellor Adolf Hitler accosted England, challenging her to pick a fight or interfere with the Reich's political aspirations. In a ceremony launching the 35,000-ton battleship Admiral von Tirpitz, Hitler spoke with fervent anger to 100,000 at Wilhelmshaven. He warned that Germany would not allow Britain to initiate a "devilish plan" of encirclement used prior to the war. He proclaimed to the crowd: "Whoever declares himself ready to pull the chestnuts out of the fire of the big powers, must expect to burn his fingers in the attempt." French observers called the speech "uncharacteristically confused" (→ 6/29).

1939

MAY

Su	Mo	Tu	We	Th	Fr	Sa
	1	2	3	4	5	6
7	8	9	10	11	12	13
14	15	16	17	18	19	20
21	22	23	24	25	26	27
28	29	30	31			

2. Detroit: Lou Gehrig ends record streak of consecutive games at 2,130 (→ 6/21).

3. Moscow: Vyacheslav Molotov named Soviet foreign minister.

3. Hungary adopts anti-Jewish law expected to expel 300,000 from country (→ 8/30/40).

4. New York: One millionth person enters World's Fair (→ 8/27).

6. Favored horse Johnstown wins Kentucky Derby with J. Stout in the saddle.

7. Spain quits League of Nations (→ 26).

8. Rome: Pope Pius asks Germany, Italy, France, Britain to attend peace talks at Vatican (→ 10/27).

10. Moscow: Soviet appoints Constantine Oumansky ambassador to U.S.

10. U.S.: Methodist Church unites for first time since 1830.

11. Boston: 38 fishermen missing as two boats collide in fog.

12. Vienna: Baron Louis Rothschild freed by Nazis after 13 months in prison.

14. Kentucky: State troops arrive in Harlan County as mines prepare to reopen (→ 7/12).

16. First local food stamp program begun in Rochester, N.Y. (→ 7/2/40).

21. Washington: It is reported that 503 million acres in U.S. remain uncharted.

23. Washington: FCC demands U.S. overseas broadcasts favorably reflect American culture.

23. British Parliament approves independence for Palestine in ten years with power divided between Arabs and Jews (→ 6/2).

25. Moscow increases military budget by 66 percent (→ 26).

26. British invite Soviet war chief Voroshiloff to attend war games (→ 7/27).

26. Madrid: Franco reports 688 executed since March (→ 8/6).

27. Sec. of State Cordell Hull asks repeal of U.S. arms embargo to countries at war (→ 7/3).

30. Wilbur Shaw takes 27th Indy 500 at 155 mph in Boyle Special.

American sub sinks; 33 saved, 26 lost

May 25. The Navy today reported the death of 26 men aboard the submarine Squalus, which sank during a training cruise in 240 feet of water off the New Hampshire coast two days ago. The 26, including one officer, 23 enlisted men and two civilian observers, were drowned in the aft section when the Squalus went down, apparently because an air valve was left open when the vessel made a routine dive.

The Navy has saved 33 officers and men who were in the forward section of the Squalus. The crew members were brought to the surface in a ten-ton rescue chamber that made four trips to the Sqaulus yesterday. Divers guided the chamber to the submarine's forward torpedo room escape hatch to free the crew members, who had been freezing in the powerless sub. The rescue chamber jammed 150 feet below the surface on its last trip yesterday but the jam was cleared by a diver.

A final trip was made to the submarine this morning, but it ended in despair when the aft section was found to be flooded.

Washington greets Nicaragua's Somoza

May 5. Twenty-one guns and a full pageant parade saluted Nicaraguan President Anastasio Somoza's arrival in Washington today. President Roosevelt, pursuing his "Good Neighbor Policy," greeted the head of the Central American republic, known as "El Yanqui" for his open sympathies for the United States and his hatred of Augusto Sandino during the Nicaraguan revolt.

Thousands lined the streets of the parade route to see the General and FDR ride by, including government employees who were excused from work early for the festivities. The city hasn't seen such a demonstration of American hospitality since King Albert of Belgium was received following the war (→ 6/29).

Stanwyck is wed

May 14. Barbara Stanwyck, 31, and Robert Taylor, 27, were married shortly after midnight at the home of San Diego friends. By obtaining the license under their true names of Ruby Stevens Fay and Arlington Spangler Brugh, they kept their plans secret. The wedding trip is delayed until he finishes making a movie with Hedy Lamarr.

Spelling Bee winner

May 29. Elizabeth Rice, 12, from Worcester, Mass., won first prize of $500 in the 15th annual National Spelling Bee, clinching the title by getting the word "canonical" right. Runner-up was Humphrey Cook, 13, from Richmond, who went out on "homogeneity." Third prize went to Mildred Kariher, 14, from Ohio, who missed out on "farcical."

May 20. Twelve years to the day after Lindbergh forged the way, Pan Am's Yankee Clipper hit the Azores, opening scheduled service to Europe.

Italy and Germany sign Pact of Steel

Flags of Italy and Reich fly together.

May 22. One of the most grandiose alliances in modern history was consummated by Italy and Germany today, creating "an invincible bloc of 300 million people." The Axis powers signed a ten-year "Pact of Steel" which binds them economically, politically and militarily with the declared objective of reorganizing Europe, promoting the two powerful nations and creating a "just peace" in the world.

At the ceremonious signing, top German and Italian officials, including Chancellor Hitler, agreed that Germany would rule on land and Italy on sea in times of war, which to many Europeans seems to be lurking on the horizon. Britain, alarmed by the event, called an extra session of Parliament to discuss the pact's ramifications (→ 6/3).

1939

JUNE

Su	Mo	Tu	We	Th	Fr	Sa
				1	2	3
4	5	6	7	8	9	10
11	12	13	14	15	16	17
18	19	20	21	22	23	24
25	26	27	28	29	30	

1. Douglas DC-4 makes first flight Chicago-New York with 40 passengers.

2. Palestine: Bomb kills five Arabs in Jerusalem; four Britons and three Jews slain on patrol (→ 3/15/40).

3. Reich trades arms for air base in Bolivia (→ 7).

5. U.S. Supreme Court voids Jersey City Mayor Frank Hague's ban on C.I.O. (→ 7/19).

7. Berlin: Estonia and Latvia sign non-aggression pact with Reich (→ 7/18).

9. Bohemia: Nazis arrest 1,000 Czechs for killing of German policeman (→ 7/6).

12. Pennslyvania: Byron Nelson wins U.S. Open golf title.

14. Moscow considers "repeal" of Mendel's genetic law for conflict with Marxist dialectics.

14. China: Japanese besiege British concession at Tientsin, demand release of Chinese accused of terrorism (→ 22).

15. French sub Phoenix sinks in Indochina; 63 killed.

21. New York: Illness forces Lou Gehrig to quit baseball (→ 7/4).

22. China: U.S. ignores Japanese order to remove destroyer Pillsbury from Swatow (→ 7/25).

23. Ankara: France, Turkey sign mutual aid pact.

24. Brazil allows entry of 3,000 German Jewish refugees.

28. New York: Joe Louis defends title, flooring Tony Galento in fourth round (→ 9/20).

28. New York: Pan Am begins regularly scheduled air service to Europe.

29. London: Viscount Halifax tells Reich Britain is ready for war (→ 8/22).

29. Managua: Anastasio Somoza promises U.S. will get canal in Nicaragua (→ 5/26/47).

BIRTH

11. Jackie Stewart, Scottish race car driver.

DEATH

26. Ford Madox Ford, British writer, editor (*12/17/1873).

907 Jews stranded; Cuba denies entry

June 6. From port to port the ship sails on, its unfortunate passengers not wanted anywhere. Some 907 Jewish refugees from Germany, more than 400 women and children, aboard the Hamburg-American liner St. Louis, were denied admission to Cuba last Friday. The government declared that 9,300 refugees are on the island already, and that the economic situation allows no more. Appeals are being made to the President and Congress to grant asylum in the United States.

Reports tell of attempted suicides aboard other refugee ships seeking haven unsuccessfully. The plight of Jews in Germany is a problem that must be solved. A plan to settle 30,000 exiles in the Philippines is being discussed (→ 24).

Judge Manton to prison; took bribes

June 20. Martin T. Manton, the former senior Judge of the Second Federal Circuit Court of Appeals, was sentenced today in New York to two years in prison and he was fined $10,000 after being convicted of exchanging "judicial favors" for cash or loans.

In passing sentence, Judge Calvin Chestnut denounced Manton as one who "has shocked the public generally and particularly the bench and bar of the country." Manton served on the bench for 22 years and had been the tenth ranking member of the nation's judiciary. Manton denied having taken any bribes in exchange for "judicial favors" and he protested that the prison term was "tantamount to a death sentence."

British King and Queen visit N.Y. Fair

June 10. King George VI and Queen Elizabeth of England toured the New York World's Fair this morning. The royal couple were escorted to the grounds by a motorcycle convoy and secret service cars. a 21-gun salute boomed, and a high school band trumpeted a welcome.

Then the royal couple went sightseeing, as bedazzled as the million people who have seen such wonders as nylon, cellophane and television for the first time. Of course, they also saw the two major structures, the Trylon and Perisphere. The "Merrie England" exhibit of the Perisphere naturally interested them. Also present were 25 girl bagpipers in kilts and midgets dressed as Grenadier Guards.

The couple's visit to the fair follows whirlwind trips to Washington, where they were hosted at the White House by President Roosevelt, and New York City proper. Despite all the activity, the queen managed a perpetual smile and alternated hands to keep the responsibility of waving from tiring her.

The King and FDR take a ride in the open air.

1939

JULY

Su	Mo	Tu	We	Th	Fr	Sa
						1
2	3	4	5	6	7	8
9	10	11	12	13	14	15
16	17	18	19	20	21	22
23	24	25	26	27	28	29
30	31					

3. FDR says U.S. arms embargo raises war peril (→ 23).

5. Kentucky: 100 killed by flash floods.

6. Berlin: Reich forces all Jews to join Union of Jews (→ 10/30).

8. Wimbledon: Bobby Riggs over Elwood Cooke 2-6, 6-8, 3-6, 6-3, 6-2; Alice Marble over Kay Stammers 6-2, 6-0.

10. Yankee Clipper lands in London, completing first passenger flight over Atlantic.

11. N.Y.: American League wins All Star baseball game 3-1.

12. Kentucky: One killed, six injured in Harlan County strike.

12. Washington: Samuel Kress donates $25 mil. art collection to National Gallery.

13. Reich leases Port of Trieste from Italy for ten years (→ 30).

16. Mass.: Fritz Kuhn, pres. of German-American Bund, arrested for drunkenness (→ 9/29).

17. Italy: 26 killed as Italians begin expelling foreigners from Tyrol.

18. Poland: 2,000 Nazi guards arrive at Danzig (→ 30).

19. Washington: Congressional inquiry asks names of WPA strikers, seeking links to Communists (→ 8/18).

21. Mexico: Pres. Cardenas offers 50 acres to each peasant.

23. FDR asks Congress to revise Neutrality Act to allow arms exports (→ 8/10).

25. China: Japan blocks British trade, closing river to Canton (→ 26).

26. U.S. renounces 1919 trade treaty with Japan (→ 8/4).

26. London: Two I.R.A. bombs kill one, injure 18 (→ 11/18).

27. Franco-British delegation sent to Moscow to discuss tripartite defense alliance (→ 8/4).

27. Bank of Basle to open U.S. branch in New York to provide haven for European capital.

30. Belgian racer Sylvere Maes wins Tour de France.

30. More Reich troops reported moving to Libya through Trieste (→ 9/1).

War threatened by crisis over Danzig

July 30. The newest flashpoint of tensions in Europe is the hotly disputed and strategic free city of Danzig. Adolf Hitler is making it quite clear he wants to absorb Danzig into the Reich. But France and Britain have both warned him the action could precipitate another war.

The warnings were contained in separate statements this month by the French Foreign Minister and British Prime Minister. Both men told Hitler that they expect him to respect the status of Danzig as mandated by the Versailles treaty.

The warnings were the strongest yet to the Fuhrer, but he shows no signs of heeding them. His military commanders have already assembled a strike force of tanks and cavalry that could easily be used in an invasion of Danzig and the arm of Poland known as "the corridor," which stretches into the Baltic.

Today, the League of Nations High Commissioner for Danzig told Reuters that Danzig is not in danger. This is the same official who has watched idly as Nazis have gradually taken control of the city (→ 8/8).

Danzig in Poland. Will Europe choose to fight over this quiet Baltic town?

July 4. Even the most calloused of ballplayers could not help but swallow hard today in Yankee Stadium as 61,808 fans honored departing Lou Gehrig. It took a tragic disease to break Gehrig's record streak of 2,130 consecutive games. The indefatigable "Iron Horse," fourth in career home runs and 18th in batting average, choked back the tears and said his friends and fellow players have made him "the luckiest man alive."

1939

AUGUST

Su	Mo	Tu	We	Th	Fr	Sa
		1	2	3	4	5
6	7	8	9	10	11	12
13	14	15	16	17	18	19
20	21	22	23	24	25	26
29	28	29	30	31		

1. India: Bombay begins Prohibition, first since U.S. law was repealed.

2. Einstein writes to FDR suggesting Atomic bomb is feasible (→ 12/2/42).

2. Washington: FDR signs Hatch Bill, preventing campaigning by federal employees.

4. London: Chamberlain threatens naval action in Far East, saying insults to Britons make his "blood boil" (→ 9/24).

4. British negotiator leaves Moscow without accord (→ 23).

6. Madrid: 53 executed as plotters after killing of army official (→ 9/12).

8. Berlin: Reich orders registration of all between five and 70 to prepare for wartime assignments (→ 16).

12. New York: 90,000 march in A.F.L. parade on Fifth Avenue.

16. Berlin: Reich reveals demands on Poland, wants both Pomorze and Danzig (→ 19).

18. Detroit: Henry Ford defies NLRB order to reinstate 24 fired during strike (→ 1/31/41).

19. Reich sends 14 U-boats to North Atlantic, calls Slovak troops to Polish border (→ 20).

20. Poland rushes troops to border to face Germans (→ 22).

22. France and Britain reaffirm pledge to aid Poland (→ 23).

22. Paris: Normandie carries full passenger load as Americans rush home fearing war.

23. Belgium proclaims neutrality (→ 5/10/40).

23. France begins war mobilization (→ 26).

24. New York: Louis "Lepke" Buchalter surrenders to FBI.

26. Reich demands Britain end Polish alliance (→ 28).

27. New York World's Fair sets daily attendance record of 306,480 (→ 11/1).

28. Holland mobilizes army to check attack (→ 29).

29. U.S.S.R.: Soviet masses soldiers in west (→ 30).

30. France: 16,000 children evacuated from Paris (→ 31).

Judy in Land of Oz delights millions

Aug 18. Frank L. Baum's children's classic "The Wonderful Wizard of Oz" had its film premiere tonight. The musical stars Judy Garland as Dorothy, the girl who sails "over the rainbow" in a tornado. Ray Bolger, Jack Haley and Bert Lahr play her friends the Scarecrow, Tin Man and the Cowardly Lion. The sounds (some songs are done by the Singer Midgets) and sights (the tornado was made by a woman's stocking) prove the real wizard is Hollywood.

"Follow the yellow brick road."

Standard to drill for Arabian oil

Aug 7. An oil concession covering the entire kingdom of Saudi Arabia was granted to the Standard Oil Company of California today by King Ibn Saud. Although the king received $1.5 million in gold and will get $750,000 annually as well as royalties on all oil found by the firm, the decision to give the concession to the American firm was based on the king's distrust of other nations.

Italy has been trying to get the lucrative concession for years and recently enlisted the help of Germany. England and France have also made bids, and Ibn Saud told an agent of Standard the Japanese had offered three times what the Americans paid for a third of the concession but had been refused.

The king said he preferred to deal with an American firm because, unlike other nations, the United States had no political designs on his country. Standard Oil has had a relatively small concession in Saudi Arabia, which it has shared with another American oil firm, the Texas Corporation. ▷

German-Russian treaty

Aug 23. Nazis and Communists shook hands today in Moscow, and they shocked the leaders of Western Europe. Germany and Soviet Russia signed a non-aggression treaty that stymies efforts in Paris and London to restrain Adolf Hitler.

The pact was signed by German Foreign Minister Joachim von Ribbentrop, Soviet leader Joseph Stalin and his Commissar of Foreign Affairs, Vyacheslav Molotov. The treaty was approved less than a week after the two countries signed a trade agreement in Berlin.

The non-aggression treaty is being praised in Berlin as an enormous victory over British efforts to form a circle around Germany with the help of France and Russia. Stalin was never very comfortable with the British, and they were never very comfortable with him. Many English diplomats believe that communism is just as great a threat to European security as Nazism.

Hitler-Stalin: Strange bedfellows?

The treaty also isolates Poland in Eastern Europe, and the diplomatic maneuvering indicates that Hitler is as determined as ever to annex Danzig and exact territorial concessions from Warsaw. German military commanders are under orders to prepare for immediate military action, and the new treaty gives Hitler more freedom to march (→ 10/29).

Europe is mobilizing for the inevitable

Aug 31. Throughout the capitals of Western Europe tonight, hope evaporated for a peaceful resolution of the conflict between Germany and Poland. Diplomacy cannot stop Adolf Hitler. Europe is on the brink of another war.

Great Britain has begun to mobilize her fleet, and the government is operating with emergency powers approved by Parliament. Thousands of school children have been evacuated from London to the safety of the countryside.

French children have also been whisked out of Paris. Military reserves have been called up, wartime censorship restrictions have taken effect and Communist newspapers have been seized. The Polish government, which had already moved many troops west to the Moravian and Slovakian frontiers, declared a general mobilization (→ 9/1).

Reich troops are poised for a speedy invasion of Europe if Hitler gives the word.

Largest peacetime order for warplanes

Aug 10. The United States War Department has announced an order for aircraft and engines totaling more than $85 million. Acting Secretary Louis Johnson issued contracts for the military equipment, the largest peacetime arms order ever, to ten corporations, six of them aircraft manufacturers and four engine producers. Consolidated Aircraft Corporation and Boeing Aircraft Company received the largest contracts, to build four bombardment planes. The contracts were submitted under the Supplemental Aircraft Appropriations Act (→ 9/5).

FDR changes date for Thanksgiving

Aug 14. President Roosevelt shattered another precedent today when he announced the move of Thanksgiving Day from Nov. 30 to Nov. 23 this year. He explained that many had urged the shift to create a holiday less close to Christmas. While retailers welcome the change, it gives football schedulers a headache. Their big day of games is now a mere Thursday in November. From Plymouth, where the first day of thanksgiving was held in 1621, comes "hearty disapproval." Since Abraham Lincoln named the last Thursday of November as the day in 1864, subsequent presidents have followed suit. Until now, that is.

1939

SEPTEMBER

Su	Mo	Tu	We	Th	Fr	Sa
					1	2
3	4	5	6	7	8	9
10	11	12	13	14	15	16
17	18	19	20	21	22	23
24	25	26	27	28	29	30

1. German troops storm Poland; Danzig ceded to Reich (→ 9).

1. Italy proclaims neutrality (→ 11/5).

1. Martial law declared across France (→ 3).

3. Britain, France declare war on Germany (→ 7).

3. British Liner Athenia sunk by U-boat torpedo; 1400 die, including 28 Americans (→ 14).

4. Pennslyvania: Australia beats U.S. to take Davis Cup.

5. New York: Stocks soar as investors predict war boom.

7. Germany: Reich troops rush west to meet French (→ 10).

9. Poland: German troops reach Warsaw (→ 16).

10. British Expeditionary Force begins to land in France (→ 19).

12. Franco forbids Spanish ships to transport arms (→ 10/23/40).

14. U-boats sink two British ships in Atlantic, bringing Allied total to 19 (→ 18).

15. Lindbergh, by radio, urges U.S. to avoid war (→ 10/2).

16. Russia invades Poland; Reich encircles Warsaw (→ 27).

17. New York: Alice Marble and Bobby Riggs take U.S. tennis titles at Forest Hills.

18. British aircraft carrier Courageous sunk by U-boat in Atlantic; 500 lost (→ 10/14).

19. London: Chamberlain says war will continue until Hitlerism is smashed (→ 10/1).

20. Detroit: Joe Louis KOs Bob Pastor in 11th round (→ 2/9/40).

22. Rumania executes scores in retaliation for yesterday's killing of Premier Armand Calinescu by Iron Guard (→ 9/6/40).

24. Japan launches drive on one million Chinese (→ 3/30/40).

26. U.S. to begin purge of Communists holding government posts.

27. Warsaw surrenders (→ 29).

29. Soviet, Reich fix border in Poland, without buffer state (→ 30).

29. New York: German-American Bund chief Fritz Kuhn jailed on $50,000 bail (→ 11/29).

Nazis invade Poland, divide country with Russia

Sept 30. After 21 years of tenuous peace, Europe is at war again. A mighty German force of 1.25 million men swept across the Polish border on the first of the month and on September 17th, Russian troops pushed in from the east. Poland has recoiled into the clutches of defeat.

The German invasion came without declaration of war and was executed by General Walter von Brauchitsch, who easily led his troops and tank brigades over the dry, warm Polish terrain. As the assault stormed on, Nazi Chief of State Albert Forster proclaimed the annexation of the free city, Danzig, to the Third Reich. Forster told the people of Danzig, "Our Fuhrer, Adolf Hitler, has freed us." Now the German flag flies over the city, capping months of Nazi planning.

After Hitler's government ignored an ultimatum from Great Britain and France to withdraw its troops or face Anglo-French involvement in the conflict, the two Western nations declared war on Germany, fulfilling their defense obligations with Poland.

Russian troops met advancing German forces on the 18th, after they easily trounced Polish defenders. Plans were made for the partition of Poland, and ten days later Soviet leader Joseph Stalin met with his Foreign Minister, Vyacheslav Molotov, and German Foreign Minister Joachim von Rippentrop in Moscow for the German-Soviet agreement to divide the beleaguered nation. According to a communique released by the two aggressors, troops will occupy Poland "to bring order to Poland and to help the Polish people, confronted with the collapse of their state."

The territorial division grants the Soviets some 76,500 square miles of the eastern region, with its population of 12.8 million. Germany received a sphere of influence encompassing Lublin in the east and most of the western portion of the country, including the capital, Warsaw—a city devastated by three weeks of nightmarish bombing.

The German campaign has exhibited the power, speed and determination of a well-trained and innovative military. Its "Blitzkrieg" or "lightning war" has impressed international observers who remember the failed trench warfare of German forces in the last war.

The invasions have elicited condemnation by almost every sovereign state. Finland appealed to the League of Nations to expel Russia from membership—which it did.

"Danzig welcomes the Fuhrer." The city's big German population greets Hitler.

In the United States, President Roosevelt has promised to keep America out of the European war, which could be long and very deadly. He answered a reporter's inquiry, "Can we keep out of it?" by saying solemnly, "I not only sincerely hope so, but I believe we can, and that every effort will be made to so do."

Meanwhile, confronted with the destruction of their nation, the Poles continue to bleed mercilessly. An estimated 60,000 Poles have been killed since the Nazi invasion, about 200,000 more have been wounded and some 700,000 soldiers are now held in captivity. In some circles, "Polish ineptitude" is to blame for the tragic and numerous losses, yet credit must be given to the fierce and impassioned German forces, spellbound by the dictatorship of Adolf Hitler.

Questions remain as to how long the German-Russian alliance will last. It has been discovered that close Nazi-Soviet relations have persisted since May, but the two powers are now neighbors, without Poland as a buffer zone, and they must work out problems destined to arise with the territorial partition of Poland (→ 10/6).

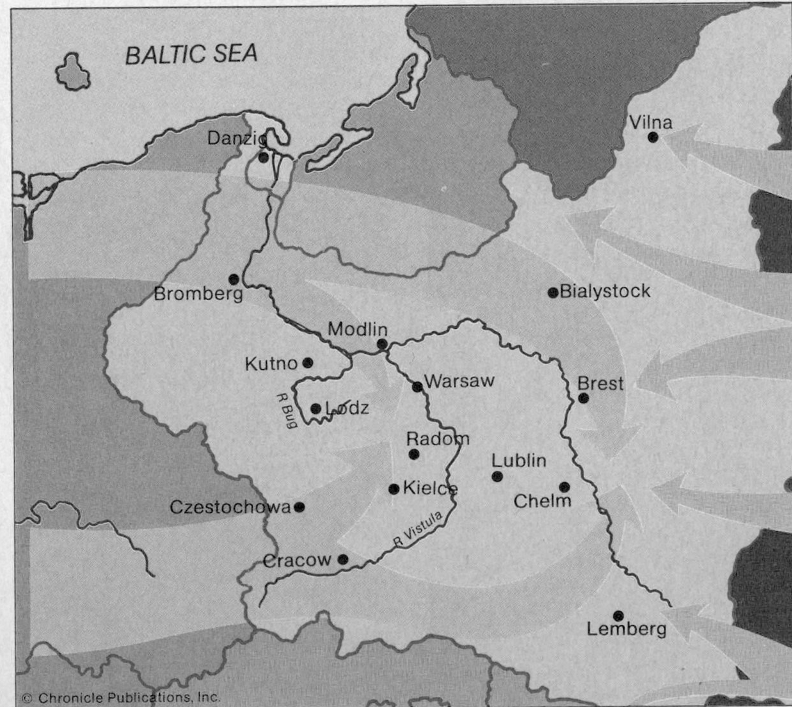

Poland is swallowed up by Reich troops pressing from the west, and Soviet forces from the east, as arranged at last month's historic meeting in Moscow.

The motorized German army swarms over Poland.

Britain and France declare war on Germany

Sept 30. Blood indelibly stained European soil this month as Great Britain and France declared war on Germany following the Nazis' lightning invasion of Poland.

Immediately after German troops blistered across the Polish border, the French and British governments issued an ultimatum to the Third Reich: "Suspend all aggressive action against Poland (and) withdraw forces from Polish territory" or the United Kingdom and France, "in fulfillment of our obligations, will come to Poland's assistance." After two days of German penetration deeper toward Warsaw, on September 3rd British Prime Minister Neville Chamberlain made his fateful, and to many, inevitable declaration that the two Western powers would fight Adolf Hitler's troops. "We shall be fighting against brute force," the British leader added. The obligations Chamberlain referred to are mutual defense treaties that Poland, France and England had signed.

Great Britain quickly announced a blockade of Germany after entering the war. Germany retaliated destructively when one of its submarines attacked and sank the British passenger liner, the Athenia, on its route from Liverpool to Montreal. One hundred and twelve people perished in the assault.

The first British attack occurred on September 4, as the English air force bombed a German fleet at the North Sea entrance to the Kiel Canal. Many of the Reich's ships were destroyed or seriously damaged, but the Germans said their anti-aircraft guns downed five English planes.

Heavy artillery fire was not the only thing unleashed from British aircraft, as Chamberlain ordered pilots to unload six million leaflets on German terrain. The leaflets, entitled, "A Warning: Great Britain to the German People," appealed to the German citizenry and explained the British position in the new and potentially long war. They described the Nazi leaders as liars, "condemning you to mass murders." The propaganda pamphlets implored the Germans to "insist upon peace" and cautioned that British strength would annihilate Germany in a protracted war.

While France and Britain declared war, scores of other nations expressed adamant wishes to stay out of the fighting. The United States denounced the German aggression, but stated it would not become engaged. President Roosevelt said, "This nation will remain a neutral nation, but I cannot ask that every American remain neutral in thought as well." Latin American countries as well as the Balkan states proclaimed their intentions to remain aloof from the war. In Italy, the course has been set for noninvolvement so decidedly that Italian trade ships resumed their normal sea commerce, despite the presence of German submarines.

German U-boat warfare has been very effective this month. In one active day, the 7th, Nazi subs sunk or fired on seven French and British vessels, including the English Manaar and the Corinthic and the French Tamara. At least two are dead and another 40 are missing from the assault on the Manaar. According to one eyewitness, four torpedoes rocked the British freighter, "the fourth one broke her in two and we watched as she up-ended and disappeared." By mid-month, 19 Allied ships had been blasted to the bottom of the sea by Nazi subs.

The French have mobilized eight million soldiers, many sent to fortify the Westwall. Early this month, the French made contact with their German opponents, but most Nazi troops were to the east, expanding their conquest of Poland. Some military observers believe a French offensive into Germany might deflate the Reich's strategic momentum, but no moves have yet been made, other than the policies of blockade and defensive preparation. Meanwhile, all the world worries that the temporary calm on the Western Front will erupt (→ 10/1).

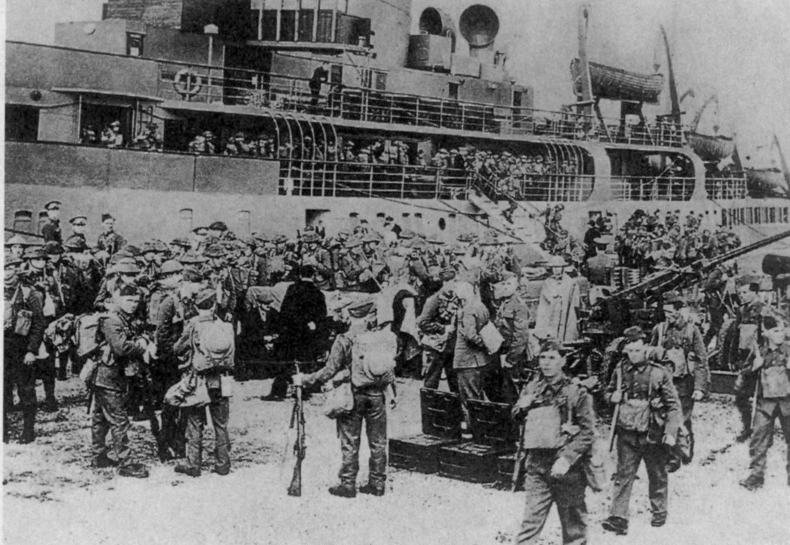

British infantry arrive in France, ready to back up the Maginot Line.

America officially neutral in Europe's war

Sept 5. President Roosevelt today proclaimed United States neutrality in the war in Europe and moved toward holding a Pan-American parley to cushion the Western hemisphere against the ravages of war.

FDR solemnly addresses the nation.

In one proclamation, the president denied United States territory and territorial waters to belligerents engaged in the European war. In another proclamation, he clamped an embargo on shipment of arms, munitions, airplanes and plane parts to all those countries in which, he said, "a state of war unhappily exists." The countries are France, Germany, the United Kingdom, Poland, India, Australia and New Zealand. Canada and South Africa were not named since the parliaments of those British dominions have not yet declared war against Germany.

The president's proclamation of neutrality was much along the lines of that issued by President Wilson at the outbreak of war in Europe in 1914, long before the United States entered that war.

Sigmund Freud: He gave us new ideas

Sept 23. The father of psychoanalysis, Sigmund Freud, has died in London at the age of 83. Freud, son of a middle-class Jewish merchant, was raised in Vienna and conducted much of his research there. He recognized the relationship between the unconscious and manifested illness. Freud thought repressed sexual memories often led to hysteria; he developed the "Oedipus complex," a theory that neurosis may be induced by a child's sexual love for a parent. Freud delved into his dreams and found meanings hidden there. He revealed himself to help us know ourselves.

Freud denied the inevitable inquiries: "Sometimes a cigar is just a cigar."

1939

OCTOBER

Su	Mo	Tu	We	Th	Fr	Sa
1	2	3	4	5	6	7
8	9	10	11	12	13	14
15	16	17	18	19	20	21
22	23	24	25	26	27	28
29	30	31				

1. London: Churchill bars peace with Hitler; Britain conscripts 250,000 more (→ 4).

2. U.S. will maintain relations with new Polish govt., but will not recognize partition (→ 3).

3. Panama City: Inter-American conference sets 300-mile security zone around continent (→ 9).

4. Germany: French rout Nazis in tank battle (→ 6).

6. Partition of Poland takes effect, at the cost, so far, of 10,500 lives (→ 4/9/40).

6. Hitler assures he is just reclaiming lands lost in 1918; nonetheless, France and Britain reject peace terms (→ 17).

8. Ohio: Yankees beat Reds 7-4 to win World Series.

9. Florida: U-boat and two tankers sighted off Key West coast (→ 11).

11. A.F.L. passes resolution proposing boycott of goods from belligerents, yet opposing U.S. entry to war (→ 18).

15. N.Y.: 325,000 watch Mayor LaGuardia dedicate North Beach airport in his own name.

16. San Francisco: Gov. Olson commutes sentence of Warren Billings, convicted of Preparedness Day bombing with Thomas Mooney.

17. Germany: Nazis attack with 100,000 on Western Front (→ 20).

18. FDR bars war subs from U.S. ports and waters (→ 27).

19. Turkey signs 15-year treaty with Allies.

25. Germany: Reich press urging bombing of Britain.

27. Washington protests seizure of American merchant ship City of Flint (→ 11/4).

27. Rome: Pope Pius, in first encyclical, condemns dictators, treaty violators, racists.

29. Soviet troops enter Latvia (→ 11/1).

29. California: Clyde Schlieper and Wes Carroll set endurance flying record at 30 days.

DEATH

23. Zane Grey, U.S. western writer (*1/31/1872).

Hitler makes peace pleas; Allies decline

Hitler and two military aides plan for war while peace is discussed in Europe.

Oct 20. Adolf Hitler is bristling at the rejection of his peace offer to London and Paris, and Germany is now vowing to fight the war to its bitter end in Western Europe.

"England and France rejected the Fuhrer's hand of peace," the German government said tonight. "They threw down the gauntlet. Germany has taken it up." The government also denied reports that Hitler would make another peace offer to the French.

Hitler made his offer in a speech to the Reichstag earlier this month, after his military victory in Poland. French Premier Daladier was the first to reject Hitler's overture. Daladier said no "real justice and lasting peace" would be possible until Hitler was defeated.

President Roosevelt also turned down an indirect appeal from Hitler to mediate an end to the war.

Hitler is also furious at the new treaty between Britain, France and Turkey. He warned Turkey it is "playing with fire," and he held urgent meetings all day about the diplomatic development (→ 11/18).

British sea losses: Royal Oak and Athenia

Oct 14. More than 800 aboard the British battleship Royal Oak are believed dead after a German submarine's torpedo struck and sank the Admiralty's ship. The sinking surprised Great Britain because most thought the Royal Oak's bulging armor would repel a torpedo. It didn't and only 396 of the crew survived the tragedy. Last month, at the outset of the war, 112 passengers aboard the British liner Athenia perished when a Nazi sub torpedoed her (→ 11/23).

Royal Oak is the latest victim of a sub war menacing merchants and warships.

British report on Nazi camp cruelties

Oct 30. Tortures and atrocities beyond imagination are visited upon Jew and non-Jew in Germany, states a report by accredited witnesses and published by the British government. It details destruction and looting by order, synagogues set afire, floggings with barbed-wire birches, brutal killinqs and more during 1938-39. In the Buchenwald camp, physical labor far beyond capacity is the order of the day. Men are forced to do knee-bends while carrying huge stone blocks.

"Tree-binding" and "merry-go-round" means that a victim's arms are bound around a tree, the feet barely touching the ground, while kicks and blows drive on a macabre dance. The "sweat box" almost guarantees a slow death. In accordance with diplomatic usage, the document is called a White Paper, but, if even partly true, it is a Black Book of horror, recalling the darkest ages in the annals of history (→ 11/18).

Patriotic Mr. Smith goes to the capital

Jimmy Stewart in Washington.

Oct 20. "Mr. Smith Goes to Washington," the latest Frank Capra romp, opened tonight at the New York Music Hall. The film is a humorous swipe at the U.S. Senate, with an underlying get-you-in-the-gut patriotism. It feels quite a bit like Capra's "Mr. Deeds Goes to Town" (1936), which centered on a naive fellow who aimed to make everyone as happy as possible.

Jimmy Stewart's Smith, like Gary Cooper's Deeds, is tall, drawling and earnest. He reacts to filibusters, hidden clauses and political intrigue with stuttering horror. Claude Rains is a senior Senator who shows Smith the ropes.

1939

NOVEMBER

Su	Mo	Tu	We	Th	Fr	Sa
			1	2	3	4
5	6	7	8	9	10	11
12	13	14	15	16	17	18
19	20	21	22	23	24	25
26	27	28	29	30		

1. New York: World's Fair closes; 26 million paid visitors.

1. Finland: For. Min. Erkko pledges resistance to Soviet bases on Finnish soil (→ 13).

4. Norway releases U.S. ship City of Flint, seized by Germans last month (→ 6).

5. Rome: Mussolini orders more troops, army reorganization (→ 3/5/40).

6. French report using U.S. planes to shoot down nine Reich fighters (→ 12/2).

9. Poland: Nazis detroy statue of Woodrow Wilson in Posen, calling it eyesore.

11. Rome: Pope Pius sends note to U.S. Catholics, denouncing education, divorce, unequal distribution of wealth.

13. After quiting Moscow parley with Soviets, Finland calls general mobilization (→ 26).

14. Venezuela: Fire sweeps oil town of Lagunillas, killing 500.

16. Indiana: General Motors found guilty in monopoly case.

18. Dutch liner Simon Bolivar sunk by mine in Atlantic; 140 dead (→ 23).

18. Germany: British royal air force raids Wilhelmshaven; 15 planes lost (→ 12/12).

18. Berlin: Reich imposes ten-hour work day to compensate for labor shortage (→ 2/21/40).

18. London: I.R.A. explodes three bombs in Picadilly Circus (→ 1/4/40).

23. Atlantic: Reich destroyer Deutschland sinks British ship Rawalpindi; 300 lost (→ 25).

24. Prague: Gestapo in Czechoslovakia executes 120 students accused of anti-Nazi plotting.

25. Nazis report four British ships sunk in North Sea; London denies (→ 12/20).

26. Soviets charge Finns with artillery attack on border (→ 28).

28. U.S.S.R. scraps non-aggression pact with Finland (→ 29).

29. N.Y.: Nazi Bund leader Fritz Kuhn found guilty of larceny (→ 12/5).

29. Finland: Soviet planes bomb airfield at Helsinki (→ 30).

Soviets attack Finland

Soviet troops, in camouflage dress, prepare for a snowbound battle in Finland.

Nov 30. The Russian invasion of Finland today by land, sea and air has left areas of Helsinki in flames after heavy bombardment by low-swooping Soviet planes.

The evacuation of Abo, Viborg and other cities is under way. In the far north, people have fled from the Petsamo port region across the Norwegian border.

Valiant Finnish troops are offering stiff resistance along the 50-mile Karelian Isthmus front, and have captured or destroyed some Russian tanks. In an appeal for international aid, Radio Finland claims that the lightning attack has been largely repulsed.

Russia is said to have delivered an ultimatum threatening to "completely destroy" Finland unless it capitulates immediately to all of Russia's previous demands, rejected by the Finnish government, which include surrender of the Karelian Isthmus, a small area of strategic importance. In Washington, President Roosevelt has appealed to both nations to refrain from bombing civilians (→ 12/2).

Rockefeller Center is open for business

Nov 1. New York's Rockefeller Center, one of the greatest urban developments ever undertaken, has been completed after eight years of construction. Designed by the firms of Reinhard & Hofmeister; Hoat, Godley & Fouilhouz; and Corbett, Harrison & MacMurray, it combines office space with recreation, broadcasting, shopping and entertainment facilities, including the fabulous art-deco style Radio City Music Hall, which opened in 1932. At the heart of the center is the RCA Building, surrounded by 13 smaller skyscrapers.

Pablo Picasso's "Night Fishing in Antibes."

U.S. ends embargo on sale of arms

Nov 4. The United States embargo against the sale of ammunition and other implements of war to the belligerent nations was lifted today when President Roosevelt signed a joint resolution passed by Congress after an historic six-week debate. However, in order to safeguard the nation's neutrality, American nationals and ships will be barred from a specified combat area in European war zones except under conditions that the president will lay down in rules and regulations to be issued next week (→ 6).

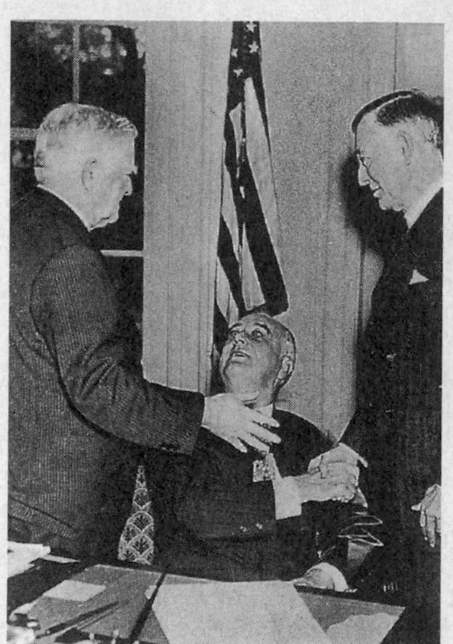

FDR greets Sen. Pittman as they confer with the V.P. Garner after signing the resolution.

Hitler escapes plot against his life

Nov 8. Six people were killed and more than 60 were injured tonight when a bomb exploded in a packed Munich beer hall. But the intended target of the attack escaped. Adolf Hitler had left the hall 15 minutes before the explosion.

Hitler departed after addressing Nazi veterans in the hall, the scene of the failed putsch 16 years ago. He was scheduled to stay later, but he reportedly left early because of pressing affairs of state. The government blamed "foreign instigators" for the assassination attempt, and newspapers claim Britain was responsible. A reward is being offered for information on the attackers.

1939

DECEMBER

Su	Mo	Tu	We	Th	Fr	Sa
					1	2
3	4	5	6	7	8	9
10	11	12	13	14	15	16
17	18	19	20	21	22	23
24	25	26	27	28	29	30
31						

2. Finland: Soviet drive halted by fierce Finnish resistance (→ 4).

2. FDR imposes "moral arms embargo" on U.S.S.R. (→ 23).

4. Moscow rejects Finnish peace proposal; refuses recognition to Premier Risto Ryti (→ 6).

5. New York: Bund leader Fritz Kuhn given two to five years for theft (→ 4/30/40).

6. London: Britain agrees to send arms to Finland (→ 14).

10. Nobel Committee offers no Peace Prize for 1939.

12. Germany: Nazis launch offensive along Rhine (→ 18).

14. Geneva: League of Nations drops U.S.S.R. (→ 25).

16. Washington: Natl. Women's Party urges immediate congressional action on E.R.A.

18. Berlin: Reich official Robert Ley says Germany aims for annihilation of Britain (→ 1/8/40).

23. U.S. and 20 nations protest violation of safety zone in Western hemisphere (→ 1/2/40).

23. Canadian troops arrive in Britain.

25. Finnish troops enter Soviet territory (→ 1/7/40).

27. Turkey: Vicious earthquakes take 11,000 lives.

CULTURAL EVENTS, 1939

Literature: James Joyce's "Finnegan's Wake"; Steinbeck's "The Grapes of Wrath"; Henry Miller's "Tropic of Capricorn"; Nathanael West's "The Day of the Locust"; William Saroyan's "The Time of Your Life."

Academia: Serge Chakotin's "The Rape of the Masses"; Swiss scientist Paul Muller discovers basis for insecticide DDT.

Music: "God Bless America"; "Three Little Fishes"; "Over the Rainbow"; "Beer Barrel Polka."

The Arts: Henry Moore's "Reclining Figure"; Anna Mary Robertson "Grandma" Moses paintings at MOMA shown; Frank Lloyd Wright's Johnson Wax building.

Film: "Gone With the Wind"; Garbo in "Ninotchka," Robert Donat's "Good-Bye Mr. Chips"; John Ford's "Stagecoach."

"Gone With the Wind" opens to cheers

Mitchell's masterpiece now a movie.

Dec 15. Rebel yells greeted the premiere of "Gone With the Wind" tonight in Atlanta. The film, based on Margaret Mitchell's sweeping novel of the Civil War South, has passed its most difficult test. Would Atlantans view the technicolor torching of their city as a smear on Southern honor? Judging by the woops and hollers of the crowd, the reply is a resounding "hell, no!"

The Atlanta Grand Theatre was dressed up to resemble Twelve Oaks, the plantation where Scarlett O'Hara and her beaus dallied. At six o'clock, the theater was roped off to keep the stars, arriving in their limousines, from being crushed by the happy mob. Clark Gable put in an appearance at 8:40 p.m. A few women fainted at the sight.

Miss Mitchell gave a speech when the three hour and 45 minute epic ended. In quavering tones she said it had "been a great thing for Georgia and the South to see the Confederates come back." Mrs. Dorothy Lamar, President of the United Daughters of the Confederacy, praised the casting of Vivian Leigh. "No one can quarrel now," she said, "with the selection of Miss Leigh as Scarlett. She is Margaret Mitchell's Scarlett to the life."

"Gone With the Wind" was directed by Victor Fleming. It also stars Leslie Howard, Olivia de Havilland and Hattie McDaniel. Max Steiner composed the film score.

Housewives glued to radio romances

"Can a girl from a little mining town in the West find happiness as the wife of a wealthy and titled Englishman?" Each episode of CBS radio's soap opera "Our Gal Sunday" begins with that question. Other popular "soaps," as they are known in the trade, include "The Romance of Helen Trent," "Backstage Wife" and "Search for Tomorrow." They are called soap operas because they are sponsored by soap manufacturers. Women working at home hear an average of 6.6 a day. The plots are gripping: Amnesia, forbidden romance and death are typical.

At night radio turns to comedy, adventure and family fare. Millions drop everything to hear the most popular show: Freeman Gosden and Charles Correll, two white men, in "Amos 'n Andy," a Negro dialect comedy. Other comedians include Burns and Allen (man and wife), Fred Allen (no kin), and Jack Benny. Among the familiar series are "One Man's Family," "The Shadow," "Jack Armstrong, the All-American Boy" and "Dick Tracy."

Trapped by British, Graf Spee scuttled

Dec 20. The commander of the German battleship Graf Spee, Captain Langsdorff, scuttled his craft off Montevideo and then placed a revolver to his head and fired. A deadly sea battle with the British cruisers Exeter, Ajax and Achilles destroyed the Graf Spee, many of her crew, the morale of the survivors and finally the skipper.

The British squadron, under the leadership of Commodore H.H. Harwood, opened fire on the German pocket battleship after the Spee had attacked the Ajax. The German ship, with its quickness and heavy armament, held off three royal navy vessels for hours but received numerous hits. Finally, after a day's worth of battling, she limped into Montevideo harbor with 36 crew members dead, 60 wounded and the ship seriously damaged.

On orders from Adolf Hitler, Langsdorff blew up one of the greatest ships in the German fleet, wrote a note to the Nazi Admiralty and ended his life (→ 1/10/40).

The Graf Spee goes down near Montevideo at the hands of its own captain.

Capt. Hornblower, a popular character

A fleet of superior novels sailed into 1939. C.S. Forester, author of the novella "The African Queen" (1935), published "Captain Horatio Hornblower," a historical novel about a fictional British navy officer serving during the Napoleonic Wars. Forester plans more works featuring this character.

John Steinbeck wrote "The Grapes of Wrath," about a family of Okies heading for what they hope is salvation in California. Richard Llewellyn is the author of "How Green Was My Valley," a semifictional remembrance of his years in a South Wales mining community. James Joyce offered a dense novel called "Finnegan's Wake." Joyce is influenced by Sigmund Freud's theories; his style of free association analyzes human relations. For the reader fed up with thinking, there is "Life With Father" to turn to. The play by Russel Crouse and Howard Lindsay is unapologetically fun.

1940–1949

1940

JANUARY

Su	Mo	Tu	We	Th	Fr	Sa
	1	2	3	4	5	6
7	8	9	10	11	12	13
14	15	16	17	18	19	20
21	22	23	24	25	26	27
28	29	30	31			

1. Pasadena: 92,000 see Southern Cal. beat Tennessee 14-0 in Rose Bowl.

2. L.I.: First anti-aircraft defense area set up at Mitchell Field, with Brig. Gen. James Chaney in charge (→ 4).

4. FDR names Atty. Gen. Frank Murphy to Supreme Court.

4. Washington: FDR asks $1.8 billion for defense, $460 million in new taxes (→ 8).

4. Dublin: Dail grants full powers to de Valera to counter I.R.A. terrorism (→ 2/7).

7. Finns smash Soviet ski attack on Karelian Isthmus (→ 11).

8. U.S. Army and Navy decide to fortify Alaska (→ 2/5).

8. Britain begins rationing sugar, meat and butter (→ 16).

10. Nazi planes attack 12 ships off British coast; three sunk, 35 dead (→ 2/15).

11. New York: Rosalind Russell opens in "His Girl Friday."

11. Stockholm: King Gustav V pledges aid to Finland (→ 12).

11. Washington: Inventor's son Charles Edison appointed secretary of Navy.

12. West Virginia: Mine explosion kills 92 in Bartley.

12. Finland: Soviet bombers raid cities in mass attacks (→ 19).

16. Hitler cancels attack in West due to bad weather and capture of German attack plans in Belgium (→ 30).

18. New York: Metropolitan Opera presents "Othello."

25. Hollywood: Metro signs Clark Gable in $2 million deal.

26. New York: Museum of Modern Art receives works by Botticelli, Raphael, Michelangelo on loan from Italy.

27. Finland: Finns trap two Soviet divisions; kill 5,000 (→ 29).

29. Soviets reported ready to negotiate with Finns (→ 2/5).

30. Berlin: Hitler warns of total war (→ 3/10).

BIRTH

21. Jack Nicklaus, American golf pro.

Fierce Finnish resistance baffles Russians

Jan 19. The skies over Finland cleared in the past week, and Russian bombers punished civilian populations in Helsinki and elsewhere. The Russians seem desperate. They have suffered large losses in this six-week-old war, and they want to teach the Finns a lesson.

Hundreds of Russians were killed in fierce fighting on the Karelian Isthmus. Soviet tanks were trapped in the snow and captured. Large numbers of prisoners were taken, many of them exhausted and suffering from frostbite.

Swedish, Norwegian and Danish volunteers have been fighting with the Finns. Their governments say the Russians will not be allowed to attack Finland from their territory.

Reports say the Russians are so angry and frustrated that they are brawling in their camps. Russian pilots are said to be fighting each other in the air. Military commanders in Moscow deny reports that scores of Red army officers have been recalled to be punished. They do not deny that secret police have been dispatched to Finland to buttress the front lines (→ 27).

Soviet soldier at war in Finland.

Fonda stars in "The Grapes of Wrath"

Fonda, deftly directed by John Ford.

Jan 4. John Steinbeck's novel "The Grapes of Wrath" came to the screen tonight in a stunning production directed by John Ford. Some of the book's language has been cleaned up, and the book's final chapter has been omitted from the screenplay. On the whole, however, it is a faithful retelling of Steinbeck's novel of Okies pushing on toward California in search of a decent livelihood.

Henry Fonda, who starred in "Young Mr. Lincoln" last year, is excellent as the fiery Tom Joad. Jane Darwell is sympathetic as his "Ma." John Ford is a visual storyteller: A few shots of tired, stained faces, abandoned farmhouses and rattling trucks, and we have seen the bottom of the Dust Bowl.

Unity Mitford fails in suicide attempt

Jan 12. It has been learned that Unity Mitford, the English friend of Adolf Hitler, tried to commit suicide last September 3. She is 25 years old and one of the six daughters of Lord Redesdale. Prince Orloff, a former broadcaster for Berlin Radio, who has since left the Reich, confirms the report. Unity Mitford has a boundless admiration for her Fuhrer. When she learned of the declaration of war between Britain and Germany last September 3, she shot two bullets into her head.

1940

FEBRUARY

Su	Mo	Tu	We	Th	Fr	Sa
				1	2	3
4	5	6	7	8	9	10
11	12	13	14	15	16	17
18	19	20	21	22	23	24
25	26	27	28	29		

1. U.S.: 600-mph barrier broken in tests of new Bell Airacobra plane.

5. Paris: Allied Supreme Council resolves to intervene in Finland and Norway (→ 11).

5. New York: Youth Congress members stage anti-war demonstration (→ 17).

7. Harvard geologists report traces of man in North America 25,000 years ago.

7. London: Britain executes two I.R.A. militants (→ 3/23).

8. New York: "Pinocchio" opens at Center Theatre.

9. New York: Joe Louis outpoints Arturo Godoy to hold heavyweight title (→ 3/29).

11. Finland: Finnish Mannerheim line pushed back by Soviets (→ 25).

12. U.S.S.R. signs trade treaty with Germany to aid against British blockade.

14. British announce merchant ships will be armed (→ 15).

15. Hitler orders British merchant ships considered warships (→ 19).

17. Sumner Welles, U.S. undersecretary of state, leaves for tour of Europe (→ 26).

19. Germans sink sixth British destroyer in Atlantic; 157 killed (→ 26).

21. Germans begin construction of concentration camp at Auschwitz (→ 9/6/41).

22. Tibet: New five-year-old Dalai Lama enthroned.

23. N.Y. Music Hall offers Sherwood's "Abe Lincoln in Illinois," with Raymond Massey and Ruth Gordon, on Washington's Birthday.

25. Copenhagen: Scandinavian states reassert neutrality in European war (→ 27).

26. Rome: Sumner Welles hands Mussolini secret message from FDR (→ 3/1).

28. Britian: Superliner Queen Elizabeth launched (→ 3/7).

BIRTH

28. Mario Andretti, American auto racer.

British seize German tanker in Norway

The Altmark lies stranded in the ice in a Scandinavian fjord.

Feb 26. British sailors from the destroyer Cossack stormed an aging German tanker in Norwegian waters and liberated more than 300 British prisoners who were locked up on board. Six Germans were killed in the assault.

It is common knowledge that Germany is preparing to invade Norway. But the country is still neutral, and Germany dared to protest what it called an act of piracy. The German tanker, the Altmark, had broken through the British blockade and dropped anchor near Bergen. It was spotted by a British agent, who communicated its position to the Admiralty by wireless. The Cossack chased the Altmark and trapped it in a fjord (→ 3/3).

New Soviet attack forces Finns back

Feb 27. The Russians have launched their biggest offensive of the war, mercilessly pounding Finnish soldiers on the Karelian Isthmus. The relentless attack has forced the Finns to abandon their positions along the all-important Mannerheim defense line. The Russians are poised to sweep down the isthmus and into the heart of the country.

Military commanders in Moscow have been embarrassed by their losses in Finland, and they have ordered their generals to throw all they have into this vicious battle. Entire companies of Russian soldiers have been chewed up by the tenacious Finnish defenders, but they are quickly replaced by reinforcements pouring in from Russia.

The fighting on the isthmus is as intense as the battles on the Somme and at Verdun, and the Finns are appealing to the world for help as they make their last stand (→ 3/5).

Death takes creator of Buck Rogers

Feb 2. The inventor of the "Buck Rogers" comic strip, Philip Nowlan, died of a stroke tonight in a Philadelphia suburb. He was 52 years old. He leaves ten children and a science-fiction legacy: Buck Rogers cartoons, radio scripts and promotional merchandise.

Nowlan attended the University of Pennsylvania, graduating in 1910. He worked for several papers, including The North American and The Retail Ledger before introducing his cartoon strip in the late 1920's. He got readers excited about the 25th century. Teens in particular do a lot of speculating about spaceships and ray guns.

A Buck Rogers serial is currently in production. It will deal with frozen animation and a voyage to Saturn. Buster Crabbe, the golden-haired Olympic swimming champion and hero of the "Flash Gordon" serial, has signed on as its star.

1940

MARCH

Su	Mo	Tu	We	Th	Fr	Sa
					1	2
3	4	5	6	7	8	9
10	11	12	13	14	15	16
17	18	19	20	21	22	23
24	25	26	27	28	29	30
31						

1. Berlin: U.S. envoy Sumner Welles meets with Hitler (→ 7).

3. Nazi air raid kills 108 on British liner in English Channel (→ 4/8).

5. British stun Mussolini, seizing seven Italian coal ships (→ 9).

5. Finns, distraught by lack of aid from Allies, send peace envoys to Moscow (→ 8).

7. Paris: Welles meets with French Premier Daladier (→ 16).

8. Hitler calls on mediating Sweden to pressure Finland into surrender (→ 13).

9. Britain frees Italian coal ships on eve of German For. Min. Ribbentrop's Rome visit (→ 18).

10. Britain begins meat rationing (→ 20).

11. New York: Arthur Rubenstein gives first recital of season at Carnegie Hall.

14. Mae West and W.C. Fields make first joint appearance in "My Little Chickadee."

14. Hollywood: Warners casts Ronald Reagan as Notre Dame's George Gipp for "Knute Rockne—All American" (→ 10/1).

15. Montevideo: World Jewish Congress Pres. Nahum Goldmann announces 90,000 Palestinian Jews are fighting with Allies (→ 11/5/44).

20. Germany: British RAF conducts all-night air raid on Nazi air base at Sylt (→ 4/3).

21. Paris: Paul Reynaud is new premier, replacing Daladier, ousted for inaction in Finland.

23. Great Britain: I.R.A. assaults Dartmoor prison in attempt to free compatriots (→ 2/18/48).

25. U.S. to give France and Britain unhindered access to American warplanes (→ 4/13).

28. New York: Joan Fontaine appears in du Maurier's "Rebecca."

29. New York: Joe Louis scores second-round KO over Johnny Paychek at Garden (→ 6/20).

30. China: Japanese set up puppet government in Nanking (→ 6/27).

31. New York: La Guardia airport officialy opens to traffic.

Welles in Europe hears crisis is near

Sumner Welles in Europe.

March 16. Sumner Welles, the American Undersecretary of State and President Roosevelt's personal emissary, came to Europe to talk about peace. What he has found is that a wider war is inevitable.

Welles has been trying without much success to convince Germany and the Allies to hold peace negotiations. On March 1, he warned Adolf Hitler that the United States would react unfavorably if Germany continues its military advances. Hitler replied by lecturing Welles at length about Germany's need to protect its borders with an aggressive policy of annexation.

Welles has also held meetings in London and Paris, but the French and British governments have been equally unsympathetic to Welles' appeal for talks to end the war. Only in Rome does Welles see any cause for hope. Italy was not ready for this war, and Benito Mussolini is encouraging Welles to do whatever he can to prevent it from dragging on (→ 25).

Spencer Tracy pilots Rogers' Rangers through the swamp in MGM's "Northwest Passage."

Finns surrender, ceding large areas

March 13. The vicious war between Russia and Finland ended this morning, three and a half months after it began. A peace treaty was signed in Moscow.

Finland was forced to surrender a large part of its territory, including the Karelian Isthmus, scene of the bloodiest fighting of the undeclared war. Thousands of Finnish and Russian soldiers are buried there beneath the snow.

Under the terms of the treaty, Finland also agreed to remove most of its submarines and warships from the Arctic Ocean. It will be allowed to maintain a small coastal defense force. Finland also agreed to lease the area around Hangoe to the Russians so that they can build a military base (→ 6/17).

Finns at the front.

Mussolini meets Hitler at Brenner

Mussolini and Hitler at Brenner.

March 18. Informed sources say that one major development of today's talks between Chancellor Hitler and Premier Mussolini will be the formation of a three-power entente between Germany, Italy and Russia.

The two leaders discussed areas of mutual interest in Mussolini's private coach, sidetracked at the railway station on the Italian side of the Brenner Pass. Germany is expected to launch immediate talks with Moscow. The entente would aim at a "new order in Europe" by assuring political and economic hegemony on the continent, dispersing the sphere of British influence and eliminating Britain as a political force in southeastern Europe and, possibly, the Near East (→ 4/2).

Parents are celebrating Disney's latest feature. Adapted from an Italian classic, "Pinocchio" bests all family efforts to teach the evils of untruth.

U.S. Census reports population at 131m

March. In 1790, by President Washington's orders, 650 men on horseback, in stage coaches and on foot added up almost four million Americans. This year, the Census Bureau did more than count 131 million noses. While the stork flew in through 6,000 windows and 4,000 souls departed this month, 120,000 enumerators asked us questions to clarify needs in housing and schools and to give legislators facts for laws dealing with unemployment and relief. The average household is now 3.8 persons and our median age lies at 28.9 years. The decade gain was the smallest in our history due to a low birth rate.

Queen Elizabeth reaches New York

Cunard's gigantic Queen Elizabeth.

March 7. The giant new British liner Queen Elizabeth slid quietly into the quarantine anchorage of Staten Island yesterday morning, terminating the strangest maiden voyage of any ocean queen. She was greeted by no rousing cheers, and no merry groups of passengers trooped down the gangway to a crowded pier. Trim and graceful in line but painted the color of the sea, the long promenade deck blacked out with paint, this 85,000-ton ship, the largest in the world, seemed like a half-manned ghost ship.

Unfinished, unready for service, she still made it safely to New York, truly the safest harbor in the world, and docked at Pier 90. She carries no guns or other defense but is equipped with Britain's latest anti-mine device. Plans are for her to remain here until the war is over.

1940

APRIL

Su	Mo	Tu	We	Th	Fr	Sa
	1	2	3	4	5	6
7	8	9	10	11	12	13
14	15	16	17	18	19	20
21	22	23	24	25	26	27
28	29	30				

1. New York: Maurice Evans returns to play in Shakespeare's "King Richard II."

2. Italy begins registration for all citizens over 14 years old (→ 29).

3. London: Winston Churchill appointed head of British Defense Council (→ 5/10).

7. Jimmy Demaret wins Masters' golf title by four strokes.

8. Norwegian waters mined by Britain and France to stop flow of ore to Nazis (→ 5/27/41).

9. Germans occupy Denmark, move on Oslo; Norway joins war against Reich.→

11. Norway: Allied ships in Skagerrak fight way to Oslo, order Germans out (→ 15).

13. Washington: FDR condemns war on Scandinavia (→ 5/15).

14. New York: "Lights Out in Europe" premieres.

14. Toronto: Maple Leafs beat Rangers to take hockey's Stanley Cup.

15. Norway: French and British troops land at Narvik (→ 20).

19. Canadian Gerard Cote shatters all records to finish first in Boston Marathon.

19. Swiss publish instructions for military mobilization in case of invasion.

20. Norway: 50,000 Allied forces advance against Nazis (→ 22).

22. German bombers smash Norwegian towns in air blitzkrieg; U.S. attache Capt. Robert M. Losey killed (→ 24).

24. Norway: Nazis gain in two battles; take Steinkjer and advance in south (→ 30).

29. Washington: FDR appeals to Mussolini to help halt war in Europe (→ 6/10).

30. Pittsburgh residents offer $1 million for capture of Hitler "alive and unhurt."

30. Norway: Nazis seize U.S. arms intended for Sweden, Finland; army advances, taking Dombaas and Stoeren (→ 5/2).

DEATH

28. Luisa Tetrazzini, celebrated Italian diva (*6/29/1871).

Nazis enter Scandinavia

A Nazi anti-aircraft gun intrudes uninvited on a clear Norwegian sky.

April 9. Suddenly, decisively and dramatically, a new theater of war opened today as German troops crossed the Danish border and occupied Copenhagen. So surprised were the Danes that they offered no resistance to the advancing Germans who came by land and sea.

Hours after the invasion, Norway declared war on Germany and fired on four Reich warships which were sailing up the Oslo Fjord. While Scandinavia is brimming with fear, the Oslo newspaper Arbejdarbladet has asked for calm amid the storm. "The situation is particularly grave for our country, but in such times we must keep our cool," it said.

German planes accompanied the land and sea invaders, but not to bomb. They dropped literature that blamed Britain for involving Northern Europe in the war. The propaganda called Britain's Winston Churchill "the century's greatest warmonger" who was planning an attack on Norway and Denmark. Germany, according to the leaflets, merely intervened to protect the two nations (→ 5/2).

Anti-war coalition organizes in U.S.

April 1. Distraught over President Roosevelt's foreign policy of recent months, a group of isolationists has formed the America First Committee. Among its members are Charles Lindbergh, Robert McCormick, publisher of the Chicago Tribune, and a few senators.

The isolationists oppose U.S. intervention in the European war and have organized to protest, picket and parade for their cause. They are diametrically opposed to the internationalists, who feel that only by banding together can the Western nations defeat fascism.

FCC is developing television rules

April 12. Saying that commercial television service could begin by September, President Roosevelt today announced the Federal Communications Commission would delay start of the service so it could develop rules preventing any group from monopolizing the new medium. The difficulties standing in the way of commercial television should be resolved by the end of the summer, the president said. While television will put many people to work, financial experts say it will not have the impact of radio or automobiles on the nation's economy.

1940

MAY

Su	Mo	Tu	We	Th	Fr	Sa
			1	2	3	4
5	6	7	8	9	10	11
12	13	14	15	16	17	18
19	20	21	22	23	24	25
26	27	28	29	30	31	

2. British yield southern Norway to Nazis, evacuating Aandalsnes (→ 6/6).

6. New York: Steinbeck awarded Pulitzer Prize for "The Grapes of Wrath."

7. Berlin: German girls reported saving hair for production of felt.

9. New York: Laurence Olivier and Vivien Leigh open in "Romeo and Juliet."

10. London: Winston Churchill replaces Neville Chamberlain as prime minister, as Reich troops storm Western Europe.→

12. London: All Germans seized to bar fifth column aid to parachutists (→ 6/17).

12. Germany: Allies bomb Krupp arms plants and Rhine areas (→ 13).

13. Belgium: French meet Nazis in clash of 1,500 tanks (→ 14).

14. Nazis take Sedan, strike at French line (→ 15).

15. Churchill sends note to FDR requesting eventual participation in war (→ 24).

15. Holland gives in after severe bombing of Rotterdam (→ 17).

16. Canadians and Americans begin construction on Niagara Bridge with two-handed shovel.

17. Nazis cut French lines on 62-mile front, take Brussels, Louvain, Namur (→ 19).

19. Paris: Gen. Maxime Weygand supplants Gen. Maurice Gamelin as Allied chief (→ 21).

21. Europe: Nazis trap Allies at Dunkirk on English Channel; Aisne River crossed, 60 miles from Paris (→ 26).

24. Earthquake hits Peru, leaving 249 dead.

26. Belgium: Allies begin to evacuate Dunkirk (→ 28).

30. Wilbur Shaw wins Indy 500 for second year in row.

30. France: British army joins French on the Somme (→ 31).

31. London: 75 percent of B.E.F. safely out of Belgium (→ 6/3).

DEATH

14. Emma Goldman, U.S. anarchist, feminist (*6/27/1869).

Churchill now in as Prime Minister

Churchill in uniform: V for Victory.

May 10. Winston Churchill, a constant critic of Britain's policy of appeasement of Adolf Hitler, walked proudly into the House of Commons today to give his first speech as Prime Minister.

"I have nothing to offer," Churchill said, "but blood, toil, tears and sweat."

Churchill was asked by King George VI three days ago to form a new government after Neville Chamberlain resigned. Chamberlain was forced out under mounting pressure from Labor and his own Conservative Party.

It was believed at first that the crisis generated by Hitler's invasion of Belgium would create new support for Chamberlain. The invasion actually served to fuel criticism of him. Chamberlain will always be remembered as the architect of appeasement at Munich.

Churchill has become the symbol of British resistance to Hitler since the outbreak of the war. He served as First Lord of the Admiralty under Chamberlain. Despite the ill feeling toward Chamberlain, he is expected to serve in the new government of Winston Churchill.

▷

Germans launch Blitzkrieg in Low Countries

Nazi tanks pour into Flanders. The speed of Hitler's attack threatens to put Europe under Reich rule in a month.

May 10. Hundreds of German planes swooped over Belgian and Dutch cities and airfields early this morning, softening defenses for an invasion of land troops, as the Nazis expanded their path of destruction.

In the Netherlands, German forces demonstrated the effectiveness of the Blitzkrieg or "lightning war." Most major airfields in and around Amsterdam were shelled hard in the pre-dawn, fast-paced terror. German parachutists, some dressed in Dutch military uniforms, dropped from the sky as land troops bolted across the border.

The swift assault did not take the Dutch completely by surprise; for a week, they readied themselves for German aggression. In fact, anti-aircraft guns downed at least six Reich planes. But the powerful, well-balanced Blitzkrieg has left the Dutch bleeding and scared. It's expected the government will soon use its unique defense mechanism—opening the flood gates of the Netherlands' elaborate dike system.

Needless to say, war was immediately declared on Germany. Holland's Queen Wilhelmina addressed the populace: "After our country, with scrupulous conscientiousness, had observed strict neutrality . . . Germany made a sudden attack on our territory without any warning." She asked the people to take up arms with "utmost vigilance and with that inner calm which comes from a clear conscience."

Other German brigades crossed the Belgian border in a similar quick and effective manner. In the early morning hours, the Nazi air force unloaded heavy artillery on Antwerp, Nivelles and Brussels. Paratroopers landed on mighty Fort Eban Emael, the northern fortress in the Belgian defense line. While defenders battled the Reich sky-to-land units, German foot soldiers surged virtually untouched over nearby Albert Canal. The Antwerp airport was struck by a barrage of bombs that didn't stop until daybreak. By then, 400 Belgians had been killed at the airport, adjacent houses burned out of control and inhabitants feared for their lives.

Belgian Premier Hubert Pierlot and Foreign Minister Paul-Henri Spaak met with King Leopold. The three leaders decreed a "state of alarm," issued a protest to Berlin and mobilized all available men. They trust France and Britain will come to their aid.

However, according to German Foreign Minister Joachim von Ribbentrop, the joint invasions were orderd for the protection of the Lowlands against Allied incursions. He said the British and French were about to use the Lowlands as stepping stones into Germany.

"The Allies were preparing an onslaught on Germany which the Reich could not tolerate," he claimed. Von Ribbentrop also issued a statement which read: "In the life and death struggle thrust upon the German people, the government does not intend to await an attack by Britain and France."

The Allied governments responded by dismissing such preposterous allegations as Nazi propaganda (→ 12).

Belgian families flee the war.

Roosevelt promises 50,000 war pilots

May 24. President Roosevelt, in an effort to prepare for the worst—direct American involvement in the European conflict—has announced plans to train 50,000 volunteer airplane pilots. The extensive training program will draw men from colleges, where the Civil Aeronautics Authority provides courses, from citizens who already have private airplane licenses and from those who simply want to join. Congress today passed a defense bill that expands the Army Air Corps in support of FDR's proposal (→ 6/3).

Holland and Belgium surrender to Nazis

May 28. Dark days have arrived in Belgium as King Leopold ordered the Belgian army to capitulate to Germany. The surrender occurred against the wishes of French Premier Paul Reynaud, who described the situation as "dark" and "grave," adding that France's "faith in victory" along the Belgian-French line is still strong.

The news of the surrender comes two weeks after the Netherlands succumbed to the relentless barrage of Germany's Blitzkrieg. On May 14, Dutch Commander-in-Chief Henri Gerard Winkelman asked his troops to give up "to prevent further bloodshed and annihilation."

While France, and Britain as well, have expressed their disdain for the Belgian and Dutch acquiescence, their harsh words mask their true emotions. Both Allied nations are frustrated, and even a bit intimidated, by the Reich's success in the Lowlands. The Nazis now stand poised at the English Channel and on the Somme-Aisne line. The Allies realize their lands are next on Hitler's invasion agenda (→ 30).

1940

JUNE

Su	Mo	Tu	We	Th	Fr	Sa
						1
2	3	4	5	6	7	8
9	10	11	12	13	14	15
16	17	18	19	20	21	22
23	24	25	26	27	28	29
30						

3. Paris hit by 1,100 bombs, from 200 Reich planes (→ 4).

3. U.S. offers surplus arms to Britain (→ 13).

5. France: Charles de Gaulle named undersecretary for natl. defense (→ 18).

6. Norway: Allies forced to evacuate Narvik (→ 10).

9. Cleveland: Lawson Little beats Gene Sarazen by three strokes for U.S. Open golf title.

10. Norwegian army capitulates to Germans (→ 7/20).

11. Mediterranean: Italians bomb British fortress at Malta (→ 7/10).

11. North Africa: British raid Libya, bomb Italian base at Tobruk (→ 8/6).

13. Military Supply Act allots $1.8 bil. for U.S. military (→ 20).

14. France: Nazis occupy Paris, drive on south (→ 15).

15. France: Reich flag raised over Versailles (→ 16).

16. France: Petain takes premiership, refuses British request to unite two countries, asks armistice of Reich (→ 18).

17. Churchill, over radio, urges Britain to conduct herself so this will be remembered as her "finest hour" (→ 7/2).

20. FDR, seeking coalition, names Republicans to Cabinet; Henry Stimson sec. of war, Frank Knox sec. of Navy (→ 27).

20. New York: Joe Louis floors Atruro Dodoy in eighth to hold heavyweight title (→ 2/17/41).

24. French sign armistice with Italians.

27. Washington: British, Australian envoys ask Cordell Hull for U.S. aid against Japan (→ 8/29).

27. FDR declares national emergency to control shipping in U.S. waters (→ 7/5).

28. U.S. Congress passes Alien Registration Act.

29. Russian troops invade Rumania (→ 7/15).

DEATH

10. Marcus Garvey, American black nationalist (*8/17/1887).

Allies are evacuated from Dunkirk

Evacuating French and British troops left the beaches of Dunkirk littered with junked war supplies.

June 4. The British royal navy has led a successful exodus of 340,000 Allied troops from Dunkirk and imminent annihilation. Throngs of cheering Britons greeted ships crossing the English Channel packed with battle-weary but rescued soldiers. The evacuation is considered one of Britain's greatest military achievements.

Pushed back by the ruthless and successful German advance, British, French and Belgian divisions were seemingly trapped at Dunkirk. Last week's surrender of Belgium by King Leopold to Nazi conquerors brought stern words from the French and British, who had rushed to the defense of the Low Countries after the German invasion. Worse, it exposes the left flank of the Allied lines. Adolf Hitler's forces took advantage and stormed through the gaping hole. According to reports, the lid was closing on the gallant but struggling defenders, among them almost all of the British Expeditionary Force.

Yet, on May 26, Hitler ordered a halt to the assault. This allowed the Allies to regroup and organize an evacuation. Dispatches fail to explain the Third Reich's rationale for temporarily halting the attack, but some speculate there was friction within the upper ranks of the German military staff.

While averting complete disaster, the Allies lost nearly 130,000 dead, wounded or captured, and thousands of guns were also destroyed. Costly supplies were left behind at Dunkirk.

Today, in a speech in the House of Commons, British Prime Minister Winston Churchill praised the combined efforts of the navy, army and particularly the royal air force, which has valiantly fought the German Luftwaffe in a deadly air war. The First French Army, which battled the Nazis at Flanders, screening the evacuation, also received Churchill's commendation. The military forces at Dunkirk achieved "a miracle of deliverance," he added.

However, the eloquent British leader warned that "wars are not won by evacuations," and he vowed to continue the battle against the Nazis, proclaiming: "We shall fight on the seas and oceans; we shall fight, with growing confidence and growing strength, in the air, we shall defend our island, whatever the cost may be, we shall fight on the beaches, we shall fight on the landing grounds, we shall fight in the fields and in the streets, we shall fight in the hills; we shall never surrender" (→ 14).

In nine days, a massive Allied effort pulled 340,000 troops across the Channel. ▷

German troops parade through Paris

Reich troops overturn history on Avenue Foch, named for the French Marshal who accepted the surrender in 1918.

June 14. To the French people, their beloved Paris is no longer the "city of light" tonight. Darkness fell over the capital today as German troops marched from Neuilly into the center of Paris, German tanks paraded through the Place de la Concorde and German armored cars swept past the trees of the Champs Elysees.

Frenchmen and women wept openly. Much of the city is deserted. Two million Parisians began streaming out of the capital as soon as the government packed up and headed to Tours four days ago.

The Germans removed French flags from government buildings and quickly replaced them with swastikas. New signs were plastered on the Eiffel Tower and the Chamber of Deputies. "Deutschland siegt auf allen Fronten," they read. "Germany conquers on all fronts."

The French military command claims it gave up Paris without much of a struggle to spare it the fate of Warsaw. Germans snicker at the excuse and retort that the French were powerless to defend their capital.

The confident German High Command claims it will occupy the rest of France within two weeks and then turn its attention to Winston Churchill and Britain. Those who accuse the Germans of arrogance are reminded that they seized Paris just ten days after the battle of France began.

The Germans claim the French were forced to abandon a large amount of military equipment when they retreated. Germany says the losses are devastating to France, since they follow so closely the disaster at Dunkirk.

The Germans also say their seizure of Paris has disrupted the economic structure of France and destroyed key communication lines that linked the French army.

To the northeast of Paris, the Germans are battering the French all along the Maginot Line and have even broken through the line at several points. The German front now extends for 300 miles, from the Rhine all the way to Le Havre.

The Germans say they seized that important port city and another 100 miles of French coastline yesterday. The victory would appear to make Britain even more vulnerable. Germany says its next prize will be Cherbourg.

The loss of Paris increases pressure on General Maxime Weygand to seek an armistice. For the time being, however, the general is trying to preserve his own honor by leaving that responsibility to the civilian government.

The government of Paul Reynaud abandoned Tours today, just several days after it installed itself next to the Loire. Reynaud will apparently move farther south and make Bordeaux his new capital.

The Cabinet ministers are not the only refugees on the road. Many civilians are also seeking a new home, and it is not easy. Human buzzards are demanding fortunes in gold to transport the Frenchmen in their cars. And German Stukas frequently sweep down from the sky to prey on the easy targets.

If the rest of France falls, Britain will be on its own. Churchill says the decisive moment has not arrived yet, but will as soon as Hitler again attacks England with his Luftwaffe. The British leader and others are wondering when that will happen. They also wonder when President Roosevelt will decide he has had enough of isolationism (→ 7/10).

U.S.S.R. occupies three Baltic states

June 17. Soviet Russia is taking advantage of the world's preoccupation with Germany's conquests in Western Europe. Moscow is flexing its own muscles. Soviet troops have occupied the Baltic states of Lithuania, Latvia and Estonia.

The Soviets seized control of the states by installing Communists in key positions, declaring the formation of "popular governments" and then forcing the small nations to allow Soviet troops to enter.

Hitler may have approved the Soviet actions during treaty negotiations last year. Soviet Foreign Affairs Commissar Vyacheslav Molotov is returning the favor by extending "his warm congratulations to Germany for its brilliant victories."

The Soviet occupation of the Baltic states returns the territories the Russians lost after the last war. It also gives them a security zone they may need later if the war spreads to Eastern Europe. Moscow's next target may be Rumanian territory (→ 29).

FDR accuses Italy of stab in the back

June 10. President Roosevelt, in a graduation address at the University of Virginia today, accused the Italian government of "a stab in the back" by allying that country with Germany in the war being waged against France and Great Britain.

"On this 10th day of June, 1940," the president said, "the hand that held the dagger has struck it into the back of its neighbor."

In view of Italy's entry into the war, the president said, the United States will give its utmost in aid to France and Great Britain, calling them "opponents of force."

The president spoke only hours after Premier Benito Mussolini of Italy announced his decision to join hands with Germany's Hitler, despite American efforts to persuade Italy to stay out of the war.

President Roosevelt reiterated his hopes that the United States will soon begin compulsory military training so as to be "equal to the task of any emergency and every defense" (→ 11).

French sign armistice

Representatives of France and Germany sign the armistice at Compiegne.

June 22. In the small town of Compiegne, the French and Germans signed an armistice today. Adolf Hitler decided not to hold the ceremony in the town's famous chateau. It was held in a rail car. And Hitler made certain it was the same rail car where he felt Germany was humiliated after its defeat in 1918.

Under the terms of the armistice, the northern half of France and the Atlantic coast will be occupied by Germany. French forces will be disarmed and demobilized. France will pay the expenses of the occupying German troops. And all German political refugees will be turned over to the Reich.

Marshal Henri Philippe Petain, the new French Premier, accepted the terms which were quickly criticized by many Frenchmen as too severe.

"Last night," wrote the French writer Andre Gide, "we were thrown into a stupor when we heard Petain speak on the radio. It must be a dirty trick. How can anyone say that France is still intact after surrendering more than half of the country to the enemy?"

Petain has been the leader of the new government for less than a week. He formed a Cabinet when Paul Reynaud resigned after refusing to sign an armistice with Hitler.

Petain chose to ignore an eloquent appeal from British Prime Minister Winston Churchill to keep up the fight against Hitler.

"If we can stand up to him," Churchill told Parliament, "all Europe may be freed and the life of the world may move forward into broad sunlit uplands. But if we fail, the whole world, including the United States and all that we have known and cared for, will sink into the abyss of a new dark age."

Churchill realized his oratory could not stop the Germans, for he also admitted that "the battle of France is over. The battle of Britain is about to begin. On this battle depends the survival of Christian civilization" (→ 7/1).

De Gaulle appeals for fight to go on

June 18. A lonely voice has spoken out, urging the French not to surrender and sign an armistice with the Germans. The voice was General Charles de Gaulle's, and he spoke from London, on BBC radio.

"I, General de Gaulle," he said, "invite French officers and soldiers who are on British territory or who are coming here, with or without arms, to join me. I also invite engineers and workers who are experts in the arms industry to join me.

"Whatever happens," de Gaulle added, "the flame of the French resistance must not go out and it will not go out."

De Gaulle's speech puts him in direct conflict with Marshal Petain, the new Premier of France. He was apparently encouraged to make the radio appeal by Paul Reynaud, who resigned as Premier rather than sign an armistice with the Germans.

De Gaulle, a graduate of the Saint Cyr military academy, served with honor in the last war. Earlier this year, he was promoted to Brigadier General. Reynaud appointed him Undersecretary of War (→ 22).

Willkie nominated to seek presidency

Willkie campaigns in native Indiana.

June 28. Wendell L. Willkie, a former Democrat who opposes the New Deal, was nominated for president by the Republicans in one of the greatest upsets in convention history. The former Wall Street lawyer was opposed by the veterans. But he defeated Thomas E. Dewey in the balloting in Philadelphia, and then topped Senator Robert Taft, the choice of the regulars (→ 7/18).

Paul Klee, imagist of a mad world, will paint no more

June 29. Paul Klee has died at Locarno of a heart attack at 61. His involvement with the musical and visual arts began early in life.

He entered the Munich Academy in 1900 and studied painting under Franz von Stuck. After he met the German Expressionist painter Wassily Kandinsky in 1912, Klee participated in the Munich exhibition of the avant-guarde Blaue Reiter (Blue Rider). Klee taught painting at the Bauhaus from 1920 to 1931 and then accepted a post at the Dusseldorf Academy. After Hitler became Chancellor in 1933, Klee, attacked by the Nazis, was treated as a corrupt foreigner. He left Germany, traveled to Italy, France and Switzerland, where he took up residence.

Klee created a new language of color, form and space. This great visionary developed an art "abstract, with memories." His work was influenced by his trips in North Africa and Europe and by his admiration for van Gogh, Paul Cezanne and Henri Matisse.

Klee's childlike "Man with a Tongue" (1932).

1940

JULY

Su	Mo	Tu	We	Th	Fr	Sa
	1	2	3	4	5	6
7	8	9	10	11	12	13
14	15	16	17	18	19	20
21	22	23	24	25	26	27
28	29	30	31			

1. French government moves from Paris to Vichy (→ 10).

2. Washington: U.S. debt reported at $43 billion (→ 10/24).

2. Reich bombers carry out first daylight raid on London (→ 3).

3. Germany: RAF bombers strike 100 cities, claim destruction of Hamburg (→ 21).

5. Hyde Park, N.Y.: FDR names conditions for just peace; disarmament, higher living standard, freedom of speech, press and religion (→ 8/18).

10. Mediterranean: British and Italian navies clash (→ 11/11).

14. Havana: Colonel Batista claims Cuban presidency.

15. Lithuania, Estonia, Latvia vote overwhelmingly for union with U.S.S.R. (→ 21).

16. Chicago: Al Jolson appears at Grand Opera House after ten-year hiatus.

16. France: Vichy govt. deprives naturalized Jews of citizenship (→ 10/18).

18. China: After accord with Japan, British close Burma Road to cut off supplies to Chinese Nationalists (→ 8/6).

20. Denmark quits League of Nations (→ 9/9/41).

21. Britain: Six RAF planes battle 80 attacking convoy in English Channel (→ 22).

21. Soviets annex Lithuania, Estonia and Lativa (→ 11/12).

22. British Special Operations Executive created to support resistance in Europe (→ 8/8).

22. British reject German peace proposal (→ 29).

24. Reich annexes Alsace-Lorraine in France (→ 29).

24. Mideast: Italian planes kill 46 in raid on British bases in Egypt and Palestine (→ 8/10).

29. Reich annexes Eupen, Malmedy, Moresnet in Belgium.

30. Cuba: Pan-American Union signs Declaration of Havana, pledging resistance to German colonial efforts (→ 9/5).

31. France: Vichy passes death sentence on all Frenchmen who join foreign army.

Aerial blitz over Britain

Londoners survey the wreckage of a bus overturned by German bombs.

July 29. German planes continue to attack the British royal air force, despite weeks of mixed results, and today the most spectacular air battle of the war lit up the skies above the English Channel.

In a half hour of heavy fighting, 17 German planes plummeted to the water, while only one RAF fighter was lost. Furthermore, the British planes kept the Luftwaffe aircraft offshore; not one Nazi bomb hit British soil in this assault.

Berlin claims three days of raids, with submarine accompaniment, have destroyed 200,000 tons of British shipping. On July 2-3, Reich bombers carried out their first daylight raid on London while the RAF hit 100 German cities (→ 8/1).

British destroy French fleet in Algeria

July 3. A tragedy has occurred in the Mediterranean that is bound to exacerbate relations between Britain and France and hurt the effort to stop Adolf Hitler. The British navy opened fire and sank a large number of French ships anchored at Mers-el-Kebir in Algeria. Some 1,000 French sailors were killed.

Winston Churchill has been concerned that French ships which have not joined General de Gaulle will be commandeered by Germany. He was not aware that the French were under orders to scuttle vessels that they could not defend against the Kriegsmarine. The British opened fire when the French rejected an ultimatum to sail for Britain or the United States (→ 10).

The French North African fleet goes up in flames, hit by British torpedoes.

Petain founds new authoritarian state

July 10. The Third Republic died today in France. A fascist and authoritarian government headed by Marshal Henri Petain took its place at Vichy.

By an overwhelming majority, the French Parliament voted itself out of existence and gave Petain the authority to form a new constitution. There will be a new Parliament in the new France, but its role will be purely advisory.

The republic is not all that died today. So did the traditional French slogan of "liberty, equality, fraternity." It will be replaced by "work, family and fatherland" as the new regime calls for a return to "traditional values."

Soldiers who deserted France after the armistice are invited to come back, and the Petain government promises to treat them with "indulgence." Some soldiers will be offered a thousand francs to ease their return to civilian life (→ 16).

FDR renominated; Farley out of post

July 18. President Roosevelt was nominated for an unprecedented third term today, soundly defeating those opposed to a break in tradition. While the president reportedly had said he did not desire to run again, Democratic delegates at the Chicago convention were sure he would accept the nomination.

The major challenge to a third term was led by the president's onetime ally, Postmaster General James A. Farley, who, polling a modest vote, moved that the president's nomination be made unanimous. Leading the third-term drive were members of FDR's inner circle, including Interior Secretary Harold Ickes, Sen. James F. Byrnes and Thomas G. Corcoran (→ 11/5).

1940

AUGUST

Su	Mo	Tu	We	Th	Fr	Sa
				1	2	3
4	5	6	7	8	9	10
11	12	13	14	15	16	17
18	19	20	21	22	23	24
25	26	27	28	29	30	31

1. British lose 359 aircraft during July (→ 8).

6. China: British pull out, leaving Shanghai in Japanese control (→ 10/1/41).

6. North Africa: Italians push into Egypt and British Somaliland (→ 11).

8. London: Britain and de Gaulle's Free French sign alliance treaty (→ 10/3).

8. 800 Reich planes storm London; 53 shot down (→ 12).

9. Turkey: Berlin-Baghdad rail line completed.

10. Britain to send tanks to Mideast (→ 29).

11. North Africa: RAF raids Italian bases in Libya (→ 19).

12. British RAF pounds Nazi strongholds with 500 planes, while 400 Reich bombers unload on British coast (→ 15).

15. British shoot down 144 out of 1,000 Nazi planes, bomb Reich oil supplies in Germany (→ 20).

18. U.S. and Canada agree to join in defense plans (→ 20).

19. North Africa: British yield Somaliland to Italy (→ 31).

19. France: Vichy dissolves Masonic lodges (→ 9/2).

20. London: U.S. and British reach accord to trade destroyers for bases (→ 23).

23. Britain offers Bermuda Great Sound for U.S. base (→ 9/3).

29. Vichy France cedes Tonkin bases in Indochina to Japanese (→ 31).

29. Mideast: Italian planes raid Suez Canal (→ 10/20).

30. Axis forces Rumanians to yield half of Transylvania to Hungary (→ 4/3/41).

31. Africa: French Equatorial Africa, Cameroons and Tahiti join with Free France (→ 9/12).

31. Indochina reported in revolt against Vichy rule (→ 9/22).

DEATHS

3. Vladimir Jabotinsky, militant Zionist leader (*10/18/1880).

18. Walter P. Chrysler, American auto tycoon (*4/2/1875).

Radar guards Britain; German planes still menace cities

Aug 20. If the British are to prevent Adolf Hitler from succeeding with Operation Sea Lion and invading Britain, their coastal radar and royal air force will have to stand up to the test. So far, both are proving to be mighty weapons.

The sophisticated radar is capable of detecting enemy aircraft at a distance of 75 miles. That gives the British enough time to put their planes in the air and meet the Luftwaffe pilots before they drop their bombs. Last month, the British lost 359 aircraft, but 653 German planes were destroyed.

Prime Minister Winston Churchill paid a special tribute to the RAF pilots in a speech to Parliament today. "Never in the field of human conflict," he said, "was so much owed by so many to so few."

On the continent, the Germans have seemed invincible. But if the British pilots do not lose their nerve and the radar does not falter, Hitler may have met his match (→ 26).

Axis bombers, a constant threat, fly in formation over British territory.

Trotsky slain, allegedly on Stalin's orders

Trotsky, at 60, in exile in Mexico.

Aug 21. Leon Trotsky, the most persistent critic of Joseph Stalin, died tonight in Mexico City. The assassin who bludgeoned him with an ax last night in his home in Coyoacan is in custody.

Stalin is suspected of ordering the murder. Last May, Trotsky accused Stalin of masterminding an unsuccessful assassination attempt.

To the very end, Trotsky spoke of Bolshevism. "I am sure of the victory of the Fourth International," he whispered on his deathbed.

The assassin, a frequent visitor to Trotsky's home, has been identified variously as a Canadian, a journalist educated in France and the son of a Belgian diplomat.

RAF hits Berlin, astonishing Goering

Aug 26. The British received an enormous psychological boost this morning and Germans had the shock of their lives as royal air force planes flew a bombing raid all the way to Berlin. More leaflets than bombs were dropped, and the damage to Berlin was minimal. But for the first time in the war, thousands of Germans cowered for hours in shelters and basements.

Prime Minister Churchill ordered the raid in retaliation for the German bombardment of London this weekend. The attack, which lasted nearly three hours, caught Adolf Hitler totally by surprise. He had been assured by Marshal Hermann Goering that British bombers could never reach Berlin (→ 9/4).

Four notables are arrested by Vichy

Aug 8. The Vichy government in France has acted quickly to arrest and jail four prominent officials who are charged with "causing the defeat of France in the war." There is apparently more to this case than meets the eye, for Germany is demanding that the Petain government "punish the defendants properly."

Those arrested are Leon Blum, the former Premier; Edouard Daladier, formerly Premier, Minister of War and Foreign Minister; Georges Mandel, who served as Minister of the Interior; and General Maurice Gamelin, who served as Commander-in-Chief of all French forces.

The defendants will be tried by the new Supreme Court of Justice, which was created just last week. Another Vichy tribunal condemned General Charles de Gaulle to death in absentia last Friday. De Gaulle, who is leading the French resistance to Germany from London, was accused of treason, plotting against the security of France and desertion in time of war. The verdict was handed down by a military court in Clermont-Ferrand (→ 19).

1940

SEPTEMBER

Su	Mo	Tu	We	Th	Fr	Sa
1	2	3	4	5	6	7
8	9	10	11	12	13	14
15	16	17	18	19	20	21
22	23	24	25	26	27	28
29	30					

2. France ordered to pay 400 mil. francs per day to maintain German troops (→ 10/18).

3. Washington: FDR tells Congress he acted on own authority in trading destroyers for bases in British colonial territory (→ 16).

4. Hitler declares all-out war on British cities in reprisal for RAF bombings (→ 9).

5. Costa Rica: Cocos Island offered to U.S. as canal defense (→ 10/13).

6. Bucharest: Rumanian King Carol II abdicates in favor of son Michael I (→ 9).

9. N.Y.: Don McNeill and Alice Marble win national tennis titles.

9. Britain: Reich planes set fire to London; 400 dead (→ 11).

9. Bucharest: King decrees anti-Semitic laws (→ 10/10).

11. New York: "Hold on to Your Hats" brings Al Jolson back to Broadway after 10-year absence.

11. London: Germans score direct hit on Buckingham Palace; royal family not hurt (→ 15).

12. Switzerland reasserts neutrality.

12. North Africa: Italian forces begin cautious offensive from Libya into Egypt (→ 25).

15. London: BBC claims 185 Reich planes downed in day (→ 30).

16. Selective Service Bill signed, requiring registration of all U.S. males aged 21-35 (→ 26).

19. Rome: Reich For. Min. Ribbentrop warns Mussolini against attack on Greece or Yugoslavia (→ 10/28).

22. Japan enters Indochina to block aid to Chinese (→ 27).

26. Washington: FDR strikes at Japan, halting steel and iron exports to all except Britain and New World nations (→ 10/3).

29. New York: Mickey Rooney and Judy Garland open in "Strike up the Band."

DEATHS

1. Lillian Wald, American child welfare reformer (*3/10/1867).

2. Sir Joseph John Thomson, 1906 Nobel in physics, discovered electron (*12/18/1856).

Battle of Britain fiercely contested

Stukas (Nazi bombers) over London.

Sept 30. Luftwaffe pilots spoke of "an ocean of flames" over London, as German aerial bombardments have dumped tons of explosives on Britain in the last two months, killing thousands. Yet, British defenders have blasted many Nazi raiders. Despite incessant, merciless air attacks, the royal air force has downed over 1,200 Luftwaffe planes; only about 700 RAF craft have been picked from the sky in this "three phase," August-September German offensive, which is being called the battle of Britain.

At the height of the raids, on the 15th, London was terrorized by waves of Nazi bombers. Much of the city has been seriously damaged. As a London correspondent reported after three days of constant attack: "Black columns of smoke are rising from many directions. The Germans are pounding and repounding their targets, reopening old wounds." Certainly, the grand city can sleep easier now, as the raids have temporarily halted.

Apparently, the Nazi war strategists have failed in their goal: to defeat Great Briatin in the air by destroying the RAF, and then to neutralize the mighty royal navy. Credit must be given to the spirited, stubborn English aerial defense.

Regardless of war objectives, many innocent people have perished, as the number of victims continues to climb. From September 7-30, during the heaviest air raids, British civilian casualties ranged from 300-600 lives lost and from 1,000-3,000 persons injured per day. On the 9th and 10th, 600 died and 2,500 were wounded (→ 10/10).

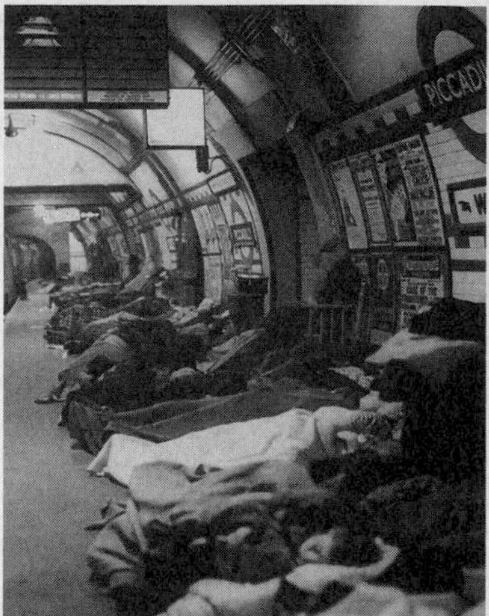

London takes shelter in the subway.

Japan joins Axis pact; enters Indochina

Sept 27. By another of those bold forays into "blitz diplomacy" with which the world is now familiar, the Reich Chancellery today presided over the birth of a tripartite military alliance as Japan formally linked its might with Germany and Italy. This development adds new weight to German and Italian leadership in forging "a new order in Europe" and Japan's right to establish "a new order in Eastern Asia." It also seems designed to effect profoundly both the course of the European war and the world in general.

While by implication the pact contains a veiled threat to Russia, that to the United States is less obscure. In pronouncing his benediction, Foreign Minister von Ribbentrop said: "Organized warmongers in the Jewish capitalistic democracies have succeeded in plunging Europe into a new war which was not wanted by Germany."

Besides drawing the United States and Great Britain closer together, the pact might also help China by making Britain reconsider its closing of the Burma Road to Chinese troops.

The pact follows by three days the Japanese invasion of French Indochina. Though casualties have been heavy, the Annamese troops are standing up well against the Japanese, who have yet to engage the main French forces. Observers said Japanese bodies were piled high along the roads and that the Japanese, pressed for time, were cutting off hands to aid them in later identification (→ 3/11/41).

Raid on Dakar fails

Sept 25. General de Gaulle, leader of the Free French, tried and failed today to land at Dakar, the heavily fortified capital of French West Africa. The Governor of the territory, who is loyal to Vichy, ordered his guns to fire on de Gaulle and the British battleships accompanying him. De Gaulle withdrew after two ships were hit (→ 10/27).

Government bldg. in ruins on Goree.

1940

OCTOBER

Su	Mo	Tu	We	Th	Fr	Sa
		1	2	3	4	5
6	7	8	9	10	11	12
13	14	15	16	17	18	19
20	21	22	23	24	25	26
27	28	29	30	31		

2. Hollywood: Warners picks Ronald Reagan and Rosemary Lane to head cast in "She Couldn't Say No."

3. U.S. Army adopts parachute troops (→ 5).

3. Paris: De Gaulle Free France posters appear for first time (→ 31).

5. U.S. Navy calls up 27,591 reserves to man new ships (→ 16).

6. Rome: Pope Pius denounces women for bowing to the "tyranny of fashion."

8. Cincinnati: Reds triumph over Detroit Tigers 2-1 to take World Series in seven games.

10. Balkans tense as Nazis move down Danube River (→ 12).

10. Luxembourg plebiscite votes 97% against Nazi occupation.

12. Rumania: Nazi troops pour into Bucharest (→ 11/26).

13. U.S. now leasing bases in Brazil and Chile (→ 11/9).

16. U.S.: Millions register for first peacetime draft (→ 29).

18. Vichy bans Jews from civil service, management positions in industry and media (→ 11/9).

20. Mideast: Italians attack Anglo-U.S. oil field in Persian Gulf (→ 4/1/41).

21. Churchill broadcasts to French people, "We are waiting for the long-promised invasion. So are the fishes" (→ 11/14).

22. Portugal bans Jews from traveling through country.

23. Berlin: Franco meets Hitler, offers to help in assault on Gibraltar, yet refuses to join war (→ 11/4).

24. U.S.: Forty-hour work week goes into effect (→ 2/3/41).

24. New York: "The Westerner" opens, with Gary Cooper and Walter Brennan.

27. North Africa: Free French occupy Gabon (→ 30).

31. London: Belgians form exiled govt., pledge resistance to Reich occupation (→ 1/1/41).

BIRTH

23. Pele, Brazilian soccer star, born Edson Arantes do Nascimento.

First draft number drawn in U.S.

Oct 29. As a band played and planes flew overhead, the first number was drawn today in America's peacetime military draft lottery by Secretary of War Henry L. Stimson. The ceremony opened with a speech by President Roosevelt.

The bowl from which the numbers were drawn had proved to be too small to hold the 8,500 capsules and had to be enlarged by an expert from the Smithsonian Institution.

After Secretary Stimson had drawn the first number, other capsules were pulled at randon from the bowl by other administration officials and members of Congress. Men in each Selective Service area of the nation whose numbers correspond to those drawn from the bowl will be called up for a year's service in the Army (→ 11/20).

FDR looks on as Secretary of War Stimson draws the fateful first number.

Hitler meets Petain and Franco separately

Petain shakes hands with Hitler; a difficult sight for France to witness.

Oct 30. Unable to invade Britain, Adolf Hitler is making dramatic changes in his war policies. And he wants France and Spain to fight with him. In the past week, the Fuhrer has held separate meetings with French Premier Petain, Vice Premier Laval and General Franco. German officials refuse to discuss the meetings, but diplomatic sources believe Hitler wants to start a new campaign against Britain at Gibraltar and in North Africa.

Petain rejected a demand from Hitler that he surrender the French navy to Germany. But Hitler insists that he be able to use French bases on the continent and in Africa. Laval was apparently more flexible than Petain with Hitler, and the Fuhrer senses he might be more open-minded about collaborating.

As he met Franco for the first time ever, Hitler asked for his help in an assault on Gibraltar. In return, Franco demands that Hitler replace the wheat and oil that would surely be cut off by Britain (→ 11/12).

German explosive drops on St. Paul's

Oct 10. The Germans demonstrated that nothing is sacred in war last night by dropping a bomb on St. Paul's Cathedral, destroying the high altar. The beloved landmark was only one of 50 targets hit as more than 200 German planes swooped low to deliver their cargo of destruction on London. The bombs that hit St. Paul's however, missed the great dome and the cathedral still stands as a symbol of British resolve, battered but erect (→ 21).

St. Paul's (left) still stands.

Italy's surprise: Invasion of Greece

Oct 28. In a sudden and startling move, Italian forces have launched a full-scale attack on Greece. At 6 a.m. the deadline expired on an ultimatum served to the Greeks by the Italians. The ultimatum called for Greece to surrender part of her territory or be subject to an invasion of Italian troops. Greek Premier Metaxas said that he thought the ultimatum to be a "declaration of war by Italy on Greece." He further exhorted the Greek people to "fight for the Fatherland, your wives, your children and sacred traditions."

The Italians additionally claimed that a Fascist military outpost on the Greek-Albanian border had been attacked by Greek soldiers. This was denied by the Greeks, who suggested that the attack may have been made by Albanian insurgents.

The Italians attacked Greece by land, sea and air, sending at least ten divisions of 200,000 troops into Greece from Albania. Some members of Greece's small army flung themselves into the path of the Italian advance, to little avail. Meanwhile, British warships are reportedly coming to the aid of the Greeks (→ 11/8).

Chaplin war satire: The Great Dictator

Charlie Chaplin's film "The Great Dictator," now in release, is as disturbing as it is hilarious. Chaplin plays a dual role as a Jewish barber and Der Phooey, Adolf Hynkel. The barber is Chaplin's friendly tramp; Der Phooey is a boor who bats about a beachball globe of the world. Chaplin began the film only a few years ago, when fascism seemed to be just a lot of empty, bombastic posturing.

Chaplin is "The Great Dictator."

1940

NOVEMBER

Su	Mo	Tu	We	Th	Fr	Sa
					1	2
3	4	5	6	7	8	9
10	11	12	13	14	15	16
17	18	19	20	21	22	23
24	25	26	27	28	29	30

3. New York: Tyrone Power opens in "The Mark of Zorro."

4. Spain annexes Tangier in North Africa (→ 2/12/41).

8. Greeks halt Italian drive on Yanina (→ 21).

9. France: Vichy dissolves all labor unions (→ 12/1).

9. Montevideo: U.S. gains naval and air bases on Uruguayan coast (→ 5/20/41).

11. Mediterranean: British attack Italian fleet at Taranto (→ 1/14/41).

12. De Gaulle appoints Felix Eboue gov. gen. of French Equatorial Africa (→ 12/9).

13. New York: Walt Disney's "Fantasia" premieres.

14. Britain: Coventry destroyed by Reich bombers in worst raid of war; 1,000 dead (→ 29).

20. Britain and U.S. agree to standardize arms and exchange technical information (→ 23).

21. Greeks storm Italians at Koritza, take heavy equipment, 2,000 prisoners (→ 30).

23. New York: British Ambassador Marquess of Lothian says Britain near end of resources, need aid for 1941 (→ 25).

24. Slovakia joins Axis.

25. 18,700 enter U.S. Army in peacetime draft (→ 12/20).

25. Washington: First inter-American shipping conference convenes.

26. Rumania: Pro-Nazi Iron Guards slay 64 of exiled King Carol's aides (→ 1/24/41).

30. Greeks take Pogradec, Italian base in Albania (→ 12/13).

30. Philadelphia: Navy blanks Army 14-0 in annual football game.

DEATH

9. Neville Chamberlain, British ex-prime minister, architect of appeasement (*3/18/1869).

18. James Welch, Native American author, "Winter in the Blood."

20. Harriot Stanton Blatch, woman suffrage activist (*1/20/1856).

Nazis hit British cities

Nov 29. The latest in a series of Nazi air attacks on British industrial cities has left fires burning in the Liverpool area, with damage to shops, movie theaters and a church.

German spokesmen have said that the destruction inflicted by the attack was comparable only with the devastating attacks over the past two weeks on Coventry, Birmingham and Bristol. Journalists in England, however, reported that although many homes in the working-class districts had been hit, the damage was not extensive and there were few casualties. British anti-aircraft fire was said to be a good deal more effective than it had been earlier this month when German planes pummeled Coventry in one of the worst air raids of the war.

Concurrent with the attack on Liverpool, German aircraft bombed London, causing scattered damage in the city (→ 2/9/41).

Civilians walk amid the remnants of Coventry's famed cathedral, only one of 60,000 buildings razed during the massive 500-bomber Reich attack.

Molotov pays his first visit to Hitler

Nov 12. Herr Hitler wined and dined the Russians this evening in hopes of bringing a new partner into the Axis alliance. Premier Molotov was met by Joachim von Ribbentrop at the Berlin train station this morning without the usual ostentatious military display, so as to downplay the importance of the meeting and mute questions of Anglo-Russian relations.

During a three-hour private meeting this afternoon, Hitler and Molotov, Stalin's right hand man, discussed the new political order in Europe and the role Japan might play in a redrawn map of Eurasia. After the meeting, Molotov and his staff were feted at a dinner for over 200 people, including 100 high-ranking Nazi officials.

Though Russia's relations with other nations were excluded from the talks, both Rome and Nazi Party members expect the talks to result in Russia joining the German-Italian-Japanese alliance. This would be quite a reversal since that pact was forged in October-November 1936, when the fascist nations agreed to defend against the spread of communism (→ 1/10/41).

General Weitel and Joachim von Ribbentrop welcome Molotov to Berlin.

Roosevelt in for 3rd term; Wallace is V.P.

Nov 5. President Roosevelt was re-elected today, the first man in American history to win a third term in the White House. Elected along with him, as Vice President, was Henry A. Wallace, who has been the Secretary of Agriculture. While the vote was much closer than the Roosevelt landslide four years ago, the president handily defeated the Republican candidate, Wendell Willkie. President Roosevelt, addresssing a crowd at Hyde Park, New York, promised to be "the same Franklin Roosevelt you have known" (→ 1/20/41).

Americans fall in love with the Jeep

Nov 11. The Jeep, developed by the U.S. Army Quatermaster Corps and built by Willys, has made its debut. Its name comes from the sound of the first letters of "general purpose." It is capable of operating on rough terrain, thanks to its high clearance and four-wheel drive. The Jeep has a great variety of military uses: command car, or ammunition and personnel carrier.

Prehistoric art found in France

Nov 1. An outstanding prehistoric cave has been discovered near Montignac in Dordogne, France. The Grotte de Lascaux was found by four boys searching for a dog. The cave has a main cavern and several galleries, all decorated with engraved and painted animals.

Nov 26. German troops have begun herding Warsaw's Jewish population behind an eight-foot wall enclosing the city's ghetto district. The area is already overcrowded, some buildings housing as many as seven in a room. The imprisoned need special passes to leave, as do non-Jews wishing to enter. Nazi spokesmen deny any anti-Semitic intent, insisting the action will give Jews a "new life" and protect Poles from diseases spread by war.

1940

DECEMBER

Su	Mo	Tu	We	Th	Fr	Sa
1	2	3	4	5	6	7
8	9	10	11	12	13	14
15	16	17	18	19	20	21
22	23	24	25	26	27	28
29	30	31				

1. Joseph Kennedy resigns as ambassador to Britain to "help the president keep the U.S out of war."

1. Vichy: Petain authorized to dismiss Parliament members (→ 16).

9. New York: Michigan's Tom Harmon gets Heismann Trophy.

9. North Africa: British seize 1,000 Italians in sudden thrust in Egypt (→ 16).

12. Berlin: Hitler issues plan for Operation Felix; drive through Spain to Gibraltar.

13. Berlin: Military staff approves Marita Plan for invasion of Greece (→ 1/20/41).

16. East Africa: British carry out air raid on Italian Somalia (→ 1/5/41).

18. Berlin: Secret plans issued for Operation Barbarossa, invasion of Russia (→ 6/11/41).

20. FDR creates Office of Production Management under William Knudsen, to organize U.S. defense industry (→ 29).

23. China: Chiang Kai-shek dissolves all Communist associations (→ 9/6/43).

CULTURAL EVENTS, 1940

Literature: Hemingway's "For Whom the Bell Tolls"; Steinbeck's "Of Mice and Men"; Graham Greene's "The Power and the Glory"; O'Neill's "Long Day's Journey Into Night"; Richard Wright's "Native Son."

Academia: Santayana's "Realms of Being"; Edmund Wilson's "To the Finland Station"; Karl Landsteiner, Alexander Wiener discover Rh factor.

Music: "You Are My Sunshine"; "When You Wish upon a Star"; Duke Ellington popularized; exodus of European composers to U.S., including Schonberg, Bartok, Stravinsky, Hindemith, Krenek, Milhaud.

The Arts: Max Beckmann's "Circus Caravan"; Edmund Duffy, 3rd Pulitzer for cartoons.

Film: John Ford's "The Grapes of Wrath"; Chaplin's "The Great Dictator"; Hitchcock's "Rebecca," Academy Award; Disney's "Fantasia."

Fitzgerald, jazz age novelist, is gone

Zelda Fitzgerald with F. Scott and "Scottie": A tumultous family life.

Dec 21. F. Scott Fitzgerald, chronicler of the 20's, has died. While his last years were spent on forgettable film scripts, he leaves very memorable novels. "The Great Gatsby" (1925) and "Tender Is the Night" (1934) are his best as well as among the best in American literature. In 1932, recalling a roaring decade "when we drank wood alcohol" and "girls all looked alike in sweater dresses," Fitzgerald wrote that "it all seemed so rosy and romantic to us who were young then because we would never feel quite so intensely about our surroundings again."

Director William "90-take" Wyler's perfectionism often frustrates stars like Bette Davis.

FDR calls America arsenal of democracy

Dec 29. In a "fireside chat" broadcast throughout much of the world, President Roosevelt tonight described the United States as being the "arsenal of democracy."

While determined to keep America out of the war, the president said the United States must send more war supplies to those "in the front lines of democracy's battle." He said no dictator or "combination of dictators" would halt America's aid to those fighting Nazi Germany.

The president ruled out any peace talks until it is certain that the "aggressor nations" abandon all thoughts of dominating or conquering the world. "The experience of the past two years," he continued, "has proven beyond doubt that no nation can appease the Nazis. No man can tame a tiger into a kitten by stroking it."

FDR told the American people that his purpose is "to keep you now, and your children later, and your grandchildren much later out of a last-ditch war for the preservation of American independence." Not since "Jamestown and Plymouth Rock has our American civilization been in such danger as now," he said, adding that that there must be more shipments of guns, planes, ships, "more of everything" (→ 1/6/41).

Mass-producing planes for Europe.

Petain seizes Laval; Germans free him

Dec 16. French Premier Petain has nipped a coup attempt in the bud by arresting Pierre Laval, the Vice Premier and Minister of Foreign Affairs. Laval was soon free, however. Adolf Hitler, infuriated by his arrest, ordered him released.

Laval was quick to denounce Petain. "Now I know where to find my friends," he announced. "Among Germans."

Over the past few weeks, Petain has been holding secret conversations with the British, assuring them he will not fight with Hitler against them. At the same time, Laval has called openly for closer collaboration with Germany.

Laval planned to seize Petain during a ceremony in Paris and then set up a new government at Versailles with Germany's support. Petain learned of the plan and ordered Laval arrested (→ 2/3/41).

Katharine Hepburn at her loveliest: The Philadelphia Story

For box office poison, Katharine Hepburn is very easy to swallow in the romantic comedy "The Philadelphia Story." For the past two years, since "Bringing up Baby," there have been rumors she drives audiences away and no director wants her. In fact, Miss Hepburn has been simply waiting for a good script to come along. She knew "Philadelphia Story" was a winner because she was brilliant in it on Broadway. She is one of several actors and actresses making comebacks or beating the odds this year.

"Star Dust" stars Linda Darnell, who is also seen in "The Mark of Zorro." Typecast as a dopey blonde, she struts some sultry talent in "Star Dust." Joel McCrea proved he could tackle a lead in "Foreign Correspondent," directed by Alfred Hitchcock. Beautiful Joan Fontaine, tagging behind her sister Olivia de Havilland unseen and unappreciated, shines in another Hitchcock film, "Rebecca."

Marlene Dietrich, who made her real comeback in "Destry Rides Again" last year, continues to ride the crest with "Seven Sinners." Miss Dietrich was recently asked by the Nazi government to return to Germany and make pictures there. She said no thank you.

As for comedy, W.C. Fields stars in and co-wrote (under the pseudonym Mahatma Kane Jeeves) "The Bank Dick." He performed a few stunts in the picture, despite his age (he is 61) and reports of ill health. Laurel and Hardy cut up in "Saps at Sea," amid rumors they are on the outs with producer Hal Roach.

The best comeback belongs to Bette Davis. She rejected recent Warner Brothers scripts; the company suspended her without pay. She sued. She is now starring in "The Letter."

An entertaining film about a talent scout discovering a star-struck girl.

"Foreign Correspondent."

Hepburn: "The Philadelphia Story."

1941

JANUARY

Su	Mo	Tu	We	Th	Fr	Sa
			1	2	3	4
5	6	7	8	9	10	11
12	13	14	15	16	17	18
19	20	21	22	23	24	25
26	27	28	29	30	31	

1. Belgium: Leon Degrelle, head of Rexist movement, calls for collaboration with Nazis (→ 3/8).

4. German actress Marlene Dietrich becomes U.S. citizen.

5. Libya: Bardia falls to British assault; 25,000 troops, six generals seized (→ 22).

6. Washington: FDR asks Congress to support lend-lease plan to supply Allies (→ 9).

9. Congress gets bill calling for "all out" anti-Axis aid; budget includes unprecedented $10.8 billion for defense (→ 18).

10. Soviet, Reich agree on East European borders, exchange of industrial equipment (→ 21).

14. Mediterranean: Three British warships hit in Axis attack (→ 16).

16. Mediterranean: Axis air strike hits British carrier Illustrious; one cruiser sunk (→ 3/29).

20. Washington: FDR inaugurated for third time.

20. Berlin: Hitler meets with Mussolini, offers aid in Albania and Greece (→ 29).

21. U.S. lifts ban on arms to U.S.S.R. (→ 3/3).

24. New York: "High Sierra," with Humphrey Bogart, opens.

24. Bucharest: Thousands die in Rumanian riots (→ 2/10).

27. U.S., Britain begin high-level military talks in Washington (→ 2/4).

28. North Africa: De Gaulle's Free French forces sack south Libya oasis (→ 2/6).

29. Athens: Greek P.M. Metaxas dies at 70; pro-Allied Alexander Korizis succeeds (→ 4/6).

31. C.I.O. strike shuts Phelps Dodge Copper plant in Elizabeth, N.J. (→ 3/25).

BIRTH

9. Joan Baez, American folk-singer, political activist.

DEATHS

4. Henri Bergson, French philosopher (*10/18/1859).

8. Robert Baden-Powell, founder of British Boy Scouts (*2/22/1857).

Italy loses Tobruk to British, Australians

Jan 22. Italian troops, unwilling to face British bayonets at close quarters after the perimeter of their Tobruk defense was cracked, have yielded the city to Allied forces.

The attack followed two nights of RAF bombing on the 20th and 21st. British forces had pushed to within eight miles of the city last night. The Italians threw up two lines of defense in a perimeter 30 miles long around the city.

Australian troops crawled out of trenches this morning, and after feints all along the line, followed as tanks forced a gap in the east. The Italians, who had trained their guns on the front, surrendered by the thousands as Australians fanned out behind them. Free French and British forces continued sporadic attacks along the line to prevent the Italians from bringing reinforcements to the site of the main assault.

The Australians were also assisted by bombing attacks from British ships and planes off the coast. The Italian government conceded the loss of the vital port city in Libya over radio in Rome today (→ 28).

Roosevelt requests lend-lease for arms

Jan 18. The lend-lease plan for providing arms to those nations now engaged in war against the Nazis was termed unjustified last night by Joseph P. Kennedy, the retiring United States Ambassador to Great Britain. Instead, Kennedy said, the United States should continue to build up its own defenses to the point where no nation dare attack it.

The bill, proposed by President Roosevelt and now pending in the Congress, would channel billions of dollars in weapons to Great Britain and France, at no cost to them, to be repaid within a reasonable time after the war in goods needed by the United States. President Roosevelt has likened the proposal to a man whose house is on fire and whose neighbor loaned him his garden hose (→ 27).

A literary puzzle: James Joyce's work

Jan 13. Author James Joyce has died in Zurich. He was 58. His work, chock full of elusive allegory, psychological symbolism and literary puns, mystified the general public. Perhaps the only obvious thing about Joyce was his genius.

Joyce was born Feb. 2, 1882 near Dublin. His years with an alcoholic father are sketched in "A Portrait of the Artist as a Young Man" (1915). He majored in modern languages at University College in Dublin and briefly studied medicine. Financial problems at home forced Joyce to quit his studies and support nine brothers and sisters.

He was a teacher in Dublin when he met a woman named Nora Barnacle. She eventually pervaded his work; many of his vivid female characters are modeled on her. She also pervaded his life; she was his mistress for 26 years and wife after that.

As his fame increased, Ireland's love for Joyce dissipated. His poems and short stories (one collection was "The Dubliners" in 1914) hardly flattered the Irish. Accordingly, Joyce made his home elsewhere, wandering like his character Leopold Blum from Paris to Zurich.

"Ulysses" (1922) explored the lives of two Dubliners. Sexually explicit and scatalogical, it was banned from the United States until 1933. Readers now know the book is not pornography, but the masterwork of the greatest writer of the century. "A man of genius makes no mistakes," Joyce once wrote. "His errors are volitional and are the portals of discovery."

1941

FEBRUARY

Su	Mo	Tu	We	Th	Fr	Sa
						1
2	3	4	5	6	7	8
9	10	11	12	13	14	15
16	17	18	19	20	21	22
23	24	25	26	27	28	

3. France: Nazis force Vichy to restore Laval to office (→ 3/10).

3. U.S. Supreme Court rules Fair Labor Standards Act (40-hour week) constitutional (→ 4/11).

4. United Service Organization (USO) formed to cater to armed forces, defense industries (→ 20).

6. Libya: RAF clears way as British take Benghazi, trapping thousands of Italians (→ 14).

9. Churchill, over radio, declares "Give us the tools and we will finish the job" (→ 12).

10. London severs diplomatic relations with Bucharest (→ 14).

10. Iceland attacked by German planes (→ 7/7).

12. Oxford: Penicillin given first successful clinical trial, by Australian Howard Florey and German Ernest Chain.

12. Germany: RAF hits Hanover industrial district in biggest British air strike yet (→ 5/12).

12. Madrid: Franco and Mussolini meet, report "identity of views" (→ 13).

13. Madrid: Ailing Alfonso XIII renounces Spanish throne in favor of son Juan (→ 9/9).

16. East Africa: Italians lose last foothold in Sudan (→ 17).

17. East Africa: Emperor Haile Selassie joins British Gen. Wingate, seeking to drive Italians out of Ethiopia (→ 26).

17. Philadelphia: Joe Louis KOs Gus Dorazio in second round to keep heavyweight title (→ 5/23).

17. Sofia: Bulgaria, Turkey sign pact, confirming Turkish reluctance to join Allies (→ 3/2).

18. Pacific: Australian reinforcements reach Singapore, now ringed by British mines (→ 21).

20. U.S. to speed war planes to Pacific (→ 3/11).

21. Tokyo: For. Min. Matsuoka threatens "countermeasures" if British do not halt moves in Southeast Asia (→ 3/11).

26. East Africa: British take Somali capital (→ 3/21).

DEATH

28. Alfonso XIII, ex-king of Spain (*5/17/1886).

Rommel's Afrika Korps in Tripoli

Rommel (left) surveys the desert.

Feb 14. Germany's General Erwin Rommel has arrived in Tripoli, and he is under orders to reverse setbacks to the Axis in Libya. The first units of his Afrika Korps went ashore today. They were specially trained by Rommel for action in the desert. He will command two divisions, one of them armored, the other motorized.

Italian forces in Libya under the command of Marshal Rodolfo Graziani have been on the run for the past few weeks. The Italians lost Tobruk last month. Benghazi was occupied last week by British forces commanded by Field Marshal Archibald Wavell. Benito Mussolini, who was infuriated by the defeats, fired his top generals (→ 16).

Bulgaria accepts Nazi occupation

Feb 14. Germany will be granted an unobstructed path through Bulgaria in the Reich's objective to control southeastern Europe. The Sofia government confirmed reports last night that it will allow German forces to march to the Greek border, despite statements expressing Bulgarian neutrality. Prime Minister Bogdan Philoff has been challenged by Britain as supporting the Axis cause.

Britain protested the decision, saying, "If Germany occupies Bulgaria, we shall have to take whatever measures the situation requires," including bombing (→ 3/1).

1941

MARCH

Su	Mo	Tu	We	Th	Fr	Sa
						1
2	3	4	5	6	7	8
9	10	11	12	13	14	15
16	17	18	19	20	21	22
23	24	25	26	27	28	29
30	31					

1. Balkans: Bulgaria joins Axis as Nazis occupy Sofia; U.S. freezes assets (→ 2).

2. Turkey closes Dardanelles to all ships without Turkish captains (→ 6/18).

2. Balkans: Secretary of U.S. officer seized in Bucharest, sent to concentration camp with 14 Britons (→ 4).

3. Moscow denounces Axis rule in Bulgaria (→ 13).

4. Balkans: Hitler meets Yugoslav Prince Paul in Belgrade, asks participation in Axis (→ 5).

5. Balkans: Britain severs relations with Bulgaria, prepares air attack (→ 25).

8. Martial law proclaimed in Holland to quell anti-Nazi protests (→ 7/19).

10. Vichy threatens to use navy unless Britain lets food reach France (→ 4/18).

11. FDR signs Lend-Lease Act, authorizing war supplies to Allies (→ 19).

11. France, under Japanese pressure, yields part of Laos and Cambodia to Thailand (→ 5/6).

13. Hitler issues edict calling for invasion of U.S.S.R. (→ 4/13).

19. Ottawa: U.S. and Canada sign St. Lawrence Seaway plan for joint defense (→ 30).

21. North Africa: Last Italian post in East Libya falls to British (→ 4/6).

22. Grand Coulee, world's largest dam, opens in Washington state.

25. Penn.: C.I.O. starts strike at Bethlehem Steel Co. (→ 4/28).

25. Balkans: Yugoslavia joins Axis (→ 27).

29. Mediterranean: British sink five Italian warships off Peloponnesus coast (→ 9/24).

30. U.S. seizes Italian, German, Danish ships in 16 ports (→ 4/4).

DEATHS

6. Gutzon Borglum, Mt. Rushmore designer (*3/25/1871).

8. Sherwood Anderson, American writer, "Winesburg, Ohio" (*9/13/1876).

Yugoslavs repudiate regime's Nazi deal

March 27. With lightning speed, the army has overthrown the government of Yugoslavia, named a general as the new Premier, put a new King on the throne and arrested the two officials who had signed a new treaty with the Axis.

Adolf Hitler is furious. His Ambassador to Yugoslavia was ejected from the Foreign Office after presenting an ultimatum from Berlin.

The new government, expecting reprisals from Hitler, ordered more than a million soldiers on full alert. Troops in Nazi-occupied Bulgaria are rushing to the Yugoslav border.

Former Premier Dragisha Cvetkovic and his Foreign Minister are both under house arrest. They were seized as soon as they returned from the treaty conference in Vienna. General Dusan Simovitch, the new premier, is acting quickly to assemble a new Cabinet. Peter II has ascended to the throne.

The dramatic developments alter the military situation in southeastern Europe. Hitler may now have to invade Yugoslavia before he tries to conquer Greece (→ 4/17).

Yugoslav patriots demonstrate against the Axis. Premier Cvetkovic was overthrown only two days after he signed the pact with Hitler in Vienna.

A sad ending for Virginia Woolf

March 28. English author Virginia Woolf met a tragic end today, drowning herself rather than face another nervous breakdown and spell of madness. Despite her overly sensitive nature, Woolf was a writer of lucid, insightful essays. Her novel "To the Lighthouse," painstakingly crafted, was groundbreaking in style and subject.

Mrs. Woolf was born Adeline Virginia Stephen in 1882. She married journalist Leonard Woolf, who nursed her through her depressions. In 1922, Mrs. Woolf wrote "Jacob's Room," an impressionistic work in which a character is seen through the eyes of his peers. In 1925, she published "Mrs. Dalloway," using a stream-of-consciousness narrative. "To the Lighthouse" (1927) explored art and mortality.

Boston Bruins win fourth straight title

March 13. The Boston Bruins exploded for five goals in the third period, defeated the New York Americans by 8-3 and became the first team ever to win a divisional championship four times in a row. The New Yorkers skated hard for two periods, but then they collapsed.

The Boston Bruins.

1941

APRIL

Su	Mo	Tu	We	Th	Fr	Sa
		1	2	3	4	5
6	7	8	9	10	11	12
13	14	15	16	17	18	19
20	21	22	23	24	25	26
27	28	29	30			

1. Mideast: Pro-Axis Rachid Ali takes power in Iraqi coup (→ 17).

3. Budapest: Premier Paul Teleki commits suicide to avoid submitting to Hungary's entry into war (→ 7).

4. FDR allows British navy to repair and refuel in U.S. ports (→ 10).

6. Balkans: German troops invade Yugoslavia, Greece (→ 9).

6. East Africa: British take Addis Ababa, Ethiopian capital (→ 5/5).

7. Balkans: Britain cuts ties with Hungary, now a base for Reich operations (→ 12).

9. New York: Bing Crosby, Bob Hope and Dorothy Lamour open in "Road to Zanzibar."

9. Greek line breaks in north; Nazis take Thessalonika (→ 21).

11. FDR extends security zone around North and South America; opens door for supplies to Suez Canal (→ 18).

12. Hungary enters war in Balkans; Soviet protests (→ 17).

13. Moscow signs non-aggression pact with Tokyo, allowing transfer of troops from Siberia to guard against Reich (→ 6/11).

17. Mideast: British troops enter Iraq (→ 5/2).

18. G.M., now producing 50% of U.S. cars, to make no changes in passenger-car models due to defense needs (→ 27).

18. Vichy France quits League of Nations (→ 5/15).

21. Nazis sink five ships evacuating British from Greece (→ 23).

21. Athens: Manuel Tsouderos named Greek premier upon death of Korizis (→ 23).

23. Greece: King George II announces transfer of capital from Athens to Crete (→ 27).

27. Singapore: U.S. military chiefs end week-long meeting with Dutch, British; plans to fight Japan concluded (→ 30).

28. U.S. Supreme Court bars employers from considering union connections in hiring (→ 5/3).

30. FDR buys first savings bond for defense fund (→ 5/3).

Greek army capitulates to Axis

Germans enter a Greek village in their sweep through the Balkans.

April 27. The Greek army collapsed today as German forces swept into Athens. German planes are still bombing isolated pockets of resistance in the port area and outside the capital.

The Greek government has already escaped to Crete. It held its first meeting in Candia. Fierce fighting is reported 25 miles west of Athens, where dogged Australian units are providing cover for the rear guard of the British Imperial Expedition. The British, battered by the Germans, are trying to escape into the Gulf of Corinth. They are attempting to evacuate most of their ammunition and supplies, but much of it has been captured. The British will presumably head for Crete and North Africa (→ 5/23).

Nazis invade Yugoslavia, smash Belgrade

German tanks drive into Yugoslavia to force capitulation to the Axis.

April 17. German forces have occupied Belgrade, about a week and a half after they attacked Yugoslavia. The first of the troops entered the capital from the south.

This undeclared war began April 6, when German planes bombed Belgrade. Adolf Hitler wants the Yugoslav army to pay for its rejection of a treaty with the Axis, and so far he has not been disappointed.

In the north, near the Italian border, German forces are consolidating earlier victories. Near Zagreb, the Germans say they have captured thousands of enemy soldiers and more than 20 generals.

Hitler apparently hopes to dismember Yugoslavia into its separate states. Croatia has already declared its independence. But a Communist named Joseph Broz Tito vows to fight Hitler to the end (→ 7/4).

U.S., fearing Nazis, occupies Greenland

April 10. The United States, concerned about recent German reconnaissance flights in the North Atlantic, will take control of Greenland to protect it and to ensure it remains a Danish colony. President Roosevelt has announced that an agreement has been reached with Danish Minister Henrick de Kauffmann establishing the right of America to develop air bases and other military facilities in the strategic area.

Greenland is an important observation point for weather conditions over the British Isles, which are currently threatened by Germany. Nazi activities in Greenland airspace prompted Washington to bring the island "within the system of hemispheric defense envisaged by the Act of Havana," according to State Department officials.

The accord was signed yesterday "on the anniversary of the day German troops invaded Denmark," Roosevelt noted. He added that he hoped for a "quick liberation of Denmark."

Great Britain expressed relief over the decision, as it explemplifies close cooperation between the United States and Britain. It's quite possible that Greenland, located between Iceland and Canada, will serve as a base for delivery of war supplies to England (→ 11).

FDR creates wage and price agency

April 11. President Roosevelt has created the Office of Price Administration and Civilian Supply and placed at its helm Leon Henderson. The iniative is necessary, according to the president, because the war is taxing the economy. It will enable the government to fix prices to prevent spiraling prices, profiteering and consumer hoarding; to stimulate provision of necessary civilian supplies; and to ensure equal distribution of products to civilians after the demands of the military have been met.

Court says Negroes can go first class

April 28. The Supreme Court has ruled unamimously that Negroes are entitled to all first-class services on railroad trains. Representative Arthur W. Mitchell brought the case to trial after he was removed from a coach car and seated in a second-class car as the train he was riding approached Arkansas. Chief Justice Charles Evan Hughes said the issue was "not a question of segregation, but one of equality of treatment," thus rejecting the claim that the laws of segregation allowed the practice.

Brecht opens play Mother Courage

April 19. Bertolt Brecht's "Mother Courage and Her Children" has opened in New York. Its theme is ethical conduct. Critics are interested; the audience seems disquieted. It is nothing new to Brecht, a German playwright specializing in the "alienation effect." The method gets an idea across by keeping the audience from focusing on the less important personal issues.

Brecht had a major success with "The Three Penny Opera" (1928). Fame hardly impresses him, however. He would rather "Mother Courage" have a short run than compromise his vision. Rewriting to please the public would be "figurative prostitution—the sell-out of one's talent and dignity."

1941

MAY

Su	Mo	Tu	We	Th	Fr	Sa
				1	2	3
4	5	6	7	8	9	10
11	12	13	14	15	16	17
18	19	20	21	22	23	24
25	26	27	28	29	30	31

2. Mideast: Iraqi troops attack British (→ 17).

3. Washington: C.I.O. gets 60 reinstated with back wages, as four-year dispute with Consolidated Edison ends (→ 6/9).

3. Twenty-six U.S. ships reach Suez Canal with supplies for British Mideast armies (→ 15).

3. Eddie Arcaro gets second victory in Kentucky Derby, on Whirlaway.

5. N.Y. Times wins Pulitzer for war reporting.

5. East Africa: Haile Selassie returns to Ethiopian throne, five years and three days after exile by Italians (→ 14).

6. Moscow: Stalin named Soviet premier after resignation of Vyacheslav Molotov (→ 8/7).

6. Tokyo: Japan and France sign trade accords for French Indochina (→ 25).

12. Reich planes bomb London, unroofing Westminster Hall in one of worst strikes yet (→ 6/22).

14. Berlin: Nazis declare Red Sea a war zone (→ 19).

15. U.S. seizes French merchant ships in American harbors, including Normandie (→ 21).

15. France: Vichy sends 5,000 Paris Jews, between ages of 18 and 40, to labor camps (→ 6/13).

17. Mideast: German planes bomb British in Iraq (→ 31).

20. Santiago: Chile seizes Nazi Socialist Vanguard on charges of plotting putsch (→ 1/15/42).

21. U.S. merchant ship Robin Moore sunk by Reich U-boat inside defense line (→ 27).

23. Greek King George II eludes Nazis, flees Crete to Egypt.

25. Hanoi: Japanese soldiers break into warehouses, steal $10 mil. in U.S. products (→ 7/24).

30. Davis and Rose win Indy 500 in Noc-Out Hose Clamp Special, averaging 115 mph.

DEATHS

18. Werner Sombart, German sociologist (*1/19/1863).

28. Max Schmeling, German ex-heavyweight boxing champ, on African front.

Hood, Bismarck sunk

The 40,000-ton Bismarck, now underwater, sunk the Hood 3 days ago.

May 27. The British royal navy, fueled by heated anger, caught up with the German warship, the Bismarck, fired and watched with revenge as it sank to the bottom of the Atlantic. The attack avenged the German naval victory three days ago when the Bismarck demolished the pride of the British fleet, the Hood. In that assault 1,300 men are believed to have died.

The two big ships met initially in the North Atlantic between Iceland and Norway, where the fateful blow to the munitions magazine on the Hood was delivered. On vows to "pursue and destroy the enemy," the royal navy chased the German flotilla for 1,750 miles before accomplishing its goal. Most of the Bismarck's 1,000-plus crew is thought to have perished in the relentless bombing. It is the worst Nazi naval defeat of the war.

Hitler aide Hess lands in Scotland. Why?

May 10. Winston Churchill and for that matter most of the British people are at a loss to explain what happened in Scotland today. A German plane crash-landed. On board was one of Hitler's most trusted confidantes, Rudolf Hess. Word is he wanted to negotiate a peace treaty.

"This is one of those cases," Winston Churchill said, "in which the imagination is baffled by the facts."

Hess was apparently on a mission to convince Britain to divide the world into two spheres of influence. Some say the idea represents the height of German arrogance. Germany says Hess is insane. Many in Britain might agree.

The wreckage of Hess' plane, vehicle for a mysterious mission, lies in Scotland.

President warns of national emergency

May 27. In a step just short of declaring war to be "imminent," President Roosevelt tonight told the nation that "an unlimited national emergency exists." Under his new proclamation, the president and Congress can commandeer many powers over labor and industries for the purpose of assuring the nation's defense as well as supplying needed arms to Great Britain.

"The delivery of supplies to Britain is imperative," he said. "This can be done; it must be done; it will be done." He said the United States would not "hestitate to use our armed forces to repel attacks" from Germany and protect territorial waters. The aim of Adolf Hitler, he said, is to dominate the high seas for an attack on the Western hemisphere and to rule the world.

President Roosevelt also noted that the Germans have been sinking merchant ships twice as fast as they are being replaced by British and American shipyards (→ 6/16).

Joe Louis wins his 17th title defense

May 23. Joe Louis continued his undefeated reign with a victory over Buddy Baer, brother of former champion Max Baer. Buddy became Louis's 17th title victim when he was disqualified in the seventh round. Nobody, it appears, can beat the "Brown Bomber."

Vichyite anti-Red poster.

Italian East Africa surrenders to British

The Emperor returns to Addis Ababa under British escort, perhaps a repayment for Britain's inaction five years ago when Italy overran Selassie's Ethiopia.

May 19. British troops have forced the surrender of Fascist strongholds in Italian East Africa. The Duke of Aosta, Viceroy of I.E.A., and his force of 38,000 soldiers waved the white flag at Alagi, Ethiopia, yesterday and will accept the terms laid down by Britain. However, these conditions were not made public.

Now, there are but two remaining areas of Ethiopia controlled by Italy. It is believed that with the surrender of the duke, who has been called "the life and soul of Italian resistance," the remaining Fascists will also acquiesce. The fall of Alagi would free British resources for the North African and Mideast fronts.

The British victory comes two weeks after the return of Haile Selassie to the throne. Selassie had been forced into exile for five years at the hands of the Fascists (→ 6/18).

British put down uprising in Iraq

May 31. Premier Rashid Ali el Gailana of Iraq ended his revolt against Britain today, as British troops surrounded Baghdad, forcing the premier to sign an armistice. The British offensive also drove German airmen and the Italian Minister at Baghdad from the Middle East. This underscores evidence that Britain was not fighting the Arab people so much as it was battling the Axis insurgents. Many credit the British troops in Crete for fighting the Nazis ferociously, thus tying up the German schedule and creating the victory in Baghdad.

Emir Abdul Illah, the former power in Iraq prior to Rashid Ali, is immediately setting up a new government and according to the terms of surrender, Britain will have access to all Iraqi highways, railroads and communication facilities. In addition, "the complete independence of the country and honor of the army will be guaranteed," as stated by the Iraqi Internal Security Commission (→ 6/8).

Welles' masterwork is Citizen Kane

May 1. "Citizen Kane" opened tonight, starring and directed by "the boy wonder," Orson Welles. This is Welles' first film, having worked for the stage and radio. He would have released "Kane" in February, but William Randolph Hearst thought the story irritably coincidental and suppressed it. "Kane" tells of a publisher rising to the top amid controversy. Welles uses a swift pace, news-reel type narrative and daring camera work. And he is a talent scout; the film stars an unknown named Rosebud.

Welles (center) in "Citizen Kane."

1941

JUNE

Su	Mo	Tu	We	Th	Fr	Sa
1	2	3	4	5	6	7
8	9	10	11	12	13	14
15	16	17	18	19	20	21
22	23	24	25	26	27	28
29	30					

2. Chief Justice Charles Evans Hughes announces retirement from U.S. Supreme Court.

8. Beirut: Captain Moshe Dayan wounded in eye by Vichy troops as bullet hits binoculars.

8. Mideast: British and Free French push into Syria (→ 13).

9. L.A.: Army seizes strike-bound plant at North American Aviation Co. (→ 20).

11. German troops reported massing on Soviet border (→ 21).

13. Syria: British, Free French encircle Damascus (→ 21).

13. Vichy says 12,000 Jews sent to camps for hindering Franco-German cooperation (→ 8/12).

16. Washington orders Berlin to close consulates in U.S. (→ 19).

17. New York: P.M. King of Canada pledges total support to British war effort.

18. North Africa: British call off three-day drive in Libya (→ 11/19).

18. Berlin: Turkey signs friendship pact with Reich (→ 3/2/44).

19. Germany and Italy expel U.S. consuls (→ 24).

20. Washington: Henry Ford gives in, signs contract with U.A.W., recognizing it as C.I.O. union; affects 130,000 across country (→ 10/10).

21. German troops drive into Russia on wide front from Arctic to Black Sea (→ 26).

22. London: RAF fighters down 26 Nazi planes (→ 3/3/42).

24. FDR pledges all possible aid to U.S.S.R. (→ 7/7).

26. Finland declares war on U.S.S.R. (→ 30).

DEATHS

1. Sir Hugh Walpole, popular British novelist (*3/13/1884).

2. Lou Gehrig, baseball great (*6/19/1903).

4. Wilhelm II, German ex-kaiser (*1/27/1859).

6. Louis Chevrolet, auto pioneer (*12/25/1878).

29. Ignace Jan Paderewski, Polish pianist and statesman (*6/11/1860).

Vichyites surrender Syria to the Allies

June 21. British and Free French troops have driven Vichy forces from Damascus, Syria, after weeks of intense fighting. Employing a familiar British tactic of encircling a target and lobbing heavy artillery, the Allied squadrons forced the evacuation of the Vichyites, who left to avoid serious casualties. The Syrian capital is now occupied by the British, who have set their sights on Beirut. Reports from London indicate the royal navy might station warships off the coast of Beirut and shell the Vichy-controlled city.

The Allies have taken seriously Vichyite resistance in this undeclared war and appear to want a quick victory regardless of the cost. The capture of Damascus is of great strategic importance and satisfies a British declaration of July 1, in which the British government vowed to prevent any hostile power from occupying Lebanon or Syria, mandated to France by the League.

British endeavors seem to be completely successful despite German assistance to Vichy troops and now, according to correspondents in Beirut, the Allies intend to attack Tadmur, an important air base along the oil pipeline in central Syria (→ 7/4).

Ickes stops sale of U.S. oil to Japan

June 16. A Japanese tanker was prevented from returning to the Orient with 252,000 gallons of lubricating oil by United States Defense Oil Coordinator Harold L Ickes. Ickes blocked the shipment because of oil shortages in America just as the tanker, Azuma Maru, was about to load up in Philadelphia. A government spokesman said the action was taken "not on a question of international oil policy, but on coordinating supplies on the East coast."

Ickes responded to complaints by the firm, Wilson and Company, which protested the shipment because its own defense work was unable to obtain adequate oil supplies. A company representative, Edward Jobbins, said, "I thought it was unfair that Japan could buy oil here at a time when we are threatened by a shortage" (→ 19).

▷

Massive Nazi attack made on Russia

June 30. The murderous tentacles of Adolf Hitler—his powerful and devoted German armies—have been thrust into the Soviet Union in a tremendous invasion stretching over 2,000 miles from the Arctic region to the Black Sea. Now, Nazi Germany and Soviet Russia are at war, as Hitler attempts to fulfill his dream of Lebensraum, or "living space" for the German people.

In a proclamation to the German people, Hitler termed the military attack the biggest in the history of the world and said Russian-British cooperation threatened the safety of Europe. The action severs the Nazi-Soviet Pact of non-aggression signed in August 1939.

The Nazis called on the Finnish and Rumanian armies to help in the awesome invasion. The potential destruction of these combined forces fighting against the vaunted Soviet military is best illustrated by gauging the manpower involved. At the start of this war, United States intelligence sources estimated the Red army of Russia at 4.11 million active troops with 3.04 million trained reserves, for a total of 7.15 million soldiers, the world's largest army at the time.

Germany had 3.5 million active troops at the war's outset, and a reserve of 3.35 million. The Rumanian army is estimated at 1.8 million and Finnish forces total 401,000.

Each side has declared victories in the first of what could be many attacks and counterattacks. Soviet dispatches claimed their alerted army (Russia expected an invasion at some point in this European nightmare) turned back advancing Germans, shot down 65 Luftwaffe aircraft and inflicted serious damage on the enemy. "Only in the districts of Grodno and Kristinople did the enemy have some tactical success," read one communique.

The German High Command issued a communique, saying the invasion was successful and that "an attempt of the enemy to fly into East Prussia was repulsed with heavy losses. German pursuit pilots shot down many Red battle planes."

As Chancellor Hitler berated Moscow—alleging Russia was about "to stab Germany in the back" while she was "engaged in a struggle for existence"—Winston Churchill talked of Nazi destruction. The British Prime Minister said Britain would help Russia in any way to obliterate the "bloodthirsty guttersnipe." Avoiding the term "alliance," and refusing to soften his stance against communism, Churchill agreed to fight alongside the Soviets, declaring, "We have but one single, irrevocable purpose . . . to destroy Hitler and every vestige of the Nazi regime."

Soviet Foreign Minister Molotov predicted the Red army would deliver a "crushing blow" to the Reich's troops. He also lambasted the "predatory assault," saying it was begun in the context of "sheer lie and provocation." And he dismissed any Soviet instigation or any violation of the 1939 non-aggression pact. Regardless of rhetoric, a protracted war between these two military giants is destined to impose grave suffering upon each nation's populace (→ 7/6).

The German army, on the move in the east, pushes rapidly through the Ukraine.

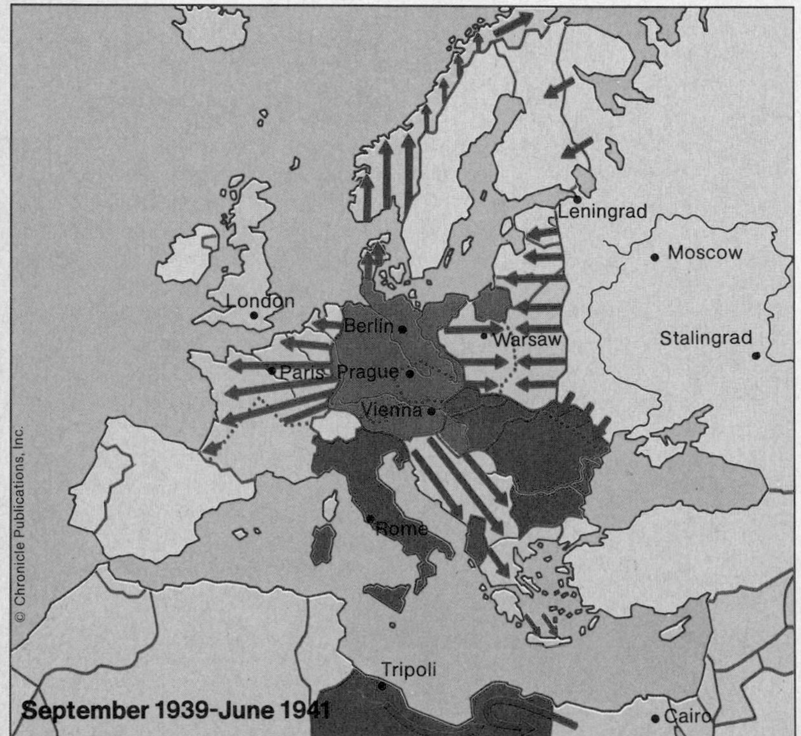

In under two years, Germany's blitzkrieg has brought Axis occupation to Poland, Denmark, Norway, Belgium, Holland, France, Yugoslavia and Greece.

1941

JULY

Su	Mo	Tu	We	Th	Fr	Sa
		1	2	3	4	5
6	7	8	9	10	11	12
13	14	15	16	17	18	19
20	21	22	23	24	25	26
29	28	29	30	31		

2. New York: Joe DiMaggio sets record, hitting safely in 45 straight games.

4. Mideast: Gen. Catroux proclaims Syrian independence on behalf of Free France (→ 8/17).

6. U.S.S.R.: Soviets slow main German drive, hurling Nazis back near Latvian border (→ 13).

8. Balkans: Germany, Italy announce plans to divide Yugoslavia; Croatia to become "independent" (→ 9/22).

11. Washington: FDR names William Donovan to head new civilian intelligence agency (→ 6/13/42).

13. Britain, U.S.S.R. pledge mutual aid for war effort (→ 16).

13. Las Vegas: William Holden and Brenda Marshall are wed.

16. U.S.S.R.: Germans smash nearer to Leningrad; Soviets report column crushed.→

19. Peru and Ecuador reach accord on border conflict.

19. London: BBC broadcasts to Europe encouraging resistance under slogan, "V for Victory" (→ 9/24).

23. German bombers attack Moscow, killing many (→ 29).

24. Indochina: Vichy yields military bases to Japanese to keep British from gaining full control of Indochina (→ 27).

25. Hyde Park, N.Y.: FDR freezes Japanese assets in U.S. (→ 26).

26. FDR nationalizes Filipino army under command of Gen. Douglas MacArthur (→ 8/4).

27. Japanese troops flood into Cambodia and Thailand under accord with Vichy (→ 10/17).

28. Las Vegas: Judy Garland and David Rose marry.

29. Britain breaks relations with Finland (→ 30).

30. Soviet restores ties with Polish govt. in London exile (→ 8/5).

DEATHS

10. Jelly Roll Morton, jazz pianist, composer (*9/20/1885).

11. Sir Arthur Evans, British archeologist, excavated Knossos (*7/8/1851).

Germans meet slight resistance in Russian drive

German soldiers carry ammunition to a tank during battle on the Eastern Front.

A Soviet tank, hit by German artillery, blackens the air with smoke.

July 16. German troops are battering Soviet forces along most of the Stalin line, and they face little resistance on their march toward Leningrad. The Germans have crossed the Luga River, the last major obstacle protecting the city.

Adolf Hitler is so confident of victory that he held a secret meeting today to discuss the reorganization of the Soviet Union. The Fuhrer's closest collaborators attended, including Martin Bormann and Hermann Goering.

Hitler plans to destroy the spirit of the Communists by razing Moscow and Leningrad and deporting or executing most high-ranking party officials. Russian peasants would work for the "glory of the Reich." And Hitler would exploit the riches of the Crimea and administer the port of Baku, the oil center.

German forces have won their largest victories along the northern and central portions of the Stalin line, the Russian defense perimeter that drops almost vertically from the eastern end of the Gulf of Finland to Odessa on the Black Sea. Finland's attack earlier this week has also put the Russians on the defensive.

German fighter planes cleared a path for the army as it closed in on Novgorod. The city is just 100 miles from Leningrad and 50 miles from the main rail line that connects Leningrad and Moscow.

One German report says that many Russian tanks have been destroyed. And Russian sharp shooters trying to protect their troops are falling like flies from the trees.

To the south, the Germans are scoring more victories after their definitive defeat of the Russians at Bialystock and Minsk, where more than 300,000 soldiers were taken prisoner and thousands of pieces of Russian artillery were captured.

A German news agency says railway stations and bridges have been smashed near Smolensk. Hundreds of trucks and tanks have been destroyed, and more than 200 planes have been shot down or destroyed on the ground.

South of Smolensk, the Russians have counterattacked near Rogachev and driven the Germans back. Resistance to the Germans is the strongest in the Ukraine. German units have been surrounded in their march toward Kiev.

German General Franz Halder is optimistic about an easy victory in Russia. But he does not agree with Hitler's tactics. The Fuhrer wants to delay an attack on Moscow so that he can capture Leningrad and the Caucasus. Halder wants to pursue all three objectives simultaneously (→ 23).

Keeping watch.

Reich soldiers invade a Soviet village, aflame from preparatory bombing. ▷

Guerrilla chief Tito organizes resistance

July 4. Joseph Broz, who calls himself Tito, has emerged as the chief leader of the resistance to the Nazis in Yugoslavia. Tito, who is a Communist, does not have the support of the Yugoslav government-in-exile. But he does have the support of many of his people.

Tito's chief rival, Draja Mikhailovich, is a Serb, resented by many Slavs for his nationalism. The different people of Yugoslavia have never been comfortable living with each other. Tito's strength lies in his support for a Yugoslav federation. His resistance movement is particularly strong in Montenegro, but he has backers all over the country.

Tito, born in Croatia, served in the Red army during Russia's civil war. He was later jailed in Yugoslavia on political charges (→ 8).

U.S. troops take charge of Iceland

July 7. President Roosevelt has informed Congress that U.S naval forces have landed in Iceland to prevent German occupation of the island. The Icelandic government invited the move, which should assure U.S. munitions deliveries to Great Britain. Some congressional members opposed the action, fearing it would lead to further involvement in the European conflict. But most approved, citing the need to clear the seas of the German menace. England applauded FDR's decision as "welcome news" (→ 25).

Whirlaway gallops to horse racing's fourth Triple Crown.

1941

AUGUST

Su	Mo	Tu	We	Th	Fr	Sa
					1	2
3	4	5	6	7	8	9
10	11	12	13	14	15	16
17	18	19	20	21	22	23
24	25	26	27	28	29	30
31						

4. U.S. makes formal commitment to supply arms to Soviets (→ 6).

5. U.S.S.R.: Smolensk falls to Germans (→ 7).

6. Tokyo offers concessions to U.S. demands on China and Indochina in return for end to freeze on Japanese assets (→ 16).

7. U.S.S.R.: Stalin becomes commander-in-chief of Soviet forces (→ 12).

12. U.S.S.R.: Germans push to Black Sea, surround Odessa (→ 16).

12. Vichy: Petain pledges French collaboration in Nazi "new order" in Europe; appoints Adm. Darlan to head Defense Ministry (→ 21).

16. Stalin agrees to Moscow talks with U.S. and Britain (→ 17).

16. Rockland, Maine: FDR declares U.S. is not nearing entry into war (→ 27).

17. Mideast: British and Soviets warn Iran to get rid of excess of German "tourists" (→ 25).

17. London and Moscow sign trade accord (→ 21).

21. France: Vichy arrests 5,000 Jews to be sent to Drancy concentration camp, opened yesterday (→ 10/3).

21. U.S.S.R.: Soviets blow up Dnieper Dam to halt German advance (→ 27).

25. Mideast: Soviet and British troops enter Iran (→ 26).

27. U.S. Sec. of State Cordell Hull warns Japan to leave Pacific open to U.S. shipping (→ 28).

28. Washington: FDR creates seven-member Supply Priorities and Allocations Board to speed arms to Allies (→ 9/4).

29. Berlin: Hitler and Mussolini meet, form plans to counter U.S. aid to Allies.

31. U.S.S.R.: Soviets launch counterattack along Dnieper River (→ 9/4).

DEATH

7. Rabindranath Tagore, Indian poet and playwright, 1913 Nobel Prize (*5/7/1861).

Atlantic Charter issued

Churchill and Roosevelt sit with their delegations aboard the USS Augusta.

Aug 14. President Roosevelt and Prime Minister Churchill, aboard the American cruiser Augusta, issued a joint declaration of "their hopes for a better future for the world," to be called the Atlantic Charter. They made eight points, similar to President Wilson's 14 Points in the Great War.

They agreed to seek no territorial gains and called for no territorial changes without the approval of the peoples concerned, the right of peoples to choose their own forms of government, equal access to trade and raw materials, international economic collaboration, freedom of the seas and abandonment of the use of force.

In the only mention of the war in Europe, the leaders said that "after the final destruction of the Nazi tyranny" they hoped for a peace offering safety and freedom for all. The charter nevertheless seemed to inch the United States of America closer to participation in the war (→ 16).

Smolensk overrun; Nazis cross Dnieper

Aug 27. Joseph Stalin's reorganized army could not stop the Germans' relentless attack on Smolensk. The important rail and industrial center has fallen after three weeks of heavy fighting.

The German army is just 200 miles from Moscow. In two months, it has advanced two thirds of the way from the border to the capital. The Germans used ingenuity and massive firepower to defeat the Russians. They crossed the Dnieper River after launching their attack from a swamp. Then they built a pontoon bridge across the river. Despite the impressive victory, the Germans are having difficulties coordinating their attack up and down the Russian front (→ 31).

British, Russians jointly invade Iran

Aug 26. Imperial British troops and Russian forces launched an attack into Iran at dawn yesterday, gaining 25 miles in two thrusts as the British attacked Iranian ships and bombed several towns. Opposition was reported heavy and Iranian planes are counterattacking.

The two powerful nations informed the government in Tehran, the Iranian capital, that their joint expedition had no designs on the Near Eastern nation but rather was aimed at throwing out German technicians and agents resident in the country. They said that their forces would be removed as soon as the threat of a German invasion, or fifth column operation, has been nullified (→ 9/16).

1941

SEPTEMBER

Su	Mo	Tu	We	Th	Fr	Sa
	1	2	3	4	5	6
7	8	9	10	11	12	13
14	15	16	17	18	19	20
21	22	23	24	25	26	27
28	29	30				

5. U.S.S.R.: Germans shell Leningrad (→ 8).

7. New York: Bobby Riggs beats Frank Kovacs to regain national tennis title at Forest Hills.

8. French Indochina: Ho Chi Minh forms League for the Independence of Vietnam (Viet Minh) (→ 3/27/43).

8. U.S.S.R.: All Volga Germans exiled to Siberia for fear of fifth column activity (→ 21).

9. British, Canadian and Norwegian troops land at Spitzbergen to destroy coal mines Nazis might use for fuel (→ 10).

9. Spain sends division to fight with Germans at Leningrad (→ 9/3/42).

10. Josef Teboven, German Commissar for Norway, invokes martial law in Oslo to quell resistance to Nazi rule (→ 10/4).

12. FDR orders U.S. Navy to shoot first if Axis raiders enter defense zone (→ 20).

16. Iran: Reza Shah Pahlevi abdicates in favor of son Mohammed, as Allied troops reach Tehran (→ 2/26/45).

20. Berlin: Reich holds two American pilots, downed while flying with RAF (→ 10/17).

21. Nazis cut off Crimean Peninsula from U.S.S.R. (→ 10/5).

22. Balkans: Reich tells Bulgaria to enter war or be occupied (→ 11/25).

24. London: French Resistance National Council formed to organize anti-Nazi efforts in Europe (→ 10/21).

24. London: Full adherence to Atlantic Charter pledged by free governments of Belgium, Free France, Czechoslovakia, Greece, Luxembourg, Holland, Norway, Poland, Yugoslavia.

24. Mediterranean: British launch operation Halbert to supply besieged Malta (→ 11/9).

26. New York: Tyrone Power opens in "A Yank in the R.A.F."

29. N.Y.: Museum of Modern Art adds van Gogh's "The Starry Night" to collection.

BIRTH

9. Otis Redding, American singer, soul (*12/10/1967).

Jews in Germany must wear Star of David

Sept 6. The German secret police published an order in the Legal Gazette today which will become effective September 19. It says in its first paragraph: "Jews who have completed their sixth year are forbidden to show themselves in public without the Jewish star. This consists of a six-pointed star, outlined with black superscription, 'Jew.' It must be worn visibly and firmly sewed to the left breast of clothing."

The order also says that Jews are not allowed to leave the area in which they reside without police permission. In addition, it proscribes a fine of 150 marks or six weeks' imprisonment for violation of the new regulations, and it covers the entire Reich as well as the protectorate of Bohemia and Moravia.

This latest action is the sharpest official measure against Jews since those introduced following the anti-Semitic outbreaks of November 9, 1938. And these regulations clear the way for further persecution.

Branded with their faith.

Unidentified sub bombs U.S. warship

Sept 4. The first attack on an American warship in the European war occurred this morning as the USS Greer was fired on by a submarine of unknown nationality in the North Atlantic near Iceland. The Greer suffered no damage and responded to the underwater torpedo assault by dropping depth charges. It is not known if the submarine, which is assumed to be German, was hit. This assumption stems from Germany's bitter reaction toward U.S. occupation of Iceland, a move authorized by President Roosevelt earlier this summer.

Washington issued no statements about the event, but Great Britain received the news with excitement and little surprise; Britons expected such attacks after American intervention in Iceland (→ 20).

Nazis encircle Leningrad; Hitler plans to starve city to death

Sept 4. Germany says it has tightened the noose around Leningrad. Troops are closing in on the city from the south, west and east, and the Finns are descending from the north along the Karelian Isthmus.

Officials in Berlin say it is unlikely that Adolf Hitler will order his soldiers to storm the city. Instead, one report says, he plans to starve the city's residents to death.

The Germans effectively surrounded Leningrad when troops which had captured Novgorod advanced north along the Volkhov Valley. They cut important rail lines, including the one to Murmansk, as they approached Schluesselburg. Russians tried to escape in boats on Lake Lagoda and the Neva River, and some of them were sunk.

From the west, the Germans advanced to Pushkino. And they overran Luga as they approached from the southwest.

In the central sector of the war, the Germans face furious Russian resistance. But the Russians are running out of new tanks. Many of their tanks are old, and they are relying instead on farm tractors.

On the southern front, the Germans seem to be facing enormous difficulties overcoming opposition in the Ukraine. The city of Odessa is still holding out (→ 5).

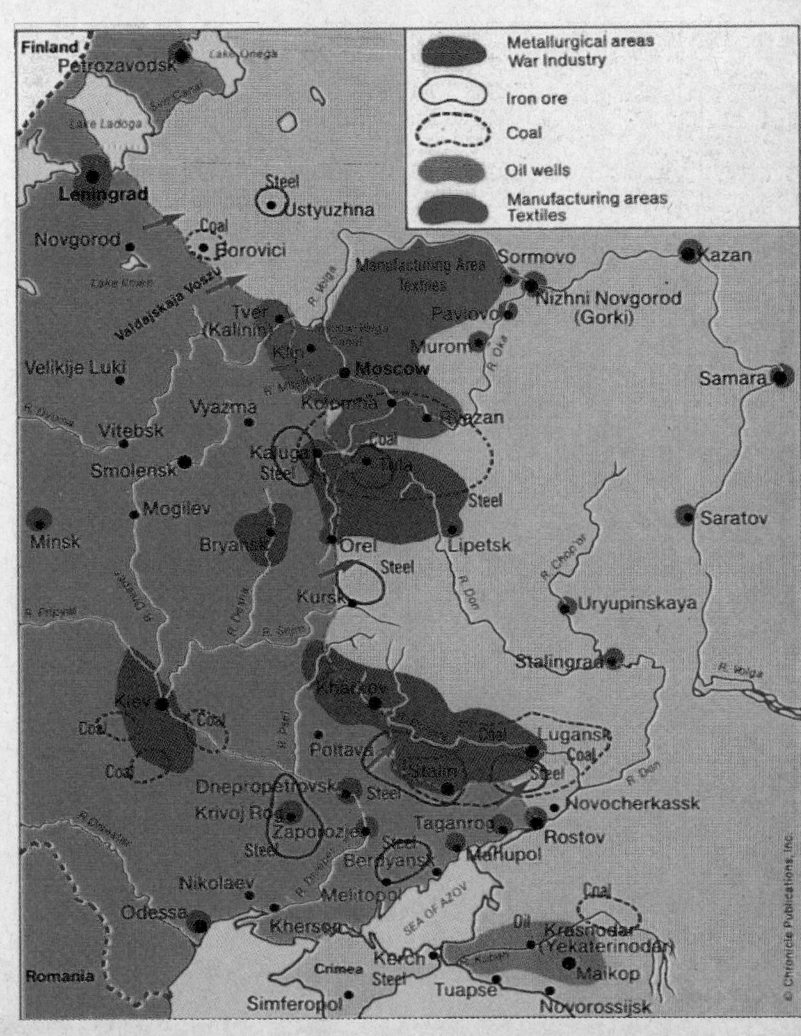

1941

OCTOBER

Su	Mo	Tu	We	Th	Fr	Sa
			1	2	3	4
5	6	7	8	9	10	11
12	13	14	15	16	17	18
19	20	21	22	23	24	25
26	27	28	29	30	31	

1. Chinese troops repel Japanese offensive at Changla (→ 4/28/43).

2. Berlin: Nazis execute Czech Premier Alois Elias.

3. Paris: Six synagogues blown up (→ 16).

4. Nazis warn Norwegian people to comply with rules under occupation or face starvation (→ 2/1/42).

5. U.S.S.R.: Red army continues strong counterattacks in Ukraine and Leningrad; claims losses at 1.1 million to Nazi's three million (→ 10).

10. Michigan: Tank output crippled by inter-union struggle as C.I.O. refuses to handle parts made by A.F.L. (→ 27).

10. U.S.S.R.: Soviets halt Nazi drive on Moscow (→ 16).

11. Washington: It is reported 2,000 Japanese will be evacuated from West Coast (→ 1/14/42).

16. U.S.S.R.: German troops take Odessa on Black Sea (→ 20).

16. France: Vichy sentences Leon Blum, Edouard Daladier, Georges Mandel, Paul Reynaud and Maurice Gamelin to life imprisonment (→ 2/19/42).

17. U.S.S. Kearney hit by torpedo off Iceland coast (→ 30).

21. Nantes: 50 French hostages slain in reprisal for assassination of German officer (→ 23).

23. "Dumbo," Disney's latest, opens in New York.

23. London: De Gaulle asks resistance to halt assassinations to protect French people from reprisals (→ 7/18/42).

25. U.S.S.R.: Kharkov falls to Germans (→ 11/13).

27. Washington: U.A.W. Pres. John L. Lewis rejects FDR's mediation, calls strike in "captive mines" (→ 11/10).

30. Washington: FDR offers $1 bil. in supplies to Soviets (→ 11/3).

BIRTH

8. Jesse Jackson, black politician, civil rights leader.

DEATH

5. Louis Brandeis, U.S. Supreme Court justice (*11/13/1856).

State of siege in Moscow

Reich heavy artillery shells Soviet positions outside of Moscow.

Oct 20. Residents of Moscow are in a state of panic as the Germans approach. Joseph Stalin has placed the city under a state of siege, despite the fact that the weather and mud are halting the German attack.

The Soviet leader also commanded civilian workers in the capital to assist the beleaguered army. Stalin told them to "keep calm and orderly and to render the Red army defending Moscow all possible help."

Stalin's order followed a warning in Izvestia. "It would be very wrong and foolish," the official government newspaper said, "to close one's eyes to the danger menacing the country. The Bolsheviks have always faced peril courageously, no matter how great. The present stage of the war involves the life and death of the peoples of the Soviet Union."

Stalin has moved his government out of Moscow and installed it in Kuibyshev, on the Volga River.

The way Adolf Hitler's spokesman describes it, the Russians are surrounded and the war is almost over. Dr. Otto Dietrich says the armies trying to defend Moscow are powerless against "Operation Typhoon." He also claims the Germans have routed the Russian armies in the south and at Leningrad. This statement was not only sensational but surprising. The Germans have been reticient to provide much detail on the war in Russia.

It is true that Kiev and Odessa have both been captured. But the Russians say the Germans have lost three million men. And they are now digging in around Moscow, ready to fight to the death (→ 25).

Two American destroyers hit, one sunk

Oct 30. Tragedy struck the United States Navy tonight as it lost its first warship in the battle of the Atlantic when Germany torpedoed and sunk the USS Reuben James. According to the Navy Department, the battleship was on convoy duty west of Iceland. Forty-four members of the crew were rescued, but the fate of the remaining 76 officers and crewmen is unknown.

This third attack on American warships has stirred passions in Washington, especially in Congress. Earlier this month, the USS Kearney survived a torpedo assault that killed 11, and last month bombs narrowly missed the Greer.

President Roosevelt, appearing before the press wearing a black armband, maintained that these disasters will not mean a break in United States-German diplomatic relations. From all indications, however, they will mean a further strengthening of Anglo-American ties. The United States has moved a long way from neutrality (→ 11/3).

Konoye resigns to be replaced by Tojo

Oct 17. A governmental crisis has Tokyo in political chaos as Premier Fumimaro Konoye and his third Cabinet resigned en bloc last night. The resignations underscore the division of the Japanese concerning international events. There are two schools of thought: one believes Japan should reach agreements with the United States; the other espouses the need to stay allied with Germany and the Axis powers.

Emperor Hirohito accepted Konoye's decision and designated General Tojo, the War Minister, to head a new government. To America, the transformation holds threatening possibilities as Konoye was much more receptive to Washington than Tojo has ever been (→ 11/3).

Bogart stars in The Maltese Falcon

Bogie, Lorre, Astor and Greenstreet.

Oct 3. It's like this, see. "The Maltese Falcon" opens. Stars Humphrey Bogart as Sam Spade, private eye. Helps some dame find a statuette. John Huston's first directing job. Mystery thriller. Check it out.

Joe DiMaggio hit safely in a record 56 straight games this year.

1941

NOVEMBER

Su	Mo	Tu	We	Th	Fr	Sa
						1
2	3	4	5	6	7	8
9	10	11	12	13	14	15
16	17	18	19	20	21	22
23	24	25	26	27	28	29
30						

3. Tokyo: U.S. Ambassador Joseph Grew cables Washington, warning of possible secret attack on U.S. positions (→ 10).

6. Soviets appoint Maxim Litvinov ambassador to U.S.

9. Mediterranean: Two Italian convoys wiped out by British navy (→ 4/16/42).

10. A.F.L. bars naval strike in San Diego (→ 11).

10. London: Churchill promises to join U.S. "within the hour" in case of war with Japan (→ 17).

11. Washington: C.I.O. men Murray and Kennedy quit wartime labor board (→ 16).

13. U.S.S.R.: Germans and Rumanians win Sevastopol battle with Red army (→ 17).

16. Five million C.I.O. members pledge solidarity with Lewis and "captive" mine strikers (→ 21).

17. U.S.S.R.: Soviets make gains in severe cold proving fatal to German troops (→ 1/7/42).

17. Washington: Japanese Ambassador Nomura begins talks with State Department (→ 26).

19. North Africa: British attack 130-mile Libyan line (→ 25).

19. Pacific: Australian cruiser Sydney sunk by German raider disguised as Dutch merchant ship (→ 1/2/42).

21. Edenborn, Penn.: 12 striking miners shot in riots (→ 22).

22. Washington: Lewis ends coal strike, submits dispute to arbitration (→ 3/24/42).

23. U.S. troops move into Dutch Guiana to guard bauxite mines.

25. North Africa: British take Gambut, major Axis supply base in Libya (→ 28).

25. Nanking Chinese and Bulgarians join Axis (→ 6/13/42).

26. Pacific: Japanese carrier force leaves base, moving east (→ 29).

26. Lebanon declares independence from French mandate.

28. North Africa: Italians surrender Gondar, last outpost of their African empire (→ 30).

29. Philadelphia: Navy defeats Army 14-6 in football.

British attack in Libya cuts supply route

Axis troops move slowly across the extraterrestrial landscape of Libya's desert.

Nov 30. British forces have sweated their way across hundreds of miles of Libyan desert and managed to cut a key Axis supply route. The British succeeded in arriving at the Gulf of Sidra, midway between Benghazi to the north and Ajedabia to the south.

The British attack sliced the important coastal route which snakes for hundreds of miles south and west from Benghazi all the way to Tripoli. Supplies had already started to thin out after the sinking of many Italian ships in the Mediterranean. The British advance may also succeed in bottling up the Axis forces that are fighting further east in Cyrenaica.

Another British force is holed up in a desert oasis 140 miles southeast of Ajedabia. It is ready and waiting to do battle with German Field Marshal Erwin Rommel.

In the major Libyan combat theater, the British are holding their own near the besieged city of Tobruk. Earlier this month, they managed to drive a wedge between German troops south of the city.

The recent British successes are creating new concerns for Rommel. The unpredictable "Desert Fox" thought it would be easy to defeat the British generals, who occasionally seem to prefer afternoon tea to combat in the desert. Today, Rommel is on the defensive (→ 1/2/42).

British carrier sunk by Italian torpedo

Nov 13. An Italian submarine torpedoed and sunk the British aircraft carrier Ark Royal 25 miles off the coast of Gibraltar, A.V. Alexander, First Lord of the Admiralty, announced today. Eighteen crewmen are reported missing, however hope remains that many of them were rescued by other British ships in the area which have not yet come to port. Because the Ark Royal could not unload her aircraft, it is thought that all 70 planes, torpedo-carriers, dive-bombers and reconnaissance planes plummeted to the ocean floor as well.

After two years of numerous rumors that German and Italian naval units had sunk the Ark Royal, creating a legend about the carrier, finally the Axis powers have succeeded. It is indeed a big blow for the British naval forces operating in the Mediterranean Sea; the planes based on the Ark Royal have destroyed over 100 German and Italian aircraft since 1938. The absence of the British ship will probably allow easier access for the Fascists to deliver arms and men to Libya.

One British lieutenant on board a sister ship witnessed the explosive hit and subsequent chaos as Ark Royal crewmen jumped ship. He remarked quietly, "That's the saddest thing I have ever seen" (→ 19).

As U.S. and Japan talk, Churchill promises British support

Nov 29. Tensions are mounting between the United States and Japan, as talks between representatives of each nation seem to be deteriorating. American leaders have cut trade agreements with the Japanese to protest Japan's aggressive expansion in French Indochina. Secretary of State Cordell Hull has offered proposals to Japanese Premier Hideki Tojo to end the hostilities. But Tojo has thus far failed to respond to these overtures.

Earlier this month, Tojo assailed American and British "exploitation" of Asiatic peoples, saying they must be "purged with vengeance." The violent rhetoric spurred British leader Winston Churchill to declare that if Japan and America go to war, Britain will quickly support the United States (→ 12/1).

Japanese division in China turns eastward to present arms to Emperor Hirohito.

1941

DECEMBER

Su	Mo	Tu	We	Th	Fr	Sa
	1	2	3	4	5	6
7	8	9	10	11	12	13
14	15	16	17	18	19	20
21	22	23	24	25	26	27
28	29	30	31			

1. Tokyo: Tojo rejects U.S. proposals for Pacific settlement as "fantastic" and "unrealistic" (→ 6).

1. Pacific: British declare state of emergence in Malaya following reports of Japanese attack (→ 7).

6. FDR issues personal appeal to Emperor Hirohito to use influence to avoid war (→ 7).

7. Pacific: Japanese planes raid Pearl Harbor in surprise attack (→ 8).

8. U.S. declares war on Japan (→ 9).

9. FDR tells Americans to prepare for long war "which we are going to win" (→ 10).

10. Pacific: Japanese troops invade Filipino island of Luzon (→ 13).

11. U.S. declares war on Italy and Germany (→ 1/30/42).

13. Pacific: U.S. troops pound Japanese on Luzon (→ 23).

19. China: Japanese land in Hong Kong, clash with British (→ 25).

22. Churchill arrives in Washington to discuss war effort (→ 5/26/42).

23. Pacific: Wake Island capitulates to Japanese (→ 31).

25. Free French occupy French Islands of St. Pierre and Miquelon off Canadian coast.

31. Pacific: MacArthur reports U.S. lines in Manila pushed back by Japanese.→

CUTURAL EVENTS, 1941

Literature: Fitzgerald's "The Last Tycoon"; Ilya Ehrenburg's "The Storm"; William Shirer's "Berlin Diary."

Music: Benjamin Britten's "Violin Concerto"; "Chattanooga Choo-Choo."

The Arts: Edward Hopper's "Nighthawks"; Paul Nash's "Bombers over Berlin"; Natl. Art Gallery in Washington.

Film: "The Two-Faced Woman," with Greta Garbo; Orson Welles' "Citizen Kane"; Hitchcock's "Suspicion"; the Marx Brothers' "The Big Store"; John Ford's "How Green Was My Valley," Academy Award.

Debacle befalls Germans at Moscow

Snow, cold and Soviet determination have stopped the Nazi blitzkrieg dead.

Dec 5. German forces that had advanced within 20 miles of Moscow have fallen back under a determined Russian counterattack. The tide turned when the Russians recaptured Kalinin, northwest of the capital. This mean war of attrition is not over, but the Russians have stopped the Nazis, and winter is on their side.

Only Adolf Hitler and his closest confidantes believed in the final assault. Hitler disregarded reports from the field that tanks were trapped in mud and soldiers were freezing in the bitter cold.

"It would be inconceivable," General Fedor von Bock dared tell Berlin, "that anyone could reasonably hope to have this operation succeed after our serious losses and our lack of officers."

But Hitler refused to listen, just as he refused to listen earlier this year when his generals in the field counseled him to make a lightning strike on Moscow. The Fuhrer vacillated and sent troops north to Leningrad and south to the Crimea.

Once Leningrad was under siege, the Russians fought back ferociously, preventing many of the German troops from joining the belated assault on Moscow.

Outside the capital, Russian troops under the command of General Georgi Khukov dug in with new weapons. They were given a new tank, the T-34, and a more powerful mortar, the Katyusha. The Russian air force zeroed in on the Luftwaffe's pilots, who were far from home and short on fuel.

Hitler is blaming his defeat on the cold, but the Russians are fighting in the same battle conditions. The Fuhrer, by ignoring his generals, has destroyed the spirit of his troops. They are hungry, exhausted and spread out over hundreds of miles of Russian territory.

Hitler's hated Gestapo have also given the Russians an enemy worth fighting against. They are appalled by the secret police, who execute Communist Party officials without trials and ship peasants back to Germany to serve as slave labor for the Nazis.

Russian partisans are creating havoc behind German lines, and Russian citizens have heeded Joseph Stalin's order to join the battle. Outside Moscow, civilians have been seen using their bare hands to dig ditches to keep the Russian tanks out.

Hitler is fuming at the new setback and he is likely to take reprisals against his generals. It was just two months ago that he announced Russia had been "struck down and will never rise again."

Britain declares war on three countries

Dec 6. Britain has declared war on Finland, Rumania and Hungary because no satisfactory replies have been received to ultimatums sent a week ago demanding their cessation of hostilities against Russia.

Rumania and Hungary are regarded as Axis puppets, but the case of Finland is special because of her long fight to remain independent of the Axis, and her friendship with the United States. By June, however, German troops had moved into that country. Eight days before Germany marched on Russia, Britain extended her blockade to include Finland, and diplomatic relations were severed in July. Soviet pressure on Britain to declare war on Finland brought a British warning that if she continued hostilities against Russia, she would be regarded as a British enemy.

Although by this week the Russians had virtually withdrawn from Finland, rendering such hostilities impossible, on November 25 Finland signed the anti-Comintern Pact in Berlin with Rumania, Hungary and others, which led the British government to issue the ultimatums.

British Hong Kong garrison gives up

Dec 25. It is an unhappy Christmas for British troops and civilians in Hong Kong. After several years of uncertainty and several weeks on the run, the British surrendered tonight to the Japanese. Threatened earlier in the month by the approach of 38 Japanese divisions, Governor Mark Young ordered the garrison to retreat to Kowloon. The Japanese infiltrated the city and bombed it intensely. This evening, Sir Mark surrendered to General Sakai.

Japanese devastate U.S. base at Pearl Harbor

December. Tragically, amid burning battleships, painfully wounded soldiers and unrecognizable corpses, America is at war.

On December 7, some 360 Japanese warplanes reached the Hawaiian Islands and pulverized the American military base at Pearl Harbor; thousands died or were wounded. And now, at month's end, the United States is violently engaged in a worldwide war, determined to emerge victorious. As President Roosevelt said the day after the deadly and explosive assault: "America was suddenly and deliberately attacked by naval and air forces of the Empire of Japan. We will gain the inevitable triumph, so help us God."

War was immediately declared on Japan after the Pearl Harbor raid with only one dissenting vote in Congress, that of Jeannette Rankin, Republican Representative from Montana. Thunderous applause interrupted the president's address in Congress as he assailed the Japanese onslaught and remarked that December 7, 1941, is a date "which will live in infamy." On the 11th, America's leaders voted to declare war on Japan's Axis partners, Italy and Germany, to "insure a world victory of the forces of justice and righteousness over the forces of savagery and barbarism."

Japan had apparently been planning the surprise assault on the Hawaiian Islands for quite some time, while pretending to negotiate with the United States over trade agreements and the recent Japanese expansion in French Indochina.

With assurances from Premier Hideki Tojo that "there is nothing to fear in this war" and that East Asia "depends on this fight," six aircraft carriers, with support from submarines and battleships and under the direction of Vice Admiral Chuichi Naguma, secretly left the Kurile Islands—destination: Honolulu and war. After 12 days, Tojo's bombers swarmed over their target.

Within two hours of unremitting attack, the Japanese planes had sunk or seriously damaged eight U.S. battleships, including the great Arizona and 14 smaller ships, obliterated 200 aircraft, killed over 2,000 seamen and almost 400 other people and wounded another 1,300. Americans are still stunned.

Tokyo's forces escaped the dramatic raid virtually unscathed; they suffered fewer than 100 casualties, lost only 29 planes and five midget submarines. The military maneuver will be regarded in Japanese history as a tremendous tactical success.

The USS West Virginia and the USS Tennessee destroyed at Pearl Harbor.

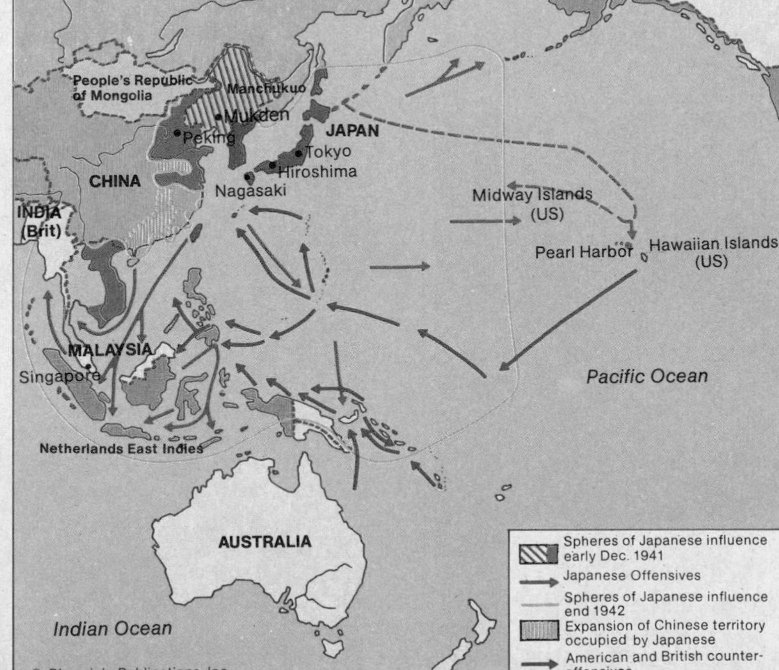

The Pacific theater.

President Roosevelt has admitted the Axis powers pulled off an amazing victory and insinuated that Germany and Italy were informed of Japanese intentions prior to the assault. FDR said, "Our enemies have performed a brilliant feat of deception, perfectly timed and executed with great skill." Yet, the president put to rest claims that the Pearl Harbor tragedy has given the Japanese supremacy in the Pacific.

It seems the strategy of the Japanese leaders is to neutralize the U.S. Pacific Fleet so as to initiate offensives throughout the Pacific. On the 10th, as American forces tried to reorganize, various Japanese divisions invaded Malaya, Hong Kong and the northern Philippines. U.S. forces were able to hit several invading planes, but as one soldier said after the battle, "Next time we'll do better, we'll give 'em hell."

American and Filipino ground forces in the Philippines total about 130,000 and are led by General Douglas MacArthur. He and his men are hopeful they can hold off the Japanese until the U.S. Fifth Fleet arrives for support.

While the war rages in both the European and Pacific theaters, many observers are trying to assess the Japanese victory and subsequent offensives. One question remains unanswered: With the violent breakdown of American-Japanese relations last month and the alarm which catapulted American troops all over the world on alert, how could the most powerful military nation in the world leave such a vast, valuable collection of ships, planes and crews so vulnerable?

Presently, no military officials are being blamed for the horror of December 7, but President Roosevelt is taking steps to gather more information. A few things are certain: the entrance of this nation into the war was caused by the devastation at Pearl Harbor, and public opinion backs the war declaration. Without the massive, tragic attack, U.S. involvement may have been resisted. Now, Americans are rallying around the flag (→ 1/24/42).

FDR signs the U.S. into the war.

1942

JANUARY

Su	Mo	Tu	We	Th	Fr	Sa
				1	2	3
4	5	6	7	8	9	10
11	12	13	14	15	16	17
18	19	20	21	22	23	24
25	26	27	28	29	30	31

1. Washington: 26 countries issue Declaration of the United Nations, affirming cooperation against Axis.

2. Pacific: Japanese troops take Manila (→ 4).

2. Libya: Bardia captured by South African troops (→ 21).

4. Pacific: British pull out of Singapore and Borneo (→ 11).

7. FDR submits biggest U.S. budget of all time—$59 bil., with $52 bil. for war (→ 16).

7. U.S.S.R.: Russians raid German troops at Sevastopol; Nazis are losing Crimea (→ 27).

11. Pacific: Japan invades Dutch East Indies at Borneo (→ 18).

14. FDR orders all U.S. aliens to register with govt. (→ 2/20).

15. Rio de Janeiro: 21 American nations resolve to break relations with the Axis (→ 3/11).

16. Jawaharlal Nehru succeeds Gandhi as head of Indian Natl. Congress (→ 3/29).

16. U.S.: War Production Board takes place of Office of Production Management (→ 22).

17. Las Vegas: 22 dead in TWA wreck; actress Carol Lombard and mother perish.

18. Pacific: General MacArthur repels Japanese in Bataan (→ 31).

20. Rogers Hornsby named to Baseball Hall of Fame.

21. North Africa: Rommel launches drive to push British eastward (→ 29).

26. American Expeditionary Force, thousands strong, lands in Northern Ireland; first since WWI (→ 30).

27. U.S.S.R.: Nazis refuse trains to survivors of 8th Italian Army pulling out of Russia (→ 3/1).

29. Libya: German and Italian troops take Benghazi (→ 4/3).

29. Office of Civil Defense established in U.S.

30. U.S.: Emergency Price Control Act allows OPA to place ceilings on prices and rents (→ 2/9).

BIRTH

17. Muhammad Ali, American boxer, first to win title three times, born Cassius Clay.

Nazis fix Final Solution

The tribulations of Jews at Auschwitz: forced labor or the gas chamber.

Jan 20. Nazi leaders met in Berlin to discuss the fate of Jews in Germany and occupied territories. Led by Reinhard Heydrich, who is called the "Hangman of Europe," the officials called their program the "final solution." It amounts to extermination and genocide.

Hundreds of thousands of Jews are believed to have been murdered by the Nazis. Adolf Hitler and his deputies say death is the only fate deserved by the "Untermenschen," or so-called sub-humans.

Many of the Jews are simply rounded up and killed like cattle in concentration camps. On the Eastern Front, Jews are treated like slaves to build new roads. German Jews who are 65 and older are sent to a special camp at Theresienstadt, along with Jews who are wounded or decorated war veterans. Men and women with only one Jewish parent may be spared from death. They are to be sterilized (→ 3/17).

Gutzon Borglum was chosen 15 years ago to carve Mt. Rushmore. And now, Presidents Washington, Jefferson, Lincoln and Teddy Roosevelt are perched in the Black Hills of South Dakota, as a monument to the United States of America's founding, philosophy, unity and expansion.

Japanese forces move into Manila

Jan 31. In the Philippines, the Japanese navy and air force are battering American and Filipino forces. General MacArthur has been forced to withdraw from Manila, but Japan's General Homma has not been able to claim a total victory. His navy cannot move into Manila Bay because MacArthur's tenacious defenders are holding the island fortress of Corregidor, and they are setting up new defense lines across the bay from Manila, on the Bataan Peninsula.

The United States is clearly worried by the Japanese advances. As Major General Jonathan Wainwright put it, "The rat was in the house, and it was no comfort."

It will be difficult for the Japanese to take Corregidor and Bataan, but their blockade of Manila is creating extraordinary problems for MacArthur. Many of his soldiers are sick and starving (→ 2/1).

Pearl Harbor probe condemns officers

Jan 24. A special presidential committee said today that high-ranking officers of the United States failed to take adequate steps to defend Pearl Harbor against the Japanese attack on December 7.

The panel, headed by Associate Justice Owen J. Roberts, said in a report to President Roosevelt that Admiral Husband E. Kimmel and Lt. General Walter C. Short had been warned by their superiors in Washington that an attack was imminent and to prepare for anything. The warnings had been sounded by General George C. Marshall, the Army chief of staff, and by Secretary of State Cordell Hull, who had alerted the secretaries of the Navy and War of the likely attack. Japanese planes, according to the report, had been heard approaching Pearl Harbor an hour before the attack.

American troops in Northern Ireland

Jan. 30. "An impressive vanguard of American military might," is how Sir Archibald Sinclair, British Air Secretary, described the landing of U.S. troops in Northern Ireland. Several thousand members of the American Expeditionary Force will guard against possible Axis aggression. Recent German air flights over the British isle have alerted the watchful eyes of the royal air force and prompted the arrival of American soldiers.

"There has been some enemy activity. Air defenses went into action," reported an RAF officer. However, no bombs have yet been dropped, leading most to believe the flights have been reconnaissance ventures. As Americans landed, Prime Minister Eamon de Valera of Southern Ireland is still demanding abolition of the border between the two parts of Ireland and also wants U.S. protection (→ 2/13).

FDR asks for biggest of budgets

Jan 22. President Roosevelt has asked Congress to raise taxes to finance the largest proposed budget in the nation's history. Of the nearly $59 billion in expenditures, about $53 billion would be earmarked for the war effort.

To help finance this huge wartime budget, the president recommended new taxes of at least $9 billion, and $2 billion increases in payments to Social Security. While he did not specify new tax levies, he suggested payroll and excise taxes, as well as higher corporate and income taxes. He reiterated his opposition to a national sales tax but left the door open, saying that "in the face of the present financial and economic situation . . . we may later be compelled to reconsider the temporary necessity of such measures."

Even with new taxes, the national debt will reach $110 billion, the president said. But he added that he was not alarmed by this figure, explaining that it could be reduced rapidly after the war. Immediate action now on his requests, he said, could head off a postwar depression (→ 30).

1942

FEBRUARY

Su	Mo	Tu	We	Th	Fr	Sa
1	2	3	4	5	6	7
8	9	10	11	12	13	14
15	16	17	18	19	20	21
22	23	24	25	26	27	28

1. Malaya: British begin withdrawal to Singapore (→ 8).

1. U.S. Pacific fleet batters Japanese bases in Marshall and Gilbert Islands (→ 8).

7. Germany: Albert Speer becomes Minister of Munitions upon Todt's death.

8. Pacific: Japanese land on Singapore (→ 14).

9. U.S. clocks turned one hour ahead for Daylight Savings Time (→ 10).

9. India: Chiang Kai-shek meets with Sir Stafford Cripps, British viceroy in India.

10. U.S.: War halts civilian car production at Ford (→ 3/14).

13. Germans kill operation Sea Lion —plan to invade Great Britain (→ 3/3).

14. Pacific: Japanese parachutists attack Sumatra (→ 15).

16. Tokyo: Tojo outlines Japan's war aims to Diet, referring to "new order of coexistence" on ethical principles in East Asia (→ 19).

19. France: Leon Blum, Edouard Daladier and General Gamelin, accused of responsibility in 1940 defeat, go on trial before Vichy govt. (→ 6/22).

19. Pacific: Port Darwin, on Australia's northern coast, bombed by Japanese (→ 20).

20. FDR authorizes internment of Japanese Americans on West Coast (→ 3/3).

20. Pacific: Lt. Edward O'Hare downs five out of nine Japanese bombers attacking aircraft carrier Lexington, earns Congressional Medal of Honor (→ 3/1).

23. San Francisco: First Axis bombs fall on U.S. mainland, at California oil field.

24. Ankara: German Ambassador Franz von Papen escapes assassination attempt.

BIRTH

5. Roger Staubach, American pro football quarterback.

DEATH

12. Grant Wood, painter of American Midwest (*2/13/1891).

Japanese take Singapore

Feb 15. The two-week siege of Singapore ended this evening. Britain's General Percival surrendered unconditionally to the Japanese, and the Allies lost control of a major waterway on the sea route which connects Europe and Asia.

Two months ago, Singapore was considered impregnable. But the Japanese air force was invincible in the skies over Malaya. And the British miscalculated badly when they assumed the jungle north of Singapore would provide them adequate protection. It didn't. Instead, it provided cover for the advancing Japanese army.

Japanese soldiers poured down the Malay Peninsula from Thailand on bicycles. They used small boats to navigate rivers and streams and land behind British positions. And they learned to live off the land while the British were always scrambling for supplies. The Japanese have taught the Allies a lesson. If they are to win this war, they must master the jungle (→ 16).

British soldiers are held by invading Japanese troops in Singapore.

Normandie burns at dock in New York

Feb 9. The most beautiful liner in the world is now a wreck. A fire broke out shortly after 2:30 this afternoon. The blaze is attributed to the sparks from a workman's torch. The French liner Normandie was built in 1935. In 1937, it held the Atlantic record, covering her 2,936-mile course in three days, 22 hours and seven minutes. Immobilized in New York since August 1939, the ship was requisitioned in December 1941 by the U.S. for conversion into a naval auxiliary.

The Normandie goes up in flames in New York harbor.

▷

Zweigs kill selves in despair over war

Feb 23. Stefan Zweig, author of numerous historical novels, committed suicide this morning with his wife. The couple were found in their Brazilian home, lying on their bed with their arms around each other. A bottle of poison stood on the bedstand. Zweig left several letters for friends and instructions for publishing remaining manuscripts.

Zweig was despondent over conditions in his native Austria. His works were burned by the Nazis on public pyres before he fled. The Nazis objected to his use of the truth in biographies about Sigmund Freud and Franz Mesmer. Zweig wrote a play called "Jeremiah" in 1939, about a prophet dishonored in his country during wartime.

Quisling is named Norway chief again

Feb 1. Vidkun Quisling has been renamed the Premier of Norway much to the delight of Norwegian Nazis and to the distaste of other countrymen. It was Quisling who left the Agrarian Party to establish the Fascist National Unity Party, and in 1940 he assisted the German preparation for the conquest of Norway on April 9.

His collaboration with Adolf Hitler produced contempt in many Allied leaders, including Prime Minister Winston Churchill who coined the word "quisling" to refer to traitors in his speech at St. James's Palace. "A vile race of quislings—to use the new word which will carry the scorn of mankind down through the centuries," he said in condemning those who collaborated with Nazism in Norway (→ 4/5).

Ronald Reagan's performance in "King's Row" shows the former sportscaster has lots of potential.

1942

MARCH

Su	Mo	Tu	We	Th	Fr	Sa
1	2	3	4	5	6	7
8	9	10	11	12	13	14
15	16	17	18	19	20	21
22	23	24	25	26	27	28
29	30	31				

1. Pacific: Japanese troops land on Java (→ 7).

1. Soviets launch counterattack in Crimea; German losses now total 1.5 million (→ 4/5).

3. New York: Exhibition "Artists in Exile" with paintings of Breton, Zadkine, Ernst, Tanguy, Chagall and Leger.

3. British RAF raids industrial suburbs of Paris (→ 4/24).

3. Madagascar: British raid Vichy base Diego Suarez (→ 5/4).

7. Pacific: Japanese troops land in New Guinea (→ 8).

7. Reich decrees Belgians may be deported to Germany to allay labor shortage.

8. Pacific: Allies capitulate to Japanese at Java, surrender 100,000 troops (→ 12).

11. Brazil confiscates Axis property in reprisal for sinking of merchant ships (→ 6/1).

14. Washington: FDR asks governors to set speed limits at 40 mph to conserve tires (→ 18).

17. Gen. Douglas MacArthur becomes Supreme Commander of United Nations forces in Southwestern Pacific (→ 4/1).

17. Nazis begin deporting Poles to Belsen camp (→ 26).

18. Washington: Third military draft begins (→ 4/14).

24. Washington: C.I.O. and A.F.L. concede premium pay for weekends and holidays (→ 26).

26. Washington: Congress gets labor's vow to ban all strikes while war is on (→ 7/16).

26. Nazis begin sending Jews to Auschwitz in Poland (→ 3/13/43).

28. France: Resistance leaders found Francs-tireurs and Partisans (FTP).

29. London: Britain offers dominion status to India after war if she cooperates now (→ 4/11).

BIRTH

2. John Irving, American novelist, "The World According to Garp."

25. Aretha Franklin, American vocalist, soul.

Philippines are captured

U.S. troops taken captive on Bataan wait to be marched off to prison camps.

March 12. Realizing that the Philippines were falling into the Axis orbit, President Roosevelt has ordered General Douglas MacArthur to leave the islands where he futilely defended Allied territory against the Japanese. Most Americans concurred with Roosevelt's decision, as Japan has concentrated great strength in the area.

MacArthur will be transferred to Australia, where he will take command of the Allied forces in the Pacific theater. On leaving the island of Baatan, the charismatic general promised the Filipino people continued American support. He said, in fact, "I shall return" (→ 17).

British raid St. Nazaire, Nazi sub base

March 27. British commandos wrecked a key Nazi port and submarine base at St. Nazaire, France, late tonight. They stormed ashore from the HMS Campbeltown, which had broken through harbor defenses and rammed the main dock. As soon as the commandos jumped overboard, five tons of explosives in the belly of the ship exploded. The royal navy mounted the operation after two German battlecruisers slipped through the Allied blockade and made it all the way to Norway. The French resistance played a major role at St. Nazaire (→ 28).

Some British soldiers were captured trying to land at St. Nazaire.

U.S. interns 100,000 Japanese-Americans

Under Army guard, Seattle's Japanese are herded off to camps in California.

March 3. In compliance with a presidential order, an area of about a quarter of a million miles of the West Coast was designated as an evacuation area from which all those of Japanese descent will be required to move.

While defining the area, Lt. General John L. DeWitt, the Western defense commander, did not order an immediate mass evacuation, saying that such a move was "impractical." However, he left no doubt that all those of Japanese descent, including American citizens, will be forced to move out eventually. The order will affect an estimated 100,000 persons.

The evacuation area, almost as large as the entire Empire of Japan, stretches for 2,000 miles, embracing-about two-fifths of the state of Oregon, two-thirds of Washington state, parts of southern Arizona and more than half of the state of California.

In announcing the creation of the military zone, General DeWitt said that those persons affected would gain "considerable advantage" by moving out of the area now and "in all probability will not again be disturbed."

British start heavy raids on German cities

Lubeck Cathedral, hit by bombs.

March 28. Britain's Bomber Command launched a devastating attack tonight on the German city of Lubeck. From the air, most of the Baltic seaport seemed to be in flames. Damage was heavy. More than a thousand buildings were destroyed, many of them homes.

The bombardment could be part of a new British campaign against entire areas of German cities. Many civilians are believed to be among the hundreds killed in the attack.

Germany is trying to play down the effectiveness of the nighttime raid, but it represented a psychological and strategic success for the British. Most of the iron ore imported by Germany from Scandinavia passes through Lubeck.

Hitler is furiously demanding that the Luftwaffe punish Britain by striking its historic cities (→ 4/29).

1942

APRIL

Su	Mo	Tu	We	Th	Fr	Sa
			1	2	3	4
5	6	7	8	9	10	11
12	13	14	15	16	17	18
19	20	21	22	23	24	25
26	27	28	29	30		

1. New York: Bob Hope opens in "My Favorite Blonde".

1. Pacific: Japanese resume major attacks at Bataan (→ 9).

3. U.S. acknowledges Free French rule in Cameroons and Equatorial Africa (→ 5/28).

3. U.S. flying fortresses bomb Japanese fleet off Burma (→ 5).

5. U.S.S.R.: German Supreme Commandant orders summer offensive on Caucasus (→ 5/8).

5. Norway: 5,000 ecclesiastics resign to show opposition to Quisling government (→ 7/10).

11. New Delhi: All-India Congress Party rejects British offer of dominion status (→ 27).

13. Augusta, Ga: Byron Nelson beats Ben Hogan to win Masters' golf title second time.

14. Detroit: Ford develops tire with only 1/16 amount of rubber formerly used (→ 26).

16. London: King George VI awards Malta the George Cross for heroism (→ 5/10).

19. Chinese join British forces in Burma (→ 29).

24. Britain: Exeter bombed by German planes (→ 29).

26. New England coastline blacked out to protect American ships from enemy subs (→ 28).

27. Oklahoma: Storm kills 100, injures 250 in Pryor.

27. Gandhi condemns stationing of U.S. troops in India (→ 7/14).

28. FDR asks American people to help win war by sacrificing, warns we will pay in "hard work, sorrow and blood" (→ 28).

28. Washington: OPA freezes prices of every major item affecting living costs (→ 6/15).

29. Japanese cut through Burma to reach Lashio, cutting off land routes to China (→ 5/9).

BIRTH

24. Barbara Streisand, versatile American actress and singer.

DEATH

18. Gertrude Vanderbilt Whitney, U.S. sculptor, Whitney Museum (*09/01/1875).

Laval is back in power in Vichy

April 18. The Vichy government has capitulated to German Chancellor Adolf Hitler and invited Pierre Laval to form a new government. It is being reported that Hitler threatened to kill French prisoners of war and cut food supplies if Marshal Petain did not recall Laval. Under the latest constitutional act, Petain is nothing more than a figurehead, and Laval has dictatorial powers. In addition to heading the government, Laval has named himself Minister of the Interior, Foreign Affairs and Information.

Laval has been traveling in German-occupied France and preaching collaboration with Berlin since he was arrested by Petain a year and a half ago for trying to stage a coup against the government. Germany ordered him released (→ 6/22).

French general escapes from Nazis

April 17. French General Giraud, the former chief of the 7th Army, captured by a German patrol, has just escaped from Koenigstein Fortress, north of Elbe. Giraud, who is 63 years old, slid down an improvised cable along a high wall. It seems that the escape was organized by Giraud's wife and Vichy bureau members. Hitler, furious, said to his staff: "This man, by himself, is worth 30 divisions."

Nazi artillery, set up on the Belgian coast, sends shells across the Channel without interruption.

36,000 taken on Bataan

April 9. Allied forces, badly outnumbered, sick and famished, have finally been crushed by the Japanese on the Bataan Peninsula after four months of savage fighting. The Americans and Filipinos, commanded by General Jonathan Wainwright, could not hold out any longer. Nearly all of the 36,000 defenders were killed or captured by an assault force of 200,000 Japanese. Several thousand Marines were apparently able to slip off the tip of Bataan into Manila Bay and escape to Corregidor. The island fortress is still in Allied hands.

Secretary of War Stimson says the Americans put up "a long and gallant defense." They had plenty of ammunition, but were very short on food. The forces had been on half-rations since January and were sharing their supplies with 20,000 civilians who had been evacuated from Luzon. "We have nothing but praise for these men," Stimson said. "I believe it to be a temporary loss. This country, in fulfillment of its pledge, will ultimately drive out the invaders" (→ 5/6).

Japanese bomb Ceylon, aiming westward

The British carrier Hermes, surprised by Japanese bombs, sinks near Ceylon.

April 5. Air raid sirens shattered the Easter Sunday calm on Ceylon this morning as Japanese bombers swept in from the Bay of Bengal. The planes attacked the harbor, airport and railway at Colombo, but the Japanese suffered heavy losses.

The Allies had been expecting this new thrust to the west, and Ceylon had been heavily fortifed by the British. At least 27 Japanese aircraft were shot down. An equal number were damaged. An undetermined number of civilians were killed when a bomb exploded in a hospital. The attack on Ceylon is the closest the Japanese have come to an assault on the Indian mainland. Since Japan occupied the Andaman Islands, 900 miles to the east, Ceylon has been strategically important for control of supply routes through the Persian Gulf and the Indian Ocean (→ 19).

Nazis launch Baedeker raids on Britain

April 29. Machine gun fire and heavy bombing ripped the streets of York, England, last night as the German "Baedeker blitz" continued. Adolf Hitler's pilots did not succeed in York as well as they have in Norwich and Bath, as five German planes were shot down by British defenders. However, the attack destroyed much of the cathedral city and fires still rage throughout every district, including oil depots in central York. The Baedeker raids on popular tourist spots have taken many lives. By the end of March, 43,822 had been killed (→ 5/20).

Doolittle's bombers hit surprised Tokyo

Doolittle sends a message to Japan.

April 18. General James Doolittle and his American flyers struck at the heart of the Japanese enemy by launching a lightning raid on Tokyo and other cities. The bombers did little damage, but the psychological victory was enormous, and it lifted spirits after the defeat at Bataan. Doolittle's B-25's took off from the aircraft carrier Hornet, protected by Admiral William Halsey's task force 600 miles off the coast of Japan. It was a dangerous mission, but all the planes left the carrier and joined the attack. Once over Japan, Doolittle said they flew so low that "one of our party observed a ball game in progress."

The bombers struck before the Japanese knew what was hitting them. They still do not know how the attack was launched. President Roosevelt is not giving them any clues. He suggests they arrived from Shangri-la.

1942

MAY

Su	Mo	Tu	We	Th	Fr	Sa
					1	2
3	4	5	6	7	8	9
10	11	12	13	14	15	16
17	18	19	20	21	22	23
24	25	26	27	28	29	30
31						

1. Moscow: Stalin promises Russia has no territorial ambitions in foreign countries (→ 26).

2. W.D. Wright rides Shut Out to victory in Kentucky Derby.

4. British forces land on Madagascar off southeast African coast (→ 7).

5. China: Japanese troops enter Yunan Province via Burma road (→ 9).

7. Vichy surrenders naval bases Diego Suarez and Antsirana to British in Madagascar (→ 30).

7. B.B. Fugate #1, Virginia's first successful oil well, opens in Rose Hill field.

8. U.S.S.R.: Germans launch offensive in oil region of Caucasus (→ 24).

9. China: Chinese forces batter Japanese in surprise attack retaking town of Maymyo (→ 15).

10. Mediterranean: Axis calls off offensive in Malta after several weeks and 11,000 missions (→ 11).

11. Mediterranean: Three British destroyers sunk by German bombers (→ 8/11).

12. New Orleans: Axis submarine sinks American cargo ship at mouth of Mississippi River, killing 27 (→ 6/21).

15. British, in retreat from Burma, reach India (→ 9/22).

15. FDR creates Women's Auxiliary Army Corps (WACs) (→ 7/30).

20. Allies adopt Harris plan for massive bombing of German industrial centers (→ 30).

20. Negro recruits allowed in U.S. Navy for first time.

24. U.S.S.R.: Soviets give up Kerch Peninsula after 15 days of stubborn resistance (→ 31).

26. London: Great Britain and U.S.S.R. sign 20-year mutual aid treaty (→ 6/12).

28. Libya: Nazi tanks push toward Tobruk (→ 6/15).

30. Japanese submarines shell Sydney and Diego Suarez naval bases in Madagascar (→ 9/10).

DEATH

29. John Barrymore, American actor (*2/15/1882).

Japanese navy battered

Enterprise, one of the carriers leading the U.S. into a new form of sea war.

May 8. The Americans and the Japanese are both claiming victory after a fierce air and naval battle in the Coral Sea. It was the first time in the history of naval warfare that the enemy ships never faced each other directly. They never even saw each other. Instead, they served as launch pads for carrier planes that carried out the attacks.

In the engagement, the Americans succeeded in stopping the Japanese from landing at Tulagi in the Solomons and Port Moresby on New Guinea. But the battle was costly to the United States.

The aircraft carrier Lexington was sunk and the Yorktown was damaged. The United States also lost a destroyer, a tanker and more than 60 planes. Most of the Lexington crew was rescued.

The Japanese lost an aircraft carrier and several cruisers and destroyers in five days of fighting. More importantly, however, they were dealt their first serious setback since Pearl Harbor. The United States proved that the Japanese are not invincible in the Pacific (→ 6/4).

Corregidor gives in after 300 air attacks

May 6. Japanese forces have prevailed despite a courageous stand by American and Filipino troops at Corregidor and other island forts in the Philippines. General Jonathan M. Wainwright, chief commander of 10,000 combined troops, has notified the War Department that "resistance of our troops has been overcome" and that the terms of surrender have yet to be determined.

Japan unremittingly bombed the islands, which many believed would fall much sooner, conducting some 300 air attacks to pave the way for landing parties to cross the three-mile strip of water separating Corregidor from the Bataan Peninsula.

The American defeat has been called one of its worst ever as the Japanese have captured about 42,000 members of the American and Philippine armies. The resounding Japanese victory will liberate military resources for Tokyo to send to other theaters of war. However, they will still have to contend with numerous guerrilla troops who continue to lurk in the island's dense jungles (→ 8).

RAF thousand-bomber raid hits Cologne

May 30. The royal air force put almost every plane that could fly into the air tonight. The target of the thousand bombers was Cologne. By the time dawn broke, the British estimated they had destroyed more than 200 factories.

The planes dropped more than 2,000 tons of bombs. In one night, the RAF figures it did more damage to Cologne than it had done in more than 1,300 previous attacks.

The British Air Marshal, Sir Arthur Harris, admits there were no specific targets in the saturation bombing. But Harris is hoping more blanket attacks will dislocate the German economy (→ 6/25).

Cologne, pounded by RAF bombs.

Soviet forces launch counter-offensive

May 31. An impressive Soviet attack has slaughtered thousands of German troops on the Kharkov front, stopping a powerful Nazi thrust. A Moscow communique claims 90,000 German soldiers have been killed or captured in the two weeks of bloody warfare. Losses on the Soviet side were severe as well, estimated at 75,000.

The counter-offensive thwarted a Nazi drive on Rostov, a strategic link to the Caucasus. According to Moscow, the military goal was accomplished: "Now that the battles are nearing their end, it can be said the main task put forward by the Soviet command—to forestall the blow of the German Fascist troops—has been completed."

Marshal Semyon Timoshenko is credited with commanding the ferocious assault. The enormity of the fighting has astounded even the most experienced military minds. Meanwhile, on the Isyum-Barvenkova front, south of Kharkov, German troops have isolated a Soviet division. Surprisingly though, the Soviet rear guard is holding its own, tying up Nazi troops that could be used in Kharkov (→ 6/15).

Nazi tank unit rests near Kharkov.

Hollywood has lost two of its greatest stars this year. Tempestous John Barrymore, beset by alcoholism, died this month, leaving a legacy of great film roles and a record 101 performances as Hamlet. In January, beloved Carole Lombard died at the peak of her career in a tragic plane crash.

1942

JUNE

Su	Mo	Tu	We	Th	Fr	Sa
	1	2	3	4	5	6
7	8	9	10	11	12	13
14	15	16	17	18	19	20
21	22	23	24	25	26	27
28	29	30				

1. Mexico declares war on Axis (→ 7/6).

4. Prague: Czech patriot kills German officer Reinhard Heydrich (→ 10).

4. Pacific: Japanese attack at Midway Island, suffer heavy losses (→ 7).

6. Japanese take Kiska and Attu in Aleutian Islands (→ 15).

7. Australia: Japanese subs shell Newcastle (→ 7/23).

12. U.S., Soviets sign Lend-Lease accord providing reciprocal defense aid and promising a "new and better world" (→ 18).

13. Balkans: U.S. bombers strike Rumanian oil fields (→ 9/4).

13. FDR creates Office of War Information with Elmer Davis as head, and Office of Strategic Services (→ 1/20/46).

15. Washington: U.S. officials open nationwide drive to salvage rubber (→ 30).

15. U.S.S.R.: Red navy shells Nazis at Sevastopol (→ 27).

15. Alaska: U.S. fliers blast six Japanese ships in Aleutians (→ 9/16).

15. North Africa: Tank war between Germans and British raging to climax in Libya (→ 19).

17. Army magazine Yank published for first time.

18. Washington: Prime Minister Churchill arrives to talk with FDR (→ 26).

19. North Africa: British forces retire to Egyptian border (→ 21).

21. Libya: Tobruk falls to Germans; 25,000 captured (→ 25).

21. San Francisco: Axis shells fall on Oregon coast near Fort Stevens.

22. France: Pierre Laval declares "I wish for a German victory" (→ 7/16).

26. Washington: Churchill and FDR agree on second front in Europe. (→ 8/17).

29. North Africa: Mussolini flies to Libya (→ 7/2).

30. Congress gives $42.8 billion for armed services; CCC collapses for lack of money (→ 9/10).

Midway: Crucial battle

June 7. After four days of savage fighting on the sea and in the air near Midway Island, Admiral Chester Nimitz has forced a badly beaten Japanese navy to withdraw. It was one of the biggest naval encounters in history. Nimitz claims to have sunk two or three enemy aircraft carriers. A dozen other Japanese vessels, including three battleships, were damaged. American losses were "inconsiderable," according to Admiral Ernest King, Commander-in-Chief of the United States fleet. The American destroyer Hammon was sunk by an enemy submarine. There are reports the aircraft carrier Yorktown had to be abandoned after it was hit.

The Japanese attack began on the 3rd, the same day Japanese planes raided Dutch Harbor in the Aleutian Islands. Admiral Yamamoto threw the bulk of his fleet into this battle, and it was clear he wanted more than Midway. Hawaii is just 1,300 miles away. While the fighting was still raging, King predicted that the outcome would alter the course of the war (→ 7/23).

The stars and stripes flutters over the wreckage of battle.

Eisenhower takes charge in Europe

June 25. Maj. General Dwight D. Eisenhower has assumed command of United States forces in the European theater of operations, with headquarters in London. It is considered likely that placing the command under General Eisenhower signals a decision to open a second front in the war, despite current setbacks in Libya and Egypt. General Eisenhower termed the creation of the command as "a logical step in coordinating the efforts of Great Britain and the United States" (→ 7/4).

Whole village razed

June 10. The Nazis have mortally punished an entire town in Czechoslovakia for the murder of a high-ranking German official. Police razed the town of Lidice and executed more than 1,300 of its civilian inhabitants in reprisal for the assassination last week of Reinhard Heydrich. Heydrich, called the "Hangman of Europe," was gunned down, presumably by Czech resistance agents. When the Nazis learned that one of the assassins may have spent the night in Lidice, they opened fire on the town and then bulldozed its 95 homes (→ 12/12/43).

British fall back as Rommel plunges 60 miles into Egypt

June 25. Field Marshal Erwin Rommel has catapulted from Libya into Egypt, scattering British forces, who are demoralized by the fall of Tobruk. Rommel seized the port city on Sunday, 17 months after it was lost by the Italians. According to latest reports from Sidi Barrani, 60 miles inside the Egyptian border, Lieutenant General Neil Methuen Ritchie is tired of running. The commander of the British Eighth Army is reorganizing his troops to make a new stand against Rommel.

The "Desert Fox," flushed with success, has been using captured American, British and French tanks in his advance. Swastikas have been painted on top of trucks seized from the Allies. Paratroopers and gliders from Crete are expected to reinforce Rommel's desert forces as he aims his sights on Alexandria (→ 29).

A German tank column rolls across the Libyan desert toward Tobruk.

1942

JULY

Su	Mo	Tu	We	Th	Fr	Sa
			1	2	3	4
5	6	7	8	9	10	11
12	13	14	15	16	17	18
19	20	21	22	23	24	25
26	27	28	29	30	31	

1. U.S.S.R.: Germans capture Sevastopol and Black Sea naval base (→ 13).

2. London: House of Commons gives Churchill and war effort 475-25 vote of confidence.

2. North Africa: British forces sweep around Axis in attack on El Alamein (→ 10).

4. London: U.S. fliers join RAF for first time, bomb Nazi bases in Holland (→ 8/1).

6. Argentina: President Castillo pledges neutrality (→ 8/22).

7. Rome: St. Peter's Cathedral now admitting women without stockings.

8. Hollywood: Actor Cary Grant marries Woolworth heiress Barbara Hutton.

10. Mussolini gives up hope of triumphant arrival in Cairo, returns to Rome (→ 25).

10. Russians pound Nazi air bases in Norway and Finland (→ 7/25/43).

13. U.S.S.R.: Nazis take Lisichansk and Kantemirovka on Don River (→ 28).

14. Indian Natl. Congress demands departure of British, agrees on passive resistance until India's independence (→ 8/9).

15. New York: Gary Cooper and Babe Ruth open in "The Pride of the Yankees."

16. American steel workers given 15% wage increase by War Labor Board (→ 8/14).

18. Belgium: Banned book list sent to all book stores (→ 8/31).

22. British reject U.S. proposal for Allied landing in Europe before end of 1942.

23. Pacific: Japanese invade East New Guinea (→ 8/7).

24. Italians strike at rebels in Yugoslavia (→ 11/3).

25. Allies agree on landing in North Africa (→ 9/1).

30. U.S. Congress creates women's naval reserves (WAVES) (→ 9/16).

BIRTH

16. Australian tennis champion Margaret Smith Court.

Nazis cross Don, head for oil fields

Germans build a bridge on the Don.

June 27. German troops intent on reaching the oil and minerals of the Caucasus are moving south in Russia and establishing bridgeheads across the Don River. But the cost is enormous. The Russians claim the river is red with the blood of Germans who have fallen victim to the blistering attacks from their dive bombers and tanks.

Five German armies are involved, assisted by armies from Italy, Rumania and Hungary. It will require more sacrifice for Germany to seize the oil depots, however. If Adolf Hitler is to succeed, he must learn to believe his own generals and accept their estimates of Russian troop strength (→ 7/1).

German saboteurs captured by FBI

June 26. Eight German saboteurs aboard submarines were seized by the Coast Guard as they attempted to land at Amagansett Beach, Long Island, and Ponte Vedra Beach, Florida, the FBI has announced. The men, who had intended to wreck vital American factories, bridges and terminals, were carrying forged draft registrations and Social Security cards, according to J. Edgar Hoover, Director of the FBI. The saboteurs could be tried in federal court or by a military tribunal (→ 7/11).

Germans in Sevastopol

July 28. Russia's great Black Sea naval base and fortress at Sevastopol finally fell under Nazi control this week after 25 days of hard fighting.

Despite the loss, a Soviet communique states that Russian troops performed magnificently at the Crimean port. "The iron steadfastness of the Sevastopol defenders has been one of the most important reasons holding up the so-called Spring Offensive of the Germans. The Germans have lost time and suffered huge losses in manpower," the announcement read.

The communique also claims that more than 300,000 Germans were killed or wounded and that what was gained after relentless bombing raids was a city of ruins. However, the valiant efforts of the Soviets also resulted in horrific bloodshed as 11,385 Russian troops were reported killed and 29,390 wounded or missing in the last three weeks of intense fighting.

According to Nazi dispatches, relatively few Soviet soldiers remain in the Chersonese Peninsula and those "face annihilation." They also claim that "the mopping up of the Sevastopol city district is being systematically continued." While declaring victory, the report admitted that Nazi troops were met with "tough enemy resistance" (→ 8/1).

Fighting in the streets of Sevastopol.

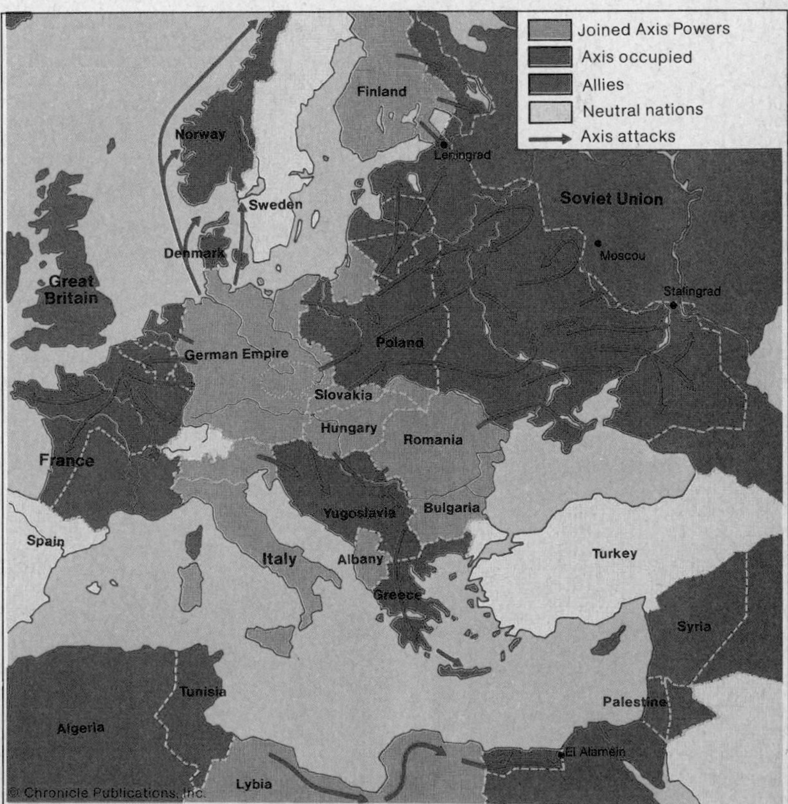

July 23. Hitler has established new war aims for Reich troops on the Eastern Front. Leningrad, under siege since September 1941, is to be taken. Troops on the Don will split into two corps, one to move on Stalingrad, the other to drive into the Caucasus and occupy the Baku oil fields.

French hold 13,000 Jews in Velodrome

July 16. At 3:00 this morning, thousands of French police officers fanned out through Paris on an unprecedented mission. They rounded up Jews, 13,000 of them, shoved them into buses and locked them up in the sports facility known as the Winter Velodrome. Among the people cowering beneath the bleachers are invalids, pregnant women and more than 3,000 children. The round-up was part of an agreement Vichy's Pierre Laval made with the Nazis. The Germans agreed not to deport any French Jews to Germany if the French arrested foreign Jews. Laval claims he can save 75,000 lives. Critics say that he has bartered with the devil (→ 10/2).

The FBI rounds up 158 more Nazis

July 11. Federal agents arrested 158 German aliens in New York City yesterday as the United States continued its crackdown on spies and saboteurs. Those arrested, including 30 women, are members of a German-American Vocational League, which has its national headquarters at 228 East 86th St. They are charged with endangering American security (→ 8/8).

July 14. De Gaulle and Eisenhower meet in London, holding the fate of Europe in their hands.

1942

AUGUST

Su	Mo	Tu	We	Th	Fr	Sa
						1
2	3	4	5	6	7	8
9	10	11	12	13	14	15
16	17	18	19	20	21	22
23	24	25	26	27	28	29
30	31					

1. U.S.S.R.: German army cuts off railway line connecting Stalingrad and Krasnodar (→ 6).

1. Germany: British bombers raid Dusseldorf, most important steel-producing center in Reich (→ 17).

5. Washington: Holland's Queen Wilhelmina pays state visit to White House.

6. U.S.S.R.: Stalingrad menaced from south as Germans advance in Pincer move (→ 23).

8. U.S.: Six German saboteurs arrested in June, executed by electrocution (→ 9).

9. Mitchel Field, L.I.: Fifth columnists found marking plowing field with arrows leading way to air base.

11. Mediterranean: Americans smash 3 of 4 cruisers in raid on Italian base in Greece (→ 10/10/43).

11. France: First prisoners of war, released under Laval-Hitler accord, arrive in Compiegne.

12. Pacific: Marines gain hold on three Solomon Islands (→ 9/15).

12. Tokyo: Premier Tojo escapes assassination attempt.

14. U.S. Navy seizes N.J. General Cable plant, orders strikers back to work (→ 11/3/43).

17. France: 8th Air Force raids Nazi-occupied Rouen in first U.S. raid on Europe (→ 19).

20. Washington: Peter Widener offers extensive collection to National Art Gallery.

22. Rio de Janeiro: After sinking of several Brazilian ships Brazil declares war on Germany and Italy (→ 6/4/43).

23. U.S.S.R.: Germans succeed in crossing Don River (→ 9/17).

26. Wendell Wilkie begins trip round world as FDR envoy to boost Allied solidarity.

26. Germany: Soviets conduct air raids over Danzig, Berlin and Stettin.

27. Holland: British and American bombers raid Rotterdam (→ 9/8).

31. Brussels: Communist spy network "Red Orchestra" broken up by Germans (→ 11/11/43).

U.S. on Guadalcanal

Aug 7. United States Marines braved Japanese snipers and bombing attacks to advance about a mile on Guadalcanal by nightfall. Within the next day or two, they hope to seize an airport the Japanese are building on the island.

The Marine attack on the Solomons started before 8:00 this morning, when the First Division landed on Florida Island. Less than two hours later, the Marines established a bridgehead on Guadalcanal. The Marines received air cover from planes that took off from three carriers, the Wasp, Saratoga and Enterprise, all commanded by Rear Admiral Frank Fletcher. Resistance on the island was thin and sporadic, but many planes were lost (→ 12).

Allied commando raid on Dieppe fails

Dieppe beach, littered with Canadian corpses and a disabled transport ship.

Aug 19. Thousands of brave Canadians have died or been taken prisoner in a daring Allied experiment on the French coast at Dieppe.

The operation was designed to attack German installations and gather intelligence on the feasibility of an Allied invasion of France. The troops learned fast it would not be easy. Some 6,000 men went ashore before dawn on landing craft that skirted a heavy concentration of German mines. Many troops died as soon as they hit the six targeted beaches. Others immobilized coastal gunners and drove the tanks they had brought with them into the center of Dieppe. Heavy fighting raged around the casino. In the air, RAF pilots tangled with the Luftwaffe. Both sides lost more than 90 planes. More Canadians were shot as they struggled back to their landing craft on the beaches.

The Allies knew this operation would be costly. They warned the French resistance beforehand not to get involved. This was not a full-scale invasion and was not worth the risk (→ 27).

Gandhi group arrested; violence results

Aug 9. Gandhi's campaign to end British rule in India has exploded into bloodshed and violence in Bombay. The British government of India used tear gas and gunfire to break up mobs. Eight persons are reported killed, 65 injured.

The All-India Congress Party is officially designated as an unlawful organization dangerous to the public peace. Gandhi, Nehru, Azad and other main All-India Congress leaders were arrested. Gandhi is detained for the sixth time in the cause of Indian independence.

On his way to prison, he said to his followers: "Remember the slogan, either we get freedom or die." In jail, he might go on a hunger strike, as he has before (→ 2/10/43).

1942

SEPTEMBER

Su	Mo	Tu	We	Th	Fr	Sa
		1	2	3	4	5
6	7	8	9	10	11	12
13	14	15	16	17	18	19
20	21	22	23	24	25	26
29	28	29	30			

1. North Africa: Rommel launches new attack in Egypt (→ 2).

2. Egypt: British hold desert defenses as fliers blast Rommel's units (→ 4).

3. U.S.S.R.: Stalingrad line pierced by Germans (→ 7).

3. Madrid: General Franco ousts Cabinet members, gets full control of govt. (→ 7/17/45).

4. North Africa: Allied forces halt Axis attack in Egypt (→ 10/1).

4. Hungary: Budapest bombed by German planes (→ 11/2).

7. U.S.S.R.: Red army pushes back German lines northwest of Stalingrad (→ 17).

8. U.S. ignores Vichy protest concerning bombing of French cities (→ 21).

10. British attack Madagascar to stop island's aid to Axis (→ 11/5).

10. Baruch Commission warns of "military and civilian collapse" due to rubber shortage in U.S. (→ 19).

15. Pacific: U.S. troops repel Japanese at Guadalcanal (→ 23).

16. Jacqueline Cochran named director of Women's Flying Training in U.S. Air Force.

16. Alaska: U.S. bombers raid Japanese base at Kiska in Aleutian Islands.

18. Paris: Nazis kill 116 for attacks on German troops (→ 10/20).

19. Washington: OPA to refuse fuel oil to plants, apartments and businesses that can and don't convert to coal (→ 25).

21. London: RAF flies 1,200 miles to raid Munich (→ 10/31).

22. Burma: British attack on Japanese front (→ 10/2).

23. Pacific: Australians attack Japanese in New Guinea (→ 27).

25. Washington: WLB orders equal pay to women as recognition of role in war.→

27. New Guinea: Japanese troops forced to withdraw by Australians (→ 10/10).

28. Tour de France replaced by reduced circuit to avoid crossing demarcation line.

British Royal Duke lost in air crash

Aug 25. The Duke of Kent, youngest brother of King George VI of England, was killed in an air crash today. He was the first member of the royal family to die in action. The duke, 39, was an air commodore in the RAF. He was bound for Iceland from Scotland in a flying boat when the plane fell, killing all aboard.

The duke, then called Prince George, was rather wild as a young man. Then he married Princess Marina of Greece, poor but very beautiful and living in exile in Paris. She bore him a third son three weeks before his death. The baby had President Roosevelt for a godfather and Franklin for one of his names.

Churchill in Russia for talks with Stalin

Aug 17. In "an atmosphere of cordiality and complete sincerity" British Prime Minister Winston Churchill has met with Soviet Premier Joseph Stalin at a four-day parley in Moscow, according to a Soviet communique. W. Averell Harriman, representing President Roosevelt, also participated in the talks. While it is not customary for military leaders to disclose the details of such conferences while engaged in war, it is believed many aspects of the war and international diplomacy were discussed, including the recently signed Anglo-Soviet Treaty. Both governments released statements condemning the tyranny of Hitler (→ 1/14/43).

Churchill, U.S. envoy William Averell Harriman and Stalin discuss war plans in Moscow.

Germans break Stalingrad line, attack city

Germans fire an anti-tank cannon amid the rubble that was once Stalingrad.

Sept 17. Stalingrad is on fire, brutalized by Nazi dive-bomber attacks. For the first time, the Russians conceded that German shock troops rammed their way into the outskirts of the city after a non-stop 26-day attack. The German command claimed its troops have crossed the Volga and barreled into the center of the city.

The Germans pierced the Russian defenses in northwestern Stalingrad. They are still attacking from the west and southwest. Their advance was steady, but artless. The infantry, helpless on its own, relied on the Luftwaffe to dive-bomb Russian forward positions in the morning. Tanks and shock troops would pour into any holes that opened. Then the planes would attack again. The battle plan was very effective until the last few days, when Russian sharpshooters, dug into trenches, learned how to punish the German fliers.

Heavy fighting is also reported in the Caucasus. Germans are said to be advancing along the coastal highway from Novorossiisk (→ 11/23).

U-boat sinks ship carrying Italian POWs

Sept 12. The commander of German U-boat number 156 thought he had quite a prize in his sights when he spotted the British transport ship Laconia through his periscope. Without a second thought, he ordered his torpedoes to fire and they scored a direct hit on the choice target. But the cheers on 156 turned quickly to gloom when it was learned the Laconia was carrying 1,800 Italian prisoners of war.

The submarine put out a distress call, but it attracted an American cutter as well as German rescue ships. The cutter opened fire on the Germans. By the time the skirmishing had ended, 2,000 men on board the Laconia were dead.

The mishap marred an impressive string of successes for German submarines. Allied losses this year have added up to five million tons. In June, a ship was being sunk every four hours. The Germans have learned how to hit and run, and they are building new subs faster than the Allies can sink them. They will have 400 in service by the end of the year.

▷

On the home front: Scarcity and sacrifice

A Victory Garden in every yard.

In the midst of war, if you are young, male, hep and not in uniform, the desired attire is a zoot suit with a real pleat, and a long watch chain looped from waist to pants pocket. The lindy hop is out and jitterbugging is in. Female jitterbugs wear swirling skirts, turned down socks and saddle shoes.

But jumping and jiving are not all there is to life in these United States. While it is by no means as grim as in Europe and the Pacific, meat, coffee, butter and shoes are scarce. Gas is also scarce in the land of the automobile, and coal has replaced fuel oil. Metal appliances have vanished from the stores. Citizens hold scrap metal, rubber and cooking fat drives, and invest billions in war bonds.

Government agencies run things: They fix wages and rents, settle labor-management disputes, try to limit racial discrimination, impose censorship, open overseas mail, and control war news reports. They are on the lookout for spies and post slogans such as "Loose Lips Sink Ships." Civil defense precautions are taken on both coasts.

A vast labor force has been mobilized. And men have been put under virtual military discipline. About two million women have also entered the work force. "Rosie the Riveter" is a national symbol. Women get equal pay for equal work in the war effort. Will this outlast the war?

"Victory Gardens" are continually springing up in backyards and vacant lots, especially in California, where two-thirds of the vegetables once were grown by Japanese-Americans, now interned. Last year, 40 percent of all vegetables in the nation came from 20 million gardens. Americans are hoeing and hoping for victory (→ 10/1).

U.S. builds 488 ships in one year

Sept 25. Prodigies of production are performed by the United States of America in supplying herself and her allies in this second great war. And no industry is more prodigious than shipbuilding.

A mass-produced cargo ship, the Liberty Ship, was designed by the Maritime Commission, aiming to build ships faster than the Germans could sink them. Today, the commission announced 488 ships had been built in the past year. Henry J. Kaiser, a West Coast industrial genius, used assembly-line methods and prefabrication to build a ship every four days.

Germans executed 207,373 until now

Sept 21. Nearly a quarter million people have been executed by the Nazis in occupied Europe, according to the Inter-Allied Information Committee, an organization set up by the Allied governments. The figure, 207,373, includes formal executions which have followed trials of court-martial and shootings of hostages and other persons held prisoner by the Germans.

Suffering the highest number is Poland, where 200,000 have been killed since the Nazi invasion three years ago. Some 100,000 were shot after German trials, 70,000 killed as hostages and 30,000 executed in concentration camps.

The committee pointed out that many more Europeans have probably been put to death by Hitler; the figures released tonight are officially confirmed. The latest victims on the increasing list were 116 Frenchmen shot last week (→ 3/13/43).

1942

OCTOBER

Su	Mo	Tu	We	Th	Fr	Sa
				1	2	3
4	5	6	7	8	9	10
11	12	13	14	15	16	17
18	19	20	21	22	23	24
25	26	27	28	29	30	31

1. FDR ends two-week trip to war plants across U.S. (→ 3).

1. North Africa: British army forces Axis from positions in region of El Alamein (→ 23).

2. France: Ex-President Herriot arrested by Vichy police (→ 20).

2. U.S. training now given to Chinese in India (→ 12/19).

3. Washington: Under new price control law, FDR freezes wages, rents and farm prices (→ 21).

3. Washington: FDR names Justice James F. Byrnes as new economic director (→ 21).

5. New York: Cardinals down Yankees to win World Series in five games.

7. Washington: FDR says U.S. will join in investigation of war atrocities after the war.

10. Australia: U.S. planes drop 40 tons of bombs on Japanese supply base at Rabaul (→ 16).

11. Omaha: Joe Louis announces "My fighting days are over" (6/19/46).

16. Bombay: Hurricane triggers flooding, leaves thousands dead.

16. Pacific: Japanese land in force in Guadalcanal (→ 11/12).

20. New York: Inauguration of "Art of this Century" exhibit, directed by Peggy Guggenheim, Max Ernst's wife.

20. Vichy, France: Laval tells French labor it must serve in Germany (→ 11/8).

21. Congress passes largest tax bill in U.S. history at $9 billion, including Victory Tax (→ 27).

23. North Africa: U.S. Gen. Mark Clark lands in Algiers to convince French to support attack (→ 24).

23. Eleanor Roosevelt visits British king and queen in London.

24. Gigantic task force led by General Eisenhower leaves for North Africa (→ 31).

26. Pacific: Japanese launch major attack on Guadalcanal, sinking two U.S. carriers (→ 11/12).

27. Washington: Economic Stabilization Director James Byrnes limits federal salaries to $25,000 (→ 11/18).

Montgomery leads British desert army

"Monty" (right) confers with aide.

Oct 31. General Bernard Montgomery is back in charge of the British Eighth Army, and Field Marshal Erwin Rommel may finally have met his match.

The "Desert Fox," who was being treated at a hospital in Germany, returned to Egypt earlier this month for the showdown with "Monty." Rommel is not optimistic. His Africa Korps has already lost at Alam Halfa, and the troops seem too exhausted and demoralized to make a strong showing at Alamein. Rommel's tanks, famed for their end runs, have bogged down in quicksand, and they are short on fuel.

When the fighting started last week, Montgomery had trouble using infantry to clear the way for his tanks, but one Australian unit fought its way to the Mediterranean coast. Montgomery says the next few days will be the turning point in the North African war (→ 11/4).

Canterbury, shrine of Anglicans, struck

Oct 31. More than 50 Nazi bombers showered the cathedral city of Canterbury this afternoon in the biggest daylight raid against England since the battle of Britain two years ago. Blasting the streets in lightning fashion, the German planes came in waves, wrecking many buildings. Casualty figures have yet to be released and it isn't known yet how badly the famous Church of England cathedral was hit. Germany did not survive the raid unscathed. British defense destroyed nine Nazi planes (→ 12/6).

1942

NOVEMBER

Su	Mo	Tu	We	Th	Fr	Sa
1	2	3	4	5	6	7
8	9	10	11	12	13	14
15	16	17	18	19	20	21
22	23	24	25	26	27	28
29	30					

3. U.S.: Republicans gain in mid-term elections.

3. Yugoslavia: Tito's partisans take Bihac, capital of Bosnia (→ 5/27/43).

5. Vichy hands over Madagascar to Allies (→ 1/8/43).

7. Led by General Dwight D. Eisenhower, American forces land in North Africa (→ 8).

8. Vichy France breaks off diplomatic relations with U.S. (→ 9).

8. Algiers, capital of French North Africa, capitulates to American forces (→ 9).

9. North Africa: Fresh German troops land in Tunisia (→ 11).

9. Canada and Mexico sever relations with Vichy (→ 12).

12. Libya: Allies recapture Tobruk (→ 23).

12. Pacific: American Flying Fortresses hit four troopships in the Solomons (→ 13).

12. London: Admiral Darlan asks Vichy fleet to go to Africa to aid Allies (→ 17).

13. Pacific: U.S. Navy downs 30 of 31 Japanese planes in Solomon Islands (→ 15).

15. Japanese lose 28 warships at Guadalcanal (→ 1/5/43).

17. France: Pierre Laval given full powers by Petain; Admiral Darlan is dismissed (→ 12/1).

18. Selective Service extended to 18-year-olds; Army strength predicted at 10 million (→ 29).

21. 1,523-mile Alcan International Highway inaugurated in Alaska.

23. U.S.S.R.: Soviets open offensive at Stalingrad; gain 40 miles and cut rail lines, killing 15,000 (→ 25).

23. West Africa: Under leadership of Admiral Darlan, Dakar joins Allies (→ 12/2).

28. Annapolis: Navy blanks Army 14-0 before home crowd.

29. U.S. begins rationing of coffee (→ 12/1).

29. London: Churchill tells Italy over radio to oust leaders or face shattering Allied air blows (→ 12/4).

Allied forces land in North Africa

American troops rescue North Africa from the Axis.

Nov 11. In just four days, American forces under the command of Lieutenant General Dwight Eisenhower have seized control of French North Africa. Admiral Francois Darlan, commander of Vichy forces, has signed a cease-fire order. American flags are flying over the major cities of Morocco and Algeria, and 100,000 G.I.'s are at the ready as Field Marshal Rommel flees west to Libya from the victorious British forces in Egypt.

In London today, the House of Commons cheered as Prime Minister Winston Churchill announced that Britain had won in Egypt. "Taken by itself, the battle of Egypt must be regarded as a historical victory," Churchill said.

The invasion of French North Africa was a delicate matter for Eisenhower. The Vichy government was not informed ahead of time. But Eisenhower made it clear as his soldiers arrived that America was at war with Germany and Italy, not France. "We come among you," he said, "to repulse the cruel invaders who would remove forever your rights or self-government, your rights to religious freedom and your rights to live your own lives in peace and security."

There was scattered resistance to the Americans, but they gained control of Algiers, Rabat and Casablanca. President Roosevelt announced triumphantly that the success in North Africa would prevent Germany and Italy from sending more troops to the area. He also said Russia will be assisted by the creation of a second front (→ 12).

French fleet scuttled at Toulon as Germans occupy South

The French greet occupying German troops with a fleet of useless ships.

Nov 27. French naval commanders were ordered to scuttle their ships today. None of them resisted.

Admiral de Laborde gave the order as German troops, which have now occupied most of Southern France, entered Toulon before dawn this morning. Most of the French navy's biggest ships had taken refuge in the harbor. Admiral Darlan had already ordered de Laborde to scuttle the fleet if it appeared the ships might fall into German hands. Many of the captains stayed on their bridges until it was clear they had succeeded. Some went down with their ships. Many crewmen stood on the docks and watched as their ships were engulfed by flames. Some wept. Others saluted.

A quarter of a million tons of shipping were sunk. It was the largest scuttling operation since the Germans sent their ships to the bottom at Scapa Flow in 1919.

Lost were the battleships Dunkirk, Provence and Strasbourg, seven cruisers and 12 submarines. Miraculously, five submarines made their way out of the harbor. ▷

British rout Rommel

Nov 4. A furious sandstorm has covered the desert of western Egypt. The sand is being kicked up by the desperate retreat of Field Marshal Rommel's Afrika Korps after a sound thrashing by the British at El Alamein. Germans and Italians are retreating west in tight formation. As they head toward Tobruk, they may provide easy targets for more of the Allied air strikes that sealed General Bernard Montgomery's victory at El Alamein.

At least 9,000 Axis troops were captured by General Montgomery's forces. Many officers were taken prisoner, including General Ritter von Thoma, commander of the Afrika Korps. More than 500 Axis tanks and guns were destroyed. Some 300 planes were shot down. And it is impossible to count the number of supply ships that were sunk in the Mediterranean Sea.

Montgomery began the battle of El Alamein with infantry, but it became a tank war. British strategy beat Rommel's magic. Once Montgomery tore a hole through German defenses west of El Alamein, he was invincible (→ 7).

Nazi dive-bomber burns in the desert.

Russians encircle Germans at Stalingrad

Nov 25. Russian soldiers are smashing through German lines west and south of Stalingrad as they tighten the noose around the 300,000 Germans occupying the city. The Russians are advancing so fast that many Germans have been shot in the back trying to retreat. An airfield controlled by the Nazis was seized before the Germans could put their planes in the air. The Russians say they have killed or taken prisoner 77,000 enemy soldiers. Many others, cut off from their supplies, are freezing to death on the steppes near the Don River.

The first major victory in the Russian counter-offensive, Moscow's biggest operation since last winter, was the recapture of Kalach, 40 miles west of Stalingrad. A short while later, Red troops seized two rail towns to the south of Kalach and cut off two rail lines that supply the Germans in Stalingrad.

Three generals of German divisions have been captured by the Russians, and the Nazi command has begun to acknowledge that some of its defenses have been penetrated. But the Germans say they are defending their positions in "savage battles" and "countermeasures" are planned (→ 12/22).

Soviet tanks, moving fast, close in on German positions at Stalingrad.

Fire and panic kill 300 in Boston club

Nov 29. A sudden fire blazed through the Cocoanut Grove Night Club in midtown Boston, killing over 300 and injuring 150 early this morning. Smoke smothered many of the victims, and screaming throngs died in the exits as they tried futilely to escape. Boston City Hospital officials said there were so many corpses lining the clinic's hallway that no attempts have been made to identify them as of yet.

The cause of the fire is unknown, but it broke out in the basement kitchen at 10:17 p.m., just as the club's performers were about to play. It spread rapidly, giving the occupants little chance for survival. The gallant efforts of Marshall Cook, a South Boston boy, saved at least 35 as he led them to safety via the roof. Many of the victims were American sailors, Marines and Coast Guardsmen visiting Boston for a weekend of rest and relaxation.

Miracle: Hero lost at sea finally found

Nov 14. "None of us had given up hope," exclaimed Captain E.V. Rickenbacker's mother when she received the extraordinary news that the lost flying ace had been rescued. Rickenbacker and his crew were forced down in the South Pacific when their Army bomber ran out of fuel on October 21. Rescued with him were Colonel Hans C. Adamson and Private John F. Bartek. They had survived for more than three weeks, drifting aimlessly in their life raft on army rations.

The Navy Catalina flying boat spotted the crew 600 miles from Somoa. Sergeant Alexander Kaczmarczyk did not survive and was buried at sea. The other members of Rickenbacker's crew were found on a small island. Now, all crewmen have been accounted for and the survivors seem to be in good health.

Earlier this month, Secretary of War Henry Stimson, who had ordered the extensive ocean search, expressed optimism that the world war hero would be found, saying Rickenbacker was "an exception to ordinary rules."

Cohan, Broadway's man of genius, dies

Nov 5. George M. Cohan died this morning in New York City. Earlier this year, when he heard a film biography was planned ("Yankee Doodle Dandy"), he asked, "Would anybody go to see it?" Who would not want to know the story of a humble composer, producer, director, actor and singer?

Cohan sang he was "born on the 4th of July." In fact it was July 3, 1878. Raised in a family vaudeville act, he produced his first musical, "The Governor's Son," in 1901. "Little Johnny Jones," "45 Minutes from Broadway" and "Little Nellie Kelly" followed. His songs, including "Give My Regards to Broadway" and "Over There," endure.

Cagney stars in "Yankee Doodle Dandy" about Cohan's life.

The 1930's marked a transition. He took a dramatic role in Eugene O'Neill's "Ah, Wilderness" (1933) and played an ebullient Franklin D. Roosevelt in "I'd Rather Be Right" (1937). In 1936, Roosevelt gave Cohan a congressional medal for his song "It's a Grand Old Flag."

German poster calls the Anglo-Soviet pact a Jewish conspiracy.

1942

DECEMBER

Su	Mo	Tu	We	Th	Fr	Sa
		1	2	3	4	5
6	7	8	9	10	11	12
13	14	15	16	17	18	19
20	21	22	23	24	25	26
29	28	29	30	31		

1. U.S.: Gas rationing goes into effect on a national scale.→

1. Adm. Darlan claims command of French govt. from Algiers, calls Petain a German prisoner (→ 24).

1. London: Beveridge report given to Commons, calling for legislative attack on poverty.

2. FDR creates Petroleum Administration for War, to be headed by Sec. of Int. Harold Ickes (→ 1/11/43).

2. North Africa: Allies repel strong attack in Tunisia (→ 18).

4. FDR closes Works Project Administration with "honorable discharge."

4. Naples: U.S. planes make first raids on Italy (→ 2/5/43).

6. Fliers of eight Allied nations strike occupied France in greatest daylight bombing raid of war (→ 1/27/43).

7. Philadelphia: U.S. launches largest battleship ever built, the U.S.S. New Jersey.

13. Washington: Redskins over Bears 14-6 for football title.

18. Germany: Hitler meets with Mussolini and Pierre Laval.

19. British advance 40 miles into Burma in drive to oust Japanese from colony (→ 2/8/43).

22. U.S.S.R.: Soviets drive German troops back 15 miles at the Don river (→ 1/8/43).

CULTURAL EVENTS, 1942

Literature: Ellen Glasgow's "In This Our Life," Pulitzer Prize; Camus' "L'Etranger"; Steinbeck's "The Moon is Down."

Academia: Erich Fromm's "The Fear of Freedom"; James Burnham's "The Managerial Revolution."

Music: Aaron Copland's "Rodeo"; Irving Berlin's "White Christmas"; "Praise the Lord and Pass the Ammunition"; "Paper Doll"; "That Old Black Magic."

The Arts: Matisse's "The Idol"; Mondrian's "New York City."

Film: Walt Disney's "Bambi"; "Holiday Inn," with Bing Crosby; Lubitsch's "To Be or Not To Be."

Atomic fission succeeds

Dec 2. A group of physicists led by Enrico Fermi has achieved the first controlled nuclear chain reaction, opening the way to both an atomic bomb and nuclear energy.

The scientists built a nuclear pile composed of uranium and graphite in the squash court of the University of Chicago. The crucial moment came at 3:45 p.m. when the removal of control rods showed that neutrons from fissioning uranium atoms split other atoms to keep the chain reaction going. The atomic pile is part of the secret Manhattan Project to build an atomic bomb. Germany is said to have begun a similar effort (→ 7/16/45).

Fermi, with model of an atom.

Boas, distinguished anthropologist, dies

Dec 21. Franz Boas, father of American anthropology, is dead. He was 84. Born and educated in physics in Germany, Boas journeyed to Baffin Island and became interested in Eskimo culture. His fieldwork among the Kwakiutl Indians of the Pacific Northwest was ground-breaking in its empirical exactitude; previously, most anthropology was done by arm-chair theorists. Boas also served as curator of ethnology at the American Museum of Natural History in New York and was until today Professor of anthropology at Columbia University. His books include "The Mind of Primitive Man" and "Race, Language and Culture."

Franz Boas in 1906.

Gas is rationed: No joy in autoland

Dec 1. Gasoline rationing has gone into effect on a nationwide basis in the United States, a move affecting 27 million passenger cars and five million buses and trucks in an effort to conserve both gas and rubber tires. Some seven million auto owners in 13 Eastern states have already had a taste of such restrictions, having been limited to three gallons of gas a week since last spring. Under the new plan, embracing the entire nation, car owners will get about four gallons each week. Last week, President Roosevelt ordered the measure, and the rationing of coffee also took effect. A War Petroleum Administration is to be established (→ 2).

Desert Fox running

Dec 18. Field Marshal Rommel has not had much time to take a breath since his disastrous defeat at El Alamein. First Tobruk and then Benghazi fell as he retreated across Libya. Rommel made a stand at Agheila, where he created a line of defense 40 miles long. "As Agheila goes, so goes the North African campaign," became the Allied byword. The Allies broke through the line on the 14th. Yesterday, the "Desert Fox" was cut off from his rear guard by a British column that sped across the desert from Agheila (→ 1/13/43).

Darlan assassinated; Giraud succeeds him

Dec 24. Admiral Jean Francois Darlan, who just last month abandoned the cause of Vichy, was assassinated today in Algiers. General Henri Honore Giraud was named immediately to succeed him as High Commissioner in French Africa.

The killer is said to be a fascist. He calls himself Morand, but his real name is Bonnier de la Chapelle. Police say he concealed a weapon in an umbrella and opened fire when Darlan walked into his office.

President Roosevelt condemned the assassination as "murder in the first degree." He conceded that Darlan was controversial, but he also said his killing complicates U.S. relations with French Africa.

Adm. Darlan and successor Giraud.

Darlan had been a supporter of Vichy's collaboration with Germany. He changed position after the Allied landing in North Africa, and he ordered resistance fighters to side with the Allies (→ 4/5/43).

1943

JANUARY

Su	Mo	Tu	We	Th	Fr	Sa
					1	2
3	4	5	6	7	8	9
10	11	12	13	14	15	16
17	18	19	20	21	22	23
24	25	26	27	28	29	30
31						

5. Pacific: Japanese begin planned withdrawal from Guadalcanal (→ 21).

8. British hand Madagascar over to Free French (→ 4/12/47).

8. U.S.S.R.: Germans besieged at Stalingrad ignore appeal to surrender (→ 11).

11. Washington: FDR calls for $100 bil. military budget (→ 20).

11. U.S.S.R.: Red army encircles Stalingrad (→ 18).

11. Great Britain and U.S. give up extraterritoriality (exemption from local law) in China.

13. Libya: Gen. Leclerc's Free French forces merge with British under Montgomery (→ 22).

14. France: Italian occupation authorities refuse to deport Jews living on their territory.

14. Morocco: FDR, Churchill and De Gaulle meet at Casablanca (→ 24).

20. Washington reports 2,600 planes shipped to U.S.S.R. to date under lend-lease. (→ 2/3).

20. Germany and Japan sign trade accord to exchange military supplies.

20. FDR made godfather to newly born daughter of Holland's Crown Princess Juliana.

21. Pacific: U.S. and Australian troops join forces in New Guinea (→ 2/9).

21. Britain: Nazi daylight air raid kills 34 in London school (→ 1/27).

22. North Africa: Axis forces pull out of Tripoli for Tunisia, destroying bases as they leave (→ 2/1).

22. France: Antoine de Saint-Exupery publishes "Pilot of War."

26. U.S.S.R.: Soviet troops defeat all but 12,000 Germans trapped at Stalingrad, free three main railways (→ 31).

27. England: First U.S. raids on Reich blast Wilhelmshaven base and Emden (→ 30).

28. Germany: Nazis mobilize women for military service.

31. London: Free French chief Giraud sends thanks to FDR for "the decisive help of the U.S."

German army gives in at Stalingrad

Jan 31. The German occupiers of Stalingrad, starving, freezing and out of ammunition, have surrendered to the Russians. Almost no supplies have reached the Nazis since the Russians encircled the city last November.

Fighting was so intense that the Germans could not reach the few supplies that were parachuted to the ground. At the end, rations had been reduced to a few ounces of bread. More than 90,000 Germans died from starvation or the cold. Another 100,000 were killed in the last three weeks of the fighting.

Hitler is furious at the surrender of Friedrich von Paulus, who had been promoted to Field Marshal in the last days of the battle because no German marshal had yet surrendered. Paulus asked several times for permission to lay down his arms, and each time Hitler said no. "Surrender is forbidden," Hitler ordered. "Sixth Army will hold their positions to the last man and last round and by their endurance will make an unforgettable contribution toward the establishment of a defensive front and the salvation of the Western world." Today, Paulus disobeyed his orders (→ 2/2).

Soviet soldiers pass by a German tank disabled at Stalingrad.

Roosevelt, Churchill, de Gaulle hold war council in Casablanca

Jan 24. American and British military strategists may not agree on everything. But President Roosevelt and Prime Minister Churchill certainly agree on the objective of the war against the Axis. At the conclusion of their ten-day meeting in Casablanca, Roosevelt said, "Peace can come to the world only by the total elimination of German and Japanese war power." That "means the unconditional surrender of Germany, Italy and Japan." It means "the destruction of the philosophies in those countries which are based on conquest and the subjugation of other people."

Roosevelt, de Gaulle and Churchill pose in the African sun at Casablanca.

Roosevelt and Churchill had some differences over the opening of a second front, but they realized that it will not be possible to invade France this year. They agreed to step up attacks on German submarines and to open a campaign in Sicily and Italy.

Churchill convinced the president to allow General Charles de Gaulle to participate in the conference at Casablanca. General Henri Giraud, despite his association with Vichy, was the major French representative (→ 3/8).

RAF and USAAF raid Berlin, key areas

Jan 30. Unintimidated by heavy Nazi defense and the bright of day, Britain's royal air force raided Berlin on two separate occasions today. New Mosquito planes, the world's fastest, zoomed over the German capital just as Reich Marshal Hermann Goering was to deliver a broadcast celebrating ten years of Adolf Hitler's regime. A second attack hit Berlin late in the afternoon, again disrupting an address, this time by Propaganda Minister Joseph Goebbels. While no official casualty reports were issued, the raids are considered a success. The RAF struck three days after the first U.S. Army Air Force attack on Germany proper destroyed key Nazi naval centers (→ 2/26).

The Swedish Embassy in Berlin crumbled under blows struck by Allied bombs.

Russians relieve Leningrad at last

Jan 18. Russian forces have cracked the German ring of steel that had choked Leningrad for 17 months. Red troops under the command of Marshals Zhukov and Voroshiloff punched a hole through the Nazi stranglehold south of Lake Lagoda. Russians recaptured key German positions, including the fortress at Schluesselburg.

News of the break in the siege was greeted with great relief all over Russia. The suffering of Leningrad has been one of the greatest tragedies of this war. Half of the city's residents died last winter. The rest stayed alive only because soldiers were able to supply them across frozen Lake Lagoda.

The end of the siege means that Russia will be able to start using the Gulf of Finland and rail lines to resupply its armies, and it gives Stalin new momentum to spring back against the Balkan states. To the south, the Russians have begun to crack Nazi defense lines in the Ukraine and Caucasus (→ 26).

Renowned Negro educator deceased

Jan 5. George Washington Carver, chemist and botanist, has died in Tuskegee, Alabama. He was born a slave in Missouri in 1861. He came to Tuskegee University with an M.A. in agriculture from Iowa State College. Carver revitalized Southern agriculture by developing new uses for soybeans, sweet potatoes, peanuts and other crops.

Carver, Negro scientist.

1943

FEBRUARY

Su	Mo	Tu	We	Th	Fr	Sa
	1	2	3	4	5	6
7	8	9	10	11	12	13
14	15	16	17	18	19	20
21	22	23	24	25	26	27
28						

1. France: Germans tear down old port of Marseilles (→ 26).

1. North Africa: American tanks and infantry battered at German positions in Fais pass (→ 15).

2. U.S.S.R.: Last of German strongholds at Stalingrad surrenders to Red army (→ 9).

3. War Dept. bans hard liquor in the U.S. Army (→ 7).

3. Finland begins talks with U.S.S.R. (→ 9/4/44).

5. New York: Boxer Jake La Motta wins unexpected victory over Sugar Ray Robinson.

5. Rome: Mussolini ousts 12 from government, including son-in-law, Count Ciano (→ 8).

7. Washington: Shoe ration put at three pairs a year, due to leather shortage (→ 21).

8. Burma: British General Wingate leads guerrilla force "Chindits" against Japanese (→ 8/1).

8. Italy: U.S. bombers smash at Naples, causing heavy damage at harbor installations (→ 3/12).

10. India: Gandhi begins hunger strike to protest imprisonment (→ 3/1).

15. North Africa: Germans break U.S. lines at Faid-Sened Sector in Central Tunisia (→ 18).

16. San Francisco: Yankee star Joe DiMaggio joins army as voluntary inductee.

18. Washington: Madame Chiang Kai-shek asks defeat of Japan in address to Congress.

18. North Africa: Rommel takes three towns in Tunisia (→ 19).

19. Art from the Netherlands seized for Hitler's Linz Gallery in Austria.

19. North Africa: U.S. troops stabilize Tunisian Line (→ 21).

21. North Africa: German tanks and two infantry battalions crack Allied line and occupy Kasserine Pass (→ 26).

22. U.S.S.R.: Outnumbered seven to one, German Gen. Manstein launches counter-attack in Caucasus (→ 3/3).

26. Germany: U.S. Flying Fortresses and Liberators pound Reich docks and U-boat lairs at Wilhelmshaven (→ 3/1).

Russians lead west, take back Kursk

Feb 9. The Soviets have retaken Kursk one year and three months after it fell to the Nazis. The city of 120,000 is a vital railroad junction where the Moscow-Crimea and Voronezh-Kiev lines meet. It was also an essential link in a chain of German outposts in the Ukraine.

Last summer, the Nazis held a series of cities stretching south from Kursk several hundred miles to the Sea of Azov. They controlled thousands of acres between the Dnieper and the Don. From this area, they launched attacks on Stalingrad and parts of the Caucasus.

Kursk freed, the Soviets hope to liberate nearby Kharkov. Rostov, southernmost city on the Nazi line, will be their last target (→ 22).

Canned food, shoes rationed in U.S.

Feb 21. At the expense of wearing out scarce shoe leather, Americans are flocking to grocery stores, buying up all the canned goods they can carry before rationing of such food tins goes into effect March 1. Shoe rationing began several weeks ago, limiting each American to three pairs of shoes a year due to a critical shortage of leather for soles. Americans purchased an estimated 450 million pairs of shoes last year.

Now that canned goods will join shoes, coffee and sugar on the list of rationed items, to be purchased only with stamps in ration books, Americans are stocking up. Mothers have wheeled away their canned goods purchases in perambulators. Young children are tugging toy wagons heaped high with the tins of food just purchased.

"Talk about your gold rush," one New York grocer exclaimed.

Canned fish and meat will not be rationed at this time but will be included in a meat ration program to begin later this spring (→ 3/1).

Japan quits Solomons

Feb 9. The six-month battle for Guadalcanal in the Solomon Islands apparently has ended in an American victory with the withdrawal of Japanese forces. Secretary of the Navy Frank Knox told reporters in Washington that all enemy resistance on the island "has apparently ceased." His statement, the first authoritative claim of victory in the long, hard-fought battle, followed an announcement by the Japanese government that some of its forces were being withdrawn from Guadalcanal and New Guinea. The conquest of Guadalcanal, with its airstrip and excellent harbor, puts American forces within striking distance of Rabaul, a major Japanese base (→ 3/5).

Yanks in tough fight for Kasserine Pass

Feb 26. American forces in central Tunisia, stung by earlier defeats to the Axis, scrambled hungrily and victoriously up the mountains of the Kasserine Pass as Field Marshal Rommel's columns retreated. The armor and dive-bombers which crushed the Americans ten days ago were nowhere to be seen. Northeast of the strategic pass, other units of the Afrika Korps are still giving the Americans a fight at Sbiba and Ousseltia. The units evacuating Kasserine will apparently try to set up new lines of defense to the east near Faid and to the south in the plains around Gafsa. But Rommel, who has taken personal command of the Korps, knows that he is in trouble. His old antagonist, General Bernard Montgomery, is approaching the Mareth line from the east. American troops are poised to the west, in Algeria. Rommel is nearly surrounded.

On the northern Tunisian front, the Germans lost the ground they had taken from the British. German tanks, infantry and paratroopers attacked several Allied positions across an 80-mile front, but Britain's Churchill tanks prevailed. The Germans were pushed back and suffered heavy losses in men and materiel. Hundreds of prisoners were taken by the British (→ 3/10).

German tanks in Libya. Desert battles often stir up man-made sandstorms.

1943

MARCH

Su	Mo	Tu	We	Th	Fr	Sa
	1	2	3	4	5	6
7	8	9	10	11	12	13
14	15	16	17	18	19	20
21	22	23	24	25	26	27
28	29	30	31			

1. British RAF conducts strategic bombing raids on all European railway lines (→ 2).

1. U.S.: Coupon books issued in new processed food rationing plan (→ 21).

1. India: Gandhi ends hunger strike (→ 6/18).

2. Germany: Center of Berlin bombed by RAF; 900 tons of bombs dropped in half hour (→ 6).

3. U.S.S.R.: Soviets capture Rzhev, Nazi strong point (→ 14).

6. Germany: 443 British RAF fliers bomb Essen and the Krupp arms works in the Ruhr (→ 4/4).

8. Adm. W.M. Standley, U.S. ambassador to U.S.S.R, charges Bolsheviks are not publicizing American aid (→ 5/11).

10. North Africa: Hitler calls Rommel back from Tunisia.→

12. Italy: Strikes break out in Genoa, Milan and Turin (→ 5/10).

12. North Africa: Rommel forces defeated at Ksar Rhilane, begin retreat (→ 18).

13. Poland: Germans close Krakow ghetto. (→ 4/19).

14. U.S.S.R.: German troops reoccupy Kharkov (→ 18).

18. Tunisia: Americans drive 42 miles, take Gafsa (→ 20).

18. U.S.S.R.: Reich calls off offensive in Caucasus (→ 7/5).

20. North Africa: Allies attack Rommel's forces on Mareth line (→ 4/2).

21. Washington: Sale of butter. lard, fats, oils halted for week (→ 4/1).

27. U.S. proposes Allied government to rule Indochina in place of French (→ 12/22/44).

31. Allied shipping losses for month reported at 120 ships (→ 5/24).

BIRTH

9. Bobby Fisher, American chess champion.

DEATH

28. Serghei Rachmaninoff, Russian composer (*1/04/1873).

Africa fight lost, Rommel goes home

March 10. Germany's Field Marshal Rommel, the so-called Desert Fox, left the desert of Africa and returned to Europe, defeated, ill and exhausted. He had lost first in Egypt and then in Tunisia, and Adolf Hitler's words at El Alamein were still ringing in his ears.

"As to your troops," Hitler said, "you can show them no other road than that to victory or death."

In Egypt, victory slipped from Rommel's grasp; the effort was so debilitating he had to enter the hospital. Four months later, British Field Marshal Montgomery proved Egypt was no fluke as he beat Rommel again in Tunisia (→ 12).

"Desert Fox" faces doubtful future.

U.S. planes sink 22 Japanese ships

March 5. In a major triumph of air power, Allied planes devastated a convoy seeking to reinforce Japanese forces on New Guinea. General MacArthur's headquarters in Australia announced that all 22 ships in the convoy, including ten warships and 12 transports, had been sunk or left sinking, and 55 Japanese fighter planes had been downed. About 15,000 troops aboard the transports were killed or drowned in the air assault, believed to be the greatest victory ever achieved by air power over naval forces. The communique issued by the MacArthur headquarters said "we have achieved a victory of such completeness as to assume the proportions of a major disaster to the enemy" (→ 4/7).

1943

APRIL

Su	Mo	Tu	We	Th	Fr	Sa
				1	2	3
4	5	6	7	8	9	10
11	12	13	14	15	16	17
18	19	20	21	22	23	24
25	26	27	28	29	30	

1. Meats, fats, cheese rationed in U.S. (→ 8).

2. North Africa: Allied air raid destroys Tunis (→ 3).

3. North Africa: Axis troops begin withdrawal from Tunisia (→ 11).

4. France: Philippe Petain denounces Allied air raids over French cities (→ 5/14).

5. France: Georges Mandel, Leon Blum, Edouard Daladier and Paul Reynaud handed over to Germans (→ 6/5).

7. Pacific: Japanese crush counterattack in Solomon Islands (→ 7/1).

8. FDR freezes prices, wages, salaries to control inflation (→ 6/26).

11. Austria: Hitler, Mussolini conclude four-day meeting in Salzburg, after discussing lost cause in North Africa (→ 5/7).

13. Washington: Jefferson Memorial dedicated.

16. Martinique and Guadeloupe agree to collaborate with Washington, but refuse to rebel against Vichy government.

17. Hungary: Hitler demands Admiral Horthy intern all Hungarian Jews (→ 3/19/44).

19. Poland: 50,000 Jews remaining in Warsaw Ghetto begin uprising against Germans.→

28. Pennsylvania: Wildcat strikes in coal mines sweep Pittsburgh area (→ 29).

28. San Francisco: Chiang Kaishek reveals that entire populations of Chinese were wiped out by Japanese for giving sanctuary to American fliers. (→ 9/6).

29. FDR threatens to invoke war powers if striking miners do not return to work (→ 5/1).

30. Allies release decoy corpse off coast of Spain, bearing false papers ordering invasion of Greece.

DEATHS

6. Alexandre Millerand, French statesman (*2/10/1859).

13. Oskar Schlemmer, German painter, sculptor (*9/4/1888).

30. Beatrice Webb, British reformer (*1/22/1858).

Desperate uprising in Warsaw ghetto

Under the iron hand of Jurgen Stroop, the SS is brutally crushing Jewish resistance in the oppressed ghetto.

April 19. Jews are fighting Nazis in Warsaw, Poland, and it is a fight to the death. The Jews know that if they do not die in their homes or in the sewers beneath the ghetto, they will certainly be gassed to death in one of the infamous concentration camps.

SS troops under the command of General Jurgen Stroop attacked the walled ghetto this morning. They are under orders to seize the 60,000 Jews still living in the area. Half a million Jews were living in the ghetto at this time last year. Most of them have been dragged away by the Nazis. Some were lucky enough to escape.

The Nazis are searching the ghetto systematically, block by block, house to house, basement to ceiling. Where there is resistance, the SS open fire with tanks, mortars and machine guns or they torch the homes with flamethrowers.

The Jews know they have nothing to lose. Guns are scarce. What they lack in firepower, they make up with ingenuity. They pass word from house to house when the Nazis approach. Some fire back. Others try to hide in attics and sewers.

Word has filtered back to the Warsaw ghetto about what happens to Jews who are carted away by the Nazis. It is no secret any more and there is nowhere to hide.

Jewish resistance fighters who have been able to keep one step ahead of Nazi search parties have returned to Warsaw with stories from the ghetto in Lublin. From their apartment windows, Jews there can see the barbed wire of the Maidanek concentration camp. They can also see the smoke rising from the large crematoriums.

A year ago, the Jewish council in Warsaw helped the Nazis organize the first evacuation of ghetto residents to the camp at Treblinka. Today, there is no cooperation. The Jews know their fate. And the Nazis have their orders. They will not leave the ghetto until all the Jews are gone (→ 5/16).

A woman and her children, famine-stricken in the streets of Warsaw.

4,000 Polish officers found in mass grave

Poles perform the odious task of pulling corpses out of the Katyn graves.

April 13. A grim discovery in the forest near Katyn, in Soviet Russia, may provide some answers to a four-year-old mystery. It has already fractured relations between Russia and the Polish government-in-exile. And it has increased the strain between Joseph Stalin and the Allies.

Buried in the forest, west of Smolensk, a mass grave was found containing the bodies of some 4,000 Polish officers. The Russians claim they were killed by Germans, but Stalin refuses to participate in an international investigation.

A German inquiry, witnessed by Polish officials, concludes the officers were killed by the Russians before the German advance to Smolensk. The Germans say the Russians tried to cover up their crime and blame it on Berlin by using captured German ammunition to shoot the Polish officers.

The Polish government in London has been demanding to know for several years what happened to an entire army that disappeared when Russia marched into Poland and divided the country with Germany in 1939.

The question remained unanswered. But it was raised again after Germany seized all of Poland and the Poles were forced into an uneasy alliance with Moscow. Under the 1941 military agreement, Russia agreed to release its Polish prisoners of war and allow many of them to form a new army on Russian soil.

Stalin was uncomfortable with both the Polish army and government because he had designs on Poland after the war was over. To prevent the new army from fighting in Europe and conceivably fighting against Russians one day in Poland, Stalin transferred the Poles to Iran.

British officers were shocked when it arrived. There seemed to be many privates, but their officers had mysteriously disappeared. The Americans and the British have little doubt the murders in the Katyn forest are the handiwork of Stalin. But they are reluctant to criticize the ally who has borne the brunt of the Nazi attack (→ 7/6).

German anti-Communist poster depicting a Soviet massacre.

1943

MAY

Su	Mo	Tu	We	Th	Fr	Sa
						1
2	3	4	5	6	7	8
9	10	11	12	13	14	15
16	17	18	19	20	21	22
23	24	25	26	27	28	29
30	31					

1. Count Fleet wins Kentucky Derby, with jockey J. Longden.

1. FDR seizes all struck coal mines (→ 2).

2. Lewis calls off coal strike minutes before FDR's radio denunciation of U.M.W. (→ 22).

3. New York: Pulitzer prize awarded to Upton Sinclair.

7. North Africa: Tunis and Bizerte captured; Axis in flight toward Cap Bon, facing death or surrender (→ 12).

10. Alaska: U.S. troops land on Attu in Aleutian Islands, held by Japan since June 1942 (→ 30).

10. Italy: Allies conduct air raid over Sicily (→ 6/11).

11. Churchill arrives in Washington for Trident parley (→ 19).

12. FDR agrees to Benes' request to expel Germans from Czechoslovakia after war.

14. Washington: Senate passes "pay-as-you-go" plan; taxes can be withheld before due date.

14. U.S. Flying Fortresses make record raid over France (→ 17).

18. U.N. Food Conference meets in Virginia, calls for equitable resource distribution after war.

19. Washington: Churchill tells Congress Allies will win total victory over Axis (→ 7/20).

22. Akron, Ohio: 40,000 strike rubber plants in protest over WLB wage award (→ 27).

24. Atlantic: German Adm. Doenitz orders halt to sub war due to heavy Axis losses since March (→ 10/12).

27. Balkans: British officers parachute into Yugoslavia to meet with Tito's resistance forces (→ 6/14).

28. FDR names James F. Byrnes to head new Office of War Mobilization (→ 6/26).

30. Alaska: Japanese report Attu is lost (→ 8/15).

31. Algiers: De Gaulle and Giraud set up Committee of Natl. Liberation to represent France until end of war (→ 6/1).

DEATH

26. Edsel Ford, president of Ford Motor Co. (*11/6/1893).

President Roosevelt ends two big strikes

May 27. More than 50,000 Akron rubber workers were back on the job tonight, heeding an ultimatum issued by President Roosevelt. C.I.O. strikers at Goodyear, Goodrich, General Tire and Firestone ended their five-day work stoppage. Full shifts were reported at the companies two hours past the 12 noon deadline set by the president.

Rubber workers, who average $1.20 an hour, sought an increase of eight cents an hour. The War Labor Board recommended no more than three cents, inciting wildcat strikes. Roosevelt's ultimatum described the union walkout as "shocking" and "inexcusable." Some rubber products such as de-icers for airplanes, life rafts and gas masks are essential for the war effort.

George H. Bass, President of the union local at Goodrich, remains optimistic. "I think the strike has achieved the results we wanted: the reopening of the War Labor Board wage case. Now we'll wait and see what they'll do with it."

The rubber worker strike is the second stoppage this month ended by presidential decree. On May 1, United Mine Workers struck to protest wage freezes. Secretary of the Interior Harold Ickes, on Roosevelt's word, arranged a government seizure of soft-coal mines to go into effect at 10 a.m. May 2. U.M.W. leader John L. Lewis canceled the strike after 24 hours (→ 6/19).

Joseph Cornell, inspired by Max Ernst, has created a unique surrealist art form, collecting everyday objects in wood boxes.

150,000 Afrika Korps troops surrender

General Ritter von Thoma, captured last year, salutes Montgomery.

May 12. The war in North Africa has ended. German tanks on Tunisia's Cap Bon peninsula, battered by six British and French divisions, surrendered. Colonel General Dietloff von Armin, who had replaced Field Marshal Rommel as commander of the Axis forces in North Africa, was captured by the British. In all, 150,000 men of the once invincible Afrika Korps have capitulated in the past week.

Bombers break two dams in Ruhr

May 17. For the second night in a row, British bombers attacked German dams in the Ruhr Valley. Lancaster bombers opened a 100-yard breach in the Mohne Dam, and its power station was swept away by the flood. The Eder Dam, the largest in Europe, was also destroyed. Reports say 1,500 people were killed. Factories, railways and entire villages were washed away. The British lost eight planes (→ 6/20).

Flood on the Eder, courtesy of RAF.

Comintern finished

May 15. The Soviet Union has dissolved its worldwide Communist organization, the Comintern. The dissolution of the international organization was prompted by the compelling need to dispell Allied notions of Soviet Communist expansion. It is seen as a cooperative war maneuver and is expected to enhance relations between Russia and the Allies. The Comintern was established by Lenin in March 1919 to organize pro-Communist trade unions, to inspire party discipline and to spread propaganda in nations where communist sympathies existed.

Warsaw ghetto ends

May 16. Resistance has collapsed in the Warsaw ghetto. There are no Jews left in the walled enclave, and the Nazis took very few prisoners. Jurgen Stroop, the SS General, says his troops killed 56,065 Jews. But not all of them died from Nazi bullets. Many committed suicide by staying in their burning homes or jumping from the roofs. Despite often fierce resistance, the Nazis needed just four weeks to crush the ghetto, and it will not be the last. Last week, Heinrich Himmler ordered the liquidation of all Jewish ghettos (→ 6/19).

1943

JUNE

Su	Mo	Tu	We	Th	Fr	Sa
		1	2	3	4	5
6	7	8	9	10	11	12
13	14	15	16	17	18	19
20	21	22	23	24	25	26
29	28	29	30			

1. Algiers: General de Gaulle insists on dismissal of all civil servants who collaborate with Vichy (→ 7/7).

3. Jean-Paul Sartre's play "Les Mouches" opens in Paris.

4. Argentina: Military coup ousts President Ramos Castillo; Juan Peron becomes minister of labor (→ 3/4/44).

5. France: Pierre Laval congratulates French volunteers fighting in U.S.S.R. with Germans (→ 8/27).

8. FDR threatens devastating bombing raids if Germans use poison gas.

11. Italian island of Pantelleria, last Axis stronghold in Sicilian strait, yields to Allied forces (→ 11).

11. FDR asks Italian people to overthrow Mussolini (→ 14).

14. U.S. Supreme Court rules unconstitutional the state practice of requiring students to salute flag.

14. Balkans: Rumania reported ready for separate peace, surrender to the Allies (→ 8/1).

18. British Marshal Archibald Wavel becomes viceroy of India (→ 5/5/44).

19. Pittsburgh: 60,000 cease work in coal mines as union and operators deliberate (→ 22).

19. Germany: Goebbels officially announces Berlin is now free from Jews (→ 8/2).

20. Lancaster shuttle system inaugurated; bombers strike Germany from Britain, and land in North Africa (→ 24).

22. John L. Lewis calls off coal strike until October 31 if Government keeps control of mines (→ 25).

24. Germany: RAF hammers Muelheim in drive to cripple Ruhr industrial base (→ 7/28).

24. Martinique joins Free French in fight against Axis.

25. Washington: Congress overrides FDR veto to pass War Labor Dispute Act, requiring 30-day notice of strikes (→ 11/2).

26. Washington: Senate bars food subsidies by vote of 46-29 (→ 7/15).

Plane shot down; Leslie Howard lost

The refined Leslie Howard.

June 1. Leslie Howard, Ashley Wilkes in "Gone With the Wind," was killed today when a plane he was aboard was shot down by German raiders. He was 50 years old. Ironically, Howard benefitted from the first world war; as a soldier he recovered from shell shock through therapeutic acting lessons.

Howard was born Leslie Stainer to Hungarian immigrants in London. Mildly successful in England, he came to prominence in American films. He played leading-man roles in "Of Human Bondage" (1934), "The Petrified Forest" (1936) and "Pygmalion" (1938). Tall and slim, he portrayed refined and intellectual gentlemen.

Howard's fateful plane trip followed a British-government sponsored lecture tour of Lisbon and cities in Spain. There are rumors he was serving on a spy mission.

▷

Troops called as 29 die in Detroit race riots

MP's patrol Detroit's Negro district in the aftermath of the riots.

June 22. Federal troops moved into Detroit yesterday to help restore order after a race riot in which 29 persons were killed and hundreds of others badly injured. It was the nation's worst racial clash since the days of Great War.

The troops in full battle regalia were ordered into Detroit on the heels of a proclamation issued by President Roosevelt, calling for peace in the stunned, industrialized city. The rioting had interfered with operation of many of the war plants in the Detroit area, with many of the workers afraid to report to work.

It is uncertain what touched off the riot. Some Negro leaders suggested it had been inspired by the Nazis, while others reported that it began as a fight between a white man and a Negro and quickly spread through the city.

Saloons were closed. Many schools failed to open. The baseball game between Cleveland and Detroit was canceled. In some sections of the city stores were looted, windows were smashed, cars overturned and burned. Federal troops used tear gas and fired more than a thousand rounds of ammunition in routing Negroes who had been sniping from upper windows. Police reported that more than 1,300 persons, most of them young Negroes, have been arrested. A 10 p.m. curfew has been ordered (→ 8/1).

British troops seize three Sicilian islands

Italian troops defend Pantelleria.

June 14. The Allies are ready for their long-awaited attack on Sicily and the "underbelly" of Europe. In the past three days, they have captured three island stepping stones between Tunisia and the Sicilian coast. The most important is Pantelleria, which surrendered to the British Friday after around-the-clock bombing raids. The island's air strips will be used with those in Malta and Tunisia by Allied planes that provide air cover for the planned assault on Sicily. Two smaller islands, Lampedusa and Linosa, also surrendered to the Allies (→ 7/10).

1943

JULY

Su	Mo	Tu	We	Th	Fr	Sa
				1	2	3
4	5	6	7	8	9	10
11	12	13	14	15	16	17
18	19	20	21	22	23	24
25	26	27	28	29	30	31

1. MacArthur launches Allied offensive in Pacific (→ 2).

2. Australia: American forces land on Rendova Island (→ 17).

5. U.S.S.R.: Germans launch drive on Kursk salient, north of Kharkov (→ 11).

6. U.S.S.R.: Mass graves discovered near Winniza.

7. General Giraud is greeted in Washington (→ 8/26).

10. Italy: Allied infantry landed on Sicilian coast (→ 16).

11. U.S.S.R.: Soviet counterattacks force Nazis back near Belgorod (→ 13).

12. Germany: Anti-Nazi opposition establishes National Committee for Free Germany.

16. Italy: Britain and U.S. drop millions of leaflets from Allied planes, warning Italy to end Fascist rule or face ruin (→ 19).

17. U.S.S.R.: Germans withdraw from Kursk; Soviets gain upper hand in Russian fight (→ 8/22).

17. Pacific: Japanese and American navies clash near Bougainville Island (→ 8/8).

19. Italy: Hitler convinces Mussolini to continue fight against Allied attack (→ 21).

19. Italy: Allied bombs blast Rome military areas, killing 1,400 (→ 21).

20. FDR orders sharing of atomic research with Britain (→ 8/13).

21. Vatican: Pope Pius XII deplores bombing of Rome (→ 22).

22. Sicily: Eighth American Army enters Palermo (→ 23).

25. Scandinavia: American planes bomb Trondheim base in Norway (→ 8/29).

28. Northern Italy hit by strikes and peace demonstrations (→ 8/5).

BIRTH

10. Arthur Ashe, first black tennis player to win major title.

DEATH

4. General Wladislaw Sikorski, Polish statesman (*5/20/1881).

Allies land in Sicily, capture Palermo

U.S. troops hit the beach in Sicily.

July 23. American troops under the command of General George C. Patton have captured Palermo two weeks after Allied forces invaded Sicily. Preceded by a week of round-the-clock bombing and under a canopy of naval gunfire, the long-awaited invasion by American and British forces took place on July 10.

General Dwight D. Eisenhower, the Allied Commander-in-Chief, described the invasion as "the first page in the liberation of the European Continent." The British Eighth Army, under Field Marshal Montgomery, landed in the southeast corner of Sicily, and the American Seventh Army under Patton landed on the southern coast. The original plan was for the American forces to protect the flanks of the British army as it drove to Messina. But when the British force was slowed down, Patton won approval to make a northern dash to capture Palermo, Sicily's largest city. German forces already had withdrawn from the city, and Italian troops were waiting to surrender (→ 25).

Count Fleet is the fifth Triple Crown winner in horse racing.

Reds hit Nazis in biggest tank battle

German tanks at Kursk. Operation Citadel was long delayed, giving the Red army time to crush Hitler's forces.

July 13. The biggest tank battle in history ended today on the Eastern Front, south of Moscow. Adolf Hitler did not surrender, but he did call it quits. His soldiers and his brand new tanks were badly beaten.

Joseph Stalin was quick to claim victory. "If the battle of Stalingrad was the beginning of the end for the Nazi army," Stalin said, "the battle of Kursk was its catastrophe."

The battle was joined last week, near a tempting bulge in the Russian line that ran east of Orel and Kharkov. The Nazis waited to attack the salient until they had massed unprecedented armor nearby. Their new Panther and Porsche tanks were the biggest ever built, the jewels of an attack force that included 27 divisions.

General von Kluge struck at the north of the salient and General von Manstein attacked from the south. At enormous cost, they breached the Russian line at several points. But, for the most part, the Russians were ready and they held fast.

The Russians could not match the size of the new German tanks, but they could match the Nazis in overall firepower on the ground and in the air. And soldiers in trenches discovered that the new tanks were vulnerable to flamethrowers that could pierce ventilation shafts.

Yesterday, the Russians counterattacked on a front north and east of Orel. They were under orders to "bleed the enemy white." It quickly became a bloodbath.

A thousand Russian tanks attacked an equal number of German tanks. Although the Germans' were bigger, the fighting was at such close range that they lost the advantage. The larger tanks were unable to maneuver, and many were disabled. The fighting and the smoke were so intense that aircraft on both sides kept at bay. They could not tell the two sides apart.

By nightfall, the Russians owned the battlefield. Hitler ordered his cease-fire today (→ 17).

Finnish troops on the Eastern Front.

Nazi gunner fires into the melee.

Mussolini deposed; Badoglio takes job

July 25. Benito Mussolini has been placed under house arrest, and Italy's King Victor Emmanuel has ordered Marshal Pietro Badoglio to form a new government.

The Allied landing in Sicily earlier this month and the bombing of Rome last week were Mussolini's final undoing. Many Italians sat by uncomfortably while the Duce allied himself with Hitler, but they rose in protest when their beloved country was invaded.

Mussolini's Fascist Party was split in the battle over his future. His opponents were encouraged by an appeal from President Roosevelt and Prime Minister Churchill to bury Fascism in Italy. Even Mussolini's son-in-law, Count Ciano, an architect of the alliance with Germany, reversed himself and appealed for peace with the Allies.

Another group of Fascists argued for an even tighter alliance with Hitler, and their hopes were raised when the Duce met with the Fuhrer last week at Feltre. Hitler urged Italy to keep fighting at his side, but many Italians were offended by his arrogant style and choice of words. Italians must be more like Germans, Hitler said, and "have a fanatical will to win."

When Mussolini appeared before the Fascist Grand Council last night, he spoke in favor of the Axis. But his speech was long and rambling. He had survived escapades in Ethiopia, in Spain and with Hitler, but he knew he could not survive the attack on his nation (→ 28).

Gary Cooper stars in the film adaptation of Hemingway's "For Whom the Bell Tolls."

French resistance chief is executed

Moulin, resistance leader.

July 8. Jean Moulin, French underground leader, is dead after a month of torture at the hands of the Gestapo. He was 44. Moulin united resistance fighters in the North and South. A traitor betrayed him.

Moulin had also been imprisoned in November 1940. At that time, he was a civil prefect at a county southwest of Paris. He refused to sign a statement blaming Senegalese soldiers for murders committed by Germans. A German soldier wrote: "I compliment you on the energy with which you defend . . . your country's honor" (→ 11/11).

Roosevelt strips Wallace of war job

July 15. His patience worn thin by their constant feuding, President Roosevelt has stripped both Vice President Henry Wallace and Secretary of Commerce Jesse H. Jones of their war economic duties.

The end of what had been called the Washington War came as the president announced creation of a new Office of Economic Warfare to be headed by Leo T. Crowley. The new agency takes over the work of the Wallace Board of Economic Warfare and the foreign subsidiaries work of the Reconstruction Finance Corporation, headed by Jones.

In a letter to the two men, the president said the move had been prompted by "the unfortunate controversy and acrimonious public debate which has been carried on between you in the public press concerning the administration of foreign economic matters." Of utmost importance, the president said, is "winning the war." He said he did not have time to determine "where the truth lies."

The vice president had accused Jones of blocking economic warfare contracts. Jones, in turn, accused Wallace of being "full of malice and misstatement" and had called for a congressional investigation. Other top government officials had tried repeatedly to heal the breach but had failed (→ 12/10).

U.S. firebombs start vast Hamburg blaze

July 28. Billowing smoke rises four miles into the air in Hamburg this morning after another American attack on the German port city. The Flying Fortresses razed seven square miles of Hamburg and claimed some 30,000 victims. Fifty German planes were shot down. British and Canadian planes dropped thousands of tons of bombs and explosives on the Krupp arms factory in Essen (→ 8/17).

Two German civilians stroll through Hamburg, razed by Allied bombers.

1943

AUGUST

Su	Mo	Tu	We	Th	Fr	Sa
1	2	3	4	5	6	7
8	9	10	11	12	13	14
15	16	17	18	19	20	21
22	23	24	25	26	27	28
29	30	31				

1. Balkans: U.S. planes bomb oil installations at Ploesti, Rumania, destroying one-third of Reich oil supply (→ 28).

1. New York: Five killed, 410 injured as rumor of murder sparks race riot (→ 4/3/44).

1. Japan declares Burma independent, announces joining with Axis (→ 2/4/44).

2. Poland: 600, interned at Treblinka, escape in uprising (→ 1/29/44).

5. Italy: The British seize Catania in Sicily (→ 13).

8. Pacific: John F. Kennedy, ex-ambassador's son, saves crew after Japanese destroyer splits PT boat in two (→ 17).

13. Quebec: FDR, Churchill and Mackenzie King meet with military advisers (→ 17).

13. New Italian regime declares Rome an "open city" (→ 17).

15. Alaska: U.S. and Canadian forces take Kiska in Aleutians.

17. Germany: Allied raid over Essen cuts Krupp arms output by 65% (→ 18).

17. Southwest Pacific: Americans take another island, Vella Lavella in the Solomons (→ 21).

21. Pacific: U.S. completes air raid on New Guinea, disabling 300 Japanese planes (→ 10/12).

21. Australia: John Curton and Labor Party win general elections.

22. U.S.S.R.: German troops evacuate Kharkov (→ 9/4).

22. Andrei A. Gromyko replaces Maxim Litvinoff as Soviet ambassador to U.S.

26. U.S. and Britain recognize de Gaulle's Committee of Natl. Liberation in Algiers (→ 11/9).

27. France: Ex-Pres. Lebrun arrested by Gestapo (→ 10/21).

28. Balkans: King Boris of Bulgaria dies of assassin's bullet wounds (→ 11/18).

29. Scandinavia: Danes revolt against Nazi rule, scuttle ships as Reich seizes govt. (→ 11/16).

BIRTH

30. Jean-Claude Killy, French skier.

Patton's army takes Messina in Sicily

Patton, avid student of war history.

Aug 17. American troops have entered Messina, completing the Allied conquest of Sicily in 38 days. The conquest of the large Mediterranean island left Allied troops separated from the Italian mainland only by the Straits of Messina, across which artillery gunfire continued to flash.

The first detachments to enter Messina were from the Third Division of General George Patton's Seventh Army. Troops of the British Eighth Army marched into the city shortly after the American infantrymen. General Patton led a drive along the mountainous northern coast, sometimes doing end runs around the defending German forces with amphibious landings.

The British army, using the same tactic of amphibious landings, drove up from the south against considerable German resistance. The Germans fought a tenacious rearguard action, trying to delay the Allied advance, while German troops and equipment were being evacuated to the Italians to man the guns. Finally, however, they surrendered in droves as resistance collapsed. The official total of Italians and Germans captured was put at 130,000 (→ 9/3).

Roosevelt and Churchill make war plans

Canadian Premier Mackenzie King, President Roosevelt, Prime Minister Churchill and British envoy Athlone pose in Quebec.

Aug 17. President Roosevelt and Prime Minister Churchill are meeting in the majesty of Quebec's Citadel, overlooking the Saint Lawrence River and the Laurentian Mountains, to map military and political strategy for the war against Germany and Japan. Both leaders are under pressure from Stalin to open a new front and relieve the burden on Russia. It is assumed they will discuss both the timing and the location of the invasion of France, which is code-named "Overlord."

Roosevelt and Churchill agreed earlier that the operation would be impossible this year, but both men think that it should be launched as soon as possible. In addition, they are expected to approve the final details of General Eisenhower's assault on Italy. They will also try to convince Stalin to attend their next meeting (→ 9/17).

British bomb Nazi secret weapons base

British Halifax bomber.

Aug 18. RAF bombers struck a top-secret Nazi weapons base on Peenemunde Island in the Baltic Sea for the second night in a row tonight. They bombed a factory that produces new planes propelled by air rushing through their engines. Some of the aircraft, called flying bombs, do not require pilots. The British also attacked the long runways that are needed for testing of the weapons (→ 9/4).

Mountbatten goes to Southeast Asia

Aug 25. Lord Mountbatten, second cousin of King George, will head the new Southeast Asia Command. The appointment follows a conference between Prime Minister Churchill and President Roosevelt. Operations will be conducted in India and Ceylon against Japan.

Lord Mountbatten.

1943

SEPTEMBER

Su	Mo	Tu	We	Th	Fr	Sa
			1	2	3	4
5	6	7	8	9	10	11
12	13	14	15	16	17	18
19	20	21	22	23	24	25
26	27	28	29	30		

2. Germany: Albert Speer takes on leadership of all war efforts.

3. Italy: Allies cross Messina straits and invade mainland (→ 8).

4. U.S.S.R.: Red army overruns 400 villages in smashing 120-mile gain (→ 26).

4. Germany: RAF blasts Berlin with 50 tons of explosives per minute (→ 16).

6. U.S. asks Chinese Nationalists to join with Communists and present unified front to Japan (→ 6/19/45).

8. Gen. Eisenhower reports Italy signed secret surrender five days ago (→ 9).

9. Italy: Badoglio's government threatens war with Germany if support is not withdrawn from Natl. Fascist Republic set up in Mussolini's name (→ 9).

9. Italy: Allied troops land at Salerno, encounter strong resistance from Reich (→ 10).

10. Italy: Nazis occupy Rome and Milan after siege (→ 12).

14. Italy: Germans abandon Salerno (→ 18).

16. France: Allied air raid on Nantes kills 1,150 (→ 10/5).

17. Washington: FDR reports agreement with Churchill on times and places for new blows in Europe and Asia (→ 10/19).

18. Mussolini asks Italians to take up arms against Allies (→ 23).

19. French rise against Axis on Corsica.

21. Fulbright Resolution adopted in House of Representatives, calling for U.S. participation in intl. peace organization.

23. Italy: Nazis wreck Naples port, sink many ships (→ 30).

25. U.S.S.R.: Red army retakes Smolensk; Germans in retreat to Dnieper (→ 26).

29. Hitler's "Mein Kampf" published in U.S.

30. Italy: Germans quit Naples as Allies close in (→ 10/1).

BIRTH

29. Lech Walesa, Polish labor and Solidarity leader.

Russians near Kiev and take Smolensk

Sept 26. The Red army blasted Nazi troops in Smolensk, once Germany's greatest Eastern Front bastion, gaining control of the city and building momentum in the battle for the Dnieper River. Soviet forces liberated Smolensk today after several days of heavy fighting, pushing the Germans out of the city block by block, finally finishing their conquest by nightfall. The fall of Roslavi, 37 miles southeast of Smolensk, was also reported.

The fall of Smolensk gives the Russians an unbroken line of 250 miles. A communique issued by Soviet Premier Joseph Stalin announced that over 4,100 Germans had been killed in 24 hours of fighting, including 1,000 in the battle at Brovary, a suburb of Kiev. The third largest city in the Soviet Union and held by the Nazis since September 1941, Kiev may well be the site of the next Russian victory.

The German defeats on the Eastern Front are being blamed on the Italian capitulation to the Allies by Berlin commentator Adolf Halfeld. He wrote: "Military and political changes by German forces have been made necessary by Italy's treason." The remark underscores the bitterness felt by most Germans over Italian acquiescence.

More than 540 localities in Russia have been wrested from German control in the last few days. A victory at Kiev will be second in strategic importance only to that at Stalingrad (→ 10/7).

Soviets, their own homeland ravaged by Nazis, delight in depicting the coming invasion of Italy.

Allies go ashore in Italy

Sept 12. American and German forces are locked in furious combat around Naples, but the Allies are encountering little resistance as they advance up the toe and across the heel of Italy's boot. The invasion of the Italian mainland began without a hitch on the 3rd. It was revealed the same day that the government of Premier Pietro Badoglio had surrendered unconditionally to a representative of General Eisenhower in a secret meeting on Sicily. Captains of many important ships in the Italian fleet soon turned their vessels over to the Allies.

British and Canadian forces under the command of the hero of North Africa, General Bernard Montgomery, crossed the Straits of Messina from Sicily before dawn on the 3rd. They quickly established a beachhead at Reggio Calabria, the most important city in the toe of the boot. Within a few days, they had advanced north through treacherous mine fields all the way to Catanzaro and established a line that runs from the Sant' Eufemia Gulf to the Ionian Sea.

Another British invasion team sliced across the heel of the boot, from Taranto to Brindisi, and seized an Adriatic port for the first time.

The American Fifth Army captured Salerno and is inching toward Naples in vicious fighting. The Germans have thrown tanks into the battle, and their pilots are engaged in non-stop dogfights with the Allies. The Americans have beefed up their beachheads, and supplies and reinforcements are streaming into the Naples area (→ 14).

Mussolini boards a German plane in the Abruzzi Mountains. After hearing of Il Duce's imprisonment at the hands of the new Italian government, Hitler ordered a commando raid, led by Otto Skorzeny, to airlift his ally to safety.

1943

OCTOBER

Su	Mo	Tu	We	Th	Fr	Sa
					1	2
3	4	5	6	7	8	9
10	11	12	13	14	15	16
17	18	19	20	21	22	23
24	25	26	27	28	29	30
31						

1. Italy: Naples and Avellino fall to Allied forces (→ 10).

5. Germany: U.S. fliers make record attack on Reich in Frankfort (→ 20).

7. U.S.S.R.: Red army cracks Nazi Dnieper River line (→ 9).

9. U.S.S.R.: Gen. Petrov drives Nazis out of Caucasus (→ 30).

10. Mediterranean: Flying Fortresses attack Greece, Crete and Rhodes for 1st time (→ 5/18/44).

10. Naples: Time bomb kills 12 in cathedral just before ranking American officers arrive for Mass (→ 12).

11. St. Louis: Yankees beat Cardinals to win World Series in five games.

12. Atlantic: Portugal opens Azores bases to Allies (→ 11/12/44).

12. Italy: U.S. Fifth Army begins drive on Rome, clashes with Nazis at Volturno River (→ 13).

12. U.S. Pacific air fleet bombs Rabaul, wrecks 177 Axis planes, 124 ships in surprise attack (→ 16).

13. Italy declares war on Germany (→ 31).

14. Eastern Poland: Over 300 Jews escape from Nazi camp at Sobibor (→ 1/29/44).

16. Pacific: Australians repel Japanese offensive in New Guinea (→ 11/1).

19. Moscow: Allied foreign ministers meet to discuss postwar plans (→ 31).

20. Germany: Flying Fortresses smash vital Luftwaffe factory in Dueren (→ 21).

21. Algerian Jews regain French citizenship in de Gaulle decree.

21. France: Resistance attack frees 14 leaders, imprisoned in Lyon (→ 11/11).

31. Moscow: U.S.S.R. Britain, U.S., China sign accord on postwar attitude to Axis (→ 11/22).

BIRTH

22. Catherine Deneuve, French actress, born Catherine Dorleac.

DEATH

31. Max Reinhard, German stage director (*9/09/1873).

Dnieper River line cracked by Soviets

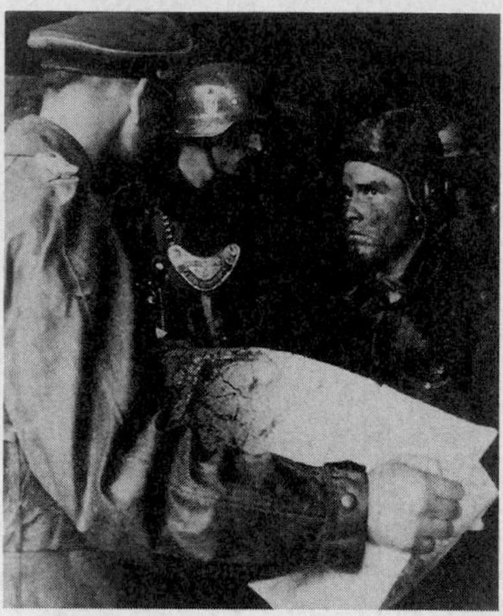

Nazis interrogate a Soviet tank crew.

Oct 30. A 25-mile long stretch of German resistance along the Dnieper River was smashed by the Red army in two blistering attacks at Dniepropetrovsk and its industrial sister city, Dnieprodzerzhinsk. Premier Joseph Stalin proudly announced the two key Russian victories, saying that Moscow would honor the victorious troops with 20 artillery salvos from 224 guns. Official reports of German losses were not issued, but some counts estimate 2,000 Nazis died in the Melitopol sector alone. After cracking the line, Russian forces captured over 40 towns (→ 11/27).

Allied drive halted by Monte Cassino

Oct 31. Allied armies, trying to inch their way up the boot of Italy, "like a bug on one leg," as Winston Churchill put it, have run into stiff resistance north of the Volturno River. The Nazis have transformed the Benedictine fortress at Monte Cassino into an almost impenetrable fortress.

The fortress has become a major impediment on the march from Naples to Rome. The Allies are short on men, and the geography is against them. The Appenines have provided the Nazis numerous locations for machine gun nests, there are few roads and the land is very marshy. Fog hampers Allied aircraft, and winter is coming. This time, the weather seems to be on the side of the Nazis (→ 1/4/44).

American bombers attack in great force

Oct 21. American Flying Fortresses annihilated an important military-industrial plant at Dueren, Germany, yesterday as the U.S. Air Force completed its seventh bombing mission of the October offensive. Last night's attack pushed the total of Allied bombs dropped on Europe in the last 100 days to 80,270 tons. Half of Germany's cities have been seriously damaged. Two German fighter planes were gunned down in the Dueren raid, bringing the October total to 475. Eight U.S. bombers were lost, boosting October downings to 174.

Earlier this month, Frankfurt, Germany, blazed like "heavy red velvet" as combined RAF and USAAF bombs ignited devastating fires. The city is a strategic rail center dotted with large industrial plants.

In mid-October, the biggest Allied air force ever assembled in the Pacific theater attacked Rabaul, New Guinea, destroying or seriously damaging 177 enemy aircraft and 123 ships. That raid dumped 350 tons of bombs and 250,000 rounds of machine gun fire and resulted in what was called "a disastrous defeat for the enemy" (→ 1/13/44).

Saint-Laurent's basilica in ruins.

Corsica is first French territory liberated

Oct 4. The island of Corsica has become the first department of France in Europe to be liberated from the Nazis. They retreated from the island today, returning freedom to the Corsicans and giving the Allies an important base for aerial and naval operations against the Germans on the continent. The Nazis' withdrawal also means they will not be able to use Corsica for U-boat attacks against the Allies.

The Allies secretly armed thousands of Corsican resistance fighters before the armistice was signed with Italy. As soon as that agreement was announced, Italian troops on Corsica joined island fighters and the French in the battle against the Nazis. Corsica has suffered much pain in the past month of fighting. German bases at Bastia and other cities on the island were heavily bombarded by Allied planes. And the Nazis aggravated food shortages by setting fire to hundreds of acres of crops and farms. But now, this small part of France is free.

"Casablanca" is more fun than real thing

You must remember this: Last spring, the American and British forces began a drive against the Germans in Morocco. Meanwhile, Humphrey Bogart and Ingrid Bergman shot a film called "Casablanca" on a Hollywood soundstage. The film is now in theaters. As time goes by, it may prove more memorable than the real thing.

Bogey plays a nightclub owner who runs into an old flame (Bergman) at his Moroccan hideaway. He sacrifices his happiness for hers while serving the Allied underground. Dooley Wilson plays a fine piano player, and Claude Rains is an unflappable chief of police. Michael Curtiz ("Yankee Doodle Dandy") directed.

"Here's looking at you, kid."

1943

NOVEMBER

Su	Mo	Tu	We	Th	Fr	Sa
	1	2	3	4	5	6
7	8	9	10	11	12	13
14	15	16	17	18	19	20
21	22	23	24	25	26	27
28	29	30				

1. Pacific: U.S. troops begin landing on Bougainville in Solomon Islands (→ 2).

2. Pacific: U.S. sinks enemy cruiser and four destroyers in Bougainville fight (→ 20).

2. Washington: Coal strike called off as Ickes grants Lewis $1.50 a day rise in pay (→ 12/27).

5. U.S. Senate passes Connally resolution calling for U.S. to support intl. peace organization after war (→ 3/21/44).

6. U.S.S.R.: Soviets retake Kiev (→ 1/4/44).

9. New York: Jackson Pollock's work first shown at Peggy Guggenheim's gallery.

9. Algiers: Gen. Giraud retires from French Committee of Natl. Liberation (→ 3/20/44).

11. France: Germans charge anti-Nazi rally in Grenoble with bayonets drawn (→ 1/10/44).

16. Scandinavia: U.S. planes hit south Norway (→ 2/22/44).

18. Balkans: German troops evacuate Bulgarian capital of Sofia (→ 29).

19. Ottawa: Ray Atherton, first U.S. ambassador to Canada, is installed.

20. Pacific: American Marines land in Tarawa (→ 23).

23. Pacific: U.S. takes Tarawa in Gilberts after losing nearly 2,700 out of 5,000 men (→ 24).

25. New York: Errol Flynn appears in "Northern Pursuit."

26. Turkey: Earthquake kills 1,800.

27. West Point: Navy shuts out Army second year in row 13-0.→

30. Italy: Badoglio government strips sovereign of titles King of Albania and Emperor of Ethiopia (→ 1/11/44).

BIRTHS

5. Sam Shepard, U.S. writer-actor, won 1978 Pulitzer.

22. Billie Jean King, American tennis star.

DEATH

22. Lorenz Hart, U.S. lyricist, teamed with Richard Rodgers (*5/2/1895).

Tito becomes boss of Yugoslav regime

Nov 29. Joseph Broz, known as Marshal Tito, has, without elaborate fanfare, become leader of the Yugoslav regime. Tito has been cooperative with Allied forces, paving the way for the Soviet armies' passage through Belgrade in September and helping the British fight Axis troops. Meanwhile, his archrival, General Draja Mikhailovich, has been disowned by the Allies for dealing with the Germans.

Tito, fierce resistant to Nazi rule.

Jailed from 1929-1934 for his involvement in the Communist Party, which was outlawed in Yugoslavia, Tito has amassed popular support among his countrymen. Some of his following stems from his constant contact with his people while serving as a recruiter for the International Brigade during the Spanish Civil War in the mid-1930's (→ 12/10).

Western leaders meet Chiang in Cairo

Nov 22. For the first time ever, President Roosevelt and Prime Minister Churchill met Chinese leader Chiang Kai-shek in Cairo. The three men reached general agreement on the offensive against the Axis and on the status of Japan and Germany after the war.

Chiang was pleased to hear that Roosevelt and Churchill will not be satisfied until Japan is forced to withdraw from Manchuria and the territory it has conquered in the South Pacific and to retreat to its home islands.

One woman was admitted to the inner circle of male leaders. Chiang speaks little English and his dashing wife served as his translator. Later, the couple was seen touring the pyramids by jeep.

The Cairo meeting has reassured Chiang about the Allies' intentions. It has also increased his prestige back at home. Many of the Chinese are tired of being treated like a third-rate power, and Chiang's role in the Cairo Conference served to legitimize China's place on the world stage (→ 28).

The Big Three debate future in Tehran

The Big Three, Stalin, Roosevelt and Churchill pose for photographers at Tehran after discussing Allied plans for the liberation of Europe.

Nov 28. Franklin Roosevelt, Winston Churchill and Joseph Stalin met for the first time in Tehran today. Their foreign ministers had already reached major agreements in Moscow on how the postwar world should be carved up. It remained for the three leaders to develop a personal relationship.

Roosevelt seemed to have a lot of fun doing just that, and he befriended Stalin by poking fun at Churchill. "I began to tease Churchill about his Britishness," the American President said, "about his cigars, about his habits. It began to register with Stalin. Winston got red and scowled and finally Stalin broke into a deep, hearty guffaw. It was then that I called him Uncle Joe."

Once a personal relationship was established, the three leaders got down to business. At the meeting in Moscow, Foreign Affairs Commissar V.M. Molotov was assured that a second front would be opened. In Tehran, the three leaders agreed that the operation, to be called "Overlord," would be launched in May of next year.

They also discussed how Germany would be divided after the war, and they reached preliminary agreement on the touchy issue of the future of Poland. Stalin was assured he would be allowed to move the Soviet Union's border west into Poland and Poland would in turn be allowed to absorb part of eastern Germany.

Stalin also told Churchill and Roosevelt about his designs on the Balkans and his desire for a warm port in the Pacific (→ 12/6).

Rolling westward, U.S. takes Gilberts

Nov 24. The Second Marine Division has seized control of the Gilbert Islands after fierce fighting with heavily fortified Japanese forces on the Tarawa Atoll. Admiral Chester W. Nimitz, Commander-in-Chief of the Pacific Fleet, announced in Pearl Harbor that Betio Island in the Tarawa Atoll had been captured after a 76-hour battle in which the Marines crushed "a desperate enemy counterattack."

The heaviest fighting in the Gilbert Islands campaign took place in the invasion of Betio Island, a small island with a landing strip that the Japanese had made into a fortress. There was no immediate information on American casualties. Radio Tokyo estimated there had been 5,000 American casualties.

The capture of the Gilbert Islands tears down what Nimitz has described as a barrier on a road to Tokyo. The westward drive across the Central Pacific has now made a big dent in the Japanese perimeter, pushing the Japanese line of defense several hundred miles northward to the Marshall Islands (→ 12/8).

War or no war Navy 13, Army 0

Nov 27. Navy's undefeated football squad chalked up another victory today, shutting out their traditional rivals Army, 13-0, at Michie Stadium in West Point, New York. Some 300 colleges have abandoned football during the war, but Army and Navy continue to battle it out.

Army and Navy on the home front.

1943

DECEMBER

Su	Mo	Tu	We	Th	Fr	Sa
			1	2	3	4
5	6	7	8	9	10	11
12	13	14	15	16	17	18
19	20	21	22	23	24	25
26	27	28	29	30	31	

8. Pacific: U.S. carriers sink two cruisers, down 72 planes in Marshall Islands (→ 17).

10. Washington: FDR signs bill to postpone draft of pre-Pearl Harbor fathers (→ 1/13/44).

10. Balkans: Allied forces bomb Sofia, capital of Bulgaria (→ 11).

11. U.S.: Secretary of State Cordell Hull demands Hungary, Rumania and Bulgaria's withdrawal from war (→ 3/18/44).

12. Moscow: Benes, president of exiled Czech govt., signs treaty with U.S.S.R. for postwar cooperation (→ 5/8/44).

17. Pacific: U.S. forces invade New Britain Island in New Guinea (→ 1/30/44).

17. U.S. Congress repeals Chinese Exclusion Acts.

26. Chicago: Bears win third football title in four years, 41-21 over Washington Redskins.

26. German battleship Scharnhorst sunk by British ships in Arctic fight.

27. Washington: Army seizes railroads on president's order, to keep trains running under threat of strike (→ 1/19/44).

DEATH

22. Beatrice Potter, author, "Peter Rabbit" books (*7/28/1866).

CULTURAL EVENTS, 1943

Literature: William Saroyan's "The Human Comedy"; Stephen Vincent Benet's poem "Western Star"; Robert Frost's "A Witness Tree," Pulitzer for poetry.

Academia: Walter Lippmann's "U.S. Foreign Policy"; Wendell Willkie's "One World"; Sartre's "Being and Nothingness."

Music: Rodgers and Hammerstein's "Oklahoma!"; Schuman wins first Pulitzer for music; "Mairzy Doats"; "Oh What a Beautiful Morning"; "Comin' in on a Wing and a Prayer."

The Arts: Mondrian's "Broadway Boogie-Woogie"; Picasso's "The Bull's Head," first "found object" sculpture.

Film: Orson Welles' "Jane Eyre"; "Casablanca," Academy Award.

Second front: Ike will run the big show

Dec 24. President Roosevelt has appointed General Dwight D. Eisenhower to lead the northern and western invasions of Europe, it was announced today. In a diplomatic maneuver, FDR praised General George C. Marshall, another candidate for the European attacks, and Admiral Ernest J. King as "military geniuses." Eisenhower has won the respect of Allied military experts and is regarded as the best strategic commander for major operations in the European theater. FDR noted that Eisenhower's "performance in Italy has been excellent" (→ 1/16/44).

General Dwight David Eisenhower.

Jane Russell in The Outlaw is a big hit

Howard Hughes' acting discovery, Jane Russell, is the star of "The Outlaw." The film concerns the exploits of Billy the Kid, but Miss Russell's cleavage somehow takes precedence over the plot. The 22-year-old actress hails from a town called Bemidji, Minn.

There was a marked drop in commercial films this year. John Ford and Frank Capra are among several directors making public relations (some say propaganda) films for the Allied governments. John Huston's only work all year was the narration and direction of a picture called "Report from the Aleutians."

Voluptuous Jane Russell.

Big Three agreed on plan to subdue Reich

Dec 6. President Roosevelt, Prime Minister Churchill and Premier Stalin announced that they had agreed on a joint military strategy to defeat Germany. Their communique provided new details on the meeting at Tehran nine days ago. The three leaders said that they had fixed the dates for a coordinated drive from the west, south and east against Adolf Hitler. They presumably reached an agreement on "Overlord," the invasion of France, but for obvious reasons no details were released.

"No power on earth," the communique said, "can prevent our destroying the German armies by land, their U-boats by sea and their warplanes from the air. Our attacks will be relentless and increasing." Observers noted that the communique differed from earlier Allied statements by not insisting upon the "unconditional" surrender of Germany. It was not clear whether the omission is significant.

Roosevelt, Churchill and Stalin also agreed to guarantee the independence and sovereignty of Iran after the war. All three leaders presently have forces in Iran.

The communique made no mention of the war against Japan. That strategy was designed at the Cairo Conference. Roosevelt and Churchill hope Stalin will turn his attention to the Pacific after Hitler is defeated. The statement also managed to sidestep the sensitive questions about the future of Poland and the Balkans (→ 1/15/44).

War books popular; so's a Brooklyn tree

War is waged in the arts. Drama, novels and non-fiction concern themselves with the reality overseas. Yet occasionally an author offers succor, perhaps in a cool cornfield or under a tree in Brooklyn.

Richard Tregaskis wrote of Marines in the Pacific in "Guadalcanal Diary" (1943). Ernie Pyle, war correspondent, produced "Here Is Your War" this year, too. "Watch on the Rhine," Lillian Hellman's play about fascism and isolationism, earned praise from critics.

Philosophers and politicians also focused on current events. Edmund Wilson's "To the Finland Station" (1940) addressed political upheaval. Pastor and Socialist Reinhold Niebuhr published "The Nature and Destiny of Man" (1941). It blamed the present on a history of greed and self-interest. Erich Fromm wrote "The Fear of Freedom" in 1942. The book claims industrial progress alienates people from themselves.

Readers found respite in the shade of "A Tree Grows in Brooklyn" (1943). The novel by Betty Smith tells of an intelligent young woman trying to rise above her life in a tenement. Emlyn Williams' play "The Corn Is Green" (1940) recounts his experiences with an inspiring teacher in a Welsh mining community. Finally, former presidential contender Wendell Willkie looked beyond today's chaos to a peaceful future when we will be "One World" (1943).

Biggest American squadron smites enemy

Paris, after an Allied air attack.

Dec 31. The heaviest and most numerous squadron of U.S. aircraft has pummeled German targets as the year draws to a close. The air raids struck a ball-bearing plant in Paris, an airfield in Cologne, the Channel coast and points in southwest Germany. The onslaught came after British planes dumped more than 2,240 bombs on Berlin, igniting towering infernos visible from 200 miles away. Over 2,000 Allied planes took part in the attacks, including 1,300 U.S. aircraft. The awesome firepower achieved its objectives: to paralyze industrial Germany and soften her for an Allied invasion.

1944

JANUARY

Su	Mo	Tu	We	Th	Fr	Sa
						1
2	3	4	5	6	7	8
9	10	11	12	13	14	15
16	17	18	19	20	21	22
23	24	25	26	27	28	29
30	31					

1. Oswald T. Avery, Colin M. MacLeod and Maclyn McCarty publish report identifying DNA as hereditary agent in a virus.

4. U.S.S.R.: Soviet troops cross former Polish border (→ 17).

4. Italy: British Fifth Army attacks Monte Cassino (→ 7).

7. U.S. Air Force announces production of first jet fighter, Bell P-59 Airacomet.

7. Italy: San Vittore taken in American drive (→ 11).

10. Lyon, France: Militia kills Victor Basch, president of Human Rights League (→ 2/13).

13. Washington: FDR presents $99.7 bil. war budget (→ 22).

13. Germany: Three Reich plane plants wrecked; 64 U.S. craft lost in air attack (→ 20).

15. European Advisory Commission decides to divide Germany into several occupation zones after war (→ 9/11).

16. London: Eisenhower assumes supreme command of Allied Expeditionary Force in Europe (→ 4/17).

17. Russia rejects Polish proposal to negotiate boundary dispute (→ 2/3).

19. Washington: Rail wage dispute ended; lines return to private ownership (→ 4/26).

22. Washington: War Refugee Board set up by FDR (→ 3/7).

26. Argentina breaks with the Axis (→ 3/4).

27. Washington announces 5,200 American prisoners have been tortured by Japanese.→

29. New York: World's greatest warship Missouri is launched.

30. Pacific: U.S. ships and planes hit atolls in savage attack on Marshall Islands (→ 31).

31. Pacific: U.S. troops under Vice Adm. Spruance land in Marshall Islands (→ 2/1).

DEATHS

6. Ida M. Tarbell, muckraking journalist (*11/5/1857).

23. Edvard Munch, Norwegian painter (*12/12/1863).

31. Jean Giraudoux, French playwright (*10/29/1882).

Bombs saturate Berlin; plane plants hit

The Lancaster bomber, a major force in RAF efforts to crush the Reich.

Jan 20. The RAF dropped 2,300 tons of bombs over Berlin today, just one week after a massive array of 1,400 American planes darkened the central German skies, unloading a barrage of bombs that obliterated three key Nazi aircraft assembly plants. Despite the loss of 59 heavy bombers and five fighter jets, the United States Eighth Air Force called its assault a "major military success" and German dispatches even acknowledged that "the enemy (was) technically superior."

The three plants hit were Oschersieben, Halberstadt and Brunswick, all important factories of war for the Third Reich. Virtually all available planes in the Luftwaffe arsenal, about 100, were used in defense. Of those, 28 were downed by American fighters (→ 2/21).

U.S. says Japanese torture Americans

Jan 27. The U.S. government has revealed that thousands of American soldiers have died at the hands of their Japanese captors in the Philippines. Americans who were captured in the fall of Corregidor and Bataan were beaten, starved and shot during a "death march" to Japanese prison camps. The reports, which have been confirmed by other sources, come from three American officers who escaped after a year in the camps.

The forced march was made under a blistering sun, and prisoners were given so little water that some went crazy. The Japanese were said to shoot stragglers, and men who went to the aid of their fallen comrades were horse-whipped. The escaped officers reported that six American and Filipino soldiers who were ill were buried alive. It is estimated that three times as many Filipinos as Americans have perished.

Yanks land at Anzio; Russians in Poland

Allied tankers unload supplies at the battered Anzio waterfront.

Jan 22. Two American divisions surprised the Germans in Italy today as they stormed ashore 60 miles behind enemy lines at Anzio. There was little resistance as German units withdrew to the south to increase defenses around the Monte Cassino fortress.

On the Eastern Front, Russian troops made their biggest advance to the west yet as they smashed through German lines in the Ukraine and captured Rakitno, ten miles inside Poland's border. The Russians say the Germans are "retreating in disorder" (→ 2/2).

Nazis planning to breed Aryan elite

Jan 29. The Nazis are taking another step toward what they call a purification of the German race. Now they hope to accelerate the reproduction of a so-called Aryan elite. The plan is the brainchild of Martin Bormann, Hitler's personal secretary. His idea of a perfect German is an SS officer.

To increase the number of what are called pure Germanic children, Bormann would reverse all societal taboos and encourage unmarried women to bear the children of the Nordic elite. The pregnant women would be cared for by the Lebensborn Society, the "Fountain of Life." By the end of the war, Bormann projects 10,000 children will be living in 22 homes administered by the society.

In addition, 200,000 children with Aryan characteristics who have been torn from the arms of their parents in Norway, Poland and Czechoslovakia will be raised as Germans. Bormann plans to finance his program of genetic selection by taxing unmarried Germans and childless couples (→ 7/12).

Ciano is shot on Mussolini's order

Jan 11. Former Italian Foreign Minister Count Galeazzo Ciano, charged with treason, has been shot to death by a firing squad. Ciano had been a member of the Fascist Grand Council that voted against Mussolini in 1943. Two days ago, Ciano was brought to trial in Verona. The Nazis were insistent that he be found guilty. His wife, Edda, daughter of Mussolini, pleaded on his behalf, yet Mussolini gave the final, fatal order (→ 22).

Giraudoux, prolific playwright, is dead

Jan 31. French dramatist Hippolyte Jean Giraudoux has died at the age of 61. Diplomat, government official and war hero (he was awarded the Legion of Honor), Giraudoux still found time to write 15 successful plays. "Amphitryon 38" (1929), "Tiger at the Gates" (1935) and "Electra" (1937) were among his best. He took themes from the Greek myths—revenge, greed and pride—and used them in allegorical settings. He leaves an unproduced play about a crazed optimist called "The Madwoman of Chaillot."

Norwegian artist Edvard Munch dies

Jan 23. Edvard Munch, a founder of Expressionism, has died outside Oslo. He was 80. Munch lived much longer than he had ever hoped. His years were wracked by depression and mental torment, yet out of those depths came original and moving art.

Munch studied in Oslo and Paris. During the 1890's, while Freud explored the psyche, he explored the emotions. His wood cuttings were violent and stark. "The Shriek" (1893) shows a person with a skull-like face shrieking at the viewer, while sea and clouds reverberate in fierce blues and reds. Works like this and "The Kiss" (1895) shocked the public. One of his shows in Berlin in 1892 closed after public outcry. His art now seems an omen of our own violent times.

1944

FEBRUARY

Su	Mo	Tu	We	Th	Fr	Sa
		1	2	3	4	5
6	7	8	9	10	11	12
13	14	15	16	17	18	19
20	21	22	23	24	25	26
29	28	29				

1. Pacific: U.S. forces take beaches on Marshall Islands (→ 3).

2. Italy: Germans stop Allied attack at Anzio (→ 15).

3. U.S. battleships shell Japanese homeland for first time—at Kurile Islands (→ 4).

3. U.S.S.R.: Red army encircles 56,000 Germans in Ukraine (→ 6).

4. Burma: Japanese attack Indian Seventh Army (→ 3/31).

4. Pacific: U.S. Marines occupy two Kwajalein Islands (→ 18).

6. U.S.S.R.: Russians take Lutsk and Rovno (→ 7).

7. Finland: Helsinki bombed twice by waves of Soviet planes (→ 26).

12. Wendell Wilkie enters American presidential race (→ 4/5).

13. Arms dropped to French resistance for first time —at Plateau des Glieres (→ 3/26).

17. Alabama: Oil discovered in commercial quantities.

18. Pacific: Army, Navy and Marines invade Eniwetok Atoll (→ 23).

19. Miami: Charles E. Bedaux, French-born former-sandhog, takes his own life while facing treason charges.

21. Tokyo: Hideki Tojo becomes chief of staff of Japanese army.

22. Stockholm bombed by unidentified planes (→ 9/10/45).

22. Washington: FDR vetoes new tax bill, calling it relief for the greedy.

23. Pacific: American bombers strike Marianas Islands bases 1,300 miles from Tokyo (→ 25).

25. Pacific: U.S. forces smash 135 planes in Marianas and Guam (→ 29).

26. Exiled Polish government refuses Curzon line as future border with U.S.S.R. (→ 3/21).

BIRTH

9. Alice Walker, black poet and author, "The Color Purple."

DEATH

1. Pieter Mondrian, Dutch painter (*3/7/1872).

Bombers blast Nazis at Monte Cassino

The city of Cassino smolders in the wake of heavy American bombings.

Feb 15. In what may turn out to be one of the most controversial operations of the war, American bombers struck mercilessly today at the fortress of Monte Cassino in Italy. Benedictine monks living in the monastery, which was built in 529, scrambled for cover. Allied troops watching the raid from below cheered the bombers on.

The Nazis claim that only two of their generals have even been inside the monastery, and they say soldiers are not permitted within a 300-yard radius. The Allies say they were forced to strike because the Germans use the ground around the monastery for surveillance and mortar attacks. Many Allied soldiers have been killed trying to seize the fortress in the past few weeks.

U.S. commanders say 200 German soldiers were seen fleeing from the fortress as the planes attacked. The raid lasted for several hours, and reports say all the buildings of the monastery were destroyed.

There are no reports on whether the monks survived the attack. It is also not clear whether the Nazis will be driven permanently from Monte Cassino, or if the destroyed buildings will only give them new cover. As of tonight, the Allies have made no progress in their effort to climb up Monte Cassino (→ 3/14).

Smashing success as U.S. bombs Reich

Feb 21. A two-day American air offensive blasted German aircraft factories early this week in the heaviest bombing raids of the war. Over 2,000 U.S. bombers struck eight strategic plane plants, knocking out 25 percent of Nazi fighter plane output. Industrial plants and airfields in northwest Germany were destroyed as Allied tactics of smashing the Nazi infrastructure resumed. The 8,000 tons of bombs whistled down shortly after the royal air force hit Leipzig with 2,240 tons. The raids were made with few Allied losses (→ 3/4).

Pieter Mondrian is dead in New York

Feb 1. Dutch painter Pieter Mondrian is deceased at the age of 71. Mondrian was known for his disciplined approach to primary colors and right angles. He often wrote about his theories, calling the style Neoplasticism in the 1920's.

Cubism had a big influence on Mondrian. He learned about it directly from Pablo Picasso and Georges Braque. In turn, Mondrian influenced the Bauhaus movement. He sought to remove his art from natural colors and shapes, creating a separate reality. He felt the old reality estranged mankind. ▷

MacArthur begins drive through Pacific islands

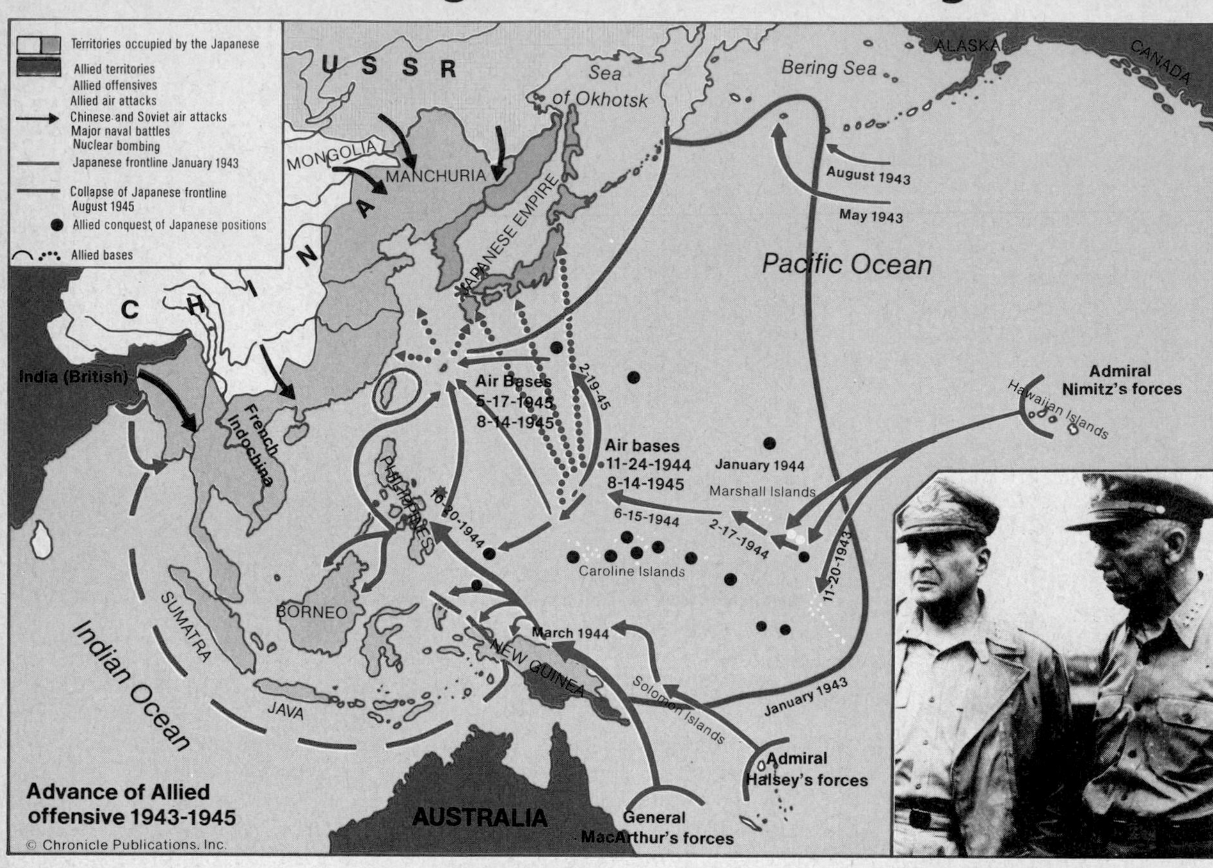

MacArthur and George Marshall (insert) are directing operations against the Japanese in the Pacific.

Feb 29. The United States forces of General Douglas MacArthur surged onto Los Negros in the Admiralty Islands today, capping a month of Allied advances in the Pacific theater that should provide impetus for even more sweeping island-hopping by MacArthur's men.

The invasion of the Admiralty Islands, known as "Operation Brewer," is of great importance to the current campaign. America knows it and so do the Japanese, who suffered severe losses in their poorly organized counterattacks to salvage some strategic points on the battered island.

Aerial bombardment by the U.S. 5th Air Force on the Admiralties prepared the area for invasion. Enemy strongholds on Momote and Lorengau islands, as well as Wewok in New Guinea, were ravaged by air bombers despite inclement weather conditions. Once sea channels were opened, MacArthur rushed troops to the Admiralties via speedy destroyers rather than the usual landing craft. MacArthur personally witnessed the landing and announced that the conquest isolates over 50,000 Japanese on the Bismarck Archipelago and clears the way for a push to the Philippines, 1,300 miles to the north. Last reports cite the general's insistence that the beachhead be held at all costs; Japanese night raids are expected to occur this evening.

American corpses litter a beach in the Pacific. Despite recent victories, landings on heavily fortified islands have taken a heavy toll in human life.

Earlier this month, in another arena in the Pacific, American bombers raided Guam, the captured U.S military base in the Marianas Islands, for the first time since Japanese forces seized the installation at the outset of the war. Admiral Chester Nimitz reported that in the assaults, which also hit air and naval bases on Saipan and Tinian, 135 Japanese planes were annihilated and 11 enemy ships were sunk or seriously damaged. Japanese defenders could do little to prevent the U.S. offensive, but did manage to down six American aircraft.

On the 18th, Admiral Nimitz announced that combined U.S. Army, Navy and Marine forces, under the command of Rear Admiral Richmond Kelly Turner, successfully invaded Eniwetok Atoll in the Marshall Islands. The onslaught was well-executed, as U.S. planes attacked Truk Island, the heart of the Japanese defense system, as a diversion for the Eniwetok assault. According to Nimitz, "The initial landings took place after strong preliminary attacks by carrier-based aircraft and heavy ships of the Pacific Fleet. The troops went ashore under the cover of battleship gunfire and with close support of low-flying naval aircraft."

Prior to the landing, Eniwetok, like most islands in the Marshall chain, had been closed to outsiders. It has excellent air facilities and large military barracks which will now serve as a staging station for American air and sea craft advancing westward.

The month began with a bang, as American forces stunned the enemy in the Kwajalein Atoll, where Rear Admiral Turner guided his troops first into the lagoons and then onto the beaches. The occupation was seen as demoralizing to the Japanese. As Turner remarked: "It should be a discouragement to the Japanese everywhere to know that when we hit, we hit hard and for keeps" (→ 3/30).

1944

MARCH

Su	Mo	Tu	We	Th	Fr	Sa
			1	2	3	4
5	6	7	8	9	10	11
12	13	14	15	16	17	18
19	20	21	22	23	24	25
26	27	28	29	30	31	

1. London: Allies cut off arms to Turkey for reluctance to fight Axis (→ 4/20).

3. French singer Yves Montand debuts in Paris.

4. Germany: Berlin gets first U.S. bombing.→

4. U.S. declares non-recognition of Argentina for collaboration with Axis (→ 3/27/45).

4. Japan begins calling up students for military service.

7. U.S.: It is reported that women comprise 42% of work force in West Coast aircraft plants (→ 4/17).

8. Wales: Miners go on strike, threatening to paralyze British war industry.

10. Irish refuse to oust Axis envoys, denying they spy on Allied troops (→ 12).

12. Britain bars travel to Ireland (→ 5/6).

12. Vatican: Pope Pius XII calls on belligerents to spare Rome (→ 24).

14. U.S.S.R. recognizes Badoglio government in Italy (→ 15).

15. Italy: Record air blow levels Cassino; tanks and troops drive in as assault renews (→ 24).

17. France: Marcel Deat named minister of labor.

17. Austria: Vienna gets first U.S. bombing (→ 4/1).

18. Balkans: Russians reach Rumanian border (→ 4/2).

20. Algiers: Vichy ex-Interior Minister Pierre Pucheu executed by Free French (→ 4/4).

21. Finland rejects Soviet armistice; Russia warns of dire fate (→ 4/10).

21. Cordell Hull gives 17-point U.S. plan calling for intl. cooperation after war (→ 29).

26. Greek resistance weakened by break between Communists and conservatives (→ 10/15/44).

29. Congress allots $1.35 billion for United Nations Relief and Rehabilitation Agency (UNRRA) (→ 8/21).

30. Pacific: U.S. fleet attacks Palau, near Philippines (→ 4/22).

Hungary's Jews sent to Auschwitz as Red army approaches

March 19. The Nazis have begun a new reign of terror in Hungary as they try to fortify the country against an inevitable Russian attack. Shortly after their invasion, the Germans began rounding up Jews and dispatching them to the gas chambers at Auschwitz.

The man in charge of the roundup is Adolf Eichmann, who told the Jewish council in Budapest, "You don't know who I am? I am a butcher thirsty for blood."

A Hungarian official says Adolf Hitler executed "a classic stab in the back" to invade Hungary. He summoned Hungarian leaders, presumably to discuss the withdrawal of their troops from Russia to increase defenses back home. As soon as the Hungarian dictator Miklos von Horthy arrived, Hitler had him arrested and the invasion began.

Hitler's invasion of Hungary is a desperation move. Ten of his divisions are bottled up in the Ukraine and in Bessarabia. The Russians' next targets are Poland, Rumania and Hungary (→ 11/30).

Soviet army on the march in the Ukraine. German defenses continue to crack under the weight of the Soviet winter offensive.

Spitfire, heroic fighter, gets more power

March 8. The airplane that held the Luftwaffe at bay and prevented an invasion of England has been given an even more powerful engine to drive the Germans back to their home bases. Prized by the RAF as the most maneuverable fighter in the air, the single-engine Spitfire knocked down so many fighters and bombers that the Germans abandoned their plans to pulverize Britain as a prelude to a land invasion. The new, powerful, yet still more compact Rolls Royce engine will be of the same type used in Malcolm Campbell's record-breaking racing car, the Bluebird.

The Spitfire was a major factor in blunting Reich air attacks on Britain.

Germans wipe out French Maquis unit

March 26. The Nazis tried to teach the French resistance a lesson today on the Glieres plateau near Annecy. The Frenchmen numbered in the hundreds, but it took thousands of Germans and the Luftwaffe to dislodge them. Some are saying it was the resistance fighters who taught the Nazis a thing or two.

The Vichy government attempted to capture the Maquis, or resistance unit, a week ago after arms were parachuted to them twice by the Allies. Vichy wanted to make an example of them, but the failure of its militiamen to seize the Maquis only infuriated the Nazis.

The chiefs of the Wehrmacht, Gestapo and Luftwaffe all gathered in Annecy to plan an assault on the resistance fighters. The Vichy militia, trying to curry favor with the Nazis, also helped in the planning.

The Luftwaffe provided air cover as 12,000 Germans stormed the plateau. The Maquis resisted furiously, but the odds were overwhelming. Some 465 Maquis fighters died. But a legend was born (→ 4/1).

War in Europe 1939 to spring 1944
© Chronicle Publications, Inc.
Iceland
5-10-1940 landing
Brit 07-41 US occupied
Area of German operations at sea since 3-18-41
Arctic Ocean
Barents Sea
Ribachi Peninsula
Murmansk
Kandalaksha
White Sea
Evacuation Sept.-Nov. 44
The Faeroes (4-11-1940 Brit. Danish after)
Shetland Islands
Norway
Sweden
Finland
Atlantic Ocean
Area of German operations at sea since 8-17-40
Great Britain
Northern Ireland
Ireland
North Sea
Baltic Sea
Copenhagen
Estonia
Latvia
Lithuania
Poland
German Empire
Netherlands
Belgium
France
Switzerland
Spain
Portugal
Andorra
Italy
Yugoslavia
Croatia
Serbia
Hungary
Slovakia
Sudeten
Prague
Ostmark
Official name of Austria from 1938 to 1945
Northern Transylvania
Rumania
Bulgaria
Albania
Greece
Black Sea
Adriatic Sea
Aegean Sea
Mediterranean Sea
Corsica
Sardinia
Sicily
Crete
Balearic Islands
Tunisia
Tripolitania
Lybia
Cyrenaica
Egypt
Algiers
Tripoli
Eisenhower 11-8-42
May 10th-June 26th 1940
Axis Powers 1939
Axis Powers allies 1939
Axis Powers allies 1941
Occupied territories 1939
Occupied territories 1940
Occupied territories 1941
Occupied territories 1942
Sequence of major advances and attacks
Front lines and positions
Withdrawal and evacuation
Grossdeutsches Reich 1942
Territories of Western Allies after 1940
Territories occupied by Allies
Sequence of major advances and attacks
Front lines and positions
Retreats
Area of Allied air-cover
Neutral nations
Frontiers after 1940
National borders and annexations
Blue and red numbers indicate war exploits
Black numbers political changes.

War on the eastern front since june 22 1941
Maximum extent of German troops since December 1941
German front line Spring 1942 following Russian Winter offensive (Territories occupied since 1941)
Maximum extent of German troops until November 1942
Unconquered Soviet territories
Territories conquered by Soviets upon 1941-42 Winter offensive
Soviet offensive Winter 1942-43
Soviet front line Spring 1943
Soviet offensive Summer 1943, Spring 1944
Soviet front line June 1944

U.S. planes bomb Berlin for first time

March 4. The war took a new and significant turn as American planes bombed Berlin for the first time. The attack was small considering the British air force dropped 2,600 tons on the city in one raid. But the American B-17 assault underscores the recent vulnerability of German air defenses. As a British-U.S. communique stated: "It is more than a year since (Berliners) were last attacked in daylight, but now they know that they have no safety there by day or night. All Germany learns the same lesson" (→ 17).

Gestapo in Rome executes innocents

March 24. Italian priests, Jews, women and two 14-year-old boys were indiscriminately arrested in Rome and shot to death by the Gestapo. They were killed in reprisal for a bomb attack that killed 33 German policemen. Adolf Hitler had demanded that 50 Italians be executed for each German who died, but German officials in Italy reduced the ratio (→ 4/17).

British hero killed in Burma operation

March 31. General Orde Charles Wingate, whose eagerness to charge into battle ahead of his men and ability to improvise tactics helped his troops route forces many times their size, has been killed in a plane crash. In 1936, he cleared Palestine of terrorists, and five years later with only a few thousand troops he captured 40,000 Italians (→ 8/4).

Guerrilla fighter Wingate.

1944

APRIL

Su	Mo	Tu	We	Th	Fr	Sa
						1
2	3	4	5	6	7	8
9	10	11	12	13	14	15
16	17	18	19	20	21	22
23	24	25	26	27	28	29
30						

1. France: SS slaughters 86 civilians in reprisal for train sabotage (→ 16).

1. Switzerland: U.S. bombers kill 50 in Shauffhausen as fliers hit wrong target (→ 6).

2. Balkans: Russians enter Rumania; deny any territorial aims (→ 15).

4. Algiers: De Gaulle takes full control of French Committee of National Liberation, appoints two Communists in promise of power-sharing after war (→ 9).

5. Wendell Willkie ends U.S. presidential campaign (→ 30).

10. Quinine—used to ward off malaria—synthesized by Robert B. Woodward and William Doering at Harvard University.

10. U.S.S.R.: Red army takes Odessa on Black Sea (→ 13).

13. Senator Maybank of South Carolina tells U.S. Senate the South won't open polls to Negroes (→ 6/3/46).

15. Balkans: U.S. fliers bomb Bucharest and Ploesti (→ 30).

17. London: Britain bans envoys' travel and code use in move to protect invasion secrets (→ 5/15).

17. Congress extends lend-lease through June 1945 (→ 5/3).

17. Italy: Badoglio Cabinet resigns (→ 22).

20. Turkey shuts off export of chrome to Germany (→ 8/2).

22. Italy: New opposition Cabinet formed under Communist Party leader Palmiro Togliatti (→ 5/11).

22. Pacific: Allies launch major attack in New Guinea (→ 24).

24. Cairo: U.S. Treasury representatives confer with British and Mideast delegates on anticipated financial problems in area.

26. Chicago: Troops seize Montgomery Ward for rejecting FDR order to extend union contract; Chmn. Sewell Avery physically removed from office (→ 1/8/45).

30. New Guinea: MacArthur rejects candidacy in U.S. presidential race (→ 6/28).

30. Balkans: Tito asks Allies to acknowledge him as head of Yugoslavia (→ 5/1).

De Gaulle becomes French forces chief

April 9. In Algiers, General Charles de Gaulle has been named Commander-in-Chief of Free French forces. But an internal dispute threatens the effort to organize French military leaders before the Allied invasion of Western Europe.

In his new role, de Gaulle displaced General Henri Honore Giraud, who has been serving in the post since 1942. Giraud charges that his ouster is illegal and scoffs at his new title of Inspector General.

De Gaulle and Giraud have served in Algiers as co-Presidents of the Committee of National Liberation since last June. It has been an uneasy alliance. De Gaulle believes Giraud is too conservative. De Gaulle also has his own ideas about the future of France.

The Americans and the British are somewhat suspicious of de Gaulle. They are also nervous about his efforts to organize and arm the French resistance. Earlier this year, it was Churchill who asked, "Can you guarantee that the resisters will obey Eisenhower and that the arms which they receive will not be turned against each other?"

The Allies are also not convinced that the resistance is all that important to the coming invasion, and they have not given de Gaulle a large role in the planning. It has been pointed out that the General in charge of the invasion of France is an American. Many of his deputies are British (→ 6/3).

April 26. Marshal Petain is acclaimed at Hotel de Ville square on his first visit to Paris since the fall of France (→ 8/20).

Russians recapture Kerch Peninsula

Soviet peasants search for friends and family among the dead on the battlefield at Kerch.

April 13. The Kerch Peninsula on the Black Sea, wrested from the Soviet Union two years ago, will soon be in Russian hands again. The Soviet army has made huge advances in the Crimea in the last two days, recapturing major coastal cities, including the vital industrial port of Odessa on April 11. Today, Russian forces stand poised a mere 11 miles away from Simferopol, the capital of Crimea.

The Soviet Black Sea fleet hinders German retreat by ferry. Soviet bombers strafe the shoreline, driving the Axis forces further inland. The Russian air force has just started bombing the Rumanian port of Costanta, 240 miles southwest of Sevastapol. As the rainy season ends, and the Crimean airfields prove dry and accessible, Soviet fliers will be in easy range of Bucharest and the Ploesti oil fields.

Harassed Axis troops have no predetermined land escape route. Associated Press and United Press estimate that 100,000 Germans are stationed in the Crimea. No one can guess, however, how many currently guard Sevastopol. That city, on the southwest Crimean tip, is an invaluable naval base. The Germans will not give it up quietly.

News of Odessa's liberation has revitalized Russian spirits. Hours after the city fell to General Rodion Y. Malinovsky's infantry, Moscow saluted the act with salvos of red, white and green flares. Malinovsky's satisfaction is personal: He is himself a native of Odessa (→ 6/11).

French serving with Nazis meet in Paris

April 16. Frenchmen who have been fighting alongside the Nazis gathered in Paris today at the Velodrome. They waved French flags and wore German uniforms, and they had only one complaint. The Nazis were not giving them enough to do. They were tired of watching roads and railway stations. They wanted to hunt resistance fighters and what they called "terrorists."

The soldiers are members of the Legion of Volunteers against Bolshevism. The group was formed one month after Hitler invaded Russia.

The soldiers left the meeting excited by the rumor of a devastating and miraculous new Nazi weapon. It is a bomber flown without a pilot and directed by electromagnetic waves. The soldiers hope the planes lead Hitler to victory (→ 6/10).

The French anti-Communist legion.

Allies launch major offensive in Netherlands New Guinea

Machine gunners in New Guinea.

April 24. In a daring 500-mile leap up the coast of New Guinea, General Douglas MacArthur's troops have bypassed Japanese strongholds at Hansa and Wewak to land and capture Humbolt and Tanahmerah bays.

MacArthur's troops have also taken the town of Hollandia and are within five miles of the airstrip outside of town. It is estimated that only a thousand Japanese are now guarding the airfield, whose capture would help extend American air control over all New Guinea and cut off supply lines to Japanese troops in the east.

MacArthur's troops received strong support from Admiral Chester Nimitz's naval attack forces, which destroyed over 100 Japanese planes and pulverized the 150-mile beachhead prior to the invasion. The carrier force had been steaming toward Palau before turning south, and the Japanese had to retreat so quickly that American troops found untouched many breakfasts that the enemy had left on the beach (→ 5/27).

Heart attack fatal to Navy Secretary

April 28. Frank Knox, the man responsible for building the U.S. Navy into the greatest fighting force ever at sea died of a heart attack at his Washington home today. Appointed by President Roosevelt to head a Navy that was thought to have been dealt a knockout blow by the Japanese at Pearl Harbor, Knox threw American industry into high gear and now, four years after he took office, hundreds of U.S. ships are beating back the Japanese in the Pacific and dogging German U-boats in the Atlantic.

Reich heavily bombed

Brunswick, victim of the ever-increasing accuracy of U.S. and RAF bombers.

April 6. American and British air forces have achieved a stunning breakthrough in the skies over Germany and Western Europe. They have achieved air superiority over the Nazis. The tactical advantage will presumably come in very handy during the long-awaited invasion.

The Allies developed the new advantage with a relentless and flexible bombing campaign. The British Lancasters have been dropping their bombs after dark. But as the Luftwaffe became more expert at nighttime defense, more of the bombing responsibility was assumed by the United States.

The American Flying Fortresses, escorted by the new Mustang fighters, attack during the day with sophisticated precision bombing. The Eighth Air Force, based in Britain, hits northern and central Germany and occupied France. The 15th Air Force strikes southern Germany and the Balkans from bases in Italy. The Allies increase their advantage by frequently rotating their planes among their bases in England, Italy and Russia (→ 5/26).

Court grants Negro voting in Texas

April 3. The United States Supreme Court has ruled that Negroes cannot be barred from voting in the Texas Democratic primaries. While the decision applied just to Texas, Southern members of Congress expressed fear that it could be extended to other Southern states. Senator James Eastland, Democrat of Mississippi, said it could "destroy state sovereignty" (→ 13).

1944

MAY

Su	Mo	Tu	We	Th	Fr	Sa
	1	2	3	4	5	6
7	8	9	10	11	12	13
14	15	16	17	18	19	20
21	22	23	24	25	26	27
28	29	30	31			

1. Balkans: Stalin threatens full-scale invasion if Bulgaria, Rumania and Hungary fail to join Allies (→ 8/23).

3. Meat rationing ends in U.S. (→ 6/22).

5. India: Mahatma Gandhi set free by British (→ 9/21/45).

6. U.S. blacklists 68 Irish firms.

6. Pensive is first in Kentucky Derby with jockey C. McCreary.

8. London: Exiled Czech govt. and U.S.S.R. conclude convention; Red army to liberate Czechoslovakia (→ 4/6/45).

9. First eyebank opened by Richard T. Paton of Manhattan Eye, Ear and Throat Hospital and John McLean of New York Hospital.

10. Washington: James Vincent Forrestal named secretary of the Navy.

11. Italy: Allies open drive on Rome, gain up to 3 miles (→ 12).

12. Italy: Allies crack Gustav line in savage fighting (→ 18).

13. Hitler gives permission for full German withdrawal from U.S.S.R. (→ 6/11).

15. Landing plans presented to British and American heads of state and army commanders-in-chief (→ 6/1).

18. Italy: German troops evacuate Monte Cassino as Allies surround it (→ 23).

18. Mediterranean: Allied ship sunk by U-boat in waning sub war (→ 6/19).

23. Italy: Allies start drive at Anzio beachhead as attacks in mountains are pressed (→ 25).

23. France: U.S. planes blast Kiel and Pas-de-Calais (→ 26).

26. France: Allies bomb Lyon, Nice, Saint-Etienne and Marseille; 3,760 killed (→ 6/6).

26. Syria: Unveiling of women causes Arab riot.→

27. Pacific: MacArthur forces land on Biak Island in New Guinea, battle foe 900 miles from Philippines (→ 6/6).

DEATH

15. Sergius, patriarch of Russia (*11/23/1867).

Rumor of unveiling causes riot in Syria

May 26. Rioters with revolvers, rifles and axes took to the streets of Damascus this afternoon, threatened by the idea of seeing women's faces. A fanatical Moslem group, hearing rumors of Syrian women removing their veils, organized vocal protests. Fears were unfounded.

Rumors were traced to a young women's culture club, the "Drop of Milk Society." Club members needed a private place to screen a film. They chose the French Officer's Club, which afforded them sufficient space—and invited rumors of abandoned veils and wild dancing.

With the increasing influence of Western ways, many Moslem men fear the emancipation of women.

Soviet army frees Crimea from Nazis

May 9. The month-long siege of Sevastopol has ended, and the fortress city of the Crimea is back in Russian hands. A Nazi rear guard kept the Russians at bay for the last few hours of the battle so that 150,000 German and Rumanian soldiers could escape by boat into the Black Sea.

Two German generals, Allmendiger and Schorner, made the final decision to evacuate Sevastopol. The action is not likely to enhance their military careers. Allmendiger's successor, General Jaenecke, was arrested and stripped of his rank when he asked Adolf Hitler for permission to surrender.

The 24-day siege took its toll on Sevastopol. Many of the buildings in the city have been reduced to rubble (→ 13).

Bing Crosby excels in one of his few dramatic roles as a Catholic priest in "Going My Way?"

Allies link up in Italy, menace Rome

May 25. American troops in Italy have shattered the stalemate at Anzio and broken out of their beachhead. Almost simultaneously, an Allied army burst through Nazi defenses at the fortress of Monte Cassino. The Germans are crumbling as the Allies march toward Rome.

The fall of Monte Cassino followed the most savage fighting of the Italian campaign. The Americans broke the spine of the Nazi defense by punishing the fortress with its largest and most powerful mobile gun, the 240-mm. howitzer.

A pincer movement by Polish and British troops did the Nazis in. The British fought their way from the south. The Poles, fighting with an intensity that matches their hatred for the Nazis, battled their way from the north.

The Allies captured 1,500 prisoners, many of them members of the elite First Parachute Division, and a large quantity of ammunition.

With Monte Cassino behind them, the Allies broke through the Gustav line, threatened the Nazis' new line of defense, called the Hitler line, and joined forces with Americans surging forth from Anzio.

The Nazis are on the run, and one report says they are ready to retreat north of Rome to set up new defenses. Another report says Nazi forces north of Rome are rushing south to defend the city (→ 6/4).

American-equipped French troops round up Germans in Castleforte.

No Exit opens: Sartre's Existentialist play

Sartre was jailed for a year by Vichy.

May 27. Jean Paul Sartre's Existentialist play "No Exit" opened tonight in Paris. Four characters appear on stage; three of them, two women and one man, are locked in a room for eternity. The message of the one-act drama can be boiled down to: "Hell is other people."

Sartre, 38 years old, burst on the literary scene last year with his book "Being and Nothingness." That work stated that consciousness sets us free, but freedom is an onerous responsibility; our many choices overwhelm us. Some critics consider Sartre a pessimistic man; others say he simply describes reality.

1944

JUNE

Su	Mo	Tu	We	Th	Fr	Sa
				1	2	3
4	5	6	7	8	9	10
11	12	13	14	15	16	17
18	19	20	21	22	23	24
25	26	27	28	29	30	

1. BBC sends first coded message to French resistance, signaling invasion is imminent (→ 5).

5. France: Rommel leaves for Germany to celebrate wife's birthday and appeal to Hitler to reinforce Normandy defenses (→ 6).

5. Italy: King Victor-Emmanuel III abdicates in favor of crown prince Umberto (→ 9).

6. Japan: U.S. B-29's drop first bombs on mainland since raid of 1942 (→ 18).

7. Belgium: King Leopold III arrested by Reich and deported to Dresden (→ 5/8/45).

8. France: Allies take Bayeux and several highways in Normandy (→ 10).

9. Rome: Ex-premier Ivanoe Bonomi chosen as Italian Premier (→ 9/30).

10. France: U.S. Armies from Omaha and Utah beaches link, begin move eastward (→ 21).

11. U.S.S.R.: Red army launches attack against German and Finnish troops on Karelian Isthmus (→ 21).

14. France: General de Gaulle lands in Normandy (→ 8/30).

16. France: Gestapo kills historian Marc Bloch, member of French resistance (→ 20).

17. Iceland proclaims independent republic.

18. Pacific: Japanese landing repelled at Saipan Island (→ 20).

19. Mediterranean: Elba surrenders to French troops.

20. France: Gestapo executes Popular Front ex-minister Jean Zay (→ 28).

20. Pacific: Japanese lose 400 planes, three carriers in Battle of Philippine Sea (→ 7/9).

21. U.S.S.R.: Soviets take Viborg on Karelian Isthmus (→ 7/4).

21. France: Americans break through Cherbourg outer defenses (→ 27).

23. U.S. and Britain recognize Bolivian government.

28. France: Vichy Minister Philippe Henriot slain in Paris by French resistance (→ 8/12).

Roosevelt signs the G.I. Bill of Rights

June 22. The G.I. Bill of Rights, granting benefits to veterans of this war, has been signed into law by President Roosevelt. Among the key provisions are these:

Unemployment benefits of $20 a week for up to 52 weeks.

A 50 percent guarantee of loans of up to $2,000, at not more than four percent interest, to establish homes or businesses.

Grants of $500 a year for four years for training and education, plus subsistence payments of $50 to $75 a month.

Up to $500 million for additional veterans' facilities (→ 8/14).

Republicans name Dewey as candidate

June 28. Gov. Thomas E. Dewey of New York won the Republican nomination for president today after Gov. John W. Bricker of Ohio withdrew from the race. Governor Bricker later won the nomination for vice president on the first ballot.

More than 25,000 Republicans, cheering loudly and waving flags and posters, greeted their new presidential nominee in the Chicago Stadium tonight. Governor Dewey, now 42 years old, first gained national recognition in his early 30's as the special prosecutor of political rackets in New York City. He later became District Attorney in New York (→ 7/11).

Ex-swimmer Esther Williams, "Queen of the Surf," has shot to stardom in "Bathing Beauty."

Allied forces enter the Eternal City

The French Expeditionary Corps amid the chaos of the Italian battlefield.

June 4. With breathtaking speed, Allied forces scattered the last of the Nazi opposition and catapulted their way into Rome tonight. They were greeted enthusiastically by many residents of the city. Rome has little strategic value for the Allies, but it is one of the capitals of the Axis powers. It is also the first European capital to be liberated from the Nazis.

One German unit made a last stand at the gates to the city, but they retreated after American General Mark Clark ordered his troops to open fire. The Allies fanned out quickly through the city, battling a rear guard at the Forum, destroying a scout car near Trajan's Column and searching for Nazi snipers who might have stayed behind.

Most of Rome was untouched in the final Allied assault, and residents cooperated in clearing the streets. The retreating Germans ignored an order from Adolf Hitler to blow up bridges over the Tiber. The city's historic sites are intact, and only the rail yards seem to have suffered major damage.

The Allies advanced 15 miles in the past 24 hours and moved so quickly that they trapped pockets of Nazis along the way. A thousand prisoners were seized, and 600 enemy vehicles were destroyed or damaged. Americans are thrilled by the capture of Rome (→ 5).

U.S. bombs a main Japanese island

June 15. American B-29 Superfortresses have bombed Japan, ushering in an all-out air war against the Japanese Empire, according to a special communique released by the War Department. The industrial guts of Kyushu, southernmost of the main Japanese islands, was hit hard by the powerful planes. The assault emphasizes a new beginning in the Pacific theater. General George C. Marshall, chief of staff, called the attack "a new type of offensive against our enemy."

No casualty figures have yet been released, but it's clear the raids have helped pave the way for an invasion of Japan, just as massive aerial warfare softened Germany for conquest. Secretary of War Henry Stimson said, "I congratulate the men who planned this action and manned the airplanes which carried it out. These pioneers have shortened our road to Tokyo" (→ 18).

Free France gets a provisional regime

June 3. France's General Charles de Gaulle is proving he is just as adept in political matters as he is in military affairs. Acting under his authority, the Committee of National Liberation in Algiers has announced that it is the new, provisional government of France. The action comes just two months after de Gaulle was named Commander-in-Chief of French forces.

The new government plans to replace the Vichy Cabinet as soon as the Allies liberate France from the Nazis. The Assembly has given its unanimous approval to the plan.

The formation of the provisional government raises troubling monetary questions: Which are the real French francs? Those printed by Vichy? Or those distributed by the Allied command? De Gaulle states that the only legitimate French currency is that which he has approved.

On the military front, de Gaulle is trying to gain control of the French resistance. Over the next few days, he hopes to discuss with the Allies what role he and the resistants will play in the coming invasion of France (→ 14).

SS massacres 642 in French town

June 10. The Nazis might call their action in the small French village of Oradour-sur-Glane today justifiable revenge. Anyone else would call it barbarism.

The Germans massacred every living person they could find in Oradour. Some 642 people were killed.

The Nazis were retaliating for the capture of an SS officer by the resistance. An unconfirmed rumor said he was executed in Oradour.

A witness says the SS circled the village, divided the men into five or six groups and herded them into barns. Women and children were locked in a church.

The men were shot first. Then smoke was seen rising from farms and houses as the SS ransacked them and set them on fire.

In the church, fires were started on the altar. When the women tried to escape into the air outside, the Germans stuck their guns through the windows and shot them all dead.

But it was not over yet. At 6:00 p.m., the Germans stopped a train and arrested all passengers bound for Oradour. They were brutally killed and then thrown into the fire (→ 16).

Oradour-sur-Glane: The victims of Nazi barbarism.

Allied forces land in great strength in Normandy

Ike instructs paratroopers in England: "Full victory —nothing else."

U.S. troops leave a Coast Guard transport to storm the beaches at Normandy.

June 6. D-Day has arrived. The long-awaited Anglo-American invasion of Europe began at sunrise. General Dwight D. Eisenhower, commander of the united forces, issued a statement stripped of any detail that the enemy might use against them: "Allied naval forces supported by strong air forces began landing Allied armies this morning on the northern coast of France."

As the day progressed, the exact number of troops remained unpublicized, but their point of disembarkment gradually became known. Many landed near Caen, 65 miles southeast of Cherbourg. A German communique put them at the mouth of the Seine.

Four waves of liberators were led by thousands of parachutists. They leaped from C-47's, ammunition and equipment strapped to their backs or hugged to their chests. Some paratroopers will serve as infantrymen behind enemy lines. Others are engineers who will seize German airfields. Failing that, they will construct new landing strips.

More than 900 tow planes and gliders of the Ninth Air Force Troop Carrier Command brought the second wave of soldiers ashore. These assault troops waded the final yards to the beaches, soaked with sea and sweat, laden with arms and supplies. Rolling alongside them were jeeps, artillery pieces and great barrels of gasoline.

The third and fourth waves of liberators, due tonight and tomorrow, will have a tougher time as German defenses stiffen. Nazi retaliation has followed lines that Eisenhower and the other commanders anticipated. Two to three percent of the Allied planes were downed, as expected. Germans increased searchlight operations, and 20-mm. guns have been moved up to meet ensuing waves. Machine guns constitute the bulk of Nazi ground defenses, but some of their methods are more primitive. Allied troops have been finding sharpened stakes half buried in coastal fields.

General Eisenhower addressed the peoples of Western Europe over the airwaves this morning. Most of his words were directed to the French, whom he acknowledged bore the brunt of the Allied offensive. He praised their military forces and then turned his attention to the French public, proclaiming:

"Citizens of France! Because the initial landing has been made on the soil of your country, I repeat to you with even greater emphasis my message to the peoples of other occupied countries of Western Europe. Follow the instructions of your leaders. A premature uprising of all Frenchmen may prevent you from being of maximum help to your country in the critical hour. Be patient. Prepare . . .

"This landing is but the opening phase of the campaign in Western Europe. Great battles lie ahead. I call upon all who love freedom to stand with us" (→ 8).

Moving inland from Omaha Beach to begin the drive on Fortress Europe.

U.S. tank dispatched at Utah Beach.

Reich gunners defend a beachhead.

Allies reach Cherbourg port, first major objective

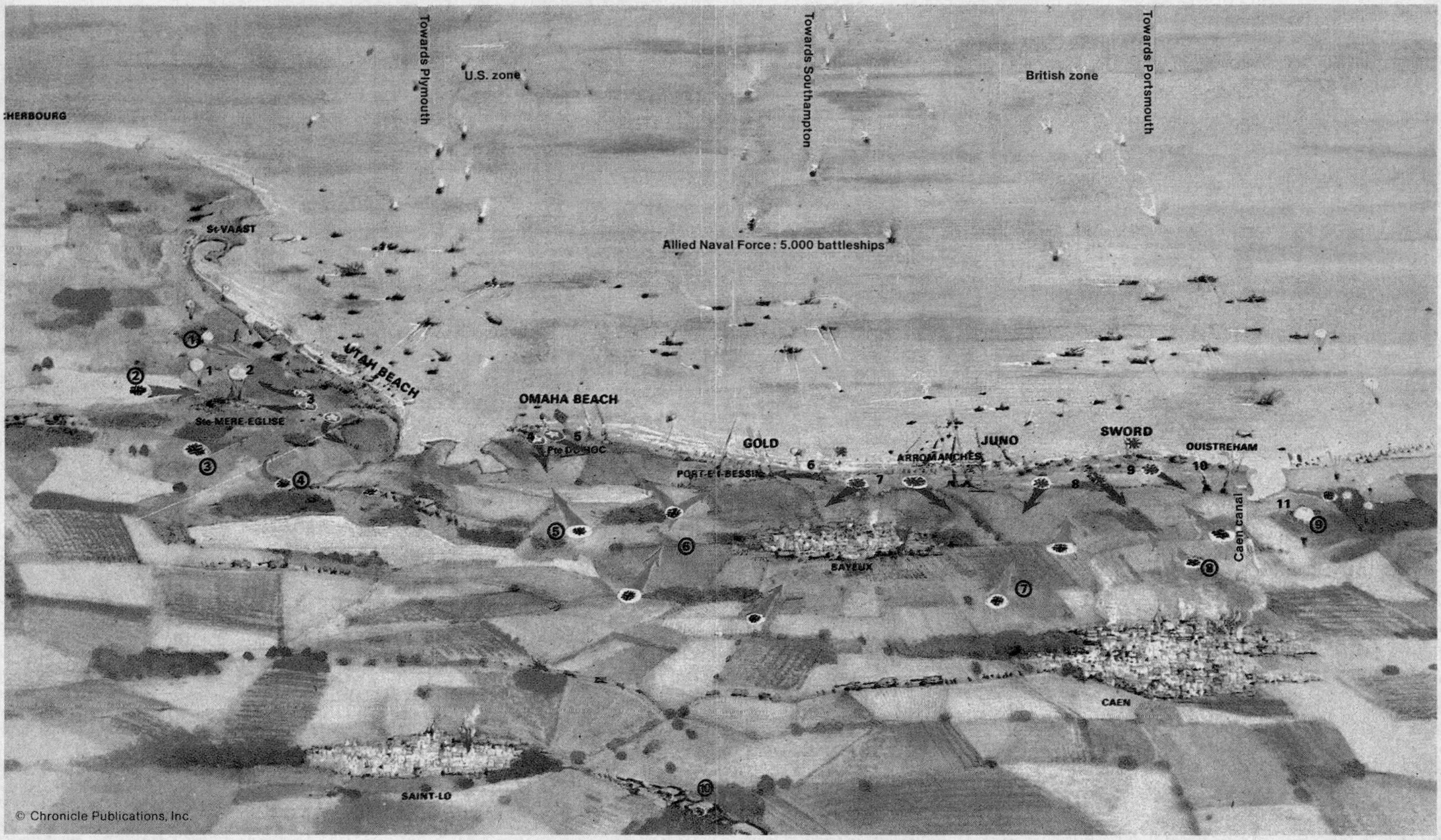

Allied forces (red arrows, uncircled numbers): 1. U.S. 82nd Airborne Division; 2. U.S. 101st Airborne Division; 3. U.S. Fourth Army; 4. U.S. Second Ranger Battalion; 5. U.S. First Army; 6. British 50th Army; 7. British Seventh Armored Division; 8. Canadian Second Army; 9. Canadian Third Army; 10. French commando unit.

German forces (blue arrows, circled numbers): 1. German 1058th Infantry Regiment; 2. German 1057th Infantry Regiment; 3. German Sixth Paratrooper Regiment; 4.and 5. German 352nd Infantry Division; 6. German 716th Infantry Division; 7. German 21st Armored Division; 9. German 711th Infantry Division; 10. Lehr Armored Division.

June 27. A tricolor stitched from red, white and blue parachutes flutters over Cherbourg this afternoon. France's third largest port is freed after a weary, week-long siege. The Allies are hailing the event as an essential first step toward the total liberation of Western Europe.

Battleships and heavy cruisers, British and American, bombarded Cherbourg's coastline. German batteries, well-armed with 450-mm. guns, answered their fire. A row of four pillboxes seemed impregnable. Troops tried to rush them with bangalore torpedoes and bazookas. Their efforts proved fatal. On June 26, the pillboxes were at last destroyed when soldiers tossed grenades through their ventilators.

That same day, Allied forces discovered a tunnel in a southern quarter of Cherbourg. Smoke from Nazi gunfire spewed out. Americans discussed plans to blast the tunnel open. The Germans must have been eavesdropping, for moments later a private emerged grasping a white flag. He told one of the American commanders that General Carl von Schlieben was within and wished to surrender. Americans accepted the offer and watched in amazement as 800 men emerged from the tunnel.

In all, perhaps 30,000 Germans were captured at Cherbourg. Nazi newspapers looked on the bright side of things, stating that "German Command has gained time through the sacrifice of troops at Cherbourg." General von Schlieben echoed these sentiments when explaining his delay at surrender.

The Allies have a right to rejoice. Cherbourg has fallen to them. Yet while one city is freed, another is enslaved. Nazis have this afternoon rolled into Helsinki (→ 7/18).

Lieutenant General von Schlieben, German commander of the Cherbourg garrison, and Rear Admiral Hennecke, Sea Defense Commander at Normandy, emerge from their hideout to surrender to Major General J. Lawton Collins and the American VII Corps at Cherbourg after five days of desperate defense.

First V-1 hits London

The V-1, a product of German scientific genius channeled into the war effort.

June 12. It is too early to tell how effective Adolf Hitler's new "miracle weapon" will be. But the British got a scare today as the first of the top-secret V-1 rockets landed and exploded in London.

The V-1, a flying bomb, is jet-propelled and pilotless. It carries a ton of explosives at a speed of up to 370 miles per hour. The Allies have been trying, with limited success, to knock out the base in the Baltic where the Nazis have been testing the V-1, or Vengeance rocket. Now, the royal air force will have to try to destroy the rockets in the air before they do damage on the ground (→ 7/6).

American planes attack Marianas Islands

June 11. Carrier planes of a powerful Pacific Fleet Task Force yesterday attacked Saipan, Tinian and Guam, Japan's heavily defended bases in the Marianas Islands. The three islands are among the most important bulwarks on the way to Admiral Nimitz's ultimate goal, the China coast and eventually the Japanese home islands.

The attack comes three weeks after carrier raids reopened the Pacific offensive by attacking Wake and Marcus Islands. The last Liberator raid on Saipan saw only 12 enemy fighters come up to meet our force. Two were shot down.

The enemy has repaired and reinforced these bases following the heavy destruction inflicted by our forces in recent months, and the carrier strike was probably designed to nullify that work.

In an attack Friday, Liberators flying from southwest Pacific bases commanded by General MacAthur destroyed 22 parked Japanese planes on Palau Island (→ 15).

1944

JULY

Su	Mo	Tu	We	Th	Fr	Sa
						1
2	3	4	5	6	7	8
9	10	11	12	13	14	15
16	17	18	19	20	21	22
23	24	25	26	27	28	29
30	31					

1. New Hampshire: 44-nation conference begins at Bretton Woods (→ 22).

4. U.S.S.R.: Russians take Minsk near Polish border (→ 20).

6. Hartford: Barnum & Bailey Circus tent catches fire, killing 168 and injuring 250.

9. Pacific: U.S. troops complete conquest of Saipan (→ 21).

11. Washington: FDR agrees to run again, saying, "I have as little right as a soldier to leave his position on the line" (→ 21).

12. Germany: Birkenau "family camp" where 12,500 Jews are imprisoned, is shut; 4,000 put to death in gas chamber (→ 31).

18. Japan drops Premier Hideki Tojo as chief of staff, as anti-war sentiment grows.

18. France: Americans win St. Lo junction, critical road linking Normandy and Brittany (→ 25).

20. N.Y.: Katharine Hepburn opens in "Dragon Seed."

21 Pacific: Americans land on Guam (→ 27).

22. Berlin: Nazis reveal plot of army officers to overthrow Hitler regime (→ 8/8).

25. France: Operation Cobra begins in drive to cut off German forces in Brittany (→ 30).

25. Hitler names Goebbels to post of Reich Plenipotentiary for the Total War Effort.

27. U.S.S.R.: Soviets drive in force to Vistula River (→ 29).

27. Pacific: Guam proclaimed under U.S. rule (→ 8/10).

29. U.S.S.R.: Soviet troops capture Brest-Litovsk (→ 30).

30. Red army begins artillery attacks on Warsaw (→ 8/18).

30. France: Nazis withdrawing entire west wing as Americans gain in Normandy (→ 8/15).

31. France: Last convoy leaves Drancy, transporting prisoners to Auschwitz (→ 8/27).

DEATHS

26. Shah Reza Pahlevi of Iran (*3/16/1878).

31. Antoine de Saint-Exupery, French pilot and writer (*6/29/1900).

2,752 are victims of V-1 flying bombs

British rescue team aids V-1 victims.

July 6. Hitler's V-1 bombs were launched too late to derail the invasion of France, but they are killing and maiming residents by the thousands in England. They strike London from Calais launch sites.

Before Parliament today, Winston Churchill revealed that 2,752 people have been killed by the pilotless flying bombs. The death toll would be even higher if half the missiles were not destroyed in flight. Women and children are being evacuated from London (→ 9/8).

The French resistance, happily freed from underground activities by Allied troops, can now devote their energies to dealing with those who chose to accept Nazi rule. These two patriots delighted in haphazardly cropping the hair of one collaborator. Similar treatments are sending the disloyal all over Northern France to their mirrors in repentance.

Allies advance widely in Normandy

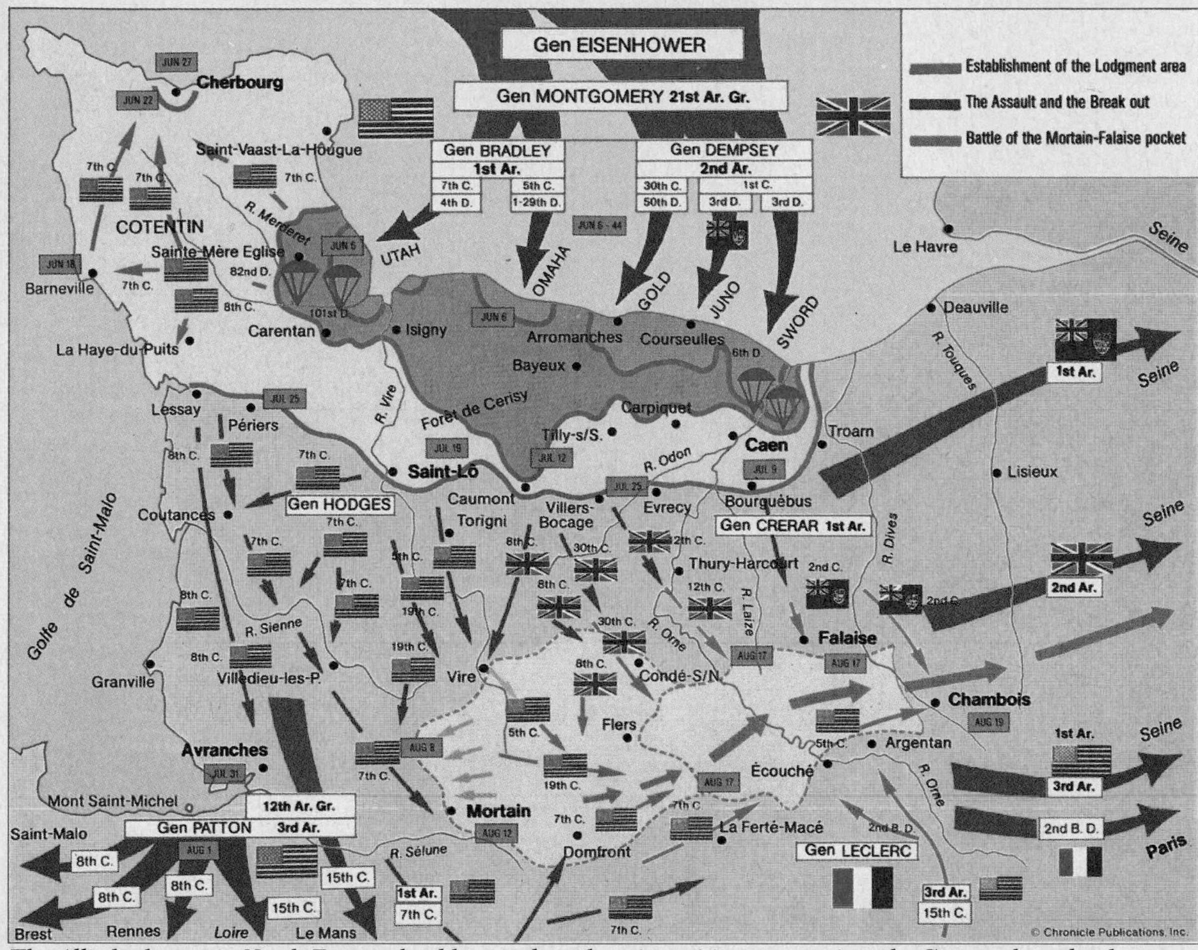

The Allied advance in North France should soon place them in position to move into the German homeland.

July 31. From Cherbourg south to St. Lo and east to Caen, the Allies have achieved stunning successes as they sweep the Nazis out of Normandy and begin to liberate France from its oppressor.

In the western sector, the Allies have chewed the Nazis to bits and forced them to abandon the entire area between the Vire River and the St. Malo Gulf.

Columns under the command of General Omar Bradley took a day of rest after advancing for five straight days. They captured St. Lo from the Germans after an eight-day siege. Then Bradley's soldiers chased the Germans from Coutances and headed south to Granville. "The advance was going well," an Allied communique said, "and we can see no possibility of more than temporary checks for some time."

Bradley's soldiers found a new ally in the weather when the clouds cleared long enough for the bombers to swoop in. The largest group of fighter jets ever to be amassed for a single attack unloaded 6,000 tons of bombs in one four-hour period. The assault was followed by an enormous artillery barrage. When General Eisenhower heard about the breadth of the bombing attack, all he could do was whistle with glee.

General Bradley's successes around St. Lo were matched by the British and Canadian advance in the eastern sector of the fighting. The Germans were squeezed out of Caen, but they managed to mine the city before they left. Thousands of civilians were killed during the final Allied assault.

The British engaged the Germans in a large armored battle in the flatlands south of Caen. Britain's 51st Infantry Division, the same unit that is credited with the spectacular victory at El Alamein, is fighting alongside the tanks.

American and British bombers helped clear the way with an unrelenting four-hour attack. There was so much smoke after the bombardment that many of the Canadians rubbed their eyes and could not see beyond their gun barrels.

The Allies have taken hundreds of German soldiers prisoner. Many have been trapped behind the advancing Allied lines. It is not clear who is in charge of the German withdrawal. The Germans say it is the wily Marshal Rommel, but reports persist in American camps that he died last month.

North of the field of battle, calm has returned to Cherbourg. Much of the deep harbor is blocked by a ship scuttled by the Germans just before their retreat, and it may take months to make the port completely operational.

The British have circumvented the problem and insured a steady delivery of vital supplies by installing a harbor on the coast that had been prefabricated in England. Concrete was dumped in the ocean to create a breakwater. A long wharf was constructed by running steel pontoons over barges (→ 8/15).

Democratic ticket: Roosevelt, Truman

July 21. Democrats chose Senator Harry S. Truman tonight as the vice-presidential nominee on a ticket in which President Roosevelt will seek a fourth term.

Senator Truman's nomination on the second ballot was an overwhelming defeat for Vice President Henry A. Wallace's bid for another term. The vice president had bested Senator Truman on the first ballot but finally was crushed, 1,100 to 66 on the second, while Associate Justice William O. Douglas polled just four votes. President Roosevelt had said he would be pleased to have either Senator Truman or Justice Douglas as a running mate.

Truman, who rose from comparative obscurity in his home state of Missouri, was sitting on the platform, eating a sandwich, when the results of the balloting were announced. Dragged to the microphone by a fellow senator, the new nominee seemed a bit stunned by his victory, making a brief, halting speech, thanking the delegates at the Chicago convention and vowing to continue efforts to shorten the war. It was the shortest speech of the day (→ 11/7).

War victim: French writer-air hero

July 31. Author of "The Little Prince," Antoine de Saint-Exupery, is assumed dead. The 44-year-old pilot disappeared while on maneuvers in Corsica. At 1:30 p.m., his plane took off with only one hour's worth of fuel. Search parties have found no sign of the craft.

Saint-Exupery was born in Lyon, the third son of a Count. He learned to fly in 1926 and worked as a commercial pilot in Europe, South America and Africa. He wrote autobiographical works about flying. "Night Flight" (1931) and "Wind, Sand and Stars" (1939) were among his books read worldwide.

None of his realistic pieces fired the imagination of adults and children like the sentimental "Little Prince." That timeless story, about a child on an interplanetary visit to Earth, celebrated a love of open skies, open land and open minds. ▷

Russians push on; bombs hit Warsaw

With Soviet troops pressing from the East, German-occupied Europe is now under attack on both fronts.

July 20. All along the Eastern Front, a powerful Russian drive, propelled by thousands of new tanks and aircraft, is forcing the Germans to retreat. The Russians are drawing a line extending from Riga in the north to Rumania to the south. And the first Russian bombs are raining down on Warsaw.

Polish partisans are attacking the Germans behind their lines, and a Committee of National Liberation was established in Lublin after the city was liberated by the Russians. The committee has distanced itself from the Polish government in London and aligned itself with Moscow.

Many Poles are excited that the Nazis are on the run, but they are nervous that the Russians have arrived. They wonder if the Nazi occupation force will simply be replaced by the Communists.

On the northern part of the long front, the Russians' target is the Baltic as they drive through Estonia and Latvia. The Russians are also trying to tighten their line that drops through "White Russia" to the Carpathian Mountains.

In Moscow, 57,000 Germans marched through the streets. They were prisoners, not conquerors. Diplomats from around the world watched as Russia boasted of its new military success.

There is no question that the tide has turned in Eastern Europe. The Russian war machine is enormous, and growing. Factories produced 16,000 planes and 14,000 tanks in the first half of the year. The new weapons are punishing German forces that have been weakened by the Allied attack in the West (→ 27).

Hitler's troops are under orders to fight to the death for the Reich.

Bombing attack on Hitler is failure

July 20. Adolf Hitler was burned and bruised yesterday at his secret headquarters when a bomb exploded, killing one and wounding 12 of his military staff.

In a broadcast a few hours later, he blamed the assassination attempt on an "officers' clique" headed by Col. Count von Stauffenberg, thus confirming recent reports of a serious rift between the Nazi High Command and the German army.

Shrieking in a maniacal rage, Hitler announced that von Stauffenberg was dead, presumably executed, and that the "criminal elements" would be exterminated (→ 22).

Nearly a grave for Adolf Hitler.

Talks end on world financial structure

July 22. The 44-member International Monetary Conference convened at Bretton Woods, New Hampshire, has ended on a promissory note, both financial and figurative, intended to solve postwar economic problems.

Plans include the establishment of two agencies, the International Monetary Fund and the International Bank for Reconstruction and Development, to administer key provisions: the stabilization of national currencies and the facilitation of long-term loans so that member nations may more readily repair war damage and restore and expand world trade.

1944

AUGUST

Su	Mo	Tu	We	Th	Fr	Sa
		1	2	3	4	5
6	7	8	9	10	11	12
13	14	15	16	17	18	19
20	21	22	23	24	25	26
29	28	29	30	31		

1. Philadelphia paralyzed by transportation strike.

1. Saranac Lake, N.Y.: Exiled Filipino Pres. Manuel Quezon dies at 65; Sergio Osmena sworn in as successor (→ 7/4/46).

2. Ankara: Turkey ends all relations with Nazis.

4. Burma: Myitkyina falls to Allies (→ 12/18).

10. Pacific: Guam completely recaptured as 500 out of 18,000 total Japanese troops surrender alive (→ 10).

10. Japan: Americans launch air raid over Nagasaki (→ 9/21).

12. France: First PLUTO (Pipe Line Under the Ocean) carries fuel from isle of Wight to Cherbourg.

12. France: Pierre Laval releases Edouard Herriot (→ 20).

14. U.S.: Production of domestic appliances resumes (→ 10/3).

15. France: Allies land in Provence, launching new front in South. (→ 16).

16. France: American paratroopers take St. Tropez (→ 19).

18. Red army reaches German border in East Prussia (→ 20).

19. France: Lt. Gen. Patton launches drive on Paris (→ 21).

20. U.S.S.R.: Soviets launch major drive in Ukraine (→ 10/22).

21. France: Americans cross Seine above Paris (→ 25).

21. Washington Conversation on Intl. Organization meets at Dumbarton Oaks Hotel to discuss world security (→ 10/9).

23. Balkans: Rumanian King Michael ousts Premier Antonescu, signs armistice with Soviets (→ 25).

25. France: Gen. Leclerc enters Paris as German Commandant Choltitz signs armistice.→

25. Rumania declares war on Germany (→ 31).

28. France: Allies force German surrender in Toulon and Marseilles, liberating Southern coastline (→ 29).

30. France: De Gaulle forms provisional govt. in Paris (→ 10/23).

French tanks lead Allies into Paris

De Gaulle leads Free French officials on their long-awaited return to Paris.

Aug 25. The French are singing the Marseillaise in the streets and cafes of Paris tonight. The tricolored flag hangs proudly from government buildings. And if there is a collaborationist left in Paris, he or she is not admitting it.

General Charles de Gaulle, fresh from his victory march in Chartres, led the tumultuous parade into Paris today. The Americans do not arrive until tomorrow. The liberation of Paris is of greater symbolic than strategic value. And the Allies decided to make this a day for the proud French.

De Gaulle had a simple answer at the Hotel de Ville when he was asked to announce officially the resurrection of the Republic. "The Republic," he replied, "never ceased to exist."

The French Second Armored Division, under the command of Major General Leclerc, was the first to enter Paris. But that was not the plan. The Allies had hoped that the resistance, fighting under the French Forces of the Interior, could liberate the city. It would be good for French morale. It would save precious ammunition for the attack on Germany. And it might spare the beautiful city of Paris from needless destruction.

But it did not work. The F.F.I faltered, and Leclerc came to the rescue. Little ammunition was used, and the city was not harmed. General von Choltitz ignored the order from Hitler to make Paris burn when he surrendered.

Parisians have been actively preparing for this day for two weeks. Workers began defying the Nazis by calling strikes, first on the rail lines, then in police stations. Collaborationist newspapers disappeared, and only Free French papers could be found at the kiosks. Vichy sympathizers were rounded up, and some of them were shot. The police headquarters was occupied and then the Hotel de Ville was liberated. Last night, bells rang in all the churches of Paris (→ 28).

Two proud French soldiers maneuver their tank gently through a crowd of jubilant Parisians.

Allies land in Southern France, move fast

Allied troops make their way carefully through a forest in Southern France.

Aug 29. If the invasion of Normandy had been as easy as the liberation of Southern France, the war against Hitler might be over by now. In just 14 days, the Allies have barnstormed across the Southern coast, from Marseilles to Nice. And American forces have scrambled across the Alps to seize Grenoble.

The German defense of the important port of Marseilles collapsed under the attack from French infantry and armor. The victory assures a flow of supplies to General Patch's Seventh American Army.

German resistance to the Seventh was described as "weak and disorganized" as it captured 17,000 German prisoners on the way to Grenoble. The army moved so quickly that it virtually cut communications between the German armies in Italy and France.

A communique from General Henry Wilson says the purpose of the thrust is to "join up with the Allied armies advancing from Normandy." At the rate the Americans are advancing, the two forces could meet within several days.

In another operation, American forces are closing in on Bordeaux, the last German enclave in southwestern France (→ 9/1).

Mass killings in Nazi camps disclosed

Aug 27. Reporters are viewing the Maidanek concentration camp in Poland today. Polish and Soviet officials estimate nearly 1.5 million people were put to death there. The victims were men, women and children, Jews and Christians, from every nation in Europe.

The 670-acre camp is carefully laid out. An electrified barbed wire fence runs around the compound. Outside the fence are 14 machine-gun turrets. Within the fenced area are neat green barracks. Beside them are hermetically sealed gas chambers and crematoriums.

Prisoners were "processed efficiently." First they went to a bath house. After they stripped, their clothes were taken away and shipped to Germany to supplement people's wardrobes there. The prisoners were then herded into the next room, sealed with the exception of holes placed high in the roof.

From these apertures cannisters of gas were tossed below. The warm showers the people took had opened their pores, allowing the gas to take effect more quickly. Prison guards watched through glass panes in the ceiling until the people were dead.

Bodies were transported to a furnace. Teeth with gold fillings were knocked out to be sold later. Bodies burned in ten or 12 minutes. The crematoriums, when used steadily, could burn 1,900 bodies a day. The ashes were then sold to German farmers as fertilizer (→ 1/27/45).

Russians capture Bucharest and oil fields

Aug 31. Russian troops sweeping through Rumania seized the capital of Bucharest today and took control of the vital oil fields at Ploesti. The loss of Rumania is a slap in the face to the Nazis. The loss of the largest oil fields in Europe could cripple their war effort.

Rumania changed sides in the war a week ago and declared war on Germany. Adolf Hitler could have prevented the startling development, but he turned down a request from Marshal Ion Antonescu to withdraw Rumanian troops from the Russian front. Antonescu thought it was time for Rumanians to start defending Rumania.

Last Friday, the Rumanian army rebelled against the Germans and allied itself with the Red army. Hitler, who was furious, ordered the bombing of Bucharest and the arrest of King Michael. He had already escaped to Switzerland.

These developments have apparently saved some Rumanian Jews from the Nazi gas chambers. Adolf Eichmann returned to Germany after the Nazi collapse (→ 9/1).

Poles rise in Warsaw; Russians hold back

Aug 31. The Polish people, encouraged by the Russians and their own government-in-exile, revolted against the Germans in Warsaw on the first of the month. Because of yet to be solved international tensions, their bid for freedom seems doomed for the worst.

As the Russians advanced on Warsaw, the commander of the Polish underground army warned his government in London that the Russians would be just another oppressor. General Bor-Komorowski viewed the committee already formed in Lublin as a puppet of Moscow. And the general figured that the revolt against the Nazis should be led by Poles, not Russians. London agreed.

Almost simultaneously, a radio broadcast sponsored by Moscow and the Lublin committee rallied the Poles. "People of Warsaw, take up your arms. A million Poles must become a million soldiers." And revolt they did, but no one came to their aid.

Stalin, who refuses to help and refuses to explain, is apparently outraged that Polish Communists are fighting side by side with loyalists of the London regime. President Roosevelt will not send help either, partly because he does not want to create a split with Stalin and partly because the Russian leader will not refuel the large American planes.

Few supplies are reaching the valiant Polish rebels. And the SS threatens to turn their rebellion into a bloodbath (→ 10/3).

Nazis arrest Petain

Aug 20. Marshal Henri Philippe Petain, head of France's collaborationist Vichy regime and the former "savior of Verdun," is on his way to Germany after his arrest by the SS.

According to reports, his personal guard was overpowered by the SS after the marshal steadfastly refused to leave Vichy. Informed he was a prisoner, he reportedly said, "You can do with me as you wish, but I will not leave this town."

The Germans then issued an ultimatum that either he leave without resistance or they would bomb Vichy. After consulting with his advisers, Petain changed his mind. He is on his way to Wiesbaden, Germany, where apartments have already been prepared for him (→ 4/24/45).

Hitler kills plotters

Aug 8. The Third Reich wasted little time executing eight men accused of plotting to assassinate Adolf Hitler. Two hours after a "people's tribunal" reached a guilty verdict, the men were hanged. Judge Roland Freisler condemned to death the men who were often scorned during the speedy trial, and told them, "You will always be schweindhunds (pig dogs)." According to some, the decision was a foregone conclusion (→ 10/14).

The global high-sign

1944

SEPTEMBER

Su	Mo	Tu	We	Th	Fr	Sa
					1	2
3	4	5	6	7	8	9
10	11	12	13	14	15	16
17	18	19	20	21	22	23
24	25	26	27	28	29	30

1. Balkans: Russian troops enter Bucharest (→ 5).

1. France: Americans storm Sedan, enter Argonne (→ 2).

1. Germany: Hermann Goering reportedly ousted by Hitler.

2. American troops enter Belgium (→ 3).

3. France: Americans capture Lyon (→ 4).

3. Belgium: British forces enter Brussels (→ 4).

4. Helsinki: Russians and Finns announce armistice.

4. British capture Antwerp, enter Holland and seal off Channel ports (→ 9).

5. Moscow: Soviets declare war on Bulgaria (→ 7).

5. London: Exiled govts. of Belgium, Holland and Luxembourg agree to customs union (Benelux) after war.

7. Balkans: Russians reach Yugoslav border to join Tito (→ 8).

8. Bulgaria delcares war on Germany (→ 13).

8. Balkans: Red army now 26 miles inside Greece (→ 13).

11. Americans enter Luxembourg (→ 12).

11. Quebec: Churchill and FDR meet for second conference, discuss strategy against Axis, and postwar world (→ 16).

12. Germany: Americans battle five miles inside Reich (→ 15).

13. Balkans: Rumania signs armistice with Allies (→ 19).

21. Belgium: Prince Charles, King Leopold's brother, appointed regent of the chamber.

21. Pacific: U.S. carrier force strikes Manila area (→ 10/12).

25. Germany: Teenagers and old men called for war service.

27. Balkans: Soviet and Yugoslav troops enter Albania (→ 10/4).

27. Holland: Allies give up Arnhem pocket; 2,000 evacuated.→

30. Italy: Germans execute 700 civilians in Marzabotto near Genes (→ 4/10/45).

Belgian cities liberated

Flags of the Allies fly again in Liege, a warm welcome for liberating troops.

Sept 9. The American First Army, having freed several Belgian cities from the Germans, has turned to the east. The army is just 20 miles from the German border. Its next target is the heavily fortified Siegfried line.

The first Allied tanks swept into Liege before dawn, and when morning broke thousands of Belgians crowded around the victorious Americans. A few days ago, they were huddled at home in fear. Today, they are slapping the Americans on the back and reading uncensored newspapers for the first time since the occupation began.

In Brussels, the scene was the same as Belgians greeted the "Tommies" almost deliriously.

The retreating Germans have tried to buy time for the defense of their homeland by flooding lowlands in both Belgium and the Netherlands. They are short on tanks and other vehicles and are desperately searching for new ones before the Allies reach their Siegfried line. The Allies are expected to attack as soon as they resupply (→ 11).

Americans break through into Reich

Sept 15. Fighting at last on German soil, General Omar Bradley's 1st Army has breached the main Siegfried line east of Aachen to stand less than 30 miles from the outskirts of Cologne on the Rhine. This puts our infantry close to the industrial Ruhr, one of the principal citadels of Germany's armed might.

Though this overshadows all other reports, the offensive to the south is also progressing well. Nancy, Charmes and Epinal, all on the right flank of General George S. Patton's Third Army, have fallen in the past 24 hours, and the German line on the Moselle River was blasted loose from its roots (→ 27).

General Omar Bradley.

Allies try and fail to seize Dutch bridge

Sept 27. A massive Allied effort to capture the Arnhem Bridge in Holland has failed tragically. Thousands of British, Polish, American and Dutch soldiers are dead following a fierce German counterattack. Allied plans to control the Rhine are altered, if not destroyed.

On September 3-4, a corps of the British Second Army under Field Marshal Bernard Montgomery pushed into Belgium, freeing Brussels and Antwerp. The troops moved northeast, joined by Polish and American forces. In a week, they were well inside Holland.

On the 14th, Montgomery gave instructions for "Operation Market Garden." Parachutists would try to take Arnhem and two other cities, Grave and Eindhoven, on the lower Rhine. Paratroopers would secure crossings for infantry, paving the way into the Ruhr Basin.

Success seemed likely. The Arnhem harbor itself was liberated; only the bridge spanning the Scheldt estuary was still guarded by the Germans. And from Belgium to Holland, German retreat had seemed steady.

Yet Nazi retaliation at Arnhem was overwhelming. A Polish brigade landing at the foot of the bridge was almost entirely wiped out. Only 50 of 3,000 paratroopers survived. Nearly 10,000 Dutch resistance fighters died. American and British casualties were high.

Today on the fields of Arnhem where years ago tulips bloomed, colorful parachutes litter the soil. Beside them lie corpses of a rotting "Market Garden" (→ 10/10).

Soviet push scares off German allies

Sept 19. Intimidated by the Red army's recent advances in Eastern Europe and the subsequent brief war with the Soviets, Bulgaria has shirked any remaining ties to Germany, signed an armistice with Russia and set up a new government this week. The new regime, led by Communist supporter Colonel Kimon Georgieff, has proceeded to exile or imprison any men responsible for allying Bulgaria with the Nazi government in Berlin. The transformation came on the heels of Soviet victories in neighboring Yugoslavia. Soviet Premier Joseph Stalin happily declared on Moscow radio: "Bulgaria has ceased to be a center of German influence in the Balkans" (→ 27).

V-2 rockets hit London

V-2, headed for London, blasts off from Peenemunde in northeast Germany.

Sept 8. The Nazis' new remote-controlled rockets, the V-2's, have been directed at London and Antwerp for the first time. They carry about the same amount of explosives as the V-1, but they are faster and deadlier. The V-2 travels at the speed of sound, and it is almost impossible to detect its approach. The Nazis abandoned the V-1 rocket when their launching pads were seized in Normandy (→ 10/14).

FDR and Winston plan shift to Pacific

Sept 16. In a series of conferences held on the Citadel on the St. Lawrence River, Prime Minister Winston Churchill and President Franklin Roosevelt agreed to re-direct war efforts from Europe to the Pacific theater, indicating the Nazis are on the edge of oblivion. A joint statement released after the meetings praised the agreement: "In a very short time, they reached decisions on all points both with regard to the completion of the war in Europe, now approaching its final stage, and the destruction of the barbarians of the Pacific."

While the two world leaders agreed to shift the focus of the war and concurred that due to the vastness of the Pacific no single person will command the operations, Churchill did have a complaint. He feels that the American press has suggested "the British wish to stint their obligation against the Japanese and throw the whole burden on the United States." He rebuffed such analysis and remarked that Britain plans to contribute more in the Pacific (→ 10/9).

1944

OCTOBER

Su	Mo	Tu	We	Th	Fr	Sa
1	2	3	4	5	6	7
8	9	10	11	12	13	14
15	16	17	18	19	20	21
22	23	24	25	26	27	28
29	30	31				

3. U.S. Congress passes Surplus War Property Act, providing for reconversion after war (→ 11/19).

3. Poland: Warsaw rebels give up after 63-day fight with Germans; almost 200,000 Poles dead.

4. Balkans: British land in Greece and take Petras (→ 7).

7. Balkans: Allied forces pour into Albania, Greece (→ 18).

9. Churchill and Eden go to Moscow (→ 20).

9. St. Louis: Cardinals take Series, beating Browns 3-1 in sixth game.

10. Germany: Americans isolate Aachen, demand surrender (→ 20).

11. New York: Lauren Bacall opens in "To Have and Have Not."

12. Pacific: 1,000 American planes attack Formosa; 71 lost (→ 14).

14. Japan: Record number of B-29's blasts Okayama (→ 20).

14. Belgium: Germans fire V-1 and V-2 rockets on Allied troops in Antwerp.

15. Greece: British troops under Gen. Scobie land in attempt to neutralize Communist faction of resistance (→ 18).

16. Germany: Hitler orders severe cut in bread rations.

18. Exiled Greek govt. returns to Athens (→ 12/3).

18. Balkans: Allies acknowledge Tito as head of Yugoslav state (→ 11/10).

20. Pacific: MacArthur lands on Leyte, fulfilling 1942 promise, "I shall return" (→ 25).

20. Moscow: Churchill and Stalin conclude agreement dividing Eastern Europe into zones of influence following war (→ 2/4/45).

23. Allies recognize de Gaulle govt. in France (→ 28).

28. France: De Gaulle decree orders disarmament of resistance (→ 11/15).

DEATH

8. Wendell Willkie, Republican leader in U.S. (*2/18/1892).

Big Four propose United Nations

Oct 9. Proposals for a world security organization are being seriously considered by the United States, Great Britain, the Soviet Union and China, according to an announcement released today. Conferees at Dumbarton Oaks in Washington D.C., called the proposed international group "The United Nations." Its purpose would be "to take such action by air, naval or land forces to maintain or restore international peace and security."

The United Nations would allocate responsibilty to the four nations to attack potential war-making countries before, rather than after, war is made.

President Roosevelt praised the conference's recommendations and said "the peace-loving nations (should) be in a position to assure that no other would-be aggressor or conquerer shall ever get started." No charter has been signed, but the four nations agree about most aspects of the proposal (→ 1/1/45).

American ballet by Graham, Copland

Oct 30. A ballet called "Appalachian Spring," celebrating the pioneer spirit, has debuted in New York. Martha Graham is the choreographer, Aaron Copland the composer. Graham's dance "Frontier" (1935) explored similar themes. Copland's "Billy the Kid" (1938) and "Rodeo" (1942) were also very American in inspiration.

MacArthur returns to the Philippines

Oct 25. General Douglas MacArthur has fulfilled his promise. He has returned to the Philippines, this time in the company of the greatest armada ever to sail the Pacific.

This afternoon, MacArthur's convoy of 225,000 men destroyed two divisions of Japan's fleet in Leyte Gulf. And at this moment, Vice Admiral Thomas Kinkaid's Seventh Fleet hotly pursues remnants of two Japanese forces.

Today, MacArthur announced that "the Japanese navy has suffered its most crushing defeat of the war." President Roosevelt agrees; he held a special press conference releasing details of the offensive. One Japanese carrier is sunk, as are numerous cruisers and destroyers.

The only serious American loss is the carrier USS Princeton, located northeast of Luzon. Badly hit by Japanese bombers, it listed in the waters until U.S. forces torpedoed it. The Americans preferred not to give the Japanese the satisfaction of sinking it. Casualties on board were light. About 134 officers and 1,227 enlisted men were saved.

The violent destruction of the Japanese fleet is newsworthy, but it will not hasten the end of the war; MacArthur's strategy may do that. When he arrived in the islands October 21, MacArthur ordered the U.S. Navy to approach areas with smaller Japanese concentrations. By snuffing out the smaller establishments, he leaves the larger ones to "wither on the vine."

Japan has been relying on Celebes, Borneo and eastern Java for oil to lubricate its war machine. As the U.S. monopolizes these regions, Japan must go further and further afield in search of raw materials. Oil will only be gotten after taking a long, circuitous route by Singapore. Japan cannot afford the time.

Conversely, as the U.S. takes the eastern Philippines, its supply route shortens. Now that the southern Marianas are under our control, the northern supply route to major battle areas is nearly sliced in half. And hundreds of abandoned airfields are now within our reach.

MacArthur will press westward toward Manila. With Manila gone, Japan's oil lifeline will be utterly severed. MacArthur has returned, and he means to stay (→ 11/12).

MacArthur, resolute and single-minded, strides ashore at Leyte.

Allies, fighting way into Aachen, take first city in Germany

A German tank near Aachen waits in the mud for the Allied advance.

Oct 20. The German city of Aachen fell to the Allies today, ten days after the American First Army dispatched a "surrender or die" ultimatum to the Germans. They elected to fight. The first German city to be seized by the Allies is a mostly empty shell.

General Omar Bradley's troops are facing similar resistance elsewhere along the heavily defended Siegfried line. Allied bombers have not been able to penetrate the clouds, tanks are trapped in the mud and the spirits of the infantry are chilled by the early winter weather.

Many residents evacuated Aachen, which is called Aix-la-Chapelle by the French. The Nazis promise to punish those who stayed behind for not opposing or even favoring U.S. occupation (→ 11/1).

Under Nazi threat, Rommel is suicide

Oct 14. Erwin Rommel, a hero of the Reich but an enemy of Hitler, died today, a victim of suicide. It was not a death he chose freely.

Rommel was implicated in the assassination attempt against the Fuhrer. Today, two of Hitler's generals offered the "Desert Fox" a choice. He could commit suicide, have a hero's funeral and spare his family disgrace. Or he could be put on trial in Berlin. Rommel agreed to swallow the poison.

Rommel was apparently aware of only the outline of the plot against Hitler. He was in a hospital recovering from wounds he suffered in Normandy when the bomb exploded in Hitler's headquarters.

Soviets in Prussia

Oct 22. The Third Belorussian and the First Baltic forces have met an entrenched line of resistance at Insterburg in eastern Prussia. The Soviet drive seems halted.

On October 16, Soviet armies crossed into eastern Prussia by way of Goldap. The Belorussian army thrashed its way through the border village of Nemersdorf and others. Reports of pillaging and some random killing leaked out of the area. French prisoners near the town of Gumbinnen were said to be afraid of their liberators. Now the Belorussian force is reinforced by Baltic troops. They are needed, for the Germans fight more vigorously than ever. They are defending their homeland (→ 1/13/45).

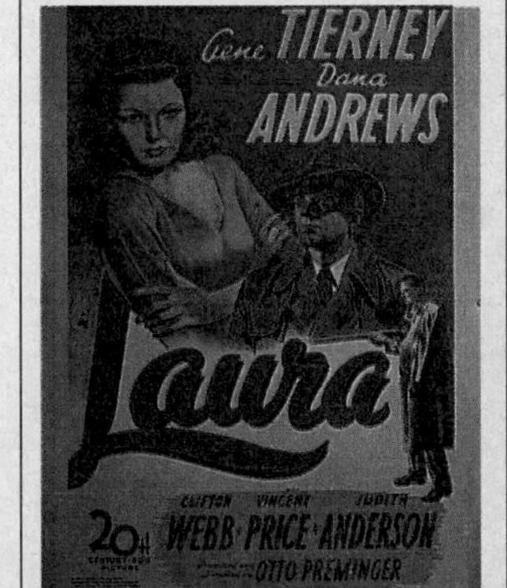

1944

NOVEMBER

Su	Mo	Tu	We	Th	Fr	Sa
			1	2	3	4
5	6	7	8	9	10	11
12	13	14	15	16	17	18
19	20	21	22	23	24	25
26	27	28	29	30		

1. Philadelphia: First quadruplets delivered by caesarean section are born to Mr. and Mrs. Joseph Cirminello.

1. Holland: British land on Dutch island Walcheren, suffer heavy losses (→ 18).

5. Cairo: Seeking independence for Palestine after war, Zionists assassinate Lord Moyne, British resident minister in Mideast (→ 9/23/45).

5. Pacific: American B-29's pound Singapore (→ 12).

7. Paris: De Gaulle demands French occupation zone in Germany (→ 6/5/45).

10. Stockholm: Nobel Peace Prize awarded to International Red Cross.

10. Balkans: Enver Hodja's Albanian govt. recognized by Allies (→ 12/26).

11. Paris: Napoleon's crown disappears from Les Invalides for second time.

12. Pacific: U.S. fliers wipe out Japanese convoy near Leyte; six destroyers, four transports, 8,000 troops (→ 24).

15. France: Ministers Council decides to nationalize Renault factories without indemnities (→ 1/16/45).

18. Germany: Allies enter Saar Basin, drive toward Ruhr (→ 23).

19. FDR opens sixth war loan drive, seeking $14 billion (→ 2/26/45).

20. Belgian resistance agrees, with Allied mediation, to surrender arms to government.

23. France: General Leclerc's troops enter Strasbourg (→ 24).

24. Japan: B-29's from Saipan bomb Tokyo by daylight (→ 12/8).

28. Belgium: First Allied supplies reach Antwerp by convoy (→ 2/23/45).

30. Balkans: Soviet troops break through German lines in south Hungary (→ 12/26).

DEATHS

7. Earl of Strathmore, father of Queen Elizabeth (*3/14/1855).

22. Joseph Caillaux, ex-premier of France (*3/30/1863).

Patton's tanks drive into the Saar Basin

U.S. tanks batter German lines in the Saar to prepare for infantry assault.

Nov 24. Lieutenant General George S. Patton's forces have burst into the Saar Basin, Germany's second most important mining and factory region. Only the Ruhr Valley could be considered more essential to Germany's war effort. The strategic advance comes as Germany's forces face enclosure by the British on the Cologne fields and by the French at Strasbourg.

The German retreat is proving to be disorganized and fearful. A week ago, when the American offensive began, U.S. soldiers found abandoned towns meticulously readied; Germans laced streets with mines and sprinkled sewers with deadly booby traps. The Germans set fire to the villages, alloting civilians a generous ten minutes to collect their belongings before striking a match.

In the past 48 hours, however, Patton and his men have found signs of panic: Two ammunition dumps and four 177-mm. guns were theirs for the taking. And the Americans took 3,000 prisoners in the last three days. Two major generals are among the captives (→ 12/2).

Tirpitz proves tough; finally sunk by RAF

Nov 12. The German battleship Tirpitz, ever a great menace to Allied shipping, was finally sunk by RAF bombers today off the coast of Norway after having been twice crippled by previous attacks.

Meanwhile, in the Philippines, "Helldivers" from Admiral Halsey's Third Fleet sank a Japanese convoy carrying an estimated 8,000 troops as it tried to ferry reinforcements to the enemy's besieged line of defense in the Ormoc Valley on northwestern Leyte Island.

The Tirpitz was the last serious German menace on the high seas.

FDR wins fourth term; Truman V.P.

Nov 7. President Franklin Delano Roosevelt won an unprecedented fourth term in office today, defeating Governor Thomas E. Dewey of New York, the Republican presidential candidate. Senator Harry S. Truman, a Missouri Democrat, was elected Vice President. Returns showed that while the president won a heavy electoral vote, he was elected by a much slimmer popular majority than he had piled up in his three earlier successful presidential races against Herbert Hoover, in 1932; Alfred M. Landon, in 1936; and Wendell L. Willkie, in 1940 (→ 1/20/45).

FDR in a classic pose.

Antwerp opened to Allied shipping

Nov 3. The grim struggle to open Antwerp in Belgium to Allied shipping is now over. British units have overrun most of Walcheren Island, and the Canadians mopped up the last of the German troops holding out south of the Scheldt River after the bulk of the German garrison surrendered this morning. With this pocket eliminated, the Scheldt is now free from German shelling and the dangerous task of minesweeping can commence. By late this month, Antwerp, the greatest port in northwestern Europe, may be open to convoys of the Western powers (→ 28).

1944

DECEMBER

Su	Mo	Tu	We	Th	Fr	Sa
					1	2
3	4	5	6	7	8	9
10	11	12	13	14	15	16
17	18	19	20	21	22	23
24	25	26	27	28	29	30
31						

2. Baltimore: Army beats Navy first time in five years, 23-7.

2. Germany: Patton's troops enter Saar valley and break through Siegfried line (→ 16).

3. Greece: Ten killed by British in Athens as leftists march defying government ban (→ 4).

4. Athens: Martial law, curfew called to combat strike (→ 25).

8. Pacific: U.S. conducts longest, most effective air raid of Pacific battle at Iwo Jima (→ 1/6/45).

17. New York: Green Bay Packers take football championship 14-7 over Giants.

18. Burma: Japanese repelled from north (→ 1/24/45).

22. Indochina: Vo Nguyen Giap founds Vietnamese People's Army (→ 3/24/45).

25. Churchill, Eden go to Athens seeking end to civil war (→ 30).

26. Balkans: Soviet troops surround Budapest (→ 1/20/45).

BIRTH

21. Michael Tilson Thomas, leading American conductor.

DEATHS

13. Wassily Kandinsky, Russian painter, originator abstract art (*12/4/1866).

30. Romain Rolland, French writer (*1/29/1886).

CULTURAL EVENTS, 1944

Literature: T.S. Eliot's "Four Quartets"; Tennessee Williams' "The Glass Menagerie"; Camus' "Caligula"; John Van Druten's "I Remember Mama"; Somerset Maugham's "The Razor's Edge"; Sartre's "No Exit."

Academia: Lewis Mumford's "The Condition of Man"; Jung's "Psychology and Religion."

Music: Aaron Copland's "Appalachian Spring"; "Swinging on a Star"; "Sentimental Journey"; "Accentuate the Positive."

The Arts: Matisse's "The White Dress"; "Art Concrete" exhibit in Basle.

Film: Olivier's "Henri V"; Carne's "Children of Paradise"; "Going My Way," Academy Award.

Germans counterattack in Ardennes

Dec 16. Adolf Hitler took the Allies by surprise as he launched a sharp counterattack in the Ardennes. He hopes to reverse his recent setbacks in Belgium and France and drive through Brussels all the way to Antwerp.

Hitler chose the daring plan over the lively protests of his generals, who favored a more limited attack.

The Fuhrer threw three armies of at least 20 divisions into the assault, all of them under the command of Field Marshal von Rundstedt. The major attack was planned on the north of the front, where panzers under General Dietrich hoped to cross the Meuse and drive on to Antwerp. An army to the south, aimed at Saint-Vith and Bastogne, was expected to support the drive to Antwerp. And a third army even farther to the south was charged with protecting the flank of the other two advancing armies.

Hitler's master plan is not working as scheduled. The northern and southern armies ran into stiff opposition after early successes. But the units in the middle plunged forth with almost alarming speed, creating a large bulge that is very vulnerable to Allied attack.

The Allies are pinning their hopes on a paratrooper unit the Germans bypassed in Bastogne during their precipitous advance. General Omar Bradley is moving infantry reinforcements to the unit so the Allies can strike at the Germans from the middle of the bulge (→ 29).

Disarmed American soldiers stand at the mercy of their German captors.

"Nuts": McAuliffe spurns surrender

Dec 29. The American expression "Nuts" as in "Nuts to you" has become the rallying cry for Allied troops besieged by Germans in the battle of the Ardennes. "Nuts" was the defiant one-word reply from Brigadier General Anthony McAuliffe when the Germans demanded that he surrender the city of Bastogne.

McAuliffe's troops, mostly paratroopers, were pinned down and encircled by five German divisions last week. In their earlier advance, the Germans had foolishly leapfrogged past Bastogne and they were trying to correct the error. Field Marshal Karl von Runstedt was convinced his enemy could not hold out any longer when he asked McAuliffe to call it quits.

Snow and clouds prevented American planes from dropping supplies, and German subterfuge made the defense of Bastogne even more difficult. A number of German soldiers confused the paratroopers by infiltrating their camp, wearing American uniforms and speaking English.

Infantry and armored divisions managed to reach Bastogne several days ago. McAuliffe's greeting was almost as laconic as his reply to the Germans. "I am very happy to see you," he said. And no doubt relieved also. Hitler had made the capture of Bastogne a top priority, and thousands of Americans died defending the city.

German soldiers, guns ready, carefully pass a burning tank near Bastogne.

Greek civil war rages; King gives up

Dec 30. King George II of Greece virtually renounced his throne in an attempt to end the civil war that is engulfing Greece. The king announced in London that he would not return to Greece unless a free election called him back to rule. As regent replacing him he designated Archbishop Damaskinos, who resisted the German occupation and is-believed to command the respect of a great majority in Greece.

The king's virtual abdication was arranged by British Prime Minister Winston Churchill and Foreign Secretary Anthony Eden, who had flown to Athens at Christmas in an attempt to end the civil strife in Greece that more and more was involving British troops.

Fighting has been raging in the Athens area between the Elas militia of the leftist National Liberation Front (EAM) and royalist troops of the British-supported government of Premier George Papandreou.

The crisis was precipitated when the EAM refused to disband its militia and called a general strike that paralyzed Athens and led to street fighting. British troops were called in to fight the leftist forces. As part of the attempt at national reconciliation, Papandreou is expected to resign (→ 1/1/45).

Glenn Miller plane is missing at sea

Glenn Miller.

Dec 16. Glenn Miller is missing. A plane carrying him and two companions disappeared en route from England to France during a USO trip. The pilot raised no distress call, and no wreckage has been spotted by British planes in the area.

A master of swing, Miller took his place alongside Duke Ellington, Benny Goodman, Artie Shaw, Tommy and Jimmy Dorsey and Count Basie. Miller plays trombone and arranges his orchestra's smooth, satisfying compositions. He is riding the crest of fame; his song "In the Mood" soared on the airwaves. The Iowa-born bandleader is only 40 years old.

Four generals get new five-star rank

Dec 15. In a unanimous vote, the Senate has agreed to create a new military rank, five-star general. Immediately after the bill's passage, four generals were promoted: George Marshall, chief of staff of the Army; Douglas MacArthur, commander in the Southwest Pacific; Dwight Eisenhower, Supreme Allied Commander in Europe; and Henry Arnold, Commanding General of the Army Air Force. The bill was sent to Capitol Hill after President Roosevelt signed the legislation authorizing the new rank.

While the bill does not specifically state that the generals wear five stars on their uniforms, it is assumed the promoted military heroes will don another star. The promotions reward these men who have dedicated their lives to the protection of the nation. The congressional act salutes the generals as the Allies appear to be close to victory in Europe.

1945

JANUARY

Su	Mo	Tu	We	Th	Fr	Sa
	1	2	3	4	5	6
7	8	9	10	11	12	13
14	15	16	17	18	19	20
21	22	23	24	25	26	27
28	29	30	31			

1. Pasadena: Southern Cal. Trojans blank Tennessee Volunteers 25-0 in Rose Bowl.

1. Hitler breaks 5-month silence to tell German people war will not end until Reich victory (→ 4).

1. France formally joins United Nations (→ 4/25).

1. Greek conflict halted by truce after 40-day battle (→ 1/21/46).

4. Belgium: Last German offensive in Bastogne fails (→ 15).

6. Pacific: B-29's strike new blows on Tokyo, Nanking (→ 7).

7. Pacific: U.S. air ace Major Thomas B. McGuire Jr. killed in battle (→ 9).

7. Hollywood: RKO radio signs Boris Karloff for parts in three horror shows.

8. Chicago: Teamsters Union asks repeal of Wagner Act and end of NLRB (→ 2/20).

9. Pacific: U.S. troops land on Luzon, 107 miles from Manila (→ 12).

12. U.S. Pacific fleet carrier planes sink 25 Japanese ships off Indochina coast (→ 2/1).

13. Red army opens offensive in south Poland, crashing 25 miles through German lines (→ 17).

15. American First Army enters Houffalize in heart of Belgian Bulge (→ 30).

17. Poland: Red army occupies Warsaw (→ 19).

19. Poland: Red army captures Lodz, Kracow and Tarnow (→ 21).

20. Washington: FDR inaugurated for fourth term (→ 4/12).

20. Moscow: Allies sign truce with Hungarians (→ 2/13).

21. Red army invades Germany in East and West (→ 31).

24. China: U.S. Mars Task Force traps Japanese along Burma Road south of Wanting (→ 28).

25. Grand Rapids, Michigan becomes first U.S. community to fluoridate water.

28. China: Chiang Kai-shek renames Burma-Ledo Road Stilwell Road, in honor of Gen. Joseph W. Stilwell.→

30. Germany: U.S. launches drive on Siegfried line (→ 2/2).

Japanese trapped on Burma Road

"Vinegar Joe" Stilwell and Lord Mountbatten talk strategy.

Jan 28. The Mars Task Force, successor to Merrill's Marauders, moved into position to entrap remnants of a Japanese army as the final push developed to clear the newly completed Ledo-Burma Road for traffic. American troops set up a barrier south of Mongyu, the junction of the Ledo and Burma Roads.

Meanwhile, the Chinese Y Army was driving the Japanese troops south toward the American position. The first convoy to use the road, one of the great engineering feats of the war, left Ledo for Kunming in China on January 12. But before the convoy of 133 vehicles could travel into China, it was necessary to remove the retreating Japanese troops.

General Chiang Kai-shek said the new overland route had broken the siege of China and announced the road would be named in honor of Gen. Joseph W. Stilwell, who first proposed the route (→ 5/2).

Guitarist Segovia in New York concert

Jan 25. Classical guitarist Andres Segovia played to a jubilant audience last night at New York Town Hall. The 51-year-old Spanish musician performed works by Gaspar Sanz, Luis Milan and others with control and finesse. Segovia's popularity has remained high in the United States since he debuted here in 1928. He is generally credited with making classical guitar a legitimate, respected instrument.

Auschwitz is liberated

When the Red army arrived at the camp in Auschwitz, a Polish industrial town, they found inscribed above the entrance, the words: "Work makes you free."

Jan 27. Soviet troops sweeping through Poland found thousands of victims of Nazi sadism today. The soldiers walked through the barbed wire of the Auschwitz concentration camp and discovered 5,000 prisoners, most of them Jews, all of them dazed and starving.

These prisoners were the lucky ones. They were survivors. Untold thousands of others were asphyxiated in the gas chambers of Auschwitz by Nazis intent on "purifying the Germanic race."

The gas was turned off last November. Earlier this month, the last of the Jewish prisoners arrived from Berlin; on the 6th, the final executions in the camp: four Jews who had been charged with hiding explosives. All of them young girls.

When the Nazis knew the advancing Russians could not be stopped, they lined up 60,000 prisoners and started a forced march in the direction of Germany. Those who could not stand the rigors of the march were beaten or killed (→ 3/12).

Day after day, behind barbed wire, imprisoned Jews awaited their bread ration.

Soviet army batters Berlin's outer defenses

Jan 31. A blinding blizzard has not deterred Soviet armies from racing through a ring of Berlin's outer cities. Marshal Georgi Zhukov's First Army stands closest to the capital. They have captured the town of Beyersdorf, only 67 miles to the northeast. Nazi broadcasts expressed fears that Zhukov was now prepared "to launch the frontal attack on Berlin."

While Zhukov poised on the brink of the city, other Red forces swirled a few hundred miles away to the east and south. One Communist army isolated the East Prussian capital of Koenigsburg. Another slashed its way to within 22 miles of the Moravian Gap, leading to Prague and Vienna. Some Western newspapers accuse the Nazis of panic, but Soviet armies report only the usual fierce opposition.

The Red forces extend 150 miles along the Oder, severing Nazi troops east and west. Those groups would have defended Frankfurt. That city may be the next in the ring around Berlin to collapse.

Running before the Soviet armies like foxes before hounds are German refugees. Some of them were settlers in Hitler's "Lebensraum," that portion of Poland Hitler appropriated. Other civilians hurry from the eastern provinces of Germany. A radio broadcast from Paris said the Soviets had rounded up 200,000 German citizens in the city of Lodz alone.

Out among those refugees are some of Hitler's leaders. Heinrich Himmler is rumored to be with those men. Hitler ordered them to the Eastern Front to "make and execute drastic decisions." Yet any decision other than surrender may prove drastic (→ 2/2).

German forces, pushed out of Russia, retreat before the Soviet offensive.

France nationalizes Renault auto firm

Jan 16. France is nationalizing the auto firm Renault and other major factories and mines. The conversion process started during the war, when the resistance government needed to modify many consumer-goods factories for wartime production. Instituting permanent nationalization is supported by patriotic labor leaders.

Most coal mines were put under state control September 27. Former company directors were suspended. Renault's expropriation should go smoothly: Defiant owner Louis Renault died December 24 (→ 6/12).

Churchill warns Reich to surrender

Jan 18. Prime Minister Churchill says Germany has less to fear in surrendering unconditionally than in continuing a hopeless war.

In a speech before the House of Commons, Churchill also called for unity among the Allies as they face the problems of peace. He scoffed at the idea that the terms of "unconditional surrender" agreed upon by President Roosevelt and himself at Casablanca were inducing the enemy to greater resistance. He also defended British intervention in Greece, saying the alternative was a Communist dictatorship.

1945

FEBRUARY

Su	Mo	Tu	We	Th	Fr	Sa
				1	2	3
4	5	6	7	8	9	10
11	12	13	14	15	16	17
18	19	20	21	22	23	24
25	26	27	28			

1. Luzon: U.S. Rangers and Filipino guerrillas rescue 513 American survivors of Bataan "death march" (→ 6).

2. Ecuador declares war on Germany (→ 3/27).

2. Pacific: American B-29's sink Singapore dock in biggest attack on naval base (→ 6).

2. Germany: Red army sweeps 15 miles closer to Berlin, taking Stettin (→ 3/30).

2. Germany: 1,200 RAF planes blast Wiesbaden and Karlsruhe (→ 3).

3. Germany: Allies drop 3,000 tons of bombs on Berlin (→ 4).

4. Germans complete evacuation of Belgium (→ 14).

4. Yalta: Big Three meet in Soviet territory to discuss war aims (→ 11).

6. Pacific: MacArthur reports fall of Manila, liberation of 5,000 prisoners (→ 10).

10. Pacific: B-29's hit Tokyo area (→ 17).

13. Balkans: Red army completes conquest of Budapest, ending 50-day siege with over 159,000 killed (→ 3/2).

17. Pacific: MacArthur's troops land on Corregidor in the Philippines.→

18. Pacific: U.S. Marines storm ashore on Iwo Jima (→ 23).

20. Washington: WLB orders minimum wage of 55 cents an hour for textile workers (→ 3/2).

23. France: First American boats arrive with food for French civilians (→ 5/12).

23. Germany: Eisenhower opens wide offensive in Rhineland (→ 28).

23. Turkey declares war on Germany and Japan.

24. Egyptian Premier Ahmed Maher Pasha killed in Parliament after reading decree declaring war on Axis (→ 9/23).

26. Midnight curfew begins throughout U.S. (→ 3/19).

26. Syria declares war on Japan and Germany (→ 5/21).

28. Germany: U.S. tanks break natural defense line west of Rhine, cross Erft River (→ 3/6).

Yalta: Big Three plan future moves

Feb 11. The Big Three adjourned their meeting in Yalta today, and one of the three leaders, Joseph Stalin, seemed bigger than ever. Russia's resounding military victories in the past several months gave Stalin a distinct advantage as he met with President Roosevelt and Prime Minister Churchill to carve up the postwar world.

The battle against Germany is not over yet, but the three men agreed it is only a matter of time. Roosevelt seemed particularly eager to conclude the American military operation in Europe and devote all his forces against Japan. To Churchill and Stalin, military considerations appeared to be of secondary importance. They were both intent on dividing the new Europe into zones of political influence.

Churchill and Stalin were not new to the game. They had already consorted like two back-room gamblers when they met in Moscow last October without Roosevelt. Using a piece of paper like a scorecard, Churchill proposed that Russia keep Rumania while Britain keep Greece. Stalin did not object, and by the time he went home he had Hungary and Bulgaria to boot.

At Yalta, Churchill and Roosevelt could not deny Stalin what he had won in Moscow. Churchill's hands were tied. And Roosevelt perceived that Stalin was now dealing from a position of strength, something he did not have when the three men met at Tehran.

The Allied triumvirate at Yalta: Churchill, Roosevelt and Stalin.

Our military heroes inspire more than the troops. The latest in ladies' fashion is a modified "Eisenhower Jacket," worn as a blouse.

To Roosevelt, the Russians were invincible as they swept through Eastern Europe toward Germany. In Western Europe, the Allies were stumbling, and there was no country powerful enough to stop Stalin. Germany was in ruins, and France was in disarray.

Roosevelt, who detests the Communist system, has a personal liking for Stalin. And he seems to trust him. All the Soviet leader wants, Roosevelt said, "is to ensure the security of his country. I think that if I give him everything I possibly can without demanding anything in return, then noblesse oblige, he will not attempt to annex anything and will work to build a peaceful and democratic world."

Stalin's influence and recent conquests in the Balkans were not challenged at Yalta. Poland presented a stickier problem. Stalin's invasion of eastern Poland was a fait accompli, and it was hard to argue against his point that residents of the area are for the most part Ukrainian and Byelorussian. Roosevelt and Churchill agreed to let Stalin move his border west to the Curzon line, but they postponed a decision on which territories Poland would reclaim from Germany.

Stalin also won a significant victory on the composition of the new Polish government. The London government-in-exile was left out in the cold, and the Lublin committee, excoriated by some as a Russian puppet, was given the job of forming the new government.

The three leaders agreed that Germany would be punished, divided, occupied and administered by the Allies after her defeat. After considerable discussion, Stalin relented and agreed to give France an occupation zone, provided it were sliced out of the American and British areas. Berlin would be jointly occupied. But Stalin refused to cooperate with the others in forming the final military strategy to be used against Germany.

On the touchy question of reparations, Roosevelt and Churchill agreed with Stalin that Germany would have to pay $20 billion, half of it to Russia.

Roosevelt, who was concerned about a possible French or British build-up in the Pacific, made a separate agreement with Stalin about the war against Japan. Stalin agreed to start fighting the Japanese three months after Germany surrendered. In return, Stalin was promised the Kurile Islands, the southern part of Sakhalin and railway rights in Manchuria. Roosevelt did not consult with another ally, Chiang Kai-shek, even though he was bartering away his possessions.

The three leaders also agreed on the formation of a new world organization, to be called the United Nations. The first meeting was scheduled for April in San Francisco.

At that meeting, the Big Three will have to smooth the feathers of those who felt arbitrarily excluded from Yalta. Gen. de Gaulle is particularly upset (→ 7/15).

Allied planes devastate Dresden, Germany's gem

Feb 14. Dresden, "the Florence of Germany," is a molten, blazing mass tonight. Allied bombs rained on the city continuously for two days. Priceless art and architecture from the 17th and 18th centuries are destroyed. More than 130,000 people, most of them civilians, are dead.

Throughout the war, Allies kept a respectable distance from Dresden. It is not an industrial town but a historic, residential city. Many of the buildings are rare examples of rococo and baroque styles. Several museums house paintings by Italian, Dutch and Flemish masters.

Last night at 10:15 respect for this art center vanished. RAF Lancaster bombers, 245 of them, battered Dresden with incendiaries and two-ton bombs. At noon today, 450 U.S. B-17's pummeled the city. This evening the RAF planes, now 550 in number, returned. The city hardly defended itself. It was never equipped for that. Exactly eight bombers were downed by German anti-aircraft.

Why was Dresden attacked? The Soviets had insisted on weakening German defense in the area. British Air Marshal Arthur Harris had also supported an offensive on the city. Yet today there is an outcry from many in the Allied nations. If we bomb Dresden, what is to stop the Luftwaffe from destroying Oxford or other treasured Allied cities? The deadliest bombing of all time fell on statues, paintings and ancient churches. These treasures belong to us all (→ 23).

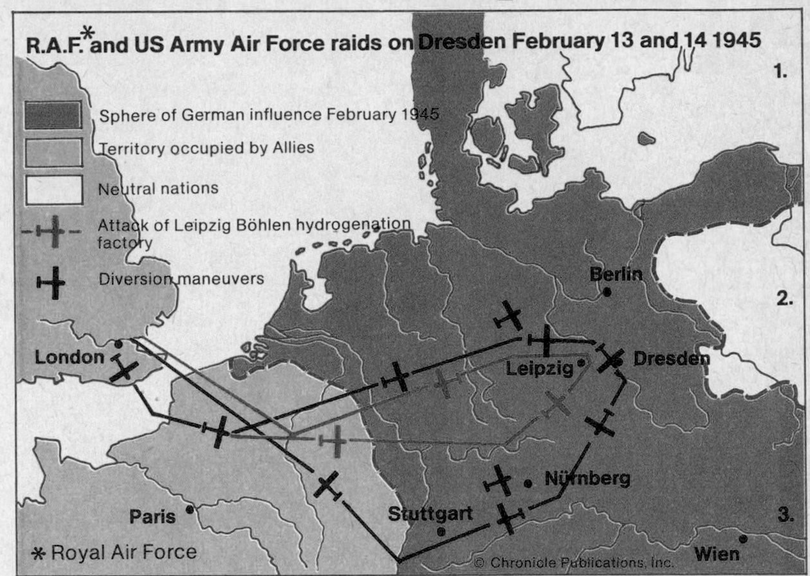

The Allies launched both diversionary and direct raids from London.

Dresden had trouble keeping its beauty intact following devastating fires in 1491 and 1685. Allied bombs will now require another rebuilding.

Stars and stripes raised over Iwo Jima

"Old Glory" at Iwo Jima.

Feb 23. After four days of bitter fighting, a Marine platoon succeeded today in reaching the top of Mount Surabachi on the southern tip of Iwo Jima and raising an American flag in triumph.

Conquest of the heavily fortified mountain had been one of the first objectives of the invasion of the small, strategic island located 750 miles south of Tokyo. The task of neutralizing the defenses and scaling the mountain fell to men in the 28th Regiment of the Fifth Marine Division. Navy Secretary Forrestal saw the flag from the beachhead and told Lt. Gen. Holland M. Smith, "The raising of that flag on Surabachi means a Marine Corps for the next 500 years" (→ 25).

5,000 POWs found in Manila; Bataan hit

Feb 17. U.S. forces liberated Manila and recaptured Corregidor, the island fortress where the United States suffered a humiliating defeat nearly three years ago. General Douglas MacArthur announced on the 6th the fall of Manila and the liberation of 5,000 prisoners of war.

The fighting for control of the Philippine capital, however, continued on for several more days as isolated groups of Japanese troops clung desperately to strongholds in Fort McKinley and Intramuros, the walled city built by the Spaniards.

While the fighting continued in Manila, General MacArthur moved to recapture Corregidor, from which he had fled in 1942. Assault troops of the 38th Division captured Mariveles on the southern tip of the Bataan Peninsula, placing American troops within seven miles of Corregidor. After several days of incessant bombing and naval gunfire, airborne troops, backed up by an amphibious landing, dropped on Corregidor and planted again the American flag after meeting only sporadic resistance (→ 18).

B-29's hit Tokyo area again and again

Feb 25. American warplanes ravaged Tokyo today, dropping 2,000 tons of bombs on its industrial sections. In the morning, 1,200 carrier-based planes ripped military installations outside the Japanese capital and then without allowing any time for recuperation, U.S. B-29 Superfortresses from the Twenty-first Bomber Command plastered the terror-stricken city.

Terrible weather conditions could not stop the assault, although it did account for errant bombs that very nearly struck one of Emperor Hirohito's imperial properties, the majestic Omiya Palace, where his mother lives. These explosions elicited irate responses from Japanese Premier Kuniaki Koiso, who expressed "anger at the enemy's arrogance and lawlessness." While the damage around the imperial areas was light, Koiso said, "I am filled with trepidation."

The second raid encountered little resistance as the heavy bombers cleared the path for the B-29's. Colonel Carl Storey remarked, "We saw no opposition and the carrier planes were probably keeping them busy." He added proudly, "We laid our bombs right down the main street of the city and that town must sure be burning tonight."

Targets in Nagoya were bombed, but Tokyo was the prize for these pilots, many of whom were making their first forays over the city. They suffered little damage as few carrier planes went down and no Superfortresses were lost (→ 3/2).

1945

MARCH

Su	Mo	Tu	We	Th	Fr	Sa
				1	2	3
4	5	6	7	8	9	10
11	12	13	14	15	16	17
18	19	20	21	22	23	24
25	26	27	28	29	30	31

2. Rumanian govt. falls under Soviet pressure; Communists appointed by King Michael (→ 6).

2. Detroit: Ten Chrysler and Briggs plants closed by strikes (→ 7/5).

2. U.S.: Raymond Massey opens in "Hotel Berlin."

2. Pacific: MacArthur raises U.S. flag on Corregidor in the Philippines (→ 10).

3. Finland declares war on Axis.

4. Germany: U.S. military government confines 30,000 Germans to homes in Neuss (→ 25).

6. Germany: Cologne falls to Gen. Hodges' First Army (→ 8).

8. Germany: U.S. First Army crosses Rhine between Cologne and Coblenz (→ 16).

10. Indochina: Tran Kim proclaims independence under Japanese (→ 24).

10. Japan: 300 B29's rain fire on Tokyo, killing 100,000 (→ 11).

11. Pacific: U.S. Marines land on Mindanao in Philippines (→ 18).

16. Germany: Saar battle won by Patton's forces; Nazis in flight to Rhine (→ 19).

17. Helsinki: Communists win Finnish elections.

18. Japan closes schools, orders all over six to war service (→ 20).

19. U.S.: OPA freezes price of clothing (→ 6/28).

19. Germany: Hitler orders scorched-earth policy (→ 23).

20. Pacific: U.S. carriers bomb Japanese fleet in lair; USS Franklin hit, killing 832 (→ 4/1).

24. France promises Indochina financial autonomy within French Empire (→ 6/9).

27. Argentina declares war on Axis (→ 4/9).

30. Poland: Russian forces take Danzig, invade Austria (→ 4/8).

31. U.S., Britain bar Soviet-supported provisional regime in Warsaw from U.N. parley in San Francisco (→ 4/21).

DEATH

26. David Lloyd George, British Liberal Party leader (*1/17/1863).

Belsen destroys brave Anne Frank

Young Anne Frank in Amsterdam.

March 12. Anne Frank has died in the Nazi concentration camp of Bergen-Belsen. Half-starved and unconscious from fever, she rolled off her bedbunk and fell lifeless to the floor. She was 14 years old.

Anne Frank kept a remarkable diary while she hid with her family in an Amsterdam attic for over a year. Every feeling, from fear over capture to joy over budding sexuality, was beautifully recorded in the book. One of her last entries described her conviction that all people are basically good (→ 4/18).

13 new declarations of war against Germany in 1945

February 2: Ecuador
February 8: Paraguay
February 13: Peru
February 14: Chile
February 16: Venezuela
February 23: Turkey
February 23: Uruguay
February 24: Egypt
February 26: Syria
February 27: Lebanon
March 1: Saudi Arabia
March 2: Finland
March 27: Argentina

Americans cross Rhine at Remagen

American tank units cross the Rhine, having found the Ludendorff Bridge before it could be destroyed.

March 8. American bravado and luck have helped our soldiers charge across the Rhine for the first time during the war. Upon hearing the unexpected news, General Omar Bradley dispatched more troops to Remagen, where the first crossing was made last night.

It happened about 10:30 p.m. Lieutenant Karl Timmerman, a commander in General Hodges' First Army, had crossed the Eifel plateau with his troops, east of the recent, vicious fighting in the Ardennes. Timmerman arrived at Remagen, a small town on the Rhine about halfway between Cologne and Coblenz.

While another unit attempted to form a bridgehead across a smaller river, the Ahr, Timmerman's men were astonished to discover that there was a bridge intact across the Rhine. It was the Ludendorff, a railway bridge, which had apparently been abandoned by the Germans in their retreat. Timmerman asked for and received permission to cross the bridge.

Suddenly, his men ducked for cover. The bridge was rattled by an explosion, set off by Germans who had booby trapped one of the supports. Miraculously, the bridge was not damaged. A second explosion also failed to destroy the span.

Timmerman and his men charged across and found a tunnel on the other side of the Rhine where soldiers and civilians were hiding. They were all taken into custody.

As soon as Timmerman radioed back news of his success, General Bradley ordered all available forces in the area to Remagen to take advantage of the crossing. The Allies must secure more bridgeheads across the Rhine, and Bradley's spirits were obviously raised by Timmerman's thrust across the river. His troops, Bradley said, are in a position to cross the Rhine "anywhere at any time."

West of the Rhine, Allied units have just about completed the mission ordered by General Eisenhower to destroy all German armies. General Patton's tanks seized Speyer, one of the last German strongholds in the area (→ 4/11).

On the 23rd, Patton's tanks crossed the Rhine on bridges built in 48 hours.

Communists take charge in Balkans

March 6. Pressure from the Soviet Union is leading Balkan nations toward Communist-controlled governments. According to a dispatch released yesterday, Marshal Tito has become the undisputed leader of Yugoslavia and, with members of Ivan Subasic's London Cabinet, has formed the Regency Council, which will be the new governing body, replacing the National Committee which has ruled the country for the last two years. Tito is expected to follow Communist teachings. Meanwhile, other Balkan nations, such as Bulgaria and Rumania, appear to favor the Soviet form of government and they are falling into the Communist orbit (→ 11/18).

German teenagers combat occupation

March 25. A band of German youths calling themselves the "Werewolves" claim responsibility for the assassination of the Mayor of Aachen today. The Hitler fanatics seek to disrupt collaboration between Germany and its "invaders." Their acts so far have been limited to lesser measures of sabotage.

The Werewolves concentrate in western territories lost to the Allies. The mayor of Aachen was a natural target. Aachen, which the French call Aix-la-Chapelle, lies within a disputed region on the Belgian border. Karl Oppenhoff, the short-lived officeholder, had just been appointed to his post by Americans.

The Werewolves worked underground; this is the first time details about them have surfaced. Allies will reinforce security measures. Any youths they capture may be tried as adults.

1945

APRIL

Su	Mo	Tu	We	Th	Fr	Sa
1	2	3	4	5	6	7
8	9	10	11	12	13	14
15	16	17	18	19	20	21
22	23	24	25	26	27	28
29	30					

1. Pacific: U.S. troops land in Okinawa, last step before Japan (→ 29).

1. Paris lights Arc de Triomphe and Cathedral of Notre Dame for first time since start of war.

5. Soviet Union renounces neutrality pact with Japan.

6. Edward Benes returns to Czechoslovakia (→ 6/10).

8. Austria: Red army drives three miles into Vienna (→ 13).

9. U.S. resumes relations with Argentina (→ 5/31).

10. N.Y. drama critics choose Tennesse Williams' "Glass Menagerie" best play of year.

10. Italy: British 8th Army tanks launch major offensive (→ 28).

11. Germany: Simpson's troops reach Elbe River at Magdeburg, 63 miles from Berlin (→ 19).

15. U.S.S.R. honors FDR, flying black-bordered flags on government offices.

18. Dachau camp liberated.→

19. U.S. First Army takes Leipzig, clearing Ruhr; 300,000 German prisoners taken (→ 20).

20. Germany: Nuremberg taken on Hitler's 56th birthday (→ 27).

21. Soviets sign pact with Poland's Communist-led Lublin government (→ 22).

22. Washington: Soviet For. Min. Molotov arrives for talks with Sec. of State Stettinus (→ 27).

23. Toronto Maple Leafs take Stanley Cup in hockey.

23. Germany: Red army plunges into heart of Berlin (→ 27).

24. Petain gives in to face treason charges in France (→ 7/23).

25. San Francisco: U.N. Conference on International Organization opens.→

27. San Francisco: Parley bars Lublin Poles; Soviet gets only three votes (→ 6/21).

29. Japanese kamikaze hits U.S. hospital ship Comfort (→ 5/11).

DEATH

22. Kathe Kollwitz, German graphic artist, sculptor (*7/8/1867).

Roosevelt dies on the eve of victory

Franklin D. Roosevelt, 1882-1945.

April 12. President Roosevelt is dead. The unexpected death of the 31st president of the United States in his clapboard cottage in Warm Springs, Georgia, stunned the nation and the world. An attending doctor said the 63-year-old president died of a cerebral hemorrhage.

The president had been at Warm Springs since March 29, resting up from the rigors of trying to bring an end to the war. His death came at a time of high triumph, for the armies and fleets under his command were at the gates of Berlin and the shores of Japan's home islands, and a gathering to frame a United Nations charter to assure world peace is scheduled to begin later this month in San Francisco.

Only hours before his death, he had been posing for a portrait by Elizabeth Shumatoff, commissioned by his longtime friend, Lucy Mercer. In early afternoon, the president murmured, "I have a terrific headache." He died a short time later and his death was announced by the White House at 5:48 p.m. Less than two hours later, Vice President Harry S. Truman was sworn in as President.

While President Roosevelt had appeared to be in declining health in recent months, the rest in Warm Springs seemed to have restored some of his vigor. No members of his family were with him at the end. Mrs. Roosevelt had been attending a Washington meeting of the Thrift Club when told to return to the White House. There, she was told of her husband's death. She sent messages to their sons, all of them in the services, saying: "He did his job to the end as he would want you to do. Bless you all and all our love. Mother."

The White House flag was lowered to half-staff, the first time marking the death of an occupant since Warren G. Harding died in 1923. As the news of the Roosevelt death spread through the city, tearful men and women gathered outside the White House and across the street in the square.

President Roosevelt, a patrician New Yorker who was educated at Groton, Harvard and Columbia, was considered one of the most remarkable men ever to occupy the White House. He was responsible for initiating the New Deal, the activist federal effort to bring the nation out of a deep depression after his election in 1932. He was reelected in a landslide in 1936 and, in a break with tradition, he sought and won an unprecedented third term in 1940, as well as a fourth term just last year.

His impact on the nation and the world was perhaps best expressed in a tribute on the Senate floor by Senator Robert A. Taft, an Ohio Republican and frequent political adversary, who termed him "the greatest figure of our time," one who died "a hero of the war, for he literally worked himself to death in the service of the American people."

Funeral services will be held later this week in the East Room of the White House, with only high officials attending, since the chamber can accommodate only 200 people. The body then will be taken to the late president's hometown of Hyde Park, New York, for burial in a plot near the Roosevelt home.

A solemn procession in the capital.

Harry S. Truman assumes the presidency

April 12. Harry S. Truman became President of the United States tonight, just hours after the death of President Roosevelt.

Truman gets the job of ending war.

Standing erect, staring straight ahead through his large glasses, the onetime farm boy from Missouri was sworn into the presidency at exactly 7:09 p.m. in the Cabinet room at the White House, as his wife and daughter Margaret and a few key Roosevelt aides stood nearby. The oath was administered by Chief Justice Harlan F. Stone.

Truman, who served a few brief months as Vice President, had no inkling of the Roosevelt death when he arrived for a gathering of the so-called Board of Education, an informal group of legislators who met in the Capitol office of Speaker Sam Rayburn. As he arrived, he was told to telephone Steve Early, the Roosevelt Press Secretary, who asked him to come immediately to the White House. Arriving there, he was told by Mrs. Roosevelt: "Harry, the President is dead."

Duce meets ignoble end

Benito Mussolini, 1883-1945.

April 28. A yellowing, disfigured face and a head riddled with bullets capped the corpse atop a pile of 12 male bodies and one female in Milan. The decaying carcass belonged to "the Father of Italian Fascism," Benito Mussolini. After a quick and expedient trial, which included cries of "Let me live and I will give you an empire!" the once seemingly invincible dictator was shot with his mistress and 11 others.

Mussolini's rise to power commenced with the establishment of the Fascist Party in 1919. With the support of rich landowners and army officiers, the Fascist movement began to grow. In 1922, after the Fascists marched on Rome, Italian King Victor Emmanuel III empowered Mussolini, and in 1926, Il Duce imposed a single party dictatorship in the country.

In the mid-1930's, Mussolini set his sights outside Italy, forming alliances with other right-wing regimes, including Franco's Spain and of course, Hitler's Germany. Italy entered the war in 1940 after Germany conquered France and appeared destined to win all Europe.

A series of military flops split the Fascists, and in mid-1943 the king had Mussolini arrested. The Nazis rescued him, but the advance by Allied troops forced Mussolini to flee. Thursday, partisan Italians caught, tried and executed him, and then brought his corpse to Milan, where he was hanged by the heels. Then, his head was propped up by a rifle butt for cameras to document his end (→ 7/14).

Rage subdued during decades of dictatorship has surfaced in Italy. Mussolini, his mistress and two compatriots hang by the heels in Milan after execution.

Hitler suicide in Berlin

Adolf Hitler, 1889-1945. The mind of a madman.

April 30. The maniacal force behind the European war is dead. Adolf Hitler, desperate and bitter, smelling Germany's demise, committed suicide today in Berlin. As Russian troops drove toward the city's center, Hitler, in his command bunker, shot his mistress Eva Braun and himself. Their bodies were set on fire outside the bunker.

In the light of history, Hitler may be seen as a demented yet determined tyrant. At the height of his unparalleled political career, he seemed invincible. He had vanquished nine nations, repulsed Europe's greatest power, devised an economic and social fabric based on the deadly subjugation of millions and hypnotically imposed his will on millions more. Over 65 million Germans glorified this demagogue as the savior of Deutschland.

The man these millions would salute as "Mein Fuhrer" was born in Braunau, Austria. His father worked as a customs official, and it's been reported, violently beat him. Young Adolf worked at painting postcards in Vienna. He embraced an intense anti-Semitism and fear of Marxism.

At the outbreak of the Great War, Hitler was lifted from obscure artist to determined soldier. He recorded in "Mein Kampf" that the war elated him. "I fell on my knees and thanked Heaven from an overflowing heart," he wrote.

After the German defeat, Hitler joined the ultra-nationalistic German Workers Party, later called the National Socialist German Workers or Nazi Party. Using his zealous oratory, he convinced some rich industrialists to back his drive to redeem Germany's humiliation at Versailles. Hitler also formed a Nazi army, the "storm troopers," and tried to oust the government at Munich. The putsch failed and Hitler was jailed. In prison, he wrote "Mein Kampf" and plotted his path to absolute power.

Following his release from jail, the Nazis and their leader grew in popularity and on January 30, 1933, Hitler was appointed Chancellor of Germany by Reich President von Hindenburg. With his new authority, the little man with the little mustache crushed all opposition, instituting a totalitarian regime.

Hitler's paramount and most dangerous ideological principle was that Germany must develop a pure Aryan race. "We must build a master class from elements of a better race," he wrote. This crazed notion, and his demonic drive to dominate Europe, ignited an inferno of horror for millions of Jews and other innocent people who died tragically in his death camps.

Hitler's military victories created in him an overconfidence which eventually derailed Nazi momentum. The Allies have been able to overrun his crumbling defenses. Now, with the end of Nazism in view, Adolf Hitler, once so mighty, is reduced to ashes.

Scenes of horror: Gates of Nazi death camps open

American troops freeing the Buchenwald concentration camp April 12 were greeted by the dead. Or so they seemed; slave laborers, laying on their barrack bunks, could barely raise their heads to see their liberators. Their muscle was eaten away. Maggots settled in the corners of their sunken eyes as they watched the G.I.'s tread silently by them. Superstition filled the soldiers, recalling warnings to step softly over graves. They were walking where some 50,000 innocent people met their deaths.

Buchenwald was founded by the Nazi Party in 1933. At that time, the camp mostly dispensed with "Juden," German Jews. The enemy list grew with the war; the 20,000 prisoners found alive April 12 included Poles, Hungarians, French, Russians, Dutch, Belgians, Yugoslavs, Austrians, Italians, Spaniards in opposition to Franco, and a few other nationalities.

A committee formed by the liberating American Army assessed conditions at Buchenwald for Allied headquarters. They described the prisoners as "the intelligentsia and leadership personnel from all of Europe." Among the inmates were four anti-Vichy members of the French Parliament.

The report went on to state that "Anyone and everyone of outstanding intellectual or moral qualifications or of democratic or anti-Nazi inclinations or their relatives" were systematically murdered at the camp. Both Jews and Christians were treated cruelly, although "Jews were given even worse treatment than the others."

Typically, prisoners were kept for six weeks, during which time their food was restricted; they were expected to lose 40 percent of their weight. During that time, prisoners never received Red Cross packages; SS personnel appropriated them for themselves. Inmates served as laborers and were subject to random beating or torture. Some were "guinea pigs" in testings of the effect of lethal germs, amputations, toxins and suspected antitoxins. Few survived these tests. Some SS personnel kept the flesh of the victims. These bits of skin, burned with tatoos, were prized possessions.

Those who lived through the six-week period were led to gas chambers and suffocated. Their bodies were transported to one of six incinerators. Each furnace could burn three bodies at a time in about 20 minutes. The corpses were fully reduced to ashes, destroying all evidence of the previous human existence—and the heinous crime.

The incinerators ran out of coal for a ten-day period in March. According to the witnesses, bodies were stacked in the camp like firewood. Eventually, 1,800 corpses lay outside the barracks. A fatigue detail of laborers was then rounded up and made to haul the bodies into trucks. They accompanied the trucks out of the camp to a nearby woods. The detail dug a large burial pit, dragged the bodies into it and refilled it with earth. They followed instructions to leave one end of the pit empty. Then SS guards shot every member of the fatigue detail and cast them into the grave.

Today, some former German prison guards are in their hometowns with family and neighbors. They witness the passing of time, sunrise to sunset. Their wives and mothers fondly call them to the dinner table, and they eat with a cherished appetite. The hunger suggests that something moves inside them, something inhales and exhales. Yet somewhere in the recesses they know their acts at Buchenwald rendered them separate and inhuman. They may be dead for the rest of their lives (→ 6/7).

Blank faces of a few Buchenwald survivors confront the prospect of freedom.

Jews were often forced to clear away the bodies of their fellow prisoners.

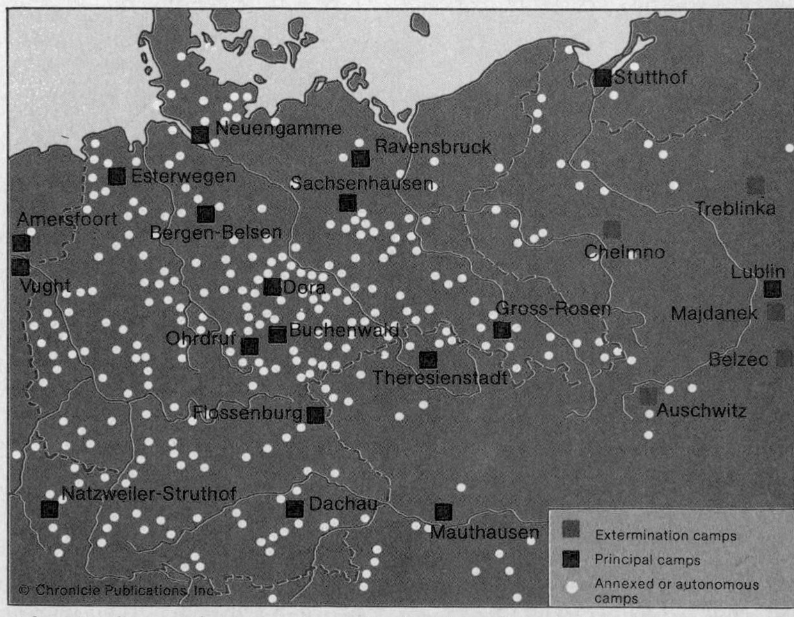

After Dachau and Oranienburg (in Berlin), the number of concentration camps multiplied steadily until the shocking discoveries of the last few months.

Reds thrust into Berlin

April 30. Soviet infantry, backed by relentless artillery and air bombardment, have nearly encircled Berlin. Only a three-mile crack west of the city remains beyond their grasp. One third of the capital is firmly under Russian control.

While a separate force held down Frankfurt, two armies, under Marshal Georgi Zhukov and Marshal Ivan Koneff, occupied four Berlin districts. Today, they claimed four more. Among their strategic captures are the metropolitan gas works and the belt railroad.

Some Nazis continue to resist. They step out of the smoking rubble waving white flags and cradling live grenades. Most of these diehards are SS members, and many of them are teens. The Soviets say most of the city only needs mopping up.

If Berlin continues its useless defense, Russian forces will advance on outlaying towns. Their bombers must use caution, however. Stray U.S. patrols are located northeast of Dresden. The U.S. First Army is stationed nine miles northeast of Leipzig. Koneff's troops are expected to rendezvous with them.

Soviet soldiers in Berlin.

Yanks and Reds join up

April 27. In the heartland of Germany, on the Elbe River, General Courtney H. Hodges of the U.S. First Army and Marshal Ivan Koneff of the First Ukrainian Army shook hands today. Their forces split Germany into two lifeless parts. Having smashed east and west, the Allies will now proceed almost leisurely north and south.

Germany's borders are under Allied control. French troops secured the Swiss frontier and reduced the Black Forest south of Stuttgart to a mopping-up operation. The British Second Army, driving in on the coast, took a radar station outside Bremen. The Polish Armored Division is also near the shore, southeast of the German naval base Emden.

An Allied rendezvous is expected in Austria today. General George Patton's Third Army will link with Ukrainian forces (→ 30).

A common foe brings a Russian major and two Americans together on the Elbe.

Vienna is now in Red army's grasp

April 13. After several days of vicious street fighting, Vienna fell to the Russians. Thousands of German soldiers were taken prisoner, and the Russians moved to block a key rail escape route.

The Germans made their last stand in the old Jewish quarter of Leopoldstadt and two commercial sectors. The Russians claim that the Germans became so desperate in the end that they turned their guns on defenseless civilians. A dispatch from Moscow characterized the German stand as "disorganized mob fighting."

More than 90,000 Germans were taken prisoner as Russian troops overran Koenigsberg, the capital of East Prussia. The Russians stormed the walls of the medieval fortress with ladders and then decimated the defenders with their modern automatic weapons. The Germans say they lost large quantities of ammunition when the city fell (→ 23).

Victorious Soviet troops march into Vienna.

2,000 art objects found in Germany

April 15. Three generals, Patton, Bradley and Eisenhower, convened in a German iron mine today to gawk. Nearly 2,000 art objects are stored there, once booty of the Nazis. The works are priceless.

Marshal Hermann Goering first seized the art of wealthy Jewish patrons. Collectors with names such as Rothschild, Kahn and Weil were stripped of their treasures. When France was invaded, French masterpieces were appropriated.

Hitler returned some works to the Louvre; he thought "lending" art to the French sent a stronger message of domination than confiscation. Yet there were some works too powerfully nationalistic to remain in French hands. Those are the paintings and sculptures the generals have the honor of seeing.

47 United Nations meet to organize

April 25. The United Nations Conference on International Organization has opened in the San Francisco Opera House in a mood of solemn deliberation with no great excitement, no ritual and very little celebration.

President Harry S. Truman set the tone of the meeting. In a short address by telephone from the White House, re-broadcast to the world, he urged the 47 members to "rise above personal interests" and create a world body which would enforce justice and make another war impossible. Stating that all nations should resort to force only in the defense of law, the president observed that "justice remains the greatest power on earth. To that tremendous power alone will we submit" (→ 5/6).

1945

MAY

Su	Mo	Tu	We	Th	Fr	Sa
		1	2	3	4	5
6	7	8	9	10	11	12
13	14	15	16	17	18	19
20	21	22	23	24	25	26
29	28	29	30	31		

1. Berlin: Reich Propaganda Minister Joseph Goebbels commits suicide.

1. Germany: Karl Doenitz proclaims himself new Fuhrer (→ 2).

2. Burma: British go ashore south of Rangoon (→ 6/14).

2. 1,000,000 Axis forces surrender in Italy and Austria (→ 2).

2. Germany: Berlin falls to Red army; 70,000 give up (→ 4).

4. Nazis surrender in Holland, north Germany, Denmark (→ 7).

5. Italy: Poet Ezra Pound, wanted for treason, seized by American forces in Genoa (→ 2/19/49).

6. San Francisco: Big Four phase of U.N. talks ends with agreement on all except Polish and trusteeship questions (→ 21).

8. Washington: Truman warns victory "is but half won" (→ 11).

8. Algeria: Nationalists rise against French rule (→ 3/16/46).

8. Leopold III declines return to Belgium after liberation.

11. Kamikaze pilot hits USS Bunker Hill, 373 killed (→ 20).

12. U.S. cuts off lend-lease to Soviet Union (→ 8/21).

13. London: Churchill says he will not let totalitarian govts. replace German tyranny in liberated Europe (→ 3/5/46).

14. U.S. and Britain tell Tito Trieste must remain under Allied control (→ 6/9).

20. Germany: Goering's $200 mil. private art collection exhibited at hotel in Berchtesgaden.

20. Pacific: U.S. troops envelop Fort Shuri in Okinawa (→ 26).

21. San Francisco: Small nations challenge big powers on veto rights at U.N. talks (→ 6/26).

21. Syria and Lebanon assert independence, breaking off negotiations with France (→ 30).

26. Tokyo devastated by B-29's; royal palaces razed (→ 6/4).

30. Syria: French seize Damascus Parliament as nationalist revolt continues (→ 12/13/45).

31. Buenos Aires: Wholesale arrests made; press silenced under war security (→ 7/21).

Germans surrender unconditionally

May 7. Europe wakes to freedom this morning. Germany capitulated to Allied demands in a ceremony at 2:41 a.m. All battlefields but those in Czechoslovakia lie silent.

The document of surrender was signed inside a little red schoolhouse at Reims. The unassuming building has been serving as headquarters for General Dwight D. Eisenhower. While Eisenhower did not witness the signing, chief of staff Lt. General Walter Bedell Smith was present. The U.S.S.R., France and Great Britain were represented. General Gustav Jodl and General Admiral Hans Friedeburg were the German delegates.

While surrender terms have not officially been released, it is believed all German forces must disarm and war criminals must submit themselves to Allied authorities. Prisoners in Allied camps may be used as a labor force to rebuild the ravaged European cities. Germany will probably be partitioned to accommodate Polish and Russian demands, but only after an extensive peace conference that may be held years from now. Meanwhile, temporary adjustments may occur.

Times Square crowds celebrate victory around a model Statue of Liberty.

Nazi soldiers on the border of Sweden are marching to Oslo to give themselves up. Forces in Norway agree to do the same, although one commander protests "we are unbeaten and in full possession of our strength." Troops in Prague were still fighting at nightfall, but were expected to desist.

The end of war with Germany was greeted with joy in the United States. However, the death of President Roosevelt still weighs heavily on hearts and minds. And no one can forget war in the Pacific rages.

Reaction in Europe was more subdued. The public, huddled in the rubble that was once their homes, are too weary to celebrate. Perhaps the only noisy festivities were held in Dublin, where Trinity College students perched on a roof, planted a Union Jack and flags of the other Allied nations and lustily sang "Rule Britannia."

German Foreign Minister Count Lutz Schwerin von Krosigk broke the news of surrender to the German people with a radio broadcast at 8:09 a.m. He expressed a hope that "the atmosphere of hatred which today surrounds Germany all over the world will give place to a spirit of reconciliation among the nations, without which the world cannot recover." An echoing cry for mercy had been expressed at the surrender at Reims.

The war in Europe lasted five years, eight months and six days. Germany has lost 2.85 million soldiers and half a million civilians. The Allies have suffered equally. It has been the second world war. May it also be the last (→ 23).

A Russian soldier hangs the hammer and sickle atop the gutted Reichstag.

Third Reich dissolves and leaders disperse

May 23. It all ended much less simply and majestically than it began. The Third Reich died today. With it collapsed the aspirations of the German people and the evil intentions of Adolf Hitler.

Grand Marshal Karl Doenitz, leader of the new rump government, and other political and military leaders were rounded up and arrested by Allied troops.

Albert Speer, the Minister of Economics and Production, was arrested at the castle where he had been living. "Yes, this is the end," Speer said, and then he added, "It is a good thing. It was just an opera anyway."

Heinrich Himmler, the evil mind behind the concentration camps, swallowed a suicide pill shortly after his arrest.

The legacy of the Germans under arrest is staggering. Nearly three million German soldiers died following their commands. Their war displaced 40 percent of the German population. And their orders sent countless millions of Jews and others to death camps (→ 6/5).

American tanks from Company B move into the devastated city of Nuremburg.

Churchill resigns and calls for election

Will Churchill win again?

May 23. With the collapse of the wartime coalition government, Prime Minister Winston Churchill resigned to force a new general election in Britain. As a result on July 5, Britain will hold its first general parliamentary election in ten years.

The general expectation is that Churchill, who formed a coalition government in 1940 with the Labor and Liberal Parties, will win reelection with a clear Conservative Party majority in Parliament.

Churchill was forced to call for general elections when the Labor Party rejected his proposal to maintain the coalition until the end of the war with Japan and he rejected Labor's counterproposal to retain the alliance until the end of October (→ 7/26).

1945

JUNE

Su	Mo	Tu	We	Th	Fr	Sa
					1	2
3	4	5	6	7	8	9
10	11	12	13	14	15	16
17	18	19	20	21	22	23
24	25	26	27	28	29	30

4. Japan: B-29's drop fire bombs on Kobe (→ 10).

6. Germany: Russians find body believed to be that of Hitler underneath Reich Chancellory.

9. Eddie Arcaro wins third Kentucky Derby, on Hoop Jr.

9. Indochina: Chinese launch drive on Japanese occupying forces (→ 8/1945).

9. Yugoslavs accept Anglo-U.S. policing of Trieste (→ 8/7).

10. Pacific: U.S. Marines on Okinawa open drive to end campaign (→ 11).

10. Czechs reported resentful over Russian "liberation" moves (→ 29).

11. Pacific: Australian troops invade Borneo (→ 19).

12. France: De Gaulle govt. halts press censorship (→ 10/21).

12. Ike made first American member of exclusive Order of Merit by British king (→ 18).

14. Burma liberated by British.

14. Germany: Joachim von Ribbentrop captured by British in Hamburg (→ 10/12).

18. Washington: Truman decorates Ike with second Oak Leaf Cluster upon arrival in U.S.

18. Chinese troops recapture port of Wenchow (→ 7/24).

19. China: Mao refuses negotiations with Chiang (→ 8/20).

19. Pacific: Marines at Okinawa push Japanese south; many jump off cliffs to avoid capture (→ 21).

21. U.S.: Pan Am announces round-the-world flight in 88 hours at cost of $700.

22. Poles get new Soviet-supported Communist govt. (→ 23).

23. San Francisco: Big Four to admit Poland to U.N. (→ 29).

24. Pacific: Hundreds of U.S. and British planes loose 1,000 tons of bombs on Borneo (→ 28).

28. Pacific: MacArthur reports liberation of all Luzon (→ 7/5).

28. Ford completes war assignment; total manufacture of 8,600 bombers, 278,000 jeeps, 57,000 aircraft engines (→ 8/15).

29. Czechs cede Ruthenia to Soviet (→ 10/18).

Germans forced to view camp cruelties

June 7. German citizens confront reality today, forced to see a film on the horrors of Belsen and Buchenwald. Military government officials ordered the townspeople of Burgsteinfurt, Germany, to attend a local theater. There they watched newsreel footage of the scene Allied troops found upon their liberation of the concentration camps.

Some in the mostly female audience wept openly. Others, even while viewing corpses piled upon each other, expressed doubt that Germans were responsible. However, there are some women who cannot doubt. Last April these healthy, well-fed SS women at Belsen were forced to bury the corpses of prisoners who starved to death.

Simon Lake, who invented sub, dies

June 23. Simon Lake, father of the modern submarine, died today in Bridgeport, Conn. at the age of 78. Lake offered his first submarine, built in 1894, to the United States Navy but took the design abroad when the offer was rebuffed. He worked in Russia for several years, returning to found the Lake Torpedo Boat Company in Bridgeport. The firm built more than 100 submarines during the Great War, 55 of them for the United States. The German U-boats that devastated Allied shipping during the war were based on Lake's designs.

Although most of Lake's submarines were war vessels, one of his major interests was to use the boats for salvage and commerce. He lost much of his fortune in the 1930's in an ill-fated effort to recover $4.8 million in gold from a ship that sank in the Hudson River in 1780.

Subs, 50 years after the first.

Okinawa battle bloody

U.S. guns, planes and artillery took over 100,000 Japanese lives on Okinawa.

June 21. The battle for Okinawa—the bloodiest land battle thus far in the Pacific war—has finally ended with an American victory, 83 days after infantrymen and Marines landed on the large, strategic island only 300 miles south of Japan.

Organized Japanese resistance came to a ritualistic end when Lt. General Mitsuri Ushijima, commander of Japanese forces on Okinawa, came out at dawn from his cave bunker and before his subordinates committed hara-kiri.

Four days earlier, Lt. General Simon Bolivar Buckner Jr., commander of American forces on Okinawa, had been killed by enemy shrapnel while watching one of the final attacks by the 8th Marine Regiment. He was the highest ranking officer to have died in combat.

The bloody battle for Okinawa began on a relatively calm note when the 1st and 6th Marine Divisions and the 7th and 96th Army Divisions landed April 1 on the southwest coast. But then the American forces ran into the Shuri defense line that Ushijima had constructed across a craggy section in the south-central sector of the island. There ensued three weeks of bitter, cave-to-cave fighting before the defense line was breached. The Japanese then slipped away for a final stand on the southern tip of the island. Meanwhile, Navy ships offshore came under desperate attack by kamikaze planes (→ 24).

A kamikaze pilot tries to direct his last dive onto a U.S. carrier off Okinawa.

United Nations formed

Sec. of State Stettinius, head of the U.S. delegation, signs the U.N. declaration.

June 26. Hailing the creation today of a charter to establish a United Nations, President Truman told a cheering throng: "Oh, what a great day this can be in history!"

Approval of the historic charter came as a climax to a 63-day conference of delegates from 50 nations, meeting in San Francisco. The new charter provides the framework for what its signers hope will be a new start on the way to a lasting peace in the world.

President Truman, who will ask the Senate next week to ratify the charter, spoke at the concluding session of the conference, telling the assembled delegates that the world must now use the new "instrument of peace." In failing to use it, he said, "we shall betray all those who have died in order that we might meet here in freedom to create it. If we seek to use it selfishly—for the advantage of any one nation or small group of nations—we shall be equally guilty of that betrayal."

The speech was loudly applauded by the 3,500 persons in the War Memorial Opera House, a gilt-walled structure dedicated to the memory of San Franciscans who died in the Great War. Truman was accompanied to the rostrum by Edward Stettinius, the Secretary of State; Alger Hiss, conference secretary; and presidential military aide Col. Harry Vaughn (→ 7/28).

The Queen Elizabeth hits N.Y., full of eligible soldiers from Europe.

Germany is divided into four zones

June 5. The Allied supreme commanders signed a declaration today in Berlin which divides Germany into four zones and imposes terms of the Reich's surrender. Formalizing the agreement, which required no German representation like that at the signing of the Treaty of Versailles, were Allied Commanders-in-Chief Dwight Eisenhower of the United States, Bernard Montgomery of Britain, Georgi Zhukov of Russia and Jean de Lattre of France. They will comprise the United Nations Control Council.

Each of the four nations will occupy a section of the German state as it existed before the Nazi expansion which began with the annexation of Austria in 1937. The division is as follows: an eastern zone for the Soviet Union; a northwestern sector for Great Britain; a southwestern area for America; and a western zone for France. The United Nations justified the action as "there is no central government in Germany capable of maintaining order."

Other provisions of the Allied declaration include complete dismantling of all armament factories in Germany, the release of prisoners of the Nazi regime, the evacuation of all occupied territories outside of Germany, the arrest of all Nazis suspected of war crimes and stern warnings against the destruction of Reich archives (→ 7/1).

Moscow forms new regime for Poland

June 21. Joseph Stalin has succeeded in establishing a new, Communist-controlled government in Poland. The final arrangements, which were made in Moscow, were delayed by the search for moderate politicians who had gone into hiding in Poland. They were all found and arrested.

The "national unity government" is headed by Osubka-Moravski. The United States and Britain recognized the government after Stanislaus Mikolajczyk was named Vice Premier. Mikolajczyk headed the government-in-exile in London, which the Russians superseded with the Lublin committee (→ 23).

1945

JULY

Su	Mo	Tu	We	Th	Fr	Sa
1	2	3	4	5	6	7
8	9	10	11	12	13	14
15	16	17	18	19	20	21
22	23	24	25	26	27	28
29	30	31				

2. Germany: First U.S. occupying units reach their zone in Berlin (→ 7/12/46).

3. Harry Hopkins resigns as Truman aide for health reasons.

5. Washington: Henry Morgenthau Jr. resigns as Treasury secretary after 11 years in office.

5. Truman orders Navy to take over Goodyear plants in Akron, Ohio, to halt strike (→ 10).

5. Manila: MacArthur reports liberation of Philippines (→ 6).

6. Japan: Superfortresses blast Honshu industries in new fire-bomb attacks (→ 13).

8. Salina, Utah: Army soldier Bertucci opens fire on German prisoners of war, killing eight and wounding 20.

10. U.S.: 19,000 on strike in coal, utility, dairy industries (→ 8/17).

13. Marlene Dietrich returns from 11-month USO tour.

13. U.S. Pacific Fleet begins first heavy bombardment of main islands of Japan (→ 18).

14. Italy declares war on Japan (→ 11/30).

15. Berlin: Truman, Churchill arrive for Big Three talks (→ 26).

16. New Mexico: First atomic bomb tested in Los Alamos desert (→ 8/6).

17. Madrid: Franco promises to restore monarchy (→ 2/9/46).

18. Tokyo: U.S. carrier planes bomb Yokusuka naval base, destroying last of foe's navy (→ 29).

21. Buenos Aires: U.S. Ambassador Braden assailed by angry Argentine crowd (→ 9/26).

23. France: Petain goes on trial in Paris (→ 31).

24. China: U.S. fliers smash 13 Japanese ships and 45 planes at Shanghai (→ 8/25).

28. U.S. Senate ratifies U.N. charter 89 to 2 (→ 12/19).

29. Japan turns down Allied surrender ultimatum (→ 8/3).

31. Pierre Laval surrenders to Americans in Austria (→ 8/14).

DEATH

20. Paul Valery, French poet (*10/20/1871).

Big Three at Potsdam

At Potsdam, Stalin (right) found himself faced with two new conferees, Harry Truman (center) and British Labor leader Clement Attlee, who was swept into power on a wave of postwar discontent, defeating Winston Churchill.

July 26. The Conference at Potsdam has failed miserably to clear the air or reduce the tensions between Russia and the Western Allies. If anything, the meeting has only highlighted differences which were ignored when the countries were fighting a common enemy.

Seemingly irreconcilable differences at the conference table divided East from West and disrupted the conference as soon as it began. President Roosevelt was not present to cajole Stalin, and Churchill was forced to pack his bags in the middle of the meeting. He returned home expecting to be re-elected but was defeated by Labor's Clement Attlee, who returned to Potsdam in his place.

Stalin refused to budge on Poland and even claimed he could not "prevent the Poles from taking over the administration of the area up to the western Neisse River." Stalin also rejected calls for free elections in Bulgaria, Rumania and Hungary, and characterized Churchill's accusations of Soviet repression in the countries as "fairy tales."

The conferees, who had trouble agreeing on minor issues, decided to act in concert to govern the new, smaller Germany through a control council. Stalin also demanded a greater share of German industry.

The leaders sent an ultimatum to Japan, demanding its immediate surrender. Otherwise, Japan "would lay herself open to complete and utter destruction." The United States has already begun to attack the home islands; Britain and Russia are to join in later (→ 1/8/46).

July 28. Nature humbled two of the modern era's technical wonders today as a B-25 bomber, lost in the fog, ripped into the Empire State Building, killing 13 people.

Wartime partners divide up Reich

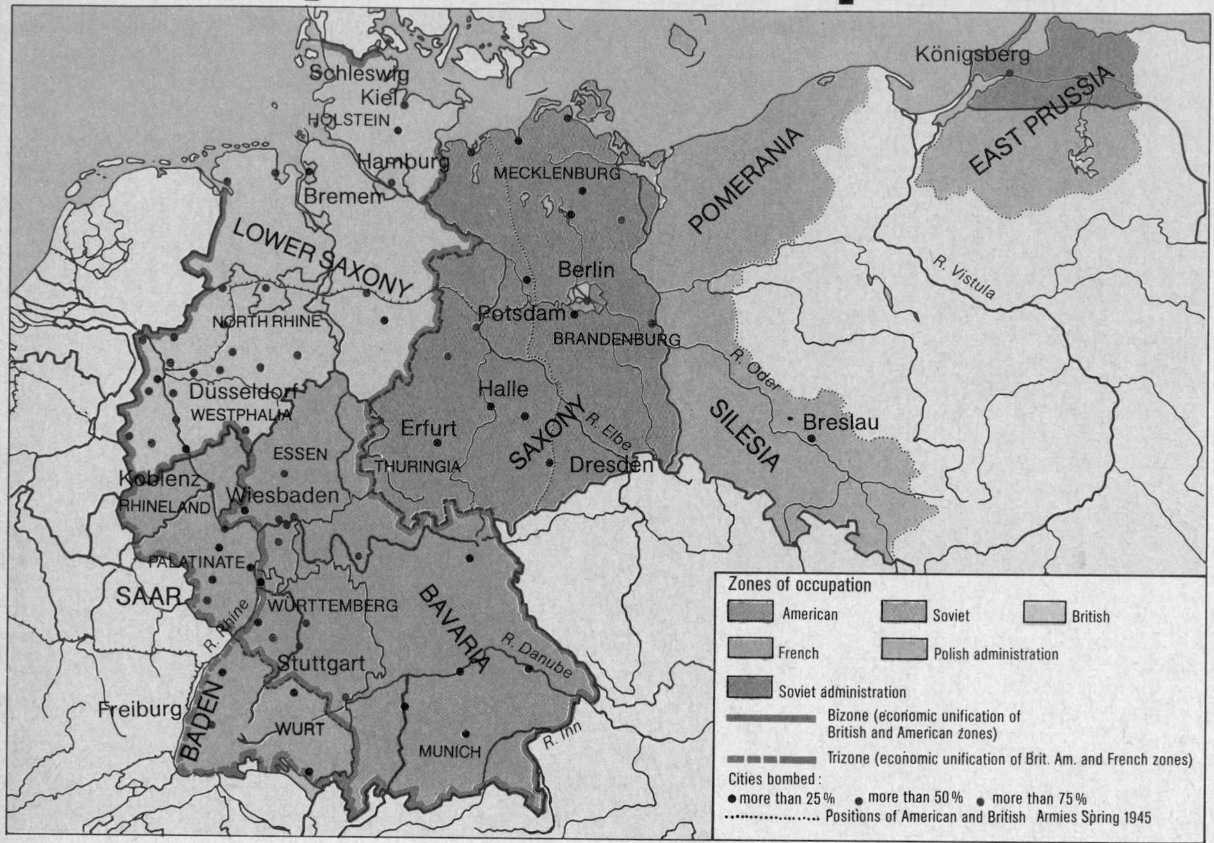

The Reich rests in Allied hands, east to Russia, north to Britain, south to the U.S. and the west to France.

July 1. The United States, Russia, Britain and France have moved into their occupation zones in Germany. And the first cracks have already begun to show in the joint administration of the former Reich.

The flashpoint is Berlin, which is jointly controlled, although it is in the middle of the Russian zone. British and American troops were almost required to use force against the Russians when they arrived to take their positions in the city.

The American and Russian zones are the largest. The Russians control the eastern portion of the country, from Mecklenburg south to Saxony. The Americans are installed in Bavaria, Hesse and northern Wurttemberg. The British control the northwestern sector, from Schleswig-Holstein south to Westphalia. The French sector, the smallest, comprises the southern Rhineland, the Palatinate and southern Baden.

On the 1st of the month, British and U.S. troops withdrew from the southern Russian sector. Hundreds of thousands of German refugees, fearful of the Russians, followed them to the west (→ 2).

Americans ride into Berlin to take up positions carved out by the Allies.

President Truman addresses the American Army in Berlin.

1945

AUGUST

Su	Mo	Tu	We	Th	Fr	Sa
			1	2	3	4
5	6	7	8	9	10	11
12	13	14	15	16	17	18
19	20	21	22	23	24	25
26	27	28	29	30	31	

3. American mines seal off Japan closing all main harbors (→ 6).

6. Japan: Atomic bomb ravages Hiroshima; U.S. War Dept. reveals three hidden cities were created to develop bomb (→ 9).

7. Belgrade: Tito bars return of King Peter II (→ 11/29).

8. U.S.S.R. declares war on Japan, attacks Manchuria (→ 13).

9. Japan: U.S. drops atomic bomb on Nagasaki, equal to 20,000 tons of TNT.→

9. Truman warns Japan: "Quit or be destroyed" (→ 10).

9. Soviets invade Korea (→ 9/8).

10. Japan offers surrender (→ 11).

11. MacArthur named to accept Japan's capitulation (→ 13).

13. Manchuria: Red army cuts Japanese rail line (→ 3/11/46).

13. 400 Superfortresses steadily resume assault on Japan (→ 15).

15. U.S.: Rationing of gas, fuel oil and oil stoves ends (→ 18).

16. Moscow: Russia, Poland sign pact fixing border (→ 4/24/46).

17. N.Y.: 100,000 laid off from war jobs as contracts end (→ 9/14).

17. Washington: Hap Arnold resigns, says another war would mean destruction of mankind.

18. Washington: 35 mph speed limit ended (→ 9/16).

19. Manchuria: Gen. Wainwright, Corregidor hero, found safe on Japanese land (→ 9/10).

20. North China: Communists clash with govt. troops (→ 28).

21. Truman orders abrupt end to lend-lease operations (→ 11/27).

21. Japanese govt. appeals to kamikazes to give in (→ 29).

22. Tokyo puts A-bomb death toll at 190,000 (→ 9/4).

25. China: Chiang forces enter Nanking and Shanghai (→ 9/16).

28. Chungking: Mao arrives for talks with Chiang (→ 10/11).

29. Pacific: Japanese troops surrender to Lord Mountbatten at Singapore (→ 30).

30. Japan: MacArthur opens headquarters in Yokohama (→ 9/2).

Atomic bombs destroy Hiroshima and Nagasaki

August. The atomic bomb, a new weapon of unprecedented destructive power, has finally ended the war. Two atomic bombs, dropped only three days apart, have destroyed the cities of Hiroshima and Nagasaki. A Japanese statement puts the toll at 60,000 dead in Hiroshima, 10,000 in Nagasaki, with 120,000 wounded, adding that "many persons are dying daily from burns sustained during the raids."

While the United States government is keeping most details secret for security reasons, it has disclosed that the atomic bomb achieves its awesome power by harnessing atomic fission, the splitting of atoms. Uranium, a rare, heavy element which is radioactive, is essential to the production of the bombs.

Work on development of the new weapon began in 1939, and some $2 billion has been spent on the project, under top-secret conditions. The War Department has disclosed that the first atomic bomb was tested successfully in New Mexico July 16.

The first weapon to be used in war was dropped on Hiroshima at 9:15 a.m. Monday, August 6, by a Superfortress named the Enola Gay (the pilot's mother's name), piloted by Col. Paul W. Tibbets Jr. The Hiroshima weapon is said to have more power than 20,000 tons of TNT, 1,000 times greater than the most powerful conventional bomb. William Parsons, one of the weapon's designers, who flew on the mission, said a bright, blinding flash was seen when the bomb was dropped and that a minute later "a black cloud of boiling dust and churning debris was 1,000 feet off the ground and above it white smoke climbed like a mushroom to 20,000 feet."

Reconnaissance flights show that the bomb wiped out 4.1 square miles of Hiroshima, 60 percent of the city of 343,000.

A second bomb was dropped on Nagasaki on August 9, after President Truman warned the Japanese that the first use of the weapon was "only a warning of things to come" and that the United States would drop more atomic bombs "until we completely destroy Japan's ability to make war." The Nagasaki bomb destroyed 30 percent of the city's industrial area, including the Mitsubishi steel and iron works, the War Department says. The Japanese offer to surrender came soon afterward.

The predominant reaction to use of the atomic bomb is jubilation the war has been brought to an end, but there is dissent. The Japanese have described the weapon as "inhuman" and the Vatican issued a statement saying it deplored use of atomic bombs. Military experts agree the atomic bomb will change the nature of war in ways that are still to be determined, but Army leaders already are saying that it will not alter the need to maintain conventional forces (→ 22).

A mushroom cloud looms over Nagasaki, spreading fear far beyond Japan.

Pilot Paul Tibbets (center) poses in the Marianas with the ground crew of the Enola Gay, not long before leaving on his fateful bombing raid over Hiroshima.

An old man, a survivor for now, plods through the wasteland of Nagasaki.

Japan surrenders; war is ended all over the world

Aug 15. The United States gave peace a tumultuous welcome today. Long-awaited V-J Day, Victory over Japan, has come. No more war.

In New York, people spontaneously danced in the streets. In San Diego, drunken sailors broke a few shop windows. On highways in the Midwest, staid and somber farmers honked their car horns as if they were teenage delinquents. Outside Naples, Italy, the Andrews Sisters had just sung "Don't Sit Under the Apple Tree" to soldiers packed in a USO hall. Maxine read the news from a slip of paper someone handed her. An instant of silence; then hats and shoes volleyed into the air.

When the boys come home, they may find the girls changed. They have worked alongside "Rosie the Riveter" at factories and plants, developing a new-found self-reliance. But the letters flying overseas have said, "Come home. Let's make the kind of home our parents had."

In Japan today, the Emperor addressed his nation over the radio. Citizens were never allowed to hear his voice before. He did not use the word surrender, but they knew the cease-fire was on Allied terms. They knew life was irrevocably changed.

The atomic bombs dropped on Hiroshima and Nagasaki and the Soviet Union's invasion of Manchuria last week forced Japan to surrender. It agrees to modified terms of the Potsdam Conference. Allied forces will occupy the nation, enforcing demilitarization.

Europe has less to celebrate today than the United States. Warsaw, Berlin, Paris, London: All have crumbled under a six-year assault. Starvation haunts Europe, Asia and Africa. Let us never forget the 50 million who died (→ 21).

Celebrating the victory in Times Square in New York.

Ho Chi Minh is master of Vietnam

Ho Chi Minh, the leader of the anti-Japanese, Communist guerrillas of Vietnam, has organized a Liberation Committee of the Vietnamese People, of which he is assured the presidency. Ho's anti-colonial guerrilla forces have taken possession of the modern armaments left by the Japanese occupation army, and they are organizing politically in Hanoi in the North as well as Saigon in the South. Ho has also forced Emperor Bao Dai, installed by the Japanese, to abdicate and he has proclaimed the Democratic Republic of Vietnam (→ 9/8).

Ho Chi Minh.

The secret is out: Story of the bomb

Aug 31. Three "hidden cities" with a total population of 100,000 were built to produce the atomic bomb, according to the United States War Department. Secrecy was so great that workers were never even told what they were making in the vast factories covering many square miles. The exact nature of the final product was not revealed either, except that tiny amounts of it were extracted from huge quantities of uranium ore.

The $2 billion project was directed by Major General Leslie L. Groves. The scientists who designed the bomb, working out practical methods for harnessing the power of atomic fission, were stationed in Los Alamos, a city built from scratch on a mesa 30 miles north of Sante Fe, New Mexico. The Los Alamos effort was led by Robert Oppenheimer, a physicist from the University of California. Oak Ridge, Tennessee, grew to a population of 75,000 to house the "Manhattan Engineer District," which operated major production facilities. Other atomic plants were built in Hanford, Washington. Some of these facilities may be used for peaceful uses of atomic energy.

Petain, once a hero, condemned to die

Aug 14. France's Marshal Petain has been found guilty of intelligence with the enemy and sentenced to death. Because of his age (the former Vichy leader is 89), the jury expressed the hope that the death sentence will be commuted.

From the first sentences of the long judgment, it became clear to all except Petain that the verdict would be "guilty." The marshal, paler than usual, leaned back in an attitude familiar during the 20-day trial, while one hand nervously stroked his mustache.

The judgment ordered the confiscation of all Petain's possessions and a proclamation of his "national unworthiness." He was further found guilty of having led astray many good citizens who had faith in him because of his heroic past. Petain is revered by many as the "savior of Verdun."

The defense had warned against a verdict that, it said, would divide the nation when unity was necessary. Summing up, it pleaded to a hushed court that if Petain were sentenced to death, "Memories of his pale face will haunt you while the people of France will beat their breasts" (→ 10/24).

Father of ballistic missile is deceased

Aug 10. Robert H. Goddard, the engineer who developed the basic inventions that made rockets usable as weapons and for space exploration, died today at his home in Baltimore at the age of 63. Goddard began working on rockets during the Great War, when he was on the faculty of Clark University, and persisted for decades although he was ignored by the government and ridiculed by the press. Goddard's inventions were adopted by the German scientists who built the V-2 rockets used in recent years in the war in Europe.

Victory kisses!

1945

SEPTEMBER

Su	Mo	Tu	We	Th	Fr	Sa
						1
2	3	4	5	6	7	8
9	10	11	12	13	14	15
16	17	18	19	20	21	22
23	24	25	26	27	28	29
30						

4. Reports indicate that A-bomb fallout in Hiroshima is still killing at least 100 a day (→ 10/3).

5. H. Corwin Hinshaw and William H. Feldman of Mayo Clinic report first successful use of streptomycin in treating tuberculosis in humans.

6. Washington: Truman gives Congress program for economic reconversion (→ 10/30).

8. Vietnam: Ho Chi Minh restores universal suffrage (→ 12).

10. Washington: Gen. Wainwright receives Congressional Medal of Honor from Truman.

10. Norway: Vidkun Quisling sentenced to death for collaboration with Nazis (→ 10/24).

12. French troops land in Indochina (→ 22).

13. Iran demands withdrawal of Allied troops (→ 11/18).

14. Detroit: Ford halts all production and lays off 50,000 workers, blaming "irresponsible labor groups" for strikes (→ 16).

16. U.S.: Ford, GM and Chrysler reject demand for 30% wage rise (→ 10/2).

16. Japanese formally surrender Hong Kong to British navy.

18. Washington: War Secretary Stimson resigns.

21. Washington: Truman approves recommendation by Stimson to designate war as "World War II."

22. Indochina: French forces occupy official buildings in Saigon (→ 11/11).

23. London: British decide to refer issue of Palestine to United Nations (→ 10/24).

23. Egyptian Cabinet demands British withdrawal, cession of Sudan (→ 2/21/46).

24. London: U.S. and Britain sign oil pact.

26. Buenos Aires: Argentina revives state of siege; all editors jailed (→ 10/17).

26. Camus' play "Caligula" has world premiere in Paris.

28. Truman orders federal control of national resources beyond continental shelf.

Japan signs unconditional surrender

Aboard the USS Missouri, MacArthur speaks of a better world.

Sept 2. The war in the Pacific officially ended this morning in a brief ceremony on the American battleship Missouri. Japan surrendered unconditionally.

It was a brief ceremony, lasting only 20 minutes. Clouds covered Tokyo Bay as Japan and the Allies signed the documents. The sun burst through the clouds as the ceremony ended.

General Douglas MacArthur, who accepted the Japanese surrender, spoke optimistically of the future. "It is my earnest hope and indeed the hope of all mankind," MacArthur said, "that from this solemn occasion a better world shall emerge out of the blood and carnage of the past."

A statement from Emperor Hirohito recognized MacArthur as Supreme Commander of the Allied forces that will occupy Japan. The American general spoke of the "grim days of Bataan and Corregidor, when an entire world lived in fear," but he also urged both sides to put the war behind them.

"It is for us, both victors and vanquished," MacArthur said, "to rise to that higher dignity which alone benefits the sacred purposes we are about to serve."

MacArthur will assume control of a country that views defeat as the highest form of dishonor. Many of Japan's leaders opposed surrender, despite the devastation of Hiroshima and Nagasaki (→ 24).

The Japanese delegation prepares to surrender.

Korea partitioned by two great powers

Sept 8. American troops have just arrived in South Korea. They mean to sit on one end of a giant, precarious seesaw; Soviet troops in North Korea are perched on the other end. The fulcrum is the 38th parallel.

The Soviets came to North Korea in August, establishing an Executive Committee of the Korean People and a revolutionary congress. The Americans will lend a balance of power. The Koreans may be used to occupation by now; Japan was their last uninvited guest. Both Americans and Russians express their intention eventually to return power to the Koreans (→ 10/1/46). ▷

Tokyo Rose arrested; broadcast to G.I.'s

Sept 8. For homesick G.I.'s in the South Pacific, cut off from everything but jungle and malaria, Tokyo Rose on the radio was an institution. They tuned in to her soft and sexy patter about home, but her appeals that they desert had little effect on morale. Now, the Los Angeles-born "Rose," alias Iva Togori, 29, has been arrested in Yokohama and will be brought here to stand trial for treason. She visited Japan in 1941 "to see a sick aunt," was caught there by Pearl Harbor and recruited by Tokyo radio for propaganda purposes (→ 10/6/49).

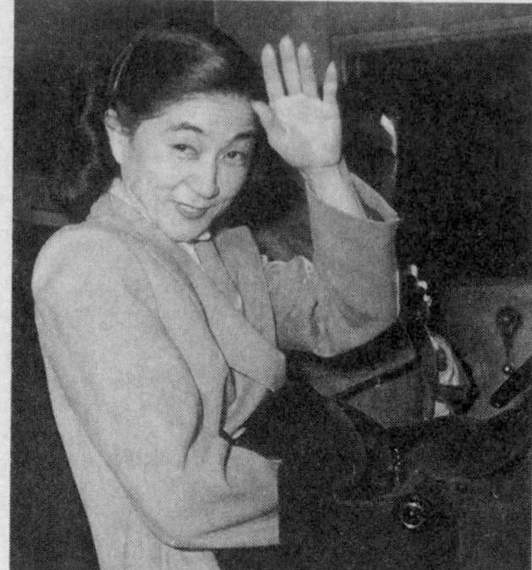

The smiling face behind the voice.

British promise India independence

Sept 21. British Prime Minister Clement Attlee pledged that steps would be taken to grant India self-government following local elections in that country this winter.

In a speech broadcast to the Indian people, Attlee said that following the election of provincial and central legislators, "positive steps" would be taken to set up a constituent assembly of Indian-elected representatives charged with drafting a constitution for self-rule. The proposal did not deal with the demands of Indian leaders for the release of political prisoners and the restoration of civil liberties. A committee of the All-India Congress has demanded that India, Burma, Malaya, Indochina and the Indonesian islands be freed from "imperialist domination."

Japanese accused of torture, massacre

Sept 5. Reports that the Japanese have brutally killed thousands of American prisoners of war have begun to flood out of the Pacific.

In Thailand, 3,500 prisoners were starved, beaten and shot to death on a 140-mile march to a prison camp. In the Philippines, 150 Americans were herded into a bunker, doused with gasoline and set afire. Torture, such as bamboo shoots thrust under the fingernails, was standard practice at the Tokyo interrogation center, and scores of Allied prisoners in Japanese hospitals are reported to have died from injections of acid and bile. Large quantities of Red Cross food and medical supplies were routinely displayed near soldiers who were dying of starvation and disease in Japanese prison camps.

G.I.'s pause to frolic with Dutch children oblivious to the trials of the last five years. Europe's collective memory, though, will be burdened by the Nazi occupation in a way America, buffered by ocean, cannot know.

Young Ford takes over; 50,000 laid off

Sept 21. The Ford Motor Company has announced that founder Henry Ford has relinquished the presidency of the company to his grandson, Henry Ford Jr., who assumes command at a crucial time. Just a week ago, Ford halted virtually all production across the country and laid off 50,000 workers, claiming "crippling and unauthorized strikes" against auto supply companies.

Nine plants supplying the auto industry have been shut down because of wage disputes centering on a demand by the United Auto Workers for a 30 percent nationwide pay raise for those suppliers. Walter Reuther, Chairman of Detroit's U.A.W., warns that if the demands are not met by winter, the strikes will spread to include the parent company itself.

The unemployment scene in Detroit is serious. Besides a total of 77,000 out of work because of strikes, an estimated 210,000 are jobless due to the cancellation of war contracts following V-J Day.

A Detroit striker, bloodied in rioting.

General Tojo shoots self; saved by doctors

Sept 24. General Hideki Tojo, Premier of Japan at the time of the attack on Pearl Harhor, arrested as a war criminal along with other members of the imperial General Staff, has tried to commit suicide by shooting himself. He has been kept alive by American doctors.

As U.S. troops began occupying Japan, General MacArthur, the Supreme Allied Commander, ordered the arrest of the first 40 persons who will be brought to trial as war criminals. The entire Tojo Cabinet at the time of Pearl Harbor was on the list, along with Lt. General Masaharu Homma, who was responsible for the Bataan "death march."

Meanwhile, General Tomoyuki Yamashita, the so-called Tiger of Malaya, surrendered the remnants of his army in the Philippines. In an interview, Emperor Hirohito said he was opposed to war as an instrument of national policy and advocated the creation of a constitutional monarchy in Japan (→ 1/1/46).

Fully decorated Hideki Tojo.

Hungarian composer Bartok dies in exile

Sept 26. Bela Bartok, a composer who could hear a symphony in a folk song, has died of leukemia. He was 64 years old. Hungarian-born Bartok spent his last five years in New York City, hired by Columbia University to transcribe a trove of Yugoslavian folk tunes.

However, Bartok will be remembered for his compositions. His "Piano Concertos 1 and 2" (1927 and 1931) and "Violin Concerto 2" (1938) are particularly memorable, infusing modern patterns with traditional rhythm and style. During his years in America, Bartok finished his "Concerto for Orchestra" (1943), a daring work of irregular chords and dissonance. Few understand it or appreciate it.

1945

OCTOBER

Su	Mo	Tu	We	Th	Fr	Sa
	1	2	3	4	5	6
7	8	9	10	11	12	13
14	15	16	17	18	19	20
21	22	23	24	25	26	27
28	29	30	31			

1. U.S., Britain, France allow occupying troops to fraternize with Germans.

2. U.S.: Coal shipments restricted in East as strikes spread (→ 4).

3. Truman suggests A-bomb ban with U.S. as monitor (→ 11/6).

4. Washington: Truman orders government seizure of 26 oil-producing companies (→ 5).

5. U.S.: Transcontinental phone service disrupted for six hours as Bell workers demonstrate nationwide strength (→ 17).

5. Vatican: Pius XII appoints Joszef Mindszenty primate of Hungary.

7. Britain recognizes Karl Renner's provisional Austrian govt (→ 12/20).

10. Chicago: Detroit Tigers defeat Chicago Cubs in final game to win World Series.

11. China: Chiang-Mao negotiations break down (→ 11/27).

12. Rome: German Gen. Anton Dostler, first tried before American commission, sentenced to death for shooting OSS men (→ 11/20).

14. California: Chuck Yeager breaks sound barrier in X-1 jet plane Glamorous Glennis.

15. Britain extends war powers to fight economic crisis following end of lend-lease (→ 11/3).

17. Washington: John L. Lewis ends coal strike (→ 11/21).

18. Prague: Pres. Benes begins nationalization of Czech industry (→ 5/26/46).

21. French elections bring left into majority (→ 11/13).

21. Venezuelan rebels gain control in Caracas.

24. Cairo: Arabs threaten oil embargo if U.S. aids Zionism (→ 11/2).

27. N.Y.: Truman bars recognition of "imposed" regimes (→ 3/5/46).

28. Indonesian Nationalists fire on British in Java (→ 11/13).

29. Brazil: Getulio Vargas resigns presidency.

30. Shoe rationing ended in U.S. (→ 11/23).

Shirtless Ones place Juan Peron in power

Peron, labor's choice in Argentina.

Oct 17. As thousands of workers demonstrated through the streets of Buenos Aires, Juan Peron regained power as the "strong man" of Argentine only eight days after he had been ousted from the government by the army. The unexpected turn of events in the Argentine political crisis came about when the "Shirtless Ones"—members of the unions that Peron had created while Secretary of Labor and Social Welfare—took over downtown Buenos Aires, demanding the release of Peron and his return to power.

At the insistence of the military, Peron had been ousted as Vice President and taken prisoner. His ouster precipitated a political crisis with the Cabinet forced to resign and the military divided over the formation of a new government. Immediately upon his release, Peron got friends and supporters named to the Cabinet and positioned himself to run for president. Peron announced he was resigning from the army and would dedicate himself to creating an indestructible union of the people, the army and the police (→ 3/28/46).

First Negro player hired for Majors

Oct 23. A Negro has been signed for the first time by a team in organized baseball. Jack Roosevelt Robinson, a Georgia-born player from the Kansas City Monarchs of the Negro League, will join the Montreal club, a Brooklyn Dodger affiliate of the International League.

A spokesman said the signing was not to be interpreted merely as a gesture toward solving racial problems. He said that Robinson, son of a sharecropper and grandson of a slave, was a four-sport star at the University of Los Angeles and made All-American as a halfback.

The signing was achieved by Branch Rickey, President and part-owner of the Dodgers, who hopes to see the 26-year-old shortstop playing soon at Ebbetts Field in Brooklyn (→ 10/9/47).

Eisenhower moves Patton second time

Oct 2. General Dwight D. Eisenhower has again removed General George S. Patton from a position of prominence to a less influential post. Patton is immediately relieved of command of the Third Army and sent to the 15th. The 15th Army has no policy-making powers; its sole purpose is to compile an academic history of World War II.

Patton's downfall is traced to comments he made a week ago. In front of reporters, he compared Nazi and non-Nazi interaction to Democratic-Republican squabbles. His first demotion followed an incident when he slapped a soldier in a hospital for what he thought was poor conduct. In fact, the man suffered from battle fatigue (→ 12/21).

Arab League begun

Oct 20. As the Middle East turns to its own internal conflicts in the wake of the war, Arab states are seeking unity in the struggle for the Holy Land. Wartime Pan-Arabism culminated today in the formation of the Arab League by Egypt, Syria, Iraq and Lebanon. Its founders warned that a Jewish state in Palestine would mean war (→ 24).

Collaborators Laval, Quisling executed

Oct 24. The two most prominent Nazi collaborators of the war—Pierre Laval of France and Vidkun Abraham Quisling of Norway—were executed for aiding German occupation of their countries.

Laval, who served as Premier of the Vichy government during the German occupation of France, was shot by a firing squad as he cried out with his last breath: "Vive la France." Beforehand, he had tried to commit suicide by taking a vial of poison that he had concealed on his person for more than a year.

Quisling, who served as head of the State Council of Norway during the five years of German occupation, had been convicted of high treason by a Norwegian court. Quisling, 58 years old, was found guilty of aiding the German invasion of Norway, of deserting from the Norwegian army, of causing the death of thousands of Norwegians, including 1,000 Jews who were deported to Germany, and of accepting money from the Nazis.

Oct 27. Pan Am opens service N.Y.-London, as a sleek, efficient new DC-4 bypasses its slower, predecessor, the 314, anchored at Port Washington.

1945

NOVEMBER

Su	Mo	Tu	We	Th	Fr	Sa
				1	2	3
4	5	6	7	8	9	10
11	12	13	14	15	16	17
18	19	20	21	22	23	24
25	26	27	28	29	30	

2. U.S.: First refrigerator plane crosses country with full load.

2. Cairo: Egyptians riot; 10 killed, 350 wounded (→ 4).

3. Britain nationalizes civil aviation (→ 2/14/46).

3. Hungary: Zoltan Tildy forms coalition government, as anti-Communist Smallholders win majority (→ 1/30/46).

4. Palestine: Tight curfew imposed by British (→ 25).

6. Moscow: Molotov insists A-bomb cannot be secret (→ 11).

7. British Meteor jet plane hits a record 606 mph.

11. British Premier Attlee asks U.S. to internationalize atom secrets under U.N. (→ 12/26).

11. Indochina: To prove nationalist sincerity, Ho's Communist Party votes its own dissolution (→ 1/6/46).

13. Indonesia: Sukarno becomes president (→ 6/29/46).

16. U.S.: 88 German scientists holding Nazi secrets arrive in U.S. aboard the Argentina.

18. Communist Fatherland Front wins elections in Bulgaria (→ 1/8/46).

18. Iran: Soviet troops aid Communist rebellion in Azerbaijan (→ 12/15).

19. Washington: Truman requests natl. health insurance.

20. Truman names Ike chief of Army staff, Chester Nimitz chief of naval operations.

21. Nationwide strike shuts G.M. plants; 180,000 out (→ 12/3).

23. Meat and butter rationing ends in U.S. (→ 12/20).

25. Palestine: Two coast guard stations blown up near Tel Aviv; Zionists suspected (→ 12/27).

27. U.S.: CARE incorporated to provide aid to Europe (→ 12/6).

29. Belgrade: Assembly proclaims Yugoslav republic, ousts King Peter (→ 12/22).

30. Christian Democrats under Gaspari win in Italy (→ 12/20).

DEATH

21. Ellen Glasgow, American novelist (*4/22/1874).

Nuremberg war crimes trial begins

Nov 20. An historic trial of 21 top Nazis accused of war crimes has opened in the Palace of Justice in Nuremberg, Germany, with representatives of four nations—United States, Great Britain, Russia and France—sitting in judgment.

Shorn of his medals and excess poundage, Hermann Goering sits in the first seat of the defendants' box. His fellow defendants include men whose names once struck terror in the hearts of so many during World War II: Rudolph Hess, Joachim von Ribbentrop, Alfred Rosenberg, Albert Speer, Julius Streicher, Hans Fritzsche and others.

The United States representatives on the International Military Tribunal are former Attorney General Francis Biddle and Judge John J. Parker of the Fourth Circuit Court of Appeals. The chief American prosecutor is Supreme Court Associate Justice Robert H. Jackson.

Front row near: Goering, Hess, Ribbentrop and Kaltenbrunner at Nuremburg.

The entire first day's session was devoted to the reading of charges to which the defendants are to plead tomorrow. The bills of particulars reviewed the bloody annals of the recent war, reviving memories of German atrocities (→ 12/4).

De Gaulle elected French President

Nov 13. Some 555 deputies have unanimously declared Charles de Gaulle President of the French provisional government a year and a half after he marched under the Arc de Triomphe and liberated Paris with his troops. The election comes four years after de Gaulle fled a defeated country and declared from England that he was head of Free France. General Petain, whose Vichy government condemned de Gaulle to death in 1940, received a death sentence last summer, which has since been commuted to life imprisonment (→ 1/20/46).

De Gaulle, hero of liberated France.

Marshall is named to mediate in China

Nov 27. President Truman has announced that he has named General George C. Marshall as his special envoy to China in an attempt to mediate the expanding civil war in Northern China between Nationalist and Communist forces.

Marshall, who only recently retired as Army chief of staff, immediately accepted the appointment, which will carry the rank of Ambassador, and said he would leave shortly for China. The president selected Marshall for the special mission shortly after Patrick J. Hurley surprised the White House by announcing that he was resigning as the U.S. Ambassador to China, a post he was named to in 1944 with the assignment of preventing the collapse of the Nationalist government of Chiang Kai-shek.

Hurley accompanied his resignation with a sharp statement accusing "professional diplomats" of undercutting U.S. policy in China. The statement said career Foreign Service officers had "openly advised" the Communists "to decline unification of the Chinese Communist army with the Nationalist army unless the Communists were given control" (→ 1/10/46)

Bob Benchley dies

Nov 21. Humorist Robert Benchley died this morning of a cerebral hemorrhage. He was 56. Benchley was witty in all media: writing for the Harvard Lampoon as a student and later editing Vanity Fair; reviewing theater for The New Yorker; penning sidesplitting radio scripts, and lately acting in films. He appears in the soon-to-be released "Road to Utopia" with Bob Hope and Bing Crosby. Benchley wrote a skit called "How to Sleep" which won an Oscar in 1935.

Roots of Abraham

Nov 3. A sickle as sharp as it was 8,000 years ago is one of many relics found at a site that may be the birthplace of civilization. An English-Iraqi excavation team has uncovered signs of domestication and farming 400 miles north of Ur. The Bible called Ur the birthplace of Abraham, father of the Jews.

The flint sickle, made to harvest grain, was found beside countless pottery fragments. By the style of the pottery and strata of earth it was buried in, excavators date the community between 5,000 and 6,000 B.C. That is 2,000 years earlier than any previous findings.

1945

DECEMBER

Su	Mo	Tu	We	Th	Fr	Sa
						1
2	3	4	5	6	7	8
9	10	11	12	13	14	15
16	17	18	19	20	21	22
23	24	25	26	27	28	29
30	31					

2. Philadelphia: Army over Navy 32-13 in football.

3. Washington: Truman asks law to curb strikes (→ 31).

4. Buenos Aires: Seven Nazi agents elude deportation by writs, illness (→ 7/16/46).

6. U.S. to write off $25 bil. of British lend-lease (→ 2/6/46).

11. B-29 Superfortress shatters all records, crossing U.S. in five hours, 27 minutes.

13. France, Britain agree to quit Syria and Lebanon (→ 5/7/46).

15. N.Y.: Baritone Robert Merrill debuts at Met.

15. Moscow announces creation of revolutionary govt. in Iranian Azerbaijan (→ 1/19/46).

16. Cleveland: Rams edge Redskins 15-14 for football title.

19. Congress confirms Eleanor Roosevelt U.S. delegate to U.N. (→ 1/30/46).

20. Tire rationing ends in U.S. (→ 2/14/46).

20. Austrian People's Party forms coalition with Socialists under newly elected President Karl Renner (→ 7/6/46).

20. Rome: Mussolini's daughter Edda jailed for two years for aiding Fascism (→ 5/9/46).

22. U.S. recognizes Tito's Yugoslav govt. (→ 1/31/46).

26. Moscow: Big Three end ten-day parley, seek atom rule by U.N. Council (→ 1/24/46).

27. Palestine: Civil investigation building blown up (→ 1/13/46).

31. Truman creates Wage Stabilization Board to replace War Labor Board (→ 1/3/46).

CULTURAL EVENTS, 1945

Literature: George Orwell's "Animal Farm"; Richard Wright's "Black Boy"; Waugh's "Brideshead Revisited"; Nancy Mitford's "The Pursuit of Love"

Music: Prokofiev's ballet "Cinderella"; Rodgers and Hammerstein's "Carousel."

Film: Rossellini's "Rome, Open City"; Eisenstein's "Ivan the Terrible"; Renoir's "The Man from the South."

Patton, master of tank warfare, killed

Dec 21. "Old Blood and Guts," America's most cantankerous war hero, has died in a Heidelberg army hospital. General George S. Patton was injured in a car accident December 9; chest wounds resulted in fatal lung congestion. He was 60.

Patton's tank units were responsible for major war victories. He led offensives in North Africa and the Western Front. His 7th Army and the British 8th Army conquered Sicily in 38 days. But his outspokenness resulted in two demotions. He once urged primary schoolchildren to study nursing and military arts to prepare for the next war.

General George S. Patton.

Cordell Hull is Peace Prize winner

Dec 12. Cordell Hull, the former Secretary of State whom President Roosevelt called "the father of the United Nations" acknowledged receipt of the Nobel Prize today by saying the struggle for peace is imperative if "the human race is to be preserved in this new and dangerous atomic age."

Central to the establishment of the U.N. was Hull's trip to Moscow in 1943. There, he got the U.S., Britain, Russia and China to agree to maintain a united front until the Axis powers had fallen and thereafter establish an organization for the maintenance of world peace. Hull then won bipartisan support for the proposal in the U.S. Congress.

Seasoned diplomat Cordell Hull.

Dreiser was a great American novelist

Dreiser, an astute social critic.

Dec 28. The author of "Sister Carrie" (1900) and "An American Tragedy" (1925) has died in Hollywood, Calif. Theodore Dreiser was 74 years old. He lived to see his work, initially reviled, venerated.

Dreiser was born in Terre Haute, Indiana. In his teens he moved to Chicago, and memories of its slums filled "An American Tragedy." The novel told the life of a murderer who goes to the electric chair. Dreiser indicted society for the crime; consequently the book was banned in Boston. H.L. Mencken wrote of Dreiser, "He stands isolated today, a figure weather-beaten and lonely, yet I can think of no American novelist who seems so secure or so likely to endure."

IMF and World Bank established

Dec 27. The International Monetary Fund and the Bank for Reconstruction and Development were born today when representatives of 28 nations ratified the Bretton Woods Agreement. Missing was the Soviet Union, expected to sign by the December 31 deadline.

The IMF is a new kind of world currency pool meant to promote healthy international trade by maintaining stable exchange rates. The bank is a medium for international risk-sharing intended to make loans more readily available for world reconstruction and development projects.

Jackson Pollock's attacks on the canvas lead the artistic revolt. Untitled.

World War II ends; will there be peace?

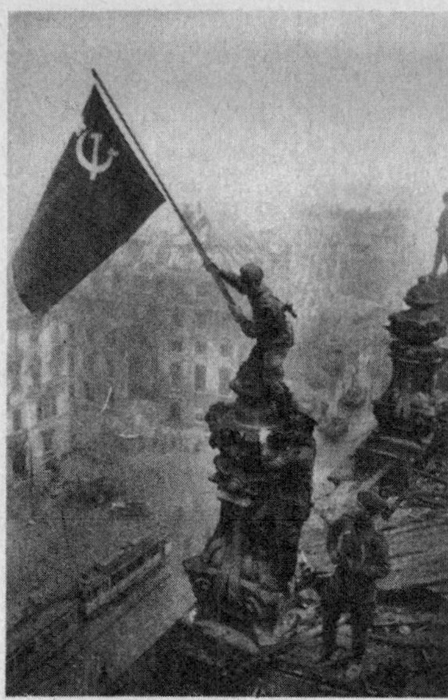

Soviet soldiers raised the hammer-and-sickle flag on the Reichstag in Berlin on April 30, 1945.

An exhausted world can pause to take a deep breath. There is more air to be had now; gone is the smoke of bombs and artillery. Gone are the fumes of propaganda drifting over the airwaves. Gone are skyscrapers, homes and churches that clogged the skyline; in their place is rubble. And gone are the 50 million people who shared this globe and breathed freely six years ago.

Since May 8, 1945, Germany has lain in ruins. Its population east of the Oder-Neisse fled before the Soviet armies. The people sought shelter in the west and found none. The German economy is in shreds.

Western European cities are occupied by military forces, many American. There is a lack of food, clothing, and of course, money. Americans send "care" packages, galling to a self-reliant people.

Since Aug. 15, 1945, war with Japan is over. Americans emerged relatively unscathed. Battles were fought on tiny islands in the South Pacific, while the continental U.S. rested peacefully. The economy is the best it has been in years. And the United States is sole possessor of the deadliest weapon ever made.

Where will the winds of power and politics blow now? China, Indochina and Indonesia, freed from Japan, face political uncertainty. And the peoples of Eastern and Western Europe ponder a legacy of power that has led them into two devastating wars.

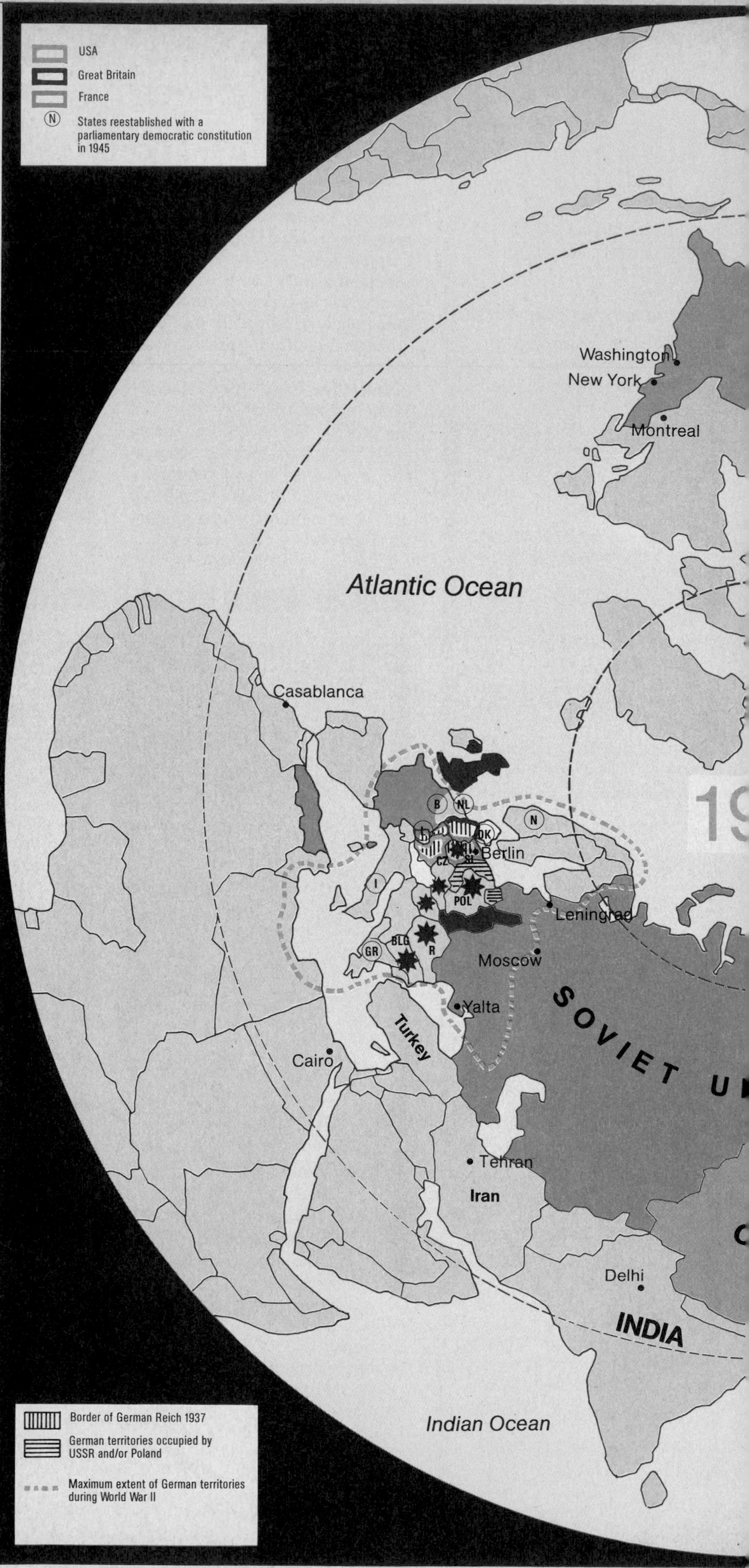

USA
Great Britain
France
N
States reestablished with a parliamentary democratic constitution in 1945
Washington
New York
Montreal
Atlantic Ocean
Casablanca
B
NL
DK
N
Berlin
CZ
POL
I
GR
BLG
R
Leningrad
Moscow
Yalta
Turkey
Cairo
SOVIET U
Tehran
Iran
Delhi
INDIA
Indian Ocean
Border of German Reich 1937
German territories occupied by USSR and/or Poland
Maximum extent of German territories during World War II

Territories annexed by USSR in 1945
Occupied territories
Territories where USSR restores or supports Communist Governments
States which became Communist

U S A
Los Angeles
San Francisco
Hawaiian Islands
Pearl Harbor
Midway Islands
Pacific Ocean
Kurile Islands
Sakhalin Islands
JAPAN
Tokyo
Hiroshima
Nagasaki
Manchuria
North Korea
Seoul
South Korea
Mongolia
Peking
Mao Tse Tung
Formosa (Taiwan)
Philippines
Indochina

Post-war Japan
Maximum extent of territory controlled by Japan during the war (until end of 1942)

On a road leading to a divided world

The Big Three —Churchill, Roosevelt and Stalin —met at Yalta in February 1945.

After the Yalta Conference in February 1945, the division of the world was overtly and tacitly understood. In the Far East, most Japanese territory would be placed under American administration. Islands off the western coast of Russia, Sakhalin and the Kuriles, would go to the Soviets. Korea would be divided North and South; each superpower would have a share.

And it will all come to pass, for the Soviet Union and the United States are the only world powers still intact. The two colonial empires of France and Great Britain have no voice to dispute it. Their possessions and strength vanished with the war. France did not even take part at the Yalta Conference or at Potsdam in July 1945.

The Soviet Union annexed the eastern half of Poland and northeast Prussia. In the Balkans and its occupied German Territory, Moscow has set up Communist regimes, supplanting previous governments. The Allies have allowed the Western nations to restore their democratic governments. The future of Germany and Berlin, where East meets West with dangerous intimacy, remains undetermined.

Just as the two superpowers imagine the world is theirs, a third voice is lifted, that of the populous nation of China. The Communist-Nationalist pairing falters, and Mao Tsetung is emerging as a formidable entity. His ideals would seem to bring him into the Soviet camp; yet can Russia happily endure a great power of any nature on its doorstep?

Until China, decades backward technologically, grows into its inevitable third place, the globe will belong to the Soviet Union and the United States. A nation not siding with one may be cajoled or forced to side with the other.

1946

JANUARY

Su	Mo	Tu	We	Th	Fr	Sa
		1	2	3	4	5
6	7	8	9	10	11	12
13	14	15	16	17	18	19
20	21	22	23	24	25	26
29	28	29	30	31		

1. Pasadena: Southern Cal., in third straight Rose Bowl, loses to Alabama 34-14.

3. Truman, in nationwide broadcast, calls on people to spur Congress to act in labor crisis (→ 16).

6. Hanoi: Ho Chi Minh wins N. Vietnamese elections (→ 3/2).

8. Truman vows to stand by Yalta accord on self-determination for Balkans (→ 3/5).

9. U.S.: Frank Stanton elected president of CBS.

10. U.S. Army Signal Corps contacts moon in radar test.

10. China: Chiang and Yenan Reds halt fighting (→ 3/11).

11. Albania: People's Republic proclaimed.

13. Palestine: British set monthly quota for Jewish immigrants at 10,500 (→ 4/27).

16. Chicago: Nation's meat output down 75% as 200,000 strike in packing plants (→ 19).

17. Britain offers U.N. trusteeships in Tanganyika, Cameroons and Togoland.

19. Pittsburgh: 800,000 steel workers begin strike (→ 25).

19. Iran charges U.S.S.R. with meddling in internal affairs; asks U.N. inquiry (→ 3/5).

20. Truman creates Central Intelligence Group (→ 7/26/47).

20. Paris: De Gaulle hands in resignation (→ 4/24).

21. London: U.S.S.R. charges British interference in Greece and Indonesia (→ 2/4).

24. London: U.N. establishes International Atomic Energy Commission (→ 3/18).

25. A.F.L. elects John L. Lewis v.p., signalling return of C.I.O. to A.F.L. fold (→ 27).

29. London: U.N. names Norway's Trygve Lie as sec. gen.

30. Hungary proclaimed a republic (→ 7/26).

31. New Yugoslav constitution inaugurated, patterned after U.S.S.R. (→ 4/18).

DEATH

9. Countee Cullen, black American poet (*5/30/1903).

U.N. holds first session

King George VI received the delegates at St. James's Palace in London.

Jan 30. The first session of the United Nations General Assembly opened on the 10th of this month, ushering in a renewed effort in the quest for world peace and cooperation. Ironically, the doors opened on the 26th anniversary of the ratification of the ill-fated League of Nations. British Prime Minister Clement Attlee welcomed the representatives of 51 nations, constituting four-fifths of the world's population. Attlee said the new venture into world diplomacy would succeed only if the nations involved brought "the same sense of urgency, the same self-sacrifice and the same willingness to subordinate self interests" with which they won the war.

The U.N.'s first problem concerned the conflict between Iran and the Soviet Union. On the 19th, Iran charged the Soviet Union with interfering in its internal affairs and asked the U.N. to investigate the matter and take necessary steps.

The U.S.S.R. had authorized its army to stop Iranian troops from occupying the Iranian province, Azerbaijan, in accordance with a treaty signed in 1942 giving Russia the right to send troops into Iran. Iran claimed it threatens her sovereignty and disrupts the flow of oil.

Yesterday, the Iranian-Russian dispute appeared to be resolved with both nations agreeing to settle their differences by direct negotiations. The Security Council retained the right to supervise (→ 10/23).

Hirohito declares his divinity is myth

Jan 1. Japanese citizens read this morning's newspapers with shock and consternation as Emperor Hirohito, in an imperial decree, declared his divinity a "false conception" founded in fiction.

Since ancient times, the emperor was believed to be descended from the Sun Goddess Amaterasu. Now, the emperor has debunked the idea. The announcement was accompanied by the following statement: "In obedience to the imperial wishes (the Japanese people) should build up a new state based on democracy, peace and rationalism."

The imperial proclamation aims to usher in a new era of modern government in Japan with the emperor regarded as an ordinary man. But traditional beliefs are not changed overnight (→ 4/10).

MacArthur, head of the American occupation, and Hirohito in Tokyo.

800,000 steel workers join millions on strike in United States

Tear gas hits strikers in L.A.; a familiar scene in postwar America.

Jan 27. To the casual observer, peacetime America appears to be encircled by one giant picket line, with millions of workers in a vast array of industries now on strike. The latest walk-out involves about 800,000 steel workers, who are on strike against the United States Steel Corporation. Elsewhere in the nation, there are costly strikes at General Motors and General Electric. Coffin makers are on strike. Phone workers are threatening to walk off the job. The nation's capital faces a taxi strike. And employees of meatpacking plants resumed work only when ordered back by the federal government (→ 2/14).

1946

FEBRUARY

Su	Mo	Tu	We	Th	Fr	Sa
					1	2
3	4	5	6	7	8	9
10	11	12	13	14	15	16
17	18	19	20	21	22	23
24	25	26	27	28		

3. Vienna: Soviet occupation army seizes Danube Steamship Company.

4. London: U.N. rejects Soviet charge that British troops in Greece threaten peace (→ 3/31).

5. U.S. recognizes Rumania (→ 7/29/47).

6. Washington: Truman orders nine steps U.S. must take to feed Europeans (→ 17).

9. London: U.N. rebukes Franco regime in Spain (→ 6/24).

9. Stalin announces new five-year plan for U.S.S.R., calling for 50% production boosts.

12. U.S. report finds Argentina gives refuge to Nazis.

12. India: 14 killed in Calcutta riots; Moslem leader Jinnah threatens civil war (→ 20).

13. London: Labor govt. repeals 1926 law banning strikes (→ 14).

14. Washington: Truman lessens wage and price controls in response to labor strife (→ 15).

15. U.S.: Steel strike settled with 18.5-cent pay raise (→ 20).

15. Ottawa: Royal Canadian mounted police seize 22 as Soviet spies (→ 3/4).

17. New Yorkers donate 2.5 mil. pounds of clothing for European relief (→ 3/29).

18. Vatican: Three U.S. prelates are made cardinals--St. Louis' John Glennon, N.Y.'s Francis Spellman, Detroit's Edward Mooney.

20. U.S.: Council of Economic Advisors created by Employment Act (→ 21).

21. Truman creates Office of Economic Stabilization under Chester Bowles, to aid in reconversion process (→ 27).

23. India: Anti-British demonstration draws 300,000 (→ 3/15).

24. Buenos Aires: Juan Peron elected Argentine president (→ 3/28).

27. New York: Bob Hope, Bing Crosby and Dorothy Lamour open in "Road to Utopia."

28. U.S. Army discloses it will use V-2 to test radar as atom-rocket defense (→ 3/18).

FDR's closest aide Harry Hopkins dies

Jan 29. Harry L. Hopkins, who was a top aide and confidante of the late President Franklin Roosevelt, died in a New York City hospital yesterday. He was 55 years old.

That he had outlived the man he had served so faithfully all those 12 years in the White House surprised friends and colleagues. Thin and wan, he was frequently ill and once underwent surgery for cancer of the stomach. Nevertheless, he put in 18-hour work days, spearheading New Deal programs, doling out billions of dollars as head of the Works Progress Administration, serving as Secretary of Commerce and later becoming a chief civilian administrator during World War II.

With the death last April of his old friend and boss, Hopkins left the government, after one final job of heading a diplomatic mission to Moscow, laying the groundwork for the Potsdam Conference of the Big Three. In recent months, he was Chairman of the Cloak and Suit Industry in New York.

A native of Iowa, Hopkins spent many years in social service work, seeking to aid the poor. His work in that field led to his appointment by Roosevelt, at that time the Governor of New York, as chief of the state's relief organization. When Roosevelt became president in 1933, Hopkins was a member of the inner circle of chief aides.

Angela Lansbury and Judy Garland star in "The Harvey Girls," about a chain of railroad-station restaurants which brings Eastern culture to the Wild West.

India erupts in anti-British demonstrations

The streets of Calcutta smolder as India explodes against British rule.

Feb 23. Some 300,000 Indians joined in anti-British demonstrations today in the wake of yesterday's violent riots in the city of Bombay.

A day of terror and rebellion saw Indian navy members turn against their British officers, firing machine guns and rifles from their barracks.

The mutiny prompted Vice Admiral John Godfrey to exclaim that the mutineers have "completely lost control of their senses." He also released a communique saying, "To continue this struggle is the height of folly when you take into account the overwhelming forces at our disposal . . . which will be used even if it means the destruction of the navy." British reinforcements finally forced the Indian sailors to surrender, but not until one man was killed and 26 hurt.

However, even worse bloodshed occurred in the streets of Bombay as anti-British protesters and riot control police clashed. Rioters looted and set ablaze grain warehouses, banks, shops and a movie theater and turned over buses and cars, completely disrupting traffic in the crowded city. The British troops responded by spraying the crowd with machine gun fire in an attempt to regain control. This resulted in tragedy as over 60 Indians were killed and more than 500 injured. Eventually, armored cars and infantry units quieted the streets (→ 3/15).

Labor nationalizes the Bank of England

Feb 14. The 250-year-old Bank of England is now under public ownership as the bill to nationalize the established financial institution became law tonight with the granting of royal assent.

This is the first major measure of the Labor government's program of socialization to pass through Parliament. In the 1945 election, both parties emphasized the need to address the domestic concerns of better housing and health care as well as full employment.

Nationalization of institutions in England is nothing new; the telegraph and telephone systems have long been run by the government, and in 1926, with the formation of a National Grid System, the state began to sell wholesale electricity. The Labor Party is expected to nationalize more institutions (→ 6/27).

The Bank of England in London.

▷

IBM introduces fast electronic calculator

The IBM 603's vacuum tubes function faster than ordinary electronic devices.

Feb 14. The U.S. War Department has announced the usage of an extremely sophisticated calculator it calls ENIAC. ENIAC (Electronic Numerical Integrator and Computer) works 1,000 times faster than any calculator ever devised. It operates by the flow of electrons in 18,000 vacuum tubes. There is not a single moving part in the machine.

ENIAC's creator is International Business Machines, a company previously known for punched card tabulating devices. The company plans to release its less ambitious electronic calculator called the 603 Multiplier. The 603 will be available for commercial use.

The vacuum tube is responsible for advancement over the adding machine. Mechanical switches are replaced by electronic pulses. Electrons flow effectively in the gas-controlled tube.

Ford strike ended

Feb 27. A wage deadlock was broken today when Ford Motor Company agreed to increase salaries by an average of 18 cents an hour. The agreement between Ford and the United Automobile Workers also provides for stringent penalties, such as job termination, against those who lead or take part in any wildcat strikes (→ 3/27).

Car after car, tire after tire . . .

Egyptians riot to protest British rule

Feb 21. British troops fired on large crowds marching and rioting through the streets of Cairo, demanding the end of British rule. At least a dozen persons were reported killed and more then 100 wounded.

The demonstrations, which turned into mob violence and then street battles between Egyptian police and British troops, took place on a day when a general strike had closed down all business and transport in Cairo. lt also had been proclaimed "evacuation day," a day of protests in support of Egyptian demands for evacuation of all foreign troops and the unification of Sudan with Egypt.

The crowds set fire to three British soldiers' clubs and attacked a royal air force installation on one of the city's main squares after British military trucks drove through a menacing crowd. Premier lsmail Sidky Pasha, in office for only four days, ordered a ban on further demonstrations (→ 5/7).

1946

MARCH

Su	Mo	Tu	We	Th	Fr	Sa
					1	2
3	4	5	6	7	8	9
10	11	12	13	14	15	16
17	18	19	20	21	22	23
24	25	26	27	28	29	30
31						

2. Hanoi: Ho Chi Minh elected president of Democratic Republic of Vietnam (→ 6).

5. U.S. sends protests to U.S.S.R. on incursions into Manchuria and Iran (→ 13).

8. Vietnam: French naval fleet arrives in Haiphong (→ 6/25).

11. Manchuria: Communists fight Nationalists in Mukden as Soviets pull out (→ 4/10).

11. Moscow: Pravda denounces Churchill as anti-Soviet warmonger (→ 10/28).

13. Detroit: Four-month strike ends at GM with pay raise of 18.5 cents per hour (→ 27).

13. Iran: Reports indicate Soviet tank units stationed 20 miles above Tehran (→ 24).

13. Tito seizes wartime collaborator Gen. Draja Mikhailovich in Yugoslav cave (→ 4/18).

15. London: Attlee offers India full independence after agreement on constitution (→ 16).

16. Algeria: Nationalist leader Ferhat Abbas, jailed for year, is set free (→ 8/9).

16. India calls Attlee's independence offer contradictory, a propaganda move (→ 6/24).

18. Bernard Baruch named U.S. member of U.N. Atomic Energy Commission (→ 6/19).

22. Britain grants independence to Transjordan (→ 5/25).

22. First U.S.-built rocket to leave Earth's atmosphere reaches 50-mile height.

23. W. Averell Harriman chosen U.S. ambassador to Britain.

29. Fiorella LaGuardia becomes director general of United Nations Relief and Rehabilitation Organization (→ 4/19).

29. Gold Coast becomes first British colony to hold African parliamentary majority.

30. Germany: Allies seize 1,000 Nazis in Frankfort, crushing attempt to revive party (→ 10/19).

31. Athens: Monarchists win Greek elections (→ 8/24).

BIRTH

12. Liza Minnelli, American singer, actress.

France recognizes Ho's Vietnam state

March 6. Ho Chi Minh, elected four days ago as the first President of the Democratic Republic of Vietnam, has struck an agreement with the French which recognizes his country as an autonomous state within the Indochinese Federation and the French Union. Tonkin, Annam and Cochin China will be united if the people so decide.

In 1911, Ho left French Indochina to work aboard a French ocean liner. After World War I, he became active in socialist politics and at the Paris peace conference pressed futilely for recognition of civil rights in his native land.

Ho learned of Lenin in France.

In 1920, Ho helped found the French Communist Party, visited the U.S.S.R. to study revolutionary tactics and from 1925-27 served in Canton, China as a Comintern agent. Ho founded the Indochinese Communist Party in 1930, and in 1941 organized the League for the Independence of Vietnam, or Viet Minh, which led resistance to the occupying Japanese. Last year in Tonkin, he proclaimed the independence of the Democratic Republic of Vietnam (→ 8).

Churchill's speech: The Iron Curtain

Churchill speaks in Fulton.

March 5. "From Stettin in the Baltic to Trieste in the Adriatic, an iron curtain has descended across the Continent," proclaimed Winston Churchill today in a speech at Fulton, Missouri. The former British Prime Minister, referring to ideological barriers, warned that differences between the Western, capitalist world and the Eastern, communist world seemed irreconcilable and that the Soviet Union desired "indefinite expansion" of its "power and doctrines." Churchill urged the United States and Great Britain to formulate an alliance to discourage possible Soviet hegemony.

Reaction to the address varied considerably. The London Times took exception to Churchill's remarks about Russia, declaring, "while Western democracy and communism are in many respects opposed, they have much to learn from each other." U.S. Senator Pepper said Churchill spoke "in his best Marlborough manner for imperialism—but it is always British imperialism." However, Senator Robertson agreed with the statesman, saying that until Russia "rolls up the iron curtain," close Anglo-American relations are essential. British Conservative Anthony Eden underlined Churchill's desire for constructive existence with Russia.

Most political observers do agree that America and Britain should continue to work together in a world so volatile (→ 11).

G.M., G.E. strikes end after 4 months

Returning to a consumer economy.

March 27. Strikes at both General Electric and General Motors have been ended with substantial wage increases for employees of both industrial giants.

The General Motors strike, lasting 113 days, was the longest and most costly in the history of the automobile industry. Workers on picket lines at hundreds of plants in 18 states, from coast to coast, gleefully greeted news of the settlement between management and the United Automobile Workers. Terms call for a wage increase of just over 18 cents an hour.

An identical wage increase will be given to 100,000 General Electric workers, whose two-month strike had held up production of a major portion of the nation's supply of electrical appliances for both home and industrial use. The settlement is subject to ratification by local unions of the United Electrical, Radio and Machine Workers in 16 states (→ 4/1).

St. Moritz hosts 1948 Olympics.

Russians announce troops leaving Iran

March 24. The Soviet Union has announced that it is withdrawing its troops from Iran, thus apparently ending an increasingly serious diplomatic confrontation with Great Britain. An announcement carried on Moscow radio said that the troop withdrawal would be completed in five to six weeks "if nothing unforeseen occurs."

The Soviet announcement was greeted with relief in the British Foreign Office, where there had been growing gloom over a likely confrontation with the Soviet Union over its continuing military presence in the Middle East. Britain had contended that the Soviet Union, by leaving its troops in Iran after March 2, had violated the British-Soviet treaty of 1942, and had been prepared to take the issue to the United Nations Security Council for a diplomatic showdown. The necessity for such a showdown has now been averted, but British officials still had their fingers crossed over whether the Soviet Union would carry out the troop withdrawal as promised.

There also were questions about what quid pro quo the Soviets might have obtained from Iran for the troop withdrawal and what now will happen in Azerbaijan, where the Russians have blocked Iranian troops from putting down a revolt. Still, it was the greatest victory yet for the new United Nations (→ 4/3).

The Shah of Iran inspects his army.

The Iron Curtain has a long history

Kaiser Wilhelm's Germany and Lenin's Russia inspired precedents for Winston Churchill's "iron curtain" metaphor in his speech at Westminster College in Fulton, Missouri. Belgium's German-born Queen Elizabeth, in 1914, saw between her birthplace and her home, "a bloody iron curtain which has descended forever." George Washington Crile saw France with "an iron curtain at its frontier" in 1915. And shortly after what he called the Bolshevik "apocalypse," Vasili Rozanov wrote: "With a rumble and a roar, an iron curtain is descending on Russian history."

Canadians uncover Soviet spy ring

March 4. A special commission reports that the Soviet Embassy in Ottawa organized a network of undercover agents to obtain secret information from the Canadian government on military matters, particularly those involving the United States. Named in the report were two women and two men, three of them employed by Canada and one by the office of the British High Commissioner. The report states that all four have admitted being involved.

Peron is formally elected President

March 28. With the overwhelming support of industrial and agricultural workers, Juan Peron has been swept into office as the President of Argentina for a six-year term. The popular vote in the election between Peron and Dr. Jose Tamborini was close, but the 50-year-old former army Colonel won a decisive margin of votes in the electoral college. The victory of Peron, who has dominated Argentine politics for more than two years, was a diplomatic setback for the United States, which had opposed his election and now faces the prospect of a hostile government in Latin America (→ 5/5).

1946

APRIL

Su	Mo	Tu	We	Th	Fr	Sa
	1	2	3	4	5	6
7	8	9	10	11	12	13
14	15	16	17	18	19	20
21	22	23	24	25	26	27
28	29	30				

1. Pittsburgh: 400,000 soft coal workers strike, demanding wage hikes, health insurance (→ 5/17).

1. Hawaii: Pacific tidal waves kill 300.

3. U.S.S.R. formally agrees to withdraw Iran troops unconditionally by May 6 (→ 7).

7. Tehran: Iran discloses accord giving U.S.S.R. 51% control of oil for 25 years (→ 5/23).

10. China: Communists launch offensive on Peking-Mukden railway in North (→ 14).

14. Chungking: Chou En-lai, Communist liason to Nationalists, declares all-out war in China (→ 28).

19. Truman orders food curbs to allow aid to Europe (→ 24).

19. Vietnam: Franco-Vietnamese talks open at Dalat (→ 7/6).

21. New York to Washington flight record set by Army P-80 in 29 minutes, 15 seconds.

22. U.S. Supreme Court bars mandatory army service for aliens with U.S. citizenship.

23. "Stalin," novel by late Leon Trotsky, published in U.S.

24. Washington gives UNRRA 100,000 tons of grain (→ 7/15).

24. France nationalizes 34 major insurance companies (→ 5/6).

24. Buenos Aires: Peron places Argentina's banks under govt. control (→ 5/5).

24. U.S. grants credits to Poland on promise of free elections (→ 6/30).

26. U.S. Navy reveals 8,000-h.p. aircraft rocket engine.

27. Palestine: British hold all of Tel Aviv responsible for murder of seven U.K. soldiers (→ 30).

28. Tokyo: Allies indict Tojo with 55 counts of war crimes and plot to rule world (→ 6/17).

28. China: Communists seize Tsitsihar, capital of Nunkiang Province (→ 7/17).

29. U.S. farm prices reach highest level since 1920.

DEATH

22. Harlan F. Stone, chief justice of U.S. Supreme Court (*10/11/1872).

U.S. accepts Tito as Yugoslav chief

Tito, Yugoslav hero.

April 18. The United States has granted recognition to the government of Yugoslavia led by Premier Tito. The American decision was based on assurances from Tito that Yugoslavia would observe existing treaties between the two nations and that the new government will "subscribe to the principles of the Declaration of the United Nations," according to a U.S. dispatch.

However, acceptance of the Tito regime "should not be interpreted as implying the approval of the policies of the regime, its method of assuming control or its failure to implement the guarantees of personal freedom promised its people." The U.S. has questioned the freedom of Yugoslav elections (→ 6/10).

Lord Keynes meets his inevitable fate

April 21. John Maynard Lord Keynes, whose efforts to restructure the theory and practice of economics won him worldwide fame, has died of a heart attack at age 63.

The Cambridge-educated British economist was married to Lydia Lopokova, the Russian ballerina, and was the center of the literary circle known as "Bloomsbury," which included Lytton Strachey, Virginia Woolf and their friends.

Keynes first achieved recognition as a brilliant thinker after publication in 1919 of his controversial book, "The Economic Consequences of the Peace," in which he warned that the harsh reparations imposed upon Germany after the First World War would prove harmful to both Germany and the victorious nations. He was subsequently proved correct, and the book has been translated into 11 languages.

In 1936, Keynes published his "General Theory of Employment, Interest and Money," in which he developed his idea that full employment should be the overriding goal of financial policy. This belief gradually took root as many nations adopted deficit-spending policies to overcome the ravages of depression.

When asked how to deal with the inflation resulting from such policies in the long run, Keynes said, "In the long run, we are all dead."

Japanese vote for liberalization policy

Women in the Diet: Unprecedented.

April 10. Japanese voters have approved a new constitution and expanded the powers of Parliament. The voters also forced Kiero Shidehara to resign and gave a plurality to the Liberal Party. Shigeru Yoshida will head the new government if he can form a coalition with progressive politicians in the Diet.

Today's elections were historic. For the first time ever in Japan, women exercised the right to vote.

Before the elections, a large demonstration was held in Tokyo to criticize Shidehara with not moving fast enough to liberalize Japan. General MacArthur, the Supreme Allied Commander, declared many former members of Parliament ineligible to run again (→ 6/17).

Big Four ministers convene in Paris

April 25. U.S. Secretary of State James Byrnes met in Paris with the foreign ministers of Britain, France and Soviet Russia to finalize the peace treaty with Germany.

The four countries have had troubles from the start with their joint occupation of Germany and Berlin, and the ministers tried to iron out some of the problems. Byrnes was most insistent that Germany remain disarmed for 25 years.

On other matters, the diplomats rubber-stamped the annexation of Transylvania to Rumania. But Russian proposals for a joint administration of the Ruhr and the return of Trieste to Yugoslavia were rejected. The diplomats also disagreed on the future of Libya.

France's Vincent Auriol, Britain's Ernest Bevin, France's Felix Gouin, Sec. of State Byrnes, Russia's Molotov and French For. Min. Georges Bidault.

1946

Two-power group bars Jewish state

April 30. The Anglo-American Committee of Inquiry on Jewish problems in Europe and Palestine has released a report urging the admission of 100,000 European Jews into the Holy Land as soon as possible, an idea proposed by President Truman. But it flatly rejects the idea of a Jewish state, together with Arab claims for dominance. It asserts Christendom's own interest in the area, and calls for guarantees of Arab civil and religious rights. The report comes in the wake of violent incidents, which took the lives of seven British soldiers. The British authorities in Palestine have imposed a curfew on the Jewish community in Tel Aviv, which they hold responsible (→ 5/3).

Jews protest the British in Jerusalem.

Musicians assess impact of television

April 30. Musicians will no longer play their instruments for television producers, at least not until it is determined how TV effects the radio industry. President of the American Federation of Musicians, James Petrillo, told union members they are temporarily banned from TV, saying telecasting must not supplant broadcasting. In the past, musicians have suffered from new technology. When Vitatone and Movietone were built into cinemas, over 18,000 musicians lost their jobs. "(The union) is determined to avoid a repetition of that tragic experience," said Petrillo. He added that television will not prosper at the expense of musicians.

MAY

Su	Mo	Tu	We	Th	Fr	Sa
			1	2	3	4
5	6	7	8	9	10	11
12	13	14	15	16	17	18
19	20	21	22	23	24	25
26	27	28	29	30	31	

2. San Francisco: Marines land on Alcatraz to battle armed convicts in attempted jail break.

2. Lana Turner opens in "The Postman Always Rings Twice."

3. Jerusalem: Arabs stone British soldiers to protest Anglo-U.S. report on Palestine (→ 30).

4. Assault is first in Kentucky Derby with jockey W. Mehrtens.

5. Peron pledges 500,000 tons of grain to UNRRA (→ 6/4).

6. French referendum rejects socialist constitution (→ 17).

7. British to quit Egypt if military alliance signed (→ 7/11/47).

9. Rome: King Victor Emmanuel III abdicates (→ 6/2).

11. First CARE packages reach Europe, at Le Havre, France.

12. AT&T announces car-phone service in St. Louis.

17. U.S. govt. seizes railroads to avert strike (→ 23).

17. France nationalizes coal mines (→ 22).

22. France votes social security for all wage earners (→ 10/13).

23. U.S.: Rail unions strike, despite govt. seizures (→ 26).

23. Soviet announces Iran was evacuated on May 9 (→ 6/13).

25. Transjordan gains independence from Britain (→ 6/2/49).

26. U.S. lifts control of railroads as accord ends strike (→ 29).

26. Prague: Communists win Czech elections (→ 1/23/48).

29. Arthur Woodbur reports Britain has developed first jet fighter plane.

30. George Robson wins Indy 500 at 114.8 mph.

30. Cairo: 7 Arab League states reject further Jewish immigration to Palestine (→ 6/18).

BIRTHS

18. Reggie Jackson, U.S. baseball star.

31. Werner Fassbinder, German film director (†6/10/1982).

DEATH

19. Booth Tarkington, American novelist (*7/29/1869).

Annie Get Your Gun: Merman belts it out

Ethel Merman is "Annie Oakley."

May 16. If Ethel Merman were a rifle and a song were a bullet, she could make bull's-eyes on a target clear across the Atlantic. Her voice and persona spell success for Irving Berlin's "Annie Get Your Gun." The musical about Annie Oakley opened tonight in New York.

Miss Merman, born Ethel Zimmerman, has starred on Broadway since 1930, her latest show being "Something for the Boys" (1943). In "Annie" her numbers include "There's No Business Like Show Business." The real "Little Sure Shot," who worked in Buffalo Bill's Wild West Show in the 1890's, could shoot a hole in a dime in mid-air while standing 90 feet away.

Coal and rail strikes bedevil the country

May 29. The 45-day coal strike ended today at the White House when John L. Lewis agreed to a new contract giving miners a daily raise of $1.85. In addition, the contract provides that mine operators will finance a welfare and retirement fund for workers. Although the coal strike is now ended, the nation still faces a grave crisis brought on by the walkout of railroad workers a week ago. The strike imperils delivery of the nation's food supplies as well as stranding those who normally use rail transportation (→ 6/11).

Trains are idle due to the strike.

Britain and France withdraw from Syria

May 7. Great Britain and France announced to the United Nations their troops have evacuated Syria 15 days ahead of schedule and that conditions of military withdrawal satisfactory to the government of Lebanon have been formalized. The Lebanese have been assured that British forces will be removed by the end of June, except for a "small liquidation party," and French troops will be pulled by August 31. The withdrawals have been ordered in accordance with decisions reached by the U.N. Security Council members after the two Mideast nations issued official complaints.

The U.S.S.R. vetoed the council vote because they felt the order lacked strong language; in short, the Russians want British and French troops off all U.N. members' soil. Meanwhile, the council has ordered the Soviets to recall their forces from Iran. The Soviet U.N. delegate, Andrei Gromyko, will probably boycott the council's upcoming meeting because he contends the U.N. demand is illegal since an agreement between Iran and Russia has already been reached (→ 3/30/49).

1946

JUNE

Su	Mo	Tu	We	Th	Fr	Sa
						1
2	3	4	5	6	7	8
9	10	11	12	13	14	15
16	17	18	19	20	21	22
23	24	25	26	27	28	29
30						

2. Italians vote republic by referendum (→ 12).

3. U.S. Supreme Court rules segregation in public transportation unconstitutional (→ 9/15).

3. South Africa adopts bill further curtailing land ownership, voting rights for Asian minority.

4. Buenos Aires: Juan Peron installed as Argentine president (→ 3/9/47).

5. Chicago: Fire in La Salle Hotel kills 58, injures 200.

10. U.S.S.R. offers aid to Yugoslav military (→ 7/17).

11. Truman vetoes bill for federal mediation in labor disputes, denies it would end strife (→ 14).

12. Rome: Full rule of Italy given to Premier Gasperi (→ 28).

13. Iran: Communist Azerbaijan province returned to govt. control (→ 4/10/48).

14. New York: Shipping paralyzed as 200,000 strike on docks (→ 7/15).

14. U.S. presents Baruch plan on atom control to U.N. (→ 19).

17. Allies bar war-crime trial for Emperor Hirohito (→ 11/3).

18. Jerusalem: Five British officers abducted, two shot; Palestine curfew imposed (→ 29).

21. Frederick Moore Vinson named chief justice of the United States.

24. N.Y.: U.N. Security Council refuses break with Franco's Spain by 7-4 vote (→ 12/11).

24. New Delhi: Congress Party rejects British plan for provisional government pending constitution (→ 8/16).

25. Ho Chi Minh goes to France for talks on Vietnamese independence (→ 7/6).

27. Britain begins bread rationing (→ 1/5/47).

30. U.S. joins United Nations Educational, Scientific and Cultural Organization.

30. Polish referendum votes one-party government, nationalization of industry (→ 2/4/47).

DEATH

6. Gerhart Hauptmann, German dramatist (*11/15/1862).

Republic wins in Italy; King quits country

President Nicola (center) and de Gasperi (to his right) surrounded by pomp.

June 28. After only 35 days on the throne, King Umberto has left Italy and the nation is now a republic.

The king lost the referendum on the monarchy last week, then made charges of voting irregularities and said it was up to the courts to verify the outcome of the referendum. The Cabinet, however, issued a statement supporting Premier de Gasperi as head of the provisional government, and when asked if he would assume the role, de Gasperi replied, "I am the head of state. There is nothing to assume."

Umberto II's departure surprised most Italians, including government officials, as he had vowed as recently as yesterday to stay and fight. Only a few airport employees were on hand to see the king off as he boarded a plane for Spain to join his family. Word of his departure brought rioting by monarchists in Rome, but most of the country accepted the news quietly.

Umberto commanded troops in World War II. If the monarchy is never reestablished, he will be the last king of Italy (→ 2/1/47).

British seek end to Palestine violence

June 29. Palestine's Jewish population remains under virtual military siege tonight as British troops launched a drive to end Palestine violence and root out the leadership of Hagana, the Jewish underground army. About 1,000 persons have been arrested for questioning, and unofficial reports claim six dead —five Jews and one British soldier.

Leaders of the Hagana have reportedly gone into hiding. With a membership of about 80,000, the Jewish underground army is distinct from the smaller extremist groups of the Irgun Zvai Leumi and the so-called Stern gang. The British military actions follow by a fortnight the kidnapping of five British officers by the Irgun. Two have been released, and the Irgun says the others will be freed (→ 7/22).

Louis kayos Conn

June 19. Joe Louis, in the 22nd defense of his world heavyweight boxing title, pounded Billy Conn for seven rounds and then finished him off in the eighth. A battered and bruised Conn said after being knocked out at two minutes 19 seconds of the eighth, "I'm quitting. This is my last fight" (→ 12/5/47).

No match for Joe Louis.

Sukarno calls for independence fight

June 29. Kidnappings, the imposition of martial law and a call for independence have marked a chaotic week on the Indonesian island of Java. Premier Sjahrir and six staff members were abducted in what most believe to be a part of a coup d'etat by President Sukarno, recently ousted as Premier by Sjahrir, who is considered a moderate, willing to work with the British and Dutch for administration of the region. Sukarno advocates complete autonomy. In order to maintain control, he has imposed martial law throughout the islands and has also asked countrymen to fight for freedom (→ 11/12).

Sukarno is welcomed in Jakarta.

U.S. asks for U.N. control of A-bomb

June 19. "World peace or world destruction"—these were the choices offered to the United Nations by American statesman Bernard Baruch in a speech this week. The United States offered to relinquish all of its secrets about the atomic bomb and destroy its store of nuclear weaponry, on the condition that the U.N. impose controls on atomic development, confining atomic research to peaceful ends. Additionally, no nation could wield veto power in this area.

The Soviets responded to the U.S. today. They would also ban using or storing A-bombs, but would retain a big-power veto on the development of atomic research. Both sides agree that without controls, an arms race will develop (→ 7/1).

1946

JULY

Su	Mo	Tu	We	Th	Fr	Sa
	1	2	3	4	5	6
7	8	9	10	11	12	13
14	15	16	17	18	19	20
21	22	23	24	25	26	27
28	29	30	31			

1. Pacific: Fourth atom bomb explodes in test off Bikini Atoll, sinking two ships, damaging 19 out of 73 (→ 25).

1. Paris: Big Four parley draws Italo-Yugoslav border as fighting rages in Trieste (→ 3/25/48).

4. Warsaw: Poles kill 26 Jews in Kielce pogrom.

6. France: Fontainbleau Conference on Vietnam opens (→ 9/10).

6. Austria: Soviet administration seizes Nazi assets; U.S. protests.

7. Wimbledon: Yvon Petra over Geoff Brown 6-2, 6-4, 7-9, 5-7, 6-4; Pauline Betz over Althea Brough 6-2, 6-4.

9. Boston: American League wins baseball All Star game.

12. Paris: Soviet Minister Molotov rejects German unity plan as Big Four adjourn (→ 8/10).

15. Truman signs British loan for $3.75 billion (→ 9/25).

15. Truman extends wartime price controls for year (→ 22).

17. China: Communists open drive on Yangtze (→ 8/19).

19. Senate kills Equal Rights Amendment (→ 1/25/50).

20. Washington: Congressional Pearl Harbor inquiry finds FDR blameless for disaster.

21. La Paz: Bolivian President Villarroel killed in uprising as new regime formed.

22. Washington: Federal Reserve reports half of U.S. yearly incomes under $2,000 (→ 8/12).

26. U.S. charges Soviets with stripping Hungary of needed resources (→ 5/31/47).

28. U.S.S.R. reported supplying Albania with arms.

29. Paris: 21 nations opposing Axis convene to consider peace treaties (→ 9/19).

30. Palestine: 20,000 British troops isolate Tel Aviv in search of Zionist guerrillas (→ 8/10).

BIRTH

19. Ilie Nastase, Rumanian tennis player.

DEATH

13. Alfred Stieglitz, New York photographer (*1/1/1864).

Irgun blasts British offices in Jerusalem

July 22. A powerful explosion has ripped through the southwestern wing of the King David Hotel in Jerusalem, which serves as headquarters for the British government. More than 100 people were killed. Irgun, the Zionist guerrilla band led by Menachem Begin, claimed responsibility for the attack.

President Truman warned the bombing might hurt the Zionist cause. And the British called it "cold-blooded murder." But Irgun blamed it on the "British tyrants," and Begin said, "The force of the explosion surpassed all our hopes."

Moderate Jews distanced themselves from the attack by branding it a "dastardly crime perpetrated by the gang of desperadoes."

Attacks on the British in Palestine have been on the rise to protest their crackdown on the illegal immigration of Jews (→ 30).

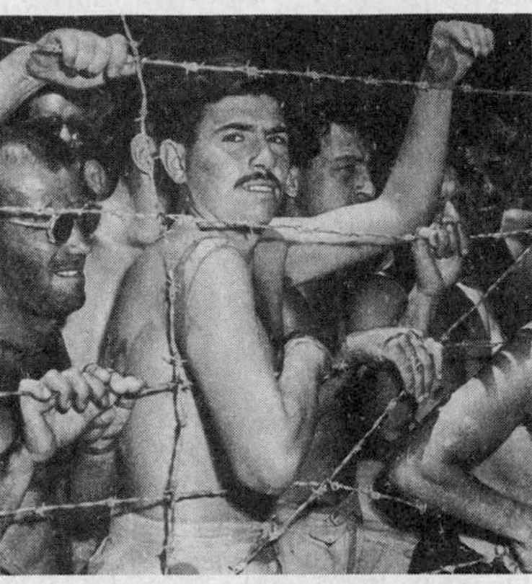

Jewish nationalists in a British camp.

Filipinos proclaim republic free of U.S.

July 4. The American flag was lowered from the Capitol building in Manila for the last time this morning. In its place, a banner emblazoned with a gold sun on a red, white and blue field was raised, marking the birth of the Philippine republic. Church bells rang throughout the islands and President Roxas, speaking of the bond between Filipinos and Americans, said, "We mark here today a forward thrust of the frontiers of freedom." President Truman sent a note renouncing claims on the Philippines and pledged massive aid for rebuilding the nation, ravaged by combat during WWII (→ 4/5/48).

Bikini is test area for new atomic bombs

The A-bomb explodes off Bikini.

July 25. Beneath the calm surface of the Pacific, off the Bikini Islands, an atomic bomb was detonated today. The blast, conducted by the U.S. military, was the first subsurface atomic explosion in history. "Bikini Helen," as Manhatten Project engineers called this bomb, exploded in a tremendous eruption, sinking 11 big Navy ships and damaging another six; the old fleet was stationed at the detonation point as part of the experiment. Meanwhile, on the beaches of Europe and America this summer, women are wearing new two-piece bathing suits, which for some reason have been dubbed bikinis (→ 8/18).

Yugoslav executed

July 17. When Marshal Tito, the Communist leader, took to the hills in 1941 to organize resistance to the Germans in Yugoslavia, he found a guerrilla army already in the field. Led by Colonel Draja Mikhailovich, it was made up of Chetnicks —bearded, long-haired Serbian patriots trained as guerrillas. Tito and the colonel met, and for a time they cooperated. In 1944, Britain and America switched their support to Tito's more aggressive partisans to defeat the Nazis. Today, with Tito in power, Mikhailovich and eight of his followers were executed for treason and collaborating with the enemy (→ 8/19).

SS convicted of Malmedy massacre

July 16. The American war crimes tribunal in Dachau convicted more than 70 members of the Nazi SS of participating in the Malmedy massacre. The court ordered 43 Germans executed, including Colonel Joachim Peiper, the SS commanding officer. Peiper and his men butchered 750 American soldiers and 150 Belgian civilians during the desperate German counteroffensive in the Ardennes in December 1944. Most of the victims died in the Belgian town of Malmedy. The SS was under orders to "act without pity" (→ 9/30).

July 7. All Rome's bells helped canonize Mother Frances Cabrini, America's first saint, founder of the Order of the Sacred Heart.

Jockey Mehrtens poses proudly in the saddle of his Triple Crown winner Assault. The Texas thoroughbred is only the sixth horse to gain American racing's finest distinction, and, at 60.5 inches, by far the smallest.

Stein, eccentric arts patron, dies in Paris

"Gertrude Stein" by Pablo Picasso.

July 27. Gertrude Stein, author and patron of the arts, has died in France at age 72. Miss Stein was raised in California but has since lived in Paris. She founded a salon there, which flourished in the 1920's, when she welcomed such writers of the "lost generation" as Ernest Hemingway and Sherwood Anderson. She wrote 40 novels; "The Autobiography of Miss Alice B. Toklas" (1933) was a best-seller.

Painters gave Stein their works; her collection was incomparable. She willed an unflattering portrait of her by Picasso to The Metropolitan Museum. In 1934, she toured the U.S., where, she wrote, "there is more space where nobody is than where anybody is. This is what makes America what it is."

July 20. An historic day in Egypt: After 64 years flying daily over the citadel in Cairo, the British flag is lowered for the last time.

1946

AUGUST

Su	Mo	Tu	We	Th	Fr	Sa
				1	2	3
4	5	6	7	8	9	10
11	12	13	14	15	16	17
18	19	20	21	22	23	24
25	26	27	28	29	30	31

1. Atomic Energy Commission created in U.S.

1. Fullbright grants for overseas academic exchange initiated by bill introduced by ex-Rhodes scholar Sěn. J. Wm. Fullbright.

4. Violent earthquake hits West Indies; Santo Domingo hit by tidal wave.

8. Washington: Truman approves $2.4 billion bill for GI leave pay.

8. Two B-17 bombers fly Hawaii to California without crew, controlled entirely by radio.

9. Algeria: Nationalist leader Ferhat Abbas proposes autonomous republic within French Union (→ 8/5/52).

10. France bars economic reunification of Germany (→ 9/16).

10. Britain vows to intercept vessels carrying illegal Jewish immigrants to Palestine (→ 13).

12. Philadelphia: Bread supply exhausted as A.F.L. strike halts bakery production (→ 9/5).

14. Wisconsin: Joe McCarthy defeats Robert La Follette for Senate seat.

16. Calcutta: Moslems, Hindus riot; 90 dead, 900 hurt (→ 18).

18. India: Death toll up to 1,000 in Calcutta riots (→ 24).

19. Yugoslavia: U.S. plane forced down near Trieste (→ 22).

21. U.S. charges U.S.S.R. proposal to share control of Dardanelles ignores U.N.

22. Yugoslavia: Tito meets U.S. demands, frees fliers, forbids firing on aircraft (→ 6/28/48).

24. U.S.S.R. accuses Greece, beset by Communist revolt, of inciting war in Balkans (→ 30).

25. Tunisia: Banned Congress of Destour demands independence from France (→ 8/5/47).

27. Pilot-ejector seat tested successfully at Wright Field.

28. U.S. to veto applications to U.N. from Soviet protege states Albania and Outer Mongolia.

29. New York: U.N. Security Council admits Sweden, Afghanistan, Iceland to U.N.

30. Greece: 21 slain in pre-election riots (→ 9/1).

Mao orders all-out war

Mao: Theorist and revolutionary.

Aug 19. Mao Tse-tung has ordered a showdown with Chiang Kai-shek. The Communist leader declared all-out war on the Generalissimo in a national radio broadcast.

Mao has more than a million soldiers in uniform and control over two million guerrillas. The Communists hope to mobilize an additional seven million fighters. Mao's order is the first full-scale declaration of war in nearly 20 years of tension and fighting. The Communists say peace talks are out of the question because of the belligerent tone of Chiang's V-J message. Chiang says peace is impossible because of the Communist siege of the city of Tatung (→ 9/14).

British confine Jewish migrants in camps

Aug 13. The Mediterranean port of Haifa ran cold with blood today when the British launched "Operation Igloo," their name for the deportation to Cyprus of illegal immigrants to Palestine.

As an angry crown surged down Mount Carmel in violation of the curfew and tried to break into the barb-wired port area, British soldiers opened fire. An 18-year-old girl was killed instantly and two of the wounded died hours later.

After being transferred from the "floating slums" that brought them from Europe, the immigrants began their trip to the Cyprus deportation camps by defiantly singing the Jewish anthem, "Hatikva" (→ 9/9).

Jewish refugees in Cyprus.

Life ends for H.G. Wells, prolific author

Wells: Science fiction or prophecy?

Aug 13. Death has come to British author H.G. Wells. He was 79. Despite credentials as a politician and historian, Wells will be remembered most for his science fiction.

Wells wrote "The War of the Worlds," "The Time Machine," "The Invisible Man" and "The First Men in the Moon." He foresaw rockets and the atomic bomb. In 1901 he wrote, "A day will come when beings who are now latent in our thoughts and hidden in our loins shall stand upon this earth as one stands upon a footstool, and shall laugh and reach out their hands amid the stars."

Nehru heads India's new native regime

Nehru and Gandhi, architects of a new India, in Bombay last month.

Aug 24. An ex-convict who spent ten years in prison has been appointed head of India's interim government. Pandit Jawaharlal Nehru, who was imprisoned nine times for non-violent resistance to British rule, was picked as Vice President of India's Executive Council by Lord Wavell, British Viceroy of India.

The council's twelve seats will include Hindu, Moslem, Sikh, Parsi and Christian representatives who will act as a sovereign government, excepting that the viceroy shall have a veto. The independent Indian Congress, of which Nehru was President four times since it declared its goal of independence from Britain in 1929, has approved all seats on the council.

The Moslem League, however, has refused the five seats allotted to it. Mohammed Ali Jinnah, President of the league, is fearful of the large Hindu majority and has staunchly insisted on dividing India into two countries, Moslem and Hindu. Mahatma Gandhi, the long-time leader of the non-violent resistance movement, maintains that this would shatter India's strength as a nation.

Earlier this month, renewed clashes between Hindus and Moslems led to the worst rioting in Calcutta's history.

One of the main goals of the interim government is to convene a constitutional assembly. It may meet soon, possibly as early as next month. Many observers fear, however, that to draft a constitution without Moslem participation would plunge the country into civil war (→ 11/27).

Einstein deplores use of atom bomb

Aug 18. In an interview with a British journal today, Albert Einstein stated regrets over use of the atom bomb. "A great majority of scientists," he said, "were opposed to the sudden employment of the bomb (on Hiroshima)." Einstein did not think Roosevelt would have used it, as he often counseled the President in nuclear matters. In March 1945, he sent him a memo urging the bomb not be used on Japan. For reasons unknown, Roosevelt never got that note (→ 10/29).

1946

SEPTEMBER

Su	Mo	Tu	We	Th	Fr	Sa
1	2	3	4	5	6	7
8	9	10	11	12	13	14
15	16	17	18	19	20	21
22	23	24	25	26	27	28
29	30					

1. Athens: Greek King regains throne in landslide plebiscite (→ 27).

5. Worst maritime strike in U.S. history freezes shipping on all coasts (→ 12).

7. U.S. Navy announces plan to build world's first atomic submarines (→ 10/29).

8. Sofia: Bulgarians reject rule of nine-year-old King Simeon in referendum (→ 9/23/47).

9. Arabs and Jews boycott London conference on Palestine (→ 10/4).

10. Paris: Fontainbleau Vietnam talks end in failure (→ 12/15).

14. China: Communists resume struggle against Chiang (→ 10/11).

15. Federal Security Agency reports annual U.S. divorces have risen 25% to 502,000.

16. U.S.: A.F.L. and C.I.O. men clash at piers over maritime strike settlement (→ 11/15).

16. Paris: Molotov rebukes U.S., insisting Polish border has not yet been fixed (→ 10/20).

18. Washington: Truman silences Sec. Wallace for criticizing U.S. anti-Communism (→ 22).

19. Paris: U.S. drops demand for full payment by war foes (→ 2/10/47).

20. N.Y.: Rock slides into Niagara Gorge; American Falls now a horseshoe.

21. Illinois: A&P food chain convicted of monopoly acts.

22. Belgian collaborator Leon Degrelle found hiding in Spain.

24. New Yorkers reported eating horse meat as prices soar (→ 27).

24. N.Y.: U.N. Security Council refuses Soviet request that U.S. and U.K. report on military bases in China, Greece and other occupied countries.

25. N.Y.: Soviet at U.N. rejects proposals for European economic unity (→ 2/21/47).

26. U.S. Navy discloses training of 140 Russians in 1944 as pary of lend-lease deal.

30. Nuremburg: Intl. tribunal to charge alleged Nazi war criminals in groups (→ 10/1).

Henry Wallace out; Harriman is in

Sept 22. In a major Cabinet change, President Truman has appointed Ambassador W. Averell Harriman as Secretary of Commerce, replacing Henry A. Wallace, who resigned at the president's request. Wallace, who once served as Vice President in the Roosevelt administration, had voiced strong differences over the Truman administration's foreign policy.

Speaking through an associate, Wallace said: "I am sure that this appointment will be received with the greatest enthusiasm by the business community." Harriman, 54, a wealthy New Yorker, has been serving as Ambassador to Great Britain. He was Ambassador to the Soviet Union during the last period of the recent war and he was a key adviser at conferences of the Allied leaders (→ 5/17/48).

Wallace, dissenter in the Cold War.

Prices lead people to eat horse meat

Sept 27. New Yorkers are eating horse flesh in increasing amounts, it was learned yesterday as supplies of standard meats stayed at a record low, black marketing spread and poultry prices soared to $1 a pound. Ceiling prices on choice cuts of horse meat are 17 and 21 cents a pound. Former Mayor LaGuardia has called the eating of horses a sign of degeneration, while Health Commissioner Weinstein says horse meat is "as nutritious and as good as any other meat" (→ 10/14).

Worst port strike hits the United States

Strikers picket Port of New York.

Sept 12. The most disastrous port strike in American history may be nearing an end, with announcement by the White House of a new plan allowing the Maritime Commission to pay wage scales set by private shipowners. The strike, affecting more than 200,000 maritime workers and some 3,000 vessels, began a week ago, freezing shipping on all U.S. coasts and tying up railroad delivery of crucial supplies to all the nation's ports. The Maritime Commission called on all those involved in the strike to provide workable refrigeration machinery on the ships so as to "prevent spoilage of thousands of tons of perishable food" (→ 16).

France holds first Cannes Film Festival

Sept 20. Film producers, directors, actors and critics gathered today on the French Riviera to attend showings of films at the first Cannes Film Festival. In the Grand Hotel gardens of the resort city, five orchestras entertained the guests. "Pastoral Symphony," "The Battle of Rail" (David Lean) and "The Lost Weekend" (Billy Wilder) are competing for the top prize, called the Golden Palm.

Finally open after Hitler so tactlessly ruined its 1939 debut by invading Poland.

Monarch returns; Greeks start fight

Sept 27. King George II has returned to his throne after six years of exile only to find the northern areas of his country embroiled in violence, as leftists continue to demonstrate their opposition to the king's return to power. It's been only three weeks since the Greek electorate voted for monarchical rule. The balloting has been challenged by those who desire a republican form of government. Yet investigations found no election fraud.

Reports from the northern frontier indicate leftists are battling government armies. The opposition seems to have strengthened since the election; many predicted the king's return would spark violence.

The British Communist Party, in support of the leftists, issued a statement which describes left-wing sentiment: "We condemn the disgraceful events, which since the liberation (from Germany), have saddled the Greek people with a government of royalist reaction" (→ 3/22/47).

Negroes are warned about communism

Sept 15. William Green, President of the American Federation of Labor, cautioned American Negroes not to fall into the deceitful hands of the Communist Party, which would use them as the "cat's-paws" of a Red revolution.

In a speech before the Sleeping Car Porter's Union, Green said the Communists were not concerned with the welfare of the Negro but only "regard Negroes as candidates for front line positions."

Green demonstrated his continued support for the passage of the anti-poll tax bill and the restoration of the Fair Employment Practice Committee. He also asserted that Communists publicly advocated these planks to kill the legislation. "By placing themselves in the forefront of the sponsors of these measures, they knew they were helping to defeat them."

The speech comes on the heels of a landmark Supreme Court decision ruling that buses must seat customers regardless of race on vehicles in interstate commerce (→ 10/29/47).

1946

OCTOBER

Su	Mo	Tu	We	Th	Fr	Sa
		1	2	3	4	5
6	7	8	9	10	11	12
13	14	15	16	17	18	19
20	21	22	23	24	25	26
29	28	29	30	31		

1. Undersec. of State Dean Acheson announces U.S. will stay in Korea until country is free and unified (→ 4/22/47).

1. Ohio: U.S. Navy plane sets record, landing in Columbus 11,236 miles from Australia.

1. Nuremburg: 9 Nazi leaders sentenced to be hanged (→ 16).

4. Truman urges Attlee to open Palestine to Jewish refugees, supports Palestine state (→ 17).

11. China: Chiang takes Kalgan, Mao base in North (→ 11/4).

13. Paris: France approves new constitution (→ 1/16/47).

14. Truman says he will cancel meat price controls (→ 15).

15. St. Louis: Cardinals win World Series in seventh game over Boston Red Sox.

16. U.S.: OPA removes margarine from price control (→ 23).

17. Saudi Arabia: King Ibn Saud charges Truman broke promise to Arabs by calling for open doors in Palestine (→ 1/2/47).

19. Washington reports lend-lease bill now $51 billion.

19. Stuttgart: Three U.S. administration buildings bombed in first organized underground aggression since war.

20. Berlin: Soviet policeman kills American for photographing elections (→ 12/2).

23. OPA frees all foods and beverages still under price controls except sugar (→ 11/9).

23. N.Y.: Truman opens U.N. General Assembly in Flushing, asks end to war fears (→ 11/14).

24. British P.M. Attlee condemns world Communism at Trades Union Congress (→ 28).

28. Soviet Kiselev says U.S. and U.K. violate U.N. Charter by keeping troops in non-enemy lands (→ 6/19/47).

29. Moscow: Stalin denies having A-bomb secrets (→ 11/28).

31. Santiago: Chilean Pres. Videla upholds pledge, giving three Communists Cabinet seats.

DEATH

12. Gen. Joseph Stilwell, hero of Burma campaign (*3/19/1883).

Nuremberg: Nine Nazi war criminals are hanged

Oct 16. One by one, the architects of Nazi policy were hanged today in a prison in Nuremberg, Germany. They had all been found guilty of war crimes.

One convicted Nazi escaped the hangman's noose. Hermann Goering, Hitler's number two man, swallowed cyanide in his cell hours before he was to be hanged.

Those executed for war crimes were Joachim von Ribbentrop, Wilhelm Keitel, Julius Streicher, Ernst Kaltenbrunner, Alfred Rosenberg, Hans Frank, Fritz Sauckel, Alfred Jodl and Arthur Seyss-Inquart. None stumbled as they walked to the gallows. Some were defiant; a few begged forgiveness. Streicher shouted "Heil Hitler" as the noose tightened around his neck.

Goering was found twitching in his cell last night, just moments after he swallowed the cyanide out of view of his guard. It is not clear how the poison made its way to his cell. The Nuremberg tribunal reserved its harshest criticism for him when it found the Nazis guilty of war crimes two weeks ago. The court called Goering a "leading war aggressor and a creator of the oppressive program against the Jews. His guilt is unique in its enormity," the court concluded (→ 2/24/47).

Hitler's henchmen await judgment at Nuremberg. Front row: Hermann Goering, Rudolf Hess, Joachim von Ribbentrop, Wilhelm Keitel, Ernst Kaltenbrunner, Alfred Rosenberg, Hans Frank, Wilhelm Frick, Julius Streicher, Walther Funk, Hjalmar Schact and Karl Doenitz. Back row: Erich Raeder, Baldur von Shirach, Fritz Sauckel, Alfred Jodl, Franz von Papen, Arthur Seyss-Inquart, Albert Speer, Konstantin von Neurath and Hans Fritzshe.

American air crash, worst yet, kills 39

Oct 3. A tragic airline accident took the lives of 39 men, women and children today. Aeronautics experts speculate "mechanical failure" caused the Berlin-bound American Overseas Airlines plane, the Erie, to nose-dive into a hill in the wilds of Newfoundland, near the town of Stephenville. Crew members of another plane, flying over the site of the wreckage, spotted the remains of the crashed craft. The pilot said the downed airliner had been ripped apart so badly that the fragments of metal didn't "even resemble" the parts of a plane.

This crash, the worst commercial air disaster in history, killed all the crew and passengers, who were American employees, or family of employees, of the U.S. War Department offices in Germany.

Americans facing severe meat crisis

Oct 15. The federal government held out hope today for an easing of the severe meat shortage that has plagued Americans for some time. Acting upon orders of President Truman, the Office of Price Administration has decontrolled meat and ended the slaughtering program which fixed monthly production quotas for individual slaughterers.

The decontrol order, which the president had called "the only remedy," was hailed by spokesmen for the livestock industry. They predicted that farmers would provide increased shipments promptly. But it is likely to be some weeks before sufficient quantities of meat reach the stores. Packers say fresh pork will probably be the first meat to become available, with fresh beef next in line.

Smoking is said to cause cancer risk

Oct 2. At a medical symposium at the University of Buffalo, scientists discussed the possibilty that cigarette smoking may be hazardous to your health. In fact, they think smoking causes lung cancer.

Men are afflicted with lung cancer six times more often than women. According to Dr. William Rienkoff, "It will be interesting, now that women are smoking, to see if the much higher ratio of the malignancy of the lung in men is decreased by an increase in the incidence in women." He believes more women will indeed get pulmonary carcinoma (lung cancer).

The doctors warn that the risk of causing phobias about cancer is less an evil than reacting with "indifference and inertia" to the possible link between smoking and cancer.

Oct 19. The repeal of order L85 legalizes long skirts, sounding the death knell for wartime austerity and a return of prosperity for fabric and clothes merchants.

1946

NOVEMBER

Su	Mo	Tu	We	Th	Fr	Sa
					1	2
3	4	5	6	7	8	9
10	11	12	13	14	15	16
17	18	19	20	21	22	23
24	25	26	27	28	29	30

3. Tokyo: Hirohito promulgates new constitution, renouncing rearmament (→ 5/2/47).

4. N.Y.: Crowds hail return of Natl. Horse show at Madison Sq. Garden, first since 1941.

4. Nanking: U.S. and China sign treaty of friendship, commerce and navigation (→ 1/29/47).

5. U.S.: Republicans regain control of Congress (→ 11).

9. California: Largest Navy plane, with capacity for 168, gets successful test flight.

11. Truman calls for "wisdom and restraint" in divided govt.

12. Holland, Indonesian nationalists sign truce (→ 7/22/47).

14. N.Y.: Six small nations say veto power makes U.N. impotent (→ 12/14).

15. John L. Lewis calls coal strike, challenges govt. to prosecute him for striking seized facilities (→ 21).

17. Thailand admitted to U.N. after ceding annexed territory back to Laos and Cambodia.

21. U.S.: 400,000 miners strike, reducing output 10% already; Justice Dept. seeking contempt citation for Lewis (→ 27).

21. Florida: Truman rides in captured German sub on naval maneuvers off Key West.

23. Vietnam: French shell Haiphong in North, killing 6,000 (→ 12/15).

25. Washington: Supreme Court grants Oregon Indians land payment right from U.S. govt.

27. Washington: Federal District Court calls Lewis strike action anarchy (→ 29).

27. London announces parley on India; Moslems accept, Hindus decline (→ 30).

28. N.Y.: Molotov agrees to intl. inspection as way to measure disarmament (→ 12/14).

29. Washington: Lewis, U.M.W. indicted for contempt (→ 12/4).

30. Philadelphia: Army edges Navy 21-18 in football.

DEATH

18. Jimmy Walker, ex-mayor of New York (*6/19/1881).

Attlee reassures Indian Moslem leader

Call for a Moslem state in London.

Nov 30. Mohammed Ali Jinnah, President of the Moslem League, "smelled a rat" when he was invited to the round table conference on India's future in London, and only British Prime Minister Attlee's personal plea convinced him to come. Pandit Jawaharlal Nehru also at first refused to attend, but then after receiving a dispatch from Attlee, he also accepted. Jinnah had become convinced that the British had secretly struck a deal with Nehru, who is Vice President of the Indian Executive Council. Only when he was shown the text of the dispatches did Jinnah change his mind. The discussions, which begin Monday, will also include Lord Wavell, British Viceroy of India (→ 2/20/47).

Joseph Stella, artist of tomorrow, dead

Nov 5. Joseph Stella, who painted a biography of New York City, died today. Born in Southern Italy in 1877, Stella came to the United States as a child. His painting "Coney Island, Battle of the Lights, Mardi Gras" (1914) was as volatile and extensive as its title suggests. A few years ago Yale University acquired his renowned "Brooklyn Bridge" (1920). On his canvas the bridge glows with a futuristic light, a transparent, Cubist structure.

Stella's "Brooklyn Bridge."

Controls reduced on wages and prices

Nov 9. President Truman tonight ended all wage, price and salary controls except ceilings on rents, sugar and rice, thus cutting the nation's economy loose from the shaky moorings of a four-year-old stabilization program.

"In short," he said, "the law of supply and demand operating in the marketplace will, from now on, serve the people better than would continued regulation of prices by the government."

The president said that the price control system had lost popular support, primarily because of the faulty control law passed by the Congress. While conceding that some prices would rise sharply, he predicted that buyer resistance to excessive costs would eventually reduce such charges.

Myrna Loy comforts returning soldier Frederick March in "The Best Years of Our Lives."

1946

DECEMBER

Su	Mo	Tu	We	Th	Fr	Sa
1	2	3	4	5	6	7
8	9	10	11	12	13	14
15	16	17	18	19	20	21
22	23	24	25	26	27	28
29	30	31				

2. U.S., Britain merge German occupation zones (→ 2/28/47).

4. Washington: Court fines Lewis $10,000, U.M.W. $3.5 million for contempt (→ 7).

10. Iran civil war erupts as four units enter Azerbaijan.

11. U.N. breaks with Spain after asking Spanish to overthrow Franco in March (→ 7/6/47).

14. U.N. votes 46-7 to take $8.5 mil. Rockefeller site in New York (→ 3/25/47).

14. U.N. adopts disarmament resolution prohibiting A-bomb (→ 1/4/47).

15. N.Y.: Chicago Bears beat Giants 24-14 for football title.

15. Hanoi: Ho sends note to new French Pres. Leon Blum, asking for peace talks (→ 20).

20. Hanoi: Viet Minh and French forces fight fiercely in Annamite section of city (→ 28).

21. Quake and Tidal wave strike Japan; 1,000 feared dead.

25. Nanking: Chiang offers new Chinese constitution, pledging universal suffrage (→ 1/29/47).

27. Melbourne: U.S. team of Jack Kramer and Ted Schroeder regain Davis Cup.

31. Truman formally ends World War II.

DEATH

25. W.C. Fields, American comedian (*1/29/1879).

CULTURAL EVENTS, 1946

Literature: Camus' "The Outsider"; Robert Penn Warren's "All the King's Men"; William Carlos Williams' "Paterson"; O'Neill's "The Iceman Cometh"; Nobel to Hermann Hesse; John Hersey's "Hiroshima."

Academia: R.G. Collingwood's "The Idea of History."

Music: Benjamin Britten's opera "The Rape of Lucretia"; Irving Berlin's "Annie Get Your Gun"; "How Are Things in Glocca-morra?"; "Zip-a-dee-doo-dah."

Film: William Wyler's "The Best Years of Our Lives"; Cocteau's "The Beauty and the Beast"; David Lean's "Great Expectations."

Vietnam uprising sparks war with French

American-made, French-supplied rifles help peasants fight raiders.

Dec 28. The French government proclaimed martial law in Vietnam tonight. Full-scale war seems to be inevitable.

French trucks equipped with loudspeakers are patrolling the streets of Hanoi, demanding that residents lay down their arms. The French warn they will shoot civilians carrying weapons, search houses not displaying a white flag and attack any house that fires at French troops or civilians.

Tension between France and Vietnam increased dramatically last week when Hanoi was bombed from the air. French garrisons outside the city were also attacked.

Ho Chi Minh, President of the Vietnamese Democratic Republic, and other officials fled after the attack, which killed French Commissioner Roger Sainteney.

Ho ordered all his people to arm themselves. "If you don't have a sword," he said, "arm yourselves with axes and sticks."

Despite the outbreak of violence, the government of Leon Blum characterizes the situation in Vietnam as "not alarming but serious." Publicly, Blum is standing by his commitment to an independent Vietnam. But he is also believed to be sending more troops to the French colony.

Major General Jacques-Philippe Leclerc arrived back in Vietnam today, ostensibly on a fact-finding mission. He is expected to buttress French defenses (→ 1/9/47).

Ford has resumed postwar passager car production in style.

W.C. Fields, irritable but hilarious, died at 66 on Christmas.

Most popular book: Spock's baby care

Bringing up baby was often brought up in literary circles this year. Dr. Benjamin Spock's revolutionary book "Baby and Child Care" reverses many of the traditional "do's and don'ts." Spock is a pediatrician and psychologist.

Hermann Hesse, German novelist, also applies psychology in his work but to different ends. He received the Nobel Prize in literature for dark, Jungian-influenced novels such as "Siddhartha" (1922) and "Steppenwolf" (1927). Robert Penn Warren's "All the King's Men" was an incisive portrait of a politician modeled on Huey Long.

In theater, Eugene O'Neill saw the production of "The Iceman Cometh," his first play in 12 years.

Nobel Prize winner Hermann Hesse.

Court curbs Lewis; he calls off strike

Dec 7. President of the United Mine Workers John L. Lewis capitulated to the Supreme Court and to the economic needs of the country by ordering all striking miners back to work. His statement came after the court agreed to hear appeal of the contempt of court case which has fined the union $3.5 million for failing to report to work. Lewis agreed to order strikers back to the job temporarily to allow the court to be "free from public pressure superinduced by hysteria of an economic crisis." Last month, a Federal District Court called the strike "anarchy," indicted Lewis for contempt and three days ago fined him $10,000. Now, it's up to the Supreme Court (→ 3/6/47).

Xerography: What is it? ask Carlson

Chester Carlson with his first model.

Every word on this page could be reproduced in a few minutes. A new device utilizing "xerography" (from the Greek for "dry writing") is capable of this miracle. And Chester F. Carlson is the miracle worker.

In 1938, Carlson was a former Bell Laboratories employee. He felt mimeographs were too slow and cumbersome for copying, photography too expensive. On October 22, in Astoria, Queens, New York, he tried an experiment.

He inked the date and place on a piece of glass. Then he electrostatically charged a chemically treated metal plate. He aimed light on the glass and plate, sprayed the plate with dye and pressed a piece of paper to the metal. When the sheet was pried off, the landmark date and place were clearly visible.

Carlson had trouble finding a backer for his electrostatic printing process. The Army Signal Corps and IBM were not interested. This year, the Haloid Company in Rochester, N.Y., invested in it. Carlson's patent will deter copy cats.

1947

JANUARY

Su	Mo	Tu	We	Th	Fr	Sa
			1	2	3	4
5	6	7	8	9	10	11
12	13	14	15	16	17	18
19	20	21	22	23	24	25
26	27	28	29	30	31	

1. Pasadena: Illinois trounces U.C.L.A. 45-14 in Rose Bowl.

1. French troops suppress rebellion in Cambodia.

2. Palestine: British attacked by guerrillas in five cities (→ 12).

3. Washington: Truman watches Congress on TV in first broadcast of session.

4. Baruch A-bomb delegation to U.N. resigns, saying work is completed (→ 2/3).

5. British nationalize coal mines (→ 13).

7. Truman names George Marshall U.S. Sec. of State as James Byrnes resigns due to ill health (→ 21).

9. Vietnam: French Gen. Leclerc breaks off talks with Ho Chi Minh (→ 19).

10. California: Stanford Univ. reports isolation of polio virus.

12. Palestine: Zionist Irgun blows up Haifa police station, ending truce (→ 31).

13. London: British troops replace striking truck drivers to save transportation (→ 23).

15. New York: James Cagney opens in "13 Rue Madeleine."

16. Paris: Vincent Auriol elected first president of Fourth Republic (→ 10/27).

19. Vietnam: French open drive on Hue, Annam capital (→ 3/5).

23. Britain considering taking displaced persons from refugee camps to allay labor shortage (→ 6/1).

27. Pittsburgh: U.S. Steel demands open shop for 1947 wage contract (→ 3/6).

29. Arthur Miller's play "All My Sons" makes U.S. debut.

30. Truman appeals to all Americans to enlist in March of Dimes charity drive.

DEATHS

3. Ogden Mills Reid, editor of New York Herald Tribune (*5/16/1882).

20. Andrew J. Volstead, father of U.S. dry law (*10/31/1860).

25. Al Capone, Chicago gangster, of apoplexy (*1/17/1899).

George Marshall named Secretary of State

General Marshall joins the Cabinet.

Jan 21. General George C. Marshall became Secretary of State today, promising that he would never seek political office. He succeeds James F. Byrnes, who resigned earlier this month on the advice of his doctors. General Marshall formerly was the Army chief of staff and chief planner of the defeat of Germany and Japan in the recent war. He now faces the task of helping to draft peace treaties. Asked whether he regarded his new job as more difficult than his military post, he replied: "Military affairs were my business, and now I am learning a new business."

Bonnard, poet with a paint brush, is gone

Jan 23. French painter Pierre Bonnard is dead at age 80. With Maurice Denis, Paul Serusier and Edouard Vuillard, Bonnard formed the group called Nabis (Hebrew for prophets), which helped to establish a new modern style of decoration that was important for the emergence of Art Nouveau in the 1920's. The influence of Japanese prints was strong on this "very Japanese Nabi." Bonnard's stylistic evolution offers a transition from Impressionism to a coloristic, abstract art.

Pierre Bonnard's "Almond Tree in Bloom." Oil on canvas (1947).

British dependents leaving Palestine

Jan 31. In the most drastic and dramatic step yet taken to combat what it terms terrorism, the British High Commissioner of Palestine has ordered an evacuation of all British women and children, 2,000 in all. Thought to be a prelude to statutory martial law, the order follows a short-lived truce which in effect muzzled the British army. The truce was shattered two weeks ago by the Irgun, which bombed a Haifa police station. About 5,000 U.S. citizens live in Palestine, but they are not considered in danger as violence has been directed against British military and government officials (→ 2/2).

Crash kills Prince and American star

Jan 26. Grace Moore, 45-year-old American opera singer and film star; Prince Gustaf Adolf, eldest son of the Crown Prince of Sweden; and 20 other persons were killed when a Dakota plane of the KLM Dutch Airline nose-dived to the ground at the airport in Copenhagen, Denmark, two minutes after takeoff, and immediately was enveloped in flames. There were no survivors. Moore, who combined opera with film since 1930, starred in "One Night of Love," which opened Hollywood's eyes to the possibilities of musical films of high standards.

America gives up China peace effort

Jan 29. The United States will abandon its peace mediations between the Chinese Nationalists and Chinese Communists as the civil war in that nation heats to a dangerous level. Most of the 12,000 American troops will be withdrawn and U.S. connection with the Committee of Three will end. The decision underscores the failure of Secretary of State Marshall's mediation attempts. Washington, however, insists it still intends to promote Chinese unity, saying, "We are hopeful but not particularly optimistic about the situation" (→ 2/2).

1947

FEBRUARY

Su	Mo	Tu	We	Th	Fr	Sa
						1
2	3	4	5	6	7	8
9	10	11	12	13	14	15
16	17	18	19	20	21	22
23	24	25	26	27	28	

1. Rome: Alcide de Gasperi forms coalition Cabinet, including Communists (→ 5/30).

2. Palestine: Jewish Agency refuses to aid British in tracking down terrorists (→ 8).

2. China: Nanking Nationalists launch drive on Communists in Shantung area (→ 15).

4. Washington: Truman greets new Polish ambassador with rebuke for violating pledge to hold free elections (→ 9/3/48).

4. Washington: Thomas Lamont donates $500,000 for restoration of Canterbury Cathedral.

5. U.S.S.R. and U.K. reject terms for U.S. trusteeship over Japanese Pacific isles (→ 4/2).

8. Arab delegates to Palestine conference reject division of Holy Land (→ 3/2).

9. Berlin: Dance-hall fire kills 150 in British zone.

12. U.S. and Canada agree to continue wartime defense collaboration.

16. Bogota: 53 bodies found in crash of Colombian Avianca airliner.

17. Reports indicate famine imperils thousands in Rumania.

20. Truman asks mandatory military training in U.S.

20. Britain pledges to quit India by June 1948 (→ 22).

21. Truman urges Congress in special message to allot $350 mil. for liberated countries.→

22. New Delhi: Nehru welcomes British independence offer, invites Moslems to join (→ 3/6).

23. Frankfort: U.S., British arrest several hundred Nazi underground organizers.

23. Washington: Ike opens drive to raise $170 mil. for relief of European Jews.

24. Nuremberg: Franz von Papen sentenced to eight years in labor camp for war crimes (→ 4/6).

26. Brussels: 50,000 Belgian veterans storm Parliament.

26. Truman names Lewis W. Douglas ambassador to Britain.

28. Britain, France draft 50-year pact to curb Germany (→ 3/31).

Truman asks aid for liberated lands

Feb 21. President Truman has asked Congress to appropriate $350 million for the relief of the destitute in liberated countries abroad. The money, he said, is needed in view of the impending end of the United Nations Relief and Rehabilitation Administration. To abandon those in need, he said, would be to replace hope with despair in the hearts of the liberated peoples and undermine spiritual and economic stability in the free world. The requested funds would be in addition to the $300 million sought in the War Department budget for the relief of destitution in Germany, Austria, Japan and Korea (→ 3/12).

Baruch says Soviets have atomic secrets

Feb 3. Members of Congress listened in shock to a report that the Soviet Union has tapped American secrets about the atomic bomb. According to Bernard Baruch, chief of the U.S. delegation that applies control policy in the United Nations Atomic Energy Commission, Soviet spies may have infiltrated American atomic plants in Canada. The elder statesman called for tighter security in all areas of atomic research. The Canadians disagree. "We believe our security measures are just as good as those in the U.S.," said one Canadian official (→ 3/5).

Chiang blames U.S. for continued war

Feb 15. Chiang Kai-shek has blamed the United States for the Chinese civil war, saying that if President Truman had continued arming the Nationalists, war with the Communists could have been averted. Chiang is convinced the only way to deal with the Communists is by force. This is even more clear after these two developments: His army captured the Communist stronghold of Lini in Shantung in a bloody battle; and, in a curt manner, he refused to accept a communique from Communist General Chou En-lai (→ 3/1).

Treaties signed with Germany's ex-allies

The scene at Paris' Palace of Luxembourg last July when the parley opened.

Feb 10. Vociferous protest was heard inside the "Gallery of Peace" at the French Foreign Ministry as treaties were signed with several countries that were formerly allied with Germany. Italy may have been the unhappiest with the arrangements that were approved.

Like the other countries, Italy must pay reparations to the Western Allies. But Italy also loses its Adriatic islands and part of Croatia to Yugoslavia. Islands in the Aegean are taken over by Greece. France also gains territory at Italy's expense. Rome loses its African colonies, and is forced to recognize Trieste as an open city. The Italian army is reduced to 300,000 men.

The other one-time German allies, Bulgaria, Rumania and Hungary, joined Italy in demanding a revision of the treaty. Greece and Yugoslavia, who benefit at Italy's expense, also complained that the terms are too harsh.

It was also agreed in Paris that Finland must cede Petsamo, or Pechenga, to Russia. Hungary returns to its 1938 borders. Rumania regains Transylvania, but loses other territory to Russia. And Bulgaria receives Dobruja in return for renouncing claims in Macedonia.

The U.S. disengages itself from a divided China. Nationalist troops pay their respects to American aviators leaving from Hsin-Hsiang's airport.

1947

MARCH

Su	Mo	Tu	We	Th	Fr	Sa
						1
2	3	4	5	6	7	8
9	10	11	12	13	14	15
16	17	18	19	20	21	22
23	24	25	26	27	28	29
30	31					

1. Nanking: Chinese Premier T.V. Soong resigns (→ 19).

4. France and Britain sign alliance treaty.

5. France: Communist leader Maurice Thorez declares support for French sovereignty over Vietnam (→ 4/25).

6. U.S. Supreme Court upholds Lewis contempt conviction (→ 7).

6. London: Churchill opposes troop withdrawal from India (→ 30).

7. Washington: Lewis declares only totalitarian regime can prevent strikes (→ 4/7).

8. Palestine: Terrorists battle troops in Tel Aviv (→ 16).

9. A.F.L. accuses Peron of using army to establish dictatorship over Argentine labor (→ 9/9).

10. Moscow: Big Four meet to discuss Germany (→ 31).

10. Warsaw: Czechs and Poles sign 20-year mutual aid pact.

13. New York: "Brigadoon" a big hit at Ziegfeld.

14. Manila: U.S. signs 99-year lease on Naval bases in Philippines (→ 4/28/49).

14. Moscow announces 890,532 German POWs held in U.S.S.R.

16. Detroit: Margaret Truman makes professional radio debut, singing with Detroit Symphony.

16. Palestine: Martial law withdrawn in Tel Aviv (→ 4/22).

22. Greek govt. imposes martial law in Laconia and southern Greece (→ 4/1).

24. U.S. Congress proposes limitation of presidency to two terms.

25. Illinois: 119 trapped in Centralia mine explosion (→ 31).

28. Philadelphia: American Helicopter Society reveals flying device that can be strapped to body.

31. John L. Lewis calls strike in sympathy with miners lost in Centralia explosion; 35,000 out.

DEATH

9. Carrie Chapman Catt, American suffrage activist (*1/9/1859).

Greece, Turkey get aid

Truman asks aid against "a militant minority exploiting want and misery."

March 12. "I believe that we must assist free peoples to work out their own destinies in their own way," President Truman declared today in a new foreign policy statement.

The president requested $400 million to aid Greece and Turkey in their fight against communism. While Truman did not mention the Soviet Union by name, it is clear that he considers the Communist state an instigator of much of the unrest in the world. The aid package is designed to prevent Soviet infiltration in these two nations undergoing economic strife.

This doctrine of intervention cuts against the grain of traditional U.S. foreign policy, which advocated neutrality until provoked. Congress admiringly listened to the president deliver such lines as, "I believe it must be the policy of the United States to support free peoples who are resisting attempted subjugation by armed minorities or by outside pressures." They responded to the speech with a standing ovation and are expected to approve the plan.

Truman also intends to send military personnel to the area to help supervise the use of the money and to train the Turks and Greeks in "special skills" (→ 4/22).

Indians warmly greet Mountbatten

March 30. Lord Mountbatten, the new Viceroy of India, has arrived in New Delhi to the delight of Indian leaders who hope the former World War II hero can help quell the riots rocking India—a nation in quest of independence.

Bombay has been the site of the worst violence; 47 people were killed in recent street fighting and another 137 were wounded. The rioting was ignited as a result of Hindu-Moslem disagreement about the role Moslems are to play in the governing of India. In Calcutta, five were killed and 42 injured as police took "deterrent action." Mountbatten has called for an end to the violence (→ 6/2).

Lord and Lady Mountbatten arrive.

Big Four parley starts slowly in Moscow

March 31. Sharp disagreement between the United States and Russia threatens to doom the foreign ministers' meeting in Moscow. In a direct attack on the Soviets, the new Secretary of State, George Marshall, criticized policies that would turn Germany into "a congested slum or an economic poor house."

Foreign Ministers Molotov of Russia, Bevin of Britain and Bidault of France have joined Marshall in an attempt to prepare peace treaties with Germany and Austria.

Marshall is pushing hard for the short-term economic reunification of Germany and the eventual political unity of the country. But he claims that Russia is trying to bleed Germany dry by demanding the payment of reparations from current production. Marshall also flatly rejects Molotov's request to share the production of the industrial Ruhr with the Western Allies.

Molotov used equally sharp language in responding to Marshall. He characterized the secretary of state's assertions as "attacks" on Russia. And Molotov insisted there would be no solution to the German problem until Russian demands for reparations are satisfied.

The disagreement between Marshall and Molotov overshadowed the statements of the French foreign minister. Georges Bidault joined Russia in opposing the creation of unified economic zones in Germany. He also objected to the formation of an autonomous central government in Germany (→ 4/9).

Rockefeller donates land for U.N. center

March 25. The East River site in New York was formally turned over to the United Nations yesterday, dedicated by its donor, John D. Rockefeller Jr., to the "hope of the people of the world." In a brief, simple ceremony in a small room on the 63rd floor of the Empire State Building, John D. Rockefeller 3rd presented his father's check for $8.5 million to Trygve H. Lie, Secretary General of the U.N., for the purchase of most of the six-block river tract north of 42nd Street. Rockefeller emphasized that "the future of this country and the lives of our children and our children's children are interwoven with the success of the United Nations" (→ 1/28/49).

1947

APRIL

Su	Mo	Tu	We	Th	Fr	Sa
		1	2	3	4	5
6	7	8	9	10	11	12
13	14	15	16	17	18	19
20	21	22	23	24	25	26
27	28	29	30			

1. Athens: King George II succumbs to heart attack; brother Prince Paul crowned (→ 7/9).

2. U.N. Council votes U.S. trusteeship of Japanese Pacific isles, as U.S.S.R., Britain give in.

4. San Francisco's Henry Grady chosen first U.S. ambassador to India.

6. Frankfurt: Nazi ex-Minister of Food Herbert Backe hangs self in prison (→ 3/13/51).

7. U.S.: 300,000 walk out in first nationwide phone strike (→ 17).

9. Moscow: U.S. Sec. of State Marshall proposes revision of Polish borders (→ 24).

10. U.S.: Tornado kills 132, hurts 1,305 in Texas, Oklahoma.

11. Washington: Senate accuses Wallace of conspiring to subvert U.S. foreign policy (→ 10/20).

12. Madagascar: French put down native revolt (→ 3/31/48).

16. Milton Reynolds ends round-world flight in record 78 hours, 55 minutes.

17. U.S. Senate committee approves full revamping of Wagner Act on labor relations (→ 20).

20. Pittsburgh: U.S. Steel and union set 15-cent hourly pay rise, setting industry pattern (→ 25).

20. Copenhagen: King Christian dies at 76; Frederick IX succeeds.

22. Washington: Senate, by 3-1 margin, passes anti-Communist aid to Greece, Turkey (→ 5/9).

22. Moscow: U.S.S.R. agrees to revival of joint Soviet-U.S. commission on Korea (→ 9/17).

22. Palestine: Guerrillas bomb troop train; eight dead (→ 30).

24. Moscow: Big Four end talks without accord on Germany; plan session for fall (→ 11/25).

25. Hanoi: Ho calls France to negotiating table (→ 5/20).

28. Iowa becomes 13th state to outlaw closed shop (→ 5/13).

30. N.Y.: Arabs defeated 8-1 in U.N. after long debate on Palestinian independence (→ 5/4).

BIRTH

16. Kareem Abdul-Jabbar, six-time MVP in NBA.

Chiang army takes Communist Yenan

March 19. The Chinese government forces of Chiang Kai-shek have seized Yenan, the former headquarters of the Chinese Communist Party. However, the military troops probably found an empty city, as reports indicate that the Communists were aware of the government's intentions and evacuated the entire area. It is not known where the Communist followers of Mao Tse-tung will set up quarters, but some suspect Manchuria might be the next Red capital. Government spokesmen have said the forced evacuation will demoralize the Communists. Meanwhile, more support for the Chiang regime is being generated in America (→ 9/19).

Palestine is partly under martial law

March 2. More than a third of Palestine's Jewish population found itself under martial law today, ringed by British soldiers, hemmed in by barbed wire and intimidated by machine gun posts. The action was taken to penalize Jewish leaders who refuse to help the British find the guerrillas who yesterday killed 20 persons in a series of coordinated attacks. Most prominent and deadly was the bombing of a British officers' club in Jerusalem. Total curfews have been placed on Tel Aviv and the Jewish sector of Jerusalem, whose residents will reportedly be granted a shopping period (→ 8).

Irgun weapons depot in Tel Aviv.

Gromyko criticizes U.S. atomic policy

Gromyko at the U.N.

March 5. Andrei A. Gromyko, the Soviet representative on the United Nations Security Council, threw cold water today on the U.S. plan for international atomic control, saying it would imperil national independence. In a long and often bitter speech at the United Nations headquarters at Lake Success, N.Y., Gromyko said that "only people who have lost the sense of reality" could believe that such a proposal could be accepted. The American plan, devised by Bernard M. Baruch, calls for international control of the crucial stages of atomic production, rather than each country developing its own atomic capabilities (→ 8/31).

President orders disloyalty inquiry

March 22. A new security program to weed out disloyal jobholders in federal posts was announced today by President Truman. While not singled out in the executive order, Communists and Communist sympathizers will be the first targets. Current jobholders who have not already undergone loyalty checks must be scrutinized by the Federal Bureau of Investigation. There have been many allegations in Congress that some Communists hold federal positions. Just this week, a House committee reported that nine alleged Communists have been fired from government jobs since July 1 (→ 4/11).

Ford, who put us all on wheels, dies

April 7. Henry Ford is dead at age 83 after one of the most astonishing careers in industrial history. At 40, Ford, born on a farm west of Detroit and a runaway at 16, was considered a failure by most, a daydreaming mechanic who would rather tinker with odd machines than hold a steady job. Later, he would say that we learn more from our failures than from our successes.

A few friends had enough faith in him to invest $28,000, and within a dozen years his Model T automobile, and then the Model A, were effecting profound changes in lives all over the world. Some 29 million Ford cars were sold before the war.

During the war, Ford directed production of four-motored Liberator bombers, tanks, tank destroyers and jeeps. He was the father of modern mass production methods, built on the assembly line and the conveyor belt system, which Joseph Stalin testified were the indispensable foundation of the Allied victory.

Ford, builder of a dynasty.

In 1914, his workers received an unprecedented $5 for an eight-hour day. Near the end, old and ill, he yielded his empire to his grandson Henry Ford II.

Texas City, Texas: Explosions kill 377

Thick, deadly smoke from burning nitrate darkens the air over Texas City.

April 19. Huge columns of black smoke stream into the Texas sky as a series of tremendous explosions and raging fires have taken 377 lives and injured an estimated 2,000 in and around the port town of Texas City, Texas. The catastrophe began when the French ship Grandcamp exploded after a fire ignited on board. Almost immediately, a second blast was triggered at the nearby Monsanto Chemical Corporation, and then, as if attached to a fuse, a chain of oil refineries exploded and caught fire.

The Red Cross headquarters resembles a war-zone hospital, as charred, unrecognizable bodies have been carried through its doors. Firefighters continue to battle the blazes, aware that other explosions could occur. But it appears the worst is over. Now, the grief of a community takes hold.

All of India is stirred by religious strife

April 30. Bloody, religious warfare is spreading rapidly through all the major cities of India. The fighting between Hindus and Moslems is particularly vicious in Calcutta, where five days of street battles claimed more than 100 lives. The British Viceroy, Lord Mountbatten, set up a blockade around the city in an effort to stop the fighting. Jawaharlal Nehru, head of the provisional government, has announced he will not oppose the formation of a Moslem state in Pakistan. Nehru also granted amnesty to 5,000 Moslem prisoners (→ 6/2).

The fight against colonialism hasn't unified an India torn by religious division.

Willa Cather dies; chronicler of frontier

April 7. Novelist Willa Cather is dead at 73. She wrote of the prairie and the immigrants who tamed it. Memories of her rough-and-tumble tomboyhood on the Nebraska Plains influenced her work.

Miss Cather's novel "My Antonia" (1918) told of a Bohemian girl confronting the elements to make a secure home for her family. "Death Comes for the Archbishop" (1927), a metaphysical story set in colonial New Mexico, won her the Pulitzer Prize. Miss Cather, who was also a literary critic, took fame lightly. "We all like to see people who do things," she wrote, "even if we only see their faces on a cigar-box lid."

Cather, a Midwesterner in N.Y.

First phone strike: 350,000 walk off job

April 25. Nineteen days ago, telephone workers en masse walked out of their offices in the first nationwide strike in the industry's history. Workers in all but nine of the 48 states are involved. And about 230,000 of the 350,000 strikers are women, the largest number of that sex ever to participate in a strike.

Long distance and toll calls are cut to 20 percent of the normal volume of 5,361,000 such calls daily from the Bell System's 26 million telephones.

The strike remains orderly and peaceful throughout the country as placards proclaim, "The girl with the smile is gone for a while."

Officials of the National Federation of Telephone Workers said tonight that the American Telephone and Telegraph Company had refused the offer to settle for a wage increase of $6 weekly, half of the original union demand. The New York Telephone Company, where an average operator earns $45 a week including overtime, has slammed the door on acceptance of the 15-cent per hour steel wage increase as a pattern for determining telephone wages.

The American Federation of Labor International Brotherhood of Teamsters has given a $10,000 check in support of the strike, promising a similar amount every two weeks. President Truman has so far refrained from commenting on the lengthy, crippling conflict (→ 28).

Mrs. McLean and the Hope diamond

April 26. Evalyn Walsh McLean, owner of the Hope diamond, who wore it everywhere, from Moscow to the movies, died tonight at 60. She spent her life and her fortune entertaining everybody from presidents to wounded war veterans. But her gaiety was marred by tragedy: Divorce, her ex-husband's madness, the death of two children, and innocent involvement in the Teapot Dome scandal and the Lindbergh kidnapping. Legend has it that the owner of the Hope diamond will have bad luck. Mrs. McLean sold things, but never the diamond.

Boulder Dam, rising 726 ft. above the Colorado, is now Hoover Dam, after the engineer-President who urged its construction.

1947

MAY

Su	Mo	Tu	We	Th	Fr	Sa
				1	2	3
4	5	6	7	8	9	10
11	12	13	14	15	16	17
18	19	20	21	22	23	24
25	26	27	28	29	30	31

1. Washington: Mexican Pres. Aleman tells Congress weak democracies inspire dictators.

2. Japan regains right to fly rising-sun flag (→ 11/12/48).

3. E. Guerin rides Jet Pilot to victory in Kentucky Derby.

7. N.Y.: U.N. recognizes Arab Higher Committee in emergency session, to meet recognition given to Jewish Agency (→ 18).

7. Rio de Janeiro: Brazil outlaws Communist Party.

9. Washington: House adopts $400 mil. bill to fight Communism in Near East (→ 14).

9. Washington: World Bank opens, giving France $250 mil. reconstruction loan (→ 8/7).

13. U.S. Senate passes Taft-Hartley labor bill by vote large enough to squelch veto (→ 6/5).

16. Washington: Senate and House agree on $350 mil. for Near East aid (→ 22).

18. Palestine: Irgun command releases 189 prisoners (→ 7/18).

20. Vietnam: Viet Minh execute Huyh Phu-so ("Mad Bonze") leader of religious sect Hoa Hao (→ 7/19).

22. Truman signs Near East aid bill as "step to peace" (→ 6/5).

25. Finland to experiment with Soviet system of collectivized agriculture (→ 5/24/48).

29. New York: Joan Crawford opens in "Possessed."

30. Italy: Premier Gaspari forms anti-Communist Cabinet—first since war (→ 12/27).

30. Mauri Rose wins 31st annual Indy 500, averaging 116.3 mph.

30. Coal mines nationalized in all Soviet occupation zones.

31. Morocco: Nationalist leader Abd el Krim escapes from 11-year imprisonment on Reunion Island (→ 12/21/50).

31. Budapest: Lajos Dinnyes installs pro-Soviet Cabinet, in first challenge to Truman Doctrine (→ 6/2).

DEATH

30. Baron Georg von Trapp, head of Austrian family singing group (*1880).

Zionists blast open Acre prison; free 251

Jewish prisoners watch the blast.

May 4. In a daring and unprecedented daylight attack, Zionist guerrillas blasted their way through the walls of a prison fortress in Acre, Palestine. They freed 251 prisoners, equally divided between Jews and Arabs.

The Irgun claimed responsibility for masterminding the jail break. This is the same group that blew up the King David Hotel in Jerusalem ten months ago.

About 100 attackers, many of them wearing stolen British army uniforms, began their well-planned attack shortly after 4:00 this afternoon. The Irgun commandos set off several explosions in the streets of Acre to divert attention from their assault on the prison.

The attackers, riding in jeeps, strafed the guard towers with heavy gunfire as they left sacks filled with explosives at the base of the fortress. When the walls crumbled, smoke bombs gave cover to the escaping prisoners, who had apparently been informed about the assault. Many of the inmates drove away in army trucks that had been stolen from the British authorities.

Fourteen Jews were killed in the attack, and several British soldiers were injured. A massive manhunt has started for the prisoners, most of whom are still on the loose. The jail break took place three weeks after four alleged terrorists were hanged in the prison (→ 7).

World's worst air crash: 40 killed

May 29. Marking the worst disaster in the history of commercial aviation, a huge four-engined United Airlines plane with 44 passengers and a crew of four crashed and burst into flames last night, just after it had taken off from LaGuardia Field on a scheduled non-stop flight to Cleveland. Forty were burned to death, eight others taken to hospitals.

One theory of the crash is that immediately after getting off the ground, the pilot (later one of the few survivors thrown clear of the wreck), while waiting to gain altitude, had not nested the retractable landing wheels, which may have hit a fence and then rammed a lighting pole. Violent downdraughts, common in thunderstorms such as the one raging yesterday, may have contributed with sudden wind changes. As the DC-4 went down in a muddy creek, flames shot 50 feet or more into the air, the heat prohibiting firefighters' immediate approach.

U.S. rushes grain to calm Germany

May 14. Alarmed by spreading unrest and food strikes in Western Germany, the U.S. War Department tonight announced emergency measures to rush more than 1.2 million tons of food, most of it grain, into the American and British occupation zones by July 31. Secretary of War Robert P. Patterson said most of the deliveries will come from the U.S., though some will be supplied by unidentified "other countries," presumably British Empire territories.

British leaders received this news with relief, as they are determined not to send any of their own scarce food to Germany and unable to spend any more dollars than those already contracted for.

Patterson said, "This is the first time that I know of in history in which conquerors have made an effort on any such scale to feed their defeated enemy," adding that the lack of actual starvation in Germany was due only to U.S. and British willingness to help (→ 16).

Army takes over Nicaraguan regime

May 26. General Anastasio Somoza, Nicaraguan President for more than ten years, has ended his 25-day respite from power by overthrowing his successor, President Leonardo Arguella, inaugurated May 1. Elected in February as Somoza's Liberal Party candidate, the 70-year-old Arguella was viewed as little more than a figurehead. Since then he has given signs of opposing the army dictator by demoting Somoza's son from Inspector General of the army to garrison chief. And in what was regarded as another anti-Somoza move, last week he granted autonomy to the University of Managua.

Yank who made good in London

May 8. Harry G. Selfridge, owner of one of Europe's largest department stores, has died in London at age 89. A poor messenger boy from Wisconsin, he rose to become a partner in Marshall Field's enterprises and moved to London in 1906. Three years after the first sale at his Selfridge & Co., Ltd., the English commercial world conceded that this Chicagoan in a top hat had "shown them how." Dubbed the "merchant prince of Oxford Street," he wrote a book, "The Romance of Commerce," and was even accepted into British high society, no mean feat for a man "in trade."

1947

JUNE

Su	Mo	Tu	We	Th	Fr	Sa
1	2	3	4	5	6	7
8	9	10	11	12	13	14
15	16	17	18	19	20	21
22	23	24	25	26	27	28
29	30					

1. London: Minister of Labor George Isaacs pleads for British women to work (→ 8/12).

2. U.S. halts $15 mil. credit to Hungary pending clarification of events in Budapest (→ 4).

2. New Delhi: Viceroy Mountbatten gives British plan for division of India into Moslem and Hindu states (→ 15).

4. Soviets bar U.S. from inspecting Hungarian army (→ 11).

5. Truman blasts Taft's views on labor relations as "fallacious and dangerous" (→ 23).

7. N.J.: Doctors say price for black-market baby now $2,500.

8. Madrid: Argentina's Eva Peron hailed with 21-gun salute on arrival in Spain.

9. Washington: Marshall gives support to unified Europe as condition for U.S. aid (→ 28).

10. Ottawa: Truman becomes first U.S. president to pay state visit to Canada.

11. Sec. of Agriculture Anderson ends household sugar rationing in U.S.

11. Washington declares Soviet guilty of meddling in Hungarian internal affairs (→ 21).

12. Gullane, Scotland: Mildred "Babe" Didrikson Zaharias becomes first American to win women's British Open golf title.

15. Truman orders Air Safety Board to investigate recent rash of aviation accidents.

15. New Delhi: All-India Congress accepts British plan for partition of India (→ 7/10).

19. London: Ernest Bevin warns U.S.S.R. period of appeasement is over (→ 21).

21. London: P.M. Attlee delivers sharp attack on U.S.S.R and European satellites (→ 9/18).

24. New York: Ike accepts post as Columbia University president (→ 6/7/48).

28. Paris: Britain, Soviet, French talks on Marshall Plan off to bad start; Molotov rejects European unity as basis for aid (→ 7/2).

DEATH

16. Bronislaw Hebermann, Polish violinist (*12/19/1882).

Marshall offers aid plan

June 5. The economic recovery of Europe is the goal of an ambitious aid plan unveiled by American Secretary of State George Marshall in an historic speech at Harvard University. He warns that Europe "must have substantial additional help or face economic, social and political deterioration of a very grave character."

A special committee established by Marshall concluded that a massive assistance plan would be beneficial to the United States, might prevent France from falling under the influence of the Communists and would invigorate the economies of France and Germany.

Marshall suggested that the Soviet Union would also be eligible to receive help from the new plan. But the secretary of state warned pointedly that the United States would not assist "any government which maneuvers to block the recovery of other countries."

It remains to be seen how the Russians will react to Marshall's idea. Foreign Minister Molotov is expected to discuss the proposal later this month (→ 9).

A French Communist poster against the Marshall Plan.

Maxwell Perkins, skilled editor, dies

June 17. Editor Maxwell Evarts Perkins died today. He is the coauthor of Thomas Wolfe's "Look Homeward, Angel." Although he is not credited as such, Perkins took the unwieldy manuscript and pared it expertly down to size.

Perkins was born in New York in 1884. A Harvard graduate, he first worked as a journalist at The New York Times. He applied to Charles Scribner's publishing firm in 1910 and remained there for more than 25 years. There, as editor and then Vice President, Perkins guided the careers of F. Scott Fitzgerald, John Phillips Marquand, Ernest Hemingway and other great writers of the 1920's and 30's.

Clang, clang went the last trolley

June 28. A streetcar named nostalgia clanged down a New York thoroughfare and turned the corner to oblivion. The borough of Manhattan retired its last trolley in a sentimental ceremony today. A horse-drawn car used in the 1850's was called out to accompany the streetcars on their final run. The fleet will be replaced by diesel buses.

Trolleys were essential urban links at the turn of the century. About 25,000 miles of track crisscrossed cities at the end of World War I; shops flourished along trolley lines the way cities burst into being along railroad tracks. The automobile, now in ascendancy, makes the trolley obsolete.

Bill curbing labor is passed over veto

"Mr. Republican" Robert Taft.

June 23. The controversial Taft-Hartley Labor Bill has become law as the Senate voted 68-25 to override President Truman's veto of the legislation. The law is the first in 12 years to restrain union power.

The Taft-Hartley Act will make unions liable to breach of contract damages in the wake of disputes, outlaw the closed shop, require a 60-day cooling-off period for strikes, grant the government power to enforce an 80-day injunction against strikes which threaten national health or safety, forbid political contributions from unions and force union leaders to take non-Communist oaths.

President Truman claims that the Taft-Hartley Law "contains the seeds of discord which will plague this nation" (→ 12/1).

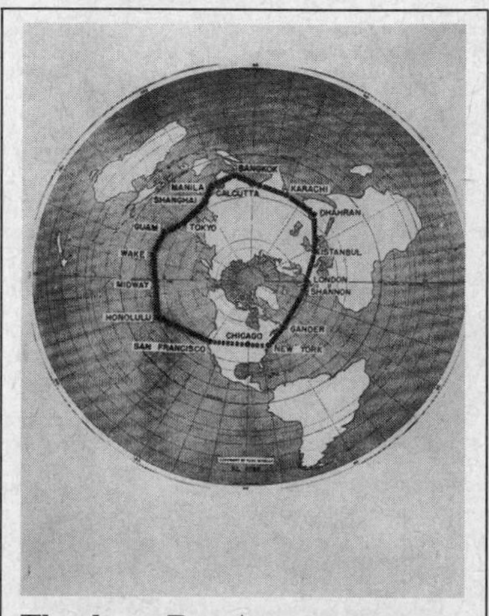

Thanks to Pan Am, you can now travel around the world thousands of feet high, seeing 17 cities in 11 countries in 13 days.

1947

JULY

Su	Mo	Tu	We	Th	Fr	Sa
		1	2	3	4	5
6	7	8	9	10	11	12
13	14	15	16	17	18	19
20	21	22	23	24	25	26
29	28	29	30	31		

2. Paris parley ends with Europe split; Molotov warns against blocs (→ 4).

4. Virginia: Truman urges end of world barriers, rejects Soviet charge that aid plan is divisive (→ 12).

6. Spain: Franco gets 80% of vote in elections (→ 10/7/48).

7. Ex-Pres. Hoover heads commission to recommend efficiency measures for executive branch.

9. Greek govt. arrests 2,800 leftists (→ 15).

11. New York: Egypt asks U.N. to end British control of Sudan (→ 8/22).

12. Paris: 16 European nations meet on Marshall Plan without participation of Communist states (→ 14).

14. Salt Lake City: Marshall urges governors' conference to help Western Europe avoid drift into Soviet sphere (→ 10/5).

15. Greek army halts drive of 2,500 guerrillas on Yanina (→ 8/16).

17. Washington: Eleanor Roosevelt accepts French military decoration for late FDR.

17. New York: Soviet informs U.N. she will not agree to Balkan borders.

17. New York: Ethiopia declines U.N. aid on grounds others need it more.

19. Hanoi: Ho Chi Minh dismisses Vo Nguyen Giap (→ 3/1/48).

19. Rangoon: Burma premier and five top aides assassinated.

20. French racer Jean Robic wins first Tour de France since war.

22. Indonesia: Dutch forces drive into eastern Java on coast of Cheribon (→ 23).

23. Indonesians burn Java cities in path of Dutch advance (→ 31).

28. New York: Girl Scouts from 22 countries pay visit to U.N.

29. Bucharest: Communist-dominated govt. dissolves Peasant Party (→ 10/7).

BIRTH

9. O.J. Simpson, American football great.

Truman calls coup in Hungary outrage

June 21. Charging that the Communist minority in Hungary forced changes in the Hungarian government with the aid of Russian army officials, President Truman today denounced the Communist coup as an "outrage" and approved a sharply worded note of protest sent to the Soviet commander in Budapest.

State department officials said the note is written in terms milder than those used by the president in his news conference. It asks the Soviets to meet their obligations to the American and British members of the Allied Control Commission, but states that the U.S. does not want to engage in recriminations.

At the same time, it implicates the Soviets in the exile and resignation of Hungarian Premier Nagy and charges the Russians with breaking the Yalta agreement. It calls on them to agree to a U.S.-Soviet-British investigation of the situation, and suggests that the U.S. might submit the case to the United Nations.

The U.S. is also suspending a $15 million credit to the Hungarian government "pending clarification of developments." The Hungarians have countercharged the U.S. with promising to aid Nagy's party in the election to create an American economic and political base in Eastern Europe. They claim that Nagy was making a show of compromise with Russia while moving slowly to the right (→ 11/3).

"Babe" Didrickson, the 1st U.S. woman to win the British Open.

British intercept Exodus

July 18. The ship which has been renamed Exodus arrived back in French waters today. On board are 4,530 Jews. They are people without a country.

The Jews, most of them refugees from Germany, left the French port of Sete last week, bound for Palestine. They changed the name of their ship from President Warfield to Exodus in the apparent hope that their crossing of the Mediterranean would be as fruitful as Moses' crossing of the Red Sea. It was not. The Jews were denied access to what they view as their Promised Land as the British refused to let them disembark at the port of Haifa. Officially, the British said, the Jews are displaced persons and illegal immigrants to the Holy Land.

The British threat to send the Jews back to Germany is being criticized in many world capitals. But no other compromise is in sight. The British government's resolve to bar the Jews from Palestine has been strengthened by the Irgun's violent attacks (→ 8/22).

The Exodus awaits its fate at Haifa.

Jinnah is appointed Governor General

Karachi greets Jinnah.

July 10. For the first time ever, Great Britain has appointed a non-white to a Governor General post in a Brittish dominion. Mohammed Ali Jinnah will become ruler of the Moslem majority of India. The news spread quickly and jubilantly through New Delhi and into every Moslem home. Jinnah, who will preside over the one million Moslems in the area, was surprised by the appointment. "I must digest the news," he said. "I've not even heard it on the radio" (→ 8/13).

Jack Kramer wins Wimbledon title

July 5. Jack Kramer, victor for the second year in a row of the United States Open tennis championship, has now won Wimbledon. He is the first American to win Wimbledon since Bobby Riggs did it in 1939, although the prestigious English tourney was discontinued from 1940-45. The women's title was taken by Margaret Osborne.

Kramer goes up for an overhead.

U.S. armed forces are unified at last

Forrestal, first Secretary of Defense.

July 26. President Truman has signed legislation that unites all branches of the armed services into one agency, the Department of Defense. And Navy Secretary James Forrestal has been approved by Congress as Secretary of Defense.

Moments later, the president flew to Missouri to visit his dying mother, Mrs. Martha Truman.

Congress had favored the new department, the aim of which is to coordinate the armed power of the nation, promote efficiency and integrate domestic, foreign and military policies.

The legislation creates another agency as well, the National Security Council, which will evaluate problems of American military power. Under its domain will be a Central Intelligence Agency to direct intelligence gathering (→ 9/17).

Indonesians resist advance of Dutch

July 31. In their determination to regain control of the republic of Indonesia, granted independence by the Japanese late in the war, the Dutch have launched a new drive into the rich tobacco and rubber region of Sumatra, the big island northwest of Java.

Knifing their way through mine fields and roadblocks, the Dutch captured the republican capital of northern Sumatra and the home of an important radio station while admittedly encountering "a certain amount of resistance."

This action follows the earlier capture by the Dutch of important sections of Java, forcing the Indonesians into a systematic scorched-earth policy as Dutch armor, aircraft and infantry began a drive on the Indonesian capital, Jakarta.

In a recent move aimed at ending the ten-day undeclared war, Australia has asked the U.N. Security Council to order both parties "to cease hostilities forthwith" and begin arbitration.

In contrast with the Australian refusal to take sides, the Indian government has accused the Dutch of having begun large-scale military action without warning at a time when the Indonesians were trying to iron out an agreement. The United States has also offered to mediate, following a Dutch proposal which suggested the idea (→ 8/1).

Dinosaurs dug up in New Mexico

July 13. Remains of the first dinosaurs inhabiting America 200 million years ago have been discovered by a team from New York's American Museum of Natural History. A quarry of complete, articulate skeletons of the reptiles was found 100 miles north of Albuquerque. Yet unnamed, the species, "the real beginning of the dinosaur," is described as small and savagely carnivorous. Probably three or four feet in length, no smaller than a chicken and no larger than a horse, they contrast sharply with their descendant, the enormous 40-ton Tyrannosaurus Rex, which roamed the earth 100 million years later.

1947

AUGUST

Su	Mo	Tu	We	Th	Fr	Sa
					1	2
3	4	5	6	7	8	9
10	11	12	13	14	15	16
17	18	19	20	21	22	23
24	25	26	27	28	29	30
31						

1. U.S. Army Air Force marks 40th anniversary (→ 10/1).

1. New York: U.N., by 8-0 vote, calls on Dutch and Indonesians to halt Java war (→ 3).

4. Austria: Soviet occupation army takes U.S. Vacuum Oil and U.K. Shell refinery as German assets.

5. Tunisia: Workers call general strike against French rule in Sfay (→ 4/18/50).

7. Washington: World Bank grants Dutch $195 mil. reconstruction loan.

11. Paraguay: Pres. Morinigo moves capital to Pilar as rebels seal off Asuncion.

12. Britain signs 20,000 refugee women from U.S. zone in Germany to help allay labor shortage in England (→ 27).

13. India: Riots sweep Lahore in Punjab; mobs stone Gandhi's house (→ 15).

16. Athens: Guerrilla leader Gen. Vafthiadis, proclaims Free Greece military govt. (→ 9/7).

17. N.Y.: U.S. women score 7-0 sweep of Wightman Cup tennis at Forest Hills.

18. New York: U.N. votes to admit Yemen and Pakistan.

20. Truman predicts U.S. govt. will end fiscal year with record surplus of $4.7 billion.

21. New York: Italy and Austria barred from U.N. by Soviet veto.

22. Jewish refugees on Exodus debark in Hamburg after refusing to enter France (→ 31).

22. Cairo: Egyptians riot against U.N (→ 4/5/48).

23. Margaret Truman makes Hollywood debut as soloist at Hollywood Bowl.

27. London imposes war curbs on food, motoring, travel (→ 7/5/48).

30. New York: 52,000 march down Fifth Avenue in American Legion parade.

31. Britain opens Harwell, her first atomic power plant (→ 9/3).

DEATHS

21. Ettore Bugatti, French car manufacturer (*9/15/1881).

Odom flies around world in 73 hours

Odom leaves Chicago.

Aug 12. American aviator William Odom has completed an encirclement of the globe in record time, 73 hours, five minutes and 11 seconds. He maintained an average cruising speed of 335 mph. The record was formerly held by Wiley Post, who made the trip in nearly 187 hours at a much slower speed.

Odom took off in Chicago, skimmed over Canada and winged through France, Egypt, India, China and Japan. His last stop was Anchorage, Alaska. Odom told reporters that on the last leg of his excursion he was falling asleep at the controls. As his lids were closing, a mountain loomed directly in his path. He shook himself awake, bypassed the mountain and sailed wide-eyed to victory.

Truce agreed on in Dutch Indies

Aug 3. Both the Dutch and the Indonesian republic announced tonight their willingness to abide by the call of the U.N. Security Council for an end to hostilities. This marked the first success by the United Nations to halt a conflict.

The question of arbitration remains to be solved. The Netherlands will accept the United States as a mediator. The Indonesians, however, desire arbitration by several nations. They have also asked the Security Council to "continuously supervise" the cease-fire and want Dutch troops withdrawn to positions held before the fighting began on July 20 (→ 1/17/48).

Britain grants independence to India and Pakistan

Aug 15. At the stroke of midnight, India won her long-awaited independence from Britain. And Moslems won a degree of freedom from Hindus. They will have their own separate dominion, Pakistan, in the British Commonwealth.

The division of India into separate states tempered the celebrations in New Delhi. Reports from the northern province of Punjab say scores of people have been killed in the past few days in fighting between Hindus and Moslems.

The real hero of India's independence was absent from New Delhi when sovereign power passed to the Indian Assembly. Mohandas Gandhi, longtime leader of the Indian National Congress, was in a modest house in Calcutta, trying to restore peace between Hindus and Moslems. Gandhi was praised by Dr. Rajendra Prasad, President of the Assembly, as "our beacon light, our guide and philosopher during the last 30 years and more."

Thousands of Indians crowded around the Council of State building as Prasad spoke. Public offices, temples and shopping centers were lit up and decorated with the new national flag, colored saffron, white and dark green.

With stiff upper lip, Lord Mountbatten declares India's independence.

At midnight, a cheer arose from the Assembly as one member blew into a conch shell, the same kind of shell used in temples to call the gods. Members of the body took an oath dedicating themselves "to the end that this ancient land attain her rightful place in the world.".

Pandit Jawaharlal Nehru, the Prime Minister of the dominion government, then informed Lord Mountbatten, who lost his title of Viceroy at midnight, that he was the newly approved Governor General of India.

Mountbatten had earlier acquired an earldom from King George, who thanked the British diplomat for his role in helping India to its independence. The king, of course, lost his title of Emperor of India.

In Pakistan, Mohammed Ali Jinnah, the Moslem leader, took his oath as Governor General of that dominion. The ceremony took place in the capital of Karachi.

The creation of two dominions on the subcontinent is viewed with considerable apprehension in some quarters. It was widely reported in Indian newspapers that astrologers had discovered an inauspicious mating of stars in the heavens. Many Hindus rely on astrology for guidance about the future.

Nehru spoke of the difficulties facing his country when he praised Gandhi before the Assembly. "The ambition of the greatest man of our generation," Nehru said, "has been to wipe every tear from every eye. That may be beyond us, but so long as there are tears and suffering, so long our work will not be over."

In Punjab tonight, there is more than tears and suffering. The province has been chopped in half and split between India and Pakistan. Moslems are fighting Hindus in the cities and in the country.

Almost all the Hindus and Sikhs who had lived in Lahore have fled from the city, but their departure has not stopped the violence. Bodies are piling up in the streets, a famous bazaar is on fire, shops are being looted and five Sikh temples are burning. Angry gun shots, not fireworks, are being fired on Pakistan's independence day (→ 9/8).

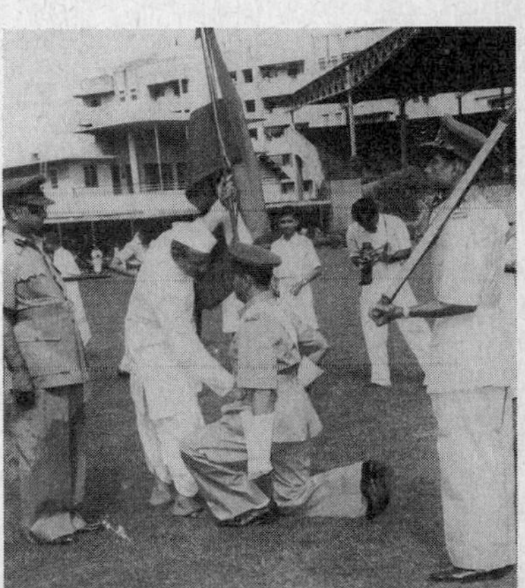

Bombay's Premier presents the flag.

U.N. proposes to partition Palestine

Aug 31. A majority of the U.N. Special Committee on Palestine has recommended termination of the British mandate and a partition of the Holy Land into two states, one Arab and the other Jewish. Jerusalem and nearby towns, including Bethlehem, would be independently administered by the United Nations. Arabs received the report with disapproval and disappointment, the Jews with pleasure and surprise. This is the first time an international body has recommended a Jewish state, the ultimate aim of Zionism. The report also provides for increased Jewish immigration into Palestine (→ 9/7).

Truman forecasts big budget surplus

Aug 21. The United States government will end the 1948 fiscal year with a surplus of $4.7 billion, according to a mid-year estimate by President Truman. This figure does not allow for expenditures of the Marshall Plan. The entire surplus will be used to reduce the national debt and as a safety deposit for emergencies here or abroad.

The extra monies were attributed to unexpected increases in national income, an equally surprising rise in prices and the continuation by Congress of the war excise tax rates. Truman criticized Congress for cutting expenditures for certain useful federal programs.

The packhorse of heavy construction: Mack's LR Off-Highway Model.

1947

SEPTEMBER

Su	Mo	Tu	We	Th	Fr	Sa
	1	2	3	4	5	6
7	8	9	10	11	12	13
14	15	16	17	18	19	20
21	22	23	24	25	26	27
28	29	30				

2. Brazil: 19 Western nations sign treaty of Rio de Janeiro on hemispheric security.

3. St. Louis: U.S. lifts ban on export of radioactive isotopes (→ 6).

5. New York: Lauren Bacall opens in "Dark Passage."

6. St. Louis: Isotope bids made by 30 nations, including U.S.S.R. (→ 11/11).

7. Athens: Greece swears in Themistocles Sophoulis as head of coalition govt. (→ 10/31).

9. Argentina grants vote to women (→ 9/24/48).

12. Pittsburgh: Eight-day steel strike ends with wage hike of 15 cents per hour.

13. N.J.: NBC votes to ban crime shows before 9:30 pm.

17. Washington: James Forrestal sworn in as first U.S. secretary of defense.

17. U.S. refers Korean independence issue to U.N. (→ 11/5).

18. New York: Soviet delegate Vishinsky tell U.N. General Assembly U.S. seeks war (→ 28).

19. Gen. Albert Wedemeyer returns from China, presents report asking five years U.S. military aid to Chiang (→ 5/20/48).

22. Douglas C-54 Skymaster makes first automatic-pilot flight over Atlantic, from London to Newfoundland.

23. Sofia: Bulgarian Agrarian Party leader Niloka Petkov hanged as traitor (→ 12/14/49).

23. N.Y.: U.N. rebukes Soviet Union, votes to consider Greece, Korea and Italy.

24. Washington: World Women's Party meets for first time since war.

28. N.Y.: U.N. asked to end Soviet control over Yugoslavia, Poland, Bulgaria, Hungary and Rumania (→ 10/5).

30. N.Y.: Canada, Argentina elected to seats on U.N. Security Council.

DEATH

20. Fiorello LaGuardia, ex-mayor of New York (*12/11/1882).

India a killing ground

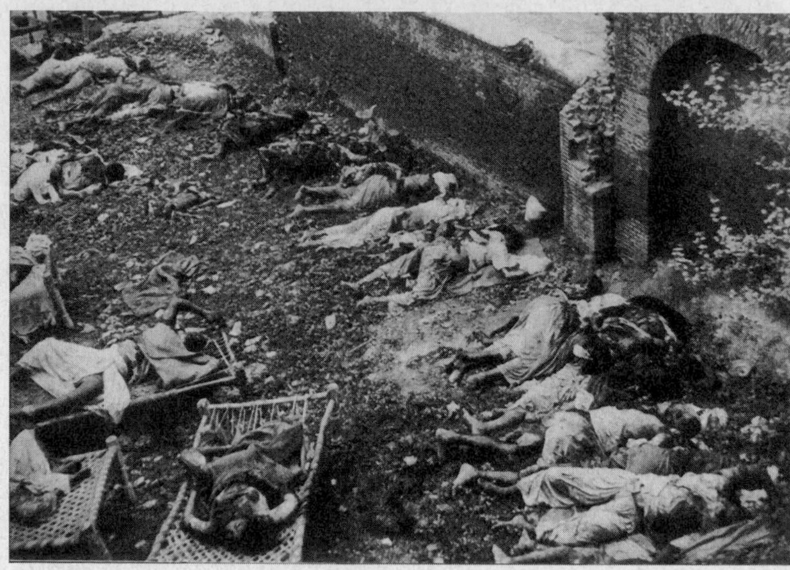

Casualties already mar the newly formed border between India and Pakistan.

Sept 8. There has been little time to celebrate independence in India and Pakistan. Large parts of the dominions are paralyzed with fear. Mobs run wild as Moslems and Hindus battle to the death and turn streets into rivers of blood.

Indian officials estimate that 150,000 people have been killed in the Punjab, which was partitioned between India and Pakistan, between Hindus and Moslems. The division has created a million refugees. Any one of them unlucky enough to be on the wrong side of the Punjab is a target for murder.

"We Hindus won't be satisfied," said one refugee, "until every Moslem has been driven out of India. They got their Pakistan, now let them go to it."

In Delhi, a curfew goes unobserved, and critics of the Indian army say they are sympathetic to the Hindu killers and looters. At least 50 Moslems were killed by Hindus and Sikhs in the New Delhi railway station. Their bodies piled up on platforms. No one was anxious to take them away (→ 10/26).

Jews from Exodus debark in Hamburg

Sept 7. The port of Hamburg was shrouded in an eerie fog at dawn as the first of the Jews from the Exodus began disembarking from a British transport ship.

Nervous German police, agitated by the delay caused by the fog, paced the docks and strained to catch a glimpse of the ship. The police were summoned by the British occupation authorities.

The Jewish passengers will be escorted to an internment camp near Lubeck.

"The brutal and inhuman treatment," Jewish leaders protested, "surpasses all the barbarism of the Middle Ages and can only be compared with the cruelties of the Hitler regime" (→ 26).

2.5m students go to college, half ex-GIs

Sept 22. More than half of the 2.5 million students matriculating this fall are war veterans, according to a new survey of 100 universities. The G.I. Bill is responsible; the government will pay $500 in tuition each year to any veteran seeking higher education. The surge in numbers puts a strain on teachers, classroom space and dormitories.

The University of California has 40,000 enrolled; half are veterans. The University of Mississippi sees a 20 percent increase in students over last year, as does the Teacher's College at the University of Cincinnati. More than 6,000 applied for 700 freshmen places at Dartmouth College. Still, the institutions will try to maintain high standards.

From the battlefield to the campus.

U.K. troops ready to leave Palestine

Sept 26. Arthur Creech Jones, British Colonial Secretary, announced to the U.N. General Assembly today that his government will end its mandate in Palestine and pull out its troops. He also warned that Britain would not impose by force of arms a settlement not acceptable to Jews and Arabs. The declaration was exactly what the Jews and Arabs want, but their distrust of Britain is so deep they suspect a trick. They think that Britain either hopes to trap them into a British solution, or hopes to lure the U.S. into sharing the administration of Palestine (→ 10/2).

1947

OCTOBER

Su	Mo	Tu	We	Th	Fr	Sa
			1	2	3	4
5	6	7	8	9	10	11
12	13	14	15	16	17	18
19	20	21	22	23	24	25
26	27	28	29	30	31	

1. U.S. Air Force becomes independent of Army.

2. N.Y.: Jewish Agency for Palestine accepts proposed partition of Holy Land at U.N. (→ 11).

5. Warsaw: Communists of nine nations form Comintern to fight U.S. "imperialist hegemony" (→ 11/18).

6. N.Y.: Yankees beat Brooklyn Dodgers 5-2 to capture World Series in final game.

7. Bucharest: Rumanian peasants strike over currency reform, cutting city supplies (→ 11/11).

11. N.Y.: U.S. proclaims support for Palestine partition (→ 13).

13. N.Y.: U.S.S.R. endorses partition of Palestine (→ 13).

13. Jerusalem: Bomb blasts U.S. Consulate (→ 11/29).

17. San Francisco: William Green elected pres. of A.F.L.

17. N.Y.: U.S. asks U.N.-supervised Korean elections (→ 11/5).

20. Washington: House Un-American Activities Committee opens inquiry into alleged radicalism in film industry (→ 23).

21. Brazil and Chile break relations with Moscow over attacks published in Pravda.

23. Screen stars Reagan, Cooper, Montgomery insist Reds do not control Actors' Guild.→

25. Truman proclaims Maine disaster area, grants federal aid after fire brings $30 mil. losses.

26. India: Kashmir, second biggest state in open revolt as Moslems, Hindus fight (→ 11/20).

27. Paris: De Gaulle calls for dissolution of Assembly, new constitution (→ 11/14).

29. Washington: Civil rights committee asks nationwide monitoring body (→ 1/12/48).

29. Brussels: Belgium, Holland, Luxembourg form customs union (Benelux).

31. Greek govt. announces drastic tax hike (→ 1/1/48).

DEATHS

4. Max Planck, German physicist, 1918 Nobel (*4/23/1858).

13. Sidney Webb, British social reformer (*7/13/1859).

House panel claims 79 subversives in films

Oct 23. Actor Ronald Reagan, President of the Screen Actors Guild, testified before the House Committee on Un-American Activities today and said that the guild is not controlled by leftists.

Yesterday, in its third day of hearings on communism in the film industry, HUAC declared it would present "at least 79" subversives in the coming days. Actor Robert Taylor testified against other stars. His deposition was not as damning as the panel may have hoped; he failed to specifically name any card-carrying Communist infiltrator.

Taylor's arrival at the session was greeted with appraising gasps by women spectators. He took a seat before a microphone and swiftly stated, "I personally believe the Communist Party should be outlawed. If I had my way they'd all be sent back to Russia."

Hollywood stars arrive in Washington for an anti-HUAC protest. Among them are Bacall and Bogart, Danny Kaye and Gene Kelly.

Reagan testifies before HUAC.

He suspected a few actors, but added sheepishly, "I don't know whether they're Communists." He noted some Screen Actors Guild members "who, if not Communists, are working awfully hard to be so." After 30 minutes of questioning, Taylor retired from the session. A matron in a red hat was heard to exclaim, "Hurray for Mr. Taylor!"

Next week, a group of Hollywood stars plan to protest the hearings. Humphrey Bogart, Lauren Bacall, Jane Wyatt, Danny Kaye and Gene Kelly are among them (→ 11/25).

"Cookie" Lavagetto connects, but the Dodgers are still "Bums." Despite Jackie Robinson's seven hits, DiMaggio, Rizzuto, Berra and the Bronx Bombers took their 11th Series. Even our boys in Moscow, glued to the radio, went wild, prompting a Soviet cop to remark, "These Americans!"

Yeager breaks sonic barrier for first time

Oct 14. Chuck Yeager is the first human being to travel faster than the speed of sound. Today, the former fighter pilot boarded a Bell X-1 rocket plane and took off from an undisclosed California Army base. Within minutes, he reached a speed over 600 mph, breaking the sound barrier. Yeager's craft, named Glamorous Glennis, was powered by a new kind of rocket engine. The fuselage is streamlined to reduce turbulence generated by faster movement; molecules would find it hard to flow around a wide-nosed plane. Other nations are trying to come up with their own Mach 1-defying aircraft (→ 2/28/48).

Yeager and Glamorous Glennis.

U.S. urgently seeks food for Europe

Oct 5. President Harry S. Truman asked the American people tonight to reduce their meat and poultry consumption, making more food available for famished Europe. He suggested Americans have no meat on Tuesdays, no poultry or eggs on Thursdays and save a slice of bread every day. Truman feels these acts will also lower inflation.

The nation's brewers will do their part. They agree to make available to the European people the 200,000 bushels of wheat they have currently in stock or under contract. In addition, brewers will seek substitutes for wheat and rice.

The charitable acts are not without political aims. The government knows hunger and revolution often go hand in hand (→ 11/8).

1947

NOVEMBER

Su	Mo	Tu	We	Th	Fr	Sa
						1
2	3	4	5	6	7	8
9	10	11	12	13	14	15
16	17	18	19	20	21	22
23	24	25	26	27	28	29
30						

3. Budapest: Hungary expels U.S. AP correspondent Jack Guinn as spy (→ 8/3/48).

3. London: Stanislaw Mikolajczyk, last Polish opposition leader arrives in British exile.

5. N.Y.: U.S. plan for Korean autonomy wins 46-0 U.N. vote; Soviets boycott (→ 1/23/48).

7. Switzerland, Hungary, Italy, Austria, admitted to UNESCO.

8. Washington: Truman committee proposes $17 bil. European recovery plan (→ 12/19).

10. Dinan, France: 27 Belgian collaborators executed.

11. Bucharest: Peasant opposition leader Juliu Maniu given life sentence for treason (→ 12/31).

14. Paris: French Communist Party disavows alliance with parliamentary Socialists (→ 30).

17. Truman asks Congress for wage and price controls.

18. Friendship train with 270 cars of food and supplies for Europe arrives in New York.

18. Chicago: Marshall warns Soviets to stop "brazen" propaganda against U.S. (→ 1/3/48).

19. Paris: Paul Ramadier resigns as French premier (→ 30).

20. New Delhi: Parliament gives Indian govt. censorship powers over press (→ 1/16/48).

22. Oxford breaks tradition, giving Marshall honorary degree.

25. London: Big Four meet to discuss Germany and European economy (→ 12/15).

26. Paris: France expels 19 Soviet citizens, charging intervention in internal affairs.

27. Australia nationalizes banks after long, divisive debate.

29. N.Y.: U.N. Assembly votes Palestine partition into Arab and Jewish states (→ 30).

29. Philadelphia: Navy shut out by Army 21-0 in football.

30. Paris: New Premier Schuman refuses to discuss new anti-strike law with labor leaders (→ 6/17/51).

DEATH

28. Philippe Leclerc, French general (*11/28/1902).

Hollywood Ten are blacklisted by movies

HUAC (Richard Nixon 2nd from rt.) passes judgment on Hollywood.

Nov 25. In an unprecedented act of self-censorship, the American motion picture industry has voted to bar ten professionals who were held in contempt of Congress. The industry, represented by the Motion Picture Association and other societies, also resolved to refuse jobs to Communists. Counsel for the Hollywood Ten likened the industry to some ignorant cattle "stampeded into surrendering" their integrity.

Fifty leaders of the film industry met in New York City's Waldorf Astoria Hotel yesterday to outline their goals. The Presidents of Paramount, United Artists and Universal were among the conferees.

Their text reads in part, "We will forthwith discharge or suspend without compensation those in our employ, and we will not re-employ any of the ten until . . . he is acquitted or has purged himself of contempt and declares under oath he is not a Communist." They add: "We are not going to be swayed by hysteria or intimidation from any source."

The ten include director Edward Dmytryk ("Farewell, My Lovely") and screenwriter Ring Lardner Jr. ("Woman of the Year"). Their chief counsel, Robert W. Kenney, said his clients "upheld the proposition that the (HUAC) committee had no right to invade the realm of ideas, whether manifested by speech, writing or association . . . I am confident the courts will rule in our favor. The Constitution is the same document that it always was, despite the present hysteria" (→ 5/19/48).

Elizabeth and Philip married in London

Elizabeth and Philip take their vows.

Nov 20. Princess Elizabeth, the daughter of King George VI and Queen Elizabeth, married her cousin Prince Philip, Duke of Edinburgh, today. Thousands of Londoners crowded the procession route, and Westminster Abbey was filled early as notables were ushered to their seats on both sides of the nave and along the choir stalls. The Archbishops of Canterbury and York and the Bishops of London and Norwich presided over the ceremony, which ended with the national anthem "God save the King." The triumphal procession returned to Buckingham Palace amidst the cheering of the crowd.

U.N. cuts Palestine into two entities

Nov 30. Yesterday's resolution by the U.N. General Assembly to partition Palestine into Jewish and Arab sectors has prompted a violent answer by the Arabs who ambushed two buses in Jerusalem, killing six Jews. It is also reported that angry mobs in Damascus, Syria, marched on the Soviet, American and French legations, tearing down and burning the American and French flags.

Dr. Hussein Khalidi, head of the Palestine Arab High Committee, rejected the partition as "a sort of declaration of war against the Arab countries" which would "lead to a crusade against the Jews." He accused the Americans of "political blackmail, power politics and economic pressure" in forcing the vote of small U.N. member nations, saying he was bitter because he had always respected what he termed American fair play.

The committee, terming the U.N. decision the start of a "serious struggle against this Zionist scheme," issued an eight-point statement calling for a three-day general strike by Palestinian Arabs followed by mass demonstrations and "non-cooperation." Elsewhere in Jerusalem, Star of David flags fluttered from windows as thousands of jubilant Jews sang and danced in the streets in celebration of a dream 2,000 years old. This was "Liberation Day" and even British soldiers joined in drinking toasts as former antagonists threw their arms around one another (→ 12/18).

Spruce Goose, Hughes plane, flies briefly

Hughes supervises the preparations for the launching of his pet project.

Nov 2. A mammoth airplane, the world's largest, rose 70 feet in the air and sustained flight for a mile today. The Spruce Goose, so called because its fuselage is made of plywood, was built and piloted by Howard Hughes. It lifted its 200-ton body off the Los Angeles-Long Beach Harbor before a cheering crowd of thousands.

The flying boat, a government wartime project, cost $25 million, of which Hughes contributed $7 million. It is under scrutiny by a congressional panel investigating war contracts. Senator Homer Ferguson, head of the panel, was not so impressed with the flight as to call off the inquiry, which is not concerned with the plane's merits.

Vishinsky implies U.S.S.R. has Bomb

Nov 11. At the 30th anniversary dinner for the Foreign Press Association tonight, the Soviet Deputy Foreign Minister Andrei Vishinsky implied the Soviet Union has now developed an atomic bomb. In a heated speech, he denounced America as a nation of "warmongers" who smugly "believe" no other country capable of the technology. He also blamed the United States for the United Nations' failure to establish controls on nuclear weaponry.

In a response, U.S. delegate to the U.N. Warren Austin expressed doubt that the Soviet Union had made a feasible atom bomb. He also insisted that it was the Soviet Union that hindered effective international control on nuclear information.

Nearly drowned out was Albert Einstein. The physicist, honored tonight for advocating peaceful uses of nuclear energy, said he was distressed by the "difficult and menacing" world situation (→ 12/1).

As reunited families seek to fill their living rooms, TV promises to be a new favorite. Sure to increase your popularity in the neighborhood, a set will bring Howdy Doody to the house to replace your babysitter. Sports lovers can root for Roller Derby, the Yankees or peroxide blonde wrestler Gorgeous George. For the serious viewer: "CBS Evening News" or "Meet the Press."

1947

DECEMBER

Su	Mo	Tu	We	Th	Fr	Sa
	1	2	3	4	5	6
7	8	9	10	11	12	13
14	15	16	17	18	19	20
21	22	23	24	25	26	27
28	29	30	31			

1. Washington: NLRB gets first union indictment for violation of Taft-Hartley Act (→ 12).

1. U.S. says Eniwetok Atoll will be A-bomb test site (→ 1/17/48).

5. N.Y.: Joe Louis outpoints Jersey Joe Walcott (→ 6/25/48).

10. Nobel Peace Prize awarded to Quaker American Friends Service Committee.

12. John L. Lewis takes U.A.W. out of A.F.L. (→ 3/15/48).

15. London: Big Four parley on Germany ends in deadlock (→ 1/20/48).

23. Truman grants pardons to 1,523 who evaded WWII draft.

27. Rome: New Italian constitution promulgated (→ 4/20/48).

28. Chicago: Cardinals take football title 28-21 over Eagles.

29. Wallace joins presidential race on third ticket (→ 5/9/48).

BIRTH

7. Johnny Bench, star catcher, pro baseball.

DEATHS

14. Stanley Baldwin, three-time British premier (*8/3/1867).

28. Victor Emmanuel III, ex-king of Italy (*11/11/1869).

30. Alfred North Whitehead, U.K. philosopher (*2/15/1861).

CULTURAL EVENTS, 1947

Literature: Malcolm Lowry's "Under the Volcano"; Theodore Dreiser's "The Stoic"; Maxim Gorky's "Mother"; Michener's "Tales of the South Pacific"; Camus' "The Plague"; Thomas Mann's "Doktor Faustus"; Mickey Spillane's "I, the Jury."

Academia: Simone Weil's "Gravity and Grace"; Willard Libby finds Carbon 14 useful for dating of archeological data.

Music: E.Y. Harburg's "Finian's Rainbow"; Pablo Casals refuses to play publicly under Franco.

The Arts: Giacometti's "The Pointing Man"; Henry Moore's "Three Standing Figures."

Film: Michael Powell's "Black Narcissus"; Chaplin's "Monsieur Verdoux"; "Gentleman's Agreement," Academy Award.

"Streetcar" is a big hit for Tennessee

Brando, Hunter and Jessica Tandy.

Dec 4. Tennessee Williams' play "A Streetcar Named Desire" made its electrifying debut in New York tonight. It describes a disintegrating Southern family irreparably torn asunder by sexual tension and lies. Marlon Brando, Jessica Tandy, Kim Hunter and Karl Malden star. Brando, mumbling and cursing in a sweaty undershirt, dominates the stage. It is his first major role; he was last seen supporting Paul Muni in "A Flag Is Born" last year.

Playwright Williams was born in Mississippi 36 years ago. He warranted praise for "The Glass Menagerie" (1945), winning the New York Drama Critics Award. Williams combines Southern dialect, tantalizing subject matter and compelling theatrical technique.

Transistor: A bit of electronic magic

It seems only a year ago that the vacuum tube was heralded as an electronic breakthrough in calculators and other devices. In fact, it was a year ago that the U.S. War Department credited vacuum tubes with powering its mighty computer ENIAC. Yet Bell Laboratories has recently developed something that may soon make the vacuum tube obsolete: the transistor.

A transistor is a solid-state electronic component. It is faster, lighter and smaller (about one 200ths the size) of an early vacuum tube. It generates less heat and requires less than one hundredth the power of an early style tube. ▷

Arabs react violently to Palestine partition

Arab volunteers, spurred by the U.N. action, train to fight for their rights.

Dec 18. As a result of the U.N. partition, Arabs have again become the aggressors in Palestine and British troops went into action against them today for the first time following an Arab attack on a Jewish settlement in the Negev. Arabs have repeatedly attacked small Jewish parties in this area, but this was the first real effort to raid a settlement. RAF fighters were also sent to reconnoiter the scene and remind the Arabs of the power in reserve.

Elsewhere, desertions by Arab "temporary police" with their arms continue, caused either by pressure from their own people or the danger of Jewish retaliation.

The Jewish press continues to revile the British for not having removed the Arab Legion from Palestine, while the Arab press accuses the British of bad faith in aiding partition. The Arabs also consider the withdrawal of British and Arab police from the Jewish areas as a step toward partition.

The Jews have also announced that 150 Jewish former police will return to Tel Aviv to serve as reinforcements for the new state (→ 1/4/49).

Eastern Europe is Red as Rumania falls

Dec 31. A Red curtain now hangs over all of Eastern Europe as Rumania's King Michael was forced to abdicate by Soviet-backed Communists. Michael, the last reigning monarch in Eastern Europe, was hastily recalled from a vacation and presented with the abdication papers by Premier Gorza. Rumanians, who have been under the heel of Soviet domination for the past three years, held no public demonstrations, but many wept behind closed doors upon hearing the news (→ 3/4/48).

Michael in England before the war.

Andre Gide wins Nobel Prize for literature

Dec 10. Andre Gide, rebellious author, received the Nobel Prize for literature tonight. Gide, 78 years old, may be France's most revered writer. His works, from "Fruit of the Earth" (1897) to "The Counterfeiters" (1925), span a quarter of a century. He examines both sides of an issue; he advocates profligacy in one novel and chastity in the next.

The Nobel Peace Prize went jointly to the Service Council of the British Society of Friends and the American Friends Service Committee. The groups work along similar lines. The American Friends was founded by Quakers in 1917 to aid relief in battle-torn Europe. Conscientious objectors, the Quakers compensated for lack of military involvement by assisting the needy. Since World War I, the society continues to offer food and medicine at international troublespots.

A Czech-American couple, Carl and Gerty Cori, won the prize for physiology. The biochemists traced the way glycogen, stored sugar, is converted into glucose. This product is essential for energy. The Coris share the prize with Bernardo Houssay, an Argentine physiologist. Houssay was a medical prodigy, taking an internship at age 13.

Sir Robert Robinson takes the chemistry prize, while Sir Edward Appleton takes the physics award. Appleton found the ionosphere reflects radio waves. Robinson studied the structure of strychnine.

Vast shipments are rushed overseas to meet urgent food crisis

On the 3rd, the Leaster left Philadelphia with grain for France and Italy.

Dec 19. Congress approved allocation of $522 million for stop-gap aid to France, Italy and Austria and $18 million for China in a late session tonight. The efforts to direct money to meet emergency food needs while curbing Communist influence encountered strong debate on Capitol Hill. It was generally agreed that the $18 million for Chiang Kai-shek amounted to a gesture of support for his fight against the Communist Party in China. Yet some members of the House questioned the need for such support, including Rep. Vito Marcantonio, who threatened to call for a full quorum vote which could have killed the measure. The call was sounded, but quorum was kept and aid will soon be sent (→ 2/10/48).

Dead Sea Scrolls reveal ancient past

One day last spring, a Bedouin shepherd boy was idly tossing stones along the cliffs of the Dead Sea. One pebble bounced out of sight and landed with an odd clink. The boy scrambled into a cave and found beside his skipping stone jars housing fragile leather scrolls. They reveal a copy of the Old Testament, dating from the 1st century B.C.

The exhausting and wonderful task of translating the scrolls of the Qumran caves continues. The Old Testament is nearly whole; the absence of the Book of Esther is balanced by two copies of Isaiah. The Essenes, ancient guardians of the Bible, also left a record of their monastic life (→ 2/7/60).

1948

JANUARY

Su	Mo	Tu	We	Th	Fr	Sa
				1	2	3
4	5	6	7	8	9	10
11	12	13	14	15	16	17
18	19	20	21	22	23	24
25	26	27	28	29	30	31

1. General Agreement on Trade and Tariffs, signed by 23 nations, goes into effect, in attempt to reduce intl. trade barriers.

3. London: Attlee accuses Soviets of threatening Europe with a "new imperialism".

4. Jerusalem: 14 killed, 98 injured in bomb blast at Arab High Committee office (→ 16).

11. Truman proposes free, two-year community colleges for all who want education (→ 2/1/49).

16. Pakistan charges India with systematic campaign to wipe out Moslems (→ 18).

17. Truman bans flying over atomic energy plants (→ 2/8).

17. Batavia: Dutch gain temporary control over Java, Sumatra in Indonesian truce (→ 10/28).

18. New Delhi: Gandhi breaks 121-hour fast after halting Moslem-Hindu riots (→ 19).

19. N.Y.: India and Pakistan accept U.N. mediation (→ 30).

19. France: Western Europe's largest dam opens on Rhone.

20. Germany: It is reported that Soviets have taken $170 mil. in art from Dresden (→ 2/3).

20. Ottawa: Mackenzie King to retire as Canadian premier.

23. Soviets refuse U.N. entry into North Korea to administer elections (→ 2/7).

23. Prague: Czech Communists take control in Slovakia, charge opponents plan revolt (→ 2/2).

27. Iraq: Saleh Jabr Cabinet resigns after 24 hours rioting; 70 killed, 300 injured.

28. Moscow sends formal protest to U.S. and U.K. on plan to reopen Mellaha air base in Libya.

31. India: Cities swept by riots in wake of Gandhi murder (→ 2/8).

BIRTH

27. Mikhail Baryshnikov, Russian ballet dancer.

DEATHS

8. Kurt Schwitters, German Dadaist poet and sculptor (*6/20/1887).

30. Orville Wright, American aviation pioneer (*8/19/1871).

Mahatma Gandhi is assassinated

Jan 30. Mohandas K. Gandhi, the spiritual leader of Indian independence, has been shot and killed by a Hindu extremist. The 78-year-old Gandhi, the Mahatma or Great Teacher to his followers, was shot at point-blank range as he was walking through a garden to a pergola, where he was to deliver his daily prayer. He died 20 minutes later.

The assassin, who had stepped out from a crowd awaiting the prayer meeting, was immediately seized by onlookers. He was identified as Nathuran Vinayak Godse, a 36-year-old Hindhu of the Mahratta tribes in Poona which have been the center of resistance to the Gandhi message of communal and religious tolerance. Only a few days ago, Gandhi had completed a five-day fast to encourage friendship.

The death of Gandhi, who for more than 20 years defied British rule with his program of civil disobedience, stunned the newly independent nation that he helped create. In a radio speech to the nation announcing the death, Prime Minister Pandit Jawaharlal Nehru, his voice quivering with grief, said, "Gandhi has gone out of our lives and there is darkness everywhere . . . The father of our nation is no more. No longer will we be able to run to him for advice and solace."

Mourners surround the beloved Gandhi, bedded in flowers in New Delhi.

The loss of Gandhi, the strongest voice for peace and unity in a turbulent new nation of 300 million persons, was an incalculable political blow to India. Throughout the nation there was an undercurrent of uncertainty about the political future and a wave of fear that his death would lead to renewed fighting between Hindus and Moslems.

The news of his death set off riots in Bombay and other cities as mobs attacked offices of the Hindu Mahasabha, the extreme anti-Moslem organization to which the assassin belonged. Nehru has appealed to Indians to turn away from violence in memory of the Mahatma, the frail, ascetic who led India to independence preaching non-violence and toleration. Gandhi's body is to be cremated according to Hindu custom (→ 31).

Truman proposes 2nd largest budget

Jan 12. The second largest peacetime budget in the nation's history was submitted to Congress today by President Truman, citing what he called an unprecedented challenge of totalitarianism abroad and the realities of domestic needs.

The proposed outlay totals just over $39.6 billion for the fiscal year beginning July 1, about $3 billion less than the previous high two years ago. About $18 billion, a major part of the proposed budget, would be earmarked for national defense and for international affairs, including the European Recovery Program. In his message to Congress, the president characterized his budget as both realistic and "hard-boiled," one that reflects the cost of the recent war and its aftermath.

Burma is independent of Commonwealth

Jan 4. Burma is an independent republic today, ending 62 years of British rule. Independence officially came at 4:20 a.m. —a time that Buddhist astrologers had chosen as most favorable for the birth of the independent nation. At dawn, the British Union Jack was hauled down from atop the Government House, to be replaced by the new Burmese flag of bright red and blue, with one large star to represent the Union of Burma and five small stars to represent the five main Burmese ethnic groups. As he raised the new flag, Premier Thakin Nu said, "Burma's period of tutelage is over."

In contrast to India, which was granted its independence five months ago after years of civil strife with the British rulers, Burma achieved its independence in friendly negotiations with the British government over ending colonial rule.

Burma becomes the second British colony in six months to gain its independence. Mountbatten (rt.) attends the raising of the new republic's flag.

Jews and Arabs fighting heavily as immigration increases

Like the Puritans who settled America, Jewish refugees bound for Palestine seek not just real estate, but a Promised Land charged with religious meaning.

With a determination hardened by the memories of Hitler's atrocities, Jews are fighting fiercely in Tel Aviv for control over the Holy Land.

Jan 16. Haifa, scene of some of the heaviest fighting in Palestine, remains in a state of general disorder, with Zionist fighters claiming they killed 82 Arabs today. Eight of those killed were children. Ranging in age from 18 months to 12 years, they died in the wreckage of their home when it was bombed.

Earlier this month, the Stern gang killed at least 34 Arabs by bombing the local Arab Higher Committee's offices, believed to be a center for Arab military planning.

The general situation in Palestine is that as time passes the fighting becomes more general and relative safety everywhere declines. Nowhere can people safely walk down a street. All sections of Haifa are virtually paralyzed as each is raked by rifle fire from other parts of town. No coherent fighting plan is discernible, but the violence continues to escalate on both sides.

The Jews were retaliating for an Arab bomb left in a truck in front of a Jewish bus station, but the Haifa killings appear as unplanned as most of the other bloodshed.

For their part, the Arabs remain intransigent in their opposition to increased Jewish immigration and the United Nations' decision to partition a country without the consent of a majority of its residents—the Arabs. Since the U.N. resolution, 2,000 casualties have resulted from the bloody tug-of-war for control of this tragic land where justice seems hard to find and peace increasingly rare (→ 2/2).

Greeks seize Konitza from Red rebels

Jan 1. The year dawned auspiciously for the Greek nationalist army, as it beat Communist troops into retreat at Konitza. Attack on the town, hid in mountainous north central Greece, was seen as a major move by General Markos Vafiades, Communist leader. His defeat can bring hope to a people who have not known civil peace since 1940.

Torrential rains kept the nationalist air force grounded. Mud and snow mired their artillery. It was the kind of weather the Communist rebels thrive on, when one man with a rifle behind a tree can gun down countless others. The Nationalist War Ministry in Athens put the number of rebels at 8,000, their own men at 2,000. Other sources put the rebel number much lower.

Guerrillas dynamited the main bridge to Konitza, and army troops were forced to use a smaller one. Tanks and armored cars slowly rolled into the town, subject to stray guerrilla gunfire. Once in Konitza, rebels abandoned hand-to-hand combat for retreat to the northeast.

A radio broadcast by General Markos denied retreat or any kind of failure. He said, "The Democratic (Communist) Army . . . will strike still harder in 1948 at the forces of the monarcho-fascists and American imperialists" (→ 5/4).

Court orders school to accept Negro

Jan 12. In a unanimous decision, the U.S. Supreme Court has ordered the state of Oklahoma to admit a Negro to the University of Oklahoma Law School. The court cited a citizen's constitutional right to equal protection under the law. The state must carry out the court's order "forthwith." The customary grace period is 25 days. The winner in the case is 28-year-old Ada Lois Sipuel. By law, the state could build a separate institution for her, but as one Justice said, as sole student she would "not receive much of a law education" (→ 2/2).

1948

FEBRUARY

Su	Mo	Tu	We	Th	Fr	Sa
1	2	3	4	5	6	7
8	9	10	11	12	13	14
15	16	17	18	19	20	21
22	23	24	25	26	27	28
29						

2. Jerusalem: Heavy explosion wrecks Ben Yehuda St., killing 33 in Jewish quarter (→ 29).

2. U.S., Italy sign pact of friendship, commerce and navigation.

2. Prague: Czech Communists threaten strike if economic demands are not met (→ 21).

2. President Harry S. Truman is hailed in the Virgin Islands as a supporter of islanders' rights.

3. Germany: 1.5 mil. Germans strike against food administration in U.S., U.K. zones (→ 3/6).

4. Chicago: Commodities, stocks and bonds take sharp dive.

4. N.Y.: U.N. finds lack of food world's worst problem.

7. U.S. Army command passes from Ike to Gen. Omar Bradley.

7. Korean Communists start strikes in South; 27 dead, 150 held in crackdown (→ 5/1).

8. Pope Pius asks A-bomb ban, calling it human mind's most terrible invention (→ 7/24).

8. New Delhi: Indian govt. bans Moslem groups Khaksars and League Natl. Guard (→ 9/11).

10. Washington: C.I.O. to be forced to purge members who oppose Marshall Plan (→ 3/1).

11. Ireland: After 16 years in power, Fianna Fail loses majority; party leader Eamon de Valera resigns (→ 18).

12. Jackson, Miss.: 4,000 "true white Jeffersonian Democrats" meet to oppose Truman civil rights program (→ 5/3).

15. "Bohemian Rapture" opens in New York.

19. Truman receives Gen. Rana, first Nepal envoy to U.S.

21. Prague: Pres. Benes bars Communist regime (→ 24).

24. Prague: Czech Communists seize ministries (→ 25).

25. Prague: Benes gives in to Red leader Gottwald (→ 26).

26. U.S., Britain and France condemn Prague coup (→ 28).

28. Prague bans 27 publications, foreign press (→ 29).

29. Palestine: 30 British soldiers die as mines rip Cairo-Haifa train (→ 3/7).

Communists stage coup against Czech regime

Some 250,000 Communists, followers of Klement Gottwald, parade through the streets of Prague shortly after police broke up an anti-Communists protest.

President Benes, one of Czechoslovakia's founding fathers, reluctantly accepts the ultimatum of Communist leader Klement Gottwald.

Feb 29. Communist Party leaders in Czechoslovakia moved to seize complete control of the country after toppling the government late last week. Political opponents of Prime Minister Klement Gottwald are being purged. Many judges have been thrown out of office. And the Communists have outlawed the creation of new political parties.

Gottwald announced to a rally of farmers and peasants that he will split up any estates that are larger than 125 acres. "The land will be the property of those who till it," he said.

Gottwald also rejected an unusual joint statement from the Western Allies that condemned the Communist coup. The prime minister said the United States, Great Britain and France do not have "the slighest legal right to intervene in Czechoslovak affairs or even to criticize. We will never take any lessons in democracy from those with Munich on their conscience, who dealt with Hitler to divide us up," Gottwald said, apparently referring to Neville Chamberlain's appeasement policy.

Moderate members of the Czech Cabinet resigned last week to protest Communist control over the police. They hoped the move would force Gottwald to quit. The plan backfired. After Communists occupied newspaper offices and threatened a general strike, Gottwald convinced a reluctant President Benes to allow him to form a "government of the workers." Benes subsequently left Prague and is likely to resign. Jan Masaryk, the populist leader, holds on to his job as Foreign Minister. He has tried to reassure the country about the Communist takeover by saying democratic institutions will not be harmed (→ 3/10).

Sweden wins Winter Olympics; U.S. 3rd

The Swiss and the Americans battle it out on the ice in St. Moritz.

Feb 8. Despite its first gold medal in figure skating, the United States placed third behind Sweden and Switzerland in the fifth Winter Olympic Games. The triumph of Dick Button in the skating event accounted for one of the nine medals captured by the Americans at St. Moritz. Sweden scored 82 points, Switzerland 77 and the United States 73.5. The Games closed on a tranquil note after a hectic beginning. The weather alternated between sun and snow and the usual political arguments abounded.

De Valera resigns as Irish Prime Minister

Feb 18. Eamon de Valera was forced to resign as Irish Prime Minister and John A. Costello was elected to replace him in a day of upheaval in the Assembly.

A new six-party coalition defeated a motion to re-elect de Valera, who had held the office for 16 years, by a 75-70 vote. Immediately following the formal resignation of de Valera came the nomination of Costello, the former Attorney General. Several supporting speeches endorsed the nomination and a vote was called. Costello won by a 75-68 margin.

In acceptance, a dignified Costello said, "The Premier of (an inter-party) government should occupy a position in political life detached from the controversial bitterness of the past." In a respectful gesture to the departing prime minister, the new leader remarked that he knew de Valera would patriotically help in the period of transition.

The new leadership in Ireland intends to cut taxes, build more housing and reduce the cost of living. Yet many feel such a splintered government will not last long enough to achieve these admirable goals (→ 11/24).

Appliances for electrified home, $2,274

Morning. The typical American housewife tosses aside her electric blanket and rises. She takes a shower in water heated by an electric furnace and dries her hair under a hairdryer. The baby is crying. The woman puts the baby's bottle in an electric sterilizer and warmer.

Breakfast. The housewife prepares a scrumptious meal with the electric waffle iron, coffee maker, egg beater, egg timer and toaster. The six-cubic-foot refrigerator is opened and closed. When the meal is over, the dishes are placed in the electric dishwasher.

Eggs beaten at the flick of a switch.

New luxuries for the kitchen-bound.

Cleaning. Washing machine and dryer are on. Iron is on. Upright vacuum cleaner is on. Housewife frequently glances at electric clock to ascertain the time. Baby is crying. Housewife stops cleaning to put electric heating pad below baby and vaporizer beside baby.

Evening. Wife is too tired to appreciate electric phonograph, electric radio, electric harpsichord or husband. She picks up a newspaper. Reads that her electric devices cost $2,274. She wonders just how long she must wait to buy an electronic maid.

Jets drive planes much faster than before

Feb 28. Four months after American Air Force Captain Chuck Yeager broke the sound barrier in his Bell X-1 experimental rocket plane, unofficial reports say the Douglas D-558 Skyrocket has been clocked at 650 mph at 35,000 feet, the speed of sound.

A jet engine makes these speeds credible. Like a cylinder, it takes in air at one end. Air is compressed, combined with fuel, and ignited. However, when the plane reaches maximum speed, the fuselage shakes dangerously; air molecules outside have not time to flow naturally. Engineers must handle this hitch, or back to propellers we go.

Sleek de Havilland Vampire jets soar in formation high in the sky.

Truman calls for an end to Jim Crow

Feb 2. Assailing "Jim Crowism," President Harry S. Truman asked Congress today to outlaw lynching and to establish a federal commission on civil rights.

"We know our democracy is not perfect," he said, "but we do know that it offers a fuller, freer, happier life to our people than any totalitarian nation has ever offered." The president's broad program of civil rights embodies the principal recommendations of a committee, headed by Charles E. Wilson, the President of General Electric Company, in a report entitled "To Secure These Rights." President Truman also proposed statehood for Alaska and Hawaii and home rule for residents of the District of Columbia (→ 12).

Soviet film genius Eisenstein deceased

Feb 11. Sergei Eisenstein, a giant in the cinemagraphic field, has died in the Soviet Union. He was 50 years old. Eisenstein directed "Potemkin" (1925), "Ten Days That Shook the World" (1928) and the three-part censored epic "Ivan the Terrible," finally shown in 1947.

Eisenstein was a linguist (Russian, French, English, German and Japanese) who ironically feared the advent of sound. His films were visual: montages, close-ups, pans, cuts, visual metaphors and rhythmic editing. Eisenstein often told stories of revolution, a natural subject for a revolutionary director.

1948

MARCH

Su	Mo	Tu	We	Th	Fr	Sa
	1	2	3	4	5	6
7	8	9	10	11	12	13
14	15	16	17	18	19	20
21	22	23	24	25	26	27
28	29	30	31			

1. Washington: Senate applauds as Sen. Vandenberg asks European relief speed to avert third world war (→ 3).

1. Vietnam: Viet Minh attack Saigon-Dalat convoy, killing 150 (→ 6/5).

3. U.S. Treasury discloses U.K. has exhausted $3.75 bil. loan (→ 31).

4. London: Rumanian King Michael breaks silence, says abdication was forced (→ 7/5/50).

6. Berlin: Western powers agree to internationalize Ruhr (→ 21).

7. Greece regains control over 50 Dodecanese Aegean Islands for first time since 1522.

7. Jerusalem: Zionist militia Haganah claims right to mobilize U.S. citizens (→ 11).

8. U.S. Supreme Court rules religious instruction in public schools unconstitutional.

15. Federal District Court nullifies Taft-Hartley ban on political spending by unions (→ 15).

15. U.S.: 200,000 miners strike for better pensions (→ 4/12).

17. Brussels: U.K., France, Belgium, Holland, Luxembourg sign 50-year mutual aid pact.

22. U.S. announces land reform plan for Korea (→ 5/1).

25. Italians ban compromise with Yugoslavia, insist on return of Trieste (→ 4/20/50).

28. Moscow accuses Sweden of offering military bases to U.S.

28. Soviet composer Dmitri Shostakovich forced to give up chair at Moscow Conservatory.

29. U.S. Supreme Court bans N.Y. state law barring sale of books of lust, crime, bloodshed.

31. Washington: House passes $6.2 bil. foreign aid bill (→ 4/3).

31. Germany: Soviets begin controlling Western trains bound for Berlin (→ 4/1).

31. France pledges Madagascar status of associate state within French Union.

DEATH

4. Antonin Artaud, French actor and playwright (*9/4/1896).

Was Masaryk suicide?

Jan Masaryk, a mysterious death.

March 10. At six a.m. this morning, three floors below an open bathroom window, an employee of Czechoslovakia's Foreign Ministry discovered the lifeless body of Foreign Minister Jan Masaryk.

The Communist administration, which seized control of the government in a coup d'etat last month, said that Masaryk was depressed over foreign criticism of his decision to join the government and had spent Sunday brooding at the grave of his father, Tomas Masaryk, cofounder and first President of the Czechoslovak republic.

Friends, however, bridle at the suggestion of suicide and contend that Masaryk was in good spirits and had a full itinerary planned for the next day. While Czech citizens puzzle over this tragedy, and wonder about the possibility that he was murdered, a spray of lillies covers the parliamentary seat Masaryk was to have assumed today (→ 6/7).

Soviets walk out of Berlin's Allied Council

March 21. Tensions between the Western Allies and Russia increased sharply after Soviet delegates walked out of the control council meeting in Berlin. There are disturbing reports that the Russians also moved more guards to the border that separates their sector of Germany from the American zone. German newspapers say the Russians are trying to stop the flow of refugees from their sector into the American area.

The new tensions were not eased by the attempted humor of a Communist politician in Berlin. "Suppose the Russians ask the Western Allies to leave Berlin and they refuse?" he wondered out loud. "Oh, we could not start a war over that."

The Russians are apparently upset that they were not briefed on recent meetings of the Western Allies. They have also expressed displeasure over the Allies' refusal to form a central German government and to allow them to share in the production of the Ruhr.

American officers in Greece, given new purpose by Truman's anti-Communist Doctrine, inspect rebel artillery seized by government troops.

Jerusalem Arabs blow up Jewish Agency

Crowds clean up the debris in Jerusalem, a city caught amid vicious rivalries.

March 11. Eleven persons were killed and 86 wounded when a powerful explosion rocked the headquarters of the Jewish Agency for Palestine in Jerusalem today. Arab guerrillas are believed to be responsible for hiding a bomb in a stolen American consul's car and then driving it into the courtyard of the building, where it exploded. The blast annihilated offices of Keren Hayesod, the foundation which solicits money to promote colonization, and seriously damaged the rest of the building. The attack seemed to be well-organized, as the headquarters were ruggedly built with concrete barriers and high wire fences to discourage terrorist assaults. The driver of the car, which has been compared to the famous Trojan horse, escaped arrest.

A fire ignited immediately after the explosion, hampering rescue efforts. Among those who perished was 72-year old Leib Jaffa, one of three joint directors of Keren Hayesod. While casualties were numerous and damage extensive, spokesmen for the agency said important agency records had been saved and placed under guard (→ 4/22).

Farouk lays cornerstone for Aswan Dam

March 27. Sporting dark glasses, a mustache and a fez, Egypt's King Farouk laid the cornerstone on his nation's ambitious new dam today. The hydroelectric plant will be built on the upper Nile, where churning flood waters are at their most powerful. Builders estimate the plant's annual output will reach as much as two million kilowatt hours.

The dam will be constructed of stone chiseled from the same quarries that created the temples and statuary of the ancient pharaohs. Those monuments took decades to build; Farouk's government predicts completion of the dam within five years. Less optimistic outside engineers put it at 12.

The first Aswan Dam was made in 1902 with British backing. The project currently underway is largely financed by a U.S.-British team. Why the long delay between dams? Egypt needs more than financial backers before it sets out to harness the longest river in the world. It needs to relocate thousands of people. It also needs to weigh the worth of some irreplacable Roman and Egyptian monuments standing in its path (→ 5/14/64).

Farouk lays the first stone.

1948

APRIL

Su	Mo	Tu	We	Th	Fr	Sa
				1	2	3
4	5	6	7	8	9	10
11	12	13	14	15	16	17
18	19	20	21	22	23	24
25	26	27	28	29	30	

1. U.S. starts flying supplies to Berlin to thwart Soviet attempt to squeeze Allies out (→ 14).

3. Truman signs Foreign Assistance Act (→ 7).

4. Albany: Governor Dewey signs bills initiating state university system.

5. Cairo: Riots rage as police strike; 25 killed by Egyptian army (→ 7/23).

6. Finns sign ten-year pact with Soviets, aggreeing to resist German drive on U.S.S.R. (→ 5/24).

7. Washington: Paul Hoffman chosen director of European Relief Program (→ 16).

7. N.Y.: World Health Organization of U.N. begins work.

8. Several Scandinavian airlines merge under name SAS.

10. Iran: 300 arrested in sudden security move; martial law in Mazandaran (→ 2/5/49).

12. Lewis ends U.S. coal strike; still faces contempt trial (→ 20).

14. Germany: Soviets move 100 tanks into Berlin area (→ 24).

14. London: Commons suspends death penalty for five years.

14. Ireland: Pan Am crash at Shannon kills 30 passengers, including 19 Americans.

15. U.S.: Merck and Company announces isolation of vitamin B-12.

15. Moscow: NBC reporter Robert Magidoff ousted as spy.

15. Manila: Filipino President Manuel Roxas dies of heart attack (→ 4/28/49).

16. Paris: European Organization for Economic Cooperation created under terms of Marshall Plan.→

22. Palestine: Haganah, Zionist militia, seizes Haifa; Arabs agree to evacuate (→ 26).

25. N.Y.: Soviets end 13-month boycott of U.N. trusteeship council.

26. N.Y.: Arabs threaten independent state if U.N. fails to establish trusteeship over Palestine (→ 30).

29. New York: "Homecoming" opens, starring Clark Gable and Lana Turner.

Arabs surrender and evacuate Haifa, as fierce fighting rages

Arab chief Abdullah of Transjordan.

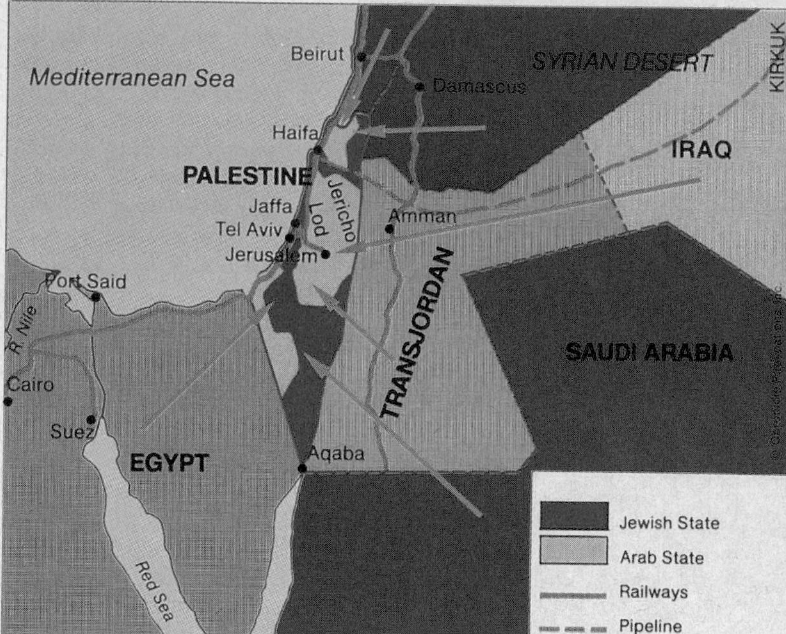

Palestine, surrounded by Arab nations, now under attack from all sides.

April 30. In the wake of this month's drive to wrest key areas from the Arabs, the Haganah today swooped down on Haifa, Palestine's only deep-water port. After a furious battle, the Arabs agreed to surrender and evacuate the city.

The Jews preceded the attack with a heavy bombardment, pouring mortar fire into Arab sectors as pillars of smoke curled over the city of 140,000 inhabitants, of whom 80,000 are Jews, and thousands of Arabs tried desperately and unsuccessfully to flee as their exit bridge was seized by the Jews.

Earlier April offensives by the Zionist militia saw the death of the Arab commander of the Jerusalem front and the massacre by the Irgun of 250 Arab civilians in the village of Deir Yasin.

The surrender terms include the laying down of all Arab arms, the deportation of all Arab fighters from Haifa and the surrender of all German and Nazi soldiers fighting in the Arab ranks.

At Lake Success, a Jewish representative told the U.N. that a Jewish state in Palestine would become a reality May 16, following the end of the British mandate, irrespective of any U.N. action regarding partition —a reference to a possible U.N. police force. President Truman at a press conference said the U.S. would willingly participate in such a force (→ 5/1).

Lewis ends coal strike, but still punished

April 20. John L. Lewis has ended the coal mine strike, but not in time to avoid heavy fines on both himself and his United Mine Workers on charges of contempt of court.

The dour head of the U.M.W. was fined $20,000 and his union was ordered to pay $1.4 million for not having obeyed an earlier court order to terminate the strike that began March 15. Lewis had won a major part of his pension demands a week ago and ordered his men back to work, but by that time the contempt proceedings were underway. Some of the 350,000 miners have refused to return to the job, despite the Lewis order, and the fines levied today may prompt still others to leave the mines.

This marked the second time in two years that heavy fines were imposed on both Lewis and the union for failing to obey court orders to end a strike. In 1946, Lewis was fined $10,000 and the union ordered to pay $3.5 million. However, the union fine later was reduced to $700,000 by the Supreme Court (→ 5/10).

Lewis, on the run after Taft-Hartley.

Associated Press is now 100 years old

April 19. The Associated Press, the worldwide news-gathering agency dedicated to the ideals of objectivity and "truth in news," is 100 years old. At its annual meeting at the Waldorf-Astoria Hotel in New York, 1,150 men and women heard journalists pay tribute to the AP.

Robert McLean, President of the AP, warned there is a trend toward creation of national news-gathering agencies, which are a threat to true information. "We cannot overlook the fact that an agency of government is serving nationalistic interest and as such has an ax to grind and the blade of such an ax is not always the blade of truth," he said. "And it is to the truth we must look to make men free."

U.S. starts flying supplies to Berlin, as Russians block trains

British liner, casualty of the Cold War, after colliding with Soviet plane.

April 24. The U.S. and Britain have mounted an airlift of food and supplies to Berlin to thwart a Soviet blockade aimed at forcing the Allies out of the former German capital. The airlift was ordered after the U.S.S.R. began imposing restrictions on the movement of trains and vehicles through the Soviet zone to Allied outposts in Berlin.

Earlier this month, the Russians refused to let American and British military trains pass through the Soviet zone to Berlin unless inspected by Soviet authorities. The United States and Great Britain rejected the Soviet inspection demands. The Soviet Union imposed similar restrictions on barge traffic and imposed inspection of all vehicles moving on the autobahn, the only highway linking Berlin with the West.

In the deepening Cold War atmosphere, the Soviet Union appeared intent on squeezing the Allies out of Berlin, which has been placed under four-power control, by cutting off their supplies. The Soviet move, however, did not prevent the use of the air routes to Berlin unless the Soviets were willing to provoke a major crisis by shooting down Allied planes. Soviet fighter planes buzzed American air transports but otherwise did not molest them. The Soviet Union apologized after a Soviet fighter collided with a British passenger plane (→ 6/7).

American states organize amid violence

April 30. Wielding machetes and guns, mobs in Bogota, Colombia, rioted on April 9 and drove the delegates of 21 countries from the Capitol building. After martial law restored order, the delegates reconvened and today signed the charter of the Organization of American States, a new international organization providing for common defense and the peaceful settlement of hemispheric issues.

The violence, which was unrelated to the conference, was touched off by the assassination of liberal leader Jorge Gaitan. More than 100 Colombians were killed and the suspected assassin was torn limb from limb in front of the presidential palace. Order was restored when the conservative administration agreed to form a coalition government, but martial law still remains in effect.

The Pan-American talks were interrupted by violence which swept the streets of Bogota following the murder of liberal leader Jorge Gaitan on the 9th.

Christian party wins big in Italy

April 20. Claiming that priests and nuns had tampered with the ballots, the Communists were sulking today as 94 percent of all eligible Italians voted overwhelmingly for democracy. Premier de Gasperi's Christian Democratic Party won 48 percent of the vote in the first election since Italy's new constitution was put into effect last January. The Communist-backed Popular Front, which called the election a clear choice between the Soviet Union and the United States, won 31 percent of the vote with right-wing Socialists taking another seven percent of the vote.

Minister of the Interior Scelba definitively stated that Communists would not be included in the new government, but most observers believe that de Gasperi will keep his coalition-based administration intact. A group of angry Communists was broken up in Milan, but elsewhere in the country, people cheered wildly at the news, and the stock market showed a strong surge. The Vatican was elated and regarded the election as a triumph of Catholicism over atheistic communism (7/14).

Truman approves foreign aid act

April 16. The countries of Western Europe are gearing up to spend the money promised by President Truman to rebuild their devastated economies. Truman signed legislation approving the European Recovery Program, which was originally proposed by Secretary of State George Marshall. Today, the Europeans signed an agreement creating a coordinating agency, the Organization for European Economic Cooperation.

Truman has already ordered that more than a billion dollars be made available immediately to the European countries. The lion's share is targeted for Britain, France, Italy, the Benelux countries and Germany. Smaller sums will be distributed to Greece, Turkey, China, Trieste and the United Nations.

The Truman administration expects that European recovery will be good for the United States. But officials also concede the aid program could harm the American economy. Paul Hoffman, the President of the Studebaker Corporation and administrator of the program, said, "Priority must be given to the maintenance of a strong, productive America. American resources are not unlimited. (The program) will of course contribute to inflationary pressures in this country."

The program also faces diplomatic pressures abroad. The Russians and most Eastern European countries are not included in the program, and Joseph Stalin is strongly opposed to the initiative.

Bogart searches the mountains of Mexico in Huston's tale of greed "Treasure of the Sierra Madre."

1948

MAY

Su	Mo	Tu	We	Th	Fr	Sa
						1
2	3	4	5	6	7	8
9	10	11	12	13	14	15
16	17	18	19	20	21	22
23	24	25	26	27	28	29
30	31					

1. Korea: Soviet-supported govt. in North adopts constitution claiming sovereignty over whole country (→ 10).

1. N.Y.: Jewish Agency demands U.N. action, as Syrian army invades Palestine (→ 14).

3. U.S. Supreme Court bans pacts barring Negroes from owning real estate (→ 7/17).

3. U.S.: Pulitzers go to Tennessee Williams for "A Streetcar Named Desire," and Michener for "Tales of the South Pacific."

4. Athens: 24 leftists executed for murder (→ 16).

9. Socialists name Norman Thomas for president (→ 6/25).

10. Korea: Six mil. go to polls in South, vote in rightists (→ 31).

13. U.S.: ERP bars aid to nations giving military aid to U.S.S.R. (→ 10/6/49).

14. Tel Aviv: State of Israel proclaimed (→ 15).

15. Egypt invades Israel, bombs Tel Aviv (→ 16).

16. Tel Aviv: Chaim Weizmann named Israeli president, as troops of five Arab nations advance in Israel (→ 20).

17. Moscow: Stalin praises presidential platform of Truman foe Henry Wallace (→ 6/25).

17. Soviet censures Tito for rebuke of Cominform (→ 6/28).

19. Congress passes Mundt-Nixon Bill, requiring Communists to register with govt. (→ 29).

20. N.Y.: U.N. Council names Count Folke Bernadotte U.N. mediator for Palestine (→ 22).

22. British down four Egyptian Spitfires over Palestine (→ 31).

24. Helsinki: Communists strike to protest dismissal of Interior Min. Yrjoe Leino (→ 8/18/49).

29. Washington: Wallace blasts Mundt-Nixon Bill as Cold War act against U.S.S.R. (→ 6/2).

31. Seoul: Syngman Rhee claims rule for all Korea (→ 8/12).

DEATHS

2. Wilhelm von Opel, German auto pioneer.

23. Claude McKay, black American Marxist poet (*9/15/1890).

State of Israel comes into existence

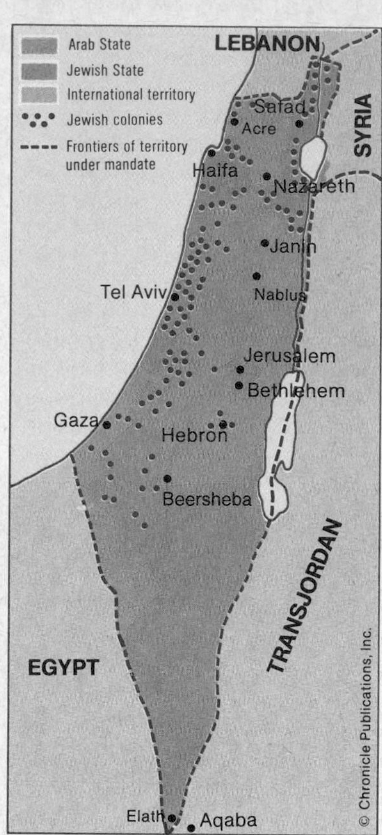

Israel after the 1947 U.N. plan.

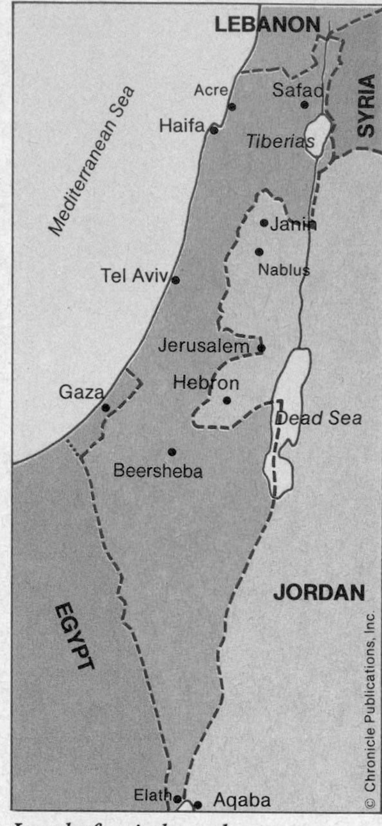

Israel after independence.

May 31. The new state of Israel, which is just two weeks old, is under siege and shrinking. It is under attack from the north, east and south by enemies intent upon forcing it into extinction. The Arab League has rejected an appeal from the United Nations for a cease-fire.

The fighting started as soon as the British mandate expired on the 15th and Israel came into existence. Troops from Syria and Lebanon attacked in the north. Forces from Transjordan and Iraq moved in from the east. And Egypt invaded from the south.

An Israeli spokesman says the country is ready to respect a cease-fire, "but we have no intention of accepting the condition, suggested in most Arab public statements, that we should abandon the Jewish state. That would be paramount to political surrender." The Arab states, for their part, refuse to even negotiate with Israel.

The military pressures on Israel are formidable. Iraq says it has cut the coastal road from the capital of Tel Aviv to Haifa. And Transjordan forces say they have defeated an Israeli effort to open the highway between Tel Aviv and Jerusalem. Tel Aviv has been bombarded from the air for two weeks.

The American Consul General, Thomas Wasson, was shot to death by a sniper in Jerusalem last week. Wasson was wounded while returning from the French Consulate, where he had been trying to arrange a truce in the fighting. A spokesman for the Haganah, the Israeli army, says Wasson was killed by an Arab sniper.

The United States was the first country to recognize the state of Israel, on May 15, just ahead of the Soviet Union. Emotions and sentiment in favor of Israel run high in parts of America. In New York, tens of thousands of people were turned away when a "Salute to Israel" rally packed Madison Square Garden. The meeting was sponsored by the American Zionist Emergency Council. Many of the speakers appealed for a lifting of the arms embargo on Israel.

This enthusiasm for Israel is not matched in Britain. After withdrawing its last High Commissioner from Palestine, the government in London refused to establish relations with Tel Aviv. "There is no need to hurry," one British official said. Britain has also made no effort to stop the Arab armies which have invaded Israel. And some British diplomats are going so far as to doubt whether the Arab invasion is an act of aggression.

The hostilities in Israel have not stopped Jews from around the world from applying for immigration to Israel. Hundreds of Jews have already arrived from France and Cyprus, where they had been interned by the British.

One of the first actions of the new Israeli government was to open its doors to all Jews. A proclamation invited Jews to join "the struggle for the fulfillment of the dream of generations, the redemption of Israel."

Prime Minister Ben Gurion read the proclamation as the Israeli flag, the Star of David, flew over his head. Dr. Chaim Weizmann was elected provisional President (→ 6/1).

Weizmann, Israel's first President.

Composition of the population of Palestine from 1922 to 1947

	Arabs	Jews	Percentage of Jews among the total population
1922	668,258	83,790	11.1%
1931	858,708	174,606	16.9%
1936	982,614	384,078	28.1%
1939	1,056,241	445,457	29.7%
1945	1,255,708	554,329	30.6%
1947	1,319,434	589,341	30.9%

Chiang is President of a dwindling China

May 20. China has a new constitution and a new President, and both are in trouble. Chiang Kai-shek's new title does not impress the Communists, who escalated the Chinese civil war after the war with Japan ended. Chiang is losing territory to the Communists, and some believe he is losing the war.

The Communists have made significant inroads in the Northern part of the country. Latest reports from the battlefield say they are fast approaching Manchuria.

Chiang, at war with Reds since 1927.

Financial difficulties are also hurting Chiang's battle against the Communists. The money pipeline from Washington has started to dry up as the United States concentrates recovery efforts on Europe. And corruption is taking its toll on Chiang's Kuomintang. In 12 years, the exchange rate of the American dollar has soared from 3.36 Chinese dollars to 12 million (→ 9/1).

213 Communists executed by Greeks

May 16. The peace which most of Europe found at the end of the war eludes the people of Greece. The Athens government, engaged in a bitter civil war with Communist guerrillas, has announced it executed 213 Communists. Some were charged with recent acts of violence. Most faced charges stemming from the rebellion in December 1944.

Lieutenant General James Van Fleet, head of the military section in the United States Mission, says more than 2,000 Communist rebels have been killed, wounded or captured in the past month. Under the Truman Doctrine, the American President has sent military advisers and funds to Greece.

On May 1, a top Greek official paid with his life for operations against the Communists. Minister of Justice Christos Ladas was allegedly assassinated by a member of Opla, a Communist execution squad. The Justice Ministry has been responsible for the executions of the Communists. Other government officials were also targeted for murder by Opla, police say. One of the latest victims of the violence is CBS correspondent George Polk, killed on his way to a meeting with a guerrilla leader (→ 11/30).

May 31. Smiling Mauri Rose sits in a Blue Crown Special after winning his second Indy 500, racing around the track at an average of 120 mph.

South African statesman Smuts resigns

May 28. The right-wing Nationalist Party, which includes Neo-Nazi elements, has pushed Jan Christiaan Smuts, Prime Minister of South Africa, from office.

Smuts, a revered guerrilla fighter during the Boer War of 1900, went on to draft the constitution that was the basis for joining British South African colonies into the Union of South Africa. As Commander-in-Chief during WWII, Smuts oversaw troops in North Africa and Italy and afterwards was instrumental in drafting the preamble to the charter of The United Nations.

Though as prime minister Smuts approved segregationist policies in South Africa, he was defeated by the Nationalist Party, which espouses the policy of apartheid or total separation of the races throughout the country.

Smuts, out after nine years in office.

Upon hearing the news of Smuts' resignation, Britain's Winston Churchill said "a great statesman has . . . been cast aside by the country he had raised to her greatest heights" (→ 1/15/49).

Rail strike is off as U.S. seizes lines

May 10. Acting upon orders of President Truman, the federal government seized the railroads today, just hours before a nationwide strike was set to begin. Railroad union officials, responding to a temporary restraining order, later canceled strike plans, but it was not certain workers would receive word immediately to stay on the job. In the meantime, the U.S. Army will operate the roads until settlement has been reached (→ 6/21).

Two auto makers grant wage rises

May 28. A 17-day strike against Chrysler Corporation ended tonight when the company granted workers a flat wage increase of 13 cents an hour. While the wage hike is two cents an hour more than that granted three days ago to employees of General Motors, the Chrysler settlement, unlike the General Motors pact, is not tied to a cost-of-living formula. The wage boost at Chrysler will increase basic pay to $1.63 an hour; at General Motors, basic pay will amount to $1.61 an hour.

Flood drives 18,500 from Oregon homes

May 31. Bursting through embankments, the Columbia River hit and submerged Vanport City north of Portland yesterday. The 18,500 residents had ten minutes warning before the muddy water poured through in high waves, crushing homes. The city is entirely afloat, and casualties cannot yet be estimated. Cresting rivers have left at least 60,000 homeless and caused $75 million worth of damage in both Washington and Oregon.

1948

JUNE

Su	Mo	Tu	We	Th	Fr	Sa
		1	2	3	4	5
6	7	8	9	10	11	12
13	14	15	16	17	18	19
20	21	22	23	24	25	26
29	28	29	30			

1. Transjordan: Israeli planes blast Amman (→ 11).

2. Washington: Thousands march to demand defeat of Mundt-Nixon Bill (→ 7/20).

2. Truman authorizes airports in Anchorage and Fairbanks.

3. California: World's biggest telescope, at 200 inches, dedicated at Mount Palomar.→

5. France signs Along Bay accords, recognizing Vietnamese independence under Bao Dai (→ 6).

6. Hanoi: Ito denounces new Bao Dai regime as "puppet govt." (→ 11/22).

7. London: U.S., Britain, France agree to keep troops in Germany "until peace of Europe is secured" (→ 15).

8. Prague: Czech Premier Gottwald signs constitution legalizing Communist Parliament (→ 7/17).

8. Frankfort: Denazification court clears Richard Strauss.

10. Chuck Yeager exceeds speed of sound in Bell XS-1 plane.

11. Israel: Arabs and Jews sign armistice (→ 15).

13. Tripoli: State of emergency declared to quell riots between Arabs and Jews.

15. Germany: Soviets halt Berlin-bound coal cars from West (→ 25).

15. N.Y.: U.N. rejects Soviet plea to send observers to Palestine (→ 7/9).

20. N.Y.: Jack Kramer beats Bobby Riggs to take 21st pro tennis title at Forest Hills.

21. U.S. Supreme Court rules unions may print views on politics (→ 11/14).

24. New York: Henry Fonda appears in "Fort Apache."

28. Prague: Cominform denounces Tito, charging he is pro-Western (→ 30).

30. Belgrade: Tito asks Balkan bloc in new blow at Cominform (→ 7/3).

DEATH

6. Louis Lumiere, French photography pioneer (*10/5/1864).

Russian command blockades Berlin

A few of the 2.5 million West Berliners eagerly greet an Allied supply plane.

West Berlin is unreachable by water.

June 25. Russian commanders have tightened the blockade around the Allied sectors of Berlin, but the Western powers say they are determined to fly in enough supplies to keep the population from starving. It will take quite an effort. There is enough food to last just one month, and the Allies estimate they will have to airlift 2,500 tons of food a day to satisfy requirements in the Western zones. At present, only six tons are flown to Berlin every day.

The Soviet Military Administration announced today it would ban all food shipments from Soviet areas into Berlin. The Russians also intercepted six barges that were bound for Berlin from Hamburg. The crackdown on canal traffic follows earlier blockades of the roads and rail lines. Ten days ago, the Soviets stopped coal shipments. They have also reduced the supply of electricity to the Allied sectors of Berlin.

In response, the Allies have outlawed food shipments to the Russian sector. This is not expected to hurt much, but the Allies believe their interruption of coal and steel shipments will have an effect. Morale in the Western sectors of Berlin remains high. The confidence is reflected in the high-riding Deutschmark, which is still worth 30 of the new Russian marks (→ 7/4).

Ike doffs his uniform for a cap and gown

June 7. "I will work. If a fellow works hard, he can't go too far wrong." That is how General Dwight D. Eisenhower summed up his feelings as he resigned his position as chief of staff of the U.S. Army to become the 13th President of Columbia University yesterday.

The general, a graduate of West Point in 1915, was commanding officer during World War I, after which he was stationed in the Panama Canal Zone and in the Philippines. His impressive performance in the 1941 army maneuvers led to his assignment as chief of operations and preceded his meteoric rise as military commander in World War II.

Ike addresses the Columbia campus.

Having spent 36 years in the military profession, the five-star general is now watching over 31,000 students. "At least I was trained for that (military) business. I'm not so sure of this ... It's been a little adjustment, but a lot of fun to try it," he commented to reporters during his brief walk to his new office at Columbia. He was installed with a hearty handshake from the former acting president of the university. Mamie, the general's wife since 1916, expressed her confidence. "Ike will be good," she said, "because he cares."

Man looks through 200-inch telescope

June 3. The world's largest telescope, with a 200-inch mirror, was dedicated and used today at Mount Palomar, 80 miles south of Los Angeles. The telescope is named for George Ellery Hale, the American astronomer whose work made its construction possible.

Hale conceived the project in 1927, when it became evident that the growth of Los Angeles was endangering the work done at the 60-inch Mount Wilson telescope. Hale died in 1938 but work continued, delayed by World War II. The 500-ton Hale telescope is so delicately balanced that a 50-pound push can move it. The observer rides in a cage at the point where light from the mirror is focused. Astronomers say the telescope will allow them to study stars at distances never before possible.

Republicans nominate Dewey and Warren

June 25. Republicans have chosen New York Governor Thomas E. Dewey as their presidential candidate and Governor Earl Warren of California as his vice-presidential running mate. In framing what could be called a "Tale of Two Coasts," Republicans meeting in Philadelphia hope to wrest control of the White House this fall from the Democrats, who have reigned since the days of Herbert Hoover. This will be Dewey's second presidential bid. He was defeated in 1944 by President Roosevelt (→ 7/9).

Dewey runs again.

Currency reform starts in Germany

June 18. Russian soldiers have stopped all traffic to and from Berlin in the wake of currency changes by the Allied forces.

In an effort to put postwar Germany on a sound economic footing, France, Britain and the United States have scrapped the virtually worthless Reichsmark and replaced it with the Deutschmark. As the Russians do not recognize the new currency, however, this step effectively suspends trade between the two sectors, and the Russians have stopped traffic to prevent an influx of Reichsmarks. The Russian authorities accuse the Allies of the switch and say its aim is the division of Germany (→ 25).

N.Y. subway fare is doubled to ten cents

June 30. Last night, New York lost the distinction of being the only large city that clung to the once universal nickel fare on its rapid transit lines, a fare that has prevailed since the city's first subway opened on October 27, 1904.

Noisily but cheerfully, New Yorkers began paying the new rates at 12:01 a.m., namely ten cents for a ride on the 239 miles of subway and elevated routes, seven cents on publicly owned surface lines (182 route miles of trolley and 133 miles of bus lines), and 12 cents for a combination ride. School children have a system of reduced fares. The normal daily passenger load of these lines is six million.

Hayworth and Welles are together at last

When would married couple Rita Hayworth and Orson Welles appear in a film together? Audiences waited breathlessly for "The Lady from Shanghai," now in release. But don't hold your breath any longer: Hayworth and Welles have already filed for divorce. And Hayworth has been seen this month hanging on the arm of Aly Kahn, son of the Moslem religious leader.

"Shanghai" is not Welles' best, but since he directed it, wrote it, produced it and co-stars in it, it is not the worst thriller ever made. In fact, the final scene is brilliant: Hayworth and actor Everett Sloane, portraying a couple united by mutual loathing, shoot at each other in a hall of mirrors. All their illusions come crashing down on them.

Playing together, only in the movies.

Benes resigns job

June 7. "Disgusted" by the new regime, Czechoslovakia's President Benes resigned today rather than sign the Communist constitution. It was Benes who with Masaryk established a Czechoslovakia independent of Austria-Hungary in 1916. After the outbreak of WWII, he established a provisional government in England and hoped that Russian liberation meant renewed freedom for his country. Benes was said to be a broken man when he realized the Soviet Union's true intentions (→ 8).

Draft act is signed

June 24. A draft act requiring men from 19 through 25 to serve in the military was signed into law today by President Truman. Registration will begin within six weeks and in the first year between 200,000 and 225,000 men will be called to duty for 21-month stints. Since those already in the National Guard and other reserve untis are exempt from the draft, the ranks of the civilian reserves have swelled rapidly in recent months. Reserve service requires weekly drills and two weeks a year in camp (→ 8/30).

June 28. A building in Fukui, ravaged by Japan's greatest earthquake since 1930, will in just a few moments be a huge pile of rubble.

June 25. Jersey Joe Walcott retreats from a barrage by champ Joe Louis. Louis scored an 11th-round knockout to retain his title (→ 3/1/49).

Georges Braque wins the grand prize at Venice

Georges Braque.

Georges Braque, the French painter who helped create the revolutionary Cubist style and then rarely strayed from it, has won first prize at the Venice art festival. The decision of the judges solidifies Braque's position as one of the most important artists of the century.

Braque moved to Paris to paint when he was 18. Like others in Montmartre, Braque was influenced by Matisse at first and he went through a Fauvist period in 1905. But it was his meeting with Picasso two years later that proved decisive. Braque was extremely impressed by Picasso's "Les Demoiselles d'Avignon," which he was painting at the time.

Braque and Picasso both rejected the direct representation of nature on their canvases. They magnified and distorted the geometry of objects and surfaces. Critics called their style "Cubism."

Despite the distortion inherent in Braque's style, his canvases were restrained, even austere. At the beginning, many of them, like "Le Gueridon" or "Cafe Table," were painted in grays and beiges. Braque experimented with another medium in 1912 by gluing paper to a work in charcoal. The paper added a new dimension to the work, and some critics believe it was one of the most important experiments of the Cubist movement. Later in his career, Braque started using color more successfully. Nine years ago, he updated his earlier work by painting "The Red Cafe Table."

Braque was born in 1882 in Argenteuil. His father was a real estate entrepreneur.

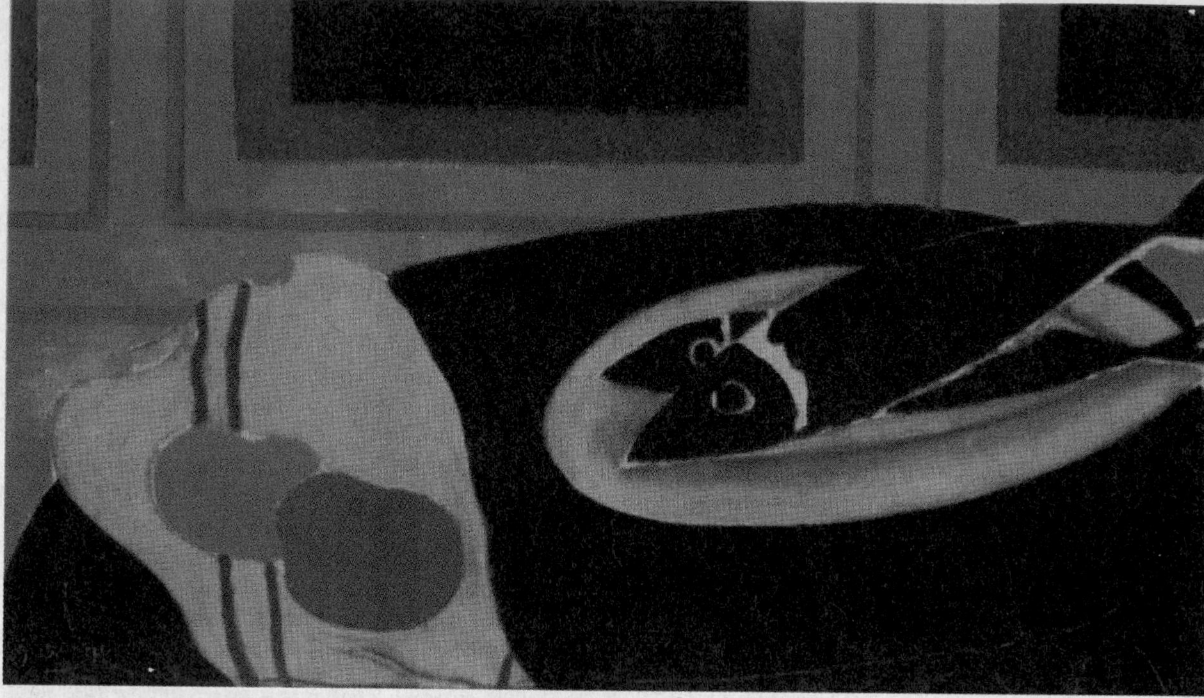

"Black Fish" (1942). Braque has recently focused predominantly on still-life studies.

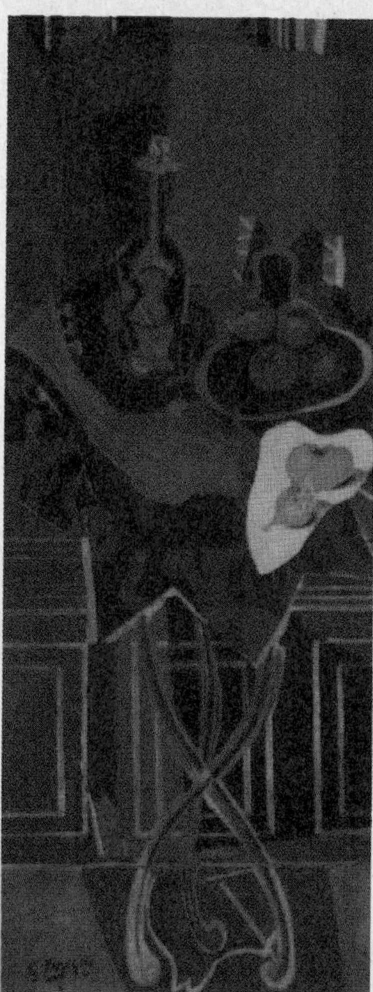

"Red Cafe Table" (1939).

"Cafe Table" (1911). Braque, with Picasso, an early Cubist innovator.

1948

JULY

Su	Mo	Tu	We	Th	Fr	Sa
				1	2	3
4	5	6	7	8	9	10
11	12	13	14	15	16	17
18	19	20	21	22	23	24
25	26	27	28	29	30	31

3. Albania orders expulsion of all Yugoslav personnel (→ 4).

4. Germany: U.S., U.K. fly 3,000 tons of food into Berlin (→ 10).

5. Britain: Natl. Health Services Act offers free "cradle to grave" medical care (→ 11/24/49).

9. Philadelphia: Ike turns down final requests to run (→ 15).

9. U.S. Census Bureau reports highest employment at 61 mil.

9. Israel: Arabs break month-long truce as Egyptians strike by air, Iraqis by land (→ 16).

10. Berlin: Soviets protest airlift as violation of air safety (→ 8/1).

14. Rome: Communist chief Togliatti shot by assassins; riots sweep Italy (→ 3/23/50).

16. N.Y.: Leo Durocher resigns as Brooklyn Dodger manager, accepts post with Giants.

16. Cairo: Arabs and Israelis, under U.N. pressure, agree to truce in Jerusalem (→ 8/25).

17. Prague: Czechs seize 71 as U.S. agents (→ 1/23/49).

17. U.S.: States' Rights Party formed by Southern Democrats, in opposition to Truman's civil rights policies (→ 26).

21. Tito charges Cominform seeks civil war (→ 12/29).

23. Cairo: State of emergency called to quell riots (→ 1/3/50).

24. Truman vows to make A-bomb deadlier while Soviets pursue intl. control (→ 10/9).

24. Philadelphia: Wallace accepts Progressive Party nomination for presidency (→ 8/2).

25. FTC warns U.S. Congress to curb growth of monopoly (→ 29).

28. Germany: Farben chemical plant blast in Ludwigshafen kills 250, injures 6,000.

29. Truman asks price-control power to fight inflation (→ 8/24).

31. N.Y.: Truman dedicates 4,900-acre New York Intl. Airport at Idlewild, Queens.

DEATHS

15. John "Black Jack" Pershing, U.S. general (*9/13/1860).

23. David Wark Griffith, American film director (*1/23/1875).

Tito breaks with Russia

July 4. Joseph Stalin may have met his match in Tito, the leader of Yugoslavia. Tito refuses to knuckle under to the Russians, and his independent brand of communism has led to a break with Moscow. The tensions have been building all year.

Tito charged Russian agents were trying to topple his government. The Russian-backed Cominform, which has its tentacles spread throughout Europe, accused Tito of deviating from the Communist line and sympathizing with the Western imperialists. Tito rejected the criticism, and Russia retaliated by ejecting Yugoslavia from the Cominform and moving its headquarters from Belgrade to Bucharest (→ 21).

Tito: Between East and West.

Army segregation ended by President

July 26. President Truman has ordered an end to discrimination in the armed forces "as rapidly as possible." Men in uniform, he said, should have "equality of treatment and opportunity" regardless of race, color, religion or national origin. The order is expected to stir up bitter opposition in the racially explosive Deep South as well as within his own Democratic Party.

In still another executive order, the president called for a fair employment policy in federal government civil service ranks, on the grounds that "merit and fitness" should be the only criteria for such employment (→ 8/4).

Satchel Paige will pitch for white team

Sidearmer Satchel Paige.

July 7. Satchel Paige, who became a baseball legend playing in the Negro leagues, has signed to pitch for the Cleveland Indians.

The Indians took on the tall, lean veteran as a relief pitcher as they stepped up their fight for the pennant. As he put on a major league uniform for the first time in his 23-year career, Paige said: "I'm starting my major league career with one thing in my favor, anyway. I won't be afraid of anybody I see in that batter's box. I've been around too long for that." Paige, who says he's 39 but could be in his 50's, said Joe DiMaggio was the toughest batter he ever faced.

12 Communists are charged with plot

July 20. A special federal grand jury in New York has indicted 12 high-ranking Communists on a charge of conspiring to overthrow the United States government. The indictments follow a year-long investigation. Among the six arrested last night in New York City were William Z. Foster, the party Chairman who has run for president several times on the Communist Party ticket; and Benjamin Davis, a New York City Councilman. Among those indicted but not yet arrested is Gus Hall, who is Chairman of the Communist Party in Ohio (→ 8/3).

Citation and Eddie Arcaro race to the finish line to capture the vaunted Triple Crown. Arcaro, who now counts four Kentucky Derbys, two Preakness races and four Belmonts among his victories, has won $645,145 on Citation, a record with a single horse.

Democrats name Truman, Barkley

July 15. President Truman, in a fighting mood, accepted the Democratic presidential nomination this morning, predicting victory this fall and saying he would call Congress back into session later this month to deal with housing, education, civil rights and other matters.

The Democratic convention, held in Philadelphia, will name Senator Alben W. Barkley of Kentucky as the vice-presidential candidate. Said the feisty president: "Senator Barkley and I will win this election and make these Republicans like it. Don't you forget that" (→ 24).

One of Billy Wilder's comic best.

1948

AUGUST

Su	Mo	Tu	We	Th	Fr	Sa
1	2	3	4	5	6	7
8	9	10	11	12	13	14
15	16	17	18	19	20	21
22	23	24	25	26	27	28
29	30	31				

1. Albert Camus' "The Plague" published in U.S.

1. Germany: French zone gets economic union with U.S. and U.K. zones (→ 5).

3. Washington: Whittaker Chambers tells HUAC of Red "underground" in federal posts, implicates Alger Hiss (→ 5).

3. Budapest: Pro-Communist Socialist Arpad Szakasits sworn in as Hungarian pres. (→ 12/26).

4. Democrats ban race segregation in natl. headquarters in bid for Negro support (→ 10/25/49).

5. Truman denounces spy inquiries in Congress (→ 25).

5. Berlin: Soviets free city funds in first truce move (→ 9/1).

6. London: American Robert Mathias wins Olympic decathlon at age 17 (→ 15).

7. China: Yang-tse flood leaves three million homeless.

12. New York: Russian teacher survives leap from third floor of Soviet Consulate (→ 25).

12. Washington grants recognition to South Korea, names John Muccio ambassador (→ 15).

15. Seoul: U.S. military govt. ends as Syngman Rhee officially proclaims republic (→ 9/9).

17. Burma declares martial law as rebels clash with govt. troops.

18. N.Y.: Soviet casts 27th veto to bar Ceylon's entrance to U.N.

19. Nanking: Chiang puts Chinese currency on gold standard.

24. U.S. consumer price index reaches record high of 173 against 1935-1939 average.

25. New York: Russian teacher Mrs. Kasenkina says she leaped to avoid returning to Russia.

25. Palestine: Israeli army halts Egyptian drive across "no man's land" (→ 9/17).

30. U.S.: 25-year-olds register for second peacetime draft.

31. Paris: Foreign Minister Robert Schuman chosen French premier.

DEATH

27. Charles Evans Hughes, 11th chief justice of U.S. Supreme Court (*4/11/1862).

U.S. wins 38 medals at London Games

Aug 15. In a dramatic counterpoint to the highly successful London Olympics, a number of Iron Curtain country athletes who competed have refused to return to their homelands. Hungarians, Czechs, Yugoslavs and Poles have made arrangements to remain in Britain or to go to the United States or Canada. There was no estimate on the number of athletes involved in the defections.

The post-Olympic defections followed the usual political controversies that have accompanied nearly every Olympics. The London Games were the first held since the highly politicized 1936 event in Nazi Germany, which became a propaganda show for Adolf Hitler.

The United States left no doubt about its continued Olympic dominance. Americans captured 38 medals and second-place Sweden was next with 17. In unofficial points, the United States scored 662 to 353 for Sweden and 230.5 for third-place France. Americans made an unprecedented sweep of the swimming events.

The highlight of the American triumph was the victory of 17-year-old Robert Mathias of Tulare, California, in the grueling decathlon. Virtually unheard of outside his home area, Mathias rolled up 7,139 points in the event. This was almost as many as he had scored in his American tryout, an amazing feat considering the miserable conditions in London: a track covered with water, slippery vaulting and jumping runways, fading light and a pelting rain.

Another thrill-producer was the 10,000-meter run, which was expected to go to Viljo Heino or some other talented Finn. Instead, a Czech, Emil Zatopek, who was not even given an outside chance, was the surprise winner. He broke all the rules of pace in setting an Olympic record of 30:11.14.

The American winners included Harrison Dillard at 100 meters, Mel Patton at 200 meters and Mal Whitfield at 800 meters. Bill Porter and Roy Cochran swept the hurdles for the United States and Guinn Smith took the pole vault. Willie Steele, a teammate, accounted for the running broad-jump gold medal.

The Olympic flame, carried all the way across Europe, arrives in London to open the Games.

Men Athletics

100 M Dash
1. Harrisson Dillard USA 10,3
2. Norwood Ewell USA 10,4
3. Lloyd LaBeach PAN 10,4

200 M Dash
1. Melvin Patton USA 21,1
2. Norwood Ewell USA 21,1
3. Lloyd LaBeach PAN 21,2

400 M Run
1. Arthur Wint JAM 46,2
2. Herbert McKenley JAM 46,4
3. Malvin Whitfield USA 46,9

800 M Run
1. Malvin Whitfield USA 1:49,2
2. Arthur Wint JAM 1:49,5
3. Marcel Hansenne FRA 1:49,8

1500 M Run
1. Henry Eriksson SWE 3:49,8
2. Lennart Strand SWE 3:50,4
3. Willem Skijkhuis HOL 3:50,4

5000 M Run
1. Gaston Reiff BEL 14:17,6
2. Emil Zatopek TCH 14:17,8
3. Willem Slijkhuis HOL 14:26,8

10,000 M Run
1. Emil Zatopek TCH 29:59,6
2. Alain Mimoun FRA 30:47,4
3. Bertil Albertsson SWE 30:53,6

Marathon
1. Delfo Cabrera ARG 2:34:51,6
2. Thomas Richards GBR 2:35:07,6
3. Etienne Gailly BEL 2:35:33,6

110 M Hurtles
1. William Porter USA 13,9
2. Clyde Scott USA 14,1
3. Craig Dixon USA 14,1

400 M Hurtles
1. Roy Cochran USA 51,1
2. Duncan White CEY 51,8
3. Rune Larsson SWE 52,2

3000 M Steeplechase
1. Thore Sjostrand SWE 9:04,6
2. Erík Elmsàter SWE 9:08,2
3. Gőte Hagstrőm SWE 9:11,8

400 M Relay
1. USA 40,6 (Norwood Ewell, Lorenzo Wright, Harrisson Dillard, Melvin Patton)
2. GBR 41,3 (John Archer, John Gregory, Alistair McCorquodale, Ken Jones)
3. ITA 41,5 (Michèle Tito, Enrico Perucconi, Antonio Siddi, Carlo Monti)

1600 M Realy
1. USA 3:10,4 (Arthur Hamden, Clifford Bourland, Roy Cochran, Malvin Whitfield)
2. FRA 3:14,8 (Jean Kerebel, Francis Schewetta, Robert Chef d'Hőtel, Jacques Lunis)
3. SWE 3:16,0 (Kurt Lundkvist, Lars Wolfbrandt, Folke Alnevik, Rune Larsson)

50 km Walk
1. John Ljunggren SWE 4:41,52
2. Gaston Godel SUI 4:48,17
3. Tebbs Lloyd-Johnson GBR 4:48,31

10 km Walk (1924, 1948, 1952)
1. John Mikaelson SWE 45;13,2
2. Ingemar Johansson SWE 45:43,8
3. Fritz Schwab SUI 46:00,2

High Jump
1. John Winter AUS 1,98
2. Bjőrn Paulson NOR 1,95
3. George Stanich USA 1,95

Pole Vault
1. Guinn Smith USA 4,30
2. Erkki Kataja FIN 4,20
3. Robert Richards USA 4,20

Long Jump
1. Willie Steele USA 7,825
2. Thomas Bruce AUS 7,555
3. Herbert Douglas USA 7,545

Triple Jump
1. Ame Ahman SWE 15,40
2. George Avery AUS 15,365
3. Ruhi Sarialp TUR 15,025

Shotput
1. Wilbur Thompson USA 17,12
2. Francis James Delaney USA 16,68
3. James Fuchs USA 16,42

Discus Throw
1. Adolfo Consolini ITA 52,78
2. Giuseppe Tosi ITA 51,78
3. Fortune Gordien USA 50,77

Hammer Throw
1. Imre Németh HUN 56,07
2. Ivan Gubijan YUG 54,27
3. Robert Bennett USA 53,73

Javelin
1. Tapio Rautavaara FIN 69,77
2. Steve Seymour USA 67,56
3. Jozsef Varsegi HUN 67,03

Decathlon
1. Robert Mathias USA 7139
2. Ignace Heinrich FRA 6974
3. Floyd Simmons USA 6950

Women Athletics

100 M Dash
1. Francina Blankers-Koen HOL 11,9
2. Dorothy Manley GBR 12,2
3. Shirley Strickland AUS 12,2

200 M Dash
1. Francina Blankers-Koen HOL 24,4
2. Audrey Williamson GBR 25,1
3. Audrey Patterson USA 25,2

80 M Hurtles
1. Francina Blankers-Koen HOL 11,2
2. Maureen Gardner GBR 11,2
3. Shirley Strickland AUS 11,4

400 Relay M
1. HOL 47,5 (Xenia Stad de Jong, Jeannette Witziers-Timmer, Gerda van der Kade-Koudijs, Francina Blankers-Koen)
2. AUS 47,6 (Shirley Strickland, June Maston, Betty McKinnon, Joyce King)
3. CAN 47,8 (Viola Myers, Nancy Mackay, Diane Foster, Patricia Jones)

High Jump
1. Alice Coachman USA 1,68
2. Dorothy Tyler-Odam GBR 1,68
3. Micheline Ostermeyer FRA 1,61

Long Jump
1. Olga Gyarmamati HUN 5,695
2. Noemi Simonetto De Portela ARG 5,60
3. Ann-Britt Leyman SWE 5,575

Shotput
1. Micheline Ostemeyer FRA 13,75
2. Amelia Piccinini ITA 13,095
3. Ine Schäffer AUT 13,08

Discus Throw
1. Micheline Ostemeyer FRA 41,92
2. Edera Gentile-Cordiale ITA 41,17
3. Jacqueline Mazeas FRA 40,47

Javelin
1. Henna Bauma AUS 45,57
2. Kaisa Parviainen FIN 43,79
3. Lily Carlstedt DEN 42,08

Men Swimming

100 M Freestyle
1. Walter Ris USA 57,3
2. Alan Ford USA 57,8
3. Géza Kadas HUN 58,1

400 M Freestyle
1. William Smith USA 4:41,0
2. James McLane USA 4:43,4
3. John Marshall AUS 4:47,4

1500 M Freestyle
1. James McLane USA 19:18,5
2. John Marshall AUS 19:31,3
3. Győrgy Mitro HUN 19:43,2

1948 London

100 M Backstroke
1. Allan Stack USA 1:06,4
2. ZRobert Cowell USA 1:06,5
3. Georges Valterey FRA 1:07,83

200 M Backstroke
1. Joseph Verdeur USA 2:39,3
2. Keith Carter USA 2:40,2
3. Robert Sohl USA 2:43,9

800 M Freestyle Relay
1. USA 8:46,0 (Walter Ris, James MacLane, Wallace Wolf, William Smith)
2. HUN 8:48,4 (Elemer Szathmari, György Mitro, Irme Nyéki, Géza Kadas)
3. FRA 9:08,0 (Joseph Bernardo, Henri Padou jun, René Corun, Alexandre Jany)

Springboard Diving
1. Bruce Harlan USA 163,64
2. Miller Anderson USA 157,29
3. Dr. Samuel Lee USA 145,52

High Diving
1. Dr Samuel Lee USA 130,05
2. Bruce Harlan USA 122,30
3. Joaquim Capilla Perez MEX 113,52

Water Polo
1. Italy
2. Hungary
3. Netherlands

Women Swimming

100 M Freestyle
1. Greta Andersen DEN 1:06,3
2. Ann Curtis USA 1:06,5
3. Marie Louise Vaessen HOL 1:07,6

400 M Freestyle
1. Ann Crustis USA 5:17,8
2. Karen-Margrete Harup DEN 5:21,2
3. Catherine Gibson GBR 5:22,5

200 M Breaststroke
1. Petronella van Viet HOL 2:57,2
2. Bèatrice Lyons AUS 2:57,7
3. Eva Novak HUN 3:00,2

100 M Backstroke
1. Karen Margrete Harup DEN 1:14,4
2. Suzanne Zimmerman USA 1:16,0
3. Judy Davies AUS 1:16,7

400 M Freestyle Relay
1. USA 4:29,2 (Marie Corridon, Thelma Kalama, Brenda Helser, Ann Curtis)
2. DEN 4:29,6 (Eva Riise, Karen Margrete Harup, Greta Andersen, Fritze Carqtensen)
3. HOL 4:31,6 (Irma Schmacher, Margot Marsman, Marie-Louise Vaessen, Johanna Termeulen)

Springboard Diving
1. Victoria Draves USA 108,74
2. Zoe Ann Olsen USA 108,23
3. Patricia Elsener USA 101,30

High Diving
1. Victoria Draves USA 68,87
2. Patricia Elsener USA 66,28
3. Birte Christoffersen DEN 66,04

Boxing

Flyweight
1. Pascual Perez ARG
2. Spartaco Bandinelli ITA
3. Soo-Ann Han KOR

Bantamweight
1. Tibor Csik HUN
2. Giovanni Battista Zuddas ITA
3. Juan Venegas PUR

Featherweight
1. Ernesto Formenti ITA
2. Denis Shepherd SAF
3. Aleksy Antkiewicz POL

Lightweight
1. Gérald Dreyer SAF
2. Joseph Vissers BEL
3. Svend Wad DEN

Welterweight
1. Julius Porma TCH
2. Horrace Herring USA
3. Alessandro D'Ottavio ITA

Middleweight
1. Laszlo Papp HUN
2. John Wright GBR
3. Ivano Fontana ITA

Light Heavyweight
1. George Hunter HUN
2. Donald Scott GBR
3. Maurio Cia ARG

Heavyweight
1. Rafael Iglesias ARG
2. Gunnar Nilsson SWE
3. John Arthur SAF

Greco Roman Wrestling

Flyweight
1. Pietro Lombardi ITA
2. Kenan Olcay TUR
3. Reino Kangasmäki FIN

Bantamweight
1. Kurt Pettersen SWE
2. Ali Mahmoud Hassan EGY
3. Halil Kaya TUR

Featherweight
1. Mehmet Oktav TUR
2. Olle Anderberg SWE
3. Ferene Toth HUN

Lightweight
1. Gustaf Freis SWE
2. Aage Eriksen NOR
3. Karoly Ferencz HUN

Welterweight
1. Gősta Andersen SWE
2. Miklos Szilvasi HUN
3. Henrik Hansen DEN

Middleweight
1. Axel Grőnberg SWE
2. Muhlis Tayfur TUR
3. Ercole Gallegati ITA

Light Heavyweight
1. Karl-Erik Nilsson SWE
2. Kaelpo Grőndahl FIN
3. Ibrahim Orabi EGY

Heavyweight
1. Ahmet Kirecci TUR
2. Tor Nilsson SWE
3. Guido Fantoni ITA

Freestyle Wrestling

Flyweight
1. Lennart Viitala FIN
2. Halit Balamir TUR
3. Thure Johanssor SWE

Bantamweight
1. Nasuh Akar TUR
2. Gerald Leeman USA
3. Charles Kouyos FRA

Light Heavyweight
1. Henri Wittenberg USA
2. Fritz Stőckli SUI
3. Bengt Fahlkvist SWE

Heavyweight
1. Gyula Bobis HUN
2. Bertil Antonsson SWE
3. Joseph Armstrong AUS

Men Fencing

Foil Individual
1. Jehan Buhan FRA
2. Christian d'Oriola FRA
3. Lajos Maszlay HUN

Foil Team
1. France
2. Italy
3. Belgium

Epée Individual
1. Luigi Cantone ITA
2. Oswald Zappelli SUI
3. Edouardo Mangiarotti ITA

Epée Team
1. France
2. Italy
3. Sweden

Sabre Individual
1. Aladar Gerevich HUN
2. Vincenzo Pinton ITA
3. Pal Kovacs HUN

Out of the blocks for the 100-meters, with eyes already on the finish line.

Featherweight
1. Gazanfer Belge TUR
2. Ivan Sjőlun SWE
3. Adolf Muller SUI

Lightweight
1. Celal Atik TUR
2. Gősta Fråndfors SWE
3. Harmann Baumann SUI

Welterweight
1. Yagar Dogu TUR
2. Richard Garrard AUS
3. Leland Merrill USA

Middleweight
1. Glen Brand USA
2. Adil Candemir TUR
3. Erik Linden SWE

Sabre Team
1. Hungary
2. Italy
3. USA

Women Fencing

Foil Individual
1. Ilona Elek HUN
2. Karen Lachmann DEN
3. Ellen Műller-Preis AUS

Modern Pentathlon
1. William Grut SWE
2. George Moore USA
3. Gősta Gårdin SWE

CHART

Weightlifting

			2 Arm Press	2 Arm Snatch	2 Arm Clean & Jerk	Total
Bantamweight						
1.	Joseph de Pietro	USA	105,0	90,0	112,5	307,5
2.	Julian Creus	GBR	82,5	95,0	120,0	297,5
3.	Richard Tom	USA	87,5	90,0	117,5	295,0
Featherweight						
1.	Mahmoud	EGY	92,5	105,0	135,0	332,5
2.	Rodney Wilkes	TRI	97,5	97,5	122,5	317,5
3.	Jaffar Salmassi	IRA	100,0	97,5	115,0	312,5
Lightweight						
1.	Ibrahim Hassan Shams	EGY	97,5	115,0	147,5	360,0
2.	Attila Hamouda	EGY	105,0	110,0	145,0	360,0
3.	James Halliday	GBR	90,0	110,0	140,0	340,0
Middleweight						
1.	Frank Spellman	USA	117,5	120,0	152,5	390,0
2.	Peter George	USA	105,0	122,5	155,0	382,5
3.	Sung-Jip Kim	KOR	122,5	112,5	145,0	380,0
Light Heavyweight						
1.	Stanley Stanczyk	USA	130,0	130,0	157,5	417,5
2.	Harold Sakata	USA	110,0	117,5	152,5	380,0
3.	Gősta Magnusson	SWE	110,0	120,0	145,0	375,0
Heavyweight						
1.	John Davis	USA	137,5	137,5	177,5	452,5
2.	Norbert Schemansky	USA	122,5	132,5	170,0	425,0
3.	Abraham Charité	HOL	127,5	125,0	160,0	412,5

Canoeing

Kayak—1 1000 M
1. Gert Fredriksson SWE 4:33,2
2. Johan Frederik Kubberup DEN 4:39,9
3. Henri Eberhardt FRA 4:41,4

Kayak—2 1000 M
1. Sweden 4:07,3
2. Denmark 4:07,5
3. Finland 4:08,7

Kayak—1 10,000 M (1936, 1948, 1952, 1956 only)
1. Gert Fredriksson SWE 50,47,7
2. Kurt Wires FIN 51;18,2
3. Ejvind Skabo NOR 51,35,4

Kayak—2 10,000 M (1936, 1948, 1952, 1956 only)
1. Sweden 46:09,4
2. Norway 46:44,8
3. Finland 46,48,2

Canadian—1 1000 M
1. Josef Holecek TCH 5:42,0
2. Douglas Bennet CAN 5:53,3
3. Robert Boutigny FRA 5:55,9

Canadian C-2 1000 M
1. Czechoslovakia 5:07,1
2. USA 5:08,2
3. France 5:15,2

Canadian-1 10,000 M (1936, 1948, 1952, 1956 only)
1. Frantisek Capek TCH 62:05,2
2. Frank Haven USA 62:40,4

Canadian-2 10,000 M (1936, 1948, 1952, 1956)
1. USA 55,55,4
2. Czechoslovakia 57:38,5
3. France 58:00,8

Canoeing Women

Kayak-1 500 M
1. Karen Hoff DEN 2:31,9
2. Alida v. d. Anker Doedans HOL 2:32,8
3. Fritzi Schwingl AUT 2:32,9

Rowing

Single Scull
1. Mervyn Wood AUS 7:24,4
2. Eduardo Risso URU 7:38,2
3. Romolo Catasta ITA 7:51,4

Double Sculls
1. Great Britain 6:51,3
2. Denmark 6:55,3
3. Uruguay 7:12,4

Pair Oars without Coxswain
1. Great Britain 7:21,1
2. Switzerland 7:23,9
3. Italy 7:31,3

Pair Oars with Coxswain
1. Denmark 8:00,5
2. Italy 8:12,2
3. Hungary 8:25,2

Four Oars without Coxswain
1. Italy 6:39,0
2. Denmark 6:43,5
3. USA 6:47,7

Four Oars with Coxswain
1. USA 6:50,3
2. Switzerland 6:53,3
3. Denmark 6:58,6

Eight Oars
1. USA 5:56,7
2. Great Britain 6:06,9
3. Norway 6:10,3

Yachting

Monotype Class Individual
1. Paul Elvstrőm DEN 5543
2. Ralph Evans jr USA 5408
3. Jacobus Hermanus de Jong HOL 5204

Star Class
1. USA 5828
2. Cuba 4949
3. Netherlands 4731

Dragon Class
1. Norway 4746
2. Sweden 4621
3. Denmark 4223

6 M Class (1908, 1912, 1920, 1924, 1928, 1932, 1936, 1948, 1952 only)
1. USA 5472
2. Argentina 5120
3. Sweden 4033

Swallow
1. Great Britain 5625
2. Portugal 5579
3. USA 4352

Cycling

Road Race Individual
1. José Beyaert FRA 5:18:12,6
2. Gerardus Petrus Voorting HOL 5:18:16,2
3. Lode Wouters BEL 5:18:16,2

Road Road Team
1. Belgium 15:58:17,4
2. Great Britain 16:03:31,6
3. France 16:08:19,4

1000 M Time Trial
1. Jacques Dupont FRA 1:13,5
2. Pierre Nihant BEL 1:14,5
3. Thomas Godwin GBR 1:15,0

Sprint (1000 M)
1. Mario Ghella ITA 12,0
2. Reginald Harris GBR
3. Axel Schandorff DEN

Tandem 2000 M
1. Italy 11,3
2. Great Britain
3. France

Team Pursuit (4000 M)
1. France 4:57,8
2. Italy 5:36,7
3. Great Britain 5:55,8

Equestrian Sports

All around Individual Competition
1. Bernard Chevallier FRA – 4
2. Frank Henry USA –21
3. Rober Selfelt SWE –25

All around Team Competition
1. USA –161,50
2. Sweden –165,00
3. Mexico –305,25

Dressage Individual
1. Hans Moser SUI 492,5
2. André Jousscaume FRA 480,0
3. Gustaf-Adolf Bolternstern Jr SUE

Dressage Team
1. France 1269,0
2. USA 1256,0
3. Portugal 1182,0

Grand Prix Jumping Individual
1. Humberto Hariles Cortes MEX –6,25
2. Rubén Uriza MEX –8/0
3. Jean Francois D'Orgeix FRA –8/4/38,9

Grand Prix Jumping Team
1. Mexico –34,25
2. Spain –56,50
3. Great Britain –67,00

Shooting

Full-Bore Rifle, 300 M
1. Emil Grűnig SUI 1120
2. Pauli Janhonen FIN 1114
3. Willy Rőgeberg NOR 1112

Small Bore Rifle, 50 M
1. Arthur Cook USA 599/43
2. Walter Tomsen USA 599,42
3. Jonas Jonsson SWE 597/44

Rapid Fire Pistol
1. Karoly Takacs HUN 580
2. Carlos Enrique Diaz Saenz Valiente ARG 571
3. Sven Lundqvist SWE 569

Free Pistol, 50 M
1. Edwin Vasquez Cam PER 545
2. Rudolf Schnyder SUI 539/60/21
3. Torsten Ullman SWE 539/60/16

Men Gymnastics

All around Individual Competition
1. Veikko Huhtanen FIN 229,70
2. Walter Lehmann SUI 229,00
3. Paavo Aaltonen FIN 228,80

All around Team Competition
1. Finland 1358,30
2. Switzerland 1356,70
3. Hungary 1330,85

Parallel Bars
1. Michael Reusch SUI 39,50
2. Veikko Huhtanen FIN 39,30
3. Josef Stalder SUI 39,10
3. Christian Kipfer SUI 39,10

Floor Exercise
1. Ferenc Pataki HUN 38,70
2. Janos Mogyorósi-Klencs HUN 38,40
3. Zdenek Ruzicka TCH 38,10

Vault Horse
1. Paavo Aaltonen FIN 39,10
2. Olavi Rove FIN 39,00
3. Janos Mogyorósi-Klencs HUN 38,50
3. Ferenc Pataki HUN 38,50
3. Léo Sotornik TCH 38,50

Sidehorse
1. Veikko Huhtanen FIN 38,70
1. Paavo Aaltonen FIN 38,70
1. Heikki Savolainen FIN 38,70
2. Luigi Zanetti ITA 38,30
3. Guido Figone ITA 38,20

Horizontal Bar
1. Josef Stalder SUI 39,70
2. Walter Lehmann SUI 39,40
3. Veikko Huhtanen FIN 39,20

Flying Rings
1. Karl Frei SUI 39,60
2. Michael Reusch SUI 39,10
3. Zdenek Ruzicka TCH 38,50

Women Gymnastics

All around Team Competition
1. Czechoslovakia 445,45
2. Hungary 440,55
3. USA 422,63

Basketball
1. USA
2. France
3. Brazil

Soccer
1. Sweden
2. Yugoslavia
3. Denmark

Field Hockey
1. India
2. Great Britain
3. Netherlands

Spy mania grips America's attention

Accused meets accuser: HUAC investigator Robert Stripling mediates between Alger Hiss (standing far rt.) and Whittaker Chambers (standing far left).

Aug 25. America is caught in the grip of a Communist spy mania, fueled by congressional probes into alleged espionage rings involving past or present federal officials.

The major focus has been on the House Un-American Activities Committee, where Whittaker Chambers, a self-confessed former spy for the Communists, accused Alger Hiss, a former top official of the State Department, of having given him secret government papers in the late 1930's. Hiss has denied the charges. Chambers is now an editor of Time magazine.

Other prominent figures, including some who served in the New Deal administration of the late President Roosevelt, have been accused in the HUAC hearings of having taken part in Red spy rings. These men, including Harry Dexter White, a former Assistant Secretary of the Treasury, and Lauchlin Currie, a top Roosevelt aide, have denied the charges.

Meanwhile, a Senate committee is investigating the effectiveness of the loyalty test given to government employees. And on the other side of the Capitol, a House committee is holding hearings on Communist influence in unions representing New York City department store workers.

President Truman has denounced what he calls the spy hunts, saying they are only a "red herring" that is designed to detract attention from his efforts to push through the Republican-controlled special session of Congress new legislation to help curb inflation. The spy mania, he said, has demoralized federal government employees and eroded public confidence (→ 9/22).

End of the line for the Sultan of Swat

Aug 23. The Sultan of Swat is dead, but he did not forget his faithful subjects. Babe Ruth left the bulk of his estate to his widow, but he remembered "the kids of America," the millions who idolized the famous home-run hitter as he dominated baseball for two decades.

Ruth's will provided for a gift of ten percent of his estate to the Babe Ruth Foundation. The foundation is "organized under the membership corporation laws of the state of New York and dedicated to the interest of the kids of America."

The will was dated August 9, one week before Ruth died of cancer. The noted slugger was 53 when he died after a two-year battle with the disease that repeatedly sent him back to hospitals.

The mighty Ruth, whose portly figure rounding the bases was a familiar sight to baseball fans, had wasted away and the once-black hair seen so often when he doffed his cap had turned to gray.

Within hours of his death, 15,000 messages were received by the hospital. They included tributes from President Truman and Cardinal Spellman.

George Herman "Babe" Ruth hit a record 60 home runs in a season in 1927, his eighth year with the Yankees. And he hit a record 714 career homers. He broke into the majors with Baltimore in 1914 and was sold that same year to the Providence farm of Boston. As a Boston hurler, he tossed a record 29 consecutive scoreless innings in a World Series.

In June, leaning on his bat, Ruth said farewell in "the house that he built."

U.S. Communists supporting Wallace

Aug 2. William Z. Foster, Chairman of the American Communist Party, endorsed the candidacy of Henry A. Wallace for president of the United States in a spirited Communist Party convention at Madison Square Garden. About 17,000 applauded the announcement and Foster's accompanying speech in which he assailed "Wall Street imperialists" as warmongers who want to rule the world.

Foster, along with 11 other Communist leaders, is currently under federal indictment for conspiring to overthrow the government by force. It is believed that the defense of those indicted will include a detailed account of how the U.S. government, not the Communist Party, is guilty of conspiracy. Eugene Dennis, another speaker at the rally, declared the Truman administration is the "force of monopoly reaction who is conspiring to launch a postwar offensive against the common people of America and the world" (→ 9/30).

West Coast gains population rapidly

MacArthur Park, a lush oasis in the thriving metropolis of Los Angeles.

Aug 8. The year 1947 proved to be the biggest single year of growth in the nation's history with births at 3.9 million and immigration at 215,000, placing the estimated 1947 population total at 143,414,000.

The Census Bureau, in a report reflecting migration between states, showed boom growth on the Pacific Coast and outward migration from the South. Leading states in population gain since 1940 are California with 9.8 million residents, a 42.1 percent increase, Oregon with a 41.8 percent gain and Washington with a 35.8 percent increase.

Some 28 states showed net losses through migration, but in most cases births made up the difference. Nine states lost population: Arkansas, Kentucky, Mississippi, Oklahoma, West Virginia, Nebraska, Montana, North and South Dakota.

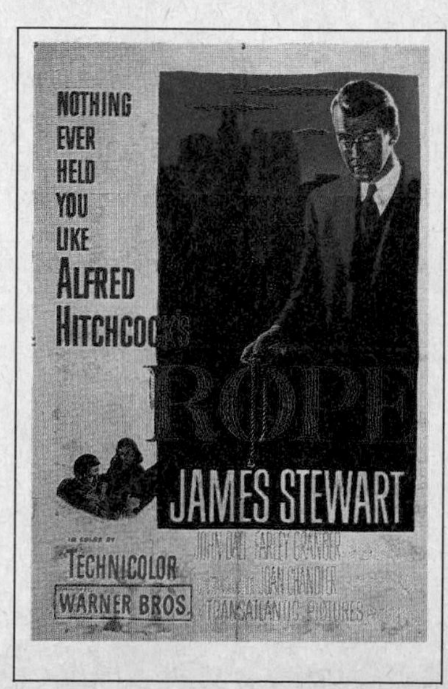

1948

SEPTEMBER

Su	Mo	Tu	We	Th	Fr	Sa
			1	2	3	4
5	6	7	8	9	10	11
12	13	14	15	16	17	18
19	20	21	22	23	24	25
26	27	28	29	30		

1. Nanking: Communist radio announces formation of North China People's Govt. (→ 26).

1. Germany: Parliamentary Council, led by Konrad Adenauer, formed in Bonn (→ 3).

2. Paris: Big Four award Italian Somaliland to Italy.

3. Berlin: Communists riot, seizing city hall (→ 9).

3. Poland: People's Workers Party chief Gomulka ousted for advocating independence from Moscow (→ 1/29/49).

4. Amsterdam: Queen Wilhelmina gives up Dutch throne to daughter Juliana.

9. Berlin: Russians fire on crowd protesting coup in Assembly (→ 26).

10. Washington: Mildred Elizabeth Gillars, alias "Axis Sally," indicted for treason.

11. Pakistan: Indian troops invade Hyderabad (→ 17).

14. U.S. scientists say world population outgrowing food supply.

17. Pakistan: Hyderabad surrenders to Indian army (→ 11/29).

17. Jerusalem: Count Folke Bernadotte, U.N. mediator for Palestine, slain by mob (→ 21).

19. Moscow announces planned withdrawal of troops from Korea by end of year (→ 10/21).

22. Truman assails HUAC as more un-American than those it investigates (→ 30).

24. Buenos Aires: Peron accuses U.S. ex-diplomat of murder plot, stirring anti-Americanism (→ 5/1/49).

26. Berlin reunification issue submitted to U.N. (→ 10/25).

26. China: Tsi-Nan taken by Mao forces (→ 10/23).

30. HUAC urges ousting Atty. Gen. Tom Clark if he fails to prosecute alleged spies (→ 10/1).

DEATHS

1. Charles Beard, American historian (*11/27/1874).

3. Eduard Benes, Czech independence leader (*5/26/1884).

11. Mohammed Ali Jinnah, first governor general of Pakistan (*12/25/1876).

Bernadotte, U.N. aide, killed in Jerusalem

Sept 21. Count Folke Bernadotte, U.N. mediator for Palestine, has been assassinated by Jewish irregulars, almost certainly members of the Stern gang, when they opened automatic fire on his car as it passed through the Israeli-held area of Jerusalem. Also killed was Col. Andre Pierre Serot, a U.N. official detached from France's Air Force.

In his final report to the U.N., received just after his slaying four days ago, Bernadotte said the U.N. must force a compromise upon the Arabs and Israelis. Recognizing the existence of "a Jewish state called Israel," he recommended radical boundary changes, with Galilee going to Israel and the Negev to the Arabs. He stated that Jerusalem "should be accorded special and separate treatment," and that "innocent people uprooted from their homes" must be assured the right of return, meaning the Arabs.

American Secretary of State George Marshall has announced that the U.S. will press the U.N. to accept Bernadotte's proposals (→ 10/15).

North Korea is made a republic

Sept 9. North Korea proclaimed independence today as the Democratic People's Republic of Korea under the leadership of Kim Il Sung. North Korea was founded on May 1 of this year; today's declaration formalizes the republic. The Communist-controlled nation, like its Southern neighbor, the Republic of Korea led by Syngman Rhee, claims jurisdiction over the entire Korean peninsula.

Pyongyang is the capital of the newly declared republic. It is expected that the new government will develop economic plans similiar to those implemented by the Soviet Union and will probably nationalize all major industries (→ 19).

Whistle Stop tour wins Truman votes

Sept 30. Politicians often travel by plane these days, but President Harry S. Truman still likes the campaign train, an American tradition. Seeking another four years in the White House, the president began traveling by train around the country in June and is still at it, visiting both the big cities and the little towns and villages called "whistle stops." He wants the voters to see him and hear him. And they seem to like what they see and hear, although every public opinion poll is against him. "Give 'em hell, Harry," one of his supporters yelled, and that has become his campaign style. His theme is, "We are going to win" (→ 10/8).

Airlift sets supply record to Berlin

U.S. C-74 Globemaster at Gatow.

Sept 18. The Allied airlift into Berlin set a new record today by flying in 7,000 tons of supplies in defiance of the three-month-old Russian blockade. Despite fog, high winds and rain, American and British planes made 895 flights into Berlin over a 24-hour period, carrying food and fuel for the Allied sectors in the jointly occupied city. To celebrate Air Forces Day, U.S. pilots flew 651 flights, carrying 5,572 tons of coal. The new record was a further demonstration that the Allied airlift would be able to supply Berlin with crucial amounts of food and fuel despite the Soviet blockade of land travel (→ 26).

Laurence Olivier brings Shakespeare to the screen. Olivier's brilliant portrayal of Hamlet's tragic dilemma is highlighted by stunning on-location film work, shot in Elsinore, Denmark.

This year's Cadillac is graced with a two-piece curved windshield, a wide rear window, tail fins inspired by Lockheed's P-38 fighter aircraft and a Hydramatic automatic transmission. Yours for only $2,833 (→ 2/1950).

1948

OCTOBER

Su	Mo	Tu	We	Th	Fr	Sa
					1	2
3	4	5	6	7	8	9
10	11	12	13	14	15	16
17	18	19	20	21	22	23
24	25	26	27	28	29	30
31						

1. Orson Welles' "Macbeth" makes U.S. premiere.

1. Washington: HUAC implicates Charlie Chaplin (→ 12/6).

4. Boston: Cleveland Indians break tie with Sox to win AL pennant in first playoff (→ 11).

4. Madagascar: French pass death sentences on two nationalist rebels.

7. Minnesota: Brecht's "The Caucasian Chalk Circle" opens.

7. Paris: U.S. bars Spain's admittance to U.N. (→ 1/19/50).

8. Cincinnati: U.M.W. backs Dewey for president (→ 11/2).

9. Paris: Premier Queuille tells France, beset by strikes, protest won't foil Marshall Plan (→ 22).

9. Wales: Churchill, in fiery speech, says only A-bomb stands between freedom and Communist domination (→ 11/4).

11. Boston: Indians win Series over Braves 4-3 in six games.

15. Israel: Arab-Israeli fighting renews, ending truce (→ 21).

21. Scotland: N.Y.-bound Dutch KLM airliner crashes at Tarbolton, killing 34 of 40 aboard.

21. Seoul: MacArthur arrives as Korean Cabinet calls emergency session to suppress Communist uprising (→ 12/8).

21. Israel: Israelis capture Beersheeba (→ 23).

22. Paris: French call army to quell strikes; two dead, 38 hurt.

23. China: Mao takes govt. centers Chengchow, Paotow (→ 30).

23. Vatican: Pius XII urges international Jerusalem (→ 28).

24. Washington: Bernard Baruch tells Senate committee "we are in the midst of a cold war which is getting warmer."

25. Paris: Soviets veto U.N. call to lift Berlin blockade (→ 11/16).

28. Indonesia: Sukarno bans Communist Party; guerrilla war continues (→ 12/19).

31. U.S. tells nationals in North China to leave area (→ 11/9).

DEATH

24. Franz Lehar, Austrian composer (*4/30/1870).

China concedes Manchuria lost to Reds

Mao's men celebrate victory with fists raised in Communist salute.

Oct 30. This is Chiang Kai-shek's birthday, but he does not have much to celebrate. The Communists have overrun Manchuria, and the losses have been devastating. The Communists say they have obliterated 12 Nationalist army divisions west of the key city of Mukden. An equal number of government troops are trying to escape from the area by sea. Some have reached Yingkow, the port on the Gulf of Liaotung which is still held by the Nationalists. But a large number of Chiang's troops are bottled up in Hulutao, on the western shore of the gulf.

The Communist rout in Manchuria makes the Nationalist troops in Northern China much more vulnerable. It is not clear how General Fu Tso-yi will respond to the threat or how the government will respond to the loss of Manchuria's coal mines and industry to the Communists. The civil war has already stretched Chiang's budget beyond the breaking point. He is meeting only a fraction of expenses (→ 31).

President supports strong, free Israel

Oct 28. Campaigning in New York City, President Truman made his strongest pro-Israel pitch in a speech tonight to the Liberal Party at Madison Square Garden.

Vowing that Israel must be "large enough, free enough and strong enough to make its people self-supporting and secure," he ignored the Bernadotte report and thus indicated a split with Secretary of State Marshall, who had endorsed it before the United Nations.

Meanwhile, the third U.N. truce in the war launched by the Arab League against the new state of Israel appears to be holding up. Peace has settled over the war-torn Negev, where the Israelis determined to take as much land as possible, captured Beersheba, shattered the Egyptian front and severed Egyptian supply lines only hours before the cease-fire, agreed upon by both sides, went into effect.

Israeli leaders are now hopeful of peace talks with the Arabs. Egypt has always been the main stumbling block to any negotiations, but the complete Israeli triumph in the Negev may well have melted Egypt's previous reluctance to negotiate (→ 11/5).

Christian Dior's "New Look" sweeps a world eager for elegance

The latest in afternoon wear, patterned after Dior's "New Look."

A year ago last spring, there was a fashion shot heard around the world. Christian Dior introduced his "New Look," and women the world over began succumbing to his romantic, young, seductive and radical silhouette.

Dior's collection at that time presented a suit that had a white silk jacket with rounded shoulders and a neatly nipped waistline, and the hips were lightly padded over a long, pleated black silk skirt that fell to about ten inches of the floor.

"What a new look," exclaimed Carmel Snow, the editor of Harper's Bazaar. The suit, called Bar, has caught on, inspiring all sorts of imitations and changes in the world of fashion, which Dior felt was due for a shake-up after 40 years of square, mannish, waistless shapes.

The new fashions, however, require a prodigious amount of fabric, presenting something of a problem to produce in countries still recovering from World War II. Shortages of all kinds, including fabric, exist all over. This has led some women to protest the "New Look." But the tremendous appeal of the elegant style from the house of Dior is proving hard to resist among women who for years had to wear dull, utilitarian clothing (→ 4/17/49).

Dior's hotel is besieged by members of the "Little Below the Knee" club.

1948

NOVEMBER

Su	Mo	Tu	We	Th	Fr	Sa
	1	2	3	4	5	6
7	8	9	10	11	12	13
14	15	16	17	18	19	20
21	22	23	24	25	26	27
28	29	30				

3. Kansas repeals Prohibition after 68 dry years.

4. Paris: U.N. approves U.S. plan for atom control, rejects Soviet proposal (→ 12/15).

5. Israel: Egyptians retreat from Negev on U.N. order; Israelis defy (→ 12/1).

8. New York: Autos force end of Hudson River Day Line after 85 years of service.

9. China: Communists break Tientsin-Pukow rail line, halting coal to Nanking (→ 10).

10. China: Martial law proclaimed in Nanking and Shanghai (→ 17).

14. A.F.L. urges U.S. Congress to repeal Taft-Hartley Act in favor of Wagner Act (→ 1/3/49).

16. Florida: Truman rejects four-power talks on Berlin until blockade is removed (→ 30).

17. U.S. to strengthen Marine force at Tsingtao on request of Chiang Kai-shek (→ 21).

19. Paris: Gary Davis, claiming to be "first citizen of the world," interrupts U.N. to call for world government (→ 9/22/49).

21. China: Communists denounce U.S. aid to Chiang as act of aggression (→ 12/1).

22. Yale elects Levi Jackson first Negro to coach football team.

22. Paris: Ho's Democratic Republic of Vietnam requests admittance to U.N. (→ 3/8/49).

24. Caracas: Venezuelan army takes over, ousting president.

24. Dublin: Dail votes independence from U.K. (→ 4/17/49).

27. Philadelphia: Army and Navy play to 21-21 tie.

29. New York: Metropolitan Opera televised for first time as season opens with "Othello."

29. India: Assembly bans discrimination against untouchables (→ 1/30/49).

30. Berlin: Communists complete division of city, installing government in Soviet sector (→ 2/13/49).

BIRTH

14. Prince Charles, heir to British throne.

Truman wins, confounding prophets

Nov 2. Confounding the prophets, President Truman has won a full term in the White House, defeating the Republican favorite, Thomas E. Dewey. The Truman victory was one of the major upsets in American political history.

Throughout the night, the Truman political fortunes waxed and waned. While leading at all times in the popular vote, the president trailed at times in the essential electoral vote until just before dawn today when he picked up Illinois.

Aside from President Truman himself, few political forecasters of either party believed that he would win. His own Democratic Party had been badly splintered by Southern insurgents who broke off to create the States' Rights Party in protest of the president's efforts to win civil rights protections. While the new party's slate of candidates, Gov. J. Strom Thurmond of South Carolina and Fielding L. Wright of Mississippi, failed to win a substantial vote, it did siphon off traditional Southern Democratic support.

Adding to the dilemma of the Democratic ticket was the existence of still another splinter party, the Progressives, whose presidential candidate was Henry A. Wallace, a former Vice President under the late President Roosevelt (→ 1/20/49).

Chicago Trib, anxious to get the scoop, ran a story that Truman proved false.

Greek struggle in north continues

Nov 30. War drags on between Nationalist Greeks and Communist guerrillas. Yugoslavia, Bulgaria and Albania increasingly aid the rebels, an act the Nationalist government asked the U.N. to condemn. Such a resolution was passed November 10 by a 48-6 vote. The "nays" came from the nations condemned, the U.S.S.R. and two Eastern-bloc nations. Resolutions are of no help to the people of San Remo, caught in the cross fire raging near the hills of Mt. Grammos in northern Greece (→ 3/31/49).

Captured by rebels in Greece.

Tojo and 7 others sentenced to hang

Nov 12. Hikedi Tojo, the man who vowed to establish "a new order in Asia," was sentenced to hang by an international tribunal today. Through assassinations and staged incidents, Tojo and his generals whipped Japan into a militaristic fervor and plunged the country into WWII, predicting that democracies such as the United States were soft and lacked the will to fight back. Of 23 other defendants on trial with Tojo, seven were sentenced to hang and 16 were given life in prison (→ 12/23).

Tojo testified in vain.

45 billion units of drug to fight V.D.

Nov 7. With 45 billion units of penicillin and hundreds of radio ads, New York is attacking 250,000 "hidden" cases of venereal disease.

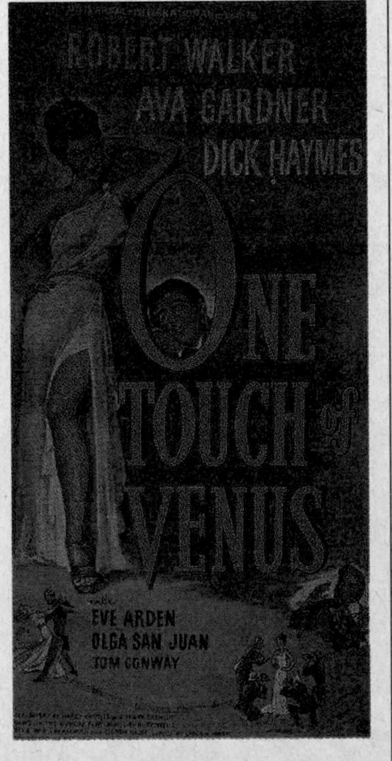

1948

DECEMBER

Su	Mo	Tu	We	Th	Fr	Sa
			1	2	3	4
5	6	7	8	9	10	11
12	13	14	15	16	17	18
19	20	21	22	23	24	25
26	27	28	29	30	31	

1. Beirut: Arab leaders name Abdullah of Transjordan King of Palestine (→ 17).

8. Paris: U.N. approves recognition of Seoul (→ 10).

9. U.S. abandons plan to deconcentrate industry in Japan.

10. China: Chiang extends martial law nationwide (→ 1/11/49).

10. Seoul: U.S. agrees to $300 mil. aid for S. Korea (→ 1/1/49).

15. French bring first nuclear reactor into service (→ 3/31/49).

17. Washington: Smithsonian accepts Wright brothers' plane Kitty Hawk.

19. Philadelphia: Chicago Bears blanked by Eagles 7-0 in pro football championship.

19. Indonesia: Dutch airborne troops seize Jakarta, imprison top leaders of republic (→ 25).

23. Tokyo: Tojo and six collaborators hanged for war crimes (→ 9/8/51).

26. Budapest: Communists arrest Joseph Cardinal Mindszenty for alleged plot against government (→ 2/1/49).

29. Belgrade: Tito declares Yugoslavia will follow own Communist line (→ 7/6/49).

CULTURAL EVENTS, 1948

Literature: Alan Paton's "Cry the Beloved Country"; Norman Mailer's "The Naked and the Dead"; Graham Greene's "The Heart of the Matter"; Ezra Pound's "The Pisan Cantos."

Academia: Churchill's "The Gathering Storm"; B.F. Skinner's "Walden Two"; Kinsey report, "Sexual Behavior of the Human Male"; George Gamow and Ralph Alpher's "The Origin of Chemical Elements," proposing Big Bang theory.

Music: Cole Porter's "Kiss Me, Kate"; "All I Want for Christmas Is My Two Front Teeth."

The Arts: Georges Braque's "The Bird"; Pollock's "Composition No. 1"; Leger's "Hommage to David."

Film: "Hamlet," with Olivier, Academy Award; David Lean's "Oliver Twist"; de Sica's "The Bicycle Thief"; Flaherty's "Louisiana Story."

Dutch encircle Jakarta, arrest Sukarno

Dutch counterinsurgency troops conduct "police operations" near Jakarta.

Dec 25. Disregarding a United Nations cease-fire order, Dutch troops captured the last Indonesian republic stronghold. The city of Madian fell, concluding a week of Dutch aggression in Java that began with a paratrooper and airborne assault on the capital, Jakarta, on the 18th. Using a tactical encircling technique, the Dutch military seized control of the infant government and arrested President Sukarno and other republic leaders.

The Dutch government, bitter about Indonesian independence and angry about alleged terrrorist attacks they claim were instigated by republic leaders, wishes to revive a new and sympathetic republican government on the islands.

The United Nations Security Council has ordered Dutch officials to terminate their fighting and release Sukarno and the other leaders. The Netherlands government has released most of its prisoners, but it seems unlikely that it will comply completely with the council's directive until they implant new leadership in Java (→ 1/28/49).

Pumpkin papers contain spy secrets

Dec 6. Tiny rolls of microfilmed documents stashed in a hollowed-out pumpkin have been found on the Maryland farm of Whittaker Chambers, a former Communist underground agent, who claims that he received these top secret papers from Alger Hiss, at that time an an important official of the State Department.

The so-called Pumpkin Papers are key evidence in a probe by the House Un-American Activities Committee into the existence of a pre-war espionage ring. The papers also will figure in a pending libel suit filed by Hiss against Chambers, and in a federal grand jury investigation in New York into communism and espionage.

Chambers, now a Senior Editor for Time magazine, claims that Hiss slipped him top secret government papers in 1937-38 for delivery to the Russians. Hiss, now President of the Carnegie Endowment for International Peace, has denied having passed on such documents.

Investigators for the House panel say that the microfilm papers found in the pumpkin shell show "definite proof of one of the most extensive espionage rings in the history of the United States" (→ 3/2/49).

T.S. Eliot wins Nobel Prize for literature

Dec 10. The author of "The Love Song of J. Alfred Prufrock" (1911) and "The Waste Land" (1922) has been given the Nobel Prize for literature. Thomas Stearns Eliot is not a prolific poet, but one of the best. He injects objectivism and modern idiom into an art grown stale. Since he came along, people no longer complacently "come and go, speaking of Michelangelo."

St. Louis-born T.S. Eliot.

Eliot was born in St. Louis, Missouri, September 26, 1888. He studied at Harvard, the Sorbonne and Oxford. Eliot took various editing jobs in England, finally becoming a British subject in 1927. He married an Englishwoman whose mental breakdown inspired some of Eliot's most wrenching poetry. (She died last year.) His friend Ezra Pound kindly hounded him to keep writing. His latest work is optimistic, reflecting a recent glad conversion to Anglo-Catholicism.

"Poetry," Eliot wrote, "is not a turning loose of emotion, but an escape from emotion; it is not the expression of personality, but an escape from personality. But, of course, only those who have personality and emotions know what it means to want to escape from these things."

U.N. votes Human Rights Declaration

Dec 10. "History will regard this proclamation as one of the most outstanding achievements of the United Nations," remarked Dr. Herbert Evatt, President of the U.N. General Assembly, on the adoption of the Human Rights Declaration. The proclamation, three years in preparation, passed the Assembly by a vote of 48-0 with the Soviet bloc, Saudia Arabia and South Africa abstaining. While details are not yet complete, it defines fundamental freedoms in an International Bill of Rights.

The assembly gave Mrs. Franklin Roosevelt a standing ovation for her tireless work on the drafting of the document. "She has raised a great name to an even greater honor," Dr. Evatt said in praising the former First Lady.

America startled by Kinsey Report on sex

A professor from the University of Indiana has published a surprising report called "Sexual Behavior of the Human Male." The author, biologist and zoologist Alfred Kinsey, had literally studied the birds and the bees before tackling the more formidable homo sapiens. He and several assistants canvassed 5,300 white males to learn about their personal sexual habits.

Men were asked about the frequency of masturbation, orgasm, oral sex, "petting" and marital and extramarital intercourse. Police occasionally tried to interfere with the questioning and hindered the final publication. Some libraries hesitated to put the book on their shelves.

Another source of controversy was the study's funding: The National Research Council and the Rockefeller Foundation were major contributors. Some people wonder if the study warranted the support, or if it was warranted at all. And some wonder how they can get a private peek at the book.

Alfred and Clara Kinsey.

Mme. Chiang in U.S. asking help

Dec 1. Mme. Chiang Kai-shek arrived in Washington at 10 a.m. aboard President Truman's former airplane, the Sacred Cow. Mme. Chiang was met at the airport by the Chinese Ambassador and Dr. H.H. Kung, her brother-in-law and once Chinese Prime Minister. There were no immediate plans to meet with the president or other officials.

Mme. Chiang comes to Washington at a crucial time for China. Civil war rages, the country rendered half-Communist, half-Nationalist. Chiang Kai-shek increasingly relies on the United States for arms and economic aid. Mme. Chiang's cool reception may reflect impatience on the part of the United States, which too often hears of Nationalist corruption and inefficiency (→ 10).

Madame Chiang and her husband.

Elizabeth names her son and heir

Dec 14. Tonight, four weeks and two days after the birth of their infant son, England's Princess Elizabeth and the Duke of Edinburgh announced their choice of the famous royal name Charles for him. The full name of the baby, second in line of succession, is His Royal Highness Prince Charles Philip Arthur George of Edinburgh. The last Charles to occupy the throne was Charles the Second, the "merry monarch," who died in 1685.

Future heir to the throne.

British team finds tsetse fly cure

Dec 29. British scientists say they have discovered a drug that prevents tsetse flies from causing sleeping sickness in cattle. The discovery is expected to open vast areas of Africa to cattle farming, now impossible because of the ravages of the tsetse fly. The drug, antrycide, was discovered and tested in Africa by a team of scientists headed by Dr. F.H.S. Curd, who tragically was killed in a railway accident just a month ago.

Israel rejected for U.N. membership

Dec 17. Israel's bid for U.N. membership has been rejected by the Security Council because of the abstention of France and Canada. The vote was five in favor (the U.S., Soviet Union, Argentina, Colombia and the Ukraine), one opposed (Syria) and five abstained (which included Britain, China and Belgium.) Since a majority of seven is needed, abstention amounts to a vote against. France and Canada think it premature to admit Israel before it sets up a demilitarized zone in the Negev and implements an armistice throughout the Holy Land (→ 1/1/49).

Americans voracious for paperback books

Paperback books are sweeping the stores, as people find reading a cheap, portable pleasure. Over 135 million of the pocketbooks were sold this year. Reaping the benefits are popular authors, including James A. Michener, Norman Mailer and Graham Greene.

Michener wrote "Tales of the South Pacific," about unlikely loves and hates during wartime. Michener's first book reveals the New Yorker's intimate familiarity with Asian culture. Mailer, a 25-year-old Harvard graduate, also published his first novel, "The Naked and the Dead." The subject matter is more concerned with the latter than the former; it is an indictment of war. Like Michener, Mailer fought in the Pacific. Prolific novelist and playwright Greene offered "The Heart of the Matter." It may be his best work since "The Power and the Glory" (1940).

Alan Paton's novel, "Cry, the Beloved Country" reveals the evils of apartheid, sanctioned this year in South Africa. Although the book is fiction, it is strongly autobiographical. Albert Camus' book "The Plague" describes the kind of rebellion that the oppression in South Africa invites.

Andrew Wyeth's haunting "Christina's World," like much of his work, is so painstakingly realistic as to appear almost surreal.

1949

JANUARY

Su	Mo	Tu	We	Th	Fr	Sa
						1
2	3	4	5	6	7	8
9	10	11	12	13	14	15
16	17	18	19	20	21	22
23	24	25	26	27	28	29
30	31					

1. Pasadena: Northwestern beats University of California 20-14 in Rose Bowl.

1. Washington formally recognizes Seoul govt. (→ 4/8).

1. Israel: Tel Aviv shelled by Egyptian ships (→ 4).

3. U.S. Supreme Court upholds Taft-Hartley Act, ruling states may ban closed shop (→ 3/2).

4. Washington: Israeli envoy says troops have left Egypt (→ 9).

7. Truman announces resignation of Secretary of State George Marshall.

9. Egypt: Israeli fighters shoot down five RAF reconnaissance planes (→ 16).

11. China: Surrender talks open with Tientsing virtually lost to Communists (→ 15).

14. Newark: U.S. brings monopoly suit against AT&T.

15. South Africa: Race riots kill 100, injure 1,000 in Durban (→ 1/29/50).

15. China: Reds occupy Tientsin after 27-hour battle (→ 19).

16. Lebanon: Israeli army gives up four Lebanese villages (→ 25).

19. China: Chiang govt. moves capital to Canton (→ 21).

19. U.S. Congress raises presidential salary to $100,000 with $50,000 expense allowance.

21. China: Chiang resigns as president to speed peace (→ 22).

22. Prague: 60 seized as agents for U.S. (→ 3/29).

23. China: Communists begin advance on Nanking (→ 3/13).

25. Israel: Ben Gurion's Mapai Party, with labor support, wins parliamentary elections (→ 29).

25. Hollywood: Ingrid Bergman to go to Italy to make film with Roberto Rosselini (→ 8/5).

28. U.N. demands Dutch withdrawal from Indonesia (→ 6/29).

29. Britain grants de facto rcognition to Israel (→ 31).

29. Poland: 200 ex-army members arrested as anti-government plotters (→ 3/18).

30. India: 100,000 pray at site of Gandhi's assassination on first anniversary of his death (→ 2/6).

China Communists occupy Peking

Mao's picture is paraded in Peking.

Jan 22. Nationalist forces have yielded control of Peking to the Chinese Communists amidst indications that the long civil war is drawing to an end. The almost polite surrender of the traditional Chinese capital, under siege for more than a month, was arranged in an agreement between General Fu Tso-yi, Nationalist commander, and the Communists that establishes a separate peace for Northern China.

Under the agreement, a coalition committee was established to supervise the transition to Communist rule. Meanwhile in the Nationalist capital of Nanking, Generalissimo Chiang Kai-shek, who has fought the Communists for more than 20 years, announced that he was retiring as President of China with the hope that his departure would bring an end to the hostilities.

Li Sung-jen, who was named acting President, announced his caretaker government was ready to negotiate a peace on the basis of terms laid down earlier this month by Communist leader Mao Tse-tung. In Tsingtao, it was announced the U.S Marine force of 8,000 would be withdrawn (→ 23).

United Nations gets Kashmir cease-fire

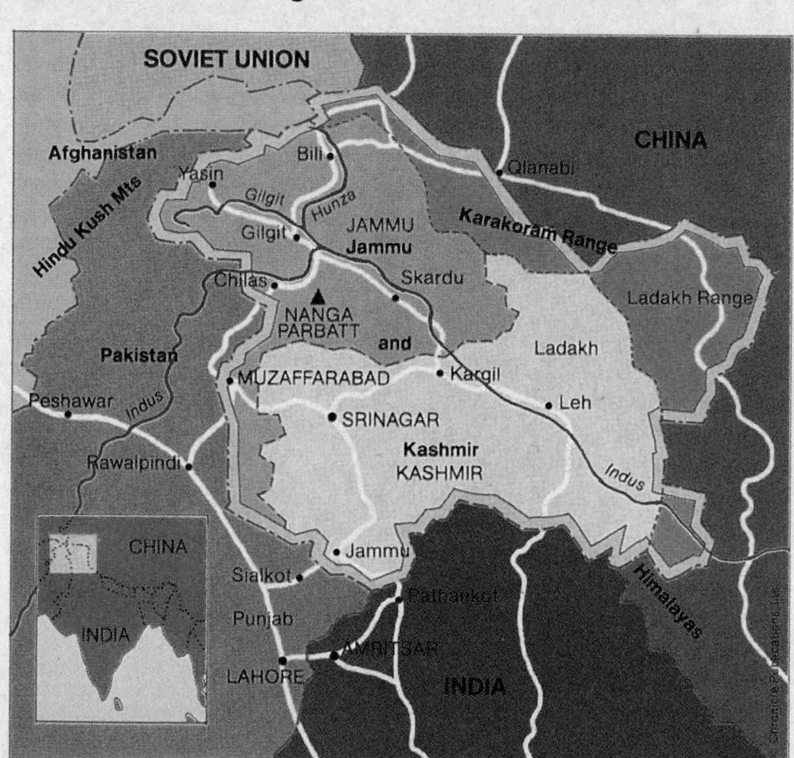

Moslem-Hindu religious tensions divide disputed Kashmir.

Jan 1. Peace returned this morning to the remote and rugged state of Kashmir. The landlocked state has been locked in civil war since India was partitioned, but now the fighting has stopped as India and Pakistan agreed to a cease-fire arranged by the United Nations.

Both dominions retain their military positions in disputed Kashmir, but they have withdrawn most of their troops. A plebiscite is being arranged so the people can decide whether their future lies with India or Pakistan.

Kashmir has been a focus of the religious rivalry between Moslems and Hindus for centuries. It was conquered by Moslems in the late 14th century. A hundred years ago, Britain installed a Hindu ruling family. Tensions festered and occasionally flared up. In 1947, Moslems attacked as soon as Pakistan was created. India, which retaliated with force, submitted the problem to the United Nations. The world organization appointed Chester Nimitz, the American Admiral, to arrange a cease-fire.

Puerto Rico swears in first Governor

Jan 2. Puerto Rico inaugurated Luis Munoz Marin, former Greenwich Village writer, as its first elected Governor today in a colorful celebration that brought out the greatest festive crowd in the history of this Caribbean island.

Munoz Marin, 50, abandoned a career as poet and journalist in New York a quarter of a century ago to enter Puerto Rican politics. In 1938, he organized and headed the Popular Democratic Party with the slogan "Bread, Land, and Liberty." He has campaigned vigorously for social and economic reform and been editor of La Democracia, a San Juan daily founded by his father.

The governor champions economic growth in cooperation with the U.S. President Truman called the election a "fine example of democracy in action" (→ 10/30/50).

Luis Munoz Marin, by popular vote.

U.N. to pay $24 million for headquarters

Jan 28. Secretary General Trygve Lie has awarded the contract for construction of the 39-story skyscraper in glass, aluminum and marble that will provide 889,000 square feet for the Secretariat of the United Nations in New York.

The $24 million contract includes complete foundations for two more buildings to be erected later, one for the General Assembly and the other for the Security Council and other U.N. agencies. Construction on these cannot start until Congress acts on a bill to appropriate the $65 million that President Truman promised as a loan. Four building companies have combined their resources to carry out the massive project on the 17-acre site.

The Secretariat building, "a manifestation of progress toward peace," will have 5,400 windows, six acres of glass "walls" and 21 high speed elevators. Under the miles of walks and roadways, coils will be installed to carry a warm liquid to melt snow and ice. The building may be ready for occupancy by the autumn of 1950 (→ 8/1950).

The Rockefeller site on the East River awaits the United Nations.

Dramatic moment on the inter-German border, sharpest line between the ever-diverging East and West: Soviet soldiers examine the papers of a group of refugees they surprised en route to the West. Everyone holds their breath, hoping they will be allowed to pass, but to no avail.

Where did Marx go wrong on America?

Karl Marx, prophet of profit.

Jan 9. Soviet economists met in Moscow today to try to figure out why the United States has not been overcome by the grave economic crisis that Marx predicted would befall all capitalist societies. America remains the envy of the world in both its productive output and socioeconomic success. The reasons for U.S. immunity to socialism are historical: America never had feudalism, which in Europe led to class consciousness; the frontier served as an escape for discontented workers; ethnic diversity prevented class solidarity; abundant resources meant vast wealth; and New Deal intervention into the depressed economy saved capitalism from itself.

Truman proposes aid to poor lands

Jan 20. Outlining a Point Four program for American leadership in the world, President Truman was inaugurated today for his first full term in the White House.

Addressing a crowd of some 100,000 persons gathered on the east plaza of the Capitol, Truman drew a sharp line between democracy and communism, saying that America would not be deluded by Soviet political philosophy.

His four cardinal points were:

Support of the United Nations.

Help European recovery through the Marshall Plan.

Military aid to freedom-loving nations to thwart aggression.

Share American industrial progress and scientific advances with those underdeveloped parts of the world (→ 10/6).

Mapai wins the first Israeli elections

Jan 31. For the first time, Israeli Jews went to the polls to vote for their nation's leaders. Prime Minister David Ben Gurion has received a strong vote of confidence from his countrymen, and his Mapai Party secured 34 percent of the balloting, which will give them 41 seats in Parliament. The oppostion Labor Party, the Mapam, collected 12 percent. The only notable surprise was the strong showing by the Communists, who captured 3.5 percent of the vote and will gain four seats in the 120-seat Assembly. Today, the U.S. granted Israel and Transjordan full recognition (→ 2/17).

President Weizmann votes.

RCA introduces a 45 rpm record

Jan 10. One day after Columbia Records made public details of the new 7-inch "micro-groove" record, RCA-Victor demonstrated its new system, involving new records, record-changers and turntables.

The records of the competitors are the same size, both made of unbreakable vinylite with hundreds of grooves an inch, but they play at different turntable speeds. The new RCA records revolve 45 times a minute, the new Columbia records 33 1/3 times a minute, while conventional shellac records, used by 16 million record-player owners, revolve 78 times a minute. The records cannot be used on competing phonographs or be played on conventional ones without an additional mechanism, resulting in confusion, even disgust, among buyers.

1949

FEBRUARY

Su	Mo	Tu	We	Th	Fr	Sa
		1	2	3	4	5
6	7	8	9	10	11	12
13	14	15	16	17	18	19
20	21	22	23	24	25	26
27	28					

1. Washington: Truman says he favors planned economy to prevent crash (→ 13).

1. Budapest: Hungary proclaimed People's Republic (→ 7).

5. Iran dissolves communist Tudeh Party (→ 3/7/51).

6. India to nationalize estate of Nizam, world's richest man — size of Conn. and Del. (→ 11/15).

7. New York: Yankees give Joe Dimaggio $90,000 for one year, highest salary in baseball.

7. Hoover Commission recommends removal of Postal Dept. from government control.

7. Budapest: Cardinal Mindszenty, primate of Hungary, gets life sentence for treason (→ 14).

12. Cairo: Moslem Brotherhood chief Hassan el Banna shot to death.

13. Ecuador: Mob burns radio station after braodcast of H.G. Wells' "War of the Worlds."

13. Berlin: Communists order "natl. state of distress" over U.S. war preparations (→ 18).

13. AMA proposes voluntary health insurance plan to oppose Truman's federal plan (→ 7/15).

14. N.Y.: U.S. charges U.S.S.R. with interning eight to 14 million in labor camps (→ 3/7).

14. Moscow: U.S. journalist Anna Louise Strong held by Soviet as spy (→ 23).

15. World oil production reported to have grown 70% in last nine years.

20. Berlin bars film version of "Oliver Twist," calling Fagan portrayal anti-Semitic.

21. Washington: Nicaragua and Costa Rica sign treaty of friendship ending border hostilities.

22. Munich: Court frees Fritz Kuhn, German-American Bund leader.

22. France: Communist leader Maurice Thorez declares party won't support war vs. U.S.S.R.

25. New Mexico: 2-stage rocket WAC-Corporal sets records — 5,000 mph, 250 miles altitude.

27. Brussels: Communists heckle Winston Churchill as he calls for European unity.

Hungarian Cardinal Mindszenty receives a lifetime sentence

Mindszenty, on trial in Budapest.

250,000 hear Pius protest the verdict.

Feb 14. Worldwide outrage has greeted the conviction and sentencing of Joseph Cardinal Mindszenty in Hungary. A court in Budapest sentenced him to life in prison after he was found guilty of treason, conspiracy to overthrow the government and changing money on the black market. Five other defendants, including three priests, were also found guilty. Mindszenty, an outspoken critic of the Communist regime, confessed to most of the charges, but Western observers say he was drugged in the showdown between church and state.

President Truman called the Hungarian judges a "kangaroo court" and he said the verdict was "infamous." New York's Mayor William O'Dwyer called it a "lynching." Pope Pius XII said the verdict was "a most serious outrage" and the Church was "crushed with most bitter grief." The Pope, in a grim announcement to the College of Cardinals, stopped short of saying Mindszenty had been drugged, but he accused Hungarian prosecutors of using a "secret influence" on the Cardinal. The court's goal, charged the Pontiff, was to "disrupt the Catholic Church in Hungary."

At his trial, Mindszenty said he was "guilty in principle of most of the accusations made," but he denied taking part in a plot to overthrow the government. The prosecution introduced as evidence a letter which it called a confession to the charges, and two handwriting experts testified that the document was genuine and written in Mindszenty's hand. The two experts have just returned to Vienna, where they reversed themselves, charged the Hungarian prosecutors with making them testify under duress and accused officials of drugging Mindszenty (→ 9/16).

Reagan earns more than the President

Feb 5. The Internal Revenue Service has released the names of wage earners who grossed $75,000 or more last year. President Truman did not make the highest-paid list. Most movie stars did.

Humphrey Bogart led the Hollywood coterie with a salary before taxes of $467,361. Bogart made only three films on his salary in 1947. Fred MacMurray ($325,000), Errol Flynn ($199,999) and Ronald Reagan ($169,000) lagged behind.

Actress Bette Davis led the women with $328,000 from Warner Brothers studios. In fact, she is the highest-paid woman in any profession. Pretty good for a woman who made no film at all in 1947. Other hefty earnings went to Deanna Durbin ($323,477) and Betty Grable ($299,333).

Acting for the movies is not the only lucrative occupation in the United States, of course. Jacob W. Schwab, a clothing maker, earned $440,542, while Joseph Pulitzer, publisher, grossed $284,712.

Jet bomber crosses U.S. in under 4 hours

Feb 8. An XB-47 jet bomber set a coast-to-coast speed record today when it flew from the Moses Lake air base in the state of Washington to Andrews Field, Maryland., in three hours, 46 minutes, averaging 607.2 mph. The six-engine jet cut 27 minutes off the record set two years ago by Col. William H. Council in an F-80 interceptor. The XB-47 is the first bomber designed for speeds over 600 miles an hour.

Major Russel E. Schleeh (left) stands before his XB-47 at Andrews Field.

Israel and Egypt sign armistice in Rhodes

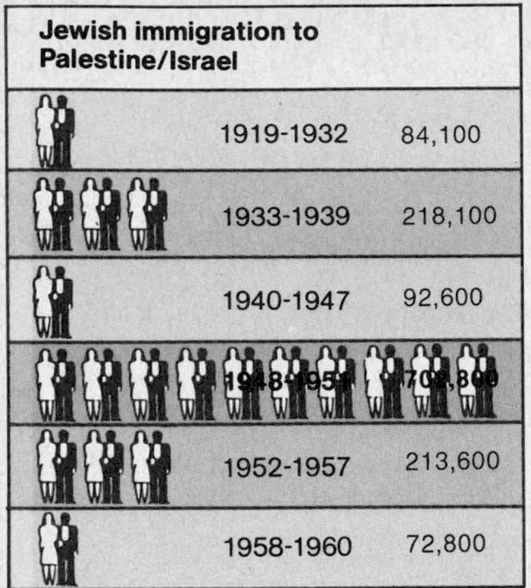

Jewish immigration to Palestine/Israel	
1919-1932	84,100
1933-1939	218,100
1940-1947	92,600
1948-1951	702,800
1952-1957	213,600
1958-1960	72,800

Feb 24. An uneasy peace has returned to the Middle East as Israel and Egypt signed an armistice on the island of Rhodes. The two countries agreed to cease hostilities, but Egypt refused to formally recognize the existence of Israel. So far, Egypt is the only Arab enemy of Israel to sign the armistice.

The agreement was reached after 42 days of difficult negotiations that nearly collapsed on several occasions. Much of the credit for the armistice must be given to Dr. Ralph J. Bunche, the mediator appointed by the United Nations. Bunche's patience and skill were taxed frequently during angry exchanges between the Israeli and Egyptian negotiators. More than once, he kept the talks alive by changing the subject of the discussions when agreement on a particular point seemed impossible. The two countries acknowledged Bunche's skill at a buffet supper on Rhodes last night.

Some 1,500 Jews, released from British camps in Cyprus, arrive in Haifa.

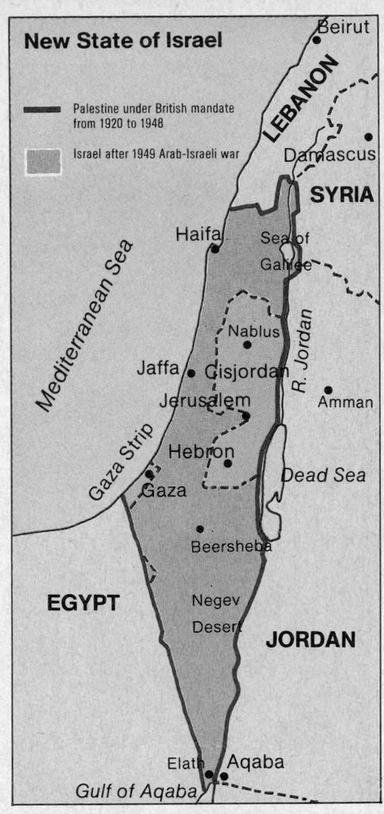

New Mideast borders set in Rhodes: Israel keeps troops in Beersheba and controls part of the Negev Desert.

One of the most bitterly contested points of the negotiations was the status of Beersheba, the strategic crossroads town of the Negev Desert. Under the terms of the United Nations partition plan, Beersheba was given to the Arabs. It has since been occupied by Israel, and Egypt wanted it back. Bunche succeeded in omitting mention of Beersheba from the armistice agreement. Its final status will be decided in negotiations with Transjordan, but it is significant that Israel has not been forced to withdraw troops from the town.

The Israelis scored another victory in the talks with Egypt when they were allowed to retain portions of the Negev captured in the offensive last October 14. Egypt had demanded the return of the area at the start of the talks.

Bunche's chief of staff, General William Riley, left Rhodes yesterday for Beirut, where he will hold more talks with the Lebanese government. Word is that Lebanon is about to agree to the armistice. Iraq, Syria and Saudia Arabia are also not far from signing. The holdout is Transjordan (→ 3/4).

Pound gets prize while locked up

Feb 19. Ezra Pound, under indictment for treason and presently in a mental hospital in Washington, won a $1,000 prize today for the best poetry published in 1948. The Bollingen Prize for Poetry was awarded his book "The Pisan Cantos," which he finished in an American Army prison camp, accused of broadcasting pro-Mussolini propaganda from Italy during the war.

Expecting to be criticized, the judges, who included Conrad Aiken, W.H. Auden, T.S. Eliot and Katherine Anne Porter, stated that "to permit other considerations than that of poetic achievement to sway the decision would destroy the significance of the award."

Idaho-born Pound, 63, has been living mostly abroad since 1911. He has disavowed any Fascist sympathies but will have to stand trial if and when he is released from the hospital, where he is reportedly translating Confucius.

Weizmann, lifelong Zionist, is President

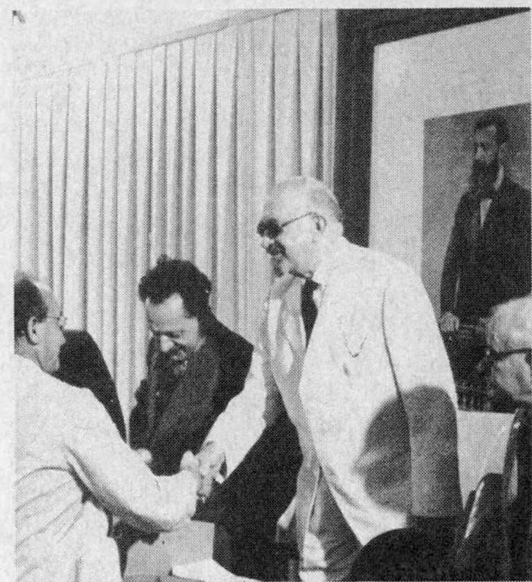

Herzl, in portrait, eyes Weizmann.

Feb 17. The Assembly has elected as Israel's first President Dr. Chaim Weizmann, elder statesman and lifelong Zionist. He has been provisional president since May 17, three days after the proclamation of Israel as the first Hebrew nation in 2,000 years, fulfilling the dream of Theodor Herzl, Zionist founder (→ 24).

Soviet Union expels Anna Louise Strong

Feb 23. For the past 28 years, Anna Louise Strong has lived in Moscow and consistently expressed pro-Soviet views, but now the 64-year-old American newspaperwoman has been arrested, charged with espionage and sabotage activities and subsequently deported.

She arrived at LaGuardia Airport today, and, as she stepped from the plane, a federal subpoena was handed to her by an FBI agent, calling for her appearance before the New York federal grand jury investigating communism. Escorted by 15 policemen, she told reporters not to "use me to inflame international friction."

Berlin airlift delivers one million tons

Feb 18. The Allied airlift, now in its eighth month, reached a total today of one million tons of cargo flown into West Berlin. The new total was set when a royal air force transport landed at Gatow Airfield in the British sector with seven and one-half tons of potatoes and food.

As has often been the case during the airlift, the plane, aided by ground controllers, made the landing despite a heavy fog that limited visibility to just a little more than one-quarter of a mile. Since the airlift began last June following a Russian blockade of land routes, 2.5 million persons in the Allied sectors of Berlin have been fed and fueled by air (→ 3/19).

Americans cheer the millionth ton to cross the "aerial bridge."

1949

MARCH

Su	Mo	Tu	We	Th	Fr	Sa
		1	2	3	4	5
6	7	8	9	10	11	12
13	14	15	16	17	18	19
20	21	22	23	24	25	26
29	28	29	30	31		

2. U.S. Communist leader Wm. Z. Foster declares party won't support war vs. U.S.S.R. (→ 23).

2. Lewis calls 2-week coal strike to protest James Boyd's appointment to Mine Bureau (→ 5/20).

4. N.Y.: Security Council votes Israel's entry into U.N. (→ 4/3).

5. N.Y.: FBI seizes three as spies, including Soviet U.N. aide.

7. U.N. votes to look into U.S. allegation that Eastern bloc holds 8-14 mil. in labor camps.

8. France signs accord with Annam ex-emperor; Tonkin, Annam, Cochin China to merge under Bao Dai as alternative to Ho's Hanoi govt. (→ 6/13).

12. Havana: Three U.S. sailors mobbed for desecrating statue of Cuban writer and nationalist rebel Jose Marti.

13. China: Mao installs regional regime north of Yangtze (→ 25).

18. Warsaw asks U.S. to recall envoy Chester Opal for calling Poland a Soviet satellite (→ 6/5).

19. Moscow calls North Atlantic Treaty a war weapon (→ 4/4).

19. Berlin: Soviet People's Council signs constitution of German Democratic Republic (→ 26).

23. New York: Ex-Communist leader Earl Browder offers to testify against 11 Communist leaders before HUAC (→ 4/30).

25. China: Mao sets up headquarters in Peking (→ 4/10).

26. Western Allies make border shifts in Germany (→ 4/8).

28. Washington: Louis Johnson replaces James Forrestal as Secretary of Defense (→ 5/22).

29. Prague: Czechs sentence two U.S. soldiers as spies (→ 6/16).

30. Damascus: Syrian army seizes power in coup (→ 8/14).

31. Boston: Churchill says only A-bomb kept U.S.S.R. from taking over Europe (→ 4/6).

31. Greece: Markos rebels attack in Thrace, Macedonia (→ 8/28).

31. Canada: Referendum makes Newfoundland 10th province.

DEATH

11. General Henri Giraud, ex-Free French chief (*1/18/1879).

Allies organize NATO

Lord Ismay takes office at London headquarters as NATO Secretary General. The 12-nation alliance, aimed at presenting a united front to the U.S.S.R. and its allies, completes the division of Europe that so many wished to avoid. The Allies, however, claim it will serve the "preservation of peace and security."

March 18. Is it a legitimate defense treaty or a militaristic plan that will only provoke the Soviet Union? Forceful arguments were made for both viewpoints as the United States and Western Europe unveiled plans for a collective defense alliance they call the North Atlantic Treaty Organization, or NATO. The Allies agreed that an armed attack on any one of them would be considered an attack against them all. Their goal is the "preservation of peace and security." They also reaffirmed support for the United Nations.

Critics say the treaty will turn Europe into an armed camp that will ignite a war with the Russians. Earlier this month, Belgian Communists adopted a resolution opposing any "war of aggression against the Soviet Union." Strong opposition to the alliance has also surfaced in left-wing circles in Italy and France. A chief backer of the treaty, Secretary of State Dean Acheson, chides critics by saying that only strength will preserve peace.

The U.S., Canada, Britain, France and the Benelux nations wrote the treaty. Italy, Norway, Denmark, Iceland and Portugal are invited to sign it next month (→ 19).

B-50 flies non-stop around the world

March 2. An American B-50 bomber, Lucky Lady II, completed the first non-stop flight around the world today when it landed at Carswell Air Force Base near Ft. Worth, Texas, at 10:31 a.m., 94 hours and one minute after takeoff. The B-50 was refueled in mid-air four times during its 23,452-mile flight. The Lucky Lady II took off just after noon on February 26, flying toward the east. It was refueled over the Azores early Sunday, over Saudi Arabia later that day, then over Manila and over Hawaii yesterday. Air Force officials say the flight demonstrates that United States aircraft can drop atomic bombs at any spot on earth at any time.

The Lucky Lady's crew greets the press in Fort Worth on their return.

Vishinsky replaces Molotov in office

March 4. To the West, he was the man who could say "no." Now, Soviet Foreign Minister Vyacheslav Molotov will no longer have that power as it was announced he will be replaced by Andrei Vishinsky. Molotov, Premier Stalin's right-hand man for so long, was known for his obstinance in East-West relations, and now political observers are attempting to gauge what impact his removal will have.

The announcement of this dramatic Soviet administration shift came with no Kremlin fanfare; nor did Soviet officials offer any explanation for the change. Yet, it's believed the recent Soviet failure in stopping the European Economy Recovery Program was a decisive factor. While some contend the move may relax Soviet rigidity in world affairs, most feel Vishinsky will continue the hard-line approach to international affairs.

Molotov's dismissal rearranges the order of succession to Premier Stalin. Now, it appears Lavrenti Beria, head of the secret police, is next in line for Soviet leadership.

Vishinsky, Molotov and Gromyko.

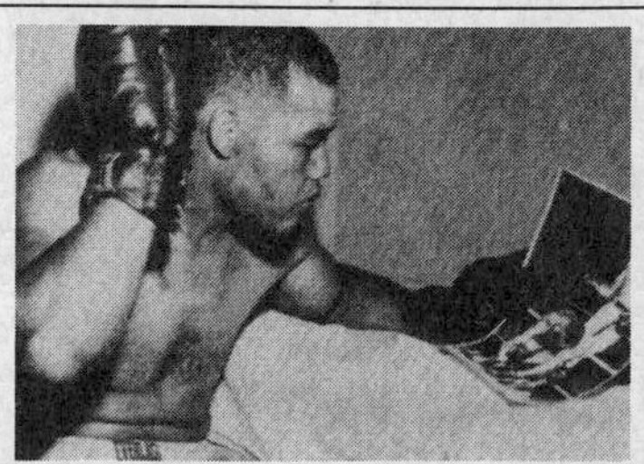

March 1. The "Brown Bomber" has quit his trade after 11 years as heavyweight champ. Son of a sharecropper who died when he was four, Joe Louis started boxing at 18, turned pro in 1934 and took the title three years later. Lightning punches won him 25 title defenses with only one loss.

1949

APRIL

Su	Mo	Tu	We	Th	Fr	Sa
					1	2
3	4	5	6	7	8	9
10	11	12	13	14	15	16
17	18	19	20	21	22	23
24	25	26	27	28	29	30

1. U.S.: Dean Martin and Jerry Lewis complete first film together, "My Friend Irma."

2. London: Advertising lights go on after ten-year restriction.

3. Rhodes: Transjordan signs armistice with Israel (→ 5/11).

4. Washington: 12 nations establish defense alliance under North Atlantic Treaty (→ 7/21).

6. Washington: Truman says he won't hesitate to use A-bomb again if necessary (→ 6/7).

8. France, Britain, U.S. to merge zones in West Germany (→ 16).

8. N.Y.: Soviet uses 30th veto to block U.N. membership for South Korea (→ 6/28).

10. China: Three Mao armies wait at Yangtze; will attack Nanking if terms denied (→ 19).

17. Dublin: Irish hail birth of Republic in South; P.M. John Costello calls on six Northern counties to join in independence from Britain (→ 5/17).

19. China: Nanking rejects Communist peace ultimatum (→ 20).

20. China: Mao forces cross Yangtze, move on Nanking (→ 23).

20. Minnesota: Scientists find method to produce cortisone in commercial quantities.

23. China: Communists enter Nanking (→ 24).

24. China: Communists surround Shanghai (→ 29).

25. Frankfort: West German constitution signed by U.S., British, French and German representatives (→ 26).

26. Moscow: Soviet offers to lift Berlin blockade if Big Four ministers meet (→ 5/4).

28. Manila: Aurora Quezon, widow of first Filipino president, slain by rebel Huk Liberation Army (→ 4/21/51).

29. New York: Leo Durocher suspended for attacking fan.

30. New York: 117,000 march in Loyalty Day parade to protest world communism (→ 6/8).

DEATH

15. Wallace Beery, American silent film star (*1/4/1886).

Plane a minute lands in Berlin every day

April 16. At a rate of one landing every 61.8 seconds, American and British planes flew nearly 13,000 tons of supplies into Berlin on this, the 294th day of the Soviet blockade of Berlin. The record-setting rate of deliveries comes at a critical time in the East-West struggle for the city and may even result in an end to the blockade. There are many in the Kremlin who believe continuing with the blockade is mere folly but that to end it now would be politically embarrassing. Some Berlin observers think the Soviets may look for a graceful way out.

Regardless of what action Russia takes, the airlift proves that with proper planning and aircraft the West can continue to feed the 2.5 million Berliners who so desperately need help (→ 25).

A Berliner has painted his impression of life and death during the airlift.

Mao orders million men to free China

April 29. A Chinese Communist army of nearly one million men launched a major offensive across the Yangtze River, under orders from Communist leader Mao Tse-tung to "liberate" all of China.

The Communist force quickly swept southward from the Yangtze Valley and captured Nanking, the Nationalist capital. As they fanned out across Southern China, the Communists bypassed Shanghai but entrapped 300,000 Nationalists between Shanghai and Hangchow.

The Communists ordered the offensive after negotiations broke down in Peking. Acting Nationalist President Li Sung-jen had rejected the Communist peace terms as "tantamount to a disposal of the conquered by the conqueror" (→ 5/24).

Refugees from Nanking.

Japanese women adopting Western ways

April 17. On the Ginza, Tokyo's main street, 80 percent of the women are wearing European dress, with long skirts. The "New Look" has become a must and to wear short skirts would be to "lose much face." Fortunes are paid for even old copies of American fashion magazines and newspapers with fashion advertisements from which styles are copied. Possession of a file of these is enough to allow the owner to set up a dress design establishment. Indeed, not only do General MacArthur's directives shape the main policies of Japan, but the presence of thousands of American soldiers with their wives is altering daily life in the nation.

While women take the lead in adopting the ways of the West and reflect most quickly the new freedom won by them since the occupation, almost everyone is affected. A new "Japanese-American language" has evolved, and couples are walking arm-in-arm in the streets, a sight never seen before the war.

Augusta, April 10. Sam Snead wins the Masters by 3 strokes.

After adorning the necks of sultans and queens, the Hope diamond has passed to N.Y. gem dealer Harry Winston upon Evalyn McLean's death.

1949

MAY

Su	Mo	Tu	We	Th	Fr	Sa
1	2	3	4	5	6	7
8	9	10	11	12	13	14
15	16	17	18	19	20	21
22	23	24	25	26	27	28
29	30	31				

1. Buenos Aires: Peron tells Congress he will continue nationalizing industry despite opposition (→ 9/28/51).

3. Tel Aviv: Israel celebrates first anniversary (→ 11).

4. N.Y.: Soviet agrees to lift Berlin blockade on May 12 (→ 8).

5. Detroit: 62,000 strike at Ford (→ 20).

8. Bonn: West German Assembly approves new constitution 53-12 (→ 12).

8. Tokyo: Army takes over all civilian jobs in Japan.

10. N.J.: Election ends 32-year reign of Frank Hague, controversial mayor of Jersey City.

12. London: Commons ratifies North Atlantic Treaty (→ 7/21).

14. London: Gerhart Eisler, U.S. Communist fugitive, carried off Polish liner Batory (→ 27).

15. Israel abolishes restrictions on immigration (→ 6/9).

17. Britain recognizes Dublin's independence; reasserts Belfast's dependence on U.K. (→ 4/6/50).

20. Cleveland: A.F.L. rejects John L. Lewis' bid for U.M.W. reaffiliation (→ 9/19).

22. Berlin: One dead, 1,000 hurt in rail strike riots.

23. Paris: Big Four ministers meet to discuss Germany (→ 30).

24. China: Communist troops enter Shanghai (→ 26).

29. China: Communist rule set up in Shanghai (→ 6/30).

29. Bolivia: 150 dead in tin strike riots; two Americans slain (→ 30).

30. Bolivia declares state of siege as labor unrest grows.

30. Bill Holland wins Indy 500, averaging 121 mph in Blue Crown Special racer.

30. Paris: U.S.S.R. rejects Western plea for reunification of Germany (→ 6/20).

31. Britain and Argentina agree on five-year trade treaty.

DEATH

5. Maurice Maeterlinck, Belgian poet and philosopher (*8/29/1862).

Berlin blockade is ended

An American car crosses from West to East for the first time in over a year, giving the German people reason to hope that reunification may come soon.

May 12. Cheers broke out in Berlin this morning as lights burned past midnight for the first time in a year. Cars roared in both directions on the autobahn connecting Berlin to the British sector of Germany. And sighs of relief were heard among overworked employees at the airport. The blockade of Berlin was over, and Berliners felt they had beaten Russia at its own game.

The Russians choked off the city last June to protest what they called intransigence by the Western Allies on the future of Berlin and Germany. They ended the blockade today after negotiations in New York under the auspices of the United Nations. The Russians also agreed to attend a new meeting of the Big Four foreign ministers, to drop their opposition to the creation of an independent West Germany and to give up their plans for a single currency for all of Berlin. The Allies and the Russians also agreed to give more autonomy to Berliners, although they retain tight control over security matters, foreign relations and the constitution.

It was the Allied airlift that punctured the holes in the Russian blockade. The operation started as soon as the blockade began, and it was costly. The Allies spent $200 million to keep the planes in the air, and 55 people lost their lives in airplane accidents (→ 23).

Germany relaxes once again: First bus from Berlin arrives in Hanover.

Airlift workers celebrate the victory of their airborne bridge.

Eisler freed after his arrest in Britain

May 27. German Communist fugitive Gerhart Eisler, who was arrested May 14 on board a Polish ship and detained in Britain, has been freed as a U.S. appeal to extradite him was rejected by a London judge. Chief Magistrate Sir Lawrence Dunne released the political activist because, by law, Britain can't allow extradition if no crime can be found. American authorities charge Eisler with perjury, but the British judge said the charge couldn't stand in England.

Eisler is regarded as a mover and shaker within the Communist movement. He once said, "I have fought in the streets, been beaten and led strikes. But these things mean nothing as personal adventures. For the Communist, they are part of normal living."

Eisler is escorted off the boat.

May 27. Rita Hayworth weds Aly Khan, Moslem playboy.

Communist forces sweep through China

A propaganda truck preaches Mao's gospel to the people of Shanghai.

May 26. One of the jewels of Chiang Kai-shek's China, Shanghai, is sparkling in Communist hands tonight. China's largest city collapsed after a month-long siege and two days of street fighting. The last units of Nationalist troops holding out at Soochow Creek surrendered and were led off to prison camps by the Communists. The American Consulate was hit in the cross fire many times yesterday afternoon. But no Americans were reported injured.

The defeat of Chiang's forces shows just how far Mao Tse-tung has expanded from his old power base in Northern China. With Shanghai and the government capital of Nanking under his command, Mao now seems poised to seize all of Southern China.

True to form, the Communists remained self-sufficent as they overran Shanghai. They did not pillage the city and even carried their wounded to field hospitals several miles outside Shanghai. The style and discipline of the Communist troops and the professionalism of their commanders have impressed Chinese peasants and convinced many to join Mao's crusade. The size of his army has doubled in a year. The Nationalists, on the other hand, have lost hundreds of thousands of soldiers (→ 29).

Mao reviews an anti-aircraft battery.

Ex-defense chief Forrestal kills himself

May 22. A brilliant career came crashing to an end early this morning. James Forrestal, former Secretary of Defense, jumped 13 stories to his death from the 16th floor of the National Naval Medical Center in Bethesda, Maryland.

On March 28, he retired as the first chief of the new Defense Department and entered the hospital on April 2. He was diagnosed as suffering from something like battle fatigue. He felt misunderstood and unfairly attacked. Before moving to Defense, he was Secretary of the Navy.

Apparently, Forrestal planned to commit suicide. He refused to take a sleeping pill and then he left beside his bed some lines from Sophocles, including these: "Comfortless, nameless, hopeless —save in the dark prospect of the yawning grave."

German Federal Republic created in Bonn

May 23. From the ashes of Nazi Germany, a new country is being formed. It will be called the Federal Republic of Germany. In Bonn, hundreds of people jammed the streets, cheering the news and waving flags colored red, black and gold, the same colors that festooned the Weimar Republic in the pre-Hitler era. There was little cheering in the Russian-controlled sector of Germany. Residents there will not be part of this new country.

Dr. Konrad Adenauer, President of the Parliamentary Council, presided over the solemn affair that proclaimed the existence of the new republic. Only twice was there any sign of emotion. The audience at the Pedagogical Institute Building broke into applause when Dr. Ernst Reuter signed the document establishing the republic. Reuter is the Mayor of Berlin and a dynamic symbol of Germany's resistance to communism. The only other drama occurred when one of the two Communist delegates was called to sign the document. "I do not sign for the splitting of Germany," Heinz Renner exclaimed. The other Communist refused to rise when called.

In a short speech, Adenauer declared, "A new Germany arises." He also said that he hoped a new constitution would reunite all of Germany. But the prospects of that happening appear slim. Once again today, the Western Allies turned down a Russian proposal aimed at reunifying Germany.

Elections for a new Parliament, the Bundestag, are expected to take place within the next few weeks. Half of the 400 deputies will be elected directly. The Bundestag will sit in Bonn, selected as the capital of the new republic (→ 31).

Israel voted into U.N. by Assembly

May 11. Israel became a U.N. member today by a General Assembly vote of 37 to 12. Nine abstentions included Great Britain. But before the applause had died away, five Arab delegations—Egypt, Iraq, Lebanon, Saudi Arabia and Yemen —walked out of the Flushing Meadow Assembly Hall in protest, complaining bitterly that Israel had not complied with U.N. resolutions calling for an international regime in Jerusalem and the repatriation of Arab refugees (→ 15).

U.S. Zionist leader Abba Silver.

Bunche refuses job in Washington

May 25. Ralph Bunche, one of the most respected diplomats of our era, has refused a job as Assistant Secretary of State in Washington. He said he did not want his family to risk indignities because of his color. Entering government service in 1941, he became the first Negro division head in the State Department in 1945, and in 1946 head of the Trusteeship Division of the United Nations. Bunche's latest effort is to restore peace in the Middle East.

Playwright Arthur Miller has won a Pulitzer Prize for his quintessentially American drama "Death of a Salesman."

1949

JUNE

Su	Mo	Tu	We	Th	Fr	Sa
			1	2	3	4
5	6	7	8	9	10	11
12	13	14	15	16	17	18
19	20	21	22	23	24	25
26	27	28	29	30		

2. Transjordan renamed Hashemite Kingdom of Jordan (→ 8/11/52).

4. French law merges Cochin China into unified govt. of Vietnam under Bao Dai (→ 13).

5. Warsaw: British Council director becomes Polish citizen, denounces Britain (→ 11/7).

7. Puerto Rico: 54 die in plane crash.

7. FBI report discloses Soviet got U.S. shipment of atomic research devices in 1947 (→ 8/22).

8. FBI names film Communists in Coplon case: Frederic March, Edward G. Robinson (→ 13).

13. Berkeley: Univ. of California to require all faculty to take anti-Communist oaths (→ 16).

13. Vietnam: Bao Dai enters Saigon to attempt to rule divided country (→ 7/1).

16. Truman denounces anti-Communist hysteria; promises dismissal of provocateurs (→ 30).

16. Prague posts guard on Archbishop Josef Beran after his refusal to permit Communist control over Church actions (→ 20).

16. Detroit: Jake La Motta KOs Marcel Cerdan to capture middleweight title.

20. Vatican: Pope excommunicates Prague leaders (→ 7/15).

20. Paris: Big Four parley ends with no resolution on reunification of Germany (→ 7/9).

22. Chicago: Ezzard Charles wins heavyweight title in decision over Jersey Joe Walcott.

28. N.Y.: Liberal Senator Robert F. Wagner resigns after 18 years.

28. Korea: Last U.S. combat troops called home, leaving only 500 advisers (→ 5/30/50).

29. Indonesia: Dutch troops pull out of Jakarta (→ 11/2).

30. China: Mao says he expects no help from West, calls Soviet China's true ally (→ 7/16).

BIRTH

22. Meryl Streep, U.S. actress.

DEATH

10. Sigrid Undset, Norwegian novelist (*5/20/1882).

Truman says nation hysterical over Reds

June 30. President Truman assured newsmen today that the nation is not going to hell, despite the wave of anti-Communist hysteria now sweeping the country in the wake of spy trials and loyalty inquiries. Responding to questions at his weekly news conference, President Truman likened the national jitters over Reds to the atmosphere that was engendered in the early days of the republic over the Alien and Sedition Acts.

Read your history, the president advised, and it will show that the hysteria over aliens of that earlier period subsided. The country did not go to hell at that time and it isn't going to do so now, he said.

The Alien and Sedition Laws were passed by Congress in the early days of the nation. The alien laws gave the president authority to deport aliens in the event of war, while the sedition laws allowed imprisonment of anyone criticizing the federal government. These laws eventually were repealed.

President Truman said that most great periods of stress, such as a war, often are followed by public hysteria. He noted that after World War I, the Ku Klux Klan engaged in what he called crazy activities, trying to clean up the country and ending up by making a mess of things.

Asked his opinion of a proposal by the House Un-American Activities Committee for screening of books taught in schools and colleges, the president said his views were summed up by a Herblock cartoon in the Washington Post, ridiculing the idea.

Meanwhile, a federal grand jury in Washington convicted Judith Coplon, a 28-year-old political analyst who worked in the Justice Department, as a spy for Russia, finding her guilty on both counts of an espionage charge that could send her to jail for 13 years.

Also this month, Alger Hiss, target of a two-count perjury indictment, testified that he was never a Communist and that he never gave State Department documents to Whittaker Chambers for transmission to a Soviet spy ring (→ 10/21).

U.S. bank helping Israel relocate Arabs

June 9. The first American bank loan to a corporation in the new republic of Israel transpired yesterday as the Bank of America National Trust and Savings Association of San Francisco sent $15 million to Keren Kayemeth L'Israel, Ltd.

The money will help compensate Arabs who lost their land in last year's Arab-Israeli skirmishes. The loan, while truly beneficial to the Arabs, will also strengthen Israel's positon in negotiations with Arab states over the issues of frontiers, Jersusalem and refugees. If many Arabs remain displaced, Israeli credibilty will be injured.

The loan is actually an advance against additional funds required to solve the immigration problems. Currently, Keren Kayemeth is administering the loan and is contacting several New York banks for more financing. Many may take part, particularly if the Bank of America successfully goes through with plans to open up a branch in Israel (→ 7/20).

An American settler in Israel.

Some 800,000 Arabs now homeless.

1949

JULY

Su	Mo	Tu	We	Th	Fr	Sa
					1	2
3	4	5	6	7	8	9
10	11	12	13	14	15	16
17	18	19	20	21	22	23
24	25	26	27	28	29	30
31						

1. Vietnam: In first decree, Chief of State Bao Dai secures full powers (→ 12/10).

3. U.S.: Enola Gay, plane that dropped A-bomb on Hiroshima, presented to Smithsonian.

6. Warsaw: Poles end trade with Yugoslavia (→ 8/2).

9. Germany: Soviet soldier killed by American in border patrol clash (→ 8/13).

15. Washington: Truman signs housing bill, alloting federal aid for construction (→ 10/26).

15. Geneva: Czech tennis pros Jaroslav Drobny and Vladimir Cernik defect (→ 11/12).

16. China: Nationalists form Supreme War Council under Chiang Kai-shek (→ 8/5).

17. China: 20 million left homeless by massive river floods.

18. Washington: Jackie Robinson refutes Paul Robeson, says Negroes will fight communism.

19. Chicago: President Truman says the Soviet Union will either destroy itself or abandon aggression.

19. Laos proclaims independence within French Union.

20. Tel Aviv: Israel and Syria sign armistice, ending 19-month war (→ 12/9).

21. U.S. Senate ratifies North Atlantic Treaty (→ 26).

24. Fausto Coppi wins 36th Tour de France.

24. Thomas Mann returns to Germany for visit after 16-year exile.

24. Tibet expels Nationalist Chinese consul (→ 5/22/50).

26. Paris: Fists fly in French Assembly as Communists try to kill N. Atlantic pact (→ 8/24).

30. West Berlin Mayor Ernst Reuter asks for immediate Marshall Plan aid.

31. Shanghai: U.S. Consulate freed in mediation offer after two-day siege by Chinese ex-employees demanding back pay.

DEATH

2. Georgi Dimitrov, founder of People's Republic of Bulgaria (*6/18/1882).

Rome will excommunicate Communists

July 13. In what amounted to a declaration of war against communism, the Vatican issued a decree threatening excommunication of Catholics who "defend and spread the materialistic and anti-Christian doctrine of the Communists."

The decree, drafted by several Cardinals under the personal direction of Pope Pius XII, also directed Roman Catholic clergy to deny the sacraments to those who "knowingly and freely" enlist in or support the Communist Party.

Vatican officials said the decree was designed to erase all doubts in the minds of Catholics as to whether they could collaborate with Communist parties or accept some aspects of Communist doctrine and still remain within the church. The pope was said to have been induced to issue the decree by persecution of the Church in Eastern Europe.

British test Comet, the first jet airliner

July 27. The world's first jet airliner, the de Havilland Comet, made its debut today in a flight at Hatfield, England. The Comet, powered by four jet engines, is Britain's bid to gain world aviation leadership by a revolutionary advance in air transport. The Comet is expected to go into service in three years, carrying 36 passengers in a pressurized cabin at 40,000 feet and a speed of 500 miles an hour, far faster than any airliner now in service.

In its first public appearance, the Comet was flown by Capt. John Cunningham, a World War II fighter ace, who rose to an altitude of 8,000 feet in the swept-wing ship. Although officials say that more than two years of testing lies ahead, de Havilland already is working on 16 Comets that have been ordered by the British government and two British airlines (→ 11/29).

Linus Pauling describes sickle-cell anemia

July 1. Linus Pauling, the celebrated chemist, reports he has found the molecular flaw responsible for the debilitating blood disease sickle-cell anemia, which afflicts American Negroes. The disease gets its name from the observation that it causes blood cells to lose their natural disc-like shape and become sickle-shaped cells that cannot easily pass through small blood vessels. Pauling's research shows the problem is in hemoglobin, an oxygen-carrying protein made of hundreds of subunits. A change in a single subunit causes the disease.

The new Buick Roadmaster, the shape of things to come?

1949

AUGUST

Su	Mo	Tu	We	Th	Fr	Sa
	1	2	3	4	5	6
7	8	9	10	11	12	13
14	15	16	17	18	19	20
21	22	23	24	25	26	27
28	29	30	31			

2. Belgrade: Tito tells Bulgarians and Albanians he would help them revolt (→ 16).

5. U.S. report blames fall of China on corruption in Chiang regime, bars more aid (→ 9/21).

10. Washington: Truman signs security bill creating Dept. of Defense (→ 11).

11. Truman appoints Omar Bradley chairman of Chiefs of Staff.

11. Strasbourg: European Council chooses Belgian ex-Premier Paul Henri Spaak as chief.

13. Germany: Three mil. ex-Nazis now eligible to vote (→ 15).

14. Damascus: Pres. Husni Zayim and Premier Mohsen el Barazi killed in military coup.

15. West German rightists win first free election since 1933 (→ 9/12).

15. San Francisco: Stunt leap off Golden Gate Bridge performed for first time.

16. Moscow: Soviet relieves envoy to Belgrade; no successor named (→ 17).

17. Washington gives Yugoslavs permission to buy U.S. steel equipment (→ 27).

18. Finns mobilize army to fight Communist-led strikes against Socialist government.

22. Washington: Gen. Carl Spaatz calls A-bomb and B-36 greatest forces for peace (→ 29).

24. Washington: Truman signs North Atlantic Treaty (→ 1/27/50).

24. U.S. Congress approves Thomas Clark for Supreme Court.

25. New York: RCA announces invention of system for broadcasting color television.

27. U.S.S.R. mobilizes three armored divisions near Yugoslav border (→ 29).

28. New York: U.S. team clinches Davis Cup.

28. Greek army takes Mt. Grammos from rebels (→ 11/4).

29. U.S.S.R. detonates first A-bomb in secret test (→ 9/23).

29. Tito asks U.S. for loan to aid against Soviet blockade (→ 9/8).

Ingrid Bergman says she's no saint

Dignified Bergman and admirers.

Aug 5. Nothing on the movie screen recently matches the events in the private life of one of the cinema's top-ranking stars. Actress Ingrid Bergman in Rome decided to tell the world that she was quitting both her marriage of 12 years to Swedish Dr. Peter Lindstrom, with whom she has a ten-year-old daughter, and her movie career.

Her involvement with Italian director Roberto Rossellini is expected to lead to marriage, but for now she pleads "exhaustion and upset" at the commotion in the press and among her until recently adoring fans. "A movie star is a ridiculous commercial product and the public tells us what to do. People saw me in 'Joan of Arc' and declared me a saint. I'm not. I'm just a woman, another human being," she said.

Bergman as "Joan of Arc."

Author of Gone With the Wind killed

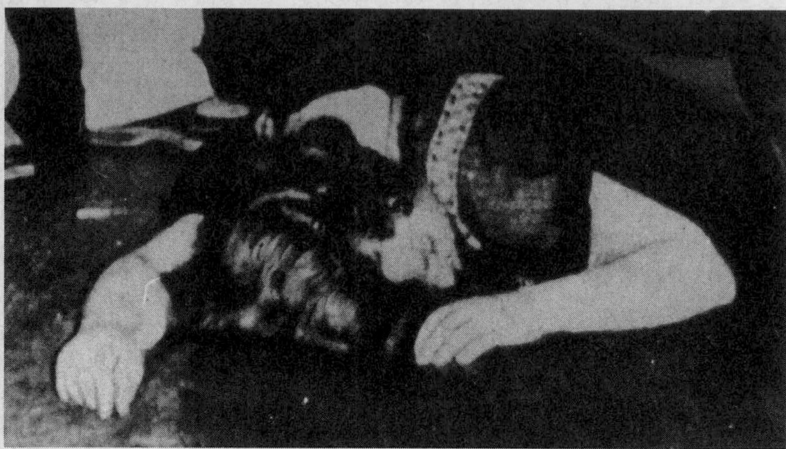

Margaret Mitchell lies unconscious on the pavement after her fatal accident.

Aug 16. Margaret Mitchell, author of "Gone With the Wind," died today at 49 from injuries received when she was struck by a speeding car in Atlanta five days ago. The publication of her 1,037-page novel brought her $1 million in royalties and movie payments and the Pulitzer Prize, but the fame disrupted her life and writing. "I haven't had time to sit down at the typewriter since 1936," she said recently.

X-1 rocket plane soars to 63,000 feet

The turbocharged, supersonic Bell X-1, spawned by the American war effort.

Aug 8. America has a new hero. He is Frank Everest, and he is appropriately named. Everest rocketed his way to new heights in the experimental Bell X-1 plane. Everest climbed to 63,000 feet, a new record.

Engineers at Bell have been developing the X-1 since early 1945, when the Air Force and National Advisory Committee for Aeronautics decided to fund a series of experimental planes. The X-1 had its first flight in January 1946. As the jet-propelled engines and turboreactors became more sophisticated, the planes kept breaking speed records and scientists had to solve a new problem. They had to create a heat shield to protect the plane during supersonic flight. Charles Yeager piloted the plane when it broke the sound barrier for the first time in October 1947.

Ecuador quake kills 4,600, destroys 4 cities

Aug 8. The death toll from an earthquake that devastated 1,500 square miles of Ecuador has risen over 4,600. The quake, which hit a region along the slopes of the Andes two days ago, has destroyed four villages. Hardest hit was Pelileo, where 3,200 of 3,500 residents perished. Property damage is estimated at $20 million. Adding to the disaster is the death of 34 persons in the crash of a mercy plane.

Vatican believes Peter's bones found

Aug 7. Did Saint Peter, "Prince of the Apostles," really live, and, if so, was he ever in Rome? Was he crucified there, and did he indeed found the Roman Catholic Church? If these contentions are confirmed, then the Bishop of Rome—the Pope —is truly his successor. The Vatican wishes to gather unmistakable proof, relying on neutral experts, before making the archeological find of bones, believed to be those of St. Peter, official. The remains were recovered in a subterranean cell 20 feet below the main altar in St. Peter's Basilica. Inscriptions on the wall and dated coins strewn on the floor may hold vital clues.

Eleanor Roosevelt in Church dispute

Aug 13. Pope Pius declared today that he believed the "delicate" controversy between Cardinal Spellman and Eleanor Roosevelt has been resolved. It concerns a bill in Congress, which would provide $300 million in federal aid to public schools. The Cardinal dubbed the bill anti-Catholic since Catholic parochial and other private schools were excluded. When Mrs. Roosevelt supported the idea in her newspaper column, the Cardinal called her attitude "unworthy an American mother." The next day, in no uncertain words, she reiterated her belief in the principle of church-state separation.

1949

SEPTEMBER

Su	Mo	Tu	We	Th	Fr	Sa
				1	2	3
4	5	6	7	8	9	10
11	12	13	14	15	16	17
18	19	20	21	22	23	24
25	26	27	28	29	30	

3. Australia: John Cade publishes results of lithium's first clinical trial on mental patients.

8. U.S. grants $20 mil. loan to Yugoslavia (→ 29).

12. West Germany: Liberal Theodor Heuss elected president of new republic (→ 15).

16. Budapest: Laszlo Rajk, resistance leader during war, admits to plotting with Tito and U.S. to overthrow Hungarian regime (→ 24).

18. Britain devalues pound 30% to fight dollar deficit (→ 19).

19. Pittsburgh: 480,000 U.M.W. members go on strike (→ 30).

19. France, Canada join 17 other nations in devaluing currency.

21. Peking: Chinese People's Political Consultative Conference convenes (→ 30).

22. U.S.: Gary Davis begins campaign to expand limits on conscientious objector status.

24. Pacific: Study shows food still radioactive from bomb test at Bikini Atoll (→ 10/18).

24. Budapest: Ex-For. Min. Laszlo Rajk sentenced to die for plotting against govt. (→ 12/29).

29. Moscow: Soviet ends friendship treaty with Yugoslavia (→ 30).

30. Pittsburgh: John L. Lewis orders miners back to work (→ 10/1).

30. Peking: Mao Tse-tung elected chairman of People's Republic of China (→ 10/1).

30. Poland and Hungary renounce friendship pacts with Yugoslavia (→ 10/1).

30. Berlin airlift officially halted after 277,264 flights (→ 10/2).

BIRTH

4. Tom Watson, U.S. professional golfer.

DEATHS

7. Jose Clemente Orozco, Mexican painter (*11/23/1883).

8. Richard Strauss, German composer (*6/11/1864).

10. Wiley Rutledge, U.S. Supreme Court justice (*7/20/1894).

Russians have the Bomb

Sept 23. President Truman's Cabinet received some shocking news at its weekly meeting this morning. "We have evidence that within recent weeks an atomic explosion occurred in the U.S.S.R.," Truman announced. The intelligence information is taken to mean that the Russians have developed an atomic bomb, according to Secretary of State Dean Acheson.

The administration moved quickly to prevent a crisis from developing. "The calmer the American people take this the better," General Omar Bradley, Chairman of the Joint Chiefs of Staff, said. "We have anticipated it for four years, and it calls for no change in our basic defense plan." Truman, who is determined to keep control of the American bomb in civilian hands, repeated his plea for international control of atomic energy.

In London, a United States Air Force spokesman said it is "quite probable" that B-29 bombers in Britain will be replaced by B-50 aircraft, which are capable of carrying atomic bombs (→ 24).

Canada has greatest ship loss since Titanic

Sept 17. Waves of fire swept away the lives of 207 people aboard a giant liner this morning. The Noronic, the largest ship on the Great Lakes, was docked at the Ontario Pier in Toronto. At 2:30 a.m. a blaze of undetermined origins gutted it in 15 minutes.

People on shore watched as terrified faces appeared and disappeared in the portholes. Passengers in party dress and sleepwear raced about or stood rooted in terror. Many stampeded to the starboard side, causing the ship to heave and crash into the pier. There was no time to lower lifeboats. Tonight, they cling charred and useless to the hull.

Surviving passengers told tales of heroism. One crew member helped passengers slip down ropes to safety while he himself stood enveloped in flames. A doctor's assistant was also credited with courage. She ran from cabin to cabin, smashing windows and freeing those within. In all, 304 survived.

The Noronic's sister ship, the Hamonic, burned in 1945. Only one person was killed.

Adenauer becomes first Bonn Chancellor

Sept 15. One of Germany's senior statesmen has been chosen to head the new Federal Republic. Dr. Konrad Adenauer, a 73-year-old centrist and a critic of the Nazi regime, was elected Chancellor. He seems to be a good choice. Adenauer is a bridge to Germany's past glories under the Weimar Republic. He is also sufficiently moderate to lead Germany to its place in the new Europe. Adenauer's support for an independent state in the Rhineland after the First World War is dismissed as a passing whim.

Adenauer's career in German politics was progressing nicely until the Nazis rose to power. A member of the Catholic Center Party, he was elected Lord Mayor of Cologne. Hitler stripped him of the job in 1933 and threw him into prison twice, but Adenauer's reputation flourished as an opponent of Hitler's regime. He was under constant police surveillance. After the war, he founded the Christian Democratic Union. In the governing of the new Federal Republic, Adenauer will be joined by Theodore Heuss, a liberal and a professor. Heuss was elected President (→ 30).

Adenauer, leader of a new Germany.

1949

OCTOBER

Su	Mo	Tu	We	Th	Fr	Sa
						1
2	3	4	5	6	7	8
9	10	11	12	13	14	15
16	17	18	19	20	21	22
23	24	25	26	27	28	29
30	31					

1. Pittsburgh: Steel strike begins; 500,000 quit (→ 11/11).

1. Bulgaria renounces friendship pact with Yugoslavia (→ 20).

2. Soviet says West German state violates Potsdam accord (→ 12).

4. U.S. Senate confirms Sherman Minton for Supreme Court.

5. N.Y.: U.N. flag raised over new headquarters (→ 8/1950).

6. Washington: Truman signs arms aid bill, alloting \$5.8 bil. for NATO Allies (→ 1/2/50).

6. San Francisco: Tokyo Rose given ten years and \$10,000 fine.

9. Boston: Harvard Law School to begin admitting women.

12. Eugenie Anderson gets post in Denmark as first U.S. woman ambassador.

15. China: Canton falls to Communists (→ 18).

17. Northwest Airlines becomes first in U.S. to serve alcoholic beverages in flight.

18. Washington: Leaked report says Truman ordered huge A-bomb expansion (→ 11/23).

18. China: Communists take Amoy, seizing whole Pacific coastline (→ 11/15).

19. Guatemala: 4,000 killed in devastating flood.

20. N.Y.: Yugoslavia elected to U.N. Security Council (→ 22).

21. N.Y.: Ten Communists get 5 years, \$10,000 fines (→ 11/2).

22. George Allen named U.S. ambassador to Yugoslavia (→ 2/17/51).

25. Mississippi: Jefferson Military College gets \$50 mil. gift on condition it teach white supremacy (→ 12/2).

26. Truman raises minimum wage from 40 to 74 cents per hour (→ 6/7/50).

28. Plane crashes in Azores; boxer Marcel Cerdan and 48 die.

BIRTH

28. Bruce Jenner, U.S. 1976 Olympic decathlon winner.

DEATH

31. Edward Stettinius, U.S. ex-sec. of state (*10/22/1900).

Sinatra still popular with bobby-soxers

Young Frank Sinatra.

Frank Sinatra, gangly crooner and darling of the bobby-sox set from Hoboken, N.J., has yet another hit song in "New York, New York." He sings it in the film "On the Town." The 33-year-old is just as popular today as when he sang "This Love of Mine" and "I'll Never Smile Again" with the bands of Tommy Dorsey and Harry James.

Robinson is named valuable player

Oct 10. The Yankees defeated the Brooklyn Dodgers by 10-6 in the fifth and final game of the World Series, but Jackie Robinson was voted the Most Valuable Player in a losing cause. Robinson batted .342 for the season, leading the league.

MVP Robinson, NL batting champ. ▷

China establishes People's Republic

Mao, forging a new Chinese future.

The optimism of a successful revolution: Peking greets Mao with open arms.

Oct 1. Cheering crowds today hailed Chinese leader Mao Tse-tung's proclamation of China's new People's (Communist) Republic and the appointment of Chou En-lai as Premier of the government.

The announcement, read to 200,000 persons at the Gate of Heavenly Peace, was hailed by a Soviet historian as one of two "stupendous events" of the year—the other was the "failure of U.S. calculations upon atomic monopoly."

Within hours of the news, the U.S.S.R. recognized the regime and asserted that the Chinese Nationalists led by Chiang Kai-shek now hold no power and that "the victory of the Chinese people deals a cruel blow to the aggressive plans of imperialists in the Pacific region."

Chou En-lai, often a representative of the Communists in negotiations with the Nationalists, will also head the Foreign Ministry, which deals with other nations. The first task ahead of him and Mao Tse-tung is to gain the world's acceptance. Mao declared in his speech: "This government is willing to establish diplomatic relations with . . . any nation willing to observe the principles of equality, mutual respect and territorial sovereignty."

The next step is to ask the United Nations to recognize a Communist Chinese representative as the legitimate delegate for China.

The establishment of a Communist republic in China comes as setback to the United States and the Western alliance, which supported the Nationalists. Official American comment is expected to be forthcoming (→ 15).

Communists in East Germany also establish a government

Oct 12. If there was ever any doubt that there are two Germanys, one in the East and one in the West, that doubt has vanished. The Russian-controlled sector now has its own government, the German Democratic Republic, with its own President and Prime Minister. Delegates to a joint meeting last week of the presidium of the Popular Council and the so-called anti-fascist bloc agreed on the formation of the government. The council created a National Front Party and turned itself into a highly centralized Provisional Assembly of the People.

Wilhelm Pieck was selected as president of the new republic. Otto Grotewohl was named prime minister. They will preside over a coalition Cabinet that is controlled by the Communist Party (→ 12/31).

Leaders of Germany's other half: President Pieck and Premier Grotewohl.

1949

NOVEMBER

Su	Mo	Tu	We	Th	Fr	Sa
		1	2	3	4	5
6	7	8	9	10	11	12
13	14	15	16	17	18	19
20	21	22	23	24	25	26
29	28	29	30			

1. Washington: 55 killed in worst U.S. air disaster as fighter plane hits airliner.

2. Cleveland: C.I.O. expels two leftist unions (→ 12/9).

2. The Hague: Round table conference decides Indonesia will get statehood (→ 12/16).

4. U.N. bans arms to Albania and Bulgaria for supplying Greek rebels (→ 4/14/50).

7. Warsaw: Konstantin Rokossovsky named defense minister (→ 4/15/50).

11. Pittsburgh: U.S. Steel signs two-year contract with unions, ending 42-day strike (→ 12/7).

12. Prague: Govt. bans church marriages (→ 5/25/50).

13. Portugal: Antonio Salazar's party wins all Parliment seats.

13. Cambodia gets independence within French Union.

15. India: Nathuram Vinayak Godse hanged for Gandhi murder (→ 26).

15. China: U.S. ship Flying Cloud shelled by Nationalists in coastal blockade (→ 23).

18. U.S. Air Force grounds B-29 after two crashes, 23 deaths in last three days.

19. Monte Carlo: Prince Ranier III crowned 30th monarch of Monaco.

20. Afghanistan: Pathan tribe sets up independent nation of Pushtunistan.

21. N.Y.: U.N. grants Libya independence in 1952.

23. Washington: David Lilienthal resigns as head of Atomic Energy Commission (→ 29).

23. China: Communists release U.S. Consul Angus Ward, order him to quit country (→ 25).

24. Britain: Iron and Steel Act nationalizes steel industry (→ 2/23/50).

25. N.Y.: Kuomintang asks U.N. to refuse recognition to Chinese Communists (→ 12/16).

26. India becomes sovereign democratic republic in new constitution (→ 4/8/50).

29. U.S. announces it will conduct atomic tests at Eniwetok Atoll in Pacific (→ 12/5).

Worst month in aviation history kills 149 in tragic accidents

Nov 29. Aviation has become a tremendous innovation, transporting people to faraway places in hours. Yet, this month, airplanes all over the world tragically failed to carry their passengers to their intended destinations.

On the 1st, a P-38 fighter plane ripped through an Eastern Airlines commercial liner, cutting it in half and killing 55 men, women and children. The accident occurred 100 feet above National Airport in Washington, D.C., as the passenger plane attempted to land. Among the victims were Helen Hokinson, the cartoonist, Representative George Bates, Republican of Mass., and former N.Y. Representative Michael Kennedy. The only survivor was the pilot of the fighter jet.

Within a three-day span, three air disasters, all involving B-29 Superfortresses, claimed 25 lives. In Stockton, Ca., two B-29's collided while on an Air Force training run. Eighteen crew members died in the fiery crash 27,000 feet up. One man who parachuted his way to safety said, "I don't know how I got out. The first thing I knew I was (out the door) and falling. Then, I pulled my rip cord." In Bermuda, the downing of a B-29 launched the biggest peacetime air-sea rescue search. After 75 hours of floating at sea, 18 of 20 men were found, delirious and weak, but alive. The other two men died in the wreck. Then, another B-29 plummeted, this time into the bay off Tampa, Fla., taking five lives. The Air Force has grounded all B-29's until they can be modernized.

Last week, a crash near Oslo, Norway, killed 34. That accident was the most tragic, as 27 of the victims were orphan children on their way to a rehabilitation center. Only a 12-year-old boy survived.

Finally, today, 28 people perished as an American Airlines plane exploded and erupted in flames at the Dallas airport, Love Field. Among the 18 survivors was pilot Captain Claude, who, after witnessing the carnage from the crash, said, "I wished I had gone too."

A bright spot amid disaster, the Comet made its first test-flight in July. Twice as fast as liners now in service, it is the first jet built to carry passengers.

G.M. to pay biggest dividend in history

Nov 7. A corporate record is about to grace American business history books as the directors of General Motors voted to pay out over $190 million in dividends to its shareholders. The large disbursements are possible because of the lucrative year the auto manufacturer is having; after nine months, it has reported a record net profit of $502 million. The profits are due to the high dollar volume of sales, the high-level production, the peacetime record of employment and payrolls of the company.

A statement from General Motors upper-level management accompanied the announcement of record profits. "General Motors," it read, "has always believed in a liberal dividend policy and dividends in the pre-war years reflected this. During the last four years, capital requirements for plant facilities and working capital increased greatly as a result of inflation which has occurred since the war."

The 436,005 shareholders can expect a fat check before the end of the month.

King of tap dancers Bill Robinson dead

Nov 28. Bojangles is gone, but the warm memories of a man who danced through life with an infectious smile linger on. Yesterday, celebrities and eight miles of crowds paid last tribute to Bill "Bojangles" Robinson, who succumbed to a heart ailment Friday. Jimmy Durante, Ethel Merman, Danny Kaye, Milton Berle and Mayor O'Dwyer were among those who spoke of his talent, wit and kind heart.

Mr. Bojangles steppin' out.

Bojangles danced for pennies as a small boy in Richmond, Va., and for $6,600 a week in movies such as "The Little Colonel." Willing to perform at benefits for others, he himself was often broke despite earnings that may have totaled a couple of millions. A "soft touch," he gave his money away, especially to schools and orphanages.

A year ago, Robinson, then 70, suffered a heart attack and had cataracts removed from his eyes, but he kept dancing. This star of Broadway and talking pictures also held a world record in running backwards. After he was admitted to the hospital, some 5,000 admirers wrote letters, including President Truman. Millions who loved Bojangles, his strut, his grin, and his taps share in the sorrow of his widow, Elaine.

Death takes patron of art Guggenheim

Arts patron Solomon Guggenheim.

Nov 3. Solomon R. Guggenheim, who was born in Philadelphia 88 years ago, has died. In this family of American industrialists, originally from Switzerland, each member seems to have chosen a different philanthropy. Solomon R. established a foundation to increase public appreciation of modern art and founded the Solomon R. Guggenheim Museum of Art in New York.

Army 38, Navy 0

Nov 26. Army rolled over Navy by 38-0 in the biggest rout of the 59-year football rivalry of the armed services teams. President Harry Truman was among 102,443 who watched in bitter cold weather.

Instead of the close battle that was predicted, the Cadets struck almost at will from the T-formation. They rolled up 27 first downs, 310 yards rushing and 149 yards passing. Army led by 13-0 at the half but missed three big scoring chances. Since the series began in 1890, Army has won 31 games and Navy 19.

Cadets celebrate exuberantly.

Louis Armstrong conquers Paris, France

Satchmo, jazz pioneer, takes the New Orleans sound to Europe.

Nov 3. Parisians speak "le jazz" as their second tongue, and they like conversing with no one so much as jazz trumpeter Louis Armstrong. Armstrong and his band performed in the City of Light tonight to standing ovations. As they did when Armstrong came to Nice last year, audience members lined up backstage seeking autographs. Some made a fad of him signing the palms of their hands.

"Satchmo" was born in 1900 in New Orleans. He learned trumpet at a school for wayward boys and turned professional under King Oliver and his Chicago band. Armstrong played piano for groups in the 20's and 30's, but when he married pianist Lil Hardin he returned to the trumpet. The instrument he has worked on the most lately is his voice, which sounds something between a bass violin and a saxophone, reverberant and mellow.

Armstrong keeps up a hammy chatter and clowns around on stage. His integrated band includes Earl Hines on piano and Barney Bigard on clarinet. They brought the house down with "Boogie-woogie on the St. Louis Blues."

Broderick Crawford, in the performance of his career, plays a charismatic, dictatorial Southern politician in "All the King's Men," Robert Rossen's film adaptation of the Pulitzer-winning novel by Robert Penn Warren.

1949

DECEMBER

Su	Mo	Tu	We	Th	Fr	Sa
				1	2	3
4	5	6	7	8	9	10
11	12	13	14	15	16	17
18	19	20	21	22	23	24
25	26	27	28	29	30	31

2. Truman bans federal housing aid where racial or religious bias exists (→ 5/12/50).

5. Washington: Uranium alleged to have been sent to U.S.S.R. in 1943 by FDR aide Harry Hopkins (→ 1/31/50).

7. London: A.F.L. and C.I.O. organize non-Communist intl. trade union (→ 2/5/50).

9. Washington: HUAC Chm. Parnell Thomas gets 6-18 months for padding congressional payrolls (→ 1/5/50).

9. N.Y.: U.N. takes trusteeship over Jerusalem (→ 21).

10. Australia: Labor defeated after eight-year rule.

10. Vietnam: 150,000 French troops mass at border to prevent Chinese invasion (→ 1/19/50).

14. Sofia: Bulgarian ex-Premier Traicho Kostov sentenced to die for treason (→ 2/21/50).

16. Java: Indonesia elects Sukarno first president (→ 28).

16. U.S.S.R.: Mao Tse-tung received at Kremlin (→ 1/1/50).

18. L.A.: Philadelphia Eagles shut out Rams 14-0 for second football title.

21. New York: Museum of Modern Art shows 200 Klee works.

29. Budapest: Hungary nationalizes all foreign and privately owned industry (→ 2/18/50).

CULTURAL EVENTS, 1949

Literature: Graham Green's "The Third Man"; Orwell's "Nineteen Eighty-Four"; Arthur Miller's "Death of a Salesman," Pulitzer Prize.

Academia: Claude Levi Strauss' "The Elementary Structures of Kinship"; Simone de Beauvoir's "The Second Sex."

Music: Bernstein's "Age of Anxiety"; Rodgers and Hammerstein's "South Pacific"; "Riders in the Sky"; "Diamonds Are a Girl's Best Friend"; "Rudolph, the Red-Nosed Reindeer."

The Arts: Chagall's "Red Sun"; Jacob Epstein's "Lazarus."

Film: Carol Reed's "The Third Man"; Rossen's "All the King's Men," Academy Award; Melville's "Les Enfants Terribles."

Nationalist China moves to Formosa

Dec 8. The Nationalist government of China, facing defeat by the Communists on the mainland, has shifted its capital to Taipei on the island of Formosa. The evacuation signified the end of effective military resistance on the mainland and probably cleared the way for many foreign governments to recognize the Communist regime in Peking as the new government of China.

On arriving in Taipei, however, Premier General Yen Hsi-shan said the Cabinet of the Nationalist government would continue to function on Formosa, which is 110 miles from the mainland. Generalissimo Chiang Kai-shek was expected shortly in Taipei along with remnants of the Nationalist staff.

125,000 leave East Germany for West

Dec 31. Thousands of East Berliners have left their half of Berlin to live in the Western section of the city. According to most figures, which are decidely difficult to gather, over 125,000 dissatisified East Berlin residents have snuck across city lines since January 1, 1949.

While the refugees seem to be of all classes, many disgruntled German professionals have fled the Communist-controlled sector of the metropolis. Included in the ranks of dissidents are doctors, lawyers and lecturers. While East Berlin authorities attempt to control the border, an adequate system to halt the exodus has yet to be devised.

Israel hurries to transfer capital to Jerusalem, defying U.N.

Dec 21. Israel plans to complete the transfer of her government from Tel Aviv to Jerusalem despite U.N. condemnation. "Operation Jerusalem is in full swing," an Israeli spokesman said, adding that it cannot be reversed.

Earlier this month, Premier David Ben Gurion announced the move to a tense Knesset (Parliament.) While he did not specifically proclaim Jerusalem as the new capital, he has arranged to move his office there, thus establishing the city as a de facto capital.

Ben Gurion also mentioned a possible return to Jerusalem by the Knesset, a reminder of the first session held there before President Weizmann's inauguration.

This sudden speed to complete what was thought to be a long-term project is generally seen as Israel's answer to the U.N. General Assembly, which has voted to internationalize the city. A transfer resolution will probably also be accepted in the Knesset without debate to show the world that Israel can present a united front.

Ben Gurion apparently watered down a statement openly proclaiming Jerusalem as the capital after receiving a note from the U.S. advising Israel against any "inflammatory" gesture that would disrupt relations between the U.S. and the Arabs or the Vatican (→ 1/23/50).

Jewish police stationed in Jerusalem.

Einstein presents gravitation theory

Dec 26. A new "generalized theory of gravitation" that attempts to unite the major forces of nature in one unified intellectual concept was published today by Albert Einstein, the discoverer of relativity theory. Just as relativity united space, time, matter and energy in one all-encompassing theory, Einstein's new achievement attempts to unite gravity and electromagnetism in one set of equations. It is the result of more than 30 years of work by the renowned physicist. However, Einstein says he has not yet developed a way that the new theory can be tested experimentally.

Dutch yield independence to Indonesia

Sukarno, finally free of Holland.

Dec 28. Sukarno is President of the newly independent republic of Indonesia. He was elected in Jakarta by the constituent assembly as Queen Juliana of the Netherlands signed documents recognizing the independence of Indonesia and the sovereignty of its six republics.

Under the agreement, by next July Dutch troops must abandon all the Indonesian islands they have occupied, with the exception of New Guinea. In return, the new Indonesian government pledges to protect Dutch economic interests. Sukarno, who led radical nationalists for more than 20 years, cooperated with the Japanese against the Dutch in the war (→ 4/5/50).

George Orwell's book foresees a grim 1984

Heroes and anti-heroes strode across stages and pages this year.

George Orwell started writing "Nineteen Eighty-Four" in 1948. He reversed the last two digits of the year to set the time for the book. Like those digits, the future Orwell depicts is familiar. Censorship, manipulation of historical fact and invasion of privacy reflect totalitarian governments of today. "1984's" hero is flabby and cowed, as anyone would be in a highly technocratic, highly paranoid society.

"The Greatest Story Ever Told," by Fulton Oursler, has been told countless times; the first version was found in the New Testament. So why did readers turn to Oursler's biography of Christ? Perhaps he told it with more immediacy. Christ the Savior seemed suddenly nearer.

Carson's McCullers' "Member of the Wedding" opened this year on Broadway. The play tenderly explores race relations and youth seeking its identity. Julie Harris starred as a 12-year-old tomboy questioning and defying society's taboos.

"Attention. Attention must be paid," says the wife of Willy Loman, hero of "Death of a Salesman." Willy is trapped in a society fond of a fast buck and friendless handshake. Playwright Arthur Miller wrote the shattering drama.

Tracy and Hepburn are together again

Tracy and Hepburn: "Adam's Rib."

Katharine Hepburn and Spencer Tracy once again tickle the public's funny bone in "Adam's Rib." The film concerns husband and wife lawyers who find themselves on opposite sides of a court case. Ruth Gordon and Garson Kanin, themselves married, wrote the nutty screenplay. George Cukor directed the cast, which includes a dizzy newcomer named Judy Holliday.

Since "Woman of the Year" (1942), Tracy and Hepburn have made three films featuring their private battle of the sexes. While often seen in each other's company, the actors are not ones to flaunt. Tracy has been married for 26 years.

The scariest Cold War crisis yet has ended peacefully. Above, the British, U.S. and S. African fliers who fed Berlin during the Soviet blockade file through London after being received by the King at Buckingham Palace.

1950–1959

1950

JANUARY

Su	Mo	Tu	We	Th	Fr	Sa
1	2	3	4	5	6	7
8	9	10	11	12	13	14
15	16	17	18	19	20	21
22	23	24	25	26	27	28
29	30	31				

1. Mao offers to discuss Sino-Soviet pact in Moscow (→ 6).

2. U.S. Commerce Dept. reports $25 bil. in foreign loans and credits since end of war (→ 3/8).

2. Pasadena: Ohio State over California 17-14 in Rose Bowl.

3. Rembrandt's "St. Peter Denying Christ" arrives from Amsterdam for first U.S. showing.

3. Cairo: Nahhas Pasha's Wadf Party wins in Egypt (→ 8/16/51).

5. Washington: Psychiatrist calls Whittaker Chambers "psychopath" at Hiss trial (→ 25).

8. Mme. Chiang Kai-shek leaves U.S. for Taiwan, pledging war to death against Mao (→ 10).

11. China: Communists land on Hainan Island (→ 14).

13. Ceylon: Commonwealth ministers agree on aid plan for Southeast Asia aimed at pact like NATO (→ 9/25).

14. Sec. of State Acheson orders U.S. consuls to leave mainland China (→ 31).

19. U.S. ready to support U.N. recognition of Spain (→ 11/4).

19. Mao recognizes Democratic Republic of Vietnam (→ 31).

21. Paul Larsen named to upgrade civil defense at head of Civilian Mobilization Office.

23. Jerusalem becomes official capital of Israel (→ 4/27).

25. U.S. Senate adopts ERA by 63-19 vote (→ 8/19/52).

27. Truman proclaims start of NATO as eight Western Europe nations sign (→ 4/1).

29. Johannesburg: Riots break out over apartheid (→ 5/29).

29. Iran: 1,500 killed by series of devastating earthquakes.

31. Paris protests Soviet recognition of Ho's Democratic Republic of Vietnam (→ 2/7).

DEATHS

2. Emil Jannings, German actor (*7/23/1884).

8. Joseph Schumpeter, Austrian economist (*2/8/1883).

15. Henry "Hap" Arnold, commander of U.S. Army Air Force (*6/15/1886).

Soviet delegate quits Security Council

The U.N. Security Council continues despite the empty chair left by Malik.

Jan 10. Boldly and bitterly, the Soviet delegate to the United Nations, Jacob Malik, has walked out of the U.N. Security Council. His exit protested the presence of Dr. T.F. Tsiang, representative of Nationalist China. A Soviet resolution to bar the Nationalists, who are no longer governors of mainland China, was denied by the council.

Malik told the council that a meeting with Tsiang presiding would be a "parody." He declared, "I, as representative of the Soviet Union, cannot participate in the work of the Security Council until the representative of the Kuomintang has been removed from membership of the Security Council."

While the Soviet position seems uncompromising, it is believed Malik will return to the U.N. on Thursday when the Soviet resolution is revived for discussion.

Clearly, the action sends a strong show of support to Mao Tse-tung and Communist China that the Soviets are sincerely allied. Reports indicate the two Communist powers have been disputing the future of Manchuria, which the Russians have long sought to acquire. The U.N. move might also be an attempt to alleviate tension (→ 11).

London recognizes Communist China

Jan 6. An intense international crisis has been provoked by Britain's recognition of the People's Republic of China. The United States and France are outraged that the British have recognized the Communists, especially since the forces of Mao Tse-tung are still at war with the Nationalist troops of Chiang Kai-shek. The United States, in particular, has been both a supporter and a supplier of Chiang during the past two years of the civil war.

In response to the indignation expressed by the Allies, Britain points out that Mao's forces have overrun almost all of mainland China. The Foreign Office also says Mao has the support of the Chinese people and is the President of the newly formed Central Committee of the People's Republic. Mao has won that support with a combination of military tenacity and a shrewd handling of China's peasantry.

Mao's Communist forces spread throughout the country from an original power base in Northern China. Most of Chiang's troops, meanwhile, have fled from the mainland to fortify the island of Formosa for a last-ditch stand against the Communists. For the past month, Mao and Foreign Minister Chou En-lai have been negotiating a new treaty with the Soviet Union. If Joseph Stalin emerges as a strong supporter of Mao, the alliance would likely create friction at the United Nations, where China is represented by the Nationalists (→ 8).

Hiss sentenced to five years in prison

Jan 25. Alger Hiss, a former top State Department official, was sentenced today to five years in prison for perjury in denying that he had passed top government secrets to Whittaker Chambers, a onetime agent for the Communists.

The stiff sentence, handed down by Judge Henry W. Goddard in New York Federal Court, came four days after a jury of eight women and four men had found Hiss guilty on two counts of perjury. An earlier trial last summer ended in an 8-to-4 hung jury.

Throughout both trials, the dapper defendant denied giving secret documents to Chambers in the late 1930's, a time when Hiss was a top assistant at State while Chambers was an underground agent for the Communists (→ 2/7).

Hiss, latest victim of Red Scare.

Nationalists keep bombing Red China

Shanghai suffers under bombs dropped from planes based on Formosa.

Jan 31. Chinese Nationalist planes carried out harassing attacks on coastal cities on the mainland in an apparent attempt to deter a Communist invasion of offshore islands. Nationalist planes based on the island of Hainan bombed and strafed the Southern port of Canton, causing considerable damage and casualties. The bombings were viewed as part of an effort to slow a Communist invasion of Hainan.

Nationalist planes based on Formosa also were attacking targets along the coast south of Shanghai. The Chinese Nationalist government has declared a blockade of shipping to the mainland, and there were reports it had mined the Yangtze River. Meanwhile, the aircraft carrier USS Boxer and two destroyers were ordered to the Far East to bolster the U.S. Seventh Fleet off the Chinese mainland (→ 2/15).

President orders hydrogen bomb built

Jan 31. President Truman says he has ordered the Atomic Energy Commission to produce the hydrogen bomb, saying that work on the weapon was necessary to be sure that the United Stated "is able to defend itself against any possible aggressor." The new weapon would be 100 to 1,000 times more powerful than the atomic bombs that destroyed Hiroshima and Nagasaki. They gained their power by splitting atoms. The hydrogen bomb would release much greater amounts of energy by fusing atoms, harnessing the energy source of the sun. Truman's decision comes only four months after the announcement that the Soviet Union successfully exploded an atomic bomb (→ 7/7).

George Orwell dead

Jan 21. George Orwell lived barely long enough to know the praise for his novel "1984," about a future ruled by claustrophobic telescreens and anesthetized behavior. Orwell, whose real name was Eric Arthur Blair, died today. He was 46.

Orwell was always preoccupied with individual rights. After fighting for the Republicans in the Spanish Civil War, he wrote "Homage to Catalonia" (1938). "Animal Farm" (1946) ribbed communism's faults.

"Third Man" a hit

Jan 13. Who is the third man? That query was on the lips of filmgoers waiting to see the British film "The Third Man," opening in America today. Exiting audiences looked like cats having swallowed canaries. This fine mystery, based on a Graham Greene novel, stars Orson Welles as a shrewd financier named Harry Lime. The mesmerizing zither score is composed by Anton Karas, and the shadowy camera work is by Robert Krasker.

1950

FEBRUARY

Su	Mo	Tu	We	Th	Fr	Sa
			1	2	3	4
5	6	7	8	9	10	11
12	13	14	15	16	17	18
19	20	21	22	23	24	25
26	27	28				

2. U.S. threatens new Berlin airlift to counter Soviet transport restrictions in Germany (→ 4/4).

3. London: Atom scientist Klaus Fuchs jailed as spy (→ 3/1).

5. U.S.: Month-old soft-coal strike spreads to 400,000 in six states (→ 11).

7. Wheeling, W. Va.: Joe McCarthy tells Republican Women's Club that Communists have infiltrated State Dept. (→ 20).

11. John L. Lewis orders miners to obey court order to go back to work; 370,000 are defiant (→ 20).

13. Albania becomes sixth Eastern bloc country to recognize Ho's Vietnamese govt. (→ 21).

18. Budapest: American Robert Vogeler tells Hungarian court he is spy, asks leniency (→ 21).

20. Washington: Court indicts U.M.W. for contempt (→ 3/2).

21. U.S. formally breaks relations with Bulgaria.

21. Yugoslavia opens diplomatic relations with Ho Chi Minh (→ 3/19).

21. Budapest: Robert Vogeler gets 15 years as spy (→ 4/21/51).

23. N.Y.: Met exhibits Vienna collection of Hapsburg art for first time in U.S.

23. London: Labor wins British general elections (→ 10/26/51).

25. U.S. abruptly freezes U.S. assets of citizens in Bulgaria, Hungary and Rumania.

28. Moscow puts ruble on gold standard, decrees price cuts.

28. Paris: French Assembly curbs sale of Coca-Cola.

BIRTHS

10. Mark Spitz, U.S. swimmer, 7 gold medals, 1972 Olympics.

22. Julius Erving, American basketball star.

DEATH

14. Karl Jansky, American engineer, initiated radio astronomy (*10/22/1905).

25. George R. Minot, American physiologist, 1934 Nobel Prize (*12/2/1885).

Two Vietnams vie for recognition

Feb 7. Two countries with the same name and the same borders have split the world between East and West. The two nations have different leaders but both are called Vietnam. This is fast becoming a new focus of tensions between the United States and the Soviet Union.

The United States recognized one of the Vietnams today, the Vietnam of Emperor Bao Dai. Britain made a similar move earlier in the day, and Australia and New Zealand are expected to follow suit. The other Vietnam, led by the extreme Nationalist and Communist Ho Chi Minh, was recognized by the Russians last week. Poland, Czechoslovakia, Bulgaria, Hungary, Rumania, Albania and North Korea also recognized Ho, who is a man with a country but not a capital. He fled underground to fight the French.

The U.S., which also recognized the kingdoms of Laos and Cambodia, has exerted pressure on France lately to lift its colonial policies in Indochina. Last week, the French National Assembly approved agreements recognizing Vietnam, Laos and Cambodia as states within the French Union. The State Department noted it supports "the peaceful and democratic evolution of dependent peoples toward self-government and independence."

British policy in Indochina has been criticized by India and Pakistan. India's Prime Minister Nehru calls Bao Dai a French "stooge" (→ 13).

Feb 7. Red Sox slugger Ted Williams, four-time home run champ who hit .406 in 1941, was unusually jovial as he told of signing a record $125,000 contract.

Stalin, Mao sign accord with secret clause

Feb 15. The Communist leaders of Russia and China shook hands early today in Moscow and told the world they are friends who will fight together if attacked. After two months of difficult negotiations, Joseph Stalin and Mao Tse-tung signed a mutual defense treaty.

Stalin agreed to return the Manchurian railroad, Port Arthur and Dairen to Mao and granted him credits worth $300 million. In two secret codicils to the treaty, Mao agreed to loan hundreds of thousands of Chinese workers to the Russians and to install Soviet officials in key positions in the Chinese army, police and Communist Party. It took so long to negotiate this treaty that rumors had begun to circulate that Mao had been taken hostage in Moscow (→ 3/18).

Stalin and a smiling Mao (standing at center) greet each other in Moscow.

One-piece windshield made for Cadillac

Feb 28. The granddaddy of American luxury cars, the Cadillac, now builds its windshields in one-piece units, the latest of many innovations that the oldest auto manufacturer in Detroit has created.

In 1908, the company won the coveted Dewar Trophy for producing perfectly interchangeable parts. Cadillac won the award again in 1912 for the invention of the electric self-starter. Lack of self-starting engines virtually excluded women from the auto world; with the new system women could drive too.

In recent times, the company, known for its cars with the latest in comfort and mechanical superiority, pioneered a new engine. In 1936, engineers designed the new 346-cubic-inch L-head motor. And now, in the postwar years, innovations like the one-piece windshield continue to steer the automaker to success.

The new Cadillac four-door sedan offers a curved, one-piece windshield.

Cold War murder on Orient Express

Feb 24. A cold-blooded murder on the elegant Orient Express has all the earmarks of a Cold War assassination. The victim's body, so battered and slashed that it was almost unrecognizable, was found in a railway tunnel south of Salzburg. His papers identified him as Eugene Karp, naval attache at the American Embassy in Bucharest. Hungarian authorities say he was something else: a spy for the U.S.

Karp was implicated in an espionage network at the trial in Hungary of one of his colleagues, Robert Vogeler. Vogeler was sentenced to 15 years in prison, and Karp apparently thought he would be next. He rushed to Vogeler's home, where he may have grabbed important documents, and sped to the Budapest train station. Karp appeared nervous, a witness said, as he made a reservation for Paris and paid for a single on the Orient Express.

He never made it to Paris. In fact, he never slept in his bed. The conductor of the sleeping car was drugged and thrown in a corner before he could even turn down the covers. Karp was grabbed, it appears, by two Hungarian agents and tossed into the tunnel in the middle of the night. His mangled body was found during the day.

McCarthy launches anti-Red crusade

Feb 20. Joseph R. McCarthy, an obscure United States Senator from Wisconsin, has aroused instantaneous national attention with a crusade against alleged communism in the federal government. McCarthy entered the Senate in 1946, but he attracted little notice.

His choice of a vehicle to fame was accidental. A Catholic priest told him the conflict with communism was the world's biggest problem. McCarthy arranged to address the Republican Women's Club of Wheeling, West Virginia, February 9. The key passage of his speech was, "I have here in my hand a list of 205 . . . members of the Communist Party . . . still working and shaping policy in the State Department." He offered no proof (→ 3/7).

1950

MARCH

Su	Mo	Tu	We	Th	Fr	Sa
			1	2	3	4
5	6	7	8	9	10	11
12	13	14	15	16	17	18
19	20	21	22	23	24	25
26	27	28	29	30	31	

2. Washington: U.M.W. found not guilty of contempt (→ 5).

3. Paris: France signs preliminary pact with Saar to gain control of mines for 50 years.

7. U.S.: Judith Coplon and Soviet consul Valentin Gubitchev found guilty as spies (→ 26).

8. Norfolk, Va.: First of $1 bil. in aid leaves for Europe (→ 25).

8. London: Czech Aja Vrzanova takes women's crown in world figure skating championships.

12. Brussels: Referendum votes return of King Leopold (→ 18).

13. G.M. reports 1949 profit of $656.4 million, a U.S. record.

16. Acheson calls for seven-point cooperation plan with Russians.

17. Berkeley: Californium, heaviest known element, discovered.

18. China: Nationalist troops land on mainland, capture Communist-held Sungmen (→ 4/23).

18. Brussels: Eyskens govt., threatened by strikes, resigns over return of king (→ 7/20).

19. Saigon: 4,000 riot over visit of two U.S. warships (→ 5/8).

23. Rome: Army called in to quell riots sparked by govt. repression; hundreds injured.

25. Truman warns economy bloc in Congress that foreign aid cuts would risk WWIII (→ 6/5).

26. McCarthy names ex-State Dept. adviser Owen Lattimore as Soviet spy (→ 30).

30. Florida: Truman denounces McCarthy as saboteur of U.S. foreign policy (→ 4/10).

DEATHS

5. Edgar Lee Masters, Chicago Renaissance writer, "Spoon River Anthology" (*8/23/1869).

6. Albert Lebrun, last president of French Third Republic (*8/27/1871).

12. Heinrich Mann, German writer (*3/27/1871).

19. Edgar Rice Burroughs, author "Tarzan" books (*9/1/1875).

24. Harold Laski, British socialist theorist (*6/30/1893).

30. Leon Blum, head of French Popular Front (*4/9/1872).

Mine strike ends after long negotiations

The recalcitrant U.M.W. rank and file are happy to return to work.

March 5. The latest coal miners' strike, a long and ugly one this time, finally ended today in the United States. The middle-of-the-winter walkout started two months ago, created serious energy shortages and sparked new tensions between the militant United Mine Workers and the Truman administration.

Incensed that negotiations could not end the strike, the administration tried to break the union by sending the Army in to mine the coal. The plan did not work. Afterwards, the union members refused to return to the mines, even though they were encouraged to do so by union President John L. Lewis. They also ignored furious harangues from conservative members of the Senate. Federal authorities arrested some of the strikers last month, but they were all eventually released.

The benefits won by the miners during this strike were not so great as the salary and pension victories of the 1940's. Under the new contract, the miners' daily pay rises from $14.05 to $14.75. The contributions of the mining companies to the workers' welfare funds also increases, from 20 to 30 cents a day.

But the miners lost some of their vacation days. And the U.M.W., already battered by heavy fines, lost public support during this cold weather strike. Some Americans are grumbling the union is run by Communists (→ 5/4).

Fuchs gets 14 years for giving away Bomb

Fuchs, never covert about his politics, has worked on the Bomb since 1943.

March 1. The modern-day Dr. Jekyll and Mr. Hyde, Klaus Fuchs, has been sentenced in London to 14 years imprisonment for divulging the most strategic secret of our time, the atom bomb, to the Soviet Union. The brilliant scientist, who was capable of turning on and off loyalty and who had confessed to charges of espionage, was convicted for violating the Secrets Act.

Fuchs left Nazi Germany in 1933 for France and then England. In 1942, he took the oath of allegiance to Britain and started work at Howell, the British atomic research center, where he had access to sensitive information which he supplied to the Soviets (→ 7/7).

RCA makes 3-color TV picture tube

March 29. The Radio Corporation of America successfully demonstrated an all-electronic color television tube today as its Chairman, David Sarnoff, proclaimed, "We are on the threshold of a new era in television—the era of color."

RCA actually demonstrated two color tubes today, one using a single electron gun, the other three guns to produce color images. Both picture tubes are the size of those in current black-and-white receivers. RCA is competing with a CBS system that uses a mechanical scanning disk to produce color images. The advantage of the RCA tube is that it is compatible with existing black-and-white transmission equipment, so that viewers could continue to use their existing home sets. The CBS system is not compatible. RCA will repeat its demonstration for industry representatives and federal officials who must decide between the two competing systems.

TV is getting in the way of school books

March 5. Children spend almost as much time, 27 hours a week, viewing TV shows as they do attending school, where a regular schedule is 27 hours and 55 minutes per week. A majority admits also that television viewing interferes with homework. The survey of youngsters, 11 to 15 years old, indicates further that Milton Berle is the most popular, followed by Ed Sullivan's "Toast of the Town," "Six-Gun Playhouse" and wrestling (→ 7/17).

A new skyline for New York City.

Eighty killed in world's worst air crash

March 12. The worst disaster in aviation history occurred today when 80 persons died in the crash of a chartered airliner in Wales. Only three passengers survived when the aircraft, a British Avro Tudor, nose-dived into a field outside the village of Sigginston near Cardiff. The toll exceeded the previous record of 55 deaths for an airplane crash, set last year when a fighter and an airliner collided near Washington, and the 73 deaths in the loss of the U.S. Navy dirigible Akron in 1933. The airliner that crashed today had been chartered by a group of Cardiff businessmen for a flight to Belfast to view a rugby match. It was about to land at Llandow Field, near Cardiff, when its nose suddenly tilted downward and the aircraft plunged straight into the ground. No cause for the accident has been determined.

The sight of disaster mars the quaint Welsh countryside around Sigginston.

1950

APRIL

Su	Mo	Tu	We	Th	Fr	Sa
						1
2	3	4	5	6	7	8
9	10	11	12	13	14	15
16	17	18	19	20	21	22
23	24	25	26	27	28	29
30						

1. The Hague: NATO ministers approve plan to counter "Soviet aggression" (→ 12/19).

4. West Berlin: Mozart girls choir of Dresden seeks sanctuary as political refugees (→ 5/1).

5. Indonesia: Rebellious soldiers capture Macassar (→ 9/28).

6. N.Y.: Irish premier arrives at Idlewild to mass protests against partition of Ireland (→ 6/13/51).

8. Soviets down U.S. Navy plane over Baltic Sea; crew lost (→ 18).

10. San Francisco: Harry Bridges given five years for concealing Communist affiliation at naturalization hearing (→ 20).

12. U.S.: Penicillin to be used to wipe out venereal disease in Haiti.

13. Cairo: Arab League signs mutual defense treaty.

14. Athens: Gen. Nicholas Plastiras replaces Sophocles Venizelos as Greek premier.

15. Italy: Iran's Princess Fatima marries American medical student, losing royal privileges.

15. Warsaw: Polish govt. signs pact with Church (→ 5/14).

18. Avro, first turbojet transport plane, flies Toronto to New York in one hour.

18. Tunisia: Habib Bourguiba proclaims Destour's independence demands (→ 11/15/51).

19. Truman authorizes economic rehabilitation plan for Navajo and Hopi Indian tribes.

20. Moscow asks removal of Anglo-American occupation troops from Trieste (→ 9/25/51).

23. N.Y. Philharmonic completes 108th season.

23. China: Chiang orders evacuation of Hainan, leaving all of mainland to Mao (→ 6/28).

27. Transcontinental and Western Air, Inc. changes name to Trans World Airlines, Inc.

27. Australia bans Communist Party.

27. Britain officially recognizes state of Israel (→ 5/25).

28. Paris: Communist Dr. Frederic Joliot Curie fired as chief of Atomic Energy Commission.

Pakistan, India agree on minority rights

Ali Khan, just off the plane in New Delhi, gets a warm greeting from Nehru.

April 5. Spurred by recent clashes in East and West Bengal between Moslems and Hindus, Indian Prime Minister Jawaharlal Nehru and Pakistani Prime Minister Ali Khan today reached agreement on a "bill of rights for minorities."

The troubles, often assuming massacre proportion, stem from 1947 with the independence of India, the establishment of Moslem Pakistan and the partition between them of Bengal and Punjab. While the partition took religion into account, it left minority pockets in each province and gave rise to religious blood-letting.

The prime ministers hope that if the minorities in each region can be made to feel secure regarding the majority of the community, other frictions will disappear.

The bill includes a provision for "drumhead justice," or summary justice to persons convicted of violating minority rights (→ 10/16/51).

Weill, master composer, passes from scene

April 3. Kurt Weill. composer of "The Three-Penny Opera" and memorable ballads like "September Song" and "Speak Low," died last night in the Flower-Fifth Avenue Hospital, at 50 years old, following a short illness.

While his music for "One Touch of Venus," "Lady in the Dark" and other hit musicals won the hearts of Broadway, his more serious work was equally hailed in concert halls throughout the world. A resident of this country since 1935, Weill was exiled from his native Germany in 1933 on stock Nazi charges of "Kultur Bolshevism."

The small composer with the enormous eyes was born in Dessau in 1900. Influenced by his father, a cantor, he began to compose while in primary school and at 18 went to Berlin to further his studies.

In 1928, Weill married the noted German soprano Lotte Lenya. The same year he teamed up with dramatist Bertold Brecht on "The Three-Penny Opera," which brought them international acclaim and ran for more than 2,000 performances in Germany. Other operas written with Brecht included "Mahagonny," also well received.

Broadway efforts included his collaboration with playwright Maxwell Anderson on "Knickerbocker "Holiday" and "Lost in the Stars."

Kurt Weill and wife Lotte Lenya.

Surgeon massages heart back to life

April 20. A New York man who was pronounced dead twice on an operating table was brought back to life both times by manual massage of his heart after it stopped beating, officials at St. John's Episcopal Hospital in Brooklyn reported today. The 65-year-old patient has made a complete recovery and will go home tomorrow, they said. Although other lives have been saved by heart massage, authorities say it has never before been used twice on the same patient. The patient's heart stopped beating during an abdominal operation. The surgeon made a chest incision and massaged it back to life, repeating the procedure when it stopped again.

Transjordan takes the name Jordan

April 24. The territory known as Arab Palestine disappeared today, and so did Transjordan. Both were swallowed up into a new country, which will be known simply as Jordan. The political move in Amman put Jordan on a collision course with Israel and the rest of the Arab League, which is on record as favoring an Arab Palestine. The move was endorsed immediately in Britain. Diplomatic sources in London say the Foreign Office favors the annexation. That means the Anglo-Jordanian military alliance will extend to both sides of the Jordan River. This is unsettling to Israel, which does not like a British presence on its border.

Soviets down U.S. bomber over Latvia

April 18. The U.S. State Department expects an immediate apology from the Soviet Union for its attack on an American Navy plane over Latvia which killed ten Americans. In a communique sent to Moscow, Washington demanded the Soviets pay "appropriate indemnity for the unprovoked destruction of American lives and property." The Soviets assert the U.S. bomber fired on a Russian fighter first.

Lattimore denies he was Communist

April 20. Innuendo or evidence? The jury in the case of accused Communist spy Owen Lattimore will have to decide which is which in the testimonies supplied by key witnesses on both sides of this dramatic trial. Louis Budenz, a former U.S. Communist leader, asserted Lattimore had served the Chinese Communists in their war against the Nationalists. Lattimore vehemently denied the accusation and his lawyer brought retired U.S. General Elliot Thorpe to the stand. Thorpe testified that during World War II Lattimore was entrusted with sensitive information and had always served America loyally, despite contrary allegations by Senator Joseph McCarthy (→ 6/9).

Nijinsky, long ill, succumbs at last

April 8. Nijinsky, perhaps the finest male dancer of the century, has died in London. He was 60. Nijinsky was a spectacular dancer and choreographer from 1909 to 1913, yet schizophrenia kept him in mental asylums for the last 31 years.

Vaslav Nijinsky was born in Kiev. He joined the Imperial Ballet in 1907 and soon met Diaghilev, the impresario, who helped him choreograph "Afternoon of a Faun" (1912) and "Rite of Spring" (1913). He was famed for the height of his leaps and breadth of ideas.

Nijinsky in "Afternoon of a Faun."

1950

MAY

Su	Mo	Tu	We	Th	Fr	Sa
	1	2	3	4	5	6
7	8	9	10	11	12	13
14	15	16	17	18	19	20
21	22	23	24	25	26	27
28	29	30	31			

1. West Berlin: 500,000 meet on May Day to denounce German Communism (→ 28).

4. Detroit: 100-day Chrysler strike comes to end (→ 8).

6. Truman asks statehood for Hawaii and Alaska to strengthen natl. security (→ 1/3/59).

6. Middleground, W. Boland up, wins Kentucky Derby.

8. U.S. Supeme Court upholds Taft-Hartley Act's requirement of non-Communist declaration from laborers (→ 23).

8. Acting on French reports of Ho-Mao pact, U.S. offers military aid to France (→ 25).

9. Schuman plan to merge German and French heavy industry drafted in Europe (→ 3/19/51).

11. Ionesco's "La Cantatrice Chauve" staged in Paris.

11. Truman dedicates Grand Coulee Dam.

14. Warsaw: Reports indicate big purge in Polish United Workers Party (→ 8/2/51).

14. Istanbul: Celal Bayar replaces Ismet Inonu as president, ending party's 27-year reign.

19. N.J.: Ammunition barges explode, killing 20, injuring 400.

22. Communist China offers autonomy to Tibet (→ 10/21).

23. Detroit: GM, U.A.W. sign five-year contract for wage rise, pensions, security (→ 2/8/51).

25. N.Y.: Brooklyn-Battery Tunnel, longest in U.S., opened.

25. U.K., France and U.S. agree to allot arms to Mideast on basis of disparity between Arab states and Israel (→ 4/5/51).

26. First whooping crane hatched in captivity born in Arkansas Natl. Game Refuge.

27. U.S. order Czechs to close consulate in N.Y. (→ 2/3/51).

28. East Berlin: 500,000 march carrying Lenin banners (→ 6/8).

29. Capetown: Non-whites plan "natl. day of mourning" to protest racial bill (→ 6/13).

30. Johnny Parsons wins Indy 500 in a Kurtis-Kraft Wynns.

30. Seoul: Syngman Rhee's party loses elections (→ 6/25).

Bowling congress lifts color bar

May 12. The American Bowling Congress has ended its 34-year-old rule that limited its membership to white males. Only a few of the 518 delegates were heard to say "nay" during the voice vote.

The counsel for the congress, Michael J. Dunn, had called the rule a threat to the supervisory structure of the bowling congress. Four states had already contested the legality of the restriction. He said that from 1895 to 1916 "there was no 'white male' in our rule book and we got along fine."

The congress was fined $2,500 in Illinois, which threatened to void the charter in that state if the restriction was not removed. The congress' decision was praised by the Rev. Charles Carow of the Catholic Youth Organization of Brooklyn, who led a six-year fight to rid bowling of racial discrimination. An official of the New York chapter of the ABC, Father Carow said that the congress would become "American not only in name but in practice."

Truman: bowler, civil rights backer.

The American Bowling Congress was organized on September 9, 1895, for the purpose of reviving the sport. The first national championship was in 1901 in Chicago (→ 6/5).

Four Viet Minh battalions attack French

May 25. French forces are feeling all the fury of the Communists in Northern Vietnam, and they are appealing to the United States for military support against the determined guerrillas. Four well-armed Viet Minh battalions attacked three French companies at the poorly defended Dong Khe outpost in Tonkin province. The Communists, trained by Chinese commanders just across the border, were armed with American howitzers seized by Mao Tse-tung's forces from the retreating Nationalists. The Viet Minh guerrillas had the French on the run until they were scattered by an intense aerial bombardment.

The French lost many men as they recaptured Dong Khe today. They have learned the hard way that the defense of northern outposts will be extremely costly.

The French have told the United States they need military equipment, particularly airplanes, as soon as possible. The request has not fallen on deaf ears. Secretary of State Dean Acheson said, "The United States government, convinced that neither national independence nor democratic evolution can exist in an area dominated by Soviet imperialism, considers the situation to be such as to warrant its according economic aid and military equipment."

The French say they need the equipment as protection against the secret military agreement the Viet Minh signed with Mao. It is no secret that a large shipment of military supplies just arrived in China from Russia (→ 10/8).

For only the 2nd time a musical has won a Pulitzer. Rodgers and Hammerstein's "South Pacific" is based on a Michener novel.

1950

JUNE

Su	Mo	Tu	We	Th	Fr	Sa
				1	2	3
4	5	6	7	8	9	10
11	12	13	14	15	16	17
18	19	20	21	22	23	24
25	26	27	28	29	30	

1. Tokyo offers to sign peace with any Allied nation that will recognize Japanese autonomy.

4. U.S.: Record 3.5 mil. enroll in Catholic schools for fall.

5. Truman authorizes $3.2 bil. for five foreign aid programs.

5. Supreme Court bars segregation in two colleges (→ 8/21).

7. Washington: First nationwide conference on aging opens at Truman's request (→ 8/28).

8. Allies grant Bonn right to set own foreign policy (→ 10).

9. Washington: Commerce Dept. official William Remington resigns to defend against disloyalty accusations (→ 14).

10. West turns down Soviet proposals for vote on German reunification (→ 15).

11. Pennsylvania: Ben Hogan, recovered from near-fatal auto accident, wins U.S. golf Open.

13. South Africa: White Assembly, representing 20% of population, votes to divide country into black and white areas (→ 20).

14. Senate group asks replacement of 13,000 aliens in U.S. diplomatic posts overseas (→ 7/20).

15. Bonn: Bundestag votes to join Council of Europe (→ 9/19).

17. Chicago: Richard G. Laoler performs first human kidney transplant.

20. Capetown: Fearing legal action, South African Communist Party dissolves (→ 3/20/52).

23. East Germans claim sovereignty over Sudeten residents.

25. N.Y.: U.N. rebukes North Koreans, asking cease-fire as 38th parallel is crossed.→

27. U.N. and U.S. agree to send troops to aid Seoul (→ 28).

28. Formosa: Chiang orders halt to attacks on mainland (→ 7/18).

28. Korea: MacArthur arrives as Seoul falls to North (→ 29).

29. Truman asserts "U.S. is not at war"; Soviets protest U.N. decision to intervene (→ 30).

30. Truman extends the draft into 1951 (→ 7/19).

30. Frankfurt: Delegates from 33 nations found new Socialist Intl.

North Korean Reds invade South

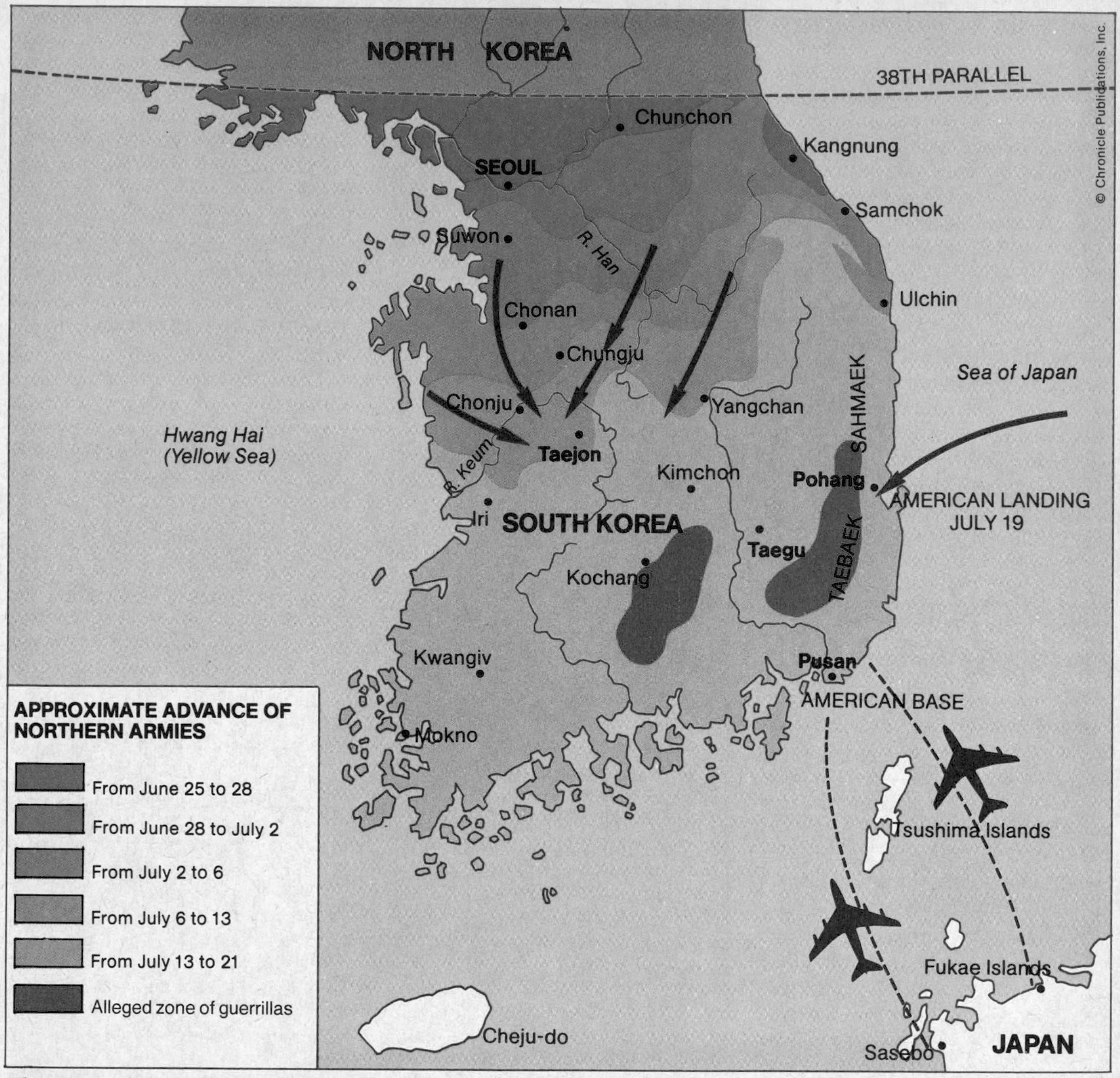

The uneasy division of Korea after the war has broken down as Northern armies swarm over the 38th parallel.

The hills of Korea looming in the background, a Southern soldier carries a wounded comrade to safety.

June 25. North Korean forces crossed the 38th parallel today and invaded South Korea. A declaration of war was broadcast on Northern Pyongyang radio. Within hours, the North Koreans were forcing South Korean border guards to retreat across a broad front. Communist units faced little resistance as they headed toward Seoul. The United States seemed surprised by the attack, which it is blaming on the Soviet Union.

President Truman, traveling in Kansas City, said he was not aware of a formal declaration of war by the North Koreans. The United States Ambassador to Seoul said there is no reason for alarm. "As yet it cannot be determined," John Muccio said, "whether the Northern Communists intend to precipitate all-out warfare." But that is precisely what they intend, acccording to a report prepared for United Nations Secretary General Trygve Lie at Lake Success. Lie received the report this morning and called the Security Council into an emergency meeting this afternoon.

In one of the sharpest resolutions it ever passed, the council accused North Korea of breaking the peace and demanded that the Communists withdraw their troops immediately. North Korea and the Soviet Union are both likely to say the vote was illegal because China is still represented on the council by the Nationalists (→ 27).

MacArthur will probably command U.N. forces preparing to fight in Korea.

Red boycott gives U.N. freedom in Korea

June 30. President Truman, acting in concert with the United Nations, authorized the use of American ground forces today to repel the North Korean invasion of South Korea. Truman acted after the Soviet Union assured the United States it has no intention of intervening militarily in South Korea.

The Security Council has already authorized the use of force by member nations to restore peace south of the 38th parallel. The council's actions have not been hindered by the Communist bloc. The Soviet delegate has refused to attend council meetings, and the Communist Chinese are not represented on the Security Council. Truman's commitment of ground forces followed the recommendations of the Defense Department and General Douglas MacArthur.

The general flew from Tokyo to South Korea yesterday and quickly perceived that the South Koreans needed more help. Truman had earlier ordered the United States Navy and Air Force to support the South Koreans south of the 38th parallel. After a report from MacArthur, Truman ordered a complete blockade of the Korean coast and air strikes when necessary against North Korea. In addition, Truman ordered a cordon around Formosa to prevent a possible Communist invasion. He dispatched more troops to the Philippines and more military supplies to the French in Vietnam.

At the United Nations, diplomats are preparing to give MacArthur command of all United Nations forces in South Korea. British Prime Minister Attlee announced today that he was placing his Asiatic fleet under MacArthur. Recent American air strikes in South Korea are helping the South Korean army hold a line south of Seoul. The fall of the capital two days ago was a demoralizing defeat. The government of President Syngman Rhee fled to the south. The 2,000 American residents of South Korea are being evacuated to Japan on ships and planes (→ 7/2).

French expedition climbs Annapurna

June 3. A French band of mountaineers has scaled Annapurna, one of the highest peaks in the Himalayas. A climber named Maurice Herzog leads the six men. Herzog began the journey with a handful of charts that later proved worthless. "The maps are wrong," he wrote. "Nothing has yet been explored."

One group member is a doctor regularly testing the men's fitness. The terrible stress they have experienced will not fade on the descent. They still breathe oxygen-depleted air (the elevation is 26,502 feet), and sub-freezing temperatures make the wind slice at them like a knife. The men wrap up every inch of their skin; their eyes peer through darkened goggles.

Because of its distinctive crest, the peak has developed a mystique perhaps greater than that of Mount Everest, highest point in the Himalayas and the world. In fact, Annapurna is not one mountain but a group of four peaks along a 35-mile long massif. Herzog's expedition ascended Annapurna I, the massif's highest and westernmost elevation.

Herzog and a bundled companion break camp on the face of Annapurna.

Another 180 lost in plane crashes

June 24. Tragic accidents continue to plague the aviation industry. The latest crash early this morning claimed 58 lives. A Northwest Airlines DC-4 plane with 55 passengers and three crew members aboard plummeted from the sky into Lake Michigan near Milwaukee. Earlier this month, a twin-engine C-46 plunged into the Atlantic off the Florida coast killing 28, but a valiant rescue effort saved 37 who had climbed onto life rafts amid swimming sharks. In France, three air disasters in as many days took the lives of 94.

Gregory Peck is "The Gunfighter," a reformed desperado from the Wild, Wild West, trying to live down his blood-stained past.

Henri Matisse, brillant colorist, wins Venice prize

Matisse's "Rumanian Blouse" (1940). Oil on canvas.

June 11. One of the great French masters of contemporary art, Henri Matisse, was honored with the grand prize at the Venice art festival. Matisse, a brilliant painter and sculptor, asked to share his prize with a colleague and friend, the sculptor Henri Laurens, who has received little public recognition for his work. The selection of the 81-year-old Matisse for the grand prize was applauded in Venice, although a number of artists and critics believe the judges of the competition overlooked Marc Chagall.

Matisse has influenced dozens of French painters for the past 50 years. He was considered the prime representative of the Fauvist school, but it is also acknowledged that Matisse broke early in his career with all formal schools and styles.

Matisse trained at the Ecole des Beaux Arts in Paris under the reclusive Gustave Moreau and had his first exhibition in 1896. At the turn of the century, Matisse drifted away to experiment with his own style and to immerse himself in a new world of bright colors.

His canvases became brighter and simpler. He was moved by his travels through Morocco, and the Arab influence can be seen in the decorations, bold lines and solid colors he painted. Slaves and concubines became favorite subjects. His attraction to the simple geometry of a line is evident in his pen and ink drawings and lithographs.

Matisse was honored in Venice while he was working on his latest project, the decoration of the Dominican Chapel of the Rosary in Vence, France. Under his direction, the walls of the chapel are painted black and white, but the somber atmosphere is relieved by the strikingly beautiful stained glass windows. Vence, a hillside town overlooking the Mediterranean near Grasse, has been the home of Matisse since the end of the war.

The artist's work is well-known in the United States. Matisse had his first big American exhibition at the celebrated New York Armory Show in 1913. More recently, his works were shown at an impressive retrospective show in Philadelphia in 1948.

The Venice festival, which is organized every two years, gives artists from around the world a chance to meet each other. For the last few years, the French have dominated the awards ceremony. Georges Braque won the grand prize at the last festival. There was much comment in Venice this year about the American exhibition. The work of the landscape painter John Marin was represented in a major retrospective. Also on view were the canvases of a new generation of artists, including Jackson Pollock and Willem de Kooning.

"Interior of a Tank for a Red Fish." Oil on canvas. Already world famous in 1914, Matisse stayed aloof from Cubism, choosing to explore the uses of color in his own Fauvist style.

"Algerian" (1908). Oil on canvas.

1950

JULY

Su	Mo	Tu	We	Th	Fr	Sa
						1
2	3	4	5	6	7	8
9	10	11	12	13	14	15
16	17	18	19	20	21	22
23	24	25	26	27	28	29
30	31					

2. U.S. asks Chiang to confer with MacArthur before sending 33,000 troops to S. Korea (→ 3).

3. Korea: U.S. forces see action for first time; Pyongyang charges "bare-faced aggression" (→ 5).

5. Korea: U.S. troops, in first major battle, stand off massive attacks on Suwon road (→ 11).

5. Rumanians expel Gerald Patrick O'Hara, acting Papal Nuncio, for espionage.

7. Truman asks $260 mil. for hydrogen bomb plan (→ 8/2).

8. MacArthur named to head U.N. force in Korea (→ 10/15).

11. Chicago: Natl. League wins baseball's All Star Game.

11. Korea: U.S. tanks enter battle as American forces fall back behind Kum River (→ 15).

15. London: Churchill warns of third world war (→ 26).

16. Uruguay wins soccer's World Cup.

16. Bastogne: Belgium inaugurates monument commemorating battle of the Bulge.

17. Univ. of Michigan study indicates half of Americans do not read books (→ 10/11).

18. British join U.S. in banning oil to Mao's China (→ 8/1).

19. Truman asks Congress for $10 bil. arms budget (→ 21).

19. Florida: Army's first attempt to launch guided missile fails.

20. Senate For. Rel. Committee rules McCarthy allegations not based in fact (→ 8/28).

20. Belgian Parliament authorizes King Leopold's return (→ 31).

21. U.S. Army calls up National Guard and reserves (→ 27).

26. Britain, Australia, New Zealand to send troops to Korea under U.N. command (→ 30).

27. U.S. Army calls 100,000 through selective service (→ 31).

30. Korea: Reds drive to win Pusan before aid arrives (→ 31).

31. Formosa: MacArthur arrives for talks with Chiang.→

DEATH

22. Mackensie King, Canadian statesman (*12/17/1874).

Truman gives military power to wage war

July 31. The powerful American war machine started its engine this month as President Truman authorized a broad military buildup for the fighting in Korea and granted the military the power to wage war.

Today, the president ordered the mobilization of Marine Corps and National Guard troops, bringing into service 114,000 American men, with another 100,000 soon to swell the military ranks via the Selective Service System. Now, all branches of the armed services have been activated. Plans also include bolstering the Army with 240,000 men, bringing its total to 834,000.

While increasing manpower, Truman also boosted funding to meet the challenges of Communist aggression, made more apparent by the Korean War. Congress approved his request of $1.2 billion to continue the Mutual Defense Assistance Program, which aids nations combatting communism.

The mobilization of money and men follows the U.N. Security Council vote on July 7 giving the United States full command of U.N. troops defending South Korea. The 7-0 vote—with Egypt, India and Yugoslavia abstaining and the Soviet Union continuing its boycott—placed "special responsibilities" on America. President Truman accepted the burden, and appointed General Douglas MacArthur chief of U.N. forces (→ 8/13).

U.S. troops debark in South Korea.

There are 150 mil. of us, census finds

July 22. The Census Bureau places the population of the continental United States at 150,520,198 persons, nearly 19 millions more than in 1940. California moved from fifth largest populated state to second, edging out Pennsylvania. New York remains number one with 14,743,210, and Manhattan is the most densely populated area in the world, squeezing 1,938,551 human beings into 22 square miles. By contrast, Nevada has an average of 1.4 persons per square mile.

Budge Patty wins Wimbledon singles

July 7. Budge Patty of California proved he has changed from playboy to serious player by beating Franck Sedgman at Wimbledon. "It's because I gave up smoking," he said. "Otherwise I wouldn't have gotten past the third round."

Patty in action on the grass.

King Leopold renounces Belgian throne

July 31. Belgium's King Leopold III has agreed to abdicate in favor of his son Baudouin. At the start of the month, 500,000 Belgians took to the streets, denouncing Leopold for his docile acceptance of Nazi occupation during the war. On July 12, strikes gripped the country's mines. Soon afterward, the Belgian Parliament gave the nod to Leopold's return to the country from exile in Austria. On the 26th, strikes spread nationwide. Today, Leopold, flanked by officials in military dress, signed abdication papers.

Baudouin's ascension to the throne is complicated by his age. He is two months shy of his 20th birthday, and the constitution demands he reach his majority before wearing the crown. The courts are debating the next step (→ 8/1).

In a somber ceremony, King Leopold abdicates in favor of his son Baudouin.

Jimmy Stewart is an Army man seeking peace with Apache Chief Cochise in "Broken Arrow."

North Koreans sweep through South unhindered

July 31. North Korean forces have swept through most of South Korea, and so far no one has been able to stop them. The South Koreans have been helpless and disorganized. American troops made a brave stand north of Taejon, but they eventually had to pull back south of the Kum River. Most of the American and United Nations forces have retreated to a heavily defended coastal strip in the southeastern part of the country.

North Korea has accused the United States of "bare-faced aggression" in the war. The Soviet Union charged that the United States is pushing the world into an "open war." And former British Prime Minister Winston Churchill warned Conservatives in his country that the conflict runs the risk of turning into a full-fledged third world war.

President Truman has responded to the new Communist threat by proposing partial mobilization. The Defense Department has ordered the Selective Service to draft 20,000 men immediately to replace the reserves who have been sent to Korea and Japan. The president asked Congress for $10 billion for rearmament, and he warned the American people that they will be called upon to fight the Communist menace through higher taxes.

The first American ground troops did not reach South Korea until Seoul and Suwon had fallen. Their mission was to protect the provisional capital of Taejon, 90 miles south of Seoul, and bridgeheads on the Kum River north of Taejon. The Americans were loaded for bear, Russian bear if need be. "If the Russkies come down, we'll fight the Russkies," General John Church told reporters.

The Russians did not come, but the North Koreans did. The United States entered the ground fighting between Suwon and Taejon. At first, a thin American line held firm against the North Korean assault, but eventually four American battalions collapsed under the thrust of three Communist divisions and an unrelenting tank attack. American commanders said shells from their powerful 105-mm. howitzers were not capable of penetrating the thick armor of the North Korean tanks.

A U.S. Eighth Cavalry soldier takes a prisoner in the hills of Korea.

Despite the recent setbacks on the battlefield, there are indications that American planes have disrupted communication lines and created havoc behind North Korean lines.

Meanwhile, the Western Allies have been pulling together in their diplomatic response to the war. Britain, Australia and New Zealand have announced that they will place ground troops under the United Nations command in Korea. Both the French President and the head of the French Socialist Party have come out in favor of the U.N. military intervention in the country. And Indian Prime Minister Nehru has told the United Nations his country will send medical supplies for relief of soldiers in Korea.

In fact, General MacArthur is now claiming the North Koreans had an opportunity, but failed, to overrun all of South Korea. "We are now in Korea in force," the commander of all United Nations forces asserted, "and with God's help we are there to stay until the constitutional authority of the republic is fully restored" (→ 8/4).

A U.S. aircraft carrier brings reinforcements to help halt the Northern drive.

American F-4-V Corsair fighter, engaged in missions over Korea.

1950

AUGUST

Su	Mo	Tu	We	Th	Fr	Sa
		1	2	3	4	5
6	7	8	9	10	11	12
13	14	15	16	17	18	19
20	21	22	23	24	25	26
27	28	29	30	31		

1. N.Y.: U.N. defeats Soviet motion to oust Nationalist China (→ 24).

1. N.Y.: U.S.S.R. readmitted to U.N. Security Council.

2. Washington: AEC picks E.I. du Pont de Nemours to take on H-bomb production (→ 12).

4. N.Y.: Soviets call for Korean cease-fire in U.N. (→ 8).

5. American Florence Chadwick swims English Channel in record 13 hrs., 23 min. (→ 8).

6. California: B-29 carrying A-bomb crashes into trailer camp, killing 17, injuring 60.

7. Ferdinand Kubler wins Tour de France.

8. Korea: U.S. line pierced along Naktong River (→ 15).

13. Republicans in Senate For. Rel. Committee denounce Truman Far East policy (→ 9/8).

15. Korea: U.S. pierces Naktong bridgehead, as 98 B-29's shell North Korean positions (→ 17).

17. N.Y.: U.S. delegate Warren Austin asks U.N. for united Korea (→ 9/1).

18. Crime inquiry reports organized crime eclipsing legitimate business in U.S.

19. Belgian Communist Party leader assassinated.

24. N.Y.: Communist China calls on U.N. to order U.S. to withdraw Seventh Fleet from Formosa patrol (→ 31).

27. U.S. govt. seizes railroads to avert nationwide strike.

28. Ex-C.I.O. counsel Lee Pressman, in deal with HUAC, names three fellow Communists (→ 28).

28. Truman adds ten mil. to Social Security roles (→ 7/18/52).

28. Hollywood: Jean Muir dropped from cast of "The Aldrich Family" after allegations of Communist connections (→ 9/23).

31. Truman pledges to withdraw Formosa fleet only after Korean conflict is settled (→ 9/19).

BIRTH

15. Anne Elizabeth Alice Louise, British princess.

Tennis admits Althea Gibson, first Negro

Aug 21. Althea Gibson will become the first Negro to compete in the United States tennis championships. The New York girl was accepted by the United States Lawn Tennis Association, a step necessary for her to compete.

Miss Gibson, a 22-year-old student at Florida A & M College, will be among 52 women seeking the grass-court title at Forest Hills next week. She was runner-up to Nancy Chaffee in the national indoors after capturing the Eastern indoor title. She also competed in important clay-court tournaments. U.S.T.A. President Lawrence A. Baker said Miss Gibson had been accepted "because of her ability" (→ 12/4).

Gibson, pioneer in a "white sport."

How to defend against atomic attack

Aug 12. A 438-page guide on civilian defense against atomic bomb attack has been released by the Department of Defense and the Atomic Energy Commission, covering effects of atomic bombs when released high in the air (as over Hiroshima and Nagasaki), low on the ground (as in the test at Alamogordo, New Mexico), and exploded underwater (as at Bikini).

By avoiding mass hysteria and panic, lives may be saved. Readers are told that in a high air burst, the danger from radiation is confined to the first minute, and the lethal radius for direct exposure to gamma rays is 4,000 feet. All buildings within a half-mile radius would be demolished with debris showering the area. It takes a blast wave seven seconds to travel two miles.

In low ground or underwater explosion, radioactive contamination presents a longer-lasting problem. People must remain in shelters two to four hours and then wash thoroughly. And they ought not to beget offspring for two to three months following exposure so as not to pass on aberrations in chromosomes (→ 9/27).

American woman sets Channel record

Aug 8. The 24-year-old Channel swimming record has been broken. Florence Chadwick of California swam the English Channel an hour faster than Gertrude Ederle did in setting the record in 1926.

Another American, Shirley May France, failed for the second time in two years to negotiate the 22-mile grind. Miss France, 17, was pulled hysterical, shivering and weeping into a pilot boat eight miles from her goal.

Miss Chadwick reached the chalk cliffs of Dover 13 hours and 20 minutes after plunging into the surf at Can Gris Nez, France.

Chadwick, the new record-holder.

Aug 1. Baudouin assumes Belgian throne, quieting those who feared his father's return would renew the evils of Nazi occupation (→ 7/16/51).

The U.N. is moving to its permanent home in N.Y. (→ 11/1).

1950

SEPTEMBER

Su	Mo	Tu	We	Th	Fr	Sa
					1	2
3	4	5	6	7	8	9
10	11	12	13	14	15	16
17	18	19	20	21	22	23
24	25	26	27	28	29	30

1. North Koreans launch assault on 50-mile front (→ 4).

3. Japan: Typhoon sweeps northern island of Hokkaido, leaving 300,000 homeless.

4. N.Y.: U.S. tells U.N. it found body of Soviet flier in plane it shot down over Korea (→ 6).

6. N.Y.: Soviets use 44th U.N. veto to bar condemnation of North Korea (→ 13).

8. Truman gets emergency economic powers in Defense Production Act (→ 10/3).

11. Pennsylvania: 33 soldiers killed in wreck of troop train.

13. Korea: U.S. and British warships shell port at Seoul (→ 15).

16. Mass.: 26,000-ton liner Constitution, "symbol of free enterprise" launched at Quincy.

16. French weather ship hits drifting WWII mine in English Channel; 51 dead in blast.

19. N.Y.: U.N. Assembly rejects Indian-Soviet proposal to admit Communist China (→ 4/29/51).

19. N.Y.: Britain, U.S., France officially recognize West Germany to bolster line against communism (→ 10/21).

20. Korea: U.S. Marines drive into Seoul (→ 22).

22. Korea: U.N. forces capture Suwon in North (→ 25).

25. Korea: Seoul retaken by U.N. forces (→ 28).

25. London: Seven Commonwealth nations draft plan for aid to Southeast Asia (→ 7/1/51).

28. Korea: MacArthur restores Seoul to Syngman Rhee (→ 28).

28. N.Y.: U.N. Assembly admits Indonesia (→ 8/10/54).

28. China: Chou En-lai threatens intervention if North Korea is invaded (→ 29).

30. U.S. State Dept. bans visas to visitors from totalitarian nations (→ 12/9).

DEATHS

11. Jan Christiaan Smuts, South African ex-president, independence leader (*8/1/1870).

21. Arthur Milne, British astrophysicist (*2/14/1876).

Inchon landing surprises the enemy

U.S. Marines climb ashore on rugged terrain near Inchon.

Americans man a rocket-launcher amid the dry underbrush of Korea.

Tired and muddy, American soldiers retreat through the village of Yongsan.

Sept 15. United Nations forces in beleaguered South Korea swung to the offensive today and surprised the Communist enemy with a daring landing from the sea at Inchon.

South Korean Marines waded ashore at Inchon, Seoul's port city, while American troops landed on the island of Wolmi, a short distance away. The attack was a big gamble by General MacArthur. As his troops broke out of Inchon and advanced toward Seoul, it looked as if the gamble was paying off.

No American Marines were killed in the operation. But some of the men, who had seen action at Guadalcanal in the last war, said this was the most difficult landing they had ever made. They had to wade through heavily mined mud flats, and they used specially constructed aluminum ladders to scramble up the steep cliffs.

As they climbed the cliffs, the Marines faced scattered resistance from the North Koreans. Some Communist units fought back tooth and nail. Others indicated their willingness to give up by stripping their commanding officer naked and raising their hands in the air.

Two days of air strikes and shelling from cruisers and destroyers had knocked out many of the enemy positions. And the B-29's did not stop in the area of Seoul and Inchon. Some pummeled Communist positions as far south as Kumchon. Others bombed as far north as Pyongyang in North Korea.

The surprise landing at Inchon was accompanied by strikes in other parts of the country. United Nations troops landed on the west coast at Kunsan, 100 miles south of Seoul. American and South Korean forces also landed behind Communist lines at two points on the east coast, northeast of Pohang and at Yongdok. Three American destroyers were slightly damaged in the assault, but the United States denies a North Korean claim that they were sunk.

The landings encouraged United Nations forces to break out of their perimeter in the southeast. MacArthur's headquarters announced that the walled city of Kasan, ten miles north of Taegu, was recaptured a week after it fell to the Communists (→ 20).

Map of the Operations

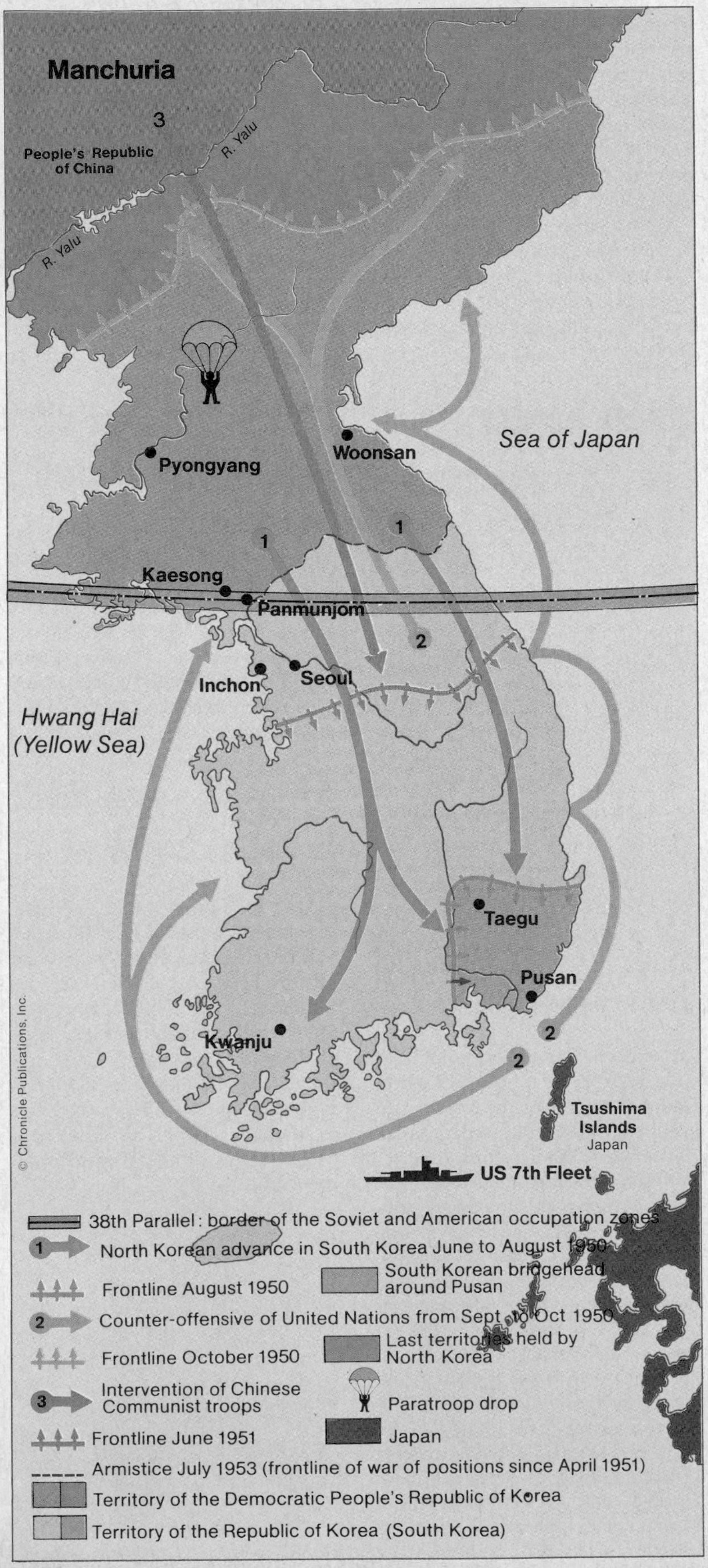

Manchuria

3

People's Republic of China

R. Yalu

R. Yalu

Sea of Japan

Woonsan

Pyongyang

1

1

Kaesong

Panmunjom

2

Inchon

Seoul

Hwang Hai (Yellow Sea)

Taegu

Pusan

Kwanju

2

2

Tsushima Islands

Japan

US 7th Fleet

38th Parallel: border of the Soviet and American occupation zones

1 North Korean advance in South Korea June to August 1950

Frontline August 1950

South Korean bridgehead around Pusan

2 Counter-offensive of United Nations from Sept. to Oct 1950

Frontline October 1950

Last territories held by North Korea

3 Intervention of Chinese Communist troops

Paratroop drop

Frontline June 1951

Japan

Armistice July 1953 (frontline of war of positions since April 1951)

Territory of the Democratic People's Republic of Korea

Territory of the Republic of Korea (South Korea)

American Marines quickly liberate Seoul

After three months, U.N. troops are finding success along the Naktong River.

Sept 29. General MacArthur returned in triumph today to Seoul, as United Nations troops recaptured the South Korean capital three months after it fell to the Communists. The general, wearing his distinctive old hat and khakis, was joined by President Syngman Rhee, who had fled from Seoul moments before the North Koreans arrived.

Much of the capital lay in ruins as Rhee warned that South Koreans would have to "pay our price" to liberate the rest of the country from the North Koreans. "I feel my bones ache and blood curdle to think that numerous innocent compatriots have been murdered by North Korean troops," Rhee said.

American troops arrived in the outskirts of Seoul on the 16th, the day after their landing at Inchon. For the first time of the war, they greatly outnumbered the North Koreans as they launched their assault. The Communists, demoralized, fled as the Americans entered Seoul on the 25th. MacArthur now hopes to repeat his victory further south (→ 10/1).

Scientists use atom to make electricity

Sept 27. Chicago scientists have discovered the first practical method for converting atomic energy into electricity without the use of boilers or dynamos, the Atomic Energy Commission disclosed today.

The method is not practical for large-scale energy production but is being used in devices that monitor atomic reactions. The technique uses wires made of dissimilar metals. When the wires are bombarded by neutrons, energy in the form of heat is released at points where the different metals meet. Details of the method have been kept secret for security reasons until now.

Patents for use of the technique have been granted to a company headed by John L. Kurantz, who worked with another physicist, Robert J. Moon, to develop the method as part of the wartime atomic bomb program (→ 11/30).

Law passed against anti-American acts

Sept 23. Congress has voted to override President Truman's veto of an anti-Communist bill, thus making the Mundt Bill a law of the land. After 22 hours of debate, the Senate voted 57-10 to override; the House voted yesterday 286-48 to override. Each chamber easily cleared the two-thirds majority required to prevail over the presidential veto.

President Truman rejected the proposed statute because he feels certain aspects of it are unconstitutional and that it will actually advance communism in America, not hinder it.

The law is designed to root out Communists, in the interests of national security, by requiring Communist organizations to identify their officers and to prove how they spend funds. The president said this was like trying to get thieves to register with the sheriff (→ 30).

1950

OCTOBER

Su	Mo	Tu	We	Th	Fr	Sa
1	2	3	4	5	6	7
8	9	10	11	12	13	14
15	16	17	18	19	20	21
22	23	24	25	26	27	28
29	30	31				

1. South Korean troops cross 38th parallel on U.S. Eight Army's order (→ 3).

3. N.Y.: India protests U.N. troops' crossing of 38th parallel (→ 7).

3. U.S. establishes Petroleum Administration for Defense under Hugh Stewart (→ 12/16).

7. N.Y.: Yankees take Series in four straight over Phillies.

7. Korea: American ground forces cross 38th parallel for first time (→ 8).

8. U.S. Defense Dept. reports Korean casualties at 1,211 (→ 9).

8. Vietnam: Viet Minh wipe out French columns at Cao Bang and That Khe (→ 16).

9. MacArthur calls on North Koreans to yield (→ 11).

11. Red China condemns U.S. invasion of North Korea (→ 19).

11. Washington: FCC authorizes CBS to begin commercial color TV broacasts (→ 11/15).

16. Vietnam: French command abandons 250 miles of Chinese border to Viet Minh (→ 11/22).

19. Korea: U.N. troops smash into Pyongyang (→ 21).

21. Prague: Eight Soviet bloc nations call on West to join in four-point plan for German reunification (→ 1/8/51).

21. Communist Chinese troops invade Tibet (→ 11/2).

21. Seoul: Syngman Rhee announces plan to control all Korea without U.N. aid (→ 22).

22. Korea: U.N. troops racing unopposed to Manchurian border (→ 26).

29. Stockholm: King Gustav V dies at age 92; son Gustav VI assumes throne.

30. San Juan: Anti-U.S. nationalists start uprising, leaving 23 dead, 15 wounded (→ 11/1).

DEATHS

19. Edna St. Vincent Millay, American poet (*2/22/1892).

20. Henry L. Stimson, sec. of war under FDR (*9/21/1867).

23. Al Jolson, American singer-actor, "The Jazz Singer" (*5/28/1883).

Truman meets MacArthur on Wake

Oct 15. Two of America's strongest personalities, General Douglas MacArthur and President Harry Truman, met on Wake Island today to discuss the Korean War and the spread of communism in the East. The two men have butted heads before, most recently in August when the general made a statement about Formosa which the president felt differed with U.S. policy, but this time they seemed to agree.

Truman expressed confidence that "we can surmount" the dangers facing U.N. forces in Korea. He also praised MacArthur and his men for their loyalty and bravery. The general said the Chinese would not enter the conflict. Truman also awarded MacArthur an Oak Leaf to add to his Distinguished Service Medal, and MacArthur returned the gesture by praising Truman in front of the press.

With characteristic flair and confidence, MacArthur told newsmen to "come on up to Pyongyang (the North Korean capital); it won't be long now," implying an expeditious U.N. victory (→ 4/5/51).

Truman, MacArthur: Uneasy allies.

U.N. troops reach the Chinese border

An oil refinery in North Korea was turned into rubble by American B-29's.

Oct 27. If South Korean troops take one more step, they will be in China. The Sixth Division met almost no resistance as it thrust through the mountains of North Korea, reached the Manchurian border and sent patrols out along the Yalu River. There is no indication that any of the forces actually crossed the border, but the stage for a major confrontation has been set.

Mao Tse-tung has said repeatedly he will not sit by idly and watch North Korea be decimated. There are reports that he has already sent up to 30,000 troops into Korea to join the fighting.

MacArthur approved the invasion of North Korea at the beginning of the month after the Communists ignored his demand that they surrender. The general made it clear he expected all North Korean troops to lay down their arms, not just those south of the 38th parallel.

Today, for the first time, MacArthur's spokesman denied reports that a buffer zone would be established between United Nations forces and the Chinese border. In the United States, President Truman said it was his understanding that South Koreans, not Americans, would patrol the border.

The United States is clearly disgusted by the tactics of the North Korean army. The bodies of 68 Americans were discovered recently near a railway tunnel in Sunchon, North Korea. All were prisoners of war, machine-gunned to death on their way to supper (→ 11/6).

World's longest oil pipeline completed

Oct 6. The world's longest pipeline, running 1,066 miles from rich United States-owned oil fields on the Persian Gulf to the town of Sidon on the Mediterranean, has gone into service. The line, which cost $250 million and took 332,000 tons of steel, was built for the Arabian American Oil Co. (→ 12/2).

After 50 years Mack is out of baseball

Oct 18. Connie Mack, 87-year-old patriarch of major league baseball, has announced his retirement as Manager of the Philadelphia Athletics. After 67 years as player, club owner and manager, the longest career in the majors, Mack revealed that he had chosen Jimmie Dykes, his protege, to succeed him as Manager. Mack said: "I'm quitting because I think the people want me to."

Connie Mack, always the teacher.

1950

NOVEMBER

Su	Mo	Tu	We	Th	Fr	Sa
			1	2	3	4
5	6	7	8	9	10	11
12	13	14	15	16	17	18
19	20	21	22	23	24	25
26	27	28	29	30		

1. Washington: Two Puerto Rican nationalists attempt to assassinate Pres. Truman (→ 2).

1. N.Y.: Despite Soviet opposition, U.N. gives Trygve Lie another term as sec. gen. (→ 2/27/52).

2. San Juan: 400 jailed as nationalist rebels yield arms after attempt on Truman's life (→ 4/6/51).

2. India rebukes Mao for invasion of Tibet (→ 7).

4. N.Y.: U.N. revokes sanctions on Franco regime (→ 12/27).

6. MacArthur says Chinese have entered Korean War (→ 9).

7. Katmandu: King Tribhubana Bir Bikram of Nepal flees palace for refuge in Indian Embassy (→ 5/27/51).

15. Chicago: Court blocks CBS color TV broadcasts on complaint of RCA (→ 5/28/51).

16. Truman reassures U.S. will take every step to avoid incursion into China (→ 20).

16. New York: Jose Ferrer opens in "Cyrano de Bergerac."

17. N.Y.: U.N. agrees on independence for Libya (→ 12/24/51).

18. Louisiana: Bureau of Mines discloses first production of oil from coal in practical amounts.

18. Washington: Roman Catholic bishops protest sex education in public schools.

19. New York: John Wayne stars in opening of "Rio Grande."

20. Korea: U.S. troops push to Yalu River within five miles of Manchuria (→ 24).

22. Viet Minh leaders hold first parley with Laotian and Cambodian rebel chiefs (→ 12/17).

24. Korea: 100,000 U.N. troops start assault in west to end war by Christmas (→ 26).

26. North Koreans and Chinese halt U.N. offensive (→ 28).

26. U.S.: Blizzards kill 250 across country.

28. Korea: 200,000 Communist troops launch attack on U.N. forces (→ 12/3).

30. Washington: Truman declares U.S. would use A-bomb to get peace in Korea (→ 1/28/51).

Chinese Reds enter the Korean War

American parachutes dot the Korean sky near the border of Manchuria.

One of the first helicopters used in combat brings reinforcements to Korea.

The jet saw its first combat on the 7th when a U.S. F-86 downed a MIG-15.

Nov 9. There is no denying it any longer. China has entered the conflict in Korea, and the United States is on the verge of a full-fledged war with the Chinese Communists. A spokesman for the Eighth Army said two Chinese divisions have thrown themselves into the fighting in the northwestern part of the country. Another five divisions are massed in Manchuria, on the other side of the Yalu River. Up to 300,000 combat-proven Communist troops are ready to move.

Chinese troops crossed the Yalu near the Supung Dam and threatened to cut off a British brigade. Allied planes struck back against the Communists as an American unit was also threatened. The Chinese attacked ferociously along the Chongchon River, just 40 miles north of Pyongyang, the former North Korean capital. Military observers said the Chinese will not be content simply to protect their border or defend electric power stations along the Yalu. They seemed to be testing United Nations positions that stand in the way of an all-out assault on Pyongyang.

Without mentioning the Chinese by name, MacArthur criticized their involvement as "one of the most offensive acts of international lawlessness of historic record." The general charged that the Communists had reopened the wounds of a war that had almost been stitched closed. And he warned obliquely that his forces are ready for a showdown with the Chinese.

MacArthur's statement was the first high-level confirmation of China's entry into the war. Mao Tse-tung's forces helped the North Koreans spring a surprise counterattack last week, but American intelligence claimed the Chinese might be volunteers with Korean ancestry.

Significantly, MacArthur signed his statement personally as Commander-in-Chief of United Nations forces. But an American diplomat at the U.N. seemed to distance himself from MacArthur by stating that more information would be needed from the battlefield before a final complaint is made to the Peking government. President Truman, who has had his differences recently with MacArthur, refused to comment on his statement (→ 16).

G.B. Shaw, preachy playwright, is dead

Nov 2. One of the most cantankerous and quotable playwrights of this century, George Bernard Shaw, has died at his home at Ayot St. Lawrence, England. He was working on a new comedy called "Why She Would Not" up to a few weeks ago. Shaw was 94 years old.

"Silence is the most perfect expression of scorn," wrote Shaw. Assuming he was right, his lifelong barrage of plays and essays must be considered most solicitous. Never did he shut up for our benefit. He lectured on socialism, manners, vegetarianism, teetotaling, economics, politics and religion. Yet he managed to serve these sermons in an appetizing way. "My method," he wrote, "is to take the utmost trouble to find the right thing to say, and then say it with the utmost levity."

Shaw was born in Dublin July 26, 1856. Success came late; his first well-received play was "Mrs. Warren's Profession" (1893). Like many Shaw works, "Mrs. Warren," about a self-satisfied prostitute, outraged the critics but pleased audiences. Among other popular works were "Caesar and Cleopatra" (1899), "Man and Superman" (1904), "Heartbreak House" (1916) and "Saint Joan" (1923).

Socialist sage George Bernard Shaw.

In 1883, Shaw helped found the Fabian Society. Socialist leanings gave way to communist ones after World War I. Now and then, he also complimented Hitler and Mussolini. Shaw had an uncanny way of seeing every side of an issue —and fairly denouncing each.

Puerto Ricans try to kill the President

Nov 1. Awakened from an afternoon nap by commotion outside Blair House in Washington, President Truman went to the window. "Get back!" yelled a guard. Outside, two Puerto Rican nationalists had just tried to shoot their way into the house to kill him. After a short, fierce gun battle, guards subdued a wounded Puerto Rican man while another lay bleeding to death on the steps. One guard was killed and two were wounded in the assassination attempt.

Oscar Collazo, the surviving assailant, said he and Giselio Torresola hatched the plot in New York last week and came down to Washington two days ago to kill the president. Truman, who is staying at Blair House during repairs to the White House, was unharmed, and after sending a letter to Mrs. Leslie Coffelt, wife of the slain guard, he kept all his previously scheduled afternoon appointments. A grand jury has begun an investigation, but many authorities are puzzled by the attempt, as Truman has strongly supported the right of Puerto Rico to determine its own relationship to the United States (→ 2).

Will drive-ins drive out movie theaters?

Recently published statistics reveal that the United States has 2,200 drive-in theaters, doubling the number in existence last year. Consequently, several sit-in cinemas are failing. Why are drive-ins driving theaters owners to despair?

The American public finds outdoor film shows very convenient. One need never step outside the car. After admission is paid, each auto is given a small speaker which is removed when the film ends. In the winter, heaters are supplied.

If one has children, one need not worry about neighboring viewers excessively hushing their antics. One need only roll up the car windows. If one is a teenager on a date with another teenager, one need not worry about peers peering from the balcony. One need only hide by squooshing further down in the seat —the front seat, parents hope.

1950

DECEMBER

Su	Mo	Tu	We	Th	Fr	Sa
					1	2
3	4	5	6	7	8	9
10	11	12	13	14	15	16
17	18	19	20	21	22	23
24	25	26	27	28	29	30
31						

1. U.S.: Drive-in theaters now total 2,200, doubling in year.

2. Philadelphia: Navy defeats Army 12-2.

2. Arabian American Oil Co. opens 753-mile pipeline from Saudi Arabia to Sidon.

3. Cleveland: Charles Bailly reports discovery of heart-lung device to revive clinically dead.

3. Korea: Chinese close in on Pyongyang; U.N. forces withdraw southward (→ 9).

4. Memphis: Univ. of Tennessee defies court rulings, rejecting five Negroes (→ 1/8/52).

8. Truman threatens to beat up critic who criticized daughter Margaret's singing.

9. Truman bans U.S. exports to Communist China (→ 24).

9. Philadelphia: Harry Gold gets 30 years for A-bomb spying during WWII (→ 1/15/51).

10. First U.S. expedition to climb Mt. Everest reaches 18,000 feet (→ 6/2/53).

17. French name Marshal de Lattre de Tassigny to command troops in Vietnam (→ 1/18/51).

21. Morocco: Marrakesh Sultan El Glaoui breaks with Sultan Ben Youssef (→ 3/21/52).

24. Cleveland: Browns edge L.A. Rams 30-28 for pro football title.

27. U.S. and Spain resume relations (→ 7/20/51).

CUTURAL EVENTS, 1950

Literature: Ray Bradbury's "The Martian Chronicles"; Clifford Odets' "The Country Girl."

Academia, Religion: Margaret Mead's "Social Anthropology"; Arthur Koestler's "The God That Failed"; Pope Pius XII's encyclical "Humani Generis," condemning Existentialism; Natl. Council of the Churches of Christ formed in U.S. with 32 million members.

Music: Loesser and Burrows' "Guys and Dolls"; "Good Night Irene"; "Mona Lisa."

The Arts: Chagall's "King David"; U.N. Building, New York.

Film: Cocteau's "Orpheus"; Kurosawa's "Rashomon"; "All About Eve," Academy Award.

Eisenhower named NATO commander

Dec 19. President Harry Truman has placed General Dwight D. Eisenhower at the head of the North Atlantic Treaty Organization (NATO). The British would have preferred to keep Northern and Mediterranean sectors autonomous —that is, under their direction— and so are not altogether pleased with Eisenhower. However, the French are glad to see a commander have control of the entire area.

Eisenhower, 60, has been President of Columbia University. During the war he was Allied commander in Europe (→ 1/7/51).

Beckmann, exiled Expressionist, dies

Dec 27. Painter Max Beckmann has died in New York. He was 66. Raised in Germany, Beckmann fled in 1937 when Nazi ethics clashed with his own.

World War I indelibly etched itself on Beckmann. He briefly served in the medical corps, only to be discharged with a nervous breakdown. Beckmann had been a structured Impressionist; war images veered him toward Expressionism. In the 1920's, he painted ghoulish scenes of torture, and the rise of fascism intensified the memories. His triptych "The Departure" (1933) was an anguished cry for release.

"The Fall" by Max Beckmann.

Emergency in America

Superfortresses rain bombs on a chemical plant in Konan, North Korea.

Dec 16. Bruised by stunning setbacks in Korea, President Truman has declared a state of emergency in the United States and urged all Americans to join the battle against "Communist imperialism." Truman warned that the "full and rich life" guaranteed by the Bill of Rights had been put in jeopardy by the Communist menace. The president called for "a mighty production effort" for defense, and he promised to defend Europe with "an arsenal of freedom."

Truman delegated many of his war powers to the new Mobilization Director, Charles Wilson. His Economic Stabilization Agency moved dramatically to impose new wage and price controls. The agency canceled recent price increases by Chrysler, Ford and General Motors. The auto industry, which had been resisting the rollbacks, promised to support the administration. Organized labor also closed ranks behind Truman, as striking railway employees went back to work.

Truman's decisive actions follow the collapse of General MacArthur's troops in North Korea. Six weeks ago, complete victory was at hand, and United Nations forces were in control of nearly all of Korea. They have since lost Pyongyang, and Chinese forces have pushed them all the way back to the 38th parallel (→ 3/31/51).

Sugar Ray ends his tour in triumph

Dec 25. With a Christmas Day knockout of Hans Stretz of Frankfurt, Sugar Ray Robinson put the tinsel on a winning European tour and set the stage for his world middleweight championship fight in February against Jake LaMotta.

Robinson put away Stretz in the fifth round only three days after he knocked out Robert Villemain of Paris in the ninth. Stretz was Robinson's fifth victim in a month; four of his wins were by knockouts. Sugar Ray opened the tour with a second-round knockout of Jean Stock in Paris and followed that with a victory over Luc Van Dam. His only decision was against Jean Walzack in Geneva (→ 2/14/51).

Sugar Ray, unbeatable in Europe.

Silent, unholy night for a Korean child

Dec 24. No Korean children, Northern or Southern, sleep calmly tonight. It is not anticipation of Christmas Day keeping them so fretfully awake, nor pleasures of any Buddhist holiday. Their bedmate, war, pries their eyes wide open.

General Douglas MacArthur had promised to "be home by Christmas." For a while it seemed possible. Northern forces, which first attacked the South June 25, were heading for retreat. But in November, Chinese Communists flooded the Korean countryside, hoisting the Northern banner. The war is now bloodier than ever. The hungriest, coldest and most innocent are the children (→ 1/1/51).

Seeking shelter from cold and war.

Bunche and Faulkner win Nobel Prizes

Dec 10. Two Americans, Ralph Bunche and William Faulkner, were among those accepting Nobel awards tonight in Oslo. Bunche, the Peace Prize recipient, is the first Negro to win a Nobel Prize. He is the U.N. mediator in Palestine; the 46-year-old can take most of the credit for peace in that region. Bunche had made his way through the University of California and Harvard by working as a janitor and doing errands for a shipping line.

Faulkner is the Mississippi-born author of "The Sound and the Fury" (1929) and "Absalom, Absalom!" (1936). His latest work is "Go Down, Moses" (1942).

Faulker (left) at the Nobel festival.

Radio stars are flocking to TV. Steve Allen, Burns and Allen (8pm Thurs.), Frank Sinatra (9pm Sat.) and Eddie Cantor can all be seen on the tube.

1951

JANUARY

Su	Mo	Tu	We	Th	Fr	Sa
	1	2	3	4	5	6
7	8	9	10	11	12	13
14	15	16	17	18	19	20
21	22	23	24	25	26	27
28	29	30	31			

1. Pasadena: Michigan blanks California 14-0 in Rose Bowl.

1. Korea: Chinese open heavy attack above Seoul, breaking 38th parallel (→ 4).

1. Jerusalem: Israel upholds censorship board in banning German language (→ 2/14).

2. Welterweight champ Sugar Ray Robinson returns to U.S. after triumphal European tour.

2. Arabian American Oil Co. agrees to share profits with Saudi Arabian government.

4. Korea: U.N. forces abandon Seoul to Communists (→ 15).

7. Paris: Hostile demonstrations welcome Ike to talks on European defense strategy (→ 2/1).

8. Bonn: Chancellor Adenauer accepts E. German proposal for talks on reunification (→ 4/2).

10. U.S.: Avro jetliner flies from Chicago to New York in one hour, 42 minutes.

15. U.S. Supreme Court curbs freedom of speech, ruling "clear and present danger" of incitement to riot is cause for arrest (→ 23).

17. MGM signs Danny Kaye for "Huckleberry Finn."

18. Brazil: Getulio Vargas again elected president as General Dutra's term ends.

21. Switzerland, Italy, Austria struck by avalanches in Alps; 217 left dead.

21. Korea: Communist troops, in 12-hour attack, force U.N. army out of Inchon (→ 24).

23. Truman creates Commission on Internal Security and Individual Rights to monitor anti-Communist campaign (→ 3/12).

24. New Delhi: Nehru assails U.S. demand for U.N. to name Peking as aggressor in Korea (→ 2/1).

26. Washington freezes prices and wages to curb inflation.

27. U.S. demands U.S.S.R. return 670 ships given to them under lend-lease.

DEATH

15. Maxence Van der Meersch, French writer, 1936 Nobel Prize (*5/4/1907).

U.N. forces halt Red drive in Korea

Jan 15. United Nations forces counterattacked in the western sector, slowing down a two-week-old major offensive by Chinese and North Korean Communist invaders. Supported by heavy air strikes and artillery fire, U.N. forces recaptured Osan and Kumyangjang, and Communist troops were reported withdrawing from the ancient walled city of Suwon, only 15 miles south of Seoul. It appeared, however, that the counterattack did not signal a general offensive against the numerically superior Communist forces but rather was a "reconnaissance in force" designed to maintain contact with enemy forces and slow down the Communist advance.

In central Korea, where there has been heavy, hand-to-hand fighting, U.N. forces withdrew from the city of Wonju, which they had attempted to hold against an encircling Communist attack.

The Communist armies launched their offensive across a broad front near the 38th parallel on January 1, quickly breaking through the U.N. defense line at several points north and northeast of Seoul. Despite constant harassment by U.S. Air Force bombers, the Communist divisions surged southward in the western and central sectors of South Korea, as the U.N. forces were forced to retreat southward in an attempt to set up a new defensive line. Four days after the offensive began, Seoul, capital of the South Korean republic, fell for the second time to Communist invaders (→ 21).

Displaced by war, refugees trek south on back roads to avoid military traffic.

B-29 bombings are beginning to take their toll on North Korean industry.

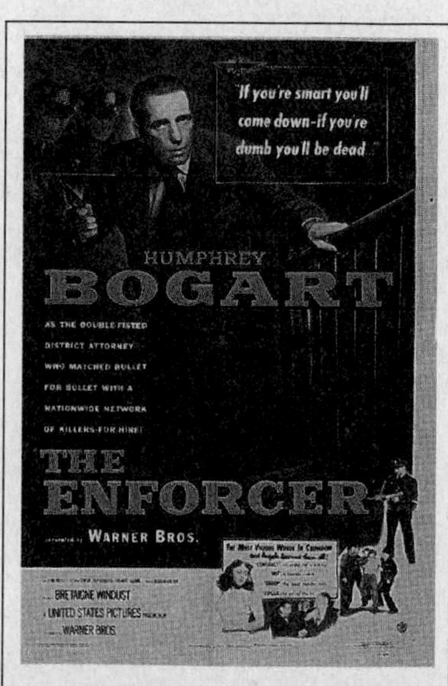

Sinclair Lewis, Babbitt's creator, deceased

Jan 10. Pulitzer and Nobel Prize winner Sinclair Lewis has died in Rome. He was 65. Lewis chronicled the 1920's, a market not quite cornered by F. Scott Fitzgerald. While Fitzgerald wrote of carefree singles and couples not too firmly tied down, Lewis described an older middle class heavily anchored by materialism and false values.

Lewis was born February 7, 1885, in Sauk Centre, Minnesota. He would immortalize the town (and irritate it) with his novel "Main Street" (1920). The book mocked and pitied small-town values.

In 1922, Lewis introduced a word to the English language. "Babbittry," from "Babbitt" (1922), means mindless conformity to bourgeois values. Character George Babbitt is a small-town real estate broker. Babbitt feels an odd void in his life; odd, for he faithfully and unthinkingly adheres to the rules of "good fellowship . . . and good business."

"Arrowsmith" (1925), about a scientist searching for a cure for commercialism, won the Pulitzer Prize. (Lewis declined to accept it). "Elmer Gantry" (1927) bitingly exposed religious revivalism. The Nobel Prize for literature in 1930 capped a decade of brilliant work.

"It Can't Happen Here" (1935), an attack on fascism, was perhaps the sole success of ten more novels. What Lewis satirized best, Small Town, U.S.A., started disappearing. Lewis' work faded with it.

Atomic tests in Nevada rattle Southwest

Jan 28. The second atomic explosion in two days at the Atomic Energy Commission's test grounds in the Nevada desert lighted up the sky across a large part of the Southwest today. In Las Vegas, 45 miles from the boundary of the test grounds, observers saw a five-second flash and felt a wind blowing through the streets of the city. In Boulder City, more than 100 miles from the explosion site, residents said the flash lit up whole rooms. Reports of seeing the explosion have come from as far away as Utah and California.

The Atomic Energy Commission issued a brief statement saying that patrols have found "no indication of any radiological hazards" from the explosion, but it has asked the Civil Aeronautics Administration to ground all local airplane flights within a 150-mile radius of the test site to allow any radioactivity in the air to dissipate. Today's explosion, visibly larger than yesterday's, is the tenth in a series of atomic tests conducted by the United States since 1945 (→ 2/1).

Ominous scene in the Nevada desert.

Mustang sets New York-London record

Jan 31. A new record of seven hours, 48 minutes for a New York-to-London flight has been set by Charles Blair Jr., an airline pilot from New York. Flying his own converted Mustang fighter plane, Blair flew across the Atlantic at an average speed of 450 mph, breaking the record established last November by an airliner of Pan American Airways, for whom he works.

Blair took off at 4:50 a.m. from Idlewild Airport in New York and arrived over London at 5:38 p.m. Greenwich mean time. He had hoped to make the trip in seven hours but ran into headwinds and icing weather that slowed his flight.

Blair said the flight was not a stunt. He flew at 37,000 feet, with the purpose of learning about the "jet stream," a high-speed wind found more than 30,000 feet above the earth. Airlines have long speculated that they could make quicker flights to Europe by taking advantage of the jet stream, but as yet they know little about it. Pan American says it will study the details of Blair's flight with great interest.

Captain Charles Blair.

French break Viet Minh attack on Hanoi

Jan 18. French troops, their low morale inflated by the daring panache of their new commander, swung to the offensive and defeated the Viet Minh guerrillas who were threatening to overrun Hanoi. General Giap was forced to retreat, leaving 6,000 Communist soldiers dead on the battlefield. Five hundred Viet Minh were taken prisoner. It was the first significant victory for the French after a string of defeats in Tonkin, and much of the credit was given to the new French High Commissioner for Indochina, General Jean de Lattre de Tassigny.

De Lattre, nicknamed "King Jean" because of his personal elegance and attachment to ceremony, flew a small plane into the besieged French outpost at Vinh-Yen. Advised that his life was in danger, the general cabled back to his staff, "Come on. Break through and get me out of here." His bravery and his nonchalance seemed to galvanize his soldiers as they charged and defeated Giap's guerrillas (→ 3/15).

De Lattre (second from rt.) attempts to locate Viet Minh positions near Hanoi.

Nessler dies; promised curls to every girl

Jan 22. The inventor of the permanent wave is dead. New Jersey resident Charles Nessler, author of the book "The Story of Hair," succumbed to a heart attack today. He was 78 years old.

The American Women's Voluntary Services organization paid tribute to Nessler two years ago for creating jobs in the beauty industry and improving women's looks. His business name, Nestle, is part of the Nestle-Le Mur Corporation. Nessler sold his firm to the Cleveland-based Le Mur Company in 1928.

Nessler started as a barber cum surgeon in Switzerland. He went to London in 1905 and nine years later used a machine for heating and waving hair. Once hair was porous enough to hold moisture, he applied hot alkali, maintaining the curl.

Soon after World War I began, Nessler opened a shop in New York. Patrons, among them President Wilson's wife, would pay up to $120 for a wave. False eyelashes, another Nessler invention, cost extra.

Porsche, designer of rear-engine auto, dies

Jan 18. Ferdinand Porsche, the German engineer who designed the Volkswagen beetle, one of the world's most successful cars, died today in Stuttgart at the age of 75.

Porsche was one of the pioneers of the automobile industry in Europe. He began his career as a construction worker in Vienna at the age of 22. Three years later, his first automobile, powered by electricity, was a feature of the 1900 Paris World Exhibition. Porsche worked for Daimler Benz from 1923 to 1929. He made his first sketch of a small, rear-engine automobile and produced a prototype in 1933. He emphasized simplicity of maintenance and operation so the car could be a "Volkauto," a people's car. The first model caught the eye of Adolf Hitler in 1935. Hitler made plans for mass production of the auto for German workers, but the car went into military service when war broke out, serving as the Wehrmacht's equivalent of the Jeep.

After the war, a modified version of Porsche's original design gained international popularity. At the present rate of world production, the Volkswagen is expected to surpass the Ford Model T as the most popular automobile ever built.

1951

FEBRUARY

Su	Mo	Tu	We	Th	Fr	Sa
				1	2	3
4	5	6	7	8	9	10
11	12	13	14	15	16	17
18	19	20	21	22	23	24
25	26	27	28			

1. Nevada: Third A-bomb tests completed in desert (→ 2).

1. N.Y.: U.N. adopts U.S. resolution to condemn China for agression in Korea (→ 11).

3. Czechs arrest Foreign Minister Vladimir Clementis (→ 25).

3. Philadelphia: Truman unveils mural dedicated to four WWII chaplains who died in war.

6. N.J.: 84 killed, 330 hurt as commuter train plunges off rails.

7. N.Y.: "Yankee Clipper" Joe DiMaggio signs $100,000 contract for third year in row.

8. Rail strikers return to work on order from U.S. Army (→ 4/8/52).

9. Actress Greta Garbo gets U.S. citizenship.

11. Korea: U.N. forces push north across 38th parallel again (→ 17).

12. Iran: Shah Mohammed Reza Pahlevi marries 19-year-old Soraya Esfandiari.

12. Washington: OPS removes price ceilings on sugar and all unprocessed farm products.

15. U.S. to send four divisions to aid in Europe defense (→ 7/23).

16. Moscow: Stalin says U.N. is becoming weapon of aggressive war.

17. Belgrade: Tito vows to resist any aggression in Europe that imperils Yugoslavia (→ 4/16/51).

17. U.S.: 1951 Packard convertible makes debut.

19. Pennsylvania Railroad indicted for manslaughter in wreck two weeks ago.

22. Washington: AEC discloses information on first atom-powered airplane.

24. Korea: Maj. Gen. Bryant E. Moore dies of hear attack after helicopter crash (→ 3/14).

26. XXII Amendment added to U.S. Constitution, limiting presidents to two terms.

DEATHS

4. Alfred A. Cohn, wrote "The Jazz Singer" (*1879).

8. Fritz Thyssen, German business tycoon (*11/9/1873).

Reds and U.N. fight over 38th parallel

Two Chinese Communists give in to the men of the First Marine Division.

Feb 17. South Korean forces on the east coast pushed north of the 38th parallel for the first time since the United Nations withdrawal from North Korea last year following the Chinese intervention in the war.

The South Korean division met little resistance as it moved up a coastal highway to Yangyang, about five miles north of the parallel, under the cover of heavy naval bombardment.

On the western front, counterattacking U.N. forces pushed north to the outskirts of Seoul and bypassed the South Korean capital to capture the port city of Inchon again. The Communist divisions, which suffered heavy casualties during the U.N. counterattack, were believed withdrawing to mountainous positions in central Korea.

In the midst of a blizzard, Communist troops marched on Chechon in central Korea, the gateway to Southern Korea. U.N. commanders believed the Communist objective was to drive down the center of South Korea, cutting off U.N. forces along the Yellow Sea (→ 24).

Feb 12. Reza Pahlevi, Shah of Iran, and his bride Soraya Esfandiari have Europe's society circles buzzing. They were wed in a Moslem ceremony, after which 2,000 guests were feted at the Gulistan Palace in Tehran. Reza Pahlevi, 31, has led Iran since Allied troops ousted his father, a German ally, in 1941. The Princess, 19, is the daughter of a rebel chieftain.

British King gets his first pay raise

Feb 8. For the first time in his 14-year reign King George VI received a pay raise today, amounting to about ten percent. The king won't get any more cash, but government departments will pay some of the royal household's bills.

The increase, announced in the House of Commons, was an official admission that living costs have gone up a tiny bit lately. Even so, the king's raise won't match the national average; the ordinary chap's wages have more than doubled since the war. There was loud laughter in the House today when Emrys Hughes, a Laborite, asked, "Is not this a case for the Minister of National Assistance?"

His Majesty King George VI.

Death takes author of Sweet Adeline

Feb 28. The man who gave the world's barbershop quartets "Sweet Adeline" is gone. Musician Henry W. Armstrong has died in the Bronx. He was 71 years old.

In 1899, Armstrong composed a song called "You're the Flower of My Heart, Sweet Rosalie." No publisher would touch it. A lyricist named Richard Husch saw an ad for opera singer Adelina Patti one day and suggested Armstrong change the name to Adelina. To cement the idea, Husch added the line, "For you I pine/Sweet Adeline." Armstrong took the song to another publisher, who argued the name Adeline did not exist. At the time he was right. There are generations of Adelines now.

Religious bloc puts Ben Gurion out

Feb 14. Israel's Socialist Prime Minister David Ben Gurion resigned tonight after his defeat in the Knesset over an ongoing conflict involving the religious education of immigrant children. Central to his fall was the inability of his unwieldy coalition Cabinet, a marriage of convenience between his own Mapai Party and the Orthodox bloc, to hammer out a compromise which would also please the opposition—the General Zionists, the pro-Soviet Mapam, the Communists, the right-wing Herut and the one-man Freedom Party of Nathan Friedman Yellin, leader of the former Stern gang (→ 11/19).

U.S. presidency is limited to two terms

Feb 26. President Franklin Roosevelt was the first and the last: the first president to serve more than two terms and, with the passage of the 22nd Amendment, he is the last.

After the state of Nevada voted for ratification, fulfilling the required three-quarters or 36 states' approval for passage, no president will be allowed to be elected for more than two terms or more than once if he has served more than two years of his predecessor's term.

Debate surrounded the proposed change. Its opponents feel the legislation would reduce a president to lame-duck status and remove accountability if he were prohibited from running for a third term. Most, however, insist it appropriately curbs presidential power.

Feb 14. Hard-hitting Sugar Ray Robinson, welterweight king for 5 years, KOs Jake LaMotta for middleweight crown (→ 7/10).

Gide the outrageous leaves exotic legacy

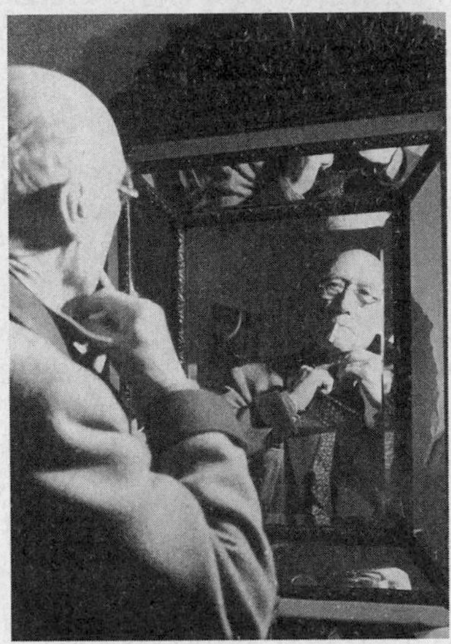

Controversial Andre Gide.

Feb 19. French novelist Andre Gide has succumbed to pneumonia at the age of 81. The French consider Gide the greatest writer of the century; Americans might credit him as the most controversial. He both defended and attacked homosexuality, capitalism, socialism and the Catholic Church.

Gide was raised by a strict Protestant family. In 1893, he spent time in a North African village, an experience instigating him against civilization's confines. His book "The Immoralist" (1902) reflected his search for ethics. In 1909, he started "The New French Revue," a paper featuring Jean Cocteau and Jean Giraudoux. His novel "The Counterfeiters" (1925) is a structural and symbolic masterpiece.

Ike opposes limiting of troops in Europe

Feb 1. If you want to keep the Cold War from turning hot, General Eisenhower told a joint session of Congress today, don't limit the number of American troops or military supplies you send to Europe.

Speaking as Supreme Commander of NATO forces, Eisenhower said that to put a cap on either would compromise the security of Western Europe against the Russians and "gravely imperil" the United States. Eisenhower also spoke to the Foreign Relations and Armed Services Committees, and Senator Wherry, who has sponsored legislation to cap the number of American troops in Europe, emerged livid from the session, exclaiming, "I don't want to say a word!" (→ 15).

Ike, advocating full commitment.

Radiation rising in East from atom tests

Feb 2. Radiation detectors in the Eastern United States have measured an increase in atmospheric radiation resulting from the atomic tests in Nevada, 2,300 miles away. But scientists making the measurements say the levels they are recording are far too low to threaten life.

Four atomic tests have occurred in the past week. Physicists say that tiny radioactive particles from the nuclear blasts apparently have been carried east by the prevailing winds to cause the increase in radiation.

The latest blast, set off at 5:45 a.m. Pacific time yesterday, rattled doors and windows in Las Vegas, 45 miles away, and was seen in Los Angeles, 250 miles distant. As always, the blast was set off without advance notice by the Atomic Energy Commission; its policy of secrecy is aimed at giving as little assistance as possible to foreign agents.

Radioactive snow has been falling all week in Rochester, N.Y., physicists there report. Radioactivity has also been measured in snow falling on Cincinnati, and traces have been found by scientists using sensitive instruments in Quebec, Brookhaven, N.Y., and Chicago.

In response to queries about the reports, the AEC has issued a statement saying that there is no evidence that the increased levels of radiation resulting from the atomic tests "could conceivably produce any damage to humans, to animals, or to water supply" (→ 3/24).

Czech ex-Foreign Minister accused of plot

Feb 25. President of Czechoslovakia Klement Gottwald has revealed a five-year-old plot designed to align his nation with the West. The plan was spearheaded by former Foreign Minister Vladimir Clementis, who has been missing since late January; some speculate he fled to Yugoslavia.

In a speech to the Communist Central Committee, Gottwald assailed his former colleague and others implicated in the plot as "traitors and conspirators." He described the conspiracy as one aimed at rupturing the infrastructure of the Czech Communist Party, changing its policies and "taking the road back toward capitalism and cooperation with the camp of imperialism." Gottwald added that the plot had been defused, and while Clementis' whereabouts are still unknown, his house, where his wife remains, is under constant surveillance.

In his address, the president assured party members that "Czechoslovakia will not be a second Yugoslavia." He was referring to the recent defection of Premier Tito's Yugoslavia from the Eastern bloc led by the Soviets (→ 3/2).

1951

MARCH

Su	Mo	Tu	We	Th	Fr	Sa
				1	2	3
4	5	6	7	8	9	10
11	12	13	14	15	16	17
18	19	20	21	22	23	24
25	26	27	28	29	30	31

2. Czechs reported purging Communist Party of Tito supporters (→ 10).

2. Groton, Conn.: U.S. Navy launches K-1, first modern sub designed to hunt enemy subs.

5. U.S.: G.M. reports record $834 million profit for 1950.

8. New York: Fred Astaire and Jane Powell appear in "Royal Wedding."

10. Prague: Archbishop Josef Beran, primate of Czechoslovakia, arrested (→ 17).

11. New York: Olivia de Haviland and Douglas Watson open in "Romeo and Juliet."

12. U.S. Supreme Court upholds perjury conviction of Alger Hiss; jail term starts in 10 days (→ 30).

12. Spain: 300,000 on strike in Barcelona to protest high cost of living.

13. Israel demands $1.5 bil. in German reparations for cost of caring for war refugees (→ 9/27).

14. Korea: U.N. troops retake Seoul without battle (→ 23).

15. Paris: Gen. de Lattre demands more troops for fight in Vietnam (→ 4/7).

17. Underground Ukranian Insurgent Army appeals to U.S. for aid in fight against Soviet govt.

17. Vatican: Pope excommunicates all involved in banishment of Prague archbishop (→ 9/8).

19. Paris: European Coal and Steel Community founded as six nations sign Schuman Plan (→ 9/10/52).

21. Marshall reports U.S. military has doubled to 2.9 mil. since start of Korean War (→ 31).

22. U.S.: "The Caine Mutiny," by Herman Wouk, is published.

23. Korea: U.S. paratroopers descend from flying boxcars in surprise attack on Reds (→ 24).

24. Buenos Aires: Peron announces Argentina has found cheap way to produce atomic energy (→ 5/12).

24. MacArthur threatens Chinese with extension of Korean War if truce not accepted (→ 29).

29. Chinese reject MacArthur's offer for truce in Korea (→ 30).

Rosenbergs found guilty

Ethel and Julius Rosenberg, escorted back to jail after their conviction.

March 30. The husband and wife team of Julius and Ethel Rosenberg have been found guilty of wartime espionage in the nation's first atomic bomb spy trial. It is likely that Judge Irving R. Kaufman, who presided over the trial in Federal Court in New York City, will impose the death penalty on the pair.

The two New Yorkers, insisting they are innocent, were charged with stealing U.S. atomic bomb secrets and giving them to the Soviet Union. Rosenberg, 32, an electrical engineer who worked for the Army-Signal Corps, and his 35-year-old wife live in Knickerbocker Village and are the parents of two young sons, Michael and Robert.

The key government witness in the trial, which began March 6, was David Greenglass, the 29-year-old brother of Mrs. Rosenberg. He has confessed his role in the spy plot and will be sentenced later. A fourth defendant, Martin Sobell, also faces sentencing. Another government witness, Harry Gold, confessed taking part in the plot and was sentenced earlier in Philadelphia to 30 years in prison.

After the verdict was handed down by a jury of 11 men and one woman, Judge Kaufman said he felt that the finding was correct. "I must say," he added, "that as an individual, I cannot be happy because it is a sad day for America." That Americans citizens would lend themselves to such a plot, he said, was shocking and loathsome (→ 4/5).

Religious fanatic kills Iran Premier

March 7. Today in Iran, a fervent nationalist who disagreed with the country's pro-Western trade policies stepped out of a crowd and put a bullet through Premier Razmara's head. The assasin, a 26-year-old carpenter, is a member of the fanatical Crusaders of Islam. Razmara was killed instantly. When asked why he fired the shot, the assassin replied, "Why do you give the country to foreigners so that I must do this deed?"

Premier Razmara was a strong administrator who expelled Russian agents from the northern territories and had begun an ambitious program to rid the government of graft. Razmara had also hoped to bolster the struggling economy by developing oil resources. He received an overwhelming vote of approval when he recenlty renewed Anglo-Iran Oil Company contracts (→ 4/27).

Gen. Ali Razmara, Iranian Premier.

Truman defers draft for better students

March 31. College students of superior scholastic standing will be subject to draft deferment under a new executive order signed by President Truman. Such action, he said, is necessary to the maintenance of the nation's health and safety.

Major General Lewis B. Hershey, director of Selective Service, will prescribe the levels of college grades or scores on an aptitude test that will permit deferment. The test will be administered by the Educational Testing Service of Princeton, N.J., in May and June. High school seniors about to enter college will not be eligible, nor will those men 26 years of age or older. It is uncertain how many of the million or so students whose grades or test scores will be examined are to be deferred. There will be no second chance for those who fail the test.

According to Hershey, Congress has been told by military leaders that "since we cannot hope to match the Iron Curtain countries in manpower, our advantage lies in our superiority in scientific and technical know-how." Therefore, he said, the immediate need is for more scientists and technicians (→ 4/5).

Iran nationalizes oil, which British exploit

March 15. Mohammed Mossadegh, the wily Premier of Iran, has sparked an international crisis and threatened a key European lifeline by nationalizing his oil fields. Britain immediately protested the move, which could lead to a complete breakdown in diplomatic relations. Under a hotly disputed and recently revised concession, the Anglo-Iranian Oil Company had exclusive rights to pump and sell Iranian oil. The action by Mossadegh, who has been riding high on a wave of fervent nationalistic sentiment, was cheered by many Iranians, including oil field workers. They left their posts in Khuzistan and went on strike to proclaim their support for the government takeover.

The output of the oil fields is likely to suffer as this latest battle between Iran and Britain is played out. That could have serious consequences for Europe. It was already importing 70 percent of its oil from the Middle East, and British oil requirements have increased sharply because of the war in Korea.

The British concession to exploit Iranian oil dates back to 1909, when the Anglo-Persian Oil Company was formed. Many Iranians grew disenchanted with the arrangement and objected to the small return they were receiving from the British. By 1933, tensions were so inflamed that the concession agreement was submitted to the League of Nations for negotiation. Five years ago, the deal was renegotiated. Under the new terms, Iran received 30 percent of the income from the oil fields (→ 4/15).

Oil workers demonstrate for nationalization. Though Iran has been formally independent, British oil companies have symbolized dependence since 1909.

Some happy Asian news: The King and I

March 29. At a point during "The King and I," the Rodgers and Hammerstein musical that opened tonight, every audience member wore a hoop skirt. Or so it seemed; Gertrude Lawrence, portraying teacher Anna Leonowens, was singing a cheerfully infectious song called "Getting to Know You" to some children. She, in 19th-century attire, billowed and swayed; the children billowed and swayed; how could the audience not be swayed?

"The King and I" is based on the true story of a British teacher who taught the 67 children of the King of Siam at the time of the U.S. Civil War. Yul Brynner, who easily assumes any ethnicity, plays the monarch. King and commoner spar over women's rights, geography, peasant's rights and the gender of elephants. Differences are tossed out the window when they waltz madly to a song called "Shall We Dance?" Other numbers include "Hello, Young Lovers," and "I Whistle a Happy Tune."

MacArthur says war may reach China

MacArthur (rt.), with aides and advisers, visits the front lines above Suwon.

March 30. United States tanks rumbled back across the 38th parallel today as the seesaw battle for control of Korea took another turn. General MacArthur, who seems increasingly isolated from the Allies and even his own President, threatens to carry the war all the way to China. Political support, however, has dwindled for MacArthur's drive back into North Korea, even though the United Nations has declared the Communists the aggressors in the war. President Truman has mixed feelings about the new offensive, and the British have told the White House that United Nations forces should not cross the 38th parallel unless attacked.

The American crossing of the frontier, just north of Seoul, came a week after the South Koreans crossed on the east coast and encountered stiff resistance from fresh Communist troops. Intelligence reports indicate the Chinese have massed 200,000 soldiers north of the border. Facing them are 160,000 United Nations troops, the great majority of them American.

The morale of the Western troops was buoyed by the recapture of Seoul for the second time on the 14th. The Eighth American Army, commanded by Lt. General Matthew Ridgway, has solidified its positions along the 38th parallel while B-29's from Okinawa bombarded Chinese supply routes across the Yalu River (→ 4/1).

G.I.'s use a quiet moment to take a few photographs for future grandchildren.

1951

APRIL

Su	Mo	Tu	We	Th	Fr	Sa
1	2	3	4	5	6	7
8	9	10	11	12	13	14
15	16	17	18	19	20	21
22	23	24	25	26	27	28
29	30					

1. Korea: U.S. forces again cross 38th parallel (→ 12).

2. Bonn: Military curbs lifted for West Germany (→ 8/12).

5. MacArthur, in letter to Congressman Joseph Martin, says "there is no substitute for victory in Korea" (→ 11).

5. Israel bombs Syria in retaliation for attacks on Israeli police (→ 5/2).

6. Washington: Puerto Rican Oscar Collazo sentenced to die for attempt on Truman's life (→ 7/25/52).

7. Hanoi: Ho drops frontal war against French (→ 9/13).

11. N.Y.: Modigliani show opens at Museum of Modern Art.

11. London: Scottish nationalists give back 336-lb. Stone of Scone (coronation stone) after stealing it four months ago.

12. Korea: U.S. Sabres destroy eight Soviet MIG's in biggest jet air battle yet (→ 5/11).

15. Abadan: Strikes and riots force closing of Anglo-Iranian Co. refinery (→ 5/22).

16. Truman authorizes $29 mil. in raw materials for Yugoslavia (→ 11/14).

17. San Francisco: MacArthur gets hero's welcome (→ 20).

21. Hungary releases Robert Vogeler, convicted of spying for U.S. (→ 6/28).

21. Manila: Five U.S. soldiers killed in ambush by Communist Huk guerrillas (→ 8/31).

25. Florida: Cuban airliner and U.S. Navy plane crash; 43 dead.

27. Tehran: In surprise move, Premier Hussein Ala resigns to Shah (→ 28).

28. Iran: Mohammed Mossadegh elected president (→ 2/15/52).

29. Chinese Premier Chou En-lai seizes assets of British Asiatic Petroleum Co. (→ 11/13).

DEATHS

14. Ernest Bevin, British ex-foreign secretary (*3/9/1881).

29. Ludwig Wittgenstein, Austrian Existentialist philosopher (*4/26/1889).

Truman fires MacArthur in Korea

April 11. President Truman has stripped General Douglas MacArthur of all his commands in the Far East, saying that he was acting with "deep regret" but had finally concluded that the general "is unable to give his wholehearted support" to the policies of the U.S. government and the United Nations.

The president immediately named Lt. General Matthew B. Ridgway to head the Far East commands, effective immediately. General Ridgway has been commander of the Eighth Army in Korea and will be replaced in that post by Lt. General James Van Fleet.

The dramatic military reshuffling, while a surprise, had been building up to a climax for some time. Just last Thursday, the House minority leader, Joseph W. Martin Jr., made public a message in which General MacArthur publicly challenged the president's foreign policy. The general urged that the United States concentrate on Asia instead of Europe and use Generalissimo Chiang Kai-shek's Formosa-based troops to open a second front on the mainland of China.

General MacArthur has been a man of many titles during the war in Korea. With his recall, he loses them all: Supreme Commander, U.N. Forces in Korea; Supreme Commander for Allied Powers, Japan; Commander-in-Chief, Far East; and Commanding General, U.S. Army, Far East.

In relieving the general of his commands, the president said that full and vigorous debate on national policies is "a vital element" in any free government. But he added: "It is fundamental, however, that military commanders must be governed by policies and directives issued to them in the manner provided by our laws" (→ 17).

MacArthur (rt.) faces his successor, Lieutenant General Matthew Ridgway.

A surprised General Eisenhower gets the news of MacArthur's dismissal.

MacArthur receives triumphal welcome

April 20. Recalling the words of an old military ballad—"old soldiers never die, they just fade away"—a tearful General Douglas MacArthur told visibly moved members of Congress yesterday: "And like the old soldier of the ballad, I now close my military career and just fade away, an old soldier who tried to do his duty as God gave him the light to see that duty. Goodbye."

Scorned by President Truman, who had stripped him of his Far East commands, but wildly applauded at the day's emotionally charged joint meeting of Congress, the general had perhaps his finest hour as he stood, ramrod straight and proud, and delivered one of the most memorable orations ever heard in the nation's capital.

Today, riding in a motorcade, he was greeted in New York City by cheering throngs and tons of ticker tape, streamers and confetti, as well as floating signs: "Welcome Home" and "Well Done."

President Truman, on April 11, removed General MacArthur from his Far East commands for publicly challenging the administration's foreign policies (→ 5/23).

MacArthur returns a hero.

Bipartisan foreign policy leader dies

April 18. U.S. Senator Arthur H. Vandenberg of Michigan, who was the chief framer of Republican foreign policy in Congress, died in his sleep tonight at his home in Grand Rapids. He was 67 years old and had been in ill health.

An isolationist before World War II, Senator Vandenberg later became chief architect of American foreign policy and was a key player in Senate ratification of the United Nations. When first elected to the Senate in 1929, he was Editor of the Grand Rapids Herald. Before the Democrats regained control of the Senate in 1948, he was chairman of the Foreign Affairs Committee and President pro tem of the Senate.

He had suffered from a heart ailment for a quarter of a century and in recent years had undergone a series of operations on his lungs and spine.

Death penalty for Rosenbergs stirs dispute

The controversial Rosenberg case is polarizing the nation.

April 5. Saying that their crime was "worse than murder," Judge Irving R. Kaufman sentenced Julius and Ethel Rosenberg to death for passing U.S. atomic bomb secrets to the Soviet Union. A fellow defendant, Morton Sobell, was sentenced to 30 years in prison.

Emanuel Bloch, chief attorney for the Rosenbergs, said they would ask the U.S. Court of Appeals to set aside the sentences and would carry the case all the way to the Supreme Court, if necessary. Noting that the Rosenbergs have said repeatedly that they are innocent, Bloch said they feel they are the victims of national political hysteria.

The defendants accepted their sentences stolidly. Just yesterday, in their cells at the Federal Courthouse, she had been heard singing "Goodnight, Irene" and "One Fine Day" from the opera "Madame Butterfly," as he sang "The Battle Hymn of the Republic" (→ 6/4).

Margaret Truman in radio acting debut

April 26. The President's daughter, Margaret Truman, made her debut as a radio actress tonight. The 26-year-old Miss Truman was featured in "Jackpot," a comedy about a contest winner who cannot come up with the tax on his winnings. Jimmy Stewart, who appeared in the film version last year, co-starred.

Margaret Truman.

Miss Truman, a professional singer, bantered comfortably with reporters before giving a flawless performance. The 375-member studio audience gave her and the ensemble a warm round of applause. The only errors of the evening were made by Stewart, who stuttered more than he intended. The National Broadcasting Company, which aired the show, also seemed self-conscious. It changed the name of one character to "Hank." The name had originally been "Harry."

Miss Truman phoned her father afterwards. She told reporters he said he had "enjoyed the play." But how did he like his daughter's acting in particular? "You'll have to find out from him," she said.

1951

MAY

Su	Mo	Tu	We	Th	Fr	Sa
		1	2	3	4	5
6	7	8	9	10	11	12
13	14	15	16	17	18	19
20	21	22	23	24	25	26
27	28	29	30	31		

1. Munich: U.S. begins broadcasting Radio Free Europe in Eastern bloc.

2. Israel: Syrian forces cross demilitarized zone, occupy two villages (→ 4).

4. Syria and Israel get cease-fire; lasts three hours (→ 7/20).

5. Count Turf wins Kentucky Derby with jockey C. McCreary.

6. Cairo: King Farouk marries Narriman Sadek, 17-year-old commoner.

7. El Salvador hit by major earthquake; at least 100 dead.

8. New York: "Stalag 17" opens at 48th Street Theater.

11. U.N. lists Communist casualties in Korea at 890,000, U.N. deaths at 248,000 (→ 18).

15. AT&T announces it has one mil. stockholders —a first in U.S.

17. Vietnam: French troop ship Adour explodes in Saigon harbor; 55 dead, 143 injured.

18. Korea: U.N. forces fall back above 38th parallel as Reds press attack on 100-mile front (→ 20).

18. New York: "Kid" Gavilan takes world welterweight title, outpointing Johnny Bratton.

22. Tehran: 30,000 Iranians jeer U.S. and Britain in rally condemning stand on oil (→ 6/18).

24. Outfielder Willie Mays, at age 20, joins N.Y. Giants.

24. Korea: U.N. armies chase foe back across 38th parallel (→ 6/10).

25. British Foreign Service officials Donald Maclean and Guy Burgess disappear (→ 6/7).

27. Vienna: Socialist Theodor Koerner elected president of Austria.

28. U.S. Supreme Court backs CBS method for transmitting TV in full color (→ 6/3).

29. Capt. Charles Blair makes first solo flight over North Pole in single-engine plane.

30. Lee Wallard wins Indy 500 in Belanger Special, averaging 126 mph.

BIRTH

23. Anatoly Karpov, Soviet chess champion.

Death takes the original Funny Girl

May 29. Fanny Brice, who gamboled across Broadway stages for two decades, has died at the age of 59. Many tried to capture her flair for dialect and mimicry, yet none would want to imitate her private life. Her time offstage was marred by intrigue and disappointment.

Miss Brice was born in New York and acted while still in her teens in Brooklyn theaters. She was in the Ziegfeld Follies in the 1910's; "Why Worry?," produced in 1918, was her first non-musical play. Her biggest year may have been 1935, when her Baby Snooks character, a big naughty girl with a bow in her hair, bowled over Broadway. Miss Brice took the act to radio. Imogene Coca and other young comediennes quickly made their own Snooks.

Nicky Arnstein, a gambler and embezzler, was Miss Brice's first husband. Producer Billy Rose was her second. Both tended to admire her for her money. Miss Brice had one serious song in her repertoire, a torch tune called "My Man." She sang it with conviction.

Full-color TV sent from Empire State

May 2. The Radio Corporation of America today broadcast color television programs from the Empire State Building. Unlike a competing CBS system, which requires special converters, the RCA pictures were received by black-and-white sets in the New York area.

Hydrogen bomb tested

Ball of fire at Eniwetok.

May 12. The United States government reports that tests of atomic weapons in the mid-Pacific have led to marked progress toward development of a hydrogen bomb.

In a statement that omitted all details about the kind of tests that were conducted, the Atomic Energy Commission and Defense Department said strides exceeding expectations had been recorded.

Alvin C. Graves of the Los Alamos Scientific Laboratory told reporters that "much useful information" has been gained about thermonuclear reactions, which are necessary for the detonation of a hydrogen bomb. Such a bomb, which would harness the basic power source of the sun, would be hundreds of times more destructive than the atomic bombs dropped on Hiroshima and Nagasaki. The government statement said that advances in atomic technology have been so rapid that tests at the Eniwetok site in the Pacific will be much more frequent than before (→ 10/3).

Two fellow generals criticize MacArthur

May 23. General Douglas MacArthur has come under heavy criticism from two fellow Army generals as a Senate committee continues an inquiry into President Truman's decision last month to recall him from his Far East command.

Both General Omar N. Bradley, the Joint Chiefs of Staff Chairman, and General George C. Marshall, who is Secretary of State, have testified they support the president's action in recalling General MacArthur, a critic of the administration's foreign policy.

Bradley said General MacArthur's Korean War strategy would have been dangerous. In his fifth day of testimony today, he was critical of the MacArthur field intelligence network, saying the general could have discovered in advance the Chinese Communist assault on his forces in Korea.

Tibet submits to Communist China

May 27. The huge, impassive Himalayas looked down on another transient change in human affairs today as Communist China "liberated" Tibet. The 16-year-old Dali Lama, temporal leader of the tiny theocratic state, sent representatives to Peking and they signed a 17-point agreement three days ago. The pact allows Tibetans to regulate their internal affairs while relinquishing control of the army and foreign affairs to the Chinese. Tibetans, who surrendered to the Chinese army last October, will be allowed to practice their religion if they sever all "pro-imperialist ties" (→ 5/1/52).

American pilot is world's first jet ace

May 20. Captain James Jabara, a World War II ace, shot down his fifth and sixth MIG's in Korea today to become the first jet ace.

Meanwhile, Chinese Communist and North Korean troops attacked across a broad front, suffering heavy casualties but forcing U.N. troops to withdraw to defensive positions. The Communists scored a breakthrough on the east coast, forcing South Korean units to retreat from positions north of the 38th parallel. U.N. officials described the situation on the east front as "fluid," but said Allied forces had repulsed Communist attacks on the northwest front around Seoul (→ 24).

1951

JUNE

Su	Mo	Tu	We	Th	Fr	Sa
					1	2
3	4	5	6	7	8	9
10	11	12	13	14	15	16
17	18	19	20	21	22	23
24	25	26	27	28	29	30

3. RCA announces it will hand over tri-color TV tube to CBS for study (→ 23).

4. U.S. Supreme Court upholds states' right to require signing of non-Communist affadavits by job applicants (→ 20).

10. Korea: U.N. forces break into Communist "iron triangle" of defense (→ 13).

12. Ford Foundation launches study to raise TV cultural level.

13. Korea: U.N. troops seize Pyongyang in North (→ 23).

14. N.J.: Television broadcasts its first human birth.

15. New York: Joe Louis KOs Lee Savold in comeback bout.

16. New Delhi: Nehru opponents found People's Party (→ 2/3/54).

18. Britain to offer Iran ten mil. pounds against future royalties for Anglo-Iranian Oil Co. (→ 21).

19. U.S.: All United Airlines flights grounded by first major pilot strike.

19. Truman extends draft to 1955, lengthens service to two years, lowers age to 18.5

22. Pan Am airliner bound for N.Y. vanishes over West African jungle with 40 aboard.

23. N.Y.: Soviet delegate Jacob Malik calls for U.N. cease-fire in Korea (→ 26).

28. Budapest: Archbishop Josef Groesz given 15 years for plot to overthrow government (→ 30).

29. U.S. invites Soviets to Korean peace talks on ship in Wonsan Harbor (→ 7/8).

30. Denver: N.Y.-bound DC-6 crashes in Rocky Mountain Park, killing all 50 aboard.

30. Vatican: Pope Pius XII excommunicates Hungarian Catholics for arrest of Archbishop Groesz (→ 12/28).

DEATHS

2. John Erskine, American writer, musician (*10/5/1879).

4. Serge Koussevitzky, director Boston Symphony Orchestra (*7/26/1874).

25. Mark Morton, co-founder of Morton Salt Co. (*1859).

British diplomats vanish; were spies

June 7. Two former top-ranking British diplomats, missing since May 25, are being sought as alleged spies for the Soviet Union. Donald Duart MacLean and Guy Francis de Moncy Burgess were employees of Great Britain's Foreign Office until June 1, when British officials suspended them for being absent without leave for a week. It is believed the men went to France and the French Surete is currently investigating the matter.

Both men held sensitive positions and had served in the British Embassy in Washington. U.S. Secretary of State Dean Acheson said that if they turn out to be "Soviet sympathizers" it would be "quite a serious matter." MacLean was believed to have "a thorough knowledge of secret Anglo-American exchanges on such subjects as the North Atlantic pact, the Korean War and the Japanese peace treaty," according to Senator Owen Brewster.

De Valera regains Irish premiership

June 13. Eamon de Valera, the Brooklyn-born Irish nationalist leader, regained the premiership of Ireland after serving for some three years in the opposition. The Dail Eireann elected de Valera Prime Minister by a narrow margin of five votes—74 to 69—after five independents deserted the ruling interparty coalition of John A. Costello. As de Valera regained the premiership that he held from 1932 to 1948, his supporters in the gallery chanted "Up Dev" (→ 3/7/57).

De Valera, veteran of Irish politics.

Soviet Union calls for Korean cease-fire

Malik asks for peace at U.N.

June 26. The Soviet Union surprised the Western Allies by proposing a cease-fire in the year-old war in Korea. The Soviet peace overture came from Jacob A. Malik, chief Soviet delegate to the United Nations, during the course of a U.N. radio broadcast. Malik suggested that as a first step toward ending the conflict, there should be discussions between the belligerents, whom he did not name, on a cease-fire to be followed by an armistice providing for withdrawal of opposing forces to each side of the 38th parallel.

The Malik proposal set off a flurry of diplomatic activity. U.N. Secretary General Trygve Lie urged immediate negotiations on a military cease-fire as the first step toward restoration of peace in Korea. American ambassadors in Moscow and at the United Nations were instructed to seek clarification of the Soviet proposal.

Secretary of State Dean Acheson reacted cautiously but positively to the Soviet overture. While the American political objective is unification of Korea, Acheson said that the military objective of the United States would be satisfied if the Communists withdrew behind the 38th parallel and gave satisfactory guarantees against renewed aggression. Such a settlement, the American official said, could be considered "a successful conclusion of the conflict" (→ 29).

Puerto Rican soldiers, fighting for the U.S. in Korea, take cover in a trench.

Television, like auto, changing social scene

June 23. Television is transforming American society to a degree unparalleled since the dawn of the automobile, according to a study published in The New York Times. Despite the fact that TV has been in commercial use only five years, it is changing how the public spends its leisure time, how it feels about politics, how much it reads, how it rears children and how it expresses itself culturally.

Television's greatest immediate impact has been on Hollywood, which reports business is off 20-40 percent. "You can't charge for mediocrity any more when everybody can get it at home for nothing," one TV watcher explains. Today, 107 TV stations are operating in 63 cities, within range of 62 percent of the U.S. population.

De Gaulle 2nd to Communists in France

June 17. Voters in France have refused to rally behind the political movement of General Charles de Gaulle. His party came in second to the Communists, even though the Communists lost considerable support since the last election. De Gaulle himself admitted that the appeal of his "Rassemblement du Peuple Francais," or R.P.F., was "limited."

Voting for the House of Deputies was calm and orderly, and few voters abstained. But counting the ballots was difficult because of a new system that permits alliances between different parties. The system was designed to frustrate the Communists and the Gaullists, who have often united in opposition to the government.

The Communists (P.C.F.) received 5,038,587 votes, or 26.5%. They lost nearly half a million votes since the last election. The Gaullists came in second with 4,134,885, or 21.7%. In third place were the Socialists (S.F.I.O), with 2,764,210, or 14.5%, a significant decline since 1946. A coalition of moderates, workers and independents received 2,496,570, or 13.1%, an improvement. They were followed by the Popular Republicans, a party of former Christian Democrats known as the M.R.P, who dropped considerably to 2,252,544, or 12.3%. The Radicals pulled up the rear with 2,194,213 votes.

Overall, the coalition of parties which supports the government is still slightly in the majority. The left was weakened. And supporters of the private school system received more votes than candidates who favor religious schools.

Gaullist propaganda is explicit: "Alert! The Communists are preparing civil war in France. And the government tolerates the criminal activity of traitors. ▷

21 Communists charged with conspiracy

June 20. A federal jury in New York has indicted 21 Communist Party leaders for conspiracy to teach and advocate overthrow of the United States government by force and violence. Sixteen of them were arrested in New York, one in Pittsburgh and four have not yet been found. Bail totaling $191,000 has been set for those arrested.

The indictments were the first since the Supreme Court, two weeks ago, upheld the constitutionality of the Smith Act, under which 11 other Communist Party leaders were convicted of the same criminal conspiracy in 1949. The 11, now free on bail, are expected to begin their three-to-five-year sentences soon.

Those indicted today hold top posts in the party's national and New York organizations. Included is Elizabeth Gurley Flynn, head of the women's commission (→ 12/13).

The 16 rounded up in New York are led off to jail for their party affiliation.

No bikinis at Wimbledon, say stern British

June 22. A year ago, tennis player Gussie Moran shocked Wimbledon officials by sporting lace underwear beneath her sporting outfit. The ensemble, designed by Britain's Teddy Tingling, was in evidence each time she swung her racket. Today, Wimbledon Chairman Sir Louis Greig said he wants to see no more "bikini bathing dresses."

British Abadan refineries seized in Iran

Premier Mossadegh, popular in Iran.

June 21. Iran has seized British oil installations in Abadan just three months after Iranian Premier Mohammed Mossadegh nationalized oil facilities. And today, he won a vote of confidence from Parliament on that decision. Mossadegh acted after the breakdown of talks with British delegates of the Anglo-Iranian Oil Company. Britain refused to agree to the Iranian injunction that it surrender its profits. The new firm controlling oil production is called the Iran National Oil Company. Mossadegh said Iran tried to work with Britain but was forced to nationalize (→ 7/5).

1951

JULY

Su	Mo	Tu	We	Th	Fr	Sa
1	2	3	4	5	6	7
8	9	10	11	12	13	14
15	16	17	18	19	20	21
22	23	24	25	26	27	28
29	30	31				

1. Cleveland Indian Bob Feller pitches third no-hitter, setting major league record.

1. Colombo Plan for cooperation and economic development goes into effect for Southeast Asia (→ 9/8/54).

5. The Hague: Intl. Court rules against Iran in dispute over seizure of British oil (→ 11).

6. Wimbledon: Dick Savitt over Ken McGregor 6-4, 6-4, 6-4; Dorothy Hart over Shirley Fry 6-1, 6-0.

7. Madrid: Church forbids scanty swim suits, opening campaign for morality in public life.

8. Korea: U.N. delegates meet with Communists in Kaesong for talks on cease-fire (→ 26).

11. Washington: Truman aide Averell Harriman to fly to Tehran to ease oil crisis (→ 15).

14. Missouri: State of emergency declared as floods leave 500,000 homeless.

15. Tehran: Nine die in riots over Iran-British oil dispute (→ 8/6).

15. J.D. Salinger's "Catcher in the Rye" published in U.S.

18. Pittsburgh: Jersey Joe Walcott KOs Ezzard Charles in seventh for heavyweight title.

23. France: Ike opens new NATO headquarters at Rocquencourt (→ 9/20).

28. Detroit: Truman warns Soviets are expanding to open new aggression "at any time." (→ 8/1)

29. Swiss racer Hugo Koblet wins Tour de France.

BIRTH

31. Evonne Fay Goolagong, Australian tennis champ.

DEATHS

13. Arnold Schoenberg, U.S. composer, twelve-tone system (*9/13/1874).

23. Robert Flaherty, U.S. documentary film director, "Nanook of the North" (*2/16/1884).

23. Henri Philippe Petain, French hero in WWI, head of Vichy government in WWII, imprisoned after war (*4/24/1856).

Sugar Ray is upset by Randy Turpin

Sugar Ray battles Turpin.

July 10. Randy Turpin, who never before had fought more than eight rounds, outboxed Sugar Ray Robinson for 15 rounds and brought the world middleweight championship to England.

In the most stunning boxing upset in 25 years—Gene Tunney outpointed Jack Dempsey for the heavyweight title—Turpin was in command all the way. He opened a gash under Robinson's eye in the seventh, bloodied his nose in the 12th and appeared on the verge of a knockout victory in the 14th.

The British crowd yelled for Turpin to finish off Sugar Ray in the 14th when he staggered him with a left hook to the jaw but Robinson, hailed as the greatest fighter of his generation, managed to stay afloat.

In fact, there were no knockdowns during the battle. Turpin, the European and British champion, emerged without a scratch. For Robinson, former welterweight champion, this was only his second loss in 133 bouts over an 11-year period (→ 9/12).

1951 Cunningham, Model C-1.

King Abdullah killed at Jerusalem mosque

July 20. Jordan's King Abdullah was shot dead today as he entered the Mosque of Omar in Jerusalem. The assassin, immediately killed by the king's guards, belonged to the Arab organization known as the Sanctuary of Struggle, linked with the Arab Higher Committee and long opposed to the king.

They felt particularly betrayed in the recent Palestinian conflict when the king diverted his troops from their drive to the coast and ordered them to storm Old Jerusalem, in the process annexing part of Palestine to the Kingdom of Jordan. The king, a mercurial figure, apparently acted after a dream in which his father commanded him to capture Old Jerusalem. The eventual successor will be Prince Talial, now being treated for a nervous breakdown in Switzerland. The only other direct heir is his 16-year-old son, Hussein (→ 8/11/52).

Abdullah, sought Arab federation.

Agenda set for Korean cease-fire talks

July 26. The two sides in the Korean War have agreed to start talking again. Now they have to reach agreement on something else: the terms of an armistice that will stop the shooting.

North Korean and Chinese negotiators retracted a key demand before the agenda for peace talks with United Nations representatives was finalized. The Communists stopped insisting on the immediate withdrawal of all foreign troops from Korea after U.S. Secretary of State Dean Acheson refused to compromise on the point.

Negotiators agreed that a demilitarized zone will separate the two Koreas along a new demarcation line that has to be drawn in the talks. Arrangements also must be made for the return of prisoners of war.

The first round of negotiations, arranged by U.S. Gen. Ridgway, North Korea's Kim Il Sung and China's Peng Tehuai, collapsed after it was learned that Kaesong, site of the talks, was still in Communist hands. United Nations negotiators insisted that the city of Kaesong be declared neutral territory (→ 8/5).

Ridgway, American leader in Korea.

CBS begins network color presentations

CBS investment in color technology may prove a bust. Last month, the network ushered in its color programming with a star-studded special hosted by Arthur Godfrey. Perhaps 30 people in the New York area owned color sets and watched. Despite further chromatic broadcasts, the audience remains tiny.

The public is in no hurry to buy available color TVs. People know the sets are noncompatible, picking up only CBS programs. RCA has developed a cheaper, compatible color system that the FCC may eventually standardize (→ 10/16).

One of the first color television sets, produced and developed by RCA.

Baudouin I, 5th Belgian King, takes oath

July 16. King Leopold III passed the crown and rule of Belgium to his 20-year old son, Baudouin, today in a dramatic royal ceremony. Both the king's speech and his son's were filled with emotion. Leopold had to struggle to keep a firm voice as he explained to his guests his reason for abdicating: to restore concord in the nation. Baudouin, choked with tears, was forced to stop halfway through his acceptance speech. His father rushed to his side and affectionately embraced him. Outside the palace, the king's supporters gathered, chanting "Long live Leopold!" Premier Joseph Pholien expressed his support for the new King.

Baudouin I is sworn in in Brussels.

Franco seeks arms and accord with West

July 20. Seeking to woo the West and end Spanish isolation, Generalissimo Francisco Franco told his newly assembled Cabinet that the two most important items on his agenda were to rearm Spain and seek friendly relations with the countries of the Americas.

Outraged by Franco's dictatorial control of Spain, many U.N. countries severed diplomatic ties in 1946. This pressure, however, banded the Spanish people together, and recently the Western powers have been favorable to Franco's staunch anti-communism. Normal diplomatic relations were resumed last year with the U.S., which has begun loaning money denied to Spain under the Marshall Plan (→ 9/26/53).

Dashiell Hammett, mystery writer, jailed

July 9. Dashiell Hammett, the noted mystery novel author, has been sentenced to six months in jail for criminal contempt of court in refusing to name those persons who contributed to a bail bond fund for four Communist leaders who have jumped bail.

Hammett is chairman of the bail fund for the Civil Rights Congress, which the attorney general says is a Communist subversive front. The author of "The Thin Man" and "The Maltese Falcon" has also been accused of links with 40 to 50 other Communist front groups. In court, he took the Fifth Amendment in declining to answer questions on the grounds his answers might incriminate him.

1951

AUGUST

Su	Mo	Tu	We	Th	Fr	Sa
			1	2	3	4
5	6	7	8	9	10	11
12	13	14	15	16	17	18
19	20	21	22	23	24	25
26	27	28	29	30	31	

1. U.S. ends tariff privileges for all Communist-dominated countries (→ 10/10).

1. Vallauris, France: Picasso quits pottery after five years, returns to painting.

2. Ystad, Sweden: 12 Polish seamen seize naval ship, seek political asylum (→ 10/31/51).

5. Korea: Gen. Ridgway suspends talks, charging violation of neutral zone (→ 10).

5. Niagara: William Hill Jr. dies shooting Falls in inner tubes.

6. Tehran: Britain, Iran open talks on oil dispute (→ 10/1).

7. New Mexico: Viking rocket climbs record 135 miles, at speed of 1,400 mph.

10. Warminster: British army displays .280 caliber automatic rifle, fires 84 rounds per minute.

10. North Koreans pledge to respect neutral zone; talks to resume (→ 9/11).

12. East Berlin: Over one million youths march for peace and Communism (→ 3/25/52).

16. N.Y.: U.S., Britain at U.N. ask Egypt to lift Suez blockade on Israel; Egypt demands removal of British troops (→ 9/1).

20. New York: Chase and Manhattan begin talks on largest merger in banking history.

24. Oakland: DC-6B luxury plane strikes hill, killing 50.

25. Belgrade: Emmanuel MacDonald runs 100-meters in record time of 10.2 seconds.

28. New York: "A Place in the Sun" opens starring Montgomery Clift.

30. Truman invokes Taft-Hartley Act to halt copper strike by injunction (→ 6/2/52).

30. U.S., Philippines sign mutual defense treaty (→ 11/11/53).

31. Dusseldorf: Deutsche Grammophone introduces first 33 LP.

DEATHS

15. Artur Schnabel, eminent Austrian pianist (*4/17/1882).

16. Louis Jouvet, French actor and director (*12/29/1887).

21. Constant Lambert, British composer (*8/23/1905).

Hearst, flamboyant news tycoon, is dead

Aug 14. A vibrant and fascinating chunk of life is gone. William Randolph Hearst, who established a vast publishing empire with earthy mass-appeal news coverage and shrieking typography, has died in Beverly Hills at age 88.

Although he at times manipulated the news, and accounts that left the truth partly behind helped drive America to war with Spain in 1898, he was not afraid to espouse unpopular causes even at great cost in money and popularity. Originally, his papers, 18 newspapers in 12 cities and nine magazines, supported public ownership, antitrust laws and labor unions. Later, he became stridently conservative. A political oracle, he was mostly unsuccessful in his political ambitions that reached as far as the presidency.

Married since 1903 and father of five sons, he lived openly with actress Marion Davies for more than 30 years, often in his castle in California, San Simeon, which houses rare art treasures. He financed several movies with the vivacious Miss Davies, 34 years his junior. They first met in 1913 and wanted to get married, but his wife refused firmly though without hostility to grant him a divorce.

Hearst at White House in the 20's.

Hearst, never one to hide his wealth, left his lavish San Simeon in 1947.

90 West Point cadets fired for cheating

Aug 23. "Duty, Honor, Country." The West Point motto was dragged in the dirt today as 90 cadets were expelled for cheating on examinations. The Army refused to provide names or details, but UPI reported that the highly successful football team "has been practically wiped out" by the scandal. Cadets are between semesters, but those involved received notices from the superintendent stating: "Balance of your leave canceled. You are to return to West Point immediately."

Cadets have been given the option of withdrawal, but this has prompted calls from Congress for stiffer punishments. Those accused not only breached academy regulations, but broke the higly vaunted honor code and will be shunned by fellow cadets. Alumni point out that the violation was reported by a cadet and contend this is a vindication of the code. No one in the class just graduated has been implicated, but some say this may be because many are serving in Korea.

Skyrocket airplane climbs to 13.7 miles

Aug 30. An experimental Douglas Skyrocket plane has broken all altitude records for flight, the United States Navy announced today. The Skyrocket was said to have also broken all aviation speed records by flying faster than 1,000 mph.

While not announcing details, the Navy said the Skyrocket had broken the 13.7-mile altitude record set in a 1935 balloon ascent and had exceeded the official airplane altitude mark of 59,445 feet set by a British Vampire jet in 1948. The Skyrocket has been flying from Edwards Air Force Base in California. It set the new records in its latest flight, on August 15. The 45-foot-long aircraft is taken aloft by a B-29 bomber and is powered by rockets that burn three tons of fuel in as many minutes.

The Skyrocket: Plane of the future?

Disputed law used to terminate strike

Aug 31. A major break in the five-day copper strike came today, just hours after President Truman invoked the national emergency section of the Taft-Hartley Act.

That the strike may be ending was signaled when Kennecott Copper Corporation, one of the nation's major producers, reached an agreement with the union to increase wages by about 15 cents an hour and improve the company's pension plan. It is considered likely that agreements may also be reached with other copper firms.

Just last night, in invoking the Taft-Hartley Act, the president named a board of inquiry, a step that could lead to the government seeking an injunction to end the strike.

Indian, denied burial, given Arlington plot

A Korean War veteran's rights have been upheld by President Truman.

Aug 29. A hero's burial in Arlington National Cemetery was arranged today by President Truman's personal intervention for a Winnebago Indian who gave his life on a Korean battlefield but was denied interment in a Sioux City, Iowa, cemetery because of his race.

The president read newspaper accounts of the burial being stopped since the cemetery was open only to "members of the Caucasian race." Immediately, he fired out angry telegrams to the Mayor of Sioux City, whose name the White House did not even bother to obtain, and to the director of the Memorial Park Cemetery. He then notified the family of Sgt. First Class John R. Rice of Winnebago, Nebraska, that the nation's full military honors will be accorded the sergeant.

Rice, 37, of the First Cavalry Division, was killed in Southern Korea on September 6, 1950, as American troops battled to hold the Naktong River bridgehead. The body was brought home recently, and Rice's non-Indian wife purchased the burial lot without noticing the race-restrictive clause.

It is likely that President Truman will attend the burial services to demonstrate anew that racial prejudice is abhorrent to the American system of democracy. He has battled vigorously for equal rights for all races and creeds throughout his tenure in office, even at the cost of splitting the Democratic Party.

Henry King's Biblical epic "David and Bathsheba" stars Susan Hayward and Gregory Peck.

Average pay $1,436

Aug 18. Americans averaged an income of $1,436 for each man, woman and child in 1950, the Commerce Department reports. Total individual income payments were divided by the total population, which means that averages were pulled up by the large incomes of the very rich. The figure represents a gain of $116, or nine percent, over 1949 and represents the highest dollar total in history, though a rise in the tax burden cut down the net gain. Federal, state and local taxes averaged $360 during the year ending June 30, 1950. Average incomes ranged from $698 in Mississippi to $1,986 in the District of Columbia.

1951

SEPTEMBER

Su	Mo	Tu	We	Th	Fr	Sa
						1
2	3	4	5	6	7	8
9	10	11	12	13	14	15
16	17	18	19	20	21	22
23	24	25	26	27	28	29
30						

1. N.Y.: U.N. Security Council asks end to Egyptian blockade on Israel (→ 10/8).

4. San Francisco: Truman opens Japanese peace treaty talks in first transcontinental TV hookup (→ 8).

6. Washington: Portugal grants U.S. rights in Azores.

8. Prague: Czech Communists purge Secretary General Rudolf Slansky (→ 11).

11. Venice: Stravinsky conducts premiere of his opera "The Rake's Progress."

11. U.N. command admits plane attacked Kaesong in Korean neutral zone in error (→ 24).

12. Washington: Marshall retires as secretary of defense.

13. Washington: Gen. de Lattre de Tassigny visits U.S. to gain support for French war in Vietnam (→ 10/3).

14. Britain: Europe's largest oil refinery opened in Fawley.

18. U.S. Congress enacts veterans' pension over Truman veto.

19. New York: "A Streetcar Named Desire," with Marlon Brando and Vivien Leigh, makes film debut at the Warner.

20. Ottawa: N. Atlantic Council agrees to admit Greece and Turkey to NATO (→ 2/20/52).

20. Swiss Parliament kills woman suffrage bill.

20. Chicago: Ford C. Frick elected commissioner of baseball for seven years.

24. Kaesong: Korean Reds quit meeting after rejecting plan to reopen truce talks (→ 10/6).

25. Washington: Italian Premier Gasperi, seeking aid on Trieste, is told U.S. favors "free" Italy over Yugoslavia (→ 3/20/52).

26. Faulkner's "Requiem for a Nun" published in U.S.

28. Buenos Aires: Army group stages revolt against Peron government (→ 11/11).

29. Athens: Gen. Nicholas Plastiras named Greek premier.

DEATH

18. Jimmy Yancey, pioneer boogie woogie pianist.

Bundestag pledges restitution to Jews

Sept 27. A repentant West German Parliament rose to its feet today and unanimously voted reparations to the Jewish people. In a remarkable speech, Chancellor Konrad Adenauer said that the German people "had the obligation to make moral and material amends . . . for the unspeakable crimes committed in the name of the German people." Even the German Party, which last week had insisted that the country should not "abase itself before Israel," joined in the demonstration in favor of payment.

An Israeli government spokesman said that the West Germans had admitted their guilt, "but no such acknowledgement has come from the East German Republic, which is under equal obligation."

Some estimates run as high as $600 million for property stolen from the Jews during WWII, but Adenauer cautioned that restitution would be based on Germany's ability to pay (→ 9/10/52).

Public kissing ban in Sweden. Sweden?

Sept 22. A Stockholm court has fined an 18-year-old sailor for kissing his girl in public, calling his offense "obnoxious behavior repulsive to public morals." The incident has profoundly shaken the Swedish capital, the hometown of Greta Garbo and Ingrid Bergman.

49-nation treaty revives Japan sovereignty

Truman offers words of caution.

Sept 8. A peace treaty has finally been concluded with Japan. The pact makes Japan a sovereign nation again, and Secretary of State Dean Acheson said the treaty was evidence of a "greatness of spirit." But the Soviet Union and other Communist countries boycotted the ceremony in San Francisco, and Foreign Minister Andrei Gromyko complained that Japan should have been treated more severely.

Under the treaty, Japan loses most of its empire. Restrictions are placed on rearmament, and U.S. Army and Navy forces will remain in Japan. "The United States," President Truman told the 49 signatories, "has not forgotten Pearl Harbor or Bataan and many of the other nations represented here have similar memories that will not be easily erased. The new Japan will not find the world entirely friendly or trusting" (→ 4/15/52).

Czech flees in train with 111 passengers

Sept 11. Refugees have climbed, tunneled and flown past the Iron Curtain. Today, they took an express train. Engineer Frazek Jarda skipped his last stop in Czechoslovakia and roared right into West Germany and freedom. "We did it because it was no longer bearable to live in an East European state," said Jarda. Some 111 passengers were on board, including Jarda's wife, two children and 21 others seeking to escape communism. The rest were captive witnesses; the Czech regime is negotiating their return.

Jarda said someone in Asch, the last stop in Czechoslovakia switched his passenger train onto a freight track. Another accomplice inside the train cut the brake lines to prevent the conductor from pulling the emergency brake and halting the flight to freedom (→ 11/27).

George VI undergoes major lung surgery

Sept 27. A bulletin describes King George's condition as satisfactory after a major lung operation Sunday. Nine physicians have convinced the British monarch to appoint five family members as counselors of state: Queen Elizabeth, Princess Elizabeth, Princess Margaret, the Duke of Gloucester and the Princess Royal (→ 2/15/52).

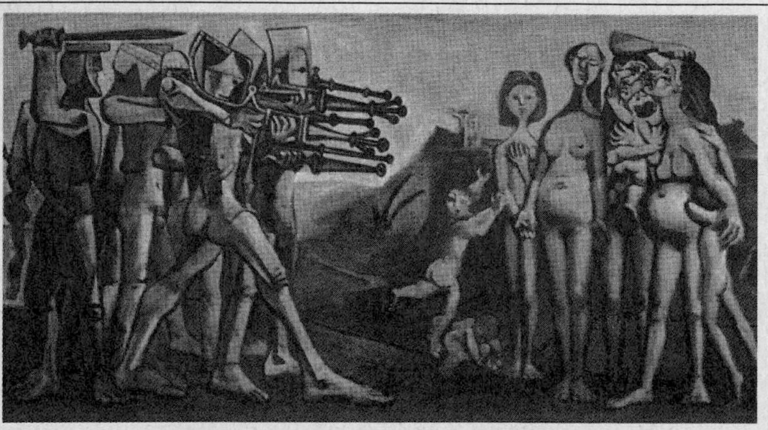

Picasso, deeply affected by the horrors of war, has painted "Massacre in Korea," reminiscent of his depiction of German atrocities at Guernica.

U.S., Australia and New Zealand allied

Sept 1. Alarmed by the growing power of Russia and China, as well as a reviving Japan, Australia and New Zealand have found security in a tripartite alliance with the United States. The pact, which was signed in San Francisco, provides for the common defense, recognizing that an attack on one threatens the security of all. The Ambassador of New Zealand drew broad implications from the treaty, saying "a true democracy must be willing to serve wherever democracy needs to be defended."

This brings to five the number of alliances the United States now has stretching around the globe, from the Arctic to Berlin to the Philippines. Agreement on the pact was considered essential for the governments of Australia and New Zealand to recognize the U.S.-sponsored treaty of reconciliation with Japan.

American Secretary of State Dean Acheson, who represented the U.S. at the ceremony, stressed that the purpose of the treaty with the two Asian nations was not offensive, but meant to send a signal "that our common desire for peace is coupled with a strong resolve to resist aggression" (→ 8/4/52).

Sugar Ray wins title

Sept 12. Sugar Ray Robinson knocked out Randy Turpin of England in the tenth round today and brought the world middleweight title back to the United States.

Turpin ducks a Sugar Ray left.

John Sloan, dean of U.S. artists, is dead

John Sloan's "Girl in Cafe."

Sept 8. Painter and teacher John Sloan has died at the age of 80. He was one of the great "Apostles of Ugliness," a member of the Ash Can School. He celebrated slums, scrubwomen and breadlines.

Sloan was born in Pennsylvania. He studied under Robert Henri in New York and gave his first exhibit when he was 29. He failed to sell a work until he was 49. Then paintings such as "6th Avenue and 20th Street" (1907) started to seem less like trash and more like realism.

In an interview last year, Sloan said, "I didn't cater to the fashion editors even when I was young. I painted my darkest, my blackest pictures . . . I'm lucky because I've never been hindered by financial success or by approval."

Little Mo wins at 16

Sept 5. Maureen Connolly, a golden-haired girl of 16, upset the veteran Shirley Fry in three sets in the final of the United States Tennis Championships and became the youngest ever to win the title.

Miss Connolly, affectionately known as "Little Mo," hit the ball with amazing velocity in capturing the Forest Hills match by 6-3, 1-6, 6-4. The San Diego shotmaker did not go to the net until the final game and the match was not settled until the final stroke. It was so nerve-wracking that Miss Connolly's coach was near collapse at the end.

Miss Fry's game was predicated on defense and the outcome might have been different had she gone to the net much earlier. Miss Fry netted the ball only three times in the one-sided second set and made only 11 errors to Miss Connolly's 30.

1951

OCTOBER

Su	Mo	Tu	We	Th	Fr	Sa
	1	2	3	4	5	6
7	8	9	10	11	12	13
14	15	16	17	18	19	20
21	22	23	24	25	26	27
28	29	30	31			

1. N.Y.: U.N. Security Council votes to take up Anglo-Iranian oil dispute (→ 8/8/52).

3. White House reports Soviets have set off 2nd A-bomb (→ 22).

3. Viet Minh launch offensive in Northwest Vietnam (→ 11/10).

3. N.Y.: Giants win pennant on Bobby Thompson's ninth inning homer, a shot heard round the world (→ 10).

6. Singapore: Sir Henry Gurney, British High Commissioner for Malaya, assassinated by Communist insurgents (→ 2/8/54).

6. Korea: U.N. troops retake "Heartbreak Ridge" (→ 14).

8. Montreal: Princess Elizabeth and Duke of Edinburgh arrive in place of sick King George (→ 16).

8. Cairo announces decrees to eject British from Suez and take control of Sudan (→ 15).

10. Truman signs Mutual Security Bill alotting $7.5 billion in foreign aid (→ 11/13).

10. Yankees over Giants in all-N.Y. Series, 4-3 in sixth game.

14. U.N. command admits raiding Panmunjom, new site for Korean peace talks (→ 11/25).

15. N.Y.: "The Lavender Hill Mob" opens, with Alec Guiness.

15. Cairo: Egypt rejects four-power plan to include her in Mideast defense pact (→ 16).

16. Americans watch Princess Elizabeth in Canada in first intl. broadcast in U.S. (→ 31).

16. U.S.: RCA demonstrates large-screen color TV (→ 19).

16. New Delhi: Pakistani Premier Leaquat Ali Khan assassinated by Moslem (→ 3/23/56).

16. Cairo: 12 die as British fight Egyptians near Suez (→ 12/3).

17. New York: James Mason appears in "The Desert Fox."

19. Washington postpones color TV due to war needs (→ 11/24).

20. Gen. Mark Clark named first U.S. ambassador to Vatican.

22. Nevada: Air Force drops first air-to-ground tactical nuclear weapon in test (→ 11/8).

31. Poland arrests Communist ex-leader Gomulka (→ 5/20/53).

Winston is back at 77

Churchill, back in power in Britain.

Oct 26. Winston Churchill, at the age of 77, has been called upon to form a new government after the Labor Party lost control of Parliament in a general election in Britain.

For Churchill, who will succeed Clement Attlee as Prime Minister, the victory was both a retribution and a challenge. Six years ago, after leading Britain through most of World War II, Churchill was ousted from office in a surprise victory by Attlee and his Labor Party.

Now, Churchill takes over once again at a time when Britain faces an economic crisis because of a growing deficit in its trade with the rest of the world. One of the first tasks of the new Conservative government will be to restore world confidence in the British pound. Churchill's mandate will be complicated by the fact that the Conservative Party will command a majority of less than 20 seats in Parliament. Liberals apparently sided with Conservatives in ousting the Labor government from 10 Downing Street.

Corn flakes maker Kellogg deceased

Kellogg and his seeing-eye dog.

Oct 6. Breakfast cereal entrepreneur Will K. Kellogg has died at the age of 91. He credited his longevity to his diet, based on Kellogg's Corn Flakes and other vegetarian foods. He developed the first wheat flake in 1894 at his brother's sanitarium in Battle Creek, Mich., and promoted the product tirelessly. He spent millions on charity.

In 1907, a conflagration engulfed one of his factories. Will Kellogg was calm. "The fire is of no consequence," he said. "You can't burn down what we have registered in the mind of the American woman."

Back-pack wings tested by U.S. Navy

Oct 22. A one-man rocket-powered helicopter that can be strapped to a man's back is being tested by the United States Navy. The 100-pound device uses rockets to turn rotors that are supposed to shoot the wearer off the ground faster than any aircraft. A man straps the device to his waist, straddles a bicycle seat, turns on the power and goes rocketing up, says Robert McGill, the inventor. The user controls direction with a stick and speed with a throttle. The device could revolutionize warfare, McGill says.

Oct 27. Rocky Marciano, 27, today stopped Joe Louis' bid to become the first to regain a heavyweight title, sending him through the ropes in the eighth with a solid right to the jaw.

Princess Elizabeth appears on U.S. TV

Royal treatment for the Princess.

Oct 31. British Princess Elizabeth and her husband, the Duke of Edinburgh, made their American television debut this week in the first international telecast ever. Officials from the U.S. welcomed them in Windsor, Ont., across the Detroit River, a victory for the Detroit Chamber of Commerce. The camera picked up amusing sidelights as an uninvited puppy's antics cheered up the tired princess, the Mayor of Windsor demonstrated a toy electric car for the royal children and the NBC announcer invoked good old American vernacular by referring to the couple as "the heiress presumptive to the throne and her sailor husband" (→ 11/2).

The agile energy of Leslie Caron and Gene Kelly make "An American in Paris" a joy to behold.

1951

NOVEMBER

Su	Mo	Tu	We	Th	Fr	Sa
				1	2	3
4	5	6	7	8	9	10
11	12	13	14	15	16	17
18	19	20	21	22	23	24
25	26	27	28	29	30	

2. Washington: Princess Elizabeth gives gift of an overmantle to Truman from King George.

8. Pairs: Vishinsky tells U.N. Soviets will never agree to West's plan for U.N. atom control (→ 2/26/52).

9. Paris: Britain, France, U.S., Turkey to pursue Mideast defense organization (→ 2/16/52).

10. Univ. of Toronto professor Heichelheim claims Romans landed on Iceland in 300 AD.

10. Vietnam: French report driving Viet Minh from 400 sq. miles near Hanoi (→ 14).

11. Buenos Aires: Peron elected to sixth term as president (→ 7/26/52).

13. Florida: Truman announces economic development plan for Near East (→ 1/5/52).

13. U.N. votes to shelve question of seating Communist China for entire Paris session (→ 7/17/52).

13. Nepal: Rana family deposed; King Tribhubana takes over.

14. Belgrade: U.S. and Yugoslavia sign military aid pact (→ 3/16/53).

14. Vietnam: French paratroopers capture Hoabinh (→ 1/11/52).

15. France turns down Tunisian request for increased autonomy (→ 29).

17. Britain reports development of world's first nuclear-powered heating system (→ 12/29).

19. Jerusalem: Knesset chooses Dr. Chaim Weizmann for second term as pres. (→ 11/9/52).

19. Egypt: British troops occupy Ismalia, kill 14 rebels (→ 12/3).

24. Kansas City: Color TV placed in medical center for daily instruction (→ 27).

25. Korea: Truce line mapped at talks in Panmunjom (→ 28).

27. FCC predicts U.S. will have 1,200-1,500 TV stations within five years (→ 4/13/52).

29. Damascus: Col. Adeeb Shishekly deposes Soviet regime in coup.

29. Tunisia: Rebels lead general strike against French presence (→ 1/17/52).

Truce reached and lines drawn in Korea

North Koreans sign the pact creating a neutral zone along the 38th parallel.

Nov 28. United Nations and Communist negotiators at the peace talks in Panmunjom reached agreement on the establishment of a truce line roughly along the 38th parallel that divides North and South Korea. Immediately after the agreement was announced, an informal cease-fire seemed to take effect on most of the Korean War front.

General James A. Van Fleet, commander of the Eighth Army, insisted that no cease-fire orders had been issued to American troops, but it appeared troop commanders were under instructions not to undertake any offensive action during a 30-day period while the negotiators attempt to reach agreement on a full armistice. Among the issues still to be resolved in the truce negotiations are enforcement of an armistice and repatriation of prisoners of war. The talks began in July (→ 12/18).

Romberg, writer of Student Prince, dies

Nov 10. Sigmund Romberg, one of the great names in the American musical theater, died yesterday in New York City. He was 64.

The man who left us "The Student Prince" briefly abandoned his natural musical talent for an engineering degree. As bridges gave way to ballads, he left Vienna and eventually landed penniless in New York, where he worked as a pianist and band leader and soon began publishing songs.

His first hits, "Maytime" and "Blossom Time," were followed in 1921 by the then-wild success of "The Student Prince," with more than 600 performances. Other hits included "The Desert Song," "The New Moon," and "Up in Central Park." In all, Romberg composed 78 musicals and some 2,000 songs, among them "When I Grow Too Old to Dream," "Lover Come Back to Me" and "Deep in My Heart."

Slansky is arrested

Nov 27. The former Secretary General of the Communist Party of Czechoslovakia, Rudolf Slansky, has been arrested as an espionage agent in Prague by the Klement Gottwald government. Slansky was relieved of his party chairmanship last September but was appointed Deputy Premier until alleged evidence led to accusing him of "spying for the enemy" (→ 12/3/52)

Truman likes Ike

Nov 11. Harry Truman, President of the United States and head of the Democratic Party, has offered to sponsor the man who led Allied forces in Europe during the war as president of the United States. General Eisenhower, to whom the offer was made, was flattered but is not expected to take advantage of Truman's offer, which is a virtual guarantee of nomination by the Democrats (→ 1/7/52).

20,000 marooned by Po River flood

Nov 18. In Italy today, 20,000 people were forced onto high ground surrounding the Adria Cathedral by the raging waters of the Po River. Their only means of communication with the outside world, a single phone line. "We are completely surrounded by the flood," said a resident, "and the water is creeping closer . . . come quickly." Gondolas, fishing and ski boats, anything that would float, was requisitioned by the government for a projected rescue attempt. Meanwhile, a relief boat reached the area this afternoon and the Pope has appealed to all Catholics to send relief funds for the victims.

A helping hand for Italy's helpless.

Nov 22. Macy's Thanksgiving Day parade down Broadway in New York City is a far cry from the sober three days of prayer and feasting observed by Plymouth's colonists in 1621. How they got by without department stores still remains a mystery.

1951

DECEMBER

Su	Mo	Tu	We	Th	Fr	Sa
						1
2	3	4	5	6	7	8
9	10	11	12	13	14	15
16	17	18	19	20	21	22
23	24	25	26	27	28	29
30	31					

1. Philadelphia: Navy trounces Army 42-7 in football.

2. N.Y.: 41st ex-employee of U.S. Radium Corp. dies of poisoning latent for 33 years.

3. Egypt: Scores killed in worst clash between British and Egyptians in Suez zone (→ 1/20/52).

10. American chemists Edwin McMillan and Glenn Seaborg win Nobels for discovery of transuranium elements.

11. N.Y.: Joe DiMaggio announces retirement from baseball.

13. Washington: Truman, after meeting with J. Edgar Hoover, pledges new effort to purge disloyal govt. workers (→ 3/3/52).

16. N.J.: 56 killed as C-46 crashes after takeoff.

18. Korean Reds give Allies list of 3,100 POWs (→ 1/10/52).

21. Illinois: Mine explosion kills 118 in West Frankfort.

23. L.A.: Rams down Cleveland Browns 24-17 for football title.

28. U.S. pays $120,000 to free four fliers convicted of espionage in Hungary (→ 8/14/52).

29. Idaho Falls: AEC produces electricity from atomic energy (→ 12/8/53).

CULTURAL EVENTS, 1951

Literature: James Jones' "From Here to Eternity"; Camus' "The Rebel"; Herman Wouk's "The Caine Mutiny"; Annemarie Selinko's "Desiree"; Sandburg's "Complete Poems," Pulitzer.

Academia: Hannah Arendt's "The Origins of Totalitarianism"; David Riesman's "The Lonely Crowd"; Barbara McClintock finds genes are in constant transformation.

Music: Vaughan Williams' opera "The Pilgrim's Progress"; Menotti's opera "Amahl and the Night Visitors"; Britten's "Billy Budd"; Rodgers and Hammerstein's "The King and I."

The Arts: Dali's "Christ of St. John on the Cross."

Film: Huston's "The African Queen"; "An American in Paris," Academy Award; Brando in "A Streetcar Named Desire"; British censors start "X certificate" classification.

Libya attains independence with U.N. aid

Dec 24. Members of the world's poorest country today greeted news of their independence in stony silence. King Idris, head of Libya's new government, in his first official act, banned a speech by Beshir Bey Sadawi, leader of the anti-Western forces within the country. Representatives of the British government said that should Sadawi win the upcoming elections, foreign bases such as the United States' big Wheelus Air Base, might be forced to close.

Libya, a former Italian colony, is the first country organized under United Nations auspices. The North African territory covers over a million acres, most of it barren desert, and its Arab inhabitants now have the lowest per capita income in the world.

Benghazi's Mayor gives the good news.

Best-loved Red, Litvinoff, is dead

Dec 31. A symbol of cooperation, former Soviet Foreign Minister Maxim Litvinoff, is dead at the age of 75. Litvinoff, crucial to East-West negotiations during the world wars, gained respect and praise from America and other democracies as a reasonable and intelligent force in Soviet foreign policy. As foreign commissar, he helped bring Russia out of isolation after the revolution, promoted American recognition of the Soviet state in 1933 and won her a seat on the League of Nations' Council. From 1941-43, he served as Soviet Ambassador to the United States and later was appointed foreign minister. He was relieved of his duties in 1946. Since then, U.S.-Soviet relations have grown tense.

Ross, founder of New Yorker, dead

Dec 6. Editor and founder of The New Yorker Harold Ross has died at the age of 59. Born in Aspen, Colorado, Ross was a high school dropout who created a magazine revered by the nation's literati. Ross debuted The New Yorker in 1925. At the outset, he established high standards for editing and fiction submissions and maintained those standards despite several lean financial years. While Ross encouraged the careers of countless writers, he gave the greatest boost to such cartoonists as William Steig, Helen E. Hokinson, James Thurber and Charles Addams.

Bagel famine threat terrifies New York

Dec 16. Is nothing sacred? That holey item, the bagel, has been denied to the residents of New York City due to a labor dispute. Members of the Bagel Bakers of America, A.F.L., and the Bagel Bakers Association have ended talks (much less baking) over contract issues. The result? Lox, the smoked salmon that languishes without a firm, white bagel beside it, is down in sales 30 to 50 percent. Seed rolls and doughnuts pathetically try to substitute for the real thing. On an average weekend, New Yorkers eat 1.2 million bagels.

An instant success: Catcher in the Rye

Teens and college students these days are clutching a small book. It is no Bible, but they swear by it. "The Catcher in the Rye," by Jerome David (J.D.) Salinger, tells of a teenager named Holden Caulfield searching for something good in this "phoney" world. Youths identify with Holden, wanting to change the world in a world where even changing a lightbulb is difficult.

"Catcher" is Salinger's first novel. Another first work is "From Here to Eternity" by James Jones. "Eternity" describes the final days before the Japanese attacked Pearl Harbor. "The Caine Mutiny" by Herman Wouk is another tale set in wartime, but now the enemy is within. A paranoid ship commander named Queeg drives his crew to desperate measures.

Carl Sandburg and Robert Frost are poets who published their first works decades ago. This year, each offers a collection called "Complete Poems." Critics are reverent.

Two books published last year which remain popular are "The Martian Chronicles" by Ray Bradbury and "Kon-Tiki" by Norwegian Thor Heyerdahl. The science-fiction "Chronicles" fluidly and lyrically describes the lives of settlers on Mars. "Kon-Tiki" was a raft made by Heyerdahl. He sailed the Pacific on it, trying to prove Peruvian Indians could have settled Polynesia. To some readers, a voyage to Mars sounds more feasible.

Dec 25. Behind front lines in Korea, G.I.'s celebrate Christmas in an improvised jungle church.

1952

JANUARY

Su	Mo	Tu	We	Th	Fr	Sa
		1	2	3	4	5
6	7	8	9	10	11	12
13	14	15	16	17	18	19
20	21	22	23	24	25	26
29	28	29	30	31		

1. Pasadena: Illinois downs Stanford 40-7 in Rose Bowl.

5. Washington: Churchill arrives to confer with Truman (→ 8).

5. New Delhi: U.S. signs five—year accord to give India $50 mil. for econ. devt. (→ 9).

7. Paris: Ike offers to accept Republican nomination for presidency.→

8. Phoenix opens cemetery to allow burial of Negro war veteran (→ 2/16).

8. U.S. agrees not to launch atomic attack on Soviet bloc without British consent.

9. Washington: Truman says U.S. must win battle against hunger in order to win Cold War (→ 6/20).

9. N.Y.: Jackie Robinson becomes highest paid player in Brooklyn Dodger history.

10. Panmunjom: U.N. delegation rejects armistice as Koreans refuse ban on building air bases in North (→ 3/4).

10. Montana: Truman dedicates 564-foot Hungry Horse Dam, third highest in world.

12. Britain's only prototype of Vickers Valiant long-range A-bomb jet crashes in test.

13. Grindewald: Jeannette Burr of Seattle wins Swiss National Women's Ski Championship.

16. Cairo: Crown Prince Ahmed Fuad born to King Farouk and Queen Narriman (→ 5/6).

17. Tunisia: Nationalist Habib Bourguiba arrested by French (→ 21).

20. Egypt: British troops occupy Ismalia (→ 26).

22. N.Y.: Ex-Sec. of War Robert Patterson and 30 others die as plane crashes into homes.

24. British appoint Vincent Massey first Canadian to serve as gov. gen. of Canada.

26. Egypt placed under martial law as anti-British riots sweep Cairo (→ 27).

27. Cairo: King Farouk ousts Premier Mustafa Nahas for failing to maintain order (→ 30).

31. "Sailor Beware" opens, with Dean Martin and Jerry Lewis.

Martial law in Egypt: King fires Premier

British police patrol an open-air prison filled with "silent protesters."

Jan 30. A week of bloody riots and political turmoil in Egypt has ended on a note of peace and conciliation. Angry at recent killings of Egyptian police by British guards and impassioned by the notion of independence, citizens of Cairo took to the streets in tumultuous rioting and seized control of the British Embassy. After the loss of some 20 lives, King Farouk took emergency measures "to save the country from destructive revolution"; he invoked martial law and enforced a shoot-on-sight curfew. He also fired Premier Mustafa Nahas Pasha and appointed Aly Maher Pasha to replace him.

The new Premier has announced, "We are ready to consider any understanding Mr. Eden might propose," referring to the British Foreign Secretary's recent reappraisal of Anglo-Egyptian relations. The new tone may help end the four-month-old rift between the two nations. The British response appeared relieved and hopeful.

Martial law has stabilized Cairo. And according to a government spokesman, "the situation is perfectly calm throughout Egypt and the government has full control of it" (→ 3/1).

Eisenhower would run as Republican

Jan 7. Army General Dwight David Eisenhower has indicated that he would accept a Republican draft as the party's nominee for president, but he made it clear he would not seek the nomination nor take part in any pre-convention activities. This marked the first time that the popular general, leader of Allied forces in Europe during World War II, publicly identified himself as a Republican. The general currently is Supreme Allied Commander in Europe. His comments on the presidency were made public in a statement issued at his headquarters in Rocquencourt, France (→ 3/11).

Bourguiba, Tunisia nationalist, jailed

Jan 21. The death toll in Tunisia jumped to 16 today as French authorities clashed with demonstrators over the arrest of Habib Bourguiba, the nationalist leader. Several members of his Neo-Destour, or New Constitution, Party were also taken into custody. More than 100 Tunisians have been wounded in violent confrontations with police in Tunis and other cities. Protesters charge that French authorities fired on them and threw grenades from rooftops without provocation. The unrest has also disrupted normally calm relations between Tunisian Arabs and Jews. Eight Jewish shops were looted in Kairouan (→ 3/26).

Nationwide drug raid brings in 500

Jan 5. Narcotics dealers have fanned out from New York City and are selling heroin and marijuana to teenagers in cities throughout the U.S. But today, that market took a steep downturn as federal agents arrested over 500 dealers nationwide. More arrests are expected at the culmination of a grand jury investigation in three weeks, but authorities declined to mention where the jury is convened. "If we even mentioned the name of the city," they said, "some of the men who are talking would be killed." The raids are part of a program initiated by President Truman to make it more costly for those who deal. Second offenders go to jail for ten years and third timers can go for up to 20.

Jacqueline Bouvier engaged to marry

Jan 20. Miss Jacqueline Lee Bouvier is engaged to marry John G.W. Husted Jr. Miss Bouvier is the daughter of Mr. John V. Bouvier 3rd and Mrs. Hugh D. Auchincloss of McLean, Va. The prospective groom is the son of Mr. and Mrs. Husted of Bedford Hills, N.Y. He is with Dominick & Dominick, a New York brokerage firm.

Miss Bouvier is an alumna of George Washington University, class of '51. She also studied at Vassar and the Sorbonne in Paris. The wedding is scheduled for June.

Captain rescued after 12 days alone on ship

The Flying Enterprise, its captain still aboard, lists near England.

Jan 10. A high seas drama ended this afternoon as the captain of an American freighter abandoned ship off the English coast, 12 days after he began a solo effort to save it from hurricane-driven waves and currents. Captain Henrik Kurt Carlsen, fighting against the elements without his crew, did not abandon the Flying Enterprise until it was listing at an 85-degree angle. The freighter had tipped over so far that water was gushing through its smokestack into the belly of the ship. Carlsen, exhausted, jumped into the frigid, turbulent waters from the funnel and tried to swim to safety. He was ultimately saved by a lifeline thrown from the Turmoil, a British salvage tug. Forty minutes later, in a final hiss of steam and explosion of fire, the freighter went to the bottom.

Carlsen's trouble began when the Flying Enterprise ran into a hurricane on Christmas, four days after leaving Hamburg. On the 26th, the freighter started to break up under the force of the wind and waves. Carlsen ordered passengers and crew to leave the ship, but he stayed on, trying valiantly to save it. The British tug managed to throw him a line last Saturday and began towing the ship toward Falmouth. But a new storm struck three days later, snapping the tow line in half. Carlsen kept hoping for a break in the weather. It never came, and he reluctantly gave up.

French hero General de Lattre succumbs

Jan 11. France is mourning the death of one of its greatest war heroes. General Jean de Lattre de Tassigny lost his battle with cancer in Paris. He was 62 years old.

The aristocratic general was a much decorated veteran of both wars, and he was honored posthumously with the title of Marshal. In the United States, de Lattre is remembered as the French representative to Germany's surrender after the Second World War.

De Lattre's most recent assignment was Vietnam, where he served as Commander-in-Chief of French forces and High Commissioner. He managed to inspire his troops with his bravery and daring, and he reversed a tide of French defeats. But de Lattre left the jungle war without defeating the Viet Minh.

A graduate of the Saint Cyr and Saumur military academies, de Lattre was decorated eight times in the First World War. He emerged as an infantry captain, served in Morocco and then was promoted to general during the Second War. De Lattre served in the Vichy army but was arrested and imprisoned for protesting the German invasion of Southern France. He managed to escape and helped command the French troops who defeated Hitler's Nazis (→ 2/24).

De Lattre, symbol of France's fading empire, is marched down Rue de Rivoli.

Guerrilla actions continue vigorously with French in Indochina

French troops in the Hoa Binh Basin, key link between North and South.

Jan 15. Communist guerrillas in Vietnam have stepped up their attacks on French troops who are numbed by the death of General de Lattre. The offensive threatens to erode the gains made by the general, particularly in Cochin China and Annam. In the South, the Viet Minh attacked military posts and communication lines. Cities, especially Saigon, have been disrupted by acts of terrorism. In the North, the guerrillas were checked as they tried to isolate the Hoa Binh Basin with a series of violent attacks. The Communists had more success infiltrating the Tonkin delta as they attempted to isolate Hanoi by cutting the road to the Gulf. The son of the late Marshal Leclerc was wounded in the fighting (→ 2/24).

Look out below in Pisa in year 2151

Jan 21. Italy's leaning tower of Pisa will lose its balance and topple over in the year 2151, according to calculations. Every 12 months, it leans one more millimeter (.039 of an inch) away from the vertical as its foundation sinks into the shifting Tuscan soil. The white marble tower, begun on August 9, 1174, has been cared for like a frail old lady with applications of splints, iron ties and counterweights. In 1934, the illustrious invalid was prescribed injections of cement; 361 holes were made around the base, and 900 tons of cement were poured in. After a seemingly steady decade, the shock from three close bombs during World War II undid the cure.

1952

FEBRUARY

Su	Mo	Tu	We	Th	Fr	Sa
					1	2
3	4	5	6	7	8	9
10	11	12	13	14	15	16
17	18	19	20	21	22	23
24	25	26	27	28	29	

5. New York adopts three-color traffic lights (→ 29).

9. Rome tells Moscow it violated peace treaty by vetoing Italy's admission to U.N.

10. N.J.: Third air crash in two months kills 42 (→ 11/15).

10. Iran: 50 killed in tribal clash.

13. Rocky Marciano KOs Lee Savold for 39th straight victory.

14. Oslo: Andrea Mead Lawrence wins giant slalom for U.S. as Olympics open (→ 20).

15. Tehran: Premier's aide Hossein Fatemi shot by Moslem youth (→ 7/17).

16. FBI seizes ten members of KKK in North Carolina (→ 17).

16. Iraq: Univ. of Chicago archeologists unearth 4,000-year-old temple for Inanna.

16. Cairo: Jordan signs Arab collective security pact (→ 8/6).

18. Goodyear becomes first rubber company to exceed $1 billion annual sales.

20. Oslo: Andrea Lawrence becomes first American to win twice in Winter Olympics.

20. Lisbon: NATO begins ninth session, stressing desire to deter aggression (→ 23).

21. London: Elizabeth Taylor weds British actor Michael Wilding.

22. U.S. signs military aid pact with Peru (→ 26).

23. Lisbon: NATO agrees to raise 50-division army in Western Europe by year end (→ 3/12).

24. Vietnam: French evacuate Hoabinh to mass for Tonkin Delta drive (→ 9/12).

26. U.S. signs military aid pact with Ecuador (→ 3/7).

27. N.Y.: U.N. committees hold first meetings in new headquarters (→ 4/4).

DEATHS

3. Harold Ickes, sec. of interior under FDR (*3/15/1874).

4. Karen Horney, American psychoanalyst (*9/16/1885).

19. Knut Hamsen, Norwegian writer, 1929 Nobel Prize (*8/4/1859).

King is dead. Long live the Queen

Feb 15. George VI, a man who never aspired to be King, was buried today among his ancestors in St. George's Chapel at Windsor Castle. His widow Elizabeth, who is now the Queen Mother, and his daughter Elizabeth II, who is England's new Queen, paid their final respects with other monarchs, presidents and dignitaries from the world over.

George became king in 1936, after his brother Edward VIII abdicated to marry "the woman I love," Wallis Simpson. George's reign was not an easy time for England, but he and his wife inspired their subjects through the dark years of the war with Hitler. They stayed in London while the city was bombed and were frequently seen contributing to the war effort.

George's elder child, Elizabeth II, will rule England in his place. The queen, who is 25, interrupted a trip to Africa when word reached her of the unexpected death of her father. Elizabeth flew back to London with her consort, the Duke of Edinburgh. The couple has two children, Charles and Anne.

In mourning: Queen Elizabeth II, Queen Mother Elizabeth and George's mother, Queen Mary.

Thousands gather in London to mourn the death of their beloved King.

Elizabeth becomes Queen on Kenya safari

Feb 8. Elizabeth of England left her country a Princess and returned a Queen. Word reached her at the Treetops Hotel, built in the branches of a giant fig tree in a Kenya game park, that her father, King George VI, had died. She returned, and today Elizabeth II took the oath of accession to the British throne and was proclaimed head of the British Commonwealth.

The 25-year-old queen is now head of her family, taking precedence over her mother, the Queen Mother Elizabeth, and her grandmother, the Queen Mary. Her son Prince Charles becomes heir apparent to the throne.

Elizabeth is expected to be queen in every sense of the word, and those who know her scoff at the idea that her consort, Philip, a Prince of Greece and Denmark, will have much influence on her judgment.

She impressed many during the war, when she was a junior subaltern (second lieutenant) in the women's services and worked as an auto mechanic. Now she holds the scepter, as Victoria, Elizabeth I and Anne did before her, and pledges to follow her father's "shining example" (→ 6/2/53).

Queen Elizabeth II.

Negro singers ban is finally ended

Feb 17. Dorothy Maynor, noted Negro soprano who sang at President Truman's inauguration, sang in Constitution Hall, Washington, D.C., today, making her the first Negro artist to perform commercially in the D.A.R. auditorium since before 1939. Fittingly, she opened her concert with Wolfgang Amadeus Mozart's aria extolling brotherhood and understanding.

The ban against commercial performances by Negro artists came about in 1939 after the D.A.R. refused permission to another Negro singer, Marian Anderson, saying the hall schedule was filled up. Since then, Negro artists have only performed at the hall at benefits. In 1947, the D.A.R. board voted to continue the "white only" clause in the contract form, in spite of claims that the board tried "very hard" to change the situation (→ 3/3).

Britain has Bomb and atomic plant

Feb 26. Britain has developed an atomic bomb and has a plant capable of producing more such weapons, Prime Minister Winston Churchill told Parliament today.

The British bomb will be tested this year in Australia, Churchill said. He added that the bomb had been developed by the Labor government of Clement Attlee, which had kept it a secret from him until he was re-elected prime minister. He accused the Labor government of practicing "Machiavellian art" by developing the bomb while denouncing atomic weapons. Churchill said he recently informed the American government of the existence of the British bomb and that "a new atmosphere was created on this subject." Churchill cited a statement by Senator McMahon of Connecticut that the development of the atomic bomb by Great Britain would contribute to the maintenance of world peace (→ 4/1).

Have you noticed Don't Walk signs?

Feb 29. New York City put up its first four "Don't Walk" signs in Times Square today, and a spot check showed that eight of every ten pedestrians obeyed them. The four signs were installed at 44th St. and Broadway and went into operation at 3 p.m. Each one displays "Walk" for 22 seconds, then flashes "Don't Walk" for ten seconds before showing a red "Don't Walk" for 58 seconds. The city also will install three-color traffic lights, with amber signals between the green and red, to help reduce accidents.

Bogart and Hepburn battle the elements, the Germans and each other in "The African Queen."

1952

MARCH

Su	Mo	Tu	We	Th	Fr	Sa
						1
2	3	4	5	6	7	8
9	10	11	12	13	14	15
16	17	18	19	20	21	22
23	24	25	26	27	28	29
30	31					

1. Cairo: Naguib forms Cabinet after resignation of Aly Maher Pasha (→ 7/23).

3. U.S. Supreme Court upholds New York's Feinberg Law banning Communist teachers (→ 20).

4. North Korea accuses U.N. forces of using germ warfare (→ 5/8).

7. U.S. signs military aid pact with Cuba (→ 15).

11. Ike defeats Taft, Kefauver beats Truman in New Hampshire primary (→ 29).

11. Famed A.S.W. Rosenbach Shakespeare collection sold to Swiss collector for over $1 mil.

12. London: Gen. Lord Ismay named secretary general of NATO (→ 5/30).

15. Rio de Janeiro: U.S. and Brazil sign military aid pact (→ 4/4).

16. New York: Toscanini sets advance sale box office record for infirmary benefit at $64,000.

17. N.Y.: Mrs. Vincent Astor, Mrs. Ogden Reid, Mrs. Sheldon Whitehouse are first female trustees of Met. Museum of Art.

19. Philippines: Erupting volcano thrusts crater 250 feet above water near Luzon.

20. Sen. William Benton likens McCarthy to Hitler (→ 26).

20. Trieste: Italians and Yugoslavs clash on border (→ 25).

21. Morocco: Sultan Sidi Mohammed requests revision of French protectorate (→ 30).

24. Seattle: James Leedom dies from infected blood given him in Defense Dept. experiments.

25. U.S., Britain, France reject Soviet proposal for armed, reunified, neutral Germany (→ 5/11).

25. Rome: Police crush student rioters demanding return of Trieste to Italy (→ 10/8/53).

26. McCarthy sues Sen. Benton for libel, conspiracy (→ 9/19).

26. France orders martial law in Tunisia, seizes premier (→ 12/6).

29. Washington: Truman pulls out of presidential race (→ 4/11).

30. Tangier: Moroccans riot against French; four killed, 60 injured (→ 4/7).

Tornadoes hit five states

Judsonia, Arkansas, in ruins.

March 22. A series of tornadoes swept down like a bomber squadron and left 200 people dead and over 2,500 injured in five Mississippi Valley states. Entire towns have been blown down and refugees clog roads leading to hospitals, armories and schools that have been turned into temporary shelters. Hail, torrential rains and severe flooding have aggravated conditions in Missouri, Tennessee, Arkansas, Alabama and Mississippi.

Thousands of Red Cross volunteers have brought food and clothing into the area, while others have begun digging out the trapped. President Truman sent agents to determine the extent of the damage and the government has declared the region a disaster area. Omer Henley of England, Arkansas, said the tornadoes sounded like "a hundred B-36's flying low" and some stranded families were reported to be using their homes for kindling to keep warm.

108 are killed in Brazil train wreck

March 4. Tragedy struck Brazil today. Passengers clinging to the outside of a grossly overcrowded train were hurled as if from a centrifuge in a horrendous train wreck that killed 108 people and left about 200 injured. The accident occurred when the engineer of a decrepit wooden freight train applied the brakes on a bridge over the Pavuna River, sending two railroad cars skidding onto nearby parallel tracks. An electric passenger train traveling at high speed from the capital then barreled into the freight train, tossing cars up against each other in a mangled wreck.

While the Brazilian government has recently been debating expenditures for new railroad equipment, fatalities have become almost a daily occurrence on the antiquated and severely overburdened system. Just last week, another freight train was wrecked in virtually the same spot. Today's accident was partly blamed on poorly maintained rails in the area.

Ambulances, rescue teams and hospital personnel were dispatched from three separate locations to aid victims of the accident and the government has sent a special train to recover the bodies and transport them to the capital.

Court allows curbs on Negro golfers

March 3. At the Miami Springs Country Club, Negroes are allowed to play golf on Monday, but every other day of the week only whites can tee off. Joseph Rice sued the city, which owns the club, for unrestricted use of the course, contending he was denied equal protection of the law. The Florida Supreme Court ruled in favor of the city and the U.S. Supreme Court refused to hear an appeal because the decision is "based upon a non-federal ground." Justices Black and Douglas voted to hear the case (→ 6/1).

Gene Kelly bounces and bounds his way through the title number in "Singin' in the Rain."

General Batista seizes power in Cuba

"Batista is the man" for Cuba.

March 10. General Fulgencio Batista, the strong man of Cuba from 1933 to 1944, regained power today in a lightning coup d'etat that ousted the government of President Carlos Prio Socarras. The coup, similar to the one that first brought him into power in 1933, began shortly before dawn when Batista followers seized control of Camp Columbia, the main army base.

Within a few hours, and with little gunfire, they had taken over police headquarters and communications. Batista, who gave himself the title of Chief of the Revolution, accused the Prio Soccaras regime of planning to create chaos through "gangster" actions so it could establish a dictatorship and cancel presidential elections set for June 1. Batista was a candidate in a three-way race in the presidential elections, and observers thought it likely he would lose. Batista suspended constitutional liberties and canceled the elections (→ 7/26/53).

Bey of Tunis gives in to French force

March 30. France, fulminating for three months over nationalist rebellion and violence in its Tunisian colony, has forcefully stomped the seeds of revolution. The French military seized the Bey of Tunis, Mohammed el Amin Pasha, and imposed martial law to show its seriousness about smashing the nationalists' push for home rule reforms.

Much to the disappointment of his followers, the 70-year-old bey has disavowed his nationalist advisers and asked for the rebels to work with France for the future of Tunisia. From his captors' quarters, he called for an end to the "dangerous paths that have gone so far as to commit actions which made their own brothers the chief victims" (→ 12/6).

It's High Noon for Cooper and Kelly

Kelly and Cooper at far right.

Gary Cooper in an Oscar-caliber performance stars in "High Noon." Cooper plays a sheriff yearning to retire, thwarted by the arrival of a gunslinger. Grace Kelly is Cooper's faithful gal. Fred Zinnemann's apt direction and composer Dimitri Tiomkin's wistful harmonica score set the clock ticking.

Malan ignores court in handling Coloreds

March 20. Premier Daniel Malan has defied the South African Supreme Court ruling that declared invalid a law placing Colored voters on separate electoral rolls. The premier called the court's decision intolerable and asked Parliament to assert its sovereignty by supporting the racial segregation legislation.

The law, called the Separate Representation of Voters Act, requires Coloreds to vote on a different register than whites for special representatives in Parliament. Four Coloreds challenged the constitutionality of the law, on grounds that it passed only by simple majority rather than a two-thirds majority which is normally required. The court unanimously ruled the law invalid.

Immediately after the court reached its decision, the irate Malan entered a packed and tense House of Assembly to call for rejection of the judgment. A majority of Parliament members agreed with Malan, but opposition party members are asking for Malan's resignation and are attempting to bring down the government (→ 11/8).

Opposition party members call for the fall of the Malan government.

Mechanical heart first used in human

March 8. A mechanical heart was used for the first time in a human patient today, officials of Pennsylvania Hospital in Philadelphia announced. They said the device was successful although the patient, Peter During, a 41-year-old steel worker from Bethlehem, Pennsylvania, died of causes unrelated to use of the mechanical heart.

The device was used during an operation to correct a condition that was blocking the flow of blood from During's heart. It sustained the patient for 80 minutes while surgeons probed to find whether a tumor or a clot was causing the obstruction. Nine doctors, five nurses and two technicians from three hospitals participated in the operation.

The mechnical heart used today is an improved version of the pump developed in 1932 by Dr. Michael de Bakey. Its function is to replace the left ventricle, the chamber of the heart that pumps oxygen-rich blood to the body. In today's operation, use of the device allowed surgeons to keep the heart free of blood while they investigated the cause of During's problem. Successful use of the mechanical heart is regarded as a step toward the long-term goal of a total artificial heart. Several research teams are working to develop such a device (→ 12/27/82).

Jackson Pollock's new ventures have earned the name "action painting."

1952

APRIL

Su	Mo	Tu	We	Th	Fr	Sa
		1	2	3	4	5
6	7	8	9	10	11	12
13	14	15	16	17	18	19
20	21	22	23	24	25	26
29	28	29	30			

1. Nevada: AEC starts third series of A-bomb tests (→ 22).

2. George Kennan named U.S. ambassador to Soviet Union (→ 10/3).

3. Dutch Queen Juliana tells Congress U.S. can give up sovereignty for world cooperation.

4. U.S. signs military aid pact with Chile (→ 17).

4. N.Y.: U.N. Security Council holds first meeting in East River headquarters (→ 10/14).

7. Spain asks control of intl. police in Tangier zone (→ 12/8).

8. Truman orders seizure of steel mills to avert strike (→ 19).

11. Puerto Rico: N.Y.-bound DC-4 crashes, killing 52.

11. La Paz: Natl. Revolutionary Party overthrows Bolivian military govt. after three-day battle.

13. FCC lifts three-year ban on new TV stations (→ 12/18/53).

15. Art world celebrates 500th birthday of Leonardo da Vinci.

16. Chicago: Sugar Ray KOs Rocky Graziano in third round to retain middleweight title.

17. U.S. signs military aid pact with Colombia.

18. L.A.: 29 killed when C-46 airliner crashes into hill.

19. Ohio Congressman George Bender asks Truman impeachment for steel seizure (→ 30).

21. Miss.: 200 police put down Jackson State Prison uprising after 20 hours of rioting.

22. One mil. see Nevada A-bomb blast on TV, twice as powerful as wartime bombs (→ 6/14).

23. Bonn: Franco-German talks on Saar break down (→ 11/30).

26. India says U.N. may disintegrate if powers block consideration of issues in small countries.

27. Azores: 176 lost as destroyer Hobson collides with aircraft carrier Wasp.

29. Germany: Air France plane attacked by Soviet MIG-15 en route from Frankfurt to Berlin.

DEATH

1. Ferenc Molnar, Hungarian playwright (*1/12/1878).

Truman signs the Japanese peace treaty

In the White House, Truman displays the treaty with Japan.

April 15. President Truman signed the Japanese peace treaty today granting Japan full sovereignty and officially ending World War II in the Pacific region. Forty-nine nations joined the United States in recognizing Japanese sovereignty—although the Soviet Union has not. The treaty, ratified unceremoniously, will restore Japan "to a position of independence, honor and equality in the world community," as stated by Truman.

The president also signed security treaties with Australia, New Zealand and Japan and a mutual defense treaty with the Philippines. The alliances will formally bind the United States and these nations militarily and economically (→ 9/17).

Picasso, super-distorter, likes Red realism

April 24. Pablo Picasso assured Communists tonight of his faith in "Socialist realism." A statement of his principles, addressed to the Secretary General of the French Communist Party, was co-signed by a few left-wing artists. The letter is a response to accusations by Communist plastic artists and critics who charged Picasso and the others with deviating from Socialist principles in their work.

Picasso, still creative in his seventies, cavorts with his young son Claude.

Steel mills seized, but strike goes on

April 30. More than 600,000 steel workers stayed off the job tonight, despite a court ruling restoring the mills to government possession. The steel mills had been seized earlier by President Truman, citing a national emergency, but Judge David Pine termed the seizure unconstitutional. A higher court has temporarily halted Judge Pine's ruling, thus placing the mills once again in goverment possession.

The walkout of union workers has slashed normal steel production from 300,000 tons a day to less than 20,000 tons, threatening defense and civilian production. The Wage Stabilization Board has proposed wage increases, but mill owners have resisted (→ 5/23).

Ike leaving NATO, presumably to run

April 11. Apparently intent on running for president, General Dwight D. Eisenhower has requested that he be returned to inactive military status on June 1. In a letter to President Truman, the general said that his work as Supreme Commander of Allied Powers in Europe had largely been accomplished.

The move would give Eisenhower time in which to present his views before the Republicans meet July 7 to choose a presidential candidate.

N.Y. Governor Dewey hailed the move, while Ohio Senator Robert Taft, who is seeking the nomination, had no comment (→ 7/12).

1952

MAY

Su	Mo	Tu	We	Th	Fr	Sa
				1	2	3
4	5	6	7	8	9	10
11	12	13	14	15	16	17
18	19	20	21	22	23	24
25	26	27	28	29	30	31

1. TWA begins first "tourist class" service, landing 95 passengers in Shannon, Ireland.

1. Tibet: Panchen lama, 15, takes office with backing from China.

2. British Overseas Airways begins first commercial jet service.

3. Eddie Arcaro takes unprecedented fifth Kentucky Derby, in the saddle of Hill Gail.

5. Herman Wouk wins Pulitzer Prize for "The Caine Mutiny."

6. Cairo: King Farouk proclaims himself direct descendant of prophet Mohammed (→ 7/23).

9. Korea: Communist prisoners on Koje Island seize U.S. camp commander Gen. Dodd (→ 6/3).

11. Essen: One killed as police fight mob of 30,000 demonstrating against Bonn pact (→ 17).

12. Washington receives its first female ambassador, India's Shrimati Vijaya Lakshmi Pandit.

13. U.N. announces huge plague of desert locusts in Mideast.

17. Bonn: Social Democrats reject plan to establish new W. German status in Europe (→ 26).

18. Chicago: Prof. W.F. Libby places age of Stonehenge at 1848 BC through charcoal analysis.

21. Tiel: Dutch Queen Juliana opens largest inland navigation lock at North Sea and Rhine.

23. Truman orders railroads handed back to owners after 21 months of army control (→ 6/2).

26. Bonn pact gives W. Germany equal status in Europe (→ 6/1).

27. U.S., U.K., France, Belgium, Italy, Holland, Luxembourg, W. Germany form European Defense Community (→ 2/25/53).

29. Greece grants vote to women.

30. Troy Ruttman wins Indy 500 in Agajanian Special at 129 mph.

30. Rocquencourt, France: Ike hands over NATO command to Gen. Ridgway (→ 4/25/53).

31. Vatican bans Andre Gide.

DEATHS

6. Maria Montessori, Italian education pioneer (*8/31/1870).

8. William Fox, American film producer (*1/1/1879).

Allies make biggest air strike in Korea

May 8. Allied fighter-bombers staged the largest air strike of the Korean War, pummeling the ancient city of Suan in North Korea from dawn to dusk with napalm, bombs and machine gun fire. The massive bombing attack seemed to have the dual purpose of wiping out a Communist supply center as well as to apply pressure on the Communists to reach an armistice.

The attack came less than a day after General Matthew B. Ridgway, Supreme Commander of United Nations forces in Korea, had served a take-it-or-leave-it notice on the Communists with a final armistice proposal. The raid thus served to underscore growing Allied impatience with Communist delaying tactics at the armistice talks in Panmunjom. The bombing could also impair the Communists' ability to resume large-scale fighting.

Suan, hit by 12,000 gal. of napalm.

In the past month, Air Force reconnaissance planes were reported to have observed a large buildup of military supplies at Suan, located 35 miles southeast of the North Korean capital of Pyongyang (→ 6/23).

Montessori, apostle of self-discovery, dead

May 6. Creator of the Montessori Method Dr. Maria Montessori has died in the Netherlands. She was 81. Dr. Montessori was Italy's first woman physician. She gave brain-damaged children "active" tasks, developing motor movement. In 1907, she applied her ideas to all children, opening a school in Rome. After decades of neglect, the Montesssori Method is having a renaissance. Preschools worldwide are emphasizing early reading and writing skills and self-discovery.

Superliner United States makes trial run

May 14. The superliner United States made its first trial run at sea today, as observers said she had a good chance of giving America the Atlantic speed record for the first time this century. The 990-foot-long liner will conclude its speed tests tomorrow and will go into service later this year. Its top speed is a secret, but it would have to average 32 knots to beat the record set by the Queen Mary, which made the Atlantic run in three days and 20 hours in 1938 (→ 7/7).

The United States is towed by tugs into its harbor at Newport, Rhode Island.

Von Braun suggests excursion to Mars

May 15. Wernher von Braun, the German rocket scientist who is now living in the United States, has never been content to dream about earthly matters. His mind has often wandered in the stars. Today, he suggested that it is time to really start wandering in space. Von Braun says the scientific community should start building a space vehicle that could transport pilots through the solar system to Mars.

The idea may seem preposterous, since the most far-sighted of American scientists are only starting to dream about putting men on the moon. But few space experts are scoffing at von Braun's idea. His dreams have a disturbing tendency to become realities.

Von Braun first started dreaming about space flight when he was 18. He joined the German Society for Space Travel more than 20 years ago and shared his fantasies with more seasoned scientists. He also started to help develop liquid-fueled rocket motors. Von Braun continued to work on the motors at the University of Berlin and at the top secret rocket center at Peenemunde, where he built the V-2 rockets that terrorized London. Since 1950, von Braun has been in charge of the U.S. Army's ballistic weapons program in Alabama.

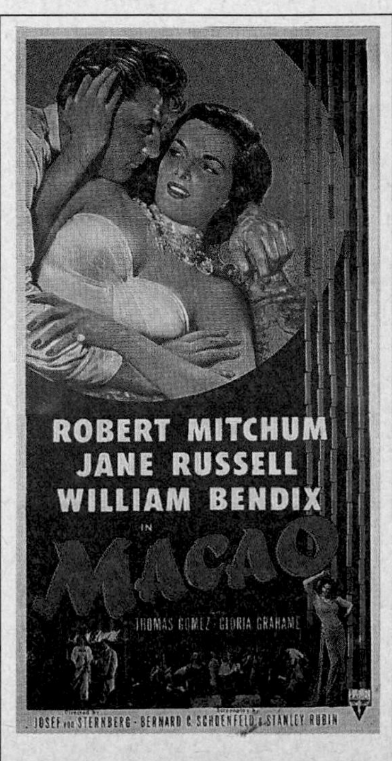

1952

JUNE

Su	Mo	Tu	We	Th	Fr	Sa
1	2	3	4	5	6	7
8	9	10	11	12	13	14
15	16	17	18	19	20	21
22	23	24	25	26	27	28
29	30					

1. Groton, exclusive boys prep school, admits first Negro (→ 9/3).

1. American Leon Fleisher wins Queen Elizabeth international music competition.

1. East Germany technically closes doors to outsiders (→ 3).

2. Bucharest: Natl. Assembly proclaims Gheorghe Gheorghiu new Rumanian premier.

3. West Berlin: British occupy Soviet radio station (→ 4).

3. Korea: Tank-led U.S. troops storm Koje POW camps, remove Communist leaders (→ 10).

4. Berlin: U.S. military policeman shot by Eastern guard on border (→ 5).

4. Britain joins U.S. in protest over Rhee's purge in South Korean Assembly.

5. Jersey Joe Walcott outpoints Ezzard Charles in 15 rounds to hold heavyweight title.

5. East Germany asks $14 mil. from U.S. for use of telephone cable from Berlin to West (→ 22).

14. Soviets name Andrei Gromyko ambassador to Britain.

15. "Anne Frank: Diary of a Young Girl" published in U.S.

16. Swedish air force plane shot down by Soviet jets over intl. waters in Baltic.

17. N.Y.: John D. Rockefeller gives Cloisters $10 mil. gift.

20. Truman signs $6.5 bil. Mutual Security Bill.

20. N.Y.: "The Winning Team" opens, with Ronald Reagan.

22. Russian and East German troops seize 40 W. German workers in disputed territory on German frontier (→ 7/2).

23. Korea: Over 500 U.N. planes smash five of North's largest hydroelectric plants (→ 8/29).

25. Olympia, Greece: Olympic torch lit in Temple of Zeus (→ 7/19).

27. U.S. Congress passes McCarran-Walter immigration quota bill over Truman veto.

DEATH

13. Emma Eames, U.S. operatic soprano (*8/13/1865).

Court rules steel seizure unconstitutional

June 2. The Supreme Court has ruled that President Truman's seizure of the steel mills earlier this year violated the Constitution by usurping powers of Congress. The president promptly ordered release of the mills to their owners, a move that prompted thousands of steel workers to walk off the job.

In the 6-to-3 ruling, the high court held that only Congress can authorize the taking of private property for public use. The president, the court maintained, "must confine himself to sending a message to Congress recommending action."

But in a dissenting opinion, Chief Justice Fred M. Vinson held that the president's move to keep the steel flowing had been warranted by a world emergency. This is no time, he said, for "timorous executive action" or for relegating the office of the president into little more than "a messenger-boy" role.

It is uncertain what the next move by the president will be. He could invoke the Taft-Hartley Act, which would require union men to return to work for 80 days while a fact-finding board investigates the wage dispute.

U.S. dedicates world's first atomic sub

June 14. President Truman dedicated the world's first atomic submarine today, calling it "the forerunner of atomic-powered merchant ships and airplanes" of the future. The sub, the Nautilus, was dedicated at the Navy submarine base at Groton, Conn. Its propulsion unit is being built at the Argonne National Laboratory near Chicago. When the vessel is completed, it will have the capability to stay submerged for almost unlimited periods and will cruise for prolonged periods at 25 to 30 knots without the need to refuel.

Truman said that successful development of compact reactors to power nuclear subs "will have as revolutionary an effect on the navies of the world as did the first ocean steamship." Development of such a reactor is well underway, under direction of Hyman Rickover of the Navy's Bureau of Ships. Completion of the Nautilus is not due until 1954, but the Navy has requested construction of another atomic sub. A dry-land reactor to produce electric power is planned (→ 9/30).

Paratroopers seize rebel Korea POWs

June 10. In a bloody battle on Koje Island, Korea, American paratroopers smashed a tough Communist prison, killing 30 of the enemy and wounding another 85. Within an hour and a half, 6,000 U.S. troops with flame-throwers and tanks ripped through Compound 76, which holds the most captives on the prison island.

Led by General Haydon Boatner, American troops scored a grand strategic and morale-building victory as they avenged an incident that occurred a month ago. Then, U.S. General Francis Dodd was held by Communists for 78 hours.

Reports indicate that prison leaders began killing captives who intended to obey Allied orders, and then many of them committed suicide. Over 6,800 prisoners were seized by U.S. troops (→ 12/14).

TV necklines rise as Congress looks

June 3. A subcommittee of the House of Representatives investigating ethics in TV fare notes that women's necklines are, unlike some Senate dealings, on the up and up. Rising necklines is the sole improvement the industry has made, following a moral code it adopted March 1. Committee members today outlined TV's moral faults.

They deplored the proliferation of violent crime shows and omnipresent beer and wine ads. However, Representative E.C. Gathings of Arkansas praised the "better apparel decorum." He said the blond star of "Broadway Open House," Dagmar, "is a most comely young lady, and I notice her apparel is a little different." When asked to be more specific, he said, "I think the waistline is a little higher." He meant to say neckline.

Famous educator John Dewey is dead

Dewey at Columbia in 1929.

June 1. Philosopher, educator and politician John Dewey died tonight of pneumonia. He was 92. Dewey believed in "learning by doing." He lived up to it. He revolutionized school systems in Chicago and New York, helped found the New School for Social Research and assisted the Civil Liberties Union.

Dewey was born to a well-established Vermont family. He studied at the University of Vermont and Johns Hopkins, followed up by teaching at the University of Michigan and other prestigious schools. In 1899, he published "The School and Society," a treatise calling for practical education. He returned from investigations in China, Japan and Russia with further appreciation for labor-related studies. His "Experience and Nature" (1925) explains his philosophy of Pragmatism.

1952

JULY

Su	Mo	Tu	We	Th	Fr	Sa
		1	2	3	4	5
6	7	8	9	10	11	12
13	14	15	16	17	18	19
20	21	22	23	24	25	26
29	28	29	30	31		

2. Palmdale, California: Starfire F-94C, new supersonic jet, makes first successful test flight.

2. Berlin: Three U.S. priests seized on crossing border into Eastern zone (→ 8/30).

4. Wimbledon: Frank Sedgman over Jaroslav Drobny 4-6, 6-2, 6-3, 6-2; Maureen Connolly over Althea Brough 7-5, 6-3.

6. Hollywood: First TV actor-producer contract signed by Screen Guild.

15. U.S. bars Soviet periodical "Amerika", and U.S.S.R. information bulletins.

17. Helsinki: Nationalist China pulls out of Olympics to protest plan to admit Peking (→ 10/25).

17. Tehran: Ahmad Ghavam replaces Mossadegh as Iranian premier (→ 22).

18. Truman places 4.5 mil. more on Social Security roles.

18. "Don't Bother to Knock," with Marilyn Monroe, opens.

19. Helsinki: Soviet flag raised at Olympics for first time on opening day (→ 27).

19. Italian racer Fausto Coppi wins Tour de France.

21. California has its second greatest earthquake, rocking 100,000 sq. miles, killing 11.

22. Tehran: Plagued by five days of riots, shah returns Mossadegh to premiership (→ 2/8/53).

23. Cairo: Naguib seizes army, appoints new premier (→ 26).

24. U.S. Steel strike ended with pay raise; 600,000 back to work after 53 days (→ 10/20).

24. U.S.: Gary Cooper appears in debut of "High Noon."

25. Puerto Rico gets self-rule, becoming first U.S. Commonwealth.

27. Helsinki: Emil Zatopek breaks marathon record to win third Olympic gold.→

30. Maryland: $45 mil. Chesapeake Bay Bridge, third longest in world, opened to traffic.

31. Scotland: Two U.S. Air Force Sikorsky H-19's end first helicopter flight over Atlantic.

31. MacArthur becomes chm. of board of Remington Rand Corp.

It's Ike and Dick for the Republicans

Ike, campaigning with Nixon (far left), gives his trademark two-arm salute.

July 12. Dwight D. Eisenhower won the Republican nomination for president on the first ballot yesterday, piling up 845 votes to outstrip his chief opponent, Senator Robert A. Taft of Ohio, the son of former President William Howard Taft. As vice-presidential running mate to the popular General, Republicans gave the nod to Richard Milhous Nixon, a 39-year-old Senator from California, who first won national attention as a member of the House Un-American Activities Committee inquiry into alleged Communist ties of Alger Hiss.

Last night, in a speech accepting the party's nomination in Chicago, General Eisenhower promised that he would wage "a great crusade" to "total victory" over a Democratic Party that, he said, has been wasteful, arrogant, corrupt and too long in power (→ 26).

Democrats choose hesitant Stevenson

Democratic hopeful Stevenson.

July 26. A reluctant Governor Adlai E. Stevenson of Illinois was nominated today for president, quoting from the Bible as he told his fellow Democrats: "If this cup may not pass away from Me, except I drink it, Thy will be done."

Stevenson's nomination came on the third ballot, after the withdrawal of Averell Harriman of New York and Senator Estes Kefauver of Tennessee. President Truman flew to Chicago to salute the party's nominee and predicted a Stevenson victory in November (→ 10/13).

Army coup takes over Egypt; Farouk out

July 26. Egypt has a new King today, and he is only seven months old. Crown Prince Ahmed Fuad was elevated to the throne after military officers overthrew his father, Farouk II. It was a bloodless coup. Strong man Mohammed Naguib Bey, who proclaimed himself Commander-in-Chief of the army, ordered Farouk to leave the country, but the two men shook hands as Farouk abdicated. Farouk is bound for Italy but hopes to settle eventually in the United States. Farouk, an internationally known playboy, left Egypt in the style to which he is accustomed, sailing on a magnificent yacht that had been outfitted from palace coffers.

A flamboyant Farouk bounces baby King on his knee with wife at left.

Naguib vows to root out corruption in Egypt, and large crowds cheered as his officers surrounded the royal palace in Cairo and the summer residence in Alexandria. Six palace aides have been forced to resign after they were accused of lining their pockets at government expense. A new Prime Minister, Aly Maher Pasha, has been installed by the military. He joined Naguib in appealing for calm on national radio. The new government is the sixth to lead Egypt in the past six months (→ 9/7).

G.M. offering cars with air cooling

July 14. General Motors has perfected an air conditioning unit for automobiles and will offer it as an added option on some of its 1953 models, C.E. Wilson, the company's President, announced today.

The unit, which works on the same principles as air conditioners in offices and railroad trains, was developed in several years of research. Tests in Arizona and Texas have shown that the unit can reduce the heat of a car that has been standing in the summer sun to comfortable levels in minutes.

Development of an automobile air conditioner was a challenging problem because it had to be small enough to fit in cars and yet achieve quick cooling, Wilson noted. The G.M. system has a sealed refrigeration unit that uses non-toxic Freon as the cooling liquid mounted under the hood of the car.

Eva Peron dies at 33; Argentina mourns

In Buenos Aires, Eva addresses workers, the Perons' main source of support.

July 26. "Our spiritual leader is gone!" Those words, broadcast at 9:42 tonight, told Argentinians that Eva Peron, their little Evita, was dead. The President's wife succumbed to ovarian cancer at age 33.

While the "descamisados," the "shirtless" poor of Argentina, prepare for a month of mourning, a few members of the middle class and opposition prepare to breathe a sigh of relief. Eva Peron was a charismatic woman, certainly more popular than her husband, Juan Peron. She was also on occasion ruthless.

Evita was born Maria Eva Ibaguren at Los Toldos. She was the illegitimate daughter of a cook. When Colonel Peron met her she was a budding 15-year-old singer and actress. He made her his mistress, not an unusual thing for the Secretary of Labor to do.

What was unusual is that he married her. In October 1945, Peron was arrested on a treason charge. Eva took to the airwaves, beseeching the masses to rally and free him. Panicky higher-ups let him go, and in thanks Peron wed Evita in December. When he became president a year later, she was by his side.

The descamisados could make a lengthy list of Evita's good deeds. She championed women, labor and the poor. She got women the vote and legalized divorce. Some of her unscrupulous acts were just petty; she kept a tremendous fur collection and practiced a little nepotism, getting her widowed sister a rather cozy job as Inspector of Schools.

But when someone disparaged Evita, punishment was swift. One comedienne impersonated Evita in her nightclub act. The performer knew the chief of police well, so she feared no reprisals. That night the police chief disappeared. The comedienne quickly left town.

As years passed, "disappearances" and cases of torture increased. Evita unofficially ran the Ministries of Health and Labor, putting her finger in every possible pie. In the summer of 1951, she "ran" for vice president. The army objected; she renounced her intentions on August 22. Evita's first defeat was her last. A nervous breakdown and physical collapse followed. She will be buried in an immaculate white dress (→ 4/15/53).

"Don't cry for me, Argentina."

The Blue Riband to The United States

July 7. The superliner United States has won the trophy coveted by all great shipowners. The Blue Riband goes to the U.S. for the first time in 68 yrs., rewarding a crossing time of three days, ten hours, 40 minutes.

Year	Ship name	Country	Propeller	Tonnage	Average speed in knots E-W	W-E
1875	CITY OF BERLIN	GBR	1	5 491	15,2	15,37
1876	GERMANIC	GBR	1	5 008	15,48	15,82
	BRITANNIC	GBR	1	5 004		15,93
1877	BRITANNIC	GBR	1	5 004	15,54	
1879	ARIZONA	GBR	1	5 147		15,95
1881	SERVIA	GBR	1	7 391	15,98	
1882	ALASKA	GBR	1	6 400		16,04
1884	OREGON	GBR	1	7 375	18,16	
	AMERIKA	USA	1	5 528		17,82
	OREGON	GBR	1	7 375		18,18
1885	ETRURIA	GBR	1	8 127	18,84	19,41
1887	UMBRIA	GBR	1	7 700	18,91	
1888	ETRURIA	GBR	1	8 127	19,57	
1889	CITY OF PARIS II	GBR	2	10 669		19,49
1891	TEUTONIC	GBR	2	9 686	20,46	
1892	CITY OF PARIS II	GBR	2	10 669	20,7	
	CITY OF NEW YORK	GBR	2	10 449		20,1
1893	CAMPANIA	GBR	2	12 950		21,33
1894	LUCANIA	GBR	2	12 952	21,82	22,01
1897	KAISER WILHELM D. GR.	GER	2	14 349		22,35
1898	KAISER WILHELM D. GR.	GER	2	14 349	22,65	
1900	DEUTSCHLAND	GER	2	16 502	23,15	23,36
1906	KAISER WILHELM II	GER	2	19 361		23,58
1907	MAURETANIA	GBR	2	31 938		23,69
	LUSITANIA	GBR	2	31 938		24,51
1908	MAURETANIA	GBR	2	31 938		24,51
1909	LUSITANIA	GBR	2	31 550	25,85	
	MAURETANIA	GBR	2	31 938	26,06	
1910	LUSITANIA	GBR	2	31 550		25,57
1911	MAURETANIA	GBR	2	31 938		25,89
1924	MAURETANIA	GBR	2	31 938		26,25
1929	BREMEN	GER	4	51 656	27,83	27,92
1930	EUROPA	GER	4	49 746	27,91	
1933	BREMEN	GER	4	51 656	28,51	
	REX	ITA	4	51 062	28,92	
1935	NORMANDIE	FRA	4	79 280	29,98	30,35
1936	QUEEN MARY	GBR	4	81 235	30,14	30,67
1937	NORMANDIE	FRA	4	83 423	30,58	31,2
1938	QUEEN MARY	GBR	4	81 235	30,99	31,69
1952	UNITED STATES	USA	4	53 329	35,95	35,59

1952 Helsinki

Aug 3. The Olympic torch lit by Finland's Paavo Nurmi has flickered; the Helsinki Games are over. After a 12-year absence, the Soviet Union's impressive team entered the Games, yet lost to the United States, 553.5 points to 614. Not merely a superpower face-off, athletes from other nations seized the spotlight and the spoils.

Emil Zatopek, a 29-year-old Czech, triumphed in the 5,000-and 10,000-meter races, always running with his face contorted. Onlookers thought he was in pain, but he only suffered from tedium. When he finished the marathon (in first place) he called it boring. He never entered a marathon before.

Zatopek's wife, Dana Ingrova Zatopek, won the javelin event, tossing the spear a distance of 165 feet, 7.05 inches, 15 feet farther than the previous Olympic record.

French swimmer Jean Boiteux entered the 400-meter freestyle event. The instant he finished in 4:30.7, his beret-topped father plunged into the pool, fully dressed, to give him a congratulatory kiss.

California-born Bob Mathias says he is going to retire now at the ripe old age of 21. He won the decathlon in 1948 and repeated the feat this year. His amazing point total of 7,887 set a world record.

Men Athletics

100 M Dash		
1. Lindy Remigino	USA	10,4
2. Herbert McKensy	JAM	10,4
3. Emmanuel McDonald Bailey	GBR	10,4

200 M Dash		
1. Andrew Stanfield	USA	20,7
2. W. Thane Baker	USA	20,8
3. James Gathers	USA	20,8

400 M Run		
1. Georges Rhoden	JAM	45,9
2. Herbert McKensy	JAM	45,9
3. Ollie Matson	USA	46,8

800 M Run		
1. Malvin Whitfield	USA	1:49,2
2. Arthur Wint	JAM	!:49,4
3. Heinz Ulzheimer	FRG	1:49,7

1500 M Run		
1. Josef Barthel	LUX	3:45,1
2. Robert McMillen	USA	3:45,2
3. Werner Lueg	FRG	3:45,4

5000 M Run		
1. Emil Zatopek	TCH	14:06,6
2. Alain Mimoun	FRA	14:07,4
3. Herbert Schade	FRG	14:08,6

10,000 M Run		
1. Emil Zatopek	TCH	29:17,0
2. Alain Mimoun	FRA	29:32,8
3. Alzksandr Anufriyev	URS	29:48,2

Marathon		
1. Emil Zatopek	TCH	2:23:03,2
2. Reinaldo Gorno	ARG	2:25:35,0
3. Gustaf Jansson	SWE	2:26:07,0

110 M Hurtles		
1. Harrison Dillard	USA	13,7
2. Jack Davis	USA	13,7
3. Arthur Barnard	USA	14,1

400 M Hurtles		
1. Charles Moore	USA	50,8
2. Yury Lituyev	URS	51,3
3. John Holland	NZL	52,2

3000 M Steeplechase		
1. Horace Ashendfelter	USA	8:45,4
2. Vladimir Kazantsev	URS	8:51,6
3. John Disley	GRB	8:51,8

400 M Relay		
1. USA	40,1	(Dean Smith, Harrison Dillard, Lindy Remigino, Andrew Stanfield)
2. URS	40,3	(Boris Tokaryev, Levan Kalyayev, Levan Sanadze, Vladimir Sukharyev)
3. HUN	40,5	(Laszlo Zarandi, Géza Varasdi, Gyōrgy Csanyi, Béla Goldovanyi)

Zatopek enters the stadium to deafening roars on the last leg of the marathon.

1600 M Relay		
1. JAM	3:03,9	(Arthur Wint, Leslie Laing, Herbert McKenley, Georges Rhoden)
2. USA	3:04,0	(Ollie Matson, Gerald Cole Charles Moore, Malvin Whitfield)
3. FRG	3:06,6	(Hans Geister, Gunter Steines, Heinz Ulzheimer, Karl-Friedrich Haas)

50 km Walk		
1. Giuseppe Dordoni	ITA	4:28:07,8
2. Josef Dolezal	TCH	4:30,17,8
3. Antal Roka	HUN	4:31:27,2

10 km Walk (1924, 1948, 1952 only)		
1. John Mikaelsson	SWE	45:02,8
2. Fritz Schwab	SUI	45:41,0
3. Bruno Yunk	URS	45:41,0

High Jump		
1. Walter Davis	USA	2,04
2. Kenneth Wiesner	USA	2,01
3. José Telles da Conceicao	BRA	1,98

Pole Vault		
1. Robert Richards	USA	4,55
2. Donald Laź	USA	4,50
3. Ragnar Lundberg	SWE	4,40

Long Jump		
1. Jèrome Biffle	USA	7,57
2. Meredith Gourdine	USA	7,53
3. Odōn Foldessy	HUN	7,30

Triple Jump		
1. Adhemar Ferreria Da Silva	BRA	16,22
2. Leonid Schtscherbakov	URS	15,98
3. Amoldo Devonish	VEN	15,52

Shotput		
1. Parry O'Brien	USA	17,41
2. Darrow Hooper	USA	17,39
3. James Fuchs	USA	17,06

Discus Throw		
1. Sim Iness	USA	55,03
2. Adolfo Consolini	ITA	53,78
3. James Dillion	USA	53,28

Hammer Throw		
1. Jozsef Csernak	HUN	60,34
2. Karl Storch	FRG	58,86
3. Imre Németh	HUN	57,74

Javelin		
1. Cyrus Young	USA	73,78
2. William Miller	USA	72,46
3. Toivo Hyytignen	FIN	71,89

Decathlon		
1. Robert Mathias	USA	7887
2. Milton Campbell	USA	6975
3. Floyd Simmons	USA	6788

At the opening ceremony, great Finnish runner Paavo Nurmi lights the Olympic flame.

After French swimmer Boiteux bested the field in the 400-meter freestyle, his elated father joined him in the pool for a celebration. He was not caught repeating the performance when his son helped the French team to a bronze medal in the 4 x 200-meter freestyle.

Christian d'Oriola (left), in battle against Italy's Spallino, won the men's individual foil tournament and went on to lead France to victory in the team competition.

Women Athletics

100 M Dash		
1. Marjorie Jackson	AUS	11,5
2. Daphné Hsasenjager-Robb	SAF	11,8
3. S. de la Hunty Strickland	AUS	11,9

200 M Dash		
1. Marjorie Jackson	AUS	23,7
2. Bertha Brouwer	HOL	24,2
3. Nadyeschda Khnykyna	URS	24,2

80 M Hurtles		
1. S. d la Hunty-Strickland	AUS	10,9
2. Maria Golubnitschaya	URS	11,1
3. Maria Sander	FRG	11,1

400 M Relay		
1. USA	45,9	(Mae Faggs, Barbara Jones, Janet Moreau, Catherine Hardy)
2. FRG	45,9	(Ursula Knab, Maria Sander, Helga Klein, Marga Petersen)
3. GBR	46,2	(Sylvia Cheeseman, June Foulds, Jean Desforges, Heather Armitage)

High Jump		
1. Esther Brand	SAF	1,67
2. Sheila Lerwill	GBR	1,65
3. Aleksandra Ischudina	URS	1,63

Long Jump		
1. Yvette Williams	NZL	6,24
2. Aleksandra Tschudina	URS	6,14
3. Shirley Cawley	GBR	5,92

Shotput		
1. Galina Zybina	URS	15,28
2. Marianne Werner	FRG	14,57
3. Klavdiva Totschenova	URS	14,50

Discus Throw		
1. Nina Romaschkova	URS	51,42
2. Yelisaveta Bagryantseva	URS	47,08
3. Nina Dumbadze	URS	46,29

Javelin		
1. Dana Zatopkova	TCH	50,47
2. Aleksandra Tschudina	URS	50,01
3. Yelena Gortschakova	URS	49,76

Men Swimming

100 M Freestyle		
1. Clarke Scholes	USA	57,4
2. Hiroshi Suzuki	JAP	57,4
3. Goran Larson	SWE	58,2

400 M Freestyle		
1. Jean Boiteux	FRA	4:30,7
2. Ford Konno	USA	4:31,3
3. Per-Olof Ostrand	SWE	4:35,2

1500 M Freestyle		
1. Ford Konno	USA	18:30,3
2. Shiro Hashizume	JAP	18:41,4
3. Tetsuo Okamoto	SWE	18:51,3

100 M Backstroke		
1. Yoshinobu Oysakawa	USA	1:05,4
2. Gilbert Bozon	FRA	1:06,2
3. Jack Taylor	USA	1:06,4

200 M Breastroke		
1. John Davies	AUS	2:34,4
2. Bowen Stassforth	USA	2:34,7
3. Herbert Klein	FRG	2:35,9

800 M Freestyle Relay		
1. USA	8:31,1	(Wayne Moore, William Woolsey, Ford Konno, James McLane)
2. JAP	8:33,5	(Hiroshi Suzuki, Yoshihiro Hamaguchi, Toru Goto, Teijiro Tanikawa)
3. FRA	8:45,9	(Joseph Bernardo, Aldo Eminente, Alexandre Jany, Jean Boiteux)

Springboard Diving		
1. David Browning	USA	205,29
2. Miller Anderson	USA	199,84
3. Robert Clotworthy	USA	184,92

High Diving		
1. Dr Samuel Lee	USA	156,28
2. Joaquim Capilla Perez	MEX	145,21
3. Gūnther Haase	FRG	141,31

Water-Polo
1. Hungary
2. Yugoslavia
3. Italy

The long stride of Jamaica's Arthur Wint brought him victory in the 400- and 800-meters.

Women Swimming

100 M Freestyle		
1. Katalin Szōke	HUN	1:06,8
2. Johanna Termeulen	HOL	1:07,0
3. Judit Temes	HUN	1:07,1

400 M Freestyle		
1. Valéria Gyenge	HUN	5:12,1
2. Eva Novak	HUN	2:54,4
3. Evelyne Kawamoto	USA	5:14,6

200 M Breastroke		
1. Eva Szekely	HUN	2:51,7
2. Eva Novak	HUN	5:54,4
3. Elen Gordon	GBR	2:57,6

100 M Backstroke		
1. Joan Harrison	SAF	1:14,3
2. Geertje Wielema	HOL	1:14,5
3. Jean Stewaet	NZL	1:15,8

400 M Freestyle Relay		
1. HUN	4:24,4	(Ilona, Novak, Judit Temes, Eva Novak, Katalin Szōke)
2. HOL	4:29,0	(Marie-Louise Linssen-Vaessen, Koosje van Voorn, Johanna Termeulen, Irma Heijing-Schuhmacher)
3. USA	4:30,1	(Jacqueline La Vine, Marilee Stepan, Joan Alderson, Evely Kawamoto)

1952 Helsinki

CHART

Weightlifting

			2 Arm Press	2 Arm Snatch	2 Arm Clean & Jerk	Total
	Bantamweight					
1.	Ivan Udodov	URS	90,0	97,5	127,5	315,0
2.	Mahmoud Namdjou	IRA	90,0	95,0	122,5	307,5
3.	Ali Mirzai	IRA	95,0	92,5	112,5	300,0
	Featherweight					
1.	Rafael Tschimischkyan	URS	97,5	105,0	135,0	337,5
2.	Nikolay Saksonov	URS	95,0	105,0	132,5	332,5
3.	Rodney Wilkes	TRI	100,0	100,0	122,5	322,5
	Lightweight					
1.	Thomas Kono	USA	105,0	117,5	140,0	362,5
2.	Yevgeny Lopatin	URS	100,0	107,5	142,5	350,0
3.	Verne Barberis	AUS	105,0	105,0	140,0	350,0
	Middleweight					
1.	Peter George	USA	115,0	127,5	157,5	400,0
2.	Gérard Gratton	CAN	112,5	112,5	155,0	390,0
3.	Sung-Jip Kim	KOR	122,5	112,5	147,5	382,5
	Light Heavyweight					
1.	Trofim Lomakin	URS	125,0	127,5	165,0	417,5
2.	Stanley Stanczyk	USA	127,5	127,5	160,0	415,0
3.	Arkady Vorobyov	URS	120,0	127,5	160,0	407,5
	Middle Heavyweight					
1.	Norbert Schemansky	USA	127,5	140,0	177,5	445,0
2.	Grigory Novak	URS	140,0	125,0	145,0	410,0
3.	Lennox Kilgour	TRI	125,0	120,0	157,5	402,5
	Heavyweight					
1.	John Davis	USA	150,0	145,0	165,0	460,0
2.	James Bradford	USA	140,0	132,5	165,0	437,5
3.	Humberto Selvetti	ARG	150,0	120,0	162,5	432,5

Springboard Diving
1. Patricia McCormick USA 147,30
2. Mady Moreau FRA 139,34
3. Zoe-Ann Jensen-Olsen USA 127,57

High Diving
1. Patricia McCormick USA 79,37
2. Paula Jean Myers USA 71,63
3. Juno Irwin-Stover USA 70,49

Boxing

Flyweight
1. Nathan Brooks USA
2. Edgar Basel FRG
3. Anatoly Bulakov URS
3. William Toweel SAF

Bantamweight
1. Pentti Hämäläinen FIN
2. John McNally IRL
3. Gennady Garbuzov URS
3. Joon-Ho Kang KOR

Featherweight
1. Jan Zachara TCH
2. Sergio Caprari ITA
3. Joseph Ventaja FRA
3. Leonard Leisching SAF

Lightweight
1. Auréliano Bolognesi ITA
2. Aleksy Ankiewiez POL
3. Erkki Pakkanen FIN
3. Gheorghe Fiat ROM

Light Welterweight
1. Charles Adkins USA
2. Viktor Mednov URS
3. Erkki Mallenius FIN
3. Bruno Visintin ITA

Welterweight
1. Zygmunt Chychla POL
2. Sergey Schtscherbakov URS
3. Victor Jörgensen DEN
3. Günther Heidemann FRG

Light Middleweight
1. Laszlo Papp HUN
2. Theunis van Schalkwyk SAF
3. Eladio Herrera ARG

Middleweight
1. Floyd Patterson USA
2. Vasile Tita ROM
3. Stig Sjölin SWE
3. Boris Nikolov BUL

Light Heavyweight
1. Norvel Lee USA
2. Antonio Pacenza ARG
3. Anatoly Perov URS
3. Harri Siljander FIN

Heavyweight
1. Hayes Edward Sanders USA
2. No Silver Medal awarded
3. Andries Nieman SAF
3. Ilkka Koski FIN

Ingemar Johansson (Sweden) was disqualified for "passivity" during the 2nd Round and therefore did not win the Silver Medal.

Greco Roman Wrestling

Flyweight
1. Boris Gurevitsch URS
2. Ignazio Fabra ITA
3. Leo Honkala FIN

Bantamweight
1. Imre Hodos HUN
2. Zakaria Chihab LIB
3. Artem Teryam URS

Featherweight
1. Yakov Punkin URS
2. Imre Polyak HUN
3. Abdel Rashed EGY

Lightweight
1. Schazam Safin URS
2. Gustaf Freij SWE
3. Mikulas Athanasov TCH

Welterweight
1. Miklos Szilvasi HUN
2. Gösta Andersson SWE
3. Khalil Taha LIB

Middleweight
1. Axel Grönberg SWE
2. Kalervo Rauhala NOR
3. Nikolay Byelov URS

Light Heavyweight
1. Kaelpo Gröndahl FIN
2. Schalva Tschikhladze URS
3. Karl-Erik Nilsson SWE

Heavyweight
1. Johannes Kotkas URS
2. Josef Ruzicka TCH
3. Tauno Kovanen FIN

Freestyle Wrestling

Flyweight
1. Hasan Gemici TUR
2. Yushu Kitano JAP
3. Mahmoud Mollaghassemi IRA

Bantamweight
1. Shohachi Ishii JAP
2. Raschid Mamedbekov URS
3. Kha-Shaba Jadav IND

Featherweight
1. Bayram Sit TUR
2. Nasser Guivehtchi IRA
3. Josiah Henson USA

Lightweight
1. Olle Anderberg SWE
2. Jaoy Thomas Evans USA
3. Djahanbakte Tovfighe IRA

Welterweight
1. William Smith USA
2. Per Berlin SWE
3. Abdullah Modjtabavi IRA

Middleweight
1. David Tsimakuridze URS
2. Gholam Reza Takhti IRA
3. György Gurics HUN

Light Heavyweight
1. Wiking Palm SWE
2. Henry Wittenberg USA
3. Adil Atan TUR

Heavyweight
1. Arsen Mekokischvili URS
2. Bertil Antonsson SWE
3. Kenneth Richmond GBR

Men Fencing

Foil Individual
1. Christian d'Oriola FRA
2. Edouardo Mangiarotti ITA
3. Manlio Di Rosa ITA

Foil Team
1. France
2. Italy
3. Hungary

Epée Individual
1. Edouardo Mangiarotti ITA
2. Dario Mangiarotti ITA
3. Oswald Zappelli SUI

Epée Team
1. Italy
2. Sweden
3. Switzerland

Sabre Individual
1. Pal Kovacs HUN
2. Aladar Gerevich HUN
3. Tibor Berczelly HUN

Sabre Team
1. Hungary
2. Italy
3. France

Women Fencing

Foil Individual
1. Irène Camber ITA
2. Ilona Elek HUN
3. Karen Lachmann DEN

Modern Pentathlon

Modern Pentathlon Individual
1. Lars SWE
2. Gabor Benedek HUN
3. Istvan Szondy HUN

Modern Pentathlon Team

1. Hungary
2. Sweden
3. Finland

Men Canoeing

Kayak-1 1000 M
1. Gert Fredriksson SWE 4:07,9
2. Thorvald Strömberg FIN 4:09,7
3. Louis Gautois FRA 4:20,1

Kayak-2 1000 M
1. Finland 3:51,1
2. Sweden 3:51,1
3. Austria 3:51,4

Kayak-1 10,000 M (1936, 1948, 1952, 1956)
1. Thorvald Stromberg FIN 47,22,8
2. Gert Fredriksson SWE 47,34,1
3. Michel Scheuer FRG 4:54,5

Kayak-2 10,000 M (1936, 1948, 1952, 1956)
1. Finland 44:21,3
2. Sweden 44:21,7
3. Hungary 44:26,6

Canadian-1 1000 M
1. Josef Holecek TCH 4:56,3
2. Janos Parti HUN 5:03,6
3. Olavi Ojanperä FIN 5:08,5

Canadian-2 1000 M
1. Denmark 4:38,3
2. Czechoslovakia 4:42,9
3. German Federal Republic 4:48,3

Canadian-1 10,000 M (1948, 1952, 1956)
1. Franck Havens USA 57,41,1
2. Gabor Novak HUN 57:49,2
3. Alfred Jindra TCH 57:53,1

Canadian-2 10,000 M (1936, 1948)
1. France 54:08,3
2. Canada (1952, 1956) 54:09,9
3. German Federal Republic 54:28,1

Women Canoeing

Kayak-1 500 M
1. Sylvi Saimo FIN 2:18,4
2. Gertrude Liebhart AUT 2:18,8
3. Nina Savina URS 2:21,6

Rowing

Single Scull
1. Yury Tyukalov URS 8:12,8
2. Mervyn Wood AUS 8:14,5
3. Teodor Kocerka POL 8:19,4

Double Sculls
1. Argentina 7:32,2
2. Soviet Union 7:38,3
3. Uruguay 7:43,7

Pair Oars without Coxswain
1. USA 8:20,7
2. Belgium 8:23,5
3. Switzerland 8:32,7

Pair Oars with Coxswain
1. France 8:28,6
2. German Federal Republic 8:32,1
3. Denmark 8:34,9

Four Oars without Coxswain
1. Yugoslavia 7:16,0
2. France 7:18,9
3. Finland 7:23,3

Four Oars with Coxswain
1. Czechoslovakia 7:33,4
2. Switzerland 7:36,5
3. USA 7:37,0

Eight Oars
1. USA 6:25,9
2. Soviet Union 6:31,2
3. Australia 6:33,1

Yachting

Individual Monotype "Racer"
1. Paul Elvström DEN 8209
2. Charles Currey GBR 5449
3. Richard Sarby SWE 5051

"Star" Class
1. Italy 7635
2. USA 7216
3. Portugal 4903

"Dragon Class"
1. Norway 6130
2. Sweden 5556
3. German Federal Republic 5352

5.5 M Class (1956, 1960, 1964, 1968)
1. USA 5751
2. Norway 5325
3. Sweden 4554

6 M Class (1908, 1912, 1920, 1924, 1928, 1932, 1936, 1948, 1952)
1. USA 4870
2. Norway 4648
3. Finland 3944

Cycling

Individual Road Race
1. André Noyelle BEL 5:06:03,4
2. Robert Grondeaers BEL 5:06:51,2
3. Edi Ziegler FRG 5:07,47,5

Team Road Race
1. Belgium 15:20:46,6
2. Italy 15:33:27,3
3. France 15:38:58,1

1000 M Time Trial
1. Russel Mockridge AUS 1:11,1
2. Marino Morettini ITA 1:12,7
3. Raymond Robinson SAF 1:13,0

1000 M Sprint
1. Enzo Sacchi ITA 12,0
2. Lionel Cox AUS
3. Werner Potemheim FRG

Tandem 2000 M
1. Australia 11,0
2. South Africa
3. Italy

Team Pursuit (4000 M)
1. Italy 4:46,1
2. South Africa 4:53,6
3. Great Britain 4:51,5

Equestrian Sports

Individual All around Competition
1. Hans von Blixen-Finecke SWE −28,33
2. Guy Lefrant FRA −54,50
3. Wilhem Büsing FRG −55,50

All around Team Competition
1. Sweden −221,94
2. German Federal Republic −235,49
3. USA −587,16

Dressage Individual
1. Henry Saint-Cyr SWE 561,0
2. Lis Hartel DEN 541,5
3. André Jousseaume FRA 541,0

Dressage Team
1. Sweden 1597,5
2. Switzerland 1579,0
3. German Federal Republic 1501,0

Grand Prix Jumping Individual
1. Pierre Jonquères d'Oriola FRA −8/0
2. Oscar Cristi CHI −8/4
3. Fritz Thiedemann FRG 8/8/38,5

Grand Prix Jumping Team
1. Great Britain −40,75
2. Chili −45,75
3. USA −52,25

Shooting

Full Bore Rifle, 300 M, 3 positions — Total
1. Anatoly Bogdanov URS 1123
2. Robert Burchler SUI 1120
3. Lev Vainschtein URS 1109

Small Bore Rifle, 50 M, Prone
1. Iosif Sirbu ROM 400/33
2. Boris Andreyev URS 400/28
3. Arthur Jackson USA 399/28

Small Bore Rifle, Combined, 3 Positions
1. Erling Kongshaug NOR 1164
2. Vilho Ylönen FIN 1164
3. Boris Andreyev URS 1163

Rapid Fire Pistol
1. Karoly Takacas HUN 579
2. Szilard Kun HUN 578
3. Gheorghe Lichiardopol HUN 578

Free Pistol, 50 M
1. Huelet Benner USA 553
2. Angel Léon de Gozalo ESP 550
3. Ambrus Balogh HUN 549

Clay Pigeon Individual
1. George Patrick Genereux CAN 192
2. Knut Holmqvist SWE 191
3. Hans Likijedahl SWE 190

Running Deer Shooting, Single and Double Shot
1. John Larsen NOR 413
2. Per Olof Sköldberg SWE 409
3. Tauno Maki FIN 407

Men Gymnastics

Individual All around Competition
1. Viktor Tschukarin URS 115,70
2. Grant Schaginyan URS 114,95
3. Josef Stalder SUI 114,75

FOR ABBREVIATIONS SEE TABLE OF CONTENTS

All around Team Competition
1. Soviet Union 574,40
2. Switzerland 567,50
3. Finland 564,20

Parallel Bars
1. Hans Eugster SUI 19,65
2. Viktor Tschukarin URS 19,60
3. Josef Stalder SUI 19,50

Floor Exercise
1. William Thoresson SWE 19,25
2. Tadao Uesako JAP 19,15
3. Jerzy Jokiel POL 19,15

Horse Vault
1. Viktor Tschukarin URS 19,20
2. Masao Takemoto JAP 19,15
3. Takashi Ono JAP 19,10
3. Tadao Uesako JAP 19,10

Sidehorse
1. Viktor Tschukarin URS 19,50
2. Yevgeny Korolkov URS 19,40
3. Grant Schaginyan URS 19,40

Horizontal Bar
1. Jack Günthard SUI 19,55
2. Josef Stalder SUI 19,50
3. Alfred Schwarzmann FRG 19,50

Flying Rings
1. Grant Schaginyan URS 19,75
2. Viktor Tschukarin URS 19,55
3. Hans Eugster SUI 19,40
3. Dmitry Leonkin URS 19,40

Women Gymnastics

Individual All around Competition
1. Maria Gorokhosvkaya URS 76,78
2. Nina Botscharova URS 75,94
3. Margit Korondi HUN 75,82

All Around Team Competition
1. Soviet Union 527,03
2. Hungary 520,96
3. Czechoslvakia 503,32

Uneven Parallel Bars
1. Margit Korondi HUN 19,40
2. Maria Gorokhovskaya URS 19,26
3. Agnès Keleti HUN 19,16

Floor Exercise
1. Agnès Keleti HUN 19,36
2. Maria Gorokhovskaya URS 19,20
3. Margit Korondi HUN 19,00

Horse Vault
1. Yekaterina Kalintschuk URS 19,20
2. Maria Gorokhovskaya URS 19,19
3. Galina Minaitscheva URS 19,16

Beam
1. Nina Botscharova URS 19,22
2. Maria Gorokhovskaya URS 19,13
3. Margit Koroni HUN 19,02

Team Exercise with Portable Apparatus (1952 and 1956 only)
1. Sweden 74,20
2. Soviet Union 73,00
3. Hungary 71,60

Basketball

1. USA
2. Soviet Union
3. Uruguay

Soccer

1. Hungary
2. Yugoslavia
3. Sweden

Handball

Demonstration

Field Hockey

1. India
2. Netherlands
3. Great Britain

The Olympic flag circles the track at the closing ceremonies.

1952

AUGUST

Su	Mo	Tu	We	Th	Fr	Sa
					1	2
3	4	5	6	7	8	9
10	11	12	13	14	15	16
17	18	19	20	21	22	23
24	25	26	27	28	29	30
31						

1. Maine, Massachusetts, South Carolina added to disaster list in drought.

3. Saskatchewan: Hundreds begin first claim-staking rush in new uranium find.

4. Honolulu: Sec. of State Acheson opens security talks with Australia, New Zealand, hails Japanese treaty as step to peace.

4. Texas: Worst U.S. bus crash takes 28 lives in Waco.

5. Algiers: Algerian Defense Front formed (→ 11/1/54).

6. Arab League denounces Israeli attempts to restore relations with Germany (→ 10/14/53).

8. Tehran: Iran demands huge indemnity from Anglo-Iranian Oil Co. (→ 30).

9. New Delhi reports 20 million Indian peasants imperiled by crop failures.

14. Budapest: Matyas Rakosi takes Hungarian premiership (→ 7/4/53).

15. N.J.: A.F.L. opens drive to bar gangsters from union rolls.

16. Washington: Truman receives Faisal II, 17-year-old king of Iraq.

17. Moscow: Chinese Premier Chou En-lai received at Kremlin (→ 9/7).

19. N.Y.: U.N. drafts convention on women's rights.

22. N.Y.: James Cagney appears in "What Price Glory."

22. Bernard Malamud's "The Natural" published in U.S.

25. New York: Ike tells Am. Legion U.S. should help nations escape "Red yoke."

25. Virgil Trucks of Detroit Tigers becomes third to toss two no-hitters in one season.

28. Dick Button, twice Olympic figure skating champ, joins Ice Capades in $150,000 deal.

29. Korea: Allied planes blast Pyongyang in heaviest attack of war (→ 10/24).

30. Tehran: Mossadegh rejects U.S.-U.K. proposal for settlement of oil dispute (→ 10/22).

30. West Berlin reports taking in 16,000 refugees from East in August (→ 6/21/53).

Hussein succeeds unstable father as King

Aug 11. Crown Prince Hussein, going on 17, was today named by Jordan's Parliament to succeed his mentally ill father, King Talial. The king's removal followed medical reports that the 41-year-old monarch, who has been treated in Swiss clinics, stood little chance for recovery.

Jordan's action comes a little more than two weeks after another Arab leader, Egypt's King Farouk, was ousted by army leaders in a clean-up of government corruption.

The new King, Hussein I, is a student at the Harrow School in England. Fond of horseback riding and driving his own car, he speaks English fluently and hopes to enter England's prestigious Sandhurst Military College upon graduation from Harrow.

Hussein, Jordan's teenage King.

Fuller designs extraordinary new dome

Aug 30. American inventor Buckminster Fuller's latest project, a Geodesic Dome House that combines light weight and strength, went on display today at the Museum of Modern Art in New York.

It consists of a framework of aluminum tubes covered by a lightweight, weatherproof plastic skin, with living areas suspended by cables from the framework. The model at the museum represents an 80-foot dome, but Fuller says domes spanning 800 feet can easily be built.

Fuller says that the triangular arrangement of the pipes that make up the framework provide unprecedented strength and lightness. While the dome of St. Peter's in Rome spans 138 feet and weighs 10,000 tons, an 800-foot-diameter geodesic dome weighs only 1,000. Such a dome can be erected anywhere and can be disassembled and reused at another location in a matter of days, Fuller says. It could also be produced at extremely low prices once factories tool up for mass production. A 49-foot geodesic dome was recently built near Montreal with only 45 man-hours of labor. The complete framework could fit in a steamer trunk and the workmen used only hand tools.

Fuller speaks amid his latest design solutions to problems of modern living.

British fly Atlantic and back in 8 hours

The Canberra long-range bomber.

Aug 26. A British Canberra twin-jet bomber made the first transatlantic round trip in a single day when it flew from Northern Ireland to Gander, Newfoundland, and back in seven hours, 59 minutes.

The plane also set an unofficial record for the fastest eastward Atlantic crossing when it completed its return journey in three hours, 25 minutes. The Canberra averaged 531 miles an hour for the round trip and 606 miles an hour for the eastward leg of the flight. The plane, with a three-man crew, took off from Aldergrove in Northern Ireland at 6:35 a.m., landed at Gander at 11:09 a.m. local time and was back at its home base at 4:35 p.m.

The flight was arranged by the plane's manufacturer to demonstrate the Canberra's abilities as a long-range bomber. The aircraft that made today's flight is a standard model of the Canberra, which went into service 18 months ago.

Aug 14. British For. Sec. Anthony Eden, expected successor to Churchill as Conservative chief, has married into the family. His bride, 23 years his junior, is the Prime Minister's niece Clarissa.

1952

SEPTEMBER

Su	Mo	Tu	We	Th	Fr	Sa
	1	2	3	4	5	6
7	8	9	10	11	12	13
14	15	16	17	18	19	20
21	22	23	24	25	26	27
28	29	30				

3. Little Rock, Ark.: Ike warns white Southerners they could lose their rights by not protecting rights of Negroes (→ 11/10).

4. India returns Peking's famine-relief aid, saying it had political strings attached.

6. London: Supersonic fighter plane DH-110 explodes at air show, killing pilot, 25 spectators.

7. Peking reports 40% of farm workers have been organized into cooperatives (→ 9/27/54).

7. N.Y.: Frank Sedgman and Maureen Connolly win U.S. tennis titles at Forest Hills.

10. Strasbourg: Six nations hold first meeting of European Coal and Steel Community (→ 3/25/57).

11. Georgetown University's Charles Hufnagel implants first artificial heart valve.

12. N.Y.: Soviets veto French proposal to admit Bao Dai's Vietnam to U.N. (→ 10/5).

16. Soviets gain accord with Peking to maintain control over Port Arthur in Korea.

17. N.Y.: Soviet delegate Malik vows not to admit Japan until American occupation ends.

18. N.Y.: Gregory Peck appears in "The Snows of Kilimanjaro."

18. Greenland: Danes and U.S. disclose building of huge air base at Thule, 930 miles from N. Pole.

19. Washington withholds visa for Charlie Chaplin pending disloyalty inquiry (→ 10/12).

20. Alfred Hershey and Martha Chase publish report confirming that DNA holds hereditary data.

24. French sub La Sybille vanishes in Mediterranean with 48 aboard.

25. Council of Europe approves Strasbourg Plan to develop European colonies as bloc against Soviet influence in Third World.

30. U.S. Army releases details on 85-ton atomic cannon (→ 10/3).

30. N.Y.: Cinerama, new film projection system with wide-angle screen, displayed to public.

BIRTH

2. James Scott Connors, U.S. tennis star.

Nixon's TV speech defends $18,000 fund

Ike commented on his running mate's performance: "Nixon was magnificent."

Sept 24. "I am not a quitter," declared Senator Richard Nixon in a television address last night in which he defended the existence of an $18,000 political fund and vowed to stay on the Republican ticket.

Recently, allegations circulated claiming the vice-presidential nominee may have misused political contributions from wealthy California businessmen. Nixon asserts the money was used for his traveling expenses, the printing of speeches, long distance telephone calls and other purposes that "permit me to carry on my fight against communism and corruption above and beyond my official duties in Washington D.C."

Dwight Eisenhower has assured supporters of his presidential campaign that he accepted Nixon's explanations and trusted the independent reviews of the fund. The Republican Party has also voiced its support for Nixon. Ike told a crowd in West Virginia, "(Nixon) is not only completely vindicated as a man of honor but, as far as I am concerned, he stands higher than ever before."

In his speech, Nixon also said that his wife, Pat, doesn't own a mink coat, "but she does have a respectable Republican cloth coat." And one gift that the senator said he would never return was "a little cocker spaniel dog" which his six-year-old daughter Tricia named "Checkers" (→ 12/10/54).

Bonn signs: Israel to get $822 million

Sept 10. Silently facing each other across a broad table, representatives of the German and Israeli governments today signed an agreement providing close to a billion dollars in reparations for Nazi crimes against the Jewish people.

The bulk of the money will go to Israel to cover the cost of absorbing Jews displaced by the war, while the rest will be distributed to other displaced Jews around the world. An agent of the Israeli government said the agreement "had moral significance for the world as a precedent for voluntary reparation." During the war, six millions Jews were killed in Nazi concentration camps.

Sept 23. Rocky Marciano ended 38-year-old Joe Walcott's reign as heavyweight champ with a paralyzing right in the 13th. Swarming fans then put Marciano in more danger than Walcott had.

Naguib assumes all power in Egypt

Sept 7. Following mass arrests of persons associated with former King Farouk's regime, General Mohammed Naguib has taken control of the Egyptian government, ending Aly Maher's brief premiership.

Naguib's newly formed civilian Cabinet is the first in Egyptian history to include a member of the Moslem Brotherhood, the uncompromising organization sworn to the advancement of Islamic principles in public and private life.

The impatient Naguib felt that Maher was taking too long to implement land reform and other far-reaching measures (→ 10/6).

"Give me 6 months to rebuild Egypt."

Santayana has died

Sept 26. George Santayana, the influential philosopher, poet and literary critic who cherished solitude and isolated himself from the social turmoil of the 20th Century, has died in a convent in Italy at 88.

Born and raised in Spain until he was eight, young Santayana came of age in Boston, graduating from Harvard, where he earned a Ph.D. and taught philosophy until 1912.

Santayana was no system builder; his view of life as an "endless flux" and his felicity of literary expression guided him to a more eclectic approach. From his sonnets (1883-1904) through "The Sense of Beauty" (1896), "Interpretations of Poetry and Religion" (1900), "The Life of Reason" (1905-06), and "Skepticism and Animal Faith" (1923) to the culminating four-volume "The Realms of Being" (1927-40), Santayana devoted himself to understanding history. "Those who cannot remember the past," he said, "are condemned to repeat it."

1952

OCTOBER

Su	Mo	Tu	We	Th	Fr	Sa
			1	2	3	4
5	6	7	8	9	10	11
12	13	14	15	16	17	18
19	20	21	22	23	24	25
26	27	28	29	30	31	

3. Britain holds first A-bomb tests off coast of Australia (→ 11/16).

5. Moscow: 19th Communist Party Congress opens (→ 16).

6. Cairo: Wafd Party ousts chief Mustafa Nahas (→ 12/10).

7. Ebbets Field: Yankees take third Series in row, beating Dodgers 4-2 in final game.

11. Ike asks repudiation of Yalta pact so U.S. can help Poland free itself of Soviet domination.

12. Chicago: 34 leading scientists attack U.S. anti-Communist visa policy as peril to science (→ 13).

13. U.S. Supreme Court rejects appeal in Rosenberg spy case (→ 23).

13. Cincinnati: Lewis and U.M.W. endorse Adlai Stevenson for president (→ 11/5).

14. N.Y.: Canadian Lester Pearson chosen president of U.N. General Assembly.→

15. Helicopter mail and parcel post service starts in New York.

16. Moscow: 36 prominent party members elected to Presidium, new body to replace Politburo.

20. U.S.: Soft coal mines struck to protest govt. order cutting 40 cents from $1.90 pay rise (→ 27).

20. Pan Am becomes first commercial U.S. airline to buy jet passenger transports.

22. New York: Gary Cooper appears in premiere of "Springfield Rifle."

22. Iran formally breaks relations with Britain over oil dispute (→ 12/5/53).

23. Chaplin's latest film "Limelight" opens in New York.

23. New York City dismisses eight teachers for alleged Communist activities (→ 1/10/53).

25. N.Y.: U.N. General Assembly, for third year, bars Communist China (→ 1/30/53).

27. U.S.: Lewis ends soft coal strike (→ 11/1).

29. Vietnam: French begin Operation Lorraine to cut off Viet Minh food supply (→ 11/7).

31. La Paz: Bolivia nationalizes three big tin companies.

If elected, Ike says, he will go to Korea

Ike has sought MacArthur's (rt.) advice on the prospects for peace in Korea.

Oct 24. As thousands cheered, General Dwight D. Eisenhower said tonight: "I will go to Korea."

His dramatic promise to seek an end to the Korean War was viewed by many as virtually clinching his election as president two weeks from now.

Speaking before a crowd of more than 5,000 in Detroit, a stop on his whistlestop train campaign, the Republican nominee said that the American people should no longer only "wait —and wait —and wait" for peace. Only by going to Korea, he said, could he learn how best to serve the people by seeking an early and honorable end of the war.

Critical of the Truman administration, General Eisenhower said the war was never inevitable, never inescapable (→ 12/17).

French troops open drive against Reds

French paratroopers in Vietnam.

Oct 5. In their first large operation in nearly a year, French Union troops have advanced into Viet Minh territory. One armored and two mobile units pushed 22 miles north of Hanoi along Route 3, the enemy's main highway for getting supplies from Communist China, and captured 16 Viet Minh soldiers.

Despite the fact that the French met little resistance in this offensive, military authorities expect an early renewal of major fighting now that the dry season has arrived. Recent movements of Viet Minh troops indicate that General Giap's Communist army may stage a new assault in the French-held Red River delta. The French say they are ready for sharp attacks (→ 29).

British take action against Mau-Mau

Oct 20. Responding to actions of the anti-white society of Kenya, the Mau-Mau, Britain has sent 800 troops to the East African colony. The Mau-Mau, dedicated to driving the British out, have the countryside ablaze with terror and destruction; they have killed 43 people, slaughtered cattle and started dozens of fires in recent weeks.

A battlion of British Lancaster Fusiliers was flown from Middle East stations to Kenya to help enforce the London-declared imposition of martial law. The directive grants the police power to detain suspects without trial. It is believed some 130 suspected Mau-Mau instigators will be arrested immediately.

The movement has the support of over 200,000 Kikuyu tribe members. Its first goal is to oust the 3,000 Britons who monopolize most of the fertile land in the "white highlands" and then to drive out the remaining whites (→ 3/22/53).

Soviets oblige U.S. to recall its envoy

Oct 3. Charging U.S. Ambassador to Moscow George Kennan with making "slanderous attacks" on the Soviet Union in a press interview in Berlin, the Kremlin has demanded his removal. America has no alternative but to yield to the Soviet demand and recall Kennan from his post.

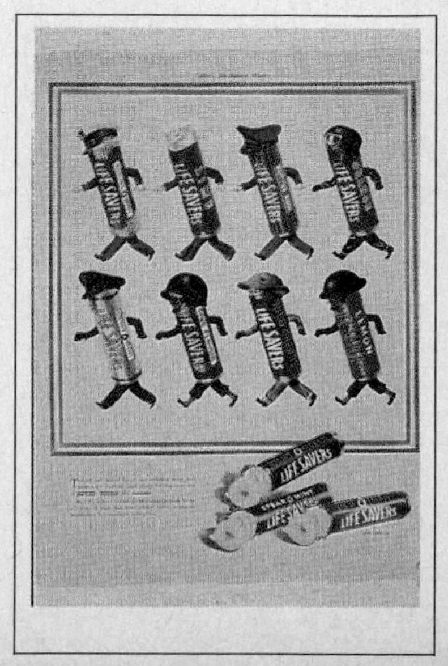

Three trains collide near London; 78 killed

Work crews try to salvage people and property from the deadly mess.

Oct 8. As commuters waited impatiently for the 8:19 train to leave Harrow for London this morning, an express train from Perth, Scotland, plowed into the back and smashed through four cars. Moments later, an express train from London hurled into the wreckage and tossed debris over six tracks. Amid the carnage, 78 were dead and more than 200 injured. Also injured were those standing on the platform, hit by flying glass, steel and pieces of wood from the trains.

Police, firefighters and hospital personnel from London and surrounding suburbs rushed to the cars which lay in a smoking pile almost 50 feet high. Blood supplies were immediatly sent to the area, and many rescue workers credit quick action by American Air Force medical personnel for saving many lives.

Both Queen Elizabeth and Prime Minister Churchill sent their condolences to families of those who died, and an immediate investigation has begun into the accident. Workmen were still cutting through the cars with torches this evening and 88 victims are on the critical list in local hospitals. One American, Donald Woodall, who was with the Air Force, was among the dead.

The worst previous rail accident in British history was the collision of two trains in Scotland in 1915 that left 227 dead.

Oct 14. The U.N. General Assembly delegates observe a minute of silence, dedicated to prayer or meditation, before opening the first session in their new home, "a workshop for peace" located in Manhattan.

1952

NOVEMBER

Su	Mo	Tu	We	Th	Fr	Sa
						1
2	3	4	5	6	7	8
9	10	11	12	13	14	15
16	17	18	19	20	21	22
23	24	25	26	27	28	29
30						

1. Washington: Soft coal owners grant $1.90 pay rise to U.M.W. (→ 25).

7. Vietnam: French Union forces cut off main Viet Minh supply route with China (→ 2/9/53).

8. South Africa: Police fire on Negro protesters in Kimberley; 14 dead, 39 hurt (→ 2/24/53).

10. U.S. Supreme Court upholds decision barring segregation on interstate railways (→ 6/2/53).

10. N.Y.: Trygve Lie resigns post as sec. gen. (→ 3/31/53).

12. Tokyo: U.S. lends Japan 68 warships to start underwriting rearmament.

13. Harvard's Paul Zoll becomes first to use electric shock to treat cardiac arrest.

15. N.J.: Newark Airport reopens after closing earlier this year due to rash of accidents.

16. Washington: AEC says H-bomb ready for use (→ 7/1/53).

18. Jerusalem: Albert Einstein tells Ben Gurion he cannot accept Israeli presidency (→ 12/8).

19. Scandinavian Airlines opens commercial route from Canada to Europe.

23. U.S. Air Force C-124 Globemaster disappears over Alaska with crew of 52.

25. Washington: George Meany replaces late William Green as A.F.L. president (→ 12/4).

29. India: First international organization for birth control founded in Bombay.

29. Philadelphia: Navy shuts out Army 7-0 in football.

30. Saar votes autonomy from Germany, alliance with France (→ 12/1).

BIRTH

5. Bill Walton, pro basketball star, MVP in 1978.

DEATHS

18. Paul Eluard, French surrealist poet (*12/14/1895).

20. Benedetto Croce, Italian socialist philosopher, historian (*2/25/1866).

21. William Green, president of A.F.L. since 1924 (*3/3/1873).

Weizmann, Israel's Washington, dead

Weizmann, Israel's founding father.

Nov 9. Israeli President Chaim Weizmann, approaching 78, died this morning in his home near Tel Aviv after a long illness. A world-famed chemist, statesman, leader of a forceful political movement, an intellectual and, above all, a great humanitarian, Dr. Weizmann was an early Zionist and the natural choice to become Israel's first president. Of humble birth in a small village near Pinsk, Russia, he lived to preside over a modern state forged by the courage of homeless, abandoned and persecuted European Jews (→ 18).

Maurras gone at 84

Nov 16. Charles Maurras, the French writer known for wielding a poison pen, died of uremia poisoning at the age of 84 today, literally with his vituperative pen in hand. A self-styled Royalist and foe of the republic who espoused "integral nationalism" and founded the Action Francaise, Maurras was a pillar of the Vichy regime. After the war, he was convicted of treason but got out of a life sentence because of illness.

The 1952 Cunningham C-3.

Eisenhower in landslide

Nov 5. Dwight D. Eisenhower was elected President of the United States, swamping his Democratic opponent, Adlai E. Stevenson, in a record turnout of voters.

The Republican landslide also swept Senator Richard M. Nixon of California into the office of Vice President as he defeated a fellow member of the Senate, Democrat John J. Sparkman of Alabama.

General Eisenhower, who until a few months ago was the Supreme Commander of Allied Forces in Europe, received word that he had won the presidential election as he mingled with Republican supporters at the Commodore Hotel in New York City.

Governor Stevenson conceded his defeat early this morning at party headquarters in Springfield, Illinois. As weeping supporters cried "No, No," the governor remarked: "My fellow citizens have made their choice and I gladly accept it." (→20).

Ike doffs his hat in victory.

Dulles and Wilson get Cabinet posts

Nov 20. President-elect Dwight D. Eisenhower has chosen three members of his Cabinet and each of the appointees promptly accepted. John Foster Dulles, a respected Republican foreign affairs expert, was designated Secretary of State. General Motors President Charles Erwin Wilson was tapped for the Secretary of Defense post. And Eisenhower selected Oregon Governor Douglas McKay to be Interior Secretary. All three of the secretaries-designate supported Ike early in the campaign (→ 1/20/53).

Dulles, a fervent anti-Communist.

John F. Kennedy wins for Senate

Nov 4. While most of the nation voted Republican in the election, one major upset occured in Massachusetts when young John F. Kennedy defeated Republican heavyweight Henry Cabot Lodge. The election stunned the Republican Party because it was the incumbent Lodge who generated the presidential nomination of Dwight Eisenhower and stirred support for the general in GOP ranks. Kennedy, 35, served three terms in the House and amassed a loyal following among Bostonians (→ 9/12/53).

"Ivanhoe," tale of fair maidens and daring knights, stars Elizabeth Taylor and Robert Taylor.

1952

DECEMBER

Su	Mo	Tu	We	Th	Fr	Sa
	1	2	3	4	5	6
7	8	9	10	11	12	13
14	15	16	17	18	19	20
21	22	23	24	25	26	27
28	29	30	31			

1. Bonn: Chancellor Adenauer refuses to recognize Saar independence vote (→ 1/1/57).

1. Mexico: Adolfo Ruiz Cordines elected president.

3. Prague: Ex-Premier Slansky and 11 others executed for treason (→ 5/16/53).

4. N.J.: Walter Reuther elected pres. of C.I.O. (→ 3/22/53).

4. N.Y.: Esther Williams opens in "Million Dollar Mermaid."

6. Tunisia: General strike called to protest murder of labor leader Farhat Hached (→ 7/1/53).

8. Casablanca: 50 die in Nationalist rioting (→ 8/21/53).

8. Jerusalem: Knesset names Itzhak Ben-Avi pres. (→ 11/5/53).

10. Cairo: Naguib cancels 1923 constitution (→ 1/16/53).

17. Yugoslavia breaks relations with Vatican.

18. Sugar Ray Robinson retires as middleweight boxing champ.

28. Cleveland: Lions take football title 17-7 over Browns.

DEATH

25. James "Dinty" Moore, U.S. restaurateur (*1879).

CULTURAL EVENTS, 1952

Literature: Ralph Ellison's "The Invisible Man"; Steinbeck's "East of Eden"; Hemingway's "The Old Man and the Sea"; Beckett's "Waiting for Godot"; Shaw's "Don Juan in Hell"; Bernard Malamud's "The Natural."

Academia: Reinhold Niebuhr's "Christ and Culture"; Norman Vincent Peale's "The Power of Positive Thinking"; Jacques Cousteau begins undersea archeology off coast of Marseilles.

Music: Bernstein's "Trouble in Tahiti"; "I Saw Mommy Kissing Santa Claus"; "It Takes Two to Tango"; "Your Cheatin' Heart."

The Arts: Jackson Pollock's "Convergence"; Jacob Epstein's "Madonna and Child."

Film: Orson Welles' "Othello"; de Mille's "The Greatest Show on Earth," Academy Award; "Moulin Rouge," with Jose Ferrer; "High Noon," with Gary Cooper and Grace Kelly.

Albert Schweitzer gets Peace Prize

Schweitzer: Scientist, humanitarian.

Dec 10. Albert Schweitzer, the Alsatian theologian and muscian who gave up a career as organist and Bach expert to establish a hospital in French Equatorial Africa, was awarded the Nobel Peace Prize today. Schweitzer was honored for setting a living example of "reverence for life," his universal concept of ethics. In addition to his theological writings, Schweitzer also is the author of a highly regarded biography of Bach and of a definitive edition of Bach's organ music. Since going to Africa in 1913, he has left only on trips to raise funds for his hospital, which is free to all who come.

Another Frenchman, Francois Mauriac, was awarded the Nobel Prize for literature in the Stockholm ceremonies. The Nobel Prize for physics was awarded to Felix Bloch and Edward Purcell of the United States, the medicine prize to Dr. Selman Waksman and the chemistry prize to Archer Martin and Richard Synge of England.

As promised, Eisenhower goes to Korea

Ike, President-elect, in Korea.

Dec 17. Amidst elaborate security precautions, President-elect Eisenhower paid a three-day visit to Korea, carrying out a promise he had made during the presidential campaign. His crowded schedule took him from the battlefields for briefings from field commanders to conferences in Seoul with diplomatic leaders and with South Korean President Syngmam Rhee.

Summarizing his conclusions before his departure, the former Army General said he had found "no panaceas, no trick solutions" to end the fighting, but that he was confident "much can be done and will be done" to improve the United Nations position. He warned that there was a danger that a definite victory could not be achieved without "enlarging the war" but said he was confident the Western Allies, despite some differences of opinion over objectives of the war, "are all here together to see it through."

On his return to the U.S., the president-elect conferred in New York with John Foster Dulles, who will become Secretary of State, and with General Douglas MacArthur, who earlier this month said he had a new "clear and definite" solution to the war. At a news conference, President Truman derided the Eisenhower visit as demagoguery and said he doubted either general knew how to end the war (→ 2/27/53).

Worst plane crash kills 84 servicemen

Dec 20. In the world's worst aviation disaster, 84 servicemen died today when the transport plane taking them home for Christmas leave crashed a few minutes after takeoff from Larson Air Force Base in the state of Washington. There were 31 survivors. The transport, a giant C-124 Globemaster, took off in light snow. It appeared to falter at the end of the runway and then smashed into a flat field at the end of the airport, bursting into flames as fuel from its tanks was ignited.

Today's accident is the latest of a series of disasters for military aviation, in which ten planes have crashed or disappeared in the past six weeks. The worst previous aviation accident was the crash of a commercial airliner that killed 80 persons in Cardiff, Wales, in 1950.

Globemaster, sheared in half, near Moses Lake in Washington.

Sex operation makes Mr. Jorgenson a Miss

Dec 15. A tall blonde with blue-gray eyes stepped off an airplane in New York last week. She is Christine Jorgenson, and a year ago the name on her passport was George. While not the first transsexual (a European could make the claim), the 26-year-old is the first to make the change very public.

George Jorgenson was a scrawny G.I. for two years before an honorable discharge. Feeling "in affections like a woman," he flew to a Copenhagen hospital to undergo 2,000 hormone injections and six operations. The result is Christine.

Some reporters at the airport thought she trotted awkwardly in heels; others gave a wolf whistle. Christine has sold her life story to American Weekly for $30,000.

Christine Jorgenson, formerly male.

Giant: Another best seller by Edna Ferber

Great quests dominated theater and literature this year. Whether people sought identity, God or financial fortunes, their goals lay just beyond their grasp. Edna Ferber's "Giant" describes two generations of Texans trying to master the land and themselves. The novel follows the success of "Showboat" (1926) and the epic "Cimarron" (1930).

Ralph Ellison's "The Invisible Man" tells of a Negro searching for self amid stereotypes. The work is rich in metaphor, symbolism and existentialism. Ernest Hemingway's "The Old Man and the Sea" differs vastly in style, purer and simpler. Yet his story of a Cuban fisherman trying to haul a huge catch to shore is another search for pride and self-worth. In John Steinbeck's "East of Eden," a boy strives to get his father's love and respect.

Samuel Beckett's "Waiting for Godot" is a purposely interminable, funny, tragic play. Two hobos stand and pace while waiting for a godlike Godot to rescue them from their lives. George Bernard Shaw's "Don Juan in Hell," extracted from "Man and Superman," came to the stage seeking some understanding between the confounded sexes. Agatha Christie's London play "The Mousetrap" has the ultimate quest—to find out who dunnit.

84 Red prisoners killed in camp riot

Dec 14. A riot erupted on the prison island of Pongam among Communist prisoners of the Korean War. United Nations guards fired on them, killing 84 and wounding another 120. The uprising involved some 3,600 of the prison population of 9,000. It is believed the violence occurred as part of a planned mass breakout. Guards were alerted to the outburst with enough time to prevent any escapes. While much blood was shed, prison authorities "maintained uncontested control of the situation."

Dec 12. The Navy's Viking 9, launched at New Mexico's White Sands Air Base, has soared a record 135 miles high at 3,900 mph.

1953

JANUARY

Su	Mo	Tu	We	Th	Fr	Sa
				1	2	3
4	5	6	7	8	9	10
11	12	13	14	15	16	17
18	19	20	21	22	23	24
25	26	27	28	29	30	31

1. Vending machines have best year in U.S., grossing $1.25 bil. in 1952.

1. Pasadena: Southern Cal. over Wisconsin 7-0 in Rose Bowl.

2. Robert Taft elected U.S. Senate Republican leader.

2. Washington: Agriculture Dept. sets standards allowing smaller holes in swiss cheese.

3. Paris: Beckett's "Waiting for Godot" makes stage debut.

6. Kingston: Reynolds announces production of bauxite in Jamaica.

7. Truman says this is age of H-bomb, warns Stalin war would mean ruin for U.S.S.R. (→ 3/17).

9. U.S. budget deficit projected at $10 billion (→ 2/22).

10. Washington: Convicted spies Julius and Ethel Rosenberg appeal to president for stay of execution (→ 2/13).

12. Vladimir Horowitz marks his silver jubilee with New York Philharmonic.

15. Rangoon: First Asian Socialist Conference agrees on alliances with West, land for peasants.

16. Cairo: Naguib dissolves all opposition parties (→ 2/12).

17. Manila: Danish Dr. Tage Ellinger reports discovery of pygmy tribe in Central Luzon.

21. New York: Yehudi Menuhin performs Bartok Sonata at Carnegie Hall.

21. Cooperstown: Dizzy Dean and Al Simmons named to Baseball Hall of Fame.

23. New York: Italy's new liner Andrea Dorea arrives to harbor fanfare.

24. N.Y.: U.N. figures show world has at least 900 cities with 100,000 or more inhabitants.

30. Ike announces he will pull Seventh Fleet out of Formosa to permit Nationalists to attack Communist China (→ 9/9/53).

DEATHS

1. Hank Williams, American country music star (*9/17/23).

7. Mrs. Cornelius Vanderbilt, New York society leader (*1869).

Nine Jewish doctors in Kremlin arrested

Jan 13. Soviet authorities have arrested nine "terrorist Jewish doctors" on charges of plotting to kill top Soviet leaders on directions from Zionist organizations and British and American intelligence agencies. According to a Soviet radio broadcast, the accused doctors confessed to killing Politburo member Andrei Zhdanov in 1948 and Alexander S. Scherbakov, an administration head in the Soviet army, in 1945. The report claims the physicians purposely misdiagnosed illnesses of the two men and then "incorrectly applied strong medicines" which killed them.

The arrests seem to substantiate reports of a growing pattern of anti-Semitism in the Soviet Union and its satellites. Last December in Czechoslovakia, 11 of the 14 tried in a major treason case were Jewish, including Rudolf Slansky, who in his confession implicated "capitalist Jewish emigrants who returned to Czechoslovakia as imperialist agents" (→ 4/4).

Millions witness Eisenhower's oath

Ike and Mamie on parade in D.C.

Jan 20. Americans from sea to shining sea had the opportunity to experience, via television, the inauguration of Dwight Eisenhower as this nation's 34th President. The popular General pledged to faithfully serve America, saying his administration would "neither compromise, nor tire, nor ever cease" in seeking an honorable world peace.

While outlining a nine-point program for the pursuit of peace, Eisenhower also rejected appeasement of aggressive intruders. As he emphatically declared: "In the final choice, a soldier's pack is not so heavy a burden as a prisoner's chains."

The ceremonies included a colorful Washington parade and the swearing-in of Vice President Richard Nixon. Then at 12:32, Ike took the oath of office that formalized the votes of 60 million Americans.

130 lost as ship sinks off Ireland

Jan 31. About 130 persons are feared to have drowned today when the motor vessel Princess Victoria sank during a savage storm off the coast of Northern Ireland.

The 2,694-ton ship, carrying 123 passengers and 54 crew members, radioed her first distress signal soon after 8 a.m. on her regular run as a ferry from Stranraer in western Scotland to Larne in Northern Ireland. She sank early in the afternoon, as tugs, naval vessels and lifeboats from both shores of the windswept North Channel raced to the rescue.

Dispatches from Belfast declare that at least 44 survivors have been brought ashore, but many went down with the ship and others drowned quickly in the heavy seas. Wind velocities as high as 113 miles an hour were recorded in Scotland.

Onassis buys out Monte Carlo casino

Jan 15. Aristotle Socrates Onassis, youthful and wealthy proprietor of 91 ships, with offices in six countries and homes in New York, Paris, Antibes, Athens and Montevideo, has added a glamorous property to his holdings.

After a year and a half of patient purchasing from 2,000 stockholders, he has acquired control of the famous casino and several hotels in Monte Carlo, Monaco. Though a frequent visitor to Monte Carlo, Onassis never gambles there. "It doesn't amuse me," says the man whose whole life has been a gamble.

Homeless, stateless and penniless, this Greek arrived at age 16 in Argentina, where his first job was as a night telephone operator. Today, his assets are estimated at $300 million. His gamble on the international scale is done with oil tankers.

Vic Seixas (left) of the U.S. in Davis Cup action. Australia and the U.S. have dominated the last nine years of cup play, with the U.S. on top 5-4.

1953

FEBRUARY

Su	Mo	Tu	We	Th	Fr	Sa
1	2	3	4	5	6	7
8	9	10	11	12	13	14
15	16	17	18	19	20	21
22	23	24	25	26	27	28

1. Britain: Storms devastate eastern coast, killing 200.

4. U.S.: Jerry Lewis appears in debut of "The Stooge."

6. Moscow: New Soviet Encyclopedia denies existence of Israel, calls Zionists agents of U.S. and British imperialism (→ 12).

7. Palm Springs: Screen star Ginger Rogers marries French actor Jacques Bergerac.

8. Switzerland: Britain's John and Jennifer Nicks take World Figure Skating Championships.

8. Tehran: Parliament approves liquor ban (→ 28).

9. Vietnam: French destroy six Viet Minh war factories hidden in jungle (→ 4/14).

11. U.S.: Walt Disney's "Peter Pan" premieres.

12. Britain and Egypt sign treaty providing for independence of Sudan in three years (→ 6/18).

12. Soviets break off diplomatic relations with Israel after bombing of Soviet legation (→ 7/20).

13. Guatemala expropriates 234,000 acres from United Fruit for land reform.

13. Pope asks U.S. for clemency in Rosenberg case (→ 17).

20. India opens $140 mil. power system modeled after TVA.

21. Mexico City: 60 dead, 90 injured in trolley car crash.

22. Washington: House Chair John Taber enlists 75 businessmen to help cut budget (→ 7/1).

24. South Africa: Parliament passes public-safety legislation giving govt. increased power to repress minorities (→ 4/16).

25. France: Gen. de Gaulle condemns European Defense Community (→ 12/8/53).

26. New York: Stravinsky conducts his own work as guest with N.Y. Philharmonic.

27. Korea: Allied F-84 Thunderjets raid North Korean base on Yalu River (→ 3/28).

28. Ankara: Greece, Yugoslavia, Turkey sign 5-year defense pact.

28. Tehran: Shah Reza Pahlevi drives Mossadegh out of home while mobs riot outside (→ 3/2).

Clemency denied to Rosenbergs, due to die

Feb 17. Death appears ever more likely for convicted atomic spies Ethel and Julius Rosenberg, as President Eisenhower rejected their appeal for clemency. The president sealed their fate, denouncing their act —giving atomic secrets to the Soviets —as one worse than murder because it could cause the death of "thousands of innocent citizens." However, the couple was granted a stay of execution through March, as the U.S. Appeals Court gave their lawyers time to prepare a new petition for Supreme Court review.

The Rosenbergs were convicted in March 1951 of espionage. They are the first Americans ever sentenced to die for espionage in peacetime. Yet, their crime was committed during the war and spying in wartime is punishable by death.

Eisenhower apparently expresses the sentiment of many citizens: The Rosenbergs were given all the rights of judicial proceedings, from District Court through the appeal process and to give them freedom would mock justice. But there are others who agree with Justice Douglas, the only Supreme Court member to vote for review, that the two deserve to have their case heard by the highest court (→ 3/30).

Polio victim, at 17, is skating champ

Feb 15. An American girl has won the world figure-skating championship for the first time and she had to overcome the dread disease of polio to do it. Tenley Albright, a 17-year-old ice ballerina from Boston, received the unanimous vote of a seven-man panel of judges in completing a U.S. sweep at Davos, Switzerland. Hayes Alan Jenkins of Ohio won the men's title. Miss Albright's win capped her six-year comeback from polio. She has been skating since age nine and was runner-up in the '52 Olympics.

Jacques Cousteau: The Silent World

Feb 3. "The Silent World," a remarkable account of an unprecedented series of underwater explorations of the world's oceans, was published today by Jacques Y. Cousteau of France. Ten years ago, Cousteau, then in the French navy, worked with an engineer, Emile Gargan, to invent the aqualung, which for the first time allowed humans to spend prolonged periods underwater. The new book, lavishly illustrated, describes underwater adventures in the Atlantic, the Mediterranean and the Red Sea. "Enough to sell a good many aqualungs," one critic says.

20th Century Fox using Cinemascope

Feb 1. The Twentieth Century Fox Film Corporation said today it would convert its entire movie-making operation to the wide-screen system called Cinemascope, a move it said was comparable to "the transfer from silent pictures to sound in 1927." The company said it will invest $25 million on 11 major Cinemascope productions, starting with a Biblical saga, "The Robe." Cinemascope uses a special wide-angle lens that allows the picture to be projected on a 145-degree, curved screen. All Cinemascope films will also have stereophonic sound, the studio says.

Oradour killers get severe sentences

Feb 13. The murderers of 652 French inhabitants of Oradour-sur-Glane in June 1944 have received stiff sentences from a military tribunal in Bordeaux. Of the seven German defendants, one was condemned to death, five to various terms of hard labor or imprisonment and one was acquitted. Thirteen Alsatians were also on trial; the Alsatians were forced to join the Nazis after the defeat of France in 1940. Of these, one, Georges-Rene Boos, who volunteered for service in the Nazi Elite Guard, was sentenced to die. The others received labor or jail terms.

Young La Follette ends his own life

Feb 24. One suicidal pistol shot ended the life of former Senator Robert La Follette Jr. His wife, Rachel, found his slumped body in their Washington, D.C., home this afternoon. He left no note, but friends said the son of Progressive Senator "Fighting Bob" La Follette, seemed despondent in recent weeks.

La Follette's career included 22 years as a senator from Wisconsin. He's probably best known for his work as Senate investigator of civil liberties during the 1930's. Before his defeat in 1946 to Joe McCarthy, he served the Senate with "inspiring heritage," in the words of Senator Alexander Wiley.

The Studebaker Starliner Coupe features sleek cat's-eye grills in front.

1953

MARCH

Su	Mo	Tu	We	Th	Fr	Sa
1	2	3	4	5	6	7
8	9	10	11	12	13	14
15	16	17	18	19	20	21
22	23	24	25	26	27	28
29	30	31				

2. Tehran: Mobs, shouting "Yankees go home," stone Americans (→ 4/6).

3. Mrs. Clare Boothe Luce takes office as U.S. ambassador to Italy.

6. Moscow: Georgi Malenkov named Soviet premier upon Stalin's death (→ 20).

10. Germany: Soviet MIG's down RAF plane, killing five above Elbe River Valley in Berlin air lane.

13. N.Y.: Soviets veto Lester Pearson for U.N. secretary general (→ 31).

15. N.Y.: Yeshiva Univ. Medical School becomes Albert Einstein Medical College.

17. U.S. Air Force charges Soviets tried to shoot down U.S. weather reconnaissance plane east of Siberian peninsula.

17. Nevada: 35th nuclear blast tests tactical weapon at Yucca Flat (→ 5/8).

18. Florida: Braves baseball club announce transfer of team from Boston to Milwaukee.

18. Turkey: Quake kills 1,000, leaves 50,000 homeless near Gonen.

20. Moscow: Khrushchev replaces Malenkov as secretary of Communist Party (→ 28).

22. N.J.: C.I.O. gives terms for merging with A.F.L. (→ 6/12).

22. Nairobi: 2,500 tribesmen arrested by police (→ 4/5).

26. Ike offers France increased aid in Vietnam (→ 4/14).

27. Charles Bohlen, despite McCarthy's opposition, named U.S. ambassador to U.S.S.R.

28. Korea: Communists accept U.N. plan for exchange of sick and injured POWs (→ 4/20).

30. Assn. of American Universities votes academic freedom, barring Communist ties (→ 4/15).

DEATHS

3. James Jeffries, heavyweight boxing champ (*4/15/1875).

14. Klement Gottwald, Czech Communist (*11/23/1896).

28. Jim Thorpe, American Indian athlete (*5/28/1888).

Joseph Stalin succumbs to stroke

Soviet leaders pose stifly around Stalin's casket: Khrushchev, Beria, Malenkov, Bulganin, Voroshilov, Kaganovich.

March 5. Joseph Stalin, the most powerful leader in the history of Russia, died tonight in Moscow. An elite team of Russian doctors, headed by Health Minister Tretyakov, worked around the clock trying to save Stalin's life after he suffered a brain hemorrhage four days ago. He died shortly before 10:00. Stalin was 73.

News of Stalin's death was withheld for six hours before it was announced on Russian radio and in Pravda, the newspaper that Stalin founded more than 40 years ago and later edited with Lenin. Black borders surrounded the front page, which printed a large picture of the Premier and a warning to Russians.

Pravda said these are "difficult days" and urged citizens to be wary and vigilant "in the struggle against internal and external foes." A portion of the obituary even read like a Communist manifesto, as Pravda announced that Soviet leaders would support "proletarian internationalism." A successor to Stalin has not been selected.

Stalin's body will lie in state for several days in the Kremlin, and he will be buried in a mausoleum near Lenin. A commission of top Soviet officials has been appointed to make the funeral arrangements. The panel is headed by Nikita Khrushchev, Secretary of the Communist Party's Central Committee.

It may be a long time before a Soviet leader acquires the skills or reaches the level that Stalin attained: his ruthlessness, his familiarity with the party bureaucracy, his shrewd diplomatic maneuvering, his tyrannical power. Stalin's transition from ally of the West in a hot war to enemy in the cold one is one of the most remarkable stories in history. Stalin was a leader who could charm a Franklin Roosevelt or mastermind the assassination of a Leon Trotsky.

Stalin was criticized by Trotsky and other opponents for joining the Communist cause too late, wrapping himself in the mantle of Lenin and pursuing policies that were counterrevolutionary. Trotsky and Stalin's two allies after the death of Lenin, Grigori Zinoviev and Lev Kamenev, complained that Stalin's economic policies were too conservative after he was elected General Secretary of the party in 1922. All three officials were purged by Stalin, along with thousands of other officials. Zinoviev and Kamenev were later executed, while Trotsky was murdered in an elaborate plot in Mexico.

Stalin was equally ruthless in his international dealings. He may have ordered the executions of thousands of Polish officers, and he allowed Polish patriots to be butchered in Warsaw. Stalin drove hard bargains not only with President Roosevelt but also with Chairman Mao. He was also a brilliant military commander who was the first to beat Hitler. Throughout Eastern Europe, the Soviet Union is still savoring the fruits of Stalin's victory (→ 6).

Amnesty is decreed

March 28. In a dramatic decree, the Soviet government has granted general amnesty to all its short-term prisoners and the Soviet Justice Department was ordered to re-examine the entire criminal code.

Only those prisoners serving long sentences for counterrevolutionary crimes, thievery and premeditated murder will remain behind bars. The action was taken "as a result of the consolidation of the Soviet social and state system, the increase in alertness and honesty of the citizens (and because) crime has considerably decreased," according to the Moscow statement. Re-examination of the criminal code is expected to occur soon (→ 7/10).

A sea of Stalins in Peking as China mourns the death of a benefactor.

Salk polio vaccine is used successfully

March 26. A vaccine against polio has been tested successfully in 90 adults and children, its developer, Dr. Jonas Salk of the University of Pittsburgh, reported today. The vaccine uses killed viruses of the kind that cause the dreaded crippling disease. The test shows that the vaccine provides protection against all three strains of the polio virus, Salk said. Salk's report, published in the Journal of the American Medical Association, called the results of the test "very encouraging" but said they do not indicate that a practical vaccine is at hand. More tests are needed to prove the vaccine's safety and effectiveness.

Salk at work in his Pittsburgh lab.

Tito first Communist chief to visit London

March 16. President Tito of Yugoslavia became the first Communist head of state ever to visit Great Britain when he arrived yesterday afternoon aboard the training ship Galeb, which anchored last night in the Thames River estuary.

And today, in the first cordial gesture of his five-day visit, the anti-Stalinist leader was greeted by Prime Minister Winston Churchill, Foreign Secretary Anthony Eden and the Duke of Edinburgh.

National defense will probably be uppermost in Tito's mind when he settles down to talk with Churchill and Eden. Though it is newly linked with Greece and Turkey in a general military treaty, Yugoslavia lacks specific guarantees of military assistance.

Despite the death of Stalin, the Yugoslavs still fear vindictive action by the Soviet Union because of their Cominform break in 1948, and they are also mindful of possible satellite reaction to the Balkan entente. Nor is Tito overlooking the threat of some new "adventures" by the Malenkov government in Moscow. Stating that a treaty is not "essential," Tito would nevertheless like some sign from Britain as to Western attitudes regarding some such possible attack from the Soviets (→ 6/3).

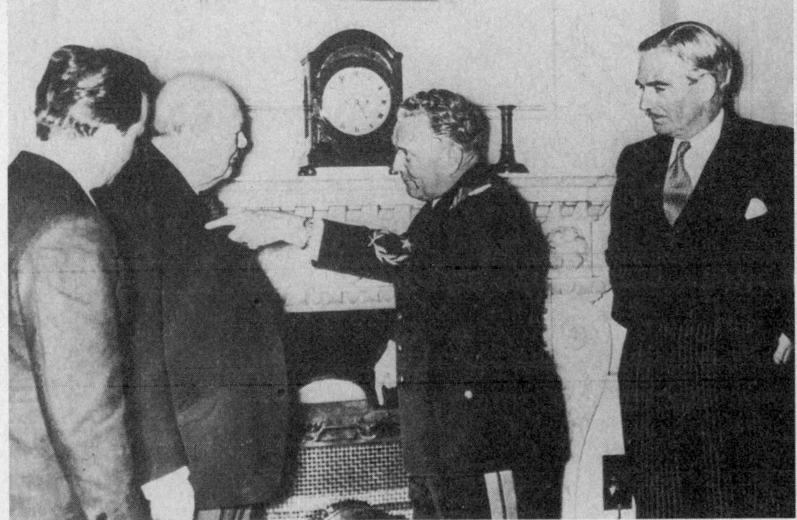

Tito greets Churchill in London, as For. Sec. Anthony Eden (rt.) looks on.

Swede becomes U.N. Secretary General

March 31. The Security Council tonight recommended Swedish Minister of State Dag Hammarskjold to succeed Trygve Lie as United Nations Secretary General.

Like the election of Lie in 1946 as the first secretary general, the surprise solution broke a deadlock between the Soviet Union and the Western powers. It is the first major action supported by both Russia and the United States since the Korean armistice negotiations.

Lie's resignation last November followed charges made by some countries that he had too readily complied with U.S. demands for the dismissal of Communists and allegedly subversive Americans on the U.N. payroll (→ 4/10).

Raoul Dufy's colorful artistry has ended

March 23. Artist Raoul Dufy has died in the French town of Forcalquier. He was 75 years old. Dufy could not be classified as a painter; he restlessly created wood cuts, textiles and stage scenery. An adherence to rich color may have been the only constant in his career.

In the early 1900's Dufy copied the Impressionists in style and subject, but a meeting with Matisse in 1905 converted him to Fauvism. A bright "Three Umbrellas" (1906) represents this era. After World War I, Dufy set his own style, painting portraits and panoramas.

The gods and modern rationalism are joined in Dufy's "La Fee Electricite."

Prokofiev, Russian composer, is dead

March 5. The composer of "Peter and the Wolf" has died near Moscow. Sergei Prokofiev was 61 years old. He created seven concertos, seven symphonies and nine sonatas. Despite government harassment, he was prolific right up to his death.

Prokofiev entered the St. Petersburg Conservatory at age 13 and composed his famed "Classical Symphony" in his early 20's. After the Russian Revolution he sailed to the United States, composing "Love for Three Oranges" for the Chicago Opera Company. He returned to Russia in 1934, offering his exquisite "Romeo and Juliet" (1940) and "Fifth Symphony" (1945) amid charges of bourgeois standards.

March 25. A few loyal subjects keeping vigil in the London fog were party to a sad note: "While sleeping peacefully, Queen Mary died at 20 minutes past 10 o'clock." At 85, she was the widow of George V and grandmother of Elizabeth II. Churchill has adjourned Parliament to express "profound sorrow and respect."

1953

APRIL

Su	Mo	Tu	We	Th	Fr	Sa
			1	2	3	4
5	6	7	8	9	10	11
12	13	14	15	16	17	18
19	20	21	22	23	24	25
26	27	28	29	30		

1. Washington: Congress creates Dept. of Health Education and Welfare (→ 11).

6. Washington: German Chancellor Adenauer arrives for talks with Eisenhower.

6. Tehran: Premier Mossadegh demands shah's power be reduced, says his life is threatened by monarch's plotters (→ 8/13).

7. Berlin: Big Four meet for first time in two years, to seek end to air clashes.

8. Bones of Sitting Bull moved from North to South Dakota after 63 years.

10. N.Y.: Dag Hammerskjold sworn in as sec. gen. of U.N.

10. Actress Hedy Lamarr becomes U.S. citizen.

11. Washington: Mrs. Oveta Culp Hobby made first sec. of Health Education and Welfare.

14. Viet Minh invade Laos with 40,000 troops (→ 28).

15. Buenos Aires: Six killed by bomb at rally addressed by President Peron (→ 4/25/54).

16. Pretoria: Premier Malan's Nationalist Party returned to power in elections (→ 5/10).

17. New York: Benny Goodman returns to Carnegie Hall after 15 years.

20. Boston: Japanese runner Keizo Yamada wins marathon in record 2:18:51.

20. Korea: POW exchange begun; 30 Americans freed (→ 21).

21. New York: Sidney Janis Gallery holds Dada exhibition.

23. New York: Leontyne Price sings Sauguet's "La Voyante" at Metropolitan Opera.

25. Washington: Sen. Wayne Morse ends longest speech in Senate history—22 hours, 26 minutes on Offshore Oil Bill.

25. Paris: NATO ends 11th session in accord on long-range arms plan, relying heavily on nuclear weapons (→ 12/8).

27. U.S. offers $50,000, political asylum to Communist pilots for delivery of MIG jet (→ 5/29).

27. Tokyo: Five killed, 60 injured as Mt. Aso erupts on island of Kyushu.

64 Yanks freed in Korean POW exchange

North Korean POWs are freed from Koje Island under terms of the armistice.

April 21. Tearful and joyous, 200 U.N. soldiers, including 64 Americans, were released from Communist captivity in the first days of the recently implemented exchange of sick and wounded Korean War prisoners. The swap, to be completed by April 30, will see the return of about 600 Allied, 5,000 North Korean and 700 Chinese prisoners.

The first moments were dramatic as the U.N. soldiers stepped from the Communist ambulances. They were well-dressed by their captors in blue coats and blue tennis shoes. The first U.S. soldier exchanged was Pvt. Carl W. Kirchenhausen of New York City. Suffering from frostbitten feet, his face was drawn and unsmiling. Meanwhile, the Communists and the Allies remain deadlocked regarding the disposition of prisoners who refuse repatriation (→ 27).

Mau-Mau chief Kenyatta jailed for 7 years

April 5. The leader of the Kikuyu tribe in Kenya, Jomo "Burning Spear" Kenyatta, has been convicted and sentenced to seven years hard labor for orchestrating the Mau-Mau rebellion, which aims to drive the British and all other whites out of the East African colony. British Magistrate R.S. Thacker handed down the verdict and sentence after a 58-day trial in a former schoolhouse in the city of Kapenguria. The charges held that Kenyatta assisted and inspired the brutal savagery of the Mau-Mau terrorists.

Kenyatta, anti-colonialist.

Five compatriots of Kenyatta were also sentenced to terms of hard labor. All the sentences are subject to review from the Kenya Supreme Court. Defense attorney D.N. Pritt, a Londoner who successfully defended German Communist Gerhart Eisler against American attempts to extradite him from Britain, will appeal the guilty verdict.

Kenyatta lived for several years in Britain with his white wife and son. He also studied for two years at the University of Moscow and returned home to initiate the Mau-Mau uprising. Great Britain announced today that it has expedited the war against the Mau-Mau, killing 21 Kikuyu tribesmen in the past 24 hours. London has also sent 1,500 combat reinforcements to Kenya (→ 5/8).

Chaplin surrenders U.S. re-entry permit

April 15. Comedian Charlie Chaplin has surrendered his U.S. re-entry permit rather than face proceedings by the Justice Department. Chaplin has been suspected of sympathizing with Communist groups. The Justice Department considered barring him from the country under a law that denies entry to aliens urging the government's overthrow.

A British subject, Chaplin makes his home in Switzerland. He made a fortune in the United States but never chose to become a citizen, explaining, "I am not a nationalist." He denies any wrongdoing. "I am a peacemonger," he adds (→ 5/25).

The sport of kings now king of sports

April 29. With attendance at other athletic events dwindling or remaining unchanged, horse racing seems ready to justify its self-proclaimed designation as the "king of sports." The crowds at thoroughbred and harness racing tracks totaled 45,880,617 last year as baseball, college football and basketball were among the spectator sports to lose fans or remain static. Baseball remained the national pastime, but in the same period its total attendance, including the minors, was down to 40,940,785. The figures were provided by Triangle Publications, which puts out horse racing periodicals.

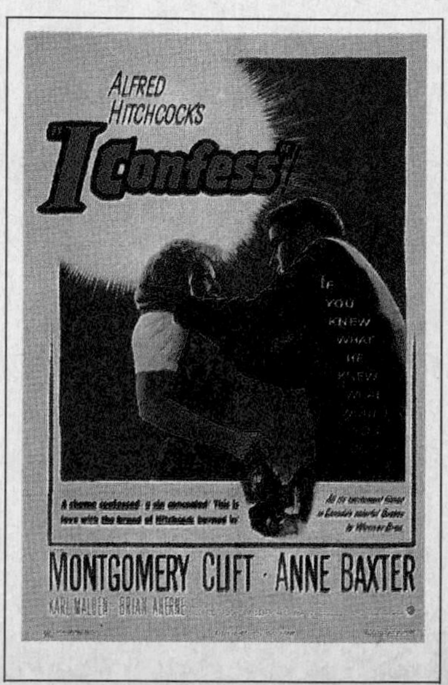

French-led forces evacuate northern Laos

French counter-insurgency troops navigate the Black River.

April 28. French forces in Laos lost another outpost in the northern part of the country to Communist guerrillas who have infiltrated the area from neighboring Vietnam. Pakseng has fallen, the fate of the French garrison unknown. The Viet Minh, allied with the sympathetic Pathet Lao, are advancing along tributaries of the Mekong River toward Luang Prabang, the royal capital of Laos. The French fear an all-out assault on the city of "The Celebrated Buddha" on May Day.

The French are still holding the Plain of Jars, where they are building a new airport. But they lost more than 2,000 soldiers when the Communists overran an outpost at Muong Khoua. The French Cabinet will decide tomorrow whether to appeal for help from the U.N. It has refrained from doing that up until now out of concern that Arab states would use the forum to attack French colonialism (→ 5/6).

Churchill becomes Knight of the Garter

April 24. Winston Churchill knelt before Queen Elizabeth II at Windsor Castle tonight and was dubbed a Knight of the Garter, the oldest and highest order of British knighthood, founded 500 years ago. He will now be called Sir Winston, and his wife Lady Churchill. After World War II, Churchill declined the offer of a dukedom because it would bar him and his heirs from the House of Commons.

Churchill in full regalia as a Knight Companion of the Order of the Garter.

DNA is described as a double helix

April 25. Writing in the journal Nature, Dr. James D. Watson and Dr. Francis H.C. Crick today suggested a new structure for deoxyribonucleic acid (DNA), the molecular basis of heredity. Refuting Linus Pauling's idea of an alpha helix structure of DNA, Watson and Crick propose a double helix model of the genetic material—two spirally wound chains consisting of complementary chemical base pairs. The new model makes it possible to envisage how genes replicate and carry information.

British West Indies agree to federate

April 30. The British West Indian colonies have announced agreement on the formation of a British Caribbean Federation which will eventually become a self-governing unit in the British Commonwealth. In 1948, a committee studied a closer association among the colonies. Their recommendations form the backbone of the federal plan, which is to include a Senate and House of Representatives in which Jamaica would have the greatest number of officials. The government capital would be in Grenada, and the chairman of the federation's Council of State would be the British Governor General.

Birth control for wives still debated

April 18. The Connecticut State Senate met today to debate a law forbidding the use of contraceptives by married or unmarried women. The legislature has met annually for 20 years to debate the issue. The state's large Roman Catholic population opposes birth control.

According to state law, "Any person who shall use any drug, medicinal article or instrument for the purpose of preventing conception shall be fined not less than $50 or imprisoned not less than 60 days nor more than one year, or be both fined and imprisoned."

Fifteen accused in Kremlin plot freed

April 4. It is not often that Soviet leaders admit they make mistakes. Today, they did just that. And Russian observers wonder if the release of 15 doctors, most of them Jewish, is a sign of things to come in the post-Stalin era. The doctors were arrested before Stalin died and accused of plotting against him. In an unusual admission, Pravda indicated that the doctors had been tortured into making confessions. Under Stalin's regime, Jews were executed for Zionist or "cosmopolitan" tendencies.

Ex-King Carol dies in Lisbon exile

April 4. The former ruler of Rumania has died at a resort outside Lisbon. King Carol II succumbed to a heart attack. He was 59.

Carol led a tempestuous life. His parents sent him to a Prussian regiment during World War I, hoping he would learn discipline. He did not. In 1918, when Germany occupied Rumania, he renounced his rights and fled to Russia to marry a commoner. He soon left her.

In June 1930, Carol retook the throne and made his latest mistress a princess. He was a dictator whose reign was marked by political unrest and economic deterioration. Carol abdicated September 6, 1940.

Pope Pius approves of psychoanalysis

April 15. Pope Pius XII has given his nod of approval to psychoanalysis, calling it another tool for modern healers but also warning of its possible abuses. In a speech to clinical psychologists, the pope encouraged the use of therapy, but cautioned counselors not to forget to remind patients that "committing material sin" produces "subjective guilt." He also stressed that analysis should not be the only means of relieving personal troubles. The address surprised many, as the Catholic Church had been hostile to psychoanalysis.

1953

MAY

Su	Mo	Tu	We	Th	Fr	Sa
					1	2
3	4	5	6	7	8	9
10	11	12	13	14	15	16
17	18	19	20	21	22	23
24	25	26	27	28	29	30
31						

2. H. Moreno rides Dark Star to victory in Kentucky Derby.

2. Calcutta: Comet jet crashes on takeoff, killing 40.

6. Laos: Viet Minh retreat as monsoon approaches (→ 8).

8. Nevada: A-bomb test, twice as powerful as wartime bombs, lights up desert (→ 25).

8. Ike announces $60 mil. in military aid for French effort in Vietnam (→ 31).

8. Nairobi: Mau Mau carry out biggest attack yet against barbed wire police camp (→ 4/12/54).

10. South Africa: Two anti-Malanist parties formed: Alan Paton's Liberals and Federal Union Party (→ 1/20/54).

12. Texas: Tornadoes hit Waco area, killing 124.

14. British experts say jet plane flights will soon damage eardrums, wreck houses.

15. Rocky Marciano retains heavyweight title, flooring Walcott in two minutes, 25 seconds.

16. Czechs free AP correspondent William Oatis, jailed as spy for two years (→ 8/13/56).

18. Nigeria: Death toll hits 32 in Moslem-Nationalist riots for independence from Britain.

20. Denmark: Polish air force pilot lands MIG-15 in Roenne, asks asylum (→ 10/18).

22. Ike signs Offshore Oil Bill, giving coastal states control over "submerged" lands.

24. Farewell party held for Empire Theater, oldest New York playhouse.

25. Nevada: Atomic cannon tested, blasting target seven miles away (→ 6/4).

25. High court denies Rosenberg appeal 3rd time (→ 6/13).

29. Seoul threatens to remove army from U.N. rule in protest over armistice terms (→ 6/10).

30. Bill Vukovich wins Indy 500 in Fuel Injection Special.

DEATHS

4. Robert Wagner, U.S. senator, liberal Democrat (*6/8/1877).

16. Django Reinhardt, Gypsy jazz musician (*1/23/1910).

Navarre takes command in Indochina; Dulles warns of domino effect in war

Navarre, hoping to rejuvenate the ailing French effort, greets his troops.

May 31. Amid internal criticism and warnings from the United States, France has appointed General Henri Eugene Navarre as Commander-in-Chief of French Union Forces in Indochina. Navarre will replace General Raoul Salan who has led French troops in the area since the death of Marshal Jean de Lattre de Tassigny last year.

The move, decided by the French Cabinet, resulted from mounting criticism in the press on the way the war is being conducted—which has been, at times, disorganized and inefficient—and of reports of corruption. Some contend the war is being purposely extended because certain French and Indochinese groups are engaged in large-scale profiteering.

The change in military leadership came while American Secretary of State John Foster Dulles emphasized how crucial the region is for the West. He says that if the Viet Minh are successful in defeating the French and can implant a Communist system, the rest of Southeast Asia will fall, like dominoes, under Soviet domination (→ 7/6).

To tear viewers away from their TVs, Hollywood has come up with a new gimmick—3D. Bespectacled audiences hide from runaway trains and monsters in thrillers like "Bwana Devils" and "House of Wax."

First woman breaks the sound barrier

May 18. Jacqueline Cochran, one of America's leading fliers, today became the first woman to fly faster than the speed of sound. Piloting a Canadian-built F-86 Sabre jet fighter over Edwards Air Force Base 100 miles north of Los Angeles, Cochran sent sonic booms thundering over the desert several times as she pulled out of steep dives at speeds over 760 miles an hour. She also set a new international speed record of 652 miles an hour for a 100-kilometer closed course, breaking a mark set in 1951.

Miss Cochran, who won the Distinguished Service Medal for her war service, is a Lieutenant Colonel in the U.S. Air Force Reserve. The previous 100-kilometer jet speed record for a woman was 540 miles an hour, set by Jacqueline Auriol, daughter-in-law of the President of France.

Cochran, a smiling daredevil.

Cousins are Kings in the Middle East

May 2. Two new monarchs related by their youth—both are 18—and their common Hashemite ancestry have assumed their thrones as King Faisal II of Iraq and King Hussein I of Jordan. The Hashemite family claims descent from the Prophet Mohammed, and this is the first time two Hashemite kings have occupied Arab thrones at the same time. Because the processions were simultaneous, neither can claim royal seniority.

"Old Man and Sea" wins Pulitzer Prize

Hemingway, now living in Cuba.

May 4. Pulitzer Prizes for Ernest Hemingway and William Inge were announced today. Hemingway's first novel was written in the 20's. Inge's first play was done in 1950.

Hemingway won for his short novel "The Old Man and the Sea." Initially published in Life magazine in September 1952, it describes a Cuban fisherman hauling a huge catch to shore. Fisherman Hemingway keeps a home outside Havana.

The drama prize went to Inge for "Picnic." Inge premiered on Broadway three years ago with "Come Back, Little Sheba." "Picnic," about a boastful man monopolizing a Kansas town, has already won the Drama Critic's Circle Award.

40 are dead in crash of Comet jetliner

May 2. Forty persons were reported dead today in the first crash of a jet airliner in commercial service. The jetliner, a British-built Comet, plunged to earth in a violent storm just a few minutes after taking off from Calcutta. It was carrying a party of rubber and tin operators from Malaya to England. There were no survivors. Two Comets have crashed before, one last October and one in March, but neither was carrying passengers.

1953

JUNE

Su	Mo	Tu	We	Th	Fr	Sa
	1	2	3	4	5	6
7	8	9	10	11	12	13
14	15	16	17	18	19	20
21	22	23	24	25	26	27
28	29	30				

2. Supreme Court bars D.C. restaurants from refusing service to Negroes (→ 5/17/54).

3. Belgrade: Tito ready to back NATO to keep peace (→ 11/28).

4. Nevada: Greatest A-bomb yet —twice the power of Hiroshima —tested in desert (→ 8/14).

4. New York: "Julius Caesar" opens with Brando, Gielgud, James Mason, Deborah Kerr.

8. Algeria: Archeologists find Ice Age artifacts thought to be man's oldest known works.

8. U.S.: Tornado strikes down 139 in Midwest.

9. U.S.: Tornado hits New England, killing 92.

10. Seoul: South Korean deputies ban U.N. truce (→ 15).

12. Pittsburgh: C.I.O. gets 8.5-cent pay rise from U.S. Steel (→ 9/10).

13. Bogota: Gen. Rojas Pinilla seizes power in bloodless coup, takes Colombian presidency.

13. U.S.: Rosenberg Judge Irving Kaufman receives death threat (→ 14).

14. N.H.: Ike, at Dartmouth, warns against "book burners," thought control (→ 19).

14. Oyster Bay, L.I.: Teddy Roosevelt's home Sagamore Hill made a national shrine.

17. Berlin: Soviet tanks fight thousands of workers rioting against E. German govt. (→ 21).

18. Japan: Globemaster transport goes down near Tokyo, killing 129 U.S. servicemen.

18. Ike sends rebuke to Pres. Rhee for releasing N. Korean prisoners against will of U.N. (→ 7/14).

20. Bangkok: Cambodian King Sihanouk returns, ending six-day exile in Thailand (→ 29).

24. Newport: John F. Kennedy and Jacqueline Bouvier announce engagement (→ 9/12).

30. Nathan Twining takes command of U.S. Air Force as Hoyt Vandenberg retires after 30 yrs.

DEATH

5. "Big Bill" Tilden, American tennis star (*2/10/1893).

Elizabeth II is crowned

Ceremony in Westminster Abbey.

June 2. A young woman who daily drove a truck during wartime was today seated in a gilded carriage. Handsome steeds drew her through London streets while her admirers surged along the thoroughfare. Her coach arrived at Westminster Abbey. She alighted, donned a heavy crown and strolled down a carpeted hall. A centuries-old incantation was recited before a thousand hushed voices. Princess Elizabeth was Queen.

Although today marks her official debut as monarch, Elizabeth has reigned since the death of her father, George VI, on Feb. 6, 1952. The intervening months were beneficial; they allowed Elizabeth to mourn her father and then prepare for the joys of coronation. The nation also had the opportunity to prepare a most glorious ceremony.

As a young child Elizabeth never imagined inheriting the throne; her uncle Edward VIII was King, and it seemed likely his children would succeed him. But Edward abdicated when Elizabeth was ten years old, and her father, next in line, was made ruler. By the time Elizabeth was a second lieutenant in the Womens' Army Corps, repairing and driving trucks, she knew she would be no mechanic but monarch.

That would account for the perfect way she conducted herself on the drive back from Westminster, waving joyously but not indecorously to her subjects. Behind the queen, in their own splendid conveyances, rode dignitaries: Premiers of India, Pakistan, Australia, New Zealand and South Africa; Sultans from Zanzibar, Brunei, Perak, Lahej and Johore. They were guarded by Canadian mounties in brilliant red coats and Malayan defense troops in sparkling white uniforms and fresh, green sarongs.

The queen addressed her empire in a radio speech. She thanked people around the world for their good wishes, and gave a special note to her husband (Prince Philip had led the peers in a pledge of loyalty). ". . . I have my husband to support me," she said. "He shares my ideals and all my affection for you."

The queen's children received more than their usual share of attention. Prince Charles and Princess Anne, four and two years old, attended part of the ceremony. As day wore on, they grew as sulky and restless as any children have a right to be, royalty or no.

The royal family waves to admirers from the balcony of Buckingham Palace. ▷

Rosenbergs executed

Ethel and Julius Rosenberg, just before their execution.

June 19. Silently, stoically and with dignity, Julius and Ethel Rosenberg walked to the electric chair. Execution assistants applied electrodes to their temples, strapped them down, and with the tug of a lever, the lives of the couple, convicted for atomic espionage, were ended. For the first time in American history, a husband and wife received the ultimate punishment.

The Rosenbergs heard early this afternoon that the Supreme Court vacated the stay given to them by Justice Douglas on Wednesday, and that President Eisenhower again refused them executive clemency. The president said their espionage activity, revealing American atomic secrets to the Soviets, jeopardized "millions of innocent people all over the world." He also reiterated his belief that they had been granted full due process of law; their various appeals spanned over two years.

Over 5,000 people gathered in Union Square in New York to protest the executions, denounce Eisenhower and pray for the couple and their two children (→ 10/23).

Egypt's new rulers proclaim republic

June 18. Formalizing a situation in existence since King Farouk's exile, Egypt's army junta has decreed the abolition of the monarchy and proclaimed Egypt a republic.

Major General Mohammed Naguib, who led the coup, was named President and Premier. The action ends the 148-year-old dynasty of Mohammed Ali, the Albanian adventurer and soldier in the Turkish army who set himself up as Viceroy of Egypt under the Ottoman Empire in 1805. Ten of his descendants ruled the country, the last being Farouk.

A statement by the revolutionary council declared that its aim from the start was to annihilate imperialism and its supporters. Citing a series of treacheries against the people "committed by the Ali dynasty," it branded Farouk as a "sinner and oppressor." Among key Cabinet changes, Colonel Gamal Abdel Nasser, organizer of the coup and still its dominant figure, was named Deputy Premier and Minister of the Interior in control of all police forces (→ 9/20).

Nasser and Naguib ride through the streets of Cairo.

Hillary scales Mt. Everest; world applauds

June 2. Mountaineer Edmund Hillary of New Zealand and his Nepalese Sherpa guide Tensing have became the first men to conquer Mount Everest, the world's tallest mountain. The two reached the pinnacle of Everest, more than 29,000 feet above sea level, at 11:30 a.m. on May 29, staying for only 15 minutes while Tensing planted the flags of Britain, Nepal, India and the United Nations and Hillary snapped commemorative pictures. Hillary has dedicated his feat to today's coronation of Queen Elizabeth II of England. He already has been knighted by the queen.

Hillary, conqueror of nature.

The successful expedition was planned by Col. C. John Hunt, who chose the 34-year-old Hillary to lead the way up Everest. The party left England in February and began its assault on Everest in May from a base camp at the 18,000-foot level. They went up the south face of the mountain. The first attempt to reach the top, on May 26, failed for lack of oxygen. A five-hour climb four days ago brought success.

Sihanouk yields country to army

June 29. Tension continues to mount in Cambodia as the army has grabbed control of Phnom Penh, the nation's capital. King Norodom Sihanouk, who earlier this month left Cambodia in self-exile, demands Cambodian independence from France. However, the king has allowed the military to take over in Phnom Penh, realizing his sphere of influence has diminished.

French forces were sent to the troubled city to protect French lives and property and to prevent the violence from escalating. Yet, their presence has stirred resentment; Cambodian officials accused French battalions of "provocation and unjustified intimidation." Sihanouk has again left the city, but still he calls for independence (→ 8/29).

South Korea balks; Red army attacks

June 15. In the biggest Korean battle since 1951, 30,000 Communist troops smashed the ill-prepared South Korean Fifth and Eighth Divisions along a 30-mile sector on the central and eastern fronts. Chinese soldiers forced back the line of South Korean control two miles, altering the truce demarcation line now being discussed by Communist and United Nations negotiators.

The American Third Infantry Division was also hit hard in the assault, suffering severe losses before stopping the thrusting enemy soldiers, who emptied some 17,000 rounds on the American defenders. Apparently, the Communists wanted to gain prestige with this offensive, before the expected cease-fire agreement is concluded (→ 18).

Soviet tanks crush surprise East Berlin uprising

Laborers, in revolt against the "worker's state," carry the black, red and gold German flag through East Berlin.

Man against tank in East Berlin.

June 21. The United States, Britain and France sharply condemned the military crackdown by Soviet authorities in East Berlin. But the Soviets shrugged off the criticism and said they would not ease martial law or reopen the city unless the Western powers "guarantee to cease sending provocateurs and other criminal elements" into East Berlin. More than 20 people have been killed and nearly 200 injured in the anti-Communist rioting that began Tuesday. The strikes started in East Berlin and quickly spread to most of East Germany.

The trouble began Monday when the government announced an increase in production quotas for construction workers. About 5,000 of the workers poured into the streets to protest. On Tuesday, the protest mushroomed to up to 50,000 workers. The government tried to rescind the new work rules, but it was too late. Rioters attacked the new Soviet Embassy, occupied political offices, shredded Red flags, tore up boundary markers between East and West Berlin and set a border shack on fire. One of East Germany's deputy premiers, Otto Nuschke, was dragged from his limousine and assaulted. Loudspeaker trucks in West Berlin urged workers to join the striking protesters in the eastern part of the city.

East Berlin police were overwhelmed by the rioters. Soviet troops were called into action, and tanks rumbled through the streets to restore calm. The Soviets sealed the border between East and West Berlin and closed a major highway to West Germany. Transportation in East Berlin ground to a halt.

Some of the Russian tanks pointed their guns at West Berlin, as if to indicate the Allied sector was the real source of the trouble. Troops in East Berlin entered apartment buildings at gunpoint, searching for leaders of the strike. Soviet trucks jammed with soldiers drove wildly through the streets and fired into the air to scare protesters back into their homes.

Martial law was declared at 1 p.m. by Major General P.T. Dibrowa, the Soviet military commandant. A curfew was established between 9 p.m. and 5 a.m.

Premier Otto Grotewohl blamed the riots on "fascist and other reactionary elements" in West Berlin. He charged that unidentified "foreign powers" had incited the protesters. The three Western Allies replied curtly that they had nothing to do with the protests. They criticized the execution of an alleged rioter from West Berlin as a "travesty of justice."

Over the past three days, it has become evident that workers in mines, factories and rail yards all over East Germany joined the strike. Many of them fought with military authorities. Others tangled with workers who stayed on the job. Premier Grotewohl urged loyal citizens to join the search for workers leading the insurrection (→ 7/10).

1953

JULY

Su	Mo	Tu	We	Th	Fr	Sa
			1	2	3	4
5	6	7	8	9	10	11
12	13	14	15	16	17	18
19	20	21	22	23	24	25
26	27	28	29	30	31	

1. Washington reports largest peacetime deficit of $9.4 billion.

1. Tunis: Prince Azzedine Bey, heir to Tunisian crown, assassinated by ex-convict (→ 10/28).

4. Wimbledon: Vic Sexias over Kurt Nielson 9-7, 6-3, 6-4; Maureen Connolly over Dorothy Hart 8-6, 7-5.

6. Paris: Vietnam and Laos accept French talks on independence (→ 17).

10. Ike asks Kremlin to let U.S. send $15 mil. in aid to East Berlin (→ 21).

13. Managua: Central American states resolve to fight communism; only Guatemala absent.

13. Louisiana: First big U.S. plant producing hydrazine opens at Lake Charles.

14. Paris: Seven killed, 130 injured as North Africans riot on Bastille Day.

14. Korea: Communists mount biggest attack in two years, advancing two miles (→ 28).

16. California: Lieut. Col. Wm. Barns breaks air speed record, traveling at 715.7 mph.

17. Vietnam: French Union paratroopers smash Viet Minh base at Lanson (→ 24).

20. Israel and Soviet Union reopen diplomatic relations.

21. U.S. Navy demonstrates Sea Dart, first jet fighter seaplane.

21. Soviets demand U.S. halt distribution of free food to East Berliners (→ 27).

22. New York: Jehovah's Witnesses, in world assembly at Yankee Stadium, baptize 4,640 in one day.

26. Louison Bobet wins Tour de France.

27. Berlin: 10,000 cross into West for free food (→ 1/1/54).

28. Rome: Premier Gasperi resigns, beaten in vote (→ 8/13).

29. U.S. B-50 downed by Soviets off Vladivostok.

DEATHS

16. Hilaire Belloc, U.K. Roman Catholic writer (*7/27/1870).

17. Maude Adams, American actress (*11/11/1872).

Korean armistice begins

In a stark setting at Panmunjom, the war comes to an end. Lieutenant General W. Harrison (left) and General Nam Il (rt.) sign the Korean armistice.

Korea is now officially ruled under two flags: South (left) and North (right).

July 28. For the first time in three years, the shooting stopped in Korea last night. An armistice took effect, and the two sides counted their losses. Nearly 25,000 American soldiers are dead. More than 100,000 were injured. More than a million South Koreans and more than a million Communists lost their lives. Millions of South Koreans are homeless.

While the shooting stopped, the war is not necessarily over. New tensions have seized the Korean peninsula. South Korea boycotted the signing ceremony at Panmunjom. President Syngman Rhee reluctantly agreed to observe the armistice "for a limited time" while Korea's new border and the return of prisoners of war are settled by a political conference.

Soviet Premier Georgi Malenkov pledged support for North Korea's effort to reunify the country. President Eisenhower asked Congress for $200 million in emergency aid for South Korea. Former President Truman said he hopes the truce means peace for Korea (→ 8/5).

Attack by Castro guerrillas repulsed

July 26. Up to 200 armed, Cuban activists attacked two army barracks near Santiago de Cuba today. Troops loyal to President Batista repelled the attackers, described by Batista as Communists and supporters of former President Prio. Some 55 people were killed. The rest were taken prisoner, including their leader, a young revolutionary and lawyer named Fidel Castro. Batista said Castro and his men launched their "crazy attempt against the armed forces" by driving 800 miles from Havana and infiltrating the Santiago area during a carnival. Castro has been linked to a terrorist group criticized by Communists for its "adventurism" (→ 10/30/54).

Cuban guerrilla leader Castro.

Soviets oust Beria as enemy of the people

Beria, secret police chief 1938-1953.

July 10. Charged with lusting for power and attempting to implant capitalism in the Soviet Union, First Deputy Premier Lavrenti Beria has been fired and will face trial for his alleged misdeeds. Beria, who is also the Minister of Internal Affairs in charge of the secret police, had been regarded as the second in command to Premier Georgi Malenkov. But now, with the surprise dismissal and indictment, his freedom and even his life are in jeopardy. Today's announcement called Beria "an agent" of imperialism and "malignant enemy of the Soviet people" (→ 9/13).

"Mr. Republican," Robert Taft, is dead

July 31. Senate majority leader Robert Taft died today of malignant tumors. The Ohio Senator's death hit the nation hard, especially Republicans who looked to the 63-year-old politician as a pillar of strength and determination. Taft, who had battled and lost to Dwight Eisenhower last year for the Republican presidential nomination, was exalted by the President as a "wise counselor and a valued friend." Son of America's 27th President, William Howard Taft, the senator was revered as "Mr. Republican."

French paratroopers envelop Lang-Son

July 24. French troops in Vietnam carried off "Operation Swallow" without a hitch. As part of the new ambitious Navarre Plan, paratroopers jumped into Lang-Son and recaptured the area in northeast Tonkin from the Communists. But General Henri Navarre, the new commander of French troops in Indochina, was disappointed by the operation. The Viet Minh melted into the jungle, and the French were not able to draw them into combat. Navarre has advised superiors in Paris that this war is like the conflict in Korea. It cannot be won. French defense officials cabled back that Navarre should do his best to protect his troops (→ 10/14).

"Operation Swallow."

Public unrest leads to change in Hungary

July 4. If the new Hungarian Prime Minister Imre Nagy can be believed, Hungarian communism is about to fulfill its billing as a "people's democracy."

Nagy, who has just replaced Matyas Rakosi, vows an easier life for farmers, consumers and just about everyone else, promising a higher standard of living mainly by subordinating heavy industry to agricultural needs.

His speech, about the most revolutionary ever heard in a Communist country, heralds an end to enforced collectivization. Individual trade is to be allowed once more, and religion controlled with a lighter hand. Internment camps are reportedly to be abolished immediately, with amnesty granted for minor offenses. And the ban on travel will be lifted.

In his dramatic appeasement of growing public unrest, Nagy declared that while Hungary plans to cultivate peace and friendship with Russia, it also envisages trade relations with capitalist as well as Communist countries (→ 4/18/55).

Gents, and others, prefer Marilyn Monroe

Marilyn Monroe and Jane Russell in "Gentlemen Prefer Blondes."

July 15. A musical comedy film, "Gentlemen Prefer Blondes," debuted tonight. Audiences entered wondering, well, do men prefer blondes? They exited with another burning question: Are diamonds, as one song purports, indeed a girl's best friend? Existential queries aside, "Gentlemen" is fluff starring Jane Russell and Marilyn Monroe.

Based on an Anita Loos story, the film follows two gals from Little Rock making the big time in Paris. Miss Monroe's character is named Lorelei Lee, a well-meaning gold-digger. "I cannot define Lorelei's character," says Miss Monroe. "I know what's in her mind."

There are several jokes in the film relating to bustlines. At one point one woman wants to exit a ship's porthole. She makes it halfway.

1953

AUGUST

Su	Mo	Tu	We	Th	Fr	Sa
						1
2	3	4	5	6	7	8
9	10	11	12	13	14	15
16	17	18	19	20	21	22
23	24	25	26	27	28	29
30	31					

5. U.S.: Burt Lancaster appears in "From Here to Eternity."

5. Korea: Communists free first 400 U.N. prisoners under terms of armistice (→ 6).

6. Washington: Gen. Mark Clark advocates using A-bomb if Koreans break truce (→ 8).

7. Ike signs bill to admit 214,000 extra immigrants to U.S. in next three years.

8. Paris: Two million walk out of jobs in protest over expected cutbacks in civil service (→ 13).

8. Seoul: Dulles and S. Korean For. Min. Pyun Yung Tai sign mutual defense pact (→ 9/20).

8. U.S.: Franklin Held sets javeline record of 267 feet.

10. NATO names Gen. Servais head of Central European army.

11. Mediterranean: Quake kills 1,000 in Ionian Islands.

13. France paralyzed by general strike.→

13. Rome: Giuseppe Pella succeeds Gasperi as premier.

13. Iran: Shah issues decree deposing Prime Minister Mossadegh (→ 16).

13. U.S.: Pianist Liberace now on WNBT on Sundays.

15. Washington: Gen. Ridgway named U.S. chief of staff.

16. Iran: Shah and empress flee to Baghdad after failed attempt to oust Mossadegh (→ 20).

20. Iran: Premier Mossadegh gives up post to Maj. Gen. Fazollah Zahedi (→ 22).

21. Moscow: Soviets ban lobotomy as inhumane.

23. Washington announces 30 million will enter school in fall, ten million too many.

24. Tehran: Premier Zahedi opens drive against banned Communist Tudeh Party (→ 9/5).

25. U.S. Air Force announces perfection of device to deliver A-bomb overseas (→ 3/1/54).

29. Paris: Jacqueline Auriol becomes second woman flier to break sound barrier.

29. France grants Cambodia control of courts and police (→ 3/2/55).

Soviet Union has the hydrogen bomb

Aug 14. The United States no longer has a monopoly on the production of the hydrogen bomb, Soviet Premier Georgi Malenkov announced today. Malenkov gave no details of the Soviet Union's success in building and testing a hydrogen bomb. He made his claim in a single paragraph of a four-hour speech delivered to the Supreme Soviet.

American politicians reacted with shock to Malenkov's statement, but nuclear scientists said Soviet success was predictable. Both nations have been in a race to develop this most powerful of weapons.

While even the smallest details of both programs are secret, some American scientists say the Soviets are ahead because their bomb is small enough to be carried by an airplane, while the hydrogen bomb exploded by the United States at Eniwetok last year is as yet too large for use in warfare (→ 25).

Move to suburbs troubles the cities

Aug 13. The loss of well-to-do residents, who are in part attracted by suburban advantages, in part repelled by city difficulties, is a basic problem for New York and other large cities. The exodus places a heavier tax burden on city inhabitants for transit, welfare, sanitation and so on. The big city must make itself more attractive to present residents by creating more light, air and open space and by re-emphasizing its own advantages.

The suburban family on wheels.

Mossadegh overthrown and Shah returns

Aug 22. Iranian troops loyal to the Shah of Iran toppled the government of Mohammed Mossadegh on Tuesday and installed Major General Fazollah Zahedi as Premier. Zahedi had been handpicked by the shah before he fled. The shah's troops and tanks fought a fierce battle with Mossadegh's household guards before bursting into his fortress home in Tehran. The eccentric Mossadegh, known to receive visitors in bed, was not receiving anyone. He was nowhere to be seen.

Shah Mohammed Reza Pahlevi flew back to Tehran from Baghdad today. It is widely believed that the American CIA helped engineer his return to the throne (→ 24).

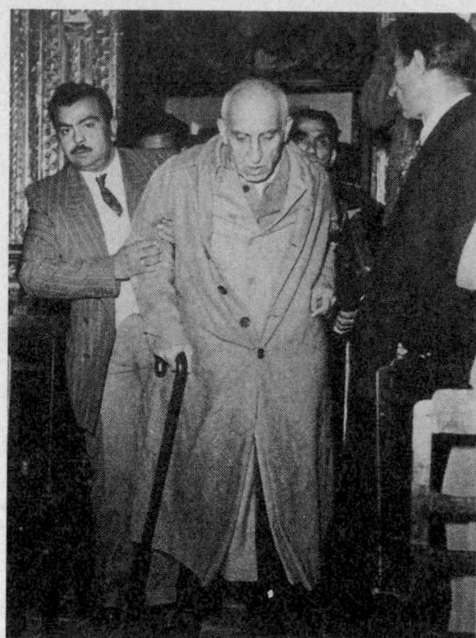

Ousted Premier Mossadegh.

Strike led by civil servants cripples France

August. This is the month almost everyone in France is supposed to go on vacation. But there are more workers on strike than there are on the beaches. A government plan to sneak through austerity measures during the peak vacation period failed miserably. Strikes spread like wildfire throughout the country, stopping rail service, interrupting mail deliveries and knocking out most telephone service. Gas pressure is low in the big cities. Electricity is in short supply.

Premier Laniel's government tried to tighten its belt to reduce an enormous budget deficit. Banking officials were warning Laniel that his budget, swollen by military spending in Indochina, might start a run on the franc. Laniel's solution was to cut the budget and push back the retirement age.

Union workers in Paris started a work slowdown. It became a full-fledged strike after postal workers in Bordeaux walked off the job. The private sector was soon affected, and four million workers were on strike. Many of them said they would not return to work until they received pay raises.

Morocco ousts Sultan; Ben Arafa succeeds

New Sultan Ben Arafa.

Aug 21. Sidi Moulay Mohammed Ben Arafa was today proclaimed Sultan of Morocco following the ouster of Sultan Sidi Mohammed Ben Youssef, exiled in Corsica.

As the sultan is expected to annouce sweeping changes which will effect the French administration of the Moroccan protectorate, Paris officials are mapping wide reforms with a view to greater independence for their North African holdings.

The former sultan owned a great deal of land, and the government plans to safeguard these interests in his name. This may be difficult, as many who demanded Ben Youssef's ouster have ideas similar to those of Egypt's President Naguib and are, accordingly, demanding drastic land reforms (→ 8/7/54).

1953

SEPTEMBER

Su	Mo	Tu	We	Th	Fr	Sa
		1	2	3	4	5
6	7	8	9	10	11	12
13	14	15	16	17	18	19
20	21	22	23	24	25	26
29	28	29	30			

1. Soviets open Moscow University.

4. California's Florence Chadwick sets English Channel swimming mark at 14 hrs., 42 min.

5. Ike announces $45 mil. U.S. grant to Iran (→ 12/21).

7. Britain claims world speed record when Hawker Hunter fighter flies 727.6 mph.

7. N.Y.: Tony Trabert beats Vic Sexias for U.S. tennis title at Forest Hills.

9. Chinese Communist warship shells British launch, killing seven, wounding five (→ 2/14/54).

10. New York: Gary Cooper appears in "Return to Paradise."

10. Martin Durkin resigns as U.S. sec. of labor over enforcement of Taft-Hartley (→ 10/1).

13. Moscow: Nikita Khrushchev elected first sec. of Communist Party (→ 12/23).

15. N.Y.: Mme. Vijaya Lakshmi Pandit chosen president of U.N. General Assembly.

16. New York: "The Robe" shown at Roxy in demonstration of Cinemascope.

20. Korea: Red pilot lands MIG-15 near Seoul and surrenders to U.S. (→ 22).

20. Cairo: 13 Farouk ex-aides seized in round-up of former monarchy (→ 2/28/54).

21. U.S.: CBS presents Orwell's "1984" as TV movie.

26. Spain signs pact giving U.S. air and naval bases (→ 1/23/55).

27. U.S.: AT&T reports 41 new TV stations in 35 cities added to Bell system (→ 10/31).

30. Washington: Negro Louis B. Toomer sworn in as Treasury register.

30. Swiss professor August Piccard dives a record 10,330 feet in self-built craft off Italian coast.

DEATHS

2. Jonathan M. Wainwright, U.S. general (*8/23/1883).

8. Frederick M. Vinson, 13th chief justice of U.S. Supreme Court (*1/22/1890).

15. Eric Mendelsohn, German architect (*3/21/1887).

23 American POWs refuse repatriation

A sight for sore eyes in Seattle.

Sept 22. As U.S. troops begin to return from Korea, 23 American war prisoners and one Briton have refused repatriation and will stay with their Communist captors, Communist correspondent Wilfred Burchett reported today. In addition, 355 South Koreans decided to remain in the Communist bloc.

Some 3,400 members of the United Nations Command are still missing and American authorities are fearful that their whereabouts may never be known.

Some 27,000 North Korean prisoners of war have refused to return to their nation. General Blackshear Bryan, U.N. chief truce commissioner, said, "These people are not in our custody. They are free. The fact that they risked their lives to avoid being returned to (North Korea) is ample demonstration of their feelings on this matter" (→ 11/23).

Wedding of the decade: Kennedy-Bouvier

Sept 12. John Fitzgerald Kennedy wed Miss Jacqueline Lee Bouvier this afternoon in Newport, R.I. Nearly 3,000 people tried to crash the affair. The new Mrs. Kennedy, until recently the inquiring photographer for the Washington Times-Herald, should have been accustomed to curious crowds; yet along with her ivory silk gown she wore a bewildered air. Her husband is the Senator from Massachusetts, a Harvard College graduate and former PT boat commander.

The newlyweds cut their wedding cake after the ceremony in Newport.

Earl Warren chosen as U.S. Chief Justice

Sept 30. Meeting President Eisenhower's requirements of honesty, experience and moderate philosophy, California Governor Earl Warren was chosen as the 14th Chief Justice. Upon likely congressional approval, he will replace recently deceased Chief Justice Vinson.

The 62-year old lawyer is known for his liberal policies, but even conservative members of Congress respect his dedication to law. He recently told reporters, "I have become devoted to the judicial processes and to the due process of law." He will have ample opportunity to exhibit this devotion and will be faced with the controversial issue of school segregation and Taft-Hartley labor questions.

Sept 24. Brawling Rocky Marciano has defended his heavyweight title. The fight was stopped in the 11th after challenger Roland LaStarza emerged from between the ropes only to meet another brutal barrage.

1953

OCTOBER

Su	Mo	Tu	We	Th	Fr	Sa
				1	2	3
4	5	6	7	8	9	10
11	12	13	14	15	16	17
18	19	20	21	22	23	24
25	26	27	28	29	30	31

1. Ike invokes Taft-Hartley Act in move to stop dock strike on North Atlantic coast (→ 12/1).

6. British rush troops to British Guiana to forestall suspected Communist rebellion.

7. Florence Chadwick sets record, swimming Bosphorus from Europe to Asia and back.

8. U.S. and Britain to pull out of Trieste, leaving Zone A to Italy (→ 11).

9. Miami: New anti-polio vaccine ready to try on children.

11. Belgrade: Tito threatens attack if Italy enters Zone A in Trieste (→ 17).

14. Germany: Sabena flight crashes near Frankfurt; 44 dead.

14. Vietnam: French Union troops begin operation Seagull in Tonkin delta (→ 11/29).

17. Rome: Premier Pella says he will resign if U.S., U.K. yield to Yugoslavia on Trieste (→ 25).

18. Poland: Catholics mass for protest over govt. dismissal of Cardinal Wyszinski (→ 4/10/56).

19. Texas: Ike and Mexican Pres. Adolfo Ruiz open Rio Grande Falcon Dam with amity pledge.

20. Tokyo: N.Y. Giants manager Leo Durocher gets key to city during 14-game Japan tour.

20. U.S.: Ray Bradbury's "Farenheit 451" published.

22. Paris: France signs pact giving Laos independence within French Union.

23. U.K. merges South Rhodesia into Federation of Rhodesia and Nyasaland (→ 2/25/59).

23. U.S. reports 1,456 forced off federal payroll in last 4 months by security inquiry (→ 11/10).

27. Bonn: Adenauer names former Nazi to Cabinet.

28. Tunisia: French put police back under civil authority to placate nationalists (→ 7/31/54).

28. Israel halts rerouting of Jordan River at U.N. request.

DEATHS

1. John Marin, American modernist painter (*12/23/1870).

8. Kathleen Ferrier, British opera contralto (*4/22/1912).

Yankees win fifth World Series in row

Oct 5. Champagne flowed freely at Yankee Stadium in the aftermath of an incredible saga of baseball history. The Yankees won their fifth straight World Series, a feat never before achieved, and the bubbly tasted even sweeter to their 63-year-old manager, Casey Stengel.

Stengel became the first manager to match five straight pennants with five successive world titles, achieved in his first five years in the American League. By finishing off the Dodgers, 4-3, in the decisive sixth game of the series, the Yanks chalked up their 16th world championship against only four defeats.

Carmen is seen on new color TV sets

Oct 31. A few homes in and about New York City with experimental TVs were treated to a splash of chromatics: Bizet's opera "Carmen" was telecast in color. The opera, seen on NBC at 5:30 p.m., was also in the usual monochrome on black and white sets. Performed at the New York Colonial Theatre, "Carmen" was a fine choice for color broadcast. Vibrant reds, from matador's cape to Carmen's gown, were stunning on stage and screen.

The FCC is due to approve specifications for commercial color TVs in a few weeks. The sets may flood shops by Christmas (→ 12/18).

Ricky, Ozzie, David and Harriet Nelson, America's favorite TV family, on the set of "Ozzie and Harriet," Friday at 8:00 p.m.

Wrangling over Trieste increases tension

Anti-Italian protests break out in Belgrade after a vehement speech by Tito.

Oct 25. The Trieste situation has heated up again as Yugoslavia denounced as "obvious hypocrisy" Italy's proposal that both nations withdraw their soldiers from the nearby frontier.

The conflict stems from 1945 when Marshal Tito's forces claimed the former Italian port city for Yugoslavia. Following that, an Italian-Yugoslovian peace treaty created the independent and neutral Free Territory of Trieste with two zones, A and B, under British, U.S. and Yugoslav control respectively. On October 8, the U.S. and Britain announced their decision to hand Zone A back to the Italians, a proposal rejected by both Yugoslovia and the Soviet Union.

In August, the Italians sent more troops to the frontier north of Trieste for fear that Yugoslovia was about to annex Zone B, a contention denied by the Yugoslavs.

Today's statement by the Yugoslavs stresses that it did not then counter the Italian move and that its own similar movements are "security measures" taken only as a result of the October 8th decision.

Yugoslav troops are in a position to seize Zone A at will. Tito has said he will do so if the U.S. and Britain follow through with their announced intentions (→ 10/26/54).

Israelis devastate Jordanian village

Oct 14. The festering tensions between Jordan and Israel exploded today in the Jordanian border village of Qibya. An Israeli army unit, enraged by a grenade attack yesterday that killed a woman and her two children in Tirat Yehuda, Israel, refused to wait for the Jordanian government to punish the terrorists. The Israelis stormed into Qibya and demolished 50 houses. Some 69 Jordanians were killed, many of them women and children who had been hiding in their homes. Prime Minister David Ben Gurion tried to convince critics that civilians, not soldiers, destroyed Qibya. But the attack was quickly condemned by the Mixed Armistice Commission and the United Nations (→ 11/9).

Aircraft carrier explodes; 37 dead

Oct 16. Thirty-seven people have burned to death in a fiery explosion on the aircraft carrier Leyte, docked in Boston's Charlestown Naval Shipyard. Another 40 were injured in the blast, but the tragedy could have been more catastrophic, as approximately 1,400 officers and crewmen and an undetermined number of civilian workers were aboard. The fire surged through the vessel so fast that Captain Thomas Akroon, the ship's commanding officer, said that within 30 seconds of the explosion his cabin was filled with thick, black smoke. An investigation has yet to determine the cause of the disaster, but officials report that the inquiry will continue (→ 11/2).

1953

NOVEMBER

Su	Mo	Tu	We	Th	Fr	Sa
1	2	3	4	5	6	7
8	9	10	11	12	13	14
15	16	17	18	19	20	21
22	23	24	25	26	27	28
29	30					

1. Czech runner Emil Zatopek sets world mark in 5,000-meters at 29:1.6.

3. Soviets insist Peking delegate be included in Big Four talks proposed by West (→ 1/31/54).

3. New York: Lillian Gish opens in "A Trip to Bountiful."

5. New York: "Kiss Me Kate," with Kathryn Grayson, opens.

5. Israel: Moshe Sharett replaces David Ben Gurion as prime minister (→ 11/2/55).

9. N.Y.: U.K., France, Greece charge Israel with death of 53 in Jordanian village (→ 14).

10. Washington: Truman gets subpoena to testify before HUAC (→ 12).

11. Cambridge, Mass.: Polio virus definitely identified and photgraphed for first time.

11. Manila: Ramon Magsaysay wins Filipino presidency (→ 5/17/54).

12. Truman refuses to testify before HUAC (→ 24).

13. Ike goes to Canada in his first state visit outside country.

14. Arab League offers U.S. choice between friendship with Arab world or loss of strategic bases in Mideast (→ 16).

16. U.S. joins in condemnation of Israel for Jordan raid (→ 3/17/54).

21. L.A.: Scott Crossfield flies at Mach II—1,327 mph—in Douglas D-588-II Skyrocket.

23. North Koreans sign ten-year aid pact with Peking (→ 27).

26. New York: 35,000 teachers to get "Permit Communist Conspirators to be teachers?" booklets (→ 12/9).

27. Taipei: Chiang and Syngman Rhee hint at alliance at dinner meeting (→ 12/26).

28. Belgrade: Yugoslavs give amnesty to 7,194 political prisoners (→ 1/17/54).

28. Philadelphia: Army over Navy 20-7 in football.

DEATH

11. Lewis Ginzberg, Jewish-American scholar (*11/28/1873).

O'Neill dies, ending great drama career

Nov 27. Eugene O'Neill, considered by many critics to be America's greatest playwright, died this afternoon in his suite at the Shelton Hotel in Boston. O'Neill, who celebrated his 65th birthday last month, had been suffering from a degenerative disorder that was so severe he was unable to sign his own name. Until recently, he was still working on a long, unpublished cycle of plays. O'Neill's first full-length play, "Beyond the Horizon," won a Pulitzer Prize in 1920. He won the prize later in his life for "Anna Christie" and "Strange Interlude." Funeral plans are private.

O'Neill, dramatist of the tormented.

Another ship blast kills 7, injures 13

Nov 2. For the second time in 17 days, a deadly blast ripped apart a ship in Boston's harbor. Today, an explosion took seven lives and injured 13 persons on board the Norwegian freighter Black Falcon. The crew on the 8,850-ton cargo ship was unpacking a load of chemicals at the Boston Army Base when a drum of sodium peroxide broke.

According to the longshoremen who survived the fire, smoke and fumes oozed out of the damaged barrel and "then there was one explosion, then another, all the time getting worse." While no official cause of the explosion has been recorded, the leaking drum is believed to have ignited the tragedy. Last month, a fire killed 37 aboard the carrier Leyte.

French paratroops land at Dien Bien Phu and organize defenses

A helicopter, latest innovation in war strategy, lands troops at Dien Bien Phu.

French paratroopers descend onto the Viet Minh-controlled plateau.

Nov 29. French paratroopers surprised the Viet Minh and captured Dien Bien Phu, a strategic plateau surrounded by mountains and rice paddies near the Laotian border. Sixty Communists were killed in "Operation Castor." The French lost 14 men. General Navarre plans on replacing the paratroopers with regular army units, who will defend the area and improve an airport built by the Japanese during their occupation. Navarre wants to extend the runway so that it will be long enough for Dakota planes to land.

Navarre, who has been pessimistic about winning this guerrilla war, thinks the capture of Dien Bien Phu is the most important action by the French in months. The general believes he can defend the area with mobile columns radiating out from the airport. Navarre hopes the base will thwart the Communists' seasonal offensives, serve as a center for pro-French resistance fighters and prevent General Giap from increasing his recent gains in Laos.

The French have received conflicting signals from Ho Chi Minh, the Communist leader, about peace talks for Vietnam. In a message published in the Swedish magazine Expressen, Ho announced that he is ready to consider a French proposal for an armistice. But in the same message, Ho criticized "American imperialists who pressure France to intensify the war." Ho predicted that the French will be weakened, defeated and ultimately replaced by American troops (→ 2/10/54).

Dylan Thomas goes into that good night

Nov 9. "Do not go gentle into that good night/ Old age should burn and rave at close of day/ Rage, rage against the dying of the light." So counseled poet Dylan Thomas who himself died today at the age of 39. Thomas preferred to rage at life, inciting brawls and drinking himself senseless. His respite and poetry lay in childhood reveries.

Thomas was born at Swansea, Wales, October 14, 1914, the son of a teacher. At age 19, he published his first obscure but well-received book, "18 Poems." Despite financial straits, he produced "25 Poems" (1936) and short story collections "Portrait of the Artist as a Young Dog" (1940) and "Adventures in the Skin Trade" (1955).

The owner of a true, expressive voice, Thomas often read his works on British radio and lectured on American campuses. A radio play and a nostalgic sketch, "Under Milk Wood" and "A Child's Christmas in Wales," have been recorded. They are due for later release.

Thomas' admirers hope he finds his lost youth in the hereafter. "Now as I was young and easy under the apple boughs/ About the lilting house and happy as the grass was green."

Campanella named as most valuable

Nov 19. Roy Campanella got an unexpected present for his 32nd birthday. For the second time in his baseball career, the Dodger catcher has been voted the National League's Most Valuable Player. Campanella, who won the honor two years ago, was overcome after being notified that he had collected 297 votes from the Baseball Writers Association. This was the highest point total since Stan Musial of the Cards won with 303 in 1948. "I hope to play baseball as long as I live," Campanella exulted.

Truman accused of aiding Communists

Wisconsin Sen. McCarthy (center).

Nov 24. The Truman administration "crawled with Communists," declared Wisconsin Senator Joseph McCarthy in a television speech last night. He accused former President Harry Truman of aiding Communists, including the late Harry Dexter White, suspected Soviet spy. It has been charged that while president, Truman promoted White, despite a report that the financial expert was an espionage agent. The Chairman of the House Un-American Activities Committee went on to blame the "Truman-Acheson regime" for fostering communism.

The speech came in reply to Truman's TV address earlier this month, when the former president refused to comply with a House subpoena for the White espionage case, citing the separation of powers doctrine as justification. Truman also assailed the investigation, warning Americans to protect themselves against "the onslaught of fear and hysteria which are being manipulated in this country purely for political purposes" (→ 26).

1953

DECEMBER

Su	Mo	Tu	We	Th	Fr	Sa
		1	2	3	4	5
6	7	8	9	10	11	12
13	14	15	16	17	18	19
20	21	22	23	24	25	26
29	28	29	30	31		

1. N.Y.: Longshoremen defy federal injuction, immobilizing ports in strike (→ 4/2/54).

5. Britain and Iran resume diplomatic relations (→ 4/10/54).

5. Italy and Yugoslavia agree to pull troops out of disputed Trieste border area (→ 10/26/54).

8. N.Y.: Ike proposes "atoms for peace" international energy stockpile (→ 1/12/54).

9. G.E. pledges to dismiss all Communist workers (→ 1/1/54).

16. White House allows press to print direct quotations from press conference for first time.

18. FCC rules color TV can go on the air (→ 2/6/54).

21. Tehran: Ex-Premier Mossadegh gets three-year jail term (→ 11/10/54).

26. U.S. to withdraw two divisions from Korea (→ 1/20/54).

27. Detroit: Lions take football title 17-16 over Cleveland.

30. Ken Rosewall defeats Vic Seixas to take fourth straight Davis Cup for Australia.

31. Hollywood: Poll rates Gary Cooper box office king for 1953.

DEATHS

2. Francis Picabia, French painter (*1/22/1878).

14. Marjorie Kinnan Rawlings, American novelist, "The Yearling" (*8/8/1896).

19. Robert Millikan, U.S. physicist, 1923 Nobel (*3/22/1868).

CULTURAL EVENTS, 1953

Literature: James Baldwin's "Go Tell it on the Mountain"; Arthur Miller's "The Crucible."

Academia: Simone de Beauvior's "The Second Sex"; B.F. Skinner's "Science and Human Behavior"; Crick and Watson's double helix model for DNA.

Music: "Doggie in the Window"; "Stranger in Paradise."

The Arts: Chagall's "Eiffel Tower"; Saarinen's General Motors Tech. Center, Michigan.

Film: Mankiewicz' "Julius Caesar"; "Roman Holiday," with Audrey Hepburn; "From Here to Eternity," Academy Award.

In Bermuda's sunshine, Big 3 affirm unity

French Council President Laniel, Eisenhower and Churchill in Bermuda.

Dec 8. Reaffirming their unity under NATO, rejecting as either "justified or permanent" the present division of Europe and approving talks with the Soviets, Britain, France and the U.S. concluded their Big Three Bermuda Conference in accord on common problems and the ways they can be solved.

An "early meeting" with the Soviet Union is planned in the hope of making some progress toward the reunification of Germany "in freedom." Also on the agenda is an Austrian state treaty.

Regarding Trieste, the United States and Britain are sticking to their decision to withdraw from Zone A and turn it over to Italy, and have drawn a new plan aimed at getting Italy and Yugoslovia to settle the dispute at a five-power parley. The communique expresses the hope that "in due course peaceful means will be found to enable the countries of Eastern Europe again to play their part as free nations in a free Europe" (→ 1/31/54).

Beria, once police boss, is executed

Dec 23. A firing squad shot to death former Soviet Deputy Premier Lavrenti Beria and six of his aides today. Beria, the second in command and former chief of the Soviet secret police, was indicted with his co-defendants in July of conspiring against the Communist Party and attempting to restore a capitalist state in Russia.

According to official Soviet statements, Beria had confessed to the charges of betrayal and received "the highest degree of capital punishment—shooting." The trial lasted six days; it was closed to the public and the Soviet press carried no information about it until the seven "traitors" were executed.

Beria allegedly led counterrevolutions against the party in 1919 and then, after entering public life, "continued and expanded his secret criminal ties with foreign intelligence services" (→ 2/7/54).

Pregnancy induced with frozen sperm

Dec 3. University of Iowa scientists announced today that they have achieved the first human pregnancies using deep-frozen sperm. The first baby conceived by insemination by frozen sperm will be born in about three months, they said.

Two other women in Iowa have also used the method successfully, but their pregnancies are not as advanced, said Drs. R.G. Bunge and J.K. Sherman of the University of Iowa Medical School. X-rays show that the babies are developing normally, they said. Frozen sperm has been widely used in agriculture, with sperm from prize United States cattle having been flown as far away as Argentina to inseminate cows.

No birth defects have been reported in the offspring resulting from frozen sperm insemination, a fact that has now led to the use of the technique to help infertile human couples achieve pregnancies.

Sir Winston the writer wins Nobel

Dec 10. British politician extraordinaire Sir Winston Churchill has been given the Nobel Prize for literature. The award is given in recognition of "historical works and biographies as well as his brilliant speeches made in the service of human valor." Churchill's wartime addresses might have warranted the drama award. "In the past we have had a light which flickered," he once said, "in the present we have a light which flames, and in the future there will be a light which shines all over land and sea."

The Peace Prize went to former U.S. Secretary of State George C. Marshall. His was the mind behind the Marshall Plan, the comprehensive strategy for the revitalization of Europe's war-ravaged economy. Other Nobel winners were Hermann Straudinger for chemistry, Frits Zernike for physics and both F.A. Lipmann and Hans A. Krebs for medicine.

Search begins for elusive Snowman

Dec 31. A British-sponsored expedition to track down the elusive Abominable Snowman has arrived in India on its way to Nepal. Edmund Hillary, who conquered Mount Everest six months ago, says he might have seen footprints of the strange, hairy beast on an earlier Himalayan expedition.

Edinburgh and the Old Vic Co. present Claire Bloom as Ophelia and Richard Burton as Hamlet.

1954

JANUARY

Su	Mo	Tu	We	Th	Fr	Sa
					1	2
3	4	5	6	7	8	9
10	11	12	13	14	15	16
17	18	19	20	21	22	23
24	25	26	27	28	29	30
31						

1. Washington: Sen. Pat McCarran says McCarthy has overstepped his bounds (→ 8).

1. Pasadena: Michigan St. over U.C.L.A. in Rose Bowl; parade broadcast in color first time.

1. West Berlin reports taking in 305,000 East Germans (1.7% of population) in 1953 (→ 2/18).

1. Haiti, second New World nation, marks 150th anniversary of independence from France.

2. Bonn: Adenauer tells 1,000 freed POWs Germany is "purified" of Hitlerism (→ 5/5/55).

3. Brazil: Second Biennial Intl. Exhibition of Modern Art opens in Sao Paulo.

7. Vatican reminds Catholics watching mass on TV does not fill religious requirements.

8. Ike proposes stripping convicted Communists of U.S. citizenship (→ 2/2).

8. N.Y.: IBM displays first use of machine as a translator.

8. AP names Maureen Connolly (for third year in row) and Ben Hogan athletes of year.

9. N.Y.: Ted Mack's "Amateur Hour" broadcast in color.

12. Avalanches kill 198 in Austria, Switzerland, W. Germany.

13. Washington: Dulles, Soviet Ambassador Zarubin discuss intl. atom energy pool (→ 3/13).

16. New York: "South Pacific" ends Broadway run of 4.5 years.

20. Korea: Over 22,000 anti-Communist prisoners turned over to U.N. forces (→ 2/1).

20. South African Labor Party backs universal franchise, regardless of race (→ 11/30).

26. U.S. Steel's 1953 earnings reported largest since 1917.

29. Rome says U.S. Ambassador Clare Booth Luce is interfering in Italy's internal affairs.

30. U.S.: Electric power now reaching 50 million, up from ten million in 1919.→

31. Belgrade: Tito rules out Soviet-style centralized government and economy (→ 5/26/55).

31. Saudi Arabia: Anglo-Iranian Oil Co. refinery at Aden to be largest, at 120,000 barrels/day.

Nautilus, first U.S. atomic sub, launched

The 340-foot atomic warship Nautilus floats in the harbor at Groton.

Jan 21. The submarine Nautilus, the first ship powered by atomic energy, was launched today at the shipyard of the Electric Boat Company in Groton, Connecticut. More than 12,000 workers and other spectators crowded into temporary bleachers to watch Mamie Eisenhower, wife of the President, break a bottle of champagne across the bow of the Nautilus in the traditional christening ceremony.

The 340-foot-long submarine, built at a cost of $55 million, is capable of cruising around the world without surfacing because its atomic engine requires no air. Its top speed of over 30 knots makes the Nautilus capable of outrunning all but the fastest surface vessels while remaining submerged.

While the Nautilus adds a potent weapon to the arsenal, speakers said she can also be influential in pointing the way to peaceful uses of atomic energy, since the reactors that power her will serve as prototypes for a generation of large civilian nuclear electric generating stations.

Adm. Rickover (left) and sub model.

The sub is due to start a series of sea tests soon and could join the fleet next year. Hyman Rickover has been nominated permanent Rear Admiral after his key role in developing the Nautilus (→ 3/1).

Dulles to talk atoms with Soviets

Jan 12. Atomic energy needs serious discussion to limit its force to peaceful purposes, says President Eisenhower. For that reason, Secretary of State John Foster Dulles will meet with Soviet Ambassador Georgi Zarubin tomorrow at the State Department for preliminary talks. A larger conference is expected if the initial talks are productive.

In a dispatch agreeing to talk about nuclear energy, the Soviet Union said it wanted a ban on the production of atomic weapons as a prerequisite to more substantial conversations. However, this is quite unacceptable to the United States, which has consistently said, in the long and protracted debates on the subject, that an effective system of international controls must be devised before it would consider a ban. In other words, before the U.S. will halt testing and production of atomic firepower, it must be sure the Soviets are doing the same.

Despite differences on the weapons issue, the preliminary talks hold hope that energy needs of the future might be met with the splitting of the atom. Some estimate that atomic energy will soon replace coal and water power as a chief source of electricity (→ 13).

Electric power has 50m U.S. customers

Jan 30. The United States continues its superiority in world power production as the 50 millionth customer was added to the nation's power lines last week. Ninety-eight percent of the population of the country is now reportedly hooked up to electric lines. In the relatively short space of one person's lifetime, the electric power industry has progressed from an experimental station built by Thomas Edison on Pearl Street in New York City to one of the cornerstones of modern civilization, indispensable to the nation's high standard of living.

Joe DiMaggio weds Marilyn Monroe

Jan 14. The Yankee Clipper has set out on the sea of matrimony with beautiful movie actress Marilyn Monroe. Former center fielder Joe DiMaggio and Miss Monroe were wed this afternoon in San Francisco City Hall. It is a second marriage for both.

Miss Monroe, born in Los Angeles as Norma Jean Baker, has starred in "Niagara" and "How to Marry a Millionaire." DiMaggio, a San Francisco native, was voted American League Most Valuable Player in 1939, 1941 and 1947. He retired in 1951 with a .325 average, 2,214 hits, 361 home runs and 1,537 runs batted in. The eighth of nine children of a fisherman, he now co-owns an eatery on Fisherman's Wharf. His business partner was best man at the wedding.

Enviable DiMaggio and his bride.

Big 4 meet on arms and other issues

The four flags adorn the center of the conference table.

Jan 31. Delegates from the four most powerful nations in the world are meeting in Berlin this week. The parley opened in West Berlin on January 25 with Soviet Foreign Minister Vyacheslav Molotov suggesting an agenda which most realized would never get Western approval. Among items he stressed for discussion were: the admittance of Communist China into power summits, the abandonment of a European defense community and a reduction of armaments.

While France, Britain and the United States recognize these issues are important to the Soviet Union, they reject most of the planks as Soviet bargaining chips. Of those offered for negotiation, the most crucial concerns atomic weaponry. The Soviets yesterday asked the West not to destroy its nuclear arsenal, to which it concedes superiority, but asked that those nations possessing nuclear bombs pledge never to use them. A similar agreement was formulated at the Geneva conventions regarding poison gas.

The Western powers are treating the proposal with skepticism. The American delegate, Secretary of State John Foster Dulles, has hinted to Molotov no more talks will be held if some agreement is not reached here. Tomorrow, the parley moves across the Iron Curtain into East Berlin (→ 2/18).

Jan 8. To celebrate turning 19 today, an obscure singer named Elvis Presley brought his guitar to a Memphis studio and paid $4 to record "Casual Love" and "I'll Never Stand in Your Way."

Djilas is removed from all positions

Jan 17. Marshal Tito may be creating his own independent brand of communism in Yugoslavia, but he made it dramatically clear today that he will not tolerate a drift toward Western-style democracy. Tito ejected Milovan Djilas from the Communist Central Committee and announced that other "enemies" would also be purged. Vice President Djilas was considered second in line to Tito and a possible successor. Djilas insists that hard-line communism is not the only road to socialism. He has also charged that Tito protects ineffective bureaucrats, and he has called for reform of the Communist League (→ 31).

1954

FEBRUARY

Su	Mo	Tu	We	Th	Fr	Sa
	1	2	3	4	5	6
7	8	9	10	11	12	13
14	15	16	17	18	19	20
21	22	23	24	25	26	27
28						

1. Korea: U.S. downs Soviet MIG while on reconnaissance flight (→ 4/17).

2. U.S. Senate votes $214,000 for McCarthy inquiry, with only Sen. Fulbright dissenting (→ 25).

3. New Delhi: Over 350 Hindus trampled to death in stampede at religious rites.

3. Sydney: Million greet Queen Elizabeth on first royal visit to Australia.

6. N.Y.C. Ballet stages Ballanchine's "The Nutcracker."

6. Kashmir Assembly accepts reunification with India.

6. TV stations now total 360 in U.S., with 231 opened in 1953 (→ 3/25).

7. Moscow: Kremlin purges reach Moldavia, Kazakhstan and Lithuania (→ 21).

8. British push Malayan Communists out to Sumatra (→ 2/8/56).

10. Ike says he can think of no greater tragedy than for U.S. to get involved in Indochina (→ 19).

11. N.Y.: 75,000-watt bulb lit at Rockefeller Center to mark 75th anniversary of Edison's first.

14. China: Nationalists drop 30 mil. leaflets on Shanghai and other coastal cities (→ 3/20).

15. French bathyscaphe dives to record 13,284 feet in Atlantic.

18. Berlin: East and West dump thousands of leaflets on each other, ending month-long truce (→ 9/23).

20. Ford Foundation gives largest grant—$25 mil.—to Fund for Advancement of Education.

21. U.S.S.R.: 3,000 Georgia party members reported purged in last two years (→ 4/26).

22. Met. Life Insurance Co. passes AT&T as world's largest private corp. with $12 bil. assets.

23. Pittsburgh: Salk's polio vaccine first given to children.

28. Damascus: Hashem al-Atassi replaces Gen. Shishekly as Syrian president.

DEATH

13. Frederick Lewis Allen, U.S. historian, editor Harper's magazine (*7/5/1890).

Frozen food sales exceed $1 billion

Feb 1. In 1953 the frozen food industry for the first time passed the billion-dollar mark with retail sales at $1.2 billion, and 3.38 billion pounds sold. The industry's chief problems are linked to rapid growth. Some 64 percent of all retail stores are now equipped with frozen food cabinets. Three-quarters of American families bought frozen foods last year, most of them in the higher income brackets, though frozen foods, particularly vegetables, tend to sell for less than their canned counterparts. Neither railroads nor truckers are as yet providing satisfactory transportation, and the rates are too high.

Bohemian poet is murdered in Village

Feb 7. Greenwich Village poet Maxwell Bodenheim was found murdered with his wife this afternoon. He had a bullet in his chest and a copy of Rachel Carson's "The Sea Around Us" over the wound. His wife had a knife in the back. Police are baffled; there was no robbery and few signs of struggle.

Bodenheim was a controversial poet in the 1920's. His titillating novel "Replenishing Jessica" was a best-seller then. Lately, he faked blindness and begged on the streets.

Leadbelly's famous folk songs released

Feb 6. Folk music fans will be happy to know that legendary Negro folksinger Leadbelly can now be heard on record. Folkway Records today released a four-record set of 94 songs, including "Irene Good Night," "Jailhouse Blues" and "On Top of Old Smokey" which were recorded several months before his death in December 1949. Born Huddie Ledbetter in 1888, Leadbelly's violent personal life—he was jailed three times for murder, attempted murder and assault—was at odds with his musical creativity, his mastery of the 12-string guitar and his role in reviving folk music.

McCarthy tackles Army

McCarthy (far right), in bringing charges against the Army, may finally have overstepped his bounds. The hearings will be televised starting next month.

Feb 25. Senator Joseph R. McCarthy, turning his investigation of alleged Communists in the government from the State Department to the Army, has set the stage for a major confrontation with the Department of the Army and indirectly with the White House.

Army Secretary Robert T. Stevens initially ordered high-ranking Army officers to ignore summons to appear before the senator's investigating subcommittee. He issued the order after he found that McCarthy, in a one-man hearing, had browbeat Brigadier General Ralph W. Zwicker, commander of Camp Kilmer in New Jersey. The much-decorated general had been called before the panel to answer questions as to who had promoted and given an honorable discharge to Major Irving Peress, an Army dentist who the senator accused of having been a Communist. When Zwicker, following orders, declined to answer questions, McCarthy told Zwicker "you are a disgrace to the uniform."

After a meeting with Republican members of the McCarthy subcommittee, arranged at White House instigation, Stevens did an abrupt about-face. In a "Memorandum of Understanding," Stevens agreed to let Army officials testify before the McCarthy panel on the Peress promotion and discharge.

When the agreement was interpreted as an Army surrender to McCarthy, Stevens, sobbing with rage and humiliation, threatened to resign and went to the White House for support. In a statement endorsed by President Eisenhower, who had tried to stay aloof from the dispute, Stevens said he would never allow Army personnel to be "browbeaten" by committees (→ 3/5).

French brace for Dien Bien Phu assault

Feb 19. French General Henri Navarre is about to get what he wants in Vietnam: a full-scale showdown with Communist guerrillas. The Viet Minh offensive across the border in Laos has ground to a halt, short of the royal capital of Luang Prabang. Many of the guerrillas in the 308th Division are sneaking back into Vietnam, and Navarre suspects that General Giap is preparing an all-out assault on the newly fortified French positions at Dien Bien Phu. Navarre believes his soldiers are better equipped than the Communists and can deal them a devastating blow.

A large chunk of the French operation in Viet Nam is being paid for by the United States. Direct and indirect aid amounts to at least $750 million. There is little opposition on Capitol Hill to the financial support, but General Eisenhower has been attacked for sending an Air Force technical mission of 200 men to support the French. Eisenhower, while justifying the war against communism, said he is trying to prevent American participation in a "hot war." The President also said he is reducing United States forces in the Far East by calling home troops from Korea. Some congressmen fear that American forces in Indochina will only encourage Communist China to become involved in the war. A Republican Senator, George Aiken of Vermont, complained that Eisenhower should have informed Congress earlier about the technical mission (→ 3/8).

A helicopter flies supplies into the French camp at Dien Bien Phu.

Egypt's Nasser challenges General Naguib

Naguib and Nasser, vying for power.

Feb 28. Egypt has had three governments in three days, but the dust has settled in Cairo as Lieutenant Colonel Gamal Nasser was reconciled with General Mohammed Naguib. Strongman Naguib quit as President and Premier on Thursday after the revolutionary council balked at giving him "absolute autocratic authority." Nasser took over as head of the council and Premier. After objections from some members of the military junta, Naguib returned as President. Nasser kept his two new titles (→ 3/9).

Cigarette industry put on the defensive

Feb 17. Seeking to counter scientific reports linking lung cancer and cigarette smoking, a group of 14 major tobacco companies announced today the formation of a Tobacco Industry Research Committee. The committee, a joint venture of tobacco growers, distributors and producers, will be in charge of "a scientist of impeachable integrity," the industry said. Concern about lung cancer is blamed for a decline in cigarette sales (→ 6/21).

Big Four and China to discuss peace

Feb 18. "At least we understand each other's position better," said British Foreign Secretary Anthony Eden about the Berlin Big Four Conference. The only real achievement of the parley between France, Britain, the Soviet Union and America was an agreement to meet with Communist China to settle the Korean question and to seek peace in Indochina. The Far East conference was arranged for April 26 in Geneva (→ 3/31).

1954

MARCH

Su	Mo	Tu	We	Th	Fr	Sa
	1	2	3	4	5	6
7	8	9	10	11	12	13
14	15	16	17	18	19	20
21	22	23	24	25	26	27
28	29	30	31			

1. Washington: Five congressmen shot by Puerto Rican nationalists in House.→

1. Caracas: U.S. convenes Organization of American States to discuss threat of communism.

1. London: Billy Graham fills Harringay Arena for opening of three-month crusade (→ 5/22).

5. Washington: McCarthy drops libel suit against ex-Sen. Benton of Connecticut (→ 10).

7. Stockholm: Soviets upset Canada 7-2 in their first world ice hockey championship.

8. U.S. signs defense pact with Japan, offering $100 mil. aid in next three months (→ 12/18/56).

8. Paris: France, Vietnam open talks on treaty to form Indochinese state (→ 14).

9. Cairo: Naguib wins back posts as premier and head of ruling military junta (→ 4/18).

10. Washington: Ike calls McCarthy peril to party (→ 12).

11. U.S. admits Marshall Islands test exposed 264 natives and 28 Americans to radiation (→ 26).

13. AEC awards Pittsburgh contract for first nuke plant to produce over 60,000 kw (→ 6/30).

14. Saigon: Viet Minh launch assault on Dien Bien Phu (→ 31).

16. New York: CBS introduces "The Morning Show" with Walter Cronkite to compete with NBC's "Today Show."

20. Ankara: Turks oust staff of World Bank.

20. Peking arrests 40, executes 13 after breaking Nationalist spy ring (→ 5/14).

22. London gold market reopens first time since 1939.

24. London: Britain opens trade talks with Hungary.

25. N.Y.: RCA begins mass production of color TV with 12" screen for under $1,000 (→ 4/1).

26. Marshall Islands: U.S. sets off second H-bomb blast in four weeks (→ 4/1).

30. Toronto opens Canada's first subway line.

31. Moscow offers to join NATO if West will join Soviet European security treaty (→ 9/30).

Murrow vs. McCarthy

CBS Newsman Edward R. Murrow.

March 12. Senator Joseph R. McCarthy has found himself under growing attack by CBS commentator Edward R. Murrow, the Army and Democrats on his investigations subcommittee. In a broadcast that evoked considerable public support, Murrow accused the Wisconsin senator of engaging in half-truths and said McCarthy's principal achievement had been in confusing the public about the internal and external threats of communism.

The Army, meanwhile, issued a 34-page report detailing charges that McCarthy and his chief counsel, Roy M. Cohn, had made threats against Army officials in an attempt to gain preferential treatment for G. David Shine, now an Army private but formerly an investigator for the McCarthy subcommittee. McCarthy replied by charging that the Army was attempting to blackmail him into dropping his investigation.

At a subcommittee hearing with McCarthy absent, Democrats, with Cohn as their target, protested against "convicting people by rumor and hearsay and innuendo." There were demands from both Democrats and Republicans on the subcommittee for an investigation into Cohn's conduct, and McCarthy found himself isolated and on the defensive in protecting his prestige and preserving the job of Cohn, a key figure in the inquiry (→ 4/22).

Puerto Ricans shoot five Congressmen

March 1. Puerto Rican fanatics opened fire in the House chamber today, injuring five Congressmen, one of them seriously. The four terrorists, three men and a woman, were disarmed by House gallery attendants and Capitol police and placed under arrest.

Most seriously injured was Rep. Alvin M. Bentley, Republican of Michigan, who was shot through the chest, stomach and liver. Others hurt by bullets sprayed from the House gallery were Reps. Ben F. Jensen, Republican of Iowa; George H. Fallon, Democrat of Maryland; Kenneth A. Roberts, Democrat of Alabama; and Clifford Davis, Democrat of Tennessee. Nearly 200 other Congressmen and House staffers on the floor at the time escaped injury (→ 7/8).

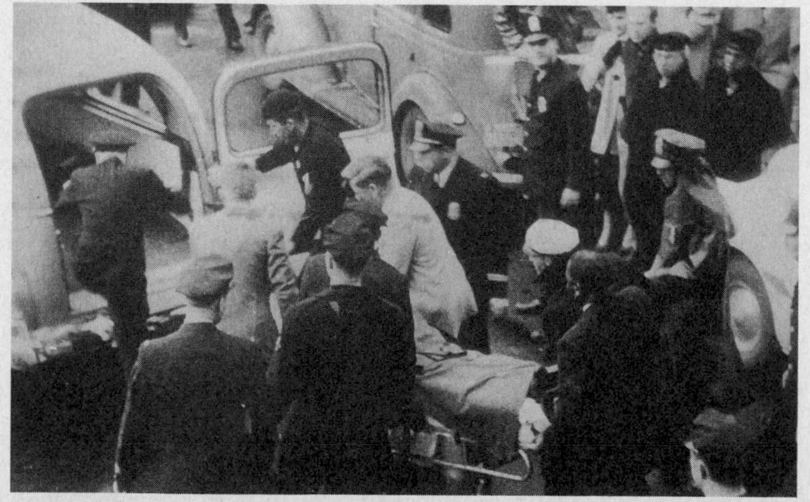

Police wheel one of the five wounded Congressmen into an ambulance.

Heavy attack made on Dien Bien Phu

Carrying the wounded to safety.

March 31. French forces in Vietnam have their backs against the wall as Communist guerrillas advance and tighten the noose around the airfield at Dien Bien Phu. The French lost several key positions after they were battered with Viet Minh artillery and infiltrated by guerrillas who slithered through barbed wire and across mine fields. Bad weather and the accuracy of Communist gunners hampered the airlift of new supplies into the besieged area. French planes did manage to drop napalm on the Communists, but the French have not been able to stop the steady stream of Russian trucks carrying supplies on resurfaced roads from China.

President Eisenhower refused to rule out the use of American ground forces in Indochina. He said that "united action" might be necessary to stop the Communists (→ 4/5).

Gen. Giap, master of guerrilla war.

H-bomb hundreds of times more powerful

March 1. The hydrogen bomb exploded by the United States at its mid-Pacific proving grounds today was hundreds of times more powerful than any previous weapon, government sources have revealed.

The detonation was so powerful that scientific measuring instruments could not record its full effects, and radioactive debris was hurled far beyond the safety zone set for the test, the sources said. The explosion is said to have jarred Kwajalein Island, 176 miles away. The bomb was believed to be 600 times more powerful than the atomic bomb dropped on Hiroshima, which released energy equivalent to 20,000 tons of TNT. The United States already is stockpiling hydrogen weapons of the type already tested and will soon explode even larger devices in its current series of tests, the sources said (→ 11).

A new, more ominous mushroom cloud fills the sky over the Marshall Islands.

New Leica, original 35mm, introduced

March 31. A new Leica 35-millimeter camera of radically different design has just been introduced, with a number of features available on no other camera. Perhaps the most significant feature is the introduction of a single-window range and viewfinder that shows the picture field as seen by the naked eye.

Among new convenience features are a bayonet thread lock that allows quick replacement of interchangeable lenses and the use of a lever rather than the old winding knob to advance the film. Instead of two dials for shutter speed, the new model has one offering a range from a tenth to a thousandth of a second. An optional exposure meter can be used for automatic selection of shutter speed. The camera opens a new era in photographic convenience, experts say.

Sinatra wins Oscar

March 25. Frank Sinatra received a best supporting actor award this evening for his role in "From Here to Eternity." The crooner tore his vocal chords in 1952; his singing career threatened, he begged for the part of Angelo Maggio in "Eternity." The film copped seven other Oscars, including best picture.

Borgnine, Lancaster and Sinatra.

Eleven Israelis slain in Beersheba ambush

A Jewish corpse on the ground, victim of smoldering Arab-Israeli tensions.

March 17. Eleven persons were machine-gunned to death today when an Israeli bus was ambushed near Beersheba. The incident was the worst of its kind since an Israeli raid killed 53 Arabs in the Jordanian village of Qibya last October 14, following which Israel was censured by the U.N. Branding the attack a "warlike act," the Jerusalem government put the blame on "the government from whose territory this unit of murderers was sent forth." No government was named, since the borders of Jordan and Egypt run close to the Beersheba area.

Israeli radio claims that "a band of Jordanians" also attacked an Israeli army unit at the foot of the Hebron Hills, north of the ambush site, but was driven off.

Stating that today's outrage brought the "series of wanton acts of hostility by the Arab states to a new climax," Israel said it would take "all necessary measures . . . to assure that the blood of Israeli citizens will not be shed with impunity." At the same time it called on the Jordanian-Israel Mixed Armistice Commission to investigate the matter immediately.

Jordan today rejected a United Nations bid for high-level talks between the two nations, as it has done twice before. Secretary General Dag Hammarskjold says he will plan the conference and fix a date, regardless of Jordanian participation (→ 2/28/55).

Giannini replaced at biggest U.S. bank

March 20. "There's your desk. Do any darn thing you want to do." Those words from the late A.P. Giannini, founder of the Bank of America, started S. Clarke Beise on the career that on April 1 will place him as President of the world's largest bank with assets of more than $8.5 billion. Giannini, who died five years ago, was the son of an Italian immigrant who went into banking in 1901. His Bank of Italy, founded in 1904, survived the San Francisco earthquake of 1906 and grew through Giannini's new system of branch banking. Beise became a bank examiner and then, in January 1936, he met Giannini. Since then, banking has been his vocation and avocation. For it, he has given up fishing, hunting, golf and other interests, though he does raise azaleas, is married and has two children.

1954

APRIL

Su	Mo	Tu	We	Th	Fr	Sa
				1	2	3
4	5	6	7	8	9	10
11	12	13	14	15	16	17
18	19	20	21	22	23	24
25	26	27	28	29	30	

1. Ike establishes U.S. Air Force Academy in Colorado.

1. U.S.: First H-bomb blast shown on national TV (→ 6/14).

2. New York: Dockworkers call off five-month strike after NLRB ultimatum (→ 6/29).

3. New Haven: Hawaii's Ford Konno wins triple crown in AAU swimming meet.

5. Sec. of State Dulles warns China U.S. will retaliate against aggression in Indochina (→ 7).

7. Ike warns Communist victory in Indochina will set off chain reaction in Asia (→ 20).

9. India reports only 43% of population speaks 15 recognized languages, noting 720 dialects, 23 tribal tongues (→ 1/14/59).

12. Memphis: Tennessee Williams finishes "Cat on a Hot Tin Roof," "Orpheus Descending."

12. AEC suspends A-bomb maker Oppenheimer as security risk (→ 29).

15. Margaret Sanger, first woman to speak in Japanese Diet, urges birth control.

16. Detroit: Red Wings take Stanley Cup over Canadiens.

17. New York: 3,000 U.S. troops return from Korea (→ 8/12).

18. Cairo: Nasser replaces Naguib as premier for second time in two months (→ 7/27).

18. U.S.: Oil companies introducing premium grade gas—hailed as greatest innovation since tetra-ethyl lead in 1920s.

20. U.S. begins flying French paratroopers to Vietnam (→ 28).

22. Senate begins inquiry into Army-McCarthy clash (→ 5/14).

22. Detroit: Hudson and Nash-Kelvinator approve merger to become American Motors.

23. Moscow breaks relations with Australia over granting of asylum to defector Petrov.

26. Geneva: Intl. parley on Indochina and Korea opens (→ 5/12).

30. Milford, Conn., inventor gets patent for snow-making device.

DEATH

10. Auguste Lumiere, French film pioneer (*10/19/1862).

Dulles warns Chinese on Indochina issue

Dulles: Dominoes in Indochina?

Chou En-lai (rt.) greets Vietnamese

April 28. Secretary of State John Foster Dulles, urging France to take a hard line with the Communists in Vietnam, accused China of "intensifying Communist aggression in Indochina." Dulles spoke amidst new speculation about American military intervention in Vietnam. The Eisenhower administration has warned that all of Indochina might fall like collapsing dominoes if the Communists defeat the French.

Peking radio replied angrily that Dulles was using lies and slander. The secretary of state, according to the broadcast, "attempted to use this vile method to deceive and hoodwink world public opinion" and to create a pretext for American intervention.

Dulles, referring to what he said was new intelligence information, said the Chinese are fighting in Vietnam, coordinating the Viet Minh assault on Dien Bien Phu and shooting down French planes. The secretary of state urged the French, in light of the new intelligence, not to open the Geneva Conference on the Far East with a request for a cease-fire in Vietnam.

The United States provided new assistance to the French by flying paratrooper reinforcements from Paris to Vietnam. The French insisted the operation did not violate American neutrality (→ 5/8).

Khrushchev plays major Moscow role

April 26. Nikita S. Khrushchev's appearance before the Supreme Soviet this week in a role that observers say was on a par with Premier Georgi Malenkov comes as a climax to a year of advancement for the First Secretary of the Communist Party of the Soviet Union. Earlier this year, on his 60th birthday, Khrushchev was given the Order of Lenin and made a Hero of Socialist Labor. Observers say Khrushchev's rise has been the result of his judicious use of his vast patronage powers in his role as head of the Communist Party (→ 2/8/55).

Khrushchev, of peasant stock.

Peron re-elected President, despite critics

April 25. As his first official act since re-election today, Argentine President Juan Peron arrested four leaders of the opposition party and threw them in jail. "Descato," or speaking disrespectfully about Peron, is a crime in Argentina. Crisologo Larralde, who received two million votes for Vice President, was taken to Mar Del Plata, the city where he made most of his campaign speeches, and also placed under arrest. Under the Peron system, the opposition Radical Party, which ran a close second in the capital, will receive only one of 15 deputy positions there. When Dr. Arturo Frondizi of the opposition party tried to inform his constituents around the country of these developments, the post office refused his telegrams.

Peron, a giant in Buenos Aires.

As Peron won a clear-cut victory, many observers are puzzled by the arrests of opposition leaders. The Interior Minister, however, said that opposition party members had "taken liberties and placed themselves beyond the pale of the law by inciting violence." Peron is thought to have won because of his anti-American stance and the wage increases he has mandated for laborers (→ 6/18/55).

Oppenheimer: Is he a security risk?

April 29. Allegations that nuclear scientist J. Robert Oppenheimer might be a security risk have made it necessary to raise "a blank wall" between him and secret information, President Eisenhower said today. Eisenhower said he admired and respected Oppenheimer, who led the wartime scientific effort to develop the atomic bomb, but said he had no regrets about suspending his security clearance last Dec. 23.

Oppenheimer, who heads the Institute for Advanced Studies in Princeton, New Jersey, has acknowledged associating with Communists but denies accusations he delayed development of the H-bomb. Secret hearings on Oppenheimer's request for restoration of his security clearance are being held before a three-man board appointed by Eisenhower. Its decision will be made public soon (→ 6/15).

Arturo Toscanini finishes 68-year career

April 4. Neither the Carnegie Hall audience nor those who heard the all-Wagner program on the radio yesterday knew they were privy to a historic if sad moment, Maestro Arturo Toscanini's swan song with the NBC Symphony Orchestra.

Concluding that his celebrated memory was not what it had been, the 87-year-old conductor had earlier tendered his resignation but wanted the news kept quiet until after the concert. Thus ended 68 years of musical lightning which began one night in 1886 when the lad of 19, a cellist with an Italian opera company touring Brazil, assumed the podium to lead from memory a performance of "Aida."

Though Toscanini was acclaimed for a variety of music, he was particularly associated with those two composers who formed the bookends of his career—Verdi and Wagner (→ 1/16/57).

Mercurial genius Toscanini.

British arrest 700 Mau-Mau as talks fail

April 12. Over 700 Mau-Mau activists were arrested in Kenya today after the collapse of negotiations for their surrender. The Mau-Mau are extremist members of the Kikuyu tribe and have been agitating against European ownership and presence in 12,000 square miles of Kenya's highlands. They have killed both Asians and Europeans, but the greatest number of dead have been Kikuyus who failed to support the Mau-Mau. The British government had been steadily increasing the number of Kenyans on the country's legislative council, but the Mau-Mau demand immediate surrender of the highlands.

The British Governor declared a state of emergency after the outbreak of terrorism in 1952, and Jomo Kenyatta, President of the Mau-Mau African Union Party, was sentenced to seven years imprisonment the following year.

General Erskine, leader of British troops in the area, vowed after the collapse of talks today "to hit these people like they've never been hit before," and the British air force continued saturation bombing of Mau-Mau jungle strongholds. The country was purchased from Zanzibar by the British in the late 19th century, named for the famous mountain in the country's interior and made a colony in 1920. Now, if the Mau-Mau have their way, the era of British domination will come to an end (→ 2/22/55).

Nicaraguan leader orders martial law

April 5. A state of martial law was imposed in Nicaragua today after an assassination attempt on President Anastasio Somoza. A spokesman for the Nicaraguan government said that on Saturday several armed men were spotted along a highway which was to be used by Somoza after departing a reception at U.S. Ambassador Thomas Whelan's home. The suspects had fled by the time National Guardsmen arrived on the scene. On Sunday, two guardsmen were killed in a clash with armed rebels at a small farm near Managua (→ 9/22/56).

Eight oil firms will work in Iran

April 10. Eight major American and European oil companies today agreed to form a combine to resume production in Iranian oil fields, suspended since former Premier Mohammed Mossadegh nationalized the industry in 1951. The United States government played a major role in intense negotiations between the oil companies and the new government of Iran. Issues that must be settled before production resumes include the length of the lease Iran will grant the combine and the degree of technical control the companies will have (→ 8/5).

Accused Kikuyus, shoeless and in rags, stand uneasily before a Nairobi court.

Rock Around the Clock is recorded

April 12. They're billed as "The Nation's Rockingest Rhythm Group," and Bill Haley and the Comets live up to the title with their new record, "(We're Gonna) Rock Around the Clock." Haley, a 29-year-old former disc jockey and veteran country-and-western singer, is finding a new sound with the Comets by adding a driving rhythm-and-blues dance beat to their music. Their last song, "Crazy, Man, Crazy," hit number 14 on the pop charts, and "Rock Around the Clock" seems set to take off with a blast (→ 6/6/55).

Price cut on first color TV to $1,110

April 1. The Westinghouse Electric Corporation has cut the suggested retail price of its 12.5-inch color TV set from $1,295 to $1,110. The only company with a color set actually on the market, Westinghouse made the cut to "maintain our leadership in color TV." The sets were introduced early in March, but only about 30 have been sold so far. RCA is producing a similar set to retail for $1,000. Larger screens are not planned, since the larger tubes necessary for them are not available. The present sets utilize RCA 15-inch tubes (→ 6/6).

The sporty Kaiser-Darrin, the perfect car on a balmy spring day.

1954

MAY

Su	Mo	Tu	We	Th	Fr	Sa
						1
2	3	4	5	6	7	8
9	10	11	12	13	14	15
16	17	18	19	20	21	22
23	24	25	26	27	28	29
30	31					

1. Determine is first in Kentucky Derby with jockey R. York.

2. St. Louis: Stan Musial hits five home runs in doubleheader, setting major league record.

2. Ceylon: Asian conference ends with plea for peace in Indochina, end of atomic tests, condemnation of colonialism.

3. Lindbergh wins Pulitzer for autobiography "The Spirit of St. Louis."

4. Gov. Gen. Massey is first Canadian leader to address both houses of U.S. Congress (→ 13).

6. Paraguay junta takes control in 10th revolution since 1948.

9. New York: "Prisoner of War" opens with Ronald Reagan.

10. New York: $30 automatic coffee makers shown, capable of brewing two cups in four min.

13. Ike authorizes construction of St. Lawrence Seaway between Montreal and Lake Erie.

13. New York: Musical "The Pajama Game" opens.

14. Seattle: Boeing displays first prototype of 707 (→ 7/19).

14. Taiwan withdraws from Olympics as Peking voted in.

15. Toronto: Dr. Wm. Mustard performs first successful heart surgery aided by hypothermia.

15. Saigon protests division of Vietnam, comparing resources of industrial North and agricultural South (→ 6/10).

16. Karachi: Pakistani labor riots take 206 lives.

17. Manila: Rebel leader Luis Taruc surrenders (→ 3/18/57).

21. U.S. Senate rejects Ike's plan for 18-year-old voting rights.

22. London: Record 120,000 hear Billy Graham end crusade.

26. Rhode Island: Blast kills 91, hurts 200 on USS Bennington.

26. Cairo: Archeologists find 4800-year-old Cheops' Ship of the Dead at pyramid.

28. New York: Hitchcock's "Dial M for Murder" opens.

29. Vatican: Pius X becomes 70th pope to be canonized.

31. Bill Vukovitch wins Indy 500 second year in row (→ 5/30/55).

Dien Bien Phu falls to Communists

Stupor in France over jungle defeat.

Worried French soldiers man the trenches at besieged Dien Bien Phu.

May 8. The brutal 55-day-long siege of Dien Bien Phu is over. French resistance collapsed as the Communists slogged through the mud, overran their trenches and captured their airfield. The French lost 4,000 men. They killed 8,000 Viet Minh, but they were all replaced by the Communist juggernaut. The Viet Minh, equipped with modern Chinese and Soviet weapons, prevented any reinforcements and supplies from reaching the beleaguered French. By the end of the struggle, likened by the French to the battle of Verdun, only one French howitzer was working.

Word of the French collapse came in a radio report from General Christian de Castries: "After 20 hours of fighting without respite, including hand-to-hand fighting, the enemy has infiltrated the whole center. We lack ammunition. The Viet Minh are now within a few meters from the radio transmitter where I am speaking." A few moments later, the radio went dead.

The Communists opened a gaping hole in the French defenses Tuesday night southwest of the airfield. Up until then, the sector had been impregnable. The Viet Minh tightened the screws from all directions, pounding the exhausted French with fresh artillery and infiltrating their last lines of defense with rested guerrillas.

General Navarre had invested the national honor of France in the defense of Dien Bien Phu, and his men fought valiantly. They lost more than a battle in the end. They may have lost the war (→ 12).

Chronology of events

Feb 1953. French and Vietnamese troops evacuate, leaving Dien Bien Phu to the Viet Minh.

Nov 29. Operation Castor. French and Vietnamese paratroopers land and retake Dien Bien Phu, begin to fortify the area.

March 15, 1954. The Gabrielle line, French outer defense, falls under Viet Minh assault.

March 23. Lt. Col. Castries' Beatrice line crumbles as the Viet Minh launch first main attack on Dien Bien Phu defenses.

March 28. General Navarre asks a brief cease-fire to evacuate wounded; Viet Minh General Giap responds with an aerial assault on French positions.

March 30. The second Viet Minh offensive is launched. In prolonged fighting, French lines Etaine and Dominique change hands six times.

May 2. Viet Minh launch the third offensive on the eve of Vietnam talks at Geneva.

May 3. France pays official tribute to the efforts of Franco-Vietnamese troops at Dien Bien Phu garrison.

May 4. The last of Franco-Vietnamese outer defenses falls in hand-to-hand combat

May 6. Viet Minh launch fourth assault, overrunning France's Isabelle line.

May 7. Franco-Vietnamese garrison at Dien Bien Phu falls to the Viet Minh under General Giap.

Dug deep in a maze of trenches, a French soldier hollows out a little shelf.

High court orders school integration

May 17. Racial segregation in the public schools of America was outlawed today by the Supreme Court. With their unanimous decision, the justices set aside the "separate but equal" doctrine handed down by an earlier Supreme Court in 1896.

Many Southerners reacted angrily to the new ruling, with some leaders in at least two states, Georgia and South Carolina, vowing that they will abolish their public schools. "The South," said Senator James O. Eastland, Democrat of Mississippi, "will not abide by nor obey this legislative decision by a political court."

The court decision could vitally affect 8.5 million white children and 2.5 million Negroes now attending segregated schools in Alabama, Arkansas, Delaware, Florida, Mississippi, Missouri, North Carolina, Oklahoma, Georgia, Kentucky, Louisiana, Maryland, South Carolina, Tennessee, Texas, Virginia, West Virginia and the District of Columbia. The ruling will not affect private schools.

Douglas, Harlan, Reed, Clark, Warren, Burton, Black, Minton, Frankfurter.

In the landmark decision, one of the most far-reaching rulings of the century, Chief Justice Earl Warren wrote: "In the field of public education, the doctrine of separate but equal has no place. Separated educational facilities are inherently unequal" (→ 6/10).

Indochina's future debated in Geneva

May 12. The French government is alarmed by an apparent shift in attitude of the United States toward Indochina. Secretary of State John Foster Dulles stunned the French by announcing yesterday that Indochina is important, but not essential, to the security of Southeast Asia.

In Geneva, the French proposed a truce, the creation of zones controlled by the French and Viet Minh and the evacuation of Communist forces from Laos and Cambodia. The Viet Minh rejected the proposal as they called for a cease-fire and independence for Vietnam, Laos and Cambodia. Westerners say independence would be a smoke screen for more Communist infiltration (→ 15).

McCarthy hearings draw 2,000 a day

May 14. A Senate subcommitee's hearings into the dispute between the Army and Senator Joseph R. McCarthy have been drawing a standing-room-only audience on Capitol Hill and a nationwide TV audience. Police estimated that more than 2,000 persons a day have trooped in and out of the Senate Caucus Room during the hearings. The hearings were abruptly recessed after President Eisenhower invoked executive privilege on disclosing certain information (→ 6/2).

Giant Brain foreshadows electronic office

Vacuum tubes, now widely used, raised calculating speed a thousand-fold.

May 24. Development of an "electronic brain" designed specifically for business use was announced today by the International Business Machines Corp. Capable of performing more than ten million operations an hour, the new device brings the all-electronic office closer to reality, the company said. Delivery of the machine will not take place until next year, but 30 of the devices already have been ordered.

The system consists of a central arithmetical and logic unit that processes data from a bank of cathode ray memory tubes. Information is fed to the machine from reels of magnetic tape, each capable of storing all the numbers in the Manhattan telephone directory. IBM says it will rent, not sell, the new machine and a typical installation will cost $25,000 a month. Insurance firms are most interested (→ 7/14).

Bannister is first to break 4-minute mile

May 6. Cross winds of 15 mph did not deter Oxford medical student Roger Bannister from breaking the four-minute mile today. Bannister ran 1,500 meters in 3 minutes and 59.4 seconds. Bannister shattered a barrier men had been trying to break for 20 years (→ 6/21).

Bannister breaks the tape at 3:59.4.

Ava Gardner and Robert Taylor in MGM's first wide-screen film "Knights of the Round Table."

1954

JUNE

Su	Mo	Tu	We	Th	Fr	Sa
		1	2	3	4	5
6	7	8	9	10	11	12
13	14	15	16	17	18	19
20	21	22	23	24	25	26
27	28	29	30			

2. McCarthy charges Communist infiltration in CIA and atomic plants (→ 17).

6. Pope opens eight-nation TV network Eurovision (→ 10/25).

10. Richmond: 12 Southern leaders agree not to comply with Court integration order (→ 25).

10. Ike calls communism global peril that cannot be checked by armed strength alone (→ 15).

12. Guatemala: United Fruit gets accord with strikers (→ 18).

14. Americans take part in nation-wide civil defense test against atomic attack (→ 11/20).

15. U.S. bars aid in Indochina until French step up military efforts (→ 16).

16. Vietnam: Bao Dai calls Diem back from exile (→ 18).

17. New York: Marciano retains heavyweight title, defeating Ezzard Charles in 15 rounds.

18. Paris: Mendes France elected premier in vote of support for Indochina peace plan (→ 28).

18. Guatemala rebels launch revolt by land, sea and air (→ 20).

20. N.Y.: Soviets veto U.S. plan to take Guatemala issue out of U.N.; U.S. warns to keep hands off Western hemisphere (→ 27).

21. San Francisco: Cancer Society says smokers over 50 have 75% higher deaths (→ 3/22/57).

21. Finland: Australian John Landy takes mile record in 3:58, becoming second to break 4:00.

24. Albany: Ike hails opening of N.Y. State Thruway as economic boost, defense asset (→ 7/12).

25. Atlanta: Two gubernatorial candidates propose ouster of Supreme Court to preserve segregation (→ 10/4).

26. New Delhi: Nehru, Chou En-lai pledge good-neighbor policy.

28. Vietnam: French troops begin to pull out of Tonkin (→ 30).

29. C.I.O., U.S. Steel sign two-year accord raising wages and welfare benefits (→ 2/9/55).

30. N.Y.: John Wayne opens in "The High and the Mighty."

30. U.S.S.R. has opened its first atomic power plant to produce over 5,000 kw (→ 8/30).

Anti-Communists in power in Guatemala

Coup leader Col. Armas (center).

June 27. A coup prompted by insurgents and anti-Communist army chiefs has forced the regime of Guatemalan President Jacobo Arbenz Guzman to come to an end. Colonel Arbenz agreed to step down in favor of a military junta.

Guatemala had been under siege for ten days, following an invasion by the forces of Colonel Castillo Armas. Two nights ago, the insurgents, broadcasting from a clandestine radio, appealed to the Guatemalan army to set up a junta and to seize President Arbenz as terms for a cease-fire. The president was informed by army officials that the present situation could not continue. The president was reportedly furious but nevertheless addressed the nation by radio to announce his resignation. His statement was immediately followed by the introduction of Colonel Diaz as the country's new President.

Throughout his term as chief executive, Arbenz reputedly walked a thin line between his Communist allies and advisers and the strongly anti-Communist army chiefs. Colonel Diaz has announced one of his first priorities will be to oppose the Communists who had infiltrated and influenced the government under Arbenz.

Rebel fighting continues. "We are figting a system, not a man," a rebel spokesman said, implying that the change in the regime's leadership is unimportant (→ 7/5).

French and Chinese agree on Indochina

June 30. French Premier Pierre Mendes France and Chinese Premier Chou En-lai, at a meeting in Berne, Switzerland, have reached agreement on the basic terms for a political settlement for Indochina.

The agreement, which represents a switch from the previous French position, would mean that the Geneva Conference, in addition to devising a military armistice in Indochina, would now work out the terms for a political settlement.

Under the French-Chinese agreement, an armistice would be followed by establishment of a unified government for Vietnam, and the French-sponsored governments in Laos and Cambodia would be given a neutral status. The agreement leaves unresolved what territory would be controlled by the Communists and French-supported forces.

France, however, finds its military control in Vietnam progressively deteriorating. In the biggest military setback since Dien Bien Phu, French troops were forced to withdraw from most of the Red River delta south of Hanoi (→ 7/10).

Army-McCarthy hearings are concluded

June 17. The Army-McCarthy hearings have ended, setting the stage for a subcommittee report to the Senate on the conduct of Senator Joseph R. McCarthy.

Throughout 36 days of hearings, the Army maintained that McCarthy and his chief counsel, Roy M. Cohn, had sought preferential treatment for Pvt. G. David Schine, a subcommittee investigator before he was drafted. McCarthy and Cohn countercharged that the Army had used Schine as a "hostage" in an attempt to "blackmail" the senator into dropping his investigation of Communists in the Army. Senator Charles E. Potter, Republican of Michigan, said there had been perjury on both sides and suggested dismissal of some Army and subcommittee employees (→ 7/19).

Oppenheimer loyal but still barred

J. Robert Oppenheimer.

June 15. A special security board today described J. Robert Oppenheimer as a "loyal" American citizen but voted 2-1 against reinstating his security clearance. The two board members who voted against Oppenheimer said they had "been unable to arrive at the conclusion that it would be clearly consistent with the security interest of the United States to reinstate Dr. Oppenheimer's clearance." The testimony regarded as most harmful to Oppenheimer included the statement by Edward Teller, "Father of the hydrogen bomb," that Oppenheimer's lack of moral support delayed development of the weapon by at least four years.

Man who perfected zipper in 1913 dies

June 21. Dr. Gideon Sundback, one of the inventors of the zipper, died yesterday at age 74. A crude version had been designed in 1893 by W.L. Judson, but in 1913 Sundback perfected a slide fastener and the machinery for its manufacture.

The Hookless Fastener Company was incorporated that year with 20 employees. Now named Talon, Inc., it has thousands of workers. Dr. Sundback was Vice President and also President of subsidiaries in Mexico and Canada. Born in Sweden and educated as an electrical engineer there and in Germany, he emigrated to the U.S. in 1903 and became affiliated with the Westinghouse Electric Co. In 1937, Allegheny College conferred upon him the degree of Doctor of Science.

1954

JULY

Su	Mo	Tu	We	Th	Fr	Sa
				1	2	3
4	5	6	7	8	9	10
11	12	13	14	15	16	17
18	19	20	21	22	23	24
25	26	27	28	29	30	31

1. El Salvador: Rebel chief Col. Castillo Armas and junta leader Col. Elfego Monzon form anti-Communist coalition govt.

3. Wimbledon: Jaroslav Drobny over Ken Rosewall 13-11, 4-6, 6-2, 9-7; Maureen Connolly over Althea Brough 6-2, 7-5.

3. Peabody, Mass: Babe Didrikson wins third U.S. women's open golf championship.

3. Britain ends meat rationing, last of wartime food controls.

5. Boeing conducts initial flight of B-52A bomber.

5. Guatemala: New regime reported to have arrested 2,000 Communists (→ 10/30).

8. Washington: Four Puerto Ricans get maximum jail terms for shooting in Congress.

10. Geneva: Mendes France arrives for final days of Indochina parley (→ 13).

11. Paraguay: Gen. Alfredo Stroessner elected president.

12. N.Y.: Ike proposes interstate highway system for general use and atomic defense.

13. Geneva: U.S., U.K., France reach accord on Indochina armistice, dividing Vietnam along 18th parallel (→ 21).

13. U.S.: GNP reaches record $365 bil. —$1 bil. per day.

14. Princeton: Computer made available for rent by private industry (→ 10/7).

16. N.Y.: Police start citywide use of "drunkometer" with chemical test apparatus.

19. Memphis: Elvis Presley records "That's All Right Mama."

24. Two Chinese MIG's down British airliner off Hainan coast.

26. Henry Cabot Lodge Jr. reappointed to head U.S delegation to U.N.

28. Britain denies Cypriot request for union with Greece, due to plans for major military base there (→ 12/18).

31. Karachi: Italian team climbs Mt. Godwin Austen, world's second highest peak.

31. Tunis: Premier Mendes France offers autonomy to Tunisia (→ 9/4).

Indochina truce signed

The Vietnamese delegation, led by Pham Van Dong, argues for Hanoi.

The last French officers begrudgingly leave Hanoi to the Vietnamese.

July 21. Admitting that it is not a perfect peace, France signed armistice agreements with the Viet Minh in Geneva early this morning. Vietnam was divided in half along the 17th parallel, with the Communists controlling the North and Emperor Bao Dai controlling the South with French support. Eventually, the country will be reunited after a referendum. During a ten-month transition, French forces will be allowed to remain in the North in the cities of Hanoi and Haiphong, and the Viet Minh may regroup in several areas in the South.

Under the agreement, the fighting is also halted in Laos, and the Viet Minh recognize the governments of Laos and Cambodia. The signing of the agreement by Cambodia was delayed because it objected to a provision that allows Communist troops to form a resistance government in two provinces of Laos. The agreement will be supervised by a commission composed of India, Canada and Poland (→ 8/16).

Boeing 707, four-engine airliner, debuts

The maiden flight of Boeing's 707 inaugurates jet transport in America.

July 19. In Seattle today, 72-year-old engineer William E. Boeing witnessed the maiden flight of Dash Eighty. The plane is a prototype of a model to be called 707. After Boeing's wife Bertha christened the Dash, it went aloft and reached a cruising speed of 600 mph. Built for intercontinental travel, the 707 can carry 219 passengers.

Cellophane creator dies in Paris at 81

July 13. Jacques Brandenberger, the Swiss-born chemist who invented cellophane, died today in Zurich at the age of 81. Trained as a dye chemist at the University of Bern, Brandenberger moved to France, where he invented the method of producing the transparent wrapping material in 1908. He founded the Societe de Cellophane in 1915 and built it into a major industrial enterprise. Brandenberger sold the United States rights for cellophane to E.I. du Pont de Nemours Company but retained the rights for his company and its subsidiaries in all other parts of the world. He was in Zurich for treatment of a kidney ailment when he died.

Newport crowded for jazz festival

July 18. Newport, the staid Rhode Island resort, was jammed and jamming this afternoon. A jazz festival was held, the first of what residents hope will be an annual event. Nearly 7,000 attended. Every variation of jazz, from Dixieland to swing to progressive to Ella Fitzgerald (who is a kind of style unto herself), was heard. The Modern Jazz Quartet and Dizzy Gillespie's Quintet were also there.

Eva Marie Saint in her film debut and Marlon Brando and Rod Steiger as brothers in the tough new film "On the Waterfront."

British end 72-year occupation of Egypt

Nasser (rt.) shows his glee as Britain's Anthony Head signs away Suez.

July 27. Britian and Egypt tonight reached agreement on a Suez Canal pact which by ending 72 years of British military occupation also closes an important chapter in British colonial history.

The accord, initialed by Egyptian Premier Gamal Abdel Nasser and Anthony Head, British Secretary of State for War, promises most immediately to calm hostilities in the Canal Zone, where a sporadic guerrilla war has cost 46 British lives and nearly 100 Egyptian lives.

The long-term provisions call for the evacuation of the 80,000-man British force from the zone within 20 months after the signing of a detailed agreement, still to be ironed out. The compromise pact also permits, for a seven-year period, the re-entry of British forces to meet an attack on Egypt, any Arab state or Turkey.

The pact may also have buoyed Nasser's hope for American foreign aid to help with Egyptian social and economic development, as the U.S. had withheld aid pending a Canal Zone settlement (→ 10/19).

Causes of noxious L.A. smog analyzed

July 31. A six-year research program has found that the eye-burning smog that afflicts the Los Angeles area is caused by the chemical action of sunlight on auto exhaust fumes and industrial emissions, the Stanford Research Institute reported today. The origin of the smog, which causes major crop damage, has been a mystery. Studies have found that ozone, a major irritant in smog, is produced when sunlight causes reactions among exhaust fume chemicals in periods of stagnant air, the institute said. Automobiles add more than 1,000 tons of noxious chemicals to the air in Los Angeles every day, contributing more than 80 percent of the total pollution, the institute adds. Research on ways to reduce smog is continuing (→ 10/22).

Roy Cohn resigns from McCarthy job

July 19. Roy M. Cohn, a key figure in the Army-McCarthy dispute, has announced that he has resigned as chief counsel of the Senate Permanent Subcommittee on Investigations headed by Senator Joseph R. McCarthy. The 27-year-old lawyer, who left a New York law practice to take up the anti-Communist crusade with Senator McCarthy, was said to believe that he was about to be made the "goat" in the subcommittee report on the Army-McCarthy controversy.

The panel was believed ready to approve dismissal of top staff members, including Cohn. McCarthy has said Cohn's departure would be a major Communist victory. His resignation has obviated any need by McCarthy or other panel members to retain Cohn (→ 8/24).

Marsh, painter of New York life, dies

July 3. Artist Reginald Marsh has died of a heart attack outside Bennington, Vermont. He was a regionalist, painting realistic scenes of New York City. Abstractionism and other movements of the past few decades failed to impress him.

Marsh was born in Paris in 1898 but was raised in Nutley, N.J. He studied in New York under John Sloan. Marsh taught at New York's Art Students' League and Philadelphia's Moore Institute of Art.

His illustrations appeared in The New Yorker, Vanity Fair and Life magazine. Recently, Marsh created drawings for a new edition of Theodore Dreiser's novel "An American Tragedy."

The artist swore by conservatism. "Critics may not know what's wrong with Picasso," he said, "but any layman can tell you. The question is, what does it mean?"

Marsh's "Broadway at 14th Street."

1954

AUGUST

Su	Mo	Tu	We	Th	Fr	Sa
1	2	3	4	5	6	7
8	9	10	11	12	13	14
15	16	17	18	19	20	21
22	23	24	25	26	27	28
29	30	31				

1. Louison Bobet wins Tour de France.

2. Ike signs Housing Act to provide 35,000 new units.

4. New York: Hitchcock's "Rear Window" has world premiere.

5. Tehran signs 25-year pact with eight intl. oil companies, restoring Iran to world leadership in oil production.

7. Morocco: 11 die in riots as nationalists demonstrate against French-appointed sultan (→ 15).

9. Taipei: Nationalist Chinese sink eight Communist gunboats in Formosa Strait (→ 11).

10. Indonesia and Holland dissolve union (→ 11/30/57).

10. Construction begins on St. Lawrence Seaway (→ 9/5/58).

11. Peking: For. Min. Chou En-lai indicates intention of attacking Taiwan (→ 17).

15. Morocco: French Legion troops seize Fez Arab quarter after riots (→ 7/17/55).

16. Haiphong: First U.S. ship arrives to evacuate refugees to South Vietnam (→ 9/17).

16. Jidda: King Saud names Prince Faisal prime minister.

17. Ike commits Seventh Fleet to protect Taiwan from invasion (→ 9/6).

17. Pope allows U.S. clergy to deliver sacraments in English.

17. Detroit: Packard and Studebaker approve merger.

18. Washington: Asst. Sec. of Labor James Wilkins is first Negro to attend Cabinet meeting.

22. Brussels: EDC talks end as France rejects German rearmament (→ 10/2).

27. Two U.S. icebrakers complete first trip through Northwest Passage, Atlantic to Pacific.

30. Ike signs Atomic Energy Act opening door to private exploitation of nuclear power (→ 9/6).

DEATHS

3. Sidonie Gabrielle Collette, French writer (*1/28/1873).

6. David Fairchild, botanist, introduced over 200,000 plants to U.S. (*4/7/1869).

French African position under pressure

Empire-juggling Mendes France.

Aug 27. The French government of Pierre Mendes France is caught in the middle between nationalists in the African protectorates who are demanding independence and conservatives in Paris who are afraid that the Premier will give the store away. For the time being, it appears that Mendes France is trying to steer a middle course by offering Morocco and Tunisia autonomy, but not independence.

In Morocco, riots erupted as demonstrators demanded the return of Sidi Mohammed Ben Youssef. The Sultan was deposed by France last year and exiled to Madagascar for advocating independence. Dozens of people were killed or wounded in riots in Port Lyautey. Some of the victims were European women, dragged into side streets by the demonstrators. To prevent a recurrence of violence in Fez, four battalions of the French Foreign Legion marched into the old quarter and surrounded two sacred mosques.

In a speech to the Assembly today, Mendes France advocated reform for Morocco, including the formation of regional assemblies and labor unions. He also promised better treatment for Youssef. Earlier, the premier flew to Tunis to recognize what he called the "internal autonomy" of Tunisia.

U.N. leaves last North Korean area

August 12. The United Nations Command withdrew from Korea today, once again leaving North and South Koreans staring at each other across a narrow strip of no-man's land. The only tangible difference after three years of war and half a million deaths was that South Korea now owns another 12,000 square miles above the 38th parallel. More importantly, it marks the first time that the U.N. as a body has banded together to resist an aggressive act by another country (→ 5/15/56).

U.N. troops on their way home.

President approves Red control law

Aug 24. A bill to destroy the Communist Party as a political and legal entity in the United States was signed into law today by President Eisenhower. The American people, the president said, are determined to protect themselves against any organization that purports to be a political party while "actually a conspiracy dedicated to the violent overthrow of our entire form of government."

As originally proposed in the Senate, membership in the Communist Party would be a crime. This feature of the bill was dropped after the president said that was going too far. But the new law does impose legal, political and economic penalties on party members. Any labor group found to be controlled by the Communists will be stripped of all rights under the Taft-Hartley Law. For instance, such labor unions will no longer be allowed to lodge any complaints against employers or other unions or seek representative rights. This is the fifth anti-subversion law placed on the books in recent days and the president is expected to sign three others soon (→ 31).

Vargas resigns under pressure, kills self

Aug 24. Brazilian President Getulio Vargas, amid growing controversy concerning his administration, committed suicide this morning, just hours after he decided to hand over his office to Vice President Joao Cafe Filho.

High-ranking Brazilian officials had counseled Vargas, re-elected in 1951, to step down in the national interest, given the steep drop in public support for his administration, which has been rocked by financial corruption and other scandals. Vargas' troubles climaxed recently when an air force major was accidentally killed by gunmen shooting at Carlos Lacerda, a crusading editor at Tribuna da Imprensa, whose articles had much to do with Vargas' fall from public grace.

In a letter to the Brazilian people discovered after his suicide, Vargas criticized "international financial groups" for conspiring against Brazil's national interests and the needs of Brazil's poor, with whom Vargas was quite popular. He first became president in 1930 and established dictatorial control.

Vargas supporters recently attacked an opposition newspaper's trucks.

Senate committee censures both sides

Aug 31. A Senate subcommittee that sat through the long Army-McCarthy hearings reached the verdict today that both sides deserved criticism. The report of the Republican majority found that Senator Joseph R. McCarthy, the subcommittee Chairman, had not sought directly to force the Army to give preferential treatment to Pvt. G. David Schine, a subcommittee investigator before being drafted. But the Republicans found that the senator had permitted Roy M. Cohn, the subcommittee's chief counsel, to pressure the Army. The report found that Army Secretary Robert T. Stevens had vacillated in dealing with Cohn. Similar conclusions were reached by Democrats in a minority report (→ 9/3).

Hidden modern art emerges in Russia

Aug 28. The Soviet public may cast its eyes upon Western modern art again, a dozen years after the government forbade it. Works by Matisse, Picasso and van Gogh are on display in a hall of the Hermitage Gallery in Leningrad. At the same time, some of the pictures have been loaned to Italy for an exhibition.

When World War II started, the art works were hidden away for "safety" reasons. They did not reappear on museum walls when the war ended, however. The government decided futuristic and Cubist paintings opposed government doctrine. Cezannes and Gauguins stayed in the closet. The new display policy does not apply to all art. Other works are still kept from public view.

1954

SEPTEMBER

Su	Mo	Tu	We	Th	Fr	Sa
			1	2	3	4
5	6	7	8	9	10	11
12	13	14	15	16	17	18
19	20	21	22	23	24	25
26	27	28	29	30		

1. Colorado: On vacation, Ike signs bill extending Social Security to ten million more.

3. U.S. Congress institutes death penalty for espionage in peacetime (→ 10/11).

4. Tunis: France lifts ban on nationalist Neo-Destour Party, as talks on Tunisian autonomy open (→ 6/1/55).

5. Siberia: Soviet jets down U.S. patrol plane over Sea of Japan.

6. Pittsburgh: Ike attends as ground is broken for first atomic power plant (→ 11/15).

6. Forest Hills: Vic Seixas, Doris Hart win U.S. singles titles.

8. Manila: Eight nations sign defense treaty creating SEATO (→ 2/1/55).

9. Algeria: Earthquake kills 1,000, leaves 10,000 homeless.

12. Ike and Security Council veto intervention in Red China-Taiwan conflict (→ 18).

17. N.Y.: Heavyweight champ Marciano takes 47th straight with KO over Ezzard Charles.

17. India outlaws bigamy.

18. Nationalist Chinese planes strike Communist oil tanker off Fukien coast (→ 11/14).

23. Berlin: East Germans arrest 400 as U.S. spies (→ 3/29/55).

27. Willie Mays wins batting title, leading N.Y. Giants to NL pennant (→ 10/2).

28. Saigon: Head of state Ngo Dinh Diem urges quicker withdrawal of French troops (→ 29).

29. U.S. announces Vietnam aid will bypass France beginning January 1955 (→ 10/10).

30. London: NATO nations reach accord on arming and admitting W. Germany (→ 10/2).

30. Asbestos, Quebec: Johns-Manville opens world's largest asbestos mill with one-third of West's capacity (→ 8/26/82).

DEATHS

7. Glenn Scobey "Pop" Warner, college football coach (*4/5/1871).

7. Harry "Bud" Fisher, creator of "Mutt and Jeff" comic strip (*4/3/1885).

China mainland and islands engage in duel

Sept 6. Squadrons of Nationalist Chinese fighter-bombers attacked Communist-held Tateng Island today, in response to the continued shelling of the Nationalist outpost of Quemoy, an island only a few miles from the Chinese mainland and the site of the first major Nationalist victory over the Communists in 1949. Chiang Kai-shek, President of Formosa, expressed fears that a Communist invasion of Quemoy was imminent, yet he expressed confidence that Nationalist forces could repel any such assault. Two U.S. Army officers were killed in the five-hour bombardment of Quemoy yesterday (→ 12).

Nationalist warship fires on Amoy.

Unexpected 250,000 flee to South Vietnam

Sept 17. Over 250,000 North Vietnamese have left their Communist-controlled homeland for South Vietnam in a grand exodus that far exceeds estimates by those at the Geneva cease-fire agreement. The U.S. Foreign Operations Administration, headed by Harold Stassen, will assist the refugees in resettling south of the 17th parallel which divides North and South Vietnam.

The latest refugee count brings the total of those who have fled to nearly 500,000, although this estimate is only speculative, as an accurate census is almost impossible.

Presently, the refugees are being housed in large U.S. Army tents. Upon reaching South Vietnamese camps, they receive clothing, bedding, hand tools for agriculture and other equipment. Eventually they will settle in newly built villages.

Over $10 million was allocated to the Foreign Operations Administration. Much of the money will be used to purchase farm animals, buffalo and oxen, which have to be imported. The funds also pay for the drilling of communal wells—the first task needing attention when establishing a new village.

Stassen has described the relocation program as "an epic in the movement of peoples." He has also noted that the Communists, bitter about the exodus, have impeded the movement of the refugees (→ 28).

North Vietnamese refugees, uncertain of the future, board boats to go south.

Mao is re-elected as Chinese Chairman

Sept 27. Mao Tse-tung was re-elected to another four-year term as Chairman of the People's Republic of China and General Chu Teh was named Deputy Chairman, the nation's second highest position. The National People's Congress nominates and votes for candidates for the offices. Neither Mao nor Chu were opposed in their election bids and therefore won unanimously. Chinese radio announced the news against a background of cheering. Crowds chanted the Eastern version of "Long live the king": "Wan Sui, Wan Sui" (10,000 years, 10,000 years). For the first time, one man, Chu, is placed directly under Mao, in succession of power. Formerly, six deputies held the second-in-command post (→ 4/4/55).

Chairman Mao.

Stunning performances by Anthony Quinn and Giulietta Massina spark Fellini's "La Strada."

1954

OCTOBER

Su	Mo	Tu	We	Th	Fr	Sa
					1	2
3	4	5	6	7	8	9
10	11	12	13	14	15	16
17	18	19	20	21	22	23
24	25	26	27	28	29	30
31						

2. Cleveland: Giants win Series in four games over Indians.

3. U.S.: TV version of "Father Knows Best" premieres.

4. White pupils march against school integration in Washington and Baltimore (→ 12/21).

5. Marilyn Monroe sues for divorce from Joe DiMaggio, citing conflicting career demands.

7. Poughkeepsie: IBM displays all-transistor calculator needing 5% the power of comparable electronic ones (→ 12/7).

11. U.S. Civil Service has fired 2,600 since Aug. under Communist Control Act (→ 11/24).

13. U.S. Air Force authorizes B-58, first supersonic bomber.

14. Bing Crosby and Danny Kaye star in "White Christmas."

14. Oxford publishes 4 vols. of Toynbee's "A Study of History."

19. Cairo: U.K. sings Suez treaty ceding canal to Egypt (→ 29).

20. N.Y.: "Peter Pan" musical opens, with Mary Martin.

22. N.Y.: 19-year-old Floyd Patterson beats Joe Gannon in first pro boxing victory.

22. Ike approves plan for intensive training of South Vietnamese army (→ 1/1/55).

22. Governor shuts L.A. oil refineries on 16th day of heavy smog (→ 4/6/60).

25. Ike conducts first televised Cabinet meeting (→ 1/19/55).

26. Trieste: U.K., U.S. end occupation, return control to Italy.

26. Detroit: Chevrolet introduces V-8 engines in new line.

28. N.J. installs automatic toll collectors on turnpike.

29. Egypt: Moslem Brotherhood dissolved after attempt on Nasser's life (→ 11/13).

30. Havana: Ramon Grau San Martin quits presidential race, charging Batista rigged vote (→ 4/29/56).

30. U.S. offers $6.5 mil. in aid to new Guatemalan Pres. Carlos Castillo Armas (→ 1/20/55).

30. Stockholm: Parliament approves natl. health care system, to take effect January 1955.

Ho Chi Minh back to rule in Hanoi

Austere Ho, the model Communist.

Oct 10. Ho Chi Minh, the Communist leader who has hidden underground for eight years, returned to Hanoi with little fanfare. He made only one well-received announcement: a plea to residents to keep the peace and go back to work. This is a time for military celebration, and Ho left the limelight to the generals. Hanoi was awash in red as General Giap and thousands of Communist soldiers paraded through sectors that were evacuated yesterday by the French under terms of the armistice. French flags were removed from buildings where they had flown for more than 70 years. Simultaneously, Viet Minh guerrillas withdrew from a stronghold in South Vietnam (→ 22).

West Germany is admitted to NATO

Oct 2. West Germany took another step in its transition from enemy to ally. The Western Allies approved its admission to NATO, despite jitters in France about rearmament. Just two months ago, France blocked West Germany's entrance into a new European Defense Community. Sir Anthony Eden, the British Foreign Secretary, and West Germany's Chancellor Konrad Adenauer were largely responsible for the agreement, which allows American and British forces to remain in West Germany (→ 12/30).

1954

NOVEMBER

Su	Mo	Tu	We	Th	Fr	Sa
	1	2	3	4	5	6
7	8	9	10	11	12	13
14	15	16	17	18	19	20
21	22	23	24	25	26	27
28	29	30				

1. U.S.: Steve Allen hosts new natl. show "Tonight," after success in local broadcasts.

2. U.S.: Democrats regain control of House and Senate in biggest mid-term voter turnout; Sam Rayburn and Lyndon Johnson to head House and Senate.

4. California: Navy demonstrates two planes; Pogo lands vertically, Sea-Dart explodes.

8. Soviet MIG's down U.S. reconnaissance plane over Japanese island of Hokkaido.

10. Tehran: Mossadegh aide Hossein Fatemi executed for plot against Shah (→ 1/22/63).

14. Communist Chinese sink Nationalist warship off Tachen Islands (→ 12/2).

15. U.S. tells U.N. it will give out fissionable material in 1955 atoms for peace plan (→ 1/9/55).

15. SAS flight saves 500 miles, from L.A. to Europe in first commercial flight over N. Pole.

19. U.S. now building Distant Early Warning radar defense net in arctic Canada.

20. Ike and administration conduct A-bomb drill (→ 2/17/55).

23. Peking: 13 U.S. fliers shot down in 1952 get four years to life for espionage (→ 5/31/55).

23. Egypt: Pharaoh Cheops' solar ship opened to light after 4,700 years.

24. Penn.: Govt. economist William Remington, in jail for Communist affiliations, dies at hands of two inmates (→ 27).

24. New York: Ed Sullivan signs 20-year contract with CBS.

27. Penn.: Alger Hiss freed after 44 months (→ 12/2).

28. Philadelphia: Navy beats Army 27-20 in football.

30. Johannesburg: Extreme nationalist Johannes Gerhardus Strydom is premier (→ 1/31/55).

DEATHS

15. Lionel Barrymore, American actor (*4/28/1878).

28. Enrico Fermi, Italian physicist, A-bomb (*9/29/1901).

30. Wilhelm Furtwangler, German conductor (*1/25/1886).

Matisse, master of pure color, is dead

Nov 3. Henri Matisse, one of the most joyous artists of the 20th Century, has died in his apartment in Nice. He was 84. Matisse freed color from the bounds of reality, letting it flow to its own limits.

Matisse was born in Picardy on December 31, 1869, the son of a grain merchant. In the late 1890's, he studied Paul Cezanne and other post-Impressionists. A decade later, he was experimenting with Fauvism, rebelling against commonplace uses of color. A portrait of his wife, "The Green Line," featured contrasting, jarring hues.

Matisse's "The Green Blouse."

The artist used many media. Matisse sculpted, designed textiles and made "decoupes," paper cutouts. "Blue Nudes," done only two years ago, is one of his finest paper constructions.

G.M. produces its 50 millionth car

Nov 23. General Motors held a nationwide celebration today as the 50 millionth car produced by the automotive giant rolled off an assembly line in Flint, Michigan. The historic car is a gold-painted Chevrolet sport coupe with 600 gold-plated parts. It took ten years after G.M. was formed in 1908 for the firm to produce its first million cars. It now makes well over a million cars a year. A message from President Eisenhower said the feat symbolizes "the industrial, scientific and creative genius of our people." ▷

Algerian independence struggle grows

Ben Bella (inset) leads the recent upsurge in Algerian nationalism.

Nov 1. Algeria is the latest target of pro-nationalist terrorists in French North Africa. They killed, pillaged and burned during the night in several attacks near the Tunisian border. At least seven French people were killed, including a school teacher dragged from his car and beaten to death. The French government, which had ignored warnings the attacks might occur, immediately dispatched 300 heavily armed mobile guards from Marseilles to Algeria. Later, Interior Minister Francois Mitterrand sent 600 Republican security troops. Premier Mendes France also announced three paratrooper battalions were on the way.

Roving bands called fellaghas carried out the attacks as new violence was also reported in the protectorates of Morocco and Tunisia. There were reports the attacks were coordinated to support Arab charges at the United Nations of French repression.

Demands in Algeria for independence have been muted if not repressed until recently. In Tunisia, French negotiators are already discussing "internal autonomy" with local officials. In Morocco, negotiations have been stymied by France's refusal to restore a deposed Sultan to the throne (→ 3/31/55).

Two new TV hosts attract attention

Nov 30. Ed Sullivan, host of "Toast of the Town," has signed a 20-year contract with CBS. Next year his program will be called "The Ed Sullivan Show." Meanwhile, Steve Allen, who began hosting NBC's "The Tonight Show" in September, is getting good reviews.

Among programs back for another year are "I Love Lucy," "Dragnet," "Topper" and "Ozzie and Harriet." "Lassie" is more enthralling than ever, now that she has had pups.

"Disneyland," new this fall, is getting good ratings. It features animation and adventure films. Five episodes on frontiersman Davy Crockett will air in December.

Tommy Rettig, Lassie and pups.

Nasser takes over full power in Egypt

Nov 13. It has been musical chairs again at the highest government levels in Egypt. This time, General Mohammed Naguib may have lost his seat for good. The President and one-time strongman was ousted by Gamal Abdel Nasser and placed under house arrest. Nasser, who up until now was Premier and head of the revolutionary council, now holds all the power.

In a confrontation earlier this year, Nasser unseated Naguib, but only for three days. A coalition of military leaders, Moslems, Communists and Wafd political leaders forced Nasser to bring him back. Since February, Nasser's influence has expanded, and he was given much of the credit for a new treaty with the British on the evacuation of the Suez Canal (→ 5/21/55).

Nasser, revolutionary since youth.

Vishinsky, purge trial figure, dies

Nov 22. The world is now without one of its more vitriolic politicians, as Soviet United Nations spokesman Andrei Vishinsky died this morning. The Soviet statesman, who has held so many key positions in the Soviet Union, was working at his desk on a speech he was to give at the U.N. General Assembly's atoms-for-peace debate, when an acute stenocardiac attack killed him. Undoubtedly, the address would have been cohesive and filled with irony, as Vishinsky was known for his keen dialectical reasoning. He honed his deadly skills as chief prosecutor in Russia's pre-war purge trials.

1954

DECEMBER

Su	Mo	Tu	We	Th	Fr	Sa
			1	2	3	4
5	6	7	8	9	10	11
12	13	14	15	16	17	18
19	20	21	22	23	24	25
26	27	28	29	30	31	

2. U.S. and Taiwan sign mutual defense treaty (→ 1/10/55).

5. Disney airs first episode in "Davy Crockett" TV series.

7. New York: IBM demonstrates NORC computer (→ 2/5/57).

10. Tenn. Gov. Frank Clement accuses Nixon, Dixon and Yates of lowering U.S. standard of public morality.

16. Ike names Nelson Rockefeller special foreign policy aide.

16. N.Y. Giant Willie Mays named National League MVP.

18. N.Y.: 26 killed in Italian Airways crash at Idlewild.

21. Jackson: Mississippi voters approve by 2-1 to continue school segregation (→ 1/7/55).

23. India: Tito, Nehru reject plan for neutral third bloc, yet insist on peaceful coexistence.

26. Cleveland: Browns trample Detroit Lions 56-10 to win pro football title.

28. Australia: Seixas and Trabert regain Davis Cup for U.S.

30. French Assembly accepts West Germany as armed ally (→ 3/22/55).

30. U.S. Post Office to halt junk mail addressed to "householder," delivered since Aug. 1953.

31. N.Y. Stock Exchange ends most active year since 1933, trading 573.4 million shares.

CULTURAL EVENTS, 1954

Literature: Ilya Ehrenburg's "The Thaw"; Kingsley Amis' "Lucky Jim"; Aldous Huxley's "The Doors of Perception."

Academia: Mortimer Wheeler's "The Indus Civilization"; Richard Wright's "Black Force."

Music: Britten's opera "The Turn of the Screw"; Menotti's opera "The Saint of Bleeker Street"; first Newport Jazz Festival held; "Mister Sandman."

The Arts: Chagall's "The Red Roofs"; Graham Sutherland's "Portrait of Churchill."

Film: Clouzot's "Diabolique"; Fellini's "La Strada"; Kurosawa's "The Seven Samurai"; "On the Waterfront," Academy Award; Hitchcock's "Rear Window."

Senate socks McCarthy

McCarthy, rebuked by fellow senators, meets the press.

Dec 2. The Senate voted 67 to 22 today to condemn Joseph R. McCarthy for conduct unbecoming a Senator. The vote—a climax to months of controversy over the tactics of the senator in his investigation of Communists in government—found the Democrats voting solidly for condemnation while Republicans were equally divided.

The resolution basically censured McCarthy for contemptuous actions against the Senate itself. It condemned him for contempt of a Senate elections subcommittee that investigated his financial affairs, for abuse of its members and for insults to the Senate itself during the lengthy censure proceedings.

Through a parliamentary maneuver, the Senate avoided a direct vote on an amendment that would have censured McCarthy for his denunciation of Brigadier General Ralph W. Zwicker as "unfit to wear an Army uniform."

To the expressed glee of McCarthy supporters, the resolution used the word condemn rather than censure to describe the disapproval of the senator's conduct, but the semantic difference did not conceal the fact that the Wisconsin Republican had been subjected to a highly unusual censure by the Senate.

McCarthy said he would resume his anti-Communist inquiry, this time in defense plants, but the consensus is that his stature has been greatly reduced (→ 1/14/55).

Cyprus Greeks riot; British open fire

Greeks demonstrate against the U.K.

Dec 18. Violence erupted during protest strikes and student demonstrations in the city of Nicosia, Cyprus, today, while in the small town of Limassol, British troops fired into rioting crowds in an attempt to restore order. It was the first such use of firearms in the British Crown Colony. This wave of protest follows in the wake of the United Nations' refusal of Greece's proposal for Cyprus' national "self-determination," and the United States delegation's decision to vote with the governments of both Great Britain and Turkey against the proposal (→ 5/24/55).

Was the universe made by Big Bang?

Dec 27. Observations of 800 galaxies show that the universe was born in a giant cosmic explosion five and a half billion years ago, astronomers reported today. Studies with the world's largest telescopes indicate that the universe has been expanding since the original explosion occurred, with countless galaxies receding from each other at speeds proportionate to their distance from one another. So far, the astronomers have been able to verify their finding for galaxies as far as 1.1 billion light years away, which are receding from the earth at one-fifth the speed of light. They plan to study even more distant galaxies soon. The cause of the giant primeval explosion is a mystery.

Nobel literary prize won by Hemingway

Dec 10. The recipient of this year's Nobel Prize for literature was unable to accept his award this evening. Ernest Hemingway was in Africa finishing up a safari. For nearly three decades Hemingway has produced novels about betrayal, brutality and courage. His novel "Across the River and into the Trees" (1950) was poorly received; it seemed the writer was in decline. "The Old Man and the Sea," however, published last year, shows him back at the top of his form.

Another American Nobel winner is Linus Pauling. He received the prize in chemistry for applying the quantum theory to chemical bonding. A Guggenheim fellow, he excels at both chemistry and physics.

"Lord of the Flies" and "... of the Rings"

Good Lord! Both "Lord of the Flies" and "The Lord of the Rings" were published this year. People who read both will never get them confused; one is a harrowing morality tale, the other a fantasy about dwarfs and dragons.

In "Lord of the Flies," by William Golding, a group of schoolboys are stranded on an island. Some turn savage, hunting wild boar with wooden spears and parading the bloodied heads on stakes. The boys who cling to civilization are preyed upon like desperate animals.

The trilogy "Lord of the Rings" by J.R.R. Tolkien follows an elf-like creature called a hobbit on a quest for a powerful ring. His habitat, Middle Earth, is described in lifelike detail. Author Tolkien teaches Old English at Oxford University.

Readers may have done another double-take. Was that "Lord Jim" by Joseph Conrad on the bookshelves? No, it was "Lucky Jim" by Kingsley Amis. "Lucky" jabs the establishment and education.

Dec 12. At a cost of $197,869,000, the U.S. Navy has launched the Forrestal, the largest aircraft carrier in the world at 1,050 feet. It is also as tall as a building with 25 stories and sports a collapsible mast for navigating under bridges. The 80,000-ton ship can race American troops and weapons to distant brush-fire conflicts at a speed of 40 knots.

1955

JANUARY

Su	Mo	Tu	We	Th	Fr	Sa
						1
2	3	4	5	6	7	8
9	10	11	12	13	14	15
16	17	18	19	20	21	22
23	24	25	26	27	28	29
30	31					

1. U.S. gives $216 million in aid to South Vietnam (→ 4/29).

1. Pasadena: Ohio State in Rose Bowl 20-7 over Southern Cal.

8. Reserpine and thorazine introduced to aid mental patients.

9. AEC announces nuclear power plants will soon be open to private ownership (→ 2/10).

10. Some 100 Communist Chinese planes raid Nationalists on Tachen Islands (→ 28).

12. Costa Rica: Nicaraguan-supported rebels strafe broad areas, including San Jose (→ 20).

13. N.Y.: Chase Natl. and Bank of Manhattan agree to merger to form second largest U.S. bank.

14. U.S. Senate votes 84-0 to continue loyalty inquiry in Civil Service (→ 9/15).

18. Yale's Albert Sabin reports he is testing live polio vaccine.

19. Washington: Ike allows press conference filmed for TV and newsreels first time (→ 12/26).

19. Selchow & Richter's new game Scrabble now on market.

20. Guatemala crushes coup, imposes state of siege (→ 7/27/57).

23. Madrid: Franco hints Prince Juan Carlos will be next head of state (→ 11/1).

25. Columbia Univ. scientists develop atomic clock accurate to within one second in 300 years.

25. U.S., Panama sign accord establishing cooperation over canal issues.

26. New York: 69-nation photo exhibit "Family of Man" opens.

28. U.S. Congress passes bill allowing mobilization if China attacks Taiwan (→ 2/5).

31. South Africa: 60,000 Negroes stage peaceful protest over govt. plan to relocate minorities outside Johannesburg (→ 2/9).

31. New York: RCA demonstrates music synthesizer.

31. Adelaide: Ken Rosewall wins Australian tennis title.

DEATH

15. Yves Tanguy, French-born Surrealist painter (*1/5/1900).

Costa Rican rebel planes strafe wide areas

Jan 20. Rebel aircraft stormed over Costa Rica earlier this month, blasting villages and taking control of government land. The aerial attack, apparently orchestrated by the Anastosia Somoza regime in nearby Nicaragua, prompted Costa Rican President Jose Figueres to condemn Somoza and prepare his country for war. Now, however, after intervention by the Organization of American States, a buffer zone has been established between the two nations to ease tensions.

Figueres, rejecting reports that the uprising was initiated by his own countrymen unhappy with his administration, said last week that Somoza was "simply trying to fool the Organization of American States by spreading propaganda about this being an internal affair." Somoza denied his country had anything to do with the assault.

After diplomatic relations were severed between Costa Rica and Nicaragua, and tempers continued to heat, Ambassador Luis Quintanilla of Mexico, President of the OAS investigating committee, met with delegates from each of the warring nations. He has successfully convinced each to agree to the demilitarized zone.

Costa Rican Civil Guard troops prepare their next move against the rebels.

Crazy man, crazy! The '55 Chevy is the hottest thing on wheels. Cruise your date to the diner or the drive-in and soar to the latest sounds. But take that V-8 where the cops don't go cause Dad ain't payin' no tickets.

Marian Anderson makes debut at Met

Versatile vocalist Marian Anderson.

Jan 7. Contralto Marian Anderson debuted at the New York Metropolitan Opera House tonight. She sang the role of Ulrica the high priestess in Verdi's "Un ballo in Maschera." Hers was a small part, but the audience applauded her as much as leads Zinka Milanov, Roberta Peters and Richard Tucker.

Miss Anderson is the first Negro to sing at the Met. Reporters from newspapers nationwide were there. Two employees of the Met bought seats and proudly listened (→ 3/21).

No-iron Dacron is put on the market

Jan 5. After nine months of development, "Fantastique," a tricot knit fabric made of DuPont polyester yarn, has debuted. It is easily laundered, fast-drying, wrinkle-resistant and requires no ironing. Now used for women's and children's garments, the Dacron fiber will be introduced into the men's shirt trade as the yarns become more available.

Inventor of first vacuum cleaner dies

Jan 14. In 1901, Hubert C. Booth watched an American carpet cleaner that made the dust fly. The Briton decided to reverse the air flow and tested his theory on his knees while breathing inward. He nearly choked, but the vacuum cleaner was born. Booth, also a designer of bridges in Europe, died today in England, 83 years old.

1955

FEBRUARY

Su	Mo	Tu	We	Th	Fr	Sa
		1	2	3	4	5
6	7	8	9	10	11	12
13	14	15	16	17	18	19
20	21	22	23	24	25	26
27	28					

1. U.S. Congress ratifies SEATO treaty (→ 23).

1. Mississippi: Tornadoes kill 29.

5. U.S. orders Seventh Fleet to Tachen Islands; U.S. fighters down 2 Communist jets (→ 9).

9. Johannesburg: First 130 Negro families moved out by force to Meadowlands (→ 6/23).

9. Peking: Military service becomes obligatory (→ 11).

10. New York: Con Ed to build first private nuclear power plant at Indian Point (→ 5/3).

10. New York: Little, Brown publishes Leonard Wibberley's "The Mouse that Roared."

10. Fort Worth, Texas: Bell Aircraft displays fixed-wing vertical takeoff plane.

11. Nationalist Chinese complete evacuation of Tachen Islands (→ 25).

11. Rochester, N.Y.: Two new nuclear particles identified, bringing total to 21.

14. Jewish couple loses fight to adopt Catholic twins as U.S. Supreme Court refuses to rule on state law.

17. Britain announces ability to make H-bombs (→ 22).

19. New Mexico: Plane goes down in snow with 16 aboard.

22. Ike proposes $101 bil. highway development plan, one-third federally financed.

22. Kenya: British troops launch drive on Mau-Mau rebels in mountains (→ 1/7/56).

22. San Diego: Maureen Connolly to retire from tennis.

23. Bangkok: Eight nations meet for first SEATO council.

23. Paris: Edgar Faure succeeds Mendes France as premier.

24. Turkey, Iraq sign Baghdad Pact military alliance (→ 9/23).

25. Nanki Island: Nationalists evacuate following Communist invasion (→ 3/2).

28. Railway line inaugurated Hanoi-Peking-Moscow-Berlin.

DEATH

23. Paul Claudel, French poet and playwright (*6/8/1868).

Bulganin replaces Malenkov as Premier

Bulganin (left) and Khrushchev.

Feb 8. The much-heralded showdown between Nikita Khrushchev, First Secretary of the Communist Party of the Soviet Union, and Georgi Malenkov finally occurred today as the latter resigned as Premier, and Marshal Nikolai A. Bulganin replaced him with the support of Khrushchev and the army.

Malenkov had been premier since the death of Joseph Stalin on March 5, 1953. In a sensational resignation statement that drew a gasp of surprise from the diplomatic and press galleries, Malenkov said his "lack of experience" held back Soviet economic development. He particularly took the blame for the poor performance of the agricultural sector, which has had "bad results." "I admit my guilt and unsatisfactory leadership," Malenkov said.

Bulganin, a popular figure who had been Defense Minister, is not a professional soldier but an old revolutionary Communist politician and administrator (→ 2/14/56).

AFL and CIO merge under George Meany

Feb 9. A formula for labor unity was approved today, leading to the merger of the American Federation of Labor and the Congress of Industrial Organizations by the end of this year. Marking the end of 20 years of conflict between the two labor giants, the merger calls for George Meany, now President of the A.F.L., to head the new union. Walter P. Reuther, President of the C.I.O., said he would be happy to step aside in Meany's favor. The plan provides that affiliated locals will respect bargaining rights of sister unions and avoid stealing members from one another (→ 7/20).

Meany and Reuther shake hands.

Poujade meetings attract thousands

Feb 24. In France, a reactionary named Pierre Poujade has turned bigotry and jingoism into an art. Today, the bedrock of the Parisian middle class, thousands of workers and shopkeepers, turned out to listen to Poujade at the Velodrome. He ripped apart statesmen who sold off the empire, "stateless homosexuals" who run the country and foreigners of every ilk who have come to live in France. Poujade saved much of his venom for former Premier Mendes France, criticized because he is not French enough, possibly because he drinks milk.

North Africa issues beat Mendes France

Feb 5. The French National Assembly has rejected the government of Premier Pierre Mendes France, voting him and his Cabinet out of office. By law, it takes an absolute majority to oust a sitting premier, and with a vote of 319 to 273, the Assembly chose to force Mendes France's resignation. His opponents objected to the premier's policy in North Africa, where nationalists are demanding independence. The premier had agreed to negotiate with the rebels. The Assembly feels the policy weakens the French republic (→ 23).

Missile with atomic warhead is tested

Missile meant to carry warheads.

Feb 22. A prototype of a guided missile with an atomic warhead was exploded today at the United States nuclear test site in Nevada. The predawn explosion was seen 400 miles away and rattled windows in Las Vegas, 75 miles distant. The Atomic Energy Commission reported slight fallout from the test northeast of Las Vegas. Troops stationed in trenches 4,000 yards from the bomb felt little heat, but some got mouthfuls of dirt when they stood up too soon, the AEC said (→ 3/10).

Israel attacks in Gaza area; 42 die

Feb 28. The relative calm of the Gaza Strip was shattered today as Israeli forces attacked Egyptian military posts near the Gaza railway station, killing 36 soldiers and six civilians. Egypt promptly protested to the U.N. Security Council against what it called an "act of aggression" in violation of the Israeli-Egyptian armistice that ended full-scale fighting in Palestine in 1949.

The strip gets its name from the spread of its 16 sandy miles along the Mediterranean. Controlled by Egypt since 1948, it serves as a way-station for 250,000 Arab refugees, 200 of whom reacted to the news by stoning the strip's U.N. headquarters, pulling down its flag and burning a Jeep.

Major General Abdullah Rifaat, Governor of Gaza, said the raid was possibly a reprisal against the hanging of two Jews as spies a month ago in Egypt (→ 4/18).

1955

MARCH

Su	Mo	Tu	We	Th	Fr	Sa
		1	2	3	4	5
6	7	8	9	10	11	12
13	14	15	16	17	18	19
20	21	22	23	24	25	26
29	28	29	30	31		

1. Washington: House raises salaries of congressmen and federal judges by 50%.

2. Ike pledges U.S. will not assist aggression by Taiwan (→ 4/23).

2. Phnom Penh: Cambodian King Sihanouk abdicates in favor of father Suramarit (→ 5/16).

6. Germany: Canada regains world hockey championship, beating U.S.S.R. 5-0 in final.

10. Ike states U.S. would use Bomb in event of war (→ 15).

12. Mexico City: Pan American Games open with 2,000 athletes (→ 18).

15. U.S. Air Force unveils self-guided missile (→ 4/14).

15. Washington: Dulles, in reversal, says U.S. retaliation will use small A-bomb in "less-than-massive" attack (→ 22).

17. Montreal: Hockey fans riot to protest NHL president's suspension of Maurice "The Rocket" Richard; 100 arrested.

18. Mexico City: U.S. runner Louis Jones sets 400-meter mark at 44.5 seconds.

20. N.Y.: "Blackboard Jungle" debuts, with Sydney Poitier.

22. Atomic fallout dusts Las Vegas, and 2,000 Marines 3,500 yards from test site (→ 4/14).

22. Honolulu: U.S. Navy DC-6 crashes, killing all 66 aboard.

22. Moscow: U.S.S.R. and seven Eastern bloc nations agree to unified military command if W. Germany is armed (→ 5/14).

25. Olympia: German archeologists find molds used to cast giant sculpture of Zeus.

28. John Marshall Harlan sworn in to U.S. Supreme Court.

29. Erich Kleiber refuses to conduct in West Berlin, charging "hostile cultural authorities" (→ 4/23).

31. France declares state of emergency in Algeria (→ 6/20).

DEATHS

11. Alexander Fleming, British biologist, discovered penicillin (*8/6/1881).

16. Nicolas de Stael, Russian-born painter (*1/15/1914).

Yalta secrets are published in U.S.

March 17. The intriguing story of the Big Three—Stalin, Churchill and Roosevelt—as they reshaped the world at Yalta in 1945 was disclosed yesterday. After much political haggling, the 400,000-word documents were released on demand by Republicans.

Allied leaders agreed on dividing Germany, but they differed on how; FDR and Stalin believed it should be sectioned into five areas. Churchill felt it should be split in two.

Britain and America granted Russia Far East territorial concessions when Stalin said the Soviets would not enter the Pacific theater without some tangible lure.

British and U.S. delegates felt uneasy toward the Russians but based their decisions on a belief that solidarity was crucial for victory.

Contrary to popular belief, Stalin did not get everything he wanted. He did not receive the concessions he desired in Iran and Turkey, nor all he wished from Germany.

Roosevelt demanded free elections in Poland, yet lacked the physical strength to ally with Churchill against Stalin; Churchill also wanted a democratic Poland, despite a quote which had him saying, "I do not care much about the Poles."

That quotation has angered Churchill, the only survivor of the three. Today, he lambasted the U.S. version of Yalta and may publish his own account to correct the "serious mistakes."

Leader of NAACP, Walter White, dies

March 21. The man who chose to be a Negro so he could fight for emancipation died last night. Walter White, Executive Secretary of the National Association for the Advancement of Colored People, was born with fair skin, blond hair and blue eyes, as his ancestry was only five-thirty-seconds Negro. It would have been easy for him to join the white majority in this nation, as 12,000 Negroes every year do. But he wanted to be recognized as a Negro and lobby against segregation laws, poll taxes and lynching.

White, 61, worked with Presidents Roosevelt and Truman on race issues, wrote books, organized rallies and worked diligently to put an end to racism (→ 4/11).

Cat on a Hot Tin Roof opens in N.Y.

March 24. Tennessee Williams' "Cat on a Hot Tin Roof" premiered tonight. As usual, a Southern family is caught up in deceit. The characters reveal themselves in simple conversation and an occasional monologue. This is Williams' truest work yet. Barbara Bel Geddes and Ben Gazzara play an anxious couple, Mildred Dunnock plays a mild mother with unexpected strengths, and Burl Ives is the family patriarch, "Big Daddy." Elia Kazan staged this splendid play.

Coonskin caps are the rage now that Davy Crockett films are on TV.

Bebop jazz artist Charlie Parker dies

Bird blows with Miles Davis (left).

March 12. Saxophone master Charlie "Bird" Parker is dead following a history of drug abuse and a recent nervous breakdown. He was 34. Parker was a seminal figure in the development of bebop, a form of jazz breaking with traditional rhythmic and harmonic patterns.

Parker was born in Kansas City. At the age of 12 he proved a capable player of the alto sax, and in his early 20's he drifted from band to band. In some larger groups, such as that of Jay McShann, his personal sound was stifled. Parker formed his own quintet; while the group was short-lived, it allowed him to compose, expand and improvise.

Ten years ago, Parker and trumpeter Dizzy Gillespie did some gigs together in New York's 52nd Street jazz joints. On their off hours they cut some records. Jazz lovers consider those recordings some of the most creative ever made.

Between birdies this month, Ike discussed tactical nuclear weapons and said the U.S. would not help Chiang attack Red China.

1955

APRIL

Su	Mo	Tu	We	Th	Fr	Sa
					1	2
3	4	5	6	7	8	9
10	11	12	13	14	15	16
17	18	19	20	21	22	23
24	25	26	27	28	29	30

2. Philippines: 200 die as earthquake hits south.

3. Mexico: Over 300 die as train falls into canyon near Guadalajara.

4. China: Manchurian party head Kao Kang purged as plotter against Mao (→ 5/25/56).

5. Chicago: Richard Daley chosen mayor as Democrats sweep city elections.

11. New York: Roy Wilkins named exec. sec. of NAACP (→ 5/31).

12. Michigan: Tests at Ann Arbor show Salk polio vaccine effective.

14. Detroit: Red Wings beat Montreal in final game to retain Stanley Cup.

14. U.S.: Loaded Nike guided missile escapes launching pad, explodes in flight (→ 5/6).

15. Moscow signs treaty with Austria, ending ten-year occupation (→ 5/15).

15. U.S.S.R. establishes permanent commission for interplanetary communications.

18. Jerusalem: Israel and Jordan set up security zone in Jerusalem area (→ 8/24).

18. Hungary: Andra Hegedus elected premier to succeed Imre Nagy, father of discredited "new course" (→ 7/16).

19. New York installs new "Don't Walk" signs at busiest intersections.

21. Laos: Government fails to gain accord in talks with rebels (→ 5/18/59).

23. East Germans seize 17 West German trucks en route to Berlin (→ 11/2).

29. Italy: Christian Democrat Giovanni Bronchi elected president with Socialist and Communist support.

DEATHS

1. Robert R. McCormick, Chicago Tribune and New York News publisher (*7/30/1880).

7. Theda Bara, American film star, top box office attraction of 1920's (*7/20/1890).

10. Pierre Teilhard de Chardin, French theologian (*5/1/1881).

Afro-Asian conference held at Bandung

Chou (left) listens to debate while a colleague discusses issues with Nasser.

April 23. Representatives of 29 African and Asian nations are meeting in Bandung, Indonesia, to promote economic and cultural cooperation and oppose colonialism.

Chou En-lai's message at the conference was direct and simple: China does not want war with the United States. The Premier of Communist China expressed the need to negotiate with Washington to alleviate tension about Formosa. His proposal for a one-on-one conference was called "hope for the future" by conference Chairman Dr. Ali Sastroamidjojo (→ 6/10).

Churchill retires as British Prime Minister

April 5. Sir Winston Churchill bowed to age today and resigned as Prime Minister, a post he held twice, first in war and then in peace. Churchill, now 80, submitted his resignation in an audience with Queen Elizabeth II at Buckingham Palace and then strode out of the palace through the cheering ranks of his countrymen. As one of his final official acts, he declined the queen's offer of a dukedom so that he could remain in the House of Commons. Churchill will be succeeded as Prime Minister by Sir Anthony Eden.

Lady Churchill (left) and Winston greet the Queen at 10 Downing Street.

Most famous savant of the age has died

April 18. Physicist and humanist Albert Einstein has died in Princeton, New Jersey. His heart, never very strong, failed him. He was 76.

Einstein was born March 14, 1879, in Ulm, Germany. An unexceptional elementary school student, he made great progress at the University of Zurich, earning a Ph.D. in 1905. That year, he published his Special Theory of Relativity and in 1915 came his General Theory of Relativity—ideas that changed the world. He stayed at German universities until anti-Semitism drove him out in 1933.

The man was an innate pacifist. Fears of German development of a nuclear bomb, however, impelled him to convince the United States to build its own. Later, he urged the weapon never be used.

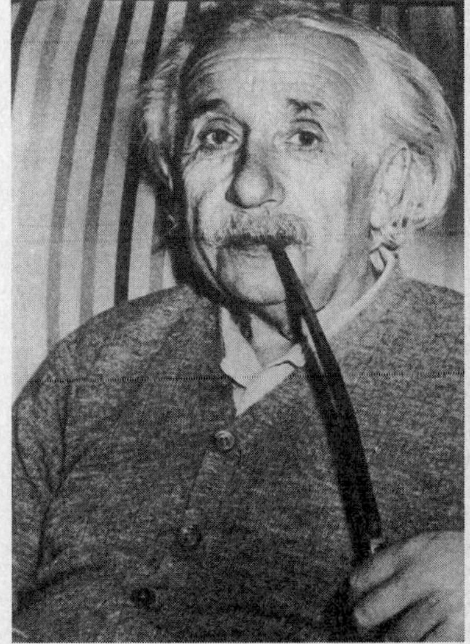

Eccentric genius Albert Einstein.

Einstein was never in awe of himself. He clowned for photographers, sticking out his tongue and wearing a Mickey Mouse hat in front of the camera. He was endearingly absent-minded. Friends said he never took walks because he had a terrible sense of direction.

A few years ago, Einstein likened faith to physics, saying, "I believe in the brotherhood of man and the uniqueness of the individual. But if you ask me to prove what I believe, I can't . . . There comes a point where the mind takes a higher plane of knowledge, but can never prove how it got there. All great discoveries have involved such a leap." ▷

Rival factions wage civil war in Saigon

Saigon, never a picture of unity, suffers under the Binh Xuyen bombing.

April 29. Civil war has erupted in the streets of Saigon. The city is on fire, confused and chaotic. Blood is splattered in the streets and on hospital walls. Dazed residents stand motionless outside as mortar shells drop nearby. The police force is split into two factions, the French and Americans are on opposite sides and Emperor Bao Dai is trying to control the situation from a villa on the French Riviera.

The trouble started when Premier Ngo Dinh Diem fired Saigon's police chief, who is a member of the Binh Xuyen faction. Binh Xuyen rebels attacked Diem's place with mortar shells, and the premier ordered his army into the streets. Some 100 people have been killed so far in the confrontation. Hundreds more were wounded, many of them women and children.

Tension has been building for months between Diem and the Binh Xuyen, onetime river pirates who supported the French in the war against the Communists. The French still favor the Binh Xuyen, but Diem is backed by the United States. And to make matters more confused, French-supported Emperor Bao Dai, who is presently living in Cannes, is distancing himself from Diem. Bao Dai summoned him to the Riviera and ordered him to give more military power to a rival (→ 5/2).

The U.S. Navy's new jet fighter, the F-7-U Chance Vought Cutlass, is equipped with air-to-air guided missiles and ready for combat.

1955

MAY

Su	Mo	Tu	We	Th	Fr	Sa
1	2	3	4	5	6	7
8	9	10	11	12	13	14
15	16	17	18	19	20	21
22	23	24	25	26	27	28
29	30	31				

3. Turkey, U.S., in atoms-for-peace pact, agree to exchange data and material for nuclear energy (→ 8/8).

5. New York: Gwen Verdon and Ray Walston star in "Damn Yankees."

6. The Hague: Britain seeks recognition of sovereignty over Falkland Islands from Intl. Court of Justice (→ 4/30/82).

7. Kentucky Derby won by Swaps, with Willie Shoemaker in the saddle.

12. New York: Last train travels Third Avenue Elevated.

14. Lawrence, Kansas: Seven-foot, two-inch Wilt Chamberlain to attend Univ. of Kansas.

15. North Vietnam: French ship Esperance leaves Haiphong, ending evacuation of troops (→ 6/14).

16. U.S. signs treaty granting military aid to Cambodia.

19. FTC says business mergers have tripled in U.S. over last five years.

21. U.S.S.R. decides to sell arms to Egypt (→ 1/16/56).

23. U.S.: Presbyterian Church votes to accept women as ministers.

23. John F. Kennedy returns to U.S. Senate after back surgery and 7 month recuperation.

24. Cyprus: Demonstrators riot, calling for annexation to Greece (→ 8/29).

27. U.S.: Tornadoes hit Southern states, killing 121.

31. U.S. Supreme Court rules states must end racial segregation "with all deliberate speed" (→ 11/20).

31. Communist China releases four U.S. airmen accused of espionage (→ 6/10).

31. Soviets agree to evacuate troops from Port Arthur, leaving it to Chinese.

DEATHS

16. James Agee, American poet and critic, "Let Us Now Praise Famous Men" (*11/27/1909).

18. Mary McLeod Bethune, black educator (*7/10/1875).

In command: Diem breaks Saigon coup

Diem, American choice in Saigon.

May 2. A coup attempt in South Vietnam has been quashed, after an international power play that extended from Saigon to the French Riviera to Washington. The clear winners are Premier Ngo Dinh Diem and the United States. The losers are France and Emperor Bao Dai, who lives in Cannes. General Nguyen Van Vy, who was supported by the emperor and the French in a bid to seize control of the army, has fled. The United States is delighted by the turn of events. General J. Lawton Chiles, President Eisenhower's special envoy to Vietnam, is flying to Saigon tomorrow. For the time being, Diem and Bao Dai are trying to patch up relations. "We are giving Bao Dai one more chance to come to his senses," Diem's brother said (→ 15).

West Germany gets its full sovereignty

May 5. After nearly ten years of Allied occupation, West Germany has gained its complete sovereignty. French and British delegates ratified the Paris agreements ending foreign occupation and granting Bonn authority to govern and rearm. However, atomic weapons production is prohibited. In a proclamation of independence, Federal Republic of Germany officials exclaimed, "We stand as free men, linked in true partnership with the former occupying powers." The Federal Republic consists of two-thirds of the territroy of Germany, with East Germany covering the other third (→ 6/7).

Austrian state treaty ends foreign control

Signatories display their accomplishment from the balcony of the castle of Belvedere: American Secretary of State Dulles (left), Austrian Foreign Minister Leopold Figl (center) and Soviet Foreign Minister Molotov (waving).

May 15. For the first time in 17 years the only troops on Austrian soil will be Austrian. The country was annexed by Hitler in 1938 and occupied by Soviet, U.S., British and French forces following WWII. Central to the treaty signed today was the provision that Austria remain a neutral buffer state between Soviet bloc nations and the democratic countries of Western Europe.

Under the provisions of the treaty, Austria may not sign any military alliance or permit any foreign military bases on her soil. The rest of the terms were favorable to Austria. She will pay no war reparations, Russia refutes all claim to her oil fields and she may rebuild her army to defend her neutrality.

U.S. Secretary of State John Foster Dulles, Soviet Foreign Minister Molotov and British Foreign Minister Macmillan were among those who signed the treaty, which stipulates that all foreign troops must be withdrawn by the end of the year. The United States had accused the Soviets of stalling during the talks in order to maintain their 45,000-troop presence in the country (→ 7/27).

Khrushchev makes up with President Tito

May 26. Immediately after arriving at the airport in Belgrade, Soviet Communist Party Secretary Nikita Khrushchev shook hands with Yugoslav President Tito and urged reconciliation in the name of Lenin and "in the interests of the international workers' movement."

The historic shift in Soviet attitude toward the independent Yugoslav leader came after seven years of severed relations between the two Communist nations. Yugoslavia was ousted from the Communist community in June 1948.

At the head of a high-ranking delegation that included Soviet Premier Nikolai Bulganin, Khrushchev called for ideological collaboration. He also apologized for past "aggravations" to Yugoslavia, attributing them to the "fabrication" of Lavrenti Beria, the former Soviet Minister of Internal Affairs, who was executed in 1953. Tito stood silently during Khrushchev's remarks, and afterwards, he did not respond to the Soviet leader.

Later, in an exchange with American Ambassador Riddleberger at a reception, Khrushchev argued the merits of socialism, expressed his dislike of capitalism and said he hoped the U.S. and U.S.S.R., once allies, would not have to fight each other in the next war (→ 6/5).

Tito (right) welcomes Khrushchev (left) and Bulganin in Belgrade.

May 30. Bill Vukovich's life, and his bid for an unparalleled third straight Indy 500 victory, ended tragically today when, at over 100 mph, he plowed into a pileup caused by swirling winds. Bob Sweikert went on to win.

Nuclear blast test held in model town

May 6. A model of a typical American community built in the Nevada desert stood up well to an atomic explosion yesterday, federal officials say, but they noted that any inhabitants outside of bomb shelters probably would have been killed. Three of ten houses one to two miles from the explosion point were ruined, while the rest suffered broken windows and battered furnishings. Dalmatian dogs left in shelters in the houses were unharmed when removed later, authorities said. The detonation, with the force of 35,000 tons of TNT, was staged in part to help civil defense officials plan for a nuclear attack (→ 8).

Hiroshima victims to get U.S. surgery

May 8. Mrs. Mitten Ishida, President of the Japanese Federation of Women Societies of San Francisco, extended a bouquet this morning to a woman stepping off a plane. She, Michiko Sako, is spokeswoman for 24 other Japanese women arriving at Travis Air Force Base. Hiroshima bomb victims, they are in the United States for plastic surgery.

The women are bound for New York's Mount Sinai Hospital. They will be housed for free at Americans' homes. Treatment will be paid by private funds. Miss Sako thanked Mrs. Ishida for the flowers, saying that Pearl Harbor was no less a tragedy than Hiroshima (→ 6/11). ▷

Eastern bloc signs military compact

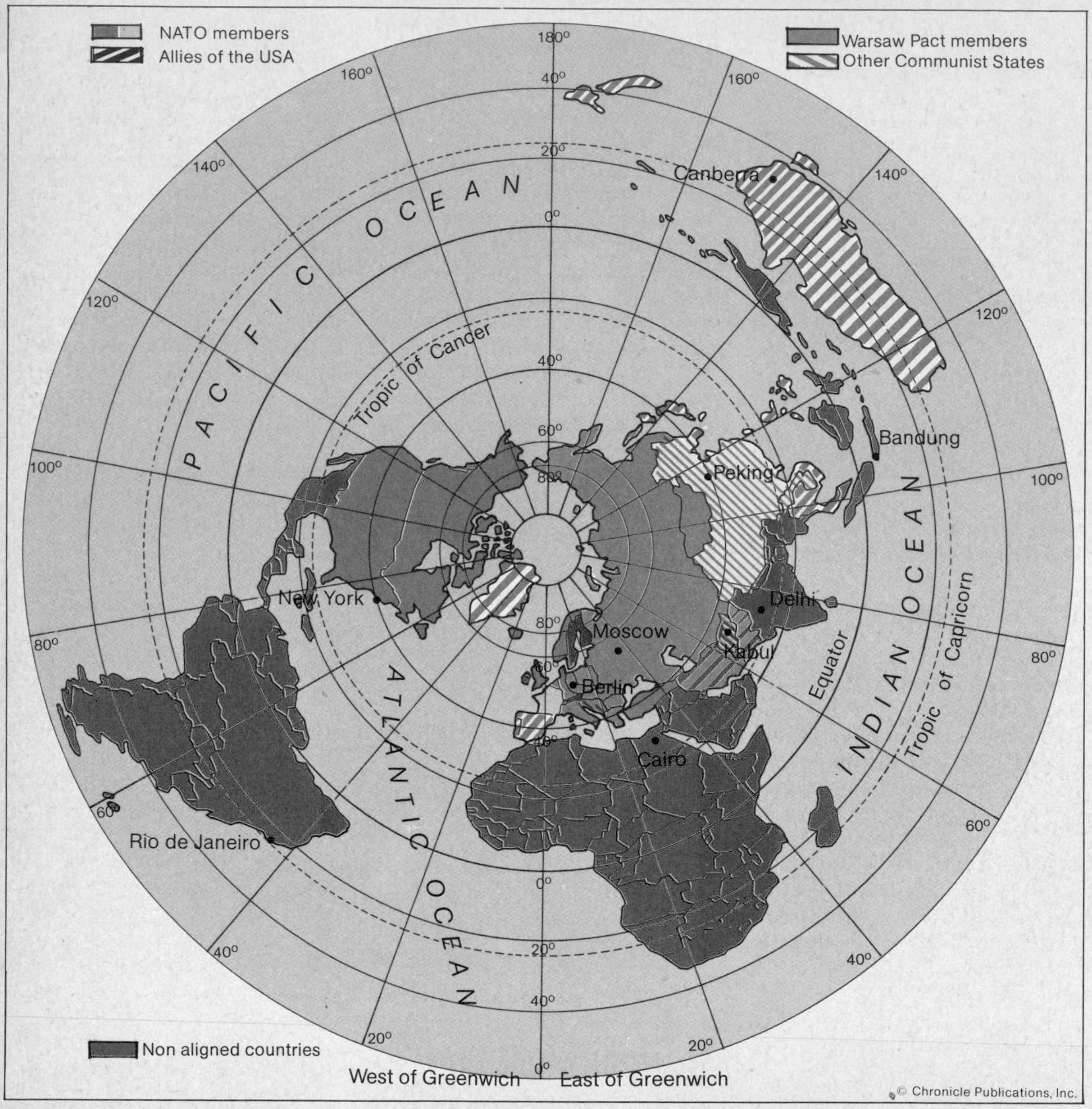

With West Germany rearming, and the signing of the Warsaw Pact, the opposition of East and West is complete.

May 14. The Warsaw Pact, unifying the Eastern bloc nations militarily, was signed this morning and Soviet Marshal Ivan S. Konev was named as the military commander of the Communist states. The treaty resembles the alliance of the North Atlantic Treaty Organization of Western nations and includes the Soviet Union, Poland, Czechoslovakia, Hungary, Rumania, Bulgaria, Albania and East Germany. The signatories agreed to abstain from the use of force in resolving international issues and vowed to collaborate for disarmament and peace. The 20-year treaty also establishes a cooperative army (→ 7/6).

Soviet representatives Molotov and Marshal Zhukov, surrounded by delegates from Eastern Europe, sign the pact creating a formal alliance against NATO.

1955

JUNE

Su	Mo	Tu	We	Th	Fr	Sa
			1	2	3	4
5	6	7	8	9	10	11
12	13	14	15	16	17	18
19	20	21	22	23	24	25
26	27	28	29	30		

1. Tunisia: Nationalist leader Bourgiba returns from exile on Groix Island (→ 3).

2. India: British party scales third highest peak Mt. Kanchenjunga, highest unclimbed peak.

5. Belgrade bars ties to Eastern bloc under Warsaw Pact (→ 6/2/56).

6. Bill Haley and the Comets' "Rock Around the Clock" hits #1 on Billboard charts.

7. Soviets invite W. German Chancellor Adenauer to Moscow to establish diplomatic and trade ties (→ 12).

10. New York: Harcourt Brace publishes Flannery O'Connor's "A Good Man Is Hard to Find."

10. Taiwan: U.S. establishes air bases to pursue struggle with Communist China (→ 8/1).

11. AEC announces ability to build cheap H-bomb of virtually limitless size (→ 15).

12. Washington: Adenauer arrives to meet with Ike (→ 30).

13. Purchase, N.Y.: First executive jet plane Beech Paris is displayed.

14. Hanoi votes law guaranteeing freedom of worship (→ 7/16).

15. Washington: Govt. moves to 30 dispersed shelters in civil defense test (→ 7/9).

15. Paris: Jean Monnet appeals for United States of Europe.

16. Washington: House extends Selective Service until 1959.

20. Algeria: 100 arrested in purge of left, including sec. gen. of Communist Party (→ 8/20).

20. Belgium to sell Congolese uranium to U.K. and U.S.

20. San Francisco: U.N. opens 10th anniversary celebration.

23. Buenos Aires: Cabinet resigns to give Peron free hand in quelling revolt (→ 7/10).

23. Johannesburg: Parliament strengthens power of ruling Nationalist Party (→ 10/24).

24. Soviet MIG's down U.S. Navy patrol plane over Bering Strait (→ 7/7).

30. U.S. begins funding of West German rearmament (→ 9/13).

Faced with revolt, Peron gives army power

Peron, Gen. Lucero in Buenos Aires.

June 18. President Juan Domingo Peron today gave the Argentine army the power "to safeguard internal order and public tranquility." This comes in the wake of last Thursday's revolt which broke out shortly after Pope Pius XII announced the excommunication of Peron. During the uprising, which was led by naval officers, air force and naval aviation fighter planes bombarded the government house and the Plaza de Mayo, killing more than 350 persons. The pope was reacting to Peron's anti-Catholic policies, including the recent expulsion from Argentina of the Auxiliary Bishop of Buenos Aires and his assistant, and the arrest of 85 priests in the last eight months (→ 23).

Tunisia autonomous as Bourguiba returns

June 3. France has formalized the autonomy of Tunisia, accepting home rule for the North African nation. After nine months of serious and difficult negotiations, French Premier Edgar Faure and Tunisian Premier Tahar Ben Ammar signed the ratification papers which assure Tunisia's internal autonomy. However, in accordance with the agreement, the French High Command will be responsible for protecting Tunisian soil and France will continue to direct the Bey of Tunis' foreign policy.

Bourguiba returns after three years.

Director Wilder emphasizes assets other than Miss Monroe's brains in "The Seven Year Itch."

80 dead at Le Mans; worst accident ever

June 11. The worst accident in the history of auto racing occurred tonight at Le Mans raceway southwest of Paris. Eighty people died and nearly 100 were injured. Three cars on the eight-mile, asphalt course sped side by side at 125 mph. But then they collided. The Mercedes on the inside track skidded into the grandstand. Hot metal severed people in half; some children were decapitated. The Mercedes team retired, but the race continued. The director of the course said, "In spite of the horror of the situation, I did not judge that the race should be interrupted. Even when a tragedy happens, the sport should be guided by its own law."

1955

JULY

Su	Mo	Tu	We	Th	Fr	Sa
					1	2
3	4	5	6	7	8	9
10	11	12	13	14	15	16
17	18	19	20	21	22	23
24	25	26	27	28	29	30
31						

1. Pittsburgh: 600,000 steelworkers get 15-cent pay raise after 12-hour strike.

6. Strasbourg: British, French foreign ministers outline plan to include Eastern bloc in new Council of Europe (→ 23).

7. New York: CBS starts new program with Johnny Carson to counter George Gobel on NBC.

7. Soviets offer indemnity for U.S. naval plane shot down in June.

9. London: Nine scientists, led by Einstein, Russell, urge war ban since Bomb threatens man's "continued existence" (→ 21).

10. Buenos Aires: Scores arrested as 1,000 Catholics protest Peron "tyranny" (→ 8/31).

10. Elmsford, N.Y.: Church holds first "drive-in" service in outdoor movie theater.

11. Colorado Springs: Air Force Academy takes first 306 cadets.

12. Milwaukee: Stan Musial hits homer in 12th inning to win All Star Game for National League.

12. New York: First shipload of 1,243 European refugees arrives under 1953 immigration act.

14. N.Y.: James Cagney, Henry Fonda star in "Mr. Roberts."

16. Hungary: Cardinal Mindszenty released under house arrest (→ 2/3/56).

16. Saigon: Diem declares South Vietnam not tied by Geneva accord (→ 10/14).

20. Washington: A.F.L. and C.I.O. agree to combine names for merged group (→ 12/5).

21. Groton, Conn.: Third U.S. nuclear sub Seawolf launched (→ 9/3).

27. Israeli airliner downed over Bulgaria; 58 passengers killed.

27. Austria formally regains sovereignty.

29. U.S. reports it will launch world's first orbiting satellite in 1957 or 1958 (→ 4/11/57).

30. Louison Bobet wins Tour de France for third time.

DEATH

23. Cordell Hull, sec. of state under FDR, champion of intl. free trade (*10/2/1871).

Disneyland is world of a child's dreams

Mickey Mouse and Walt Disney.

July 18. Disneyland, a steel-and-concrete "Never-Never Land" for youngsters, has come to life at Anaheim, California. Walt Disney, who gave the nation Mickey Mouse, has let a fantastic kingdom drop out of a cloud onto 160 acres 22 miles outside of Los Angeles. There a child can drive the car of the future, ride in a Mississippi stern-wheeler, romp through a medieval castle or walk down Main Street, U.S.A.

The super amusement park cost some $17 million and kept 2,500 workers toiling to the last minute on "Peter Pan Fly-Through," rocket trips to the moon, Old West trains and much more. Disney's real-life dream world is expected to attract five million callers a year. Is this a people trap built by a mouse?

Chuck Berry has given the blues a rocking new sound with his hit "Maybellene," cut this month.

Big Four summit at Geneva a success

The Big Four in Geneva: Bulganin, Eisenhower, Mendes France and Eden.

July 23. The Big Four summit meeting has ended in Geneva, with the leaders of the United States, Britain, France and the Soviet Union calling it a success. They did not reach agreement on the future of Germany, European security or disarmament. And they barely discussed the Far East. But they decided their foreign ministers would discuss most of these problems in October in what might be called the "spirit of Geneva."

On the subject of Germany, French Prime Minister Edgar Faure argued that it could be reunited only through the framework of NATO. Soviet Premier Nikolai Bulganin replied that the biggest obstacles to reunification are the rearmament of West Germany and the presence of American troops.

On the question of disarmament, the final communique did not mention President Eisenhower's "open sky" proposal. The president suggested that the United States and Soviet Union exchange defense blueprints and allow aerial inspection of defense installations.

British Prime Minister Anthony Eden said the summit established a better atmosphere among the leaders. Bulganin said it was "a beginning," but would have been more successful if the questions of Asia, Formosa and Communist China had been discussed (→ 8/13).

Martial law halts Moroccan riots; 56 dead

July 17. The city of Casablanca has been placed under martial law as a result of the fierce fighting between Europeans and native Moroccans for the past two days.

On Thursday, July 14 (Bastille Day), a bomb exploded outside a crowded cafe, killing six Europeans and wounding 35 others. Since then, at least 50 persons have been killed in the violence, including eight Moroccans who were fired upon by French Foreign Legionnaires and mobile gendarmes.

These clashes have been fueled by the growing nationalist sentiments of many native Moroccans, as well as the fears of some Europeans of nationalist gains, which have even been championed by Gilbert Grandval, the French Resident General (→ 8/20).

French guards try to quell riots sparked by the arrival of Res. Gen. Grandval.

Hundred Germans make U.S. rockets

July 6. More than 100 German scientists and specialists are developing guided missiles for the United States at the Redstone Arsenal in Huntsville, Alabama, the Army has disclosed. They are working under Wernher von Braun, developer of the German V-2 rocket that rained destruction on London during World War II.

Von Braun now is Director of the Guided Missile Development Division at Redstone, a secret installation that has produced at least one missile, which is named for the installation. The Army referred to von Braun and his colleagues as "former Germans," saying that many have become U.S. citizens and the rest are willing to qualify.

The Army also announced that a new member of the Redstone group is Hermann Oberth, a German rocket pioneer, who is said to have rebuffed Communist invitations to go to East Germany. Oberth, who in 1923 wrote a pioneering work on liquid-fueled rockets, did some of the supporting research for the V-2 rocket. He continued his research on rockets on his own after the war.

1955

AUGUST

Su	Mo	Tu	We	Th	Fr	Sa
	1	2	3	4	5	6
7	8	9	10	11	12	13
14	15	16	17	18	19	20
21	22	23	24	25	26	27
28	29	30	31			

1. Geneva: Peking frees 11 U.S. fliers as talks with U.S. begin (→ 9/10).

2. U.S. Congress votes to build 45,000 public housing units.

2. Massapequa, L.I.: Mrs. Sheldon Robbins named first woman cantor at Temple.

8. Geneva: Scientists from 62 nations open conference on atomic energy (→ 8).

8. AEC approves plans for private nuclear reactors in Chicago and Detroit areas (→ 10).

10. Geneva: British announce reactor that produces twice the fuel it consumes (→ 10/18).

11. Two U.S. Air Force planes collide over West Germany, killing 66 servicemen.

12. Ike increases minimum wage to $1 per hour.

13. Moscow announces troop reduction of 650,000 because tension has eased (→ 10/27).

19. U.S.: Floods strike Northeast, killing 179.

20. Morocco: Rebels kill 49 French on anniversary of Sultan Ben Youssef's deposition (→ 22).

20. Portugal breaks relations with India after invasion of Goa by Indian nationalists.

23. British Canberra jet flies London to N.Y. in under 14.5 hours, setting speed record.

24. Cairo: Egypt pulls out of talks with Israel on Gaza border conflicts (→ 29).

25. Chamonix: World's highest cable car inaugurated.

25. Morocco: French Resident General Gilbert Grandval resigns in crisis (→ 9/12).

27. Forest Hills: Australia, led by Ken Rosewall, retakes Davis Cup from U.S.

29. U.K., Turkey and Greece open Cyprus parley (→ 9/6).

29. Egyptian and Israeli jets meet in clash over Gaza (→ 31).

31. Buenos Aires: Peron briefly offers resignation amid student protests (→ 9/1).

DEATH

17. Fernand Leger, French painter (*2/4/1881).

Algerian rebels launch big attack

French Union official Jacques Soustelle dicusses matters with Algerian leaders.

Aug 20. Hundreds of nationalist rebels killed and pillaged in northeastern Algeria today. Their murderous attack was apparently coordinated with terrorists in Morocco who massacred dozens of Europeans. The Algerian insurrectionists, led by former town councilman Zirout Youssef, struck in 25 towns, bombing French command posts, police stations, town halls and train stations. At the same time, several thousand men and women from peasant villages attacked the homes of Europeans and massacred the residents. In Philippeville, French Moslems were targeted as 60 people were killed by a mob. French security forces, on alert since yesterday, were quick to strike back and razed entire villages suspected of harboring the rioters (→ 9/11).

North Africa incurs serious death toll

Aug 22. Violence in Algeria and Morocco has already cost more than 1,000 lives since fighting broke out two days ago. The French attribute the unrest in both Algeria and Morocco to nationalist groups intent on forcing France out of North Africa. Attacks by terrorist bands began on the second anniversary of the ousting of the pronationalist Moroccan Sultan Sidi Mohammad Ben Youssef.

As the French attempt to crush the uprisings, a conference between the French and leaders of various Moroccan factions opens today in Aix-les-Bains. The French may be willing to make concessions to the Moroccan nationalists, but they strongly oppose any nationalist movement in Algeria (→ 25).

Master novelist Thomas Mann deceased

Aug 12. One of the masters of the 20th Century is dead. Author Thomas Mann has died in Zurich, Switzerland. He was 80 years old.

Mann was born to an upper-class German family. In 1901, he wrote "Buddenbrooks," a novel relating his family's financial decline. Dark, romantic and at times funny, the book was praised throughout Europe. Other works include "The Magic Mountain" (1924) and a tetralogy about the Biblical Joseph.

Nazism and anti-Semitism repelled Mann. (He married a Jewish woman and they had six children.) "God help our darkened and desecrated country," he wrote, "and teach it to make its peace with the world and with itself."

Mann came to the United States in 1938 at the invitation of Princeton University, where he lectured against totalitarianism. Reporters visiting him on his 80th birthday found him absorbed in writing.

In Lubeck just before his death, Mann went out with his wife Katia.

Cease-fire halts Israeli-Egyptian battle

Aug 31. Though the crackle of gunfire can still be heard, the Gaza Strip conflict is winding down as Egypt today agreed to a proposed U.N. cease-fire. Israeli agreement is expected shortly.

Earlier, the Israeli military claimed to have driven off four Egyptian planes which they said had penetrated Israeli air space. Egypt claims the reverse. This was believed to be the first encounter between Egyptian and Israeli jet fighters since the 1948 armistice.

Meanwhile a wave of terror has engulfed central Israel where assassins, hunting their victims from the thicket-like cover of orange groves, have murdered seven in the past two days. The killers are thought to belong to an Egyptian terrorist group called Al Fedayeen (The Self-Sacrificers), formed originally to fight the British in the Suez Canal Zone before the evacuation took place (→ 9/3).

Aug 17. French painter Fernand Leger is dead. Trained in architecture, he was interested in geometric shapes. Above: "Les Loisirs" (1949).

1955

SEPTEMBER

Su	Mo	Tu	We	Th	Fr	Sa
				1	2	3
4	5	6	7	8	9	10
11	12	13	14	15	16	17
18	19	20	21	22	23	24
25	26	27	28	29	30	

1. Buenos Aires placed under state of siege due to student rioting (→ 16).

3. Philadelphia: Army stages mock atom raid for visiting Soviets (→ 11/26).

3. Israel accepts cease-fire along Gaza frontier (→ 25).

4. Col. Talbott flies Super Sabre jet, first supersonic combat plane cross-country in 3 hrs., 48 min.

6. Turkey: Anti-Greek riots spread out in Istanbul and Smyrna (→ 9).

7. Peru grants voting rights to women.

9. Britain announces home rule plan for Cyprus (→ 1/10/56).

10. Peking agrees to free all remaining U.S. civilians in Communist China (→ 7/7/56).

11. Paris: French draftees protest at train station, refusing to leave for Algeria (→ 10/1).

12. Paris: Deputies approve plan to pacify Morocco by reinstating Sultan Ben Youssef (→ 30).

13. Moscow: U.S.S.R. and W. Germany agree to re-establish diplomatic ties (→ 11/12).

15. U.S.: 360 citizens ask Supreme Court to ban Internal Security Act of 1950 (→ 2/18/57).

16. Argentina: Military revolt erupts against Peron (→ 19).

18. Soviets pledge to liquidate bases on foreign soil.

18. Soviet Vladimir Kuts sets 5,000-meter record at 14:46.8.

19. Buenos Aires: Peron overthrown by rebels (→ 24).

21. N.Y.: Marciano KOs Archie Moore in fifth to retain title.

23. Israel celebrates discovery of oil.

23. Pakistan joins Baghdad Pact (→ 11/21).

25. U.S. offers weapons to Egypt to offset Soviet aid (→ 10/11).

26. N.Y.: Stock Exchange has $44 mil. one-day loss, heaviest in history.

26. N.Y.: Actress Debbie Reynolds marries Eddie Fisher.

30. Rabat: Moroccan Sultan Ben Arafa resigns throne under pressure from France (→ 10/2).

Peron ousted and exiled

Sept 24. Rather than turn former President Juan Peron into a martyr through trial and punishment, Argentina's new military junta recognized "the right of asylum" and packed him off to Paraguay.

Peron had been hiding out on a Paraguayan gunboat in the Buenos Aires harbor since a four-day-old revolution swept him from office on Monday. The power base for Peron's ten-year-old regime began to crumble when he courted business over labor, stepped up his attacks on the Catholic Church and agreed to let Standard Oil of California develop Argentine resources. Rebel forces seized control of the army and navy and brought the government to its knees when they threatened the capital with bombardment.

News of Peron's downfall bought wildly cheering crowds out into the rain on Monday, and statues of Eva Peron, the dictator's late wife, were dragged through the streets. The junta now has most of the country within its grasp, but isolated pockets of Peronists continue to fight on (→ 10/2).

Primitive painter Grandma Moses is 95

Grandma Moses hard at work in her starkly furnished New England home.

Sept 7. "Anybody can paint," says Grandma Moses. She would probably add, "and at any age." Mrs. Moses, world-famous primitive artist, started painting in her seventies. She is 95 years old today.

Anna Mary Robertson was born on a farm in the hills of New York state. She worked as a hired girl until she was 27, marrying another hired worker, Thomas Moses. Mrs. Moses, like her mother before her, bore ten children. Her hands would scrub floors, milk cows and can fresh vegetables. By her late 70's arthritis ruled out those tasks. So she reached for a paintbrush.

Now, Grandma Moses' art is in museums worldwide. She uses bright colors for unabashedly happy scenes: farmers carrying logs for a fire, blacksmiths shoeing horses and youngsters bellywhopping down snowy slopes (→ 12/13/61).

Eisenhower hospitalized for heart attack

Sept 24. President Eisenhower suffered a "mild coronary thrombosis" in his sleep last night and has entered Fitzsimons Army Hospital near Denver. He has withstood the attack well, though he has been placed in an oxygen tent as a precaution. His wife Mamie is at his side, and Vice President Nixon flies in tomorrow. The illness of the popular president, who will be 65 on October 14, may lead him to decide against seeking re-election, to the dismay of his supporters (→ 11/11).

James Dean, idol of youth, is killed

Dean in "Rebel Without a Cause."

Sept 30. Teen idol James Dean died tonight in a car crash. Dean was killed instantly when his coupe, a Porsche Spider, careened off a road between Los Angeles and Salinas. He had been on his way to an auto rally. He was 24 years old.

Indiana-born Dean starred in only three films: "East of Eden," "Giant" and "Rebel Without a Cause." (The latter two have not yet been released.) His performance in "Eden" was enough to earn near-idolatry from teens. He portrayed restless, inarticulate youth. His mumble was his trademark.

Leo Durocher quits

Sept 24. Leo Durocher has resigned as Manager of the New York Giants to enter private business. He began as Dodgers Manager in 1939, and took over the Giants in 1948.

Durocher: "Nice guys finish last."

1955

OCTOBER

Su	Mo	Tu	We	Th	Fr	Sa
						1
2	3	4	5	6	7	8
9	10	11	12	13	14	15
16	17	18	19	20	21	22
23	24	25	26	27	28	29
30	31					

1. France boycotts U.N. General Assembly after vote to consider Algerian crisis (→ 2/1/56).

1. Athens: Constantin Caramanlis elected president of council.

2. Peron arrives in Paraguay to begin life in exile (→ 11/2).

2. Morocco: French fight off tribesmen near Fez (→ 31).

2. Old Mystic, Conn.: All-white Methodist church installs Negro as pastor.

4. Georgia: Bell Telephone uses light of sun to power phone call for first time (→ 11/1).

6. U.S. Army commissions first male nurse.

6. United Airlines plane hits mountain in Wyoming; 66 dead.

7. N.Y.: Navy launches USS Saratoga.

11. Israel asks U.S. aid to counter Egyptian aid from Czechoslovakia (→ 16).

11. Korea: Soviets evacuate Port Arthur, leaving it under Chinese control.

11. Canada, U.S.S.R. give each other most-favored-nation status in trade accord.

13. U.S.: "The Deer Park," by Norman Mailer, published.

14. New Delhi: Colombo Plan conference issues plea for technological aid to Asia.

14. France signs first trade agreement with Hanoi (→ 24).

16. Sinai: Israeli and Egyptian forces clash in El Auja demilitarized zone (→ 19).

18. U.C. Berkeley, AEC find new atomic particle called negative proton (→ 3/15/56).

19. Egypt, Syria, Jordan decide to unify military commands (→ 12/11).

23. Saar, by 66% vote, rejects plan for "European" rule.

24. France recognizes Diem govt. in S. Vietnam (→ 1/1/56).

27. Geneva: Big Four conference opens (→ 1/25/56).

DEATH

18. Jose Ortega y Gasset, Spanish essayist and philosopher (*5/9/1883).

South Africa walks out of U.N. debate

Oct 24. Upset over a debate focusing on "the racial conflict in South Africa resulting from the policies of apartheid," W.C. du Plessis, the South African United Nations representative walked out of a General Assembly committee meeting. Du Plessis cited a section in the U.N. Charter which forbids interference in domestic affairs of another nation as justification for his protest. He said that considering the assembly's "flagrant intervention" in South African affairs and its "repeated infringement" of charter resolutions, he was instructed to leave the discussion. Yet, before his dramatic exit, du Plessis told his colleagues South Africa would reserve the right to return if a vote is called on any measure concerning South Africa and its policies.

A U.N. committee on human rights was set up in 1952; its current report denounces apartheid, declaring it "continues to constitute a serious threat to national life within the Union and to be a seriously disturbing factor in international relations." South Africa has refused to cooperate with the panel, which has asked to get a closer look at apartheid's implementation.

The South African walkout occurred on United Nations Day, supposedly a "happy occasion" in which nations are to focus their efforts to cooperate (→ 2/1/56).

Jubilant in a moment of freedom, S. African Negroes occupy a segregated train.

Brooklyn Dodgers win first Series

Oct 4. The Bums have beaten the Bombers to win their first World Series ever. The Brooklyn Dodgers won 4 games to 3 on a final shutout pitched by southpaw Johnny Podres. Podres' comment after the final 2-0 score? "Wow, wow, wow!"

The Dodgers have lost the series eight times—the last five times against the Yanks. This year, they lost the first two games but went on to win the big four. No team ever did that before. In the 4th inning today, Roy Campanella went home on a single by Gil Hodges, who also sent shortstop Pee Wee Reese home in the 6th. Brooklyn is delirious.

Wife kills racing notable Woodward

Oct 30. The wife of horsebreeder William Woodward Jr. shot her husband this morning, mistaking him for a prowler. He received one bullet to the temple. An autopsy is scheduled for tomorrow.

Woodward, 35, was a banker and owner of the racehorse Nashua. He and his wife, Ann Eden Crowell Woodward, 33, lived in Oyster Bay, Long Island. At a party last night (given in honor of the Duchess of Windsor), Woodward expressed to partygoers his concern over some recent tampering with door locks.

The Woodwards returned from the party at 1 a.m. and promptly slept. Mrs. Woodward woke at 2 a.m. by a sound downstairs. She grabbed a rifle and aimed at a shape she said she "failed to recognize." Police found her bent over the naked lifeless form of her husband.

Children are all ears for Mouseketeers

A late afternoon television show that premiered last month has children donning mouse ears and chanting M-I-C-K-E-Y. Walt Disney's new program "The Mickey Mouse Club" is a an hour of entertainment and education. The Mouseketeers, its troupe of dancing and singing children, are already receiving fan mail—and love letters.

In between Pluto cartoons and documentaries on Eskimos, the Mouseketeers romp in T-shirts emblazoned with their first names. Female fans often have a crush on sincere, friendly Mouseketeer Bobby; male fans suffer intensely at the sight of dark-eyed Annette.

Triumphal return of Moroccan Sultan

Oct 31. "With guns and bombs we have regained our King." So went the thankful prayers of Moroccans today, greeting the return of their Sultan after a two-year absence. The French government had deposed and exiled Sidi Mohammad Ben Youssef in August 1953, following nationalist unrest.

If France had trouble policing its protectorate before the sultan's exile, it had a worse time afterward. Moroccans burned down foreign-owned stores and stoned Europeans in the streets. France hopes the restoration of the sultan will be viewed as a form of rapprochement rather than appeasement (→ 11/21).

The late James Dean and Natalie Wood speak for the younger generation's growing alienation in "Rebel Without a Cause."

1955

NOVEMBER

Su	Mo	Tu	We	Th	Fr	Sa
		1	2	3	4	5
6	7	8	9	10	11	12
13	14	15	16	17	18	19
20	21	22	23	24	25	26
27	28	29	30			

1. Arizona: Parley on solar power opens in Tuscon (→ 9/30/58).

1. Madrid: Franco and U.S. Sec. of State Dulles affirm close ties.

2. N.Y.: Liberace appears in first film, "Sincerely Yours."

2. Israel: David Ben Gurion returns as premier (→ 6/17/56).

2. Geneva: Soviet Molotov insists Bonn and Berlin join talks on German reunification (→ 16).

2. Juan Peron ends Paraguayan exile, enters Nicaragua (→ 13).

11. Ike arrives back in Capital after heart attack (→ 6/9/56).

11. Brazil: Army seizes power in quick, bloodless coup.

13. Buenos Aires: Provisional Pres. Lonardi overthrown by Gen. Pedro Aramburu (→ 16).

16. Boulder City, Nevada: Donald Campbell drives Bluebird to water speed record of 216 mph.

16. Geneva: Big Four talks on German reunification end in failure (→ 5/1/56).

16. Buenos Aires: Tank-supported Marines seize Argentine labor headquarters (→ 26).

20. Maryland National Guard ordered desegregated (→ 25).

20. Washington: Talks open on financing of Aswan Dam across Nile (→ 7/19/56).

21. Morocco: French authorities get orders to suppress all outbreaks of violence (→ 4/4/56).

21. Baghdad: U.K., Iraq, Iran, Pakistan, Turkey to set up common defense on Soviet border (→ 6/3/57).

25. ICC orders end to segregation on trains and buses crossing state lines by Jan. 10 (→ 12/1).

26. Buenos Aires: Anti-Peron groups cover statues of ex-leader and wife in burlap (→ 6/10/56).

26. Philadelphia: Army takes Navy 14-6 in football.

DEATHS

4. Cy Young, baseball pitcher, record 511 wins (*3/29/1867).

5. Maurice Utrillo, French painter (*12/26/1883).

27. Arthur Honegger, Swiss composer (*3/10/1892).

How-to pioneer Dale Carnegie dies

Pop psychologist Dale Carnegie.

Nov 1. Author of "How to Win Friends and Influence People," Dale Carnegie has died after a long illness. He was 64. Missouri-born Carnegie was poor most of his life, and he failed at most jobs, including a brief acting stint. In his mid 20's, he found his forte, teaching public speaking at YMCA's nationwide.

Carnegie's book came out in 1936. In the depths of the Depression, people hungry for work were anxious to seem better than other prospective employees; they bought millions of copies. To date, 4.9 million copies have been sold. Critics fault the book's equation for success, which adds up to nothing much more than: smile a lot and don't argue.

New German army starts in a garage

Nov 12. The new West German army was created today as 101 men received their certificates in a casual ceremony inside a Bonn garage. Defense Minister Theodor Blank presided as the assemblage of army, navy and air force inductees ended more than ten years of German de-militarization. The formation of the army sparked little interest; newspapers even downplayed the event, probably because of the memory of over 4.5 million German servicemen who perished in World War II. Tomorrow, citizens will acknowledge those losses when they observe Volkstrauertag, West Germany's Memorial Day (→ 5/15/56).

U.S.S.R. explodes powerful H-bomb

Nov 26. The Soviet Union has confirmed reports that it recently exploded its "most powerful" hydrogen bomb. Although the power of the weapon was not officially disclosed, Nikita Khrushchev said it was equal to one million tons of TNT—a megaton. The Soviet statement hinted at development of even more destructive weapons by saying its scientists were continuing to test "new types of atomic and thermonuclear weapons." The statement said the Soviet Union was carrying out the tests "in the interest of guaranteeing her security" and reiterated Soviet proposals for the prohibition of nuclear weapons "with establishment of effective international control" (→ 1/5/56).

Robert Sherwood, playwright, is dead

Nov 14. Four-time Pulitzer winner Robert E. Sherwood died of a heart attack this morning. He was 59. Sherwood was born into a humorous family—his father founded the Harvard Lampoon—but he excelled at both comedy and drama.

Rejected for infantry during the war (too tall at 6'7"), Sherwood worked at the Office of War Information. He met Roosevelt, wrote some of his speeches and got the Pulitzer for his book "Roosevelt and Hopkins" (1949). Three plays produced in succession, "Idiot's Delight," "Abe Lincoln in Illinois" and "There Shall Be No Night" all won Pulitzers, yet possibly his greatest work, "The Petrified Forest" (1935) did not. That play exposed false hopes of the Depression.

Brando is cool but seems out of his element in the lavish new musical comedy "Guys and Dolls."

1955

DECEMBER

Su	Mo	Tu	We	Th	Fr	Sa
				1	2	3
4	5	6	7	8	9	10
11	12	13	14	15	16	17
18	19	20	21	22	23	24
25	26	27	28	29	30	31

1. Montgomery, Alabama: Rosa Parks defies state law, refusing to give up seat on front of bus to white person (→ 5).

1. India: Khrushchev delivers speech condemning British colonialism (→ 1/11/56).

5. Montgomery: Bus boycott begins under leadership of Rev. Martin Luther King Jr. (→ 1/9/56).

5. Washington: Ike, at official merger, bids AFL-CIO heed minority political rights (→ 6/4/56).

8. New York: "Kismet" opens at Radio City Music Hall.

8. Roy Campanella of Dodgers named National League MVP.

9. U.S.: Sugar Ray Robinson KOs Carl Olson to regain world middleweight title (→ 5/2/57).

11. Israel raids Syrian positions on Sea of Galilee (→ 1/13/55).

14. U.N. admits 15 nations, excluding Mongolia and Japan.

14. London: Hugh Gaitskell succeeds Attlee as Labor chief.

15. N.Y. Thruway completed as Tappan Zee Bridge opens.

19. Jordan: Pro-West Premier Mahali quits in dispute over joining Baghdad Pact (→ 1/7/56).

26. U.S.: RKO sells film library for TV distribution (→ 2/25/56).

26. L.A.: Rams trounce Browns 38-14 for pro football title.

CULTURAL EVENTS, 1955

Literature: Kafka's "The Trial"; Graham Greene's "The Quiet American"; Dylan Thomas' "Quite Early One Morning."

Academia: Walter Lippmann's "The Public Philosophy"; James Baldwin's "Notes of a Native Son"; Dorothy Hodgkin finds composition of Vitamin B-12.

Music: Adler and Ross' musical "Damn Yankees"; Cole Porter's "Silk Stockings"; "The Yellow Rose of Texas"; "Davy Crockett"; "Tutti-Frutti."

The Arts: Dali's "The Lord's Supper"; "The New Decade" Modern Art exhibit, New York.

Film: Bergman's "Smiles of a Summer Night"; "Marty," Ernest Borgnine, Academy Award; Olivier's "Richard III."

Attlee quits as Labor chief, becomes Earl

Attlee, welfare statesman.

Dec 7. Clement Attlee, who as Prime Minister from 1945 to 1951 presided over the establishment of the welfare state in Britain, resigned today as leader of the Labor Party. Attlee, 72, said he was retiring to help resolve uncertainty over the future leadership of the ideologically divided Labor Party, which he has headed for 20 years. There are three principal candidates vying for leadership of the party: Hugh Gaitskell, Herbert Morrison and Aneurin Bevan, with Gaitskell the apparent favorite. Queen Elizabeth II conferred an Earldom on Attlee, entitling him to sit in the House of Lords.

Two baseball greats die: Young, Wagner

Dec 6. Baseball has lost two of its earliest stars. Cy Young, the legendary pitcher, and Honus Wagner, possibly the greatest shortstop the game has known, have died. The right-handed pitcher, whose name was Denton True Young, compiled a record of 511 victories, including three no-hitters. He was elected to the Hall of Fame in 1937. The heavy-set Flying Dutchman, who was born John Peter Wagner, was deceptively fast and won eight National League batting championships. He was elected to the Hall of Fame in 1936.

Pop artist Jasper Johns takes aim

"Target with Four Faces" (1955).

A 25-year-old artist from Augusta, Ga., is driving Abstract Expressionists to distraction. Like his hero Marcel Duchamp, Jasper Johns "finds" objects and puts them together for startling statements. His "Target with Four Faces," finished this year, is newspaper on canvas with blue and yellow concentric circles. Atop the target are four eyeless faces. Is it painting? Is it sculpture? And what is Johns aiming at?

Johns, Robert Rauschenberg and a handful of other artists settled in New York are popularizing Pop Art. Using the weapons of graffiti artists —spray guns and acrylic paint— they alternately lampoon and enshrine what is quick and callous in modern society. Or at least they give it their best shot.

Girls, girls, girls: Eloise, Lolita, Marjorie

Females are featured in three best-sellers this year, but the characters have no more in common than their gender. "Eloise," "Lolita" and "Marjorie Morningstar" are the books. Eloise is rambunctious, Lolita randy and Marjorie rebellious.

Kay Thompson's Eloise is a little girl who lives in the Plaza Hotel. Her adventures, told in comic-book style, include manipulating the hotel elevator, releasing a mouse in the dining room and decorating the halls with a crayon. She makes a glorious nuisance of herself.

Vladimir Nabokov's Lolita is a sexually precocious youngster who seduces a stodgy university professor. Nabokov is himself a teacher (at Cornell University) but far from staid. His novel is daring and funny, bereft of moralizing lectures.

Herman Wouk's book "Marjorie Morningstar," on the other hand, does have ethical underpinnings. Miss Morningstar is a young Jewish woman who tries to deny her heritage and fails. Wouk apparently feels reaction against traditional limits is warranted but doomed.

Among other best-sellers, Mackinlay Kantor's "Andersonville" is Pulitzer Prize material. It recounts a shocking Civil War trial. Sloan Wilson's "The Man in the Gray Flannel Suit" jabs the suburban commuter set. And satirist Evelyn Waugh's "Officers and Gentlemen" suggests one cannot properly be both at the same time.

R.K.O. films sold for television viewing

Dec 26. The entire film output of R.K.O. has been sold for $15 million. The buyer is C & C Super Corporation, a New York-based firm intending to sell the motion pictures to television. An executive said returns of $43 million were expected within five years.

Among the 740 features are "Citizen Kane," "Gungha Din," "The Hunchback of Notre Dame" and eight musicals starring Ginger Rogers and Fred Astaire. R.K.O. no longer produces film, expanding into other media. However, this sale raises the possibility of film companies competing against their own previously released material.

The new Mercedes Benz six-cylinder, seven-litre "Gullwing."

For the private pilot, Cessna this year unveiled its 172 Skyhawk, a single-engine, light aircraft billed as "the world's most popular airplane."

1956

JANUARY

Su	Mo	Tu	We	Th	Fr	Sa
1	2	3	4	5	6	7
8	9	10	11	12	13	14
15	16	17	18	19	20	21
22	23	24	25	26	27	28
29	30	31				

1. Pasadena: Michigan State over U.C.L.A. 17-14 in Rose Bowl.

1. Khartoum: Sudan proclaimed independent republic.

1. Saigon: Pro-Western Diem regime wins in first National Assembly election (→ 5/11/57).

5. U.S. installs first long-distance Nike missiles in West Germany (→ 4/23).

7. Kenya: It is reported British have killed 10,173 Mau-Mau rebels since Oct. 1952 (→ 27).

7. Jordan: Mobs damage U.S. property, trample flag (→ 3/4).

9. Virginia sanctions state funding of private schools, thus enabling segregation (→ 2/6).

10. U.K. orders 1,600 paratroopers to Cyprus (→ 3/9).

11. U.S. Sec. of State Dulles says East and West "are in a contest in the field of development of underdeveloped countries... Defeat... could be as disastrous as defeat in the arms race" (→ 2/1).

13. Syria and Lebanon sign mutual defense pact against Israel (→ 19).

16. Egyptian govt. makes Islam state religion (→ 6/13).

18. Berlin: Parliament approves creation of East German People's Army (→ 6/21).

19. N.Y.: Security Council condemns Israeli raid on Syrian military posts last month (→ 2/21).

22. L.A.: Two commuter trains derail, killing 30, injuring 140.

25. Moscow: Khrushchev says he believes Ike is sincere in efforts to abolish war (→ 28).

26. Italy: Winter Olympics open in Cortina d'Ampezzo (→ 2/2).

27. Austria celebrates Mozart on bicentennial.

28. Washington: Ike turns down Soviet bid for 20-year friendship pact, citing U.N. ties (→ 4/18).

DEATHS

23. Alexander Korda, Anglo-Hungarian film director (*9/16/1893).

31. A.A. Milne, British author, created "Winnie the Pooh" (*1/18/1882).

Queen visits calm Nigeria as Kenya rebels

Princess Margaret presents flag.

Jan 27. Queen Elizabeth II, her husband the Duke of Edinburgh and Princess Margaret are in Nigeria for a ceremonial tour. The visit may hold political significance as well in light of the recent Soviet denunciations of British colonialism in Africa. The Soviet Union has accosted British rule in an effort to spark anti-colonial revolutions like the one now occurring in Kenya. British troops have killed 10,173 members of the Mau-Mau organization in Kenya since October 1952.

Nigeria is one of the more loyal British colonies, partly because in 1954 Parliament granted it a degree of autonomy. So, the people of Lagos are ready to greet the royal visitors with open arms. The streets are gaily adorned and will be packed with residents hoping to get a peek at the queen, duke and princess as they are escorted through town.

The tide of nationalism has not swept into Nigeria, but some Englishmen are worried that the Moslems in the northern sections may stir revolutionary passions. The queen's visit is expected to solidify loyalty to the British crown.

The great iconoclast, Mencken, is gone

Jan 29. "The great artists of the world are never Puritans, and seldom even ordinarily respectable." Despite those words, Henry Louis Mencken earned a very respectful following as a major editor and author of the 1920's. He died this morning of heart failure. The longtime Baltimore resident was 75.

Mencken criticized the phlegmatic middle-class, what he called the "booboisie," and championed writers who sided with him. While editor of The Smart Set (1914-24) and the Mercury (1924-33), he published Sinclair Lewis, Theodore Dreiser, Edgar Lee Masters and other opponents of complacency. George Jean Nathan helped him write some biting essays.

Mencken's popularity declined in the 30's. He opposed Roosevelt's policy but offered no alternatives. A stroke in 1948 silenced him.

Mencken once wrote, "The plain fact is that I am not a fair man and don't want to hear both sides. On all subjects, from aviation to xylophone playing, I have fixed and invariable ideas."

For years at the Baltimore Sun, Mencken tore at complacency in all forms.

French enchanted by Lionel Hampton

"Hamp" plays the vibes.

Jan 19. Orchestra leader Lionel Hampton performed tonight at the Olympia theater in Paris. He won accolades; jazz is popular in France, and Hampton is one smooth jazzman. A highlight of the evening was his performance on the vibraphone, a kind of xylophone having resonant, motor-driven metal bars. Coolly dressed in a neat suit and tie, he beat out some red-hot notes.

Hampton was born in Louisville, Kentucky, in 1913. His sound, like that of Bix Beiderbecke, Gene Krupa and others, came out of Chicago in the 1920's. He was one of Benny Goodman's quartet in the 1930's, playing two-finger piano and drums in addition to the vibes. He formed his own group in 1940.

Solved at last: The Brink's robbery

Jan 12. The FBI has identified the men behind the $2.7 million holdup on January 17, 1950, in Boston, when seven armed men in Halloween masks walked into the armored car company's headquarters, bound and gagged five employees, emptied the vault and left, all in less than 20 minutes. Today, six men were arrested, two others are in prison on other charges, one is dead and two are at large. Brinks Inc. had put up a $100,000 reward, but FBI agents cannot accept such rewards, and this was their case all the way. To this day, not a penny of the loot has been traced or recovered.

1956

FEBRUARY

Su	Mo	Tu	We	Th	Fr	Sa
			1	2	3	4
5	6	7	8	9	10	11
12	13	14	15	16	17	18
19	20	21	22	23	24	25
26	27	28	29			

1. Washington: Ike and British Premier Eden sign declaration warning Third World against taking aid from U.S.S.R.

1. Algeria: Gen. Catroux replaces Jacques Soustelle as French resident general (→ 6).

1. Paris: Socialist Guy Mollet chosen French premier.

1. South Africa demands Soviets close consulates, charging agitation of minorities (→ 8/25).

2. Italy: Tenley Albright of U.S. takes Olympic gold in women's figure skating.

3. U.S. bans travel to Hungary, calls off proposed talks with Budapest govt. (→ 3/23).

6. Tuscaloosa: Univ. of Alabama suspends its first Negro student for "safety" reasons (→ 21).

8. British set tentative August 1957 date for Malayan independence (→ 8/3/57).

8. U.S. bars launching of weather balloons due to Soviet complaints.

12. A.F.L. film union asks boycott of "Daniel Boone," filmed in Mexico with non-union staff.

14. Moscow: Khrushchev, at opening of XXth Party Congress, states communism can exist without violence (→ 21).

15. Helsinki: Premier Urho Kekkonen elected Finnish pres.

21. Montgomery: Grand jury indicts 115 in Negro bus boycott (→ 24).

21. Tel Aviv: Ben Gurion asks 150,000 volunteers to dig air-raid shelters against Arab attack (→ 3/4).

21. Moscow: Hungarian revolutionary Bela Kun vindicated at party congress (→ 25).

25. N.Y.: Closed-circuit TV for instruction installed in Schenectady public school (→ 4/14).

25. Moscow: Stalin secretly disavowed by Khrushchev at party congress (→ 3/23).

27. Washington: Italian Pres. Gronchi arrives for state visit.

DEATH

8. Connie Mack, grand old man of baseball (*2/22/1862).

Negroes boycott buses

Quietly determined Rosa Parks occupies territory forbidden for decades.

Feb 24. Tension is mounting in Montgomery, Alabama, where the arrests of 115 Negroes on charges of boycotting the city's buses have triggered large, dramatic protests. In fact, religious leaders across the nation have called for a "National Deliverance Day of Prayer" to protest Alabama's mass arrests.

Two months ago, a brave and defiant Montgomery woman, Rosa Parks, refused to move from the front, whites-only section of a city bus to a seat in the rear, protesting bus segregation laws. She was promptly arrested, fined and eventually jailed when she told the presiding judge she would not pay the fine and intended to appeal his decision. Since then, thousands of Negroes have boycotted the bus lines, in violation of an Alabama statute outlawing organized boycotting.

Rev. Ralph Abernathy, one of 20 ministers arrested, has called for a mass pilgrimage through the streets of Montgomery "to pray to Almighty God and get into the hearts of Montgomery's people so that justice may be done."

Ministers in Montgomery have asked the federal government to intervene, urging Washington to "exhaust every effort to give relief to these citizens whose civil rights have been violated." Federal officials have reacted slowly to the South's racial strife (→ 29).

14-year-old wins $100,000 in quiz

Feb 4. By correctly identifying a song hit of the 20's, "Me and My Shadow," and then singing its chorus, George L. Wright 3rd, 14, completed the sixth part of the final question from last week and won $100,000 on the TV quiz show "The Big Surprise." The scholarship student at St. Agnes Roman Catholic High School in Manhattan plans to first of all buy a tipple, a sort of ukulele, with his fortune, which after taxes will amount to between $30,000 and $50,000. His parents will put 75 percent of the sum into a trust for George's education.

University ordered to accept Negro

Feb 29. "That girl sure has guts," remarked NAACP lawyer Thurgood Marshall, referring to Autherine Lucy, the University of Alabama's first Negro. A federal court ruled today that the university must re-admit Miss Lucy. She had been suspended after riots erupted over her initial admittance on campus. The college was accused of succumbing to mob rule when it suspended the co-ed. But officials claim they acted to prevent her from suffering "great bodily harm."

Angry crowds "greeted" Miss Lucy by throwing a barrage of eggs and rocks at her. She barely escaped without serious injury. When she returns, the college must furnish her adequate protection (→ 3/1).

Miss Lucy enters a new world.

Mob attacks French Premier in Algiers

Feb 6. Guy Mollet, France's new Premier, was pelted with tomatoes and flower pots by a mob in Algiers today. Heavily armed security police charged the demonstrators, who screamed, "Mollet to the gallows. Algeria is French." The protesters, who were Frenchmen, called "pied noirs," were concerned Mollet would give too much autonomy to Algeria. As soon as word of the attack reached Paris, General Georges Catroux resigned from the Cabinet and quit his new job as Resident Minister for Algeria. Catroux, derided as "the liquidator" by French Algerians, played a role in the French withdrawal from Lebanon and Syria and the return of the deposed Moroccan Sultan (→ 4/11).

1956

MARCH

Su	Mo	Tu	We	Th	Fr	Sa
				1	2	3
4	5	6	7	8	9	10
11	12	13	14	15	16	17
18	19	20	21	22	23	24
25	26	27	28	29	30	31

1. Univ. of Alabama ousts Negro Autherine Lucy, saying she made libelous accusations (→ 5).

2. France grants independence to Morocco (→ 4/4).

5. U.S. Supreme Court affirms ban on segregation in public schools (→ 21).

5. Syrian gunners down Israeli plane on northeast front (→ 7).

7. Ike rejects Israeli arms request (→ 4/4).

8. New York: Met displays Steuben glass etchings of Japan's Suekichi Akaba.

10. Exile of Archbishop Makarios sparks general strike in Cyprus, riot in Athens (→ 14).

11. "Richard III," with Olivier, has U.S. premiere on TV and at New York's Bijou.

14. Nicosia: British police sergeant killed by Greek Cypriots (→ 6/16).

15. London: Soviet ex-Premier Malenkov arrives for tour of British power plants (→ 5/4).

20. Westinghouse Electric workers end 156-day strike.

21. Ike states, "It is incumbent on all the South to show some progress" toward integration (→ 22).

23. Pakistan becomes first Islamic republic, though still within British Commonwealth (→ 10/27/58).

23. Soviet students strike at Tiflis Univ. in protest over campaign to desanctify Stalin (→ 5/4).

23. Hungary vindicates Lazlo Rajk, executed in 1949 (→ 10/23).

24. Tunisia: Bourguiba back in Monastir to seek votes (→ 4/9).

26. W.Va.: Canadian, Mexican heads of state meet for first time.

27. IRS closes leftist journal Daily Worker for tax evasion.

28. Reykjavik: Parliament calls for withdrawal of U.S. troops from Iceland.

28. U.S. Post Office installs electric stamp sellers.

DEATH

17. Irene Joliot-Curie, French chemist, from radiation-induced leukemia.

King guilty in boycott

March 22. Rev. Dr. Martin Luther King Jr. has been found guilty of orchestrating the Montgomery, Alabama, bus boycotts, but he vows to continue the protest by using "passive resistance and the weapon of love." King's conviction follows a hectic month of developments in race relations in the South.

On March 1, the board of trustees at the University of Alabama "permanently expelled" Autherine Lucy, the Negro co-ed who by federal court order was granted admission to the school. The trustees, in defiance of the court, ousted Miss Lucy on the grounds that she made "outrageous, false and baseless accusations" against college officials. The trustees charged educational discipline would be jeopardized if Miss Lucy was allowed to accost them verbally with impunity.

On March 5, the Supreme Court ruled that its 1954 Brown v. Board of Education decision, which outlawed segregation in public schools, extends to tax-supported colleges. The civil rights decision came after the University of North Carolina refused to admit three Negroes on the basis of their race.

Rev. King, raising Negro awareness.

And after criticism from minority leaders that he has failed to act on civil rights, President Eisenhower, in yesterday's news conference, said, "It is incumbent on all the South to show some progress toward racial integration" (→ 4/10).

Morocco, Tunisia gain independence

March 20. In just three weeks, France has lost both of its protectorates in North Africa. An agreement was signed in the Foreign Ministry in Paris today that virtually gives Tunisia its independence. On the 2nd, France recognized the independence of Morocco. The fate of Algeria, lodged between Tunisia and Morocco and seething with violent, nationalist sentiment, remains to be decided.

The agreement with Tunisia nullifies a 75-year-old treaty that established the protectorate. The negotiations were difficult and punctuated by terrorist attacks. At one point, French and Tunisian troops had to join forces to repel invaders from Libya. Elections for the new constituent assembly are scheduled for next week, and the French are concerned extremists will gain the upper hand over moderates. The agreement with Morocco solidified the position of Mohammed V, the Sultan France once removed from the throne (→ 24).

"My Fair Lady" is ecstatically received

March 15. "I've grown accustomed to her face!" groans confirmed bachelor Henry Higgins. He realizes he's in love; but who would not fall for "My Fair Lady"? The Lerner and Loewe musical opened this evening on Broadway.

Alan Jay Lerner has adapted George Bernard Shaw's "Pygmalion," the tale of Professor Higgins (Rex Harrison) making a lady out of a Cockney flower seller (Julie Andrews). Effervescent tunes by Frederick Loewe include "Loverly" and "I Could Have Danced All Night." Moss Hart directed.

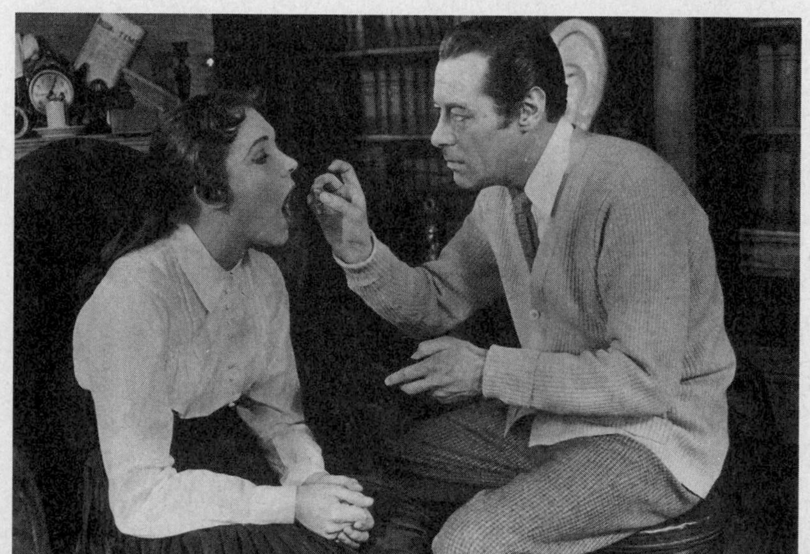

Professor Higgins teaches Eliza to speak like a proper British lady.

No more laughter

March 17. Former radio great Fred Allen died of a heart attack tonight while on a stroll near his New York apartment. The comedian was 61. He leaves his wife and broadcast partner, Portland Hoffa.

"Town Hall Tonight" was a popular program in the 1930's. One out of every three homes tuned in. Allen made zingy one-liners and zany characters with names like Senator Claghorn and Titus Moody. Since 1955, he was a regular on the TV show "What's My Line?"

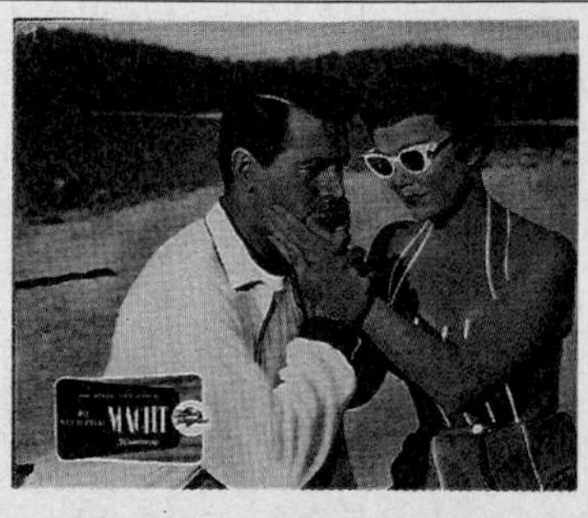

Young Rock Hudson and Jane Wyman are scandalous lovers in "All That Heaven Allows."

Greek Archbishop driven from Cyprus

Rebellious Archbishop Makarios.

March 9. British authorities on Cyprus, acting with stunning speed, have arrested and deported Archbishop Makarios. He was charged with supporting terrorists in the Cypriot separatist movement. Several other Greek church officials were also seized. As soon as word spread of the deportations, bombings shook Cyprus and British patrols were attacked. Britain has 50,000 soldiers and policemen on the island. In Athens, crowds rioted in opposition to the British action, and Greece recalled its Ambassador to Britain. In London, the opposition Labor Party criticized the government for arresting Makarios when he was trying to board a plane for Athens. The party warned the move would harm relations with Greece (→ 10).

Hussein dismisses Arab Legion chief

March 4. In a startling move, Jordan's 20-year-old King Hussein has dismissed Lieutenant General John Bagot Glubb, the veteran British commander of the Arab Legion, or Jordanian army.

The ouster follows an anti-Western campaign among Arab nationalists to remove British elements from the Legion, partially financed by Britain. The campaign gained momentum several weeks ago when the Legion helped put down Arab riots against the Western-sponsored Baghdad Pact of Britain, Iraq, Iran, Turkey and Pakistan that Jordan has been asked to join. In turn, the new Arab alliance of Saudi Arabia, Egypt and Syria is bitterly opposed to the Baghdad Pact, and Hussein's precipitate act is seen as an attempt to ease the pressure being brought to bear by these various extremists.

British officials fear the Mideast may move closer to war without the restraining influence of Glubb, who repeatedly warned Jordan, and indirectly the other Arab nations, that they stood no chance of defeating the Israeli army.

Glubb, better known to his Arab soldiers as Glubb Pasha, had commanded the Legion since 1939 and turned it into the Arab world's most efficient fighting force. Since WWII, it has changed its Arab chargers for tanks, and now comprises 35,000 bedouin soldiers led by 450 British and Arab officers (→ 5).

"The Kitchen of Tomorrow," as envisioned by Frigidaire.

1956

APRIL

Su	Mo	Tu	We	Th	Fr	Sa
1	2	3	4	5	6	7
8	9	10	11	12	13	14
15	16	17	18	19	20	21
22	23	24	25	26	27	28
29	30					

4. N.Y.: U.N. Sec. Gen. Dag Hammarskjold to go to Mideast to seek end to hostilities (→ 11).

4. Spain: Moroccan sultan arrives to seek end to Spanish rule in northern Morroco (→ 7).

7. Franco signs Moroccan accord, giving up control of Rif area (→ 10/7).

9. Tunisia: Voters elect Habib Bourguiba first premier of independent nation (→ 6/15).

10. Birmingham: Whites attack Nat King Cole as he sings to white audience (→ 23).

11. Ike signs Colorado River Bill alloting $760 mil. for power and irrigation.

11. French dissolve Algerian Assembly (→ 5/18).

11. Tel Aviv: Arab guerrilla raid kills four, wounds 16 (→ 19).

14. Chicago: AMPEX displays device to record TV shows on magnetic tape (→ 6/10).

16. U.S. exhibits Lockheed Starfighter, 1,500-mph jet built to carry nuclear bombs.

16. Bulgaria: Premier Chervenkov ousted in anti-Stalin drive.

17. Cominform, intl. coalition of Communist parties, is dissolved.

18. London: Khrushchev and Bulganin arrive for talks on international issues (→ 6/7).

19. Jerusalem: Hammarskjold reports Israeli-Egyptian agreement on cease-fire (→ 21).

21. Egypt signs military pact with Saudi Arabia and Yemen (→ 5/10).

23. U.S. Supreme Court upholds lower court ban on intrastate bus segregation (→ 24).

23. London: Khrushchev says Soviets can make intercontinental missile with H-bomb warhead (→ 5/1).

25. Elvis Presley has #1 hit with "Heartbreak Hotel."

28. New York: The Coliseum at Columbus Circle opens.

28. Mass.: 8,000-lb. telescope, largest in U.S., dedicated at Harvard.

29. Havana: Ex-Pres. Carlos Pri Socarras arrested, charged with starting armed revolt (→ 11/30).

Rocky Marciano retires undefeated

Marciano: 43 KOs in 49 fights.

April 25. Rocky Marciano, the son of a New England shoemaker who earned a fortune with his fists, has retired as the undefeated heavyweight champion of the world.

Marciano said his decision was final, despite the prevalence of "comebacks" by champions. "I thought it was a mistake when Joe Louis tried a comeback, "said Marciano. "Barring poverty, the ring has seen the last of me." The so-called Brockton Blockbuster said he wanted to devote more time to his family.

Speculation has Archie Moore as the likely heir to the throne, but Moore doubts that Marciano is serious about retirement. "Rocky loves the jingle of the American dollar too much," said Moore. Marciano has 43 knockouts and three decisions to his credit. He defeated Jersey Joe Walcott for the title in 1952.

Bus lines are integrated

Backed by the Supreme Court, Negroes in Virginia ride with equal rights.

April 24. Bus companies in the South can no longer force Negroes to sit at the back of the bus, as the Supreme Court ruled yesterday that segregation in public transportation is unconstitutional. The court upheld a lower court's decision that a South Carolina bus segregation law was in violation of the First Amendment. By refusing to review an appeal of the ruling, because it would "needlessly consume our time," the court will require South Carolina and 12 other states with similar laws to remove the whites-only signs from the fronts of buses.

While minority leaders hailed the court's decision, they also hope for strict and consistent enforcement of the ruling. In the South however, opponents of integration called in an infringement of states' rights. Governor Marvin Griffin of Georgia called the decision "another example of an overt usurpation of the liberties of the people."

In Montgomery, Alabama, the site of months of bus boycotting by Negro residents, the decision took on special significance. Yet the boycott will continue, according to Dr. Martin Luther King Jr., organizer of the protests. He told reporters, "Two of our original proposals have been met, but we are awaiting word on the third—employment of Negro bus drivers for predominantly Negro routes" (→ 5/2).

Gomulka is freed by Polish regime

April 10. Soviet leaders gave new evidence today that the worst horrors of the Stalinist era are over. De-Stalinization spread to Poland. Wladyslaw Gomulka, the Polish political leader who was arrested in 1951 for deviations from the party line and pro-nationalism, was released and rehabilitated. The Communist Party said that Gomulka had made mistakes, but his arrest and incarceration were not justified. The party also rehabilitated the "patriotic Polish army," which helped defeat Hitler's forces in 1944. Stalin believed that elements of the army were aligned with the Polish government-in-exile and therefore reactionary. The release of more political prisoners is expected (→ 6/29).

Saratoga in service; biggest of warships

April 14. The nuclear-powered aircraft carrier Saratoga, largest and most powerful warship in the world, was commissioned at the Brooklyn Navy Yard. Built at a cost of $207 million, the Saratoga is more than 1,000 feet long and will carry a force of 100 jet aircraft. It is slightly larger than the Navy's first nuclear carrier, the Forrestal, commissioned last year. Five other nuclear carriers are under construction, and the Navy has asked for seven more. The Saratoga is scheduled to begin sea trials next month.

Prince of Monaco marries Grace Kelly

The royal couple kneels in reverence.

April 19. Monaco, the miniature monarchy, was the scene of a royal wedding today. Prince Rainier II wed actress Grace Kelly in a Roman Catholic ceremony. Over 1200 guests attended, including dignitaries from 25 nations. The groom wore a uniform of his own design, a black suit with gold cuffs. The bride wore ivory taffeta and a 125-year-old lace veil. The gown will be sent to the Museum of Art in Philadelphia, the bride's hometown. The Princess starred in a few Hitchcock films. One was "To Catch a Thief," made in Monaco last year. There she met the prince, somehow overlooking Cary Grant.

1956

MAY

Su	Mo	Tu	We	Th	Fr	Sa
		1	2	3	4	5
6	7	8	9	10	11	12
13	14	15	16	17	18	19
20	21	22	23	24	25	26
27	28	29	30	31		

1. Washington: Sec. of Defense Charles Wilson concedes Soviets lead in H-bomb planes (→ 21).

1. Berlin: 100,000 march for German reunification (→ 11/27/58).

2. Minneapolis: Annual conference of Methodist Church bars racial segregation (→ 6/1).

4. Moscow: Supreme Soviet curtails powers of internal security organs (→ 29).

4. AEC approves private nuclear reactor at Indian Point, N.Y. (→ 10/17).

5. Kentucky Derby won by Needles, with jockey D. Erb.

8. N.Y.: Eugene O'Neill's "The Iceman Cometh" opens at Circle in the Square.

9. British Togoland votes annexation to Ghana.

10. N.Y.: Hammarskjold reports acceptance of unconditional cease-fires by Israel, Egypt, Jordan, Syria, Lebanon (→ 24).

15. West Germany receives first large-scale shipment of heavy arms from U.S. (→ 7/9).

15. Seoul: Syngman Rhee elected to third term as president.

21. Bikini Atoll: U.S. tests powerful A-bomb from plane over island of Namu (→ 6/12).

23. Paris: Mendes France resigns from Cabinet, opposing govt. crackdown in Algeria (→ 27).

24. Egypt, Israel agree to allow U.N. observation post along Gaza Strip (→ 9/25).

25. Peking: Propaganda chief Lu Ting-Yi promises liberalization of intellectual life in "Speech of the 100 Flowers" (→ 4/27/57).

27. Algiers: Casbah sealed off as 5,000 French troops search for hidden weapons (→ 6/22).

28. Ike signs farm bill allowing govt. to store agricultural surpluses.

28. Swiss team scales Everest, and, 1st time, twin peak Lhotse.

29. Moscow: Soviets execute four aides of late Lavrenti Beria for treason (→ 6/1).

30. Pat Flaherty wins Indy 500, averaging 128.5 mph in John Zink Special.

Nineteen French soldiers killed in Algeria

May 18. The French government has recoiled in horror at the latest atrocity in Algeria. An entire army unit was wiped out, massacred by rebels. No one survived to describe what happened. And there are no bodies to bury.

The unit of 19 soldiers was based in the mountain village of Beni Amrane. Most of them were green, having arrived just last week from a barracks outside of Paris. Charged with watching the road between Algiers and Constantine, they set out on patrol at 6:25 this morning. By the middle of the day, when nothing was heard from the unit, French authorities became nervous and sent a company out to look for the missing soldiers. The search party, walking with guns pointed straight ahead, had no luck at first, checking every bush and wall in an isolated area of the Ahmed Mountains. Near the entrance to a Moslem tent community, the searchers found a pool of blood near a silo. Inside were the bodies, decapitated and hacked into unrecognizable pieces. In remote Algeria, there are no limits to cruelty (→ 23).

French soldiers in Algeria.

Suburban housing boom underway in U.S.

People, plug your ears. First came the Baby Boom. Now comes the Housing Boom. Married couples are thundering into suburbia.

When war veterans came home to America, they sought security. They met nice women and went "steady." When that failed to prove steady enough, they married. In a couple of years, the couples had a couple of kids. The former G.I.'s wanted to give their children plenty of fresh air and sunshine. On to the commuter paradise, the suburbs.

Only a few years old, the suburban world has already established a peaceful if banal image for itself. It is a land of swing sets, garden hoses and charcoal briquets. Mothers get behind the steering wheels of wood-paneled station wagons to drive their kids from ballet classes to Scout meetings to piano lessons. Everybody seeds, weeds, mows and waters ungrateful lawns. Apparently even paradise requires upkeep.

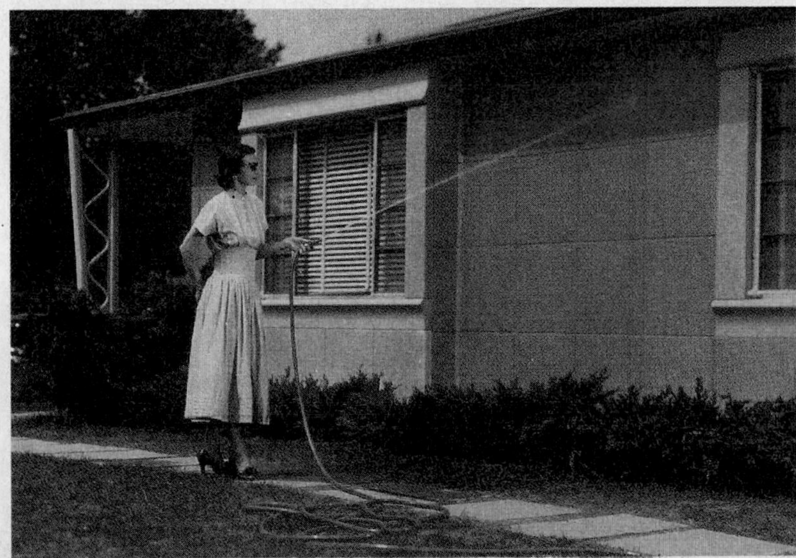

The garden hose also keeps your house cleaner than the one next door.

1956

JUNE

Su	Mo	Tu	We	Th	Fr	Sa
					1	2
3	4	5	6	7	8	9
10	11	12	13	14	15	16
17	18	19	20	21	22	23
24	25	26	27	28	29	30

1. State court orders NAACP to stop operating in Alabama (→ 8/31).

1. Moscow: Molotov resigns as foreign minister (→ 5).

2. Moscow: Tito arrives for state visit (→ 20).

4. Washington: Ike speaks at opening of new AFL-CIO headquarters.

7. Soviet Premier Bulganin asks U.S. to match Soviet military cut of 1.2 million troops (→ 7/12).

10. Buenos Aires: 40 Peronist counterrevolutionaries put to death for attempted revolt (→ 2/24/58).

11. Chicago: At AMA meeting, Jonas Salk predicts polio will be eliminated in three years.

12. Washington: Scientists report radiation harms descendants of those exposed (→ 8/21).

13. U.S. Army gets its first official flag.

15. Paris and Tunis sign accord confirming Tunisia's autonomy in foreign affairs (→ 2/18/57).

16. Nicosia: U.S. vice consul killed by Cypriot rebel bomb in restaurant (→ 3/28/57).

17. Tel Aviv: Golda Meir replaces Moshe Sharett as foreign minister (→ 12/30/57).

18. Windsor: Anthony Eden and Clement Attlee made knights of the Order of the Garter.

20. Moscow: Soviet-Yugoslav paper issued, recognizing many routes to socialism (→ 11/15).

21. East Germany reports release of 19,000 political prisoners in past week.

23. Cairo: Nasser elected Egyptian president (→ 7/26).

26. Guatemala imposes state of siege due to alleged Communist plot.

30. U.S.: 650,000 steel workers go out on strike.

BIRTH

6. Bjorn Borg, Swedish tennis star, Wimbledon champ '76-'80.

DEATH

27. Clifford Brown, American jazz musician (*10/30/1930).

Developer of IBM, Watson, is deceased

IBM mastermind Watson.

June 19. Thomas J. Watson Sr., who built the International Business Machines Corporation into the world's dominant computer company, died of a heart attack today in New York at the age of 82. Watson became President of what was then the Computing-Tabulating-Recording Company, which had 400 employees, in 1914. He oversaw its expansion for nearly 40 years, setting up corporate laboratories to develop new technologies. Although IBM was not the first company to move into computers after World War II, its success in marketing the devices quickly outdistanced all competitors. One of Watson's achievements was to coin the slogan, "Think," found in all IBM offices.

June 29. Two artists were wed today in London, for sultry Marilyn Monroe, her third, for playwright Arthur Miller, his second.

Stalin is denounced by Khrushchev

June 5. Joseph Stalin was a brutal, psychologically deranged torturer, who committed atrocious acts of mass murder in creating and sustaining his powerful reign of terror. Westerners have believed this for years. But now, so do high-ranking Soviet officials—men who were previously forced by fear to praise the mad dictator—including Soviet leader Nikita Khrushchev who recently denounced Stalin in a long speech to the Twentieth Congress of the Communist Party.

The United States State Department obtained a copy of Khrushchev's shocking February 24 address to his comrades and has released it for public perusal.

The party Chairman's 50-page speech includes many revelations about the savage despot, including: Stalin's paranoia, which led to the 1937-38 purges of many Soviet officials; Stalin's secret plots to murder critics and even friends; his erroneous military decisions, which cost the lives of thousands; and various examples of Stalin's cowardice and panic during World War II.

Khrushchev also accused Stalin of planning to assassinate Foreign Minister Vyacheslav Molotov and First Deputy Premier Anastas Mikoyan, telling the Twentieth Congress "neither Comrade Mikoyan nor Comrade Molotov would be here today" if Stalin hadn't died on March 5, 1953.

Stalin reportedly slumped into deep psychotic depression when he was finally convinced that Nazi troops had invaded the Soviet Union in 1941; he refused to talk to anyone and gave no orders.

According to Khrushchev, Russia would have been better off if its World War II leader had remained out of strategic decision-making; because of military stupidity, Stalin almost lost the war. The worst blunder occurred in the attempt to encircle Kharkov in 1942-43. Hundreds of thousands of Soviet soldiers died as a result. Stalin visited the battle front only once during the war. That was in a relatively safe zone near Moscow, where Soviet forces had pushed back weakened German troops.

Much of Khrushchev's attack centered on the Stalin-ordered executions of hundreds of Bolsheviks in the late 1930's, when Stalin chose the path of repression and physical annihilation not only against actual enemies, but also against individuals who had not committed any crimes against the Soviet government. "Here we see no wisdom but only a demonstration of the brutal force which had once so alarmed V.I. Lenin," Khrushchev said.

In fact, of the seven Politburo members in 1920, all but Lenin were purged by Stalin, who perpetrated "odious falsifications and criminal violations of revolutionary legality" that enabled him to kill the Bolsheviks. He apparently wanted to replace the old guard with young party leaders who would flood him with flattery. He also twisted law to gain convictions based on confessions he had directed his henchmen to extract forcefully.

Khrushchev confirmed reports of Stalin's personality flaws. Lenin's wife once complained of Stalin's "unusually rude outbursts." As well, the Eastern member of the Big Three was depicted as childish, insecure and unduly suspicious.

Stalin was also charged with jeopardizing relations between China and the U.S.S.R., which could have threatened the solidarity of the Communist bloc. The most famous alienation of a Communist supporter was that of Yugoslav leader Marshal Tito; after friction developed between the two, Stalin proclaimed he would "get rid of Tito with the shake of my little finger." Stalin shook his finger, Khrushchev recounted, but "nothing happened."

The revelations came as a shock to many American observers unaccustomed to such Soviet self-criticism. But members of President Eisenhower's administration consider the address to be propagandistic—to create an illusion of Soviet liberalization. The U.S. claims Khrushchev condemned Stalin's "cult of personality" only because his brutality was directed at party members when it was unnecessary.

The text of the speech released to the American press was first obtained from an unspecified Eastern European nation and is believed to be a "sanitized" version, cleaned up to avoid embarrassing current Soviet leaders and as an information guide for Soviet satellite countries. And State Department officials stressed that state-sponsored murder, mass arrests and physical and mental torture continue to exist in the Soviet Union.

Despite official U.S. downplaying of the speech, it is regarded by some to be a significant step in Soviet self-analysis; never before has the Communist government assailed one of its own popular leaders. It also may signal a truly different path of Soviet governing. One thing is certain. The address substantiates what most knew to be true: Joseph Stalin was a monstrous tyrant.

"Comrades, I wish to disclose a very important secret: Stalin was a pig." The cartoon, from a conservative Italian magazine, is based on George Orwell's "Animal Farm," ruled by pigs, where "all pigs are equal, but some pigs are more equal than other pigs"—a satire on Stalin's U.S.S.R.

In 1950, Stalin was photographed in the ritual of casting his ballot in an election. In the Soviet Union, there is one name for each office, chosen by the Communist Party. The voter cannot substitute another name.

Britain gives up Suez after 72 years

June 13. As the last token force of British officers and men sailed out of Port Said this morning—five days before the June 18 deadline—Britain's 72-year occupation of the Suez Canal Zone came quietly to an end. Egypt now assumes full responsibility for defending the great East-West waterway.

For some time the Egyptians have been preparing for a five-day gala celebration. A week ago, Premier Nasser told them they would awaken on June 19 to "a bright new era" in which Egypt would no longer be under "the domination of the imperialists." The British, sensitive to the melting away of another vital iink in their empire, preferred not to take part. Said one officer, "We decided we did not want to make a song and dance of our final departure."

Britain keeps an active military supply base in the zone and may reactivate it in defense of an attack against Turkey or other Mideast countries (→ 23).

TV networks facing monopoly charges

June 10. A Senate panel is preparing to look into charges of monopoly by the three television networks. CBS, NBC and ABC are accused of hindering development of other VHF (Very High Frequency) channels. Should the panel allow other such channels to be established, it could mean the shouldering out of UHF (Ultra High Frequency).

The President of each network will testify. Each man will justify his company's grip on production, distribution and exhibition of television programs. Just such a grip was broken a few years ago, when the film industry's right to theater ownership was wrenched away by government anti-trust action.

Should the government allow stations to take the remaining ten VHF channels, UHF could very possibly fail. Conceived as a solution to the crowded airwaves, UHF has never been popular; few TV owners bother to buy converters for it. UHF's future may be determined by a fateful spin of the dial (→ 7/24/57).

Poznan's anti-Red riots

A Polish army tank patrols the streets of Poznan to hold rioters in check.

June 29. Tanks were sent into Poznan in an attempt to quell violent demonstrations against Poland's Communist-led government. Poznan, whose population exceeds 300,000, is one of Poland's largest cities. One of the targets of the crowd was the headquarters of the Polish United Workers (Communist) Party.

The demonstrations began yesterday when workers from the Stalin engineering works walked off the job, demanding higher pay. They were soon joined by other workers. The rioters tore down red banners that carried Communist slogans and chanted "We want bread." Poland suffers from many shortages, especially of bread. Several hundred Westerners in Poznan for the annual international trade fair are witnesses to the protests. Recent events in the Soviet Union, including the anti-Stalin campaign, as well as admissions by Polish Communist Party leaders that living standards are lower than they should be, undoubtedly contributed to the demonstrations (→ 9/27).

Battle for Algiers begins

June 22. A violent and deadly explosion wrecked three buildings in the Casbah of Algiers shortly after midnight. Some 70 bodies were found in the rubble. The bombing is the latest in a series of attacks in a city divided by politics, hate and fear. Nearly 50 people were killed in the past three days, apparently in revenge for the execution of two nationalist rebels. Church authorities begged for their pardon, but the French refused. One of the rebels had been convicted of taking part in an ambush on a tourist bus that killed eight people, including a seven-year-old girl. Both rebels were sent to the guillotine. Tensions are high in Algiers. More violence is likely (→ 9/30).

The Casbah in Algiers is being ruined by violence.

Post-Stalin reforms begin in U.S.S.R.

June 2. The Soviet government has announced that it is abolishing the centralized Justice Ministry, transferring judicial functions to the 16 republics. The intention of this is to avoid a repeat of the abuses by the police and judicial authorities under Joseph Stalin. The decentralization, recommended by Soviet leader Nikita Khrushchev, is considered a major liberal reform.

Similar restructuring has occurred in the economic arena. Now, more power will be given to local authorities in light industry, agriculture, highways and retail trade. Soviet spokesmen say the development of technical and managerial staffs within republics made the reforms possible (→ 7/2).

Eisenhower is sent to hospital again

June 9. President Eisenhower successfully underwent surgery to relieve an intestinal obstruction early today, the White House has announced. It was the second medical crisis in less than a year for the president, who suffered a major heart attack last September. The decision to perform the operation was made by surgeons at Walter Reed Army Hospital at 2 a.m. today. The president was brought to the hospital when he complained of persistent stomach discomfort. X-rays were taken, and the surgeons decided that exploratory surgery was necessary. The nature of the president's illness has not been described, but Press Secretary James Hagerty says it is not cancer (→ 7/15).

Over $33 billion voted for highways

June 29. A bill authorizing more than $33.4 billion for a nationwide network of highways linking most major cities in the United States was signed into law today by President Eisenhower. Secretary of Commerce Sinclair Weeks immediately authorized distribution of $1.1 billion for the first year of what he called "the greatest public works program in history." The main feature of the program is a 41,000-mile network of limited access highways between 90 percent of all cities with populations over 50,000. The federal share of the cost will be financed by an increase in highway user taxes. The interstate highway program will create an estimated 150,000 new construction jobs.

Yul Brynner, star in 1,246 Broadway performances of "The King and I," has brought his act to Hollywood. The cryptic actor from Sakhalin Island is brilliant as the stubborn ruler who charms a widowed teacher (Deborah Kerr) into falling in love with him.

1956

JULY

Su	Mo	Tu	We	Th	Fr	Sa
1	2	3	4	5	6	7
8	9	10	11	12	13	14
15	16	17	18	19	20	21
22	23	24	25	26	27	28
29	30	31				

2. Moscow: Soviet chiefs deny fearing Stalin, say he was too popular to oust (→ 2/15/57).

2. U.S.: Steel strike starts affecting nation; rail lines forced to lay off 30,000.

6. Wimbledon: Lew Hoad over Ken Rosewall 6-2, 4-6, 7-5, 6-4; Shirley Fry over Angela Buxton 6-3, 6-1.

7. Taipei: Nixon gives Chiang note from Ike pledging unwavering U.S. support (→ 10/11).

9. West Germany reinstates military service (→ 8/17).

10. London: Lords reject Commons bill to ban death penalty.

12. London: 15 in Supreme Soviet arrive to see British cultural, political institutions (→ 6/2/57).

12. Pakistan asks U.S. to set up permanent food bank to fight famine in Asia.

13. West Germany: Seven Hungarian student defectors land hijacked airliner.

15. Ike returns to White House after operation (→ 11/26/57).

19. U.S. withdraws offer to help Egypt build Aswan Dam, citing Cairo ties to U.S.S.R. (→ 20).

19. Brioni Island: Nasser meets with Nehru and Tito.

20. Britain rescinds offer to help build Aswan Dam (→ 21).

20. U.S.: "Lady Sings the Blues," by Billie Holiday, is published.

20. France: Prehistoric art found in Rouffignac grotto, Dordogne.

21. Moscow claims it will not aid in building Aswan Dam (→ 22).

22. U.S. rebukes Egypt for bluffing Soviet aid to influence Americans (→ 10/23/58).

22. Panama: American states sign five-point anti-Communist declaration outlining philosophy of Western hemisphere.

22. India: Quake shatters town of Anjar; 117 dead, 800 missing.

28. Roger Walkowiak wins Tour de France.

28. London: British freeze Egyptian assets in U.K. (→ 8/1).

31. Burma: Chinese occupy 1,000 square miles after clashes on border.

Nasser takes over Canal

A convoy of merchant ships crosses the waterway now owned by Egypt.

July 26. In a highly emotional speech, President Nasser announced today that his revolutionary regime was nationalizing the Suez Canal Company, and thus seizing full control of the canal itself.

Since the canal was opened 87 years ago, the company has been run by foreign interests, largely British and French. Nasser said a new company will be formed, adding with a shout, "And it will be run by Egyptians!" No sooner was the statement made than the company's Cairo headquarters was taken over by Egyptian company officials and a squad of police.

Proceeds from the waterway will be used to build the High Dam at Aswan, and Nasser's action was his heated and angry answer to the withdrawal by the U.S., Britain and the World Bank of offers to help finance the $1.3 billion project to harness the Nile River. The offers fell through last week when the U.S. announced that recent developments had led it to conclude that Egypt was incapable of carrying out the project. Nasser's move also made it apparent that he has given up any hope of getting a Soviet counter-offer.

Nasser said that Suez Canal Company stockholders would be repaid at the prevailing price on the Cairo stock market. What action the company, or countries involved, might take could not be determined, but a Western official said the case might be laid before an international court (→ 28).

The suburbanite, not self-sufficient or conveniently close to necessities, is foresaking the corner store for the stores which corner the market.

Two liners collide but hundreds saved

July 27. Shortly after 11:00 last night, the Swedish ocean liner Stockholm sliced through the fog off Nantucket and right into the Italian liner Andrea Doria. The collision left the Doria listing badly and she foundered 12 hours later. Several ships responded to her SOS and have rescued most of her passengers and crew. The Stockholm's bow was crumpled, but she is limping into port under Coast Guard surveillance. Both ships were equipped with radar, and authorities are puzzled as to the cause of the accident that left up to 52 people dead or missing.

Wreckage of the Andrea Doria.

Planes crash over canyon, killing 128

July 1. Beth Davis, 24, recently won a college scholarship and had decided to quit being a TWA stewardess. But today, she and 127 other people perished in history's worst civilian air disaster.

A TWA plane and a United Air Lines plane, on parallel flight paths out of Los Angeles, collided over the Grand Canyon and plunged to the floor below. A helicopter that reached the site after an intensive air search reported no survivors.

Minutes before the crash the TWA pilot received permission to fly above the storm, and it is believed that he climbed into the path of the United plane. The last radio transmission was a frantic three-word message from the United plane: "We are going . . ."

The government reports that there are an average of four near-collisions every day in the skies over America.

1956

AUGUST

Su	Mo	Tu	We	Th	Fr	Sa
			1	2	3	4
5	6	7	8	9	10	11
12	13	14	15	16	17	18
19	20	21	22	23	24	25
26	27	28	29	30	31	

1. London: U.K., France, U.S. hold talks on Suez Canal (→ 2).

1. Salk polio vaccine made available to public.

2. Britain mobilizes forces on Suez (→ 5).

3. Damascus: Pres. Shukri el-Kuwatly deposed by Syrian military (→ 8/7/57).

5. Portsmouth: British carrier Theseus leaves for Suez loaded with paratroopers (→ 9).

6. China: Nearly 2,000 reported killed, 1,200 injured by typhoon in Chekiang province.

7. Bridgeport, Conn.: Mechanics and Farmers Savings Bank opens first drive-up window.

8. Japan launches world's largest oil tanker—780 feet long, weighing 84,730 tons.

9. Cairo: Nasser proclaims formation of new national liberation army (→ 12).

12. Egypt rejects West's invitation to London parley on Suez Canal (→ 21).

13. Czechs grant 160,000 ethnic Germans right to emigrate to West Germany (→ 11/19/57).

17. West Germany bans Communist Party (→ 9/15/57).

21. London: Egypt to negotiate on Suez if France and Britain pull out of Mideast (→ 23).

21. Bonn: Adenauer comes out against American nuclear arms buildup (→ 10/9).

23. Moscow says it will send volunteers if West attacks in Egypt (→ 26).

25. Johannesburg: Over 100,000 non-whites ousted from homes under new law (→ 10/27/58).

26. Cairo: Nasser agrees to five-nation mission to discuss Suez (→ 29).

27. Storrs: Univ. of Conn. traces plant life back two bil. years.

29. New Delhi: India gets $360 mil. loan as food aid.

31. Mansfield: Texas Rangers called to quell riots over Negroes enrolling in high school (→ 9/2).

DEATH

25. Alfred Kinsey, American sexologist (*6/23/1894).

Eisenhower and Nixon team renominated

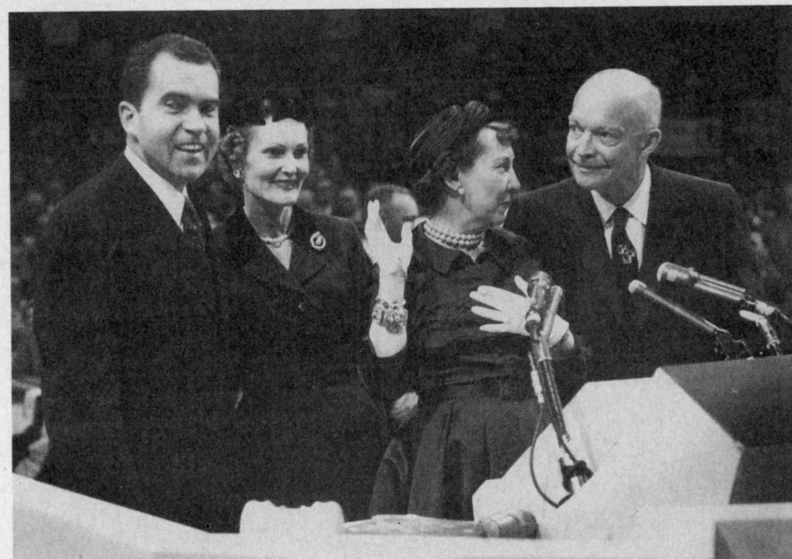

The Nixons and the Eisenhowers on top at the convention in San Francisco.

Aug 22. A "dump Nixon" move collapsed tonight, clearing the way for Republicans to choose unanimously President Eisenhower and Vice President Richard Milhous Nixon as their candidates in the fall election.

It was a moment of both triumph and tragedy for the vice president, who was at the bedside of his critically ill father, Francis A. Nixon, near Los Angeles.

Leading the move to replace the vice president on the ticket by nominating Governor Christian Herter of Massachusetts was Harold E. Stassen of Minnesota. However, the governor declined to run and later nominated Nixon, calling him "a great vice president" who had made his office "more significant, more influential, more useful than ever before in our history."

President Eisenhower, who was nominated without opposition, had declined to say whether he thought Nixon was the strongest candidate the Republicans could select for the second spot on the ticket.

The convention, in San Francisco, was marked by a moment of levity when a Nebraska delegate sought to place in nomination for president the name of "Joe Smith." The Chairman, Rep. Joseph W. Martin Jr., ignored him (→ 11/6).

Stevenson, Kefauver named, not Kennedy

Kefauver and Stevenson.

Aug 17. Democrats closed ranks today after naming Tennessee Senator Estes Kefauver as vice-presidential running mate to Adlai E. Stevenson, the party's candidate for president. Kefauver edged out Senator John F. Kennedy of Massachusetts for the second spot on the ticket.

Stevenson, who lost the presidency four years ago, was given another run at it by defeating Governor Averell Harriman of New York on the first ballot yesterday at the convention in Chicago.

Former President Truman, who had said earlier that Stevenson was "too defeatist to win," appeared on the convention platform tonight with the winning slate and appealed for party unity (→ 22).

Britain, France plan Suez Canal venture

Aug 29. The latest in a series of moves by Britain and France to pressure Egypt's President Nasser to negotiate control of the Suez Canal came today when France received British permission to station her troops on Cyprus.

Earlier this month, Britain announced the call-up of 500,000 reserves. Royal navy and air force units have also been ordered to the Mideast, and part of the French navy has been massed at Toulon, including two aircraft carriers and a battleship.

The word has thus been clearly sent to Nasser that if he refuses to back down from his nationalization program, an invasion is definitely in the wind with the Canal Zone the main target.

A joint statement issued by the Big Three questions Egypt's right to nationalize the canal because of its international use. Nasser has agreed to meet in Cairo next week with a five-nation delegation appointed by the recent Suez Canal Conference, which will present a U.S. proposal to internationalize the canal. Nasser has said he will reject this idea but would consider an Indian proposal setting up an advisory board of "user nations" to supervise Egyptian operations.

The United States has tried to exert a moderating influence in the belief that the threat of force will make it difficult for Nasser to come to terms and also stir up anti-Western feelings in the developing world (→ 9/9).

Marilyn Monroe shocks, teases and titillates and also proves that she can act in "Bus Stop."

Brecht, renowned in theater, is dead

Aug 14. Playwright and Communist theorist Bertolt Brecht has died in Berlin. He was born in Bavaria in 1898. In the mid-20's, he met composer Kurt Weill and they adapted John Gay's "The Beggar's Opera" to make the extremely successful "Three Penny Opera."

When fascism spread, Brecht fled first to Russia then America. The United States failed as a refuge when in 1947 the House Committee on Un-American Activities accused him of communism. Brecht returned to Germany, directing his own Berliner Ensemble.

Aside from "Three Penny," Brecht had little commercial success. It hardly mattered. He left his mark on other writers who study his ideas of encouraging social change.

Expressionist artist killed in car crash

Aug 11. Abstract painter Jackson Pollock was killed today in a car crash on Long Island. He was 44. His large canvases of dripped and swirling paint were a revolt against conventional methods and subject matter. Studies in the 1930's with Thomas Hart Benton flowed into unconscious exercises, as in the dynamic "Full Fathom Five" (1947).

Years ago, Pollock and fellow Action painters such as Willem de Kooning, Mark Rothko and Robert Motherwell met weekly in Greenwich Village. There they shared their ideas. When fame came Pollock's way, he told critics to check out his friends' work. As Willem de Kooning said, "Jackson broke the ice for us."

The U.S. Navy F-84 Crusader.

1956

SEPTEMBER

Su	Mo	Tu	We	Th	Fr	Sa
						1
2	3	4	5	6	7	8
9	10	11	12	13	14	15
16	17	18	19	20	21	22
23	24	25	26	27	28	29
30						

1. Ike salutes U.S. labor force for creating economy so strong it is "the terror of any who would be our enemies."

2. Clinton: Tennessee National Guard halts riots over admission of 12 Negroes to schools (→ 4).

4. Clinton: Nine of 12 Negroes admitted to school (→ 6).

4. Afghanistan confirms it gets Soviet military aid.

6. Sturgis, Ky.: Natl. Guard charges mob with bayonets to open schools to Negroes (→ 8).

9. Cairo: Suez talks fail as Nasser bars intl. control (→ 12).

12. London: Eden says U.S., U.K., France will create authority to operate Suez Canal (→ 14).

14. Watts and Freeman, at George Washington Univ., perform first prefrontal lobotomy.

14. Cairo: Egypt takes over full operation of Suez Canal with all Egyptian personnel (→ 15).

15. Egypt: Soviet ship pilots arrive with promise to help solve dispute on Egypt's terms (→ 19).

22. Managua: Pres. Anastasio Somoza gravely wounded by assassin (→ 23).

23. Managua: 200 in opposition held in Somoza shooting (→ 29).

25. First cross-Atlantic phone cable opens, 2,250 miles, Newfoundland to Scotland.

25. Tel Aviv: Israelis report raiding Jordanian posts, police station, killing 50 (→ 11/10).

27. U.S. Air Force Bell X-2, world's fastest and highest-flying, crashes, killing test pilot.

27. Poznan: Trials begin for June riots; fairness stressed (→ 10/8).

30. First FLN bombs placed in European cafes by Algerian nationalists (→ 10/22).

BIRTH

29. Sebastian Coe, British middle-distance runner.

DEATHS

27. Mildred "Babe" Didrikson Zaharias, star American athlete (*6/26/1914).

28. William Boeing, pioneer in plane technology (*10/1/1881).

Elvis the Pelvis gains record TV audience

Teen idol Elvis Presley.

Sept 9. Elvis Presley gyrated his way into millions of American homes tonight, as his frenetic, hip-shaking performance style captured a record TV audience.

Singing over the hysterical shrieks of a mostly teenaged studio audience on Ed Sullivan's "Toast of the Town" show, the 21-year-old rock-and-roller performed "Hound Dog" and "Love Me Tender," two songs that helped catapult him on his recent meteoric rise to fame. A survey revealed the show was viewed by 82.6 percent of the total television audience, or an estimated 54 million people.

Presley, who just two years ago drove a truck in Tennessee, scored a string of hits this year, including "Heartbreak Hotel," "Blue Suede Shoes" and "Don't Be Cruel." Adult critics have attacked his singing as "hillbilly howling" and called his energetic stage manner "deeply disturbing." But as tonight's triumph attests, Elvis Presley's hold on millions of record-buying teenagers appears very much intact. As one female fan explained: "He's just one big hunk of forbidden fruit."

Egyptians operating Canal; war threatens

Sept 19. The 18-member Suez Canal Conference of user-nations opened today in London marked by a disagreement as to what the group will do and a reluctance by certain nations to join it at all. The group generally aims at keeping pressure on Egypt to negotiate a settlement acceptable to the West by planning its own regulations and routes, using its own pilots and paying tolls to the association rather than the Egyptians. Secretary of State Dulles has also broached the possibility of a shipping boycott.

Eden, seeking intl. control of canal.

Condemning the group, President Nasser called it a "horrible conspiracy" and threatened war to the bitter end if the West tries to force the association on Egypt.

Earlier, the mass resignations of foreign pilots forced Egypt to assume full control with its own largely inexperienced personnel and led to their quick acceptance of an offer by the Soviet Union to send trained pilots (→ 10/1).

White mobs oppose Negroes in schools

Sept 8. Amid chants of "Negro, go home," swinging fists and flying bricks, 12 Negro youths entered, under police guard, the previously all-white Sturgis High School in Kentucky. Over 500 Sturgis townspeople gathered in violent protest of the integration of the school, prompting Governor A.B. Chandler to call in the state police force and the National Guard. Twelve whites were arrested in the disturbances.

In Clinton, Tennessee, similar riots erupted and Clinton Sheriff Glad Woodward has declared a state of emergency in the area. He also asked every able-bodied man to come forward to assist in keeping law and order, especially after the National Guard leaves (→ 11/13).

Somoza is victim of assassin's bullet

Sept 29. General Anastasio Somoza, President of Nicaragua, died today in the Canal Zone, from wounds received September 22. Somoza was in Panama to take part in inauguration celebrations for President Ernest de la Guardia Jr. He was shot by Nicaraguan Rigoberto Lopez Perez, who was killed immediately after shooting Somoza.

Nicaragua's Congress has unanimously elected Luis Somoza Debayle to serve out his father's presidential term, which ends May 1. Somoza Sr. was educated in the U.S. and pursued a military career upon returning to Nicaragua, eventually heading the National Guard. He became president in 1937 after seizing power from President Juan Bautista Sacasa (→ 2/4/57).

Hot-rodders make drag-racing popular

Sept 16. Speeding up abandoned airport runways and unused roads, hyped-up cars are racing one another at more than 100 miles per hour in what has been recognized as "drag-racing." Once shunned as rebellious, dangerous entertainment for American teenagers, high speed auto-racing on a quarter-mile strip has evolved into a sophisticated sport. Over 350,000 hot-rodders now engage in the thrills, frills and sometimes spills of the popular pastime. And with a million fans watching, drag-racing is leaving its mark on America.

1956

OCTOBER

Su	Mo	Tu	We	Th	Fr	Sa
	1	2	3	4	5	6
7	8	9	10	11	12	13
14	15	16	17	18	19	20
21	22	23	24	25	26	27
28	29	30	31			

1. London: Suez Canal Users Assn. formally inaugurated by 15 member nations (→ 7).

7. Israel: For. Min. Golda Meir says U.N. failure has necessitated Israeli action in Egypt (→ 17).

7. U.S. renounces extraterritorial rights in Morocco (→ 8/11/57).

8. Poznan: Polish youths get light four-year terms for riots, murder of secret police (→ 20).

9. Ike blasts Stevenson plan for H-bomb ban as idealistic "cheap and easy" peace (→ 1/10/57).

11. Hong Kong: Despite British police, Communist-Nationalist clash leaves 40 dead (→ 1/7/57).

17. U.K. opens world's largest nuke plant at Calder Hall (→ 26).

17. Tel Aviv: Ben Gurion tells Parliament Israel's greatest danger is "Fascist" Nasser (→ 29).

19. Moscow normalizes relations with Japan.

20. Soviet leaders rush to Poland to demand pro-Moscow regime; stopped at border (→ 24).

22. Paris: Morocco and Tunisia recall ambassadors in rebuke for French action in Suez.

23. Budapest: Police fire on revolting Hungarians (→ 25).

24. Warsaw: Thousands of youths demonstrate against Soviet influence (→ 1/20/57).

25. Budapest: Premier Nagy launches dawn attack to put down revolt (→ 27).

26. N.Y.: Ike offers 11,000 lbs. of Uranium 235 to IAEC at U.N. (→ 3/5/57).

27. Budapest: Premier Nagy says Russians will leave; as mass burial held for 85 students and workers killed in revolt (→ 30).

29. Egypt: Israeli forces thrust into Sinai peninsula (→ 30).

30. Budapest: Cardinal Mindszenty set free.→

30. Britain, France veto U.S. and Soviet demand for Israel-Egypt cease-fire (→ 31).

31. Ike tells nation U.S. will stay out of Mideast hostilities.→

BIRTH

18. Martina Navratilova, Czech-American tennis star.

Hungarians fight Reds

Oct 30. Anti-Soviet protests in Hungary have turned into a full-scale war. On one side are most of the Hungarian people. On the other are Soviet troops who have shown little restraint trying to quell the rebellion.

The first shots were fired last week by Hungarian police who were trying to control a crowd outside the Budapest radio building. The students, intellectuals, office workers and even soldiers were demanding the withdrawal of Soviet troops from Hungary. They also clamored for the return to office of Imre Nagy, the pro-consumer former Premier forced out by the Soviets.

Budapest radio called the protesters "fascist reactionary elements." They were also condemned by Erno Gero, the chief of the Hungarian Communist Party. Gero charged that the demonstrators were trying to replace communism with a bourgeois system. "Our decision," Gero said, "is definitely to abide by Socialist democracy. We must defend it."

A new member of the Hungarian Politburo put it more bluntly. Janos Kadar accused the protesters of "trying to bring back capitalism. They must capitulate," Kadar said, "or we will crush them."

Other party leaders preferred to compromise with the hundreds of thousands of rebels who were marching through the streets of Budapest. At an all-night meeting on the 23rd, they relented and returned Nagy to office.

The new Premier was quickly compromised, however, because he did not object as Soviet troops moved in to assist the clearly overwhelmed Hungarian police. Soon, it was Nagy himself who was directing the Soviet troops against his supporters. The rebels, disgusted, said Nagy was no Gomulka, referring to the rehabilitated foe of Stalin who is pursuing a more moderate course in Poland as the new Communist Party leader.

The fighting spread from Budapest across the country. In the western industrial town of Gyor, the rebels established an "independent Hungarian government." In Budapest, soldiers joined the protest and helped arm the rebels. They destroyed Soviet tanks and planes. Russians shot back at thousands of demonstrators, most of them unarmed. Witnesses to the violence say hundreds of people have been killed in the capital. An all-day curfew was declared by the Nagy government last Friday. Factories were ordered to close.

The United States, Britain and France protested to the United Nations over the Soviet intervention in Hungary. The Soviets responded that the Western powers were supporting the rebels (→ 11/2).

Budapest rioters, lashing out at Soviet domination, climbed a 23-foot statue of Stalin erected by the Russians after their 1945 victory and decapitated it. ▷

British, French and Israelis move on Suez Canal

In the canal region, villages have been devastated by French and British aerial bombs. Here, an Egyptian woman searches the ruins of her house.

Oct 31. Following the concerted attack on Egypt by Israeli, French and British forces, the U.N. tonight called an emergency session of the General Assembly. U.N. Secretary General Dag Hammarskjold expressed the general mood when he indirectly condemned the aggressor nations by deploring the French-British veto of U.S. and Soviet resolutions for a cease-fire.

In a bitterly divided House of Commons, Labor Party leader Hugh Gaitskell charged Prime Minister Eden with an act of "tragic folly" as that body went on to endorse the action by a majority of 52.

The orchestrated invasion was launched by Israel two days ago when its army cut through Egypt's Sinai Peninsula to within miles of the causus belli, the Suez Canal.

Yesterday, Cyprus-based British bombers hit Egyptian military targets with an aim to crippling the Egyptian air force in preparation for the landing of a seaborne invasion force of British and French units headed south from Cyprus and backed by the largest naval concentration in the Mediterranean since World War II. Their goal is the capture of Port Said, Ismailia and Suez and the withdrawal of Egyptian forces from the Canal Zone. The British navy also recorded its first victory when the cruiser Newfoundland sank an Egyptian frigate in the Gulf of Suez, taking survivors aboard.

President Nasser, vowing his nation will fight any foreign intervention, has rejected a French-British appeal for an Egyptian-Israeli cease-fire. Israel has tentatively accepted the appeal and agreed to pull back its forces ten miles from the canal with the proviso that Egypt also accept. If not, Israel will feel free to continue her Sinai offensive.

Washington is convinced that a major war can be avoided. There is also a genuine belief among U.S. officials that, with the East European satellites in revolt and the U.S. and the Soviets both opposed to the British-French intervention in Egypt, it might be possible to reopen serious negotiations for the reunification of Germany and an all-European security pact (→ 11/2).

French and British planes from Cyprus strafed and bombed Egyptian airports and installations near Suez. Ironically enough, the British opposed the building of the canal in the 1860's; now they are willing to fight for the right to use it.

1956

NOVEMBER

Su	Mo	Tu	We	Th	Fr	Sa
				1	2	3
4	5	6	7	8	9	10
11	12	13	14	15	16	17
18	19	20	21	22	23	24
25	26	27	28	29	30	

2. Hungarian Premier Nagy renounces Warsaw Pact as Soviet troops pour into Budapest (→ 4).

2. N.Y.: U.N. Assembly approves cease-fire plan for Egypt fighting (→ 3).

3. Egypt: Israeli troops take Gaza Strip, control Sinai (→ 4).

4. Hungary: Soviets hit Budapest with 1,000 tanks, arrest Premier Nagy (→ 5).

4. London: Laborites protest in Trafalgar Sq., demanding Eden resign over Suez action (→ 5).

5. British and French invade Egypt by air (→ 6).

5. India: Nehru breaks silence, condemning Soviets for repression in Hungary (→ 18).

6. British and French, at U.N. bid, halt drive in Egypt (→ 7).

7. N.Y.: U.N. Assembly, 65-1, asks invading powers to quit Egypt (→ 15).

10. Tel Aviv: For. Min. Meir states Gaza Strip is integral part of Israel (→ 1/23/57).

13. U.S. Supreme Court kills Alabama law requiring segregation on city buses (→ 12/24).

13. N.J.: Atlantic City report ties lung cancer to air pollution.

15. Italy: First of U.N. force leaves for Egypt (→ 29).

15. Belgrade: Tito speech charges Soviets divided on policy toward E. Europe (→ 8/3/57).

17. U.S. Navy icbreaker reports Antarctic iceberg twice size of Connecticut.

18. New York: Hungarian patriot puts Hungarian flag on Statue of Liberty (→ 21).

21. U.N. demands halt to mass deportations of Hungarians (→ 23).

22. Melbourne: XVIth Summer Olympic Games open.

30. U.S. offers emergency oil to Europe to counter Arab ban (→ 12/16).

30. Cuba: Exiled student leader Fidel Castro heads rebel attack on rural guard posts (→ 12/2).

DEATH

4. Art Tatum, American jazz pianist (*10/13/1910).

Sabin will test oral polio vaccine

Sabin at University of Cincinnati.

Oct 6. A new polio vaccine that can be taken by mouth will soon be tested in humans, its developer, Dr. Albert B. Sabin of the University of Cincinnati, announced today. If the tests succeed, the Sabin vaccine could replace the currently used Salk vaccine, which must be given by injection. The Salk vaccine induces immunity against polio by using killed viruses. The Sabin vaccine contains strains of virus that have been systematically weakened so that they stimulate the body's immune defenses without causing illness. Plans already have been made to produce two million doses of the new vaccine. Large-scale tests, starting with convict volunteers, will begin next year.

The beauty of the St. Tropez coastline is rivaled only by that of 22-year-old Brigitte Bardot, in Roger Vadim's new film "And God Created Woman."

French capture Algerian leadership

Oct 22. In a daring move, French authorities seized five leaders of the National Liberation Front in Algeria today. The rebels were arrested on a plane bound for Tunisia that French officials managed to reroute to an airport in Maison-Blanche, Algeria. Rabah Bitat, Mohammed Boudiaf, Hocine Ait Ahmed, Mohammed Khider and Ahmed Ben Bella were flying from a meeting with Morocco's Sultan to a summit conference in Tunis when their plane was intercepted. The French started tracking the aircraft as soon as it left Morocco (→ 1/31/57).

Perfect no-hitter pitched in Series

Oct 10. Breathless, spine-tingling baseball history was made two days ago as Don Larsen threw the World Series' only no-hit game. In fact, the New York Yankee was perfect, conquering every Brooklyn Dodger hitter he faced. Asked after the 2-0 victory if he had made any special preparations the night before, the big right-hander said, "Why, no. I did just like I always do. Had a few beers and went to bed around midnight." The Yankees captured their 17th World Series today with a 9-0 win over their crosstown rivals.

Birdseye, frozen food inventor, dies

Oct 9. Clarence Birdseye, whose invention of a quick-freezing process for food made his name a household word and helped change the way Americans live, died today in New York at the age of 69. Birdseye developed his food-freezing method after spending time in Labrador as a fur trader. He noticed that foods frozen quickly in the winter remained fresh when kept at low temperatures, and worked at home to commercialize a method of freezing food in packages. He formed a company to market frozen fish in 1924 and sold the rights to his process four years later for more than $22 million to what is now the General Foods Corporation.

Americans still like Ike as President

Eisenhower, in for a second term.

Nov 6. President Eisenhower won a second term in the White House today in a landslide victory over Democrat Adlai E. Stevenson. The 66-year-old hero of the Normandy invasion is the first Republican in this century to win two successive presidential elections. He won 41 states to seven carried by former Illinois Governor Stevenson and he polled 25 million votes to the 18.3 million cast for his opponent. The Eisenhower landslide—the largest since Franklin D. Roosevelt swamped Republican Alfred M. Landon in 1936—swept Richard M. Nixon into another term as Vice President (→ 1/21/57).

Patterson takes heavyweight title

Nov 30. Floyd Patterson, at the tender age of 21, has become the youngest man ever to hold the world heavyweight boxing title. Patterson knocked Archie Moore down twice before the referee stepped in to halt the bout in Chicago Stadium. The time was two minutes, 27 seconds of the fifth round. Patterson put Moore away with a textbook left hook. Moore stirred at the count of 6 and got to his feet at 9, but he had nothing left. Patterson pelted him with a furious barrage and it was all over. The two were fighting for the right to succeed Rocky Marciano as world heavyweight champion. Last April, Marciano retired undefeated.

Soviet tanks crush Budapest revolt

Hungarian hopes were destroyed along with their inadequate tools of revolt.

Kadar, a traitor to the rebels.

Nov 23. To the Western world, they were freedom fighters. To the Soviet Union, they were rebels who went too far challenging the Communist system. In Hungary this month, that challenge came to an end. Now it is the Soviet Union that is being accused of going too far in crushing the rebellion and the spirit of the Hungarian people. Soviet tanks turned Budapest into a war zone. They demolished buildings, destroyed boulevards and taught the Hungarians a lesson.

Soviet troops from Russia, Rumania and Czechoslovakia began their attack on Hungary before dawn on the 4th. News of the assault on Budapest was broadcast on state radio. "Soviet troops attacked the Hungarian capital with the open purpose to overthrow the legal government," Premier Imre Nagy announced. "The Hungarian troops are in combat and the Hungarian government is on its post."

A short while later, there was an even more dramatic appeal from a Hungarian radio announcer. "We don't have much time," he said breathlessly. "You know what is happening. Help the Hungarian nation, help its workers, its peasants and its intellectuals. Help! Help! Help!" It was the last report.

Russian planes roared over Budapest as up to a thousand tanks rumbled into the city, most of them from the south and southeast. Armored detachments and troop transports sped through the suburbs and secured guard posts blocking Danube River crossings. Tanks and infantry stormed into the center of Budapest and opened fire on public buildings. The Hungarian army was overwhelmed and powerless. Soviet troops overran the Parliament building at 9:00 and took Nagy and most of his government prisoner.

A half hour later, Soviet tanks opened fire on the United States Embassy. Taking shelter inside, along with American diplomats, was Joseph Cardinal Mindszenty. The outspoken defender of Hungarian liberty had been released just several days earlier after spending seven years in prison.

A rescue official said the Soviets committed "barbarous butchery" as they fanned through Budapest. He said they killed up to 10,000 Hungarians. At least 30,000 people were wounded. The troops were apparently helped by local undercover authorities. "The Russians are not the most hated people in Hungary," the official said. "The most hated are members of the secret police."

In the middle of the Russian attack, Janos Kadar changed stripes. Just a few days ago, the new First Secretary of the Hungarian Communist Party was promising to negotiate with the Soviet Union about the withdrawal of its troops. Now he announced that he had formed a new government that wanted the Russians to help end the counter-revolution.

Top Soviet officials have also been accused of treachery in carrying out their well-planned attack. The night before it was launched, a commission of top Hungarian military officers left Budapest for talks with the Russians about pulling out their troops. The generals never returned. Presumably, they are still under arrest somewhere in the Soviet Union.

Premier Nagy himself was also kidnapped by Soviet security police. Yugoslav officials, criticizing the Soviet government, say Nagy was snatched outside their embassy in Budapest. The Yugoslavs said today they had been guaranteed that Nagy would be given safe passage back to his home.

Yugoslavia was not the only Communist country to take issue with the Soviets over their brutal repression in Hungary. An article in the Polish Communist newspaper accused Russian leaders of reverting to "Stalinist tactics." At the U.N. Security Council, nine countries approved an American resolution censuring the Soviet Union. It was vetoed by Moscow (→ 12/1).

Soviet tanks dominate the scene along the streets of Budapest.

Dorsey, master of smooth jazz, dies

"Sentimental Gentleman of Swing."

Nov 26. Tommy Dorsey the velvet trombonist and leader of the popular swing band, died today in Greenwich, Connecticut, at 51. After co-leading a band with his brother Jimmy, Tommy formed his own group. It hit its peak in the early 1940's and was hailed by one critic as "the greatest all-around dance band of them all." Because of his mellifluous playing, Dorsey became known as "the Sentimental Gentleman of Swing." His style was highly influential. Frank Sinatra, who sang with Dorsey in his early years, has said he learned more about phrasing from the smooth trombonist than from any singer he ever heard.

Sartre breaks with Communist Party

Nov 9. Jean Paul Sartre, the leading French philosopher and novelist and a very visible Communist, split with the Communist Party today.

Sartre was appalled by the way the Soviets crushed the rebellion in Hungary. It was only this year that Sartre wrote, "Carried along by history, the Communist Party manifests an extraordinarily objective intelligence: it rarely makes a mistake." Today, Sartre changed his tune. He said his friendship for the Soviet Union has been replaced by "horror" for the actions of its bureaucratic leaders. Sartre plans to devote an issue of his Modern Times magazine to the martyrs of Hungary.

Under U.N. pressure, Suez operation is ended

French paratroopers from the Foreign Legion prepare to move into battle after landing at Port Said despite explicit warning from the United Nations.

British soldiers brandish an Egyptian flag taken in combat at Port Said; the British too have sustained heavy losses, in international support as well as lives.

An Egyptian soldier bails out into a barrage of gunfire as his truck, riddled with bullets from British rifles, begins to burst into flame.

Nov 29. Called by the Egyptians "the Anglo-French aggression," the brief Suez Canal war is over, ended November 6 by a United Nations cease-fire. The U.N. has also called for the withdrawal of all invading forces, and the first units of a U.N. emergency international police force are already arriving in the heavily damaged Canal Zone.

An invasion November 5th took place in defiance of a U.N. resolution calling for the abstention of military action by Britain and France when British and French paratroopers dropped on Port Said at the northern end of the zone.

It followed heavy preliminary attacks by fighters and bombers of the RAF and French air force as they pounded Egyptian air bases to neutralize the Egyptian air force, an aim quickly realized. More than 100 Egyptian planes were destroyed or damaged on the ground, a high number of them Soviet-built MIG-15 fighters and Ilyushin-28 bombers.

The attack next shifted to the destruction of Egyptian army bases and supply centers and included the blasting of Cairo and outlying villages. According to an Egyptian report, 100 persons were killed in one town alone.

Meanwhile the Israeli army, commanded by Major General Moshe Dayan, completed its lightning conquest of the Sinai Peninsula, taking 12,000 prisoners, killing or routing another 18,000 and capturing 150 tanks, mostly Russian T-34's.

Since the cease-fire, the invaders have dragged their heels over the U.N. call for a troop withdrawal. Though President Eisenhower has personally cabled Israeli Premier David Ben Gurion urging compliance, the premier has flatly rejected the stationing of the U.N. emergency force, "no matter how called," on Israeli territory or Israeli-occupied areas. In his answer to the U.N. request that Israel pull her troops back to the 1949 Egyptian-Israeli armistice line, Ben Gurion declared that the line was no longer valid because "the armistice agreement with Egypt is dead and buried and cannot be restored to life."

The French and British governments, meanwhile, have said that they would comply with the resolution as soon as the U.N. police force reached adequate strength. Other terms for their troop withdrawals are the speedy clearance of the canal and the prospect of negotiations regarding the canal's future operation.

In related news, demonstrators in London have denounced the British action, and the Soviet government newspaper Izvestia, branding Israeli leaders as "an irresponsible handful of adventurers," says that the Israeli invaders should be tried as war criminals. Iraq had ordered full mobilization of its army in the event of an Israeli attack on Jordan, and an Israeli U.N. official has declared that the possibility of an attack on Israel from Syrian soil was implicit in the repeated Soviet charges against his country.

The Israelis have grown anxious of late over heightened tensions along the borders that Israel shares with Syria and Jordan. The United States has also voiced "concern" over Soviet arms shipments to Syria, and the British are worried about the possibility of a Soviet drive in the Middle East (→ 30).

French Foreign Legion gunners guard their position in front of a huge merchant ship sunk by the Egyptians, seeking to close the canal to all traffic.

The canal, closed at Port Said, is littered with wrecked ships. Many of the 46 sunken vessels are noticeable only by a smokestack piercing the water's surface.

1956 Melbourne

Dec 8. The Soviet Union came out on top "down under" in this year's Olympics. The Games—in Melbourne, Australia—have concluded with Russia leading 68 other countries as well as the former champion, the United States. The U.S.S.R. surpassed the U.S. 712 points to 593, claiming 30 more medals. Still, individual U.S. athletes scored private victories.

In the hammer throw, two mild and massive schoolteachers, American Harold Connolly and Russian Mikhail Krivonosov, dueled for the gold. Connolly won on his final heave. The Bostonian has been dating Czech discus thrower and fellow gold winner Olga Fikotova. Marriage rumors are in the air.

Odds takers had put their money on New Yorker George Breen in the 1,500-meter freestyle swim. In a recent practice heat, he set a world record of 17:52.9. Yet it was Aussie Murray Rose who won out. Rose, a blond teenage vegetarian who gulps kelp for energy, swam for all he was worth, leaving Breen wallowing in third place. Rose's real competitor was Japanese Tsuyoski Tamanaka. The pair were neck-and-neck instants before Rose won.

In another disappointment for the U.S., high diver Gary Tobian finished with a bronze medal instead of gold. Many observers blame consistently low scores given by judges from two Soviet bloc nations; they tended to award Tobian points in the range of 7.3 when other judges scored him much higher. The gold winner, Mexican Juan Capilla, magnanimously called Tobian a better diver than himself.

Blood was thicker than water in a semi-final aquatic polo match between the Hungarians and Russians. Hungary, still seething from the Soviet Union's recent invasion, had a particularly aggressive team. A few minutes into the match, a Russian player smacked a Hungarian, cutting him on the head. The Hungarians retreated to one end of the pool and seemed to hold a deep discussion. The nervous Russians forfeited the game.

Other Soviet wins in soccer, Greco-Roman wrestling and gymnastics have also gotten Americans wondering just how much training and financing a country owes its athletes. And how can poorer nations prevail against wealthier ones? The Russians may think the questions are nothing but sour grapes.

After running 26 miles in 2:25, marathon winner Alain Mimoun approaches the finish line.

At 21 years of age, Frenchman Michel Rousseau is the Olympic cycling champion.

Men Athletics

100 M Dash			
1.	Robert Morrow	USA	10,5
2.	Thane Baker	USA	10,5
3.	Hector Hogan	AUS	10,6
200 M Dash			
1.	Robert Morrow	USA	20,6
2.	Andrew Stanfield	USA	20,7
3.	W. Thane Baker	USA	20,9
400 M Run			
1.	Charles Jenkins	USA	46,7
2.	Karl-Friedrich Haas	FRG	46,8
3.	Voitto Hellsten	FIN	47,0
3.	Ardalion Igantyev	URS	47,0
800 M Run			
1.	Thomas Courtney	USA	1:47,7
2.	Derek Johnson	GBR	1:47,8
3.	Audun Boysen	NOR	1:48,1
1500 M Run			
1.	Ron Delany	IRA	3:41,2
2.	Klaus Richtzenhain	FRG	3:42,0
3.	John Landy	AUS	3:42,0
5000 M Run			
1.	Vladimir Kuts	URS	13:39,6
2.	Gordon Pirie	GBR	13:50,6
3.	Derek Ibbotson	GBR	13:54,4
10,000 M Run			
1.	Vladimir Kuts	URS	28:45,6
2.	Jozsef Kovacs	HUN	28,52,4
3.	Allan Lawrence	AUS	28,53,6
Marathon			
1.	Alain Mimoun	FRA	2:25:00,0
2.	Franjo Mihalic	YUG	2:26:32,0
3.	Veikko Karvonen	FIN	2:27:47,0
110 M Hurdles			
1.	Lee Calhoum	USA	13,5
2.	Jack Davis	USA	13,5
3.	Joel Shankle	USA	14,1
400 M Hurdles			
1.	Glen Davis	USA	50,1
2.	Eddie Southern	USA	50,8
3.	Josh Culbreath	USA	51,6
3000 M Steeplechase			
1.	Christopher Brasher	GBR	8:41,2
2.	Sandor Rozsnyoi	HUN	8:43,6
3.	Ernst	NOR	8:44,0
400 M Relay			
1.	USA 39,5 (Ira Murchison, Leanon King, Thane Baker, Robert Morrow)		
2.	URS 39,8 (Boris Tokatyev, Vladimir Sukharyev, Leonid Bartenyev, Yury Konovolov)		
3.	FRG 40,3 (Lothar Knörzer, Leonhard Pohl, Heinz Füttrer, Manfred Gennar)		
1600 M Relay			
1.	USA 3:04,8 (Louis Jones, Jesse Mashburn, Charles Jenkins, Thomas Courtney)		
2.	AUS 3:06,2 (Leon Gregory, David Lean, Graham Gipson, Kevin Gosper)		
3.	GBR 3:07,2 (John Salisbury, MIchael Wheeler, F. Peter Higgins, Derek Johnson)		
20 km Walk			
1.	Leonid Spirin	URS	1:31:27,4
2.	Atanas Mikenas	URS	1:32:03,0
3.	Bruno Yunk	URS	1:32:12,0
50 km Walk			
1.	Norman Read	NZE	4:30:42,8
2.	Yevgeny Maskinskov	URS	4:32,57,0
3.	John Ljunggren	SWE	4:35:57,0
High Jump			
1.	Charles Dumas	USA	2,12
2.	Charles Porter	AUS	2,10
3.	Igor Kaschkarov	URS	2,08
Pole Vault			
1.	Robert Richards	USA	4,56
2.	Robert Gutowski	USA	4,53
3.	Georgios Roubanis	GRE	4,50
Long Jump			
1.	Gregory Bell	USA	7,83
2.	John Bennett	USA	7,68
3.	Jorma Valkama	FIN	7,48
Triple Jump			
1.	Adhemar Ferreira Da Silva	BRA	16,35
2.	Vilhjalmur Einarsson	ISL	16,26
3.	Vitold Kreyer	URS	16,02
Shotput			
1.	Parry O'Brien	USA	18,57
2.	William Nieder	USA	18,18
3.	Jiri Skobla	TCH	17,65
Discus Throw			
1.	Alfred Oeter	USA	56,36
2.	Fortune Gordien	USA	54,81
3.	Desmond Koch	USA	54,40
Hammer Throw			
1.	Harold Connolly	USA	63,19
2.	Mikhail Krivonosov	URS	63,03
3.	Anatoly Samotsveyetov	URS	62,56
Javelin			
1.	Egil Danielsen	NOR	85,71
2.	Janusz Sidlo	POL	79,98
3.	Viktor Tsybulenko	URS	79,50
Decathlon			
1.	Milton Campbell	USA	7937
2.	Rafer Johnson	USA	7587
3.	Wassiliy Kuznyetsov	URS	7465

Women Athletics

100 M Dash			
1.	Betty Cuthbert	AUS	11,5
2.	Christa Stubnick	FRG	11,7
3.	Marlène Matthews	AUS	11,7
200 M Dash			
1.	Betty Cuthbert	AUS	23,4
2.	Christa Stubnick	FRG	23,7
3.	Marlène Matthews	AUS	23,8
80 M Hurdles			
1.	Shirley de la Henty	AUS	10,7
2.	Gisela Köhler	FRG	10,9
3.	Norma Thrower	AUS	11,0
400 M Relay			
1.	AUS 44,5 (Shirley de la Hunty, Norma Croker, Fleur Mellor, Betty Cuthbert)		
2.	GBR 44,7 (Anne Pashley, Jean Scrivens June Paul-Foulds, Heather Armitage)		
3.	USA 44,9 (Mae Gaggs, Margaret Matthews, Wilma Rudolph, Isabelle Daniels)		
High Jump			
1.	Mildred McDaniel	USA	1,76
2.	Maria Pissaryeva	URS	1,67
3.	Thelma Hopkins	GBR	1,67
Long Jump			
1.	Elzbieta Krzesinska	POL	6,35
2.	Willye White	USA	6,09
3.	Nadveschda Dvalischvili	URS	6,07
Shotput			
1.	Tamara Tyschkevitsch	URS	16,59
2.	Galina Zybina	URS	16,53
3.	Marianne Werner	FRG	15,61
Discus Throw			
1.	Olga Fikotova	TCH	53,69
2.	Irina Boglyakova	URS	52,54
3.	Nina Ponomaryeva Romaschkova	URS	52,02
Javelin			
1.	Inese Yaunzennz	URS	53,86
2.	Marlène Ahrens	CHI	50,38
3.	Nadyeschda Konyayeva	URS	50,28

Men Swimming

100 M Freestyle			
1.	Jon Henricks	AUS	55,4
2.	John Devitt	AUS	55,8
3.	Gary Chapman	AUS	56,7
400 M Freestyle			
1.	Murray Rose	AUS	4:27,3
2.	Tsuyoshi Yamanaka	JAP	4:30,4
3.	George Brenn	USA	4:32,5
1500 M Freestyle			
1.	Murray Rose	AUS	17:58,9
2.	Tsuyoshi Yamanaka	JAP	18:00,3
3.	George Breen	USA	18:08,5
100 M Backstroke			
1.	Davis Theile	AUS	1:02,2
2.	John Monckton	AUS	1:03,2
3.	Frank McKinney	USA	1:04,5
200 M Breastroke			
1.	Masaru Funukawa	JAP	2:34,7
2.	Masahiro Yoshimura	JAP	2:36,7
3.	Charis Yunitschev	URS	2:36,8
200 M Butterfly Stroke			
1.	William Yorzik	USA	2:19,3
2.	Takashi Ishimoto	JAP	2:23,8
3.	Gyorgy Tumpek	HUN	2:23,9
800 M Freestyle Relay			
1.	AUS 8:23,6 (Kevin O'Halloran, John Devitt, Murrsay Rose, Jon Henricks)		
2.	USA 8:31,5 (Richard Hanley, George Breen, William Woolsey, Ford Konno)		
3.	URS 8:34,7 (Vitaly Sorokin, Vladimir Struchanov, Gennady Nikolayev, Boris Nikitin)		
Springboard Diving			
1.	Robert Clotworthy	USA	1159,56
2.	Donald Harper	USA	1156,23
3.	Joaquin Capilla Perez	MEX	150,69
High Diving			
1.	Joaquin Capilla Perez	MEX	152,44
2.	Gary Tobian	USA	152,41
3.	Richard Connor	USA	149,79
Water Polo			
1.	Hungary		
2.	Yugoslavia		
3.	Soviet Union		

Women Swimming

100 M Freestyle			
1.	Dawn Fraser	AUS	1:02,0
2.	Lorraine Crapp	AUS	1:02,3
3.	Faith Leech	AUS	1:05,1
400 M Freestyle			
1.	Lorraine Crapp	AUS	4:54,6
2.	Dawn Fraser	AUS	5:02,5
3.	Sylvia Ruuska	USA	5:07,1
200 M Breastroke			
1.	Ursula Happe	FRG	2:53,1
2.	Eva Székely	HUN	2:54,8
3.	Eva-Maria Ten Elsen	FRG	2:55,1
100 M Backstroke			
1.	Judith Grinham	GRB	1:12,9
2.	Karin Cone	USA	1:12,9
3.	Margaret Edwards	GBR	1:13,1

1956 Melbourne

100 M Butterfly Stroke
1. Shelley Mann USA 1:11,0
2. Nancy Ramey USA 11:11,9
3. Mary Sears USA 11:14,4

400 M Relay
1. AUS 4:17,1 (Dawn Fraser, Faith Leech, Sandra Morgan, Lorraine Crapp
2. USA 4:19,2 (Sylvia Ruuska, Shelley Mann, Nancy Simons, Joan Rosazza)
3. SAF 4:25,7 (Jeanette Myburgh, Suzan Roberts, Ntalie Myburgh, Moira Abenathy

Springboard Diving
1. Patricia McCormick USA 142,36
2. Jeanne Stunyo USA 125,89
3. Irene MacDonald CAN 121,40

High Diving
1. Patricia McCormick USA 84,85
2. Juno Irwin-Stover USA 81,64
3. Paula Jean Myers USA 81,58

Boxing

Flyweight
1. Terence Spinks GBR
2. Mircea Dobrescu ROM
3. John Caldwell IRL
3. René Libeer FRA

Bantamweight
1. Wolfgang Behrednt URS
2. Soon-Chun Song KOR
3. Frederick Gilroy IRL
3. Claudio Barrientos

Featherweight
1. Vladimir Safronov URS
2. Thomas Nicholls GBR
3. Henryk Niedzwidezki POL
3. Pentti Hämäläinen FIN

Lightweight
1. Richard McTaggart GBR
2. Harry Kurschat FRG
3. Anthony Byrne IRL
3. Anatoly Lagetko URS

Light Welterweight
1. Vladimir Yengibaryan URS
2. Franco Nenci ITA
3. Henry Loubscher SAF
3. Constantin Dimitrescu ROM

Welterweight
1. Nicolae Linca ROM
2. Frederick Tiedt IRL
3. Kevin John Hogardth AUS
3. Nicholas Gargano GBR

Light Middleweight
1. Laszlo Papp HUN
2. José Torres USA
3. John McCormack GBR
3. Kbigniew Pietrzykowski POL

Middleweight
1. Gennady Schatkow URS
2. Ramon Tapia CHI
3. Gilbert Chapron FRA
3. Victor Zalabar ARG

Light Heavyweight
1. James Felton Boyd USA
2. Gheorghe Negrea ROM
3. Romualdas Murauskas URS
3. Carlos Lucas CHI

Heavyweight
1. T. Peter Rademacher USA
2. Lev Mukhin URS
3. Daniel Bekker SAF
3. Giacomo Bozzano ITA

Greco-Roman Wrestling

Flyweight
1. Nikolay Solovyov URS
2. Ignazio Fabra ITA
3. Durum Ali Egribas URU

Bantamweight
1. Konstantin Vyrupayev URS
2. Edvin Vesterby SWE
3. Francisc Horvat ROM

Featherweight
1. Rauno Mäkinen FIN
2. Imre Polyak HON
3. Roman Dzneladze URS

Lightweight
1. Kyosti Lehtonen FIN
2. Riza Dogan TUR
3. Gyula Toth HUN

Welterweight
1. Mithat Bayrak TUR
2. Vladimir Maneyev URS
3. Per Berlin SWE

Middleweight
1. Givy Kartoziya URS
2. Dimiter Dobrev BUL
3. Rune Jansson SWE

Light Heavyweight
1. Valentin Nicolayev URS
2. Petko Sirakov BUL
3. Karl-Erik Nilsson SWE

Heavyweight
1. Anatoly Parfenov URS
2. Wilfried Dietrich FRG
3. Adelmo Bulgarelli ITA

CHART

Weightlifting

		2 Arm Press	2 Arm Snatch	2 Arm Clean & Jerk	Total
Bantamweight					
1. Charles Vinci	USA	105,0	105,0	132,5	342,5
2. Vladimir Stogov	URS	105,0	105,0	127,5	337,5
3. Mahmoud Nandjou	IRA	100,0	102,0	130,0	332,5
Featherweight					
1. Isaac Berger	USA	107,5	107,5	137,5	352,5
2. Yevgeny Minayev	URS	115,0	100,0	127,5	342,5
3. Marian Zielinski	POL	105,0	102,5	127,5	335,0
Lightweight					
1. Igor Rybak	URS	110,0	120,0	150,0	380,0
2. Rafael Khabutdinov	URS	125,0	110,0	137,5	372,5
3. Chang-Hee Kim	KOR	107,5	112,5	150,0	370,0
Middleweight					
1. Pyodor Bogdanovsky	URS	132,5	122,5	165,0	420,0
2. Peter Georges	USA	122,5	127,5	162,5	412,5
3. Ermanno Pignatti	ITA	117,5	117,5	147,5	382,5
Light Heavyweight					
1. Thomas Kono	USA	140,0	132,5	175,0	447,5
2. Vasily Stepanov	URS	135,0	130,0	162,5	427,5
3. James George	USA	120,0	130,0	167,5	417,5
Middle Heavyweight					
1. Arkady Vorobyov	URS	147,5	137,5	177,5	462,5
2. David Sheppard	USA	140,0	137,5	165,0	442,5
3. Jean Dubuf	FRA	130,0	127,5	167,5	425,0
Heavyweight					
1. Paul Anderson	USA	167,5	145,0	187,5	500,0
2. Humberto Selvetti	ARG	175,0	145,0	180,0	500,0
3. Alberto Pigaiano	ITA	150,0	130,0	172,5	452,5

Freestyle Wrestling

Flyweight
1. Mirian Tsalkalamanidze URS
2. Mohamed-Ali Khojastehpour IRA
3. Mikhail Schakhov URS

Featherweight
1. Shozo Sasahara JAP
2. Joseph Mewis BEL
3. Erkki Pentilä FIN

Lightweight
1. Emamali Habibi IRA
2. Shigeru Kasahara JAP
3. Alimbeg Bestayev URS

Welterweights
1. Mitsuo Ikeda JAP
2. Ibrahim Zengin TUR
3. Vakhtane Balavadze URS

Middleweight
1. Nikola Stantschev BUL
2. Daniel Hodge USA
3. Georgy Skhirtladze URS

Light Heavyweight
1. Gholam-Reza Takhti IRA
2. Boris Kulayev URS
3. Peter Steele Blair USA

Heavyweight
1. Hamit Kaplan TUR
2. Hussein Mekhmedov BUL
3. Taisto Kangasniemi FIN

Men Fencing

Foil Individual
1. Christian d'Oriola FRA 6
2. Giancarlo Bergamini ITA 5
3. Antonio Spalino ITA 5

Foil Team
1. Italy
2. France
3. Hungary

Epée Individual
1. Carlo Pavesi ITA 5/1/2
2. Guisepee Delfino ITA 5/1/1
3. Edouardo Mangiarotti ITA 5/1/0

Epée Team
1. Italy
2. Hungary
3. France

Sabre Individual
1. Rudolph Karpati HUN 6
2. Jerzy Pawlowski POL 5
3. Lev Kuznyetsov URS 4

Sabre Team
1. Hungary
2. Poland
3. Soviet Union

Women Fencing

Foil Individual
1. Gillian Sheen GBR 6+1
2. Olga Orban ROM 6
3. Renée Garilhe FRA 5

Modern Pentathlon

Individual
1. Lars Hall SWE
2. Olavi Mannonen FIN
3. Väinö Korhonen FIN

Team
1. Soviet Union
2. USA
3. Finland

Field Hockey

1. India
2. Pakistan
3. German Federal Republic

Men Canoeing

Kayak-1 1000 M
1. Gert Fredrikson SWE 4:12,8
2. Igor Pissaryev HUN 4:15,3
3. Lajos Kiss HUN 4:16,2

Kayak-2 1000 M
1. German Federal Republic 3:49,6
2. Soviet Union 3:51,4
3. Austria 3:55,8

Kayak-1 10,000 M
(1936, Shigeru Kasahara 1948, 1952, 1956 only)
1. Gert Fredriksson SWE 47:43,4
2. Ferenc Hatlaczky HUN 47:53,3
3. Michel Scheuer FRG 48:00,3

Kayak-2 10,000 M
(1936, 1948, 1952, 1956 only)
1. Hungary 43:37,0
2. German Federal Republic 43:40,6
3. Australia 43:43,2

Canadian-1 1000 M
1. Lèon Rotman ROM 5:05,3
2. Istvan Hernek HUN 5:06,2
3. Gennady Bukharin URS 5:12,7

Canadian-2 1000 M
1. Romania
2. Soviet Union
3. Hungary

Canadian-1 10,000 M (1948, 1952, 1956 only)
1. Léon Rotman ROM 56:41,0
2. Janos Parti HUN 57:11,0
3. Gennady Bukharin URS 57:14,5

Canadian-2 10,000 M
(1936, 1948, 1952, 1956 only)
1. Soviet Union 54:02,4
2. France 54:48,3
3. Hungary 55:15,6

Canoeing Women

Kayak-1 500 M
1. Yelisaveta Dementyeva URS 2:18,9
2. Thérèse Zenz FRG 2:19,6
3. Tove Söby DEN 2:22,3

Rowing

Single Scull
1. Vyatscheslav Ivanov URS 8:02,5
2. Stuart Mackenzie AUS 8:07,7
3. John Kelly jun. USA 8:11,8

Double Sculls
1. Soviet Union 7:24,0
2. USA 7:32,2
3. Australia 7:37,4

Pairs Oars Without Coxswain
1. USA 7:55,4
2. Soviet Union 8:03,9
3. Austria 8:11,8

Pair Oars with Coxswain
1. USA 8:26,1
2. German Federal Republic 8:29,2
3. Soviet Union 8:31,0

Four Oars without Coxswain
1. Canada 7:08,8
2. USA 7:18,4
3. France 7:20,9

Four Oars with Coxswain
1. Italy 7:19,4
2. Sweden 7:22,4
3. Finland 7:30,9

Eight Oars
1. USA 6:35,2
2. Canada 6:37,1
3. Australia 6:39,2

Yachting

Finn Monotype Class Individual
1. Paul Elvström DEN 7509
2. André Nelis BEL 6257
3. John Marvin USA 5953

Star Class
1. USA 5876
2. Italy 5649
3. Bahamas 5223

Dragon Class
1. Sweden 5723
2. Denmark 5723
3. Great Britain 4547

5.5 M Class (1952, 1956, 1960, 1964, 1968)
1. Sweden 5527
2. Great Britain 4050
3. Australia 4022

Sharpie Class (1956 only)
1. New Zealand 6086
2. Australia 6086
3. Great Britain 4859

Cycling

Individual Road Race (187,73 km)
1. Ercole Baldini ITA 5:21:17,0
2. Arnaud Geyre FRA 5:23:16,0
3. Alan Jackson gbr 5:23:16,0

Team Road Race (1912, 1920, 1924, 1928, 1948, 1952, 1956 only)
1. France 22
2. Great Britain 23
3. German Federal Republic 27

100 M Sprint
1. Léandro Faggin ITA 1:09,8
2. Lasdilav Foucek TCH 1:11,4
3. Alfred Swift SAF 1:11,6

1000 Time Trial
1. Michel Rousseau FRA 11,4
2. Guglielmo Pesenti ITA
3. Richard Ploog AUS

2000 M Tandem
1. Australia 10,8
2. Czechoslovakia
3. Italy

Team Pursuit 4000 M
1. Italy 4:37,4
2. France 4:39,4
3. Great Britain 4:42,2

Equestrian Sports

Individual All-around Competition
1. Petrus Kastenman SWE
2. August Lütke-Westhues PRG
3. Frank Weldon GBR

All-around Team Competition
1. Great Britain 355,48
2. German Federal Republic 475,91
3. Canada 572,72

Individual Dressage
1. Henri Saint-Cyr SWE 860,0
2. Lis Hartel DEN 850,0
3. Liselott Linsenhoff PRG 832,0

Team Dressage
1. Great Britain 2475
2. German Federal Republic 2346
3. Switzerland 2346

Grand Prix Jumping Individual
1. Hans Günther Winkler PRG -4
2. Raimondo D'Inzeo ITA -8
3. Piero d'Inzeo ITA -11

Grand Prix Jumping Team
1. German Federal Republic -40,00
2. Italy -66,00
3. Great Britain

Shooting

Full-Bore Rifle, Combined, 3 positions
1. Vassily Borissov URS 1138
2. Allan Erdman URS 1137
3. Vilho Ylönen FIN 1128

Small-Bore Rifle, 50 M, Prone
1. Gérard Raymond Ouellette CAN 600
2. Vassily Borissov URS 599
3. Gilmour Stuart Boa CAN 598

Small-Bore Rifle, Combined, 3 positions
1. Anatoly Bogdanov URS 1172
2. Otakar Honnek TCH 1172
3. Nils Johan Sundberg SWE 1167

Rapid-Fire Pistol, 50 M
1. Stefan Petrescu ROM 587
2. Yevgeny Tschrkassov URS 585
3. Gheorghe Lichiardopol ROM 581

Free Pistol, 50 M
1. Pentti Limosvuo FIN 556/26
2. Makhmud Umarov URS 556/24
3. Offutt Pinion USA 551

Clay Pigeon
1. Galliano Rossini ITA 195
2. Adam Smelczynski POL 190
3. Alessandro Ciceri ITA 188/24

Running Deer Shooting, Single and Double Shot (1952 and 1956 only)
1. Vitaly Romanenko URS 441
2. Per Olof Sköldberg SWE 432
3. Vladimir Sevryugin URS 429

Men Gymnastics

All-around Individual Competition
1. Viktor Tschukarin URS 114,25
2. Takashi Ono JAP 114,20
3. Yury Titov URS 113,80

All-around Team Competition
1. Soviet Union 568,25
2. Japan 566,40
3. Finland 555,95

Paralellel Bars
1. Viktor Tschukarin URS 19,20
2. Massami Kubota JAP 19,15
3. Tabashi Ono JAP 19,10
3. Masao Takemoto JAP 19,10

Floor Exercise
1. Valentin Muratov URS 19,20
2. Nobuyuki Aihara JAP 19,10
2. William Thoresson SWE 19,10
2. Viktor Tschukarin URS 19,10

Horse Vault
1. Helmut Bantz PRG 18,85
2. Valentin Muratov URS 18,85
3. Yury Titov URS 18,75

Sidehorse
1. Boris Schakhlin URS 19,25
2. Takashi Ono JAP 19,20
3. Viktor Tschukarin URS 19,10

Horizontal Bar
1. Takashi Ono JAP 19,60
2. Yury Titov URS 19,40
3. Masao Takemoto JAP 19,30

Flying Rings
1. Albert Azaryau URS 19,35
2. Valentin Muratov URS 19,15
3. Masao Takemoto JAP 19,10
3. Masami Kubota JAP 19,10

Women Gymnastics

All-around Individual Competition
1. Larissa Latynina URS 74,933
2. Agnes Keleti HUN 74,633
3. Sofia Moratova URS 74,466

All-around Team Competition
1. Soviet Union 444,80
2. Hungary 443,50
3. Romania 438,20

Uneven Bars
1. Agnès Keleti HUN 18,966
2. Larissa Latynina URS 18,833
3. Sofia Muratova URS 18,800

Floor Exercise
1. Agnès Keleti HUN 18,733
2. Larissa Latynina URS 18,733
3. Elena Leustean ROM 18,700

Horsevault
1. Larissa Latynina URS 18,833
2. Tamara Manina URS 18,800
3. Ann-Sofi Colling SWE 18,733
3. Olga Tass HUN 18,733

Beam
1. Agnès Keleti HUN 18,800
2. Tamara Manina URS 18,633
3. Eva Bosakova TCH 18,633

Team Exercise with Portable Apparatus (1952 and 1956 only)
1. Hungary 75,20
2. Sweden 74,20
3. Poland 74,00

Basketball

1. USA
2. Soviet Union
3. Uruguay

Football

1. Soviet Union
2. Yugoslavia
3. Bulgaria

Four years after winning the 5,000-, 10,000-meters and the marathon, Emil Zatopek finished sixth in the marathon this year.

1956

DECEMBER

Su	Mo	Tu	We	Th	Fr	Sa
						1
2	3	4	5	6	7	8
9	10	11	12	13	14	15
16	17	18	19	20	21	22
23	24	25	26	27	28	29
30	31					

1. U.S. opens door to 21,500 more Hungarian refugees (→ 5).

1. Philadelphia: Army and Navy play to 7-7 tie in football.

5. Hungary rejects Hammarskjold request for visit to Budapest (→ 12).

6. Thailand: Benny Goodman and King Phumiphol Aduldet get together for impromptu jazz jam session.

12. U.N. calls for immediate Soviet withdrawal from Hungary (→ 22).

16. Egypt: U.N. troops occupy Port Said (→ 24).

18. Japan admitted to U.N. (→ 6/30/57).

22. Ohio: Columbus Zoo reports first gorilla born in captivity.

24. Tallahassee, Florida: Negroes defy city laws, occupying front bus seats (→ 1/1/57).

25. Czech radio halts nightly playing of Soviet natl. anthem.

29. Ike asks Congress for authority to oppose "Soviet aggression" in Mideast (→ 1/21/57).

DEATH

21. Lewis Terman, U.S. pioneer of IQ test (*1/15/1877).

CULTURAL EVENTS, 1956

Literature: John F. Kennedy's "Profiles in Courage"; Grace Metalious' "Peyton Place."

Academia: Colin Wilson's "The Outsider"; William H. Whyte's "Organization Man"; neutrino detected at Los Alamos.

Music: Bernstein's musical comedy "Candide"; Lerner and Loewe's "My Fair Lady"; Douglas Moore's opera "The Ballad of Baby Doe"; Maria Callas debuts in Bellini's opera "Norma"; "Blue Suede Shoes"; "Hound Dog"; "On the Street Where You Live"; "Don't Be Cruel."

The Arts: Barbara Hepworth's sculpture "Orpheus."

Film: Bergman's "The Seventh Seal"; Elia Kazan's "Baby Doll"; King Vidor's "War and Peace"; "Around the World in 80 Days," Academy Award; Preminger's "The Man with the Golden Arm"; "The Ten Commandments"; "The King and I."

Castro in Cuba; Batista claims he's killed

Castro, wanted dead or alive.

Dec 2. Cuban planes strafed the coast of Oriente province tonight, killing 40 revolutionaries, including their leader Fidel Castro, according to government accounts. Castro, self-exiled in Mexico after a failed effort to take power, had returned to Cuba to overthrow President Fulgencio Batista's regime.

The 30-year-old rebel once declared he would lead a "fight to the death of the last combatant" against Batista and called on "all democratic people of the continent" to support "the Cuban people in their heroic struggle." Now, it appears Castro's uprising will have to continue without him, his brother and comrades Raul and Jose Manuel Merco, also rebel leaders reportedly killed by government troops.

The rebels wear olive-green uniforms with the phrase "26 de Julio" blazoned across their sleeves. On July 26, 1953, Castro's forces killed 100 soldiers at the Moncada army post. This act symbolized the genesis of the revolution (→ 2/23/57).

British and French troops leave Suez

Dec 24. Though France and Britain completed their troop withdrawals two days ago, the heavy damage remains. In the United Nations today, Egypt submitted a resolution calling for "adequate compensation." In return for its withdrawal, Great Britain expects the U.N. to clear the Suez Canal immediately and support untrammeled traffic. It has also suggested that the Gaza Strip be evacuated by Israeli troops and made a U.N. responsibility. The salvage operation in the canal, held up by Cairo's previous refusal to permit French and British ships to help out, will begin shortly as Egypt today agreed to such assistance.

Egypt suffered greatly during the fighting. Port Said was all but leveled, the canal is now unusable and casualties were high. Yet it gained a major victory. While the British hollowly claim to have thwarted Soviet Mideast plans and ended the conflict between Israel and Egypt, they failed in their main objectives. They did not topple the Nasser regime nor force upon it international control of the Suez Canal (→ 1/4/57).

Janos Kadar seeking coalition in Hungary

Dec 22. As Christmas approaches in Hungary, the country is still split by political turmoil. Janos Kadar, the new hard-line Communist Premier, is trying to reach out to more moderate elements to form a coalition government. It is not likely, however, that former Premier Imre Nagy will agree to cooperate with Kadar. Nagy reportedly believes that only free elections can save Hungary. Even if Nagy did agree to compromise, it is unlikely that the Soviets would allow him back into the government.

Resistance to the Soviets' occupation of Hungary has been growing since their attack on Budapest last month. Today, Kadar's government conceded that workers' strikes and slowdowns in the coal mines are continuing. The job actions have already crippled most of Hungarian industry, and they have even attracted the sympathy of some Russian soldiers. Five Russians were shot by superiors last week when they refused to fire into a crowd of demonstrators in Tokaj.

Workers' councils set up before the Soviet crackdown are still functioning in parts of Hungary like local governments. Kadar, charging that the councils are counterrevolutionary, has failed in attempts to dissolve them (→ 1/13/57).

John Osborne vs. Organization Man

Middle-class morals were mauled and mocked in literature and drama this year. John Osborne, W.H. Whyte and Grace Metalious were among authors taking on the subject. Methods of attack varied.

Osborne's first play "Look Back in Anger" champions the struggling working class. Its anti-hero protagonist Jimmy Porter rails against the smug, false values of the middle and upper classes. If his voice rings true, it may be because Osborne himself is an "Angry Young Man," one of Britain's crusading writers.

W.H. Whyte's non-fiction work "The Organization Man" uses a less visceral, more analytical approach in condemning the white-collar world. He explains step by step how individualism is squeezed out of employees for the ends of furthering inanimate corporations. Whyte suggests the ultimate victim is the company itself; without the creativity of individuals, it will fail.

Grace Metalious' "Peyton Place" rises a bit over other popular pulp fiction. She exposes the hypocrisy in small-town life, opening people's closets and giving the skeletons within a good rattle. Within weeks of its publication, there was talk of making the book into a movie.

Readers tired of cynicism picked up Senator John F. Kennedy's "Profiles in Courage." Its biographies of leaders who lived by their convictions are immediately inspiring.

1957

JANUARY

Su	Mo	Tu	We	Th	Fr	Sa
		1	2	3	4	5
6	7	8	9	10	11	12
13	14	15	16	17	18	19
20	21	22	23	24	25	26
27	28	29	30	31		

1. Tallahassee: Gov. Collins halts bus service to stop integration efforts (→ 2/14).

1. Saar becomes 10th state of West Germany under 1956 treaty with France.

1. Pasadena: Iowa trounces Oregon State in Rose Bowl.

1. Honduras: Constitutional govt. formed under Liberal Pres. Ramon Villeda Morales.

4. Colliers Magazine and 85-year-old Woman's Home Companion fold.

5. U.S.: Jackie Robinson announces he will retire from baseball.

7. Moscow: Chinese Premier Chou En-lai arrives for talks with Soviet leaders (→ 6/28).

8. Washington: Sen. John F. Kennedy wins Foreign Relation Committee seat over Estes Kefauver (→ 1/31/60).

10. Ike proposes intl. control of space missile, satellite development for arms control (→ 4/5).

13. Hungary: Death penalty instituted for strikes and other opposition acts (→ 4/8).

15. Egypt nationalizes French and British banks (→ 3/9).

18. California: Three Air Force Stratofortresses end 45-hour round-world trip at average speed of 500 mph.

19. Cairo: Egypt, Saudi Arabia, Syria sign accord to replace British aid to Jordan (→ 3/13).

20. Polish election law modified to give people wider choice (→ 6/7).

25. Kashmir becomes Indian state.

26. Taiz: Isolated kingdom of Yemen beginning to open doors to outside world.

30. Washington: Saudi Arabian King Saud and son arrive for state visit (→ 2/8).

BIRTH

23. Princess Caroline of Monaco.

DEATH

10. Gabriela Mistral, Chilean poet (*4/7/1889).

French General takes action in Algiers

Jan 31. The commander of a parachute unit in Algeria, General Massu, has been given extraordinary powers by the French Governor General to restore peace to Algiers. Leaders of the separatist National Liberation Front protested the action and called a general strike, but to no avail. Massu's paratroopers, acting like policemen, landed in helicopters at the gates to the Casbah, shot lookouts and fanned out in the old quarter looking for terrorists. Governor Lacoste says he had no choice in the matter. Last Saturday, two bombs exploded in the center of Algiers, one at the Otomatic bar, the other at the Coq Hardi cafe. European witnesses were so outraged they lynched two innocent Moslems (→ 2/26).

Massu, Frenchman in a hostile land.

Suez Canal partly opened; clearing goes on

Oil tanker Statue of Liberty, one of 13 vessels freed by U.N. salvage efforts.

Jan 4. As U.N.-sponsored salvage crews clear wreckage left by the Suez Canal conflict, passage was opened today for medium shipping halfway down the waterway.

The main impediment was the Firdan railway bridge whose 164-foot east tower, a tangled web weighing over 350 tons, was nudged over to the west bank by two German tugs and their sister salvage vessels Ausdauer and Energie, the most powerful craft of their kind.

The next major obstacle is the 1,400-ton Egyptian LST Akka, lying on her side south of Ismailia in Lake Timsah and blocking passage to the southern half of the canal. The Akka is loaded with scrap iron and cement, which has hardened into a solid block. Efforts will begin tomorrow to move some 13 ships stranded in the Ismailia area north by tugboat out and through the obstructed Port Said harbor where one French and five British ships are working to clear 12 sunken craft blocking all but a slender channel between the canal and the open sea (→ 15).

Macmillan replaces Eden as Premier

Jan 10. Harold Macmillan, a leader of the right wing of the Conservative Party, was chosen today by Queen Elizabeth II as the new Prime Minister of Britain. Macmillan, the 62-year-old former Chancellor of the Exchequer, will succeed Anthony Eden, who resigned because of ill health. Sir Winston Churchill was reported to have interceded with the queen to select Macmillan over R.A. Butler, a spokesman for the moderate and liberal wings of the Conservative Party. One of Macmillan's first tasks will be to restore the traditionally close relationship with the United States that was severely strained by the Suez invasion.

Ike is inaugurated; will defend Mideast

Jan 21. President Eisenhower was sworn in for a second term today, just two weeks after he issued a clear warning to the Soviet Union and Egypt, and asked Congress to authorize him to use U.S. armed forces against Communist aggression in the Middle East.

Appearing before a joint session of Congress earlier this month, the president said he would use troops only if requested by those under attack, that he would keep in close contact with Congress and would act only in keeping with recommendations of the United Nations.

Ike's appeal was heard in troubled silence, indicating that Congress has reservations about possible involvement in the Mideast. But Congress is likely to accede (→ 2/8).

Pomp and splendor in Washington.

Israel to hold Gaza for the time being

Occupying Israeli troops interrogate Arab peasants in the Gaza Strip.

Jan 23. Reaffirming Israel's determination to hold the Gaza Strip "for the good of the inhabitants and their neighbors outside it," Israeli Premier David Ben Gurion today outlined the conditions for Israeli withdrawal from the Gaza area and Sharm el Sheikh. The latter controls the Strait of Tiran's entrance to the Gulf of Aqaba.

The U.N. has demanded a complete and unconditional Israeli withdrawal behind the 1949 armistice lines. While responding that the armistice agreement "has been violated and broken beyond repair," the premier noted that an absence of peace with Egypt was not the same thing as a state of war, and that Israel was prepared to sign with Egypt a pact of "non-belligerency and mutual nonaggression."

Israel's main condition for a withdrawal is that Egypt would not use these areas for hostile actions. Calling for assurances that the Strait of Tiran, and thus the Gulf, would never again be blockaded, Ben Gurion has asked for a treaty with those nations bordering it—Egypt, Saudi Arabia and Jordan. He also insisted on Israel's right to use the Suez Canal (→ 2/2).

Americans are taking to the air with such voracity that their facilities cannot keep up. LaGuardia, New York's busiest airport, though the last to modernize, will be equipped—at the cost of $30 mil.—to handle heavy turbine planes and an expected yearly traffic flow of 6.5 mil. by 1960.

Tough guy Bogart defeated by cancer

Jan 14. Actor Humphrey Bogart has died of throat cancer at age 57. He is survived by his wife, actress Lauren Bacall, and their two children. Bogie specialized in cons and gangsters, but in real life he was the prep school-educated son of a surgeon. After a stint in the Navy, where a lip wound gave him his distinctive lisp, Bogart got a few small stage roles. His breakthrough was playing a lowlife in Robert E. Sherwood's "The Petrified Forest" in 1934. Films followed, including "The Maltese Falcon," "High Sierra," "Casablanca" and "The Caine Mutiny." He won an Oscar for work in "The African Queen."

Bogey, model of cynical self-reliance.

Toscanini's baton put down forever

Jan 16. Arturo Toscanini died today in his Riverdale, New York, home three months short of 90. While the century's most celebrated conductor was of slight build, his uncompromising standards and incandescent purity earned him an immeasurable stature. If in his perfectionist quest he rode his musicians to the breaking point, he drove no one harder than himself. And if his reputed temper tantrums and enraged shouts of "Vergogna!" ("For shame!") made his musicians cringe, his evident integrity and wholehearted dedication also aroused feelings of devotion, affection and love. The result, as one player said, was that "he made us play better than we could."

1957

FEBRUARY

Su	Mo	Tu	We	Th	Fr	Sa
					1	2
3	4	5	6	7	8	9
10	11	12	13	14	15	16
17	18	19	20	21	22	23
24	25	26	27	28		

2. N.Y.: U.N. again calls on Israel to quit Egypt (→ 9).

4. Managua: Luis Somoza elected Nicaraguan president (→ 6/1/59).

5. Cambridge researchers report new cryotron device to revolutionize computers—so small, 100 fit in thimble (→ 8/1981).

6. Boston: Ted Williams now highest-paid player, signing $100,000 contract with Red Sox.

7. Moscow orders two U.S. diplomats expelled on spy charges.

8. U.S. promises military aid to Saudi Arabia in exchange for use of base at Dhahran airfield (→ 3/9).

9. Jerusalem: Thousands of Israelis protest U.N. demand for withdrawal from Gaza (→ 3/1).

12. New York: Communist Party votes to remain independent from Soviet control.

12. G.E. research labs report production of man-made material as hard as diamond.

14. Georgia Senate outlaws interracial athletics (→ 4/29).

16. U.S. flag flown for first time over outpost in Wilkes Land, Antarctica.

18. Washington: Grand jury indicts playwright Arthur Miller for contempt in HUAC inquiry (→ 5/2).

18. Tunisia: Premier Bourguiba asks evacuation of French troops (→ 7/25).

21. James Stewart stars as Lindbergh in premiere of "The Spirit of St. Louis."

24. Vatican: Pope Pius grants use of pain reliever if "advantage of higher worth" is gained.

25. Supreme Court places pro football under anti-trust laws.

26. U.S. Senate opens hearings on corruption in Teamsters union (→ 3/13).

DEATHS

9. Miklos von Horthy, first regent of independent Hungary (*6/18/1868).

10. Laura Ingalls Wilder, author "Little House on the Prairie" (*2/7/1867).

Gromyko takes job as Foreign Minister

Gromyko, party member since 1931.

Feb 15. Andrei Gromyko, who enjoyed great fame at the United Nations in the Stalin era, has replaced Dmitri T. Shepilov as Soviet Foreign Minister. The State Department says this means the position will be considerably less important politically, but other experts interpret the shake-up to mean the Soviet Union is headed toward a harder policy line both domestically and diplomatically. Shepilov, a former editor of Pravda, the Soviet Communist newspaper, has been reassigned to do party work as Secretary of the Soviet Communist Party's Central Committee (→ 5/7).

Castro is alive and well in mountains

Feb 23. Cuban rebel leader Fidel Castro is not only alive but is fighting President Fulgencio Batista's troops with tenacity and strength from a secret jungle outpost.

Last December, President Batista claimed his troops killed the charismatic revolutionary. But a New York Times correspondent has made exclusive contact with Castro and his men. According to reporter Herbert Matthews, Castro is waging a successful guerrilla war against the Batista regime and has generated much popular support among his countrymen. Castro's comrades are dedicated to ousting Batista. "I'd rather be here fighting for Fidel, than anywhere in the world," said one rebel (→ 7/27).

Humanite reports torture in Algeria

Feb 26. French authorities in Paris shut down L'Humanite after the Communist daily printed a shocking eyewitness account about torture by the French in Algeria. The article, "Christian Testimony," quoted from letters written by a man named Jean Muller before he died in combat in Algeria. "Ten officers, four subordinates and a unit of recruits do the torture," he wrote. "It is the only way to get information. At the Tablat camp, 150 prisoners are interrogated; electric current is applied to their ears, they are left outside in the sun in cages, they must sit naked on a pole, hands and feet tied . . . their hands are slammed in doors . . . it reminds you of Nazi barbarity" (→ 3/30).

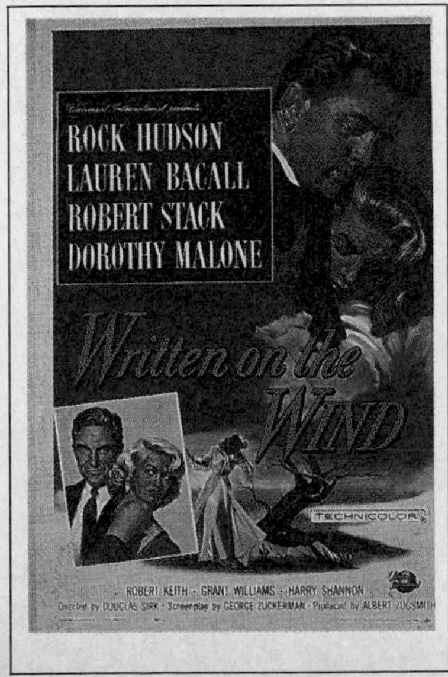

Bruce Dern insists on Elvis sideburns

Feb 8. Taking a stand against conformity, University of Pennsylvania track star Bruce Dern opted today to resign from the team rather than shave his Elvis Presley-style sideburns. "It doesn't make you a hoodlum just by wearing sideburns," said Dern, 20. The journalism and acting student may have gained some of his individualist spirit by playing the role of Caleb recently in a stage production of "East of Eden," which in a movie version starred another rebel, James Dean.

1957

MARCH

Su	Mo	Tu	We	Th	Fr	Sa
					1	2
3	4	5	6	7	8	9
10	11	12	13	14	15	16
17	18	19	20	21	22	23
24	25	26	27	28	29	30
31						

1. Israel agrees to prompt removal of troops from Gaza Strip (→ 7).

3. Accra: Nixon arrives to represent U.S. at birth of Ghana as independent nation (→ 6).

5. Britain adopts plan to triple nuclear energy production by 1965 (→ 4/11).

7. Egypt: Gaza Strip goes under U.N. administration (→ 3/30/58).

7. Dublin: Eamon de Valera swept back into power as prime minister (→ 1/8/59).

9. Cairo: Nasser bars U.N. plans to share tolls for use of Suez Canal (→ 4/10).

10. Saudi oil pipeline to Bahrein reopens.

13. U.S.: FBI arrests Teamsters V.P. Jimmy Hoffa on bribery charges (→ 29).

13. Anglo-Jordanian treaty of 1948 ends; British to withdraw in six months (→ 4/14).

18. Philippine Pres. Magsaysay found dead in plane crash on island of Cebu (→ 19).

19. Manila: Carlos Garcia takes oath as president (→ 6/15/60).

20. Bermuda: Ike and British Premier Macmillan meet to strengthen relations strained over Suez crisis.

21. Nixon returns to U.S after three-week tour of Africa (→ 24).

22. San Francisco hit by heaviest earthquakes since 1906.

24. CBS presents "The Black Star Rises," on Nixon's trip to Africa.

28. British release Cypriot Archbishop Makarios, but bar him from Cyprus (→ 6/15/58).

30. Paris: Rightists demonstrate in support of French army in North Africa (→ 4/5).

30. Rabat: Tunisia and Morocco sign friendship treaty.

31. Israel offers to negotiate with Arabs on refugees (→ 4/11).

DEATHS

11. Adm. Richard Byrd, U.S. explorer, first to fly over North and South Poles (*10/25/1888).

26. Edouard Herriot, French statesman (*7/5/1872).

Ike's Middle East policy takes effect

March 9. In signing a congressional resolution today, President Eisenhower passed into law his own Mideast doctrine. It permits the president to send U.S. armed forces to the aid of any Mideast nation desiring such help. It also allows him to spend $200 million in foreign aid for special military and economic projects in the area, and aims expressly at bolstering the ability of Mideast nations to defend themselves against Communist infiltration, subversion and overt aggression (→ 6/3).

Rumanian sculptor Brancusi deceased

March 16. Rumanian sculptor Constantin Brancusi is dead in Paris. He was 81. Brancusi worked in wood, marble and bronze, preserving natural characteristics of the material. By keeping shapes simple, his sculpture was simply beautiful. Brancusi studied throughout Europe before briefly meeting Auguste Rodin in 1906. On his own, he studied primitive art. Around 1912, he abandoned modeling for carving, making graceful human torsos and soaring birds.

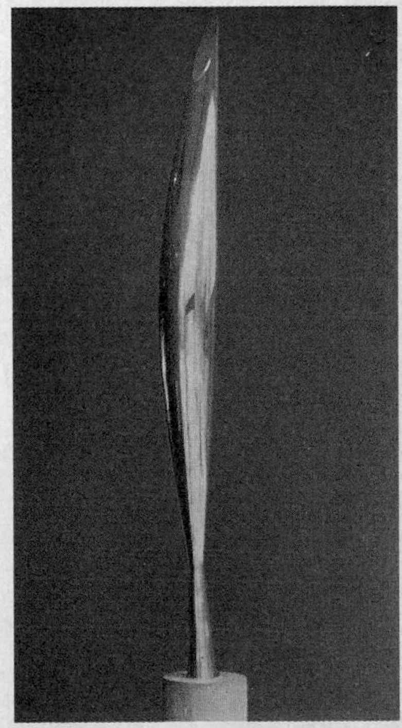

Brancusi's "Bird in Space."

European Common Market treaty signed in Rome

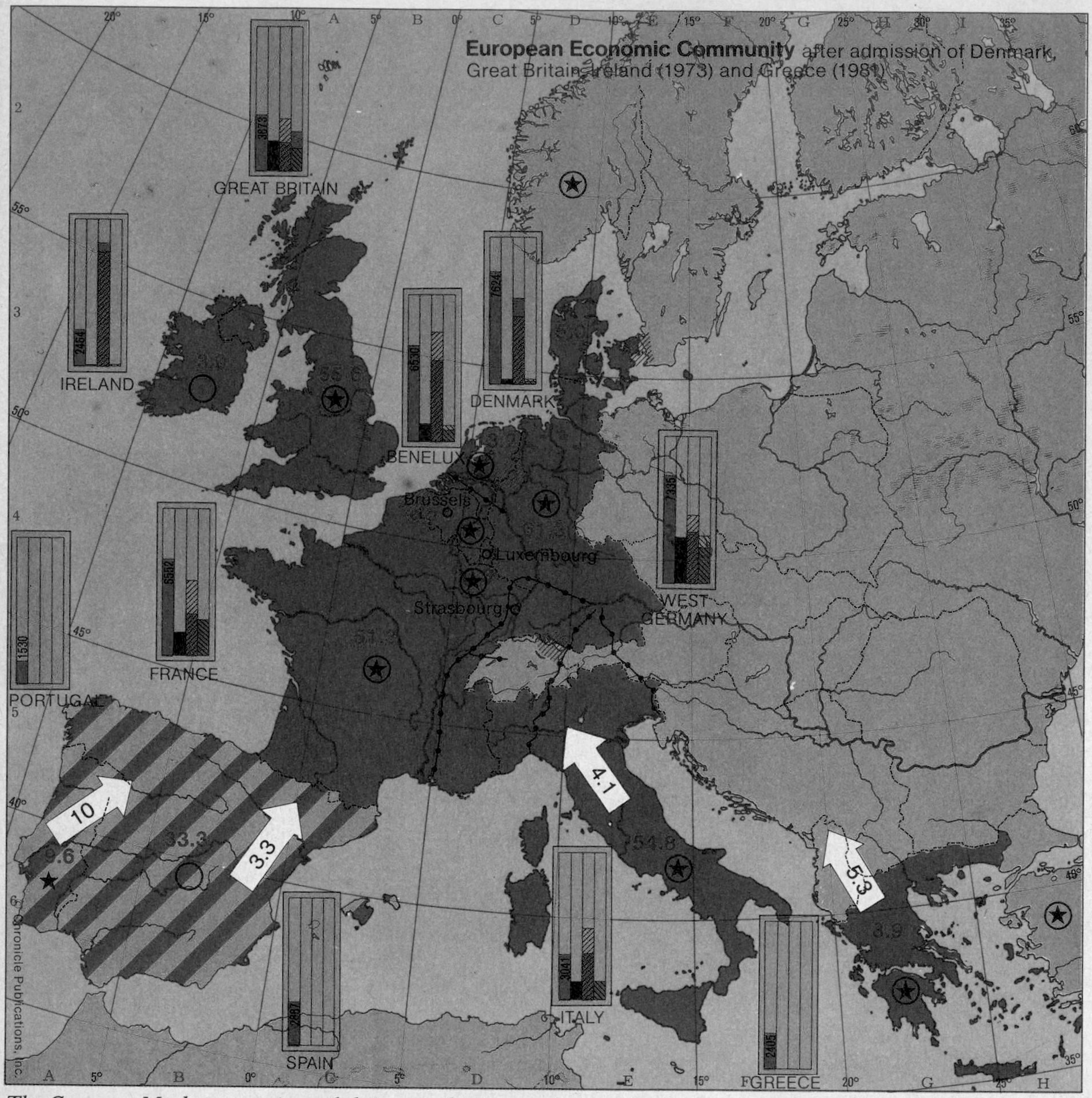

The Common Market countries and their contributions to the organization.

March 25. The countries of Western Europe took a major step in Rome today to merge into one unified economy. France, West Germany, Italy, Luxemburg, Belgium and the Netherlands signed a treaty establishing the European Economic Community. They signed a separate agreement setting up Euratom, an organization designed to develop peaceful uses for nuclear energy.

The goal of the economic agreement is to create a "common market" for all products and services, and coal in steel in particular. A new international agency, called the European Commission, will administer treaty provisions. Eventually, customs barriers among the member countries will be eliminated for most products. In the short term, they will adjust their individual import taxes so that they are all the same. Regulations on agricultural products are more complicated so that farm income will not be jeopardized. This was the most difficult part of the negotiations, and the countries agreed to many exceptions from the general rules.

The Treaty of Rome also establishes a new European Investment Bank which will assist underdeveloped countries with aid and credits.

The movement toward a European economic union has political roots that were planted after the First World War. After the Second War, a European council was established to distribute Marshall Plan funds. The new economic pact complements the military agreement finalized in NATO (→ 8/4/61).

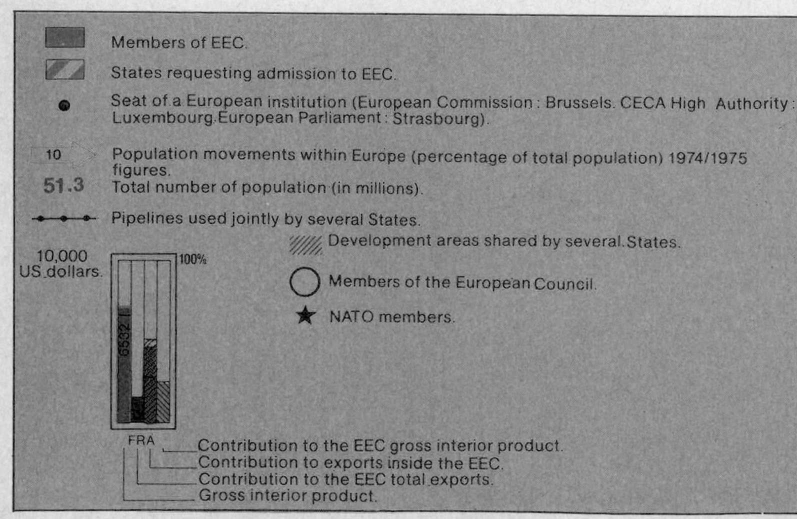

The European delegates make history in Rome at the signing of the treaty.

Ghana, formerly Gold Coast, independent

March 6. Ghana, the former British colony of the Gold Coast, achieved its independence today as a new nation in Africa. Prime Minister Kwame Nkrumah told the last session of the colony's legislative assembly that the "chains of imperialism and colonialism which hitherto have bound us to Britain" had been broken and Ghana, the name of an ancient African empire, had recovered "her lost freedom."

Representatives of more than 50 nations, including Vice President Nixon representing the United States, attended the independence celebrations that saw thousands of Ghanians marching through Accra. The independence was achieved without any significant violence after riots in 1948 (→ 7/1/60).

Nkrumah arrives at Parliament.

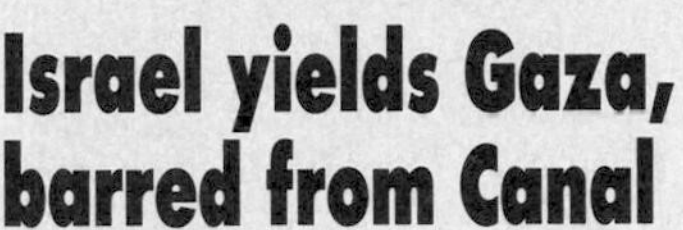

Israel yields Gaza, barred from Canal

March 5. President Nasser today decided to deny Israel the use of the Suez Canal, and Saudi Arabia declared the same regarding Israeli rights in the Gulf of Aqaba. These events followed by days Egypt's announced intention to retake the Gaza Strip, controlled by U.N. forces since Israel's recent withdrawal. Waiting until Gaza Arabs provoked a shooting incident, President Nasser demanded the immediate restoration of Egyptian rule, leaving the light U.N. force with no real choice in the matter (→ 7).

Hoffa indicted for trying to get files

March 29. James R. Hoffa, a Vice President of the Teamsters union, has been indicted by a federal grand jury for bribery, conspiracy and obstruction of justice in attempting to obtain information from the files of a Senate committee investigating improper activities in the labor and management fields. The 44-year-old labor leader, the likely heir to the union presidency now held by Dave Beck, faces up to 13 years in prison and a fine of up to $69,000 if he is later convicted on all three of the counts (→ 7/19).

False advertising comes under attack

March 31. The Federal Trade Commission has accused three makers of arthritis pain relief formula of false advertising. The companies' radio and TV. ads claim their products "penetrate below the skin," providing "deep relief." Consumers lobbied the FTC, protesting that the ointments did neither. The companies must respond to the complaints within 30 days. Other complaints arose over misstatements of prices and misrepresentation of sponsor's status. Some companies have misled viewers over qualities of competing products.

Smoking is shown to promote cancer

March 22. Cigarette smoking causes lung cancer, a committee of experts appointed by the American Heart Association, the American Cancer Society and the National Heart and Cancer Institutes reported today. Their report is the first to say that scientific evidence "establishes beyond reasonable doubt" that there is a direct cause-and-effect relationship between smoking and lung cancer. The seven-member panel said more research is needed on the nature of the link but the evidence justifies public health measures against smoking.

1957

APRIL

Su	Mo	Tu	We	Th	Fr	Sa
	1	2	3	4	5	6
7	8	9	10	11	12	13
14	15	16	17	18	19	20
21	22	23	24	25	26	27
28	29	30				

2. New York: Metropolitan Museum celebrates 152nd birthday of Hans Christian Andersen.

4. Cairo: Canadian Ambassador Herbert Norman, accused of Communist ties, kills self.

5. Soviets test another H-bomb to warn Western Europe against nuclear war (→ 12).

5. France establishes commission to monitor human rights abuses in Algeria (→ 5/26).

8. Budapest: Three leaders of uprising sentenced to death (→ 22).

9. Italian auto Fiat to enter American market.

10. Egypt: First passenger ship since fall transits canal (→ 19).

11. N.M.: Navy rocket Aerobee-Hi climbs 126 miles with satellite instruments (→ 5/2).

11. Saudi Arabia reports it will bar Israel from use of Gulf of Aqaba (→ 3/30/58).

12. Bonn: Leading German physicists drop all work connected with nuclear weapons (→ 22).

14. "Twelve Angry Men," with Henry Fonda, premieres in U.S.

14. Jordan: King Hussein, in military coup, ousts pro-Egyptian elements in govt. (→ 29).

19. Egypt: First British ship to pay Egyptian toll crosses Suez Canal (→ 5/22).

20. Plymouth, England: Mayflower II sails for Plymouth, Mass., in reenactment of original journey (→ 6/13).

22. Budapest: Govt. dissolves Writer's Association as instigators of last year's revolt (→ 1/27/58).

24. Olympic winners Harold Connolly and bride Olga Fikotova arrive in U.S. after Czech govt. approved emigration.

29. Ft. Belvoir, Virginia: Army Sec. Wilbur Brucker dedicates first U.S. nuclear power reactor (→ 7/29).

29. Washington: House passes weakened civil rights bill after internecine struggle (→ 6/13).

30. Washington: Five named to Senate Hall of Fame: Henry Clay, Daniel Webster, John Calhoun, Robert La Follette and Robert A. Taft.

Atomic missiles to guard U.S. cities

April 22. New York and other large American cities will soon be defended by new missiles with atomic warheads, the Army Air Defense Command reported yesterday. The new Nike Hercules missiles will be installed to replace existing Nike Ajax defense systems, which have conventional warheads.

A spokesman said the nuclear-tipped missiles in the New York system will be installed as far north as the Kensico Reservoir near White Plains and as far south as Monmouth County in New Jersey. There will be one installation in the city, at Fort Tilden in Queens.

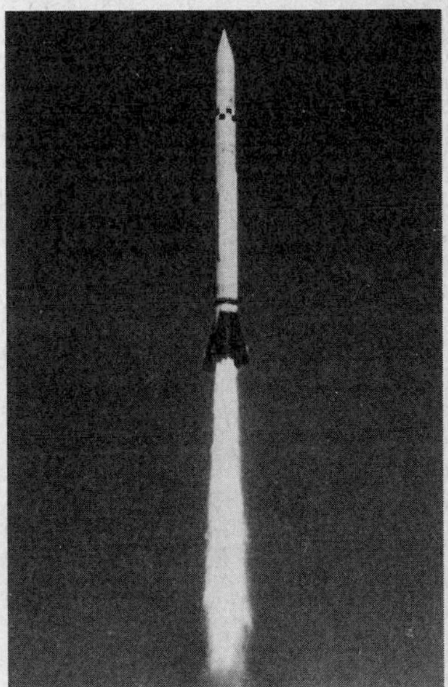

Test flight of a guided missile.

Other major industrial cities to be defended with the nuclear missiles include Bridgeport, Hartford, Providence, Boston and Buffalo. The storage of atomic warheads near the cities poses no danger, the spokesman said, and fallout from an air explosion if the missiles are used would be "negligible" (→ 5/16).

Hussein drives out pro-Egyptian elements

April 29. Having survived the shakiest month of his youthful rule, 21-year-old King Hussein today accepted $10 million in U.S. foreign aid to help him in his struggle to rid Jordan of Communists and other extremists and give his country a moderate government.

The king has also vowed to purge the conspiracy, reportedly run by Egypt, which earlier this month tried to topple him and impose a pro-Soviet revolutionary regime modeled after that of Egyptian President Nasser.

The crisis erupted when the king ousted Premier Suleiman Nabulsi, a moderate leftist who headed Jordan's powerful National Socialist Party. Pro-Egyptian elements in the Jordanian army answered with a coup, quickly put down by the loyal, British-trained Arab Legion. Nabulsi and a number of army officers were reportedly arrested.

The king's moves are as much pro-Iraqi as anti-Egyptian. Iraq, ruled by Hussein's cousin King Faisal, is allied with the West in the anti-Communist Baghdad Pact, anathema to Syria and Egypt. Determined to thwart their efforts to turn Jordan into an anti-Western satellite, the king seems to have emerged from this test as a mature, grim, implacable battler (→ 6/16).

Russia begins using largest accelerator

April 11. Soviet scientists today said they have moved into the forefront of physics research by placing into operation the world's most powerful particle accelerator. The new machine, the largest scientific instrument yet built, is capable of accelerating protons to an energy of ten million electron volts. It is in Dubna, one of the Soviet Union's new science cities. It uses magnets weighing 38,700 tons to whirl the protons around a circle with a radius of 100 feet, then smashes them into targets. By analyzing the particles produced in the collisions, physicists can learn more about the basic nature of matter and energy.

The Soviet Union's lead in particle accelerators is expected to be short-lived, since more powerful machines are planned for Geneva and Brookhaven, New York. The one at Geneva will have an energy of 28 million volts (→ 29).

Henry Fonda (right) plays a rebel juror seeking mercy in justice in the film "Twelve Angry Men."

Hundred flowers plan still blossoms

April 27. The leadership of Communist China, not to be outdone by destalinization in Russia, is urging critics of the regime to come forward and explain their disenchantment. The internal reform policy was launched a year ago by China's propaganda chief, who said the country could tolerate "100 flowers opening, 100 rival schools." The liberalization is Mao Tse-tung's response to labor strikes, student demonstrations and peasant protests. Party members have been stoned, and government ministers who are not Communists have complained their role is symbolic (→ 7/15).

Britain cuts back on defense resources

April 4. The sun is setting on the British Empire. In a major change in defense policy, the government has announced it will reduce its conventional forces and rely in the future upon a nuclear deterrent force of bombers and missiles. As part of the defense realignment, dictated as an economy measure, the strength of the armed forces will be reduced by half and troops will be withdrawn from British garrisons around the world. The traditional British force of battleships will also be scrapped, to be replaced by aircraft carriers and an airborne strategic reserve based in Britain.

1957

MAY

Su	Mo	Tu	We	Th	Fr	Sa
			1	2	3	4
5	6	7	8	9	10	11
12	13	14	15	16	17	18
19	20	21	22	23	24	25
26	27	28	29	30	31	

2. Bonn: Dulles tells NATO U.S. will keep military force in Western Europe (→ 3/7/59).

2. U.S.: Two stages of rocket for satellite launch tested (→ 6/1).

2. Sugar Ray Robinson regains middleweight title fourth time, defeating Gene Fullmer.

3. N.Y.: O'Neill's "A Moon for the Misbegotten" opens.

4. Alan Freed hosts "Rock 'n' Roll Show," first prime-time network special on rock music.

4. Iron Liege wins Kentucky Derby with jockey W. Hartack in the saddle.

6. Pulitzer to O'Neill for "Long Day's Journey into Night," JFK for "Profiles in Courage."

7. Moscow: Khrushchev, in move to decentralize, divides industry into 92 regions (→ 7/3).

11. Washington: Ike and South Vietnamese Pres. Ngo Dinh Diem meet, pledge resistance to communism (→ 10/22).

15. New York: Billy Graham opens evangelist crusade at Madison Sq. Garden (→ 7/20).

16. Groton: Skate, third U.S. atomic sub, launched (→ 16).

16. Tokyo: Japanese protest at British Embassy against nuclear tests (→ 6/14).

19. CBS airs documentary on Cuban revolution with Castro interview.

20. Dave Beck expelled from AFL-CIO for fund misuse.

21. Spirit of St. Louis II flies Atlantic in 6.7 hrs., marking Lindbergh flight's 30th anniversary.

22. Egypt: Destroyer McGowan is first U.S. ship to use canal since reopening (→ 4/29/58).

24. Taipei: Riots protesting release of accused American killer quelled by Chinese tanks.

26. France: Algerian V.P. killed by Algerian nationalist during soccer game (→ 7/2).

28. Chicago: Brookyn Dodgers and N.Y. Giants get permission to move to L.A., San Francisco.

29. Kirk Douglas appears in "Gunfight at the OK Corral."

30. Sam Hanks wins Indy 500 at 135.6 mph in Belond Special.

All-American boy Pat Boone is a hit

Boone (center), picture of purity.

May 31. Just as the fever-pitched rock-and-roll craze seemed to have put many parents in a state of panic, along comes clean-cut Pat Boone, with his polished manners, gleaming smile and white buckskin shoes.

The 22-year-old singer, who is a straight-A Ivy League student and father of two, has three million-selling records: "I'll Be Home," "I Almost Lost My Mind" and "Ain't That a Shame."

Though much of his music jumps with a rock-and-roll dance beat, Boone, a descendant of frontiersman Daniel Boone, shuns the pelvic shakes of recording-rival Elvis Presley. He instead stands still and croons in an even-toned Nashville-flavored tenor. Some teenagers complain the star has forsaken the rebellious energy that draws them to rock and roll, but a huge new audience seems to favor his more wholesome approach.

Says Churchill of Graham Sutherland's portrait, "It makes me look half-witted." And Lady Churchill's burning of it, says the artist, is "an act of vandalism unequalled in the history of art."

McCarthy dead after short, sharp career

May 2. Controversial, pugnacious, a true patriot, a madman—Senator Joseph McCarthy, the man who was called all of these during his brief but active career, has died at the age of 48. As leader of the Senate anti-Communist investigations, the Wisconsin Republican gained a reputation for rooting out Communists in America, often at the expense of ruining the lives of innocent victims. It was in Wheeling, West Virginia, in 1950 when he began his flamboyant hunt for Reds, with the famous claim: "I have here in my hand a list of 205 that are known . . . as being members of the Communist Party."

While stirring the passions of many Americans with his queries for four years, McCarthy finally became too reckless for all but his most loyal supporters. Eventually, acting on a motion of censure, the Senate voted 67-22 to "condemn" him. Nevertheless, the Senate will hold rites for him Monday (→ 6/17).

Army takes control as Haitians strike

May 25. The sparks of civil war have ignited in Haiti with throngs of angry islanders looting and burning buildings in the streets of Port-au-Prince. The riots have forced Haitian leader General Leon Cantave to call in the army to halt the violence. The troops resorted to firing rifle shots at the crowds to get them to disperse. Casualty figures have not been released.

An attempted coup by Cantave foe Lieutenant Pierre Armand was also stopped by the army. Since December, when a general strike forced the deposition of President Paul Magliore for trying to extend his term, the Haitian people have seen ten presidential candidates vying for power. Two of the candidates were overthrown because they were accused of trying to rig the June elections. Cantave took control after he ousted the Haitian Executive Council, saying he wanted to save the country from anarchy and destruction. It's not certain how long the disgruntled masses will remain calm (→ 9/23).

1957

JUNE

Su	Mo	Tu	We	Th	Fr	Sa
						1
2	3	4	5	6	7	8
9	10	11	12	13	14	15
16	17	18	19	20	21	22
23	24	25	26	27	28	29
30						

1. Soviets announce they are ready to launch first satellite (→ 11).

2. U.S. Khrushchev, on TV, says U.S.S.R. ready to seek disarmament (→ 1/6/58).

3. U.S. enters Baghdad Pact to fight communism in Iraq, Iran, Pakistan, Turkey (→ 1/21/58).

5. U.S.: American Medical Assn. votes to study use of stimulants in athletics.

7. U.S. agrees to give Poland $48.9 mil. in surplus farm equipment (→ 30).

13. Washington: Nixon meets with Martin Luther King to discuss racial problems (→ 8/2).

13. Plymouth, Mass.: Mayflower II reaches harbor in 54 days from England.

14. Paris: Gauguin's "Still Life with Apples" sells for $255,000, highest paid for modern art.

14. Soviets agree to Western plan for atomic test ban (→ 7/7).

16. Jordan closes embassy in Cairo (→ 8/7).

17. Supreme Court frees five California Communists jailed under Smith Act (→ 6/16/58).

26. Soviet scientists say they will send first radio-guided rocket to moon in early 1960's (→ 10/4).

27. Mideast: Great Mecca pilgrimage Dhu al Hijjah begins with appearance of new moon.

28. Dulles reiterates U.S. refusal to recognize Red China, insists govt. is temporary (→ 8/3/58).

28. Lake Charles, Louisiana: Hurricane smashes Gulf of Mexico, killing 500.

30. Japan: American occupation headquarters dissolved (→ 12/6/58).

30. Tito, on U.S. TV, asserts he backs Mao's new line.

30. Warsaw pledges to restore free market in crops for peasants (→ 10/3/57).

DEATHS

12. Jimmy Dorsey, American jazz clarinetist (*2/29/1904).

24. Frantisek Kupka, Czech painter credited with first totally abstract work (*9/23/1871).

Atlas 5,000-mile missile explodes in test

June 11. The first test of an Atlas intercontinental missile ended in failure today when it exploded shortly after takeoff from the Air Force test center at Cape Canaveral, Florida. Thousands of spectators watching from nearby beaches saw the explosion. Onlookers said the missile began wobbling off course moments after liftoff, flopped over at 5,000 feet and then plunged into the sea. The Atlas was to have gone 5,000 miles in the test. Today's crash was the fifth failure in a recent series of missile tests. The Air Force said there were no casualties and the tests will continue (→ 26).

Atlas before takeoff at Canaveral.

After 22 years rightists will rule Canada

Diefenbaker to rule in Ottawa.

June 17. For the first time in 22 years, a Conservative Party leader, John Diefenbaker, was invited tonight to become Prime Minister of Canada. Bowing to the will of the people, as expressed in last Monday's election, Prime Minister Louis St. Laurent, 75-year-old "grand old man" of Canadian politics and leader of the Liberal Party, resigned, an action not legally demanded since neither party had a majority. But the majority of the Cabinet deemed it unwise to remain in power with nine of their members defeated in the election.

Diefenbaker's party holds 109, the biggest single bloc, of the 265 seats in the House of Commons. Neither party can rule without support from the minority parties —the right-wing Social Credit and the moderately left-wing Cooperative Commonwealth Federation. St. Laurent said the Liberals will not attempt "any obstruction" to the new government's program, though their views will be expressed fully (→ 6/18/62).

Court won't protect obscene matter

June 24. Obscenity is not protected by the constitutional guarantee of free speech, according to a decision by the Supreme Court today. The ruling upholds a federal law prohibiting the sale of obscene literature. The court stated that sex per se differs from indecency in that the latter encourages "overt antisocial conduct." Justices William O. Douglas and Hugo Black dissented, insisting an injunction against the sale of books without prior hearing was "censorship at its worst."

1957

JULY

Su	Mo	Tu	We	Th	Fr	Sa
	1	2	3	4	5	6
7	8	9	10	11	12	13
14	15	16	17	18	19	20
21	22	23	24	25	26	27
28	29	30	31			

2. Iran: Earthquakes rock Caspian Sea, killing nearly 2,000 in coastal towns.

6. Wimbledon: Lew Hoad over Ashley Cooper 6-2, 6-1, 6-2; Althea Gibson over Darlene Hard 6-3, 6-2 (→ 11).

7. New York: Army Redstone ballistic missile displayed in Grand Central Station (→ 16).

10. Ft. Worth, Tex.: Supersonic B-58 bomber tested successfully.

13. Geneva: From white satin throne, Aga Khan IV, grandson of late Aga Khan III, proclaims start of reign as Moslem leader.

15. China: Mao Tse-tung denounces campaign of the "100 flowers" (→ 2/11/58).

15. Khrushchev pledges boost in Soviet living standard: "Marxism-Leninism will taste better with butter" (→ 8/31).

16. Sec. of Def. Wilson orders reduction in U.S. military force by 100,000 troops (→ 8/21).

17. Sultan Said of Muscat and Oman calls for British help in quelling civil war (→ 24).

19. Washington: Jimmy Hoffa acquitted on bribery charges (→ 10/4).

20. Tour de France won by Jacques Anquetil.

24. Persian Gulf: RAF jets raid rebel fort to put down uprising against sultan of Muscat, Oman.

25. Tunisia: Bourguiba ousts bey of Tunis, proclaims republic with self as president (→ 8/13).

27. Guatemala: U.S.-installed Pres. Carlos Castilla Armas assassinated by palace sentry (→ 11/13/60).

27. Cuba: Castro raids army post with force of 200 rebels (→ 8/2).

29. Washington: IAEC created to advance peaceful development of atomic energy (→ 8/17).

29. New York: Floyd Patterson retains heavyweight title, beating Tommy Jackson in ten.

30. Great Britain grants autonomy to Nigeria.

DEATH

11. Aga Khan III, Moslem spiritual leader (*11/1/1880).

Khrushchev foils coup

Khrushchev, consolidating power.

July 3. Nikita S. Khrushchev, the Soviet leader, has foiled a plot to remove him. And instead, he has removed those who were plotting against him.

Recently, in his absence, a special meeting of the Presidium of the Soviet Communist Party's Central Committee was convened. He was voted out of office 8 to 4. When he was informed, he protested that he could legally be removed only by a vote of the full Central Committee. With the help of Marshal Georgi K. Zhukov, the Defense Minister, who had fleets of aircraft at his disposal, he rounded up the committee. It met from June 22 through 29.

It decided to remove Vyacheslav Molotov, Georgi Malenkov and Lazar Kaganovich, all Stalinists, from the Presidium and Central Committee, and to discipline their ally, Dmitri P. Shepilov. Essentially, they were all accused of wanting to restore Stalinism, which Khrushchev denounced in a speech last year (→ 15).

Kennedy urges America to aid Algerians

July 2. Senator John F. Kennedy urged the administration today to cease its support of what he called France's colonial repression in Algeria. The United States, he said, should begin working for Algerian independence instead of backing the French war in that country.

In a speech on the Senate floor, the Massachusetts Democrat criticized what he called the administration's "head-in-the-sand' attitude on the Algerian question. The senator is Chairman of a Senate subcommittee on United Nations affairs. The Kennedy speech was greeted coolly by Secretary of State John Foster Dulles, who said that the conflict in Algeria is primarily a French problem (→ 11/22).

July 12. If New York is hit by a nuclear attack, civil defense officials say 2,339,012 will perish. In the nation's 4th such drill, Ike holed up in a mountain while students hid from H-bombs under their desks (→ 8/21).

Parade staged for Harlem tennis star

Gibson is greeted on Broadway.

July 11. Althea Gibson, a Negro woman who learned to play tennis in the asphalt jungle of New York and went on to win Wimbledon, was saluted joyfully in her hometown.

Thousands cheered as she drove up Broadway in an open car to receive a City Hall welcome from Mayor Wagner. Ticker tape swirled from the office buildings.

Mayor Wagner described the tall Harlemite as "an humble New York girl who learned the game here."

"If we had more women like you," he told her, "the world would be a better place."

Miss Gibson, who defeated Darlene Hard by 6-3, 6-2 in the Wimbledon final last week, responded that this was her finest hour. "This victory was won through the help of all your encouragement and all you well-wishers," she said. "With God's help," she went on, "I hope to wear this crown that I have attained with honor and dignity." She also won the national singles title.

Fred Astaire brings out the fun-loving soul of Cyd Charisse in the new MGM hit "Silk Stockings."

100,000 crowd stadium for Billy Graham

July 20. The largest crowd in Yankee Stadium's history, 100,000 people, jammed the place last night to hear the Rev. Dr. Billy Graham call sinners to repentance. The earlier record was set in 1935 when 88,150 watched the Joe Louis-Max Baer heavyweight fight. Among the 300 persons on the platform was Vice President Richard M. Nixon, introduced as "one of the hardest working men in the U.S."

The rally was to be the evangelist's farewell to New York, but his campaign was extended three more weeks. He reviewed the ills of the world, declaring that "Christ is the only answer." From opening night on May 15 through projected closing on August 10, the crusade will cost about $2.14 million, including TV time. As of Friday, the campaign recorded 35,228 "decisions for Christ" plus an unknown number "saved" by watching TV at home (→ 9/1).

Billy Graham calls for repentance.

Television is having its toughest season

July 24. Television may face its first unprofitable season in its ten-year history. Inflation and the escalating costs of producing programs are blamed for the lack of air-time buyers this summer. All three networks stand to lose millions of dollars if their remaining time slots are not purchased before September.

ABC, CBS and NBC have an average of three hours of unsold weekly prime time. The hours would normally bring in $3.5 million to $5 million. Network executives blame the industry slump on outside trends, noting that the auto industry and firms producing major appliances are also doing poorly.

Next season's shows will shun big budgets and cling to tried and true formulas. Westerns and situation comedies will predominate. Few insiders have suggested that the business slump may be traced to boring programs, although few of the shows introduced last season are expected back this fall.

In San Francisco tonight, the American Federation of Television and Radio Artists meets to discuss yet another threat to profitability: pay TV. The federation fears if pay TV ever manifests itself, it will command bigger budgets and audiences. As one member said, viewers would have a choice: "good things on pay television and mediocre products on free television" (→ 2/7/58).

"Father Knows Best" (Wednesdays at 8:30 p.m.) has reached great popularity after a slow start in 1954.

Andy Williams joins Dale Evans and Roy Rogers, guarding the good guys from villains and varmints on one of the kids' favorite television shows.

1957

AUGUST

Su	Mo	Tu	We	Th	Fr	Sa
				1	2	3
4	5	6	7	8	9	10
11	12	13	14	15	16	17
18	19	20	21	22	23	24
25	26	27	28	29	30	31

2. Ike tells Senate he prefers no civil rights bill to one weakened by Senate amendments (→ 7).

3. Belgrade: Tito and Khrushchev meet, pledge closer ties (→ 9/7).

3. Malaya: Sir Abdul Rahman elected first head of state of independent nation (→ 31).

5. San Juan, Puerto Rico: Cellist Pablo Casals, 80, weds 20-year-old student Marta Montanez.

7. U.S. Senate approves weakened Civil Rights Bill 72-18 (→ 16).

7. Moscow: Syrian delegation arrives to establish close ties to Soviet Union (→ 13).

11. Moroccan Sultan Mohammed V becomes king, abandoning traditional title (→ 11/25).

11. Quebec: Chartered plane carrying Canadian vets home from Britain crashes, killing 79.

13. Syria asks eviction of three U.S. Embassy officials for plotting overthrow of govt. (→ 9/9).

13. Tunisia: Pres. Bourguiba refuses to ban arms smuggling to Algerian rebels (→ 11/15).

16. Levittown: First Negro family moves into white suburb under police guard (→ 29).

17. Geneva: First European particle accelerator (600 billion volts) opens (→ 1/24/58).

21. Ike signs Niagara power bill, authorizing construction of hydroelectric dam on river.

21. Ike offers to suspend nuclear bomb tests for two years (→ 26).

23. U.S.: Tyrone Power appears in "The Sun Also Rises."

23. Hoffa gets 48-point indictment from U.S. Senate (→ 10/4).

26. Detroit: Ford reveals the Edsel, latest model.

27. Wisconsin: Democrat William Proxmire chosen for U.S. Senate in special election.

28. David Beck, ex-head of AFL-CIO, charged with tax evasion.

29. N.Y.: Doris Day, John Raitt open in "The Pajama Game."

31. Moscow: Molotov, purged as foreign minister, named envoy to Outer Mongolia (→ 11/3).

Soviet spymaster is caught in Brooklyn

Aug 7. A federal grand jury has indicted the most important Soviet espionage figure ever caught in America. A seemingly harmless, unobtrusive man, Rudolf Ivanovich Abel is charged on three counts of divulging U.S. defense secrets from his small Brooklyn apartment to an intelligence center in Moscow.

Abel entered the country illegally in 1948 and operated his spy network for nine years across from the federal court where today he was indicted. Police believed they were only dealing with a violator of immigration laws until a search uncovered radio and photographic equipment in Abel's home. If convicted, the spymaster could receive the death sentence (→ 2/10/62).

Exasperated Oliver, Stan's pal, is dead

Ollie and Stan, bedfellows no more.

Aug 7. Oliver Hardy, rotund partner of Stan Laurel, died this morning of complications following a stroke. Laurel, who has also suffered a stroke, was very moved at his passing, saying Hardy was "like a brother." Laurel and Hardy made successful silent and sound-filled comedies in the 20's and 30's. The public rediscovered them when their films came to television.

Hardy was born in Georgia in 1892. A brief attempt at law school was following by a singing stint on a showboat. He appeared in film shorts throughout the early 1920's, playing alternately villains and second bananas. In 1927, Hal Roach paired Hardy with Stan Laurel in a short called "Duck Soup." The rest is hilarious history (→ 2/23/65). ▷

Youth crime growing problem world over

Eight members of a Boston gang are lined up for assaulting a police officer.

Aug 14. The problem of juvenile delinquency has reached epidemic proportions throughout the world. Experts have traced the crisis to the worldwide breakdown of order that followed in the wake of World War II, and point out that the juvenile delinquent most often lacks a suitable home environment.

In New York, persons under 21 comprise 50 percent of those arrested for robbery and 60 percent of those arrested for burglary. In Chicago, crimes committed by youths are becoming more serious in nature. In Los Angeles, 20 percent of all crimes are committed by persons under 18 years of age. In London, gangs of "teddy boys" roam the streets while San Francisco, Rome and Melbourne report no gangs. Youth's favorite crime is auto theft.

Social workers cite a decline in corporal punishment, distorted ideas of freedom, and materialism as causes of the spreading malaise.

Malaya independent, elects first ruler

Aug 31. Malaya is free. The last of Britain's major Asian colonies won its independence today and will join the Commonwealth. The nation will be led by Sir Abdul Rahman, who was elected to serve a five-year term earlier this month in anticipation of the emancipation. His first task will be to quell the country's Communist rebellion. He said he hoped the "men of the jungle" would stop their fight (→ 9/5).

Aug 26. After three years and $250 million worth of research, Ford presents the long, low dimensions of the Edsel. Prices have not come out yet, but the Ranger, the Pacer, the Citation and the Corsair (above) should run between $2,400 and $3,800. Will the Edsel, with a V-8 under its hood, bring Ford's line up to a par with G.M. and Chrysler? (→ 11/19/59).

Soviet Union tests long-range missile

Aug 26. The Soviet Union has announced that it successfully tested an intercontinental ballistic missile. The announcement said the missile "covered a huge distance in a brief time" and "landed in the target area." United States military officials refused official comment on the Soviet statement, but said unofficially that the successful test added urgency to the American effort to develop ballistic missiles. The only American test thus far ended in failure on June 11. The Soviets have recently tested atomic and hydrogen bombs that presumably could be carried by their new intercontinental missiles (→ 9/6).

New act to protect Negro voting rights

Aug 29. The first major civil rights bill since the Reconstruction Era cleared the Senate today and was sent to the White House for the President's signature. Final approval of the voting rights measure came as Senator Strom Thurmond, the right-wing South Carolina Democrat, abandoned his record-setting filibuster in which he had held the floor for more than 24 hours. Final approval of the measure was a major victory for Senator Lyndon B. Johnson of Texas, Democratic leader. The bill, designed to assure voting rights for Negroes and other minorities, creates a Civil Rights Commission (→ 9/2).

Civil rights are lost as Cuba is besieged

Aug 2. President Fulgencio Batista has suspended all constitutional guarantees throughout Cuba for 45 days in response to outbreaks of anti-government violence. Press censorship begins immediately. Rebel forces led by Fidel Castro attacked two Cuban military posts, Bueycito and Minas. A general strike is in progress in Santiago de Cuba, the center of the movement against Batista, to protest the killing of two members of Castro's 26th of July Movement (→ 9/5).

1957

SEPTEMBER

Su	Mo	Tu	We	Th	Fr	Sa
1	2	3	4	5	6	7
8	9	10	11	12	13	14
15	16	17	18	19	20	21
22	23	24	25	26	27	28
29	30					

1. New York: 200,000 pack Broadway in farewell rally for Rev. Billy Graham.

2. Little Rock, Ark.: Gov. Orval Faubus calls state police as school integration begins (→ 4).

4. Little Rock: Militia bars nine Negroes from white high school on governor's orders (→ 7).

5. Cuban soldiers join Castro rebels in fighting south of Havana (→ 13).

5. N.Y.: Federation of Malaya approved for U.N. membership.

6. London: Disarmament talks end in failure (→ 19).

7. Ike sees Atty. Gen. Brownell concerning integration crisis in Little Rock (→ 9).

7. Yugoslavia: One of first U.S.-type supermarkets in Eastern bloc opens at Zagreb.

9. Birmingham: Negro minister beaten trying to enter daughter and others in school (→ 10).

9. Jordan: U.S. planes land to block Syrians (→ 2/1/58).

10. Nashville: Bomb rips school that admitted Negroes (→ 14).

14. Providence, R.I.: Arkansas Gov. Faubus meets with Ike on school integration (→ 23).

15. Bonn: Adenauer wins election by landslide (→ 4/25/58).

17. Bangkok: Thai army seizes power in coup.

19. Nevada: First underground nuclear test set off (→ 10/22).

23. Little Rock: Mobs force nine Negroes out of school (→ 24).

23. U.S.: Carmen Basilio beats Sugar Ray Robinson to take world middleweight title.

23. Haiti: Francois Duvalier elected president (→ 7/31/58).

24. Little Rock: Ike sends troops and federalizes Arkansas National Guard (→ 25).

26. U.S.: Joanne Woodward appears in "Three Faces of Eve."

29. N.Y.: Fans chase Giants to clubhouse, steal souvenirs on last game before move to Calif.

DEATH

21. King Haakon VII of Norway (*8/3/1872).

Troops sent to Little Rock schools

Sept 25. Arkansas Governor Orval Faubus, staunch opponent of racial integration, defied federal law earlier this month when he ordered state militia troops to Little Rock to stop Negro students from entering a white high school. The action has triggered racial violence and forced a showdown with federal officials.

Faubus sent the Arkansas National Guard to Little Rock's Central High School on September 2 to prevent violence and bloodshed, he claimed. The following day, the troops barred nine Negro students from entering the school, while an angry mob of 400 whites yelled, "Go home niggers!" As Faubus declared that the situation was growing "more explosive by the hour," Mayor Woodrow Mann of Little Rock denounced the governor's "interference." Mann said the governor called on troops to "put down trouble where none existed." He added resentfully, "If any racial trouble does develop the blame rests squarely on the doorstep of the governor's mansion."

Trouble did develop, both for Little Rock and the governor. First, a federal district court directed Faubus to comply with integration plans, and after meeting with President Eisenhower, the governor reluctantly agreed to observe "the supreme law of the land." Yet, not until Eisenhower angrily threatened to use "whatever force was necessary" to enforce the law, were Negroes able to attend the school.

Federal troops, armed for another civil war, escort nine Negroes into school.

Despite the court order, and an irate president, violent white agitators continued to gather outside Central High School. Today, federal troops, on orders from Washington, converged on Little Rock, determined to enforce the directive to integrate. With bayonets pointed to deter opposition, they saw to it that Negroes were admitted into the school building; not without incident, however. About 1,500 whites descended on the school. At least seven were arrested and one man was struck down, after trying to wrestle away a soldier's rifle.

After initially berating Eisenhower for having "no guts," jazz great Louis Armstrong praised Ike's show of force in Little Rock. Meanwhile, Governor Faubus intends to appeal the federal intervention in Arkansas (→ 1/18/58).

Sonorous Sibelius, music master, dead

Sept 20. Composer Jean Sibelius has died of a cerebral hemorrhage. The Finn was revered for his majestic Fifth and Seventh Symphonies and stirring anthem "Finlandia." His last birthday, his 92nd, was marked by dedicatory concerts in Helsinki, New York and London.

Sibelius was born to an upperclass family. Despite their wishes, he abandoned law school for music training in Vienna. Critics found his early works somber or unfeeling. The Fourth Symphony, finished in 1911, was ridiculed as discordant. By the mid 1940's, however, his genius was unquestioned.

Sibelius, the pride of Finland.

Levittown, suburbia for the masses, is thriving after ten years

Levittown, Long Island, from the air: A masterwork of suburban planning.

After ten years of existence, Levittown, Long Island, has not become a slum nor have its inhabitants become assimilated clones. These two trends had been predicted by sociologists when 300 families moved into identical, four-room Cape Cod houses a decade ago. The purpose of the development was to meet the severe housing shortage which followed World War II; ex-servicemen and their families moved into the dwellings.

Levittown is now a thriving community of 7.3 square miles, comprising 21,000 homes and a population of 81,000, making it the largest town in Nassau County, New York. And much to the surprise of the experts, Levittown has fostered a populace that strives to be different from the guy next door, not to mention an increase in property values.

Batista will not ask for re-election

Sept 13. Cuban President Fulgencio Batista will not be a candidate in next June's elections. He announced his decision in an interview with the National Broadcasting Company taped several weeks ago but just shown in the United States. Tomorrow, Batista will sign a decree renewing the suspension of constitutional rights and censorship of the press for another 45 days, the fifth such suspension in Cuba since last December 2.

The September 5 uprising at Cienfuegos probably influenced the president's decision not to run for re-election. In the NBC interview, Batista admitted some of his own military units had taken part in the revolt led by Fidel Castro and ex-President Prio (→ 1/14/58).

1957

OCTOBER

Su	Mo	Tu	We	Th	Fr	Sa
		1	2	3	4	5
6	7	8	9	10	11	12
13	14	15	16	17	18	19
20	21	22	23	24	25	26
27	28	29	30	31		

3. Warsaw: Poles demonstrate against ban on student newspaper "Po Prostu" (→ 4/14/58).

4. Miami Beach: Hoffa elected president of Intl. Brotherhood of Teamsters (→ 24).

7. Khrushchev says Soviets willing to bring earth satellite and all pilotless missiles under intl. control in pact with U.S. (→ 11).

10. Milwaukee Braves beat Yankees to take World Series.

10. Ike apologizes to Ghana finance minister for Delaware restaurant's refusal to serve him (→ 1/18/58).

11. N.Y.: 22 nations back U.S. plan to limit outer-space to peaceful purposes only (→ 15).

12. Canada: Queen Elizabeth II arrives to open Parliament (→ 17).

13. Syria: Egyptian troops land to block possible Israeli-Turkish attack (→ 21).

15. U.S. fails in three attempts to fire rocket 4,000 miles into space for altitude mark (→ 11/3).

15. American Bible Society presents Ike with 500,000,001st Bible.

16. Virginia: Queen Elizabeth in Williamsburg for festival of first British settlement (→ 17).

18. Bonn breaks relations with Yugoslavia for recognizing East Germany on 15th (→ 11/27/58).

21. Turkey accepts Saudi Arabian mediation in Turkish-Syrian dispute (→ 11/11).

22. U.S.: Intermediate-range ballistic missile Jupiter tested successfully (→ 11/15).

22. Saigon: 13 U.S. servicemen, five civilians injured by unclaimed bomb (→ 7/9/59).

25. New York: Umberto Anastasia, master killer for Murder, Inc., gunned down by two men.

26. Moscow: Marshal Georgi Zhukov relieved as defense minister for promoting "cult of personality" (→ 11/3).

DEATHS

25. Henry van der Velde, Belgian architect (*4/3/1863).

29. Louis B. Mayer, American film producer (*7/4/1885).

Sputnik launching surprises the world

Oct 4. The Soviet Union has announced that it has successfully launched the world's first man-made satellite into orbit around the earth. Officials in the United States said they were astonished not only by the Soviet first but also by the size of the satellite, whose weight was given as 184 pounds—eight times heavier than the satellite the U.S. plans to launch early next year.

The Soviet announcement said the satellite, a sphere 22 inches in diameter, was orbiting the earth once every hour and 35 minutes at a maximum altitude of 560 miles and was broadcasting continuous signals on two frequencies. Receiving stations in the United States and Europe confirmed that they had picked up the signals. The orbit is at a 65 degree angle to the equator, which brings it over Moscow twice a day. The Soviets gave no details of the rocket that launched the satellite but said it had left the ground at a speed of five miles per second; they said the launch opened the way to interplanetary travel.

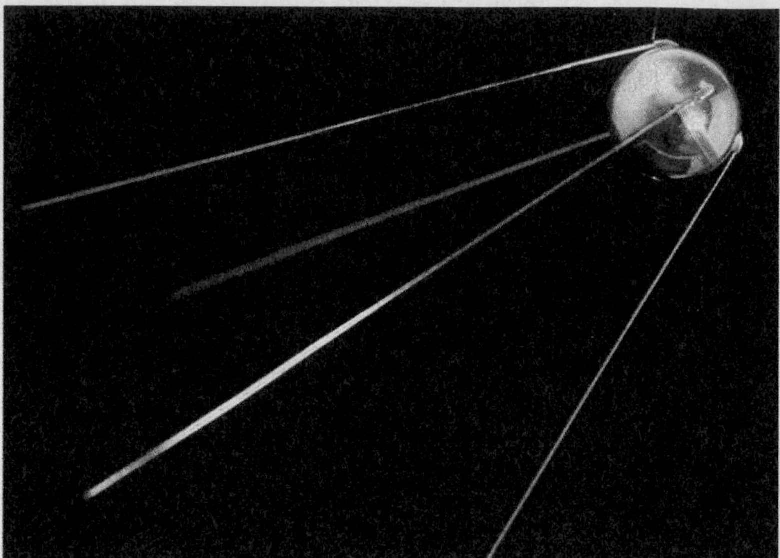

A model of Sputnik I, only 22 inches in diameter, but an historic achievement.

The Soviet launch, like the United States satellite program, is a part of the International Geophysical Year, a coordinated effort to explore the earth and its atmosphere. Experts in the United States said the Soviet satellite had no immediate military applications but that it indicated a Soviet edge in the exploration of space. Soviet scientists had made low-keyed announcements about their plans to launch a satellite and insisted they were not in a space race with America (→ 7).

Queen in Canada and U.S. for state visits

Queen greets Ike at Brit. Embassy.

Oct 17. Britain's Queen Elizabeth II was given a royal welcome as she arrived in Washington today for a state visit, the third stop on a trip in which she opened the Canadian Parliament in Ottawa and explored America's colonial past in historic Williamsburg. Hailing the ties that bind Great Britain and the United States, the queen praised leaders of the American Revolution in which the colonies won independence from her own country. Tonight, she and Prince Philip were honored at a state dinner by President and Mrs. Eisenhower.

Hoffa heads Teamsters; is out of A.F.L.

Oct 24. Organized labor's high command voted today to suspend the International Brotherhood of Teamsters, which has been accused of widespread abuses and corrupt influences. The principal target of the AFL-CIO leaders is James R. Hoffa, who was elected President of the Teamsters earlier this month in Miami Beach. Unless the 1.5-million-member union cleans up its act, and gets rid of Hoffa, labor leaders said that they will recommend that the Teamsters be expelled from the AFL-CIO later this year. Upon learning of the action, Hoffa stormed out of the meeting, angrily refusing to answer all questions posed by news reporters (→ 12/6).

Dior, the dean of Paris couture, dead

Oct 24. Designer Christian Dior has died in Italy at the age of 52. In 1947, just when it looked as if Paris would be replaced by New York as the world's couture capital, Dior introduced his "New Look." The narrow-waisted, heavily petticoated dresses were instantly the rage. France gave Dior the Legion of Honor for reviving the industry.

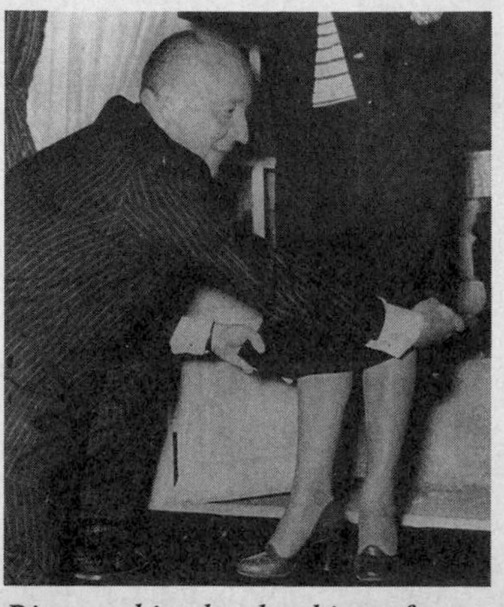

Dior, working hard at his craft.

Everlys wake up Little Susie on TV

The Everlys on the Sullivan Show.

October. Rock and roll has found a softer blend with Nashville-style harmonies on the Everly Brothers' new hit, "Wake Up Little Susie." Moving to an infectious guitar rhythm, the record features the resonant lead vocal of Don Everly, 20, and the lilting harmonies of brother Phil, 18. The duo introduced the song at Nashville's Grand Ole Opry and sang it again this month on "The Ed Sullivan Show." Like their earlier hit, "Bye Bye Love," the record is climbing both the country and pop top-ten charts.

The Everlys' distinctive vocal sound comes from years of singing together while growing up in Shenandoah, Iowa, and learning from their parents, country singers Ike and Margaret Everly. Judging from the stir their sons' records have created, it seems they taught them well.

Joanne Woodward stars, playing three parts in one character, in "The Three Faces of Eve."

1957

NOVEMBER

Su	Mo	Tu	We	Th	Fr	Sa
					1	2
3	4	5	6	7	8	9
10	11	12	13	14	15	16
17	18	19	20	21	22	23
24	25	26	27	28	29	30

5. London: Govt. announces women will sit in House of Lords first time in history (→ 2/14/63).

7. Washington: Ike names James R. Killian Jr. special aide for space technology (→ 12/6).

11. Damascus: Thousands of Palestinian refugees demonstrate for death of King Hussein.

14. U.S.: Hank Aaron of Milwaukee Braves named MVP of National League.

14. London: Queen Elizabeth II abolishes presentation at court for debutantes.

15. France demands halt to Anglo-American arms shipments to Tunisia (→ 2/8/58).

15. Khrushchev asserts Soviet superiority in missiles, challenges U.S. to rocket-range shooting match (→ 19).

19. New York: Leonard Bernstein named musical director of N.Y. Philharmonic.

19. Prague: Antonin Novotny elected Czech pres. upon death of Zapotocky (→ 10/3/63).

19. U.S. presents plan to install intermediate-range missiles in Western Europe (→ 21).

21. Washington: Air Force wins right to produce Thor intermediate-range missile (→ 12/17).

21. Rabat: Mohammed V and Tunisia's Bourguiba ask French to end Algerian War (→ 22).

22. Algeria: French attack rebels in Sahara, killing 42 (→ 12/10).

25. Moroccan King Mohammed arrives in U.S. (→ 4/20/58).

26. Washington: Ike suffers mild stroke (→ 3/1/58).

30. Remains of Capt. Bligh's Bounty found off Pitcairn Isle.

30. Jakarta: Indonesian Pres. Sukarno escapes assassin's grenade; seven killed (→ 12/1).

30. Philadelphia: Navy blanks Army 14-0 in football.

DEATHS

12. Antonin Zapotocky, Czech president (*12/19/1884).

24. Diego Rivera, Mexican mural painter (*12/8/1886).

28. Aleksei Remizov, Russian symbolist poet (*7/6/1877).

A dog named Laika makes space history

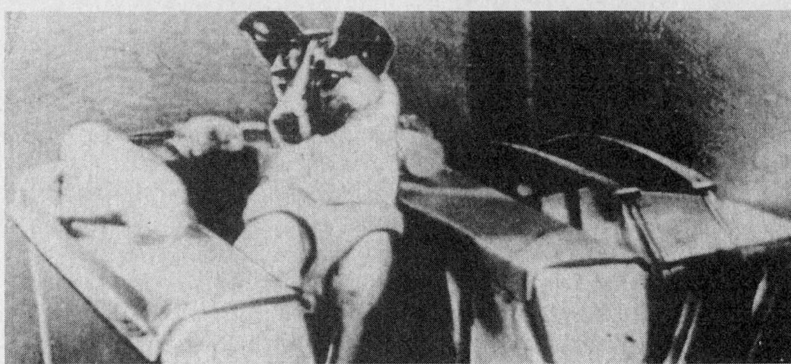

Laika, perhaps conscious of her historic role, poses for posterity.

Nov 3. The Soviet Union announced today the launching of its second space satellite, this one carrying a dog. The announcement said radio signals indicated the dog was alive in the satellite, which at 1,100 pounds is six times heavier than the original Sputnik, launched last month and still in orbit. The new satellite is orbiting the earth once every hour and 42 minutes at a height of 937 miles and completed its first trip around the earth this morning, Moscow said.

In addition to equipment to monitor the condition of the dog, named Laika, the satellite also carries instruments for measuring cosmic rays, temperature and pressure. The Soviets said they planned to launch several more earth satellites and that "it is completely realistic to speak about the launching of a satellite which will exist for tens and hundreds of years." President Eisenhower has dismissed the military significance of the Soviet feat, saying he is not worried "an iota" (→ 7).

Zhukov, hero in WWII, fired by Soviets

Nov 3. Marshal Georgi Zhukov, a Soviet hero in World War II, was dismissed last week from his post as Defense Minister and today was removed from all his top positions in the Soviet Communist Party. Furthermore, the party's Central Committee deflated Zhukov's war achievements as mere self-aggrandizement at the expense of the Soviet people and the party cause. The committee reported he "violated the Leninist party principles guiding the armed forces." This is believed to mean that he interfered with governmental control of the military. In Washington, officials say the ousting of Zhukov shows the "stresses and strains" currently plaguing the Soviet Union (→ 3/27/58).

Oppenheimer, head of gem firm, dies

Nov 25. Diamond king Sir Ernest Oppenheimer has died of a heart attack in Johannesburg. He was 77. Oppenheimer was one of the richest men in the world and one of the most powerful. He held a seat in the South African Parliament.

German-born Oppenheimer bought the famed De Beers mines, built a profitable little city for its miners and became boss of a cartel owning 95 percent of the world's diamond products. During the Depression, he held diamonds off the market to keep prices high.

Nov 22. Yankee Mickey Mantle, though on the losing side in the Series, is now the AL's MVP.

1957

DECEMBER

Su	Mo	Tu	We	Th	Fr	Sa
1	2	3	4	5	6	7
8	9	10	11	12	13	14
15	16	17	18	19	20	21
22	23	24	25	26	27	28
29	30	31				

1. Indonesian govt. starts day-long strike against Dutch enterprises to protest rule in West New Guinea (→ 2/12/58).

5. Leningrad: First nuclear ice-breaker Lenin launched.

6. AFL-CIO ousts Teamsters in corruption scandal (→ 3/25/58).

6. Cocoa Beach, Florida: Test satellite Vanguard blows up two seconds after firing (→ 2/1/58).

10. U.N. implicitly recognizes FLN rebels in Algeria (→ 1/11/58).

16. New York: First $2 million day in department store history recorded at Macy's.

26. Anti-Western crowds stir Cairo as Afro-Asian Solidarity Conference convenes.

27. Australia beats U.S. for third straight Davis Cup.

29. Detroit: Lions capture pro football title, trouncing Chicago Bears 59-14.

30. Jerusalem: Premier David Ben Gurion's coalition government falls (→ 1/26/58).

CULTURAL EVENTS, 1957

Literature: Lawrence Durrell's "Justine"; Simone de Beauvoir's "The Mandarins"; Ayn Rand's "Atlas Shrugged"; Nevil Shute's "On the Beach"; Bernard Malamud's "The Assistant"; Jack Kerouac's "On the Road"; O'Neill's "Long Day's Journey into Night," Pulitzer; Dr. Seuss' "The Cat in the Hat."

Academia: Noam Chomsky's "Syntactic Structures"; Isaacs and Lindenmann describe interferon's role in building up immunity against viruses.

Music: Bernstein's "West Side Story"; Meredith Willson's "The Music Man"; Britten's "The Turn of the Screw"; "Love Letters in the Sand"; "Young Love"; "Maria"; "Tonight."

The Arts: Francis Bacon's "Screaming Nurse"; Pier Luigi Nervi's UNESCO Conference Hall, Paris.

Film: "The Bridge on the River Kwai," Alec Guinness (Academy Award); Wilder's "Love in the Afternoon"; Preminger's "Bonjour Tristesse"; Chaplin's "A King in New York."

Atomic weapons in Europe agreed upon

Dec 19. The North Atlantic Treaty Organization has agreed upon the stationing of American nuclear weapons in Europe, including intermediate-range ballistic missiles. The agreement was reached at an unusual heads-of-state meeting of the North Atlantic Council, called to heal a widening breach between the United States and the Allies over the direction of the alliance and its policy toward the Soviet Union. The Europeans acceded to U.S. suggestions that the military side of the alliance should be strengthened by the addition of nuclear weapons. The U.S. endorsed a more flexible approach to the Soviets on disarmament (→ 1/13/58).

U.S. loses satellite; Atlas missile flies

Dec 17. The United State successfully fired the Atlas intercontinental ballistic missile on a 500-mile flight from Cape Canaveral today. The success made up somewhat for the ignominious failure on December 6 of America's first attempt to launch an earth satellite. The Vanguard rocket carrying the satellite exploded only two seconds after takeoff from Cape Canaveral. The four-pound satellite, undamaged, lay beeping on the ground. Its launch had been rushed by United States officials in an effort to match the Soviet Union's space successes (→ 19).

Albert Camus wins Nobel for novels

Algerian-born Albert Camus.

Dec 10. French author Albert Camus has received the Nobel Prize for literature. Camus' life seems to negate the statement of his work. His novels suggest that life, inevitably leading to death, is absurd; yet Camus is relentlessly productive. His book "The Stranger" (1942) and play "Caligula" (1948) are popular Existentialist works.

Chinese-Americans Tsung Dao Lee and Chen Ning Yang won the physics prize for findings on elementary particles. Briton Alexander Todd won the chemistry award for research on Vitamin B-12, and Swiss doctor Daniele Bovet took the medicine prize for studies on curare. Canadian Foreign Minister Lester Pearson earned the Peace Prize for efforts during the Suez crisis.

Alec Guinness, in "Bridge on the River Kwai," plays a British POW, living by discipline and the Geneva Convention. Done by blacklisted writers, the script is credited to novelist Pierre Boulle, who speaks no English.

Kerouac depicts the Beat Generation

People hitherto out of step with the Beat Generation are catching up by reading "On the Road" by Jack Kerouac. He writes about a cross-country car trip taken with a buddy named Neal Cassady. Through California and Mexico they meet people, try drugs and talk non-stop.

The beatniks have a lot to say, and they say it with the rhythm and idiom of jazz. They like bongo drums. They don't like middle-class obsession with objects and conformity; they expand their minds with drugs or religion (many check out Zen Buddhism). They like New York and San Francisco. They don't like the suburbs.

Poets Allen Ginsberg and Lawrence Ferlinghetti write about Beat feelings. Ferlinghetti uses striking images in "Pictures of the Gone World" (1955), and Ginsberg cries for his generation in "Howl" (1956).

"Cat in the Hat" and all of that

A man named Geisel who called himself Seuss wrote a very nice book —but what was the use? No publishers liked it, they turned it down flat. "Who on earth wants to read about a cat in a hat? The pictures are odd, the rhymes even worse," said the publishers condemning each line of each verse.

The good doctor persisted, and this year on the shelves are hundreds of copies adults buy for themselves. But if you confront them they'll go all to pieces and lie that they bought them for nephews and nieces . . .

The theater had a fine year, too. John Osborne's "The Entertainer" premiered. The play focuses on three generations of vaudeville performers, the last being a cynical dancer named Archie Rice. Novelist Gore Vidal wrote a drama called "A Visit to a Small Planet," about an alien investigating the peculiar politics of the earth. "Endgame" by Samuel Beckett is a play concerning a wheelchair-bound man named Hamm and his aide, Clov. It seems an apocalyptic war has killed everyone but them. And that is that.

1958

JANUARY

Su	Mo	Tu	We	Th	Fr	Sa
			1	2	3	4
5	6	7	8	9	10	11
12	13	14	15	16	17	18
19	20	21	22	23	24	25
26	27	28	29	30	31	

1. Pasadena: Ohio State over Oregon 10-7 in Rose Bowl.

2. Venezuela: Army crushes revolt; rebel leaders flee to Colombia (→ 10).

3. Everest climber Edmund Hillary reaches South Pole with expedition from New Zealand.

3. Holland nationalized banking.

3. British create West Indies Federation with Lord Hailes as governor general.

5. Cameroon: French troops crush Communist-led uprising.

6. Moscow announces reduction of armed forces by 300,000.

10. Caracas: Pres. Jimenez dismisses two of most powerful aides at army's demand (→ 17).

13. N.Y.: Linus Pauling presents petition of 9,000 scientists asking U.N. to halt nuclear tests (→ 28).

14. Cuba: Rebels raid port area of Manzanillo (→ 2/23).

15. Washington: Postmaster Gen. Arthur Summerfield says those whose dogs bite mailmen will have to get their own mail.

15. Gallup poll shows Eleanor Roosevelt most admired woman in U.S.

16. Ottawa: Lester Pearson is new leader of Canadian liberals.

17. Caracas police attack women protesters with machetes (→ 23).

18. N.C.: Raid by 500 Indians breaks up KKK rally (→ 4/4).

21. Moscow: Soviet Union calls for ban on nuclear arms in Baghdad Pact countries (→ 29).

26. Moshe Dayan resigns as Israeli army commander (→ 4/24).

27. Washington: U.S. and Soviets agree to widen cultural exchanges (→ 2/2).

27. Hungary: Ferenc Munnich replaces Janos Kadar as premier (→ 6/16).

28. Florida: Air Force successfully tests Thor missile (→ 2/22).

28. New York: Roy Campanella paralyzed in car crash.

29. U.S. to give $10 mil. to Baghdad Pact nations (→ 2/11/59).

30. Paris: Yves St. Laurent, 22, hailed as heir to Christian Dior in first showing.

Fighting continues along Algerian border

Jan 11. French troops in Algeria are under attack from guerrillas who hit and then run with impunity to their bases across the border in independent Tunisia. In the latest incident, 15 French infantrymen were killed by National Liberation Front forces who crossed into Algeria from Sakiet Sidi Youssef. The 350 guerrillas, backed by heavy artillery, pinned down the French until they were scattered by an air strike. The rebels jumped back across the border, and French officers, using binoculars, watched helplessly as four of their soldiers who had been taken prisoner were loaded into Tunisian army trucks.

French commanders have complained to higher authorities that they are sitting ducks along the border. Guerrillas in Tunisia, they charge, even launch mortar attacks into Algeria and fire on French planes. The commanders have asked for permission to chase the guerrillas across the border, but Habib Bourguiba, President of Tunisia, says he will not tolerate French intervention in his land (→ 4/30).

French counterinsurgency forces seek out the FLN in the Djurdjura Mts.

100 million degrees produces fusion

Jan 24. British and American scientists created more than a little heat as they succeeded in bashing two light atoms together to create a third heavier atom. The atoms were warmed up to 100 million degrees, the temperature of a hydrogen bomb explosion, to create the nuclear fusion. The breakthrough research was announced by Sir John Cockcroft of Britain and Lewis Strauss of the United States (→ 2/8).

Vidor's "A Farewell to Arms."

Venezuelan regime overthrown in riots

Jan 23. The dictatorship of General Marcos Perez Jimenez was overthrown early today. More than 100 persons were killed or wounded in two days of fighting in Caracas. A civilian rebel group under the command of the Patriotic Junta has claimed victory. Although the revolt was centered in Caracas, large uprisings also occurred in Maracay, Barinas and Cabimas. Perez Jimenez has reportedly fled by plane for an unknown destination. He seized power in 1948, ruling for two years as part of a three-man junta before emerging as the dominant force in the government.

Suspect arrested in ten murder cases

Jan 29. A 19-year-old trash collector named Charles Starkweather is being held in the deaths of ten people. His girlfriend, 14-year-old Caril Fugate, had an as yet undetermined role in the murders. The pair were seized outside Douglas, Wyoming, following a 110-mph car chase with police. Most of the ten victims lived in or around Lincoln, Nebraska. Three of them were members of Fugate's family: her mother, step-father and step-sister. Caril Fugate and Starkweather were photographed outside their jail cells in Douglas. Both grinned broadly for the camera (→ 11/21).

Daily Worker shut; editor quits party

Jan 13. The Communist Party is "a futile and impotent political sect," proclaimed John Gates as he resigned from the party and quit his position as editor of The Daily Worker yesterday. His dissatisfaction and renunciation of communism and subsequent job resignation further splinters the party and closes the newspaper; it will be the first time in nearly 40 years that Communists in this country don't have their own daily publication. Gates also said, "The isolation and decline of the Communist Party have long been apparent."

1958

FEBRUARY

Su	Mo	Tu	We	Th	Fr	Sa
						1
2	3	4	5	6	7	8
9	10	11	12	13	14	15
16	17	18	19	20	21	22
23	24	25	26	27	28	

1. Calif.: 47 die as two military planes collide in midair.

1. Cairo: Syria and Egypt declare alliance, forming United Arab Republic (→ 14).

2. Moscow: Bulganin asks Ike for summit meeting (→ 6).

3. The Hague: Benelux countries sign treaty abolishing 97% of trade curbs.

5. Florida: Vanguard satellite launching fails again, exploding in flight (→ 7).

6. Washington: New Soviet Ambassador Mikhail Menshikov arrives in U.S. (→ 3/16).

7. Washington establishes first U.S. space body, Advanced Research Projects Agency (→ 9).

7. Hollywood: Paramount sells TV rights to pre-1948 movies for $50 million (→ 3/10).

8. Tokyo: Japan achieves its first nuclear fusion reaction (→ 9/13).

9. Texas: Donald Farrell begins week of simulated space flight (→ 3/2).

11. Peking: Chou En-lai resigns as foreign minister (→ 5/3).

12. Jakarta warns U.S. to stay out of Indonesian affairs (→ 15).

14. Amman: Jordan, Iraq sign union, following example of Egypt and Syria (→ 5/1).

15. Indonesian rebels proclaim regime defying Jakarta (→ 22).

20. Tunisia forces French consuls to quit posts (→ 4/16).

20. Chicago: Nathan Leopold receives parole for 1924 murder.

22. U.S. to install 60 Thor nuclear missiles in Britain (→ 3/11).

22. Indonesians bomb two rebel centers, silencing radios (→ 26).

23. Cuban rebels seize Argentine auto racing champ Juan Manuel Fangio (→ 25).

24. Argentina: Dr. Arturo Frondizi elected president (→ 11/12).

26. Indonesian army takes rebel center Gorontalo (→ 3/12).

27. Washington: Ex-Pres. Herbert Hoover says current recession is temporary.

BIRTH

24. Plastic Bertrand, Belgian rock star, born Roger Jouret.

America's Explorer I satellite is launched

The Jupiter, power for Explorer I.

Feb 1. The United States launched its first space satellite into orbit around the earth today. The 30.8-pound Explorer satellite was put into orbit by a Jupiter-C rocket that lifted off from Cape Canaveral, Florida, at 10:48 a.m. President Eisenhower received word of the launching over a direct telephone line to the White House and announced the feat shortly after 1 p.m.

The satellite is in an orbit that takes it around the earth every 114 minutes, at a maximum height of 2,000 miles and a minimum altitude of 230 miles. Radio signals from Explorer's transmitter were picked up in California only minutes after launch. The satellite is equipped to measure cosmic radiation found in space and send data back to earth. Although Explorer has a peaceful mission, its launch was made possible by a modified military rocket developed by an Army missile team headed by Wernher von Braun, a former German rocket scientist. The first American effort to launch a satellite failed December 6 (→ 5).

French make reprisal raids on Tunisia

Feb 8. The frustration and fury of French authorities in Algeria finally boiled over today, as they approved an air raid on separatist rebels operating from inside Tunisia. More than two dozen bombers and fighters struck a rebel sanctuary at Sakiet Sidi Youssef after a French plane was forced down by an artillery barrage from the camp. About 70 people were killed and 130 were wounded, many of them civilians, according to Tunisian authorities. Red Cross trucks were hit while delivering supplies to the camp.

Jacques Chaban-Delmas, French Defense Minister, justified the reprisal raid as "legitimate defense." Tunisia's President Habib Bouguiba, saying "our relations can no longer be normal ones," recalled his Ambassador from Paris. His Cabinet demanded the withdrawal of French forces from Tunisia (→ 20).

In a move sure to inflame international opinion, French bombers hit Red Cross trucks carrying supplies to the village of Sakiet Sidi Youssef.

Rouault, painter of deep faith, dies

Feb 13. Painter Georges Rouault is dead in Paris at the age of 86. He was an artist haunted by the image of a suffering Savior. One of his most admired paintings is "Christ Mocked by Soldiers."

Frenchman Rouault was poor for the first few decades of his life. In debt, he sold all his paintings to an art dealer in exchange for room and board. He later sued the dealer and won possession of them again in 1947. Rouault promptly burned over 300 of the works; he did not consider them his best, and so they were unworthy of existence. Following a conversion to Roman Catholicism in 1895, Rouault strived to arrive at a perfect depiction of Christ's perfect sorrow.

Rouault also painted landscapes.

U.S. arrests Cuban planning invasion

Feb 25. Former President of Cuba Carlos Prio Socarras was arrested last week in Miami on charges that he had violated the neutrality laws of the United States. Prio and eight other Cubans were indicted by a federal grand jury for conspiracy to equip a military expedition to invade Cuba. If convicted, Prio could be sentenced to five years in prison and fined $10,000.

Prio, who was overthrown in 1952 by Fulgencio Batista, reportedly planned to train soldiers and pilots at camps in the United States and purchase ships, aircraft and armaments for the invasion. Fidel Castro accused the United States of making a secret agreement with Batista, trading a return of constitutional guarantees in Cuba for action against Cuban rebels in the United States (→ 3/12).

1958

MARCH

Su	Mo	Tu	We	Th	Fr	Sa
						1
2	3	4	5	6	7	8
9	10	11	12	13	14	15
16	17	18	19	20	21	22
23	24	25	26	27	28	29
30	31					

1. Washington: Doctors report Ike fully recovered from stroke.

1. Turkey: At least 220 die as ferry sinks.

2. Werner von Braun declares U.S. space research is several years behind U.S.S.R. (→ 5).

5. Florida: Second U.S. satellite Explorer lost after successful launching (→ 17).

8. N.J.: Navy, after decommissioning Wisconsin, is without a battleship first time since 1895.

10. Report indicates U.S. has two-thirds of world's TV sets, 47 million (→ 2/20/59).

11. U.S. unemployment now at highest mark since 1941 (→ 4/1).

11. S.C.: B-47 injures six, accidentally dropping unarmed A-bomb on farm home (→ 20).

12. Jakarta drops paratroopers on Sumatra to seek rebels (→ 23).

12. Havana: Batista suspends constitutional rights to fight rebels; Cabinet resigns (→ 27).

16. Moscow: U.S. team observes 130 mil. Soviets vote (→ 7/3).

17. Florida: Vanguard, second successful U.S. satellite, reaches orbit at 2,513 miles (→ 26).

20. Bonn: Chancellor Adenauer defers to NATO on nuclear arms in West Germany (→ 31).

22. Missouri: Harry Truman conducts K.C. Philharmonic.

23. Sumatra: Indonesian army drives rebels out of U.S. oil center (→ 5/4).

25. U.S. Senate committee calls Hoffa boss of "hoodlum empire" (→ 1/20/59).

25. Chicago: Sugar Ray Robinson recaptures middleweight title for fifth time.

26. Florida: Army orbits third satellite, Explorer III (→ 27).

27. U.S. announces plan to explore space near moon (→ 7/26).

27. Texas: U.S. seizes 35 New Yorkers on way to join Castro rebels in Cuba (→ 4/2).

30. Syrian and Israeli forces clash at border (→ 8/16).

31. Moscow declares halt on atomic tests, asks other nations to follow (→ 4/2).

Khrushchev Soviet Premier; Bulganin out

March 27. "We shall conquer capitalism with a high level of work and a higher standard of living," promised Nikita Khrushchev today as he accepted the leadership of the Soviet Union. Khrushchev replaces Nikolai Bulganin, who had resigned, as Premier of this nation of 200 million, while remaining First Secretary of the Communist Party. Not since Joseph Stalin has a Soviet leader held both positions. It is not known whether most Russians approve of this consolidation of power (→ 8/15).

Volatile Khrushchev, now Premier.

Elvis is now just U.S. 53310761 in Army

March 24. Elvis Presley traded in his rock-and-roll crown for a set of Army fatigues this morning when he reported to Local Draft Board 86 in Memphis, Tennessee.

The 23-year-old singer, who stands at the pinnacle of recording and movie stardom, arrived in the drizzling rain at 6:35, accompanied by his parents and manager, Colonel Tom Parker. He was met by hordes of newsmen, photographers, and teenaged fans distraught over the prospect of losing the pop idol to the armed services for the next two years.

Presley's monthly earnings will plummet from more than $100,000 to just $83.20. But the star, who sold over 40 million records in the past two years and just finished his fourth movie, seemed unperturbed. "I'm looking forward to serving in the Army," he remarked. "I think it will be a great experience for me."

Presley in uniform, ready to exchange his guitar for a gun.

Handy was the man who made the blues

March 28. "The blues comes from the man furthest down, the blues comes from nothingness, from want, from desire . . ." So wrote W.C. Handy, a prolific composer who died today in New York. He was 84. Handy wrote "Memphis Blues," "St. Louis Blues" and many other enduring melodies.

Handy was born dirt poor in Alabama to a strict Methodist family that frowned on music. At age 31, recalling lean years as a trumpeter in St. Louis, he wrote his immortal song about the city. A film on Handy's life is due out April 7.

Why did he drop bomb? Truman tells

March 14. Harry S. Truman said today that the dropping of two atomic bombs on Japan in 1945 saved thousands of Japanese and American lives. In a letter to the Chairman of the Hiroshima City Council, the ex-President explained that 1.5 million soldiers would have been needed to invade the Japanese islands and that at least 250,000 of those men, plus 250,000 Japanese, would have died. "The need for such a fateful decision," he added, "never would have arisen had we not been shot in the back by Japan at Pearl Harbor in December 1941."

March 22. Mike Todd died today in an air crash that would have taken wife Liz Taylor had she not stayed home with a timely cold.

1958

APRIL

Su	Mo	Tu	We	Th	Fr	Sa
		1	2	3	4	5
6	7	8	9	10	11	12
13	14	15	16	17	18	19
20	21	22	23	24	25	26
27	28	29	30			

1. Ike signs emergency $1.8 mil. emergency housing bill to bolster flagging economy.

1. France crippled by 24-hour strike of public workers.

2. Ike calls Soviet halt on atom tests "a gimmick" (→ 4).

2. U.S. embargoes arms shipments to Cuba (→ 3).

3. Havana: Batista decrees Cubans may kill inciters (→ 6/29).

4. London: 5,000 attend anti-nuclear rally at Trafalgar Sqare (→ 11).

4. Malcolm X frees Harlem Negro beaten by police during arrest for fighting (→ 6/21).

5. Canada: Marine hazard Ripple Rock destroyed with 1,375 tons of explosive, one of largest non-atomic explosions ever.

6. Georgia: Arnold Palmer wins Masters golf title.

11. U.S. Navy announces first test-firing of Polaris missile from submerged sub (→ 5/4).

14. Poland: Gomulka declares strikes illegal; unions to submit to Party rule (→ 11/9/64).

16. Paris: Premier Felix Galliard resigns over Tunis talks, 23rd to fall since WWII (→ 2/17/59).

19. Belgrade: Soviet bloc to boycott Seventh Congress of Yugoslav Communists (→ 4/7/62).

20. Rabat demands Spain withdraw all troops from Moroccan territory (→ 9/14).

22. Trinidad: Princess Margaret inaugurates first Parliament of West Indies Federation.

24. Jerusalem: Israel holds military parade to celebrate tenth anniversary (→ 7/5/59).

25. Bonn signs trade pact with Moscow (→ 7/1/59).

27. Trinidad: Nixon begins tour of South America (→ 5/7).

28. Paris: Walls of Iris Clert gallery bare for Yves Klein show "Emptiness Exhibited."

30. Tangier: Tunisia, Morocco, Algerian representatives call for exiled Algerian govt. (→ 5/13).

DEATH

8. George Nathan, dean of Broadway critics (*2/14/1882).

Van Cliburn wins Moscow piano contest

Young virtuoso Van Cliburn.

April 13. A young American pianist has broken the ice at a kind of Cold War party. Van Cliburn, 23 years old, is the winner of the Soviet Union's international Tchaikovsky piano competition. A panel of 16 Soviet judges chose Cliburn over eight other contestants, including three Russian performers.

The pianist, christened Harvey Lavan Cliburn, was born in Shreveport, La. His mother, a concert pianist, was his first teacher, guiding him to a Carnegie Hall recital in 1947. When he was 17, Cliburn practiced with Rosina Levhinne at Juilliard. Performances nationwide hindered his postgraduate study.

Cliburn has a fluid command of works by the late Romantics. Chopin, Tchaikovsky and Liszt are among his favorite composers. His passionate rendition of Rachmaninoff's Piano Concerto No. 3 was a highlight of the competition.

The pianist is 6'4", blond and youthful. The Soviet press calls him "Malchik." It means "little boy."

Millionth visitor at Brussels World's Fair

April 26. A Dutch-born Belgian woman, hair slightly mussed by a brisk wind and steady rain, was the millionth visitor to the Brussels World's Fair. Incredibly, the exposition has been open only ten days. Pavilions from 51 countries attract great crowds, rain or no rain.

The fair's centerpiece is the huge Atomium. The building is a magnified recreation of an iron crystal, 200 thousand times actual size. It symbolizes the safe and peaceful uses of atomic energy. Escalators connect restaurants and display shows housed inside.

The Atomium symbolizes the safe, peaceful uses of atomic energy.

Ezra Pound freed from treason charge

April 18. Poet and critic Ezra Pound is free to return to Italy now that charges of treason have been dismissed. An insanity plea led to the dropped charges. During the war, Pound made over 300 radio broadcasts in support of dictator Benito Mussolini. Among others he helped are the worthy writers T.S. Eliot and William Butler Yeats.

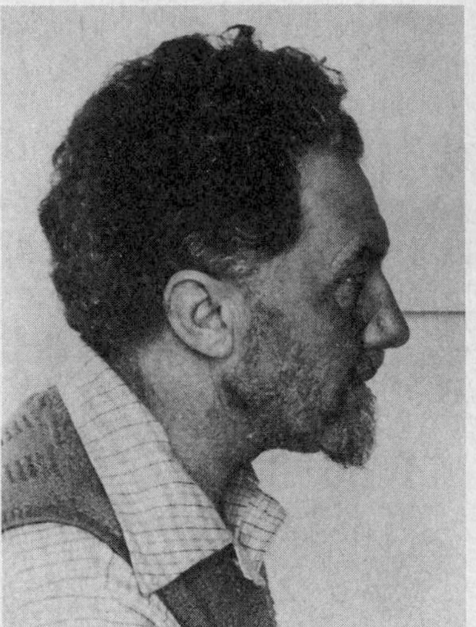

Haggard Pound, a Fascist poet?

Egypt agrees to pay $81 million for Suez

April 29. In a preliminary agreement signed today in Rome, Egypt has agreed to pay, in a five-year installment plan, more than $81 million to Suez Canal Company stockholders in compensation for Egypt's seizure of the canal. Forty percent of the stock is held by the British government, the rest by 130,000 French people (→ 1/1/59).

Lana Turner's child stabs boyfriend

April 11. Cheryl Crane, 14, daughter of Lana Turner and her ex-husband, restaurateur Stephen Crane, has been found by an inquest to have committed "justifiable homicide" in stabbing to death her mother's paramour, Johnny Stompanato, 32, as the Hollywood hoodlum threatened the star with serious injury or death if she left him.

1958

MAY

Su	Mo	Tu	We	Th	Fr	Sa
				1	2	3
4	5	6	7	8	9	10
11	12	13	14	15	16	17
18	19	20	21	22	23	24
25	26	27	28	29	30	31

1. Nasser, in U.S.S.R., signs accord committing Egypt to support Soviet foreign policy if Moscow works for liberation of Asian, African peoples (→ 6/10).

3. Kentucky Derby won by Tim Tam, jockey I. Valenzuela up.

4. Sumatra: Indonesian army take rebel capital of Bukittinggi (→ 7/5/59).

4. U.S. rejects Polish plan for nuclear-free zone in Central Europe (→ 22).

7. Lima: Nixon greeted by 1,000 Peruvians shouting "Out with Nixon" (→ 13).

9. Moscow: Mikhail Botvinnik retakes world chess title.

13. Algeria: French troops take control of Algiers, call for return of Charles de Gaulle.→

13. Caracas: U.S. sends troops to Caribbean as Venezuelan mobs attack Nixon (→ 14).

15. N.Y. holds retrospective performance of works of John Cage.

19. Canada and U.S. establish North American Air Defense Command (NORAD).

19. Paris: De Gaulle gives press conference, denying intent to impose self as dictator (→ 23).

22. N.J.: Eight Nike missiles explode at base, killing ten (→ 7/1).

23. Algiers: Gen. Raoul Salan gives formal recognition to Algerian juntas (→ 24).

24. Corsica: French army rebels take power (→ 25).

24. N.Y.: United Press and Intl. News Service merge into U.P.I.

25. Paris: Premier Pierre Pflimlin decrees full press censorship (→ 28).

28. Paris: Leftists hold massive protest in support of republican goverment (→ 31).

30. Virginia: Unknown soldiers from WWII, Korea enshrined at Arlington National Cemetery.

30. Indy 500 won by Jimmy Bryan at 133.8 mph; Pat O'Connor dies in 13-car crash.

DEATH

29. Juan Ramon Jimenez, Spanish poet (*12/24/1881).

Algerian French assault government

May 13. While political pandemonium prevailed in Paris, mobs of Frenchmen took to the street in Algiers. Concerned that the French Cabinet will knuckle under to the demands of Algerian nationalists, protesters seized French government buildings in Algiers. Security forces threw a few token tear gas canisters at the rioters. But it was no secret that sympathetic French paratroopers lent the protesters trucks to break down the doors.

Thousands of demonstrators gathered in front of the Algiers post office and yelled abuse at the policies of Premier Pierre Pfimlin. Two groups sent telegrams to French President Rene Coty to express a lack of support for the Cabinet.

A soap opera atmosphere prevailed in Paris, as the government debated its policy in Algeria. From the left came cries of "Fascism will not prevail." "Algeria is French" was the response from the right.

By nightfall, the French military, given special powers by the government, had control of most of Algiers. Their sympathy was with the demonstrators, and not with Premier Pfimlin. General Raoul Salan broadcast a message saying "the destinies of French Algeria" were in his hands. But the very popular General Jacques Massu said only one man is capable of restoring peace to Algeria and ensuring "the everlastingness of French Algeria, an integral part of France." That man, said Massu, is Charles de Gaulle, and he urged him to come out of seclusion and form a new government (→ 19).

Angry Frenchmen in Algeria occupy the French radio station in Oran, expressing the fear that Paris has given up the fight for French colonialism.

Protesters ransack files of the French administration in Algiers.

Nixons stoned, spat on, threatened on Latin American tour

May 14. Stoned and shoved in Caracas, booed and spat on in Lima, Vice President Richard M. Nixon and his wife landed in San Juan tonight, cutting short a turbulent tour of Latin America. Venezuelans and Peruvians had lined Nixon parade routes to protest United States policies in Latin America.

Holding signs that read "Nixon is a viper!" students at Lima's San Marcos University protested U.S. economic policies which threaten to place tariffs on lead and zinc, key exports for Peruvians. The Communist Party is believed to have instigated the demonstrators and their chants of "Death to Yankee imperialism!" However, editorials in Lima's La Tribuna, the official organ of the American Popular Revolutionary Alliance, usually a moderate group, have suggested the anti-American sentiment is not confined to Communist factions. The paper said the "bitterness" felt by Latinos stems from traditional U.S. support for Latin American dictatorships.

In Venezuela, the United States military had to be called in to protect the Nixons as they toured the nation amid violence. Yet, this action was criticized by U.S. politicians as provocative and unwise. Senator Estes Kefauver said the presence of U.S. troops just "makes matters worse" and "gives the Communists a lot to talk about."

The tour seems to have been counterproductive to U.S.-Latin relations. The purpose of the trip was to enhance lines of communication. Instead, however, American dominance over the Southern hemisphere has become more apparent. ▷

French recall de Gaulle

De Gaulle, for a French Algeria?

May 31. French government leaders, paralyzed by indecision in the crisis over Algeria, have agreed to return Charles de Gaulle to power and give him the "exceptional" authority he demands. One by one, the leaders of all political parties except the Communists met with the General today in a small hotel off the Champs Elysees in Paris. Even though de Gaulle is known to believe that political parties are the root of many of France's problems, most of the leaders assured him of their support when he is invested as Premier tomorrow.

One politician, the Socialist Francois Mitterrand, withheld his support out of concern de Gaulle will become a dictator. "It is not," Mitterrand told de Gaulle, "that I do not recognize your authority or that I mistrust your aspirations. But the expanded powers for the presidency, even if you do not abuse them, how can we be sure, after you are dead, of your successors?"

Ever the expert at repartee, de Gaulle replied, "At the bottom of everything, Mr. Mitterrand, there is only one thing that interests you, and that is my death. It is true, I am mortal, but you are not going to put me to my death right away." In recent negotiations, de Gaulle has silenced most Socialist critics. A few may even be appointed to his new Cabinet (→ 6/1).

Powell is charged with tax evasion

Powell, hero of Harlem.

May 19. It has been a grueling month for Rep. Adam Clayton Powell Jr. First, a federal grand jury indicted the New York Democrat on tax evasion and tax fraud. If convicted, Powell faces up to five years imprisonment and fines of $30,000. The indictments have jeopardized his political career. Yesterday, the National Association for the Advancement of Colored People charged the Congressman of "extreme racism." Furthermore, Manhattan Borough President Hulan Jack has accused Powell, who is also a minister, of "preaching hatred" (→ 4/20/60).

Great leap forward planned for China

May 3. "The achievements of a single night surpass those of several millenia!" So claim Chinese propagandists, announcing what they call the Great Leap Forward, the biggest and most ambitious experiment in human mobilization in history.

The Leap is supposedly the spontaneous idea of the masses, but actually it stems from Mao's conviction that the only way to modernize China is through the mobilization of its sole resource—people. In the countryside, millions of peasants are to be deployed in "people's communes" in which all private property is confiscated. Formed into military brigades, they will be shifted from fields to "backyard" steel furnaces amid slogans urging them to work around the clock and perform modern economic miracles.

"As much as we may brag about our large population and our thousands of years of history and culture, our country is no better than Belgium," says Mao, impatient with the slight progress he has seen on the industrial front (→ 4/27/59).

1958

JUNE

Su	Mo	Tu	We	Th	Fr	Sa
1	2	3	4	5	6	7
8	9	10	11	12	13	14
15	16	17	18	19	20	21
22	23	24	25	26	27	28
29	30					

1. Paris: Gen. de Gaulle named premier of France; he asks six months of rule by decree (→ 3).

3. Paris: Assembly enacts de Gaulle's emergency reforms under threat of resignation (→ 4).

6. Brooklyn: 60,000-ton carrier Independence christened.

7. U.S. expels Soviet diplomat Nikolai Kurochkin as spy.

9. Washington: Ike meets with British Premier Macmillan on world affairs (→ 10).

10. Washington: U.S., U.K. agree to send 50 jets to Iran, Jordan and Lebanon (→ 12).

12. London to send paratroopers to reinforce security in Jordan (→ 25).

15. Athens severs military ties to Turkey in Cyprus issue (→ 8/4).

16. U.S. Supreme Court bans passport denials to suspected Communists (→ 19).

18. Tokyo: Japanese break tradition, letting Price Akihito choose his own bride.

18. New York: Wilt Chamberlain signs contract with Harlem Globetrotters.

19. Washington: Nine entertainers refuse to answer questions on ties to communism (→ 26).

21. Arkansas: Federal judge lets Little Rock delay school integration (→ 29).

21. Two Americans, Linus Pauling and Detlev Bronk, elected to Soviet Academy of Science.

22. N.Y.: Seven police injured at Soviet U.N. delegation by Hungarians protesting execution of Imre Nagy (→ 11/30/59).

24. Geneva: U.S.S.R. authorizes Intl. Labor Organization to study Soviet labor practices.

24. Washington: Ike meets with premier of Afghanistan.

25. Beirut: Lebanon asks U.S. to help stop flow of arms from United Arab Rebublic to Lebanese rebels (→ 9/23).

29. Birmingham: Rev. Fred Shuttleworth, civil rights activist, escapes as bomb explodes outside church (→ 8/21).

29. Sweden: Brazil takes World Cup 5-2 over Sweden in soccer.

Cuban rebels seize American Marines

June 29. Cuban rebel forces, led by Fidel Castro, seized 28 U.S. naval personnel, mostly Marines, near the American naval base at Guantanamo. A day earlier, the rebels had kidnapped ten Americans and two Canadians at a mining site in Oriente province, the center of the rebel activity against the regime of President Fulgencio Batista. The rebels said they were retaliating against the U.S. for giving assistance to Batista forces by refueling Cuban military planes at Guantanamo. The rebels dropped hints the Americans would be freed (→ 7/18).

Robeson gets his passport at last

June 26. Actor, singer, lawyer and activist Paul Robeson has been permitted a passport after a seven-year struggle. He had been denied the document on charges of Communist sympathies following trips to the Soviet Union and other Socialist nations. Robeson thanked the Supreme Court and well-wishers "of all races and creeds" for their legal and emotional support.

Robeson was one of the first Negroes to attend Rutgers University and Columbia Law School. In the 1920's he starred in "The Emperor Jones" and other brave new plays. Lately, he speaks out against segregation. The U.S.S.R. gave him the Stalin Peace Prize in 1952 (→ 8/7).

De Gaulle sows confusion in Algiers

Algerians greet Premier Charles de Gaulle, hoping he will solve the crisis.

June 4. The streets of Algiers were packed with cheering supporters of Charles de Gaulle as the General arrived to take charge of the crisis in North Africa just three days after rising to the office of Premier. The cheers continued as de Gaulle walked out onto a balcony of the government offices, proclaimed, "I understood you" and raised two fingers in a victory sign. But some people scratched their heads and there were even a few boos as de Gaulle started to speak.

Not once did the premier use the phrase dear to the hearts of many in the crowd. He never said "French Algeria." Instead, he confused some supporters and angered others when he said, "In all of Algeria, there are only Frenchmen, with the same rights and the same duties." Most Europeans in Algeria hate the nationalist rebels and would never deign to call them French. They blanched when de Gaulle called the separatists courageous fighters.

De Gaulle also said that all Algerians will vote as Frenchmen to elect representatives who will determine their future. "With these elected representatives, we will see what remains to be done," he said.

Army officials are displeased with two members of de Gaulle's Cabinet, Max Lejeune and Louis Jacquinot. They were not allowed on the balcony and locked in a room. The two were called "remnants of the old regime" (→ 8/23).

Suspension bridge is world's longest

June 28. The world's longest suspension bridge, part of a five-mile span linking Michigan's upper and lower peninsulas, was dedicated today. The suspension portion of the new Mackinac Bridge measures 8,614 feet, about 2,000 feet longer than the Golden Gate Bridge at San Francisco, although the Golden Gate's center span is longer. The complete Mackinac Bridge is 26,444 feet long. Built at a cost of $100 million, the bridge is intended to stimulate industrial development of the isolated upper peninsula, which now subsists primarily on mining and the tourist trade.

Hungary executes Nagy, ex-Premier

June 16. Imre Nagy, the Hungarian Communist who was twice Premier, was executed during the night by the pro-Soviet regime. Nagy was born a Bolshevik, but he became a moderate. He was returned to office in 1956 by the force of the anti-Soviet revolution. Less than a month later, when Russian tanks rolled into Budapest, Nagy was kidnapped by Soviet security police. He was arrested, transferred to Rumania, tried behind closed doors, found guilty and returned to Hungary to be hanged. Executed with the former premier was General Pal Maleter, former Defense Minister (→ 22).

Pele the Great wins world soccer cup

Pele moves the ball upfield.

June 28. His name is Edson Arantes do Nascimento, but after the 1958 World Cup matches he is simply known as Pele, King of Soccer.

The lithe "Black Pearl" of the world's most popular sport scored two goals for Brazil in its final match against Sweden for the cup, but that was only part of his accomplishment. Along the way, he booted three goals against France in the semi-finals and was the star, although he didn't score, in Brazil's qualification triumph over the Soviet Union. With the 5-2 win over Sweden in the final, Pele returned to his regular spot on Brazil's Santos team.

Weapons like the Rascal pilotless bomber, developed in fierce competition with the Soviets, make nuclear war portable and ever more threatening.

1958

JULY

Su	Mo	Tu	We	Th	Fr	Sa
		1	2	3	4	5
6	7	8	9	10	11	12
13	14	15	16	17	18	19
20	21	22	23	24	25	26
27	28	29	30	31		

1. Geneva: Intl. talks begin on detection of atomic tests (→ 9).

2. Washington: Vito Genovese pleads Fifth Amendment 150 times in Senate Mafia inquiry.

3. New England industrialist Bernard Goldfine admits giving X-mas checks to 33 White House aides (→ 9/22).

3. U.S. envoy gets 15-minute spot on Soviet TV (→ 2/23/59).

5. Wimbledon: Ashley Cooper over Neale Fraser 3-6, 6-3, 6-4, 13-11; Althea Gibson over Florence Mortimer 8-6, 6-2.

9. Florida: U.S. fires ICBM 6,000 miles in record test (→ 19).

10. Ottawa: Canada, U.S. set up new defense link at Cabinet level.

12. Moscow: U.S. sect leader, sitting in Red Square, proclaims himself king of Russia.

14. Baghdad: Iraqi army deposes King Faisal; Britain mobilizes 6,000 troops (→ 15).

15. Ike sends 5,000 U.S. Marines into Lebanon (→ 17).

17. Jordan: Two British battalions land at Amman (→ 20).

18. Cuba: Rebels free last 14 U.S. servicemen held (→ 28).

19. Florida: First Atlas three-stage rocket explodes after two minutes in air (→ 8/17).

19. Charly Gaul wins Tour de France.

20. Moscow: Khrushchev tells Nasser Soviet volunteers are ready for Mideast service (→ 23).

23. Moscow: Khrushchev accepts U.S. plan for Mideast summit at U.N. (→ 31).

26. Florida: U.S. launches fourth satellite Explorer IV to explore cosmic ray data (→ 29).

26. London: Queen Elizabeth gives Prince Charles title of Prince of Wales.

28. Cuba: U.S. troops land to aid Batista against rebels (→ 9/10).

29. NASA created by bill alotting million for U.S. space program (→ 8/17).

BIRTH

30. Daley Thompson, British athlete, Olympic decathlon winner 1980 and 1984.

Iraq coup kills King, Prince and Premier; Eisenhower sends 5,000 troops to Beirut

Faisal II, late King of Iraq.

July 31. The bloody coup d'etat in Iraq has done much more than overturn the pro-Western regime. It has unleashed new tensions in the Middle East cauldron and put the United States and the Soviet Union on a new collision course.

Baghdad radio announced on the 14th that the Iraqi army had risen against King Faisal. It was subsequently learned that the King, the Crown Prince and the Premier of Iraq had all been executed. The army had opposed Faisal's efforts to help Jordan and Lebanon quash internal rebellions, and the new leaders immediately aligned themselves with the anti-Western, pan-Arab policies of Egypt's General Gamal Abdel Nasser.

President Eisenhower dispatched troop transport planes to Europe. British Prime Minister Macmillan put some of his troops on alert. Lebanon's President Camille Chamoun issued an urgent appeal to the Western powers to seal his border with Iraq. Jordan's King Hussein also asked for help.

The next day, President Eisenhower acted. Conceding risks were involved, the president sent more than 5,000 Marines into Lebanon. "We could not in honor stand idly by in this hour of Lebanon's grave peril," Eisenhower said. The Marines easily took control of the Beirut airport. On the 17th, Macmillan sent a parachute brigade to Jordan.

In a blistering attack on the United States, the Soviet Union condemned the movement of Marines as "open aggression" that is "extremely alarming and dangerous to world peace." Eisenhower retorted that Soviet Premier Nikita Khrushchev's fear of general war was "extravagantly expressed."

"The real danger of war," Eisenhower said, "would come if one small nation after another were to be engulfed by expansionist and aggressive forces supported by the Soviet Union" (→ 8/2).

American Marines conduct debarking operations off the Lebanese coast.

Duvalier helps put down Haiti revolt

Papa Doc, being sworn in last year.

July 31. President Francois Duvalier led his palace guard to put down an insurgency by Haitian exiles. The rebel force, led by two former army captains, had landed near St. Marc and then advanced on Port-au-Prince, where it seized control of army barracks across the street from the Presidential palace. Supported by the palace guard and top army officers, Duvalier was reported to have led a counterattack and "wiped out" the rebel force of about 100 men.

Haitian officials charged that the revolt had been organized by Louis Dejoie, who was defeated in the presidential elections last fall, and former President Paul Magloire, both of whom are in exile in the United States. Following the abortive revolt, the Haitian Congress granted Duvalier his request to rule by decree for six months, making him a virtual dictator (→ 8/24/59).

Chennault, Flying Tigers leader, is dead

July 27. Lt. Gen. Claire L. Chennault, the pioneering aviator who led the Flying Tigers to fame over China, died today in a New Orleans hospital of lung cancer at 67. At his bedside was his wife Anna, a Chinese newspaperwoman who served as a nurse for the Flying Tigers.

The son of a Louisiana cotton farmer, Chennault became an Army aviator in World War I and quickly showed a talent for the tactics of fighter planes. During the 1930's, he was the leader of an aerial acrobatic team, known as "The Men on the Flying Trapeze," as he developed the concept that fighter planes were more effective flying in formation than alone, as in World War I.

In 1938, Mme. Chiang Kai-shek hired him to reorganize the Chinese Nationalist Air Force. With tacit approval from Washington, he organized the American Volunteer Group—Americans flying American-made planes for the Chinese—that came to be known as the Flying Tigers. Between its first flight in December 1941 and its incorporation into the Army Air Force in July 1942, the group was credited with shooting down 250 Japanese planes.

The Flying Tiger, immortalized by Lt. Gen. Claire Chennault.

Thousands besiege embassy in Moscow

July 18. Bricks and bottles bounced off the United States Embassy in Moscow today, as tens of thousands of irate Soviet citizens besieged the American building on Tchaikovsky Street. They were venting their anger over recent U.S. actions in the Middle East; the protesters demanded that the Eisenhower administration withdraw its troops from Lebanon. While no injuries were reported in the demonstration, several windows were broken and furniture in the building was damaged. American Ambassador Llewellyn Thompson registered a strong protest against the attack with the Soviet government and has requested compensation for damages.

July 28. U.C.L.A.'s tall and husky Rafer Johnson generated his own cult of personality in Moscow this week, setting a decathlon record of 8,302 points. His triumph could not prevent a narrow U.S. loss in the dual meet.

1958

AUGUST

Su	Mo	Tu	We	Th	Fr	Sa
					1	2
3	4	5	6	7	8	9
10	11	12	13	14	15	16
17	18	19	20	21	22	23
24	25	26	27	28	29	30
31						

2. U.S. recognizes new Iraqi regime (→ 2).

2. Amman: Hussein dissolves Jordan's union with Iraq (→ 10).

3. New York: 250,000 attend Jehovah's Witness rallies at Yankee Stadium, Polo Grounds.

4. Cyprus: Greek rebels call truce with Turks and British (→ 3/1/59).

7. U.S.: Court reverses conviction of Arthur Miller for contempt of Congress (→ 5/13/60).

9. U.S. reaffirms refusal to recognize Red China (→ 23).

10. Amman: Jordan uncovers large pro-Nasser spy ring (→ 13).

13. Ike presents Mideast plan at U.N., pulls 1,700 troops out of Lebanon (→ 1/2/59).

14. Dutch plane crashes off Ireland; 99 lost, 51 Americans.

15. Moscow: Ex-Premier Bulganin demoted to provincial post (→ 7/15/64).

16. Tel Aviv: 14 Israelis seized as Syrian spies (→ 10/16).

17. Florida: First U.S. moon shot fails when rocket explodes at 50,000 feet (→ 9/26).

17. Soviets to supply Peking with nuclear weapons (→ 21).

18. "Lolita" published in U.S.

19. Groton: Triton, world's largest sub, is launched.

21. Arkansas Gov. Faubus bars compliance with Supreme Court integration order (→ 9/5).

21. Denmark bars entry of U.S. nuclear sub Skate as a atomic hazard (→ 9/30).

23. Taiwan: Peking shells Quemoy in record attack (→ 9/8).

24. Britain: Race riots erupt in Nottingham.

28. Paris: 3,000 Algerians arrested in police dragnet (→ 9/19).

BIRTHS

4. Mary Decker, U.S. middle-distance runner.

29. Michael Jackson, American pop singer.

DEATH

14. Frederic Joliot-Curie, French physicist (*3/19/1900).

De Gaulle outlines plan for colonies

In charge: De Gaulle in Brazzaville.

Aug 23. French Premier Charles de Gaulle indicated very strongly today that he will not stand in the way of former colonies that are striving for complete independence.

De Gaulle spoke in Brazzaville, the latest stop in his nine-day, 13,000-mile tour of what used to be the French Empire. The premier proposed that the residents of the Congo choose their own future through a referendum, and he gave them a choice: "yes" to the French Community and cooperation with Paris or "no" to France as a decisive step toward independence. "I guarantee you," de Gaulle told a large crowd, "that an important threshold has been crossed in France in the process of decolonization."

De Gaulle flew on his Superstarliner plane to the Congo from Madagascar. The premier is delivering a similar message to ten other cities in French Africa (→ 28).

Sub sails under polar ice

Nautilus, world's first atomic sub, blazing new trails for war and peace.

Aug 27. The crew of the nuclear submarine Nautilus was honored by a New York ticker-tape parade today for making history's first undersea voyage across the North Pole. The voyage took place last summer, but it was disclosed by the White House only this month.

The Nautilus began its historic trip on July 23 at Pearl Harbor and cruised north through the Bering Strait. It went under the polar ice cap at Point Barrow, Alaska, and remained submerged thereafter, sending its periscope up only once to check its bearings. The Nautilus passed beneath the polar ice pack at the North Pole at 11:45 a.m. August 3. Its trip across the polar region took four days, and the Nautilus ended its voyage at Iceland on August 7. Cmdr. W.R. Anderson, skipper of the Nautilus, was given the Legion of Merit medal, and all 116 crew members and observers were honored with citations.

Experts say the Nautilus' polar voyage, which broke all records for submarine travel, has immense strategic significance, since it could open the Arctic for launching guided missiles from submarines. The trip also has potential commercial implications. It blazed a path that could be followed by cargo-carrying submarines. New Yorkers viewing today's parade cheered not only the submarine's crew but also Rear Admiral Hyman Rickover, the man given most credit for bringing the Navy's nuclear submarine fleet into existence (→ 10/6).

Khrushchev meets Mao for talks in Peking

Mao greets Khrushchev in Peking.

Aug 3. Nikita Khruschchev and Mao Tse-tung, the two head Reds, got together today to iron out the kinks in communism. Khrushchev is visiting Peking to mollify Chinese concern over an upcoming summit meeting arranged by the United Nations. The Communist Chinese do not recognize the U.N. because of Nationalist Chinese membership. The two leaders did agree that communism was a "great success" and that the chief threat to world peace was from Western "imperialist war maniacs" (→ 9).

1958

SEPTEMBER

Su	Mo	Tu	We	Th	Fr	Sa
	1	2	3	4	5	6
7	8	9	10	11	12	13
14	15	16	17	18	19	20
21	22	23	24	25	26	27
28	29	30				

2. Natl. Defense Education Act signed to provide student loans and aid for technical education.

5. Alabama: Martin Luther King, arrested for loitering, fined $14 for refusing to obey police (→ 12).

5. New York: Two-nation ceremony starts power flow from St. Lawrence station (→ 4/25/59).

7. New York: Ashley Cooper, Althea Gibson win U.S. tennis titles at Forest Hills.

8. Taiwan transport, escorted by U.S., sunk by Communist China (→ 8).

8. Moscow: Khrushchev asks Ike to recognize Peking (→ 18).

10. Florida: Customs agents seize 31 heavily armed on boat bound for Cuba (→ 17).

13. Geneva: Second intl. atomic energy talks end; France offers U-235 secrets (→ 1/16/59).

14. U.S. agrees to progressive evacuation of Morocco military bases (→ 12/22/59).

18. Taiwan claims five MIG-17's and three Communist torpedo boats (→ 24).

21. Boston: Ted Williams hits woman in head with hurled bat after strikeout.

23. Beirut: Gen. Fouad Chehab now Lebanese pres. as Sami es-Solh flees to Turkey (→ 10/25).

24. Taiwan shoots down ten MIG-17's (→ 10/20).

26. Florida: Navy orbits 20-inch Vanguard satellite (→ 10/12).

26. Rhode Island: U.S. wins America's Cup in four straight.

28. U.S. Air Force selects Thor over Jupiter for mass production as ICBM (→ 30).

29. Supreme Court bans "evasive schemes" to thwart school integration (→ 10/5).

30. Mass.: Army opens test solar furnace (→ 3/16/60).

30. Washington: AEC reports U.S.S.R. has resumed atomic testing in Arctic (→ 10/31).

DEATH

25. John B. Watson, American psychiatrist, spokesman for behaviorism (*1/9/1878).

Guinea repudiates French Community

Toure says "no" to France.

Sept 28. After 70 years, the French flag no longer flies in Guinea and a new nation is born. Today, the West African territory alone voted to reject the constitution for a new French Community. Premier Sekou Toure, an outspoken nationalist, had expressed his opposition to the plan beforehand. In the seven other West African territories and the four in Equatorial Africa, in Madagascar, Somaliland, the Comoros, Polynesia, New Caledonia, and St. Pierre and Miquelon, the constitution was accepted. As a warning to these former colonies, Premier de Gaulle told Toure his nation would no longer receive financial aid (→ 1/21/61).

Rebels name team for Algeria regime

Sept 19. Ferhat Abbas, an Algerian pharmacist, announced a new prescription today for the ills of Algeria. He established a rebel government-in-exile in Egypt. The provisional government was immediately recognized by Libya, Iraq, the United Arab Republic, Tunisia and Morocco. In Paris, the Cabinet of General de Gaulle dismissed the rebel government as "artificial."

Abbas, 59 years old, is one of the oldest members of the rebel government. Most of the ministers, and there are 16 of them, are under 40. The military leader of the separatist rebels, Belkacem Krim, was named Vice President and Minister of the Armed Forces (→ 28).

French vote for de Gaulle's 5th Republic

Sept 28. General Charles de Gaulle was a big winner, and French Communists and Algerian rebels were big losers as an overwhelming majority in France and the overseas territories voted for the new constitution. Nearly 80% of the voters approved the document, which establishes the Fifth Republic, enhances the powers of de Gaulle and reduces the authority of the Parliament. Communists suffered their worst setback since the Second World War.

Algerians ignored the rebels, who demanded a boycott, and flocked to the polls. Some 96% of the voters approved the constitution. Moslem women voted for the first time, and many of them told a New York Times reporter that they had "voted for peace" or "voted for de Gaulle."

In all overseas territories except French Guinea, the vote was against independence and for participation in the new French Community, which will grant more autonomy than the former Union (→ 11/22).

Sherman Adams, Ike's assistant, ousted

Adams prepares to step down.

Sept 22. Sherman Adams, he of vicuna coat fame, resigned his top White House post today, saying he had been the victim of a "campaign of villification" designed to destroy him and embarrass President Eisenhower and the Republican Party.

His resignation came in the wake of disclosures by a House panel that he had received an Oriental rug and a vicuna coat from a New England textile magnate, Bernard Goldfine, for whom he had made inquiries at two federal agencies. According to the committee, Goldfine also paid $3,000 worth of hotel bills for Adams.

"I have done no wrong," Adams said in announcing his resignation in a radio and television speech. He was leaving the job, he said, so as not to embarrass the president or endanger Republican chances for gaining control of Congress. President Eisenhower accepted the Adams resignation "with sadness" and told his top aide that "you will be sorely missed."

Castro's guerrillas launch offensive

Sept 17. From his mountain stronghold in western Cuba, Fidel Castro launched his promised offensive against the army troops of the Batista government. The rebel radio said six columns had left the mountains and "are penetrating into the territory of the republic." At least two of the columns were reported driving into the northern and southern sections of Camaguey province in the middle of Cuba. The group along the southern coast was said to be led by Che Guevara, an Argentine physician who has become a chief aide to Castro. Leading other columns was Raul Castro, brother of Fidel (→ 10/13).

Faubus shuts Little Rock's high schools

Sept 12. For the second year in a row, Little Rock, Arkansas, high schoolers look at the fall term with trepidation and uncertainty. The Supreme Court unanimously voted today to reject an appeal by the Little Rock school board for a delay in racial integration of Central High School. Governor Orval Faubus, upset with the ruling, ordered four Little Rock high schools closed next Monday when the new term is to commence. The governor's reply sets in motion a new political battle between the federal and state governments, the outcome of which will determine the future of school integration in the South (→ 29).

1958

OCTOBER

Su	Mo	Tu	We	Th	Fr	Sa
			1	2	3	4
5	6	7	8	9	10	11
12	13	14	15	16	17	18
19	20	21	22	23	24	25
26	27	28	29	30	31	

2. Detroit: U.A.W. gets three-year pacts with Chrysler, G.M.

3. N.Y. Port Authority opens Idlewild to jet airliners.

5. Tenn.: Dynamite wrecks Clinton High School, integrated in 1956 (→ 12).

6. Groton: Seawolf surfaces after setting 60-day underwater mark.

9. Milwaukee: Yankees defeat Braves 6-2 to win World Series.

10. National Congolese Movement founded by Patrice Lumumba (→ 12/28).

12. Atlanta: Synagogue destroyed by bomb blast (→ 1/20/59).

13. Cuba: Castro proclaims on radio, candidates for Nov. 3 elections will be executed for treason (→ 26).

16. Israel sentences eight border police for murder of 43 Israeli Arabs (→ 9/24/59).

19. Brussels: World's Fair closes with 41 mil. total visitors.

20. Thailand: Military chief Sarit Thanarat seizes power in bloodless coup.

20. Taiwan: Chinese Communists resume shelling of Quemoy after two-week truce (→ 11/3).

21. Florida: Truman accuses Ike of surrendering to Communists in 1952.

22. New York: 3,000 mark 75th anniversary of Metropolitan Opera.

23. Nova Scotia: Underground rock shift traps 96 miners.

25. Beirut: Last U.S. troops leave Lebanon (→ 11/10).

26. Cuba: Castro warns U.S. to stay out of revolt (→ 11/29).

27. South Africa: Negro women demonstrate against identity cards required of minorities (→ 3/22/60).

27. Pakistan: Iskander Mirza resigns; Mohammed Ayub Khan new president.

27. Pecos County, Tx.: World's deepest oil well reaches 25,340 feet before being abandoned.

31. Geneva: U.S., U.S.S.R., Britain reach accord on draft of nuclear test ban (→ 11/15).

Pasternak refuses Nobel for his novel

Pasternak, Soviet critic.

Oct 31. Author Boris Pasternak has been coerced into refusing the Nobel Prize for literature. While his letter to the Swedish Academy calls it "voluntary refusal," Westerners believe the Soviet government pressured him to decline. His novel "Doctor Zhivago," set at the time of the Russian Revolution, criticizes Soviet ideals.

Pasternak, 68 years old, has been a popular poet and translator. When he completed "Doctor Zhivago" earlier this year, he approached a Russian publisher, who rejected it on political grounds. Pasternak then had it released by an Italian firm. The book is basically a love story upholding Christian morals. Today, at a rally in Moscow, a leader of the Young Communist League denounced Pasternak as "a pig" (→ 2/15/59).

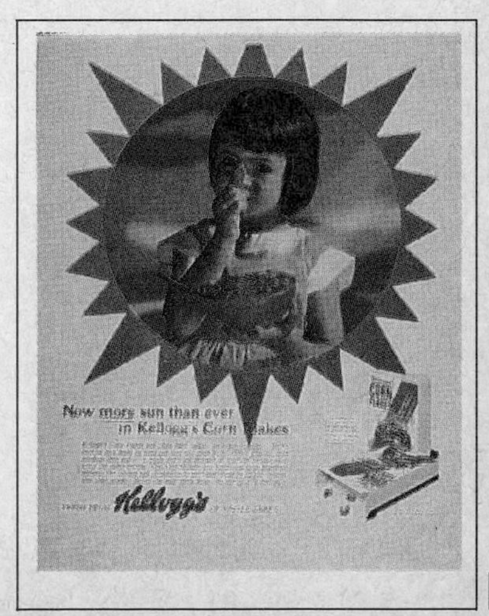

John XXIII will replace late Pius XII

Oct 28. Shortly before 5:00 this afternoon, white smoke rose from a small chimney above the Sistine Chapel at the Vatican. A new Pope had been elected. An hour later, he appeared on a balcony of St. Peter's Basilica as a large crowd of the faithful shouted "Viva il Papa!" Angelo Giuseppe Cardinal Roncalli, Patriarch of Venice, had been elevated to the papacy. He selected the name of John XXIII.

Thousands of Italians and tourists braved a taxi strike and rushed to St. Peter's Square when they saw the white smoke. They sang hymns and kneeled as Pope John gave his first blessing. Women held their children in the air above the crowd.

The Cardinals convened at the Vatican to elect a new pope after Pius XII died on the 9th. Pius placed major emphasis on the celebration of the mass and the Blessed Virgin Mary. John is regarded as a humble priest and an unassuming man. As Cardinal, he met with Italian Communists to discuss the problems of poverty and working conditions. Few expected that he would become pope, but he was elected on the 11th ballot after a relatively short enclave (→ 11/4).

Pope John XXIII in Vatican rites.

United States shows off X-15 rocket plane

The tiny X-15, resembling a mechanical bee, can soar at 4,500 mph.

Oct 15. The X-15 rocket plane, built to carry man higher and faster than ever before, was rolled out for its first public appearance today. The X-15, due to make its first flight in February, will reach a maximum speed of 4,500 miles an hour at altitudes between 100 and 150 miles. There is speculation that a more advanced model might be able to carry a pilot on an orbiting flight around the earth. Vice President Nixon, speaking at the Los Angeles rollout, said completion of the X-15 means that the United States leads in the race to outer space (→ 9/17/59).

Pioneer satellite fails to reach moon

Oct 12. A Pioneer satellite launched yesterday in an effort to orbit the moon burned up in the earth's atmosphere today after a 43-hour trip that took it only a third of the way to its goal. But United States officials said the spacecraft set a record by reaching an altitude of 68,800 miles above the earth and that it made valuable observations of the intense band of radiation around the earth. It also set a space speed record of 23,450 miles an hour. The flight failed because of a slight error in the initial angle of launch, officials said (→ 11/8).

Pioneer I at launching pad.

Russia lends money to build Aswan Dam

Oct 23. Stepping in to fill a gap left by withdrawal of Western aid, the Soviet Union said today it would loan Egypt money for construction of the Aswan High Dam. Premier Nikita Khrushchev said his government would lend up to 400 million rubles, $100 million at the official rate of exchange, and would also make available specialists, materials and tools.

The Aswan project is a centerpiece of a program by President Gamal Abdel Nasser to revitalize his country. It would increase Egypt's irrigated acreage by one third and add major electric generating capacity. The United States decision not to finance the project, announced two years ago, led to Nasser's seizure of the Suez Canal, which precipitated a British-French attack on Suez. Conceding that the Soviet announcement gave it increased leverage in the Mideast, the U.S. State Department said the Soviet involvement in the Aswan project could be a source of difficulties. The dam, largest ever planned, will cost $1.3 billion and will take about 20 years to build (→ 11/8/59).

Pan Am puts first 707 on Atlantic route

Oct 26. Pan American World Airways began regular transatlantic jet airliner service today when a Boeing 707 flew from New York International Airport to Paris. Pan American will also start jet service to Rome in two days, in what is regarded as the beginning of mass travel by jet airliner. Pan Am is the second airline to open regular transatlantic jet service. British Overseas Airways began New York-to-London service on October 4, the day after noise rules that had prevented use of jet aircraft at New York airports were changed. The jet flight takes seven hours, a third less than the fastest propeller plane (→ 1/25/59).

An upbeat marching band sends the 707 off on its inaugural N.Y.-Paris flight.

1958

NOVEMBER

Su	Mo	Tu	We	Th	Fr	Sa
						1
2	3	4	5	6	7	8
9	10	11	12	13	14	15
16	17	18	19	20	21	22
23	24	25	26	27	28	29
30						

3. Paris: Inauguration of UNESCO building.

3. Taiwan: Communist Chinese hit Quemoy with 38,000 shells (→ 2/7/59).

4. U.S.: Democrats gain 15 Senate seats, 48 in House; Nelson Rockefeller governor of N.Y.; JFK re-elected sen. from Mass.

4. Vatican: Pope John XXIII crowned as 262nd pontiff (→ 1/25/59).

6. Paris: Churchill given Cross of Lorraine by de Gaulle.

8. Florida: Third Air Force moon shot hits only 1,000 miles before falling to earth (→ 12/6).

10. Amman: King Hussein claims his plane was attacked by Syrian MIG's (→ 12/23).

12. Argentina, under martial law, foils plot laid to vice president; 700 seized (→ 1/20/59).

15. Ike rejects Soviet proposal for nuclear test ban (→ 28).

17. Americans Richard Cushing and John O'Hara now cardinals.

22. Algeria: Rebels to boycott election (→ 4/19/59).

24. Sudan: Coup leader Ibrahim Abboud, in power for week, proclaims independent republic.

27. Soviets threaten to cut lines to West Berlin if U.S. doesn't demilitarize (→ 2/16/59).

27. London: Nixon hosts Queen Elizabeth at U.S. Embassy for Thanksgiving dinner.

28. U.S. reports first full-range firing of ICBM (→ 12/19).

28. Africa: In five days, Mali, Mauritania, Senegal, Chad, Gabon, Congo-Brazzaville have all proclaimed republics (→ 12/18).

29. Philadelphia: Army beats Navy 22-6 in football.

29. Havana: Cuba arrests 30 officers who refuse to join new offensive against rebels (→ 12/30).

DEATHS

15. Tyrone Power, American actor (*5/5/1914).

15. Samuel Hopkins Adams, American journalist (*1/26/1871).

25. Charles F. Kettering, U.S. inventor (*8/29/1876).

The Hope diamond to the Smithsonian

Nov 8. There was once a 112-carat steel-blue diamond embedded in a statue of a Hindu god. In 1642, a thief stole it and he was promptly mauled to death by wild dogs. Marie Antoinette owned the jewel but did not wear it to the chopping block. A British banking family named Hope had it in the 1800's before their financial ruin.

Around 1900, a Turkish Sultan's courtesan wore the item before her untimely death. A former owner of the Washington Post had it before his son died in a car crash, his daughter committed suicide and he himself expired in a mental asylum. Today, jeweler Harry Winston gave the $1.5 million Hope diamond (now reduced to 44.5 carats) to the Smithsonian. With relief.

Starkweather's gal is sentenced to life

Nov 21. A 15-year-old girl named Caril Ann Fugate sobbed bitterly in a Lincoln, Nebraska, courthouse today. It was hard to tell if she cried from fear or relief: A jury of seven men and five women had just sentenced her to life in prison. She had been spared the electric chair.

Fugate and her boyfriend Charles Starkweather drove through Wyoming and Nebraska last January in a random killing spree. Eventually they claimed 11 victims. At his trial last May, Starkweather at first exonerated Fugate, saying she was his helpless hostage. He then recanted; her innocence was "hogwash." Witnesses insist that when the pair were arrested Fugate still seemed deeply attached to Starkweather. Fugate is guilty of murder in the first degree. Her lawyers will probably appeal the verdict.

1958

DECEMBER

Su	Mo	Tu	We	Th	Fr	Sa
	1	2	3	4	5	6
7	8	9	10	11	12	13
14	15	16	17	18	19	20
21	22	23	24	25	26	27
28	29	30	31			

1. Chicago: 90 die in tragic school fire.

6. Florida: Moon rocket with scientific instruments rises 65,000 miles before falling to earth (→ 1/4/59).

6. Japan: World's largest oil tanker, capacity one mil. barrels, launched at Kure (→ 1/19/60).

9. Two U.S. jets set records: N.Y.-to-London in 5:56; N.Y.-to-Paris in 6:16.

18. Africa: Since beginning of month, republics proclaimed in Central Africa, Nigeria, Upper Volta, Ivory Coast, Dahomey.

19. Geneva: Arms control talks end with little gain (→ 1/26/59).

23. Egypt: Nasser accuses Syrian Communists of opposing Arab nationalism (→ 1/25/59).

28. N.Y.: Colts beat Giants 23-17 in overtime for NFL title.

28. Congo: Lumumba declares independence a right, not a privilege (→ 11/1/59).

30. New York: Batista's sons arrive with reports Cuba's fall is near (→ 1/1/59).

31. Australia: U.S. retakes Davis Cup first time in three years.

CULTURAL EVENTS, 1958

Literature: Boris Pasternak's "Dr. Zhivago"; Leon Uris' "Exodus"; Harold Pinter's "The Birthday Party"; Lorraine Hansberry's "A Raisin in the Sun"; Truman Capote's "Breakfast at Tiffany's"; William Carlos Williams' "Paterson."

Academia: John Kenneth Galbraith's "The Affluent Society"; Levi Strauss' "Structural Anthropology"; Bondi, Gold and Hoyle fully propound steady state theory of universe.

Music: Samuel Barber's opera "Vanessa," Pulitzer; "Chanson d'Amour"; "Chipmunk Song"; "The Purple People Eater"; "Catch a Falling Star."

The Arts: Frank Lloyd Wright's Guggenheim Museum, N.Y.; Jasper John's "Three Flags."

Film: "Cat on a Hot Tin Roof," Elizabeth Taylor; "Me and the Colonel," Danny Kaye; Jacques Tati's "Mon Oncle"; "Gigi," Academy Award.

New law says work expands to fill time

"Work expands to fill the time for its completion." "Parkinson's Law," a best-seller by historian Cyril Parkinson, has other such axioms on business and bureaucracy. Another popular book examining life with a little less levity is "The Affluent Society," by John Kenneth Galbraith. Galbraith indicts Western economies when he writes that "wealth is the relentless enemy of understanding." He blames social imbalance on financial trends. Among noted fiction this year were Truman Capote's "Breakfast at Tiffany's," about an unusual ingenue, and Leon Uris' "Exodus," exploring the founding of Israel.

Drug causes horrid defects to 7,000

A major epidemic of severe, deforming birth defects is being linked to thalidomide, a drug sold in Europe as a sleeping pill and treatment for morning sickness during pregnancy. About 7,000 babies have been born with flipper-like arms and legs and other major deformities because their mothers took thalidomide during pregnancy, officials say. Most of the deformed babies have been born in West Germany and England. Thalidomide was kept off the market in the United States because Dr. Frances Kelsey, a medical officer with the Food and Drug Administration, had suspicions about its safety for pregnant women.

The Lincoln Continental.

1959

JANUARY

Su	Mo	Tu	We	Th	Fr	Sa
				1	2	3
4	5	6	7	8	9	10
11	12	13	14	15	16	17
18	19	20	21	22	23	24
25	26	27	28	29	30	31

1. Pasadena: Iowa defeates California 38-12 in Rose Bowl.

1. Egypt: Nasser arrests 200 Communists (→ 1/20/65).

1. Havana: Castro seizes power; Batista flees Cuba (→ 3).

3. Havana: Castro named head of Cuban army (→ 7).

4. Soviet rocket passes moon, signals 343,750 miles out (→ 27).

6. British jet Lightning P-1 flies double speed of sound.

7. U.S. recognizes new Cuban government (→ 16).

8. Dublin: Eamon de Valera resigns as premier to seek presidency (→ 5/27/64).

14. New Delhi: Nehru daughter Indira Gandhi emerges as leading choice for president (→ 2/2).

16. U.S.: AEC displays atomic generator smaller than man's hat (→ 7/21).

19. Buenos Aires: Transport workers stage general walkout, crippling nation (→ 20).

20. Texas Sen. Lyndon Johnson commits influence to passing civil rights bill (→ 2/2).

20. Washington: Sen. John F. Kennedy offers labor bill to drive out racketeers (→ 9/4).

20. Argentine Pres. Arturo Frondizi arrives in U.S. for state visit (→ 3/24/60).

25. Amman: Jordanian King Hussein says he will end feud with Egypt's Nasser (→ 3/10).

25. American Airlines begins first coast-to-coast jet service, N.Y.-L.A. on Boeing 707.

25. Vatican: Pope John XXIII, seeking unity between Catholics and others, calls ecumenical council (→ 4/13).

26. Geneva: U.S., U.K. offer Soviets guarantees for impartial intl. control of test ban (→ 2/6).

27. Moscow: Khrushchev proclaims rocket success shifts power balance to Soviets (→ 27).

27. NASA selects 110 candidates for first U.S. space flight (→ 2/17).

DEATH

3. Edwin Muir, Scottish poet and critic (*5/15/1887).

Fidel Castro's forces conquer Cuba

Castro, charismatic rebel leader, marks a new era in Cuban history.

Jan 16. Cuban revolutionaries have completely supplanted the government of Fulgencio Batista, replacing him with rebel leader Fidel Castro's choice of Manuel Urrutia as provisional President. The Cuban leader resigned to "prevent further bloodshed" and has sought refuge in the Dominican Republic. While Castro and his men have seized power, they will remain on "war footing" until they are sure the remaining members of Batista's junta accept the change of leadership.

When news of the change in power reached the masses, people stormed into the streets to celebrate. The red and black flag of the rebels was displayed on buildings and cars. In some areas, violence broke out, and the office of El Tiempo, a newspaper owned by a close friend of Batista, was set ablaze. People in Cuba are both elated and scared by the success of the revolution.

The first official order of the new administration was to lift the suspension of constitutional rights imposed by Batista during the two-year rebellion and to allow freedom of the press. President Urrutia and Castro, who was named to head the military, also claim that they intend to restore Cuba's economy, refurbish its democracy and oppose dictatorships in Latin America.

The United States government moved swiftly in recognizing the new government; within days of Castro's takeover of Havana on the 1st, the State Department sent a note of recognition to President Urrutia. Normally, America waits for a new nation to become fully established and for several Latin American countries to recognize a new regime first. But upon hearing that the Cuban regime will honor international agreements, United States officials apparently felt no need to delay (→ 2/10).

De Gaulle takes office as French President

Jan 8. Charles de Gaulle has been both General and Premier in his long and illustrious military and political career in France. Today, he has a new title, and it is not a ceremonial one. As President of the Fifth Republic, De Gaulle has more authority than any French leader since Emperor Napoleon III. At his inaugural ceremony at the Elysee Palace in Paris, de Gaulle indicated he will use that authority to "impose" his will upon the government.

De Gaulle, who received more than 78% of the vote in the election last month, was honored at the ceremony by the outgoing President of the Fourth Republic, Rene Coty. "The first among Frenchmen is now the first in France," Coty said.

De Gaulle was swept back to power by the crisis in Algeria, but he managed to skirt the issue of Algeria's future in his inaugural address. The new president said that Algeria, colonized since 1830, has a "choice place" in the new French Community and will be able to develop "closely associated with France." What that association will be, de Gaulle did not say. It could mean continued "integration" as a department of France. Or it could mean more autonomy.

De Gaulle enters Elysee Palace.

End comes for great director of epics

Jan 21. Cecil B. De Mille, master of "colossal" and "stupendous" movie spectacles, died of a heart ailment today in his Hollywood home. Born in Massachusetts in 1881 to actor parents, he went on stage at 17. In 1913, he joined Jesse Lasky and Sam Goldwyn to make "The Squaw Man," one of the earliest four-reel features, in a Los Angeles stable. His "Ten Commandments" in 1923 was a huge hit so he made it again in 1956.

De Mille produced more than 70 major films and won an Academy Award in 1953 for "The Greatest Show on Earth." Among his many honors are Knight of the Legion of Honor (France) and the Most Exalted Order of the White Elephant (Thailand). At the time of his death, he was preparing "On My Honor" about the Boy Scout movement and its founder, Lord Baden-Powell. De Mille was lavish with gifts to educational institutions.

Soviets send rocket hurtling past the moon

The Lunik, miracle of Soviet science.

Jan 5. A "cosmic rocket" carrying a hammer-and-sickle emblem and Lunik satellite has flown past the moon and is on its way to a permanent orbit around the sun, the Soviet Union has announced. At 4 a.m. Moscow time, the rocket was reported to be 343,750 miles from earth, traveling at a speed of at least 5,500 miles an hour. Its weight was given as 3,238 pounds, including 795 pounds of instruments to measure the moon's magnetic field, cosmic radiation and interplanetary space. The rocket was launched Friday and passed over Hawaii before heading for outer space. Soviet spokesmen say the failure of the U.S. to match their nation's space feats means the balance of power is shifting in their favor (→ 27).

Alaska becomes 49th and largest state

Jan 3. Alaska became a state today at two minutes past noon in the White House. In Juneau, capital of the 49th state, it was 9:02 a.m., as President Eisenhower signed the document of proclamation as well as an executive order setting a new design of 49 stars for the official flag of the United States: seven staggered rows of stars, seven stars in each row, plus the traditional 13 stripes. The president then made a brief informal greeting to the people of Alaska, while their Democratic congressional delegation stood beside his chair in the White House.

History was thus made with a minimum of ceremony and no pomp. Today's proclamation came almost as an anti-climactic end to a 42-year struggle for statehood, finally approved by the Senate last June, 64 to 20. Last time a statehood proclamation was signed was by President Taft for Arizona on February 14, 1912. Alaska, a U.S. territory since 1912, is nearly one-fifth the size of the rest of the U.S., making it the largest but the least populous state in the union.

"Hug the hoop to the backside, push hard with the right hand, now rock, swing it, sway it . . . you got it." So goes the advice given by Wham-O to its 30 million Hula Hoop users. Stolen from the Australians by J. Russell and D. Reynolds, the fad may fade as fast as it unfolded; prices are down from $2.79 to $.50. But a Belgian expedition to Antarctica took 20 along.

1959

FEBRUARY

Su	Mo	Tu	We	Th	Fr	Sa
1	2	3	4	5	6	7
8	9	10	11	12	13	14
15	16	17	18	19	20	21
22	23	24	25	26	27	28

2. Virginia: Arlington, Norfolk peacefully desegregate public schools (→ 18).

6. Cape Canaveral: Titan ICBM fired for first time (→ 3/18).

7. Soviets sign pact with Peking to aid in Chinese industrial expansion (→ 5/28).

10. Havana: Electoral age reduced to 30; Castro now eligible for presidency (→ 16).

11. Iran turns down Soviet aid in favor of U.S. proposal (→ 3/2).

15. Moscow: Boris Pasternak, ousted for "Dr. Zhivago," seeks return to Soviet Writer's Union.

16. U.S. rejects Soviet plan for 28-nation talks on Germany, asks meeting of Big Four (→ 24).

16. Havana: Castro takes oath as Cuban premier (→ 3/22).

17. U.S. launches first weather station in space, Vanguard II satellite (→ 3/1).

17. Tunis: Bourguiba to oust French military base if Algerian War continues (→ 7/19/61).

18. Front Royal, Virginia: White students boycott school as 22 Negroes enter (→ 5/25).

19. U.K., Greece, Turkey agree on Cypriot autonomy (→ 3/1).

20. U.S.: FCC applies equal time rule to TV newscasts of political candidates (→ 9/1959).

20. Acapulco: Ike, Mexico Pres. Lopez Mateos agree to build Diablo Dam on Rio Grande.

23. British premier in Moscow first time since war; U.K. and Soviets to expand trade and cultural relations (→ 26).

24. Moscow: Khrushchev rejects Western plan for Big Four parley on Germany (→ 5/10).

25. Rhodesia proclaims state of emergency, dissolves African nationalist parties (→ 4/13/64).

26. N.Y. Philharmonic to go to U.S.S.R. in summer (→ 7/25).

BIRTH

16. John Patrick McEnroe, American tennis star.

DEATH

1. Willie Hoppe, legendary U.S. billiards player (*10/11/1887).

Rock and rollers die in small plane

Feb 3. A small plane carrying rock-and-roll singers Buddy Holly, J.P. "Big Bopper" Richardson and Richie Valens crashed early today near Mason City, Iowa, killing all three and sending millions of teen-aged fans into mourning.

The aircraft, headed for Fargo, North Dakota, where the performers were scheduled to appear tonight, took off in light snow at about 1:00 a.m. It hit the ground within minutes, also killing the pilot. Authorities blamed weather conditions for the crash.

The singers had each scored million-selling hit records in recent months: Holly, 22, with "Peggy Sue" and "That'll be the Day"; Richardson, 24, with "Chantilly Lace"; and Valens, 17, with "Donna" and "La Bamba."

Indira Gandhi to lead Indian party

Feb 2. Family tradition still counts for something in Indian politics. Indira Gandhi, the only daughter of Prime Minister Jawaharlal Nehru and the granddaughter of a statesman, has been elected President of the Congress Party in India. Mrs. Gandhi will be installed into her new office next Sunday, and her job is not expected to be an easy one.

The Congress Party has been wracked by internal dissension and has been on the verge of collapse. It is hoped that Mrs. Gandhi, who is 41, will breath some new life into the party. Most of the politicians who have been arguing about the future of their party and country are fairly old. Mrs. Gandhi, who is known for her leftist sentiments, is expected to act quickly to put her own mark on party policies.

1959

MARCH

Su	Mo	Tu	We	Th	Fr	Sa
1	2	3	4	5	6	7
8	9	10	11	12	13	14
15	16	17	18	19	20	21
22	23	24	25	26	27	28
29	30	31				

1. Calif.: Air Force receives signals from Discoverer satellite launched yesterday (→ 4).

1. Cyprus: Archbishop Makarios returns after three-year exile (→ 12/14).

2. Iran renounces 1921 treaty with Soviet Union (→ 5).

4. Pioneer IV speeds past moon for orbit around sun (→ 17).

5. U.S. pledges continued military aid to Iran, Pakistan and Turkey (→ 24).

7. France to pull Mediterranean fleet out of NATO in case of war (→ 6/5).

10. Iraqi air assault reported in Syria (→ 8/14).

14. Italy: Aldo Moro chosen head of Christian Democrats.

17. U.S.: Scientists write off Discoverer I as missing, doubt it was ever in orbit (→ 19).

18. Ike signs bill to make Hawaii 50th state (→ 8/21).

18. U.S. reveals nuclear tests at unparalleled 300-mile altitude last September (→ 21).

19. Anthony Perkins and Audrey Hepburn appear in "Green Mansions."

19. Westford, Mass.: First known radar contact made with Venus (→ 4/14).

20. Lhasa: Tibetans battle Chinese, resisting attempt to seize Dalai Lama.→

21. Washington: Radioactive strontium 90 reported greatest in U.S. (→ 6/9).

22. Havana: Castro bars pledge to join U.S. in Cold War against U.S.S.R. (→ 4/3).

24. Iraq pulls out of Baghdad Pact after revolution (→ 6/1).

DEATHS

3. Lou Costello, American comedian, partner of Bud Abbott (→ 3/6/1908).

15. Duncan Hines, American gourmet (*1880).

15. Lester Young, American jazz tenor player (*8/27/1909).

26. Raymond Chandler, American writer, detective novels (*7/23/1888).

Dalai Lama leaves Tibet to Chinese rule

March 20. For the first time, officials of the Indian government are confirming reports of widespread resistance to the Chinese occupying forces in Tibet. Open warfare has erupted in the capital city of Lhasa, and the Dalai Lama, the spiritual leader of Buddhist Tibetans, has disappeared. There have been reports he was arrested by the Chinese forces. But it is widely believed the Dalai Lama has escaped and will seek political asylum in India.

India's Prime Minister Jawaharlal Nehru has avoided confirming reports of the violence in Tibet, partly because he is concerned about offending the Chinese. Nehru is also reluctant to allow India to become a refuge for the Khamba tribesmen, who are badly outnumbered in their fight against the Chinese.

The trouble in Lhasa apparently began ten days ago, during celebrations of the Tibetan New Year. As the festivities got out of hand, the Chinese moved to arrest the Dalai Lama. Angered by the threat, residents of Lhasa fought with the Khambas against the Chinese. Some 2,000 of the foreign troops were killed, but reinforcements quashed the rebellion (→ 4/18).

Gomulka addresses Communist nations

Marx, Lenin and Gomulka.

March 10. In a speech before Communists from 42 nations, Polish leader Wladyslaw Gomulka said Soviet intercontinental missiles had "bankrupted" Western policy. He remarked at the opening session of the Congress of Polish Unity Workers that the awesome strength of Soviet firepower puts the West into an arms race that depletes its financial resources and frustrates policy-makers. Capitalism, he claimed, is an ill institution.

Gomulka, in his boisterous oratorical style, also stressed that while Poland would not return to the repression of the Stalin era, it would suppress "anti-Socialist activities." He used much of his seven-hour speech to warn of the threat of a strengthened West Germany. He said if the government in Bonn refused to sign a peace treaty with Poland, his nation would sign a comprehensive separate pact with East Germany.

Broadway gets two contrasting hits

March. Two powerful plays arrived on Broadway this month. "A Raisin in the Sun" by Lorraine Hansberry opened March 11 to excellent reviews. "Sweet Bird of Youth" by Tennessee Williams was shown a day earlier to similar raves.

"Raisin" follows a Negro family in Chicago. The matriarch (Claudia McNeil) awaits $10,000—her late husband's life insurance premium. She tries to keep her children's hopes and goals high. Sidney Poitier plays her driven son.

"Sweet Bird" alights on a Hollywood has-been and her young male companion. The unlikely couple (Geraldine Page and Paul Newman) return to an unwelcoming Southern town. When the forces clash, the feathers fly.

"Rio Bravo": Wayne is a small-town sheriff trying to keep crime off the streets and in his jail.

1959

APRIL

Su	Mo	Tu	We	Th	Fr	Sa
			1	2	3	4
5	6	7	8	9	10	11
12	13	14	15	16	17	18
19	20	21	22	23	24	25
26	27	28	29	30		

3. Havana: Castro demands U.S. restore Cuba's former sugar quota (→ 17).

3. U.S. begins study of nuclear fallout from tests (→ 6/9).

7. Britain passes $1 bil. tax cut to foster economic expansion.

7. Oklahoma, by referendum, ends 51 years of Prohibition.

7. Los Alamos: AEC announces first conversion of energy from atomic reactor directly into electricity (→ 7/21).

10. Tokyo: Michiko Shoda weds Crown Prince Akihito, first commoner to marry heir to throne.

13. Vatican: Pope John bans Catholic vote for any pro-Communist (→ 7/2).

14. U.S. launches recoverable satellite Discoverer II (→ 5/28).

14. France: Left-wing Gaullists form Democratic Work Union.

15. Castro arrives in Washington for 11-day U.S. visit (→ 17).

16. Cairo: Arab nations meet for first oil conference.

18. Ike names Christian Herter sec. of state to succeed Dulles, out due to health (→ 5/27).

18. Peking: Premier Chou En-lai insists Tibetan Dalai Lama was abducted to India (→ 9/9).

18. India, Pakistan sign one-year pact on Indus River irrigation.

19. Lamar, Missouri: Truman's birthplace dedicated as state shrine.

19. Algiers: Eight slain, 20 abducted as voting starts in Algeria (→ 7/23).

22. Vatican: Princess Margaret and Queen Mother Elizabeth visit Pope John.

25. St. Lawrence Seaway opens, links Great Lakes to Atlantic.→

27. Peking: Liu Shao-chi, leading theoretician, succeeds Mao as head of state.→

28. U.S. Senate confirms Clare Booth Luce as ambassador to Brazil; husband asks her to resign due to criticism (→ 5/1).

DEATH

20. Edward Johnson, Canadian operatic tenor, manager of Metropolitan Opera (*8/22/1881).

Wright dies: Iconoclast among architects

April 9. Frank Lloyd Wright, who considered himself "the greatest living architect," died today after emergency surgery to remove an intestinal obstruction. The Wisconsin native was 89 years old.

The man who pleaded for a curb to America's "lust for ugliness" created not only great buildings but controversy his whole life. He was a supreme egotist. When on May 28, 1953, he was awarded the Gold Medal of the National Institute of Arts and Letters, he said: "I feel coming on me a strange disease—humility." As a gift, he would offer to rearrange a friend's furniture.

Wright's parents were intensely religious, and from them he developed his strong sense of individuality and rebelliousness. He left the University of Wisconsin in his last year for Chicago, where he studied under Louis Sullivan, the "father of the skyscraper." Wright came to detest steel, stone cities, declaring "a box is more of a coffin for the human spirit than an inspiration."

His own philosophy was that form should follow function. He won fame with his low terrain-conforming "prairie homes"; the Falling Water House in Pennsylvania; and the Imperial Hotel in Tokyo, the only large structure to survive the 1922 earthquake. Not bad for a high school dropout (→ 10/21).

The dean of American architects.

Bolshoi Ballet arrives for tour of States

April 12. For the fourth time in nearly 200 years, Moscow's Bolshoi Ballet has ventured outside Russia. The troupe is in New York, first leg of an eight-week tour of the United States and Canada. Most of the 216 members spent their first night here munching frankfurters and seeing a circus at Madison Square Garden. The dancers will jete and plie in the same arena a few days hence.

The most enthusiastic hot dog eater was soloist Maya Plisetskaya. Many balletomanes predict that the graceful 33-year-old will be the company's next prima ballerina.

Bolshoi dancers in "The Doves."

Castro visits U.S.; denies Red influence

April 17. "I have said very clearly that we are not Communists," declared Cuban Premier Fidel Castro in a speech before the American Society of Newspaper Editors. The new leader, who seized power on January 1, made several points to his audience and judging from the volume of applause after his address, it seems he impressed them. Castro said his main concern is to develop the island-nation's industry and to curb its high unemployment.

He also promised to sustain the agreement which grants America the right to hold a naval base at Guantanamo Bay in Cuba and to maintain Cuba's membership in a mutual defense treaty with the U.S. and 21 Western hemisphere republics. Earlier, Castro met with members of the Senate and House, assuring them as well that his rebellion was devoid of Communists (→ 5/2).

British ballet star arrested by Panama

April 20. The tale is as dramatic as any staged by the Royal Ballet. Dancer Margot Fonteyn is held tonight on suspicion of fomenting a revolt against Panama's government. Officials are searching for her husband, Roberto Arias. The son of a former Panamanian President, he is charged with planning an attack on a government garrison. The couple spent the day on their yacht in the Gulf of Panama. The government says Arias was planning his coup aboard the ship. He eluded capture by leaping to a passing shrimp boat. Rumors are he is now at his family's cattle ranch.

Liu Shao-chi named as Mao's successor

April 27. Liu Shao-chi has been named by the Chinese Communist Party to succeed Mao Tse-tung as head of state. A stalwart of the party since its founding in 1921, Liu was renowned as a labor organizer. He became a member of the Central Committee in 1927, and in 1934 was promoted to the Politburo. He became the party's leading expert on organization and its chief theoretician, second only to Mao in political authority. His manual "How to Be a Good Communist" (1939) is used as the orthodox text for the indoctrination of new party members (→ 9/17).

NASA has chosen 7 astronauts (l to r): Scott Carpenter, Gordon Cooper, John Glenn, Gus Grissom, Walter Schirra, Alan Shepard, Deke Slayton.

April 25. The Atlantic and the Great Lakes are linked, consummating Jacques Cartier's 1535 dream. The St. Lawrence Seaway, open after five years of construction, was a major joint U.S.-Canadian project (→ 6/26).

1959

MAY

Su	Mo	Tu	We	Th	Fr	Sa
					1	2
3	4	5	6	7	8	9
10	11	12	13	14	15	16
17	18	19	20	21	22	23
24	25	26	27	28	29	30
31						

1. New York: The Texas Co. changes name to Texaco Inc.

2. Castro calls on U.S. for $30 bil. over ten years to make Latin Am. safe for democracy (→ 18).

2. Shoemaker gets second victory in Kentucky Derby, on Tommy Lee.

10. Rome: Archeologists find ruins of Nero's gardens.

10. Moscow: First census in 20 years puts Soviet population at 208.8 million.

10. Geneva: Soviets propose participation of East and West Germany in Big Four talks (→ 11).

11. Geneva: Big Four meet to discuss German reunification (→ 4/22/60).

13. Florida: New epidemic of land fever sweeping state; lots being sold by mail.

14. New York: Ike breaks ground at Lincoln Center for new Performing Arts Center.

18. Laos: Fighting breaks out between royal troops and Pathet Lao in Jarres Valley (→ 7/31).

18. Cuba: U.S. sugar mills to lose plantations by new law (→ 23).

20. U.S.: Japanese-Americans regain citizenship lost in WWII.

20. Ford wins battle to call new cars Falcon, registering name 20 minutes before Chrysler.

22. U.S. agrees on nuclear cooperation with Canada.

22. Vatican: Pope sees King Paul in first meeting with Greek ruler since 1439.

22. U.S.: Benjamin O. Davis first Negro to gain rank of maj. gen.

23. Havana: Govt. to take over seven Cuban airlines (→ 6/12).

25. U.S. Supreme Court outlaws Louisiana ban on fights between white, Negro boxers (→ 6/18).

28. Munich: Olympics bar Taiwan in favor of Peking (→ 9/22).

28. Big Four ministers have first major airborne intl. conference en route back to Geneva.

30. Rodger Ward is victor in Indy 500, averaging 138.6 mph in Leader Card 500 Special.

31. NASA to use satellites for transcontinental radio (→ 6/2).

Two monkeys survive American space trip

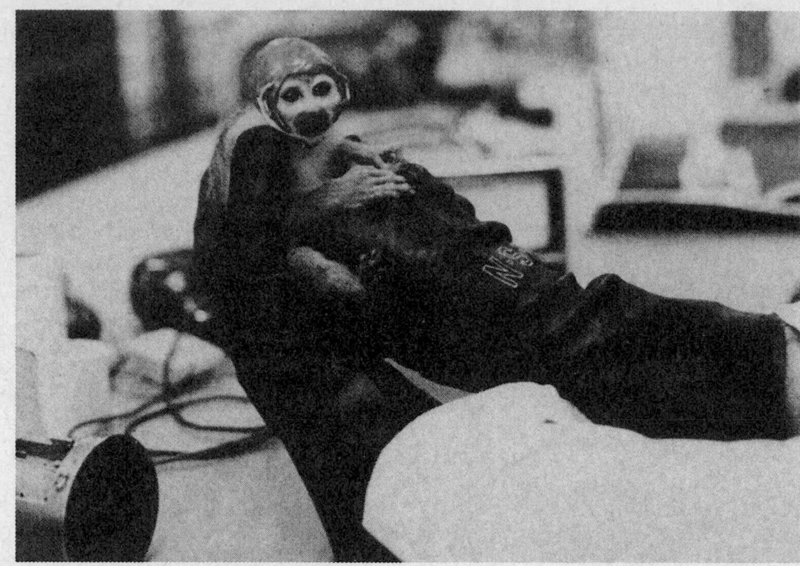

A NASA scientist prepares little Baker for his debut as an astronaut.

May 28. Two monkeys were picked up alive from the Atlantic Ocean today after a 1,700-mile space trip that took them to a height of 360 miles in the nose cone of a Jupiter rocket. The monkeys' flight is a prelude to the first manned United States space flight, expected in about two years. Seven candidates for the mission have been picked by the National Aeronautics and Space Administration.

Today's trip was made by a seven-pound rhesus monkey named Able and a one-pound squirrel monkey named Baker, both heavily wired to gather data about the effects of space flight on living beings. Able was also trained to tap a telegraph key when a red light flashed to see whether acceleration to a maximum speed of 10,000 miles would affect performance on basic tasks. The U.S. plans to get more data by sending four mice into orbit next week. The Soviets sent the dog Laika into orbit aboard Sputnik 2, but she did not return to earth alive (→ 31).

Brinksman Dulles, ex-Secretary, is dead

May 27. Former Secretary of State John Foster Dulles, known as a fighter all his life and the man who defined brinksmanship as the fine art of almost going to war, today lost the battle he had waged against cancer for two years.

Dulles, man on the brink.

The architect of America's Cold War policy, Dulles accused the Democrats of being soft on communism and threatened to use nuclear bombs to meet Soviet aggression. At the Republican convention in 1952, he urged the liberation of Soviet-dominated countries but abandoned that stance after the Allies failed to come to Hungary's aid during the 1956 uprising.

Dulles' messianic opposition to communism drew mixed reviews from the Allies; the obituary in England's Daily Telegraph typified world reaction. Dulles' attitude, it said, "may have denied the West advantageous moments for negotiation ... but without this crusading approach it is doubtful whether the peoples of the West could have maintained the will to go on fighting the Cold War." Dulles received the Medal of Freedom last month.

Clare Luce resigns ambassadorial post

May 1. Clare Boothe Luce resigned today as Ambassador to Brazil, a post she was appointed to on April 28. In a letter to President Eisenhower, she said criticism of her by Senator Wayne Morse had "poisoned" the climate of goodwill necessary for the success of the mission. After trying to dissuade her, the president accepted "with regret" her decision. Morse has carried on a one-man battle against Luce's nomination, calling her "unqualified," "emotionally unstable" and worse. Henry R. Luce, Editor-in-Chief of Time, Life, and Fortune, advised his wife to resign, feeling strongly that much of the criticism was aimed at him and his position.

Bright-eyed Clare Boothe Luce.

Blue Whale fading

May 15. The blue whale, one of the largest mammals ever known on earth, could be extinct in five years unless restrictions are placed on the international whaling industry, scientists warned today. In fact, the blue whale population has dropped so low that individual whales now have difficulty finding other members of their species for mating.

Records of the whaling industry show a steady decline in the blue whale population. In the 1931-32 season, blue whales were 82.1% of the total catch. In 1957, only 4.6% of the catch consisted of blue whales. The scientists recommend immediate adoption of strict controls on the catch at the next International Whaling Commission meeting, to be held next month in London. The whales are hunted primarily for their oil.

1959

JUNE

Su	Mo	Tu	We	Th	Fr	Sa
	1	2	3	4	5	6
7	8	9	10	11	12	13
14	15	16	17	18	19	20
21	22	23	24	25	26	27
28	29	30				

1. Nicaragua: National Guard hunting armed invaders in southwest (→ 11/11/60).

1. Badhdad: Iraq bars U.S. military aid due to conflict with new policy of neutrality (→ 10/9).

3. U.S. recovers mice from earlier space shot (→ 7/6).

3. Singapore gains self-govt. within British Commonwealth.

5. London: Queen Elizabeth convenes NATO nations, assembled to reaffirm unity (→ 12/21/62).

9. U.S. launches George Washington, first nuclear sub with ballistic missiles (Polaris) (→ 11).

11. Ike advises Congress he will send nuclear arms to Greece (→ 9/22).

11. U.S. Postmaster General bans "Lady Chatterley's Lover" from U.S. mails.

11. London: New land-sea vehicle Hovercraft unveiled.

12. Brigitte Bardot is married to Jacques Charrier.

12. Havana: Five Cuban ministers resign in dispute with Castro over land reform (→ 25).

15. N.Y. Stock Exchange reports 13 mil. Americans own stocks.

16. U.S. Defense Dept. reports two MIG jet fighters with Soviet markings attacked Navy patrol plane over Sea of Japan.

18. Federal court annuls Arkansas law allowing schools closings to prevent integration (→ 7/12).

22. Tallahassee: Four white youths get life terms for raping Negro co-ed.

23. London: Dr. Klaus Emil Fuchs, jailed for giving Soviets A-bomb secrets, is released.

24. British collector Leonard Koetser pays $770,000 for Reubens' "Adoration of the Magi."

25. Cuba seizes 2.35 mil. acres under new agrarian reform law (→ 30).

26. Milan: TWA airliner crashes in thunderstorm, killing 68.

26. Quebec: Queen Elizabeth II and Ike dedicate St. Lawrence Seaway.

30. Ike raises federal debt ceiling to $295 billion.

Quarrels break out in Castro regime

June 30. An agrarian reform bill, instituted by Fidel Castro, has ruptured the new government of Cuba. Five Cabinet ministers resigned as a result of the new law which breaks up large landholdings, confiscating thousands of acres from Cuban and foreign property owners.

In Washington, the administration voiced "serious concern" that compensation be paid to Americans who owned some of the lucrative sugar-producing land. According to Castro, the policy is at the heart of the revolutionary sentiment. He also asserted the resignations do not splinter his regime. "The revolutionary government is as solid as a rock and is treated with respect by the great and the small," he said.

In a related note, the chief of Cuba's air force has resigned. Major Pedro Diaz Lanz quit today, citing Communist infiltration of the armed services as his rationale. "The Communist elements have exerted pressure to carry out a certain plan of indoctrination," he said. Castro has repeatedly denied Communist affiliation (→ 7/12).

Host of Mafiosi conclave is dead

June 17. Joseph Barbara, the man whose home played convention center to the Mafia, eluded the police just as he had most of his life when he slipped away due to natural causes last night.

In November 1957, 60 luminaries of the underworld, sporting gold watches, diamond belt buckles and over three thousand dollars in cash, met at Barbara's house in Apalachin, New York. Over 40 of the "delegates" who were arrested by the police claimed they were paying their respects to the ailing Barbara and "just happened" to show up on the same day. Police speculate that the real reason for the meeting was to discuss jurisdiction in various crime operations and the assassination of Mafia leader Albert Anastasia. Barbara, who had a wine and soft drink company, was suspected of four murders by the police, but his only conviction was for illegally procuring sugar.

Johansson of Sweden conquers Patterson

June 26. Ingemar Johansson struck down Floyd Patterson with fists like the hammer of Thor and became the first non-American to hold the world heavyweight championship in 25 years. The lightly regarded Swede, in becoming the first native-born Scandinavian ever to win the title, floored Patterson seven times before the referee halted the fight in the third round. Patterson, who had ascended to the title by beating Archie Moore in 1956, was knocked out at two minutes, three seconds of the third with a right-hand punch that Johansson later boasted about but few people had seen (→ 6/20/60).

Patterson, down and out in the 3rd.

Ethel Barrymore, stage royalty, dies

All warmth and dignity on stage.

June 18. "That's all there is, there isn't any more," Miss Ethel Barrymore once explained to an audience demanding an encore. Theatergoers today learned there will be no more forever: The great actress has died in Beverly Hills at age 79.

Miss Barrymore was born in 1879 in Philadelphia to a family of prominent thespians. She appeared on stage at age 14 but was not hailed until she played in "Captain Jinks of the Horse Marines" in 1901. Among ensuing triumphs were "The Corn Is Green" in 1940.

Miss Barrymore's rich, full voice and stately walk earned her a regal reputation. "The Royal Family," a play by Edna Ferber and George S. Kaufman, is based on the lives of Miss Barrymore and her volatile brothers, John and Lionel.

Space monkey loses life after returning

June 2. One of the two monkeys that circled the earth last week has died of causes unrelated to the flight. Able, a seven-pound rhesus monkey, was having its cerebral electrode removed in an operation last night when it expired. An Army representative at the Fort Knox, Ky., hospital said the animal probably received too much anesthesia. An autopsy is expected.

Able and her partner Baker, a tiny squirrel monkey, flew in the nose cone of a Jupiter ballistic missile. Electrodes recorded their heart rate, temperature and other data. No ill effects were noted at the end of their 1,700-mile journey. Today, Baker had its electrode removed without anesthesia. The animal seems in fine spirits (→ 3).

1959

JULY

Su	Mo	Tu	We	Th	Fr	Sa
			1	2	3	4
5	6	7	8	9	10	11
12	13	14	15	16	17	18
19	20	21	22	23	24	25
26	27	28	29	30	31	

1. Bonn: Dr. Heinrich Luebke elected president of West Germany (→ 2/17/63).

2. Vatican: Pope John XXIII, in first encyclical, urges all steps be taken toward world peace.

3. Wimbledon: Alex Olmedo over Rod Laver 6-4, 6-4, 6-4; Maria Bueno over Dorothy Hard 6-4, 6-3 (→ 16).

5. Jakarta: Sukarno issues decree reinstating repressive 1945 constitution (→ 8/17/60).

5. Jerusalem: Premier David Ben Gurion resigns in crisis over arms sale (→ 1/31/61).

6. Soviets report bringing two dogs and a rabbit back safely from upper atmosphere (→ 8/7).

8. Washington: Ike says Catholicism should be no bar to presidency (→ 12/30).

9. Bienhoa, South Vietnam: Two U.S. soldiers killed by Communist guerrillas (→ 10/26/60).

12. Havana: Castro denounces U.S. for giving asylum to Cuban air force ex-chief (→ 18).

14. U.S.: Unemployment up by 1.4 million from mid-May.

15. U.S.: 500,000 steel workers strike for new contract (→ 10/9).

16. Chicago: Wimbledon winner Olmedo thrown out of national clay courts for listless play.

18. Spanish racer Federico Bahamontes wins Tour de France.

18. Havana: Castro ousts Urrutia, takes presidency (→ 8/12).

20. Spain joins Western European trading community.

21. Camden, N.J.: U.S. launches world's first atomic merchant ship, Savannah (→ 3/23/60).

23. Algeria: France lands sea and air forces to begin offensive in Kabylia region (→ 8/27).

27. U.S. celebrates centennial of first American oil strike, Edwin Drake's well at Titusville, Penn.

31. Laos: Jungle fighting between govt., Pathet Lao spreads to second province (→ 8/20).

DEATH

6. George Grosz, German-American artist (*7/26/1893).

The Kitchen Debate: Nixon vs. Nikita

Nixon shows Khrushchev the domestic perks of a consumer economy.

July 25. Vice President Richard Nixon and Soviet Premier Nikita Khrushchev publicly argued the virtues of capitalism and communism yesterday in Moscow. The vice president was formally opening the American National Exhibition when the sharp exchanges took place in the model kitchen of the exhibit. While neither world leader seemed angry, each seemed unwilling to back down in this verbal confrontation of one-upmanship, which included a potpourri of subjects—from the merits of washing machines and free exchange of ideas to summit meetings and rockets.

Khrushchev at one point told Nixon, "You don't know anything about communism except fear of it." After a lengthy discourse, in which he seemed to be gaining momentum, the Soviet leader's sails were trimmed when Nixon accused him of "filibustering."

Today, Nixon warded off a shower of remarks, as hecklers challenged him on the issue of free speech, while being escorted on a tour of Moscow (→ 8/1).

Lady doesn't sing the blues anymore

July 17. A few weeks ago police arrested Billie Holiday on charges of illegal narcotics possession. They didn't know they had arrested a dying woman. The life of Lady Day, once the finest singer of the blues, ended today. She was 44.

Miss Holiday was born in Baltimore, Maryland, an illegitimate child of a jazz musician. She was raised by her mother in New York, where she sang in nightclubs at an early age. In the 1930's her fame took a sudden upswing when she recorded torch songs such as "My Man" and "Mean to Me." In the 40's she performed with the bands of Count Basie and Paul Winter, singing out her personal despair.

Lady Day and Sid Catlett on drums.

NAACP cites end to lynching and stronger rights for Americans

July 12. For 50 years, the National Association for the Advancement of Colored People has fought diligently to undo the shackles of injustice strapped to American Negroes and others. Today, in a parley marking the golden anniversary of the NAACP, 2,000 delegates met at the New York Coliseum to examine the organization's achievements.

Wilkins and ex-chief Walter White.

Executive Secretary Roy Wilkins opened the meeting, praising the efforts of the association, which has put an end to the lynching of Negroes and also instituted constitutional safeguards for all Americans.

Wilkins was asked about an incident in which Dr. Ralph Bunche, Under Secretary for Special Political Affairs at the United Nations, and his son were refused membership in the West Side Tennis Club at Forest Hills, Queens, because they are Negroes. Wilkins commended Bunche for putting the incident into perspective as an insignificant embarrassment compared to the denial of the right to vote and other rights refused Negroes for years. "Let us not be too emotional on this problem," Wilkins said. "Nothing in the Constitution says people can't get together and make jackass rules for themselves." He described the action as "a terrible reflection on those who seek to deny the rights of others, but you can't prevent these people from being poisonously discriminatory if they wish to do so."

The NAACP was founded in 1909 on the same "principles on which this country was organized." Its inception made big headlines, because Negroes and whites were meeting together. "This was news in 1909," Wilkins remarked, when New York was "not as liberal as it is today" (→ 8/12).

1959

AUGUST

Su	Mo	Tu	We	Th	Fr	Sa
						1
2	3	4	5	6	7	8
9	10	11	12	13	14	15
16	17	18	19	20	21	22
23	24	25	26	27	28	29
30	31					

1. Nixon, on Moscow TV, proclaims end of fear depends on Khrushchev tactics (→ 15).

7. U.S. puts paddle-wheeled satellite into orbit (→ 13).

12. Santiago: O.A.S. denounces "anti-democratic regimes" in Latin America (→ 14).

13. New York: Ground broken for $320 million Verrazano Narrows Bridge.

13. Vandenberg Air Force Base: Discoverer V launched into orbit (→ 9/14).

14. Jordan and United Arab Republic reopen diplomatic relations (→ 6/6/61).

15. Moscow: Soviets bar Nixon's request to see missile factory during visit (→ 22).

17. Massive power failure hits Manhattan, blacking out over half a million.

20. Laotian govt. reports rebels moving through six provinces toward South Vietnam (→ 26).

22. Moscow: Leonard Bernstein and N.Y. Philharmonic given ovation by traditionally conservative Soviet listeners (→ 23).

23. Washington announces 400 U.S. schools will offer Russian this fall (→ 9/15).

24. Haiti asks Pope recall Rev. Francois Poirier for criticizing Pres. Duvalier (→ 4/29/63).

25. New Delhi: Premier Nehru declares India will defend Bhutan and Sikkim if attacked by China (→ 29).

26. Bonn: Ike hailed by West Germans chanting "we stand by your side" (→ 9/2).

29. India sends troops to Tibet border to block Chinese (→ 10/21).

31. New York: Police commissioner shifts 1,400 to fight increasing youth crime.

31. Forest Hills, N.Y.: Neale Fraser defeats Barry McKay to take Davis Cup for Australia.

DEATHS

8. Don Luigi Sturzo, founded Italian Christian Democratic Party (*11/26/1871).

19. Sir Jacob Epstein, British sculptor (*11/10/1880).

Hawaii formally proclaimed 50th state

Ike helps unfurl the new American flag, 50th star added for Hawaii.

Aug 21. "The paradise of the Pacific," as the eight Hawaiian islands and numerous islets with their coral beaches, colorful vegetation and cloud-covered volcanic peaks have been called, became the 50th state of the union today, so proclaimed by President Eisenhower at bipartisan White House ceremonies.

These were followed by the unfurling of the new 50-star flag with the stars arranged in nine alternate staggered rows of six and five stars each, the 20th design since the United States was formed. The historic occasion was the second time within a year that a new state was welcomed. As territories, both Hawaii and the 49th state, Alaska, were represented by non-voting delegates in the House of Representatives; now they will have Senators and Congressmen.

On the islands of Hawaii, joyous celebrations burst forth as the long fight for statehood came to an end. Some Southerners in Congress had taken a dim view of the mixed racial strains of its population; more ethnic and cultural groups are represented there than in any other state. Others cited its distance from the mainland as a drawback. Hawaii adds 585,000 people, including 183,000 registered voters, and 6,345 square miles to the U.S. (→ 7/4/60).

Aug 15. Radiation-free living for the nuclear family, only $1,195. A fallout shelter has been tested at Princeton. Cooking by candle, reading by flashlight, the Powners survived two weeks and liked it. "I got to know my children better," said Mr. Powner. Of course, they were aided by tranquilizers, whiskey and a copy of "Lady Chatterly's Lover" (→ 9/22).

Communists ready to attack in Laos

Aug 26. Communist North Vietnamese troops have been slipping into Laos to join forces with the Pathet Lao and are said to be massing for an attack. President Eisenhower has increased financial aid to the Laotian government but has refused to send military equipment, hoping that the problem can be resolved by the United Nations. The U.S. Defense Department said the Pathet Lao seek to regain the northern provinces they occupied before joining forces with the Laotian army two years ago.

The town of Muong Penn has already fallen and Communist troops have saturated Samneua province and been spotted in six other provinces. The head of the royal Laotian government received deafening cheers from a crowd of 6,000 in the capital city when he vowed to resist the Communists. Laos won its independence from France in 1954, but has since been locked in a power struggle with the Pathet Lao, which is backed by both the Chinese and North Vietnamese. Currently, the U.S. is paymaster for nearly all the royal Laotian army (→ 8/9/60).

After 8 centuries, Paris market going

Aug 9. Les Halles, Paris' famous central wholesale market and rendezvous for tourists with a yen for early morning onion soup, now appears certain to disappear from the site it has occupied for more than 800 years on the Right Bank.

It took a big market fire last Wednesday, in which six persons died, to clarify the government's intentions regarding what has long been criticized as one of the world's most inefficient and costly market distributing centers. Artichokes grown in Brittany, for example, must pass through it before they can be sold in their home province.

Les Halles, which Emile Zola called the "belly of Paris," may be divided into two parts, one in the northern section of the city and one to the south. However, such a transfer will probably take at least five years to be realized. ▷

Little Rock restrains mob as school opens

White students stare as nine Negroes, books in hand, enter under heavy guard.

Aug 12. A hostile crowd of 250 persons gathered outside Central High School in Little Rock, Arkansas, to protest school integration. Two Negroes walked through the front doors of the school amid the jeering, white demonstrators who were held back by police and firemen using clubs and water hoses. Twenty-one protesters were arrested for violence or refusing to obey police orders. But compared to the riots at Central High two years ago, this outburst was contained.

Despite a clearly defined court order to integrate, the state's Governor, Orval Faubus, an outspoken segregationist, condemned the admittance of the Negroes. "The sun is hot out there, where the police are on duty. This enforcing of illegal orders will grow burdensome," Faubus said as he asked segregationists to "continue the struggle" (→ 9/7).

Castro's opponents under heavy attack

Aug 14. The government of Fidel Castro in Cuba has launched a counter-offensive against elements within the island-nation that have been attempting to overthrow the revolutionary leader's authority. Since last Friday, over 4,500 people have been arrested as suspects in the anti-Castro conspiracy. Most of those detained are believed to be former soldiers of the Fulgencio Batista regime. The penalty for anti-government action can be death.

Yesterday, Castro's troops lured a counterrevolutionary plane, loaded with men and arms, into a deadly trap. When the plane landed it was pummeled with bullets, killing two of the ten men aboard. In a speech to his citizenry, Castro accused Generalissimo Rafael Trujillo of the Dominican Republic of triggering the revolt (→ 10/16).

De Gaulle visiting forces in Algeria

Aug 27. France's President Charles de Gaulle is in Algeria, trying to solidify his support in the French army. But de Gaulle is still refusing to guarantee that Algeria will remain linked to France. The president even told one Moslem leader that Algerians could have their choice: participation in the French Community, autonomy or independence. General Jacques Massu warned de Gaulle that Algeria might go the way of French Guinea and vote for independence, but the president told him that was unlikely to happen.

De Gaulle, hoping to rally American support for the French position in Algeria, will meet with President Eisenhower next week in Paris. The United Nations is about to vote on a resolution favorable to the Algerian nationalists (→ 9/3).

1959

SEPTEMBER

Su	Mo	Tu	We	Th	Fr	Sa
		1	2	3	4	5
6	7	8	9	10	11	12
13	14	15	16	17	18	19
20	21	22	23	24	25	26
27	28	29	30			

2. Paris: Ike welcomed by one million French.

3. French Pres. de Gaulle to offer Algeria elected govt. (→ 1/5/60).

4. Labor Reform Act passes U.S Congress, restricting power of unions to curb racketeering (→ 5/18/62).

7. Washington: Civil Rights Commission asks Ike for federal registrars to monitor voting in South (→ 23).

7. United Council of Churches reports 64% of Americans are church members.

9. N.Y.: Dalai Lama asks U.N. for immediate intervention against Chinese in Tibet.

15. Americans give big but quiet welcome to Khrushchev, here on state visit (→ 18).

17. Peking: Maoists strengthened with naming of Lin Piao as defense minister (→ 10/1).

18. N.Y.: Khrushchev at U.N. bids nations to disarm down to police units in four years (→ 25).

22. N.Y.: U.N. bars entry to Communist China (→ 6/4/60).

22. Groton: Second U.S. missile-firing sub, USS Patrick Henry, is launched (→ 11/10).

22. First telephone cable linking Europe and U.S. is inaugurated.

23. S.F.: George Meany denounces AFL-CIO's only Negro v.p. in debate over union Jim Crow practices (→ 2/1/60).

24. N.Y.: Israeli For. Min. Golda Meir at U.N. denounces U.A.R. for barring Israeli ships from Suez Canal (→ 2/1/60).

25. Maryland: Ike and Khrushchev begin Camp David talks (→ 28).

26. Colombo: Ceylon's Premier S.W.R.D. Bandaranaike killed by Buddhist monk.

27. Tokyo: Worst typhoon since 1945 kills over 1,000; 1,457 still missing.

28. U.S. paddle-wheel satellite Explorer VI takes first TV pictures of earth (→ 10/4).

DEATH

21. Abraham Flexner, American reformer medical education (*11/13/1866).

TV: Gumshoes and gunslingers on top

Roger Smith (rt.) asks Kookie to lend him his comb on "77 Sunset Strip."

If the final TV season of this decade is any indication, the 60's will be overrun with gumshoes. Last year's hit "77 Sunset Strip," with Efrem Zimbalist Jr. and Roger Smith as private eyes and Ed Byrnes as their comb-wielding car hop assistant Kookie, has spawned a pack of copycat shows. "Bourbon Street Beat," "Hawaiian Eye" and "Surfside Six" have more detectives slinking through exotic locales.

"77 Sunset Strip" is a copycat itself, nothing but a modern western. Kookie et al, in running down some hood, are doing exactly what Matt Dillon of "Gunsmoke" has been doing since 1955. His imitators, "Cheyenne," "The Rifleman," "Rawhide," "Wagon Train," "Maverick" and an entry new this season called "Bonanza" are doing great.

As the decade progressed, there were fewer live programs or variety shows. "Lawrence Welk's Dodge Dancing Party" is one of the few still clinging to life. And the future may not bode well for the situation comedies: Lucy and Desi are contemplating a divorce (→ 12/7).

James Arness (left) plays Sheriff Matt Dillon on "Gunsmoke."

Nikita in movieland; misses Disneyland

Sept 28. The tranquility of Camp David seems to be having a calming effect on Nikita Khrushchev. It is a good thing he did not meet with President Eisenhower in Hollywood. The Soviet Premier's temper exploded on a movie set after security officials told him it would be too dangerous to visit Disneyland. "What is it? Do you have rocket launching pads there? Is there an epidemic of cholera there or something? Or have gangsters taken hold of the place that can destroy me?"

Khrushchev's mood had not improved a short time later, when he delivered a shockingly blunt speech on the possibility of nuclear war. By the time the premier went east to Camp David, he had calmed down a bit and even reached an agreement with Eisenhower on the future of Berlin. Perhaps we'll learn some day how the president turned on the charm. With a picture of Mickey Mouse perhaps? (→ 11/24)

Khrushchev at 20th Century Fox.

U.S. X-15 flies under own power

Sept 17. The X-15 rocket plane made its first powered flight today, climbing ten miles above the Mohave Desert at 1,400 miles an hour, twice the speed of sound. The X-15 was carried aloft from Edwards Air Force Base near Los Angeles under the wing of a B-52 jet bomber and was released at an altitude of seven miles. A three-minute burn of its rocket engine then sent the X-15 on a 100-mile trip that ended when it coasted to a landing on the desert floor. Test pilot Scott Crossfield said the plane flew "perfectly with no surprises." The X-15 is scheduled for a series of gradually extended test flights. The goal is a 125-mile, 3,600-mile-an-hour flight that will be a prelude to manned orbital rocket voyages (→ 28).

X-15 (below) and mother ship.

Soviet Lunik II hits moon after 35 hours

Sept 14. The Lunik II spacecraft launched by the Soviet Union has made mankind's first trip to the moon. The spacecraft crashed into the moon just after midnight yesterday, according to Leonid Sedov, the Soviet scientist who is President of the International Astronautical Federation. The trip from earth to moon took 35 hours, and the instrument package of Lunik II transmitted data to earth until impact, he said. The spacecraft also carried emblems marked with the hammer and sickle. The moon mission apparently was timed for the visit by Soviet Premier Khrushchev to the United States this week (→ 17).

Lunik's sphere, now on the moon.

1959

OCTOBER

Su	Mo	Tu	We	Th	Fr	Sa
				1	2	3
4	5	6	7	8	9	10
11	12	13	14	15	16	17
18	19	20	21	22	23	24
25	26	27	28	29	30	31

1. Sixty-eight World Bank nations approve new Intl. Development Association.

4. U.S. fires "Little Joe" booster rocket with model of capsule for first manned launch (→ 27).

6. Ike invokes Taft-Hartley Act to end dock strike.

8. London: Macmillan's Conservatives double majority in House of Commons.

8. Chicago: L.A. Dodgers take World Series over White Sox.

8. France: Nine Gaullist deputies leave UNR Party over de Gaulle's speech on Algerian independence (→ 1/5/60).

9. Washington: Baghdad Pact ministers end first meeting under new name, Central Treaty Organization (CENTO).

9. Ike invokes Taft-Hartley Act against steel strikers (→ 27).

10. Nixon dedicates Dales Dam on Columbia River between Oregon and Washington.

11. Vatican: Pope announces Mother Elizabeth Anne Seton will be first American-born to be beatified by Catholic Church.

15. France: Francois Mitterrand escapes assassination attempt.

15. Twelve nations vow to bar war from Antarctica (→ 12/1).

16. U.S. opposes sale of British jets to Cuba (→ 22).

21. Chinese and Indian troops clash on border at Ladakh (→ 8/6/62).

22. Havana: Cuban workers pour into streets to protest terrorist attack killing two and injuring 45 (→ 23).

23. Castro charges U.S. planes bombed Havana in secret attack (→ 11/13).

27. U.S. Appeals Court upholds Ike's petition for 80-day injunction in steel strike (→ 11/7).

27. Bonn returns West German Volkswagen factories to private ownership.

DEATHS

14. Errol Flynn, American actor (*6/20/1909).

15. Mario Lanza, American opera singer (*1/31/1921).

Quiz shows fixed reportedly for years

Oct 19. Faked emotions, rigged questions and phony games of chance; the tangled web of television quiz shows began to unravel today when producer Dan Enright gave subpoenaed testimony before Congress. Enright, who at one time ran six game shows, said that the purpose of the deception was to increase tensions and boost ratings.

Tactics included providing questions and answers on "Tic Tac Dough," a rigged money machine on "Dotto" and humming songs before the show on "Name That Tune." CBS, which carried most of Enright's shows, has dropped all the programs he was associated with. These practices apparently ran smoothly for years until a Tennessee preacher said he "had been fed an answer" on the "$64,000 Question."

Charles Van Doren, a distinguished Columbia University professor who won $129,000 on "Twenty-one" did not respond to the invitation to testify before the committee and a substitute teacher has taken over his classes (→ 11/1).

Van Doren (rt.) on rigged show.

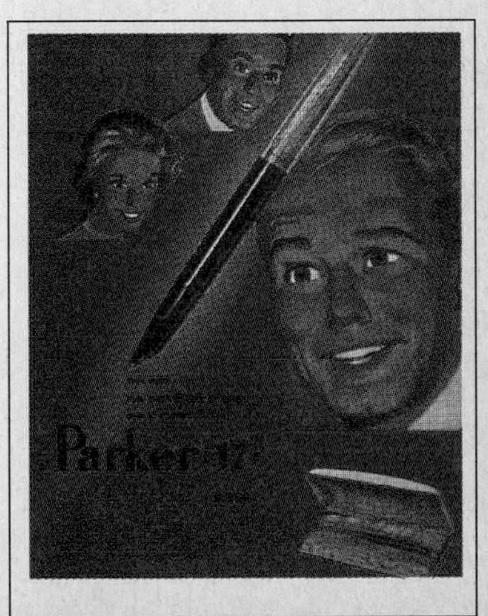

Communist China observes 10th birthday

Khrushchev and the Third World's leading revolutionaries, Mao and Ho.

Oct 1. The Chinese celebrated the tenth anniversary of the Communist takeover with a vast display of military force that has made them a pre-eminent Asian power and helped subjugate an entire people.

Economically and militarily the country has made significant strides, but the price for these steps has been high. The Communists maintain rigid control of the press and education, have virtually eliminated private property, have killed untold numbers of people and have forced tens of millions into compulsory labor. Mao Tse-tung's avowal of China's love of peace has been betrayed by the seizure of Tibet in 1951 and continued fighting with India (→ 12/4).

Wright's Guggenheim Museum opened

Oct 21. A modern art museum has opened in New York. The Guggenheim, named for magnate Solomon Guggenheim, is the creation of the late Frank Lloyd Wright. Critics say art and architecture do not complement each other; they are not even on speaking terms.

The building is a multi-story cylinder ascended by a spiral staircase. Paintings float outward from the walls, suspended by metal bars. Viewers are impelled to move on rather than linger and admire the canvases. Artists call the design arrogant, but then, Wright once said he preferred "honest arrogance" to "hypocritical humility."

The space-age Guggenheim houses Kandinskys, Chagalls, Klees and others.

Lunik III photographs back side of moon

Oct 27. The first picture of the far side of the moon, taken by the Lunik III spacecraft, was released today by the Soviet Union. The Soviet news agency Tass said the picture was one of a "considerable number" taken by the spacecraft when it flew past the moon 20 days ago.

The picture showed a vast white area with a number of hazy dark spots, eight of which have been given names by a special committee of the Soviet Academy of Sciences. One of the largest features to be named is a depression 187 miles across, now known as the Moscow Sea. Tass said the 600-pound spacecraft had succeeded in taking pictures of 70 percent of the far side of the moon in bright sunlight. The pictures were developed on board Lunik III and were transmitted to earth October 18. Most of the area in the pictures has never been seen by astronomers because the moon always keeps the same side toward earth. The pictures show the far side of the moon is "more monotonous" than the side turned toward earth, the Soviets say (→ 12/4).

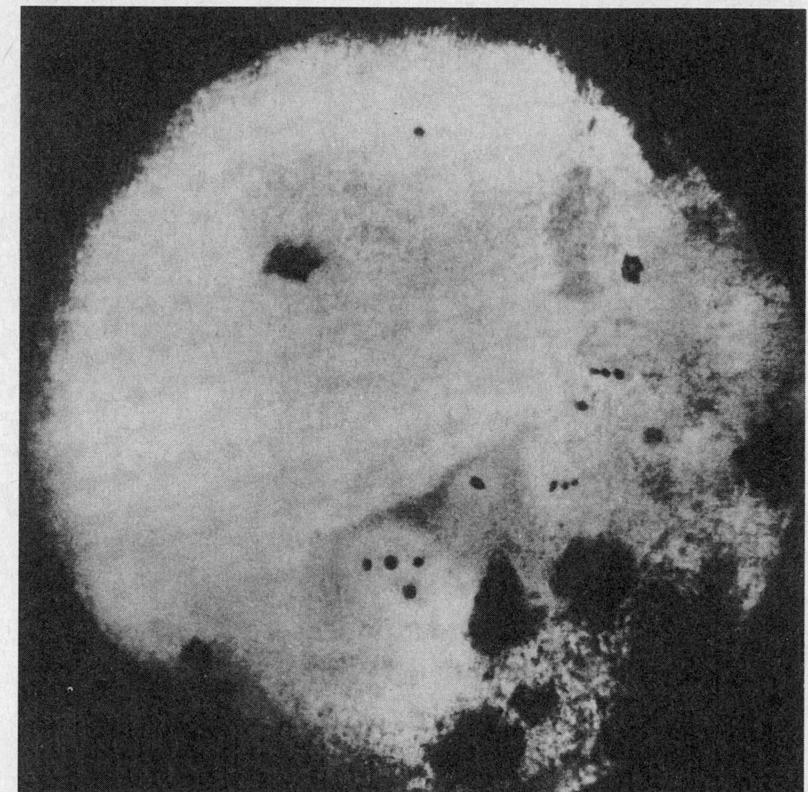

The mysterious far side of the moon, captured on film for the first time.

General Marshall of World War II dead

Oct 16. General George Catlett Marshall died today at the age of 78. During World War II, Marshall served as chief of staff of the Army. He was recalled from retirement to serve as President Truman's emissary in an unsuccessful attempt to mediate the Chinese Civil War. He served as Secretary of State and Secretary of Defense in the Truman administration. He will always be remembered for the Marshall Plan, which rebuilt war-torn Europe.

Berenson, famous art expert, is dead

Oct 7. Renaissance art connoisseur Bernard Berenson has died in Florence, Italy, at the age of 94. He led a quiet life of discovery. It was his job to discern an authentic antique from a modern fake or a Giorgione from a Titian. His findings saved—or cost—collectors millions of dollars. Berenson studied art authentication at Harvard and Oxford. "Aesthetics and History" was one of several books on his theories.

1959

NOVEMBER

Su	Mo	Tu	We	Th	Fr	Sa
1	2	3	4	5	6	7
8	9	10	11	12	13	14
15	16	17	18	19	20	21
22	23	24	25	26	27	28
29	30					

1. U.S.: TV quiz show scandals start FTC drive to bar misrepresentative ads (→ 12/7).

3. Panama: Anti-American riots break out over U.S. control of Canal Zone (→ 29).

3. Jerusalem: Ben Gurion's party, Mapai, gains in legislative elections (→ 1/31/61).

5. France removes 200 import curbs.

7. New York: British Gilbert and Sullivan actor Martyn Green has leg amputated after elevator accident.

10. Groton: Triton, largest nuclear sub yet, commissioned by U.S. Navy (→ 20).

13. Havana: Castro denies U.S. charge Cuba is deliberately trying to jeopardize relations (→ 21).

15. Hilo: Kilauea Ike crater erupts, spurting lava 200 feet in air.

20. Stockholm: Europe's outer seven nations form free trade region: Britain, Sweden, Norway, Denmark, Switzerland, Austria and Portugal.

20. U.N. calls on France to refrain from projected nuclear bomb production (→ 2/13/60).

20. Washington: National Shrine of Immaculate Conception is dedicated.

21. Cuba approves new oil law to reduce size of claims for exploration (→ 26).

23. Tehran: Shah of Iran announces engagement to Farah Dibah.

24. U.S., Soviets sign accord for cooperation in science, sports and culture (→ 4/18/60).

27. Tokyo: Demonstrators march to protest defense treaty with U.S. (→ 1/19/60).

28. Philadelphia: Navy trounces Army 43-12 in football.

29. Panama: U.S. troops quell riots at Canal Zone (→ 1/9/64).

30. Budapest: Hungarian Party Congress opens, Khrushchev presiding (→ 8/19/62).

DEATH

17. Heitor Villa-Lobos, Brazilian composer (*3/5/1887).

Lumumba arrested in Congo after riots

Nov 1. Patrice Lumumba, the nationalist leader in the Congo, is under arrest after Stanleyville and Mangobo were both rattled by deadly riots. Lumumba is charged with inciting the violence with public statements he made after a conference of nationalist parties. The conference approved a plan for a boycott of elections, the "immediate liberation" of the Congo and "mobilization to end the Belgian occupation." In a speech afterwards, Lumumba went even further, using violent language as he criticized Belgian authorities and Congolese moderates. He also condemned any collaboration with Belgium and urged residents of the Congo to use mass civil disobedience.

Shortly after Lumumba spoke, a disturbance erupted inside the prison at Stanleyville. Congolese inmates refused to return to their cells and threw stones at European prisoners. Police had to be called in to break up the riot with tear gas. In Mangobo, several thousand people, armed with sticks, spears, bows and arrows, ran through the streets and fought with police as they yelled, "Independence! Attack the white man!" About 20 of the rioters were killed and 100 were injured. Fourteen of the policemen were hurt in the violent disorders (→ 12/26).

No pinstripes for banker Che Guevara

Young Che with leader Fidel.

Nov 26. The financial policies of Cuba will now be set by Major Ernesto "Che" Guevara who was appointed President of the National Bank of Cuba. Guevara replaces Felipe Pazos, regarded as a moderate in the Fidel Castro Cabinet. The new financial chief, an Argentine doctor, fought closely with Castro during the recent revolution and is considered to be anti-American and a radical leftist.

The bank, established in 1949, controls imports and exports of the nation and the foreign exchange involved. Guevara will also direct the industrial division of the Agrarian Reform Institute, which oversees the expropriating and redistributing of land and also forms various cooperatives. In Washington, the appointment is seen as detrimental to U.S.-Cuban relations. It is believed other moderates in the Havana government will also soon be replaced.

A new law was passed in Havana today. The Ministry of Labor can intervene in any business disrupted by striking employees (→ 12/1).

Charlton Heston stars in movie of Ben Hur

"Ben Hur," Heston at right.

"Ben Hur," an Oscar-caliber picture, is in theaters. Charlton Heston, who was Moses in "The Ten Commandments," (1956) assumes the title role. The plot (two friends become rivals in ancient Palestine) is a bit moralistic, but the film offers plenty of distractions. Director William Wyler makes a sea battle into a spectacle of blood, bodies and brine. And a chariot race is rendered excruciating when the sound of the wheels colliding resembles fingernails on a blackboard. Hugh Griffith and Martha Scott co-star.

Egypt, Sudan share waters of the Nile

Nov 8. A 30-year rivalry, sparked by economic competition and aggravated by political differences, ended today as Egypt and the Sudan formally agreed to share the waters of the Nile. The agreement also paves the way for Egypt to build the contested Aswan Dam. Egypt will pay the Sudan $43 million to compensate for land that will be covered by the water of the new dam. Egypt also agreed to relocate 50,000 Sudanese who will lose their homes.

President Nasser will receive substantial financial aid from the Soviet Union to build the Aswan Dam. The United States, hoping to reverse the pro-Soviet drift in Cairo and aspiring to create an anti-Soviet bloc in the Middle East with a coalition of Egypt, Jordan and Saudi Arabia, assisted in the delicate negotiations between Egypt and the Sudan (→ 1/7/60).

Ford drops Edsel as auto failure

Nov 19. Ford has discontinued production of the Edsel, a revolutionary car whose time has not yet come—if ever. The Edsel was introduced last year to compete with medium-priced autos such as the Oldsmobile and De Soto. When sales lagged, its price was reduced, but fewer than 100,000 were sold.

The Edsel had as much chance as any Ford. Its name (Henry's son's first name) was test-marketed. The publicity photos were dazzling, highlighting discrete sections. But the Edsel has a fault: progress. It has push-button automatic transmission, narrow horizontal taillights, a detailed grill and other futuristic features. In other words, it's ugly.

Today, Ford announced discontinuation of the auto, stating a steel shortage hastened the decision. At the same time, Ford offered to sell two million more shares of stock.

Navy beats Army 43-12 in stunning upset

The Cadets drive downfield toward Navy territory, a rare scene today.

Nov 28. The season heroics of Army quarterback Joe Caldwell were expected to carry over into the Navy game and virtually assure the Cadets of victory over their service rivals from Annapolis. But when the academies clash, past performances mean nothing and Navy rolled to the most lopsided victory in the history of the long rivalry, 43-12. Caldwell, who entered the game with 99 completions in 165 attempts for a 60 percent average, was held to four for 69. The hero, instead, turned out to be the Navy quarterback, Joe Tranchini.

"Sound of Music" heard on Broadway

Nov 16. When a show has an advance sale of $2,325,000, it had better not flop. "The Sound of Music," which opened tonight on Broadway, could not fail if it wanted to. Composer Richard Rodgers, lyricist Oscar Hammerstein and librettists Howard Lindsay and Russel Crouse have put together an inescapable crowd-pleaser. It is as if the show were arrived at by a perfect mathematical equation.

Like "The King and I," "Sound of Music" is based on a true story, about an Austrian nun named Maria who married a widower named von Trapp. It is also another musical heaped with children; "King" had a couple dozen, but this latest entry has only seven.

Maria, played by Mary Martin, teaches von Trapp's children to sing. They escape from their Nazified country by spewing tunes as if they were bullets. Among the numbers are "Edelweiss," "Something Good" and the title song.

Steel strike order is upheld by Court

Nov 7. President of the United Steelworkers of America, David McDonald, will be forced to order his union members back to the mills, as the Supreme Court ruled to halt the 116-day steel strike. In an 8-1 decision, the court upheld the constitutionality of the emergency procedure of the Taft-Hartley Act.

Under the applicable clause in Taft-Hartley, the employees must report back to work for a maximum of 80 days, because the strike "imperils the national health or safety." After the 80th day, if no resolution between labor and management has been reached, the union may strike again. Then, the matter would be decided by Congress.

Justice William O. Douglas dissented. He felt the case should be returned to trial court to determine why the entire industry should be reopened for national safety and not just a few plants. The strike was the longest in the steel industry's history.

1959

DECEMBER

Su	Mo	Tu	We	Th	Fr	Sa
		1	2	3	4	5
6	7	8	9	10	11	12
13	14	15	16	17	18	19
20	21	22	23	24	25	26
27	28	29	30	31		

1. Washington: 5 Cuban exiles arrested loading bombs into Cuban-bound plane (→ 2/4/60).

4. Florida: Monkey Sam survives trip to space, charting way for humans (→ 1/27/60).

4. Peking pardons Pu Yi, ex-emperor of China and of Japanese puppet state Manchukuo (→ 3/27/60).

7. U.S.: FCC opens hearings on TV crime, standards (→ 6/1/60).

18. New York: 20 believed to be mob bosses convicted of obstructing justice.

19. Houston: Reputed last Civil War veteran Walter Williams dies at age 117.

22. Ike and King Mohammed announce U.S. forces will leave Morocco by 1963 (→ 9/1/60).

26. Congo: Civil war reported hindering plans for independence (→ 1/20/60).

27. Baltimore: Colts over Giants 31-16 for NFL title.

30. Sen. Hubert H. Humphrey first to enter Democratic presidential race (→ 1/31/60).

30. Groton: USS George Washington, first of new undersea dreadnoughts, commissioned.

CULTURAL EVENTS, 1959

Literature: William Burroughs' "The Naked Lunch"; Ionesco's "Rhinoceros"; Vance Packard's "The Status Seekers"; Ian Fleming's "Goldfinger"; James Michener's "Hawaii"; Philip Roth's "Goodbye, Columbus"; Allen Drury's "Advise and Consent"; Gunter Grass' "The Tin Drum."

Academia: Pierre Teilhard de Chardin's "The Phenomenon of Man"; Mary Leakey finds Australopithecus skull in Tanzania.

Music: Richard Rodgers' "The Sound of Music"; "He's Got the Whole World in His Hands"; "Tom Dooley"; "Everything's Coming up Roses"; "Mack the Knife."

The Arts: Miro's murals for UNESCO building, Paris.

Film: Preminger's "Anatomy of a Murder"; Resnais' "Hiroshima, Mon Amour"; Fellini's "La Dolce Vita"; "Ben Hur," Oscar.

Eisenhower tours three continents

Dec 23. President Eisenhower returned to Washington yesterday after an 11-nation, three-continent journey in which he delivered the American Christmas message of "peace and friendship in freedom."

In Italy, the president asked for help in pursuing "policies aimed at reducing the burden of armaments throughout the world." Ike greeted a sea of humanity, in the first visit by an American leader to India, by wishing the nation of 450 million that it realize its goals of peace and prosperity. Over 500,000 flocked to Eisenhower's parade route in Athens, Greece, as the president saluted "the country responsible for much that belongs to Western civilization." Despite the trip's length, Ike seemed rejuvenated by his tour.

Young student is Shah's third bride

Dec 21. A former shepherdess is Iran's Empress today. Farah Dibah has wed Mohammed Reza, Shah of Iran, in his palace in Tehran. It is his third marriage and her first. He is 40, she about half that.

Marriage to the shah may not prove tranquil. His rule, since 1941, has been turbulent. In 1949, he barely escaped assassination by a member of the leftist Tudeh Party. In 1953, he briefly fled a usurper.

The nuptial ceremony called for three special items: a Koran, a three-branched candelabra and a handful of consecrated soil.

The Shah and bride Farah Dibah.

Pact makes Antarctic science preserve

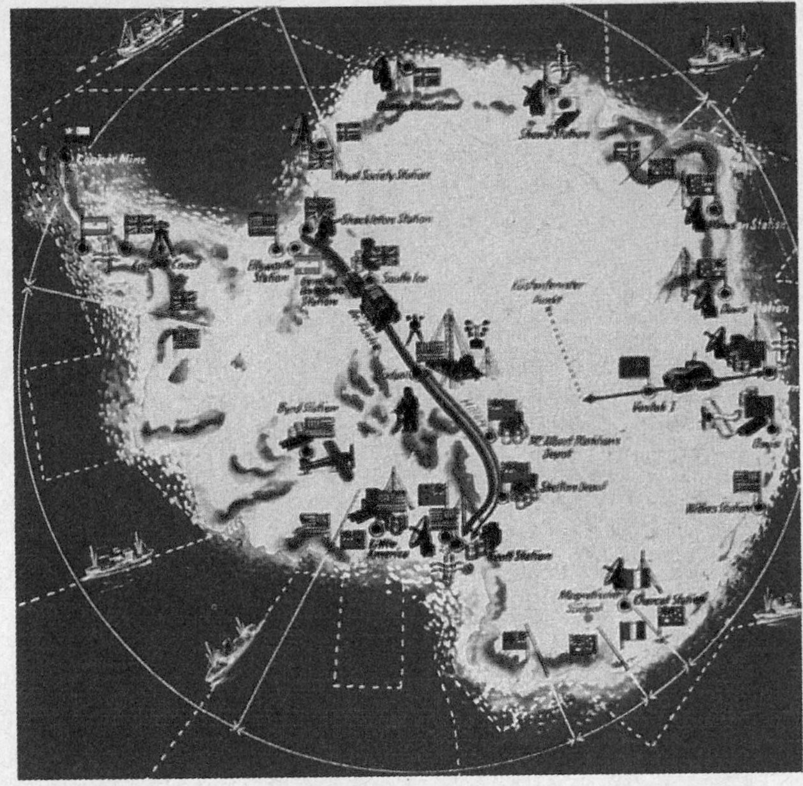

Antarctica: A frozen international laboratory for scientific research.

Dec 1. In an unprecedented international agreement, 12 nations have signed a treaty setting the Antarctic continent aside as a preserve for scientific research. The signers included the United States, the Soviet Union and all other nations with claims on Antarctica. The treaty freezes all such claims. It also bans all nuclear explosions and the dumping of radioactive waste in Antarctica. All 12 nations must ratify the treaty before it becomes effective, but the document provides that it will then remain in force indefinitely and can be changed only by unanimous agreement of all the signers. It allows free access to all parts of Antarctica to scientists of all nations (→ 8/10/60).

Archbishop Makarios President of Cyprus

Dec 14. A priest who headed a group at war must now lead a nation in peace. Archbishop Makarios beat his Turkish Cypriot opponent by a two to one margin today to win the presidency of Cyprus.

As head of the Greek Cypriots, Makarios was exiled by the British in 1956. They let him return the following year when EOKA, the Greek Cypriot military organization, suspended the attacks which had ravaged the island. The Greek Cypriots have been agitating for "enosis" or union with Greece while the Turkish Cypriots have favored partition. Greeks outnumber Turks eight to one. Under an agreement reached by the Turkish and Greek governments with the approval of the British, Cyprus will become a republic in July of 1960. Foremost on Makarios' agenda is a new constitution (→ 8/16/60).

U.N. envoy Bunche and Makarios.

Rock and roll just keeps on rolling along

Dismissed as a passing teenage fad from its first defiant rumblings, rock and roll, despite some setbacks, appears destined to rule the pop charts well into the next decade.

In 1955, Bill Haley and the Comets' "(We're Gonna) Rock Around the Clock" struck an explosive chord with young audiences from small towns to Ivy League campuses. That chart-topper was followed by the phenomenal success of Elvis Presley, and rock and roll was suddenly the major force in popular music of the 1950's. Joining in the takeover of the airwaves were the likes of Little Richard, Chuck Berry, Fats Domino and Jerry Lee Lewis, among many others.

The driving rhythms and uninhibited performances of the new stars sparked raging debates over what many saw as the music's negative effect on America's youth. This reached a peak in 1957 with Presley's third appearance on "The Ed Sullivan Show," when television cameras censored the wild movements of his hips.

Overshadowed by such attention was the music itself. A hybrid by its very nature, rock and roll proves the perfect meeting-ground for a variety of American forms. And the music seems sure to grow as new performers continue to inject influences as diverse as country, rhythm-and-blues, gospel, jazz and Chicago-style blues.

This year, three major stars died in a plane crash and Presley remains in the Army. And though naysayers again proclaimed the end of a craze, at the close of the decade the hits keep coming and the audiences are still rocking to a lively beat that is transforming the American social and music scene.

Every soda shop worth hanging out in has a jukebox with Presley, Berry, Haley, and before their untimely deaths, Big Bopper, Buddy Holly and Richie Valens.

1960–1969

1960

JANUARY

Su	Mo	Tu	We	Th	Fr	Sa
					1	2
3	4	5	6	7	8	9
10	11	12	13	14	15	16
17	18	19	20	21	22	23
24	25	26	27	28	29	30
31						

1. Cameroon proclaims independence from France (→ 4/14).

5. France: Newspaper Le Monde publishes Red Cross report on torture in Algeria (→ 24).

5. West Germany: Cologne anti-Semitic rioters arrested by Bonn government.

7. Egypt: Nasser lays cornerstone for Aswan Dam (→ 5/14/64).

9. Nixon declares candidacy in presidential race (→ 3/8).

12. Kenya ends seven-year state of emergency (→ 7/8).

19. U.S. signs mutual defense treaty with Japan (→ 6/11).

19. Sabena Airlines inaugurates Boeing 707 service.

22. Boston: Paul Pender outpoints Sugar Ray Robinson to take middleweight title.

23. Frenchman Auguste Piccard descends record 3,350 feet in Trieste bathyscape.

24. Algiers: Armed European mobs rise against de Gaulle's moves toward independence for Algeria (→ 25).

24. Washington reports GNP record set last year at $400 billion before steel strike.

24. German racers Schock and Moll win Monte Carlo Rally in Mercedes 220.

25. Paris: Ionesco play "Rhinoceros" premieres.

25. Algiers: French premier and paratroopers arrive as European uprising widens (→ 29).

25. Rochester: Swedish boxer Ingemar Johansson is first foreigner to be chosen S. Rae Hickok Pro Athlete of the Year.

26. Antarctica: First heavy transport plane equipped with skis lands at Byrd Station base.

26. San Francisco: Outfielder Willie Mays signs with Giants for $85,000.

31. Monterey: Nobel Prize winner Dr. Linus Pauling rescued, trapped on coastal cliff for 24 hours.

DEATH

24. Edwin Fisher, noted Swiss pianist (*10/6/1886).

Europeans launch uprising in Algiers

Jan 29. The crisis that swept Charles de Gaulle back into power in France has erupted again to create the first major test of his presidency. Military leaders in Algeria are revolting against his policy of self-determination. The Home Guard, which possesses arms supplied by the French government, took up those weapons against de Gaulle's forces in Algiers. Thousands of European settlers also filled the streets. At least 19 people died when fighting broke out Sunday night. Scores were injured. Today, de Gaulle sent in the army.

Calling the rioting in Algeria "a bad blow against France," de Gaulle pledged decisive action to quell the disturbance. "If I fail in my task," de Gaulle said, "the prestige, the fate of France will be compromised." Critics charge that de Gaulle himself ignited the latest uprising by removing the very popular General Jacques Massu from his post as commander of French forces in Algeria. Massu, one of the generals who was behind the recall of de Gaulle in 1958, had upset the President by criticizing his new policies in Algeria (→ 2/1).

European rebels and frightened spectators, separated by barricades in Algiers.

Soviet professional women in majority

Jan 30. According to the official Soviet paper Izvestia, most Russian professional specialists are women. An article printed today contains a speech by a high-ranking party member who offered several statistics on Soviet women's role in the economy. Miss Yekaterina Furtseva said that while women take up only 45 percent of the total labor force, they hold a majority of the professional employment positions.

The Soviet Union has 110,000 women scientists, 233,000 women engineers and 300,000 women physicians. About 85 percent of all medical personnel are women. In the nation's schools, 1,283,000 women are teachers at all levels.

While it is official policy in the Soviet Union to expand job opportunities for women, the nation also employs women out of necessity. Millions of men previously in the labor force died in World War II.

Albert Camus killed in auto accident

Jan 4. Algerian-born Existentialist author Albert Camus has died in a car crash 70 miles southeast of Paris. His auto struck a tree and rolled over, the metal body nearly shredding in half. Those who know of Camus' nihilist inclinations might imagine the event a suicide. This is unlikely; Camus was a passenger in the vehicle, not the driver.

During World War II, Camus joined the French resistance in Paris and was principal editor of the underground newspaper Combat. In these years, he formulated and presented his philosophy in "The Stranger" and "The Myth of Sisyphus," both published in 1942. After the war, he lost some of his pessimism; where before he had thought the world an absurd circus of relative values, in the novel "The Plague" (1947) he advocated a moderate search for dignity. Camus won the 1957 Nobel Prize in literature.

Doctors introduce artificial kidney

Jan 29. An artificial kidney that can operate continuously without human monitoring was described today by Dr. Belding H. Scribner of the University of Washington Medical School. In its first three months, the device has helped save the lives of eight persons with kidney failure, he said. It prevents the build-up of urea and other waste products whose accumulation can be fatal.

Blood flow to the artificial kidney is established by implanting a tube in the patient's arm. The blood flows through a cellophane envelope immersed in a fluid that contains all normal blood chemicals but urea. The urea flows from the blood into the fluid through pores in the cellophane that let it pass but are too small to allow loss of proteins and other blood elements. More experiments are needed before an artificial kidney can be built for general use, Scribner said.

M14, faster than a machine gun, in use

Jan 30. The Army this week began issuing its versatile new rifle, the M14, to all American troops. The M14 will replace several weapons, including the famous M1 Garand rifle and the Browning automatic rifle. Weighing just ten pounds, the M14 has a 20-round magazine and can fire at a rate of 250 shots a minute, faster than the Army's .30-calibre machine gun. By comparison, the M1 Garand used in World War II and Korea has only an eight-round magazine.

First to get the new weapon were units of the 101st Airborne Division at Fort Campbell, Kentucky, part of the Army's strategic readiness force. The entire division will be equipped with the M14 by the end of the year and deliveries will begin soon to other units. Contracts for production of 70,000 M14s have already been issued.

New, more valuable franc in France

Jan 1. Anything that cost 300 francs in Paris yesterday has a price tag of three francs today. A piece of furniture in Marseilles that cost 50,000 francs is going for 500. But buyers are not flocking to the stores. This is not a post-Christmas national sale. It's called devaluation.

The French franc has been losing its buying power since the First World War. Reconstruction, inflation, high budgets and Algeria have all taken their toll. Consumers got dizzy looking at all the zeroes in prices, so effective today the government devalued the franc and lopped two zeroes off prices. The French can exchange 100 old francs for one new one, or they can use their old francs as new centimes.

It's hard to break tradition, though. In Paris cafes, prices are still being quoted in old francs.

The new French 500-franc note.

Roundtable on Congolese freedom begins

King Baudouin speaks with skeptical Congolese visitors at his Brussels palace.

Jan 20. "You are here, gentlemen of the Congo, to talk with us. Speak without fear, we want to know what is at the bottom of your hearts." In this way, Belgian Prime Minister Gaston Eyskens welcomed 82 Congolese delegates to a conference in Brussels. The parties hope to reach some accord on the issue of the Belgian Congo's government. The entire African continent is looking for something positive to emerge.

Leopoldville, the Belgian Congo's capital, has been the scene of anti-Belgian riots since January 1959. Native Africans have no say in the colony's administration. They are used as cheap labor in the nation's paper and textile mills and copper mines. Black Africans have only been allowed secondary education in the last few years.

Many Congolese would like to see a government headed by Patrice Lumumba, the firebrand leading the nationalist movement. Violence followed a series of speeches Lumumba gave last November, yet on record Lumumba has advocated peaceful civil disobedience. He is among the delegates at the conference in Brussels today.

Pope opens synod on Church discipline

Jan 24. Pope John XXIII inaugurated today the first synod, or diocesan ecclesiastical council, ever held in Rome. Those recommendations of the synod that the pope approves will become a "constitution," the fundamental law of Rome, with dioceses throughout the world expected to follow suit.

A tightening of discipline for both clergy and laity is expected. It is recommended that priests be forbidden to smoke in public. They may not attend any theater or motion pictures. They should not buy or drive automobiles without permission from superiors.

As for the laity, women in Rome with bare arms or wearing male clothing will be denied the sacraments. Catholics will be urged to attend religious rites with greater fervor and not to watch motion pictures, stage shows or television programs not considered "safe" by ecclesiastical authorities. They may not read publications inspired by Protestantism, illuminism, Existentialism, atheism or materialism, nor are they allowed to take part in sessions of spiritism, magic or divination. They would be liable to excommunication if they join or vote for political parties or persons promoting heretical ideas or doctrines.

Satellite that can change orbit shown

Jan 27. A rocket engine that can enable satellites to change orbit in space was demonstrated today by the Lockheed Missiles and Space Division. The engine can loft heavy satellites into orbit, shut down and then be restarted to change the orbit path. It is an advanced version of the Lockheed Agena, a single-firing liquid-fuel rocket that has been used as a second stage in six successful launches. The new rocket's ability to fire more than once means that it will be able to orbit heavier satellites and put them in higher orbits that have military significance, spokesmen said. It develops 15,000 pounds of thrust and could be used for moon missions (→ 3/13).

Senator Kennedy to seek presidency

Jan 31. Senator John F. Kennedy tossed his hat into the ring of presidential hopefuls early this month. At month's end, he had campaign offices opened throughout the U.S. Democrat Hubert Humphrey currently trails him in most polls. While Kennedy failed to win the vice-presidential post at the last Democratic convention, the move at least got him national exposure. Poorly known outside Massachusetts, he must expand his base, especially in the West.

Maynard G. Krebs, TV beatnik, and his "good buddy" Dobie Gillis and Zelda on "The Many Loves of Dobie Gillis," Tuesdays at 8:30 on CBS.

1960

FEBRUARY

Su	Mo	Tu	We	Th	Fr	Sa
	1	2	3	4	5	6
7	8	9	10	11	12	13
14	15	16	17	18	19	20
21	22	23	24	25	26	27
28	29					

1. N.C.: Four Negro students stage sit-in at segregated Greensboro lunch counter (→ 2).

1. Israelis invade Syrian base in demilitarized zone in biggest action since 1956 (→ 3/17/62).

1. Algiers: Insurgents surrender; de Gaulle seeks rule by decree (→ 10).

2. U.S. Senate approves 23rd Amendment calling for ban on poll tax (→ 8).

4. Havana: Soviet envoy Mikoyan signs accord with Castro to buy sugar barred by U.S. (→ 10).

8. Durham, N.C.: Blacks demonstrate against stand-up service only at lunch counters (→ 9).

9. Little Rock: Bomb explodes at home of Carlotta Walls, one of Negroes at Central High (→ 17).

10. Havana: Military court convicts 104 govt. foes in largest mass trial yet in Cuba (→ 17).

10. Golden, Colorado: Adolph Coors, brewer, kidnapped.

11. New Delhi: Khrushchev, on Asian tour, hails Indian neutrality, urges disarmament (→ 3/2).

16. Ike asks Congress for $4.1 billion in continued foreign aid.

17. Ike approves CIA training of Cuban exiles to overthrow Castro govt. (→ 21).

17. Atlanta: Martin Luther King arrested on perjury charges in Alabama bus boycott (→ 23).

21. Havana places all Cuban industry under direct control of government (→ 3/4).

23. N.C.: Whites join Negro students in sit-in at Winston-Salem Woolworth store (→ 23).

23. Chattanooga: Rioting hits lunch counter sit-in; seven whites arrested (→ 27).

23. New York: Iron ball demolishes Ebbets Field, home of Dodgers from 1913 to 1957.

24. U.S.: Study finds venereal disease on rise, especially among teenagers.

26. New York: Full-scale model of build-it-yourself fallout shelter displayed in bank for $105.

29. Washington: White House report finds U.S. children getting too fat.

Negro sit-ins integrate lunch counters

Seeking lunch in Greensboro, a white lady found she wasn't ready for change.

Feb 27. Lunch counter sit-in protests by Negroes seeking to be served have spread throughout much of the South, resulting in rioting in some major cities and numerous arrests.

The sit-ins began earlier this month in Greensboro, North Carolina, when Negro students from Agriculture and Technical College and Bennett College marched into a variety store and took seats at the lunch counter. White waitresses refused to serve them.

Within days, the passive resistance movement spread to Raleigh and Charlotte and finally to other cities such as Atlanta, Birmingham, Little Rock, Nashville and Montgomery. The protests have been held largely in variety stores, such as S.H. Kress and Co. and Woolworth's, which offer inexpensive lunchtime meals. Many lunch counters have been closed. No similar sit-ins have been staged at the more expensive restaurants.

Taking a seat at a lunch counter in Charlotte, Joseph Charles Jones, a Negro college graduate, said that he and others were seeking "God-given" rights. "All I want is to come in and place my order and be served and leave a tip if I feel like it," he said.

In Chattanooga, Tennessee, there were angry clashes between Negroes and whites in one variety store. Dishes, flower pots and other items were hurled at the Negroes as the store management sought to close the lunch counter. In Rock Hill, South Carolina, a Negro was knocked from a lunch counter stool, another struck by an egg (→ 3/1).

Algiers insurgents surrender; de Gaulle orders wide reforms

Feb 10. The latest rebellion in Algeria against President de Gaulle's policies is over. But there is likely to be another one in the future. Residents who believe the territory should be French forever are bristling at the president's reforms, which crack down on dissident military elements and tighten de Gaulle's control over Algeria.

Jo Ortiz, the right-wing leader of the French National Front, fled from Algeria as the army quashed the revolt. It's believed he took refuge in Spain. Pierre Lagaillarde, the military official who led the rebellion, was whisked to the airport, where he was saluted as a hero, and flown to Paris, where he was thrown into prison. Three generals were stripped of their commands.

De Gaulle abolished the Home Guard and a political and psychological warfare section of the army. Both were accused of participating in the revolt last month. The president also shook up his Cabinet in Paris. The moves are not sitting well with hard-liners. One ousted Cabinet member, Jacques Soustelle, issued a blistering attack on de Gaulle, who threatened to eject him from the party (→ 3/3).

Insurgents guard occupied quarters.

Barricades in the streets, a tactic the troops appropriated from the French left.

More Biblical texts uncovered in Israel

Feb 7. About 1,700 years ago, a small band of Hebrews in revolt against Roman occupation hid in caves in the Judean Desert. There they sewed clothes, made pottery and hunted game. And they kept their faith alive by transcribing the Bible on rolled pages of parchment. Now, centuries later, those parchments have been discovered by Israeli archeologists.

The priceless scroll fragments bear 16 verses from the Book of Exodus. Besides being a bit frayed they are in excellent condition. It is a miracle they exist at all; when time fails to destroy ancient artifacts, marauding robbers often do. The archeologists found the scrolls in small, inaccessible caves. Nearly a foot of dust hid them from view.

This find is only slightly less spectacular than the uncovering of the Dead Sea Scrolls in 1947. Those documents, from caves in Jordanian territory, were far more extensive. The Old Testament then was found nearly in its entirety.

That first find raised the question of dating. Some scientists put it at 100 B.C.; others at 700 B.C. or earlier. This latest discovery may offer a clue: A coin found near a scroll was struck in the days of the Roman Emperor Trajan, who died in the year 117 A.D (→ 4/2/61).

Soviet Union wins Winter Olympics

Feb 28. For a while it seemed as if there would be no Winter Olympics. Torrential rains washed snow off Squaw Valley, Idaho, peaks and even Piute Indian dancers couldn't stop the downpour. But when the weather cleared, the show went on and the Soviet shussed off with the unofficial point honors.

The Soviet rolled up 165.5 points to 71.5 for Sweden and 71 for the United States. But the Americans scored a stunning upset over the Czechs in the hockey final (with the help of a Russian tip to use oxygen), and Carol Heiss and David Jenkins won their respective figure-skating championships. The U.S. lost a probable gold medal when Penny Pitou fell in the giant slalom.

"Viva Eeke!" Brazilians yell at Ike on tour

Surrounded by gray-suited secret servicemen, Ike greets Buenos Aires.

Feb 29. Wildly cheering crowds greeted President Eisenhower today in Santiago, Chile, the third stop on his four-nation South American tour in which he is seeking to cement U.S. relations with Latin-American republics.

Earlier in the tour, in a speech in Rio de Janeiro, Brazil, the president said that the United States would "consider it intervention" in the internal affairs of South American countries if any power denied freedom of choice to any republic in the Western hemisphere. Such intervention, he said, might come about by invasion, coercion or subversion.

In Rio, the president addressed a joint session of the Brazilian Congress. As he rode through the city, he was showered with a blizzard of confetti and cheered by hundreds of thousands Brazilians, shouting "Viva Eeke!"

At times during the grueling tour, President Eisenhower has seemed to tire. Just yesterday, he returned from a fishing trip in Argentina, looking pale and drawn. He went to bed immediately, but an hour later he was off again for a meeting with President Arturo Frondizi.

Asked about the state of the president's health, Press Secretary James C. Hagerty said: "I think he is feeling fine. As for looking tired, I can tell you I am awfully tired. Have you ever tried fishing in a stream for two and a half hours?"

Today, President Eisenhower met in Santiago with Chilean President Jorge Alessandri Rodriguez, asking him to assist in the East-West summit meeting, which is scheduled to begin in Paris in May. Saying he was too realistic to expect miracles, Eisenhower said he hoped that the summit "will lessen the tensions that divide and vex the world" (→ 3/2).

G-man who trapped Dillinger is suicide

Feb 29. Melvin Purvis, 56, the special agent in charge of the FBI Chicago office when John Dillinger was trapped and slain on July 24, 1934, committed suicide today.

Purvis, who had been depressed and in poor health recently, shot himself with an automatic in his home. His wife, Rosanne, was in the garden when the shot rang out.

Purvis was also the leader of the spectacular raid on October 22, 1934, when "Pretty Boy" Floyd was killed. The following year, Purvis left the FBI to follow careers in law and broadcasting.

The Dillinger case broke on a woman's tip. Anna Sage was being investigated for deportation when she told police that she knew Dillinger. On that July night, she and another woman went to the movies with John Dillinger, and she wore a red dress to point out the disguised bandit to Purvis and 23 FBI agents and policemen, who closed in on him. The "woman in red" was later deported and died in Rumania.

French test first atomic device in Sahara

Feb 13. A large cloud billowed skyward from the sands of southern Algeria today. And France's President de Gaulle was rejoicing. It was an atomic explosion, a first for France as it joined the elite club of atomic powers in the world.

"Hurray for France," de Gaulle said in a cable to scientists near Reggan, in the Sahara. "France is stronger and prouder. Our defenses have been strengthened." Development of the bomb has become, for de Gaulle, a major expression of his country's independence. "France must have allies and friends," the president remarked, "but she does not need a protector." De Gaulle ordered the continuation of the A-bomb program, despite strong protests from the United States. He also ignored the formal opposition of the United Nations.

French scientists were quick to point out that the experimental bomb had a strength of 60-70 kilotons, three times more powerful than the first U.S. and British bombs. The other member of the atomic club is the U.S.S.R. (→ 26).

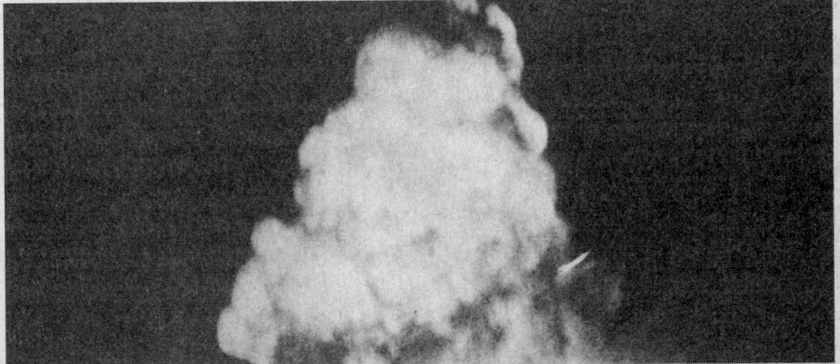

The desert sky is beclouded as France becomes the fourth nuclear nation.

1960

MARCH

Su	Mo	Tu	We	Th	Fr	Sa
		1	2	3	4	5
6	7	8	9	10	11	12
13	14	15	16	17	18	19
20	21	22	23	24	25	26
27	28	29	30	31		

1. Montgomery: 1,000 Negro students pray and sing national anthem on steps of old Confederate Capitol (→ 7).

2. Montevideo: Uruguayans march with pro-Castro banners on Ike's arrival.

3. Algiers: De Gaulle insists on French victory before independence (→ 10/5).

3. Vatican: Pope names as Cardinals an African, a Japanese and a Filipino.

4. Vancouver, B.C.: Carol Heiss of U.S. wins fifth straight world figure-skating title.

5. Havana: Castro denounces U.S., charging complicity in munitions ship blast (→ 4/20).

6. Swiss grant women right to vote in municipal elections.

7. Houston: White youths beat Negro with chains, carve six "K's" in his chest (→ 9).

9. N.Y.: MOMA opens "Claude Monet: Seasons and Moments."

9. Boston: Celtics crush Knicks for record 59th win in season.

15. Geneva: Ten nations meet in disarmament talks; Soviet bloc cool to Western plan (→ 27).

16. N.Y.: Car displayed with battery recharged by solar cells.

22. Sharpeville: South African police open fire on Africans protesting pass law; 50 killed (→ 30).

23. Los Alamos scientists report thermonuclear fusion (→ 9/20).

24. Argentine army arrests 500 Peronists after assassination attempt on army major (→ 3/20/62).

27. Cocoa Beach: Navy's revolutionary Polaris missile undergoes crucial tests (→ 4/1).

28. U.S. Supreme Court, Douglas dissenting, refuses to investigate govt. plan to spray DDT.

30. Marshall, Tex.: Police break up Negro protest at lunch counters with fire hoses (→ 4/15).

31. Johannesburg: 300 jailed under martial law; four shot (→ 31).

31. U.S. capital in South Africa reported at $350 million (→ 4/7).

DEATH

11. Roy Chapman Andrews, U.S. naturalist (*1/26/1884).

Massacre in Sharpeville

March 30. The South African government declared a state of emergency after demonstrations led to the deaths of more than 50 Africans from police gunfire. The bloodiest incident took place at Sharpeville, where police fired on thousands of Africans demonstrating outside a police station against a government requirement that Africans carry identification passes.

Apartheid shows its brutal face.

A smilar clash between protesting Africans and police took place in the non-white town of Langa.

Official reports said 56 Africans had been killed at Sharpeville, where police fired sub-machine guns into the front ranks of the demonstrators, and six at Langa.

Prime Minister Verwoerd at first relaxed the pass requirement but then proclaimed a national emergency as Africans continued mass demonstrations against the official policy of white supremacy. The government arrested 234 political opponents (→ 31).

100,000 Afghans hail Khrushchev on tour

March 2. A smiling Premier Nikita Khrushchev was showered with confetti as he rode an open car through the streets of Kabul this afternoon. A hundred thousand Afghans lined the thoroughfare to greet Khrushchev on this, his most receptive stop on his Asian tour. The Soviet Union, sharing a 1,458-mile border with Afghanistan, invests millions in the grateful nation.

Premier Mohammad Daud was on hand to welcome Khrushchev. Daoud realizes the Soviet Union has the capacity to overwhelm Afghanistan militarily but does not anticipate interference. Russia has spent $300 million modernizing the Afghan armed forces. Its goodwill can also be gauged by the Soviet-built cars and trucks milling the streets and by a Soviet-built silo soaring on the Kabul skyline.

Why would a Moslem nation deal with an atheistic one? Afghanistan's likelier trade partner, neighboring Pakistan, feuds with Afghanistan over sea trading routes. And the U.S. refuses to spend more than a few million dollars on the country.

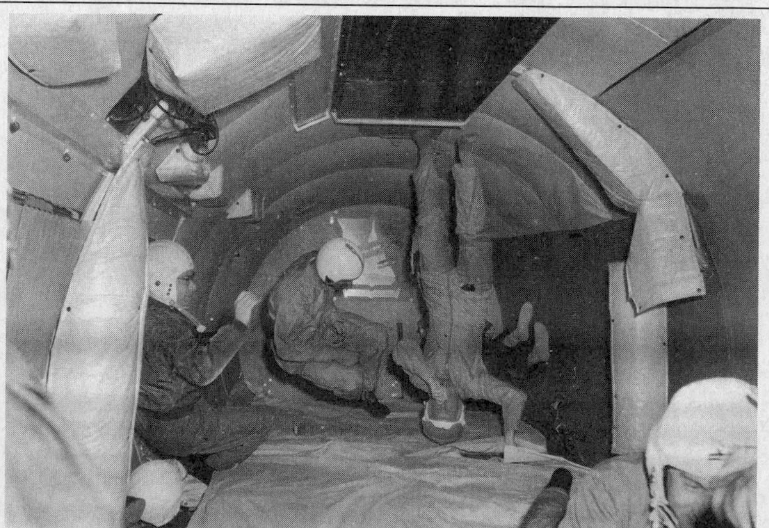

Preparing for space flight: Four of the seven chosen as America's first astronauts learn to function without gravity at 18,000 feet in the high-pressurized cabin of a C-131 transport, based in New Mexico (→ 4/2).

'Quakes virtually destroy Agadir

Extracting a survivor at Agadir.

March 1. Two earthquakes that triggered a tidal wave and fire that destroyed the city of Agadir, Morocco, may have killed more than 1,000 persons, authorities said today. Most of Agadir's 45,000 inhabitants have been left homeless. The first quake struck the port city just before midnight and the second came an hour later. The tidal wave, which swept 300 yards into the city, came between the two quakes, and fires broke out while rescue work was in progress. About 80 percent of Agadir is in ruins, including the old quarter, Tal Borj, and the Casbah, an ancient fortress that was a favorite tourist site.

Mao's ideas being spread to masses

March 27. Communist Party and government officials in Red China have been ordered to begin an intensive campaign to spread the Marxist theories of Mao Tse-tung to the masses. The Socialist re-education or propaganda effort maintains that Mao's ideas provide answers to every problem in China and calls Mao "the world's greatest contemporary theoretician of Marxism-Leninism." Vast numbers of books containing Mao's writings are being printed for mass distribution. "The law of social development should not be mastered by a small number of people," one newspaper said, "but by millions" (→ 4/1966).

75 killed as Cuban arms ship explodes

March 4. Seventy-five to 100 persons are dead in Cuba after a French freighter loaded with ammunition exploded in Havana harbor today. The vessel, named La Courbre, had docked and crew members were unloading her cargo, ammunition and explosives for the Cuban military when the blast occurred. A series of eruptions ensued. More than 200 people were injured. Cuban Premier Fidel Castro declared 24 hours of national mourning for the victims of the tragedy and appropriated $1 million to the families of those killed. Castro also hinted that foul play was involved and implied that the United States might be responsible (→ 4/20).

Kennedy drives on at one-third mark

March 8. The traditional "one-third of the way" mark in the preconvention race is the country's first primary, traditionally held in New Hampshire. Senator John F. Kennedy of Massachusetts triumphed in the Democratic Party primary. And Republican contender Richard Nixon won his party's primary, but only by a 5-to-4 margin. Kennedy, opposed by only one other member of his party, a Chicago pen manufacturer named Paul Fisher, encountered criticism in the Republican state. Governor Wesley Powell accused him of being "soft on communism," and an editorial in a major newspaper judged him unfit to deal with the Soviets (→ 4/10).

Satellite is heard at 409,000 miles

March 13. United States tracking stations today reported receiving signals from the Pioneer V spacecraft, launched two days ago and now 409,000 miles away from the earth. Pioneer V was launched on a path that will take it a maximum distance of 186 million miles from earth, far enough for it to cross into true interplanetary space. Its transmitters are capable of sending across 50 million miles of space. The spacecraft's mission is to explore the solar system. It carries instruments capable of measuring the radiation and magnetic fields found in outer space. Its path will take it close to the planet Venus, 18 million miles from earth, on August 9 (→ 4/2).

Negroes gather at Confederate Capitol

King, urging federal intervention.

March 9. A thousand Negro students gathered on the steps of the former Confederate Capitol building in Montgomery, Alabama, last week to protest against segregation. The demonstration was peaceful; in fact, protest organizer Elroy Embry warned that "if anyone thinks they cannot be orderly, they can help us better" by not taking part. However, racial tension in the city remains high. Negro leader Dr. Martin Luther King has asked President Eisenhower to intervene. "We feel this terror (in Montgomery), violating elementary constitutional rights, requires immediate federal action," he said (→ 30).

Adenauer meets Ben Gurion for first time

Ben Gurion and Adenauer at the Waldorf: An historic reconciliation.

March 14. An historic step toward mitigating the heritage of the Holocaust took place today when Chancellor Konrad Adenauer and Premier David Ben Gurion sat down to talk about German-Jewish relations and world conditions—the first meeting ever between West German and Israeli leaders.

After a friendly conversation at the Waldorf-Astoria, Dr. Adenauer said he was "deeply moved" and that the German people were deeply satisfied that their war restitution has helped "the process of rehabilitation in Israel." Thus far, the Germans have paid more than $1.43 million in restitution.

Stating that he was glad to meet the chancellor, Ben Gurion replied that "the Germany of today is not the Germany of yesterday. We remember the past not in order to brood upon it but in order that it shall never reoccur." The main issue between the two nations—renewed diplomatic relations—was not discussed.

Baritone drops dead on stage at Met

March 4. One of America's finest opera singers, Leonard Warren, died tonight at the Met during a performance of Verdi's "La Forza del Destino." The baritone, 48 years old, had just finished an aria and was preparing to exit when he suddenly pitched forward on his face. Members of the public imagined he had tripped, but his wife, present in the audience, sensed tragedy and rushed to his aid. A stroke claimed his life in minutes.

Frank Sinatra hires blacklisted writer

March 20. Singer and actor Frank Sinatra has hired a blacklisted writer for his production company's next film. Albert Maltz, one of the Hollywood Ten imprisoned for contempt of Congress 12 years ago, will be the author of a screen version of "The Execution of Private Slovik." Sinatra plans the picture to be his directorial debut. The hiring of Maltz was not announced by Sinatra himself but leaked from another source. Some believe Sinatra wanted to keep the fact quiet until after the Democratic national convention. The singer is a strong Kennedy backer, making "High Hopes" his campaign song.

Thursdays, 9:30 on ABC, watch Eliot Ness, played by Robert Stack, lead "The Untouchables" into battle against Al Capone's Prohibition-era gangsters.

1960

APRIL

Su	Mo	Tu	We	Th	Fr	Sa
					1	2
3	4	5	6	7	8	9
10	11	12	13	14	15	16
17	18	19	20	21	22	23
24	25	26	27	28	29	30

1. Sahara: French explode second A-bomb on eve of Khrushchev-de Gaulle talks (→ 18).

5. Hollywood: "Ben Hur" gets record ten Oscars.

6. Sacramento: California Legislature approves nation's first state smog-control bill.

7. Cape Town: South African police seize 1,500 in raid (→ 9).

14. Cameroon: Rebels kill hundreds in new republic (→ 11/13/61).

15. White House picketed by students protesting racial segregation, use of nerve gas (→ 19).

18. London: 75,000 protest nuclear weapons, call for unilateral British disarmament (→ 28).

18. W. Va.: JFK states, "I don't think my religion is anyone's business" (→ 23).

18. Moscow: Sell-out crowd gives U.S. troupe standing ovation for "My Fair Lady" (→ 5/1).

19. AFL-CIO pledges support to Negro boycotts (→ 21).

19. Seoul: Police kill 80 rioters at Pres. Rhee's palace, draw U.S. rebuke of South Korea (→ 27).

20. Harlem Congressman Adam Clayton Powell charged with tax fraud and perjury (→ 11/23/66).

20. Cuba moving thousands from slums to modern homes (→ 5/1).

21. U.S. Congress sends Civil Rights Bill to White House after long internecine battle (→ 25).

22. South Africa says 1,575 held in state of emergency (→ 9/12).

23. Washington: Nixon tells editors' convention of centrist economic aims, termed "progressive conservatism" (→ 5/17).

25. Iran: Earthquake kills 1,500 in town of Lar.

27. Seoul: Pres. Syngman Rhee quits; regime under fire (→ 28).

27. New York approves plans for Shea Stadium in Flushing.

28. Cape Canaveral: Titan ICBM fired over 3,000 miles in limited test (→ 29).

28. Lome: Togoland declares independence from Britain.

29. Geneva: Arms talks end in deadlock (→ 5/20).

Kennedy beats Humphrey in Wisconsin

JFK, bidding to be youngest Pres.

April 10. A coalition headed by Senator Robert C. Byrd of West Virginia formed today to "stop Kennedy," following his success in the Wisconsin primary April 5. Byrd, a staunch Johnson backer, is joined by Pennsylvania Governor David L. Lawrence and other Democrats faulting Kennedy's youth and inexperience. As Lyndon Johnson is not entered in West Virginia's primary next month, Byrd urges votes for Senator Hubert Humphrey instead.

The unspoken issue is Catholicism. One of the reasons Kennedy scored a victory in Wisconsin was that state's unique religious makeup; it is 32 percent Catholic, versus the average state's 23 percent. Only one out of 20 West Virginians is Catholic, the rest being Protestant. Besides any personal animosity Byrd may hold for Kennedy—on the record he is cordial—he may fear Kennedy's failure in his state could weaken the party.

Kennedy plans to tackle the religious issue head on in West Virginia, making it plain that while he firmly believes in the separation of church and state, he will make no apologies for his faith. The primary will be held next month (→ 18).

Canadiens win Cup five times in a row

April 14. Hockey fans who were stunned last year when the Montreal Canadiens won their fourth straight Stanley Cup have had their minds boggled by even more startling news: The Canadiens have run their consecutive cup streak to five, a feat never achieved before in the National Hockey League.

They made a four-game sweep of the cup series, shutting out the Maple Leafs by 4-0 in the finale. The star of the victory was Jean Beliveau, who got two of the goals.

The Flying Frenchmen needed only four games to knock off their semi-final rivals, the Chicago Black Hawks. The Detroit Red Wings, in 1952, were the only other squad to sew up the cup in eight games since the NHL was founded. Henri Richard and Doug Harvey each got a goal in the final game. "Boom Boom" Geoffrion failed to score but he was credited with three assists.

Korean President ousted; 115 dead in riots

April 28. Syngman Rhee, one of the fathers of the Republic of Korea, resigned the presidency yesterday after the National Assembly unanimously approved a resolution demanding he leave office immediately. The United States had called on Rhee to resign in order to end South Korea's political crisis. Foreign Minister Huh Chung will head a caretaker government until new elections are held in the nation.

Nationwide protests began because of alleged irregularities in the March 15 elections, which returned the unopposed Rhee to office for a fourth term. Over 100,000 students from Seoul took to the streets last week, angered by Rhee's disregard for the democratic process. More than 115 persons have been killed in the uprisings (→ 5/29).

"Bye Bye Birdie"

April 14. What's the story, morning glory? "Bye Bye Birdie," a musical starring Dick Van Dyke, Chita Rivera and a flock of teens opened tonight on Broadway. All are crazy for a singer named Birdie (Dick Gautier) who looks like Elvis. And that's the tale, nightingale.

White man wounds South African leader

Dutch immigrant Verwoerd.

April 9. Prime Minister Hendrik F. Verwoerd, a champion of white supremacy in South Africa, was shot and seriously wounded by a white man as he was attending an exposition honoring the 50th anniversary of the formation of the Union of South Africa. The 58-year-old Verwoerd, who has extended the policy of apartheid since becoming prime minister in 1958, was reported "resting well" following an emergency operation. The would-be assassin was described as a middle-aged cattle breeder of English extraction. The shooting threw the nation into turmoil just as racial tensions were abating (→ 22).

Aug 11. Arnold Palmer has won the Masters. Ike joined him today for a round, launching his spring holiday on a sporting note.

Super-modern city becomes Brazil's capital

The Senate buildings at Brasilia were designed by architect Oscar Niemeyer.

April 21. Rio de Janeiro may be the playground of Brazil, but it is no longer the capital. In a stunning move, the government of the South American country has packed its bags and moved to the hinterlands to a brand new city, Brasilia, which was erected magically on a central plateau 600 miles from the coast.

Modern buildings, temples of government, rise from the plateau. But the new city also has the aura of a country fair. Government bureaucrats were forced to move to Brasilia, but visitors and future residents are also streaming there in droves, fascinated by the country's leap into the 20th Century.

Brasilia appears to have been built overnight, but it has roots in the last century. The "Father of Brazilian independence," Jose Bonifacio de Andrada e Silva, first dreamed of moving the capital to the interior in 1822. The move was not approved until 1955. The city map was designed by Lucio Costa. The architect was Oscar Niemeyer. Both men worked to organize the city around two intersecting axes. On one side are offices, on the other, apartments. The public buildings have a very modern, almost plastic, unifying theme.

Ten shot in race riot in Biloxi, Mississippi

April 25. Violence gripped Biloxi, Mississippi, yesterday as the worst race riot in the state's history resulted in the shooting of eight Negroes and two whites. The trouble started when a group of Negroes gathered on a section of the Biloxi beach, usually reserved for whites only. A group of whites converged on the scene, a gun was pulled and shooting and rioting began.

Anthony Ragusin, a city Chamber of Commerce leader, accused the National Association for the Advancement of Colored People of instigating the riot. An NAACP spokesman denied the charge and assailed the city's law enforcement and judicial systems (→ 5/6).

First weather lab launched into space

April 2. The first artificial satellite capable of taking pictures of the earth's weather systems has been sent into orbit by the United States. Its first pictures, distributed by the National Aeronautics and Space Administration, showed the cloud cover over the northeast United States and part of Canada. The earth's curvature was clearly visible in the pictures, which were taken from an altitude of 450 miles. The 270-pound satellite, Tiros I, gives meteorologists their first chance to see global weather patterns on a large scale. It is the prototype of satellites expected to provide 24-hour weather coverage of the entire globe in a few years (→ 8/20).

One million watch de Gaulle parade

April 26. The sky of lower Manhattan was filled with ticker tape and a million people stood twelve deep on Broadway as the city of New York saluted France's President Charles de Gaulle this afternoon. The General waved from an open car as the bells at Trinity Church struggled with "The Marseillaise." "Vive de Gaulle," people in the large crowd shouted. "Hi ya, Charlie," yelled someone else with typical New York reserve.

All the demonstrators were not friendly when de Gaulle attended receptions at the French Consulate on Fifth Avenue and the Seventh Regiment Armory on Park Avenue. "Freedom for Africa," chanted sympathizers for the rebels in Algeria and nationalists in French Africa.

The French president alluded to the situation in Algeria for the first time in his trip to the United States during a luncheon at the Astor Hotel. De Gaulle said France is committed to self-determination for Algeria. "Nothing will deflect her from it, I can assure you," he said. The general is believed to have discussed Algeria and Africa with President Eisenhower at the White House and Camp David. The two presidents were preparing for the Big Four summit next month.

First families at the White House.

East Germans crowd into West Berlin

April 22. The flow of East German refugees into West Berlin has jumped sharply this month, apparently caused by the Communist government's policy of collectivization. In the week since Good Friday, 6,478 East Germans have been received at the Marienfelde refugee reception center. On Good Friday alone, 1,336 refugees were recorded. The number of refugees is more than double the average weekly inflow last year and is approaching the levels of the mass exodus following the bloody uprising in 1953.

Western authorities believe the upsurge in refugees reflects a protest against the forced collectivization policies recently imposed by the Communist German Democratic Republic. This analysis is supported by the comments of the refugees. "I got my nose full of the collectivization," is a common explanation given for fleeing East Germany. In the past three months, private farmers, who controlled nearly half the agricultural land in East Germany, have been forced to put their property into government-managed cooperatives (→ 1/2/61).

House committee looks into payola

April 27. Host of "American Bandstand" Dick Clark has been paying disk jockeys to play records he has invested in. That is the charge of a House panel investigating payola in the music field. Today, an editor of a major music magazine testified defending Clark, saying song-plugging was a tradition in the music business (→ 5/19).

Lucy and Desi have filed for divorce, ending a marriage portrayed on television since 1951.

1960

MAY

Su	Mo	Tu	We	Th	Fr	Sa
1	2	3	4	5	6	7
8	9	10	11	12	13	14
15	16	17	18	19	20	21
22	23	24	25	26	27	28
29	30	31				

1. Havana: 250,000 in May Day protest rail against U.S. (→ 14).

1. Soviets down American U-2 plane invading Soviet airspace; U.S. calls it weather plane (→ 7).

2. San Francisco: Caryl Chessman executed after ten years on death row, denying guilt to end.

4. Washington: Ike signs wheat pact with India for largest U.S. food sale.

6. Washington: Ike signs Civil Rights Act of 1960 (→ 10).

6. London: Princess Margaret married to Anthony Armstrong Jones at Westminster Abbey.

7. Venetian Way, W. Hartack in saddle, wins Kentucky Derby going away.

7. U.S., for first time, admits U-2 flight was spy plane (→ 14).

9. FDA approves contraceptive pill for public use (→ 12/1960).

10. Tenn.: Nashville integrates six lunch counters in first such action in South (→ 28).

13. San Francisco: 52 seized by police in riot over HUAC inquiry into alleged Communist activities (→ 6/5/61).

14. N.Y.: 200 supporters and opponents of Castro clash at Cuban Consulate (→ 6/29).

16. Paris: Big Four summit opens with Ike, Macmillan, Khrushchev, de Gaulle (→ 17).

17. Paris: Summit breaks up over U-2 incident; Khrushchev bars Ike from U.S.S.R. (→ 26).

20. U.S. fires Atlas ICBM record 9,000 miles (→ 24).

24. U.S. Air Force orbits 5,000-pound Midas I satellite designed to detect nuclear attack (→ 6/10).

28. Montgomery: Martin Luther King Jr. acquitted of perjury charges stemming from 1956 bus boycott (→ 7/12).

29. Seoul: Ex-Pres. Syngman Rhee flees to Hawaii (→ 5/18/61).

DEATHS

14. Lucrezia Bori, Spanish opera star, made Met debut opposite Caruso in 1912 (*12/24/1887).

29. Boris Pasternak, Russian poet and novelist, "Dr. Zhivago" (*2/10/1890).

U-2 spy plane breaks up Big 4 summit

Nikita Khrushchev looks over some debris from the demolished U-2.

The Soviet journal Trud published this photo of the U-2 wreckage. The debris underwent severe secrutiny for any evidence of espionage activities.

May 26. Diplomatic furor over the American spy plane shot down by the Russians has driven East-West relations into a tailspin, broken up the Big Four summit, jeopardized the disarmament conference in Geneva and provoked some dangerously ugly charges at the United Nations. At the Security Council today, Soviet Foreign Minister Andrei Gromyko charged that the United States could push the world to "the brink of war" by continuing its policy "of military espionage and sabotage against the Soviet Union." American Ambassador Henry Cabot Lodge called Gromyko's statement a "fantastic allegation."

When Soviet Premier Nikita Khrushchev announced on the 5th that the U-2 reconnaissance plane had been shot down on the 1st, diplomats started scrambling to prevent the disruption of the Big Four summit in Paris. The Allies of the United States did not quibble with the mission of the plane, taking pictures of Soviet military installations. Getting caught was another story. The Allies viewed it as a diplomatic disaster, which became progressively worse as the United States equivocated on the mission of pilot Francis Gary Powers. The State Department denied at first that Powers was on a spy mission. Then officials conceded that he was, and they ended up by saying the mission was justified.

Khrushchev was enraged. By the time he reached Paris on the 14th, however, his attitude seemed to have cooled. British Prime Minister Harold Macmillan was appointed as go-between to soothe relations between the Soviet premier and President Eisenhower. Hopes rose when Eisenhower agreed to announce the cancellation of future U-2 flights. They plummeted when he refused to knuckle under to Khrushchev and apologize for the Powers mission. The summit collapsed on the 17th.

Macmillan and France's President Charles de Gaulle fell in line behind the United States when the summit failed. They issued a joint communique expressing "complete disgust" at the attitude of the Soviet delegation. A group of Soviet editors responded that the summit had been "torpedoed" by the "aggressive actions" of the United States.

In Geneva, talks on disarmament and a nuclear test ban have been unsettled by the Soviet-American friction. The only beneficiary of the new tension appears to be NATO. The organization has been strengthened by the rift between Washington and Moscow (→ 7/8).

Israel captures Eichmann, death camp chief

May 23. In a daring international operation, Israeli agents have spirited away one of the Nazis most hated by Jews and brought him to Israel to stand trial for war crimes.

Adolf Eichmann, who headed the SS Jewish section and allegedly masterminded the extermination of millions of Jews, was discovered living in Argentina under the name of Ricardo Clement. It has been revealed that Israeli agents kidnapped him at work in Buenos Aires, held him under guard in a suburb of the capital and then hid him in a plane that was returning to Israel with a delegation that had attended Argentine independence celebrations. Argentina was apparently never asked to extradite Eichmann. So far, the government has had no reaction to the unusual methods used by Israel to capture the former SS leader.

In the past, Israeli Supreme Court judges have called Eichmann a "bloodthirsty criminal" and a "monster." He is widely accused of engineering the so-called Final Solution during the Second World War. If convicted under a 1950 war crimes statute, Eichmann could be sentenced to death (→ 6/10).

May 11. Mme. de Gaulle baptized the liner France today.

Military coup removes Premier in Turkey

May 27. In a move that came as a complete surprise to United States State Department officials, Premier Adnan Menderes of Turkey was ousted by the armed forces in a bloodless coup today.

Lieutenant General Gemal Gursel, who led the army, navy, and air force officers involved in the takeover, has assured the Turkish people by radio that he does not intend to institute a military dictatorship, and he promised "free and fair elections for the formation of constitutional and democratic government."

Menderes, after a foiled escape, was reported to be safely in custody, along with other members of his administration. A spokesman for the military junta remarked that Menderes would be put on trial "if there is a well-founded complaint against him."

The coup marks the climax of several months of political unrest, focusing on the attempts of Menderes to ban all political activity of the opposition, the Republican Party, led by former President Ismet Inonu. This week cadets, sympathetic to student protesters, led a demonstration in Ankara against the government. Foreign policy experts generally agree that Turkey, under the junta, will remain a staunch ally of the United States and NATO (→ 3/27/61).

Students demonstrate in the streets for the overthrow of the government.

Humphrey quits as Kennedy wins again

May 17. Senator Humphrey conceded the Democratic race to Senator Kennedy last week, bowing to a string of primary results favoring the other candidate. A Kennedy victory in Wisconsin in April was followed by ones in Nebraska and West Virginia May 10. In the Maryland primary today, Kennedy swept 70 percent of the vote, opposed only by Oregon Senator Wayne Morse.

Immediately upon the close of the West Virginia primary, Kennedy told a television audience, "I think we are going to be nominated." The Protestant state was the Catholic candidate's acid test: If he survived in that state's primary, he could survive anywhere. He often found himself reminding voters that an official customarily swears to uphold division of church and state.

But Kennedy emphasized that such an oath was made on the Bible. "And if he breaks his oath," he told the West Virginians, "he is not only committing a crime against the Constitution—for which Congress can impeach him and should impeach him—but he is committing a sin against God." With these words he effectively defended his quest for public office and his faith.

Kennedy's campaign manager, his brother Robert, has gained Humphrey's promise of support. Their only opposition now is the Republican kind: specifically, Vice President Richard Nixon (→ 7/15).

Congo tribes fight in capital streets

Congolese confront Belgian troops.

May 13. The African quarter of Leopoldville, in the Belgian Congo, was occupied by military officials who are trying to stop the worst tribal warfare in more than a year. Five people were killed as warriors of the Lulua and Baluba tribes battled in the streets with knives, spears and machetes. Residents fear there is worse to come. Two other tribes, the Bakongo and Bayaka, are also gearing up to fight.

The Congo is scheduled to gain its independence at the end of next month, and Governor General Henri Cornelis warned that tribal warfare could lead to a military dictatorship. It appears that many Congolese would prefer a dictator to the blood-curdling screams they have been hearing (→ 6/14).

Eight arrested for taking radio payola

May 19. A district attorney has accused disk jockey Alan Freed and eight others of taking over $100,000 in bribes from record companies in return for plugging songs. Freed and another broadcaster will plead not guilty. Trial is set for Sept. 19. The disk jockeys allegedly played records excessively in return for royalties or a $25 per play fee. Freed is charged with playing the same tune as many as eight or nine times on his four-hour program. Currently with KDAY in Los Angeles, 38-year-old Freed previously championed rock and roll at New York stations WINS and WABC.

Rockefeller Jr. dies; gave away millions

May 11. John D. Rockefeller Jr. died today in the Tucson Medical Center. The 86-year-old philanthropist, one of the world's richest men, made a career of giving away the ever-growing millions that accrued from the vast fortune he had inherited. At first, he did help to direct the destinies of corporate giants such as Standard Oil and U.S. Steel, but from age 36 he concentrated on mammoth contributions, among them the East River site for the United Nations and Rockefeller Center. Donations reached more than 50 nations and aided those of many creeds and colors.

May 30. Jim Rathmann has won amid tragedy at the Indy 500. Just before the race, a makeshift scaffold fell, hurling at least 100 spectators onto others below and killing two. While rescuers sought out the 70 or so injured, the hardiest fans merely jockeyed for better viewing positions.

1960

JUNE

Su	Mo	Tu	We	Th	Fr	Sa
			1	2	3	4
5	6	7	8	9	10	11
12	13	14	15	16	17	18
19	20	21	22	23	24	25
26	27	28	29	30		

1. New York: Natl. Council of Churches assails sex and violence on TV and radio (→ 5/1/62).

2. N.Y.: 22 Broadway shows closed in Actors Equity strike (→ 13).

4. Taiwan: Peking hits Quemoy isles with 500 shells (→ 14).

10. N.M.: Army announces first known interception of one guided missile by another (→ 27).

10. N.Y.: Argentina to file complaint at U.N. if Israel fails to return Eichmann (→ 4/11/61).

11. Tokyo: Marine helicopter rescues U.S. officials from car besieged by rioters; Ike visit in jeopardy (→ 16).

13. N.Y.: Broadway theaters reopen after ten-day strike.

14. Washington: JFK, in major foreign policy speech, favors bringing Peking into Geneva arms talks (→ 18).

14. Lumumba claims votes to form Congo government (→ 17).

15. Manila: Million greet Ike, who blasts communism in talk at legislature (→ 10/5/64).

16. Tokyo: 20,000 leftists storm Parliament; 870 injured (→ 17).

17. Tokyo: Japan cancels Ike trip, saying safety cannot be guaranteed (→ 19).

17. Leopoldville: Joseph Kasavubu named to form first Congolese government (→ 30).

18. Denver: Arnold Palmer wins U.S. Open golf championship.

18. Taiwan: Ike hailed, pledges U.S. aid; Communists shell Quemoy in welcome (→ 12/15/61).

19. Tokyo: Parliament ratifies defense pact with U.S. as 300,000 march in protest (→ 7/17).

21. Zurich: German Armin Hary runs 100-meters in record ten seconds flat.

21. Texas: Study says Catholic couples use birth control as much as Protestants and Jews.

21. Linus Pauling risks contempt of Congress, refusing to name scientists who helped him ask U.N. for atom test ban in 1958.

27. Geneva: Soviets leave arms talks, blaming U.S. (→ 7/21).

Congo celebrates freedom amid disputes

Dancing free in the streets, 75 years after Belgian rule was recognized in Berlin.

June 30. Thousands of flags were waving in Leopoldville today as the treaty establishing the independence of the Congo from Belgium was presented to the new Parliament. King Baudouin of Belgium was given a warm welcome yesterday as he was greeted by President Joseph Kasavubu and Premier Patrice Lumumba. The irony was not lost on some spectators who remember that Lumumba was jailed twice by the Belgians, once for inciting violence with a nationalistic speech. But the only hitch to King Baudouin's arrival occurred when one overly enthusiastic Congolese snatched his ceremonial sword and started dancing in the street. The man was promptly arrested.

It is the fear of swords that are more than ceremonial that dampened some of the enthusiasm at the independence celebrations. Political tensions and the threat of tribal warfare threaten two provinces, Katanga and Kasai. The Lulua and Baluba tribes are ready to take to the streets again in Kasai.

Lumumba sent word to the Belgian commander of Congolese forces to maintain order in the troubled areas. Under the terms of the new treaty, Belgian troops will remain in the Congo for an unspecified period of time. Belgium has agreed to give financial aid to the new republic and represent the Congo in international affairs until it creates a diplomatic service (→ 7/8).

Jubilant tribeswomen, painted for the occasion, celebrate Congo independence.

Patterson is first to regain lost title

June 20. Floyd Patterson avenged a humiliating defeat he had suffered at the hands of Ingemar Johansson and at the same time has become the first boxer ever to regain the world heavyweight championship.

A blinding left hook at 1:51 of the fifth round sent the Swede down for the count and Patterson again held the title he had lost last June 26.

It was a left hook also that stunned Johansson earlier in the fifth, but he rose at the count of 9. Johansson's defeat was his first in 23 fights. Patterson got his 36th victory in 38 bouts. Among the fighters who failed to win back the crown were James J. Corbett, Jim Jeffries, Jack Dempsey and Joe Louis.

Who has best IQ? Could it be dolphin?

June 20. Research has shown that the bottle-nosed dolphin has a brain that is at least equal, and perhaps superior, to that of man, marine scientist John C. Lilly said today. The Navy-sponsored research shows that dolphins can talk to each other with high-pitched whistles, mimic human speech and help each other in moments of distress, Lilly said. He added that his five-year study has raised the possibility that as more is learned of the dolphins' language, it may become possible for humans to speak with them.

Hootenanny ends Newport folk show

June 26. The Newport Folk Festival concluded tonight with a hootenanny, as audience members were invited to come on stage to hoot and holler. The amateurs were allowed to do one song each. The evening ended on this freewheeling note, despite some sad tributes paid to the ailing songwriter Woody Guthrie. Professional performers at the three-day festival included Lester Flatt and Earl Scruggs, teenager Joan Baez and the workingman's pal Pete Seeger. Yesterday, a large audience attended a discussion on folk's new popularity (→ 7/2).

Cuba takes Texaco to refine Russian oil

June 29. Cuban leader Fidel Castro ordered the seizure of the Texaco Company oil refinery at Santiago de Cuba after the plant's officials refused to refine petroleum the Cuban government had purchased from the Soviet Union. Cuba and the U.S.S.R. have agreed on a pact wherein the Soviets will trade their oil for Cuban sugar. A spokesman in Washington protested the seizure, saying it was "in contravention of the norms of conduct by responsible governments." Castro attacked a bill pending in Washington which would curtail U.S.-Cuban sugar sales. In a speech before sugar mill workers, he assailed "Yankee imperialism" (→ 7/6).

Japan cancels Ike; Taiwan cheers him

June 20. President Eisenhower was greeted with shouts of "Aloha" in Honolulu today at the end of a nine-day Far Eastern goodwill trip in which he was cheered in Taiwan but canceled in Japan.

The president's scheduled visit to Japan had been postponed when officials of that country said they could not guarantee his safety from Communist agitators.

The Communist presence in that part of the world was quite evident in recent days as the president arrived to a friendly, tumultuous welcome in Taipei, Taiwan. Just hours before his visit, the Chinese Communists fired about 86,000 rounds at the Nationalist offshore islands.

City bars Nazi rallies after leader mobbed

"Fuhrer" Rockwell speaks.

June 22. New York Mayor Robert F. Wagner emphatically denied the American Nazi Party the right to hold a rally on July 4 at Union Square. Basing his decision on grounds that the Nazis' purpose was to incite a riot by preaching "race hatred and violence," the mayor made the announcement just after Nazi leader George Lincoln Rockwell was mobbed outside the State Supreme Court. Rockwell was being interviewed by television reporters, when 150 people converged on the scene, shouted obscenities and attempted to attack him. Security guards rushed Rockwell to protective custody.

Court disallows use of illegal evidence

June 27. The U.S. Supreme Court today overthrew the "silver platter doctrine" by holding that federal courts not admit evidence seized by state officers in violation of the Constitution. The rule, first laid down by the high court in 1914, allowed federal prosecutors to use illegal evidence given to them "on a silver platter." Today's decision found the court divided, 5 to 4, with Justice Potter Stewart writing the majority opinion. Justice Felix Frankfurter termed the majority view a "juridical somersault."

Hitchcock reaches his horror-filled best with "Psycho." Perkins runs the Bates Motel, with 12 rooms and 12 vacancies, and in turn is run by his "mother." Janet Leigh is a victim. Don't close your eyes in the shower.

1960

JULY

Su	Mo	Tu	We	Th	Fr	Sa
					1	2
3	4	5	6	7	8	9
10	11	12	13	14	15	16
17	18	19	20	21	22	23
24	25	26	27	28	29	30
31						

1. Palo Alto, Calif.: John Thomas sets high jump mark of 7 feet, 3.75 inches in Olympic trials.

1. Accra: Ghana becomes republic in British Commonwealth, Kwame Nkrumah is president.

1. Mogadishu: Somalia proclaims republic (→ 8/21).

2. Wimbledon: Neale Fraser over Rod Laver 6-4, 3-6, 9-7, 7-5; Maria Bueno over Sandra Reynolds 8-6, 6-0.

2. Miami Beach: First U.S. Negro competes in Miss Universe contest, representing Ohio.

4. Philadelphia: Fifty-star flag makes official debut at Independence Hall.

6. Ike cuts Cuban sugar imports by 95% for "deliberate policy of hostility toward the U.S."; totals $92.5 million (→ 8).

8. Congo army rebels riot, dismiss all Belgian officers; European civilians fleeing (→ 11).

8. Nairobi: Kenyan police seize 100 as Mau-Mau aides (→ 2/28/61).

8. Khrushchev threatens rocket attack if U.S. fights in Cuba, offers to buy 700,000 lbs. sugar to make up for U.S. cuts (→ 8/7).

11. Congo: Katanga Premier Tshombe proclaims independence, asks Belgian aid (→ 15).

11. Eugene, Oregon: Rafer Johnson breaks decathlon record, lifting U.S. Olympic hopes.

12. L.A.: Democrats adopt strong civil rights plank over Southern protests (→ 8/15).

14. Guatemala: 200 inmates die in asylum fire.

16. Warsaw to pay $40 mil. for U.S. property seized in Poland.

17. Italian racer Gastone Nencini wins Tour de France.

17. Tokyo: Ikeda replaces Kishi as Japanese premier (→ 10/11).

21. Cape Canaveral: Sub completes first Polaris missile underwater launch (→ 9/24).

21. Puebla, Mexico: 30,000-yr.-old fossil pushes man's existence in hemisphere back 20,000 yrs.

28. Leopoldville: U.N. chief Dag Hammarskjold arrives in Congo (→ 8/14).

Gary Powers of U-2 indicted as a spy

Francis Gary Powers, U-2 pilot.

July 8. Soviet Premier Nikita Khrushchev stepped up his anti-American rhetoric today as Francis Gary Powers was formally charged with espionage against the Soviet Union. Powers will go on trial next month. His U-2 reconnaissance plane was shot down by the Soviets in May.

It was Cuba that formed the focus of Khrushchev's attack against the United States. The premier said President Eisenhower is strangling the island with an economic blockade, and he threatened to retaliate with rockets if the U.S. intervenes militarily in Cuba. "One should not forget now that the United States is no longer at an unreachable distance from the Soviet Union as it was before," he said (→ 8/17).

Soldiers stop riots at Newport Festival

July 2. The seventh annual Newport Jazz Festival was marred by violence tonight as over 100 police, Marines and National Guardsmen were called in to quell riots. Ruffian youths in Bermuda shorts protested the lack of tickets to the music fair. Beer cans and epithets were hurled. Some of the youths seized and refused to relinquish seats bought by paying concertgoers. Stores in the area were vandalized, forcing police to shoot tear gas into the mob. After more than 100 arrests were made, the concert resumed.

Kennedy named; Johnson takes 2nd place

Raving Kennedy supporters take over the convention hall in Los Angeles.

July 15. Launching what he called his "New Frontier," Senator John F. Kennedy accepted the Democratic nomination for president today, and, in a surprise move, chose Senator Lyndon B. Johnson of Texas as his vice-presidential running mate.

In his acceptance speech at the final convention session in Los Angeles, the 43-year-old nominee from Massachusetts said that the nation must move beyond the New Freedom and New Deal of past Democratic administrations.

"Woodrow Wilson's New Freedom promised our nation a new political and economic framework," Senator Kennedy said. "Franklin Roosevelt's New Deal promised security and succor to those in need. But the New Frontier of which I speak is not a set of promises—it is a set of challenges."

The presidential nominee's choice of Senator Johnson as his running mate was the major surprise of the convention, for Johnson, a major leader in the Senate, had waged a vigorous campaign for the top spot on the ticket, leveling harsh attacks on Kennedy recently.

While angered at the Johnson attacks, the Kennedy strategists felt that Senator Johnson might prove to be the key to uniting the party, helping to assure victory in the South (→ 28).

Nixon and Lodge put on Republican ticket

July 28. Vice President Richard M. Nixon handily won the Republican nomination for president last night on the first ballot. And today, in the final session of the convention in Chicago, he chose Henry Cabot Lodge to be his vice-presidential running mate.

The Nixon victory came as his only opponent, Senator Barry Goldwater of Arizona, withdrew from the race and, in a dramatic speech, called upon all conservatives to support Nixon so as not to aid those Democrats "dedicated to the destruction of this country."

In a stern lecture to his fellow conservatives, Senator Goldwater said: "Let us put our shoulders to the wheel of Dick Nixon and push him over across the line." He said conservatives must "grow up" and get to work "if we want to take this party back some day—and I think we can."

Nixon is the first vice president in the history of the modern two-party system to win a presidential nomination in his own right. He has served for nearly eight years under President Eisenhower.

Lodge, chief U.S. delegate to the United Nations, accepted the second spot on the Nixon ticket, saying his party would strengthen the nation's military power so as to guarantee "that no nation will ever dare attack us" (→ 9/26).

Eisenhower has a laugh with Lodge and Nixon, the Republican team for '60.

Copper-rich Katanga splits off from Congo and civil war begins

Europeans rush to leave the Congo.

July 15. United Nations forces started arriving in the Congo today as peace in the newly independent republic was shattered by mutiny, revolution and vicious attacks on European residents. Moise Tshombe, the political leader of mineral-rich Katanga, proclaimed the independence of his province from the rest of the Congo. Almost immediately, Belgium, which still controls the copper mines in Katanga, announced it would send more troops to the republic. Belgium claimed the Congolese government had asked for the military assistance.

But today, Premier Patrice Lumumba charged the troops had been sent to topple his government, and he demanded their immediate withdrawal. Describing the new treaty between Belgium and the Congo as a worthless "scrap of paper," Lumumba also ordered all Belgian diplomats out of the country.

Congolese soldiers in the republic's army mutinied against white, Belgian officers a week ago. They attacked Europeans in the streets, looking for arms. Women were raped. Among the victims were nuns at the convent in Mbanza-Boma. Thousands of European refugees fled across the Congo River from Leopoldville to Brazzaville until troops closed the route.

Lumumba appealed to Moscow for help, and Premier Khrushchev obliged by warning Western countries to keep "their hands off" the Congo. The United States called his remark "irresponsible" (→ 28).

Englishman sails Atlantic by himself

July 21. A 59-year-old British adventurer sailed into New York harbor alone in his 39-foot sloop, the winner of a one-man boat race across the Atlantic Ocean.

"Have you heard anything from the others?" Francis Chichester called as his Gipsy Moth II sailed into port. The answer was negative. The "others" were three Englishmen and a Frenchman who were competing single-handed as well. Chichester, a map publisher, trimmed by 16 days the previous west-bound transatlantic record of 56 days. He left Plymouth, England, on June 11 and lost a day making repairs as a result of winds from a two-day gale off Halifax.

Ceylon has world's first woman leader

Bandaranaike, 1st woman Premier.

July 21. Mrs. Sirimavo Bandaranaike, a newcomer to politics, was sworn in today as Prime Minister of Ceylon. She will also be Foreign Minister and Minister of Defense.

The socialist Sri Lanka Freedom Party she led in yesterday's election won an overwhelming victory at the polls. It had been led by her husband, who was assassinated by a Buddhist monk in September.

The attractive 44-year-old widow and mother of three children is the first woman premier of a modern parliamentary regime. Her Freedom Party is committed to nationalization and to the state's taking over schools run by religious denominations. The election gave the Freedom Party 75 seats, the United National Party 30, the Tamil Federalists 16, the Trotskyites 12, and Communists 5 seats with 19 independents or splinter party members.

Lancaster is a charlatan evangelist in the film adaptation of Sinclair Lewis' "Elmer Gantry."

1960

AUGUST

Su	Mo	Tu	We	Th	Fr	Sa
	1	2	3	4	5	6
7	8	9	10	11	12	13
14	15	16	17	18	19	20
21	22	23	24	25	26	27
28	29	30	31			

4. Calif.: X-15 rocket plane sets manned record of 2,150 mph at Edwards Air Force Base (→ 12).

10. Philadelphia: Wilt Chamberlain gets record contract with 76ers.

10. U.S. Senate ratifies 12-nation Antarctic Treaty.

12. Calif.: X-15 rocket plane sets altitude record of 25 miles.

14. Congo: U.N. forces replace Belgians in Katanga (→ 15).

15. Virginia: Richmond, Roanoke enroll their first Negroes in white schools (→ 10/19).

15. Brazzaville: Congo Republic declares total independence from France (→ 16).

15. Laos: Neutralist Prince Souvanna Phouma replaces Tiao Somsanith as premier (→ 9/16).

16. Leopoldville: Lumumba decrees martial law in Katanga secession crisis (→ 9/14).

17. Indonesia severs releations with Holland (→ 12/19/61).

17. Moscow: U-2 trial opens; Powers pleads guilty to spying charges (→ 19).

18. Hamburg, West Germany: Beatles give first public performance, in striptease bar.

20. Russians retrieve satellite with two live dogs (→ 10/4).

21. Somalia and Ethiopia clash in bloody border fighting (→ 11/10/63).

23. Ike requests cut in sugar imports from Dominican Republic after OAS breaks relations (→ 1/5/61).

24. Washington: FDA approves Sabin polio vaccine for use.

25. Rome: XVII Olympics open before 75,000 (→ 29).

28. San Jose, Costa Rica: OAS condemns Communist intervention in Hemisphere; Cubans walk out (→ 9/26).

29. Rome: Tobian, in diving victory, wins first U.S. gold (→ 31).

31. Rome: Nieder breaks Olympic record in U.S. sweep of shot put medals (→ 9/5).

DEATH

24. Aly Maher Pasha, four-time Egyptian head of government.

Castro nationalizes all American property

Castro has joined Khrushchev and Mao as a leader of Third World workers.

Aug 7. American-owned property in Cuba has been seized by Cuban leader Fidel Castro in a dramatic retaliatory move against U.S. "economic aggression." American oil refineries, sugar mills, utility plants and other properties worth hundreds of millions of dollars were nationalized with the force of the Cuban military. Castro said the action vindicates recent Eisenhower administration economic sanctions against the island-nation, particularly the Washington decision to reduce Cuban sugar sales to the U.S.

The expropriated property will be compensated for with bonds over the next 50 years at two percent interest, according to Castro. The premier also denounced all treaties with the U.S. He told a cheering crowd, "Cuba does not feel tied to the warlike merry-go-round of the United States" (→ 28).

Dead: Hammerstein, master of the musical

Aug 23. Winston Churchill once told Parliament he was glad to see the United States and Britain working together. He said their union was mighty as the Mississippi and would "just keep rolling along." Churchill, generally a quotable man, cannot take credit for this line. It comes from "Old Man River," written by Oscar Hammerstein.

Hammerstein died today of cancer at age 65. Through the 20's with composer Jerome Kern, through the 40's and 50's with Richard Rodgers, he penned the words the music longed for. One energetic tune demanded the title "June Is Bustin' Out All Over." A dreamy melody called for "The Last Time I Saw Paris." "I'm as corny as Kansas in August" Nellie Forbush sang in "South Pacific," as any "cock-eyed optimist" would.

The lyricist was proud that his words could further a plot. In "The Sound of Music" (1959), the novice Maria asked the Reverend Mother what to do with her life. A librettist might have made her reply forgettable, but Hammerstein had her sing "Climb every mountain." Three words worth three hundred.

Eastwood: "Rawhide." Today's strong, silent heroes prompted a critic to laud the Rocky Mountains as best actor in such shows.

Souvanna Phouma takes Laos after coup

Aug 9. Prince Souvanna Phouma will head the new government in Laos and will pursue a neutralist policy. He believes that a coalition government in his country is the only way to achieve peace.

Souvanna Phouma was briefly Prime Minister in 1957-58 when he formed a coalition with the pro-Communist Lao Patriotic Front. Except for that period, Laos has been ruled since 1954 by right-wing, pro-Western governments. In April, the army under General Phoumi Nosavan gained control of the government by fraud in the elections for the National Assembly.

Today's coup, which overthrew the military regime, was carried out by a rebel faction of the army led by neutralist Captain Kong Le. The pre-coup regime claimed to be neutral, but was anti-Communist and maintained strong ties to Western nations, especially France and the United States. Last year, the U.S. spent over $18 million to support the 30,000-man Laotian army and a village militia of 20,000 (→ 15).

Souvanna Phouma, new Laos chief.

Cyprus independent as British rule ends

Aug 16. Cyprus became a republic today as, beneath slowly turning ceiling fans, British, Turkish and Greek officials signed in Nicosia a charter formally granting independence to the embattled island.

The proclamation by the British Governor was followed outside by a 21-gun salute, a cause for nervous smiles inside as gunfire is not unfamiliar to the island's 500,000 people. The independence ends four years of almost constant violence which saw 502 persons killed in a three-way tug of war between the contending British, Turkish and Greek communities. Cooperation among them is a must if the agreements are to work. Among other things, they called for general community cooperation, the protection of Turkish minority rights and a mutual defense pact.

As it has since it first became a British protectorate in 1878—and a crown colony in 1925—Cyprus will continue to serve the strategic interests of Britain, which retains two military enclaves encompassing 99 square miles (→ 12/21/63).

Pres. Makarios rides triumphantly through the streets of independent Cyprus.

Powers guilty, gets ten-year sentence

Aug 19. Francis Gary Powers was found guilty of espionage against the Soviet Union and handed a ten-year prison and work farm sentence today. Powers, the pilot of the U-2 spy plane shot down near Sverdlovsk, showed no emotion in the packed Moscow courtroom. An appeal is not permitted, but Powers' family says it will ask Premier Nikita Khrushchev for a reprieve. Powers could have received the death penalty, but the court said he had expressed "sincere repentance and confession of his guilt."

At the beginning of the trial, three days ago, Powers pleaded guilty to the espionage charge, said he was "sincerely sorry" and noted that he was only following orders from the Central Intelligence Agency. In closing arguments, both prosecution and defense condemned the United States (→ 6/4/61).

Eleven new states created in Africa

Aug 17. One after another, former European colonies in Africa are forming independent governments. The entire map of the continent is being redrawn. This month alone, eight new states were created out of territory in French West Africa and French Equatorial Africa.

Dahomey led the way, becoming an independent republic on the 1st, with its 1.7 million inhabitants and an area of 44,000 square miles. On the 3rd, the republic of Niger was declared (2.5 million people, 459,000 square miles). On the 5th, the republic of Upper Volta (3.3 million people, 106,000 square miles). On the 7th, the Ivory Coast (2.5 million people, 127,500 square miles). On the 11th, the republic of Chad (2.5 million people, 501,000 square miles). On the 13th, the Central African Republic (1.1 million people, 238,000 square miles). On the 15th, the Republic of the Congo, formerly the French Congo (760,000 people, 132,000 square miles). And today, the republic of Gabon, (470,000 people, 102,000 square miles). The former Belgian Congo, Somalia and Madagascar also became independent this year.

1960

SEPTEMBER

Su	Mo	Tu	We	Th	Fr	Sa
				1	2	3
4	5	6	7	8	9	10
11	12	13	14	15	16	17
18	19	20	21	22	23	24
25	26	27	28	29	30	

1. Rabat: French sign pact with Morocco, calling for evacuation of military bases (→ 2/26/61).

5. Rome: U.S. sweeps 110-meter high hurdles; Wilma Rudolph takes 200-meters; U.S. boxers, including Cassius Clay, win three golds (→ 6).

6. Rome: Rafer Johnson wins Olympic decathlon.→

7. New York: Grandma Moses celebrates 100th birthday.

12. U.S: Hurricane Donna hits East Coast, called worst on record.

12. South Africa: Johannesburg Anglican bishop exiled for criticism of apartheid (→ 10/5).

14. Iraq, Iran, Kuwait and Saudi Arabia form OPEC.

14. Leopoldville: Congolese army takes power under Colonel Mobutu.→

16. Laos: Pro-Communists of Pathet Lao invade north (→ 12/9).

16. Jordan and Syrian troops gather on both sides of common border.

18. New York: 2,000 cheer Castro on arrival for U.N. session (→ 26).

20. New York: U.N. General Assembly opens with many heads of state in attendance.

20. Vienna: Fourth conference of Intl. Atomic Energy Agency opens (→ 4/5/63).

23. New York: Khrushchev demands U.N. leave U.S., oust Hammarskjold (→ 10/12).

24. Newport News, Virginia: Enterprise launched, first nuclear aircraft carrier (→ 10/21).

27. Mexico nationalizes all utilities.

30. New York: 15 new African nations admitted to U.N.

DEATHS

1. Francis Everett Townsend, American physician, activist for social security (*1/13/1867).

7. Wilhelm Pieck, East German statesman (*1/3/1876).

14. Sir Arthur Fleming, British engineer, pioneer in radar technology (*1/16/1881).

American Negroes star at the Rome Olympics

Sept 11. The Soviet Union carried off unofficial point honors in the Rome Olympics, but the Americans dominated the events they considered the most important—track and swimming.

Just as in Melbourne four years ago in its second Olympic appearance, the Soviet Union was first in medals with 43 gold, 33 silver, 30 bronze and a total of 807.5 points.

The Americans won 34 gold, 21 silver and 16 bronze for 564 points. They were hurt by their weak showing in gymnastics and Greco-Roman wrestling and trailed the Russians as well in weightlifting, shooting and rowing.

The Americans scored a stunning sweep of the 110-meter high hurdles, beating the world record-holder from Germany, Martin Lauer. Three American Negroes, Lee Calhoun, Willie May and Hayes Jones, all outran Lauer.

Another American Negro, Otis Davis, took the 400-meter run and an Ohio State grad, Glenn Davis, won the 400-meter hurdles. A Negro woman from the U.S., Wilma Rudolph, scored a notable triumph in the 100-meter final. Her time of 11 seconds bettered the existing record but was disallowed because of a light following wind.

An 18-year-old Negro from Louisville was one of three Americans to take gold medals in boxing. Cassius Clay defeated Ziggy Pietrzykowski, an experienced Polish Olympian, in the 178-pound final. The other winning Americans were Willie McClure of Toledo and Eddie Crook, an Army sergeant.

The two-day decathlon went to Rafer Johnson, a Negro from California. "I wanted this one real bad," said Johnson on becoming the so-called world's greatest athlete. "But I never want to go through that again—never."

Abebe Bikila, a barefoot Ethiopian, won the marathon and said, "I could have gone around the course again without any difficulty."

Gary Tobian and Sam Hall finished one-two in the springboard dive and a California girl, Carolyn Schuler, scored a surprise by winning the 100-meter butterfly in Olympic record time. Bill Mulliken just missed a record in taking the 200-meter breaststroke.

Armin Hary (extreme left), closing in on the 10-second mark, finishes the 100-meters in 10.2. He is the first German to win a gold medal in the event.

Wilma Rudolph, the "black gazelle," swept three golds in sprint events for the Americans: The 100-and 200-meters, and the 4 x 100-meter relay.

The equestrian gold medals in the team jumping competition went to the Germans. Left to rt.: Theidemann, Winkler and Schockemohle, on Meteor, Halla and Ferdl.

Though the Americans won the 4 x 400 relay, their favored 4 x 100 team dropped the baton. The West German sprinters, led by Armin Hary, went on to win. From left to rt.: Bernd Cullmann, Hary, Walter Mahlendorf and Martin Lauer.

Men Athletics

100 M Dash
1. Armin Hary FRG 10,2
2. David Sime USA 10,2
3. Peter Radford GBR 10,3

200 M Dash
1. Livio Berruti ITA 20,5
2. Lebster Carney USA 20,6
3. Abdoulaye Seye FRA 20,7

400 M Run
1. Otis Davis USA 44,9
2. Carl Kaufmann FRG 44,9
3. Malcolm Spence SAF 45,5

800 M Run
1. Peter Snell NZL 1:46,3
2. Roger Moens BEL 1:46,5
3. George Kerr ANT 1:47,1

1500 M Run
1. Herbert Elliot AUS 3:35,6
2. Michel Jazy FRA 3:38,4
3. Istavan Rozsavōlgy HUN 3:39,2

5000 M Run
1. Murray Halberg NZL 13:43,4
2. Hans Grodotzki FRG 13:44,6
3. Kazimierz Zimny POL 13:44,8

10,000 M Run
1. Pyotr Bolotnikov URS 28:32,2
2. Hans Grodotzki FRG 13:44,6
3. David Power AUS 28:38,2

Marathon
1. Abebe Bikila ETH 2:15:16,2
2. Rhadi Ben Abdesselem MAR 2:15:41,6
3. Barry Magee NZL 2:17:18,2

110 M Hurdles
1. Lee Calhoun USA 13,8
2. Willie May USA 13,8
3. Hayes Jones USA 14,0

400 M Hurdles
1. Glenn Davis USA 49,3
2. Clifton Cushman USA 49,6
3. Richard Howard USA 49,7

3000 M Steeplechase
1. Zdzislaw Kryskowiak POL 8:34,2
2. Nicolai Sokolov URS 8:36,4
3. Seymon Czichine URS 8:42,2

400 M Relay
1. FRG 39,5 (Bernd Cullman, Armin Hary, Walter Mahlendorf, Martin Lauer)
2. URS 40,1 (Gusman Kosanov, Leonid Barteniev, Yuri Konovalov, Edvin Ozolin)
3. GBR 40,2 (Peter Radford, David Jones, David Segal, Neville Withehead)

1600 M Relay
1. USA 3:2,2 (Jack Yerman, Earl Young, Glenn Davis, Otis Davis)
2. FRG 3:2,7 (Hans-Joachim Reske, Mandfred Kinder, Johannes Kaiser, Carl Kaufmann)
3. ANT 3:4,0 (Malcolm Spence, James Wedderburn, Keith Gardner, George Kerr)

20 km Walk
1. Vladimir Golubnichiy URS 1:34:07,2
2. Noel Freeman AUS 1:34:16,4
3. Stanley Vickers GBR 1:34:56,4

50 km Walk
1. Donald Thompson GBR 4:25:30,0
2. John Ljunggren SWE 4:25:47,0
3. Abden Pamich ITA 4:27:55,4

High Jump
1. Robert Chaviakadzo URS 2,16
2. Valery Brumel URS 2,16
3. John Thomas USA 2,14

Pole Vault
1. Donald Bragg USA 4,70
2. Ronald Morris USA 4,60
3. Eeles Lendstroem FIN 4,55

Long Jump
1. Ralph Boston USA 8,12
2. Irvin Roberson USA 8,11
3. Igor Ter-Ovanesian URS 8,04

Triple Jump
1. Jozef Schmidt POL 16,81
2. Vladimir Gorsav URS 16,63
3. Vitold Kreer URS 16,43

Shotput
1. William Nieder USA 19,68
2. Parry O'Brien USA 19,11
3. Dallas Long USA 19,01

Discus Throw
1. Alfred Oerter USA 59,18
2. Richard Babke USA 58,02
3. Richard Cochran USA 57,16

Hammer Throw
1. Vasily Rudenkov URS 67,10
2. Gyula Zsivotzky HUN 65,79
3. Tadeusz Rut POL 65,64

Javelin
1. Viktor Cybulenko URS 84,64
2. Walter Krueger FRG 79,36
3. Gergely Kulcsar HUN 78,57

Decathlon
1. Rafer Johnson USA 8392
2. Chuang Kwang Yang TAI 8334
3. Vassily Kusnnetsov URS 7809

Women Athletics

100 M Dash
1. Wilma Rudolph USA 11,0
2. Dorathy Hyman FRG 11,3
3. Giuseppina Leone ITA 11,3

200 M Dash
1. Wilma Rudolph USA 24,0
2. Juta Heine FRG 24,4
3. Dorathy Heyman GBR 24,7

800 M Run
1. Ludmila Chevzova URS 2:04,3
2. Brenda Jones AUS 2:04,4
3. Ursula Donath FRG 2:05,6

80 M Hurdles
1. Irina Press URS 10,8
2. Carol Qunton GBR 10,9
3. Gisela Birkemeyer-Koehler FRG 11,0

400 M Relay
1. USA 44,5 (Martha Hudson, Lucinda Williams, Barbara Jones, Wilma Rudolph)
2. FRG 44,8 (Martha Langbein, Annie Biechl, Brunhilde Hendrix, Juta Heins)
3. POL 45,0 (Tereza Wieczorek, Barbara Janiszewska, Celina Jesionowska, Halina Richter)

High Jump
1. Iolanda Bales ROM 1,85
2. Jaroslawa Iozwiakowska POL 1,71
3. Dorothy Shirley GBR 1,71

Long Jump
1. Vera Krepkina URS 6,37
2. Elzbieta Krzesinska POL 6,27
3. Hildrun Claus FRG 6,21

Shotput
1. Tamara Press URS 17,32
2. Johanna Luettge FRG 16,61
3. Earlene Brown USA 16,42

Discus Throw
1. Nina Ponoereva URS 55,10
2. Tamara Press URS 52,59
3. Lia Manoliu ROM 52,36

Javelin
1. Elvina Ozolina URS 55,98
2. Dana Zatopkova TCH 53,45
3. Birute Kaledene URS 53,45

Men Swimming

100 M Freestyle
1. John Devitt AUS 55,2
2. Lance Larson USA 55,2
3. Manuel Dos Santos BLA 55,4

400 M Freestyle
1. Murray Rose AUS 4:18,3
2. Tsuyoshi Yamanaka JAP 4:21,4
3. John Konrads AUS 4:21,8

1500 M Freestyle
1. John Konrads AUS 17:19,6
2. Murray Rose AUS 17:21,7
3. George Breen USA 17:30,6

100 M Backstroke
1. David Theile AUS 1:01,9
2. Franck Mac Kinney USA 1:02,1
3. Robert Bennett USA 1:02,3

200 M Breaststroke
1. William Mulliken USA 2:37,4
2. Yoshihiko Osaki JAP 2:38,0
3. Wieger Emile Mensonides HOL 2:39,7

200 M Butterfly Stroke
1. Michael Troy USA 2:12,8
2. Neville Hayes AUS 2:14,6
3. J. David Gillanders USA 2:15,3

800 M Freestyle Relay
1. USA 8:10,2 (George Harrisson, Richard Blick, Michael Troy, F. Jeffrey Farell)
2. JAP 8:13,2 (Makoto Fukui, Hiroshi Ishii, Tsuyoshi Yamanaka, Tatsuo Fujimoto)
3. AUS 8:13,8 (David Dickson, John Devitt, Murray Rose, John Konrads)

400 M Medley Relay
1. USA 40:05,4 (Frank Mac Kinney, Paul Hait, Lance Larrson, F. Jeffrey Farell)
2. AUS 4:12,0 (David Theile, Terry Gathercole, Neville Hayes, Geoffrey Shipton)
3. JAP 4:12,2 (Kazuo Tomita, Koichi Hirakida, Yoshihiko Osaki, Keigo Shimizu)

Springboard Diving
1. Gary Tobian USA 170,00
2. Samuel Hall USA 167,08
3. Juan Botella MEX 162,30

High Diving
1. Robert Webster USA 165,56
2. Gary Tobian USA 165,25
3. Brian Eric Phelps GBR 157,13

1960 Rome

Water-Polo
1. Italy
2. Soviet Union
3. Hungary

Women Swimming

100 M Freestyle
1. Dawn Fraser AUS 1:01,2
2. Susan Christine von Seltza USA 1:02,8
3. Nathalie Steward GBR 1:03,1

400 M Freestyle
1. Susan Christine von Saltza USA 4:50,6
2. Jane Cederquvist SWE 4:53,9
3. Cathairna Lagerberg HOL 4:56,9

200 M Breaststroke
1. Anita Lonsbrough GBR 2:49,5
2. Wiltrud Urselman FRG 2:50,0
3. Barbara Goebel FRG 2:53,6

100 M Backstroke
1. Lynn Burke USA 1:09,5
2. Nathalie Steward GBR 1:10,8
3. Sakoto Tanaka JAP 1:11,4

100 M Butterfly Stroke
1. Carolyn Schuler USA 1:09,5
2. Marianne Heemskerk HOL 1:10,4
3. Janice Andrew AUS 1:12,2

400 M Freestyle Relay
1. USA 4:08,9 (Joan Spillane, Shirley Stobs, Carolyn Wood, Susan Christine von Saltza)
2. AUS 4:11,3 (Dawn Fraser, Ilsa Konrads, Lorraine Crapp, Alva Colqhoun)
3. FRG 4:19,7 (Christel Seffin, Heidi Pechstein, Gisela Weiss, Ursula Brunner)

400 M Medley Relay
1. USA 4:41,1 (Lynn Burke, Patty Kempner, Carolyn Schuler, Susan Christine von Saltzqa)
2. AUS 4:45,9 (Marilyn Wilson, Rosemary Lassig, Janice Andrew, Dawn Fraser)
3. FRG 4:47,6 (Ingrid Schmidt, Ursula Kueper, Baerbel Fuhrmann, Ursel Brunner)

Springboard Diving
1. Ingrid Kreemer FRG 155,81
2. Paula Jean Pope-Meyers USA 141,24
3. Elizabeth Ferris GBR 139,09

High Diving
1. Ingrid Kreemer FRG 91,28
2. Paula Jean Pope-Meyers USA 88,94
3. Ninel Krutova URS 86,99

Boxing

Flyweight
1. Gyula Török HUN
2. Sergei Sivko URS
3. Kioshy Tanabe JAP
3. Abdelmoneim Elquindi EGY

Bantamweight
1. Oleg Grigorev URS
2. Primo Zamparini ITA
3. Oliver Taylor AUS
3. Brunon Bendig POL

Featherweight
1. Francesco Musso ITA
2. Jerzy Adamski POL
3. Jorma Limmonen FIN
3. William Meyers SAF

Lightweight
1. Kazmierz Pazdior POL
2. Sandro Loppolo ITA
3. Richard Mac Taggart GBR
3. Abel Laudonio ARG

Light Welterweight
1. Bobumil Nemecek TCH
2. Clement Quartey GHA
3. Quincy Daniels USA
3. Marian Kasprzyk POL

Welterweight
1. Giovanni Benvenuti ITA
2. Yuri Radoniak URS
3. Leszek Drogosz POL
3. James Lloyd GBR

Light Middleweight
1. Wilbert Mac Cure USA
2. Carmelo Bossi ITA
3. Boris Lagutin URS
3. William Fisher GBR

Middleweight
1. Edward Crook USA
2. Tadeusz Walesek POL
3. Ion Monea ROM
3. Yevgeny Feofanov URS

Light Heavyweight
1. Cassius Clay USA
2. Zbigniew Pietrzykowski POL
3. Giulio Saraudi ITA
3. Antony Madigan AUS

Heavyweight
1. Franco de Riccoli ITA
2. Daniel Bekker SAF
3. Guenter Siegmund FRG
3. Josef Nemec TCH

Field Hockey

1. Pakistan
2. India
3. Spain

CHART

Weightlifting

			2 Arm Press	2 Arm Snatch	2 Arm Clean & Jerk	Total
Bantamweight						
1.	Charles Vinci	USA	105,0	107,5	132,5	345,0
2.	Yoshinobu Miyake	JAP	97,5	105,0	132,0	337,5
3.	Esmail Elm Khah	IRA	97,5	100,0	132,5	330,0
Featherweight						
1.	Yevgeny Minaev	URS	120,0	110,0	142,5	372,5
2.	Isaac Berger	USA	117,5	105,0	140,0	362,5
3.	Sebastiano Manniron	ITA	107,5	110,0	135,0	352,5
Lightweight						
1.	Viktor Bouchouev	URS	125,0	122,5	150,0	397,5
2.	Howe-Liang Tan	SIN	115,0	110,0	155,0	380,0
3.	Abdul Wahid Aziz	IRK	117,5	115,0	147,5	380,0
Middleweight						
1.	Aleksandr Kurynov	URS	135,0	132,5	170,0	437,5
2.	Thomas Kono	USA	140,0	127,5	160,0	427,5
3.	Gyözö Veres	HUN	130,0	120,0	155,0	405,0
Light Heavyweight						
1.	Ireneusz Palinski	POL	130,0	132,5	180,0	442,5
2.	James George	USA	132,5	132,5	165,0	430,0
3.	Jan Bocenek	POL	130,0	120,0	170,0	420,0
Middleweight						
1.	Arkady Vorobiev	URS	152,5	142,5	177,5	472,5
2.	Trofim Lomakin	URS	157,5	130,0	170,0	457,5
3.	Louis Martin	GBR	137,5	137,5	170,0	445,0
Heavyweight						
1.	Yuri Vlasov	URS	180,0	155,0	202,5	537,5
2.	James Bradford	USA	180,0	150,0	182,5	512,5
3.	Norbert Schemansky	USA	170,0	150,0	180,0	500,0

Greco Roman Wrestling

Flyweight
1. Dimitru Pirvulescu ROM
2. Osman Sayed EGY
3. Mohamed Paziarye IRA

Bantamweight
1. Oleg Karavayev URS
2. Ion Cernea ROM
3. Petrov Dinko BUL

Featherweight
1. Müzahir Sille TUR
2. Imre Polyak HUN
3. Konstantin Vrupaev URS

Lightweight
1. Avtandil Korize URS
2. Branislav Martinovic YUG
3. Gustav Freij SWE

Welterweight
1. Mithat Bayrak TUR
2. Günther Maritschnigg FRG
3. René Schiermeyer FRA

Middleweight
1. Dimiter Dobrev BUL
2. Lothar Metz FRG
3. Ion Taranu ROM

Light Heavyweight
1. Trefik Kis URS
2. Krali Bimbalov FRG
3. Bohumil Kubat TCH

Freestyle Wrestling

Flyweight
1. Ahmet Bilek TUR
2. Masayki Matsubara JAP
3. Mohamad Saifpour Sadabadi IRA

Bantamweight
1. Terence MacCann USA
2. Nedschet Zalev BUL
3. Tadeusz Trojanowski POL

Featherweight
1. Mustafa Dangistanli TUR
2. Stantcho Ivanov BUL
3. Vladimir Rubashvili URS

Lightweight
1. Shelby Wilson USA
2. Vladimir Sinjavski URS
3. Enyu Dirnov BUL

Welterweight
1. Douglas Blubaugh USA
2. Ismail Ogan TUR
3. Muhammed Bashir PAK

Middleweight
1. Hasan Güngör TUR
2. Georgy Skhirtladse URS
3. Hans Yngve Antonsson SWE

Light Heavyweight
1. Ismet Ali TUR
2. Gholam-Reza-Takhti IRA
3. Anatoly Albul URS

Heavyweight
1. Wilfried Dietrich FRG
2. Hamit Kaplan TUR
3. Savkus Dzarasov URS

Men Fencing

1. Viktor Zdanovitch URS
2. Yuri Sisikine URS
3. Albert Axelrod USA

Foil Team
1. Soviet Union
2. Italy
3. German Federal Republic

Epée Individual
1. Giuseppe Delfino ITA
2. Allan Jay GBR
3. Bruno Khabarov URS

Epée Team
1. Italy
2. Great Britain
3. Soviet Union

Sabre Individual
1. Rudolf Karpati HUN
2. Zoltan Horvath HUN
3. Wladimiro Calarese ITA

Sabre Team
1. Hungary
2. Poland
3. Italy

Women Fencing

Foil Individual
1. Heidi Schmid FRG
2. Valentine Rastvorova URS
3. Marina Vicol ROM

Foil Team
1. Soviet Union
2. Hungary
3. Italy

Modern Pentathlon

Individual
1. Ferenc Nemeth HUN
2. Imre Nagy HUN
3. Robert L. Beck USA

Team
1. Hungary Ferenc Nemeth, Imre Nagy, Andras Balczo
2. Soviet Union Igor Novikov, Nikolai Tatarinov, Hanno Selg
3. USA Robert L. Beck, Jack Daniels, George Lambert

Men Canoeing

Kayak-1 1000 M
1. Erik Hansen DEN 3:53,00
2. Imre Szöllösi HUN 3:54,02
3. Gert Frederiksson SWE 3:55,89

Kayak-2 1000 M
1. Sweden 3:34,73
2. Hungary 3:34,91
3. Poland 3:37,34

Canadian-1 1000 M
1. Janos Parti HUN 4:33,93
2. Aleksandr Silaev URS 4:34,41
3. Leon Rotman ROM 4:35,87

Canadian-2 1000 M
1. Soviet Union 4:17,94
2. Italy 4:20,77
3. Hungary 4:20,89

2000 M Kayak-1 Relay (1960 only)
1. FRG 7:39,43 (Paul Lange, Gunther Perleberg, Friedhelm Wenzke, Dieter Krause)
2. HUN 7:44,02 (Imre Szöllösi, Imre Kemecsey, Andras Szente, György Meszaros)
3. DEN 7:46,09 (Helmuth Sorensen, Arne Hoyer, Erling Jessen, Erik Hansen)

Women Canoeing

Kayak-1 500 M
1. Antonina Seredina URS 2:08,08
2. Therese Zenz FRG 2:08,22
3. Daniela Walkowiak POL 2:10,46

Kayak-2 500 M
1. Soviet Union 1:54,76
2. German Federal Republic 1:56,66
3. Hungary 1:58,22

Rowing

Single Scull
1. Vatcheslav Invanov URS 7:13,86
2. Achim Hill FRG 7:20,21
3. Teodor Kocerka POL 7:21,26

Double Sculls
1. Czechoslovakia 6:47,50
2. Soviet Union 6:50,49
3. Switzerland 6:50,59

Pair Oars without Coxswain
1. Soviet Union 7:02,01
2. Austria 7:03,69
3. Finland 7:03,80

Pair Oars with Coxswain
1. German Federal Republic 7:29,14
2. Soviet Union 7:30,17
3. USA 7:34,58

Four Oars without Coxswain
1. USA 6:26,26
2. Italy 6:28,78
3. Soviet Union 6:29,62

Eight Oars
1. German Federal Republic 5:57,18
2. Canada 6:01,52
3. Czechoslovakia 6:04,84

Yatching

Finn Monotype Class
1. Paul Elvstrôm DEN 8171
2. Aleksandr Tchutchelov URS 6250
3. André Nelis BEL 5934

Star Class
1. Soviet Union 7619
2. Portugal 6665
3. USA 6269

Flying Dutchman Class
1. Norway 6774
2. Denmark 5991
3. German Federal Republic 5882

Dragon Class
1. Greece 6733
2. Argentina 5715
3. Italy 5704

5,5 m (1952, 1956, 1960, 1964, 1968 only)
1. USA 6900
2. Denmark 5678
3. Soviet Union 5122

Cycling

Individual Road Race
1. Viktor Kapitonov URS 4:20:37,0
2. Livio Trapè ITA 4:20:37,0
3. Willy van der Bergen BEL 4:20:57,0

100 km Team Time Trial
1. Italy 2:14:33,53
2. German Federal Republic 2:16:56,31
3. Soviet Union 2:18:41,67

1000 M Time Trial
1. Sante Gaiardoni ITA 1:07,27
2. Leo Sterckx BEL 1:08,75
3. Rostilav Vargashkin ITA 1:08,86

1000 M Sprint
1. Sante Gaiardoni ITA 11,1
2. Leo Sterckx BEL
3. Valentino Gasparella ITA

2000 M Tandem
1. Italy 10,7
2. German Federal Republic
3. Soviet Union

Team Pursuit 4000 M
1. Italy 4:30,90
2. German Federal Republic 4:35,78
3. Soviet Union 4:34,05
(During the race held to determine 3rd place, the Soviets scored better than the Germans).

Equestrian Sports

All-around Individual Competition
1. Lawrence Morgan AUS
2. Neale Lavis AUS
3. Anton Bühler SUI

All-around Team Competition
1. Australia -128,18
2. Soviet Union -386,02
3. France -515,71

Individual Dressage
1. Sergei Filatov URS 2144,0
2. Gustav Fischer SUI 2087,0
3. Josef Neckermann FRG 2082,0

Grand Prix Jumping Individual
1. Raimondo d'Inzeo ITA -12
2. Piero d'Inzeo ITA -16
3. David Broome GBR -23

Grand Prix Jumping Team
1. German Federal Republic -46,50
2. USA -66.00
3. Italy -80,50

Shooting

Full-Bore Rifle, 300 M, 3 positions
1. Hubert Hammerer AUT
2. Hans Spillmenn SUI
3. Vassily Borisov URS

Small-Bore Rifle, 50 M, Prone
1. Peter Kohnke FRG 590
2. James Hill USA 589
3. Enrie Forcella Pellicioni VEN 587

Small-Bore Rifle, Combined 3 Positions
1. Viktor Shamburkin URS 1149
2. Marat Myasov URS 1145
3. Klaus Zähringer FRG 1139

Rapid-Fire Pistol, 25 M
1. William Mac Millan USA 587/147
2. Pentti Linnosvuo FIN 587/139
3. Aleksandr Zabelin URS 587/135

Free Pistol, 50 M
1. Alexei Gustchin URS 560
2. Makhmud Umarov URS 552/26
3. Yoshilisa Yoshikawa JAP 552/20

Clay Pigeon
1. Ion Dimitrescu ROM 192
2. Galliano Rossini ITA 191
3. Sergei Kelinin URS 190

Men Gymnastics

All-around Individual Competition
1. Boris Chakline URS 115,95
2. Takashi Ono JAP 115,90
3. Yuri Titov URS 115,60

All-around Team Competition
1. Japan 575,20
2. Soviet Union 572,70
3. Italy 559,05

Parallel Bars
1. Boris Chakline URS 19,400
2. Giovanni Carminucci ITA 19,375
3. Takashi Ono JAP 19,350

Floor Exercise
1. Nobuyuki Alhara JAP 19,450
2. Yuri Titov URS 19,325
3. Franco Menicelli ITA 19,279

Horse Vault
1. Boris Chakline URS 19,350
2. Takashi Ono JAP 19,350
3. Vladimir Portnoi URS 19,225

Sidehorse Vault
1. Boris Chakline URS 19,375
2. Eugen Ekman FIN 19,375
3. Shuji Tsurumi JAP 19,150

Horizontal Bar
1. Takashi Ono JAP 19,600
2. Masao Takemoto JAP 19,525
3. Boris Chakline URS 19,475

Flying Rings
1. Albert Azaryan URS 19,725
2. Boris Chakline URS 19,500
3. Takashi Ono JAP 19,425
3. Velik Kaspazov BUL 19,425

Women Gymnastics

1. Soviet Union 382,320
2. Czechoslovakia 373,323
3. Romania 372,053

All-around Individual Competition
1. Larissa Latynina URS 77,031
2. Sofia Muratova URS 76,696
3. Polina Astakhova URS 76,164

Uneven Bars
1. Polina Astakhova URS 19,616
2. Larissa Latynina URS 19,416
3. Tamara Ljukmina URS 19,399

Floor Exercise
1. Larissa Latynina URS 19,583
2. Polina Astakhova URS 19,532
3. Tamara Ljukmina URS 19,400

Horse Vault
1. Margarita Nikolayeva URS 19,316
2. Sofia Muratova URS 19,043
3. Larissa Latynina URS 19,014

Beam
1. Eva Bosakova URS 19,283
2. Larissa Latynina URS 19,233
3. Sofia Muratova URS 19,232

Basketball

1. USA
2. Soviet Union
3. Brazil

Soccer

1. Yusgoslavia
2. Denmark
3. Hungary

Kennedy and Nixon meet in first TV debate

Kennedy and Nixon, lighted for TV cameras, face the panel in Chicago.

Sept 26. Vice President Richard M. Nixon and Senator John F. Kennedy clashed mildly tonight in the first nationally televised debate between presidential candidates. To many viewers questioned after the one-hour show, the encounter ended in a draw, with most saying that their minds had not been changed or that they were still undecided which man to vote for in the upcoming November 8 election.

While not generating any real heat, the debate was not all sweetness and light. Nixon accused his Democratic opponent of being a spendthrift at the expense of the taxpayers, saying that his program would cost many billions of dollars. In turn, Kennedy accused the vice president of giving only "lip service" to an increase in the minimum wage to a dollar an hour; expanding school construction; and providing medical care for the aged.

The debate, held in a television studio in Chicago, was carried by all major TV and radio stations. The two candidates were questioned by Sander Vanocur of NBC; Stuart Novins of CBS; Charles Warren of Mutual Broadcasting; and Robert Fleming of ABC. Howard K. Smith of CBS was moderator (→ 10/7).

Poet Leopold Senghor is Senegal President

Sept 5. Leopold Senghor, a brilliant man of letters and leader of his nation's independence movement, is the first President of the new republic of Senegal, a former French colony in West Africa.

Senghor, apostle of African culture.

The son of a wealthy landowner, Senghor was so gifted in literature that he won a scholarship to study at the Sorbonne in Paris in the 1930's. There, he met writers Aime Cesaire and Leon Damas and together they formulated the concept of Negritude, which asserted the evils of colonialism and the cultural importance of their black African heritage. All three began writing poetry to express their pride.

In World War II, Senghor served as an officer in the French army and was captured by the Germans. Afterwards, he represented Senegal in the French legislature until 1958.

Among his works are "Songs of the Shade" (1945) and "Ethiopiques" (1956). He is working on a book about African socialism.

Castro addresses U.N., speaks over 4 hours

Sept 26. Cuban Premier Fidel Castro bombastically assailed the United States before the U.N. General Assembly today and cautioned developing nations against American "monopolists" and "imperialists" who wish to exploit them. After suggesting his address would be brief, the bearded revolutionary leader spoke for over four hours. The purpose of the speech seemed not to request U.N. intervention in the U.S.-Cuban conflict but to gather international support for Cuba's "struggle."

While praising the Soviet Union for opposing colonialism, he accused American leaders of having "decreed the destruction" of his government on the supposition that

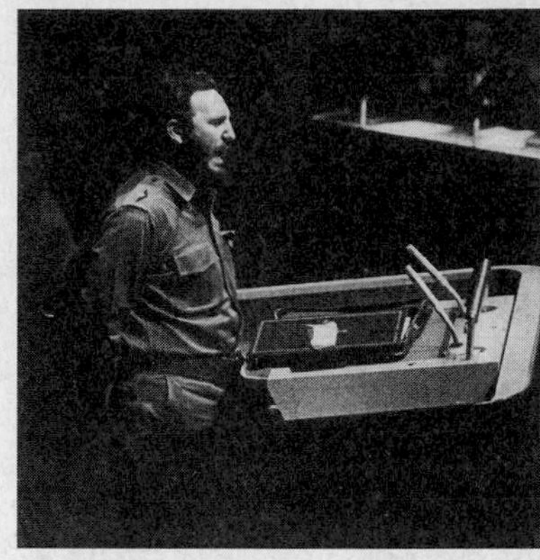

Castro sermonizes at the U.N.

Cuba is Communist-controlled. He asserted Washington is punishing Havana for trying to pave its own economic avenues (→ 10/14).

Congo army takes over under Mobutu

Sept 14. The army seized control of the Congo tonight, and Colonel Joseph Mobutu announced that the military would remain in power until the end of the year so that political leaders could restore peace to the ten-week-old country. Mobutu said it was not a coup d'etat, but it was reliably reported that Premier Lumumba had fled from Leopoldville. Lumumba has been locked in a power struggle with President Kasavubu from the moment the Congo became independent from Belgium. Earlier today, Kasavubu announced he had named Joseph Ileo to replace Lumumba as Premier. Lumumba claims the support of the army, but Col. Mobutu is known to support Kasavubu (→ 11/21).

Ted hits last homer

Sept 28. Ted Williams has left baseball with a bang. In his final turn at bat, the star of the Boston Red Sox poled a 420-foot home run against the Baltimore Orioles and said he was quitting the sport. Williams was supposed to end his career after a final three-game series against the Yankees but decided to leave with a flourish after his 521st career homer. He received a standing ovation. Williams' career home run total is exceeded only by Babe Ruth (714) and Jimmy Foxx (534).

Emily Post, arbiter of etiquette, is dead

Sept 25. What is the proper way to express condolences to the family of Emily Post? Mrs. Post was the nation's grande dame of etiquette, politely providing social do's and don'ts for nearly 60 years. She died today in New York at age 86.

Although her name was synonymous with fastidiousness, Mrs. Post was actually a proponent of common sense, starting with her first best-seller "Etiquette," published in 1922. When a reader wrote asking how to dunk a doughnut neatly, she replied that there was no need to take pains. Doughnuts are not served at sophisticated occasions but at picnics, where "short of smearing wet doughnuts from ear to ear," nearly anything goes.

1960

OCTOBER

Su	Mo	Tu	We	Th	Fr	Sa
						1
2	3	4	5	6	7	8
9	10	11	12	13	14	15
16	17	18	19	20	21	22
23	24	25	26	27	28	29
30	31					

1. Lagos: Nigeria becomes independent nation within British Commonwealth.

4. U.S. launches first active telecommunications satellite, Courier I-B (→ 11/12).

5. France: 200 intellectuals sign manifesto in favor of French rule in Algeria (→ 12/19).

5. South Africa: Whites vote to become a republic, with support of rural Afrikaners, opposition from urban Britons (→ 3/15/61).

7. Washington: Nixon and Kennedy, in second TV debate, clash over Taiwan (→ 13).

11. Japan: Militant rightist student assassinates Socialist leader Inejir Asanuma (→ 2/9/62).

13. New York: Nixon, Kennedy battle in third TV debate (→ 21).

14. Cuba nationalizes banks and all major companies (→ 16).

16. Havana: Two more Americans shot as Cuban invaders (→ 19).

17. East Pakistan: 3,000 killed by cyclone and tidal wave.

18. New York: Casey Stengel let go as manager of Yankees.

19. U.S.: Martin Luther King arrested for Atlanta sit-in (→ 25).

19. U.S. places embargo on goods to Cuba (→ 11/14).

19. U.S. and Canada agree to build hydroelectric plant on Columbia River.

19. Islamic Republic of Mauritania gains independence from France.

21. New York: Nixon, Kennedy hold fourth TV debate (→ 11/9).

21. Britain launches her first nuclear-powered sub (→ 11/15).

22. Louisville: Cassius Clay fights first bout as professional.

24. U.S. and Mexico agree to build dam across Rio Grande.

25. Georgia: Martin Luther King gets four months in prison for sit-in (→ 26).

26. Robert Kennedy calls Coretta Scott King to discuss husband's imprisonment (→ 11/14).

26. South Vietnam: NLF guerrillas and govt. troops meet in bloody clash (→ 11/5).

Nikita bangs desk with shoe at U.N. session

Khrushchev, shoe in right hand, draws attention (and smirks) at the U.N.

Oct 12. When Nikita Khrushchev came to the West, he must have decided to start acting like a cowboy. The Soviet Premier did it again today. He disrupted a meeting of the United Nations General Assembly. Instead of using invective or a clenched fist, he picked up his shoe and did a little undiplomatic banging on his desk.

Khrushchev was enraged, or at least pretended to be, by the speech of a Philippine diplomat. Lorenzo Sumulong accused the Soviet Union of having "deprived" Eastern Europe nations of "political and civil rights," and he warned they would soon be "swallowed up by the Soviet Union." To express his displeasure, Khrushchev pulled off his right shoe, brandished it at Sumulong and then began to pound it on the table. The Soviet premier also shouted abuse at the Philippine diplomat, calling him a "kholui," which translates as a "lackey."

The Soviet premier interrupted the General Assembly several more times during the day. He shouted, waved his fist and even removed his shoe again when Assistant Secretary of State Francis Wilcox was speaking. Soviet Foreign Minister Andrei Gromyko, one of the few people in the hall to be amused by Khrushchev's antics, smiled and winked at the premier.

Earlier in the session, Khrushchev used his fist to bang his desk when Secretary General Dag Hammarskjold spoke. He also shouted at Harold Macmillan. The British Prime Minister, outwardly unperturbed, said he would need a translation if Khrushchev continued.

Combative Kirk Douglas leads rebel slaves against Rome in Kubrick's spectacular "Spartacus."

Pirates win Series; Yanks drop Stengel

Oct 18. The Yankees told him he was too old to continue managing, but Casey Stengel believes he was dropped as Yankee Manager because of his demand for continued authority over player personnel.

Stengel, who in 12 years brought ten American League pennants and seven World Series championships to New York, was released because he had reached the mandatory age of 70, the Yankees said.

Left unsaid was the fact that Stengel had failed to capture another world championship for the Bombers. Only four days ago, the Pittsburgh Pirates completed a seven-game triumph over the Yankees with a 10-9 victory on a ninth-inning homer by Bill Mazeroski in the decisive game.

Rumors of Stengel's departure have persisted since Pittsburgh captured its first World Series in 35 years. "I was told my services were no longer desired," said Stengel. He made it clear that he would have stayed if his demands had been met.

Star of McCarthy hearings deceased

Oct 6. Joseph N. Welch, the Boston lawyer who rose from obscurity to challenge Senator Joseph R. McCarthy in the nationally televised Army-McCarthy hearings in 1954, died today in the Cape Cod Hospital. He was 69 and had been hospitalized with a heart ailment.

A member of the Boston law firm of Hale & Dorr, Welch was hired as counsel for the Army in the Senate committee hearings into whether McCarthy had sought preferential treatment from the Army for one of his aides, G. David Schine.

With his dry wit, facial expressions and courtroom dramatics, he enthralled the nationwide TV audience and turned the tide of public opinion against Senator McCarthy.

A dramatic climax to the confrontation between the Yankee lawyer and the senator came when McCarthy suggested a young lawyer in Welch's law firm had been a member of a Communist organization. "Senator," Welch asked. "Have you no decency?"

1960

NOVEMBER

Su	Mo	Tu	We	Th	Fr	Sa
		1	2	3	4	5
6	7	8	9	10	11	12
13	14	15	16	17	18	19
20	21	22	23	24	25	26
27	28	29	30			

3. Pakistan: Second cyclone in two weeks hits; tidal wave and winds kill 4,000.

3. Geneva: Cameroons opposition leader Felix Mounie assassinated.

5. South Vietnam: U.S. official ambushed by guerrillas (→ 11).

5. Belgium: New Single Law text published, asking austerity in economic recovery plan (→ 12/29).

11. Saigon: Ngo Dinh Diem crushes army revolt (→ 12/20).

11. Rebels based in Costa Rica invade Nicaragua (→ 2/5/67).

11. Moscow: Albanian leader Enver Hodja walks out of intl. Communist Party Congress.

12. Calif.: Discoverer XVII shot into orbit from Vandenberg Air Force Base (→ 1/31/61).

12. Shechem, Israel: Important artifacts unearthed at Biblical temple site.

13. Guatemala: Fuentes crushes brief army uprising (→ 3/9/62).

14. New Orleans integrates two white schools (→ 16).

14. U.S.: O'Neill play "The Iceman Cometh," starring Robert Redford and Jason Robards, premieres on TV.

14. Ike orders U.S. naval units to Caribbean after Guatemala and Nicaragua charge Castro with instigating uprisings (→ 1/3/61).

15. Charleston, S.C.: George Washington, first sub with nuclear missiles, goes to sea (→ 22).

16. New Orleans: 2,000 riot in streets against integration (→ 1/6/61).

21. Congo: Congolese army battles U.N. forces for first time (→ 22).

22. New York: Congo's Kasavubu wins U.N. seat; Lumumba excluded (→ 24).

26. Philadelphia: Army goes down to Navy 17-12 in football.

27. Ivory Coast: Felix Houphouet-Boigny elected president of republic.

DEATH

5. Mack Sennett, film pioneer, developed slapstick, directed Charlie Chaplin (*1/17/1880).

Kennedy elected by narrow margin

Nov 9. A younger generation of American politicians moved into power yesterday with the election of 43-year-old John Fitzgerald Kennedy as President of the United States.

After a night of uncertainty as to the election outcome, final returns showed that the young Senator from Massachusetts had narrowly eked out a victory over his Republican opponent, Vice President Richard Milhous Nixon of California. Kennedy won 303 electoral votes to 219 for Nixon. However, Kennedy topped Nixon by less than 120,000 in the popular vote.

In addition to being the youngest man ever elected to the nation's highest political office, Senator Kennedy broke new ground by becoming the first man of the Roman Catholic faith chosen as president. His religious affiliation had been an issue in the campaign, but far less so than when Alfred E. Smith, another Democrat of that faith, had lost the presidency to Republican Herbert C. Hoover in 1928.

As running mate on the Kennedy ticket, Senator Lyndon B. Johnson of Texas was elected Vice President.

Early this afternoon, Senator Kennedy walked into the Cape Cod armory at Hyannis, Massachusetts, to accept his election. With him was his wife, Jacqueline, who is expecting a baby within the next month. Flashing his now famous grin, the president-elect said: "So now my wife and I prepare for a new administration and a new baby."

An hour earlier, Vice President Nixon had formally conceded the election. However, he had all but conceded shortly after midnight as he told several thousand supporters in a Los Angeles hotel ballroom that it appeared he had lost. Standing by his side was his teary-eyed wife, Pat. Supporters repeatedly cried, "We want Nixon" and "You're the best man" as he spoke.

For the new president-elect, the scion of a wealthy, political family, Election Day opened as he and his wife entered the polling booths in the basement of a public library in what Bostonians call "the back side of Beacon Hill," a once elegant residential area that is now a slum. From Boston, the Kennedys flew to their Cape Cod summer home in Hyannisport. There, the senator played with his young daughter, Caroline, and tossed a football with his brothers, Robert and Teddy.

Youthful Kennedy, America's most inspiring new leader since FDR.

That night, surrounded by other members of the Kennedy clan and such close friends and advisers as Pierre Salinger, William Walton, and William Haddad, the senator listened to election returns at his home, then retired while the final outcome was still in doubt.

This morning, he was greeted by daughter Caroline, saying: "Good morning, Mr. President."

Senator Kennedy had long sought higher political office. While still in his 30's, he had hoped to win the vice-presidential nomination on the 1956 ticket of Adlai E. Stevenson but was defeated by Senator Estes Kefauver of Tennessee.

Not long after the defeat of that ticket, the young Massachusetts senator began thinking of going for the top spot this year. Winner of several presidential primaries earlier this year, including one in which he crushed Minnesota Senator Hubert H. Humphrey, he went on to win the nomination in Los Angeles in July, topping his nearest opponent, Senator Johnson, in a first ballot vote of 806 to 409 (→ 1/20/61).

Gable, the very model of a movie star, dies

Nov 16. Clark Gable has died in Hollywood at the age of 59. A heart ailment which long troubled him was aggravated by stunts he insisted on performing in his last film, "The Misfits." He leaves his fifth wife, Kay Spreckels, who is pregnant with his first and only child.

Gable was Hollywood's humble king, reigning most powerfully in the 1930's. His popularity took a hiatus during WWII because he wasn't making any films. He was a U.S. Major flying bomb missions.

Casting directors in the late 20's could never imagine William Clark Gable as the star of "It Happened One Night," "Mutiny on the Bounty" or "Gone With the Wind." His ears stuck out too much. Gable denied ever pinning them back.

"I can't emote worth a damn," Gable once said. But then, kings don't have to.

Clark Gable, "King of Hollywood." ▷

Richard Wright dies; wrote "Native Son"

Wright, at work in his Paris home.

Nov 29. Richard Wright, literary spokesman for two American minorities, has died in Paris exile at 52. In Chicago during the Depression, Wright looked to the Communist Party for two things: a haven from racism and recognition as a writer. He found his race and talents used as political tools, and wrote about it bitterly in "The God that Failed." Wright stayed a leftist after breaking with the party in 1944. His writing from Paris deals with racism and the plight of the Third World. "Native Son" (1940), story of a Negro murderer victimized by white society, and "Black Boy" (1945), tales of growing up Negro in the South, are his masterworks.

U.S. Navy building a nuclear sub fleet

Nov 22. The United States Navy today launched its most powerful atomic submarine, the 6,900-ton Ethan Allen, which will be able to fire 16 nuclear-tipped Polaris missiles 1,500 miles. The launching came exactly a week after the beginning of the first sea mission of a nuclear-armed atomic submarine, the George Washington. It is armed with an earlier generation of Polaris missiles whose range is 1,200 miles.

The George Washington will soon be joined by two sister boats, each carrying weapons equal in destructive power to all the bombs dropped in WWII. The Navy hopes to have a fleet of 45 nuclear-armed submarines in service by 1965. President Eisenhower issued a statement saying the nuclear submarines "possess a power and relative invulnerability which will make suicidal any attempt by an aggressor to attack the free world by surprise."

Experts say the George Washington can remain at sea for two years, submerged most of the time and virtually undetectable. Both today's launch and the beginning of the George Washington's mission were the target of protests by pacifists. Nine members of an anti-war group that has been holding demonstrations were arrested today, two of them when they swam out and boarded one sub (→ 1/17/61).

Kasavubu in U.N. seat; Lumumba vanishes

Nov 24. Joseph Kasavubu, President of the Congo, left New York tonight after his delegation was seated at the United Nations as the official representative of the war-torn country. Kasavubu won a bitterly contested vote in the General Assembly even though troops loyal to him battled with United Nations forces in Leopoldville Monday night. The Soviet bloc argued unsuccessfully that Patrice Lumumba, ousted as Premier by Kasavubu, should head the delegation. Lumumba, who has reportedly received funds from Moscow, has gone undercover in the Congo, even though his home is guarded by United Nations forces.

The fighting between United Nations and Congolese forces began outside the home of Ghana's Ambassador. Kasavubu's government has tried to deport the diplomat because he supports Lumumba (→ 12/2).

Lumumba, ousted and undercover.

1960

DECEMBER

Su	Mo	Tu	We	Th	Fr	Sa
				1	2	3
4	5	6	7	8	9	10
11	12	13	14	15	16	17
18	19	20	21	22	23	24
25	26	27	28	29	30	31

2. Congo: Lumumba arrested; Mobutu orders him tried (→ 7).

6. Moscow: New Soviet-Chinese ideological compromise published after three-week congress of Communist leaders.

9. Laos govt. flees to Cambodia; Vientiane engulfed in war (→ 18).

10. Nobel for physics goes to American Donald Glaser, Peace Prize to South Africa's Albert John Luthuli.

12. Kennedy names Dean Rusk secretary of state (→ 1/20/61).

14. U.S. B-52 bomber sets 10,000-mile, non-stop record without refueling.

17. Ethiopia: Emperor Haile Selassie returns after brief ouster at hands of son.

18. Laos: Rightist govt. installed under Prince Boun Oum; U.S resumes arms shipments (→ 29).

20. South Vietnam: National Liberation Front formed by guerrillas fighting Diem regime (→ 3/15/61).

26. Philadelphia: Eagles beat Green Bay Packers 17-13 for NFL title.

29. Brussels: Socialist-led strike against govt. austerity plan in 11th day of mounting violence.

CULTURAL EVENTS, 1960

Literature: Harper Lee's "To Kill a Mockingbird"; Camus' "The Plague"; Robert Bolt's "A Man for All Seasons"; Lillian Hellman's "Toys in the Attic"; John Updike's "Rabbit, Run."

Academia: William Shirer's "The Rise and Fall of the Third Reich"; Vance Packard's "The Waste Makers"; Paleolithic fossils found in northern Greece; British surgeons develop pacemaker for human heart.

Music: Britten's "Midsummer Night's Dream"; Lionel Bart's "Oliver!"; "Itsy Bitsy Teenie Weenie Yellow Polka Dot Bikini"; "Let's Do the Twist"; "Never on Sunday."

The Arts: Sidney Nolan's "Leda and the Swan" series; Picasso exhibit at Tate Gallery, London.

Film: Hitchcock's "Psycho"; Preminger's "Exodus"; "The Apartment," Academy Award.

Birth control pill to go on sale in U.S.

This year, the Food and Drug Administration gave its approval to an oral contraceptive to be marketed in the United States next spring. The pills will be sold under the brand names Enovid and Norlutin. Price for a month's supply of protection will be around $10.

Planned Parenthood spearheaded testing in Puerto Rico in 1956. Initially, pills used progesterone to suppress the development of ova. Recently, other hormone combinations at lower dosages proved just as effective. The progesterone alternative is less expensive.

The Worcester Foundation for Experimental Biology, based in Shrewsbury, Massachusetts, has been monitoring the women in the Puerto Rican study for adverse effects. One in five report weight gain and/or nausea. There has been no sign of cancer; in fact, preliminary findings show a reduction in breast and uterine cancer. Fertility usually returns a month or two after discontinuation of the pills.

Airliners collide over city, killing 127

Dec 16. Two airliners flying in fog and sleet collided over New York City, killing 127 passengers and crew members. Another five persons were killed when one of the airliners crashed in Brooklyn, setting off a seven-alarm fire. It was the worst aviation disaster in American history.

The collision occurred between a United Airlines jetliner with 77 passengers and a crew of seven flying from Chicago and a Trans World Airlines Lockheed Super-Constellation with 39 passengers and five crew members arriving from Columbus, Ohio. The only survivor was an 11-year-old boy on the United jet who was thrown clear of the wreck and landed in a snowbank.

The United jet crashed in the crowded Park Slope section of Brooklyn, demolishing a church. Fuel from its tanks ignited to set the neighborhood ablaze. The TWA jet crashed 11 miles to the southeast, on Staten Island. It missed several houses by a few hundred feet.

Faced by violence, de Gaulle leaves Algiers

Paris as well as Algiers is inflamed over the Algerian question.

Dec 19. France's President Charles de Gaulle, booed by Frenchmen and cheered by Moslems, cut short a visit to Algeria after the streets of Algiers became a battlefield once again. At least 60 people were killed in clashes between paratroopers and right-wing French residents on one side and Moslems on the other. Despite the ugly confrontation, de Gaulle remained committed to his policy of self-determination for Algeria. "All of us feel," he said, "after so many trials, how necessary it is to make peace here."

Violence was feared during de Gaulle's visit, but no one foresaw the spectacle that occurred during his airport arrival. The usual flags were in evidence. "Down with de Gaulle, Algeria is French" competed with "Long live de Gaulle, Algeria for Algerians." Noting the favorable banners, de Gaulle descended from his plane, waded through his French opponents and shook hands with the Moslems (→ 1/8/61).

Individualists crowd the literary scene

Soloists on spiritual sojourns dominated drama and literature this year. Robert Bolt's play "A Man for All Seasons" described Thomas More, the 16th-century churchman who clashed with Henry VIII. As Lord Chancellor, More refused to recognize Henry as supreme leader of the Church of England. More's faith in his principles earned him a beheading in 1535.

Englishman Allan Sillitoe wrote "The Loneliness of the Long Distance Runner," a novel about a lower-middle-class man seeking self-worth. Harper Lee's "To Kill a Mockingbird" concerns a Southern lawyer who defends a Negro, alienating his community while earning his children's respect.

John Updike, former staff writer for the New Yorker, introduced a harassed, middle-class suburbanite in "Rabbit, Run." "Rabbit" thinks sex may be the answer to his problems—at least it couldn't hurt.

1st black African is Peace Prize winner

Dec 10. South African civil rights leader Albert John Luthuli is this year's recipient of the Nobel Peace Prize. The slim, 62-year-old minister who adheres to the teachings of Gandhi is a pacifist violent only in his speech. He has told the apartheid government that his people "shall never rest" until black Africans are accorded the same rights as the nation's Europeans.

Luthuli has tried to arrange full citizenship rights for black South Africans through peaceful lobbying. A Zulu chief, he joined the African National Congress in 1945. (The congress was outlawed this year.) A native of Natal, Luthuli represented his province in the congress in 1951. A year later, he was elected President-General.

Luthuli will not be present at award ceremonies tonight. The South African government, considering him dangerous, has forbidden him to leave the country since 1959.

Lumumba captured and will be tried

Dec 7. The arrest of ousted Premier Patrice Lumumba and other incidents in the Congo have convinced three countries to withdraw from the United Nations force there. Yugoslavia, Ceylon and the United Arab Republic have pulled out in protest. Indonesia and Ghana are considering withdrawal.

In the Congo, President Joseph Kasavubu, who dismissed Lumumba in September, placed Oriental province under martial law. The province is Lumumba's stronghold. Col. Joseph Mobutu, head of the army regime, said the former premier was arrested on the 1st while trying to reach Oriental province. He was brought to Leopoldville and treated like a common criminal, his hands tied behind his back. Lumumba is accused of inciting the army to rebel (→ 2/12/61).

Pathet Lao fights pro-Western troops

Dec 29. Three factions are battling for control of the small Southeast Asian nation of Laos. The United States supports the current right-wing government which came to power by overthrowing the short-lived neutralist regime of Souvanna Phouma. Government troops have been battling pro-Communist guerrillas called the Pathet Lao.

British newspapers have accused the United States of prolonging the fighting by refusing to support a neutralist government. Communist China has suggested reviving the International Control Commission to investigate and try to end the conflict. The commission, made up of Canada, India and Poland, was created in 1954 to oversee implementation of the Geneva agreement that ended French involvement in Indochina (→ 3/17/61).

Dec 15. All of Belgium was enthralled today, watching the marriage of its King on TV for the first time. Baudouin's Spanish bride Dona Fabiola de Mora y Aragon is the country's first Queen since the death of Astrid in 1935. As one paper observed, "So ends twenty-five years of mourning."

1961

JANUARY

Su	Mo	Tu	We	Th	Fr	Sa
1	2	3	4	5	6	7
8	9	10	11	12	13	14
15	16	17	18	19	20	21
22	23	24	25	26	27	28
29	30	31				

2. Pasadena: Washington upsets Minnesota to win Rose Bowl.

2. Bonn reports 2,820 from East Germany between Christmas and New Year's (→ 6/10).

3. Washington breaks diplomatic ties to Cuba (→ 4/1).

5. OAS votes sanctions against Dominican Republic leader Hector Trujillo for aggression against Venezuela (→ 5/30).

6. Federal court orders Univ. of Georgia to admit Negroes, including Charlayne Hunter (→ 3/28).

6. Nigeria breaks relations with France over continued nuclear tests in Sahara (→ 4/25).

7. Casablanca: African heads of state meet, announce plan for common defense.

12. Oslo: Princess Astrid marries commoner, yields right of succession to throne.

16. British intelligence uncovers biggest Soviet spy network since war.

18. Moscow: Central Committee approves Khrushchev plan for agricultural decentralization.

20. Mali demands evacuation of French troops.

21. Guinea: Sekou Toure elected president of republic.

22. U.S.: ABC airs "The Red and the Black," documentary on Soviet influence in Africa.

23. Caribbean: Portuguese ship with 900 aboard seized by Salazar foes.

25. U.S.: Presidential press conference televised live first time.

29. New York: Associated Press names Wilma Rudolph female athlete of year for 1960.

29. Ruanda declares independence from Belgium as republic.

31. Cape Canaveral: Chimpanzee Ham completes successful one-day flight in test of Mercury space capsule (→ 2/5).

31. Paul-Henri Spaak resigns as secretary general of NATO.

DEATH

31. Dorothy Thompson, American foreign correspondent and columnist (*7/9/1894).

Youngest President sworn in, urges service

Despite snow and frigid temperatures, JFK declined to wear an overcoat.

Jan 20. Over half a foot of pristine snow blanketed Washington last night, leaving the air this morning bitterly cold and pure. Some 20,000 people in coats and scarves massed before the East Portico of the Capitol, prepared for the swearing-in of the nation's 35th President. They expected the typical inauguration speech of rehearsed guarantees and praise for the constituency. John F. Kennedy, however, promised nothing and demanded everything.

"In your hands, my fellow citizens, more than mine, will rest the final success or failure of our course," Kennedy said. "Now the trumpet summons us again . . . against the common enemies of man: tyranny, poverty, disease and war itself." In the war against war, Kennedy intimated he was ready to negotiate with the Soviets on the inspection and control of nuclear arms. He praised NATO and the U.N. for their peace-keeping efforts.

"The torch has been passed to a new generation of Americans," he said. Some listeners imagined he compared himself to the departing Eisenhower, nearly a generation older than he. But Kennedy meant more. "And so, my fellow Americans," he said, "Ask not what your country can do for you—ask what you can do for your country."

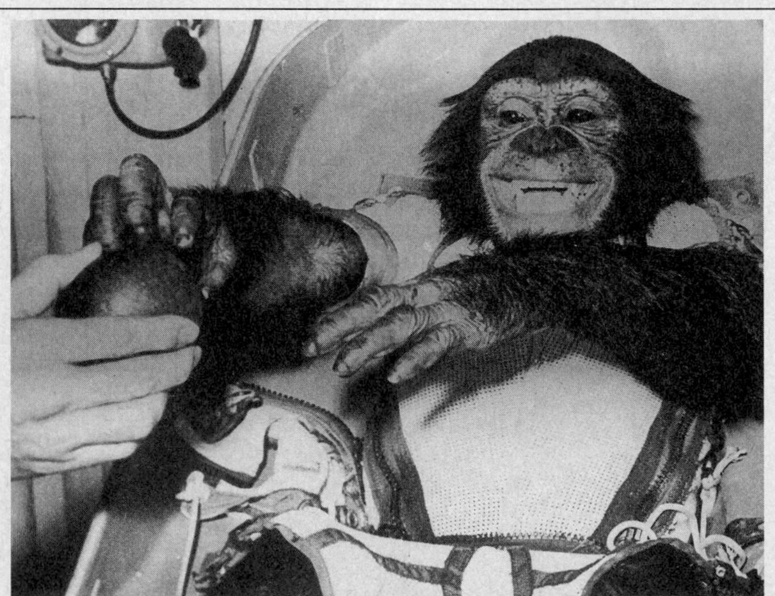

Jan 31. Ham, America's first astrochimp, and probably the largest animal ever to visit outer space, was rewarded with an apple after returning safe and sound after an 18-minute flight taking him 150 miles above the earth. His flight is a direct step toward putting a man in orbit (→ 2/5).

Ike warns against military complex

Jan 17. In his farewell speech tonight, President Dwight D. Eisenhower warned the nation against a growing "military-industrial complex." Many listeners were surprised that an old soldier should bite the hand that feeds him. In fact, Ike cautioned against the military's potential for wrongdoing without reference to its past record.

"The potential for the disastrous rise of misplaced power," Eisenhower stated, "exists and will persist." He foresees the possibility of public policy becoming "the captive of a scientific-technological elite," noting that for "every old blackboard there are now hundreds of new electronic computers." He advocated a decentralization of federal control of research.

Eisenhower concluded his speech with thoughts on world peace, which he sadly felt was not in sight. Still, he offered a prayer that "peoples of all faiths, all races, all nations" might live together in "mutual respect and love" (→ 2/1).

3 French out of 4 favor free Algeria

Jan 8. France's President de Gaulle and his policy of self-determination for Algeria have won decisive victories in France. Freedom for Algeria was approved by 75.3% of the continental voters. Many leftists abstained. Early returns indicate the measure was accepted by about 67% of the voters in Algeria. As many as 40% of the eligible Algerian electorate did not vote, apparently obeying orders from nationalists to boycott the process.

De Gaulle made a remarkable appearance on French television Friday night to urge support of the referendum. The strong vote for approval amounts to a vote of confidence in his presidency, but it also creates a dilemma for de Gaulle. Should he plunge ahead and install a provisional government in Algeria? Or should he do something he has so far refused to do and negotiate with the rebel government-in-exile that Ferhat Abbas has established in Tunis? (→ 4/14)

Violent demonstrations in Belgium subside

Jan 23. Little by little, Belgian workers are returning to their jobs after a month of strikes, riots and political turmoil. Streets are being cleared of debris, but jail cells are still full of anti-government protesters who are accused of committing more than 1,300 acts of sabotage.

The strikes started three days before Christmas, when the Belgian Assembly was considering a revision of budget and tax laws that included a controversial proposal to deduct workers' income taxes from their pay checks. By Christmas Eve, Belgium was paralyzed by strikes. Deputies were fighting in the aisles of the Assembly. On Christmas Day, as people ate their meals by candlelight, Prime Minister Gaston Eyskens urged workers to end their strikes. Things only got worse. Leftists demanded the overthrow of the government. Severe accidents were caused as truckers blocked the roads and threw nails on the pavement. Liege was in a state of siege as rioters ransacked the train station, set cars on fire and threw steel projectiles at police. Outside of Liege, a police patrol was surrounded and opened fire. Despite the violence, the Assembly approved the new tax law. Now the government can use the receipts to clean up the country (→ 2/13).

Mounted police clear the Brussels streets of leftist demonstrators.

Dashiell Hammett's last novel written

Jan 10. If Dashiell Hammett's writing had a fault, it was too exciting, the plots too thrilling to qualify for great literature. Yet Hammett's works permeated radio, stage and screen, and he singlehandedly revolutionized the mystery novel genre. Hammett died today in New York at age 66. His longtime companion, dramatist Lillian Hellman, will deliver a eulogy at his funeral.

Hammett wrote "The Maltese Falcon" (1930) and "The Thin Man" (1934). His detectives, Sam Spade and Nick and Nora Charles, were not the meticulous sleuths of old but flawed and human. Their methods were based on Hammett's practices as a Pinkerton man.

Spy case wrecks Israeli government

Jan 31. Israeli Premier Ben Gurion resigned today in the wake of his unpopular refusal to absolve Pinchas Lavon of spy charges despite the finding by a special committee of Lavon's innocence. Although shrouded by Israeli censorship, the case involves an Israeli espionage ring operating in Cairo, several members of which were hanged by the Egyptians after its discovery in 1954 when Lavon was Minister of Defense. Lavon has always insisted on his ignorance of the affair. Ben Gurion's resignation is seen as a test of will, and it is expected that he will be asked to form a new government and resume the leadership of Israel (→ 5/21/63).

1961

FEBRUARY

Su	Mo	Tu	We	Th	Fr	Sa
			1	2	3	4
5	6	7	8	9	10	11
12	13	14	15	16	17	18
19	20	21	22	23	24	25
26	27	28				

1. Florida: First Boeing Minuteman ICBM tested.→

4. U.S.: Heaviest snow storm since 1947 ties up Northeast coast.

5. Soviets launch Sputnik V, heaviest satellite at 7.1 tons (→ 12).

12. Congo: Katanga leader Patrice Lumumba is assassinated.→

12. Colomb-Bechar: French launch rocket Veronique (→ 13).

13. Soviets fire rocket toward Venus from Sputnik V (→ 21).

13. Belgium: Senate passes Single Law austerity program.

15. Belgium: 18 in U.S. figure-skating team lost in air crash.

15. N.Y.: Most violent riot in U.N. history halts debate.

16. Paris: African students demonstrate against presence of Belgian troops in Congo (→ 19).

19. Cairo: Students ransack Belgian Embassy after disclosure of Lumumba murder (→ 25).

21. French rocket Veronique, with rat on board, recovered after reaching height of 95 miles (→ 4/12).

24. Tanganyika: Leakeys unearth bones of earliest human, Australopithecus.→

25. Washington: JFK names Kissinger national security adviser.

25. New York: Ralph Boston sets indoor broad jump mark at 26 feet, 6.25 inches.

25. United Arab Repbulic breaks relations with Belgium over Congo (→ 4/4).

26. Rabat: Hassan II becomes new Moroccan king upon father's death.→

27. Daytona Beach: Marvin Panch sets world record in 500-mile auto race, averaging over 150 mph.

28. Nairobi: Tom Mboya wins in Kenyan elections (→ 8/21).

DEATHS

20. Percy Grainger, Australian composer (*7/8/1882).

26. Mohammed V, king of Morocco (*8/10/1909).

Hassan, 31, is new King of Morocco

New King Hassan II.

Feb 26. King Mohammed V of Morocco, who has occupied the throne since 1927, died today after minor surgery. His heart stopped beating shortly after an operation on his nose, and the ten doctors in attendance were unable to revive him. The king had selected his son, Crown Prince Moulay Hassan, 31, to succeed him. He will rule the North African country of ten million people as King Hassan II.

After World War II, Mohammed V actively supported the nationalist movement in Morocco. At that time the country was partitioned into sections controlled by France and Spain. The French deposed him in 1953 but restored him to the throne in 1955 in an effort to quiet the growing unrest in North Africa.

In 1956, the French gave up their territory and by 1958 the Spanish had too. Mohammed V was in the process of converting the sultanate into a modern constitutional monarchy; in 1957, he changed his title from Sultan to King (→ 3/27/63).

Disney, who added a TV series to his movies in 1954, has a new film hit with "101 Dalmations."

Leakeys unearth earliest human bones

Dr. Leakey in Tanganyika.

Feb 24. A British scientist said today he had discovered the bones of the oldest member of the human race known to science. The bones, those of an 11-year-old child, were found by Louis S.B. Leakey, an anthropologist who has been digging in the Olduvai Gorge of Tanganyika for 30 years.

Leakey said he could not yet give an exact age for the bones, but they were much older than those of his previous find, the 600,000-year-old Zinjanthropus Bosei, or "Nutcracker Man," so called because of its huge crushing molars and until now considered the earliest man.

The latest find includes the skull, parts of the hands and a foot and a collarbone. The brain size of the child was larger than that of Zinjanthropus and its teeth were markedly different, indicating that "we are dealing with a hominid with a somewhat larger brain capacity and less specialized than Zinjanthropus."

The fact that the skull had fractures radiating from a sharp nick indicates that the child might have been murdered by a blow. The discovery was made when Leakey and his son Jonathan began digging in an area where they found the jaw of a sabertooth tiger. Leakey said he will go on digging in the Olduvai Gorge, where early humans lived for many thousands of years.

Lumumba, Congolese leader, murdered

Feb 12. Patrice Lumumba, the deposed Premier of the Congo, has been killed in questionable circumstances. Moise Tshombe, President of Katanga and a rival of Lumumba, claimed he was killed after escaping from prison in Elizabethville. The explanation was viewed with some skepticism in the Congo and at the United Nations, which has ordered an investigation.

Tshombe refused to cooperate on the grounds that the death of Lumumba is "solely an internal Katanga matter." Tshombe also said he would not meet with Iyassu Mengasha, the Ethiopian who is investigating Lumumba's murder as chief of staff of United Nations forces in the Congo. In recent months, Lumumba had been a vocal opponent of Belgium, Congolese President Kasavubu, Strongman Joseph Mobutu and Tshombe (→ 16).

Dejected Lumumba, held by Mobutu's soldiers before his death.

First U.S. solid-fuel missile is launched

Feb 1. A military milestone was reached at the Eastern Test Range in Florida today, when the Strategic Air Command launched the first solid-fuel rocket, the Minuteman, an intercontinental ballistic missile. The Boeing Company was awarded the government contract in October 1958. The test marks the first time a multi-stage missile has been fired with all stages "live," and using its own internal guidance system on an initial launch. Military personnel expressed their satisfaction over the successful test.

President Kennedy, in his State of the Union address, stressed the need to boost American missile experimentation and development, to increase airlift capacity and to speed up the Navy's Polaris submarine program. With today's test, it appears the modernization program is proceeding according to plan, despite claims that the United States has fallen behind Soviet military research and development (→ 4/3).

The Minuteman takes to the skies.

18 U.S. skaters lost in single air crash

Feb 15. A Sabena Airlines Boeing 707 jet en route from New York crashed near the Brussels Airport today, killing all 72 aboard, 49 of whom were Americans, and a farmer in the field. Among the passengers were the 18 members of the U.S. figure-skating team on its way to a world championship meet in Prague. Nothing seemed wrong as the plane circled the airfield twice at about 600 feet in a cloudless sky and then suddenly fell at a 70-degree angle, bursting into flames.

1961

MARCH

Su	Mo	Tu	We	Th	Fr	Sa
			1	2	3	4
5	6	7	8	9	10	11
12	13	14	15	16	17	18
19	20	21	22	23	24	25
26	27	28	29	30	31	

7. Los Angeles: Maj. Robert White sets record of 2,650 mph in X-15 rocket plane.

8. Miami: Max Conrad in Piper Aztec circles globe in record time of eight days, 18 hours, 49 minutes.

12. Austro-German team lead by Toni Hiebeler climb Mount Eige for first time in history.

14. New York: Randall Jarrell, Conrad Richter and William Shirer receive National Book Awards.

14. Miami Beach: Floyd Patterson KOs Ingemar Johansson in the sixth to retain heavyweight title.

15. Saigon reports Viet Cong killing 200-250 per month, greater than Laos (→ 21).

16. New York: "The Agony and the Ecstasy" by Irving Stone is published.

16. Florida: 2,342-pound, 22-foot-long python crushes handler to death.

16. Saudi Arabia ends pact on U.S. base at Dharan.

17. Washington: U.S. increases military aid and technicians to Laos (→ 26).

24. Paris: Fire from explosion devastates Palais Bourbon.

26. Washington: JFK meets with British Premier Macmillan to discuss increased Communist involvement in Laos (→ 31).

27. Turkey abolishes ban on opposition parties (→ 9/17).

28. Jackson, Miss.: Club-swinging police with dogs rout 100 Negroes from courthouse (→ 5/4).

29. New York: "A Raisin in the Sun" opens in new film version.

29. Twenty-third Amendment added to U.S. Constitution, allowing D.C. residents to vote in presidential election.

31. London: Laotian leader Souvanna Phouma ties Soviet aid halt to U.S. halt in aid to right-wing rebels (→ 4/1).

DEATH

8. Sir Thomas Beecham, British conductor and composer (*4/29/1879).

Kennedy increasing aid to Southeast Asia

President Kennedy tells the press of new advances by the Pathet Lao.

March 21. Vowing to "back the royal Laotian government to the hilt" in its battle against Communist-led rebel forces, President Kennedy is increasing military aid to Laos and has sent additional advisers to help train the Laotian army, doubling the 100 already there.

Though recent increases in American aid to Laos have been connected with the flow of Soviet arms to the rebels, U.S. officials stress they are not engaged in an arms race with the Soviets and that the new aid is rather meant to counter heightened rebel activity.

Meanwhile, South Vietnam is embroiled in a war claiming greater casualties than the more publicized struggle in Laos. The Communist Viet Cong kill several hundred South Vietnamese every month in their drive to topple the Pro-Western government or President Ngo Dinh Diem and reunify Vietnam under the Hanoi Communist regime of President Ho Chi Minh, and their disruption of life in the delta rural area south of Saigon has thus far been highly successful.

Officials loyal to Diem are assassinated, schools forced to close, farmers punished for accepting Diem's crop loans and village health officers killed or kidnapped. Coupled with damage to communications and railway lines, this activity has vividly advertised Diem's inability to provide security where the Viet Cong operate (→ 4/10).

Americans help to train Laotian soldiers in the art of jungle warfare.

X-15 reaches new speed and height

March 30. The X-15 rocket plane set a world altitude record of 31.25 miles today, three days after it established an unofficial speed record of 2,650 miles an hour. Both marks were set in flights from Edwards Air Force Base in the Mohave Desert of California. Major Robert M. White set the speed record in a nine-minute flight testing a new high-thrust engine for the X-15. The altitude record was established even though the plane's engine failed immediately after it was launched from its B-52 mother ship. The pilot, Joseph A. Walker, succeeded in restarting the engine after a few moments and then brought the X-15 in for a safe landing at Edwards.

Plan for progress proposed to Latins

March 13. President Kennedy tonight outlined his ten-point, ten-year economic and social development program for Latin America, fulfilling his campaign pledge to put new vigor into Franklin D. Roosevelt's "Good Neighbor" policy. "Our motto is what it has always been—Progress, yes! Tyranny, no!—Progresso, si! Tiranuia, no!"

Kennedy's ten-point plan is comprehensive. Within the next ten years the program will help each nation in Latin America achieve self-sustaining growth, in the process raising living standards, providing a basic education and ending hunger. To deal with current emergencies, the United States will increase the Food for Peace program. In addition, Kennedy will ask Congress to approve the $500 million in aid promised last year by the Eisenhower administration.

The plan will also establish educational exchange programs for both teachers and students, and will enable Latin American scientists to work in the United States. The United States renewed its promise to defend any Latin American nation whose independence is endangered. President Kennedy also expressed the hope that both Cuba and the Dominican Republic would "soon rejoin the society of free men" (→ 8/17).

Peace Corps to help developing nations

March 1. President Kennedy announced today the formation of a U.S. Peace Corps to aid developing nations. The president's brother-in-law, Sargent Shriver, organized the temporary agency. The president has asked Congress to make the corps and Shriver's post permanent should the program prove successful. Kennedy envisions volunteers, mostly youths just out of college, going to less advantaged countries and teaching secondary school, assisting in health education or advising on agricultural matters. "It will not be easy," Kennedy admitted during a press conference. Among immediate volunteers was athlete Rafer Johnson (→ 9/22).

South Africa quits British community

March 15. South African Prime Minister Hendrik Verwoerd announced today that his country would withdraw from the British Commonwealth of Nations. After ten heads of state within the Commonwealth assailed South Africa's policy of apartheid, Verwoerd surprised many and pulled South Africa out. He blamed those critical of the segregation system of meddling in South Africa's affairs (→ 4/5).

The master has married his model. Pablo Picasso, still active at 79, was wed amid great secrecy this month to Jacqueline Roque, only 42 years his junior.

1961

APRIL

Su	Mo	Tu	We	Th	Fr	Sa
						1
2	3	4	5	6	7	8
9	10	11	12	13	14	15
16	17	18	19	20	21	22
23	24	25	26	27	28	29
30						

1. Moscow: Soviets join U.S. in seeking Laos cease-fire (→ 5/2).

1. Miami: 50,000 Cuban refugees straining economy, creating explosive situation (→ 8).

3. London: Thousands demonstrate against U.S. Polaris missiles (→ 25).

4. Congo: Katanga mobs attack U.N. force holding airfield (→ 26).

5. N.Y.: U.S. at U.N. opposes anti-apartheid sanctions against South Africa (→ 7).

6. Hong Kong: American Robert McCann released after ten years in Chinese prison.

8. N.Y.: Anti-Castro Cubans in U.S. call on Cubans to overthrow Castro (→ 15).

9. Persian Gulf: British liner Dara burns, killing 100.

10. Augusta, Georgia: Gary Player wins Masters by a stroke.

14. Algeria frees 700 nationalist political prisoners (→ 22).

15. New York: Fellini's "La Dolce Vita" premieres in U.S.

15. Cuba: Anti-Castro forces bomb three government air bases (→ 17).

17. Cuba: 1,400 armed exiles, organized by CIA, land at Bay of Pigs (→ 19).

19. Cuba: Castro strikes rebels on beach with MIG's and tanks; JFK warns Soviets (→ 25).

19. Angola: Portuguese reinforcements rushed into battle against rebels.

21. Peace Corps to help local technicians develop roads in Tanganyika in first project.

22. Algeria: Algiers seized by French army insurgents (→ 26).

25. Sahara: French explode their fourth atomic bomb (→ 8/31).

27. NASA launches Explorer XI satellite, carrying telescope to hunt gamma rays (→ 28).

28. Florida: Final test flight, Little Joe 5B, proves Mercury escape system infallible (→ 5/5).

DEATH

9. Ahmed Zogou, Albania's ex-King Zog I (*10/8/1895).

Soviet Union puts first man in space

Yuri Gagarin, smiling and boyish.

April 12. The Soviet Union today won the race to place a man in space by sending 27-year-old air force Major Yuri Gagarin into orbit and bringing him safely back to earth.

A brief announcement by the official press agency, Tass, said Gagarin had orbited the earth in a 10,395-pound sputnik named Vostok, or East. It said the spacecraft's orbit had a maximum altitude of 187.75 miles and a minimum of 109.5 miles, and that each revolution around the earth took 89.1 minutes.

The first official word of the flight came when a Moscow radio announcer broke into a program just before 10 a.m. local time and said emotionally, "Russia has successfully launched a man into space." The announcement was repeated three times, after which the station played patriotic music.

Gagarin applied a braking device and landed less than an hour later in what was described as the "prescribed area" of the Soviet Union. Tass said that after the landing, Gagarin said, "Please report to the party and the government, and personally to Nikita Sergeyevich Khrushchev, that the landing was normal. I feel well, have no injuries or bruises." The only statement attributed to him during his historic flight was: "Flight is proceeding normally. I am well."

Gagarin was described by Tass as an industrial technician who is married. Other sources said he probably has been trained as a test pilot. He was reported to have received pre-flight training similar to that of the seven astronauts who will fly the United States' first manned missions, scheduled for later this year.

Tass said the Vostok was sent into orbit by a multistage rocket from the Soviet launch site at Tyura Tam and that constant radio contact was maintained with Gagarin during the mission. It said his condition was monitored continually by radio telemetering devices and television.

Rumors of an impending manned space flight had been circulating in Moscow for the past 24 hours. Several sources said the Soviet Union had sent a man into space and brought him back successfully last week, a report that led to speculation that something had gone wrong with an earlier mission (→ 28).

The Vostok, or East, first vehicle to take a human being into space.

Army rises again in Algeria and fails again

April 26. The curtain fell on the latest uprising in Algeria shortly after midnight. Some say the confrontation between France's President de Gaulle and his rebellious generals had all the elements of high drama. Others say it was a farce not worthy of the Comedie Francaise.

Four retired French generals mutinied and seized control of Algiers early on the 22nd. Paratroopers surrounded government buildings. They were led by General Maurice Challe, a former NATO commander in Central Europe and head of French forces in Algeria until he was relieved of his command for disagreeing with de Gaulle's policy in North Africa. Challe thinks Algeria should be forever French.

The last time generals revolted in Algeria, de Gaulle was swept back to power. This time, he had no sympathy for their cause. Thousands of right-wing Frenchmen turned out with weapons to support the generals, but they were overwhelmed by de Gaulle's gendarmes. The generals fled, and they are likely to be arrested. De Gaulle's talks with nationalist rebels are still on track (→ 5/20).

U.N., 83-0, assails South Africa policy

April 7. The United Nations General Assembly, by a 83-0 vote, assailed South Africa's policies and racial practices in the territory of Southwest Africa. South Africa administers the territory under an old League of Nations mandate and has refused to place it under a United Nations trusteeship. The United States joined African and Asian nations in supporting the resolution, which calls on South Africa to desist from its policy toward Southwest Africa (→ 10/11).

Bay of Pigs landing in Cuba is fiasco

April 25. Anti-Castro exiles invaded their Cuban homeland last week in a failed attempt to overthrow the Fidel Castro government. The invasion of the Bay of Pigs sparked international tension as Soviet leader Nikita Khrushchev accused U.S. President John Kennedy of orchestrating the military raid.

Unrest among Cuban exiles, particularly those of the Cuban National Revolutionary Council, led by Dr. Jose Miro Cardona, has grown within the past few months. Miro Cardona issued a call to arms on April 8, urging Cubans to back his anti-Castro movement. "To arms, Cubans!" he declared. "We must conquer or we shall die choked by slavery." With such proclamations, Castro's military prepared for a counterrevolutionary attack.

It's been no secret that the Kennedy administration has hoped for the fall of Castro's government. During the last presidential campaign debate with Richard Nixon, Kennedy proposed that America support Cuban exiles in an invasion. Remembering such talk and hearing reports that U.S. planes were used in the mistake-ridden raid, Khrushchev assailed America. "The organizers of the aggression against Cuba are encroaching on the inalienable right of the Cuban people to live free and independently," he said. He also vowed to support Cuba if the attacks continue. Yet, Cuba's military seems to need little help as they easily warded off the insurgents, dealing the anti-Castro movement a serious blow (→ 5/1).

Anti-Castro Cuban counterrevolutionaries storm the beach at the Bay of Pigs.

Castro, cigar in hand, rushes to meet the first major challenge to his revolution.

Tshombe, refusing to yield, is arrested

April 26. President Moise Tshombe of Katanga was arrested briefly today after he walked out of a meeting of Congolese leaders at Coquilhatville. It was not immediately clear whether Congolese President Kasavubu ordered the arrest, but it is certain to widen the breach which exists between Katanga secessionists and other leaders in the Congo. The two sides came close to a compromise last month, when Tshombe agreed to end secession and join a confederation of Congolese states. The meeting broke down today after Tshombe insisted that the powers of the central government should be limited. He also demanded the withdrawal of United Nations forces from the Congo (→ 6/22).

Diem sweeps to victory in Vietnam

April 10. In a decisive electoral victory, South Vietnam's President Ngo Dinh Diem was swept back into office with about 78 percent of the total vote. More than 90 percent of all registered voters cast ballots and the result was seen as a resounding defeat for Communist agitators who had urged voter abstention. Nor did expected Communist violence materialize except for one minor isolated incident. Diem's landslide stems largely from his control of the government machinery and the country's marked prosperity under his rule (→ 5/13).

Adolf Eichmann goes on trial in Jerusalem for anti-Jewish acts

Eichmann testifies under guard.

April 11. The trial of Adolf Eichmann, the former Nazi official, began today in Jerusalem. The indictment charges him with having handed over more than six million Jews to extermination camps during the Second World War, when he was chief of the Gestapo's Jewish section. If convicted, he faces the death penalty.

Eichmann was led from his cell into an auditorium in the Beit Haam (House of the People), where he was placed in a bullet-proof glass booth. Amid a crowd of more than 750 reporters, foreign representatives and Israeli citizens, Supreme Court Justice Moshe Landau, one of the three presiding judges, read the 15 charges of the indictment in Hebrew. Eichmann seemed composed, even impassive, throughout the reading.

Eichmann's lawyers are expected to challenge the Israeli government's right to try their client in their opening statements. Eichmann was apprehended in Argentina by Israeli agents last May. Then, he was secretly placed on an Israeli airliner and flown to Jerusalem to stand trial (→ 6/23).

Forty more scrolls found in Palestine

April 2. The Dead Sea caves have yielded more ancient scrolls. These latest findings are not religious papers, however, but legal documents. The discoverer, a professor of archeology at Hebrew University, lauded the manuscripts for "beauty of script and wealth of detail." The scrolls, about 45 documents, were probably penned by followers of a Jewish rebel. Dating from the second century A.D., they are in Greek, Aramaic and an ancient Semitic language.

1961

MAY

Su	Mo	Tu	We	Th	Fr	Sa
	1	2	3	4	5	6
7	8	9	10	11	12	13
14	15	16	17	18	19	20
21	22	23	24	25	26	27
28	29	30	31			

2. New York: "All the Way Home," based on Pulitzer-winning novel "To Kill a Mockingbird," wins Pulitzer for drama.

2. Laos: Cease-fire halts fighting in critical zone (→ 16).

2. Ottawa: One of largest Canadian grain sales sends six million tons to Communist China.

4. Freedom Rides to desegregate buses begin in South (→ 14).

5. U.S.: JFK signs Fair Labor Standards Act, raising minimum wage to $1.15 in Sept. (→ 6/30).

5. Alan Shepard Jr., in 15-min. suborbital flight, becomes first U.S. man in space (→ 25).

7. Carry Back, favorite, wins Kentucky Derby with jockey John Sellers up.

13. U.S. agrees to increase arms to South Vietnam (→ 28).

14. Birmingham: White mob attacks integrationist Freedom Riders at bus station (→ 20).

16. Geneva: International Conference on Laos opens (→ 10/8).

18. Seoul: Anti-Communist junta, in coup, proclaims victory over Gen. Chang regime (→ 7/3).

20. Montgomery: Freedom Riders hit by white mob of 1,000; 20 beaten with clubs (→ 22).

20. Evian, France: 30-day truce declared as talks with Algerian rebels open (→ 6/13).

22. Montgomery: 400 National Guardsmen battle white mob besieging Rev. King and 1,500 others in church (→ 24).

24. Jackson, Miss.: 27 bi-racial Freedom Riders jailed as integration campaign widens (→ 24).

24. U.S. Justice Dept. bars Alabama police from interfering with interstate travel (→ 25).

27. Calif.: Ralph Boston sets broad jump mark at 27'5".

28. Miss.: 17 more Freedom Riders jailed, defying federal injunction (→ 7/11).

30. A.J. Foyt Jr. wins 45th Indy 500 at 139.1 mph.

DEATH

4. Maurice Merleau-Ponty, French phenomenologist (*3/14/1908).

First American in space for 15 minutes

May 25. Following up America's first manned space flight, President Kennedy has asked Congress to approve a program to send men to the moon. The moon project, estimated to cost from $7-9 billion, may "hold the key to our future on earth," Kennedy said, maintaining that the United States "must take a leading role in space achievement."

His proposal came 20 days after 37-year-old Navy Cmdr. Alan B. Shepard Jr. made a 15-minute flight that took him 115 miles above the earth and made him the first American in space.

Shepard was launched in a Freedom 7 capsule by a Redstone rocket at 10:34 a.m. on May 5 from Cape Canaveral. During the flight, he exclaimed, "What a beautiful view!" and said, "Everything A-OK," a rocket engineer's term for perfect.

He landed in the Atlantic near the Bahamas, 302 miles from Cape Canaveral, at 10:49 a.m. A Marine helicopter lifted him to the aircraft carrier Lake Champlain, where doctors reported him in "excellent" condition, suffering no ill effects.

Although Shepard went only a fraction of the distance logged by Yuri Gagarin, the first Soviet in space, and his capsule had a top speed only a quarter as great as Gagarin's, he did maneuver his craft in space by firing small rockets, an achievement the Soviets have not claimed (→ 7/21).

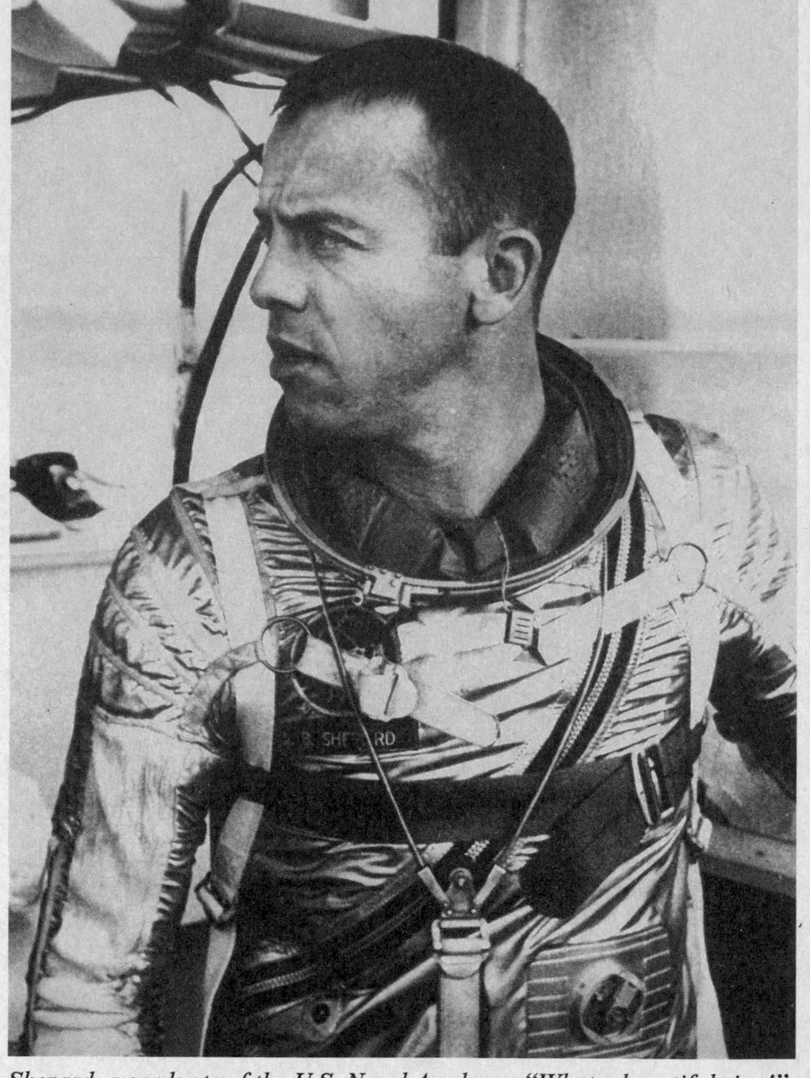

Shepard, a graduate of the U.S. Naval Academy: "What a beautiful view!"

President Kennedy accompanies Jackie to Paris; French enchanted

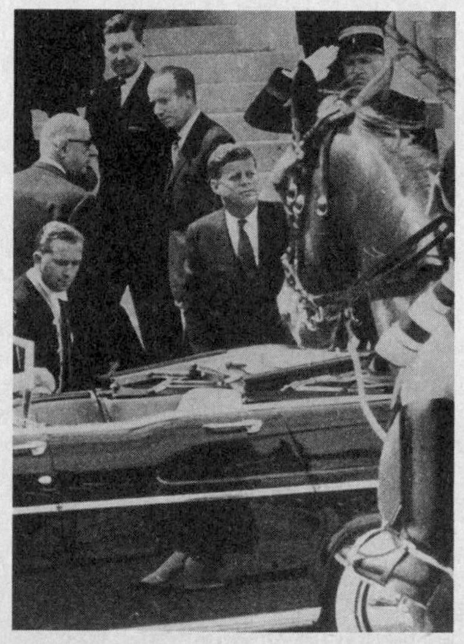

De Gaulle and JFK in Paris.

May 31. A million French men and women lined the streets of Paris today as President Kennedy arrived for talks with President de Gaulle. The two leaders had weighty affairs of state to discuss, but many of the spectators were concentrating on something else. They wanted a glimpse of the elegant American First Lady with the French heritage, and Jacqueline Bouvier Kennedy did not let them down. De Gaulle himself welcomed her as "the gracious Mrs. Kennedy." At one point, newsmen chuckled as the relaxed President Kennedy joked that his real mission in Paris was to "escort Jacqueline Kennedy."

On more serious matters, Kennedy and de Gaulle agreed that Western leaders would act together to resist any Soviet threat to West Berlin. "American forces," Kennedy said, "will remain in Europe as long as they are required." The two leaders also discussed problems in Algeria, Laos and the rest of Southeast Asia. Throughout the day, in his public comments, Kennedy seemed respectful of de Gaulle. The president called him "a captain in the field in defense of the West for more than 20 years."

Kennedy combined humor with praise when he said, "A few years ago it was said that the optimists learned Russian and the pessimists learned Chinese. I prefer to think that those with vision study French and English."

Freedom Riders beaten

May 25. "This is an ugly situation," said one Montgomery, Alabama, policeman. The city has erupted in racial violence as Negro and white Freedom Riders, testing segregation policies on state and interstate buses, have been attacked and arrested. Mobs of angry white segregationists, including members of the Ku Klux Klan, descended on Montgomery. Governor John Patterson imposed martial law in an attempt to quell the race riots.

In the most violent outburst, over 1,000 whites attacked a busload of Freedom Riders last week. At least 20 people were hurt as mob members used their fists and clubs to beat the protesters. The riders were subsequently arrested for contempt of an injunction banning this form of protest. The mob also assaulted news reporters and cameramen covering the riot, beating them, smashing cameras and destroying notes.

Federal marshals were ordered to the city by U.S. Attorney General Robert Kennedy to protect a Negro church mass meeting, where integration leader Rev. Martin Luther King Jr. spoke. Despite the presence of armed guards, hundreds of whites gathered and shouted obscenities toward the church. Rev. King said Negroes would "continue the struggle for freedom" (→ 28).

Freedom Riders defiantly board another bus in Montgomery, Alabama.

Tall and taciturn star, Gary Cooper, dies

May 13. "'Yup' is a convenient word," actor Gary Cooper once said, noting it discourages personal questions. The private Gary Cooper died of cancer today in Los Angeles. He had just turned 60 years old.

Cooper won two Oscars, one for the title role in "Sergeant York" (1941) and the other a dozen years later for the beleaguered sheriff in "High Noon." He never considered himself much of an actor and refused to play Shakespeare, saying he looked foolish in tights.

Montana-born Cooper was a traveling salesman in 1925 when friends told him Hollywood was looking for men who could ride. As a fledgling western star Cooper was a lothario, romancing Lupe Velez, Clara Bow and other actresses. In 1934, he married and settled down—a bit. His movie career prospered.

Cooper got his start in B westerns.

Dominican dictator Trujillo is assassinated

May 30. The dictator of the Dominican Republic, Generalissimo Rafael Leonidas Trujillo Molina, was assassinated Tuesday night. It was reported that army General Juan Tomas Diaz, an enemy of Trujillo, organized a group of seven men to ambush Trujillo as he left his home in San Cristobal. Since his rise to power, Trujillo has been notorious for maintaining an almost absolute hold on the small Caribbean nation by ruthless terrorist methods. He is reputed to have ordered the deaths of over 1,000 Dominicans in 1930 (his first year in power), 15,000 Haitian squatters in 1937 and many rivals (→ 11/19).

Trujillo on a U.S. destroyer.

Du Pont must sell all shares in G.M.

May 22. In 1957, General Motors bought all the paint and fabric for its automobiles from Du Pont. The Supreme Court decided that choice was no accident because Du Pont owned 25 percent of G.M., and found the firm in violation of antitrust law. Today, the Supreme Court ordered Du Pont to sell all $3 billion worth of its G.M. stock. Du Pont had argued in favor of passing on all the voting rights to its shareholders while retaining ownership of the stock. But a 4-to-3 decision headed by Chief Justice Warren found that the surest way to break up a potential for monopoly was a complete divestiture of all stock. Justices Clark and Marshall abstained from the vote.

Castro makes Cuba Socialist; ends vote

May 1. Cuban leader Fidel Castro shouted out to an enthusiastic crowd this question: "Do you need elections?" They screamed back, "No!" With that, Castro declared there would be no more voting for political officials. He also told his people that Cuba now officially aligns itself with the Soviet Union and the Communist bloc. In the May Day speech, amid parades and banners of Karl Marx, he said, "If Kennedy does not like socialism, we don't like imperialism" (→ 8/24).

U.S. helps Vietnam stop infiltration

May 28. While admitting there is little possibility of preventing outright the use of Laotian bases by subversive Communist forces, the U.S. is undertaking new steps aimed at impeding Communist raids into South Vietnam and Thailand. The South Vietnam army, with the help of American military advisers, is setting up a system of village-based operations against the Viet Cong guerrillas moving in through the Laotian corridor from North Vietnam, and the U.S. is expanding its Military Advisory Group. U.S. officials are cautiously optimistic that these new anti-guerrilla moves will prove effective, and cite encouraging progress reports from the first phase (→ 10/2).

1961

JUNE

Su	Mo	Tu	We	Th	Fr	Sa
				1	2	3
4	5	6	7	8	9	10
11	12	13	14	15	16	17
18	19	20	21	22	23	24
25	26	27	28	29	30	

5. Supreme Court upholds anti-Communist laws within U.S. (→ 5/21/62).

6. United Arab Republic charges U.S.S.R. with imperialistic aims in Arab world (→ 9/28).

7. London: JFK pays state visit to Prime Minister Macmillan.

10. Bonn: Soviets propose six-month moratorium on Berlin crisis (→ 7/17).

10. New York: Archie Moore, now in 40's, retains light-heavy-weight title over Rinaldi.

13. France: Evian parley between French and FLN suspended (→ 7/5).

13. New York: Jump in birth rate recorded nine months after four-hour black-out.

19. Britain relinquishes protectorate over oil-rich Kuwait; will still give military aid (→ 26).

19. U.S. Supreme Court bars evidence seized illegally by states.

22. Congo: Tshombe, freed by Mobutu, denounces pact, refusing to end Katanga secession (→ 8/1).

23. Paris: Rudolf Nureyev, only a week after defection, performs in "Sleeping Beauty."

23. Calif.: X-15 sets speed record, traveling over 3,000 mph at Edwards Air Force Base.

23. U.S.-Cuban exchange—tractors for prisoners—collapses (→ 8/24).

23. Jerusalem: Eichmann claims he spared Jews (→ 12/15).

25. New York: Frank Budd streaks to record of 9.2 seconds in 100-yard dash.

26. Washington: JFK invokes Taft-Hartley Act in ship walkout.

26. Kuwait: Vote opposes Iraqi annexation plans (→ 7/1).

28. New York: AMA delegates back Sabin polio vaccine over Salk (→ 8/17).

30. JFK signs Housing Act of 1961 (→ 2/6/62).

DEATH

25. Miriam "Ma" Ferguson, ex-Gov. of Texas (*1875).

Soviet-American summit

In Vienna, Khrushchev sizes up the new, young American President.

June 4. No one banged any shoes on the table, and no one stomped out of the room in anger. In the field of diplomacy, that represents progress. President Kennedy and Premier Khrushchev may not have agreed on much in their two-day summit meeting in Vienna. But at least the United States and the Soviet Union are talking again. That's an improvement over the failed summit in Paris.

Kennedy and Khrushchev apparently disagreed sharply over the status and future of Berlin. The Soviets have been threatening to turn control of East Berlin over to East German authorities. The move could disrupt the flow of supplies to the Allied command in West Berlin. President Kennedy warned Khrushchev about the consequences of Soviet intervention in West Berlin. The president reminded the premier that the United States had gone to war twice this century to protect Western Europe.

The two leaders reached a limited agreement on the sovereignty of Laos. The regime there has been threatened by Communist guerrillas supported by Moscow (→ 7/8).

Jung, psychiatric pioneer, succumbs

June 6. Carl C. Jung, one of the great pioneers in modern analytic psychiatry, died today in Switzerland at the age of 85. After training with Sigmund Freud, who maintained that most mental problems were due to sexual conflicts in infancy and regarded religion as unimportant, Jung established his own theory, which stressed the importance of a natural impulse toward religion. Jung maintained that individuals could draw on collective experiences of the human race recorded in the subconscious mind for support. The theory led Jung to explore folklore and tribal religious rites as keys to mankind's thinking and subconscious processes.

Theater wizard Kaufman is dead

June 2. George S. Kaufman was a congenial gent. He might have been able to write a Pulitzer Prize play by himself but he always chose to do it with a friend. "Of Thee I Sing," his first Pulitzer winner, was co-authored with Morrie Ryskind and Ira Gershwin in 1931. His second, "You Can't Take It With You," was done with Moss Hart. The screenplays for "The Solid Gold Cadillac" and "Silk Stockings" were also collaborations, the latter written with his wife. Kaufman managed to be simultaneously a critic for The New York Times and a dramatist without offending either side's sensitivity. Kaufman died today at 71. He will be missed.

Soviet ballet star Nureyev defects

June 16. Pleading "Protect me!" Rudolf Nureyev broke from his Soviet guards this morning and raced toward a group of Paris policemen. The 23-year-old ballet dancer was at Le Bourget Airport ready to board a plane and join his fellow dancers when he made the dramatic defection. Authorities say his asylum request will likely be granted.

Nureyev has danced since age 13, joining the Kirov as a soloist in 1958. He was made lead male dancer last year. Arguably the best male dancer in the Soviet Union, he is certainly the best in the West.

Nureyev has superb technique, power, and evidently gumption. He defected even though he knew Soviet officials knew what he was up to. The Paris Opera currently performs "Sleeping Beauty." Perhaps Nureyev will appear in it (→ 23).

Nureyev, dancer and defector.

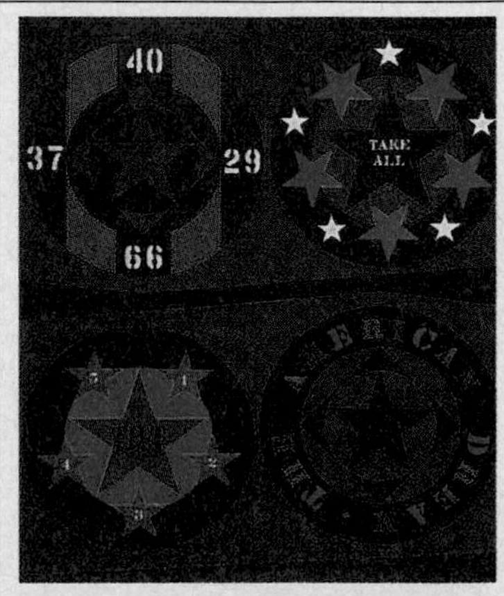

"The American Dream," by Robert Indiana, Robert Clark till he took the name of his home state.

1961

JULY

Su	Mo	Tu	We	Th	Fr	Sa
						1
2	3	4	5	6	7	8
9	10	11	12	13	14	15
16	17	18	19	20	21	22
23	24	25	26	27	28	29
30	31					

1. Kuwait: British troops land to aid against Iraqi threats (→ 11/30).

3. Seoul: Korean leader Gen. Chang resigns; Gen. Pak heads junta (→ 6/3/64).

5. U.S.: "The Making of the President," by Theodore White, is published.

5. Algiers: Nationalists riot against French plan to leave Sahara out of future Algeria; 80 killed, 266 wounded (→ 20).

6. Moscow: Soviets sign ten-year military aid pact with North Korea.

7. Wimbledon: Rod Laver over Chuck McKinley 6-3, 6-1, 6-4; Florence Mortimer over Christine Truman 4-6, 6-4, 7-5.

8. Moscow: Khrushchev halts troop reduction, increases defense budget (→ 25).

9. Moscow: Soviets display new jet fighters and big bombers.

11. Washington: White Citizens Council and Louisiana county registrar charged in federal court on black voting rights (→ 9/25).

14. U.S.: James Baldwin's "Nobody Knows My Name" is published.

14. Pope, in encyclical "Mater et Magistra," urges aid to poor nations without colonialism.

15. Moscow: U.S.-Soviet track and field teams meet at Lenin Stadium.

16. Jacques Anquetil wins Tour de France for second time.

19. Tunisian troops besiege French at Bizerte (→ 20).

19. Stuttgart, Germany: Wilma Rudolph sets women's record of 0:11.2 in 100-meter dash.

20. France: Algerian talks resume at Lugrin Castle in Haute-Savoie (→ 9/9).

22. Berkeley: Radioactive dating adds million years to man's existence.

22. Louisville: Cassius Clay defeats Alonzo Johnson in heavyweight bout.

BIRTH

1. Carl Lewis, U.S. track and field star, four golds at 1984 Olympics.

Hemingway commits suicide with shotgun

Hemingway, rugged individualist.

July 2. Author Ernest Hemingway was found dead this morning at his Ketchum, Idaho, home. He had been wounded in the head by a shotgun blast. Some friends described Hemingway as despondent; others thought him in good spirits. His wife issued a statement saying Hemingway accidentally killed himself while cleaning the firearm.

Hemingway won the Nobel and Pulitzer Prizes, influencing two generations of writers. His novels included "The Sun Also Rises" and "For Whom the Bell Tolls." He used a terse style and brutal themes.

Hemingway was a risk-taker. He was a big-game hunter. He was a war correspondent who reported from the front lines. And he walked away from two plane crashes. Hemingway may have inherited some of his daring from his father, an ambitious man who committed suicide.

U.S.S.R. and U.S. plan bigger defense

July 25. President Kennedy and Soviet Premier Khrushchev, calling each other aggressors, are both ordering sharp increases in military spending. Kennedy, addressing the nation on television tonight, plans to boost the Pentagon budget by almost $3.5 billion. It has not escaped attention that the figure matches Khrushchev's increase almost exactly. Kennedy also said he will double the military draft and add 217,000 men to the armed forces in order to counter a "worldwide" Soviet military threat. "We do not want to fight," Kennedy said, "but we have fought before."

In justifying his hike in military spending, Khrushchev pointed to the crisis in Berlin and accused the West of "paying lip service to the idea of disarmament" (→ 2/10/62).

Gus Grissom follows Shepard into space

July 21. Air Force Capt. Virgil I. "Gus" Grissom became the second American in space today, in a flight that was marred when his Mercury capsule sank in the Atlantic with valuable films aboard. Grissom was launched from Cape Canaveral at 8:20 a.m. and landed 302 miles away in the Atlantic Ocean 16 minutes later after a flight that took him 116 miles into space. Minutes after the landing, explosive bolts blew out the side hatch of the capsule before a waiting helicopter could hook on and lift it upright. The capsule flooded, and Grissom had to swim for more than two minutes before a second helicopter plucked him from the sea. He said the dunking left him "a bit uneasy," but doctors said he suffered no harm (→ 8/7).

Korean War veteran Grissom.

French entangled with Tunisian forces

July 20. French forces, embroiled in another North African dispute, broke the siege of the naval base at Bizerte today and then moved into the Tunisian city. The French attacked at dawn with planes, tanks and machine guns. More than 100 Tunisians were killed. At the United Nations, Tunisia demanded that France remove its troops from the Mediterranean base. The battle follows new troubles in Algeria, where Moslems clashed with French security forces (→ 8/12).

Ty Cobb, baseball immortal, is deceased

July 17. Ty Cobb, the first player ever elected to Baseball's Hall of Fame, has died at the age of 74. He had suffered from prostate cancer, diabetes and heart disease.

Cobb still holds 16 major league records. He was known as one of the meanest competitors in the game during his 22 years with the Detroit Tigers and Philadelphia Athletics. He was chosen for the Hall of Fame in 1936, beating out Babe Ruth by seven votes.

The so-called Georgia Peach was feared by rival players for his deadly use of spikes on the basepaths. He won 12 batting championships in the age of the "dead" ball and stole more bases (892) than any other player. He scored 2,244 runs in his 3,033 games. And his .367 lifetime batting average is the highest ever.

Thousands of East Germans fleeing

July 17. There are thousands of them every week, 3,000 just this past weekend—refugees fleeing from the Communists in East Germany. Fleeing to freedom in West Berlin, they say, before it is too late. Officials say the refugees are suffering from "Torschlusspanik," panic or fear that the door will slam in their face. Rumors are flying in the East that the Russians will seal the border between the two Berlins as soon as they sign a separate peace treaty with East Germany (→ 8/8).

1961

AUGUST

Su	Mo	Tu	We	Th	Fr	Sa
		1	2	3	4	5
6	7	8	9	10	11	12
13	14	15	16	17	18	19
20	21	22	23	24	25	26
27	28	29	30	31		

1. Leopoldville: Kasavubu names Socialist Cyrille Adoula Congo premier (→ 9/13).

4. London: Parliament approves govt. request to join European Common Market (→ 22).

6. Ogden, Utah: Gene Fullmer retains middleweight title against Fernandez of Cuba.

8. West Berlin: 1,741 East Germans arrive in 24 hours, spurred by Khrushchev speech warning of military buildup (→ 13).

12. France: Anti-Franco Basques seized over French border.

12. Frankfort: Assassins kill Tunisian opposition leader Salah Ben Youssef (→ 25).

13. Berlin: East Germans close East-West border (→ 14).

14. Berlin: Battle-ready Soviet divisions encircle city, backing border sealing (→ 16).

16. West Berlin Mayor Willy Brandt urges U.S. take political action in crisis (→ 20).

17. Uruguay: Alliance for Progress meets first time at Punta del Este, drafts charter of economic cooperation (→ 12/16).

17. U.S. Public Health Service licenses Sabin oral polio vaccine.

20. Berlin: East Germans erect five-foot concrete wall on border (→ 23).

22. Sweden, following tradition of non-alignment, refuses to join EEC (→ 12/7).

23. Berlin: West deploys 1,000 troops, tanks on border (→ 31).

24. N.Y.: Cuba in U.N. challenges U.S. right to retain Guantanamo Bay naval base (→ 1/2/62).

25. France institutes decrees to liberalize education.

25. New York: U.N. condemns France in Bizerte clashes with Tunisia (→ 7/20/62).

26. Burma becomes world's first Buddhist republic.

31. Soviets resume atomic tests (→ 9/12).

DEATH

18. Learned Hand, served longest term, 52 years, as U.S. federal judge (*1/27/1872).

Berlin cut in two by Communist wall

Countrymen or ideological foes? East (front) and West face off over the wall.

The wall culminates 13 years of hostilities, launched by the blockade of 1948.

Aug 31. A harshly impersonal monument to the Cold War, evidence of the insoluble problems between East and West, slices like a rapier through the heart of Berlin. A wall, constructed with astounding speed from prefabricated blocks of concrete, is the Communists' answer to the Germans who have snubbed their system and fled to the West. It is hard to bypass the wall. East Berliners need a special permit and East German soldiers do not bend the rules for anybody.

East German soldiers, armed with machine guns, threw barbed wire across the line that divides East and West Berlin early in the morning of the 13th. It was the first step toward sealing the border. Emigration to the West had become embarrassing. Some 2,000 refugees were leaving every day. The border guards reinforced the eastern side of the Brandenburg Gate, the main exit point in the flight to freedom. The guards also stopped the 50,000 East Berliners who were used to earning a pay check, capitalist style, in West Berlin every week.

After the wall went up, there were only seven crossings to West Berlin, down from 80. The Communists also insisted on a 110-yard-wide no man's land on the western side of the new wall, but they backed down when Allied tanks and soldiers appeared inside the zone, their weapons pointed at East Berlin. The Allies have called these actions "illegal, brutal and callous." They can call them anything they want. Words will not tear down this wall. It has been built to stay (→ 10/26).

Soviet cosmonaut orbits 17 times

Aug 7. Cosmonaut Gherman S. Titov, the second Soviet in space, made a safe landing today after orbiting the earth 17 times in 25 hours and 17 minutes. Moscow radio said the five-ton Vostok II carrying the 26-year-old cosmonaut landed close to the site where Yuri Gagarin, the first Soviet in space, landed on April 12. Titov, who was seen on Soviet television, ate lunch and dinner in space and slept for more than seven hours during his flight (→ 9/13).

British free Kenya nationalist Kenyatta

Aug 21. After spending nine years behind bars for leading the Mau-Mau rebellion, Kenya nationalist Jomo Kenyatta was granted his freedom. African nationalists, who recently won majority rule in the legislative council, say they wish to have Kenyatta as their prime minister when they gain their independence. Great Britain categorized Kenyatta a Communist in 1952, but recently he denied he was either a Communist or anti-white. He says he intends to work for equal rights for all races in Kenya (→ 5/27/63).

Kenyatta, free after nine years.

1961

SEPTEMBER

Su	Mo	Tu	We	Th	Fr	Sa
					1	2
3	4	5	6	7	8	9
10	11	12	13	14	15	16
17	18	19	20	21	22	23
24	25	26	27	28	29	30

1. Chicago: 78 killed in plane crash outside city.

1. Yugoslavia: Tito invites 25 nations to attend non-aligned conference (→ 4/7/62).

5. U.S. makes airline hijacking a federal offense.

5. U.S. Agency for Intl. Development (USAID) created under Foreign Assistance Act.

5. Paris: De Gaulle acknowledges Sahara as part of Algeria (→ 9).

10. Monza, Italy: Racer Count von Trips and 11 spectators killed in Grand Prix crash.

10. Forest Hills: Roy Emerson beats Laver for U.S. tennis title.

12. Soviets detonate series of A-bombs, detected by U.S. long-range equipment (→ 12).

12. London: Bertrand Russell jailed over atom protest (→ 15).

13. U.S.: "Franny and Zooey," by J.D. Salinger, published.

13. Cape Canaveral: Unmanned Mercury capsule orbited and recovered in test for first manned flight (→ 11/29).

15. U.S. resumes atom tests with underground blast (→ 10/16).

17. Istanbul: Turkish ex-Premier Adnan Menderes hanged.

20. Rhodesia: U.N., Tshombe agree on cease-fire in Katanga (→ 11/14).

22. JFK signs congressional act formally establishing Peace Corps.

25. U.S.: Rev. King opens Negro vote drive in South (→ 12/11).

26. New York: Warner Bros. offers $5 million for film rights to "My Fair Lady."

26. N.Y.: Roger Maris hits 60th homer of season to tie Babe Ruth's 1927 record (→ 10/1).

28. Damascus: Military revolts against Egyptian domination of Syrian region of UAR (→ 30).

DEATHS

22. Marion Davies, American film actress.

24. Sumner Welles, FDR aide, Latin American diplomacy (*10/14/1892).

U.N. Secretary General dies in plane crash

Hammarskjold prepares to board the plane that would take him to his death.

Sept 18. Dag Hammarskjold's elusive search for peace in the war-torn Congo ended today when he died in a suspicious plane crash in Northern Rhodesia. Twelve other passengers and crew members, including three Americans, were killed with the United Nations Secretary General. The lone survivor of the crash, an American security guard, said he heard several explosions before the plane plummeted to the ground near the airport in Ndola, Northern Rhodesia. The plane was apparently circling the airport when it crashed.

Hammarskjold was flying to a meeting with the President of Katanga, Moise Tshombe, who had fled to Northern Rhodesia after United Nations forces overran his troops and returned control of Katanga to the Congolese regime. Tshombe was holding a news conference when word reached him that Hammarskjold was dead. He appeared to be shocked. Tshombe, who had earlier criticized U.N. policy in the Congo, said he had hoped to talk to the secretary general about a "settlement that would leave Katanga free" (→ 11/3).

Bob Dylan plays in Greenwich Village

Sept 28. A surprising young talent with a frayed appearance and compelling stage presence is generating the kind of excitement in a Greenwich Village cafe normally reserved for grizzled veterans of the folk music scene.

Bob Dylan, 20, who is appearing this week at Gerde's Folk City, strikes a vocal blend between the nasal drawl of Depression-era folksingers and the deep-throated growl of Southern blues. He accompanies himself with a driving guitar and harmonica. Dylan's repertoir includes a variety of folk styles, and his original material reveals an already-powerful facility with words that may have just started to mature.

Self-taught Dylan, hit in the Village.

U.N. takes Katanga, ending secession

Sept 13. United Nations forces seized control of Elisabethville today and proclaimed an end to Katanga's secession from the rest of the Congo. But it was not easy. The international forces battled with Katangese soldiers who were armed with machine guns and dug in around the post office. At least 30 soldiers were killed in vicious hand-to-hand combat. The President of Katanga, Moise Tshombe, is apparently in hiding. Some members of his rebel government have been arrested. Others fled to Northern Rhodesia. Shortly after the fighting ended, Dag Hammarskjold, Secretary General of the United Nations, arrived in Leopoldville (→ 18).

Syrians rebel and end tie to Egypt

Sept 30. Syria staged a military revolt to end its political union with Egypt in the United Arab Republic. Acknowledging defeat, President Gamal Abdel Nasser in Cairo called back Egyptian forces sent to crush the revolt by Syrian army officers.

In Damascus, a new civilian government was established, headed by Mahmoun al-Kuzbari, a 48-year-old conservative lawyer. Syria's reestablishment of its independence was widely regarded as a devastating setback to Nasser's dream of creating an Arab state that would represent all of the Arab world. As a step toward Arab unity, Nasser in 1957 merged Egypt and Syria into the United Arab Republic (→ 10/5).

Attempt made on de Gaulle near Paris

Sept 9. France's President de Gaulle narrowly escaped an assassination attempt last night as he was driving from Paris to his country home at Colombey-les-Deux-Eglises. An explosive charge misfired, sending a wall of flame across a country road, but failing to ignite nine pounds of plastic explosives. An unidentified young man was arrested nearby. He has already been linked to a militant right-wing group that opposes de Gaulle's policies in Algeria. Immediately after the incident, de Gaulle stopped and left his car to make certain no one in his motorcade was hurt. He said the bungled assassination attempt was a "joke in bad taste" (→ 10/20).

1961

OCTOBER

Su	Mo	Tu	We	Th	Fr	Sa
1	2	3	4	5	6	7
8	9	10	11	12	13	14
15	16	17	18	19	20	21
22	23	24	25	26	27	28
29	30	31				

1. N.Y.: Roger Maris hits record 61st homer of season (→ 9).

2. Saigon: Diem says struggle with Viet Cong has become a war in last year (→ 16).

5. Cairo: Nasser formally gives up claims to Syria (→ 2/12/62).

5. Peking signs accord defining China-Nepal border.

8. Laos: Prince Souvanna Phouma named to head provisional coalition (→ 1/6/62).

10. U.S.: Joseph Heller's "Catch-22" is published.

11. Calif.: X-15 sets flight record flying 40 miles over Edwards Air Force Base at 3,477 mph.

11. New York: U.N. General Assembly votes to censure South Africa (→ 11/22/62).

16. Quincy, Mass.: Bethlehem Steel displays first nuclear-powered surface warship, USS Long Beach (→ 23).

16. Moscow: Khrushchev welcomes Chou En-lai to 22nd Party Congress (→ 17).

17. Moscow: Khrushchev banishes Albania from Communist bloc (→ 12/10).

20. Paris: Police put down Algerian FLN protests (→ 31).

20. U.S.: U.A.W. ends first company-wide strike against Ford after 17 days.

23. U.S.S.R. explodes record-sized 30-megaton bomb (→ 30).

24. Great Britain grants Malta autonomy in Commonwealth.

26. Berlin: Soviet tanks move into East Berlin, face off with U.S. force (→ 28).

27. Outer Mongolia and Mauritania join U.N.

30. Soviets detonate enormous 50-megaton H-bomb (→ 11/9).

31. Algiers: 86 dead, 150 wounded in riots marking seven years of rebellion (→ 1/4/62).

DEATHS

4. Max Weber, Russian-American painter (*4/18/1881).

30. Luigi Einaudi, Italian president '48-'55 (*3/24/1874).

31. Augustus John, British portrait artist (*1/4/1878).

American and Soviet tanks face each other

Soviet and U.S.: On the brink of war.

Oct 28. Soviet and American tanks confronted each other today across the border between East and West Berlin in a dispute over border-transit rights. The confrontation, which lasted 16 hours, began when Soviet tanks wheeled into position at the Friedrichstrasse crossing point on the Berlin boundary. U.S. tanks then took up position 100 yards away on the other side of the crossing point. The Soviet tanks were the first to withdraw, easing the tensions but apparently leaving unresolved the issue of the right of U.S. officials to cross into the Communist sector of Berlin.

The confrontation of the tanks developed after the United States challenged the right of East German guards to check on the credentials of American officials in civilian clothes crossing into East Berlin under a military police guard. In Moscow, the American Ambassador protested the East German action violated the Berlin occupation agreement (→ 4/9/62).

Stalin is removed from Lenin's tomb

Oct 30. The body of Joseph Stalin, interred beside Lenin with great pomp in 1953, has been quietly taken away from the great mausoleum in Red Square. The Soviet Communist Party voted for the removal following revelations of Stalin's mass purges in the 1930's and 40's. Half the public, once victimized by the dictator, rejoiced at news of his posthumous fall. However, a few students in Georgia, Stalin's birthplace, decried the action (→ 11/10).

Diem says Vietnam now engaged in war

Oct 16. With a renewed Viet Cong offensive expected during the upcoming dry season, South Vietnam's President Diem declared today that the struggle against Communist insurgents was "no longer a guerrilla war but a real war waged by an enemy who attacks us with regular units." The conflict has taken on a new dimension in the last 12 months, he said, following the Communist failure at political subversion (→ 11/9).

Maris exceeds the Babe's total by one

Maris, in Ruth's footsteps, hits #61.

Oct 9. Roger Maris wasn't much help to the New York Yankees as they won the World Series for a record 19th time, but he could point to his own home-run record as proof of a successful season.

Maris got only two hits in the five-game series against Cincinnati, but he finished the regular season with 61 homers. The final one, the blast that propelled him one ahead of Babe Ruth for a single season, came in the final game of the season. The reticent Maris had to be forced to take a bow.

The Yankee outfielder demolished a mark that had stood for 34 years against a 21-year-old Boston rookie whose name will live in trivia, Tracy Stallard. However, Ruth got his 60 in a 154-game season. Maris needed the extended 162-game season to hit his 61.

Chubby Checker has us all doing the twist

"Come on, baby, let's do the twist."

Oct 18. Once reserved for gyrating teenagers only, the rock and roll dance craze, led by Chubby Checker's irrepressible hit "The Twist," has even shimmied its way up the social ladder. In recent weeks, throngs of Jet Set socialites have jammed the dance floors of such once-staid bastions of New York cafe society as the Stork Club and Peppermlnt Lounge, not only to twist but to jerk, poney, wiggle wobble and frug till the wee hours. Checker, 19, has embarked on a European tour, and one can only wonder if the new dance sensation is headed for the British royal palace.

Augustus John, the portraitist, is dead

Oct 31. Augustus John, one of Britain's most eminent and colorful painters, died today, 83 years old, at his home in Fordingbridge, Hampshire. An exceptional portrait painter, he knew and painted most everyone, from G.B. Shaw to William Butler Yeats to James Joyce. In 1942, the prestigious Order of Merit was awarded to him. It was said of this aristocratic Bohemian that he was not a snob; he simply wished everyone had a title. He visited the United States often and found it "an orgy of color, noise, smartness and multitudinous legs."

1961

NOVEMBER

Su	Mo	Tu	We	Th	Fr	Sa
			1	2	3	4
5	6	7	8	9	10	11
12	13	14	15	16	17	18
19	20	21	22	23	24	25
26	27	28	29	30		

3. New York: U Thant of Burma elected interim secretary general of U.N. (→ 14).

4. Camden, N.J.: Crimson Satan takes Garden State Stakes, world's richest horse race.

7. New York: Argentine team wins Nations Cup in National Horse Show.

9. Albany: Gov. Rockefeller wins legislative approval for major fallout shelter plan (→ 24).

9. Calif.: X-15, from Edwards Air Force Base, shatters speed records, hitting 4,070 mph.

9. U.S. sending 200 Air Force instructors to S. Vietnam (→ 14).

10. Soviets rename Stalingrad Volgograd (→ 11).

13. Washington: Cellist Pablo Casals plays at the White House.

13. Cameroons: State of Emergency proclaimed to quell rebellion (→ 3/13/62).

14. N.Y.: U.N. reports Tshombe and Kasavubu collaborated in Lumumba murder (→ 16).

15. N.Y.: Met buys Rembrandt's "Aristotle Contemplating the Bust of Homer for $2.3 million.

16. Leopoldville: Mutinous Congolese murder 13 Italians from U.N. (→ 12/5).

17. France: Henri Manoury, de Gaulle murder plotter, arrested.

19. Dominican Republic: Restoration of Trujillo regime averted with U.S. Navy patrolling off coast; Trujillo family leaves (→ 1/5/62).

20. Algeria: Ben Bella and fellow nationalists granted political prisoner status after hunger strike (→ 1/4/62).

24. U.N. adopts bans on nuclear arms over U.S. protest (→ 28).

28. Geneva: Soviet test ban without international inspection rejected by U.S. (→ 1/29/62).

29. Cape Canaveral: NASA orbits chimp named Enos twice and recovers him (→ 1/26/62).

30. New York: Soviets veto U.N. seat for Kuwait, pleasing Iraq.

DEATH

2. James Thurber, American humorist (*12/8/1894).

U.S. advisers in Vietnam raised to 16,000

Nov 14. U.S. Army training personnel in South Vietnam, currently at 700, will soon be joined by 200 Air Force instructors in an accelerated effort to strengthen that country's air force. It was also announced today that U.S. military advisers to South Vietnam will be increased over the next two years to a level of 16,000. Whether U.S. airmen might fly tactical missions was not disclosed, and the full extent of U.S. participation in the fighting awaits a decision by President Kennedy on the fact-finding mission led by General Maxwell D. Taylor, his special military adviser.

The program includes U.S. bombers, fighters, helicopters and the massive movement of equipment. American Globemasters have been flying in cars, trucks, radar equipment, generators, Quonset huts and other material needed to operate a number of medium bombers soon to arrive. And a U.S. ground crew of 20 men has set up at Bienhoa, an airfield just northeast of Saigon (→ 12/22).

JFK confers with Green Beret Cmdr.

Mr. Sam, the former Speaker, is gone

Nov 16. "I always say without prefix, without suffix and without apology that I am a Democrat," Sam Rayburn once said. Rayburn, Speaker of the House for 17 years, died of cancer today. He was 79.

Rayburn held the Speaker's position longer than anyone and had an extraordinary ability to pass bipartisan legislation, utilizing his powerful but honest persuasion techniques. He prided himself on being able to lead as well as follow, when others demonstrated quality leadership talents. He lobbied hard and won support for many Democratic programs, including the Marshall Plan, the New and Fair Deals and civil rights legislation. His veracity, integrity, professionalism and earthy sense of humor will be missed on Capitol Hill.

California heavily damaged by fire

Nov 6. The most destructive fire in Southern California's history raged unchecked through the Hollywood Hills tonight. The blaze, fanned by high winds, destroyed at least 186 homes, damaging and endangering hundreds of others, many valued above $100,000 and some containing rare works of art. At least 1,300 men fought the flames in a 6,000-acre area of winding, narrow canyons, but winds up to 40 miles an hour sped the fire storm through Bel Air and surrounding suburbs.

Destroyed homes include those of Burt Lancaster, comedian Joe E. Brown and Zsa Zsa Gabor. Homes threatened or damaged include mansions belonging to Cary Grant, Red Skelton, Kim Novak, Maureen O'Hara, Fred MacMurray, Ginger Rogers, Marlon Brando, Robert Stack and Greer Garson.

Former Vice President Richard Nixon was working on his book "Six Crises" when he noticed flames outside his rented Brentwood home. He went up on the roof and sprayed water with a hose until the fire crept within 200 yards and firemen ordered him to leave. Schools in a large area were evacuated, one was destroyed, but there have been no reports of deaths or serious injuries.

Dead: The gentlest of writer-artists

Nov 2. In one James Thurber cartoon there is a man and a woman on a couch at a party. The man, in conservative bow tie and glasses, is looking skeptically at the woman as she says, "I think of you as being enormously alive." Thurber was a bit skeptical about women's intentions, and probably had doubts about his talent, but most readers were enormously pleased with him.

Thurber died today in New York at age 66. He recently underwent surgery for a blood clot on the brain. He had grown increasingly blind in one eye, and the other eye had been useless since a boyhood accident.

It may seem strange that a nearly sightless man should have a career as a cartoonist, and be a cartoonist at the most prestigious magazine, The New Yorker. An editor proudly called Thurber a "third-rate artist." The fact was he could hardly draw pictures at all. What he drew were human foibles and anxieties, difficult things to illustrate indeed.

Thurber wrote a play called "The Male Animal," spoofing football rituals, and co-wrote a book with E.B. White called "Is Sex Necessary?" His daydreaming alter-ego Walter Mitty was brought enormously to life in a film with Danny Kaye.

Soviet party expels three top Stalinists

Nov 11. Khrushchev's revisionist policies went one step further today as three former Stalinists were ousted from the Soviet Communist elite. Georgi M. Malenkov, Lazar Kaganovich and Vyacheslav Molotov have been stripped of their party rights. They are expected to appeal.

Molotov is on his way to the Soviet Union from Austria, where he has represented the U.S.S.R. at the International Atomic Energy Agency. Malenkov was exiled to a Siberian electric plant in the late 1950's and he is still there. In 1953, after Stalin's death, he had briefly run the country as Premier. Nikita Khrushchev had removed him from power. Kaganovich resides in Moscow, living on a retirement pension.

Yesterday, the city of Stalingrad was renamed Volgograd. An imposing statue of the dictator there was toppled and hauled off. Today, the site where it stood is occupied by a smooth patch of concrete.

1961

DECEMBER

Su	Mo	Tu	We	Th	Fr	Sa
					1	2
3	4	5	6	7	8	9
10	11	12	13	14	15	16
17	18	19	20	21	22	23
24	25	26	27	28	29	30
31						

2. Philadelphia: Navy over Army 13-7 in football.

4. Toronto: Patterson retains boxing title against McNeeley.

5. Congo: U.N. forces launch assault in Katanga (→ 21).

7. EEC admits 18 African nations as associates (→ 1/14/63).

9. Tanganyika proclaims independence (→ 12/9/62).

10. Moscow closes Albanian Embassy in warning to China (→ 1/13/62).

10. Dag Hammarskjold gets posthumous Nobel Peace Prize.

11. U.S. Supreme Court voids first integration sit-in convictions (→ 4/20/62).

15. U.N. denies seat to Peking in victory for U.S. (→ 5/17/62).

16. Caracas: JFK begins South American tour to cheers (→ 18).

18. Bogota: 500,000 greet JFK on Alliance for Progress tour (→ 1/1/62).

19. Portuguese Goa surrenders to Indian troops.

19. Indonesia: Sukarno orders mobilization to attack Dutch New Guinea (→ 1/15/62).

31. Green Bay: Packers blank N.Y. Giants 37-0 for NFL title.

31. Lebanon crushes right-wing army coup.

CULTURAL EVENTS, 1961

Literature: Gunter Grass' "The Tin Drum"; Saul Bellow's "Herzog"; James Baldwin's "Nobody Knows My Name"; Irving Stone's "The Agony and the Ecstacy"; Robert Heinlein's "Stranger in a Strange Land."

Academia: B.F. Skinner's "Walden Two"; "The New English Bible"; Harry Hess explains continental drift by offering theory of "sea floor spreading."

Music: "Moon River"; "Love Makes the World Go Round"; "The Lion Sleeps Tonight"; "Runaround Sue."

The Arts: Motherwell's "Elegy to the Spanish Republic."

Film: Truffaut's "Jules and Jim"; Fellini's "Boccaccio '70"; "Judgment at Nuremberg"; "West Side Story," Oscar.

Grandma Moses, artist of rural life, dies

Rural America on canvas: "Joy Ride," painted by Grandma Moses in 1953.

Dec 13. Artist Grandma Moses has died in Hoosick Falls, N.Y., at the age of 101. She caught the public's fancy in the 1950's, when her paintings began to sell well in the United States and Europe. As a child she sketched with wild berries and grapes; as an adult she wielded a paintbrush and oils.

Grandma Moses captured simple times with direct strokes, choosing bright, undaunted hues. She could not point to any painter who inspired her. As she always lived on a farm, it is unlikely any other artist had a chance to influence her.

Among favorite Grandma Moses works are "Catching the Thanksgiving Turkey" and "Sugaring Off in the Maple Orchard." In her autobiography (published at age 92), Grandma described "sugaring off," tapping maple trees with her family. Children had "a gay time" pouring syrup on dishes of snow and eating their fill.

Eichmann sentenced to death in Israel

Dec 15. There will be no mercy for Adolf Eichmann. An Israeli court decided the former Nazi does not deserve any. In Jerusalem today, the head of the SS Jewish section was sentenced to death by hanging for his role in the extermination of millions of Jews. Eichmann, who was snatched by Israeli agents in Argentina last year, was convicted of "crimes against the Jewish people." The presiding judge said he was guilty of "1,000 premeditated murders" every time he sent a train packed with 1,000 Jews to the death camps. Eichmann, appearing pale but standing straight and almost defiantly, rejected the sentence as unfair. He admitted that Jews were persecuted "with avidity and fervor," but he said he was only following orders from political leaders.

1st American slain by Viet Cong forces

Dec 22. James Davis today became the first U.S. soldier killed in Vietnam when he and three Vietnamese soldiers were ambushed west of Saigon. The news put other U.S. advisers on their toes as they cautiously prepare for Christmas in lonely jungle bases (→ 1/4/62).

Tshombe agrees to unification of the Congo

Dec 21. President Moise Tshombe of Katanga agreed to end his secession from the Congo today. After United Nations forces had seized control of Elisabethville for the second time, Tshombe sat down with the Premier of the Congo, Cyrille Adoula, and agreed to reunite his wealthy province with the rest of the republic. The arrangement may end months of violence in Africa, but it has provoked a divisive argument in the U.S.

Tshombe, Katangese leader

The Kennedy administration helped arrange the agreement and supported United Nations military operations in the Congo. Undersecretary of State George Ball said international policy in Africa had prevented a confrontation between the West and the Communist world and "the horrible firestorm of nuclear devastation." Former President Herbert Hoover charged that the U.N. had thwarted Katangese efforts to be free from Communist domination (→ 11/27/62).

Scientist explains continental drift

Dec 31. A revolutionary new theory of continental drift has been developed by an American geologist, Harry Hess of Princeton University. He proposes that the continents move because they float on huge plates of heavier rock that make up the earth's crust. His theory is based on studies showing that hot rock rises continually from the earth's interior and spreads from the center of the oceans. The idea of continental drift was proposed in 1912 by a German, Alfred Wegener, but geologists have rejected it until now because there was no explanation of what made the continents move. Hess' theory could make the idea acceptable.

Outsiders dominate literature this year

Literature this year explored the theme of aliens, aliens of another skin, another mind, or another planet. Yossarian, the protagonist of Joseph Heller's novel "Catch 22," considers himself an outsider due to a personal quirk: He wants to live. No one else in his bomber squadron seems interested in the idea. The pilot alone battles World War II bureaucracy, feigning ills, physical and mental, in a dark comedy struggle for survival.

James Baldwin's essays, "Nobody Knows My Name," explore the Negro search for identity. The tone of his writing is more poignant than radical, but Baldwin makes no bones about his demands for civil rights. In "Stranger in a Strange Land," Robert Heinlein describes a visitor to a planet very different from his own. The tone of Heinlein's science fiction is generally optimistic, as if the future will make the universe more unified.

Irving Stone brought artist Michelangelo from the ceiling of the Sistine Chapel down to earth in "The Agony and the Ecstasy." And Henry Miller is no longer an outsider: His erotic masterpiece "Tropic of Cancer" (1934) was legally published in the United States this year.

Henry Miller, now off banned list.

Moss Hart, writer, had the last word

Dec 20. Indefatigable Moss Hart died of heart failure this morning in Palm Springs. He was 57. Hart wrote and directed for theater and film, and when that bored him he wrote a book about the experiences. That autobiography, "Act One," was a best-seller. A film based on his life is due for production.

Hart co-wrote some of Broadway's funniest plays with George S. Kaufman, among them "Once in a Lifetime" and the Pulitzer-winning "You Can't Take It With You." These works and "The Man Who Came to Dinner" jabbed at the human personality. "I'd Rather Be Right" took a stab at politics.

The duo failed at serious drama, but in 1947 Hart wrote the very serious screenplay for Laura Z. Hobson's "Gentleman's Agreement," exploring anti-Semitism. Hart's friends could understand how he could write weighty material—he had a rough childhood, quitting school in the 8th grade to support his family—but none could determine his comedic inspiration.

Hart staged the musical "My Fair Lady" in 1956. Last year, he directed "Camelot." Other projects were waiting in the wings.

Edith Wilson, widow of President, dies

Dec 28. Edith Wilson, whom some called the "First Woman President," died tonight in Washington. She was 89. Mrs. Wilson was the wife of Woodrow Wilson. She had considerable sway during his second term, particularly after he suffered a debilitating stroke.

Mrs. Wilson was born Edith Bolling in Virginia in 1872. Miss Bolling married a Washington jeweler, and even though she said she could not tell "an asset from a liability," she managed his company after his death. She met Wilson in 1915 after the recent loss of his wife. He was 58, she 45, when they wed.

After expressing reservations about her capabilities, the new Mrs. Wilson enthusiastically aided the war effort. She was the first to sign a homemaker's pledge to conserve limited goods. She decoded secret messages and even attended the Paris peace talks in her husband's stead.

Wilson's stroke paralyzed him in the autumn of 1919. She and his aides ran the White House while they kept him in seclusion. After his death, Mrs. Wilson usually only appeared in public for projects honoring her husband. In the last election, she cast her vote for John F. Kennedy.

Tiffany's is scene of Truman Capote movie

The film may be called "Breakfast at Tiffany's," and Truman Capote's novel is called likewise, but very little noshing goes on at that jewelry shop. "Tiffany's" stars Audrey Hepburn as Holly Golightly, a Southern girl who goes to New York and goes mod. Director Blake Edwards dwells little on Capote's sobering asides, keeping the picture frothy. Henry Mancini's theme song "Moon River" sets the mood.

Hepburn and Peppard: "Tiffany's."

Stanley Kramer directed "Judgment at Nuremberg," a story of the trial of German war criminals. Included in the all-star cast are Burt Lancaster, Judy Garland, Montgomery Clift and William Shatner. Spencer Tracy plays a judge, Maximilian Schell a lawyer and Marlene Dietrich a soldier's widow.

Tracy and Dietrich: "Nuremberg."

Romeo and Juliet are Italian and Puerto Rican in "West Side Story." Robert Wise and Jerome Robbins directed, Robbins responsible for the vibrant choreography as well. Natalie Wood, who also stars this year in "Splendor in the Grass," can hardly sing a note of the Leonard Bernstein-Stephen Sondheim score. But supporting actress Rita Moreno can—and she can dance, too. She shines in the spirited number "(I Like to Be in) America."

"West Side Story."

Paul Newman is cooler than a cucumber in "The Hustler." Robert Rossen directed the picture about a disillusioned pool shark. George C. Scott and Piper Laurie give excellent supporting performances, and Jackie Gleason virtually embodies Minnesota Fats.

Paul Newman is "The Hustler."

Alistair MacLean's short novel "The Guns of Navarone" came to the screen under the direction of Jack Lee Thompson. Gregory Peck stars as the leader of an Allied force assigned to destroy a German outpost in the Mediterranean during World War II. The international cast includes David Niven, Irene Papas and Gia Scala.

Among other popular pics this year was "Fanny," an offbeat romance starring Leslie Caron, Charles Boyer and Maurice Chevalier. Sophia Loren silenced critics forever with her powerful work in "Two Women." Vittorio DeSica directed the painful story of a mother and daughter raped during wartime. Tennessee Williams' "Summer and Smoke" stars Geraldine Page as an unrequited wooer.

Peck in "The Guns of Navarone."

1962

JANUARY

Su	Mo	Tu	We	Th	Fr	Sa
	1	2	3	4	5	6
7	8	9	10	11	12	13
14	15	16	17	18	19	20
21	22	23	24	25	26	27
28	29	30	31			

1. Pasadena: Minnesota over U.C.L.A. 21-3 in Rose Bowl.

1. Lebanese army arrests 400 for plotting to overthrow govt.

1. Venezuela: Saboteurs blow up four U.S. oil pipelines (→ 3/19/63).

2. U.S. publishes report condemning Cuban military build-up, Soviet ties (→ 30).

4. Algeria: Banned rightist Secret Army Organization (O.A.S.) appeals openly for revolution against France (→ 22).

5. Dominican junta seizes property of ex-Pres. Trujillo (→ 18).

6. Geneva: U.S.S.R. and U.K. invite three rival Laos princes to Geneva to form coalition (→ 12).

9. JFK asks congressional leaders to raise debt ceiling.

12. U.S. resumes aid to Laotian regime (→ 19).

13. Peking: China and Albania sign pact for economic and technical cooperation (→ 7/2).

15. New Guinea: Two Indonesian torpedo boats sunk by Dutch off coast (→ 8/15).

18. Dominican junta of Rafael Rodriguez Echavarria ousted (→ 12/20).

18. South Vietnam: U.S. sprays foliage with pesticide to reveal Viet Cong guerrillas (→ 2/8).

19. Moscow: Soviets accuse Israeli diplomats of using synagogues for espionage activities.

22. Paris: O.A.S. bomb attack at French Foreign Ministry kills one, injures 13 (→ 31).

23. New York: Jackie Robinson elected to Baseball Hall of Fame.

26. Cape Canaveral: U.S. rocket Ranger 3 strays off path, misses moon by 20,000 miles (→ 2/20).

27. New Zealand: Peter Snell sets mile record of 3:54.4.

29. Geneva: U.S., U.S.S.R., U.K. suspend 39-month-old arms talks indefinitely (→ 2/22).

30. Uruguay: Organization of American States, at U.S. request, bans Cuba (→ 2/4).

DEATH

16. R.H. Tawney, British economic historian (*11/30/1880).

Saigon gets new aid; U.S. Army units added

JFK reviews the Immediate Ready Force, on constant alert for overseas service.

Jan 4. As a sign of faith in the future of a free South Vietnam, the U.S. announced today it is backing a "broad economic and social" program to raise living standards in that country. Complementing recent substantial military aid increases, the program would cost appreciably more than last year's $136 million. Military aid expenditures are a secret.

Covering public health, education, agriculture and industry, the 11-point plan is part of the larger effort to strengthen South Vietnam against Communist guerrilla attack. It should also enhance President Diem's popularity. President Kennedy has also announced the immediate activation of two new regular Army divisions "to demonstrate in unmistakable terms our determination to resist Communist aggression" (→ 18).

MERSEYSIDE'S OWN ENTERTAINMENTS PAPER

The name for Records, Amplifiers, Transistor Radios, Also Pianos and Organs

HANOVER STREET, LIVERPOOL 1

MERSEY BEAT

NEMS

WHITECHAPEL AND GREAT CHARLOTTE STREET

THE FINEST RECORD SELECTIONS IN THE NORTH

Open until 6-0 p.m. each day (Thursday and Saturday 6-30 p.m.)

Vol. 1 No. 13 | JANUARY 4-18, 1962 | Price THREEPENCE

Beatles Top Poll!

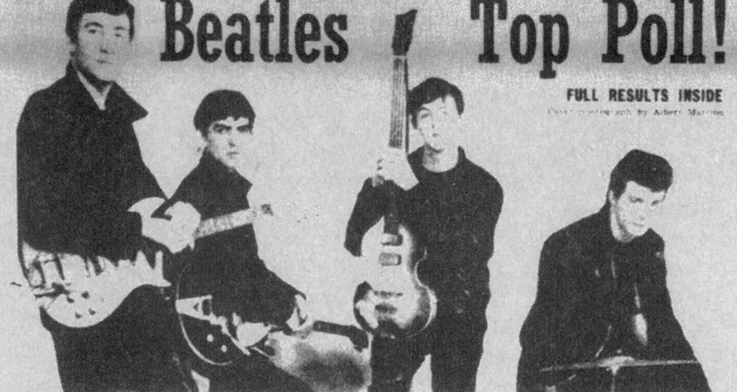

FULL RESULTS INSIDE

JOHN LENNON GEORGE HARRISON PAUL McARTNEY PETE BEST

Despite their success on the Liverpool music scene, the Beatles have been rejected by Decca, a major British recording studio. Their audition early this month, set up by manager Brian Epstein, convinced experts that the four would never make it on the music charts. After a hard day's night, Epstein and his proteges decided to produce their first album themselves.

St. Laurent makes hit with first show

Designer Yves Saint-Laurent has opened a house of fashion in Paris, displaying his own flowing creations for women. YSL had worked under Christian Dior until the latter's death in 1957, and Dior groomed him for succession. When the 21-year-old took over the Dior industry, he was not afraid to try a few experiments. He shocked many former Dior admirers with an above-the-knee skirt in 1959.

Algerian-born Saint-Laurent is a nearsighted and well-groomed man with long, tapered fingers. He believes in women looking elegant, an effect he maintains by clothing them in A-line dresses, choosing fabrics that hang and drape flatteringly.

Yves St. Laurent dresses a model.

Van Doren is guilty in quiz show fix

Jan 17. Charles Van Doren and nine other former contestants on rigged TV quiz shows pleaded guilty yesterday to perjury charges and received suspended sentences from Justice E.F. Breslin, who said the humiliation was evident in their faces. Van Doren, 35, a former professor at Columbia University and member of a distinguished literary family, won $129,000 on the show "Twenty-One." He denied at first that he had received advance answers to difficult questions but later admitted his lies and was charged with perjury. Appearing gaunt and nervous, Van Doren stated his wish to drop out of the limelight and resume teaching (→ 5/1).

Secret Army strikes widely in France itself

"The O.A.S. strikes where it wishes, when it wishes, as it wishes."

Jan 31. The war of terror against French President de Gaulle's policies in Algeria spread across the Mediterranean to France itself this month. The message was simple. The underground Secret Army Organization (O.A.S.) will stop at nothing to prevent the independence of Algeria from France.

In one of the latest attacks, one man was killed and at least a dozen people were injured when a bomb exploded on the 22nd at the Foreign Ministry in Paris. A mailroom worker was killed unloading a truck where the bomb had been hidden. The blast shattered windows, wrecked offices and set sensitive documents on fire. The same day, a Deputy who supports de Gaulle's policies was kidnapped from his home. He was later released.

Earlier in the month, a former Communist adviser to the Algerian nationalists was gunned down at his home in Alencon, 120 miles west of Paris. Three men opened fire on the headquarters of the Communist Party in the capital. From the 18th to the 23rd, 35 bombs exploded in Paris to mark the anniversary of the uprising in Algiers. There is no end in sight, and no one knows who the next victim will be (→ 2/8).

Two of the Flying Wallendas killed

Jan 30. Two members of the Flying Wallendas, the high-wire circus act, lost their lives tonight as the troupe performed in Detroit. One member apparently lost his footing, confusion followed, and four of the seven plunged 50 feet to the floor, while three clung to safety. Fatally injured were Richard Faughan, 29, and Dieter Shoep, 33. Shoep's sister Jane, 19, and Mario Wallenda, 22, were seriously injured. Panic threatened to spread, but a circus clown calmed the spectators. The act has been an international attraction since it was formed by Karl Wallenda in Germany in 1923. There have been numerous accidents but no fatalities until now.

Ernie Kovacs, famed TV comic, is killed

Jan 13. Ernie Kovacs, the cigar-chomping comic whose zany TV antics rocketed him to stardom, was killed shortly before 2 a.m. this morning when his station wagon skidded across wet pavement and smashed into a power pole in West Los Angeles. He had attended a baby shower in honor of the wife of comedian Milton Berle. Kovacs and his wife, singer Edie Adams, left the party in separate cars for the ten-minute trip from the house of their host, director Billy Wilder, to their 17-room mansion, which Miss Adams reached, unaware of the crash. Kovacs, who would have been 43 in ten days, was the father of three children, aged 15, 13 and 2.

Death toll is 3,000 in Peru landslide

Jan 11. A wall of ice and snow thundered down the slopes of Mt. Huascaran late yesterday, devastating several mountainside villages and burying possibly more than 3,000 persons. The ice and snow piled up into a mass 30 feet high and half a mile wide at the bottom of the slide. The villages hit by the avalanche had a total population of 3,100, none of whom is known to have escaped. Only one body has so far been recovered from the icy tomb. Huascaran, a 22,205-foot extinct volcano 30 miles north of Huaraz, a city 175 miles northwest of Lima, is Peru's tallest mountain and one of the highest in the towering Andes chain.

Merger of two vast rail lines proposed

Jan 12. The Pennsylvania and New York Central Railroads have proposed a $4 billion merger. Spokesmen for the railroads say the lines had been serving some of the same areas, duplicating efforts. Fierce competition from the trucking industry was another factor in their move. The new railroad, should merger be approved, would extend as far east as Boston and as far west as St. Louis (→ 4/27/66).

Major rackets boss dies natural death

Jan 26. Salvatore Luciano was 14 when he took his first job as a $5 a week clerk, but after winning $250 in a floating crap game, he turned to crime and eventually became head of the U.S. Mafia. Better known as "Lucky" Luciano, he controlled prostitution, narcotics and gambling rings, was a partner in Murder Inc. and took over most of Al Capone's operations. Arrested 25 times, Luciano went to prison only twice but was deported from the United States in 1946. Luciano continued to run a highly profitable drug ring from Italy, but died of a heart attack today on his way to discuss a movie of his life with a Hollywood producer.

3 Laotian Princes agree on coalition

Jan 19. The Princes of Laos reached agreement in Geneva today on a new coalition government that one of them called "a firm basis for future peace." Prince Souvanna Phouma's neutralists will have majority control over the Cabinet, which will have Communist and right-wing ministers. The agreement was reached after the United States threatened Prince Boun Oum, the right-wing Premier, with a cutoff of military aid. Boun Oum and Prince Souphanouvong, the pro-Communist, will each control four seats in the 18-member Cabinet. A treaty is being drafted in Geneva to guarantee the neutrality and independence of Laos (→ 5/6).

O'Toole stars as legendary Lawrence

Now on the wide screen seeming wider than ever is "Lawrence of Arabia." The camera meanders over endless panoramas of sand and sunsets. Monotony is broken by Peter O'Toole on a jolting camel.

T.E. Lawrence was a WWI British intelligence agent who led the Arab revolt and sabotaged German outposts. His philosophical book "Seven Pillars of Wisdom" is a kind of classic. O'Toole puts in a classic performance himself in this, his first starring film role. Before playing the eccentric Lawrence he was in the Bristol Old Vic troupe.

David Lean ("Bridge on the River Kwai") directed. Robert Bolt ("A Man for All Seasons") wrote the screenplay and veteran Freddie Young did the photography.

O'Toole is Lawrence of Arabia.

1962

FEBRUARY

Su	Mo	Tu	We	Th	Fr	Sa
				1	2	3
4	5	6	7	8	9	10
11	12	13	14	15	16	17
18	19	20	21	22	23	24
25	26	27	28			

2. New York: American John Uelses becomes first to pole vault over 16 feet.

3. New York: 42 arrested at Times Square peace rally (→ 16).

4. Switzerland: Hilti von Allmen and Walter Etter become first to climb north face of Matterhorn in winter.

6. JFK, in school aid plea, asks Congress for $5.6 bil. (→ 4/26).

7. Germany: Mine blast kills 249; 146 missing.

8. U.S. Defense Dept. reports creation of Military Assistance Command in S. Vietnam (→ 14).

8. Argentina breaks diplomatic ties with Cuba (→ 3/29).

9. Tokyo: Robert Kennedy debates Japanese leftist Akira Iwai; invites him to U.S. to see value of capitalism (→ 9/1/63).

12. Damascus: New Syrian regime seeking aid from Soviet bloc (→ 13).

13. Washington: JFK and King Saud confer on U.S. air base in Saudi Arabia.

14. JFK defends role in Vietnam, says men are "not combat troops in the generally understood sense of the word" (→ 18).

17. Hamburg: Hurricane and floods leave over 100 dead.

18. Saigon: RFK says troops will stay until communism defeated in Vietnam (→ 27).

20. John Glenn, in Friendship 7, becomes first American to orbit earth (→ 26).

22. U.S. again turns down Soviet bid to new Geneva arms talks (→ 25).

24. Algiers: Terrorists kill 25 in suburbs (→ 3/18).

24. Bronx: Police seize $20 million worth of heroin.

25. London: Bertrand Russell calls atomic tests "butchery" (→ 3/2).

27. Saigon: Two planes bomb presidential palace; Ngo Dinh Diem safe (→ 28).

DEATH

17. Bruno Walter, German-American conducter, founder of Salzburg festival (*9/15/1876).

Glenn is first American to orbit earth

Glenn, veteran of World War II.

Feb 26. The United States is hailing Lt. Col. John H. Glenn Jr., first American to orbit the earth. Despite heavy rain, tens of thousands turned out in Washington today to cheer Glenn in a parade up Pennsylvania Ave. to the Capitol, where he addressed a joint meeting of Congress. Three days ago, President Kennedy flew to Cape Canaveral to present Glenn with a medal and praise him for "unflinching courage" and "extraordinary ability."

Glenn's three-orbit flight took place on February 20, after ten delays caused by bad weather and poor sea conditions in the recovery site area. Glenn's Mercury spacecraft, the Friendship 7, lifted off from launch complex 14 at Cape Canaveral at 9:47 a.m., after a last-minute delay caused by a power failure in a computer at Bermuda. Hundreds of thousands of spectators on Florida beaches watched the launch, and tens of millions more saw it on television. An Atlas rocket put him in an orbit 99 miles above the earth 11 minutes later.

On his first orbit, Glenn reported seeing the lights of Perth, Australia, whose residents turned on all their house lights for the occasion. Completing the first orbit, Glenn reported seeing thousands of luminous particles near the capsule in the sunrise over the Pacific. Experiencing some minor difficulty with the spacecraft's altitude control system, Glenn switched to manual control and reported it to be "smooth and easy." After considering whether the flight should be cut short, Mission Control gave a go-ahead for a full three orbits.

The most serious problem occurred just before re-entry, when Glenn was told ground instruments indicated a possible loosening of the spacecraft's heat shield, whose failure would result in incineration of the capsule as it plunged into the atmosphere. A decision was made not to jettison the crafts retro rockets, which slow the capsule for re-entry. The spacecraft descended safely, landing close to the destroyer Noa, the recovery ship, at 2:43 p.m. "My condition is excellent," Glenn said as he went aboard (→ 4/3).

Cape Canaveral, 9:47 a.m.: An Atlas rocket sends Glenn, in Friendship 7, hurtling toward outer space.

Upon Glenn's return, New Yorkers covered him with more confetti than the city had seen since WWII's end.

Secret Army blamed for ten Paris bombs

Paris: Finally fed up with O.A.S.

Feb 8. Left-wing protesters in Paris had a deadly clash with police today as they demonstrated against French policy in Algeria and the latest bombing spree by right-wing terrorists. The underground Secret Army Organization was blamed for exploding ten bombs yesterday at the homes of Cultural Affairs Minister Andre Malraux, a Senator and military officers. Six people were hurt, including a young girl who may lose her eye as a result of the explosion at the Malraux home. In Paris today, the leftist protest overflowed from the Bastille to the Charonne subway station, where the leftists were rushed by French security forces. Eight protesters were crushed to death when they were pushed by the crowd against the closed doors of the station (→ 24).

U-2 pilot traded for spymaster Abel

Feb 10. The Soviet Union released American pilot Francis Gary Powers in exchange for the freedom of Soviet spy Rudolf Abel, convicted in 1957 for espionage against the United States. The trade occurred after months of negotiation and was orchestrated by New York attorney James Donovan. Powers was flying a U-2 over the Soviet Union as part of a reconnaissance operation in May 1960, when Russian ground forces downed his plane and held him captive. He pleaded guilty to spy charges and received a ten-year prison term. Abel, convicted of conspiring to pass U.S. defense and military secrets to the Kremlin, served four and a half years of a 30-year sentence (→ 3/8).

Jackie guides TV White House tour

Feb 14. Millions of television viewers went through the White House last night with Mrs. John F. Kennedy leading the way. In an hour-long program, she explained the restoration she has made in the interior of the Executive Mansion.

She proved to be a virtuoso among guides. Softly and without faltering, she presented historical facts and human details, was a subtle art critic, a knowing antiquarian and a poised TV narrator.

Wearing a simple wool suit and three strings of pearls, Mrs. Kennedy strolled through room after room, showing the magnificence of the State Dining Room and the rich warmth of the Red Room, pointing out details on a battered old Lincoln chair plucked from a warehouse and many of the antiques and paintings recently donated to the White House in response to her pleas. Her effortless familiarity with names and dates attested to homework well done. She praised past contributions of Theodore Roosevelt and James Monroe. She recalled that Grant's renovation of the East Room had been called a unique mixture of ancient Greek and "Mississippi River Boat."

Jackie, Queen of Washington.

After the tour, the President appeared briefly to second his wife's efforts to impart a sense of taste to the White House. All in all, "A Tour of the White House with Mrs. John F. Kennedy," carried simultaneously by CBS and NBC, gave a personal flavor to history.

RFK says U.S. stays until Viet Cong beaten

Feb 28. Robert F. Kennedy, who was in Saigon last week on a month-long world tour, said that American troops are committed to staying in Vietnam until the Viet Cong are beaten. But the U.S. Attorney General did not say what his brother's administration intends to do about the internal problems plaguing the South Vietnamese regime itself.

Today, South Vietnam's presidential palace came under non-Communist fire when two fighter bombers of the country's own air force subjected it to 50 minutes of bombing, strafing, rockets and napalm, leaving one wing in flames.

Neither the 61-year-old bachelor President Diem nor his close confidantes, his brother Ngo Dinh Diem and sister-in-law Mme. Nhu, were present. A report that the attack was launched by rebels of the South Vietnam air force stems from the eventual crash of one of the planes, whose pilot was captured.

U.S. officials regard the bombing as an isolated incident, and maintain that Diem is in full control.

Family talk at the White House.

The attack follows by 15 months an attempted coup by Diem's own paratroopers, who had announced plans to set up a more liberal regime to replace what they termed the "totalitarian, authoritarian and nepotistic" Diem regime. That uprising was crushed (→ 3/17).

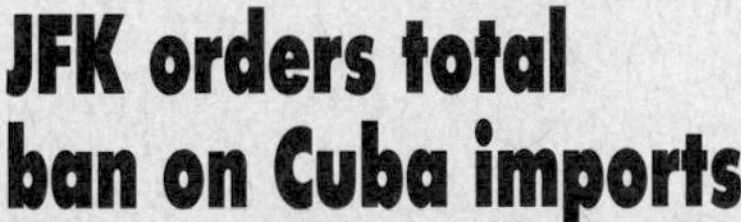

JFK orders total ban on Cuba imports

Feb 4. President Kennedy banned all trade with Cuba yesterday, depriving the Fidel Castro government of $35 million in annual income. The embargo will limit Cuba's capacity to subvert other nations in the Americas, the White House asserted.

Castro lashed out at Kennedy in a TV speech today, tagging the ban on imports from Cuba "another (act of) economic aggression." He called Kennedy "a shameless person," and asked Cubans to triple their industrial and agricultural production to overcome the U.S. "blockade." With determination and sacrifice, declared Castro, the troubled Cuban economy will prosper. "We will laugh at the desperation of the imperialists," he said.

The ban will also hurt Americans, particularly the Tampa, Florida, cigar industry, which depends exclusively on Cuban tobacco. JFK directed Labor Secretary Arthur Goldberg to assist the 6,000 industry employees who will lose their jobs when tobacco reserves are depleted by year's end (→ 8).

March for peace held in Washington

Feb 16. Hundreds of college students are braving the Washington winter to march for peace outside the White House. The demonstration was organized by students from Harvard, but the marchers are arriving from all over the country. President Kennedy was apparently impressed by the protest. He sent an urn of coffee to the students and invited some of them into the White House to meet with top aides. One of the officials called the students "a nice balance to the cold warriors." The students called for disarmament, a halt to atmospheric testing of nuclear weapons and the cancellation of the civil defense program.

The demonstration, which continues tomorrow, threw off sparks only once. Some of the students were annoyed at the off-handed way they were treated at a State Department briefing. One of them said he was told to go and picket in the Soviet Union. Another delegation met with Congressmen on Capitol Hill. Police turned back a group that tried to picket outside the Soviet Embassy (→ 2/19/65).

1962

MARCH

Su	Mo	Tu	We	Th	Fr	Sa
				1	2	3
4	5	6	7	8	9	10
11	12	13	14	15	16	17
18	19	20	21	22	23	24
25	26	27	28	29	30	31

2. Burmese army takes over country in coup.

2. U.S. to begin atmospheric A-bomb tests in April unless Soviet sign test ban (→ 14).

5. U.S. Supreme Court rules airports must compensate neighbors for noise and vibrations.

8. U.S., Soviets expand cultural exchanges, Benny Goodman and Bolshoi Ballet (→ 5/30).

9. Guatemala: Students strike, protesting 1961 election of Pres. Miguel Ydigoras Fuentes (→ 19).

13. JFK meets with Cameroon President Ahmadou Ahidjo.

14. Geneva: Arms talks begin anew, France absent (→ 16).

16. Florida: Titan 2 rocket makes maiden flight, hits target 5,000 miles away (→ 28).

17. Moscow asks U.S. to pull out of South Vietnam (→ 4/1).

17. Syria: Israeli border raid kills 30 Syrians (→ 4/6).

18. France: French, Algerians sign truce ending war (→ 20).

19. Guatemala: Army imposes state of siege (→ 3/31/63).

20. Argentina Pres. Frondizi to form coalition with military, barring Peronists (→ 29).

20. Algiers: 80 Moslems killed in internecine fighting (→ 26).

27. Syrian regime ousted by army; junta in power (→ 4/13).

28. U.S. Air Force now researching use of lasers to intercept missiles and satellites (→ 4/24).

29. Argentina: Ex-Pres. Frondizi, deposed yesterday, jailed by army (→ 4/24).

29. Havana: Cuba opens trial of Bay of Pigs invaders (→ 4/8).

30. JFK names Byron White to replace Charles E. Whittaker on Supreme Court.

30. Boston: Edward Kennedy admits ouster by Harvard for cheating on exams.

DEATHS

15. Arthur H. Compton, U.S. physicist, 1927 Nobel, developed A-bomb (*9/10/1892).

24. Auguste Piccard, Swiss oceanographer (*1/28/1884).

Algeria war ends; combatants sign truce

Blood-spattered French flag at her side, an Algerian girl hopes for peace.

March 26. In the week since French and Algerian representatives signed a cease-fire, they have learned a major lesson. There will be no real peace in Algeria until the right-wing leaders of the Secret Army Organization are arrested and put in jail. As soon as the truce was signed, General Raoul Salan, director of the O.A.S., urged his supporters to keep fighting against independence for Algeria. "I order our fighters," Salan said on television, "to harass enemy positions in the large cities of Algeria. I ask members of the armed forces, Moslem and European, to join us." Within days of Salan's appeal, scores of people were dead as street battles erupted in Algiers and Oran.

Under the terms of the cease-fire agreement, Algerians will go to the polls in several months to decide whether they want to remain part of France, gain more autonomy or win complete independence. A provisional government is in the process of being selected (→ 4/8).

Wilt Chamberlain scores 100 in game

March 2. In an awesome offensive display unmatched in professional basketball, Wilt Chamberlain scored 100 points for the Philadelphia Warriors against the New York Knickerbockers. Many records were toppled along the way, including the point total for the Warriors' 169-147 victory at Hershey. Wilt the Stilt used his 7-foot 3-inch height to advantage in getting a record 36 field goals, most points for a quarter (31) and most points for a half (59). He also set a league record by making 28 of 32 free throws. The collegiate scoring record is also 100. Chamberlain had held the previous pro record of 78.

Jackie, on world tour, visits Gandhi shrine

March 12. Mrs. John F. Kennedy received a glowing welcome as she arrived in New Delhi today for a two-week goodwill tour of India and Pakistan, the 32-year-old First Lady's first such trip without the President. She is accompanied by her sister, Princess Radziwill.

Jackie rides in style the Asian way.

India at her springtime best with thousands dressed in their finest clothes flocking to the roadsides, tossing flower petals, gave not a hint of its other side, that of an underdeveloped, poor country of 483 million people. Jackie was met by Prime Minister Jawaharlal Nehru and his daughter, Indira Gandhi, at the airport. She visited President Prasad and then rode to a memorial on the shore of the Jumna River where the body of Mahatma Gandhi was cremated in January of 1948. She placed a sheaf of white roses on the spot.

Before India, Mrs. Kennedy went to Rome where she was received in private audience by Pope John XXIII. They conversed in fluent French and exchanged gifts; rosaries for her family, her husband's book, "To Turn the Tide," for him.

Conservatives hold rally for Goldwater

Barry, conscience of conservatism.

March 7. Thousands of conservative Americans unanimously applauded Republican Senator Barry Goldwater and vehemently booed the name of John Kennedy at a mass gathering at Madison Square Garden last night. Arranged by the Young Americans for Freedom, the rally raised $80,000 for conservative causes, one of which may be a presidential campaign for Goldwater in 1964. Amid red, white and blue balloons, streamers and banners, Goldwater assailed President Kennedy and Communist aggression and praised political right-wingers. He proclaimed: "Conservatism is young, virulent and alive . . . the wave of the future."

Three crashes kill 312, G.I.'s included

March 15. The third air disaster in two weeks killed 107 tonight when a Flying Tiger Super Constellation plane dropped into the Pacific on a flight from Guam to Manila. Of those on board, 93 were soldiers, en route to Saigon as part of the growing number of American military men assisting the South Vietnamese in their war against Communist guerrillas.

A British airliner crashed in the remote jungles of West Africa on March 5. The wreck claimed the lives of 110 South Africans, Rhodesians and Europeans. The plane, an American-made DC-7, was flying from Mozambique in East Africa to Luxembourg via Cameroon.

On the 1st, 95 persons died in the deadliest, single commercial airplane crash in the nation's history. Mysteriously, an American Airlines 707 nose-dived into Jamaica Bay, Queens, just after takeoff for Los Angeles. Ironically, the crash occurred on the first bright, sunny day in weeks in New York.

Critic of American society deceased

March 20. C. Wright Mills, the prominent American social critic, and Professor of Sociology at Columbia University for the past 17 years, was only 45 years old when he died today.

Basing his ideas on the classical theories of Karl Marx and Max Weber, Mills authored "White Collar" (1951), "The Power Elite" (1956), "The Sociological Imagination" (1959) and "The Marxists" (1962). He firmly believed that social scientists should take an active, responsible role in society.

Mills' best-known work is "The Power Elite," in which he proposed the thesis that arbitrary, self-interested power in American society is wielded by a ruling business and military elite, popularly known as the military-industrial complex. This idea has gained such wide currency that even former President Eisenhower, in his farewell address last year, warned his countrymen against the dangers of such an institutional arrangement.

1962

APRIL

Su	Mo	Tu	We	Th	Fr	Sa
1	2	3	4	5	6	7
8	9	10	11	12	13	14
15	16	17	18	19	20	21
22	23	24	25	26	27	28
29	30					

1. South Vietnam: Govt. troops penetrate Viet Cong territory in Binhdinh province (→ 15).

3. U.S. Air Force announces first satellite TV broadcast (→ 23).

6. New York: Brazil Pres. Joao Goulart gets ticker tape parade.

6. New York: U.S., U.K. ask U.N. to censure Israel for attack on Syria last month (→ 8/11/63).

7. Belgrade: Milovan Djilas, ex-Tito aide, arrested for book on Stalin (→ 5/14).

8. Havana: Bay of Pigs invaders get 30 years; Castro offers exchange for $62 million (→ 14).

8. French ratify Algerian truce by 90% majority (→ 21).

9. Georgia: Arnold Palmer wins Masters golf tournament.

9. Berlin: Two East Berliners escape to West by smashing truck through wall (→ 5/27).

13. Syria: Pres. Nazam el-Kodsi returns to office (→ 2/8/63).

14. Paris: Georges Pompidou succeeds Michel Debre as French prime minister.

15. South Vietnam: 400-man U.S. helicopter unit joins war against Viet Cong (→ 5/16).

15. New York: 500 attend memorial services on 50th anniversary of Titanic sinking.

18. Boston: Celtics win fourth straight NBA title.

19. Boston: Eino Oksanen wins Boston Marathon for third time.

20. New Orleans: Segregationists offer Negroes free one-way bus transport to Northern cities (→ 5/28).

20. Britain to release political prisoners after IRA peace offer (→ 5/27/64).

21. Florida: JFK opens Seattle World's Fair by remote control.

23. U.S., Soviets agree to cooperate on weather satellites (→ 26).

24. JFK orders resumption of atmospheric atom tests (→ 5/4).

24. Argentina: Pres. Jose Guido nullifies provincial vote to bar Peronist victories (→ 11/15/63).

26. U.S. rocket Ranger IV, launched four days ago, crashes on dark side of moon (→ 5/24).

Cuba sentences invaders, asks for ransom

Bay of Pigs invaders are lined up to be flown back to the United States.

April 14. A Cuban military tribunal has convicted 1,179 Cuban exiles who participated in the failed Bay of Pigs invasion last year. The five-man jury found the defendants guilty of "crimes committed against the nation in connivance with a foreign power." That "foreign power" is the United States via the Central Intelligence Agency, which, according to Cuban officials, masterminded the assault. The anti-Castro invaders were sentenced to 30-year prison terms. However, they will be released on payment of $62 million.

This prison-for-ransom verdict has attracted American interest and U.S. delegates are to fly to Havana tomorrow to negotiate. However, it's doubtful the Kennedy administration will pay anything for the prisoners' release. (Last year, Washington turned down Castro's offer to trade the prisoners for 500 tractors.) U.S. officials will probably encourage private citizens and Cuban-exile groups to raise the ransom money (→ 8/25).

Furious Kennedy gets steel price rollback

April 26. President Kennedy played hardball with steel industry giants this month, and won.

On April 10, United States Steel, the nation's largest steel producer, announced price increases of six dollars a ton, calling the large hike a "catchup" adjustment. Company President Leslie Worthington cited mounting production costs and competitive pressure from foreign steel imports as reasons for the increase. Bethlehem Steel followed U.S. Steel with a similar price hike. Within three days, five more industrial heavyweights followed suit.

However, an enraged Kennedy used full executive clout to thwart what he considered would be a damaging blow to the nation's economy. By verbally attacking the companies, opening legal proceedings with possible anti-trust action and ordering the Defense Department to divert contracts to those steel manufacturers which didn't raise prices, JFK forced U.S. Steel and the others to roll back their prices.

Today, Bethelem, U.S. Steel and two other companies were indicted on price-fixing charges, in violation of anti-trust laws (→ 8/20).

Secret Army loses leadership; Salan is held

April 21. General Raoul Salan, leader of the much feared terrorist group that is opposed to independence for Algeria, was indicted in Paris today for crimes against the state. Salan, head of the Secret Army Organization, or O.A.S., was locked up in a Paris prison. His capture in Algiers yesterday dealt a devastating blow to the terrorist group which has killed and maimed hundreds of people in Algeria and France. Salan was the last of four generals to be arrested after their abortive coup against President Charles de Gaulle in Algeria.

Two of the four generals, Maurice Challe and Andre Zeller, were arrested last year and sentenced to 15 years in prison. Edmond Jouhaud, second in command to Salan in the O.A.S., was condemned to death last week by a jury of civilians and military officials. The sentence cannot be appealed. Salan was sentenced to death in absentia while he hid underground in Algeria. Under French law, however, he must be tried again. The trial is scheduled for next month (→ 5/2).

Pablo Picasso gets Lenin Peace Prize

April 30. Artist Pablo Picasso and four others of international repute have been given the Lenin Peace Prize. Picasso professes socialist inclinations, and his painting of a peaceful dove has been adopted as a Communist symbol. The majority of his work, failing to uphold Socialist Realism, is denied display in the Soviet Union.

Arcaro, winner of 4,779 races, retires

April 3. Eddie Arcaro, a jockey for 31 of his 46 years, has retired as the greatest money-winning rider in the history of horse-racing. With earnings of $30 million from his mounts—of which he received the jockey's share of ten percent—Arcaro is quitting to become a consultant for a company that makes equipment for betting machines.

Charismatic Kennedy at popularity peak

April 22. Publishers in New York today for the annual Press Week find the President at the height of his popularity. His foreign policy program and handling of the steel crisis were cited as reasons for the upswing. Another factor, intangible but real, is Kennedy's charisma.

Newspaper executives noted public approval of Kennedy's evenhandedness with the Soviets. An officer from the Des Moines Register said anything Kennedy does this year will make him look better than last year, when events in Laos and Berlin gave him bad press. Two editors from Midwest papers called last year's Cuban affair a "fiasco" and a "disaster" for Kennedy.

The public was pleased the president was harsh with steel unions threatening to raise prices. Some newspaper people wondered whether Kennedy would deal similarly with other labor unions, and if the public would continue to admire such tactics. An officer from The Louisville Courier-Journal confided he was "delighted" that Kennedy "showed the iron" in dealing sternly with the steel companies.

Yet, what really pleases the nation are images fleeting and peaceful: The president with 18-month-old John-John and 4-year-old Caroline romping in the Oval Office; Kennedy at the helm of a boat, wind streaming through his hair, with Jackie at his side; and the whole family playing touch football at their summer home on Cape Cod.

Jack and Jackie at Hyannisport.

1962

MAY

Su	Mo	Tu	We	Th	Fr	Sa
		1	2	3	4	5
6	7	8	9	10	11	12
13	14	15	16	17	18	19
20	21	22	23	24	25	26
27	28	29	30	31		

2. Algiers: Rightist terrorists slay 91 Moslems (→ 20).

4. Pacific: U.S. explodes fourth atom bomb in ten days (→ 6/1).

5. Decidedly wins Kentucky Derby; jockey W. Hartack gets third Derby win.

6. Laos: Pathet Lao rebels capture Nam Tha, royal govt. stronghold (→ 10).

8. Groton: Jackie Kennedy christens Lafayette, world's largest submarine.

10. JFK orders ships and 1,800 Marines to Indochina to counter Communist gains in Laos (→ 11).

11. Pathet Lao forces govt. troops out of northern Laos (→ 15).

14. Belgrade: Milovan Djilas sentenced to nine years for book on Stalin (→ 4/7/63).

15. U.S. orders 4,000 troops to Thailand (→ 17).

16. South Vietnam: Diem bans public gatherings without police authorization (→ 29).

17. JFK calls U.S. troops in Indochina a "diplomatic solution" (→ 6/11).

17. Hong Kong erects barbed-wire fence to bar illegal Chinese immigrants (→ 21).

18. U.S. indicts Jimmy Hoffa for accepting $1 mil. illegally from Detroit truck line (→ 2/13/63).

21. U.S. Supreme Court voids contempt convictions of six who pleaded Fifth in congressional loyalty inquiries (→ 12/22/63).

21. Taiwan offers to accept refugees from China (→ 6/26).

27. Berlin: East and West soldiers fight gun battle over attempted escapee (→ 8/17).

28. New York: Stock prices take sharpest dive since 1929.

28. NAACP sues Rochester, N.Y., schools for de facto segregation (→ 6/4).

30. Moscow: Khrushchev, at Benny Goodman concert, is pleased but puzzled (→ 7/6).

DEATH

13. Franz Kline, American Abstract Expressionist painter (*5/23/1910).

Salan is sentenced to life in prison

Salan, crusader for a French Algeria.

May 23. Cheers of joy and relief resounded through a Paris courtroom today as General Raoul Salan was sentenced to life in prison. It was widely expected that the former leader of the Secret Army Organization would be condemned to the gallows for his abortive coup against President de Gaulle and the terrorist acts of his Algerian organization. It was Salan's lawyer, Jean-Louis Tixier Vignancour, who saved the general from execution.

In a long and emotional summation, the lawyer told the court that Salan helped sweep de Gaulle back into power and was tricked into believing that Algeria would remain French forever. When it became clear that the president actually favored independence for Algeria, the lawyer said, Salan had no choice but to work underground for the honor of France (→ 6/5).

Public TV to get $32m federal fund

May 1. President Kennedy today signed a bill authorizing $32 million to expand educational television facilities throughout the country. The funds are to be distributed on a matching basis over a five-year period to educational institutions and non-profit groups, bringing greater opportunities for cultural growth to all Americans. Wide distribution of the funds is provided by a limitation of $1 million in grants to a state. In the last decade, the FCC has reserved 273 channels for educational television. Thus far, only 62 are in use (→ 7/11).

U.S. sends forces into Thailand to aid Laos

May 29. The Kennedy administration ordered 4,000 troops, including a Marine battalion, into Thailand to counter an expanding military offensive by pro-Communist forces in neighboring Laos. President Kennedy said the military move was necessary "to help ensure the territorial integrity" of Thailand, with which the United States has a mutual defense treaty.

The military show of force, however, was regarded as part of a diplomatic effort to preserve the neutral, independent status for Laos agreed upon by Kennedy and Soviet Premier Khrushchev at their summit meeting in Vienna last year.

The year-long cease-fire in Laos was broken earlier this month when pro-Communist Pathet Lao forces captured a royal government stronghold near the Communist Chinese border and seized most of northwest Laos. In Saigon, Defense Secretary McNamara said American military aid to South Vietnam will level off (→ 6/16).

Training under U.S. supervision.

Israel hangs Eichmann for death camp acts

May 31. Inside a fog-enshrouded Israeli prison, a noose was placed around the neck of Adolf Eichmann just before midnight tonight. His last appeal for mercy had been rejected. Eichmann's ankles and knees were tied. He said a few last words and then a black trap door sprang open in the floor. Eichmann, the man who sent millions of Jews to their deaths in Nazi concentration camps, was dead.

"Long live Germany. Long live Argentina," Eichmann said before he was executed. Argentina was the country where he hid until he was kidnapped by Israeli security agents. "I had to obey the rules of war and my flag. I am ready," were the mass murderer's final words.

In denying Eichmann's appeal for mercy, the Israeli Supreme Court said he had shown no repentance for his crimes, which it said he had committed with "genuine joy and enthusiasm." The justices also called the death sentence "inadequate compared to the millions of deaths in the most diverse ways he inflicted on his victims." In rejecting Eichmann's claim that he was only following orders, the justices said the man given "the task of dealing with the final solution of 11 million Jews is no mere screw, small or large, of a machine propelled by others. He is himself one of those who propel the machine."

Eichmann (left), 20 years later, is brought to justice before the Star of David.

Europeans fleeing to France from Algeria

The post-colonial exodus.

May 20. Scores of cars filled with panicked Europeans are backed up at the airport in Algiers. Luggage is piling high as thousands of people prepare to leave the violence of Algeria. Military officials have been forced to assume control of the airport, and today they began an emergency airlift to France. Sixteen planes left for Paris. Others are boarding boats for the journey. In Algiers, terrorists of the right-wing Secret Army Organization attack at will, gunning down Moslems who want independence for Algeria and Europeans who line up at police stations for exit visas. The arrest of General Salan may have deprived the terrorists of a leader, but it has also ignited their fury (→ 23).

Carpenter orbits, misses landing, rescued

May 24. M. Scott Carpenter today made the second American manned orbital flight, giving the nation an hour of anxiety when his Mercury spacecraft landed 250 miles beyond the designated recovery point. The flight ended happily when Carpenter was located by a Navy search plane and picked up by a rescue helicopter.

The overshoot was the only flaw in Carpenter's three-orbit flight, which began when an Atlas rocket carried his spacecraft, Aurora VII, aloft at Cape Canaveral at 8:45 a.m., 45 minutes behind schedule. Carpenter was lifted into an orbit whose high point was 167.4 miles and low point was 99 miles. The capsule landed at 1:41 p.m., after traveling 81,000 miles. Space agency officials explained that it overshot the designated Caribbean landing point because the nose of the spacecraft was tipped too high when it re-entered the earth's atmosphere (→ 8/12).

May 30. Rodger Ward sped to victory today in the Indy 500. Powering his Leader Card Roadster around the track at an average of 140.3 mph, Ward duplicated his 1959 effort, becoming Indy's sixth two-time winner.

1962

JUNE

Su	Mo	Tu	We	Th	Fr	Sa
					1	2
3	4	5	6	7	8	9
10	11	12	13	14	15	16
17	18	19	20	21	22	23
24	25	26	27	28	29	30

1. Pentagon announces first federal construction plans for fallout shelters (→ 7/7).

1. Iraq: Kurds ask U.N. to acknowledge right to autonomy.

4. U.S. Supreme Court voids convictions of six Freedom Riders (→ 7/10).

5. Paris: Gen. Edmond Jouhad, in plea bargain with French, asks O.A.S. to halt terrorism (→ 7).

7. Algiers: O.A.S. explodes three phosphorous bombs at Algiers University (→ 14).

11. Hollywood: 20th Century Fox shelves film due to Marilyn Monroe's absenteeism (→ 8/5).

11. Laos: Three feuding princes form coaltition regime (→ 7/26).

12. San Francisco: Three convicts dig way out of Alcatraz with spoons.

14. Paris: 30 arrested in plot to kill de Gaulle (→ 7/3).

17. African common market established.

17. Pennsylvania: Jack Nicklaus wins U.S. Open golf title.

18. Ottawa: Canadian Conservatives beaten due to mounting economic problems (→ 24).

22. West Indies: 112 killed as French airliner hits hill.

24. Ottawa: U.S., U.K. loan Canada $1 billion to halt economic slide (→ 2/5/63).

25. Moscow: Soviets give five death sentence for speculation in gold and foreign currency.

26. U.S. says it will not back Taiwanese attack on mainland China (→ 9/9).

26. U.N. vote assures Ruanda and Urundi of independence.

29. Mexico City: One million cheer JFK on visit.

30. Los Angeles: Sandy Koufax hurls no-hitter to beat Mets 5-0.

DEATHS

2. Victoria Sackville-West, British writer, member of Bloomsbury Set (*3/9/1892).

4. William Beebe, U.S. naturalist, oceanographer (*1877).

6. Yves Klein, French painter (*4/28/1928).

Court bans official prayers in schools

June 25. Justice Black firmly stated a Supreme Court opinion today: "In this country, it is no part of the business of government to compose official prayers for any group of the American people to recite." With that, the court ruled that a prayer written by the New York Board of Regents and read aloud in public schools violates the "establishment of religion" clause of the First Amendment. The landmark decision will affect an estimated 30 percent of public schools which conduct some form of prayer. The ruling builds the "wall of separation" between church and state, that Thomas Jefferson referred to, higher and sturdier.

121 from a single city die in air crash

June 3. An Air France Boeing 707 jet crashed and burned while taking off from Orly Airport, Paris, killing 130 persons. The only survivors were two stewardesses. All of the victims except eight were Americans, and most were from Atlanta. A group of 121 had come to Europe on an art-appreciation tour sponsored by the Atlanta Art Association and had chartered the plane for the return flight. The plane gathered speed, rose about six feet and then faltered. It careened crazily as it ate up the remaining yardage of the runway. Crashing through a fence, the jet engines scraped the earth, and two muffled explosions were heard as the jet fuel —20,000 gallons of it—ignited.

Kubrick directs James Mason and Sue Lyon in a bizarre film version of Nabokov's "Lolita."

Brazil keeps world trophy in soccer

Czech goalie blocks a Brazilian goal.

June 17. Soccer star Pele was on the sidelines, but his muscle injury did not prevent Brazil from winning the final against Czechoslovakia 3-1 and retaining the World Cup championship in Chile. A new forward, Amarildo, picked up the slack created by Pele's absence, and Garrincha kept getting better in every game that he played. The Czech goalie, Schroif, was brilliant, but he could not stop Brazil's forward line. Third place in the championship went to Chile after the team slipped past Yugoslavia 1-0. Police had to be called onto the field in Chile's earlier game against Italy. Fans got out of hand, and the Italians had to be given a police escort at the end of the game.

Two Americans die in Vietnam ambush

June 16. Two U.S. Army officers were killed when Communist guerrillas ambushed an armored convoy on a highway 35 miles north of Saigon. The entire convoy of seven vehicles was destroyed in the skillfully planned ambush carried out by at least 200 Viet Cong guerrillas, and at least 15 South Vietnamese soldiers were killed. Meanwhile, South Vietnamese army units, transported by American helicopters, launched an offensive against a Communist stronghold, known as Zone D, in the jungles 50 miles north of Saigon (→ 7/15).

1962

JULY

Su	Mo	Tu	We	Th	Fr	Sa
1	2	3	4	5	6	7
8	9	10	11	12	13	14
15	16	17	18	19	20	21
22	23	24	25	26	27	28
29	30	31				

1. Convicted Soviet spy Robert Soblen slashes wrists on extradition flight from Israel to U.S.; hospitalized in London.

2. Moscow: Khrushchev says U.S.S.R. would defend China against any attacker (→ 9/20).

6. U.S. lifts curbs on travelers from U.S.S.R. (→ 12/12).

7. Nevada: U.S. conducts first atom test within own territory since 1958 (→ 9).

7. Wimbledon: Rod Laver over Martin Mulligan 6-2, 6-2, 6-1; Karen Susman over Vera Sukova 6-4, 6-4.

9. Pacific: H-bomb test lights up night sky from Hawaii to New Zealand (→ 19).

10. Georgia: Rev. King jailed for leading protest march without permit (→ 28).

13. Texas: Court declares Billie Sol Estes, controversial land financier, bankrupt (→ 3/28/63).

15. Washington: Report links premature births to smoking during pregnancy.

15. Jacques Anquetil wins his third Tour de France.

15. South Vietnam: Communists down helicopter with five Americans (→ 11/25).

17. Calif.: Robert White, from Edwards Air Force Base, pilots X-15 to record 59-mile altitude.

18. Peru: Army seizes power, arrests Pres. Prado; U.S. breaks ties (→ 8/17).

19. Pacific: U.S. anti-missile missile makes first successful interception of ICBM (→ 8/5).

20. France and Tunisia restore diplomatic ties (→ 1/16/63).

20. Gen. Maxwell Taylor succeeds Gen. Lauris Norstad as head of U.S. Joint Chiefs of Staff.

22. Pennsylvania: Gary Player wins PGA championship.

23. Australia: Dawn Fraser becomes first woman to swim 100-meters in under 1:00.

25. Washington: House passes bill for equal pay regardless of sex.

28. Georgia: Rev. King in jail as riots persist; Negro lawyer beaten, 37 arrested (→ 8/10).

Algeria is independent

July 3. Thousands of jubilant Algerians filled the streets of Algiers today and welcomed the arrival of their new government at the airport. Premier Benyoussef Ben Khedda and his entourage flew from Tunisia to Algiers just a few hours after President Charles de Gaulle proclaimed Algeria's independence from France. De Gaulle took just two days to transfer sovereignty to Algeria. The Algerian electorate voted for independence nearly unanimously on Sunday. The final vote was 99.72% De Gaulle's action today ended 132 years of French colonial rule.

Independence does not mean an end to Algeria's problems, however. Vice Premier Ahmed Ben Bella refused to participate in the ceremonies today and flew to Cairo for urgent talks with Egypt's President Nasser. Almost all of the military commanders of Algeria's zones have also withdrawn their support from Ben Khedda because he approved amnesty for members of the hated Secret Army Organization. The terrorist group fought against Algeria's independence (→ 8/20).

Algerian flag flies free of France.

Faulkner, chronicler of decadence, is dead

July 6. "The writer in America isn't part of the culture of this country. He's like a fine dog. People like him around, but he's of no use." So said William Faulkner, pessimistic about his role in America's literary history. But President Kennedy marked his passing by comparing him to Henry James, hailing his work as an enduring monument. Faulkner died today at age 64.

The writer spent his last year in Oxford, Mississippi. He was never far from the town in his thoughts, even while he lectured at the University of Virginia or traveled elsewhere. He needed Oxford. He drew upon its residents, the refined and the unpolished, to fill his novels and short stories with characters.

The town resented his mental intrusions. When he came to main street to patronize the drugstore or mail a letter at the post office, Oxfordians often avoided his gaze. When he left, they would say he was drunk. He often was.

Faulkner, Southern recluse.

Faulkner was a Pulitzer and Nobel winner. His most popular novels were "Absalom, Absalom," "The Sound and the Fury" and "As I Lay Dying." The books tended to deal with death and decay, in sentences that wound themselves endlessly around paragraphs. His writing style was often parodied, and more frequently envied.

Satellite sends first worldwide TV show

July 11. Americans saw their first live television pictures from Europe tonight when signals from France and Britain were transmitted via the Telstar communications satellite. The first transmission came at 7:35 p.m. Eastern daylight time when France broadcast a seven-minute program including a song by Yves Montand. The British broadcast, made on the satellite's next orbit, consisted of test patterns and an official government greeting.

The signals were bounced off Telstar and picked up by a 384-ton antenna in Andover, Maine. The successful transatlantic television broadcast has prompted the U.S. government to begin a study exploring the opportunities and problems arising in a new era of global electronic communications (→ 4/4/64).

Technicians "mate" Telstar to the third stage of the Delta rocket.

Accord reached on neutrality for Laos

July 26. Prince Souvanna Phouma, who has been reinstated as Premier of Laos, flew to Washington today to make arrangements for the aid promised his neutral, coalition government. The final agreement on the new Laotian Cabinet was signed this week in Geneva. Phouma, a centrist, will share power with the right-wing and pro-Communist Pathet Lao parties.

The welcoming ceremony for Souvanna Phouma at National Airport was restrained. It was less than two years ago that he was chased from office in a coup approved by President Eisenhower. The move backfired when the prince was replaced by a right-wing regime headed by Prince Boun Oum. The country plunged into a civil war that did not end until the United States and the Soviet Union agreed to support the formation of a neutral government.

Souvanna Phouma has meetings scheduled with President Kennedy, Secretary of State Dean Rusk and officials at the Treasury, Pentagon and U.S. Agency for International Development (→ 4/20/63).

Russian sets world high jump record

July 22. Valeri Brumel of the Soviet Union, with a leap of 7 feet, 5 inches, set a world high jump record at Palo Alto, surpassing his own record by one inch. The American men outscored the Soviet team, 128-107, but the United States lost the women's competition, 66-41, for the fourth straight time.

Brumel joins a host of Soviet athletes excelling with profuse state support.

1962

AUGUST

Su	Mo	Tu	We	Th	Fr	Sa
			1	2	3	4
5	6	7	8	9	10	11
12	13	14	15	16	17	18
19	20	21	22	23	24	25
26	27	28	29	30	31	

1. Ghana: Pres. Nkrumah escapes assassination attempt; bomb kills four, injures 56 (→ 1/2/64).

5. Soviets resume atmospheric atom tests on day before Hiroshima anniversary (→ 18).

6. Jamaica gets independence after 307 years as British possession.

6. Peking agrees to talks with India to settle border disputes (→ 10/11).

7. Columbia: Leon Valencia elected president of republic.

7. Soviets announce gradual abolition of one-family houses in urban communities.

13. East Berlin guards use tear gas to disperse Western protests at wall (→ 20).

14. France: Tunnel under Mont Blanc completed.

15. Dutch sign pact giving Indonesia rule over New Guinea (→ 5/18/63).

17. U.S. resumes diplomatic relations with Peru.

18. Groton: Polaris sub Alexander Hamilton launched despite pacifist attempts to interfere (→ 9/10).

19. Budapest: Hungarian chief Janos Kadar ousts 25 in purge of Stalinists (→ 10/23/64).

20. U.S. national debt exceeds $300 billion for first time (→ 2/14/63).

20. West Berliners fight own police in riots at wall (→ 9/14).

20. Algiers: Army now controls over one-third of Algeria's first Constituent Assembly (→ 9/25).

25. Havana suburb shelled in sea raid by Cuban exiles (→ 9/2).

26. Cape Canaveral: U.S. launches Mariner II space probe to explore Venus (→ 10/3).

30. Trinidad-Tobago mark passing from colonies to independent nation.

DEATHS

5. Marilyn Monroe, American film star (*6/1/1926).

26. Vihjalmur Stefansson, Canadian Arctic explorer (*11/3/1879).

Marilyn, beautiful but damned, kills herself

Marilyn, the one and only.

Aug 5. Marilyn Monroe has been found dead in her Los Angeles home, a vial of sleeping pills beside her. She was only 36. While police hesitate to call it a suicide, her psychoanalyst says she has tried to kill herself twice before, rescued only by placing a call in time. This morning, she was found in bed, her arm limply stretched to a phone beside her.

Marilyn had a phenomenal career as a sex symbol, starring in films such as "The Prince and the Showgirl" and "The Seven Year Itch." She had serious aspirations, studying under Lee Strasberg in New York. The public, who could not see beyond her sex kitten persona, thought her ambitions absurd. They did not know she was a voracious reader, in her way as much an intellectual as her third husband, playwright Arthur Miller.

Marilyn fudged a line in "Some Like It Hot" a dozen times. The script called on her to knock on a door and say, "It's me, Sugar." Instead she said over and over, "It's Sugar, me." No cast member, no director, no producer, asked her what drug confused her mind so thoroughly or what drove her to take it. And no one stopped to ask if Sugar's life was truly sweet.

First man is killed climbing the Wall

Aug 17. Peter Fechter, 18 years old, lay in a pool of blood for an hour this afternoon while East German police watched. The youth was attempting to defect over the six-foot-high Berlin Wall when he was machine-gunned in the back. Helpless West Berlin police could only toss him bandages. He cried out for help a few times before sinking into silence. His body was finally removed by East Berlin police. A friend who had fled with the victim successfully scaled the wall, only scarred by barbed wire.

Fechter, dead at the base of the wall.

Nobel winner Hesse dies in Switzerland

Aug 9. Ascetic examiner of humanity Herman Hesse has died in southern Switzerland. He was 85. Hesse was better known and more appreciated in Europe, a fact that inadvertently besmirches the intellectual capacity of Americans. Hesse wrote difficult books, works that explored spiritual alternatives in our materialistic times.

Hesse was born in Germany to missionaries. An open-minded couple, they often had visitors of other faiths. Exposure to Eastern religions is reflected in Hesse's "Siddhartha" (1922), a novel based on the Buddha's early years.

In his late 30's Hesse reached a mental crisis, alleviated through Jungian analysis. "Demian" (1919) and later works centered on introverted characters finding themselves through psychology. In the 1920's Germany considered Hesse's books a mirror of the nation's turmoil, and he was heralded as the country's conscience. The masterpieces "Steppenwolf" (1927) and "Narcissus and Goldmund" (1930) were denounced by Hitler's regime.

King convicted but freed in Georgia

Aug 10. City officials in Albany, Georgia, avoided a mass demonstration today by releasing Dr. Martin Luther King and the Rev. Ralph Abernathy after two weeks in jail. The two had led 26 anti-segregationists to the steps of City Hall after eight months of promised meetings with officials failed to materialize.

When told the Mayor was not in, Abernathy replied, "Then we'll just pray until they see fit to see us." After a short prayer, Chief of Police Pritchett said they were creating a disturbance and had the group carried off to jail. Local leaders had promised to bring in hundreds from out of state for a parade and to integrate public places to protest the jailing. This marks the third time since January that King and Abernathy have been arrested in Albany for protesting segregation (→ 9/13).

King, apostle of civil disobedience.

Malden and Lancaster star in a pensive study of a convict's obsession, "Birdman of Alcatraz."

Soviet spacecraft orbit the earth in tandem

Vostok's cabin measures 23 feet in length including the last stage of the rocket.

Aug 12. The Soviet Union has set another space first by sending two manned spacecraft into orbit side by side. The first Vostok ship, with cosmonaut Andrian G. Nikolayev, was launched two days ago. The second spacecraft, carrying cosmonaut Pavel R. Popovich, was sent aloft yesterday. Today, the two ships were flying in adjacent orbits, while their pilots conversed with each other by radio telephone.

In a message to earth, Nikolayev reported that he could see the spacecraft of his fellow cosmonaut, although Moscow radio gave no indication of how close the two ships came. Nikolayev already has set a new record for manned flight in space, traveling more than 750,000 miles in 31 orbits. The two astronauts were seen on Soviet television in flickering pictures sent from their spacecraft. Both agreed they were in "a wonderful mood."

Although the official purpose of the mission given by the Soviets is to test tandem flight in earth orbit, Western experts believe that the Vostok spacecraft might be practicing orbital rendezvous techniques in preparation for an eventual Soviet flight to the moon. No comparable American tests are expected for at least two years. A statement issued today by President Kennedy congratulated the Soviets on "this exceptional technical feat" (→ 26).

De Gaulle escapes crossroads killer

Aug 22. For the second time in a year, gunmen tried to kill France's President Charles de Gaulle after he had left Paris for his country home at Colombey-les-deux-Eglises. This time, they nearly succeeded. It happened on a road near Versailles. Bullets punctured three of the tires of de Gaulle's Citroen D.S., but his driver plunged his foot on the accelerator and tried to keep going. At the Petit-Clamart crossroads, a black car with a white roof careened into the intersection and sprayed the president's motorcycle escort with machine gun fire. One officer was hit in the helmet. The last assassination attempt was mounted by the O.A.S., the terrorist group. In all likelihood, so was this one.

Goldberg replaces Frankfurter on court

Aug 29. President Kennedy today announced the appointment of Labor Secretary Arthur Goldberg to the Supreme Court to replace Justice Felix Frankfurter. Frankfurter resigned because of poor health, after 23 years on the bench.

Leaders of both parties expressed their approval of Goldberg. He brings years of labor law experience to the court. It is not certain who will replace him in the Department of Labor, but Under Secretary W. Willard Wirtz and Joseph Keenan, secretary of the electrical workers union, are both candidates.

Kennedy praised Frankfurter, saying, "Few people have made as significant and lasting an impression upon the law."

1962

SEPTEMBER

Su	Mo	Tu	We	Th	Fr	Sa
						1
2	3	4	5	6	7	8
9	10	11	12	13	14	15
16	17	18	19	20	21	22
23	24	25	26	27	28	29
30						

1. Washington: Report indicates world's population now over three billion.

2. Iran: Some 20,000 killed in country's worst earthquake.

2. Soviets announce they will arm and train Cuban military (→ 4).

4. Washington: JFK pledges to use any step to bar Cuban aggression in West (→ 24).

8. Moscow: Khrushchev meets with Robert Frost.

9. China: Communists down U-2 reconnaissance plane owned by Taiwan (→ 1/1/63).

10. U.S. nuclear test schedule revised in fear over recently formed radiation belt (→ 11/4).

13. Mississippi Gov. Ross Barnett defies federal court order to integrate Univ. of Miss. (→ 17).

14. Berlin: 29 escape to West through tunnel under wall (→ 12/26).

17. U.S. Justice Dept. files first federal suit to end racial segregation in public schools (→ 22).

20. Peking asks U.S.S.R. to close three remaining consulates in China (→ 1/21/63).

22. Washington: Ceremony at Lincoln Memorial marks centennial of Emancipation Proclamation (→ 24).

24. Jackson: Univ. of Miss. agrees to admit James Meredith (→ 25).

25. Miss. Gov. Ross Barnett bars Univ. of Miss. from admitting James Meredith (→ 29).

25. Algeria: Ferhat Abbas elected pres. of Assembly, proclaims People's Democratic Republic (→ 29).

26. Italy: Flood kills 333 in Barcelona.

26. U.S. to supply Israel with short-range missiles.

27. Yemen: Iman Amhad assassinated after one week on throne (→ 11/15).

29. JFK federalizes Mississippi National Guard, orders state to yield on integration (→ 30).

29. Algeria: Ben Bella elected president of the council, pledges neutral socialist state (→ 10/8).

Rod Laver achieves tennis Grand Slam

Laver loses racquet but not balance.

Sept 10. In 1938, when Don Budge vanquished the competition at Forest Hills to win the first Grand Slam in men's tennis, Rod Laver was six weeks old. The "Rocket" has come of age. His four-set victory over fellow Aussie Roy Emerson in the finals of the U.S. championships makes Laver the first to follow in Budge's footsteps. Vicious ground strokes and an impeccable court sense make the affable Laver and his iron wrist the undisputed master of tennis. Emerson, who fell to the lefty in the last round of the Italian, French and Australian, praised Laver's "fantastic record," adding, "He has beaten some great players in the finals."

Sept 25. Sonny Liston disappointed all but himself tonight in Chicago. Two minutes into round one, he dealt Floyd Patterson a crushing blow, and then walked off world heavyweight champ.

Rioting erupts as Ole Miss admits Negro

Sept 30. The admission of a Negro student to the University of Mississippi has stirred violent passions of segregationist whites, resulting in riots and pushing Governor Ross Barnett and President John F. Kennedy into confrontation. Despite the controversy, James Meredith has become the first Negro to enroll in the all-white institution.

The university Board of Trustees agreed a week ago to adhere to federal law prohibiting segregation, allowing Meredith to enroll. The decision infuriated Barnett, who vowed to fight the board and the government to sustain school segregation. Kennedy and the governor negotiated on the phone, but Barnett would not budge. Kennedy, citing obstruction of justice, sent U.S. troops to the area to force compliance with the law. In previous attempts to register Meredith, state troopers blocked his path.

Meredith, first Negro at Ole Miss.

Tonight, after Meredith enrolled, a massive riot erupted. Mobs of angry whites stormed onto campus to protest. At least three people have died in the fighting and 50 have been injured. Troops are now attempting to restore order (→ 10/1).

Nixon seeks to be California governor

Sept 12. Richard Nixon opened his drive for California's governorship today by accusing Governor Edmund G. Brown of ignoring the threat of communism in the state.

The race for governor brings Nixon back to the campaign trail for the first time since narrowly losing the presidency two years ago to John F. Kennedy. A native of California, and a Republican, Nixon had earlier served eight years as Vice President under President Eisenhower.

In this latest political race, Nixon has revived an issue—namely, "soft on communism"—that had been something of a trademark in his successful campaigns for the House and Senate some years ago. At his kick-off rally in Pomona, he promised that, if elected governor, he would deal effectively with "the Communist threat" (→ 11/7).

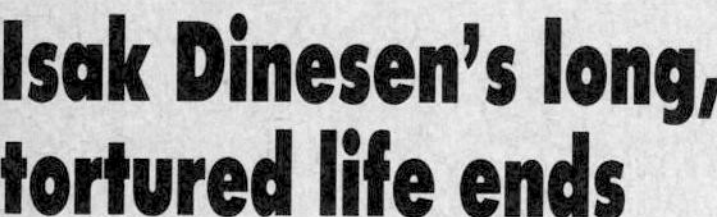

Isak Dinesen's long, tortured life ends

Sept 7. Author Isak Dinesen, 77, has died in Copenhagen, Karen Dinesen was her maiden name, Isak a pen name and Baroness von Blixen-Finecke her married name. Her most popular book was "Out of Africa," about her years on a coffee plantation. She wrote of tragedy: her divorce, the loss of her lover and years of illness. She began writing, in English, after going home to Denmark in 1931. Despite her illness, she entertained often and traveled widely.

death ends career of e.e. cummings

Sept 3. American poet edward estlin cummings had a style punctuated by colons and hyphens. He did not disdain the uppercase "I" for its strong individuality; he just thought capitals superfluous. Cummings wrote of childhood and mortality. "for life's not a paragraph," he wrote, "and death I think is no parenthesis." His readers are grieved to learn this individualist died today at age 67. Among other works he leaves "95 Poems" (1958).

War talk focuses on Cuba situation

Sept 24. Cuba has become the main concern of the foreign policy of the Kennedy administration, and today Congress granted the President power to call up 150,000 military reserves, if he decides it's necessary. The House passed the legislation 342-13; recently, the Senate voted for the bill unanimously. Essentially, the measure eliminates the need for the chief executive to declare a national emergency before mobilizing military reserves.

The legislation passed so decisively, in part, because of the recent threat by the Soviet Union that any American attack on Cuba would mean nuclear war. The Kremlin issued the warning on Sept. 11, in response to Kennedy's request for call-up power. In that statement, the Soviets called JFK's move "an act of aggression" against Cuba.

Earlier this month, Secretary of State Dean Rusk met with 19 Latin American envoys to explain U.S. determination to halt the export of communism from Cuba. The Allies were informed of recent reports that the Castro government was receiving Soviet missiles and military personnel. All envoys agreed with the policy of containment (→ 10/7).

Wanted in the U.S., spy kills himself

Sept 11. Dr. Robert A. Soblen died today in London after having taken a massive overdose of barbiturates last week. Soblen, a Lithuanian-born American psychiatrist, had been convicted in the United States on charges of spying for the Soviet Union. He became entangled in British politics last July, when he was removed from an El Al flight to New York, after stabbing himself. The Home Secretary ordered Soblen's deportation last month.

48 years later, Igor Stravinsky in Russia

Sept 21. The conquering hero was elderly and slight, wielding no weapon mightier than a baton. Still, Igor Stravinsky was home, back tonight in the Soviet Union after an absence of 48 years. The government has invited him to lead two concerts in Moscow. Tonight, he will conduct the "Orpheus" ballet suite, the second half of a program. The first piece will be "The Rite of Spring." Stravinsky composed both, in 1947 and 1913 respectively.

1962

OCTOBER

Su	Mo	Tu	We	Th	Fr	Sa
	1	2	3	4	5	6
7	8	9	10	11	12	13
14	15	16	17	18	19	20
21	22	23	24	25	26	27
28	29	30	31			

1. Jackson: James Meredith attends first classes; 200 arrested in riots (→ 11/20).

2. U.S.S.R. withdraws from 1964 World's Fair.

3. Cape Canaveral: Walter Schirra orbits earth six times in Sigma 7 (→ 10).

6. South Vietnam: Three Americans killed in helicopter crash.

7. Cuba broadcasts "Radio Free Dixie" program praising Negro revolt in South (→ 21).

7. Yemeni troops clash with Saudi Arabians on Yemen border.

8. Algeria joins U.N. (→ 11/29).

9. Uganda gains independence in Commonwealth (→ 2/22/66).

10. U.S.: Mariner II data reveals presence of solar winds (→ 11/1).

11. Chinese, Indian troops clash on border; 50 dead (→ 20).

14. Brussels: 60,000 Flemish march to demand proportional representation; 19 injured in clash with French (→ 5/26/63).

15. Amnesty International created to monitor human rights.

16. San Francisco: Yankees beat Giants to win World Series in final game.

16. Brazil seizes U.S.-owned phone system.

17. Saudi Arabia: King Saud names Prince Faisal premier.

20. Chinese push Indians back in heavy border fighting (→ 26).

21. Washington: JFK and high officials in conference all weekend; U.S. forces maneuver off Puerto Rico (→ 22).

22. U.S. reveals missile sites in Cuba, imposes arms blockade (→ 23).

23. Castro mobilizes as U.S. orders interception of 25 Soviet vessels in defiance of Moscow threat (→ 24).

24. Khrushchev suggests summit to avoid nuclear war, orders ships to avoid blockade (→ 27).

27. Moscow: Khrushchev offers to remove bases in Cuba if U.S. removes bases in Turkey (→ 28).

28. U.S. pledges to rush arms to India (→ 11/19).

Cuban missile crisis: The week that shook the world

Castro speaks with a smiling Khrushchev, who bailed Cuba out of economic crisis by convincing the Warsaw bloc to buy sugar exports cut off by the U.S.

Soviet cargo ship Krasnograd, crossing the Caribbean, was photographed by a U.S. plane. (Long white shapes in the bow were identified as jet fighters.)

An aeriel view shows one of the Cuban sites ready for missile installation.

Oct 28. A new agreement between President Kennedy and Premier Khrushchev has broken the extraordinary tension that has gripped the world for seven days and eased the United States and the Soviet Union back from the brink of nuclear devastation. After a week of high-stakes, showdown diplomacy, it was Khrushchev who blinked. He agreed to stop work on missile sites in Cuba and ship all the weapons back to the Soviet Union. In return, Kennedy agreed not to invade Cuba and to end the American blockade of the island.

Rumors of the impending crisis started to leak out in Washington last weekend. President Kennedy interrupted his congressional campaigning. A spokesman said he had a cold. The Joint Chiefs of Staff were asked not to leave the Washington area. The public explanation: There was pressing work to be done on the budget. Off the island of Vieques, near Puerto Rico, the Navy and Marine Corps began one of the biggest joint military maneuvers in memory. From the White House, there was no explanation as lights burned around the clock in the offices of key Kennedy aides.

On Monday night, in one of the most blunt speeches of his presidency, John Kennedy gave the country the explanation it had been awaiting. Kennedy said the Soviet Union had broken its promise, lied to the United States and started to build offensive missile and bomber bases in Cuba. Soviet statements that the bases were merely defensive were false, Kennedy said. The president asserted that some of the missile sites were built to accommodate intermediate-range weapons that could strike "most of the major cities in the Western hemisphere."

Calling the construction of the bases a "clandestine, reckless and provocative threat to world peace," Kennedy announced he would impose a naval and air "quarantine" on Cuba to stop the shipment of more offensive military equipment. He demanded the withdrawal of all offensive weapons from the island. And he threatened to retaliate against the Soviet Union if missiles were launched from Cuba against any country in the Americas.

Within hours of Kennedy's radio and television address, Premier Fidel Castro announced the mobilization of thousands of Cuban forces. A Havana television commentator denied that Soviet intermediate-range ballistics missiles were in Cuba, and he called Kennedy's blockade an act of war.

On Tuesday, Kennedy received a letter from Khrushchev. Its contents were not revealed.

On Wednesday, shortly after the blockade went into effect, Khrushchev proposed a summit meeting with Kennedy to reduce the risk of nuclear war. In a letter to Bertrand Russell, the British pacifist, Khrushchev also threatened to retaliate against the United States for the blockade. From the Atlantic, however, came word that several Eastern bloc ships bound for Cuba had changed course to avoid a confrontation with the United States.

Thursday, Khrushchev agreed to a United Nations proposal to stop sending missiles to Cuba if the United States ended its blockade. The proposal was made by Acting Secretary General U Thant. Kennedy agreed only to allow American representatives to talk with Thant.

On Friday, tensions escalated sharply. The White House made public an intelligence report showing that work was speeding up on the Cuban missile bases to make them operational "as soon as possible." Kennedy administration officials met to consider their next move in the crisis.

Yesterday, the Pentagon revealed that a U-2 spy plane was missing over Cuba. Several other planes were fired on, and Defense Department officials warned they were ready to shoot back. More than 14,000 Air Force reservists were called to active duty. Kennedy said Khrushchev had made an offer to end the crisis, but proceeded to back off by linking the dismantling of Soviet missiles in Cuba to the removal of U.S. weapons in Turkey. Rumors flew that Cuba was bolstering its defenses out of fear it would be "sold out" by Khrushchev.

Today, the agreement between Kennedy and Khrushchev was announced. It apparently meets all of Kennedy's demands, but there has been too much tension for much jubilation in Washington (→ 11/8). ▷

Indians and Chinese clash on their border

Oct 26. Heavy fighting flared up between India and Communist China in their three-year-old dispute over border lines in the Himalayas.

Each side accused the other of initiating the fighting that began along the Tibetan border early this month, but in New Delhi authoritative sources predicted that Indian forces would move to oust Chinese troops from disputed territory.

Initially, Indian troops pushed back Chinese units along the northeastern frontier between India's Assam state and Chinese-occupied Tibet. Fighting also broke out in the northwestern border between Sinkiang and the Ladakh region of Kashmir. As the fighting continued, however, Chinese troops took the offensive. India lost its main posts of Dhola and Khinzemane near the Tibetan border to a large force of Chinese troops. On the northwest frontier, Indian troops retreated from outposts in Ladakh.

Chinese troops threatened Bomdila, an administrative headquarters on the northeast frontier, and appeared poised to strike at Tazpur in northern Assam. Faced with defeat and a possible Chinese invasion into Indian territory, India declared a state of emergency (→ 28).

Oct 11. In Saint-Peter's Basilica, Pope John convenes Vatican II amid all the splendor the Church can offer. The Ecumenical Council, unlike others, was not called to attack the heresies of modernity. The Bishops will confront the Church's need to adapt to changing conditions, addressing issues like lay participation and use of the vernacular (→ 6/21/63).

1962

NOVEMBER

Su	Mo	Tu	We	Th	Fr	Sa
				1	2	3
4	5	6	7	8	9	10
11	12	13	14	15	16	17
18	19	20	21	22	23	24
25	26	27	28	29	30	

1. U.S.S.R. launches rocket to Mars (→ 12/14).

4. U.S. halts atmospheric tests, urges world ban (→ 12/11).

6. U.S.: Democrats gain in largest voter turnout for non-election year; Edward Kennedy wins Mass. Senate seat.

7. California: Defeated gubernatorial candidate concedes, proclaiming, "You won't have Nixon to kick around anymore."

7. Texas: Billy Sol Estes found guilty of real estate swindle.

8. U.S. announces all known missile bases in Cuba have been dismantled (→ 15).

10. Belgium: Jury acquits five in euthanasia of thalidomide baby.

15. Cuba threatens to down U.S. planes on reconnaissance flights (→ 20).

15. Yemen declares war on Saudi Arabia (→ 8/24/65).

19. New Delhi: Nehru asks more U.S. aid as China drives into India (→ 21).

20. JFK bars religious or racial discrimination in federally funded housing (→ 1/25/63).

22. South Africa: Eight die in race riot as U.N. debates sanctions (→ 6/20/63).

25. Paris: De Gaulle supporters win control of National Assembly.

25. South Vietnam: 109 Viet Cong slain in abortive attempt to seize govt. outposts (→ 1/2/63).

27. Peru: U.S.-bound jet crashes, killing 97.

27. U.S., Belgium threaten economic sanctions if Katanga refuses cession to Congo (→ 12/30).

28. Paris: De Gaulle commutes death sentence of Gen. Jouhaud to life imprisonment.

29. Algeria bans Communist Party (→ 9/15/63).

DEATHS

7. Eleanor Roosevelt, ex-first lady, reformer, envoy to U.N. (*10/11/1884).

26. Albert Sarraut, ex-premier of France (*7/28/1872).

28. Queen Wilhelmina of Netherlands (*8/31/1880).

An era is ended as Mrs. Roosevelt dies

Eleanor Roosevelt.

Nov 10. As Eleanor Roosevelt was laid to rest beside her husband this afternoon, the New Deal era came to a quiet close. Dignitaries from around the world came to Hyde Park to pay their respects. It was a time for reflection.

Born in 1884, Mrs. Roosevelt was one of those rare beings who grow steadily in spirit long after most people's ideals have waned. When she married her cousin Franklin D. Roosevelt in 1905, she was a shy, some would say awkward, young woman. When he entered the Oval Office, she was his outspoken assistant. When polio struck him, she was often his guide. When he died, she served the public on her own.

While her husband was President, Mrs. Roosevelt gave frequent press conferences and wrote a popular newspaper column called "My Day." In 1945, she became a delegate to the United Nations, a post she held until 1952. There, she helped draft the U.N. Declaration of Human Rights. In 1961, President Kennedy requested her to serve the U.N. once more. In intervening years she was a self-appointed goodwill ambassador, traveling extensively and seeking rights for minorities and women.

The gathering at her funeral mirrored the world's affection for this woman. Former Presidents Truman and Eisenhower were present, as was President Kennedy. Condolences were whispered in dozens of languages by U.N. representatives. The Roosevelt family had requested no flowers but there were plenty, roses, daffodils and lillies. One of the most beautiful bouquets was sent by the Soviet Union.

Soviet Union closing Cuban missile bases

Nov 20. President Kennedy ordered an end to the month-old United States blockade of Cuba after he was assured that the Soviet Union had removed all of its offensive missiles from the island. Missile and bomber bases have also been dismantled. The final obstacle to a lifting of the "quarantine" of Cuba was cleared this afternoon. Kennedy received a communication from Premier Khrushchev that some 30 aging IL-28 Soviet jet bombers would be shipped out of Cuba soon.

The United States had insisted that the planes were offensive weapons that had to be removed from Cuba as part of the agreement between Kennedy and Khrushchev. The Soviets said the aircraft were defensive in nature, but they reversed their position after ten days of difficult negotiations. Cuba's Premier Fidel Castro, who had claimed the planes were Cuban property, abandoned his position after strong pressure from Khrushchev. Castro is still threatening to shoot down any American planes that enter Cuban airspace. Kennedy said today, however, that reconnaissance flights will continue to verify that new weapons systems are not built in Cuba (→ 12/25).

Bohr, who helped with A-bomb, is dead

Nov 18. Niels Bohr, the Danish scientist who was ranked second only to Albert Einstein among 20th-Century physicists, has died in Copenhagen at the age of 77. One of Bohr's major achievements was to develop the modern concept of the atom, in which electrons move around the nucleus in restricted orbits. After working abroad early in life, he returned to Denmark in 1916 to head an Institute for Theoretical Physics that quickly became a major world center. He won the Nobel Prize in physics in 1922. Flown out of Denmark in a British military plane in 1943, Bohr did much of the theoretical work that made the atomic bomb possible.

Bohrs on their 50th anniversary.

Boeing 727 flies

Nov 27. Up, up and away! The Boeing Company let sail the 727 Trijet at its testing center today. The giant plane is expected to receive Federal Aviation Administration certification soon.

The Boeing 727 Trijet.

India is beaten; war with China ends

Nov 21. Communist China announced a cease-fire in its border war with India and said it would withdraw its troops 12 miles behind the boundary lines that existed in 1959. China said it was making the move to end the hostilities and to implement proposals it had made in October to settle the border dispute. Before the cease-fire, Chinese troops had seized the Indian headquarters at Bomdila near Tibet and were threatening the Indian state of Assam. Faced with defeat on the border and a Chinese invasion, the Indian government said it would "respond positively" to the Chinese offer of a cease-fire (→ 12/6).

1962

DECEMBER

Su	Mo	Tu	We	Th	Fr	Sa
						1
2	3	4	5	6	7	8
9	10	11	12	13	14	15
16	17	18	19	20	21	22
23	24	25	26	27	28	29
30	31					

1. Philadelphia: Navy defeats Army 34-14 in football.

5. London: Heavy smog kills 55.

6. India closes consulates in Communist China (→ 8/1/63).

11. Montana: First 20 Minuteman missiles become operational at Malmstrom Air Force Base (→ 1/20/63).

12. JFK endorses emergency communications link, Washington to Kremlin (→ 4/5/63).

13. Borneo: British crush revolt against plan to create Federation of Malaysia (→ 9/16/63).

16. Cape Canaveral: Explorer 16 launched, first satellite only for meteorite studies (→ 5/7/63).

20. Dominican Republic: Pro-American Juan Bosch Gavino wins presidency (→ 9/28/63).

21. Nassau: U.S., U.K. plan joint NATO atom force (→ 1/30/63).

25. Miami: Bay of Pigs captives, just ransomed, vow to return and topple Castro (→ 1/13/63).

26. Berlin: Eight escape to West, crashing through gates in armor-plated bus (→ 1/17/63).

30. New York: Green Bay Packers beat Giants 16-7 to keep NFL championship.

CULTURAL EVENTS, 1962

Literature: Anthony Burgess' "A Clockwork Orange"; James Baldwin's "Another Country"; John Barth's "The Sot-Weed Factor"; Albee's "Who's Afraid of Virginia Woolf?"; Faulkner's "The Reivers"; Solzhenitsyn's "One Day in the Life of Ivan Denisovich"; Ken Kesey's "One Flew Over the Cuckoo's Nest."

Academia: Levi-Strauss' "The Savage Mind"; Thomas Kuhn's "The Structure of Scientific Revolutions"; Marshall McLuhan's "The Gutenberg Galaxy."

Music: Britten's "War Requiem"; "Green Onions"; "Go Away, Little Girl"; "Blowin' in the Wind."

The Arts: Warhol, Roy Lichtenstein, Jasper Johns, Robert Indiana launch Pop Art in N.Y.

Film: John Huston's "Freud"; Welles' "The Trial"; "Cleopatra," Taylor, Burton; "Lawrence of Arabia," Academy Award.

Horizons widening for current novels

After a couple of years of books dealing with solitary figures, writers in 1962 started considering the community. Novels now have multiple voices, speaking up on issues current and eternal.

"Ship of Fools" is short-story writer Katherine Anne Porter's long-awaited novel. Her boat, the Vera, is a German liner sailing from Mexico to Germany in the summer of 1931. The passengers are an ethnic and social mix, and Porter carefully reveals their interactions.

Ken Kesey's novel "One Flew Over the Cuckoo's Nest" is set in an insane asylum. A half-Indian narrates the story, and one inmate named McMurphy stands out, but "Cuckoo's Nest" is about an isolated, oppressed group. The sufferings and shenanigans of mental patients are unflinchingly brought to light.

Anthony Burgess' "A Clockwork Orange" is a satirical but harrowing look at a Sovietized, Americanized society gone mad—a futuristic distopia where teenagers run wild until their minds are controlled.

"Letting Go," by Philip Roth, follows in the steps of his 1959 "Goodbye, Columbus." He still discusses the Jewish-American community and its crises domestic and financial in a half-humorous vein. James Baldwin's "Another Country" uses explicit language to describe Negroes and whites in Harlem and Greenwich Village.

Cartoonist Charles M. Schulz wrote the heartwarming book "Happiness Is a Warm Puppy," peopled with wise small fry and a huggable beagle called Snoopy.

U.N. forces invade Katanga; Tshombe flees

Blue U.N. helmets in Katanga.

Dec 30. For the third time in 16 months, United Nations forces are on the move in Katanga. This time, the troops are under orders not to stop fighting until they end once and for all Katanga's secession from the rest of the Congo. Two previous agreements were later reversed. Katangese President Moise Tshombe, who fled to Salisbury, Southern Rhodesia, accused the United Nations of forcing its will on Katanga and creating "a new Algeria" there. "We have always been prepared to negotiate," Tshombe said, "but if they wish to force a solution on us, all Katangians, including myself, prefer to die."

Last Friday, United Nations forces announced they had captured the headquarters of Tshombe's security forces in the capital of Elisabethville. The international troops were given more flexibility to use their weapons as they cleared roadblocks set up by the gendarmes. "If they shoot at us, we will shoot back," one official said. United Nations planes strafed Kolwezi and Jadotville, centers of the extremely profitable mining operations still run by a Belgian company. The airport at Kolwezi was destroyed. U.N. forces also seized Kamina, northeast of Elisabethville, and Kipushi, which sits on the Northern Rhodesian border (→ 1/2/63).

Tanganyika a republic; Nyerere is leader

Dec 9. Exactly one year after it gained its independence from Great Britain, Tanganyika, a former United Nations Trust Territory, is a republic. Although it has broken all direct ties with the crown, the new nation remains in the British Commonwealth.

The occasion was marked by a stirring ceremony at the National Stadium in Dar-es-Salaam, as the new nation's green, black and gold flag was unfurled before 75,000 elated spectators. The flag was simultaneously raised on the summit of Mount Kilimanjaro, the highest peak in Africa. Delegates from 17 nations were on hand to witness a festive display of dancing by Masai, Wamakonde and Wasumkuma tribesmen.

Earlier, 50,000 persons lined the beaches to bid farewell to Richard Turnbull, the departing British Governor General, and his wife, Lady Turnbull.

Julius Nyerere, the former schoolteacher who led the independence movement, was sworn in as

Nyerere pled his case at the U.N.

Tanganyika's first President. Nyerere said that his nation's new constitution would advance "the implementation of democracy in an African context." Rashidi M. Kawasawa, the former Prime Minister, was named Vice President of Tanganyika (→ 10/29/64).

Steinbeck wins Nobel Prize for literature

Dec 10. The Nobel Prize for literature has gone to John Steinbeck, author of "The Grapes of Wrath" and "East of Eden." Steinbeck's latest book is "Travels With Charley: In Search of America." Charley is Steinbeck's French poodle.

Linus Pauling received the Peace Prize for his efforts against nuclear arms. The renowned chemist persuaded over 11,000 scientists to sign an anti-war petition and gave the paper to the U.N. In 1958, he wrote a tract called "No More War!"

Lev Landau of the U.S.S.R. got the physics prize for studies in condensed states of matter. John Kendrew and Max Perutz share the chemistry prize for their findings on hemoproteins. And an Anglo-American team won in physiology for exploring the structure of DNA.

Footlights out for Laughton, a prime actor

Charles Laughton.

Dec 15. Character actor Charles Laughton has died, leaving his widow, actress Elsa Lanchester. He was 63. Once a gold-medal student at the Royal Academy of Dramatic Art, Laughton in later years tackled his roles with hammish abandon.

Laughton and his wife left Britain for the United States in the 30's. He played a huffy butler in "Ruggles of Red Gap" (1935) and an unloved bellringer in "The Hunchback of Notre Dame" (1939). Laughton may be best remembered for his implacable Captain Bligh in "Mutiny on the Bounty" (1935).

Spacecraft sends close-up photos of Venus

Dec 14. The Mariner 2 spacecraft gave mankind its first close-up observations of another planet today as it flew by Venus and beamed data from its instruments across 36 million miles of space to earth.

The signals contained data on the temperature and atmosphere of Venus, a mysterious cloud-shrouded planet whose surface temperature might be hot enough to melt lead.

Mariner 2 was launched at Cape Canaveral 109 days ago and followed a trajectory covering 180 million miles toward its rendezvous with Venus. The success of the mission was endangered as the spacecraft became increasingly hot as it flew closer to the sun. Twice during the early morning hours, an automatic timer aboard Mariner failed to turn on instruments that were to make the temperature readings. Radio signals from earth finally turned on the instruments. Those signals traveled three minutes to reach Mariner, setting a record in interplanetary communications. The instruments made the measurements five hours later, during a 40-minute period when Mariner flew within 21,100 miles of the surface of Venus.

James E. Webb, head of the National Aeronautics and Space Administration, called Mariner's flight an "historic scientific event" and an "outstanding first in space for our country and the free world" (→ 16).

Iconoclastic Leonard Bernstein, musical renaissance man, has conducted the New York Philharmonic Orchestra since 1958.

New nations proclaimed in Africa, Asia and the Caribbean

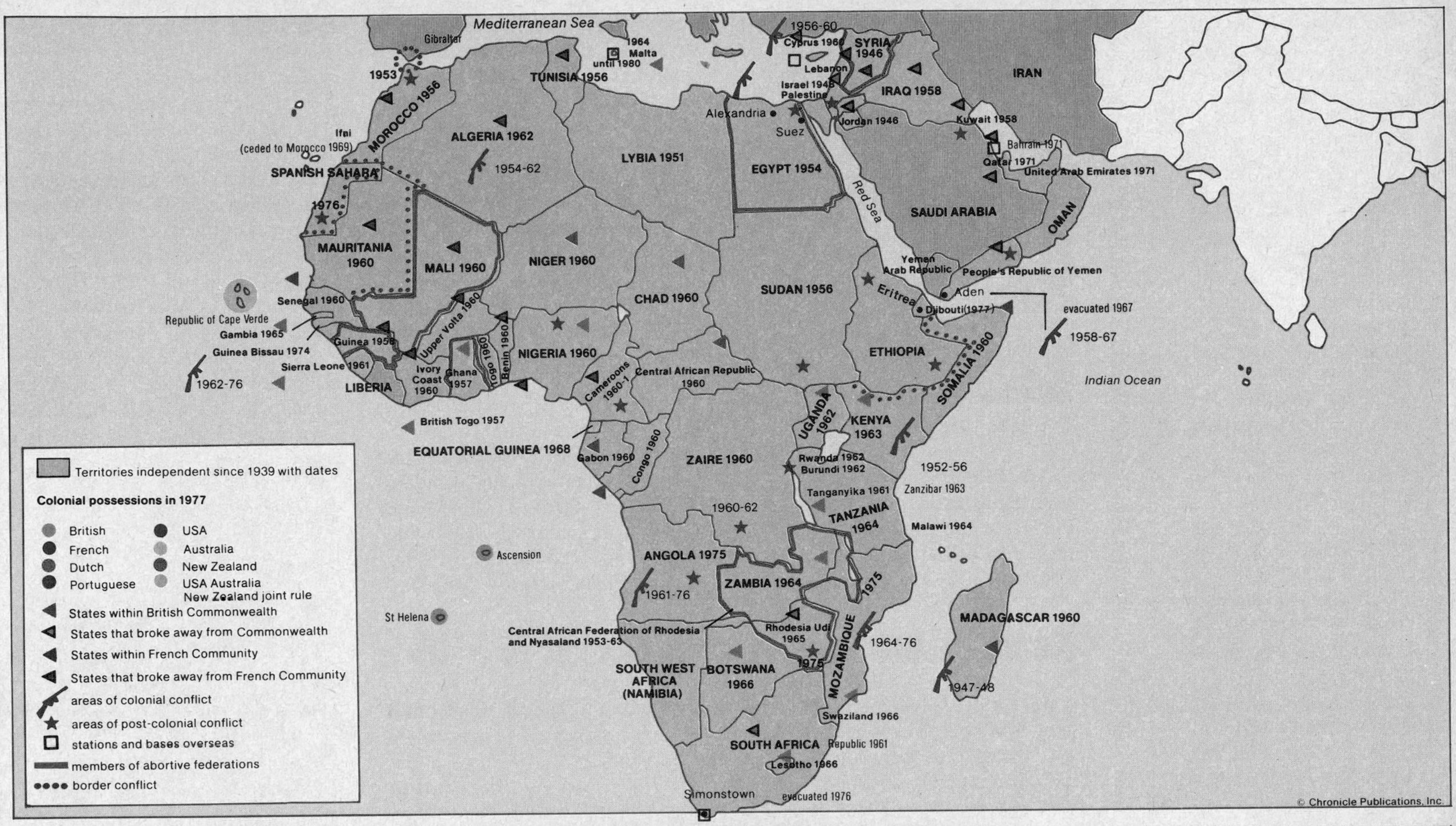

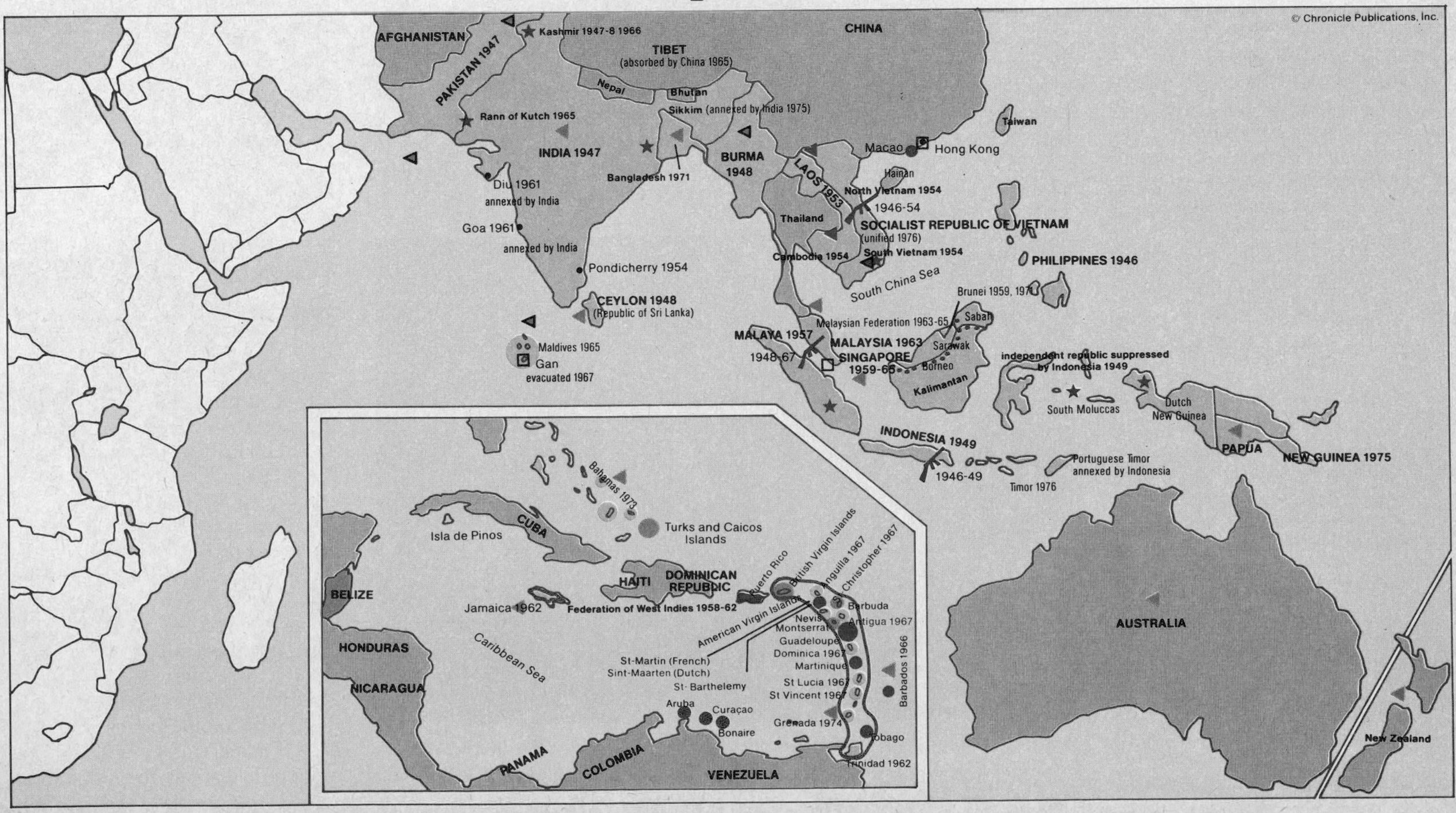

Territories independent since 1939 with dates

Colonial possessions in 1977

- British
- French
- Dutch
- Portuguese
- USA
- Australia
- New Zealand
- USA Australia New Zealand joint rule
- States within British Commonwealth
- States that broke away from Commonwealth
- States within French Community
- States that broke away from French Community
- areas of colonial conflict
- areas of post-colonial conflict
- stations and bases overseas
- members of abortive federations
- border conflict

Mediterranean Sea
Gibraltar
1953
MOROCCO 1956
Ifni
(ceded to Morocco 1969)
SPANISH SAHARA
1976
ALGERIA 1962
1954-62
TUNISIA 1956
1964 Malta until 1980
LYBIA 1951
Alexandria
Suez
EGYPT 1954
1956-60
Cyprus 1960
SYRIA 1946
Lebanon
Israel 1948 Palestine
Jordan 1946
IRAQ 1958
IRAN
Kuwait 1958
Bahrain 1971
Qatar 1971
United Arab Emirates 1971
SAUDI ARABIA
OMAN
Red Sea
Yemen Arab Republic
People's Republic of Yemen
Aden
evacuated 1967
1958-67
Djibouti (1977)
Eritrea
MAURITANIA 1960
MALI 1960
NIGER 1960
CHAD 1960
SUDAN 1956
ETHIOPIA
SOMALIA 1960
Republic of Cape Verde
Senegal 1960
Gambia 1965
Guinea Bissau 1974
1962-76
Guinea 1958
Sierra Leone 1961
LIBERIA
Ivory Coast 1960
Upper Volta 1960
Ghana 1957
Togo 1960
Benin 1960
NIGERIA 1960
Cameroons 1960-1
Central African Republic 1960
British Togo 1957
EQUATORIAL GUINEA 1968
Gabon 1960
Congo 1960
ZAIRE 1960
UGANDA 1962
KENYA 1963
1952-56
Zanzibar 1963
Rwanda 1962
Burundi 1962
Tanganyika 1961
TANZANIA 1964
Malawi 1964
1960-62
Indian Ocean
Ascension
ANGOLA 1975
1961-76
ZAMBIA 1964
MOZAMBIQUE 1975
1964-76
MADAGASCAR 1960
1947-48
St Helena
Central African Federation of Rhodesia and Nyasaland 1953-63
Rhodesia Udi 1965
1975
SOUTH WEST AFRICA (NAMIBIA)
BOTSWANA 1966
Swaziland 1966
SOUTH AFRICA Republic 1961
Lesotho 1966
Simonstown
evacuated 1976

AFGHANISTAN
Kashmir 1947-8 1966
PAKISTAN 1947
CHINA
TIBET (absorbed by China 1965)
Nepal
Bhutan
Sikkim (annexed by India 1975)
Rann of Kutch 1965
INDIA 1947
Bangladesh 1971
BURMA 1948
Diu 1961 annexed by India
Goa 1961 annexed by India
Pondicherry 1954
CEYLON 1948 (Republic of Sri Lanka)
Maldives 1965
Gan evacuated 1967
Taiwan
Macao
Hong Kong
Hainan
LAOS 1953
North Vietnam 1954
1946-54
Thailand
SOCIALIST REPUBLIC OF VIETNAM (unified 1976)
Cambodia 1954
South Vietnam 1954
PHILIPPINES 1946
South China Sea
Brunei 1959, 1971
Sabah
Malaysian Federation 1963-65
MALAYA 1957
1948-67
MALAYSIA 1963
SINGAPORE 1959-65
Sarawak
Borneo
Kalimantan
independent republic suppressed by Indonesia 1949
South Moluccas
Dutch New Guinea
INDONESIA 1949
1946-49
Portuguese Timor annexed by Indonesia
Timor 1976
PAPUA NEW GUINEA 1975
AUSTRALIA
New Zealand

Bahamas 1973
Isla de Pinos
CUBA
Turks and Caicos Islands
HAITI
DOMINICAN REPUBLIC
Puerto Rico
British Virgin Islands
Anguilla 1967
St Christopher 1967
BELIZE
Jamaica 1962
Federation of West Indies 1958-62
American Virgin Islands
Barbuda
Nevis
Montserrat
Antigua 1967
Guadeloupe
Dominica 1967
Martinique
St Lucia 1967
St Vincent 1967
Barbados 1966
St-Martin (French)
Sint-Maarten (Dutch)
St-Barthelemy
Caribbean Sea
HONDURAS
NICARAGUA
Aruba
Curaçao
Bonaire
Grenada 1974
Tobago
Trinidad 1962
PANAMA
COLOMBIA
VENEZUELA

1963

JANUARY

Su	Mo	Tu	We	Th	Fr	Sa
		1	2	3	4	5
6	7	8	9	10	11	12
13	14	15	16	17	18	19
20	21	22	23	24	25	26
27	28	29	30	31		

1. Pasadena: U.S.C. over Wisconsin 42-37 in Rose Bowl.

1. Taiwan: Chiang reveals sending agents to foster revolt on mainland, predicts Peking's fall (→ 10/21).

2. New York: U.N. rejects Tshombe's call for truce talks (→ 7).

2. Viet Cong down five U.S. helicopters in Mekong Delta; 30 reported dead (→ 5/9).

6. Peru: Junta arrests 800 in drive on Communists.

7. Congo: Central govt. takes over Katanga on interim basis (→ 9).

7. U.S. raises postage for first-class letters to five cents.

8. Washington: JFK attends unveiling of "Mona Lisa."

9. Katanga: U.N. places Tshombe under house arrest (→ 15).

13. Miami: 100 U.S. citizens arrive from Cuba (→ 2/6).

16. Tunisia gives death sentence to 13 for plotting assassination of Bourguiba (→ 5/12/64).

17. Berlin: Khrushchev visits Berlin Wall (→ 5/4).

20. Moscow offers to allow on-site inspection of nuclear testing (→ 2/13).

21. Berlin: East German Party Congress ends; Ulbricht, with Soviet support, condemns Chinese invasion of India (→ 3/13).

22. Washington: 12 Iranian students sit in at Iranian Embassy to protest Shah (→ 6/6).

24. U.S.: Cold wave kills 150 across nation.

25. New Orleans: Tulane admits its first five Negroes (→ 2/25).

29. New York: G.M. reports record income of $1.4 bil. in 1962.

30. De Gaulle vetoes Anglo-American plan for multilateral NATO atom force (→ 6/21).

DEATHS

5. Rogers Hornsby, U.S. baseball great (→ 4/27/1896).

18. Hugh Gaitskell, British labor leader (*4/9/1906).

30. Francis Poulenc, French composer (*1/7/1899).

Tshombe ready to join Katanga and Congo

Tshombe, forced to give in.

Jan 15. The long, bloody battle over the secession of Katanga from the rest of the Congo may finally be over. Moise Tshombe, President of Katanga, agreed to reunite the province with the republic, provided that he and his followers are granted amnesty. The agreement, based on a proposal from United Nations Secretary General U Thant, was hammered out over the past 36 hours.

Establishing a formula for the division of Katanga's enormous mining profits was the most difficult part of the talks. Tshombe, who has been under virtual house arrest since returning to Katanga from Southern Rhodesia, was urged to end his secession by more than 30 newly independent African countries. They all approved of United Nations policies in the Congo. For the last few days, Tshombe has had a steady stream of visitors, including Robert Denard, the former French Legionnaire who was the underground commander of mercenaries in Katanga (→ 11/21).

Kennedy proposes 3-year tax cut of $10b

Jan 14. President Kennedy today proposed a net tax cut of $10 billion over the next three years, saying this would stimulate economic growth and reduce unemployment in the United States. He said enactment of his proposal this year "overshadows all other domestic problems."

The president's appeal for tax reduction and reform came in his State of the Union address to a joint session of Congress. He won loud applause, but it is uncertain if Congress will approve the plan unless the president agrees to reduce federal spending.

While taxes on corporations would be reduced to some extent, most of the tax cut would benefit individual taxpayers. For example, a family of four with an income of $3,000 a year would pay a tax of $42 instead of $60. For a family of four making $10,000 a year, there would be a reduction of $304 on the present tax of $1,375.

A week before his speech, JFK welcomed the famed "Mona Lisa" to the National Gallery of Art. French Cultural Minister Andre Malraux, also present, lauded the U.S. for saving the painting, not to mention France itself, in 1945.

No more miles to go: Robert Frost is dead

Jan 29. Four-time Pulitzer winner Robert Frost has died at age 88. Among his mourners are President Kennedy, who had asked Frost to read a new poem at his inauguration. When a brisk wind whipped the pages of the work into illegibility, Frost recited an older one, "The Gift Outright," instead. "The land was ours before we were the land's," he said, seizing the American spirit.

Like Kennedy, Frost loved New England. His images were often rural, as in "Stopping By the Woods on a Snowy Evening." And the line from "Mending Wall," "Something there is that doesn't love a wall," has come to refer to Berlin. Last year, Frost recited it calmly in the U.S.S.R.

Frost, poet of the wilderness.

France bars Britain from Europe market

Jan 14. France's President de Gaulle startled other members of the Common Market by calling a press conference in Paris to oppose the admission of Great Britain to the organization. De Gaulle fears that Britain's lower food prices and cash subsidies to farmers would threaten the cohesion of the market. Europe would run the risk of being absorbed by "an enormous Atlantic community dependent upon the direction of the United States" if England were admitted, de Gaulle said. Foreign ministers of the other market countries are already beginning to object to de Gaulle's comments (→ 2/25/64).

1963

FEBRUARY

Su	Mo	Tu	We	Th	Fr	Sa
					1	2
3	4	5	6	7	8	9
10	11	12	13	14	15	16
17	18	19	20	21	22	23
24	25	26	27	28		

1. U.S.S.R. and France sign trade pact.

1. Federation of Rhodesia and Nyasaland broken up; Nyasaland to be independent under Hastings Banda.

5. Ottawa: Coalition ousts minority Conservative govt. led by Premier Diefenbaker (→ 4/17).

6. U.S. reports all Soviet offensive arms out of Cuba (→ 21).

7. N.Y.: "Mona Lisa" shown at Metropolitan Museum of Art.

9. Boeing continues flights of 727 aircraft.

13. L.A.: Jimmy Hoffa accuses RFK of waging vendetta against him (→ 11/20).

13. U.S. announces plan to sell plutonium to France (→ 4/15).

14. JFK proposes jobs program, including creation of Youth Conservation Corps (→ 1/8/64).

15. Venezuelan Communists seize American freighter, seek asylum in Brazil.

17. Willy Brandt re-elected mayor of West Berlin (→ 10/16).

19. Baghdad: Kurds, fighting for autonomy, begin peace talks with Iraqis (→ 2/10/64).

20. San Francisco: Willie Mays signs $100,000 contract for one year with Giants.

21. JFK cautions Cuba as MIG's fire rockets near American shrimp boat (→ 22).

22. Moscow warns U.S. attack on Cuba would mean war (→ 27).

22. Libya: Earthquakes kill 300, leave 12,000 homeless.

25. New Delhi: Nehru refuses to recognize China-Pakistan border pact (→ 3/2).

25. U.S. Supreme Court frees 187 Negroes convicted in protest in South Carolina (→ 3/1).

26. New York: U.N. dispatches Ralph Buche to Yemen to head off Arab crisis (→ 8/24/65).

27. U.S.S.R. says 10,000 troops will remain in Cuba (→ 28).

27. New York: Mickey Mantle signs one-year, $100,000 contract with Yankees.

28. Paris: Nine arrested in plot to kill Premier Pompidou.

Soviet missiles out of Cuba; troops will stay

Robert Strange McNamara.

Feb 28. Tensions between the Soviet Union and the United States heated up this month over the Soviet military presence in Cuba. At month's outset, U.S. Defense Secretary Robert S. McNamara assured Americans that Soviet offensive weapons have been removed from the island as Soviet Premier Khrushchev vowed to do last fall. But he vehemently asserted that America "will not tolerate the use of Cuba as a base for the export of aggression and subversion."

That tough rhetoric, combined with other complications, including a stepped-up Washington effort to combat Cuban-directed subversion in Latin America, did not sit well in the Kremlin. The Soviets countered by warning that if the U.S. attacked Cuba, the Soviets would come to its defense, even if it meant world war.

Additionally, the Soviets said that while their missiles may be out of the area, they would continue to maintain troops in Cuba (→ 4/27).

Wilson elected British Labor Party chief

Feb 14. The British Labor Party today elected Harold Wilson, its foreign affairs spokesman, to succeed the late Hugh Gaitskell as party leader. Wilson once opposed Gaitskell for his stand against unilateral nuclear disarmament. In selecting Wilson, at 46 the youngest leader in its history, the opposition party chose a man it felt would have the widest appeal in the general elections predicted by many to be held later this year. The suave and witty Wilson, a middle-class intellectual who graduated from Oxford with honors, is one of the party's most experienced politicians and its most skilled debater (→ 10/17/64).

Wilson at party offices, London.

Metal tennis racquet

Feb 22. A revolutionary tennis racquet with a frame of steel rather than wood has been patented by the former French champion, Rene Lacoste. Lacoste's lawyers have arrived in Washington with a sample racquet, which was made in England. In the patent, he expresses a preference for an extruded tubular frame. The strings are passed around regularly spaced hoops like inverted U's. The ring is held in place by a wire passed through the U's and wrapped tightly around the frame. The inventor designed the Lacoste alligator sports shirt.

Abd el Krim is dead

Feb 6. Abd el Krim, the "Wolf of the Rif" and fiery father of Moroccan nationalism, died today in Egyptian exile at 81. He had not been in his native land in 37 years. In the early 20's, his nationalist army of soldiers of fortune and tribesmen swept out of the mountains and inflicted a crushing defeat on a vastly superior Spanish colonial army. But in May 1926, he surrendered to the French and was exiled to the island of Reunion. He escaped to Egypt in 1947 and was awarded the title of national hero by the King of Morocco in 1958.

Iraqi leader ousted in military coup

Feb 8. Described by some as a pro-Nasserite coup and by others as a purge of Communists, a revolt led by the Iraqi air force toppled Premier Abdul Karim Kassim. General Kassim came to power as leader of the 1958 revolution when his troops seized the palace and murdered King Faisal. His policies in Iraq since then have never been very clear-cut. At first favoring cooperation with Egypt, he turned toward the Soviet Union but has recently purged Communists in his government (→ 3/8).

Five taken in plot to kill de Gaulle

Feb 15. Another plot to kill the President of France was uncovered early this morning, just hours before it was to be carried out in Paris. Three men and two women were arrested. Sources say they planned to shoot President de Gaulle in the courtyard of the Ecole Militaire. A rifle with a telescope was found in the apartment of one of the conspirators after police were tipped off by informers. The suspects may be linked to the defendants on trial for the last attempt on de Gaulle's life and to other military officials who blame General de Gaulle for the independence of Algeria.

Alexander Calder's "The Pregnant Whale," finished this year.

1963

MARCH

Su	Mo	Tu	We	Th	Fr	Sa
					1	2
3	4	5	6	7	8	9
10	11	12	13	14	15	16
17	18	19	20	21	22	23
24	25	26	27	28	29	30
31						

1. Greenwood, Miss.: Voter registration drive launches Emancipation Proclamation centennial protests (→ 27).

2. China reports troops have left disputed are in India (→ 8/1).

3. Peru: Landslide kills 300.

3. Peru: Junta chief Ricardo Gody ousted by Gen. Nicolas Lindley Lopez.

4. Paris: Six get death sentence for plot to kill de Gaulle.

5. U.S.S.R. ignores tenth anniversary of Stalin's death (→ 7/15/64).

9. French O.A.S. member Georges Bidault asks political asylum in Germany (→ 6/8/68).

10. Iraq asks Syria to join United Arab Republic (→ 14).

13. China invites Khrushchev to visit Peking (→ 5/9).

14. Cairo: Syrian delegation arrives for unity talks (→ 4/17).

14. Vatican absolves Juan Peron after eight-year excommunication (→ 10/17/64).

15. Washington: Buckminster Fuller gets patent on underwater submarine base.

17. Bali: Volcanic eruption kills 11,000.

17. Rome: Elizabeth Seton becomes first American-born to be beatified.

19. Costa Rica: JFK, six Latin American presidents pledge to fight communism (→ 11/11).

20. Algiers: Premier Ben Bella insists French ban atom tests in Sahara.

23. American Henry Carr runs 200-meters in record 0:20.3.

24. Poland agrees to let some Germans back into territory taken at end of WWII.

25. L.A.: Davey Moore dies of injuries from featherweight bout with Sugar Ramos.

27. U.S.: William Levitt refuses plots to Negroes in test of housing discrimination ban (→ 4/2).

27. Washington: JFK meets with King Hassan II of Morocco (→ 6/7/65).

31. Guatemala: Pres. Miguel Fuentes overthrown by military.

N.Y. newspapers struck for 114 days

March 31. New York newspapers rolled off the presses today for the first time since some unions went on strike 114 days ago. Said one union leader: "This should be the strike to end all newspaper strikes."

Avid readers, happy to end the fast, eagerly snatched up the still ink-wet editions at newsstands. There were cheers, too, at the eight newspapers whose 19,074 employees had been idled by the longest and costliest newspaper blackout in New York's history. It was estimated that the economic losses in circulation and advertising totaled between $190 million and $250 million, while employees of the affected newspapers lost more than $50 million in benefits and wages.

Court decides poor must have lawyers

March 18. The U.S. Supreme Court held today that states must supply free legal services to all poor persons facing criminal charges. The case involved Clarence Earl Gideon, convicted of breaking and entering a poolroom in Florida and sentenced to prison. His request for a lawyer during his trial had been denied. The new Supreme Court ruling, one of the most important in the current term, overturned a 1942 decision of the high court that had held that the United States Constitution required appointment of counsel only in cases involving the death penalty or in such special circumstances as an illiterate defendant.

Syria has eighth revolt since 1945

March 8. Claiming to have won control of the country "without a drop of bloodshed," Syrian army rebels today overthrew their government in a move that met with no serious resistance. The new Syrian leader is identified as Col. Louai Atassi. While the officers in the coup incline toward the Egyptian brand of nationalist socialism, they also appear to favor the more independently minded regime that took charge in Iraq last month. Iraq and the United Arab Republic have threatened war against any country interfering in Syria, a warning believed aimed at Jordan which persists in its opposition to President Nasser. Today's was the eighth revolt in Syria since 1945 (→ 10).

The Rock, Alcatraz, no longer a prison

March 21. The federal prison on Alcatraz Island in San Francisco Bay became a hollow, echoing shell today with the removal of the last 27 prisoners. An Army prison in 1909 and a federal prison since 1934, the Rock has nearly succumbed to the wear of weather and winds. Its walls, from a fort built in the 18th century, have huge cracks and the concrete itself is badly decomposed. This is where federal convicts too difficult to keep in other prisons have been tucked away, such men as Al Capone, Alvin Karpis and other incorrigibles. It was the most expensive prison in the U.S.: $13 a day per prisoner as opposed to $5.40 average elsewhere.

Hitchcock directs Jessica Tandy and a vicious flock of feathered extras. The behind-scenes shot masks the terror instilled by "The Birds" in the film's tiny California town, not to mention audiences across the country.

Poet-doctor William Carlos Williams dies

Williams: "No ideas but in things."

March 4. William Carlos Williams delivered 2,000 babies and dozens of poems. The physician cum poet died today from a cerebral hemorrhage. He was 79 years old.

Williams, who practiced and died in Rutherford, N.J., immortalized the neighboring town of Paterson in a long poem (five books long) of the same name. He was usually more interested in close-ups of nature, more concerned with the petal of a flower than the flower entire.

He studied medicine at the University of Pennsylvania and shortly afterward toured Europe. There, he met fellow student Ezra Pound, who urged him to publish his first book of poetry in 1910.

Billie Sol Estes is guilty of mail fraud

March 28. Billie Sol Estes was convicted today of mail fraud that involved swindling a dozen major finance companies of $24 million worth of mortgage deals. He faces up to 25 years in prison. Estes, a 38-year-old Texan, was accused by the federal government of using non-existent fertilizer tanks as security for the mortgages that he sold to the finance companies. While convicted on four charges, he was acquitted by a federal jury in El Paso, Texas, of eight other counts of mail fraud and of transporting fraudulent documents (→ 4/15).

1963

APRIL

Su	Mo	Tu	We	Th	Fr	Sa
	1	2	3	4	5	6
7	8	9	10	11	12	13
14	15	16	17	18	19	20
21	22	23	24	25	26	27
28	29	30				

2. Birmingham: Rev. King launches new non-violent campaign to end segregation (→ 12).

3. Washington: John L. Lewis retires as president of United Mine Workers of America.

5. Geneva: U.S.S.R. approves hot line to U.S. for emergency communications (→ 6/20).

5. AEC gives Fermi Prize to Robert Oppenheimer for research in nuclear energy (→ 6/17/66)

7. Belgrade: Tito to rule for life under new constitution (→ 10/17).

9. JFK makes Winston Churchill a U.S. citizen.

12. Birmingham: King arrested for leading protest march (→ 14).

14. Alabama: 30 arrested as violence erupts between Negroes and police (→ 25).

15. Texas: Billie Sol Estes given 15 years for mail fraud and conspiracy (→ 6/7/65).

15. London: 70,000 march in A-bomb protest (→ 5/23).

17. Ottawa: Diefenbaker resigns as prime minister (→ 22).

17. Cairo: New United Arab Republic proclaimed by Egypt, Syria and Iraq (→ 27).

20. Madrid: Spain executes top Communist Julian Grimau Garcia, despite Khrushchev pleas.

20. Laos: Pro-Communist forces capture airport stronghold of pro-West troops (→ 4/19/64).

27. Philadelphia: Brian Sternberg sets pole vault mark at 16 feet, 5 inches.

27. Moscow: Castro arrives for visit with Khrushchev (→ 5/1).

27. Baghdad: Palestinian students storm Jordanian Embassy, shouting "Death to King Hussein" (→ 7/19).

29. Port-au-Prince: Haitian police withdraw from Dominican Embassy after besieging 22 Duvalier foes in refuge (→ 8/17).

30. New Hampshire legalizes nation's only sweepstakes.

DEATH

23. Itzhak Ben-Zvi, Israeli president (*11/24/1884).

Wallace adamant on race as Negroes resist

April 25. School desegregation has forced a political showdown between Alabama Governor George Wallace and U.S. Attorney General Robert Kennedy. Kennedy met with the governor to try to convince Wallace to abide by federal integration orders. Wallace, a segregationist, refused to retreat on his threat to defy U.S. law. Kennedy left the meeting frustrated, saying, "It's like a foreign country. There's no communication."

On April 12, Dr. Martin Luther King Jr. and Dr. Ralph Abernathy, two prominent Negro leaders, led a march down the streets of Birmingham, Alabama, to protest the city's racial barriers. Although the demonstration was peaceful, the two ministers and 58 others were arrested for parading without a permit.

Wallace, at war with Washington.

The arrests triggered violence as 2,000 Negroes battled police in a protest for their release. Many people were hurt while the protesters sang "We Shall Overcome" (→ 5/2).

American sub is lost with crew of 129

April 10. The atomic submarine Thresher with 129 men aboard has sunk in the Atlantic, the Navy announced. It is the U.S. Navy's worst peacetime submarine disaster. The cause of the sinking is not known. The Thresher, newest of a class of nuclear attack submarines, went to sea early today for deep diving tests after an overhaul at the Portsmouth, New Hampshire, Navy Yard. She was accompanied by the submarine rescue ship Skylark, which lost contact after the Thresher dived at 9 a.m. today about 200 miles east of Boston. The ocean is 8,400 feet deep in that area, a depth at which the Navy says rescue attempts would be "absolutely out of the question."

Football stars are rapped for betting

Packer running back Hornung.

April 17. The National Football League has been rocked by a betting scandal and the suspension of two of its star players. Paul Hornung of the Green Bay Packers and Alex Karras of the Detroit Lions were barred indefinitely for betting on league games and associating with gamblers or "known hoodlums."

Fines were imposed on five other players for wagering on the 1962 league championship game, and the Detroit club was also fined for ignoring reports of the gambling.

Football Commissioner Pete Rozelle said Karras made at least six significant bets on league games since 1958. Hornung was fined for giving out betting information.

Celtics win fifth straight NBA title

April 24. Bob Cousy could not have ended his 13-year career on a happier note. The littlest Celtic led Boston to its fifth straight National Basketball Association championship by beating the Los Angeles Lakers, 112-109, in the finale of the four-of-seven series. Cousy got only 18 points and was outscored by his teammate, Tom Heinsohn, with 22. But it was his leadership quality that rescued the Celtics when they most needed it. While he was on the bench in the fourth quarter, the Lakers narrowed the gap to 100-99, but his return sparked them to win.

Pearson becomes Canadian Premier

April 22. Liberal Party leader Lester B. Pearson is now the Prime Minister of Canada. He accepted a request by Governor General Georges P. Vanier to form a new Liberal government after John Diefenbaker's Progressive Conservative Party lost seven parliamentary seats, and all possibility of forming a majority coalition, in the general elections on April 8. Pearson, a Nobel Peace Prize winner and former diplomat, has selected his Cabinet members, and announced his hopes for a rejuvenated Canadian economy (→ 5/11).

The brand new T-bird, sleek and trim, is the coolest set of wheels since the '57 Chevy. Slide into the front seat on a spring day and flick a switch to turn on the air conditioner or open the windows. Then lean back and let those fabulous new wheels take you wherever you want to go.

1963

MAY

Su	Mo	Tu	We	Th	Fr	Sa
			1	2	3	4
5	6	7	8	9	10	11
12	13	14	15	16	17	18
19	20	21	22	23	24	25
26	27	28	29	30	31	

1. Moscow: U.S. envoy boycotts May Day ceremonies due to presence of Castro (→ 7/24).

2. Birmingham: 500 arrested in Negro protest march; police disperse crowd with firehoses (→ 6).

4. Chateaugay wins Kentucky Derby, jockey B. Baeza up.

4. Berlin: U.S. Army Captain Alfred Svenson defects to East Germany, asks asylum (→ 6/26).

6. Birmingham: 1,000 arrested in civil rights march (→ 12).

7. Cape Canaveral: Second Telstar satellite launched (→ 16).

9. Saigon: Diem agrees to spend $17 mil. on moving villagers into "strategic hamlets" to isolate them from Viet Cong (→ 6/10).

9. Peking agrees to hold talks with U.S.S.R. on ending ideological rifts (→ 6/24).

11. Premier Pearson agrees to take U.S. warheads in Canada (→ 4/20/68).

12. JFK sends federal troops to Birmingham after riots (→ 16).

14. New York: Kuwait admitted as 111th U.N. member.

16. Washington: Malcolm X scores JFK racial policy (→ 18).

18. Indonesia: Sukarno's self-appointed delegates to Congress make him pres. for life (→ 9/20).

20. U.S. Supreme Court legalizes sit-ins in cities enforcing segregation (→ 21).

21. Federal court orders University of Alabama to admit two Negroes (→ 31).

21. Schneor Zalman Shazar becomes 3rd Israeli pres. (→ 6/16).

22. Soviets bar payment of U.N. dues, charging pro-West bias.

23. Oregon: Portland bans civil defense program, citing uselessness in nuclear war (→ 31).

26. Belgium: 15,000 Walloons demonstrate for separate state.

27. Jomo Kenyatta elected first Kenya prime minister (→ 12/12).

30. Parnelli Jones wins Indy 500.

31. Mississippi: Police jail 600 Negro children (→ 6/1).

31. U.S. report says Soviet, U.S. 1962 atom tests doubled world's radioactive debris (→ 7/20).

Kennedy sends troops to calm Alabama

May 18. In an effort to reestablish order in Alabama, President Kennedy has sent federal troops to the racially divided area. On May 6, about a thousand Negroes were arrested in Birmingham after a protest march against the state's segregation policies. Violence erupted, prompting JFK to use U.S. troops. U.S. Attorney General Robert Kennedy continues his efforts to orchestrate negotiations between Negro and white leaders; in one proposed deal, Negroes were asked to halt their demonstrations until the new city administration officially takes office. Yet, Negro leader Rev. Martin Luther King Jr. considers such plans to be "too little, too late."

Malcolm X, a more radical Negro spokesman, assailed the Kennedy administration for its inaction and its condemnation of Black Muslims, saying, "Instead of attacking the Ku Klux Klan and the White Citizens' Committee, Kennedy attacked Islam, a religion."

Malcolm X, militant in Negro fight.

The president returned to Washington today after a one-day tour of the South, where he hailed the civil rights struggle and asked for Negroes to fight peacefully (→ 20).

Cooper makes 22 orbits, lands safely

May 16. Major L. Gordon Cooper today completed America's longest manned space flight when he piloted his Mercury capsule to a landing in the Pacific after 22 orbits of the earth. Cooper, who had to take manual control of the spacecraft for the landing when the automatic system failed, guided it to within four miles of the aircraft carrier Kearsarge, the recovery ship, 115 miles east of Midway Island. His flight of 34 hours, 20 minutes carried him 600,000 miles and lasted almost four times longer than the longest previously flown by an American astronaut. Soviet cosmonauts have flown longer missions, of three and four days.

Dr. Charles Berry, head of the space flight medical team, said Cooper showed only minor changes in blood pressure on landing, although he experienced some dizziness. Cooper spent seven hours asleep, drawing curtains over the windows of his Faith 7 spacecraft at 10:30 p.m. and awakening at 6 a.m. as he flew over Australia. He landed at 7:24 p.m. and was greeted minutes later by a phone call from President Kennedy, who said, "That was a great flight" (→ 6/19).

African states form unity organization

May 25. Leaders of 30 independent African states have adopted a charter creating an Organization of African Unity, which will try to establish political, economic and defense links. The African leaders taking part also pledged their support to anti-colonial movements, agreeing to set up a fund to assist freedom fighters in areas still under foreign control.

Nelson Rockefeller: Divorced and wed

May 4. Potential presidential candidate Nelson Rockefeller wed a divorcee today, following his own divorce from his wife of 31 years. Rockefeller and Mrs. Margaretta Fitler Murphy were married in a brief ceremony in Pocantico Hills, New York. They will honeymoon at one of Rockefeller's estates, a Venezuelan pleasure ranch. Republican leaders disagreed on the New York Governor's chances of winning his party's nomination next year. One West Virginia official thought Rocky's image was now badly tarnished in that state.

Churchill retiring after long career

May 1. Sir Winston Churchill will not run again for Parliament. His long political career will end when the next general election takes place, at the latest in October 1964. Sir Winston has served in the House of Commons since he was first elected in 1900, except for the two years from 1922-24. He guided Britain through the critical years of World War II, becoming Prime Minister in 1940 and inspiring his country's resistance to the Nazis. His party was defeated after the war, and he led the opposition until the Conservatives regained power in 1951. He resigned as prime minister in 1955 in favor of Anthony Eden.

Soviets give death penalty to a spy

May 11. Oleg Penkovsky, formerly a Soviet government official, who had confessed to spying on his nation for the United States and Britain, today received his sentence: death. As a Soviet judge read the sentence, the crowded Moscow courtroom erupted in applause. Hearing this, Penkovsky maintained the same tough exterior he had shown throughout the trial. His co-defendant, a British businessman, Greville Wynne, was given three years in prison and five at hard labor for his part as courier of secret military information.

Ursula Andress and Sean Connery join to battle "Dr. No" as James Bond takes to the screen.

1963

JUNE

Su	Mo	Tu	We	Th	Fr	Sa
						1
2	3	4	5	6	7	8
9	10	11	12	13	14	15
16	17	18	19	20	21	22
23	24	25	26	27	28	29
30						

1. Birmingham: Gov. Wallace vows to defy injunction to integrate Univ. of Alabama (→ 9).

9. New York: Martin Luther King denounces JFK's civil rights policy (→ 11).

10. Saigon: Buddhist monk Ngo Quang Duc dies by self-immolation to protest persecution by Diem government (→ 13).

12. Mississippi: NAACP leader Medgar Evers shot dead in ambush (→ 15).

12. Washington: JFK establishes President's Advisory Council on the Arts.

16. Jerusalem: Ben Gurion resigns as Israeli premier and defense minister (→ 6/1/67).

17. U.S. Supreme Court bans required reading of Lords Prayer and Bible in public schools.

18. Alabama: 450 Negroes arrested for defying injunction against sit-ins (→ 24).

18. London: Cassius Clay KOs Henry Cooper in fifth, just as he predicted (→ 2/20/64).

20. Geneva: U.S., U.S.S.R. agree on hot line between Washington and Moscow (→ 8/30).

20. South Africa: Report indicates one out of 236 in total population are jailed (→ 8/2).

20. New York: Arthur Ochs Sulzberger named president and publisher of N.Y. Times.

21. St. Louis: Bob Hayes sets record in 100-yard dash, 0:09.1.

21. Paris: France annouces it will withdraw from NATO fleet in North Atlantic (→ 5/13/64).

23. Massachusetts: Julius Boros wins U.S. Open golf title.

24. Rev. King, James Baldwin, Malcolm X, on TV, call JFK's leadership inadequate (→ 7/4).

24. Moscow: Kremlin rebukes Communist leadership in China (→ 7/21).

27. Henry Cabot Lodge appointed U.S. ambassador to South Vietnam (→ 7/15).

30. New York: Ken Rosewall wins U.S. Pro tennis title.

30. Rome: Pope Paul VII crowned in St. Peter's Square.→

Kennedy at Berlin Wall

Kennedy speaks at the Berlin Wall: "Ich bin ein Berliner" (I am a Berliner).

June 26. President Kennedy was treated to the most extraordinary welcome of his life today as more than a million West Berliners turned out to cheer him in the streets of the divided city. Kennedy did not let them down. "Ich bin ein Berliner" (I am a Berliner), the president declared, expressing his solidarity with the isolated people of this city, who live surrounded by the Communist bloc. The crowd of 150,000 at City Hall roared their approval. "All free men, wherever they may live, are citizens of Berlin," the president said.

Kennedy also made a strident denunciation of Communist philosophy. "There are some who say in Europe and elsewhere, 'we can work with the Communists.' Let them come to Berlin," the president said. "And there are even a few who say that it's true that communism is an evil system but it permits us to make economic progress. Let them come to Berlin."

Later, in a speech at the Free University of Berlin, Kennedy clarified his apparent rejection of dealing with Communists. The president indicated he was criticizing movements which try to combine democratic and Communist elements.

Kennedy was scheduled to get his first look at East Berlin at the point where the wall joins the Brandenburg Gate. East Berlin authorities had blocked the view, however, by hanging large red flags from the gate. The president got a better look at Checkpoint Charlie, the crossing point to East Berlin controlled by the United States. The Communists had hung signs condemning what they called a fascist and militaristic revival in West Germany. Kennedy was cheered by a small group of East Berliners from their side of the wall (→ 8/7).

Khomeini arrested during Iran rioting

June 6. More than 30 Moslem religious leaders were arrested in Iran as riots spread from Tehran to other cities. One of those arrested was the Ayatollah Khomeini. Iranian security officials say Khomeini and others were trying to topple the regime of Shah Mohammed Reza Pahlevi. The fighting in Tehran became so intense that the shah and his family took refuge at the summer palace in Saadabad. Shiite mobs were allegedly recruited and paid by the religious leaders, who are opposed to the shah's land reforms and new rights for women. Three unveiled women were massacred by one mob (→ 1/26/65).

Soviet Union puts first woman in space

June 19. Chalk up another first for the Soviets in outer space. Junior Lieutenant Valentina Tereshkova has become the first woman to blast off and circle the globe. She came back to earth today after her Vostok VI capsule made 48 revolutions in just under three days. Tereshkova was called "my space sister" by a male astronaut, Lt. Col. Valery Bykovsky, who was circling the earth at the same time in another capsule. The two flights are apparently part of the Russian plan to dock two capsules together in outer space.

A large part of Tereshkova's flight was broadcast on television to the Soviet Union and Eastern Europe. Premier Khrushchev spoke to her by radio. Many Muscovites were proud of the mission. "Valya my love," sang one young man with a harmonica, "you are higher than even the Kremlin" (→ 1/29/64).

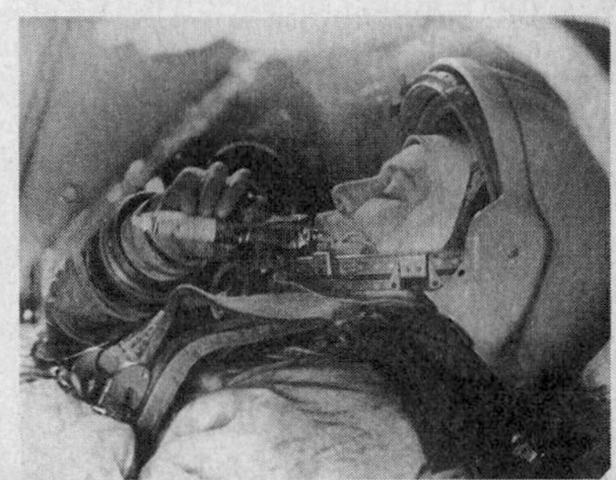

Valentina Tereshkova, in training.

John XXIII dies; Pope Paul VI crowned

June 30. It has been a tumultuous month for Roman Catholics, as a much-beloved Pope is mourned, and a new Pope is crowned. Pope John XXIII, born Angelo Roncalli in 1881, died on June 3, after a long struggle with stomach cancer. He was said to be in considerable pain but lucid in his last hours, as family and Church officials gathered around his bedside to pray. His body was interred in the catacombs of St. Peter's Basilica two days later.

Pope John, popular among non-Catholics too, was hailed by world leaders and religious figures as a tireless champion of the cause of peace and religious unity, and was acknowledged as a powerful force for "modernization" in the Church.

On the 21st, the College of Cardinals, in one of the shortest conclaves on record, elected Giovanni Battista Montini, Archbishop of Milan, as the 262nd occupant of the throne of St. Peter. He has chosen the name Paul VI, and his resplendent coronation took place at the Vatican today.

Pope Paul is generally believed to be a theological liberal, one who is committed to the process of aggiornamento, or reform, begun by John XXIII. He is expected to reopen the Ecumenical Council, which was suspended during his predecessor's illness (→ 7/2).

Funeral services for John XXIII.

Pope Paul VI is crowned.

Sniper kills Medgar Evers, Negro leader

June 15. Ten days before his death, Negro civil rights leader Medgar Evers calmly said, "If I die, it will be in a good cause." On June 12, the National Association for the Advancement of Colored People Field Secretary lay slumped and bleeding in front of his Jackson, Mississippi home from a sniper's rifle bullet. The murder sparked rioting in the South. Hundreds of Negroes took to the streets in Jackson after the funeral for Evers. Police arrested 27 in the brick-throwing melee. The Federal Bureau of Investigation joined local authorities in the hunt for the killer. The NAACP is offering a $10,000 reward for information leading to the arrest and conviction of the slain leader's assassin (→ 18).

Wallace forced to take Negro students

June 11. Alabama Governor George Wallace temporarily abandoned his fight to prevent the enrollment of two Negro students at the University of Alabama. On orders from President Kennedy, National Guardsman were sent to the scene to ensure admission of Vivian Malone and James Hood to Foster Auditorium for school registration.

Wallace pledged in his gubernatorial campaign "to stand in the schoolhouse door" to stop the resumption of desegregation in the Alabama educational system. He did, but was forced to step aside. Wallace said he would continue to raise constitutional questions about federal "interference" in his state. The students' enrollment is seen as a political defeat for Wallace (→ 12).

Buddhist holds fiery protest in Saigon

June 13. Buddhist protests in Vietnam reached a peak three days ago when a monk in Saigon immolated himself. Convinced that South Vietnam's heavily Buddhist population is being unfairly treated, the United States has warned President Diem it will officially condemn his oppression of the Buddhists unless he promptly moves to redress their grievances. Diem, a Catholic, heads a predominately Catholic regime. His quarrel with the Buddhists became prominent in May when Vietnamese soldiers fired on a Buddhist demonstration in Hue, killing nine persons.

According to Washington, Saigon cannot beat the Viet Cong unless it first inspires confidence among its mainly Buddhist people, and the current religious conflict is seen as being possibly an irreparable blow to Diem's reputation (→ 27).

Martyrdom, fiery challenge to Diem.

Sex scandal forces out British war minister

June 17. "Resign!" cry Laborites, but British Prime Minister Harold Macmillan and the Conservative Party tenuously hold on to the government. Today, his party has a slim majority—69 votes—in the House of Commons. Macmillan's credibility has crumpled since the revelations of the Profumo scandal.

Until a few weeks ago, John Dennis Profumo was an illustrious politician. He had been a respected member of Parliament and held several prestigious offices, the latest being Secretary of War. He and his wife, a former actress, often took well-publicized state trips together.

On June 5, Profumo resigned his office. He was charged with having sex with a 21-year-old prostitute named Christine Keeler. Miss Keeler was having a concurrent affair with a Soviet naval officer who returned to Moscow in December.

Another name sullied in the scandal is that of osteopath Dr. Stephen Ward. Ward is accused of introducing Profumo and Miss Keeler after having told the woman to elicit top security information for the Soviets. Ward is in custody; Profumo, merely disgraced, is living in comfortable seclusion.

Macmillan was slow to investigate the Profumo case. He admits it is "very unfortunate" that secret service agents delayed presenting him with the evidence (→ 7/31).

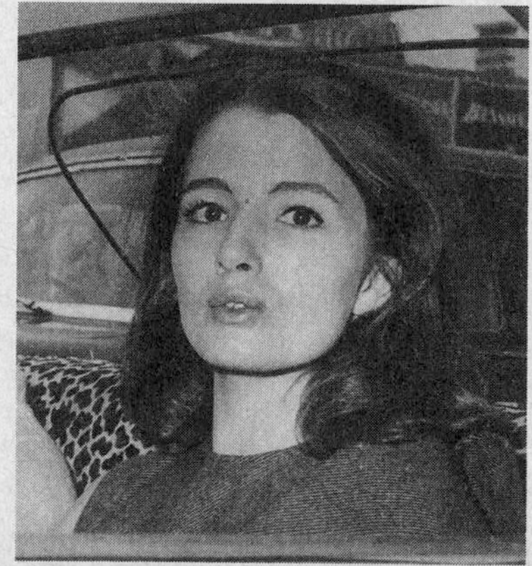

Temptress Christine Keeler . . .

and toppled politician Profumo.

1963

JULY

Su	Mo	Tu	We	Th	Fr	Sa
	1	2	3	4	5	6
7	8	9	10	11	12	13
14	15	16	17	18	19	20
21	22	23	24	25	26	27
28	29	30	31			

1. U.S. ousts Soviet diplomat Gennadi Sevastyanov for trying to recruit CIA agent.

1. U.S. postmaster general inaugurates zip code.

2. Rome: JFK confers 40 min. with Pope Paul VI (→ 11/2).

6. Wimbledon: Chuck McKinley over Fred Stolle 9-7, 6-1, 6-4; Margaret Smith over Billie Jean Moffitt 6-3, 6-4.

12. Miss. Gov. Ross Barnett says JFK aiding Communist plot to divide U.S. in racial strife (→ 21).

12. Ecuador: Newly installed junta bans Communist Party.

14. Jacques Anquetil wins Tour de France for fourth time.

14. Washington: Sen. Thomas Dodd claims Ghana has become first Soviet satellite in Africa.

15. South Vietnam: Buddhist leaders announce renewal of struggle against Diem (→ 30).

15. Moscow: U.S., U.S.S.R. open talks on nuclear test ban treaty (→ 20).

19. Syria executes 12 pro-Nasser rebels after yesterday's attempted coup (→ 4/28/64).

20. Moscow: U.S. and Soviets reach tentative accord on atom test ban (→ 26).

20. Indonesia announces it will rename Indian Ocean to call it Indonesian Ocean.

21. JFK names Negro Howard Jenkins to National Labor Relations Board (→ 8/18).

22. Las Vegas: Sonny Liston KOs Floyd Patterson in first to retain heavyweight title.

23. JFK asks Congress to abolish immigration quotas.

24. Havana: Govt. expropriates U.S. Embassy building and grounds (→ 9/6).

26. Yugoslavia: Earthquake hits Skoplje, killing over 1,000.

26. JFK calls test ban treaty "a victory for mankind" (→ 8/5).

30. South Vietnam: 60,000 Buddhists march in protest against Diem govt. (→ 8/13).

DEATH

23. Alexander Gerassimov, Russian painter (*8/12/1881).

British name Kim Philby as Soviet spy

July 1. The British government disclosed today that Kim Philby, a newspaper correspondent and former diplomat, is a Soviet agent and was the "third man" in the Burgess-Maclean spy case of the 1950's. Philby, who disappeared in January from Beirut, Lebanon, where he was a correspondent for The Observer of London, is presumed to be behind the Iron Curtain. The security service has since discovered that Philby was working for the Soviets prior to 1946.

Donald Maclean and Guy Burgess were working as Foreign Office diplomats when they vanished in 1951, only to appear in the Soviet Union, where they still live. In 1955, the British government made public its suspicions that the two had been working as Soviet spies. Philby was asked to resign from the Foreign Service because of his "Communist associations." However, at that time there was no evidence that Philby was the one who had warned Burgess and Maclean that the security service was aware of their spy activities.

Philby, villain in British spy case.

Doctor in Profumo case takes overdose

July 31. Osteopath Dr. Stephen Ward lies in a coma tonight, hours after a jury found him guilty of running a prostitution ring. Ward was accused of arranging trysts between a call girl and former British Secretary of War John Profumo, who has since resigned. Ward apparently tried to commit suicide with an overdose of barbiturates.

Ward has not been formally charged with any form of treason, but it is understood in political circles that he also arranged an affair between the prostitute and a Soviet naval officer. Theoretically, his "employee," Miss Christine Keeler, could have traded secrets between the officer and Profumo. The London judge in the case will postpone sentencing until Ward recovers. He could get up to 14 years (→ 8/3).

Peking, Moscow fail to resolve differences

July 21. Communist China and Soviet Russia have failed to resolve their ideological differences after two weeks of secret meetings in Moscow, in which national representatives discussed "important questions of principles concerning contemporary world developments, the international Communist movement and Soviet-Chinese relations."

The main ideological point of contention between the Communist powers concerns relations with the West. The Soviet Union advocates "peaceful coexistence" and charges that China is flirting with a war it could not survive. The People's Republic of China views this stand as an abject surrender to capitalism.

Throughout the talks, the Russians and Chinese continued to lambast each other's ideas in the press, leading Western observers to believe that the battle of ideas could lead to a formally declared split in the international Communist movement. A worldwide meeting to prevent such a split has been suggested.

The evils of drink: President tossed out

July 11. Toppled after tippling, Ecuador President Carlos Arosemena Monray has been ousted by the military. Army leaders said Arosemena was "frequently drunk, spotted the national honor and sympathized with communism." A four-man junta replaces him. Arosemena came to power in November 1961 with an air force coup. He advocated relations with Cuba over strong military protest.

Noted minister held in integration move

July 4. Rev. Eugene Carson Blake, head of the United Presbyterian Church, joined hundreds of protesters pushing for integration of an all-white amusement park near Baltimore, Maryland. He and 287 others were arrested. Among them were 12 Protestant, Catholic and Jewish clergymen. This is the first time a large group of clergy from all three faiths joined in a confrontation against race discrimination. Despite the protest, the park's owners refuse to allow in Negroes, claiming their white customers like the segregationist policy (→ 12).

Yugoslav earthquake claims 1,000 lives

July 26. A death toll of more than 1,000 is feared from an earthquake that struck the city of Skoplje in Yugoslavia today. More than 80 shock waves rocked the city for nearly three hours this morning, destroying 85 percent of Skoplje's living quarters, rebuilt after severe damage in World War II. Officials say more than half of the city's 170,000 residents have been made homeless. The United States and Sweden are flying in emergency medical supplies as officials warn of a possible typhus epidemic. At least 500 bodies have been recovered from the ruins and as many are still buried.

Young girl sits atop her ruined home.

1963

AUGUST

Su	Mo	Tu	We	Th	Fr	Sa
				1	2	3
4	5	6	7	8	9	10
11	12	13	14	15	16	17
18	19	20	21	22	23	24
25	26	27	28	29	30	31

1. Soviets offer India arms to block China (→ 12/30/64).

2. New York: U.S. tells U.N. it will halt arms sales to South Africa (→ 8/12/64).

3. London: Dr. Stephen Ward, convicted in prostitution scandal, dies of drug overdose.

5. Utah: Craig Breedlove sets world land speed record at 407.45 mph (→ 10/5/64).

5. Moscow: U.S., U.S.S.R., U.K. sign test ban treaty (→ 9/24).

7. West Germany reports 16,456 have escaped from East in two years since Berlin Wall (→ 11/6).

11. Cairo: Nasser calls Israel threat to Arab world (→ 23).

13. Saigon: 17-year-old Buddhist monk burns self to death (→ 21).

17. Haiti: Govt units attack rebel base near Dominican border (→ 23).

18. Birmingham: James Meredith gets diploma from University of Mississippi (→ 20).

20. JFK says he opposes job quotas based on race (→ 28).

21. Saigon: Army arrests over 100 Buddhist monks (→ 22).

22. Washington: South Vietnamese ambassador resigns to protest Saigon's treatment of Buddhists (→ 25).

23. N.Y.: Syria, Israel accept U.N. cease-fire in fighting north of Sea of Galilee (→ 1/17/64).

23. Haiti suspends all rights to fight rebels (→ 6/14/64).

25. South Vietnam: 1,000 protesting students arrested after schools closed yesterday (→ 26).

26. Washington: Last three Vietnamese diplomats leave U.S. over Saigon actions (→ 27).

27. Cambodia severs ties to South Vietnam (→ 29).

29. Saigon: U.S. Ambassador Henry Cabot Lodge refuses to give up Buddhists in U.S. mission (→ 9/7).

DEATHS

1. Theodore Roethke, American poet (*5/25/1908).

2. Oliver La Farge, writer, "Laughing Boy," 1929 Pulitzer (*12/19/1901).

Martin Luther King: "I have a dream"

Aug 28. More than 200,000 peaceful demonstrators filled Washington today to demand the passage of civil rights legislation. It was the largest protest of its kind in the history of the capital. Solemn speeches were given at the Lincoln Memorial, and leaders of the mostly black protesters met with President Kennedy and congressional leaders. But the huge demonstration had the aura of a large country fair until the Rev. Dr. Martin Luther King Jr. spoke. It was the President of the Southern Christian Leadership Conference who transformed the day from an outing to a crusade. It was King who gave the protesters a mission and the nation a goal.

King speaks of justice and equality, "a dream rooted in the American dream."

"I still have a dream," said King, his voice rising and falling in the spirit and tradition of a Biblical orator. "It is a dream chiefly rooted in the American dream. I have a dream that one day this nation will rise up and live out the true meaning of its creed: 'We hold these truths to be self-evident, that all men are created equal.'" At the end of each thought, King paused and the crowd was silent. "I have a dream," he would begin again, and the crowd roared with approval. A dream that "the sons of former slaves and the sons of former slave owners" would sit together at "the table of brotherhood" in Georgia. A dream that freedom and justice would replace oppression in Mississippi. A dream that his people would be "free at last, free at last, thank God Almighty, free at last."

Some 200,000 crowd the Mall.

Roy Wilkins of the NAACP, John Lewis of the Student Nonviolent Coordinating Committee and other civil rights leaders also spoke, generally in words that were more harsh and less inspired than King's.

Bob Dylan, the young folksinger, sang about "the day Medgar Evers was buried from a bullet that he caught." Singer Joan Baez promised, "We shall overcome," and baseball player Jackie Robinson pledged, "We cannot be turned back." Peter, Paul and Mary wondered, "How many times must a man look up before he can see the sky?" Singer Josephine Baker flew from Paris to announce, "You are on the eve of a complete victory."

The politicians in Washington are not convinced. Senate Democratic leader Mike Mansfield said he was not certain that the protest would speed passage of civil rights legislation. Republican leader Everett Dirksen agreed. Until Congress does act, King's dreams will remain just that (→ 9/2).

Kennedy baby lost; best efforts fail

Aug 8. The day-and-a-half-old son of President and Mrs. Kennedy has died of respiratory distress due to the lungs not being fully developed. He was placed in a high-pressure oxygen chamber, but the struggle to keep breathing became too much for his heart. Five and one-half weeks premature, he was delivered by Caesarean section and weighed four pounds, ten ounces. He was christened immediately and given the name Patrick Bouvier Kennedy. Mrs. Kennedy received a two-pint blood transfusion.

Georges Braque, Cubist painter, is dead

Aug 31. The first artist to raise the painter's canvas to a higher plane—and a lower one—has died in France. Georges Braque, with Pablo Picasso, founded the Cubist style. He exposed an object's many layers, mingling time with vision.

Braque was born May 13, 1882. Like most painters at the turn of the century, he was impressed by the Impressionists. Like others, he flowed into a Fauve period, favoring loose shapes and shimmering hues.

In 1907, he met Picasso at a Cezanne retrospective in Paris. Both of them admired Cezanne's geometry, his way of rendering distant hillsides into pale pyramids. They experimented on their own. Braque painted still lifes, tableware and musical instruments. In the 30's he turned to beach scenes. The last 20 years birds were his passion.

"Still Life with Playing Cards."

Greatest train robbery

Aug 14. More than $5 million in cash and jewelry were snatched in 15 minutes from a British train this morning. A dozen bandits clutching crowbars and guns made off with the booty. They may have pulled off the world's greatest heist.

In the wee hours of the morning, laden with $2.8 million in British pound notes, a train was making its regular Glasgow-to-London run. As it approached Cheddington, a tiny town on the outskirts of London, the train got a "slow" warning on the signal lights. It eased to a stop as the signal turned red.

The co-engineer stepped out to a railroad phone, but found the wires cut. He looked around and found himself staring down a gun barrel. Pushed back to the engine, he found the driver slumped, unconscious from a head wound. The bandit, handkerchief over his face, told the co-engineer to keep quiet. Or else.

The thieves uncoupled the engine and first two cars from the rest. Mail sorters in the rear cars innocently kept on sorting. The front cars were driven to a side track, where the money and gems were stashed into a waiting truck. Detectives suspect an inside job. Otherwise, they have no clues (→ 3/26/64).

Moscow-Washington hot line working

"The direct . . . link between Washington and Moscow is now operational."

Aug 30. A diplomatic "hot line," designed to reduce the risk of accidental war, went into operation between Moscow and Washington today. The opening was announced in a one-sentence Defense Department statement: "The direct communications link between Washington and Moscow is now operational." Instead of an exchange of official messages, the link was opened when Americans sent a standard test signal over the line and received one from the Soviet end. From now on, the line will be used only in times of emergency, for messages between the two heads of government.

The link consists of a teletype line running from machines in the Pentagon to a facility near the office of Premier Khrushchev in the Kremlin. The Americans will send messages in English, the Soviets in Russian. Each message will be encoded to prevent its interception along the 10,000-mile line. American and Soviet negotiators agreed to establish the hot line when delays hindered communications in last year's Cuban missile crisis.

W.E.B. Du Bois to be buried in Ghana

Du Bois, civil rights pioneer.

Aug 27. William Edward Burghardt Du Bois, the father of the Negro intelligentsia and of African liberation, born in Great Barrington, Massachusetts, 95 years ago, will be laid to rest in Ghana, West Africa, fulfilling a final wish.

In 1961, when the great Negro scholar left the United States forever to live in Ghana, and applied for membership in the Communist Party, he wrote: "My great-grandfather was carried away in chains from the Gulf of Guinea. I have returned so that my dust shall mingle with the dust of my forefathers."

Throughout his life, Du Bois, the first Negro to earn a Harvard Ph.D., was instrumental in the civil rights movement, from the founding of the NAACP to tomorrow's march on Washington. In one of his poems, he wrote: "I heard the Song of Children, crying/"Free!"/I saw the face of Freedom/And I died."

Odets, dramatist of the Depression, dies

Clifford Odets, dramatist of the left.

Aug 14. The author of "Waiting for Lefty," Clifford Odets, has died at the age of 57. Odets wrote protest plays of the 30's, denouncing the capitalist machine and championing labor unions. In the 50's he ostensibly "sold out," writing for Hollywood. However, although his story themes changed from the political to the personal, he consistently sought reform.

Philadelphia-born Odets was a member of New York's social-conscious Group Theater. He was its outstanding playwright. After the immediate success of "Lefty" in 1935, he saw his optimistic "Awake and Sing" come to the stage. In 1937, he wrote "Golden Boy," about a violinist turned boxer.

Among Odets works that came to film was "Country Girl," starring Bing Crosby and Grace Kelly. That picture focused on a wife trying to help her alcoholic husband.

Times Square, the crossroads of the nation, the "Great White Way," illuminated at night by a profusion of enormous electrical signs.

1963

SEPTEMBER

Su	Mo	Tu	We	Th	Fr	Sa
1	2	3	4	5	6	7
8	9	10	11	12	13	14
15	16	17	18	19	20	21
22	23	24	25	26	27	28
29	30					

1. Japan: 100,000 protest visit of U.S. nuclear subs (→ 11/9/64).

2. Alabama: Gov. Wallace calls state troopers to Tuskegee H.S. to prevent integration (→ 3).

3. Public schools begin integration in South Carolina and Louisiana (→ 5).

5. Birmingham shuts schools scheduled for integration (→ 10).

6. Cuba accuses U.S. of raid on air force base (→ 8).

7. Saigon: Police arrest 800 teenagers in protest (→ 11).

8. Havana: Castro calls JFK "the Batista of his time" (→ 1/23/64).

10. Alabama: Schools integrate as JFK federalizes Alabama National Guard (→ 15).

10. Washington: JFK halts draft for married men.

11. U.S. tells Diem to oust brother Nhu or face cut in aid (→ 21).

15. Algeria: Ben Bella elected president, plans to nationalize European settlers' land (→ 23).

16. Malaysia formed as Malaya, Singapore, Sarawak and North Borneo unite (→ 18).

17. Britain: $1 mil. anti-missile system goes into operation.

18. Jakarta: Mob of 10,000 burn British Embassy in protest over formation of Malaysia (→ 1/23/64).

20. Indonesia announces takeover of all British companies (→ 3/25/64).

23. Algiers: Ben Bella says French atom test in Sahara will accelerate nationalization plans in Algeria (→ 3/13/64).

24. U.S. Senate ratifies test ban treaty (→ 10/15).

28. Dominican Republic: Ex-President Juan Bosch sent into exile (→ 4/25/65).

29. Alabama: Two arrested in in church bombing (→ 30).

30. South Carolina: Two anti-segregation protests broken up; 189 Negroes seized (→ 1/23/64).

DEATH

4. Robert Schuman, French statesman, advocate of European unity (*6/29/1886).

Valachi names Genovese as boss of bosses

Sept 27. Joseph M. Valachi, a convicted killer-for-hire, testified before the Senate Investigations Committee today, where he named the men who he said were the leaders of organized crime in the United States. Valachi admitted to being a member of a New York crime syndicate headed by Vito Genovese, whom he called the "boss of bosses." Other underworld organizations are headed by Carlo Gambino and Thomas Luchese, according to Valachi.

Valachi described organized crime as an association of "borgatas" (families) that had distinct levels of rank, from "bosses" to "lieutenants" to "soldiers." Valachi, who claimed he wished to "destroy" organized crime through his testimony, recounted in grim detail the episodes of murder, extortion and assault that are common in organized crime, or the "Cosa Nostra" as it is called by its members. Valachi has also claimed that Genovese ordered his death when the two of them were in prison together, and it has since been reported that the syndicate has offered $100,000 for his assassination.

Valachi during Senate investigation.

Genovese, "King of the Rackets."

Bombing of church kills 4 Negro girls

Sept 15. Tragedy rocked Birmingham, Alabama, again today, when a bomb exploded during a Sunday church service, killing four Negro girls. The terrorist act ignited racial rioting in which two Negro boys were shot to death.

Local authorities requested and received state guardsmen, who attempted to control the various shootings, fires and street fighting throughout the city. Birmingham Mayor Albert Boutwell, in a television speech, pleaded with residents to end "this senseless reign of terror." Sheriff Melvin Baily called the day of bloodshed "the worst in the history of Birmingham."

The tension in Alabama has centered around desegregation. Governor Wallace has repeatedly defied integration laws and at the start of the school year, he ordered police to prevent the opening of certain high schools. He said the action was directed "to preserve the peace." However, the schools opened a week later with the admission of Negroes when President Kennedy, through the force of federal troops, ordered Wallace to obey (→ 29).

George Grosz work shown in New York

Sept 25. Two New York galleries begin exhibits today on the work of George Grosz. Grosz, who died in 1959, was a Marxian painter. With savage detail he satirized Germany during WWI and throughout its decadent, corrupt postwar years.

"Nightmare," by George Grosz.

Red China accused of 5,000 incursions

Sept 22. Hostility between the two superpower Communist states has heated, as the Soviet Union accused China of some 5,000 border violations, and today the Kremlin issued a strong warning to the Chinese Communists. Western political experts who examined the long document sent to Mao Tse-tung were surprised by its rhetorical harshness. The statement charged the Chinese had "betrayed" the international Communist cause. It asserted that unless Peking stopped its border incursions and its recent verbal attacks on Moscow, "the most decisive rebuff on the part of the Soviet Communist Party and the entire Soviet people" will be taken.

American analysts seem uncertain what form "a decisive rebuff" would take. The most extreme diplomatic sanction would be to sever formal political relations. Most agree this is unlikely (→ 7/13/64).

U.S. advises Diem to dismiss brother

Sept 21. The Kennedy administration, concerned about the strength of the South Vietnamese government, advised President Ngo Dinh Diem to remove his brother Ngo Dinh Nhu from office. As chief of the secret police, Nhu is responsible for the crackdown on Buddhist leaders following Buddhist demonstrations against the Diem regime.

Through Henry Cabot Lodge, Ambassador in Saigon, the administration also warned Diem that rising congressional criticism of repressive measures by his government could lead to a reduction in military and economic aid. Reflecting the administration's growing concern over developments in Saigon, President Kennedy ordered Defense Secretary Robert S. McNamara and General Maxwell Taylor, Chairman of the Joint Chiefs, to fly to South Vietnam, to review the military effort (→ 10/2).

1963

OCTOBER

Su	Mo	Tu	We	Th	Fr	Sa
		1	2	3	4	5
6	7	8	9	10	11	12
13	14	15	16	17	18	19
20	21	22	23	24	25	26
27	28	29	30	31		

1. Nigeria proclaimed a republic; Nnamdi Azikiwe first president (→ 1/16/66).

1. Washington: JFK meets with Ethiopian Emperor Haile Selassie.

2. New York: Sandy Koufax sets World Series strike-out record with 15 in one game (→ 6).

2. U.S. predicts victory in Vietnam by 1965 (→ 11/2).

3. Honduras: Army ousts Pres. Ramon Villeda Morales; Gen. Lopez Arellano takes power.

3. Prague: Czechs release five Cardinals, including Primate Josef Beran, jailed since 1949 (→ 11/12/64).

5. London: 1,000 hurl eggs at British Nazi leader Colin Jordan and bride after wedding.

6. L.A.: Dodgers beat Yankees to win Series in four straight.

6. Haiti: Hurricane strikes, taking nearly 4,000 lives (→ 13).

9. Italy: Flood kills 2,000 as dam malfunctions.

13. Cuba: Castro says 1,000 died in hurricane Flora.

14. U.S.: Pan Am and TWA order 21 supersonic passenger planes.

15. New York: 17 nations call for U.N. to ban arms in space (→ 26).

15. Algeria mobilizes army to meet Moroccan attack (→ 18).

16. New York Mirror folds.

17. Washington: JFK meets with Yugoslav chief Tito (→ 6/1/69).

18. Morocco charges Algeria with border attacks (→ 27).

21. New York: U.N. votes to bar Communist China (→ 1/27/64).

23. New York: Guggenheim announces gift of 34 Picassos.

25. U.S.: Northeast put on alert for air pollution.

26. Nevada: AEC detonates 12-kiloton warhead underground (→ 4/20/64).

27. Morocco: Army seizes 200 Algerian prisoners (→ 30).

30. Mali: Algeria and Morocco signs cease-fire (→ 2/20/64).

31. Indianapolis: Blast at ice show kills 63, injures hundreds.

President signs treaty for atomic test ban

JFK signs the treaty in Washington.

Oct 7. President Kennedy today approved the treaty to limit nuclear testing, using 17 pens to sign his name to four leather-bound documents, thus moving the historic pact one step closer to the end of the diplomatic maze through which treaties must pass. The ceremony took place in the newly renovated Treaty Room in the White House, the first event there of international significance since the signing of a peace protocol in 1898 ending the Spanish-American War. The room was used for Cabinet meetings from 1865 to 1902.

$250m wheat sale made to U.S.S.R.

Oct 9. President Kennedy announced today the sale of some 150 million bushels of wheat to the Soviet Union at a price tag of $250 million. Kennedy asserted the sales agreement does not radically alter Soviet-American trade relations. "But," he said, "it does represent one more hopeful sign that a more peaceful world is both possible and beneficial to us all." The grain sale will help American farmers, as well as shippers and the entire agricultural complex. Furthermore, it will reduce the American balance-of-payments deficit.

Khrushchev, in need of U.S. wheat.

Macmillan resigns; Home is Premier

Oct 17. British Prime Minister Harold Macmillan, who announced his resignation from office last week, has recommended to the Queen that the Earl of Home, Britain's Foreign Secretary, be named as his successor. The 69-year-old Macmillan surprised Conservative Party leaders when he decided to retire because of poor health. His decision to pass party leadership to Lord Home reflects the infighting between R.A. Butler, Viscount Hailsham and Reginald Maudling to succeed Macmillan as prime minister (→ 10/16/64).

Adenauer retires and Erhard named

Oct 16. Ludwig Erhard, credited by many West Germans for their country's spectacular postwar economic renaissance, was elected Chancellor yesterday. Konrad Adenauer retired after 14 years as head of the government. Adenauer, an outspoken anti-Nazi during the Hitler regime and a fervent anti-Communist after the war, warned again of the dangers of a rapprochement between East and West as he delivered his last speech to the Bundestag. Adenauer's hard anti-Communist line has become less popular in recent years, and the political battle over his successor divided the Christian Democrats. The party finally decided to close ranks behind Erhard (→ 2/16/64).

Paris in mourning for Piaf and Cocteau

Piaf, Parisian street singer at 15.

Oct 11. "When she sang it was more than a voice, it was like an April nightingale." That is how Jean Cocteau described Edith Piaf this morning, having heard she had passed away. Seven hours later, Cocteau himself died. France has lost movers of the mind and heart.

They were both frail in body, but that is where similarities between Cocteau and Piaf end. He was raised by a lawyer; after the best education money can buy, he toured Europe. She, born Edith Gassion ("piaf" is French for sparrow), was raised by her grandmother (a brothel owner) and her acrobat father. She sang on the streets until a gangster put her in a black dress and put her on a nightclub stage.

Cocteau wrote plays (one specifically for Miss Piaf), directed films ("Beauty and the Beast" in 1947) and staged avant-garde shows. Miss Piaf sang "La Vie en Rose" and other torch songs. He died at age 74. She was only 47.

Cocteau, avant-garde playwright.

1963

NOVEMBER

Su	Mo	Tu	We	Th	Fr	Sa
					1	2
3	4	5	6	7	8	9
10	11	12	13	14	15	16
17	18	19	20	21	22	23
24	25	26	27	28	29	30

2. In unprecedented move, pope admits five women as delegates to Vatican II (→ 1/5/64).

5. Newfoundland: Archeologists find Viking ruins predating Columbus by 500 years.

6. East Germany: Under protests from West, Soviets release U.S. convoy, held for 41 hours (→ 12/20).

7. U.S. recognizes new regime in Saigon (→ 1/30/64).

9. Japan struck by disaster; three-train pile up kills 164; mine blast kills 327, injures 348.

10. Somalia bars Western aid for larger Soviet plan (→ 2/8/64).

11. Brazil: Pres. Joao Goulart questions effect of Alliance for Progress on Latin American economic problems.

12. Moscow: Yale professor Frederick Barghoorn arrested on spy charges (→ 14).

14. Moscow: Steinbeck, Edward Albee denounce arrest of Frederick Barghoorn (→ 16).

14. Greece to free hundreds jailed in Communist uprising of 1944-1950.

15. Argentina voids all foreign oil contracts (→ 10/17/64).

16. Moscow releases Barghoorn, still insisting he was spy.

19. Ike rededicates Gettysburg cemetery on 100th anniversary of Gettysburg Address.

20. Nashville: Hoffa's lawyer disbarred for trying to bribe juror (→ 3/12/64).

21. Congo ousts Soviet aides, suspends ties to Moscow (→ 7/10/64).

26. New York: Stocks up $15 bil. in biggest one-day rally.

28. Cape Canaveral renamed Cape Kennedy (→ 29).

29. Montreal: 119 die as Trans-Canada jetliner crashes.

30. Beatles' "She Loves You" hits third on charts (→ 2/12/64).

DEATHS

22. Aldous Huxley, British novelist, essayist, "Brave New World" (*7/26/1894).

22. C.S. Lewis, British Christian scholar, writer (*11/29/1898).

John F. Kennedy shot dead in Dallas

The final moments: JFK in Dallas.

Nov 22. President Kennedy was killed today by an assassin's bullet as he rode in a motorcade in Dallas.

Just 99 minutes after the Kennedy death, Vice President Lyndon B. Johnson was sworn in as the 36th President of the United States in the presidential jet plane as it stood on the runway at Love Field. The plane, bearing the body of the slain head of state and the 55-year-old new president, then took off for Washington, D.C.

Shortly after the fatal shooting, police arrested Lee Harvey Oswald and charged him with murder. The 24-year-old Oswald once defected to the Soviet Union and has been active in the Fair Play for Cuba Committee. He is believed to have fired at least three shots from a rifle as he stood in the Texas school book depository where he was employed.

The assassination occured shortly after noon. Cheering crowds lining the streets had been stunned when shots rang out and the 46-year-old president crumpled in the seat of the open limousine, a massive, gaping wound in his head. The car was driven immediately and at high speed to Parkland Hospital, where the president died 30 minutes later without regaining consciousness. Two priests administered last rites to the fallen leader, who was a Roman Catholic.

Jacqueline Kennedy, who had been seated beside her husband in the motorcade, was not injured but her stockings were splattered with his blood as she stood beside the new president as he took the oath of office on Air Force One. Her face was sorrowful. She still wore the raspberry-colored suit in which she had greeted welcoming crowds in Fort Worth and Dallas, but she had taken off the matching pillbox hat and her dark hair was wind-blown and tangled. Her hand rested lightly on her husband's coffin as it was taken by hearse from the hospital to the plane.

Johnson, who had been in another car in the motorcade but who was not injured, took the oath of office in the presence of his wife, Mrs. Kennedy and about 25 others who crowded into the presidential cabin on the plane. Judge Sarah T. Hughes, who was appointed to the court in 1961 by President Kennedy, was red-eyed from weeping as she administered the 34-word presidential oath to the onetime Texas farm boy who taught school before going into politics.

Gov. John B. Connally Jr. of Texas, riding in the same car as the Kennedys, was severely wounded in the chest, ribs and arm. He is in serious but not critical condition.

There had been no inkling of what horror the day would bring when the Kennedys arose this morning in Fort Worth. Addressing a crowd in a parking lot near his hotel, President Kennedy was smiling as he said: "Mrs. Kennedy is organizing herself. It takes longer, of course, she looks better than we do when she does it."

Later, at a breakfast gathering in Fort Worth, the president noted his wife's presence by saying: "Two years ago, I introduced myself in Paris by saying that I was the man who had accompanied Mrs. Kennedy to Paris. I am getting somewhat that same sensation as I travel around Texas. Nobody wonders what Lyndon and I wear."

From Fort Worth, the Kennedys and their party flew on to Dallas, an eight-minute flight. Vice President Johnson flew in a separate plane. The president and vice president do not travel together, out of fear of a double tragedy.

In Dallas, the motorcade wound its way along a ten-mile route. Mrs. Kennedy, who seldom accompanied her husband on political outings, appeared to be enjoying herself. As the motorcade neared its end, heading for the Merchandise Mart where the president was scheduled to speak, the shots rang out.

"Oh, no," Mrs. Kennedy cried, cradling her husband's body as he slumped in his seat as the car sped to the hospital.

In the speech that he did not live to deliver, President Kennedy was going to assail right-wing conservatives, saying that voices are being heard in the land, "voices preaching doctrines wholly unrelated to reality, wholly unsuited to the sixties, doctrines which apparently assume that words will suffice without weapons, that vituperation is as good as victory and that peace is a sign of weakness" (→ 24).

LBJ takes the oath aboard Air Force 1, with grief-stricken Jackie at his side.

Moments of sheer terror recorded in amateur movie

An amateur film, blurred like the perception of bystanders, pictures Mrs. Kennedy climbing out of the car seat where her husband lies dying.

A secret serviceman runs toward the car . . .

. . . and, car still moving, climbs aboard . . .

too late to save JFK. already fatally wounded. ▷

Lee Harvey Oswald killed as millions watch on TV

Lee Harvey Oswald's captors appear paralyzed by shock as Jack Ruby unloads his pistol into their prisoner at point-blank range.

Nov 24-26. One .38 caliber bullet pierced Lee Harvey Oswald's left side and the accused killer of President Kennedy fell dead to the concrete floor of the basement of a Dallas jail. Jack Ruby, a Dallas nightclub owner and admirer of the slain president, fired his snub-nosed revolver into Oswald as the alleged assassin was escorted by police from one jail to another. As the shot echoed through the building, a policeman who knew Ruby shouted, "Jack, you son of a bitch." Millions witnessed the murder on television and many are wondering if Ruby acted to keep Oswald from talking.

Today, two days later, a Dallas grand jury indicted Ruby on charges of killing Oswald "voluntarily and with malice aforethought." If convicted he could be sentenced to death. Ruby's attorney, Tom Howard, said his defendant would plead not guilty on grounds of insanity.

Howard offered his version of how Ruby was able to gain access to the municipal building where Oswald was to be moved from. Ruby approached the exit ramp of the basement garage unobserved. As a policeman left his post to talk to another officer, Ruby walked down the ramp and joined the 50 reporters and policemen in the basement.

The transporting of Oswald to a tighter security prison was to be conducted by the county Sheriff. But a last minute change of plans had the city police move the prisoner. To thwart any attempt on Oswald's life, authorities were to use a bullet-proof van for transport; Oswald didn't make it that far.

Speculation that Ruby killed Oswald to prevent him from telling a jury all he knew about the Kennedy assassination prompted President Johnson to order the Federal Bureau of Investigation to conduct a thorough analysis of the shooting.

Ruby was described by his lawyer as a "very emotional man" who killed out of sympathy for Jackie Kennedy; Ruby said he didn't want the former First Lady to have to endure a distressing trial of Oswald. The trial of Ruby is expected to begin in mid-January (→ 25).

Kennedy buried at Arlington; whole nation mourns

Nov 25. A boy played soldier this afternoon and all the world watched and wept. Three-year-old John-John Kennedy saluted along with the honor guard as the body of his father, John Fitzgerald Kennedy, passed before them. America's youngest and possibly most loved President has been laid to rest.

The day dawned clear. Shortly before 11 a.m. the President's widow, Jacqueline, and Robert and Edward Kennedy entered the Capitol's East Rotunda. The three of them kneeled before the coffin and prayed. The casket was raised high upon a catafalque, the same that supported the stilled form of Abraham Lincoln nearly 100 years ago.

After a few moments, the Kennedys retreated quietly toward the East Plaza. Eight bearers in military dress lifted the casket and carried it carefully down the Rotunda steps. They then placed it upon a caisson pulled by six gray horses.

Along Pennsylvania Avenue the caravan rolled, making its slow way toward St. Matthew's Cathedral. Behind the casket walked Mrs. Kennedy, the Kennedy brothers to either side of her. A few yards behind them stepped President Johnson and his wife, Lady Bird. Foreign delegations in loose array followed.

More than 1,100 family members and guests came into the church. When all were seated, a rapt silence was heightened by a dirge played by a bagpipe corps outdoors. Around 12:30, the Most Reverend Philip M. Hannon started the eulogy. His own words failed him; he quoted the former president, reminding the congregation that "the torch has been passed to a new generation of Americans," as Kennedy promised in his inauguration speech.

At 1:15 the service ended. Kennedy family members entered several limousines, Mrs. Kennedy and President Johnson riding together. Ahead, the caisson rolled down Connecticut Avenue, past the Lincoln Memorial, on toward Arlington. Crowds lined the route, solemn and somehow bewildered.

Two hours later, the final speeches, the final prayers, were ended. But never the sadness. Throughout the day, Mrs. Kennedy had stood proud and erect. Her face had been hid by a black veil, while tears glistened in privacy (→ 28).

Gloom hangs over the Kennedys after Requiem Mass. Jackie is flanked by brothers-in-law Edward and Robert. Son John, 3, with daughter Caroline, 6, salutes his father's coffin, parroting a gesture familiar in Washington.

The solemn funeral procession makes its way slowly through the capital.

▷

Coup topples Diem; suicide reported

Nov 2. President Ngo Dinh Diem of South Vietnam was toppled by a swift military coup during the night in Saigon. Units of the South Vietnamese army, air force and marines seized key points in Saigon, forcing President Diem and his influential brother Ngo Dinh Nhu to flee the presidential palace. The coup leaders reported later over Saigon radio that the two had committed suicide.

The insurrectionists were regarded as pro-Western and anti-Communist and to have staged the coup in protest of the repressive measures of the Diem regime that were weakening its popular support. The expectation in Washington was that the military junta would be replaced by a new civilian government, perhaps headed by Vice President Nguyen Ngoc Tho, a highly regarded Buddhist leader. Mme. Ngo Dinh Nhu, currently in the United States on a visit, accused the Kennedy administration of having incited the military coup against her husband (→ 7).

Warren is to head JFK death inquiry

Nov 29. President Johnson has appointed Chief Justice Earl Warren as head of a special commission to investigate the assassination of President Kennedy. Johnson issued a statement tonight instructing the panel "to evaluate all available information concerning the subject."

One reason for the creation of this commission is to stave off competing inquiries from Capitol Hill, so as to give Americans a single, comprehensive report. Congress seems to agree with LBJ. Senate Judiciary Chairman James Eastland said, "You couldn't have both a Senate investigation and a presidential commission at the same time."

The other members of the panel are: Sen. Richard Russell, Democrat of Georgia; Sen. John Sherman Cooper, Republican of Kentucky; Rep. Gerald Ford, Republican of Michigan; Rep. Hale Boggs, Democrat of Louisiana; former Director of the Central Intelligence Agency Allan Dulles; and John McCloy, a former aide to Kennedy (→ 12/9).

1963

DECEMBER

Su	Mo	Tu	We	Th	Fr	Sa
1	2	3	4	5	6	7
8	9	10	11	12	13	14
15	16	17	18	19	20	21
22	23	24	25	26	27	28
29	30	31				

7. Philadelphia: Navy over Army 21-15 in football.

8. Maryland: Jet crash kills 81.

10. Zanzibar regains independence after 73 years as British protectorate (→ 1/12/64).

12. Kenya gets independence in Commonwealth; Jomo Kenyatta prime minister (→ 12/12/64).

18. Moscow: 500 Africans battle police; one protest sign reads, "Moscow, a second Alabama."

20. Berlin: 4,000 cross wall to visit relatives under 17-day Christmas accord (→ 10/1/64).

21. Cyprus: Turk minority riots to protest anti-Turkish revisions in constitution (→ 1/1/64).

22. Paul Robeson returns to U.S. after five-year exile to escape Red Scare persecution (→ 5/24/65).

24. N.Y.: Idlewild renamed John F. Kennedy Airport (→ 1/14/64).

29. Chicago: Bears beat New York Giants 14-10 for NFL title.

DEATHS

12. Theodore Heuss, first pres. of West Germany (*1/31/1884).

14. Dinah Washington, American blues vocalist (*8/8/1924).

25. Tristan Tzara, French poet, father of Dadaism (*4/4/1896).

28. Paul Hindemith, German composer (*11/16/1895).

CULTURAL EVENTS, 1963

Literature: Sylvia Plath's "The Bell Jar"; John Le Carre's "The Spy Who Came in From the Cold"; William Carlos Williams' "Pictures from Brueghel."

Academia: Hannah Arendt's "Eichmann in Jerusalem: A Report on the Banality of Evil"; Barbara Tuchman's "The Guns of August," Pulitzer; Betty Freidan's "The Feminine Mystique"; scientists define quasars.

Music: Peter, Paul and Mary's "Puff the Magic Dragon" and "Blowin' in the Wind"; Bobby Vinton's "Blue Velvet"; Martha and the Vandellas' "Heat Wave."

The Arts: Art Nouveau revived worldwide.

Film: Kubrick and Sellers' "Dr. Strangelove"; Hitchcock's "The Birds"; "Tom Jones," Oscar.

FBI says Oswald acted alone in shooting

Dec 9. The Federal Bureau of Investigation has concluded that Lee Harvey Oswald acted alone in assassinating President Kennedy last month in Dallas.

In its report sent today to the special commission investigating the Kennedy assassination, the FBI also concluded there was no link between Oswald and Jack Ruby, the nightclub owner who killed Oswald in the Dallas police department garage two days later.

Among the FBI findings that point to Oswald as the lone assassin are bits of clothing found on the rifle used in killing the president and fingerprints on wrapping paper that covered the rifle when it was taken into the Dallas school depository from which the fatal shots were fired on November 22. The rifle was identical to one ordered by Oswald under an assumed name (→ 24).

Linus Pauling wins second Nobel Prize

Dec 10. In a ceremony readied a year ago today, Linus Pauling was awarded the Nobel Peace Prize. Pauling's name was picked in 1962, but the Nobel Committee, waiting on the results of a test ban meeting last July, decided to postpone the award-giving. Pacifist Pauling won the chemistry prize in 1954. The literature prize went to George Seferis, the first Greek ever to win the award. A former Ambassador to Britain, the poet juggles the modern with the mythological.

Frank Sinatra Jr. snatched, ransomed

Dec 11. Frank Sinatra Jr. is safe in his parents' Los Angeles home tonight. The 19-year-old son of the famed performer was kidnapped from a Lake Tahoe casino three nights ago. He was drugged, blindfolded and shoved from one car trunk to another. His father paid $240,000 ransom at an undisclosed location. As yet the FBI has not named any suspects. To avoid reporters, Sinatra Jr. took one last ride in a car trunk—in the police car that took him home (→ 2/11/64).

877 saved from liner; 159 may be lost

Dec 23. The first distress calls were heard in Portugal and Morocco. Ships off Madeira rushed to the Greek liner Lakonia after fire broke out on board, but scores of people were trapped by the flames. Some 159 people are missing; 877 were rescued by Belgian, Argentine and English ships. A specially equipped American plane assisted in the rescue effort. The Lakonia was on a two-week holiday cruise.

Heavy clouds of smoke linger around the gutted superstructure of the Lakonia.

1964

JANUARY

Su	Mo	Tu	We	Th	Fr	Sa
			1	2	3	4
5	6	7	8	9	10	11
12	13	14	15	16	17	18
19	20	21	22	23	24	25
26	27	28	29	30	31	

1. Pasadena: Illinois beats Washington 17-7 in Rose Bowl.

1. Cyprus: Makarios announces he will abrogate treaties with U.S., Greece, Turkey (→ 3/16).

2. Ghana: Pres. Kwame Nkrumah escapes fifth assassination attempt (→ 2/5).

8. Washington: LBJ pledges "war against poverty" in State of Union message (→ 2/1).

9. Panama: U.S. forces kill six Panamanian students protesting in canal zone (→ 10).

10. Panama breaks ties with U.S., demands revision of canal treaty (→ 4/3).

11. Toronto: Picasso's never before seen art exhibited.

12. Zanzibar: Nationalists oust Arab govt.; Abeid Karume proclaims people's republic (→ 16).

13. India: 200 die in Hindu-Moslem riot in Calcutta (→ 3/21).

14. Jaqueline Kennedy, on natl. TV, thanks nation for expressing sympathy (→ 3/14).

14. New York: Jackson Pollock exhibit opens.

15. L.A.: "Whiskey-a-Go-Go," nation's first disco, opens on Sunset Strip.

16. Zanzibar: New govt. seizes U.S. consul at gunpoint (→ 6/6/65).

17. Cairo: 13 Arab nations agree to bar Israel from diverting waters of Jordan to irrigate Negev (→ 5/28).

18. New York: Plans disclosed for World Trade Center.

23. South Dakota ratifies 24th amendment, banning poll tax (→ 26).

23. Indonesia and Malaysia agree to cease-fire (→ 8/9/65).

26. Atlanta: 84 held in segregation protest; six hurt (→ 3/3).

27. France opens ties with Communist China (→ 6/30/65).

28. Soviets down U.S. jet over East Germany, killing three.

29. Innsbruck: Ninth Winter Olympics begin (→ 2/9).

30. Cape Canaveral: Ranger spacecraft launched to moon with six TV cameras (→ 2/2).

Pope in Holy Land; sees Greek Patriarch

Athenagoras, Patriarch of Constantinople, receives Pope Paul VI.

Jan 5. Pope Paul VI is braving the tensions and divisions of the Middle East to make an emotional and historic visit to Jerusalem. The pope flew first to Amman, where he met with Jordan's King Hussein. He then drove to Jerusalem, visiting the Jordanian sector of the divided city first. Tears welled in his eyes as he prayed at the Church of the Holy Sepulcher above the tomb of Jesus. Soldiers restrained enthusiastic crowds as he visited the Stations of the Cross.

Pope Paul took decisive steps toward mending five centuries of religious schism and antagonism. He met the Orthodox Patriarch of Jerusalem, and today he also received Athenagoras, spiritual leader of the Eastern Orthodox Church (→ 8/9).

29 die as Panama seeks canal changes

Jan 14. Anti-American demonstrations in Panama have resulted in 29 deaths and injuries to over 70 persons. The bloody protests were ignited after American students waged their own demonstrations over Panamanian restrictions on their display of the American flag in the Canal Zone. However, growing resentment of the U.S. presence in Panama is the chief reason for the violence; many in Panama want more control over the canal. The deaths caused a break in relations between the two nations, but today it was announced that diplomatic ties have been resumed and negotiations are to begin to resolve differences (→ 4/3).

Fidel and Nikita wheel and deal

Jan 23. Cuban Premier Fidel Castro and Soviet leader Nikita Khrushchev have tightened their ideological and commercial links this month. Castro flew to Moscow for political business and to accompany Khrushchev on a hunting trip. Their dealings solidified Cuba's support for the Soviet Union in its recent dispute with China, brought about the inclusion of Cuba in the multi-nation treaty on limiting atomic testing to underground explosions and granted Cuba additional Soviet aid (→ 2/6).

Military dissidents oust Vietnam junta

Jan 30. The military junta that deposed South Vietnamese President Ngo Dinh Diem in November was thrown out of power in another military coup. This one was led by Major General Nguyen Khanh, commander of the Vietnamese army's I Corps. He promptly proclaimed himself chief of state, replacing Major General Duong Van Minh who led the November coup, as Chairman of the Military Revolutionary Council. He said he seized power to thwart a French plot for a neutralist Vietnam (→ 2/1).

British put down 3 African mutinies

Jan 25. At the request of the governments of three former colonies, British armed forces acted to overcome mutinies by African soldiers. It was the first British military operation in Africa since the 1956 Suez crisis. In Tanganyika, 60 helicopter commando units subdued 800 mutineers in a 40-minute assault. In Nakuru, Kenya, an army strike was dispersed by Royal Horse Artillery, and in Uganda, a rebel base near Lake Victoria was seized by members of the Staffordshire regiment.

Curb on cigarette ads is projected

Jan 18. Severe limits on cigarette advertising are being planned by the Federal Trade Commission in response to a Surgeon General's report linking cigarettes to lung cancer and other diseases. The long-awaited report, issued two days ago, said cigarettes cause bronchitis, emphysema and other lung diseases and also increase the risk of heart attacks. It called for "appropriate remedial action." The FTC is proposing warning messages on cigarette packs and an end to advertisements that make use of endorsements by athletes (→ 6/24).

Saturn rocket lifts its heaviest payload

Jan 29. A Saturn rocket today put into orbit a ten-ton payload, heaviest in history, enabling America to surpass the Soviet Union for the first time. The launch of the Saturn came six years to the day after the orbiting of the first United States satellite, which weighed 31 pounds. The liftoff was shown on national television. The key to the Saturn's success was its liquid hydrogen upper stage, which worked perfectly in its first test. A ten-ton dummy version of the Apollo moon capsule is scheduled to be put into orbit by the Saturn in three months (→ 30).

Jan 11. "Oh, goodie," said Peggy Fleming, 15, upon making the Olympic figure skating team.

1964

FEBRUARY

Su	Mo	Tu	We	Th	Fr	Sa
						1
2	3	4	5	6	7	8
9	10	11	12	13	14	15
16	17	18	19	20	21	22
23	24	25	26	27	28	29

1. LBJ picks Sargent Shriver to head anti-poverty drive (→ 26).

1. LBJ rejects de Gaulle's plan for neutral Vietnam (→ 3/29).

2. U.S. spacecraft Ranger 6 crashes on moon, fails to send back pictures (→ 4/8).

2. Innsbruck: Lidiya Skoblikova becomes first to win four golds at one Olympics (→ 9).

5. U.S. calls home ambassador to Ghana to protest anti-American campaign (→ 2/24/66).

6. Cuba blocks water supply to Guantanamo Naval Base in rebuke for U.S. seizure of four Cuban fishing boats (→ 18).

6. London and Paris agree to build rail tunnel under English Channel.

7. New York: 25,000 greet Beatles at JFK airport (→ 12).

8. Somalia, Ethiopia clash at border; 100 killed, 200 injured.

10. Iraq gets cease-fire with Kurdish rebels.

11. Cambodia: Prince Sihanouk blames U.S. for S. Vietnamese air raid on village (→ 3/11).

11. L.A.: Defense attorney says Sinatra kidnapping was publicity stunt (→ 3/7).

16. Bonn: Willy Brandt elected president of Social Democrats (→ 11/20/66).

18. U.S. cuts military aid to five nations in reprisal for trading with Cuba (→ 3/20).

19. French troops restore govt. in Gabon after one-day military coup.

20. Rabat: Morocco, Algeria agree to end border conflict.

20. Malcolm X visits Cassius Clay's training camp (→ 25).

23. U.S. and Britain recognize new Zanzibar government.

25. European Coal and Steel Community and Euratom merge with EEC (→ 7/6/65).

26. LBJ signs tax bill with $11.5 bil. in cuts (→ 3/16).

DEATH

6. Emilio Aguinaldo, hero of Philippine independence struggle (*3/22/1869).

Beatles invade America

Ringo, George, Ed, John and Paul rehearse for the Sullivan show.

Feb 12. A mass shriek of delight erupted yesterday afternoon at Kennedy Airport the moment the Beatles' plane touched down, and the frenzied adulation from fans never ceased during the Liverpool quartet's first day in America. The British rock and rollers—John Lennon, 23; Paul McCartney, 21; George Harrison, 21; and Ringo Starr, 23—rose steadily to the peak of pop stardom in Europe the past year. Their latest record, "I Want to Hold Your Hand," has now skyrocketed to number one on this side of the Atlantic, and judging from the scene yesterday, it appears Beatlemania is conquering the U.S.

Thousands of teenagers overwhelmed the airport yesterday morning, as disk jockeys offered constant updates on the flight and non-stop sets of Beatles music. Police struggled to contain a wild surge in the crowd at 1:20 p.m., when the plane finally landed, and again soon after, when the group, their shaggy hair tousled by the breeze, emerged to wave.

The pandemonium followed the musicians into Manhattan, where a huge gathering outside the posh Plaza Hotel, where the group is staying, waved banners proclaiming "Beatles We Love You" and chanted "We Want The Beatles" on into the evening.

During their stay in New York City, the Beatles will appear live on "The Ed Sullivan Show," which may prove as big a boost to their careers as it once did for Elvis Presley, and perform two sold-out shows at Carnegie Hall (→ 7/6).

The long-haired "Fab Four" pose in a promo for their American tour.

Clay TKOs Liston for world title

Feb 25. The brash, cocky kid, incredibly, kept his word. Cassius Clay left a bleeding, wounded Sonny Liston in his wake as he ascended to the world heavyweight boxing championship.

Only three of the 46 sportswriters were present who thought Clay could fell the giant Liston. And yet, after six rounds, Liston was the victim of a 22-year-old upstart who had bragged he would "float like a butterfly, sting like a bee."

It was Liston himself who said he could not come out for the seventh. He seemingly favored one shoulder while missing punches in the first round, and state-appointed doctors affirmed that an injury had prevented him from defending himself against Clay. An aide said Liston had hurt his arm in training (→ 3/6).

Clay gets tagged by a Liston left.

Innsbruck is host to Winter Olympics

Feb 9. The United States was snowed under by the Soviet Union and a half-dozen other nations in the Winter Olympics, yet managed to pull off the biggest upset at Innsbruck, Austria. A 23-year-old barber from Michigan, Terry McDermott, beat the world's greatest skater, Yevegni Grishin of the Soviet Union, in the grueling 500-meter race. McDermott won the only gold medal that the Americans were able to gain against the Russians, who netted 11, and the Nordic nations. The only other notable achievement for the U.S. was a second and third place finish by Billy Kidd and Jimmy Heuga behind the Austrian, Josef Steigler, in the slalom.

1964

MARCH

Su	Mo	Tu	We	Th	Fr	Sa
1	2	3	4	5	6	7
8	9	10	11	12	13	14
15	16	17	18	19	20	21
22	23	24	25	26	27	28
29	30	31				

3. New York: 464,000 Negro and Puerto Rican students boycott public schools in segregation protest (→ 4/20).

6. New York: Cassius Clay changes name to Cassius X Clay (→ 5/25/65).

7. L.A.: Two men get life sentences for kidnapping of Frank Sinatra Jr.

10. U.S. reconnaissance bomber shot down over East Germany.

11. Cambodia: Protesters riot in demonstrations against U.S. and Britain (→ 15).

13. Paris: Ben Bella meets de Gaulle in surprise visit to France (→ 5/6).

15. Phonom Penh: Cambodia receiving military aid from Communist China (→ 4/26/65).

16. LBJ submits $1 bil. war on poverty program to Congress (→ 8/20).

16. U.N. forces land in Cyprus (→ 8/8).

19. Italy: Tunnel of Grand Saint-Bernard opens in Alps.

20. Key West: Two Cuban hijackers land military helicopter, ask political asylum (→ 25).

21. India rushes troops to east to quell anti-Moslem violence.

23. Supreme Court rules U.S. cannot legally question foreign expropriation of property.

25. For. Rel. Committee Chairman J.W. Fulbright tells Senate U.S. should relax Cold War, recognize Castro (→ 4/30).

25. Indonesia: Pres. Sukarno tells U.S., "To hell with your aid" (→ 1/21/65).

26. London: Ten found guilty in $7 mil. train robbery (→ 8/12).

27. Alaska: Earthquake hits Anchorage; 60-100 dead.

28. Saudi Arabia: King Saud stripped of power; Faisal takes full control (→ 6/21/66).

29. U.S. to add $50 mil. a year to South Vietnam aid (→ 4/18).

DEATHS

20. Brendan Behan, Irish playwright (*2/9/1923).

23. Peter Lorre, Hollywood actor (*8/26/1904).

Jack Ruby is given sentence of death

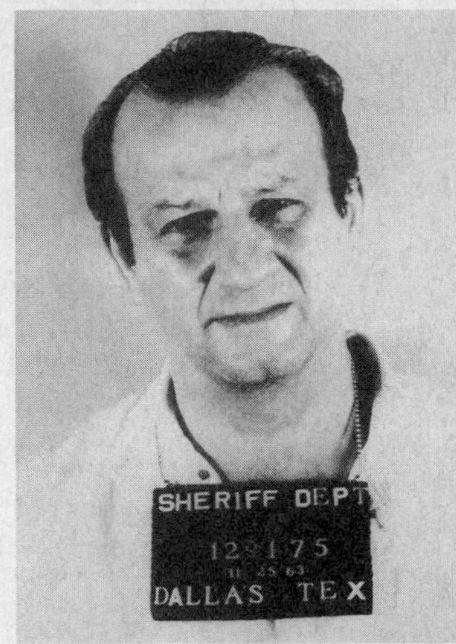

Ruby will go to death row.

March 14. "We find the defendant guilty of murder with malice as charged in the indictment and assess his punishment as death," announced the jury in the trial of Jack Ruby, killer of President Kennedy's accused assassin Lee Harvey Oswald. Ruby's lawyers lambasted the jury before a television audience of millions, calling the verdict "a violent miscarriage." Melvin Belli, chief defense attorney, declared he would appeal the decision outside of Dallas "where there is justice." The prosecution thanked the jury for a fair verdict (→ 9/27).

Malcolm X breaks with Black Muslims

March 8. Negro activist leader Malcolm X has announced he is splitting from the Black Muslim movement led by Elijah Muhammad to form the "black nationalist party." He expressed his dissatisfaction with the Muslims, saying their perspectives are too limiting and offer little prospect for change. He declared the new party will persuade Negroes to replace non-violence with active self-defense against white supremacists. Malcolm, in a passionate style, bellowed cries of revolt: "I shall tell (Negroes) what a real revolution means. There can be no revolution without bloodshed, and it is nonsense to describe the civil rights movement as a revolution" (→ 4/19).

Neighbors ignore cries; woman slain

March 27. Two weeks ago, 37 people witnessed a murder in the making and did nothing to prevent it. New York police revealed this shocking fact today, relating the events of a woman's agonizing death and the reactions of her indifferent neighbors. The murder took place in one of the better middle-class neighborhoods of Queens.

On the night of March 13, Kitty Genovese, 28 years old, was returning home from her job managing a bar. A man approached and knifed her. She screamed for help. Neighbors turned on their lights and peered out; the man slinked off. When people turned out their lights again, he returned to finish the job.

Hoffa is sentenced for jury tampering

March 12. James R. Hoffa, the President of the International Brotherhood of Teamsters, was fined $10,000 and sentenced to eight years in prison today, after his conviction last week on charges of jury-tampering.

Hoffa and three of his associates were found guilty of trying to fix a jury for a conspiracy case against Hoffa in Nashville in 1962: at that time, Hoffa was accused of sharing in a $1 million kickback from a trucking firm. A hung jury led to the dismissal of that case as a mistrial. U.S. District Judge Frank W. Wilson blasted the controversial union leader, saying that Hoffa was "tampering with the soul of the nation." Hoffa plans to appeal the decision (→ 8/17).

Union boss Hoffa—guilty.

Greece's new King faces difficult task

Constantine, 23, assumes the throne amid mounting anti-monarchism.

March 6. The new King of Greece is only 23 years old and he is short on experience to face the difficulties dividing his country. It was only two weeks ago that Constantine was named regent by his father, King Paul. Days later, the king was dead after a serious operation on his stomach. The regent was elevated to king. Constantine faces a country that is increasingly anti-royalist in sentiment. After parliamentary elections last month, Premier Papandreou won the authority to unite republicans and liberals in a new government (→ 9/18).

Wiener, theorist of automation, dies

March 18. Norbert Wiener, the onetime child prodigy who became the father of modern automation, died today at the age of 69. Wiener, a mathematician on the faculty of the Massachusetts Institute of Technology, died during a trip to Europe. He coined the term "cybernetics," from the Greek for "steersman," to describe a system of automated controls of machinery, and used the concept to develop a theory to cover controls and communications in living organisms as well. Born to a Harvard professor, Wiener knew the alphabet at 18 months and received his doctorate at 19. He was considered to be one of the world's leading mathematicians, linguists and philosophers.

1964

APRIL

Su	Mo	Tu	We	Th	Fr	Sa
			1	2	3	4
5	6	7	8	9	10	11
12	13	14	15	16	17	18
19	20	21	22	23	24	25
26	27	28	29	30		

2. Brazil: Pres. Joao Goulart exiled in army revolt; Raniri Mazilli installed (→ 15).

3. U.S. and Panama resume ties after canal dispute (→ 12/18).

4. New York: Home TV recorder demonstrated.

8. First U.S. Gemini test flight orbits earth three times (→ 5/29).

13. White Supremacist Rhodesian Front Party names Ian Smith prime minister (→ 10/27).

13. New York: Michelangelo's "Pieta" arrives in U.S. for World's Fair.

15. Brazil: New Pres. Humberto Branco pledges moderate, democratic line.

16. German Geraldine Mock becomes first woman to complete solo round-world flight.

17. N.Y.: Shea Stadium opens; traffic jams clog Long Island.

18. LBJ orders study to assess need for draft (→ 24).

19. Malcolm X makes hajj (pilgrimage) to Mecca (→ 6/28).

19. Laos: Vientiane seized by army rightists; Souvanna Phouma's coalition ousted (→ 22).

20. Cleveland school boycott gets participation of 86% of Negro students (→ 6/11).

20. Belgian Aurele Vandendriessche wins Boston Marathon for second straight year.

20. U.S. and U.S.S.R. sign pact to cut production of fissionable material for arms (→ 5/23).

22. Laos: Junta asks Prince Souvanna Phouma to head new coalition (→ 5/27).

23. Houston: Ken Johnson is first pitcher to lose no-hitter.

24. Vietnam: Viet Cong fire wounds six on plane of Gen. Westmoreland (→ 5/1).

25. Copenhagen: Head stolen from statue of "The Little Mermaid" (→ 6/1).

26. Boston: Celtics wins sixth consecutive NBA title.

28. Syria abdicates pact of military union with Iraq (→ 5/8).

30. Havana: Castro says Cuba will shoot at U.S. reconaissance planes flying over Cuba (→ 6/2).

Gen. Douglas MacArthur just fades away

Rows and rows of Cadets stand at attention one last time for Gen. MacArthur.

April 5. General of the Army Douglas MacArthur, who led the Allied victory over Japan in World War II, died today at the age of 84. His death, following a series of operations, seemed to fulfill his observation in a farewell speech to Congress in 1951 that "old soldiers never die—they just fade away."

His illustrious military career that ended with a presidential dismissal spanned nearly a half-century. He won the Medal of Honor in World War I, served as chief of staff of the Army in the 1930's before becoming Governor General of the Philippines, commanded Allied forces in the Pacific in World War II and in the Korean War, and directed the postwar occupation that reshaped Japan.

A man of military brilliance and imperious pride, he was relieved of command by President Truman in 1951 for openly questioning the administration's Korean strategy. As a final tribute, his body is to lie in state in the Capitol.

Arnold Palmer wins his fourth Masters

April 12. The suspense is over for Arnold Palmer. Forget the 11 straight tournaments he lost. General Arnie reassured his army that he still had his touch by winning the prestigious Masters for the fourth time. Palmer posted a final-round 70 for a six-stroke victory with a total of 276, only two shots over the record set by Ben Hogan in 1953. The winning purse of $20,000 was welcome, but Palmer was more comforted by the fact that his long slump was over. His nemesis, Jack Nicklaus, finished in a two-way tie for second with Dave Marr.

Palmer clubs his way out of trouble.

April 23. Civil Rights activists yesterday turned the opening of the New York World's Fair into a political forum. Police arrested at least 300 at President Johnson's speech, as hecklers scored Washington's hesitant pursuit of integration. Aided by rain, civil disobedience cut attendance to 92,000 from a projected 250,000.

Death takes the author of "Silent Spring"

April 14. Rachel Carson, the biologist whose book "Silent Spring" started a national debate on the effects of pesticides, died today in Silver Spring, Md., at the age of 56.

Intending to become a writer, Carson became fascinated with biology while in college and did graduate work in the subject at Johns Hopkins University. After teaching for several years, she took a job with the federal Bureau of Fisheries.

An article about the sea led to her first book, "Under the Sea Wind," published in 1941. A later book, "The Sea Around Us," has been printed in 30 languages. But it was the publication of "Silent Spring" in 1962 that made her famous.

The book, which described pesticides as "the sinister and little-realized partners of radiation" in damaging nature, was bitterly attacked by the chemical industry, which described her criticisms as exaggerated. Some vindication of her stand came last year when the President's Science Advisory Committee warned against indiscriminate use of pesticides and said more research was needed on their potential health hazards.

Carson, opposed pesticides.

1964

MAY

Su	Mo	Tu	We	Th	Fr	Sa
					1	2
3	4	5	6	7	8	9
10	11	12	13	14	15	16
17	18	19	20	21	22	23
24	25	26	27	28	29	30
31						

1. Vietnam: USS Card sunk by Viet Cong; all crewmen escape (→ 9).

2. Northern Dancer wins Kentucky Derby.

3. Geneva: Kennedy Round talks on tariff reductions open; 37 nations in attendance.

4. N.Y.: Pulitzer committee decides no fiction, music or drama worthy of Prizes this year.

6. Moscow gives Algeria loan for technical assistance (→ 6/15).

8. Cairo: Khrushchev arrives in United Arab Republic (→ 24).

9. Saigon: Ngo Dinh Can, brother of late Pres. Diem, executed by junta (→ 6/20).

11. Philippines: 74 die as U.S. military plane goes down.

12. France suspends aid to Tunis in retaliation for land seizures (→ 8/13/66).

13. Paris: Manlio Brosio elected to succeed Kirk Stikker as head of NATO (→ 5/30/65).

22. Tokyo opens big Picasso exhibition.

23. Africa: U.S. error spreads 2.2 lbs. plutonium worth $1 mil. into atmosphere (→ 9/24).

24. Cairo: U.S.S.R. extends new loan of $227 mil. to United Arab Republic (→ 3/1/65).

25. New York: Museum of Modern Art opens with new wings.

27. Washington: LBJ meets with Irish President Eamon de Valera (→ 1/14/65).

27. U.S. reports sending aircraft to Laos for use against Pathet Lao rebels (→ 1/13/65).

28. Jerusalem: Palestine Natl. Congress meets to form PLO (→ 1/20/65).

31. Bolivia: Pres. Victor Paz Estensoro wins election to third term.

31. Paris: De Gaulle attends ceremony marking 800th anniversary of Notre Dame.

DEATHS

1. Spike Jones, U.S. composer, band leader (*12/14/1911).

30. Leo Szilard, U.S. physicist, writer, created nuclear fission with Fermi (*2/11/1898).

Ford introduces sporty new Mustang

Ford's sporty new Mustang.

April. Have you driven a Mustang lately? Not likely; Ford's latest car has only just rolled into showrooms. It may not stay there long, though, having an enticing sticker price of just $2,368.

Ford built the Mustang to attract the new youth market. Designers, under Ford Division General Manager Lee Iacocca, studied the most brazen car around —the Falcon. They used some of its features, such as major chassis components, and made them a touch more sporty. It has plenty of standard features and up to 50 available options.

The Mustang isn't perfect: There isn't much leg room in the back seat, and trunk space isn't much. Still, it looks great. A model now on display at the New York World's Fair is eliciting a lot of ogling.

Poitier wins Oscar

April 13. The first Negro to win an Oscar for Best Actor accepted his prize tonight, saying "it has been a long journey . . ." Sidney Poitier starred in "Lilies of the Field." The last Negro to win a major prize was Best Supporting Actress Hattie McDaniel in "Gone With the Wind."

Poitier in "Lilies of the Field."

Aswan Dam in service; menaces Abu Simbel

The relics of ancient Egypt make way for technological progress: Dismantling the temple of Abu Simbel, threatened by flooding from the new dam.

May 14. The waters of the Nile were diverted from their normal channel today to begin the next stage of construction of the Aswan Dam. Soviet Premier Khrushchev and Gamal Abdel Nasser, President of the United Arab Republic, jointly pressed a button setting off an explosive charge that opened a new channel for the Nile. The explosion marked a significant step toward completion of the billion-dollar power and water project, which is designed to foster agriculture and industry in the United Arab Republic, a union of Egypt and Syria. The dam is not scheduled to be completed for another four years.

The diversion channel that was opened today and a temporary coffer dam are steps toward the erection of the High Dam, which will raise the level of the Nile nearly 200 feet and will create an artificial lake nearly 300 miles long. Archeologists already have expressed fear about loss of Egypt's ancient sites to flooding, but the mood today was festive. Khrushchev called the dam the "eighth wonder of the world" and named Nasser a Hero of the Soviet Union for conceiving it.

May 30. A.J. Foyt today added another Indy 500 title to his 1961 victory.

Nehru, India's chief, dies

May 28. A slow-moving funeral cortege containing the body of Jawaharlal Nehru inched through the streets of New Delhi today. A million and a half Indians lined the route to pay final respects to their beloved leader. Nehru, who died of a heart attack yesterday at 74, led India since it won its independence from Britain. He suffered a stroke in January, but resumed a full-time schedule against the advice of his doctors. A search for a new Prime Minister has already begun. Nehru's only daughter, Indira Gandhi, is a leading contender.

Nehru, India's first Prime Minister.

In the cortege, Nehru's body was surrounded by flowers and partly covered by the Indian flag. His white, high-collared jacket had the trademark red rose in the buttonhole. The procession moved past the former symbols of British authority, including the palace where the viceroys lived. Nehru refused to tamper with these symbols. He thought they represented an important part of Indian history. The last Viceroy, Lord Mountbatten, stood near the funeral pyre. He called Nehru "one of the greatest friends of my life." And U.S. Secretary of State Dean Rusk called him "one of the greatest historic figures of our time" (→ 6/1).

B-70 flies three times the speed of sound

May 11. The 2,000-mile-an-hour B-70 bomber, relegated to research status before it got off the ground, made its formal debut today at the North American Aviation plant in Palmdale, California. Only one more B-70 is scheduled to be built in an Air Force program that has cost $1.34 billion. Designed to fly 6,000 miles at an altitude of 70,000 feet, the B-70 sets new standards for aircraft performance. But critics said its technology is obsolete.

Its supporters retorted that the B-70 pioneered in the use of the lightweight metal titanium, six tons of which are used in the aircraft's forward areas. The 275-ton B-70, believed to be the heaviest aircraft ever built, is powered by six jet engines with air inlets big enough for a six-footer to stand upright. The B-70 will begin test flights this summer. Data gathered from flight testing will be used to help design a commercial transport plane that will fly at up to three times the speed of sound.

The obsolete B-70, $1.34 billion victim of an unparalleled technological boom.

Stampede kills 300 at Peru soccer game

May 24. An unpopular decision by a referee touched off a riot at a soccer game between Argentina and Peru that left 300 persons dead and 500 injured. The government proclaimed a state of emergency and suspended constitutional guarantees. Incensed Lima fans spilled out of the bleachers and broke stadium windows. They overturned cars, looted stores and set buildings afire. Mounted policemen threw tear gas bombs and turned dogs loose on the crowd of 45,000. Most of those killed were trampled to death.

Lady Astor, first woman M.P., dies

May 2. When Lady Astor, the former Nancy Langhorne of Virginia who married Waldorf Astor of the $110 million Astor fortune in 1906, became the first woman to sit in the British House of Commons in 1919, some were amused. After a quarter of a century, she having won in seven consecutive elections, many were in awe of her.

Her career was marked by an unceasing opposition to the liquor interests, and she also did much for women and child welfare. In 1944, when she and her husband were 65 (they were born on the same day), she gave up her seat, and the Astors' political and literary gatherings became famous. Her husband died at age 73. She, who would have been 85 on May 19, remained active until suffering a stroke two weeks ago.

Soviet Union is now using spy satellites

May 29. The Soviet Union is using spy satellites to photograph American military bases and installations, Premier Khrushchev disclosed today. Speaking with former Senator William Benton in Moscow, Khrushchev said, "If you wish, I can show you photographs of military bases taken from outer space. I will show them to President Johnson if he wishes." Half-jokingly, he offered to exchange spy satellite pictures with the U.S. (→ 7/31).

1964

JUNE

Su	Mo	Tu	We	Th	Fr	Sa
	1	2	3	4	5	6
7	8	9	10	11	12	13
14	15	16	17	18	19	20
21	22	23	24	25	26	27
28	29	30				

1. India: Lal Bahadur Shastri elected prime minister (→ 8).

1. Copenhagen: "The Little Mermaid" re-erected with new head, stolen five weeks ago.

2. Havana: Three executed as spies for CIA (→ 29).

3. Seoul under martial law as 10,000 riot (→ 4/16/65).

4. Philadelphia: Sandy Koufax pitches 3rd no-hitter (→ 9/9/65).

8. India: Shastri names Indira Gandhi minister of information and broadcasting (→ 1/19/66).

11. Florida: Rev. King and 17 others jailed for trying to integrate restaurant (→ 25).

13. New York: 100 protest arrest of Lenny Bruce (→ 16).

14. Haiti: Francois Duvalier is decreed pres. for life (→ 8/23).

15. Last French troops leave Algeria; 10,000 left in Mers El-Kebir and Sahara (→ 6/20/65).

18. Japan, U.S. linked by underwater communications cable.

19. Mass.: Ted Kennedy severely injured in plane crash (→ 12/16).

20. Washington: Ken Venturi wins U.S Open golf title.

20. Gen. Westmoreland succeeds Gen. Paul Harkins as head of U.S. forces in Vietnam (→ 23).

21. N.Y.: Jim Bunning pitches perfect game, first since 1958.

23. Henry Cabot Lodge resigns as envoy to Vietnam; Maxwell Taylor to succeed (→ 7/12).

24. FTC announces it will require health warnings on all cigarette packages (→ 1/11/65).

28. Malcolm X founds Org. for Afro-American Unity to seek independence for Negroes in Western Hemisphere (→ 2/14/65).

29. Castro's sister defects, accuses Castro of selling Cuba out to "Russian imperialism" (→ 7/2).

DEATHS

9. Louis Gruenberg, American composer, opera "Emperor Jones" (*8/3/1884).

18. Giorgio Morandi, Italian painter (*7/20/1890).

24. Stuart Davis, American artist (*12/7/1894).

Three rights activists missing in Mississippi

June 25. President Johnson ordered 200 naval personnel to Mississippi to assist in the search for three civil rights workers missing since Sunday. Yesterday's discovery of the workers' automobile, burned and demolished, has aroused serious concern over the men's fate and stepped up the manhunt operation.

The men, James E. Chaney, 21, a Negro; Michael Schwerner, 24; and Andrew Goodman, 21, were arrested for speeding, incarcerated, fined and released. That was the last anyone has seen of them. If they have been harmed, it is expected large-scale rioting will erupt.

Congressman John Bell Williams denounced the president's decision to send federal troops to the area. He stated that the case is receiving preferential treatment, noting that for the 188 cases of missing persons listed in New York City, 12,600 federal troops should be sent to the city. Williams said LBJ has succumbed to the wishes of "every left-wing agitator."

Despite the criticism, Johnson stood behind his decision and plans to commit whatever manpower is necessary to find the men (→ 7/2).

Beaverbrook, London press lord, deceased

June 9. Lord Beaverbrook, press baron and champion of the British Empire, died today in Surrey, England, at age 85. Born as Max Aitken, the son of a Presbyterian minister in Canada, he left school at 14, amassed a fortune and founded an empire of sensational newspapers of vast circulation (The Daily Express, The Sunday Express, The Evening Standard, The Glasgow Evening Citizen). He became a power in the British government and as Minister of Aircraft Production in Churchill's war Cabinet he played a crucial role in the World War II effort.

Lord Beaverbrook.

Lenny Bruce, comic, on trial for obscenity

June 16. Nightclub comedian Lennie Bruce goes on trial today in a New York City court on charges of obscenity. It is not new for Bruce, who faced similar accusations in Chicago and Los Angeles. The cities take exception less to his subject matter than to his vocabulary; he uses expletives to describe everyday occurrences. His lawyer, who successfully defended the novel "Lady Chatterly's Lover," will hold forth alone. The 37-year-old comic, a known heroin-user, is ill.

Bruce, expelled from U.K. last year.

Pole vault mark set

June 5. Fred Hansen pole vaulted 17 feet, 1 inch in setting a new world record at the United States championships today. The former Rice University star brushed the bar as he went over, but it stayed intact after a quiver. The former mark of 17 feet, .75 inch was set by John Pennel in Miami last year. Hansen's nearest competitor, Billy Pemelton of Abilene, vaulted 16 feet, 1.5 inches. Hansen just missed at 17 feet, 3.75 inches (→ 25).

1964

JULY

Su	Mo	Tu	We	Th	Fr	Sa
			1	2	3	4
5	6	7	8	9	10	11
12	13	14	15	16	17	18
19	20	21	22	23	24	25
26	27	28	29	30	31	

2. Washington reports Castro's sister has been CIA informant for four years (→ 6).

3. Wimbledon: Roy Emerson over Fred Stolle 6-4, 12-10, 4-6, 6-3; Maria Bueno over Margaret Smith 6-4, 7-9, 6-3.

6. London: Beatles first film, "A Hard Day's Night," released in Britain (→ 8/18).

6. Castro offers to halt aid to Latin American rebels if U.S. halts subversive activities (→ 25).

8. Geneva: Intl. Commission of Jurists scores Soviet repression of Jews.

13. Peking charges Khrushchev with seeking capitalist rule (→ 8/30).

14. Jacques Anquetil wins his fifth Tour de France.

14. U.S. sends 600 more troops into Vietnam (→ 21).

15. Moscow: Anastas Mikoyan becomes Soviet president (→ 10/17).

16. New York: McCarthy aide Roy Cohn acquitted of perjury in second trial.

18. Harlem: Thousands riot, break windows, loot stores; 30 arrested (→ 21).

20. NASA tests first successful electric rocket engine.

21. LBJ orders full FBI inquiry into Harlem riots (→ 27).

21. Saigon: French Embassy ransacked on tenth anniversary of Geneva accord (→ 27).

24. Algiers: 100 on UAR ship killed in blast while unloading munitions.

25. L.A.: Fred Hansen sets pole vault mark at 17'4".

25. Washington: Org. of Am. States (OAS) votes 14-5 to impose sanctions on Cuba (→ 9/8).

27. U.S. to send 5,000 more advisers to Vietnam (→ 8/1).

27. London: Churchill pays last visit to Commons (→ 1/30/65).

31. Ranger 7 sends first close-up photos of moon (→ 10/13).

DEATH

12. Maurice Thorez, head of French Communist Party for 30 years (*4/28/1900).

Great groups make Motown their home

Supreme songstresses.

July 18. "Where Did Our Love Go," by the Supremes, has popped into the top 40. Put a bullet on it; their number "When the Lovelight Starts Shining Through His Eyes" came out last December and stayed on the charts seven weeks. The Supremes are three Negro women named Mary Wilson, Florence Ballard and Diana Ross. They, the Miracles (led by Smokey Robinson), Stevie Wonder, Marvin Gaye, and the Temptations are all under the same label, Motown.

Motown is the brainchild of Berry Gordy Jr., a Negro entrepreneur who saw a market for contemporary Negro music among white listeners. Gordy set up Motown (short for Motor Town, a nickname for Detroit) in 1960 and did his best to give his acts songs that stick. Business is booming, but as the Beatles encroach, where will their sound go?

Peter Sellers plays the bumbling Inspector Clouseau in Blake Edwards' "The Pink Panther."

LBJ signs Civil Rights Act

July 2. The most sweeping civil rights legislation in the history of the nation became law today with the stroke of President Johnson's pen. In approving the Civil Rights Act of 1964, the president, in a television address, asked all citizens to help "eliminate the last vestiges of injustice in America."

The law prohibits racial discrimination in employment, places of public accomodation, publicly owned facilities, union membership and federally funded programs. Congress made certain modifications in the proposed law and sent it along for executive signature.

Johnson, and President Kennedy before him, lobbied hard for the legislation, which seems likely to replace the barricade of inequality with the avenue of fair opportunity for the 22 million Negroes living in America. Johnson told the viewing audience that the days of denying inalienable rights to Negroes are over. "Let us close the springs of racial poison," he added (→ 18).

LBJ signs in the East Room.

Conservative Goldwater named by GOP

July 15. Senator Barry Morris Goldwater of Arizona was nominated for president tonight at the 28th Republican national convention, held at the Cow Palace in San Francisco. His victory signals the rise of a new conservative sentiment among Republicans.

Goldwater handily captured the nomination on the first ballot, with 883 votes. His only serious challenger, Governor William Scranton of Pennsylvania, received 214 votes. There was little doubt that this convention would overwhelmingly opt for Goldwater after Senator Everett Dirksen's nominating speech was followed by 29 minutes of thunderous applause.

Republicans have been actively challenging Goldwater's reputation as a right-wing extremist. Senator Dirksen remarked: "It is the fashion of our critics to sneer at patriotism, to label positions of strength as extremism, to find other nations' points of view right more often than our own" (→ 8/17).

Goldwater: "Extremism in the defense of liberty is no vice . . ."

Negroes riot; troops called in Rochester

July 27. Racial violence ripped Rochester, New York, last night and today, prompting Governor Nelson Rockefeller to send 1,000 National Guardsmen to quell the first serious race riots in the North. Molotov cocktails exploded, rifle fire blasted and stores were looted in the center of the Negro section. Over 120 rioters were arrested. Earlier this month in Harlem, crowds of Negroes rioted after a rally protesting the police shooting of a 15-year-old Negro boy. By the time police arrived, scores of people had already been hurt (→ 8/4).

Vietnam Reds win biggest battle yet

July 12. In apparently the biggest battle yet, Viet Cong forces inflicted a serious defeat on South Vietnamese government troops in the Mekong Delta region. A Communist guerrilla force of more than 1,000 men attacked Vinh Cheo, one of the government's last remaining footholds in Chuong Thien province, killing, wounding or capturing over 200 South Vietnamese soldiers. The Communists successfully ambushed a large government relief force sent to rescue the outpost. Meanwhile, regular North Vietnamese troops were reported to have engaged in attacks on enemy positions in the North (→ 14).

Tshombe becomes big boss of Congo

July 10. There has been yet another shake-up in the government of the Congo. Moise Tshombe, the former secessionist from Katanga, was named Premier by President Kasavubu. Cyrille Adoula, forced out as Premier, delayed the transition of power by refusing to countersign Kasavubu's decree. The deadlock was broken when a new constitution was approved, allowing Tshombe to take over without Adoula's consent. The constitutional referendum passed handily despite opposition to a clause denying women suffrage (→ 8/12).

1964

AUGUST

Su	Mo	Tu	We	Th	Fr	Sa
						1
2	3	4	5	6	7	8
9	10	11	12	13	14	15
16	17	18	19	20	21	22
23	24	25	26	27	28	29
30	31					

1. South Vietnam: Guerrillas attack village four miles from Saigon (→ 2).

2. South Vietnam: Communist PT boats reportedly fire on U.S. destroyer in Tonkin Gulf (→ 4).

4. U.S. planes hit bases in North Vietnam; two U.S destroyers sunk in Tonkin Gulf (→ 5).

4. Mississippi: Bodies of three missing civil rights workers found (→ 8/13).

5. North Vietnam reports downing five U.S. planes as air raids continue (→ 7).

8. Cyprus: Turks bomb north coast to halt attacks on Turkish Cypriots (→ 10).

9. Vatican: Pope Paul signs first encyclical, calling for dialogue with non-Christians (→ 9/15).

10. New York: Turkey, Greece agree to U.N. cease-fire call (→ 4/19/65).

12. U.S. sends four planes to Congo to aid Tshombe (→ 9/8).

12. South Africa barred from Tokyo Olympics in rebuke for apartheid policy (→ 7/18/66).

12. London: Raid frees British train robber from top-security prison.

13. N.J.: Three days of race riots end in Patterson and Elizabeth (→ 10/4).

17. Washington: Jimmy Hoffa gets five years, $10,000 fine for defrauding union (→ 3/7/67).

22. U.S. agrees to give up Wheelus Air Force Base in Libya.

23. Mass executions reported in Haiti (→ 4/21/71).

25. Zambia: Kenneth Kaunda elected pres. as nation nears independence (→ 10/24).

27. Saigon: Nguyen Khanh agrees to share power; triumvirate of generals to lead (→ 9/14).

30. Peking accuses Moscow of backing U.S. intervention in Vietnam (→ 9/2).

DEATHS

3. Flannery O'Connor, novelist, American South (*3/25/1925).

21. Palmiro Togliatti, Italian Communist leader, a founder of Eurocommunism (*3/26/1893).

Communist boats reported to attack U.S. ships

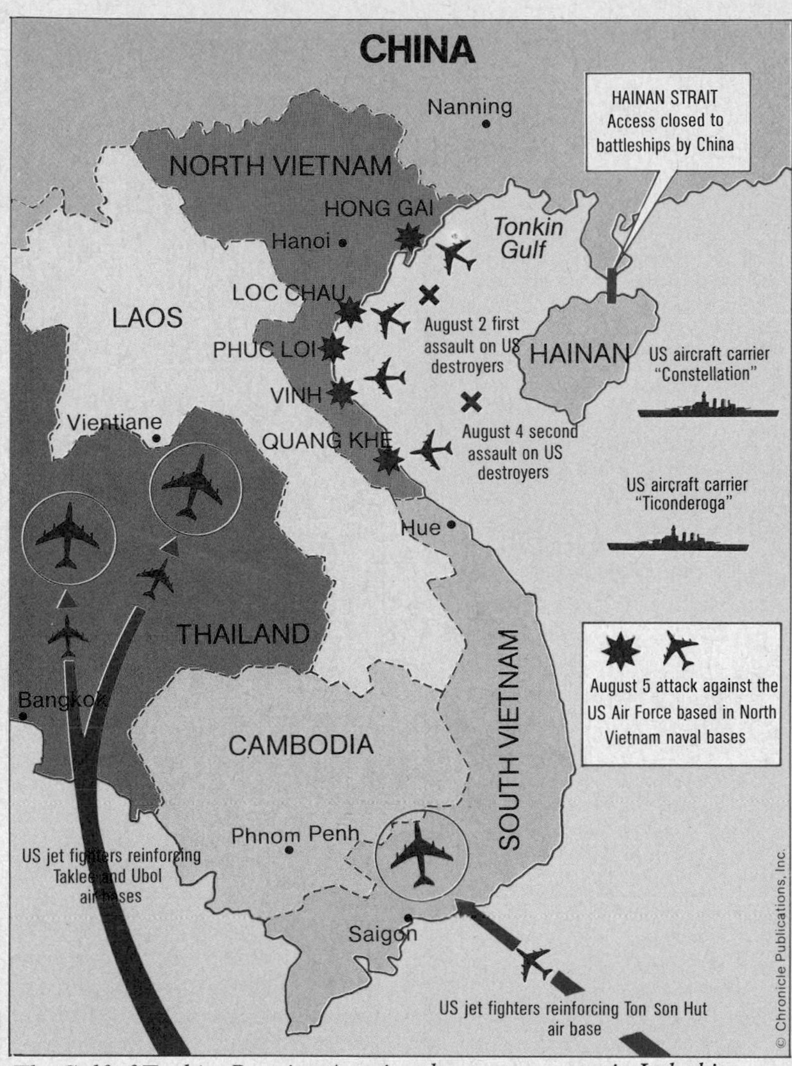

The Gulf of Tonkin: Drawing America closer to open war in Indochina.

Aug 7. The Senate and the House of Representatives voted almost unanimously today to give President Johnson greater authority to strike back against the Communists in North Vietnam. The president appealed for the support after he said that North Vietnamese patrol boats had made unprovoked attacks on American ships in the Gulf of Tonkin. Many of the Congressmen who approved the resolution today expressed their misgivings about the deepening American military involvement in the Vietnam War.

The Defense Department reported on Sunday that North Vietnamese PT boats had fired torpedoes and shells at the destroyer Maddox while it was on a routine patrol in the gulf, southeast of Hanoi. The Maddox was not damaged, and Secretary of State Dean Rusk says it struck back immediately. "The other side got a sting out of this," Rusk said. "If they do it again, they'll get another sting." The Defense Department said three Communist boats were damaged by the Maddox and by F-8 aircraft from the USS Ticonderoga. Pentagon officials insisted that the Communist attack did not create a crisis.

On Tuesday night, at 11:30, President Johnson went on television to announce that he had ordered air strikes against the PT boats and Communist coastal facilities following new attacks on American destroyers. The president characterized the counterattacks as a "limited and fitting" response to "open aggression on the high seas."

Defense Secretary Robert McNamara held a news conference Wednesday morning to say that American planes from the carriers Ticonderoga and Constellation had struck along 100 miles of North Vietnamese coastline. He claimed 25 patrol boats and an oil depot had been destroyed or seriously damaged. The secretary said two American planes were lost and two others were damaged. McNamara did not dispute a report from Hanoi that an American pilot had been captured.

Johnson asked for congressional passage of a resolution assuring support "for all necessary action" to defend U.S. forces in Southeast Asia. The House passed the measure 416-0. After a nine-hour debate, the Senate vote was 88-2. The two Democrats voting no, Sens. Wayne Morse of Oregon and Ernest Gruening of Alaska, claimed the resolution was unconstitutional.

Some approving the measure feared it would be used to commit U.S. troops to a war that should be avoided. "I am still apprehensive," Vermont Republican George Aiken said. "As a citizen, I feel I must support our president whether his decision is right or wrong" (→ 27).

World's population booming, U.N. says

Aug 30. Not only is the world's population soaring, but the rate of increase is accelerating. The annual increase now amounts to a high 2.1 percent a year, the United Nations reports. Midway through 1962 the earth's population was 3.1 billion. The annual increase is 63 million, more than the population of France and Czechoslovakia. This could defeat the battle against poverty in developing nations. For Europe the increase rate is 0.9 percent, for North America 1.6 percent, while many underdeveloped areas show increases of three to five percent. At least 20 percent of the world's population lives in the country with the most people—Communist China.

Beatles return to U.S. as movie opens

Aug 18. Hot on the heels of their new movie "A Hard Day's Night," the Beatles arrived in San Francisco this afternoon, amid the usual hysterical reception from fans, to begin a 23-city concert tour. Since their last visit, in February, the Beatles have exploded into a pop music phenomenon; at one point all top five slots on the Billboard record chart were taken by Lennon and McCartney songs. "A Hard Day's Night," which brought the teen frenzy of Beatlemania into hundreds of movie houses when it opened earlier this month, appears to have even won over the critics, who have acclaimed it as a whale of a comedy (→ 6/11/65).

Ian Fleming, creator of James Bond, is dead

Aug 12. Ian Fleming, who created James Bond, Agent 007 of the British Secret Service, died today on his son Caspar's 12th birthday after suffering a heart attack. He was 56. Of the 12 books he wrote, all but two were about Bond. They sold more than 18 million copies and were translated into ten languages, earning Fleming $2.8 million. Three have become successful movies.

Educated at Eton and Sandhurst, he planned a diplomatic career but became a journalist and was Reuters' correspondent in Moscow from 1929. In 1935, he became a stockbroker. During the war, he did intelligence work and afterwards was the foreign manager of the Sunday Times of London, spending vacations writing novels. Some felt he made Bond a thinly disguised projection of himself, a firearms expert, a lover of fast cars, golf, gambling and gourmet cooking.

Fleming, mastermind behind 007.

Democrats go all the way with LBJ and HHH

Humphrey and LBJ, all smiles.

Aug 17. "The Democratic Party," came the declaration from the podium at Convention Hall in Atlantic City, "nominates President Lyndon Baines Johnson for the Democratic candidacy for president of the United States of America." With that announcement, banners waved, bands played and the crowd screamed as the president saluted his ecstatic party.

In his opening remarks, LBJ evoked laughter when he graciously greeted the press, chiding the Republicans who assailed the media at their convention. After paying tribute to President Kennedy, the party platform and delegates, Johnson nominated his running mate.

Passing over the choices of many party members, he named Senator Hubert H. Humphrey as his selection for vice president. Johnson, in picking the Minnesota New Dealer, said balancing the ticket was not his concern; he said he simply wanted "the best man for the job." LBJ added that his choice has the complete backing of the party. On hearing the choice, the crowd exploded with applause (→ 9/23).

President signs anti-poverty legislation

Aug 20. In the first legislation to originate exclusively from his administration, a happy and proud President Johnson signed his $947.5 million anti-poverty bill today. The program will assist the estimated 30 to 35 million citizens who live in poverty. Specifically, the federal funds will be used for job training and rudimentary education of the nation's impoverished youth; to lend to low-income farmers and businessmen; for the creation of employment programs; and for ghetto improvement projects.

Refuting Republican claims that the legislation will uselessly throw money at the poor, perpetuating the poverty cycle, the president said, "We are not content to accept the endless growth of relief rolls or welfare rolls. We want to offer the forgotten fifth of our people opportunity and not doles" (→ 10/9).

Zany Gracie Allen, a.k.a. Mrs. Burns, dies

Gracie, determined to attend college and earn a sheepskin in "College Swing." Her major? Logic, what else?

Aug 28. To understand better the art of comedienne Gracie Allen, you should get to know her uncle, the one who eats concrete. That's right, he was invited for dinner once but he said no thanks, he'd prefer to eat up the road. Miss Allen had a lot of relatives who were peculiar to most of us but not to her, oh no. She always defended them in front of her always reposed cigar-puffing partner/husband George Burns.

Miss Allen died today of a weak heart. She was 58. She and Burns began their act in 1922 and wed in 1925. Their adopted boy and girl starred with them on their TV show. "Gracie was Gracie," Burns said. Say goodnight, Gracie.

1964

SEPTEMBER

Su	Mo	Tu	We	Th	Fr	Sa
		1	2	3	4	5
6	7	8	9	10	11	12
13	14	15	16	17	18	19
20	21	22	23	24	25	26
27	28	29	30			

2. U.S.S.R.: Pravda denounces Chinese territorial claims in Siberia (→ 10/28).

4. Chile: Moderate Eduardo Frei Montalva chosen president over People's Front candidate Salvador Allende (→ 10/22/69).

8. Uruguay breaks ties with Cuba; Mexico now only holdout in OAS (→ 17).

8. Congo: People's Republic proclaimed by rebels under Gbenye (→ 11/5).

13. N.Y.: Roy Emerson, Maria Bueno repeat Wimbledon wins with victories at Forest Hills.

14. Saigon: Lam Van Phat coup crushed by govt. (→ 16).

15. Vatican, Hungary sign accord on church rights (→ 11/20).

16. Saigon: Nguyen Khanh arrests five leaders of attempted coup (→ 18).

17. Havana: Castro announces Cuba will reduce buying in non-Communist countries (→ 22).

18. Vietnam: U.S. destroyers fire on hostile targets in Tonkin Gulf (→ 10/24).

20. Malta gains independence in British Commonwealth.

20. Tokyo: Taiho (Great Bird) wins world sumo wrestling title.

21. Rhode Island: U.S. wins America's Cup in 4-0 sweep.

22. New York: Nine indicted for conspiring to arrange student tour of Cuba (→ 12/11).

23. Dallas: Pres. candidate Barry Goldwater calls military power the key to peace (→ 11/3).

24. Florida: First Minuteman II ICBM tested (→ 10/16).

24. Berlin: Willi Stoph named East German premier upon death of Otto Grotewohl.

25. Detroit: G.M. struck by 260,00 in U.A.W. (→ 10/25).

25. U.S. Senate approves $1.6 billion in aid for Appalachia.

29. India: 1,000 reported dead as reservoir bursts.

DEATH

5. Elizabeth Gurley Flynn, head of American Communist Party (*8/7/1890).

Sean O'Casey, Irish dramatist, is dead

Sept 18. Sean O'Casey, whose Irish eyes smiled under unkempt beetle brows, has died in an English coastal town. He was 84. O'Casey wrote some of the most lilting plays in the English language, featuring characters with bluster and blarney.

Along with William Butler Yeats and Lady Gregory, O'Casey created the Irish Literary Renaissance. At the Abbey Theater he wrote "The Shadow of a Gunman" (1923) and "Juno and the Paycock" (1924). "The Plough and the Stars" (1926) outraged early audiences, who said it was a disrespectful retelling of the 1916 Easter Rebellion. The next generation found it quite patriotic.

Sergeant York, hero of Great War, dies

Sept 2. Sgt. Alvin C. York, the heroic World War I infantryman and winner of the Medal of Honor, died this morning at the age of 76 in Nashville's Veterans Administration Hospital. On October 8, 1918, York, whose pacifist religious convictions originally kept him from combat, single-handedly overcame an entire German machine-gun battalion, a feat which Marshal Ferdinand Foch of France called "the greatest thing accomplished by any private soldier of all the armies of Europe."

Sept 18. King Constantine has married Princess Anne-Marie, joining the nations of Greece and Denmark in royal matrimony.

Warren inquiry finished

Sept 27. The Warren Commission investigating the assassination of President Kennedy has issued a report calling for a sweeping revision of the Secret Service so as to tighten up protection of a head of state. It also recommended that the killing of a President or a Vice President be made a federal crime.

The final report of the panel that was headed by Chief Justice Earl Warren was highly critical of the Secret Service for failing to make adequate preparation for the visit to Dallas last November by John F. Kennedy. The commission report also reprimanded the FBI for failing to supply the Secret Service with information on the presence there of Lee Harvey Oswald, the accused assassin who once defected to the Soviet Union and who was active in the Fair Play for Cuba Committee. Oswald was killed in a prison garage by Jack Ruby, a nightclub owner, two days after the assassination of the president.

The report provides poignant details of Mrs. Kennedy's reactions at the time of the shooting. As shots rang out, according to the report, Jacqueline Kennedy cried: "Oh my God! They've shot my husband. I love you, Jack." Seeing her husband's skull torn open by a bullet, she cradled his body in her arms as the limousine sped toward the hospital (→ 11/22).

Bobby Kennedy resigns to run for Senate

Sept 3. Stepping down from the position of Attorney General to which he was named by his late brother, President Kennedy, nearly four years ago, Robert F. Kennedy today tendered his resignation to President Johnson the better to turn his complete attention to a Capitol Hill career. Kennedy is the Democratic candidate in New York's upcoming senatorial race. He will be running against Kenneth B. Keating, a Republican, and Henry Paolucci, a Conservative.

Kennedy will be succeeded, at least temporarily, by his deputy, Nicholas deB. Katzenbach. It is speculated that President Johnson may name a new attorney general after the November election, and Leon Jaworski, a prominent Houston attorney, has been mentioned for the post (→ 11/3).

RFK and LBJ, no love lost.

Chagall's bold colors enliven Paris Opera

Chagall's work, done at no charge to France, was solicited by Andre Malraux.

Sept 23. A stunning new ceiling, painted by the artist Marc Chagall, was unveiled tonight at the Paris Opera. Many spectators found it enchanting, but others were displeased. They discussed it at the gala opening of "Daphnis and Chloe," the ballet by Maurice Ravel, with sets also by Chagall.

Work on the ceiling, Chagall's first project commissioned by the state, was ordered by Andre Malraux, the writer and Minister of Cultural Affairs. The ceiling is simultaneously flamboyant, colorful, dreamlike and lyrical. Characters from operas written by Debussy, Mozart, Rameau and Wagner wander among the monuments of Paris. The Eiffel Tower is clearly visible. So is the Arc de Triomphe.

Few of the spectators tonight doubted that the ceiling is a formidable piece of artwork. That was not questioned. But critics of Chagall's handiwork wondered aloud whether it was not out of place among the gilt, Second Empire carvings in the cupola of the Opera. Chagall did not harm or even obscure any of the intricate detail that was already in place in the dome. But critics found his style and that of Lenepveu discordant and even contradictory. Chagall offered his work on the ceiling as a gift to France. The artist, a Russian Jew, was naturalized in France in 1937.

Togliatti's last word was: Decentralize

Sept 4. Italy's Communist Party has made public the testament of its leader Palmiro Togliatti, who died last month. Known as a staunch supporter of the Kremlin, Togliatti's final words are surprising. He advocated the decentralization of authority, a polycentric basis for communism in which national Communist parties would be more independent of Moscow. Khrushchev had eulogized Togliatti as an outstanding Communist, "unbending anti-fascist and great friend of the Soviet Union."

71-year-old crosses the Pacific on a raft

Sept 9. William Willis, a 71-year-old American explorer and author, has completed a two-stage, 9,800-mile drift across the Pacific Ocean, beaching his raft, named Age Unlimited, near Tully in northern Queensland. The journey began from Peru July 4, 1963. Willis arrived in Samoa 128 days and 7,400 miles later. He left for Australia and covered 2,400 miles in 72 days. He was forced to land at Tully because of a severe back injury that left him paralyzed from the waist down for six days.

Harpo's whistle and rippling music silenced

Sept 28. Harpo Marx, the silent, blond-wigged member of the Marx Brothers comedy team, died today at the age of 70. According to an official at Mount Sinai Hospital, the comedian, whose given name was Arthur, died at 8:30 p.m., after undergoing heart surgery. He was renowned for the zany pantomime which he performed in movies with his brothers Groucho, Chico and Zeppo. The team began as a vaudeville act in 1918 and made movies until 1949. Harpo's trademark was a harp, which he played with musical and comic virtuosity. He never spoke a word throughout his screen career and, even his whistle, horn and harp are silent now.

Harpo, master of pantomime, displays his disapproval of Brendan Behan's antics. The Irish playwright also died this year, in March.

1964 Tokyo

Oct 24. For the first time, an authentic American hero who was not a track or field star emerged from the Olympics. Don Schollander won four swimming gold medals and stole some luster from his track teammates, who totaled ten firsts in 24 events.

Schollander won the 100-meter and 400-meter freestyle events in world-record times and added two gold medals in the relays.

Billy Mills won only one gold, but it was one never before taken by an American. He broke the Olympic record in the 10,000-meter run by racing 50 seconds faster than he had ever gone before.

Mills was a Marine and has some Sioux Indian blood. After the race, the world champion from Australia, Ron Clarke, was asked if he worried about Mills during the race.

"Worry about him?" said Clarke. "I'd never even heard of him."

Bob Hayes won his 100-meter semi-final in 9.9 seconds, an incredible time that was disallowed because of the wind. He tied the world record of ten seconds in the final.

There were other stirring track victories, by Henry Carr and Mike Larrabee in the sprints; Hayes Jones and Rex Cawley in the hurdles; Dallas Long in shotput and Al Oerter in discus, but the swimmers kept apace.

Donna deVarona led a U.S. sweep in the 400 medley and four California girls splashed to a world record in the 800-meter relay.

In all, American male swimmers won nine of 12 events, set seven world records, equalled another and picked up medals in losing races. The women won seven of ten and set four world records.

In other notable Olympic performances, Peter Snell of Australia won the metric mile after taking the 800 meters, a double achieved for the first time in 44 years. And the barefoot Ethiopian, Abebe Bikila, was back to take the marathon, this time in a world record of two hours, 12 minutes, 11 seconds.

Bob Hayes breaks the tape in the 100-meters in 10.0. He also anchored the victorious U.S. 4 x 100 relay team.

Men Athletics

100M Dash
1. Robert Hayes USA 10,0
2. Enrique Figuerole CUB 10,2
3. Harry Jerome CAN 10,2

200 M Dash
1. Henry Carr USA 20,3
2. Otis Paul Drayton USA 20,5
3. Edwin Roberts TRI 20,6

400 M Run
1. Michael Larrabee USA 45,1
2. Wendell Mottley TRI 45,2
3. Andrzej Badenski POL 45,6

800 M Run
1. Peter Snell NZL 1:45:1
2. William Crothers CAN 1:45:6
3. Wilson Kiprugut KEN 1:45:9

1500 M Run
1. Peter Snell NZL 3:38,1
2. Josef Odlozil TCH 3:39,6
3. John Davies NZL 3:39,6

5000 M Run
1. Robert Schul USA 13:48,8
2. Harald Norpoth FRG 13:49,6
3. William Dellinger USA 13:49,8

10,000 M Run
1. William Mills USA 28:24,4
2. Mohammed Gammoudi TUN 28:24,8
3. Ronald Clarke AUS 28:25,8

Marathon
1. Abebe Bikila ETH 2:12:11,2
2. Basil Heatley GBR 2:16:19,2
3. Kokichi Tsuburaye JAP 2:16:22,8

110 M Hurdles
1. Hayes Jones USA 13,6
2. Harold Blaine Lindgren USA 13,6
3. Anatoly Mikhailov URS 13,7

400 M Hurdles
1. "Rex" Warren Cawley USA 49,6
2. Johnd Cooper GBR 50,1
3. Salvatore Morale ITA 50,1

3000 M Steeplechase
1. Gaston Roelants BEL 8:30,8
2. Maurice Herriott GBR 8:32,4
3. Yvan Belaiev URS 8:33,8

400 M Relay
1. USA 39,0 (Otis P. Drayton, Gerald Ashworth, Richard Stebbins, Robert Hayes)
2. POL 39,3 (Andrzej Zielinski, Wieslaw Maniak, Marian Foik, Marian Dudziak)
3. FRA 39,3 (Paul Genevay, Bernard Laidebuer, Claude Piquemal, Jocelyn Delecour)

1600 M Relay
1. USA 3:00,7 (Ollan Cassell, Michael Larrabee, Ullis Williams, Henry Carr)
2. GBR 3:01,6 (Timothy Graham, Adrian Metcalfe, John Cooper, Robbie Brightwell
3. TRI 3:01,7 (Edwin Skinner, Kent Bernard, Edwin Roberts, Wendell Mottley)

20 km Walk
1. Kenneth Matthews GBR 1:29:34,0
2. Dieter Lindner FRG 1:31:13,2
3. Wladimir Golubnichy URS 1:31:59,4

50 km Walk
1. Abdon Pamich ITA 4:11:12,4
2. Paul Vincent Nihill GBR 4:11:32,1
3. Ingvar Petterson SUE 4:14:17,4

High Jump
1. Valery Brumel URS 2,18
2. John Thomas USA 2,18
3. John Rambo USA 2,16

Pole Vault
1. Fred Hansen USA 5,10
2. Wolfgang Reinhardt FRG 5,05
3. Klaus Lehnertz FRG 5,00

Long Jump
1. Lynn Davies GBR 8,07
2. Ralph Boston USA 8,03
3. Igor Ter-Ovanesian URS 7,99

Triple Jump
1. Jozef Schmidt POL 16,85
2. Oleg Fedoseiev URS 16,58
3. Viktor Kravchenko URS 16,57

Shotput
1. Dallas Long USA 20,30
2. Randel "Randy" Matson USA 20,20
3. Vilmos Varju HUN 19,39

Discus Throw
1. Alfred Oerter USA 60,52
2. Ludvik Danek TCH 60,52
3. David Weill USA 59,49

Ethiopian Abebe Bikila finishes the marathon in four minutes ahead of the competition.

"We swear that we will take part . . . in loyal competition . . . for the honor of our country and for the glory of sport."

Hammer Throw
1. Romuald Klim URS 69,74
2. Gyula Zsivotsky HUN 69,09
3. Liwe Beyer URS 68,09

Javelin
1. Pauli Nevala FIN 82,66
2. Gergely Kulcsar HUN 82,32
3. Janis Lusis URS 80,57

Decathlon
1. Willi Holdorf FRG 7887
2. Rein Aun URS 7842
3. Hans-Joachim-Walde FRG 7809

Women Athletics

100 M Dash
1. Wyomia Tyus USA 11,4
2. Edith Mac Guire USA 11,6
3. Eva Klobukovska POL 11,6

200 M Dash
1. Edith Mac Guire USA 23,0
2. Irena Kirzenstein POL 23,1
3. Marilyn Black AUS 23,1

400 M Run
1. Betty Cuthbert UAS 52,0
2. Anne Packer GBR 52,2
3. Judith Amoore AUS 53,4

800 M Run
1. Ann Packer GBR 2:01,1
2. Maryvonne Dupureur FRA 2:01,9
3. Ann Chamberlain NZL 2:02,8

80 M Hurdles
1. Karin Balzer FRG 10,5
2. Tereza Ceipla POL 10,5
3. Pamela Kilborn AUS 10,5

1600 M Relay
1. POL 43,6 (Tereza Ciepla-Wieczorek, Irena Kirszenstein, Halina Gorecka-Richter, Eva Klobukovska)
2. USA 43,9 (Willye White, Wyomia Tyus, Marilyn White, Edith Mac Guire)
3. GBR 44,0 (Janet Simpson, Mary Rand, Daphne Arden, Dorothy Hyman)

High Jump
1. Iolande Balas ROM 1,90
2. Michele Brown-Mason AUS 1,80
3. Taisiya Chenchik URS 1,78

Long Jump
1. Mary Rand GBR 6,76
2. Irena Kirszenstein POL 6,60
3. Tatiana Chelkanova URS 6,42

Shotput
1. Tamara Press URS 18,14
2. Renate Garisch FRG 17,61
3. Galina Zybina URS 17,45

Discus Throw
1. Tamara Press URS 57,27
2. Marta Rudas HUN 58,27
3. Lia Manoliu ROM 56,97

Javelin
1. Mihaela Penes ROM 60,54
2. Marta Rudas HUN 58,27
3. Yelena Gorchkova URS 57,06

Pentathlon
1. Irina Press URS
2. Mary Rand GBR
3. Galina Bystrova URS

Men Swimming

100 M Freestyle
1. Donald Schollander USA 53,4
2. Robert Mac Gregor GBR 53,5
3. Hans Joachim-Klein FRG 54,0

400 M Freestyle
1. Donald Schollander USA 4:12,2
2. Frank Wiegand FRG 4:14,9
3. Allen Wood AUS 4:15,1

1500 M Freestyle
1. Robert Windle AUS 17:01,7
2. John Nelson USA 17:03,0
3. Allan Wood AUS 17:07,7

200 M Backstroke
1. Jed Graef USA 2:10,3
2. Gary Dilley USA 2:10,5
3. Robert Bennett USA 2:13,1

200 M Breaststroke
1. Ian O'Brien AUS 2:27,8
2. Geogy Prokopenko URS 2:28,2
3. Chester Jastremski USA 2:29,6

200 M Butterfly Stroke
1. Kevin Berry AUS 2:06,6
2. Carl Robie USA 2:07,5
3. Fred Schmidt USA 2:09,3

400 M Medley
1. Richard Roth USA 4:45,4
2. Roy Saari USA 4:47,1
3. Gerhard Hetz FRG 4:51,0

400 M Freestyle Relay
1. USA 3:33,2 (Stephen Clark, Michael Austin, Gary Ilman, Donald Schollander)
2. FRG 3:37,2 (Horst-Loffler, Frank Wiegand, Liwe Jacobsen, Hans Joachim Klein
3. AUS 3:39,1 (David Dickson, Peter Doak, John Ryan, Robert Windle)

800 M Freestyle Relay
1. USA 7:52,1 (Stephen Clark, Roy Saari, Gary Ilman, Donald Schollander)
2. FRG 7:59,3 (Horst-Gunther Gregor, Gerhard Hetz, Frank Wiegand, Hans Joachim Klein)
3. JAP 8:03,8 (Makoto Fukui, Kunihiro Iwaski, Toshio Shoii, Yukiaki Okabe)

400 M Medley Relay
1. USA 3:58,4 (H. Thompson Mann, William Craig Fred Schmidt, Stephen Clark)
2. FRG 4:01,6 (Ernst-Joachim Kuppers, Egon Henniger, Horst-Gunther Gregor, Hans-Joachim Klein)
3. AUS 4:02,3 (Peter Reynolds, Ian O'Brien, Kevin Berry, David Dickson)

Springboard Diving
1. Kenneth Sitz Berger USA 159,90
2. Francis Gorman USA 157,63
3. Larry Andreasen USA 143,77

High Diving
1. Robert Webster USA 148,58
2. Klaus Dibiasi ITA 147,54
3. Thomas Gompf USA 146,57

Water-Polo

1. Hungary
2. Yugoslavia
3. Soviet Union

Abbreviations on table of contents

Women Swimmming

100 M Freestyle
1. Dawn Fraser AUS 59,8
2. Sharon Stouder USA 59,9
3. Kathlenn Ellis USA 1:00,8

400 M Freestyle
1. Virginia Duenkel USA 4:43,6
2. Marilyn Ramenofsy USA 4:44,6
3. Terri Lee Stickles USA 4:47,2

200 M Breaststroke
1. Galina Prozumenschchikova URS 2:46,4
2. Claudia Kolb USA 2:47,6
3. Svetlana Babanina URS 2:48,6

100 M Backstroke
1. Cathy Ferguson USA 1:07,7
2. Christine Caron FRA 1:07,9
3. Virginia Duenkel USA 1:08,0

100 M Butterfly Stroke
1. Sharon Stouder USA 1:04,7
2. Ada Kok HOL 1:05,6
3. Kathleen Ellis USA 1:06,0

400 M Medley
1. Donna De Varona USA 5:18,7
2. Sharon Finnernan USA 5:24,1
3. Martha Randall USA 5:24,2

400 M Freestyle Relay
1. USA 4:03,8 (Sharon Stouder, Donna De Varona, Lillian "Pokey" Watson, Kathleen Ellis)
2. HOL 4:37,0 (Robyn Thorn, Janice Murphy, Lynette Bell, Dawn Fraser)
3. HOL 4:12,0 (Paulina van der Wildt, Catherina Beumer, Winnie Weerdenburg, Erica Tepstra)

400 M Medley Relay
1. USA 4:33,9 (Cathy Rerguson, Cynthia Goyette, Sharon Stouder, Kathlean Ellis
2. HOL 4:37,0 (Cornelia Winkel, Klena Bimolt, Ada Kok, Erica Tepstra)
3. URS 4:39,2 (Tatiana Saveleva, Svetlana Babanina, Tatiana Deviatova, Natalia Oustinova)

Springboard Diving
1. Ingrid Engel Kramer FRG 145,00
2. Jeanne Collier USA 138,36
3. Mary Willard USA 138,18

High Diving
1. Lesley Bush USA 99,80
2. Ingrid Engel-Kramer FRG 98,45
3. Galina Alexeyeva URS 97,60

Boxing

Flyweight
1. Fernando Atzori ITA
2. Artur Olech POL
3. Stanislav Sorokin URS
3. Robert Carmody USA

Bantamweight
1. Takao Sakurai JAP
2. Shin-Cho Chung KOR
3. Juan Fabila Mendoza MEX
3. Washington Rodriguez URU

Featherweight
1. Stanislav Stepashkin URS
2. Anthony Villanueva PHI
3. Henz Schulz FRG
3. Charles Brown USA

Lightweight
1. Jozef Grudzien POL
2. Velikton Baranniko URS
3. James Mac Court IRL
3. Ronald Harris USA

Light Welterweight
1. Jerzy Kulej POL
2. Yevgeny Frolov URS
3. Eddie Blay GHA
3. Habib Galhia TUN

Welterweight
1. Marian Kasprzyk POL
2. Ritchardas Tamulis URS
3. Pertti Purhonen FIN
3. Silvano Bertini ITA

1964 Tokyo

Light Middleweight
1. Boris Lagutin URS
2. Joseph Gonzales FRA
3. Nojim Maiyegun NGA
3. Jozef Grzesiak POL

Middleweight
1. Valery Popenchko URS
2. Emil Schulz FRG
3. Franco Valle ITA
3. Tandeusz Walasek POL

Light Heavyweight
1. Cosimo Pinto ITA
2. Alexei Kiseliov URS
3. Aleksandar Nikolov BUL
3. Zbigniew Pietrzykowski POL

Heavyweight
1. Joseph Frazier USA
2. Hans Huber FRG
3. Giuseppe Ross ITA
3. Vadim Yemelyanov URS

Greco Roman Wrestling

Flyweight
1. Tsutomu Nanahara JAP
2. Angel Kerezov BUL
3. Dumitru Pirvulescu ROM

Bantamweight
1. Masamitsu Ichiguchi JAP
2. Vladlen Trostiansky URS
3. Ion Cernea ROM

Featherweight
1. Imre Polyak HUN
2. Roman Rurua URS
3. Branislav Martinovic YUG

Lightweight
1. Kazim Ayvaz TUR
2. Valeriu Bularca ROM
3. Davis Gvantseladze URS

Welterweight
1. Anatoly Koletzov URS
2. Cyril Todorov BUL
3. Bertil Nyström SWE

Middleweight
1. Branislav Simic YUG
2. Jifti Komanik TCH
3. Lothar-Metz FRG

Light Heavyweight
1. Alexanrov BUL
2. Per Svensson SWE
3. Heinz Kiehl FRG

Heavyweight
1. Istvan Koszna HUN
2. Anatoly Roschin URS
3. Wielfried Dietrich FRG

Freestyle Wrestling

Flyweight
1. Yoshikatsu Yoshida JAP
2. Chang Sun Chang KOR
3. Said Aliaakbbbar Haydari IRA

Bantamweight
1. Yojiro Uetake JAP
2. Hüseyin Akbas TUR
3. Aydyn Ibrajimov URS

Featherweight
1. Osamu Watanabe JAP
2. Stantscho Ivano BUL
3. Nodar Khokhashvili URS

Lightweight
1. Dimov BUL
2. Klaus-Jurgen Rost FRG
3. Iwao Horiuchi JAP

Welterweight
1. Ismail Ogan TUR
2. Guliko Segaradze URS
3. Mohamad-Ali Sanatkaran IRA

Middleweight
1. Prodan Gardschev BUL
2. Hasan Gungör TUR
3. Daniel Brand USA

Light Heavyweight
1. Aleksandr Medved URS
2. Ahmet Ayik TUR
3. Sherifov BUL

Heavyweight
1. Aleksandr Ivanitsky URS
2. Lyutvi Dschüber BUL
3. Hamit Kaplan TUR

Judo

Lightweight
1. Takehide Nakatani JAP
2. Eric Hänni SUI
3. Oleg Stepanov URS
3. Aron Bogolubov URS

Middleweight
1. Isao Okano JAP
2. Wolfgang Hofmann FRG
3. James Bregman USA
3. Eui-Tac Kim KOR

Heavyweight
1. Isao Inokuma JAP
2. Alfred Harold Rogers CAN
3. Anzor Kiknadze URS
3. Parnaoz Chikviladze URS

All Categories
1. Antonius Geesink HOL
2. Akio Kaminaga JAP
3. Klaus Glahn FRG
3. Theodore Boronovskis AUS

CHART

Weightlifting

			2 Arm Press	2 Arm Snatch	2 Arm Clean & Jerk	Total
	Bantamweight					
1.	Alexei Vakhonine	URS	111,0	105,0	142,5	357,5
2.	Imre Földi	HUN	115,0	102,5	137,5	355,0
3.	Shiro Ichinoseki	JAP	100,0	110,0	137,5	347,5
	Featherweight					
1.	Yoshinobu Miyake	JAP	122,5	122,5	152,5	397,5
2.	Isaac Berger	USA	122,5	107,5	152,5	382,5
3.	Mieczyslaw Nowak	POL	112,5	115,0	150,0	377,5
	Lightweight					
1.	Waldemar Baszanovski	POL	132,5	135,0	165,0	432,5
2.	Vladimir Kaplounov	URS	140,0	127,5	165,0	432,5
3.	Marian Zielinski	POL	140,0	120,0	160,0	420,0
	Middleweight					
1.	Hans Zdrazila	TCH	130,0	137,5	177,3	445,0
2.	Viktor Kourentsov	URS	135,0	130,0	175,0	440,0
3.	Masashi Ohuchi	JAP	140,0	135,0	162,5	437,5
	Light Heavyweight					
1.	Rudolf Plyukfelder	URS	150,0	142,5	182,5	475,0
2.	Geza Toth	HUN	145,0	137,5	185,0	467,5
3.	Gyözö Veres	HUN	155,0	135,0	177,5	467,5
	Middle Heavyweight					
1.	Vladimir Golovanov	URS	165,0	142,5	180,0	487,5
2.	Louis Martin	GBR	155,0	140,0	180,0	475,0
3.	Ireneusz Palinski	POL	150,0	135,0	182,5	467,5
	Heavyweight					
1.	Leonid Jabotinsky	URS	187,5	167,5	217,5	572,5
2.	Yuri Vassov	URS	197,5	162,5	210,0	570,0
3.	Norbert Schemansky	USA	180,0	165,0	192,5	537,5

Men Fencing

Foil Individual
1. Egon Franke POL
2. Jean-Claude Magnon FRA
3. Daniel Revenu FRA

Foil Team
1. Soviet Union
2. Poland
3. France

Epée Individual
1. Grigory Kriss URS 2+1
2. Henry Hoskyns GBR 2
3. Guram Khostava URS 1+1

Epée Team
1. Hungary
2. Italy
3. France

Sabre Individual
1. Tibor Pésza HUN 2+1
2. Claude Arabo FRA 2
3. Umar Mavlikhanov URS 1+1

Sabre Team
1. Soviet Union
2. Italy
3. Poland

Women Fencing

Foil Individual
1. Ildiko Ujlaki-Retjöol HUN 2+2
2. Helga Meca FRG 2+1
3. Antonella Ragno ITA 2

Foil Team
1. Hungary
2. Soviet Union
3. German Federal Republic

Modern Pentathlon

Individual
1. Dr. Ference Török HUN
2. Igor Novikov URS
3. Albert Mokeev URS

Team
1. Soviet Union
2. USA
3. Hungary

Men Canoeing

Kayak-1 1000 M
1. Rolf Peterson SWE 3:57,13
2. Mihaley Hesz HUN 3:57,28
3. Aurel Vernescu ROM 4:00,77

Kayak-2 1000 M
1. Sweden 3:38,54
2. Netherlands 3:39,30
3. Federal Republic 3:40,69

Kayak-4 1000 M
1. Soviet Union 3:14,67
2. Germany Federal Republic 3:15,39
3. Romania 3:15,51

Canadian-1 1000 M
1. Jürgen Eschert FRG 4:35,14
2. Andrei Igorov ROM 4:37,89
3. Yevgeny Penaiev URS 4:38,31

Canadian-2 1000 M
1. Soviet Union 4:04,64
2. France 4:06,52
3. Denmark 4:07,48

Women Canoeing

Kayak-1 500 M
1. Ludmila Khvedosyuk URS 2:12,87
2. Hilde Lauer ROM 2:15,35
3. Marcia Jones USA 2:15,68

Kayak-2 500M
1. German Federal Republic 1:56,95
2. USA 1:59,16
3. Romania 2:00,25

Rowing

Single Scull
1. Vyatcheslav Ivanov URS 8:22,51
2. Achim Hill FRG 8:26,24
3. Gottfried Kottmann SUI 8:29,68

Double Sculls
1. Soviet Union 7:10,66
2. USA 7:13,16
3. Czechoslovakia 7:14,23

Pair Oars without Coxswain
1. Canada 7:32,94
2. Netherlands 7:33,40
3. German Federal Republic 7:38,63

Pair Oars with Coxswain
1. USA 8:21,23
2. France 8:23,15
3. Netherlands 8:23,42

Four Oars without Coxswain
1. German Federal Republic 7:00,44
2. Italy 7:02,84
3. Netherlands 7:06,46

Eight Oars
1. USA 6:18,23
2. German Federal Republic 6:23,29
3. Czechoslovakia 6:25,11

Yachting

Finn Monotype Class Ind.
1. Wilhelm Kuhweide FRG 7638
2. Peter Barrett USA 6373
3. Hennig Wind DEN 6190

Star Class
1. Bahamas 5664
2. USA 5585
3. Sweden 5527

Flying Dutchman
1. New Zealand 6255
2. Great Britain 5556
3. USA 5158

Dragon Class
1. Denmark 5854
2. German Federal Republic 5826
3. USA 5523

5,50 M Class (1952, 1956, 1960, 1964, 1968 only)
1. Australia 5981
2. Sweden 5254
3. USA 5106

Cycling

Individual Road Race (194.83 km)
1. Mario Zanin ITA 4:39:51,63
2. Kjell Akerstrom Rodian DEN 4:39:51,65
3. Walter Godefroot BEL 4:39:51,74

100 km Time Trial
1. Netherlands 2:26:31,19
2. Italy 2:26:55,39
3. Sweden 2:27:11,52

1000 M Time Trial
1. Patrick Sercu BEL 1:09,59
2. Giovanni Pettenella ITA 1:10,09
3. Pierre Trentin FRA 1:10,42

1000 M Sprint (last 200 Meters)
1. Giovanni Pettenella ITA 13,69
2. Sergio Bianchetto ITA
3. Daniel Morelon FRA

2000 M Tandem (last 200 Meters)
1. Italy 10,75
2. Soviet Union
3. German Federal Republic

Individual Road Race 4000 M
1. Jiri Daler TCH 5:04,75
2. Giorgio Ursi ITA 5:05,96
3. Preben Isaksson CAN 5:01,90

Team Pursuit Race 4000 M
1. German Federal Republic 4:35,67
2. Italy 4:35,74
3. Netherlands 4:38,99

France's lone gold medal winner this year was Pierre Jonqueres d'Oriola. Riding the graceful Lutteru B, he swept to a first place finish in the individual jumping competition.

Equestrian Sports

All-around Individual Competition
1. Mauro Checcoli ITA
2. Carlos Moratorio ARG
3. Fritz Ligges FRG

All-around Team Competition
1. Italy +85,80
2. USA +65,86
3. German Federal Republic +56,73

Individual Dressage
1. Henri Chammartin SUI 1504
2. Harry Boldt FRG 1503
3. Sergei Filatov URS 1486

Team Dressage
1. German Federal Republic 2558,0
2. Switzerland 2526,0
3. Soviet Union 2311,0

Grand Prix Jumping Individual
1. Pierre Jonqères d'Oriola FRA -9
2. Hermann Schridde FRG -13,75
3. Peter Robeson GBR -16,0

Grand Prix Jumping Team
1. German Federal Republic -68,50
2. France -77,75
3. Italy -88,50

Shooting

Full-Bore Rifle, 300 M, 3 positions
1. Gary Anderson USA 1153
2. Schota Kveliashvili URS 1144
3. Martin Gunnarson USA 1136

Small-Bore Rifle, 50 M Prone
1. Laszlo Hammerl HUN 597
2. Lones Wigger USA 597
3. Tommy Pool USA 596

Small-Bore Rifle, Combined, 3 positions
1. Lones Wigger USA 1164
2. Velitchko Khristov BUL 1152
3. Laszlo Hammerl HUN 1151

Rapid-Fire Pistol, 25 M
1. Pentti Linnosvuo FIN 592
2. Ion Tripsa ROM 591
3. Lubomir Nacovsky TCH 590

Free Pistol, 50 M
1. Väine Markkanen FIN 560
2. Franklin Green USA 557
3. Yoshilisa Yoshilawa JAP 554,26

Clay Pigeon
1. Ennio Mattarelli ITA 198
2. Pavel Senichev URS 194,25
3. William Morris USA 194,24

Men Gymnastics

All-around Individual Competition
1. Yukio Endo JAP 115,95
2. Shuji Tsurumi JAP 115,40
3. Viktor Lisitsky URS 115,40
3. Boris Chakline URS 115,40

All-around Team Competition
1. Japan 577,95
2. Soviet Union 575,45
3. German Federal Republic 565,10

Parallel Bars
1. Yukio Endo JAP 19,675
2. Shuji Tsurumi JAP 19,450
3. Franco Menichelli ITA 19,350

Floor Exercise
1. Franco Menichelli ITA 19,450
2. Viktor Lisitsky URS 19,350
3. Yukio Endo JAP 19,350

Horse Vault
1. Haruhiro Yamashita JAP 19,600
2. Viktor Lisitsky URS 19,325
3. Hannu Rankatari FIN 19,300

Sidehorse
1. Miroslav Cerar YUG 19,525
2. Shuji Tsurumi JAP 19,325
3. Yuri Tsapenko URS 19,200

Horizontal Bar
1. Boris Chakline URS 19,625
2. Yuri Titov URS 19,550
3. Mirosalv Cerar YUG 19,500

Flying Rings
1. Takuji Hayata JAP 19,475
2. Franco Menichelli URS 19,425
3. Boris Chakline ITA 19,400

Women Gymnastics

All-around Individual competition
1. Vera Caslavska TCH 77,564
2. Larissa Latynina URS 76,998
3. Polina Astakhova URS 76,965

All-around Team Competition
1. Soviet Union 380,890
2. Czechoslovakia 379,989
3. Japan 377,899

Uneven Bars
1. Polina Astakhova URS 19,332
2. Katalin Makray HUN 19,216
3. Larissa Latynina URS 19,199

Floor Exercise
1. Larissa Latynina URS 19,599
2. Polina Astakhova URS 19,500
3. Aniko Janosi HUN 19,300

Horse Vault
1. Vera Caslavska TCH 19,483
2. Larissa Latynina URS 19,283
3. Birgit Radochla FRG 19,283

Beam
1. Vera Caslavska TCH 19,449
2. Tarmara Manina URS 19,399
3. Larissa Latynina URS 19,382

Phillip K. Shinnick dances his way through the long jump on a rainy day in Tokyo.

Basketball

1. USA
2. Soviet Union
3. Brazil

Football

1. Hungary
2. Czechoslovakia
3. German Federal Republic

Field Hockey

1. India
2. Pakistan
3. Australia

Men Volleyball

1. Soviet Union
2. Czechoslovakia
3. Japan

Women Volleyball

1. Japan
2. Soviet Union
3. Poland

1964

OCTOBER

Su	Mo	Tu	We	Th	Fr	Sa
				1	2	3
4	5	6	7	8	9	10
11	12	13	14	15	16	17
18	19	20	21	22	23	24
25	26	27	28	29	30	31

1. Berlin: First from West visit East under new accord (→ 5).

5. Utah: Art Arfons sets land speed record, 434.02 mph (→ 15).

5. Berlin: 57 flee to West through tunnel; pursuer killed (→ 4/7/65).

5. Washington: LBJ meets with Pres. Diosdado Macapagal of Philippines (→ 11/12/65).

9. N.Y.: Dr. George James calls poverty the number three cause of death in U.S (→ 1/4/65).

9. Venezuela: Terrorists kidnap U.S. Col. Michael Smolen.

10. Tokyo: XVIIIth Olympics inaugurated.

10. New York: Ravi Shankar performs at Town Hall.

10. Paris holds Toulouse Lautrec exhibit on centennial of his birth.

12. Montana: LBJ equates John Birch Society with KKK.

13. U.S.S.R.: Three Soviet astronauts land after orbitiing 16 times in 24 hours (→ 1/19/65).

15. St. Louis: Cardinals beat Yankees 7-5 to win World Series in final game.

17. Buenos Aires: Scores injured at rally for exiled Juan Peron (→ 12/2).

23. Tokyo: Three Hungarians defect to U.S. at Olympics.

24. Northern Rhodesia becomes Republic of Zambia, ending 73 years of British rule.

24. Saigon: Civilian Phan Khac Suu installed as head of state by military junta (→ 11/1).

25. Detroit: U.A.W. strike at G.M. ends.

27. London appeals to Rhodesia to force resignation of Prime Minister Ian Smith (→ 5/7/65).

27. Utah: Art Arfons breaks Breedlove's land speed record, hitting 536.71 mph (→ 11/7/65).

28. Peking: Chou En-lai praises Soviet shifts, hopes for better relations (→ 11/1).

29. Tanganyika, Zanzibar united into Republic of Tanzania.

DEATH

15. Cole Porter, American composer and lyricist (*6/9/1892).

Brezhnev replaces deposed Khrushchev

Brezhnev chats with Kosygin.

Oct 17. Nikita Khrushchev has been ousted by the Soviet Union's Communist Party and replaced by Leonid Brezhnev, who will take Khruschev's job as First Secretary, and Aleksei Kosygin, who will take over as Soviet Premier.

The change in leadership happened quickly, surprising most Western observers. Initially, spokesmen at the Kremlin said Khrushchev was leaving because of poor health, but today Pravda, the official news agency, ripped into the deposed leader, which clearly indicates he fell from grace in the party. Pravda called Khrushchev's leadership one of "harebrained scheming, immature conclusions and hasty decisions and actions divorced from reality." It also suggested he had promoted his own "cult of personality," for which he had criticized Joseph Stalin.

The shift is not considered to change significantly the direction of East-West relations; Brezhnev and Kosygin will continue to pursue their predecessor's policy of "peaceful coexistence" with the United States. However, it is expected that the new Soviet leaders will try to end the friction between China and the Kremlin. Khrushchev took a hard line toward Peking, straining relations between the Communist neighbors. Some believe this contributed to his fall (→ 3/22/65).

Japan, intent on offering technological prowess to Olympic visitors, has finished a revolutionary monorail. Brainchild of Swedish engineer Axel Leonard Wenner-Gren, it covers eight miles, linking Tokyo and its airport. The Japanese are hoping to dominate electronics in the future.

Shoemaker rides to 5,000th victory

The Shoe in the saddle.

Oct 22. It was just another race on the Aqueduct program, but it proved to be a milestone for jockey Willie Shoemaker. The Shoe rode the 5,000th winner of his career on a horse named Slapstick. Only Johnny Longden, with nearly 6,000, has ridden more winners. Longden, at 57, is still riding too.

Star of India stolen in daring burglary

Oct 29. Priceless and irreplaceable gems, among them the famed Star of India, 563.35 carats and 2.5 inches in diameter, were stolen last night from the American Museum of Natural History's 4th floor in a daring burglary. An alarm system was discontinued years ago as was the all-night guard in the gem hall, both for reasons of economy. The jewels were uninsured due to high-priced premiums (→ 1/8/65).

Labor Party leader Wilson is Premier

Oct 16. Harold Wilson is Britain's new Prime Minister, succeeding Sir Alec Douglas-Home. Wilson is confident that his Labor government will be effective in spite of its small majority of four seats in the 630-seat House of Commons. Labor's plans include renationalization of the steel industry. Labor opposes British participation in West European integration and is against taking part in the U.S. plan for a nuclear fleet (→ 3/31/66).

Great career ends for Eddie Cantor

Oct 10. Entertainer Eddie Cantor, famous for his comedy and antics on stage, in movies, radio and television, died today at the age of 72 of a coronary occlusion. Born Isidor Iskowitch, the vaudevillian grew up in the tenements and poolrooms of New York's Lower East Side, beginning his career on stage as a blackface comedian. He later appeared in the Ziegfeld Follies and as a featured player with Will Rogers, W.C. Fields and other stars. He made many movies in the 1940's, was an active philanthropist and a writer in his later years.

Cantor in "Roman Scandals."

Land speed record is set by Breedlove

Breedlove displays jet car model.

Oct 15. No one expects a jet car driver on the Bonneville Salt Flats to die by drowning, but Craig Breedlove can almost prove otherwise. The 28-year-old Californian set his second world record in two days, but he almost drowned when his two-ton racer went into a pond. The accident occurred minutes after Breedlove had become the first man to surpass 500 mph on land. His average two-run time of 526.28 mph was 57.56 mph faster than his earlier record. He said "the brakes must have turned to ashes" when he applied them, and the water was up to his nose when he swam to safety (→ 27).

Oct 26. England's self-styled "Newest Hitmakers" have hit the U.S. The Rolling Stones played tunes from their new album "12 x 5" on "The Ed Sullivan Show." Raunchier than the Beatles, the Stones are helping to widen the generation gap. From left: Charlie Watts (drums), Keith Richard (lead), Mick Jagger (vocals), Brian Jones(rhythm), Bill Wyman(bass).

Chinese explode their first atomic bomb

Oct 16. Communist China has announced that it exploded its first atomic bomb, but said it would never be the first to use nuclear arms. A communique said the test was conducted at 3 p.m. Peking time. No location was given, but Western sources said the test site was in Sinkiang, a province bordering the Soviet Union in western China.

While China now is the world's fifth nuclear power, following the United States, Soviet Union, Britain and France, American experts say it is not yet a first-class military power because it will take several years for the Chinese to build a delivery system for atomic weapons. The withdrawal of Soviet technicians in 1960 disrupted Peking's program to build ballistic missiles.

The official Chinese statement said the aim of its nuclear weapons program was to protect its people "from the danger of the United States launching a nuclear war." The statement also called for China and the Soviet Union, now bitter enemies, to "unite on the basis of Marxism-Leninism and proletarian nationalism." The Soviet press agency Tass printed a three-line announcement of the Chinese nuclear test but did not mention that the Chinese statement called for a ban on nuclear weapons (→ 8/9/65).

Two are indicted in civil rights deaths

Oct 4. Two residents of Philadelphia, Mississippi, have been indicted and arrested for the slayings of three civil rights workers in the Southern town. The victims had been missing since late June until an extensive search uncovered their bodies on August 4. Five other area residents, four of them law enforcement officials, were arrested yesterday on charges of depriving seven Negroes of their civil rights by unlawfully detaining and physically abusing them. The charges are not related to the murders. Early this morning, dynamite exploded in a Negro church in Vicksburg, Mississippi, killing two. The building was being used as a voter registration center (→ 11/18).

Julie Andrews is "Mary Poppins," the "practically perfect" nanny who transforms the Banks family and steals the heart of carefree Dick Van Dyke. Disney spares no charm in this film. Score by Richard and Robert Sherman leaves you humming.

Hoover dies, ending worldwide career

Oct 20. Herbert Clark Hoover, President of the United States from 1928 to 1932, died yesterday at the age of 90. Born in a small Iowa town, Hoover was, throughout his life, an exponent of what he called "rugged individualism." During and after World War I, Hoover directed relief efforts to help the starving masses of Europe. Prior to being elected President in 1928, he served as Secretary of Commerce in the administrations of Presidents Harding and Coolidge. Hoover's detractors have blamed him for the stock market crash of 1929 and the subsequent Depression, but some later judgments suggest that he was the victim of events which coincided with his tenure.

"The rain in Spain falls mainly in the plain." Hepburn and Harrison: "My Fair Lady," the movie.

1964

NOVEMBER

Su	Mo	Tu	We	Th	Fr	Sa
1	2	3	4	5	6	7
8	9	10	11	12	13	14
15	16	17	18	19	20	21
22	23	24	25	26	27	28
29	30					

1. South Vietnam: Viet Cong attack major U.S. base, destroy six B-57's (→ 10).

1. Moscow: New Soviet leaders call for Communist unity in message to Peking (→ 5).

3. Robert Kennedy elected Senator from N.Y. (→ 3/16/68).

4. Bolivia: Pres. Paz Estenssoro flees; military junta takes over.

5. Moscow: Chou En-lai arrives to mark 47 years of Bolshevik Revolution (→ 11/28/65).

5. Congo: 2,000 troops open attack on rebels (→ 22).

9. London: Judy Garland and Liza Minnelli give mother-daughter concert.

9. Warsaw: Writer Melchior Wankowicz, U.S. citizen, gets jail term as slanderer (→ 1/30/66).

9. Tokyo: Eisaku Sato elected premier of Japan (→ 6/17/71).

10. Australia begins draft to fill commitment in Vietnam (→ 19).

12. Prague: Antonin Novotny re-elected Czech president (→ 6/28/67).

14. Italian scientist says Tower of Pisa may fall at any time.

18. J. Edgar Hoover calls Martin Luther King "most notorious liar in the country (→ 12/1).

20. Vatican approves exoneration of Jews for guilt in crucifixion of Jesus (→ 23).

21. Sudan: Revolt spreading throughout south.

22. Virginia: 40,000 at Arlington pay tribute to JFK on first anniversary of death (→ 7/4/66).

22. Congo: Belgian paratroopers land in Stanleyville (→ 24).

23. Vatican abolishes Latin as official language of Roman Catholic liturgy (→ 12/2).

24. Congo: 20 to 30 hostages killed as Belgian paratroopers begin rescue operations (→ 26).

25. Eleven nations offer $3 bil. to rescue value of British pound.

25. Saigon imposes martial law to halt student riots (→ 12/12).

28. Moscow: Student protesters, angered over Congo aid, attack U.S. Embassy (→ 1/8/65).

South Vietnam starts biggest attack of war

South Vietnamese troops and American advisers are airlifted to battlefield.

Nov 19. South Vietnamese forces initiated the largest attack of the war, striking at a Communist guerrilla stronghold in a forest 40 miles northwest of Saigon. Supported by 105 U.S. Army helicopters, supplied by the American Military Assistance Command, 7,000 Vietnamese troops were airlifted for the attack on an area near Thudaumot. The Vietnamese troops made no immediate contact with the enemy, and it appeared the guerrilla force of about 300 men had quietly withdrawn from the area about three days before the operation began.

High-ranking American officers had expressed reservations about such a large-scale attack against the elusive guerrilla forces but found themselves drawn into cooperating with an operation planned by the new military high command headed by Major General Nguyen Khanh, the former Premier. Tran Van Huong, the new Premier, has pledged "total war against the Communists." Early in the month, Viet Cong guerrillas attacked the American air base of Bienhoa near Saigon, killing four Americans and destroying six B-57 jet bombers (→ 25).

The Verrazano-Narrows Bridge has opened. The longest suspension bridge in the U.S. stretches 4,260 ft., linking Brooklyn and Staten Island.

Johnson landslide buries Goldwater

The First Family.

Nov 3. Lyndon Johnson will again serve America in the nation's highest office, as he defeated Barry Goldwater in one of the most lopsided elections in American history. LBJ called his victory and vice-presidential candidate Hubert Humphrey's "a mandate for unity, for a government that serves no special interest." Democrats secured majorities in both houses of Congress. Robert Kennedy will be among those Democrats in the Senate, as he defeated Republican Senator Kenneth Keating in New York (→ 1/20/65).

Belgians free 211 hostages in Congo

Nov 26. Belgian paratroopers, flown on American Air Force planes, liberated 211 white hostages in Paulis, the Congo, today. The rescue effort came too late for thousands of Congolese, more than 20 Belgians and an American missionary. They were all slaughtered, many of them clubbed to death by rebel followers of Christian Gbenye. Many of the victims were allies of former Premier Cyrille Adoula. Gbenye has ordered the deaths of all whites in rebel hands. On Tuesday, 18 whites, including at least two Americans, were slaughtered in Leopoldville. American embassies were attacked in Cairo, Nairobi and Prague today by demonstrators protesting American assistance to the Belgians (→ 28).

1964

DECEMBER

Su	Mo	Tu	We	Th	Fr	Sa
		1	2	3	4	5
6	7	8	9	10	11	12
13	14	15	16	17	18	19
20	21	22	23	24	25	26
27	28	29	30	31		

1. Washington: J. Edgar Hoover meets with Martin Luther King (→ 10).

2. Brazil sends Juan Peron back to Spain, foiling effort to return to native land (→ 6/28/66).

2. India: Pope Paul VI greeted by millions (→ 10/4/65).

11. New York: Cuban exiles fire bazooka at U.N. as Che Guevara speaks (→ 2/6/66).

12. Kenya becomes a republic (→ 7/5/69).

12. Saigon: Three Buddhist leaders begin hunger strike to protest government (→ 24).

18. LBJ announces U.S. willing to renegotiate Panama Canal treaty (→ 9/24/65).

21. London: Commons votes to ban death penalty (→ 12/18/69).

24. Saigon: U.S. headquarters hit by bomb; two officers dead (→ 1/2/65).

25. Indian Ocean: Hurricane kills 4,000 in Ceylon, 3,000 in Indian province of Madras.

27. Cleveland: Browns win NFL title, blanking Baltimore 27-0.

30. India: 500 seized as Chinese spies (→ 9/11/67).

CULTURAL EVENTS, 1964

Literature: Gore Vidal's "Julian"; Saul Bellow's "Herzog"; Chinua Achebe's "Arrow of God"; Hemingway's "A Moveable Feast."

Academia: Hofstadter's "Anti-Intellectualism in American Life"; Eric Berne's "Games People Play"; Marshall McLuhan's "Understanding Media."

Music: Jerry Herman's "Hello Dolly"; Jerry Bock's "Fiddler on the Roof"; The Beatles' "I Want to Hold Your Hand"; Dionne Warwick's "Walk On By"; Martha and the Vandellas' "Dancing in the Street."

The Arts: Picasso's "The Painter and his Model"; Op Art gains first admirers.

Film: Peter Brook's "Lord of the Flies"; Cacoyannis' "Zorba the Greek"; Stevenson's "Mary Poppins; "My Fair Lady," Academy Award; "Goldfinger" (James Bond); The Beatles' "A Hard Day's Night."

Busy Dr. King collects Nobel Peace Prize

Dec 10. A man J. Edgar Hoover once called "the most notorious liar in the country" accepted the Nobel Peace Prize tonight. Dr. Martin Luther King Jr., a peaceful warrior for civil rights, took the prize expressing "abiding faith in America." At age 35, the minister is the youngest Nobel recipient.

The month has been particularly active for King. On Dec. 1 he met with Hoover, who regretted his earlier outburst and assured King the FBI would get the killers of three civil rights activists in Mississippi. On Dec. 6 the minister preached at St. Paul's Cathedral in London, sounding off against separatism.

Dorothy Hodgkin took the chemistry prize for findings on Vitamin B-12. Konrad Bloch and Feodor Lynen won in medicine for studies on cholesterol. Charles Townes, Nikolai Basov and Aleksandr Prokhorov won in physics for developing lasers. And Jean Paul Sartre got the literature prize—at last.

Minister of peace accepts his prize.

Free speech leader detained by police

Dec 7. Thousands of students and professors at the University of California at Berkeley watched in shock today as a student leader was grabbed by campus police and dragged from the microphone at a large outdoor university meeting. Mario Savio, leader of the Free Speech Movement, was briefly detained and then allowed back onto the podium to speak to the audience of 13,000. The incident gave new life to Savio's movement and threatened to disrupt a compromise over on-campus political activity. A dispute erupted in September at Berkeley after students were barred from politicking at university property on Bancroft Way. The rule has since been overturned.

Savio speaks out at Berkeley.

Kennedy is walking again after crash

Dec 16. Massachusetts Senator Edward Kennedy strode out of a Boston hospital today, a leather brace concealed under his jacket. Kennedy broke his lower spine in a plane crash six months ago. A close aide died in the accident. Flight has been cruel to the Kennedys. Edward's brother Joe died on a bombing mission in WWII and his sister Kathleen died in a crash in Europe. The senator will recuperate in Miami. He will fly there (→ 7/19/69).

Basketball career loses to education

Dec 20. Bill Bradley, Princeton basketball star, has turned down a chance to turn pro to attend Oxford as a Rhodes scholar. The tall, lean collegian probably would have been the first choice of the New York Knickerbockers in the draft next spring. Instead of commanding at least $20,000 as a pro, he has opted for the $2,500 annual stipend at Oxford. He said that athletes "retire at 30 with nothing more than a scrapbook of their clippings."

21 arrested in civil rights murder case

Dec 10. Twenty-one men, including a sheriff and deputy, have been arrested by federal agents in connection with the brutal slayings of three civil rights workers near Jackson, Mississippi. All are members of the Ku Klux Klan or White Knights, segregationist lynch mobs. The accused law officers allegedly detained the three men last June on trumped-up traffic charges, and then released them to the KKK. Today, a federal judge dismissed 19 of the defendants on grounds that the FBI improperly obtained a confession from Horace Barnette, one of the accused (→ 1/16/65).

Tom Wesselmann's "Still Life Painting, 30," like most Pop Art, loudly satirizes contemporary values in living, almost blinding color.

1965

JANUARY

Su	Mo	Tu	We	Th	Fr	Sa
					1	2
3	4	5	6	7	8	9
10	11	12	13	14	15	16
17	18	19	20	21	22	23
24	25	26	27	28	29	30
31						

1. Pasadena: Michigan over Oregon State 34-7 in Rose Bowl.

2. Miami: Joe Namath signs first pro contract—three years, $427,000 with N.Y. Jets.

2. South Vietnamese lose six-day battle at Binh Gia (→ 6).

3. Syria nationalizes main industries (→ 3/4).

4. LBJ outlines goals for Great Society in State of Union address (→ 17).

8. Congo: 500 rebels reportedly executed in last six weeks (→ 11/25).

11. Washington: Interagency Council on Smoking Health says 125,000 Americans will die from cigarettes in 1965 (→ 2/8).

13. Laos: Two U.S. planes shot down on combat mission (→ 9/17/69).

14. Belfast: Premiers of North Ireland and Republic of Ireland meet for first time (→ 3/8/66).

15. London: Churchill suffers stroke; condition grave (→ 30).

16. Mississippi: 18 arrested in murder of three civil rights workers (→ 2/1).

17. Washington: LBJ announces 88 anti-poverty projects (→ 20).

19. Cape Kennedy: Unmanned Gemini 2 launched after weather delays (→ 2/16).

20. West Germany begins shipping $80 mil. in military aid to Israel (→ 2/12).

20. Cairo: Nasser takes nomination for 3rd presidency (→ 3/15).

21. New York: Indonesia formally pulls out of U.N. (→ 2/26).

23. Colorado: 100 cadets charged in Air Academy cheating scandal.

26. Iran: Premier Hassan Ali Mansour dies of assassin's bullet wounds (→ 4/10).

27. Saigon: Military leaders oust civilian govt. of Tran Van Huong (→ 2/6).

28. Cairo: Sophia Loren movies banned in Arab states.

DEATH

24. Winston Churchill, British statesman and world leader (*11/30/1874).

Sir Winston Churchill, 1874-1965

Churchill was in the bath in 1945 when told that Britain was voting Labor: "There may well be a landslide and they have a perfect right to kick us out. That is democracy. That is what we have been fighting for. Hand me my towel."

Churchill, renowned in Britain for 65 years, lies in state in London.

Jan 30. Sir Winston Churchill, who rallied his nation and the world to the cause of freedom in World War ll, has died at the age of 90. Sir Winston was laid to rest in a small cemetery near his family's ancestral home at Blenheim Palace following an extraordinary state funeral in London that included representatives of 110 nations. It was the final tribute to a man who stood as a giant among the statesmen of the 20th Century. For Britain, its imperial glories already fading, his death seemed to be the symbolic end of a proud era. For the world as a whole, it was the departure of a brilliant statesman who with his determination and eloquence stood as a symbol of defiance to Hitler.

In the darkest hours of World War II, when the German armies were overruning Europe, it was to Sir Winston that Britain turned in 1940 as Prime Minister. Grimly, he told the House of Commons that "I have nothing to offer but blood, toil, tears and sweat." ln the forbidding months when Britain stood alone in the war, fearing a German invasion and battered by German bombers, Churchill stood as a symbol of perseverance, a cigar typically in his mouth and two fingers raised in the signal of victory.

With America's entry into the war following Pearl Harbor, he provided the leadership and cohesion for the alliance of Britain, the United States and the Soviet Union that finally crushed the Axis powers.

In his long career of public service, stretching back to the turn of the century, he suffered his most bitter personal setback in 1945, when, with the war won in Europe, he was defeated in a national election by the Labor Party.

In the postwar period, he was one of the first voices to warn of Soviet expansion, declaring in a 1946 speech in Fulton, Missouri, that an "iron curtain" was descending across the continent. He was reelected Prime Minister in 1951, a post he held until 1955, when he retired because of failing health.

A graduate of Sandhurst, he began his career as army officer and war correspondent. He was first elected to Parliament in 1901 and shortly before World War I was made First Lord of the Admiralty.

Stolen gems found; Murph the Surf held

Jan 8. Jack "Murph the Surf" Murphy, 27, and a companion were arrested in Miami as suspects in the theft of $410,000 in rare gems from the American Museum of Natural History in October of last year. The world's largest sapphire, the Star of India, and eight of the other 22 stolen gems were returned to New York in an attorney's coat pocket, having been recovered in two water-logged suede pouches from a Miami bus terminal locker with the help of a third suspect. The three describe themselves as "beach boys." Murphy is a sometime aquatic clown, but mainly they are notorious jewel thieves. Murphy is also accused of pistol-whipping actress Eva Gabor and stealing jewels worth $50,000 from her a year ago.

136 Americans died in Vietnam in 1964

Jan 6. The total number of American combat casualties suffered by military advisers in South Vietnam in 1964 was made public today by the United States military mission in Saigon. From among the Army, Navy, Air Force and Marine Corps personnel stationed there, 136 were killed and 1,022 were wounded. Eleven Americans are listed as missing in action. There are currently at least 16,000 men serving in the various units under the U.S. Military Assistance Advisory Group Command, and this year's figures represent an increase over the previous two. According to the Saigon military mission, 32 Americans were killed in 1961-62, while 76 were reported killed last year (→ 27).

Johnson installed; stresses Great Society

LBJ takes oath from Warren as Lady Bird and V.P. Humphrey look on.

Jan 20. Lyndon Baines Johnson officially begins his first full term as President of the United States today. After being sworn in by Chief Justice Earl Warren, LBJ addressed the thousands who braved frigid weather to witness the inaugural ceremonies. His speech, praised by Democrats and Republicans alike, emphasized his war on poverty and denounced the horrors of racism.

Noting that "we are all passengers on a dot of earth," Johnson remarked, "How incredulous it is that in this fragile existence we should hate and destroy one another." He described his notion of a "Great Society" as "the excitement of becoming . . . always trying and always gaining." America, he said, seeks "no dominion over our fellow man, but man's dominion over tyranny and misery."

Last week, Johnson announced the creation of 88 new anti-poverty projects at a cost of $101 million. The funds will provide education, employment and job training for the nation's destitute, particularly poor urban youths (→ 4/11).

Life of distinction ends for T.S. Eliot

Jan 4. "I should have been a pair of ragged claws/Scuttling across the floors of silent seas." Happily, T.S. Eliot rejected a crustaceous career for a lifetime of writing poems. His work "The Waste Land" (1922) and others are classics. The writer died today at the age of 76.

Two nations claimed Eliot: England (he studied at Oxford and spent many years in London) and the United States (he was born in St. Louis). His poem "The Lovesong of J. Alfred Prufrock" (1909) and play "Murder in the Cathedral" (1935) were praised for their expert phrasing. "Things have a terrible permanence when people die," Eliot wrote. Elliot's permanent place among the literary greats is assured.

Eliot, father of Modernist poetry.

Noted Negro lady playwright is dead

Lorraine Hansberry.

Jan 12. "What happens to a dream deferred?" asks a Langston Hughes poem. Playwright Lorraine Hansberry's dreams are deferred eternally by her untimely death from cancer. She was only 34.

Miss Hansberry, daughter of a wealthy Negro banker, took another line from a Hughes poem for the title of her first play, "A Raisin in the Sun." The work, given the 1959 New York Drama Citics Award, was criticized and praised. Miss Hansberry had dared to show Negroes without stereotype. Her play "The Sign in Sidney Brustein's Window" is now on Broadway.

A bunch of kids balanced on skateboards cruise the streets of the suburbs before an audience of old-fashioned but envious bike riders.

1965

FEBRUARY

Su	Mo	Tu	We	Th	Fr	Sa
	1	2	3	4	5	6
7	8	9	10	11	12	13
14	15	16	17	18	19	20
21	22	23	24	25	26	27
28						

1. Alabama: Rev. King and 770 others arrested in protest against voter discrimination (→ 3).

1. Auckland: Australian Ron Clarke runs 5,000-meters in record 13:33.6.

3. Alabama: 1,000 more held in voting rights drive (→ 10).

6. Vietnam: Seven U.S. G.I.'s killed in Viet Cong raid on base at Pleiku; 126 wounded (→ 7).

7. North Vietnam: U.S. jets hit Don Hoi guerrilla base in reprisal for Viet Cong raids (→ 9).

8. New York: 84 die as DC-7 crashes off Jones Beach.

8. Britain bans cigarette ads on television (→ 6/2/67).

9. Moscow: U.S. Embassy stoned by Chinese, Vietnamese students (→ 11).

12. West Germany, under Arab pressure, halts military shipments to Israel (→ 5/12).

14. New York: Malcolm X home firebombed; no injuries (→ 21).

15. Ottawa: Canada's maple leaf flag raised for first time.

16. Cape Kennedy: First Pegasus satellite launched to study meteoroids and other conditions important to Apollo (→ 20).

16. N.Y.: Four held in plot to blow up Statue of Liberty, Liberty Bell, Washington Monument.

18. Gambia gains independence within British Commonwealth.

19. New York: 14 Vietnam protesters arrested for blocking U.N. doors (→ 4/17).

20. Ranger 8 hits moon, radios 7,000 photos to U.S. (→ 3/18).

26. Bronx: Norman Butler arrested in Malcolm X murder (→ 2/28/66).

26. Indonesia seizes rubber plants of U.S. firms (→ 28).

28. Jakarta: 500 Indonesian students invade home of U.S. ambassador (→ 3/21).

DEATHS

13. William Kilpatrick, U.S. philosopher, father of progressive education (*11/20/1871).

22. Felix Frankfurter, ex-Supreme Court justice (*11/15/1882).

Hundreds of protesting Negroes arrested

King looks to Montgomery, with marchers toting signs, "We need bail money."

Feb 10. Mass arrests of Negroes protesting segregation and voting rights violations continue in the turbulent South. In Selma, Alabama, February 1, civil rights leader Rev. Dr. Martin Luther King Jr. and 770 others were arrested for picketing a county courthouse for elimination of discriminatory voting requirements. At the rally, King said, "If Negroes could vote, there would be no oppressive poverty directed against Negroes, our children would not be crippled by segregated schools and the whole community might live together in harmony."

More than 1,000 Negro schoolchildren were arrested two days later for truancy or unlawful assembly, as the Selma protest campaign spread to nearby Marion. King directed the demonstration from his Selma jail cell.

Today, Sheriff James Clark and several deputies forced 165 Selma Negro youths to march. Applying cattle prods and swinging clubs, the officers pushed the crowd to a makeshift jail (→ 3/9).

Malcolm X is shot to death by Negroes

Feb 21. In a dramatic shooting before an audience of 400, Negro leader Malcolm X was killed by assassins. Malcolm X, born Malcolm Little, was for a number of years a minister and one of the principal spokesmen of the Black Muslim organization led by Elijah Muhammad. Following disagreements with Muhammad, Malcolm split with the Black Muslims and founded his own group, The Organization for Afro-American Unity. The two groups waged a feud which ultimately culminated in the shooting; he was unprepared for the attack which occured as he was beginning a speech to followers (→ 26).

X is wheeled off to the hospital.

U.S. launches air strikes on North Vietnam

Feb 11. The Johnson administration has ordered air strikes against targets in North Vietnam in retaliation for guerrilla attacks directed by Hanoi against American military installations in South Vietnam. The first strike by Navy carrier planes at what was described as a Viet Cong staging area in the southern part of North Vietnam was ordered after Communist guerrillas staged coordinated attacks against U.S. installations at Pleiku in the Central Highlands of South Vietnam. Eight G.I.'s were killed and 108 wounded.

When the Viet Cong then attacked a U.S.Army barracks in the coastal city of Quinhon, both Air Force and Navy planes, in the biggest air attack of the war, struck at coastal supply depots in the southern part of North Vietnam.

The White House said the air strikes were in response to "provocations ordered and directed by the Hanoi regime." President Johnson said that "we seek no wider war" but cautioned that "whether or not this course can be maintained lies with the North Vietnamese aggressors." Amid growing tension, Johnson sent an American battalion equipped with Hawk anti-aircraft missiles into South Vietnam to protect an air base at Danang (→ 25).

G.I.'s help a fellow soldier to safety.

Stan Laurel, the weepy one, is dead

Feb 23. Stan Laurel of the Laurel and Hardy team has died in Santa Monica, Calif. He was 74. The men made nearly 150 slapstick comedies in the 20's and 30's. Laurel wrote most of the gags (when they weren't improvising) and scrupulously edited the film. He did not believe in retakes, which may surprise his four wives: He wed each woman twice.

Oddly enough, although their association spanned decades, Laurel and Hardy had only recently gotten to know each other well. On a ship bound for a publicity tour in England, the men found enough time on their hands to do more than talk shop. They talked about their love of singing, their wives, their childhoods. Laurel ended public appearances after Hardy died in 1957. He lost an old partner and a new friend.

1965

MARCH

Su	Mo	Tu	We	Th	Fr	Sa
	1	2	3	4	5	6
7	8	9	10	11	12	13
14	15	16	17	18	19	20
21	22	23	24	25	26	27
28	29	30	31			

1. Cairo: UAR signs $100 mil. aid pact with E. Germany (→ 4).

2. Vietnam: 160 U.S. and Saigon planes bomb two bases in North in first of "Rolling Thunder" raids (→ 6).

4. Syria nationalizes nine oil companies, two of U.S. (→ 9/16).

6. U.S. announces it will send 3,500 troops to Vietnam (→ 31).

9. Selma: King and 1,500 others blocked with clubs and tear gas on march to Montgomery (→ 11).

11. Selma: White civil rights activist Rev. James Reeb dies of beating by whites (→ 17).

15. Cairo: Nasser re-elected Egyptian president (→ 2/15/66).

17. Alabama: Federal judge authorizes civil rights march to Montgomery (→ 20).

19. London: Rembrandt's "Titus" sold for $2.2 million.

20. Texas: LBJ orders 4,000 troops to protect Selma-Montgomery marchers (→ 21).

21. Indonesia nationalizes Goodyear and four U.S oil companies (→ 10/1).

21. Alabama: 3,200 begin freedom march from Selma to Montgomery (→ 24).

21. Cape Kennedy: U.S. launches Ranger 9, last in series of lunar explorations (→ 24).

22. Soviets say Khrushchev underestimated Marxism (→ 5/8).

24. Alabama: Freedom marchers reach Montgomery (→ 25).

24. U.S.: Ranger 9 moon photos shown on live TV (→ 4/6).

25. Alabama: Viola Liuzzo, white, shot to death transporting freedom marchers (→ 26).

26. Alabama: FBI arrests four Klan members for murder of Viola Liuzzo (→ 27).

27. Alabama: KKK leader Robert Shelton calls civil rights murders Communist plot to destroy U.S. right wing (→ 28).

29. U.S. Supreme Court rules business can shut down to avoid unionism.

DEATH

17. Farouk, ex-king of Egypt (*2/11/1920).

Khanh is deposed by Vietnam military

Feb 25. Lt. Gen. Nguyen Khanh, the military strongman who seized power 13 months ago, has been overthrown in a coup by junior officers. His ouster followed a week of events more confusing than usual. South Vietnamese army and marine units had marched on Saigon and announced the ouster of Khanh, who has been serving as Commander-in-Chief of the armed forces. For a few days, it appeared that Khanh had regained control, but eventually he was forced to accept the post of Ambassador-at-Large and leave the country. The events were a setback to President Johnson's effort to portray progress in Vietnam (→ 3/6).

Nat King Cole, the sweet singer, dies

Feb 15. A voice that was three parts fog to one part frog resulted in a hoarse, honey-cured quality that sustained Nat "King" Cole as a top singer for a quarter of a century and racked up $50 million in record sales. Nathaniel Adams Coles from Alabama, the son of a Baptist minister, began by tickling the ivories in small barrooms, formed his own trio and started singing by accident. Songs kept uncurling from his cavernous mouth, each vowel savored, as he flashed those yard-wide smiles. He has succumbed to lung cancer, only 45 years old, but he has left us a legacy of haunting romantic ballads and swinging jazz tunes.

Cole and wife in Hollywood.

Alabama freedom walk

March 28. After several short-distance protest marches, marked by violence and mass arrests, 25,000 civil rights demonstrators embarked on a 50-mile walk for freedom from Selma, Alabama, to the state Capitol in Montgomery. With passion in their hearts and justice on their minds, they reached their destination and challenged Alabama to end racial discrimination.

The marchers, led by Rev. Dr. Martin Luther King Jr., requested and received a court order allowing them to proceed along U.S. Route 80 without interference. Federal Judge Frank Johnson ordered Governor George Wallace to refrain from "harassing or threatening" the protesters along their historic trek. Wallace, a staunch segregationist, has often ordered the arrests of thousands of Negro and white civil rights activists, despite reprimands from President Johnson.

King and Abernathy (rt.) lead way.

On reaching the Capitol steps, King told the massive crowd, "We are on the move and no wave of racism will stop us!" (→ 4/25).

Marines land; bomb rips Saigon Embassy

March 31. In the first commitment of combat troops, the Johnson administration has ordered two battalions of U.S. Marines into South Vietnam to help protect a major air base at Danang. The arrival of the Marines appeared to mark a distinct change in the American military role in the Vietnam War. There already are 23,500 American servicemen in South Vietnam, but their role has been to serve as advisers to the South Vietnamese armed forces. The Marines, in contrast, will engage in military patrols to protect the Danang air base.

Meanwhile, the Johnson administration escalated the air war against North Vietnam. Early in the month, more than 100 United States planes bombed a North Vietnamese munitions depot at Xombang. For the first time, the air raid was not directly linked as a reprisal for a Viet Cong attack against American military installations. Near the end of the month, a huge bomb, apparently planted by the Viet Cong, exploded at the American Embassy in Saigon, causing scores of casualties and killing two Americans (→ 4/2).

Marines wade ashore near Danang to face the elusive Viet Cong.

Soviet cosmonaut floats outside spacecraft

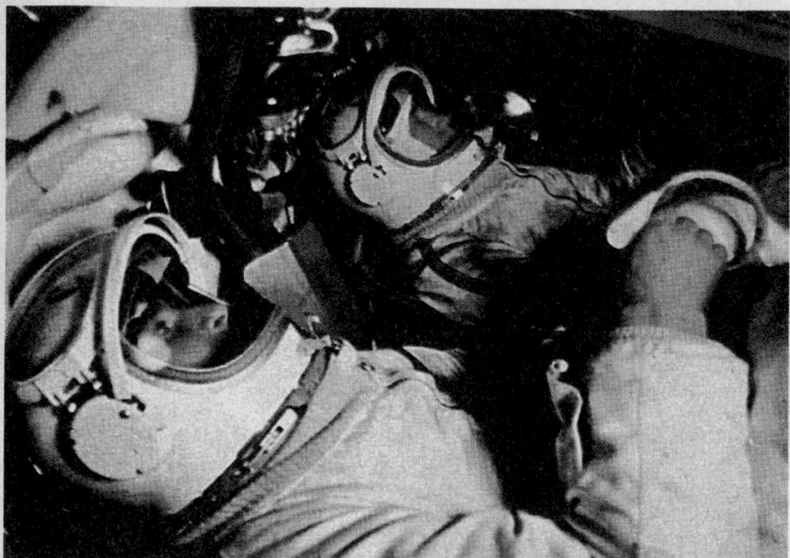

Beliaiev (left) and Leonov in Voskhod 2 before Leonov's space acrobatics.

March 18. Soviet cosmonaut Aleksei A. Leonov today became the first man to leave an orbiting spacecraft and float in space. Leonov opened the hatch of the two-man Voskhod 2 spacecraft as it passed over the Soviet Union and spent ten minutes in space. He was tethered to the spacecraft by a five-yard rope and wore a space suit specially equipped to shield him from the intense heat of the sun. Television viewers in the Soviet Union and Europe watched Leonov emerge from the capsule and do a somersault in space (→ 21).

Quinn and Andrews are Oscar contenders

Both Anthony Quinn and Julie Andrews are up for Oscars, but there their similarities end. Quinn, of Irish-Mexican heritage, has been in pictures since the mid 1930's. Until the 50's he tended to play heavies, especially ethnic ones (he could pass for Peruvian or Serb). Last year, he put in a stirring performance as "Zorba the Greek."

English-born Miss Andrews stars in the current songfest "The Sound of Music." She is an Oscar contender for her role as the levitating nanny in "Mary Poppins." That movie was her motion picture debut.

Andrews frolics in the Austrian Alps.

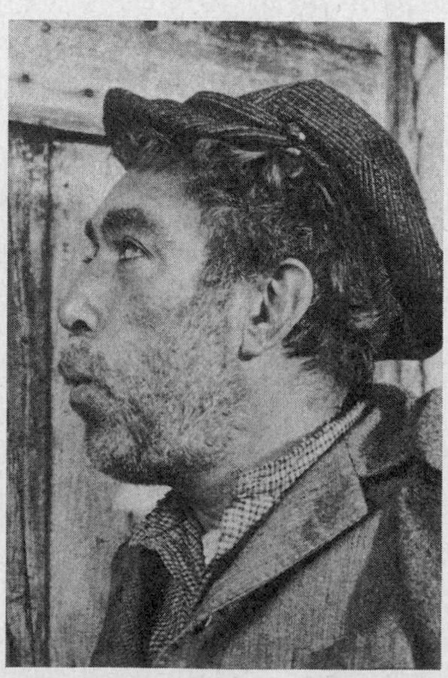

Anthony Quinn: "Zorba the Greek."

1965

APRIL

Su	Mo	Tu	We	Th	Fr	Sa
				1	2	3
4	5	6	7	8	9	10
11	12	13	14	15	16	17
18	19	20	21	22	23	24
25	26	27	28	29	30	

2. U.S. to increase men, money and supplies to Vietnam (→ 4).

4. Vietnam: Two Hanoi MIG's down two U.S. jets in first air clash (→ 15).

4. New York: 3,000 protest Soviet curbs on Jews (→ 7/25).

6. Cape Canaveral: NASA launches Early Bird, world's first commercial satellite (→ 23).

7. Berlin: East German jets harass Bundestag as Parliament meets there first time in seven years (→ 10/7/66).

10. Iran: Shah escapes attempt on his life (→ 12/11).

11. Texas: LBJ signs bill for $1.3 bil. in aid to education (→ 7/30).

11. Georgia: Jack Nicklaus wins Masters with record 271.

12. U.S.: Tornadoes ravage Midwest; 239 dead in six states.

15. South Vietnam: 230 planes strike Viet Cong in biggest raid yet (→ 19).

16. Korea: Troops rushed to Seoul as students riot for fifth day (→ 10/17/72).

18. New York: Marian Anderson sings farewell at Carnegie Hall.

19. Turkey to deport 3,000 Greek nationals in dispute over mistreatment of Turks in Cyprus (→ 9/9/67).

19. South Vietnam: Nine Americans killed in helicopter by Viet Cong ground fire (→ 5/16).

19. Boston: Morio Sigematsu wins Boston Marathon.

23. U.S.S.R.: Soviets launch their first communications satellite (→ 5/2).

25. Dominican Republic: U.S.-supported govt. deposed in military coup (→ 28).

26. Cambodia: 20,000 attack U.S. Embassy (→ 5/3).

28. LBJ sends Marines to Dominican Republic (→ 30).

29. Commissioner of Education Francis Keppel orders all public schools desegregated by fall of 1967 (→ 5/7).

29. Australia, despite public opposition, announces decision to send 800 troops to Vietnam (→ 5/16).

Murrow, CBS News patron saint, dies

April 23. "This—is London." With these words, broadcast on CBS Radio during the battle of Britain in the early years of WWII, young Edward R. Murrow made a name for himself that to this day and hereafter is synonymous with integrity and excellence in journalism. Murrow, who reportedly smoked four packs of cigarettes a day, has died of lung cancer, four days short of his 57th birthday.

A North Carolina native who grew up in Washington state and graduated from Washington State College, Murrow joined CBS in 1935. In 1948, his "Hear It Now" radio program became "See It Now" on television. Although he won praise, he grew to distrust TV's commercialism. From 1961-63, Murrow was JFK's Director of the United States Information Agency.

Murrow, pioneer in TV journalism.

World's largest air cooled park opened

April 9. The Houston Astrodome, the world's biggest air-conditioned arena, opened today as President Johnson attended an exhibition baseball game between the New York Yankees and the Houston Astros—the first ever played indoors. Built on what was once grazing land, the Astrodome is 208 feet high and can seat 50,000 spectators. The only flaw is that the clear plastic panels at the top of the dome do not allow outfielders to see fly balls. Orange baseballs are being tested, but it may be necessary to replace the plastic panels.

Coup deposes Dominican President

April 30. President Donald Reid Cabral has been thrown out of office in the Dominican Republic. A new military junta seized control of the government and reportedly called for American support to help fight leftist rebels. President Johnson was quick to oblige. An additional 1,000 Marines and 2,500 men from the 82nd Airborne Division started arriving on the war-torn Caribbean island. Their mission is to protect American citizens and property and to prevent a Communist takeover. The arrival of the American troops was assailed by Cuba's Premier Fidel Castro.

Hundreds of people have died in this civil war. One Marine was killed and about 18 Marines and airborne soldiers were hurt today in skirmishes with rebels (→ 5/2).

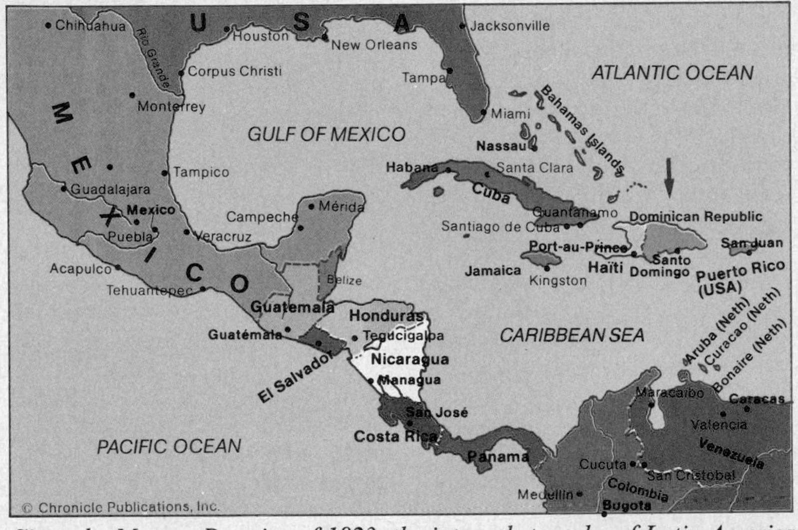

Since the Monroe Doctrine of 1823, the internal struggles of Latin America and the Caribbean have been treated as direct risks to U.S. national security.

Marines patrol the streets of Santo Domingo, in an effort to ensure the advancement of American interests.

American planes reported dropping napalm bombs in Vietnam

April 15. American and South Vietnamese bombers mounted the biggest aerial attack of the war today, dropping 1,000 tons of explosives on a Viet Cong stronghold in South Vietnam near the Cambodian border. American planes are reportedly dropping napalm, a highly inflammable chemical substance that turns jungle into desert. Tayninh, the scene of the bombing attack, is heavily wooded. American commanders, who suspect it is the military and political headquarters of the Viet Cong, have declared it "a free bomb zone." Civilians have been urged to move away. Napalm does not make any distinctions between soldiers and civilians.

The bombing raid today comes less than two weeks after a sharp increase in the American military commitment to South Vietnam by President Johnson. He apparently hopes that new bombing raids will convince the Viet Cong to participate in peace negotiations (→ 29).

An American soldier lends aid to a wounded South Vietnamese. The unique perils of guerrilla war are producing numerous civilian casualties.

15,000 protesters picket White House

April 17. The man they came to impress had left for the weekend. That did not stop 15,000 students from marching outside the White House today, demanding a withdrawal of American troops from Vietnam. They jammed the sidewalk on Pennsylvania Avenue as they demonstrated peacefully and carried signs calling for an end to the Vietnam War. President Johnson neither saw nor heard the students. He had flown to his Texas ranch. The protesters, organized by the left-leaning Students for a Democratic Society, paraded in the bright sunshine to the Washington Monument and then marched to Capitol Hill (→ 5/15).

Maddox organizes segregation march

April 25. Segregationist Lester Maddox and a band of 2,000 supporters are responding to civil rights protest marches by marching through the heart of Atlanta. They were forced to detour when someone tossed a smoke bomb in their path. Maddox told the crowd, many of whom belong to the Ku Klux Klan and other radical anti-integrationist groups, that "deadly, bloody and ungodly communism threatens our very existence." The turnout was far below the expected crowd of 10,000 (→ 29).

Merchant of beauty Rubinstein is dead

April 1. Helena Rubinstein, multimillionaire beauty expert and cosmetics manufacturer, died yesterday in New York. She always tried to keep her age a secret, but associates said that she was 94. Born in Krakow, Poland, she studied medicine briefly in Switzerland, then went to Australia and began treating skin, soon opening salons in the United States. Twice-married Rubinstein collected Picassos and Matisses but brought her lunch in a bag. Hard-working and eccentric, she never lost interest in the 110 products that bore her name.

1965

MAY

Su	Mo	Tu	We	Th	Fr	Sa
						1
2	3	4	5	6	7	8
9	10	11	12	13	14	15
16	17	18	19	20	21	22
23	24	25	26	27	28	29
30	31					

1. Shoemaker, on Lucky Debonair, wins third Kentucky Derby.

2. LBJ says Communists took over Dominican uprising, raises invasion force to 14,000 (→ 13).

2. U.S. Early Bird satellite begins transmission, linking Europe and North America (→ 6/3).

3. Cambodia breaks ties with U.S. (→ 5/1/66).

7. Alabama: Klansmen indicted for Viola Liuzzo murder get mistrial (→ 6/14).

8. Texas: Randy Matson hits 70'7" in shot put, first over 70'.

8. Moscow gives first public praise of Stalin since 1956 (→ 12/9/65).

9. New York: Vladimir Horowitz returns to stage at Carnegie Hall after 12-year absence.

11. Pakistan: Cyclone kills up to 5,000; five mil. homeless.

12. West Germany opens diplomatic ties with Israel (→ 14).

14. Nine Arab nations break ties with West Germany (→ 27).

15. New York: Sit-in halts Armed Forces Day parade on Fifth Avenue (→ 31).

16. South Vietnam: Chain of blasts kill 21 Americans, destroy 40 planes (→ 6/5).

22. Rome: Very Reverend Pedro Arrupe named head of Jesuits.

24. U.S. Supreme Court voids law curbing Communist propaganda in mails (→ 11/15).

24. Britain adopts metric system.

27. Israelis raid Jordan, claiming retaliation for Jordanian border strikes (→ 2/5/66).

28. India: Mine blast kills 200.

30. French refuse active role in 1966 NATO exercises (→ 9/11).

31. New York: Columbia valedictorian booed for deploring student protests (→ 6/8).

31. Jim Clark wins Indy 500 at 150.7 mph in Lotus.

DEATHS

7. Charles Sheeler, American painter, industrial landscapes (*7/16/1883).

23. David Smith, American sculptor, painter (*3/9/1906).

14,000 U.S. troops in Dominican Republic

Straw-hatted and armed for battle.

May 13. Both sides broke the eight-day-old cease-fire in the civil war that has divided the Dominican Republic. Efforts to set up negotiations failed. Warplanes of the military junta backed by the United States strafed a rebel radio station. Rebel forces allied with Col. Francisco Caamano Deno fired from their positions in the streets. At least one American paratrooper was killed. There are now 14,000 Americans bogged down in this chaotic, confusing and deadly civil war.

President Johnson made a televised speech on the 2nd to announce that he was doubling U.S. forces in the island-nation. Their mission is to "prevent another Communist state in this hemisphere." Johnson charged that the democratic revolution on the island had taken a sharp turn to the left under the command of Communist conspirators. "We must use every resource at our command to prevent the establishment of another Cuba," Johnson said.

Juan Bosch, former Dominican President, disputes LBJ's charge that Communists are behind the rebellion. The allegation, he said, reminds him of "a great big elephant afraid of a little mouse" (→ 9/26).

Ralph Boston leaps 27 feet, 5 inches

Boston soars to a world record.

May 29. Ralph Boston and Hal Connolly set world records at the California Relays. Boston leaped 27 feet, 5 inches in the broad jump and Connolly won the weight-throw with a distance of 233 feet, 2 inches at Modesto. Boston broke the record he set a year ago by three-quarters of an inch.

Frances Perkins was 1st woman in Cabinet

May 14. Frances Perkins is dead at 83. President Roosevelt appointed her Secretary of Labor in 1933, the first woman Cabinet member in American history, and she presided over the department for 12 turbulent years, a champion of such sweeping social legislation as the Public Works Administration, the National Recovery Act and the Social Security Act. She wrote "The Roosevelt I Knew" as well as books on labor problems. A handicap being a woman? "Only when climbing trees," said the warmly admired lady with the Boston accent.

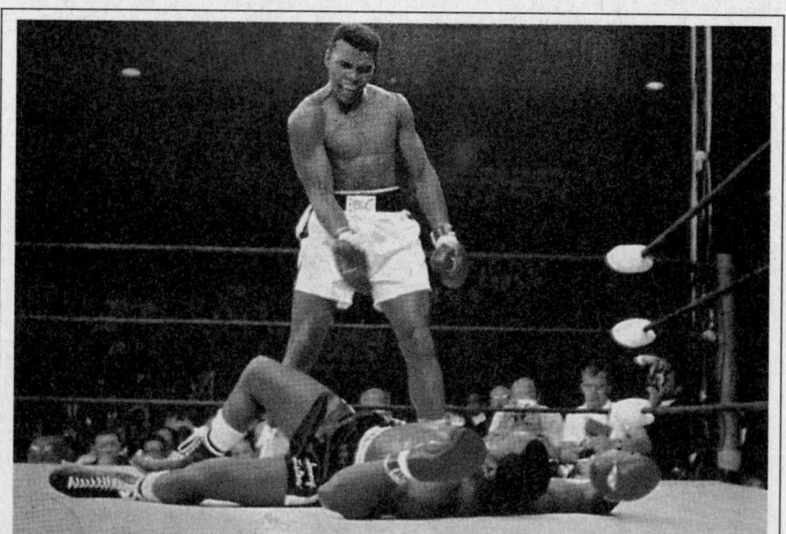

May 25. "I told you I had a surprise," said Cassius Clay after flooring Sonny Liston in 48 seconds to shouts of "Fake, fake, fake!" from the crowd of 4,280. Clay, now a Moslem, wore a robe marked Muhammad Ali and called his victory a triumph of the "righteous life" (→ 11/22).

Ian Smith's party wins in Rhodesia

May 7. Rhodesian Prime Minister Ian Smith won a decisive victory today, as his Rhodesian Front Party took all 50 parliamentary seats contested in the general election. Smith's routing of the opposition party strengthens his resolve to win the self-governing colony's independence from Great Britain and to consolidate his racially exclusive political policies.

Although Smith has an overwhelming amount of support among Rhodesia's 217,000 white voters, few of Rhodesia's four million blacks have the legal right to vote. Only 15 black Africans were elected to Parliament this election, making the opposition, for the first time in the colony's history, entirely black. Smith's government was condemned in the United Nations Security Council, and a number of African states had lobbied unsuccessfully to get Britain to stop the election. But Smith and his colleagues believe they know what is best for Rhodesia (→ 10/8).

1965

JUNE

Su	Mo	Tu	We	Th	Fr	Sa
		1	2	3	4	5
6	7	8	9	10	11	12
13	14	15	16	17	18	19
20	21	22	23	24	25	26
27	28	29	30			

1. Albany: Gov. Rockefeller signs bill ending death penalty in New York (→ 5/3/71).

1. Japan: Mine blast takes 236 lives.

5. U.S. State Dept. admits for first time U.S. troops in Vietnam have combat role (→ 8).

6. Zanzibar: Chou En-lai greeted by big crowds, attacks U.S.

7. U.S. Supreme Court bars curbs on birth control.

7. U.S. Supreme Court voids conviction of Billie Sol Estes because trial was televised against his wishes.

7. Morocco: Hassan II restores absolute monarchy (→ 10/30).

8. LBJ authorizes commanders in Vietnam to commit U.S. ground forces to combat (→ 14).

8. New York: 17,000 attend antiwar rally at Madison Square Garden (→ 7/4).

8. U.S.: Frito-Lay, Inc. and Pepsi-Cola merge to form PepsiCo., Inc.

11. London: Queen Elizabeth includes Beatles in birthday honors list (→ 7/29).

14. Jackson: 472 arrested on civil rights march (→ 8/6).

14. Saigon: Military triumvirate takes control of South Vietnam (→ 16).

16. Washington: Def. Sec. MacNamara says U.S. will add 21,000 to Vietnam force (→ 17).

17. South Vietnam: 27 B-52's hit Viet Cong; two planes lost (→ 19).

21. Saigon: Communist Tran Van Dong executed in Saigon square (→ 29).

25. California: Military transport plane goes down; 84 die.

27. Cairo: Nasser meets with Chou En-lai and Sukarno.

30. U.S. ends economic aid to Taiwan (→ 10/13).

DEATHS

13. Martin Buber, Jewish philosopher, theologian (*2/8/1878).

22. David O. Selznick, American film producer, "Gone With the Wind" (*5/10/1902).

U.S. forces authorized to fight in Vietnam

Americans traverse a beachhead before plunging into the inscrutable jungle.

June 29. For the first time in the Vietnam War, American troops are fighting in a combat role tonight next to soldiers of the Saigon regime. It is a "search and destroy" mission aimed at Zone D, a Communist stronghold 20 miles northeast of Saigon. At least one American serviceman was killed by a Viet Cong mortar attack. Communists have been dug into the thick jungle of Zone D since the end of the war with France. South Vietnamese forces have not been able to penetrate the area for 20 years.

Four Marines were killed and several were injured in another clash with Communist guerrillas south of Danang.

Earlier this month, the State Department revealed that President Johnson had authorized a wider combat role for American troops in South Vietnam. General William Westmoreland, commander of United States troops in Vietnam, was given the authority to commit men to the battlefield if the Saigon government requested the assistance. Until this month, the Americans were authorized only to provide "perimeter defense" of installations, but it was widely known that they were venturing at great distances beyond those perimeters to pursue Communist forces (→ 7/8).

June 3. Edward White takes a stroll 100 miles above the earth, untethered for 20 minutes while James McDivitt stayed in the capsule of Gemini 4. They plan the longest U.S. space flight yet at four days (→ 7/15).

Thieu names Ky as Premier in Vietnam

June 19. Vowing to mobilize all able-bodied men in the war against the Viet Cong, Air Marshal Nguyen Cao Ky today became South Vietnam's new and youngest Premier. The 34-year-old Ky, commander of the Air Force, was named to the post by the ten-man Military National Leadership Committee headed by Major General Nguyen Van Thieu. Though the militant Buddhists would prefer a civilian government, they seem willing for now to accept Ky. The flamboyant, mustached Ky received part of his training in the United States and has personally led air strikes against North Vietnam (→ 21).

Ky, 34, new Premier in Saigon.

Baruch, adviser to Presidents, is dead

June 21. A financier, philanthropist and adviser to Presidents, Bernard M. Baruch died last night of a heart attack at the age of 94. Baruch had made and lost millions of dollars in Wall Street speculation. By the time he was 31, he had amassed $100,000 for each year of his age. Accordingly, his views on economic matters carried considerable weight with the public and with heads of state. Baruch engaged in extensive correspondence with nine Presidents of the United States and was an especially important adviser to Presidents Wilson, Roosevelt and Eisenhower. He frequently wrote letters to newspapers and made his opinions known on many topics. ▷

Boumedienne takes power in Algeria

Ex-army chief Boumedienne.

June 20. A coup d'etat in Algeria has toppled the government of President Ahmed Ben Bella. The new man in charge is Houari Boumedienne, formerly Vice President of the Council and Minister of Defense. In the war against France, he was commander of the army of national liberation. News of the coup was broadcast to a startled country on Algiers Radio this morning. The report said Ben Bella "had become a traitor and would be punished in a manner befitting a despot." He was arrested at his home under orders from the Revolutionary Council signed by Boumedienne.

The coup d'etat comes just nine days before the opening of the Third World Conference, which will be hosted by Algeria. Some 50 Kings and Presidents are expected to attend. The meeting will provide a test of Boumedienne's leadership. Egypt might be reluctant to support the new President because Ben Bella is a personal friend of Gamal Abdel Nasser (→ 7/29).

"Come listen to a story 'bout a man named Jed, poor mountaineer barely kept his family fed."

1965

JULY

Su	Mo	Tu	We	Th	Fr	Sa
				1	2	3
4	5	6	7	8	9	10
11	12	13	14	15	16	17
18	19	20	21	22	23	24
25	26	27	28	29	30	31

3. Wimbledon: Roy Emerson over Fred Stolle 6-2, 6-4, 6-4; Margaret Smith over Maria Bueno 6-4, 7-5.

4. Washington: Martin Luther King calls for end of Vietnam War (→ 8/4).

5. Missouri: Harry Truman says the United States is "still the greatest country."

6. France withdraws delegate from EEC (→ 5/11/67).

8. South Vietnam: Maxwell Taylor resigns U.S. ambassadorship (→ 14).

14. Felice Bimondi wins Tour de France.

14. North Vietnam: U.S. jets hit target 40 miles from China (→ 24).

15. Mariner 4 sends first close-up photos of Mars back to U.S. (→ 8/29).

18. U.S.S.R.: Soviets launch rocket into solar orbit (→ 8/29).

19. France charges U.S. plane photographed atomic site.

20. LBJ appoints Arthur Goldberg to replace Adlai Stevenson as U.S. delegate to U.N.

21. Athens: Police battle 10,000 students asking return of Premier Papandreou, ousted week ago for attacks on army (→ 8/5).

24. North Vietnam: 16 U.S. planes hit bomb plant (→ 28).

25. Newport: Bob Dylan booed off stage at folk festival for using electric instruments.

25. Moscow: U.S. rabbis speak in Soviet pulpit (→ 2/19/71).

28. LBJ appoints Abe Fortas to replace Arthur Goldberg on Supreme Court.

28. London: Edward Heath named head of Conservatives.

29. London: Beatles' second film "Help," produced by Richard Lester, opens in U.K. (→ 8/15).

29. Algiers: France, Algeria sign pact for joint exploitation of Sahara resources (→ 2/24/71).

DEATH

19. Syngman Rhee, first pres. of South Korea (*4/26/1875).

30. Junichiro Tanizaki, Japanese writer (*7/24/1886).

Johnson signs Medicare in Truman library

LBJ signs in the presence of Lady Bird, Humphrey, Bess and Harry Truman.

July 30. President Johnson flew to the Harry S. Truman library in Independence, Mo., today to sign the medicare Social Security bill in a moving tribute to former President Truman, the first president to propose a federal program of health insurance under Social Security.

"The people love and voted for Harry Truman," LBJ said, "not because he gave them hell but because he gave them hope." The 81-year-old Truman was visibly moved.

The bill expands the 30-year-old Social Security insurance program to provide hospital care, nursing home care, home nursing services and out-patient diagnostic services to all Americans over 65 years old. It covers 17 million persons eligible for Social Security and two million others, who do not qualify under the present old-age, survivors and disability insurance program (→ 9/9).

LBJ sends 50,000 more troops to Vietnam

July 28. In a nationally televised news conference, President Lyndon B. Johnson today announced he was sending 50,000 more men to South Vietnam "almost immediately," increasing American troop strength from the present 75,000 to 125,000. Monthly draft calls will be raised from the current 17,000 to 35,000. Johnson also called on the United Nations to work harder on Vietnam peace efforts, and said the U.S. was willing to discuss North Vietnamese peace proposals. The president said the United States was involved in Vietnam because "we have learned at a terrible and brutal cost that retreat does not bring safety and weakness does not bring peace" (→ 8/13).

Adlai Stevenson, Ambassador to U.N., dies

July 14. United States Ambassador to the United Nations Adlai Stevenson suffered a heart attack and died today on a London street. He was often characterized as a man who arrived on the political scene at the wrong time. A Democrat, he ran twice for president against Eisenhower and was soundly defeated. Later, he lost the Democratic nomination to John F. Kennedy, who appointed him to the U.N. post. "A wise man," he once said, "does not try to hurry history" (→ 20).

Stevenson at the Security Council.

1965

AUGUST

Su	Mo	Tu	We	Th	Fr	Sa
1	2	3	4	5	6	7
8	9	10	11	12	13	14
15	16	17	18	19	20	21
22	23	24	25	26	27	28
29	30	31				

3. Amherst, Mass.: Three New England colleges found experimental Hampshire College.

4. LBJ hails college students as "fellow revolutionaries" (→ 9).

5. Athens: George Athanasiadis-Novas resigns as premier (→ 20).

9. Washington: 350 Vietnam protesters arrested (→ 27).

9. Arkansas: Fire in Titan II missile silo traps workers; 53 bodies removed (→ 10/29).

9. Singapore, with large Chinese population, splits with newly founded Malaysia, becomes independent state (→ 8/11/66).

10. New York: 70,000 hear N.Y. Philharmonic in Central Park.

11. L.A.: Vicious race riots break out in Watts, Newton (→ 15).

11. U.S.S.R. buys $450 mil. in Canadian wheat.

13. North Vietnam: Five Navy planes downed in raids (→ 18).

14. N.Y.: Brooklyn Navy Yard launches its last ship.

15. N.Y.: Beatles play to 55,000 at Shea Stadium (→ 9/26).

16. Indian troops cross Kashmir line, seizing two Pakistani outposts (→ 9/1).

17. Britain: Robert Manry ends Atlantic crossing in 13.5-ft. boat.

18. South Vietnam: Marines trap 2,000 Viet Cong, kill hundreds (→ 28).

20. Athens: 21,000 leftists riot as new govt. installed (→ 4/21/67).

27. LBJ bans draft exemption for married men (→ 10/16).

28. South Vietnam: Viet Cong unit routed in Mekong Delta; over 50 killed (→ 31).

29. Gemini 5 splashes down in Atlantic, as Charles Conrad and Gordon Cooper end record eight-day space flight (→ 11/26).

30. New York: Casey Stengel steps down as manager of Mets.

31. Saigon: U.S. to pay G.I.'s in military scrip to curb black market (→ 9/8).

DEATH

8. Shirley Jackson, American writer, "The Lottery" (*12/14/1919).

Race riots rage in Watts for five days

Aug 15. The racial tension which has plagued the nation for years exploded in a bloodbath of rioting, looting and arson in the Negro section of Watts in Los Angeles this month. Authorities, with assistance from some 20,000 National Guardsmen, have finally restored order, but not until five days of violence left about 30 dead, hundreds injured, over 2,200 arrested and millions of dollars of property damaged. The streets of the L.A. ghetto now resemble a ravaged war zone.

The arrest of a Negro on drunken driving charges and subsequent alleged police brutality triggered the riots. But temperatures had been climbing to the boiling point for some time, as disgruntled and impoverished Negroes and police had clashed in several minor skirmishes. Cornell Henderson, a Negro worker for the Congress of Racial Equality, described those involved. "There were a lot of young hoods and agitators. But there were a lot of others who were just discontented and took advantage of the situation for emotional release," he said. Henderson also pointed to instigation from Black Muslims, who have preached hate and disorder, as a cause of the violence.

Chaos reigns in Watts, the scorching summer sun obscured by heavy smoke.

While fires raged and snipers rattled the streets, police and riot-control squads were debilitated in their efforts to establish peace. The riot spread quickly, forcing California Governor Edmund Brown to call in federal troops and issue an 8 p.m.-to-sunrise curfew in a 35-mile area around the center of the storm.

President Johnson lashed out at the violence and its causes. "It is not enough to simply decry disorder. We must also strike at the unjust conditions from which disorder largely flows," he said. The chief executive has advocated and legislated for ghetto restoration. Now, with the smoke still smoldering, Los Angeles and the nation are even more alarmed by urban deterioration and racial strife (→ 9/2).

Le Corbusier, innovative architect, is dead

Aug 27. Le Corbusier, the architect whose influence was rivaled only by Frank Lloyd Wright and Mies van der Rohe in modern times, died of a heart attack while swimming at the Riviera. He was 77.

Born Charles-Edward Jeannert-Gris in Switzerland, he moved to Paris in 1917. Le Corbusier adopted his pseudonym, the family name of his maternal grandmother, to keep his careers as architect and painter separate. His first major fame came in the 1920's, when his plan for the League of Nations building in Geneva was selected twice by architectural juries but was turned down both times on technicalities by League officials.

Le Corbusier helped design the U.N.

His total output was less than 100 buildings, but they had a major impact both on architecture and city planning. His design for a Ministry of Education building in Rio de Janeiro, using breeze-admitting window panes, was widely copied, and many adopted ideas from his design for the new capital of the Punjab. His only building in the U.S., the Visual Arts Center at Harvard, was completed in 1963. Le Corbusier became increasingly aloof after World War II, but his influence on modern architecture continued to grow until his death.

Voting rights bill is signed into law

Aug 6. President Johnson has signed the Voting Rights Act of 1965, saying, "Today we strike away the last major shackle of those fierce and ancient bonds." The legislation, rigorously debated before congressional passage, prohibits states from using poll taxes, literacy tests or other impediments which deny minorities their right to vote. It also grants Congress the power to send federal examiners to those areas where voting discrimination is believed to exist. Tomorrow, in an effort to enforce the new statute, the Justice Department will specify which regions have discriminated against voters.

It is expected that Southern politicians will challenge the law on constitutional grounds that it unlawfully limits states' rights. It is also believed the large influx of Negro voters will alter the complexion of traditionally conservative Southern politics (→ 11).

Americans seeing things: UFOs in 4 states

Aug 2. Authorities in Texas, New Mexico, Oklahoma and Kansas were besieged last night and early today by reports of unidentified flying objects. The Oklahoma Highway Patrol said officers in three cars had seen the objects fly in a diamond-shaped formation for 30 minutes and that Tinker Air Force Base had tracked four unidentified objects on radar at 22,000 feet.

In Kansas, the Sedgewick County Sheriff's office said the Weather Bureau had tracked objects at altitudes of 6,000-9,000 feet. One observer said the objects "were red and exploded in a shower of sparks." The Air Force dismissed the importance of the sightings, saying they were "astronomical in nature."

Viewers probably saw the planet Jupiter or the stars Rigel, Capella, Betelgeuse or Aldebaran, which were in the part of the sky where the sightings were reported, the Air Force said.

Egypt and Saudis agree to end Yemen war

Aug 24. A new agreement to end the bitter Yemeni civil war was signed today, after two days of negotiations between President Gamal Abdel Nasser of the United Arab Republic and King Faisal of Saudi Arabia. The two Arab nations have fought on opposite sides in the conflict since 1962. The accord stipulates that an immediate cease-fire must take effect. It also provides for the institution of a new caretaker government in Yemen, the withdrawal of Egyptian troops and the cessation of Saudi aid to Yemeni royalists (→ 5/1/66).

Ancient Moslem village in Yemen.

Times they are a-changin' for Bob Dylan

Aug 27. He emerged from the New York folk music scene to pen a series of protest anthems that stirred the conscience of millions, but Bob Dylan now appears to be striking out for new musical territory. The enigmatic 24-year-old, who hails from the small mining town of Hibbing, Minnesota, changed his name from Zimmerman and wandered into Greenwich Village in 1961 with just a guitar and the clothes on his back. He quickly astounded the folk world with such rallying cries against injustice as "Blowin' in the Wind" and "The Times They Are A-Changin'."

Dylan and Joan Baez, an early fan who has recorded many of his songs.

Dylan's recent material has revealed a more introspective outlook, a flowing use of poetic imagery and the startling use of electric rock instruments. An outcry from folk purists, who see Dylan turning his back on the protest movement, reached a peak last month when he was widely booed during a performance with a rock band at the Newport Folk Festival. But the success of new songs like "Mr. Tambourine Man" and "Like a Rolling Stone," and his continued deep influence on other performers, shows that a huge audience will follow Dylan wherever his inspiration leads.

1965

SEPTEMBER

Su	Mo	Tu	We	Th	Fr	Sa
			1	2	3	4
5	6	7	8	9	10	11
12	13	14	15	16	17	18
19	20	21	22	23	24	25
26	27	28	29	30		

1. Kashmir: Indians battle Pakistanis in air and on ground (→ 6).

2. Mississippi: Natchez civil rights march called off as troops move in (→ 10/22).

3. Dominican Republic: Hector Garcia Godoy assumes power as provisional president (→ 26).

6. Indian troops invade Lahore; Pakistani paratroopers raid Punjab (→ 7).

7. U.S. suspends military aid to India and Pakistan (→ 22).

9. LBJ signs bill creating Dept. of Housing and Urban Development (HUD) (→ 9/23/66).

10. New York: News Guild ends 25-day strike at N.Y. Times.

11. Paris: De Gaulle demands control of NATO bases in France (→ 10/16).

16. Casablanca: 12 Arab nations sign solidarity pact (→ 11/20/66).

17. Saigon: U.S. forces told to curb civilian killings (→ 20).

20. Vietnam: Seven U.S. planes downed in one day (→ 10/5).

21. England: Ted Erikson swims English Channel both ways.

22. N.Y.: India, Pakistan agree to cease-fire at U.N. (→ 28).

24. Philadelphia: Sugar Ray Robinson wins decision over Jersey Joe Walcott (→ 12/10).

24. LBJ says new pact will give Panama share in canal (→ 3/26/68).

26. Dominican Republic: Violence marks return of exiled Pres. Juan Bosch (→ 4/28/66).

26. London: Queen decorates Beatles with the Order of the British Empire (→ 8/23/66).

27. Japan launches 150,000-ton tanker, world's largest.

28. Philippines: Volcano erupts near Manila, killing hundreds.

30. U.S. govt. gives Lockheed $2 billion defense contract.

DEATHS

10. Father Divine, black cult leader, founder of Peace Mission (*1877).

26. Clara Bow, U.S. actress, "The It Girl" (*1/29/1905).

Koufax sets record with four no-hitters

Koufax, blazing speed, dazing curve.

Sept 9. Sandy Koufax of the Los Angeles Dodgers has pitched a perfect game, in which no rival player reaches first base. En route to his 1-0 victory over the Chicago Cubs, he also became the first in baseball history ever to pitch four no-hitters.

With his fourth no-hit game in four years, Koufax surpassed the record for multiple no-hitters held by Cy Young, Bob Feller and Larry Corcoran. There was only one hit given up in the entire game, that by Bob Hendley in a brilliant duel of lefthanders. While retiring 27 Cubs in order, Koufax struck out 14 and raised his total to a league-leading 332.

The 29-year-old Dodger, whose career almost ended three years ago because of a circulatory ailment, pitched the eighth perfect game in history and the first since Jim Bunning of Philadelphia did it last year. The only other such game pitched in the National League was by Harvey Haddix, then with Pittsburgh (→ 11/18/66).

Tony Curtis (rt.) plus Jack Lemmon and Peter Falk star in Blake Edwards' "The Great Race."

Albert Schweitzer, healer-musician, dies

Sept 4. "Humanitarianism," said Dr. Albert Schweitzer, "consists in never sacrificing a human being to a purpose." Until the moment of his death today at 90, he lived that credo of "reverence for life" and believed that such a code of ethics would reconcile the drives of altruism and egoism and demand the highest development of the individual's resources.

In 1906, the 31-year-old doctor of philosophy, theology and music, distinguished organist and Bach authority, announced that he would become a doctor of medicine and go to Equatorial Africa. Seven years later, he established his hospital in Lambarene, Gabon. An idol of millions, he received the Nobel Peace Prize in 1952. His life illustrates that moral splendor can be chosen and absolute love can be lived.

Schweitzer, Renaissance man.

India-Pakistan hostility erupts into war

Sept 28. The simmering dispute between India and Pakistan, between Hindus and Moslems, has erupted again in Kashmir. Fighting was also reported today in the Indian province of Rajasthan. China, which supports Pakistan in the dispute, has massed troops on its border with Kashmir. Indian troops in the protectorate of Sikkim have exchanged fire with Chinese forces in neighboring Tibet.

At the United Nations today, Pakistan's Foreign Minister Zulfikar Ali Bhutto called for the withdrawal of Indian and Pakistani forces from Kashmir and a plebiscite. Secretary General U Thant has sent observers to Kashmir in a so far fruitless effort to keep the peace. Under a 1949 agreement, Pakistan and India divided Kashmir, with India receiving the larger and wealthier portion (→ 2/15/66).

Viking map of New World to be shown

Scholars at Yale University are plotting to disrupt Columbus Day revelries. Since 1957, historians have been scrutinizing a map of Leif Ericson's 11th-century voyage to a new land he called "Vinland." Finally validated, it will go on display in New Haven, Conn., on the very day reserved to honor Columbus.

Ericson's travels were recounted orally for 200 years before being written down in the 1200's. Vinland on the 1440 map appears to be the American continent, thought by the Vikings to be part of an island. Ericson's visit is backed up by discoveries of a Norse sword in Nova Scotia; an archaic stone tower near Newport, Rhode Island; a stone with runic characters in Minnesota and a 1,000-year-old settlement in Newfoundland (→ 4/13/69).

108,000 troops in Vietnam; 650 killed

Sept 8. The U.S. military headquarters in Saigon today released last week's casualty figures. Twenty-six Americans were killed, 44 wounded and three missing or captured, raising the number of Americans killed in action in Vietnam since 1961 to about 650.

The number of U.S. servicemen, just past the 100,000 mark, will soon reach President Johnson's goal of 125,000. Few observers believe that troop increases will stop there, especially if the Viet Cong put on new pressure. The figure does not include the Seventh Fleet, technically not stationed in South Vietnam. South Vietnamese casualties last week were 180 men killed to the Viet Cong's 420, a "kill ratio" in the government's favor but lower than usual (→ 17).

1965

OCTOBER

Su	Mo	Tu	We	Th	Fr	Sa
					1	2
3	4	5	6	7	8	9
10	11	12	13	14	15	16
17	18	19	20	21	22	23
24	25	26	27	28	29	30
31						

1. Indonesia uncovers Communist plot against Sukarno (→ 18).

3. New York: LBJ says doors are open to all Cuban exiles (→ 11).

5. Saigon: G.I.'s get permission to use tear gas (→ 28).

6. Luxembourg: Patricia Harris, first U.S. Negro ambassador, takes office.

7. Aden: Police use tear gas to rout students, rioting against British rule (→ 7/3/67).

8. Washington: LBJ doing well after gall bladder operation.

8. London: Talks on Rhodesian independence fail (→ 11).

9. Uruguay imposes state of siege to end labor agitation.

11. N.Y.: U.N. demands Britain curb Rhodesian revolt threatened by Ian Smith (→ 27).

11. Florida: Third boat of Cuban refugees arrives (→ 12/1).

13. U.S.: Sen. RFK suggests Peking send delegate to Geneva arms talks (→ 3/14/66).

14. Minnesota: Dodgers beat Twins 2-0 in final game to capture World Series.

16. New York: 10,000 march in anti-Vietnam protest (→ 18).

16. Pentagon says U.S. is dropping plan for NATO nuclear fleet (→ 3/18/66).

22. Alabama: All-white jury acquits Collie Leroy Wilkins in Viola Liuzzo murder (→ 12/3).

28. Pentagon lowers standard for military volunteers (→ 11/2).

28. Vietnam: Six G.I.'s killed by U.S. gunfire (→ 30).

29. Alaska: U.S. explodes 80-kiloton H-bomb over Aleutian Islands (→ 11/25).

30. Vietnam: U.S. jets bomb friendly village, killing 48 civilians, wounding 55 (→ 11/15).

31. Washington: Ex-Army intelligence agent says he bugged Eleanor Roosevelt's hotel room.

DEATHS

11. Dorothea Lange, American documentary photographer (*5/26/1895).

15. Randall Jarrell, American poet (*5/16/1914).

Draft card burned; FBI arrests owner

Oct 18. A quiet college student was arrested by the FBI in Vermont today and charged with burning his draft card at an anti-Vietnam rally in New York last Friday. David Miller, a member of a pacifist group called Catholic Worker, is the first person to be arrested under a new federal law signed by President Johnson. If convicted, he could be sentenced to five years in jail and fined $10,000. "I think the draft is wrong," Miller said. "I am opposed especially to this war." Thousands of demonstrators marched against the Vietnam War on Saturday in New York and around the country (→ 28).

Sukarno puts down Communist revolt

Oct 18. The Communist Party of Indonesia was placed under a government ban today, as civil unrest continues to plague the Southeast Asian nation. The violence began on October 1, when an attempt to overthrow the government of President Sukarno was foiled by General Abdul Nasution. Since then, there have been numerous armed clashes between Communist guerrilla units and army loyalists around Jakarta. Sukarno vowed to create a new Communist Party, less influenced by China (→ 1/12/66).

Oct 4. Che Guevara, doctor and master guerrilla, has left Cuba, according to Castro, "to fight imperialism abroad"—rumor has it in Bolivia (→ 9/21/67).

Paul VI brings his peace call to U.N.

Oct 4. Pope Paul VI, the first pontiff to visit the Western hemisphere since the Church was founded, arrived in New York today and made an urgent appeal for peace. Millions of people watched on television around the world as the pope told the United Nations General Assembly, "The real threat to peace does not come from progress or science but from man himself."

Earlier in the day, Paul held an historic meeting with President Johnson in a suite at the Waldorf Astoria Hotel. The president called their conversation "stimulating and inspiring." The pope ended the day with an ecumenical sermon delivered during a mass at Yankee Stadium. The ball park was packed with 90,000 spectators (→ 28).

Catholic positions issued, one on Jews

Oct 28. In St. Peter's Basilica today, Pope Paul VI formally approved five documents drawn up by the Ecumenical Council over the past five years. One decree extends the friendship of the Church to the other major religions and specifically criticizes anti-Semitism. It disassociates Jews from guilt for the crucifixion of Jesus and demands that Catholics not treat Jews as "rejected by God or accursed." In New York, the head of the American Jewish Committee called the decree "an act of justice long overdue." Some 250 prelates voted against language in the document, but the Vatican took pains to point out that they were primarily concerned that conversion efforts might be hurt by the ecumenical language (→ 12/7).

Ian Smith to fight for freedom from Britain

White supremacist Ian Smith.

Oct 27. Police dogs were loosed upon black demonstrators in the Rhodesian capital of Salisbury, as they protested the attempt of Prime Minister Ian Smith to consolidate his white supremacist government. Negotiations between British Prime Minister Harold Wilson and Smith concerning Rhodesian independence broke down on October 8, when Wilson insisted upon black majority rule in Rhodesia. Smith would not agree to that, and he was quoted as saying that a unilateral declaration of independence from Britain was an imminent possibility (→ 11/11).

Foundation donates $85m to orchestras

Oct 21. The Ford Foundation has announced grants and endowment funds totaling $85 million to about 50 symphony orchestras throughout the United States. The sum is the largest any foundation has ever allocated at one time to one of the arts. The objectives are to strengthen orchestras by lengthening their seasons, to improve the low financial state of musicians, to increase quality and to attract more talented young people to professional careers in music.

Moroccan dissident kidnapped in Paris

Oct 30. Kidnapped or arrested? That is the question being asked in Paris this morning about El-Mehdi Ben Barka, a well-known leftist opponent of Morocco's King Hassan. He disappeared at noon yesterday in the middle of chic St. Germain des Pres. At first it was called a kidnapping. Then another story emerged from a police informant who may have been freelancing for Hassan's agents. It is beginning to appear that Ben Barka was nabbed by French police (→ 1/20/66).

1965

NOVEMBER

Su	Mo	Tu	We	Th	Fr	Sa
	1	2	3	4	5	6
7	8	9	10	11	12	13
14	15	16	17	18	19	20
21	22	23	24	25	26	27
28	29	30				

2. John Lindsay elected mayor of New York City.

2. Washington: Quaker Norman Morrison burns to death at Pentagon in anti-war protest (→ 9).

9. New York: Roger LaPorte, 22, immolates himself at U.N. to protest Vietnam War (→ 27).

12. Manila: Ferdinand Marcos claims victory in Philippines presidential election (→ 12/30).

13. Bahamas: Liner Yarmouth Castle sinks; 91 lost, 459 saved.

13. N.Y.: Africans at U.N. ask boycott against Rhodesia (→ 16).

15. U.S. admits rejecting 1964 Hanoi peace talk offer (→ 24).

15. U.S. Supreme Court voids law requiring Communists to register with govt. (→ 19).

16. Rhodesia: 4,000 black postal workers refuse oaths of loyalty to Ian Smith govt. (→ 12/16).

18. Pope Paul VI initiates beatification of John XXIII, Pius XII.

19. U.S. Communist Party fined $230,000 for failing to register as agent of U.S.S.R. (→ 8/22/66).

24. Vietnam: U.S. dead sets one-week record of 240 (→ 12/15).

25. N.Y.: U.S. rejects 35-nation plea at U.N. to stop underground atom tests (→ 1/17/66).

26. Sahara: France puts its first satellite into orbit (→ 2/3/66).

27. Washington: 50,000 march in peace demonstration (→ 30).

27. Philadelphia: Army, Navy play to 7-7 tie in football.

28. Moscow: Soviets say Peking is threat to international communism (→ 29).

29. Peking: Chou accuses Soviets of undermining world revolutionary struggle (→ 10/7/66).

DEATHS

6. Edgar Varese, French-American composer, pioneer electronic music (*12/22/1883).

16. William Cosgrave, 3rd pres. of Irish Free State (*6/6/1880).

16. Harry Blackstone, popular American magician.

18. Henry A. Wallace, liberal politician, v.p. under FDR (*10/7/1888).

Mobutu overthrows Kasavubu in Congo

Rebellious General Mobutu.

Nov 25. Political leaders come and go in the Congo, but Joseph Mobutu has been the strongman from the beginning. Today, the army chief stepped into the political arena, deposing President Joseph Kasavubu and installing himself as head of the government. The latest upheaval in the Congo started when Kasavubu dismissed Premier Moise Tshombe and placed Evariste Kimba in the office. At first, Tshombe took his dismissal in stride and vowed to fight Kasavubu in the next elections. Last week, however, Tshombe charged the president was using "repression and intimidation" to reach his goals. By today, Mobutu had had enough as he took over the government and declared a state of emergency (→ 6/2/66).

Formal fashions for a couple of young mod bods who have not yet outgrown the haven of suburbia.

Anti-war protesters immolate themselves

Nov 30. What happened in South Vietnam in 1963 is beginning to happen in the United States. It is the ultimate protest against the politics of war. Like the Buddhist monks of Saigon, opponents of the Vietnam War are burning themselves to death in public places.

It started at the beginning of the month when a 32-year-old Quaker, the father of three children, set himself on fire in front of a Pentagon entrance. Norman Morrison of Baltimore was holding his year-old daughter when his clothes caught fire. He dropped her, and she was rescued by a passer-by just in time. Morrison's wife said later he was very upset "over the great loss of life and human suffering" in the war.

A week later, on the 9th, a former seminarian set himself on fire outside the United Nations. Roger Allen LaPorte, a member of the Catholic Worker movement, said it was a protest against "war, all war."

These extreme protests occurred as moderate Americans appeared to be joining the anti-war movement. At a large rally in Washington on the 27th, there were just as many mothers, fathers and professionals as there were students protesting the Vietnam War (→ 12/3).

Arfons leads in speed rivalry at 576 mph

Breedlove's "Spirit of America" breezes over the Bonneville Flats at 555 mph.

Nov 7. Art Arfons regained the world speed record with a wild ride in which his car went out of control and careened across the Bonneville Salt Flats before rolling to a stop with a blown-out tire.

His jet racer was going 576 miles an hour when Arfons lost control, but he walked away without injury. He was almost overcome in the cockpit but pried open the canopy and released the smoke.

With an average speed of 576.553 mph, he regained the record from Craig Breedlove, who four days earlier had sped across the flats at 555.127.

Arfons, who escaped serious injury twice last year in accidents, was unable to handle his car as it swerved from one side of the speedway to the other and broke metal markings along the south end of the course. The air speed indicator showed approximately 600 mph when the trouble began. By the time the car stopped, the right rear tire was blown to shreds and the front right tire frayed. The right rear wheel well was blown apart. Also, one of the parachute compartments used for stopping the jet racer was blown away and there was damage to the undercarriage. Breedlove also survived one crash last year and nearly had another this year.

"I've never had to work so hard for a record in my life," Arfons said. Breedlove, who surpassed the mark that had been set by Arfons at 536.71 last year, has broken the record four times (→ 11/17/66).

Greatest power failure strikes nine states

Nov 9. Nine Northeastern states and parts of Canada descended into sudden darkness tonight during the worst power failure in history. Off-duty police officers and National Guardsmen were ordered into metropolitan streets to regulate traffic and protect stores from burglary. Most of the 24 million people weathered the dark good-naturedly.

At 5:17 p.m., a switch at a station near Niagara Falls inexplicably failed. Cities in northern New York state blacked out. Massachusetts was hit next; Connecticut, Rhode Island, Vermont, Maine, New Hampshire and two Canadian provinces followed. Parts of New Jersey and Pennsylvania were hit too.

Traffic signals gave out; intersections jammed. Skyscraper elevators halted between floors. As of midnight, untold numbers were still trapped in them. Operating rooms went dark, relighted by generators owned by the hospitals or loaned from civil defense offices. Airplanes circled darkened landing strips.

Some romantic couples, finding themselves in a warm, cozy place, took advantage of the situation. A baby boom may be due nine months from now. And a third grader from Cos Cob, Conn., wrote of the blackout, "It was dark! We had popcorn at the fireplace! It was fun!"

Nov 11. Since 1890 when the British South African Company rode into South Rhodesia, the country has been ruled by whites. Prime Minister Ian Smith today signed a secession decree to keep it that way. The U.N. and Britain seek black majority rule as a condition of independence (→ 13).

Nov 22. Ali suggested Floyd Patterson get a new hat to fit his "lumped up" head after the fight. Good advice, but for 12 rounds before the merciful end, Patterson faced Ali's jabs and taunts of "No contest" (→ 2/17/66).

1965

DECEMBER

Su	Mo	Tu	We	Th	Fr	Sa
			1	2	3	4
5	6	7	8	9	10	11
12	13	14	15	16	17	18
19	20	21	22	23	24	25
26	27	28	29	30	31	

1. Miami: 75 Cuban exiles arrive on first air exodus (→ 2/6/66).

3. Wisconsin: Natl. Council of Churches asks U.S. to halt bombings in N. Vietnam (→ 21).

6. James Lovell, on Gemini 7, is first to fly in space in underwear, without protective gear (→ 15).

7. Rome: Mutual excommunication of Roman Catholic and Orthodox Churches is ended as Vatican II closes (→ 3/18/66).

9. Moscow: Nikolai Podgorny succeeds Anastas Mikoyan as Soviet chief of state (→ 3/29/66).

10. New York: Sugar Ray Robinson, at 45, retires from boxing.

11. Tehran: Shah denies Iran depends on U.S. (→ 2/19/67).

15. North Vietnam: U.S. drops 12 tons of bombs on industrial center near Haiphong (→ 29).

16. N.Y.: 24 African delegations walk out over Rhodesia issue as British Premier Harold Wilson speaks at U.N. (→ 17).

17. Britain imposes oil embargo on Rhodesia (→ 28).

20. Georgia: 209 lbs. heroin seized in largest U.S. bust yet.

21. N.Y.: 4 pacifists indicted for burning draft cards (→ 1/6/66).

28. U.S. bars oil sales to Rhodesia (→ 4/16/66).

31. California becomes largest state in population this year.

CULTURAL EVENTS, 1965

Literature: Norman Mailer's "An American Dream"; Hesse's "Steppenwolf"; John Berryman's "77 Dream Songs," Pulitzer poetry; Henry Miller's "The Rosy Crucifixion."

Academia: Herbert Marcuse's "Culture and Society"; Arthur Schlesinger, Jr.'s "A Thousand Days," Pulitzer biography; Nader's "Unsafe at any Speed."

Music: Bernstein's "Chichester Psalms"; "King of the Road"; Beatles' "A Hard Day's Night."

The Arts: Picasso's "Self-Portrait"; Michaelangelo's "Pieta" exhibited in New York.

Film: Olivier's "Othello"; David Lean's "Dr. Zhivago"; The Beatles' "Help!"; "The Sound of Music," Academy Award.

Two American craft rendezvous in space

Gemini 7 in orbit above the earth, captured on film by Gemini 6.

Dec 15. American astronauts today steered two Gemini spacecraft to a rendezvous in orbit. The two capsules flew side by side only six to ten feet apart for two orbits as high as 195 miles above the earth. The rendezvous was made by astronauts Walter P. Schirra Jr. and Thomas P. Stafford aboard Gemini 6 and Frank Borman and James A. Lovell Jr. aboard Gemini 7.

Their success is a major step toward a manned moon flight, scheduled for 1969, which will require a rendezvous in space.

Gemini 7 was launched from Cape Canaveral 11 days ago. Gemini 6 went aloft at 8:37 a.m. today, as its sister ship passed overhead. At the end of its first orbit, Gemini 6 fired an 18-second burst of its rockets to lift it toward Gemini 7's higher orbit. Schirra, Gemini 6's pilot, repeated the maneuver several times over the next two orbits. The meeting came on the fourth orbit, when the spacecraft met over the Pacific. After four hours in formation, Gemini 6 was maneuvered to a lower orbit; it will return to earth tomorrow. Gemini 7 is to remain in orbit for three more days (→ 2/3/66).

Maugham, who was skilled writer, dies

Dec 16. "I would sooner read a timetable or a catalog than nothing at all. They are much more entertaining than half the novels that are written." The always critical Somerset Maugham said this in 1938, long after his own literary reputation was secure. Maugham died of a stroke today on the French Riviera. He was 91 years old.

Maugham wrote drawing room stage comedies while in his 20's. In his 40's he wrote the novels "Of Human Bondage" (1915) and "The Moon and Sixpence" (1919), attacking people who would attack art. A bit of a misogynist, an agnostic to his dying day, Maugham allowed pessimism to permeate his work.

Somerset Maugham at 87.

De Gaulle is re-elected, only after runoff

Dec 19. Charles de Gaulle has done it again, but it was not so easy this time. The General was re-elected to a seven-year term as President of France, but he needed two rounds at the polls. After the first try, the polls showed a drop in de Gaulle's popularity, but he gathered momentum for the second go-round, as he defeated an old nemesis, Francois Mitterrand, 55% to 45%. Mitterrand headed a coalition which called itself the Federation of the Democratic and Socialist Left.

De Gaulle, founder of 5th Republic.

De Gaulle is now the first president of France to be elected by universal suffrage since Louis Napoleon Bonaparte won the office in 1848. In 1958, de Gaulle was selected by an electoral college. This election was a bitter one, and the minority National Party threw its support to Mitterrand at the last minute. Mitterrand refused to congratulate de Gaulle when it was over. Another opponent said de Gaulle's victory was temporary.

3 Klansmen guilty of killing woman

Dec 3. Three members of the Ku Klux Klan were convicted in Montgomery, Alabama, by an all-white federal jury today for the brutal murder of civil rights worker Viola Gregg Liuzzo. The jury was deadlocked for a day and a half before Judge Frank Jonhnson sent them back to the jury room with firm orders to return with a verdict. The Klansmen received ten-year jail sentences. Yesterday, another white vigilante, Robert Strange, was sentenced to ten years for killing Willie Brewster, a Negro. President Johnson, on hearing of the convictions, said, "The whole nation can take heart that there are those in the South who believe in justice in racial matters" (→ 2/21/66).

Christmas truce is observed in Vietnam

Two Marines and a Vietnamese soldier get a respite from battle. U.S. troops in S.E. Asia now number 154,000; U.S. combat deaths since 1961 total 1,636.

Dec 29. The spirit of Christmas is raising hopes ever so slightly that something can be done to end the war in Vietnam. The halt in American bombing entered its sixth day today, as President Johnson tries again to prod the North Vietnamese to the bargaining table. Both sides observed a truce in ground fighting on Christmas Day.

In a Christmas sermon, Pope Paul VI said he hoped the truce would bring about "a just and brotherly peace." It was revealed today, however, that Ho Chi Minh had sent the pope a message saying that "United States leaders want war, not peace." Ho reiterated his hard-line stand that peace will come to Vietnam only if American forces are withdrawn. The State Department has not dismissed Ho's message because it was sent at the same time that a new diplomatic offensive to end the war was beginning.

United Nations Representative Arthur Goldberg met with the pope at the Vatican, Ambassador-at-Large Averell Harriman had meetings in Warsaw and Vice President Hubert Humphrey met with officials in Tokyo and Manila (→ 1/2/66).

Marcos inaugurated Philippine President

Dec 30. With the kind of panache the Filipinos love—strutting horses, blaring bands and the honorific passes of jet fighters—Ferdinand E. Marcos, a lawyer who bolted the Liberal Party and won election on a National Party ticket, was sworn in today as the Philippine republic's sixth President before an ecstatic crown of 80,000 in Manila's Luneta Park bordering the bay. Men in the crowd were dressed in their best sheer white barong tagalags —the country's formal outer shirt —while the women sported brilliantly colored silk and cotton frocks.

Marcos also wore a barong tagalag, and when the cheering stopped he led the salute to the flag while the national anthem was played. Waiting in the grandstand was the president's wife, Imelda, resplendent in a cream-colored silk dress with butterfly-sleeves. Seated behind her was President Johnson's personal envoy, Vice President Humphrey, taking time out from his Asian tour. No stranger to such events, Humphrey was seen to sweat profusely in the tropical heat (→ 9/14/66).

Marcos and wife Imelda, an avid socialite, are toasted in Tokyo.

The Byrds, branching out from bluegrass roots, blend the melodies and lyrics of folk with a heavy electric sound into hits like "Mr. Tambourine Man" and "Turn! Turn! Turn!." The band is now recording "Eight Miles High," a psychedelic poem of the drug culture. Leader Jim McGuinn (rt.) has changed his name to Roger because it sounds like his mantra.

UNICEF is awarded Nobel Peace Prize

Dec 10. Food. Water. Health care. These are some of the things the United Nation's Children's Fund has delivered around the world since the organization's inception 19 years ago. A UNICEF representative accepted the Nobel Peace Prize in Oslo tonight.

Mikhail Sholokhov received the award for literature. The Russian wrote the war novel "And Quiet Flows the Don." The physics prize went to Julian Schwinger, Sinitiro Tomonaga and Richard Feynman for studies in quantum electrodynamics. American Robert Woodward got the chemistry award for findings on organic growth. Three French biologists shared the medicine prize for work on enzymes.

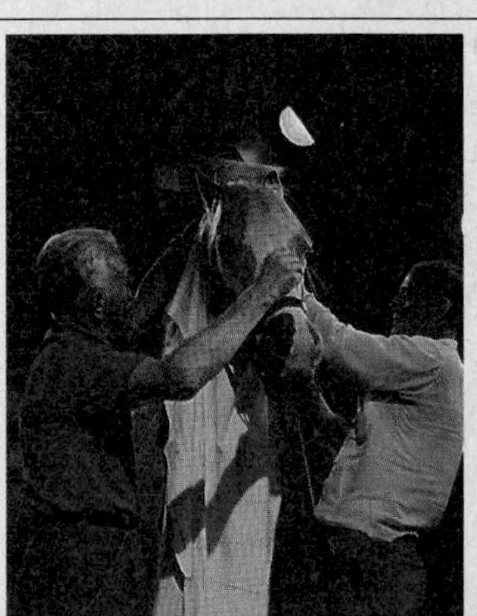

Architect Wilbur Post and his wife Carol found a surprise waiting for them when they moved into their new home—Mr. Ed, "the playboy horse of L.A.," and the greatest conversationalist of the animal world . . . if we are to believe American television.

1966

JANUARY

Su	Mo	Tu	We	Th	Fr	Sa
						1
2	3	4	5	6	7	8
9	10	11	12	13	14	15
16	17	18	19	20	21	22
23	24	25	26	27	28	29
30	31					

1. Pasadena: U.C.L.A. edges Michigan 14-12 in Rose Bowl.

1. Central African Republic: Pres. David Dacko ousted; new chief Bokassa expels Chinese Communists (→ 12/4/77).

2. South Vietnam: G.I.'s move into Mekong Delta for first time (→ 3).

2. Green Bay: Packers beat Cleveland 23-12 for NFL title.

3. New York: Cambodia warns U.N. of retaliation unless U.S., S. Vietnam end intrusions (→ 8).

12. Indonesia: 100,000 Communists reported killed in last three months (→ 3/13).

16. Nigeria: Army chief Johnson Aguiyi-Ironsi takes over in coup; premier kidnapped (→ 8/1).

17. Washington: Sargent Shriver quits as head of Peace Corps.

19. Saigon: 50 officers arrested for plot to topple regime (→ 25).

20. Boston: Ted Williams elected to Baseball Hall of Fame.

20. France issues warrant for arrest of Moroccan interior minister for kidnapping of rebel leader Ben Barka (→ 24).

24. France: Air India jet hits Mont Blanc; 117 killed.

24. Paris: Gaullist deputy linked to kidnapping of Moroccan rebel Ben Barka (→ 10/19).

25. Vietnam: 47 G.I.'s die in crash of transport plane (→ 31).

30. Warsaw: Stefan Cardinal Wyszynski says Polish Church will not be vanquished (→ 5/3).

31. U.S.: Storm kills 166 on Eastern seaboard.

31. Vietnam: U.S planes resume bombing of North after 37-day pause (→ 2/7).

DEATHS

1. Vincent Auriol, French Socialist, first president of Fourth Republic (*8/27/1884).

5. Marguerite Higgins, Pulitzer Prize-winning U.S. journalist (*9/3/1920).

11. Lal Bahadur Shastri, Indian prime minister (*10/2/1904).

14. Sergei Korolev, designer of Soviet space program since 1954 (*12/30/1906).

Nehru's daughter Indira becomes Premier

New Prime Minister Indira Gandhi.

Jan 19. When she today became India's third Prime Minister, Mrs. Indira Gandhi, no relation to Mohandas Gandhi, became only the second woman in modern history to head a government. The other was Mrs. Sirimavo Bandaranaike, Ceylon's recently deposed leader.

Though technically her election was only for the leadership of the Congress Parliamentary Party, India's leading party, as leader she is automatically prime minister. At the news conference which followed, the first and perhaps inevitable question, "How does it feel to be the first woman prime minister of India?" received a cool reply. "I am," she answered, "just an Indian citizen and the first servant of my country." She might have added that more than 50 women sit in the Indian Parliament and that several others hold key government posts.

Asked what message she had for the nation, the 48-year-old Mrs. Gandhi recalled that of her father, Pandit Jawaharlal Nehru, the country's first Prime Minister for 17 years: "Create a climate of peace" (→ 2/26).

8,000 G.I.'s launch war's biggest attack

G.I.'s debark on burned-out terrain.

Jan 8. American troops have launched their biggest offensive of the war, striking at a Communist stronghold 20 miles northwest of Saigon. About 8,000 U.S. Army soldiers were involved in the operation, designed to sweep the Viet Cong out of a jungle area known as the Iron Triangle. The attack was preceded by B-52 bombing strikes and artillery barrages of an intensity not previously seen in the war. And the American offensive was conducted independently of the South Vietnamese government.

Officials said the operation was kept secret from the South Vietnamese army for fear it might be disclosed by Viet Cong agents in the army. Earlier this month, U.S. Army troops for the first time made a strike into the Mekong Delta area, another Viet Cong stronghold. Previously, American fighting was to the north of Saigon (→ 19).

Student groups pledge Vietnam support

Jan 6. President Johnson has been hearing a lot recently from students who say it is time to get out of Vietnam. Today, he received a different message. A scroll representing nearly half a million students who support the administration's war policy was presented to Vice President Hubert Humphrey.

The ceremony was organized by the National Student Committee for the Defense of Vietnam. Another student organization announced it will hold two days of rallies to support Johnson's Vietnam policies. The demonstrations are being sponsored by a splinter group of the conservative Young Americans for Freedom. The first rally is scheduled to be held in Boston tomorrow night. The widow of an officer killed in Vietnam will help kick off a pro-war rally at the Statue of Liberty on Saturday (→ 2/10).

U.S. plane loses H-bomb over Spain

Jan 17. It might seem hard to believe, but it happened in the skies over Almeria, Spain. An American B-52 bomber, carrying nuclear weapons, collided with a K-C 135 fuel re-supply plane in mid-air. Eight of the 14 crew members were killed, and an H-bomb was dislodged from the bomber. It fell into the Atlantic Ocean and is still missing. Red-faced officials at the Pentagon dispatched planes from the Strategic Air Command and 1,000 soldiers to look for the bomb. So far, no luck (→ 3/8).

1,000 protest ban on Negro legislator

Jan 14. About a thousand persons marched on the state Capitol in Atlanta today to protest the ouster of Julian Bond, a Negro pacifist, from the State House of Representatives. The House voted, 184 to 12, earlier this week not to seat the 26-year-old Bond after he endorsed a Student Nonviolent Coordinating Committee statement critical of U.S. involvement in Vietnam. The Rev. Dr. Martin Luther King, who addressed the rally, had left by the time a scuffle took place as some demonstrators sought to force their way into the Capitol.

Jan 18. The nine-foot "Tall Figure, Number IV," by Albert Giacometti, who died on the 11th, has been bought for $60,000.

1966

FEBRUARY

Su	Mo	Tu	We	Th	Fr	Sa
		1	2	3	4	5
6	7	8	9	10	11	12
13	14	15	16	17	18	19
20	21	22	23	24	25	26
27	28					

3. Soviet Luna 9 achieves soft landing on moon (→ 26).

4. Tokyo: Japanese 727 crashes in Tokyo Bay; 133 dead.

5. U.S. to sell 200 tanks to Israel to balance Soviet and American shipments to Arabs (→ 4/2).

6. Castro accuses China of trying to subvert revolution by breaking rice trade pact (→ 10/19).

10. New York: David Miller convicted of burning draft card (→ 3/4).

11. V.P. Hubert Humphrey begins tour of Vietnam (→ 12).

12. South Vietnamese win two big battles in Mekong Delta (→ 16).

15. Pakistan: Humphrey tells nation U.S. will resume aid (→ 6/15).

15. Cairo: 46 Moslem extremists charged with plot to kill Nasser (→ 8/29/67).

16. Geneva: World Council of Churches urges immediate peace in Vietnam (→ 19).

17. Kentucky: Muhammad Ali reclassified 1-A by draft board (→ 3/29).

19. Washington: RFK suggests U.S. offer Viet Cong role in governing S. Vietnam (→ 3/8).

21. Alabama: White man shoots five Negroes during segregation protests (→ 3/15).

26. Cape Canaveral: First Apollo test flight a success (→ 28).

26. India: 34 national leaders charge Gandhi's rule is "constitutional dictatorship" (→ 3/27).

27. Switzerland: Peggy Fleming wins gold in world championship figure skating.

27. Florida: Richard Petty wins Daytona 500.

28. St. Louis: Gemini 9 astronauts Elliott M. See Jr. and Charles Bassett killed in jet crash during training (→ 3/1).

28. New York: Talmadge Hayer confesses guilt in slaying of Malcolm X (→ 3/10).

DEATH

20. Adm. Chester Nimitz, commanded U.S. Pacific Fleet in WWII (*2/24/1885).

Nkrumah loses his job while away in China

Nkrumah: "Africa must unite!"

Feb 24. The President of Ghana has learned the hard way that domestic problems have to come first. Kwame Nkrumah was flying to Peking on a Vietnam peace mission today when his government was toppled back home. Military leaders led the coup and seized power after a short battle with Nkrumah's personal guard outside his heavily defended residence in Accra. A self-declared National Liberation Council, made up of army and police officers, suspended the constitution and ordered the release of all political prisoners. Nkrumah, who had ruled as a dictator, has been blamed for corruption which has kept many Ghanians poor despite a wealth of national resources (→ 3/1).

Hollywood loses Hedda and her hats

Feb 1. After 28 years as reigning queen of gossip in Hollywood, Hedda Hopper, 75, died today of pneumonia with heart complications. With frequent disdain for grammar, logic and accuracy, Hedda in her outrageous hats kept movie stars insecure, as she wrote about pregnancies, romances, scandals and career twists in her gossip column. A small-town girl from Pennsylvania, she ran off to become a chorus girl, married DeWolf Hopper, a leading actor in his day, and appeared in more than 100 films. She leaves her son, William, who plays detective Paul Drake on the Perry Mason television show.

Hedda, gossip queen of Hollywood.

LBJ and Ky talk about winning war

Feb 7. President Johnson told South Vietnamese leaders in Honolulu today that they must carry out economic and social reforms to win the war against the Communists. Johnson also emphasized "our resolution and determination to see this thing through." Premier Nguyen Cao Ky agreed that both sides must search for peace, but he also suggested that his government would never deal with the Viet Cong. In Washington, Senate Foreign Relations Committee Chairman Fulbright warned that China might enter the war if it is not ended soon (→ 11).

Obote seizes all power in Uganda

Feb 22. Cutting off the possibility of a coup, Prime Minister Milton Obote jailed five of his Cabinet ministers and seized "all the powers of the government of Uganda" today. The threat to Obote's rule began last week when Daudi Ocheng, the opposition leader, said Obote had split with two other Cabinet ministers more than $300,000 from the sales of gold captured during the 1964 border rebellion. Obote said the charges were a "frame up," and a panel "whose members I shall name later" would conduct an investigation (→ 9/8/67).

Sophie Tucker was a great singer

Feb 8. Her theme song, "One of These Days (You're Gonna Miss Me, Honey)," today became a fact when Sophie Tucker, 79, passed from the scene in her Park Avenue home. Born in a Russian farmhouse of a Jewish family, the "Last of the Red Hot Mamas" became a vaudeville star after they moved to the United States. For nearly 60 years, the flamboyant singer belted out songs, in her brassy and decidedly unsophisticated way, whose titles preserve a bygone era: "I May Be Getting Older Every Day (But Getting Younger Every Night.)"

Longtime favorite Buster Keaton dies

Feb 1. When Buster Keaton was in his parents' vaudeville act, he was a human broom. His folks would pick him up, sweep the floor with him and a good minute later he would gravely say "ouch." That was Keaton's shtick, stoicism and reticence. He died in Hollywood today of lung cancer. He was 70. Keaton was best known for his silents "The Navigator" (1924) and "The General" (1927). In the next decades, he became an alcoholic and lost his fortune. Cameo roles in the 50's and re-release of his films put his career on the rebound.

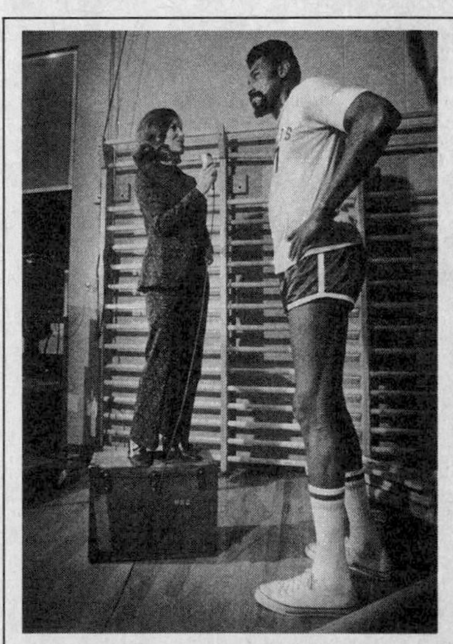

Feb 15. Wilt "The Stilt" Chamberlain, all 7'3" of him, broke the NBA's career scoring record last night. With 20,884 points, he has surpassed in only seven seasons Bob Pettit's total for 11 years.

1966

MARCH

Su	Mo	Tu	We	Th	Fr	Sa
		1	2	3	4	5
6	7	8	9	10	11	12
13	14	15	16	17	18	19
20	21	22	23	24	25	26
27	28	29	30	31		

1. Moscow reports space probe has crashed on Venus, first contact with another planet (→ 17).

1. Ghana expels Soviet advisers (→ 4).

4. New York: James Wilson gets two-year suspended sentence for burning draft card (→ 12).

4. Washington: Ghanian regime recognized by U.S. (→ 8/30/69).

5. Japan: British 707 crashes into Mount Fujiyama, killing 130.

8. France: Private art collection of Claude Monet found.

8. Spain: U.S. Ambassador Duke swims in Mediterranean near where A-bomb was lost (→ 17).

8. Australia announces it will triple troops in Vietnam (→ 16).

9. India yields to Sikh demand for Punjab-speaking state.

10. N.Y.: All three found guilty in slaying of Malcolm X.

12. U.S.: 41 govs. declare support for Vietnam policy (→ 24).

14. China denounces Humphrey's friendship offer as "kiss of Judas" (→ 8/21/67).

15. Los Angeles: Watts riot kills two, injures 25 (→ 4/5).

15. Iran opens oil terminal at Kharg Island (→ 8/17/85).

16. Saigon: Buddhist Gen. Thi ousted; 10,000 march to protest corruption in Ky govt. (→ 4/1).

18. Washington: 14 Allies reject French demand for control of NATO bases in France (→ 4/12).

18. Vatican: Pope cancels excommunications of Catholics wed by non-Catholics (→ 4/9).

21. N.Y.: Herald Tribune, Journal American, World Telegram announce merger (→ 8/15).

24. U.S.: Selective Service announces college deferments based on performance (→ 31).

27. Washington: Indira Gandhi meets with LBJ (→ 2/8/67).

29. Toronto: Ali outpoints George Chuvalo (→ 5/21).

31. London: Labor wins 97-seat majority in Parliament (→ 7/25).

DEATH

30. Maxfield Parrish, American poster artist (*7/25/1870).

Auto critic Nader gets apology from G.M.

Consumer crusader Nader.

March 22. The President of General Motors has apologized before a congressional committee for a company-ordered investigation of the private life of Ralph Nader, a crusader for safer cars. James M. Roche agreed with Sen. Ribicoff that the investigation was "most unworthy of American business."

Nader became a target of the auto industry after publishing a book, "Unsafe at Any Speed," that questioned the safety of American cars. Roche said he had not known about the investigation, in which private detectives questioned 50 to 60 of Nader's friends and relatives about his sex habits, political beliefs and attitudes toward Jews. Ribicoff told Nader today, "You and your family can be proud. They have put you through the mill and they haven't found a damned thing wrong with you." Nader, who appeared with Roche before the committee, accepted the apology but held to his stand, saying that General Motors should alter current models of the Corvair to remedy defects (→ 4/15).

Brezhnev becomes top Soviet leader

March 29. Leonid Brezhnev has become the First Secretary of the Soviet Communist Party and in his speech, which opened the 23rd Congress, he condemned the American "policy of aggression" against Vietnam. While assailing U.S. military intervention in Southeast Asia, the top leader also spoke in a moderate tone, leaving open a path for conciliation with the United States.

Brezhnev started his political career as chief of a trade union and quickly worked his way up the party ranks. In World War II, he was appointed a Major General. Following the war, he worked under Nikita Khrushchev in the Ukraine. After Joseph Stalin's death, Brezhnev was elevated to the Presidium and, with Khrushchev's removal, he became the most likely choice for party leader (→ 8/2).

Indonesia regime orders Reds wiped out

Suharto, staunch anti-Communist.

March 13. As his first official act since taking control of Indonesia last night, General Suharto told the military to wipe out all traces of the Communist Party. The order follows six months of bloody reprisals that have left over 100,000 Communists dead since an attempted coup last September. Though the Communists failed, their attempt shook Sukarno's government and led to the military takeover. Groups of Moslems who suffered during the rise of the Communist Party formed vigilante groups to carry out the executions (→ 7/6).

Lost H-bomb found off coast of Spain

March 17. The sighs of relief at the State Department were heard across the Atlantic in Spain today after a midget submarine found the H-bomb that has been missing for two months. The weapon, which fell off a B-52 bomber, is said to be intact. Its disappearance embarrassed the United States and panicked Spaniards about a possible radiation leak. American officials plunged into the frigid Atlantic surf recently to demonstrate that the water is still safe (→ 5/9).

Dublin's Nelson Column hit; blame I.R.A.

March 8. Dublin's Nelson Column, symbol of British rule over Ireland, was demolished in an early morning explosion that rocked downtown Dublin. Police blamed the outlawed Irish Republican Army, or a splinter group of the I.R.A., for the bombing in the heart of the capital. The blast brought down the top 60 feet of the 103-foot masonry column as well as the 20-foot statue of Lord Nelson, the British naval hero at the 1805 victory over the French at Trafalgar.

The statue, a near-duplicate of the one that stands in London's Trafalgar Square, was erected in 1809 and recently has become the targeted symbol of British oppression for Irish extremists. The explosion coincided with growing I.R.A. activity as Ireland approaches the 50th anniversary of the 1916 Easter Rebellion that led to the independence of Southern Ireland from Britain. In Washington, Rep. Barrett O'Hara, Democrat of Illinois, commended the Irish bombers for their example of "instant urban renewal" (→ 1/4/69).

Paris: Nureyev, Fonteyn dance Petit's "The Praise of Folly."

1966

APRIL

Su	Mo	Tu	We	Th	Fr	Sa
					1	2
3	4	5	6	7	8	9
10	11	12	13	14	15	16
17	18	19	20	21	22	23
24	25	26	27	28	29	30

1. LBJ halts all congressional trips to Vietnam (→ 19).

2. U.S. State Dept. to sell jets to Jordan (→ 8/15).

3. Saigon: 3,000 troops lead protest against Ky regime (→ 8).

4. Soviets announce Luna 10 is orbiting moon (→ 6/5).

5. Mississippi: Police rout 1,000 civil rights demonstrators with gas and clubs (→ 5/27).

5. Ottawa: Canada votes to retain death penalty.

7. Dakar holds first worldwide exhibit of African art.

8. Vietnam: U.S. jets sink 12 junks supplying Viet Cong (→ 19).

9. Vatican abolishes index of banned books (→ 7/29/68).

12. Paris: U.S. Sec. of State Dean Rusk says France not vital to NATO (→ 7/1).

14. Switzerland: Sandoz Corp. suspends distribution of LSD.

14. Lebanon: Iraqi Pres. Abdel Salam Arif killed in plane crash.

15. U.S.: Paul Parkman, Harry Myer develop rubella vaccine.

16. Rhodesia breaks relations with Britain (→ 3/6/68).

17. New York: Vladimir Horowitz plays Carnegie Hall.

18. Detroit: Ford recalls 30,000 1966 autos to test brakes (→ 28).

19. Boston: Kenji Kimihara wins Boston Marathon.

19. North Vietnam: U.S. jets hit power plant at Haiphong (→ 26).

21. London: Queen opens Parliament, first shown on television.

23. N.Y.: Memorial to Eleanor Roosevelt dedicated at U.N.

27. ICC sanctions merger of Penn. and N.Y. Central Railroads, largest in U.S. history.

28. U.S. Supreme Court rules G.M. violated anti-trust laws.

28. Dominican Republic: U.S. troops shoot seven protesters on first anniversary of intervention (→ 7/1).

DEATH

2. C.S. Forester, British writer (*8/27/1899).

Veterans fight with anti-war protesters

Skull-masked demonstrators.

March 31. The parades and protests against the Vietnam War are getting bigger. They are also becoming violent. The march down Fifth Avenue in New York on Friday was the largest demonstration yet against the war. More than 20,000 people took part. Counter-demonstrators, some of them veterans of other wars, threw eggs from the sidewalk, and several dozen fought with the protesters at 86th Street. Police say they made seven arrests.

Thousands of other protesters marched in Washington, the Midwest and California. In Boston today, 50 high school students shouted, "Kill them, shoot them," as they fought with anti-Vietnam protesters after four of them burned their draft cards (→ 5/5).

Two craft achieve 1st docking in space

March 17. The Gemini 8 astronauts made the first docking in space but then had to make an emergency landing when they suddenly lost maneuverability of their craft. Astronauts Neil A. Armstrong and David R. Scott guided their Gemini capsule to dock with an Agena spacecraft on the fifth orbit of their planned three-day mission. Half an hour later, the Gemini capsule began to spin and roll uncontrollably. One of the spacecraft's 12 small thruster rockets had started firing, for an unknown reason. The astronauts separated their craft from the Agena and made a successful landing in the Pacific (→ 4/4).

Influential German drama theorist dies

March 30. Theatrical innovator Erwin Piscator is dead at age 72. Ulm, Germany, was his birthplace (it was Einstein's as well) and he died in West Germany, but Piscator spent the 1940's in New York. There, he directed the Dramatic Workshop at the New School for Social Research, bringing radical politics to American drama. Piscator introduced Brecht to "alienation," favoring sirens, blinding lights and other devices to shake up an audience. He freely used multimedia, enlivening a play with film and animated cartoons.

March 10. Dutch Princess Beatrix wed German ex-diplomat Claus von Amsberg amid protests by leftists and pacifists today in Amsterdam.

Artificial pump is implanted in heart

April 26. Marcel L. de Rudder, who had lived for nearly five days with an implanted heart pump, has died in a Houston hospital. Dr. Michael E. de Bakey, the surgeon who implanted the heart pump, said death was caused by a ruptured lung and was not related to use of the device. But de Bakey said he would modify the artificial heart before using it again. The device took over the function of the left ventricle, the chamber that pumps blood to the body. De Bakey said a perfected device eventually could be used to help at least 75 percent of the 900,000 Americans who die of heart disease each year (→ 12/21/67).

Henry Ford knocks auto safety critics

April 15. Only a few days after General Motors recalled 1.5 million Chevrolets to correct a throttle defect, Henry Ford II today cautioned Congress not to do anything "irrational" about automobile safety. Speaking at a factory dedication, Ford acknowledged that the industry was "being attacked on all sides" for its safety record but said critics such as Ralph Nader "don't really know anything about safety." Congress is considering legislation that could establish the first nationwide safety standards for cars sold in the United States (→ 18).

April 11. Jack Nicklaus: First to win two consecutive Masters.

Mao launches Cultural Revolution in China

Vibrant posters inspire Mao's attempt to revive revolutionary zeal in China.

"A revolution is not a dinner party, or writing an essay, or painting a picture, or doing embroidery; it cannot be so refined, so leisurely and gentle, so temperate, kind, courteous, restrained and magnanimous. A revolution is an insurrection, an act of violence by which one class overthrows another." These words, written by Mao Tse-tung in 1927 at the start of the Chinese Revolution, are being taken to heart again by the Chinese masses as their "infallible leader" prepares them for what is being called The Great Proletarian Cultural Revolution.

The new campaign, which intends to revive the revolutionary zeal which proved victorious in 1949, takes many forms. Within the Communist Party apparatus, Mao and his followers aim to purge the entrenched power-holders who resist his ideas. In artistic and educational institutions, renewed efforts to "criticize bourgeois reactionary thinking" are underway. And in the army, "the chief instrument of the dictatorship of the proletariat in China," a drive to recruit loyal revolutionaries is beginning.

The moment has arrived to translate into action Mao's latest poem: "Seize the day, seize the hour!/ Away with all the pests!/Our force is irresistible!" (→ 5/6).

LSD advocate Leary held in drug case

April 17. Former Harvard psychology professor Timothy Leary was arrested just after midnight on charges of narcotics possession. The 45-year-old confessed LSD user was at his Dutchess County, New York, home when police made a raid, finding a small amount of marijuana in a bedroom. Leary said he did not know how it got there.

Police also found about 30 men and women lolling on mattresses in Leary's 64-room mansion. Some tapes they were listening to were confiscated, as was an as yet unidentified substance. Three of Leary's guests were taken into custody, including a 46-year-old Hindu priest and his wife (→ 10/11).

Waugh, a crochety, clever writer, dies

April 10. Satirist Evelyn Waugh has died in Somerset, England. He was 62. Waugh was a dandy who criticized aristocracy, a Catholic who lampooned suicide, a conservative who wrote about sexual romps in detail. He feared driving a car but flew planes in wartime.

Waugh's most-read works are "Vile Bodies" (1930), a story of a breezy, careless society circle living in the future; "Put Out More Flags" (1942), about England's stumbling preparations for World War II; and "The Loved One" (1948) about morticians in California. "Brideshead Revisited" (1945) seriously studies the effects of Catholicism on an upper-crust British family.

First major Negro coach joins Celtics

April 18. Bill Russell has been named the first Negro coach in professional sports and will receive from the Boston Celtics the highest salary ever paid to any coach or manager—$125,000 a year. Russell will continue to play for the Celtics, eight-time champions of the National Basketball Association, as he takes over the managerial chores from Arnold "Red" Auerbach, who will devote his full time to serving as General Manager.

Beloved Met closes doors after 83 years

April 16. "Arrivederci! Auf Wiedersehen!" basso buffo Fernando Corena boomed tonight, taking his leave of no lady but the New York Metropolitan Opera House. After 83 years it is closing its doors. Farewell ceremonies featured Lotte Lehman, Marian Anderson, Alexander Kipnis, Leopold Stokowski, Anna Moffo, Roberta Peters, Zubin Mehta and many more. In all, 57 stars performed works by Wagner, Donizetti, Verdi and Strauss.

U.S. deaths exceed Vietnamese first time

April 26. American combat deaths exceeded those of South Vietnam last week for the first time in the Vietnamese War. A U.S. military spokesman reported that 95 Americans and 67 Vietnamese were killed during the week and that 504 Americans were wounded and four were listed as missing. No figures were given on South Vietnamese wounded or missing. The figures may reflect a letup in South Vietnamese military activity during the latest political crisis in Saigon.

During the last week, the ruling military junta moved some combat units out of battle zones into Saigon against the threat of Buddhist demonstrations. Meanwhile, North Vietnam for the first time sent Soviet-built MIG-21's—its most advanced fighter plane—into combat against American aircraft. One MIG-21 was shot down northeast of Hanoi (→ 5/8).

Bullet-torn helmet and its ex-owner.

Sophia Loren finally wed to Carlo Ponti

April 9. The tale of their romance reads like a script written in Hollywood. Sophia Loren and Carlo Ponti tied the knot again today in a discreet civil ceremony outside Paris. It all looks a little more legal the second time around, but authorities in Italy are not convinced. They still insist the director is married to his first wife.

Loren and Ponti were married for the first time in Mexico in 1957. Ponti was immediately accused of bigamy in Italy. He and Loren had the Mexican marriage annulled and were naturalized as French citizens so Ponti could get a divorce in France. The divorce is not recognized in Italy. The reception today was for close friends only.

Newlyweds Ponti and Loren.

1966

MAY

Su	Mo	Tu	We	Th	Fr	Sa
1	2	3	4	5	6	7
8	9	10	11	12	13	14
15	16	17	18	19	20	21
22	23	24	25	26	27	28
29	30	31				

1. U.S. troops shell Cambodia first time, after taking fire from across Caibac River (→ 8/5).

1. Cairo: Nasser threatens to invade Saudi Arabia in Yemen dispute (→ 11/5/67).

3. Poland: 300,000 celebrate 1,000 years of Christianity (→ 8).

5. Senator Fulbright insists U.S. is "succumbing to the arrogance of power" in Vietnam (→ 12).

7. Kauai King wins Kentucky Derby with D. Brumfield in the saddle.

8. Vietnam: U.S. bombers sever four main rail links to Hanoi (→ 9).

9. China detonates its third nuclear bomb (→ 10/27).

9. South Vietnam: U.S. planes drop 7,200 lbs. tear gas powder on Viet Cong base (→ 16).

11. Spain: Barcelona police beat 100 priests protesting police brutality.

12. University of Chicago students seize administration building (→ 13).

13. New York: 150 students take over administration building at City College (→ 15).

15. Washington: 8,000 anti-war activists circle White House for two hours (→ 19).

15. California: Bob Seagren sets pole vault mark at 17'5.5".

16. Saigon: Buddhists ask LBJ to help oust Nguyen Cao Ky (→ 23).

18. Philadelphia: Harry Gold, convicted atom spy, released from jail after 16 years.

19. White House bars draft for civilian service (→ 28).

21. London: Ali TKOs Henry Cooper in sixth to retain title (→ 8/6).

23. South Vietnam: 400 dissidents give in at Danang (→ 25).

25. Saigon: Tear gas used to rout anti-U.S. protests (→ 6/1).

26. British Guyana becomes independent nation of Guyana.

27. Chicago: Rev. King disassociates self from separatist stand of Stokely Carmichael (→ 6/6).

30. Graham Hill wins 50th Indy 500 at average of 144.3 mph.

Opposition to Vietnam War keeps growing

May 28. On American campuses students picket, march, chant and sometimes riot. On the White House lawn, moderate protesters urge the President to "cool it." In Saigon, Buddhists set themselves ablaze in fiery suicides. At defense contractors' corporate offices, scores denounce the production and use of napalm. Everywhere, it seems, the anti-war movement, in all its various forms of expression, grows in intensity as record numbers of Americans die in Vietnam.

About 350 students seized control of administration offices at the University of Chicago, protesting the college's cooperation with the Selective Service. A similar demonstration at City College in New York obstructed campus activities. Thousands more students are seeking draft deferments.

A crowd of 8,000 "intellectuals" gathered in Washington, voicing their opposition to what many are calling the "unwinnable war." A group of 75 yelled, "Nazi ovens in '44, U.S. napalm in '66," in front of Dow Chemical headquarters. And three days ago, tear gas was used to rout anti-American protests in Saigon itself (→ 6/4).

Not only the young are anti-war.

Schlesinger wins 2nd Pulitzer Prize

May 2. Arthur M. Schlesinger jr. won his second Pulitzer Prize today, this time in biography, for "A Thousand Days: John F. Kennedy in the White House." In this work, he drew on his three-year experience as special assistant to President Kennedy. In 1946, Schlesinger won the Pulitzer Prize in history for his book, "The Age of Jackson."

The history prize this year went to the late Perry Miller, the fiction prize to Katherine Anne Porter and the poetry prize to Richard Eberhart. The Boston Globe won for its campaign against a federal judge confirmation, the Los Angeles Times' staff for its coverage of the Watts riots. In drama, for the third time in four years, no play was considered worthy of the prize; some jury members proposed "Man of La Mancha," a musical based on Cervantes' "Don Quixote."

Nader criticizes even Rolls-Royces

May 5. General Motors today announced a production cutback because of declining sales that have been attributed to the current controversy over auto safety. Even the Rolls-Royce is not immune from criticism. Auto safety crusader Ralph Nader yesterday called it "overrated and overpriced" and said it had poorly designed latches that allowed the doors, hood and trunk to pop open in a crash (→ 9/9).

Polish primate is hailed by 300,000

May 8. Poland's besieged Roman Catholic Church in the person of Stefan Cardinal Wyszynski registered a great victory today when most of Krakow's half-million residents thunderously acclaimed the Cardinal as he strode the red-draped streets of the ancient royal capital. It proved that the Cardinal, the target of a virulent government campaign, remains Poland's most magnetic figure.

Collector gives vast array of art to U.S.

May 11. A Greenwich, Conn., resident is contributing a $35 million modern art collection to the United States. News of Joseph Hirshhorn's gift was leaked from a government source tonight. The paintings and sculpture, by artists from Thomas Eakins to Ben Shahn, will be cared for by the Smithsonian Institution. The Smithsonian will consider building a sculpture garden expressly for the collection.

Missing on May Day, Mao has weak heart

May 6. Mao Tse-tung's health has been the subject of speculation in the West in recent weeks, fueled by his absence from public functions and celebrations. A former Communist newsman in Hong Kong was quoted today as saying that Mao is recuperating from a heart condition and soon may be well enough to appear in public. The 72-year-old Chairman of the People's Republic of China is said to be on a rigid diet and under doctors' orders to avoid all strenuous activity (→ 7/11).

Mafia chief turns up after 19 months

May 17. Joseph Bonnano, 61, the Mafia leader hunted around the world for 19 months, walked into the courthouse at Foley Square, New York, yesterday, and gave himself up. He had disappeared Oct. 21, 1964, the eve of his appearance before a grand jury. Followers of Bonnano have tried to keep control of his underworld operations, while others have chosen Gaspare Di Gregorio as their gangster king. This has resulted in bloody conflicts and unrest in Mafia circles.

The Beach Boys, so named after 1st hit "Surfin' Safari," are topping charts with "Sloop John B."

1966

JUNE

Su	Mo	Tu	We	Th	Fr	Sa
			1	2	3	4
5	6	7	8	9	10	11
12	13	14	15	16	17	18
19	20	21	22	23	24	25
26	27	28	29	30		

1. Saigon: Junta agrees to admit ten civilians to National Leadership Committee (→ 6/14).

2. Congo: Four ex-ministers hanged for attempted coup (→ 3/13/67).

4. U.S.: 6,400 sign appeal against Vietnam War, largest political ad ever published (→ 8).

5. Eugene Cernan, on Gemini 9, floats two hours in space (→ 7/18).

6. Miss.: James Meredith shot in back on civil rights march (→ 9).

7. California: Ronald Reagan wins Republican nomination for governor (→ 11/8).

8. New York: 130 students, faculty walk out of N.Y.U. graduation as Robert McNamara gets honorary degree (→ 8/27).

9. Miss.: Rev. King and 208 others take up protest march begun by James Meredith (→ 23).

14. Washington: Marine pilot testifies he shot two S. Vietnamese while on drugs (→ 29).

14. LBJ signs Coulee Dam bill to give U.S. world's largest power plant.

15. U.S. resumes full economic aid to India and Pakistan (→ 2/19/68).

15. Amsterdam: Three days of anti-establishment youth riots end.

17. TVA awards contract to G.E. for world's largest nuclear power plant (→ 5/20/67).

21. Washington: LBJ meets with King Faisal of Saudi Arabia (→ 1/9/75).

23. Miss.: Civil rights marchers dispersed by tear gas (→ 25).

26. New York: U.S. Communist Party elects Gus Hall secretary general.

28. Argentina: Junta ousts Pres. Illia; Gen. Ongania takes over; U.S. suspends ties (→ 7/15).

29. North Vietnam: U.S. shells gas depots near Hanoi (→ 30).

29. Iraq offers 12-point plan for peace in Kurdistan (→ 3/11/70).

DEATH

7. Jean Hans Arp, French avant-garde artist (*9/16/1887).

Unmanned space ship films moon surface

The protective capsule of the satellite prevents docking with Gemini 9.

June 6. The U.S. space program had one small failure and one large success this month. Astronauts Eugene Cernan and Thomas Stafford were unable to dock Gemini 9 with a satellite, but Cernan did float in space for two hours, and they splashed down safely today.

Meanwhile, Surveyor 1 landed safely on the moon on the 2nd and sent back pictures showing a rubble-strewn but smooth surface. The landing was a significant step in the American program to land men on the moon by 1970. The 144 photographs sent to earth by Surveyor in its first hours on the moon showed that the lunar surface is both level and strong enough to support a manned landing craft.

The success of Surveyor 1 was a bonus for the scientists who designed and built the spacecraft. They had said it would take three or four flights to get the performance achieved today. "This, in my opinion, puts the Surveyor program ahead at least a year," said Robert F. Garbarine of the National Aeronautics and Space Administration.

Surveyor used radar, a computer and four rockets to settle down gently on its three legs. Obtaining electrical power from large panels of solar cells, it is expected to send back hundreds of photos daily (→ 5).

June 13. Despite harsh dissent, the Supreme Court has ruled 5-4 in the case of convicted rapist Ernesto Miranda (rt.) that confessions are invalid if obtained before a suspect has been informed of his rights (→ 1/20/67).

Meredith is shot on civil rights march

June 25. James Meredith, who braved taunts, threats and hostility to break the color barrier at all-white "Ole Miss" University in 1962, was shot in the back June 6 as he marched for civil rights in Mississippi. The first Negro admitted to the segregated college fell in a pool of blood along U.S. Highway 51. His companions rushed him to a nearby hospital where surgeons removed shrapnel from his neck, shoulders and back. Immediately after the shooting, police arrested a suspect, a 40-year-old white man, who admitted to the ambush but could not explain his motive. Today, fully recovered, Meredith joined the marchers near Jackson as they continue the struggle to end racial discrimination (→ 7/15).

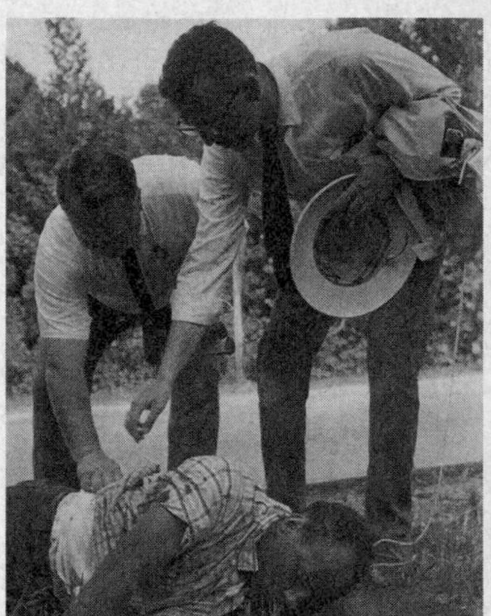

Meredith, attended to at roadside.

U.S. forces focus on Hanoi's fuel dumps

June 30. American bombers have destroyed more than five, large fuel storage areas in Hanoi over the past two days, reducing North Vietnam's vital oil-storage capacity by 50 percent. The raids mark a departure from previous restrictions that had kept U.S. planes away from the major city. Meanwhile, antiwar protests continued at home this month. At commencement exercises, students and some faculty members at Amherst College and N.Y.U. walked out when Defense Secretary Robert McNamara was awarded honorary degrees (→ 7/7).

1966

JULY

Su	Mo	Tu	We	Th	Fr	Sa
					1	2
3	4	5	6	7	8	9
10	11	12	13	14	15	16
17	18	19	20	21	22	23
24	25	26	27	28	29	30
31						

1. France pulls armed forces out of NATO (→ 9/26).

1. Dominican Republic: Pres. Balaguer sworn in.

2. Wimbledon: Manuel Santana over Dennis Ralston 6-4, 11-9, 6-4; Billie Jean King over Maria Bueno 6-3, 3-6, 6-1.

4. Israel: Monument to JFK unveiled (→ 10/5).

6. Indonesia: Sukarno, stripped of lifetime presidency, disputes Suharto's right to rule (→ 9/28).

6. Nyassaland becomes Malawi, independent in Commonwealth.

7. Warsaw Pact nations offer volunteers to aid Hanoi (→ 12).

9. Jack Nicklaus wins British Open golf championship.

11. China restricts foreign visitors during purges (→ 8/1966).

11. Moscow: Soviets boycott track meet to protest U.S. war in Vietnam.

12. N. Vietnam threatens to try U.S. pilots for war crimes (→ 17).

14. Lucien Aimar wins Tour de France.

15. Chicago: Troops quell race riots; two dead, 57 hurt (→ 21).

15. U.S. recognizes Argentine junta (→ 5/28/69).

17. California: Jim Ryun sets mark in mile at 3:51.3.

17. Hanoi: Ho Chi Minh orders partial mobilization (→ 30).

18. Gemini 10 launched; links up with satellite Agena (→ 8/14).

18. The Hague: Intl. Court bars Liberian, Ethiopian protest on apartheid in S.W. Africa (→ 9/6).

21. Cleveland: Police wound Negro mother and 3 kids (→ 31).

23. L.A.: J. Pennel sets pole vault mark of 17' 6.25" (→ 6/24/67).

25. London: Parliament votes to nationalize steel (→ 11/30).

30. London: England 4-2 over W. Germany for World Cup.

30. Vietnam: U.S. planes bomb demilitarized zone between North and South (→ 8/7).

DEATH

25. Frank O'Hara, American poet, art critic (*6/27/1926).

One man accused of murdering eight nurses

July 19. The sole survivor of the mass slaying of eight student nurses in Chicago identified Richard F. Speck today as the murderer. "That is the man," Corazon Amurso said, pointing to Speck as she stood in the doorway of his hospital room at the Cook County Jail.

Speck, a 24-year-old ex-convict, was arrested in a transient hotel in Chicago. He was bleeding profusely from self-inflicted cuts on his right wrist and left elbow. A laborer and former seaman, Speck once served a three-year prison sentence for burglary and forgery in Dallas. He has now been charged with murder, but it is uncertain when he might stand trial because of his frail condition.

The student nurses were brutally slain a week ago in a row house that served as a dormitory for the South Chicago Community Hospital. Miss Amurso, a Filipino exchange student, escaped death by rolling under a bed and then groping her way to a window ledge. There, she began screaming: "They are all dead! They are all dead! My friends are all dead! Oh, God, I'm the only one alive" (→ 8/1).

Corazon Amurso (left), sole survivor.

Sinatra and Mia are wed; go to London

July 19. Entertainer Frank Sinatra kept his ol' blue eyes on Mia Farrow today, as the two were wed in a five-minute ceremony in Las Vegas. He is 50, she 21. "We decided to be married 20 minutes ago," Sinatra laughed. Miss Farrow is a star on the soap opera "Peyton Place." She is the daughter of director John Farrow and actress Maureen O'Sullivan. The slim bride, who recently cut off her long, blond hair, wore a white silk dress for the ceremony. She and Sinatra plan to honeymoon in England.

Young bride Mia Farrow.

Clift dies at peak of his movie career

Clift during the making of "Freud."

July 23. Intense and melancholy actor Montgomery Clift has died of a heart attack. He was only 45, but in some ways he seemed older. His face, scarred by a car accident early in his career, left his face craggy and battered. Four years ago, he had cataracts removed from his eyes. And his fears, whispered to friends like Elizabeth Taylor, too often had to do with death. Nebraska-born Clift premiered in summer stock at age 14. He had strong roles in "From Here to Eternity" (1953), "Judgment at Nuremberg" (1961) and "Freud" (1962).

Negroes battle cops in three big cities

July 31. The streets of Chicago, New York and Cleveland seared with racial unrest this month; many have been killed and injured in firebomb attacks, sniper gunfire and clashes between white and Negro gangs and police.

Over 4,000 National Guardsmen were called into Chicago to quiet an ongoing war between police and Negro snipers. Two Negroes were killed in the shooting and six policemen were wounded. Fifty-one others were inflicted with minor injuries from flying glass and rocks. A community leader expressed the sentiment of many angry ghetto dwellers. "We need jobs," he said. Today, 54 people were hurt when angry whites hurled bricks at civil rights protesters marching through an all-white neighborhood.

The situation in the East New York section of Brooklyn has turned so ugly that an additional 1,000 policemen were sent to the area. Bands of Negroes, whites and Puerto Ricans sparred in the streets for nearly a week, resulting in scores of injuries and at least two deaths. Mayor John Lindsay has pleaded with leaders of the gangs to try to negotiate their differences. "It won't do any good to demonstrate violently in the streets," he said.

In Cleveland, a young Negro mother was killed by police gunfire. The incident triggered more rioting, which had already taken two lives and injured 30 others (→ 8/26).

"The Godfather of Soul" James Brown, (and private jet): "It's a Man's Man's Man's World."

1966

AUGUST

Su	Mo	Tu	We	Th	Fr	Sa
	1	2	3	4	5	6
7	8	9	10	11	12	13
14	15	16	17	18	19	20
21	22	23	24	25	26	27
28	29	30	31			

1. Nigeria: Lt. Col. Yakubu Gowon takes over in military coup (→ 5/30/67).

1. Chicago: Richard Speck pleads not guilty to killing eight nurses (→ 4/15/67).

2. Soviets re-elect Aleksei Kosygin premier (→ 11/14/69).

5. U.S. praises Prince Sihanouk for keeping Cambodia neutral (→ 1/10/68).

6. U.K.: Ali KOs Brian London in 3rd to keep title (→ 9/10).

7. North Vietnam: Seven U.S. planes lost, most in one day (→ 11).

10. U.S. Treasury halts printing of $2 bills.

11. Vietnam: U.S. planes attack U.S. Coast Guard cutter, killing two (→ 26).

11. Indonesia, Malaysia end three-year war, call for referendum in Sabah and Sarawak on cession to Indonesia.

13. Tunis: Pres. Bourguiba outlaws miniskirts.

14. Lunar Orbiter 1 becomes first U.S craft to orbit moon (→ 18).

15. Israel downs two Syrian MIG's over Sea of Galilee (→ 10/14).

18. First pictures of earth taken from moon orbit are sent back to U.S. (→ 25).

22. Washington: Scientists say evidence used to convict Rosenbergs was invalid (→ 11/3/71).

23. N.Y.: 45,000 see Beatles at Shea Stadium (→ 8/27/67).

25. Cape Kennedy: Apollo test craft makes successful 18,000-mile flight (→ 9/15).

26. Chicago: Ten-point accord on housing reached; Rev. King calls off marches (→ 9/4).

26. South Vietnam: U.S. planes napalm battalion of U.S. G.I.'s; 20 killed (→ 9/16).

27. Ohio poll shows 54% think U.S. role in Vietnam a mistake (→ 9/1).

DEATH

3. Lenny Bruce, American comedian, of narcotics overdose (*10/13/1926).

Sniper on tower terrorizes campus, slays 12

Woman hides from barrage of bullets; man who was not so lucky lies at left.

Aug 1. An architectual honor student, perched atop a 27-story tower at the University of Texas in Austin, shot 12 persons to death and wounded 33 others before he was killed by police today.

Charles J. Whitman, 25, a former altar boy and Eagle Scout, also is believed to have killed his wife and mother at their homes before going to the university campus to begin his shooting rampage shortly before noon.

University officials were at a loss to explain Whitman's actions. They said he had never been treated at the student health center for psychiatric disorder and had no record of being disciplined. However, he had an unusually heavy study schedule and also was working part-time as a collector for a finance firm. He was a former Marine who received an honorable discharge in 1964.

The mass shootings on campus took place after Whitman carried a trunkful of guns, food and water to the top of the tower. There, he crouched on a ledge and sprayed the area below with bullets for more than an hour as students, visitors and professors ran for cover in the 98-degree heat.

The sniper was finally killed by an off-duty policeman, Romero Martinez, who inched his way around a wall at the top of the tower and fired six bullets.

Old salt sets out to circle the earth

Aug 27. Not just anyone can sail around the world alone. But Sir Francis Charles Chichester is not your average guy with average goals. The 64-year-old English yachtsman, adventurer and author of "The Lonely Sea and Sky" set sail today from Plymouth, England, on his 13,750-mile journey around the globe. The voyage should take eight months. Chichester is not an inexperienced thrill-seeker; in the 30's, he earned international acclaim for his solo air flights, and now sets out for the lonely sea (→ 12/12).

Lone yachtsman Francis Chichester.

Chinese Communists proclaim widespread Cultural Revolution

August. "The Great Proletarian Cultural Revolution now unfolding is a great revolution that touches people to their very souls." So proclaims a communique issued by the Central Committee of the Chinese Communist Party after its 11th plenary session. It also declared that Peking would continue its militant revolutionary policies at home and abroad, endorsed the leadership of party Chairman Mao Tse-tung, who presided over the session, and praised the ideological contributions of Defense Minister Lin Piao.

Public spectacle: Remolding China.

Lin, at 58 the youngest member of the Politburo, has emerged as the most influential deputy of the 72-year-old Mao after recent purges, which are an essential part of the Cultural Revolution. Mao and his loyalists have vowed to continue their attack on "the handful of anti-party, anti-Socialist rightists."

The revolution also consists of Red Guards, mostly bands of teenagers, pressing to remove all old and foreign influences from Chinese life. In huge demonstrations, they are parading with portraits of Mao, Marx, Lenin and Stalin; carrying little, red books of quotations from Mao's works; and shouting in unison slogans attacking "Soviet revisionism and U.S. imperialism" (→ 11/23).

Maoist doctrine in pocket size.

The Herald Tribune ceases publication

Aug 15. The New York Herald Tribune, a newspaper with a proud history which ran into financial difficulties in recent years, has announced it will cease publication. In an attempt to survive, The Herald Tribune merged in March with two other New York newspapers. The company planned to publish a morning newspaper, to be called The Herald Tribune, and an afternoon and a Sunday paper. A protracted labor dispute prevented publication and precipitated the decision to close The Herald Tribune.

Mays is now second on home run list

Aug 17. Willie Mays belted his 535th home run and moved into second place among career homer-hitters. Only Babe Ruth, with 714, has hit more than the 35-year-old Giant outfielder. Ruth, of course, was a left-handed batter, while Mays moved one ahead of Jimmy Foxx as the premier right-handed slugger. His fourth-inning shot helped the San Francisco Giants beat the St. Louis Cardinals by 4-3. Mays, who has led the National League in homers four times, raised his season output to 30 (→12/1973).

Starfighter crashes cause furor in Germany

Aug 25. A crisis over American-built Starfighters has thrown the German air force into a tailspin and created an enormous controversy in the government. Sixty of the fighter jets sold to Germany by the United States have already crashed on training missions, and a number of high-ranking officers in the Federal Ministry of Defense were forced to resign. Word of the trouble with the aircraft leaked out when the Inspector General of the air force blew the whistle. In a newspaper interview, Werner Panitzki vehemently criticized the Defense Ministry for its role in the affair. Panitzki was suspended almost immediately by Defense Minister von Hassel.

Von Hassel's troubles did not stop in the air force. The Inspector General in the army, Heinz Trettner, quit before he could be fired over his opposition to an order from von Hassel banning union activities within the armed forces. Von Hassel punished two high-ranking officers in the army by dumping them into the reserves. He also quickly replaced Trettner with a new Inspector General.

American-built Starfighters: 60 lost since the Germans have been using them.

1966

SEPTEMBER

Su	Mo	Tu	We	Th	Fr	Sa
				1	2	3
4	5	6	7	8	9	10
11	12	13	14	15	16	17
18	19	20	21	22	23	24
25	26	27	28	29	30	

1. Cambodia: De Gaulle condemns U.S. involvement in Vietnam (→ 7).

3. Pennsylvania: LBJ calls for 100-nation talks on lack of water.

6. South Africa: Prime Minister Hendrik Verwoerd assassinated in Parliament by whites (→ 13).

7. N.J.: Pvt. Dennis Mora gets three years hard labor for refusing Vietnam service (→ 10/9).

9. LBJ signs car safety bill; names William Haddon director of National Traffic Safety Agency (→ 1/6/67).

10. Germany: Muhammad Ali KOs Karl Mildenberger in 12th to keep title (→ 11/14).

12. Miss.: Police allow mob to attack Negroes trying to integrate Grenada schools (→ 17).

14. Washington: LBJ meets with Ferdinand Marcos (→ 1/22/67).

16. New York: New Metropolitan Opera House opens.

16. China charges new U.S. raid on border area (→ 18).

17. Miss.: 13 whites arrested in Grenada for harassing Negro protesters (→ 19).

18. New York: U Thant tells U.N. force cannot solve Vietnam problem (→ 28).

23. LBJ signs bill for $1.60/hour minimum wage.

26. Washington: LBJ and Bonn chief Erhard confer on cost of defending Europe (→ 4/3/69).

27. Alabama: Jury clears Klansman Eugene Thomas in slaying of Viola Liuzzo (→ 10/24).

28. South Vietnam: U.S. accidentally bombs friendly village, killing 28 (→ 10/6).

28. Indonesia returns to U.N. after 20-month absence (→ 2/22/67).

30. Africa: Bechuanaland becomes independent Commonwealth nation of Botswana.

30. London: Lord Thompson buys Times of London.

DEATHS

21. Paul Reynaud, ex-premier of France (*10/15/1878).

29. Bernard Gimbel, department store magnate (*4/10/1885).

Early advocate of birth control is dead

Sept 6. Margaret Sanger was a fortunate visionary. Unlike other great women such as Susan B. Anthony, who never saw women get the vote, Mrs. Sanger saw her dreams realized. In her lifetime, new, effective forms of birth control were developed, radically enriching the lives of millions of women—and men. Mrs. Sanger made it happen.

Mrs. Sanger died today at the age of 82. She was born Margaret Higgins, raised in New York state by a heavy-drinking socialist father and a mother worn out by bearing more than a dozen babies. Margaret became a nurse and witnessed the ugly effects of self-induced abortions.

Sanger, birth control pioneer.

She swore to end them.

The nurse raised three children (one died young) and raised hell sending birth control information through the mails. She went to France to study contraceptives there; she came back with pessaries, diaphragms and jellies. In 1916, she opened a birth control clinic in Brooklyn. It was swiftly shut down. She attacked laws against birth control step by step until in 1953 she was President of the International Planned Parenthood Federation.

Her greatest coup was the birth control pill. After reading studies in medical journals implying its feasibility, she urged scientists to make the oral contraceptive a reality.

Critics might blame the pill and indirectly Mrs. Sanger for the present sexual revolution. Mrs. Sanger would probably argue that men and women now are not having any more sex than they used to—they are simply enjoying it more. ▷

Gemini joins with satellite; soars 850 miles

Gulf of Aden, as seen from Gemini 11, nearly 400 miles above the earth.

Sept 15. Astronauts aboard the Gemini 11 spacecraft have set an altitude record of 850 miles and created artificial gravity in space by spinning in tandem with a companion Agena spacecraft at the end of a 100-foot tether. Astronauts Charles Conrad Jr. and Richard F. Gordon Jr. rendezvoused and docked with the Agena on the first orbit after their launch, a maneuver that is essential for the planned manned flights to the moon.

With the primary objective of the flight achieved, they then used the Gemini's rockets to head for an altitude that gave them a view of the earth Conrad called "fantastic." By flying with only a rope between the Gemini and Agena spacecraft, the astronauts showed that craft can stay in formation in orbit using little or no maneuvering rocket fuel. The Gemini 11 mission is due to end tomorrow morning, after 44 orbits of the earth in 71 hours (→ 11/15).

Breton, the creator of Surrealism, dead

Sept 28. The babbling of madmen inspired French poet and theorist Andre Breton. When he was a medical student during World War I, Breton worked in military psychiatric wards. There, he noticed the connection between the inmates' wild musings and poetry, between dreams and splendid realities. His "Manifesto of Surrealism" (1924) guided decades of art and politics. Breton died today at age 70.

Raised in Normandy, at age 17 Breton befriended avant-garde poet Guillaume Apollinaire. After his stint at the army hospitals, Breton conferred with Freud. He then wrote his manifesto, calling for an end to control and inhibitions.

Artists such as Salvador Dali and Rene Magritte heeded the call. Anarchists and Marxists embraced the philosophy, not always to Breton's liking. In the 50's and 60's other movements outpaced Breton, making his anti-church and free-love stance seem outdated.

Home for American art is established

Sept 27. A bomb threat at the gala opening of the New York Whitney Museum last night did not spoil the party. Police combed the building and, finding nothing, ushered patrons back to the displays of American art. The Whitney, conceived and financed by the late Mrs. Gertrude Vanderbilt Whitney, opens to the general public tomorrow.

Baez leads Negro children to school

Sept 19. Like a solemn pied piper, civil rights activist and singer Joan Baez led a small group of Negro children to the door of an all-white school today. State patrol officers denied them entry to the Grenada, Miss., elementary school. Grenada, population 8,000 and 48 percent Negro, is targeted for integration by Dr. Martin Luther King Jr. and other civil rights marchers (→ 27).

Hecklers at civil rights march face bayonets

Sept 4. Both Negro activists and their white antagonists are increasingly facing the sharpened edges of bayonets. Some 12 persons were injured today as a march for open housing in an all-white suburb of Chicago ended in a clash between white hecklers and National Guard troops carrying bayonets. Roving gangs of whites threw rocks, eggs and cherry bombs at the marchers, shouting "Kill 'em!" "Tar and feather 'em." As guardsmen moved in, police loudspeakers blared: "Watch out! Bricks on the left flank. Pop bottles on your right flank."

Three months ago, 225 Negroes in a civil rights march on City Hall in Prichard, Alabama, faced National Guard bayonets (→ 12).

Vorster replaces slain South African leader

Verwoerd, helped set up Bantustans.

Sept 13. Balthazar Vorster has been appointed Prime Minister one week after Hendrik Verwoerd was brutally stabbed to death by a messenger on the floor of the South African Parliament. Dimitri Stifianos, the messenger, was a drifter who complained that Verwoerd was helping blacks at the expense of whites. Verwoerd, a pro-Nazi during WWII, was the architect of the country's strict apartheid laws. During the war, he railed against "British Jewish liberalism" and protested when the goverment gave Jews refuge. Vorster is expected to follow in his footsteps (→ 10/27).

Negro activists come up against the sharpened edge of the establishment.

1966

OCTOBER

Su	Mo	Tu	We	Th	Fr	Sa
						1
2	3	4	5	6	7	8
9	10	11	12	13	14	15
16	17	18	19	20	21	22
23	24	25	26	27	28	29
30	31					

4. Africa: Basutoland becomes independent nation of Lesotho.

5. Texas Appeals Court voids conviction of Jack Ruby (→ 12/21).

6. New York: Hanoi insists U.S. end bombing before peace talks begin (→ 24).

7. Moscow expels all Chinese students in reprisal for Peking act last month (→ 11/7).

7. Berlin: Four dig under wall to flee to West (→ 3/19/70).

9. Baltimore: Orioles beat Dodgers 1-0 to sweep World Series.

9. U.S. reports Vietnam War now costing $2 bil. per month (→ 28).

11. New York: Dr. Timothy Leary arrested on narcotics charge (→ 5/19/69).

14. New York: Israel at U.N. accuses Syria of plot to destroy nation (→ 11/13).

18. New York: Bodies of 12 firemen taken from burned building in worst disaster in department's 101-year history.

19. State Dept. lets U.S. chess team go to Cuba (→ 9/24/67).

19. Paris: Moroccan secret police chief surrenders in kidnapping of Ben Barka (→ 9/26/69).

24. Miss.: 200 arrested for protesting harassment of Negro students in Grenada (→ 11/8).

24. New Delhi: India, Yugoslavia, UAR call on U.S to stop bombing of N. Vietnam (→ 25).

25. Manila: U.S., Allies pledge to leave S. Vietnam six months after Hanoi halts war (→ 26).

27. Peking, Hanoi reject Manila plan for ending war (→ 11/12).

27. China explodes A-bomb borne by guided missile (→ 1/27/67).

27. U.N. ends South African mandate over Southwest Africa (Namibia) (→ 2/4/67).

28. New York: Stokely Carmichael vows not to serve in armed forces (→ 12/1).

30. New York: Police seize 20 men and tons of weapons in raid on right-wing group Minutemen.

30. Italy: Social Democrats and Socialists merge.

LBJ pays a surprise visit to the boys in 'Nam

LBJ, sweating in the Vietnamese heat, shares a jovial moment with G.I.'s.

Oct 26. American soldiers in South Vietnam were surprised by a distinguished guest today: President Lyndon Johnson. LBJ unexpectedly flew into Camranh Bay to salute his troops; he was on a scheduled 17-day visit to the South Pacific, but for security purposes his stop in the war zone was kept secret.

The president decorated many of the men and women, joked, dined and thanked them. He promised support and told the combined military forces, "You know what you are fighting against: a vicious and illegal aggression across this little nation's frontier."

General William Westmoreland arranged the two-and-a-half-hour stopover and received from his boss a surprise Distinguished Service Medal for courage and leadership. Secretary of State Dean Rusk, accompanying Johnson on the trip, reassured the soldiers that the Johnson administration is seeking a peaceful, victorious end to the war.

As he boarded his plane for Bangkok, LBJ told the troops to come home "safe and sound."

Oct 1. Albert Speer (rear left), the Nazi architect who designed the stadium at Nuremberg and who, as Minister of Armaments, organized slave labor to build Hitler's war machine, leaves Spandau prison with Baldur von Schirach after serving the 20 years given them at Nuremberg.

Hurricane Carter arrested in killings

Oct 15. Police have arrested Hurricane Carter, a former top-ranked middleweight boxer, and charged him and John Artis in the murder of a bartender and two customers in a Paterson, New Jersey, tavern. Carter and Artis were riding in a car that was similar to the one reported at the scene of the killings. The two men were released and then rearrested, reportedly as a result of information supplied by a witness.

Carter, now 29 years old, admitted that he had spent one-third of his life in jail. He came close to achieving fame in the ring when he fought Joey Giardello for the middleweight championship but lost on a decision. That was two years ago. He lost his last fight in Argentina August 5 (→ 9/26/74).

Carter (left) and Artis at N.J. court.

Red Dean no longer bugs establishment

Oct 22. Known as the Red Dean for his support of communism, former Dean of Canterbury Dr. Hewlitt Johnson died today. The man variously described as a crank, "Commie" and a saint was 92.

Johnson drew disdain from the traditional British political and clerical establishment for his outspoken espousal of Marxism. He stirred quite a furor when he remarked during a sermon that if Jesus Christ were alive today, he would be a Communist. The Archbishop of Canterbury, Dr. Michael Ramsey, said that while he disagreed with the political views of the Red Dean, he respected Johnson's compassion for human life.

1966

NOVEMBER

Su	Mo	Tu	We	Th	Fr	Sa
		1	2	3	4	5
6	7	8	9	10	11	12
13	14	15	16	17	18	19
20	21	22	23	24	25	26
27	28	29	30			

2. Vienna: Simon Wiesenthal accuses Austria of laxity in trying ex-Nazis (→ 2/12/67).

3. LBJ signs bill requiring food labeling to identify contents.

3. India: Hurricane strikes Bengal, killing 1,000.

4. Washington: U.S., U.S.S.R. sign accord for direct air service from Washington to Moscow.

6. N.Y.: Soviet poet Yevgeny Yevtushenko begins tour of U.S.

7. India: Riots over slaughtered cow leave seven dead.

7. Moscow: Chinese quit Bolshevik anniversary celebration second day in row (→ 8/13/67).

12. Saigon: Corruption taking up to 40% of U.S. aid (→ 12/24).

13. Israel, Jordan fight fierce battle in Hebron area (→ 24).

14. Houston: Ali TKOs Cleveland Williams in third to retain heavyweight title (→ 1/12/67).

15. Atlantic: James Lovell, Edwin Aldrin end Gemini 12 flight, last in program (→ 12/24).

17. Utah: Art Arfons badly hurt in 585-mph car crash.

20. West Germany: Ultra-rightist Natl. Democratic Party wins 15 of 204 Bavaria seats (→ 12/1).

20. Beirut: Arab League votes to boycott Coca-Cola and Ford (→ 11/27/70).

21. Mississippi: Aubrey Norvell pleads guilty to shooting James Meredith (→ 2/28/67).

22. Washington: Episcopal Church affirms support of federal birth control aid.

23. N.Y.: Adam Clayton Powell ignores court order to serve 30 days for contempt (→ 1/9/67).

24. Jordan: Protesters riot against King Hussein's policy of moderation with Israel (→ 25).

25. New York: U.N. censures Israel for raid on Jordan (→ 26).

26. Philadelphia: Army over Navy 20-7 in football.

26. Jordan: Hussein calls draft of all between 18 and 40 (→ 12/11).

30. Barbados gets independence.

30. London: P.M. Wilson urges European strength to avoid U.S. economic domination.

Invaluable art damaged in Florence flood

A rubber raft carrying Florentines through the deluge passes a disabled car.

Nov 5. The Door of Paradise has been flung wide, ripped from its hinges and swept away. The bronze door to the cathedral Il Duomo is one of many treasures of Florence ravaged by a devastating flood. Centuries-old paintings, sculpture and books have been annihilated. The Mayor of Florence calls the cost of the damage "incalculable."

Winds up to 90 miles per hour and rain for days whipped the Arno River high above its banks. Waters battered but did not collapse the 14th-century Ponte Vecchio, the only bridge in Venice that Germans in World War II failed to destroy. Some shops on the bridge, however, were smashed and washed away.

Thousands of ancient books in the National Library lie submerged. Furniture and archives, some 400 years old, were ruined in the Strozzi Palace. In the cellar of the Uffizi Gallery, 130,000 photo negatives of art work were obliterated. The original masterpieces, stored on an upper floor, are miraculously intact.

Red Guards accuse President Liu Shao-chi

Liu, heretic in secular China.

Nov 23. Chinese Red Guards, whipped into a frenzy during the continuing Cultural Revolution, have denounced Liu Shao-chi, chief of state, and at one time Mao Tse-tung's designated heir apparent. Representing the party stalwarts opposed to Mao's personal rule, Liu is now one of the "walking wounded," prominent Chinese leaders who have been condemned by wall posters but not by name in the official press. He has lost most but not all of his power and slipped down in the hierarchy because of his opposition to the Cultural Revolution and adherence to "bourgeois revisionism." Liu is said to have confessed his political sins (→ 1/8/67).

Arthritis forces Koufax retirement

Nov 18. Sandy Koufax has decided to retire from baseball rather than risk permanent injury to his left arm because of arthritis. The pain in his arm has grown progressively worse, the star pitcher of the Los Angeles Dodgers said, since it first began three years ago. He tried to ignore the pain as his salary soared to $125,000 a year, the highest of any pitcher in baseball. "I'm doing the right thing and don't regret one minute of the last 12 years," he said.

Koufax has pitched four no-hitters—one a perfect game—more than any other man. He set a major league record of 382 strikeouts in one season (1965) and won the Cy Young Award as the outstanding pitcher in 1963, 1965 and 1966. Since the pain began, Koufax has kept pitching with the help of pills, shots and therapeutic treatments.

California elects Reagan as Governor

Nov 8. Ronald Wilson Reagan, the ruggedly handsome former movie star turned politician, was elected the Governor of California today, defeating his Democratic opponent, Gov. Edmund G. "Pat" Brown, in a heavy turnout of voters. A conservative Republican who was once a liberal Democrat, the 55-year-old Reagan, an Illinois native, scored in his first bid for public office (→ 9/12/67).

Reagan's next act: Governor.

First Negro Senator elected by popular vote

Nov 8. State Attorney General Edward W. Brooke won a seat in the U.S. Senate today, the first Negro ever chosen by the electorate to serve in that body. He will succeed another Massachusetts Republican, Leverett Saltonstall, who did not seek re-election.

When he takes his seat in January, he will be the first Negro member of the Senate in 85 years. The first two, Hiram R. Revels and Blanche Kelso Bruce, both from Mississippi, were elected at that time by the state legislature, not the voters. In that era, following the Civil War, state legislatures in the South were controlled largely by Northern carpet-baggers.

Brooke easily defeated Endicott Peabody, his Democratic opponent who once served as Governor of Massachussetts. A native of Washington, D.C., Brooke was editor of the Law Review while a student at Boston University (→ 21).

Brooke, formerly Mass. Atty. Gen.

Sheppard acquitted after nine years in jail

Nov 16. Samuel H. Sheppard broke into sobs today as a jury in Cleveland, Ohio, found him not guilty of killing his pregnant wife, Marilyn, 12 years ago in the bedroom of their suburban home in Bay Village.

Sheppard, a 42-year-old osteopath, served nine years in prison after an earlier jury found him guilty of the murder of his wife. The Supreme Court last year granted him a new trial in what has been one of the more celebrated murder cases in America.

F. Lee Bailey, the defendant's chief attorney, said later that he thinks that Sheppard's acquittal will mean that his license as an osteopath will be restored.

With Sheppard as the jury verdict was announced was his second wife, with whom he began corresponding while he was in prison. They were married two days after his release from prison. In ordering the new trial, the Supreme Court held that "prejudicial publicity" and "a carnival atmosphere" at the earlier trial had tainted the conviction.

The miniskirt: Men can't believe their eyes

Take an ineffably skinny teen model, don her in minimum garb, and you have a fashion frenzy. Twiggy, nee Leslie Hornsby, is popularizing the miniskirt. British Miss Twiggy "rounds out" the look with thick false eyelashes and colorful fishnet stockings.

Fashion observers trace the maximum mini trend to British designer Mary Quant. But what gave Miss Quant the idea? Perhaps she sees our times something like the 1920's, when women, free to smoke, drink and curse, did so in flimsy flapper gowns. Today, sure to keep her shape as long as she is on the pill, woman is again feeling free. The mini is complemented by headbands, beads and plastic boots.

Miniskirts trouble Twiggy, yardstick of fashion. Stockings, bereft of support, tend to gravitate to her ankles.

1966

DECEMBER

Su	Mo	Tu	We	Th	Fr	Sa
				1	2	3
4	5	6	7	8	9	10
11	12	13	14	15	16	17
18	19	20	21	22	23	24
25	26	27	28	29	30	31

1. California: 5,000 boycott Berkeley classes to protest Navy recruitment (→ 5).

1. Bonn: Kurt Kiesinger sworn in as chancellor (→ 4/25/67).

3. New York: Judy Collins plays at Carnegie Hall.

11. Cairo: Arab League votes to put troops in Jordan to face Israelis (→ 22).

16. Maryland: LBJ has successful operations for hernia and throat polyp.

22. U.S. announces allocation of 900,000 tons of grain to fight famine in India (→ 9/14/67).

22. U.S. to send arms to Jordan to aid in defense against Israel (→ 1/25/67).

24. Vietnam: U.S. cargo plane crashes into village, killing 125 civilians (→ 26).

24. Soviet research station soft-lands on moon (→ 1/27/67).

28. Australia beats India for third straight Davis Cup.

CULTURAL EVENTS, 1966

Literature: John Fowles' "The Magus"; Truman Capote's "In Cold Blood"; Bernard Malamud's "The Fixer"; Jacqueline Susann's "Valley of the Dolls"; Mario Vargas Llosa's "The Green House"; Graham Greene's "The Comedians."

Academia, Religion: James Cameron's "Witness," on Vietnam War; Chemical structure of DNA revealed; U.S. Catholics allowed to eat meat on Friday, except during Lent.

Music: Samuel Barber's "Antony and Cleopatra" opens new Metropolitan Opera House; Burton Lane's "On a Clear Day You Can See Forever"; Mitch Leigh's "Man of La Mancha"; "Born Free"; Sinatra's "Strangers in the Night"; Beatles' "Eleanor Rigby."

The Arts: Chagall's "The Triumph of Music," in Metroplitan Opera, New York.

Film: Hitchcock's 50th, "Torn Curtain"; John Huston's "The Bible"; Truffaut's "Farenheit 451"; Lewis Gilbert's "Alfie"; "Who's Afraid of Virginia Woolf?," Taylor and Burton; "A Man for All Seasons," Oscar.

U.S. admits hitting civilians in Vietnam

Dec 26. The Defense Department acknowledged that some civilian areas may have been hit accidentally during the bombing of military targets in North Vietnam. A Pentagon statement said U.S. policy was to attack only military targets and that "all possible care is taken to avoid civilian casualties." The statement added, however, "it is impossible to avoid all damage to civilian areas," particularly since North Vietnam deliberately places air defense sites, oil storage dumps and radar in populated areas.

The official U.S. statement was issued in response to a dispatch from Hanoi by Harrison Salisbury, a New York Times correspondent, reporting bombing damage to civilians in two North Vietnamese towns. Meanwhile, it was reported that the Soviet Union has supplied 100 new MIG fighters to Hanoi, doubling the size of its air force (→ 1/6/67).

Another grieving civilian.

Book about JFK's death causes suit

Dec 21. Mrs. Jacqueline Kennedy has dropped her suit against Look magazine. The publication, in turn, agrees to excise a few pages from a serialization of "The Death of a President." William Manchester's original version gave an unflattering portrait of Mrs. Kennedy.

In the unaltered manuscript, Mrs. Kennedy was described as wrestling with a nurse to gain entry to her husband's hospital room after he had been shot. Other material related to her distraught behavior following his death. In a statement, Mrs. Kennedy said she was sure "history will deal fairly and justly" with these events (→ 1/3/67).

Walt Disney is gone but his talent lives on

Disney's "Bambi" was based on a novel by Hungarian author Felix Salten.

Dec 15. The name Walt Disney is synonymous with creativity. "Snow White," the world's first animated feature-length cartoon, was his brainchild. The 1964 film "Mary Poppins" demonstrated his genius. Disneyland in Anaheim, California, reflected his ideas. Yet Walter Elias Disney never drew ears, tail or any part of Mickey Mouse; his partner Ubbe Iwerks did.

The man who made millions with the mouse is dead. Walt Disney died of lung cancer this morning in Los Angeles. He was 65.

Chicago-born Disney was one of many animators in the 1920's vying for attention. Animal characters were popular, but most types were already claimed. Felix the Cat ruled out other felines; Oswald the Rabbit (conceived in part by Disney) ruled out other bunnies. Disney decided on a mouse, which his wife dubbed Mickey. Disney supplied the fellow's voice in his first audio cartoon "Steamboat Willie" in 1928. Further feats won Disney honorary degrees from Harvard and Yale and 20 Academy Awards.

American writers this year make a killing

When writers committed pen to paper this year, murder and suicide often flowed forth.

Truman Capote's "In Cold Blood" recounts the story of two drifters who murdered a Kansas farm family for no apparent reason. The book is innovative, using the techniques of fiction to tell a factual tale.

William Manchester analyzes the most infamous homicide of the century in "The Death of a President." He describes Kennedy's assassination and the ensuing panic.

"Papa Hemingway" is about a notorious suicide—that of novelist Ernest Hemingway. Author A.E. Hotchner knew Hemingway for his last 13 years, and his biography is full of brawny exploits.

Jacqueline Susann's "Valley of the Dolls" is not great literature, but an undeniable best-seller. Miss Susann, a former actress, introduces three women clawing ahead in a glitzy world. One woman squeaks by, another goes mad and the third kills herself. The book has been attacked for its profanity and explicit description of breast cancer.

Bernard Malamud and Robert Heinlein wrote about prisoners. Malamud's hero in "The Fixer" is a Jewish handyman unfairly convicted of murder. Heinlein's cons in "The Moon Is a Harsh Mistress" are in a lunar colony in the 21st century. If Heinlein's sci-fi work is correct, cruelty is here to stay.

Lone sailor makes his longest voyage

Dec 12. Bruised, emaciated and weary, Francis Chichester was helped ashore in Sydney, Australia, after making the longest solo sea voyage in history, a 13,750-mile sail in 107 days. The British adventurer and magazine publisher received a hero's welcome on his arrival from Plymouth, England, in his 53-foot ketch, the Gipsy Moth IV. Sydney was the halfway point of his planned around-the-world voyage.

The lean 65-year-old sailor swigged a glass of English beer on his arrival and vowed: "I shall go on." He failed in his goal of reaching Sydney in 100 days. In 1961, he entered the first single-handed race across the Atlantic. At 57, and minus a lung lost to cancer, Chichester not only entered the race but also won it.

Gregory goes to Hanoi, defying U.S.

Dec 5. Despite federal warnings, comedian Dick Gregory is en route to Hanoi, North Vietnam. Gregory, known for his offbeat, intelligent humor, plans to work out details with the North Vietnamese government for a return trip at Christmas to perform for captured American soldiers. The State Department telegraphed Gregory, warning that his passport might be revoked if he went to Hanoi. North Vietnam is labeled a "restricted area" to U.S. travelers by government officials. Other nations that are restricted include Communist China, Cuba, North Korea and Albania.

The trip was arranged by British philosopher Bertrand Russell and by Gregory, who had met with members of the Hanoi government in London (→ 1/15/67).

At the movies: History and contemporary

Scofield in "A Man for All Seasons."

Actor Paul Scofield repeats his stage success in the film "A Man for All Seasons." Scofield plays Sir Thomas More, the 16th-century statesman who butts horns with Henry VIII over formation of the Church of England. Orson Welles and Wendy Hiller co-star. Fred Zinnemann ("High Noon") directed the opulent production.

From the sublime to the subcutaneous: "Fantastic Voyage" is a sci-fi film about a microscopic medical team battling viruses and bacteria inside the body. Raquel Welch and Stephen Boyd star. Richard Fleischer (Walt Disney's "20,000 Leagues Under the Sea") directed.

"Georgy Girl" focuses on a pudgy Lynn Redgrave looking for love in unlikely places. The theme song sets the funny, pathetic mood. Miss Redgrave's sister Vanessa is featured in "Morgan!," playing a wife who divorces a madcap artist.

Who is afraid of an Edward Albee script? Not Richard Burton and Elizabeth Taylor, portraying a married couple in "Who's Afraid of Virginia Woolf?" Their lies and fantasies ensnarl another couple (Sandy Dennis and George Segal) in a memorably terrifying night. The picture is the first directed by theater wunderkind Mike Nichols.

In another film, Michael Caine plays a Cockney playboy who discards women the way most of us dispense with used facial tissue. What's it all about, "Alfie"?

Welch et al: "Fantastic Voyage."

1967

JANUARY

Su	Mo	Tu	We	Th	Fr	Sa
1	2	3	4	5	6	7
8	9	10	11	12	13	14
15	16	17	18	19	20	21
22	23	24	25	26	27	28
29	30	31				

1. Connecticut: Nation's first fluoridation law goes into effect.

2. Pasadena: Purdue beats U.S.C. 14-13 in Rose Bowl.

6. Detroit: G.M. recalls 269,000 1967 cars for safety (→ 2/21).

6. South Vietnam: 16,000 U.S., 14,000 Vietnamese troops start biggest attack, on Iron Triangle, northwest of Saigon (→ 19).

8. China: Red Guard foes take over Nanking (→ 23).

9. Democrats oust A.C. Powell as committee chairman (→ 3/1).

11. Moscow: New U.S. Ambassador Llewellyn Thompson arrives with note from LBJ.

15. New Haven: 462 on Yale faculty call for end to bombing of North Vietnam (→ 2/15).

16. Alabama: Lurleen Wallace, incumbent's wife, sworn in as governor.

20. New York: Confessed murderer Charles Wright freed for police failure to read rights.

21. Bahamas: First black government takes power.

22. Manila: 20 killed by police at anti-Marcos rally (→ 7/26/69).

25. Jerusalem: Israelis, Syrians reaffirm armistice (→ 4/7).

27. Washington: 62 nations sign pact to curb arms in space (→ 2/12).

28. N.Y.: Marc Chagall gives eight stained glass windows to church in Pocantico Hills.

29. Blasts rock Yugoslav diplomatic premises in New York, Chicago, S.F., Ottawa, Toronto.

29. Vietnam: 31 civilians killed by U.S. helicopter attack (→ 31).

30. Florida: Last words of Apollo astronauts reported: "Get us out of here!" (→ 31).

30. Paris: Two-month Dada exhibit closes.

31. Texas: Wm. Bartley and Richard Harmon killed by fire in spacecraft simulator (→ 4/19).

31. Vietnam: Civilian deaths top Saigon army's for week (→ 2/15).

DEATH

18. Evelyn Nesbit, American actress (*1885).

Three astronauts killed

Jan 27. Astronauts Virgil I. Grissom, Edward H. White 2nd and Roger B. Chaffee were killed tonight in a flash fire that engulfed their Apollo 1 spacecraft. The three died on the ground during a full-scale simulation of the scheduled February 21 launching that was to put them in earth orbit for 14 days.

Officials of the National Aeronautics and Space Administration said an electrical spark must have ignited the pure oxygen inside the cabin of the Apollo spacecraft. The astronauts were seated abreast, just as they would have been during a flight, atop a Saturn 1 rocket on launching pad 34 at Cape Kennedy when the fire broke out at 6:31 p.m.

They were trapped behind closed hatches, unable to use the Apollo escape system because it was blocked by a gantry. Emergency crews tried to reach them but were blocked by dense smoke that rolled out of the cabin. The Air Force and NASA have impounded all data related to the fire. Officials say the loss of the men and the spececraft has dealt a serious blow to the Apollo program, which has been struggling to stay on deadline for a lunar landing by the end of the decade in the face of budget cuts (→ 30).

Grissom, White and Chaffee, first American casualties of the race to space.

Jan 15. In an L.A. stadium only two-thirds full, Bart Starr methodically tore apart Kansas City in the first Super Bowl, hitting 16 of 23 and using back Jim Taylor (above) well. Final score: Packers 35, Chiefs 10.

U.S. suffers highest weekly casualties

Numbers of dead, wounded mount.

Jan 19. Two records were set in South Vietnam last week. The Pentagon is not very proud of one of them. The casualty toll of American servicemen was the highest of the war: 144 men were killed; 1,044 were wounded. Six are listed as missing in action. The casualty totals are stark evidence of the deepening American involvement in Vietnam. They also point to the treacherous, insidious nature of guerrilla warfare. Most of the men were killed or wounded by mines and booby traps when they were out on small patrols.

The other record was set by American pilots last Thursday. They flew 549 missions; most were aimed at Communists who are dug in 25 miles north of Saigon (→ 29).

Draft board refuses exemption for Ali

Jan 12. A Louisville draft board has refused to consider Cassius Clay's request for exemption from military service as a Black Muslim minister. "Cassius Clay is still 1-A," said the board, of the 24-year-old world heavyweight champion, who prefers the name Muhammad Ali. The Kentucky Selective Service Board of Appeals earlier had turned down Clay's appeal to the National Selective Service Director and, if neccessary, to the United States Supreme Court. Clay was originally classified 1-Y for having failed the Army's aptitude test. When the standards were reduced because of Vietnam, his status was raised to 1-A. "I ain't got no quarrel with them Viet Congs," Clay protested (→ 2/6).

China in upheaval; bloody battles rage

Red Guards, agents of revolution.

Jan 23. China's Cultural Revolution has taken the lives of 54 "counterrevolutionaries" as well as Red Guards loyal to Chairman Mao Tse-tung after bloody battles between rival factions raged in Nanking, a city now in the grip of terror. Some 60,000 prisoners on both sides of the conflict reportedly underwent torture. They had "fingers and noses chopped off while girl students had their clothes ripped off," a Japanese newspaper reported. Violent incidents have been reported in other cities and rail service has been suspended, as opposition grows to Mao's Cultural Revolution from followers of Liu Shao-chi and other "capitalist roaders" (→ 2/11).

Stamp society pays forger to stop it

Jan 5. Stamp collectors around the world rested easier today when Raul de Thuih, prompted by the American Philatelic Society, resigned from "the art of making Philatelic rarities for those who wanted something unique." Translation: stamp-forging. Operating out of Merida, Mexico, the 76-year-old native Belgian has sold his work to unsuspecting collectors and experts for millions of dollars. To ease his retirement, the society is paying the artist an undisclosed lump of unforged cash.

We are older than we thought, folks

Jan 13. A discovery that seems to push the history of man back to 2.5 million years before the present has been made public by Harvard University. An elbow bone found in Kenya has been identified as that of a human-like creature living 750,000 years earlier than the until now oldest known human-like fossil. Less than a decade ago, the history of man was thought to have begun 600,000 years ago. When Dr. Louis S.B. Leakey found remains 1.75 million years old, the world of anthropology was shocked. He called it Homo habilis because the creature was a user of stone tools. The new find is classified as a man on the grounds that the body structure was more similar to that of a modern man than to an ape.

High court gives more press freedom

Jan 9. The Supreme Court has ruled 5 to 4 to extend the constitutional guarantees of freedom of the press to invasion-of-privacy cases. In voiding a judgment against Life, the court ruled plaintiffs could not collect damages for articles or broadcasts that contain errors that give a false impression of a person unless proof was offered that the falsehoods were published deliberately or recklessly. The case extends the landmark libel decision of New York Times v. Sullivan of 1964.

Jack Ruby, who killed Oswald, dies

Jan 3. He wandered from shabby obscurity into epic tragedy. He fired the shot that frustrated the world, then the mists of his mind swirled up and no one could be sure why Jack Ruby killed Lee Harvey Oswald on November 24, 1963. Now this unlikely avenger of President Kennedy, an ex-Chicago hustler and Dallas strip-joint proprietor, the ward of Dallas officials for three years, has succumbed to an extensive cancer that left his body weak and his mind filled with violent hallucinations (→ 10/20/68).

1967

FEBRUARY

Su	Mo	Tu	We	Th	Fr	Sa
			1	2	3	4
5	6	7	8	9	10	11
12	13	14	15	16	17	18
19	20	21	22	23	24	25
26	27	28				

1. U.S. drops plans to build dams in Grand Canyon.

1. Spain: Top matador Manuel Benitez announces retirement.

4. South Africa bars leave for U.S. crew on carrier FDR because of apartheid laws (→ 21).

5. Nicaragua: Gen. Anastasio Somoza Debayle elected president (→ 3/14/72).

6. Houston: Ali beats Ernie Terrell in 15-round decision to keep title (→ 3/22).

8. India: Indira Gandhi hit in face by stone while addressing crowd (→ 9/14).

9. U.S.S.R. agrees to sell part of Czarist art treasure collection.

12. Mexico: 21 Latin nations approve final text of nuclear test ban treaty (→ 3/29).

12. Austria: Neo-Nazi party National Democrats founded in Linz.

15. Vietnam: 13 U.S. helicopters downed in one day (→ 15).

15. Vietnam: South Korean army kills 242 Viet Cong (→ 23).

18. Washington: Natl. Art Gallery agrees to buy a Da Vinci for record $5 million.→

19. Tehran: Iran to buy $110 mil. in arms from Soviets (→ 8/22).

21. Detroit: Ford recalls 217,000 cars to check brakes and steering (→ 10/24).

21. N.Y.: U.S.S.R. at U.N. calls U.S. hypocritical in policy to South Africa (→ 2/26/68).

22. Indonesia: Sukarno turns over authority to Gen. Suharto (→ 7/28/69).

22. Report from Africa indicates world's first white gorilla found.

23. Vietnam: U.S. troops begin largest offensive of war, near Cambodian border (→ 26).

28. Mississippi: 19 indicted in 1964 slayings of three civil rights workers (→ 5/17).

DEATHS

15. William Bullitt, first U.S. ambassador to Soviet Union (*1/15/1991).

18. Robert Oppenheimer, American physicist, pioneer in atom bomb research (*4/22/1904).

Death, as it must, comes to Henry Luce

Feb 28. Magazine magnate Henry R. Luce has died in Phoenix, Ariz. He was 68 years old. Luce was the founder of Time magazine, Fortune and Sports Illustrated. He and his wife, diplomat and dramatist Clare Boothe Luce, designed Life magazine on their honeymoon.

Yale-educated Luce started Time with former schoolmate Briton Hadden in 1923. Articles in the weekly soon had a reputation for reversing the ho-hum order of words and grasping for alternatives to the verb "said." The New Yorker once parodied the style, concluding "Where it will all end, knows God!"

The reporting angle reflected Luce's personal prerogatives. The son of a missionary, he demanded a column on faiths, "The World's Great Religions." A Republican, he insisted on investigation of excess public spending. He made no apologies for allowing his feelings to sway Time. "Show me a man who claims he is objective," he said, "and I'll show you a man with illusions."

If possible, Fortune magazine held an even dearer place in Luce's heart. On Time, Hadden had made most of the editorial decisions (he died in 1929) and Luce was more the businessman. Fortune, a financial publication, combined Luce's interests in a neat package. The first issue premiered in 1930.

When news of Luce's death was released to the press, the first condolences Mrs. Luce received were from President Johnson.

Publishing giant Henry R. Luce.

Red China's army takes control of capital

Mao is welcomed by loyal troops.

Feb 11. Peking has been placed under military rule as the Chinese army under Chairman Mao's chosen heir Lin Piao continues to extend its power throughout China. Its mission is to ensure "the maintenance of revolutionary order."

Peking has been a trouble spot since the beginnings of the Cultural Revolution, Mao's campaign to purge all those who favor "the capitalist road" or who are accused of supporting Soviet communism.

Meanwhile, a wall poster put up today said primary schools were to reopen Monday. All schools were closed last spring to permit the drafting of new curricula based on Mao's ideas in the framework of the Cultural Revolution (→ 4/2).

U.S. starts biggest assault of Vietnam War

Feb 26. In the largest assault of the war, American troops drove into a jungled area near the Cambodian border in search of a secret Viet Cong headquarters. More than 25,000 men were committed to the operation in a fan-shaped area near Cambodia known as War Zone C. Their mission was to find and destroy the headquarters of the Central Office South Vietnam, the control post for all insurgents in South Vietnam. Meanwhile, U.S. Navy planes started dropping mines in rivers in the southern part of North Vietnam to impede junk traffic. President Johnson emphasized that he would not stop the bombing of North Vietnam until Hanoi reduced its military actions (→ 3/10).

Search and destroy.

Dissenting women storm the Pentagon

Feb 15. About 2,500 women demanding to see "the generals who send our sons to die" stormed the Pentagon today. Defense Secretary Robert McNamara refused to meet with the women but sent an aide. Some of the women, carrying signs such as "Drop Rusk and McNamara, Not the Bomb," wept while demonstrating against the Vietnam War. The action was organized by Women Strike for Peace, which often protests at the White House, the Capitol and the Pentagon (→ 3/6).

Line of executive succession is fixed

Feb 10. The 25th Amendment became part of the U.S. Constitution today. It enables the Vice President to act as the President in the event the chief executive becomes physically or mentally unable to carry out the duties of his office. It also gives the President power to nominate a Vice President if the No. 2 post becomes vacant, either by death or resignation. Until now, the office of Vice President remained vacant until the next presidential election.

CIA ordered to stop aid to collegians

Feb 14. President Johnson intervened in a controversy over Central Intelligence Agency subsidies to the National Student Association and instructed the CIA to close out all secret programs of aid to student groups. He also called for a review of all other programs intended to combat Communist activities in private organizations. It is believed the CIA provides clandestine aid to anti-Communist labor unions, publications, and radio and television stations (→ 5/7).

Gallery pays record $5m for da Vinci

Feb 18. The National Gallery of Art in Washington has agreed to buy a portrait by Leonardo da Vinci from Prince Franz Joseph II of Liechtenstein for between $5 million and $6 million, the highest price ever paid for a painting. The Leonardo, believed to have been painted between 1474 and 1480, is called "Ginevra dei Benci." The 16.5-inch by 14.5-inch oil portrait on poplar wood of a young patrician woman of Florence has been called the counterpart of the "Mona Lisa."

Man said to be Boston Strangler recaptured

DeSalvo leaves press conference.

Feb 25. Two men working at a small clothing store in Lynn, Mass., watched a customer enter their shop this afternoon. Looking tired and distressed, wearing an ill-fitting Navy uniform, the man asked to use a phone. After he hung up, one of the workers screwed up some courage and asked him, "Are you DeSalvo?" The con calmly nodded, police were called and the Boston Strangler was again behind bars.

Albert DeSalvo, confessed killer of 13 women, escaped yesterday from the mental ward of a nearby correctional institution. He broke out with two other inmates who were also apprehended. DeSalvo will now complete his life sentence in a maximum security prison.

Feb 13. Picasso's "Three Musicians" (1921). In the last three months, 603,132 persons attended a show in Paris honoring the 86-year-old master.

1967

MARCH

Su	Mo	Tu	We	Th	Fr	Sa
			1	2	3	4
5	6	7	8	9	10	11
12	13	14	15	16	17	18
19	20	21	22	23	24	25
26	27	28	29	30	31	

1. Adam Clayton Powell ousted from House by vote (→ 5).

4. Vienna: Peggy Fleming retains women's world figure skating championship.

6. Texas: LBJ announces plan to establish draft lottery (→ 23).

7. Penn.: Jimmy Hoffa begins eight-year jail term (→ 8/20/71).

10. North Vietnam: U.S. jets conduct first bombing of major industrial installation (→ 15).

10. Mexico City: Couple has first confirmed octuplets.

13. California: Nixon authorizes Nixon for President Committee (→ 2/1/68).

13. Congo: Tshombe given death sentence in absentia (→ 8/4).

15. LBJ names Ellsworth Bunker to replace Henry Cabot Lodge as Saigon ambassador (→ 21).

15. Poland, East Germany sign 20-year mutual aid treaty.

20. French Somaliland: French troops crush riots with machine guns; 11 Somalis dead.

21. Vietnam: Outnumbered G.I.'s crush Viet Cong attack, killing 423 (→ 24).

22. N.Y.: Ali KOs Zora Folley in 7th to keep title (→ 4/17).

23. Atlanta: Rev. King calls Vietnam War biggest obstacle to civil rights movement (→ 4/4).

24. South Vietnam: Viet Cong ambush truck convoy, damaging 82 out of 121 trucks (→ 4/3).

25. Kentucky: UCLA beats Dayton 79-64 in NCAA basketball final.

29. France launches Redoutable, its first nuclear sub (→ 9/18).

31. LBJ signs Consular Treaty with Moscow; first bilateral pact since Bolshevik Revolution (→ 5/22/72).

DEATHS

5. Mohammad Mossadegh, Iranian leader (*1880).

6. Zoltan Kodaly, Hungarian composer (*12/16/1882).

11. Geraldine Farrar, American operatic soprano (*2/28/1882).

30. Jean Toomer, Harlem writer, "Cane" (*12/26/1894).

Stalin's daughter defects

Stalin's daughter, Svetlana Alliluyeva, meets the Western press.

March 9. At first, American officials thought her story was too incredible to be true. A woman walked into the United States Embassy in New Delhi, India, and said she was Svetlana Alliluyeva, daughter of the late Soviet dictator. After a short conversation, Ambassador Chester Bowles confirmed her identity. She said she wished to defect.

At any other time, the defection of Stalin's daughter would have represented a major propaganda coup for the United States. But the Johnson administration hopes the times are changing. The State Department is pursuing a policy of "peaceful engagement" with the Soviet Union. Both nations are in the middle of sensitive negotiations on Vietnam and nuclear non-proliferation. Svetlana's defection to the U.S. would hurt more than help.

With the apparent help of the CIA, Svetlana Alliluyeva was whisked away to Rome and hidden in a suburban apartment. She was later flown to Switzerland, where she will reportedly be granted asylum. Svetlana is expected to visit the United States. Perhaps she'll even write a book and unravel some of the secrets that still surround her father's terrifying regime (→ 4/21).

Wrecked tanker spreads vast oil slick

March 28. A gigantic oil spill threatens a large portion of the French coast, from Brittany to the Cotentin Peninsula. Thousands of birds, their feathers slick with crude oil, have been plucked from the black sea. The accident happened when the supertanker Torrey Canyon went aground off Cornwall, England. Mechanical failures and bad weather are blamed. British authorities, convinced the ship was lost, ordered the royal air force to bomb it in the hope that the oil would catch on fire. The plan failed, and the oil was driven by the currents to the French coast. Residents there are trying to fight back with sandbags, oil booms and pumps, but they are fighting a losing battle. It will take years for nature to clean up the mess and repair the damage.

The supertanker Torrey Canyon spews oil into the water off Britain.

10,000 hippies rally at New York Be-In

All you need is love.

March 26. A swarm of 10,000 hippies gathered in Central Park, holding a kind of ecstatic spelling bee. "L-O-V-E!" they chanted, releasing kites, balloons, bubbles and smoke rings from burning banana skins into the air. Police reported no violence of any kind.

Four New Yorkers, a fledgling actor, a rock magazine editor, a poet and an arts administrator organized the Be-In, modeling it on a Be-In held in San Francisco last winter. They plastered the city with ads and invited all to come as they are. They came. Most were under 30, or so they said. They sported Day-Glo paint, daisies, buttons and guitars. The over-30 set went to the Fifth Avenue Easter Day parade instead.

The folks still love Adam up in Harlem

March 5. At the Abyssinian Baptist Church in Harlem, New York, 4,500 Negroes rallied in support of Adam Clayton Powell. Powell lost his seat in the 90th Congress last week when House members voted 307-116 to exclude the controversial Manhattan Democrat, who is also a Baptist minister. The vote of exclusion marks only the third time in history that U.S. legislators have rejected a duly elected member. Most adversaries of Powell cite his use of public funds for unauthorized expenses as grounds for exclusion (→ 4/11).

1967

APRIL

Su	Mo	Tu	We	Th	Fr	Sa
						1
2	3	4	5	6	7	8
9	10	11	12	13	14	15
16	17	18	19	20	21	22
23	24	25	26	27	28	29
30						

2. Peking: Hundreds of thousands demonstrate against Mao foe Liu Shao-chi (→ 8/22).

3. U.S. State Dept. says Hanoi may be brainwashing American prisoners (→ 4).

4. N.Y.: Rev. King urges boycott of war by seeking conscientious objector status (→ 10).

4. Vietnam: U.S. loses 500th plane of war (→ 6).

6. South Vietnam: 1,500 Viet Cong attack Quangtri, freeing 200 prisoners (→ 20).

7. Israel reports downing six Syrian MIG's (→ 5/18).

10. New York: NAACP votes against Rev. King's stand on Vietnam War (→ 5/13).

11. New York: Adam Clayton Powell wins back seat in House in special election (→ 3/23/68).

15. Illinois: Richard Speck found guilty of murdering eight student nurses (→ 6/5).

17. U.S. Supreme Court bars Ali's request to block induction into Army (→ 30).

19. Surveyor 3 lands on moon, sends photos back to U.S. (→ 24).

20. North Vietnam: U.S. jets knock out power plant in attack on Haiphong (→ 5/10).

21. New York: Svetlana Stalina arrives in U.S. to "seek self-expression" (→ 11/2/84).

21. Athens: Army colonels take over, install Constantine Kollias as premier (→ 24).

24. S.F.: Philadelphia 76ers beat Warriors 125-122 for NBA title.

24. Soviet astronaut Vladimir Komarov dies as craft crashes with tangled parachute (→ 9/10).

24. Athens: New Greek regime bans miniskirts (→ 29).

25. Colorado: Gov. John Arthur signs nation's first law legalizing abortion (→ 7/1/70).

27. Montreal: Prime Minister Lester Pearson lights flame to open Expo 67 (→ 5/1967).

DEATHS

13. Luis Somoza Debayle, Nicaraguan ex-pres. (*11/18/1922).

19. Konrad Adenauer, West German leader (*1/5/1876).

Adenauer, father of West Germany, is dead

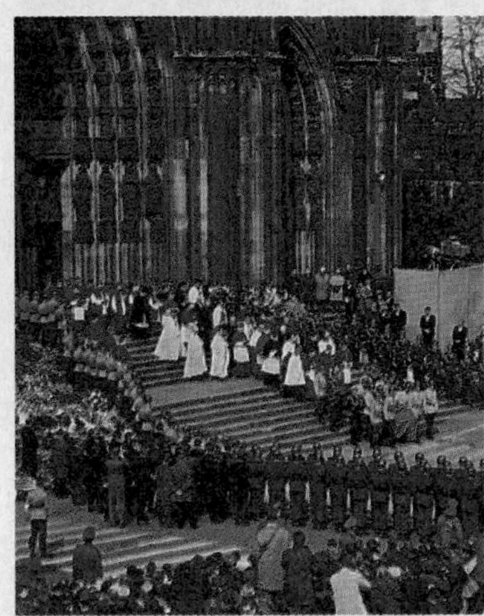

Requiem mass for Adenauer.

April 25. Konrad Adenauer, the German leader affectionately called "the old man" by some and "the old fox" by others, was laid to rest today in a churchyard near his home in Rhondorf. Adenauer, who was 91, died last Wednesday. President Johnson, France's President de Gaulle and British Prime Minister Wilson were among the dignitaries attending the elaborate services for Adenauer, who was West Germany's first postwar Chancellor. He is credited with leading his country back to economic prosperity and transforming Germany from enemy to partner of the Western Allies.

The government of Chancellor Kurt Georg Kiesinger paid its tribute to Adenauer this morning at ceremonies in the Bundestag. Adenauer's old chair was festooned with flowers. Kiesinger conceded that Germany had not reached one of the former chancellor's goals, reunification. "He left this to us as a great legacy," Kiesinger said. "May we be worthy of it."

A requiem mass for Adenauer was celebrated this afternoon at the cathedral in Cologne. Then his body was taken by ship for a last trip down the river he loved, the Rhine. Adenauer was buried next to his wife in Rhondorf (→ 3/5/69).

Greek colonels rebel, fail to get King's help

April 29. King Constantine of Greece appeared in public for the first time since military leaders swept out the government and established dictatorial powers for themselves last week. The king, who has refused to sign the decree suspending constitutional freedoms, was cheered by a large crowd as he entered the Athens Cathedral for Orthodox Easter services.

The ruling junta has proceeded to tighten its control despite the obvious disapproval of the king. Their first steps were to place armored personnel carriers in front of the Parliament. They arrested the king's secretary and many government officials. Most of the moderate politicians are still in jail. A state of siege and a nighttime curfew were declared. Boys were ordered to cut their hair, girls were warned not to wear miniskirts and all young people were told to go to church. Today, the Democratic Left, which succeeded the banned Communist Party, was outlawed.

The junta installed a new Premier, Constantine Kollias. But Brigadier Stylianos Patakos, Interior Minister, and Col. George Papadopoulos, assigned to the premier's office, hold the real power (→ 5/4).

A troop transport looms ominously in front of Parliament in Athens.

Ali won't serve; loses boxing title

May have to stick to shadow boxing.

April 30. Cassius Clay, who prefers the name Muhammad Ali, was stripped of his world heavyweight boxing championship today when he refused to be inducted into military service. The 25-year-old boxer balked at taking the one step forward in Houston that would have constituted induction into the service. The boxing associations stripped him of his title and criminal prosecution is expected to follow.

Said Ali: "I have searched my conscience and I find I cannot be true to my belief in my religion by accepting such a call." He has claimed exemption as a minister of a Black Muslim sect. Ali faces a minimum jail sentence of five years and a fine of $10,000 if convicted.

Ali first came to world attention in 1960 when he won the Olympic light-heavyweight championship. He beat Sonny Liston for the world heavyweight title in 1964, and since then has been a very popular "fighting champion" (→ 5/8).

Burton and Taylor are good in Zeffirelli's colorful film of "The Taming of the Shrew," notwithstanding Shakespeare purists.

1967

MAY

Su	Mo	Tu	We	Th	Fr	Sa
	1	2	3	4	5	6
7	8	9	10	11	12	13
14	15	16	17	18	19	20
21	22	23	24	25	26	27
28	29	30	31			

4. Greece: New regime deports 6,000 foes to Yaros island (→ 9).

6. Proud Clarion wins Kentucky Derby, jockey R. Ussery up.

7. Washington: CIA leader admits giving cash to anti-Communist labor leaders.

8. Houston: Muhammed Ali indicted for draft evasion (→ 6/20).

9. Athens: Greek junta bans bearded tourists (→ 8/26).

10. Stockholm: Intl. Tribunal on War Crimes, convened by Bertrand Russell, finds U.S. guilty of "systematic" bombing of civilians in Vietnam (→ 19).

11. Britain, Ireland, Denmark ask admission to EEC (→ 16).

11. Miss.: Natl. Guard called to quell Negro student riots (→ 17).

12. Cannes: Antonioni film "Blow Up" awarded Gold Palm.

13. New York: 70,000 march to support Vietnam War (→ 8/16).

14. New York: Mickey Mantle hits 500th home run.

16. Paris: De Gaulle vetoes Britain's entry to EEC (→ 11/27).

17. Houston: Policeman shot to death as Negroes riot at Texas Southern University (→ 6/4).

18. U.N. force, at Nasser's request, quits Israeli border (→ 21).

18. Tennesse Gov. Ellington repeals "Monkey Law," upheld in 1925 Scopes trial.

18. U.S.: G.E. recalls 90,000 TV sets for possible radiation leaks.

19. North Vietnam: U.S. jets bomb downtown Hanoi for first time (→ 7/7).

20. U.S.S.R.: Soviets display world's largest atom smasher, near completion (→ 12/10).

21. Cairo: UAR orders mobilization of 100,000 reserves (→ 26).

26. Cairo: Nasser pledges to destroy Israel if she provokes war (→ 30).

29. Rome: Pope Paul VI names 27 new Cardinals, including Karol Wojtyla, archbishop of Krakow (→ 10/23/78).

DEATH

30. Claude Rains, British actor (*11/10/1890).

Nasser threatens Israel as U.N. withdraws

Nasser, ready to fight in Mideast.

May 30. War fever is boiling up in the Middle East cauldron. United Nations emergency forces have left the border between Israel and Egypt at President Nasser's request. Nasser warned Israel it risks all-out war if it attacks his country or Syria. "Our main objective," the president of the United Arab Republic said, "will be the destruction of Israel."

Today, Nasser concluded a surprise military alliance with Jordan's King Hussein, who had been a bitter enemy. Nasser said Syria, Iraq, Kuwait and Algeria are ready for war. Syria's Defense Minister said a "punishing blow" should be dealt to Israel, and he warned his country is ready to "explode Zionist existence." Iraq's Vice Premier said it is time to "get rid of the Zionist cancer." The Palestine Liberation Organization is said to be preparing new attacks against Israel.

Israel, angered by Nasser's blockade of the southern port of Elath, threatened to use force to open the harbor. Israel has also threatened to retaliate against Syria for infiltrating its northern border. Some troops have already been mobilized. Reserves were called up after the United Nations forces left the Sinai and Gaza Strip (→ 6/5).

Biafra, Eastern region of Nigeria, secedes

May 30. Lieutenant Colonel Odumegwu Ojukwu, the Military Governor of Eastern Nigeria, announced the secession of the region today, and declared its independence as the republic of Biafra.

Lieutenant Colonel Yakubu Gowon, head of Nigeria's federal government, condemned the secession as treasonous, instituted severe economic sanctions against Biafra and promised a swift military response. At least two Nigerian army batallions are reported to be on Biafra's northern border.

Nigeria has long been plagued by regional tensions between the Moslem Northerners, predominantly members of the Hausa tribe, and the animist and Christian Easterners, who are mostly members of the Ibo tribe (→ 7/7).

May 15. Edward Hopper painted America with tenacious realism after it was out of style. He is dead at 84. Above: "Lighthouse at Two Lights."

Elvis and Priscilla tie the knot in Vegas

Just married: Priscilla and Elvis.

May 1. When the king of rock and roll, Elvis Presley, singer and film actor, croons "Love Me Tender," a chorus of sighs can be heard from female throats around the world. Today, in Las Vegas the idol of millions promised his tender and true love to his longtime girl friend, Priscilla Beaulieu. They took their marital vows before 14 friends, then entertained 100 guests at a champagne breakfast. Presley, 32, wore a tuxedo, and the bride, 21, was attired in a white chiffon gown embroidered with tiny pearls and a full chiffon veil. The couple met in 1959 in Germany, while he was serving with the U.S. Army, and she, the daughter of an Air Force Lieutenant Colonel, attended high school in Frankfurt. Both are from Memphis.

May 30. A.J. Foyt, in his Sheraton-Thompson Special, has outraced the field at the Indy 500. With victories in 1961 and 1964, he is the third driver in Indy's 57 years to win the race three times.

Chichester ends solo sea sail in triumph

After seven and a half months at sea, the weary sailor returns to Plymouth.

May 28. From the silence of the open sea to a noisy, tumultuous welcome at Plymouth, England, Sir Francis Chichester has completed his voyage alone around the world. He appeared tired but fit. The 65-year-old adventurer completed a 28,500-mile voyage that began August 27, 1966. Today, he sailed into a welcoming flotilla of 200 pleasure boats in Plymouth harbor. Nearly 40,000 onlookers cheered from the grassy harbor where Chichester started out last August. "Welcome home" read a message from Queen Elizabeth II. And Prime Minister Harold Wilson hailed Chichester for his "epic voyage."

Canada's Expo '67 is a marvel

By the end of May, seven million people will have visited Canada's Expo '67—and walked on the moon. The United States lunar exhibit is one of the most popular displays at the international fair. A 123-foot-high escalator takes viewers by a simulated lunar landscape.

Expo '67 opened April 27 in Montreal. The fair covers 700 acres, the largest exhibit being the Canadian complex. The granite, canvas and steel structure borders on La Ronde amusement park, where teens can go-go dance and children can ride tamed zebras.

Prime Minister Pearson lights flame at Place des Nations to open Expo '67.

1967

JUNE

Su	Mo	Tu	We	Th	Fr	Sa
				1	2	3
4	5	6	7	8	9	10
11	12	13	14	15	16	17
18	19	20	21	22	23	24
25	26	27	28	29	30	

1. Israel: Moshe Dayan named defense minister (→ 3/17/69).

2. FCC orders TV, radio stations that advertise cigarettes to air health warnings (→ 1/17/73).

4. Boston: Nine injured as Negro youths smash windows, set fires (→ 12).

5. Sinai: Heavy fighting breaks out between Israeli and Egyptian forces (→ 6).

5. Illinois: Richard Speck gets death sentence for murder of eight student nurses.

6. Egypt closes Suez Canal, breaks ties with U.S., as Israel seizes Gaza (→ 7).

7. Israelis occupy Old Jerusalem (→ 8).

8. Sinai: Israelis accidentally attack U.S. ship, killing ten and injuring 100 (→ 9).

9. Israeli forces drive deep into Syria (→ 10).

10. Moscow severs ties with Israel (→ 11).

11. New York: Israel, Syria accept U.N. cease-fire; Israeli war dead at 679 (→ 28).

12. U.S. Supreme Court rules states cannot ban interracial marriages (→ 28).

17. New York: 135,000 attend free Barbra Streisand concert at Central Park.

20. Houston: Ali gets five years in jail, $10,000 fine for evading draft (→ 7/6/68).

23. California: Jim Ryun runs mile in record 3:51.1.

23. U.S. Senate censures Thomas Dodd for using campaign funds for private benefit.

24. California: Paul Wilson hits record 17'8" in pole vault (→ 4/8/72).

25. Washington: Natl. Heart Institute gives 16 contracts for artificial heart research (→ 12/21).

28. N.Y.: 14 shot on second day of race riots in Buffalo (→ 7/4).

28. Prague: Czech writers sign petition calling for liberalization of Communist govt. (→ 1/5/68).

DEATH

29. Primo Carnera, Italian ex-boxing champ (*10/25/1906).

LBJ and Kosygin meet in Glassboro

Kosygin (left), Gromyko and LBJ.

June 23. President Johnson and Soviet Premier Kosygin got to know each other at their summit meeting in Glassboro, New Jersey, today. They apparently did not make major progress on important issues, but they did agree to meet again Sunday. Kosygin insisted that no real peace will come to the Middle East until Israel withdraws from occupied territories. Johnson said something must be done now to prevent the spread of nuclear weapons. Little if any progress was made on the Vietnam issue. Kosygin, pleased by his reception in Glassboro, stopped his car to say he wants "friendship with the American people." The local theater operator returned the favor by changing tonight's feature to "The Russians are Coming, the Russians are Coming."

The Beatles have joined the drug culture with their new "Sgt. Pepper's Lonely Hearts Club Band." ▷

Israel smashes Arabs in Six Day War

Israeli Def. Min. Moshe Dayan.

Israeli tanks storm into action in the arid land around Rafa junction.

June 28. Israel bore the fruit of its victory over its Arab enemies in the Six Day War today. The city of Jerusalem was formally reunited under Israeli control. Jews streamed into the walled Old City, which was controlled by Jordan before the war. Many of them wept openly. Soldiers armed with machine guns and grenades bent in prayer before the Wailing Wall. The man who led Israel to glorious victory over Egypt and its Arab allies, Defense Minister Moshe Dayan, told the soldiers, "We have returned to the holiest of our holy places, never to depart from it again."

The biggest loser of this war is Egypt. Its army and air force were humiliated by Israel. Gamal Abdel Nasser gambled and he lost. Even U Thant, the usually neutral Secretary General of the United Nations, blamed Egypt for the build-up which led to the outbreak of hostilities on the 5th. Thant stopped short of saying who actually fired the first shot early that Monday morning. Israel and Egypt are still blaming each other.

Israel met strong resistance from Egyptian forces in the opening hours of the fighting. The tide turned quickly however, and within 72 hours, it was a rout. Israeli forces swept through Gaza and catapulted across the Sinai peninsula all the way to the Suez Canal. Paratroopers and naval units overran Sharm el Sheikh and broke Egypt's blockade of the Gulf of Aqaba and the port of Elath. "The strait of Tiran is now open," said Itzhak Rabin, Israeli chief of staff.

On the first day of fighting, the Israelis destroyed 50 Egyptian tanks, many of them Russian-built. On Tuesday, another 150 were disabled in the Sinai. More than 400 of Nasser's planes were shot down. "This is beyond my wildest dreams," Mordechai Hod, an air force commander, said. He called Israeli pilots "the best in the world. We made mincemeat of their air forces. We are now making mincemeat of everything on the ground."

Jordan, Nasser's latest ally, was pleading for mercy by Tuesday. Jerusalem had fallen. So had Bethlehem and Jericho. The West Bank of the Jordan River was in Israeli hands. Most of Jordan's soldiers had become Israel's prisoners.

On Israel's northern front, Syrian artillery pounded several Israeli towns in the first three days of the war. Israel denied a Syrian claim that it had captured Shear-Yashuv and was advancing on Safad. Rabin's forces struck back ferociously, and by Saturday, they rolled over the top of the Golan Heights, Syria's staging grounds for attacks into northern Israel. "If you ask me, we will never give back this ridge," said one Israeli. Some observers say the Israeli tanks could have rolled all the way to Damascus, but they stopped at El Quneitra. A cease-fire was signed on Sunday the 11th.

This war was an enormous victory for Israel, but a defeat without honor for the Arab world. Political problems led to the war. New political problems have been created. Israeli forces now occupy territories four times bigger than Israel itself. In the larger international arena, the United States and the United Arab Republic broke diplomatic relations after Nasser charged that American planes attacked his country. The United States denied the charge. All these problems have to be solved somewhere. The United Nations was virtually powerless in these six days in June (→ 7/2).

Israeli gunners on Suez patrol.

An Arab peasant pleads for peace.

Spencer Tracy, one of the finest, is gone

June 10. When actress Katharine Hepburn stepped into the kitchen of Spencer Tracy's home today to wish him good morning, he was sitting at the kitchen table, turned from her, head bowed. She knew without knowing that her dear friend, one of America's finest actors, was gone.

Tracy was known as an actor's actor. He wasn't pretty, he wasn't chummy and he wouldn't know a trend if it spat in his eye. He won Oscars two years in a row (for "Captains Courageous" and "Boys Town") without moving in the "right" Hollywood circles. Laurence Olivier said he learned more about acting by watching Tracy than by watching anyone else.

Tracy was born in Milwaukee in 1900. A strong part in a stage prison drama landed him a role in a John Ford cops-and-robbers picture, "Up the River." Until the mid-30's his weathered face limited him to tough-guy roles. After "Courageous" he was given free rein.

In 1942, he met Miss Hepburn; he separated from his wife but did not divorce her, helping her found a school for the deaf named after their deaf son. Tracy and Hepburn made nine films together, fighting a loving battle of the sexes to the end.

Dorothy Parker, writer and wit, dies

June 7. The woman who said, "Men seldom make passes at girls who wear glasses," has passed on. Dorothy Parker was 73. She was a frequent contributor to The New Yorker magazine and Vanity Fair, writing prize-winning short stories and a long-running book column.

But Miss Parker was best at repartee, which she honed at the literary roundtable at the Algonquin Hotel. At a party once, a young man yearned for a sample of her wit. After a long evening without a clever word from her, he said he was leaving. "That's all right," she said, "but do me a favor. When you get home, throw your mother a bone."

"Scratch a lover and find a foe," Miss Parker wrote. She wed three times when she had an itch to marry the second man twice.

Monterey Pop Festival draws 50,000 kids

Hendrix, acid king of the electric guitar, has a growing legion of fans.

June 18. California's hippie subculture converged into a mass of long hair, flowers and rock music this weekend, as 50,000 flowed into the fairgrounds of the Monterey International Pop Festival. The event featured the largest collection of major rock acts ever assembled; thousands of fans had to be turned away from the sold-out concert.

Established artists such as the Byrds, Jefferson Airplane, Otis Redding, and the Mamas and the Papas received the expected ovations from the huge audience. But the response was equally enthusiastic for performances by Indian sitar master Ravi Shankar and new talents Janis Joplin, the Who, and Jimi Hendrix, a young man who plays the electric guitar like nobody else.

The Who's Pete Townshend.

Jayne Mansfield meets tragic end in auto

Mansfield, an untimely death.

June 29. Curvaceous actress Jayne Mansfield has died in a car crash outside New Orleans. She and three of her children were being driven in a limousine to a TV studio when their car plowed into a truck. Miss Mansfield was decapitated; her children, sleeping on the back seat, survived with minor injuries.

Miss Mansfield succeeded Jane Russell as pin-up queen, making a splash in a revealing red swimsuit. She made several B films, breaking briefly from the dumb blonde mold for a good role in John Steinbeck's "The Wayward Bus" in 1957.

1967

JULY

Su	Mo	Tu	We	Th	Fr	Sa
						1
2	3	4	5	6	7	8
9	10	11	12	13	14	15
16	17	18	19	20	21	22
23	24	25	26	27	28	29
30	31					

2. Israelis, Egyptians exchange fire across Suez Canal (→ 17).

3. Aden: British troops recapture Arab quarter of port (→ 11/30).

4. Miss.: James Meredith finishes "march against fear" (→ 5).

5. California: Congress of Racial Equality drops "multiracial" in describing membership (→ 16).

7. Saigon: Gen. Westmoreland asks Robert McNamara for more troops in Vietnam (→ 28).

7. Nigeria: Govt. troops invade Biafra in attempt to end secession (→ 8/10).

8. Wimbledon: John Newcombe over Wilhelm Bungert 6-3, 6-1, 6-1; Billie Jean King over Adrienne Jones 6-3, 6-4.

16. Newark: Death toll in four days of race riots hits 26; 1,500 hurt, 1,000 arrested (→ 20).

17. LBJ signs bill for injunction to end railroad strike.

17. Israel: U.N. team begins Suez observation (→ 8/7).

18. Boston: Scientists announce discovery of Akrotiri, Minoan city on Greek isle of Thera.

20. Newark: 400 attend largest gathering of civil rights leaders held in U.S. (→ 24).

23. Frenchman Robert Pingeon wins Tour de France; racer Tom Simpson killed.

23. Puerto Rico: 60% in referendum bar independence or statehood for commonwealth status.

24. Detroit: Race riots sweep city; 19 killed, 700 arrested as federal troops intervene (→ 26).

26. Detroit: Troops quell riots; death toll hits 31 (→ 26).

26. Virginia: SNCC head H. Rap Brown arrested for inciting riots (→ 27).

28. North Vietnam: U.S. loses eight planes (→ 29).

29. Vietnam: Fire on U.S. aircraft carrier Forrestal ruins 29 planes; many dead (→ 30).

DEATHS

20. Albert Luthuli, South African civil rights leader, 1961 Nobel Peace Prize (*1898).

21. Basil Rathbone, British actor (*6/13/1892).

De Gaulle: "Long live a free Quebec"

De Gaulle: "Vive Quebec Libre."

July 31. France's President de Gaulle is not saying how far he will go, but he is causing quite a controversy on both sides of the Atlantic with his clarion call for the liberation of French Canadians. The General is not sending in the troops, and he says he has no territorial ambitions in Canada. But de Gaulle is promising the support of France to Canadians who are short on "liberty, equality and fraternity." De Gaulle's statement has further shocked the Ottawa government. Prime Minister Lester Pearson had criticized de Gaulle for saying "Long live a free Quebec" in Montreal last week. The declaration also created a furor in Paris, but it's likely to die down during the traditional August exodus (→ 10/5/70).

"BIFF!" "BAM!" "ZOWEE!" "Holy Guadalcanal, Batman, what now?!" Tune in tomorrow, "same bat-time, same bat-channel." They just may die this time.

Vicious race riots ravage major U.S. cities

White policemen line up suspected looters against the wall of a Detroit store.

July 27. President Johnson tonight announced he has named a special commission to investigate the wave of race riots sweeping across the U.S. this summer. The commission will be headed by Governor Otto Kerner of Illinois, while New York Mayor John Lindsay will serve as the Vice Chairman.

At the same time, the president said he has ordered Secretary of Defense Robert S. McNamara to issue new training standards for riot control to all National Guard units so as to prepare them effectively for future violence.

Just days ago, the president rushed 4,700 paratroopers into Detroit, which had been nearly paralyzed by race riots. The death toll there, in the nation's fifth largest city, stands at 38 while damage by fire and looting has been estimated at more than $150 million. At the height of the rioting, Detroit Mayor Jerome P. Cavanagh said: "It looks like Berlin in 1945."

There have been race riots, too, in other cities. Just this week, two persons were killed and others were injured when thousands of Puerto Rican youths looted stores and set cars on fire in New York City before police moved in to quell the riot. Reinforced police units also have been sent in to handle rioting in Toledo, Ohio; Grand Rapids, Michigan, and elsewhere (→ 8/1).

U.S. General wants more men in Vietnam

July 30. "The war is not a stalemate," asserted General William Westmoreland as he requested more U.S. troops for duty in Vietnam. "We are winning slowly but steadily. North Vietnam is paying a tremendous price with nothing to show for it," he added. It is believed Westmoreland asked Defense Secretary Robert McNamara for an additional 100,000 men; currently, about 464,000 Americans are serving in Vietnam.

A "tremendous price" was paid by Americans yesterday in the war effort when an accidental fire raged on board the U.S. aircraft carrier the Forrestal in the Gulf of Tonkin. At least 70 men died and 89 others are missing (→ 8/3).

Westy wants to fight a general's war.

Carl Sandburg, truly American poet, dies

July 22. Author Carl Sandburg died today in North Carolina at age 89. If anyone writes his biography, it won't be with half the care Sandburg used on his six-volume life of Abraham Lincoln. That task took 16 years and a quarter million more words than the Bible. Sandburg loved Lincoln's simplicity and honesty, loved the state of Illinois (both men were raised there) and loved poems written without pretension of rhyme. He won a Pulitzer in 1940 for prose and one in 1950 for poetry.

Cops nab notables

July 11. Dame Margot Fonteyn, 48, and Rudolf Nureyev, 29, stars of Britain's Royal Ballet, were arrested early today with 16 other persons in a raid on a noisy hippie party in San Francisco. Both tried to flee when the police burst in but were found hiding on nearby rooftops. The police said that 12 marijuana cigarettes had been found in the flat of the party, but there were no grounds to prosecute the internationally famous ballet stars.

Sad end for Vivien Leigh, a great beauty

July 8. The actress who breathed life into the fictional Scarlett O'Hara has died. Vivien Leigh, 53 years old, has succumbed to tuberculosis. She was in London preparing for a return to the stage following a five-year absence.

Miss Leigh was born to British parents in Darjeeling, India. After a convent education she pursued theater work, meeting her future husband Laurence Olivier in the film "Fire Over England" in 1937. They wed in 1940 after her success in "Gone With the Wind," and have since divorced. She won an Oscar for her Scarlett and for her Blanche du Bois in "A Streetcar Named Desire." Her triumphs were marred by episodes of mental illness.

Leigh with husband Olivier in 1951.

Jazz scene loses Coltrane on sax

July 17. John Coltrane's angered horn was prematurely silenced today when the tenor sax man, one of the most gifted of jazz musicians, died in a Long Island hospital. He was only 40 years old. Born in Hamlet, North Carolina, Coltrane traveled a long road in a short time. He developed an abrasive style that led him, according to New York Times critic John S. Wilson, to "long, hard-bitten, rapid, rising and falling runs that had the cumulative effect of an aural battering ram." In 1965, Coltrane was named Down Beat magazine's "Jazzman of the Year" and elected to their Hall of Fame.

A British court has canceled jail for Jagger, convicted for "pep pills," and Keith Richard, for having an "Indian Hemp" party.

1967

AUGUST

Su	Mo	Tu	We	Th	Fr	Sa
		1	2	3	4	5
6	7	8	9	10	11	12
13	14	15	16	17	18	19
20	21	22	23	24	25	26
27	28	29	30	31		

1. Havana: Stokely Carmichael calls for black revolution in the United States.→

3. LBJ announces plan to send 45,000 more to Vietnam (→ 23).

4. Congo: U.S. ends military airlifts to govt. troops (→ 21).

6. Havana: Hijackers land Colombian DC-4 with 78 passengers (→ 2/21/68).

7. Jerusalem: Arabs hold general strike to resist Israel (→ 9/2).

10. Nigeria: Rebels seize mid-western region (→ 10/4).

13. Chinese release seized Soviet freighter Svirsk after protest by Kosygin (→ 3/2/69).

16. Michigan: Couple returns LBJ's letter of sympathy on son's war death (→ 10/16).

21. China downs two U.S. Navy planes; one pilot seized (→ 11/28).

21. Congo: Mobutu and rebels declare cease-fire (→ 6/4/69).

22. Peking: Red Guards sack British Consulate and attack staff (→ 10/31/68).

22. Washington: LBJ welcomes shah of Iran on two-day visit (→ 10/20).

23. North Vietnam: U.S. planes bomb Hanoi suburbs, killing more than 100 (→ 28).

26. Athens: Ex-Premier Andreas Papandreou indicted for high treason (→ 12/13).

28. U.S. election observation team leaves for Saigon (→ 30).

29. Cairo: 150 military officers arrested in plot to overthrow Nasser (→ 9/14).

30. South Vietnam: Viet Cong strike jail in Quangngai, freeing 1,200 (→ 31).

31. Saigon: Gen. Westmoreland says Hanoi lies about casualty figures (→ 9/3).

DEATHS

24. Henry Kaiser, American industrialist (*5/9/1882).

30. Ad Reinhardt, American painter, art theoretician, Abstract Expressionism (*12/24/1913).

31. Ilya Ehrenbourg, Soviet writer (*1/27/1891).

Black power advocates call for revolution

Brown (left) with Stokely Carmichael at SNCC changing of the guard in May.

Aug 1. Stokely Carmichael, former Chairman of the Student Nonviolent Coordinating Committee, has called for a black revolution in America. At a conference for Latin-American Solidarity in Havana, he said, "They taught us to kill (in Vietnam). Now the struggle is in the streets of the United States."

"We have no alternative but to use aggressive armed violence in order to own the land, houses and stores inside our communities, and to control the politics of those communities," Carmichael added.

These sentiments were echoed by Adam Clayton Powell, who said from his self-imposed exile in Bimini that the riots in Detroit and other American cities "are a necessary phase of the black revolution."

In Alexandria, Virginia, H. Rapp Brown, current SNCC Chairman, who was arrested last month as a fugitive wanted on charges of inciting riots and arson, said, "We stand on the eve of a black revolution."

One change that is revolutionary for many Americans is the use of the word 'black' instead of 'Negro.' For some time, black militants have used the designation, but it is now being used by ordinary black and white Americans, too (→ 10/20).

First black gets Supreme Court seat

Aug 30. By a 69-11 majority the Senate appointed Thurgood Marshall as the first black to the Supreme Court today, despite charges by Southern Senators that he is too liberal. Typical of the opposition, Democrat Robert Byrd said Marshall would favor criminal over defendant's rights. Republican support would have been unanimous except for the vote of Strom Thurmond. Prior to his current position as Solicitor General, Marshall was chief legal officer for the National Association for the Advancement of Colored People and won 29 out of 32 cases before the Supreme Court. His most famous case, Brown v. the Board of Education, overturned legal segregation of schools (→ 10/2).

Promoter of the Beatles dies at 32

Aug 27. Brian Epstein, the man who discovered the Beatles in a dingy Liverpool club and engineered their ascendancy to worldwide stardom, is dead. He was 32.

Found in his London home by a housekeeper, Epstein apparently took an overdose of sleeping pills. The Beatles returned immediately from a spiritual retreat in Wales with the Maharishi, an Indian guru.

Epstein first saw the group while he was managing a record store, in 1961. Though they had "very little stage presentation," he once said, "they seemed to me to be full of possibilities." Two months ago, the Beatles released "Sgt. Pepper's Lonely Hearts Club Band," their best album yet (→ 2/1968).

Sniper kills leader of U.S. Nazi Party

Aug 25. George Lincoln Rockwell, leader of the American Nazi Party, was shot and killed today by a sniper's bullet in Arlington, Virginia. A former assistant to Rockwell, John Patler, is being charged with the murder. Patler was forced out of the party earlier this year after he caused dissension in the Nazi ranks between light-skinned and dark-skinned party members; he referred to fair-skinned Nazis as "blue-eyed devils." Rockwell's successor, Matt Koehl, called the slaying a defeat for whites and said, "Whoever did it, it is of benefit only to the blacks and Jews of this country."

Avowed racist Rockwell.

Aug 15. Belgian Surrealist Rene Magritte, a onetime commercial artist influenced by de Chirico, is dead at 68. Above, his dreamlike "The Red Model" (1935).

1967

SEPTEMBER

Su	Mo	Tu	We	Th	Fr	Sa
					1	2
3	4	5	6	7	8	9
10	11	12	13	14	15	16
17	18	19	20	21	22	23
24	25	26	27	28	29	30

2. Sudan: Arab summit agrees on aid to Egypt and Jordan, bars compromise with Israel (→ 24).

5. Saigon: Election loser Truong Dinh Dzu charges fraud (→ 23).

6. Detroit: U.A.W. strikes Ford (→ 10/22).

8. Uganda is proclaimed a republic (→ 12/19/69).

9. Turkey: Greek and Turkish leaders confer on Cyprus dispute (→ 12/8).

10. Surveyor 5 soft-lands on moon, sends photos back to U.S. (→ 10/18).

10. Forest Hills: John Newcombe, Billie Jean King win U.S. national tennis titles.

11. China and India exchange artillery fire on Sikkim-Tibet border (→ 4/15/76).

14. U.S. announces plan to give India $1.3 million to buy contraceptives (→ 12/20).

14. Cairo: Egyptian ex-army chief Abdel Hakim Amer commits suicide (→ 11/26).

15. U.S.S.R.: Polish sprinter Ewa Klobukowska banned from meet for failing to pass sex test.

17. Turkey: 42 killed, 600 injured in riots at soccer game.

18. Rhode Island: U.S. sweeps America's Cup in four straight.

18. San Francisco: McNamara announces U.S. commitment to $5 bil. ABM system of Nike and Spartan missiles (→ 1/22/68).

21. Washington: Che Guevara reported commanding guerrilla operations in Bolivia (→ 10/10).

23. Soviets sign pact to send more aid to Hanoi (→ 26).

24. Washington: OAS ministers adopt new anti-Cuban policies (→ 1/28/68).

24. Israel: Premier Levi Eshkol announces plan to settle areas seized from Arabs (→ 10/5).

26. Hanoi rejects peace proposal from U.S. Ambassador Arthur Goldberg (→ 28).

28. LBJ denies military victory is U.S aim in Vietnam (→ 10/17).

DEATH

14. Earl of Iveagh, head Guinness Brewery (*3/29/1884).

Thieu is President of South Vietnam

Sept 3. During this crucial phase in the war, the Vietnamese people have elected a military man as President. Lt. General Ngyuen Van Thieu, who headed the military junta that has run the country for the past two years, said he would seek to instigate peace talks with the North by asking the U.S. to stop bombing for one week. Though he beat his closest opponent by a two-to-one margin, less than half the eligible voters turned out, and analysts believe the low showing will give sustenance to his political opponents (→ 5).

Reagan urges more effort to win war

Sept 12. Ronald Reagan wants America to win the Vietnam War. The California Governor told news reporters that "full technological resources" should be employed quickly to end the war victoriously. He suggested leaking to the Viet Cong that America is ready to use nuclear weapons. He recounted a statement by President Eisenhower about U.S. strategy in the Korean War: "(Ike) said one of our great mistakes was in assuring the enemy of our intention not to use (the Bomb), that the enemy should still be frightened that we might" (→ 1/7/69).

Buchenwald Beast hangs self in prison

Sept 2. Ilse Koch, known as the Beast of Buchenwald, strangled herself with a bedsheet in her German prison cell last night. She was serving a life sentence for atrocities she committed at the Buchenwald death camp. She was the wife of the camp commandant, Karl Koch. Mrs. Koch had been investigated by the United States, West Germany and her own fellow Nazis. In 1943, SS officers deemed her excessively cruel. She had starved, beaten and murdered hundreds of camp prisoners and had lampshades made of the skin of her victims.

Death takes writer Carson McCullers

Sept 29. One day in 1934 Carson McCullers lost her wallet on a New York subway. She was devastated—gone was every dollar destined for a music education at Julliard. Luckily, she abandoned the piano for a rewarding career in writing.

Frail, wheelchair-ridden Miss McCullers died tonight. She was 50. Miss McCullers wrote strange tales of her native South, her characters cripples or misfits imbued with unanticipated strengths. "The Heart Is a Lonely Hunter" (1940) and "The Ballad of the Sad Cafe" (1951) are among her best novels.

Sept 20. As the Queen Mary makes her last voyage, Britain is launching the QE2 (Queen Elizabeth 2), above. Scots, who don't recognize Elizabeth I, Queen when Scotland was independent, are angry about the name.

1967

OCTOBER

Su	Mo	Tu	We	Th	Fr	Sa
1	2	3	4	5	6	7
8	9	10	11	12	13	14
15	16	17	18	19	20	21
22	23	24	25	26	27	28
29	30	31				

2. Thurgood Marshall takes seat on U.S. Supreme Court.

3. California: X-15 rocket plane sets speed record of 4,534 mph.

4. Biafra: Govt. troops seize Enugu, capital of seccessionist region (→ 5/19/68).

5. Jerusalem: Rosh Hashanah celebrated at Wailing Wall for first time in 20 years (→ 13).

11. New York: First major show of Picasso sculpture opens.

12. Boston: St. Louis Cardinals beat Red Sox 7-2 to win World Series in final game.

13. Cairo says U.S. intelligence helped Israel win war (→ 21).

17. Vietnam: 58 G.I.'s slain in battling 2,900 Viet Cong (→ 30).

18. Moscow: Data from Venus 4 space capsule shows conditions cannot support life (→ 30).

20. Miss.: Jury acquits seven of 18 in 1964 slaying of three civil rights workers (→ 1/2/68).

21. Sinai: Egyptians sink Israeli destroyer Elath off coast (→ 24).

22. N.Y.: Thousands march to support Vietnam G.I.'s (→ 27).

22. Detroit: U.A.W. and Ford reach accord, ending 46-day work stoppage.

23. N.J.: Pittsburgh Pipers beat Jersey Americans 110-107 in first game of ABA.

24. G.M. recalls 1.1 mil. Chevrolets for faulty steering (→ 31).

24. Egypt: Israelis hit oil refineries in Suez exchange (→ 11/8).

29. New York: Norman Thomas makes last public appearance (→ 12/19/68).

29. Mexico: Pres. Diaz gives titles for 2.5 mil. acres to 9,600 peasant families.

30. Two Soviet satellites achieve first unmanned docking in space (→ 11/9).

30. Saigon: Lt. Gen. Nguyen Van Thieu sworn in as South Vietnamese president (→ 11/1).

31. Detroit: Ford recalls all 1967 Mustangs (→ 2/26/69).

DEATH

8. Clement Attlee, British Labor Party leader (*1/3/1883).

Protesters storm Pentagon; Mailer jailed

Armed federal troops in shiny helmets surround demonstrators at the Pentagon.

Oct 21. A peaceful rally in Washington against the Vietnam War turned violent this afternoon as thousands of protesters crossed the Potomac and stormed the Pentagon. They yelled obscenities as they rushed lines of soldiers and federal marshals who were armed with rifles and bayonets. No shots were fired, but many of the demonstrators were bashed over the head with nightsticks and rifle butts. Blood dripped on the sidewalk. Some 250 protesters were arrested, including novelist Norman Mailer and David Dellinger, Chairman of the group that organized the rally, the National Mobilization Committee to End the War in Vietnam. The violence ebbed as darkness fell, but hundreds of protesters continued to mill about, setting bonfires and burning draft cards.

The protest started when 50,000 anti-war demonstrators congregated around the Lincoln Memorial. Some banners said to be Viet Cong flags fluttered in the air, but the rally was for the most part peaceful. Shortly after 2 p.m., marchers started crossing the Potomac. There were so many protesters that it took three hours for all of them to walk across Memorial Bridge (→ 22).

Oct 20. Tehran erupted in ceremony as Mohammed Reza Shah Pahlevi was crowned King of Kings and Sun of the Aryans. Some 15,000 soldiers lined the way to his marble palace. The shah, a moderate, proclaimed a general amnesty for political prisoners filling Iran's jails (→ 5/31/72).

Che Guevara killed leading Bolivian rebels

Oct 10. Ernesto Che Guevara, the underground revolutionary leader and hero to popular movements in Central and South America, has been reported dead or captured several times since he disappeared two years ago. Today, military authorities in Bolivia confirmed that Guevara was killed Sunday when his guerrilla band was overrun by government forces. Six other guerrillas were also killed, including four Cubans. Guevara's body was displayed at a news conference in Valle Grande, Bolivia.

The death of the revolutionary is likely to set back efforts by Cuba's Premier Fidel Castro to export his revolution to the Americas. Guevara's whereabouts have been a mystery since 1965, but he has been linked to guerrilla activity in Argentina, Brazil, Colombia, Peru and Venezuela. Guevara, formerly Minister of Industries and number two man in Cuba, warned in 1961 that a decade of revolution was about to come to Latin America (→ 11/17).

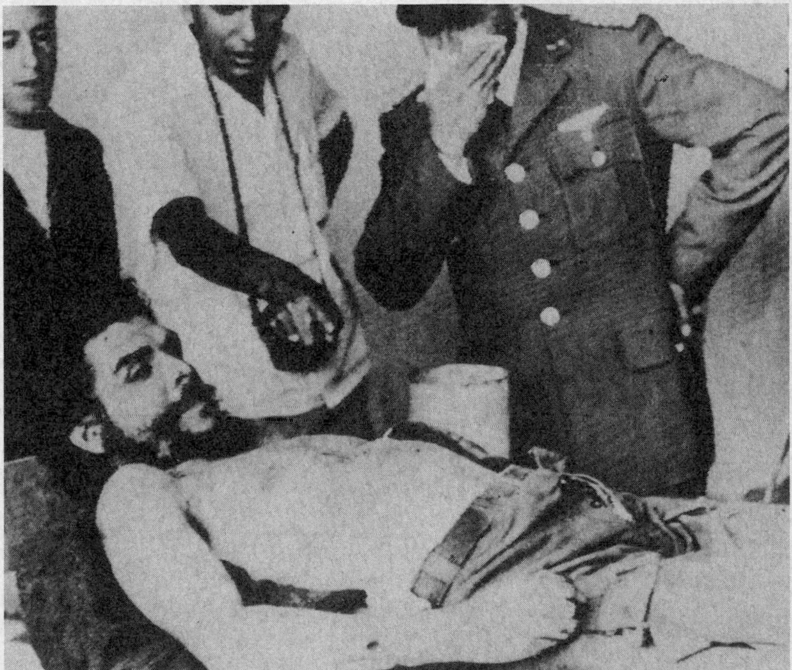

Guevara's post-mortem revealed he had been shot to death after capture.

Woody Guthrie, activist-folksinger, dies

Oct 3. Woodrow Wilson Guthrie, the pioneering folksinger and song writer better known as Woody, died today after a 13-year bout with Huntington's chorea. He had been bed-ridden for the past nine years, and was 55 years old.

The raspy-voiced activist for the downtrodden began life in Okemah, Oklahoma, during the Dust Bowl. He left at 15 for the life of a wandering minstrel, singing at labor union halls, supporting striking farmers and writing articles of social protest. Out of his travels came songs like "So Long It's Been Good to Know You," "Blowing Down this Old Dusty Road" and 1,000 others. He also sang out for America's beauty. The folksinger Odetta once suggested that "This Land is Your Land," perhaps his best-known song, should become the national anthem.

Woody, itinerant folksinger.

Joan Baez is held in anti-war protest

Baez, mixing politics and song.

Oct 16. Singer Joan Baez was one of thousands of anti-war protesters demonstrating throughout the nation today. Anti-draft rallies were held in Chicago, Philadelphia, Boston, Cincinnati and Portland, Oregon. Draft cards were turned in or set on fire at churches and federal offices. Little violence was reported. Miss Baez was among 119 demonstrators at the Selective Service Center in Oakland, California. Despite their efforts to block the doors to the induction center, the usual number of draftees, about 300, were processed. Miss Baez sang for reporters and was then arrested, charged with disturbing the peace (→ 21).

Renowned French writer Maurois dies

Oct 9. The prolific biographer Andre Maurois has died in France. His last successful work, an examination of the life of Balzac, was done two years ago at the age of 80. The book capped a 45-year career. Maurois investigated writers whose lives or ideas somehow paralleled his own. He studied the poet Shelley because he came, as Maurois did, from an unsympathetic family. Disraeli was the subject of scrutiny because he was, like Maurois, a Jew asserting himself in a Christian world. Byron and Victor Hugo represented a romantic age he may have wished to know. Surprisingly, Maurois' own "Memoirs" (1948) are relatively unrevealing.

Three pour blood on U.S. draft files

Oct 27. A Roman Catholic priest and two other men demonstrated their disgust with the Vietnam War today by splattering blood over Selective Service files in Baltimore, Maryland. Father Philip Berrigan and two accomplices asked to see their own draft records, then opened briefcases and tossed a mixture of their own and duck's blood over the open drawers. Berrigan said they were demonstrating the blood that would be spilled, both American and Vietnamese, and called on others to "move with us from dissent to resistance." All three waited at the office for FBI agents to arrest them (→ 11/14).

Lords will lose its legislative powers

Oct 31. Britain's ancient, unelected, largely hereditary House of Lords was informed today it would lose its legislative power. The word came from Queen Elizabeth II in her speech at the opening of Parliament, a speech written by the Labor government. It said the "hereditary basis" of the House would be eliminated. By the Parliament Act of 1911, the House of Lords' power was reduced to delaying legislation for two years, later cut to one. In 1958, non-hereditary life peerages were created, and since 1963 peers have been allowed to renounce their titles and sit in the House of Commons.

Head of FDA says pot as bad as booze

Oct 18. The Commissioner of the Food and Drug Administration, Dr. James L. Goddard, yesterday equated the dangers of marijuana use with those of alcohol and called for the removal of criminal penalties for possession of the drug. He cautioned, however, that more research was needed, because "we don't know what the long-term effects are," and he added that marijuana "distorts your perception of reality, so it's dangerous if you are driving a vehicle."

1967

NOVEMBER

Su	Mo	Tu	We	Th	Fr	Sa
			1	2	3	4
5	6	7	8	9	10	11
12	13	14	15	16	17	18
19	20	21	22	23	24	25
26	27	28	29	30		

1. Malaysia: Humphrey, on Asia tour, says U.S. is winning war in Vietnam (→ 6).

5. Yemen: Pres. Abdullah Salal ousted in bloodless military coup.

6. North Vietnam: U.S. bombs biggest supply depot (→ 13).

8. Cairo: Egyptian official says nation guarantees Israel's right to exist (→ 1/11/68).

9. Cape Kennedy: NASA sends Apollo 4 capsule into orbit in successful test of Saturn V rocket (→ 17).

13. Japanese report four Americans have deserted from aircraft carrier Intrepid (→ 16).

16. North Vietnam: Haiphong shipyard hit by U.S. planes for first time (→ 21).

17. Surveyor 6 makes six-second flight on moon, first lift-off on lunar surface (→ 1/9/68).

20. U.S. census reports population at 200 million.

20. Cincinnati: TWA jet crashes, killing 62.

21. LBJ signs air quality act, alloting $428 million to fight pollution.

23. U.S., considering blockade, orders study on Viet Cong use of Cambodia (→ 1/10/68).

26. Portugal: 250 die in flooding near Lisbon.

26. Cairo bars Soviet military bases in Egypt (→ 12/20/69).

27. Paris: De Gaulle again vetoes Britain's entry into Common Market (→ 12/2/69).

27. LBJ appoints Robert McNamara to presidency of World Bank.

28. N.Y.: U.N. rejects plea to admit Peking (→ 1/12/68).

28. N.Y.: Timothy Leary weds ex-aide Rosemary Woodruff.

30. Mass.: David Eisenhower announces engagement to Julie Nixon (→ 12/22/68).

DEATHS

7. John Nance Garner, v.p. under FDR (*11/22/1898).

20. Casimir Funk, Polish-American biochemist, coined term "vitamin" (*2/23/1884).

Rusk says bigger war is unavoidable

Protesting for peace in New York.

Nov 14. Anti-war protesters collided with police in New York City tonight as Secretary of State Dean Rusk said there is no turning back from Vietnam. Rusk told the Foreign Policy Association that the United States must continue its policy of escalation. Several thousand protesters milled outside the New York Hilton, where the secretary was speaking. Hundreds of them threw stones and eggs at police, blocked traffic and harassed theatergoers in Times Square. Rusk's speech followed a statement by Vice President Humphrey that the United States is winning the war. In Washington, many administration officials say they suspect Humphrey is correct. An inter-agency group is studying the military situation to determine whether their suspicions are correct (→ 12/5).

Big arms show marks 50th Soviet birthday

An imposing Vostok missile is raised skyward in the Soviet Union.

Nov 7. Opening an elaborate celebration of the 50th anniversary of the Russian Revolution, Soviet Communist Party leader Leonid I. Brezhnev warned both the United States and China that his nation's armed forces were prepared to attack from any direction.

Speaking to an audience of the leaders of world communism in the Kremlin Palace of Congresses, Brezhnev said: "The Soviet people would not flinch if someone will be mad enough to make an attempt on the security of the Soviet Union and our allies. This attempt wherever it might come will encounter the all-conquering might of our armed forces. No shields and no distances are too great for this might."

In a huge military parade in Red Square, five new types of missiles were unveiled. The biggest, 110 feet long, was equal in size to any ever seen before. Other armaments, marked with such inscriptions as "Power to the Soviets" and "Capital is the enemy," were also on display.

In 50 years, the Soviets have made progress—such as building the world's largest hydroelectric generators and other technological marvels. But these have come at great cost. Recent scholarly works claim Stalin was responsible for the deaths of over 20 million persons.

The Doors, whose "Light My Fire" hit top 40 for 14 weeks this year, blend rhythm and blues, acid rock and the Freudian lyrics of leader Jim Morrison into an often eery, always infectious sound. Morrison's antics draw whole police forces to his shows along with the thousands of feverish fans.

Che's French ally gets 30-year term

Nov 17. Regis Debray, the young French philosopher and revolutionary author who became the confidante of Fidel Castro, was sentenced to 30 years in prison in Bolivia today. A military tribunal found Debray guilty of participating in the guerrilla activities of the late Che Guevara. Debray was also found guilty of murder. The court said Guevara's guerrilla band killed 20 Bolivian soldiers in two separate ambushes. Debray, who was dispatched to Bolivia by Castro himself, said he was tried criminally for what were actually political charges. "I am not a murderer or a thief," Debray said.

Guerrilla warrior Regis Debray.

British leave Aden, colony for 128 years

Nov 30. As helicopters whisked the last few British troops out of South Yemen today, Arabs surged into the port city of Aden to celebrate the end of 128 years of colonial rule. Qantan al-Shaabi, who is expected to be elected president, blasted the departing troops after failing to secure $140 million in economic assistance. "Britain is not giving us independence; we have achieved it through blood and sacrifice." Al-Shaabi, however, agreed to accept $24 million and to maintain diplomatic ties with Britain. The East India Tea Company seized control of Aden in 1839 to stop pirate attacks on shipping to India. Rebellion broke out in 1963 and independence talks were concluded just two days ago in Geneva. Over 1.5 million people inhabit the county, with deserts covering much of its 112,000 square miles.

U.S. on offensive in Vietnam campaign

Dropping supplies to a G.I. camp.

Nov 21. U.S. Air Force and Navy planes have accelerated the air war against North Vietnam, striking at targets near Hanoi and Haiphong that previously had been off-limits. Air Force planes based in Thailand bombed a large military supply depot at Giathuong, three miles from the center of Hanoi. Carrier-based Navy planes struck a shipyard on the outskirts of Haiphong. Meanwhile, U.S. troops were engaged in fierce fighting in the Central Highlands near the Cambodian border. Paratroopers of the 173rd Airborne Brigade suffered heavy casualties as they fought up the slopes of Hill 875 against fierce North Vietnamese resistance (→ 12/8).

British devalue the pound to $2.40

Nov 18. Britain's Labor Party government conceded failure today by devaluing the pound 14.3 percent. The official value yesterday was $2.80; it is now $2.40. The British hope to increase exports overseas and reduce their purchases of foreign goods. Unfortunately for the average Briton, many necessities, from foodstuffs to textile fabrics, must be imported. Gasoline rates may go up more than 12 percent.

Peugeot 204 all-terrain racer.

1967

DECEMBER

Su	Mo	Tu	We	Th	Fr	Sa
					1	2
3	4	5	6	7	8	9
10	11	12	13	14	15	16
17	18	19	20	21	22	23
24	25	26	27	28	29	30
31						

1. London: $1.4 mil. paid for Monet's "La Terrasse a St.-Adresse," record for Impressionist.

2. Philadelphia: Navy beats Army 19-14 in football.

5. N.Y.: 246 arrested in protest at draft induction center (→ 30).

8. South Vietnam: 365 Viet Cong killed in biggest battle yet in Mekong Delta (→ 12).

8. Greek troops begin withdrawal from Cyprus under terms of pact with Turkey (→ 2/25/68).

9. Rumania: Nicolae Ceausescu elected president (→ 2/29/68).

10. N.M.: World's first commercial nuclear blast detonated by El Paso Natural Gas (→ 1/11/72).

12. U.S. ends biggest airlift, landing 6,500 men in Vietnam (→ 23).

15. Washington: LBJ signs meat bill in presence of Upton Sinclair.

20. India: Gandhi gets powers to outlaw groups that question sovereignty (→ 8/24/69).

24. Athens: Junta frees ex-Premier Papandreou (→ 9/29/68).

DEATHS

10. Otis Redding, American soul singer (*9/9/1941).

29. Paul Whiteman, "The Jazz King" (*3/28/1890).

CULTURAL EVENTS, 1967

Literature: Chaim Potok's "The Chosen"; William Styron's "The Confessions of Nat Turner"; Solzhenitsyn's "Cancer Ward"; Tom Stoppard's "Rosencrantz and Guildenstern are Dead"; Gabriel Garcia Marquez's "One Hundred Years of Solitude."

Academia: Galbraith's "The New Industrial State"; Desmond Morris' "The Naked Ape."

Music: Beatles' "Penny Lane," "All You Need Is Love"; Rolling Stones' "Ruby Tuesday"; Young Rascals' "Groovin'"; Gerry Dorsey changes name to Engelbert Humperdinck.

The Arts: Chagall's "The Blue Village."

Film: Antonioni's "Blow Up"; Chaplin's "The Countess from Hong Kong"; Warhol's "The Chelsea Girls"; Schlesinger's "The Taming of the Shrew."

The first heart transplant

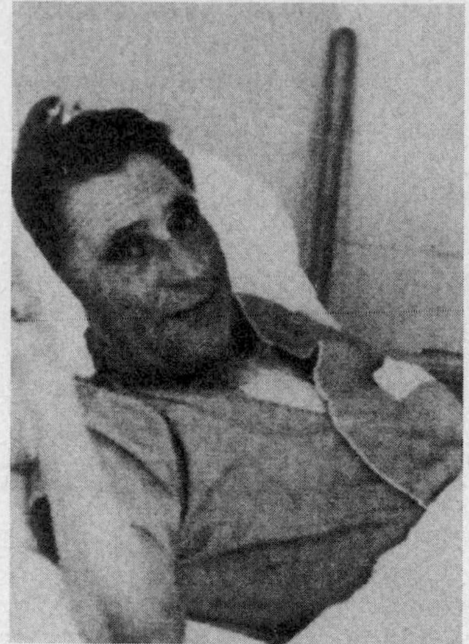

Recipient Washkansky . . .

and miracle-worker Barnard.

Dec 21. Louis Washkansky, the world's first heart transplant patient, died in Cape Town, South Africa, today after living for 18 days with the heart of a 25-year-old woman who was killed in an auto accident. Doctors at Groote Schuur Hospital said the 53-year-old grocer died after a steady deterioration that began when he developed lung complications several days ago. The transplanted heart continued to beat strongly until the end.

Washkansky's transplant was performed on December 3 by a five-surgeon team headed by Dr. Christiaan N. Barnard, who trained in the United States and continued animal experiments on heart transplants in South Africa. The operation was performed when Washkansky, who had suffered a series of heart attacks, was so weakened that he would have lived only a few days.

After explaining the procedure to Washkansky and his wife, surgeons told him the night before the operation that a suitable heart was available and asked him if he wanted to go ahead. "He made up his mind in two minutes," Mrs. Washkansky said. The surgeons later described their emotion when the transplanted heart began beating again in Washkansky's chest. Washkansky made good progress until the appearance of the lung problems that led to his death (→ 1/2/68).

Dec 11. The Concorde, a joint British-French venture and the world's first supersonic airliner, was unveiled in Toulouse. Said a British official, in reference to French intransigence on EEC issues: "Maybe the inspiration of cooperation here will have some influence on our heads of state."

546 arrested for protesting the draft

Dec 30. Opponents of the Vietnam War changed tactics this month. They tried to close down an armed forces induction center in New York City. At least 546 people were arrested in two days of protests. Among those taken into custody were Dr. Benjamin Spock, the famed pediatrician and author, and the poet Allen Ginsberg. Police lines surrounding the draft center were so strong that Spock pleaded to be let through so that he could be arrested. Other protesters gave up and blocked traffic in the area. In Hanoi today, Ho Chi Minh sent a message to American opponents of the war. "We shall win," said Ho, "and so will you" (→ 1/5/68).

Daisies, a wilting symbol of peace.

King Constantine's counter-coup fails

Dec 13. As a 24-hour-old counter-coup sputtered out today, Greece's King Constantine grabbed his family and fled to Rome. In a dramatic radio announcement yesterday, Constantine dismissed the junta that seized power last April and called everyone "on the side of democracy" to assist him. Apparently the military was not listening and by nightfall the few generals on his side had surrendered. Col. Papadopoulos labeled the attempt "a criminal conspiracy" and claimed the king had been misled by power seekers to "turn against the national revolution" (→ 24).

Johnson visits troops again as war rages on

LBJ urges G.I.'s at Cam Ranh Bay to ignore anti-war protests back at home.

Dec 23. President Johnson today visited the scene of his greatest frustration and anguish. Taking time from his trip to Australia, the Commander-in-Chief went to the largest base in Vietnam to confer, console and wish the troops a Merry Christmas. Many who had expected that Johnson would use the holiday to announce a lull in the bombing were surprised when Johnson said the Viet Cong had met their match and the U.S. would not "shimmy" in its resolve. Referring to the protests back in the U.S., Johnson said "the slogans and signs" could not diminish the pride Americans felt in their troops. The speech was greeted with restrained applause.

The visit follows a recent meeting in Australia, where South Vietnamese President Thieu rejected Johnson's request that he negotiate with representatives from North Vietnam. "Our position is very clear," said Thieu. "We never recognize the National Liberation Front or anything else, but if one of them is willing to come over to our side we are willing to talk to them."

Two weeks ago, government sources reported that South Vietnamese forces crushed two Viet Cong battalions, killing 365 enemy troops. The battle was the second serious blow to the Viet Cong that week, as American troops killed over 235 in the Mekong Delta.

Fast food at home: 1st microwave oven

Cooks are wondering how popping frozen food in an oven and seeing it sizzle in an instant can be appealing.

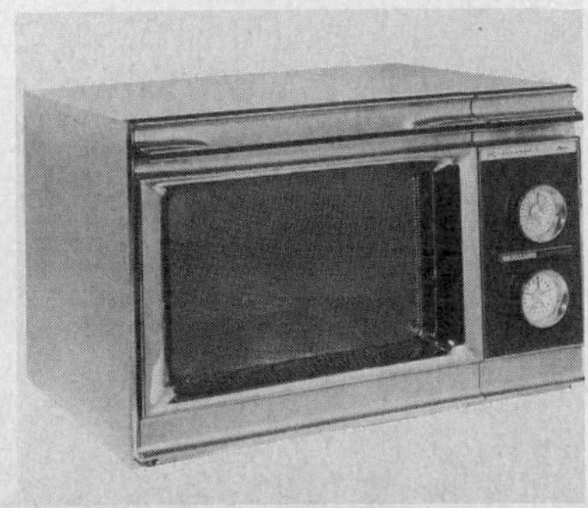

New microwave oven.

Spellman, powerful prelate, passes on

Dec 7. "Grant him mercy and peace everlasting," pronounced the Pope's representative as the body of Cardinal Spellman was lowered in the Archbishop's Crypt below St. Patrick's Cathedral in New York. The Cardinal, dynamic and powerful in his leadership of Roman Catholics, died Saturday at the age of 78. President Johnson, amid tight security, flew into New York unannounced to attend the funeral services for Spellman, which included words from the pope. His Holiness sent his prayer: "May his brave, Christlike, priestly soul rest in peace."

Best of '67 include Dustin, Faye and Warren

"The Graduate" may send every filmmaker scurrying back to school. Everything about it, from acting to direction to soundtrack, is daringly innovative. And fearfully funny.

The comedy stars newcomer Dustin Hoffman as an earnest young man bumbling his way into an affair with a seductive older woman (Anne Bancroft) and her daughter. Director Mike Nichols gleefully slams icons, while the Simon and Garfunkel score, wistfully asking where Joe DiMaggio has gone, seems to be seeking them.

"Bonnie and Clyde" breaks all the rules too, but goes to the head of the class. Arthur Penn has directed Faye Dunaway and Warren Beatty in a quirky gangster picture about a pair of quirky 30's outlaws, Bonnie Parker and Clyde Barrow. Their deaths (they are riddled with bullets) are depicted in eerily effective slow motion.

Rod Steiger has a gritty role as a police officer in "In the Heat of the Night." Sidney Poitier plays a big-city cop trying to help him solve a murder in a redneck Southern town. Norman Jewison ("The Russians Are Coming, the Russians Are Coming") directed.

Katharine Hepburn and Spencer Tracy play a liberal couple taking liberal pains to accept a black (Sidney Poitier) as their son-in-law. "Guess Who's Coming to Dinner" also features Katharine Houghton, Miss Hepburn's niece.

"Cool Hand Luke" is laid-back con Paul Newman. He and fellow prisoner George Kennedy plot escape, revenge and practical jokes.

"If you could talk to the animals ..." begins a song in "Doctor Dolittle," listing the advantages of inter-species conversation. Rex Harrison stars in the lavishly filmed picture.

Roger Vadim made his former wife Brigitte Bardot into a sex symbol in "And God Created Woman." He seems to be trying to do the same with his current wife, Jane Fonda, but just to cover himself he is placing her in a foolishly camp sci-fi pic called "Barbarella." The film is due for release next year.

Faye, Warren: "Bonnie and Clyde."

"In the Heat of the Night."

Dustin Hoffman is "The Graduate."

Jane Fonda will play "Barbarella," already banned by the Church.

1968

JANUARY

Su	Mo	Tu	We	Th	Fr	Sa
	1	2	3	4	5	6
7	8	9	10	11	12	13
14	15	16	17	18	19	20
21	22	23	24	25	26	27
28	29	30	31			

1. Pasadena: U.S.C. beats Indiana 14-3 in Rose Bowl.

2. Mississippi seats its first black legislator in 74 years, Robert Clark (→ 2/10).

2. Capetown: Dr. Christiaan Barnard performs second successful heart transplant (→ 6).

4. Newark: Militant black writer Leroi Jones given three years in jail on gun charge.

6. California doctor performs first successful heart transplant in U.S. (→ 21).

9. Surveyor 7, last of five unmanned U.S. flights to moon, soft-lands on moon (→ 4/4).

10. Cambodia: Prince Sihanouk agrees to bolster border guard against Viet Cong (→ 19).

11. Israel expropriates 838 acres of Old Jerusalem (→ 2/15).

12. China charges U.S. pirate planes raided Yunnan province (→ 3/20/69).

13. U.S. reports shifting most air targets from North Vietnam to Laos (→ 31).

13. Sweden: Three U.S. military deserters ask asylum (→ 18).

19. Cambodia charges U.S. and South Vietnamese crossed border, killed three Cambodians (→ 10/4).

21. L.A.: Mike Kasperak, first U.S. heart transplant recipient, dies after 15 days (→ 3/16).

22. Greenland: U.S. B-52 with four H-bombs crashes in bay (→ 28).

23. North Korea seizes U.S. intelligence ship Pueblo, holds 83 in crew as spies (→ 27).

25. LBJ orders 14,787 reserves to active duty (→ 29).

27. New York: U.N. Security Council begins private talks on Pueblo incident (→ 30).

27. Mediterranean: French sub Minerve disappears with 52.

28. Havana announces it will try nine members of pro-Soviet dissident group (→ 2/3).

29. LBJ presents record $186 bil. budget to Congress (→ 2/8).

31. Indian Ocean: Island of Mauritius gains independence from Britain.

Vietnam Reds launch Tet offensive

Jan 31. Communist guerrillas in Vietnam shattered the lunar New Year truce and shocked the United States and South Vietnam by launching a broad offensive that spread from the cities of the Mekong Delta to Saigon and north to the highlands. The Tet, or New Year, attack was aimed at more than 100 cities. President Johnson nervously demanded more details as word reached Washington that even the American Embassy in Saigon was under attack.

The assault on the embassy was part of a broader drive into Saigon by thousands of Viet Cong commandos. Defense of the capital was recently transferred by the United States to South Vietnamese authorities to demonstrate confidence in their abilities. Just before 3:00 this morning, a team of guerrillas blasted a hole through the embassy wall and started shooting. Four American soldiers were killed. The Viet Cong squad held parts of the embassy for six hours before they were repulsed. Ambassador Ellsworth Bunker was spirited away from his nearby home as a security measure.

Another group of commandos tried and failed to break into the presidential palace in a suicide mission. The headquarters of General William Westmoreland at the Saigon airport was also attacked. A guerrilla band seized control of the studios at a Saigon radio station, but technicians thwarted their efforts to broadcast revolutionary messages. At Bienhoa, a Communist division assaulted an American base. In the Mekong Delta, the Communists carried out well-planned attacks against 13 provincial capitals.

MP's lie dead in the U.S. Embassy.

Shocked Saigon residents, their city turned into a battleground, flee the war.

The shocking move of the Viet Cong out of the jungle and into the cities is being seen on television in millions of American living rooms. Westmoreland said the Communists' "well-laid plans went afoul," but their attack shows the cities are not invincible. Television coverage also shows Americans and South Vietnamese in disarray (→ 2/1).

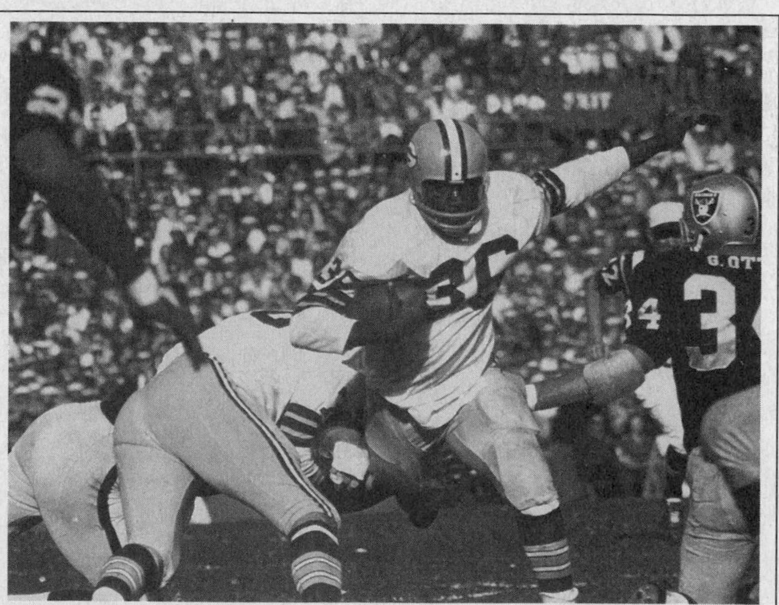
Jan 14. Green Bay over Oakland 33-14 for their 2nd straight Super Bowl.

Vince Lombardi looks to retirement

Jan 12. Vince Lombardi, whose dedication to winning has made him a football legend, has indicated that he will step down as Coach of the Green Bay Packers but remain as their General Manager. Lombardi dropped the hint at a news conference in Miami Beach before the Packer-Raider game in the Super Bowl. But he hedged by saying, "I haven't decided. I really have not. I do know that in pro football today it is almost impossible to be a coach and general manager and do a good job at both." The 54-year-old Lombardi has been telling friends for weeks he seriously expects to end his 30-year coaching career.

North Korea captures U.S. surveillance ship

Jan 30. North Korea seized a U.S. Navy intelligence ship on a surveillance patrol of the North Korean coast and took the vessel and its 83 crew members into the port of Wonsan. The seizure of the Pueblo provoked a tense confrontation between the U.S. and North Korea, and American forces in South Korea were placed on military alert.

The Defense Department said the Pueblo was 25 miles off the coast of North Korea and in international waters when it was boarded by armed sailors from North Korean patrol boats. But the Pentagon declined to give the Pueblo's position when it was first accosted two hours earlier by the patrol boats.

A State Department spokesman said the Pueblo had remained outside the 12-mile territorial limit at all times, but a North Korean radio broadcast said the ship had "intruded into the territorial waters of the republic and was carrying out hostile activities."

It was unclear whether the Pueblo, which is armed with only two 50-caliber machine guns, had resisted the seizure, but the Defense Department said four crew members had been wounded, apparently by gunfire from the North Korean patrol boats. The Pueblo, commanded by Commander Lloyd M. Bucher, is a 906-ton ship equipped to monitor electronic signals (→ 12/24).

Liberal Dubcek takes over Czechoslovakia

Jan 5. The Communist Party in Czechoslovakia now has a new leader in Alexander Dubcek. Dubcek, considered by Westerners as a liberal reformer, takes over as the First Secretary of the party after his successful drive to oust Antonin Novotny, although the deposed leader was appointed President of the nation and praised for his accomplishments while leading the party.

Dubcek (left), liberal leader.

Dubcek, a well-regarded party official who began his political career working with the Communist underground during World War II, is the first Slovak to gain supreme power in Prague. He will probably attempt to industrialize the economy of his home area, Slovakia, which is the least industrialized region in Czechoslovakia. He is also expected to relax controls on the press, initiate a foreign policy independent of the Soviet Union and pursue a gradual democratization of Czech political life (→ 3/13).

Plane with 4 H-bombs crashes in Greenland

Jan 28. A U.S. Air Force B-52 bomber carrying four hydrogen bombs crashed into ice off Greenland while attempting to make an emergency landing. The Defense Department said the bombs were "unarmed so that there is no danger of a nuclear explosion at the crash site," near the U.S.air base at Thule.

It was not immediately clear what had happened to the bombs after the crash—whether they had been scattered across the surface or had plunged through the ice with parts of the bomber into 800 feet of water. The Pentagon said one crew member, the co-pilot, had been killed but that the other six crew members had safely parachuted from the burning airplane.

The plane had been attempting to make an emergency landing at Thule after a fire broke out in the navigator's compartment. The B-52, which had taken off from the Air Force base in Plattsburgh, N.Y., was on an airborne alert maintained by the Strategic Air Command to protect its bombers against a surprise missile attack. On such patrols, a B-52 normally carries four H-bombs, which can only be armed to detonate after a series of steps by the crew (→ 2/1).

Britain to withdraw from east of Suez

Jan 16. Prime Minister Wilson told the House of Commons today that Britain will withdraw its military forces from east of Suez by 1972 and abandon its role as peacekeeper in the area. Britian's unfavorable balance of payments and devalued currency will force the closing of bases in the Persian Gulf and Singapore. Wilson was moved to cite Kipling's "Recessional": "Far called, our navies melt/away;/On dune and headland sinks the fire:/Lo, all our pomp of yesterday/Is one with Nineveh and Tyre!"

Spock indicted for his anti-draft advice

Jan 5. Benjamin Spock, the baby doctor who counseled mothers in the 1950's, was indicted today for counseling their children to resist the draft. The famous pediatrician and author could receive five years in prison and said he hoped "100,000, 200,000 or even 500,000 young Americans would refuse to be drafted or obey orders if in the military service." Also indicted was Rev. William Sloan Coffin, Yale chaplain, who together with Spock collected draft cards in Washington to be returned to the government.

Eartha Kitt speaks out at White House

Jan 18. Nerves and chinaware were rattled at a White House luncheon this afternoon, as entertainer Eartha Kitt spoke out against the Vietnam War. Miss Kitt was one of about 50 white and black women invited by Mrs. Lyndon B. Johnson to discuss urban crime. Miss Kitt linked the crime rate with the escalation of the war. "You send the best of this country off to be shot and maimed," she said. "They rebel in the street." She described first-hand knowledge of the Watts section of Los Angeles. Although Mrs. Johnson was visibly upset by Miss Kitt's outburst, they parted cordially (→ 25).

Clark Clifford is named to Defense

Jan 20. Clark Clifford has been in and out of the White House since 1946, advising three Presidents Starting today, he has to dispense more than advice. President Johnson has nominated the urbane, well-connected Washington lawyer to succeed Robert McNamara as Secretary of Defense. Clifford, regarded as a hawkish supporter of the Vietnam War, said tonight that he is "not conscious of falling under any of those ornithological divisions." In announcing the nomination, Johnson tried to quash speculation he had forced McNamara to resign by saying he had "never known a more competent public official."

Frisco's Haight-Ashbury is a hippie haven

They call it the Haight—a section of San Francisco now reserved for the disaffected products of middle-class life. Crash pads and free clothes are available to runaways. Rock and roll is a form of protest here, as is everything parents abhor. Chet Helms fills the Avalon Ballroom with Day-Glo painted freaks milling around vats of Kool-Aid mixed with LSD. The Jefferson Airplane, the Grateful Dead and Janis Joplin all started with Helms and moved on to Bill Graham's Fillmore West to find a wider audience. Last year's "summer of love" brought media attention, but the area remains the center of a counterculture of sex, drugs and music where it is advised "to hang loose."

Haight's oldest resident and friend.

1968

FEBRUARY

Su	Mo	Tu	We	Th	Fr	Sa
				1	2	3
4	5	6	7	8	9	10
11	12	13	14	15	16	17
18	19	20	21	22	23	24
25	26	27	28	29		

1. New Hampshire: Nixon enters presidential race (→ 8).

1. Saigon: Pres. Thieu declares martial law (→ 5).

1. Washington: McNamara reports Soviets doubled ICBM force in 1967 (→ 7/1).

3. Havana: Pro-Soviet Castro critic Anibal Escalante gets 15-year sentence (→ 9/23/70).

5. Vietnam: U.S. troops divide Viet Cong at Hue; Saigon to arm loyal civilians (→ 13).

6. Grenoble: 60,000 see de Gaulle open 19th Winter Olympics (→ 17).

7. Austria: Capital punishment abolished.

8. Washington: George Wallace enters presidential race (→ 3/16).

8. Washington: RFK says U.S. cannot win Vietnam War (→ 16).

10. Newark: Riot inquiry calls police action excessive (→ 4/4).

11. Paraguay: Alfredo Stroessner re-elected president.

13. U.S. sends 10,500 more combat troops to Vietnam (→ 18).

15. Newark: Henry Lewis becomes first black to head symphony orchestra in U.S.

15. Israelis use jets in day-long clash with Jordanians (→ 3/3).

16. LBJ curbs draft deferments for graduate students (→ 29).

18. Washington: Three U.S. pilots freed by Hanoi arrive in U.S. (→ 20).

19. Geneva: Arbitration group gives 300 sq. miles of Cutch region to Pakistan (→ 4/4/71).

20. Vietnam: Hue army chief orders looters shot on sight (→ 24).

25. Cyprus: Archbishop Makarios re-elected pres. (→ 7/15/74).

26. Congo: 32 African nations agree to boycott Olympics due to admittance of S. Africa (→ 4/21).

29. Budapest: Rumania walks out of Intl. Communist Congress to protest Soviet tactics.

DEATHS

5. Neal Cassady, beatnik, hero of counter-culture.

22. Peter Arno, American cartoonist (*1/8/1904).

American forces blunt Tet offensive

Khesanh, still under siege.

Feb 24. South Vietnamese troops received the glory today. But it was the might of three United States Marine battalions which enabled them to liberate Hue. Capture of the city was one of the Viet Cong's greatest victories of the Tet offensive. Sounds of grenades exploding were heard as the South Vietnamese regained control of the imperial palace in Hue. But the grenades were hardly needed. Most of the 1,000 Communists occupying the area around the palace had disappeared quietly in the night, just as quickly as they came at the beginning of the Tet attack on January 31.

It has been more than three weeks since President Johnson declared at a news conference in Washington that the Tet offensive was a "complete failure." He discounted the Communists' successes in a number of cities, including Hue. "A few bandits can do that in any city," the president told reporters. "It looks like somebody has paid a very dear price for the temporary encouragement that some of our enemies had," Johnson said.

Johnson was obviously speaking for domestic consumption. The widespread ferocity of the Communist attack shocked some American military commanders in South Vietnam. The president also spoke before the Viet Cong's brutal attack on Khesanh.

The Communist body count was up to 20 times the number of American and South Vietnamese soldiers killed in the Tet offensive. But the attacks also convinced Johnson that he needed to send more men to Vietnam. He dispatched another 10,500 combat troops to the war, raising the total American commitment above the half-million mark. The president also abolished most graduate school deferments from the draft.

Johnson says the Communists were beaten back in Tet. But he appears frustrated about what to do next. Last week, at a news conference, he said North Vietnam appears no more ready to negotiate now than it was three years ago. The president said American offers for peace talks have gone "as far as honorable men could go" (→ 3/2).

U.S. troops liberate Hue, central Vietnam, a major target of the Tet offensive.

Major politicians speak against war

Feb 29. New York's two Senators are now in the forefront of the opposition to the Vietnam War. Senator Robert Kennedy, a Democrat, issued a blistering attack on the war by charging there is not "any prospect" for victory. "It is time for the truth," Kennedy said as he wondered why more than a million American and South Vietnamese soldiers could not protect one major city in the Tet offensive. Republican Senator Jacob Javits, calling military victory "illusory," said it is time "to end the Americanization of this war" (→ 3/17).

The Beatles, bored with Western fame and fortune, are seeking "absolute bliss consciousness" on the Ganges with Maharishi Mahesh Yogi. George, says their guru, has "the most Indian taste" (→ 10/21/69).

Jean-Claude Killy wins three medals

Killy (rt.), king of the slopes.

Feb 17. The French call him "le Superman" and Jean-Claude Killy lived up to their expectations. The handsome customs officer scored a sweep of the Olympic Alpine ski events at Grenoble, France. The triple was achieved only once before, by Toni Sailer of Austria in 1956. Killy had to overcome a protest by the irate Austrians before he was declared victor in the spine-tingling slalom, final leg of the triple. It was at first thought that Karl Schranz of Austria was the winner because of his faster time but, after a two-hour lapse, he was disqualified for having missed a gate. Peggy Fleming of Colorado was an easy winner of the women's figure skating championship at Grenoble.

American jetliner hijacked to Cuba

Feb 21. A Delta airliner destined for Miami was hijacked to Havana, Cuba, this afternoon by an armed man wearing a white hat. The hijacker said he was South American and indicated he did not want to hurt anyone, although he did grab a stewardess and held her at gunpoint for the entire flight.

Upon landing in Havana, the man disembarked and, according to stewardess Joy Beil, "disappeared right away." Miss Beil, the hostage, said the man was facing the death penalty and was desperate. No one on board was hurt and the crew and passengers were greeted in Miami by a cheering crowd. Pilot J.D. Gainey, praised for his poise, passed along the credit, saying Beil is "the bravest girl I've ever met" (→ 3/12).

1968

MARCH

Su	Mo	Tu	We	Th	Fr	Sa
					1	2
3	4	5	6	7	8	9
10	11	12	13	14	15	16
17	18	19	20	21	22	23
24	25	26	27	28	29	30
31						

2. Georgia: LBJ watches as Lockheed Galaxy, world's largest plane rolls off assembly line.

2. Geneva: Peggy Fleming wins world figure skating title.

2. Vietnam: 48 G.I.'s killed in ambush near Saigon (→ 9).

3. Beirut: Nasser pledges UAR will regain land seized by Israel during six-day war (→ 24).

3. Puerto Rico: Oil tanker with 5.7 mil. gallons splits in half in San Juan harbor.

6. Rhodesia defies Britain, hanging three black Africans (→ 8/9).

8. Rome: Pope Paul VI names Terence Cooke to succeed Spellman as archbishop of New York.

8. Warsaw: Polish students protest, chanting "Down with censorship," "Long live Czechoslovakia" (→ 4/8).

9. Westmoreland asks 206,000 more troops in Vietnam (→ 16).

12. Miami: Gunmen hijack Natl. Airlines DC-8, force crew to fly to Havana (→ 7/17).

13. Prague: Censorship curbed; ex-head of secret police Mamula arrested (→ 4/15).

16. Washington: RFK joins presidential race.→

16. LBJ decides to send 35-50,000 more combat troops to Vietnam (→ 22).

16. Cape Town: Philip Blaiberg leaves hospital 74 days after heart transplant (→ 4/8/69).

17. London: 200 held in anti-war protest at U.S. Embassy (→ 18).

18. Madison: War protesters make graveyard with 400 crosses for graduating class (→ 4/23).

22. LBJ names Gen. Westmoreland Army chief of staff (→ 28).

23. New York: Cheering crowds welcome Adam Clayton Powell back to Harlem (→ 1/3/69).

23. L.A.: U.C.L.A. beats N. Carolina 78-55 for NCAA basketball title.

24. N.Y.: U.N. condemns Israel for raids on Jordan (→ 5/2).

DEATH

27. Yuri Gagarin, Soviet astronaut, first man in space, in plane crash (*3/9/1934).

Johnson wins in N.H.; McCarthy does well

Anti-war candidate McCarthy spawned the slogan, "Come clean for Gene."

March 16. The presidential nominating race heated up this week as President Johnson won the New Hampshire Democratic primary, despite a strong showing by Senator Eugene McCarthy of Minnesota, who collected 40 percent of the vote running on an anti-war platform. In the state's Republican balloting, former Vice President Richard Nixon trounced his only opponent, New York Governor Nelson Rockefeller, a write-in candidate. Nixon captured 80 percent of the vote.

Today, New York Senator Robert Kennedy shook up the Democratic race by declaring his candidacy and attacking Johnson. Kennedy said he seeks the presidency because the nation's "disastrous, divisive policies" in Vietnam can only be changed by a change in the White House. With two strong challengers to an incumbent president seeking re-election, some Democratic leaders fear the worse: A split in the party which would strenghten Republican support. Yet, others feel three prominent contenders show Democratic strength (→ 31).

Prison notes of black radical: "Soul on Ice"

Eldrige Cleaver, in "Soul on Ice," provides a telling account of the personal effects of racism on black lives. His essays are social commentary seen through the prism of introspection found only in prison. He claims marijuana, for which he was jailed at age 19, was a necessity to bolster young blacks against onslaughts on their manhood. Returned to jail for raping a white woman, Cleaver converted to Islam. Though disavowing separatism, he devotes his most passionate prose to a eulogy of Malcolm X.

The most provocative essays of "Soul on Ice" paint a complex picture of sexual relations as the archetype of black oppression. The black man, he charges, has been emasculated. Denied the economic means to support a family, he is rejected by the black woman. Yet the white woman, symbol of his oppression, is taboo. Economics and politics do resurface in Cleaver's comparison of the black cause to colonial struggles throughout the world.

Radical Panther leader Cleaver.

▷

Johnson won't run again

Early this month, Vietnam chief Westmoreland (left), frustrated by restraints from political dissent at home, asked 206,000 more troops. He got 35-50,000.

March 31. In a decision that stunned political friends and foes alike, President Johnson announced tonight: "I shall not seek and I will not accept the nomination of my party as your president."

Acknowledging that there was "division in the American house," the president said he was withdrawing in the name of national unity.

By taking himself out of this year's presidential race, the president left the field open to the only two men who have declared as candidates for the Democratic nomination: Sens. Robert F. Kennedy of New York and Eugene J. McCarthy of Minnesota. Vice President Hubert H. Humphrey also is likely to seek the presidential nomination.

The president's decision was made in a nationally televised address on the war in Vietnam. Ending his prepared speech, he went on to quote Franklin D. Roosevelt: "Of those to whom much is given, much is asked." Continuing solemnly, the president spoke proudly of what he had accomplished in the White House and then he dropped his political bombshell by saying that he had concluded "that I should not permit the presidency to become involved in the partisan divisions that are developing."

Just today, a Gallup Poll showed that only 26 percent of those questioned favor President Johnson's handling of the war in Vietnam (→ 4/27).

Panama's President refuses to quit office

March 26. Impeached and embattled, President Marco Robles held firmly onto his office today with the help of Panama's National Guard. Members of the National Assembly, which is led by the opposition party, were tear-gassed by the guard when they tried to go to their offices. Robles called the impeachment "a parliamentary coup d'etat" and has appealed to the Supreme Court for a ruling. General Vallarino, who controls the guard, cited the appeal as a pretext for protecting Robles (→ 10/12).

First F-111 lost in combat in Vietnam

March 28. The U.S. lost its first aircraft in Vietnam today when an F-111 fighter-bomber vanished on a combat mission. In a broadcast, the North Vietnamese claimed they shot it down. Based in Thailand where they landed last week, the swing-wing F-111's, capable of 1,500 mph, began flying missions over North Vietnam four days ago. Today, no enemy MIG's were sighted, anti-aircraft fire was light to moderate and enemy surface-to-air missiles were reported to be off target (→ 4/5).

1968

APRIL

Su	Mo	Tu	We	Th	Fr	Sa
	1	2	3	4	5	6
7	8	9	10	11	12	13
14	15	16	17	18	19	20
21	22	23	24	25	26	27
28	29	30				

4. Memphis: Martin Luther King shot by assassin (→ 5).

4. Cape Kennedy: Unmanned Apollo 6 launched in test of Saturn V booster rockets (→ 8/2).

5. U.S.: Race riots sweep cities; LBJ orders troops into capital; seven killed in Chicago (→ 5).

5. Vietnam: Operation Pegasus breaks 76-day Viet Cong siege of U.S. base at Khe Sanh (→ 10).

5. Memphis: Ralph Abernathy succeeds King at S. Christian Leadership Conference.→

8. Memphis: Coretta Scott King leads memorial march (→ 9).

8. Poland: Party leaders crush brief rebellion (→ 12/23/70).

10. LBJ names Gen. Creighton Abrams commander of U.S. troops in Vietnam (→ 11).

11. U.S. calls 24,500 reserves to active duty (→ 5/3).

12. Berlin: Students, police clash after shooting of leftist student leader Rudi Dutschke.

15. N.Y.: Trading exceeds 16.4 mil. first time since Oct. 1929.

17. N.C.: Five inmates killed, 78 injured in battle with guards.

21. Switzerland: Olympics, in reversal, votes to bar South Africa (→ 1/28/70).

23. New York: 300 protesting Columbia students barricade office of college dean (→ 25).

23. U.S. Army adds 10,000 to anti-riot units (→ 24).

24. Blacks occupy Boston Univ. administration building to demand black history major (→ 29).

25. New York: Columbia closes campus as protest grows (→ 26).

26. New York: 200,000 college and high school students cut classes in war protest (→ 30).

27. Washington: Humphrey joins presidential race (→ 5/7).

29. Prague: Soviets halt wheat aid to Czechoslovakia (→ 5/9).

DEATHS

1. Lev Landau, Soviet scientist, predicted existence of neutron stars, 1962 Nobel (*1/22/1908).

16. Edna Ferber, American novelist (*8/15/1887).

Civil rights measure becomes law in U.S.

April 11. President Johnson signed the Civil Rights Act of 1968 today while pleading for an end to the rioting which has erupted since the slaying of civil rights leader Rev. Dr. Martin Luther King Jr. The law's major provision makes it illegal to discriminate on the basis of race in the renting and sale of houses and apartments. In 1966, LBJ proposed the Fair Housing Act during a White House meeting with King.

The president called for a halt to the rioting, saying, "We all know that the roots of injustice run deep, but violence cannot redress a solitary wrong or remedy a single unfairness." He also promised to fight for other programs to aid minorities and the poor (→ 19).

French-Canadian is nation's leader

April 20. Pierre Trudeau was sworn in as Canada's 15th Prime Minister today, succeeding Lester Pearson, who had retired. Trudeau, virtually unknown to Canadians three years ago, was a professor of law until appointed as Minister of Justice last year by Pearson. He may call a general election for the summer, in hopes of changing the Liberal minority in Parliament into a majority; currently, the Liberals hold 130 of the 235 House of Commons seats. After meeting with his Cabinet, Trudeau reported that no decision on the election had been reached. A Liberal Parliament, in tandem with a Liberal leader, could greatly alter the political complexion of Canada (→ 3/24/69).

Popular Trudeau greets supporters.

Martin Luther King killed

April 5. The Rev. Dr. Martin Luther King was fatally shot last night as he leaned over the second-floor balcony railing just outside his room at the Lorraine Motel in Memphis, Tennessee.

The death of the 39-year-old civil rights leader sent shock waves throughout much of the city and the nation. Governor Buford Ellington of Tennessee ordered 4,000 National Guard troops into Memphis to keep order and a curfew was imposed on residents, 40 percent of whom are blacks.

The assassin, who managed to escape, is believed to be a white man who was staying in a flophouse about 50 to 100 yards from the motel. Police believe that he fled in a late model white Mustang. Found about a block from the scene of the crime was a high-powered rifle.

Dr. King, noted for preaching non-violence and racial harmony, was leaning over the rail to talk with his fellow civil rights activist, Jesse Jackson, who was standing below. Dr. King had just asked a Jackson friend, a musician, to play a Negro spiritual, "Precious Lord, Take My Hand," at a rally scheduled to begin two hours later in support of the striking Memphis sanitationmen. Dr. King was rushed unconscious to St. Joseph's Hospital, where he died.

Top associates of the slain civil rights leader sought to calm his black followers, reminding them of his messages of peace, but rioting broke out in parts of the city before National Guardsman arrived to restore order.

King, martyr to the black struggle.

Later, the Rev. Andrew Young, who is Executive Director of Dr. King's Southern Christian Leadership Conference, recalled there had been some talk two days ago about possible harm to Dr. King. He said Dr. King had told him such reports did not bother him, that he had "reached the peak of fulfillment with his non-violent movement."

Indeed, Dr. King was something of a fatalist as he spearheaded the drive for racial equality. He had suffered beatings and was once stabbed in the left chest ten years ago in a Harlem department store. A few years ago, after shots were fired into nearby houses as he preached in a small Georgia church, he remarked: "It may get me crucified. I may even die. But I want it said even if I die in the struggle, that 'He died to make me free'" (→ 8).

Coretta Scott King, her sadness veiled, leaves for the funeral on the 9th.

Prague Spring: Czechs are liberalizing

April 15. Winter has come and gone in Czechoslovakia, and more than the ice has thawed. There is a new sense of political freedom in Prague. Hope lights up the faces of citizens. In central squares where people used to walk with a resigned step, Czechs yell out, embracing each other and debating. Teenagers who are too young to remember the Emperor wear buttons stamped with a picture of Franz Joseph. Students acclaim the moderate policies of Communist Party leader Alexander Dubcek, who believes it is possible to reconcile Marxism with personal liberty—"socialism with a human face."

The most welcome surprise is the return of the newspapers, which are no longer content to reprint Communist Party propaganda. Reminiscent of Kafka, they tell stories of horror and expose the excesses of the secret police. One described the transfer of prisoners in tour buses to a work camp, where they extracted uranium from the ground. None of them was protected from the dangerous radioactivity.

The Czechs are trying to rewrite history. "The last few years," said President Novotny, "are a blot on our postwar existence" (→ 29).

Blacks riot in four cities

The nation's capital smolders in anger over the death of Martin Luther King.

April 9. The death of Rev. Dr. Martin Luther King Jr. has enraged the nation's blacks, triggering riots in major cities. Four cities, Chicago, Baltimore, Washington and Cincinnati, have been hit the hardest by arson, looting and violence.

In Chicago, 5,000 federal troops were dispatched to contain rioters who have caused havoc along a 28-mile stretch of West Madison Street. So far, 11 have died and 300 were injured from sniping gunfire, street fighting and raging fires; over 125 major fires have caused millions of dollars of property damage.

Five have died in Baltimore, and Governor Spiro Agnew has ordered 6,000 National Guardsmen into the center of the storm. However, looters, seemingly undaunted by the troops, continue to smash store windows, grab armfuls of goods and run. Police have arrested over 500, including a suspect charged with one of the killings.

A white graduate student was pulled from his car and stabbed to death while attempting to drive through a black section of Cincinnati. Bands of black youths have set fires and looted stores, despite the presence of federal troops, who have finally quelled most of the rioting.

In the nation's capital, eight have died in riots. Many parts of Washington have been reduced to smoldering piles of rubble. In all, 31 persons have died in the violence nationwide (→ 11).

Student protesters trash Columbia campus

SDS leader Mark Rudd speaks.

April 30. New York City police swarmed onto the Columbia University campus early this morning to evict students who had occupied five buildings. Many students were asleep when the police moved in at the request of the Columbia administration. University President Dr. Grayson Kirk, who canceled classes Friday and again yesterday, has refused to guarantee any of the students amnesty. But he is willing to negotiate some of their demands.

The protest began on the 22nd when the students, led by Mark Rudd, head of the Columbia chapter of Students for a Democratic Society, held the dean of the college hostage in his office for 24 hours. The protesters also surrounded Kirk's office. Rudd demanded that Columbia stop work on a new gymnasium in Morningside Heights. He said the project was "racist" because it would deprive the Harlem community of recreational space. Rudd also insisted that Columbia end its ties with the Institute for Defense Analysis because of its alleged connection with the Vietnam War.

Off-campus protesters and black leaders joined the protest, and by yesterday thousands of people were milling in front of Low Memorial Library. The Columbia faculty rejected Rudd's demand on the defense institute, but supported him on the new gymnasium. On Friday, Mayor Lindsay ordered a halt on construction there; the project may be dead for good (→ 5/18).

King's heir plans Poor People's Walk

April 29. The man chosen to succeed the slain Rev. Dr. Martin Luther King Jr. as President of the Southern Christian Leadership Conference, Rev. Ralph Abernathy, has taken charge of the Poor People's Campaign. The campaign, initiated by King, will center around a massive march on Washington D.C. planned for June.

Abernathy and King both held a philosophy on civil rights so similar that a fellow associate once remarked, "Ralph and Martin always thought alike. You had the feeling that he (King) and Ralph functioned as one mind." Always by his colleague's side, Abernathy cradled King in his dying hour after a sniper's bullet pierced the charismatic leader's neck. Both began their passionate struggle for equality in Montgomery, Alabama, as ministers. Their dedication spread contagiously to their congregations and beyond. Most agree Abernathy is the natural successor to lead the freedom crusade (→ 5/2).

FBI names assassin as James Earl Ray

April 19. The Federal Bureau of Investigation said today that it is seeking an escaped convict, James Earl Ray, for the murder of the Rev. Dr. Martin Luther King, the civil rights leader.

According to the FBI, Ray now goes by the alias of Eric Starvo Galt. He was pictured as a trouble-prone drifter with a long record of erratic and violent behavior, who escaped from Missouri State Penitentiary last year where he was serving a 20-year sentenced for car theft and armed robbery.

Now 40 years old, a native of Alton, Illinois, Ray dropped out of school in the tenth grade. After drifting from job to job, he served in the Army as an infantryman and as a military policeman, most of the time in Germany, before receiving a general discharge in late 1948 for "ineptness and lack of adaptability to military service." While in the Army, he spent three months at hard labor for drunkenness and resisting arrest (→ 23).

1968

MAY

Su	Mo	Tu	We	Th	Fr	Sa
			1	2	3	4
5	6	7	8	9	10	11
12	13	14	15	16	17	18
19	20	21	22	23	24	25
26	27	28	29	30	31	

2. Memphis: 1,000 begin Poor People's March on Washington (→ 22).

2. Jerusalem: Israel, jeopardizing peace talks, holds biggest military parade to celebrate 20th anniversary (→ 6/4).

3. U.S. and N. Vietnam agree to begin formal talks in Paris (→ 6).

3. Paris: 500 students arrested at Sorbonne as students riot (→ 6).

4. R. Ussery rides Dancer's Image to his second straight Kentucky Derby victory.

6. New York: William Styron wins Pulitzer for "The Confessions of Nat Turner."

6. Saigon: Four newsmen killed as Viet Cong press attack (→ 13).

6. Paris: 40-50 hurt as police battle New Left students (→ 13).

7. Indiana: RFK wins his first presidential primary (→ 28).

8. Oakland: Catfish Hunter pitches perfect game.

11. Montreal: Canadiens beat St. Louis Blues 3-2 for Stanley Cup.

11. Paris: Three biggest French labor federations call general strike to support students (→ 13).

13. Paris: Hundreds of thousands march against de Gaulle and "police repression" (→ 17).

17. France: 100,000 workers occupy dozens of industrial plants across country (→ 20).

18. New York: 117 arrested in Columbia Univ. sit-in (→ 24).

19. Nigeria claims vital Biafran city Port Harcourt (→ 8/15).

20. France near paralysis as millions of workers occupy factories, mines, offices (→ 26).

22. New Orleans: Black power advocate H. Rap Brown gets five years on weapons charge (→ 29).

23. Vietnam: Record 1,100 G.I.'s killed in last two weeks (→ 6/10).

26. Paris: Striking French workers get 35% hike in minimum wage (→ 30).

29. Washington: Protestors from Poor People's Campaign storm Supreme Court building (→ 6/8).

30. Bobby Unser wins Indy 500, averaging 152.9 mph in Rislone Special.

U.S. and Vietnam begin Paris talks

May 13. American and North Vietnamese diplomats opened formal talks in Paris today aimed at ending the war in Vietnam. The negotiators, introduced by French protocol officers wearing white gloves, took their own gloves off as soon as they started talking. They jabbed at each other with acrimonious language. The Communist delegate, Xuan Thuy, accused the United States of "monstrous crimes." W. Averell Harriman, the chief American delegate, charged the North Vietnamese with "aggression." One hopeful sign did emerge from the session on the Avenue Kleber. Thuy indicated he would not break off the negotiations if the United States continues to drop bombs on the Viet Cong (→ 23).

McCarthy outruns Kennedy in Oregon

May 28. Senator Eugene J. McCarthy won a stunning upset victory over Senator Robert F. Kennedy in the Oregon presidential primary today. The defeat of Kennedy, his first in three primaries, slows his drive for the Democratic nomination for president and could endanger his chances in the California primary, to be held next week. Senator McCarthy told cheering supporters tonight: "I think we've demonstrated who has the real staying power, the real strength, the real commitment" (→ 6/5).

France nearly paralyzed by protesters

French display support for de Gaulle.

May 30. The trains are not running in France, and the airports are closed. Millions of workers have barricaded themselves inside factories and offices. Mail is not being delivered, and it is almost impossible to make a telephone call. Universities are closed, and hundreds of thousands of students say they will not open again until their demands are met. The government and the country are crippled by strikes, and one leading politician warns France is on the brink of civil war.

President Charles de Gaulle, furious at striking workers and students, dissolved the National Assembly today, postponed a national referendum and vowed to use force if necessary to prevent what he called a Communist dictatorship. "I have made my resolutions," de Gaulle said. "I shall not withdraw. I have a mandate from the people. I shall fulfill it."

Hundreds of thousands of Parisians turned out to support de Gaulle, but his speech was sharply criticized by Francois Mitterrand. The head of the Federation of the Left charged that the president had "committed an action that is a call to civil war."

De Gaulle's speech was heard on radio and heard, but not seen, on television. Because of a television strike, a still picture of the president was broadcast while he spoke.

Students, led by Daniel Cohn-Bendit, ignited the strikes when they occupied the Sorbonne at the beginning of the month. Hundreds of them were arrested and many were injured when riot police charged onto the campus on the 3rd. The Sorbonne was closed for the first time in its 700-year history. The Nanterre campus, in suburban Paris, was also closed as students agitated for more control of the university and the overthrow of the "capitalist establishment." On the 13th, hundreds of thousands of students jammed the streets of Paris, calling de Gaulle an "assassin."

New Left leader Cohn-Bendit.

Near-revolution in the streets.

Labor unions, distressed by sagging wages, called a general strike on the 11th. On the 15th, an aircraft construction plant was occupied in Nantes and managers were held hostage. By the 20th, millions of workers had seized their factories. On the 26th, the government raised the minimum wage by 35 percent.

De Gaulle is relying on the armed forces to help him restore order to France. There are rumors in Paris tonight that tens of thousands of troops are returning to France from West Germany (→ 6/16).

Students swarm the streets in spontaneous revolt against the establishment.

Anti-colonialists on the march.

Soviet army active on Czech border

May 9. The Soviet Union has launched a new war of nerves against Czechoslovakia. Russian troops are reported to be massing near the Czech border in both Poland and East Germany. Western diplomats have been ordered not to leave Warsaw for the Polish countryside, so it is difficult to verify the extent of the Soviet buildup.

Czech and Western observers in Prague discount the possibility of a Soviet invasion of Czechoslovakia, but it is apparent that hard-line leaders in Moscow and the rest of the Eastern bloc are dissatisfied with the reforms of Alexander Dubcek. The Czech Communist Party leader was summoned to Moscow for meetings last weekend. The communique issued at the conclusion of the talks indicated that Dubçek and the Soviets still had sharp differences. Communist leaders from Bulgaria, East Germany, Hungary and Poland traveled to Moscow yesterday, possibly to discuss joint action against Dubcek (→ 7/15).

Berrigan sentenced for bloodying files

May 24. Two defendants in a Baltimore courtroom received a standing ovation today after a judge sentenced them to six years apiece in a federal penitentiary. Father Philip Berrigan and Thomas Lewis of Artists Concerned About Vietnam were found guilty of destroying federal property for pouring duck's blood over draft files at Baltimore's Selective Service headquarters last October. Judge Edward Northrup said the two had gone beyond civil disobedience and were trying to "bring down this society."

Berrigan called the act "sacrificial and constructive" and charged at the time that America would "rather protect its empire of oversea's profits than welcome its black people, rebuild its slums and cleanse its air and water." A scuffle followed the decision when marshals subdued a protester passing out peace pamphlets. One other defendant in the case has already received a three-year sentence, while a fourth still awaits trial (→ 6/14).

1968

JUNE

Su	Mo	Tu	We	Th	Fr	Sa
						1
2	3	4	5	6	7	8
9	10	11	12	13	14	15
16	17	18	19	20	21	22
23	24	25	26	27	28	29
30						

4. Israel, Jordan fight battle across Jordan River with artillery and planes (→ 7/17).

5. L.A.: RFK shot, critically wounded; Sirhan Sirhan held (→ 8).

8. Paris: Ex-O.A.S. member Georges Bidault returns from exile; given freedom (→ 15).

9. Washington: Ralph Abernathy names Sterling Tucker to head Poor People's Campaign (→ 19).

10. Saigon: Westmoreland calls military victory unlikely in face of political restraints (→ 29).

14. Boston: Dr. Spock, three others found guilty of conspiring to counsel draft evasion (→ 7/10).

15. Paris: De Gaulle frees Raoul Salan and 13 others convicted for O.A.S. terrorism.

16. Texas: Lee Trevino wins U.S. Open golf championship.

16. Paris: Clashes erupt as police evacuate students from Sorbonne (→ 30).

19. Washington: 50,000 march in support of Poor People's Campaign (→ 24).

20. Jim Hines sets mark for 100-meters at 0:9.8.

21. Florida: Hugo Vihlen completes 84-day Atlantic crossing in six-foot boat.

23. Argentina: 73 killed in stampede at soccer game.

24. Washington: Natl. Guard ordered out as looting breaks out in black section of city (→ 25).

26. LBJ names Abe Fortas to succeed Earl Warren as Supreme Court chief justice (→ 10/10).

29. Saigon: Premier Tran Van Truong to dismiss 50-100 district chiefs (→ 7/20).

30. France: With electorate fearing Communist take over, Gaullists win overwhelming majority in National Assembly (→ 7/8).

30. U.S. jet with 214 servicemen intercepted by Soviets, forced to land in Kurile Islands.

DEATHS

6. Robert Kennedy, U.S. senator, ex-atty. general (*11/20/1925).

14. Salvatore Quasimodo, Italian poet, 1959 Nobel (*8/20/1901).

Bobby Kennedy is killed

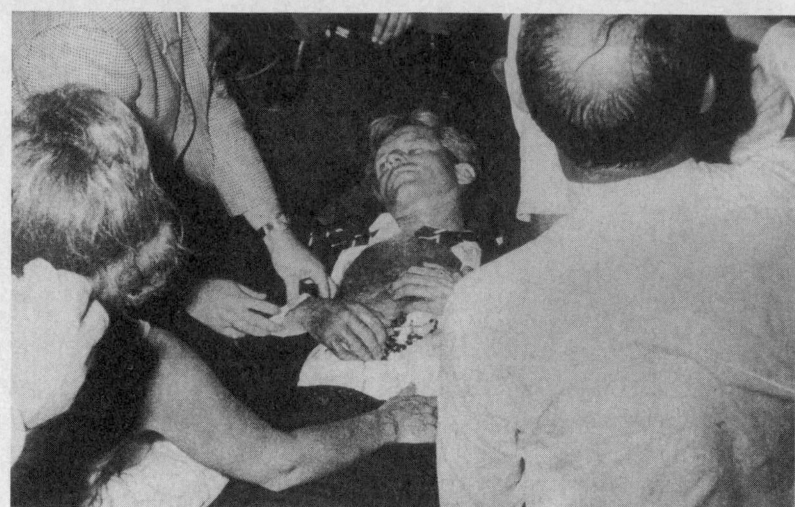

Robert Kennedy, the presidency just beyond his grasp, lies dying in L.A.

June 8. "Oh God, it can't happen to this family again!" They were the disbelieving, anguished cries of a bystander in the back of the Embassy Room of the Ambassador Hotel in Los Angeles. Just minutes before, Senator Robert F. Kennedy had completed a statement claiming victory in the California primary.

Amid cheers and V-for-Victory signs, the New York senator exited into an anteroom. Seconds later, he was lying on the cement floor of a kitchen corridor. He had been shot twice in the head, once in the forehead and once near the right ear.

Robert Francis Kennedy died at 1:44 a.m., June 6, 20 hours after the attack and four and a half years after his brother, President John F. Kennedy, was assassinated.

Yesterday, hundreds of thousands of mourners filed past the senator's closed coffin in New York. Millions more will pay their respects as a train carries the body to Arlington cemetery, where he will be buried.

At the funeral today, in a moving tribute to his brother, Senator Edward Kennedy of Massachusetts, his voice so choked with grief he could barely keep back the tears, said, "My brother need not be idealized or enlarged in death beyond what he was in life. He should be remembered simply as a good and decent man, who saw wrong and tried to right it, saw suffering and tried to heal it, saw war and tried to stop it.

"As he said many times, in many parts of this nation, to those he touched and who sought to touch him: 'Some men see things as they are and say why. I dream things that never were and say, why not'" (→ 7).

Somber and stalked by tragedy, the Kennedy family arrives for the funeral.

Young Arab is held for Kennedy murder

June 7. Sirhan Bishara Sirhan was indicted today by a Los Angeles grand jury on a first-degree murder charge in the assassination of Senator Robert F. Kennedy. The 24-year-old Jerusalem-born Jordanian had been seized at the scene of the fatal shooting in the Ambassador Hotel, where Kennedy was celebrating his victory in the California presidential primary (→ 8/2).

Accused assassin Sirhan Sirhan.

James Earl Ray is arrested in London

Ray tries to avoid prying cameras.

June 8. James Earl Ray, accused of the assassination of the Rev. Dr. Martin Luther King Jr., in April, was arrested this morning at the London Airport as he disembarked from an airliner bound from Portugal to Belgium. He was traveling on a Canadian passport under the name of Ramon George Sneyd. Ray is accused of killing Dr. King in Memphis, Tennessee (→ 9).

50,000 march in capital for poor people

Marchers cool off in the reflecting pool in front of the Lincoln Memorial.

June 25. Pleading for deliverance from poverty and discrimination, over 50,000 people marched a mile in the hot, humid Washington D.C. sun earlier this week. At first, the crowd respected the wishes of Rev. Ralph Abernathy and other march organizers by remaining peaceful. Abernathy denounced violence as a means for change. The U.S. government "believes in firepower, and those who believe in violence should join the Army and follow them. But Ralph Abernathy will rely on soul power," he declared to the people.

However, by week's end, hundreds staying in the wood shanty community called "Resurrection City" grew angry. Vandalism disrupted what had been a peaceful assembly. Troops were called to the area and Abernathy was arrested. Today, the minister pleaded "no contest" to charges of unlawful assembly. Regardless, march leaders agreed, light was shed on the masses living in abject poverty and shackled by discrimination (→ 7/22).

Warhol is shot by actress he hired

June 3. The founder of S.C.U.M. (Society for Cutting Up Men) shot artist Andy Warhol this afternoon. The woman, Valeria Solanis, had placed an ad for her organization in a newspaper. Warhol read it and, thinking it a joke, hired her to act in his surreal films. Miss Solanis shot Warhol because, she said, he refused to film a script she wrote.

Warhol was on the phone at his New York studio when Solanis fired two bullets in his chest and abdomen. He is now in a hospital.

Warhol's pop posters of soup cans and Marilyn Monroe have established his reputation as one of the most avant of the avant garde. Three years ago, he started concentrating on films featuring nudity, profanity and boredom. The motion picture "I, a Man" featured the 28-year-old Miss Solanis.

Helen Keller's life in the spotlight ends

June 1. Shifting shadows of leaves upon a bedroom wall was the only sight Helen Keller could recollect. Deaf and blind since 18 months of age, Miss Keller led a life of astonishing accomplishment. She died in her sleep this afternoon in Westport, Conn. She was 87 years old.

If the debilitating fever had never struck her, Helen Keller might have grown up to be a Southern belle in the Scarlett O'Hara tradition. She was feisty and rebellious, an unkempt girl of six when her first teacher, Miss Anne Sullivan, met her at her family's Alabama plantation. A few months and fistfights later, the girl was signing with her fingers and reading a little Braille.

Miss Keller graduated from Radcliffe cum laude. She learned to speak, ride horses, waltz, loved German and Greek, and inspired us all.

1968

JULY

Su	Mo	Tu	We	Th	Fr	Sa
	1	2	3	4	5	6
7	8	9	10	11	12	13
14	15	16	17	18	19	20
21	22	23	24	25	26	27
28	29	30	31			

1. Moscow: 36 nations sign nuclear non-proliferation treaty (→ 8/12).

2. Soviets release U.S. airliner with 214 G.I.'s.

6. Ali asks U.S. Supreme Court to void conviction for draft evasion (→ 2/16/70).

7. New York: Communist Party names black woman Charlene Mitchell for president (→ 8/5).

8. Paris: Armed police remove 17 demonstrators from Univ. of Paris Medical School (→ 10/8).

10. Boston: Dr. Spock and three others get two years for counseling draft evasion (→ 8/26).

13. Britain: Gary Player wins British Open golf title.

15. Moscow: Commercial flights to U.S. begin.

15. Prague demands revisions of Warsaw Pact to provide more equality for members (→ 20).

17. Miami: Natl. Airlines DC-8 with 64 passengers hijacked to Cuba (→ 11/23).

17. Iraq: Rightist army officers oust Pres. Arif, call for liberation of Palestine (→ 8/4).

20. Honolulu: LBJ assures Pres. Thieu U.S. will pursue Vietnam War at present pace (→ 8/10).

20. Prague: Czech leaders reject Soviet call for Moscow parley (→ 30).

21. Dutch racer Jan Janssen wins Tour de France.

22. Memphis: James Earl Ray pleads not guilty to murdering Martin Luther King (→ 25).

23. Algiers: Algerians detain 21 Israelis on hijacked El Al jet (→ 27).

25. Cleveland: Mayor Carl Stokes orders National Guard back to slum areas (→ 9/8).

27. Algeria releases ten of 21 Israelis on hijacked jet (→ 8/31).

29. Rome: Papal Encyclical bans artificial birth control (→ 8/22).

DEATHS

21. Ruth St. Denis, modern dance pioneer (*1/20/1878).

28. Otto Hahn, German physicist, pioneer in nuclear fission (*3/8/1879).

Billie Jean wins 3rd Wimbledon title

July 6. The tennis version of perpetual motion, little Billie Jean King, raced to her third straight Wimbledon championship today. She thus became the first woman to win the title three times since Maureen Connolly achieved the feat in 1952-54. The feisty 24-year-old Californian, who won as an amateur in 1966-67, put away Judy Tegart in the final. She also combined with Rosie Casals to win the women's doubles. Mrs. King's aggressiveness is changing women's tennis. In the all-Australian men's doubles final, John Newcombe and Tony Roche outlasted Ken Rosewall and Fred Stolle in five sets.

King's volley, devastating this week.

Soviets, Czechs talk as army builds up

July 30. An unprecedented meeting of Soviet bloc leaders broke up today in a small town in eastern Czechoslovakia as the Soviet Union massed more troops in Poland and East Germany. From the terse communique issued at the end of the meeting in Cierna, it was apparent that Kremlin leaders made little headway in their effort to convince Alexander Dubcek to abandon his democratic experiment in Czechoslovakia. All but two members of the Soviet Politburo attended the conference. They were led by Communist Party chief Leonid Brezhnev, Premier Aleksei Kosygin and President Nikolai Podgorny.

Two fresh Soviet divisions have been dispatched to the Czech border, and they seem ready for combat. They are equipped with tanks, artillery and rockets (→ 8/21).

1968

AUGUST

Su	Mo	Tu	We	Th	Fr	Sa
				1	2	3
4	5	6	7	8	9	10
11	12	13	14	15	16	17
18	19	20	21	22	23	24
25	26	27	28	29	30	31

2. L.A.: Sirhan pleads not guilty to RFK murder (→ 1/7/69).

2. Mariner 6 data show Mars atmosphere much different than earth (→ 9/22).

2. Manila: Earthquake strikes, killing at least 400.

4. Jordan: Israeli jets attack alleged terrorist center (→ 9/4).

5. Miami: Ronald Reagan joins presidential race (→ 8).

5. Spain suspends civil rights in Basque province (→ 12/30/70).

9. Rhodesia: High court validates nation's legal status despite British opinion (→ 10/13).

10. Washington: Sen. McGovern to run for presidency (→ 20).

10. Vietnam: Eight G.I.'s killed in strafing error by U.S. (→ 19).

12. Texas: LBJ to let Bikinians return to island (→ 24).

14. India: Week-long flood death toll reaches 1,000.

15. Nigeria turns down Red Cross plan to airlift food to starving Biafrans (→ 18).

16. Washington: Dwight Eisenhower has seventh heart attack.

19. Detroit: LBJ rules out further de-escalation during his term unless Hanoi joins in (→ 9/14).

20. Chicago: Gov. Shapiro calls Natl. Guard for protection at Democratic Convention (→ 28).

21. Soviets and four Warsaw Pact nations invade Czechoslovakia (→ 22).

22. Bogota: Paul VI is first pope to visit S. America (→ 6/10/69).

23. Moscow: Czech Pres. Svoboda arrives for talks (→ 9/1).

24. Pacific: France explodes her first H-bomb (→ 9/3).

26. Natl. Student Assn. reports 221 major college protests since start of year in U.S. (→ 10/23).

27. New York: SEC accuses Merrill Lynch of insider trading.

28. Chicago: 178 arrested as police battle protesters (→ 29).

28. Guatemala: U.S. Ambassador John Gordon Mein slain in ambush.

30. Chicago: Police raid offices of Sen. McCarthy (→ 9/17).

Soviet tanks invade defiant Prague

One Soviet tank, decorated angrily with a swastika, succumbed to the fierce Czech desire for self-determination.

Aug 22. Words could not convince Alexander Dubcek to abandon his liberal experiment in Czechoslovakia. Tonight, Soviet tanks are patrolling Prague, and angry Czechs are fighting back with guns, sticks and even their bare hands. They managed to set some of the Soviet tanks and munitions trucks on fire. Explosions are rattling the previously quiet Czech capital.

Several hundred thousand Soviet troops crossed the border into Czechoslovakia Tuesday night. Czechs were astounded. The troops, commanded by the Soviet Vice Minister of Defense, General Ivan Pavlovsky, came from the Soviet Union, Poland, Hungary, Bulgaria and East Germany. At first, there was little resistance as the troops entered Czechoslovakia from all directions. Weapons and soldiers streamed into Prague in a massive airlift. The skies of the capital were filled with the roar of Soviet planes.

Fighting erupted when the Soviets tried to storm the national radio station in Prague. Thirty Czechs were killed; more than 300 were injured. As the station fell to the Soviets, a Czech announcer urged residents of the city to remain loyal to Communist Party leader Dubcek and President Ludvik Svoboda. "These may be the last reports you will hear," the announcer said, "because the technical facilities in our hands are insufficient." A short while later, the transmitter went dead. Czechs turned to underground radios for the latest information.

Rude Pravo, the official newspaper of the Czech Communist Party, reported that Dubcek and other top officials were whisked away in an armored car, presumably for more arm-twisting by Soviet officials. Their location is unknown. Earlier, the Central Committee offices on the Vitava River were surrounded by Soviet tanks and paratroopers as Dubcek held a strategy session with his leadership and demanded the withdrawal of Soviet troops. There is no indication that Dubcek is ready to heed Soviet demands to abandon his democratic reforms or crack down on the press.

A series of Eastern bloc leaders tried and failed to convince Dubcek to do just that. Over the past two weeks, he was visited by Tito of Yugoslavia, Walter Ulbricht of East Germany and Nicolae Ceaucescu of Rumania (→ 23).

Sticks, stones and determination seem to be no match for Soviet armor. Resistance continues, as Dubcek meets with leaders of the Eastern bloc.

Police battle mobs as Democrats meet

Aug 29. Divisions over the Vietnam War exploded in Chicago tonight as demonstrators were bludgeoned, beaten and maced outside the convention center where Hubert Humphrey was nominated for president. Humphrey won on a plank supporting the war, but his candidacy may have been mortally wounded by what Senator Ribicoff called Mayor Daley's "gestapo tactics" against the protesters.

The most violent rioting erupted when hundreds of policemen, brandishing night sticks, charged as organizers tried to lead a march out of Grant Park to the convention center four miles away. Amid the tear gas and blood, over 100 were injured, including children, the elderly and members of the press who were watching when police turned on them.

The strong-arm tactics spilled into the convention hall itself as two candidates were dragged from the floor, and CBS correspondent Mike Wallace was punched in the face by a guard. One delegate interrupted the proceedings by seizing a microphone and asking if "Mayor Daley can be compelled to end the police state of terror."

Vice President Humphrey's nomination victory over Eugene McCarthy and George McGovern signalled a defeat of the minority plank, which called for an immediate halt to the bombing of North Vietnam. Pierre Salinger drew a roar of applause earlier in the evening when he said Robert Kennedy would have supported the minority plank and called the majority position indistinguishable from the Republican platform. Missouri Gov. Hearnes countered that the peace plank would "jeopardize the lives of American servicemen in Vietnam." Millions of Americans witnessed the turmoil in the streets and on the convention floor on TV (→ 30).

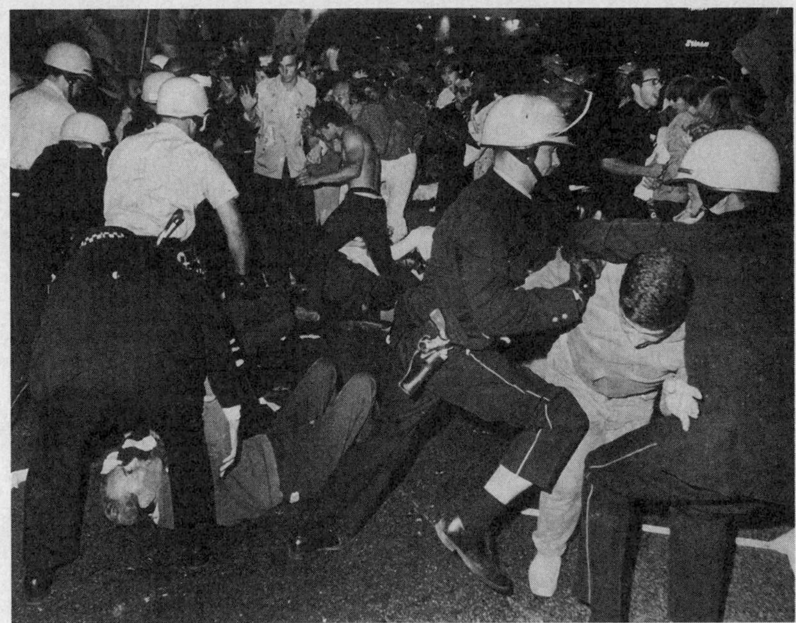

As cameras roll, protesters battle to escape the clubs of Daley's riot police.

Humphrey, chosen amid chaos.

Republicans name Nixon and Agnew

Aug 8. Richard M. Nixon, the "old pro" of the Republican Party, was nominated for president today on the first ballot, and, to the dismay of some supporters, chose Governor Spiro T. Agnew of Maryland as his vice-presidential running mate.

In an address to the cheering delegates at the GOP convention in Miami Beach, Nixon pledged that his "first priority foreign policy objective" would be "to bring an honorable end to the war in Vietnam." He also promised a tough crackdown on crime.

Taking note of the battle over the nomination of Governor Agnew, he said it had been a healthy thing for the party and that Republicans now "stand united before the nation."

Earlier in the day, as the Nixon choice for vice president was made public, there was grumbling by many delegates, particularly those in the moderate wing of the party and from big urban states, who felt that a Southern-oriented ticket could not win this fall. Despite their misgivings, Governor Agnew won 1,128 votes to just 186 for Governor George Romney of Michigan.

Nixon is only the eighth man ever nominated by the Republicans after having lost a presidential election. He was narrowly defeated in 1960 by John F. Kennedy (→ 10).

El Al jet hijacked to Algeria, later released

Aug 31. The tense drama is over: Algerian hijackers have released the 12 remaining hostages aboard the Israeli airliner seized on July 23. The terrorists allowed a French crew to return the $7.5 million El Al Airlines plane to Rome, where it will be inspected for damages and then flown back to Tel Aviv.

The scheduled Rome-Tel Aviv flight was taken over by Arab nationalists and forced to land in Algiers. The hijackers, calling themselves the Popular Front for the Liberation of Palestine, immediately released passengers of various nationalities but detained 21 Israeli passengers and crew. They demanded the release of several Palestinian commandos held by Israel since the Arab-Israeli War of 1967. They also claimed that El Al was responsible for running weapons and mercenaries to Israel.

The Tel Aviv government quickly denounced the action as "airborne piracy" and demanded that the Algerian government pressure the terrorists to give up. Algerian officials denied suggestions that they were involved in the hijacking. The Red Cross in Rome accepted the task of negotiating for the release of the hostages; today, Israel thanked them for their efforts.

Pilot Oded Abarbanall, after reaching safety, told of the abuse and horror his captors inflicted. "For 40 days we enjoyed no political or human rights." he said. "Without being military men, we were treated like war prisoners."

Biafra turns down Nigeria's peace program

Aug 18. As 1,000 people met in prayer before the United Nations yesterday as a plea for member nations to move food to Biafra's starving children, no progress is reported in the Addis Ababa peace talks between warring Nigeria and secessionist Biafra, slowly being starved into submission by Nigeria's food blockade.

While recent Nigerian terms seem more conciliatory than formerly, they call for the disarming of the Biafran army and a repudiation of Biafra's independence proclamation of May 1967. Biafra, previously Nigeria's Eastern region, insists that only autonomy can save it from more of the Nigerian massacres that led it to secede in the first place (→ 9/29).

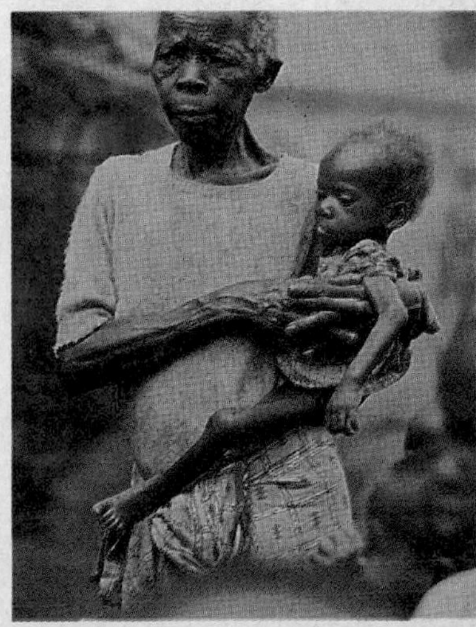

The pressure of civil war led Nigeria to turn down a Red Cross plan to airlift food to famine-torn Biafra.

1968

SEPTEMBER

Su	Mo	Tu	We	Th	Fr	Sa
1	2	3	4	5	6	7
8	9	10	11	12	13	14
15	16	17	18	19	20	21
22	23	24	25	26	27	28
29	30					

1. Iran: Earthquake in northwest kills at least 8,000.

1. Prague: Czech party, defiant, adds liberal leaders (→ 7).

3. Bikini Atoll: Nine native men return to ex-atom test site (→ 3/14/69).

4. Tel Aviv: Bomb blasts stir mob attack on Arabs (→ 11/2).

6. Swaziland gains independence from Britain.

7. Belgrade: Yugoslav and Italian Communist leaders meet to discuss Prague invasion (→ 10).

10. Illinois: 300 black students arrested in protest at Univ. of Illinois (→ 11/13).

10. Prague: Czech govt. issues proclamation assuring protection of individual rights (→ 13).

11. France: 95 die as French jet burns, falls into Mediterranean.

14. Vietnam: 400 Viet Cong killed in 24-hour battle (→ 11/1).

17. Texas: American Party nominates George Wallace for president (→ 11/6).

19. Mexico City: Army seizes Natl. Univ. to end student protests; 18 killed (→ 22).

19. Prague: Czech Foreign Minister Jiri Halek resigns over Soviet demands (→ 25).

21. New York: 150 militant students halt registration at Columbia University (→ 10/23).

22. Mexico City: Hundreds arrested as police put down student demonstrations (→ 30).

22. Soviets recover lunar spacecraft Zond 5 after landing in Indian Ocean (→ 10/22).

25. Bonn: Chancellor Kiesinger urges defense build-up in wake of Prague invasion (→ 10/4).

26. Portugal: Marcelo Caetano replaces Salazar, in coma for ten days, as premier.

29. Nigeria: Red Cross DC-4 crashes, killing 55 Nigerian soldiers (→ 1/11/69).

30. Mexico City: Troops evacuate campus of National University (→ 10/3).

DEATH

19. Chester Floyd Carlson, U.S. inventor of Xerox (*2/8/1906).

Ashe first black male to win big tennis title

Ashe on way to win at 1st U.S. Open.

Sept 9. Arthur Ashe has broken a color barrier in sports. The young Army Lieutenant became the first black male to win a major tennis tournament when he captured the United States Open championship.

The 25-year-old officer served a total of 26 aces in defeating Tom Okker of the Netherlands in the inaugural of the tourney at Forest Hills, New York. As an amateur, Ashe was ineligible to collect the $14,000 first prize in the $100,00 event, richest ever in tennis.

The slim, serious Ashe grew up in a middle-class area of Richmond, Va., the son of a park attendant. He won a scholarship to UCLA, where he was given the job of tending the tennis courts. Ashe continued his winnings ways and on August 25 won the United States amateur title. Althea Gibson, a product of Harlem, was the first black woman ever to win major titles, including the prestigious Wimbledon.

As Czechs give in, Soviet troops leave

Sept 13. Alexander Dubcek has found it very difficult to argue with Soviet tanks. The defiance of the Czech Communist Party chief has ebbed, and he now realizes he has no choice but to capitulate to the Soviets and curtail his democratic experiment. The Soviets have assured him that they will withdraw many of their troops from Czechoslovakia. Most units have already left Prague and other large cities.

Dubcek's acquiescence has been reluctant and gradual. At the beginning of the month, the party was still keeping its distance from Moscow. Until recently, its only concession was the admission of two orthodox Communists (→ 19).

Sept 9. Caroline Kennedy, daughter of the late President, today in Virginia handed over the nuclear-powered aircraft carrier John F. Kennedy, largest in the world, to the United States Navy.

Placido Domingo makes debut at Met

Sept 29. Spanish tenor Placido Domingo's Metropolitan Opera debut was moved up by four days when a hoarse throat forced Franco Corelli to drop out of last night's "Adriana Lecouvreur" less than an hour before curtain time. Domingo received the call at 7:20 at his home in Teaneck, New Jersey, and 8 p.m. found him at the Met, quickly dressing and preparing. Domingo was to have made his Met debut in the same opera, but a different role. The evening found him in fine voice—fresh, clear, more lustrous than on previous city appearances—and in all a commendable partner for Miss Renata Tebaldi, who was also in good voice.

Greek colonels get 91.9 percent vote

Sept 29. The ruling military junta in Greece solidified its position and expanded its powers in a new constitutional referendum that was approved overwhelmingly. The referendum, written by the government of Prime Minister Papadopoulos, virtually guts the powers of the Parliament. The controversial measure was approved by nearly 92 percent of the voters. More than 20 percent of the electorate opted to abstain from the voting (→ 10/21).

Huey Newton found guilty in shooting

Panthers protest outside courthouse.

Sept 8. Huey Newton, leader of the Black Panther Party, was convicted today on charges of voluntary manslaughter in the death of John Frey, an Oakland policeman. Later this month, the 26-year-old black activist will be sentenced; he faces two to 15 years in prison. Two other charges, kidnapping and assault, were dropped.

The verdict was considered by the prosecution a defeat. However, defense attorney Charles Garry failed to see any victory. "I am prepared to take (this case) to the highest court in the land," he said. "We are tremendously disappointed. The verdict makes no sense."

The case has received national attention; many activists feel the Oakland police engage in brutality toward blacks. A "Free Huey" movement was generated by Newton's supporters (→ 10).

Sept 14. Denny McLain of Detroit wins his 30th this year, first to do so since Dizzy Dean in 1934.

1968

OCTOBER

Su	Mo	Tu	We	Th	Fr	Sa
		1	2	3	4	5
6	7	8	9	10	11	12
13	14	15	16	17	18	19
20	21	22	23	24	25	26
29	28	29	30	31		

2. St. Louis: Bob Gibson sets World Series record with 17 strikeouts in opener (→ 10).

3. Mexico City: Deaths put at 49 as troops fire on students.

4. Cambodia admits Viet Cong use country for sanctuary (→ 3/13/70).

5. New York: Panel on Columbia Univ. riots says police used excessive force (→ 23).

8. France: Faure plan to decentralize university system passed in Natl. Assembly (→ 4/19/69).

9. New York: Norton Simon pays $1.55 mil. for a Renoir, record for Impressionist work.

10. St. Louis: Detroit Tigers become World Series champs, beating Cardinals 4-1 in final game.

12. Mexico City: 100,000 attend opening of Olympics (→ 14).

12. Panama: Bloodless coup ousts Pres. Arias (→ 12/16/69).

13. Gibraltar: British-Rhodesian talks end in failure (→ 3/1/70).

14. Mexico: Jim Hines, Randy Matson win first gold medals for U.S. (→ 15).

15. Mexico: Al Oerter sets record, winning fourth consecutive gold in discus (→ 18).

18. Mexico: Tommie Smith and John Carlos ousted for raising fists in black power salute while getting medals (→ 19).

19. Mexico: Bill Toomey wins gold in decathlon (→ 20).

20. Mexico: Dick Fosbury wins gold in high jump with Fosbury flop.

21. U.S. resumes arms to Greece after 17-month ban (→ 4/15/70).

22. Atlantic: Apollo 7 splashes down after "perfect mission" (→ 11/18).

23. California: Students seize office building on Berkeley campus (→ 2/13/69).

28. Prague: Tens of thousands of Czechs rally to protest Soviet occupation (→ 11/7).

DEATHS

1. Marcel Duchamp, French painter (*7/28/1887).

11. George White, Broadway producer, director (*1890).

Army in power in China

The jubilant images of revolutionary optimism should fade from view in China.

Oct 31. With the Chinese Communist Party shattered from top to bottom, the army is firmly in control in China. After two and a half years, Mao's Cultural Revolution is winding down, although it will take years for the people to recover.

Mao's campaign to purge his enemies and renew revolutionary zeal led to such widespread chaos and violence that the army was the only force capable of restoring order. Many persons have died at the hands of wild, vicious Red Guards.

Addressing Red Guard leaders in July, Mao expressed what he could no longer hide. "You have let me down," he said, "and moreover, you have disappointed the workers, peasants and soldiers of China."

Czechs ending reforms; Red troops stay

Oct 4. Alexander Dubcek flew back from Moscow to Prague tonight a defeated man. Under pressure from the Soviets, the Czech Communist Party leader agreed to shelve his democratic reforms and toe Moscow's inflexible line. Dubcek agreed with leaders at the Kremlin to outlaw all other political parties, eliminate liberals from the party and the government and subject newspapers, radio and television to strict controls. To add insult to injury, Soviet troops will be stationed indefinitely inside Czech borders. Most of them will apparently be posted along the German frontier. The agreement will be clearly spelled out in a new treaty that Czech Premier Oldrich Cernik told reporters should be signed within the next few days (→ 28).

Jackie weds Greek millionaire Onassis

Newlyweds Ari and Jackie.

Oct 20. For Greeks, rain on a wedding day is good luck. Luckily for the former Jacqueline Kennedy, today it poured. On the island of Skorpios the 39-year-old widow of John F. Kennedy wed Aristotle Onassis, shipping magnate. Onassis claims to be 62 years old; his passport says 68. The couple will divide their time between New York, Athens, Paris, Montevideo, Monte Carlo and the Greek islands.

Fortas ends fight to head high court

Oct 10. To halt what he called "destructive and extreme assaults upon the court," Associate Justice Abe Fortas has abandoned his fight to become chief justice of the United States. Fortras' October 2 withdrawal left President Johnson with the opportunity to select another appointee to the chief justice seat, left empty by Earl Warren's resignation. However, LBJ announced today that he would allow the next President to submit a nominee to the Senate.

Fortas pulled out after supporters of his nomination failed to stave off a filibuster by his opponents in the Senate. The balloting was shy by 14 votes of the two-thirds majority needed to cut off debate. Because Congress plans to adjourn for the year in a week or so, the vote to continue debate was considered a final blow to Fortas.

The associate justice was accused of lacking judical propriety because he accepted a $15,000 lecturer's fee, and because he continued to advise Johnson while serving on the high bench. Republicans also criticized him for voting with the liberal Warren Court on such issues as obscenity and criminal defendants' rights (→ 5/15/69).

Oct 3. Yippie leader Jerry Rubin arrives at HUAC's inquiry into the August riots with a toy M-16 and a red, blue and yellow cape resembling the Viet Cong flag.

1968 Mexico

Oct 27. The Olympics in Mexico City survived student riots, the banning of black militant demonstrations and other obstacles before settling down to another tour de force for the United States.

American athletes won 45 gold, 28 silver and 34 bronze medals. The Soviet Union collected 30 gold medals. American men set 11 Olympic and three world swimming records while women from the United States broke 12 Olympic and two world records in 14 water events.

The United States continued its domination of basketball but this time against stiff odds. For one reason or another—some in black protest—such stars as Alvin Hayes, Westley Unseld and Bob Lanier were missing from the team.

George Foreman, a black heavyweight from Houston, Texas, won the boxing gold medal with a knockout of Russian Ionas Chepulis.

There were two stunning track and field performances by Americans. Bob Beamon and Lee Evans amazed the crowd with breakthroughs that were likened to the first four-minute mile and the first 17-foot pole vault.

Evans posted a time of 0:43.8 in the 400-meter run, a fraction under the world record, and Beamon flew 29 feet, 2.5 inches in the long jump, almost two feet beyond the world mark.

Evans and two other Americans who finished second and third in the 400, Larry James and Ron Freeman, wore black berets at the award ceremony in a black power protest, but they avoided the official wrath incurred by two teammates.

Tommie Smith and John Carlos, gold and bronze medalists in the 200-meter sprint, were suspended from the Games and expelled from the Olympic village for using the victory celebration as a black power vehicle. They wore black scarves and black gloves and raised their clenched fists in the black power salute as the American national anthem was played. They were protesting the treatment of blacks in the United States.

On the lighter side was the advent of the "Fosbury Flop," an unorthodox style of high-jumping that enabled Dick Fosbury of Oregon State University to beat Russia's Valeri Brummel for the title. Fosbury twisted his body over the crossbar and flopped over backwards, landing safely on his neck.

However, the American coach issued a warning against imitating the new style. "Kids imitate champions and if they try to imitate Fosbury," he remarked, "he will wipe out an entire generation of high jumpers because they all will have broken necks."

Men Athletics

100 M Dash			
1.	Him Hines	USA	9,9
2.	Lennox Miller	JAM	10,0
3.	Charlie Green	USA	10,0
200 M Dash			
1.	Tommy Smith	USA	19,8
2.	Peter Norman	AUS	20,8
3.	John Carlos	USA	20,0
400 M Run			
1.	Lee Evans	USA	43,8
2.	Larry James	USA	43,9
3.	Ronald Freeman	USA	44,4
800 M Run			
1.	Ralph Doubell	AUS	1:44,3
2.	Wilson Kiprugut	KEN	1:44,5
3.	Thomas Farrell	USA	1:45,4
1500 M Run			
1.	Kipchoge Keino	KEN	3:34,9
2.	Jim Ryun	USA	3:37,8
3.	Bodo Tummler	FRG	3:39,0
5000 M Run			
1.	Mohamed Gammoudi	TUN	14:05,0
2.	Kipchoge Keino	KEN	14:05,2
3.	Naftali Temu	KEN	14:06,4
10,000 M Run			
1.	Naftali Temu	KEN	29:27,4
2.	Mamo Wolde	ETH	29:28,0
3.	Mohamed Gammoudi	TUN	29:34,2
Marathon			
1.	Mamo Wolde	ETH	2:20:26,4
2.	Kenji Kimihara	JAP	2:23:31,0
3.	Michael Ryan	NZL	2:23:45,0
110 M Hurdles			
1.	Willie Davenport	USA	13,3
2.	Ervin Hall	USA	13,4
3.	Eddy Ottoz	ITA	13,4
400 M Hurdles			
1.	David Hemery	GBR	48,1
2.	Gerhard Hennige	FRG	49,0
3.	John Sherwood	GBR	49,0
3000 M Steeplechase			
1.	Amos Biwott	KEN	8:51,0
2.	Benjamin Kogo	KEN	8:51,6
3.	George Young	USA	8:51,8
400 M Relay			
1.	USA 38,2	(Charles Greene, Melvin Pender, Ronnie-Ray Smith, Jim Hines)	
2.	CUB 38,3	(Hermes Ramirez, Juan Morales, Pablo Montes, Enrique Figuerola)	
3.	FRA 38,4	(Gerard Fenouil, Jocelyn Delcour, Claude Piquemal, Roger Bambuck)	
1600 M Relay			
1.	USA 2:56,1	(Vincent Matthews, Ronald Freeman, Larry James, Lee Evans)	
2.	KEN 2:59,6	(Daniel Rudisha, Munyoro Vyamau, Natali Bon, Charles Asati)	
3.	FRG 3:00,5	(Helmar Muller, Manfred Kinder, Gerhard Hennige, Martin Jellinghaus)	
20 km Walk			
1.	Vladimir Golubnichy	URS	1:33:58,4
2.	Jose Pedraza	MEX	1:34:00,0
3.	Nicolai Smaga	URS	1:34:03,0
50 km Walk			
1.	Christoph Hohne	GDR	4:20:13,6
2.	Antal Kiss	HUN	4:30:17,0
3.	Larry Young	USA	4:31:55,4
High Jump			
1.	Dick Fosbury	USA	2,24
2.	Ed Caruthers	USA	2,22
3.	Valentin Gavrilov	URS	2,20
Pole Vault			
1.	Bob Seagren	USA	5,40
2.	Claus Schiprowski	FRG	5,40
3.	Wolfgang Nordwig	GDR	5,40
Long Jump			
1.	Bob Beamon	USA	8,90
2.	Klaus Beer	GDR	8,19
3.	Ralph Boston	USA	8,60

Bob Beamon soars to victory in the long jump, apparently over the heads of several Olympic officials.

Triple Jump			
1.	Viktor Saneiev	URS	17,39
2.	Nelson Prudencio	BRE	17,27
3.	Giuseppe Gentile	ITA	17,27
Discus Throw			
1.	Alfred Oerter	USA	64,78
2.	Logher Milde	GDR	63,08
3.	Lazar Lovasz	HUN	69,78
Shotput			
1.	Randy Matson	USA	20,54
2.	George Woods	USA	20,12
3.	Eduard Guchchine	URS	20,09
Hammer Throw			
1.	Gyula Zsivotsky	HUN	73,36
2.	Romuald Klim	URS	73,28
3.	Lazar Lovasz	HUN	69,78
Javelin			
1.	Janis Lusis	URS	90,10
2.	Jorma Kinnunen	FIN	88,58
3.	Gergely Kulcsar	HUN	87,06
Decathlon			
1.	Bill Thomey	USA	8193
2.	Hans-Joachim Walde	FRG	8111
3.	Kurt Bendlin	FRG	8064

Women Athletics

100 M Dash			
1.	Wyomia Tyus	USA	11,0
2.	Barbara Ferrell	USA	11,1
1.	Irana Szewinska-Kirzenstein	POL	11,1
200 M Dash			
1.	Irena Szewinska-Kirzenstein	POL	22,5
2.	Raelene Boyle	AUS	22,7
3.	Jennifer Lamy	AUS	22,8
400 M Run			
1.	Colette Besson	FRA	52,0
2.	Lillian Board	GBR	52,1
3.	Natalya Pechenkina	URS	52,2
800 M Run			
1.	Madeleine Manning	USA	2:00,9
2.	Ilenea Silai	ROM	2:02,5
3.	Maria Gommers	HOL	2:02,6
80 M Hurdles			
1.	Maureen Caird	AUS	10,3
2.	Pam Kilborn	AUS	10,4
3.	Chil Cheng	TAI	10,4
400 M Relay			
1.	USA 42,8	(Barbara Ferrell, Margaret Bailes, Mildrette Netter, Wyomia Tyus)	
2.	CUB 43,3	(Marlene Elejado, Fulgencia Romay, Violetta Quesada, Migueline Cobian)	
3.	URS 43,4	(Ludmila Zharkova, Galina Burkharina, Vera Popkova, Ludmila Samotesove)	
High Jump			
1.	Miloslava Reskova	TCH	1,82
2.	Antonina Okorokova	URS	1,80
3.	Valentina Kozyr	URS	1,80
Long Jump			
1.	Viorica Viscopoleanu	ROM	6,82
2.	Shelia Sherwood	GBR	6,68
3.	Tatiana Talycheva	URS	6,66
Shotput			
1.	Margitta Gummel-Helmboldt	GDR	19,61
2.	Maritta Lange	GDR	18,78
3.	Nadejda Tchichova	URS	18,19
Discus Throw			
1.	Lia Manoliu	ROM	58,28
2.	Liesel Westermann	FRG	57,76
3.	Jolan Kleiber	HUN	54,90
Javelin			
1.	Angela Nemeth	HUN	60,36
2.	Mihaela Penes	ROM	59,92
3.	Eva Janko	AUT	58,04
Pentathlon			
1.	Ingrid Becker	FRG	
2.	Liese Prokop	AUT	
3.	Annamaria Toth	HUN	

Men Swimming

100 M Freestyle			
1.	Michael Wenden	AUS	52,2
2.	Ken Walsh	USA	52,8
3.	Mark Spitz	USA	53,0
200 M Freestyle			
1.	Michael Wenden	AUS	1:55,2
2.	Donald Schollander	USA	1:55,8
3.	John Nelson	USA	1:58,1
400 M Freestyle			
1.	Michael Burton	USA	4:09,0
2.	Ralph Hutton	CAN	4:11.07
3.	Alain Mosconi	FRA	4:13,3
1500 M Freestyle			
1.	Michael Burton	USA	16:38,9
2.	John Kinsella	USA	16:57,3
3.	Gregory Brough	AUS	17:04,7
100 M Backstroke			
1.	Ronald Matthes	GDR	58,7
2.	Charles Hickcox	USA	1:00,2
3.	Ron Mills	USA	1:00,5
200 M Backstroke			
1.	Roland Matthes	GDR	2:09,6
2.	Mitchel Ivay	USA	2:10,6
3.	Jack Horsley	USA	2:10,9
100 M Breaststroke			
1.	Donald Mac Kenzie	USA	1:07,7
2.	Vladimir Kosinsky	URS	1:08,0
3.	Nicolai Pankin	URS	1:08,0
200 M Breaststroke			
1.	Felipe Munoz	MEX	2:28,7
2.	Vladimir Kosinsky	URS	2:29,2
3.	Brian Job	USA	2:29,9
100 M Butterfly Stroke			
1.	Douglas Russell	USA	55,9
2.	Mark Spitz	USA	56,4
3.	Ross Wales	USA	57,2
200 M Butterfly Stroke			
1.	Carl Robie	USA	2:08,7
2.	Martin Woodroffe	GBR	2:09,0
3.	John Ferris	USA	2:09,3
400 M Medley			
1.	Charles Hickcox	USA	2:12,0
2.	Gregory Buckingham	USA	2:13,0
3.	John Ferris	USA	2:13.3
800 M Medley			
1.	Charles Hickcox	USA	4:48,4
2.	Gary Hall	USA	4:48,7
3.	Michael Holthaus	FRG	4:51,4
400 M Freestyle Relay			
1.	USA 3:31,7	(Zachary Zorn, Stephen Rerych, Mark Spitz, Kenneth Walsh)	
2.	URS 3:34,2	(Semyon Belitz-Geiman, Viktor Mazanov, Georgy Kulikov, Leonid Ilitchev)	
3.	AUS 3:34,7	(Gregory Rogers, Robert Windle, Robert Cusack, Michael Wenden)	
800 M Relay			
1.	USA 7:52,3	(John Nelson, Stephen Rerych, Mark Spitz, Don Schollander)	
2.	AUS 7:53,7	(Gregory Rogers, Graham White, Robert Windle, Michael Wenden)	
3.	URS 8:01,6	(Vladimir Bure, Semyon Belitz-Geiman, Georgy Kulikov, Leonid Ilitchev)	
400 M Medley Relay			
1.	USA 3:54,9	(Charles Hickcox, Donald Mac Kenzie, Douglas Russell, Kenneth Walsh)	
2.	GBR 3:57,5	(Roland Matthes, Egon Henninger, Horst-Günther Gregor, Frand Wiegand)	
3.	URS 4:00,7	(Yuri Gromak, Vladimir Kosinsky, Vladimir Nemchilov, Leonid Ilitchev)	
Springboard Diving			
1.	Bernie Wrightson	USA	170,15
2.	Klaus Dibiasi	ITA	159,74
3.	James Henry	USA	158,09
High Diving			
1.	Klaus Dibiasi	ITA	164,18
2.	Alvaro Gaxiola	MEX	154,49
3.	Edwin Young	USA	153,93
Water-Polo			
1.	Yugoslavia		
2.	Soviet Union		
3.	Hunary		

Women Swimming

100 M Freestyle			
1.	Jan Henne	USA	1:00,3
2.	Susan Pedersen	USA	1:00,3
3.	Linda Gustavson	USA	1:00,3
200 M Freestyle			
1.	Debbie Meyer	USA	2:10,5
2.	Jan Henne	USA	2:11,0
3.	Jane Barkman	USA	2:11,3
400 M Freestyle			
1.	Debbie Meyer	USA	4:31,8
2.	Linda Gustavson	USA	4:35,5
3.	Karen Moras	AUS	4:37,0
800 M Freestyle			
1.	Debbie Meyer	USA	9:24,0
2.	Pamela Kruse	USA	9:35,7
3.	Maria Teresa Ramirez	MEX	9:38,5
100 M Breaststroke			
1.	Djurdjica Bjedov	YUG	1:15,8
2.	Galina Prozumenschikova	URS	1:15,9
3.	Sharon Wichman	USA	1:16,1
200 M Breaststroke			
1.	Sharon Wichman	USA	2:44,4
2.	Djurdica Bjedov	YUG	2:46,4
3.	Galina Prozumenschikova	URS	2:47,0
100 M Backstroke			
1.	Kaye Hall	USA	1:06,2
2.	Elaine Tanner	CAN	1:06,7
3.	Jane Swagarty	USA	1:08,1
200 M Backstroke			
1.	Pokey Watson	USA	2:24,8
2.	Elaine Tanner	CAN	2:27,4
3.	Kaye Hall	USA	2:28,9
100 M Butterfly Stroke			
1.	Lynette Mac Clements	AUS	1:05,5
2.	Ellie Daniel	USA	1:05,8
3.	Susan Shields	USA	1:06,2
200 M Butterfly Stroke			
1.	Ada Kok	HOL	2:24,7
2.	Helga Lindner	GDR	2:24,8
3.	Ellie Daniels	USA	2:25,9
200 M Medley			
1.	Claudia Kob	USA	2:24,7
2.	Susan Pedersen	USA	2:28,8
3.	Jan Henne	USA	2:31,4
400 M Medley			
1.	Claudia Kob	USA	5:08,5
2.	Lynn Vidali	USA	5:22,2
3.	Sabine Steinbach	GDR	5:25,3
400 M Freestyle Relay			
1.	USA 4:02,5	(Jane Barkman, Linda Gustavson, Susan Pedersen, Jan Henne)	
2.	GDR 4:05,7	(Gabriele Wetzko, Roswsitha Krause, Uta Schmuck, Martina Grunert)	
3.	CAN 4:07,2	(Angela Coughlaw, Marilyn Corson, Elaine Tanner, Marion Lay)	
400 M Medly Relay			
1.	USA 4:23,3	(Kaye Hall, Catie Ball, Ellie Daniel, Susan Pedersen)	
2.	AUS 4:30,0	(Lynette Watson, Lynette Mac Clements, Judy Playfair, Janet Steinbeck)	
3.	FRG 4:36,4	(Angelika Kraus, Ute Frommater, Keite Hustede, Heidi Reineck)	
Springboard Diving			
1.	Sue Gossick	USA	150,77
2.	Tamara Pogozheva	URS	145,30
3.	Keals O'Sullivan	USA	145,23
High Diving			
1.	Milena Duchkova	TCH	109,59
2.	Natalia Lobanova	URS	105,14
3.	Ann Peterson	USA	101,11

Boxing

Light Flyweight		
1.	Francisco Rodriguez	VEN
2.	Yong-ju Jee	KOR
3.	Harlan Marbley	USA
3.	Hubert Skrypezak	POL
Flyweight		
1.	Ricardo Delgado	MEX
2.	Artur Olech	POL
3.	Servilio Olivera	BRE
3.	Lee Rwabwago	UGA

FOR ABBREVIATIONS SEE TABLE OF CONTENTS

1968 Mexico

CHART

Weightlifting

			2 Arm Press	2 Arm Snatch	2 Arm Clean & Jerk	Total
	Bantamweight					
1.	Mohamad Nasiri	USA	112,5	105,0	150,0	367,5
2.	Imre Földi	HUN	122,5	105,0	140,0	367,5
3.	Henryk Trebicki	POL	150,0	107,5	135,0	357,5
	Featherweight					
1.	Yoshinobu Miyake	JAP	122,5	117,5	152,5	392,5
2.	Dito Shanidze	URS	120,0	117,5	150,0	387,5
3.	Yoshiyuki Miyake	JAP	122,5	115,0	147,5	385,0
	Lightweight					
1.	Waldemar Baszanovski	POL	135,0	135,0	167,5	437,5
2.	Parviz Jalayer	IRA	125,0	132,5	165,0	422,5
3.	Marian Zielinski	POL	135,0	125,0	160,0	420,0
	Middleweight					
1.	Viktor Kurentsov	URS	152,5	135,0	187,5	475,0
2.	Masashi Ohuchi	JAP	140,0	140,0	175,0	455,0
3.	Karoly Bakos	HUN	137,5	132,5	170,0	440,0
	Light Heavyweight					
1.	Boris Selitsky	URS	150,0	147,5	187,5	485,0
2.	Viktor Belaiev	URS	152,5	147,5	185,0	485,0
3.	Norbert Ozimek	POL	150,0	140,0	182,5	472,5
	Middle Heavyweight					
1.	Kanto Kangasniemi	FIN	172,5	157,5	187,5	571,5
2.	Jan Talts	URS	160,0	150,0	197,5	507,5
3.	Marek Golab	POL	165,0	145,0	185,0	495,0
	Heavyweight					
1.	Leonid Jabotinsky	URS	200,0	170,0	202,5	572,5
2.	Serge Reding	BEL	185,0	147,5	212,5	555,0
3.	Joe Dube	USA	200,0	145,0	210,0	555,0

Bantamweight
1. Valeri Sokolov URS
2. Eridari Mukwanga UGA
3. Eiji Morioka JAP
3. Kyou-Chull Chang KOR

Featherweight
1. Antonio Roldan MEX
2. Albert Robinson USA
3. Philipp Waruingi KEN
3. Ivan Michailov BUL

Lightweight
1. Ronald Harris USA
2. Jozef Grudzien POL
3. Calistrat Cutov ROM
3. Zvonimir Vujin YUG

Light Welterweight
1. Jerzy Kulej POL
2. Enrique Requel Feros CUB
3. Arto Nilsson FIN
4. James Wallington USA

Welterweight
1. Manfred Wolke GDR
2. Joseph Bessala CAM
3. Vladimir Mussalinov URS
3. Mario Guilloti ARG

Light Middleweight
1. Boris Lagutin URS
2. Rolando Garbey CUB
3. John Baldwin USA
3. Günther Meier FRG

Middleweight
1. Christopher Finnegan GBR
2. Alexei Kiselev URS
3. Agustin Zaragoza MEX
3. Alfred Jones USA

Light Heavyweight
1. Dan Pozniak URS
2. Ion Monea ROM
3. Georgy Stankov BUL
3. Stanislav Dragan POL

Heavyweight
1. George Foreman USA
2. Ionas Chepulis URS
3. Giogio Bambini ITA
3. Joaquin Rocha MEX

Greco Roman Wrestling

Flyweight
1. Petar Kirov BUL
2. Vladimir Bakulin URS
3. Miroslav Zeman TCH

Bantamweight
1. Janos Varga HUN
2. Ion Baciu ROM
3. Ivan Kochergin URS

Featherweight
1. Roman Rurua URS
2. Hideo Fujimoto JAP
3. Simeon Popescu ROM

Lightweight
1. Munji Mumemura JAP
2. Stevan Horvath YUG
3. Petros Galaktopoulos GRE

Welterweight
1. Rudolf Vesper GDR
2. Daniel Robin FRA
3. Karoly Bajko HUN

Middleweight
1. Lothar Metz GDR
2. Valentin Olemik URS
3. Branislav Simie YUG

Light Heavyweight
1. Boyan Radev BUL
2. Nicolai Yakovenko URS
3. Nicolae Martinescu ROM

Heavyweight
1. Istvan Kozma HUN
2. Anatoly Roshin URS
3. Petr Kment TCH

Freestyle Wrestling

Flyweight
1. Shigeo Nakata JAP
2. Richard Sanders USA
3. Surenjav Sukhbaatar MON

Bantamweight
1. Yojiro Uetake JAP
2. Donald Behm USA
3. Abutaleb Gorgori IRA

Featherweight
1. Masaaki Kaneko JAP
2. Enyu Todorov BUL
3. Shamseddin Seyed-Abassy IRA

Lightweight
1. Abdollah Movahed Ardabili IRA
2. Enyu Valtchev BUL
3. Sereeter Danzandarjae MON

Welterweight
1. Mahmut Atalay TUR
2. Daniel Robin FRA
3. Dagvasuren Purev MON

Middleweight
1. Boris Gurevitch URS
2. Munkbat Jigjid MON
3. Prodan Gardehev BUL

Light Heavyweight
1. Ahmet Ayik TUR
2. Schota Lomidze URS
3. Joszef Csatari HUN

Heavyweight
1. Aleksandr Medved URS
2. Osman Douraliev BUL
3. Wilfried Dietrich FRG

Men Fencing

Foil Individual
1. Ion Drimba ROM 4
2. Dr Jeno Kamuti HUN 3
3. Daniel Revenu FRA 3

Foil Team
1. France
2. Soviet Union
3. Poland

Epee Individual
1. Gyozo Kulcsar HUN 1 + 2
2. Grigory Kriss URS 4/10/8
3. Gianluigi Saccaro ITA 4/10/7

Epee Team
1. Hungary
2. Soviet Union
3. Poland

Sabre Individual
1. Jerzy Pawlowski POL 4 + 1
2. Mark Rakita URS 4
3. Tibor Pezsa HUN 3/16

Sabre Team
1. Soviet Union
2. Italy
3. Hungary

Women Fencing

Foil Individual
1. Yelena Novikova URS 4
2. Pilar Roldan MEX 3/14
3. Ildiko Ujlaki-Retjö HUN 3/16

Foil Team
1. Soviet Union
2. Hungary
3. Romania

Modern Pentathlon

Individual
1. Björn Ferm SWE
2. Andras Balezo HUN
3. Pavel Lednev URS

Team
1. Hungary
2. Soviet Union
3. France

Men Canoeing

Kayak-1 1000 M
1. Mihaly Hesz HUN 4:02,63
2. Aleksandr Chaparenko URS 4:03,58
3. Erik Hansen DEN 4:04,39

Kayak-2 1000 M
1. Soviet Union 3:37,54
2. Hungary 3:38,44
3. Austria 3:40,71

Kayak-4 1000 M
1. Norway 3:14,38
2. Romania 3:14,81
3. Hungary 3:15,10

Canadian-1 1000 M
1. Tibor Tatai HUN 4:36,14
2. Detlef Lewe FRG 4:38,31
3. Vitaly Galkov URS 4:40,42

Canadian-2 2000 M
1. Romania 4:07,18
2. Hungary 4:08,77
3. Soviet Union 4:11,30

Women Canoeing

Kayak-1 500 M
1. Ludmila Pinaeva Khedosyuk URS 2:11,09
2. Renate Breuer FRG 2:12,71
3. Viorica Dimitru ROM 2:13,22

Rowing

Single Scull
1. Henri Jean Wienese HOL 7:47,80
2. Jochen Meissner FRG 7:52,00
3. Alberto Demiddi ARG 7:57,19

Double Sculls
1. Soviet Union 6:51,82
2. Netherlands 6:52,80
3. USA 6:54,21

Pair Oars without Coxswain
1. German Democratic Republic 7:26,56
2. USA 7:26,71
3. Denmark 7:31,84

Pair Oars with Coxswain
1. Italy 8:04,81
2. Netherlands 8:06,80
3. Denmark 8:08,07

Four Oars without Coxswain
1. German Democratic Republic 6:39,18
2. Hungary 6:41,64
3. Italy 6:44,01

Four Oars with Coxswain
1. New Zealand 6:45,62
2. German Democratic Republic 6:48,20
3. Switzerland 6:49,04

Eight Oars
1. German Federal Republic 6:07,00
2. Australia 6:07,98
3. Soviet Union 6:09,11

Yachting

Monotype Finn Class
1. Valentin Mankin URS 11,7
2. Hubert Raudaschi AUT 53,4
3. Fabio Albarelli ITA 55,1

Star Class
1. USA 14,4
2. Norway 43,7
3. Italy 44,7

Flying Dutchman
1. Great Britain 3.0
2. German Federal Republic 43,7
3. Brazil 48,4

Dragon Class
1. USA 6,0
2. Denmark 26,4
3. German Democratic Republic 32,7

5,50 M (1952, 1956, 1960, 1964, 1968 only)
1. Sweden 8,0
2. Switzerland 32,0
3. Great Britain 39,8

Cycling

Individual Road Race
1. Pierfranco Vianelli ITA 4:41:25,24
2. Leif Mortensen DEN 4:42:49,71
3. Gösta Petterson SWE 4:43:15,24

100 km Time Trial Team
1. Netherlands 2:07:49,06
2. Sweden 2:09:26,60
3. Italy 2:10:18,74

Men Volleyball

1. Soviet Union
2. Japan
3. Czechoslovakia

Tommy Smith and John Carlos, first and third in the 200-meters, were suspended for accepting medals with the black power salute.

100 M Time Trial
1. Pierre Trentin FRA 1:03,91
2. Niels-Christian Fredborg DEN 1:04,61
3. Janusz Kierzkowski POL 1:04,63

1000 M Sprint
1. Daniel Morelon FRA 10,68
2. Giordano Turrini ITA
3. Pierre Trentin FRA

2000 M Tandem
1. France 9,83
2. Netherlands
3. Belgium

Individual Road Race 400 M
1. Daniel Rebillard FRA 4:41,71
2. Mogens Frey Jensen DEN 4:42,43
3. Xaver Kurmann SUI 4:39,42

The scores of the race held to determine 3rd place were better than those of the initial race.

Team Pursuit Race 4000 M
1. Denmark 4:22,44
2. German Federal Republic 4:18,94
3. Italy 4:18,35

The West German team was the winner but was at first disqualified for having been pushed at the start and then placed second.

The scores of the race held to determine third place were better than those of the initial race.

Equestrian Sports

All-around Individual Competition
1. Jean-Jacques Guyon FRA
2. Derek Althusen GBR
3. Michael Page USA

All-around Team Competition
1. Great Britain -175,93
2. USA -245,87
3. Australia -331,26

Individual Dressage
1. Ivan Kizimov URS 908 + 664-1 572
2 Josef Neckermann FRG 948 + 598-1 546
3. Dr. Reiner Klimke FRG 896 + 641-1 537

Team Dressage
1. German Federal Republic 2699
2. Soviet Union 2657
3. Switzerland 2547

Grand Prix Jumping Individual
1. William Steinkraus USA -4
2. Marion Coakes GBR -8
3. David Broome GBR -12/0/35,3

Grand Prix Jumping Team
1. Canada -102,75
2. France -110,50
3. German Federal Republic -117,25

Shooting

Full-Bore Rifle, 300 M, 3 positions
1. Gary Anderson USA 1157
2. Vladimir Kornev URS 1151
3. Kurt Muller SUI 1148

Small-Bore Rifle, 50 M prone
1. Jan Kurka TCH 598
2. Laszlo Hammerl HUN 598
3. Ian Ballinger NZL 597

Small-Bore Rifle Combined, 3 positions
1. Bernd Klingner FRG 1157
2. John Writer USA 1156
3. Vitaly Parkhimovich URS 1154

Rapid-Fire Pistol
1. Josef Zapedski POL 593
2. Marcel Rosca ROM 591/147
3. Renart Suleimanov URS 591/146/148

Free Pistol, 50 M
1. Grigory Kossykh URS 526/30
2. Heinz Mertel FRG 526/26
3. Harald Vollmar GDR 560

Clay Pigeon
1. John Robert Braithwaite GBR 198
2. Thomas Garrigus USA 196/25/25
3. Kurt Czekalla GDR 196/25/23

Skeet
1. Yevgeny Petrov URS 198/25
2. Romano Garagnani ITA 198/24/25
3. Konrad Wirmhier FRG 198/24/23

Men Gymnastics

All-around Individual
1. Sawao Kato JAP 115,90
2. Mikhail Voronine URS 115,85
3. Akinori Nakayama JAP 115,65

All-around Team Competition
1. Japan 575,90
2. Soviet Union 571,10
3. German Democratic Republic 557,15

Parallel Bars
1. Akinori Nakayama JAP 19,475
2. Mikhail Voronine URS 19,425
3. Vladimir Klimenko URS 19,225

Floor Exercise
1. Sawao Kato JAP 19,475
2. Akinori Nakayama JAP 19,400
3. Takeshi Kato JAP 19,275

Horse Vault
1. Mikhail Voronine URS 19,000
2. Yukio Endo JAP 18,950
3. Sergei Diomidov URS 18,925

Sidehorse
1. Miroslav Cerar YUG 19,325
2. Olli Eino Laiho FIN 19,225
3. Mikhail Voronine URS 19,200

Horizontal Bar
1. Mikhail Voronine URS 19,550
2. Akinori Nakayama JAP 19,550
3. Eizo Kenmotsu JAP 19,375

Flying Rings
1. Akinori Nakayama URS 19,450
2. Mikhail Voronine JAP 19,325
3. Sawao Kato JAP 19,225

Women Gymnastics

All-around Individual Competition
1. Vera Caslavska TCH 78,25
2. Zinaida Vononina URS 76,85
3. Natalia Koutchinskaia URS 19,425

All-around Team Competition
1. Soviet Union 382,85
2. Czechoslovakia 382,20
3. German Democratic Republic 379,10

Uneven Bars
1. Vera Caslavska TCH 19,650
2. Karin Janz GDR 19,500
3. Zinaida URS 19,425

Floor Exercise
1. Larissa Petrik URS 19,675
2. Vera Caslavska TCH 19,675
3. Natalia Koutchinskaia URS 19,650

Horse Vault
1. Vera Caslavska TCH 19,775
2. Erika Zuchold GDR 19,625
3. Zinaida Voronina URS 19,500

Beam
1. Natalia Koutchinskaia URS 19,650
2. Vera Caslavska TCH 19,575
3. Larissa Petrik URS 19,250

Basketball
1. USA
2. Yugoslavia
3. Soviet Union

Field Hockey
1. Pakistan
2. Australia
3. India

Women Volleyball
1. Soviet Union
2. Japan
3. Poland

Soccer
1. Hungary
2. Bulgaria
3. Japan

NOVEMBER

Su	Mo	Tu	We	Th	Fr	Sa
					1	2
3	4	5	6	7	8	9
10	11	12	13	14	15	16
17	18	19	20	21	22	23
24	25	26	27	28	29	30

2. Jerusalem: Israel seizes 15 Arab shops (→ 12/7).

4. U.S.: Pan Am begins first helicopter service from JFK to Newark.

4. W. Berlin: 150 hurt as police battle students protesting disbarment of their defense lawyer.

5. U.S.: Protesters demonstrate nationwide on election day (→ 6).

7. Prague: Crowds burn Soviet flags and battle police (→ 17).

8. London: Bruce Reynolds, last in great train robbery, arrested after five-year search.

12. U.S. Supreme Court voids Arkansas law banning teaching of evolution in public schools.

13. Miss.: Judge fines KKK and three men $1 mil. for slaying of black (→ 27).

14. New Haven: Yale announces plan to go co-ed.

17. Prague: Students occupy university buildings to support progressive reform (→ 1/16/69).

18. Soviets recover Zond 6 spacecraft after flight around moon (→ 12/27).

20. Bonn: Leaders of ten non-Communist European nations meet on currency crisis (→ 25).

21. Nigeria signs $140 mil. credit accord with Soviets (→ 1/11/69).

23. Miami: Four seize U.S. jet with 87 passengers and force it to Cuba (→ 1/8/69).

24. Bronx: Co-op city dedicated, largest U.S. housing cooperative.

25. European currency crisis subsiding following strong restrictive measures.

27. California: Warrant issued for arrest of Eldridge Cleaver for parole violation (→ 3/11/69).

28. New York: Jimi Hendrix attracts huge crowd to Philharmonic Hall.

DEATHS

1. George Papandreou, three-time premier of Greece (*2/13/1888).

6. Charles Munch, American conductor (*9/26/1891).

25. Upton Sinclair, American novelist, "The Jungle" (*9/20/1878).

Nixon and Agnew team wins close election

Agnew and Nixon, the winning team, despite 11th-hour push by Humphrey.

Nov 6. Richard Milhous Nixon was elected President of the United States yesterday, succeeding in a quest in which he had failed just eight years ago.

The California Republican and his vice-presidential running mate, Governor Spiro T. Agnew of Maryland, edged out the Democratic ticket headed by Vice President Hubert H. Humphrey by more than 500,000 votes. It was a remarkable political comeback for Nixon, a former Vice President in the Eisenhower years, who lost his first presidential bid in 1960 to John Fitzgerald Kennedy. Nixon suffered a further blow in 1962 when he lost his bid to become governor of California (→ 1/20/69).

First black woman is elected to House

Nov 5. For the first time in American history a black female will serve in the House of Representatives. Democrat Shirley Chisholm, who campaigned as an "unbought and unbossed" candidate, defeated James Farmer in the 12th Congressional District in Brooklyn, New York. The district includes one of the nation's worst ghettos.

Chisholm (right) with Julian Bond.

Beate Klarsfeld calls Kiesinger Nazi

Nov 7. Beate Klarsfeld, 29, hit Chancellor Kurt Georg Kiesinger in the left eye shortly before noon today at the closing of his Christian Democratic Union's national congress in West Berlin. The back-of-the-hand blow caused slight damage to the mucous membrane lining the inner surface of the eyelid.

Mrs. Klarsfeld was dismissed two years ago as secretary of the French-West German youth service after she had published an article describing Kiesinger as a "Nazi" and "murderer." She is married to a Parisian employed by the Paris newspaper Combat. She provoked two other incidents in the last year, shouting "Nazi!" and "Criminal!" at Kiesinger in Bonn and Paris. The chancellor was a nominal member of the Nazi Party while working in the German Foreign Ministry during WWII. Mrs. Klarsfeld asserted that the reason for her action was his "continuing fascist attitude."

LBJ calls halt to bombing in Vietnam

Nov 1. President Johnson told the nation in a televised speech that he has ordered a stop to all American air, naval and artillery bombardments in North Vietnam, in hopes it will lead to progress at the Paris peace talks. LBJ said, "What we now expect—what we have a right to expect—are prompt, productive, serious and decisive negotiations in an atmosphere conducive to peace." In exchange for the bombing halt, Hanoi has agreed to allow the South Vietnamese government participation in Paris. Despite claims that Johnson acted to enhance Vice President Humphrey's election chances, many have hailed the move (→ 12/8).

TV viewers aghast: game cut for Heidi

Nov 17. A little Swiss ophan girl named Heidi manhandled two professional football teams and knocked them off television in millions of homes. NBC terminated its telecast of the Jets-Raider game to put on the heroine of the Johanna Spyri novel. There was one minute left in the game, with the outcome in doubt. Thousands of irate fans jammed NBC switchboards, causing one to break down. Those who couldn't get through called the Police Department or local newspapers. The network said it was sorry and it wouldn't happen again.

Join the Peace Corps.

1968

DECEMBER

Su	Mo	Tu	We	Th	Fr	Sa
1	2	3	4	5	6	7
8	9	10	11	12	13	14
15	16	17	18	19	20	21
22	23	24	25	26	27	28
29	30	31				

6. French Communists issue declaration asserting policy independence from Soviet Union.

7. Israel severely curbs travel by Israeli Arabs (→ 27).

8. Paris: Saigon V.P. Ky arrives for peace talks (→ 1/5/69).

10. Philadelphia: Frazier outpoints Oscar Bonavena to retain title held in 5 states (→ 2/16/70).

11. U.S. Dept. of Labor reports unemployment at 3.3%, lowest rate in 15 years.

16. Spain voids 1492 law expelling Jews.→

26. Australia: U.S. tennis team regains Davis Cup.

27. U.S. agrees to sell 50 F-4 Phantom jets to Israel (→ 28).

28. Beirut: Israel attacks airport, smashing 13 planes (→ 1/28/69).

DEATHS

9. Karl Barth, Swedish theologian (*9/10/1886).

11. Arthur Hays Sulzberger, N.Y. Times owner (*9/12/1891).

30. Trygve Lie, first secretary general of U.N. (*7/16/1896).

CULTURAL EVENTS, 1968

Literature: Jerzy Kosinski's "The Painted Bird"; Arthur Hailey's "Airport"; Tom Wolfe's "Electric Kool-Aid Acid Test"; John Updike's "Couples"; Kurt Vonnegut's "Welcome to the Monkey House."

Academia: Herbert Marcuse's "Psychoanalysis and Politics"; Will and Ariel Durant, Pulitzer for "The Story of Civilization"; Watson's "The Double Helix."

Music: Beatles' "Hey Jude"; Marvin Gaye's "I Heard it Through the Grapevine"; Otis Redding's "The Dock of the Bay"; Simon and Garfunkel's "Mrs. Robinson."

The Arts: Saarinen's Gateway Arch, St. Louis; "Dada, Surrealism and Their Heritage" exhibit, at MOMA in New York.

Film: "The Odd Couple," Lemmon and Matthau; "Funny Girl," Streisand; "The Lion in Winter," Hepburn and O'Toole; Kubrick's "2001: A Space Odyssey"; "Oliver!," Oscar.

First astronauts orbit moon, return safely

The Apollo 8 team, first astronauts ever to orbit the moon. Left to rt.: James A. Lovell, William Anders and Frank Borman, captain of the mission.

Dec 27. The three Apollo 8 astronauts have returned safely to earth after becoming the first men to orbit the moon. Launched from Cape Kennedy on December 21, astronauts James A. Lovell, William Anders and Frank Borman reached the moon on Christmas Eve, providing a moment of high emotion when they read verses from the Bible across the 250,000 miles of space separating earth from the moon.

In all, they made ten orbits of the moon before traveling back to a splashdown in the Pacific Ocean between Hawaii and Samoa. The most important parts of their mission were seen via direct television transmissions by people all over the world. Their feat was given added meaning by the recent successful lunar orbital flights by Zond spacecraft, which the Soviet Union say are trailblazers for a manned moon voyage. Apollo 8 keeps America's lunar plans on target (→ 1/9/69).

Frogmen board Apollo 8, afloat in the Pacific after splashdown.

Pueblo crew comes home from Korea

Dec 24. The families of the crew from the Navy ship Pueblo got the best Christmas present of all today when their husbands, sons and fathers were released from 11 months of captivity by the North Koreans. "They are heroes among heroes," said Rear Admiral Rosenberg, who nevertheless acknowledged that the crew would have to undergo an investigation into the seizure of their intelligence ship.

North Korea has insisted that the Pueblo was spying within their 12-mile territorial limit, and Commander Bucher of the Pueblo and several crew members later "confessed" to this. But after his release today, Bucher maintained that he had never been closer than 13 miles and was 15 miles out when the ship was seized.

More damaging than the "confessions" was the capture of sensitive surveillance and coding equipment which Bucher acknowledged they did not have time to destroy. Negotiations for the crew's release took place at Panmunjom, where the crew crossed the Bridge of No Return to freedom today (→ 1/23/69).

Popular Socialist Thomas is deceased

Dec 19. Norman M. Thomas, the social critic and six-time candidate for president on the Socialist Party ticket, died today at the age of 84.

Thomas began his public career in 1911, when he was ordained a Presbyterian minister and became a pastor of the East Harlem Church, a parish in one of the poorest sections of New York City. His work there convinced him that the problems of poverty, injustice and war could not be solved within the political status quo.

After resigning his ministry and joining the Socialist Party, Thomas ran for governor of New York, twice for mayor of New York City, and six times for the U.S. presidency. He was also Associate Editor of the weekly magazine The Nation, a leader of the League for Industrial Democracy, and one of the founders of the American Civil Liberties Union. ▷

Final journey for novelist John Steinbeck

Chronicler of the dispossessed.

Dec 20. "Man . . . grows beyond his work, walks up the stairs of his concepts, emerges ahead of his accomplishments." When John Steinbeck wrote this in "The Grapes of Wrath" (1939), was he thinking of himself? Perhaps not; but his novels, awakening Americans to the plight of immigrants and the restlessness of youth, rose above his initial hopes. If the man outpaced his accomplishments, he ascended to a lofty place indeed.

Steinbeck died today in New York City. He was 66 years old. Among his best-selling novels were "Of Mice and Men" (1937) "The Pearl" (1947) and "East of Eden" (1952). Many books were translated for stage and film. The writer earned a Pulitzer and Nobel Prize.

Steinbeck explored the country while centering most works on his native rural California. An ardent Democrat, he took his party's failure in the last election very hard. Still, in "America and the Americans," published in 1966, he expressed faith in the nation's future.

Tallulah, toast of 2 continents, is gone

Dec 12. Tallulah Bankhead was never at a loss for words, printable or unprintable. Friends and enemies could never find enough to say about her: tempestuous, tantalizing, talented, an Alabama beauty, aristocrat and actress. She triumphed in London, New York and Hollywood. Her finest hours were spent in Lillian Hellman's "The Little Foxes" on the stage and Hitchcock's "Lifeboat" on the screen. Today, she died.

Woman flouts rule of marrying rapist

Dec 4. Franca Viola did not wed the man who raped her, earning the wrath of her Sicilian village. The 20-year-old woman married instead an accountant who wooed her by respectable means. Italy's President Giuseppe Saragat was a happy witness at the wedding today. Sicilian custom dictates that rape dishonors a woman, rendering her unfit to wed any but the rapist. In Miss Viola's case, the offender was an admirer whom she had spurned.

On the eve of the Paris talks, the U.S. has halted attacks north of the DMZ. Above, some of the 536,000 G.I.'s enjoy a little holiday diversion.

Lots of beginners' luck in this year's movies

Hepburn in "The Lion in Winter."

Fledgling actors and directors seized their share of spoils in this year's films. The woman who may spoil others' chances of winning the Best Actress award next spring is Barbra Streisand. The 26-year-old stage performer makes her film debut in "Funny Girl," giving a tour de force as vaudevillian Fanny Brice. William Wyler directed.

Miss Streisand faces stiff competition from Katharine Hepburn in "The Lion in Winter." She plays Eleanor of Acquitaine, an ambitious Queen frequently imprisoned by her husband Henry II. Henry (Peter O'Toole) contemplates a successor, a touchy subject as he has three sons vying for the honor. "Lion" is only the second directing job for Anthony Harvey.

"The Thomas Crown Affair" is a classy caper starring Steve McQueen as a millionaire robber. Faye Dunaway is the insurance investigator leisurely tracking him down. Norman Jewison directed.

"Oliver!" features a bunch of boys who never saw a camera in their lives. Director Carol Reed manages them nicely, retelling Dickens' "Oliver Twist" with panache. "Consider Yourself" is among the musical's rousing tunes. Other young unknowns are in "Romeo and Juliet." Franco Zeffirelli cast two teens as the eternal duo. Nino Rota wrote the lovely musical score.

Paul Newman excels in his first directing job. "Rachel, Rachel" stars his wife, Joanne Woodward, as a spinster teacher trying to creep out of her fragile shell.

"Funny Girl" Barbra Streisand takes a bath in a first-rate musical.

Faye Dunaway and Steve McQueen star in "The Thomas Crown Affair."

Julie Nixon weds David Eisenhower

Dec 22. At a political function a decade ago, the families of Dwight D. Eisenhower and Richard Nixon were photographed on a balcony. Dwight David Eisenhower 2nd, the former President's grandson, and Julie Nixon, the President's younger daughter, were seen leaning over the balcony, ardently trying to get a good look at each other. They have plenty of time for that now. David and Julie, both 20, wed today at a New York church. Dr. Norman Vincent Peale performed the Dutch Reformed ceremony.

Spain voids law of 1492 banning Jews

Dec 16. Four hundred and seventy-six years ago, King Ferdinand and Queen Isabella banished Jews from Spain. Today, that order was rescinded. A gathering of 700 Spanish, Jewish and other officials heard the proclamation at the opening of a Madrid synagogue—the first built in Spain in 600 years. Dr. Solomon Gaon, a rabbi, said, "We witness a historic moment when past and present meet . . . May this mean the beginning of a new time of moral and spiritual progress for all the people of this land."

1969

JANUARY

Su	Mo	Tu	We	Th	Fr	Sa
			1	2	3	4
5	6	7	8	9	10	11
12	13	14	15	16	17	18
19	20	21	22	23	24	25
26	27	28	29	30	31	

1. Pasadena: Ohio State over U.S.C. 27-16 in Rose Bowl.

3. Washington: House seats Adam Clayton Powell, fines him $25,000 (→ 6/16).

4. Spain returns Ifni province to Morocco (→ 9/26).

5. New York: Nixon appoints Henry Cabot Lodge negotiator at Paris parley (→ 4/3).

6. U.S.: Presidential salary raised from $100,000 to $200,000.

7. L.A.: RFK murder trial opens, Sirhan Sirhan accused (→ 2/28).

7. California: Gov. Reagan asks Legislature to "drive criminal anarchists and latter-day Fascists" off campuses (→ 3/3/71).

8. Cuba: 81 Cubans shoot way past guards at Guantanamo base and fly to Florida (→ 19).

9. Washington: NASA picks Edwin Aldrin, Neil Armstrong for first moon landing (→ 10).

10. New York: Apollo 8 astronauts honored in ticker tape parade (→ 16).

12. London: Fighting breaks out as 5,000 protest racial violence.

14. Pacific: Blast on U.S. carrier Enterprise kills 24, injures 85.

15. Lebanon: Rashid Karami forms 16-man coalition Cabinet.

16. N.Y.: Ten paintings at Met defaced, including a Rembrandt.

16. Prague: Czech student Jan Palach immolates self to protest Soviet regime (→ 4/17).

17. U.S. accuses IBM of monopolizing computer market.

17. New York: Ex-McCarthy aide Roy Cohn indicted for bribery, conspiracy, extortion.

19. Paris: Viet Cong flag placed on steeple of Notre Dame.

25. New York: NASA unveils moon landing craft (→ 3/3).

26. Kenya: Police evict all 1,200 students at Nairobi University (→ 7/5).

26. California declared disaster area after two days of flooding and mud slides; at least 11 dead.

26. New York: LBJ sells rights to memoirs for $1.5 million.

31. New York: Marty Liquori wins Wanamaker Mile.

Pueblo captain admits signing confession

Commander Bucher leaves inquiry.

Jan 23. Commander Lloyd M. Bucher, captain of the intelligence ship Pueblo seized by North Korea a year ago, testified today he signed a confession that his ship was engaged in espionage to save the lives of the 82 surviving crew members.

In a choked and sobbing voice, the 41-year-old officer with 16 years of naval service told a Navy court of inquiry, "I was not prepared to see my crew shot." He described in detail how before signing the confession he had been beaten repeatedly by his North Korean interrogators and threatened with death.

Earlier, the court of five admirals had warned Bucher that he faced possible court-martial for surrendering his ship without offering resistance. He had testified that he surrendered the Pueblo without a fight "because it was nothing but a slaughter out there and I couldn't see killing the entire crew for no reason." He described how he had requested help but received no guidance from United States naval headquarters (→ 4/15).

Oil well blowout threatens Santa Barbara

Jan 28. Some of California's finest coastline was threatened with major pollution today when a well drilled from an offshore platform near Santa Barbara blew out, spewing thousands of gallons of oil into the ocean each hour. The blowout occurred at the Union Oil Company's platform A, about five miles offshore.

Geologists said the blowout apparently took place when the drill penetrated an underground fault, rupturing it and letting loose an underwater geyser of reddish-brown crude oil. A major oil slick has formed at the site of the blowout and is drifting toward beaches.

Union Oil immediately began efforts to contain the slick using plastic sea curtains floating on foam pillows. Ships also are being brought in to scoop up as much of the oil as possible, while efforts to seal the leaky well have also begun.

Ecologists say the blowout is reason to end oil production in the Santa Barbara Channel, where 14 firms have paid $603 million for leases, and to prompt passage of laws to combat pollution (→ 2/3).

Jan 12. Joe Namath (handing off to Emerson Boozer) led his Jets to the first AFL Super Bowl win, 16-7 over the heavily favored Baltimore Colts.

Starving Biafrans receive food gifts

Saving lives in Biafra.

Jan 11. Cartons and shopping bags of beans, rice and canned meat piled up on the steps of St. Patrick's Cathedral yesterday as thousands of New Yorkers donated food for the starving Biafrans. Mrs. Richard M. Nixon joined Archbishop Cooke, Senators Charles E. Goodell and Jacob K. Javits, and Mayor John V. Lindsay for a ceremony where 500 people gathered in the bitter cold.

Mrs. Nixon's appearance was a "humanitarian gesture," not an expression of the President-elect's attitude toward the Nigerian-Biafran dispute. Abie Nathan, an Israeli jet pilot, has arranged in the Netherlands for the charter of the Norwegian ship Forra to take the food from Brooklyn to the Portuguese island of Sao Tome off the African coast for airlifting to Biafra. Volunteers are loading trucks provided by transport firms (→ 2/7).

Satevepost, aged 141, comes to end

Jan 10. The final issue of the Saturday Evening Post eased off the presses tonight, marking the end of the 141-year-old magazine. At its height in the late 50's, circulation was over six million. This year, the number was a little over half that. Norman Rockwell covers set the journal's tone: folksy, rural, not too highbrow—or so non-readers believed. But over the decades, subscribers read riveting works by Edgar Allan Poe, Jack London, Gertrude Stein, Saul Bellow, John Updike, Graham Greene and others. ▷

Cuban skyjackings becoming epidemic

Jan 19. In addition to serving coffee, tea and milk, stewardess Joan Tognola had to act as interpreter today for a Hispanic man who pressed a grenade to her back. But Captain R.D. Smith, pilot of the Eastern Airlines flight to Miami, didn't need any translation of where the man wanted to go.

"Cuba, Cuba!" yelled the hijacker as he burst into the cockpit. This makes seven planes commandeered this month, including a second, Ecuadoran plane today. Hijackings have become so frequent that Cuban maps have become standard issue to pilots, and Miami airport officials have opened a hot line to Cuba.

All passengers have returned safely, but Captain Smith had to calm the hijacker down. "I don't want to die either" said the man as he strapped himself in for landing at Havana's airport (→ 9/19).

Communal violence rages in Ireland

Jan 4. Communal violence erupted again in Northern Ireland as Protestant militants stoned and harassed university students marching in support of voting rights for Catholics. As the four-day march from Belfast neared an end in Londonderry, 200 Protestants, wielding sticks and stones, charged the line of about 100 marchers, chasing them into the fields and beating them with sticks. By nightfall, 136 persons, including 26 policemen, had been treated for injuries.

The march, approved by British authorities, was conducted by students from Queens University in Belfast demanding "one man, one vote" in Ulster and abolishment of the property qualification for voting. The opposition to the civil rights march was led by the Rev. Ian Paisley, self-styled leader of the Free Presbyterian Church (→ 4/17).

Soviet astronauts link up spaceships

Jan 16. Two Soviet Soyuz spacecraft docked in orbit today and remained joined for four hours while cosmonauts transferred from one to another by taking a walk in space.

The linkup between Soyuz 4, with a one-man crew, and Soyuz 5, with three cosmonauts aboard, produced what the Soviet Union described as the "world's first experimental space station." The two spacecraft began their docking maneuver at 10:47 a.m. Moscow time and linked up less than an hour later. There was no internal passage between the two ships, so the astronauts went into space to transfer from one to the other. During the hour-long space walk, they also performed some assembly tasks and scientific experiments. Today's feat is regarded as a step toward establishment of a permanent manned space station by the Soviets (→ 25).

Iraqis kill nine Jews; U.S. cautions Israel

Jan 28. Following the recent execution by Iraq of nine Iraqi Jews charged with spying for Israel, the United States has urged Israel to refrain from retaliation. State Department officials are fearful of a move against the 20,000 Iraqi troops stationed in Jordan similar to that of last December when Israel was provoked into launching a series of heavy air strikes.

In Washington's view, such action would only ignite once again the Mideast tinderbox and worsen tensions at a time when Gunnar V. Jarring, United Nations representative in the Middle East, stands ready to resume his promotion of a peaceful settlement between the Israelis and the Arab nations. Iraq has announced more spy trials are in the offing. An Egyptian report of one in progress says the defendants spied for the CIA (→ 2/2).

Aborigine is chosen Aussie of the Year

Jan 18. For the first time, the honor of being named "Australian of the Year" has gone to a member of the aboriginal race that once populated the entire Australian continent and now survives in greatly reduced numbers, mostly in poverty. The title has been awarded to Lionel Rose, 20, the bantamweight boxing champion of the world, who fought his way to national adulation from squalid surroundings near Melbourne and won the world title last year from Masahiko Harada of Japan. Rose, who has won 32 of his 34 professional bouts, was also chosen "Fighter of the Year" by the World Boxing Council in 1968.

Bob Fosse directs Shirley MacLaine, who plays a soft-hearted prostitute in "Sweet Charity."

Former CIA chief Dulles is deceased

Jan 30. Allen W. Dulles, the man who oversaw many of America's postwar clandestine operations, died today at the age of 75. Like his older brother, former Secretary of State John Foster Dulles, he was a successful lawyer, diplomat and statesman. Yet, unlike his brother, he moved away from the public limelight and into the shadowy world of secret politics as Director of the Central Intelligence Agency.

In World War II, Dulles worked for the Office of Strategic Services. He organized an intelligence network in Switzerland, assisted the anti-Nazi German underground and was instrumental in the defeat of Nazi troops in Italy in 1945.

In 1953, President Eisenhower drew on Dulles' espionage expertise and appointed him CIA director. With John Foster constructing U.S. foreign policy aboveboard and Allen implementing it covertly, the brothers launched a fierce crusade against communism, which critics say helped propel the Cold War. Allen Dulles resigned in 1961 after the Bay of Pigs invasion of Cuba and other events revealed the controversial role of the CIA.

Use finally found for Maginot Line: Housing

Jan 2. Did you ever hanker to sink a bundle in a bunker? The French government is selling some 30-year-old forts for just a fraction of their original cost. The pillboxes and bunkers along the Maginot Line are going for $125 to $1,000.

The Maginot Line was a string of defenses set up near the German border, developed to keep the Nazis out. It did not. Because it is associated with national embarrassment, the French public is somewhat reluctant to buy the small, semi-subterranean edifices.

A spokesman for the Property Office, who in the past has made used prisons sound like choice real estate, said the forts might make fine vacation homes, adding "there are actually some nice views across the Rhine . . ."

Jan 20. Richard Nixon was sworn in today as anti-war protests made known the nature of his mandate. LBJ and Humphrey, toppled largely by opposition to the war, watched as the guard changed (→ 2/9).

1969

FEBRUARY

Su	Mo	Tu	We	Th	Fr	Sa
						1
2	3	4	5	6	7	8
9	10	11	12	13	14	15
16	17	18	19	20	21	22
23	24	25	26	27	28	

2. Israel: Police quell riot of Arab girls; 90 hurt (→ 3).

6. Lima: Peru announces seizure of all holdings of International Petroleum Company.

7. Biafra: Market struck by bombs; 200-300 killed (→ 5/29).

8. California: Oil leak causing huge spill is located and plugged (→ 18).

8. Boeing 747, largest commercial plane, makes first flight.

9. Washington: LBJ admits he failed to gain trust of youth.

10. New York: 14 dead, 68 hurt as city digs way out of biggest snowstorm in seven years.

12. Israel shoots down Syrian MIG-21 (→ 18).

17. Lima: Soviets and Peru sign first trade accord (→ 6/24).

18. California to sue federal govt. and Union Oil Co. for $1.6 billion in oil spill.

18. Zurich: Six on El Al jet wounded in Arab attack (→ 19).

19. Iraq: Seven executed as spies for Israel (→ 21).

20. Bucharest bars Warsaw Pact military maneuvers in Rumania.

21. Rome: Univ. of Rome closed in student unrest (→ 27).

22. Washington: Gallup Poll shows steady growth of isolationism in U.S. (→ 4/5).

25. London: Nixon meets with Queen Elizabeth (→ 27).

26. Detroit: G.M. recalls 4.9 million cars for defect check (→ 3/18).

27. Rome: Thousands of students, leftists protest as Nixon arrives (→ 28).

28. L.A.: Court refuses Sirhan Sirhan's request to be executed (→ 3/3).

DEATHS

14. Vito Genovese, American Mafia boss (*11/27/1897).

23. King Saud of Saudia Arabia (*1/15/1902).

25. Levi Eshkol, Israeli premier (*10/25/1895).

26. Karl Jaspers, German Existentialist philosopher (*2/23/1883).

Yasir Arafat leads Palestinian forces

Arafat wants Palestinian state.

Feb 3. The sound trouncing of the Arab world in the Six Day War did not convince Palestinian terror groups to renounce their claims on Palestine or abandon their attacks on Israel. But their hit and run attacks, launched mostly from Syria and Jordan, have not been unified, and the guerrillas lacked political clout. Today, they united under the umbrella of the Palestine Liberation Organization. At a Cairo conference, Yasir Arafat was acknowledged as leader of the PLO. One radical group, the Popular Front for the Liberation of Palestine, refused to support Arafat, who founded Al Fatah in 1963 (→ 12).

Bomb rips largest Jerusalem market

Feb 21. Bottles and canned goods flew like shrapnel today when a terrorist bomb ripped apart the rear of Jerusalem's largest supermarket, killing two Israelis. The blast came during the store's peak period, the hours before the Sabbath, as hundreds of customers did their weekend shopping. The attack follows by three days the machine-gunning by four Arab terrorists in Zurich of an El Al Boeing 720 on its way from Amsterdam to Tel Aviv. Six were wounded. The Popular Front for the Liberation of Palestine, based in Jordan, has claimed responsibility for that attack (→ 3/1).

Protesters face guardsmen at Wisconsin U.

Feb 13. Mention Wisconsin and most people think of cows, farming and quiet, but the idyllic vision was shattered by tear gas and bayonets today as 900 National Guardsmen moved to quell disturbances at the Univ. of Wisconsin at Madison.

The disruptions began last Friday after the administration agreed to include more black students and teachers in the university, but decided against amnesty for demonstrators. During the past week, roving bands of students moved from one building to another seeking to close classes and draw other students to their side.

This afternoon, troops with gas masks and night sticks waded into a crowd of 1,500 protesters who were trying to prevent students from entering buildings. About 1,000 more troops are due to arrive tomorrow. Madison Mayor Otto Fetge requested the National Guard when 600 local police complained of exhaustion after two straight days of guarding the 34,000-member campus. Guardsmen kept classes open today, but tonight 5,000 torch-bearing students marched on the Capitol five blocks away, yelling "on strike, shut em down!"

The administration blamed "white radicals" from Students for a Democratic Society for stirring up the unrest. A similar but more violent protest rocked the University of North Carolina today when 1,000 white and black students battled police over black rights. The melee ended after two hours, but 500 National Guardsmen are on alert at an armory (→ 22).

Karloff, sinister but kindly, is dead

Karloff, Frankenstein's better half.

Feb 3. Frankenstein, the boogey man, Dr. Jekyll and Mr. Hyde, the mummy and other ghouls are dead. Or rather, the gentle British actor who portrayed them all is gone. Boris Karloff was 81 years old.

Karloff, born William Pratt, was the son of a civil servant. He emigrated to Canada as a young man, where he drove a truck when stage work was hard to find. He made his film debut (in a small part) with Anna Pavlova in 1916. Karloff's role as the daisy-picking, murdering monster in "Frankenstein" (1931) made him a household name.

Strangely, in the 1930's Karloff played several Chinese criminals. One of his last projects was narrating an animated cartoon based on a Dr. Seuss story, "How the Grinch Stole Christmas."

All drilling halted at Santa Barbara

Feb 3. Oil companies have agreed to suspend drilling in the Santa Barbara Channel of California because of an oil slick that threatens the area's beaches, Secretary of the Interior Walter J. Hickel said today. Hickel said the suspension would continue "until it can be determined whether corrective measures are necessary." The Coast Guard said the oil slick, which is more than ten miles long, is being kept "under reasonable control" (→ 8).

Feb 28. President Nixon, on tour to greet the Allied heads of state, meets de Gaulle in Paris.

1969

MARCH

Su	Mo	Tu	We	Th	Fr	Sa
						1
2	3	4	5	6	7	8
9	10	11	12	13	14	15
16	17	18	19	20	21	22
23	24	25	26	27	28	29
30	31					

1. Florida: Mickey Mantle announces baseball retirement.

1. Cairo: Nasser predicts fourth war unless Israel withdraws from occupied territory (→ 9).

2. Siberia: Chinese, Soviets clash on border; 31 Soviets dead (→ 7).

3. L.A.: Sirhan Sirhan testifies he killed Robert Kennedy (→ 6).

3. Cape Kennedy: Apollo 9 launched in first test of lunar module (→ 13).

5. Gustav Heinemann elected West German pres. (→ 9/28).

6. L.A.: Sirhan Sirhan tells court he doesn't remember killing Robert Kennedy (→ 4/23).

7. Moscow: Windows of Chinese Embassy smashed in protest (→ 19).

9. Egypt: Israeli shell kills army chief Abdel Riad (→ 26).

14. Nixon asks Congress to approve new "Safeguard" ABM system (→ 6/17).

16. Venezuela: Over 150 die as jet crashes in suburb.

16. London: Coretta Scott King becomes first woman to speak from pulpit of St. Paul's.

18. Detroit: G.M. recalls 1.1 mil. cars for brake check (→ 4/7).

19. U.S.S.R.: Poet Yevgeny Yevtushenko denounces Mao (→ 29).

20. Washington: Sen. Edward Kennedy calls on U.S. to close bases in Taiwan (→ 9/15).

20. Egypt: Air crash kills 91.

22. Kentucky: UCLA wins NCAA basketball title.

22. Anguilla: Hundreds protest British invasion, block U.K. commissioner from office.

24. Washington: Nixon meets with Canadian Prime Minister Trudeau (→ 5/8/74).

26. Jordan: 18 killed, 25 wounded in Israeli air raid (→ 4/1).

31. Britain: George Harrison and wife fined $1,500 for possession of marijuana.

DEATHS

24. Joseph Kasavubu, Congolese independence leader (*1910).

25. Max Eastman, American leftist writer (*1/4/1883).

First flight of Concorde

The French-British Concorde noses its way into flight for the first time.

March 2. "Finally the big bird flies," the pilot said with a large smile creasing his face. "And I can say that it flies pretty well."

And what a bird! With its sharply pointed beak turned down to give a view of the runway, the sleek flying machine known as the Concorde jetted into the air in Toulouse, France, today on its maiden flight. It climbed abruptly as its French and British co-developers crossed their fingers, and smoke poured from its four Rolls-Royce-Olympus engines. Some 28 minutes later, the triangular airplane glided successfully back to earth.

Eventually, the British and French hope the Concorde will cross the Atlantic in three and a half hours at twice the speed of sound. Today, pilot Andre Turcat was content with a top speed of just under 300 miles per hour.

Airline companies are taking a wait-and-see attitude toward the Concorde. Development costs have already quadrupled the budget of $500 million. Critics also worry that the Concorde is too heavy to take a full load of passengers across the Atlantic. If these problems can be overcome, service could start as early as 1974 (→ 10/1).

Career of triumph ends for Eisenhower

March 28. Dwight David Eisenhower, who led the Allies to victory in World War II, and in 1952 was elected 34th President of the United States, died today at Walter Reed General Hospital in Washington, D.C. The former five-star General, who suffered from chronic coronary disease, was 78 years old.

After a three-day state funeral, Eisenhower will be interred at a cemetery in his native Kansas. President Nixon, who served Ike as Vice President, said, "General Eisenhower held a unique place in America's history, and in its heart, and in the hearts of people the world over."

Dwight David Eisenhower.

Israel's Golda Meir is nation's Premier

March 17. Golda Meir, a woman who once taught public school in Milwaukee, Wisconsin, was sworn in as Israel's fourth Premier today. In her formal speech, the 71-year-old Mrs. Meir said she would push for "face-to-face talks" with the Arabs, adding that as long as they thought "there might be a solution without negotiations, the solution is only obstructed." The approval of her coalition Cabinet saw one surprise as David Ben Gurion abstained, claiming the new members included people who had "split the nation." Mrs. Meir was also opposed by Agudat Israel, a religious party whose adherents counsel Jewish men not to look at "strange women" (→ 10/3).

Barnard co-eds try to integrate dorms

March 9. A sleep-in is underway tonight at Columbia University. Nearly 100 Barnard women seeking co-educational living have settled into dormitory rooms vacated by male students. They plan to remain for three days. "When you isolate people you only accentuate the differences," said one Barnard student, explaining her wish to share living quarters with the men. "Psychologically and educationally, it's a more natural way to live," another added. They will be taking single rooms. The men will use separate bathrooms. The women's presence has not been sanctioned by either Barnard or Columbia, but their actions do not violate visiting rules (→ 6/25/70).

Ray pleads guilty; jailed for 99 years

March 11. James Earl Ray pleaded guilty to killing Rev. Dr. Martin Luther King Jr. and today he arrived at the Tennessee State Prison, where he will serve a 99-year jail sentence. While prosecution and defense attorneys agreed there was no evidence linking Ray to a conspiracy plot, the assassin refused to accept their findings. "Your honor," Ray said after entering his plea, "the only thing I have to say is that I can't agree with Mr. Clark." He was referring to former Attorney General Ramsay Clark, who, with FBI chief J. Edgar Hoover, concluded after one investigation that Ray had acted alone. Ray's testimony, it seems, will perpetuate conspiracy speculation (→ 4/2).

1969

APRIL

Su	Mo	Tu	We	Th	Fr	Sa
		1	2	3	4	5
6	7	8	9	10	11	12
13	14	15	16	17	18	19
20	21	22	23	24	25	26
27	28	29	30			

1. N.Y.: U.N. censures Israel for air attacks on Jordan (→ 8).

2. New York: 21 Black Panthers indicted for plot to kill policemen (→ 19).

3. Vietnam: U.S. deaths, now 33,641, pass Korea total (→ 24).

3. Ottawa: Trudeau announces plan to reduce Canadian NATO forces (→ 9/16/74).

5. New York: Thousands march against Vietnam War down Avenue of the Americas (→ 10).

5. Four Britons reach North Pole after 407-day dog sled journey (→ 5/30).

7. Britain: Rolls-Royce recalls at least 5,000 cars (→ 8/13/70).

8. Washington: Nixon confers with King Hussein on Mideast settlement (→ 24).

10. Mass.: 400 police remove 300 students from occupied buildings at Harvard (→ 14).

12. Washington: Nixon cuts $4 billion from budget.

14. Chicago: 13 found guilty of violating police order during '68 Democratic convention (→ 29).

15. North Korea says it downed U.S. reconnaissance plane with crew of 31 (→ 21).

17. Prague: Alexander Dubcek replaced by Gustav Husak as sec. of Czech Party (→ 6/20).

17. London: 21-year-old Irish student activist elected to House of Commons (→ 20).

18. Houston: Astronauts simulate moon activity (→ 5/18).

19. France exiles student leader Daniel Cohn-Bendit to West Germany (→ 28).

20. Belfast: British send 1,000 troops as bus station and nine post offices fire-bombed (→ 22).

21. U.S. fleet enters Sea of Japan to protect planes off coast of North Korea (→ 5/6).

22. Houston: Doctors perform first transplant of human eye.

24. U.S. agrees to sell 18 F-104 jets to Jordan (→ 6/18).

29. Mass.: MIT bars government research projects (→ 5/1).

30. N.Y.: Radical students seize two Columbia buildings (→ 5/1).

China charges Soviet attacks across border

March 29. A disputed island in the middle of a frozen river is the newest flashpoint of tensions between China and the Soviet Union. Both countries claim the island, which lies along their border, in the middle of the Ussuri River. China calls it Chenpao, and the Soviets call it Damansky. Some countries in the Soviet bloc fear that Moscow will use the quarrel as the pretext for a larger attack against China.

Moscow asserts and Peking concedes that Soviet troops are in control of the island. Chinese diplomats charge that Russian troops have used the island as a staging ground for artillery attacks "deep within Chinese territory" into Manchuria. The Soviets claim that the Chinese have escalated tensions by attacking troops guarding Damansky Island.

The Russians said the Chinese killed 31 of their soldiers in an assault on the island on the 2nd. An undetermined number of Chinese were killed. Fighting flared again on the 14th and 15th. China charged that the Soviet troops on the island advanced across the frozen Ussuri and attacked Chinese border guards with "armored vehicles, tanks and armed troops."

Demonstrations have erupted outside Russia's Embassy in Peking and China's Embassy in Moscow. The Soviets have urged a resumption of talks, but again blamed China for the fighting (→ 8/13).

Soviet troops guard frozen wasteland along the Ussuri River on China's border.

In moon landing test, two space ships link

March 13. The Apollo 9 spacecraft returned safely to earth today after a ten-day mission that successfully accomplished the space rendezvous necessary for a landing on the moon. During the mission, astronauts James A. McDivitt, David R. Scott and Russell L. Schweickart separated the lunar module that will make the landing from the command ship, rocketed 100 miles away and maneuvered the two ships together again, as will happen in a moon mission. National Aeronautics and Space Administration officials say the Apollo 9 success opens the way to a landing on the moon this summer after one more lunar orbital flight (→ 4/18).

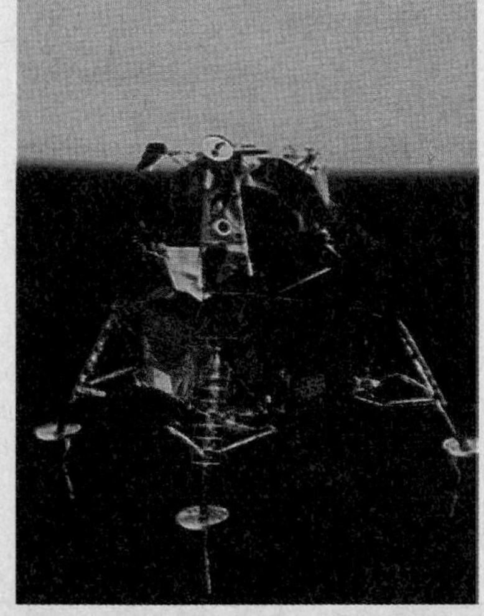

The lunar module from Apollo 9.

Irish firebrand in her London debut

Devlin (center), activist and M.P.

April 22. Bernadette Devlin, a diminutive, 21-year-old Irish woman just elected to Parliament, held the House of Commons spellbound today with her maiden speech deploring the oppression of both Roman Catholics and Protestants in Northern Ireland. With quiet eloquence, Miss Devlin told the House, "There is no place for us, the ordinary peasant, in Northern Ireland. It is a society of the landlords" (→ 8/16).

Artificial heart is implanted first time

April 8. The world's first implant of a total artificial heart was performed four days ago by a team headed by Dr. Denton A. Cooley of St. Luke's Episcopal Hospital in Houston. The recipient, Haskell Karp, 47, of Skokie, Illinois, was reported in satisfactory condition afterwards, but today he died. Cooley said the half-pound plastic and metal device was implanted as a temporary measure before a transplant could be performed (→ 8/27).

Say it ain't so, Chris: Columbus a pirate?

April 13. According to a Spanish historian, Columbus was a Basque pirate. Current wisdom has him born in Genoa, Italy, but records are vague, and Columbus himself was not the most reliable source of his own history. Columbus-stalking is sort of a sport in Southern Europe, almost rivaling bullfights. A disbelieving Yale professor said, "Every little village in Italy thinks he was born there." The professor happens to hail from Genoa. ▷

Thousands protest as war deaths mount

Nixon under fire after three months.

April 24. American B-52 bombers launched their biggest attack of the Vietnam War today, and antiwar activists vowed to keep protesting until it stops. They plan to spread their demonstrations to more than 40 cities. Thousands marched up Sixth Avenue in New York this month in the first protest against the young Nixon administration. Some of the marchers, who wore civilian clothes, said they were servicemen on leave. Other demonstrations occurred in Atlanta, Chicago and California. More American soldiers have now died in Vietnam than were killed in the Korean War. The death toll rose to 33,641 this month (→ 5/20).

CBS kills Smothers show as controversial

April 4. "The Smothers Brothers Comedy Hour" has been canceled. CBS charges that the brothers failed to submit tapes to network executives for previewing. The brothers insist CBS always receives their tapes but is afraid to acknowledge its objections to the show's content. Because the program was signed for renewal next season, the brothers will probably pursue litigation.

CBS censors cringed at the show's anti-establishment humor. Guest comedian David Steinberg and cast member Pat Paulsen routinely knocked the Vietnam War and the Nixon administration. Acts starring war protester Harry Belafonte and others were often cut.

Tommy Smothers, canned by CBS.

Blacks at Cornell seize Student Union

April 19. Families visiting Cornell for parent's weekend got a rude surprise this morning when 100 black students seized the Student Union where they were sleeping and gave them ten minutes to get out. The activists, from the University's Afro-American society, also took control of the airwaves of the student radio station, but an engineer at the transmitter five miles away cut power after a few minutes.

This afternoon, members of the Delta Upsilon fraternity, angered by the administration's handling of the affair, tried to retake the Student Union, but were repulsed after fistfights broke out with the occupiers.

Activists charge the university with racism and demand the establishment of a separate black college. And the Afro-American group said they would not relinquish the building until charges against their members for a protest last December were dropped.

Cornell University campus guards broke up the Afro-frat brawl. And campus officials have not called in the police, but the President of the University, James Perkins, had to cancel his planned parent's day address on "The Stability of the University" (→ 5/4).

French say no to de Gaulle; he leaves office

April 28. An era came to an end in France very abruptly at 11 minutes past midnight. President Charles de Gaulle announced from his country home that he would formally step down later in the day. De Gaulle is not obligated to quit. But he had promised he would if the French electorate turned down a referendum on decentralization and reform of the Senate. The measure lost by five percentage points.

Two weeks ago, de Gaulle put his personal prestige on the line when he told a television interviewer that he would leave office if the referendum failed. His stance put a number of allies in an awkward position. They were for de Gaulle but against the referendum. They hoped something might change the president's mind. Nothing did. For de Gaulle, personal prestige and national honor are one and the same.

Alain Poher, President of the Senate, will act as interm President until new elections are held. In the next few weeks, France will witness quite a debate. There is no shortage of presidential candidates (→ 6/20).

Sirhan convicted of killing Robert Kennedy

April 23. A Los Angles jury today sentenced Sirhan Bishara Sirhan to death in the gas chamber for the murder last year of Senator Robert F. Kennedy.

Convicted of first-degree murder last week by the same jury, the 25-year-old Palestinian Arab sat impassively as the panel announced the death penalty. Later, he told one of his attorneys: "Even Jesus Christ couldn't have saved me."

It is possible, however, that the presiding Judge, Herbert V. Walker, could reduce the sentence to life imprisonment at the time of formal sentencing.

Robert Kennedy, the brother of the slain President Kennedy, died last June 6 of wounds inflicted the night before as he and his friends celebrated his victory that day in the California presidential primary. Five supporters near the senator in the crowded Los Angeles hotel were wounded.

The Sirhan Sirhan trial opened on January 7. The state based most of its case of premeditated murder on notebooks, found in Sirhan's room, in which the defendant had written that Senator Kennedy and others must die. Sirhan testified that he did not remember the shooting and did not recall writing in any notebooks. However, he did express his hatred of Senator Kennedy for supporting Israel and for having said he would send jet bombers to Tel Aviv if elected president.

"Don't make a mistake! Say yes." But France has said no to its leader.

1969

MAY

Su	Mo	Tu	We	Th	Fr	Sa
				1	2	3
4	5	6	7	8	9	10
11	12	13	14	15	16	17
18	19	20	21	22	23	24
25	26	27	28	29	30	31

1. N.Y.: Students quit Columbia buildings after warrants issued for their arrest (→ 3).

3. New York: Six Students for a Democratic Society members arrested for disrupting ROTC drill (→ 13).

3. It's Majestic Prince in Kentucky Derby as jockey W. Hartack wins his fifth.

4. New York: Black militant James Forman interrupts Riverside Church service to read list of demands (→ 6/21).

4. St. Louis: Canadiens beat Blues 2-1 to retain Stanley Cup.

6. Washington: Sec. of Navy bars disciplinary action against crew of Pueblo (→ 6/5/70).

13. Nixon calls for draft lottery with 19-year-olds first (→ 15).

14. Canada legalizes abortion and homosexuality in omnibus criminal code bill.

15. Abe Fortas quits U.S. Supreme Court, first to leave under public criticism (→ 21).

15. California: Police disperse Berkeley demonstrators with shotguns and tear gas (→ 20).

20. Calif.: Natl. Guard helicopter rains skin-stinging powder on student protesters (→ 22).

20. Washington: Kennedy assails U.S. tactics on Vietnam (→ 6/8).

26. Florida: Stafford, Cernan end 8-day "dress rehearsal" for lunar landing in Apollo 10 (→ 5/28).

27. Bogota: Bolivia, Chile, Colombia, Ecuador, Peru join to form Andean Common Market.

28. Argentina calls state of siege amid student unrest and general strike (→ 31).

29. New York: Bruce Mayrock immolates self at U.N. to protest genocide in Biafra (→ 1/12/70).

30. Arctic: British team completes first recorder trek across frozen Artic Ocean.

31. Argentina: Death toll hits 23 as general strike ends (→ 6/26).

DEATHS

2. Franz von Papen, German chancellor, 1932 (*10/29/1879).

19. Coleman Hawkins, U.S. jazz sax player (*11/21/1904).

Anti-war activists seize college campuses

May 22. From New York to California, students have occupied college campuses to protest the Vietnam War and to demand greater involvement in university affairs.

At Columbia, 100 students fled from two buildings they had occupied after warrants were issued for their arrests. The protesters, members of Students for a Democratic Society, were demanding an end to on-campus military recruiting, the abolition of the Reserve Officers Training Corps and the establishment of a black studies program. At Queens College in New York, students went on a rampage as they demanded greater control over a minority program. At Cornell, six SDS members were arrested after they tried to disrupt an ROTC drill.

In California, Governor Ronald Reagan dispatched the National Guard to Berkeley after students clashed with authorities about the status of university land they had renamed "People's Park."

Police collar a Berkeley activist.

The student protests grew as Democratic Senator Edward Kennedy called tactics in Vietnam "senseless and irresponsible." The Canadian government has offered to allow American military deserters to settle in Canada (→ 7/11).

Timothy Leary wins in Supreme Court

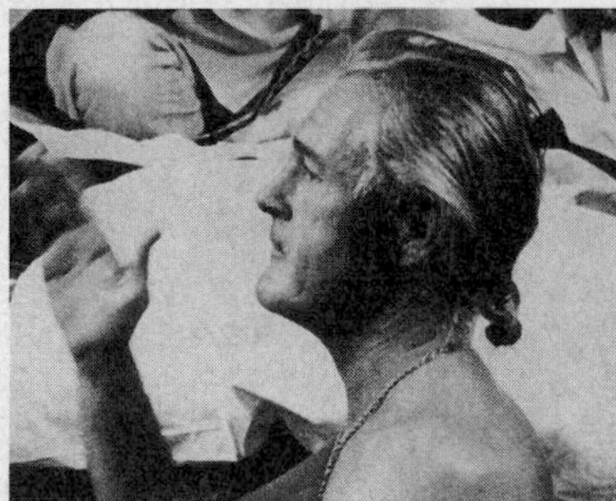

Drug guru Leary, freed by court.

May 19. The Supreme Court voted unanimously today to overturn the conviction of drug guru Dr. Timothy Leary, thereby voiding two federal anti-marijuana laws. Leary was convicted in 1966 after crossing the Mexican border into Texas with several ounces of marijuana. The court determined that two laws used in the conviction—which required one to notify authorities and pay a tax when purchasing or importing the drug—violated the Fifth Amendment privilege against self-incrimination. All other state and federal laws in the United States against the drug still stand, however (→ 3/2/70).

Celtics are champs, defeating Lakers

May 5. The Boston Celtics rolled to their 11th National Basketball Association title in 13 years but the Los Angeles Lakers forced them into a seventh game before losing. Even in the deciding game in the best 4-of-7 series, the Celtics were forced to hold off a closing Laker rally before walking off with the 108-106 victory.

The "aging" Celtics, who finished only fourth in the regular season, were at their very best for the showdown. They had to overcome the hot hand of Jerry West, who scored 42 points despite a leg injury. He set a playoff record by getting 556 points in the 18 games the Lakers played after the regular season.

West only began to find the range after the Celtics had spurted to a 24-12 lead on the sharp outside shooting of Sam Jones, John Havlicek and Em Bryant. The Lakers took the momentum in the second half and tied at 60-60, but then their offense died and they were unable to get a point in five minutes. The Lakers' Wilt Chamberlain drew his fourth personal foul at that point and played defensively.

Burger nominated as Fortas resigns

May 21. A shift toward a more conservative Supreme Court was virtually assured today with the nomination by President Nixon of Warren Burger as chief justice to succeed Earl Warren, a liberal who is to retire from the court's top post in June. The new nomination comes just a week after another liberal Justice, Abe Fortas, resigned from the court under heavy public pressure. It had been disclosed that he had arranged to receive a yearly fee of $20,000 for services to the family foundation of Louis E. Wolfson, now in prison for selling unregistered securities (→ 6/23).

Rockefeller gives Met art collection

May 8. New York Governor Nelson Rockefeller has given his $20 million collection of primitive sculpture to the Metropolitan Museum of Art. A new wing will be added to the building to accommodate the huge exhibit. The walls must be unusually high; some of the African and pre-Columbian totem-like figures stand 17 feet tall. The wing will be named after the governor's son Michael, lost on an expedition to New Guinea in 1961.

May 18. Earthrise: Vietnam's DMZ and the frontiers of Israel vanish in the first live color TV pictures of earth from space, courtesy of Apollo 10 (→ 26).

1969

JUNE

Su	Mo	Tu	We	Th	Fr	Sa
1	2	3	4	5	6	7
8	9	10	11	12	13	14
15	16	17	18	19	20	21
22	23	24	25	26	27	28
29	30					

1. Belgrade boycotts Intl. Communist Congress (→ 7/29/71).

2. South China Sea: Australian carrier cuts U.S. destroyer Frank Evans in two; 73 lost.

4. Mexico: 79 die in air crash, including tennis star Rafael Osuna.

4. Congo-Kinshasa: 100 students killed as Mobutu's troops break up demonstration (→ 8/4/70).

6. New York: Joe Namath quits football after Pete Rozelle order to sell interest in bar (→ 7/18).

8. Midway: Nixon meets with Pres. Thieu, says he will pull out 25,000 troops by August (→ 18).

9. U.S. licenses rubella vaccine.

10. Paul VI becomes first pope to visit Geneva since 16th century (→ 2/9/70).

16. U.S. Supreme Court rules barring of Adam Clayton Powell by House was illegal.

17. U.S. concludes Soviets not trying to gain first-strike nuclear capability (→ 11/17).

18. Jordan: Israeli jets carry out five-hour bombing raid (→ 24).

20. Prague: Czech students' union dissolved (→ 8/21).

21. South Carolina: Civil rights leader Rev. Ralph Abernathy jailed on riot charges (→ 7/3).

23. Earl Warren turns over center seat on Supreme Court to Warren Burger.

24. Arab saboteurs blow up oil pipeline from Haifa (→ 7/2).

24. Peru to seize all major tracts of privately owned land.

26. Argentina: Chain of Rockefeller-owned stores fire-bombed three days before arrival of Nelson Rockefeller (→ 6/8/70).

27. Salvador, Honduras sever ties in soccer dispute (→ 7/18).

28. Cape Kennedy: NASA puts 14-lb. monkey in orbit (→ 7/8).

DEATHS

8. Robert Taylor, American movie actor (*8/5/1911).

21. Maureen "Little Mo" Connolly, U.S. tennis star (*9/17/1934).

29. Moise Tshombe, Congo independence leader (*11/10/1919).

Nixon orders 25,000 out; he plans more

Clark Clifford, urging withdrawal.

June 18. Clark Clifford, former Defense Secretary in the Johnson administration, has urged President Richard Nixon to scale down military operations in Vietnam.

The advice comes just ten days after Nixon, following a meeting with South Vietnamese President Nguyen Van Thieu at Midway Island, announced that the U.S. would withdraw 25,000 soldiers, the equivalent of a combat division, from Vietnam by the end of August.

Nixon held out the hope for further reductions in the 540,000-man American force as South Vietnamese troops prove capable of taking over the ground battle.

Nixon described the withdrawal as a "significant step forward" toward peace in Vietnam. Aside from placating domestic critics, the troop withdrawal appeared designed to put pressure on North Vietnam in the Paris peace talks. Differences between the U.S. and South Vietnam on the goals of the peace talks must also be ironed out (→ 7/8).

Judy has found the end of the rainbow

June 22. Judy Garland has been found dead in her London apartment. She was 47. While suicide is not yet proven, it is known she tried to take her life 20 times before. Why would such a talented woman despise herself? Her devoted fans do not know; they always showered her with loving applause.

Born Frances Gumm in Grand Rapids, Minn., Judy went from a family stage act to film at age 13. She starred in Andy Hardy pictures with Mickey Rooney and some of the best musicals of the 40's. She wed five times and had three children. Pills to settle her nerves and seesawing weight left her a shadow with a marvelous voice.

Judy Garland in "A Star is Born."

Pompidou succeeds President de Gaulle

Pompidou takes over in Paris.

June 20. Georges Pompidou, an intellectual comfortable in the world of politics and poetry, has succeeded Charles de Gaulle as President of France. In elections, he defeated acting President Alain Poher. Pompidou, who headed de Gaulle's Cabinet, must strike a new course without alienating the Gaullists. He has asked a conservative to be Finance Minister, but he named liberal Jacques Chaban-Delmas as Premier (→ 1/31/70).

1969

JULY

Su	Mo	Tu	We	Th	Fr	Sa
		1	2	3	4	5
6	7	8	9	10	11	12
13	14	15	16	17	18	19
20	21	22	23	24	25	26
29	28	29	30	31		

2. Egypt: Israelis down three MIG-21's in dogfight (→ 8).

3. N.Y.: Stokely Carmichael resigns from Black Panthers (→ 7).

5. Wimbledon: Rod Laver over John Newcombe 6-4, 5-7, 6-4, 6-4; Adrienne Jones over Billie Jean King 3-6, 6-3, 6-2.

5. Kenya: Min. of Economic Affairs Tom Mboya assassinated.

8. Honolulu: Bonny the space monkey dies 12 hours after emergency splashdown (→ 16).

8. Vietnam: 84 of 543,400 leave Saigon in first of U.S. troop withdrawals (→ 8/12).

8. Israel downs seven MIG-21's in clash over Syria (→ 10).

9. U.S. Dept. of Agriculture suspends use of DDT pending results of study (→ 6/14/72).

10. Egyptian troops attack Israeli positions at Port Taufik, killing or wounding 40 (→ 27).

11. Boston: U.S. Appeals Court voids convictions of Dr. Spock and three others (→ 8/25).

14. N.Y.: "Easy Rider" opens.

16. Cape Kennedy: Apollo 11 launched to put first man on moon (→ 20).

18. N.Y.: Joe Namath agrees to sell bar and return to Jets (→ 8/1/72).

19. Mass.: Ted Kennedy drives off Chappaquiddick bridge, killing Mary Jo Kopechne (→ 30).

20. Belgian racer Eddy Merckx wins Tour de France.

22. Madrid: Franco names Juan Carlos successor (→ 12/30/70).

26. Manila: Nixon confers with Pres. Marcos (→ 1/26/70).

28. Jakarta: Nixon becomes first U.S. president to visit Indonesia (→ 7/3/71).

31. Mariner 6 sends close-ups of Mars back to U.S. (→ 11/14).

DEATHS

5. Walter Gropius, German architect, founder Bauhaus school of design (*5/18/1883).

7. Brian Jones, guitarist with Rolling Stones (*2/28/1944).

25. Otto Dix, German painter (*12/2/1891).

Mankind makes its greatest leap: To the moon

July 20. Men landed on the moon today. Two American astronauts, Neil A. Armstrong and Edwin E. Aldrin Jr., piloted their Apollo lunar module, named Eagle, to a landing on the Sea of Tranquillity at 4:17 p.m. Eastern daylight time, then walked on the lunar surface six hours later. The first words from the moon, spoken by Armstrong moments after the module set down, were, "Houston, Tranquillity Base here. The Eagle has landed." And as Armstrong stepped down from the landing craft at 10:56 p.m. to become the first man to set foot on the moon, he told the hundreds of millions who were watching the scene on television, "That's one small step for man, one giant leap for mankind."

Armstrong was joined 19 minutes later by Aldrin, while the third member of the Apollo 11 team, Michael Collins, orbited the moon aboard the command ship. Armstrong and Aldrin set up a television camera away from the lunar module, planted an American flag, collected soil and rock samples and set up scientific instruments. Both men moved about easily in the lunar gravity field, only one-sixth as strong as the earth's, despite the bulky spacesuits they wore. Armstrong reported he was "very comfortable" and described the surface of the moon as "fine and powdery," saying that his boots sank in "only a small fraction of an inch."

Their work was interrupted when President Nixon congratulated them from the White House in what he said "certainly has to be the most historic telephone call ever made." Black-and-white television pictures showing them hopping and loping on the moon were transmitted to earth with amazing clarity. The astronauts returned to the lunar module two hours and 21 minutes after they had opened its hatch. They were asleep soon afterward.

The historic flight of Apollo 11 began four days ago with a liftoff from launching pad 39-A at Cape Kennedy. After a trouble-free three-day flight, the linked command ship and module went into orbit around the moon yesterday. The astronauts were awakened at 7 a.m., on their tenth lunar orbit. Armstrong and Aldrin entered the lunar module on the next orbit and after receiving the go-ahead from mission control, undocked from the command ship at 1:50 p.m. Collins fired the command ship's maneuvering rockets to move two miles away from the lunar module a few minutes later.

The descent to the moon began at 3:08 p.m., when the lunar module was behind the moon and out of touch with the earth. Tension built until 3:46 p.m., when contact was reestablished with Collins, who reported that "things are going just swimmingly, just beautiful." By then, the lunar module's on-board computer had made the 29.8-second rocket burn that sent the craft toward its designated landing area. At 50,000 feet above the moon, the engine built up thrust to lower the rate of descent. There was a moment of high tension when the craft reached an altitude of 300 feet and the astronauts saw that the computer was guiding them toward a crater filled with boulders that could wreck the ship. Armstrong took over control and landed the module safely on a flat surface 120 miles southwest of the crater Maskelyn, on the east side of the moon. Aldrin told mission control it was a "very smooth touchdown."

Armstrong brought a flag to the moon, crediting the U.S with the effort, yet his words ". . . one giant leap for mankind" offer benefits to all.

Meanwhile, all the world was in the moon's grip. From Australia to Norway, from Kansas City to Warsaw, people pressed their ears to radios or watched the momentous event on television. The TV audience was estimated at 600 million persons, one-fifth of the earth's population. Even in unfriendly nations, the mission was reported favorably or at least impartially.

Cairo radio called the Apollo moon landing "the greatest human achievement ever." "Absolutely bloody marvelous," was the way a solicitor's clerk in London described it. "Nothing in show business," said Gina Lollobrigida, the actress, "will ever top what I saw on television today."

The first trip to the moon is scheduled to last less than a day. The lunar module is due to lift off the moon at 1:55 p.m. tomorrow. It will be jettisoned before the command ship begins its return to earth (→ 26).

Lunar pioneers (left to rt.) Neil Armstrong, Michael Collins and Edwin Aldrin.

Woman drowned in car driven by Kennedy

The late Mary Jo Kopechne.

July 30. Senator Edward M. Kennedy has decided to remain in Congress, despite his involvement in the recent drowning death of Mary Jo Kopechne on tiny Chappaquiddick Island in Massachusetts.

The accident occurred when a car, driven by the senator, plunged off a bridge as the two drove away from a cookout attended by a group of persons who had been active last year in the late Robert Kennedy's presidential campaign.

Several days ago, Senator Kennedy pleaded guilty to the charge of leaving the scene of an accident. He was given a two-month suspended sentence and placed on probation for one year. He said in a televised speech that he sought to rescue the 28-year-old secretary and that at one point felt that he was drowning. He has denied any romantic link to Miss Kopechne.

The dramatic, and still mysterious, accident cast a cloud over the young Massachusetts senator's political career and he had thought at one point of leaving the Senate. While deciding to remain in Congress, he apparently has decided not to seek the Democratic nomination for president in 1972 (→ 4/7/70).

A biracial town elects black Mayor

July 7. Charles Evers was sworn in today as the first Negro Mayor of a biracial town in Mississippi since Reconstruction. Three-quarters of Fayette, Mississippi's 1,700 residents are black, but until the Voting Rights Act of 1968, they were unable to get enough names on the registration books to elect Negro officials. In the election last spring, Evers defeated the incumbent Mayor by 386 to 255 votes.

Some white residents have been shaken up by the change, a number of them leaving town. Although asked to stay by Evers, 15 of 16 City Hall staff members have quit their posts. The new mayor, brother of slain civil rights leader Medgar Evers, said the law would be enforced impartially and assured both blacks and whites that all would have a home in Fayette (→ 15).

Countries go to war over soccer match

July 18. The undeclared war between Honduras and El Salvador that erupted four days ago over a disputed soccer match and took the lives of 1,000 persons may be drawing to a close. Both governments have accepted a four-point peace plan drafted by the Organization of American States.

The plan calls for a cease-fire effective tonight, mutual troop withdrawals within four days, guarantees of safety for citizens of each nation and the presence of observers to guard against violations.

The violence reflects deep-seated economic and social hostilities between the two nations. Hondurans deeply resent the influx of Salvadorans across the border into their more sparsely populated farmland, and El Salvador has accused Honduras of persecuting these settlers.

Planes of Egypt and Israel duel over Canal

July 27. The Arab-Israeli conflict took to the air again this month when Israeli dogfights with Syrian jets and attacks on Egyptian army bases were followed by winged Egyptian reprisals. July 8th saw clashes over the Golan Heights as Israeli French-made Mirage fighters downed seven Syrian MIG-15's in just 30 minutes. This morning, Egyptian planes hit back at Israeli army positions in the Sinai Peninsula—the third such Egyptian attack this week and unusual in that it was a clear attack unlike the earlier retaliatory raids.

In recent weeks, the Israelis have attacked enemy aircraft at an unprecedented rate, downing 16 Egyptian and Syrian jets in the last 15 days. Since the 1967 Six Day War, they claim 41 enemy jets while losing eight of their own. Newly elected French President Georges Pompidou has stated that he will continue former President Charles de Gaulle's embargo on the 50 Mirage fighter-bombers already purchased by the Israelis from France (→ 8/3).

Boeing's 747, first double-decker passenger jet, rolled off the production line this year. Pan Am is expected to schedule flights for early 1970.

Two black power figures leave scene

July 15. Eldridge Cleaver and Stokely Carmichael, two prominent black activists, have withdrawn from the American spotlight,and today from Algeria, Cleaver condemned his former ally.

Carmichael resigned earlier this month as Prime Minister of the Black Panther Party. He called the party's principles "dogmatic," assailed the militant group for its alliance with radical, white leftists and characterized its methods as "dishonest and vicious." The former Chairman of the Student Nonviolent Coordinating Committee now lives in self-exile in Conakry, Guinea, studying French at the Institute for Languages.

Cleaver, former leader of the Panthers, fled America, violating his parole, to take refuge in Algeria. Cleaver was arrested after a Panther clash with the Oakland, California, police April 6, 1968. The fugitive released a vehement open letter to Carmichael, blasting him for his condemnation of the party. Cleaver said oppressed people need solidarity in a "revolution (based on) principles rather than skin color." He also thanked Algeria's government for allowing him entry (→ 8/20).

Scientists get first look at moon rocks

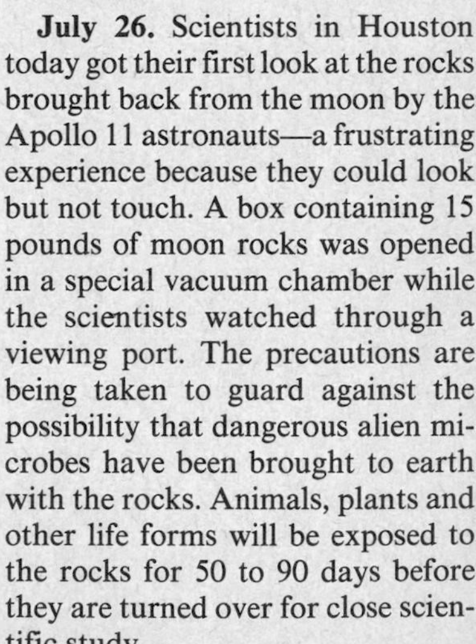

July 26. Scientists in Houston today got their first look at the rocks brought back from the moon by the Apollo 11 astronauts—a frustrating experience because they could look but not touch. A box containing 15 pounds of moon rocks was opened in a special vacuum chamber while the scientists watched through a viewing port. The precautions are being taken to guard against the possibility that dangerous alien microbes have been brought to earth with the rocks. Animals, plants and other life forms will be exposed to the rocks for 50 to 90 days before they are turned over for close scientific study.

The scientists said most features of the rocks were hidden by a coating of blackish, fine-colored dust. The rocks will have to be scrubbed before they can be studied (→ 31).

1969

AUGUST

Su	Mo	Tu	We	Th	Fr	Sa
					1	2
3	4	5	6	7	8	9
10	11	12	13	14	15	16
17	18	19	20	21	22	23
24	25	26	27	28	29	30
31						

2. Rumania: Nixon becomes first U.S. president in 25 years to visit Communist country.

3. Israel announces plan to keep Golan Heights, Gaza Strip and most of Sinai Peninsula (→ 11).

4. Bonn: Pres. Heinemann extends statute of limitations on war crimes from 20 to 30 years.

6. Saigon: Robert Rheault, ex-Green Beret head, and seven others charged with murder (→ 14).

8. Washington: Nixon proposes welfare overhaul, work or job training required (→ 7/12/71).

11. Lebanon: Israeli jets strike in reprisal for alleged terrorist acts (→ 23).

13. China and U.S.S.R. fight battle along Central Asian frontier (→ 4/19/70).

14. Saigon: Green Berets up for murder reported to have ties to CIA (→ 28).

15. N.Y.: 200,000 arrive in small town of Bethel for Woodstock Music Festival (→ 17).

17. Miss.: 200,000 flee as Hurricane Camille hits; 300 dead.

21. Prague: Tanks suppress protests on first anniversary of Soviet invasion (→ 9/28).

22. Saigon: Premier Tran Van Huong resigns to make way for broader regime (→ 9/4).

23. Cairo: Nasser calls for war on Israel for fire at Al Aksa mosque in Jerusalem (→ 26).

24. India: V.V. Giri sworn in as president (→ 3/11/71).

26. N.Y.: U.N. condemns Israel for raid on Lebanon (→ 30).

27. South Africa: Christiaan Barnard implants artificial arteries in child (→ 7/25/71).

30. Ghana: Progressives win first free election since 1956.

DEATHS

6. Theodor Adorno, German Marxist philosopher (*9/11/1903).

17. Otto Stern, German-American physicist, 1943 Nobel Prize (*2/17/1888).

31. Rocky Marciano, U.S. boxer, only heavyweight champ to retire undefeated (*9/1/1923).

Thousands overwhelm Woodstock festival

Richie Havens strums and thumbs his guitar, and sings about freedom.

Aug 17. A massive gathering of young people, estimated at close to 400,000, survived endless traffic jams, food and water shortages and torrential downpours this weekend to proclaim the Woodstock Music and Arts Fair a fantastic success.

The crowd was more than twice as large as anyone had expected, and roads for 20 miles around the site were reported at a standstill. Thousands abandoned cars and swarmed through the small town of Bethel, New York, near Woodstock, toward the festival, held on a 600-acre dairy farm loaned for the event by owner Max Yasgur.

The crowd behaved peacefully the entire weekend despite light security, inadequate facilities and an abundance of what a doctor at the festival site called "bad LSD trips." Cases of nudity were also reported.

Festival-goers were drawn by a list of performers that read like a pop music Who's Who, including Richie Havens; Jefferson Airplane; Grateful Dead; Crosby, Stills, Nash and Young; Creedence Clearwater Revival; the Who; the Band; Janis Joplin and Jimi Hendrix.

Anti-war paint at the festival.

Exodus from Bethel begins as 400,000 end weekend of music, love and peace.

Five brutally slain in actress' home

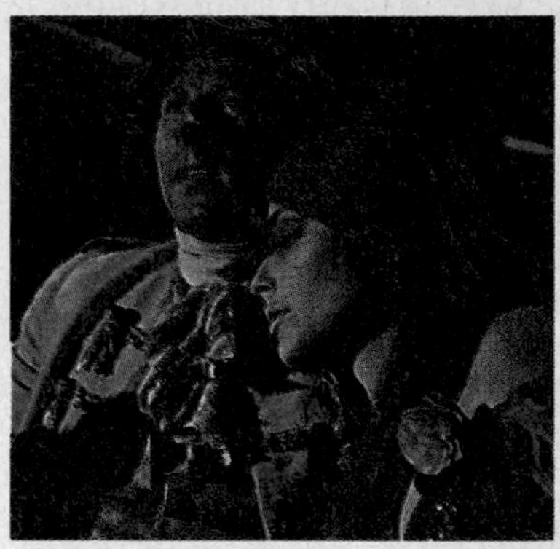

Sharon Tate and Roman Polanski.

Aug 9. Actress Sharon Tate, wife of director Roman Polanski, has been found bloodily murdered in her Beverly Hills home. Three guests were also killed. Polanski, who has directed ghoulish films such as "Rosemary's Baby," broke down at the news and said he would fly to Los Angeles at once.

Last night, a person or persons got past a barbed wire fence, severed phone wires and entered the house. Miss Tate, eight months pregnant, was stabbed. A nylon rope clung to her neck, as if a hanging had been planned and abandoned. A man lay beside her, cut open. Two other guests were stretched upon the lawn, their futile escape cut short. A fifth victim, a neighbor, was slumped in a car out front. No weapons were found in the area, although the killers left a calling card, the word "pig" smeared in blood on a door (→ 12/24).

Company A soldiers refuse official order

Aug 25. After five days of fierce fighting in a maze of Vietnamese trenches and bunkers, Company A of the 196th light infantry balked at a command today. "My men refuse to go. We cannot move out," reported Lt. Eugene Shurz over his radio. Sgt. Blankenship, who arrived with Major Richard Waite to "kick their butts" and get them going again, told the men "another company is down to 15 men and they're still moving," adding later, "I lied to them." The soldiers picked up their rifles and followed him back into battle (→ 9/19).

▷

Rioting, burning beset Belfast three days

Armored truck turns its water cannon on burning barricades in N. Ireland.

Aug 16. Belfast was torn by three days of rioting, shooting and burning until armed British troops intervened to establish order. British troops with armored cars carrying machine guns set up barricades around the Roman Catholic areas in the western section of Belfast that was the center of the rioting. During the three days of violence, eight persons, all Catholics, were killed, and 236 persons were injured.

The continuing violence widened the policy rift between Britain and Northern Ireland. Prime Minister Chichester-Clark of Northern Ireland charged the violence was fomented by Irish Catholics to end the partition of Ireland. British Prime Minister Harold Wilson, meanwhile, has been pressing the Protestant-controlled government in Belfast to compromise with the Catholics (→ 10/5).

Influential architect van der Rohe dies

Aug 17. Mies van der Rohe, one of the great figures of 20th-Century architecture, died in Chicago this evening. He was 83. Van der Rohe was a leading designer of the glass-walled skyscrapers that have come to typify modern architecture. His philosophy was summed up in an often-quoted remark: "More is less," meaning that useless ornamentation detracts from the beauty of a building. He was widely copied.

One of his innovations was the ribbon window, which has become standard in skyscrapers. A concrete villa he designed in 1924 is regarded as the forerunner of the California ranch house. Born in Germany, he apprenticed himself to a modern architect in 1909. After army service in World War I, van der Rohe achieved continuing success. In 1930, he became head of the Bauhaus, a laboratory of architecture that was closed as "degenerate" by the Nazis in 1933. Van der Rohe came to the United States in 1937, building another successful career. The Seagram Building on Park Avenue in New York is regarded as his masterwork.

1,450 Vietnamese slain in 24 hours

Aug 12. More bodies piled up in South Vietnam today. The great majority of them are reported to be North Vietnamese and Viet Cong. After the heaviest fighting in three months, 1,450 enemy soldiers were killed. Some 90 Americans and 107 South Vietnamese died. Nearly 900 Allied troops were wounded. "It's probably the beginning of their fall campaign," an American military spokesman said, "but there is no indication how long they'll be able to sustain it." President Nixon's Press Secretary, Ronald Ziegler, warns the Communist offensive may lead to a slowdown in the withdrawal of U.S. forces. A week ago, Hanoi radio reported the release of three U.S. POWs (→ 9/4).

One side's victory is another's pain.

Syrians free all but Israelis and hijackers

Aug 30. Some 96 of the 113 persons aboard the TWA jet hijacked to Damascus, Syria, yesterday, arrived in Athens today aboard an Italian airliner after having been released by Syrian officials. In all, 105 were freed. Nine Americans remain of their own volition, including an injured woman and the pilot of the damaged Boeing 707 jet. The Syrians detained the two hijackers, members of the PLO who are now thought to be in jail, and six Israelis, four of them women. The PLO has said the Israelis will be kept as hostages for "the release of Syrian comrades in Israeli torture prisons." Western officials think the four women will be freed soon.

In Tel Aviv, Israeli Premier Golda Meir warned that "it would be best advised" for the Syrians "to think twice about their future moves" (→ 9/1).

4 Green Berets in murder case linked to CIA

Aug 28. The Central Intelligence Agency has mounted a rare public relations campaign to deny that it had anything to do with the murder of a South Vietnamese civilian suspected of being a double agent for the Communists. Thai Khac Chuyen vanished at the beginning of June. Reports have spread that he was killed and his body dumped off the South Vietnamese coast. Eight members of the Army's Special Forces, or Green Berets, are suspects in the apparent murder of Chuyen. Four of the Green Berets have been linked to the CIA.

Sources say the soldiers worked in a Special Operations Group which is authorized by intelligence officials to kidnap and "eliminate" enemies in North and South Vietnam, Laos and Cambodia (→ 9/29).

Black Panther chief arrested in murder

Aug 20. Federal agents in Berkeley, California, arrested Bobby Seale, National Chairman of the Black Panther Party, for the murder of former Panther Alex Rackey. Rackey reportedly disagreed with party policies, was put on "trial" and killed. His mutilated body was found in Connecticut last May. Seales' attorney, Francis McTernan, accused the Justice Department of waging a harassment campaign against the Panthers. With Seale's arrest, most of the party's leadership is now in jail, out on bail or residing outside the country.

Bail was set and made at $25,000, which McTernan termed "ridiculously high." Some believe the arrest will invigorate the party. One member told reporters, "The idea of the Black Panthers has caught on and every revolution has proven that you can't kill ideas with the arrests of its leaders" (→ 9/21).

Heart patient dies

Aug 17. Philip Blaiberg, the second man to receive a heart transplant from Dr. Christiaan N. Barnard and the world's longest surviving heart recipient, died in Cape Town, South Africa, today. Blaiberg, a 60-year-old retired dentist, had lived for 19 months and 15 days with the transplanted heart.

Saved last year only by a deluge of praise from devotees, "Star Trek" is off the air after 3 years.

1969

SEPTEMBER

Su	Mo	Tu	We	Th	Fr	Sa
	1	2	3	4	5	6
7	8	9	10	11	12	13
14	15	16	17	18	19	20
21	22	23	24	25	26	27
28	29	30				

1. Cairo: Four Arab nations open conference to coordinate action against Israel (→ 9).

3. Washington: Marine chief Leonard Chapman orders halt to racial violence in corps.

6. U.S. formally recognizes new regime in Libya (→ 1/16/70).

7. Brazil: Kidnappers release U.S. Ambassador C. Burke Elbrick, held three days, in exchange for 15 political prisoners.

9. Indiana: 83 die as airliner and small plane collide.

9. Egypt: Israeli task force crosses Gulf of Suez to destroy Egyptian coast positions (→ 11).

11. Israel downs 11 Eyptian jets in raids over canal (→ 10/24).

12. Nixon orders resumption in bombing of N. Vietnam (→ 16).

13. Aden: Eritrean guerrillas hijack Ethiopian airliner with 66.

13. Albania announces intention to withdraw from Warsaw Pact.

15. New York: U Thant asks inclusion of Peking in disarmament talks (→ 11/11).

16. Nixon announces new troop withdrawal of 35,000 (→ 24).

17. Laos: U.S.-backed govt. forces take rebel areas (→ 11/23).

19. Nixon cuts draft call by 50,000 this year (→ 10/9).

19. Cuba enacts law allowing extradition of hijackers (→ 8/2/70).

20. Cleveland: U.S. tennis team retains Davis Cup.

21. Mass.: Harvard opens program in black studies (→ 27).

24. Hanoi: Ton Duc Thang elected to succeed Ho Chi Minh as president (→ 10/6).

26. Morocco: Hassan II decries Arab terrorism (→ 8/16/72).

27. Washington: Martin Luther King's family halts talks with Nixon on memorial, citing indifference to blacks (→ 10/29).

28. Bonn: Christian Democrats win at polls (→ 10/21).

28. Prague: Dubcek ousted from Presidium (→ 10/9).

29. U.S. drops murder case against Green Berets as CIA bars agents from testifying.

Rod Laver wins second tennis Grand Slam

Laver flashes his U.S. Open trophy.

Sept 8. Rod Laver has captured the United States Open tennis championship, becoming the first man to win the Grand Slam of tennis twice.

The 31-year-old Australian outlasted his countryman, Tony Roche, 7-9, 6-1, 6-2, 6-2, and won $16,000, the richest prize in the sport. His triumph completed a second sweep of the Australian, French, British and American titles. "Winning this grand slam was a lot tougher because of all the good players," said Laver. The courts were still soggy from a morning rain. Laver, who switched from sneakers to spiked shoes, has proved he's the best player on any surface.

Libya King ousted; Khadafy in power

New Libyan ruler Col. Khadafy.

Sept 1. In a bloodless coup, a revolutionary council has overthrown the 18-year regime of King Idris I. While the 79-year-old Idris was in Turkey, undergoing medical treatment, Crown Prince Hassan al-Rida announced he would relinquish all powers to the junta.

Spokesmen for the revolution have stated that one of the main aims of the takeover was to solve Libya's underdevelopment problems, but observers see this as an inadequate reason since King Idris was known for his efforts to develop the country both socially and economically. The coup is considered to be a further symptom of a current wave of radicalism in the Arab world. There have been three other such revolutions in Arab countries in the last year. Military officers Col. Shwirrib and Col. Khadafy are known to have led this revolt (→ 6).

Ho Chi Minh, shrewd Vietnamese chief, dies

Sept 4. President of North Vietnam Ho Chi Minh is dead at the age of 79. He had been in critical condition and under the care of a team of doctors for several weeks before succumbing to a heart attack.

Ho had been a prime mover in the revolution which gave North Vietnam its independence from French rule in 1954 and, although a Communist, he enjoyed prestige even among anti-Communist Vietnamese. Under the North Vietnamese constitution, Ho Chi Minh will be succeeded by the Vice President, Ton Duc Thang. United States officials have said that Ho's death and the change in leadership would probably not alter the course of the war in South Vietnam or affect the peace talks in Paris (→ 12).

Ho, a Communist for 50 years.

Episcopal Bishop Pike dies in Judean desert

Sept 7. In the same wasteland where Jesus endured 40 days and 40 nights of temptation, ex-Episcopal Bishop James Pike has died. His body was located in the Judean desert today by Israeli police. Pike and his wife were driving in the area three days ago when their car broke down. Mrs. Pike sought and found help while her husband stayed behind. A fall from a cliff killed him.

Pike, a Catholic turned agnostic turned Episcopal bishop turned layman, alienated many churchgoers. He doubted the Holy Trinity, a literal virgin birth and salvation through faith in Christ alone.

Bishop Pike, speaking about peace.

Police bust hippies

Sept 21. Tensions between the leisure and working classes boiled over in London this week, except this leisure class wasn't rich. They were 200 squatters who had occupied a house and refused to work. "You're a disgrace!" yelled one housewife who was part of a group that came to harass the hippies down the block. The police routed them all, but a quick tour revealed that though they may have had little money or food they had kept a very tidy house. One youth said he believed the neighborhood residents were jealous, because they had to work and he didn't.

1969

OCTOBER

Su	Mo	Tu	We	Th	Fr	Sa
			1	2	3	4
5	6	7	8	9	10	11
12	13	14	15	16	17	18
19	20	21	22	23	24	25
26	27	28	29	30	31	

1. Sweden: Olof Palme elected leader of Social Democrats, in effect next premier (→ 10/5/78).

1. France: Concord breaks sound barrier for first time.

3. Milwaukee: Golda Meir visits elementary school she attended (→ 11/7).

6. Pres. Thieu declares Saigon ready for cease-fire (→ 11/8).

9. Chicago: Natl. Guard called out to quell SDS protests (→ 11).

9. Prague: Czechoslovakia bans travel by individuals to Western nations (→ 5/29/75).

11. Washington: Heads of 79 colleges appeal to Nixon to speed up Vietnam pullout (→ 13).

13. Washington: Nixon vows not to be swayed by anti-war protests (→ 15).

15. U.S. Congress votes to coin new dollar honoring Ike.

21. Bonn: Social Democrat Willy Brandt elected West German president (→ 4/25/74).

22. Chile: Failed coup prompts demonstrations in support of regime (→ 9/5/70).

23. St. Louis: Large doses of monosodium glutamate found to produce brain damage in mice.

23. New York: Cartier pays record $1.05 mil. for diamond.

24. Israel: Deputy Premier Yigal Allon threatens war if Lebanon invaded by Arabs (→ 25).

25. Beirut: 300 in PLO invade Lebanon (→ 28).

28. Syria: PLO leader Arafat asks Lebanese to support him against Beirut govt. (→ 31).

29. U.S. Supreme Court orders desegragation at once, superceding "with all deliberate speed" ruling (→ 11/5).

31. Lebanon: Guerrillas claim victory in battle (→ 11/2).

31. Gunman takes plane from San Francisco to Rome in first transatlantic hijacking.

DEATHS

12. Sonja Henje, Norwegian figure skater (*4/8/1912).

21. Jack Kerouac, U.S. writer, Beat Generation, "On the Road" (*3/12/1922).

New York Mets win their first World Series

Oct 16. The Mets did it. After seven years of playing the buffoon of baseball, the New York team swept the Baltimore Orioles in the World Series and made believers of those who had ridiculed them.

The Mets beat the Orioles in the fourth series game by 5-3 and set off a celebration the likes of which has never been seen in the Big Apple. Ticker tape drifted from skyscrapers, schools suspended classes and traffic all but stopped. Isaac Stern, the violinist, summed it up: "If the Mets can win the Series, anything can happen—even peace."

The Mets, rated 100-1 to win before the season began, went on to take the pennant in a three-game sweep of the Atlanta Braves. Said a joyous Ron Swoboda, "It's the first one and the sweetest, and because it's the first, nothing can be that sweet again."

Pandemonium strikes at Shea Stadium as fans swarm their amazing Mets.

Cyclamates banned as a sweetener

Oct 18. In a major blow to the diet food industry, the government today banned the use of cyclamates as artificial sweeteners. Officials said the ban, to be fully effective early next year, was ordered because of animal tests indicating that cyclamates might cause cancer. Cyclamates now are used in over 250 foods and soft drinks.

McCartney is dead? Rubbish, agent says

Oct 21. A Beatle spokesman today dismissed rumors of Paul McCartney's death as "a load of old rubbish," but fans everywhere continued to search for cryptic messages in songs and on album covers. The hoax took off after a Detroit disk jockey played a Beatle record backwards to reveal what he said were voices chanting "Paul is Dead." Thousands have claimed recently to have uncovered other such hidden evidence, but as the spokesman insisted today, the musician is "alive and well" (→ 11/25).

Anti-war protest spreads across U.S.

Oct 15. The Vietnam Moratorium, the largest protest in the history of the anti-war movement, was a complete success. Throughout the United States, in small towns and big cities, in every region of the country, millions of students, laborers, executives, housewives, schoolchildren, the young and the old, the black and the white, the rich and the poor, showed their opposition to the Vietnam War in diverse peaceful ways. Many of the participants wore black armbands in silent protest. As the first nationally coordinated demonstration, it was unique. But will it end the war in Vietnam?

The Presidents of 79 colleges have appealed to President Nixon "for a stepped up timetable for withdrawal from Vietnam" while Governor Francis W. Sargent of Massachusetts, a World War II combat veteran, said simply, "This war is costing America its soul" (→ 11/15).

British fire tear gas at Belfast militants

Oct 5. British troops fired tear gas to disperse a group of militant Protestants marching in Belfast in defiance of a government ban on public processions. The confrontation with troops came after five hours of street fighting between Protestants and Catholics that ended before dawn this Sunday morning.

First, The Royal Ulster Constabulary and then the British troops tried to disperse the Protestant group headed by the Rev. Ian Paisley marching to a church. When the parade continued, the British troops used tear gas to disperse the crowd.

The latest violence comes on the first anniversary of the sectarian rioting that broke out last year in Londonderry and then spread last spring to Belfast. The Protestant government is considering various reform measures, but neither side believes that they will lead to peace (→ 12/22).

Aga Khan, Harvard man, wed in Paris

Oct 28. Aga Khan, spiritual leader of millions of Moslems, a millionaire and a Harvard graduate, was married in his home in Paris today. His bride is a beautiful English woman, Sarah Crocker Poole. She has converted to the Islamic religion and will henceforth use the name Begum Salima. The ceremony was performed by the head of the Moslem Institute in Paris.

Aga Khan and Begum Salima.

1969

NOVEMBER

Su	Mo	Tu	We	Th	Fr	Sa
						1
2	3	4	5	6	7	8
9	10	11	12	13	14	15
16	17	18	19	20	21	22
23	24	25	26	27	28	29
30						

2. Lebanon: Cease-fire reached with PLO guerrillas (→ 6).

3. New York: Census places city population at 7,964,200.

4. New York: John Lindsay re-elected city mayor.

5. Chicago: Black Panther leader Bobby Seales given four years for contempt of court (→ 12/4).

6. Cairo: Nasser says only Arab course is "fire and blood" (→ 12/21).

7. Israel allows TV broadcast on Sabbath first time (→ 1/23/70).

8. North Vietnamese troops strike bases deep in Mekong Delta (→ 20).

11. New York: U.N. refuses seat to Peking 20th year (→ 12/19).

14. Cape Kennedy: Apollo 12 launched by NASA (→ 19).

16. South Vietnamese villagers claim G.I.'s slew 567 unarmed peasants at My Lai (→ 19).

17. Helsinki: U.S. and U.S.S.R. begin SALT arms talks (→ 24).

19. Apollo 12 astronauts walk on moon, set up research station (→ 21).

19. Washington: U.S. sergeant says he saw G.I.'s massacre women and children at My Lai (→ 24).

20. Henry Cabot Lodge resigns as U.S. delegate to Paris peace talks (→ 12/15).

21. Cape Kennedy: First British radio satellite launched into orbit by U.S. (→ 24).

23. Saigon: Officials report U.S. is stepping up air raids on Laos (→ 3/8/70).

24. Georgia: U.S. orders murder trial for G.I. William Calley (→ 30).

24. Nuclear non-proliferation treaty signed by Podgorny and Nixon (→ 7/17/70).

25. London: John Lennon returns Order of British Empire award to protest U.K. support for Vietnam War (→ 4/10/70).

25. Washington: Nixon renounces germ weapons, orders destruction of stocks.

27. New York: Rolling Stones play Madison Square Garden.

250,000 war protesters march in capital

Peace symbols in Washington as 250,000 protesters fan out from the Capitol.

Nov 15. Inside the Justice Department and the Pentagon, hundreds of paratroopers stood at alert this morning with rifles loaded. They did not need them. The large rally in Washington demanding an end to the Vietnam War was for the most part orderly and peaceful. When a few splinter groups caused trouble after nightfall, it was tear gas and not bullets that dispersed them.

At least 250,000 protesters marched from the Capitol up Pennsylvania Avenue to the Washington Monument. Some carried coffins printed with the names of American war dead. Only one person was arrested. A young man from Buffalo was seized for drawing a peace symbol on the monument. Most of the demonstrators insisted that President Nixon's policy of gradual withdrawal was not good enough. "Tyranny has always depended on a silent majority," one sign said. "I'm an effete intellectual snob for peace," said another that was aimed at Vice President Agnew.

One Republican Senator spoke to the protesters. "We are not here to break a President or even a Vice President," New York's Charles Goodell said. "We are here to break the war and begin the peace." Goodell was joined by Democrats Eugene McCarthy and George McGovern, Coretta King, Arlo Guthrie, Dick Gregory, Leonard Bernstein, and Peter, Paul and Mary.

Parade marshals kept the demonstrators in order and were even criticized for being too firm with some protesters. After nightfall, a small group of young radicals pelted the Justice Department with rocks and bottles. At least 93 people were arrested. An equal number was injured, mostly by tear gas (→ 12/1).

U.S. ship makes 2nd landing on the moon

Nov 24. Mankind's second trip to the moon ended successfully today when the Apollo 12 astronauts landed safely within sight of the recovery ship USS Hornet in the South Pacific. Astronauts Charles Conrad Jr., Richard F. Gordon Jr. and Alan F. Bean took off from Cape Kennedy ten days earlier, with Conrad and Bean landing on the moon for a 32-hour stay on November 19.

On the 20th, they left the lunar module Intrepid for two excursions totaling more than eight hours that took them more than 1,000 feet from their spacecraft. On their second moon walk, the astronauts went to the inner surface of a nearby crater to collect parts of an unmanned spacecraft, Surveyor, that had been resting there for more than three years. They also collected 50 pounds of moon rocks and set up a battery of scientific instruments.

The one major flaw of the trip was the malfunction of a camera that was supposed to televise pictures of the moon-walking astronauts back to earth. But they lifted off the moon exactly on schedule and made a virtually flawless return trip, splashing down in the Pacific at 3:58 p.m. Eastern standard time. Aboard the Hornet, the astronauts, all Navy officers, were called by President Nixon, who told them they had all been given promotions (→ 1/13/70).

Royalty finds palace costly, Philip says

Nov 9. Prince Philip of Britain, pleading that the royal family is sorely pressed financially, said today on the "Meet the Press" TV show that he and Queen Elizabeth may have to move from Buckingham Palace to smaller quarters unless Parliament increases the queen's allowance. When crowned in 1952, she was granted an annual allowance of 475,000 pounds ($1.03 million); he was allotted 40,000 pounds ($95,000) a year. He said they have had to sell a yacht, and he might have to give up playing polo. Most of the allowance is allocated for particular purposes and the queen may only spend a small part on what she wants, he said. ▷

567 massacred at Mylai

Nov 30. An ugly, 20-month-old story is emerging from a small hamlet in South Vietnam called Mylai. Some 567 residents of the community were reportedly slaughtered by an American platoon. Survivors say many of the victims were women and children as young as two years old. First Lt. William Calley, the alleged platoon leader, has been implicated in the murders of more than 100 of the villagers. He will be given a general court-martial on charges of premeditated murder. If convicted, he could be executed.

The platoon swept into Mylai, a hamlet of Songmy, on March 16, 1968. Sgt. Michael Bernhardt, who was in the platoon, refused to identify its commander. But he did tell The New York Times that the commander ordered his men to destroy the village and the occupants. "He said they were all V.C. and there were no innocent civilians in the area," Bernhardt said, but "they were women and children and old men mostly. I didn't notice any military-age males there." He said it took "15 to 20 minutes" to wipe out the village.

An Army private told the London Times, "They had them in a group standing over a ditch, just like a Nazi-type thing." An ex-photographer told the Cleveland Plain Dealer he recalls a man holding two small children when the soldiers approached. "They saw us and were pleading. The little girl was saying 'No, no.' Then all of a sudden a burst of fire and they were cut down." Capt. Ernest Medina, described by the Army as the company commander at Mylai, said he never gave orders to shoot innocent civilians (→ 3/10/70).

Lt. Calley, charged with murder.

Bombings spread fear in New York City

Nov 13. A wave of terror has engulfed much of New York City in the wake of at least eight bombings in midtown Manhattan in recent weeks. Some of the buildings have been severely damaged and scores of others have been evacuated.

Today, the FBI announced it had arrested and charged three men and one woman with terrorism involving at least eight bombings and said that a fifth suspect, a young woman, is being sought in connection with the alleged conspiracy. Authorities say letters sent by the conspirators to various newspapers in recent days indicated a vendetta against the so-called establishment.

Several days ago, bombs exploded in the early morning in the RCA Building in Rockefeller Center; the General Motors Building on Fifth Ave.; and Chase Manhattan Plaza, headquarters of Chase Manhattan Bank. There have been explosions, too, at a United Fruit Company pier, the Criminal Courts Building, the Marine Midland Grace Trust Company and several other federal and corporate buildings. No one was killed but several persons were injured (→ 3/22/70).

Joe Kennedy, who drove sons to glory, dies

Nov 18. Joseph P. Kennedy, the patriarch of a political dynasty beset by tragedy, died quietly today at the family's summer home in Hyannisport, Massachusetts. The 81-year-old former Ambassador to Great Britain in the Roosevelt administration suffered a number of heart attacks in recent years.

At his bedside when he died was his wife, Rose, to whom he had been married for 55 years, and their only surviving son, Senator Edward M. Kennedy, a Massachusetts Democrat. Also present were Mrs. Jacqueline Onassis, the widow of another son, President John F. Kennedy, who was assassinated in 1963; and Ethel Kennedy, widow of still another son, Senator Robert F. Kennedy, who was slain in 1968 while celebrating victory in a presidential primary in California. Also present were three Kennedy daughters, Mrs. Eunice Shriver, Mrs. Jean Smith and Mrs. Patricia Lawford.

Solzhenitsyn calls U.S.S.R. a sick society

Nov 14. Aleksandr Solzhenitsyn has bitterly described his native land as a "sick society." In a letter to the writer's union of the Russian Federated Republic, which expelled him four days ago, the Soviet author castigated those who stripped him of his official status as a writer for their action and for not even giving him a chance to defend himself.

Dissenting writer Solzhenitsyn.

"The blind lead the blind, " Solzhenitsyn wrote. "In this time of crisis of our seriously sick society, you are not able to suggest anything constructive, anything good, only your hate-vigilance. Shamelessly flouting your own constitution, you expelled me in feverish haste and in my absence, without even sending me a warning telegram, without even giving me the four hours to travel to Moscow to be present."

Solzhenitsyn, the 51-year-old author of such anti-Stalinist novels as "One Day in the Life of Ivan Denisovich," "The Cancer Ward" and "The First Circle," has been silent for two years. His works have been banned in the Soviet Union since 1966, though the latter two have become best-sellers in the West.

"Publicity and openess, honest and complete—that is the prime condition for the health of every society, and ours too," he concluded in his letter (→ 11/27/70).

Senate turns down Nixon's Court choice

Nov 21. In a setback for President Nixon, the Senate today rejected the nomination of Judge Clement F. Haynsworth of South Carolina as an associate justice of the United States Supreme Court. It was the first time since 1930 that a court nominee had been rejected. The 55-to-45 vote was announced in the hushed chamber by Vice President Spiro T. Agnew, who said solemnly: "The nomination is not confirmed."

Critics had accused the nominee, who is Chief Judge of the U.S. Court of Appeals for the Fourth Circuit, of opposing civil rights and labor causes and of failing to separate his judicial and business interests.

President Nixon expressed deep regret over the Senate action and pledged that he would submit the name of another candidate who would "restore the proper balance" to the high court (→ 1/19/70).

Uninhibited Danes put on sex fair

Nov 1. They came from five continents to see for themselves that the Danes have ripped down the bars on the dirty-word-and-picture business. While some Americans are demanding stiffer rules, the Danes are boldly taking the opposite tack.

After a study that involved medical, psychiatric, sociological and church experts, Parliament voted in June to repeal the prohibitions (146 votes for, 25 against) and legalize pornography. This does not mean that they approve of it. They simply feel that prohibition stimulates interest, and that it is smarter to make pornography more legitimate and less tantalizing.

Actually, since the law change, sales of porno material are down. So, to stimulate foreign buyers, a six-day fair was held in the Copenhagen Sports Palace—with the emphasis on joyful sex, not sex combined with violence and sadism.

1969

DECEMBER

Su	Mo	Tu	We	Th	Fr	Sa
	1	2	3	4	5	6
7	8	9	10	11	12	13
14	15	16	17	18	19	20
21	22	23	24	25	26	27
28	29	30	31			

1. U.S.: First draft lottery since 1942 is held (→ 21).

2. The Hague: EEC nations agree to talks with U.K. (→ 5/10/71).

12. Milan: Terrorist bomb kills 13, injures 85 at National Bank.

15. Nixon announces 3rd round of Vietnam withdrawals (→ 30).

19. U.S. eases curbs on trade with Peking (→ 5/20/70).

20. Cairo: Nasser names Anwar Sadat vice pres. (→ 9/28/70).

21. Rabat: Arab leaders open conference (→ 1/7/70).

21. Montreal: U.S. draft evaders gather for holiday dinner (→ 2/14/70).

22. Belfast: Bernadette Devlin given six months in jail for part in Aug. 13 riots (→ 6/27/70).

31. Congo-Brazzaville declared a people's republic.

DEATH

22. Joseph von Sternberg, German film director (*5/29/1894).

CULTURAL EVENTS, 1969

Literature: Philip Roth's "Portnoy's Complaint"; John Fowles' "The French Lieutenant's Woman"; Mario Puzo's "The Godfather"; Vonnegut's "Slughterhouse-Five"; Norman Mailer's "Armies of the Night," Pulitzer.

Academia: Rene Dubos' "So Human an Animal," Pulitzer; Erik Erikson's psychobiography "Gandhi's Truth"; Thor Heyerdahl recreates Egyptian voyage N. Africa-Barbados in Ra II.

Music: "1776"; "Hair"; Tommy James & The Shondells' "Crimson and Clover"; Sly & The Family Stone's "Everyday People"; Peter, Paul & Mary's "Leaving on a Jet Plane"; Beatles' "Come Together."

The Arts: Oldenburg's monumental sculpture "Lipstick."

Film: Hopper's "Easy Rider"; "Bullitt," Steve McQueen; "Butch Cassidy and the Sundance Kid," Newman and Redford; Fellini's "Satyricon"; "Isadora," Vanessa Redgrave; Ken Russell's "Women in Love"; "They Shoot Horses Don't They," Jane Fonda; "Midnight Cowboy," Oscar.

Hippie group arrested in movie murders

Manson, eyes of a crazed killer?

Dec 24. "A sad, tragic mistake" is how Los Angeles Judge William Keene has termed the decision of Charles Manson to represent himself in court. Manson and four members of his commune have been indicted in the Tate-LaBianca murders. Manson will probably enter a plea of innocent.

Last August, actress Sharon Tate, the wife of director Roman Polanski, was brutally slain at her Beverly Hills home. Three guests and a passerby were also murdered. The following night, a similar attack occurred when Leno and Rosemary LaBianca, owners of a prosperous supermarket chain, were killed at their nearby home. On both occasions epithets were smeared in blood on the house walls.

Manson's hippie family lived in a ramshackle commune about 20 miles outside Los Angeles. Neighbors believed the cult worshipped both God and the devil. Drugs, especially LSD, were omnipresent. Even at their arraignment today, Manson and his followers had eerily bright eyes, as if something unnatural still raced through their veins.

Most commune members are young women who adore Manson like a divine prophet. From a distance, in long hair, beard and mustache, he may look one. Up close he is just a slight, 35-year-old ex-con who has crept in and out of reformatories and prisons since he was 13.

The prosecution will scramble for motives in the murders. Nothing was stolen, the accused did not know the victims and the evidence lies helter-skelter (→ 8/4/70).

British put an end to capital punishment

Dec 18. The British Parliament has voted to outlaw capital punishment. Three days ago, the House of Commons approved the resolution, and today the House of Lords passed it by voice vote. An amendment to permit executions up to July 31, 1970, was squelched.

Britain's only form of execution has been hanging. As of 1957, the punishment was applied to murder committed during a robbery, a killing committed while resisting arrest or murder of a police officer. Increasingly, offenders have been given life sentences instead.

An era in British history has gone with the gallows. The scaffold was a lurid, recurring image in novels by such authors as Dickens, who disapproved of the practice. The public spectacle went private and became more efficient; in the late 1800's trap doors were developed to allow victims' necks to snap quickly.

In America, hundreds of criminals are sentenced to the gas chamber or electric chair every year, but none have been executed since 1967.

Melodies make motion pictures memorable forever and ever

Hum a few bars of Tara's theme and you're looking at a Southern plantation. Soundtracks for the 1969 films have the same effect; hear the theme song from "Midnight Cowboy" and you see Dustin Hoffman and John Voight hustling in the streets of New York. Director John Schlesinger ("Billy Liar") has made a funny, moving film about a stud and his pseudo-pimp.

Hear Steppenwolf's "Born To Be Wild" and you're on the road with Dennis Hopper and Peter Fonda in "Easy Rider." Jack Nicholson plays a drunken lawyer joining the hip duo on their American journey.

Askew and Fonda in "Easy Rider."

Listen to "Raindrops Keep Fallin' on My Head" and you're astride a wobbly bicycle with Paul Newman and Katharine Ross. "Butch Cassidy and the Sundance Kid" stars Newman and Robert Redford as the infamous pair of bank robbers on the lam. George Roy Hill ("The World of Henry Orient") directed this truly unwestern western.

Hoffman in "Midnight Cowboy."

"You can have Paris, or London, or Rome" sings Petula Clark, but what the showgirl seems to want is a stuffy old professor. "Goodbye, Mr. Chips" stars Peter O'Toole as the oddly charismatic instructor.

Sydney Pollack directs exhausted dancers trotting to 1930's tunes in "They Shoot Horses, Don't They?" Jane Fonda stars. Maggie Smith makes her students sing and obey in "The Prime of Miss Jean Brodie."

And Barbra Streisand stars in "Hello, Dolly!" It's so nice to have her back where she belongs—in a movie musical.

"Sundance" and "Butch."

Samuel Beckett wins Nobel literature prize

Beckett, dramatist of the absurd.

Dec 10. A playwright of few words has won the Nobel Prize for literature. Samuel Beckett, 63, was recognized for "Waiting for Godot" (1953), "Krapp's Last Tape" (1959) and "Happy Days" (1961). The Irishman lives in Paris and often writes in French. He was once secretary to James Joyce.

Beckett explores sweet memory and the stultifying present. His characters babble to their subjective and objective selves. They live in wheelchairs, trashcans and mounds of sand. Like us, they are trapped.

Briton Derek H. Barton and Norwegian Odd Hassel shared the chemistry prize for studies on discrete compounds. American Murray Gell-Mann won in physics for work on behavior of elementary particles. Americans Max Delbruck, Alfred Hershey and Salvador Luria got the medicine award for findings on the genetic structure of viruses.

The International Labor Organization won the Peace Prize for improving workers' safety worldwide, and the first economics award was given to Norwegian Ragnar Frisch.

Our radical writers skewer the system

The sixties closed with a literary bang while the establishmentarians whimpered. The war machine, politics and that most exclusive of old-boy networks, the Mafia, were shot down in novels and non-fiction.

"Slaughterhouse-Five," by Kurt Vonnegut Jr., is a masterful anti-war novel. An innocent named Billy Pilgrim wanders through the horrors of World War II. He eases in and out of a sci-fi land, seeking respite that earth doesn't offer.

"The Collapse of the Third Republic" is a scholarly yet dramatic account of France before the Nazi invasion. William Shirer studies 70 years of a nation's fatal errors.

Norman Mailer's "Armies of the Night" aims to keep America from committing similar mistakes. He describes the 1967 peace march on the Pentagon and the public's wish for withdrawal from Vietnam.

"The Selling of the President" ridicules Richard Nixon's use of TV in his election campaign. Joe McGinnis quotes the man and details his methods of patent manipulation.

Mario Puzo invents a ruthless Mafia family in "The Godfather." The hub of the clan's vicious circle is Don Vito Corleone, a man who makes offers you can't refuse.

Panama's leader out and in again

Dec 16. Brig. Gen. Omar Torrijos, the commander of Panama's ruling military junta, was restored to power today, only one day after he was deposed in a bloodless coup by rival National Guard officers.

Yesterday, when Torrijos was visiting Mexico City, Colonels Ramiro Silvera and Amado Sanjur usurped the leadership of the Panamanian National Guard. The radio and television broadcasts which announced the overthrow justified it by citing the "cult of personality" that had grown around Torrijos, and the extreme concentration of power in his hands. The junta said that elections for an assembly to draft a new constitution would be held next December, although there was no mention of a new presidential election.

This morning, however, word of Torrijos' immediate return was spread, and, according to Colonel Luis Segura, "that was all that the troops needed to know to overthrow the usurpers." Silvera and Sanjur were arrested without any resistance. This incident follow a recent meeting between Torrijos and Governor Nelson Rockefeller of New York state on the subject of free elections in Panama (→ 10/11/72).

Willie Sutton is no longer doing time

Dec 24. Willie Sutton will enjoy a priceless Christmas gift tomorrow: his freedom. The bank robber was released from Attica prison tonight after two recent court decisions reduced 30- and 20-year sentences handed down in 1952. Sutton has been behind bars for 20 years.

Now a bent, whited-haired man of 68, Sutton was once a debonair thief known as "The Actor." He donned elaborate disguises for his robberies and dressed to the nines for his court trials. Sutton escaped from Sing Sing in 1932 and "blasted" his way out of a Pennsylvania jail in 1947 with a wooden rifle.

Sutton was on the lam from 1947-52, when a salesman named Arnold Schuster recognized him on a Brooklyn subway. Schuster turned him in and two weeks later turned up dead. Neither Sutton nor anyone else was ever charged with his mysterious murder. When asked why he robbed banks, Willie once said, "Cuz that's where the money is."

Willie "The Actor" Sutton.

U.S. presents a list of 1,406 MIA's

Dec 30. American officials issued a list to the North Vietnamese of 1,406 names of U.S. soldiers missing in action in Southeast Asia. Philip Habib, head of the American delegation at the Paris peace talks, presented the compilation to the Communist delegates in hopes "that your side, even at this late date, will indicate which men are prisoners and whom you know to be dead, as a matter of humanitarian concern for their families," he said.

North Vietnamese and Viet Cong representatives did not say what they would do with the list. Instead, they bitterly denounced the U.S. government, demanding that the United States withdraw its troops from Southeast Asia (→ 3/31/70).

Gunman in Uganda shoots down Obote

Dec 19. Uganda's President Milton Obote was shot and wounded tonight as he left the annual convention of his political party, the Uganda People's Congress.

A spokesman said that Obote, 44, had closed the convention and left the Lugogo stadium conference hall when three shots were fired. He was then taken to Kampala's Mulago Hospital, where his condition was said to be "not serious." A gunman is reported to have been arrested for the shooting. The convention which Obote had addressed had called for one-party rule. Shortly after the shooting a state of emergency was declared, and Uganda's opposition Democratic Party was banned (→ 1/25/71).

Chicago cops shoot up Black Panther gang

Dec 4. Two high-ranking members of the Black Panthers were killed today by the Chicago police in a pre-dawn raid on the group's Illinois headquarters. Fred Hampton, the Panther's Illinois Chairman, and Mark Clark, a party leader in Peoria, died and two female members were wounded in a wild shoot-out on Chicago's west side.

For weeks, the city's black community and the police have clashed in bloody confrontations; police shot and killed several black youths under controversial circumstances and blacks have fired on patrolmen. The deaths of Hampton and Clark bring the total to 28 Panthers who have died in battles with the police in the last two years. Hampton was called one of the most active organizers in the party, which has seen many of its leaders killed, arrested or forced into hiding (→ 1/24/70).

The 60's: Decade of Challenge and Change

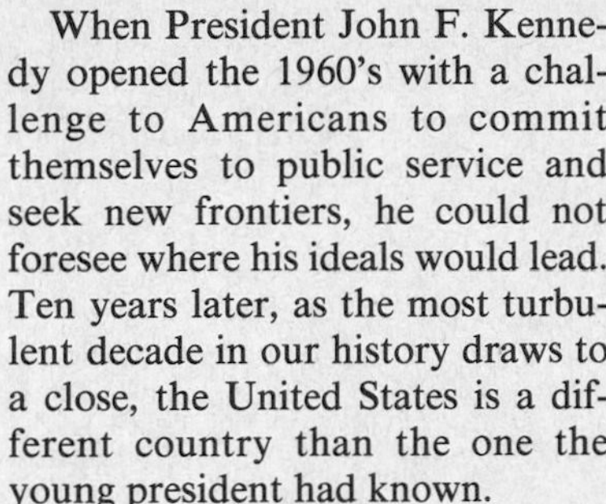

When President John F. Kennedy opened the 1960's with a challenge to Americans to commit themselves to public service and seek new frontiers, he could not foresee where his ideals would lead. Ten years later, as the most turbulent decade in our history draws to a close, the United States is a different country than the one the young president had known.

It was, above all, a decade of dissent. The civil rights and antiwar movements drew millions of people into the streets, where public protests raged. Bloody riots erupted, and cities and flags burned. But new rights were also won and the troops, Kennedy's "watchmen on the walls of freedom," are beginning to come home from Vietnam.

It was a decade of dynamic change for the nation's youth, the new generation to whom JFK said "the torch has been passed." Long hair, mod dress, drugs, sexual freedom and anti-establishment ideas were hard to find ten years ago; now they are everywhere, as affluent kids embrace a counterculture fueled by rock music and a sincere yearning for brotherhood and peace.

It was a decade of tragic death, not only for the soldiers in Southeast Asia but also for John Kennedy, Martin Luther King and Robert Kennedy. Who can forget when Martin was killed, and Bobby tried to console a crowd in Indianapolis by explaining that his brother had been killed by a white man too.

"What we need in the United States," he said, "is love and wisdom and compassion toward one another, and a feeling of justice toward those who still suffer within our own country, whether they be white or they be black." Two months later, Bobby was dead.

Despite its problems, the nation endures. It was an unforgettable, exciting era. It was, like another period of upheaval, simply the best of times and the worst of times.

1970-1979

1970

JANUARY

Su	Mo	Tu	We	Th	Fr	Sa
				1	2	3
4	5	6	7	8	9	10
11	12	13	14	15	16	17
18	19	20	21	22	23	24
25	26	27	28	29	30	31

1. Pasadena: U.S.C. over Michigan 10-3 in Rose Bowl.

7. Israeli pilots ("Moshe's Marauder's") attack military targets in Egypt (→ 23).

13. NASA announces it will cut 50,000 jobs (→ 4/11).

15. U.S. Sec. of Defense Melvin Laird announces defense reductions will cut 1.25 million jobs.

16. Tripoli: Col. Muammar Khadafy becomes premier of Libya (→ 7/21).

20. New York: Rocky Marciano KO's Muhammad Ali in 13th in computer-simulated bout.

22. Pan Am flies 747 New York to London first time, with 330 passengers.

22. Paris: Playwright Eugene Ionesco elected to French Academy.

23. Jerusalem: High court rules children may be registered by nationality rather than religion (→ 29).

24. Philadelphia: Nixon gives Medal of Freedom to conductor Eugene Ormandy.

26. Manila: Mr. and Mrs. Marcos attacked by protesters throwing stones, bottles (→ 30).

27. U.S. Senate passes bill allowing FBI to enter without warning or ID during drug raids.

28. Egypt: Israeli jets attack suburbs of Cairo (→ 2/1).

29. Israel: Cabinet reverses court ruling allowing definition of Jew by nationality (→ 1/20/72).

30. Manila: Two killed as 2,000 storm presidential palace protesting corruption in Marcos government (→ 3/3).

31. Washington: David Eisenhower breaks family tradition by joining Navy.

31. Louisiana: LSU star Pete Maravich breaks collegiate basketball scoring record.

31. France reports eight high school students have immolated selves in protests this month (→ 5/28).

DEATH

27. Erich Heckel, German Expressionist painter (*7/31/1883).

Biafra gives in to Nigeria after 30 months

Jan 12. Biafra, with its last defenses crumbling and its supplies of food and ammunition exhausted, capitulated today to the Nigerian government. The flag of independence was first raised on May 30, 1967. On July 7 that year, the Biafrans were plunged into a brutal, bewildering civil war. Only five nations recognized the secessionist state, for which international groups tried to raise funds. President Nixon has authorized an additional allocation of $10 million in food and medicine for Biafran relief.

In Europe, governments and agencies await authorization from Nigeria for a large-scale relief program and seek, with the U.S., to prevent reprisals against the defeated and starving Ibo people of Biafra.

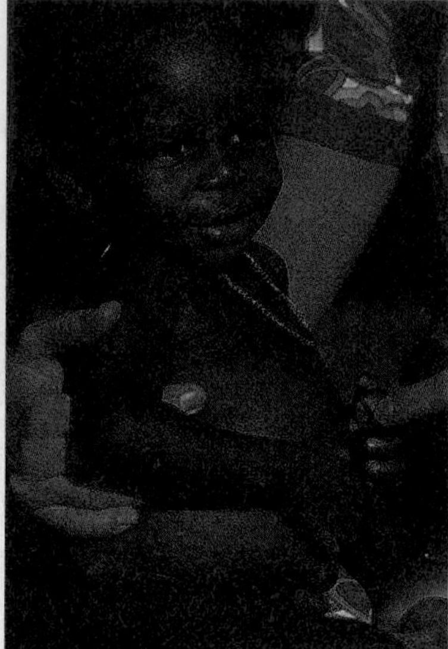

War may be over but hunger persists.

Radical Chic party raises cash for Panthers

Jan 24. Mr. and Mrs. Leonard Bernstein's gatherings on behalf of the New York Panther 21 Legal Defense Fund are rapidly becoming the most talked-about in town. "Not parties," says Mrs. Bernstein. "We have serious meetings, involving civil liberties." They range from 5-7 p.m. cocktail debates to buffet suppers with speakers, where celebrities mix with Panthers and others.

"The question is of a fair trial, of justice—not the Panther philosophy," says Mrs. Peter Duchin, one of those moved by Mrs. Lee Berry's story. Her husband is a Panther, a Vietnam veteran and an epileptic. It is claimed that he was taken from the hospital, handcuffed and put in the Tombs, as one of 21 black New Yorkers charged with plotting to kill policemen and dynamite public places. The disabled Berry is said to have been beaten and denied proper medication. "We seek information," says Mrs. Sidney Lumet.

One Panther wife says she feels no envy when invited to Park Avenue apartments. "I do wonder that one segment of the population has so much and the others don't have hot water and heat." The questions sometimes surprise her. "It's like nobody's heard of us" (→ 5/1).

Jan 11. Quarterback Len Dawson holds as Jan Stenerud kicks a field goal in this year's Super Bowl. The Chiefs vanquished coach Bud Grant's Minnesota Vikings 23-7 in New Orleans for football's highest honors.

Waiting for Brody, who never shows up

Jan 17. A lot of itchy palms are left empty tonight, as millionaire Michael Brody failed to show up with the bucks. A week ago Brody, son of a New York businessman who invested in oleomargarine, told reporters he was going to give his inheritance to needy people. Word traveled, and soon even down-and-out Parisians were demanding to know where their shares were. Tonight, Brody was aboard a jet bound for Puerto Rico. He had signed about $60,000 in checks, most of which were no good. The 21-year-old, guitar-toting "philanthropist" has estimated his fortune at $25 million, while insiders put it closer to $2 million.

Another named to Court by President

Jan 19. President Nixon today nominated Judge G. Harrold Carswell of Florida to a seat on the Supreme Court. The 51-year-old Southern conservative currently serves on the U.S. Court of Appeals for the Fifth Circuit. This marks the second time the president has sought to fill the seat vacated last year by Associate Justice Abe Fortas. Two months ago, the Senate turned down the president's first choice, Judge Clement Haynsworth of South Carolina, accusing him of racial and labor bias (→ 4/8).

South Africa bars Ashe, black athletes

Jan 28. Arthur Ashe, third-ranking tennis player in the United States, has been denied a visa to play in South Africa because of the black athlete's view on apartheid. The Minister of Sport said that Ashe would be barred only as an individual but would be permitted to compete as a member of the United States Davis Cup team. Ashe had applied for a visa to play in the South African Open and to tour the country. Had he been admitted he would have been the first black ever to compete against whites in South Africa (→ 2/20).

1970

FEBRUARY

Su	Mo	Tu	We	Th	Fr	Sa
1	2	3	4	5	6	7
8	9	10	11	12	13	14
15	16	17	18	19	20	21
22	23	24	25	26	27	28

1. Golan Heights: Israel, Syria clash in worst fighting since Six Day War (→ 6).

2. Munich: Nerve transplant performed first time in history.

6. Gulf of Suez: Israelis sink 700-ton Egyptian minelayer in reprisal for sinking of two ships at Elath (→ 6).

6. U.S. to sell jet aircraft and other weapons to Israel (→ 12).

9. Rome: Vatican calls on priests to affirm celibacy yearly (→ 8/26/78).

12. Cairo: Israeli jets attack scrap metal plant, killing 70 (→ 21).

13. Detroit: G.M. reported redesigning autos to run on unleaded fuel.

14. Chicago: Four defendants on trial for Democratic convention riots get long sentences for contempt (→ 15).

15. Chicago: Defense attorney William Kunstler gets four years on contempt charges (→ 18).

16. New York: Joe Frazier KOs Jimmy Ellis to solidify claim to heavyweight title (→ 10/26/70).

18. Chicago: All seven in trial for convention violence acquitted of conspiracy to incite riots (→ 20).

19. Baseball suspends Denny McLain for gambling ties.

20. Chicago: Five convicted in conspiracy trial get five years for crossing state lines with intent to incite riots (→ 28).

20. South Africa: 22 blacks accuse police of torture (→ 2/22/71).

21. Switzerland: Blast and crash kill 47 on Israel-bound Swiss jet (→ 22).

22. Israel calls for world aid in stopping attacks on civilian airplanes (→ 3/28).

25. New York: Van Gogh's "Cypress and Blossoming Tree" and one other sold for $2.1 million.

26. Saigon: Five Marines arrested on charges of murdering 11 S. Vietnamese women, children.

DEATH

17. Samuel Joseph Agnon, Israeli writer, 1966 Nobel Prize (*7/17/1888).

Unruly trial ends for Chicago Seven rioters

A Panther leader (left) greets Kunstler, Abbie Hoffman, Dellinger, Rubin.

Feb 28. The seven defendants in the Chicago conspiracy trial and their lawyers walked out of a Federal Appeals Court on bail today. Another round of their circus trial was at an end, but there is more to come. The Chicago Seven are appealing their convictions.

After a trial that was almost as divisive as the street fighting before the 1968 Democratic convention, the jury reached a split verdict. All the defendants were found not guilty of plotting to incite a riot at the convention. Five of them, David Dellinger, Rennie Davis, Thomas Hayden, Abbie Hoffman and Jerry Rubin, were found guilty of crossing state lines with intent to incite a riot. Two other defendants, John Froines and Lee Weiner, were acquitted.

After disrupting the trial frequently, the seven defendants and their lawyers, William Kunstler and Leonard Weinglass, were sentenced by Judge Julius Hoffman to terms of up to four years for contempt. One of the defendants objected that it was the court that was "in contempt of human life, dignity and justice." Dellinger told Hoffman, "You want us to be like good Jews, going quietly to concentration camps while the court suppresses the truth. That's a travesty of justice." Dellinger's supporters yelled, "Right on!" after he spoke. A defense lawyer screamed at the judge, "You are a racist, a fascist and a pig" (→ 3/2).

Rothko, celebrated artist, is a suicide

Feb 25. Painter Mark Rothko has been found dead in his New York studio, his wrists slashed. He recently suffered a heart attack, leaving him despondent. He was 66.

Russian-born Rothko was a disciplined Abstract Expressionist who used muted color and universal shapes to evoke common emotions, especially dread and anxiety. After brief instruction under painter Max Weber, Rothko met regularly with other Greenwich Village artists such as Barnett Newman, Arshile Gorky and Willem de Kooning.

At his death, Rothko's ideas were being accepted by the mainstream. One of his last works was commissioned by a church in Texas.

Maddox hands out ax handles in D.C.

Feb 24. Georgia Governor Lester Maddox stirred a furor on Capitol Hill today. Maddox argued with Senator Birch Bayh of Indiana, after Bayh suggested Georgia denies blacks their right to vote. He accused Michigan Rep. Charles Diggs, a black, of behaving "more like a baboon than a member of Congress." And he distributed ax handles in a congressional restaurant. Years ago, Maddox caught the public eye by wielding ax handles to prevent blacks from entering his Atlanta restaurant.

Bertrand Russell, versatile scholar, is dead

Russell, ended career protesting war.

Feb 3. Bertrand Russell, the renowned philosopher, mathematician, and political activist, died last night at his home in Wales. He was 97 years old. Russell had been Professor of Philosophy at Trinity College, Cambridge, and was the author of many books, including the classic "Principia Mathematica." He won the Nobel Prize for literature in 1950, and was a member of the British Order of Merit. The third Earl Russell was an ardent opponent of nuclear weaponry, and recently organized the Stockholm War Crimes Tribunal, which condemned American policy in Vietnam.

Avalanche kills 39

Feb 10. A huge avalanche in Val d'Isere, a town in the French Alps, has killed 39 people. Sixty others were injured. The victims, aged 15 to 24, were staying at a youth hostel.

Avalanche casualties in Val d'Isere.

1970

MARCH

Su	Mo	Tu	We	Th	Fr	Sa
1	2	3	4	5	6	7
8	9	10	11	12	13	14
15	16	17	18	19	20	21
22	23	24	25	26	27	28
29	30	31				

1. Salisbury: Rhodesia severs last ties with Britain (→ 9).

2. U.S. Supreme Court rules draft evaders can't be penalized after five years (→ 4/2).

2. Houston: Timothy Leary given ten years for smuggling marijuana (→ 10/20).

3. Manila: Police prevent 1,000 from marching on U.S. Embassy (→ 8/21/71).

4. Mediterranean: 57 lost as French sub Eurydice sinks.

8. Nixon administration discloses deaths of 27 Americans in Laos (→ 1/19/71).

9. U.S. to close consulate in Rhodesia (→ 8/15/72).

11. Paris: Picasso donates 800 of works to museum in Barcelona.

11. Iraq grants autonomy to Kurds, ending nine years of war.

13. Cambodia orders Hanoi and Viet Cong troops out (→ 18).

15. Osaka: Japan opens Expo 70.

17. Washington: Army charges 14 officers with suppression of My Lai facts; West Point chief Samuel Koster resigns (→ 4/1).

18. U.S.: Mail service paralyzed by first postal strike (→ 24).

18. Cambodia: Prince Sihanouk ousted in coup by premier (→ 27).

19. Berlin: Willy Brandt and Willi Stoph meet in first East-West Germany summit (→ 8/12).

21. Maryland: UCLA beats Jacksonville 80-69 for fourth straight NCAA basketball title.

22. New York: 15 hurt by bomb at East Village nightclub Electric Circus (→ 28).

23. New York: Mafia "Boss of Bosses" Carlo Gambino arrested for plotting $3 million theft.

28. Turkey: Earthquake strikes, killing 600.

28. Syria reports seizing 21 Israeli positions in Golan Heights (→ 4/5).

31. Vietnam: U.S. downs MIG-21, first since Sept. 1968 (→ 5/2).

DEATH

29. Anna Louise Strong, U.S. Communist writer, aided revolution in China (*11/24/1885).

New York townhouse bomb plant blows up

March 28. Two deadly explosions rocked apartment houses in New York City this month. The first occurred in a Greenwich Village townhouse, killing three people. Police are looking for Kathy Boudin and Cathlyn Wilkerson, two young women presumed to be radical terrorists of the Weathermen ultramilitary faction, who fled the scene of the explosion. An investigation determined the townhouse contained 57 sticks of dynamite, blasting caps, several homemade pipe bombs and other explosives.

Another massive explosion in a Manhattan apartment, which was being used to manufacture munitions, killed one man and seriously wounded another. Among the debris from the blast, police discovered live bombs, bomb-making materials, guns, a picture of Malcolm X and literature of the Black Panther political party. The men are believed to be responsible for some of the many recent bombings that have rocked New York City.

In recent weeks, the New York Police Department has received 2,246 bomb scares. On March 12, three separate bombs damaged office buildings in midtown. Then, on the 22nd, 15 people at a popular nightclub, The Electric Circus, were injured when a bomb erupted on the main dance floor. Local authorities have called in the FBI to help apprehend the terrorists responsible for the blasts (→ 10/30).

Army accuses five in Mylai massacre case

Capt. Medina and lawyer F. Lee Bailey (rt.) face a battery of microphones.

March 10. Captain Ernest Medina and four other men were formally accused by the Army today of murder and other crimes at Mylai in 1968. Medina was the commander of the company of soldiers that allegedly massacred hundreds of Vietnamese civilians in the hamlet of the village of Songmy.

It has been disclosed that Medina, commander of Company C, First Battalion, 20th Infantry, was charged with four murders, assault and maiming. A second Captain, Eugene Kotouc, was slapped with similar charges. At least one of the victims allegedly killed by Medina and Kotouc reportedly died during interrogation. If convicted, both men could be sentenced to death.

Three other soldiers were hit with charges ranging from murder to rape. In all, it is believed that 37 men are being investigated in connection with the massacre at Mylai; 22 of them have already left the armed services, and it is not clear how the Army will proceed with possible charges against them. Two men, including First Lt. William Calley, have been ordered to face courts-martial.

Last fall, it was reported that 567 residents of Mylai had been massacred by an American platoon in March 1968. Last November, Medina said he never gave orders to shoot civilians (→ 17).

Sihanouk removed; S. Vietnamese enter

Sihanouk, on a happier occasion.

March 27. Prince Norodom Sihanouk, who tried to steer a neutralist course for his nation, was ousted as chief of state of Cambodia in a coup by anti-Communist military leaders. Power was seized by Lt. Gen. Lonister, who had been urging a firmer stand against the presence of Communist troops in Cambodia.

Within ten days of the coup, South Vietnamese troops conducted their first major operation into Cambodia, sweeping through an area near the border known to be a Viet Cong sanctuary. Two American helicopter gunships supported the operation, but American military advisers did not accompany the South Vietnamese units. Sihanouk as well as the new leaders have been concerned about Communist use of Cambodia as a sanctuary (→ 4/17).

The costliest stamp: $280,000 for a cent

March 24. A collector from Wilkes-Barre, Pennsylvania, has paid $280,000 for a useless stamp—useless for mail delivery but very handy for inflation protection. The one-cent 1856 Guiana stamp may double in price in ten years. The tiny red scrap with the image of a sailing vessel upon it was printed in British Guiana (present-day Guyana). It is the only one of its kind. Coincidentally, a massive U.S. mail strike is crippling post office deliveries nationwide.

1970

APRIL

Su	Mo	Tu	We	Th	Fr	Sa
			1	2	3	4
5	6	7	8	9	10	11
12	13	14	15	16	17	18
19	20	21	22	23	24	25
26	27	28	29	30		

1. Washington: Army charges Capt. Ernest Medina in My Lai massacre (→ 5/4).

2. Mass.: Gov. Frances Sargent signs bill to force legality test in court for Vietnam War (→ 10).

5. Israel bars Nahum Goldmann, pres. of Intl. Jewish Congress, from meeting with Nasser in Cairo (→ 5/13).

7. Mass.: Dukes County grand jury closes Mary Jo Kopechne case (→ 1/21/71).

8. U.S. Senate 51-45 rejects Harrold Carswell for Supreme Court (→ 14).

10. Senate For. Rel. Committee votes to repeal Gulf of Tonkin Resolution (→ 21).

11. Cape Kennedy: Apollo 13 launched on third moon trip (→ 13).

13. Oxygen leak forces Apollo 13 astronauts to abandon ship and return in lunar module (→ 17).

15. France: 15 West European nations accuse Greece of torturing prisoners (→ 3/20/73).

17. Pacific: Apollo 13 splashes down safely after failed mission (→ 24).

17. Cambodia: It is reported govt. troops slaughtered 100 Vietnamese civilians (→ 30).

17. Washington: Johnny Cash plays at White House.

18. Moscow: Census puts Soviet population at 241.7 million.

19. Moscow: Rumania bars aid if Soviets attack China (→ 5/18).

21. New York: Fugitive priest Philip Berrigan held for pouring blood on draft files (→ 23).

22. Trinidad: U.S. flies in load of weapons to aid in quelling revolt inspired by black power groups.

23. Nixon bans occupational draft deferments and deferments for fathers (→ 29).

24. China launches its first space satellite (→ 6/19).

26. Master and Johnson publish "Human Sexual Inadequacy."

29. Ohio: Seven shot in student rioting at Ohio State (→ 30).

30. Ohio: Natl. Guard disperses students with tear gas, shot guns; 73 hurt, 100 arrested (→ 5/4).

Nixon sends combat units into Cambodia

G.I.'s march through now familiar-looking jungle terrain in a new country.

April 30. President Nixon has announced that he has sent American combat troops into Cambodia to destroy Communist military sanctuaries in that country. In a televised speech to the nation, the president described the action as "not an invasion of Cambodia" but rather a necessary extension of the Vietnam War designed to protect the lives of American servicemen and shorten the war.

As the president spoke, several thousand American troops were moving across the border to attack Communist staging areas in the area of Cambodia that juts into South Vietnam 50 miles northwest of Saigon. The president's action provoked an outcry of protest from congressional critics of the war. Senators John Sherman Cooper and Frank Church prepared an amendment that would bar the use of any funds for military operations in Cambodia (→ 5/5).

Millions march for ecology on Earth Day

April 22. Millions of Americans marched and participated in rallies today to mark the nation's first celebration of Earth Day. In New York, part of Fifth Avenue was closed to traffic for two hours. In Washington, Congress recessed and 10,000 persons joined in a rally at the Washington Monument. The Earth Day idea originated with conservationists in Congress and was organized by youth activist groups. Its purpose is to heighten awareness of ecological problems. Supporters say that Earth Day will become an annual event (→ 12/31).

Gypsy Rose, up from burlesque, is gone

Legendary Gypsy Rose Lee.

April 27. Gypsy Rose Lee left the stage forever last night, claimed by cancer at the age of 56. Before she died, she carved out a niche indisputably her own, moving the recondite H.L. Mencken to coin the word "ecdysiast" for what her more earthy fans were content to call the striptease. More than another burlesque queen, Miss Lee was a literate and charming woman whose books include the memoir "Gypsy," turned into a Broadway musical and a movie.

McCartney splits, breaking up Beatles

April 10. Paul McCartney marked the end of an era today when he announced he was leaving the Beatles, thereby disbanding the most successful pop group in history. McCartney said the split was the result of "personal differences, business differences, musical differences—but most of all because I have a better time with my family." The Beatles appeared to be drifting apart recently, as members pursued individual projects. The vastly influential and innovative group, which also included John Lennon, George Harrison and Ringo Starr, will release its swan song later this month, an album titled "Let It Be."

George, Ringo, Paul and John.

Blackmun named; replaces 2nd reject

April 14. President Nixon has named his third choice for the empty Supreme Court seat, Judge Harry Blackmun. Blackmun, from Minnesota, is a member of the U.S. Court of Appeals for the Eighth Circuit and is regarded as scholarly and rather conservative. While he is expected to go through extensive Senate scrutiny, most court observers believe he will be confirmed—unlike Nixon's two other nominees, Clement Haynsworth and Harrold Carswell (→ 5/12).

1970

MAY

Su	Mo	Tu	We	Th	Fr	Sa
					1	2
3	4	5	6	7	8	9
10	11	12	13	14	15	16
17	18	19	20	21	22	23
24	25	26	27	28	29	30
31						

1. Conn.: Police use tear gas to disperse rally of 12,000 Black Panther supporters (→ 8).

2. North Vietnam: 128 U.S. jets carry out heavy raid (→ 6/22).

4. Ohio: Natl. Guard shoots four students dead at Kent State protest rally (→ 6).

5. Peking: Sihanouk forms govt. in Chinese exile (→ 6/17).

6. Sec. of Int. Hickel complains Nixon is ignoring youth's abhorrence for Vietnam War (→ 8).

8. Chicago: Court frees 7 Black Panthers who survived shoot-out with Chicago police (→ 12).

8. New York: Helmeted construction workers beat up anti-war protesters (→ 9).

9. Washington: Rally asks U.S. pull out of Cambodia (→ 18).

12. Georgia: Six blacks shot dead in back at rally (→ 15).

12. U.S. Senate approves Harry Blackmun for Supreme Court.

13. Lebanon: Israeli forces leave after 32-hour strike at guerrilla bases; 30 Arabs killed (→ 6/12).

15. Miss.: Two dead, 12 wounded as police open fire on women's dorm at Jackson State (→ 17).

15. Nixon nominates first two women for general, Elizabeth Hoisington, Anna May Hays.

17. Miss.: Blacks begin boycott of white-owned businesses over recent police killings (→ 23).

17. Morocco: Thor Heyerdahl sails for Latin America in papyrus boat Ra II to prove Egyptians made journey 4,000 years ago.

18. Moscow accuses Mao of seeking rule over Asia (→ 7/2).

20. Mao calls for world revolt against U.S. imperialism (→ 7/10).

23. Atlanta: Five-day march against racism ends (→ 29).

25. N.Y.: Stocks fall 20 points to seven-year low (→ 8/25/71).

28. Paris: Maoist students battle police for second day (→ 6/26).

29. Calif.: Court voids conviction of Panther leader Huey Newton for manslaughter (→ 6/29).

30. Al Unser wins Indy 500 in Johnny Lighting 500 Special.

Kent State shootings shock the nation

National Guardsmen advance at Kent State just before the fatal shootings.

May 18. National Guardsmen fired into a crowd of Kent State University student protesters, killing two women and two men and wounding eight others. The May 4th shootings have created a furor as angry Americans try to comprehend the cause of such a tragedy.

Kent State has traditionally been a politically apathetic school. However, as many American campuses have risen up in opposition to the Vietnam War, students at Kent State joined in. Expecting trouble from a planned student rally against the U.S. incursion in Cambodia, university officials called in the National Guard. The federal troops broke up a demonstration at a college square. Some students, enraged over their presence, began yelling and tossing stones at the soldiers. The guardsmen, on previous orders to shoot if attacked, unloaded a burst of rifle fire at the crowd.

The incident comes on the heels of statements by politicians on how to control campus unrest, including California Governor Ronald Reagan, who said about protesters, "If it takes a bloodbath, then, let's get it over with." Education Secretary Robert Finch has said that such rhetoric heated the climate which led to the Kent State slayings.

Today, Soviet poet Yevgeny Yevtushenko published a commemorative poem to Allison Krause, a victim of the shootings (→ 6/24).

Knicks beat Lakers

May 8. The New York Knickerbockers have joined the Mets and Jets in the championship ranks. The Knicks won their first National Basketball Association title and became the third New York team in 16 months to dominate its sport. They joined the football Jets and baseball Mets by beating the Los Angeles Lakers, 113-99, in the seventh game in the final round of playoffs. The individual honors went to Walt Frazier, who got 36 points.

Bruins are champs

May 10. It took them nearly 30 years to do it, but the Boston Bruins finally won another Stanley Cup. They completed a four-game sweep of the St. Louis Blues by winning the clincher in overtime, 4-3, on a goal by Bobby Orr. The Bruins last won the cup in 1941 and they had finished last in seven of the eight years before 1967, when their new era dawned. Then the General Manager, Milt Schmidt, told his scouts, "If your prospects can fit through the door, we don't want them."

Hard hats uphold U.S. war policy

May 11. For the second time in three days, New York's hard-hatted construction workers showed their support for the Vietnam War by attacking several onlookers, snarling traffic and vocally abusing Mayor Lindsay. "Lindsay is a bum," they chanted as they marched beneath signs which read, "Impeach the Red Mayor."

Earlier, they had stormed and nearly taken over City Hall, beating up students and cowing officials into raising the American flag to full staff. It had been at half-mast in mourning for the four students killed a week ago at Kent State University. At Pace College, workers had also smashed windows and assaulted students. And in the city itself, they tore down a Red Cross banner and tried similarly to sully the flags of an Episcopal Church, apparently mistaking them for Viet Cong flags.

Yesterday's demonstration drew applause from the Wall Streets crowds, but one woman was heard to mutter in disgust, "The new Nazis—they're here."

Freelancer gets a Pulitzer for Mylai

May 4. Seymour Hersh, freelance reporter who broke the story of the Mylai massacre, has been named for the Pulitzer Prize in international reporting. Hersh circulated his articles through the Dispatch News Service in fall 1969. He has since worked on a book titled "Mylai 4."

Mylai is a hamlet in South Vietnam. On March 16, 1968, a U.S. Army unit entered the town seeking Viet Cong sympathizers. Over 350 unarmed civilians, including elderly women and newborns, were shot to death and tossed into a common grave. No one breathed a word about it until one sickened soldier confessed to a government official.

A shamed America blames division leader Lt. William Calley, who faces a court-martial and murder charges (→ 6/23).

1970

JUNE

Su	Mo	Tu	We	Th	Fr	Sa
	1	2	3	4	5	6
7	8	9	10	11	12	13
14	15	16	17	18	19	20
21	22	23	24	25	26	27
28	29	30				

1. Peru: Devastating earthquake kills over 30,000.

3. Madison: Hars Gorbind Khorana of Univ. of Wisconsin synthesizes first artificial gene (→ 11/12).

4. Tonga gains independence from Britain.

5. North Korea sinks armed U.S. spy ship in its territorial waters.

6. Pakistan: 191 govt. officials ousted for corruption.

8. Argentina: President Juan Carlos Ongania ousted in military coup (→ 8/27).

12. Jordan: King Hussein gains cease-fire with Palestinian guerrillas (→ 7/19).

16. Brazil: Kidnappers free Bonn envoy after obtaining release of 40 political prisoners.

17. Cambodia: North Vietnamese troops cut last operating rail line (→ 29).

19. London: Edward Heath becomes prime minister as Conservatives win majority in Parliament (→ 2/21/71).

19. U.S.S.R.: Soyuz 9 astronauts land safely after record 17 days in space (→ 9/21).

21. Mexico: Pele leads Brazil to third World Cup in soccer.

22. U.S. suspends use of defoliants in Vietnam (→ 10/12).

23. U.S. Army exonerates three officers in My Lai cover-up charges (→ 8/15).

24. Senate 81-10 repeals Gulf of Tonkin resolution (→ 7/23).

25. N.Y.: Judge orders McSorley's to serve women (→ 8/10).

26. Paris: Jean Paul Sartre and Simon de Beauvoir held for role on Maoist weekly (→ 11/24).

27. Belfast: Four dead, 100 hurt in rioting between Protestants and Catholics (→ 7/3).

29. Cincinnati: NAACP charges Nixon administration is racist (→ 7/9).

DEATHS

11. Alexander Kerensky, headed provisional Russian government in 1917 (*4/22/1881).

21. Ahmed Sukarno, Indonesian ex-president (*6/6/1901).

Thousands of homosexuals protest in N.Y.

Gay rights demonstrators in N.Y.

June 28. Beneath bright multicolored banners and chanting, "Say it loud, gay is proud," thousands of young men and women homosexuals marched from New York's Greenwich Village to Central Park yesterday in what one organizer called "a new militancy among homosexuals." Asserting "the new strength and pride of the gay people," they arrived from all over the Northeast, and the march was more than a token demonstration, their aim being to rescind laws that make homosexual acts illegal between consenting adults. They are also protesting the social stigma that often bars them from keeping jobs and renting apartments (→ 6/27/71).

Eighteen fixed by law as voting age

June 22. For years the cry has been heard: "We are old enough to die for our country, but we cannot vote!" Today, President Nixon silenced that refrain by signing into law a historic measure reducing the voting age from 21 to 18. The president immediately called for a court challenge to the new legislation to determine its constitutionality. The act was attached to a bill that extends the Voting Rights Act of 1965, which cut into racial discrimination. If the act passes the court test, and most experts agree it will, 11 million new, young voters will go to the polls.

E.M. Forster, esteemed British writer, dies

June 7. Before contemplating a trip to Italy or India, take an E.M. Forster novel along. Although it may have been written over 40 years ago, it will be a perfectly up-to-date guide, capturing the region's eternal rhythms and passions. Forster has died in England at age 91. His books "A Room With a View" and "A Passage to India" explored the tensions and delights that ensue when different cultures collide. He professed to doubt that people (of like culture or no) could ever really understand each other. "Only connect!" he entreated.

Edward Morgan Forster.

U.S. troops pulled out of Cambodia

June 29. The last American soldiers in Cambodia retreated to South Vietnam today, ending two months of U.S. military expansion in Southeast Asia. At its apex, the operation saw 18,000 U.S. troops maneuvering in Cambodia. Political opposition to the incursion pressured President Nixon to pull them out of the area, where Vietnamese Communists took refuge. Last week, the Senate voted 81-10 to repeal the 1964 Gulf of Tonkin resolution, regarded as the equivalent of a declaration of war in Vietnam. But Nixon has said the resolution does not guide his policy (→ 8/23).

Laurence Olivier first actor named Lord

June 12. Sir Laurence Olivier has been named by Queen Elizabeth as a Baron, Lord Olivier of Brighton, and a member of the House of Lords. Many luminaries of the theater have been made knights, beginning with Henry Irving in 1895, but few have been named to the peerage. Aside from Sir Laurence, only two playwrights have been so honored—Lord Willis in 1963 and Lord King Hall in 1966.

Lord Olivier of Brighton.

The 63-year-old Olivier is well-known for his performances in Shakespearean productions, most recently as Shylock in "The Merchant of Venice." Some 711 other people received honors from the queen as part of the celebration of her birthday. Most of the awards went to little-known people for service in community organizations, but Richard Burton, the actor, and John Schlesinger, the director, were included in the list (→ 3/24/71).

Bearden's "Patchwork Quilt."

1970

JULY

Su	Mo	Tu	We	Th	Fr	Sa
			1	2	3	4
5	6	7	8	9	10	11
12	13	14	15	16	17	18
19	20	21	22	23	24	25
26	27	28	29	30	31	

2. New York: Greek Orthodox vote to use vernacular in liturgy.

3. Spain: British plane crashes; 112 believed dead.

3. Belfast: Police battle snipers; five dead, 50 wounded (→ 13).

4. Wimbledon: John Newcombe over Ken Rosewall 5-7, 6-3, 6-2, 3-6, 6-1; Margaret Court over Billie Jean King 14-12, 11-9.→

5. Mexico: Luis Echevarria Alvarez elected president.

7. New Jersey: 46 shot in rioting in Asbury Park.

7. Bucharest signs 20-year friendship pact with U.S.S.R.

9. U.S. Justice Dept. sues Mississippi to force school integration in fall (→ 8/2).

10. China frees U.S. bishop James Walsh after 12 years in prison (→ 10/13).

11. New York: Two-year-old boy dies of LSD overdose.

12. Scotland: Jack Nicklaus wins British Open golf title.

13. Belfast: 100,000 march in favor of Protestant rule (→ 10/21).

16. London: State of Emergency declared as 47,000 dockworkers go on strike.

17. Belgian racer Eddy Merckx wins Tour de France.

17. Washington reports Israel may have A-bomb (→ 12/18).

18. Italy: On sixth day of riots, youths set fire to Reggio Calabria police station.

19. Israel conducts air raids on Egypt, Jordan, Lebanon (→ 23).

21. Libya confiscates property of Jews, Italians, claiming it was usurped in WWII (→ 4/2/71).

23. Cairo: Nasser accepts U.S. proposal for three-month cease-fire on Israeli border (→ 28).

27. Chicago: Three shot in riot at Sly and Family Stone concert.

28. Egypt frees 80 Jews; French diplomacy credited (→ 31).

29. Calif.: Cesar Chavez, United Farm Workers gain contracts with 26 grape growers (→ 12/4).

31. Israeli Cabinet, joining Jordan and Egypt, accepts U.S. plan for Mideast settlement (→ 8/7).

Aswan Dam is completed with Soviet help

The dam, 2.3 miles long, is 17 times larger than the Great Pyramid at Giza.

July 21. The final engine was switched on today at Gamal Abdel Nasser's dream project on the Nile. The Aswan Dam is finished, and the Soviets are being given much of the credit. They spent hundreds of millions of dollars on the project, and 5,000 Russian workers helped build it. Soviet Ambassador Sergei Vinogradov was smiling as the 6,400-foot dam was officially dedicated. Before the project was completed, the temple of Abu Simbel and four huge statues of Ramses were raised 200 feet so they would not be submerged.

Abortions numerous under liberal law

July 1. Hospitals report that 147 pregnancy terminations were performed in New York today, as the state's new, and the nation's most liberal abortion law went into effect. In New York City alone, 1,263 applications for abortions have been filed. Costs for the operation range from $300 to $500.

While eight of New York's Roman Catholic hospitals have maternity wards, they are not allowed to perform abortions. Catholic Bishops abhor the operations on moral grounds and have issued guidelines prohibiting any doctors or nurses in Catholic hospitals from assisting in pregnancy terminations anywhere.

New York City's Health Department directs family planning projects to prevent unwanted pregnancies. The department chief stressed the need for such projects, saying, "If we had done a good job in family planning, we wouldn't need abortions" (→ 1/22/73).

FBI finds shooting not needed at Kent State

July 23. An extensive Justice Department report has concluded the National Guard had no cause to fire on students at Kent State University last May. Guardsmen shot and killed four students during a protest against American military involvement in Cambodia.

Prosecution of those who shot into the crowd could occur if the situation is not legally classified as a riot. The analysis indicates the demonstration was not a riot and that the 200 protesters heckling the guardsmen could have been repelled by tear gas. The FBI recommended that alternatives to prosecution be explored. It also dismissed rumors that Communists instigated the protest (→ 8/11).

China-Russia accord

July 2. Relations between China and the Soviet Union seem to be stabilizing as Peking has accepted Vladimir Stepakov, the new Soviet Ambassador to China. The Communist superpowers have not had ambassadors in each other's capitals since 1966, when border disputes and ideological rifts caused a split in Sino-Soviet relations (→ 3/2/79).

Salazar, ruler of Portugal 40 years, is dead

Salazar, Premier since 1932.

July 27. Dr. Antonio Salazar, Portugal's authoritarian ruler for nearly 40 years, died today in Lisbon of a heart attack at the age of 81. Last September, Salazar was replaced as Premier by Marcello Caetano, after having suffered a stroke. Salazar's doctors never informed him of the transfer of power, and insulated him from newspapers, radio and television for fear the news of his replacement might prove fatal. Salazar's political policies, like those of Spain's Francisco Franco, were fervently right-wing. In his early years, he was a professor of political economy and deeply religious (→ 4/25/74).

July 4. John Newcombe wins at Wimbledon 5-7, 6-3, 6-2, 3-6, 6-1 over fellow Aussie Ken Rosewall.

1970

AUGUST

Su	Mo	Tu	We	Th	Fr	Sa
						1
2	3	4	5	6	7	8
9	10	11	12	13	14	15
16	17	18	19	20	21	22
23	24	25	26	27	28	29
30	31					

2. Miss.: First known interracial marriage in state's history is conducted (→ 29).

4. Washington: Nixon meets with Congo President Joseph Mobutu (→ 10/27/71).

5. Mass.: Robert Kennedy Jr. and Robert Shriver III facing marijuana charges.

7. Israel: 90-day cease-fire goes into effect along Egypt-Israeli border (→ 9).

9. Peru: 99 die in plane crash; 54 from U.S.

9. Lebanon: Israeli planes bomb guerrilla bases for five hours (→ 28).

11. N.Y.: Prisoners in Tombs riot for second day; city vows to investigate conditions (→ 10/4).

12. Washington: Nixon makes Post Office independent govt. agency.

12. Moscow: Soviets sign non-aggression pact with W. Germany; Bonn keeps right to work for reunification (→ 1/31/71).

13. Detroit: G.M. settles with Ralph Nader for $425,000 for invasion of privacy (→ 3/29/71).

14. Washington: FCC orders TV to give prime time to critics of Vietnam War (→ 24).

15. Saigon: U.S. Marine gets five years for murdering 15 Vietnamese (→ 10/19).

23. Guam: Agnew, on S.E. Asian tour, says U.S. cannot pull out of Vietnam if Cambodia falls to Communists (→ 1/22/71).

24. Wisconsin: One killed in bombing at Army Mathematics Research Center (→ 9/28).

27. Argentina: Terrorists kill major leader of trade union movement (→ 11/17/72).

28. Jordan: Palestinian National Council rejects U.S. peace plan for Mideast (→ 9/7).

29. Florida: Black Vietnam vet Pondexteur Williams buried in white cemetery under court order (→ 31).

30. Cleveland: U.S. tennis team retains Davis Cup.

31. Philadelphia: Police raid three Black Panther centers; three policemen shot (→ 4/20/71).

10,000 women observe 50 years of voting

Aug 26. A throng of 10,000 women paraded up New York's Fifth Avenue tonight, celebrating the 50th anniversary of the passing of the 19th Amendment. The march capped a day of activities for the women's movement across the U.S. Not content to rest on their laurels, women were demanding passage of the Equal Rights Amendment and other pro-feminist changes.

In New York, Betty Friedan, Kate Millett, Bela Abzug and Gloria Steinem spoke out for day care centers, non-sexist advertising and revision of some Social Security laws. Members of the National Organization of Women visited businesses to urge promotions and equal pay for women workers. "Man is not the enemy," Ms. Friedan said, "man is a fellow victim."

The vote is not enough 50 years later.

McSorley's opens to women, reluctantly

Aug 10. A 116-year-old bar in New York admitted its first female quaffer this afternoon, following the Mayor's signing of a bill forbidding sexual discrimination in public places. The pub is one of hundreds of formerly male-only establishments that must now admit women. Only a half-dozen females tipped an elbow at McSorley's today.

Lucy Komisar, NOW Vice President, was pushed and shoved trying to enter the bar. A waiter refused to serve her, unconvinced she was of drinking age. She quarreled with a male patron wearing an undershirt who was later evicted. The bartender asked Ms. Komisar if she had had a good time. "Not particularly," she said (→ 10/12/71).

Fugitive priest is arrested by the FBI

Aug 11. The Rev. Daniel Berrigan, a 49-year-old Jesuit priest who was convicted of destroying draft records to protest the Vietnam War, was arrested today by FBI agents at Block Island, Rhode Island. Berrigan, one of the so-called Catonsville Nine, was apprehended at the home of Anthony Towne and William Stringfellow, two prominent antiwar activists, after having eluded authorities since last April. Berrigan's brother, Rev. Philip Berrigan, is currently serving a six-month sentence for his part in the incident. The Berrigans have long been involved in a variety of causes (→ 14).

Daniel Berrigan, activist priest.

Nixon says Manson guilty, but retracts

Aug 4. Charles Manson gleefully displayed a newspaper this morning with the headline "Nixon Declares Manson Guilty" before the jurors on his case. The paper was confiscated and the judge asked the jurors if the headline would influence their opinions. All said it would not. Yesterday at a conference, President Nixon said Manson was "guilty directly or indirectly, of eight murders without reason." Minutes later he "clarified" the comment, saying a defendant should be presumed innocent unless proven otherwise. Last night, the remark was retracted altogether (→ 1/25/71).

Boy stowaway gets free ride to Paris

Aug 5. Next time you want to fly from Melbourne to Paris for free, look young and sound plaintive. It worked for 14-year-old Charles Semo-Tordjman, a Parisian-raised schoolboy who didn't like his family's move to Australia. Last weekend, he went to the Sydney airport, cried "Wait for me!" after a family of strangers, and was soon eating salmon in first class. He is staying with an uncle in Paris until his father can afford his return fare.

Jumbo jet with 379 aboard is skyjacked

Aug 2. Fidel Castro personally rolled out the welcome mat when a 747 jet landed in Havana this morning. The plane was hijacked by a beret-clad passenger shortly after it started its New York-to-San Juan flight. No one was injured, and some passengers even slept through most of the event. Castro walked around the plane and admired it; it was the largest ever to land in Cuba. He asked the pilot about its capacity and speed, and the pilot cheerfully supplied the answers. After a 53-minute wait on the ground, the plane and 379 passengers returned to Miami for refueling (→ 9/24).

1970

SEPTEMBER

Su	Mo	Tu	We	Th	Fr	Sa
		1	2	3	4	5
6	7	8	9	10	11	12
13	14	15	16	17	18	19
20	21	22	23	24	25	26
29	28	29	30			

1. N.Y.: World's first computer chess tournament opens.

1. Jordan: Hussein escapes assassination attempt (→ 7).

5. Chile: Salvador Allende becomes first elected Socialist president in Western hemisphere (→ 10/9).

7. Jordan: Arab commandos hold 150 hostages in desert on two N.Y.-bound jets (→ 9).

9. Jordan: Arab guerrillas hijack British jet, bringing hostage total to 300 (→ 12).

12. Jordan: Arabs blow up three jets after removing passengers; free 260, hold 40 (→ 14).

15. Detroit: U.A.W. begins strike against G.M.; 240,000 out (→ 11/11).

17. Jordan: Hussein's tanks clearing guerrillas out of Amman; U.S. orders Sixth Fleet to Mideast (→ 20).

20. Jordan: Syrian tanks invade second day in row (→ 21).

21. Soviet Luna 16 scoops up rocks on moon and lifts off for earth (→ 24).

21. Jordan: All cities in North except Amman now in hands of PLO (→ 26).

23. Cuba reports killing eight armed mercenaries from U.S. (→ 5/21/71).

24. U.S.S.R.: Luna 16 lands, ending first unmanned round trip to moon (→ 11/17).

24. Cuba returns hijacker to U.S. for first time (→ 2/6/72).

26. Jordan: Arabs release 32 Americans as Hussein and PLO agree on cease-fire (→ 27).

28. Ohio: Students burn draft cards in memorial at Kent State (→ 10/16).

28. Rhode Island: Intrepid wins America's Cup 4-1.

DEATHS

3. Vince Lombardi, Green Bay football coach (*6/11/1913).

22. Alice Hamilton, pioneer in occupational medicine (*2/27/1869).

25. Erich Maria Remarque, German writer, "All Quiet on the Western Front" (*6/22/1898).

Heart attack takes Nasser, Egypt's hero

Sept 28. Cries of "Nasser! You are in our hearts," reverberated in Cairo as word spread that the Egyptian leader was dead. Gamal Abdel Nasser, 52, succumbed to a heart attack just hours after presiding over negotiations between Jordan and Palestinian guerrillas. Nasser will be remembered as the feisty revolutionary who overthrew King Farouk, allied himself with Moscow and ignited a war against Israel. Fidel Castro called his death a blow to Arab revolutionary movements. But Nasser was a man who was not opposed in the end to talks with Israel. France's Foreign Minister called him a man of peace (→ 10/5).

An Arab hero is mourned in Cairo.

Jordan ends Palestinian takeover attempt

Tanks patrol Amman.

Sept 27. Jordan's King Hussein and Palestine Liberation Organization chief Yasir Arafat both had guns strapped to their waists when they shook hands in Cairo and agreed to stop fighting each other.

The agreement came just 11 days after Hussein proclaimed martial law in Jordan and installed a new military government to fight the Palestinian guerrillas who were threatening to take over the entire country. At one point, the guerrillas had overrun all of northern Jordan and were on the outskirts of Amman. In desperation, Hussein appealed to the United States for help, and American forces were put on alert.

Hussein and Arafat agreed to turn their attention to a common enemy, Israel. But Hussein has yet to solve another problem. Palestinians disavowed by Arafat are now holding 50 hostages in the desert; Israel refuses to meet their demands (→ 10/23).

Arabs hijack 5 planes, blow up 3 in desert

Sept 14. More than 50 airline passengers from five countries are still being held hostage in the stifling heat of the Jordanian desert by a Palestinian splinter group that is demanding the release of hundreds of prisoners. The passengers, from the United States, Israel, Britain, West Germany and Switzerland, have been held at gunpoint for a week by terrorists belonging to the Popular Front for the Liberation of Palestine. On Saturday, the gunmen blew up the three planes that the passengers had boarded in Europe. A TWA Boeing 707, a Swissair DC-8 and a British Overseas Airways Corporation DC-10 were all destroyed. A Pan Am 747 jumbo jet was blown up in Cairo last week after it was hijacked on a flight from Beirut. Two commandos tried to hijack an El Al 707 from Amsterdam last week, but the two terrorists were seized on board. One of them was killed. The PFLP is demanding the release of the other hijacker and hundreds of prisoners held by Israel, Great Britain, Switzerland and Germany (→ 17).

Drugs finish Jimi Hendrix, rock star

Sept 18. Jimi Hendrix, a musician whose searing guitar solos and flamboyant, sensual performing style revolutionized rock, died today in London of drug-related causes. He was only 27 years old. Born in Seattle, Hendrix spent years as a sideman before creating an instant stir in England leading his own group, the Experience, in 1967. His wildly imaginative guitar sounds, ranging from primal blues to innovative, high-decibel electronic wails, stretched the boundaries of rock to previously uncharted limits.

"Excuse me while I kiss the sky."

Margaret Court wins tennis Grand Slam

Sept 13. Margaret Court completed a Grand Slam of women's singles titles with a three-set victory over Rosie Casals in the United States Open tennis championships. The British star became the first woman grand-slammer since Maureen Connolly in 1953. The Grand Slam also includes the Australian, French and Wimbledon titles.

Ken Rosewall of Australia won the men's Open title by defeating Tony Roche. Only two men, Rod Laver and Don Budge, have completed the Grand Slam. The 35-year-old Rosewall delighted the Forest Hills crowd with his comeback. Not since Bill Tilden won the 1929 Amateur has a player of so "advanced" an age been able to stand the 12-day grind on grass.

1970

OCTOBER

Su	Mo	Tu	We	Th	Fr	Sa
				1	2	3
4	5	6	7	8	9	10
11	12	13	14	15	16	17
18	19	20	21	22	23	24
25	26	27	28	29	30	31

4. N.Y.: Tombs prisoners free 17 hostages as Mayor Lindsay threatens to use force; riots now in four city prisons (→ 9/9/71).

5. Montreal: Quebec separatists kidnap British envoy, demand release of 12 prisoners (→ 10).

7. Bolivia: Leftist General Juan Torres takes power as president (→ 8/22/71).

9. Chile: Leftists and moderates reach accord assuring Allende's installation as pres. (→ 11/3).

10. Fiji gains independence after 96 years of British rule.

10. Montreal: Two kidnap Quebec's Min. of Labor and Immigration Pierre Laporte (→ 18).

11. New York: Minister at St. John the Divine's urges legalization of marijuana.

12. Nixon announces pullout of 40,000 more Vietnam troops by Christmas (→ 11/21).

13. Ottawa: Canada opens ties with Peking, drops relations with Taiwan (→ 4/10/71).

16. Ohio: 25 indicted in Kent State shootings; none are National Guards (→ 11/9).

19. New York: World Trade Center, under construction, becomes world's tallest.

20. Algeria grants asylum to Timothy Leary (→ 4/20/76).

21. Ireland: Bernadette Devlin freed from prison (→ 2/8/71).

23. U.S. agrees to sell 180 tanks to Israel (→ 6/9/71).

26. Atlanta: After three-year absence, Ali TKOs Jerry Quarry in third round (→ 2/23/71).

28. Washington: Federal court bars U.S. from publishing list of radicals (→ 11/3/71).

30. N.Y.: Bombs hit two armories and police station (→ 11/2).

30. New York: Angela Davis sues city to release her from solitary confinement (→ 12/22).

DEATHS

10. Edouard Daladier, French ex-premier 1930's, Radical Party leader (*6/18/1884).

22. John T. Scopes, accused teacher in Tennessee "monkey trial" (*8/3/1900).

Trudeau acts firmly against Quebec revolt

Trudeau, keeping Canada united.

Oct 18. Canada's Prime Minister Pierre Trudeau, calling a band of French separatists "insurrectionists," has invoked emergency war powers to quell their rebellion. Hundreds of suspects were rounded up almost immediately in Montreal, Quebec and other cities.

The police crackdown did not come quickly enough to save Labor Minister Pierre Laporte, who had been kidnapped by French extremists. His body was found crumpled in the trunk of a car. Nothing is known of the fate of James Cross, a senior British consular official. He was kidnapped at gunpoint on the 5th by members of the Front for the Liberation of Quebec. It is not known whether the terrorists have heeded an appeal from the diplomat's wife. She has urged them to give Cross the life-saving medication he needs twice a day to treat his high blood pressure.

The extremists are demanding $500,000 in gold, the rehiring of fired postal workers and flights to Cuba or Algeria for 23 inmates they call political prisoners. Trudeau, calling the prisoners "bandits," has rejected the demands (→ 3/13/71).

Witness testifies he saw Calley kill civilians

Oct 19. Dramatic testimony at a Texas court-martial linked First Lt. William Calley and another defendant to the slaughter of helpless Vietnamese civilians in the hamlet of Mylai. Charles Sledge, the radioman in Calley's platoon, testified that he was rarely more than a few feet from Calley's side. Sledge said that he saw Calley and Sgt. David Mitchell herd women, children and elderly men into a ditch before they opened fire. There was a lot of screaming, Sledge said, "and a lot of blood falling."

Sledge and another witness, Dennis Conti, said they did not see or hear hostile fire in Mylai. The civilians "screamed as they were getting shot up," Conti said. "I saw Lt. Calley fire, and I saw a woman get hit in the head and a piece fly off." Calley is charged with murdering 109 civilians at Mylai (→ 11/12).

Angela Davis, back in East, caught by FBI

Disguised Davis arrested in N.Y.

Oct 13. Angela Davis, 26, a former acting assistant professor of philosophy at UCLA, who has been hunted for nearly two months on murder and kidnap charges, was arrested yesterday at a midtown Manhattan motel by FBI agents. She and a male companion were unarmed and offered no resistance. The charges grew out of a kidnap-escape drama in a San Rafael courtroom in August, when a California Superior Court judge and three others were killed. Miss Davis is not alleged to have been at the scene but is charged as an accomplice for having bought a 12-gauge shotgun used in the killings (→ 30).

Janis Joplin falls victim to drugs

Sad but soulful Janis Joplin.

Oct 4. Janis Joplin, known for her passionate, bluesy vocal style, died today in Hollywood of a drug overdose. She was just 27 years old. Miss Joplin, called "Pearl," was raised in Port Arthur, Texas, but later moved to San Francisco, where she gained fame in 1967 as lead singer of Big Brother and the Holding Company.

Sadat succeeds Nasser as President

Oct 5. Anwar Sadat, Gamal Abdel Nasser's Vice President, has been elected President of the United Arab Republic. Nasser's funeral on the 1st was an extraordinary gathering of dignitaries. Sobbing women cried out, "Gamal, my beloved, what have we done to you to make you leave our house?" (→ 1/4/71).

Moderate Sadat, new chief in Cairo.

1970

NOVEMBER

Su	Mo	Tu	We	Th	Fr	Sa
1	2	3	4	5	6	7
8	9	10	11	12	13	14
15	16	17	18	19	20	21
22	23	24	25	26	27	28
29	30					

1. France: Fire in nightclub kills 142.

2. New York: Six weathermen arrested as bomb plotters (→ 12/4).

3. New York: Nelson Rockefeller re-elected governor.

3. Cleveland: Jane Fonda charged with smuggling pills and kicking police officer.

3. Chile: Allende sworn in as president (→ 1/1/71).

9. Supreme Court refuses to hear Mass. challenge on legality of Vietnam War (→ 3/21/71).

11. Detroit: G.M. and U.A.W. agree on terms of pact, ending two-month strike.

11. London: Govt. gives $100 mil. grant to struggling Rolls-Royce Co. (→ 2/4/71).

12. Buffalo: Scientists report first artificial synthesis of living cell (→ 1/6/71).

12. Georgia: Lt. Calley court-martial opens in Mylai massacre case (→ 20).

13. Syria: Def. Min. Gen. Hafez al-Assad seizes power in coup.

17. Soviets now operating Lunar 17—self-propelled, eight-wheel vehicle—on moon (→ 1/31/71).

20. Texas: Sgt. David Mitchell acquitted on Mylai charges (→ 12/7).

21. North Vietnam: U.S. planes conduct widespread bombing raids (→ 23).

23. Washington says rescue team landed 23 miles from Hanoi but failed to find POW's (→ 12/24).

24. Paris: Alain Geismar, hero of New Left students, gets two-year sentence for illegal political activities (→ 6/18/71).

27. Syria joins pact linking Libya, Egypt and Sudan (→ 8/12/71).

28. Philadelphia: Navy over Army 11-7 in football.

30. Washington: Census puts U.S. population at 204,765,770.

DEATHS

26. Benjamin Davis, first black U.S. general (*7/1/1877).

30. Nina Ricci, French fashion designer (*11/14/1881).

France mourns de Gaulle

De Gaulle, embodiment of France.

Nov 12. Charles de Gaulle, who represented like no other man the grandeur of France, was buried today in a simple country ceremony near his home in Colombey-les-Deux-Eglises. Kings and heads of state had paid their respects in Paris. They were not invited to Colombey. De Gaulle had requested that "neither President, nor ministers, nor Assembly committees, nor public authorities" come to the funeral. There were no orations, no speeches. But tens of thousands of ordinary Frenchmen did come, squeezing into the square and streets around the Church of Notre Dame to catch a glimpse of de Gaulle's coffin as it was driven from his home to the funeral mass in a simple military vehicle.

Twelve boys from the village carried the coffin into the church. Several pews were reserved for veterans of the resistance, including Andre Malraux. The rest of the church was filled by family and villagers. Large wreaths sent by Mao Tse-tung covered one of the walls. The parish priest, a Bishop and de Gaulle's nephew offered the mass and gave communion to Mrs. de Gaulle and her family. The young pall bearers then removed the casket to de Gaulle's resting place. He was buried next to the grave of Anne, his retarded daughter. "She was not like the others," remembered a chaplain from the resistance. "And when she was buried there, de Gaulle told his wife, 'Now she is like the others.' Well, now de Gaulle is like the others."

At Notre Dame in Paris this morning, the mood was more formal and worldly. Some 80 Emperors, Kings and heads of state had come from around the world. Among those paying their respects were President Pompidou, President Nixon, Soviet leader Nikolai Podgorny, the Shah of Iran, Emperor Haile Selassie, Prince Rainier of Monaco and many African leaders.

Political animosities were forgotten at the majestic funeral. Socialist leader Francois Mitterrand said, "No one can love France more than he loved it." The Times of London called de Gaulle the "spokesman, conscience and personification of France." Nixon said, "The clarity of his vision allowed him to recognize the great movements of history while others could only see the events of the day."

Dignitaries gather in Paris to honor the controversial French leader.

Wave sweeps away 150,000 victims

Nov 19. The death toll from the cyclone and tidal wave that struck the Ganges Delta in Pakistan a week ago has been put at 150,000 by government officials. A government spokesman said that a million survivors face death if relief supplies cannot be delivered to them soon. The 120-mile-an-hour cyclone swept a tidal wave more than 20 feet high over the East Pakistani coast and more than 100 nearby islands. Bhola, the island that took the brunt of the storm, suffered an estimated 100,000 deaths. Mass burials of 5,000 persons were reported in several communities.

Nobel Prize winner won't pick it up

Nov 27. Aleksandr Solzhenitsyn says he will not go to Sweden for "personal" reasons, and the Nobel Committee knows what they are: If he picked up his prize for literature, the Soviet Union would personally see to it that he never comes back. The writer does not want to risk being permanently separated from his family (his wife is often under medical treatment). His anti-Stalinist books "One Day in the Life of Ivan Denisovich," "The First Circle" and others irk Soviet officials. They are published only outside the U.S.S.R. (→ 4/4/72).

Japanese novelist commits hara-kiri

Nov 25. Japanese novelist Yukio Mishima burst unannounced into Tokyo defense headquarters today, stepped out on a balcony and exhorted a crowd of hundreds to revivify the militarized state. When boos and jeers erupted, he retreated inside to commit hara-kiri. The 45-year-old author of "Confessions of a Mask" and other works advocated a return to imperial glory. His books, lyrical if macabre, lauded the tradition of suicide. Mishima was a martial artist who organized a private army of youths with Japanese government consent, a government now sent reeling.

1970

DECEMBER

Su	Mo	Tu	We	Th	Fr	Sa
		1	2	3	4	5
6	7	8	9	10	11	12
13	14	15	16	17	18	19
20	21	22	23	24	25	26
27	28	29	30	31		

2. U.S. Senate votes to give 48,000 acres of New Mexico back to Taos Indians.

4. New York: Six Weathermen arrested for attempting to blow up bank (→ 7/8/80).

7. Texas: G.I. testifies Lt. Calley shot civilians at Mylai for one hour (→ 14).

8. Washington: Gen. Westmoreland ends Army practice of playing reveille in morning.

10. Detroit: Lee A. Iacocca named Ford pres. (→ 7/14/78).

18. Nevada: Atomic leak forces hundreds to flee test site (→ 2/11/71).

22. California: Angela Davis, extradited from N.Y., booked for murder, kidnapping, criminal conspiracy (→ 2/23/72).

24. Vietnam: Nine G.I.'s killed, nine wounded by U.S. artillery fire (→ 1/1/71).

30. Madrid: Franco, under pressure in Europe, voids death sentences of 6 Basques (→ 11/3/73).

31. Nixon signs bill to cut auto fumes 90% by 1977 (→ 4/14/71).

CULTURAL EVENTS, 1970

Literature: Eudora Welty's "Losing Battles"; Neil Simon's "Last of the Red Hot Lovers"; Richard Bach's "Jonathan Livingston Seagull."

Academia: Theodore Roszak's "The Making of a Counter-culture"; archeologists find Buddha-like statue in Guatemala dating to 700-300 B.C.

Music: Sondheim's "Company"; "Applause," with Lauren Bacall; Burt Bacharach, Academy Award for "Butch Cassidy and the Sundance Kid" score; Simon and Garfunkel's "Bridge over Troubled Water"; Beatles' "Let It Be"; Jackson 5's "ABC," "I'll Be There"; Smokey Robinson & The Miracles' "The Tears of a Clown"; George Harrison's "My Sweet Lord."

The Arts: Met buys Velasquez's "Portrait of Juan de Paraja," for $5 mil.; Robert Smithson's "Spiral Jetty," environmental art.

Film: "True Grit," John Wayne; Mike Nichols' "Catch-22"; Hitchcock's "Topaz"; Wadleigh's "Woodstock."

Cesar Chavez jailed for lettuce boycott

Chavez pleads for a peaceful strike.

Dec 4. "Boycott the hell out of them!" yelled Cesar Chavez as he was led to jail today. The Mexican-American labor leader received a ten-day jail term for organizing an illegal nationwide boycott of lettuce on behalf of workers who do not have contracts with unions. Superior Court Judge Gordon Campbell, in Salinas, California, demanded that the defiant and influential Chavez call off the boycott.

Chavez, leader of the United Farm Workers Organizing Committee, claimed "sweetheart" contracts were arranged between the Teamsters union and many of the lettuce producers, neglecting the concerns of farm workers. Chavez vows to fight the ruling (→ 2/29/72).

Million cans of tuna are recalled by FDA

Dec 15. The Food and Drug Administration today ordered the recall of more than one million cans of tuna fish because of mercury contamination. The agency said the recall was precautionary and that the tuna fish was safe to eat even though about 23 percent of the cans contained amounts of mercury that are considered excessive. The recall came after tests in which an average of .37 parts per million of mercury were found in 138 cans that were tested. The cause of the mercury contamination remains a mystery. The loss to the canning industry is an estimated $84 million.

Polish riots drive Gomulka from job

Dec 23. A decade of discontent and a week of rioting forced the Polish government to dump Communist Party chief Wladyslaw Gomulka for the popular Edward Gierek. The economy has been depressed for some time, but drastic increases in food, fuel and clothing prices in the week before Christmas turned anger to action as looting and rioting left hundreds injured and 60 dead. Gierek, a party official who was credited with ending last year's meat shortage, shortly after taking office said recent events "have reminded us the party must always maintain a close link with the working class" (→ 10/29/77).

Hijacking sends 11 to prison in U.S.S.R.

Dec 31. Although on December 24 a Soviet court found all 11 defendants accused of attempting to hijack a plane on June 18 guilty and sentenced two of them to death, the decision was eased today, sparing the lives of the two and lightening the terms of some of the others. Of the 11, nine were Jews who said they were trying to escape anti-Semitism in the Soviet Union. Foreign protests were seen as a major factor in deciding to ease the sentences. The hijackers allegedly planned to fly the single-engine aircraft to Sweden. It has not been revealed how the Soviet agents knew about the hijacking plot or why 20 other Jews were arrested at the same time in various places throughout Russia.

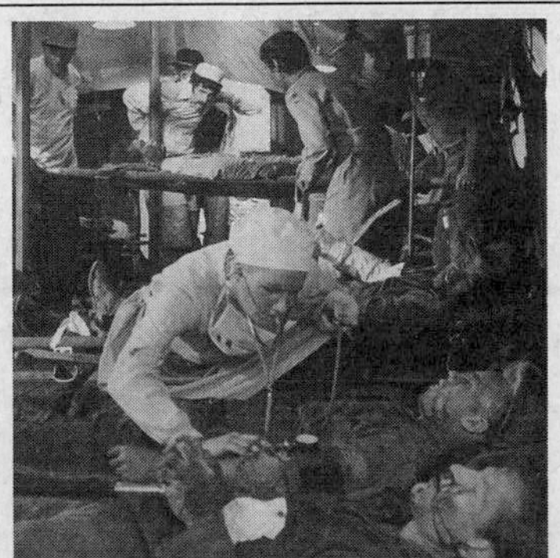

"M*A*S*H," poking fun at war, the gravest of issues, is black comedy at its irreverent best.

G.I. says officer had ordered massacre

Dec 14. Defense witnesses at the Mylai murder trial of Lt. William Calley testified today that they believed a commanding officer had given them the go-ahead to kill every living human being in the Vietnamese hamlet. Capt. Ernest Medina, they testified, wanted everyone dead. When Sgt. L.G. Bacon was asked if that included women and children, he replied "Yes" twice. Last week, a witness shocked the defense when he testified that Calley shot women and children and dumped them in a ditch for over an hour. Today's testimony was designed to show that Calley was simply following orders (→ 1/22/71).

Borlaug gets Nobel for aid to hungry

Dec 10. Norman Borlaug, the Iowa-born crop expert whose research on new strains of high-yielding rice and wheat has led to a Green Revolution in developing countries, was awarded the Nobel Peace Prize today. Working at the International Maize and Wheat Improvement Center of Mexico since 1944, Borlaug, 56, has directed a team of agronomists working on development of new crop plant strains that have allowed Third World farmers to multiply yields dramatically. His organization has trained farm technicians from 29 countries, including India, Pakistan and Turkey, enabling them to move steadily toward the goal of self-sufficiency in food production.

George C. Scott may be infuriating but he is also unforgettable as eccentric warrior "Patton."

1971

JANUARY

Su	Mo	Tu	We	Th	Fr	Sa
					1	2
3	4	5	6	7	8	9
10	11	12	13	14	15	16
17	18	19	20	21	22	23
24	25	26	27	28	29	30
31						

1. Pasadena: Stanford beats Ohio State 27-17 in Rose Bowl.

1. U.S. begins second decade of involvement in Vietnam (→ 6).

1. Chile nationalizes banking (→ 2/17).

4. Cairo: Sadat admits six Soviet soldiers aiding Egypt were killed in Israeli raid (→ 5/13).

5. Washington: Nixon names Robert Dole chairman of Republican National Party.

6. Calif.: Berkeley chemists announce first synthetic production of growth hormones (→ 4/5/73).

14. Brazil frees 70 political prisoners in exchange for kidnapped Swiss envoy.

19. New York: Police end six-day strike.

19. Saigon: Officials report U.S. is flying helicopter missions for Laos troops (→ 2/8).

21. Washington: Robert Byrd ousts Edward Kennedy as assistant majority leader of Senate (→ 9/23/74).

22. Georgia: Army clears last four enlisted men in Mylai case (→ 29).

22. Cambodia: Communists shell Phnom Penh for first time (→ 5/11).

23. New Haven: Oil tanker runs aground, spilling 385,000 gallons into Long Island Sound.

24. Guinea sentences 92 to death in treason trial.

29. Washington: Army dismisses Mylai charges against Maj. Gen. Samuel Koster.→

29. New York: Marty Liquori wins Wanamaker Mile for third time.

30. Washington: U.S. signs accord on fishing dispute with Ecuador after rebuke from OAS.

31. Cape Kennedy: Apollo 14 launched on moon mission (→ 2/5).

31. Berlin: Telephone service links East and West for first time in 19 years (→ 5/12/72).

DEATH

6. Sonny Liston, American boxer, ex-heavyweight champ.

Manson and three women guilty of murder

Jan 25. A grueling 121-day trial for Charles Manson and three codefendants has ended with a verdict of guilty. When the jury filed into the Los Angeles courtroom to deliver its decision, uniformed police and plainclothesmen sifted into the spectator's section. They kept their eyes on the glassy-eyed defendants.

Manson was found guilty of planning the murders of the actress Sharon Tate and four others at her Beverly Hills home in August 1969. He was also found guilty in the deaths of the LaBiancas, a Los Angeles couple. In the latter case, Manson strolled on the beach munching peanuts while his hippie family carried out his instructions.

During the trial, Manson ranted about an impending war between blacks and whites. His lawyers were often fined for their unrestrained outbursts. The female co-defendants, all in their early 20's, showed no emotion when the first-degree charge was handed down. "You won't outlive this, old man," Manson told Judge William Older. The accused himself is 36 years old.

In California, first-degree murder leads to life imprisonment or death in the gas chamber. The prosecution seeks the latter (→ 3/29).

Idi Amin seizes power in Uganda

Amin, fought with British in WWII.

Jan 25. President Milton Obote of Uganda was not in the country today when rebels toppled his government. He was lucky. The insurrectionists, led by Maj. Gen. Idi Amin Dada, left a bloodbath in their wake, murdering all troops and officials who were loyal to Obote.

Idi Amin, who rose in the military ranks from private to commander of the army, gave himself dictatorial powers. He declared a nighttime curfew, and soldiers in Kampala were shooting their weapons into the air tonight to discourage anyone from breaking the curfew. Workers considered to be essential were given military escorts to their jobs. Amin is expected to solidify his control over the government by dissolving Parliament and outlawing political parties (→ 9/14/72).

McGovern campaign pledges end of war

McGoverns, seeking White House.

Jan 18. Senator George McGovern of South Dakota opened his campaign for the Democratic presidential nomination today, pledging that he would withdraw all U.S. troops from Vietnam if he is elected. A persistent critic of the war in Southeast Asia, Senator McGovern is the first announced candidate for the nation's top elective office to be decided 22 months from now. His early announcement signalled his awareness that he trails the party's front-runner, Senator Edmund Muskie of Maine, who has not yet formally announced his candidacy. Muskie said today that Senator McGovern's announcement came as "no surprise" (→ 8/5).

Coco Chanel, fashion revolutionary, is dead

Jan 10. Famed fashion designer Gabrielle "Coco" Chanel has died in Paris. When Katharine Hepburn appeared in a biographical play last year, Chanel sneered that Miss Hepburn was too old for the part. The actress was 60, the couturier 86.

For 50 years Miss Chanel uncluttered women's wardrobes. She used comfortable fabrics in subdued beige, black and gray. One day in the 1920's, after her hair got terribly dirty, she bobbed it. Millions of women followed suit, dirty hair or no. In the 30's, she came back from a vacation sporting a deep tan and slacks. Another trend was on. Miss Chanel called her famous perfume No. 5 because a fortune teller told her that was her lucky number.

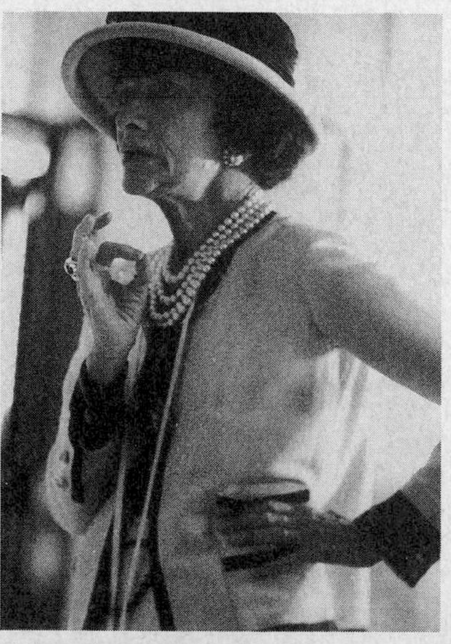

"Grande Dame" of fashion.

Long Red hair legal

Jan 7. "Oh say can you see, my eyes, if you can, then my hair's too short." Sung to the tune of the "The Star Spangled Banner," this refrain is popular with young American men who sport long hair. But their counterparts in the Soviet Union have had a more difficult time letting their locks flow. Until recently, long-haired Soviets could be arrested for such fashion. Now, First Deputy Prosecutor General Mikhail Malyarov, replying to a young woman who asked for help after seeing her shaggy boyfriend hauled off to jail for his appearance, said police may not incarcerate long-haired comrades. No matter how revolting the fad is, the official said, it violates no Soviet law.

1971

FEBRUARY

Su	Mo	Tu	We	Th	Fr	Sa
	1	2	3	4	5	6
7	8	9	10	11	12	13
14	15	16	17	18	19	20
21	22	23	24	25	26	27
28						

2. Washington: Nixon names William Casey chairman of SEC.

3. Georgia: Blast at arms plant kills 24; 33 hospitalized.

3. OPEC decides to set oil prices without consulting buyers (→ 1/31/73).

4. N.Y.: Mayor Lindsay visits Serpico in hospital (→ 12/14).

5. Two Apollo 14 astronauts walk on moon (→ 4/24).

7. Switzerland gives women right to vote in federal elections.

8. South Vietnamese invade Laos with U.S. air support to attack Ho Chi Minh Trail (→ 13).

8. Belfast: Five-year-old girl run over by army car; four teens shot in ensuing riots (→ 27).

11. Washington: U.S., U.S.S.R. sign treaty banning nuclear weapons on seabed (→ 11/6).

14. Moscow publicizes new five-year plan geared to expanding consumer production (→ 4/27/73).

16. Saigon: U.S. Air Force Col. Gerald Kehrli given three years for smoking marijuana (→ 3/14).

17. Chile: Peasants seize farms despite govt. warnings to wait for land reform (→ 25).

19. Moscow: Soviets warn Jews against espousing Zionism (→ 11/5).

20. Athens: Youths protest forced shearing of long hair.

21. London: 100,000 march in protest against Conservative labor policies (→ 3/1).

22. Britain decides to sell helicopters to S. Africa (→ 8/4).

23. Miami: Muhammad Ali surprises fans, sparring ten rounds in silence (→ 3/8).

24. Algeria seizes French oil assets (→ 4/12/75).

25. Chile to sell copper directly to China (→ 3/26).

27. Belfast: Gunmen kill two police, wound four (→ 3/20).

27. Bogota: State of siege declared after riots kill eight.

28. Florida: Jack Nicklaus wins his second PGA golf title.

28. Lichtenstein: Male electorate refuses vote to women.

Drive against drugs ordered in Vietnam

Jan 6. Reports of "stoned" American soldiers have caused concern among high-ranking officers about drug abuse in Vietnam. General Creighton Abrams, commander of U.S. forces in Vietnam, has ordered officers to conduct searches to weed out marijuana growers and smokers in Southeast Asia. An estimated 65,000 G.I.'s were involved in drug abuse last year. Besides marijuana, American soldiers also use LSD, amphetamines and heroin. Abrams believes drug abuse is hampering military performance (→ 2/16).

All G.I.'s cleared in Mylai massacre

Jan 29. "Dismissal of the charges was in the best interest of justice." That was the opinion of Lt. Gen. Albert O. Connor as he threw out charges against the last enlisted men accused in connection with the Mylai massacre. The men cleared are Pvt. Max Hutson, Pvt. Gerald Smith, Sgt. Esequiel Torres and Specialist 4 Robert T'Souvas. One of the defense attorneys said "the Army has decided to stop trying to place the blame on a few enlisted men." The defendants insisted that they were only following orders at Mylai. Today, the Army dropped charges against Maj. Gen. Samuel Koster, the division commander who had been accused of trying to cover up the massacre (→ 2/23).

Hells Angel freed in Altamont death

Jan 14. Allan Passaro, a member of the Hell's Angels motorcycle gang, was found not guilty today of a slaying at a December 1969 Rolling Stones concert at Altamont Speedway, near San Francisco. The British rock band hired the motorcycle gang as a security force at the free concert, attended by 300,000 people. But violence erupted throughout the day and was capped by the stabbing of Meredith Hunter, 18. The not-guilty verdict was reached despite filmed evidence of the killing.

In two years Army spied on 18,000

Jan 17. North Carolina's Senator Sam Ervin has scheduled hearings on a possibly unprecedented domestic intelligence operation run by the Army. From mid-1967 through the fall of 1969, the Army spied on some 18,000 Americans. Ervin, who is not convinced that the spying has ended, said military officials must disclose in full "what has to be done to ensure that it will never happen again." The intelligence operation apparently centered on radicals, opponents of the Vietnam War and black militants. Subjects' names were stored in Army computers. The NAACP, the John Birch Society, the Black Panthers and Students for a Democratic Society were among the groups investigated.

Jan 17. Miami hosted a comedy of errors ending in defeat for Dallas, as the Colts won the Super Bowl 16-13 with a last-minute field goal.

Mideast oil prices expected to increase

Feb 14. The threat of an oil production stoppage was removed in Iran today with an agreement between 23 oil companies and six Persian Gulf states. The settlement increases the payments of oil companies by a total of $10 billion to Iran, Iraq, Saudi Arabia, Kuwait, Abu Dhabi and Qatar. Dr. Jamshid Amouzegar, chief negotiator for the states, said after the signing of the accord, "I was so happy I had tears in my eyes." So might American consumers when they see the expected gas price hike.

One-third of U.S. students tried pot

Feb 1. A federal survey of marijuana use on college campuses has revealed that 31 percent of students have tried the drug and 14 percent are regular smokers. The figures, released by the National Institute of Mental Health, were based on questionnaires distributed to 10,000 students at 50 colleges across the nation. The report concluded that the percentages showed a "substantial increase among college students" from previous surveys. But it found that in some areas, such as San Mateo County, California, use of the drug may have "crested," a trend which the report predicted may eventually spread elsewhere. The report did not record whether use of other drugs is increasing.

American ingenuity at its best: A clear umbrella for wind and rain.

Thousands of Vietnamese pour into Laos

Feb 13. Supported by American planes and artillery, thousands of South Vietnamese troops crossed into Laos in an attempt to cripple Hanoi's supply line down the Ho Chi Minh trail. In announcing the operation, President Nguyen Van Thieu described the attack as an "act of legitimate self-defense" in view of North Vietnam's use of neutral Laos as a supply line to support military operations in the South. He said the military operation would be "limited in time and space," but military sources said plans call for the operation to last at least five months.

With U.S. ground troops being withdrawn, President Thieu reportedly argued that the time had come to strike a decisive blow at Communist supply lines in Laos. The United States agreed to artillery support, fired from South Vietnam, and air support in Laos, but the U.S. military command emphasized that no U.S. ground troops or advisers would enter Laos. Over 12,000 South Vietnamese troops, gathered in the northern province of Quangtri, crossed into Laos, some transported in the early phases of the attack by U.S. helicopters (→ 3/7).

U.S. helicopters transport troops.

Major earthquake hits L.A., killing 51

Feb 10. The list of dead in yesterday's major earthquake rose to 51 today, as the Los Angeles area began pulling itself together. Little hope is held for ten persons, still buried in the wreckage of a Veterans Administration hospital. About 80,000 are still kept away from their homes as a precautionary measure, since dams have been seriously weakened by the tremor, the worst to hit the region in 38 years.

The original quake measured 6.6 on the Richter scale, and a series of aftershocks last night and today reached as high as 5. The police report 880 injured, 39 seriously. The property damage will exceed $1 billion. However, the time of the quake—6 a.m.—saved many lives, including those of schoolchildren.

J.C. Penney, known to all, dies at 95

Feb 12. J.C. Penney, the founder of the department store chain of the same name, died yesterday of complications following a fall that he suffered during the Christmas holidays. James Penney, who gave himself the middle name Cash to emphasize the cash-and-carry aspect of his stores, was one of a few 20th-Century merchants who created vast empires from virtually nothing.

He began in the retail business as an employee in a local dry-goods store earning $25 a year. In 1902, he borrowed money and bought an interest in a small store. Today, the J.C. Penney chain has 1,660 retail outlets, which all operate, as Penney taught, on the Golden Rule, a policy of humanity to employees and customers.

Rolls-Royce company declares bankruptcy

Feb 4. In what politicians described as "a major national tragedy," Rolls-Royce, Ltd., Britain's symbol of quality for automobiles, declared bankruptcy today. The company said it had been driven to the action by the huge losses incurred in developing a new jet engine for the Lockheed Aircraft Corporation's new Tristar airliner.

The British government quickly announced that it would take over the Rolls jet engine activities essential for national defense and major international projects, including development of the engines for the British-French Concorde supersonic jetliner. Bankruptcy will not interfere with the manufacture of Rolls-Royce automobiles, which set a world standard for luxury but account for only five percent of the company's sales. Rolls-Royce makes only 2,000 automobiles a year, most of which are sold in the United States. Its more important role is as the centerpiece of the British aircraft industry.

Rolls engines power most British military and commercial aircraft. Rolls-Royce's downfall came when it agreed to produce the new jet engines for Lockheed at a price that turned out to be too low (→ 3/5).

Vintage Rolls-Royce autos are even more expensive than newer models.

Calley admits Mylai, but rejects blame

Feb 23. Lt. William Calley, charged with murdering more than 100 men, women and children at Mylai, admitted on the witness stand that he had killed civilians. But he said he was only following orders. "They were all enemy," he said. "They were all to be destroyed." Yesterday, he testified he had learned to hate all Vietnamese. This was not a war where he could give "candy and chewing gum and things to children." Calley said children were dangerous and "very good at planting mines" (→ 3/31).

U.K. changes pound to decimal system

Feb 15. Let's see. Twelve pence make a shilling, and 20 shillings make a pound. If a shirt in London costs eight pounds two shillings sixpence, how much does that make in dollars? That's the way it used to be. For 1,000 years the English pound was divided into 240 pence. Today, the pound was decimalized —100 pence to the pound. Now that shirt simply costs 8.45 pounds. The world's most complicated currency has now become one of the simplest.

Agnew's golf balls hit three spectators

Feb 13. Vice President Spiro Agnew managed to steal the spotlight away from Arnold Palmer and other top golf pros at the Bob Hope Classic. He hit three spectators with his first two shots. Disgusted, Agnew dropped his driver, jumped into his golf cart and rode off.

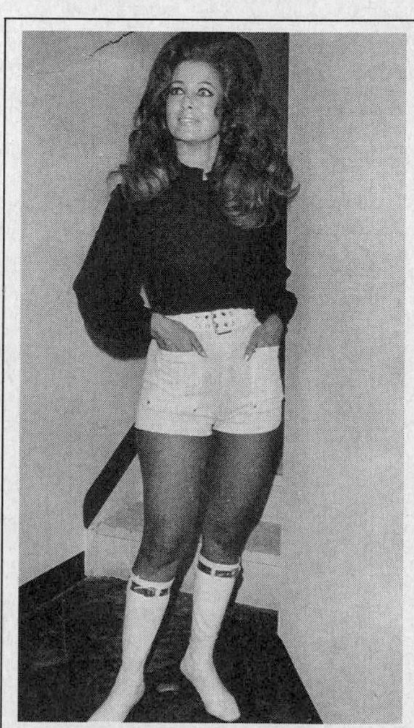

Feb 16. Women longing for summer filled Alexander's in N.Y. today for a "hot pants" show.

1971

MARCH

Su	Mo	Tu	We	Th	Fr	Sa
	1	2	3	4	5	6
7	8	9	10	11	12	13
14	15	16	17	18	19	20
21	22	23	24	25	26	27
28	29	30	31			

1. Britain: One million industrial workers strike to protest bill curbing unions (→ 3/4/74).

3. California: Gov. Reagan urges huge cutbacks in welfare rolls (→ 3/8/75).

5. Britain offers Rolls-Royce $144 million in aid.

6. London: 4,000 march for women's rights.

7. Saigon: 1,000 U.S. planes bomb Cambodia, Laos (→ 18).

11. India: Indira Gandhi wins majority in Parliament (→ 3/12/72).

12. Ankara: Turkish regime ousted by military promising to curb civil strife (→ 3/30/72).

13. Montreal: Paul Rose gets life sentence for part in slaying of Juan Laporte (→ 11/16/76).

14. Washington: Sen. Kennedy estimates 25,000 Vietnamese civilians killed in 1970 (→ 7/7).

18. N.Y.: Whitney Museum acquires 1,500 works by Edward Hopper.

18. Laos: U.S. helicopters airlift 1,000 South Vietnamese soldiers out of country (→ 24).

20. Belfast: James Clark, Irish premier, resigns under pressure from Protestants (→ 8/9).

21. Vietnam: Two U.S. platoons refuse orders to advance (→ 4/24).

23. U.S. Senate cuts off funds for supersonic SST.

24. London: Sir Laurence Olivier takes seat in House of Lords.

26. Chile signs contract to buy Bethlehem iron mines (→ 27).

27. Houston: UCLA wins fifth straight NCAA basketball title.

27. Chile: Allende promises to bar any base that imperils U.S. (→ 4/4).

29. Detroit: Ford recalls all Pintos for engine defect (→ 12/4).

DEATHS

8. Harold Lloyd, Hollywood comedian (*4/20/1893).

16. Thomas Dewey, Republican politician, N.Y. gov., two-time pres. candidate (→ 3/24/1902).

Calley is convicted of killing 20 at Mylai

March 31. The longest war crimes trial in American history came to an end today. Lt. William Calley was sentenced to life at hard labor for his role in the Mylai massacre. A military tribunal at Fort Benning, Georgia, found him guilty of killing at least 20 civilians. Calley had been accused of murdering more than 100 men, women and children, but there was conflicting testimony about how many people were actually killed at Mylai.

Outside the courtroom, about 100 spectators gathered to support Calley. "He's been crucified," one woman said. "Lt. Calley killed 100 Communists single-handedly. He should get a medal. He should be promoted to general."

George Latimer, Calley's lawyer, said he will appeal the verdict. He called it a "horrendous decision for the United States, the United States Army and my client." Latimer, a retired military judge, said, "This boy is a product of the system. He was taken out of his own home, given automatic weapons, taught to kill. They ordered him to kill. And then the same government tries him for killing and selects the judge, the court and the prosecutor."

Calley is the first of 25 officers and enlisted men charged in connection with the Mylai massacre to be convicted. Charges have been dropped against 19. Two were acquitted. Three still face trial, including Capt. Ernest Medina, commander of Calley's platoon. Medina allegedly instructed Calley to use captured Vietnamese as guides across suspected mine fields. Calley says he had them shot because they walked too slowly (→ 4/1).

Manson group is sentenced to death

Charles Manson, marked for death.

March 29. "It's going to come down hard!" Susan Atkins threatened the jury before being evicted from the Los Angeles courtroom. Much more menacing is the reality of her sentence: death. She, Charles Manson, Leslie Van Houten and Patricia Krewnwinkel are condemned to the gas chamber. The four were found guilty of first-degree murder in one of the most sensational trials of the century. Many mainstream Americans now fear the counterculture, Manson representing the flower child gone to very bad seed.

Internal quarrels cause Pakistan tension

March 2. Violence erupted in Pakistan as a Parliament was elected by universal suffrage for the first time since the country gained its independence from India. Old passions have been reignited, and blood is being spilled. The formation of a new government seems to be almost impossible.

In Eastern Pakistan, the Awami League of Sheik Mujibur Rahman won an overwhelming victory. Zulfikar Ali-Khan Bhutto, leader of the People's Party, won big in Western Pakistan. The politics of the two leaders are radically different. Rahman demands independence. Ali Bhutto wants to preserve the unity of Pakistan. Yahya Khan, President of Pakistan, also wants to keep his country unified. Hoping to force Ali Bhutto, Rahman and political leaders from Bengal to the bargaining table, the president sent in troops to keep the peace. But the plan has backfired (→ 4/5).

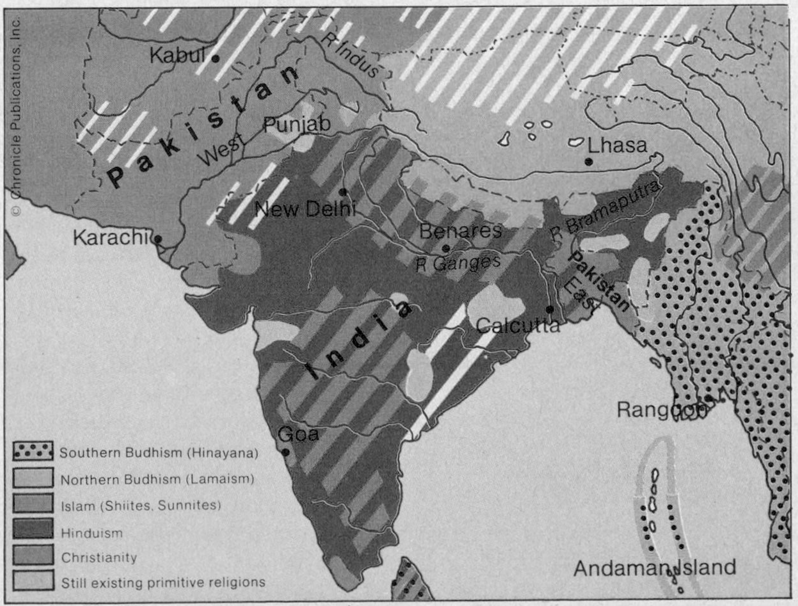

East Pakistan lies 1,000 miles from the Pakistani seat of government and shares almost nothing with West Pakistan except a common Moslem faith.

South Vietnamese fail in Laos effort

March 24. In the face of heavy Communist resistance, South Vietnam was forced to end prematurely its military operation against enemy supply lines in Laos. The withdrawal came 44 days after South Vietnamese troops, supported by American air power and artillery fire, swept into Laos in an attempt to disrupt the Communist supply line, known as the Ho Chi Minh Trail. At the height of the operation, more than 20,000 South Vietnamese troops were in Laos. South Vietnam suffered heavy casualties, with 1,146 killed. The United States lost 89 helicopters and 51 Americans were killed (→ 8/2).

Frazier outpoints Ali to retain title

March 8. A hammer-like left hook in the 15th and final round by Joe Frazier nearly finished off Muhummad Ali and helped to send him to his first defeat. Frazier won the fight on points and retained his heavyweight championship, but that one blow symbolized the crushing humiliation of the once-invincible Cassius Clay. The battle was so exciting that one man in the Madison Square Garden crowd died of a heart attack. Ali was taken to a hospital after the fight to have his severely swollen jaw X-rayed, but he was later released (→ 6/28).

Pierre Trudeau weds young bride

March 4. Prime Minister Pierre E. Trudeau married Margaret Sinclair, 22, today in a Roman Catholic ceremony in North Vancouver, British Columbia. The surprise announcement of the 51-year-old bachelor's nuptials, when he officially was off skiing, came in the name of the bride's parents, her father a longtime force in the Liberal Party, now led by Trudeau. Born Oct. 18, 1919, and called to the Quebec bar in 1943, Trudeau has risen quickly in Canadian politics. He has dated many women since becoming Prime Minister in 1968, among them Barbra Streisand.

Senate chamber is blasted by bomb

March 1. In the first serious act of sabotage against a federal building in recent years, a bomb exploded in the Senate wing of the Capitol, causing damage throughout the building, but no injuries. A half-hour before the blast, a telephone call to the Capitol switchboard warned that the bomb would go off in protest of United States military action in Laos. Windows were shattered, tables overturned, walls and floors cracked, and doors were blown off their hinges. Nevertheless, the Senate and House were able to meet, as were the Capitol's guided tours.

1971

APRIL

Su	Mo	Tu	We	Th	Fr	Sa
				1	2	3
4	5	6	7	8	9	10
11	12	13	14	15	16	17
18	19	20	21	22	23	24
25	26	27	28	29	30	

1. Washington: Nixon orders Lt. Calley freed while conviction is reviewed (→ 6).

2. Tripoli: Western oil companies sign five-year pact with Libya (→ 12/7).

4. Pakistan reports seizure of nine Indian army vehicles (→ 5).

4. Chile: Allende coalition wins 49.5% of vote in local elections (→ 9/28).

5. U.S. Supreme Court upholds federal law against possession of unregistered gun.

5. East Pakistan: Hundreds of foreigners being airlifted out as rebellion grows (→ 13).

7. Nixon pledges withdrawal of 100,000 more from Vietnam by December (→ 12).

8. New York: OTB opens with $2 bet by Mayor Lindsay.

10. China: U.S. table tennis team arrives (→ 11).

11. Peking: Three U.S. newsmen enter China (→ 14).

12. North Vietnam: U.S. drops 7.5 tons of bombs on Hanoi troops (→ 5/9).

13. East Pakistan: Rebels form Cabinet of state they call Bangladesh (→ 25).

14. Nixon eases trade embargo on Communist China to allow non-strategic exports (→ 19).

14. Washington: Sen. Muskie says FBI spied on 1970 Earth Day ecology rallies (→ 6/14/72).

15. California: "Patton" wins seven Oscars, including Best Picture and Best Actor.

20. U.S. Supreme Court 9-0 backs busing to end segregation in public schools (→ 5/25).

21. New York: Eleven mayors warn of collapse of U.S. cities.

24. U.S.S.R.: Soyuz 10 links with orbital laboratory, then lands (→ 5/30).

25. New Jersey: 1,000 war protesters block N.J. Turnpike four hours; 100 arrested (→ 5/3).

26. Washington: Presidential commission suggests U.S. seek China's entry to U.N. (→ 6/10).

27. Atlanta: Hank Aaron joins Babe Ruth, Willie Mays at 600+ home run mark (→ 4/4/74).

Bangladesh established

Waves of refugees flee Eastern Pakistan, the scene of wholesale slaughter.

April 25. The government of West Pakistan refuses to admit that secessionists even exist in Eastern Pakistan. But they do. They have formed a new Cabinet, and they have given themselves a new name. It is Bangladesh, or Bengal Nation. Tajuddin Ahmed, who has acted as deputy to the political leader Skeik Mujibur Rahman, is the Prime Minister and Minister of Defense. Sheik Rahman has been named President, although it is conceded that he is a prisoner in West Pakistan.

You cannot read about any of these developments in West Pakistani papers, and authorities there are reluctant to allow foreign journalists to travel in the East. But reports indicate that troops from the West are using brutal, unrestrained force to eliminate political dissidents in the East. There has been a wholesale slaughter of students, professors, professionals and intellectuals. Entire villages suspected of harboring Rahman's sympathizers have been burned to the ground. Tens of thousands of people have been killed (→ 5/31).

700 veterans toss medals at Capitol

April 24. "To President Nixon, I send you greetings," said one Vietnam veteran as he and about 700 vets tossed away their war medals in vehement and moving protest at the Capitol yesterday. Those participating in the emotional display were members of the Vietnam Veterans Against the War. They came to Washington to tell the world of the horrors of battle.

Today, over 200,000 anti-war demonstrators rallied on Capitol Hill carrying placards which read: "Enough—out now." The message was intended to speed President's Nixon's plan of U.S. withdrawal from Vietnam. But he did not hear the plea, as he was at his Camp David retreat. The protest lived up to its promise to be peaceful; only ten arrests were made (→ 25).

Nixon frees Calley while guilt assayed

April 6. Lt. William Calley is back in his apartment at Fort Benning, Georgia, tonight. He was ordered released from the stockade while President Nixon decides his fate. The president acted to short-circuit the military appeals process after 50,000 telegrams arrived at the White House. Most of them objected to Calley's conviction and life sentence for his role in the Mylai massacre. A new poll shows that 79% of the American public is opposed to the verdict.

John Ehrlichman, Nixon's domestic adviser, indicated the controversial case presents more than legal questions. He said Nixon will look into his heart to decide what should happen to Calley. The military tribunal that convicted Calley criticized Nixon's action (→ 8/20). ▷

Igor Stravinsky, modern music master, dies

April 6. Igor Stravinsky, arguably this century's greatest composer, died yesterday of heart failure in his New York apartment at 88. The Russian-born musician is still best known for "The Rite of Spring." Its 1913 Paris premiere rocked the musical world and its scorching rhythms all but buried Romanticism. Yet, Stravinsky proved an eclectic genius whose evolving styles incorporated and made inimitably his own all the great periods that preceded him, including the Schonberg Twelve-Tone School. Tributes have been reverential. To Leonard Bernstein, he was music's "great old man"; and to Georg Solti, "the last musical genius of the 20th Century."

Eclectic maestro of modern music.

Ping-Pong initiates China-U.S. contact

April 19. A small, featherweight, white ball is bringing a relaxation in tensions between two great nations, as an American table tennis team is soon to visit Communist China to play the Ping-Pong wizards of Peking. The group will be the first Americans to travel to China since the mid-1950's. Today, President Nixon eased a 20-year-old embargo on trade with China to help improve Sino-U.S. relations (→ 26).

U.S.S.R. wins ninth world hockey title

April 3. For the ninth consecutive time, the Soviet Union has won the world hockey championship. The Soviets scored four goals in the third period and defeated Sweden by 6-3. Sweden was able to salvage third place in the tournament as Czechoslovakia took the silver medal. The Czechs would have been champions if the Swedes had defeated the Soviets. The United States squad finished in sixth place.

Papa Doc Duvalier dies; Baby Doc succeeds

April 22. President-for-Life of Haiti, Francois Duvalier, died last night at the age of 61. Within a matter of hours after his death, Jean-Claude Duvalier, his son, had been sworn in as the new dictator of the impoverished black republic.

Baby Doc and Tontons Macoutes.

Francois Duvalier, or Papa Doc, as he enjoyed being called, styled himself as a simple country doctor but was known to the world as a dictator ruthless with his enemies.

Elected to the presidency by an overwhelming majority in 1957, Papa Doc immediately began recruiting the Tontons Macoutes, his private army which held the island-nation in a reign of terror. In subsequent elections, Duvalier's party was the only one allowed to participate. In 1964, he declared himself president-for-life. Baby Doc, as the Haitians call Jean-Claude, is a 19-year-old law student who was appointed to succeed to the presidency by his father. In spite of the change, Haitians are apathetic (→ 1/31/86).

1971

MAY

Su	Mo	Tu	We	Th	Fr	Sa
						1
2	3	4	5	6	7	8
9	10	11	12	13	14	15
16	17	18	19	20	21	22
23	24	25	26	27	28	29
30	31					

1. New York: Whitney Museum opens Andy Warhol exhibit.

1. Canonero II wins Kentucky Derby, G. Avila in the saddle.

3. U.S. Supreme Court rules 6-3 juries can impose death penalty (→ 2/18/72).

3. Tennessee: Martin L. King killer James Earl Ray captured in abortive jail break.

3. Berlin: Erich Honecker replaces Walter Ulbricht as head of East Germany.

8. Brussels: Finance ministers in EEC meet to discuss dollar crisis.

9. Hanoi accuses U.S and South Vietnam of 51 cease-fire violations (→ 7/1).

10. Brussels: French ease terms for U.K. entry into EEC (→ 21).

13. Cairo: 91 arrested in purge of opposition to Sadat (→ 27).

18. Chicago: Montreal Canadiens win Stanley Cup with 3-2 win over Black Hawks.

19. Moscow: Canadian Prime Minister Trudeau signs amity pact with Kosygin.

19. U.S.: Vote in Congress kills nationwide rail strike.

21. Paris: Pompidou and British Premier Heath reach accord on U.K. entry into EEC (→ 10/28).

21. Paris: Sixty Western intellectuals, including Sartre, denounce Castro for treatment of poet Herberto Padilla (→ 7/11/72).

22. Turkey: Earthquake strikes east, killing 600.

24. Prague: Communist leaders gather for Czech Party Congress.

25. Conn.: Judge drops murder charges against Black Panthers Bobby Seale, Ericka Huggins, citing undue publicity (→ 7/17).

26. Calif.: Juan Corona arrested for murder of 12 migrant workers (→ 28).

27. Cairo: Egypt and U.S.S.R. sign 15-year friendship treaty (→ 7/18/72).

28. New York: 727 jet hijacked at LaGuardia, forced to Nassau in Bahamas (→ 2/6/72).

30. Cape Kennedy: Mariner 9 launched for orbit of Mars (→ 6/30).

Who said "candy is dandy," et cetera?

May 19. If you never heard of Ogden Nash, you could readily make his acquaintance through his poem "Reflections on Ice-Breaking": "Candy is dandy/But liquor is quicker." The comedic poet, author of the book "Bed Riddance," has died in Baltimore at age 68.

Nash started out at an ad agency. One day he doodled some verses at at his desk and mailed them to the New Yorker on a whim. He saw the lines in print soon after, and a career was born, for better or verse. Nash wrote his own glad epitaph: "Here lies my past. Goodbye, I have kissed it. Thank you, kids. I wouldn't have missed it."

Queen's request for money causes furor

May 31. A controversy involving the British royal family has erupted since Queen Elizabeth II asked Parliament to increase her annual grant of $1.14 million. The matter was looked into discreetly until Richard Crossman, ex-Labor minister and now Editor of The New Statesman, exploded the headline "The Royal Tax Evaders." He said one of the world's richest women ought not to burden taxpayers.

Angkor Wat temple damaged in fighting

May 11. Angkor Wat, Cambodia's magnificent temple and national treasure, was damaged, it has been learned, in an artillery barrage about three months ago. Built in the 12th century, the great temple covers nearly a square mile and includes a moat, vast courtyards and a wall 6,000 yards around.

When Viet Cong and North Vietnamese troops occupied the temple last June, the Cambodians were hesitant to attack, fearing they would destroy it; but finally they were forced into firing the artillery. Damage was caused to a gallery and to the famous frescoes, considered an outstanding example of bas-relief art, which depict the history of the Khmer people (→ 10/20).

Washington holds nearly 10,000 marchers

May 3. The anti-Vietnam protesters who call themselves the Mayday Tribe did not succeed in shutting down the government in Washington this morning. But they did disrupt the capital for several hours as they battled with police and littered the streets with garbage.

Thousands of demonstrators, including Chicago Seven defendant Rennie Davis, were arrested. They were herded into temporary detention centers near Robert F. Kennedy Stadium. About half of them were still being held tonight. The others were treated like traffic offenders and released. Davis is still being held. Federal government managers asked employees to come to work early this morning to avoid the protest. Many government workers obliged. Those who did not got caught in the traffic for up to three hours (→ 8/13).

21st of murdered migrants is found

May 28. In Sutter County, Calif., sheriff's deputies uncovered the 21st body today in the peach orchards outside the Sacramento Valley farming center. Shortly before 4:30 a.m., Juan V. Corona, 37, a farm labor contractor, was arrested in connection with the slayings. Two sales receipts made out to him were found in the shallow grave of one man, dead less than 48 hours. Others have been dead for six or seven weeks.

The deputies also found an 18-inch bolo machete, a two-and-a-half-foot wooden club and a crowbar in Corona's home. The victims, 20 white and one black, seem to have been drifters, aged 40 to 65.

Corona, who comes from a rural area near Jalisco, Mexico, and is the father of four young daughters, has a history of mental illness. He was committed to a state mental hospital in 1956 but declared cured and released after three months (→ 6/2).

Cholera epidemic strikes Bangladesh

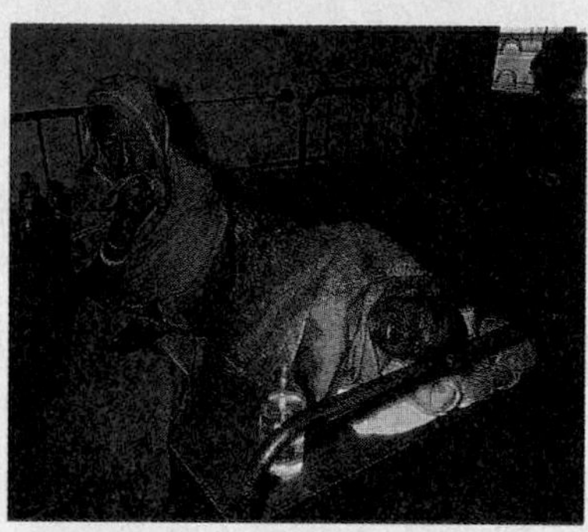

The world's newest nation in peril.

May 31. First they were forced to flee from their homes, and now they are deathly ill. The civil war in Bangladesh, or East Pakistan, has turned two million people into refugees. Many of them are suffering from cholera and smallpox. The authorities of West Pakistan refuse to care for them, and India cannot afford to. Indira Gandhi is calling for international help (→ 8/1).

May 29. Three out of four years, the track at Indy has belonged to the Unsers. Al has won his second in a row, adding to Bobby's 1968 victory.

1971

JUNE

Su	Mo	Tu	We	Th	Fr	Sa
		1	2	3	4	5
6	7	8	9	10	11	12
13	14	15	16	17	18	19
20	21	22	23	24	25	26
29	28	29	30			

1. Washington: Nixon pledges national drive against drug addiction (→ 30).

2. Calif.: Juan Corona pleads not guilty to murder of 23 migrant workers (→ 9/11/72).

6. Honduras: Ramon Cruz elected president.

9. U.S. cites Israeli settlements in Jordanian Jerusalem as violation of Geneva Convention (→ 9/18).

10. Washington: Nixon ends 21-year-old trade embargo on Peking (→ 7/15).

10. Mexico City: Ten students killed in riots; 130 injured.

13. New York: 19 police injured as radical groups interrupt Puerto Rican Day Parade.

13. Paris: Francois Mitterrand named to head Socialist Party (→ 18).

14. Washington: Atty. Gen. John Mitchell asks N.Y. Times to stop publishing Pentagon Papers; Times refuses (→ 15).

15. Washington: Judge halts Times from printing Vietnam series for four days (→ 26).

17. U.S. signs pact to return Okinawa to Japan (→ 9/16).

17. Moscow: Mack Trucks signs contract to build Soviet plant.

18. Paris: Jean-Paul Sartre indicted for libeling police (→ 4/2/74).

21. Pennsylvania: Lee Trevino wins U.S. Open golf title.

26. Washington: Justice Dept. issues warrant for Daniel Ellsberg, accused of giving away Pentagon Papers (→ 30).

26. Oregon: John Smith sets mark in 440-yard dash, 0:44.5.

27. New York: 5,000 march for gay rights to rally in Central Park (→ 12/15/73).

28. U.S. Supreme Court votes 8-1 to forbid states from reimbursing parochial schools.

30. Washington: Nixon says Turkey agrees to curb production of opium poppies (→ 11/20).

DEATH

15. Wendell Meredith Stanley, U.S. biochemist, first to crystallize a virus (*8/16/1904).

Mafia boss gunned down; killer is dead

June 28. Reputed mob chieftan Joseph A. Colombo Jr. was shot and critically wounded yesterday, less than an hour before an Italian-American civil rights rally in New York City's Columbus Circle was scheduled to begin. Colombo's alleged assailant, a 25-year-old, black, Brooklyn man named Jerome A. Johnson, was shot dead at the scene, although it was not clear whether he was killed by police, Colombo's associates or a third party. Colombo, who underwent five hours of brain surgery, has a 50 percent chance of survival. Police officials have insisted that the attack on Colombo was planned.

3 cosmonauts found dead in spaceship

June 30. Three cosmonauts who set a world endurance record orbiting the earth were found dead when their Soyuz spacecraft returned to earth, the Soviet Union announced today. The Soviet news agency Tass said the cause of their death is unknown. Cosmonauts Viktor L. Patsayev, Vladislav N. Volkov and Georgi T. Dobrovolsky were sent into orbit on June 6, linking their Soyuz 6 spacecraft to an orbiting Salyut laboratory. They reboarded the Soyuz last night and made an apparently normal re-entry this morning, but were dead when a recovery team reached the landing site in Kazakhstan, Tass said (→ 7/31).

June 12. Nixon's daughter Tricia weds Edward Finch Cox today.

Printing of Pentagon Papers is upheld

June 30. The Supreme Court has overruled government attempts to stop The New York Times and The Washington Post from publishing articles based on a secret Pentagon study of the Vietnam War. The government thus failed in the first attempt in American history to restrain newspapers from publishing information on grounds of national security.

By a 6-3 vote, the court held that any attempt by the government to impose "prior restraint" on publication of information by newspapers bears "a heavy presumption against its constitutional validity" under the First Amendment.

In a brief, unsigned opinion, the court said the government "thus carries a heavy burden of showing justification for the imposition of such a restraint," and it found in the Pentagon Papers case that the government "had not met that burden." The decision left The Times and other newspapers free to resume publication of the text and articles drawn from the Pentagon study that includes many documents stamped "secret" and "top secret."

When The Times, which had obtained the study from undisclosed sources, began publishing articles earlier this month, Attorney General John N. Mitchell asked the newspaper to refrain from further publication of the documents on the grounds the disclosures would cause "irreparable injury to the defense interests of the United States."

When The Times refused to halt publication voluntarily, the Justice Department went into the courts seeking an injunction against further publication. The Times and The Washington Post won at the District Court level, but there was a division between two Appeals Courts, and the matter was quickly brought before the Supreme Court.

In an usual diversity of views, all nine Justices wrote separate opinions, so there was no majority opinion to provide precedent for the future, only the brief statement, approved by a 6-3 vote, endorsing lower court decisions against enjoining publication of the information. There was some disgreement among legal scholars, therefore, on how important a landmark had been established by the court for freedom of the press cases.

One three-man bloc held that the courts lacked power to suppress any press publication under the First Amendment, particularly since Congress twice had rejected such powers for the courts. Another three-man bloc held that the government had not demonstrated that publication of the information would cause irreparable damage. The third group found the courts could support the executive branch but had not been given enough time to resolve the issues (→ 5/1/72).

"All the News That's Fit to Print"

The New York Times

LATE CITY EDITION

NEW YORK, TUESDAY, JUNE 15, 1971

15 CENTS

MAYOR'S BUDGET OF $8.8-BILLIONS AVOIDS LAYOFFS

COURT SAYS CITIES MAY CLOSE POOLS TO BAR RACIAL MIX

MITCHELL SEEKS TO HALT SERIES ON VIETNAM BUT TIMES REFUSES

Vietnam Archive: Study Tells How Johnson Secretly Opened Way to Ground Combat

COURT STEP LIKELY

Return of Documents Asked in Telegram To Publisher

ATTRITION ON JOBS

Losses Put at 14,320 And 5,013 Vacancies Due to Go Unfilled

JERSEY APPROVES AIRPORT RAIL LINK

FACTORY OUTPUT CLIMBED IN MAY

Italian Neo-Fascists Make Gains in Regional Voting

U.S. SUES SUBURB ON HOUSING BIAS

The Times covers its own battle for the right to air the secret war in Vietnam.

Getty Museum buys Titian for $4 million

June 28. The J. Paul Getty Museum of Malibu, California, has purchased Titian's "The Death of Actaeon," the 16th-century masterpiece, for $4,032,000, the second highest auction price for a work of art. It may become part of a loan exchange program with the National Gallery in London. Last November, Velasquez's portrait of his assistant was sold at Christie's for a record sum of of $5,544,000 to the Metropolitan Museum of Art in New York. The Getty Museum, mainly financed by the oil billionaire, has eight galleries of European paintings, sculptures and antiques.

Lukacs, humanist Marxist, dead at 86

June 4. Gyorgy Lukacs has died a natural death in Vienna, outliving countless Marxists who angered Joseph Stalin. Lukacs was born in Hungary. His conversion to Marxism in 1917 was almost religious, a gestalt switch which informed his view of revolution as a transformation of consciousness. Works such as "History and Class Consciousness" (1923) fathered a school of thought that resurrected the humanist and libertarian in Marx, facets that embarrassed Stalin. Harassed for advocating the freedom of art and thought from politics, Lukacs escaped persecution by disowning his own ideas time and again.

Old Blue Eyes says it's time to retire

June 14. Sounding as good as he ever has, Frank Sinatra typically charmed the audience gathered to hear his farewell appearance at the Los Angeles Music Center yesterday as he wandered down memory lane with "I've Got You Under My Skin," "Angel Eyes," "My Way" and other songs he has made his own during the past 30 years. Once the idol of bobby soxers, the 55-year-old singer said he was "serious" about his retirement, adding, "There are lots of things I want to do that I haven't done."

Women's crime rate outrunning men's

June 13. In Los Angeles County last year, male arrests went up ten percent while female arrests went up 23 percent. The FBI reports that from 1960 to 1969 female arrests for major crimes increased 156.2 percent, compared with an increase among males of 61.3. And in New York City this morning, a women's correctional center with a 400-bed capacity was closed down. Why? Overcrowding. Experts tend to blame drug use and the emancipation of women for the rise in female crime.

Court decides for Ali on army service

June 28. Four years after he was convicted and stripped of his heavyweight title for refusing Army induction, Muhummad Ali has been cleared by the United States Supreme Court. By an 8-0 vote, with one abstention, the court decided that Ali, then known as Cassius Clay, was improperly drafted in the first place. The Justice Department was accused in the court opinion of having misled Selective Service authorities by having advised them Ali's claim as conscientious objector was unwarranted (→ 11/17).

June 3. Yehudi Menuhin entertained at Sotheby's yesterday. Today, the 250-year-old Stradivarius sold for a record $200,000.

1971

JULY

Su	Mo	Tu	We	Th	Fr	Sa
				1	2	3
4	5	6	7	8	9	10
11	12	13	14	15	16	17
18	19	20	21	22	23	24
25	26	27	28	29	30	31

1. Paris: Viet Cong agree to trade POW's for U.S. withdrawal before end of year (→ 7).

3. American Pat Matzdorf sets new high jump mark at 7'5.5".

3. Indonesia holds first natl. elections since 1955 (→ 12/20/77).

7. FDA recalls Bon Vivant canned foods due to botulinum contamination (→ 8/22).

7. Washington: Saigon Gen. Ngo Dzu accused in Congress of trafficking in heroin (→ 22).

10. Morocco: Soldiers fail to seize power in attack on king's palace (→ 13).

10. Britain: Lee Trevino wins British Open golf title.

12. Nixon signs first public employment legislation since WPA in 1930's (→ 8/25).

13. Morocco: Army executes ten leaders of attempted coup.

14. U.S.: 400,000 phone workers go on strike.

15. Washington: Nixon says he will visit Peking in May to seeking opening of ties (→ 28).

17. Washington: Agnew chides U.S. black leaders (→ 9/9).

18. Belgian Eddy Merckx wins his third Tour de France.

23. Sudan executes four charged in attempted coup.

24. U.S., U.K. back military build-up in Iran (→ 5/31/72).

25. Vienna: Freudian analysts hold first international meeting in Freud's home.

25. Cape Town: Christiaan Barnard transplants man's heart and lungs (→ 1/25/74).

27. Washington: Nixon presents first Eisenhower silver dollar to widow Mamie Eisenhower.

28. U.S. suspends spy flights over Communist China (→ 8/2).

29. Belgrade: Tito re-elected to five-year term (→ 9/25).

30. Japan: 162 die in worst plane crash on record.

DEATH

3. Jim Morrison, rock and roll vocalist, lyricist, The Doors.

26. Diane Arbus, American photographer (*3/14/1923).

U.S. astronauts take a spin on the moon

The LRV, a sort of lunar dune buggy, takes a solo joy ride on the moon.

July 31. Apollo 15 astronauts David R. Scott and James B. Irwin today took mankind's first ride on the moon, steering their four-wheeled moon rover for several miles through craters and boulders on the rough lunar surface. Scott and Irwin became the seventh and eighth men to walk on the moon and the first to ride in a vehicle.

They landed on the moon's Sea of Rains yesterday and left their lunar module, Falcon, at 9:25 a.m. Eastern time today. Minutes later, they detached the rover from the spacecraft and set off on their exploratory trip. The rover's front steering did not function, but the vehicle was designed to be maneuvered with the rear wheels only and worked well.

When the astronauts made their first stop at the rim of Elbow Crater, a mile from the lunar module, mission control in Houston turned on the rover's television camera, which transmitted color pictures of remarkable sharpness to earth. Viewers could watch the astronauts evaluate and collect rock samples. At one point, they exclaimed, "There's some beautiful geology out here."

Their ride lasted two hours and took them five miles before their return to the lunar module. Scott and Irwin are scheduled to make more trips on the lunar rover tomorrow and the day after. They will join the third Apollo 15 astronaut, Alfred M. Worden, in the command ship for the return trip (→ 11/13).

Louis Armstrong, jazz virtuoso, dies

July 6. "My life has been my music," Louis Armstrong once said. This was the day the music died. He was 71. Satchmo (the nickname Satchelmouth nicked further) was raised in a bordello. He learned cornet at a school for truant boys, moved on to trumpet and caught a second wind to sing. "Hello, Dolly" was a recent hit. One of his firsts was Fats Waller's "Ain't Misbehavin'." Black militants called his goodwill concerts in Africa "Uncle Tomish," but he refused to play in his native New Orleans until the Civil Rights Act was passed.

No more encores for Satchmo.

Weekly death toll drops to five-year low

On the 9th, G.I.'s turned over their last base along the DMZ to Saigon.

July 22. The continued withdrawal of American troops and the low level of combat has brought the weekly Vietnam death toll to its lowest level since 1965. Only 11 American deaths were reported, as compared with the more than 300 deaths which occurred weekly when the fighting was at its peak.

Some 230,000 U.S. troops remain in South Vietnam. The highest number of troops, 534,000, was reached in mid-1969. The recent deaths brought the total number of Americans who have died in Vietnam and Cambodia since 1961 to 45,384, according to the official record. Total South Vietnamese military deaths number 130,366; North Vietnamese and Viet Cong deaths are listed at 759,816 (→ 8/18).

Graceful Goolagong

July 2. The daughter of an Australian aboriginal sheep-shearer has defeated the world's premier woman tennis player with ease. Evonne Goolagong, 19, breezed past England's Margaret Court by 6-4, 6-1 to win the Wimbledon title.

This is the end

July 3. Victim of the rock-and-roll spotlight, Jim Morrison of The Doors is dead in Paris of a probable drug overdose. Both plagued and inspired by LSD, alcohol and star worship, Morrison, son of a Navy man, often shocked audiences by stripping on stage. He died a self-proclaimed misunderstood poet. But his songs may become classics.

1971

AUGUST

Su	Mo	Tu	We	Th	Fr	Sa
1	2	3	4	5	6	7
8	9	10	11	12	13	14
15	16	17	18	19	20	21
22	23	24	25	26	27	28
29	30	31				

2. Washington: CIA admits it has 30,000-man army in Laos (→ 3/18/72).

2. U.S. officially backs U.N. seat for Communist China (→ 5).

3. Jamaican runner Don Quarrie sets mark in 200-meters, 0:19.8.

4. South Africa accepts Malawi Ambassador Joe Kachingwe, first black recognized by Pretoria regime (→ 10/4/74).

5. Alabama: George Wallace says he will run for president in 1972 (→ 1/25/72).

5. Turkey opens ties with Peking; drops Taiwan (→ 10/25).

6. Britain: Clay Blyth ends first solo, non-stop sea voyage around world in westerly direction.

9. Ulster invokes emergency powers as 12 die in riots (→ 25).

9. India and U.S.S.R. sign non-aggression treaty.

11. New York: Mayor Lindsay switches party enrollment from Republican to Democrat.

12. Syria severs ties to Jordan in support of PLO (→ 4/6/72).

13. Atty. Gen. John Mitchell drops Kent State case (→ 12/26).

18. Australia, New Zealand announce they will pull troops out of Vietnam this year (→ 9/3).

20. Georgia: Lt. Calley's sentence cut to 20 years (→ 9/19).

20. U.S. Parole Board denies parole to James Hoffa (→ 12/23).

21. Manila: Terrorists kill ten at rally of opposition Liberal Party (→ 29).

22. Texas: Campbell's recalls chicken soup, detecting botulin in some cans.

22. Bolivia: Military crushes resistance, installs Gen. Hugo Banzer Suarez (→ 11/7/79).

26. N.Y.: Football Giants say they will move to N.J. in 1974.

29. Manila: Opposition leader Benigno Aquino leaves on campaign tour (→ 9/23/72).

DEATHS

14. Georg von Opel, German car manufacturer (*5/18/1912).

28. Bennet Cerf, New York publisher (*5/25/1898).

Crisis in Northern Ireland

Fire from an I.R.A. bomb rages in a burned-out section of war-torn Belfast.

Aug 25. Violence has erupted in Northern Ireland after the government invoked emergency powers of preventive detention to arrest suspected leaders of the Irish Republican Army. Prime Minister Brian Faulkner, who also imposed a six-month ban on parades, said that the emergency measures were necessary to protect life and property in Northern Ireland.

There was a bitter reaction, however, from the Roman Catholic minority. Within hours after 300 men were seized by British army and police patrols, street fighting, gun battles and bombings erupted in Belfast and other cities of Northern Ireland. Within the past three days, 21 civilians and two soldiers have been killed, and downtown Belfast now resembles a ghost city, littered with the hulks of cars and buses (→ 9/2).

Photographer Margaret Bourke-White dies

Aug 27. Photographs made the world visible to America for the first half of this century and wherever the big events or personalities were, Margaret Bourke-White was there with her camera. In a time when most women were chained to a typewriter, she rode shotgun with bomber crews, descended thousands of feet into a South African gold mine and wriggled on the floor for a new angle on Stalin.

Margaret Bourke-White.

Already recognized in her twenties as a photographer whose lens turned American factories and machinery into objects of art, Henry Luce brought her to Fortune where she documented the Dust Bowl with future husband, playwright Erskine Caldwell. Her picture of the immense Ft. Peck Dam in Montana spanned the cover of Life's first issue in 1936, and later she covered Gandhi's hunger strikes and revealed the horrors of Buchenwald in the pages of the magazine.

Her slim good looks and aggressive manner were a worldwide visa. Churchill and FDR were among those she photographed. Three decades of brilliant work were stopped by Parkinson's disease, and today she died at her Connecticut home.

Nixon orders wage and price freeze

Aug 25. President Nixon has ordered sweeping economic changes in an effort to curb inflation and strengthen the dollar, but organized labor has so far refused to cooperate. Nixon demanded a 90-day freeze on wages and prices, asked Congress to cut taxes and increase business deductions and announced a ten percent surcharge on many imports. To prevent a run on the dollar, the president said the United States would no longer convert dollars abroad into gold. George Meany, President of the AFL-CIO, said he had "absolutely no faith in the ability of President Nixon to successfully manage the economy of this nation" (→ 10/4).

Rock stars raise cash for Bangladesh

Aug 1. Former Beatle George Harrison led an all-star entourage of rock talent through two sold-out shows at New York's Madison Square Garden tonight, in a benefit for Bangladesh refugees. More than 40,000 attended the concerts, and Harrison hopes to donate $250,000 to the cause. The shows opened with sets of Indian music by sitarist Ravi Shankar, then moved through songs featuring Harrison, Eric Clapton, Billy Preston, Leon Russell, and another ex-Beatle, Ringo Starr. But the evening's most ecstatic ovations were reserved for the unexpected appearance of Bob Dylan (→ 11/7).

Eagles found dead

Aug 3. Federal officials have found the bones of a large number of bald and golden eagles buried on a ranch owned by a Wyoming stockman. They are among an estimated 500 eagles that have been killed by local ranchers in recent months in defiance of federal law protecting eagles. The ranchers say the eagles kill their livestock, a charge denied by environmentalists. Herman Werner, owner of the ranch where the bones were found, faces federal penalties of $500 in fines or six months in jail for each bird killed.

1971

SEPTEMBER

Su	Mo	Tu	We	Th	Fr	Sa
			1	2	3	4
5	6	7	8	9	10	11
12	13	14	15	16	17	18
19	20	21	22	23	24	25
26	27	28	29	30		

2. Belfast: Bombs injure 39, ruin Unionist Party offices (→ 10/23).

3. Saigon: Nguyen Cao Ky, barred from ballot, threatens coup if election proceeds (→ 21).

4. Alaska: 109 die as jetliner hits mountain.

7. London: BBC bars "Sesame Street" because of alleged authoritarian aims (→ 8/16/73).

9. New York: Convicts revolt at Attica, hold 32 guards (→ 11).

9. Michigan: Six KKK members arrested for ten school bus bombings in Pontiac (→ 10/13).

11. N.Y.: Black Panther leader Bobby Seale brought in to negotiate with Attica convicts (→ 13).

12. Mongolia: Ex-Mao aide Lin Piao, seeking refuge in U.S.S.R. after failed coup, dies in plane crash (→ 7/27/72).

13. New York: Nine hostages, 28 prisoners killed as 1,000 police storm Attica (→ 30).

13. Leningrad goes wild over Duke Ellington on Soviet tour.

15. New York: Stan Smith wins U.S. Open tennis title.

16. Tokyo: Three police killed, 150 hurt as students battle police at airport (→ 10/9).

17. Hugo Black retires from U.S. Supreme Court (→ 23).

18. Israel and Egypt exchange fire over Suez Canal after 13-month truce (→ 11/26).

21. U.S. reveals eight unanswered 1945 letters from Ho Chi Minh seeking aid against French colonial rule (→ 10/1).

23. John Harlan retires from U.S. Supreme Court (→ 10/21).

24. London expels 105 Soviets for espionage (→ 10/8).

25. Belgrade: Tito, Brezhnev sign declaration asserting Yugoslav independence (→ 7/23/76).

28. Budapest: Cardinal Mindszenty, after 15-year confinment in U.S. Embassy, accepts exile in Rome.

28. Chile bars payment for seized copper mines (→ 11/12).

DEATH

24. Hugo Black, retired Supreme Court justice (*2/27/1886).

Police crush convict revolt at Attica prison

Sept 30. A nine-member citizens committee was appointed today to investigate the Attica prison riot in which ten hostages and 32 prisoners were killed earlier this month.

The panel, named at the request of Governor Nelson Rockefeller of New York, will be headed by Robert B. McKay, Dean of the law school at New York University. One of the members, Amos Henix, is a former convict who once served time for attempted assault, forgery and narcotics violations.

The uprising, one of the worst in American history, began September 9 when more than 1,000 prisoners at Attica State Correctional Facility in New York state seized 32 guards as hostages and took control of part of the prison. Fires were set, fire hoses shredded and windows were broken before police and New York state troopers stormed the prison and quelled the rampage four days later.

Prisoner demands included better medical care, a minimum wage, freedom of religion and political activities, and what they termed "realistic rehabilitation." Many of the demands were granted, but state officials refused prisoner demands that they not be put on trial for killing the guards and fomenting the riot (→ 12/30/76).

Medina is cleared of Mylai charges

Sept 22. According to his defense lawyer, Capt. Ernest Medina was a disciplined commander "who honored and loved the uniform." To the prosecution, Medina was a murderer, the company commander with overall responsibility for the Mylai massacre. In Georgia today, a jury of five combat officers sided with the defense. Cheers broke out as Medina was acquitted of murder and manslaughter charges in the deaths of "no less than 100 Vietnamese civilians." Medina was the last man to face a murder charge in the Mylai incident (→ 9/2/72).

Nikita Khrushchev dies in obscurity

Sept 11. Nikita Khrushchev died in Moscow today, but Russians did not know about his death until they heard the news on their short-wave radios. Hours passed before the Kremlin made an official announcement. The former head of the Soviet Communist Party has been a non-person since he was purged seven years ago. Only Khrushchev's wife, Nina, and one of his daughters were at his side as he succumbed to a heart attack. It is unlikely that the once powerful Soviet party boss will be given a state funeral.

Khrushchev will be remembered by Russians as the man who denounced Stalin and tried to rehabilitate his enemies. In the United States, Americans remember the man who banged his shoe on the table at the United Nations.

Bernstein's "Mass" opens JFK Center

Sept 8. The $70 million John F. Kennedy Center for the Performing Arts opened tonight to the strains of a modern, haunting "Mass." Mrs. Rose Kennedy and other members of her clan, dressed in glittering finery, came to Washington for the performance. Yet Jacqueline Kennedy Onassis, who personally asked Leonard Bernstein to compose the work in memory of her husband, did not choose to attend.

The national cultural center was conceived 13 years ago when Congress realized the capital was bereft of a home for theater, music or dance. Not a stone was laid until President Kennedy was assassinated; then the center was seen as the perfect place to honor him. Rose Kennedy termed the evening a "religious" experience.

Look magazine fails in television era

Sept 16. Management announced at noon that Look was folding. The final issue will reach newsstands October 19. Rising postal costs, poor advertising revenue and competition from TV were blamed for the demise of the 34-year-old journal. Lyndon Johnson's memoirs, slated for publication in Look, have been sold to The New York Times. The country "can only support one quality photo-journalism magazine," a Look executive sighed. He was referring to Life (→ 12/29/72).

Perhaps the tumult of the sixties is drawing to a close. Or maybe the Disney empire has just found a fun and profitable escape. Walt Disney World is open in Florida.

U.S. Army drops murderous training slogan

Troops training in Vietnam.

Sept 19. Bob Dylan was right when he wrote the song, "The Times They Are A-Changin'." In a drastic departure from tradition, the U.S. Army has changed its bayonet drill slogan of "Kill! Kill!" to "Yah! Yah!" In the hand-to-hand combat drill, sweating young recruits brutally slam the blades of their bayonets into an enemy dummy. Army training specialist Col. W.C. Carter said of the move: "We're trying to keep things modern and in good taste" (→ 22).

1971

OCTOBER

Su	Mo	Tu	We	Th	Fr	Sa
					1	2
3	4	5	6	7	8	9
10	11	12	13	14	15	16
17	18	19	20	21	22	23
24	25	26	27	28	29	30
31						

1. Saigon: Police attack Buddhist anti-Thieu rally (→ 3).

2. Utah: Snowmobile speed record set at 140.6 mph.

3. Saigon: Thieu, only candidate running, re-elected to four-year term as president (→ 31).

4. Labor leader George Meany urges Congress to take control of economy from Nixon (→ 18).

7. Tel Aviv: Israel bars 21 U.S. black Jews (→ 1/20/72).

8. Moscow ousts four British aides in reprisal action.

10. North Carolina: U.S. tennis team clinches Davis Cup.

12. Washington: House passes ERA 354-23 (→ 3/22/72).

15. Japan agrees to curb flow of textiles into U.S. (→ 11/19).

16. New York: Black militant H. Rap Brown wounded in shooting after armed robbery (→ 12/28).

17. Washington: First comparative study shows Hispanic families earn more than blacks.

17. Baltimore: Pirates take Series over Orioles in final game.

18. Washington: House orders Nixon not to cut funds for school lunch programs (→ 11/14).

20. Cambodia: Premier Lon Nol declares state of emergency as revolt grows (→ 3/10/72).

21. Washington: Nixon names Lewis Powell, Wm. Rhenquist to Supreme Court (→ 1/7/72).

23. Ulster: British soldiers kill five in rioting, including two sisters (→ 11/10).

24. Detroit: Charles Hughes becomes first player to die during pro football game.

24. New York: Pablo Casals conducts concert at U.N.

25. New York: U.N. to seat Peking, oust Taiwan (→ 26).

26. Taipei: Chiang calls U.N. ouster vote illegal (→ 11/1).

27. Congo renamed Zaire (→ 9/27/75).

31. Saigon begins release of 1,938 Hanoi POWs (→ 11/12).

DEATH

25. Philip Wylie, American essayist, novelist (*5/12/1902).

Britain will join the Common Market

Oct 28. Shouts erupted in the British Parliament tonight as the House of Commons ended a 14-year debate and approved membership in the European Common Market.

Polls show that a majority of the English oppose entering the market, but the 356-244 vote was seen as a victory for Prime Minister Heath and his Conservative Party. It also split the opposition Labor Party down the middle. Labor leader Harold Wilson favored membership in the Common Market when he was Prime Minister, but he led the attack on the terms negotiated by Heath. Wilson's deputy, Roy Jenkins, led a group of Laborites who bolted and sided with Heath. Jenkins was hissed by some members of his party as he walked out of Parliament tonight. The vote by the House of Commons brings Europe one step closer to economic and political union (→ 1/22/72).

Largest cargo plane recalled for defects

Oct 12. The Air Force has grounded all of its C-5A cargo planes, the world's largest planes, because of a possible defect in engine mountings.

The order grounding the 47 C-5A's came after one of the four jet engines fell off an aircraft as it was preparing to take off from Altus Air Force Base in Oklahoma two weeks ago. After cracks were discovered in the engine mounting of another C-5A, the Air Force said it would ground seven aircraft that had a particularly large amount of flying time. The order was extended to the entire C-5A fleet when cracks were discovered in the same part of the engine mounting of yet another aircraft. The grounding is the latest problem for the C-5A, which has suffered from huge cost overruns and a number of technical malfunctions. The C-5A has cost Lockheed, its manufacturer, more than $200 million in losses.

Hirohito tours Europe, gets mixed reaction

Oct 9. "We cannot pretend that the relations between our two peoples have always been friendly," said Queen Elizabeth during a lunch for visiting Emperor Hirohito, "but this experience should make us all the more determined never to let it happen again." Others seem unable or unwilling to forget the past. Would she have Hitler or Mussolini to lunch, asked one British newspaper.

There was a warm reception in Brussels, but thousands stood mute on the streets of London and Paris as the Japanese emperor paraded past. In Holland, protestors booed, burned Japanese flags and carried signs that said, "Hirohitler go home." Many believe the emperor sees this as a trip of penance, but are puzzled why Hirohito, who has never mentioned the war during his visit, doesn't, as one journalist put it, "just apologize."

Hirohito, in London, lays a wreath at Britain's tomb of the unknown soldier.

London Bridge up in Arizona of all places

Oct 10. In an extravagant splash combining ancient pageantry and modern press-agentry, London Bridge was opened today in the middle of the Arizona desert. The Lord Mayor of London and the Governor of Arizona pulled on a red silk ribbon, releasing balloons, pigeons, skydivers and rockets. Last night, a banquet for 800 duplicated the one for King William IV at the inauguration of the bridge in 1831. The unique purchase was oil millionaire Robert P. McCulloch's idea. He has invested $10 million to bring tourists and their money to Arizona's Lake Havasu City.

Southern students fight over Dixie flag

Oct 13. A brawl broke out at a St. Petersburg, Florida, high school over the use of a Confederate flag as the school's banner. Black students have deplored the use of the flag since the school was integrated last year. This morning, black and white students clashed in front of Dixie Hollins High with sticks and bottles. Thirteen black students led the attack and were arrested, according to police reports. Several students were injured in the melee and black pupils not jailed boycotted classes. An election will be held to choose a new banner (→ 16).

Vasectomy fair is big success in India

Oct 23. If India's "vasectomy fairs" had hawkers, they might cry, "Come one, come all—all one billion." India faces a population of one billion by the year 2000. To hold down that number, the government is offering money ($13 to each man) and gifts (a sari for his wife) to those willing to be sterilized. Thirteen dollars is more than three times what an average village worker can earn in one month. In December, a fair held at Kerala attracted 15,000 men. Just seven months later, a fair in the same town received 63,000. Doctors operated in ten-hour shifts.

1971

NOVEMBER

Su	Mo	Tu	We	Th	Fr	Sa
	1	2	3	4	5	6
7	8	9	10	11	12	13
14	15	16	17	18	19	20
21	22	23	24	25	26	27
28	29	30				

1. New York: Chinese flag raised at U.N. for first time (→ 15).

2. India: Hurricane and ensuing tidal wave takes 6,000 lives.

3. U.S. to deny passports to those who refuse to take oath of allegiance (→ 8/4/75).

5. U.S. agrees to sale of $136 mil. in grain to U.S.S.R. (→ 5/22/72).

5. Moscow: New surge of emigration by Soviet Jews is reported (→ 1/17/72).

6. Alaska: U.S. conducts underground atom test despite vocal protests (→ 1/5/72).

7. India admits forces entered Bangladesh to silence artillery (→ 22).

10. Belfast: Two women tarred and feathered for dating British soldiers (→ 12/4).

12. Nixon announces withdrawal of 45,000 more from Vietnam by February (→ 1/25/72).

12. Chile: Castro speaks to students on revolution (→ 12/8).

14. U.S. enters "Phase II" of Nixon's economic program (→ 3/28/72).

17. Houston: Ali wins 12-round decision over Buster Mathis (→ 1/15/72).

19. Tokyo: 1,785 arrested in demonstrations against U.S. bases in Okinawa (→ 4/27/72).

20. U.S. to give Turkey $35 mil. for farmers who stop growing opium poppies (→ 2/18/72).

22. India opens full-scale attack on Bangladesh (→ 12/6).

25. London: Half of Carnaby Street sold for $8.5 million.

26. Dallas: Rod Laver becomes first tennis millionaire.

26. Saudi Arabia: King Faisal agrees to let Israeli Moslems visit Mecca (→ 28).

26. London outlaws caning of students as punishment in schools.

27. Philadelphia: Army beats Navy 24-23 in football.

28. Cairo: Jordan Premier Wasfi Tal assassinated by Palestinian Black September (→ 2/5/72).

28. Anglican Church ordains its first two women priests.

China in United Nations

Chinese flag is raised at the U.N.

Nov 15. The People's Republic of China made its formal entry into the United Nations, as chief delegate Chiao Kuan-hua rebuked its members for allowing the superpowers "to manipulate and monopolize" the international organization.

The six-member delegation that arrived in New York last Tuesday was the first group of Chinese officials to visit the United States since 1950, when diplomats from Peking participated in a United Nations debate on the Korean War.

In his welcoming address to the Chinese delegation at the General Assembly, the U.S. Ambassador to the U.N., George Bush, remarked that although member nations were sharply divided on the issue of Taiwan's expulsion, nearly all countries, including the U.S., "agreed that the moment in history has arrived for the People's Republic of China to be in the United Nations."

In his address, Chiao, clad in a blue Mao tunic, criticized Japanese and U.S. efforts "to create two Chinas in the United Nations," and reiterated his nation's determination to "liberate Taiwan." He also pledged support to Arab nations opposed to "Israeli Zionism," condemned the U.S. military presence in Vietnam and vowed that "under no circumstances will China be the first to use nuclear weapons."

In a bid for leadership of the Third World, Chiao went on to remark that his nation opposed "the power politics of big nations bullying small ones or strong nations bullying weak ones . . . Countries want independence, nations want liberation and the people want revolution," the new Chinese delegate declared (→ 2/22/72).

Chinese delegates bring Mao to N.Y.

Mariner 9 placed in orbit around Mars

Nov 13. Mariner 9, a 300-pound spacecraft launched by the United States more than five months ago, was successfully placed in orbit around Mars today. Obeying instructions radioed from earth, Mariner fired a rocket to put itself in an orbit that brings it as close as 800 miles from the Martian surface. Mariner carries two cameras that will enable it to make a detailed photographic map of Mars, the first such map of any planet but earth. It will also study the two moons of Mars and measure the planet's temperature, surface composition and atmosphere (→ 1/5/72).

French agent guilty on heroin charges

Nov 16. Roger de Louette, a former French intelligence agent, pleaded guilty today to charges of smuggling $12 million worth of heroin into the United States. De Louette also accused Colonel Paul Fournier, another high-ranking French counter-espionage officer, of being the mastermind behind the conspiracy, and then he cited a contact in the French Consulate in New York, whose name was not disclosed at the arraignment in federal court. De Louette, who was indicted yesterday along with Fournier, faces up to 20 years imprisonment on his plea (→ 20).

Led Zeppelin, said one poll, surpassed the Beatles in popularity last year. This month they cut their second album, featuring "Stairway to Heaven."

Gene Hackman is a maverick detective and reckless driver obsessed with busting a heroin ring in "The French Connection."

1971

DECEMBER

Su	Mo	Tu	We	Th	Fr	Sa
			1	2	3	4
5	6	7	8	9	10	11
12	13	14	15	16	17	18
19	20	21	22	23	24	25
26	27	28	29	30	31	

4. Detroit: G.M. to recall 6.7 million Chevrolets.

4. Belfast: 13 killed, 19 hurt as blast destroys pub (→ 1/30/72).

6. U.S. bars aid to India for aggression against Pakistan (→ 17).

7. Libya nationalizes British Petroleum Co. (→ 3/4/72).

10. Nobel Peace Prize to Willy Brandt; literature to Chile's Pablo Neruda.

20. Pakistan: Zulfikar Ali Bhutto sworn in as pres. (→ 1/2/72).

21. N.Y.: Kurt Waldheim named to replace U Thant as U.N. sec. gen. (→ 12/7/76).

23. Nixon commutes sentence of Jimmy Hoffa (→ 9/7/72).

28. U.S. Justice Dept. sues Mississippi officials for ignoring ballots of blacks (→ 3/17/72).

31. Iraq expels thousands of Iranians (→ 2/10/74).

DEATHS

9. Ralph Bunche, U.S. envoy to U.N. (*8/7/1904).

18. Bobby Jones, American golf champion (*3/17/1902).

CULTURAL EVENTS, 1971

Literature: John Updike's "Rabbit Redux"; E.M. Forster's "Maurice"; Herman Wouk's "The Winds of War"; Erich Segal's "Love Story"; Sylvia Plath's "The Bell Jar"; Jerzy Kosinski's "Being There."

Academia, Religion: Analysis of Australian meteorite indicates conditions for life exist in space; Anglican and Roman Catholic Churches end 400 years of discord, agreeing on "essential meaning" of Eucharist.

Music: "Jesus Christ Superstar"; Bernstein's "Mass"; closing of Fillmore East and West; Janis Joplin's "Me and Bobby McGee"; Three Dog Night's "Joy to the World"; Rod Stewart's "Maggie May"; Carole King's "It's too Late"; Osmonds' "One Bad Apple"; Dance Theater of Harlem established.

The Arts: Conceptual art becomes fad in U.S.

Film: Kubrick's "A Clockwork Orange"; Warhol's "Trash"; "The French Connection."

Bangladesh gives in to India, ending war

Dec 17. President Yahya Khan of Pakistan changed his position dramatically today and announced he would accept a cease-fire with India. Only yesterday, after his forces in East Pakistan surrendered unconditionally, Yahya Kahn vowed to keep fighting in the West against his political enemy. His reversal today undermines his administration, and there are growing indications he will step down as head of the military government.

Yahya has already been criticized for his brutal repression of the Bengali separatist movement, which has renamed East Pakistan Bangladesh. India was quick to recognize the rebel government, and the conflict between East and West Pakistan was a major cause of this latest war. It appears that the separatists may actually benefit from the fighting, because India has managed to defeat most of Yahya's military forces in East Pakistan.

This war has also created new frictions between the United States and India, which was supported by the Soviet Union. Prime Minister Indira Gandhi has objected to President Nixon's support of Yahya, and tensions flared this week when the aircraft carrier Enterprise steamed toward the conflict (→ 1/8/72).

Bengali peasants disrupted by war.

Serpico spills guts in police graft probe

Dec 14. Detective Frank Serpico, deaf in one ear from a bullet wound in the head, told the Knapp Commission of his efforts to tell high-ranking New York City officials of police corruption. For five months, Serpico complained to Jay Kriegel, a close aide to Mayor John Lindsay, and to City Commissioner of Investigation Arnold Fraiman, of his fellow officers' dealings in the city's underbelly. But they failed to act on the allegations of corruption.

Whitman Knapp heads the commission that Serpico helped create to wage his war against scandalous police activity. Serpico testified to various instances of policemen taking "nuts"—police jargon for illegal payoffs. Several officers are likely to be indicted for the illegal acts uncovered by Serpico.

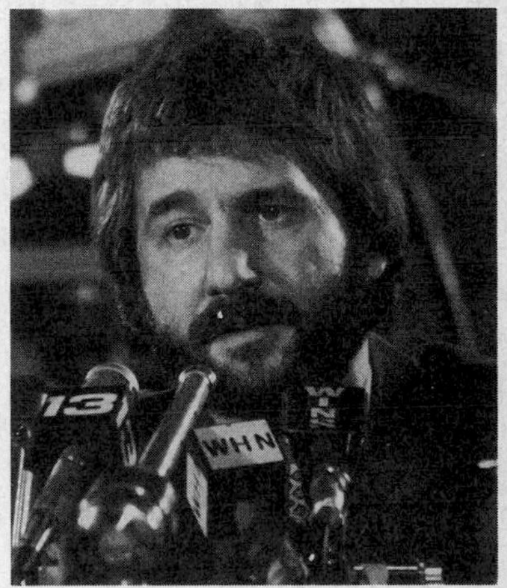

Serpico before Knapp Commission.

Allende acts to quell women's food riots

Dec 8. President Salvador Allende of Chile announced today that the government will take over the distribution of food in his nation. The move comes on the heels of a revolt by women aligned with right-wing military commander Augusto Pinochet. The women embarked on a "March of the Empty Pots" to protest Chile's food shortages. Chile's Communist newspaper contends the U.S. Central Intelligence Agency organized the revolt. Violence erupted during the demonstration, forcing Allende to declare a state of emergency.

Chile's economic problems have plagued Allende's Marxist administration. Now, an anti-Marxist coalition is threatening the stability of the country. The president, at a rally to honor visiting Cuban Premier Fidel Castro, warned of the radical right-wing opposition. "The germs of fascism" are at work in Chile, he asserted. He blamed the Christian and National Parties for exploiting the troubled economy and asked for citizens to exercise discipline during the lean times.

He said he respects the opposition if they "remain within the law." An opposition rally planned for next week will be allowed, he said, but he urged government supporters to show their colors too (→ 4/12/72).

Vets take Liberty

Dec 26. A band of Vietnam veterans have seized the Statue of Liberty in a dramatic anti-war statement. Sixteen men entered the statue with a group of tourists late this afternoon, hid in the basement after it closed and evicted a watchman. They then barricaded entrances and telephoned the news media. The National Park Service seemed almost sympathetic to the vets. "We'll let them stay the night," a representative said quietly. Meanwhile, in Philadelphia 25 demonstrators occupied the home of Betsy Ross to protest what they called "indiscriminate bombing of the peoples of Indochina" (→ 1/26/72).

Media mogul Sarnoff signs off forever

Brigadier General David Sarnoff.

Dec 12. David Sarnoff, who pioneered both radio and television broadcasting, died in New York today at the age of 80. Starting as a telegraph operator, Sarnoff rose to head the Radio Corporation of America, which played a major role in popularizing radio in the early 1920's. In 1926, he founded the National Broadcasting Company and within two years was experimenting with television. He saw video become a major new force before retiring from RCA in 1970.

1972

JANUARY

Su	Mo	Tu	We	Th	Fr	Sa
						1
2	3	4	5	6	7	8
9	10	11	12	13	14	15
16	17	18	19	20	21	22
23	24	25	26	27	28	29
30	31					

1. Pasadena: Stanford edges Michigan 13-12 in Rose Bowl.

2. Pakistan nationalizes ten industries (→ 2/1).

3. Liberia: William Tolbert inaugurated president; Pat Nixon in attendance.

5. Washington: Nixon signs bill allotting $5.5 billion to begin work on space shuttle (→ 2/26).

5. Groton: Error by nuclear sub leaks 500 gallons coolant into river (→ 8/3).

7. Washington: Lewis Powell and William Rehnquist sworn in as Supreme Court justices.

8. Pakistan: Bengali chief Mujibur Rahman freed after nine months in prison (→ 12).

11. New York: AEC asks for test run at Indian Point nuclear power plant (→ 9/21/74).

12. Bangladesh: Mujibur Rahman becomes premier (→ 17).

15. New Orleans: Joe Frazier KO's Terry Daniels in fourth to retain title (→ 3/31).

15. Copenhagen: Margrethe proclaimed Queen of Denmark.

17. Bangladesh: Sheik Mujibur Rahman orders Bengali rebels to surrender arms (→ 24).

17. Israel: 350 Soviet Jews arrive in El Al 747 (→ 3/15).

24. Moscow recognizes Bangladesh sovereignty (→ 30).

24. Nixon proposes budget with largest deficit of $25.5 billion.

25. New York: Shirley Chisholm announces candidacy for president as Democrat (→ 2/15).

25. Nixon airs eight-point peace plan for Vietnam, asking POW release for withdrawal (→ 2/13).

26. Washington: Anti-war leader Rev. Daniel Berrigan paroled (→ 2/12).

28. N.Y.: Biographer Clifford Irving says wife transferred money from Howard Huges into Swiss account (→ 2/11).

30. Londonderry: British troops kill 13 as riots break out against British rule (→ 2/22).

DEATH

14. King Frederick IX of Denmark (*3/11/1899).

Mujibur becomes Premier of Bangladesh

Sheik Mujib, father of Bangladesh.

Jan 30. Surviving a harrowing arrest and months of tortuous imprisonment, Sheik Mujibur Rahman has become the Prime Minister of the newly independent nation of Bangladesh. The charismatic leader was released from his West Pakistani jail cell on January 10, returned to his homeland and swiftly moved into political action. He adopted a provisional constitution, shuffled Cabinet officials around, and now figures to lead the national agenda in Bangladesh's parliamentary, democratic government.

Pakistani soldiers arrested Sheik Mujib last March for leading the Bengali liberation movement in East Pakistan. While imprisoned, his captors told Mujib he would die and that the blame would be placed on the Bengalis. But when Zulfikar Ali Bhutto took power in West Pakistan, he reversed plans for Mujib's execution and then freed him.

However, the release of Mujib was arranged for political purposes; execution of the Bengali leader would only incite his followers. Bhutto has tried to link up with the Mujib regime, but Mujib has rejected him, fearing Bengali liberation would be threatened (→ 2/29).

Jewish-born atheist denied change of status

Jan 20. The running battle in Israel over "Who is a Jew?" recently surfaced again when the high court refused to let a Jewish-born atheist change his status. Israel recognizes both citizenship and nationality. Only Jews can be both; a 1970 law upheld rabbinic law which states that Jews by definition have Jewish mothers.

Enter Dr. Georges Tamari, born Jewish but an avowed atheist. Charging that the 1970 law is racist, Tamari asked the court to change his status from Jewish by nationality to that of plain Israeli citizen by virtue of his atheism. The court refused, ruling that the desire by such Jews to separate from the greater Jewish nation would be divisive. In other words, Israeli Jews may not alter their religious "nationality" despite religious beliefs to the contrary (→ 5/7/73).

Jan 16. Roger Staubach's Cowboys rout Miami 24-3 in Super Bowl.

Four more countries in Common Market

Britain enters the EEC.

Jan 22. After ten years of difficult negotiations, the European Common Market was enlarged today to include Britain, Ireland, Denmark and Norway. With the signing of the Treaty of Brussels, the ten-nation community in principle becomes one of the world's great economic powers. The enlarged community has a population greater than the United States or the Soviet Union, accounts for 41 percent of world trade and has a gross national product of $700 billion a year.

While the European Economic Community still lacks centralized political powers, the sponsors hope that the treaty, particularly the inclusion of Great Britain, will represent a major step toward fulfillment of the postwar dream of a united Europe (→ 2/11/75).

Coke recalls three million unsafe cans

Jan 12. The Coca-Cola Bottling Company of New York has pulled more than three million cans of soft drinks off the market in the last month because some of the aluminum lids on the cans were found to be contaminated. The Food and Drug Administration, which revealed the recall today, said the contamination did not present a serious health problem. It said the contamination occurred when an oven in a manufacturing plant malfunctioned and failed to bake off all the solvent on the lids.

Gospel singer's fine voice is silenced

Jan 26. Mahalia Jackson's favorite songs said a lot about her. "Move on Up a Little Higher" was one; "Just Over the Hill" was another. So were "How I Got Over" and "What a Friend I Have in Jesus." Miss Jackson, who died today of heart failure, always looked up to the Lord. And it was a happy gaze; no blues for her. Gospel all the way.

Miss Jackson was heard in black and white churches, on stages in Israel and France, and on million-selling records. Before Martin Luther King talked about his dream at the Lincoln Memorial in 1963, Mahalia Jackson sang it. She was there.

The singer was born in 1901 in New Orleans to a strict Baptist family. In 1928, she moved to Chicago and did church solos. She began performing elsewhere, any place liquor was not served. President Nixon called her "an exemplary servant of her God."

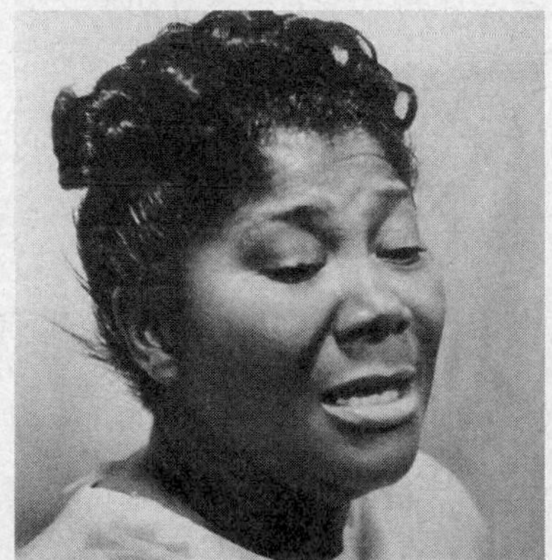

Mahalia Jackson sings the gospel.

Chevalier tips his hat for the last time

Debonair Chevalier does cabaret.

Jan 1. Maurice Chevalier was blessed with poor pipes. He said if he had been a smooth-voiced balladeer, he might never have been driven to "sing from the heart." It set him above many other chanteurs.

Chevalier died in Paris tonight. He was 83. People all over the world could do an impression of Chevalier. It merely involved singing one of his songs ("Valentine," "Ma Louise," "Thank Heaven for Little Girls," for example) in a thick French accent while tipping a straw hat. Chevalier adopted the beloved boater and tuxedo in 1919.

The ninth child of a house painter, Chevalier tried to make money in his teens doing acrobatics. A fall ended that career, but he was headlining the Folies-Bergere at age 21. He was still singing at age 76.

Jan 8. Britain's pride of the seas is no more. The Queen Elizabeth, first launched in 1934, carried troops in war and vacationers in peace. In 1969 it was sold. Renamed Seawise University by a Chinese investor, it was housing students in Hong Kong harbor when fire ravaged the aging ship.

1972

FEBRUARY

Su	Mo	Tu	We	Th	Fr	Sa
		1	2	3	4	5
6	7	8	9	10	11	12
13	14	15	16	17	18	19
20	21	22	23	24	25	26
27	28	29				

1. Peking: Pakistani Pres. Bhutto meets with Mao (→ 2/24/75).

2. Tokyo: Winter Olympics begin.

5. Washington: It is reported U.S. has agreed to sell 42 F-4 Phantom jets to Israel (→ 3/31).

6. U.S. airlines set up hijacking screens (→ 6/19).

11. Life cancels plan to print Irving's "autobiography" of Howard Hughes (→ 15).

12. Washington: Sen. Kennedy advocates amnesty for Vietnam draft resisters (→ 4/23).

13. Vietnam: Enemy attacks decline for third day as U.S. continues intensive bombing (→ 24).

15. N.Y.: Warrant issued for arrest of Edith Irving, wife of Hughes "biographer" (→ 3/13).

15. Atty. Gen. John Mitchell resigns to direct Nixon's re-election campaign (→ 5/16).

18. California Supreme Court voids death penalty (→ 6/29).

18. Washington report calls alcohol abuse nation's biggest drug problem.

22. Peking: Nixon meets with Mao Tse-tung one hour (→ 28).

22. Britain: I.R.A. bombing kills seven at officers mess (→ 23).

23. San Jose: Angela Davis freed on $102,500 bail (→ 28).

24. Paris: Hanoi walks out of peace talks to protest U.S. air raids on N. Vietnam (→ 3/23).

26. Soviets recover Luna 20 with cargo of moon rocks (→ 3/2).

27. New York: 100 injured as attack frees five hostage guards held at Rikers Island.

28. San Jose: Angela Davis murder trial begins (→ 3/29).

29. Florida: Cesar Chavez signs state's first contract for migrant farm workers (→ 3/10/77).

29. Bangladesh: Premier Mujibur Rahman flies to Moscow for goodwill trip (→ 3/3).

DEATHS

5. Marianne Moore, American poet and critic (*11/15/1887).

20. Walter Winchell, father of gossip column (*4/7/1897).

Mob burns British Embassy in Dublin

Feb 23. The British Embassy has been firebombed and destroyed by demonstrators protesting the killing of 13 persons by British paratroopers in Northern Ireland.

What had started as an orderly parade of protest through the streets of Dublin turned to violence when the large crowd reached the British Embassy. Outnumbered police stood passively by as the demonstrators hurled stones and then firebombs at the Georgian building in Merrion Square. The Irish government had declared the day to be one of national mourning for the 13 persons shot by British troops during a demonstration in Londonderry.

Later in the month, after the bombing of a paratrooper officers mess near London, the lrish government cracked down on the lrish Republican Army by arresting eight leaders of the outlawed group (→ 3/24).

West Germans pay $5m to hijackers

Feb 25. Bonn paid the hijackers of a jumbo jet $5 million for the release of passengers today, after Arab terrorists issued an ultimatum. Germany has never paid a skyjacker ransom before. The United States hopes to see a decline in hijackings, having started random searches at Kennedy International Airport two weeks ago.

Brando is the magnanimous Don Corleone in "The Godfather."

Pres. Nixon visits China

Nixon attends a dinner in Peking, an unsusual sight adorning the rear wall.

Feb 28. President Nixon is flying home from Shanghai today, convinced that his week-long visit to China has helped build a new "generation of peace." Premier Chou En-lai gave the president, Secretary of State William Rogers and adviser Henry Kissinger a warm farewell, but he refused to characterize his 15 hours of talks with Nixon. Chou said he would let the joint communique "speak for itself."

Throughout Nixon's visit, both sides recognized that American recognition of Taiwan has been a major stumbling block in relations. In the communique, the United States said the problem should be resolved "by the Chinese themselves." Nixon also committed himself to the "ultimate objective of the withdrawal of all United States forces and military installations from Taiwan." Privately, however, administration officials said Nixon has no intention of abandoning Nationalist China. The Americans and the Chinese stopped short of saying when they might establish diplomatic relations, but they did promise to increase informal contacts. They also noted their differences on the future of Vietnam and Korea.

Nixon's trip began almost as successfully as it ended. He had a surprise meeting with Chairman Mao Tse-tung on his first afternoon in Peking, and he exchanged gracious toasts that night with Chou while a Chinese band struck up "Home on the Range" and "America the Beautiful" (→ 3/12).

Mao, the father of Third World revolution, welcomes Nixon to Peking.

1972

MARCH

Su	Mo	Tu	We	Th	Fr	Sa
			1	2	3	4
5	6	7	8	9	10	11
12	13	14	15	16	17	18
19	20	21	22	23	24	25
26	27	28	29	30	31	

3. Moscow: Pakistani premier signs joint policy declaration with Kosygin (→ 3/19).

4. Moscow: Soviets gain accord with Libya to help develop and refine Libyan oil (→ 6/11).

10. Vienna: Jury frees Walter Dejaco, man who designed Auschwitz gas chambers.

10. Cambodia: Premier Lon Nol nullifies nearly completed constitution (→ 9/8).

12. U.K, China agree to establish full diplomatic relations (→ 7/5).

12. India: Vote gives Indira Gandhi 70% of regional seats (→ 4/8/73).

15. Washington: Jewish Defense League member pours blood on head of Soviet diplomat Alexander Yevstafyev (→ 8/13).

16. Colombia: Man said to be Nazi war criminal Martin Bormann seized.

17. Nixon asks Congress to halt busing to achieve desegregation (→ 2/27/73).

18. Washington: Sen. Kennedy charges civilian aide to Laos goes to CIA (→ 2/15/73).

19. Dacca: India, Bangladesh sign 20-year mutual aid pact (→ 26).

22. U.S. Senate passes Equal Rights Amendment (→ 1/20/74).

23. Paris: U.S. calls halt to peace parley on Vietnam (→ 30).

25. L.A.: UCLA wins sixth straight NCAA basketball title.

26. El Salvador: Govt. says 100 were killed in failed revolt yesterday (→ 2/20/77).

26. Dacca: Bangladesh nationalizes main industries (→ 4/4).

27. Sudan: Arab Moslems in north and black Christians sign peace, ending 17-year conflict.

28. Labor chief Meany says "Phase II" of Nixon economic plan failed America (→ 1/11/73).

30. Hanoi launches heaviest attack in four years, crossing DMZ (→ 4/2).

30. Turkey: Leftists slay three foreign hostages as police storm building, killing ten (→ 7/25/75).

31. Tokyo: Ali outpoints Mac Foster in 15 rounds (→ 5/1).

Irving admits hoax on Hughes book

March 13. Author Clifford Irving confessed in a New York court this morning that his "autobiography" of Howard Hughes was phony. One of the most elaborate swindles in years has failed, its details not failing to entertain the public.

Last year, Irving submitted a manuscript to McGraw-Hill. He said he had held about a hundred taped interviews with the secretive Howard Hughes, conversations he transcribed by hand. Some of it, he added, was in Hughes' own hand.

The publishing world went mad. McGraw-Hill and Time Inc. put $1 million into publicizing the work (and paying Irving $750,000). Paperback and book club rights were sold at exorbitant sums.

Clifford and Edith Irving in N.Y.

Then a phone rang. It was Howard Hughes. He said he would not know Clifford Irving from Adam.

Irving and a research assistant had collected facts about Hughes at his former companies and then taken turns talking into a tape player, making up Hughesian comments.

They transcribed the tapes; some of the handwriting was forged from a sample of Hughes' scrawl photographed in a magazine. Irving's real blunder was underestimating Hughes. As a court prosecutor said, Irving thought the 66-year-old eccentric was either dead "or not of sufficient mental or physical capacity to denounce" the book. Irving will be sentenced in June (→ 6/16). ▷

Britain imposes direct rule on North Ireland

March 24. Britain's Prime Minister Heath took dramatic steps today to stop the sectarian violence that has flared up again in Northern Ireland. He suspended the provincial government and Parliament and established direct rule over the troubled area. William Whitelaw was appointed Secretary of State for Northern Ireland. Some 4,000 additional British soldiers were put on standby. And 15,000 are already stationed in Northern Ireland. Protestant leaders condemned Heath's moves as surrender to "terrorist violence." Catholics applauded the abolition of the Protestant-dominated provincial government.

A firebomb blazes in Belfast.

Heath acted after two powerful bombs exploded this week in central Belfast. The worst daylight bombing in 30 months killed six people in the shopping district on Monday. Seventy people were hurt when a bomb blew up in a railway station parking lot on Wednesday (→ 5/29).

Phantoms go to both Israel and Jordan

March 31. The United States has agreed with Jordan's King Hussein, currently on a visit to America, to help modernize that country's air force with 24 F-5 Phantom fighters, 12 to be delivered in the next two years. The action closely follows last month's agreement to sell Israel 42 F-4 Phantoms and 90 A-4 Skyhawks over the next two to three years. The two transactions are not considered related, and analysts stress that they could not upset the Mideast balance of power. Israel now has about 400 warplanes as compared with Jordan's 35 jet fighters. The F-5's are also inferior to the F-4's in speed, payload and operational range (→ 5/9).

Jackie is suing to avoid photographer

March 6. Mrs. Aristotle Onassis spelled out in federal court yesterday what she terms "aggressive actions" toward her by freelance photographer Ronald E. Galella. She told of him "lunging" at her outside her apartment at 1040 Fifth Avenue and in a theater; of being followed when shopping, seeing friends and bicycling with her son John Kennedy Jr.; of Galella calling her "Jackie" or "baby" and always taking photos. She seeks an injunction to keep him 200 yards from her residence and 100 yards from her anywhere else. Her action is a countersuit. Galella is suing her for $1.3 million, charging interference with his livelihood (→ 7/5).

Spacecraft is launched to explore Jupiter

March 2. The United States today launched the Pioneer 10 spacecraft on what is planned to be the longest and most far-reaching interplanetary voyage of the space age—a 21-month journey that will take it to the planet Jupiter.

The launching took place at 8:50 p.m., after a last-minute delay caused by a technical problem. Officials say the spacecraft is on course, traveling at 31,413 miles an hour. It weighs 570 pounds and has four nuclear generators to provide electricity for its systems and instruments. It is equipped to measure the planet's hydrogen-rich atmosphere, cloud cover and radiation belts.

Pioneer 10 will also take the first close-up pictures of the planet, largest in the solar system, when it arrives in December 1973. Pioneer's trajectory will take it within 100,000 miles of Jupiter for four days of close observations which will allow it to photograph two-thirds of the planet's surface.

After its encounter with Jupiter, Pioneer will shoot toward the outer edge of the solar system, eventually becoming the first spacecraft to enter outer space. It carries a record containing greetings from earth and information about our planet directed at extraterrestrial beings who might intercept it in space (→ 4/27).

An artist's rendering of Pioneer 10 spacecraft in orbit around Jupiter.

Angela Davis denies aiding prison break

March 29. In an emotional declaration of innocence, Angela Davis told a court in San Jose, Calif., she bought guns to protect herself, not to be used to try to free George Jackson from prison. "For a black person growing up in violence-filled Alabama," she said, "guns were a normal way of life." She spoke for two hours, after a delay to gauge what effect an attempted jailbreak in a nearby building, involving hostages and a killing, reminiscent of the shootout from which the charges against Miss Davis stem, would have on the jury (→ 6/4).

Howard Hughes meets with Somoza

March 14. Increasingly unreclusive Howard Hughes met cordially with Nicaraguan President Somoza tonight, thanking him for his hospitality. Hughes came to Managua after a long stay in the Bahamas. Since Hughes held a phone conference January 9 to debunk the Irving "biography," the press has noted his comings and goings. He was in seclusion for over a decade, spending many of those empty years in a Las Vegas hotel. Eyewitnesses say he is trim, fit and has fingernails of normal length (→ 12/28/74).

Ball is held for Cuban social exiles

March 5. More than 900 Cuban exiles paid $25 each to dine and dance at the Sonesta Beach Hotel in Key Biscayne, Florida, last night. All the waiters and hotel help were Cubans, but not all partygoers had been rich and not all waiters poor in Cuba. A former lawyer served a prosperous Miami store owner who was a sales clerk in pre-Castro Havana. An hour-long show with 18 elaborate tableaus from Columbus to the present day ended with the entire cast of 170 bursting into a rock dance, giving a touch of reality to a night of nostalgia.

Bob Fosse's "Cabaret" captures the sultry side of pre-war Berlin. Liza Minnelli, Joel Grey star.

1972

APRIL

Su	Mo	Tu	We	Th	Fr	Sa
						1
2	3	4	5	6	7	8
9	10	11	12	13	14	15
16	17	18	19	20	21	22
23	24	25	26	27	28	29
30						

2. South Vietnam: Hanoi takes half of Quangtri province (→ 15).

3. N.Y.: Charlie Chaplin returns to U.S. after 20-year absence.

4. U.S. extends diplomatic recognition to Bangladesh (→ 8/25).

4. Stockholm: Soviets refuse Swede visa to give Nobel Prize to Solzhenitsyn (→ 12/28/73).

6. Cairo severs ties with Jordan over Hussein's plan for federation with Palestinians (→ 8/2).

8. Texas: Kjell Isaksonn sets mark in pole vault, 18'1" (→ 5/29/76).

9. Soviets sign anti-Zionist, anti-colonial pact with Iraq (→ 6/1).

9. Augusta, Ga.: Jack Nicklaus wins fourth Masters golf title.

10. Moscow: 70 nations sign pact banning biological weapons.

12. Chile: 200,000 anti-Marxists stage protest march (→ 18).

13. Chicago: First mass strike in major league baseball settled after two weeks.

15. North Vietnam: U.S. begins massive bombing of Haiphong area (→ 30).

15. Ottawa: Nixon, Trudeau sign pact to clean up Great Lakes.

18. Chile: Allende to ask Congress to nationalize ITT property in Chile (→ 10/11).

23. N.J.: 23 held trying to block loading of munitions ship (→ 25).

25. N.Y.: 14 hurt as police charge Columbia protesters (→ 30).

27. Japan paralyzed by strike of 1.6 million (→ 5/15).

28. Oxford: Five colleges break 750 years of tradition, deciding to admit women in 1974.

30. New York: Seven nuns arrested in anti-war protest at St. Patrick's Cathedral (→ 5/11).

DEATHS

4. Adam Clayton Powell, controversial Harlem congressman (*11/29/1908).

9. James Byrne, ex-Supreme Court justice, sec. of state under FDR (*5/2/1879).

27. Kwame Nkrumah, first pres. of Ghana (*9/21/1909).

North Vietnamese launch invasion of South

South Vietnamese women recruits move out to meet the Communist attack.

April 30. Thousands of North Vietnamese and Viet Cong troops are tightening the noose around the besieged provincial capital of Quangtri. If the city collapses, Hue and Danang could fall next. South Vietnamese forces in the northern part of the country have been on the run since early this month, when the equivalent of two Communist divisions launched a major attack across the demilitarized zone.

Advancing under heavy cloud cover, the Communists have been almost immune from American and South Vietnamese air attacks. Supported by heavy artillery and tanks, the Communists managed to seize half of Quangtri province within a couple of days. American B-52's finally took to the air and dropped hundreds of tons of bombs through the clouds, but the raids did little to halt the Communist advance.

Motivated by political as well as military concerns, President Nixon ordered B-52 raids on North Vietnam for the first time in four years. The huge, slow-moving bombers, protected by faster F-4 fighter jets, struck fuel dumps, warehouses and transportation centers around Haiphong, 60 miles east of Hanoi. Hanoi radio reported that 11 American planes were shot down.

Nixon hopes to show the North Vietnamese that he is committed to his policy of "Vietnamizing" this war. Through their offensive, the Communists are trying to upset that policy, whip up anti-war sentiment in the United States and convince Moscow and Peking not to make a separate deal with Nixon to end the war. In Paris today, Le Duc Tho, the Communist delegate, said he wants "a just and equitable peaceful solution" of the war (→ 5/1).

G.I. watches as a hamlet, attacked by invaders, burns to the ground.

Moon exploration ends successfully

April 27. Apollo 16, carrying more than 200 pounds of rocks from the moon, splashed down in the Pacific today after an 11-day lunar exploration mission. Astronauts John W. Young and Charles M. Duke Jr. spent a record 71 hours on the moon while the third crew member, Thomas K. Mattingly, orbited in the command ship. "You got your money's worth on this one," Young said of the mission (→ 7/26).

Joey Gallo is killed in gangland war

April 7. Joseph Gallo, the organized crime figure known as "crazy Joe," was assassinated yesterday morning outside a restaurant in the Little Italy section of New York City. He was shot by an unknown assailant while celebrating his 43rd birthday with his wife and sister.

Man and woman row across Pacific

April 22. Two Britons, John Fairfax, 33, and Sylvia Cook, 31, landed at Hayman Island off Australia today in good shape but with blistered hands. The first ever to row across the Pacific Ocean, they began the 8,000-mile trip in San Francisco a year ago in a $5,000 rowboat filled with food and water.

Hsing-Hsing and Ling-Ling, a gift from China to the U.S.

1972

MAY

Su	Mo	Tu	We	Th	Fr	Sa
	1	2	3	4	5	6
7	8	9	10	11	12	13
14	15	16	17	18	19	20
21	22	23	24	25	26	27
28	29	30	31			

1. N.Y. Times gets Pulitzer for Pentagon Papers (→ 4/27/73).

1. Vancouver: Ali wins decision over George Chuvalo (→ 25).

1. South Vietnam: Quangtri, northernmost province, abandoned to Hanoi troops (→ 3).

3. Nixon names Patrick Gray director of FBI.

3. South Vietnam: 150,000 evacuating Hue as North Vietnamese troops approach (→ 8).

5. U.S. Congress hears report wiretaps up 37% in past year.

6. Kentucky Derby won by Riva Ridge, Ron Turcotte riding.

7. L.A.: Lakers beat N.Y. Knicks for NBA title.

8. Nixon orders ports in North Vietnam mined to cut off supplies to Hanoi (→ 10).

10. Saigon: Thieu imposes martial law, as U.S. continues bombing in North (→ 13).

12. New York: Guggenheim opens Kandinsky show.

12. Berlin: East, West Germany sign first pact, agreeing on all traffic but air transport (→ 6/3).

15. Tokyo: U.S. returns control of Okinawa to Japan in formal ceremony (→ 6/17).

16. Washington: George Schultz replaces John Connally as secretary of the Treasury.

19. Washington: Bomb explodes in Air Force section of Pentagon (→ 6/28).

22. Moscow: Nixon, first U.S. president to visit Soviet leader, meets with Brezhnev (→ 29).

22. Ceylon gains independence as Sri Lanka, after 24 years as British Dominion.

25. Omaha: Joe Frazier KO's Ron Stander in fifth to retain heavyweight title (→ 6/27).

27. Mark Donahue wins Indy 500 in Sunoco McLaren.

29. Dublin: IRA orders end to armed action in Ulster (→ 7/10).

29. N.C.: Gunman Harvey McLeod opens fire in shopping mall, killing three, then himself.

31. Tehran: Bomb explodes at tomb of shah's father hour before visit of Nixon (→ 6/27/74).

Nixon talks in Moscow

Nixon, continuing a year of firsts for U.S. diplomacy, is hailed by Brezhnev.

May 29. President Nixon and Soviet Communist Party leader Leonid Brezhnev wrapped up a week of historic talks in Moscow today. In a joint communique, the two men acknowledged their major differences on the Vietnam War, but they agreed to "do their utmost to avoid military confrontations." They also endorsed the idea of "reciprocal reductions" of forces in Central Europe. Soviet leaders accepted an invitation from Nixon to travel to the United States, but no date was set. At the end of his official visit to Moscow, the first ever by an American president, Nixon flew on to Kiev, Iran and Poland.

The president's adviser on national security, Henry Kissinger, told newsmen tonight that the United States will continue to bomb North Vietnam and to mine Haiphong's harbor. Asked if Brezhnev had persuaded Nixon to change his military strategy in Vietnam, Kissinger said, "We do not intend to take unilateral action" (→ 7/7).

Hoover, first head of FBI, is deceased

May 2. J. Edgar Hoover, who directed the Federal Bureau of Investigation for 48 years, died today at the age of 77. Right up until the time of his death, he was in firm personal control of the agency that he built into a dominant force in American law enforcement. He presided over the FBI during its crackdown on gangsters in the 1930's, the search for spies in World War II and the postwar campaign against Communists. In an unusual tribute to a man who was both respected and feared, his body will lie in state in the rotunda of the Capitol (→ 3).

Hoover, soul of the FBI for 48 years.

Belgian engineer tricks hijackers in Flemish

May 9. A tense 23-hour hijacking drama ended this afternoon when a dozen Israeli paratroopers, disguised as maintenance workers, stormed a Sabena plane in Tel Aviv. The Israelis shot two male hijackers to death and captured two women. All of the 100 passengers and crewmen were rescued, although five passengers were wounded. Premier Golda Meir said that the incident should be turned into a movie script. If it is, the Belgian flight engineer will be sure to play a major role. Raised in Morocco, the officer understood Arabic and communicated in Flemish the hijackers' plans to the control tower (→ 6/13).

Security forces fan out around the hijacked jet at the far end of Lod Airport.

Japanese shoot up Israel's Lod Airport

May 30. Some 25 persons were killed and 72 wounded when three Japanese terrorists armed with automatic rifles and hand grenades attacked a terror-stricken crowd of 300 people last night at Tel Aviv's Lod International Airport. The attack, begun soon after the gunmen debarked from an Air France jet, sent the screaming crowd in the waiting room scurrying for cover.

Victims included 11 Puerto Ricans on a Holy Land pilgrimage, and a two-year-old girl. One of the terrorists was apparently killed by gunfire from his two companions, and one committed suicide with a grenade. The third, who was captured, said he belonged to The Army of the Red Star, a left-wing Japanese group allied with the Arab guerrilla movement. In Beirut, the militant PLO claimed responsibility for the attack (→ 7/17).

King who gave up throne for love is dead

The Duke and Duchess of Windsor.

May 28. The Duke of Windsor, who gave up the British throne in 1936 to marry Wallis Simpson, a twice-divorced American, has died in his home near Paris at 77. The duke, who reigned for 325 days as King Edward VIII, was born June 23, 1894, eldest son of George V. The popular Prince of Wales attended Royal Naval College and served in the Grenadier Guards in WWI.

In 1930, he met Mrs. Simpson, whom he called "fiercely independent, complex and elusive," but she was unacceptable as queen. Rather than give her up, he abdicated and was succeeded by his brother, George VI. The duke married his Wallis June 3, 1937, and they have lived in virtual self-exile. During WWII, he was Governor of the Bahamas.

Americans heavily bomb Hanoi, Haiphong

May 13. President Nixon ordered his military commanders to step up B-52 raids around Hanoi and Haiphong as his latest peace proposals were rejected by the Communists in Paris. Soviet-built MIG fighters rose to attack the American planes on Thursday. The Pentagon says ten of the MIG's were shot down. Three American planes were lost, and four crewmen are missing. The Communists claim they shot down 16 American planes.

The American command in Vietnam said today that it knocked out a major target on the bombing raids, a bridge on a supply line that runs northeast of Hanoi to China. The Communists had no reaction to the American statement, but they did charge that United States planes hit dikes outside of Hanoi. Much of the capital has been evacuated, according to Canadian officials.

In South Vietnam, President Nguyen Van Thieu has imposed martial law after several stunning defeats to the Communists. Quangtri was lost on the 2nd, and tens of thousands of South Vietnamese have left Hue in panic. North Vietnamese forces are also close to capturing Anloc, which is just 60 miles north of Saigon (→ 6/8).

Stalker shoots down Wallace during speech

May 16. The sight was all too familiar to Americans: A political leader on the ground, bleeding from an assailant's bullet. Governor George Wallace was shot yesterday while campaigning in Laurel, Md. The attacker pumped bullets into the stomach, shoulders, arms and spine of Wallace. Today, the governor was taken off the critical list, but doctors say he may be permanently paralyzed from the waist down.

Police grabbed the gunman, Arthur Bremer, moments after he fired his crippling shots. He had apparently been stalking Wallace; Bremer turned up in film footage of other recent Wallace rallies. Investigation revealed Bremer had a fixation about Wallace; police found a notebook in the suspect's home containing such passages as, "Happiness is having George Wallace arrested for a hit-and-run accident."

Despite the possibility of living the rest of his life in a wheelchair, Wallace said he would continue his quest for the White House, and today he won his first Democratic primary, in Michigan (→ 6/17).

Hanoi youths search the wreckage of an area devastated by American bombs.

Deranged man attacks Pieta with hammer

May 21. "I am Jesus Christ!" the assailant screamed, battering the image of the Virgin Mary with a hammer. Onlookers were frozen with horror. A guard ran up, seized the man by his long red hair and wrenched him away from his crazed attack. The damage was done: Michelangelo's centuries-old sculpture the Pieta was in pieces.

Whitsunday worshippers strolled through St. Peter's Basilica this morning admiring its Renaissance art. The Pieta, the Madonna cradling the prostrate Jesus, was encircled as always by a hushed group. Lazlo Toth, a Hungarian native, seemed a typical tourist until he lifted the hammer. The Madonna's left arm was severed, her veil and nose smashed. Most pathetic of all was the disfigurement of her left eye, ending the tender gaze she had cast on her son for nearly 500 years.

After Toth was delivered to Italian authorities, Pope Paul visited the site. He knelt in prayer and spoke of the "serious moral damage." A large red cloth was placed over the sculpture.

Vatican art experts met to assess the harm. While the affected areas are in many pieces, it should be possible to restore the sculpture's form, if not its pristine beauty.

Toth is dragged away from the Pieta.

Court overturns Chicago 7 verdict

May 11. A courtroom or a three ring circus in the United States of America? At times, it was hard to tell during the trial of the Chicago 7, but today a district court decided that Judge Julius Hoffman had erred in citing the defendants for contempt and granted a new trial.

Tom Hayden, Abbie Hoffman, Jerry Rubin and four others were arrested for their alleged role in inciting riots at the Democratic convention in 1968. At times, the trial disintegrated into a yelling match between the defendants and Judge Hoffman. Black Panther Bobby Seales was bound and gagged during the proceedings and was eventually given a separate trial. Today, however, the court ruled that Hoffman waited too long to impose sentencing (→ 19).

Experts drop into ocean to aid liner

May 18. A bomb threat was phoned into Cunard offices today, but officials were at a loss as to how to evacuate people from the intended target, the QE2, in the middle of the Atlantic. Instead, they parachuted bomb experts into the ocean where they were picked up by launches from the ship. The passengers were told of the threat after the team had conducted a preliminary survey. "Their examination proved negative," said the captain over a loudspeaker. Victor Mathews, Chairman of Cunard, said, "I think it is probably a hoax . . . but I cannot take the risk." The caller demanded a $1 million ransom, but did not tell officials where to leave the money. Some 2,300 people are aboard the ship, which is supposed to dock in Cherbourg tomorrow.

1972

JUNE

Su	Mo	Tu	We	Th	Fr	Sa
				1	2	3
4	5	6	7	8	9	10
11	12	13	14	15	16	17
18	19	20	21	22	23	24
25	26	27	28	29	30	

1. Iraq nationalizes Western-owned consortium Iraq Petroleum Company.

3. Berlin: Four WWII victorious powers sign first comprehensive accord on Berlin (→ 11/8).

6. Rhodesia: Underground explosion kills 422 miners.

8. South Vietnamese drop napalm on own troops and group of civilians (→ 22).

11. Libya: Premier Khadafy says Libya is aiding Irish revolutionaries in Ulster (→ 6/11/73).

13. Israeli, Egyptian planes clash over Mediterranean first time in 22 months (→ 21).

14. Washington: EPA Director Ruckelshaus bans nearly all use of DDT (→ 2/1/73).

15. Texas: 75,000 attend Billy Graham rally billed as "religious Woodstock."

16. N.Y.: Hughes biographer Irving gets 2.5 years for fraud; wife Edith gets $10,000 fine.

17. Tokyo: Eisaku Sato announces retirement as Japanese premier (→ 7/5).

17. N.Y.: "Fiddler on the Roof" sets Broadway record with 3,225 straight performances.

18. Calif.: Jack Nicklaus wins U.S. Open, tying Bobby Jones' record with 13 major titles.

18. Britain: 118 die in nation's worst air disaster.

19. U.S.: Pilots halt overseas flights to protest need for better fight against hijacking (→ 24).

20. Nixon names Gen. Creighton Adams commander-in-chief of U.S. armed forces.

22. Saigon: It is reported police seized thousands as Communists in last two months (→ 8/11).

26. St. Louis: Air Force unveils new F-15 jet fighter.

26. New York: Roberto Duran wins lightweight title with KO in 13th over Ken Buchanan.

27. Las Vegas: Ali TKO's Jerry Quarry in seventh (→ 7/19).

28. Nixon says no new draftees will be sent to Vietnam (→ 7/27).

30. New York: Agnew calls McGovern one of greatest frauds ever to run for president (→ 7/1).

Court bars death penalty as now used

June 29. The Supreme Court handed down an historic decision today by ruling the death penalty unconstitutional. The majority in the ruling determined that capital punishment in modern-day America violates the Eighth Amendment, which prohibits "cruel and unusual" punishment. The decision will spare 600 convicted criminals currently sitting on death row. They will now serve life prison sentences. A close 5-4 vote brought passionate dissent from the minority, including Chief Justice Burger, who believes the electric chair acts as a deterrent to crimes such as murder and kidnapping (→ 3/13/74).

Angela Davis freed on serious charges

June 4. After just 13 hours of deliberations, an all-white jury in San Jose, Calif., found black militant Angela Davis not guilty of murder, kidnapping and criminal conspiracy charges. She broke into sobs after the verdict. Davis, 28, attracted nationwide attention in 1969 when she was dismissed from teaching at the Univ. of Calif. at Los Angeles for being a Communist. The charges against her were lodged in August 1970, because guns used in a San Rafael court escape-murder drama were registered in her name.

Glittery and androgynous, Britain's David Bowie has cut "The Rise and Fall of Ziggy Stardust and the Spiders from Mars."

Israeli armor hits southern Lebanon

June 21. Following yesterday's resumption of raids on Israel by Lebanese-based Palestinian guerrillas after a four-month lull, Israel retaliated today with a three-pronged attack. As jets and artillery hammered the area in southeastern Lebanon from which the guerrillas are known to operate, an Israeli armored column struck into southern Lebanon territory, capturing a Lebanese officer, three military policemen as well as five Syrian officers. The latter came as a surprise and was cited by an Israeli officer as "evidence of joint Syrian-Lebanese planning against Israel" (→ 9/5).

Skyjacker bails out with large ransom

June 24. Tonight, thousands of pilots are saying, "I told you so." A hijacker bailed out of an American Airlines plane over Indiana at 4 o'clock this morning. He had a shovel in one hand and a $502,000 ransom in the other. Search parties have found no sign of the as yet unidentified culprit. Last week, commercial pilots in more than 30 countries went on strike to protest the skyrocketing number of skyjackings. Not very effective in America, the action shut down European travel for days (→ 8/29).

Eminent American critic Wilson is dead

Edmund Wilson, man of letters.

June 12. Edmund Wilson, critic, historian, novelist and journalist is dead, depriving America of perhaps its last great man of letters. Raised in the classical tradition, he spoke or read eight languages, and never tired of jabbing at the unlearned. Wilson's America had rejected intellectual values for the profits of pragmatism. But Wilson, who courted Marxism during the Depression, did not ignore "lowbrow" culture. He wrote about it. Adding to studies of Joyce, Faulkner and Henry James, he wrote of etiquette columns, detective novels, miners in Harlan County and his travels in the Soviet Union. There was not much, in fact, in 20th-Century culture that eluded his sagacious mind.

Five burglars caught in Watergate offices

June 17. Five men were arrested early this morning and charged with breaking into the executive quarters of the Democratic National Comittee in the Watergate apartment complex in Washington, D.C.

Police said that the men, all well-dressed and wearing gloves, were discovered on the sixth-floor site of the Democratic offices. In their possession, according to the police, were walkie-talkies, cameras, burglary tools and some electronic surveillance equipment.

One of the men, James W. McCord of Rockville, Md., identified himself as a retired employee of the Central Intelligence Agency. The others, including two who claimed past ties to the CIA, are Bernard L. Barker, alias Frank Carter; Frank Angelo Fiorini, alias Edward Hamilton; Eugenio L. Martinez, alias Gene Valdes; and Raul Godoy, alias V.R. Gonzales (→ 30).

The Watergate, Washington, D.C.

1972

JULY

Su	Mo	Tu	We	Th	Fr	Sa
						1
2	3	4	5	6	7	8
9	10	11	12	13	14	15
16	17	18	19	20	21	22
23	24	25	26	27	28	29
30	31					

3. Iceland: Bobby Fischer arrives late after British banker adds $125,000 to world chess championship purse (→ 12).

5. Tokyo: Kakuei Tanaka chosen premier by party caucus (→ 9/21).

5. U.S. grants license for Boeing to sell 727's to China (→ 9/29).

5. Washington: Judge bars photographer Ronald Galella from going near Jackie Onassis.

7. Moscow: U.S., Soviets sign accord for cooperation in science and technology (→ 8).

8. Soviets agree to buy U.S. grain for $750 million (→ 4/12/73).

9. Wimbledon: Stan Smith over Ilie Nastase 6-3, 6-3, 4-6, 7-5; Billie Jean King over Evonne Goolagong 6-3, 6-3.

10. Britain orders 1,200 more troops into N. Ireland (→ 14).

11. Cuba now full member of Soviet economic bloc (→ 9/6/74).

12. Iceland: Bobby Fischer loses first game in world title chess match (→ 9/3).

14. Miami: McGovern names Thomas Eagleton as running mate (→ 25).

14. Belfast: British troops battle I.R.A.; nine killed (→ 21).

15. Scotland: Lee Trevino wins British Open golf title.

17. Census Bureau reports median U.S. income at $10,285.

17. Israel: Japanese Kozo Okamoto gets life sentence for airport massacre.

19. Dublin: Ali TKO's Al Lewis in 11th round (→ 9/20).

21. Belfast: Bomb attacks kill 13, injure 130 (→ 11/25).

24. N.Y.: 20,000 see Rolling Stones at Madison Sq. Garden.

25. South Dakota: Eagleton admits he has had shock therapy on two occasions (→ 31).

26. NASA gives multibillion dollar space shuttle contract to North Am. Rockwell (→ 30).

27. Nixon calls Kurt Waldheim naive for opposing Vietnam War (→ 8/8).

28. India and Pakistan sign Simla Pact, settling border dispute in Kashmir.

Democrats name McGovern; Eagleton quits

Eagleton, Humphrey, Chisholm, McGovern, Jackson, Muskie and Sanford.

July 31. Senator Thomas F. Eagleton of Missouri bowed out tonight as the vice-presidential running mate to fellow Senator George McGovern, the Democratic candidate for president.

The McGovern-Eagleton ticket was chosen 18 days ago at the Democratic convention in Miami. But six days ago, Senator Eagleton, in a surprise announcement, said he had undergone electric shock therapy for depression on two occasions.

At first, Senator McGovern said he was determined to keep Senator Eagleton on the ticket. But tonight, as the political storm continued to mount, the two senators met in the Marble Room, just off the Senate floor. There, Senator McGovern asked Senator Eagleton to withdraw and thus end a national debate over his health. While gaunt and red-eyed, the 42-year-old deposed vice-presidential candidate had his armed draped over the shoulder of Senator McGovern as they parted.

In announcing the decision at a news conference, McGovern said that "health was not a factor" but that the issue had "dominated the political dialogue of the country" and threatened to obscure the real issue of the campaign (→ 8/4).

Mao says Lin Piao died in plane crash

July 27. After months of official silence, Mao Tse-tung has revealed the fate of former Defense Minister Lin Piao. According to Mao, Lin, whose name has not appeared in any Chinese document or report in nearly a year, died when a Chinese Trident jetliner crashed in Mongolia on September 13, 1971. In statements to Ceylon's Prime Minister and the French Foreign Minister, Mao said that Lin was fleeing the country in the wake of an attempted coup, aimed at replacing the civilian regime in China with a military dictatorship, when the plane crashed. It was not revealed how the alleged plot was uncovered (→ 2/4/74).

Lin Piao compiled "little red book."

Egypt orders Soviet advisers to leave

July 18. An announcement by the President of Egypt, Anwar el-Sadat, ordered the immediate withdrawal of Soviet "military advisers and experts" from his country. Until Sadat's speech today, there were 5,000 Soviet advisers in Egypt, as well as 10-15,000 combat personnel and pilots. Although it was not made clear whether the order applies to all of these personnel, it is suspected that it does. The speech also specified that all military installations established within Egyptian borders following the Six Day War of June 1967 will be the exclusive property of the Arab Republic of Egypt. Observers say the move will improve Egypt's relations with the West (→ 1/3/73).

Mitchell is leaving Nixon's committee

July 1. John N. Mitchell resigned today as President Nixon's campaign manager, responding to his wife's demand that he choose either her or politics. In recent days, Martha Mitchell has given interviews saying that her husband must leave politics if he wished for their marriage to survive.

Mitchell, one of the most powerful men in Washington, explained in his resignation letter to the president that "the happiness and welfare of my wife and daughter" must come first. Named to succeed Mitchell as the campaign director to re-elect the president was Clark MacGregor of Minnesota, a former member of the House of Representatives (→ 14).

Stamps and medals smuggled to moon

July 30. The Apollo 14 astronauts carried 200 silver medallions coined by a private mint to the moon on their 1971 mission without informing federal officials, the National Aeronautics and Space Administration disclosed today. Although they were given no money, the astronauts were allowed to keep 150 of the medals for their private use. The disclosure follows a space agency reprimand of the Apollo 15 astronauts for smuggling 400 first-day covers to the moon on their mission. A German dealer has placed 100 of the covers on the market. The Apollo 14 astronauts have not been reprimanded because none of the medals have been placed on the market, federal officials say (→ 12/19).

1972

AUGUST

Su	Mo	Tu	We	Th	Fr	Sa
		1	2	3	4	5
6	7	8	9	10	11	12
13	14	15	16	17	18	19
20	21	22	23	24	25	26
29	28	29	30	31		

1. N.Y.: Namath signs record contract with Jets; $500,000 for two years (→ 5/22/75).

2. Cairo: Sadat and Khadafy agree to set up "unified political leadership" (→ 9/18).

3. U.S. Senate ratifies ABM treaty with U.S.S.R. (→ 10/3).

4. Maryland: Arthur Bremer given 63 years for shooting George Wallace (→ 5).

4. Peking: Han Dynasty tomb reported found; milestone in archeology.

8. Washington: Pat Nixon rebukes Jane Fonda for anti-war stance: "She should ask Hanoi to stop their aggression" (→ 23).

11. Last U.S. ground unit in Vietnam deactivated (→ 12).

13. Jerusalem reports Soviets will let 35,000 Jews emigrate to Israel annually (→ 8/21/73).

14. Berlin: 156 killed as plane crashes in suburb of East Berlin.

15. Munich: Ethiopia pulls out of Olympics, protesting presence of Rhodesia (→ 22).

17. Hanoi: Editorial rebukes Soviets, China for letting relations with U.S. weaken support (→ 20).

20. South Vietnam: District capital of Queson abandoned to North Vietnamese (→ 22).

22. Miami: Republicans renominate Nixon-Agnew (→ 9/15).

22. Saigon: Thieu bans elections for posts in 10,775 hamlets (→ 9/22).

22. Munich: Olympic Committee ousts Rhodesia (→ 7/6/73).

23. Miami: Police arrest 900 anti-war demonstrators (→ 9/5).

25. N.Y.: China's first U.N. veto bars Bangladesh (→ 1/29/74).

26. Munich holds Olympic opening ceremonies (→ 31).

30. New York: John Lennon and Yoko Ono perform at Madison Square Garden.

31. Munich: Mark Spitz becomes second to win five gold medals in one Olympics (→ 9/4).

DEATH

26. Sir Francis Chichester, U.K. yachtsman, first to sail solo around the world (*9/17/1901).

B-52's stage biggest raid on North Vietnam

Agents of destruction are loaded up at an air base in South Vietnam.

Aug 12. American ground combat forces are streaming out of South Vietnam, but bomber pilots are trying to take up the slack. In the past 24 hours, B-52 bombers delivered the heaviest raids of the entire war against North Vietnam. Most of the targets were supply routes around the city of Donghoi. Bombers also struck in northern South Vietnam, near Quangtri, and in the Mekong Delta south of Saigon, where the Communists are believed to be opening another front.

One high-ranking American official openly questioned the effectiveness of the bombing raids around Quangtri. "It is evident," he said, "the Communists are moving their heavy guns very skillfully, often concealing them in caves and otherwise keeping them out of the way of our air strikes."

The last American ground combat unit in South Vietnam was deactivated yesterday. Members of the Third Battalion of the 21st Infantry packed up and left Danang. President Nixon is still hoping to "Vietnamize" the war, but he can call on tens of thousands of American troops stationed in Thailand and on ships off the Vietnam coast.

First Lady Pat Nixon defended her husband's war policy and attacked recent statements by Jane Fonda as she held a rare news conference at the White House. Instead of criticizing American bombing raids, Mrs. Nixon said Fonda should have told the North Vietnamese "to stop their aggression." Fonda said recently the U.S. is bombing dikes near Hanoi (→ 17).

The U.S. combat role ended when the Marines evacuated Danang on the 11th.

Two airline firms to examine luggage

Aug 29. Trans World Airlines and American Airlines will soon inspect the baggage of passengers before they board planes. Officials from the companies said the procedure would not only deter hijackings but encourage the return of travelers who had stayed away from the somewhat unfriendly skies. The examination process may add 30 minutes to average travel time. Meanwhile, passengers should be leery of gifts from strangers, especially gifts given before boarding. On August 16, two British women on an El Al jet were hurt when a last-minute token from Arab acquaintances blew up (→ 9/2).

Shriver takes place on Democratic slate

Aug 5. Senator George McGovern reached into the Kennedy clan today by choosing Sargent Shriver as his vice-presidential running mate on the Democratic ticket. Shriver was the first Director of the Peace Corps under his brother-in-law, the late President Kennedy. The No. 2 spot on the party ticket had been vacant since Senator Thomas F. Eagleton dropped out a week ago, following disclosure that he had twice undergone electric shock therapy for depression. Senator Edmund S. Muskie of Maine later declined the McGovern suggestion that he fill the slot (→ 22).

Air force fires on King Hassan's plane

Aug 16. In a surprise attack, Moroccan air force jets fired on a plane that was carrying King Hassan II of Morocco. At the same time, other jet fighters piloted by rebels strafed and fired rockets at the royal palace and airport. The rebellion was led by a Major Kouera, commander of the base at Kenitra where the planes took off. There were several injuries inflicted by the attacks, but no deaths, and the king was unharmed. Troops loyal to Hassan suppressed the rebels without bloodshed (→ 10/16/75).

1972

SEPTEMBER

Su	Mo	Tu	We	Th	Fr	Sa
					1	2
3	4	5	6	7	8	9
10	11	12	13	14	15	16
17	18	19	20	21	22	23
24	25	26	27	28	29	30

2. U.S. Army ends inquiry into Mylai massacre, punishes three more.

2. U.S. widens hijacking curbs to include foreign airlines operating in U.S. (→ 10/29).

5. Penn.: Philip Berrigan gets eight years for smuggling letters out of jail (→ 11/21).

5. Munich: 11 on Israeli Olympic team slain by four Arab terrorists; four Arabs killed (→ 8).

6. London: Amnesty Intl. accuses Brazil of torturing political prisoners.

7. Washington: 25 generals forced to retire; Al Haig named to second highest military post.

7. U.S. cancels Jimmy Hoffa's permit to go to Hanoi on peace seeking mission (→ 8/3/75).

8. Phnom Phenh: Rioters loot markets, looking for rice (→ 3/17/73).

10. Munich: Frank Shorter is first American to win Olympic marathon since 1908.

11. California: Mass murder trial of Juan Corona begins (→ 1/18/73).

13. GOP files countersuit against ex-Democratic natl. chairman for making issue of Watergate (→ 15).

14. U.S. halts $3 mil. loan to Uganda after Idi Amin praises Hitler (→ 18).

18. Uganda halts small army of invaders from Tanzania (→ 10/5).

18. Egypt and Libya agree on Cairo as joint capital (→ 7/21/77).

20. New York: Ali KO's Floyd Patterson in seventh (→ 11/21).

21. Mass.: Mitsubishi donates $1 million to Harvard for chair in Japanese studies (→ 3/3/73).

23. Manila: Martial law declared after attack on minister (→ 25).

25. Manila: Chief of opposition party arrested (→ 10/22).

27. Moscow: Three pilots freed by Hanoi refuse U.S. aid to come home.

29. Peking: China, Japan agree to resume relations; Japan severs ties with Taiwan (→ 10/27).

Arabs massacre 11 Israeli Olympians

The Olympic flag flies at half-mast in memory of victims of the attack.

Sept 8. Israeli jets streaked deep into Lebanon and Syria today, bombing and strafing Palestinian guerrilla bases in retaliation for the bloody massacre at the Olympic Games. In Munich, the Games went on without Israeli athletes.

The terrorist assault on the Israeli compound in Munich began early Tuesday morning, the 5th. Black September guerrillas, members of the same group that hijacked a Belgian jet last spring, infiltrated the area where 10,000 athletes are staying. At five o'clock, the commandos broke into the Israelis' building. A coach managed to sound an alarm, allowing some members of the team to escape. Two Israelis were shot to death. They were later identified as Joseph Romano, a weightlifting coach, and Moshe Weinberg, a wrestling coach. Nine Israelis were taken hostage.

By 9:00 in the morning, the Olympic Village was surrounded by 12,000 police officers and two dozen sharpshooters. At noon, the terrorists announced their demands: the release of 200 Palestinians from Israeli jails and safe passage out of West Germany. Tense negotiations followed. From time to time, a terrorist, shrouded by a mask, was seen on one of the balconies.

Talks continued, but Israel refused to release any prisoners. The terrorists refused to alter their demands or allow German officials to replace Israeli athletes as hostages. They also turned down money.

A little before midnight, the terrorists and their hostages were flown by helicopter to the Munich airport where a plane was waiting, purportedly to fly them to Cairo. Soon after two of the guerrillas emerged onto the tarmac, German sharpshooters opened fire. The terrorists fired back. All nine Israeli hostages were killed. So were four of the seven guerrillas and a German police officer. The helicopter pilot was critically wounded.

In its reprisal raids today, Israel dropped bombs and fired rockets at ten bases identified as Al Fatah training camps. Black September is believed to be part of Al Fatah. Israel claims to have killed scores of guerrillas during the raids in Lebanon and Syria. Arab sources say 30 people were killed (→ 10/29).

A German guard helps to block the escape of terrorists in the Olympic Village.

One photographer caught a haunting glimpse of a masked terrorist.

Burned-out helicopter at Munich airport, a graveyard for nine hostages.

Mark Spitz of U.S. wins 7 gold medals

Spitz holds 5 of 7 gold medals.

Sept 4. Mark Spitz, a native-born Californian, has won a record seven gold medals at the Munich Olympics. No other athlete has ever dominated the Games as did the 22-year-old American swimmer. Spitz's stunning performance included winning the 100- and 200-meter freestyle and butterfly events and swimming as a member of two freestyle relay teams and one medley relay team.

The United States won its first Olympic marathon since 1908. Frank Shorter's running victory removed some of the sting from the first loss ever suffered by the United States in Olympic basketball. The Americans failed in a basketball protest and the victory went to the Soviet Union, 51-50. In overall medals, the Soviets captured 99, the United States 94. East Germany finished a surprising third with 66 (→ 10).

Combat deaths drop to zero in one week

Sept 22. Last week, no American soldiers died in combat in Southeast Asia. This is the first time since March 1965 that no U.S. deaths were reported in the Vietnam conflict. However, the South Vietnamese reported 409 combat deaths and 1,170 wounded. Since 1961, 45,857 Americans have died in action in Southeast Asia. Another 10,274 died from non-combat, accidental or natural causes (→ 10/1).

Bobby Fischer is world chess champ

Sept 3. The unpredictable Bobby Fischer won the world championship of chess by defeating the Russian master, Boris Spassky, and then showed up an hour late for the award ceremony.

The 29-year-old American not only upset the timetable of the strange Icelandic setting but also replayed with Spassky the decisive 21st game before they went onto the dais to get their prizes.

Spassky insisted at the replay that he had sealed the wrong move and should have sealed K-R3 instead of Q-B7. Fischer said that Spassky was doomed no matter what he had done. He then pulled out a pocket chess set and they replayed the final move.

Chess mastermind Bobby Fischer.

Dr. Max Euwe, President of the International Chess Federation, said Fischer had given new life to the game with his inventive approach. However, Spassky got the greater applause from the crowd.

After 1,500 years new haircut allowed

Sept 14. Pope Paul VI today abolished the tonsure, the circular shaving of the head of aspirants to the priesthood. Although it has been a symbolic "renunciation of the world" for seminarians since the end of the fifth century, the Vatican document indicated that it had become "an empty ritual" and henceforth it would be a voluntary option for individual priests and their orders.

Seven in Watergate break-in are indicted

Sept 15. Two former White House aides, E. Howard Hunt and G. Gordon Liddy, were among the seven men indicted in Washington today on charges of conspiring to break into the Democratic national headquarters in the Watergate complex three months ago.

Liddy was a former presidential assistant on domestic affairs and at the time of the break-in was counsel to the finance committee for the President's re-election. Hunt once served as a White House consultant.

The five others indicted in U.S. District Court were seized by police during the break-in. A spokesman for the White House said there is "absolutely no evidence" that any others were involved (→ 10/4).

Liddy, after pleading not guilty.

Bomb kills 22 in Montreal nightclub

Sept 2. A bomb explosion followed by a flash fire in a Montreal nightclub filled with about 200 people killed at least 22 persons and injured 60 to 75 others last night. Three men, who were thrown out of the Blue Bird Cafe, a country-and-western club, returned and threw one more firebomb up the stairway into the second-floor dance hall. The rear door had been bolted shut, preventing escape. The suspects were picked up about 40 minutes after the blast. Police officials say that they could be involved in a protection racket.

Jet hits ice cream parlor, killing 22

Sept 24. A privately owned jet, a former warplane, crashed into an ice cream parlor in Sacramento, Calif., killing 22 persons, ten of them children, and injuring at least 26. Witnesses say the F-86 Sabre jet was never airborne. It roared down the runway, hit an old river levee beyond it, catapulted across the highway into a shopping center parking lot and exploded into a ball of fire. About 100 customers, including families celebrating birthdays, were inside the parlor when the jet hit. The pilot survived and is reported in fair condition.

Sept 28. People got out however they could when Paris' Le Drugstore caught fire tonight. All 300 watching an Israeli film above the store were saved. Terrorists claimed the fire, but police say it started accidentally.

1972 Munich

Men Athletics

100 M Dash
1. Valeri Borzov URS 10,14
2. Robert Taylor USA 10,24
3. Lennox Miller JAM 10,33

200 M Dash
1. Valeri Borzow URS 20:00
2. Lerry Black USA 20:19
3. Pietro Mennea ITA 20:30

400 M Run
1. Vincent Matthews USA 44,66
2. Wayne Collet USA 44,80
3. Julius Sang KEN 44,92

800 M Run
1. David Wottle USA 1:45,9
2. Evgueni Arzhanov URS 1:45,9
3. Mike Boit KEN 1:46,0

1500 M Run
1. Pekka Vasala FIN 3:36,3
2. Kipchoge Keino KEN 3:36,8
3. Rod Dixon NZL 3:37,5

5000 M Run
1. Lasse Viren FIN 13:26,4
2. Mohammed Gammoudi TUN 13:27,4
3. Ian Stewart GBR 13:27,6

10,000 M Run
1. Lasse Viren FIN 27:38,4
2. Emiel Puttemans BEL 27:39,6
3. Merus Yifter ETH 27:41,0

Marathon
1. Frank Shorter USA 2:12:19,8
2. Karel Lismont BEL 2:14:31,8
3. Mamo Wolde ETH 2:15:8,4

400 M Hurtles
1. John Akii-Bua USA 47,82
2. Ralph Mann USA 48,51
3. David Hemery GBR 48,52

110 M Hurtles
1. Rodney Milburn jr. USA 13,24
2. Guy Drut FRA 13,34
3. Thomas Hill USA 13,48

3000 M Steeplechase
1. Kipchoge Keino KEN 8:23,6
2. Benjamin Jincho KEN 8:24,6
3. Tapio Kantanen FIN 8:24,8

400 M Relay
1. USA 38,19 (Larry Black, Robert Taylor, Gerald Tinker, Eddie Hart)
2. URS 38,50 (Alexandr Korneliuk, Vladimir Lovetski, Yuri Silov, Valeri Borzov)
3. FRG 38,79 (Jobst Hirscht, Karlheinz Klotz, Gerhard Wucherer, Klaus Ehl)

1600 M Relay
1. KEN 2:59,8 (Charles Asati, Hezahiah Nyamau, Robert Ouko, Julius Sang)
2. GBR 3:00,5 (Martin Reynolds, Alan Pascoe, David Hemery, David Jenkins)
3. FRA 3:00,7 (Gilles Bertould, Daniel Valasques, Francis Kerbiriou, Jacques Carette)

20 km Walk
1. Peter Frenkel GDR 1:26:42,4
2. Vladimir Golubnichyi URS 1:26:55,2
3. Hans Reimann GDR 1:27:16,6

50 km Walk
1. Bernd Kannenberg FRG 3:56:11,6
2. Veniamin Soldatenko URS 3:58:24,0
3. Larry Young USA 4:00:46,0

High Jump
1. Yuri Tarmak URS 2,2
2. Stefan Junge GDR 2,21
3. Dwight Stones USA 2,21

Pole Vault
1. Wolfgang Nordwig GDR 5,50
2. Robert Seagren USA 5,40
3. Jan Johnson USA 5,35

Long Jump
1. Randy Williams USA 8,24
2. Hans Baumgartner FRG 8,18
3. Arnie Robinson USA 8,03

Triple Jump
1. Viktor Saneiev URS 17,35
2. Jorg Drehmel GDR 17,31
3. Nelson Prudencio BRE 17,05

Shotput
1. Wladyslaw Komar POL 21,18
2. George Woods USA 21,17
3. Harmut Briesenick GDR 21,14

Discus Throw
1. Ludvik Danek TCH 64,40
2. Jay Silvester USA 21,17
3. Richard Bruch SWE 63,40

Hammer Throw
1. Anatoli Bondarchuk URS 75,50
2. Jochen Sachse GDR 74,96
3. Vasili Khmelevski URS 74,04

Javelin Throw
1. Klaus Wolfermann FRG 90,48
2. Ianis Lusis URS 90,46
3. William Schmidt USA 84,42

Decathlon
1. Nicolai Avilov URS 84,54
2. Leonid Litvinenko URS 80,35
3. Ryszard Katus POL 79,84

Women Athletics

100 M Dash
1. Renate Richter GDR 11,07
2. Raelene Boyle AUS 11,23
3. Silvia Chivas CUB 11,24

200 M Dash
1. Renate Stecher GDR 22,40
2. Raelene Boyle AUS 22,45
3. Irena Szewinska POL 22,74

400 M Run
1. Monika Zehrt GDR 51,08
2. Rita Wilden FRG 51,21
3. Kathy Hammond USA 51,64

800 M Run
1. Hildegard Falck FRG 1:58,6
2. Niele Sabaite URS 1:58,7
3. Gunhild Hoffmeister GDR 1:59,2

1500 M Run
1. Ludmila Bragina URS 4:01,4
2. Gunhild Hoffmeister GDR 4:02,8
3. Paola Cacchi ITA 4:02,9

100 M Hurtles
1. Annelie Ehrardt GDR 12,59
2. Valeria Bufanu ROM 12,84
3. Karin Balzer GDR 12,90

400 M Relay
1. FRG 42,81 (Christiane Krause, Ingrid Mickler, Annegret Richter, Heide Rosendahl)
2. GDR 42,95 (Evelyn Kaufer, Christina Heinich, Barbel Struppert, Renate Stecher)
3. CUB 43,36 (Marlene Elejarde, Carmen Valdes, Fulgencia Romay, Silvia Chivas)

1600 M Relay
1. GDR 3:23,0 (Dagmar Kasling, Rita Kuhne, Helga Seidler, Monika Zehrt)
2. USA 3:25,2 (Mable Fergeson, Madeline Manning, Cheryl Toussaint, Kathy Hammond)
3. FRG 3:26,5 (Anette Ruckes, Inge Bodding, Hildegard Falck, Rita Wilden)

High Jump
1. Ulrike Meyfarth FRG 1,92
2. Yordanka Blagoeva BUL 1,88
3. Ilona Gusenbauer AUT 1,88

Long Jump
1. Heide Rosendhal FRG 6,78
2. Diana Yorgova BUL 6,77
3. Eva Suranova TCH 6,67

Shotput
1. Nadezhda Tchichova URS 21,03
2. Margitta Gummel GDR 20,22
3. Ivenka Christova BUL 19,35

Discus Throw
1. Faina Melnik URS 66,62
2. Argentina Menis ROM 65,06
3. Vassilika Stoeva BUL 64,34

Javelin
1. Ruth Fuchs GDR 63,88
2. Jacqueline Todten GDR 62,54
3. Kathy Smith USA 59,94

Pentathlon
1. Mary Peters GBR 48,01
2. Heide Rosendahl GDR 47,91
3. Burglinde Pollack GDR 47,68

Men Swimming

100 M Freestyle
1. Mark Spitz USA 51,22
2. Jerry Heidenreich USA 51,65
3. Vladimir Bure URS 51,77

200 M Freestyle
1. Mark Spitz USA 1:52,18
2. Steven Genter USA 1:53,73
3. Werner Lampe FRG 1:53,99

400 M Freestyle
1. Bradford Cooper AUS 4:00,27
2. Steven Genter USA 4:01,94
3. Tom Mac Breen USA 4:02,64

1500 M Freestyle
1. Michael Burton USA 12:52,58
2. Graham Windeatt AUS 12:58,48
3. Douglas Northway USA 16:09,25

100 M Backstroke
1. Roland Matthes GDR 56,58
2. Mike Stamm USA 57,70
3. John Murphy USA 58,35

200 M Backstroke
1. Roland Matthes GDR 2:02,82
2. Mike Stamm USA 2:04,33
3. Mitchell Ivey USA 2:04,33

100 M Breaststroke
1. Nobutaka Taguchi JAP 1:04,94
2. Tom Bruce USA 1:05,43
3. John Hencken USA 1:05,61

200 M Breaststroke
1. John Hencken USA 2:21,55
2. David Wilkie GBR 2:23,67
3. Nobutaka Taguchi JAP 2:23,88

100 M Butterfly Stroke
1. Mark Spitz USA 54,27
2. Bruce Robertson CAN 55,66
3. Jerry Heindereich USA 55,74

200 M Butterfly
1. Mark Spitz USA 2:00,70
2. Gary Hall USA 2:02,86
3. Robin Backhaus USA 2:03,23

200 M Medley
1. Gunnar Larson SWE 2:07,17
2. Tim Mac Kee USA 2:08,37
3. Steven Furniss USA 2:08,23

400 M Medley
1. Gunnar Larson SWE 4:31,98
2. Tim Mac Kee USA 4:31,98
3. Andras Hargitay HUN 4:32,70

400 M Freestyle Relay
1. USA 3:26,42 (Dave Edgard, John Murphy, Jerry Heindereich, Mark Spitz)
2. URS 3:29,12 (Vladimir Bure, Viktor Mazanov, Viktor Aboimov, Igor Grivennikov)
3. GDR 3:32,42 (Roland Matthes, Wilfried Hartung, Peter Bruch, Lutz Unger)

800 M Freestyle Relay
1. USA 7:35,78 (John Kinsella, Frederick Tyler, Steven Genter, Mark Spitz)
2. FRG 7:41,69 (Klaus Steinbach, Werner Lampe, Hans-Gunter Vosseler, Hans Fassnacht)
3. URS 7:45,76 (Igor Grivennikov, Viktor Mazanov, Georgy Kulikov, Vladimir Bure)

400 M Medley Relay
1. USA 3:48,16 (Mike Stamm, Tom Bruce, Mark Spitz, Jerry Heindenreich)
2. GDR (Roland Matthes, Klaus Katzur, Hartmut Flockner, Lutz Unger)
3. CAN (Eric Fish, William Mahnony, Bruce Robertson, Bob Kasting)

Springboard Diving
1. Vladimir Vasin URS 594,09
2. Franco Cagnotto ITA 591,63
3. Craig Lincoln USA 577,29

High Diving
1. Klaus Dibiasi ITA 504,12
2. Richard Rydze USA 480,75
3. Franco Cagnotto ITA 475,83

Water Polo
1. Soviet Union
2. Hungary
3. USA

CHART

Weightlifting

			Press	Snatch	Clean & Jerk	Total
Flyweight						
1.	Zygmunt Smalcerz	POL	112,5	100,0	125,0	337,5
2.	Lajos Szuecs	HUN	107,5	95,0	127,5	330,0
3.	Sandor Holczreiter	HUN	112,5	92,5	122,5	327,5
Bantamweight						
1.	Imre Foeldi	HUN	127,5	107,5	142,5	377,5
2.	Mohamed Nassiri	IRA	127,5	100,0	142,5	370,0
3.	Gennadi Chetine	URS	120,0	107,5	140,0	367,5
Featherweight						
1.	Novair Nourikian	BUL	127,5	117,5	157,5	402,5
2.	Dito Chanidze	HUN	127,5	120,0	152,5	400,0
3.	Janos Benedek	URS	125,0	120,0	145,0	390,0
Lightweight						
1.	Mukharbi Kirzhinov	URS	147,5	135,0	177,5	460,0
2.	Mladen Koutchev	BUL	157,5	125,0	167,5	450,0
3.	Zbigniew Kaczmarck	POL	145,0	125,0	167,5	437,5
Middleweight						
1.	Yordan Bikov	BUL	160,0	140,0	185,0	485,0
2.	Mohamed Trabulsi	LIB	160,0	140,0	172,5	472,5
3.	Anselmo Silvino	ITA	155,0	140,0	175,0	470,0
Light Heavyweight						
1.	Leif Jenssen	NOR	172,5	150,0	185,0	507,5
2.	Norbert Ozimek	POL	165,0	145,0	187,5	497,5
3.	Gyoergy Horvath	HUN	160,0	142,5	192,5	495,0
Middle Heavyweight						
1.	Andon Nikovov	BUL	180,0	155,0	190,0	525,0
2.	Atanass Chopov	BUL	180,0	145,0	192,5	517,5
3.	Hans Bettembourg	SWE	182,5	145,0	185,0	512,5
Heavyweight						
1.	Yan Talts	URS	210,0	165,0	205,0	580,0
2.	Alexandre Kraitchev	BUL	197,5	162,5	202,5	562,5
3.	Stefan Grutzner	GDR	185,0	162,5	207,5	555,0
Super Heavyweight						
1.	Vassili Alexeiev	URS	235,0	175,0	230,0	640,0
2.	Rudolf Mang	FRG	225,0	170,0	215,0	610,0
3.	Gerd Bonk	GDR	200,0	155,0	217,5	572,5

Young Ulrike Meyfarth, a tall and angular West German, won the gold in the women's high jump with a best of 6'6".

Women Swimming

1\. 100 M Freestyle
1. Sandra Neilson USA 58,59
2. Shirley Babashoff USA 59,02
3. Shane Gould AUS 59,06

200 M Freestyle
1. Shane Gould AUS 2:03,56
2. Shirley Babashoff USA 2:04,33
3. Keena Rothhammer USA 2:04,92

400 M Freestyle
1. Shane Gould AUS 4:19,04
2. Novella Calligaris ITA 4:22,44
3. Gudrun Wegner GDR 4:23,11

800 M Freestyle
1. Keena Rothhammer USA 8:53,68
2. Shane Gould AUS 8:56,39
3. Novella Calligaris ITA 8:57,46

100 M Breaststroke
1. Catherine Carr USA 1:13,58
2. Galina Stepanova URS 1:14,99
3. Beverley Whitfield AUS 1:15,73

200 M Breaststroke
1. Beverley Whitfield AUS 2:41,71
2. Dana Shoenfield USA 2:42,05
3. Galina Stepanova URS 2:42,36

100 M Backstroke
1. Melissa Belote USA 1:05,78
2. Andrea Gyarmati HUN 1:06,26
3. Susie Atwood USA 1:06,34

200 M Backstroke
1. Melissa Belote USA 2:19,19
2. Susie Atwood USA 2:20,38
3. Donna Marie Gurr CAN 2:23,22

100 M Butterfly Stroke
1. Mayumi Aoki JAP 1:03,34
2. Roswitha Beier GDR 1:03,73
3. Andrea Gyamati HUN 1:03,73

200 M Butterfly Stroke
1. Karen Moe USA 2:15,57
2. Lynn Colella USA 2:16,34
3. Ellie Daniel USA 2:16,74

200 M Medley
1. Shane Gould AUS 2:37,07
2. Kornelia Ender GDR 2:23,59
3. Lynn Vidali USA 2:24,06

400 M Medley
1. Gail Neall AUS 5:02,97
2. Leslie Cliff CAN 5:03,57
3. Novella Calligaris ITA 5:03.99

400 M Freestyle Relay
1. USA 3:55,19 (Sandra Neilson, Jennifer Kemp, Jane Barkman, Shirley Babashoff)
2. GDR 3:55,55 (Gabriele Wetzko, Andrea Eife, Elke Sehmisch, Kornelia Ender)
3. FRG 3:57,93 (Jutta Weber, Heidemarie Reineck, Gudrun Beckmann, Angela Steinbach)

400 M Medley Relay
1. USA 4:20,75 (Melissa Belote, Catherine Carr, Deena Deardurff, Sandra Neilson)
2. GDR 4:24,91 (Christine Herbst, Renate Vogel, Roswitha Beier, Kornelia Ender)
3. FRG 4:26,46 (Silke Pielen, Verena Eberle, Gudrun Beckmann, Heidi Reineck)

Springboard Diving
1. Micki King USA 450,03
2. Ulrika Knape SWE 434,19
3. Marina Janicke GDR 430,93

High Diving
1. Ulrika Knape SWE 390,00
2. Milena Duchkova TCH 370,92
3. Marina Janicke GDR 360,54

Boxing

Light Flyweight
1. Gyoergy Godo HUN
2. U Gil Kim PRK
3. Ralph Evans GBR
3. Enrique Rodriguez ESP

Flyweight
1. Gheorgi Kostadinov BUL
2. Leo Rwabwogo UGA
3. Leszek Blazynski POL
3. Douglas Rodriguez CUB

Bantamweight
1. Orlando Martinez CUB
2. Alfonso Zamora MEX
3. George Turpin GBR
3. Ricardo Carreras USA

Featherweight
1. Boris Kousnetsov URS
2. Philip Waruinge KEN
3. Andras Botos HUN
3. Clemente Rojas COL

Lightweight
1. Jan Szoepanski POL
2. Laszlo Orban HUN
3. Samuel Mbuga KEN
3. Alfonso Perez COL

Light Welterweight
1. Ray Seales USA
2. Anghel Anhelov BUL
3. Zvonimir Vujin YUG
3. Isaaka Daborg NIG

Welterweight
1. Emilio Correa CUB
2. Janes Kadji HUN
3. Jesse Valdez USA
3. Dick Tiger Murunga KEN

Light Middleweight
1. Dieter Kottysch FRG
2. Wieslaw Rudkowski POL
3. Alan Minter GBR
3. Peter Tiepold GDR

Middleweight
1. Viatchesiav Lemechev URS
2. Reime Vitanen FIN
3. Marvin Johnson USA
3. Prince Amarrey GHA

Light Heavyweight
1. Mate Parlov YUG
2. Gilberto Carillo CUB
3. Janusz Gortat POL
3. Isaac Ikhouria NGA

1972 Munich

Heavyweight
1. Teof. Stevenson CUB
2. Ion Alexe ROM
3. Peter Hussing FRG
3. Hasse Thomsen SWE

Greco Roman Wrestling

Light Flyweight (48 kg)
1. Gherge Berceanu ROM
2. Rahim Aliabadi IRA
3. Stefan Anghelov BUL

Flyweight
1. Petar Kirov BUL
2. Koichiro Hirayama JAP
3. Giuseppe Bognani ITA

Bantamweight
1. Rustem Kazasov URS
2. Hans Jurgen Veil FRG
3. Risto Bjoerlin FIN

Featherweight
1. Gheorghi Markov BUL
2. Heinz Helmut Wenling GDR
3. Kazimierz Lipien POL

Lightweight
1. Shamil Krhisamutdinov URS
2. Stoyan Apostolav BUL
3. Gian Matteo Ranzi ITA

Welterweight
1. Vitezslav Macha TCH
3. Petros Galaktopoulos GRE
3. Jan Karlsson SWE

Middleweight
1. Csaba Hegedus HUN
2. Anatoli Nazarenko URS
3. Milan Nenadic YUG

Light Heavyweight
1. Va leri Rezantsev URS
2. Josip Corak YUG
3. Czeslaw Kwiecinski POL

Heavyweight
1. Nicolas Martinescu ROM
2. Nicolai Iakovenko URS
3. Ferenc Kiss HUN

Super Heavyweight
1. Anatoly Roshin URS
2. Alexandre Tomov BUL
3. Victor Dolipschi ROM

Freestyle Wrestling

Light Flyweight
1. Roman Dimitriev URS
2. Ognian Nikolov BUL
3. Ebrahim Javadpour IRA

Flyweight
1. Kiyomi Kato JAP
2. Arsen Alakhverdiev URS
3. Hyong Kim Gwong PRK

Bantamweight
1. Hideaki Yanagida JAP
2. Richard Sanders USA
3. Laszlo Klinga HUN

Featherweight
1. Zagalav Abdulbekov URS
2. Vehbi Akdag TUR
3. Ivan Krastev BUL

Lightweight
1. Dan Gable USA
2. Kikuo Wada JAP
3. Ruslan Ashuraliev URS

Welterweight
1. Wayne Wells USA
2. Jan Karlsson SWE
3. Adolf Seger FRG

Middleweight
1. Levan Tediashvili URS
2. John Peterson USA
3. Vassile Jorga ROM

Light Heavyweight
1. Ben Peterson USA
2. Gennadi Strakhov URS
3. Karoly Bajko HUN

Heavyweight
1. Ivan Yarigin URS
2. Khorloo Baianmunkh MON
3. Jozsef Csatari HUN

Super Heavyweight
1. Alexandr Modved URS
2. Osman Douraliev BUL
3. Chris Taylor USA

Judo

Lightweight
1. Takao Kawaguchi JAP
2. Bakhsaavaa Buidaa* MON
3. Yong Ik Kim PRK
3. Jean-Jacques Mounier FRA

*Buidaa lost his medal for use of drugs.

Welterweight
1. Toyakazu Normura JAP
2. Anton Zajkowski POL
3. Dietmar Hotger GDR
3. Anatoli Novikov URS

Middleweight
1. Shinobou Sekine JAP
2. Seung-Lip Oh PRK
3. Jean-Paul Coche FRA
3. Brian Jacks GBR

Light Heavyweight
1. Shota Chochoshvili URS
2. David Colin Starbrook GBR
3. Chiaki Ishii BRE
3. Paul Barth FRG

Heavyweight
1. Wim Ruska HOL
2. Klaus Glahn FRG
3. Motoki Nishimura JAP
3. Givi Onashvili URS

Open Category
1. Wim Ruska HOL
2. Vitali Kusnetzov URS
3. Jean-Claude Brondani FRA
3. Angelo Parisi GBR

Men Fencing

Foil Individual
1. Witold Woyda POL
2. Dr. Jenoe Kamuti HUN
3. Christian Noel FRA

Foil Team
1. Poland
2. Soviet Union
3. France

Epée Individual
1. Dr. Csaba Fenyvesi HUN
2. Jacques la Degaillerie FRA
3. Gyoezoe Kulcsar HUN

Epée Team
1. Hungary
2. Switzerland
3. Soviet Union

Sabre Individual
1. Viktor Sidiak URS
2. Peter Maroth HUN
3. Vladimir Nazlymov URS

Sabre Team
1. Italy
2. Soviet Union
3. Hungary

Women Fencing

Foil Individual
1. Antonella Ragno-Lonzi ITA
2. Ildiko Bobis HUN
3. Galina Gorokhova

Foil Team
1. Soviet Union
2. Hungary
3. Romania

Modern Pentathlon

Individual
1. Andreas Balczo HUN 5412
2. Boris Onichenki URS 5335
3. Pavel Lednev URS 5328

Team
1. Soviet Union 15958
2. Hungary 15348
3. Finland 14812

Men Canoeing

Kayak-1 1000 M
1. Aleksandr Shaparenki URS 3:48,06
2. Rolf Peterson SWE 3:48,35
3. Geza Csapo HUN 3:49,38

Kayak-2 1000 M
1. Soviet Union 3:31,23
2. Hungary 3:32,00
3. Poland 3:33,83

Kayak-4 1000 M
1. Soviet Union 3:14,02
2. Romania 3:15,07
3. Norway 3:15,27

Canadian-1 1000 M
1. Ivan Patzaichin ROM 4:08,94
2. Tamas Wichmann HUN 4:12,42
3. Detlef Lewe FRG 4:13,63

Canadian-2 1000 M
1. Soviet Union 3:52,60
2. Romania 3:52,63
3. Bulgaria 3:58,10

Kayak Slalom
1. Siegbert Horn GDR 268,56 363,20
2. Norbert Sattler AUT 270,76 270,76
3. Harald Gimpel GDR 277,95 298,11

Canadian Slalom
1. Reinhard Eiben GDR 315,84 327,50
2. Reinhold Kauder FRG 327,89 350,31
3. Jamie Mac Ewan USA 335,95 421,52

Canadian Two-Man Slalom
1. GDR 310,68 445,51
2. FRG 311,90 316,96
3. FRA 315,10 362,05

Women Canoeing

Kayak-1 500 M
1. Yulia Ryabchinskaya URS 2:03,17
2. Mieke Jaapies HOL 2:04,02
3. Anna Pfeffer HUN 2:05,50

See Table of Contents for Abbreviations

Kayak-2 500 M
1. Soviet Union
2. German Democratic Republic
3. Romania

Canadian Slalom*
1. Angelika Bahamnn GDR 364,50 413,07
2. Gisela Grothaus FRG 398,15 521,10
3. Magdalena Wunderlich FRG 400,50 515,40

Rowing

Single Scull
1. Yuri Malishev URS 7:10,12
2. Alberto Demiddi ARG 7:11,53
3. Wolfgang Güldenpfennig GDR 7:14,45

Double Sculls
1. Soviet Union 7:01,77
2. Norway 7:02,58
3. German Democratic Republic 7:05,55

Pair Oars without Coxswain
1. German Democratic Republic 6:53,16
2. Switzerland 6:57,06
3. Netherlands 6:58,70

Pair Oars with Coxswain
1. German Democratic Republic 7:17,25
2. Czechoslovakia 7:19,57
3. Romania 7:21,36

Four Oars without Coxswain
1. German Democratic Republic 6:24,17
2. New Zealand 6:25,64
3. German Federal Republic 6:28,41

Four Oars with Coxswain
1. German Federal Republic 6:31,85
2. German Democratic Republic 6:33,30
3. Czechoslovakia 6:35,64

Eight Oars
1. New Zealand 6:08,94
2. USA 6:11,61
3. German Democratic Republic 6:11,67

100 km Team Time Trial
1. Soviet Union 2:11:17,8
2. Poland 2:11:47,5
3. Netherlands 2:12:27,1

The Dutch team lost their medal for use of drugs.

1000 M Time Trial
1. Niels Fredborg DAN 1:06,44
2. Daniel Clark AUS 1:06,87
3. Jurgen Schutze GDR 1:07,02

Sprint
1. Daniel Morelon FRA 11,69/11,25
2. John Michael Nicholson AUS -/-
3. Omari Phakadze URS -/12,12/11,34

2000 M Tandem
1. Soviet Union -/10,52/10,60
2. German Democratic Republic 10,68/-/-
3. Poland 10,76/10,67

Individual Pursuit (4000 M)
1. Knut Knudsen NOR 4:45,74
2. Xaver Kurmann SUI 4:51,96
3. Hans Lutz FRG 4:50,80

Team Pursuit (4000 M)
1. German Federal Republic 4:22,14
2. German Democratic Republic 4:25,25
3. Great Britain 4:23,78

Equestrian Sports

All around Individual Competition
1. Richard H. Meade GBR 57,73
2. Alassandro Argenton ITA 43,33
3. Jan Johnsson SWE 39,67

All around Team Competition
1. Great Britain 95,53
2. USA 10,81
3. German Federal Republic -18,00

Individual Dressage
1. Liselott Linsenhoff FRG 1229,00
2. Elena Petishkova FRG 1185,00
3. Josef Neckermann URS 1177,00

Tiny Olga Korbut, near perfection in her craft, soars off the uneven bars in a dazzling dismount.

Yachting

Finn Monotype Class
1. Serge Maury FRA 58,0
2. Ilias Hatzipavlis GRE 71,0
3. Victor Potapov URS 74,7

Star Class
1. Australia 28,1
2. Sweden 44,0
3. German Federal Republic 44,4

Flying Dutchman Class
1. Great Britain 22,7
2. France 40,7
3. German Federal Republic 51,1

Soling Class
1. USA 8,7
2. Sweden 31,7
3. Canada 47,1

Dragon Class
1. Australia 13,7
2. German Democratic Republic 41,7
3. USA 47,7

Cycling

Individual Road Race
1. Hennie Kuiper HOL 4:14:37,0
2. Kevin Clude Sefton AUS +27,0
3. Jaime Huelamo ESP

*As per *in search of excellence.*

Team Dressage
1. Soviet Union 5095,0
2. German Federal Republic 5083,0
3. Sweden 4849,0

Grand Prix Jumping Individual
1. Graziano Mancinelli ITA
2. Ann Moore GBR
3. Neal Shapiro USA

Grand Prix Jumping Team
1. German Federal Republic -32,00
2. USA -32,25
3. Italy -48,00

Shooting

Full-Bore Rifle, 300 M, 3 Positions
1. Lones Wigger USA 1155
2. Boris Melnik URS 1155
3. Lajos Papp HUN 1149

Small-Bore Rifle, 50 M, Prone
1. Ho Jung Li PRK 599
2. Victor Auer USA 598
3. Nicolas Rotaru ROM 598

Small-Bore Rifle, Combined, 3 Positions
1. John Writer USA 1166
2. Lany Bassham USA 1157
3. Werner Lippoldt GDR 1153

Moving Target
1. Lakov Zhelezniak URS 569
2. Helmut Bellingrodt COL 565
3. John Kynoch GBR 562

Clay Pigeon (Trench)
1. Angelo Scalzone ITA 199
2. Michel Carrega FRA 198
3. Silvano Bassigni ITA 195

Skeet
1. Konrad Wirnhier FRG 195
2. Evgeni Petrov URS 195
3. Michael Buchheim GDR 195

Rapid Fire Pistol, 25 M
1. Jozef Zapedzki POL 595
2. Ladislav Faite TCH 594
3. Victor Torshin URS 593

Free Pistol, 50 M
1. Ragnar Skanaker SWE 567
2. Dan Iuga ROM 562
3. Rudolf Dollinger AUT 560

Men Archery

1. John Williams USA 2528
2. Gunnar Jarvil SWE 2481
3. Kyoesti Laasonen FIN 2467

Women Archery

1. Doreen Wilber USA 2424
2. Irena Szydlowska POL 2407
3. Imma Gaptchenko URS 2403

Men Gymnastics

All around Individual Competition
1. Sawao Kato JAP 114,650
2. Eizo Kenmotsu JAP 114,575
3. Akimori Nakayama JAP 114,325

All around Team Competition
1. Japan 571,25
2. Soviet Union 564,05
3. German Democratic Republic 559,70

Parallel Bars
1. Sawao Kato JAP 19,475
2. Shigeru Kasamatsu JAP 19,375
3. Eizo Kenmotsu JAP 19,025

Floor Exercise
1. Nicolai Andrianov URS 19,175
2. Akimori Nakayama JAP 19,125
3. Shigeru Kasamatsu JAP 19,025

Horse Vault
1. Klaus Köste GDR 18,850
2. Viktor Klimenko URS 18,825
3. Nicolai Andrianov URS 18,800

Sidehorse
1. Viktor Klimenko URS 19,125
2. Sawao Kato JAP 19,000
3. Eizo Kenmotsu JAP 18,950

Horizontal Bar
1. Mitsuo Tsukahara JAP 19,725
2. Sawao Kato JAP 19,525
3. Shogeru Kasamatsu JAP 19,450

Flying Rings
1. Akinori Nakayama JAP 19,350
2. Mikhail Voronine URS 19,275
3. Mitsuo Tsukahara JAP 19,225

Women Gymnastics

All around Individual Competition
1. Ludmila Touritcheva URS 77,025
2. Karin Janz GDR 76,875
3. Tamara Lazakovich URS 76,850

All around Team Competition
1. Soviet Union 380,50
2. German Democratic Republic 376,55
3. Hungary 368,25

Uneven Bars
1. Karin Janz GDR 19,675
2. Olga Korbut URS 19,450
3. Erika Zuchold GDR 19,450

Floor Exercise
1. Olga Korbut URS 19,575
2. Ludmila Touritcheva URS 19,550
3. Tamara Lazakovich URS 19,450

Horse Vault
1. Karin Janz GDR 19,525
2. Erika Zuchold GDR 19,275
3. Ludmila Touritcheva URS 19,250

Beam
1. Olga Korbut URS 19,400
2. Tamara Lazakovich URS 19,375
3. Karin Janz GDR 18,975

Hand-Ball

1. Yougoslavia
2. Czechoslovakia
3. Romania

Soccer

1. Poland
2. Hungary
3. GDR

Field Hockey

1. Germany
2. Pakistan
3. India

Men Volleyball

1. Japan
2. GDR
3. Soviet Union

Basketball

1. Soviet Union
2. USA
3. Cuba

Women Volleyball

1. Soviet Union
2. Japan
3. North Korea

1972

OCTOBER

Su	Mo	Tu	We	Th	Fr	Sa
1	2	3	4	5	6	7
8	9	10	11	12	13	14
15	16	17	18	19	20	21
22	23	24	25	26	27	28
29	30	31				

1. New York: Freed POW says treatment in Hanoi camps was humane (→ 11).

3. New York: Bloomingdale's celebrates 100th anniversary.

4. Washington: Judge John Sirica puts gag rule on Watergate break-in case (→ 11/8).

5. Somalia: Uganda, Tanzania announce settlement of dispute (→ 7/5/73).

6. Mexico: 147 killed in train crash; 700 injured.

6. Berlin: E. Germany announces political amnesty expected to free thousands (→ 11/3).

11. Chile: Massive strikes begin against Allende govt. (→ 31).

11. Hanoi: French Mission destroyed by U.S. bombing raid (→ 26).

11. Panama: Gen. Omar Torrijos obtains full powers in new constitution (→ 5/5/76).

12. Scotland: Hundreds of students shouting obscenities mob Queen Elizabeth at university.

14. Moscow: 170 killed in worst jet crash on record.

15. Bucharest: U.S. beats Nastase and Rumanian team, keeping Davis Cup fifth straight year.

17. Seoul: Pres. Park Chung Hee declares martial law (→ 12/23).

18. Soviets agree to pay $722 mil. lend lease debt to U.S.

22. Cincinnati: Oakland A's beat Reds 3-2 in final game of World Series.

22. Philippines: Govt. troops put down rebel attack in south (→ 1/17/73).

27. Washington: Nixon announces $18 mil. sale of corn to Communist China (→ 3/12/73).

29. Texas: Four hijackers kill airport employee, hijack plane with 29 to Cuba (→ 11/10).

30. Washington: Nixon signs bill expanding social security $5 bil.

31. Chile: Cabinet resigns to give Pres. Allende free hand in curbing civil unrest (→ 3/20/73).

DEATH

24. Jackie Robinson, U.S. baseball great, first black in major league (*1/31/1919).

Nixon and Gromyko sign arms limit treaty

Oct 3. President Nixon signed an arms agreement with the Soviet Union today that he hopes will increase the chances of peace and his own chances of being re-elected. In an ornate ceremony in the East Room of the White House, Nixon and Soviet Foreign Minister Andrei Gromyko signed two separate agreements. The more important of the two limits the United States and the Soviet Union to 200 defensive missiles, to be installed at two sites. The second is an interim treaty which limits each side's offensive land and submarine missiles. Under the agreement, the Soviets will continue to have superiority in total number of missiles, but the United States will have more multiple-missile warheads.

Nixon and Gromyko also agreed to open a new round of talks in Geneva to limit offensive weapons. Nixon called the agreements today a "first step" to a broader treaty. Gromyko agreed and called the new accords "a significant achievement in restraining the arms race."

Nixon's talks with Gromyko began at the White House yesterday and continued at Camp David later in the day and this morning. White House Press Secretary Ronald Ziegler says the two men also discussed Vietnam, the Middle East, European security and the reduction of forces in Central Europe.

Nixon attempted to draw as much political advantage as possible from the new treaty. He held a separate signing ceremony Saturday of a congressional resolution supporting the accord (→ 5/18/74).

Kissinger declares peace is at hand

Kissinger, harbinger of peace?

Oct 26. Henry Kissinger, President Nixon's adviser on national security, broke the administration's silence on the Paris peace talks today and declared that "peace is at hand" in Vietnam. He predicted that a cease-fire could be arranged in just one more negotiating session. Nixon, campaigning in Kentucky, promised he would achieve "peace with honor and not peace with surrender." Democratic challenger George McGovern said anti-war activists, not Nixon, would be credited with ending the war (→ 11/1).

Arabs rescue 3 terrorists by hijacking plane

Oct 29. Another round has been lost in the international battle against terrorism. Palestinian guerrillas who hijacked a Lufthansa jet forced West Germany to release three terrorists who participated in the Munich massacre.

The Boeing 727 jet was commandeered on a flight from Beirut to Ankara. It was refueled in Nicosia, Cyprus, and Zagreb, Yugoslavia, and headed for Munich after West Germany agreed to release the prisoners. At the last moment, the hijackers decided not to land in Munich. They returned to Zagreb, where another plane flew the prisoners from Germany. They flew on to Tripoli, where the Lufthansa passengers were released unharmed. Israel condemned West Germany by saying, "Every capitulation encourages the terrorists to continue their criminal acts" (→ 11/1).

Helicopter's developer, Igor Sikorsky, dies

Oct 26. Igor Sikorsky, the aviation pioneer who developed the first practical helicopter, died today at his home in Easton, Connecticut. He was 83. Sikorsky's other aviation firsts included the multiple-engine aircraft and the flying boat, but he said the most significant event of his career occurred on September 14, 1939, when he successfully flew the VS300, the helicopter he designed and built. Sikorsky Aircraft, the company he founded, has since built 5,000 helicopters.

Sikorsky in an early helicopter.

Sikorsky began dreaming of a helicopter when he read the science fiction of Jules Verne as a boy in Russia. He was already a successful aircraft designer when he went to France and later the United States after the Russian Revolution.

Sikorsky's first American success was the four-engine S40, a flying boat used by Pan American. Later, the Sikorsky firm, which became part of United Aircraft, concentrated on production of helicopters.

Sex therapy clinics spread nationwide

"A man and a woman need each other more . . . than ever before," said Dr. William Masters of the Masters and Johnson psychoanalysis team, referring to the deterioration of the extended family. Still, the phrase could serve as a kind of advertising slogan for the hundreds of sex clinics springing up nationwide. While some so-called clinics are simply brothels, others are run by trained therapists. Treatment often involves removing couples to hotels to escape daily worries. There, they rediscover each other's bodies; emphasis is put on kissing and touching non-erogenous zones. With less emphasis placed on intercourse, problems surrounding the act often fade away.

1972

NOVEMBER

Su	Mo	Tu	We	Th	Fr	Sa
			1	2	3	4
5	6	7	8	9	10	11
12	13	14	15	16	17	18
19	20	21	22	23	24	25
26	27	28	29	30		

1. Saigon: Thieu calls cease-fire draft "surrender to Communists" (→ 7).

1. Tripoli: Libya refuses to try or extradite Palestinians who hijacked German jet (→ 10).

3. Berlin: East Germany frees 30,000 political prisoners.

4. New York: Communist Party headquarters is firebombed.

6. Britain freezes wages and prices to fight inflation.

8. Berlin: East and West Germany sign treaty to normalize relations (→ 6/22/73).

9. San Diego: 130 refuse to join ship in Navy's latest racial incident.

9. California: Human origins pushed back million years by African bones found by Leakeys.

10. Cleveland: Hijackers divert jet to Detroit; demand $10 mil. and ten parachutes (→ 12).

12. Havana: Cuba seizes three hijackers, returns 31 on hijacked plane (→ 15).

13. London: BBC celebrates 50th anniversary.

17. Baton Rouge: Police admit mistake in shooting deaths of two young blacks yesterday.

17. Buenos Aires: Thousands cheer Juan Peron on return after 17-year exile (→ 7/13/73).

18. Moscow: Sakharov heads 51 human rights leaders asking amnesty for political prisoners (→ 1/2/74).

21. Chicago: Judge voids five convictions in 1968 Chicago seven trial (→ 29).

21. Nevada: Ali KO's Bob Foster in eighth round (→ 1/22/73).

25. Dublin: I.R.A. chief Sean MacStiofain jailed for belonging to illegal group (→ 26).

26. Dublin: Eight gunmen foiled in attempt to free Sean MacStiofain (→ 12/1).

28. Vietnam: U.S. attack kills 19 civilians (→ 12/18).

29. Washington: Rev. Philip Berrigan paroled (→ 8/3/73).

DEATH

1. Ezra Pound, American poet (*10/30/1885).

It's Nixon by a landslide

A reassuring Richard Nixon.

Nov 8. President Richard M. Nixon piled up a huge majority yesterday to win a second term in the White House, losing only Massachusetts and the District of Columbia to Senator George S. McGovern, the Democratic candidate.

Nixon's victory was reminiscent of the landslide triumphs of Franklin D. Roosevelt in 1936 and Lyndon B. Johnson in 1964.

In a televised address from the White House tonight, the president summoned the nation "to get on with the great tasks that lie before us" and pledged to secure not only "a peace with honor in Vietnam" but also "a new era of peace" in the world. Also re-elected on the Republican ticket was Vice President Spiro T. Agnew (→ 1/15/73).

500 Indians seize Washington bureau

Nov 2. Angry American Indians seized control of the Bureau of Indian Affairs in Washington today to protest injustices against Indians. Over 500 Native Americans traveled to the capital to demonstrate against the failure of the government to honor promises made to them. The leaders of the "Trail of Broken Treaties" are demanding action to provide proper food and housing on Indian reservations.

The Nixon administration sent police to encircle the bureau building, but indicated they will listen to the protesters' demands. A 71-year-old Pawnee summed up the protesters' sentiments toward Washington politicians, saying, "They'll steal you blind" (→ 2/28/83).

Letter bombs arrive at Jewish companies

Nov 10. The Arab Black September group continues to terrorize through the mail. Eighteen letter bombs mailed from India reached Jewish companies and individuals in Geneva and London, where one exploded in the hands of a diamond company official, wounding him. Eleven other bombs, unexploded, came to light at various London addresses and five were intercepted in Geneva. Scotland Yard thinks the bombs are part of a consignment mailed throughout the world to prominent Jews whose names are culled by the Arabs from Who's Who, the Zionist yearbook and pro-Israeli ads (→ 1/12/73).

U.S. B-52's set one-day bombing record

Nov 7. There is still talk in the air of a cease-fire in Vietnam, but the air above South Vietnam is full of American bombers. The B-52's set a record for bombing a single province today. Aerial attacks against the North tapered off. The bombers dropped their deadly payloads as American voters were deciding between Nixon and McGovern. In the closing days of the campaign, Nixon said he would not be stampeded into signing a truce. But it is also known he is trying to convince South Vietnam to accept a tentative agreement worked out in Paris (→ 28).

American B-52 bombers strike again, as American citizens go to the polls.

Cuba and America to seek hijacking curb

Nov 15. The United States and Cuba are making diplomatic moves to block the high incidence of hijacking that has afflicted the two nations. Bolstering security and working out extradition rights are two measures Havana and Washington hope to achieve in their talks. The initiative comes after last week's hijacking of a Southern Airways jet to Havana in which 31 hostages were terrorized by three gunmen. Premier Fidel Castro said the hijackers will be tried in Havana (→ 1/5/73).

500 sex changes done in past 6 years

An estimated 500 sex-change operations have been done in the United States since Johns Hopkins University performed its first in 1966. Many patients, once on the verge of suicide, report increased happiness and self-esteem. Many marry people of normal gender. Medical centers get hundreds of requests for sex changes every year (there are an estimated 7,500 would-be transsexuals in the United States, most men wanting to be women). Applicants must live as members of their desired sex for several months before surgery is done.

1972

DECEMBER

Su	Mo	Tu	We	Th	Fr	Sa
					1	2
3	4	5	6	7	8	9
10	11	12	13	14	15	16
17	18	19	20	21	22	23
24	25	26	27	28	29	30
31						

1. Dublin: Irish Parliament votes bill to crush I.R.A. (→ 2/3/73).

2. Philadelphia: Army beats Navy 23-15 in football.

2. Australia: Labor govt. voted out after 23 years.

3. Canary Islands: 155 die in crash of Spanish jet.

12. FTC charges Xerox with monopoly on office copiers.

15. Australia: Commonwealth orders equal pay for women.

18. White House says bombing of North Vietnam will resume until accord is reached (→ 24).

20. N.Y. police report 300 pounds of seized narcotics stolen in last week (→ 1/31/73).

21. Nixon names James Schlesinger to replace Richard Helms as director of CIA.

23. Seoul: Pres. Park re-elected to six-year term (→ 1/8/74).

24. Hanoi bars peace talks until air raids stop (→ 30).

DEATHS

27. Lester Pearson, Canadian ex-premier, 1963 Nobel Peace Prize (*4/23/1897).

29. Joseph Cornell, American collage artist (*12/24/1903).

CULTURAL EVENTS, 1972

Literature: Eudora Welty's "The Optimist's Daughter"; Richard Adams' "Watership Down"; Yukio Mishima's "Spring Snow."

Academia: Lithium found to aid in treating manic depression.

Music: Robert Moog patents Moog Synthesizer; Don McLean's "American Pie"; Neil Young's "Heart of Gold"; Roberta Flack's "The First Time Ever I Saw Your Face"; Johnny Nash's "I Can See Clearly Now"; Helen Reddy's "I Am Woman."

The Arts: Norton Simon pays $3 mil. for Raphael's "Madonna and Child."

Film: Bob Fosse's "Cabaret," Liza Minnelli; Coppola's "The Godfather"; Hitchcock's "Frenzy"; Woody Allen's "Play it Again Sam"; "Klute," Jane Fonda; "The French Connection," Oscar; Bunuel's "The Discreet Charm of the Bourgeoisie."

Last, longest Apollo moon visit ends

Apollo 17 heads for the moon.

Astronauts in LRV and landing craft; the moon's last human visitors?

Dec 19. America's Apollo moon program ended today when the crew of Apollo 17 splashed down in the Pacific Ocean after the longest lunar mission of the series. Two of the astronauts, Eugene A. Cernan and Harrison H. Schmitt, spent a total of 75 hours roaming the moon's surface while the third crew member, Ronald E. Evans, circled the moon in the command ship.

Schmitt, a geologist, was the first scientist to go to the moon. He and Cernan made their lunar landing on December 11, after a three-day trip from earth. In their three visits to the surface, they drove the lunar roving vehicle, or LRV, among boulders at the foot of a mountain and to a crater that had given signs of volcanic activity. They also planted seismometers to measure any moonquakes that might occur, gravity meters, a cosmic ray detector and other scientific instruments.

Their most striking finding was the discovery of glassy orange soil, believed to contain a number of elements rare on the moon, which scientists believe might indicate that the now-barren lunar surface had water some time in the past.

In a ten-minute ceremony, Cernan and Schmitt unveiled a plaque fixed to the part of their landing craft that will remain on the moon. Signed by the Apollo 17 astronauts and President Nixon, it reads: "Here man completed his first exploration of the moon, December 1972, A.D. May the spirit of peace in which we came be reflected in the lives of all mankind."

The Apollo program, which cost $25 billion, resulted in six manned trips to the moon. A seventh mission, Apollo 13, nearly ended in disaster when an oxygen tank ruptured. Its astronauts rigged emergency equipment that enabled them to orbit the moon and return safely to earth. In all, Apollo astronauts returned from the moon with 836 pounds of rocks and a vast amount of scientific information. No U.S. astronauts are expected to return to the moon for years (→ 5/14/73).

Quake levels city; 10,000 lives lost

Dec 25. The Nicaraguan government has cut off food supplies to force survivors to leave the earthquake-shattered capital of Managua, where 75 percent of the buildings have been destroyed and the death toll is expected to reach 10,000. Most of the survivors in the city of 325,000 have fled, but the government fears for those who refuse to leave their homes. The two-and-a-half-hour series of quakes early yesterday touched off explosions and fires. Some likened it to "the end of the world." Howard Hughes, the industrialist, was among the 3,000 Americans in Managua when disaster struck. He is reported to be safe (→ 12/31).

U.S. population at sub-zero growth

Dec 17. If recent trends remain, the U.S. population in the year 2000 could fall 20 million short of previous projections. The Census Bureau released a revised projection today based on the current sub-zero growth pattern. The present U.S. population is 209.3 million; new estimates put the future number between 251-300 million. The average family now has 2.08 children. The no-growth rate is 2.1. The drop is due in part to the poor economy, more single and working women, effectiveness of contraception and legalization of abortion. Smaller families mean a higher living standard and countless more social and political changes.

Smuggler chooses lesser of two evils

Dec 1. A heroin smuggler prefers to be sentenced to 80 years in an American prison than be extradited to France —where the guillotine awaits. Christian David, who with a partner handled ten percent of the globe's heroin market, pleaded guilty to the crime in a New York court today. He was at once given the maximum sentence of 20 years without parole; another 60 years could result from other charges. The 41-year-old kingpin has operated in Brazil, Argentina, Uruguay and the United States. He is wanted in his native France for murdering a police officer there in 1966. His two suicide attempts (one by swallowing pieces of metal) failed.

Survivors of plane crash report cannibalism

Dec 26. Survivors of an air crash in the Andes Mountains admitted to eating the bodies of other passengers during a 69-day ordeal. Most of the 16 who lived were in Santiago, Chile, yesterday to attend a Christmas mass. A priest there told the men their lives were "a gift of God."

On October 13, their Uruguayan air force plane crashed. Twenty-nine aboard were killed at once or in a later avalanche. Of the survivors, eight were hardy rugby players. They lived on dried fruit and candy they had brought with them, and on a soup made of lichens. Temperatures sinking below zero, their food gone, they despaired. Cannibalism was a last resort.

The survivors camp out in the Andes.

Harry S. Truman has taken his last walk

Dec 26. Harry S. Truman, the 33rd President of the United States, died this morning in a Kansas City hospital. He was 88 years old.

The outspoken, decisive Democrat from Missouri, nicknamed "Give 'Em Hell, Harry" along his winning campaign trail in 1948, succumbed to lung, heart, kidney and other ailments. President Nixon has declared a national day of mourning later this week, the day of the state funeral in Independence.

The onetime farm boy moved on to become Senator, Vice President and finally, upon the death of Franklin D. Roosevelt, the president who left a lasting mark as a world leader, helping to end World War II and presiding over postwar America. In recent years, he enjoyed taking walks.

Truman at 85 in Independence.

Nixon orders an end to bombing in North

Dec 30. After two weeks of heavy bombing raids on North Vietnam, President Nixon has halted the American air offensive and agreed to resume peace negotiations with Hanoi representaive Le Duc Tho.

The news came amid much speculation that bombing north of the 20th parallel had hindered more than it helped the U.S. war effort. In the raids, 15 American B-52's and 12 other aircraft were shot from the sky. Ninety-three airmen have been killed, captured or are missing since the start of the campaign on December 18. One military official, who has generally supported a hard-line approach in Vietnam, said, "Is bombing going to be effective? I don't see any reason why it would."

However, another officer believed the decision to stop the air attacks is counter-productive to ending the war. "Even if the bombs don't coerce the enemy into successful peace talks," he said, "they're destroying his will to fight."

International and domestic pressures to stop the raids are believed to have figured into the decision, although the president did not cite these as a factor. Nor has he commented on the recent criticism from Pope Paul VI, who denounced the "painful delay" in attaining peace.

Secretary of State Henry Kissinger will resume peace talks with Tho on January 8 in Paris (→ 1/2/73).

In a moment of peace, G.I.'s observe mass in the hills of South Vietnam.

Heinrich Boll is Nobel Prize winner

Boll, anti-militarist writer.

Dec 10. The author of "Billiards at 9:30" has won the Nobel Prize for literature. Heinrich Boll, 54, is a former prisoner of war who repudiates aggression. The West German will share his $100,000 award with jailed writers worldwide.

Americans John Bardeen, Leon Cooper and John Schrieffer share the physics prize for findings on metal conduction of electricity. Americans Christian Anfinsen, Stanford Moore and William Stein get the chemistry award for studies on enzymes. Briton Rodney Porter and Gerald Edelman from the U.S. take the medicine prize for work on antibodies. American Kenneth Arrow and Briton John Ilicks get the economics prize for their welfare theory. No Peace Prize was given.

Baseball hero dies in rescue effort

Dec 31. Roberto Clemente, who overcame illness and injury to become one of baseball's outstanding players with the Pittsburgh Pirates, is missing and feared dead in the crash of a plane on a mercy mission. As honorary chairman of a Puerto Rican committee to help earthquake victims in Nicaragua, Clemente responded to an emergency call that the city of Managua had no water. He boarded an overloaded, old DC-10 that crashed just outside San Juan. Clemente got his 3,000th hit in 1972 just before his 38th birthday. He hit .362 in the two World Series in which he participated.

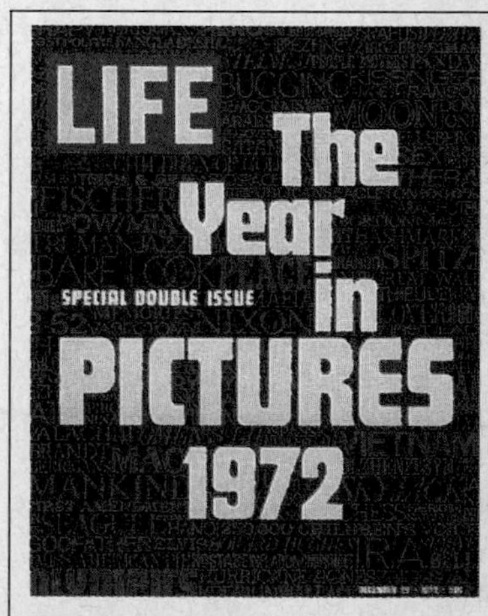

Dec 29. The last issue of the weekly Life magazine (above) was published today, advertisers having fled for the lure of TV.

1973

JANUARY

Su	Mo	Tu	We	Th	Fr	Sa
	1	2	3	4	5	6
7	8	9	10	11	12	13
14	15	16	17	18	19	20
21	22	23	24	25	26	27
28	29	30	31			

1. Pasadena: U.S.C. trounces Ohio State 42-17 in Rose Bowl.

2. U.S. admits accidental bombing of Hanoi hospital (→ 23).

3. Cairo: Thousands of riot police use tear gas to put down student protesters (→ 2/2/74).

6. New York: Carl Sagan says life is possible on Saturn moon.

9. Brazil bans sale of Picasso's erotic prints.

11. Nixon ends mandatory wage, price controls except in food, health, building (→ 6/13).

11. N.Y.: American League baseball to allow designated hitters to bat for pitchers.

12. Mideast: Arafat re-elected head of PLO (→ 2/21).

15. Washington: Four of six remaining defendants plead guilty to Watergate spying (→ 20).

17. Washington: Public Health Service links smoking to fetal and infant risks (→ 10/17/75).

17. Manila: Marcos extends own rule indefinitely (→ 29).

20. Washington: Nixon sworn in, exhorts, "Ask not just what will the govt. do for me, but what can I do for myself?" (→ 23).

22. Nigeria: Jet returning from Mecca pilgrimage crashes; 180 feared dead.

23. Washington: Mitchell linked to $199,000 payment to Liddy in Watergate inquiry (→ 30).

23. Washington: Nixon says Vietnam peace reached in Paris; POW's home in 60 days (→ 27).

25. Paris: Work begins on intl. plan to preserve Venice.

28. Detroit: William Nolde identified as last American killed in Vietnam (→ 2/5).

29. Manila: Marcos orders crackdown on campus activism (→ 8/27).

31. N.Y.: Police report one-fifth of narcotics seized since 1961 has been stolen.

31. Washington: Nixon aides warn of coming oil shortage (→ 3/6).

DEATH

26. Edward G. Robinson, American actor (*12/12/1893).

U.S. agrees to stop fighting in Vietnam

Jan 27. On paper at least, the fighting stopped in Vietnam tonight. A cease-fire went into effect at seven o'clock.

The truce agreement was signed earlier in the day in Paris. It was raining outside, and the atmosphere was just as gloomy inside the Hotel Majestic. There were no smiles as both sides signed the documents to end the most divisive war in American history.

The fighting by Americans may have stopped, but the conflict in Vietnam has not ended. The agreements are full of language that means different things to different people. If the United States hopes that the conflict will move from the battleground to the polling place, there was little reason to be hopeful at the Majestic. Two separate signing ceremonies had to be arranged, because South Vietnam refuses to even recognize the existence of the Viet Cong. In the morning ceremony, the United States, North Vietnam, South Vietnam and the Viet Cong participated. All references to the Provisional Revolutionary Government of the Viet Cong were excised from the documents and included in separate papers that were signed in the afternoon by the United States and North Vietnam alone.

The U.S. assumed a full combat role in Vietnam in 1965. It started counting casualties in 1961. The Pentagon says 45,997 Americans were killed in combat; 10,928 died from non-combat causes; 303,640 were wounded. Nearly 600 were captured; more than 1,300 are still missing. The cost? $109.5 billion.

The last American to die was an Army career officer from Michigan, Lieut. Col. William Nolde. He was killed by an artillery shell at An Loc. Nolde's widow, Joyce, says she is not bitter. "The war has ended," she said. "That's what he wanted." In a letter, Nolde wrote, "We tend to think only in terms of what this war has cost us, but by comparison to what it has cost so many Vietnamese, our price pales."

More than 183,000 South Vietnamese were killed in this war. The Communist death toll is said to approach one million (→ 28).

Delegates in Paris, safely separated by a mammoth table, prepare for signing.

Kissinger (left) and Le Duc Tho.

Jan 14. The Miami Dolphins, led by QB Bob Griese, ended a perfect season with a 14-7 Super Bowl victory over the Washington Redskins.

Corona is convicted of killing migrants

Jan 18. A Fairfield, California, jury has convicted Juan V. Corona, a 38-year-old Mexican man, of brutally murdering 25 migrant farm laborers. A week in deliberation, the jurors considered evidence provided by 116 witnesses called by the prosecution and over 900 pieces of evidence. The defense called no witnesses. Corona was found guilty of killing the migrants, most with a heavy sharp object, mutilating the bodies and burying them in the peach orchards of Yuba City, California. Due to ill health, Corona is in a state prison hospital (→ 12/2).

Liddy and McCord guilty in Watergate

Jan 30. G. Gordon Liddy and James W. McCord Jr., former aides to the Nixon political organization, were convicted today of plotting to spy on the Democrats during last year's presidential campaign.

McCord, a former official of the Central Intelligence Agency, was one of five men who broke into the offices of the Democratic National Committee in the Watergate apartment and office complex in Washington last June. He was a security official of the Republican National Committee.

Liddy, a lawyer, was counsel to the Committee for the Reelection of the President and head of its financial panel. Judge John J. Sirica has not yet passed sentence (→ 2/2).

Police in helicopter shoot killer of ten

Jan 9. After a day of terror that left ten dead and 13 wounded, New Orleans policemen in a helicopter shot and killed the sniper atop the 17-story Howard Johnson's Motor Lodge. He was Mark Essex, 23, of Emporia, Kansas, described as a "quiet boy" from an ordinary black family. In Jan. 1969, he joined the Navy and was discharged in Feb. 1971 for "character and behavior disorders." His pastor in Emporia says that "something happened in the Navy. After it, he just hated white folks." A second sniper may have been involved. Ballistics tests show that the rifle used by Essex was the same that killed one police cadet and wounded a policeman in New York on New Year's Eve.

State laws denying early abortions voided

Jan 21. State laws forbidding abortion during a pregnancy's first trimester have been overturned by the Supreme Court. By a 7-to-2 vote today, the court ruled states cannot prohibit or restrict a woman's right to abortion during her first three months of pregnancy. Tighter restrictions remain on abortions attempted at later months.

The dramatic decision affected the Catholic Church and pro-choice groups predictably. Cardinal Krol of Philadelphia, President of the National Conference of Catholic Bishops, called the ruling an "unspeakable tragedy." Members of Planned Parenthood praised the move as courageous.

On record President Nixon has opposed abortion. Three of his four Supreme Court appointees, however, sided with the majority. Justices William Rehnquist and Byron White alone dissented. White wrote that he rejects a morality that values the "convenience of the pregnant mother more than the ... life or potential life which she carries."

The court leaves the decision to terminate a pregnancy in the first trimester up to a woman and her doctor. In the second trimester, a state may regulate the operation "in ways that are reasonably related to maternal health." As for the last ten weeks, when a fetus can live outside the womb, any state may reserve the right to prohibit abortions.

Hawaii, Washington, Alaska and New York have laws coinciding with the court ruling. All other states have a great deal of revisions ahead of them (→ 2/15/75).

LBJ, a hard-driving man, driven no more

Jan 22. Former President Lyndon B. Johnson died of an apparent heart attack today in Texas. Johnson, who had been fighting heart disease for 18 years, was stricken at his ranch in Johnson City. He was rushed by private plane to San Antonio, where he was declared dead at 4:33 this afternoon. He was 64. Johnson's body will lie in state at his library in Austin and the Capitol rotunda in Washington. Funeral services will be held in Washington, and the former president will be buried on his Texas ranch.

Johnson was a New Dealer who originated the Great Society program. He will be remembered and honored for his innovations and reforms in civil rights, Social Security, housing and education. But he has also been vilified for presiding over the most divisive war in our history.

Johnson's presidency began with the tragedy of John Kennedy's assassination and ended with the tragedy of Vietnam. One tragedy forced him into the presidency. The other forced him out. Ironically perhaps, Johnson died as American involvement in Vietnam was coming to an end.

LBJ, 36th President of the United States, lies in state in the Capitol rotunda.

Airports begin to screen all clients

Jan 5. At all 531 airports in the U.S., boarding passengers will now be subject to thorough inspection. Every item of luggage will be examined; a few airlines provide X-ray machines to speed the process. Passengers may be "patted down" at random. Airports at Los Angeles, Atlanta, Chicago and elsewhere have made "sterile concourses," which passengers enter through metal-detector gates. The detectors are so sensitive they can pick up a few coins in a pocket (→ 2/15).

Jan 22. Joe Frazier fell victim to the heavy hands of George Foreman today in Jamaica, losing his title in a 2nd-round KO (→ 3/31).

Hitler's car brings $153,000 at sale

Jan 7. In Scottsdale, Arizona, this afternoon, Earl Clark got the auto of an autocrat. He purchased a Mercedes once owned by Adolf Hitler. Clark paid $153,000, $60,000 more than any price paid for a car at auction. He will display it at his Pennsylvania amusement park. Hitler and pals such as Mussolini toured Berlin in the back seat of the 770-K 1940 Mercedes. Its bulletproof glass and armor plates made them feel at ease, cruising three miles with each gallon of gas.

Archie Bunker and his family battle over bigotry on TV's "All in the Family," producer Norman Lear's popular sit-com.

1973

FEBRUARY

Su	Mo	Tu	We	Th	Fr	Sa
				1	2	3
4	5	6	7	8	9	10
11	12	13	14	15	16	17
18	19	20	21	22	23	24
25	26	27	28			

1. Washington: Court bars EPA from delaying air pollution clean-up (→ 8/4/78).

2. Washington: Sirica to revive Watergate inquiry (→ 8).

3. Belfast: Six dead, 17 hurt as police battle I.R.A. gunmen (→ 3/1).

4. Switzerland: Innsbruck, Austria, chosen for 1976 Winter Olympics.

5. Washington: Bill Nolde, last killed in Vietnam, buried at Arlington Natl. Cemetery (→ 14).

5. Nixon administration admits impounding $8.7 bil. alotted for federal programs.

9. Washington: Nixon signs bill ending Penn Central strike.

12. U.S. devalues dollar 10% to improve trade balance (→ 3/2).

13. Uruguay: Armed forces take power in coup.

14. U.S., Hanoi set up group to channel U.S. reconstruction aid to Hanoi.→

15. Washington: U.S., Cuba sign pact to curb hijacking.

15. Washington: Pentagon reports increase in air raids on Laos (→ 21).

16. Washington: U.S. Army review court upholds conviction of Lt. Calley in Mylai massacre.

17. Nixon names Patrick Gray director of FBI (→ 4/5/73).

18. Florida: Richard Petty wins Daytona 500.

21. Laos: Two sides sign pact aimed at ending war (→ 4/16).

21. Sinai: Israel shoots down Libyan passenger jet, killing 74 (→ 24).

22. Washington: U.S. and China agree to set up offices in each other's capitals (→ 3/12).

26. Washington: Publisher and ten reporters subpoenaed to testify on Watergate (→ 3/7).

27. U.S. Supreme Court rules Virginia pool club can't bar blacks who are local residents (→ 7/9).

DEATH

6. Elizabeth Bowen, Irish writer (*6/7/1899).

Indians seize Wounded Knee and hostages

Members of the militant American Indian Movement at Wounded Knee.

Feb 28. About 250 members of the American Indian Movement occupied a trading post and church at the Pine Ridge Sioux Reservation last night, and today they hold at least ten persons hostage. Federal marshals and FBI agents have exchanged gunfire with the militants, but so far there are no reports of injuries. The Native Americans are demanding the Senate start a full-scale inquiry into government treatment of Indians in the U.S.

In 1890, the Oglala Sioux lost their last tragic battle with the U.S. cavalry at Wounded Knee. Afterwards, one Indian said, "As I look back from this high hill of my old age, I can still see the butchered men, women and children as clear as I saw them with eyes still young. And I can see that something else died and was buried in the blizzard. A people's dream died there. It was a beautiful dream. Now the nation's hoop is broken and scattered. There is no center any longer. And the sacred tree is dead" (→ 3/2).

First planeload of POWs home from war

Feb 14. On this Valentine's Day, 20 former POWs, symbols and victims of a decade of agonizing war in Southeast Asia, came home. The first returning prisoner to touch the U.S. mainland was Capt. Jeremiah A. Denton Jr. of the Navy, who recalled they used to signal good news to each other by whistling "California Here I Come." Now they did, arriving at Travis air base in California. The man held longest in captivity among them is Cmdr. Raymond A. Vohden, whose plane was downed in North Vietnam on April 3, 1965 (→ 3/17).

Sgt. William Robinson, once again a free man, is greeted by his family.

Watergate inquiry likely to continue

Feb 8. The federal prosecutor in the Watergate case said today that all seven defendants will be ordered to appear before a grand jury in an attempt to explore possible high-level involvement in the break-in of Democratic headquarters. Earl J. Silbert's remarks were apparently prompted by Federal Judge John J. Sirica's charge just a few days ago that he had grave doubts that the recent trial of the men involved in the break-in last year had gotten to the bottom of what has now become a potentially politically explosive case (→ 26).

Israel shoots down Libyan jet in error

Feb 24. Israeli Defense Minister Moshe Dayan admitted today that his country made an "error of judgment" when it shot down a Libyan passenger jet on Wednesday. Dayan's statement was the first concession from Israel that it bore any responsibility for what Libya has branded a "criminal act."

At least 106 people were killed when Israeli fighter jets shot down the Libyan Arab Airlines plane. It crashed into the Israeli-occupied Sinai Desert. The plane, which was off course and apparently having radio problems, did not acknowledge Israeli ground transmissions. It also ignored signals from Israeli jets to land. Israel says its pilots did not open fire until the Libyan pilot disregarded all signals (→ 4/21).

Feb 19. Evel Knievel, shown above last year in S.F., jumped 52 wrecked cars today in L.A. after a demolition derby.

1973

MARCH

Su	Mo	Tu	We	Th	Fr	Sa
				1	2	3
4	5	6	7	8	9	10
11	12	13	14	15	16	17
18	19	20	21	22	23	24
25	26	27	28	29	30	31

1. Ireland: Fianna Fail Party of John Lynch defeated after 16 years (→ 8).

2. S.D.: Federal forces encircle occupied Wounded Knee; FBI car hit by gunfire (→ 11).

2. Banks in Japan, W. Europe close to cope with monetary crisis caused by dollar devaluation.

3. Sudan: Arab terrorist gives up after killing two U.S. hostages yesterday.

3. Japan discloses first defense plan since WWII (→ 11/19/74).

4. Calif.: Scientists report rings of Saturn composed of large chunks of solid matter.

6. Nixon reimposes price controls on oil and gas (→ 4/18).

7. Washington: Nixon's lawyer says he gave $30,000 to Donald Segretti who headed Watergate break-in (→ 22).

11. S.D.: FBI agent shot by Indians at Wounded Knee (→ 4/5).

12. Conn.: John Downey returns to U.S. after 20 years as prisoner in China (→ 9/4/74).

17. Cambodia: 20 killed in bombing aimed at President Lon Nol (→ 4/10).

17. Hanoi: POW's cleared out of Hanoi Hilton first time in eight years (→ 29).

20. Britain releases White Paper advocating pro-Catholic reforms in Northern Ireland (→ 4/16).

20. Athens: Police storm university to end sit-in of 800 students (→ 5/28).

22. Washington: FBI chief Gray testifies John Dean probably lied to FBI about Watergate (→ 23).

23. Washington: McCord says he was under political pressure to plead guilty (→ 28).

26. Penn.: William Prater found guilty in 1969 slaying of mine union leader Abe Yablonski.

31. San Diego: Ken Norton wins split decision over Ali (→ 9/10).

DEATHS

6. Pearl S. Buck, American writer (*6/26/1892).

26. Sir Noel Coward, U.K. playwright, actor (*12/16/1899).

CIA, ITT acted against Allende election

Allende speaks to Chilean youth.

March 20. A Senate subcommittee heard shocking testimony today about an apparent conspiracy by International Telephone and Telegraph and the Central Intelligence Agency to disrupt the political process in Chile in 1970. William Merriam, a Vice President of ITT, testified that the goal of the venture was to prevent Salvador Allende, a Marxist, from being elected President of Chile. The plan failed, and Allende was elected.

Merriam told the committee that the CIA agreed to a plan by ITT to provide anti-Allende propaganda and even incite violence that might provoke an anti-Marxist coup in Chile. The collaboration between the private firm and the intelligence agency grew out of a meeting between Harold Geneen, President and Chairman of ITT, William Broe, Director of CIA clandestine activities in Latin America, and Merriam. The Senate panel, headed by Democrat Frank Church, is investigating activities of multinational corporations (→ 6/21).

Theatergoers lose a playful dramatist

Noel Coward, author of 27 plays.

March 26. The urbane dramatist, songwriter and showman Noel Coward has died at his Jamaican villa. He was 73. He leaves just as he was being appreciated—again. There have been many revivals of his plays "Private Lives" (1930), "Design for Living" (1933), "Blithe Spirit" (1941) and others.

Coward was born in a town outside London. In his teens he starred in a stage production of "Peter Pan." At age 26, he had three shows on the London stage. Characters in his plays were spoiled, peevish, witty, jaded and kind. So was Coward.

His plays dealt with bickering but loving heterosexual couples; Coward himself, as revealed in "A Song at Twilight," a drama he wrote at age 66, was homosexual. He had been reticent about it in public but made no apologies in private. His honesty won him friends such as Sir Winston Churchill and Lord Olivier. Coward was knighted in 1970.

Two bombs rattle London, injure 234

March 8. Two bombs, planted by terrorists, exploded in London near Trafalgar Square and at the Old Bailey criminal court today, killing one and injuring 234. A provisional arm of the Irish Republican Army is believed to be responsible for the blasts. The explosions had been timed to coincide with Northern Ireland's referendum to decide if the province should remain under British rule. The I.R.A. adamantly opposes British control. Telephone warnings of the bombs prevented more casualties (→ 20).

Political element in Watergate laid bare

March 28. The Watergate affair took on political overtones today as a key witness told a closed Senate hearing that John N. Mitchell, the former Attorney General and head of the Nixon re-election committee, had prior knowledge of the break-in at Democratic headquarters last June. The testimony came from James W. McCord, Jr., recently convicted of conspiracy in the break-in at the Watergate complex. Mitchell resigned his party post two weeks after McCord and four others were arrested (→ 4/3).

Walton leads UCLA to seventh straight title

March 27. Bill Walton, with a 44-point spree, led UCLA to its seventh straight National Collegiate Athletic Association basketball title. Stoic even in victory, Walton refused to talk about his future as a professional. "When that game ended," he said of the 11-point victory over Memphis State, "I stopped being UCLA's No 32 for this season." Walton got 21 field goals in 22 shots and two successful free throws out of five in each half as UCLA won its 75th basketball game in a row.

Walton, 6'11", battles for a rebound.

United States ends war role in Vietnam

March 29. After a decade of fighting in Vietnam, United States troops have withdrawn from the war-torn area and the North Vietnamese have released the last American prisoners of war. There was little celebration as American involvement in the unpopular, divisive war came to an end. A special North Vietnamese prison for American POWs, called the Hanoi Hilton, is empty now for the first time in eight years (→ 7/17).

1973

APRIL

Su	Mo	Tu	We	Th	Fr	Sa
1	2	3	4	5	6	7
8	9	10	11	12	13	14
15	16	17	18	19	20	21
22	23	24	25	26	27	28
29	30					

1. Washington: FDA decides to recall diet drugs containing amphetamine.

1. India opens drive to save tiger from extinction.

3. Washington: Liddy given 18 months for refusing to answer jury's questions (→ 16).

5. S.D.: Indians and U.S. sign accord in 37-day confrontation (→ 17).

5. Washington: Nixon withdraws Patrick Gray as nominee for FBI director.

5. Washington: Scientists produce human blood cells in living mouse (→ 8/28/76).

8. India takes control over Sikkim after anti-government riots (→ 5/2/74).

10. Cambodia: U.S. begins airlift to besieged Phnom Penh (→ 5/11).

11. Bonn: West Germany closes file on Nazi war criminal Martin Bormann.

12. Moscow: U.S.S.R. and Occidental Petroleum sign largest private contract in history of Soviet-U.S. trade (→ 6/16).

16. Washington: Martha Mitchell calls Nixon's claim that he and John Mitchell didn't meet 4/4, "god blessed lie" (→ 19).

16. Laos: U.S. bombs village, claiming Hanoi broke truce (→ 5/14/75).

16. Dublin: I.R.A. chief MacStiofain freed from jail (→ 5/31).

17. S.D.: Indian at Wounded Knee critically wounded by FBI bullet (→ 5/8).

18. Nixon offers plan to avert energy crisis (→ 10/21).

19. Washington: John Dean insists he will not be made "a scapegoat" on Watergate (→ 30).

21. New York: U.N. denounces Israeli raids on Lebanon (→ 6/3).

21. Siberia-to-Eastern Europe pipeline begins pumping oil.

27. Moscow: Andropov, Gromyko get full Politburo membership in first major shake-up since Khrushchev ouster (→ 1/2/74).

29. Washington: It is reported Pentagon spends millions yearly to aid failing companies.

Four top Nixon aides quit over Watergate

April 30. Four top aides to President Nixon resigned today in the wake of allegations that the White House had sought to cover up what has become known as the Watergate affair.

Meanwhile, President Nixon, in a televised address to the nation, said he accepted responsibility for what happened in the Watergate case but that he had no knowledge of any political espionage or attempts to cover it up.

Among those resigning today were H.R. "Bob" Haldeman, the austere chief of staff; and John D. Ehrlichman, the chief presidential adviser on domestic affairs. They said their ability to carry out their duties had been undermined.

John W. Dean 3rd, the White House counsel, who has threatened to implicate his superiors, resigned at the request of the president. He will be succeeded, at least for now, by Leonard Garment.

Also resigning was Attorney General Richard G. Kleindienst, who said that some of his close friends had become Watergate suspects and that "impartial enforcement of the law" ruled out his role in the matter. Named to succeed him was Elliot L. Richardson, who has been Secretary of Defense. Richardson will be in charge of investigations into the break-in at Democratic offices at the Watergate complex and allegations of later cover-ups by top aides or party officials (→ 5/1).

Haldeman, chief of staff.

Ehrlichman, domestic adviser.

White House tried to lift Ellsberg records

April 27. A federal judge disclosed today that two White House aides convicted as Watergate conspirators had broken into the office of a psychiatrist to Daniel Ellsberg, charged with stealing the Pentagon Papers and leaking them to the press. A Justice Department memorandum made public by Judge William Matthew Bryne Jr. said that E. Howard Hunt Jr. and G. Gordon Liddy had broken into the psychiatrist's office in mid-1971 when the government was investigating the disclosure of the Pentagon Papers. Judge Byrne immediately raised the question of whether Ellsberg's constitutional rights had been violated (→ 5/11).

Vatican purportedly knew of Nazi evils

April 4. Today, the Vatican released documents which show that aides to Pope Pius XII, and probably the pope himself, knew of the Nazis' extermination of millions of Jews. The revelation has renewed the controversy over why the pope never spoke out publicly against the holocaust. The secret documents include a report by Archbishop Roncalli, the future Pope John XXIII, sent to Monsignor Montini, then Pius' secretary and now Pope Paul VI, which tells of a meeting with one of Hitler's envoys, where Roncalli alluded to the extermination camps in Poland. This suggests that the camps were known to the Vatican.

Picasso: He changed our point of view

The master, active until the very end.

April 8. The century's greatest artist is dead. Pablo Picasso has died at his estate in Southern France. He was 92 years old.

An entire museum could be built around Picasso's work, as extensive and varied as it was. When Picasso finished one exploration he moved on, flowing from a "Blue" period to a "Rose" at the turn of the century, experimenting with Cubism into the early 20's, investigating Surrealism in the 30's and pondering mythological symbols in the last decades. The son of an art professor, Picasso grew less from studying nature than from studying peers and predecessors.

"Les Demoiselles d'Avignon" (1907) and "Guernica" (1937) are two masterworks among many. He had completed 201 paintings since October 1970, paintings of a vision growing steadily calm and serene.

"The Painter at Work," created with a steady hand at the age of 90.

1973

MAY

Su	Mo	Tu	We	Th	Fr	Sa
		1	2	3	4	5
6	7	8	9	10	11	12
13	14	15	16	17	18	19
20	21	22	23	24	25	26
29	28	29	30	31		

1. Washington: Panel reports evidence of Watergate cover-up by top Nixon aides (→ 10).

5. Secretariat wins Kentucky Derby in record time, Ron Turcotte in the saddle (→ 19).

7. Jerusalem: Thousands march in parade marking Israel's 25th anniversary (→ 3/10/74).

8. S.D.: Indians end occupation of Wounded Knee (→ 8/23/74).

10. Washington: John Mitchell and Maurice Stans indicted for perjury (→ 17).

10. Calif.: N.Y. Knicks beat L.A. Lakers for NBA title.

11. White House vows to continue with "right policy" of bombing Cambodia (→ 12).

12. U.S.: Poll shows Americans oppose 2-1 bombing of Laos and Cambodia (→ 31).

14. Cape Kennedy: U.S. puts Skylab into orbit (→ 25).

17. Senate panel begins public hearings on Watergate.→

18. Archibald Cox named Watergate prosecutor (→ 22).

19. Baltimore: Secretariat wins Preakness (→ 6/9).

19. Bonn: Brezhnev, Brandt sign ten-year cooperation pact on trade, technology (→ 4/25/74).

22. Nixon, citing national security, admits White House role in Watergate cover-up (→ 6/5).

24. London: House of Lords leader Earl Jellicoe resigns in growing sex scandal.

26. New York: 70,000 see Carole King play in Central Park.

28. Athens to try 35 navy officers for rebellion (→ 6/1).

28. Indy 500 postponed after 12-car accident at start (→ 30).

30. Gordon Johncock wins Indy 500 in race shortened by rain.

31. U.S. Senate halts funds for bombing of Cambodia (→ 6/27).

31. Dublin: Erskin Childers elected pres. of Roman Catholic Republic of Ireland (→ 6/24).

DEATH

18. Jeannette Rankin, pacifist, first woman in U.S. Congress (*6/11/1880).

Senate panel begins Watergate hearings

Baker, Ervin, Sam Dash all ears.

May 17. A Nixon campaign official was the first witness as a special Senate committee opened hearings today into the plot to spy on the Democrats last year and administration efforts to cover it up.

Testifying in the ornate Senate Caucus Room, Robert C. Odle Jr. said Jeb Stuart Magruder, the deputy director of the President's re-election committee, had ordered that a file, apparently containing political intelligence, be removed from his desk, only hours after the break-in last year at Democratic headquarters in the Watergate complex. Odle said that he suspected the file contained "things which have no place in a political campaign."

In opening the hearings, Senator Sam J. Ervin Jr., a courtly Democrat from North Carolina, said that the committee he heads is determined to uncover all relevant facts "and spare no one, whatever his station in life may be." Those who broke into the Democratic offices, he said, "were in effect breaking into the home of every citizen of the United States." His determination to discover the facts was echoed by Senator Howard H. Baker Jr. of Tennessee, who is the committee's vice chairman. He said the final verdict must be rendered by the American people (→ 18).

Washington Post is honored for Watergate

May 7. The Washington Post has been awarded the Pulitzer Prize for public service in journalism for its investigation of the Watergate case, the affair that began with an attempt to bug Democratic National Committee headquarters last June and grew into a national scandal last month. While the newspaper received the prize, much of the credit for the series of investigative stories went to two reporters on the metropolitan staff—Carl Bernstein, 29, and Bob Woodward, 30.

The two young reporters were assigned to check into the break-in at Democratic Party offices in the Watergate complex in Washington, and the five suspects who were arrested. At first it seemed like a routine case of burglary. As they continued their investigation, however, relying upon an unidentified source known only as "Deep Throat," they uncovered the existence of a Republican espionage network, a secret fund and links to high administration officials.

Watergate whistle-blowers Woodward and Bernstein (rt.) at work at The Post.

Ellsberg is freed in the Pentagon affair

Ellsberg, target of the White House.

May 11. A federal judge in the Pentagon Papers case dismissed all charges against Dr. Daniel Ellsberg on the grounds of "improper government conduct." Ellsberg, along with Anthony J. Russo Jr., had been charged with espionage, theft and conspiracy for stealing and copying the classified Pentagon Papers, which were then printed by The New York Times and other newspapers.

In dismissing the charges on the 89th day of the trial, Judge William Matthew Byrne Jr. said government misconduct had made a fair trial impossible. He cited the break-in to the office of Ellsberg's psychiatrist by a "special unit" reporting to the White House as well as the wiretapping of Ellsberg's telephone by the FBI with no record of authorization (→ 9/5).

May 25. Joseph Kerwin, Charles Conrad and Paul Weitz are rocketing their way toward Skylab (above), first U.S. space station. They carry replacement parts for broken solar panels (→ 6/7).

1973

JUNE

Su	Mo	Tu	We	Th	Fr	Sa
					1	2
3	4	5	6	7	8	9
10	11	12	13	14	15	16
17	18	19	20	21	22	23
24	25	26	27	28	29	30

1. Athens: Premier Papadopoulos bars monarchy, proclaims republic (→ 16).

3. Jerusalem: Israel exchanges 56 Arab POW's for three captured Israeli pilots (→ 7/13).

5. Washington: Ehrlichman says Mitchell chose three bugging sites, including Watergate (→ 6).

6. Washington: Papers reveal Nixon approved "partly illegal" '70 internal security plan (→ 12).

7. Skylab astronauts Conrad, Kerwin fix broken solar panel, gaining electricity (→ 22).

9. U.S. asks Costa Rica to extradite fugitive financier Robert Vesco (→ 12/12).

11. Tripoli: Khadafy nationalizes U.S. oil company (→ 9/1).

12. Washington: John Dean pleads Fifth Amendment at Watergate hearing (→ 14).

13. Nixon orders 60-day freeze on all retail prices (→ 7/14/74).

14. Washington: Jeb Magruder links Dean, Mitchell to Watergate bugging, Haldeman to cover-up (→ 25).

16. Washington: Brezhnev arrives for nine-day visit (→ 25).

16. Athens: Greece announces it will seize property of King Constantine (→ 8/19).

19. Tokyo: Erotic Picasso prints exhibited after censoring.

21. Washington: Senate finds ITT and U.S. at fault for meddling in Chile election (→ 29).

22. Pacific: Skylab astronauts splash down safely after record 28 days in space (→ 8/4).

22. N.Y.: U.N. Security Council approves admission of West and East Germany (→ 10/6/79).

23. Rome: Pope opens Vatican gallery of modern art.

25. Washington: Dean tells panel Nixon, Haldeman, Ehrlichman all took part in cover-up.→

27. Nixon vetoes Senate ban on Cambodia bombing (→ 30).

29. Chile: Revolt crushed as army backs Allende (→ 7/5).

DEATH

10. William Inge, Midwestern playwright, suicide (*5/3/1913).

Dean accuses Nixon and two chief aides

June 25. John W. Dean 3rd told a Senate committee today that President Nixon had taken part in the Watergate cover-up for as long as eight months.

Dean, who was fired as White House counsel recently, testified he had warned the president that covering up the break-in of the Democratic offices at Watergate was "a cancer growing on the presidency." But Dean said that the president "did not realize or appreciate at any time the implications of his involvement."

In his explosive testimony before the Senate committee investigating the Watergate affair, Dean said that the prime orchestrators were two recently resigned top White House aides, H.R. Haldeman and John D. Ehrlichman. Dean acknowleged he had taken part in some aspects of the cover-up but said he had not known of the break-in before it took place last year (→ 7/30).

Dean tells of White House wrongs.

Brezhnev pays visit to France and U.S.

June 25. Soviet leader Leonid Brezhnev was greeted by the President of France, Georges Pompidou, today as he arrived in Paris for two days of talks. Brezhnev was still beaming over his successful week-long trip to the United States, where he held long conversations with President Nixon, met Hollywood stars at a pool party in California and addressed the American people on television. The joint communique from Nixon and Brezhnev called their meetings a "further milestone" toward improved relations. It also indicated that the two superpowers still have major differences, notably in the Middle East (→ 6/27/74).

Pompidou (right) greets Brezhnev.

Supreme Court sets obscenity standards

June 21. The Supreme Court gingerly handed the hot potato issue of obscenity to the states today, leaving the decision of to censor or not to censor up to them. By a 5-to-4 vote, the court ruled states may forbid works "which appeal to the prurient interest in sex, which portray sexual conduct in a patently offensive way and which ... do not have serious literary, artistic, political or scientific value." Chief Justice Burger wrote, "People in different states vary in their attitudes ... and this diversity is not to be strangled by the absolutism of imposed uniformity."

June 9. Tiny jockey Ron Turcotte steers sinewy Secretariat across the finish line at the Belmont Stakes to capture horse racing's coveted Triple Crown.

De Valera resigns as President of Ireland

June 24. The oldest head of state in the world retired today. Eamon de Valera, 90, President of Ireland, ended his 57-year political career at the place where it all began: Boland's bakery. In 1916, de Valera commanded an Irish Republican Army battalion, which was stationed at the bakery. Throughout his life, he struggled for the union of Ireland and today he predicted his wish will come true (→ 11/15).

Rebels open strong drive in Cambodia

June 30. Communist rebels have begun a major offensive in Cambodia, pushing closer to the nation's capital at Phnom Penh. The insurgent forces have seized control of Highway 4, which is the only overland route to the strategic port of Kompong Sum on the Gulf of Siam. With the loss of the road, the government of Lon Nol clings precariously to power in the nation. One Cambodian officer described the assault: "The situation is bad. This is the worst attack we've ever had to deal with." President Nixon appealed to Congress to halt its opposition to U.S. bombing in Cambodia, suggesting the nation would fall without U.S. support (→ 7/20).

Soviet SST explodes in Paris, killing 6

June 3. The Soviet Union's Tu-144 supersonic airliner exploded during a flight at the Paris air show today, killing its crew of six. The Tu-144 was the first commercial supersonic airliner. Its crash was a major blow to Soviet aviation plans.

Soviet Tu-144 in ruins in Paris.

1973

JULY

Su	Mo	Tu	We	Th	Fr	Sa
1	2	3	4	5	6	7
8	9	10	11	12	13	14
15	16	17	18	19	20	21
22	23	24	25	26	27	28
29	30	31				

5. U.S. bars ambassador to Uganda for Idi Amin insult to Nixon on Watergate (→ 11).

5. Chile: Allende names new Cabinet in biggest shake-up since taking office (→ 9/11).

6. Rhodesia: Guerrillas kidnap 278 from Roman Catholic mission (→ 12/8/74).

7. Wimbledon: Jan Kodes over Alex Metreveli 6-1, 9-7, 6-3; Billie Jean King over Chris Evert 6-0, 7-5.

9. Atlanta: Ralph Abernathy resigns as head of Southern Christian Leadership Conference (→ 10/3).

11. Uganda: 112 in Peace Corps ousted by Idi Amin (→ 7/1/75).

11. Paris: 122 killed as Brazilian jet crashes just short of airport.

11. India frees 438 Pakistani prisoners on medical grounds (→ 8/28).

13. Argentina: Pres. Hector Camporas to resign to make way for election of Peron (→ 8/23).

13. New York: Kurt Waldheim to go to Mideast to seek Arab-Israeli settlement (→ 26).

15. Detroit: Nolan Ryan pitches second no-hitter of season.

17. U.S. Senate 77-20 approves plan for Alaskan pipeline.

17. Afghanistan: Mohammad Zahir Shah overthrown; new republic proclaimed (→ 4/27/78).

17. Britain recognized Hanoi government (→ 21).

20. Washington: Pentagon admits falsifying Cambodia bombing reports to Congress (→ 8/7).

21. Washington: Air Force colonel admits planned bombing of Viet Cong hospital (→ 9/3).

26. N.Y.: U.S. vetoes U.N. measure criticizing Israel (→ 8/17).

28. Watkins Glenn: 600,000 attend biggest U.S. rock concert.

DEATHS

6. Otto Klemperer, German conductor (*5/14/1885).

13. Lon Chaney Jr., American actor (*2/10/1906).

24. Capt. Eddie Rickenbacker, American WWI flying ace (*10/8/1890).

All Nixon's official discussions on tape

July 30. H.R. Haldeman told a Senate committee today that secret White House tapes failed to show that either he or President Nixon had any knowledge of the break-in at Democratic headquarters in the Watergate complex last year.

The existence of tape-recorded conversations between Nixon and various aides was disclosed in dramatic testimony two weeks ago by Alexander P. Butterfield, who was a deputy assistant to the president until a few months ago. Butterfield testified before the Senate committee investigating the Watergate affair that nearly all Oval Office conversations had been taped since early 1971 (→ 8/8).

Bahamas become independent of U.K.

July 10. "We are prepared to shoulder our responsibilities, and despite the ups and downs, we know that we are going to make it," declared Prime Minister Lynden Pindling of his newly independent nation, the Bahamas. After more than 300 years of British rule, the island chain will shed the shackles of colonialism and govern itself. The Bahamas has applied for membership within the U.N.; if admitted, it will become the 135th member of the world group. England's Prince Charles handed over documents of independence to Pindling at the jubilant liberation celebration.

Like the Broadway musical, the film "Jesus Christ Superstar" brings Jesus into the Rock Era.

1973

AUGUST

Su	Mo	Tu	We	Th	Fr	Sa
			1	2	3	4
5	6	7	8	9	10	11
12	13	14	15	16	17	18
19	20	21	22	23	24	25
26	27	28	29	30	31	

3. U.S. Justice Dept. reopens case of Kent State shootings (→ 3/29/74).

4. Houston: Astronomers pierce clouds of Venus with radar for first time (→ 9/24).

5. Athens: Arab gunmen kill three, wound 55 in airport lounge.

7. Cambodia: U.S. plane accidentally bombs village, killing 400 civilians (→ 14).

9. Texas: Elmer Wayne Henley admits role in 25 killings.

12. Cleveland: Jack Nicklaus wins his third PGA golf title.

14. Washington officially ends bombing of Cambodia (→ 26).

17. Syria-Lebanon border reopens three months after PLO crisis (→ 9/13).

19. Athens: Pres. Papadopoulos ends martial law, vows to free all political foes (→ 11/17).

21. Moscow: 20 Soviet Jews attacked at Moscow University games (→ 9/30).

23. Buenos Aires: Police battle anti-Peronists; 100 arrested (→ 9/23).

24. Moscow: U.S. basketball team beats Soviets in world games final.

25. London: Doctors report using first CAT scan.

26. Cambodia: Phnom Penh reports supply lines cut off by rebels (→ 11/19).

27. Manila: Benigno Aquino refuses to defend himself against subversion charges (→ 8/14/75).

28. India, Pakistan sign accord paving way for release of 90,000 Pakistanis (→ 11/30/74).

28. Mexico: 500 die in earthquake; toll still rising.

29. Washington: Sirica calls for surrender of Watergate tapes; Nixon refuses (→ 9/8).

DEATHS

4. Eddie Condon, American jazz guitarist (*11/16/1905).

6. Fulgencio Batista, Cuban ex-dictator, in Spanish exile (*1/16/1901).

17. Conrad Aiken, American writer, critic (*8/5/1889).

Rogers resigns and Kissinger gets job

Shuttle diplomat Henry Kissinger.

Aug 22. Secretary of State William P. Rogers has tendered a letter of resignation to President Nixon. The president announced he would accept the resignation with "personal regret" and would nominate White House adviser on national security Henry A. Kissinger to the Cabinet position. This will mean little change in foreign policy, as Kissinger has already been handling the responsibilities of the post with Rogers holding the job in name only. Kissinger will also retain his present position, thus tightening White House control over 12,000 State Dept. workers (→ 12/23/73).

Agnew discloses he's under scrutiny

Aug 8. Vice President Spiro Agnew has disclosed that he is under investigation on charges of taking kickbacks from government contractors in Maryland.

The vice president, who had previously served as Governor and as County Executive in Maryland, immediately went on national television to denounce the charges as "damned lies." Agnew, insisting that he had "nothing to hide," said that he did not expect to be indicted by a federal grand jury in Baltimore and that he had no intention of resigning from office. The vice president is being investigated for bribery, extortion, tax fraud and conspiracy (→ 18).

Moscow warns of imperialist Sesame Street

Big Bird, Oscar and the gang.

Aug 16. "One of these things just doesn't belong here" goes a "Sesame Street" song teaching children to differentiate shapes. The Kremlin sings a similar tune, murmuring "nyet" to the broadcast of "Sesame Street" in the Soviet Union. The program is "veiled neocolonialism."

The Children's Television Workshop, producer of the PBS program, is dumbfounded. Since its debut in 1969, "Sesame Street" strives to destratify society. The black and white cast dresses casually and rarely discusses work. They live in a peaceful, unspecified urban area.

Even Jim Henson's Muppets, hand and life-size puppets, are green, orange and other value-free colors. The most popular Muppet is a towering canary-yellow Big Bird.

What the Soviets may be objecting to are the "commercials," quick, slick cartoon lessons on numbers and letters. Even the producer admits they are mesmerizing.

East German leader Walter Ulbricht dies

Aug 1. Walter Ulbricht, former head of state of the German Democratic Republic, died today at his home in Dollnsee after suffering a stroke. The East German leader was 80 years old.

Ulbricht rose to power in 1960, when he assumed the posts of head of state and chair of the National Defense Council. He was responsible for the construction in 1961 of the infamous Berlin Wall, a barrier designed to stem the flow of refugees to the Western sector. Ulbricht was removed from power two years ago, when he was replaced as Secretary of the Socialist Unity Party, having fallen out of favor with the Soviets.

John Ford, master movie maker, dies

Aug 31. Actors called him "Pappy"; he called actors "unborn children." John Ford, the indomitable director, has died in Palm Desert, California. He was 78 years old.

Ford won Oscars for five films out of a lifetime total of 130. The winners were "The Informer," "The Grapes of Wrath," "How Green Was My Valley," "The Quiet Man" and a World War II documentary. No other director won so often. Ironically, although his finest films were westerns, none won him Oscars. "Stagecoach," starring John Wayne, was a vivid, thrilling picture. Equally ironic, Ford, who created red, white and blue movies, was raised in greenest Ireland.

Aug 18. A poll has found 44% "not at all" convinced by Nixon's recent TV address on Watergate; 27% were satisfied. Most say he should turn over tapes, and 58% reject his allegation that civil disobedience led to Watergate.

Streisand is a political activist, Redford the antithesis, but they are in love: "The Way We Were."

1973

SEPTEMBER

Su	Mo	Tu	We	Th	Fr	Sa
						1
2	3	4	5	6	7	8
9	10	11	12	13	14	15
16	17	18	19	20	21	22
23	24	25	26	27	28	29
30						

1. Cairo: Libya to nationalize all foreign oil firms (→ 12/2/79).

3. Saigon imprisons heads of three unions (→ 10/27).

5. L.A.: Ehrlichman, three others indicted for stealing Ellsberg's psychiatric records (→ 6/3/74).

8. Washington: Agnew says worst of Watergate is over (→ 16).

9. New York: John Newcombe, Margaret Court win U.S. Open singles titles.

10. Calif.: Ali wins 12-round decision over Ken Norton (→ 1/28/74).

11. Chile: Allende ousted in military coup; police say he committed suicide (→ 13).

11. New York: West Point ends tradition of giving silent treatment to honor code violators.

12. Cairo: Egypt reopens relations with Jordan (→ 7/21/77).

13. Mediterranean: Israeli and Syrian jets fight major battle; Israel claims 13 MIG's (→ 10/6).

13. Chile: New junta breaks relations with Cuba (→ 17).

15. Sweden: Gustaf dies; crown prince becomes King Carl XVI.

17. IBM guilty in anti-trust suit, told to pay Telex $325.5 million.

17. Chile: Junta to try 5,200 civilians by court-martial (→ 19).

19. Mexico: Mrs. Allende says husband was murdered (→ 21).

20. New York: Willie Mays announces retirement.

21. New York: Jackson Pollock painting sold for $2 million, record for American work.

24. Pacific: Second Skylab crew —Alan Bean, Owen Garriott, Jack Lousma —return from 59-day mission (→ 11/16).

28. New York: Bomb devastates part of Latin American section of ITT building (→ 10/11).

30. Austria, forced by hijackers to bar emigration of Soviet Jews, asks U.S. to share burden of taking immigrants (→ 1/14/75).

DEATH

2. J.R.R. Tolkein, British writer, "Trilogy of the Rings" (*1/3/1892).

Juan Peron elected to presidency again

Juan Peron, in power again after 18 years, this time with wife Isabel.

Sept 23. In a unique political comeback, Juan Peron was elected President of Argentina today. He returns to rule Argentina for the second time, having been ousted from power in 1955 by a military coup. Peron's wife ran with him as Vice President on the Justicialist Liberation Front Party ticket. Isabel Peron is now the first woman vice president in Latin American history. They claim they will embark on a program of social justice and economic freedom (→ 10/9).

Martha says John Mitchell has left

Sept 16. Martha Mitchell said tonight that her husband, once a top aide to President Nixon, has walked out on her. "He walked out, yes," she said. "But I've been trying to get him out. If you've got a man 24 hours a day, I couldn't stand it. He was watching the football games."

John N. Mitchell is under federal indictment on a charge of having obstructed a fraud investigation of Robert L. Vesco, the fugitive financier, in exchange for a secret $200,000 cash contribution to the Nixon 1972 campaign. Mitchell is a former Attorney General and he was a Nixon campaign director.

Mrs. Mitchell also said reports that her husband had been trying to get her to undergo psychiatric care were "a goddamned lie." She said that they never even had a fight (→ 10/12).

1973

OCTOBER

Su	Mo	Tu	We	Th	Fr	Sa
	1	2	3	4	5	6
7	8	9	10	11	12	13
14	15	16	17	18	19	20
21	22	23	24	25	26	27
28	29	30	31			

Chile coup ousts Allende, leaving him dead

Sept 21. Chilean President Salvador Allende Gossens was brutally killed in a violent takeover of the government by Chile's armed forces earlier this month, and now the Marxist leader's wife believes the United States sponsored the coup.

Declaring devout dedication to freeing Chile "from the Marxist yoke," a military junta, led by General Augusto Pinochet Ugarte, captured the presidential palace, killed Allende and proclaimed a state of siege. Initial reports indicated Allende committed suicide. Yet, based on new information, Mrs. Allende is convinced her husband was murdered, and she feels America financed and helped plan the coup. "We often heard the (U.S.) State Department did not want Allende in power," she said. "Financial interests always predominate." Allende had seized the property of several U.S. corporations which had previously profited.

Elected president in 1970, Allende vowed to turn the nation to socialism within a democratic framework. However, growing opposition from the middle class, propelled by anti-Marxist military leaders, barricaded his path. In his last speech, he asserted he would not resign, even at the cost of his life; he would teach a "lesson in the ignominious history of those with strength but no reason" (→ 28).

Chilean troops, said to have U.S. backing, control the streets of Santiago.

Sept 20. Woman has triumphed in "the battle of the sexes." King over Riggs in straight sets.

Two great poets, Auden and Neruda

Sept 28. Englishman W.H. Auden died tonight in Vienna, only five days after the death of Chilean Pablo Neruda. Neruda won the Nobel Prize in 1971; Auden won every other honor available, including the Pulitzer in 1948. Both poets were prolific until their deaths, at age 66 and 69 respectively. Neruda, recently Ambassador to France, was a fervent leftist. Auden denied serious socialist leanings, but at least one poem he wrote in the 1930's chafed against the rise of fascism: "In the nightmare of the dark/All the dogs of Europe bark,/And the living nations wait,/Each sequestered in its hate."

1. Houston: Leo Durocher to retire from baseball.

3. Boston: Six blacks burn white woman to death (→ 3/26/74).

6. Mideast: Egypt crosses Suez, Syria attacks Golan Heights in worst fighting since 1967 (→ 7).

7. Sinai: Israel launches counterattack (→ 9).

9. Syria: Israeli jets hit Damascus; 100 civilians killed (→ 11).

9. Argentina: Fourth labor leader assassinated since Peron's election (→ 6/29/74).

10. New York: Miro exhibit opens at MOMA.

11. Chile: 2,000 reported killed since junta took power (→ 14).

11. Israeli troops push six miles across Syrian border (→ 13).

13. Jordan begins moving troops into Syria (→ 15).

14. Chile bans seven parties that supported Allende (→ 11/11).

15. U.S. supplying Israel to offset Soviet arms to Arabs (→ 22).

15. Thailand: Students oust military govt. leaders in exile.

19. Washington: Nixon rejects Appeals Court demand to turn over Watergate tapes (→ 20).

20. Nixon fires Cox as special prosecutor; congressional leaders talk of impeachment (→ 22).

21. Oakland: A's beat Mets 5-2 in final game of World Series.

22. Washington: AFL-CIO votes to ask Nixon resignation (→ 23).

23. Paris: Le Duc Tho rejects Nobel Peace Prize, citing situation in Vietnam.

25. U.S. puts military on world alert in Mideast conflict (→ 27).

26. California: Alcatraz opened to public.

27. Saigon: Viet Cong say U.S. keeps 20,000 military in Vietnam in civilian guise (→ 2/21/74).

28. Toronto: Secretariat wins last race of career.

DEATHS

2. Paavo Nurmi, Finnish long-distance runner (*6/13/1897).

22. Pablo Casals, Spanish cellist (*12/29/1899).

Agnew resigns; Ford is chosen to succeed

Agnew, the day after his resignation.

Oct 12. Spiro Agnew resigned as Vice President after agreeing not to contest a government charge of income tax evasion. President Nixon immediately nominated Gerald R. Ford, the 60-year-old Republican leader of the House, to succeed Agnew as vice president.

Under an agreement with the Justice Department to avoid imprisonment, Agnew pleaded no contest to a government charge that he had failed to report $29,500 of income in 1967 while he was Governor of Maryland. Heeding a Justice Department plea that "leniency is justified," Federal District Judge Walter E. Hoffman fined Agnew $10,000 and sentenced him to three years probation.

Under the recently adopted 25th Amendment, the Ford nomination must be approved by both houses of Congress. He is expected to be quickly confirmed (→ 19).

Ford joins an ailing administration. ▷

Yom Kippur attack surprises Israel

Egyptian tanks crossed the Suez Canal and captured most of the east bank.

Oct 22. The heaviest fighting since 1967 erupted in the Middle East this month, and for a short period of time the Egyptians and Syrians were able to batter the invincible Israeli war machine. They launched a surprise attack on the 6th in the middle of Yom Kippur, the most religious holiday of the year. Egyptian forces crossed the Suez Canal and quickly controlled most of the eastern bank. Syrian artillery attacked in the Golan Heights, and Syria said its forces recaptured Mount Hermon for the first time since 1967.

Israel acted quickly to mobilize its ground forces, but it was the air force that prevented an Arab rout. Israeli jets struck deep into Syria and Egypt on the 7th. They scored their biggest successes along the Suez Canal, where they knocked out nine bridges Egypt had constructed. Some 400 Egyptian tanks were trapped on the east bank.

As more Israeli soldiers rushed to the two fronts, Egypt and Syria were pushed back to the 1967 cease-fire lines. Fierce fighting raged in the Golan Heights, and Israel attacked again with punishing air raids. Syria charged that 100 civilians were killed in a raid on Damascus. Iraq and Jordan rushed to assist Syria, but Israeli forces broke out of the Heights and began advancing on Damascus.

President Nixon and Soviet leader Brezhnev exchanged messages on the fighting. Secretary of State Kissinger flew to Moscow for meetings. The United Nations called for a cease-fire. Israeli Premier Golda Meir rejected a truce on the 16th, saying, the enemy had not been "beaten enough."

In the next few days, the premier changed her mind about Egypt. A cease-fire went into effect tonight along the Egyptian front. Fighting continues in Syria (→ 11/6).

Saturday Night Massacre: Three legal eagles shot down by Nixon

Oct 23. President Nixon, faced with possible impeachment, agreed today to turn over Watergate tapes. But in the aftermath of what has been dubbed "the Saturday Night Massacre," his troubles appear far from over.

Controversy over release of the tape recordings of conversations with White House aides concerning the break-in of Democratic offices last year had led to the president's abrupt dismissal Saturday night of his special Watergate prosecutor, Archibald Cox, who felt that the tapes were essential evidence in the case.

Cox, out as special prosecutor.

That same night, Attorney General Elliot Richardson resigned after having refused the president's demand that he fire Cox. President Nixon then discharged William D. Ruckelshouse, the Deputy Attorney General, who also refused to fire Cox.

The dramatic exodus of top Nixon legal officials prompted renewed calls by some members of Congress for an inquiry into the possible impeachment of Nixon.

The demand that the president turn over the crucial tapes had been made by both the U.S. Court of Appeals and by a special Senate panel investigating the Watergate affair. Until today, Nixon had said he would turn over only edited summaries of the tapes.

Ex-Attorney General Richardson.

But today, faced with a possible contempt citation from Judge John J. Sirica, the president reversed his decision after what he termed "very painful and anguished discussions" with advisers, including his chief of staff, General Alexander M. Haig. The general said that there had been much "misinformation" (→ 11/1).

Nixon places troops on worldwide alert

Oct 27. Detente between the United States and the Soviet Union seemed to evaporate as both sides traded vituperative charges about the military alert called by President Nixon on Thursday. Nixon explained yesterday that he had believed the Soviets were sending "a very substantial force" to the Middle East. It was reported the Russians might try to assist the thousands of Egyptian soldiers trapped behind Israeli lines. Tass replied today that Nixon's explanation was "absurd" and designed to "intimidate the Soviet Union." After ordering the alert, Nixon postponed a news conference where he was to explain his actions in the Watergate tapes controversy (→ 11/7).

Arabs' non-friends suffer oil embargo

Oct 21. An Arab embargo on oil shipments to the United States became complete today when four Persian Gulf nations joined all the other Middle East oil-producing countries who are protesting America's support of Israel. Saudi Arabia and other leaders of the embargo also said they would cut production and sales steadily until Israel evacuated the land it captured in the 1967 war. Countries that assist the Arab cause will not suffer from the sales cuts, the Arabs said (→ 11/8).

That drumming man Gene Krupa is gone

Oct 16. Gene Krupa, the first jazz drummer to become a star in his own right, died yesterday at his Yonkers home. He was 64 and had suffered the past ten years from benign leukemia. Krupa began with the Benny Goodman band but later formed his own. Those who ever saw him will remember the electric vision of a man possessed, hunched over his drums, sweat dripping, sticks hammering with machine-gun speed. The roar that followed was as loud as the drumming, and thanks to Krupa drum solos became standard fare.

1973

NOVEMBER

Su	Mo	Tu	We	Th	Fr	Sa
				1	2	3
4	5	6	7	8	9	10
11	12	13	14	15	16	17
18	19	20	21	22	23	24
25	26	27	28	29	30	

1. Nixon names Leon Jaworski special prosecutor, William Saxbe attorney general (→ 26).

3. Barcelona: 113 anti-France leaders arrested (→ 12/29).

6. Tel Aviv: Israel reports 1,854 killed in war; 1,800 injured (→ 7).

6. New York: Abraham Beame elected 104th N.Y. mayor.

7. Washington: House and Senate override Nixon veto of curb on war powers.

7. Cairo: U.S., Egypt announce resumption of ties, severed since war in 1967 (→ 11).

8. N.J.: Tollway speed limits reduced to 50 mph to save fuel (→ 27).

11. Geneva: Soviets kicked out of World Cup soccer for refusing to play Chile (→ 3/11/76).

11. Egypt and Israel sign cease-fire agreement (→ 1/5/74).

13. Gulf and Ashland Oil Co. plead guilty to charges of illegal gifts to Nixon campaign (→ 26).

15. London: Eight I.R.A. members given life sentences for London bombings (→ 22).

16. Cape Kennedy: Skylab 3 astronauts dock with Skylab, begin 84-day mission (→ 29).

16. New York: Peter Max holds sixties reunion party.

17. Greece imposes martial law to quell student revolt (→ 25).

19. New York: Stock market takes sharpest drop in 19 years.

19. Cambodia: Lon Nol's palace bombed by Air Force fighter plane (→ 12/26).

20. Australia: 12 on rafts cross Pacific in 17 days.

22. Britain announces plan for moderate Protestants and Catholics to share power in Northern Ireland (→ 12/9).

24. Australia grants vote to Aborigines.

27. Washington: Nixon signs Emergency Petroleum Allocation Act of 1973 (→ 30).

29. Pioneer 10 reports Jupiter's magnetism 40 times greater than earth's (→ 12/3).

29. Japan: Department store fire kills 100.

Military coup in Greece; curfew in effect

Students, linked arm in arm, march in protest down the streets of Athens.

Nov 25. President George Papadopoulos of Greece was ousted today in a military coup. The president was put under house arrest and replaced by Lieut. Gen. Phaidon Gizikis, who was an active participant in the 1967 coup. Premier Spyros Markezinis was dismissed and other supporters of Papadopoulos were purged.

Leaders of the coup said they had acted to save Greece from "chaos and catastrophe." They are known to believe Papadopoulos was moving too quickly to restore democracy. The military leaders have also blamed him for recent violent demonstrations by students and workers. A 24-hour curfew has been put into effect (→ 7/23/74).

Nixon orders oil measures; gas prices rise

Nov 30. Leading American oil companies today announced large gasoline price increases on the eve of anticipated widespread closing of service stations throughout the country. President Nixon has asked gas stations to close voluntarily on Sundays as one measure to reduce oil consumption in response to the oil embargo imposed by Arab nations. Nixon has also ordered a cutback in home heating oil deliveries, a 15 percent cut in gas production and a lowering of speed limits to 50 mph for cars to help conserve oil.

The gas price increases announced today ranged from 2 to 3.2 cents a gallon and are expected to push the retail price of gasoline over 50 cents a gallon for the most expensive grades.

Nixon acted under authority given him by an oil allocation law he had long opposed but which he signed when the embargo became effective. He said the measures he proposed would cut the expected shortage of oil from 17 percent of the nation's needs to 7 percent. Officials say Americans must cut gasoline consumption, a goal they hope to reach without rationing (→ 12/2).

Nixon's secretary admits spoiling tape

Nov 26. President Nixon's personal secretary, Rose Mary Woods, testified today that through some "terrible mistake" she had caused an 18-minute "gap" in one of the Watergate tape recordings.

Testifying in federal court, Miss Woods said she had pressed the wrong button on her tape recorder. She said she told the president of her

Woods: "Accidental" erasures?

error minutes after it occurred last Oct. 1 and that he assured her it did not matter, that it was not one of the subpoenaed tapes. But it turned out to be one of those tapes subpoenaed in the ongoing inquiry into the break-in at the Democratic national headquarters last year. The partially erased tape had recorded a conversation of the president and a key aide, H.R. Haldeman, three days after the break-in (→ 1/15/74).

Nov 14. Princess Anne and Capt. Mark Phillips wed in London ceremony.

1973

DECEMBER

Su	Mo	Tu	We	Th	Fr	Sa
						1
2	3	4	5	6	7	8
9	10	11	12	13	14	15
16	17	18	19	20	21	22
23	24	25	26	27	28	29
30	31					

1. Philadelphia: Army routs Navy 51-0 in football.

1. Cleveland: Australia takes Davis Cup away from U.S.

2. U.S.: 99% of gas stations close voluntarily to save fuel (→ 6).

2. Calif.: Mass murderer Juan Corona stabbed 32 times in jail.

9. Britain, Ireland reach accord; Northern Ireland to get coalition govt. with Protestants and Catholics (→ 3/13/74).

10. Kissinger, Le Duc Tho share Nobel Peace Prize.

13. Britain cuts work week to three days to save energy supply.

17. Rome: Arab guerrillas kill 31 on U.S. jetliner, fly to Athens with hostages.

23. Washington: Kissinger reported taking full control of U.S. foreign policy.

25. Skylab astronauts take seven-hour walk, photograph comet Kohoutek (→ 2/8/74).

26. Cambodia: Long Boret appointed premier (→ 1/9/74).

28. Paris: Solzhenitsyn's "Gulag Archipelago" out (→ 1/2/74).

30. Peru nationalizes U.S.-owned mining concern.

CULTURAL EVENTS, 1973

Literature: Erica Jong's "Fear of Flying"; Lillian Hellman's "Pentimento"; Gore Vidal's "Burr"; Vonnegut's "Breakfast of Champions"; Grass' "From the Diary of a Snail."

Academia: Frances Fitzgerald's "Fire in the Lake"; David Halberstam's "The Best and the Brightest"; bone tool found in Yukon, dating human life to 27,000 B.C. in New World.

Music: Britten's "Death in Venice"; Roberta Flack's "Killing Me Softly with His Song"; Marvin Gaye's "Let's Get it On"; Stevie Wonder's "You Are the Sunshine of My Life"; Tony Orlando and Dawn's "Tie a Yellow Ribbon 'Round the Old Oak Tree."

Film: Woody Allen's "Sleeper"; Bertolucci's "Last Tango in Paris," Brando; "The Sting," Academy Award; "A Touch of Class," Glenda Jackson; "Save the Tiger," Jack Lemmon.

Oil embargo causes acute economic trouble

Dec 31. The Arab oil embargo has led to plans for gas rationing in the United States, crippling oil price increases for industrialized and Third World countries and a three-day work week in Great Britain.

The disruption caused by the embargo has led the British government to announce it was shifting from a goal of economic growth to one of survival. It said the oil shortage made the three-day week necessary despite its dire effects on British industry.

In the U.S., Federal Energy Director William Simon has announced a standby gas rationing program that would limit most motorists to about eight gallons a week. He has called for self-rationing to prevent a formal program. Prices in the U.S. already have risen $1 a barrel for crude oil, and decisions announced by oil-producing nations will lead to a 60-80 percent increase.

Most oil-producing nations have posted prices over $10 a barrel. The highest price, $18.77 a barrel, has been posted by Libya. The increases are expected to have the most serious effects on development efforts of the poorer countries (→ 1/2/74).

Psychiatrists say homosexuality not illness

Dec 15. The American Psychiatric Association has just approved a resolution calling for "civil rights legislation ... that would ensure homosexual citizens the same protections guaranteed to others." The association adopted this proposal after nearly a hundred years of classifying homosexuality as a mental illness. The group now believes that "by itself, homosexuality does not meet the criteria for being a psychiatric disorder."

In Washington today the association redefined "sexual orientation disturbance" as applying to "individuals whose sexual interests are directed toward people of their own sex and who are either disturbed by, in conflict with or wish to change their sexual orientation."

Psychiatrists hope homosexuals with problems unrelated to their sexual orientation will now seek help, knowing doctors will not try to modify their sexual inclinations. The National Gay Task force lauds the resolutions (→ 3/1974).

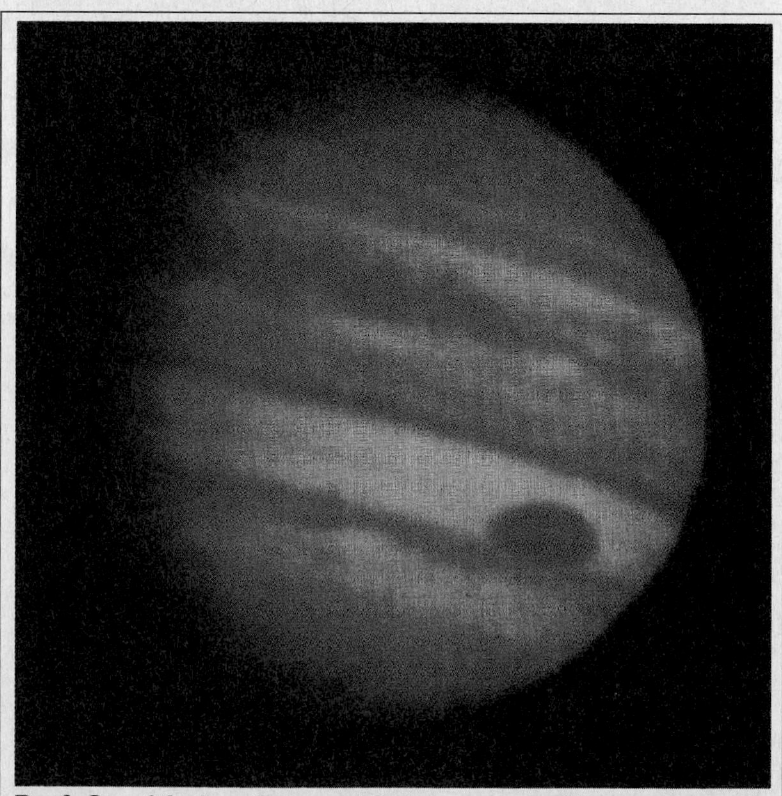

Dec 3. One of the first close-ups of Jupiter, courtesy of Pioneer 10 (→ 25).

Getty heir freed; oil executive still held

Paul Getty walks free after release.

Dec 14. John Paul Getty III, grandson of the American oil tycoon, has been freed after six months of captivity at the hands of kidnappers in Italy. At one point, they cut off the young man's right ear and sent it through the mail. The ransom was about $750,000.

Meanwhile, in Argentina, a $10 million ransom will be paid for the release of a kidnapped oil executive. Exxon agrees to pay the sum in exchange for the safe return of American Victor S. Samuelson, who was seized nearly a week ago at a refinery outside Buenos Aires.

The guerrillas want the ransom spent on food, clothes and building materials to be distributed in poor Argentine communities. They explain the act is "a partial reimbursement to the Argentine people for the copious riches extracted from our country by the company in long years of imperialist exploitation."

O.J. Simpson sets year's rushing mark

Dec 16. O.J. Simpson of Buffalo became the first pro football player ever to rush more than 2,000 yards in a season. Four other players topped the 1,000-yard mark. The offensive surge by runners has been credited to the increasing use of zone defenses, which discourage long passes. There is no telling how many more yards Jim Brown of the Cleveland Browns might have gained under the increased use of the zone defense. Brown, who retired after 1965, was the rushing leader from 1957 through 1961 and 1963 through 1965.

Spain's Premier victim of Basque blast

Dec 29. Nine days have passed since the Premier of Spain was killed by a powerful bomb explosion in Madrid. No arrests have been made in the case, but the regime of Generalissimo Francisco Franco indicated again today that it will deal harshly with the Basque separatists who have been linked to the murder. Franco appointed Interior Minister Carlos Arias Navarro to succeed the late Luis Carrero Blanco as Premier. Arias, a former prosecutor and police official, is a strong advocate of law and order.

Franco's government also showed in the courts that it will strike back firmly at political dissidents. Ten labor leaders were given prison sentences of up to 20 years. The defendants were accused of running labor commissions that have ties to the Communist Party.

Spanish authorities say the six Basques who killed Carrero Blanco hid a bomb in a tunnel beneath a Madrid street. The bomb exploded when he emerged from church. Spanish police have sealed the border with France in an attempt to prevent the Basque suspects from leaving the country (→ 7/19/74).

Past and future are present in 1973 movies

Woody Allen in "Sleeper."

Newman and Redford: "The Sting."

Max von Sydow in "The Exorcist."

People are vaguely dissatisfied with the present day, if the settings of 1973 films are any indication.

In "Sleeper," Woody Allen plays a frozen 20th-Century man thawed in the future. He escapes mad scientists by dressing as a robot and dallying with Diane Keaton.

In "The Sting," director George Roy Hill again pairs Robert Redford and Paul Newman, so popular in "Butch Cassidy and the Sundance Kid." Now they're considerate con men operating in Chicago in the 30's. Their scams are set against a Scott Joplin ragtime score.

"The Exorcist" harkens to a simpler age when there was no mental illness, just Satan butting into minds. Max Von Sydow plays a priest succoring the possessed Linda Blair. William Friedkin directs.

"American Graffiti" recalls 1962 with hot rods and newborn rock tunes. George Lucas directs Richard Dreyfuss and Ron Howard.

"The Way We Were" is a real weeper. Barbra Streisand and Robert Redford star in a love story stretching from the 30's to the 50's. Sydney Pollack ("Jeremiah Johnson") directs. And "Paper Moon" shines on Tatum O'Neal and her father Ryan as petty Depression-era crooks. Peter Bogdanovich directs. Tatum is a nine-year-old who doesn't look a day over ten. Apparently time has been kind to her.

Ben Gurion, first Israeli Premier, is dead

Ben Gurion, father of Jewish state.

Dec 1. David Ben Gurion, modern Israel's first Premier and one of its founding fathers, died in Tel Aviv today from a brain hemorrhage at the age of 87. A Zionist guerrilla fighter in his youth, Ben Gurion's later years were devoted to study, writing, correspondence and the study of languages. Though he had little formal education, he was a serious student of the Bible. At 56, he learned Greek so that he could read the Greek version of the Old Testament, and at the age of 68 he began studying Sanskrit better to understand the dialogues of Buddha. Throughout his life, he professed socialist, Zionist ideals.

High tech has come to downtown Manhattan in the form of the twin towers of the World Trade Center, completed this year at a cost of $750 million. The towers are 110 stories high, making the structure second only to Chicago's Sears Tower, which will be 104 feet higher—the tallest building in the world—when it is completed some time next year.

Arab states taking money out of West

Dec 6. The Arab "money war" with the United States promises to heat up as economists at the Cairo meeting of the Arab League have agreed on a "gradual withdrawal" of funds from Western banks to fund Arab development projects. In total funds the Arabs hold on deposit in Western banks the equivalent of about $10 billion, $1.5 billion of which is in British pounds. With a report that the Arabs were selling pounds as well as dollars, London stocks took their worst losses since World War II. A Western economist mitigated the gloom by observing that "the Arabs have a monopoly on oil, but we have a monopoly on where they invest their money" (→ 13).

After 21 years with the Giants and one with the Mets, Willie Mays has retired with 660 home runs, 3,283 hits, one Rookie of the Year and two MVP awards.

1974

JANUARY

Su	Mo	Tu	We	Th	Fr	Sa
		1	2	3	4	5
6	7	8	9	10	11	12
13	14	15	16	17	18	19
20	21	22	23	24	25	26
29	28	29	30	31		

1. Pasadena: Ohio State routs U.S.C. 42-21 in Rose Bowl.

2. Nixon signs bill for 55 mph ceiling on speed limit (→ 23).

2. Moscow calls Solzhenitsyn's "Gulag Archipelago" slander (→ 2/12).

4. Laguna Beach, Calif.: Nixon rejects subpoenas for 500 tapes and papers (→ 15).

5. Kissinger and Israeli Def. Min. Moshe Dayan end two days of talks (→ 17).

8. Seoul: Pres. Park bans opposition to constitution in response to rising discontent (→ 8/15).

9. Cambodia: Govt. troops open drive to avert insurgent attack on Phnom Penh (→ 2/2).

11. New York: Blue Cross and Blue Shield announce merger plans.

11. U.S.: Susan and Colin Rosenkowitz give birth to sextuplets.

13. U.S. eliminated from Davis Cup in earliest defeat ever.

15. Washington: Experts tell Sirica 18-minute gap in Watergate tape due to erasures (→ 23).

15. Associated Press names Billie Jean King female athlete of the year.

16. U.S.: "Jaws" by Peter Benchley is published.

17. Egypt, Israel reach accord on separation of Suez forces, opening of canal (→ 2/18).

19. Chinese troops seize Paracel Islands from South Vietnam.

21. U.S. Supreme Court rules pregnant teachers can't be forced to take long leaves (→ 8/22).

25. Cape Town: Dr. Christiaan Barnard transplants first human heart without removal of old one (→ 12/27/82).

28. New York: Ali outpoints Joe Frazier in non-title bout at Madison Sq. Garden (→ 3/26).

DEATHS

1. Charles Bohlen, U.S. diplomat, expert on Soviet Union (*8/30/1904).

25. U Thant, Burmese educator, third secretary general of U.N. (*1/22/1909).

Women moving into business mainstream

Jan 20. Despite obstacles, American women are reaching the higher rungs of the corporate ladder.

Women won't hack it, some male executives said. They won't go on business trips or relocate, they said. They won't learn the business lingo, run with the ball or be a team player. They won't swear or be sweared at, they said. But damn it! They do.

Legislation makes it happen. In 1964, Title 7 of the Civil Rights Act forbade sex discrimination in the workplace. Longtime secretaries finally got promoted. The Equal Opportunity Commission, which received enforcement powers in March 1972, has been taking noncomplying companies to court, forcing AT&T to give $38 million in back pay to women and minorities.

And individuals are suing. In the last fiscal year, 24,300 complaints were filed against companies. Corporations are now rushing to hire members of the aggrieved groups to fend off potential litigation.

White female job seekers often compete with black men. For reasons not too clear, many women are promoted over black men in brokerage and banking institutions. Black women should have the best opportunities, but many are reporting a sad isolation at their jobs.

Women are advancing. Can they reach the top? Says an oil company manager: "The United States will have a woman President before (our) company does" (→ 21).

Bangladesh has 7 born every minute

Jan 29. Seven babies are born each minute in Bangladesh, 10,000 a day. The populatlon of 75 million is expected to double in two decades in the eighth most populous nation in the world with the highest population density: more than 1,300 per square mile. Three years after the creation of this impoverished nation out of a wing of Pakistan, the population explosion is its most crucial problem. Fatalistically, people have many children, expecting several to die. The World Bank plans a multimillion dollar health center project. The United States is expected to make a grant of about $3 million, mostly for contraceptives (→ 2/22).

Exxon is profiting from the oil embargo

Jan 23. Exxon Corporation, the world's largest oil company, yesterday reported a profit increase of 59 percent for the 1973 fourth quarter, when the Arab oil embargo against the United States was imposed. "I am not embarrassed," said J.K. Jamieson, Exxon's Chairman. The company was criticized by Senator Henry Jackson, who said it had cut supplies to U.S. armed forces on orders of Saudi Arabia during the crisis. Jackson described the action as a "flagrant case of corporate disloyalty to the United States government" (→ 2/11).

As high prices fatten returns, investment in exploration is sure to rise.

Experts find five erasures on tape

Jan 23. A court-appointed panel of experts reported that a 18-and-a-half-minute gap on a key Watergate tape was caused by five separate erasures and not by accident, as the White House has contended. The tape, recording a conversation between President Nixon and H.R. Haldeman, White House chief of staff, in which the president ordered a public relations offensive in the Watergate case, had been subpoenaed by the special Watergate prosecutor (→ 2/6).

Jan 13. Manny Fernandez blocks a Tarkenton pass to help the Dolphins to their second straight Super Bowl in a 24-7 win over Minnesota.

Picture pioneer Sam Goldwyn dies at 91

Jan 31. Film producer Samuel Goldwyn has died in Los Angeles. He was 91. Goldwyn oversaw the details of many Oscar-caliber pictures, including "The Best Years of Our Lives" and "Guys and Dolls."

Goldwyn's malapropisms were famous. It seems unlikely, however, he ever said, "I'll tell you in two words: im - possible!" —an expression credited to him. For how could a man who was born in Warsaw, emigrated to America at age 13 without a dime, became a rich glove manufacturer, started a film company with a brother-in-law as naive as himself, who made movies until he was 78, call anything impossible?

1974

FEBRUARY

Su	Mo	Tu	We	Th	Fr	Sa
					1	2
3	4	5	6	7	8	9
10	11	12	13	14	15	16
17	18	19	20	21	22	23
24	25	26	27	28		

1. Sao Paulo: 170 die as fire wrecks Brazilian office building.

2. Cairo: Sadat ousts powerful Mohammed Hassanein Heykal as top Egyptian editor (→ 4/18).

2. Nixon tells Cambodian Premier Lon Nol U.S. will provide maximum possible aid (→ 11).

4. Peking: Mao proclaims new cultural revolution (→ 10/31).

5. Berkeley: Patty Hearst kidnapped at gunpoint by white woman, two black men (→ 12).

6. House votes 410-4 to give judiciary committee broad powers to investigate Nixon (→ 3/1).

8. U.S.: Skylab 3 astronauts Gerald Carr, Edward Gibson, William Pogue return from record 84-day trip (→ 3/29).

9. Britain: 269,000 miners begin strike over wage dispute (→ 3/6).

10. Iranian, Iraqi troops clash on border; 70 dead (→ 3/6/75).

12. Berkeley: Symbionese Liberation Army asks Hearsts for $230 mil. in food for poor (→ 18).

12. Moscow: Solzhenitsyn arrested by Soviet police (→ 15).

15. U.S.: Gas stations threaten to close in protest over federal fuel policies (→ 3/13).

17. Florida: Richard Petty wins Daytona 500.

18. Washington: Kissinger gets four-nation Arab plan for truce in Golan Heights (→ 23).

18. S.F.: Randolph Hearst to give $2 mil. in free food to open talks for his daughter (→ 23).

20. U.S.S.R. offers visas to Solzhenitsyn family without barring citizenship (→ 3/29).

21. Washington: Report claims U.S. use of defoliants has scarred Vietnam for century (→ 3/22).

22. Pakistan extends recognition to Bangladesh (→ 1/25/75).

23. New York: Moslem nations at U.N. denounce U.S. support for Israel, demand withdrawal from occupied territory (→ 4/6).

26. Ethiopia: Dissident troops seize Asmara, second largest city (→ 28).

28. Ethiopia: Selassie names new premier in attempt to placate mutinous army troops (→ 9/12).

Daughter of publisher Hearst is abducted

Feb 23. Ransom demands spiral ever higher for the release of Patty Hearst, daughter of millionaire publisher Randolph Hearst. Today, the Symbionese Liberation Army, her captors, demanded $4 million worth of foodstuffs be distributed to the poor in exchange for her release. Hearst, who spent $2 million on a similar demand a week ago, vows to seriously consider the request.

Patty Hearst, a 19-year-old art student at the University of California at Berkeley, was kidnapped from her apartment Feb. 4 by two black men and a white woman. They have since been identified as members of the Symbionese Liberation Army, a leftist group intent on redistributing America's power and wealth. The SLA was linked to the murder of a prominent black school superintendent in Oakland Nov. 6.

Hearst has received several taped messages from his daughter. She assures him she is unharmed but is a "prisoner of war," not unlike, she adds, two SLA members who are now in a federal prison (→ 3/3).

Kidnapped: Patty Hearst.

Soviet Union expels author Solzhenitsyn

Feb 15. Soviet author Aleksandr I. Solzhenitsyn arrived in Switzerland today following his expulsion from the U.S.S.R. two days ago. The Nobel Prize-winning writer was banished from his home country as a result of the publication of his huge new work on the Soviet prison system, "The Gulag Archipelago, 1918-1986." With almost no warning, the 55-year-old Solzhenitsyn was issued a decree demanding his exile to West Germany. He has continued on to Zurich where he was offered political asylum. This follows a long history of dissidence, including an 11-year prison term (→ 20).

Solzhenitsyn arrives in Zurich.

Gasoline shortage gets worse than ever

Feb 11. A "gasoline gap" caused by exhaustion of January allocations and blocked deliveries of the February supply because of a drivers' strike has caused the worst day of the energy crisis for motorists, federal officials say.

In the New York area, more than half the service stations were closed for lack of gasoline, with lines up to six miles long at open stations.

Panic buying has been eased by adoption of a plan that limits gasoline sales to odd-numbered days for cars whose plates end in odd numbers and even-numbered days for even plates. The plan, mandatory in New Jersey, has been adopted voluntarily in New York, Massachusetts and other states. Many stations are limiting purchases to $2 or $3 per automobile. Word that February allocations will be even lower than January's has caused some motorists to spend hours in line for a few gallons of gas (→ 15).

Insurgents mow down 139 in Cambodia

Slaughter in Phnom Penh.

Feb 11. Communist-led rebels showered artillery fire into a crowded section of Phnom Penh today, killing 139 and wounding 46. The bloody shelling in the Cambodian capital came after an eight-day lull in this nation's civil war; it was the heaviest attack in almost two years. Officials estimate 73 bombs were launched in the half-hour midday barrage. Fast, dry winds swept flames from the explosions onto the wooden, brittle houses in the rather poor district of the city. Before firefighters could control the flames, nearly a quarter-mile section of the neighborhood had been severely burned (→ 1/4/75).

Stolen 'copter lands at the White House

Feb 17. A crazed soldier stole an Army helicopter today, zoomed from Fort Meade, Md., to Washington D.C., and landed in a barrage of shotgun fire 100 yards from the White House. Private Robert Pearson swiped the aircraft from his Fort Meade base and out-raced a Maryland state police helicopter. He hovered near the Washington Monument, and then headed directly toward the White House before Executive Protection Service agents fired at the craft, forced it down and wrestled Pearson to the ground. He was taken to a mental hospital for psychiatric care.

1974

MARCH

Su	Mo	Tu	We	Th	Fr	Sa
					1	2
3	4	5	6	7	8	9
10	11	12	13	14	15	16
17	18	19	20	21	22	23
24	25	26	27	28	29	30
31						

1. Washington: Grand jury indicts seven Nixon aides for conspiracy on Watergate (→ 2).

2. Washington: Grand jury concludes Nixon involved in Watergate cover-up (→ 15).

4. London: Harold Wilson, after Labor victory in natl. elections, takes over as premier (→ 10/11).

6. London: Miners end strike, getting 35% pay raise.

7. N.C.: USS Monitor, Civil War boat sunk in first battle of iron-clad warships, located off coast.

7. Washington: Cardinals testify on abortion, ask amendment to protect fetus (→ 2/15/75).

10. Jerusalem: Golda Meir re-elected Israeli premier (→ 4/10).

13. U.S. Senate votes 54-33 to restore death penalty (→ 5/17).

13. Arab nations decide to end oil embargo on U.S. (→ 16).

13. Dublin: Premier Cosgrave, in landmark declaration, acknowledges N. Ireland as province under British control (→ 4/20).

15. Washington: Federal judge orders U.S. to stop paying for sterilization of children and mentally incompetent.

16. Vienna: 12 oil exporting nations reject reduction of crude oil prices (→ 19).

22. Johannesburg: Racing driver Peter Revson dies in auto crash.

22. Viet Cong propose new truce, general elections (→ 5/18).

26. Washington: House votes to bar courts from ordering busing to end segregation (→ 9/3).

26. Caracas: George Foreman keeps boxing title, stopping Ken Norton in second (→ 10/29).

27. U.S.: "The Great Gatsby" premieres, starring Robert Redford and Mia Farrow.

29. Cleveland: Grand jury indicts Natl. Guard members in Kent State shootings (→ 9/16).

29. Mariner 10 takes first close-ups of Mercury (→ 8/27).

29. Zurich: Sohlzhenitsyn and family reunited (→ 9/15).

DEATH

4. Adolph Gottlieb, American painter (*3/4/1903).

Nixon named co-conspirator in Watergate

Nixon, on the defensive.

March 15. A federal grand jury has concluded that President Nixon joined in a conspiracy to cover up White House involvement in the Watergate break-in of Democratic Party offices.

The finding that Nixon was a co-conspirator in the Watergate cover-up was contained in a sealed report from the grand jury, which issued conspiracy indictments against seven former White House and Nixon re-election campaign officials. The report was given to Federal Judge John J.Sirica with the recommendation that it be shown to the House Judiciary Committee, which is considering impeachment proceedings against the president.

In a speech before business executives in Chicago, Nixon declared that he would not resign because that would be a "cop-out" and weaken the presidency. "It would lead to weak and unstable presidencies in the future," he said, "and I will not be a party to the destruction of the presidency of the United States of America" (→ 4/3).

Oil embargo lifted; prices remain high

March 19. A ban on Sunday gasoline sales and other restrictions on oil use will be lifted because of the end of the Arab embargo, President Nixon has announced. Arab oil-producing nations agreed three days ago to end their embargo on sales to the United States but rejected a reduction in crude oil prices. Saudi Arabia argued at a meeting of the Organization of Petroleum Exporting Countries for a cut in prices, up by more than 300 percent since the embargo began, but most other nations called for an increase. OPEC's members will earn more than $100 billion this year because of the price increases (→ 1/21/77).

Hearsts appeal to daughter's kidnappers

March 3. Randolph and Catherine Hearst pleaded for their daughter's release this afternoon, nearly one month since she was abducted and ten days since her last message. Patty Hearst was kidnapped in Berkeley February 4 by a leftist organization calling itself the Symbionese Liberation Army. The group makes ever-increasing demands, the latest of which Hearst says he will reject until his daughter is released. At their Hillsborough, California, home, Mr. and Mrs. Hearst faced television cameras and begged for a reassuring word. "Patty, we kind of missed you on your birthday," Hearst said. Miss Hearst turned 20 three weeks ago (→ 4/3).

Worried Hearst parents in S.F.

345 killed as jumbo jet falls in Paris

March 3. A Turkish DC-10 jumbo jet plunged into a forest 26 miles from Paris today, killing all 345 persons aboard. It was the worst disaster in aviation history. Turkish officials said the cause of the crash was unknown but sabotage could not be ruled out. They said some passengers might have been guerrillas who carried bombs on board the aircraft. The three-engine jetliner was fully loaded when it took off for London from Orly Airport. It crashed only a few minutes later. The wreckage of the plane and the bodies of its passengers were strewn in a half-mile valley of pine trees near the town of Senlis. The death toll was almost double that of the worst previous crash.

Chet Huntley, popular news anchor, is dead

Worldwatcher Chet Huntley.

March 20. Chet Huntley, who as a co-anchor helped introduce America to television network news, died today of cancer at the age of 62. Beginning in 1956, Huntley, a rangy Westerner, teamed up with David Brinkley, a droll Easterner, to co-anchor NBC's Nightly News. Their conclusion of "Good night, David—Good night, Chet," became familiar to millions of Americans. His last good night came in 1970 when he retired and returned to his native Montana, where he was preparing to dedicate a $25 million recreational complex called Big Sky.

DC-10 remains litter the forest.

Sol Hurok, great impresario, is gone

March 5. Sol Hurok, the famed impresario whose attractions read like a Who's Who of 20th-Century artists, died yesterday of a heart attack at the age of 85. Arriving in the U.S. from his native Russia in 1906 with $1.50, Hurok began his presentations soon thereafter. Early triumphs included Eugene Ysaye, Pavlova and Madame Schumann-Heink, but on the great Chaliapin he lost $150,000. His presentation of Isadora Duncan in Boston, where she bared a breast, later led him to observe, "If they're not temperamental, I don't want them. It's in the nature of a great artist to be that way."

More Americans are trying bisexuality

Sociologists and psychologists believe bisexuality is on the rise. Based on the Kinsey reports of the 50's and more recent data, it is estimated 12 percent of women have bisexual experiences, as compared with twice that percentage for men. Doctors are only beginning to ask about its causes and "healthiness."

Some experts say the women's movement "frees" formerly heterosexual women from dependency on men. Others say the new assertive woman sends would-be heterosexual men scurrying into the closet. Still others say feminism encourages homosexual men to love women. One psychiatrist says, "There are more views on bisexuality than there are bisexuals" (→ 3/29/76).

Coppola wrote the script for the film version of Fitzgerald's "The Great Gatsby." Redford stars.

1974

APRIL

Su	Mo	Tu	We	Th	Fr	Sa
	1	2	3	4	5	6
7	8	9	10	11	12	13
14	15	16	17	18	19	20
21	22	23	24	25	26	27
28	29	30				

3. Patty Hearst, in tape-recorded message, says she will stay with SLA (→ 15).

3. Nixon announces he will pay $432,787 in back taxes (→ 11).

4. Cincinnati: Hank Aaron ties Babe with 714th homer (→ 8).

6. Golan Heights: Israeli jets hit Syrian force that crossed cease-fire line (→ 11).

9. New Delhi: India, Pakistan, Bangladesh reach pact to exchange prisoners of 1971 war.

11. Judiciary committee subpoenaes Nixon to produce tapes for impeachment inquiry (→ 28).

11. Israel: Three Arab guerrillas kill 18 in Qiryat Shemona (→ 13).

13. Jerusalem: Moshe Dayan threatens to clear out South Lebanon if govt. aids PLO (→ 14).

14. Washington: Crime study finds N.Y. safest of 13 cities.

14. Augusta, Ga.: Gary Player wins Masters golf title.

14. Israel, Syria fight heavy battle atop Mt. Hermon (→ 19).

15. Washington: Report shows drop in U.S. birth rate to lowest point in history.

19. Golan Heights: Syria, Israel fight first air battle here since October war (→ 5/16).

21. Moscow: Sen. Kennedy tries opinion poll at university, gets hostile response on whether Soviets should spend less on arms.

22. Israeli Mapai (Labor) Party picks Itzhak Rabin for premier (→ 6/3).

22. Bali: Pan Am jetliner crashes with 107 aboard; most reported dead.

25. Lisbon: Army takes over, ousting Premier Caetano (→ 27).

25. Bonn: Brandt aide Gunter Guillaume arrested as East German spy (→ 5/6).

27. Leningrad: Soviet airliner burns after takeoff, 100 killed.

30. President Nixon in TV speech presents edited transcripts of tapes (→ 5/1).

DEATH

24. William "Bud" Abbott, U.S. comedian (*10/2/1895).

Patty Hearst joins captors, helps rob bank

April 15. This morning, Patricia Hearst pointed a rifle not at one of her captors but at a bank teller. The newspaper heiress assisted the Symbionese Liberation Army in its hold-up of a San Francisco bank. The FBI is not sure if Miss Hearst acted on her own free will or "under duress and coercion." Another SLA member was seen pointing a gun in her direction.

Since her abduction by the SLA February 4, Miss Hearst has apparently embraced the group's ideals. On April 3, she sent her parents a message that said she would join the war for "the freedom of oppressed people." The words accompanied a photo of her posed before a cobra-emblazoned SLA flag (→ 5/18).

Patty, now called "Tania."

Hank Aaron hits 715th homer, besting Ruth

Aaron watches the historic #715.

April 8. Skyrockets burst in the rain above Atlanta Stadium as Henry Aaron hit his 715th home run and passed Babe Ruth as the greatest slugger in baseball history.

In his second time at bat, the 40-year-old outfielder of the Braves smote a powerful drive in the fourth inning off Al Downing of the Dodgers and the ball cleared the left-center fence 385 feet away.

Aaron, who began his career with the Indianapolis Clowns of the Negro League, broke the 39-year-old mark set by Ruth four days after he tied the Babe in the season's opener.

What did he think about when he hit the record-breaker? "All I could think about was that I wanted to touch all the bases," he said. So shaken were the Dodgers they made six errors and lost 7-4 (→ 10/10/76).

Irish terrorists kill 1,000 in five years

April 20. James Corbett, a Roman Catholic resident of Belfast, became a grisly statistic today: He was the 1,000th person killed in the terrorist violence that has plagued Northern Ireland since the summer of 1969. The civil unrest in Ulster which claimed Corbett's life has accelerated since the practice of detention without trial was introduced by the government in August 1971 (→ 5/3).

TV networks reduce violence on screen

The television networks have announced they are dropping several shows that rely on gunfights and fisticuffs for fun, replacing them with family-oriented fare. The fall season will feature "The Waltons," "Happy Days" and other programs of their ilk. While the networks say the cuts come in reponse to disturbing findings by a Senate communications subcommittee, many of the shows had low ratings anyway.

Portuguese army to end dictatorial rule

Rebel troops sport red flowers.

April 27. When military leaders seize control of a government, they generally suspend the constitution and civil liberties. Just the opposite seems to be happening in Portugal. A seven-man junta has thrown Premier Marcello Caetano out of office and promised to end 40 years of dictatorial rule. Flowers were thrown at soldiers patrolling the streets of Lisbon, and civilians even emerged from liquor stores offering them bottles of wine.

General Antonio de Spinola, leader of the junta, exiled Caetano to Madeira. Spinola promised democratic reform and free elections for a president and a national assembly within a year. The general said that a provisional civilian government would be named within a week.

Conservatives are resisting Spinola. He is also learning that freedom of expression can lead to violent dissent. A leftist mob sacked a right-wing newspaper in Lisbon. Liberals put themselves on a collision course with Spinola by calling for an end to the war in Africa. Spinola, true to his military tradition, said he will not withdraw troops from Portuguese Guinea, Mozambique and Angola (→ 6/9).

Long illness conquers Pompidou of France

April 2. Georges Pompidou, the President of France, died tonight at his home in Paris. The government did not release the cause of death, but it has been known for some time that Pompidou was seriously ill. His face often seemed bloated and his complexion was pale. Pompidou tried to joke about his health when he talked with Secretary of State Henry Kissinger. "Every time someone shakes my hand," he said, "I think they're trying to take my pulse." On another occasion, he said that every politician has his problems. "Nixon has Watergate, and I am going to die."

Whoever succeeds Pompidou is likely to break with Gaullist policies. Pompidou began the transition away from General de Gaulle's programs by favoring the enlargement of the Common Market and by devaluing the franc (→ 5/6).

World leaders attend Pompidou's funeral in the Cathedral of Notre Dame.

Golda Meir resigns as Israel's Premier

April 10. Israeli Premier Golda Meir tonight resigned in view of an ongoing schism within her own Labor Party regarding errors in Israeli military planning prior to last October's war. The Labor Party comprises three factions, two of which favored placing the blame on Defense Minister Moshe Dayan and removing him from his post.

Although an official report last week cleared Dayan of any responsibility, calls for his resignation persisted amid a growing desire by many Israelis for new leadership as well as new policies. Rather than dismiss Dayan and thus knuckle under to opposition demands, Mrs. Meir decided to quit herself (→ 22).

Egypt ends reliance on Russian arms

April 18. Eighteen years of Egyptian reliance on Soviet arms has ended with President Anwar el-Sadat's dramatic announcement that Egypt will henceforth buy arms from other sources. Though these sources weren't named, Sadat probably has in mind the Arab oil-producing nations, some of which are making huge arms purchases in the West. Saudi Arabia is buying U.S. Phantom jets; Abu Dhabi, Kuwait and Libya are buying French fighters; and Saudi Arabia may buy French-British tanks (→ 6/14).

Mitchell and Stans free in Vesco case

April 28. Former Attorney General John N. Mitchell and former Commerce Secretary Maurice H. Stans were acquitted of conspiracy charges involving a contribution to the Nixon re-election campaign. The two were charged with impeding a Securities and Exchange Commission investigation of financier Robert L. Vesco in return for a secret $200,000 campaign contribution. The jury acquittal eliminated a key issue in a House committee's inquiry into impeachment of President Nixon (→ 30).

1974

MAY

Su	Mo	Tu	We	Th	Fr	Sa
			1	2	3	4
5	6	7	8	9	10	11
12	13	14	15	16	17	18
19	20	21	22	23	24	25
26	27	28	29	30	31	

1. Washington: Judiciary committee rejects edited transcripts as substitute for tapes (→ 2).

2. Annapolis: Appeals Court orders disbarment of Agnew for tax evasion (→ 21).

2. New Delhi: 700 union leaders arrested in move to avert rail strike (→ 6/12/75).

3. Dublin: I.R.A. threatens destruction of $20 mil. in stolen art masterpieces if political prisoners are not released (→ 17).

6. Paris: Socialist Mitterrand, conservative Giscard d'Estaing nominated for presidency (→ 19).

6. Bonn: Chancellor Brandt resigns in spy scandal (→ 16).

7. S.F.: League of Women Voters decides to admit men.

8. Ottawa: Trudeau's Liberals lose confidence vote in Commons on budget policy (→ 7/8).

12. Milwaukee: Boston Celtics beat Bucks for NBA title.

13. Rome: Italians vote 60% to keep three-year-old law allowing divorce in Catholic country.

17. N.Y.: Gov. Wilson signs bill to restore limited death penalty (→ 7/2/76).

17. Dublin: Three auto bombs kill 23, injure 80 at height of rush hour (→ 29).

18. U.S. Defense Dept. admits making rain in Indochina to slow Hanoi troops (→ 1/7/75).

19. Philadelphia: Flyers win Stanley Cup.

21. Washington: Jeb Magruder, deputy dir. of re-election campaign, given 10 months for break-in and cover-up (→ 29).

25. N.Y.: Frances, only pregnant white whale in captivity, dies of poisoning at N.Y. Aquarium.

26. Johnny Rutherford comes from 25th place to win Indy 500 at 158 mph in McLaren racer.

28. Italy: Bomb hidden in garbage bag kills six, injures 94 at Brescia anti-Fascist rally.

29. Washington: Nixon agrees to turn over 1,200 pages of edited Watergate transcripts (→ 30).

29. Israel and Syria, with Kissinger's aid, accept pact for truce in Golan Heights (→ 6/16).

France elects Giscard d'Estaing President

Giscard d'Estaing, aristocrat.

May 19. France's Valery Giscard d'Estaing turned back the most effective challenge from the left ever as he defeated Francois Mitterrand for the presidency. Giscard d'Estaing received 50.8% of the vote, compared to the 49.2% received by Mitterrand from Socialists, Communists and other leftists. The President-elect acknowledged the power of the left by saying, "You want changes, politically, economically and socially. You won't be disappointed." Mitterrand beat Giscard in the first round of the race, but he failed to win a majority in a field of 14 candidates. "Keep faith with your cause," he told supporters. "Something has started which won't stop soon" (→ 8/25/76).

Police storm house, kill Hearst captors

May 18. The charred bodies of five Symbionese Liberation Army members were identified this morning, following a bloody raid on their hideout by police. Symbionese chief "Cinq," Donald deFreeze, is among the dead. Patty Hearst, the guerrillas' hostage for 104 days, was not with them and is presumed alive. Yesterday, the radicals holed up in a Los Angeles home on the fringe of the Watts section. Police sprayed the place with gunfire and tear gas. A gas canister or other device set off a blaze, engulfing the house in minutes and asphyxiating those inside. The location of the other SLA recruits is unknown (→ 9/18/75).

Arabs seize school; 26 die in relief effort

May 16. No place is sacred in the gruesome conflict between Arabs and Israelis. Yesterday, Arab guerrillas ambushed a car, killing one and wounding ten, drove to Maalot, Israel, where they seized a school and held 90 children hostage. They demanded the release of 20 imprisoned comrades. The Tel Aviv government refused to yield to the terrorists. Instead, Israeli troops stormed the school, killing many of the captors but also 26 students. Today, amid angry, vengeful cries from citizens, the Israeli government ordered planes to strafe and bomb Palestinian refugee camps and guerrilla hideouts (→ 29).

Nixon turns over tape transcripts to House

May 30. Exactly one month after President Nixon went on television to release edited transcripts of Watergate tapes, the possibility of his impeachment has increased.

The House Judiciary Committee today warned Nixon that his refusal to turn over actual Watergate tapes subpoenaed by the panel "might constitute a ground for impeachment." The warning, joined in by eight of the 17 Republicans on the committee, was a further indication of an erosion of support for Nixon within the committee. The White House has contended that the defiance of the committee subpoena was based on the constitutional power of executive privilege (→ 6/11).

Nixon, transcripts in background.

India has the Bomb: First test succeeds

May 18. A powerful underground explosion rocked India's desert of Rajasthan today, making India the sixth nation in history to set off a nuclear device. The blast, which took place at a depth of 330 feet, was in the range of 10-15 kilotons, smaller than the bomb exploded by the U.S. at Nagasaki in WWII. India is signatory to the 1963 test ban treaty, and thus was prohibited from exploding the device on land or in the air. Prime Minister Gandhi claimed the purpose of the test was peaceful and said such explosions may have their use in mining operations (→ 11/24).

Protestant strike closes down Belfast

May 29. In a smashing defeat for moderate forces in Northern Ireland, its coalition government collapsed today in the wake of a general strike organized by extremist Protestant groups. In London, the government of Prime Minister Harold Wilson announced the suspension of the Ulster provincial assembly and the reinstitution of direct rule by the British government. The strike, which was organized by the Ulster Worker's Council, interrupted many vital services. The strikers opposed the increased representation of Catholics in Ulster's government (→ 6/15).

Brandt resigns; Schmidt is Bonn Chancellor

Brandt, a 1971 Nobel winner, out.

May 16. West Germany's Finance Minister, Helmut Schmidt, was named by Parliament today to succeed Willy Brandt as Chancellor. Brandt resigned ten days ago in the middle of a large spy scandal. A top member of his staff, Gunter Guillaume, was arrested and charged with being a spy for East Germany. German authorities say Brandt's aide for party affairs has confessed to espionage charges. An associate of Brandt says he decided to quit rather than fire one or two Cabinet ministers. Brandt thought that "would have been cowardly and dishonest," the friend said.

Maker takes Dalkon Shield off market

May 15. A.H. Robins Company has yielded to pressure from the U.S. Food and Drug Administration and agreed to take its intrauterine contraceptive device off the market. The Dalkon Shield has produced a high pregnancy rate (10% compared with 3% for most other IUD's). What is worse, more than 100 of the women who got pregnant contracted serious uterine infections. Seven women died. Of the three to five million women using IUD's, two million have been using the Dalkon Shield.

May 4. Duke Ellington, 75, most prolific jazz composer, is dead.

1974

JUNE

Su	Mo	Tu	We	Th	Fr	Sa
						1
2	3	4	5	6	7	8
9	10	11	12	13	14	15
16	17	18	19	20	21	22
23	24	25	26	27	28	29
30						

1. U.S.: 110,000 clothing workers start nationwide strike.

3. Washington: Nixon aide Charles Colson pleads guilty to obstructing justice in Ellsburg case (→ 21).

3. Israel: Yitzhak Rabin succeeds Golda Meir as premier (→ 11/10).

5. N.Y.: Sly Stewart and Kathy Silva wed in rock-and-roll ceremony at Madison Sq. Garden.

5. India: Smallpox sweeping nation, fatal to 10,000.

9. Moscow reopens ties with Portugal, broken since 1917 (→ 9/30).

11. Salzburg: Kissinger threatens to resign unless cleared of wiretapping allegations (→ 17).

13. London: Prince Charles makes maiden speech at House of Lords, first such royal speech in 90 years.

14. Cairo: Nixon, Sadat report U.S. to supply Egypt with nuclear reactors (→ 10/26/75).

14. N.Y.: Stolen Regents exams being sold in Metropolitan area.

15. London: I.R.A. scratches two-foot high letters in Ruben's "Adoration of the Magi" (→ 17).

16. Mamaroneck, N.Y.: Hale Irwin wins U.S. Open golf title.

16. Damascus: Nixon, Assad announce resumption of U.S.-Syrian relations (→ 7/8).

16. Mogadishu: Somalia to close schools for year so students can help teach nomads.

17. Nixon ex-lawyer Kalmbach given 6-18 months for illegal fund-raising activities (→ 7/19).

21. Colson given 1-3 years in Ellsberg case after insisting he acted on Nixon orders (→ 7/12).

23. Vienna: Socialist Rudolf Kirshschlager elected president.

27. Paris: Iran gains $4 bil. accord with France for five nuclear reactors (→ 5/21/75).

29. Buenos Aires: V.P. Isabel Peron becomes acting president as husband Juan falls ill (→ 7/1).

DEATH

24. Darius Milhaud, French composer (*9/4/1892).

Baryshnikov, Soviet ballet star, defects

Baryshnikov leaps to the West.

June 30. Mikhail Baryshnikov, leading Soviet ballet dancer, fled from the touring Bolshoi troupe in Toronto last night, apparently to continue dancing in the West. The dancers were walking toward a chartered bus after a reception when Baryshnikov turned toward a waiting car. He was pursued by persons said to be from the KGB, the Soviet security apparatus, but was assisted into the vehicle by Canadian police. Critics place Baryshnikov, 26, in the topmost ranks of male ballet dancers. Born in Latvia, he was a favorite pupil of the late Alexander Pushkin and has won gold medals in ballet contests. Other defecting Soviet dancers include Rudolph Nureyev in 1961 and Natalia Makarova in 1970.

Ancient London hall hit by terror bomb

June 17. The Irish Republican Army has struck again. This time the I.R.A. planted a bomb inside the most historic section of the Houses of Parliament, the 900-year-old Westminister Hall. A man with an Irish accent called police six minutes before the bomb was to explode. Authorities rapidly evacuated the building, but 11 people were injured when the blast occurred and the chamber suffered some damage. As smoke curled around Big Ben, a fire from the explosion destroyed the hall's annex. Parliamentary leader Robert Mellish said the terrorists seem determined "to destroy this major part of our heritage" (→ 11/21).

Nixon, on tour, goes to a Soviet summit

June 27. Despite being immersed in the sludge of Watergate, President Nixon has triumphed in what some say may be his last world tour as chief executive. The president met with Egyptian President Anwar el-Sadat in Cairo earlier this month. The two leaders signed an accord, in which the United States will supply Egypt with nuclear technology to be used for peaceful purposes. Nixon also asked Sadat to pursue a path of peace in the Mideast.

Today in Moscow, Soviet chief Leonid Brezhnev warmly greeted Nixon for a third summit meeting between the two superpower leaders. They will embark on serious arms negotiations over the next five days for the "strengthening of universal peace," according to a Washington spokesman (→ 10/24).

Nixon and Sadat at an historic site.

Heimlich describes anti-choking move

June 14. A new method for saving the life of a person choking on food or other objects has been developed by Dr. Henry M. Heimlich of Xavier University in Cincinnati. The "Heimlich Maneuver" consists of standing behind a choking victim and pressing a fist sharply into the person's abdomen to compress the lungs, forcing a flow of air that causes the object to pop out of the throat. Heimlich says the maneuver, if widely used at the first sign of choking, could save the lives of the estimated 3,000 to 4,000 Americans who choke to death each year, many of them in restaurants.

Condo craze alters housing in America

June 1. A "condominium craze" is bringing fundamental changes to American housing. In 25 metropolitan areas, 40.3 percent of new units for sale in 1972 were condos. They are cheaper than detached houses, mortgage interest payments offer tax advantages and joint ownership makes pools and tennis courts obtainable. However, there are increasing complaints of shoddy construction and unfair maintenance fees. Consumer protection provisions after a sale are primitive.

Mrs. King killed as son was by gunman

June 30. A gunman yelled "I'm tired of all this. I'm taking over," and fired wildly inside an Atlanta church, killing a church deacon and the organist, Mrs. Martin Luther King Sr., mother of the slain civil rights leader. The assailant also seriously injured a churchgoer. Marcus Wayne Chenault, a black 21-year-old, was then tackled to the floor by congregation members in the famed Ebenezer Baptist Church. Later, he told police he had received orders from his god to kill Martin Luther King Sr. But instead he shot Mrs. King "because she was nearest" to him.

June 16. Bjorn Borg, 18, is the youngest French Open winner, beating Manuel Orantes in five.

1974

JULY

Su	Mo	Tu	We	Th	Fr	Sa
	1	2	3	4	5	6
7	8	9	10	11	12	13
14	15	16	17	18	19	20
21	22	23	24	25	26	27
28	29	30	31			

1. Turkey defies U.S., resuming sale of opium (→ 7/25/75).

1. Guatemala: Kjell Laugerud Garcia chosen president in elections of questionable validity.

6. Wimbledon: Jimmy Connors over Ken Rosewall 6-1, 6-1, 6-4; Chris Evert over Olga Morozova 6-0, 6-4.

7. Munich: West Germany defeats The Netherlands to take World Cup soccer final.

8. Ottawa: Premier Trudeau and Liberal Party win elections in landslide (→ 5/22/79).

8. Lebanon: Israeli naval commandos raid three southern ports, sink 30 vessels (→ 10/28).

12. Washington: Ehrlichman, Liddy and two others convicted of conspiracy and perjury in Ellsberg break-in (→ 31).

13. Scientists trace continental drift to Icelandic volcano.

13. St. Annes, England: Gary Player wins British Open.

15. Cyprus: Greek army officers lead Cypriot troops to power in coup (→ 16).

16. Malta: Deposed Cyprus Pres. Makarios arrives safely, escaping coup (→ 20).

19. House Judiciary Committee recommends Nixon stand trial in Senate on any of five impeachment charges (→ 24).

20. Cyprus: Turkey invades by sea and air (→ 22).

22. New York: U.N. reports Cyprus cease-fire (→ 8/13).

24. U.S. Supreme Court rules 8-0 Nixon must surrender Watergate tapes (→ 27).

27. House panel 27-11 asks impeachment of Nixon for obstruction of justice (→ 29).

29. Washington: Ex-Treasury Secretary John Connally indicted for bribery, perjury and obstructing justice (→ 30).

31. Ehrlichman given 20 months to five years (→ 8/2).

DEATHS

3. John Crowe Ransom, U.S. poet, critic (*4/30/1888).

11. Dizzy Dean, U.S. baseball pitcher (*1/16/1911).

Nixon loses in Court; impeachment begins

July 30. The Supreme Court, in a 8-to-0 decision, ruled that President Nixon must turn over additional tape recordings sought by the special Watergate prosecutor for the cover-up trial of six former Nixon aides. Nixon, who had sought to withhold the tapes on the grounds of executive privilege, announced he would abandon his challenge to the court's jurisdiction and turn over the information.

In announcing the historic decision, Chief Justice Warren Burger said presidential power of executive privilege was not absolute and was outweighed by the interests of fair administration of criminal justice.

The court's decision, coming on top of the televised hearings of the House Judiciary Committee, chaired by Rep. Peter Rodino, appeared to have tipped the balance in favor of impeachment of the president. By a 27-11 vote, the House committee recommended impeachment of the president on grounds that he had obstructed justice in the investigation of the Watergate burglary (→ 8/2).

Rodino, head of House committee.

Inflation replaces energy as concern

July 14. Inflation has replaced the energy crisis as the chief concern of Americans, the latest Gallup Poll shows. In the poll, 48 percent of those questioned listed the high cost of living as the nation's biggest problem. Another 15 percent named "lack of trust in government" and 11 percent cited "corruption in government," or Watergate.

Middle-income Americans, earning between $10,000 and $15,000 a year, expressed the highest degree of concern about inflation. The rising cost of living has bothered Americans in the 1970's, polls have found, but it was replaced briefly as the number one concern last January, when 46 percent of those questioned placed energy at the top of the list.

Many of the 1,509 persons questioned in the poll expressed puzzlement about why prices have risen so sharply in recent years (→ 8/12).

Peron, twice chief of Argentina, dies

July 1. One of the most powerful and controversial figures of 20th-Century Latin America is dead. The passing of President Juan Domingo Peron has left Argentina in grave uncertainty. Peron rose to power in 1943 and ushered in a new era of social and labor reform. But he alienated many Argentines with his dictatorial style of governing. Dissatisfaction among his countrymen forced Peron into self-exile, where he waited for 18 years before he was called back last year to lead his nation again. His wife, Isabel, who was Vice President, now assumes the presidency (→ 7/8/75).

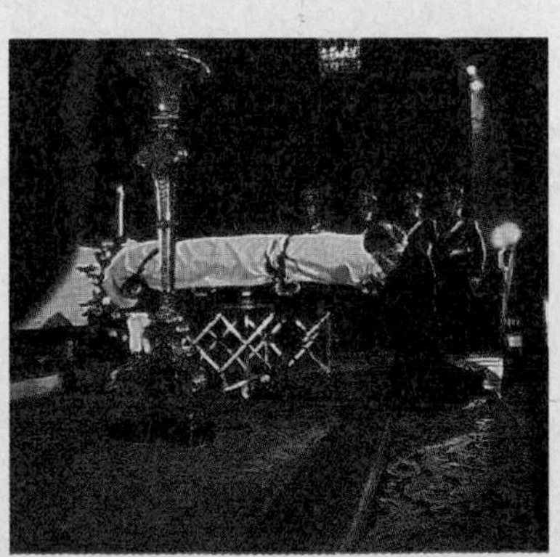

Isabel mourns at husband's casket.

Warren, innovative Court chief, is dead

July 9. Earl Warren, 83, ex-Chief Justice of the United States, died tonight. During the Warren years, the previously conservative Supreme Court became a force for such liberal reforms as the 1954 decision ending segregation in the public schools, the one man-one vote rulings and new rights for those accused of a crime. The Los Angeles-born liberal judge was appointed by conservative President Eisenhower.

Caramanlis takes over again in Greece

July 23. Military leaders of Greece, paralyzed by economic stagnation at home and the political crisis on Cyprus, have returned the government to civilian control. Constantine Caramanlis was sworn in as Premier and head of a new coalition government. Caramanlis has been living in exile in Paris since serving as premier from 1955-63. Thousands of Greeks lined the streets of Athens to cheer Caramanlis as he promised "the return of the country to normalcy" (→ 8/1).

Franco gives rule to Prince Juan Carlos

July 19. Generalissimo Francisco Franco, his health deteriorating, has turned over the reign of Spain to his designated successor, Prince Juan Carlos de Borbon. The 81-year-old chief of state, ruler of Spain for 35 years, steps down amid mixed reactions among the populace. Many, bitter with Franco's tyrannical rule, hope for a new era, while others are fearful the change will create havoc and violence (→ 9/2).

Juan Carlos, heir to Spanish throne.

1974

AUGUST

Su	Mo	Tu	We	Th	Fr	Sa
				1	2	3
4	5	6	7	8	9	10
11	12	13	14	15	16	17
18	19	20	21	22	23	24
25	26	27	28	29	30	31

1. Greece restores 1952 constitution protecting civil rights (→ 10/23).

3. Texas: Two inmates, two hostages killed in escape attempt at Huntsville prison.

5. Nixon admits he ordered cover-up for political as well as national security reasons (→ 6).

6. Nixon to let legal process decide his fate, despite opposition from Cabinet (→ 8).

10. Portugal announces two-year plan for Angolan independence (→ 1/16/75).

12. Washington: Ford calls for bipartisan effort to cut spending, limit inflation (→ 24).

13. Cyprus fighting resumes as peace talks collapse (→ 14).

14. Greece pulls out of NATO, blaming Allies for allowing Turk advance in Cyprus (→ 16).

15. South Korea: Assassins kill wife of Park Chung Hee in attempt on president (→ 2/15/75).

19. Nicosia: U.S. Ambassador Rodger Davies shot to death during Greek Cypriot protest at embassy (→ 22).

22. Ford names Aug. 19 Women's Equality Day (→ 1/1/75).

22. Turkey offers to fill gaps in Mediterranean defense left by Greek withdrawal (→ 11/1).

23. Washington: George Steinbrenner pleads guilty to illegal use of corporate funds for campaign contributions.

24. Washington: Ford signs bill creating special agency to monitor wages and prices (→ 9/20).

26. Portugal signs accord granting independence to Portuguese Guinea on September 10.

27. Soviet Soyuz 15 spacecraft put in orbit headed for meeting with space station (→ 11/30).

28. Ford says Nixon has been punished enough for Watergate, suggests pardon (→ 9/8).

31. New Zealand: Premier Norman E. Kirk dies of heart attack.

DEATH

26. Charles A. Lindbergh, U.S. aviator, first non-stop solo flight across Atlantic (*2/4/1902).

Nixon quits, first President to do so

Aug 8. President Nixon, faced with impeachment in Congress, has announced he is resigning, to be succeeded by Vice President Ford.

Less than two years after his landslide re-election victory, Nixon found himself so entangled in the Watergate scandal that he was forced to become the first president in history to resign from office. Only one other president, Andrew Johnson, has faced impeachment; the attempt to remove him in 1868 came to a Senate vote but failed.

Nixon's combative language of the past was gone as he told the nation in a conciliatory speech that he was resigning with the hope that his departure would start a "process of healing that is so desperately needed in America." Speaking to the nation from the Oval Office, the president, in tones more of sadness than bitterness, expressed regret for any "injuries" caused by his actions and acknowledged that some of his judgments had been wrong.

In describing his personal pain at leaving office, Nixon said, "I have never been a quitter. To leave office before my term is completed is opposed to every instinct in my body." But he said he had decided to put "the interests of America first."

Only three days before the resignation speech, the president, in releasing additional tapes of White House conversations, had acknowledged that six days after the Watergate burglary, he had ordered a halt to the investigation of the break-in for political and national security reasons and had withheld the information from his lawyers and the House Judiciary Committee.

In his resignation speech, the president conceded he no longer had the votes to avoid impeachment in the House and conviction in the Senate. To continue to fight for personal vindication, he said, would absorb the time of the president and Congress "when our entire focus should be on the great issues of peace and prosperity" (→ 9).

Nixon, in a sign usually reserved for victory, turns thumbs up after resigning.

A final farewell as he bows out.

Dean and Ehrlichman jailed for misconduct

Aug 2. "A shameful episode in the history of this country," as Judge Gerhard Gesell said of the Watergate scandal, has claimed two more victims: Presidential aides John Dean and John Ehrlichman have been sentenced to jail terms.

Ehrlichman, formerly President Nixon's chief adviser on domestic affairs, received 20 months to five years imprisonment for his involvement in the break-in of Daniel Ellsberg's psychiatrist's office and for lying to a grand jury about the break-in. Before hearing his sentence, Ehrlichman professed his innocence. "I am the only one in this room who really knows whether I am guilty or not guilty of the charges against me. Your Honor," he declared, "I am innocent." Judge Gesell replied flatly that "the Constitution was ignored, the rights of the citizens were abused," and he handed down the sentence.

John Dean, former legal counsel to Nixon, was sentenced to a minimum of one year and a maximum of four years in jail for his admitted cover-up of Watergate transgressions. Judge John Sirica listened to the futile appeals by Dean for "compassion" before levying the sentence without comment. Dean had hoped for additional immunity in exchange for his cooperation with the prosecution; he has set White House personnel on fitful edge with his revealing testimony. But the immunity granted to Dean did not extend to all of the charges against him, so off to jail he went (→ 5).

Marshals break up Wounded Knee trial

Aug 23. Heated tensions finally exploded today in the trial of American Indian leaders for their part in last year's armed occupation of Wounded Knee Indian Reservation. U.S. marshals arrested two defense attorneys and sprayed debilitating chemical mace on disruptive spectators in a St. Paul, Minn., courtroom. The lawyers vehemently disputed cross-examination proceedings of a star prosecution witness. Judge Fred Nichol threatened to throw the lawyers out of court for their outbursts. When attorney William Kunstler said, "I don't care," the judge cited him and his partner, Mark Lane, for contempt and had them arrested (→ 6/26/75).

Ford assumes presidency

Ford takes the oath of office as wife Betty, the new First Lady, looks on.

Aug 9. For the first time in American history a man has become President without winning a national election. Gerald Rudolph Ford, appointed Vice President by President Nixon after Spiro Agnew left the position in disgrace, takes control of the Oval Office after Nixon resigned in shame from the Watergate scandal. Ford, sworn in today by Chief Justice Warren Burger, declared to the nation: "Our long national nightmare is over."

Ford's first task is to rekindle public trust in the White House. The former Speaker of the House and longtime Congressman vowed to return honor to the presidency and pledged candor in all his activities as president. He also acknowledged his unique entry into the nation's highest office. "I am acutely aware that you have not elected me as your president," he said in a television address. "So I ask you to confirm me as your president with your prayers."

Ford bade an emotional farewell to Nixon, his friend and colleague for 25 years. Ford's Press Secretary, J.F. terHorst, suggested that, despite the men's closeness, Ford would probably not pardon Nixon from criminal prosecution (→ 20).

Ford chooses Rockefeller as vice president

Aug 20. Former New York Governor Nelson Rockefeller was nominated to be America's 41st vice president by President Ford today. Ford said he felt Rockefeller would be a "good partner for me and a good partner for our country."

The 66-year-old multimillionare gracefully accepted the nomination and hailed Ford for ushering in a renewed era of "faith and hope" in American leadership. Rockefeller must be confirmed, under the 25th Amendment, by a simple majority in both houses of Congress. His nomination is expected to sail through confirmation procedures.

Ford consulted many Republicans before choosing the man who is "a heartbeat away from the presidency." George Bush, GOP National Chairman, and Illinois Representative John Anderson were among those considered (→ 28).

Rocky, multimillionaire politician.

Turks invade Cyprus, cut island in two

Aug 16. Tens of thousands of refugees clogged the roads of Cyprus today as victorious Turkish invaders split the island in two. The northern third of the island is controlled by some 30,000 Turkish troops who began an all-out offensive against Greek Cypriots on Wednesday. A cease-fire went into effect at six o'clock tonight.

The situation on Cyprus has splintered the Atlantic alliance. Greece, complaining that its NATO partners have refused to help in the struggle against Turkey, withdrew its forces from the alliance on Wednesday. Constantine Caramanlis, the Premier of Greece, refused an offer from Turkey tonight to resume the Cyprus peace talks in Geneva. He also rejected an invitation from President Ford to visit Washington. Caramanlis said it would be ridiculous for Greece to "negotiate under the pressure of a fait accompli." Secretary of State Kissinger said he is willing to visit Cyprus to help arrange a political settlement.

Cyprus has been in turmoil since it achieved independence from Britain 14 years ago. Greek and Turkish Cypriots have been fighting on the island for most of the past decade. Greeks outnumber the Turks four or five to one, and thousands of Greeks are now trapped behind Turkish lines in the north. Similarly, there are many Turkish Cypriots in the south who are trying to move to the north. The Turkish line has split the capital of Nicosia in half. Heavy fighting raged along the Green Line in Nicosia until the cease-fire went into effect. Five United Nations soldiers have been killed in the fighting (→ 19).

Turkish tank, invader in Cyprus.

Teenage basketball star to earn $3m

Aug 29. Moses Malone became the first player to go from high school into pro basketball and the move made him the highest salaried teenage athlete in the U.S. Malone, who is 19, has the potential of earning $3 million instead of playing for the University of Maryland, one of the 300 colleges in the nation that offered him scholarships.

The young Virginian had agreed to attend Maryland, but the offer of the Utah Stars of the American Basketball Association —$150,000 a year beefed up by fringe benefits —proved too inviting. Malone had only a C average in high school. Even then, as one teacher explained, "he needed a lot of tutoring."

Malone's mother works as a meatpacker in a market for $100 a week. As for his move directly into the pros, she said, "It's his life. He has to make his own decision."

Lee Trevino wins PGA championship

Aug 11. Lee Trevino interrupted his usual clowning long enough to capture the Professional Golfers' Association championship with a one-stroke victory over Jack Nicklaus. Trevino said he would pull out all the stops in his effort to win the $45,000 victor's share of the $225,000 purse. He went out and shot a 69 for a 276 total that was four strokes under par.

Tied for third at 279 were Sam Snead, at 62 a three-time PGA winner; Bobby Cole of South Africa, David Hill and Hubert Green.

When Trevino three-putted the 17th green for his only bogey of the round, Nicklaus was only one shot back. Trevino needed a par four to stave off Nicklaus, and he got it with ease. Nicklaus, meanwhile, needed a birdie to send the match into an 18-hole playoff, but he fell short.

1974

SEPTEMBER

Su	Mo	Tu	We	Th	Fr	Sa
1	2	3	4	5	6	7
8	9	10	11	12	13	14
15	16	17	18	19	20	21
22	23	24	25	26	27	28
29	30					

1. U.S. Air Force pilot James Sullivan flies N.Y.-London in 1:55:42 in SR-71 jet.

2. Spain: Franco reassumes full power after illness (→ 9/27/75).

3. N.J.: Newark orders curfew, bans street protests to curb racial strife (→ 10/15).

4. Washington: Ford names GOP head George Bush as U.S. envoy to China (→ 6/7/75).

6. Panama, Colombia, Costa Rica, Venezuela asks OAS to lift sanctions against Cuba (→ 27).

8. Washington: Ford grants pardon to Nixon (→ 16).

9. N.Y.: Jimmy Connors, Billie Jean King win U.S. Open singles crowns at Forest Hills.

15. Moscow: Bulldozers, fire hoses used to break up outdoor exhibit of nonconformist art (→ 11/12/75).

16. Washington: Ford offers conditional amnesty to draft evaders who agree to work two years in public service (→ 12/21).

16. Alexander Haig appointed NATO commander in Europe (→ 10/20/80).

18. The Hague: Three Japanese terrorists free hostages at French Embassy, take off in jetliner.

20. Honduras: Cyclone Fifi hits, killing 10,000.

20. U.S.: Consumer Price Index up record 1.3% in Aug. (→ 23).

21. AEC orders 21 of 50 nuclear reactors shut to check for cracks in cooling systems (→ 4/6/77).

23. Sen. Edward Kennedy pulls out of 1976 presidential contest.

25. Nixon suffers lung damage from blood clot in leg phlebitis.

26. Paterson, N.J.: Data turns up challenging conviction of Hurricane Carter for murder seven years ago (→ 3/20/76).

27. Havana: Senators Javits and Pell arrive under objections of U.S. to meet Castro on resumption of relations (→ 3/9/75).

28. Betty Ford undergoes surgery for breast cancer.

DEATH

4. Creighton Abrams, U.S. military commander (*9/15/1914).

Ford gives Nixon pardon

Sept 16. Although mounting evidence indicates former President Nixon may have engaged in criminal acts in the Watergate scandal, he will not be tried on any charges as President Ford, earlier this month, granted full and unconditional pardon to his predecessor. Today, Ford also granted immunity to Vietnam-era draft evaders.

In his proclamation pardoning Nixon, Ford said the former chief executive, who is in ill health, has already "paid the unprecedented penalty of relinquishing" the presidency. He said the act will spare Nixon and the nation additional grief in this "American tragedy."

The reaction from politicans and citizens has ranged from outright anger to full support of Ford's historic move. Many believe, as Ford enunciated, that the former president has suffered enough and that obtaining a fair trial by jury would be nearly impossible. Others feel the pardon does a disservice to justice and sets a dangerous precedent (→ 10/1).

Evel Knievel fails in leap across canyon

Sept 8. Evel Knievel's attempt to rocket 1,600 feet across a canyon in Idaho ended in near-death for the stuntman. Knievel's vehicle went streaking 1,000 feet above the Snake River when a tail parachute opened prematurely on takeoff. The craft floated into the canyon and landed nose-down on a rocky river bank; it was feared it might fall into the crowd below. A rescue team pulled Knievel from the wreck. He suffered only minor cuts and scrapes.

Haile Selassie deposed after 58 years

Sept 12. Emperor Haile Selassie, who ruled Ethiopia for 58 years, largely in regal and opulent splendor, was driven away from his palace today in a very unregal Volkswagen. His reign was at an end. The military leaders who ousted Selassie accuse him of tolerating corruption and forcing most of the country to live in abject poverty. The coup was bloodless, and its leaders invited Selassie's son, Crown Prince Asfa Wossen, to return to Addis Ababa and serve as a figurehead king. A provisional military regime will rule Ethiopia until elections are held. Military leaders, who say Selassie hoarded vast sums of cash and gold in Europe, promise to return "the land to the people" (→ 1/31/75).

Selassie, Lion of Judah.

Aerosol gases said to threaten earth

Sept 25. Freon gases released from aerosol spray cans are destroying the ozone layer that protects the earth from lethal ultraviolet radiation, scientists reported today. Unless use of Freon is reduced, about 15 percent of the ozone layer, ten to 15 miles aloft in the earth's atmosphere, will be destroyed by the year 2000, researchers Michael McElroy and Steven Wofsy wrote in the journal Science. Breakdown of the ozone layer could cause a major increase in skin cancer and unpredictable changes in the earth's weather patterns, they said. Freon-using companies disputed the report as "largely hypothesis" (→ 9/13/76).

Portuguese leader quits, warning of chaos

Spinola, ousted by young rebels.

Sept 30. In an emotional farewell speech, President Antonio de Spinola resigned as leader of Portugal, warning the public that the nation was steered toward chaos and "new forms of slavery." The surprise resignation comes amid an increase in power of leftist forces, including Communist elements. General Francisco de Costa Gomes, a close associate of Spinola, will replace the president who ruled for a brief five months during the Portuguese revolution.

Rifts between Spinola and the young leaders in the Armed Forces Movement frustrated the president, prompting his resignation. It is assumed friction between the leftists and the conservatives will result in political upheaval (→ 3/14/75).

Sept 9. Gritty Jimmy Connors added the U.S. Open to his Wimbledon and Australian titles.

1974

OCTOBER

Su	Mo	Tu	We	Th	Fr	Sa
		1	2	3	4	5
6	7	8	9	10	11	12
13	14	15	16	17	18	19
20	21	22	23	24	25	26
29	28	29	30	31		

1. Washington: Watergate cover-up trial begins (→ 12).

1. Washington: Hirshhorn Museum opens.

3. Cleveland: Indians name Frank Robinson first black manager in major league baseball.

4. India in apartheid protest refuses to play South Africa in Davis Cup finals (→ 11/12).

8. Ford calls on Americans to cut driving 5% and use cold water for wash to combat energy crisis (→ 21).

11. London: Labor Party led by P.M. Harold Wilson wins second general election (→ 2/4/75).

12. Washington: Leon Jaworski resigns as special prosecutor in Watergate inquiry (→ 17).

17. Washington: Ford defends pardon before House panel, saying there was "no deal" with Nixon (→ 11/21).

17. Oakland: A's defeat L.A. Dodgers 3-2 in fifth game to win World Series.

21. Ford meets with Mexican Pres. Luis Echeverria Alvarez to discuss new oil findings for world use (→ 12/6).

22. Canada, concerned over changing racial patterns, tightens immigration controls.

23. Moscow awarded 1980 Summer Olympics.

23. Athens: Ex-Premier Papadopoulos and four other leaders of 1967 coup exiled (→ 11/18).

24. Moscow: Kissinger meets with Brezhnev for six hours on major issues (→ 10/20/75).

25. Washington: Civil rights leaders, including Jesse Jackson, state that Ford comment on Boston school violence encourages whites to break law (→ 5/10/75).

25. U.S. Air Force fires ICBM successfully from plane.

28. Rabat: Arab heads of state call for creation of independent Palestinian state (→ 29).

DEATHS

4. Anne Sexton, American poet, suicide (*11/9/1928).

13. Ed Sullivan, CBS variety show host (*9/28/1902).

U.S. officials warn of world depression

Sept 23. President Ford and Secretary of State Kissinger said yesterday that a continuation of escalating oil prices set by producing countries will lead to a worldwide depression and, in Ford's words, "the breakdown of world order and safety."

Speaking in Detroit at the ninth World Energy Conference, the president said that in the face of clear danger, he was optimistic that oil-producing and consuming nations would cooperate to find a solution, and the United States would reach its goal of energy independence.

In a gloomy speech to the United Nations General Assembly, meanwhile, the secretary said "the early warning signs of a major economic crisis are evident.

"Rates of inflation unprecedented in the past quarter century are sweeping developing and developed nations" he said. "The world's financial institutions are staggering under the most massive movements of reserves in history. And profound questions have arisen about meeting man's fundamental needs for energy and food" (→ 10/8).

Millions lose favorite author and fantasies

Sept 21. Novelist Jacqueline Susann has died in New York after a 12-year battle with cancer. She was 53 years old. Miss Susann wrote some very popular pulp fiction laced with drugs, sex and four-letter words. Her latest, written last year, was titled "Once Is Not Enough."

Miss Susann's first book was printed in 1962, the same year she found she had breast cancer. Those who did not know about her illness thought she brought up the subject in her novels merely to shock; they did not know that writing about it was a kind of therapy for her.

Two of her novels have been made into poorly received films. One, "The Love Machine," starred Dyan Cannon.

Susann charts lives of her characters.

Green Revolution could double food yield

Sept 2. Agricultural scientists at the International Maize and Wheat Improvement Center in Mexico have produced several new plant varieties that could enable farmers to fill the present gap between food production and demand around the world. By crossing different strains of a plant species, they have been able to combine desirable traits such as disease resistance and richer protein content. Further plant-breeding programs should make it possible to double the global yield of food, preventing a mass famine that some predict to be the inevitable result of the population explosion.

Scientists at the center, led by Nobel laureate Norman Borlaug, are attempting to duplicate on a global scale the success achieved in Mexico. Borlaug was brought in by the Mexican government in 1944 to make the country self-sufficient in food production by developing high-yielding strains of wheat. At that time, many Mexican fields were yielding six to ten bushels an acre.

By the 1950's, with the help of better seed and fertilizer, yields rose to 50 to 60 bushels an acre. Mexico grew all the food it needed and the techniques developed by Borlaug began to spread around the world, in what has become known as the Green Revolution. Scientists from the center now travel constantly to developing countries to bring farmers new plant varieties and to train them in the methods needed to get maximum yields, in a race against worldwide starvation.

Troops summoned in Boston dispute

Oct 15. Racial violence in Boston's public schools has erupted again and Governor Francis Sargent today called President Ford, requesting federal troops to curb the fighting. However, Ford said the city should first exhaust all its riot enforcement resources and that federal guards "should be used only as a last resort."

Seven students were hurt in racial fighting at Hyde Park High School, one of the many schools troubled by court-ordered busing to achieve integration. Police were summoned after a white girl was attacked by 20 black students, resulting in a gang fight with knives and clubs.

Governor Sargent, disappointed that Ford denied him use of the National Guard, said he will continue to request federal help (→ 25).

Blood clot causes concern for Nixon

Oct 3. Former President Nixon was in critical condition today after massive internal bleeding that followed an operation to prevent a blood clot in his upper thigh from breaking loose and traveling to his lungs, where it could be fatal. But Nixon's surgeons said a "stable condition" had been established after his blood pressure dropped to dangerously low levels because of the bleeding. The operation was done at a hospital in Long Beach, California, when Nixon's doctors discovered the clot in the leg. They said immediate surgery was necessary because part of the clot might break off at any time despite blood-thinning drug therapy (→ 11/6).

Pacino is the Don, DeNiro, his father as a young man. "The Godfather Part II" is rare: a sequel equal to its predecessor.

Ali regains his world heavyweight title

Foreman takes a punishing right from Ali in the sweltering heat of Zaire.

Oct 29. In an unlikely setting in Zaire, under an African moon a few hours before dawn, Muhammad Ali knocked out George Foreman and became the second man in boxing history to regain the world heavyweight championship. The other was Floyd Patterson. The 32-year-old Ali floored his 25-year-old rival with a stinging left and a chopping left in the eighth round of what was to have been a 15-round bout. "Ali, kill him," most of the 60,000 fans chanted as Ali took Foreman's most powerful punches and came back stronger than before (→ 1/1/75).

Chinese confirm the death of Liu Shao-chi

Oct 31. The death of Liu Shao-chi, once China's chief of state, was confirmed today by Hong Kong's official Communist newspaper, Ta Kung Po. Rumors of Liu's death have circulated since 1968, when he was formally purged from China's ruling elite during the Cultural Revolution. Liu, who was thought to be Mao Tse-tung's obvious successor, was denounced by China's Red Guards as "China's Khrushchev," a revisionist deviating from the true Communist path.

The paper also confirmed the death of Lin Piao, who succeeded Liu as Mao's heir, but was rumored to have died in a plane crash in 1971 during an escape attempt to the Soviet Union after he had reportedly failed in a plot to overthrow Chairman Mao (→ 1/8/76).

Arabs agree on aid to frontline countries

Moroccan King Hassan in Rabat.

Oct 29. At an Arab League summit in Rabat, Morocco, billions of dollars were pledged to Arab countries that have borne the brunt of the wars with Israel. Egypt and Syria will each receive a billion dollars a year for four years. The Palestine Liberation Organization was promised $50 million, to be paid by Saudi Arabia and Kuwait. The PLO was also recognized "as the sole legitimate representative of the Palestinian people" and the eventual administrator of any land Israel might give up on the West Bank (→ 11/4).

1974

NOVEMBER

Su	Mo	Tu	We	Th	Fr	Sa
					1	2
3	4	5	6	7	8	9
10	11	12	13	14	15	16
17	18	19	20	21	22	23
24	25	26	27	28	29	30

1. Cyprus: Turkish Cypriots now resettling Greek sections of island (→ 12/7).

2. S.F.: J.D. Salinger breaks silence of 20 years, announces new works.

4. New York: Over 100,000 rally at U.N. against PLO participation in Mideast debate (→ 13).

5. Hartford: Ella T. Grasso is first elected woman governor without husband preceding.

6. Nixon, recovering from blood clot surgery, develops pneumonia.

10. Tel Aviv: Rioting flares in protest against rise in food prices (→ 4/8/77).

11. U.S. Little League World Series, won by Taiwan last four years, now limited to U.S.

14. Jane Alpert, militant radical, gives up four years after jumping bail in 1969 N.Y. bombings.

18. Athens: Premier Constantine Caramanlis wins in first free election in over decade (→ 12/8).

19. Tokyo: Ford greeted by Hirohito on state visit (→ 5/17/77).

20. U.S. files antitrust suit to break up AT&T (→ 1/8/82).

20. Nairobi: West German jumbo jetliner crashes, killing 59.

21. Washington: Watergate tape shows Nixon asked aides to help protect him (→ 12/10).

21. London: 17 die as bombs destroy two crowded pubs; I.R.A. suspected (→ 1/16/75).

22. New York: Mayor Beame to freeze hiring, cut 1,510 city jobs to save $100 mil. (→ 10/29/75).

23. Morris Udall is first Democrat to officially open presidential campaign (→ 12/12).

23. Tunis: Palestinian hijackers kill German banker, hold 27 for release of prisoners in Cairo (→ 2/9/75).

30. Pioneer II, nearing Jupiter, sends many photos (→ 1/8/75).

30. India, Pakistan decide to end ten-year trade ban (→ 5/14/76).

DEATH

24. Cornelius Ryan, Irish-American writer, WWII popular history (*6/5/1920).

Arafat, toting a gun, addresses the U.N.

Arafat demands a Palestinian state.

Nov 13. Yasir Arafat, who for the moment only dreams of having his own state, was treated like the head of a government at the United Nations in New York. The head of the Palestine Liberation Organization was also allowed the privilege of speaking to the world community with a gun strapped to his waist.

In his speech, Arafat called for the establishment of a Palestinian state, where Moslems, Christians and Jews would all be welcome. "I have come bearing an olive branch and a freedom fighter's gun," Arafat said in what appeared to be a threat to the United Nations. "Do not let the olive branch fall from my hands." Israel's delegate, Yosef Tekoah, said Palestinians are free to form a government in Jordan. He charged that Arafat's plan would destroy Israel (→ 23).

H.L. Hunt can't take it with him

Nov 29. H.L. Hunt, the militant anti-Communist and ultraconservative oil billionaire, died today in Dallas, Texas, at 85. He left the family farm in Illinois at 16, working as a logger, harvester and railroad hand. In 1921, by then a professional gambler, he showed up in El Dorado, Arkansas, and may have won his first oil well in a game of five-card stud. One of the world's richest men, he spent little on himself; drove old, battered cars; made no munificent gifts to worthy causes; opposed all welfare legislation and supported General Douglas MacArthur and later George C. Wallace as presidential candidates.

Ford and Brezhnev get tentative accord

Nov 24. President Ford and Soviet leader Leonid Brezhnev have reached a tentative agreement limiting the numbers of strategic nuclear weapons and delivery systems. Following groundwork laid down by Secretary of State Henry Kissinger last month, President Ford arrived in the Soviet Union this week for his first meeting with the Soviet leader since becoming president.

Ford and Brezhnev left the meeting optimistic that, as Ford said, "a sound basis for a new agreement that will constrain our military competition over the next decade" had been set. The numbers of weapons and delivery systems agreed upon will remain secret until Ford has a chance to brief Congress, but it is well-known that both nations have enough missiles to destroy each other several times over (→ 4/23/75).

Ford and Brezhnev in frigid Siberia.

U.N. vote rebukes South Africa 91-22

Nov 12. The United Nations General Assembly erupted in applause today upon hearing the announcement of the decision to suspend South Africa's participation in the current session. By a vote of 91-22, South Africa, condemned by most member nations for its policy of apartheid, will lose its right to take seats, vote, make proposals or speak in the world organization in this term which ends December 17. The United States and Britain unsuccessfully challenged the decision. The campaign against South Africa was led by several African nations which abhor its racial policies (→ 6/16/76).

1974

DECEMBER

Su	Mo	Tu	We	Th	Fr	Sa
1	2	3	4	5	6	7
8	9	10	11	12	13	14
15	16	17	18	19	20	21
22	23	24	25	26	27	28
29	30	31				

3. Washington: Rep. Wilbur Mills enters hospital after removal from House committee in sex and alcohol scandal.

6. U.S. Dept. of Labor reports jobless rate at 6.5%, highest since 1961 (→ 1/3/75).

7. Cyprus: Pres. Makarios returns, vowing to resist Greco-Turkish partition (→ 2/13/75).

8. Greece votes to abolish 142-year-old monarchy (→ 8/24/75).

8. Zambia: Factions in Rhodesian black liberation movement unite (→ 11).

10. Washington: Ehrlichman, crying, tells how Nixon made him quit (→ 19).

11. Salisbury: Premier Ian Smith announces cease-fire with black nationalists (→ 3/3/76).

12. Atlanta: Carter joins presidential race (→ 7/8/75).

18. FDA to approve food coloring despite warnings against Red Dye No. 2 (→ 10/22/76).

19. Rockefeller sworn in as v.p. after House vote (→ 1/1/75).

21. Washington: CIA accused of illegal spying on anti-war movement under Nixon (→ 1/5/75).

23. U.S.: B-1 bomber makes first test-flight successfully.

24. Japan: Nation's largest oil spill pollutes 1,600 sq. miles of scenic Inland Sea.

29. Pakistan: Earthquake kills 4,700, injures 15,000.

CULTURAL EVENTS, 1974

Literature: John Le Carre's "Tinker, Tailor, Soldier, Spy"; Studs Terkel's "Working"; Peter Benchley's "Jaws"; Tom Stoppard's "Travesties."

Academia: Solzhenitsyn's "The Gulag Archipelago: 1918-1956"; Fogel and Engerman's "Time on the Cross."

Music: Streisand's "The Way We Were"; John Denver's "Sunshine on my Shoulders"; Eric Clapton's "I Shot the Sheriff."

Film: Roman Polanski's "Chinatown"; Coppola's "The Godfather, Part II," Academy Award; Paul Mazursky's "Harry and Tonto"; "Alice Doesn't Live Here Anymore," Ellen Burstyn.

Bomb explodes in Harrod's in London

Dec 21. Christmas shoppers at Harrod's, one of London's most exclusive department stores, had ten minutes to evacuate before a bomb exploded. A potential tragedy was averted when an anonymous caller warned police that an explosive had been placed in the store; only one minor injury resulted from the blast. The explosion and subsequent fire considerably damaged Harrod's, known worldwide as an elegant and expensive place to shop.

The bombing was the second in three days in London. Thursday, another West End store was damaged after a bomb rocked the building. Both acts of terrorism are believed to be the work of the Irish Republican Army. Britain outlawed the I.R.A. last month following an explosion that killed 22 and wounded 182 (→ 1/16/75).

Lippmann, leader of journalists, dies

Dec 14. Political commentator and onetime editor of The New Republic Walter Lippmann has died at 85. For 36 years, his syndicated column "Today and Tomorrow" examined every side of political, social and moral issues, Lippmann being his own devil's advocate. Harvard-educated Lippmann wrote Pulitzer Prize books in 1958 and 1962. "Public Opinion" (1922) and "A Preface to Morals" (1929) were written during his early, liberal years. Of leadership, he wrote, "The final test of a leader is that he leaves behind him in other men the conviction and will to carry on."

Gate crasher fails

Dec 25. The serenity of Christmas morning was disturbed when Marshall Fields crashed his car through a White House gate, stationed himself near the mansion and held off police for four hours. He finally surrendered to authorities, who had believed he was carrying explosives; but the suspicious load on his back was only emergency warning flares. He had recently made threats against U.S. officials.

Fine comedian Jack Benny dies at 80

Dec 21. Jack Benny, America's favorite tightwad, died today in Beverly Hills at the age of 80 from cancer of the pancreas. Although he became a success on television, Benny was, during its heyday, one of radio's most enduring stars, and 7 o'clock on Sunday night became his special preserve.

Benny's perennial running gags would make a long list, but they included his trips to the cellar vault to check his money; his run-ins with his masterful valet, Rochester; his feud with Fred Allen; and violin lessons which reduced his teacher, Monsieur Le Blanc, to a suicidal depression. Ever 39, ever stingy and second to none, Benny will be remembered as the man who, when once held up, took seemingly forever to agonize over the demand, "Your money or your life."

Leftists seize 20 at Managua party

Dec 28. Left-wing rebels stormed a Christmas party in Managua, Nicaragua, killing three guards and capturing 20 hostages to be exchanged for the release of political prisoners. President Somoza, in the United States at the time, flew back to his nation and declared martial law. The guerrillas released 17 of the hostages, including Nicaragua's Ambassador to America and its U.N. delegate. But they continue to hold three other government officials. The leftists are members of the Sandinista Front, which vehemently opposes the autocratic rule of the Somoza regime (→ 3/1/77).

"Phantom of the Paradise" is an offbeat rock-and-roll remake of "Phantom of the Opera." The score was done by Paul Williams, the set design by Sissy Spacek.

1975

JANUARY

Su	Mo	Tu	We	Th	Fr	Sa
			1	2	3	4
5	6	7	8	9	10	11
12	13	14	15	16	17	18
19	20	21	22	23	24	25
26	27	28	29	30	31	

1. Washington: Haldeman, Ehrlichman, Mitchell convicted in Watergate cover-up (→ 2/21).

1. Malaysia: Ali wins 15-round decision over Joe Bugner in title fight (→ 3/24).

1. U.N. proclaims beginning of Woman's Year (→ 5/2).

3. Labor Dept. reports U.S. unemployment up to 7.1% (→ 27).

4. Phnom Penh: Khmer Rouge launches newest assault in five-year war (→ 16).

5. Ford names Rockefeller commission to investigate domestic spying by CIA (→ 6/23).

7. South Vietnam: Hanoi troops take Phuoc Binh in new full-scale offensive (→ 3/18).

9. U.S. gets $750 mil. contract to sell 60 jet fighters to Saudi Arabia and train pilots (→ 2/8).

10. Rome: Ugandan Bernadette Olowo becomes first female ambassador to Vatican.

11. Soviet spacecraft Soyuz 17 launched, links up with space lab (→ 4/19).

14. U.S. voids 1972 trade accord with Soviets over restrictions on Jewish emigration (→ 11/12).

16. Belfast: I.R.A. calls end to 25-day cease-fire (→ 2/9).

21. Montreal: 13 murdered in tavern; mob suspected.

24. N.Y.: Bomb kills four, injures 44 in Fraunces Tavern; blast laid to Puerto Rican nationalists.

25. Bangladesh adopts constitution giving Mujibur Rahman authoritarian powers (→ 8/15).

27. U.S. Dept. of Labor reports 9.3% jobless rate, highest since Depression (→ 2/5).

29. U.S.: "Alice Doesn't Live Here Anymore" opens, with Ellen Burstyn.

31. Ethiopia: Rebellion breaks out in Asmara (→ 2/2).

DEATHS

8. Richard Tucker, leading tenor with Met 30 years (*8/28/1914).

19. Thomas Hart Benton, American regionalist painter (*4/15/1889).

28. Antonin Novotny, Czech leader (*12/10/1904).

Insurgents launch new attack in Cambodia

Cambodia, a killing ground.

Jan 16. An insurgent drive against Phnom Penh and its environs, launched New Year's Day, has thrown government troops into confusion and retreat. The hospitals are full, bomb and artillery explosions have become deafening, the number of refugees has swelled and tens of thousands more have been killed in this five-year war.

Today, the United States Embassy announced that there is an emergency contingency plan to use the U.S. Air Force to operate a large supply airlift into Cambodia to keep Phnom Penh from falling to the Communists. The rebels have effectively cut the Mekong River, which normally is used for 80 percent of the city's supplies. Congress has cut military aid to Cambodia by $200 million this year, and Secretary of State Kissinger believes this has encouraged the rebels (→ 2/6).

Portugal grants Angola independence

Jan 16. A nation was born today. After centuries of foreign rule and 13 years of struggle, the people in the Portuguese territory of Angola have gained their sovereignty. The actual date for independence is November 11, but an agreement signed today seals Angolan liberation.

Portugal lost control of its power in what is one of its last colonial territories in Africa when a military coup ousted the authoritarian regime in Lisbon last April. Differences were set aside at a banquet for Portuguese and Angolan officials celebrating today's accord.

A ten-month transitional government, comprised of an equal number of representatives from Angola's three rival liberation movements, will be established. The accord calls for an election among the three factions to set up a constituent assembly. This gives Portugal confidence that a strong, stable government will be in place before formally relinquishing control.

Portuguese President Francisco da Costa Gomes said, "This accord is a fundamental step in the decolonizing process generously conceived by the men of the armed forces in the clandestine nights that preceded the revolution" (→ 6/21).

Jan 12. The Steeler defense held Tarkenton and the Vikings to a standstill today in New Orleans, leading Pittsburgh to a 16-6 Super Bowl victory.

Panel will study CIA domestic spying

Jan 15. The Director of the Central Intelligence Agency admitted today that his organization had infiltrated dissident political groups inside the United States, but he denied any massive illegality.

Director William Colby of the CIA testified before a Senate committee just days after President Ford had named a commission headed by Vice President Nelson Rockefeller to investigate domestic spying by the agency.

The New York Times reported last month that the CIA had conducted massive and illegal spying operations against anti-war radicals in the late 1960's and early 1970's, at the time when Richard Helms was head of the agency (→ 3/5).

Auto makers offer rebates to buyers

Ford's latest compact, Pinto Pony.

Jan 20. Mired in one of their worst slumps since World War II, the Big Three American auto makers are offering rebates to customers in an attempt to spur sales of new cars. Chrysler was the first to offer rebates of $200-$400 on new cars. It was followed by Ford and then G.M., which is offering rebates as high as $500 on some models.

Until this month, the Big Three had opposed even rebates, but a growing backlog of unsold cars forced them to offer the price reductions. More than 200,000 auto workers have been laid off because of the sales slump, which is attributed to the companies' overestimate of the demand for compact and subcompact cars that was generated by last winter's gasoline shortage. The rebates generally are limited to slow-selling small cars.

1975

FEBRUARY

Su	Mo	Tu	We	Th	Fr	Sa
						1
2	3	4	5	6	7	8
9	10	11	12	13	14	15
16	17	18	19	20	21	22
23	24	25	26	27	28	

4. London: Edward Heath withdraws from Conservative Party leadership after losing one round voting to Thatcher (→ 11).

5. Washington: 10,000 auto workers rally to demand jobs and end to recession (→ 26).

6. Ford asks Congress for $497 mil. in aid to Cambodia (→ 3/7).

6. Rome: Two invaluable Francescas, one Raphael stolen from Ducal Palace.

8. Private contractor reported to have recruited hundreds of Americans to train Saudi troops to protect oil fields (→ 3/25).

9. U.S.: Kissinger leaves for Mideast to seek interim accord between Egypt and Israel (→ 21).

9. Dublin: I.R.A. renews cease-fire in Northern Ireland and Britain (→ 8/29).

11. Brussels: EEC opens all nine nations to doctors from any member country (→ 5/28/79).

12. U.S.: "The Stepford Wives," with Katharine Ross, opens.

13. Cyprus: Turks proclaim autonomous state in Turkish-occupied area (→ 8/3/77).

14. Northern Marianas Islands made a U.S. Commonwealth in first territorial acquisition since West Indies in 1917 (→ 6/17).

15. Seoul: Pres. Park Chung Hee announces amnesty for all political prisoners except Communists (→ 3/12/76).

17. Milan: $5 mil. in art by Cezanne, Gauguin, Renoir, van Gogh stolen from Municipal Museum.

21. U.N. censures Israel for anti-Arab acts in occupied territories (→ 3/29).

24. U.S. lifts ten-year embargo against Pakistan (→ 3/7/77).

26. U.S. Congress approves $22.8 billion tax cut (→ 4/26).

DEATHS

14. Sir Julian Huxley, British scientist, author, humanist (*6/22/1887).

24. Nikolai Bulganin, Soviet ex-premier (*6/11/1895).

25. Elijah Muhammad, American spiritual leader of Black Muslims (*10/7/1895).

Three sentenced in Watergate case

Feb 21. Three top aides to former President Richard Nixon were sentenced to prison today for their roles in the Watergate cover-up.

Each of the three men—John N. Mitchell, H.R. Haldeman and John D. Ehrlichman—was sentenced to serve two and one-half to eight years in prison by Judge John J. Sirica of Federal District Court. A fourth, Robert C. Mardian, was sentenced to ten months to three years.

The four men were convicted on New Year's Day of conspiring to obstruct justice in the Watergate investigation through such means as paying "hush money" to those who broke into the Democratic headquarters in the Watergate complex on June 17, 1972.

Mitchell is a former Attorney General; Haldeman and Ehrlichman were top White House assistants; and Mardian was an Assistant Attorney General (→ 7/8/76).

Mitchell, a lawyer, will do time.

British Tories get first woman leader

Thatcher, a grocer's daughter.

Feb 11. Britain's Conservative Party has elected its first woman leader. Former Minister of Education Margaret Thatcher defeated former Prime Minister Edward Heath and four others for the post. "I am very, very thrilled," she said with uncharacteristic ardor.

Mrs. Thatcher, 49, is the daughter of a grocer. She won scholarships at a public school and studied chemistry at Oxford. She eased into politics, marrying, raising a boy and a girl (twins) and earning a law degree before entering Parliament.

She favors tight reins on public spending and curbs on trade union demands. Familiar with national politics, she has little exposure to the international scene. Party leadership is often but one step away from the Prime Ministry (→ 6/13).

Asmara is captured after hard fighting

Feb 2. For the past day, the Addis Ababa government of Ethiopia has been fighting in earnest against secessionist guerrillas in Eritrea province. The Ethiopian military now holds the Eritrean capital of Asmara, 450 miles north of Addis Ababa. While the inhabitants of Asmara remained indoors under curfew, columns of Ethiopian tanks, armored cars and troops moved in. Roaring overhead, Ethiopia's two American-built F-5A fighter planes dropped bombs on a suspected rebel stronghold ten miles north of the city. About 75 persons have been killed and 200 wounded.

The Addis Ababa troops are controlled by a military junta which deposed Emperor Haile Selassie last September. They are battling two rebel groups, the Eritrean Liberation Front and the Marxist Popular Liberation Front, both financed by Arab nations (→ 3/21).

Women train to defend the state.

Doctor is convicted of killing a fetus

Feb 15. A Boston physician has been found guilty of manslaughter in the death of a fetus. Dr. Kenneth Edelin committed the crime during an abortion at a Boston hospital in October 1973. He was accused of depriving the fetus of oxygen while it was still in the womb. According to a Supreme Court ruling passed in January 1973, states may impose certain restrictions on abortions done during a woman's second trimester, that is, her fourth through sixth month of pregnancy. In the Edelin case, the woman was six months pregnant (→ 11/8/76).

World's only Hindu King crowned in Nepal

Feb 4. King Birendra, ending a jubilant day of coronation ceremonies, urged Nepal to enter a "new age" and erase the poverty and illiteracy engulfing the small Himalayan country. The bespectacled 29-year-old king, heir to the world's only Hindu throne and the first formally educated (at Eton, Harvard and Tokyo University) Nepalese monarch, told his subjects that he wants the government to make primary education free to every child. Less than 13 percent of the 12 million inhabitants are literate.

As he seeks to advance Nepal, he will also maintain the firm dominance of the crown in the land-locked, feudal nation, where political parties are forbidden. Birendra Bir Bikram Shah Dev is the tenth king to rule in the present dynasty.

Lavish coronation in Katmandu.

1975

MARCH

Su	Mo	Tu	We	Th	Fr	Sa
						1
2	3	4	5	6	7	8
9	10	11	12	13	14	15
16	17	18	19	20	21	22
23	24	25	26	27	28	29
30	31					

2. Shelton, Conn.: Three claiming to be Weathermen blow up million-dollar rubber factory.

4. London: Charlie Chaplin knighted by Queen Elizabeth.

5. Washington: CIA admits it had dossier on Bella Abzug for 20 years (→ 8/27).

6. Iran, Iraq announce border dispute settled (→ 9/20/80).

7. Cambodia: Govt. troops lose last beachhead on lower Mekong River (→ 11).

8. Washington: Reagan blasts Ford statement that Republican Party should include moderates and liberals (→ 8/25/77).

9. Alaska oil pipeline begun at Sheep Creek Camp (→ 11/29).

9. Iraq launches offensive against rebellious Kurds (→ 31).

11. Phnom Penh: Pres. Lon Nol ousts army commander, asks Premier Long Boret to form new Cabinet (→ 4/1).

11. Texas: Fossil hunters find wing of reptile Pterosaur believed to be 60 million years old.

14. Lisbon: Military govt. ousts leftists, decrees nationalization of banks (→ 4/11).

18. South Vietnam: Saigon abandoning most of Central Highlands to Hanoi (→ 21).

21. South Vietnam: Hue and other northern towns being evacuated under Hanoi advance (→ 25).

21. Ethiopia calls end to monarchy (→ 7/13/76).

24. Richfield, Ohio: Ali retains title, flooring Chuck Wepner in 15th round (→ 10/1).

25. South Vietnam: Hue lost, Da Nang imperiled; U.S. orders big refugee airlift (→ 30).

29. Cairo: Sadat to reopen Suez Canal on June 5 (→ 4/13).

30. Saigon: Desperate soldiers mob rescue jet (→ 31).

DEATHS

14. Susan Hayward, Hollywood actress (*6/30/1918).

16. Aaron "T-Bone" Walker, American blues guitarist, vocalist (*5/28/1910).

Turmoil in Vietnam: Hue and Danang taken

Viet Cong, triumphant in Hue.

March 31. North Vietnamese forces swept toward Saigon today as South Vietnamese troops retreated in confusion before the Communist offensive. The hope of the government of President Nguyen Van Thieu was to draw a defensive line around Saigon, but this seems increasingly impossible in view of the growing demoralization of the South Vietnamese army.

The Communist offensive began on March 10 when North Vietnamese troops attacked Ban Me Thuot, capital of Dariac province, 150 miles northeast of Saigon. With the capture of the town against little resistance from the South Vietnamese defenders, it was clear that the entire northern part of South Vietnam was in danger of falling into Communist hands.

Supported by large numbers of tanks, the North Vietnamese forces began pushing southward, crossing the Thach Han River that had formed the demarcation line since the cease-fire in January 1973. Despite public pledges by President Thieu "to hold the line," South Vietnamese troops, offering little resistance and beating a disorderly retreat, abandoned the northern half of the country to the invaders.

The former imperial capital of Hue was evacuated as the North Vietnamese troops pressed southward to capture Danang, the second largest city in South Vietnam and once the headquarters for the United States Marines.

Tens of thousands of panicky refugees, sometimes fired upon by North Vietnamese artillery and rockets, fled toward the coastal cities, compounding the confusion overtaking South Vietnam's forces. The United States initially sent naval ships to help in the evacuation of the refugees, but this proved impossible as North Vietnamese troops moved down the coastline.

By month's end, the South Vietnamese army is in virtual disarray. Intelligence estimates are that about half the army is on the run, has deserted or has been captured by the victorious North Vietnamese army. And as a Communist attack is awaited on the capital, Saigon is overwhelmed by a mood of defeatism. Radio Hanoi said the Viet Cong are ready to talk with a government that excludes President Thieu (→ 4/2).

North Vietnamese tank, hit by artillery, burns among companions in Saigon.

Iraq makes attack on rebellious Kurds

Kurdish leader Mustafa al-Barzani.

March 31. A new agreement this month between Iran and Iraq has given Baghdad forces greater freedom to fight Kurdish rebels in northern Iraq. Six Iraqi divisions assaulted the Kurds in an effort to end once and for all the fighting that has lasted for 20 years. A million Kurds live in the rebel area. Tens of thousands of them have been fighting Iraq under the leadership of General Mustafa al-Barzani. The general has lost Iran's military support, but there is speculation he will seek refuge in Tehran.

The agreement between Iran and Iraq, meanwhile, could lead to yet another realignment in the Middle East. The Shah has made recent visits to Jordan and Egypt in an effort to close the breach between Iran and the Arab world.

Mafia reportedly asked to kill Castro

March 9. If two former aides to the late Robert Kennedy are right, the American government wanted Cuban Premier Fidel Castro dead. According to Adam Walinsky and Peter Edelman, their boss Attorney General Kennedy found out the Central Intelligence Agency asked a Mafia crime family to assassinate Castro in the early 1960's. The two aides said Kennedy played a major role in halting the assassination plans. Asked about the allegations, a high-ranking official at the CIA declined to offer comment (→ 6/20).

King Faisal killed by crazed nephew

March 25. The Middle East was jolted today with the news that King Faisal of Saudi Arabia was assassinated in Riyadh. He was gunned down at a palace reception by a nephew with a history of mental illness. Hundreds of Saudis, dressed in white robes, gathered outside the palace to mourn the death of the 70-year-old Faisal and to express their support for the monarchy. Crown Prince Khalid was quickly named to succeed Faisal, but the new Crown Prince, Fahd, is expected to wield the real power. Faisal was seen as an opponent of Israel, but a voice of moderation in the search for peace (→ 10/14/81).

Faisal, moderate in the Arab world.

Onassis, shipping magnate, passes on

March 15. Aristotle Onassis, the Greek shipping magnate, died of bronchial pneumonia in Paris today after months of suffering from myasthenia gravis. The tough, vital, self-made multimillionaire, known around the world as Ari, lived lavishly and was the prime mover of the jet set. He had two children, Christina and Alexander, with his first wife, Tina, who divorced him due to his decade-long relationship with opera diva Maria Callas. In 1968, Ari married Jacqueline Bouvier Kennedy. He will be buried on his private island of Skorpios, next to his son who was killed in an airplane crash two years ago. Onassis never recovered from the shock of his son's death (→ 6/7).

Lovely star, Susan Hayward, is dead

A life as sad as her film roles.

March 14. The star of the 1958 film "I Want to Live!" has died in Beverly Hills. Susan Hayward suffered a seizure, a complication of a brain tumor. She was 55 years old.

Brooklyn-born, red-haired Miss Hayward graduated from modeling to films. In 1947, she got the first of five Oscar nominations for meaty roles in tearjerkers. "I Want to Live!" was based on a true story of a prostitute framed for murder and sent to the gas chamber. Miss Hayward's real life was too harsh for the screen, involving a messy divorce, a sudden death of a second husband and a suicide attempt.

U.S. ship picks up piece of Soviet sub

March 18. A deep-sea salvage vessel whose construction was financed by the Central Intelligence Agency has recovered about a third of the wreckage of a Soviet submarine that sank in the Pacific Ocean in 1968, it was revealed today. But the effort failed in its main goal, recovery of hydrogen-warhead missiles and code books from the submarine. The ship, the Glomar Explorer, was constructed for the CIA by Howard Hughes, the reclusive billionaire, who said it would be used for deep-sea mining.

1975

APRIL

Su	Mo	Tu	We	Th	Fr	Sa
		1	2	3	4	5
6	7	8	9	10	11	12
13	14	15	16	17	18	19
20	21	22	23	24	25	26
29	28	29	30			

1. Phnom Penh: President Lon Nol flees country (→ 11).

2. South Vietnam: Viet Cong issue call for uprising against Saigon government (→ 3).

3. Ford tells Allies not to interpret Vietnam as sign U.S. won't honor other commitments (→ 8).

3. Soviet Anatoly Karpov named world champion chess player as Bobby Fisher withdraws.

8. Saigon: Thieu's palace attacked by South Vietnamese plane (→ 21).

11. Lisbon: Six major parties sign away power to participate in drafting of constitution (→ 7/17).

11. U.S. shuts embassy in Phnom Penh as Khmer Rouge approach military victory (→ 13).

12. Algeria: Giscard first French pres. to visit Algeria since independence (→ 12/27/78).

13. Beirut: Right-wing Lebanese open fire on bus, killing 22 Palestinians (→ 15).

13. Phnom Penh: Khmer Rouge open big attack on capital (→ 17).

19. New Delhi: First Indian satellite shot into space atop Soviet rocket (→ 7/15).

21. Saigon: Pres. Thieu leaves office, denouncing U.S. as untrustworthy (→ 22).

22. U.S.: First Vietnamese refugees arrive on West Coast (→ 29).

23. Los Alamos scientists report development of lasers to aid nuclear weapons output (→ 11/24).

26. Washington: Tens of thousands of union members march for jobs (→ 5/29).

29. Ford orders emergency evacuation of all Americans left in South Vietnam (→ 30).

DEATHS

5. Chiang Kai-shek, Nationalist Chinese leader, last of WWII Allied Big 4 (*10/31/1887).

10. Walker Evans, U.S. photographer, "Let Us Now Praise Famous Men" (*11/3/1903).

14. Frederick March, American actor (*8/31/1897).

19. Raymond Aron, conservative French sociologist (*5/25/1896).

Chiang Kai-shek's checkered life ends

Chiang, embattled political warrior.

April 5. Generalissimo Chiang Kai-shek died of a heart attack tonight on Taiwan, the island where he has been forced to live in exile since 1949. The President of Nationalist China, who was 87, died without seeing his dream of a united China fulfilled. Vice President C.K. Yen was named to succeed Chiang, but the real power is expected to rest with the late President's son, Premier Chiang Ching-kuo. No plans were announced for the funeral.

In his last testament, Chiang urged his countrymen to "recover the mainland and to restore our national culture." The Nationalist Chinese are no closer to doing that today than they were when they were driven off the mainland by Mao Tse-tung's Communists 26 years ago.

April 12. Josephine Baker, model of 1920's hedonism, led a host of black Americans to Paris in search of artistic freedom. Dead at 68, she leaves 12 adopted kids she called her "rainbow tribe."

Saigon surrenders to the Communists

April 30. Shortly after noon today, the Viet Cong flag was raised over the presidential palace in Saigon. Duong Van Minh, President of South Vietnam for only nine days, surrendered unconditionally to the Communists. Saigon was quickly renamed Ho Chi Minh City. American forces were gone, two decades after they had first arrived.

Scores of tanks from North Vietnam and trucks built in China rolled into the capital. Some Saigon residents cheered the arrival of the Viet Cong. Others raced to pillage the American Embassy that had propped up two regimes against the Communists. Everything was stolen, from filing cabinets to the kitchen sink. A bronze plaque with the names of five Americans killed at the embassy in 1968 was thrown on the floor.

Thousands of South Vietnamese soldiers, unable to find space on American helicopters, begged for seats on river boats to speed them from Saigon. Many did not make it. As they were rounded up, the Communists cut off communications with the outside world. Speaking in Paris, a representative of the Provisional Revolutionary Government called the collapse of Saigon "a victory of historic significance for the Vietnamese."

The departure of the Americans seemed as disorganized as their war effort. Up until the past few days, the Ford administration had been sharply divided about whether to remove Americans from Saigon. President Ford finally ordered the emergency helicopter evacuation after the airport was closed by gunfire. The operation, the largest of its kind in American history, ended last night. It took 19 hours, five times longer than the Pentagon had estimated. At 7:52 p.m., 11 Marines were lifted off the roof of the embassy. They were the last soldiers to be evacuated after the most divisive war in American history.

A total of a thousand Americans and more than 5,000 South Vietnamese judged to be in danger were airlifted to carriers in the South China Sea. Many more people fled from the country in small boats. Secretary of State Henry Kissinger estimated that 70,000 South Vietnamese may eventually have to be resettled in the United States.

Marines help South Vietnamese onto an Army helicoper at the U.S. Embassy.

The United States Ambassador to South Vietnam, Graham Martin, criticized American policy as soon as he was evacuated from Saigon to the safety of a Navy ship. "If we had done as a nation the things I think we said we would do," Martin said, "if we had kept our commitments, we wouldn't have to evacuate." Martin, who is viewed as a firm supporter of former President Nguyen Van Thieu, refused to answer when a reporter asked if he were ashamed of his country.

Thieu, who was forced to resign by the Communists before they would even negotiate with South Vietnam, had few good things to say about the United States. Although he was supported by Washington for ten years, Thieu called America untrustworthy. He singled out Secretary of State Kissinger for the "acceptance of the continued presence of North Vietnamese troops in South Vietnam."

President Ford had "no comment" today about the surrender of the South Vietnamese government. Yesterday, he said the evacuation of Americans "closes a chapter in the American experience." The president also appealed to the country "to close ranks, to avoid recrimination about the past, to look ahead to the many goals we share."

Last week in New Orleans, Ford was cheered when he said the war in Indochina was finished "as far as America is concerned." The president came close to calling the American experience a defeat. "Some seem to feel," he said, "that if we do not succeed in everything everywhere, then we have succeeded in nothing anywhere." Ford called that "polarized thinking" (→ 5/3).

100 Vietnamese orphans are killed in crash

April 4. An American Air Force transport taking 243 Vietnamese orphans to refuge in the U.S. crashed and burned shortly after takeoff from Saigon today. More than 100 of the children and at least 25 of the accompanying adults were killed. This was the first in an airlift series to bring 2,000 orphans to be adopted by American families. The tragedy began when a sudden depressurization in the four-engine Galaxy C-5A jet blew out the rear door which struck the tail.

Innocent victims of a brutal war.

Zoologists observe World Whale Day

April 28. World Whale Day was observed around the globe today. The event was staged to publicize zoologists' concern over the killing of whales by Japan and the Soviet Union. Five species of whales are in danger of extinction, and the numbers of several others have been reduced to dangerously low levels. The species that appear to be in most danger are the fin whale, found in the Antarctic, and humpback whales, only a few thousand of which are known to exist. Right whales, protected by international agreement since 1935, and grey whales, protected since 1947, are believed to be stable or increasing in number in recent years (→ 6/27).

John B. Connally is acquitted of bribery

April 17. John Connally, who eluded death from an assassin's bullet twelve years ago, today escaped a bribery conviction. The former Texas Governor was found not guilty of accepting illegal gifts from the dairy industry. The case cut short Connally's bid for the presidency, but after the trial he said, "I hope I never lose the desire to participate in public affairs." In 1963, Connally was hit by bullets from the same gun that killed President Kennedy, but he fully recovered.

Drinking water in 79 cities is polluted

April 18. The drinking water of 79 American cities is polluted with traces of organic chemicals, including some suspected of causing cancer, the Environmental Protection Agency reported today. "People should not react with any sense of panic but they should know there is a problem," said Russell E. Train, the agency's administrator. Only parts per billion of the chemicals were found in the water of most cities, and the health consequences of the pollutants are unknown, he said. The survey began when 66 chemicals were found in the New Orleans water supply (→ 8/4/78).

Reds capture Cambodia

Cambodians are fleeing to countryside under orders of Communist patrols.

April 17. Communist-led forces have seized control of the capital city of Phnom Penh, ending a five-year civil war in Cambodia. The new military government supported by the United States surrendered without a major fight after it became apparent that the Communist-led insurgents were prepared to attack the city. As white flags fluttered over downtown buildings, Communist patrols moved through the city warning residents to evacuate to the countryside.

As it became evident that Phnom Penh was about to fall to the Communists, personnel in the United States Embassy, including Ambassador John Gunther Dean, were evacuated by Marine helicopters to Thailand. This also marked the end of an American airlift bringing supplies into the beleaguered capital.

As a last-minute gesture, the American Embassy had proposed the return from Peking of Prince Sihanouk, the nominal leader of the insurgents who was overthrown in 1970 by the Lon Nol regime that was supported by the U.S. The proposal was rejected by the military leaders that had taken control of the government in recent days. It was not immediately clear what had happened to Premier Long Boret, who was on a Communist list of "traitors," but it was believed he had fled to Thailand (→ 5/8).

Donald Sutherland stars in the film of Nathanael West's "The Day of the Locust," a disturbing tale of emptiness and fanaticism in Depression-era Hollywood.

Jack Nicklaus wins his fifth Masters

April 13. No one can accuse Jack Nicklaus of making it look easy. He provided one of the most exciting finishes in Masters history while taking the coveted golf championship the fifth straight time.

The victory was determined by the last two putts on the final green and Jack walked off with a final-round 68 for a 72-hole total of 276, the third best score in Masters history. Tom Weiskopf and Johnny Miller finished a shot behind Nicklaus after missing putts on the 18th. They had seen their chances crumble when Nicklaus sank a 40-foot birdie putt on the 16th (→ 4/13/86).

Palestinians fight Christian militia in Beirut

April 15. As bombs exploded and machine gun fire rattled the windows of Beirut, the little nation of Lebanon was troubled for the third straight day by the battle between Palestinian guerrillas and the Phalangist militia, which took a toll of ten dead for the day and about 100 altogether.

The right-wing Christian Phalangist Party has a strong base in a country whose equally divided Moslem-Christian population is similarly divided over the Arab-Israeli conflict. The Phalangists have been critical of Palestinian attacks on Israel from Lebanese soil and the main issue in this battle involves the future home of Palestinian guerrillas, driven out of Jordan in 1970-71 by King Hussein (→ 5/20).

Streets of Beirut a battleground.

Freedom Train on its way to 80 cities

April 1. More than 30,000 persons visited the Freedom Train in Stanton, Delaware, today in its first stop on a nationwide tour to 80 cities in 21 months. A private, tax-exempt, nonprofit project funded with $5.6 million in corporate donations, the train is the first major enterprise in the Bicentennial celebration. It is a traveling historical museum of Americana, featuring more than 750 artifacts—from George Washington's copy of the Declaration of Independence to Judy Garland's dress from "The Wizard of Oz" (→ 7/4/76).

Seven to nine will be family viewing time

April 9. Responding to an FCC mandate, the National Association of Broadcasters has voted to designate early evening viewing hours "family time." In the fall, networks will schedule programs low in sexual innuendo and violence from 7 to 9 p.m. (6 to 8 p.m. Mountain and Central time). Objectionable programs will air later in the evening. Since few present shows meet the new criteria (NBC's "Little House on the Prairie" and "The Wonderful World of Disney" might), several programs will have to be developed in a hurry.

Audiences scream as movie Jaws is shown

Just when you thought it was safe to go into a theater, "Jaws" snaps to your attention. The film is based on the popular Peter Benchley novel concerning a placid New England beach and a gargantuan shark. Roy Scheider as a beleaguered cop, Robert Shaw as a shark expert and Richard Dreyfuss as a bearded, bespectacled icthyologist try to kill the fangish fish. The tense scenes were well-edited by Verna Field, and the edge-of-your seat score was composed by John Williams. The director is 27-year-old Steven Spielberg, whose only success has been "The Sugarland Express."

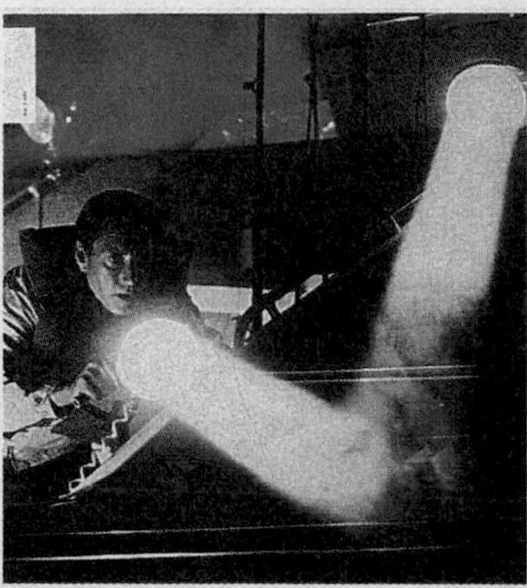

Roy Scheider, a local cop, searches anxiously for the toothy giant.

1975

MAY

Su	Mo	Tu	We	Th	Fr	Sa
				1	2	3
4	5	6	7	8	9	10
11	12	13	14	15	16	17
18	19	20	21	22	23	24
25	26	27	28	29	30	31

3. Foolish Pleasure, ridden by Jacinto Vasquez, wins 101st Kentucky Derby.

3. Saigon radio announces Hanoi undertaking vast reconstruction program in South (→ 5).

5. Ford asks Congress for $507 million to resettle 150,000 refugees from South Vietnam (→ 7).

8. Cambodia: Khmer Rouge reported uprooting millions in peasant revolution (→ 12).

11. Saigon: New leadership to hold nationwide vote (→ 6/8).

12. Gulf of Siam: U.S. merchant ship Mayaguez fired on by Cambodian naval vessel (→ 15).

12. New York: Met opens new section housing Robert Lehman art collection.

14. Laos: Demonstrators ransack U.S. missions in Luang, Prabang, Savannakhet (→ 8/23).

15. Ford announces Marines have retaken Mayaguez from Cambodians (→ 16).

16. Thailand recalls ambassador to U.S., citing sovereignty violation in Mayaguez rescue (→ 21).

20. Vienna: Kissinger, Gromyko agree to cooperate in reopening Geneva talks on Mideast (→ 23).

21. Tehran: Rebels kill two U.S. Air Force officers (→ 2/28/76).

22. Joe Namath rejects $4 mil. offer to play for Chicago in World Football League.

23. Beirut: Pres. Franjieh names first military Cabinet since independence in 1963 in attempt to restore order (→ 6/5).

27. Washington: Bolshoi Ballet makes first U.S. appearance in ten years, at JFK Center.

27. Philadelphia Flyers capture hockey's Stanley Cup.

29. Ford vetoes $5.3 billion jobs bill (→ 6/30).

DEATHS

6. Joseph Cardinal Mindszenty, exiled primate of Hungary (*3/29/1892).

8. Avery Brundage, American pres. of Olympic Committee for 20 years (*9/28/1887).

28. Ezzard Charles, American ex-heavyweight boxing champ.

Marines rescue ship seized by Cambodians

May 21. The White House has released figures revealing that 15 men have died trying to rescue the Mayaguez, an American-registered merchant vessel. An additional 23 men died when a helicopter crashed in Thailand, en route to the rescue operation.

The Mayaguez incident began May 12, when commercial radio operators received a Mayday signal from the ship. The message, relayed to the State Department, said that the ship had been fired upon and boarded by Cambodian forces and that it was being towed to an unknown port.

Rescue ship Coral Sea on the way.

President Ford met with the National Security Council and issued an appeal to China for aid in releasing the ship and its 39 crew members. The following day, American forces reached the island of Tang, where the Mayaguez was being held, sinking Cambodian vessels which would have removed the hostages to the mainland. By evening, an assault force had arrived, including a thousand Marines. An hour later, American troops boarded the Mayaguez, but found it empty.

The White House released a statement demanding the release of the crew. Cambodia immediately released the hostages, but more U.S. warplanes were already on the way and it was a half-hour before bombardment ceased (→ 9/9).

Boston is ordered to bus 21,000 children

May 10. Federal District Court Judge W. Arthur Garrity ordered the implementation of a new integration plan in Boston's racially troubled public schools today. The plan calls for the busing of 21,000 students in the coming school year, more than half of them in grades one through five. It replaces this year's temporary busing order, which caused sporadic racial violence in the classroom and numerous anti-busing demonstrations by white parents.

Under Judge Garrity's order, the Boston School Department must prepare a comprehensive transportation plan by July. Boston School Committee Chairman John McDonough reiterated the committee's long-standing opposition to busing, and he said that the plan would be appealed to the Supreme Court (→ 7/28).

Despite widespread resistance, busing promises a ray of hope for race relations.

Ford declares end to Vietnam effort

Troops arrive home from Saigon.

May 7. President Ford in effect has declared an end to the Vietnam War by signing a proclamation terminating wartime veteran's benefits. "America is no longer at war," the president said in a statement proclaiming the end "of the Vietnam era." The proclamation was issued two years after the withdrawal of American combat forces from Vietnam and one week after the fall of Saigon to the Communists.

The Defense Department earlier had ordered the withdrawal of U.S. Navy ships that had been picking up refugees fleeing from South Vietnam in small boats. The House of Representatives rejected an administration bill that would have authorized $327 million in aid for the Vietnamese refugees and use of combat troops to assist in the evacuation. President Ford was described as "damned mad" at the widespread opposition to resettlement of 130,000 refugees (→ 11).

May 25. The Unser racing dynasty has added yet another trophy to the family shelf. Bobby caught up to brother Al today with his second victory at Indy. The 500-mile race, plagued by the memory of a 12-car accident in 1973, was shortened to 435 miles due to rain-slickened pavement.

Trial of German terrorists begins

May 21. The trial of the alleged terrorist group known as the Baader-Meinhof gang was adjourned in West Germany today almost as quickly as it began. The defendants rejected their court-appointed attorneys and accused them of violating the confidential lawyer-client relationship. Extraordinarily tight security has been put in effect around the Stuttgart prison where the accused terrorists are being held. They are charged with unleashing a series of terrorist acts since 1968, when leader Andreas Baader was convicted of starting a fire in a Berlin department store (→ 5/9/76).

Women join Army in record numbers

May 2. Women are joining the U.S. Army in record peacetime numbers, integrating hundreds of previously male-only soldiering jobs, from fixing tanks to flying helicopters, and moving closer to the last bastion of male exclusivity—combat. Their ranks have tripled in four years to 35,000, only 4.5 percent of the Army's force of 780,000, but the highest number in history. The highest-ranking military woman, Major General Jeanne M. Holm, predicts that women will soon fly Air Force fighter planes, serve aboard Navy warships and even participate in combat (→ 6/3).

Japanese is first woman on Everest

May 16. A woman has conquered Mount Everest for the first time. Junko Tabei, 35, of Japan reached the 29,028-foot summit of the world's highest peak at 12:30 p.m. local time today. Escorted by a male Sherpa guide, she arrived at the summit about five hours after leaving the 24,885-foot camp of 15 Japanese women. Mrs. Tabei is the leader of the expedition. Everest has been climbed by 35 men over the past 22 years, since Sir Edmund Hillary and Tensing Norkal of Nepal were the first to scale the Himalayan peak on May 29, 1953.

1975

JUNE

Su	Mo	Tu	We	Th	Fr	Sa
1	2	3	4	5	6	7
8	9	10	11	12	13	14
15	16	17	18	19	20	21
22	23	24	25	26	27	28
29	30					

2. France: Prostitutes occupy church in Lyons to protest police repression.

3. HEW releases new regulations aimed at equalizing opportunities for women in schools and colleges (→ 9/16).

4. Ethiopia: Severe drought bringing famine to more than 800,000 (→ 12/26/77).

7. Taiwan: U.S. removes last combat aircraft (→ 12/1).

7. Athens: Onassis will provides $250,000 per year for Jackie (→ 9/19/77).

8. North Vietnamese Natl. Assembly urges Hanoi be capital of unified nation (→ 8/11).

12. New Delhi: Allahabad court voids Gandhi's election as premier, citing corruption (→ 26).

15. Paris: Bjorn Borg wins French Open at Roland Garros.

16. Italy: Communists gain 33.4% of vote to Christian Democrats' 35.3% (→ 1/7/76).

17. Mariana Islands: Referendum ratifies pact to become U.S. commonwealth.

21. Nairobi: Divided Angolan liberation movements rework pact for independence from Portugal (→ 11/11).

23. Washington: Appeals Court requires warrant for wiretaps by executive branch (→ 8/27).

23. U.S., Soviets near accord outlawing techniques to alter weather for military purposes.

24. N.Y.: Eastern 727 crashes on landing at JFK, killing 109.

25. Mozambique gains independence from Portugal after 470 years; Marxist Samora Machel takes over.

26. S.D.: Two FBI agents killed making arrests at Oglala Sioux Reservation (→ 7/15/78).

27. London: Intl. Whaling Commission bars hunting of finback whale (→ 6/1976).

30. Ford signs bill allowing unemployed to receive benefits for 65 weeks (→ 9/10).

DEATH

2. Sato Eisaku, ex-premier Japan, 1974 Nobel for fighting nuclear proliferation (*3/17/1901).

Indira Gandhi convicted of election fraud

June 26. Indian Prime Minister Indira Gandhi's election to Parliament was invalidated today by the high court of Allahabad on the grounds of corrupt election practices. She is prohibited from running for any public office for the next six years. Although she is legally permitted to retain her present position, many observers believe that she will resign.

Mrs. Gandhi was convicted of illegally retaining the services of a government official as a campaign organizer in her 1971 election bid. Her opponent in that election, Socialist Raj Narain, filed the lawsuit which led to the court's decision (→ 11/7).

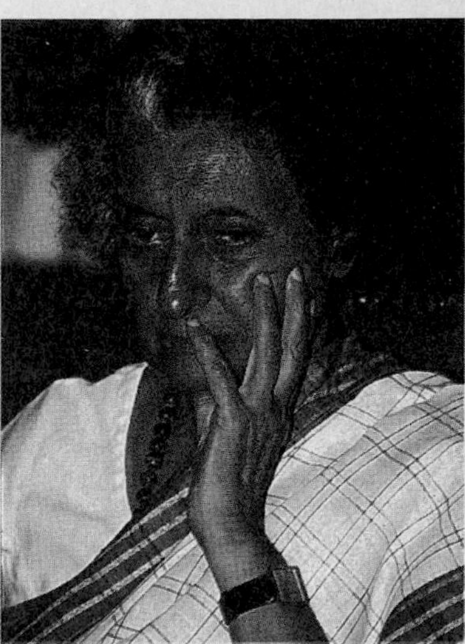

Troubled Indian leader Gandhi.

British inflation reaches 25 percent

June 13. Harold Wilson's beleaguered government, already under fire because of rising inflation, suffered a further blow today with newly released figures showing a record annual inflation rate of 25 percent, the highest in Europe. Prime Minister Wilson has relied on persuasion, rather than legal curbs, to restrain trade union demands, but this glum news only underscores a general feeling that voluntary wage restraint is not working. Admitting there is no magic formula, Wilson's aides hope that the fear of unemployment may yet lower union expectations (→ 11/3).

Mental patients win certain legal rights

June 26. The Supreme Court ruled today that mental patients are free to leave psychiatric institutions if they wish, providing they are not dangerous and can survive on their own. The unanimous decision will result in the release of 250,000 patients. Justice Potter Stewart asked rhetorically, in the court opinion, "May the state fence in the harmless mentally ill solely to save its citizens from exposure to those whose ways are different?" Kenneth Donaldson, who spent 15 years in an institution and brought the case before the court, called the ruling "a victory in common sense."

Belgium buying American F-16 jet fighters

June 7. The Belgian government today said it would buy 102 F-16 jet fighters from the General Dynamics Company, rather than the French-made Mirage F-1. Belgium joins three other European countries—Norway, Denmark and the Netherlands—in choosing the American-designed plane. The four countries will buy 306 of the fighters, with options on another 28.

The U.S. Air Force has ordered 650 F-16's, and some officials predict a potential market of 3,000 to 4,000 planes, worth up to $20 billion. As part of the deal, the engines and some of the electrical equipment for the aircraft will be made in Europe. The Belgian decision was made in the face of a statement by French President Valery Giscard d'Estaing that refusal to buy the Mirage could put the progress of European unity in question.

The F-16, bound for Belgium.

Suez Canal reopened after eight years

International traffic freely transits Suez for the first time in eight years.

June 5. Ship sirens let out long blasts and tens of thousands of spectators cheered in Port Said today as Egypt reopened the Suez Canal. A convoy passed through the strategic waterway eight years to the day after it was closed in the 1967 Arab-Israeli War. President Anwar el-Sadat said the opening of the canal was a gesture of peace, but he also pledged that Egypt would "liberate" the Sinai, the Golan Heights and Palestine from Israel. Privately, however, it is reported that Sadat has agreed with President Ford to resume piecemeal negotiations with Israel on the future of the Sinai. Up until now, Sadat has been insisting on a full-blown international peace conference in Geneva (→ 15).

Rockets are fired at Israeli beach resort

June 15. "An eye-for-an-eye" continues to characterize the Middle East conflict as Arab and Israeli reprisals swiftly succeed each other. Following a Palestinian attack on a frontier village home and its subsequent liberation by Israeli soldiers, which saw two Israelis and the four guerrillas killed, the Israeli air force retaliated by bombing targets in Lebanon. In reply to that, Palestinians next fired three rockets into Nahariya, an Israeli coastal resort (→ 7/13).

Pele has signed with the N.Y. Cosmos for $7 mil. over 3 years.

Mob boss tied to Castro plot is slain

June 20. Sam Giancana, a Chicago organized crime figure who was reputed to have participated in a failed CIA plot to assassinate Fidel Castro, was gunned down last night outside his suburban home in Oak Park, Illinois. Vincent Inserra, head of the FBI's Organized Crime Squad in Chicago, said that the murder was probably "a professional hit" stemming from recent friction between Giancana and rival syndicate bosses. Giancana, who was 65, returned to the U.S. last year after a nine-year stay in Mexico, after he refused to testify before a federal grand jury (→ 8/21).

1975

JULY

Su	Mo	Tu	We	Th	Fr	Sa
		1	2	3	4	5
6	7	8	9	10	11	12
13	14	15	16	17	18	19
20	21	22	23	24	25	26
29	28	29	30	31		

5. Wimbledon: Arthur Ashe over Jimmy Connors 6-1, 6-1, 5-7, 6-4; Billie Jean King over Evonne Goolagong 6-0, 6-1.

8. Washington: Ford to seek re-election in 1976 (→ 11/12).

8. Buenos Aires: Isabel Peron yields to wage demands to stop general strike (→ 10/5).

8. West Germany: Yitzhak Rabin arrives for first visit by Israeli head of state.

13. Carnoustie, Scotland: Tom Watson wins British Open golf title.

13. Lebanon: Israeli planes raid largest Palestinian refugee camp; Arabs retaliate with rockets (→ 9/1).

15. Apollo and Soyuz blast into orbit from U.S. and U.S.S.R., head for rendezvous (→ 17).

17. Apollo and Soyuz dock in space; Stafford and Leonov complete first intl. handshake in space (→ 19).

17. Portugal: Army rulers dissolve coalition govt. as two moderate parties pull out (→ 18).

18. Portugal: Military on alert as conflict between Communist Party and rivals heats up (→ 25).

20. Bernard Thevenet wins Tour de France.

22. U.S. Congress restores citizenship of late Confederate General Robert E. Lee.

23. Canada closes Atlantic ports to Soviet fishing trawlers.

25. Turkey takes over American bases to protest U.S. refusal to end arms embargo (→ 5/1/77).

28. Congress extends Voting Rights Act seven years, bringing Hispanics under protection (→ 9/8).

29. Lagos: Gen. Yakubu Gowon deposed in Nigerian bloodless coup (→ 2/13/76).

31. Helsinki: 33 heads of state open largest summit in European history (→ 8/1).

DEATHS

15. Charles Weidman, pioneer in American modern dance (*7/22/1901).

30. Jimmy Hoffa, American labor leader (*2/13/1914).

Triumvirate takes power in Portugal

July 25. The Armed Forces Movement, which has governed Portugal since it seized power in a bloodless coup over a year ago, has announced that the nation will shift the emphasis of its government from a 30-man high council to a triumvirate of army generals. The action resulted from conflicts between the country's three main parties, the Communists, the Socialists and the Popular Democrats. The triumvirate said it intended to slow the pace of the revolution and the move toward socialism, a decision conciliatory to the parties and to the Western Allies (→ 8/29).

Idi Amin pardons Briton facing death

July 1. Idi Amin, the President of Uganda, reversed himself again today and announced that he would not execute Denis Cecil Hills. The Briton's head has been on and off the chopping block since he enraged Amin by calling him a tyrant in an unpublished manuscript. The unpredictable Amin, who has accused Britain of interfering in Uganda's affairs, originally said Hills would be executed unless Foreign Secretary James Callaghan made a personal visit to Kampala. Amin later threatened to kill all 700 Britons still living in Uganda (→ 2/7/77).

July 27. Customized vans, 5,000 of these "sin bins," carried a variety of vagabonds into Bowling Green, Kentucky, today for the third annual Truck-in. "Tricked out" vans allow the modern rugged individualist to seek out new frontiers without leaving all the comforts of home behind. Despite the energy crisis and the high cost of gas, Americans still seem to love the open road.

Americans and Russians meet in space

July 19. American and Soviet astronauts ended an unprecedented two-day international mission in space today as they undocked their Apollo and Soyuz spacecraft and went into separate orbits. The Soviets will return to earth tomorrow, the Americans in five days.

The joint mission began when the two spaceraft, each carrying three astronauts, were launched four days ago. The Soviets broke their habitual secrecy by showing the launch of Soyuz live on TV. The spacecraft linked together two days ago about 140 miles over the Atlantic Ocean.

"Glad to see you," Aleksei A. Leonov, the Soviet commander, said in English. Thomas P. Stafford, the American commander, replied in Russian. The commanders shook hands through the hatches of their spacecraft, then traded gifts as the Americans entered the Soviet ship.

During the next two days, the six crew members shared meals and cooperated on scientific experiments as they moved from one craft to the other. Then they flew in formation for two orbits to make observations of the sun and the earth. The Apollo-Soyuz test project, as the mission is called, was agreed to at a meeting in Moscow three years ago. American and Soviet officials say exploratory talks about future cooperative space ventures have been held (→ 10/22).

Apollo and Soyuz join in space, human counterparts Leonov, Slayton in insert.

China finds 2,000-year-old pottery army

Life-sized warriors of clay, 2,000 years old, lined up in battle formation.

July 11. Chinese archeologists have announced the uncovering of a three-acre burial mound concealing a massive "army" of funerary figures. Hsinhua, the official news agency, states that the site (in Shensi province, northwestern China) contains 6,000 clay statues of warriors and their regalia. Some of the 2,000-year-old figures are shattered but well-preserved.

The finding dates from 221 to 206 B.C., the reign of the first Chin Emperor, Shih Hwang-ti. He centralized government, shifting society from slavery to feudalism, and simplified trade by establishing uniform weights and measures. Barbarians to the north were deterred by construction of the Great Wall.

The clay warriors, their horses, spears and arrows, bring the era to life. Indeed, the soldiers are life-size, standing nearly six feet tall. Their swords, Hsinhua asserts, "remain stainless and shiny." Implements and ornaments of gold and jade litter the ground at their feet.

Hsinhua believes the soldiers, driving chariots pulled by teams of four proud horses, recreate a symbolic battle. The phalanx evokes "the sublime scene of Shih Hwang-ti fighting across the country to wipe out the forces of slave owners and unify China as whole." The newspaper goes on to praise the artisans who built the army, a working class as resourceful as the working class of modern China. Laborers made the historic find while digging for well water.

Jerusalem market is hit by terror bomb

July 4. Bodies were hurled in the air, buildings scorched and windows shattered for blocks around when a bomb hidden in an old refrigerator left on the sidewalk blasted Jerusalem's main Zion Square during the busiest hours of the pre-Sabbath shopping period. The city's worst terrorist incident since Israel was founded left 13 dead and 72 wounded. Egypt and Israel are currently trying to reach an interim peace agreement. The attack was presumably an attempt by the PLO to remind the negotiators that no true peace can ignore their movement (→ 13).

Mauna Loa erupts after 25 quiet years

July 6. Hawaii's Mauna Loa volcano erupted last night after 25 years of inactivity. Lava fountains up to 200 feet high broke out just before midnight in the oval-shaped crater of the volcano, which is on the island of Hawaii, largest in the Hawaiian chain. Mauna Loa erupted sporadically before 1950 but has been quiet since then. Scientists said the eruption was no threat to life or property because the crater is far from inhabited areas. Meanwhile, geologists say Mount Baker in the state of Washington shows signs of new volcanic activity after six decades of dormancy.

The luxurious Queen Elizabeth 2 sets New York harbor aglow on the eve of its first round-the-world cruise. The last of her kind, the QE2 set out in January with 1,250 passengers for the farthest reaches of the globe.

1975

AUGUST

Su	Mo	Tu	We	Th	Fr	Sa
					1	2
3	4	5	6	7	8	9
10	11	12	13	14	15	16
17	18	19	20	21	22	23
24	25	26	27	28	29	30
31						

2. Poland opens door for 120,000 Germans to emigrate to West Germany.

2. New York: Billy Martin replaces Bill Virdon as manager of Yankees.

3. FBI opens investigation on disappearance of Jimmy Hoffa.

3. N.Y.: Staten Island Ferry hikes fare from five to 25 cents.

3. Agadir: Jetliner carrying Moroccan workers home from France crashes, killing 188.

4. Alger Hiss, convicted in HUAC investigations, readmitted to Massachusetts bar.

10. New York: Samuel Bronfman, 21-year-old son of Seagram CEO, kidnapped (→ 17).

10. Calif.: David Frost reports he has bought rights to Nixon's "TV memoirs."

11. N.Y.: U.S. vetoes entrance of Vietnam to U.N. (→ 9/13/76).

12. Goteborg, Sweden: New Zealand's John Walker, at 3:49.4, is first to break 3:50 in mile.

14. Philippines: Moro Liberation Front accepts cease-fire with govt. (→ 12/7).

16. Dacca: New Bangladesh govt. moves to take nation out of India political orbit (→ 10/2/77).

21. U.S. lifts 12-year ban on exports to Cuba (→ 11/20).

23. New York: Met buys 13th-century Japanese art collection for $5.1 million.

24. Greece: Athens court voids death sentences of colonels who led 1967 putsch (→ 3/10/85).

25. Lima: Non-aligned nations hold fifth parley; Vietnam, Panama, North Korea and PLO join.

26. FDA warns birth control pills raise heart attack risk.

27. Cleveland: Federal jury clears Gov. Rhodes and 27 Natl. Guardsmen in 1970 Kent State shootings (→ 9/25).

29. Lisbon: Pro-Communist Premier Vasco Goncalves dismissed by president (→ 11/13).

DEATH

27. Haile Selassie, last emperor in 3,000-year-old Ethiopian monarchy (*7/23/1892).

35 nations affirm peace and human rights

Delegates assemble in Helsinki.

Aug 1. President Ford stressed the importance of human rights as he joined the Soviet Union and 33 other countries in signing the Helsinki agreement. The pact recognizes the sovereignty of the individual nations in Europe and rejects the use of force. But the idealistic goals of the document were undermined by sharp exchanges at the podium.

In an apparent challenge to the Soviets, Ford said that people are tired "of having their hopes raised and then shattered by empty words and unfulfilled pledges. We had better mean what we say," the president said. Soviet leader Brezhnev suggested that the Helsinki charter would have supported the invasion of Czechoslovakia in 1968.

The President of Rumania, Nicolae Ceausescu, insisted that noninterference is more important than all the "talk about humanitarian problems." And international talks to solve the crisis on Cyprus collapsed when the Premier of Turkey walked out and flew home.

Pathet Lao seizes power in Vientiane

Aug 23. The Communist-led Pathet Lao took over control of Laos, culminating the Communist ascension to power in Indochina. The months-long transition to Communist rule in the former French colony ended with a rally in Vientiane, the Laotian capital, to "welcome the people's revolutionary administration" in Vientiane province. Left unclear was the status of Premier Souvanna Phouma, a neutralist leader who two years ago worked out an agreement for a coalition government that would include both rightists and the Pathet Lao. The rightists progressively lost political support in the countryside.

De Valera, durable Irish patriot, dies at 92

Aug 29. Since his critical role in the 1916 Easter Rebellion, Eamon de Valera has been a national hero to the people of the Republic of Ireland. Yesterday, the 92-year-old former Prime Minister, President and statesman died of bronchial pneumonia and cardiac failure. Despite de Valera's lifelong struggle to see all 32 counties in Ireland united, the land and its people remain divided. On his deathbed, he painfully uttered his last words to a nursing nun: "All my life I have done my best for Ireland; now, I am ready to go" (→ 10/2).

De Valera, in Irish politics 62 years.

Mujibur is killed in Bangladesh coup

Aug 15. Sheik Mujibur Rahman, President of the young nation of Bangladesh, was overthrown and killed today in a military coup. Martial law was declared and a 24-hour curfew was imposed. A former ally of Sheik Mujib, Khondaker Moshtaque Ahmed, installed himself as President. One of the original leaders of the independence movement, Sheik Mujib called himself the father of the nation. But in recent months his rule became increasingly autocratic (→ 16).

Ransom is paid for Bronfman, regained

Aug 17. After nine days of captivity, Samuel Bronfman II, the heir to the Seagram's fortune, was rescued by New York City police and FBI agents today. His alleged kidnappers, Mel Patrick Lynch, a city fireman, and Dominic Byrne, who ran a limousine service, were arrested in the raid on an apartment in Flatbush, Brooklyn. Byrne claimed that he and Lynch were forced at gunpoint to abduct Bronfman from his Purchase, New York, mansion by "two strangers." The $2.3 million in ransom, paid by Bronfman's father yesterday, was also recovered by the federal agents (→ 12/10/76).

Soviet composer Shostakovich dies

Aug 10. The Soviet Union lost its most celebrated composer yesterday when Dmitri Shostakovich died from a lingering heart ailment at the age of 68. Shostakovich first burst on the international scene with his First Symphony, an incredibly fine, mature work from the pen of one who was then but 19 and still a student at the Leningrad Conservatory. A committed Communist, he was nevertheless alternately in and out of grace with the Communist Party for music it often deemed "bourgeois decadence," but the undeniable power of his best works gradually lifted him above the political fray.

Even dear old Dad joins the T-shirt fad

Anyone wearing a T-shirt this summer that does not advertise a product or make a political statement might very well feel naked. Plain T-shirts a la Marlon Brando are out; shirts lauding beer, sex, Beethoven, running shoes, the environment and The Fonz are in. The fad began when Budweiser started selling emblazoned T's in the early 60's. They caught on at hot Florida and California beaches, where youth publicized their proclivities. Airlines, sporting goods manufacturers and other businesses gave it a try. Now many cities have T-shirt shops, where personal messages are printed while-u-wait.

1975

SEPTEMBER

Su	Mo	Tu	We	Th	Fr	Sa
	1	2	3	4	5	6
7	8	9	10	11	12	13
14	15	16	17	18	19	20
21	22	23	24	25	26	27
28	29	30				

1. Alexandria: Israel and Egypt initial pact on Sinai pullout, use of Suez Canal (→ 4).

4. Geneva: Israel and Egypt sign interim peace pact (→ 18).

5. Sacramento: Lynette Alice "Squeaky" Fromme arrested after agents save Ford by pulling gun from her hand (→ 22).

6. N.Y.: Czech tennis star Martina Navratilova asks asylum in U.S.

6. Turkey: Earthquake in east takes at least 1,000 lives.

7. New York: Manuel Orantes and Chris Evert win U.S. Open titles at Forest Hills.

8. Boston: Schools open under heavy guard as integration busing begins (→ 4/23/76).

9. Cambodia: Prince Sihanouk returns from exile (→ 9/28/77).

10. Congress, in blow to Ford anti-inflation policy, overrides veto on $7 billion education bill (→ 10/6).

14. Amsterdam: Rembrandt's "The Night Watch" slashed by man with bread knife.

14. Rome: Mother Elizabeth Ann Seton becomes first U.S.-born saint.

16. U.S.: Rhodes Scholarship administrators to offer fellowships to women (→ 6/28/76).

18. Beirut: Heavy fighting breaks out; govt. warns residents to stay off streets (→ 24).

19. Greece: Undersea explorers find wreckage of early Bronze Age ships off coast.

24. Israeli For. Min. Allon and Soviet Gromyko meet in rare talk on Mideast (→ 11/10).

25. U.S. Senate makes public 238 illegal FBI burglaries against dissident groups (→ 3/10/76).

27. Madrid: Five Basques executed despite protests througout Europe (→ 28).

27. Zaire: Leo Tindemans welcomed in first visit by Belgian premier since 1960 (→ 3/10/77).

28. Spain: Police shoot six in Basque demonstration against executions (→ 29).

29. Spain: Thousands strike to protest executions (→ 10/1).

Beirut torn by civil war

Palestinians, intent on retaking Israeli-occupied lands, now fight in Beirut.

Sept 16. Civil war is tearing the country of Lebanon apart, turning streets of Beirut into walls of flame and threatening the government. Battles between heavily armed Moslems and Christians have left bodies and debris piled on the sidewalks. The cost of the damage has risen sharply to eight billion pounds. Foreign capital is fleeing from the once elegant and opulent capital.

Fighting erupted in Tripoli earlier this month. Today, it flared in Beirut. Moslems and Christians battled for control of different neighborhoods, fighting from building to building and then barricading themselves inside. Shopkeepers and residents ducked for cover.

The fighting has split the coalition government, which was already wracked by internal divisions. The Phalangist Party, composed of Christians and Lebanese nationals, opposes Moslem and Palestinian elements. Prime Minister Rashid Karami seems undecided about how to stop the street battles. A Moslem, Karami is reluctant to send in the national army. A majority of the soldiers are Christian, and Karami fears they will only make a bad situation worse.

In southern Lebanon, Israeli warplanes have mounted reprisal raids against Palestinian guerrilla bases. Syria has been asked to provide help against Israel (→ 24).

Mighty Casey Stengel has struck out at last

"The Old Professor" of baseball.

Sept 29. Casey Stengel is dead. The garrulous, wrinkled baseball wizard who led the New York Yankees to new heights and the Mets to their earliest depths, succumed to lymph cancer at his Glendale, California, home at age 85.

Forget that he owned Texas oil wells or that he was a millionaire real estate dealer. It was his down-home humor and skill at managing baseball teams that lifted Stengel to worldwide fame.

Stengel was a player, coach or manager for 17 baseball teams, four of them in New York. Three of them dropped him as manager along the way, but his Yankees won ten pennants and seven world championships between 1949 and 1960.

Two attempts made on President Ford

Sept 22. For the second time in 17 days, President Ford escaped possible assassination today when a woman fired a gun as he stepped out of a hotel in San Francisco. His assailant was identified as Sara Jane Moore, a 45-year-old activist.

Another woman in the same state pointed a pistol at President Ford from close range as he neared the state Capitol in Sacramento on September 5. She was identified by police as Lynette Alice "Squeaky" Fromme, 26, who was a follower of Charles Manson, the leader of the group convicted of killing Sharon Tate, the actress, and six others in 1969 (→ 11/26).

Family asks to turn off woman's lifeline

Sept 27. The parents of Karen Anne Quinlan, a 21-year-old New Jersey woman who has been in a coma for five months, have gone to court for permission to have her life-sustaining respirator turned off. The parents say the suit is necessary because St. Clare's Hospital in Denville, New Jersey, refused to turn off the respirator although doctors said Karen Anne had suffered irreversible brain damage. They say they want their daughter to die "with grace and dignity" (→ 9/13/76).

Patty Hearst found; faces crime charges

Sept 18. A red-haired, gum-chewing waif answering to the name of Tania was apprehended in San Francisco today. Patty Hearst was with the Symbionese Liberation Army for more than one year and seven months, first as a hostage and then as an accomplice. She faces bank robbery and other charges. When Miss Hearst was taken from her Berkeley apartment in February 1974, she went kicking and screaming. Yet with time she embraced the SLA's radical ideals, taking the name Tania and dying her hair before lopping most of it off. In court this afternoon, she raised a fist in cheerful salute (→ 1/14/76).

1975

OCTOBER

Su	Mo	Tu	We	Th	Fr	Sa
			1	2	3	4
5	6	7	8	9	10	11
12	13	14	15	16	17	18
19	20	21	22	23	24	25
26	27	28	29	30	31	

2. Belfast: I.R.A. kills 12 in series of terrorist attacks (→ 1/5/76).

4. France: 100,000 youths demonstrate against unemployment.

5. Congress acts to halt strip mining in Death Valley.

5. Buenos Aires: 26 killed as leftist guerrillas attack army headquarters (→ 3/26/76).

6. Ford proposes $11 bil. in tax reductions for 1976 (→ 1/19/76).

6. New York: Diana Nyad, 25, swims around Manhattan Island on second attempt in 11 days.

6. N.Y.: African, Arab members denounce Daniel Moynihan at U.N. for referring to terrorists as "racist murderers."

7. U.S.: John Lennon wins court battle, barring deportation by immigration officials.

16. Marrakesh: King Hassan II announces he will lead 350,000 unarmed Moroccans into Sahara to claim territory (→ 11/6).

17. Washington: Govt. files suits against six cigarette manufacturers for inadequate display of health warnings (→ 11/22/77).

20. U.S. to give Soviets six mil. tons grain in exchange for ten mil. tons oil (→ 2/24/76).

21. Madrid: Franco stricken with heart attack (→ 30).

22. Boston: Cincinnati Reds win World Series, defeating Red Sox 4-3 in final game.

22. Soviet spacecraft Venera 9 lands on Venus, sends photos (→ 7/20/76).

26. Sadat, first Egyptian president to visit U.S., arrives seeking military aid (→ 3/14/76).

30. Madrid: Prince Juan Carlos assumes powers as Franco nears death (→ 11/22).

DEATHS

19. Hans Bellmer, German painter, sculptor (*3/13/1902).

27. Rex Stout, American detective novelist, created Nero Wolfe (*10/27/1975).

27. Georges Carpentier, French boxer, ex-middleweight champ (*1/21/1894).

30. Guy Mollet, French ex-premier (*12/31/1905).

Toynbee, chronicler of civilization, dies

Toynbee, a prolific scholar.

Oct 22. On September 17, 1921, Arnold Toynbee, an Oxford-educated classical scholar, had an idea. He decided he would chronicle the rise and fall of civilizations. He began the task in 1929. Forty years, 12 volumes and three and a half million words later, "A Study of History" was finished. "The most provocative work on historical theory written in England since Marx's "Das Kapital," Time magazine said.

Toynbee not only recorded, he interpreted. In comparing 26 civilizations, he rejected the idea that "life is just one damn thing after another." And unlike Marx, he proposed that spiritual rather than material forces shape history. The end of history is the Kingdom of God and history is "God revealing himself." Toynbee died today at age 86. "The most obvious way of reconciling oneself to death," he said, "is to make sure of enjoying life before death snatches it from us."

Oct 1. Ali won the "Thrilla in Manila" by a TKO, surviving 14 rounds of punishment from challenger Joe Frazier (→ 2/20/76).

New York City faces grave fiscal crisis

Oct 29. President Ford threatened today to veto any bill proposing that New York City be bailed out of its fiscal crisis by the federal government. Instead, he sent Congress a proposed bill to enable the city to file for bankruptcy and maintain its essential services, perhaps with some financial aid from the federal government. In a speech at the National Press Club, the president castigated city and state officials of New York for their management tactics. His comments were decried by New York officials and by some of the city's leading bankers and securities officials (→ 11/26).

Basque executions cause great furor

Oct 1. Northern Spain has been overcome by tens of thousands of angry Basque strikers this week. They are protesting the execution last Saturday of five Basque separatists who were convicted of killing policemen. Three more policemen were shot and killed at a pro-Franco rally today in Madrid. Protest demonstrations against the executions were held in several European nations, and the governments of Britain, Norway, East and West Germany, Denmark and the Netherlands have recalled their ambassadors from Spain (→ 21).

Spanking of pupils OK, high court says

Oct 20. Spare the rod no longer, teachers. The Supreme Court has ruled that states may allow, at their discretion, spanking in the schools. According to the decision, as long as a teacher gives a child fair warning and gives preference to lesser punishments, paddling is all right. Spanking may even be administered over the protestations of a parent.

The mother of a sixth grader wanted justice when her son was paddled after some class roughhousing. She thought spanking violated the 14th Amendment, which gives parents the right to oversee disciplining of their children.

Man may have lived 3.75 million years

Mary Leakey and her son Richard continue her late husband's work.

Oct 30. At a news conference organized by the National Geographic Society in Washington, Dr. Mary Leakey announced the discovery of human remains dating back 3.75 million years. While older fossils of transitional ape-men have been found, these are the oldest known remains of true genus homo. Scientists now deduce that ape and human parted ways more than five million years ago.

Dr. Leakey made the finding 25 miles south of Olduvai Gorge in Tanzania. There, she and her late husband Louis B. Leakey had dug up more and more evidence pointing to the extreme age of humankind. At the new location, Mary Leakey uncovered jaws and teeth of 11 ancient skeletons.

Oct 11. The gutsy, street-wise sound of Bruce Springsteen and his E-Street Band has hit the top 40 with "Born to Run."

1975

NOVEMBER

Su	Mo	Tu	We	Th	Fr	Sa
						1
2	3	4	5	6	7	8
9	10	11	12	13	14	15
16	17	18	19	20	21	22
23	24	25	26	27	28	29
30						

2. Ford dismisses Sec. of Defense James Schlesinger and William Colby, director of CIA.

6. Sahara: Thousands of Moroccans enter desert in attempt to annex Spanish Sahara (→ 9).

7. New Delhi: Indian Supreme Court validates election of Indira Gandhi (→ 1/29/76).

8. New York: Comoro Islands become 143rd member of U.N.

11. Angola gains independence from Portugal; rival govts. proclaimed in Luanda and Huambo (→ 12/7).

12. Montgomery: Gov. George Wallace enters presidential race (→ 20).

12. Moscow: Sakharov denied visa to receive Nobel Peace Prize in Oslo (→ 12/10).

13. Lisbon: Pres. Gomes calls for unity as workers imprison Premier de Azevedo in home (→ 25).

14. Washington: Berlin Opera makes U.S. debut at JFK Center with Wagner's "Lohengrin."

14. Madrid: Spain agrees to abandon Spanish Sahara by March.

17. Rome: Italian and French Communist Parties, two largest in W. Europe, issue declaration disavowing violent revolution.

20. Miami: Reagan joins presidential campaign (→ 7/15/76).

24. Washington: Defense Dept. foresakes Safeguard ABM system after $5.7 bil. investment (→ 1/21/76).

25. Lisbon: Army goes into rebellion against govt. (→ 2/26/76).

25. Surinam gains independence from Dutch.

26. Sacramento: "Squeaky" Fromme found guilty of attempt on Ford's life (→ 12/17).

26. Ford asks $2.3 bil. loan for N.Y.C. to help avert default (→ 12/28/76).

DEATHS

6. Lionel Trilling, American critic, educator, novelist (*7/4/1905).

20. Generalissimo Francisco Franco, ruler of Spain 36 years (*12/4/1892).

Juan Carlos ascends throne as Franco dies

Franco, dictator in Spain 36 years.

Juan Carlos and wife are married.

Nov 22. Spain has a new leader today. He has a tough act to follow, and it is not clear how he will proceed. Juan Carlos de Borbon was proclaimed King two days after Generalissimo Francisco Franco died in Madrid. In a posthumous message, Franco appealed for unity in the country and warned that the "enemies of Spain and Christian civilization are watching."

Juan Carlos, who was handpicked by Franco, swore that he would remain faithful to his principles. He also acknowledged, however, the pressure for reform. Without committing himself to change, Juan Carlos said he would encourage "far-reaching improvements." The audience, some of whom wore the distinctive blue shirts of the semi-fascist Falange, applauded only once, when the king called indirectly for the recapture of Gibraltar. Juan Carlos faces a more immediate problem in the Sahara.

President Ford promised to continue "excellent relations" with Spain. But a group of 25 historians and officials urged him to reconsider policy toward what they called a "totalitarian regime" (→ 1/19/76).

Britain counting on oil to aid economy

Nov 3. Britain's Queen Elizabeth formally opened the first underwater pipeline today to oil reserves in the North Sea. The oil will be transported 100 miles to the coast of Scotland and then bypass Aberdeen and Dundee to a refinery on the Firth of Forth.

Britain is hoping North Sea oil will be an economic bonanza and free it from the clutches of the Persian Gulf producers. British Petroleum, a nationalized company, is already talking about a new economic era and energy independence in the 1980's. Two years ago, the expense of tapping North Sea reserves did not make sense. Then came the Arab oil embargo. Some 14 promising oil fields have been discovered in the past year. Britain hopes to find more (→ 2/19/76).

CIA plotted deaths of foreign leaders

Nov 20. A Senate select committee reported today that American officials plotted to kill, through the Central Intelligence Agency, two foreign leaders and were involved in plots to kill three others. Patrice Lumumba of the Congo (now Zaire) and Cuban Premier Fidel Castro were targets in plots originating in Washington. Ngo Dinh Diem of South Vietnam, Gen. Rene Schneider of Chile and Rafael Leonidas Trujillo of the Dominican Republic were killed in plots in which U.S. officials played a part. But the panel found no evidence directly linking the CIA with the murders.

This is the first time a congressional investigation has ever determined that assassination was employed as an instrument of U.S. foreign policy (→ 2/28/76).

U.N. vote declares Zionism is racist

Nov 10. In related moves, the United Nations General Assembly tonight adopted a resolution branding Zionism as "a form of racism and racial discrimination," and also one calling for the participation of the PLO in Mideast peace talks. Israel's chief delegate, Chaim Herzog, charged that the text was born "of a deep pervading feeling of anti-Semitism." Daniel Patrick Moynihan, the American delegate, said that the United States "will never acquiesce in this infamous act." The text resulted from Arab maneuvers after their earlier failure to oust Israel from the U.N. (→ 12/2).

Moroccan marchers try to occupy Sahara

Nov 9. Even the supporters of Morocco's King Hassan are wondering what is on his mind. For weeks, he has been whipping up support for his ambitious plan to seize control of the Spanish Sahara from Madrid. About 350,000 Moroccans heeded his call, and half of them marched across the border. Not a shot was fired, and there was no resistance from Spanish troops.

Today, without explanation, Hassan called the marchers home and said the dispute over the Spanish Sahara would be resolved by diplomacy. "Spain is not only a friend," Hassan said, "but also a neighbor." Officials of the Spanish government were visibly relieved. They had already beefed up forces in the Sahara and in the Canary Islands. Algeria, which has its own ideas about the Sahara, was also pleased. The matter is likely to move to the U.N. (→ 14).

Moroccans march for rule in Sahara. ▷

Douglas quits Court after 36 years there

Douglas, scourge of conservatives.

Nov 12. Failing health has forced Justice William O. Douglas to retire from the Supreme Court, after serving on the bench longer than anyone —36 and a half years. Ironically, Douglas notified President Ford of his intentions to quit; in 1970, Ford led the last of three failed attempts to impeach Douglas.

Appointed by President Roosevelt in 1939, Douglas became a controversial and powerfully persuasive justice. He consistently upheld his commitment to a liberal interpretation of the Constitution, particulary on issues involving the First Amendment and civil liberties. His retirement means Ford can now appoint a new justice, which could significantly alter the complexion of the high court.

Unheard-of action taken in Australia

Nov 11. John Kerr, the Governor General of Australia, stepped out of his largely ceremonial role today and fired Prime Minister Whitlam. Scandals and a poor economy had plagued the Whitlam administration, but the whole country was shocked by his dismissal, the first in the country's 75-year history. The opposition party's refusal to pass Whitlam's budget sparked the crisis; Kerr has called for new elections. But Whitlam said the action would provoke a constitutional crisis and claimed to have the majority of Parliament on his side (→ 12/14).

Ford says Alaska's oil liberates U.S.

Nov 29. President Ford toured the trans-Alaska pipeline today and hailed the project as a weapon in the fight to "liberate" the United States from "unreliable" foreign sources of oil. During an overnight stop on a trip to China, Ford cited the pipeline as proof that the United States has "the physical resources, the economic resources, the ingenuity and the national will" to achieve energy independence. He said construction of the pipeline "has proven to be an outstanding example of how ecology can be preserved while energy needs are met" (→ 1/21/77).

Jack Nicholson opens in Cuckoo's Nest

Nicholson in "Cuckoo's Nest."

In one of his earliest films, "The Little Shop of Horrors," Jack Nicholson played a man who liked dentists to molest his molars. Pain was just marvelous. In the current "One Flew Over the Cuckoo's Nest," Nicholson is again offbeat, but aching to free others from torture. He is outstanding as a mental patient leading fellow inmates in rebellion.

Milos Forman, a Czech director with little experience in the United States, also elicits fine work from actress Louise Fletcher, who plays a calculating nurse. Will Sampson portrays a giant, silent Indian. Producer Michael Douglas bought the rights to Ken Kesey's book almost ten years ago, waiting for just the right talent to come along.

1975

DECEMBER

Su	Mo	Tu	We	Th	Fr	Sa
	1	2	3	4	5	6
7	8	9	10	11	12	13
14	15	16	17	18	19	20
21	22	23	24	25	26	27
28	29	30	31			

1. China: Ford arrives on state visit to expand new relationship (→ 2/16/78).

2. Lebanon: Israeli jets hit Palestinian refugee camps (→ 8).

2. The Hague: South Moluccans seize train in Holland, killing two, taking 50 hostages (→ 7).

6. Nairobi: World Council of Churches elects two women.

7. Manila: Ford arrives to cheers of 100,000 (→ 1/30/76).

7. Timor: Capital Dili falls to pro-Indonesian forces (→ 19).

8. U.S. vetoes U.N. resolution condemning Israeli air raids in Lebanon (→ 1/22/76).

14. Canberra: Australian voters sweep Premier Malcolm Fraser's Liberals into office.

19. U.S. Senate, in blow to Ford, cuts off covert aid to Angolan rightist rebels (→ 1/27/76).

23. Mexico City: Raul Ramirez wins Davis Cup for Mexico, beating Connors in final match.

30. U.S. lifts ban on foreign competition in Little League World Series.

DEATHS

4. Hannah Arendt, German-American philosopher (*6/14/1906).

7. Thornton Wilder, U.S. writer, "Our Town" (*4/17/1897).

CULTURAL EVENTS, 1975

Literature: Saul Bellow's "Humboldt's Gift"; James Clavell's "Shogun"; Edward Albee's "Seascape"; Thomas Mann's notebooks opened at his wish, 20 years after his death.

Academia: Eugene Genovese's "Roll, Jordan Roll"; Robert Nozick's "Anarchy, State and Utopia."

Music: Beverley Sills makes Metropolitan Opera debut; Elton John's "Lucy in the Sky with Diamonds"; Bee Gees' "Jive Talkin'"; Doobie Brothers' "Black Water"; Earth, Wind & Fire's "Shining Star."

Film: Spielberg's "Jaws"; Altman's "Nashville"; "The Story of Adele H," Isabelle Adjani; "The Sunshine Boys," George Burns.

Wife accepts Nobel Prize for Sakharov

Dec 10. The official Soviet news agency Tass makes no mention of Yelena Bonner receiving the Nobel Peace Prize in her husband's name tonight. Yet it happened; the wife of dissident Andrei Sakharov was in Oslo to accept a gold medal and a check for $143,000. Sakharov was denied an exit visa ostensibly because, as a thermonuclear physicist, he could divulge military secrets. Sakharov supports nuclear disarmament and increased civil liberties in the U.S.S.R. In 1968, he issued an appeal for understanding between East and West (→ 10/25/76).

Sakharov, prisoner of conscience.

Two who imperiled Ford both guilty

Dec 17. Two women accused of seeking to assassinate President Ford this year have been sentenced to life imprisonment.

Lynette Alice Fromme, now 27, was accused of pointing a gun at the president on September 5 as he walked from his hotel to the state Capitol in Sacramento, California. She was a follower of Charles Manson, the mass murderer. During her trial in Sacramento, "Squeaky" Fromme, as she is called by some, created a stir by hurling one of her breakfast apples at the U.S. attorney, knocking his glasses off.

Sara Jane Moore, a 45-year-old radical activist, acknowledged in court in San Francisco this month that she had knowingly attempted to kill President Ford as he stepped out of the St. Francis Hotel in that city on September 22.

South Moluccan siege ends in Amsterdam

Dec 19. Two terrorist incidents, both the work of South Moluccan separatist groups, were successfully foiled by Dutch government officials this week.

A 16-day siege at the Indonesian Consulate in Amsterdam ended today, as seven South Moluccan terrorists surrendered without incident to police.

On December 12, a train hijacking 90 miles from Amsterdam ended with the release of 23 hostages and the surrender of their six captors. The train was overtaken December 2 by the terrorists, who were demanding independence for their island homeland east of Indonesia. The engineer and two male passengers were shot to death in that incident.

A hostage held by South Moluccans.

The Prime Minister of the Netherlands, Joop den Uyl, appealed for "peaceful coexistence" with the 40,000 Moluccans (many of them political refugees) living in Holland, but warned that "the Moluccans must have no illusions that the Dutch government will support a free Moluccan state in Indonesia" (→ 5/23/77).

Plays and novels going to the dogs, cats etc.

There were paws in print and hoofing on stage this year. Richard Adams' novel "Shardik," about a bear considered a god by a primitive people, follows the success of last year's "Watership Down," about a society of rabbits. (Some called that hefty book "Warren Peace.") Peter Matthiessen's "Far Tortuga" describes turtle hunters sailing off the Cuban coast. "Dog Soldiers," by Robert Stone, is not about canines but small-time heroin smugglers working out of Vietnam.

Peter Shaffer's drama "Equus" probes the mind of a troubled youth who blinds a team of horses. Edward Albee's play "Seascape" concerns a couple on a beach watching sea creatures evolve into humans. Albee's work won a Pulitzer for its anthropomorphic allegory.

Arabs seize oil ministers, quickly give up

Dec 23. The pro-Palestinian terrorists who broke into OPEC headquarters two days ago and captured 11 oil ministers released their hostages today when their demands concerning a jetliner were not met.

Although three persons were killed and eight wounded when the six terrorists began firing into the conference room of the world oil cartel in Vienna, no one was harmed as the captors fled with their hostages and then surrendered during a seven-hour stopover in Algiers. The international terrorist Carlos was spotted at Algiers airport.

The terrorists claimed to represent "the arm of the Arab revolution" and made demands for a Palestinian share in the oil industry and for irradication of U.S. influence. The PLO disavowed any involvement in the terrorist incident.

Intl. terrorist Carlos (in beret).

Cubans with Soviet arms turn tide in Angola

Dec 7. Russian arms in Cuban hands tipped the scales of civil war toward the Popular Movement for the Liberation of Angola (MPLA) today. Fighting erupted when the Portuguese departed November 11, leaving a power vacuum that opposing factions rushed to fill.

The fomer colony was granted provinicial status in 1951, but the MPLA led a revolt a decade later. Shortly thereafter, two pro-Western groups formed to fight the Portuguese. They combined against the MPLA last month after attempts to form a coalition government failed. Led by heavily armed Cubans, the MPLA has pushed 50 miles north within the past week. The President of one pro-Western faction said, "This is a war of men against weapons. We have the men and they have the weapons" (→ 19).

Luanda tank, center of attraction.

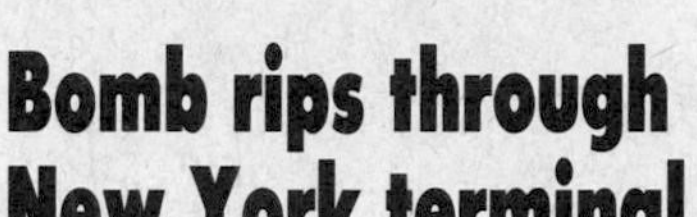

Bomb rips through New York terminal

Dec 30. A tragic explosion killed 14 and wounded more than 70 others at New York's LaGuardia Airport last night. A bomb had been planted in the baggage claim area in the main terminal, where crowds of holiday travelers had gathered. Smoke and flames raced through the terminal as rescue workers rushed to aid those caught in the blast. Officials at the Port Authority of New York and New Jersey, which runs the airport, have closed down service to passengers until at least late this evening so that investigators can examine the scene.

Research finds daily diet causes cancer

Dec 3. Scientists have reported new evidence that ingredients of the daily diet may be responsible for half of all cancers among women and 30 percent of those in men. A 300-page report issued this week in the journal Cancer Research says that such dietary factors as animal fat, alcohol and contaminants, as well as deficiencies of vitamin A and C, are related to cancer of the colon, stomach, esophagus, breast and liver. The National Cancer Institute will spend more than $4 million this year to study the relationship between diet and cancer.

Ford visits Mao; 100,000 hail him in Manila

Dec 7. President Ford completed his tour of China and the South Pacific today with a stop in the Philippines, where a crowd of 100,000 cheered his arrival. He visited Manila to meet with President Ferdinand Marcos and renew the terms of arrangement for the use of strategic American air and naval bases in the islands. Ford agreed to grant the Marcos administration sovereignty over Clark Air Base, allowing the Filipinos to gain income from it, in exchange for continued U.S. control of the facilities.

At month's outset, Ford arrived in China to meet with Chairman Mao Tse-tung. The two superpower leaders discussed American detente with the Soviets.

Ford and aging Mao Tse-tung.

1976

JANUARY

Su	Mo	Tu	We	Th	Fr	Sa
				1	2	3
4	5	6	7	8	9	10
11	12	13	14	15	16	17
18	19	20	21	22	23	24
25	26	27	28	29	30	31

1. Pasadena: UCLA beats Ohio State 23-10 in Rose Bowl.

1. Saudi Arabia: 82 die as Lebanese jet crashes in desert.

3. Tripoli: 400 armed Lebanese assault prison, freeing 100.

4. U.S.: National Airlines ends 127-day strike.

5. Ulster: Ten Protestant workmen shot dead (→ 2/12).

6. Washington: CIA reported to have given Italian anti-Communists $6 million (→ 7).

7. Rome: Italian Cabinet resigns as support ends (→ 5/17).

11. Philadelphia: Soviet team walks off ice to protest rough tactics of Flyers.

13. Argentina ousts British envoy in dispute over Falkland Islands (→ 4/2/82).

14. S.F.: Patty Hearst takes witness stand first time; says she is not proud (→ 2/23).

19. Washington: Ford appeals to nation for "new realism" cuts in tax and spending (→ 28).

19. Madrid: Spain drafts 70,000 railmen to halt strikes (→ 4/4).

21. Moscow: Brezhnev and Kissinger meet to discuss SALT (→ 2/29).

24. Washington: Pearl Bailey makes farewell performance in "Hello Dolly!" at JFK Center.

27. Washington: House bars aid to right-wing Angolan rebels (→ 2/10).

28. Washington: Senate overrides veto on $45 bil. bill for social spending (→ 12/10/77).

29. New Delhi: Parliament approves permanent govt. censorship of newspapers (→ 2/25).

30. U.S. Supreme Court bans spending limits in campaigns, equating funds with freedom of speech.

30. Manila: Troops arrest 200 in crackdown on strikers (→ 4/1).

31. Arizona: Ernesto Miranda, famous from Supreme Court ruling, stabbed to death.

DEATH

10. Howling Wolf, American blues vocalist, born Chester Burnett (*6/10/1910).

Beirut factions reach peace agreement

Beirut, once the financial capital of the Mideast, now torn by violence.

Jan 22. A Syrian-drawn peace accord was signed today by both opposing factions in Lebanon's civil war. While details have yet to be released, officials in Beirut announced that "all parties" had accepted "an all-embracing political settlement." It seems some of the Moslem demands for sharing more political power were met while maintaining the rights of the minority Lebanese Christians.

The accord was reached two days after reports indicated Palestine Liberation Army troops had crossed the border in Syria to assist the Lebanese Moslems. The inclusion of the PLA into an already violent, bloody and vindictive conflict worried Syria, chief arbitrator in the peace efforts. However, fighting has tapered off since word of the agreement reached the front. The High Military Committee, comprised of Syrian, Lebanese and Palestinian officials, expects the ceasefire, scheduled to take effect tonight at 8:00, will be honored.

Leftist leader Kamal Jumblat, who has bitterly fought the Christians on the side of the Moslems, said his faction accepts the accord and expressed his gratitude for "the efforts exerted by sister Syria so that we may all get out of this bloodshed and crisis" (→ 3/15).

Jan 18. Pittsburgh's Lynn Swann dives for a Bradshaw bomb as the Steelers defeated Tom Landry's Dallas Cowboys 21-17 in Super Bowl X.

Chou En-lai, China's top diplomat, dies

Jan 8. Chou En-lai, the Prime Minister of China since the Communists won power in 1949, is dead of cancer at the age of 78. Hsinhua, the official Chinese press agency, released the information about Chou's death in the early hours of the morning, some 18 hours after the premier's death. Although the press release described Chou's death as a "gigantic" loss to the Communist Party, there was little reaction on the streets, activities being conducted as usual. Chou En-lai was among the most influential in the government, second in power only to Chairman Mao, who played the role of revolutionary, while Chou was the pragmatist (→ 2/7).

Chou En-lai, China's pragmatist.

Vatican releases documents on Jews

Jan 23. The Vatican has released a 688-page volume from its archives which deals with its controversial role in World War II. The document claimed that the public silence of the Holy See concerning the wartime atrocities of the Nazis and the plight of the Jews was intended to avoid disruption of quiet diplomacy on behalf of the Jews. Pope Pius XII was often criticized for not speaking out against the Nazis, but this document suggests that he tried to maintain relations with the Germans for the purpose of influencing them. The volume also reveals that the Church opposed a Jewish nation in Palestine.

Life ends for one who dealt in death

Jan 12. Dame Agatha Christie, the English writer who created two of the most distinctive sleuths of detective fiction—the astute Jane Marple and the dapper Hercule Poirot—died yesterday in her home west of London. She was 85 years old. This shy but regal person, who set out to be an opera singer, began to write on a dare from her sister and turned out 60 detective novels, six romantic novels under the name Mary Westmacott, 19 volumes of short mystery stories, 14 plays, two works of non-fiction and a book of verse. She was married to archeologist Sir Max Mallowan, often accompanying him on Middle East digs.

Canadian rapist accepts castration

Jan 15. A rapist and murderer has asked to be castrated to prevent further crimes. The mental patient, 26-year-old Henry Williams, made the request at his trial in Ottowa today. He was being sentenced to his third life term, having murdered and raped his latest victim, a 19-year-old college student, in 1972. A psychiatrist for the defense said a study of 900 castrations done in Denmark showed "desired results" 90 percent of the time.

Jodie Foster, on the streets in Scorsese's gory "Taxi Driver."

Kate Rothko gains control of fortune

Jan 16. Kate Rothko, daughter of the late painter Mark Rothko, has been named sole administrator of her father's estate. A New York court gave the second-year medical student executor power, but she will share half of the $30 million fortune with a 12-year-old brother. The other $15 million will go to a charitable artists' organization. Mark Rothko was one of America's finest Abstract Expressionists. He died by his own hand in February 1970 at the age of 66.

The song is ended: Paul Robeson dies

Robeson, career ruined in the 50's.

Jan 23. One of black America's most influential performers and political figures passed from the scene yesterday when Paul Robeson died in Philadelphia at the age of 77. Tall and built like the all-American football star he had been at Rutgers University, Robeson was a commanding figure, one of the best baritone singers of his day and an equally impressive actor, best remembered in the role of Othello.

An advocate of socialism, Robeson went to Spain during the civil war there and sang for members of the International Brigade. Because of his socialism, his open admiration for the Soviet Union and his acceptance of the Stalin Peace Prize in 1952, he became ostracized in his own country during the Cold War and the period of the McCarthy hearings.

1976

FEBRUARY

Su	Mo	Tu	We	Th	Fr	Sa
1	2	3	4	5	6	7
8	9	10	11	12	13	14
15	16	17	18	19	20	21
22	23	24	25	26	27	28
29						

1. New York: Moslem temple renamed for Malcolm X in sign of acceptance of ex-leader.

2. Washington: Daniel Moynihan resigns as U.S. envoy to U.N.

4. Innsbruck: Winter Olympics open (→ 13).

4. Guatemala: Devastating quake kills 12,000, leaves over one million homeless.

6. Washington: Lockheed confirms payments of $1.1 mil. to Dutch Prince Bernhard, $2 mil. to Japanese officials (→ 5/18).

7. Peking: Hua Kuo-feng named Chinese premier (→ 4/7).

10. Angola: Leftist rebels take two seaports (→ 17).

12. I.R.A. militant Frank Stagg dies after long hunger strike (→ 3/5).

13. Nigeria: Head of state Murtala Rufai Mohammed killed in failed coup.

17. Paris: France recognizes leftist MPLA in Angola (→ 7/10).

19. London: Britain slashes welfare spending (→ 3/5).

20. Puerto Rico: Ali KO's Jeanne Pierre Coopman in fifth to retain title (→ 4/30).

23. Calif.: Patty Hearst pleads fifth 42 times, citing peril to self and family (→ 3/20).

24. Moscow: Brezhnev says detente aids Soviet growth (→ 2/25).

25. Washington: Supreme Court rules state may ban hiring of illegal aliens (→ 12/4/81).

25. India announces plan to penalize parents who have more than two children (→ 10/27).

26. Portugal: Party leaders sign pact to end military rule (→ 4/25).

28. Florida: Ford calls Castro an "international outlaw" (→ 4/26).

28. N.Y.: Iran accused of torture, repression (→ 8/7).

DEATHS

1. Werner Heisenberg, German physicist, formulated "uncertainty principle" (*12/5/1901).

13. Lily Pons, French coloratura soprano (*4/12/1904).

Sunbelt leads U.S. in population growth

Feb 7. The Census Bureau reports that the metropolitan areas of the South and Southwest were the only ones experiencing substantial population growth since 1970.

Most urban centers of the North and East lost population or gained only marginally. The New York area dropped by 313,600 persons, or 1.8 per cent. Even Los Angeles, after decades of heady growth, shows signs of having passed a peak. California, however, remains the most populous state in the nation.

This underscores a dramatic reversal in American population trends. After a generation of migration by the millions into big cities and their suburbs, rural and small-town areas are growing faster than urban areas. The chief exceptions are in the South and Southwest. All but two of the 13 fastest-growing metropolitan regions are in Florida, Texas and Arizona—parts of the so-called Sunbelt. The two others are in Colorado, a mountain state also attracting new population.

People are shifting away from the Northeastern states, the base of population and power since the nation's birth, though the industrial North remains a dominant bloc of economic and voting power. Major factors in the emergence of the Sunbelt, consisting of 14 states plus Southern California, are high technology and aerospace installations.

Feb 13. Dorothy Hamill: gold at Innsbruck in women's freestyle.

World spends $300 billion a year on arms

Feb 29. Worldwide recession and inflation have hurt many companies, but one group of entrepreneurs is definitely not in the red. Arms manufacturers are earning vast sums of money. Their profits come from what a new study calls "an arms race out of control," worth $300 billion a year. Military spending skyrocketed nearly 45% over and above inflation in the past 15 years, and the countries that can least afford to buy arms have some of the fastest growing appetites. The U.S. and the Soviet Union are purchasing 60% of the arms produced, but military spending in developing countries has doubled since 1960. In the Mideast, arms purchases are up 800% (→ 3/15).

Africans at odds over Western Sahara

Feb 26. Talks among African officials in Addis Ababa, Ethiopia, are focusing on rival claims by Mauritania, Morocco and the Algerian-backed Polisario liberation movement over control of the Western Sahara. Spain granted Mauritania and Morocco control of the area (formerly called Spanish Sahara), but the Polisario group claims it has the right to administer the disputed desert region, and it has recently battled military troops of the two nations.

Mauritanian troops in the Sahara.

Soviets beamed microwaves at embassy

Feb 25. Soviet officials have finally admitted that they have transmitted microwaves at the American Embassy in Moscow, but justify it as a means to disrupt U.S. eavesdropping equipment. For 15 years, Washington officials have queried Moscow about beams of low-level electromagnetic radiation, like those produced by radio transmitters. But not until now has Moscow conceded existence of the rays.

Listening devices on the roof of the embassy often pick up conversations of Soviet officials riding in their limousines, despite attempts to jam communication lines. Relatively harmless, the beams are irritating to diplomats, and the U.S. has asked the Soviets to stop (→ 6/1/78).

Linda Carter is "Wonder Woman," TV's feminist superheroine.

Eskimos lay claim to fifth of Canada

Feb 27. Canadian Eskimo leaders presented a 61-page proposal to Canadian Premier Pierre Trudeau today, in which they claimed over 250,000 square miles of northern Canada. In addition, the Eskimos want special rights to another 500,000 square miles of Canada's soil and 800,000 square miles of ocean. Those rights include a request for three percent royalty on any natural resources. The government is expected to respond to the proposal within three months, but Trudeau indicated that a final decision would take longer.

1976

MARCH

Su	Mo	Tu	We	Th	Fr	Sa
	1	2	3	4	5	6
7	8	9	10	11	12	13
14	15	16	17	18	19	20
21	22	23	24	25	26	27
28	29	30	31			

3. Mozambique shuts border with Rhodesia (→ 8/10).

4. Boston: Pan Am indicted, first airline charged with criminal negligence in crash.

5. London: British pound drops below $2 first time (→ 16).

5. Britain gives up on Ulster talks, will retain rule in Northern Ireland indefinitely (→ 7/21).

8. Yugoslavia: Simon Wiesenthal says 62 Nazi war criminals believed living in U.S.

10. Washington: Nixon testifies Kissinger picked targets for wiretaps (→ 28).

11. Washington: Nixon testifies he ordered CIA to foil election of Allende in Chile (→ 9/21).

12. Seoul: Govt. ousts 400 university professors (→ 9/17/80).

13. Washington: Natl. Science Foundation reports U.S. lead in science is slipping.

14. Cairo: Sadat ends '71 friendship pact with Soviets (→ 9/16).

15. Lebanon: Two armored columns head for mansion of Pres. Franjieh (→ 4/9).

15. Washington: CIA says Israel has 10-20 A-bombs (→ 5/28).

16. London: Premier Harold Wilson resigns (→ 4/5).

20. N.J.: Hurricane Carter released on bail to await new trial (→ 12/21).

21. Thailand: U.S. ends all military operations at bases.

27. Washington D.C. opens subway system.

28. Washington: Files released showing FBI raided leftist offices 92 times 1960-1966 (→ 4/28).

29. U.S. Supreme Court rules states may prosecute people for homosexual acts.

29. Philadelphia: Indiana over Michigan 106-92 for NCAA basketball title.

DEATHS

14. Busby Berkeley, American choreographer (*11/29/1895).

17. Luchino Visconti, Italian film director (*11/2/1906).

24. Field Marshal Montgomery, British war hero (*11/17/1887).

Military overthrows Argentine President

Peron, faces corruption charges.

March 26. Two days after a bloodless coup toppled the administration of Argentinian President Isabel Martinez de Peron, Lieutenant General Jorge Rafael Videla was selected to be President of the new military government.

Mrs. Peron, who succeeded her husband, the late Juan Peron, as president in 1974, was arrested and deposed by the junta after she refused to resign under pressure from the armed forces. She is being held in custody, and she is expected to be tried on charges of official corruption.

Since the coup, the junta has imposed martial law, threatened Peronist guerrillas with death and abolished the labor code which gives labor leaders immunity from arrest (→ 4/2).

Patty Hearst guilty of armed robbery

March 20. Patricia Hearst, former hostage of the radical group called the Symbionese Liberation Army, has been found guilty of assisting its members in a bank heist. The jury in the San Francisco courtroom did not sympathize with the arguments of her lawyer, F. Lee Bailey, who contended the accused was coerced. According to Bailey, Miss Hearst spent weeks locked in closets, bombarded by propaganda. The jury may have sided with the prosecution in part because Miss Hearst often took the Fifth Amendment, refusing to testify (→ 8/9).

1976

APRIL

Su	Mo	Tu	We	Th	Fr	Sa
				1	2	3
4	5	6	7	8	9	10
11	12	13	14	15	16	17
18	19	20	21	22	23	24
25	26	27	28	29	30	

1. Manila: Ex-Pres. Macapagal denounces Marcos as dictator (→ 12/4).

2. Argentina: New conservative recovery program reversing Peronist policies (→ 3/20/81).

4. Madrid: Police attack protesters with rifle butts, tear gas, rubber bullets; hold 200 (→ 8/4).

9. Lebanon: Syrian troops cross border (→ 12).

12. West Bank: Arabs gain in local elections in Israeli-occupied territory (→ 5/9).

13. Washington: RFK's Justice Dept. accused of ignoring recommendations to investigate Frank Sinatra.

15. India announces it will send envoy to Peking, first time in 15 years.

17. Chicago: Mike Schmidt hits four home runs in one game.

18. New York: "A Chorus Line" sweeps Tony awards.

20. San Diego: Timothy Leary out of prison on parole.

20. Japan: Public transport in chaos as rail strike begins.

22. Bonn: Volkswagen announces plan to build plant in U.S. (→ 8/15/77).

23. Boston: Tens of thousands protest racial violence day after bomb injures 21 in courthouse (→ 11/14).

26. Washington: Senate panel calls for curbs on covert action in foreign policy as CIA inquiry ends (→ 4/28/77).

26. Pan Am inaugurates nonstop New York-to-Tokyo service on Boeing 747.

27. Vatican: Pope Paul VI names 21 new Cardinals, majority from Third World.

28. Washington: Senate panel says FBI and other agencies violated citizens' rights (→ 8/24).

30. Maryland: Ali retains title with 15-round decision over Jimmy Young (→ 5/24).

DEATHS

1. Max Ernst, German-born French painter (*4/2/1891).

25. Sir Carol Reed, British film director (*12/30/1906).

Hua becomes China Premier, Mao's heir

April 7. In an organized demonstration of support for the recent changes in China's leadership, more than 100,000 people marched in Tien An Men Square carrying red flags and chanting approved slogans. The marchers showed little emotion, only relief that the shake-up of top-level government officials following the death of Chou En-lai had finally been resolved.

When Chou died of cancer on January 8, his apparent successor was Deng Hsiao-ping, the Deputy Prime Minister. The Communist Party's Central Committee, however, issued an announcement yesterday linking Deng with the riots which have recently occurred and removed him from the government.

Appointed to the post of Prime Minister was Hua Kuo-feng, a man unconnected with any political movements in China. Hua will also succeed Mao Tse-tung as Chairman in the event of his death (→ 9/18).

Socialist Soares is now Portuguese Premier

April 25. Socialists and Communists in Portugal united behind Mario Soares as the Socialist leader was elected Premier. His astounding victory comes almost two years after a military coup, engineered by liberals, threw off the shackles of 40 years of totalitarian rule in Portugal. The coup leaders promised democratic reform, but it took longer than expected for rival military factions to agree on a plan for elections. Major progress was achieved when the army was removed from political discussions. In parliamentary elections, Soares received just under 35% of the vote. Communist support gave him the majority he needed (→ 7/14).

Soares holds a rose aloft in victory.

James Callaghan succeeds Wilson as P.M.

April 5. A change of command took place at the top of the Labor Party in Britain today, and the new leader automatically became the new Prime Minister. Foreign Secretary James Callaghan was elected leader in the third round of balloting. He immediately presented his credentials to Queen Elizabeth. Employment Secretary Michael Foot, who came in second, graciously accepted defeat. He is expected to be a key member of the new Cabinet.

Callaghan, facing flagging economy.

The party election was forced by the unexpected resignation of Prime Minister Harold Wilson last month. Callaghan is expected to follow most of Wilson's policies. On television tonight, the new prime minister said his "first and most vital job is driving down the rate of inflation." It reached 26% last year. To win approval of an austerity budget and to keep a lid on wage increases, Callaghan needs support of all Laborites. The center and the right-wing Manifesto group are expected to back Callaghan, but he may face opposition from a leftist group called the Tribune (→ 3/28/79).

Eccentric Hughes, leaving $1.5b, dies

April 5. An emaciated body was wheeled on a stretcher off a Lear jet this afternoon and guided to the morgue of a Houston hospital. Police stood guard, as if Howard Hughes in death craved privacy as much as he did in life. The billionaire recluse died of a stroke aboard his plane at 1:27 p.m. today. He was 70 years old.

Hughes was born in Texas to a family already rich with profits from a tool company. In the 20's and 30's, he tried his hand at making movies, producing "Scarface" and other box office hits. Jane Russell was among his discoveries. Hughes studied aviation, designing planes and setting speed records. Investments in Las Vegas casinos raised his fortune to $1.5 billion. Of late, he fled from continent to continent, perhaps seeking something he had lost inside himself.

Barbara Walters weighs a $1m deal

April 20. The first woman newscaster to reach a position of national prominence has been offered a $1 million-per-year contract. ABC offers Miss Barbara Walters a five-year contract to co-host the nightly news. NBC, her home for 12 seasons, proffers a similar deal. Miss Walters has been hosting the "Today" show, an early-morning grind she publicly deplores. Still, it has made her insights and delivery (tinged by a slight lisp) recognized nationwide.

Walters: Journalist or celebrity?

1976

MAY

Su	Mo	Tu	We	Th	Fr	Sa
						1
2	3	4	5	6	7	8
9	10	11	12	13	14	15
16	17	18	19	20	21	22
23	24	25	26	27	28	29
30	31					

1. Bold Forbes wins Kentucky Derby, jockey A. Cordero up.

3. Washington: Howard Hughes to give plane Spruce Goose to General Services Admin.

3. New York: Saul Bellow wins Pulitzer for "Humboldt's Gift."

5. Panama blocks two U.S. vessels in canal for illegal fishing (→ 10/7).

9. Israel decides to ask settlers to quit site on West Bank (→ 6/1).

9. Stuttgart: German terrorist Ulrike Meinhof commits suicide in jail cell.

10. London: Top British Liberal Jeremy Thorpe resigns over allegations of homosexuality.

11. Paris: Bolivian Ambassador Joaquin Anaya killed in reprisal for death of Che Guevara.

13. New York: Nets beat Denver Nuggets 112-106 for ABA title.

14. Pakistan and India agree to resume diplomatic ties.

15. New York: Hundreds parade through Central Park smoking marijuana.

16. Philadelphia: Canadiens beat Flyers 5-3 to sweep Stanley Cup.

17. Rome: Vatican calls on Italian voters to shun Communists (→ 7/4).

18. Canada cancels contract with Lockheed in wake of bribery scandal (→ 7/27).

19. N.J.: Mario Jascalevich, "Dr. X," indicted in five curare deaths.

20. Texas: Pres. Giscard arrives on Concorde, opening commercial SST transport from France to U.S. (→ 9/23/77).

23. N.Y.: West Point acknowledges widespread cheating.

24. Munich: Ali TKO's Richard Dunn in fifth to retain heavyweight title (→ 9/28).

28. New York: Ellis Island officially reopened.

28. U.S., U.S.S.R. sign pact limiting atomic tests (→ 10/10).

29. Kansas: Earl Bell sets world pole vault record at 18'7.25" (→ 6/22).

31. New York: Martha Mitchell, wife of ex-attorney general, dies.

'Quake-prone area in Italy has another

Remains of home in Northern Italy.

May 6. Entire towns in northeast Italy disappeared tonight as a severe earthquake struck along the border with Yugoslavia. First reports from the Interior Ministry said at least 95 people were killed. That number could climb into the hundreds and even thousands. Officials said 1,000 people were injured and 80,000 may be homeless.

The earthquake was measured variously on the Richter scale from 6.5 to 8.9. Even the lower figure can cause severe damage. The epicenter was reportedly near Udine, where a spokesman said hundreds of people may be trapped under the debris. The tremor was felt to the south in Rome, east to Trieste, west to Turin and in five other countries. But the major damage occurred in the towns located in the foothills of the Alps near Yugoslavia.

Earthquakes are not new to the area. At least 27 were recorded between 1896 and 1963. But, once again, no one was ready for this one. About 10,000 volunteers are trying to help, but a police officer in Forgaria said, "We lack equipment for rescue work. We have no power. It is not possible to estimate the dead."

May 30. Johnny Rutherford, adding to his 1974 victory, is now two-time champ of the Indy 500.

Heidegger, German philosopher, is dead

Heidegger, the "sense of being."

May 26. Martin Heidegger, widely acknowledged as one of the most important continental philosophers of the 20th Century, died today at the age of 86 in Messkirch, West Germany, the town of his birth.

Heidegger, born September 26, 1889, studied philosophy at the University of Freiburg under Edmund Husserl, the founder of the phenomenological movement. In 1923, he was appointed to his first chair at Marburg, where his colleagues included the theologian Paul Tillich. He returned to Freiburg in 1928, where he was appointed Husserl's successor. He was made rector of the university in 1933, during the rise of the Nazis, but resigned a year later. His brief relationship with the Nazis, and his subsequent break with them, plagued his reputation for the rest of his life, in part because of his resolute silence on the issue.

Although he denied the label, Heidegger's meditations on "the being-question" inaugurated the Existentialist movement, and his work "Being and Time" was a major influence upon Jean-Paul Sartre.

Redford and Hoffman are dogged reporters on trail of Watergate: "All the President's Men."

1976

JUNE

Su	Mo	Tu	We	Th	Fr	Sa
		1	2	3	4	5
6	7	8	9	10	11	12
13	14	15	16	17	18	19
20	21	22	23	24	25	26
29	28	29	30			

1. Lebanon: Syria sends troops and tanks into center of country (→ 8).

3. Washington: Britain lends original Magna Carta to U.S. for Bicentennial (→ 7/4).

6. Phoenix: Boston Celtics beat Suns for their 13th NBA title.

8. Lebanon: Syrian troops cut off Beirut (→ 16).

8. Nebraska: Caril Ann Fugate, who accompanied Charles Starkweather on murder rampage, freed on parole.

13. Paris: Adriano Panatta beats Harold Solomon 6-1, 6-4, 4-6, 7-6 in French Open final.

15. Minn.: Twins get Vida Blue from Oakland A's for $1.5 mil., highest price for baseball player.

16. Beirut: U.S. Ambassador Francis Meloy, aide Robert Waring killed by kidnappers (→ 18).

16. South Africa: Six die in race riot after student protest in Soweto (→ 19).

17. Albany: Appeals Court voids New York's blue laws.

17. Massachusetts: NBA, ABA basketball leagues merge.

18. Washington: Ford orders Americans evacuated from Lebanon (→ 20).

21. New York: 110-foot model of King Kong dropped off World Trade Center for movie remake.

22. Oregon: Dave Roberts sets pole vault record at 18'8.25".

24. London: Anonymous American gives Britain $1.2 mil. to buy site of Battle of Hastings.

28. Col.: First women enter Air Force Academy (→ 11/4/77).

28. Seychelles Islands get independence after 162 years under British rule.

29. Uganda: Hijackers with 256 hostages demand freedom for 53 PLO prisoners (→ 7/3).

DEATHS

10. Adolph Zukor, founder of Paramount movie empire (*1/7/1873).

25. Johnny Mercer, U.S. songwriter, "That Old Black Magic" (*11/18/1909).

A world without tigers, eagles and elephants?

The bald eagle nests high off the ground to protect its long-helpless young.

The tiger, victim of forest clearing.

Humankind has wiped out a little over one percent of the world's species since 1900. While that figure may not sound too dire, Dr. Lee Taylor of the President's Council on Environmental Quality can put the estimate into perspective. If the rate of extinction keeps up, he says, 4,062 species of mammals will be gone in 30 years. The only species left will be the 4,063rd: Man.

In the 1970's, a few governments and private organizations are trying to halt the deadly stampede. It is a near-impossible task. As long as the human population expands, animal habitats will shrink; as long as animals continue to grow fur on their backs, horns on their heads or meat on their ribs, people will value them more dead than alive.

Gorilla, territorial but vegetarian.

In 1973, the Convention of International Trade in Endangered Species of Fauna and Flora took a step to preserve the dwindling numbers, naming 216 species it considered at greatest risk. The bald eagle, the symbol of America, was on the list. So was the tiger.

Even the elephant, whose shape is meshed in our childhood memories with the alphabet's letter "e," is threatened. The Trade Convention specified the Asian species, but its big-eared cousin, the African elephant, is no better off. A survey from 1975 showed about 15,000 are slaughtered each year.

The international community felt all 216 species were in trouble, but the U.S. Department of the Interior did not. It agreed to protect only 159 of them, the other 57 species seeming less desirable. The California sea otter, for example, competes with fishermen for abalone. The glacier bear, says Interior, is "only the uncommon color variety of the black bear." In other words, it is not quite glamorous enough to be worth the fuss.

Yet, desirable creatures are permitted to fade away, too. The Save the Whales movement has grown of late in response to over-zealous whale hunting. Whales are prized for their oil and meat, especially in Japan where the steak is a delicacy. Five species of whales teeter on extinction, and continuing the rate of killings would make those steaks very rare indeed.

In 1972, the U.N. passed a resolution calling for a ten-year moratorium on commercial whaling. A year later, Japan and Russia said they would set their own quotas instead. They had better take care; whale populations replenish themselves very slowly, an adult female usually giving birth to just one calf every other year.

While some justification can be made for hunting for food (Japan claimed whale meat is an important protein source for the average Japanese), hunting rare game for sport seems pathetically foolish. In the early 1970's, members of Kenya's ruling family, the Kenyattas, were reported to hunt elephant for fun. Bad publicity brought the practice to a halt, but it would have ended sooner or later when no more elephants wander into firing range. Kenya vows to make amends by outlawing all big-game hunting.

Most wildlife experts say pleasure hunters are less a threat than poachers seeking ivory and hides. In one six-month period in Kenya, poachers killed hundreds of elephants, rhinoceroses and leopards.

Kenya can afford to thwart hunters and poachers because they interfere with a profit-making business: tourism. No animals, no tourism, no profits. But what happens when the profit motive and animal survival do not so nicely coincide? This year, the Tennessee Valley Authority proposed a dam called Tellico. A tiny perch called a snail darter stands, or swims, in its way. Conservationists are searching for other places where the fish might thrive, while swatting away public ridicule.

The United States passed an Endangered Species Act in 1973. Most threats to wildlife, however, cannot be solved by legislation. Urban encroachment is inexorable; tropical habitats are eroding at an awesome rate. Colombia plans to set aside 5.5 million acres for parks in a brave move which, on the huge stage of the ecosystem, is a tiny gesture.

Man-made pollution endures. DDT, banned in 1972, is still being detected in the bodies of migratory songbirds, and acid rain continues to render lakes in the United States, Canada and Europe lifeless.

It is said the lion is king of beasts. Humankind seems a sorry pretender to the throne (→ 5/19/77).

Coveted ivory of giant tusks mark the elephant as a target of fortune hunters. ▷

Violence in South Africa

White vs. black in Soweto.

June 19. The worst racial violence in 15 years has swept through the black townships outside Johannesburg. Police, who were under orders from Prime Minister John Vorster to restore order "at all costs," refused to release casualty figures. Unconfirmed reports say at least 100 people were killed. A picture on the front page of a South African newspaper this morning showed a 12-year-old girl dead in the street. Police say she had been rioting.

The trouble started Tuesday when 10,000 black students marched in Soweto to protest a government order to teach them the Afrikaans language. It is viewed as a symbol of the white minority government. Police say the marchers began to riot, attacking government buildings, trains and buses. In confrontations between protesters and police, most of the valuable property in Soweto was destroyed. On some blocks, only hovels that are home to blacks remain (→ 8/4).

Syrians enter Lebanon; Americans leave

June 20. The U.S. Navy evacuated 263 Americans from Beirut today to avoid becoming entangled in the Lebanese civil war. Syrian troops entered the multi-factioned war last week, seizing control of most lines of transportation. Syria had been acting as the peace negotiator, but now is taking military steps to end the conflict.

The recent killings of American Ambassador Francis Meloy and his economic adviser Robert Waring prompted Washington to advise Americans in Lebanon to leave. However, over 1,500 U.S. citizens refused the Navy escort out of Beirut, choosing to stay and complete the various forms of work that sent them to the Mideast. The evacuation, code-named "Operation Fluid Drive," was ordered by President Ford. Some have sarcastically referred to the rescue effort as "Operation Iowa Primary," suggesting Ford was politically motivated in removing Americans from danger before the primary (→ 29).

Billionaire J. Paul Getty dies in Britain

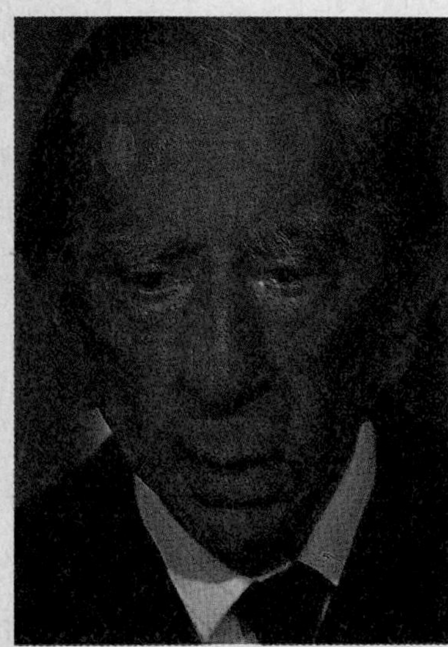
Getty had his first million at 23.

June 6. J. Paul Getty, 83, symbol of oil, wealth and power, has died at his mansion near London. The son of a Minneapolis oilman, he made his first million buying and selling oil leases 60 years ago.

His most daring coup was obtaining an oil concession near Saudi Arabia, paying King Saud $9.5 million in cash and $1 million per year, a gamble that paid off in 1953.

A bit of a restless eccentric with a pay phone in his mansion, he married five times and divorced five times. Seldom did he give away money; he felt that being accustomed to "passive acceptance of money" corrupts people. He leaves $4 billion, three sons and priceless collections of works of art.

1976

JULY

Su	Mo	Tu	We	Th	Fr	Sa
				1	2	3
4	5	6	7	8	9	10
11	12	13	14	15	16	17
18	19	20	21	22	23	24
25	26	27	28	29	30	31

2. U.S. Supreme Court rules death penalty not cruel or unusual punishment (→ 10/4).

3. Wimbledon: Bjorn Bjorg over Ilie Nastase 6-4, 6-2, 9-7; Chris Evert over Evonne Goolagong Cawley 6-3, 4-6, 8-6.

3. Uganda: Israeli raid frees hostages at Entebbe airport (→ 4).

4. Rome: Pietro Ingrao is first Communist president of Italian Parliament (→ 3/16/78).

6. Supreme Court limits power of federal courts to void state convictions for illegal evidence.

8. New York: Court disbars Nixon for Watergate (→ 10/28).

8. New Guinea: Earthquake takes at least 9,000 lives.

10. Angola: Four mercenaries executed; three British, one American (→ 3/19/84).

11. California: Frank Sinatra marries Barbara Marx.

13. Ethiopia: 18 put to death for plotting coup (→ 2/3/77).

14. Lisbon: Gen. Antonio Ramalho Eanes sworn in as president (→ 7/27/78).

18. Montreal: Nadia Comaneci scores ten on uneven bars, first in Olympic gymnastics.

18. Van Impe wins Tour de France.

20. Thailand: U.S. completes withdrawal of G.I.'s.

21. Dublin: British Ambassador Christopher Ewart-Biggs killed by mine (→ 8/27).

23. Belgrade: American Laszlo Toth, accused of spying, freed by Yugoslavs (→ 1/20/80).

24. Beirut: Lebanese rightists get cease-fire with PLO (→ 27).

25. Montreal: Edwin Moses sets record in 400-meter hurdles.

27. Tokyo: Ex-Premier Kakuei Tanaka arrested for taking bribes from Lockheed (→ 8/26).

27. Lebanon: U.S. Navy evacuates 308 from Beirut (→ 8/3).

30. Montreal: American Bruce Jenner wins gold in decathlon.

DEATH

6. Chu Teh, Chinese military chief under Mao (*12/18/1886).

Democrats choose Carter and Mondale

July 15. Jimmy Carter of Georgia, named yesterday as the presidential nominee of the Democratic Party, wooed the liberal wing today with his choice of Senator Walter F. Mondale of Minnessota as his vice-presidential running mate. The choice of Senator Mondale, a liberal, came after a methodical search for the best man by Carter, a former Governor of Georgia, who is the first major-party nominee from the Deep South since Zachary Taylor in 1848. "It's now a time to heal," Carter told Democrats at their convention in Madison Square Garden in New York (→ 8/19).

Carter, a "born-again" Baptist.

Enormous loss of life in China 'quake

July 29. A French visitor in China described the devastating earthquake that has killed thousands this way: "It was horrible. We were lost, like an ocean . . . an ocean (with) everything moving." The earthquake that virtually destroyed the city of Tangshan registered 8.2 on the Richter scale, making it the strongest 'quake in the world since 1964. It was followed by a second tremor which hit 7.9 on the scale. Millions were forced to sleep in the streets amid reports that aftershocks might occur. Hundreds of thousands have been left homeless as officials continue to assess casualties and property damage.

Nation has a glorious 200th birthday

Celebration in the nation's capital.

July 4. From one coast to the other, this has been a day of tall ships, sizzling hamburgers and unrestrained fireworks displays. The United States celebrated its 200th birthday today, and millions showed up for the public festivities. Many more drove to beaches, mountains and parks to spend peaceful times with their families.

The celebrations started on a mountain in Maine called Mars Hill, where dawn first reached the country. As daylight broke in Baltimore, the national anthem was sung at Fort McHenry. Fireworks exploded around the clock from South Carolina to California, and parties were just getting started on American islands in the Pacific as the rest of the country was fast asleep.

True to tradition, this was a day for records to be set. The nation's first President might have developed indigestion from the cherry pie baked in the town of George, state of Washington. It was 60 square feet. On a hillside in Sheboygan, Wisconsin, 1,776 frisbees whirled through the air. A pancake in Boston was 76 inches across, and a cake there weighed 69,000 pounds. More than 10,000 people were naturalized as citizens in mass ceremonies held in Chicago, Detroit and Miami.

Washington had the largest fireworks celebration, with a price tag of $200,000. But it was New York that hosted the most spectacular event of the day. Fifteen tall ships and more than 200 smaller ones sailed through the Upper Bay and up the Hudson River. Hundreds of thousands of New Yorkers and visitors jammed river banks and rooftops to catch a glimpse of the ships.

President Ford had one of the best vantage points. He flew onto the aircraft carrier Forrestal and then took a helicopter to the deck of the USS Nashville, anchored in the middle of the Hudson. New York was the last stop for the president, who made earlier appearances in Valley Forge and Philadelphia.

Ford warned the country not to be content with its past and to look to the future to increase its freedoms and improve its quality of life. Vice President Nelson Rockefeller struck a somber note as he admitted in Washington, "We face today what seem like insurmountable problems."

A tall ship in "Operation Sail."

Celebrations elsewhere were more restrained. Minutemen fired a salute over the grave of John Hancock in Massachusetts, and the President of Boston University delivered a speech entitled "Counterfeits of Democracy." By the end of the day, however, almost everyone in the United States had caught the spirit. And a million people cheered after the Washington fireworks when laser guns fired the message, "1776-1976, Happy Birthday, U.S.A." (→ 12/27).

The attraction of the tall ships made New York harbor the place to be today.

Viking 1 lands on Mars, sends photos

July 20. A Viking spacecraft landed on Mars today and sent back two spectacularly detailed pictures showing a rocky, surprisingly earth-like desert terrain. The three-legged, six-foot-high spacecraft landed on the Chryse Plain of Mars at 7:53 a.m. Eastern daylight time after an 11-month journey from earth. A major part of its mission will be to analyze the Martian soil for signs of water and life. In eight days, if all goes well, a mechanical arm will reach out from the Viking lander and scoop up soil samples that will be tested in three separate instruments for activity that could reveal the presence of living things. A sister ship is scheduled to land on a different part of Mars in less than three months (→ 8/7).

Viking 1, a pioneer on Mars.

Daring Israeli raid at Entebbe succeeds

July 4. Israeli commandos staged a daring raid late last night to free 105 hostages held by pro-Palestinian hijackers at the Entebbe Airport in Uganda. The terrorists had threatened to start shooting the mostly Israeli and Jewish hostages later today. They were whisked onto transport planes and flown to Israel. Preliminary reports say at least two of the hostages may have been killed. All of the hijackers were reportedly killed.

The commandos flew more than 2,000 miles from Israel to Entebbe on three planes. After landing, they set off several explosive devices at one end of the airport to distract Ugandan forces. The troops and President Idi Amin had reportedly been cooperating with the hijackers and had even furnished them with fresh weapons. The shoot-out took place in the old passenger terminal where the Arab, Palestinian and German terrorists had been holed up all week with the hostages.

The commando raid came as a surprise to many Israelis, who believed the government was negotiating with the hijackers. After commandeering the Air France jet last Sunday on a flight from Athens to Paris, the guerrillas demanded the release of 53 Palestinian and pro-Palestinian prisoners from jails in Israel and Europe. The Israeli Cabinet offered to release some of the prisoners. It is not clear yet if it was just buying time for the raid (→ 24).

1976 Montreal

The star of the Montreal Olympics was only 14 years old, barely five feet tall, weighed 83 pounds and wore pigtails. But Nadia Comaneci of Rumania whirled and danced her way into the hearts of millions of televiewers and presented the image of perfection to the judges.

Wee Nadia more than succeeded the talented Olga Korbut of 1972 gymnastics fame. Olga won only two gold medals at Munich, but Nadia captured three golds and also posted the first perfect 10.0 score in Olympic history.

East Germany dominated the women's track events with nine firsts in 14 events, but the men's honors were divided fairly evenly. The East German women also were nearly invincible in swimming, taking 11 of 13 golds.

With 22 black African countries out of the competition in protest of a rugby tour by New Zealand in South Africa, such recordholders as John Akki-Bua in the 400-meter hurdles and Filber Bayi in the 1,500-meter run were absent.

The closest thing to an American hero in track was 26 years old, six feet, two inches tall and weighed 195 pounds. He was Bruce Jenner of San Jose State, winner of the decathlon. He Admitted his earlier interest in the decathlon was aided-by the chance to make a lot of post-Olympic money through testimonials and personal appearances.

But as he completed his victory lap, Jenner was handed a little American flag by a small boy, and he said afterward; "I did all the work, sure, but I grew up in a country that allows you to do what you want to do."

The American aquatic star was John Nabor, who won both backstroke events in world record time. American women swimmers scored an upset in taking the 400-meter freestyle relay.

Men Athletics

100 M Dash		
1. Hasely Crawford	TRI	10,06
2. Donald Quarrie	JAM	10,08
3. Valéri Borzov	URS	10,14

200 Dash		
1. Donald Quarrie	JAM	20,23
2. Millard Hampton	USA	23,29
3. Dwayne Ewans	USA	20,43

400 M Run		
1. Alberto Juantorens	CUB	44,26
2. Fred Newhouse	USA	44,40
3. Hermann Frazier	USA	44,95

800 M Run		
1. Alberto Juantorens	CUB	1:43,50
2. Iva Vandamme	BEL	1:43,86
3. Richard Wolhuter	USA	1:44,12

1500 M Run		
1. John Walker	NZL	3:39,17
2. Ivo Vandamme	BEL	3:39,27
3. Paul-Heinz Wellmann	FRG	3:39,33

5000 M Run		
1. Lassa Viren	FIN	13:24,8
2. Dick Quax	NZL	13:25,2
3. Klaus-Peter Hildenbrand	FRG	13:25,4

10,000 M Run		
1. Lasse Viren	FIN	27:40,4
2. Carlos Lopez	POR	27:45,2
3. Brendan Foster	GBR	27:54,9

Marathon		
1. Waldemar Cierpinski	GDR	2:09:55,0
2. Frank Shorter	USA	2:10:46,80
3. Kavel Lismont	BEL	2:11:26,0

110 M Hurdles		
1. Guy Drut	FRA	13,30
2. Alejandro Casanas	CUB	13,33
3. Willie Davenport	USA	13,38

400 M Hurdles		
1. Edwin Moses	USA	47,64
3. Michael Shine	USA	48,69
3. Jevgenij Gavrilenko	URS	49,45

3000 M Steeplechase		
1. Anders Gaerderud	SWE	8:08,02
2. Bronislaux Malinovski	POL	8:09,11
3. Frank Baumgartl	GDR	8:10,36

400 M Relay	
1. USA	38,34
2. German Democratic Republic	38,66
3. Soviet Union	38,78

1600 M Relay	
1. USA	2:58,56
2. Poland	3:01,14
3. German Federal Republic	3:01,98

20 km Walk		
1. Daniel Bastia	MEX	1:24:40,4
2. Hans Reimann	GDR	1:25,13,7
3. Peter Frenkell	GDR	1:25:29,3

High Jump		
1. Jacek Wszola	POL	2,25
2. Greg Joy	CAN	2,23
3. Dwight Stones	USA	2,21

Pole Vault		
1. Tadensz Slusarski	POL	5,50
2. Autti Kalliomacki	FIN	5,50
3. David Roberts	USA	5,50

Long Jump		
1. Arnie Robinson	USA	8,35
2. Randy Williams	USA	8,11
3. Frank Wartenberg	GDR	8,02

Triple Jump		
1. Viktor Saneiev	URS	17,29
2. James Butts	USA	17,18
3. Jao de Oliveira	BRA	16,90

Shotput		
1. Udo Beyer	GDR	21,05
2. Jevgeni Mironov	URS	21,03
3. Alexander Barychnykov	URS	21,00

Discus Throw		
1. Marc Wilkins	USA	67,50
2. Wolfgang Schmidt	GDR	66,22
3. John Powell	USA	65,70

Hammer Throw		
1. Juvi Sedyh	URS	77,52
2. Alexei Spiridonov	URS	76,08
3. Anatoli Bondarchuk	URS	75,48

Javelin		
1. Miklos Nemeth	HUN	94,58
2. Hanun Siitonen	FIN	87,92
3. Gheorghe Megelea	ROM	87,16

Decathlon		
1. Bruce Jenner	USA	8618
2. Guido Kratschmer	FRG	8411
3. Nicolai Avilov	URS	8369

Modern Pentathlon

Individual		
1. Janusz Pyciak-Peciak	POL	5520
2. Pavel Lednev	URS	5485
3. Jan Bartu	TCH	5466

Team	
1. Great Britain	15 559
2. Czechoslovakia	15 451
3. Hungary	15 395

Women Athletics

100 M Dash		
1. Annegret Richter	FRG	11,08
2. Renate Stecher	GDR	11,13
3. Inge Helten	FRG	11,17

200 M Dash		
1. Bäbel Eckert	GDR	22,37
2. Annegret Richter	FRG	22,39
3. Renate Stecher	GDR	22,47

400 M Run		
1. Erena Szewinska	POL	49,29
2. Christina Bremer	GDR	50,51
3. Ellen Streidt	GDR	50,55

800 M Run		
1. Tatiana Kanzankina	URS	1:54,94
2. Nicolina Chtereva	BUL	1:55,42
3. Elfie Zinn	GDR	1:55,60

1500 M Run		
1. Tatiana Kazankina	URS	4:05,5
2. Gunhild Hoffmeister	GDR	4:06,0
3. Ulrike Kepezinski	GDR	4:06,1

100 M Hurdles		
1. Johanna Schaller	GDR	12,77
2. Tatiana Anisimova	URS	12,78
3. Natalia Lebedeva	URS	12,80

400 M Relay	
1. German Democratic Republic	42,55
2. German Federal Republic	42,59
3. Soviet Union	43,09

1600 M Relay	
1. German Democratic Republic	3:19,23
2. USA	3:22,81
3. Soviet Union	3:24,24

High Jump		
1. Rosemarie Ackermann	GDR	1,93
2. Sara Simeoni	ITA	1,91
3. Joardanka Blagoeva	BUL	1,91

Long Jump		
1. Angela Voigt	GDR	6,72
2. Kathy McMillan	USA	6,66
3. Liajia Alfeiva	URS	6,60

All-American boy Bruce Jenner topped his fellow decathletes by more than 200 points.

Shotput		
1. Ivanka Christova	BUL	21,16
2. Nadeja Tchivova	URS	20,96
3. Helena Fibingerova	TCH	20,67

Discus Throw		
1. Evelyn Schlaak	GDR	69,00
2. Nadeja Tchivova	URS	68,30
3. Maria Vergova	BUL	67,30

Javelin Throw		
1. Ruth Fuchs	GDR	65,94
2. Marion Becker	FRG	64,70
3. Kathy Schmidt	USA	63,96

Pentathlon		
1. Sigrun Siegl	GDR	4745
2. Christine Laser	GDR	4745
3. Burglinde Pollack	GDR	4740

Men Swimming

100 M Freestyle		
1. Jim Montgomery	USA	49,99
2. Jack Babashoff	USA	50,81
3. Peter Nocke	FRG	51,31

200 M Freestyle		
1. Bruce Furniss	USA	1:50,29
2. John Naber	USA	1:50,50
3. Jim Montgomery	USA	1:50,58

400 M Freestyle		
1. Brian Godell	USA	3:51,93
2. Tim Shaw	USA	3:52,54
3. Vladimir Raskatov	URS	3:55,76

Nadia's initial exercise on the uneven bars drew the first perfect ten in Olympic history.

1500 M Freestyle		
1. Brian Godell	USA	15:02,40
2. Boby Hackett	USA	15:03,21
3. Stephen Holland	AUS	15:04,66

100 M Backstroke		
1. John Naber	USA	55,49
2. Peter Rocca	USA	56,34
3. Roland Matthes	GDR	57,22

200 M Backstroke		
1. John Naber	USA	1:59,15
2. Peter Rocca	USA	2:00,55
3. Dan Harrigan	USA	2:01,35

100 M Breaststroke		
1. John Hencken	USA	1:03,11
2. David Wilkie	GBR	1:03,43
3. Avidas Ivozaitis	URS	1:04,23

200 M Breaststroke		
1. David Wilkie	GBR	2:15,11
2. John Hencken	USA	2:17,26
3. Rick Collela	USA	2:19,20

100 M Butterfly Stroke		
1. Matt Vogel	USA	54,35
2. Joe Bottom	USA	54,50
3. Gary Hall	USA	54,65

200 M Butterfly Stroke		
1. Mike Bruner	USA	1:59,23
2. Steve Gregg	USA	1:59,54
3. Bill Forester	USA	1:59,56

400 M Medley Relay		
1. Rod Strachan	USA	4:23,68
2. Tim MacKee	USA	4:24,62
3. Andrei Smirnov	URS	4:26,90

800 M Freestyle Relay	
1. USA	7:32,22
2. Soviet Union	7:27,97
3. Great Britain	7:32,11

400 M Medley Relay	
1. USA	3:42,22
2. Canada	3:45,94
3. German Federal Republic	3:47,29

Springboard Diving		
1. Phil Boggs	USA	619,05
2. Giorgio Cagnotto	ITA	570,48
3. Alexander Kosenkov	URS	567,24

High Diving		
1. Klaus Dibiasi	ITA	600,51
2. Gregory Louganis	USA	576,99
3. Vladimir Aleynik	URS	548,61

Water Polo
1. Hungary
2. Italy
3. German Federal Republic

Women Swimming

100 M Freestyle		
1. Kornelia Ender	GDR	55,65
2. Petra Priemer	GDR	56,49
3. Enith Brigitha	HOL	56,56

200 M Freestyle		
1. Kornelia Ender	GDR	1:59,26
2. Shirley Babshoff	AUS	2:01,22
3. Enith Brigitha	HOL	2:01,40

400 M Freestyle		
1. Petra Thumer	GDR	4:08,89
2. Shirley Babashoff	USA	4:10,46
3. Shannon Smith	CAN	4:14,60

800 M Freestyle		
1. Petra Thumer	GDR	8:37,14
2. Shirley Babashoff	USA	8:37,59
3. Wendy Weinberg	USA	8:42,60

100 M Breaststroke		
1. Hennelore Anke	GDR	1:11,16
2. Ljubov Rusanova	URS	1:13,04
3. Marina Koshevaia	URS	1:13,30

200 M Breaststroke		
1. Marina Koshevala	URS	2:33,35
2. Marina Turchenia	URS	2:36,08
3. Ljubov Rusanova	URS	2:36,22

100 M Backstroke		
1. Ulrike Richter	GDR	1:01,83
2. Birgit Treiber	GDR	1:03,41
3. Nancy Garapick	CAN	1:03,71

200 M Backstroke		
1. Ulrike Richter	GDR	2:13,43
2. Birgit Treiber	GDR	2:14,97
3. Nancy Garapick	CAN	2:15,60

100 M Butterfly Stroke		
1. Kornelia Ender	GDR	1:00,13
2. Andrea Pollack	GDR	1:00,98
3. Wendy Boglioli	USA	1:01,17

200 M Butterfly Stroke		
1. Andrea Pollack	GDR	2:11,41
2. Ulrika Tauber	GDR	2:12,50
3. Rosemarie Gabriel	GDR	2:12,86

400 M Medley		
1. Ulrike Tauber	GDR	4:42,77
2. Cheryl Gibson	CAN	4:48,10
3. Becky Smith	CAN	4:50,48

400 M Medley Relay	
1. German Democratic Republic	4:07,95
2. USA	4:14,55
3. Canada	4:15,22

400 M Freestyle Relay	
1. USA	3:44,82
2. German Democratic Republic	3:45,50
3. Canada	3:48,81

Springboard Diving		
1. Jennifer Chandler	USA	506,19
2. Christa Kohler	GDR	469,41
3. Cynthia MacIngvale	USA	466,83

High Diving		
1. Elena Vaytsekhovskaia	URS	406,59
2. Ulrike Knape	SWE	402,60
3. Deborah Wilson	USA	401,07

Boxing

Light Flyweight (48kg)	
1. Jorge Hernandez	CUB
2. Byong Uk Li	PRK
3. Orlando Maldonado	PUR
3. Payo Pooltarat	THA

Flyweight (51 kg)	
1. Leo Randolph	USA
2. Damon Duvalon	CUB
3. David Torosyan	URS
3. Leszek Lazynski	POL

Bantamweight (54 kg)	
1. Yong Jo Gu	PRK
2. Charles Money	USA
3. Patrick Cowdell	GBR
3. Victor Rybakov	URS

Featherweight (57 kg)	
1. Angel Herrera	CUB
2. Richard Nowakowski	GDR
3. Leszek Kosadowski	POL
3. Juan Parades	MEX

Lightweight (60 kg)	
1. Howard Davis	USA
2. Simon Cutov	ROM
3. Vassily Solomin	URS
3. Ace Rusevski	YUG

Light Welterweight (63,5 kg)	
1. Ray Leonard	USA
2. Andres Aldema	CUB
3. Vladimir Kolev	BUL
3. Kazimier Szczerba	POL

Welterweight (67 kg)	
1. Jochen Bachfeld	GDR
2. Pedro Gamarro	VEN
3. Reinhard Skrice	FRG
3. Victor Zilbermann	ROM

Nadia Comaneci, dazzlingly talented at 14, scored three perfect tens on her way to a gold on the balance beam.

1976 Montreal

Light Middleweight (71 kg)
1. Jerzy Ribicki POL
2. Tdija Kacar YUG
3. Victor Savchenko URS
3. Rolando Garbey CUB

Middleweight (75 kg)
1. Michael Spinks USA
2. Rufat Riskiev URS
3. Alec Nastac ROM
3. Louis Martinez CUB

Light Heavyweight (81 kg)
1. Leon Spinks USA
2. Sixto Soria CUB
3. Costica Dafinoui ROM
3. Janusz Gortat POL

Heavyweight (more than 81 Kg)
1. Teofil Stevenson CUB
2. Mircea Simon ROM
3. Johnny Tate USA
3. Clarence Hill BER

Weightlifting

Flyweight (52 kg)
1. Alexander Voronine URS 242,5
2. Gyoergy Koszegi HUN 237,5
3. Mohammed Nassiri IRA 235,0

Bantamweight (56 kg)
1. Nourair Nourikian BUL 262,5
2. Grzegorz Cziura POL 252,5
3. Kenkichi Audo JAP 250,0

Featherweight (60 kg)
1. Nicolai Kolesnikov URS 285,0
2. Georgi Todorov BUL 280,0
3. Kazamasu Hirai JAP 275,0

Lightweight (67.5 kg)
1. Zbigniev Kaczmarek POL 307,5
2. Poitr Korol SOV 305,0
3. Daniel Senet FRA 300,0

Middleweight (75 kg)
1. Yordan Mikov BUL 335,0
2. Wartan Militosyan URS 330,0
3. Peter Wenzel GDR 327,5

Light Heavy weight (less than 82.5 kg)
1. Valri Shary URS 365,0
2. Blagoi Blagoev BUL 362,0
3. Trendufil Stoichev BUL 360,0

Middle Heavyweight (less than 90 kg)
1. David Rigert URS 382,5
2. Lee James USA 362,5
3. Atanas Chopov BUL 360,0

Heavyweight (110 kg)
1. Valentin Khristov BUL 400,0
2. Juri Zaitsev URS 385,0
3. Krastic Semerdjiev BUL 385,0

Super Heavyweight (more than 110 kg)
1. Vassily Alexeiev URS 440,0
2. Gerd Bonk GDR 405,0
3. Helmut Losch GDR 387,5

Greco Roman Wrestling

Light Flyweight (48 kg)
1. Alexei Shumakov URS
2. Georghe Berceanu ROM
3. Stefan Anghelov BUL

Flyweight (53 kg)
1. Vitaly Konstantinov URS
2. Nieu Ginga ROM
3. Kochira Hirayama JAP

Bantamweight (57 kg)
1. Pertti Ukkola FIN
2. Ivan Fric YUG
3. Farhat Mustafin URS

Featherweight (62 kg)
1. Kazimier Lipien POL
2. Nelson Davidian URS
3. Laszlo Reczi HUN

Lightweight (68 kg)
1. Suren Nalbadiann URS
2. Stefan Rusu ROM
3. Heinz Helmut Wehling GDR

Welterweight (74 kg)
1. Anatoli Bykov URS
2. Vitezlav Macha TCH
3. Karl-Heinz Helbing GDR

Middleweight (82 kg)
1. Momir Petkovic YUG
2. Vladimir Tchebokcharov URS
3. Ivan Kolev BUL

Light Heavyweight (90 kg)
1. Valeri Rezantsev URS
2. Ivano Mikolov BUL
3. Czeslaw Kwiecinski POL

Heavyweight (100 kg)
1. Nicolai Balbochine URS
2. Andrzey Skrzylewski POL
3. Kamen Goranoff BUL

Super Heavyweight (more than100 kg)
1. Alexander Kelchinski URS
2. Roman Codreanu ROM
3. Alexander Tomov BUL

Freestyle Wrestling

Light Flyweight (48 kg)
1. Kassan Issaev BUL
2. Roman Dimitriev URS
3. Akiva Kudo JAP

Randy Williams soared nearly 26.5 feet and still came in second to teammate Arnie Robinson in the broad jump.

Flyweight (Less than 52 kg)
1. Yuji Takado JAP
2. Alexander Ivanov SOV
3. Hae-sup Jeon COR

Bantamweight (less than 57 kg)
1. Umin URS
2. Hans-Dieter Bruchert GDR
3. Masoo Arai JAP

Featherweight (less than 62 kg)
1. Jum-mo Yang COR
2. Zevgden Oidov MON
3. Jean Davis USA

Lightweight (less than 68 kg)
1. Pavel Pinigin URS
2. Lloyd Kaeser USA
3. Yasabavo Sugawara JAP

Welterweight (less than 74 kg)
1. Juchivo Date JAP
2. Mansouv Barzegar IRA
3. Stanley Dzledzle USA

Middleweight (less than 87 kg)
1. John Peterson USA
2. Viktor Novojoilov URS
3. Adolf Seger FRG

Light Heavyweight (less than 90 kg)
1. Levan Tediashvili URS
2. Benjamin Peterson USA
3. Stelica Morcov ROM

Heavyweight (less than 100 kg)
1. Ivan Yarygin URS
2. Russel Helickson USA
2. Dimo Kostov BUL

Super Heavyweight (more than 100 kg)
1. Soslan Andiev URS
2. Josef Balla HUN
3. Ladislav Simon ROM

Judo

Lightweight (less than 63 kg)
1. Hector Rodriguez CUB
2. Eunk Zunk Chang COR
3. Joseph Tuncsik HUN
3. Felice Mariani ITA

Welterweight (less than 70 kg)
1. Vladimir Nevzorov URS
2. Koji Kuamoto JAP
3. Patrick Vial FRA
3. Marian Talaj POL

Midleweight (less than 80 kg)
1. Isamu Sonoda JAP
2. Valeri Dvonikov URS
3. Slavko Obadov YUG
3. Yungchul Park KOR

Light Heavyweight (less than 95 kg)
1. Kazuhiro Niyomina JAP
2. Ramaz Kharshiladze URS
3. David Starbrook GBR
3. Jorg Rothlisbeger SUI

Heavyweight (less than 95 kg)
1. Sergei Novikov URS
2. Gunther Neureuther FRG
3. Allan Coage USA
3. Sumio Endo JAP

Open
1. Haruki Usmura JAP
2. Keith Remfri GBR
3. Shota Chochishvili URS
3. Jeaki Cho KOR

Men Fencing

Foil Individual
1. Fabio Dal Zotto ITA
2. Alexander Romankov URS
3. Bernard Talvard FRA

Foil Team
1. German Federal Republic
2. Italy
3. France

Epee Individual
1. Alexander Pusch FRG
2. Jurgen Hehn FRG
3. Gyoso Kulcsar HUN

Epee Team
1. Sweden
2. German Federal Republic
3. Switzerland

Sabre Individual
1. Viktor Krovopouskov URS
2. Vladimir Mazlimov URS
3. Viktor Sidiak URS

Sabre Team
1. Soviet Union
2. Italy
3. Romania

Women Fencing

Foil Individual
1. Ildiko Schwarzenberger HUN
2. Consolata M. Collino ITA
3. Elena Belova URS

Foil Team
1. Soviet Union
2. France
3. Hungary

Men Canoeing

Kayak-1 500 M
1. Vasile Diba ROM 1:46,41
2. Zoltan Sztanity HUN 1:46,95
3. Rudiger Helm GDR 1:48,30

Kayak-2 500 M
1. German Democratic Republic 1:35,87
2. Soviet Union 1:36,81
3. Romania 1:37,43

Kayak-4 1000 M
1. Soviet Union
2. Spain
3. German Democratic Republic

Canadian-1 500 M
1. Alexander Rogov URS 1:59,23
2. John Wood CAN 1:59,58
3. Matija Ljubak YUG 1:59,60

Canadian-2 500 M
1. Soviet Union 1:45,81
2. Poland 1:47,77
3. Hungary 1:48,25

Canadian-1 1000 M
1. Yugoslavia
2. Soviet Union
3. Hungary

Canadian-2 1000 M
1. Soviet Union
2. Romania
3. Hungary

Women Canoeing

Kayak-1 500 M
1. Carola Zirzov GDR 2:01,05
2. Tatiana Korchunova URS 2:03,07
3. Klara Rajnai HUN 2:05,01

Kayak-2 500 M
1. Soviet Union 1:51,15
2. Hungary 1:51,69
3. German Democratic Republic 1:51,81

Men Rowing

Single Scull
1. Pertti Karppinen FIN 7:29,03
2. Peter-Michael Kolbe FRG 7:31,67
3. Joachim Dreifke GDR 7:38,03

Double Sculls
1. Norway 7:13,20
2. Great Britain 7:15,26
3. German Democratic Republic 7:17,45

Pair Oars without Coxswain
1. German Democratic Republic 7:23,31
2. USA 7:26,73
3. German Federal Republic 7:30,03

Pair Oars with Coxswain
1. German Democratic Republic 7:58,99
2. Soviet Union 8:01,82
3. Czechoslovakia 8:03,28

Four Oars without Coxswain
1. German Democratic Republic 6:37,42
2. Norway 6:41,22
3. Soviet Union 6:42,53

Foar Oars with Coxswain
1. Soviet Union 6:40,22
2. German Democratic Republic 6:42,70
3. German Federal Republic 6:46,96

Eight Oars
1. German Democratic Republic 5:58,29
2. Great Britain 6:00,29
3. New Zealand 6:03,51

Women Rowing

Single Sculls
1. Christina Scheiblich GDR 4:05,56
2. Joan Lind USA 4:06,21
3. Elena Antonova URS 4:10,86

Double Sculls
1. Bulgaria
2. GDR
3. Soviet Union

Four Oars with Coxswain
1. GDR
2. Bulgaria
3. Soviet Union

Quadruple Sculls with Coxswain
1. GDR
2. Soviet Union
3. Romania

Pair Oars without Coxswain
1. Bulgaria
2. GDR
3. RFA

Four Oars without Coxswain
1. GDR
2. Bulgaria
3. Soviet Union

Eight Oars
1. GDR
2. Soviet Union
3. USA

Yachting

Finn Monotype Class
1. German Democratic Republic 35,4
2. Soviet Union 39,7
3. Australia 46,4

Flying Dutchman Class
1. German Democratic Republic 34,7
2. Great Britain 51,7
3. Brazil 52,1

Soling Class
1. Denmark 46,7
2. USA 47,4
3. German Democratic Republic 47,4

Tempest Class
1. Sweden 14,0
2. Soviet Union 30,4
3. USA 32,7

470 Class
1. German Federal Republic 42,4
2. Spain 49,7
3. Australia 57,0

Tornado Class
1. Great Britain 18,0
2. USA 36,0
3. German Federal Republic 37,7

Cycling

Individual Road Race
1. Bernt Johansson SWE 4:46,52
2. Giuseppe Martinelli ITA a 31 Sec.
3. Mieczyl Nowiki POL a 31 Sec.

100 Km Team Time Trial
1. Soviet Union 2:08,53
2. Poland 2:09,13
3. Denmark 2:12,20

1000 M Time Trial
1. Klaus-Jurgen Grunke GDR 1:05,92
2. Nichel Varten BEL 1:07,51
13. Niels Fredborg DEN 1:07,61

Sprint
1. anton Tkac TCH
2. Daniel Morelon FRA
3. Hans-Jurgen Geschke GDR

4000 M Individual Pursuit
1. Gregor Braun FRG 4:47,61
2. Hermann Ponsteen HOL 4:49,72
3. Thomas Huschke GDR 4:52,71

400 M Team Pursuit
1. German Federal Republic 4:21,06
2. Soviet Union 4:27,15
3. Great Britain 4:22,41

Equestrian Sports

All Around Individual Competition
1. Edmund Coffin USA -144,99
2. John Plumb USA -125,65
3. Karl Schultz FRG -129,45

All Around Team Competition
1. USA -451,00
2. German Federal Republic -584,60
3. Australia -599,54

Individual Dressage
1. Christine Stuckelberg SWE 1486
2. Harry Boldt FRG 1435
3. Reiner Klimke FRG 1395

Team Dressage
1. German Federal Republic 5155
2. Switzerland 4684
3. USA 4647

Grand Prix Jumping Individual
1. Alwin Schockemohle FRG 0
2. Michel Vaillantcourt CAN –12
3. Francois Mathy BEL –12

Grand Prix Jumping Team
1. France
2. German Federal Republic
3. Belgium

Shooting

Small-Bore Rifle, 50 M Prone
1. Karlheinz Smieszek FRG 599
2. Ulrich Lind FRG 597
3. Gennadi Luschikov URS 595

Small-Bore, Combined, 3 Positions
1. Lanny Bassham USA 1162
2. Margareth Murdock USA 1162
3. Werner Seibold FRG 1160

Rapid-Fire Pistol, 25 M
1. Norbert Klaar GDR 597
2. Jurgen Wiefel GDR 596
3. Roberto Ferrais ITA 595

Skeet
1. Josef Panacek TCH 198
2. Eric Swinkels HOL 198
3. Weslaw Gawlikowski POL 196

Free Pistol 50 M
1. Uwe Potteck GDR 573
2. Harald Vollmar GDR 567
3. Rudolf Dollinger AUT 562

Clay Pigeon Individual
1. Donald Haldemann USA 190
2. Armando Silva Margues POR 189
3. Ubaldesc Baldi ITA 189

Moving Target
1. Alexander Gazov URS 579
2. Alexander Kedyarov URS 576
3. Jerzy Greskiweicz POL 571

Men Archery

1. Darrel Pace USA 2571
2. Hiroshi Michinaga JAP 2502
3. Giao Carlo Ferrari ITA 2495

Women Archery

1. Luann Ryon USA 2499
2. Valentina Kovpan URS 2460
3. Zebiniso Rustamova URS 2407

Men Gymnastics

All around Individual Competition
1. Nicolai Andrianov URS 116,650
2. Sawao Kato JAP 115,650
3. Mitsuo Tsukahara JAP 115,575

All around Team Competition
1. Japan 576,8
2. Soviet Union 567,4
3. German Democratic Republic 564,6

Parallel Bars
1. Sawao Kato JAP 19,675
2. Nicolai Andrianov URS 19,500
3. Mitsuo Tsukahara JAP 19,475

Floor Exercise
1. Nicolai Andrianov URS 19,450
2. Vladimir Marchenko URS 19,425
3. Peter Korman USA 19,300

Horse Vault
1. Nicolai Andrianov URS 19,450
2. Mitsuo Tsukahara JAP 19,375
3. Horishi Kajiyama JAP 19,275

Sidehorse
1. Zoltn Magyar HUN 19,700
2. Eizo Kenmotsu JAP 19,575
3. Nicolai Andrianov URS 19,525

Horizontal Bar
1. Mitsuo Tsukahara JAP 19,675
2. Eizo Kenmotsu JAP 19,500
3. Eberhard Ginger FRG 19,475

Flying Rings
1. Nicolai Andrianov URS 19,650
2. Alexander Didiatin URS 19,550
3. Dan Grecu ROM 19,500

Women Gymnastics

All around Individual Competition
1. Nadia Comaneci ROM 79,375
2. Nelli Kim URS 78,675
3. Ludmila Touritcheva URS 78,625

All around Team Competition
1. Soviet Union 390,35
2. Romania 387,15
3. German Democratic Republic 385,10

Uneven Bars
1. Nadia Comaneci ROM 20,000
2. Teodora Ungureanu ROM 19,800
3. Marta Egervari HUN 19,775

Floor Exercise
1. Nelli Kim URS 19,850
2. Ludmila Touritcheva URS 19,820
3. Nadia Comaneci ROM 19,750

Horse Vault
1. Nelli Kim URS 19,800
2. Ludmila Touritcheva URS 19,650
3. Carola Dombeck GDR 19,650

Beam
1. Nadia Comaneci ROM 19,950
2. Olga Korbut URS 19,725
3. Teodora Ungureanu ROM 19,700

Men Basketball

1. USA
2. Yugoslavia
3. Soviet Union

Women Basketball

1. Soviet Union
2. USA
3. Bulgaria

Soccer

1. German Democratic Republic
2. Poland
3. Soviet Union

Men Hand-Ball

1. Soviet Union
2. Romania
3. Poland

Women Hand-Ball

1. Soviet Union
2. GDR
3. Hungary

Field Hockey

1. New Zealand
2. Australia
3. Pakistan

Men Volleyball

1. Poland
2. Soviet Union
3. Cuba

Women Volleyball

1. Japan
2. Soviet Union
3. Korea

1976

AUGUST

Su	Mo	Tu	We	Th	Fr	Sa
1	2	3	4	5	6	7
8	9	10	11	12	13	14
15	16	17	18	19	20	21
22	23	24	25	26	27	28
29	30	31				

1. Colorado: 139 killed in flash flood at recreation area.

3. Beirut: Red Cross begins removing injured from besieged Palestinian camp (→ 12).

3. Philadelphia: Death toll hits 20 in mysterious Legionnaires disease; 115 ill (→ 26).

4. South Africa: Police open fire on rioting students (→ 11).

4. Sudan: 81 executed for attempted coup.

4. Spain pardons 90% of political prisoners (→ 12/22).

7. Viking spacecraft tests strengthen hint of life on Mars (→ 9/17).

7. Tehran: U.S., Iran announce $10 bil. arms deal (→ 28).

10. Mozambique: Rhodesian troops raid guerrilla bases, killing 300 (→ 9/24).

11. South Africa: 17 blacks killed, 50 hurt as police break up riots near Cape Town (→ 9/2).

12. Beirut: Christians seize Tell Zaatar Palestinian camp after two-month siege (→ 11/15).

16. Maryland: Dave Stockton wins PGA golf title.

17. Philippines: Earthquake and tidal wave sweep coast, killing at least 3,100.

18. North Koreans kill two Americans at DMZ (→ 19).

20. Non-aligned nations end fifth Colombo conference, call for rearrangement of intl. economic relations.

20. Argentina: Extremists kill 46 in two mass murders.

24. Seattle: American Legion boos Jimmy Carter as he promises to pardon draft resisters (→ 1/21/77).

25. Paris: Raymond Barre becomes premier upon resignation of Jacques Chirac (→ 3/25/77).

27. London: European Commission on Human Rights accuses Britain of torture in N. Ireland (→ 6/16/77).

28. Tehran: Three U.S. civilians killed by guerillas (→ 11/15/77).

DEATH

2. Fritz Lang, German film director (*12/5/1890).

28 die of mystery Philadelphia virus

Aug 26. The death toll from a mysterious flu-like disease that broke out in Philadelphia over the July 4 holiday has reached 28, federal officials reported today. The malady is being called Legionnaire's disease because most of the cases occurred at a state American Legion convention. Another 149 patients have survived, although two are in critical condition. Scientists do not know the cause of the disease, but some tests indicate that nickel carbonyl, a highly toxic substance, may have been responsible. The disease resembles a severe viral pneumonia, doctors say (→ 9/4/77).

Bribery charged against Tanaka and Prince

Takeo Miki, Tanaka's successor.

Aug 26. Prince Bernhard of the Netherlands has resigned from his military and business posts after a government commission criticized his dealings with the Lockheed Aircraft Corporation. The prince denied receiving any money from the aircraft manufacturer, but the commission reported that he may have accepted over $162,000 as bribes designed to ensure Dutch purchases of Lockheed airplanes.

This follows the recent indictment of former Prime Minister of Japan Kakuei Tanaka for having accepted $1.6 million from Lockheed to arrange the purchase of Lockheed L-1O11 aircraft by Japan's largest airline (→ 6/15/78).

Laboratory makes a synthetic gene

Aug 28. The first synthesis of a complete, functioning gene was reported today by biologists at the Massachusetts Institute of Technology. Leading geneticists said the feat by Dr. Har Gobind Khorana and his colleagues was a major step toward understanding how genes, the basic units of heredity, regulate the growth and functioning of living things. It took nine years for Khorana's group to synthesize the gene by painstakingly assembling chemical subunits to reproduce the sequence of a natural gene extracted from bacteria (→ 9/7/78).

Bloody fight occurs in Korean DMZ

Aug 19. A North Korean officer yelled "kill" to his troops. They did, storming a group of American and South Korean soldiers with axes and metal spikes, killing two and wounding four Americans and injuring five South Koreans. The attack took place in the demilitarized zone near the Bridge of No Return. President Ford called the assault "brutal and cowardly," asserting the North Korean government would be held responsible for "the consequences." North Korea has claimed it was the "U.S imperialist troops" who attacked.

Ford and Dole are Republican team

Aug 19. President Ford surprised his fellow Republicans today by choosing Senator Robert J. Dole of Kansas as his vice-presidential running mate. His choice of the conservative senator came after a post-midnight meeting between the president and Ronald Reagan, who had been his closest rival for the presidential nomination. Reagan, when asked to comment on a list of prospects, had spoken warmly of Senator Dole. The president won nomination for a full term by a vote of 1,187 to Reagan's 1,070 at the Kansas City convention (→ 9/23).

Harrises guilty of kidnapping Patty

Aug 9. William and Emily Harris, the last known Symbionese Liberation Army members, have been found guilty of kidnapping Patricia Hearst in 1974. They could receive a maximum life sentence. Mr. Harris looked grim as the verdict was read in the Los Angeles courtroom. Mrs. Harris looked faint.

For 16 months, the couple lived underground, robbing a bank to pay bills, stealing autos to travel. The car owners, kidnapped, went along for the rides. Mrs. Harris was once a schoolteacher; he was a Marine. A prosecution lawyer called them "mindless terrorists" (→ 9/24).

Renee Richards wins first match as woman

Richards, should she play as a she?

Aug 21. Renee Richards, who never achieved much recognition as a male tennis player, has won her first tournament match as a woman. A former Navy officer and baseball star scouted by the Yankees as a man, she underwent a sex change and is trying to establish herself in women's tennis. In what amounted to a media circus, Dr. Richards won the first set against Kathy Beene at Orange, New Jersey, 6-0, and the second, 6-2, after nerarly collapsing from exhaustion. Dr. Richards, father of a young son as Richard Raskind, played some matches in California under the name of Renee Clark before making her official debut as a woman player.

1976

SEPTEMBER

Su	Mo	Tu	We	Th	Fr	Sa
			1	2	3	4
5	6	7	8	9	10	11
12	13	14	15	16	17	18
19	20	21	22	23	24	25
26	27	28	29	30		

2. South Africa: 3,000 blacks clash with police in Cape Town (→ 10/18).

6. Tokyo: Soviet pilot lands highly advanced MIG-25, asks political asylum in U.S.

7. Washington: La Scala debuts in U.S. with Verdi's "Macbeth" at JFK Center.

7. Corsica: Militants blow up French jet.

8. California: Christo unveils $2 mil., 24-mile environmental art work "The Running Fence."

10. Yugoslavia: 176 killed as two planes collide.

12. N.Y.: Connors beats Borg, Evert over Goolagong for U.S. Open singles titles.

13. U.S. announces it will veto Vietnam's U.N. bid (→ 11/12).

14. Michigan: 165,000 members of UAW strike Ford.

16. Egypt: Sadat re-elected (→ 1/19/77).

17. California: Space shuttle is unveiled (→ 2/18/77).

19. Turkey: Jet hits mountain, killing 146.

19. Washington: Sun Myung Moon ends four-year U.S. ministry with anti-Communist speech (→ 11/1).

20. Brussels opens subway.

21. Washington: Chilean opposition leader Orlando Letelier slain by bomb in car (→ 1/4/78).

23. Philadelphia: Ford and Carter hold first debate (→ 10/6).

24. California: Patty Hearst sentenced to seven years for armed robbery (→ 11/19).

24. Rhodesia: Smith accepts plan calling for biracial regime, black rule in two years (→ 26).

26. Five African presidents denounce plan for black rule in Rhodesia (→ 2/7/77).

28. New York: Ali wins decision over Ken Norton to retain heavyweight title (→ 5/16/77).

29. New York: Record $3.25 million paid for a Rembrandt.

DEATH

9. Mao Tse-tung, Communist Chinese leader (*12/26/1893).

Mao Tse-tung dies at 82

Sept 18. Eight hundred million Chinese stood silent for three minutes today as the sirens of ships, trains and factories sounded in tribute to Mao Tse-tung, a giant among the giants of the 20th Century, who died nine days ago at the age of 82.

In Peking, after an army band played a funeral march, the national anthem and the Internationale, Hua Kuo-feng saluted Mao as the "founder and wise leader of the Communist Party of China, the Chinese People's Liberation Army and the People's Republic of China."

"It was under Chairman Mao's leadership that the Chinese people, who had long suffered from oppression and exploitation, won emancipation and became masters of the country. It was under Chairman Mao's leadership that the disaster-plagued Chinese nation rose to its feet," the top senior official said in eulogizing the man who led the Communist takeover in 1949 and then dominated the nation as he guided it from underdevelopment and isolation to a nuclear power with an expanding industrial base, defying Soviet hegemony, purging rivals, opening a relationship with the U.S. and winning a seat in the U.N. "The Chinese people love, trust and esteem Chairman Mao from the bottom of their hearts."

Eight days of mourning and official ceremonies have come to an end, but it may be millenia before China and the world forget Mao.

Mao, father of Chinese Revolution.

He may have had more influence on more people than any other figure of the 20th Century. In China, the masses have been instructed to carry on his cause. Throughout the Third World, millions of peasants digest his thoughts while their leaders study his tactics on guerrilla warfare. In the West, scholars reflect on his undeniable failures as well as contributions to Marxist theory, his belief in the major role of the peasantry in revolution in particular. Marx had considered peasants ignorant "sacks of potatoes."

Throughout it all, Mao professed an abiding faith in people. "I have witnessed the tremendous energy of the masses," he said. "On this foundation it is possible to accomplish any task whatsoever" (→ 10/12).

Intellectual, political and spiritual leader of the Chinese people for 27 years.

Science group backs curbs on aerosol

Sept 13. Limits on the use of fluorocarbon gases as propellants in aerosol spray cans are needed to save the earth's protective ozone layer, a committee of the National Academy of Sciences said today. The committee said it could not yet recommend when limits should be imposed but said there is strong evidence that the fluorocarbons, called Freons, enter the atmosphere and release chlorine that attacks the ozone layer. About three-quarters of fluorocarbon production goes into aerosol spray cans, but the chemicals also are used in air conditioners and refrigerators (→ 1/29/78).

California enacts 1st right-to-die law

Sept 13. The California State Legislature today approved the nation's first right-to-die law. The Natural Death Act stipulates that a terminally ill person may register a desire to avoid life-prolonging treatment by signing a "directive to physicians" that is effective for five years. Doctors must obey the request if patients file such a document at least 14 days after being told they have a terminal condition. Otherwise, the directive is not mandatory. A number of other state legislatures are considering similar right-to-die legislation.

Swedish Socialists lose after 44 years

Sept 19. Prime Minister Olof Palme's Social Democrats received a stunning defeat in Sweden. A victorious coalition of center, liberal and moderate parties is expected to back Thorbjorn Falldin as the new Prime Minister. For the first time in 44 years, Sweden will not be governed by a Socialist coalition. The new Cabinet is unlikely to disassemble the elaborate welfare state the Socialists constructed, but it is likely to improve relations with the United States. They deteriorated in 1972 when Palme compared the bombings in North Vietnam to Nazi massacres (→ 10/5/78).

1976

OCTOBER

Su	Mo	Tu	We	Th	Fr	Sa
					1	2
3	4	5	6	7	8	9
10	11	12	13	14	15	16
17	18	19	20	21	22	23
24	25	26	27	28	29	30
31						

1. Mexico: Hurricane Lizzie hits, leaving 2,500 dead, 14,000 injured and 40,000 homeless.

4. Washington: Sec. of Agriculture Earl Butz resigns over racist remark.

4. U.S. Supreme Court lifts ban on death penalty in murder cases (→ 11/5).

7. U.S., Panama agree on new canal negotiations (→ 8/10/77).

9. Nepal: Two Americans reach top of Mount Everest.

10. American student publishes article detailing how to build atomic bomb (→ 11/6).

10. N.J.: $68 mil. football stadium opens at Meadowlands.

10. Tokyo: Sadaharu Oh ties Babe Ruth's home run record in Japan's pro league (→ 4/11/80).

12. Peking: Gang of Four seized for plotting coup; Hua Kuo-feng named prime minister (→ 16).

12. Paris says it will sell nuclear technology to Pakistan.

12. U.S.: Swine flu vaccinations halted in nine states as three die after getting shots (→ 12/16).

13. Bolivia: U.S. 707 crashes in main street of Santa Cruz, killing 102 and injuring 105.

15. Atlantic: Cargo ship with 37 vanishes in Bermuda Triangle.

16. Shanghai: Crowds assail effigies of Mao's widow (→ 23).

18. Pretoria: Premier Vorster says he "cannot foresee such a day" when blacks will share power in S. Africa (→ 6/13/77).

21. New York: Reds win Series in four straight over Yankees.

22. FDA bans use of Red Dye No. 4.

23. Annapolis: Tony Dorsett sets college football rushing record.

25. Moscow: 30 Jewish activists arrested in protest (→ 2/22/77).

25. Alabama: Gov. Wallace pardons Clarence Morris, last survivor of Scottsboro case.

27. India: Premier Gandhi admits some died in riots over sterilization (→ 2/2/77).

28. Washington: John Erlichman begins jail sentence for Watergate (→ 4/12/77).

Mao's widow, three others jailed in China

Oct 23. Millions of Chinese, encouraged and no doubt organized by the Peking government, paraded through the streets of the capital and other cities today to celebrate the jailing of the so-called Gang of Four. Mao Tse-tung's widow and three other "Shanghai radicals" were reportedly purged for plotting a coup. Their ouster apparently means that the new party Chairman, Hua Kuo-feng, will try to steer a more moderate course.

Mao's widow, Chiang Ching, helped him to radicalize music, art and literature. To many Chinese, "radical" meant boring. At work, it meant longer hours and less pay. An official news agency report today called Chiang Ching and her associates "bourgeois revisionists and fascists." The report said the gang members were "filthy and contemptible like dog's dung" (→ 24).

Public hostility let loose in Peking.

Hua assumes full power in Peking

Oct 24. At an enormous rally of more than one million people yesterday, Hua Kuo-feng was proclaimed Chairman of the Chinese Communist Party. An official editorial said that Hua had been chosen for the post 17 days ago at the expressed wish of Mao. "With you in charge," it quoted Mao as having written last April, "I'm at ease."

A year ago, Hua was an obscure party functionary, virtually unknown. Following Chou's death in January, he was named Premier. As head of the Military Affairs Commission, he is the first man in China to hold three top spots at one time.

Hua, hand-picked heir to Mao.

At today's rally, however, he downplayed his role by not speaking, and there were no cheers of "Long live Chairman Hua!" indicating he is not trying to build a personality cult as Mao had (→ 1/16/77).

Thailand military takes over after rioting

Oct 6. Rioting and chaos in Thailand have led to a coup. This morning, a new goverment was in control and the constitution had been abolished. Admiral Sa-ngad Chaloryu declared himself President, then banned the press and imposed a curfew on the country.

Chaloryu said he stepped in because the six-month-old government was unable to control student protests that he claims were backed by Communists. A student revolt toppled the country's military regime in 1973, and Thailand has been a democracy for the past three years. The recent protests broke out when Field Marshal Kittikachorn, an ex-dictator, returned to Thailand three weeks ago. Sa-ngad said, "We set our sights too high as far as democracy was concerned."

Ford in debate denies Soviet power in East

Oct 7. Call it a misstatement. Call it a gaffe. Call it creative interpretation. President Ford seemed to befuddle listeners in his debate with Democratic presidential nominee Jimmy Carter last night when he said, "There is no Soviet domination in Eastern Europe and there never will be under a Ford administration." His statement obviously ignores the entrenched control the Soviets have in the Eastern bloc nations. Carter was quick to respond to the remark: "I would like to see Mr. Ford convince Polish-Americans and Czech-Americans . . . that those countries don't live under the domination and supervision of the Soviet Union behind the Iron Curtain" (→ 11/2).

Carter and Ford at the scene of the President's gaffe on Eastern Europe.

According to data from Viking 1, scientists say, the terrain and atmosphere of Mars might possibly support some form of life.

1976

NOVEMBER

Su	Mo	Tu	We	Th	Fr	Sa
	1	2	3	4	5	6
7	8	9	10	11	12	13
14	15	16	17	18	19	20
21	22	23	24	25	26	27
28	29	30				

1. Washington: Sun Myung Moon denies allegations he is agent of Seoul CIA (→ 3/24/77).

2. N.J. approves Las Vegas-style casinos for Atlantic City.

3. Britain: Nobel laureate Sir Martin Rye, fearing alien attack, urges scientists to keep life on earth secret.

5. Utah: Gary Gilmore asks for death sentence (→ 15).

5. N.Y.: Queens student killed by bayonet in ROTC fraternity hazing rite.

6. London: Exiled Soviet scientist says atomic blast killed hundreds in U.S.S.R. in 1958 (→ 26).

12. Paris: U.S. and Vietnam begin first talks since fall of Saigon (→ 1/6/77).

12. Washington: Chrysler gets $4.9 billion contract to build tanks for U.S. Army.

14. Georgia: Jimmy Carter's church drops ban on blacks (→ 7/11/77).

15. Utah: Gilmore and girlfriend overdose on barbiturates in apparent suicide pact (→ 30).

15. Lebanon: Syrian peace force takes control of Beirut (→ 21).

19. Calif.: Patty Hearst freed on $1.5 million bail (→ 5/15/78).

19. Brazil: Catholic bishops denounce military regime (→ 10/16/78).

21. Lebanon: Key ports taken by Syrian troops (→ 1/15/77).

21. Bucharest: U.S., Rumania sign ten-year trade pact.

26. Bucharest: Warsaw Pact proposes pact to bar first use of nuclear arms (→ 12/9).

27. Philadelphia: Navy beats Army 38-10 in football.

30. Utah: Board of Pardons grants Gilmore's request for execution (→ 1/17/77).

DEATHS

11. Alexander Calder, American sculptor (*7/22/1898).

18. Man Ray, American Dadaist painter, photographer (*8/27/1890).

20. Trofim Denisovich Lysenko, Soviet biologist, agriculturalist (*9/29/1898).

Carter elected President; credits debates

Carter acknowledges his victory.

Nov 2. Jimmy Carter was elected President today, sweeping his native South and some Northern industrial states to defeat President Ford, a Republican, in a close election.

A former Governor of Georgia, Carter is the first man from the Deep South to be elected president in a century and a quarter. President Ford, the nation's first appointive head of state, is the first incumbent to lose a presidential election since Herbert Hoover in 1932. Carter, a 52-year-old peanut farmer from the little town of Plains, Georgia, gave much of the credit for his victory to his showing in the televised debates between the two candidates (→ 1/20/77).

High court sanctions Medicaid abortions

Nov 8. The Supreme Court has ruled that a law which blocks the use of federal funds for abortions is unconstitutional. The decision will enable hospitals performing abortions to continue to accept payment from Medicaid funds. The ruling is seen as a victory for women on welfare who wish to terminate their pregnancies but without such federal monies could not afford to. Opponents of abortion view the ruling as a temporary setback and have vowed to fight federally funded abortions and the 1973 court decision which allows women to terminate their pregnancies with certain limitations (→ 8/31/78).

'Quake kills 3,000, ruins 80 villages

Nov 24. The death toll from a major earthquake that struck a mountainous area of eastern Turkey today could be over 3,000, government officials say. The earthquake, with a magnitude of 7.9 on the Richter scale, was the worst in Turkey since a 1939 tremor that killed 30,000. Its epicenter was near Muradiye, a town close to the Soviet border, where 95 percent of the buildings were reported leveled. It was also felt in the Armenian Republic of the Soviet Union, but no casualties were reported there. The United States and other nations are rushing relief supplies to the devastated region.

Independence party wins Quebec election

Levesque, Premier with 41% of vote.

Nov 16. The victory of the independence movement is being celebrated all over Quebec today. In Montreal, Trois-Rivieres and many small towns, the red and white Canadian flags with maple leaves have been replaced by blue Quebec banners emblazoned with fleurs-de-lis. The Parti Quebecois, headed by 54-year-old Rene Levesque, won 41% of the vote and 89 of the 110 seats in the Assembly. Levesque is the new Premier. The Liberal Party was the big loser. Levesque plans to hold a referendum on the question of sovereignty-association for Quebec (→ 11/3/77).

Malraux, man of many talents, dies

Nov 23. Renaissance man Andre Malraux has died in Paris. He was 75. Malraux was a writer, a politician and a war hero. He held a lifelong fascination for Asian culture and archeology.

Having attended a college for Asian languages, Malraux went to Cambodia intending to bring back and sell native art. Instead, he was jailed for stealing state property. His resentment of government propelled him toward Marxism, and when Nazis invaded France he defied fascism by serving the underground. After the war, Malraux was De Gaulle's Minister of Culture, a post Marxists frowned on.

His esthetic book "Man's Fate," exploring the role of self-sacrifice in the Chinese revolt of 1927, has been equated with Proust's best work.

Malraux, shaper of French culture.

Simpson in one day rushes 273 yards

Nov 25. O.J. Simpson broke his own one-game record of 250 yards by running 273 in a losing cause against the Detroit Lions. With the Michigan crowd chanting "Juice! Juice!" Simpson ran for touchdowns of 48 and 12 yards that brought standing ovations. However, they failed to save his Buffalo Bills from a 27-14 defeat. This was the fifth 200-yard game of Simpson's nine-year career, another National Football League record. He also passed the 1,000-yard mark for the fifth straight season.

1976

DECEMBER

Su	Mo	Tu	We	Th	Fr	Sa
			1	2	3	4
5	6	7	8	9	10	11
12	13	14	15	16	17	18
19	20	21	22	23	24	25
26	27	28	29	30	31	

1. Mexico: Jose Lopez Portillo sworn in as president.

4. Manila: Marcos rejects accord tying $1 bil. in U.S. aid to use of military bases (→ 11/25/77).

6. Washington: Democrats elect Tip O'Neill speaker of the House.

6. Georgia: Billy Carter loses mayoral election in Plains (→ 2/25/79).

9. Brussels: NATO rejects no-first-strike pledge (→ 3/30/77).

10. N.Y.: Mel Lynch, Dominic Byrne guilty of extortion, but not kidnapping Samuel Bronfman.

16. U.S.: Nationwide swine flu program suspended, vaccination linked to paralysis.

20. Rome: Cardinals approve canonization of Bishop John Neumann, first U.S. male saint.

25. Red Sea: 100 Moslems returning from pilgrimage die as boat sinks.

28. Georgia: Carter pledges not to let N.Y.C. go bankrupt (→ 6/8/78).

30. New York: Gov. Carey pardons seven inmates to close book on Attica uprising.

CULTURAL EVENTS, 1976

Literature: William Gaddis' "JR"; Alex Haley's "Roots"; Leon Uris' "Trinity"; Kurt Vonnegut's "Slapstick"; Gore Vidal's "1876"; Gabriel Garcia Marquez's "The Autumn of the Patriarch."

Academia: Michael J. Arlen's "Passage of Ararat"; Hedrick Smith's "The Russians"; earliest bronze work—3600 BC—found in Thailand; first functioning gene synthesized, at M.I.T.

Music: Gian-Carlo Menotti's opera "The Hero"; Rod Stewart's "Tonight's the Night"; Elton John & Kiki Dee's "Don't Go Breaking My Heart"; Wings' "Silly Love Songs."

The Arts: Several Michelangelo wall drawings found in Medici Chapel; photorealism gains popularity in painting.

Film: "All the President's Men," Redford, Hoffman, Robards; "Rocky," Talia Shire, Stallone; "Taxi Driver," De Niro; "Face to Face," Liv Ullmann.

Daley, who really ran Chicago, is dead

Daley, with family, thanked supporters for an unequalled sixth term in 1975.

Dec 20. He was loved. He was hated. He was feared. But nobody could deny that Mayor Richard Daley of Chicago held the reins of government firmly in hand. Daley died today, plunging the Second City into grief and praise for the man who is considered the last of the old-time big city bosses.

Mayor Daley ran the Chicago Democratic political machine for over two decades; he was mayor from 1955 until his death. Rising through the Cook County political ranks, he served in the state Legislature from 1936-46. He amassed a strong following with his persuasive skills and ability to attend swiftly to state business. After his entry into Chicago mayoral politics, Daley controlled many political decisions for all of Illinois.

Daley gained national recognition in the 1960 presidential election when his administration was suspected of tinkering with ballots to support fellow Democrat John Kennedy. Daley also hit the national spotlight in 1968 when his police force brutally attacked protesters at the Chicago Democratic presidential nominating convention.

Plaintive Palestinian child calls for peace in Lebanon, ravaged by civil war for more than a year.

Spanish vote 94 percent for reform

Dec 22. The people of Spain overwhelmingly voted in support of the Adolfo Suarez government's political reform program. The clear-cut victory of the national referendum, which proposes conversion to a parliamentary democratic form of government, signals an end to the General Franco-era of autocratic rule.

However, the election does not end domestic difficulties in Spain. Today, Prime Minister Suarez ordered the arrest of Santiago Carrillo, the Spanish Communist Party leader. Suarez has vowed to enforce a law which makes the Communist Party illegal. Coupled with opposition from the right, the Communist influence has dampened some of the government's satisfaction with the election (→ 1/25/77).

Nobel Prize goes to Milton Friedman

Dec 10. Americans took Nobel Prizes in every category but peace this year. Milton Friedman, who favors a laissez-faire economy, won the Nobel Prize for economic science. Burton Richter and Samuel Chao Chung share the award for physics. The chemistry prize goes to William N. Lipscomb. Saul Bellow, author of "Humboldt's Gift," accepted the literature honors.

Betty Williams and Mairead Corrigan from Northern Ireland were given the Peace Prize. After the deaths of three of Miss Corrigan's relatives, the pair organized the Community of Peace People, a group opposing sectarian violence.

Conservative economist Friedman.

Fragments of 1776 Declaration turn up

Dec 27. The first two pages of what may be the long-lost final draft of the Declaration of Independence, handwritten by Thomas Jefferson with quill pen and ink, have been found in a Boston attic. "I don't have any doubt that it's the document lost 200 years ago," says the Rev. James K. Allen, who discovered the document among old papers given to him by a friend.

It will take time for experts to determine the authenticity of the yellowed, frayed pages. Nobody knows where the last two pages of this document, drafted by Jefferson with help from John Adams, Roger Sherman and John F. Livingston and changed by members of the Continental Congress, then approved on July 4, 1776, may be.

Literature and drama sift the sands of time

Writers this year aimed at turning points in history. "The Final Days," by Carl Bernstein and Bob Woodward, traces Watergate from the firing of John Dean in 1973 to Richard Nixon's resignation. The book focuses on the President's last two pathetic weeks in office.

Lillian Hellman recalls her interrogations during the McCarthy era in "Scoundrel Time." Her radical stance left her nearly penniless for years. Hedrick Smith describes "The Russians" more than 50 years after their revolution. New York Times Bureau Chief for Moscow from 1971 to 1974, Smith gives an intimate portrait of the people.

Tom Stoppard's comedy "Travesties" zooms in on a significant (and silly) hypothetical moment, when James Joyce, Tristan Tzara (founder of the Dadaist movement) and Lenin met. In David Rabe's play "Streamers," Vietnam vets consider death in an army barracks.

In Alan Ayckbourn's "The Norman Conquests," Norman is a wild-maned romantic whose quadrangle (he loves three women) is examined from every angle. "A Chorus Line," by Michael Bennet, centers on the tense and jubilant moments of a Broadway audition.

Gore Vidal's novel "1876" relives the times of Ulysses S. Grant. And Alex Haley's "Roots," which will air as a miniseries, has made this bicentennial year rich in history for black and white alike (→ 2/1/77).

Libya buys tenth of Fiat for $415m

Dec 1. Today, the Libyan government purchased ten percent of the Fiat Corporation, the financially strapped Italian automobile manufacturer. Giovanni Agnelli, the Chairman of Fiat, announced that the purchase of new stock by the oil-rich government of Libya will yield $415 million in capital for the automobile manufacturing giant. Fiat, which has 185,000 workers, is Italy's largest private employer.

Jury convicts two men second time

Dec 21. A jury in Paterson, New Jersey, has for the second time convicted Rubin "Hurricane" Carter, a former middleweight contender, and a companion in the murder of three persons ten years ago. Carter and John Artis had been found guilty but offered new evidence beneficial to the defense that their lawyers said had been withheld by the prosecution in the first trial in 1967. Both defendants have served nine years of life terms (→ 2/9/77).

Kurt Waldheim gets second term at U.N.

Waldheim will serve U.N. again.

Dec 7. Kurt Waldheim, the 57-year-old diplomat from Austria, has been backed by the United Nations Security Council for a second term as Secretary General of the international assembly. The move assures his re-election by the General Assembly and will allow him to continue in his post for another five years. Waldheim, rather than initiating bold diplomatic moves, has followed a policy of quiet perseverance. His neutral status has been both an asset and a source of criticism. He has been blamed for letting the U.N. slip from popular awareness. His neutrality, however, has been of great benefit to the Mideast negotiations in Geneva, which may not have even begun without his presence (→ 3/5/86).

Macho 1976 films get off to a Rocky start

Stallone, writer and star: "Rocky."

Faye Dunaway in "Network."

Virile deeds dominated film in 1976, but a few women got their two cents in. "Rocky" stars the heavy-lidded Sylvester Stallone as a dumb boxer who punches his way to glory. Stallone wrote the script, and John G. Avildsen directed.

Dustin Hoffman is a runner running into unscheduled dental work in "Marathon Man." A convoluted plot has Hoffman evading a former Nazi played by Laurence Olivier. John Schlesinger directed.

Faye Dunaway shoulders aside the male competition in "Network." She plays an aggressive TV executive in a mad media world. Peter Finch is a suicidal newscaster, William Holden is a nearly sane management head. Paddy Chayefsky wrote the wild script.

"The Enforcer" is Dirty Harry Callahan, back by popular demand. Eastwood plays the cop with a little less gunplay than usual. Tyne Daly co-stars as a lady cop.

"All the President's Men" seem to be up to no good in the Alan J. Pakula film. Dustin Hoffman and Robert Redford are Carl Bernstein and Bob Woodward, who stumble onto the biggest scandal in history.

Who could be more macho than "King Kong"? Ask Jessica Lange, who fills the Faye Wray role. Director Dino D. Laurentis thought it was time to redo the classic beauty-beast tale, improving it (he thought) with a 40-foot mechanical ape. Jeff Bridges co-stars (but not as Kong).

Martin Scorsese's chilling "Taxi Driver" was an unexpected box office success. Robert DeNiro portrays an alienated, increasingly disturbed cab driver. When an affair with an idealistic young woman (Cybill Shepherd) fails, he turns to a prostitute, a girl barely into her teens (Jodie Foster). Bernard Herrmann composed the haunting musical score.

Two spooky pics rounded out the year. In "The Omen," a little boy sired by the devil makes things a bit uncomfy for his adoptive parents. Gregory Peck and Lee Remick star. Sissy Spacek is "Carrie," a teen with telekenetic powers. When she is made to look a fool at her high school prom, she wreaks vengeance by burning all her schoolmates to death. So watch out, guys.

Dustin Hoffman: "Marathon Man."

Clint Eastwood is "The Enforcer."

1977

JANUARY

Su	Mo	Tu	We	Th	Fr	Sa
						1
2	3	4	5	6	7	8
9	10	11	12	13	14	15
16	17	18	19	20	21	22
23	24	25	26	27	28	29
30	31					

1. Pasadena: U.S.C. over Michigan 14-6 in Rose Bowl.

1. Indianapolis: Rev. Jacqueline Means becomes first female Episcopal priest.

6. A.P. votes Nadia Comaneci and Bruce Jenner athletes of the year.

6. World Bank sends its first mission to Vietnam (→ 7/3).

9. Paris: Abu Daoud, alleged architect of 1972 Olympics attack, arrested.

10. Prague: Writer Pavel Kohout, whose "Poor Murderer" just closed on Broadway, arrested for involvement in human rights (→ 10/23/79).

12. U.S.: Steve Cauthen, 16-year-old jockey, takes 15 wins at apprentice horse racing meet.

15. Hussein and Sadat call for separate Palestinian delegation in Geneva talks (→ 2/18).

16. China: Thousands demand return of Deng on first anniversary of Chou's death (→ 7/22).

19. Cairo: Curfew imposed after riots kill 44, injure 600 (→ 5/21/78).

21. Carter urges 65 degrees as maximum heat in homes to ease energy crisis (→ 4/18).

21. Carter pardons draft resisters, orders study of deserters (→ 7/12).

25. Madrid: Tens of thousands strike day after murder of three Communist labor chiefs (→ 4/9).

29. L.A.: Comedian Freddie Prinze dies of self-inflicted gunshot wound.

DEATHS

2. Erroll Garner, U.S. jazz pianist, composed "Misty" (*6/15/1923).

6. William Gropper, American artist (*12/3/1897).

12. Henri-Georges Clouzot, French film director (*11/20/1907).

14. Anais Nin, American writer (*2/21/1903).

14. Sir Anthony Eden, British statesman (*6/12/1897).

14. Peter Finch, British actor (*9/28/1916).

Let's do it, says Gary Gilmore, and it's done

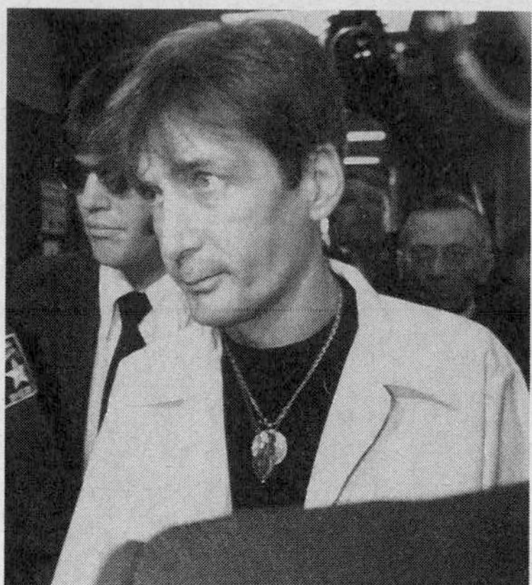

Gilmore after hearing of death date.

Jan 17. "Let's do it," said Gary Gilmore. Seconds later, the convicted killer was dead, the first in ten years to be executed in the United States. Gilmore had been convicted of the murders last year of two students of Brigham Young University, but a stay of execution had been won by foes of the death penalty. The stay was overturned by the U.S. Court of Appeals for the Tenth Circuit today and Gilmore, his head covered by a black hood, was taken to a warehouse and executed by a firing squad at Utah State Prison (→ 8/6/82).

Rupert Murdoch expands his empire

Jan 7. Rupert Murdoch, the man who made full-page photos of desirable young women an essential element of journalism, has purchased the New York Magazine Company. And last week, he bought The New York Post, a respected photo-journalistic tabloid he will no doubt make more sensational. Aussie Murdoch is reviled by some publishers for lowering journalistic standards. He does raise circulation, however. Employees at two New York Magazine Company publications, New York magazine and The Village Voice, threaten to quit but admit that with or without them the papers will likely thrive.

Air is alive with the sound of CB

Jan 22. "Breaker, breaker, one-niner, this is Highway Host. You got a smokie at 297 on the double nickle." Translated from Citizen Band radio lingo, this means, "Attention listeners on channel 19, my code name is Highway Host and I'm warning you of a state trooper radar trap at mile marker 297 on Interstate 55." CB radios have become so popular that they are now causing a national fuss. It seems unsolicited voices from highway airwaves are, because of electronic quirks, infiltrating radio and TV lines. Congress and CB manufacturers are at odds over what to do about the problem.

Jan 9. Minnesota's Fred McNeill blocks an Oakland punt during Super Bowl XI in Pasadena. The Raiders went on to trounce the Vikings 32-14.

Carter sworn in; walks down avenue

Jan 20. President Carter took his oath, made his speech and then, to the astonishment of the crowds, proceeded to walk home to the White House today. In a city hooked on security, the new president's jaunty amble down Pennsylvania Avenue, accompanied by his wife, Rosalynn, and daughter, Amy, was a sight to behold and there were cheers and shouts of "Jimmy! Jimmy!" from large crowds along the parade route. The president's walk dramatized the tone of his inaugural address in which he pledged to aid Americans in regenerating a spirit of trust.

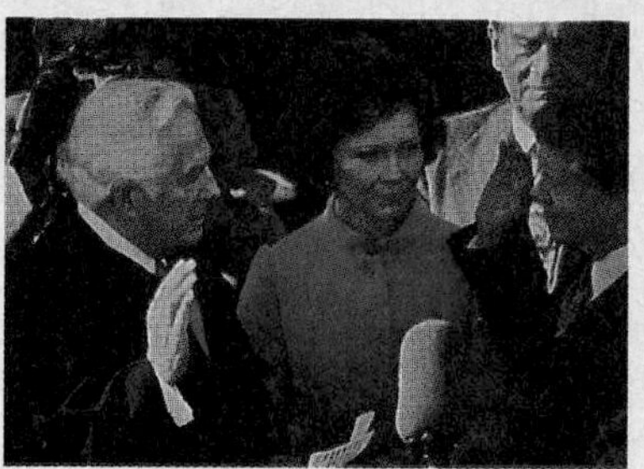

Rosalynn watches Jimmy take oath.

Pollution threatens Athens Acropolis

Parthenon at Acropolis in Athens.

Jan 10. The Acropolis has withstood 24 centuries of wind, rain and occasional military bombardment, but not half a century of car exhaust and factory fumes. Those 20th-Century pollutants are harsh indeed, and today the Director General of UNESCO stood by the pitted, crumbling edifices in Athens and appealed for donations for a rescue effort. While pollution is the main culprit, tourists have not helped. Souvenir hunters have been caught pocketing rubble and chipping the walls with chisels.

1977

FEBRUARY

Su	Mo	Tu	We	Th	Fr	Sa
		1	2	3	4	5
6	7	8	9	10	11	12
13	14	15	16	17	18	19
20	21	22	23	24	25	26
27	28					

2. India: Jaglivan Ram, Cabinet member 30 years, resigns to protest emergency rule, causing split in Congress Party (→ 3/21).

3. Addis Ababa: Ethiopian chief of state and six other leaders killed (→ 11).

6. London: Queen Elizabeth marks Silver Jubilee.

7. Rhodesia: Seven white missionaries slain in raid by black guerrillas (→ 23).

7. Amnesty Intl. charges Idi Amin with execution of thousands in Uganda (→ 16).

8. U.S.: Hustler editor Larry Flynt given seven years for engaging in organized crime.

9. N.J.: Hurricane Carter gets life term in retrial (→ 11/7/85).

11. Ethiopia: Lt. Col. Mengistu Haile-Mariam becomes head of state (→ 4/23).

12. Sacramento: Gov. Brown names Rose Elizabeth Bird as chief justice.

16. Uganda: Anglican Archbishop Luwum and two govt. officials, held for plot, reported dead (→ 25).

17. U.S.: Kissinger signs with NBC-TV to consult on news programs for five years.

18. Washington: It is reported that CIA made secret payments to Jordan's King Hussein for 20 years (→ 3/6).

20. Rocky Flats, Co.: U.S. unveils six windmills in test as source of power for farms.

20. El Salvador: Gen. Carlos Humberto Romero elected pres.; opposition charges fraud (→ 26).

22. U.S.: Boy Scouts, concerned about image with females and minorities, changes name to Scouting/USA.

22. Carter sends letter of support to dissident Soviet physicist Andrei Sakharov (→ 5/24).

23. Rhodesia opens industrial zones, shopping areas to blacks (→ 7/18).

26. El Salvador declares state of siege to quiet rioters protesting electoral fraud (→ 5/8/79).

27. Eric Heiden becomes first American to win three world speed skating titles in year.

Roots draws 80 million, largest audience

Haley: The roots of black America.

Feb 1. More people watched the final episode of "Roots" tonight than saw the first half of "Gone With the Wind" at its recent airing. The ABC miniseries reached a record 80 million viewers and was shown eight nights in a row, an unprecedented scheduling feat.

"Roots," based on the family tree of author Alex Haley, traced the lineage of Kunta Kinte, a West African youth enslaved in America. LeVar Burton, Cicely Tyson and John Amos were among the series' stars. Its gritty, moving plot has all Americans intensely interested.

It is ironic "Roots" outdrew "Gone With the Wind." Both are Civil War tales, but the black experience in the Scarlett O'Hara epic was flatly ignored (→ 4/18).

Idi Amin holds 240 American hostages

Feb 25. President Idi Amin of Uganda has detained 240 Americans in his nation until they meet with him. The action, viewed in Washington as equivalent to hostage-taking, expresses Amin's anger at recent denunciations by President Carter of events in the African nation, including the suspicious death of Uganda's Anglican Archbishop Janani Luwum.

Amin sent a letter to Carter telling him that the United States should deal with its own human rights problem before interfering in Uganda's affairs. He warned that his military forces could defeat any effort by American troops to rescue the hostages and accused the Central Intelligence Agency of plotting against him. Carter, faced with his first international crisis, sent word to Amin that his aggressive move would not be tolerated (→ 3/1).

Petulant dictator Idi Amin.

Pompidou Center: factory or museum?

The innovative Pompidou Center.

Feb 2. Traditionalists who like the 18th-century courtyards of Paris and zinc counters in cafes are likely to despise the brand new Pompidou Center. It does not look like an annex of the Jeu de Paumes or the Louvre. In fact, with its exposed, brightly colored pipes, tubes and funnels, it may appear to some as a place to punch a time clock. All of the art world does not agree, however. Light streams through the glass walls of the structure, which serves as a museum of modern art, a public library and a research institute. Mrs. Georges Pompidou, widow of the late President, said her husband "wanted art to return to Paris and wanted Paris to have an extraordinary art center, like nowhere else in the world." On that point, even the critics agree.

Space shuttle rides piggyback on 747

The space shuttle hitches a ride.

Feb 18. The space shuttle, designed to be America's spaceplane of the 1980's, made its first flight today atop a Boeing 747 jumbo jet.

The flight, made from Edwards Air Force Base in California, was made to test the stability of the 747-shuttle combination, which will be used to transport the shuttle from its landing site to launch areas when it makes its first orbital flights, scheduled for 1979. Ten more 747-shuttle test flights will be performed before the craft is cut free from the jet for the first time so it can glide back to earth. The landing will simulate the return to earth of the shuttle from orbital flights.

On its first missions, it will be rocketed into space from Cape Canaveral and will land at Edwards. Later, it will land at a special strip being built at Cape Canaveral. Because the shuttle orbiter is reusable, officials say it will reduce the cost of going into space (→ 8/12).

Violation of rights brings aid reduction

Feb 24. Underlining the Carter administration's dedication to international human rights, Secretary of State Cyrus Vance announced today reductions in U.S. foreign aid to three nations guilty of human rights violations. Aid to Uruguay, Ethiopia and Argentina will be decreased; the amount cut is relatively small, but Carter hopes the action will carry a significant symbolic message. While Vance noted that many nations ignore the basic rights of their citizens, including South Korea, he said America would not reduce financial support to strategically placed allies.

1977

MARCH

Su	Mo	Tu	We	Th	Fr	Sa
		1	2	3	4	5
6	7	8	9	10	11	12
13	14	15	16	17	18	19
20	21	22	23	24	25	26
29	28	29	30	31		

2. Beverly Hills: Bette Davis is first woman to get Life Achievement Award of American Film Institute.

4. Rumania: Earthquake kills 750, injures 5,642.

6. Israeli Premier Yitzhak Rabin arrives in U.S. for talks with Carter (→ 12).

7. Saudi Arabia announces it is allocating $1 billion in aid to black Africa.

7. Pakistan: Ali Bhutto's party wins legislative elections (→ 4/21).

8. Washington: Army announces U.S. has conducted 239 open-air tests of germ warfare.

8. Biloxi, Miss.: Black Bishop Joseph Howze named by Pope Paul VI to head new diocese.

10. Calif.: Teamsters, United Farm Workers sign pact ending decade of conflict over organizing migrant farm workers.

10. Washington: Moslem terrorists release 150 hostages after killing one, injuring 15.

12. L.A.: Roman Polanski arrested for rape.

12. Cairo: Sadat says Egypt must have all Israeli-occupied Arab territory back (→ 16).

15. U.S. to send arms to Zaire to help repel invading forces from Angola (→ 4/4).

19. Congo: Pres. Marien Ngouabi killed by suicide commando.

22. Washington: Carter proposes abolition of Electoral College.

24. New Delhi: Morarji Desai, just out of jail as political prisoner, chosen to be India's fourth premier (→ 10/3).

25. Paris: Jacques Chirac elected mayor (→ 5/10/81).

27. New York: Chris Evert beats Sue Barker to win $50,000 Virginia Slims Championship.

29. U.S.: Studies find birth control pills riskier for smokers over 30 years of age.

30. U.S.: Natl. Aeronautics and Space Admin. reports Uranus encircled by at least five rings.

30. Moscow: Arms talks between Vance and Brezhnev break down (→ 7/31).

Aircraft disaster kills 574

Bystanders watch in horror as the two 747's are engulfed in flames.

March 28. In the Canary Islands, the death toll from the near-head-on collision of two chartered 747 jumbo jets jumped to 574 today. It is the worst aviation disaster in history. Seventy survivors, some of them in critical condition, are being treated in Tenerife, where the accident occurred yesterday. All of the 248 vacationing passengers and crew members on the KLM jet died. And 326 people died on the Pan Am aircraft, which was on a charter from Los Angeles. The KLM jet was barreling down the fog-covered runway to takeoff when it rammed into the Pan Am jet. The American plane was taxiing for takeoff. It is not clear yet who was responsible for the accident.

Angolan forces penetrate southern Zaire

March 10. The Zaire government radio said today that three of its cities had been bombed and invaded by mercenaries from Angola. Zaire, the former Belgian Congo, is one of the richest nations in black Africa, rich in copper and other minerals. During the Angola Civil War, Zaire aided the Western-backed National Front for the Liberation of Angola, which eventually lost to the Soviet-backed and Cuban-bolstered Popular Movement for the Liberation of Angola (→ 15).

Shaba, Zaire: New front in a continent torn by ethnic and political divisions.

Churchmen charge Managua atrocities

March 1. The Nicaraguan government of President Anastasio Somoza has been charged by the country's Roman Catholic Bishops with systematic torture, rape and executions of civilians in their continued fight against the leftist guerrilla group known as the Sandinist National Liberation Front. Church documents list hundreds of peasants who have been murdered or have mysteriously disappeared, and government forces are accused of having carried out mass executions since December of 86 civilians, including 29 children. A spokesman for Somoza said that the charges were either false or exaggerated (→ 1/10/78).

Moonies returned to parents by judge

March 24. The Unification Church of the Rev. Sun Myung Moon, a Korean industrialist, received a major setback when a San Francisco State Superior Judge ordered five adult members, aged 21 to 26, placed in temporary custody of their parents, who seek to have them "deprogrammed." The judge refused to bar attempts to reverse alleged "brainwashing," though the parents must be present at all times. The church claims infringement on the young adults' freedom of speech and religion, speaking of "legal kidnapping" (→ 6/26/81).

It's a trend: Living alone and liking it

March 19. "No roommate, no spouse," says a growing legion of Americans. The number of adults under 35 living alone has more than doubled since 1970, which affects housing, schools, and even puts a pinch on supermarkets. Americans now spend one of every three food dollars in restaurants and fast-food shops. The trend is to leave home early and marry late. A new wariness about marriage, easier credit and more career opportunities for women contribute to more persons choosing alternative lifestyles.

1977

APRIL

Su	Mo	Tu	We	Th	Fr	Sa
					1	2
3	4	5	6	7	8	9
10	11	12	13	14	15	16
17	18	19	20	21	22	23
24	25	26	27	28	29	30

2. Geneva: 107-nation talks on huge fund to stabilize commodity prices end in failure.

3. Washington: Sadat arrives to talk with Carter on peace terms in Mideast (→ 25).

4. Zaire breaks ties with Cuba, charging complicity in invasion of Shaba (→ 5/26).

6. Carter aides say U.S. will halt work on nuclear breeder reactors (→ 5/2).

8. Tel Aviv: Rabin stuns Israel, dropping try for 2nd term under fire about deposits in U.S. (→ 17).

9. U.S.: Supermarkets reported in trouble due to rising popularity of eating out.

9. Spain legalizes Communist Party (→ 5/13).

11. Irving Howe's "World of Our Fathers" wins National Book Award in history.

12. Carter reduces Liddy's 20-year sentence, making him eligible for parole in July (→ 5/4).

12. L.A.: TRW employee Christopher Boyce indicted for giving defense secrets to Soviets.

17. Jerusalem: Lea Rabin, wife of premier, fined $27,000 for illegal accounts in U.S. (→ 5/18).

18. Alex Haley gets special Pulitzer for "Roots."

21. New York: Musical "Annie" opens.

21. Islamabad: Premier Bhutto puts three cities under martial law to halt opposition (→ 6/14).

23. North Sea: Blowout on well sends 20-sq.-mile oil slick drifting toward Norway (→ 30).

25. Washington: Jordan's King Hussein arrives to discuss admitting PLO to Geneva (→ 5/24).

28. Washington: HEW bans discrimination against 35 mil. disabled Americans.

28. U.S. and Cuba reach accord on fishing rights in overlapping zones (→ 6/3).

28. West Germany: Terrorist Andreas Baader and two others given life in prison.

DEATH

11. Jacques Prevert, French poet (*2/4/1900).

Defeated at polls, Mrs. Gandhi quits

March 21. The Indian people have delivered a stinging rebuke to the woman who had ruled them without the benefit of a constitution for the past 19 months by dumping her from office in a landslide election. After 11 years of rule, Indira Gandhi has resigned, and in an uncharacteristically humble statment said she "accepted the verdict unreservedly" and promised "constructive cooperation" with the new government. The heads of the victorious parties immediately dropped the year-and-a-half-old state of emergency, freed political prisoners and began negotiations over who would head the new government (→ 24).

Druse chief Kamal Jumblat is killed

March 16. Machine gun fire from unidentified assailants ripped through the car of Kamal Jumblat today, killing the Druse chieftain, his driver and bodyguard on a mountain road south of Beirut. During the 19-month civil war that ended in November, Jumblat led an alliance of 11 leftist and Moslem militias against right-wing Christian fighters. Following the assassination, Jumblat's former adversaries were quick to eulogize him as a "great man" amid widespread fears that the killing might ignite further reprisals (→ 4/3).

Idi Amin tells U.S. citizens they're free

March 1. Ugandan President Idi Amin, after twice postponing a meeting with 240 Americans he had detained, today said they were free to travel inside or outside the country. He did meet with a small group of the hostages, most of whom were pilots and airline workers, telling them that Ugandans were their "brothers and sisters." He also assured President Carter that none of the Americans was in danger. Carter breathed easier, as this dilemma, his first international test, seems to be resolved (→ 11/2/78).

North Sea oil well blows, creating vast slick

Cleanup efforts attempt to halt the flow of oil into the North Sea.

April 30. A North Sea oil well that shot out of control eight days ago was brought under control today after it dumped more than 7.5 million gallons of crude oil to create a slick 45 miles long and 30 miles wide in the ocean between Norway and Britain. Norwegian and American workers succeeded in closing the gusher by sealing it with hydraulically operated rams of a type that had failed to hold two days ago. They held this time because greater pressure was applied, officials said.

The Norwegian government said the giant slick was drifting slowly to the northwest, toward Scotland, but that there was "no real chance" it would reach the coast. Officials said its effect on marine life would be "relatively small." Most of the visible oil slick is expected to disappear in the next few days because of weather and wave action. But remnants could drift ashore for two years, experts say.

Ethiopia ejects U.S. officials, missionaries

April 23. The Ethiopian government today ordered the closing of three United States government offices and an American military mission. Their personnel have been ordered to leave the country within four days. The agencies are: the Military Assistance Advisory Group, a naval medical research unit, the United States Information Service and the Kagnew communications station in Asmara. Approximately 330 Americans are affected by the government order.

The expulsion is the latest indication of increased tensions between the United States government and Ethiopia. Washington had retained close ties with Ethiopia's late Emperor Haile Selassie, and has been the main supplier of arms to the Ethiopian military.

In 1974, Selassie was deposed in a military coup. The junta's leadership has become increasingly Marxist under the leadership of Lt. Col. Mengistu. In February, the Carter administration decided to restrict aid to Ethiopia on the grounds of human rights violations. This, along with U.S. support of the Sudan, which is aiding rebel forces in Ethiopia's Eritrea province, prompted the expulsion order (→ 5/25).

Mengistu seized power in February.

Carter says U.S. must treat oil crisis like war

April 18. President Carter warned tonight that the U.S. faces a national catastrophe unless it responded with a "moral equivalent of war" to dwindling energy supplies. In his televised speech to the nation, the president proposed stringent conservation of fuels, higher energy prices and penalties for waste.

The president, speaking from the Oval Office of the White House, said the nation would begin to run short of energy supplies in the 1980's unless its citizens changed their "wasteful" use of fuels. He will ask Congress this week for legislation calling for higher prices, higher taxes and a halt in the unlimited increases in energy consumption. His program, he said, is aimed at reducing gasoline consumption by ten percent below its current level by 1985.

"Ours is the most wasteful nation on earth," the president said. "I am sure each of you will find something you don't like about the specifics of our proposal. It will demand that we make sacrifices and changes in our lives" (→ 10/13).

Wrigley dies but his gum sticks around

April 12. Philip K. Wrigley, 82, Chairman of the company that sold billions of chewing gum sticks each year and owner of the Chicago Cubs baseball team, died today. He took over both from his father, a Philadelphia soap salesman who handed out free sticks to his customers.

Chewing gum became to many a symbol of the U.S., as did baseball. But while the baseball team declined in the World War II years, Wrigley's produced 600 million sticks of gum a month at the height of the war—and all went to the armed forces. Wrigley's personal wealth rocketed to over $100 million and his real estate includes virtual ownership of Santa Catalina, a resort island off the Pacific Coast near Los Angeles.

Woody Allen trains his wit on the politics of relationships. Diane Keaton is "Annie Hall."

Policies on women cadets to change

April 16. Officials of the U.S. Military Academy at West Point have decided to introduce broad changes in recruitment, testing and training of women, based on an assessment of their first year at what once was an all-male institution. Among their findings: Women from the Deep South are poor prospects; college students are more likely to drop out than women who recently graduated from high school; and few recruits had any idea of the grueling physical and mental stress they would encounter. Of the 119 women appointed last summer, 89 are still at the academy. Officials said some of the physical tests will be discarded and that women will be graded on a different scale from the men.

Life in transition at West Point.

1977

MAY

Su	Mo	Tu	We	Th	Fr	Sa
1	2	3	4	5	6	7
8	9	10	11	12	13	14
15	16	17	18	19	20	21
22	23	24	25	26	27	28
29	30	31				

1. Istanbul: 39 killed in clash on May Day (→ 9/27/78).

4. Washington: Nixon says he "let the American people down" by lying in Watergate (→ 6/22).

7. London: U.K., Canada, Germany, France, Italy, Japan, U.S. meet on global recession.

14. Montreal beats Boston Bruins for hockey's Stanley Cup.

16. Ali retains heavyweight title with unanimous decision over Alfredo Evangelista (→ 9/29).

17. Japan agrees to curb TV exports under threat of hike in U.S. tariffs (→ 1/13/78).

19. Nairobi: Kenya bans hunting of big game to conserve wildlife.

20. Orient Express takes its last trip.

22. Indianapolis: Janet Guthrie becomes first woman to qualify for Indy 500 (→ 29).

23. Brussels: Fire sweeps Duc de Brabant Hotel, killing 302.

23. Assen: S. Moluccan nationalists seize Dutch school and hijack train with 161 (→ 29).

24. Washington: Saudi Crown Prince Fahd praises Carter for supporting idea of Palestinian homeland (→ 7/26).

24. Moscow: Podgorny ousted from Soviet Politburo (→ 6/16).

25. U.S. says Cuba has military advisers in Ethiopia.

25. Tel Aviv: Moshe Dayan to serve as for. min. in coalition headed by Begin (→ 4/19/78).

26. Zaire officially reports end of Shaba War (→ 5/14/78).

27. Ottawa: Trudeau and wife announce they are separating; he will keep children.

28. Southgate, Kentucky: Nightclub fire kills 160, injures 130.

29. Glimmen: S. Moluccan nationalists hold 56 Dutch hostages at gunpoint, refuse to free pregnant captive (→ 6/11).

30. Mrs. Rosalynn Carter begins tour of seven Caribbean and Latin American nations.

DEATH

9. James Jones, U.S. WWII novelist, "From Here to Eternity" (*11/6/1921).

La Pasionaria comes home after 38 years

La Pasionaria, Communist legend.

May 13. Dolores Ibarruri, a living Communist legend from the Spanish Civil War, has slipped back into her homeland after 38 years in exile, mainly in Moscow. La Pasionaria, as she was called, was a fiery orator who rallied the spirits of the republic against the advancing armies of Francisco Franco, shouting, "It is better to die on your feet than live on your knees!"

Now, 18 months after Franco's death and 34 days after the legalization of the Communist Party, the frail-looking woman in black, as always, was greeted by youths crying "Dolores!" and straining to glimpse a founding member of the party (1920), who left in 1939, before most of them were born.

Ibarruri, 81, heads the Communist list in June's parliamentary elections. Despite a reputation as a Stalinist, she formally protested the Soviet Union's invasion of Czechoslovakia in 1968 (→ 6/15).

Human fly climbs 110-story building

May 26. A 27-year-old toymaker delighted thousands of New Yorkers by scaling one 110-story World Trade Center tower, but he then found the police to be less than thrilled on his descent. George Willig was arrested and given three summonses for his early morning adventure. That was followed by a $25,000 lawsuit by the City of New York. Willig, using equipment that he designed and built in secret at night, said, "I just wanted the prize of getting to the top"—which was only 1,350 feet above the street level.

Race driver A.J. Foyt wins 500 fourth time

May 29. A.J. Foyt breezed home "talking to the Lord and praying" as he won the Indianapolis 500-mile auto race for a record fourth time.

His prayers apparently canceled out any that Gordon Johncock was saying for it was more the latter's failure than Foyt's speed that won the race. With 15 laps to go, Johncock's engine blew while he was in the lead, and then Foyt took over. Ol' Super Tex whisked ahead and finished 28 seconds ahead of Tom Sneva. Al Unser, a two-time winner, salvaged third just as his fuel ran out on the cool-off lap.

Foyt posted an average time of 161.331 miles an hour. The 42-year-old grandfather also had to beat out the first woman ever to race in the Indianapolis 500. Janet Guthrie of New York was plagued by engine problems and retired after 27 laps and eight pit stops. Her presence changed the traditional introduction to: "In company with the first lady ever to qualify at Indianapolis, gentlemen start your engines." The 29-year-old Miss Guthrie vowed: "I'll be back."

A.J. Foyt, unprecedented success at Indy, 16 years after his first victory.

First protest staged at nuclear plant

May 2. More than a thousand of the demonstrators who have vowed to stop construction of a nuclear generating plant were arrested today by New Hampshire state police. The protesters, who call themselves the Clamshell Alliance, occupied the site of a proposed $2.5 billion, twin-tower nuclear plant in Seabrook, New Hampshire, yesterday, vowing to remain until plans for the plant were abandoned.

The Seabrook facility has become a symbol of the growing debate in the United States about the use of nuclear energy as a power source.

Protesters scored one victory when the federal Nuclear Regulatory Commission halted construction work after environmentalists protested that the plant's cooling system would harm marine life, but the halt is expected to be temporary. More than 100 protesters were arrested in a demonstration at the site last August. Today's demonstration drew a crowd of 2,000.

"If they keep building, we'll come back with 18,000," said one alliance leader. Those arrested, most of them young people carrying backpacks, were brought to a local court in buses and processed in batches of ten into the evening (→ 6/30/78).

Labor beaten; Begin takes over in Israel

Begin led Irgun guerrillas, 1943-48.

May 18. Menachem Begin yesterday became Israel's new Premier when the Likud Party, which he heads, emerged from 29 years of opposition to hand the hitherto dominant Labor Party, led by Shimon Peres, a surprising defeat. Likud's victory has stunned both foreign and domestic officials because of its hawkish stance regarding any compromise solution to the Arab conflict. Begin seems to have considered this by calling immediately for a national unity of "all Zionist parties." The Likud win apparently stems from its strong showing among the Sephardic Jews of North Africa and the Mideast, who now form the bulk of Israel's population (→ 25).

Joan Crawford dies; great at the box office

May 10. She was Texan Lucille Le Sueur, and she could do a snappy Charleston. She danced her way to a Broadway chorus line and then an MGM film contract. But her name didn't sit well with producers, and they flung a contest at the public: Name this woman with the broad shoulders, arched brows and dark eyes, they said. The people said she looked like a Joan Crawford.

Crawford starred in over 80 films.

Miss Crawford died today at age 73. Not particulary interpretative or versatile (despite an Oscar for her tear-jerking role as a sacrificing mother in "Mildred Pierce"), Miss Crawford created her stardom as much offscreen as on. She was married to three actors (Douglas Fairbanks Jr., Franchot Tone, Philip Terry) and one fan, Pepsi-Cola Chairman Alfred Steele. In the 60's, after Steele died, she became a Pepsi board member.

A part in a particular horror movie made with Bette Davis in 1962 had former fans asking, Whatever happened to baby Joan?

Five are killed when helicopter breaks up

May 16. Five persons were killed today when the landing gear of a helicopter atop the Pan Am building in midtown New York gave way, throwing a huge rotor blade free. The blade killed four people on the rooftop heliport. Part of it plunged to the ground, killing a woman walking on East 43rd Street. Seven other people were injured, five seriously, by the blade or fragments of a window that it struck.

Carrie Fisher (center) and others take a back seat to C-3PO (rt.) and R2-D2 in "Star Wars," George Lucas' tale of good and evil in the skies.

1977

JUNE

Su	Mo	Tu	We	Th	Fr	Sa
			1	2	3	4
5	6	7	8	9	10	11
12	13	14	15	16	17	18
19	20	21	22	23	24	25
26	27	28	29	30		

3. Cuba to free ten of 30 American prisoners (→ 11/5/78).

4. Paris: Anne Morrow Lindbergh arrives for 50th anniversary of husband's flight.

5. Chicago: Humboldt Park hit by rioting, leaving two dead.

5. Seychelles: Leftist rebels oust pro-Western govt. of President James Mancham.

10. Tenn.: Martin L. King killer James Earl Ray breaks out of Brushy Mt. state prison (→ 13).

13. Petros, Tenn.: James Earl Ray captured, returned to jail.

13. Johannesburg: Three blacks break into police headquarters, kill two whites (→ 10/19).

14. Pakistan: Bhutto and opposition agree to elections (→ 7/5).

14. N.Y.: Three armed Croatian nationalists invade Yugoslav mission to U.N.

16. Cincinnati: Tom Seaver traded to Reds after 11 years with New York Mets.

16. Moscow: Brezhnev, head of party, named first Soviet president (→ 1/26/78).

16. Dublin: Jack Lynch's Fianna Fail Party sweeps to victory in legislative elections (→ 8/10).

19. Rome: Pope Paul VI declares Bishop John Nepomucene Neumann first U.S. male saint.

23. Moscow: Pravda denounces Eurocommunism for seeking power through Parliament.

24. Tanzania: Activist Bishop Josiah Kirbira becomes first black and first African to head Lutheran World Federation.

27. French Somaliland gains independence as Djibouti (→ 9/20).

28. U.S. Supreme Court upholds public control of Nixon papers and tapes (→ 7/12).

28. New York: Police, in hunt for Son of Sam killer, tracing all Charter Arms Bulldogs guns ever made (→ 7/31).

30. Carter declares opposition to B-1 bomber.

DEATH

3. Roberto Rossellini, Italian film director (*5/8/1906).

Trans-Alaskan oil pipeline finally opened

June 20. Oil started flowing into the trans-Alaskan pipeline today, marking the completion of the $7.7 billion project that runs 799 miles from Prudhoe Bay in the north to Valdez on Alaska's southern coast. It will take 30 days for the first oil to reach Valdez, where it will be loaded into tankers. Production in Alaska's North Slope oil fields is expected to reach 1.2 million barrels a day by autumn, nearly ten percent of the United States' daily consumption. The North Slope has an estimated 9.7 billion barrels.

America's lifeline in the wilderness.

Britain celebrates Elizabeth II's jubilee

The Queen and Duke in St. Paul's.

June 5. On a February morning in 1952, Princess Elizabeth awoke in an African game lodge to find herself Queen Elizabeth II. This week, the celebration of her 25 years on the throne climaxes with six days of imaginative pomp and pageantry. In a sense, Britons are celebrating being better off now than then, when war damage was visible everywhere and few had luxuries. Today, there are nine times as many TV sets, three times as many cars, four times as many telephones and infant mortality has been cut in half.

Spain holds its first free vote in 41 years

June 15. Democracy returned to Spain today as voters resoundingly elected the center-right coalition of Prime Minister Adolfo Suarez. The last free elections in Spain were held in 1936; they were suspended with the victory of Generalissimo Francisco Franco's forces in the Spanish Civil War.

With approximately 70 percent of the vote counted, Suarez's Democratic Center coalition led with approximately 35%, and was followed by the Socialists' 26%, the right-wing Popular Alliance's 8% and the Communists' 7%. This would give the Democratic Center coalition 170 seats in Spain's 350-member lower house, or six short of a majority. Suarez was appointed Prime Minister by King Juan Carlos last year, after the young Spanish king removed Carlos Arias Navarro (→ 10/8).

Mitchell goes to prison in style

June 22. Prisoners at a Montgomery, Alabama, prison crowded the jail's entrance to see their most recent "roommate" leave a big blue Cadillac to join them. Former Attorney General John Mitchell, whose portrait once hung respectfully in the prison, began serving his 30-month jail term for conspiracy, obstruction of justice and perjury in the Watergate cover-up.

Mitchell, who arrived in Alabama aboard a private jet, said as he was rushed through the prison gates, "It's nice to be back in Alabama." The facility, called the Federal Prison Camp, has had plenty of illustrious criminals; two other Watergate figures, Charles Colson and Frederick Lerue, have served time at the minimum security jail. In all, 25 people have been imprisoned for their illegal involvement in the Watergate scandal (→ 28).

Train, school taken from Asian captors

June 11. A three-week hostage drama in the Netherlands ended today as Dutch commandos stormed a hijacked train and a school where children had been taken hostage. On the train, six of the nine terrorists and two hostages were killed; 51 hostages were released. At the school, all four children were released unharmed and four gunmen were arrested. The terrorists were South Moluccans demanding release of Moluccan prisoners in the Netherlands and freedom for their South Pacific homeland from Indonesia (→ 3/13/78).

Von Braun, pioneer rocketeer, is dead

June 16. Wernher von Braun, the German-born rocket scientist who became a technological leader of the American space program, died in Alexandria, Virginia, today of cancer. He was 65 years old.

Born in East Prussia, von Braun became a space travel enthusiast early in life. His early experiments made him the German army's top civilian rocket specialist at the age of 20. He continued his work under the Nazis, establishing a secret base at Peenemunde on the Baltic Sea. His group developed the V-2 rocket that devastated London at the end of the war. Surrendering to Americans, von Braun and his group went to work for the U.S. Army. He transferred to the civilian space program to lead development of the Saturn rockets that carried Apollo astronauts to the moon.

June 11. Seattle Slew and jockey J. Cruguet race to victory and the Triple Crown at Belmont.

1977

JULY

Su	Mo	Tu	We	Th	Fr	Sa
					1	2
3	4	5	6	7	8	9
10	11	12	13	14	15	16
17	18	19	20	21	22	23
24	25	26	27	28	29	30
31						

2. Wimbledon: Bjorn Borg over Jimmy Connors 3-6, 6-2, 6-2, 5-7, 6-4; Virginia Wade over Betty Stove 4-6, 6-3, 6-1.

3. U.S. State Dept. asks White House to admit 15,000 Indochinese refugees (→ 12/3).

8. Nice: Artist Marc Chagall celebrates 90th birthday.

8. Alaska: Pump station on Alaska oil pipeline hit by blast, killing one, injuring six.

9. U.S.: Early retirement reported as growing trend.

10. Helsinki: Soviet airliner hijacked with 72 aboard.

11. Washington: Carter gives Coretta Scott King Medal of Freedom in honor of husband (→ 6/28/78).

12. Ohio: Police remove 194 in sit-in to bar gym on site of Kent State killings (→ 4/10/78).

12. U.S.: Liddy granted early release from Watergate sentence (→ 10/4).

14. New York: Power restored after massive blackout; 3,300 arrested for looting.

18. Rhodesia: Ian Smith on TV announces dissolution of Parliament for new elections (→ 8/6).

21. Cairo: Egypt reports major border clash with Libya (→ 24).

21. Sri Lanka: Sirimavo Bandaranaike, premier 12 years, defeated in national elections.

22. China: Gang of Four barred from party (→ 6/3/78).

24. Bernard Thevenet wins his second Tour de France.

24. Cairo: Sadat orders halt to fighting with Libya (→ 9/10/80).

27. Santa Barbara: Brush fire destroys 185 homes as drought worsens in Southwest.

31. Brooklyn: Son of Sam killer wounds 12th and 13th victims (→ 8/10).

31. France: One killed, 20 injured in clash with police at Creys-Malville anti-nuclear protest (→ 9/21).

DEATH

9. Alice Paul, militant in U.S. fight for women's suffrage (*1/11/1885).

Army arrests Bhutto; Zia ul-Haq in power

Zia ul-Haq, army ruler in Pakistan.

July 5. In a move impervious to political lines, the Pakistani army staged an apparently bloodless coup this morning, arresting Prime Minister Ali Bhutto and other prominent officials regardless of their political leanings. Following four months of civil unrest, the coup seems like an effort to stem further violence initially triggered by Bhutto's lopsided victory in last March's national elections.

As Butto was charged with fraud and corruption, protest demonstrations led to bloody rioting, with some 300 persons killed. Prime Minister Bhutto arrested most of the opposition leaders and put major cities under martial law.

Bhutto's downfall, after five years in office, was ironic in that he had already admitted to some irregularities, had agreed to new elections and was trying to iron out an election agreement with the opposition. To the army, which ruled Pakistan from 1958-71, his conciliatory posture was apparently too little and too late. It is reported that General Zia ul-Haq will head up the new government (→ 9/3).

California ravaged by drought and fire

July 28. A runaway box kite becoming entangled in high-voltage lines, forcing an electrical arc, may have caused an explosive brush fire last night that destroyed more than 185 homes in Montecito and Santa Barbara, California, devastating large parts of the scenic communities. The blaze began in a hilly region that, like most of California, is tinder dry from the second consecutive year of drought. The flames swept seaward, mowing down trees, brush and homes like a nightmarish scythe. More than 3,000 people had to be evacuated.

Parched earth in California's expanding desert testifies to drought.

3 West Bank towns get Begin's sanction

July 26. Israeli Prime Minister Menachem Begin snubbed President Carter and put himself on a collision course with his Arab neighbors today. Begin gave his official approval to three Israeli settlements on the West Bank of the Jordan River. The State Department was quick to criticize Begin's decision. It said it was "deeply disappointed" by a move which created "an obstacle to the peacemaking process."

In their talks in Washington last week, Carter urged Begin not to legalize the settlements. They are all located on land seized in the 1967 war. The United States wants Israel to return at least some of the land to Jordan and believes the status of the settlements could be resolved at a Middle East peace conference. Begin says the West Bank was "liberated," not "occupied," by Israel. He points out that the area, which he calls Judea and Samaria, is part of the ancient Jewish homeland.

The Israeli action is likely to inflame tensions between Jews and Arabs on the West Bank. There have been frequent anti-Israeli demonstrations in the towns of Nablus and Ramallah. There are likely to be more (→ 8/14).

Nabokov, notable novelist, deceased

Nabokov, also a butterfly expert.

July 2. It is wrong to be miffed with the dead, but the passing of novelist Vladimir Nabokov breeds resentment. Why didn't he write in Russian? Did he have to write so well in his adopted language, showing up all its natural speakers the way Joseph Conrad rubbed it in a century earlier? And why did Nabokov write wildly funny satires instead of dull theses, as a Cornell don ought?

Nabokov was born April 23, 1899, to an aristocratic Russian family. He learned English and French and pursued interests in soccer, butterflies, chess and poetry. His family emigrated to England, and he attended Cambridge, studying Romance and Slavic languages.

In the 20's and 30's he spun about Paris and Berlin, writing plays and stories under the pen name V. Sirin. "Laughter in the Dark" (1938) came from this era. In 1940, he moved to the United States to teach at a few colleges. "Lolita" (1958), about a nymphet and a professor, disclosed his comic talents.

Liza Minnelli and DeNiro in "New York, New York," Scorsese's Big Band-era musical.

1977

AUGUST

Su	Mo	Tu	We	Th	Fr	Sa
	1	2	3	4	5	6
7	8	9	10	11	12	13
14	15	16	17	18	19	20
21	22	23	24	25	26	27
28	29	30	31			

1. Calif.: Francis Gary Powers, U-2 spy shot down in 1960, dies in helicopter crash.

3. New York: Blasts kill one, injure seven in two midtown offices; 100,000 leave buildings.

3. Cyprus: Archbishop Makarios, president 17 years, dies of heart attack (→ 11/15/83).

6. Plains, Ga.: Carter asks new welfare system with emphasis on work (→ 12/10).

6. Salisbury: 11 Rhodesians killed in bomb blast at crowded variety store (→ 31).

6. Paris: U.S., 13 other nations agree to lend $10 bil. to poor countries hit by oil recession.

10. N.Y.: David Berkowitz held in Son of Sam murders (→ 30).

10. U.S., Panama agree on basic elements of pact to transfer control of canal (→ 9/1).

10. Northern Ireland: Queen Elizabeth II makes first royal visit in 11 years (→ 2/18/78).

12. Calif.: Space shuttle Enterprise passes first flight test in Mojave Desert (→ 20).

14. Israel extends govt. services to inhabitants of West Bank and Gaza Strip (→ 9/18).

15. Evangelist Billy Graham accepts invitation to visit Hungary.

17. Soviet nuclear icebreaker Arktika reaches N. Pole, first surface ship to break ice pack.

19. Indian Ocean: Earthquake hits 7.7-8.9 on Richter scale; believed to be strongest ever.

20. Cape Kennedy: First Voyager 2 launched for Jupiter, Saturn, maybe Uranus (→ 3/2/78).

25. U.S.: Reagan urges Senate to reject Panama Canal treaties (→ 11/13/79).

28. Oregon: N.Y. Cosmos win American Soccer League title.

31. Washington: Grand Jury indicts Tongsun Park in South Korean influence-buying.

31. Rhodesia: Ian Smith re-elected with 80% majority, 15,000 of 6.2 mil. blacks voting (→ 11/24).

DEATH

4. Ernst Bloch, German Marxist philosopher (*7/8/1885).

Elvis Presley, singer and cult figure, is dead

Aug 16. Millions of fans mourned today for the singer they called "The King," after Elvis Presley, one of America's most dynamic and successful pop musicians of the last 20 years, died in Memphis. He was 42 years old.

Presley was found unconscious in the bedroom of his sprawling mansion, known as Graceland, this afternoon. He was rushed to a nearby hospital but pronounced dead within the hour from what doctors termed "cardiac arrhythmia," or irregular heartbeat. As news of the performer's death spread, thousands descended around the Graceland perimeter to weep openly for their fallen idol.

Presley's career had been mostly erratic since his stunning triumphs of the 50's and early 60's. Once an object of adulation to millions of screaming, fainting teenaged girls, he had battled a severe weight problem in recent years and been publicly accused by former employees of being addicted to amphetamines and barbiturates. But to legions of grieving fans, he was and will forever remain "The King."

28 gold records; 106 hits in top 40.

Son of Sam caught; held unfit for trial

Aug 30. On August 10, police arrested David Berkowitz, who is believed to be Son of Sam, the .44-caliber killer of six young people in a yearlong New York City murder spree. After authorities charged Berkowitz with the murders and assaults that injured seven others, and read him his rights, he said flatly, "Well, you've got me." Yesterday, two court-appointed psychiatrists declared the suspect, described as a bizarre loner, clinically paranoid and unfit for trial. A new hearing has been scheduled for October 4 (→ 10/21).

Berkowitz, a N.Y. postal worker.

VW is phasing out Bug in United States

What will next year's Volkswagen Beetle look like? If it were anything like last year's Beetle, it would look just like the Beetles of the preceding 25 years. However, next year's Bug will not exist. It is being phased out in favor of the squarish Volkswagen Rabbit. The Bug fails standards for emissions (it is a lead guzzler) and safety (in an accident it folds like origami paper). Yet owners say the Beetle has personality; the Rabbit is a bore.

Groucho Marx dies

Aug 19. The man of the painted mustache and unlit stogie is gone. Julius "Groucho" Marx was 77. He was the last of the three Marx Brothers (Chico died in 1961, Harpo in 1964), but lesser-known clan member Zeppo survives. Groucho played leaders, from captains to veterinarians, in "Animal Crackers," "Duck Soup" and other comedy films. He was the intellectual of the group, the one who rolled his eyes skyward meditatively while feeling the plump derriere of actress Margaret Dumont.

1977

SEPTEMBER

Su	Mo	Tu	We	Th	Fr	Sa
				1	2	3
4	5	6	7	8	9	10
11	12	13	14	15	16	17
18	19	20	21	22	23	24
25	26	27	28	29	30	

1. Stockholm: Panamanian Leopoldo Aragon immolates self at U.S. Embassy to protest signing of canal treaty (→ 7).

1. U.S., Japan reach accord to allow opening of Japanese nuclear fuel reprocessing plant.

3. Lahore, Pakistan: Bhutto arrested in murder plot (→ 2/28/78).

4. Ohio: Four cases of mysterious Legionnaires disease confirmed (→ 1/18/78).

5. Senators Percy, Ribicoff urge resignation of Bert Lance for financial illegalities (→ 21).

11. N.Y.: Vilas beats Connors, Evert beats Turnbull in U.S. Open finals at Forest Hills.

15. Washington: House approves hikes in minimum wage, rejects lower wage for youth.

18. Washington: Moshe Dayan arrives for new round of talks on Mideast (→ 25).

19. Calif.: Roman Polanski given three months in jail for rape.

20. Washington: Govt. study finds birth rate among girls 15-17 rising.

20. New York: Djibouti admitted to U.N.

21. Washington: Carter accepts resignation of Bert Lance (→ 5/23/79).

21. London: 15 nuclear-exporting nations reach accord to curb proliferation (→ 4/3/78).

23. U.S. government backs landings by Concorde in 13 cities (→ 10/19).

25. Jerusalem: Israeli Cabinet approves U.S. plan for single Arab delegation, including Palestine, at Geneva (→ 26).

26. Israel announces cease-fire on Lebanese border (→ 10/1).

29. N.Y.: Ali wins decision over Earnie Shavers (→ 2/15/78).

DEATHS

1. Ethel Waters, Broadway actress, singer (*10/31/1900).

4. E.F. Schumacher, British economist, "Small is Beautiful" (*8/16/1911).

8. Zero Mostel, American comic actor (*2/28/1915).

Treaty gives Panama future control of canal

Carter and Torrijos sign the pact to end U.S. control of the canal in 1999.

Sept 7. Transfer of the Panama Canal to the control of Panama in the year 1999 moved a step closer today at a ceremony marking the signing of two treaties. Still ahead, however, is a possibly bruising fight in the United States Senate over ratification of the canal transfer.

The treaties were signed by President Carter and Brigadier General Omar Torrijos Herrera, head of Panama's government, in the presence of 16 other heads of state assembled in the Washington headquarters of the Organization of American States. Also present were former President Gerald R. Ford and Mrs. Lyndon B. Johnson, widow of the President under which the negotiations were begun in 1964.

If ratified, the new accords would revoke the 1903 treaty under which the U.S. built one of the world's engineering marvels across a strip of territory it obtained from the new Panama republic. Enduring pride in that achievement, as well as strong feelings by many that retention of the canal is vital to U.S. security, could make the fight over ratification by the Senate the most dramatic battle of its kind since the Senate blocked U.S. membership in the League of Nations (→ 4/18/78).

Pol Pot, Cambodian leader, visits Peking

Sept 28. The leader of Cambodia, Pol Pot, arrived in Peking today to meet with Chinese Prime Minister and Communist Party Chairman Hua Kuo-feng. The visit is the first the mysterious Pol Pot has taken outside Cambodia since the end of the Indochina war. Because of the Cambodian regime's maintenance of secrecy, little is known about Pol Pot. Some suspect he is a French-educated intellectual named Saloth Sar. Others claim he was a rubber plant worker who climbed the political ranks during the war.

Pol Pot, mystery man.

Cambodia just recently announced it had a Communist Party and that Pol Pot is head of the organization. The meeting in Peking underscores speculation that China and Cambodia are developing an alliance under communism. China has sent technicians to Cambodia to help repair electric power facilities, roads and agricultural production plants in the war-torn nation. Additional aid will be discussed at the meeting (→ 1/3/79).

Death takes Stokowski, stylish conductor

Sept 13. The long, lyrical line that was Leopold Stokowski's life ended yesterday when the 95-year-old conductor died of a heart attack in his English home. The fascinating and flamboyant musician was a man of mystery, glamor and genius.

Born and bred in London, his undeniable but inscrutable European accent was as puzzling as his meteoric rise as a conductor, at 27 with the Cincinnati Symphony, with scarcely any experience. Ever an admirer of feminine beauty, he had a much-publicized liaison with Greta Garbo, and married Gloria Vanderbilt, then 21, when he was 63, siring two sons. He also served as musical adviser on Disney's "Fantasia." His music-making was intriguing and exotic, and his years with the Philadelphia Orchestra secured his deserved fame.

Flamboyant genius Stokowski.

Magnetic, volcanic Callas is no more

Callas, capricious coloratura.

Sept 16. Maria Callas, one of the most celebrated and exciting singers of our time, died yesterday at her Paris home of a heart attack at the age of 53. If her vocal pre-eminence was questioned, her aim often exceeding her grasp, her spine-tingling coloration was not, and she could project a haunting beauty unlike few others. The stunning blend of voice and drama readily mesmerized audiences and made her unique.

Tall, aristocratically beautiful and a Prima Donna supreme, she moved naturally in high society with billionaires and king-makers. Her first marriage to an Italian tycoon was annulled six years later in the midst of her front-page romance with Greek shipping magnate Aristotle Onassis.

Jackie gets $20m from Ari's estate

Sept 19. Jacqueline Onassis has negotiated a settlement with her late husband's daughter Christina, 23, under which the widow will receive $20 million in return for abandoning all further claims on his multimillion dollar estate. This is more than double what she would have received under the terms of Aristotle Onassis' will, namely $250,000 a year, $50,000 of which was earmarked for her children, Caroline and John F. Kennedy Jr., and seven times the alleged settlement, $3 million, had rumored divorce proceedings been actualized.

"Happy Days," TV's answer to "American Graffiti," showcases real talent in Ron Howard as Richie and Shakespearean actor Henry Winkler as The Fonz.

1977

OCTOBER

Su	Mo	Tu	We	Th	Fr	Sa
						1
2	3	4	5	6	7	8
9	10	11	12	13	14	15
16	17	18	19	20	21	22
23	24	25	26	27	28	29
30	31					

2. Dacca: Junior officers oust Bangladesh military govt (→ 5/30/81).

3. New Delhi: Indira Gandhi arrested on charges of official corruption (→ 4/12/78).

4. Washington: Sirica reduces sentences of Mitchell, Haldeman and Erlichman (→ 7/20/78).

5. New York: Musical "Hair" is revived.

7. Baltimore: Gov. Marvin Mandel given four years in mail fraud and racketeering case.

8. Madrid: Basque province chief assassinated after banning Guernica protests (→ 7/29/79).

11. North Yemen: Pres. Ibrahim al-Hamdi killed in military coup (→ 6/24/78).

13. Carter attacks U.S. oil industry for opposing energy plan (→ 12/21).

14. Dubai: W. German jet seized with 91 aboard; hijackers ask release of 13 terrorists (→ 18).

14. Washington: California ex-Congressman Richard Hanna indicted for taking bribes from South Korean CIA.

18. New York: Yankees beat L.A. Dodgers 8-4 in sixth game to take World Series.

19. Johannesburg: Govt. closes black newspaper, arrests editor in major crackdown (→ 27).

19. Ecuador: 220 killed in riots during sugar refinery strikes.

21. New York: Son of Sam killer David Berkowitz found fit for trial (→ 5/8/78).

24. U.S.: 17-year-old Steve Cauthen becomes first jockey to ride for $5 mil. in purses in year.

26. Penn.: Bethlehem Steel reports $477 mil. loss in third quarter, largest in U.S. history.

27. Washington: Carter says U.S. will support U.N. arms embargo on S. Africa (→ 11/10).

29. Poland: Cardinal Wyszinski sees Edward Gierek in first meeting with party leader in 20 years (→ 7/3/80).

DEATH

27. James M. Cain, U.S. suspense novelist, "The Postman Always Rings Twice" (*7/1/1892).

Commandos storm jetliner, save hostages

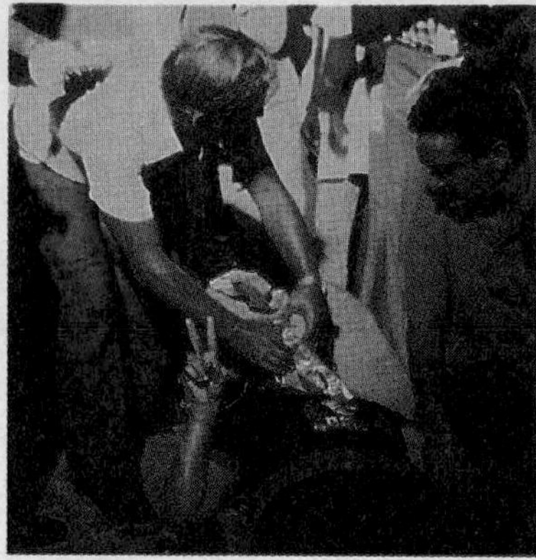

German commando, hurt in raid.

Oct 18. First Entebbe. Now Mogadisho. West German commandos stormed a hijacked Lufthansa jet in Somalia today and freed 86 hostages just an hour and a half before terrorists had threatened to blow up their plane. None of the hostages was harmed; all four of the hijackers were reportedly killed. They had been demanding the release of 11 members of the Baader-Meinhof gang in Germany and two Palestinians in Turkey.

The successful conclusion to the five-day hijacking ordeal was seen as a victory for the government of Chancellor Helmut Schmidt. "The government had no real choice," a spokesman said. "Releasing these 11 terrorists would have led only to new crimes. We weighed the risks as thoroughly as we could."

The hijacking began last Thursday, when the 737 jet was overtaken during a flight from Majorca to Frankfurt. It made refueling stops in Rome, Cyprus, Dubai, Aden and Mogadisho.

Earliest form of life is found in Africa

Oct 23. Remains of the earth's earliest life forms, one-celled fossils that are 3.4 billion years old, have been found in South African rocks. The discovery pushes back the age of the first evidence of life on earth by 100 million years. The microscopic cells, which are nearly as old as the earliest known rocks on earth, are remarkably similar to blue-green algae that exist today, said their discoverer, paleontologist Elso S. Barghoorn of Harvard University. Their existence indicates that the earth provided the conditions for life in its earliest times, he said.

Weekend marriages are the latest trend

Oct 31. A growing group of American couples live apart by choice, usually to pursue independent careers but maintain a marriage. These "commuter," "weekend" or "long-distance" marriages are becoming more common as women attain higher status in the labor market and are offered attractive positions away from their families. The trend is accompanied by a tendency to remain childless indefinitely, a lessening of employment and credit discrimination against women and a greater acceptability of divergent lifestyles in society.

Oct 19. The Concorde, formerly banned from N.Y., lands at Kennedy for the first time, "a vulture spewing black smoke," according to a resident.

U.S. and Soviets set joint Mideast goals

Oct 1. In a joint proclamation, the Soviet Union and the United States have set the guidelines for peace in the Middle East. The declaration states that any peace conference about the area should ensure "the legitimate rights of the Palestinian people" and promote "normal peaceful relations." Both superpowers compromised: America agreed to recognize the existence of rights for Palestinians and the Soviets accepted the exclusion of the Palestine Liberation Organization from the statement (→ 11/9).

Bing dies in place he loved, a golf course

Crosby, America's favorite crooner.

Oct 14. Crooner Harry "Bing" Crosby has died after collapsing on a golf course near Madrid. He was 73. Crosby loved golf, the perfect sport for a very mellow man.

Born in Tacoma, Wash., Bing left law school to sing with the Paul Whiteman orchestra. He co-wrote "Where the Blue of the Night," his signature song. And his renditions of "White Christmas" and "Silent Night" are reported to be the most popular recordings ever made.

Crosby segued from singing roles in movies to light drama ("The Bells of St. Mary's") to comedy (the road pictures with Bob Hope) to heavy drama (playing an alcoholic in "The Country Girl"). He married twice and raised the second family on orange juice, an investment advertised in recent TV ads.

1977

NOVEMBER

Su	Mo	Tu	We	Th	Fr	Sa
		1	2	3	4	5
6	7	8	9	10	11	12
13	14	15	16	17	18	19
20	21	22	23	24	25	26
27	28	29	30			

1. U.S. quits the International Labor Organization.

1. Carter signs minimum wage increase from $2.30 to $3.35 an hour by 1981.

3. Paris: Pres. Giscard gives Legion of Honor to Quebec premier, endorsing right to self-determination (→ 5/20/80).

4. U.S.: Ex-CIA Director Richard Helms fined $2,000 for misleading testimony.

8. New York: Edward Koch elected mayor (→ 12/12).

9. Beirut: Israeli jets hit Lebanon in bombing raids, killing at least 60 civilians (→ 14).

10. Pretoria: Police arrest 626 blacks in sweep through township (→ 14).

13. Somalia orders all Soviet advisers out, breaks relations with Cuba (→ 2/7/78).

14. Cairo: Sadat says he is ready to address Israeli Knesset (→ 15).

14. Pretoria: Police deny they assaulted Stephen Biko, but admit they left him shackled, naked for two days (→ 12/2).

15. Washington: Shah of Iran disturbed by tear gas used to quell protests during his speech at White House (→ 1/9/78).

15. Jerusalem: Begin asks Sadat to speak at Knesset (→ 20).

20. Jerusalem: Sadat offers Israel "peace with justice," calls for return of occupied lands (→ 21).

20. India: Cyclone hits Andhra Pradesh, killing 10,000.

22. Civil Aeronautics Board bans cigar and pipe smoking on U.S. airliners (→ 1/11/79).

24. Salonika: Greeks announce finding tomb of King Philip II, father of Alexander the Great.

24. Rhodesia: Ian Smith ready to concede majority rule (→ 26).

26. Rhodesia: Black nationalist leader Bishop Abel Muzorewa agrees to talks with Smith based on universal suffrage (→ 28).

DEATHS

5. Guy Lombardo, American band leader (*1902).

18. Kurt Schuschnigg, Austrian ex-leader (*12/12/1897).

Sadat addresses Knesset

Sadat, in an historic moment, offers "peace with justice" to the Israeli Knesset.

Nov 21. Egypt's President Anwar el-Sadat ended an astounding visit to Israel today, joining hands with Prime Minister Menachem Begin and pledging "no more war." Noting that Israel and Egypt are technically still at war, Begin praised Sadat for making "this momentous visit." As he flew back to Cairo, Sadat was escorted part of the way by Israeli jet fighters.

The highlight of Sadat's visit occurred yesterday, when he made an unprecedented address to the Knesset and announced that he accepts the existence of Israel. "If you want to live with us in this part of the world," Sadat told the Parliament, "in sincerity I tell you that we welcome you among us with all security and safety." Sadat emphasized, however, that Israel would have to recognize the rights of Palestinians and withdraw from occupied Arab lands, including East Jerusalem.

In his speech, Begin praised Sadat but rejected his call for withdrawal from Arab territories. Israel, Begin said, "will not be put within range of fire for annihilation."

Despite all the talk of peace, it was clear that Sadat and Begin have many differences. Begin would prefer to negotiate with Sadat and other Arab leaders one by one. Sadat is pushing for a Middle East peace conference. In a surprise development today, both men announced that Begin's expected visit to Cairo will be postponed. Sadat needs time for the furor over his visit to die down in the Arab world (→ 12/5).

Women win $1.5m in equality action

Nov 4. The Reader's Digest has settled in one of the nation's biggest sex discrimination cases. The little magazine agrees to pay 2,600 female employees (both currently and formerly on the payroll) $1.5 million. Of that amount, $1,375,000 will consist of back pay, the rest going into salary increases for women still on the job. Eight women brought the lawsuit, charging discrimination in hiring and promotion. Reader's Digest must also pay their lawyers' fees (→ 7/9/78).

Smith now ready to talk majority rule

Nov 28. Fighting continues in Rhodesia in spite of an announcement by Prime Minister Ian Smith that he is prepared to concede the principle of full voting rights for Rhodesia's black majority.

Although Rhodesian-based black leaders, who are supported by 80 percent of the nation's black population, have agreed to negotiate with Smith, nationalist guerrillas based in the neighboring country of Mozambique have denounced the prime minister's proposal and have continued their raids against the white-led Rhodesian forces. A recent attack by government forces reportedly has killed 1,200 guerrillas, nearly a fifth of the entire guerrilla forces (→ 1/7/78).

Filipino Aquino is sentenced to death

Nov 25. Former Philippine Senator Benigno Aquino was sentenced to death by firing squad on charges of subversion, murder and illegal possession of firearms. Aquino, who is the main rival of Philippine President Ferdinand E. Marcos, has been in prison for four years while the military court reviewed the charges. He has been accused of contributing to the efforts of anti-government guerrillas, possessing weapons illegally and complicity in a murder. He says he is not guilty and the charges stem from his rivalry with Marcos (→ 4/9/78).

Spielberg's "Close Encounters of the Third Kind," with Richard Dreyfuss, makes contact with our most treasured fantasies of life in space.

1977

DECEMBER

Su	Mo	Tu	We	Th	Fr	Sa
				1	2	3
4	5	6	7	8	9	10
11	12	13	14	15	16	17
18	19	20	21	22	23	24
25	26	27	28	29	30	31

4. Singapore: Hijacked Malaysian airliner crashes, killing 100.

5. Tripoli: Hard-line Arab nations fail to unite against Sadat peace moves (→ 16).

16. Washington: Begin agrees to give Sinai back to Egypt (→ 21).

20. Indonesia frees 10,000 political prisoners arrested in 1975 (→ 5/15/84).

21. Cairo: Sadat bars Israeli military presence on West Bank of Jordan (→ 1/4/78).

21. Caracas: OPEC conference decides to freeze price of barrel at $12.70 (→ 1/5/79).

26. West Africa: Famine spreading widely again in sub-Saharan countries (→ 6/8/80).

31. Cambodia breaks relations with Vietnam (→ 1/3/78).

DEATHS

7. Peter Carl Goldmark, Hungarian-born U.S. inventor of LP record (*12/2/1906).

10. Adolph Rupp, American basketball coach (*9/1/1901).

26. Howard Hawks, American film director (*5/30/1896).

CULTURAL EVENTS, 1977

Literature: John Cheever's "Falconer"; Jerzy Kosinski's "Blind Date"; Colleen McCullough's "The Thorn Birds"; J.R.R. Tolkien's "The Silmarillion"; Nadine Gordimer's "Guest of Honor"; Michael Cristofer's "The Shadow Box," Pulitzer drama.

Academia: Writing traced to 10,000 B.C. in Mesopotamia; rings of Uranus discovered.

Music: Soviet Union adopts new lyrics for natl. anthem, not sung legally for 20 years because it glorified Stalin; Debby Boone's "You Light up My Life"; Emotions' "Best of My Love"; Stevie Wonder's "Sir Duke"; Eagles' "Hotel California."

The Arts: Public sculpture: Oldenberg's "Batcolumn," Chicago; Carl Andre's "Stone Field," Hartford, Conn.

Film: George Lucas' "Star Wars"; Woody Allen's "Annie Hall"; "Julia," Vanessa Redgrave; "Saturday Night Fever," John Travolta.

U.S. wishes to admit 10,000 boat people

Vietnamese refugees, seeking a new life, brave high seas in a rickety boat.

Dec 3. The State Department proposed the emergency admission to the United States of 10,000 more Vietnamese refugees who in increasing numbers are fleeing their nation in small boats. The monthly rate of "boat people" fleeing Vietnam has grown to 1,500, apparently stimulated by fears that the Communist authorities in Vietnam were about to confiscate privately owned boats to stop the exodus.

The United States last summer approved the emergency admission of 15,000 Indochinese refugees, including 7,000 Vietnamese boat people and 8,000 drawn from 100,000 refugees, largely Laotians, in Thailand. Since the fall of Saigon in 1975, the United States has approved the emergency admission of 165,000 Indochinese refugees, including 145,000 Vietnamese, 17,500 Laotians and 7,500 Cambodians, under special powers given the Attorney General (→ 3/30/78).

Police absolved in death of African

Dec 2. A South African magistrate has exonerated the security police in the death of black leader Stephen Biko.

Biko, who was arrested during a government crackdown on black dissidents, was, according to police testimony, forced to spend 19 days naked in a cell and 50 continuous hours shackled by handcuffs and leg irons. On September 7, the police claim, the prisoner attempted to throw a chair at his interrogator and had to be restrained forcibly.

After this incident, Biko began exhibiting bizarre symptoms, alternating between rational behavior and a total inability to communicate, but police thought he was "shamming" and doctors were unable to detect anything seriously wrong. He was eventually found lying on the floor of his cell, foaming at the mouth. The police then drove him 700 miles, by Landrover and with no medical care, to a prison hospital where he died from massive head injuries. It is feared that the exoneration of the police will be interpreted as a license to abuse black dissidents with impunity (→ 1/22/78).

Tractors and trucks roll through Washington in farm protest

Dec 10. Angry farmers rolled into Washington today aboard massive trucks and tractors, blocking intersections and snarling traffic as they moved toward the Capitol in columns stretching for several miles. The display of farm power was a prelude to a nationwide farmers' strike later this week to protest what the nation's growers say are grave economic conditions pushing many of them to near-bankruptcy and threatening their way of life.

Braving bitter cold and a piercing wind, the farmers flocked into the capital city from Maryland and Virginia. There were similar demonstrations and tractor motorcades in Atlanta, Denver, Topeka and more than 30 other state capitals around the country.

Few farm-state Representatives and Senators are optimistic that Congress would act on demands of the farmers that 100 percent parity be paid for their products. A two-year decline in grain prices, coupled with a severe drought in many areas of the nation, prompted demands for the strike.

"Jimmy's a good 'ol boy," one farmer said today, a reference to President Jimmy Carter, a Georgia peanut farmer, who had left earlier in the day for the presidential retreat at Camp David. "But there's no place in Washington for boys. We need men" (→ 3/29).

Anti-Carter signs and angry farmers on tractors invade urban Washington.

Death ends career of comic genius Chaplin

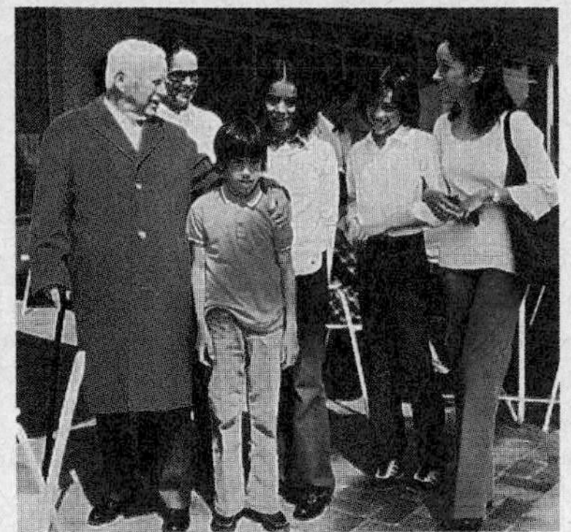
Aging genius Chaplin and family.

Dec 25. The Little Tramp has ambled into his final sunset. Charlie Chaplin died peacefully at his estate in Switzerland today. He was 88.

Charles Spencer Chaplin was born April 16, 1889, in south London to a poor vaudeville family. In his teens, he sang off-color songs and learned the value of mime from working before French audiences. Producer Mack Sennett asked him to appear in the film "Making a Living" (1914), after which he never returned to the stage.

Among Chaplin's great films were "The Gold Rush" (1925) and "Modern Times" (1936). Early on they were recognized as true art, innovative and subtle.

Chaplin once said, as John Lennon of the Beatles echoed later, that he was better known than Jesus. Unlike Lennon, Chaplin never heard people disagree too strongly (→ 3/2/78).

Long life ends for Baroness Churchill

Lady Churchill during WWII.

Dec 12. Lady Spencer-Churchill, the widow of Sir Winston Churchill, died today at 92. The former Clementine Ogilvy Hozier met the young politician in 1904; they married in 1908 when she was 23 and he 33, and from that moment she was the widely admired "perfect wife." Churchill called his marriage to his darling Clemmie "the most fortunate and joyous event . . . in the whole of my life." During 57 years of marriage to a brilliant but difficult man, Lady Churchill cheered him on, raised five children (only two survive) and was at her husband's side during many important events of WWII, refusing to leave London or him during the blitz.

Koch sworn in as Mayor of New York

Dec 12. The 105th Mayor of New York City was sworn into office today. Edward Koch took the oath and now has the difficult task of repairing a city devastated by financial problems. Koch defeated his toughest opponent, Liberal Party candidate Mario Cuomo, by about 100,000 votes in November's election. He takes over from Abraham Beame, whom many blame for the severe fiscal situation of the city; New York has wavered on the brink of bankruptcy in recent years.

After his victory, Koch pledged to "confront the fiscal crisis, the quality of our schools, the need to protect our citizens and the declining conditions of our neighborhoods—not with the words of an election campaign, but with the action these problems demand."

Koch, plucky New York Mayor.

Bokassa gives himself a gaudy coronation

Bokassa, backed by an imperious bronze eagle, is crowned in Bangui.

Dec 4. The coronation of Jean Bedel Bokassa, a former Captain in the French colonial army, as Emperor of the newly named Central African Empire today was full of contradictions. Bokassa's throne sat in the lap of a bronze eagle and his crown had 5,000 diamonds, but the ceremony was held in a decorated sports stadium. The music of Mozart was used for the coronation, but tribal drum beats were heard in the distance. The party Bokassa threw for himself reportedly cost $30 million, but his country is one of the poorest in the entire world.

The contradictions do not stop there. Bokassa's country is independent, but France still pays his bills. The emperor has a reputation for being ruthless, but he is apparently loved by his people. And there seems to be a method to his madness; he hopes publicity about his coronation will attract tourists from all over the world (→ 1/18/79).

Peace Prize goes to Amnesty International

For "securing the ground for freedom," as the award committee put it, Amnesty International has been given the Nobel Peace Prize. The London-based group was established in 1961 by lawyer Peter Benenson to petition the freedom of prisoners of conscience. Amnesty International does not assist those who use or have advocated violence.

In physics, the winners were Nevill Mott of Great Britain, Philip Anderson and John Van Vleck of the United States for improving electronic solid-state circuitry. Americans Rosalyn Yalow, Roger Guillemin and Andrew Schally took the medicine prize for developing the radioimmunoassay test, which can detect minute amounts of enzymes and other organic substances. The chemistry award went to Belgian Ilya Prigogine for studies on thermodynamics.

Swede Bertil Ohlin and Briton James Meade received the economics prize for work on international capital movements. Vicente Aleixandre of Spain was the recipient of the literature honors. Poet Aleixandre's best-known work is "Destruction of Love" (1933).

Travolta struts across the floor in "Saturday Night Fever."

1978

JANUARY

Su	Mo	Tu	We	Th	Fr	Sa
1	2	3	4	5	6	7
8	9	10	11	12	13	14
15	16	17	18	19	20	21
22	23	24	25	26	27	28
29	30	31				

1. India: Airliner with 213 explodes over Arabian Sea; no survivors.

2. Pasadena: Washington Univ. beats Michigan 27-20 in Rose Bowl upset.

3. Cambodia: Vietnamese troops reportedly occupying 400 square miles (→ 1/7/79).

4. London: Said Hammani, PLO envoy in Britain, assassinated (→ 12).

7. Rhodesia puts strict new censorship laws in effect (→ 2/16).

9. Iran: 60 killed in rally for Khomeini in holy city of Qom (→ 2/18).

10. Nicaragua: Pedro Joaquim Chamorro, La Prensa editor and Somoza critic, murdered (→ 12).

12. Managua: Riots erupt after funeral of dissident editor (→ 28).

12. Rome: Moshe Dayan meets with Pope Paul VI to discuss Mideast (→ 2/2).

13. Tokyo: U.S., Japan reach accord on easing trade tensions (→ 1/11/80).

18. Atlanta: Centers for Disease Control isolates cause of Legionnaire's disease (→ 9/8).

19. Washington: William Webster named head of FBI.

21. Las Vegas: Roberto Duran takes lightweight title with KO of Esteban DeJesus in 12th.

22. South Africa: 23 journalists detained after anti-government meeting (→ 5/4).

24. Canada: Soviet atomic spy satellite re-enters atmosphere and disintegrates (→ 30).

26. Moscow: Protesting workers announce formation of unofficial labor union (→ 5/18).

27. Illinois: State Supreme Court rules Nazis can display Swastika in Skokie march (→ 6/12).

29. Sweden becomes first nation to curb aerosol sprays to halt destruction of Ozone.

DEATHS

13. Hubert Humphrey, v.p. under LBJ (*5/27/1911).

14. Kurt Godel, Czech-born American mathematician (*4/28/1906).

Death of anti-Somoza editor causes rioting

Jan 28. President Anastasio Somoza Debayle has invoked emergency powers in an attempt to deal with disturbances protesting the slaying of a prominent newspaper editor who was critical of the regime. The death of Pedro Joaquin Chamorro Cardenal, Editor of La Prensa, was followed by rioting in Managua and a nationwide strike organized by government critics demanding the resignation of Somoza. Relying on the emergency powers, Somoza prohibited radio and TV stations from mentioning the strike and threatened fines against businesses that refuse to reopen. In a speech, Somoza said he had no intention of leaving office until his term expires in 1981 (→ 2/23).

Nicaragua: Beginnings of civil war?

Carter ends world tour in Normandy

Jan 5. President Carter traveled to Normandy today for the last stop on a seven-nation tour marked by a full agenda and sharply contrasting scenery. In the past few days, Carter has flown from nation to nation, meeting with leaders in an effort to solve such world problems as the situation of Palestinians in the Middle East. Today, he met with French President Giscard d'Estaing and laid a wreath on the beach where Allied soldiers went ashore in the D-Day invasion of 1944, vowing that "Europe's freedom will never again be endangered."

Soviet spy in sky drops on Canada

Jan 30. Searchers have found the impact crater of a major part of the Soviet nuclear-powered spy satellite that fell in northern Canada last week, the Canadian government announced today. The Cosmos 954 satellite, whose descent from orbit was monitored for days, created a nine-foot-wide crater, the government said. The Soviet Union has confirmed that the satellite, sent up to track United States naval units, carried a reactor with 100 pounds of radium that has left a radioactive trail across northern Canada (→ 2/5).

Jan 15. Ed "Too Tall" Jones smothers Denver quarterback Craig Morton en route to a 27-10 Dallas victory over the Broncos in Super Bowl XII.

Pinochet wins 75% in Chile plebiscite

Jan 4. President Augusto Pinochet emerged a big winner today in a vote of confidence in Chile. He won 75 percent approval. The plebiscite was called after the United Nations condemned the military government for human rights violations. In Washington, the State Department discounted the vote on the grounds that "normal political activities are banned in Chile." Many anti-Pinochet workers apparently voted for the president out of fear of losing their jobs. Pinochet announced he will write a new constitution for an "authoritarian democracy." There will be no more elections in Chile until 1986 (→ 9/2).

Pinochet, 45 years in Chilean army.

Financier MacArthur dies; leaves a billion

Jan 6. John D. MacArthur, the Florida insurance magnate, died yesterday at age 80. A minister's son and an eighth grade dropout, he built one of the nation's largest fortunes by selling dollar-a-month insurance policies door to door, creating the Bankers Life and Casualty Corporation from scratch in the Depression. "Wealth from others' calamities," commented MacArthur, whose vast holdings included banks, textiles, oil and real estate, but who lived no life of lofty elegance. He drove an old Cadillac, favored drip-dry shirts, never flew first class and frowned on the idea of servants, chauffeurs and public relations people. Most of his wealth goes to charity and public service foundations.

1978

FEBRUARY

Su	Mo	Tu	We	Th	Fr	Sa
			1	2	3	4
5	6	7	8	9	10	11
12	13	14	15	16	17	18
19	20	21	22	23	24	25
26	27	28				

2. U.S. Jewish leaders bar meeting with Sadat (→ 26).

5. Canada: Highly radioactive piece of Soviet satellite found.

6. Washington: Hubert Humphrey's wife Muriel sworn in to fill his Senate seat.

6. Chad severs ties with Libya to protest support for Moslem guerrillas fighting in Chad.

7. Ethiopia mounts counterattack against Somalia (→ 11).

9. Canada expels 11 Soviet aides in spying case.

12. Paraguay: Gen. Stroessner, head of state since 1954, re-elected with 90% of vote.

12. New York: Eric Heiden wins world speed skating title.

16. Rhodesia: Black and white leaders announce accord on future of country's army (→ 3/3).

16. China, Japan sign $20 bil. trade pact, most important move since 1972 resumption of diplomatic ties (→ 10/24).

18. Iran: Troops break up protests in Tabriz (→ 5/11).

18. Cyprus: Gunmen kill editor of leading Cairo paper, take 30 hostages to airport (→ 19).

18. Belfast: Police arrest 20 in I.R.A. for restaurant bombing (→ 8/27/79).

19. Cyprus: 15 Egyptians killed in freeing hostages on jet (→ 22).

22. New York: Reggie Jackson introduces the Reggie Bar.

23. Managua: Protesters, troops clash; many left dead (→ 3/9).

23. Japan: Fishermen club 1,000 dolphins to death.

26. Washington: Vladimir Horowitz performs, marking 50th anniversary of American debut.

26. Senegal: Pres. Leopold Senghor re-elected.

26. Israel: Cabinet decides to expand Sinai settlements despite U.S. opposition (→ 3/11).

28. Pakistan: Political activity banned for one month (→ 3/18).

DEATH

11. James Conant, U.S. chemist, educator, pres. of Harvard for 20 years (*3/26/1893).

Leon Spinks takes title from Ali on decision

Spinks is champ in Vegas after becoming the first boxer to strip Ali of a title.

Feb 15. The legend that was Muhummad Ali has been destroyed by Leon Spinks, a brash 24-year-old heavyweight. Spinks, so lowly regarded that Las Vegas bookmakers would not accept bets on him, won a split decision and became the new world boxing champion.

Ali, sharply honed for his 36 years, tried his rope-a-dope and his peek-a-boo, but these tried-and-true ploys of another era did not work. And when Ali tried to goad and intimidate Spinks, the former Marine just laughed. Ali was nonplussed. "I want to be the first man to win the championship back for the third time," said the man who won it back for a second time from George Foreman (→ 6/19).

15 Egyptians killed freeing jet hostages

Feb 22. Egypt broke diplomatic relations with Cyprus today as it buried 15 soldiers killed Sunday in a wild shoot-out with Cypriot troops at the Larnaca Airport. The Egyptian commandos were trying to free 15 hostages from a hijacked jet. At funeral services in Cairo today, tens of thousands of Egyptians swarmed the cortege and shouted, "Down with Cyprus" and "Slaughter all Palestinians."

The hijacking drama began in Nicosia on Saturday after two Arab terrorists shot an Egyptian newspaper editor to death. The gunmen seized hostages and commandeered a Cypriot Airways DC-8. The plane took off for Djibouti but later returned to Cyprus after Arab countries refused it landing permission. Egyptian commandos tried to storm the plane, but 15 of them were shot dead by Cypriot forces. At least 38 were captured. So were the two hijackers. The 15 hostages were released unharmed.

Calvin Klein pays ransom for child

Feb 4. All but $100 of a $100,000 ransom paid by designer Calvin Klein has been recovered, report FBI agents. Klein's 11-year-old daughter Marci was lured off a New York street into a car yesterday and held for ten hours. The girl, briefly gagged and bound, is unharmed. A babysitter is a suspect (→ 9/24).

To buy or not to buy

Feb 23. Alas, poor Yorick. China knew him and "Hamlet" well 30 years ago, when the play was widely read in translation. With the coming of the Cultural Revolution, it was banned along with other Western literature. Today, the work was back on sale, and the line of people waiting to buy it started at a spot 300 feet outside the bookstore. Each copy sold for 20 cents. Other authors soon to be rediscovered by the Chinese include Tolstoy, Hugo, Cervantes and Balzac.

Oldest humanoid footprints are found

Feb 24. Footprints that appear to be those of a human ancestor who lived 3.5 million years ago have been found at the bottom of an African watering hole, their discoverer, Mary D. Leakey, announced today. The prints were made by a creature about four feet tall. Each footprint is six inches long and 4.5 inches wide. Study indicates that the being that made them moved slowly and took very short steps, Mrs. Leakey said, adding that she was "75 percent sure" that the footprints were made by an ancestor of the human race. They were preserved by a layer of volcanic lava that covered them as soon as they were made.

Somalia mobilizes against Ethiopia

Feb 11. Somalia is mobilizing its armed forces and will dispatch troops into the Ogaden region of Ethiopia. Somalia's policy in the past has been to supply guerrillas fighting Ethiopian forces, but not to involve itself in the fighting.

The policy change follows U.S. Secretary of State Cyrus Vance's statement yesterday accepting Soviet assurances that Ethiopia does not plan to invade Somalia. Ethiopia receives Soviet and Cuban military assistance. Somalia broke off ties with the Soviets last November and would like to obtain arms from the United States. But Vance's comments made it clear that the United States will maintain its policy of neutrality (→ 3/8).

Bruce Dern, Jane Fonda and Jon Voight star in powerful anti-Vietnam War film "Coming Home."

1978

MARCH

Su	Mo	Tu	We	Th	Fr	Sa
			1	2	3	4
5	6	7	8	9	10	11
12	13	14	15	16	17	18
19	20	21	22	23	24	25
26	27	28	29	30	31	

2. U.S.S.R.: Czech pilot Vladimir Remek becomes first non-Russian or American in space (→ 6/27).

3. Salibury: Rhodesian leaders sign pact providing for majority rule (→ 7).

6. Washington: Carter invokes Taft-Hartley Act in effort to get miners back to work (→ 24).

7. Zambia: Rhodesia attacks guerrilla base, killing 38 (→ 21).

8. Somali troops agree to leave Ogaden.

9. Nicaragua: Natl. Guard Chief Gen. Raynoldo Perez Vega assassinated (→ 7/19).

11. Israel: 30 die in gun battle as Palestinians seize bus (→ 14).

13. Netherlands: S. Moluccan gunmen seize 72 in govt. building, demand release of comrades (→ 14).

14. Lebanon: Israeli force of 22,000 invades south Lebanon, hitting PLO bases (→ 22).

14. Netherlands: Dutch raid frees hostages; three terrorists seized.

16. Rome: Leftists seize ex-Premier Aldo Moro, ask release of Red Brigade radicals (→ 19).

17. Washington: Ex-Congressman Richard Hanna pleads guilty to conspiring with Seoul CIA to defraud U.S. govt.

17. France: U.S. oil tanker splits off coast, spilling 24 million gallons (→ 19).

18. Pakistan: Ex-Premier Bhutto sentenced to death for murder (→ 2/9/79).

19. Rome: Italians to continue trials of Red Brigade despite Moro kidnapping (→ 4/15).

22. Puerto Rico: Karl Wallenda, 73, dies in 100-foot fall from tight rope.

24. U.M.W. agrees to contract, ending longest strike of 109 days.

24. Lebanon, Syria announce ban on aid to PLO (→ 4/7).

27. St. Louis: Kentucky over Duke 94-88 for NCAA basketball title.

30. U.S. opens doors to 25,000 Indochinese refugees per year (→ 11/11).

U.S. tanker causes huge oil spill off France

Last of the Amoco tanker goes under in the Channel off the coast of Brittany.

March 19. More than 100,000 gallons of crude oil have poured out of the tanker Amoco Cadiz, which went aground off the Brittany coast in what has become the worst oil spill in history, marine pollution experts said today. There are fears that heavy seas may break up the tanker, spilling even more of the 230,000 barrels of oil it carried.

Already, oil has seriously fouled 70 miles of the Brittany coastline, and a slick about ten miles long and seven miles wide is moving up the English Channel toward the islands of Jersey and Guernsey. The Standard Oil Company of Indiana, which owns the tanker, plans to pump the remaining oil to smaller ships, but that work cannot start for three or four days, until pumpers reach the grounded vessel. French officials are investigating charges that the disaster was caused by an argument about financial terms between the captain of the Amoco Cadiz and the master of a West German tug called to the rescue after the ship's steering broke in heavy seas. During the argument, the towline broke and the Amoco Cadiz drifted onto the rocks. The captains of the tanker and the tug have been taken into custody by French police.

The worst previous oil spill was the loss of 100,000 barrels from the Torrey Canyon, which went aground off Britain 11 years ago.

Carter offers farm aid after protest

Protesting to save a dying way of life.

March 29. Giving in to pressure by Congress, President Carter today proposed increasing federal aid to the nation's farmers, some of whom have threatened to strike if farm subsidies are not doubled. The new plan calls for paying corn and cotton farmers to let a small part of their land lie idle this spring and to pay wheat farmers a higher subsidy if they do not harvest part of what they have already planted. Just two weeks ago, the Carter administration opposed paying for any land diversion. While today's move represented a major step in meeting farmer demands, restive farm bloc members of Congress are expected to push for still more aid in this election year (→ 7/4).

Rhodesians agreed on rule by blacks

March 21. The first step in Rhodesia's transition to majority rule was taken today when three black nationalists were sworn in as joint leaders of the country's new interim government. The black leaders—Bishop Abel Muzorewa, the Rev. Ndabaningi Sithole and Chief Jeremiah Chirau—will share executive power with Ian D. Smith, who will retain his title of Prime Minister. The black majority government scheduled to be installed by December 31 does not have the backing of the Patriotic Front, a loose alliance of black nationalist guerrillas led by Robert Mugabe and Joshua Nkomo (→ 6/23).

Hustler owner shot; testified on smut

March 16. Larry Flint, 35, owner of Hustler magazine, was critically wounded today after testifying at his trial in Lawrenceville, Georgia, on yet another obscenity charge. President Carter's evangelist sister Ruth, credited by Flynt for his conversion as a "born-again Christian," flew to pray at his bedside. The assailant is reported to be one of two white males who fled in a car after he walked up to Flynt on the street, jammed a pistol into his stomach and fired once.

Chris Evert, no. 1 since 1974, inspires a new generation with her methodical backcourt play. She will try for her 5th straight U.S. Open in September (→ 9/11).

Israel hits Lebanon after attack on bus

March 22. Neither in Washington nor the Mideast does the Israeli-Arab conflict seem any closer to a peaceful solution. President Carter and Israeli Prime Minister Menachem Begin ended two days of talks described as "grim" with no sign of compromise over U.N. Resolution 242, which calls for an Israeli withdrawal from all Arab lands occupied in 1967.

The Israelis claim the resolution does not apply to the West Bank. The U.S. insists that it does. In southern Lebanon, the first members of a 4,000-man U.N. peacekeeping force arrived to begin occupation of the territory seized by the Israelis during their recent thrust to root out the terrorist bases along the border.

The invasion followed the attack on a bus outside Tel Aviv by Palestinian terrorists which killed 30 and wounded 80 Israeli civilians. In retaliation, thousands of Israeli troops struck across the border at guerrilla bases, killing scores of guerrillas and seizing a "security belt" about 60 miles long and five miles deep. The Israelis will withdraw their troops once the U.N. force is in place (→ 24).

Chaplin's coffin is lifted from cemetery

March 2. The coffin of the late Charlie Chaplin has been spirited from its grave. Police in the village of Corsier-sur-Vevey, Switzerland, report the body was taken from a small public cemetery last night or early this morning. The Chaplin family has not received any ransom notice yet, ransom being the only motive officials could give for the bizarre theft.

Chaplin died Christmas Day at the age of 88 and was buried two days later. A village resident who assisted at the burial said the casket was extremely heavy, requiring four men to lift it. Marks in the earth show the coffin was dragged several feet before being heaved to a truck.

The theft is not unprecedented. In August 1977, two men tried to steal the body of Elvis Presley from its Memphis shrine (→ 5/17).

1978

APRIL

Su	Mo	Tu	We	Th	Fr	Sa
						1
2	3	4	5	6	7	8
9	10	11	12	13	14	15
16	17	18	19	20	21	22
23	24	25	26	27	28	29
30						

3. Washington: Aides say Carter will veto neutron bomb (→ 7).

3. Calif.: Woody Allen's "Annie Hall" wins four Oscars.

7. U.S. says Israel used cluster bombs in Lebanon, breaking pledge (→ 30).

7. N.Y.: Gutenberg Bible bought for $2 million, most ever paid for a book.

9. Augusta, Ga.: Gary Player wins Masters golf title.

9. Manila: 600 seized in protest over vote counting (→ 9/7/79).

10. Washington: Ex-FBI Director Patrick Gray and two aides indicted for conspiracy in search for radicals (→ 1/4/79).

10. Washington: Top Soviet U.N. official Arkady Shevchenko defects (→ 11).

12. India: After several state victories, Congress Party-I (for Indira) is recognized as official opposition (→ 7/22).

14. Britain: WWII bomb defused near London.

15. Rome: Italian terrorists say Aldo Moro will die (→ 20).

17. Boston: Bill Rodgers wins Boston Marathon.

19. Israel: Yitzhak Navon elected president (→ 9/30/80).

20. Soviets force down Korean 707 over Soviet airspace; two killed, 13 injured.

24. Calif.: Supreme Court refuses to review Patty Hearst case.

25. Moscow: Brezhnev says Soviets will also defer production of neutron bomb (→ 10/19).

27. W.Va.: 51 killed as scaffolding collapses at power plant.

27. Afghanistan: Pres. Mohammad Daud killed in coup as Gen. Taraki seizes power (→ 30).

28. Washington: Gen. John Singlaub agreees to retire after second attack on Carter policies.

30. N.Y.: Begin arrives in U.S. to meet with Carter (→ 6/13).

DEATHS

16. Gen. Lucius Clay, leader of Berlin airlift (*4/23/1897).

16. Richard Lindner, American artist (*11/11/1901).

Senate ratifies pact giving canal to Panama

Many fear a national security risk.

April 18. Marking what President Carter termed "the beginning of a new era," the Senate has voted to turn over the Panama Canal to Panama on December 31, 1999.

By a vote of 68 to 32, the Senate action settles an issue that has existed since Panama seceded from Colombia in 1903 and entered into a treaty with the United States. It also ends 13 years of negotiations, although some financial details remain to be resolved by Congress, probably next year.

President Carter hailed the vote, saying: "This is a day of which Americans can always feel proud; for now we have reminded the world and ourselves of the things we stand for as a nation" (→ 7/31/81).

Afghan President is killed in bloody coup

April 30. President Mohammad Daud of Afghanistan was shot and killed Friday by rebel troops who captured the presidential palace in the capital city of Kabul. The military has set up a new government in what they are calling the Democratic Republic of Afghanistan.

The Revolutionary Council, which will rule by martial law, will be headed by a civilian, Nur Mohammad Tarakki, who will also be Prime Minister. Tarakki has never held office, but is an important member of the Afghan Communist Party. The Soviets have reportedly recognized the new government.

Although Daud was considered progressive for his attempts to modernize Afghanistan, he belonged to the small ruling elite. He took power in 1973 by overthrowing his first cousin and brother-in-law, King Mohammad Zahir Shah. He subsequently closed the Parliament.

Afghanistan is a landlocked country about the size of Texas, bordered by the Soviet Union on its north, Pakistan on its south, Iran on its west and China on its east. The Soviet Union is its principal trading partner (→ 12/5).

Captors threaten Moro, offer to swap him

April 20. The Italian government is again faced with the agonizing decision of whether it should negotiate with the kidnappers of former Prime Minister Aldo Moro. He was seized five weeks ago. Today, the Red Brigades released a photograph purporting to show Moro alive. The terrorist group also accused the government of Prime Minister Giulio Andreotti of circulating false reports that Moro was dead.

The government has so far refused to negotiate with the Red Brigades, who are demanding the release of Communist prisoners. In Milan, the guerrillas struck again today and killed the deputy commander of a prison. It was their ninth killing this year (→ 5/5).

Aldo Moro, dead or alive?

High Soviet official in U.N. is defector

April 11. The Soviets have accused United States intelligence agents of holding Arkady N. Shevchenko "under duress." Shevchenko, who as Under Secretary General in charge of the Department of Political and Security Council Affairs is the highest-ranking Soviet at the United Nations, yesterday renounced his Soviet citizenship and refuses to return to Moscow as ordered. In a meeting with Shevchenko, Soviet U.N. Ambassador Oleg Troyanofsky and Soviet U.S. Ambassador Anatoly Dobrynin were unable to convince him to return.

Making of neutron bomb is deferred

April 7. President Carter said today he had "decided to defer" production of the controversial neutron bomb, but said the decision could be reversed if the Soviet Union failed to exercise restraint in future arms deployment. Carter said he had ordered continued development of artillery and short-range missiles capable of using neutron warheads, which emit lethal doses of radiation but cause relatively little blast damage. Officials said the decision was based on failure of the European Allies to express support for development of the neutron bomb (→ 25).

First Volkswagen is produced in America

April 10. The first American-made Volkswagen automobile rolled off the assembly line of a Pennsylvania plant today, opening an era in which more foreign manufacturers are expected to produce cars in the United States. Volkswagen says it built the plant because the declining value of the dollar has caused constant price increases in German-made autos. The new plant will use engines and drive-trains made in Germany, with other parts made in the United States. Honda already has agreed to make motorcycles and perhaps cars in an Ohio plant, and other Japanese manufacturers are studying U.S. facilities.

1978

MAY

Su	Mo	Tu	We	Th	Fr	Sa
	1	2	3	4	5	6
7	8	9	10	11	12	13
14	15	16	17	18	19	20
21	22	23	24	25	26	27
28	29	30	31			

1. Vietnam: Thousands of Chinese reported fleeing nationalization of businesses (→ 7/3).

1. Naomi Uemura reaches N. Pole after 54-day trek by sled.

4. Angola: South African troops cross border to attack SWAPO guerrillas (→ 6).

5. Rome: Red Brigade announces it will kill Moro (→ 7).

6. Affirmed wins Kentucky Derby, Steve Cauthen up (→ 6/10).

6. U.N. condemns South African raid as violation of Angolan sovereignty (→ 17).

7. Rome: 26 arrested in drive to find Aldo Moro (→ 9).

8. New York: David Berkowitz pleads guilty to six Son of Sam killings (→ 6/12).

9. Rome: Bullet-riddled body of Aldo Moro found; family bars officials from funeral (→ 13).

11. Iran: After four days rioting, Moslem chiefs ask halt to modernization, return of Mosque lands seized for land reform (→ 16).

13. N.J.: 52,000 attend Christian rally at Giants Stadium.

14. Zaire reports attack by Communist-backed Katanga (→ 19).

15. Calif.: Patty Hearst returns to jail to finish term (→ 1/29/79).

16. Cincinnati: Tom Seaver pitches his first no-hitter.

16. Peking: Juan Carlos makes first visit to China by European king.

17. Switzerland: Charlie Chaplin's coffin found in Noville.

17. South Africa closes case of Stephen Biko (→ 9/29).

18. Moscow: Dissident physicist Yuri Orlov gets 7 years (→ 27).

21. Egypt: Vote backs Sadat's purge of opposition (→ 26).

26. Egypt: Sadat calls home 130 journalists to face disloyalty charges (→ 4/20/79).

27. Fourth group of U.S. scientists cancels trip to U.S.S.R. to protest Orlov sentence (→ 7/14).

29. Guatemala: Indian peasants rise in Panzos; 100 killed.

30. Washington: Ballet Nacional de Cuba makes U.S. debut at JFK Center.

As Katangans attack, 3 nations aid Zaire

A European soldier confronts suspected Katangan rebels on the battlefront.

May 19. French and Belgian paratroopers dropped into the besieged town of Kolwezi in southern Zaire today in an attempt to free 3,000 foreigners trapped by Communist-backed rebels. French Foreign Legion officials said they found the bodies of 44 Europeans who had been massacred by Katangese rebels. President Carter dispatched 18 Air Force C-141 transport planes to Zaire to assist in the evacuation.

The United States involvement is the biggest military operation to date of the Carter administration. The White House is making a very public show of its commitment to counter the Cuban and Soviet forces it says are backing the rebels. Secretary of State Cyrus Vance raised the issue today with the Soviet Ambassador, Anatoly Dobrynin. American officials are also questioning the assertion of Fidel Castro that he is not backing the rebel cause. The Cuban leader summoned the top American diplomat in Havana to his office Tuesday night and insisted that he is not supporting the rebels.

The invasion of Zaire's southern province of Shaba, formerly named Katanga, began last week. Zaire's President Mobutu Sese Seko said that Katangese rebels based in Angola infiltrated his country from Zambia. Mobutu charged that the rebels were supported by the Soviet Union, Cuba, Algeria and Libya. The United States accused Cuba of training the rebels and supplying them with weapons made in the Soviet Union (→ 6/2).

Moro's body found; Pope attends requiem

Supporters march at Moro's funeral.

May 13. Pope Paul VI presided over a requiem mass today for Aldo Moro, the former Prime Minister of Italy who was assassinated this week by terrorists. The pope and Moro were friends. This was the first time in history that a pontiff had attended a requiem service for anyone other than a Cardinal.

Moro's body was found crumpled in the back seat of a small Renault on Tuesday, nearly eight weeks after he was kidnapped in a blaze of gunfire by Red Brigade terrorists. The guerrillas demanded the release of Communist prisoners, but the government refused to negotiate with them. Moro was buried Wednesday in a small ceremony that was closed to public officials (→ 6/23).

Shah facing strongest political opposition

May 16. Shah Mohammed Reza Pahlevi faces mounting opposition to his 37-year rule as bloody riots swept through major Iranian cities. Apparently unperturbed by the demonstrations, the shah said he intends to continue his policies and flew off to Bulgaria for a state visit.

The shah's confidence seems to be based on a conviction that his opponents cannot challenge his power, which is backed by a well-equipped army. Some of the shah's supporters, however, believe that the continuing protests demonstrate a coalescing of the opposition that could lead to a revolutionary uprising against him. The most powerful group opposing the shah is that of the Moslem traditionalists loyal to Ayatollah Khomeini, the exiled religious leader (→ 7/22).

Caroline of Monaco marries a commoner

May 27. Princess Caroline of Monaco, 21 years old, has married Philippe Junot, a French businessman. Junot, who is considerably older than Caroline, will retain his nationality. She retains her title.

Caroline is the oldest child of the royal Grimaldi clan. Prince Albert and Princess Stephanie are not yet of marriageable age, Albert a college student in the United States and Stephanie just 13 years old. It is assumed Princess Grace and Prince Rainier will want better mates for them when the time comes. Philippe Junot is a reputed lady-killer and gambler. The press gives the match two years (→ 10/9/80).

Caroline and Philippe Junot.

Abortion is legalized in Catholic Italy

May 18. Roman Catholic Italy has voted to legalize abortion, despite the Vatican calling it homicide. As the legislation stands, women 18 and over may have state-provided abortions for the first 90 days of a pregnancy. Those under 18 must have parental approval. Some legal specialists think women will still go to back-alley practitioners, afraid government-run facilities would betray their privacy.

May 28. Al Unser is now the fifth driver to capture three Indy 500 titles.

1978

JUNE

Su	Mo	Tu	We	Th	Fr	Sa
				1	2	3
4	5	6	7	8	9	10
11	12	13	14	15	16	17
18	19	20	21	22	23	24
25	26	27	28	29	30	

1. Moscow: U.S. reports finding wiretaps in U.S. Embassy (→ 7).

2. U.S. announces airlift to get French paratroopers out of Zaire (→ 13).

3. China calls for flexible interpretation of Maoist ideology by armed forces (→ 5).

5. China: 110,000, detained since 1957 crackdown, reported freed (→ 12/19).

7. Seattle: Baltimore Bullets beat Seattle Supersonics 105-99 for NBA title.

7. Carter tells Soviets to choose between cooperation and confrontation; Soviets reaffirm detente, call Carter's attitude "strange" (→ 4/23/81).

8. Washington: House supports New York with $2 bil. bond.

9. Nevada: Larry Holmes beats Ken Norton for WBC heavyweight title.

11. Paris: Borg wins French Open for third time.

11. Ohio: Nancy Lopez wins fourth straight tournament, LPGA championship.

12. New York: David Berkowitz gets 25 years to life in each of six Son of Sam slayings (→ 7/6).

13. Lebanon: Israelis withdraw last of invading forces in south Lebanon (→ 7/1).

13. Brussels: Zaire agrees to control by IMF in exchange for economic assistance.

15. Italy: Pres. Leone resigns, charged with embezzlement in Lockheed affair (→ 10/11/83).

19. Moscow: Muhammad Ali meets with Brezhnev (→ 9/17).

23. Rome: Red Brigade trial ends; 29 sentenced, 16 cleared (→ 7/8).

24. North Yemen Pres. Ahmed Hussein al-Ghashmi assassinated (→ 26).

25. Argentina: Argentina beats Netherlands 3-1 for World Cup soccer title.

26. South Yemen: Head of state Salem Robaya executed, succeeded by pro-Soviet Ali Nasser (→ 2/24/79).

27. Soviets put Polish astronomer in orbit on Salyut 6 (→ 8/28).

Proposition 13 wins at California polls

June 6. Californians have voted in favor of an amendment to the state constitution which will cut $7 billion off the amount of property tax revenue. The referendum, called Proposition 13, sends a message to politicians that citizens are concerned about excess government spending and the diminution of personal income. Such a "tax revolt" has been brewing for some time, and not only in the Golden State.

Sick of taxes? Vote them down.

Californians, led by Howard Jarvis and Paul Mann, authors of the proposal, may set a new trend in government fiscal frugality. Many states have examined Proposition 13 and, if the cutback in collected taxes does not adversely affect services, are likely to follow the California initiative.

June 10. Affirmed (inside) wins the Belmont Stakes by a nose to take the Triple Crown with 18-year-old phenom Steve Cauthen.

Rebels kill white teachers and children

White students gather in Salisbury.

June 23. A terrorist attack on a mission school in Vumba, Rhodesia, last night has left 12 people dead, including teachers and their young children. A group of black nationalists beat and bayonetted the 12 whites to death. One woman was found alive but critically injured. Only one white resident of the school escaped unharmed—by hiding after a black servant alerted him to the arrival of the terrorists.

Before the killings took place, the terrorists assembled the school's 250 black students and teachers and told them that they were freedom fighters from the Mozambique-based Zimbabwe African National Union (ZANU).

Missionaries are more and more the targets of terrorist violence in Rhodesia's civil war, in part because farmers are armed and have fortified their property against attack. A total of 21 missionaries had been slain by terrorists before yesterday's attack, five within the past month (→ 7/30).

Bakke wins right to enter med school

June 28. The Supreme Court affirmed today by a 5-to-4 vote the constitutionality of college admissions programs favoring minorities to help remedy past discrimination against them. But the court also ruled that would-be medical student Alan P. Bakke, twice rejected by the University of California Medical College at Davis, must be admitted, the program having been unjustifiably biased against him, a white applicant. Sixteen of 100 places were set aside for racial minorities and he charged he was more qualified than some of those admitted (→ 8/10).

Blacks given equal rights as Mormons

June 9. The 148-year-old policy of excluding black men from the Mormon priesthood was struck down by Church leaders yesterday. Spencer W. Kimball, President of the 4.2 million members of the worldwide Church of Jesus Christ of Latter Day Saints, said from Church headquarters in Salt Lake City that the decision was the result of a revelation. By Mormon custom, it is the duty of "every worthy, faithful man" to take on the functions of priests from age 12. The Church exclusion of women from all priestly functions remains intact.

Big Ford LTD II, one of many American "gas guzzlers" despite oil crisis.

U.S. stops building Seabrook nuclear plant

Alternative energy exhibits gave a positive aspect to the Seabrook protest.

June 30. Public opposition has forced the Nuclear Regulatory Commission to order a halt in the construction of the controversial nuclear power plant at Seabrook, New Hampshire. By a two-to-one vote, the federal agency asserted that the indefinite construction delay will allow time and "freedom to decide on alternatives to the Seabrook site," according to the NRC's public statement.

For seven years, the $2.3 billion plant has faced public opposition from environmentalists wary of the potential danger nuclear energy facilities present. Announcement of the NRC decision received elated cheers from the hundreds of protesters who had been demonstrating outside the agency's headquarters.

The commission said alternative sites for the plant should be considered. The construction design at Seabrook calls for reactors to be cooled with ocean water. Radiated water would then return to the Atlantic. The NRC anticipates the Environmental Protection Agency will soon rule this type of system illegal, as it is potentially dangerous to the environment (→ 3/9/79).

Wing of Versailles is struck by bomb

June 26. A bomb planted by terrorists exploded in the Versailles Palace outside Paris today. Three rooms containing artwork from the time of Napoleon were destroyed. Paintings were ripped to shreds, and an official said they would have to be "assembled like a jigsaw puzzle." Restoration and repairs could take up to a year. The most famous rooms of the palace, including the Hall of Mirrors, were not harmed by the explosion. Three groups have claimed responsibility for the blast, including Breton separatists, the International Organization of the Jobless, and the Revolutionary Workers. Police are skeptical of the claims (→ 11/30).

Court rules Nazis may stage parade

June 12. In a decision which may strike terror in the hearts of the thousands of concentration camp survivors who live in the Chicago suburb, the Supreme Court has cleared the way for American Nazis to march through Skokie, Illinois. Although the National Socialist Party of America argued that it had a constitutional right to peaceful assembly, the heavily Jewish town asked Justice John Paul Stevens to intervene. The Supreme Court, in today's ruling, upheld the rights of the Nazis. Justices Blackmun and Rehnquist dissented, saying the decision conflicted with a 1952 ruling supporting the censorship of "hate literature" (→ 7/9).

1978

JULY

Su	Mo	Tu	We	Th	Fr	Sa
						1
2	3	4	5	6	7	8
9	10	11	12	13	14	15
16	17	18	19	20	21	22
23	24	25	26	27	28	29
30	31					

1. Beirut: 22 killed in fighting between Syrian troops and Christian militia (→ 23).

3. Peking cancels aid to Vietnam over alleged mistreatment of ethnic Chinese (→ 11/3).

4. Washington: Study shows machinery and manufactured goods have overtaken oil as #1 U.S. import (→ 10/20).

6. New York: David Berkowitz committed to psychiatric center.

8. Wimbledon: Bjorn Borg over Jimmy Connors 6-2, 6-2, 6-3; Martina Navratilova over Chris Evert 2-6, 6-4, 7-5.

8. Italy elects first Socialist pres., 82-year-old Alessandro Pertini (→ 4/4/81).

9. Washington: 100,000 march for ERA extension (→ 10/6).

14. Detroit: Lee A. Iacocca resigns as pres. of Ford (→ 11/2).

15. Washington: Hundreds of American Indians end five-month march to protest proposed legislation.

17. Bonn: U.S. and six allies to cut air links to countries that shelter hijackers.

18. Sudan: 30 nations attend Organization of African Unity summit at Khartoum.

19. Managua: 24-hour general strike called to force resignation of Somoza (→ 8/22).

20. Washington: John Mitchell released on parole (→ 9/3/79).

22. Iran: 40 killed in anti-govt. riots in Meched (→ 9/8).

22. India: Gandhi charged with criminal misconduct during 1977 campaign (→ 12/26).

23. Bernard Hinault wins Tour de France.

23. Jerusalem: Begin rejects Egyptian request to turn over El Arish and Mount Sinai (→ 30).

27. Portugal: Govt. collapses as president dismisses Premier Soares (→ 7/19/79).

28. London: Gold exceeds $200 per ounce first time in Europe.

30. Cairo: Sadat bars meeting with Israelis now (→ 8/3).

30. Mozambique: Rhodesians hit guerrilla bases in major offensive (→ 10/22).

First test-tube baby is born in London

July 25. The first baby to be conceived outside the human body was born today to a British couple, Lesley Brown and her husband, John. The baby weighed five pounds, 12 ounces and was delivered by Caesarian section at Oldham General and District Hospital. She has been named Louise, and she is normal.

Mrs. Brown was unable to conceive because of a defect in the Fallopian tubes, which carry an egg from the ovaries to the uterus each month. Dr. Robert G. Edwards and Patrick C. Steptoe, the two British researchers who pioneered the so-called test-tube baby technique, removed an egg surgically from an ovary, fertilized it with sperm in a laboratory dish, and implanted the embryo in Lesley Brown's uterus, where it developed normally. The birth of the Brown baby was the first success for Steptoe and Edwards, who have worked on the technique for 12 years and have had a number of failures. It is estimated that the method could be used to help one-fifth to one-half of infertile women achieve pregnancy (→ 8/19).

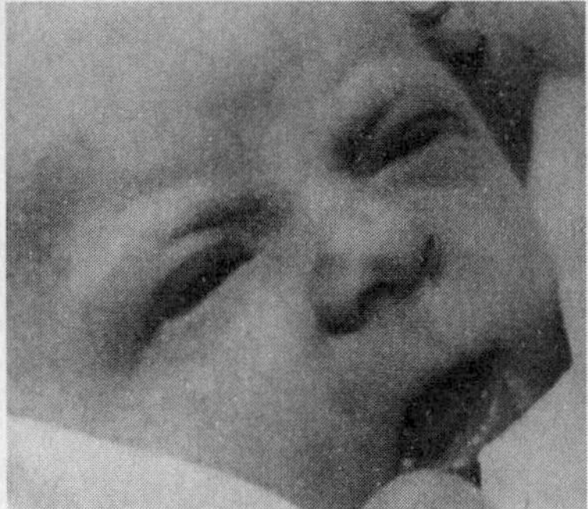

Louise Brown, tiny but healthy.

3 Soviet dissidents get long jail terms

July 14. Angry protests in Western Europe and the United States accompanied the sentencing by the Soviet Union of three dissidents. The best known, Anatoly Shcharansky, who had led a Jewish immigration movement, got 13 years in prison. Aleksandr Ginzburg, a fundraiser for the families of political prisoners, was handed eight years in prison and labor camps. In Lithuania, Viktoras Petkus received a ten-year prison term to be followed by five years of internal exile. Petkus had headed a watchdog committee which publicized Soviet violations of the 1975 Helsinki human rights accord. Shcharansky and Ginzburg were similarly active in Moscow (→ 4/27/79).

Mauritania is taken over by military

Soldiers direct an execution.

July 10. The military has toppled the government of the West African country of Mauritania in a reportedly bloodless coup. President Moktar Ould Daddah was arrested this morning. Daddah was Prime Minister under the French colonial system and has been Mauritania's leader since independence in 1960. Algerian-backed Polisario guerrillas have been trying to gain independence for the Western Sahara, which is currently partitioned between Mauritania and Morocco. The French are interested in protecting iron-ore mines in the disputed area.

Campsite explosion kills 200 in Spain

July 11. A horrible tragedy occurred on the coast of Spain today. A truck loaded with inflammable liquid gas flipped over on a road 50 miles south of Barcelona, exploded and tumbled into a campground. Nearly 200 summer campers were killed instantly. Some of them were thrown by the force of the explosion 150 yards into the Mediterranean. The blast leveled 100 trailers and houses at the Los Alfaques campsite. Hundreds of campers were burned, many of them seriously. An official at a hospital that admitted 40 burn victims said, "Most of them are in critical condition. I don't think many will survive."

Reporter won't give up notes, is jailed

July 24. M.A. Farber, a reporter for The New York Times, was sent to jail today for contempt of court for refusing to turn over his notes for possible use in the murder trial of Dr. Mario E. Jascalevich. Farber later was released, pending a hearing by the New Jersey Supreme Court, which also will determine the validity of a $100,000 fine that was imposed against The Times today in the same case. Farber's articles in The Times on 13 mysterious deaths at Riverdell Hospital in Oradell, New Jersey, in the mid-1960's helped lead to reopening of the case and the trial of Dr. Jascalevich (→ 10/25).

Police arrest 72 at Nazi rally in Chicago

July 9. In Chicago's Marquette Park this afternoon, more than 2,000 people milled around, shouting racial slurs and chanting Nazi slogans. The event was a rally sponsored by the National Socialist Party of America, a white supremacist organization based on Adolf Hitler's Nazi Party. Four hundred police officers were on duty to protect the Nazis and to turn counter-demonstrators away from the park.

The volatile situation broke out into frequent scuffles which led to at least 72 arrests, but out-and-out rioting was averted. Represented by the American Civil Liberties Union, the Nazis fought a long legal battle to demonstrate in Marquette Park and in the Chicago suburb, Skokie, Illinois. Last month, the Supreme Court ruled that the Nazis do have rights to peaceful assembly. Nazi leader Frank Collin called off the rally in Skokie, a largely Jewish town, saying he had used the threat of a Skokie rally to win the right to demonstrate in Marquette Park.

1978

AUGUST

Su	Mo	Tu	We	Th	Fr	Sa
		1	2	3	4	5
6	7	8	9	10	11	12
13	14	15	16	17	18	19
20	21	22	23	24	25	26
29	28	29	30	31		

1. Atlanta: Pete Rose ends hitting streak at 44 games.

3. Tel Aviv: Bomb kills one, wounds five; Israeli jets strike Lebanon in reprisal (→ 14).

4. New York: First families begin leaving Love Canal (→ 7).

8. Philadelphia: One policeman killed in eviction of radical group MOVE; 18 hurt (→ 11/8/83).

10. Atlanta: Sen. Julian Bond files suit to end use of word "nigger" on radio, TV (→ 9/13).

10. Chrysler sells European subsidaries to Peugeot-Citroen.

13. Florida: Police burn record marijuana seizure of 100 tons.

14. Tel Aviv: Israeli Cabinet approves five new military settlements on West Bank (→ 29).

15. Athens: Christina Onassis, just wed to Serguei Kausov, goes to Moscow to rejoin husband.

18. Chicago: Two Croatian nationalists hold hostages six hours in West German Consulate.

19. Bucharest: Chinese leader Hua Kuo-feng makes first state visit to Communist-bloc country.

19. N.Y: Court awards woman $50,000 after hospital destroys test-tube embryo (→ 10/7).

22. Nicaragua: 100 rebels, led by Eden Pastora, seize 2,000 hostages in National Palace (→ 25).

25. Managua: Sandinistas fly to freedom after taking hostages at National Palace (→ 30).

28. Soviet and first East German astronaut dock with Salyut 6 orbital laboratory (→ 9/21).

29. Syria completes sweep of Christian militia strongholds in northwest Lebanon (→ 9/18).

31. Kentucky: First woman on trial for self-induced abortion found not guilty on insanity (→ 7/2/79).

DEATHS

6. Pope Paul VI (*9/26/1897).

21. Charles Eames, U.S. architect, designer (*6/17/1907).

22. Jomo Kenyatta, Kenyan nationalist leader, born Kamau Johnstone (*10/20/1891).

23. Ignazio Silone, Italian writer (*5/1/1900).

Nicaragua rebels seize hostages in palace

Sandinista Commander Zero.

Aug 30. Leftist guerrillas seeking the overthrow of President Anastasio Somoza Debayle seized Nicaragua's National Palace earlier this month, taking hundreds of government officials as hostages. The raid into the heart of the Nicaraguan capital by the guerrilla force known as the Sandinist National Liberation Front confronts Somoza with the most serious challenge he has yet faced to his authoritarian rule in the Central American republic.

The crisis finally was resolved by the Somoza government acceding to the guerrillas' demands for ransom money, the release of a number of political prisoners and safe passage out of the country. The capitulation, however, symbolized the weakening control of Somoza, who has steadfastly rejected demands that he resign from office. He faces a growing opposition that includes conservative businessmen, Christian Democrats and Marxist-oriented guerrillas who have been organizing strikes and demonstrations for the past year (→ 9/3).

Paul VI dies; new Pope will be John Paul I

Pope Paul VI lies in state.

Aug 26. Albino Cardinal Luciani, the Patriarch of Venice, was elected the 263rd pontiff of the Roman Catholic Church today, succeeding the late Pope Paul VI, who died on August 6.

Giovanni Battista Montini, who had served as Pope Paul VI since 1963, was felled by a heart attack at the papal summer residence of Castel Gandolfo. Pope Paul, who was 80, had long suffered from chronic arthritis, insomnia, and complications from prostate surgery. After lying in state in St. Peter's for three days, his body was interred in the crypt below the basilica.

The conclave of Cardinals, which convened earlier this morning, elected Luciani on the fourth ballot, one of the quickest papal elections in modern history. Cardinal Luciani chose the name John Paul I, in homage to his two immediate predecessors on the throne of St. Peter.

John Paul I is generally considered to be a moderate, agreeing with his predecessor's disapproval of divorce and artificial contraception, but supportive of the goals of ecumenism and Vatican II, convened by Pope John XXIII and continued by Pope Paul. His election, by more than two-thirds of the 111 voting Cardinals, seems to indicate that he was a candidate acceptable to both liberal and conservative churchmen (→ 9/30).

John Paul I to reign in the Vatican.

Balloon sets record in Atlantic crossing

Double Eagle soars over the Atlantic.

Aug 19. Three Americans have made the first transatlantic balloon crossing, setting an endurance record of 138 hours and six minutes in the air in the process. The balloon touched down in a field west of Paris carrying Ben Abruzzo, Max Anderson and Larry Newman, all of Albuquerque, New Mexico. Abruzzo said he hoped to land next to the Eiffel Tower but missed by 60 miles. The balloonists will return next week to the United States, where they have been invited to the White House. Abruzzo says they already are planning to make a 30-day balloon trip around the world.

Families begin to leave Love Canal

Aug 7. Emergency state and federal aid has been pledged to residents of the Love Canal area of Niagara Falls, New York, forced to leave their homes by leakage of dangerous chemicals from an abandoned dump. Fifteen families already have moved out, following recommendations that young children and pregnant women leave the site. High rates of birth defects and miscarriages have been reported in Love Canal residents. Hooker Chemicals, which used the area as a dump years ago, will help pay for a cleanup program (→ 5/16/80).

1978

SEPTEMBER

Su	Mo	Tu	We	Th	Fr	Sa
					1	2
3	4	5	6	7	8	9
10	11	12	13	14	15	16
17	18	19	20	21	22	23
24	25	26	27	28	29	30

2. Chile: State of emergency imposed in north; 13 arrested for labor agitation (→ 8/27/80).

3. Managua: Somoza strips nation's top political group of charter (→ 15).

6. Doctor in California develops successful method of choosing a child's sex.

7. S.F.: Scientists produce insulin through genetic engineering (→ 1/16/80).

8. New York: Pan Am and Natl. Airlines agree to $350 million merger.

8. Iran: Martial law sparks riots; opposition claims 2,000 victims as police open fire (→ 10/6).

8. New York: Four more cases of Legionnaires disease confirmed; one fatality.

11. New York: Connors beats Borg; Chris Evert over Pam Shriver for U.S. Open titles.

13. California: Mandatory busing begins (→ 6/27/79).

15. Managua: Somoza mobilizes National Guard to fight rebels in seven cities (→ 20).

16. Iran: Vicious earthquake kills at least 25,000.

17. New Orleans: Ali in decision over Leon Spinks becomes first to win heavyweight title three times.→

20. Nicaragua: National Guard seizes Esteli; many civilian casualties reported (→ 29).

20. Jordan says it is not bound by Camp David (→ 10/11).

21. Two Soviet astronauts set space endurance record at 96 days (→ 11/2).

21. Nigeria: State of emergency lifted after 12 years (→ 8/1/79).

24. New York: Babysitter who kidnapped Calvin Klein's daughter says Klein paid her to do it for publicity.

27. Carter ends three-year ban on arms to Turkey (→ 3/29/80).

29. South Africa: Pieter Botha chosen to succeed Vorster as prime minister (→ 4/12/79).

DEATH

19. Etienne Gilson, French Thomist historian (*6/13/1884).

Somoza struggles to hang on in Nicaragua

Insurgent peasants, tired of 45 years of iron rule, destroy a statue of Somoza.

Sept 29. President Anastasio Somoza struggled this month to put down an armed insurrection led by the leftist Sandinist National Liberation Front. Since the bloody fighting broke out, more that 1,500 persons are believed to have been killed, with the casualties largely among the small rebel force that is battling Somoza's National Guard and police force.

The Sandinista force, which started off as a small Marxist revolutionary group demanding the ouster of Somoza, appears to have gained widespread popular support as it battled government troops in a half-dozen Nicaraguan cities. As the fighting expanded, an emissary of President Carter urged Somoza to accept mediation by Latin American states to find a peaceful solution to the crisis. There was speculation that as part of the solution the Carter administration was urging Somoza to resign (→ 10/14).

Ali floats and stings to third boxing title

Sept 17. Muhammad Ali once again wears the heavyweight boxing crown after defeating Leon Spinks in tonight's grueling 15-round bout. Ali now holds the title for the third time, unprecedented in boxing history. Some experts claim that Ali didn't necessarily win the bout as much as Spinks lost it. After the decision, Spinks admitted, "My head wasn't in it." But credit must go to the 36-year-old boxing legend whose dancing, jabbing style reminded fans of his glory days when he vowed to "float like a butterfly and sting like a bee" (→ 6/26/79).

John Paul I dies after just a month as Pope

Catholics mourn again.

Sept 30. Pope John Paul I, who was elevated to the papacy on August 26, died of a heart attack in his room at the Vatican last night. He would have been 66 on October 17. The pope was found early this morning by his secretary, Rev. John Magee, who said he seemed to have been reading a book when he was stricken. John Paul has had a lifetime history of poor health. John Paul's reign was the second shortest in Church history: only that of Stephen II, who died two days after his election in 752, was shorter (→ 10/17).

Collision of 727 jet, small plane kills 150

Sept 25. At least 150 people have died in one of America's worst air disasters when a private plane collided with a Pacific Southwest Airlines jetliner over San Diego. All 135 persons aboard the 727 airliner and the pilot of the light plane died immediately, and an undetermined number of persons died on the ground when flaming wreckage crashed into a residential neighborhood. The collision occurred after both pilots were warned that other aircraft were dangerously close.

Investigators say the pilot of the light plane was a student who was practicing instrument landings and that he might not have seen the jetliner because he could have been wearing a hood to simulate foul weather conditions. The crash has caused airlines to renew their demands for installation of collision warning equipment on all aircraft. Federal Aviation Authority officials say existing equipment is not reliable enough.

The 727 plummets earthward . . .

and crashes in a residential area.

Sadat, Begin, Carter at Camp David summit

Camp David: Begin, Carter, Sadat.

Sept 18. Israel's Prime Minister Begin and Egypt's President Sadat came down from the mountain last night to announce that they had reached agreement at Camp David. President Carter, who shuttled tirelessly between the two often hostile delegations for 13 days, appeared exhausted. But the president was smiling. He had helped fashion two remarkable agreements.

Carter acknowledged that the accords were only a beginning. "There are still great difficulties that remain," he said, "and many hard issues to be settled." Sadat, who appeared almost stiff at White House ceremonies, praised Carter and spoke hopefully of the "spirit of Camp David." Begin was effusive in congratulating Carter for achieving "a great victory," and he said the summit should be called the "Jimmy Carter Conference." The prime minister said, "He worked harder than our forefathers did in Egypt building the pyramids."

Sadat and Begin signed two separate documents. The first is called "Framework for Peace in the Middle East." It calls for more negotiations to determine the future of the West Bank and the Gaza Strip. Israel agreed to withdraw almost all of its forces from the two areas and not to build any more settlements on the West Bank during the negotiations. The document does not guarantee the creation of a Palestinian state in the area, but one report says Begin did agree to "recognize the legitimate rights of Palestinians."

The unanswered question is whether Jordan's King Hussein will join the future talks between Egypt and Israel. At one point during the deliberations, hopes were raised and then dashed over speculation that a representative of Hussein was on his way to Camp David.

The second agreement is entitled "Framework for the Conclusion of a Peace Treaty Between Egypt and Israel." Under the accord, both countries agree to move toward normal diplomatic relations and Israel agrees to withdraw its forces from the Sinai. Still to be negotiated is the status of Jewish settlements built in the Sinai.

These extraordinary talks almost collapsed a week ago. Begin and Sadat did not meet face to face for days. Both men say it was President Carter who made the agreements possible by his shuttle diplomacy and his perpetual motion between Sadat's Dogwood Lodge and Begin's Birch Lodge (→ 20).

Sept 16. The Grateful Dead, seeking perfect sound and immortality, perform at Egypt's Pyramids.

The Ewings, tormented Texas tycoons, bring soap opera to prime time on new CBS show "Dallas."

1978

OCTOBER

Su	Mo	Tu	We	Th	Fr	Sa
1	2	3	4	5	6	7
8	9	10	11	12	13	14
15	16	17	18	19	20	21
22	23	24	25	26	27	28
29	30	31				

2. Guatemala paralyzed by general gtrike; 30 killed, 1,000 arrested (→ 1/31/80).

5. Sweden: Conservatives asking freedom for nuclear energy oust premier Falldin (→ 3/23/80).

6. U.S. Senate extends deadline for ERA (→ 1/13/79).

7. India: Birth of world's second test-tube baby announced.

10. Geneva: Los Angeles approved as site of 1984 Summer Olympics.

11. Beirut: Soviets begin evacuation of embassy (→ 12).

12. Washington: Egypt-Israeli peace talks open (→ 21).

14. Washington: Carter signs first major revision of U.S. civil service laws in 20th Century.

14. Nicaragua: Somoza extends martial law six months (→ 2/8/79).

14. N.J.: Two Soviet U.N. employees convicted of spying.

16. Brazil: Joao Batista Figuerido elected pres. (→ 10/4/79).

17. Rome: Polish Cardinal Karol Wojtyla becomes first non-Italian pope in 455 years (→ 23).

19. Carter orders production of elements for neutron bomb (→ 11/17).

20. N.Y.: Dow Jones has worst week in history, down 59 points (→ 11/1).

21. Washington: Mideast peace talks come to end (→ 11/5).

25. London: Poll shows one in three think royal family out of touch with reality.

25. N.J.: Dr. Mario Jascalevich (Dr. X) acquitted of three murder charges.

27. New York: Guggenheim opens Rothko exhibit.

29. Paris: Andrei Gromyko calls award of Nobel Prize to Sadat and Begin "something of a joke" (→ 12/10).

30. Iran: Thousands clash with police in nationwide oil strike (→ 11/6).

DEATH

21. Anastase Mikoyan, Soviet statesman (*11/25/1895).

Karpov keeps title, defeating Korchnoi

Karpov studiously eyes the board.

Oct 19. Anatoly Karpov of the Soviet Union defeated a defector from his homeland, Viktor Korchnoi, and retained the world chess championship. The 27-year-old Karpov got the title by default three years ago from Bobby Fischer of the United States. Karpov was asleep when his rival conceded and was spirited away to a private villa before he could be interviewed. Korchnoi foundered on the 22nd game of the three-month series, which went to the first player to win six games. There were 21 draws. Korchnoi frequently charged that hostile Soviet thought waves, yogurt signals and favoritism were used to thwart him.

Belgium's popular songster, Brel, dies

Oct 10. The flippant would say Jacques Brel is no longer alive and well and living in Paris. The Belgian balladeer, who has died of cancer at age 49, could be a bit sarcastic himself. His attacks, however, usually aimed at bigotry, hypocrisy and overly inflated national pride. He is remembered more for love songs written in the 1950's, "Tendresse," "Ne me Quitte Pas" (Don't Leave Me) and "Marijke" among them. Brel kept his own loves discreet; he leaves three daughters, none by his wife. Feeling that his songs were going somewhat stale, Brel turned to stage and film acting in the 1960's and 1970's.

New Pope is first non-Italian in 455 years

Oct 23. John Paul II, the first non-Italian to be elevated to the papacy in over four centuries, was inaugurated in a mass at St. Peter's Square today. More than 100,000 people attended the ceremony, many of whom were from the new Pope's native Poland.

Karol Cardinal Wojtyla, Archbishop of Krakow, was elected to the papacy on the eighth ballot of a conclave which ended on October 17. Like his predecessor, John Paul I, he is a theological conservative and a social progressive. And at 58, he is the youngest man to become pope in this century, and the first non-Italian leader of the Catholic Church since Hadrian VI, a Dutchman who died in 1523 (→ 1/25/79).

John Paul II, Polish ex-Archbishop.

Iraq expels Iranian Ayatollah Khomeini

Oct 6. The French government has injected itself dramatically into a Middle East quarrel by agreeing to grant refuge to the Ayatollah Khomeini. The Iranian religious leader was agitating against the Shah of Iran from a base in Iraq until the Baghdad regime expelled him as a gesture of peace to Iran. Khomeini had nowhere to go until 100 Iranian imams prevailed on French President Giscard d'Estaing "to accord the necessary respect and honor" to the ayatollah.

Giscard's critics are shocked. Khomeini has stated brazenly: "No satisfying solution to the Iranian political problem is possible without the disappearance of the Pahlevi dynasty." Supporters of the shah are concerned that Khomeini will continue his revolutionary activities from France (→ 30).

Khomeini in exile in France.

Rhodesia reports killing 1500 rebels

Oct 22. Rhodesian forces have killed as many as 1,500 guerrillas during four days of bold raids on rebel camps in Zambia.

Cross-border raids against guerrilla encampments in Zambia, where Joshua Nkomo's Zimbabwe African People's Union (ZAPU) is based, have been infrequent. However, Rhodesian forces often cross into Mozambique where Robert Mugabe and his Zimbabwe African National Union (ZANU) are based. Last November, 1,200 of Mugabe's men were killed in a raid.

The raid into Zambia took place while leaders of Rhodesia's government were meeting in Washington to discuss possible peace talks with the rebels. Estimates of guerrilla strength place 8,000 rebels in Rhodesia and 22,000 in Mozambique and Zambia (→ 1/30/79).

Troops of white Rhodesia on guard.

Japan and China declare friendship

Oct 24. In an ebullient ceremony in Tokyo today attended by Chinese Deputy Premier Deng Hsiao-ping and Japanese Premier Takeo Fukuda, the respective foreign ministers ushered in a new era in Sino-Japanese relations by elegantly brushing their signatures on an historic peace and friendship pact.

The 500-word treaty, initially signed in Peking after a six-year delay by Japan, marks a final rapprochement between the former World War II enemies. In a meeting with 77-year-old Emperor Hirohito, Deng suggested that "bygones be bygones." The emperor answered with an indirect apology for the Japanese invasion of China.

After champagne toasts and hugs, Deng and Fukuda lauded the treaty with phrases like "profound historic significance" and "progress in the flow of history." The Soviet Union may be less enthusiastic. The pact opposes "hegemony" by a third power, a Chinese code word for Soviet saber-rattling, and Deng, the second most powerful man in China, was clearly sent to Tokyo to cement Chinese relations with its industrially mighty neighbor.

Observing that Japan had the right to the protection of the 1953 U.S.-Japan security pact, Deng also implied that Japan should similarly defend itself against possible Soviet aggression (→ 12/18).

Two Bergmans, no relation, make film

Avant-garde director Bergman.

Bergman, meet Bergman. Actress Ingrid Bergman has just completed "Autumn Sonata," a film directed by Ingmar Bergman. Miss Bergman wanted to work with Mr. Bergman, writing him pleading letters for 13 years before, he says, he found the proper role for her.

"The Seventh Seal" (1957), "Wild Strawberries" (1957) and "Cries and Whispers" (1972) are among Mr. Bergman's personal, occasionally surreal films. He earns parody and praise from directors Francis Coppola and Woody Allen.

Miss Bergman has starred in "Casablanca" (1943), "Notorious" (1946) and "Stromboli" (1949). She thinks "Sonata" may be her last film because, she says, roles for women her age (she is 65) are hard to find. She denies any rumors of serious illness holding her back.

Sid Vicious, punk star, kills girlfriend

Oct 13. Sid Vicious, bass guitarist for the now-defunct Sex Pistols, the British band at the center of the rebellious maelstrom known as punk rock, was arrested and charged with the death of his girlfriend in Manhattan today. Vicious, 21, who changed his name from John Simon Richie, often performed in a drug- and alcohol-induced daze, sometimes bleeding from self-inflicted cuts. He called police early this afternoon to report that his girlfriend, Nancy Spungen, 20, had been stabbed once in the stomach (→ 2/2/79).

Nancy and Sid at court in February.

1978

NOVEMBER

Su	Mo	Tu	We	Th	Fr	Sa
			1	2	3	4
5	6	7	8	9	10	11
12	13	14	15	16	17	18
19	20	21	22	23	24	25
26	27	28	29	30		

1. Tokyo: U.S. dollar hits post-war low of 175 yen (→ 12/16).

2. Soviet cosmonauts Kovalenok and Ivanchenkov end record 140-day space trip (*3/7/79).

2. Uganda: Idi Amin says he has annexed 710 sq. mile strip of Zambia (→ 3/4/79).

2. Chrysler announces it will hire Lee A. Iacocca (→ 11/1/79).

3. Vietnam reports repulsing two Chinese attacks (→ 2/17/79).

5. Rome: Women terrorists firebomb apartment of obstetrician.

5. Cuba to free 3,000 political prisoners for emigration to U.S. (→ 9/10/79).

5. Baghdad: Arab League calls on Egypt to renounce accord with Israel (→ 12/10).

6. Iran: Shah puts military in control after two days of rioting; Khomeini, in Paris, calls for revolution.→

8. Iran: Shah in purge orders arrest of ex-premier (→ 10).

10. Iran: Strikers demand expulsion of all foreigners with oil jobs (→ 13).

13. Iran: Threatened with dismissal, most oil workers return to jobs after two-week strike (→ 12/4).

15. Sri Lanka: 189 Moslem pilgrims die in jet crash.

16. Washington: House committee concludes James Earl Ray was paid to kill Rev. King.

17. Moscow: Brezhnev says Soviets have tested neutron bomb (→ 3/9/79).

18. Guyana: Congressman Leo Ryan missing on visit to Jonestown sect (→ 20).

20. Guyana: Official reports 400 found in mass suicide (→ 26).

22. Malaysia: 200 Vietnamese refugees die when boat capsizes (→ 7/20/79).

26. Guyana: U.S. troops leave Jonestown; death toll 909 (→ 29).

30. France: Two given 15 years for June bombing of Versailles.

DEATH

20. Giorgio de Chirico, Italian Surrealist painter (*7/10/1888).

909 die in mass suicide

The deadly Kool-Aid (top right) does its work on members of the Peoples Temple.

Nov 29. The last of the bodies have been flown out of Guyana and returned to the United States. Legal authorities, diplomats, psychologists and families are all wrestling with the troubling questions. They want to know why more than 900 American followers of a fanatical Californian committed suicide in the jungle of South America.

The bodies of the cultists, dressed in gaudily colored clothes, were found sprawled on the grounds of the so-called Peoples Temple in Jonestown, Guyana. Survivors say temple members took part in a mass suicide rite by swallowing a concoction of Kool-Aid and cyanide. The deadly potion was ladled into the mouths of infants. Small children were ordered to help themselves. Adults swallowed the punch willingly and collapsed in a death embrace, their arms wrapped around other cult members. The body of their leader, James Warren Jones, alias Rev. Jim Jones, was found on the altar in the commune, a bullet wound in his head.

One follower said Jones wanted everyone to believe he was God. Others described him as paranoid, sex-crazed and power-hungry. He was apparently infuriated by the visit of California Congressman Leo Ryan to Jonestown on the 18th. Ryan had flown to Guyana to investigate complaints that cult members were being held against their will, forced to give up their worldly possessions and compelled to participate in bizarre sexual rites.

Jones allegedly ordered cult members to ambush Ryan and his party at the Port Kaituma airport, eight miles from Jonestown. The congressman's body was found sprawled on the dirt airstrip. Nearby were the bodies of NBC reporter Don Harris, cameraman Robert Brown, photographer Gregory Robinson and Patricia Parks. Brown kept filming after the shots rang out and did not stop until a bullet struck him in the head.

Eyewitnesses say Jones ordered his followers to commit suicide after he learned that some members of Ryan's party had escaped. Jones had said earlier that he would destroy the community if it were ever attacked. He had trained his followers in a suicide ritual, and few of them resisted. Apparently brainwashed, they followed Jones when he proclaimed, "The time has come to meet in another place" (→ 12/3).

Jones, worshipped until the end.

2,517 on Hai Hong roam hostile seas

Nov 11. The Hai Hong drifts on the South China Sea with 2,517 aboard. They are the "boat people," refugees fleeing the Communist Vietnamese regime. Day after day, they crouch shoulder to shoulder, too tired to complain of the little food and the relentless sun. One woman begs for the boat to turn around; if they go back now, she says, they will only serve six months of hard labor in prison. The Hai Hong has been at sea for weeks, turned aside first by Malaysia, then Indonesia. These neighboring countries take in over 10,000 refugees a month and say they have reached their limits (→ 22).

The Hai Hong hunts for a home.

Scholar suggests Rubaiyat is dubious

Nov 3. An English professor at Cambridge University believes one of the famous manuscripts of Omar Khayyam's poem "The Rubaiyat" is a phony. The university bought the manuscript in the 1950's, thinking it was 1,200 years old. The scholar, Arthur Owen, feels the copy of the mystical love poem is not more than a century old. University members grew suspicious when other fake "Rubaiyat's" were surfacing. Scotland Yard and the London Institute of Archeology were called in for some tests. They showed that the manuscript pages contain a combination of chemicals not available before 1860.

1978

DECEMBER

Su	Mo	Tu	We	Th	Fr	Sa
					1	2
3	4	5	6	7	8	9
10	11	12	13	14	15	16
17	18	19	20	21	22	23
24	25	26	27	28	29	30
31						

1. Alabama: Ex-Sheriff James Clark, symbol of resistance to civil rights, given two years for smuggling marijuana.

2. Philadelphia: Navy blanks Army 28-0 in football.

3. Guyana: Pan Am bars transport of Jonestown survivors without armed U.S. escort.

4. Iran: Anti-shah strikes cutting oil production 30% (→ 11).

5. Moscow: Soviets sign 20-year friendship pact with Afghanistan (→ 2/14/79).

11. Tehran: Millions march against shah (→ 29).

16. Cleveland becomes first U.S. city to default since Depression (→ 2/5).

18. Washington: Goldwater questions constitutionality of ending Taiwan pact (→ 1/1/79).

26. India: Gandhi released after week in jail for refusing to testify on corruption (→ 1/6/80).

28. Illinois: 21 bodies found buried at home of John Gacy.

30. Washington: House committee concludes conspiracy likely in murder of Rev. King.

CULTURAL EVENTS, 1978

Literature: Herman Wouk's "War and Remembrance"; D.L. Coburn's "The Gin Game"; Howard Nemerov's "Collected Poems," Pulitzer and National Book Award; Iris Murdoch's "The Sea, The Sea"; John Irving's "The World According to Garp"; James Michener's "Chesapeake."

Academia: Barbara Tuchman's "A Distant Mirror"; Theodore White's "In Search of History."

Music: Penderecki's opera "Paradise Lost"; Fats Waller musical "Ain't Misbehavin'"; Bee Gees' "Night Fever," "Stayin' Alive"; Streisand and Diamond's "You Don't Bring Me Flowers";

The Arts: 2,000-year-old Egyptian Temple of Dendur shown at Metropolitan Museum of Art.

Film: "Grease," Travolta, Olivia Newton-John; "Animal House," John Belushi; Woody Allen's "Interiors"; Bergman's "Autumn Sonata"; "The Deer Hunter," Robert de Niro.

Rockwell, nation's favorite illustrator, dies

Nov 8. Illustrator Norman Rockwell has died at his Stockbridge, Massachusetts, home. He was 84. Rockwell alienated some people by his optimism. His 317 covers for the Saturday Evening Post featured cheery occasions (Thanksgiving dinner, little boys fishing, a child confiding in a friendly cop), which delighted the public but earned scorn from fellow artists.

Rockwell was born in New York on February 3, 1894. At age 21 he did his first Post cover: A boy dejectedly wheeling a baby carriage past pals suited up for a ball game. "I unconsciously decided," Rockwell said, "that if it wasn't an ideal world, it should be, and so painted only the ideal aspects of it . . ."

Rockwell's "Triple Self-Portrait."

Shah puts military in charge of Iran

Nov 6. The Shah of Iran put his country under military control today in an effort to master the revolutionary chaos that has shaken Iran for the past ten months. At least a thousand people have been killed in the violence. Troops fanned out through Tehran and shut down newspapers, radio and television networks. Later, in a conciliatory speech, the shah promised free elections after order is restored. In Washington, the shah's moves were endorsed by the Carter administration. But in Paris, they were criticized by the exiled Ayatollah Khomeini. The Shiite Moslem leader threatened to start a civil war to topple the shah (→ 12/8).

Two Frisco officials victims of assassin

Nov 27. Mayor George Moscone of San Francisco was shot to death in his City Hall office this morning. Within minutes, Supervisor Harvey Milk, the city's first acknowledged homosexual official, was shot and killed in the same building. An hour later, Dan White, 32, who resigned as Supervisor November 10 but sought to withdraw his resignation, surrendered to police. Dianne Feinstein, President of the Board of Supervisors, was sworn in as Mayor to serve until a replacement is selected. As supervisor, White, a former fireman, saw himself as the defender of home, family and religious life against homosexuals, pot smokers and cynics (→ 5/21/79).

Noted anthropologist Margaret Mead dies

Nov 15. Margaret Mead, expert on primitive cultures and modern society, has died of cancer at 76. Dr. Mead revolutionized anthropology when she wrote "Coming of Age in Samoa" in 1928. Her observations of teen love were much more subjective than anything previous researchers had done, and while some experts objected they had to admit she boosted public awareness. The American Association for the Advancement of Science voted Dr. Mead its President when she was a feisty, at times acerbic, 72.

Cultural anthropologist Mead.

Golda Meir, heroine of Israel, deceased

Meir, Prime Minister from 1969-74.

Dec 8. Golda Meir, Israel's first woman Prime Minister, died this afternoon at the age of 80 from viral hepatitis following a 12-year bout with leukemia. Because the announcement was made after the Sabbath had begun, there was little public reaction in the largely deserted streets of Tel Aviv and other cities, but informed Israelis expressed the deepest grief.

Shimon Peres, Chairman of Mrs. Meir's own Labor Party, called her a "stalwart lioness" and "one of the great women in Jewish and world history." And Egyptian President Anwar el-Sadat, said to receive the news in Cairo "with sorrow," described the former prime minister as a "first-class political leader" and praised her as "an honest foe" who had started "efforts for peace."

"Superman," with Christopher Reeve, mixes the best of adventure, special effects and satire.

Begin and Sadat jointly win Peace Prize

Begin (left), being congratulated.

Dec 10. Israel's Prime Minister Begin and Egypt's President Sadat are the joint winners of the Nobel Peace Prize. Because of security concerns, the medals were awarded inside an Oslo fortress. Outside the Akershus Castle, demonstrators criticized the awards and demanded a homeland for Palestinians.

Sadat, who was meeting in Egypt with Secretary of State Vance, did not attend the ceremony. His spokesman did not mention Begin by name, and he indicated that profound differences continue to exist between Egypt and Israel, particularly on the Palestinian issue. It is known that Sadat wants to revise the Camp David agreement to include self-rule for Palestinians. Begin stressed that he is satisfied with the agreement as is. He also distanced himself from Sadat by referring to Jerusalem as "the eternal capital of Israel" (→ 1/19/79).

Rare disease takes President of Algeria

Dec 27. Houari Boumedienne, the President of Algeria, died early this morning after a long struggle with a rare blood disease. He had been in a coma for several weeks with Waldenstrom's disease. It is believed Boumedienne was 46.

Boumedienne was a leading commander in the war to end French colonial rule in Algeria. He seized power from Ahmed Ben Bella in 1965 and was re-elected in 1976 with 99.5% of the vote. Boumedienne was an outspoken supporter of developing nations and critic of the Camp David agreement. He also backed the rebels in the Western Sahara (→ 7/4/79).

Coke is it, the real thing, in China now

Dec 19. Coca-Cola, to many the one product most symbolic and symptomatic of the American way of life, is going to China. The Coca-Cola Company starts selling the popular soft drink next month, the first American consumer product to hit that market since the Communist regime took power. The Chinese ideographs on the bottles translate as "tastes good, tastes happy," and they may signal a new era. Boeing announced a $156 million agreement with Peking for three 747 aircraft, Pan Am is petitioning to fly between San Francisco and Peking, and McDonalds is talking hamburgers (→ 4/4/79).

Millions march against the Shah in Tehran

Dec 29. Month-long protests have eroded the power of the Shah of Iran. Tonight, the imperial palace was forced to release a statement denying a report that the shah has decided to leave the country. The report was circulated by Shahpur Bakhtiar, the opposition leader selected by the shah to head a new civilian government. Thousands of foreign diplomats and workers have streamed out of Iran. President Carter is trying to decide whether to dispatch an aircraft carrier to the Persian Gulf as a show of support for the embattled monarch.

Strikes have reduced Iran's oil output by 90 percent, and there is barely enough for domestic consumption. The government has imposed rationing. Strikes have also shut down banks, stores and airlines. The shah is hoping that Iranians inconvenienced by the strikes will turn against the opposition National Front. Its leaders insist, however, that the strikes will not end until the shah leaves Iran.

Anti-shah protests, organized by Shiite Moslem leaders, intensified this month. Millions of protesters shouting "Death to the Shah" have filled the streets of Tehran and many other cities (→ 1/6/79).

A nationalist hero is lost: "Algeria cries over Houari Boumedienne."

Military reconsiders homosexual policy

Dec 7. Guided by a U.S. Court of Appeals decision, America's military forces have begun reviewing their policy of forbidding homosexuals to join their ranks. The ruling requires the Defense Department to accept homosexuals unless the military offers "some reasoned explanation" for exclusion. The victorious defendant said this is "the first time a federal court has recognized the existence of homosexuals in the military" (→ 8/14/79).

DeNiro in Deer Hunter recreates Vietnam

Like a bruise that blackens long after the wound, artistic reaction to the Vietnam War has been slow in coming. It is surfacing now, in films both current and under production. "The Deer Hunter" and "Coming Home" premiered this year; Francis Coppola's "Apocalypse Now" is still in the making.

"The Deer Hunter" traces the lives of small-town Pennsylvania youths before and after Vietnam. Robert DeNiro, having tackled tough roles in "Bang the Drum Slowly," "The Godfather Part II" and "Taxi Driver," puts in a steely performance as a vet who comes to terms with the war. A violent, graphic picture, it is Michael Cimino's first major directing job.

Hal Ashby's "Coming Home" is a bit more subdued, centering on a paraplegic veteran (Jon Voight) and the woman who comes to care for him (Jane Fonda).

Man is not guilty of raping his wife

Dec 27. John Rideout was found not guilty of raping his wife. An Oregon jury handed down the decision after a three-hour deliberation. "I don't think justice was done," said John's wife, Greta.

Greta Rideout charged her husband with beating her and forcing her to have sex. Rideout admitted he beat his wife, but said the sex had been voluntary. The jury sided with him, unsure whom to believe.

The case was the first one in which a wife charged a husband with rape while still living under the same roof. A defense lawyer said these kinds of conflicts do not usually end up in court but "in one of two ways—homicide or suicide."

Hayes out; punched another team's man

Dec 31. Ohio State's legendary football coach, Woody Hayes, lost his composure during Friday's Gator Bowl game and now he has lost his job. Hayes was fired after he punched Clemson University player Charlie Bauman. Bauman intercepted a pass in the last minute of play in the 17-15 Clemson win and was pushed out of bounds near the Ohio State bench when Hayes went after him, fists flying. Despite his impressive 205-61-10 won-lost-tie record at Ohio State, Hayes was quickly dismissed. College President Harold Enarson said, "There is not a university in this country that would permit a coach to physically assault a college athlete."

1979

JANUARY

Su	Mo	Tu	We	Th	Fr	Sa
	1	2	3	4	5	6
7	8	9	10	11	12	13
14	15	16	17	18	19	20
21	22	23	24	25	26	27
28	29	30	31			

1. New York: Doctors reattach leg of 11-year-old girl run over by train.

1. Pasadena: U.S.C. beats Michigan 17-10 in Rose Bowl.

1. Peking: U.S., China formally resume relations (→ 28).

4. Ohio: State official approves out-of-court settlement of $675,000 in Kent State killings (→ 9/23/81).

5. U.S. govt. sues nine of nation's largest oil companies for overpricing in last five years (→ 5/5).

6. Iran back under civilian rule as Bakhitar takes office; Shah says he will "take a rest" (→ 8).

8. U.S. in reversal advises shah to get out of Iran (→ 13).

11. U.S.: Surgeon general's report leaves no doubt smoking causes lung cancer (→ 5/23/84).

13. U.S.: 23 resign from Natl. Advisory Committee of Women to protest Carter's dismissal of Bella Abzug (→ 5/21/80).

13. Paris: Khomeini says he has formed council to assume duties of shah of Iran (→ 16).

15. N.Y.: Soviets veto U.N. call for withdrawal of Vietnamese troops from Cambodia (→ 5/14).

16. Shah leaves Iran (→ 19).

18. Central African Republic: Troops crush riot against required school uniforms (→ 4/17).

19. Lebanon: Israelis kill 40 Palestinians in raid (→ 22).

19. Tehran: Million rally for Khomeini in streets (→ 30).

22. Beirut: Abu Hassan, alleged planner of 1972 Munich raid, killed by bomb (→ 3/20).

25. Santo Domingo: Pope arrives at site of first Christian mass said in New World (→ 28).

28. Washington: Deng Hsiao-ping, Chinese deputy premier, arrives in U.S. (→ 31).

29. Carter commutes sentence of Patty Hearst (→ 2/1).

30. Rhodesia: Whites vote to accept limited rule by black majority (→ 2/20).

DEATH

5. Charles Mingus, American innovator in jazz (*4/22/1922).

Shah flees insurgent Iran

The Shah, ousted after 37 years.

Jan 30. The Shah of Iran has been forced to leave the country, and the Ayatollah Khomeini is coming back. The shah had no choice, and the ayatollah rejected any restrictions on his return.

The shah departed on the 16th after an emotional farewell at Mehrabad Airport. "I hope the government will be able to make amends for the past and also succeed in laying the foundation for the future," the shah said. His eyes welled with tears as two members of his imperial guard knelt to kiss his shoes. The shah called his departure a vacation, but many doubt that he will ever return to the country that he ruled for 37 years.

In Tehran today, Prime Minister Shahpur Bakhtiar approved the return of Khomeini from his exile in Paris. Bakhtiar was forced to drop his insistence that the ayatollah not form a rival, revolutionary government. "We will have to wait until he is here and hope we can succeed then," a spokesman said (→ 2/1).

United States and China resume relations

Jan 31. President Carter and the Deputy Prime Minister of China, Deng Hsiao-ping, today signed agreements to provide a framework for a new era in Chinese-American relations. The signing of the two scientific and cultural exchange accords took place in the East Room of the White House.

While hailing the agreements as providing "a new and irreversible course in relations between the two nations," President Carter noted that the two sides do not always concur on broad, global problems. He said heads of the two countries have agreed to consult regularly on matters of "common global interest." Resumption of formal diplomatic relations between China and the U.S. ends nearly three decades of estrangement that followed the setting up of a new regime in Taiwan by Chiang Kai-shek (→ 3/1).

Jan 21. Terry Bradshaw may be on the ground, but the Super Bowl MVP passed for 318 yards and four TDs in the Steelers' 35-31 win over Dallas.

Vietnam forces take over in Cambodia

Jan 7. Vietnamese troops, supported by Cambodian insurgents, have seized control of Phnom Penh, the capital city, toppling the pro-Chinese government of Prime Minister Lon Nol.

Within a day after capture of the Cambodian capital, Hanoi Radio announced that a group calling itself the Cambodian National United Front for National Salvation had set up a council headed by Heng Samrin to govern the country. Vietnamese forces, however, controlled only the southeastern section of the country, and it appeared Cambodia might be headed for a long siege of guerrilla warfare. Analysts believed that Hanoi's objective, in launching the fight in late 1977, was to topple the government of Pol Pot, who with Communist aid seized power in 1975 from a right-wing government supported by the United States. Lon Nol, however, then aligned himself with China (→ 15).

Vietnamese tanks in Phnom Penh.

Nelson Rockefeller meets unusual end

Jan 26. Former Vice President Nelson A. Rockefeller, 70, died last night after suffering a heart attack. The four-time Governor of New York and three-time presidential hopeful had returned to his Rockefeller Center office after dinner with his wife, Happy, and their sons, Nelson Jr., 15, and Mark, 12. He was stricken at 10:15 p.m., and there were reports he died in the arms of a young, female friend while supposedly working on a book on art, one of his favorite subjects. As governor, he expanded state services in education, transportation, housing and environmental control. ▷

Guadeloupe summit covers Soviet issues

Schmidt, Carter, Giscard d'Estaing and Callaghan in Guadeloupe.

Jan 5. Extraordinary security was put into effect in Guadeloupe as Western leaders arrived for a summit meeting today. President Carter, Britain's Prime Minister James Callaghan and West Germany's Chancellor Helmut Schmidt were all greeted by Valery Giscard d'Estaing, the President of France. The goal of the meeting is to devise a common strategy to be used against the Soviet Union. It is possible the leaders will agree to improve relations with China. The summit is expected to be an unusually intimate affair because each leader is accompanied by a small delegation. Most of the discussions are expected to take place in the Hamak Hotel in the town of Saint Francois.

Conrad Hilton, hotel magnate, checks out

Jan 4. Conrad Hilton, 91, "King of Innkeepers," died last night at St. John's Hospital in Santa Monica, Calif., after a three-day battle with pneumonia. Born in New Mexico, where his father rented out rooms, he bought his first hotel in Cisco, Texas, in 1919. He ran his international hotel chain until just a few weeks ago. One of his three wives was Zsa Zsa Gabor, and he was Elizabeth Taylor's father-in-law.

Pope John Paul II pays holy visit to Mexico

John Paul II speaks in Mexico.

Jan 28. Pope John Paul II is convinced that the future of the Roman Catholic Church lies in Latin America. Aware that one-half of all Catholics will be living in the region by the year 2000, John Paul has chosen Mexico for his first trip overseas since ascending to the papacy. The pontiff arrived Friday to a very warm welcome. In Notre Dame de Guadalupe, Guadalajara and Oaxaca, John Paul has been greeted by pageantry and festive dancing. Today, in Puebla, he attends the opening of a large meeting of Bishops from South America. Some 900 prelates have arrived to participate in the conference (→ 6/2).

1979

FEBRUARY

Su	Mo	Tu	We	Th	Fr	Sa
				1	2	3
4	5	6	7	8	9	10
11	12	13	14	15	16	17
18	19	20	21	22	23	24
25	26	27	28			

1. Tehran: Millions greet Khomeini on arrival in Iran (→ 8).

4. The Hague: Beth Heiden joins brother Eric as world champion speed skater.

5. Washington: 3,000 farmers clog traffic with tractors to demand higher price supports (→ 3/31/80).

8. Tehran: Over a million march to demand resignation of Premier Shahpur Bakhtiar (→ 11).

9. Brezhnev, Pope plead for life of Pakistani ex-Premier Bhutto, sentenced to die by Zia (→ 4/5).

10. N.Y.: Met announces first major theft in 110-year history, $150,000 Greek marble head.

11. Iran: Bakhtiar resigns as military withdraws support (→ 14).

14. Afghanistan: U.S. Ambassador Adolph Dubs shot to death (→ 9/16).

14. Washington: Two leaders of Cuban exile group convicted of murdering Chilean dissident Orlando Letelier.

14. Tehran: Armed guerrillas attack U.S. Embassy (→ 16).

15. New York: Jim Rafferty wins second race up stairs of Empire State Building.

16. Calif.: Eamonn Coghlan sets mark in indoor mile at 3:52.6.

16. Tehran: Four of shah's generals executed (→ 26).

17. Chinese troops and planes strike in force on Vietnamese border (→ 27).

18. Richard Petty wins Daytona 500 as leaders crash on last lap.

20. Rhodesia: Rebels attack Salisbury airport for first time (→ 4/13).

24. Border war breaks out between North and South Yemen (→ 3/7).

24. Carter names Gen. Bernard Rogers commander of U.S. forces in Europe.

DEATHS

2. Sid Vicious, British punk rocker.

8. Dennis Gabor, British inventor of holography (*6/5/1900).

13. Jean Renoir, French film director (*9/15/1894).

China and Vietnam at war on border

Feb 27. Chinese troops, in what Peking described as a counterattack, struck at Vietnamese positions along the 480-mile-long border. Hsinhua, the Chinese news agency, said China did "not want a single inch of Vietnamese territory" and attacked only after Vietnam had "ignored China's repeated warnings" and had "continually sent armed forces to encroach on Chinese territory and attack Chinese frontier guards and inhabitants."

Aside from border incidents, the Chinese invasion appeared designed to serve a warning on Hanoi, which has been taking an increasingly anti-Chinese stance as it consolidates its control over Southeast Asia. The Chinese attack came six weeks after Vietnam toppled the Lon Nol government in Cambodia that had been supported by China and 15 weeks after Vietnam signed a treaty of cooperation with the Soviet Union.

Vietnamese artillery near China.

Chinese Deputy Prime Minister Deng Hsiao-ping told American reporters in Peking that China cannot "tolerate the Cubans of the Orient to go swashbuckling unchecked in Laos, Cambodia or even China's border areas."

The Soviet Union, stating that it would honor its treaty obligations to Vietnam, warned Peking to stop the invasion "before it is too late." The United States urged China to withdraw its troops and advised the Soviet Union not to retaliate against China (→ 3/23).

Khomeini in Iran, greeted by millions

Shiites celebrate Khomeini's return.

Feb 26. The triumphant return of the Ayatollah Khomeini to Iran has unleashed a revolutionary fervor that was checked for years by the forces of the departed Shah. It has also posed a direct threat to the interests of the United States. Millions of Shiite Moslems and other followers of the ayatollah jammed the streets of Tehran for his long motorcade at the beginning of the month. Within a matter of days, the new government put in place by the shah before he left was toppled. The United States Embassy was attacked. And scores of Iranians who backed the Pahlevi regime were lined up and shot to death.

Every day, Iranian newspapers printed the names of the officials executed. Many of them were officers in the shah's army and secret police, Savak. It is also known, however, that certain members of Savak have been tapped by Khomeini forces to provide their unique torture services in the new regime.

The ayatollah returned to Tehran from Paris on the 1st; 15 years of exile had come to an end. Exultant banners greeted Khomeini at the airport. "The flag of the revolution is in your hands," one banner proclaimed. "You are our religious, political, military, economic and social leader."

Khomeini, dressed in a turban and robe, told supporters he would act quickly to cleanse Iran of undesirable elements. "Our final victory will come when all foreigners are out of the country," he said. "I beg God to cut off the hands of all evil foreigners and all their helpers."

Government officials were conspicuously absent from the airport ceremonies, which were watched by millions on television. At one point, the transmission was cut by the army and replaced by a picture of the shah. As the ayatollah was driven to the center of Tehran, thousands of soldiers patrolled the streets. Prophetically, perhaps, some army units had carnations tucked in the muzzles of their guns.

Prime Minister Shahpur Bakhtiar had warned the ayatollah that he would use "strong action" to prevent the establishment of an Islamic republic. "I will not allow the country to be governed by any force other than legitimate authority," Bakhtiar said. But events quickly passed out of his control. In less than a week, a top official admitted the government was not working. "Ministers are blocked from doing their jobs," he said. "The military is so divided that I don't think it can be counted on any longer." Large rallies were held across Iran in support of Khomeini. A few days later, opposition leader Mehdi Bazargan announced the formation of a new Cabinet that had the support of the ayatollah. Bakhtiar disappeared underground. Reports circulated that he was under arrest. "A great Satan has fled in ignominy," Khomeini's backers proclaimed.

On the 14th, an armed band attacked the United States Embassy.

The Ayatollah returns after 16 years.

Two guerrillas were shot to death. Two Marines were wounded. Ambassador William Sullivan and 100 staffers were trapped inside for two hours. "They attacked from three sides," Sullivan said. "They shot up my home, my office and the chancery." American diplomats credited Sullivan for bringing the incident to a close without further bloodshed. Sullivan thanked officials in the ayatollah's regime for persuading the attackers to withdraw.

At the State Department, plans were announced to evacuate thousands of Americans from Tehran. A top official rejected the use of force. "We just have to wheedle them out the best we can," he said (→ 3/10).

Moslem crowds pack the streets of Tehran to welcome their spiritual leader.

Sentence cut, Patty Hearst quits prison

Feb 1. A beaming Patricia Hearst strolled out of a California prison this morning, waving a white piece of paper with a golden seal. The document was a clemency order signed by the President, releasing her from a seven-year prison sentence after serving 22 months. Greeting reporters and family members, Miss Hearst savored the air of freedom—something she has not really tasted in nearly five years.

Miss Hearst was kidnapped by the radical Symbionese Liberation Army on Feb. 4, 1974. A hostage turned accomplice, she assisted in a bank holdup and in a few lesser crimes. She now plans to marry her bodyguard, Bernard Shaw, in April.

Washington breaks ties with Nicaragua

Feb 8. The United States cut off military ties with Nicaragua after President Anastasio Somoza Debayle rejected a three-nation proposal for ending the civil strife in his country. The Carter administration had been warning General Somoza for months that failure to cooperate in the mediation effort could lead to the severing of American ties with the Nicaraguan government. The United States, the Dominican Republic and Guatemala had proposed a plebiscite on whether Somoza should leave office (→ 6/1).

President disavows Billy's vulgar words

Feb 25. President Carter has disassociated himself from rude and injudicious remarks made recently by his brother, Billy Carter. At a reception given by the Libyan delegation to the United Nations, Billy was asked about Jewish criticism of his friendship with the Libyans. He replied, "They can kiss my ass as far as I'm concerned." The president was quoted as telling a close associate that "Billy doesn't tell me what to say and I don't tell him what to say . . . those comments don't reflect my feelings. I want to be disassociated from them" (→ 4/23).

1979

MARCH

Su	Mo	Tu	We	Th	Fr	Sa
				1	2	3
4	5	6	7	8	9	10
11	12	13	14	15	16	17
18	19	20	21	22	23	24
25	26	27	28	29	30	31

1. China agrees to pay 41 cents on the dollar for U.S. assets seized in 1949 (→ 1/24/80).

4. Uganda: Invading Tanzanian forces near capital (→ 29).

7. U.S. sends arms and advisers to North Yemen (→ 1/24/86).

9. Milwaukee: U.S. judge bars use of article on how to build H-bomb (→ 4/6).

9. N.H.: Hundreds protest delivery of reactor at Seabrook nuclear power plant (→ 13).

11. Washington: Andres Segovia performs at White House.

13. Washington: NRC orders five atomic plants shut (→ 28).

13. Grenada: Socialist Maurice Bishop seizes power in coup (→ 2/24/82).

18. N.J.: 20 tons hashish seized in largest bust in U.S. history.

20. Israel: Begin bars Palestinian state in occupied area (→ 26).

21. Washington: Report Mary Leakey has discovered world's oldest known biped footprints.

22. The Hague: British Ambassador to Netherlands Richard Sykes is slain.

23. Nevada: Larry Holmes retains title with TKO of Osvaldo Ocasio in seventh round.

26. Utah: Michigan State beats Indiana State for NCAA basketball title.

26. Washington: Begin and Sadat sign formal treaty, ending 30 years of war (→ 27).

27. Baghdad: Arab League agrees on steps against Egypt for signing of peace treaty (→ 31).

28. Britain: Callaghan Labor government ousted by vote in Commons (→ 5/3).

28. Pennsylvania: Accident at Three Mile Island reactor releases radiation (→ 30).

30. Iran: Referendum establishes 98% support for Islamic Republic (→ 4/7).

30. Washington: NRC reports danger of meltdown at Three Mile Island (→ 31).

DEATH

16. Jean Monnet, French architect of EEC (*11/9/1888).

Egypt, Israel sign treaty

Sadat, Carter and Begin enjoy a moment of triumph at the White House.

March 31. Egypt's President Anwar el-Sadat has made history by signing a peace treaty with Israel. He has also managed to isolate himself in the Arab world. The foreign ministers of 18 Arab countries moved in Baghdad today to cut diplomatic and economic relations with Cairo. Their agreement was also approved by the Palestine Liberation Organization. It calls for the immediate recall of ambassadors from Egypt, a complete termination of diplomatic relations within a month, an end to all financial aid and the imposition of economic sanctions. Egypt receives a billion dollars a year from other Arab countries, mainly Saudi Arabia.

Sadat indicated he was aware of the risks when he signed the peace agreement with Israel's Prime Minister Begin at the White House on Monday. Sadat also recognized its historic importance, and he praised President Carter for his role in masterminding the accord. "Without any exaggeration, what he did constitutes one of the greatest achievements of our time," Sadat said.

Carter, who signed the agreement as a witness, said it proved that "peace has come." Carter also said, "We have won, at last, the first step of peace, a first step on a long and difficult road."

Just how long and difficult it will be was clear in the remarks of Prime Minister Begin. He said the agreement meant "no more war, no more bloodshed, no more bereavement." But Begin also indicated he will resist a key demand from Sadat to relinquish control over eastern Jerusalem. The Israeli prime minister spoke emotionally of the day "when Jerusalem became one city and our brave, perhaps most hardened soldiers, the parachutists, embraced with tears and kissed the ancient stones of the remnants of the wall destined to protect the chosen place of God's glory."

The Israeli-Egyptian agreement took months to negotiate, and diplomats worked past midnight on the day it was signed to finalize the language. The last stumbling block was the timetable for Israeli withdrawal from oil fields in the Sinai. Sadat and Begin agreed they would be returned to Egypt seven months after the treaty is ratified (→ 4/2).

Sadats and Carters at Pyramids.

Chinese forces will evacuate Vietnam

March 23. China has announced it will withdraw its troops from Vietnam. A Chinese official said Peking had "attained the goals set" in the 17-day border conflict. The Vietnamese had refused to negotiate with China on peace terms until the superpower pulled its military. Peace talks are still not certain, as a Vietnamese report said the Chinese offer to withdraw only veils a planned military attack. Vietnamese-supported insurgents ousted the Chinese-backed Pol Pot government in Cambodia. And today, a friendship treaty between Laos and Cambodia was signed, completing the formation of an Indochinese union headed by Vietnam (→ 3/2).

Some Iran women protest new curbs

March 10. "In the dawn of freedom, there is absence of freedom!" These words were chorused by Iranian women today, protesting the restrictions, actual and anticipated, that Islamic rule will bring them. About 15,000 women marched on Tehran's Palace of Justice, lines of sympathetic men flanking them to fend off angry onlookers, some of whom were cursing women wearing the traditional chador, or veil. The protesters demanded the right to wear attire of their choosing and a guarantee of their legal rights and liberties (→ 30).

Treat Williams breaks up a society party in Milos Forman's "Hair," reviving some of the joyous irreverence of the sixties. Choreography by Twyla Tharp.

3-Mile Island atomic leak

Skyline of danger: Three Mile Isle.

March 31. The worst nuclear accident in United States history is being brought under control, federal officials said today, but they added the possibility of a core meltdown at the Three Mile Island nuclear generating plant in Pennsylvania could still not be ruled out. The plant began emitting radiation two days ago when problems with its cooling system exposed part of the core, causing a shutdown.

Governor Dick Thornburgh has advised the evacuation of pregnant women and children from a five-mile radius around the plant, but federal officials say a general evacuation probably will not be necessary. The major problem now is a bubble of hydrogen and other gases that has formed within the reactor containment vessel, said Harold Denton, the federal official overseeing safety measures. If the hydrogen exploded, it could breach the plant's containment and release large amounts of radioactivity. But Denton said there is "no imminent problem of explosion."

A core meltdown that could breach the reactor containment is even more unlikely, Denton said. Water is being infused into the reactor to cool the core, and gases are being vented slowly from the containment vessel.

Investigators have not determined what caused the accident, but a preliminary study indicates it was a combination of equipment failure and human error involving the cooling system that is supposed to keep the plant's radioactive core constantly submerged in water. Some valves failed to function properly and others were mistakenly opened by technicians, exposing part of the core and causing uranium containing fuel rods to melt.

Only a small amount of radiation was released outside the plant, federal officials say, but there is a substantial contamination problem inside the reactor building because of the partial meltdown. It will take several more days to bring temperatures inside the reactor core down to safe levels, Denton said.

President Carter has announced plans to visit the scene for a personal inspection. Opponents of nuclear power will hold a protest rally tomorrow at the state Capitol (→ 4/6).

Idi Amin Dada, Uganda ruler, driven out

March 29. Idi Amin Dada, the President of Uganda, charged with widespread atrocities, has fled the capital city and is reportedly headed north with what is left of the Ugandan army. Ugandan rebels and Tanzanian troops have held Kampala under siege for three days and are ready to take it over. Anti-Amin forces already control Entebbe and its airport. The Uganda National Liberation Front has said its forces will take no prisoners, and there is speculation they have postponed capturing Kampala to allow remaining Amin troops to escape, avoiding a slaughter (→ 4/13).

Idi Amin, butcher of Kampala.

Soviet calls China most serious threat

March 2. In a wide-ranging speech on domestic and foreign policy, Soviet leader Leonid I. Brezhnev branded the People's Republic of China "the most serious threat to peace in the whole world." The allegation stems from China's February 17 invasion of Vietnam, which Brezhnev called an "unprecedentedly brazen bandit attack" against the Socialist Republic of Vietnam. The Soviet leader stopped short of pledging military support to Vietnam and he adopted a conciliatory tone toward the United States, describing the strategic arms treaty as virtually completed. Both Hanoi and Peking have recently shown a willingness to open talks about the border raid (→ 5/2).

Lee Marvin's former companion sues him

Latest front in the battle of sexes.

March 10. Actor Lee Marvin, 55, has been sued for "palimony" by Michelle Triola Marvin, 46, who took his last name but never was married to him. She contends she abandoned a promising singing career to serve as his cook, companion and confidante, entitling her to up to half of the $3.6 million he made while they were living together from 1964-70. Mel Torme, Gene Kelly and other celebrities are testifying on behalf of Marvin, an Academy Award winner in 1965 for "Cat Ballou." Many follow the trial since similar suits have been filed by other non-married companions (→ 4/18).

Photos show thin ring around Jupiter

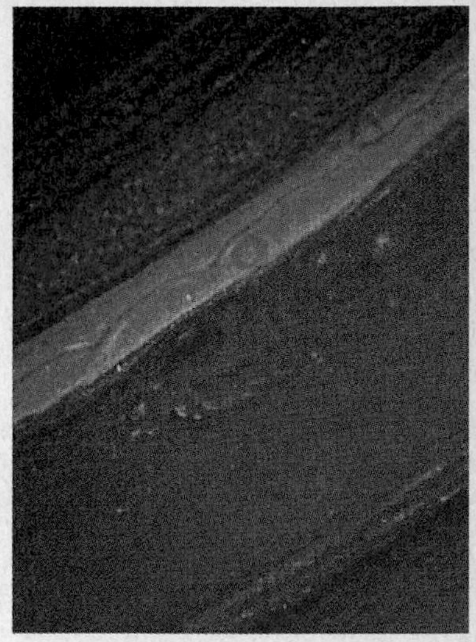

Voyager 1 photo of Jupiter.

March 7. The Voyager 1 spacecraft has detected a faint ring of rocky debris around the planet Jupiter, scientists at the Jet Propulsion Laboratory in Pasadena, California, announced today. The discovery was the first major surprise of the Voyager 1 mission to Jupiter. In an 11-minute exposure photograph made 16 hours before the spacecraft's closest approach to Jupiter, the ring shows up as a fuzzy white streak. It is only 18 miles thick and more than 5,000 miles wide, scientists estimate. Jupiter thus joins Saturn and Uranus on the list of ringed planets. Astronomers have known about Saturn's rings since 1610. Uranus' rings were detected in 1977 (→ 7/11).

Halston collection for spring.

1979

APRIL

Su	Mo	Tu	We	Th	Fr	Sa
1	2	3	4	5	6	7
8	9	10	11	12	13	14
15	16	17	18	19	20	21
22	23	24	25	26	27	28
29	30					

1. Staten Island: 700 gravestones vandalized at Jewish cemetery.

2. Cairo: Begin becomes first Israeli prime minister to visit Egypt (→ 7).

2. Malaysia: 100 Vietnamese refugees drown as boat capsizes (→ 7/20).

3. Chicago: Jane Byrne elected mayor.

4. Peking: Four arrested putting up posters critical of Chinese bureaucracy (→ 12/6).

6. U.S. says eight reactors by Babcock & Wilcox, makers of Three Mile Island, may keep operating (→ 10).

6. U.S. cuts aid to Pakistan over evidence of nuclear arms plan (→ 19).

7. Tehran: Ex-Premier Amir Abbas Hoveida executed (→ 5/26).

7. Egypt to block attempts to move Arab League headquarters from Cairo to Tunis (→ 26).

12. South Africa ousts three U.S. Embassy aides as spies (→ 6/4).

13. Zambia: Rhodesian raiders attack in attempt to kill guerrilla leader Joshua Nkomo (→ 24).

15. Augusta, Ga.: Fuzzy Zoeller wins Masters golf title.

16. N.Y.: Sam Shepard wins Pulitzer for "Buried Child."

17. Bangui: Bokassa orders slaughter of 100 schoolchildren (→ 9/22).

18. Calif.: Lee Marvin to pay $104,000 in palimony suit.

19. Washington: Report indicates Ike told AEC to keep public confused on atom testing and fallout (→ 6/7).

20. Cairo: Sadat wins landslide vote for peace treaty (→ 9/5/81).

23. Calif.: Billy Carter vows not to drink again (→ 7/14/80).

25. NRC recommends closing all nine Babcock & Wilcox reactors until safety assured (→ 5/6).

26. Lebanon: Israel and PLO agree to U.N. truce (→ 6/24).

27. U.S. frees two spies for five dissidents jailed by Soviets (→ 29).

29. N.Y.: 100,000 march in rally for Soviet Jews (→ 1/22/80).

Pakistan's former Premier Bhutto hanged

Bhutto, martyred in Pakistan.

April 5. Pakistani newspapers reported that the once suave and urbane Ali Bhutto, formerly Prime Minister, was led to the gallows yesterday as fellow inmates on death row chanted a traditional dirge. Bhutto was convicted last year of trying to murder a political opponent in 1974. President Zia, the General who toppled Bhutto in 1974, had wavered before a flood of clemency petitions from world leaders including President Carter, Leonid I. Brezhnev and Pope John Paul II. The hanging of the popular Bhutto led to violent demonstrations amid shouts of "Zia is a dog!" (→ 9/22).

Tanzania installs new Uganda regime

April 13. Yusufu K. Lule was sworn in as head of Uganda's provisional government today. In his speech, he acknowledged the role played by Tanzania in overthrowing Idi Amin. In addition to providing military support to anti-Amin forces, Tanzania convinced the factious Ugandan exile groups to unite. Tanzania's President, Julius K. Nyerere, is a close friend of former Ugandan President Milton Obote, who was overthrown by Amin in 1971. Lule was named President because he was acceptable to all exile groups (→ 7/28/85).

Muzorewa's party wins Rhodesian election

April 24. Bishop Abel Muzorewa's United African National Council will control 51 seats out of 100 in Rhodesia's first biracial Parliament. Muzorewa, a nationalist educated in the United States, will become the country's first black Prime Minister. He interpreted his victory as a rejection of the Patriotic Front, which boycotted the elections and has promised to overthrow the new government.

Rhodesia's first black P.M.

Rev. Ndabaningi Sithole, whose party only won 12 seats, is contesting the election. Although Sithole's accusations of election-tampering are not supported by other parties, they could make it harder for the new government to win international recognition. The United States and Britain never accepted the internal agreement leading to black majority rule because the guerrilla groups were not included, and because they thought the whites retained too much power in Rhodesia (→ 12/21).

Carter says America needs atomic power

April 10. President Carter today expressed continuing support for nuclear power despite the recent accident at the Three Mile Island power plant in Pennsylvania. "There is no way for us to abandon the nuclear supply of energy in our country in the foreseeable future," said Carter, who added that he would continue to press for faster licensing of nuclear generating plants. But the Director of the federal Nuclear Regulatory Commission told a Senate subcommittee that "we cannot have an acceptable nuclear power program in this country if there is any appreciable risk" of major accidents (→ 25).

2:09.27 is new record for Boston Marathon

Rodgers crosses the line in 2:09:27.

April 16. They call it Heartbreak Hill, a steep grade that has crushed the hopes and aspirations of thousands of runners in the Boston Marathon. Bill Rodgers took the heartbreak out of the hill in 1976 and did it again, this time in record time. With a time of two hours, nine minutes, 27 seconds, he lowered the American record he set four years earlier. Rodgers has almost won permanent possession of the slice of Commonwealth Avenue that contains the hill and that would be appropriate, since he lives nearby. Japan's Toshihiko Seko finished second in 2:10.12, also considered good time in view of the rain.

Woody Allen and Diane Keaton take a walk in "Manhattan."

1979

MAY

Su	Mo	Tu	We	Th	Fr	Sa
		1	2	3	4	5
6	7	8	9	10	11	12
13	14	15	16	17	18	19
20	21	22	23	24	25	26
27	28	29	30	31		

1. Washington: George Bush joins presidential race (→ 11/13).

2. Peking says losses in Vietnam were 20,000 killed and wounded (→ 6/15).

5. Kentucky Derby won by Spectacular Bid, jockey R. Franklin in the saddle.

5. Carter orders gradual end to oil price controls (→ 6/1).

6. Washington: 65,000 march in rally to halt nuclear plants (→ 18).

8. San Salvador: Police open fire on demonstrators; 24 slain (→ 10).

10. San Salvador: 20,000 march in funeral procession for slain protesters.→

14. New York: U.N. calls Cambodian food shortage tragic (→ 8/3).

21. S.F.: Dan White found guilty of murdering Mayor Moscone and Harvey Milk (→ 22).

21. Montreal: Canadiens over N.Y. Rangers 4-1 in Stanley Cup.

22. S.F.: 140 injured in violence following murder conviction of ex-Supervisor Dan White.

22. Canada: Conservatives win plurality in Commons; Trudeau bows to Joe Clark (→ 2/18/80).

22. Leningrad: Fans mob Elton John at concert.

23. Atlanta: Ex-Carter aide Bert Lance and three others indicted in bank conspiracy (→ 4/30/80).

23. Bonn: Ex-Nazi Karl Carstens elected West German president (→ 10/5/80).

25. Chicago: 272 die in worst U.S. air accident as DC-10 crashes just after takeoff (→ 29).

27. Rick Mears wins Indy 500 at average of 159 mph.

28. Greece to be admitted to EEC in 1981 (→ 1/1/81).

DEATHS

11. Barbara Hutton, Woolworth heiress (*11/14/1912).

16. A. Philip Randolph, black American labor leader (*4/15/1889).

29. Mary Pickford, American film actress (*4/8/1893).

Mrs. Thatcher first British woman Premier

May 3. Margaret Thatcher became Europe's first woman Prime Minister as she and her Conservative Party won a decisive victory today in Great Britain's general election. An Oxford-educated chemist and lawyer, Mrs. Thatcher first entered Parliament in 1959. In campaigning for prime minister, she promised a government that "would stop trying to step in and make decisions for you that you should be free to take on your own." A dedicated Tory, she has frequently said "free choice is ultimately what life is about," and she promised to cut personal income taxes and restrain unions (→ 11/10/80).

A woman of steely confidence.

Silkwood estate gets $10.5m award

May 18. A federal jury in Oklahoma City today awarded $10.5 million in damages to the estate of Karen Silkwood, a 28-year-old laboratory technician, for radiation contamination she suffered in 1974 at a Kerr-McGee plutonium plant. The verdict was a setback for the nuclear industry because it made companies responsible for the escape of low-level radiation. Kerr-McGee lawyers said they would appeal the verdict. Silkwood died in a car crash in 1974 on her way to talk to a reporter about safety violations at the plant (→ 6/3).

Troops kill 24 at Salvador cathedral

May 10. Some 20,000 mourners walked through the streets of San Salvador today in the funeral procession for 17 of the 24 persons killed by police and soldiers two days ago when they opened fire on a crowd of 300 peacefully demonstrating outside the Metropolitan Cathedral. The group had been showing its support for the members of the anti-government Popular Revolutionary Bloc, who occupied the cathedral and also the Costa Rican and French Embassies, where they held six hostages. Mentioning previous massacres, a woman said "this is the first time they've fired on a cathedral" (→ 9/25).

Khomeini blames U.S. for attempt on aide

To Moslem fundamentalists, decades of American influence were injurious.

May 26. Iran's Ayatollah Khomeini issued a blistering attack against the United States today and charged the Carter administration with trying to kill a top member of his government. The State Department rejected the charge. Ayatollah Hashemi Rafsanjani, believed to be a member of the ruling Revolutionary Council, was shot and wounded at his home last night. In a radio address, Khomeini blamed "America and other superpowers" for the attack. The ayatollah said Washington "must know that Iran's revolution is alive. Such idiotic attempts cannot kill our revolution." A State Department spokesman replied, "It is totally false to link the United States in any way with this reprehensible act."

In Tehran, no arrests have been reported in the attack on Rafsanjani. Newspaper reports say that rightists have claimed reponsibility for the shooting. Two other Khomeini aides have been killed in the past six weeks.

In addition to criticizing the United States, Khomeini has tried to remove Western influences from Iran. He has ordered women to wear veils and long robes in public. Women who ignored the edict were stoned and called whores by revolutionary guards. In Chiraz, a woman accused of adultery was beaten with sticks. Men and women have been prohibited from playing tennis together. And thousands of dollars worth of alcohol was destroyed by guards at Tehran hotels (→ 7/5).

273 die in worst U.S. air disaster

May 29. The government today ordered the grounding of all DC-10 airliners because it said a flaw that caused the death of 273 persons in a crash four days ago appears to be widespread. Investigators said the crash, the worst disaster in United States aviation history, occurred because an engine ripped from the wing of an American Airlines DC-10 as it was taking off from O'Hare International Airport in Chicago. Inspections have found weaknesses in many DC-10 engine mounts, making the grounding necessary, officials said (→ 6/6).

1979

JUNE

Su	Mo	Tu	We	Th	Fr	Sa
					1	2
3	4	5	6	7	8	9
10	11	12	13	14	15	16
17	18	19	20	21	22	23
24	25	26	27	28	29	30

1. Carter denounces Mobil for opposing decontrol of oil prices (→ 28).

1. Nicaragua: Sandinistas open long-awaited offensive (→ 6).

2. Washington: Assassination inquiry final report backs theory of plot on JFK.

2. Warsaw: Pope John Paul II welcomed to homeland (→ 10).

3. New York: 15,000 protest at Shoreham nuclear plant; 600 arrested (→ 10/14).

3. Paris: Borg beats Victor Pecci in French Open final.

4. South Africa: President Vorster resigns (→ 1/25/80).

6. U.S. halts all DC-10 flights pending safety inquiry (→ 7/13).

6. Managua: Somoza declares state of siege (→ 17).

7. Carter approves MX missile program (→ 18).

9. Carter's approval rating hits all-time low of 30% in poll.

12. American Bryan Allen pedals plane across English Channel.

15. Malaysia to put 70,000 Vietnamese refugees back out to sea (→ 7/20).

16. Calif.: Evelyn Ashford breaks 11-second barrier in women's 100-meter dash.

17. Managua: Rebels name five to form provisional govt. (→ 23).

19. New York: Ed "Too Tall" Jones to quit football and take up boxing.

22. New York: Larry Holmes KO's Mike Weaver in 12th round to keep title.

23. Washington: OAS calls for ouster of Somoza (→ 29).

24. Lebanon: Israel bombs eight towns after blast in Tel Aviv (→ 27).

26. Newark: Ali announces retirement (→ 10/2/80).

27. U.S. Supreme Court upholds affirmative action (→ 8/9).

27. Lebanon: Israeli, Syrian planes clash first time in five years (→ 7/25).

28. Geneva: OPEC raises oil prices 16%, now up 50% in last year (→ 7/15).

Pope says mass for million in native Poland

Polish Catholics welcome the Pope.

June 10. Pope John Paul II ended his unprecedented nine-day trip to his native Poland today with a mass attended by over one million people. It was the first pontifical visit ever to a Communist country, which is officially atheist.

The political tone of the pope's speeches was muted in today's sermon, in which John Paul exhorted the Polish people to be "strong with the strength which comes from faith." Today's mass commemorated Poland's patron saint, St. Stanislaus. Because the government refused to allow the pope to visit on the saint's actual anniversary, the Polish Catholic Church officially delayed the feast until the pope arrived (→ 9/29).

Brezhnev, Carter sign SALT II pact

East and West, a shaky love affair.

June 18. President Carter and Soviet leader Leonid Brezhnev exchanged American-style handshakes and Russian-style embraces as they signed a new arms control agreement in Vienna. Carter warned that "a nuclear arms competition without shared rules . . . would be an invitation to disaster."

For the first time, the United States and the Soviet Union are limited to a maximum number of long-range missiles and bombers. The pact does allow them, however, to produce an unlimited number of warheads. Both leaders pledged to improve the pact in the future. First, this accord has to overcome Senate opposition. And Brezhnev, who looked pale in Vienna, has to overcome his illness (→ 9/7).

First elections held for Europe assembly

June 10. Socialists and Social Democrats won the largest number of seats in the first direct elections ever for a European Parliament. They each captured 25% of the vote as elections were held in nine countries. Conservative parties, Communists and liberals trailed behind. The first President of the Parliament is a woman, Simone Veil, formerly Minister of Health in France.

The actual power of the organization in the Common Market will be fairly limited, but it will consult with the Council of Europe on fairly important matters. Many voters in Europe seemed to yawn their way through these elections. In Great Britain, nearly 70% of the eligible electorate did not bother to vote. Absenteeism was 40% in France. By comparison, West Germans streamed to the voting booth.

European Parliament in Strasbourg.

Somoza states he is ready to resign

June 29. General Anastasio Somoza Debayle offered yesterday to resign as President of Nicaragua, but rebel leaders rejected the proposal today. They also accused the United States of meddling in Nicaragua's internal affairs. Somoza has insisted that the National Guard and the Liberal Party be given a role in a transitional government. But opposition groups demanded Somoza be replaced once and for all. For the past month, civil war has ripped Nicaragua in half; and Somoza's forces have been on the defensive (→ 7/16).

The Duke is dead: Star of great westerns

June 11. The Duke is dead; long live the memory of John Wayne, who starred in countless westerns and epitomized the strong, silent man. Wayne died in Los Angeles this afternoon at the age of 72. He had suffered from lung and stomach cancer, a bout well-publicized.

Marion Morrison became John Wayne when his mentor, John Ford, renamed him. He rode in B westerns until Ford cast him in the brilliant "Stagecoach" in 1939.

Conservative Wayne invested millions in "The Alamo," in which Mexicans are bad guys, Americans all good. Ironically, all three of the Duke's wives were Hispanic.

The Duke, archetypal western hero.

1979

JULY

Su	Mo	Tu	We	Th	Fr	Sa
1	2	3	4	5	6	7
8	9	10	11	12	13	14
15	16	17	18	19	20	21
22	23	24	25	26	27	28
29	30	31				

3. Bonn: Parliament abolishes statute of limitations on war crimes.

5. Iran nationalizes most remaining heavy industry (→ 9).

7. Wimbledon: Borg over Roscoe Tanner 6-7, 6-1, 3-6, 6-3, 6-4; Navratilova over Evert Lloyd 6-4, 6-4.

11. Australia: Skylab, detroyed by re-entry, sinks in ocean off coast (→ 8/19).

12. Spain: 71 killed, 47 hurt in hotel fire.

12. New York: Mob boss Carmine Galante slain.

13. U.S.: FAA ends grounding of DC-10's.

15. Ankara: PLO gunmen end siege at Egyptian Embassy; release nine hostages.

16. Managua: Somoza retires 100 senior officers (→ 17).

17. Carter's Cabinet and all members of senior staff offer resignations (→ 19).

17. Oslo: Sebastian Coe sets mile record at 3:49.0.

17. Nicaragua: Somoza overthrown; exiled to U.S. (→ 25).

19. Portugal gets first woman president, Maria de Lourdes Pintassilgo (→ 4/25/83).

20. Geneva: Vietnam urges U.S. to accept more refugees as talks open (→ 21).

21. Geneva: Vietnam to try to halt exodus of refugees (→ 28).

22. Bernard Hinault wins Tour de France second time.

23. Iran: Khomeini bans broadcast music, charging it corrupts youth (→ 8/7).

25. Israel turns over another part of Sinai to Egypt (→ 9/24).

28. U.S. to double quota for Indochinese refugees (→ 11/24).

29. Madrid: Blasts at airport and rail stations kill four, injure 113; claimed by Basques (→ 10/25).

DEATHS

10. Arthur Fiedler, conductor of Boston Pops (*12/17/1894).

22. "Two Ton" Tony Galento, heavyweight boxer, knocked down Joe Louis (*3/12/1910).

Somoza ousted; Nicaragua in ruins

July 25. Under pressure from guerrillas at home and the United States abroad, General Anastasio Somoza Debayle resigned as President of Nicaragua and flew into exile. Under a plan worked out by the U.S. between the Somoza government and the Sandinista rebels, Somoza, whose family has ruled Nicaragua since 1933, was to be succeeded in power by a five-man junta controlled by the Sandinistas.

A momentary hitch developed in the plan when Francisco Uryco Malianos, the President of the Chamber of Deputies who was to serve as a transitional President, at first declined to surrender power to the junta.

Somoza, who said he had been driven from power by a Communist conspiracy, left behind a nation devastated by civil war with fighting continuing in several regions of the country. Several thousand persons were believed to have been killed in the fighting in the past two months and 500,000 persons—one fifth of the country's population—have been displaced from their homes.

Within days after the revolutionary junta had taken power, fissures began developing in the unusual coalition of conservative businessmen and Marxist rebels that had opposed the authoritarian Somoza regime. A business group expressed concern that the new government would not fulfill its pledge to encourage private enterprise (→ 8/21).

Jubilant Sandinistas hoist their flag over a government building in Managua.

Somoza, last in 46-year-old dynasty.

Rebel wrecks remnant of regime.

Limit proposed on oil imports by U.S.

July 15. President Carter tonight proposed a six-point package of energy measures, including a limit on oil imports, designed to save 4.5 billion gallons of oil a day by 1990. His televised speech was a response to a 50 percent price increase over the past year by the Organization of Petroleum Exporting Countries. Carter assailed what he called a "crisis of confidence" among Americans as he announced "the most massive peacetime commitment of funds and resources in our nation's history" to reduce American dependence on foreign oil (→ 11/26).

Major shifts made in Carter Cabinet

July 19. A dramatic reshuffling of his Cabinet was announced today by President Carter in Washington. Joseph A. Califano Jr. was forced out as Secretary of Health, Education and Welfare, to be succeeded by Patricia Roberts Harris, now the Secretary of Housing and Urban Development. Treasury Secretary W. Michael Blumenthal resigned, to be replaced by G. William Miller, Chairman of the Federal Reserve Board. And Attorney General Griffin B. Bell resigned. His replacement will be Benjamin R. Civiletti (→ 8/3).

Marcuse, father of New Left, is dead

July 29. Marxist philosopher Herbert Marcuse has died at age 81. The German-American college professor was embraced by 60's radicals for his opposition to the "repressive monolith," American society. He advocated the use of violence, but only as "counterviolence" to an oppressive, non-negotiating force. Many scholars scoffed at his prescriptions for a revolution led by a coalition of urban blacks, radical students and white intellectuals, but few could deny his brilliance. "One Dimensional Man" and "Eros and Civilization" are his best works. ▷

Isle of Man Parliament is 1,000 years old

Millenial celebrations: Norsemen conquered the Isle of Man in the 9th century.

July 5. The Parliament of the Isle of Man has passed only 18 laws this year. It hasn't been hampered by filibusters; there simply aren't many things left to legislate after 1,000 years of operation. Queen Elizabeth II and dignitaries from several democracies attended a ceremony today marking the birthday of the oldest continuous Parliament.

Manxmen, whose island lies nearly equidistant from Scotland, Ireland and England, had arbitrarily designated this their Parliament's millenium. It is not known exactly when a band of Vikings landed on the windswept shores and formed a ruling body they called Tynwald.

Now the Tynwald recognizes the queen as its sovereign, and some islanders petitioned her today, seeking a retention of birching or corporal punishment. The European Court of Human Rights has forbidden the practice, but 75 percent of Manxmen find it jolly good.

Algeria frees Ben Bella, held for 14 years

July 4. This was liberation day in Algeria for Ahmed Ben Bella. The hero of Algerian independence and former President was freed after 14 years of house arrest. The once fervent nationalist is 62, and much of the country seems to have forgotten him.

Ahmed Ben Bella, led 1954 revolt.

Ben Bella was a key leader in Algeria's struggle to win its freedom from France. In 20 years, he rose from a sergeant in the army to president in 1963. Ben Bella drifted toward Moscow, improved ties with Peking and became a spokesman for the non-aligned countries. He continued to criticize France, but still managed to win $200 million in aid from Paris every year.

Houari Boumedienne deposed Ben Bella in 1965 and ordered him arrested. He was too popular and too threatening. In recent years, the status of Ben Bella has been something of an embarassment to Algeria. Yugoslavia's President Tito and Cuba's Fidel Castro have often inquired about him. Algeria's new President, Chadli Benjedid, apparently thinks Ben Bella is too old to do any harm.

Chrysler Corp. asks U.S. for $1 billion

July 31. The Chrysler Corporation reported the largest quarterly loss in its history today and said it was asking the federal government for $1 billion in cash over the next 18 months to keep the company afloat. Chrysler's Chairman, John J. Riccardo, said he was confident the government would help the company to avoid the possible loss of 250,000 jobs by its auto workers. Chrysler lost $207 million in the latest quarter and has run out of cash, Riccardo said. The company has no recourse but to ask the government for aid, said Lee Iacocca, who was recently named President of the troubled company (→ 8/8).

Court removes bar to minors' abortions

July 2. "Please, ma, can I have an abortion?" That unlikely request need never be made, now that the Supreme Court has ruled a minor may seek an abortion without parental consent. The 8-to-1 decision shoots down a Massachusetts law requiring unmarried girls under age to get permission for an abortion from parents or a court judge. Justice Byron White gave the only dissenting vote, saying it seemed "inconceivable . . . that the United States Constitution forbids even notice to parents when their minor child who seeks surgery object to such notice" (→ 3/23/81).

Amnesty is granted to many Iranians

July 9. Ayatollah Khomeini, faced with growing resistance to his regime, declared a general amnesty today for Iranians who committed crimes when the Shah was in power; 3,000 political prisoners are expected to be freed. The amnesty does not cover Iranians accused or convicted of murder and torture. The ayatollah's announcement is intended to discourage further attacks against his supporters. There has been widespread dissatisfaction in Iran to the executions of 200 people since Khomeini returned (→ 23).

1979

AUGUST

Su	Mo	Tu	We	Th	Fr	Sa
			1	2	3	4
5	6	7	8	9	10	11
12	13	14	15	16	17	18
19	20	21	22	23	24	25
26	27	28	29	30	31	

1. London: Thatcher assails Nigeria's nationalization of British oil interests (→ 8/8/80).

3. U.N. reports 2.5 mil. starving in Cambodia; relief efforts stalled by rival governments (→ 19).

7. Tehran: Leading newspaper closed in crackdown (→ 12).

8. Detroit: Chrysler lays off 4,600 more workers (→ 12/20).

8. Iraq: 21 officials executed for plotting revolt.

9. Alabama: Klansmen begin 50-mile "white rights" march Selma to Montgomery (→ 10/18).

11. India: Dam in Goudjerat bursts, killing hundreds.

12. Tehran: Hundreds injured in riots over closing of major newspaper (→ 10/22).

14. U.S. drops rule barring suspected homosexuals from entering country (→ 8/17/84).

14. Britain: 18 drown in storm during yacht race.

15. Zurich: Sebastian Coe sets record in 1,500-meters at 3:32.1.

19. Soviet cosmonauts Lyakhov and Ryomine end record 175-day space trip (→ 7/18/80).

20. Florida: Diana Nyad swims 60 miles from Bahamas to U.S.

21. Iran executes 18 Kurdish rebels (→ 9/2).

21. Nicaragua: Sandinistas ban capital punishment, restore human rights laws (→ 10/17).

21. New York: Two men steal $2 mil. from Brink's truck.

22. Puerto Rico: U.S. basketball coach Bobby Knight given six months for assaulting policeman.

24. Washington: Carter aide Hamilton Jordan denies taking cocaine at Studio 54 (→ 9/26).

27. Ireland: Lord Mountbatten killed by IRA bomb on fishing boat (→ 30).

30. New York: 11 banks robbed in one day placing total for month at 137.

DEATHS

2. Thurman Munson, N.Y. Yankee catcher (*6/7/1947).

21. James Farrell, American realist writer (*2/27/1904).

I.R.A. blows up Mountbatten, war hero

Britons mourn death of a war hero.

Aug 30. Earl Mountbatten of Burma, a World War II hero and the last British Viceroy in India, was killed when Irish terrorists exploded his family fishing boat off the coast of Ireland. The Provisional Wing of the Irish Republican Army immediately took credit for the killing, which it described as "an execution" designed to further "the noble struggle to drive the British intruders out of our native land."

Three days later, Irish police arrested two members of the I.R.A. and charged them with the murder of Mountbatten.

Mountbatten's 29-foot fishing boat exploded as he was setting off on a family fishing trip near his summer home in northwestern Ireland. Two other persons, one a 14-year-old grandson, were killed, and four other passengers were seriously wounded. The I.R.A. killing of Mountbatten, probably the boldest in a long campaign of terrorism, set off shock waves of indignation against the I.R.A in both Britain and Ireland (→ 11/23).

Cambodia condemns Pol Pot for genocide

Pol Pot's genocidal legacy.

Aug 19. At the Choeung Ek mass grave site in Cambodia, hundreds of skulls eerily dot the ground as a gruesome reminder of the reign of Pol Pot, the Khmer Rouge and their atrocities. Millions of Cambodians died from 1975, when Pol Pot came to power, to January of this year, when he was finally ousted. The grave site is one of the many traces of genocide left behind by one of the century's most brutal rulers.

Today, Cambodia's government sentenced to death Pol Pot and his accomplice, Leng Sari, for the horrors for which they were responsible. Yet, the two maniacal leaders were nowhere to be found, although some reports suggest Pol Pot is hiding in the jungles of Thailand.

While chaos now reigns in Cambodia, most citizens agree the mass murderer will never be allowed to return to power. As one young Cambodian said, "Pol Pot can never come back." The disdain for the former leader runs so deep that an annual "Day of Hatred of Pol Pot" is being planned (→ 9/21).

Young resigns as U.N. Ambassador

Young (left), human rights champ.

Aug 15. Outspoken Andrew Young submitted his resignation as the American delegate to the United Nations today, saying that he could not guarantee he would stay out of controversies which might embarrass President Carter. Yesterday, Young was reprimanded for holding an unauthorized meeting with a member of the Palestine Liberation Organization. Currently, American policy abides by the Israeli decision not to negotiate with the PLO.

Young has been wrapped in controversy in his 30 months of service at the U.N., beginning the day after he took office. Then, he stirred a furor in Washington by saying the Cubans had brought "a certain stability and order to Angola."

Diefenbaker, Canadian conservative, dies

Aug 16. Former Prime Minister John G. Diefenbaker, one of the most colorful and combative figures in Canadian politics, died today at his home after suffering a heart attack. He was 83 years old.

Just yesterday, in apparent good health, he had visited the National Press Club in Ottawa to inaugurate a billiard table. And he had planned to visit China next month.

The only Progressive Conservative to win power since World War II until the election last month of Joe Clark, Diefenbaker remained active in politics after his defeat as prime minister in 1963. His constituents, who called him Dief, elected him to the House of Commons for the 13th time just three months ago.

While in the nation's top job, he launched development of the vast Arctic lands, calling it "a new vision of a Canada of the North, adventure to the nation's utmost boundaries." After leaving as prime minister, he continued to be a favorite among colleagues in the House.

France has sold the liner that carries the country's name. Its Scandinavian owner will fix the aging boat and rename it, appropriately, the Norway.

First black woman remains in Cabinet

Harris sworn in by Justice Marshall.

Aug 3. The first black female to occupy a Cabinet post in a presidential administration was sworn in again today. Patricia Harris took the oath as Secretary of Health, Education and Welfare (retitled Health and Human Services), replacing ousted Joseph Califano. Ms. Harris, a lawyer, former Dean of Howard University Law School, former Ambassador to Luxembourg and onetime alternate delegate to the United Nations, was sworn in by Thurgood Marshall, the first and only black Supreme Court Justice. Ms. Harris became the first black woman ever to hold a Cabinet position in the United States when she became Secretary of Housing and Urban Development in 1977.

1979

SEPTEMBER

Su	Mo	Tu	We	Th	Fr	Sa
						1
2	3	4	5	6	7	8
9	10	11	12	13	14	15
16	17	18	19	20	21	22
23	24	25	26	27	28	29
30						

2. Iran: Kurds repel 400 govt. troops from rebel center.

2. Dominican Republic: Hurricane David hits, killing 400, leaving 15,000 homeless (→ 12).

3. Calif.: Nixon holds reunion of White House staff at San Clemente (→ 5/14/83).

6. Carter commutes sentences of four Puerto Ricans in 1950's shootings in Washington.

7. Carter announces plan to deploy 200 MX missiles (→ 10/29).

7. Philippines: Ex-Pres. Macapagal arrested for sedition and rumor-mongering (→ 1/17/81).

9. New York: Tracy Austin and John McEnroe win U.S. Open singles titles.

10. Moscow: Soviets say troops in Cuba are advisers, denying combat role (→ 17).

10. Britain to end production of MG sportscar.

16. Afghanistan: Pres. Taraki killed in coup; Premier Hafizullah Amin takes over (→ 12/26).

17. Cuba releases last four U.S. citizens held as political prisoners (→ 10/12).

21. N.Y.: U.N. seats Cambodian regime of Pol Pot (→ 11/14).

22. Pakistan: Pres. Zia denies A-bomb charges, urges U.S. to resume aid (→ 11/21).

24. Lebanon: Israelis down four Syrian fighter planes (→ 24).

24. Tunis: Arab League relocates from Cairo in rebuke for Egypt-Israeli treaty (→ 29).

25. El Salvador: Seven killed as troops open fire on guerrillas (→ 10/15).

26. Calif.: Woman who says she saw Hamilton Jordan use cocaine changes story.

27. U.S. Congress approves Dept. of Education.

28. Nevada: Larry Holmes retains heavyweight title with KO over Earnie Shavers in 11th.

29. Ireland: Pope arrives, pleads for peace, says mass to crowd of two million (→ 10/2).

29. Lebanon: Jesse Jackson confers with Yasir Arafat (→ 10/21).

Brock steals 938th, more than anybody

Speedster Brock shows how it's done.

Sept 23. Lou Brock made his farewell to New York baseball a memorable one by stealing his 938th base, a major-league record.

In his last New York appearance as a player, the Cardinal speedster drew a walk in the fifth inning and then broke the base-stealing record. He surpassed the career total of 937 achieved by Billy Hamilton from 1888 through 1901. However, a runner was credited with a stolen base until 1898 for advancing on a throw to another base or for other reasons. In 1977, Brock broke Ty Cobb's modern base-stealing record of 892.

Brock will be able to tell President Carter all about his accomplishments tomorrow. He was invited to the White House after getting his 3,000th hit earlier this season.

Two hurricanes hit Caribbean and U.S.

Sept 12. Mother Nature has been hard on mankind this month, sending two devastating hurricanes through the Gulf of Mexico. President Carter ordered the National Guard to assist in the cleanup effort in Puerto Rico, which was socked by fierce Hurricane David.

In Mobile, Alabama, the 100 mile-per-hour winds of Hurricane Frederic plowed through the port city, causing extensive damage. Over 400,000 people in low-lying areas all along the coast between Louisiana and Florida were forced to evacuate. The storm has been called the worst ever to hit Alabama, but thanks to modern meteorology, most residents have taken cover.

Bokassa's empire becomes a republic

Sept. 22. Emperor Jean-Bedel Bokassa of the Central African Empire was deposed in a bloodless coup last Thursday. David Dacko, a former President who was overthrown by Bokassa in 1965, seized power and declared the country a republic. Dacko secretly planned the coup with the help of France and some friendly African countries. Bokassa is claiming French citizenship and is now at a French military airport, but the government does not appear willing to let him stay in the country.

A sad ending for a life like a movie

Sept 8. The body of actress Jean Seberg, 40, was found today in the back seat of her car in an exclusive section of Paris. She had been dead for several days. Ahmed Hasni, 29, her recent and fourth husband, said that she disappeared ten days ago, wearing only a blanket and carrying barbiturates.

At 17, Iowa-born Seberg was chosen from 80,000 applicants for the title role in "Saint Joan." In spite of bad reviews, she appeared in some 25 more movies, mainly in France, and earned raves for her role in "Breathless." She leaves a son, Diego, by Romain Gary, her second husband. Their daughter died three days after birth, causing a lasting depression. Seberg detailed her life in the book, "Blue Jeans."

Unforeseen rise and sudden fall.

1979

OCTOBER

Su	Mo	Tu	We	Th	Fr	Sa
	1	2	3	4	5	6
7	8	9	10	11	12	13
14	15	16	17	18	19	20
21	22	23	24	25	26	27
28	29	30	31			

1. Detroit: Phillip Caldwell succeeds Henry Ford II as CEO of Ford Motor Co.

2. New York: Pope speaks at U.N., says mass to 80,000 at Yankee Stadium (→ 6).

4. Brazil: Report indicates police routinely torture suspects to get confessions (→ 1/15/85).

6. East Berlin: Brezhnev says Soviets will pull 20,000 troops out of E. Germany in year (→ 6/25/84).

6. Washington: John Paul II becomes first pope to be received at White House.→

14. Bonn: 100,000 march against nuclear energy (→ 6/29/80).

17. Baltimore: Pittsburgh Pirates take World Series in fifth game over Orioles.

17. Nicaragua nationalizes insurance companies (→ 11/3).

18. Boston: Racial violence disrupts high schools for third straight day (→ 11/3).

21. Bill Rodgers and Grete Waitz win N.Y. Marathon.

21. Israel: Moshe Dayan resigns as for. min. in dispute with Begin over occupied lands (→ 11/13).

23. Prague: Six human rights activists jailed for subversion.

25. New York: Frederick Church's "Icebergs" sold for $2.5 mil., a U.S. record.

25. Spain: 85% vote autonomy for Basque lands and Catalonia (→ 3/9/80).

26. Seoul: Pres. Park Chung Hee assassinated (→ 29).

27. Washington: U.S. debut of Vienna State Opera features "Fidelio" at Kennedy Center.

29. San Salvador: 24 killed by police in anti-govt. protests (→ 3/7/80).

31. Mexico City: 74 die as DC-10 crashes on runway.

DEATHS

1. Roy Harris, U.S. composer, "When Johnny Comes Marching Home" (*2/12/1898).

23. Merle Oberon, movie actress (*2/19/1911).

27. Charles Coughlin, 1930's radio priest (*10/25/1891).

Pope pays first U.S. visit, travels widely

Pope speaks to thousands in Chicago.

Oct 6. Pope John Paul II came to the United States this month to cheering crowds in several major cities, preaching peace, dedication to human rights and condemning liberal sexual values and abortion.

In Boston, the pope extolled traditional moral beliefs, telling the nation's young to resist "temptations, fads and every form of mass manipulation." First Lady Rosalynn Carter greeted John Paul there and hailed him as a "champion of the vision that unites mankind—our Creator's vision of a world of justice."

Visiting Philadelphia, the pope led a mass attended by hundreds of thousands of followers. In his address, he stressed basic human freedoms while upholding the Vatican's strong opposition to abortion and divorce. And in his visit to Chicago, the pontiff denounced modern birth control. His seven-day tour also included stops in New York and Washington, where he drew praise for his adamant support of a decrease in the arms race (→ 11/30).

Shah is brought to New York hospital

Oct 22. Mohammed Reza Pahlevi, the deposed Shah of Iran, was flown to New York today for key medical tests. A spokesman for the State Department said that Iran's former ruler, who has been living in Mexico since his monarchy fell earlier this year, was quite sick. The nature of his illness was not known.

The shah, who is 59 years old, and his wife left Iran January 16 in an unsuccessful attempt to defuse the revolutionary movement being led by Ayatollah Khomeini. The shah first traveled to Egypt, then to the Bahamas and finally to Mexico. He has now been allowed to enter the U.S., sources say, only because it alone can provide the medical attention needed (→ 11/4).

Castro, at U.N., asks for Third World aid

Castro speaks for the Third World.

Oct 12. Cuban President Fidel Castro spoke today before the General Assembly of the United Nations, saying that the United States and other "imperialists" should pay $300 billion to help develop the poor Third World nations. Castro demanded that this fund be managed by the United Nations and warned that "if there are no resources for development, there will be no peace . . . the future will be apocalyptic."

Although claiming he was not there to "denounce . . . the attacks to which our small but worthy country has been subjected for 20 years," he nevertheless singled out the United States as the source of many world problems, condemning the U.S. for, among other things, supporting "Israeli aggression at the expense of the Palestinian Arab people." He also accused the U.S. of "direct or indirect collaboration in the maintenance of South Africa's criminal policy and racist oppression."

Castro's visit to New York disrupted the area around the Cuban Mission at 38th and Lexington and required 2,000 policemen to keep both anti- and pro-Castro demonstrators in line (→ 4/6/80).

Hispanics speak against Castro.

1,045 arrested at Wall Street rally

Oct 29. Police today arrested 1,045 anti-nuclear demonstrators who tried unsuccessfully to shut down the New York Stock Exchange. The protesters, chanting "No nukes," linked arms and attempted to block entrances to the exchange on the 50th anniversary of the 1929 Crash. Leaders of the group said the action was aimed at companies who were heavily invested in the nuclear industry. More than 800 policemen began arresting demonstrators at 7 a.m., carrying many of them away on stretchers when they went limp (→ 11/10).

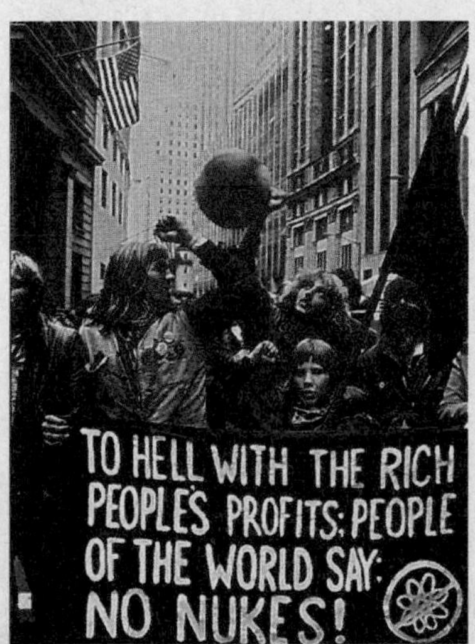

Blast the business of building arms.

Korean chief killed; KCIA boss suspected

Oct 29. At first attributed to an "accidental argument," the murder of South Korean President Park Chung Hee two days ago by Kim Jae Kyu, head of the Korean CIA, is now being called part of a premeditated plot. Kim reportedly shot the 62-year-old president because of policy disagreements. The president's bodyguard, Cha Chi Chol, was also killed because he apparently had blocked most of Kim's reports from reaching the president. Kim had also opposed Park's use of force to combat student protests (→ 5/27/80).

S.J. Perelman dies, leavin' 'em laughin'

Oct 17. Humorist S.J. (Sidney Joseph) Perelman has died in New York. He was 75. "Why anyone would want to live with a small container of stagnant water populated by a half-dead guppy is beyond me," Perelman once wrote of aquariums. He was very serious about humor, as William Shawn, his editor at The New Yorker, averred. Perelman wrote somber scripts for "Around the World in 80 Days" and the Marx Brothers films "Horse Feathers" and "Monkey Business."

U.S. hears atomic blast; sub suspected

Oct 27. A loud, underwater blast near South Africa was detected by the United States, stirring suspicion. According to American intelligence officers, special equipment aboard satellites indicated an explosion had occured last month. The blast leads some experts to speculate that perhaps South Africa has secretly joined the nuclear club. The South African government has rejected such talk and suggested to United States officials that an accident aboard a Soviet nuclear submarine may have caused the explosion.

Salvador military removes President

Oct 15. As business and traffic continued undisturbed in the city of San Salvador, capital of the nation of El Salvador, a coup led by leaders of the Salvadoran military deposed President Carlos Romero and set up a civilian-military junta in his place. The coup was apparently a response to increased violence in the nation from both extreme right- and left-wing groups. The new leaders appealed to both factions to lay down their arms and accept a peaceful role in the government (→ 29).

1979

NOVEMBER

Su	Mo	Tu	We	Th	Fr	Sa
				1	2	3
4	5	6	7	8	9	10
11	12	13	14	15	16	17
18	19	20	21	22	23	24
25	26	27	28	29	30	

1. Detroit: Lee A. Iacocca succeeds John Riccardo as CEO of Chrysler Corp.

3. N.C.: Four shot to death at Greensboro anti-Klan march (→ 4).

3. Nicaragua: Mining industry nationalized (→ 9/17/80).

4. Tehran: Students seize U.S. Embassy, hold hostages (→ 7).

7. Tehran: Civil govt. out, conceding power to Khomeini; hostages face death threat (→ 9).

9. U.N. urges Iran to free hostages; marchers in Tehran chant "death to the Americans" (→ 14).

10. Washington reports computer error brought military close to taking action against false missile attack (→ 12/12).

12. Ontario: Toxic gas leaks from derailed train; 250,000 evacuate.

14. Carter freezes billions in Iranian assets (→ 17).

14. U.N. demands Vietnam pull out of Cambodia (→ 6/28/80).

16. American Airlines fined $500,000 for improper DC-10 maintenance (→ 28).

17. Tehran: Khomeini orders students to release black and female hostages (→ 26).

20. Mecca: Gunmen seize Grand Mosque (→ 24).

21. Pakistan: Hundreds storm U.S. Embassy; one Marine killed (→ 1/13/80).

23. Dublin: Thomas MacMahon convicted in murder of Lord Mounbatten (→ 1/16/81).

24. U.S. admits thousands of troops in Vietnam were exposed to Agent Orange (→ 1/24/82).

26. Venezuela: Oil deposit equaling OPEC reserves is found (→ 12/16).

28. Antarctica: 257 killed as DC-10 crashes into mountain.

30. Nevada: Sugar Ray Leonard KOs Wilfredo Benitez in 15th for welterweight title.

30. Istanbul: John Paul II is first pope in 1,000 years to attend Orthodox mass (→ 5/2/80).

DEATH

1. Mamie Eisenhower, ex-first lady (*11/14/1896).

Angered by U.S., Iran seizes embassy

Nov 26. The hostage crisis at the United States Embassy in Tehran has deteriorated sharply, and the State Department is concerned about the well-being of Americans in other Moslem countries. Ayatollah Khomeini made an angry, public speech condemning the Carter administration and supporting the students who continue to hold 49 hostages. Khomeini repeated the students' threat that the hostages would be destroyed if the embassy is attacked. "This is not a struggle between the United States and Iran," the ayatollah said. "It is a struggle between Iran and blasphemy." Khomeini also urged the students to remain firm. "Why should we be afraid?" he asked. "We consider martyrdom a great honor."

The State Department is concerned about ripple effects of Khomeini's Islamic Revolution throughout the Moslem world. In a period of three weeks, the Tehran embassy was overrun and the embassy in Islamabad, Pakistan, was stormed and destroyed. Today, the State Department urged Americans in ten Moslem countries to leave.

The Tehran siege began on the 4th, one year to the day after the Shah's forces shot students at the university. Enraged that the shah was permitted to enter the United States for medical treatment, a mob stormed the embassy and took the occupants hostage. Students hung a banner reading, "Khomeini struggles, Carter trembles."

The Carter administration said Iranian officials had promised their support to free the hostages, but it quickly became apparent that Khomeini supported the students. His son visited the embassy and announced that Iran should cut all ties with the United States. On the 6th, the relatively moderate government of Prime Minister Bazargan was dissolved. The ayatollah was in complete command.

On the 19th and 20th, the students released black and female hostages, but they threatened to put some of the remaining hostages on trial for espionage. The White House ordered all Iranian assets in the United States frozen. Demonstrators in Iran had a simple, but chilling response. "Margh bar Carter! Death to Carter!" (→ 12/7).

Shiite students set fire to an American flag atop the embassy in Tehran.

At Khomeini's behest, four women and six blacks were freed on the 20th.

Iranian government troops parade across the flag at the American Embassy.

Gang takes Islam's holiest sanctuary

Nov 24. With armored personnel carriers circling the holiest site in Islam, Saudi government troops retook the Grand Mosque in Mecca after a "dramatic and violent" battle. The mosque had been seized five days ago by a group of what Saudi officials called "religious renegades"—members of Iran's Moslem Shiite branch. Its leader, calling himself a Mahdi, or Prophet, had urged the Saudi government to ban radio, television, soccer and prohibit women from holding business jobs. The group apparently got away in the fighting.

In Tehran, where hostages held by Islamic students in the American Embassy entered their third week of captivity, Ayatollah Khomeini laid the attack to "the U.S.-Israeli conspiracy" and charged President Carter with a failure to "comprehend the depth of the contemporary Islamic movement" (→ 1/9/80).

Bolivia has another coup, plus a strike

Nov 7. In the wake of major strikes protesting his military junta, Col. Alberto Natusch Busch, who proclaimed himself President after a coup last Thursday, suspended martial law and censorship of the press, and promised free elections.

In what was the third military takeover in 14 months and about the 200th coup in the nation's history, Col. Busch overthrew the government of President Walter Guevara Arze, who was elected to that office by Bolivia's Congress last August.

Guevara, who led the first civilian government in Bolivia in more than a decade, announced from his refuge that his government would function "underground" and seek a return to power.

The coup, which observers believe to be motivated by the ambitions of Col. Busch, was condemned as "a major step backwards" by the United States, which suspended $21.5 million in aid and $6 million in military credits. The general strike, which has crippled Bolivia's vital mining industry, was called by union leaders to protest the junta.

Reagan, Kennedy seeking presidency

Nov 13. Former Governor of California and screen star Ronald Reagan has announced his candidacy for the Republican presidential nomination. He joins Democratic Senator Edward Kennedy and President Carter as the leading names in the 1980 presidential race. Kennedy said earlier this year he would seek to dethrone the incumbent Carter as the Democratic nominee.

In a nationally televised speech, the 68-year-old politician, the tenth Republican officially to enter the race, invoked the phraseology of a famous Democrat. Reagan said America had a "rendezvous with destiny," echoing the words of Franklin Roosevelt. Reagan criticized President Carter, saying the nation has lost confidence in its leaders. His address also underlined his commitment to traditional American values, free enterprise and a strong military (→ 2/26/80).

Kennedy greets supporters in Boston.

Al Capp, founder of Dogpatch, is gone

Nov 5. Cartoonist Al Capp has died. He was 70. Capp founded Dogpatch, a fictional hick town where characters Daisy Mae and Mammy and Pappy Yokum lived. It was also home to Li'l Abner, a hulking, dimwitted hero.

Capp, born Alfred Caplin in New Haven, Connecticut, co-wrote the "Joe Palooka" strip before soloing with "Li'l Abner" in 1934. He satirized America with it, skewering conservatives and radicals in yokel guise. The long-running television series "The Beverly Hillbillies" drew on Capp's backwoods images.

West Bank mayors all resign posts

Nov 13. Yesterday's arrest and threatened deportation of a Palestinian mayor by the Israeli military led today to protest resignations by other West Bank Palestinian mayors. Conflicting reports put the numbers between five and 16.

While one PLO faction favored the resignations, another, Al Fatah, said they only helped Israel remove prominent radical voices from the West Bank political stew.

The arrested Mayor, Bassam al-Shaka of Nablus, was one of the West Bank's most outspoken Arabs and had recently in private conversations with Israeli military officers expressed an understanding of Arab terrorist motives. His comments were leaked to an Israeli newspaper, and exaggerated. Though the mayor's remarks disgusted some Israeli officials, they regarded the arrest as rash. Tensions on the West Bank have been inflamed (→ 2/4/80).

13,000 lose jobs as U.S. closes plants

Nov 26. United States Steel will close 15 plants and mills in eight states, putting 13,000 production and white-collar employees out of work. The retrenchment, announced today, is one of the most sweeping in the nation's history. It will reduce the company's workforce by eight percent. U.S. Steel executives also said the company would report a "sizable loss" in the current quarter because of the closings. Industry analysts say the loss could exceed $400 million.

The company, the nation's largest steel producer, has been losing money on many of its older plants despite rising demand for steel. Chairman David Roderick warned that more plants would be closed unless the company could make steel operations "an attractive business investment." He said the steel industry's problems were caused by the Environmental Protection Agency's demands for installation of expensive pollution control equipment, which he said made American steel uncompetitive with low-priced imports, and by a lack of government aid to the industry.

Four are shot dead in anti-Klan march

To the Klan, Hitler is a martyr.

Nov 4. Four persons were killed and eight others wounded when two carloads of white men opened fire yesterday on demonstrators who were opposing the Ku Klux Klan in Greensboro, North Carolina. Police arrested 12 men they said were associated with the Klan and charged them with four counts of first-degree murder and one count of conspiracy to commit murder.

The deaths were the first Klan violence in at least five years, according to an official of the Southern Regional Council, a group that follows social and economic trends in the area. The latest shootings, which took place during what had been billed as a "Death to the Klan" march, occurred against the backdrop of increasing activity by the Klan in recent years.

Greensboro was the city in which the first lunch-counter sit-ins took place in 1960. However, the city has had a relatively untroubled racial climate in recent years (→ 5/19/80).

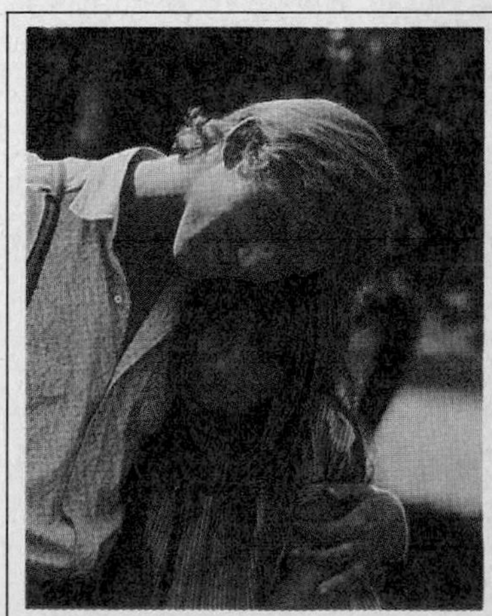

"The Waltons" brings the therapeutic myth of small-town, tight-knit America to a country beset by a nostalgic sense of loss.

1979

DECEMBER

Su	Mo	Tu	We	Th	Fr	Sa
						1
2	3	4	5	6	7	8
9	10	11	12	13	14	15
16	17	18	19	20	21	22
23	24	25	26	27	28	29
30	31					

2. Libya: 2,000 storm U.S. Embassy; 12 employees escape safely (→ 5/6/81).

3. Cincinnati: 11 dead, eight hurt in rush to see The Who at rock concert.

7. Paris: Mustapha Chafik, nephew of shah is slain (→ 11).

11. Washington: Judge halts immigration checks on 50,000 Iranian students in U.S. (→ 15).

12. NATO countries, France and Greece dissenting, agree to take 572 U.S. cruise missiles (→ 6/26/80).

18. Iran: Khomeini aide Hojatol-islam Mohammed Mofateh assassinated (→ 1/25/80).

25. Egypt undertaking major restoration of Sphinx.

26. Soviets fly 5,000 troops into Afghanistan conflict (→ 31).

DEATHS

22. Darryl Francis Zanuck, U.S. film producer (*9/5/1902).

23. Peggy Guggenheim, U.S.-born international arts patron and collector (*8/26/1898).

CULTURAL EVENTS, 1979

Literature: V.S. Naipaul's "A Bend in the River"; William Styron's "Sophie's Choice"; Margaret Atwood's "Life Before Man"; David Attenborough's "Life on Earth"; Sam Shepard's "Buried Child," Pulitzer drama.

Academia: Elaine Pagel's "Gnostic Gospels"; Edward O. Wilson's "On Human Nature," Pulitzer.

Music: Joseph Schwantner's "Aftertones of Infinity," Pulitzer; Doobie Brothers' "What a Fool Believes"; Billy Joel's "52nd Street"; Dionne Warwick's "I'll Never Love This Way Again"; The Knack's "My Sharona."

The Arts: Performance art in vogue.

Film: Coppola's "Apocalypse Now"; "The Deerhunter," Robert DeNiro; Fassbinder's "The Marriage of Maria Braun"; "Kramer vs. Kramer," Academy Award, Dustin Hoffman; "Being There," Peter Sellers; "Norma Rae," Sally Field.

Russians in Afghanistan

Afghani rebels shell Soviet positions.

Dec 31. President Carter accused Soviet leader Leonid Brezhnev today of not telling the truth about the invasion of Afghanistan. Carter used unusually blunt language in criticizing the Soviet intervention, saying it "would severely and adversely affect the relationship now and in the future between ourselves and the Soviet Union." Carter's comments reflected a new focus on Afghanistan by an administration that has been preoccupied with the hostage crisis at the United States Embassy in Tehran.

In a television interview on ABC today, Carter rejected Brezhnev's assertion that Soviet troops had been invited to Afghanistan by the government that was subsequently toppled in a coup. Carter accused the Soviets of engineering the coup, shooting President Hafizullah Amin and installing a new President, Babrak Karmal.

In the past few days, Soviet troops have swarmed across the border into Afghanistan. Their numbers have mushroomed to 40,000. The Soviets increased their military presence because they were convinced that Amin was unable to quell opposition to his Marxist regime. The late president rejected an offer of assistance from the Soviets earlier this month. Officials in Moscow were apparently concerned Moslem fundamentalists might emerge in Afghanistan, as they already have in nearby Iran.

In Kabul today, fierce fighting broke out again between Soviet troops and Afghan rebel forces, called mujahedeen. Gunfire was heard through much of the capital. The tank and machine gun battles were intense around the radio station and presidential palace, where Amin was shot on Thursday.

The United States is not the only world power criticizing Soviet intervention in Afghanistan. The Chinese Foreign Ministry said the action "poses a threat to China's security," and it demanded the withdrawal of Soviet troops. Pakistan, which has supported the anti-Communist forces in Afghanistan, also condemned the Soviet invasion. Pakistan and other Third World countries are clamoring for a meeting of the United Nations Security Council to censure Moscow (→ 1/2/80).

Mujahedeen, though backed by much of the Arab world, are poorly supplied.

Curtain comes down on a musical wizard

Dec 30. Composer Richard Rodgers has died at his New York home. He was 77. Among Rodgers' lyricists were Lorenz Hart, Oscar Hammerstein and Stephen Sondheim. Their jobs were easy. Rodgers' tunes for "Pal Joey," "Babes in Arms," "Oklahoma," "South Pacific," "Do I Hear a Waltz" and 34 other Broadway shows practically wrote themselves. In fact, Rodgers was his own lyricist for the show "No Strings" in 1962. Librettist Alan Jay Lerner said, "Dick's got that pipeline to heaven that goes through him." In other words, his music sounded divine.

Rodgers, "pipeline to heaven."

Five OPEC members raise prices again

Dec 16. Libya has become the fifth major oil producer in less than a week to announce hefty price increases. On the eve of the OPEC meeting in Caracas, Libya said prices will rise $4 to $30 a barrel. The action will have an almost immediate effect on gas prices because the United States imports large quantities of crude oil from Libya. Last Thursday, price increases of up to a third were announced by Saudi Arabia, Venezuela, the United Arab Emirates and Qatar. Earlier this year, prices skyrocketed by almost 85%. The new increases, coming at the beginning of the winter heating season, are expected to aggravate inflation and the recession expected next year (→ 1/25/80).

Mother Teresa, a living saint, wins Nobel

Dec 10. A woman frail of body but frail of nothing else accepted the Nobel Peace Prize tonight. Mother Teresa is founder of a charitable empire now stretching to 700 shelters and clinics. Born in Albania in 1910, she moved to a Calcutta convent when she was 18. She left its relative comfort in 1946 to pursue more direct work with India's poor.

The literature prize went to the Greek Odysseus Alepoudelis, who pens surreal poems under the name of Elytis. Elytis, 68 years old, writes in a positive vein about his life and Greek history. His major work is "Seemly It Is," published in Greek in 1959 and only translated into English five years ago.

Mother Teresa, empress of charity.

Democracy Wall in Peking is no longer

Dec 6. For years, Democracy Wall in Peking was a place for Chinese dissidents to express their desires for more democratic freedoms. Recently, so many people, unhappy with their leadership, have postered the wall with anti-Communist slogans that officials have decided to prohibit posters on the 200-yard wall. The move came in response to complaints that the wall was a "gathering place for lawbreakers to sow disorder" (→ 9/7/80).

Shah leaves U.S. for stay in Panama

Dec 15. Shah Mohammed Reza Pahlevi, the former ruler of Iran, secretly left the U.S. this morning for exile in Panama. His departure opened a new phase in the 42-day crisis in which 50 Americans are being held hostage in Iran by militants who say their prisoners will not be released until the shah is returned to Iran for trial. The shah has been under medical treatment, reportedly for cancer, in New York City since October (→ 18).

House and Senate vote Chrysler aid

Dec 20. The Senate today approved $1.5 billion in federal loan guarantees to save the Chrysler Corporation from bankruptcy. The House approved the loans yesterday and the bill is expected to be signed by President Carter by Christmas.

The rescue package requires Chrysler workers, banks and others with a stake in the company's future to make $2.1 billion more available in loans, stock purchases and wage givebacks. Chrysler and the United Auto Workers had lobbied heavily for the bill, warning that a bankruptcy could result in 700,000 layoffs, setting off a recession or even a depression. Opponents argued against using tax dollars to help a private company (→ 7/31/80).

7-year Rhodesian war brought to end

Dec 21. Robert Mugabe, Joshua Nkomo and Bishop Abel Muzorewa today signed agreements ending Rhodesia's seven-year civil war. The three men, representing the factions involved in the war, pledged to observe a cease-fire and have agreed to a new constitution and carefully monitored elections.

The cease-fire agreement, which was reached December 17 after 14 weeks of difficult negotiations, provides for British administration of the country for an interim period. Elections will be held during this period, followed by independence. In response, the United Nations Security Council has lifted the economic embargo it imposed against Rhodesia 13 years ago (→ 1/27/80).

1979: Directors make magnificent movies

"The China Syndrome."

Hoffman in "Kramer vs. Kramer."

The John Fords and Frank Capras of tomorrow are here—with names like Robert Benton, James Bridges and Francis Ford Coppola. Coppola, who made the great "Godfather" films, directed this year's "Apocalypse Now," loosely based on Conrad's "Heart of Darkness." Martin Sheen plays a U.S. agent sent to root out a mercenary (Marlon Brando) from Vietnam's jungle.

In Benton's "Kramer vs Kramer," a woman sets out to find herself, leaving her son with a father who does not even know how to make french toast. The story of fatherhood and divorce stars Dustin Hoffman and Meryl Streep.

All is not well at the nuclear plant in James Bridges' "The China Syndrome." Jane Fonda portrays a TV reporter, Jack Lemmon a harried executive. The picture is bereft of musical score, heightening tension.

New director Ridley Scott disturbs the bellies of viewers with "Alien." Sigourney Weaver stars as a space traveler battling a beast that likes to nestle in one's innards.

Sylvester Stallone, who let John G. Avildsen direct him before, handles "Rocky II" himself. Stars Talia Shire, Carl Weathers and Burgess Meredith are back in the ring.

Blake Edwards, responsible for the "Pink Panther" films, turns irresponsible with "10." Bo Derek is the beautiful woman Dudley Moore decides to dump for Julie Andrews.

Woody Allen is back on familiar turf with "Manhattan." He plays a comedy writer whose neurotic admirers include Diane Keaton, Meryl Streep and Mariel Hemingway.

Werner Herzog ("Aguirre the Wrath of God") has made one of the best vampire films of all time. His unique Dracula (Klaus Kinski) of "Nosferatu" carries his coffin under one arm when he is on the go.

Gary Nelson, working for the Disney studios, directed a not-too-terribly plausible script for "The Black Hole." The sci-fi pic stars Anthony Perkins.

"Time After Time," another sci-fi entry, is directed by Nicholas Meyer. H.G. Wells (Malcolm McDowell) hops into his time machine to pursue Jack the Ripper as he flees into the 1970's. Directors Steven Spielberg ("1941") and Robert Wise ("Star Trek") got mixed reviews. There will be a "Star Trek II"—but no "1942."

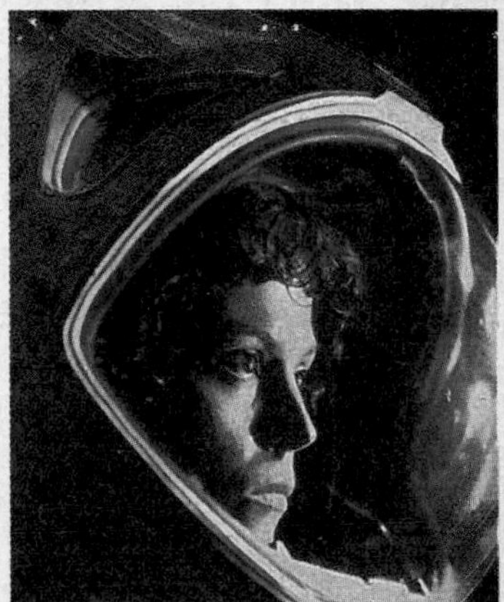

"Alien," horror in outer space.

Horror on earth: "Apocalypse Now."

1980-1989

1980

JANUARY

Su	Mo	Tu	We	Th	Fr	Sa
		1	2	3	4	5
6	7	8	9	10	11	12
13	14	15	16	17	18	19
20	21	22	23	24	25	26
29	28	29	30	31		

1. Pasadena: U.S.C. edges Ohio State 17-16 in Rose Bowl.

2. Carter asks Senate to delay arms treaty ratification in response to Soviet action in Afghanistan (→ 14).

3. Oakland: Ex-Black Panther leader Eldrige Cleaver given probation for 1968 assault.

6. India: Gandhi gains majority in legislative elections (→ 2/17).

11. Honda to build Japan's first U.S. passenger-car assembly plant in Ohio (→ 11/26/82).

13. U.S. offers Pakistan two-year aid plan to counter Soviet threat in Afghanistan (→ 2/21/85).

14. U.N. votes 104-18 to deplore Soviet Afghan acts (→ 20).

16. Boston: Scientists produce interferon, natural virus-fighting substance, through genetic engineering (→ 6/16).

18. New York: Gold, up $159 in week, soars to $802 (→ 25).

20. Belgrade: Tito's left leg amputated to avoid spread of gangrene (→ 5/4).

24. U.S., in rebuff to Soviets, will sell arms to China (→ 30).

25. U.S.: Exxon reports $.3 bil. net in 1979, a record (→ 4/2).

25. Iran: Abolhassan Bani-Sadr named prime minister (→ 29).

25. Pretoria: Three blacks take 25 hostages in suburban bank, ask freedom for political prisoners; all die in rescue (→ 6/13).

25. U.S.: 1979 inflation rate highest in 33 years (→ 3/14).

27. Salisbury: Rebel leader Robert Mugabe returns to Rhodesia after five-year exile (→ 2/10).

30. N.Y.: First-ever Chinese Olympic team arrives for Winter Games (→ 7/10).

31. Guatemala: 36 die as police break siege of Spanish Embassy (→ 1/10/82).

DEATHS

14. Andre Kostelanetz, popular American composer (*1902).

18. Cecil Beaton, British designer, photographer (*1/14/1904).

19. William O. Douglas, U.S. Supreme Court justice (*10/16/1898).

Islam asking Soviets to leave Afghanistan

Mujahedeen, Islamic warriors.

Jan 29. Islam and communism collided head-on today as the Soviet Union was rebuked sharply for its invasion of Afghanistan. The Islamic Conference, representing 36 countries and 900 million Moslems, adopted a resolution condemning the Soviet intervention. Agha Shahi, Pakistan's Foreign Minister, said the resolution was without precedent. He also said its wording was surprising because many of the signatories have friendly relations with the Soviet Union.

The Soviets were not the only target of the Islamic Conference. Iran was criticized for continuing to hold hostages at the American Embassy in Tehran. The issue arose when Iranian delegates were trying to push through a resolution criticizing American economic sanctions. Led by Saudi Arabia and Iraq, several foreign ministers demanded an immediate end to the hostage siege. Prince Saud al-Faisal, Saudi Arabia's Foreign Minister, said it was important for Iran to turn its attention from the embassy siege to the Soviet invasion of its Afghan neighbor. But Iran rejected a suggestion that the Islamic Conference mediate the crisis between Tehran and Washington. "No compromise," said Iran's Deputy Foreign Minister. "We are not men of compromise. We will release the hostages when America returns the Shah."

Several conferees doubted the debate would lead to the release of the American hostages because the Iranians attending the meeting were low-level officials with little access to Ayatollah Khomeini (→ 20).

Jan 20. Lynn Swann flies for a Bradshaw bullet. Steelers over Rams 31-19 in Super Bowl XIV.

Mecca raid causes 63 to lose heads

Jan 9. Earlier claims by both Saudi and United States officials that last November's attack on the Grand Mosque in Mecca was undertaken by Iranian Shiite Moslems were contradicted today when 63 persons were beheaded for their role in the sensational attack.

None were Iranians and the leader, a self-professed prophet, was a Saudi, Juseiman bin Seif, the military commander who led the extremist group in what was in effect a Saudi rebellion.

Of the 63 executed, 41 were Saudis, ten Egyptian, six from Southern Yemen, three from Kuwait and one each from Yemen, the Sudan and Iraq. Nor was the attack launched by a small group. According to Saudi figures, more than 700 took part in the rebellion. In the fighting which led to the government's recapture of the mosque, 117 rebels were killed and 143 captured. Government losses were put at 127 dead and 451 wounded.

The official statement said that a number or prisoners who supplied the rebels with weapons and otherwise aided them during the attack would undergo "religious re-education" during their two-year terms.

Spy called Falcon escapes from prison

Jan 22. Christopher John Boyce, 26, who was convicted in 1977 of selling American military secrets to the Soviet Union, escaped last night from the maximum security prison at Lompoc, Calif., where he was serving a 40-year term. Boyce was hired in mid-1974 by the TRW Co., a principal supplier of surveillance satellites. His father, a former FBI agent, helped him to get the job. Soon Boyce and Andrew Daulton Lee, a childhood friend, sold documents to Soviet agents in Mexico City. The story of the two youths is the subject of a book, "The Falcon and the Snowman," written by reporter Robert Lindsey.

Dissident Sakharov is exiled to Gorki

Jan 22. Nuclear physicist and political dissident Andrei Sakharov has been ousted from his Moscow home and exiled to Gorki. Sakharov and his wife, Yelena Bonner, were given just two hours to pack for the move. At six p.m. they were shuttled aboard a plane bound for Gorki, 250 miles to the east. Earlier this month, Sakharov spoke out against the Soviet presence in Afghanistan, asking the United States to pressure the Soviet Union into a withdrawal (→ 10/23).

Laetrile tests on humans authorized

Jan 3. The National Cancer Institute today was given permission to conduct trials of the controversial substance laetrile in human cancer patients. Jere Goyan, head of the Food and Drug Administration, said the human tests had been approved although "all the data to date suggests that laetrile has no effect on cancer." Thousands of cancer patients are taking laetrile, an extract of peach pits, although most medical authorities say it is worthless. The cancer institute trials, to be conducted at four medical centers, will be the first scientifically controlled tests of laterile in advanced cancer cases.

Veteran laborite Meany dies at 85

Jan 10. George Meany dedicated his life to bolstering the rights of American laborers through tough talk and decisive action. Meany died tonight in Washington at the age of 85. Never one to mince words, the former President for nearly 25 years of the AFL-CIO, America's most powerful labor group, challenged presidents, intellectuals and judges in leading strikes and collective bargaining battles. As he saw it, his job was to promote the economic welfare of the union's 13.6 million members. Meany once described his tactics for successful lobbying: "Never threaten, never be intimidated, tell the truth."

Durante says good night for last time

"Everybody's gettin' into de act."

Jan 29. Jimmy Durante, a comedian of irrepressible goodwill, died today in Santa Monica at the age of 86 from pneumonitis. The lovable wacko with the penguin walk will be remembered for a nose that earned him the nickname "Schnozzola," his running raids on the English language, the way he maniacally assaulted the piano with such standbys as "Inka Dinka Doo." Durante-isms include "Am I mortified, Everybody's gettin' into de act" and "I'm surrounded by assassins." Then there was the way he forever ended his shows, "Good-night, Mrs. Caleabash, wherever you are," as he walked out of the spotlight.

Americans flee Iran in Canadian guise

Jan 29. Six Americans who had been in hiding in Tehran ever since the U.S. Embassy was seized three months ago have escaped from Iran, posing as Canadian diplomats. The whereabouts of the six embassy employees had been kept a tight secret ever since they escaped out the back door when the embassy was seized and took refuge in the Canadian Embassy. Their escape was arranged by the Canadian government, giving them diplomatic passports, and the Central Intelligence Agency, forging Iranian visas in the passports. They flew by commercial airliners out of Tehran to West Germany (→ 3/6).

Afghan reprisals are taken by Carter

Jan 20. The Olympics could be the next casualty of the Soviet Union's invasion of Afghanistan. President Carter threatened a United States withdrawal from the Games unless they are moved out of Moscow, postponed or canceled. Earlier this month, Carter asked the Senate to delay consideration of the new arms agreement with the Soviet Union. The president also imposed economic sanctions, cut trade and recalled Ambassador Thomas Watson from Moscow (→ 2/4).

Henry Miller, no Puritan, is dead

Jan 7. The author of "Tropic of Cancer" and "Tropic of Capricorn" has died. At 87, Henry Miller outlived most of his critics, and they were many. His works were considered obscene when they were first published. Today, they are thought breakthroughs in the use of realistic language and sensual image.

Miller was born in New York to a stifling bourgeois family. He went to Paris, writing "Cancer" (1934) and "Capricorn" (1939) there. Europe welcomed the books; the United States banned them until 1961. His celebration of Greek culture, "The Colossus of Maroussi" (1941), won over his severest critics.

1980

FEBRUARY

Su	Mo	Tu	We	Th	Fr	Sa
					1	2
3	4	5	6	7	8	9
10	11	12	13	14	15	16
17	18	19	20	21	22	23
24	25	26	27	28	29	

4. Beirut: Syria withdrawing peacekeeping force (→ 17).

4. Tehran: Khomeini condemns Soviet intervention in Afghanistan (→ 21).

10. Salisbury: Rebel leader Mugabe narrowly escapes second assassination attempt as bomb explodes behind car (→ 3/4).

11. Oman, Kenya and Somalia agree to give U.S. forces access to military facilities.

12. N.Y.: Lake Placid Winter Olympics open (→ 21).

16. Miami: FBI indicts 55 for pornography and film piracy.

17. Cairo: Israeli diplomats arrive to open first embassy in Arab world (→ 4/7).

17. New Delhi: Indira Gandhi dissolves nine state assemblies led by opposition (→ 8/16).

18. Canada: Trudeau's Liberal Party gains legislative majority in voting (→ 4/17/82).

19. Calif.: 16 dead in flooding; Gov. Brown declares state of emergency in four counties.

20. U.S. Supreme Court rules faculties at private universities are managerial employees, barring govt. protection of unions.

21. Lake Placid: Eric Heiden becomes only man to take four golds in Winter Games (→ 23).

21. Kabul: Afghani stores shut in protest over Soviet presence (→ 22).

22. Kabul: Martial law proclaimed as at least three die in anti-Soviet rioting (→ 3/2).

23. Lake Placid: Eric Heiden sets record, winning 10,000-meters for fifth gold (→ 24).

25. Surinam: Leftist officers seize power in military coup.

27. Colombia: Guerrillas seize Dominican Republic Embassy in Bogota (→ 28).

DEATHS

17. Graham Sutherland, British portrait painter (*8/24/1903).

22. Oscar Kokoschka, Austrian painter and printmaker (*3/1/1886).

26. Alexander Brook, American realist painter (*7/14/1898).

Americans are hell on ice at Olympics

Heiden, unprecedented five golds.

Feb 24. Eric Heiden of the U.S. won his fifth gold medal in Olympic speed-skating competition yesterday, and today a victory by the United States hockey team in the Olympic final touched off patriotic celebrations throughout the nation.

When the Americans defeated Finland by 4-2 after a stunning 4-3 victory over the incumbent Soviet squad, thousands of spectators charged onto Olympic Driveway chanting "We're No. 1." At Radio City Music Hall in New York, the audience began singing the "Star Spangled Banner" when the musical version of "Snow White" was interrupted to announce the result.

The celebrations were particularly vocal in Minnesota, whence most of the American players came. Even in staid Avery Fischer Hall in Lincoln Center, violinst Alexander Schneider announced, "We beat the Finns, 4 to 2!"

In winning only the second American gold medal in hockey in 24 years, the team made strong use of body checks. They also moved faster and utilized longer passes than their rivals.

Put the champagne on ice.

Bogota leftist rebels take 80 hostages

Feb 28. The Colombian urban guerrillas who seized the Dominican Republic Embassy in Bogota yesterday have exchanged 13 of the 80 hostages for supplies and food. Numbering about ten men and women, they belong to the radical left-wing April 19 Movement. Pretending to play soccer on a nearby field, they stormed the embassy with automatic guns and grenades. Their demands include the release of political prisoners, 311 to be named by the guerrillas, and a ransom payment of $50 million. Among the hostages are 14 ambassadors, including the American, and the papal nuncio (→ 4/27).

Reagan wins big in N.H. primary race

Feb 26. Ronald Reagan won a landslide victory over George Bush in the Republican presidential primary in New Hampshire today. Senator Howard H. Baker Jr., finished third in the race and Rep. John B. Anderson was fourth. The Reagan victory reestablishes him as the Republican favorite after his upset defeat in the Iowa primary last month. However, the most recent victory was clouded to some extent by his ouster of John P. Sears, his campaign chief, who has been bitterly opposed by conservatives in the Reagan ranks (→ 6/10).

Phony sheiks assist FBI in bribe inquiry

Feb 2. Agents of the Federal Bureau of Investigation, posing as Arab shieks and businessmen, have conducted a two-year sting operation involving several Congressmen. The agents, dressed in sheik clothing, offered bribes to the politicians in exchange for political favors. The operation, code-named "Abscam," short for "Arab Scam," is part of a new effort to weed out political corruption. Senator Harrison Williams and seven U.S. Representatives may have criminal charges brought against them for accepting large bribes (→ 6/13).

1980

MARCH

Su	Mo	Tu	We	Th	Fr	Sa
						1
2	3	4	5	6	7	8
9	10	11	12	13	14	15
16	17	18	19	20	21	22
23	24	25	26	27	28	29
30	31					

2. Islamabad: Soviet and Afghan troops begin attack on rebel strongholds (→ 21).

6. Tehran: Islamic militants say they will turn over hostages to Revolutionary Council (→ 10).

6. Paris: French Academy elects novelist Marguerite Youcenar, first woman since founding in 1635.

7. El Salvador declares state of siege, decrees nationalization of banks, coffee, sugar (→ 24).

9. Spain: Basques elect autonomist regional Parliament (→ 20).

10. Tehran: Khomeini lends support to militants holding U.S. hostages (→ 23).

10. Salisbury: Mugabe names Joshua Nkomo as minister of home affairs (→ 4/18).

13. Detroit: Henry Ford III resigns as chairman, leaving Ford without family member at helm.

14. Warsaw: Polish jet crashes, 87 die, including 22 U.S. boxers.

20. Spain: Catalonia chooses autonomist regional Parliament (→ 2/23/81).

23. Sweden: Referendum comes down 58.2% in favor of building nuclear power plants (→ 5/11).

23. Panama: Shah leaves for Cairo day before Iran was to request extradition (→ 4/7).

24. El Salvador: Archbishop Oscar Arnulfo Romero killed by sniper at mass (→ 30).

25. N.Y.: Jean Harris indicted for murder in Herman Tarnower killing (→ 2/24/81).

29. Ankara: U.S. gains accord to use Turkish air base in return for military, economic aid (→ 9/11).

30. Salt Lake City: Mormon Church celebrates 150th anniversary.

31. Carter deregulates banking industry (→ 5/2).

DEATHS

26. Roland Barthes, French philosopher (*11/12/1915).

29. Annunzio Paolo Mantovani, condutor of popular orchestras.

31. Jesse Owens, American track star (*9/12/1913).

Sniper kills Salvadoran Archbishop at mass

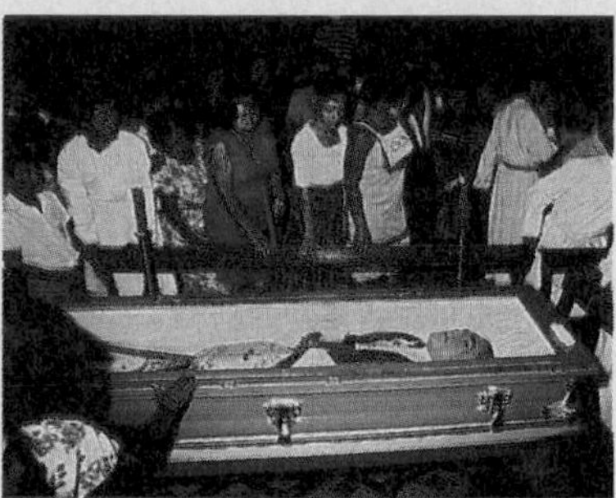

Archbishop is mourned in Salvador.

March 30. A wave of violence has swept El Salvador this week, as Archbishop Oscar Romero, an outspoken human rights advocate, was assassinated while saying mass at a hospital chapel in San Salvador.

Romero, a vocal critic of El Salvador's right- and left-wing extremists, and a champion of economic and political reform, was shot on March 24, during his sermon on peace and justice, at a mass in honor of Jorge Pinto, a well-known opposition journalist. The archbishop is believed to be the victim of a right-wing paramilitary group; he had received a number of death threats recently.

Today, at Romero's funeral at the plaza in front of the Metropolitan Cathedral in San Salvador, explosions and gunfire set off a stampede which killed 26 and wounded over 200 of the 30,000 mourners. Jose Napoleon Duarte, a government spokesman, blamed leftist guerrillas for the violence (→ 11/29).

Fashionable doctor slain by mistress

March 11. Dr. Herman Tarnower, author of the best-selling "Complete Scarsdale Medical Diet," was shot to death in his Westchester County home tonight. Mrs. Jean Harris, 56-year-old headmistress of a prestigious Virginia girls school, is being held in the murder. Mrs. Harris, a divorcee, and the bachelor Tarnower, 69, knew each other for 14 years. A credit in his diet book thanks her for her assistance. Tarnower was found in the bedroom of his Purchase, New York, home. Mrs. Harris was stopped trying to drive away from the estate (→ 25).

Budget is cut $13b because of inflation

March 14. Saying that America's soaring inflation requires a new program of "pain" and "discipline," President Carter announced today he would cut federal spending by $13 billion in order to achieve a balanced budget by next year. He also said he would impose a fee on imported oil, aimed at raising gas prices ten cents a gallon; and he joined with the Federal Reserve Board in applying new curbs on the use of credit cards, check overdraft plans and other forms of consumer credit as a way of restraining individual spending (→ 31).

Mugabe to organize black majority rule

Mugabe partisans rally in Salisbury.

March 4. Robert Mugabe, leader of Rhodesia's largest guerrilla army, will become Prime Minister of what will soon be the independent state of Zimbabwe. Mugabe's party won 57 seats in the 100-seat Assembly. Mugabe has offered a role in his administration to his partner in the Patriotic Front alliance, Joshua Nkomo, and has hinted that some whites will be asked to join the government. In the past, Mugabe has appeared to favor a Marxist transformation of the country, but since his victory, he has made it clear that he is a moderate socialist who does not plan to do away with private property (→ 10).

Mount St. Helens spews out steam and ash

March 28. Mount St. Helens, a volcano in southeastern Washington state that has been dormant since 1857, has begun emitting steam, ash and small boulders from its crater and vents on its sides. Scientists from the United States Geological Observatory are monitoring the emissions and have ordered the evacuation of 100 persons from areas that could be reached by lava flows or mudslides. It is the first volcanic activity in the continental U.S. since the eruption of Mount Lassen in California in 1917.

In 1979, a Geological Survey report described Mount St. Helens as "especially dangerous" and said "explosive eruptions can be expected sometime in the future." The main immediate danger is from flooding and mudslides caused by melting of the mountain's snowpack, but geologists say a more violent eruption is possibile (→ 4/22).

First signs of activity since 1857.

Carter tells athletes we'll skip Olympics

March 21. The United States will not take part in the Moscow Olympics, President Carter told a group of athletes that he had summoned to the White House. Carter sought the support of the past and present Olympians for his boycott plan designed to protest the Soviet intervention in Afghanistan. The athletes listened quietly and applauded him only at the end of his 20-minute talk. Carter is trying to get other nations to join the boycott. The U.S. Olympic Committee has indicated it will accede to Carter's request and pass up the Games (→ 6/22).

Teacher and thinker Erich Fromm dies

March 18. Philosopher and psychoanalyst Erich Fromm has died days short of his 80th birthday. Fromm, who most recently taught at New York University, held that the pursuit of communism or fascism is an "Escape from Freedom," as one of his books put it. On the other hand, his idea that workers become estranged from themselves in industrial society is a theory any Marxist would willingly embrace. "Man for Himself" (1947), "The Art of Loving" (1956) and "The Anatomy of Human Destructiveness" (1970) were well-received.

Lowenstein, noted politician, is killed

March 14. A mentally unstable gunman walked into the law office of Allard Lowenstein, former U.S. Congressman from Long Island, and fired five bullets into his heart and lungs. The assailant, Dennis Sweeney, reportedly shot Lowenstein and then waited calmly for the police to come and arrest him. Sweeney said Lowenstein had pressured his family in a lawsuit, which he claims resulted in the heart attack death of his stepfather. Lowenstein was best known for his successful effort to block the 1968 re-election bid of President Johnson.

Oil platform is hit in North Sea storm

March 28. An oil field platform with more than 200 people on board collapsed in a North Sea storm last night, and more than 60 people are missing. The platform was operated by the Phillips Petroleum Company in the Norwegian section of the North Sea oil field. It was reported to have overturned in a gale of near-hurricane force and to be adrift upside down today. At least 20 ships were in the area of the platform, but rescue operations were hampered by poor visibility and high seas. Only 91 persons have been rescued thus far.

1980

APRIL

Su	Mo	Tu	We	Th	Fr	Sa
		1	2	3	4	5
6	7	8	9	10	11	12
13	14	15	16	17	18	19
20	21	22	23	24	25	26
27	28	29	30			

1. New York: 33,000 transit workers strike as talks fail.

2. U.S. Windfall Profits Tax imposed on oil industry (→ 6/10).

6. Havana: 10,000 surround Peruvian Embassy, demanding right to leave country (→ 14).

7. U.S. cuts ties with Iran, imposing sanctions for Khomeini's backing of captors (→ 9).

7. Misgav Am: Israelis retake kibbutz, killing five who seized hostages yesterday (→ 6/4).

9. Tehran: Militants say hostages die if U.S. tries even smallest military action (→ 17).

12. Liberia: Pres. William R. Tolbert Jr. killed in army coup.

13. Spaniard Severiano Ballesteros becomes youngest and only second foreigner to win Masters golf title.

14. New York: Off Broadway play "Talley's Folly," by Lanford Wilson, wins Pulitzer.

16. Alaska ends state income tax.

17. Carter says military action is only choice left to U.S. if Iran fails to free captives (→ 20).

17. Washington: John Anderson prepared to run for president on independent ticket (→ 6/10).

20. Tehran: Revolutionary Council closes universities to combat unrest (→ 24).

21. Boston: Bill Rodgers wins third straight Boston Marathon.

22. Washington: Mount St. Helens erupts again after four-week silence (→ 5/18).

24. White House announces eight U.S. deaths in failed rescue attempt in Iran (→ 26).

26. Tehran: Hostages to be moved to several cities (→ 28).

27. Bogota: Rebels end 61-day siege at Dominican Embassy.

30. U.S.: Bert Lance cleared on nine counts of fraud.

30. London: Three gunmen seize Iranian Embassy, hold 20 hostages (→ 5/5).

DEATH

30. Luis Munoz Marin, first popularly elected governor of Puerto Rico (*2/18/1898).

Gordie Howe at 52 hangs up his skates

Howe: 1,850 career points in NHL.

April 30. The durable Gordie Howe has retired again—this time for good. At 52, the former Detroit Red Wing, who in 1973 resumed his career with the Houston Aeros of the World Hockey Association, has hung up his skates. In 25 years with the Wings, Howe set National Hockey League records for the most games played (1,687), most goals (801), most assists (1,049) and most points (1,850).

As Juliana leaves, Beatrix takes crown

April 30. Queen Juliana of the Netherlands abdicated today on her 71st birthday, and her daughter Beatrix, 42, known for her liberal views, became the nation's sixth sovereign. At this time, her 13 million subjects are divided on political and religious issues, and rock-throwing squatters protested housing conditions during the ceremony.

Beatrix is crowned in Amsterdam.

Hostage rescue is fiasco

Disaster in the desert: Helicopter wreckage after the failed rescue attempt.

April 28. President Carter's effort to free the American hostages in Tehran collapsed in the Iranian desert Friday. Today, the president received another jolt. Secretary of State Vance resigned out of disagreement with the rescue mission.

A grim-faced president went on television early Friday morning to announce that the mission had failed and eight American servicemen were dead. Carter said that he took full responsibility. Eight helicopters full of commandos had been dispatched to Iran to free the hostages, but they were called back after three had technical failures. The choppers landed in the desert to refuel. The eight servicemen were killed when one of the helicopters collided with a transport plane.

Questions were raised immediately about the failed mission because of the Iranians' threat to kill the hostages if the United States took military action. Lawmakers on Capitol Hill closed ranks behind the president, but it is not clear how long their support will last. The day before the mission, the Senate Foreign Relations Committee moved to discourage Carter from taking military action against Iran without first consulting Congress (→ 5/24).

Jean-Paul Sartre, Existentialist, is dead

April 15. Paris mourns philosopher Jean-Paul Sartre, who has died at the age of 74. He leaves Simone de Beauvoir, his lover and intellectual sparring partner of 50 years.

Mourners fill the streets of Paris.

He also leaves a plethora of nonfiction and fiction, including the treatise "Being and Nothingness" and the disturbing play "No Exit."

Sartre was born to a bourgeois family that never really appreciated his intellectual capacity. He learned to read before he was four and at an early age decided words were "the quintessence of things." By the time he was in his 60's, a Marxist joining the street protests of May 1968, his view was altered. "Commitment is an act," he said, "not a word."

In 1933, he studied philosophy under Martin Heidegger, who enlarged his ideas on being and perception. Sartre, in turn, urged his readers to be self-determining, to free themselves from others' expectations and truly feel alive.

Rhodesia takes African name Zimbabwe

April 18. At midnight, Rhodesia became the independent state of Zimbabwe. Britain's Prince Charles presented Zimbabwe's new President, the Rev. Canaan Banana, with documents signed by Queen Elizabeth II granting independence to the colony. Blacks celebrated the end of years of struggle to obtain majority rule as the new green, yellow, black and red flag replaced the Union Jack. Only four months ago, Britain negotiated a cease-fire and set up an interim colonial government, which prepared for elections.

Former guerrilla leader Robert Mugabe, whose party won a majority in March's parliamentary elections, was sworn in as Prime Minister of Zimbabwe's first black majority government at the ceremony.

Smith (center) bows out to Mugabe.

Representatives of 104 nations were present. Former Prime Minister Ian D. Smith had declared independence from Britain in 1965 rather than accept a proposed transition to black rule. In his speech today, Mugabe stressed the importance of reconciliation between blacks and whites in Zimbabwe (→ 8/27).

Cuban refugees to be admitted to U.S.

April 14. After a bus full of Cubans smashed its way into the Peruvian Embassy in Cuba, killing a Cuban guard, Fidel Castro withdrew his guards from the embassy and announced that any Cubans who wished to emigrate to Peru could go to the compound. Some 10,000 Cubans flocked into the embassy grounds, quickly overwhelming the facilities. President Carter has agreed to admit 3,500 into the U.S. and urged other nations to provide aid to the refugees as they flee Cuba by air and sea (→ 6/1).

Rarest of stamps is sold for $850,000

April 5. Within 50 seconds, the world's rarest stamp was auctioned at the Waldorf Astoria Hotel with a price tag of $850,000. In fact, the anonymous purchaser paid closer to $935,000, ten percent of which went for fees to the auctioneer. Ten years ago, the one-cent British Guiana 1856 magenta fetched a mere $280,000. On that occasion the buyer was Irwin Weinberg, the investor who sold the stamp today. Weinberg was about the ninth owner of the one-of-a-kind item, found by a British Guiana teen in 1873 who sold it for about $1.50.

Hitchcock, master of suspense, is dead

April 29. Alfred Hitchcock, who died today at age 80 in Los Angeles, left us his anxiety. As a lad, he was locked for five minutes in a jail cell by his father to learn what happens to bad boys, and he grew up with a plethora of phobias. Heights ("Vertigo") and open places (the crop duster scene with Cary Grant in "North by Northwest") were among his fears. He profited by them. The director was nominated for Oscars five times, winning with "Rebecca" in 1940. He was recently knighted by Queen Elizabeth.

Hitchcock, in famous profile.

1980

MAY

Su	Mo	Tu	We	Th	Fr	Sa
				1	2	3
4	5	6	7	8	9	10
11	12	13	14	15	16	17
18	19	20	21	22	23	24
25	26	27	28	29	30	31

2. U.S.: Jobless rate now at 7%, largest in three years (→ 1/29/81).

2. Pope John Paul II begins African tour (→ 4).

3. Genuine Risk, Jacinto Vasquez riding, becomes 2nd filly in history to win Kentucky Derby.

4. Belgrade: President Tito dies after four-month illness (→ 8).

8. World Health Organization announces worldwide eradication of smallpox.

9. St. Petersburg: 32 killed as ship tears 1,000-foot section of bridge, dropping bus and four cars into Tampa Bay.

11. Sweden: Two weeks of strikes end as pay raise is granted (→ 9/19/82).

12. London: Picasso's "Saltimbanque" sold for record $3 mil.

16. EPA finds evidence of chromosome damage in residents of Love Canal area (→ 19).

18. Washington: Eight dead as Mt. St. Helens erupts (→ 19).

19. Niagara Falls, N.Y.: Homeowners at Love Canal hold EPA official five hours, demanding evacuation of area (→ 20).

19. Miami: 18 killed, 400 injured in three days of riots sparked by acquittal of four police charged with murdering black (→ 7/25).

21. Jean Marie Bulter becomes first woman to graduate from U.S. service academy (→ 6/30/82).

21. U.S.: "Star Wars" sequel "The Empire Strikes Back" opens.→

22. New York: Met opens Picasso show.

24. New York Islanders win hockey's Stanley Cup.

24. The Hague: World Court orders release of all U.S. hostages held in Iran (→ 29).

27. South Korea: Govt. troops retake Kwangju, foiling coup (→ 8/16).

29. Fort Wayne, Indiana: Vernon Jordan, pres. of Natl. Urban League, shot in back.

29. Britain, after long holdout, imposes sanctions on Iran (→ 7/5).

Tito, who told off Stalin, dead at 87

Tito lies in state in Belgrade.

May 8. Leaders from 115 countries paid their respects to Joseph Broz Tito in Belgrade today. Yugoslavia's independent-minded President-for-Life died four days ago, just three days short of his 88th birthday. Vice President Mondale represented the United States at the funeral. Also attending were two antagonists who had never met, Soviet leader Leonid Brezhnev and Chinese party chief Hua Kuo-feng.

In a eulogy, Stevan Doronjski, the new Yugoslav party head, recalled with pride Tito's break with Stalin in 1948. A statement from the Central Committee praised Tito for uniting the diverse elements in Yugoslavia. "He knew well," it said, "that it is our destiny to be interlinked, that for centuries we fought against foreign invaders, that our feeling is that everybody must be master in his own house."

Quebec rejects idea of separate nation

May 20. Residents of Quebec voted overwhelmingly today against a move to put that predominantly French-speaking province on the road out of the Canadian federation. The vote was a victory for Canadian Prime Minister Pierre Elliott Trudeau and Claude Ryan, leader of the Quebec Liberal Party. In urging against breaking up Canada, the two men had promised to work for constitutional changes. Sovereignty forces failed to win a majority of French-speaking voters who make up 80 percent of Quebec's 6.2 million residents. About 54 percent of those French voters joined with the non-French minority in voting no (→ 7/1).

710 families will leave Love Canal

May 20. New York state and federal officials have agreed on evacuating the 710 families remaining in the Love Canal area of Niagara Falls. They have not agreed on how the cost will be shared or whether the evacuation will be permanent, but they have decided that health hazards are great enough to remove residents whose homes are near the site of an abandoned chemical dump. Scientists say they have detected chromosome damage in 11 of 36 Love Canal residents whose cells were tested (→ 4/18/81).

Pope touring Africa; rush to mass kills 9

Pope spreads the Word in Africa.

May 4. Pope John Paul II was unaware this afternoon that crowds attending his open-air mass in Kinshasa, Zaire, trampled to death seven worshippers. About 1.5 million Zaireans thronged the plaza of the people's palace to hear the pope on this, the first stop of an extensive African tour. Seven women and two children were crushed in the excitement, as reported by the state-run radio station.

The pope greeted the people in four dialects and consecrated seven bishops. And he spent much of the five-hour mass on a bamboo and ebony throne. The globe-trotting pope supports the Third World's poor in their struggle against exploitation, but he has warned the clergy against taking political roles. He visits the Congo, Kenya and Ghana later this week (→ 11/15).

Here's Johnny! for three more years of gab

Carson got his start as a magician.

May 6. Johnny Carson has signed a three-year contract with NBC-TV to continue as star of the "Tonight Show" in a format that will be reduced from one and a half hours to one hour in September, and at a salary said to be in excess of $5 million a year. Carson, 54, will host the program four nights a week, leaving Mondays and vacation periods to guest hosts and reruns. The show, which he has hosted since 1962, is among the network's most profitable, and is seen by an average of 15.5 million viewers when Johnny himself is there. Carson will also develop and produce other projects for NBC.

Darth Vader is back for another crack at Luke, Han and the Princess in "The Empire Strikes Back." Judging from box office receipts, director George Lucas may be the one with The Force.

British storm Iran's Embassy, freeing 19

May 5. The explosions and gunfire of a combat zone rattled an elegant section of London, as British commandos and police fought their way into the Iranian Embassy to free 19 hostages who had been held there for five and a half days.

The situation began when gunmen identifying themselves as members of Iran's Arab minority burst into the embassy, overpowering an officer of Scotland Yard and taking as hostages Iranian diplomats and workers. At least three Britons were also taken captive, an embassy clerk, a British Broadcasting Corporation technician who had been applying for a visa, and the police officer. The building was immediately surrounded by British police.

The gunmen identified themselves to the police and issued a series of demands, including the release of 91 political prisoners said to be held by the Iranians. Over the next few days, the Arabs released five hostages. The raid to free the hostages came after the gunmen suddenly announced that they would begin killing their captives unless their demands were met. Two hostages were shot to back up the threat. At that point, the British police stormed the building amid flames and explosions. Three of the five gunmen were killed in the raid, but the remaining hostages were freed.

Eight are killed as Mt. St. Helens blows

Ashes this time drifted 500 miles.

May 19. At least eight persons died today when Mount St. Helens erupted, sending up a 60,000-foot tower of ash that darkened the skies as far east as Walla Walla, 160 miles away. The long-dormant volcano had been monitored for weeks by geologists after it began emitting steam and ash. It erupted at 8:39 a.m. today with an explosion that blew the top off the 9,677-foot peak and was felt 100 miles away.

Most of the deaths occurred when the eruption sent flood waters and mudslides down the Toutle River Valley, inundating the few residents who had not been evacuated. Forests around the volcano were hit with dozens of fires burning out of control. Geologists said the eruption probably was triggered by two earthquakes that occurred before the volcano blew (→ 10/17).

May 25. Johnny Rutherford waves to the crowd after becoming the sixth driver to win the Indy 500 three times. Rutherford won in 1976 and 1974.

1980

JUNE

Su	Mo	Tu	We	Th	Fr	Sa
1	2	3	4	5	6	7
8	9	10	11	12	13	14
15	16	17	18	19	20	21
22	23	24	25	26	27	28
29	30					

4. West Bank: Protest strike fails as Israelis compel shops to open (→ 8/19).

5. U.S.: Gulf and Western announce new battery that will run electric car.

8. UNICEF predicts 20 million African lives are threatened by famine and war (→ 10/18/83).

10. Reagan, who would be oldest president if elected, vows to resign if White House doctors find him unfit to serve (→ 7/17).

10. U.S.: John Travolta and Debra Winger star in opening of "Urban Cowboy."

10. Algiers: 13 OPEC ministers hike oil prices up to $32 per barrel (→ 23).

13. Washington: Congressman John Jenrette indicted for conspiracy in Abscam case (→ 8/29).

13. South Africa discloses major raid on Namibian rebels in Angola (→ 17).

13. Chicago: AT&T fined $1.8 bil. in antitrust conviction.

16. U.S. Supreme Court rules 5-4 that new life forms created in lab can be patented (→ 6/18/81).

17. Soweto: At least eight killed as police break up black protest (→ 1/30/81).

20. U.S. Congress deregulates trucking industry.

22. Soviets announce partial withdrawal of troops in Afghanistan (→ 9/16).

26. France announces testing prototype of neutron bomb (→ 8/5).

28. Fighting on Thailand-Cambodian border disrupting U.N. famine relief efforts (→ 1/7/85).

29. Penn.: Full-scale release of Krypton gas begins at Three Mile Island (→ 1/31/81).

DEATHS

7. Philip Guston, American painter (*6/13/1913).

24. Clyfford Still, U.S. Abstract Expressionist, largest one-person show at Met (*11/30/1904).

25. David Burpee, mail order seed catalogue founder.

Cuban refugees riot at Arkansas camp

June 1. Protesting the slow pace at which the relocation center was processing their cases, Cuban refugees at the Fort Chaffee Army Reserve Base in Arkansas threw stones at police and soldiers after bursting out the front gate.

About 18,000 Cuban refugees now occupy the Fort Chaffee relocation center. Today's riot was only the latest in a series of incidents in which up to 1,000 refugees have banded together to demand their freedom from the center. This was the first time, however, that police and soldiers were forced to use tear gas and clubs to quell the disturbances. About 25 people were injured, at least 15 of whom were police officers (→ 10/13).

Pryor nearly killed by drug explosion

Pryor, victim of cocaine freebasing.

June 10. Prize-winning comedian Richard Pryor is in critical condition today after a volatile mixture of ether and cocaine exploded in his face. Pryor was concocting the substances to produce free base, a powerfully euphoric cocaine derivative. Authorities are not sure what sparked the blast; perhaps a cigarette ignited the flammable liquid.

Pryor, known for his hilarious stand-up comedy acts and his movie roles, ran screaming for nearly a mile with his clothes ablaze until he got help. He suffered extensive burns over his upper torso and the polyester shirt he was wearing melted to his body.

Leaders pledge to seek new energy sources

"We must break the link between economic growth and consumption of oil."

June 23. President Carter and leaders of the other industrial countries disagreed sharply about international politics during two days of meetings in Venice. But they did agree on the need for energy independence. Faced with sharply rising OPEC prices, the leaders said they could reduce oil consumption by up to 20 million barrels a day by the end of the decade. "We must break the existing link between economic growth and consumption of oil," they said in a joint declaration.

Carter and the leaders of West Germany, Britain, France, Italy, Canada and Japan agreed that they could replace oil by doubling coal production and developing more nuclear and synthetic sources. The agreement put Carter on a collision course with his own Democratic Party, which adopted a convention platform to "retire nuclear plants in an orderly manner."

On other matters, it was clear that Carter had sharp disagreements with some leaders about their reaction to the Soviet invasion of Afghanistan. It also seemed that Carter has shifted his position in recent weeks. Last month, he was very critical of the meeting in Warsaw between Soviet leader Brezhnev and France's President Valery Giscard d'Estaing. Carter was also skeptical about the upcoming visit of West Germany's Chancellor Helmut Schmidt to Moscow. Today, President Carter said that contacts between Western leaders and Moscow might be useful in stressing their opposition to Soviet activities in Afghanistan (→ 2/16/82).

June 20. The stone hands of Roberto Duran, brawler from the Panama slums, have stripped previously unbeaten Sugar Ray Leonard of his welterweight title.

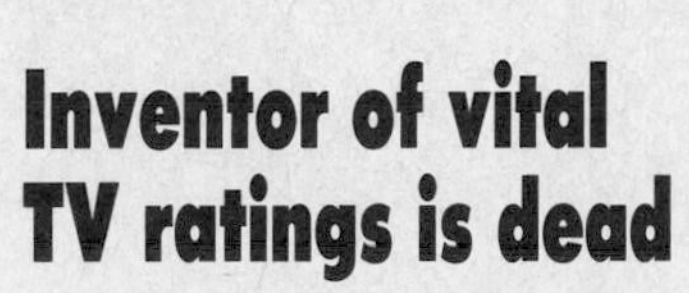

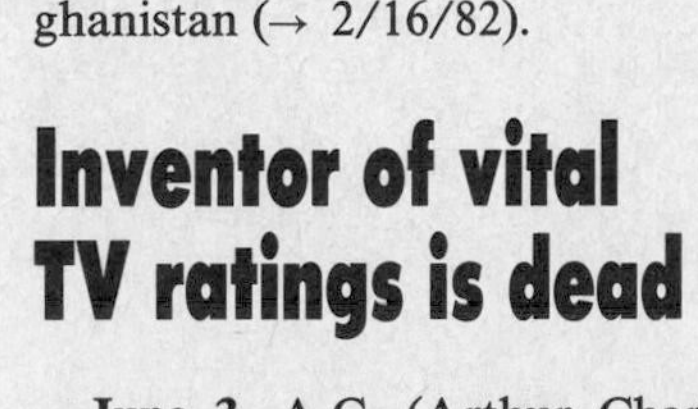

Inventor of vital TV ratings is dead

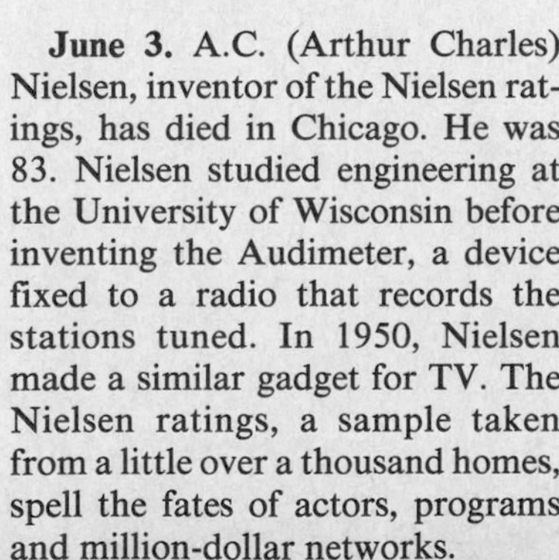

June 3. A.C. (Arthur Charles) Nielsen, inventor of the Nielsen ratings, has died in Chicago. He was 83. Nielsen studied engineering at the University of Wisconsin before inventing the Audimeter, a device fixed to a radio that records the stations tuned. In 1950, Nielsen made a similar gadget for TV. The Nielsen ratings, a sample taken from a little over a thousand homes, spell the fates of actors, programs and million-dollar networks.

1980

JULY

Su	Mo	Tu	We	Th	Fr	Sa
		1	2	3	4	5
6	7	8	9	10	11	12
13	14	15	16	17	18	19
20	21	22	23	24	25	26
27	28	29	30	31		

1. Canada proclaims national anthem in effort to enhance unity (→ 4/13/81).

2. Carter signs bill for draft registration at age 18 (→ 18).

3. Warsaw: Unannounced increase in price of meat brings work stoppages (→ 8/14).

5. Tehran: Women protest at president's office over Islamic dress code (→ 11).

5. Pope John Paul II warns against manipulation of mind by radio and television.

9. U.S.: Harper's Magazine bought by two foundations to forestall bankruptcy.

10. Tokyo: Carter meets with Hua of China to solidify ties against Soviet threat (→ 10/22).

11. Bonn: Richard Queen, released by Iran for illness, arrives in West Germany (→ 14).

14. Tehran: 26 executed by firing squads (→ 18).

14. Billy Carter registers as agent of Libyan govt., discloses he received $200,000 in payments.

17. Marjorie Matthews, Methodist minister, becomes first woman bishop of U.S. church.

18. Washington: Federal court voids Selective Service Act for excluding women (→ 19).

18. India becomes sixth nation to put satellite into orbit (→ 10/11).

18. France: Shah of Iran's last premier, Shahpur Bakhtiar, unhurt in attempt on life (→ 27).

19. Supreme Court Justice William Brennan rules draft registration may begin (→ 11/3/81).

21. Joop Zoetemelk wins Tour de France.

25. Chattanooga: Civilian patrols used to quell racial rioting (→ 4/19/81).

28. Lima: Fernando Belaunde Terry sworn in as president, ending 12 years military rule.

31. Detroit: Chrysler reports largest loss ever by U.S. car maker, $536.1 million.

DEATH

1. C.P. Snow, British novelist, physicist, civil servant (*10/15/1905).

Brezhnev opens boycotted Olympics

Opening ceremonies in Moscow.

July 19. The Games of the 22nd Olympiad were opened in Moscow, but the talented athletes of the United States, West Germany and Japan were not in attendance.

The boycotting countries were protesting the military intervention of the Soviet Union in Afghanistan. There was even a military tone to the Olympic preparations as the Soviet capital was sealed off and normal traffic barred from the streets hours before the opening ceremony.

Leonid I. Brezhnev, the party Chairman, declared the Games open after policemen and soldiers formed a wall around Lenin Stadium to control the thousands of athletes and spectators arriving for the Games. The 81 teams on hand marked the lowest number since the Melbourne Olympics of 1956.

Before Brezhnev arrived, two Americans in the stands unfurled the stars and stripes and stretched it over their heads. People in the 103,000-seat stadium applauded. Sixteen teams chose to fly the Olympic flag rather than their national banners to protest Afghanistan.

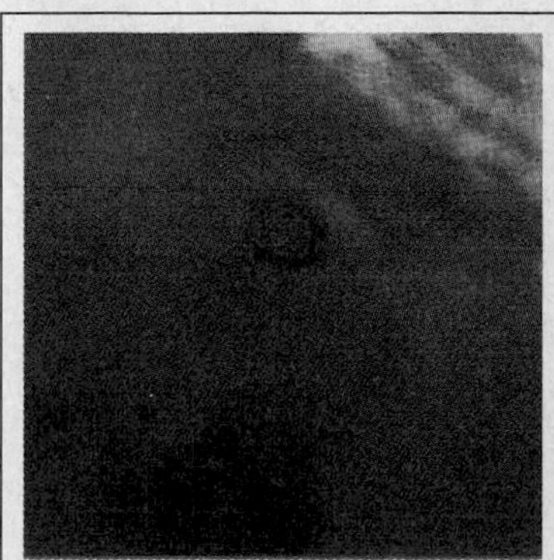

July 13. A five-million-sq.-mile section of the Tharsis Ridge volcanic region of Mars, as seen today from Viking Orbiter I.

1980 Moscow

Men Athletics

100 M Dash
1. Allan Wells GBR 10,24
2. Silvio Leonard CUB 10,25
3. Petyr Petrov BUL 10,39

200 M Dash
1. Pietro Mennea ITA 20,19
2. Allan Wells GBR 20,21
3. Donald Quarrie JAM 20,29

400 M Run
1. Viktor Markin URS 44,60
2. Rick Mitchell AUS 44,84
3. Franck Shaffer GDR 44,87

800 M Run
1. Steven Owett GBR 1:45,4
2. Sebastian Coe GBR 1:45,9
3. Nicolai Kirov URS 1:46,0

1500 M Run
1. Sebastian Coe GBR 3:38,4
2. Jurgen Straub GDR 3:38,8
3. Steven Owett GBR 3:39,0

5000 M Run
1. Miruts Yifter ETH 13:21,0
2. Suleiman Nyambui TAN 13:21,6
3. Kaarlo Maaninka FIN 13:22,0

10,000 M Run
1. Miruts Yifter ETH 27:42,7
2. Kaarlo Maaninka FIN 27:44,3
1. Mohammed Kadir ETH 27:44,7

Marathon
1. Waldemar Cierpinski GDR 2:11,03
2. Gerald Nijboer HOL 2:11,20
3. Satymk Dzhumenazarova URS 2:11,35

110 M Hurdles
1. Thomas Munkelt GDR 13,39
2. Alejandro Casanas CUB 13,40
3. Alexander Puchkov URS 13,44

400 M Hurdles
1. Volker Beck GDR 48,70
2. Vassili Arkhipenko URS 48,86
3. Gary Oakes GBR 49:11

3000 M Steeplechase
1. Bronislaw Malinowski POL 8:09,7
2. Filbert Baya TAN 8:12,5
3. Eshetu Tura ETH 8:13,6

400 M Relay
1. URS 38,26 (Vladimir Muraviov, Nicolai Sidorov Alexander Aksinin, Andrei Prokofiev)
2. POL 38,33 (Krzystof Swolinski, Zenon Liczerski, Leszck Dunecki, Marian Woronin)
3. FRA 38,53 (Antoine Richard, Pascal Barre, Patrick Barré Hermann Panzo)

1600 M Relay
1. URS 3:01, (Remigius Valiusis, Michail Linge, Nicolai Chernetsky, Victor Markin)
2. GDR 3:01,3 (Klaus Thiele, Andreas Knebel, Frank Schaffer, Volker Beck)
3. ITA 3:04,3 (Stefano Malinverni, Mauro Zuliani, Roberto Tozzi, Pietro Mennea)

20 km Walk
1. Maurizio Damilano ITA 1:23:35
2. Poitr Pochinchuk URS 1:24,45

50 km Walk
1. Hartwig Gauder GDR 3:49,24
2. Jorge Llopart ESP 3:51:25
3. Jewgeni Ulvchenko URS 3:56:32

High Jump
1. Gerd Wessig GDR 2,36
2. Jacek Wszola POL 2,31
3. Jorg Freimuth GDR 2,31

1. Pole Vault
1. Wladyslaw Kozakiewicz POL 5,78
2. Konstantin Volkov URS 5,65
3. Tadeusz Slusarski POL 5,65

Long Jump
1. Lutz Dombrovski GDR 8,54
2. Frank Paschek GDR 8,21
3. Valeri Podluzny URS 8,18

Triple Jump
1. Jaak Uudmas URS 17,35
2. Vikter Saneiev URS 17,24
3. Joao Carlos de Oliveira BRA 17,22

Shotpput
1. Vladimir Kiseliev URS 21,35
2. Alexander Barichnikov URS 21,08
3. Udo Beyer GDR 21,06

Discus Throw
1. Viktor Raschupkin URS 66,64
2. Imrich Bugar TCH 66,38
3. Luis Delis CUB 66,32

Hammer Throw
1. Juri Sedykh URS 81,80
2. Sergei Litvinov URS 80,64
3. Juri Tamm URS 78,96

Javelin
1. Dainis Kula URS 91,20
2. Alexander Makarov URS 89,64
3. Wolfgang Hanisch GDR 86,72

Decathlon
1. Daley Thompson GBR 8495
2. Juri Kutsenko URS 8331
3. Sergeo Zhelanov URS 8135

Women Athletics

100 M Dash
1. Ludmila Kondratieva URS 11,06
2. Marlies Gohr GDR 11,07
3. Ingrid Auerswald GDR 11,14

200 M Dash
1. Barbel Wockel GDR 22,03
2. Natalia Bochina URS 22,19
3. Merlent Ottey JAM 22,20

400 M Run
1. Marita Koch GDR 48,88
2. Jarmila Kratochvukiva TCH 49,46
3. Christine Lathan GDR 49,66

800 M Run
1. Nadejda Olizarenko URS 1:53,5
2. Olga Minieva URS 1:54,9
3. Tatiana Providokhina URS 1:55,5

1500 M Run
1. Tatiana Kazankina URS 3:56,6
2. Christiane Wartenberg GDR 3:57,8
3. Nadejda Olizarenko URS 3:59,6

100 M Hurdles
1. Vera Komisova URS 12,56
2. Johanna Klier GDR 12,63
3. Lucyna Langer POL 12,65

400 M Relay
1. RDA 41,60 (Ingrid Auerswald, Marlies Gohr, Romy Muller, Barbel Wockel)
2. URS 42,10 (Vera Komisova, Vera Anisimova, Ludmila Maslakova, Natalia Bochina)
3. GBR 42,43 (Heater Hunte, Kathryn Smallwood, Beverley Goddard Sonia Lannaman)

1600 M Relay
1. URS 3:20,2 (Tatiana Prorochenko, Tatiana Goistchik, Nina Suskova, Irina Nasareva)
2. GDR 3:20,4 (Gabriele Lowe, Barbara Krug, Christina Lathan, Marita Koch)
3. GBR 3:27,5 (Linsey MacDonald, Michelle Probert, Joslyn Hoyte-Smith, Janine Mac-Gregor)

200 M Freestyle
1. Sergei Kopliakov URS 1:49,81
2. Andrei Krylov URS 1:50,76
3. Graenie Brewer AUS 1:51,60

400 M Freestyle
1. Vladimir Salnikov URS 3:51,31
2. Andrei Krylov URS 3:53,24
3. Iwar Stukolkin URS 3:53,95

1500 M Freestyle
1. Vladimir Salkinov URS 14:58,27
2. Alexander Chaev URS 15:14,30
3. Max Metzker AUS 15:14,49

100 M Backstroke
1. Bengt Baron SWE 56,63
2. Viktor Kuznetsov URS 56,99
3. Vladimir Dolgov URS 57,63

200 M Backstroke
1. Sandor Wladar HUN 2:01,93
2. Zoltan Verraszto HUN 2:02,40
3. Mark Kerry AUS 2:03,14

100 M Breaststroke
1. Duncan Goodhew GBR 1:03,34
2. Arsen Miskarov URS 1:03,82
3. Peter Evans AUS 1:03,96

200 M Breaststroke
1. Robertas Julpa URS 2:15,85
2. Alban Vermes HUN 2:16,93
3. Arsen Miskarov URS 2:17,28

100 M Butterfly Stroke
1. Par Arvidsson SWE 54,92
2. Roger Pyttel GDR 54,94
3. David Lopez ESP 55,13

200 M Butterfly Stroke
1. Sergei Fesenko URS 1:59,76
2. Philipp Hubble GBR 2:01,20
3. Roger Pyttel GDR 2:01,39

400 M Medley
1. Alexander Sidorenko URS 4:22,89
2. Sergei Fesenko URS 4:23,43
3. Zoltan Verraszto HUN 4:24,24

800 M Freestyle Relay
1. URS 7:23,50 (Sergei Kopliakov, Vladimir Salnikov, Ivan Stukolkin, Andrei Krylov)

Colorful pageantry failed to mask the absence of the United States, West Germany and a number of other teams, using the Games as a forum to protest the Soviet invasion of Afghanistan.

High Jump
1. Sara Simeoni ITA 1,97
2. Urszula Kielan POL 1,94
3. Jutta Kirst GDR 1,94

Long Jump
1. Tatiana Kolpakova URS 7,06
2. Brigitte Wujak GDR 7,04
3. Tatiana Skachko URS 7,01

Shotput
1. Ilona Slupianek GDR 22,41
2. Svetlana Krachvskaya URS 21,42
3. Margitta Pufe GDR 21,20

Discus Throw
1. Evelin Jahl GDR 69,96
2. Maria Petkova-Vergova BUL 67,90
3. Tatiana Lesovaya URS 67,40

Javelin
1. Maria Caridad Colon CUB 68,40
2. Saida Gunba URS 67,76
3. Ute Hommola GDR 66,65

Pentathlon
1. Nadejda Tkachenko URS 5083
2. Olga Rukavishnikova URS 4937
3. Olga Kuragina URS 4875

Men Swimming

100 M Freestyle
1. Jorg Woithe GDR 50,40
2. Per-Alvar Homertz SWE 50,91
3. Per Johansson SWE 51,29

2. GDR 7:28,60 (Frank Pfutze, Jorg Woithe, Detlev Grabs, Rainer Strohbach)
3. BRA 7:29,30 (Jorge Luiz Fernandes, Marcus Mattioli, Ciro Marques Delgado, Djan Garrido Madruga)

400 M Medley Relay
1. AUS 3:45,70 (Mark Kerry, Peter Evans, Mark Tonelli, Neil Brooks)
2. URS 3:45,92 (Victor Kuznetsov, Arsen Miskarov, Jevgeni Seredin, Sergei Kopliakov)
3. GBR 3:47,71 (Gary Abraham, Duncan Goodhew, David Lowe, Martin Smith)

Springboard Diving
1. Alexander Portnov URS 905,025
2. Carlos Giron MEX 892,140
3. Giogio Cagnotto ITA 871,500

Water-Polo

1. Soviet Union
2. Yugoslavia
3. Hungary

See Table of contents for abbreviations

Women Swimming

100 M Freestyle
1. Barbara Krause GDR 54,79
2. Caren Metschuk GDR 55,16
3. Ines Diers GDR 55,65

200 M Freestyle
1. Barbara Krause GDR 1:58,33
2. Ines Diers GDR 1:59,64
3. Carmela Schmitt GDR 2:01,44

400 M Freestyle
1. Ines Diers GDR 4:08,76
2. Petra Schneider GDR 4:09,16
3. Carmela Schmitt GDR 4:10,86

800 M Freestyle
1. Michelle Ford AUS 8:28,90
2. Ines Diers GDR 8:32,55
3. Heike Dane GDR 8:33,48

100 M Breaststroke
1. Ute Geweniger GDR 1:10,22
2. Elvira Vasilkova URS 1:10,41
3. Susanne Schultz-Nielsson DEN 1:11,16

200 M Breaststroke
1. Lina Kachuschite URS 2:29,54
2. Svetlana Varganova URS 2:29,61
3. Julia Bogdanova URS 2:32,39

100 M Backstroke
1. Rica Reinisch GDR 1:00,86
2. Ina Kleber GDR 1:02,07
3. Petra Riedel GDR 1:02,65

200 M Backstroke
1. Rica Reinisch GDR 2:11,77
2. Cornelia Polit GDR 2:13,75
3. Birgit Treiber GDR 2:14,14

100 M Butterfly Stroke
1. Caren Metschuk GDR 1:00,42
2. Andrea Pollack GDR 1:00,92
3. Christiane Knacke GDR 1:01,44

200 M Butterfly Stroke
1. Ines Geissler GDR 2:10,44
2. Sybille Schonrock GDR 2:10,45
3. Michelle Ford AUS 2:11,66

400 M Medley
1. Petra Schneider GDR 4:36,29
2. Sharon Davies GBR 4:46,83
3. Agnieszka Czopek POL 4:48,17

400 M Freestyle Relay
1. GDR 3:42,71 (Barbara Krause, Caren Metschuk, Ines Diers, Sarina Hulsenbeck)
2. SWE 3:48,93 (Carina Ljundal, Tina Gustafsson, Agneta Martensson, Agneta Erikson)
3. HOL 3:49,51 (Cornelia van Bentum, Wilma van Velsen, Reggie de Jong, Annelies Maas)

400 M Medley
1. GDR 4:06,67 (Rica Reinisch, Ute Geweninger, Andrea Pollack, Caren Metschuk)
2. GBR 4:12,24 (Hellen Jameson, Margaret Kelly, Ann Osgerby, June Croft)
3. URS 4:13,61 (Jelena Kruglova, Elvira Vasilkova, Askyonova, Klevakina)

Springboard Diving
1. Irina Kalinina URS 725,910
2. Martina Proeber GDR 698,895
3. Karin Guthke GDR 684,245

High Diving
1. Martina Jaschke GDR 595,250
2. Serward Emirzyan URS 576,465
3. Liana Tsotadze URS 575,925

Boxing

Light Flyweight (less than 48 kg)
1. Shamil Sabirov URS
2. Hipolito Ramos CUB
3. Ismail Mustafov BUL
3. Byonk Uk Li PRK

Flyweight (less than 51 kg)
1. Petyr Lessov BUL
2. Victor Mirochnichenko URS
3. Janos Varadi HUN
3. Hugh Russel IRL

Bantamweight (less than 54 kg)
1. Juan Bernardo Hernandez CUB
2. Bernardo Jose Pinango VEN
3. Michael Anthony GUY
3. Dumitriu Cipere ROM

Featherweight (less than 60 kg)
1. Rudi Fink GDR
2. Adolfo Horta CUB
3. Krysztof Kosedovski POL
3. Viktor Ribakov URS

Lightweight (moins de 57 kg)
1. Angel Herrera CUB
2. Viktor Demianenko URS
3. Richard Nowakowski GDR
3. Kazimierz Adach POL

Light Welterweight (less than 63.5 kg)
1. Patrizio Oilve ITA
2. Serik Konakbaev URS
3. Anthony Willis GBR
3. Jose Aguilar CUB

Welterweight (less than 67 kg)
1. Andres Adalma CUB
2. John Mugabi UGA
3. Karl Heinz Kruger RDA
3. Kazimierz Szczerda POL

Light Middleweight (less than 71 kg)
1. Armando Martinez CUB
2. Alexander Kochkin URS
3. Detlef Kastner GDR
3. Jan Franek TCH

Middleweight (less than 75 kg)
1. Jose Gomez CUB
2. Victor Savchenko URS
3. Valentin Silaghi ROM
3. Jerzy Rybieki POL

Light Heavyweight (less than 81 kg)
1. Slbodan Kacar YUG
2. Pavel Skrzecz POL
3. Hebert Bauch GDR
3. Ricardo Rojas CUB

Heavyweight (more than 81 kg)
1. Teofilo Stevenson CUB
2. Piotr Zaev URS
3. Istvan Levai HUN
3. Jurgen Fanghanel GDR

Weightlifting

Flyweight (less than 52 kg)
1. Kanybek Osmolaliev URS 245,00
2. Ho Bong Zol PRK 245,00
3. Han Gyong Si PRK 245,00

Bantamweight (less than 56 kg)
1. Daniel Nunez CUB 275,00
2. Jurik Sarkissian URS 270,00
3. Tadeusz Denbonczyk POL 265,00

Featherweight (less than 60 kg
1. Viktor Mazine URS 290,00
2. Stefan Dimitrov BUL 287,50
3. Marek Seweryn POL 282,50

Lightweight (less than 67.5 kg)
1. Yanko Roossev BUL 342,50
2. Joachim Kunz GDR 335,00
3. Mintcho Pachov BUL 325,00

Middleweight (less than 75 kg)
1. Assen Zlatev BUL 360,00
2. Alexander Pervyi URS 375,50
3. Nedeltcho Kolev BUL 345,00

Middleweight (less than 75 kg)
1. Jurik Vardanian URS 400,00
2. Blagoi Blagoev BUL 372,50
3. Dusan Poliacik TCH 367,50

Light Heavyweight (less than 82.5 kg)
1. Peter Baczako HUN 377,50
2. Rumen Alexandrov BUL 375,00
3. Frank Mantek GDR 370,00

Heavyweight (less than 100 kg)
1. Ota Zaremba TCH 395,00
2. Igor Nikitan URS 392,50
3. Alberto Blanco CUB 385,00

Heavyweight (less than 110 kg)
1. Leonid Taranenko URS 422,50
2. Valentin Christov BUL 405,00
3. Gyorgy Szalai HUN 390,00

Super Heavyweight (more than 110 kg)
1. Sultan Rakhmanov URS 440,50
2. Jurgen Heuser GDR 410,50
3. Tadeusz Rutkowski POL 407,50

Greco Roman Wrestling

Light Flyweight (48 kg)
1. Saksylik Uchkenplirov URS
2. Constantin Alexandru ROM
3. Ferenc Seres HUN

Flyweight (less than 52 kg)
1. Wachtang Blagidze URS
2. Lajos Racs HUN
3. Mladen Mladenov BUL

Bantamweight (less than 57 kg)
1. Chamil Serikov URS
2. Jozef Lipien POL
3. Benni Ljungbeck SWE

Featherweight (less than 62 kg)
1. Stylianous Nijiakis GRE
2. Istvan Toth HUN
3. Boris Kramorenko URS

Lightweight (less than 68 kg)
1. Stefan Rusu ROM
2. Andrezj Supron POL
3. Lars-Erik Skiold SWE

Welterweight (less than 74 kg)
1. Ferenc Kocsis HUN
2. Anatoly Bjkov URS
3. Mikko Huhtala FIN

Middleweight (less than 82 kg)
1. Gennadi Korban URS
2. Jan Dolgowicz POL
3. Pavel Pavlov BUL

Light Heavyweight (less than 90 kg)
1. Norbet Nottny HUN
2. Igor Kanygin URS
3. Petre Dicu ROM

Heavyweight (less than 100 kg)
1. Georgi Raikov BUL
2. Roman Bierla POL
3. Vasile Andrei ROM

Super Heavyweight (more than 110 kg)
1. Alexander Kolchinski URS
2. Alexander Tomov BUL
3. Hassan Bschra LIB

1980 Moscow

Freestyle Wrestling

Flyweight (48 kg)
1. Claudio Pollio ITA
2. Se Hong Jang PRK
3. Sergei Kornilaev URS

Bantamweight (less than 57 kg
1. Sergei Beloglazov URS
2. Ho Hyong Li PRK
3. Dugassuren Ouinbold MON

Featherweight (less than 62 kg
1. Mahomed Hasan Abuchev URS
2. Micho Doukov BUL
3. Georges Hazionides GRE

Lightweight (less than 68 kg)
1. Saipullah Absaidov URS
2. Ivan Yankov BUL
3. Saban Sejdi YUG

Welterweight (less than 74 kg)
1. Valentin Raitchev BUL
2. Jamtsying Davaajav MON
3. Dan Karatin TCH

Middleweight (less than 82 kg
1. Ismail Abilov BUL
2. Mahomet Aratsilov URS
3. Istvan Kovacs HUN

Light Heavyweight (less than 90 kg)
1. Saganar Oganesyan URS
2. Uwe Neupert GDR
3. Alexander Cichon POL

Heavyweight (less than 100 kg)
1. Ilja Mate URS
2. Slavtcho Tchervenkov BUL
3. Julius Strnisko TCH

Super Heavyweight (more than 100 kg)
1. Soslan Andiev URS
2. Joszef Balla HUN
3. Adam Sandurski POL

Judo

Extra Lightweight (less than 60 kg)
1. Theirry Rey FRA
2. Jose Rodriguez CUB
3. Tibor Kineses HUN
3. Arambu Emizh URS

Half Lightweight (less than 64 kg)
1. Nicola Soloduchine URS
2. Zemjing Damdin MON
3. Ilian Nedkov BUL
3. Janusz Pawlowski POL

Lightweight (less than 71 kg)
1. Enzio Gamba ITA
2. Neil Adams GBR
3. Karl-Heinz Lehmann GDR
3. Ravdan Davaadalai MON

Half Middleweight (less than 78 kg)
1. Shota Khabareli URS
2. Juan Ferrer CUB
3. Bernard Tchoullouyan FRA
3. Harald Heinke GDR

Middleweight (less than 86 kg)
1. Jurg Rothlisberger SUI
2. Isaac Aszcuy CUB
3. Detlev Ultsch GDR
3. Alexander Iatskevitch URS

Half Heavyweight (more than 95 kg)
1. Robert van de Walle BEL
2. Tengis Khubuluri URS
3. Dietmar Lorenz GDR
3. Henk Numan HOL

Heavyweight (more than 95 kg)
1. Angelo Parisi FRA
2. Dimitar Zaprianov BUL
3. Vladimir Kocman TCH
3. Radomir Kovacevic YUG

Open Category
1. Dietmar Lorenz GDR
2. Angelo Parisi FRA
3. Andras Ozsvar HUN
3. Arthur Mapp GBR

Men Fencing

Foil Individual
1. Vladimir Smirnov URS 4 victories before tiebreak
2. Pascal Jolyot FRA 4 victories before tiebreak
3. Alexander Romankov URS 3 victories before tiebreak

Foil Team
1. France
2. Soviet Union
3. Poland

Epée Individual
1. Johan Harmenberg SWE 4 v.
2. Emo Kolczonay HUN 3 v. (19:23)
3. Philippe Riboud FRA 3 v. (17:20)

Epée Team
1. France
2. Poland
3. Soviet Union

Sabre Individual
1. Viktor Krovopuskov URS 4 victories before tiebreak
2. Michael Burtsev URS 4 victories before tiebreak
3. Imre Gedovari HUN 3 victories before tiebreak

Sabre Team
1. Soviet Union
2. Italy
3. Hungary

Women Fencing

Foil Individual
1. Pascale Trinquet FRA 4 v.
2. Magda Maros HUN 3 v.
3. Barbara Wysosanska POL 3 v.

Foil Team
1. France
2. Soviet Union
3. Hungary

Modern Pentathlon

Individual
1. Anatoli Starostin URS 5568
2. Tamas Szombathelyi HUN 5502
3. Pavel Lednev URS 5382

Team
1. Soviet Union
2. Hungary
3. Sweden

Men Canoing

Kayak-1 500 M
1. Vladimir Parfenovich URS 1:43,43
2. John Sumegi AUS 1:44,12
3. Vasile Diba ROM 1:44,90

Kayak-1 1000 M
1. Rudiger Helm GDR 3:48,77
2. Alain Lebas FRA 3:50,20
3. Ion Birladeanu ROM 3:50,49

Kayak-2 500 M
1. Soviet Union 1:32,38
2. Spain 1:33,65
3. German Democratic Republic 1:34,00

Kayak-2 1000 M
1. Soviet Union 3:26,72
2. Hungary 3:28,49
3. Spain 3:28,66

Kayak-4 1000 M
1. German Democratic Republic 3:13,76
2. Romania 3:15,35
3. Bulgaria 3:15,46

Canadian-1 500 M
1. Sergei Postrekhin URS 1:53,37
2. Lubomir Lubenov BUL 1:53,49
3. Olaf Heukrodt GDR 1:54,38

Canadian-1 1000 M
1. Lubomir Lubenov BUL 4:12,38
2. Sergei Postrekhin URS 4:13,53
3. Eckhard Leue GDR 4:15,02

Canadian-2 500 M
1. Hungary 1:43,39
2. Romania 1:44,12
3. Bulgaria 1:44,83

Canadian-2 1000 M
1. Romania 3:47,65
2. German Democratic Republic 3:49,93
3. Soviet Union 3:51,28

Women Canoeing

Kayak-1 500 M
1. Birgit Fischer GDR 1:57,96
2. Vania Ghecheva BUL 1:59,48
3. Antonina Melnikova URS 1:59,66

Kayak-2 500 M
1. German Democratic Republic 1:43,88
2. Soviet Union 1:46,91
3. Hungary 1:47,95

Men Rowing

Single Scull
1. Pertti Karppinen FIN 7:09,61
2. Wassili Yakusha URS 7:11,66
3. Peter Kersten GDR 7:14,88

Double Sculls
1. German Democratic Republic 6:24,33
2. Yugoslavia 6:26,34
3. Czechoslovakia 6:29,07

Pair Oars without Coxswain
1. German Democratic Republic 6:48,01
2. Soviet Union 6:50,50
3. Great Britain 6:51,40

Pair Oars with Coxswain
1. German Democratic Republic 7:02,54
2. Soviet Union 7:03,35
3. Yugoslavia 7:04,92

Quadruple Sculls
1. German Democratic Republic 5:49,81
2. Soviet Union 5:51,47
3. Bulgaria 5:51,38

Four Oars without Coxswain
1. German Democratic Republic 6:08,17
2. Soviet Union 6:11,81
3. Great Britain 6:16,58

Four Oars with Coxswain
1. German Democratic Republic 6:14,51
2. Soviet Union 6:19,05
3. Poland 6:22,52

Eight Oars
1. German Democratic Republic 5:49,05
2. Great Britain 5:51,92
3. Soviet Union 5:52,66

Rowing Women

Single Scull
1. Sanda Toma ROM 3:40,69
2. Antonina Makhina URS 3:41,65
3. Martina Schroter GDR 3:43,54

Double Sculls
1. Soviet Union 3:16,27
2. German Democratic Republic 3:17,63
3. Romania 3:18,91

Pair Oars Without Coxswain
1. German Democratic Republic 3:30,49
2. Poland 3:30,95
3. Bulgaria 3:32,39

Four Oars with Coxswain
1. German Democratic Republic 3:19,27
2. Bulgaria 3:20,75
3. Soviet Union 3:20,92

Quadruple Sculls
1. German Democratic Republic 3:15,32
2. Soviet Union 3:15,73
3. Bulgaria 3:16,10

Eight Oars
1. German Democratic Republic 3:03,32
2. Soviet Union 3:04,29
3. Romania 3:05,63

Yachting

Monotype Finn Class
1. Esko Rechardt FIN 36,7
2. Wolfgang Mayrhofer AUT 46,7
3. Andrej Balaschov URS 47,4

Flying Dutchman Class
1. Spain 19,0
2. Ireland 30,0
3. Hungary 45,7

Soling Class
1. Denmark 23,0
2. Soviet Union 30,4
3. Greece 31,1

Star Class
1. Soviet Union 24,7
2. Austria 31,7
3. Italy 36,1

470 Class
1. Brazil 36,4
2. German Democratic Republic 38,7
3. Finland 39,7

Tornado Class
1. Brazil 21,4
2. Denmark 30,4
3. Sweden 33,7

Cycling

Individual Road Race
1. Sergei Soukhorouchenkov URS 4:48,28
2. Czeslaw Lang POL 4:51,25

Sebastian Coe (far left) beat his British teammate Steve Ovett in the 1,500-meters, finishing in 3:38.4. Ovett had earlier edged Coe by .5 of a second in the 800-meters.

3. Juri Barinov URS 4:51,25

100 Km Team Time Trial
1. Soviet Union 49-,4-38 km/h
2. German Democratic Republic 48-,8-26 km/h
3. Czechoslovakia 48-,8-12 km/h

Sprint
1. Lutz Hessligh GDR
2. Yave Cahard FRA
3. Sergei Kopylov URS

1000 M Time Trial
1. Lothar Thoms GDR 1:02,955
2. Alexander Panvilov URS 1:04,845
3. David Weller JAM 1:05,241

Individual Pursuit (4000 M)
1. Robert Dill-Bundi SUI 4:35,66
2. Alain Bondue FRA 4:42,96
3. Hans-Erik Orsted DEN 4:36,54

Team Pursuit (4000 M)
1. Soviet Union 4:15,68
2. German Democratic Republic 4:19,68
3. Czechoslovakia

Equestrian Sports

All Around Individual Competition
1. Federico Roman ITA -108,70
2. Alexander Blinov URS -120,80
3. Juri Salnikov URS -151,60

All Around Team Competition
1. Soviet Union -457,00
2. Italy -656,20
3. Mexico -1171,85

Individual Dressage
1. Elisabeth Theurer AUT 1370
2. Juri Kovshov URS 1300
3. Victor Ugryumov URS 1234

Team Dressage
1. Soviet Union 4384,0
2. Bulgaria 3580,0
3. Romania 3346,0

Individual Grand Prix Jumping
1. Jan Kowalczyk POL -8
2. Nicolai Korolkov URS -9,50
3. Joaquin Perez de las Heras MEX -12
3. Osvaldo Mendez Her bruger GUA -12

Team Grand Prix Jumping
1. Soviet Union -20,25
2. Poland -56,00
3. Mexico -59,75

Shooting

Small-Bore Rifle, 50 M, Prone
1. Karoly Verga HUN 599
2. Hellfried Heilfort GDR 599
3. Petyr Saprianov BUL 598

Small-Bore Rifle, Combined, 3 Positions
1. Viktor Vlassov URS 1173
2. Bernd Hartstein GDR 1166
3. Sven Johansson SWE 1165

Rapid Fire Pistol, 25 M
1. Corneliu Ion ROM 596+443
2. Jurgen Wiefel GDR 596+442
3. Gerhard Petritsch AUT 596+146

Free Pistol
1. Alexander Melentev URS 581
2. Harald Vollmar GDR 568
3. Lubtcho Diakov BUL 565

Clay Pigeon (Trench)
1. Luciano Giovanetti ITA 198
2. Rustam Iambulatov URS 196
3. Jorg Damme GDR 196

Skeet
1. Hans-Kjeld Rasmussen DEN 196
2. Lars-Goran Carlsson SWE 196
3. Roberto Castillo CUB 196

Moving Target
1. Igor Sokolov URS 589
2. Thomas Pfeffer GDR 589
3. Alexander Gasov URS 587

Archery

Men Archery
1. Tomi Poikalainen FIN 2455
2. Boris Isachenko URS 2452
3. Giancarlo Ferrari ITA 2449

Women Archery
1. Keto Losaberidze URS 2491
2. Natalia Butuzova URS 2477
3. Paivi Marilouto FIN 2479

Men Gymnastics

All-Around Individual Competition
1. Alexander Didiatin URS 118,650
2. Nicolai Andrianov URS 118,255
3. Stojan Deltchev BUL 118,000

All-Around Team Competition
1. Soviet Union 589,60
2. German Democratic Republic 581,15
3. Hungary 575,00

Parallel Bars
1. Alexander Tkatchev URS 19,775
2. Alexander Didiatin URS 19,750
3. Roland Bruckner GDR 19,650

Floor Exercise
1. Roland Bruckner GDR 19,750
2. Nicolai Andrianov URS 19,725
3. Alexander Didiatin URS 19,700

Horse Vault
1. Nicolai Andrianov URS 19,825
2. Alexander Didiatin URS 19,800
3. Roland Bruckner GDR 19,775

Sidehorse
1. Zoltan Magyar HUN 19,925
2. Alexander Didiatin URS 19,800
3. Michael Nicolai URS 19,775

Horizontal Bar
1. Stojan Deltchev BUL 19,825
2. Alexander Didiatin URS 19,870
3. Nicolai Andrianov URS 19,675

Flying Rings
1. Alexander Didiatin URS 19,870
2. Alexander Tkatchev URS 19,725
3. Jiri Tabak TCH 19,600

Women Gymnastics

All-Around Individual Competition
1. Jelena Davidova URS 79,150
2. Nadia Comaneci ROM 79,075
3. Maxi Gnauck GDR 79,075

All-Around Team Competition
1. Soviet Union 394,90
2. Romania 393,50
3. German Democratic Republic 392,55

Uneven Bars
1. Maxi Gnauck GDR 19,875
2. Emilia Eberle ROM 19,850
3. Maria Filatova URS 19,775
3. Steffi Kraker GDR 19,775
3. Melita Ruhn ROM 19,775

Floor Exercise
1. Nadia Comaneci ROM 19,875
2. Nelli Kim URS 19,875
3. Natalia Chapochnikova URS 19,825
3. Maxi Gnauck GDR 19,825

Horse Vault
1. Natalia Chapochnikova URS 19,725
2. Seffi Kraker GDR 19,675
3. Melita Ruhn ROM 19,650

Beam
1. Nadia Comaneci ROM 19,800
2. Jelena Davidova URS 19,750
3. Natalia Chapochnikova URS 19,725

Men Basketball

1. Yugoslavia
2. Italy
3. Soviet Union

Women Basketball

1. Soviet Union
2. Bulgaria
3. Yugoslavia

Soccer

1. Czechoslovakia
2. German Democratic Republic
3. Soviet Union

Men Handball

1. German Democratic Republic
2. Soviet Union
3. Romania

Women Handball

1. Soviet Union
2. Yugoslavia
3. German Democratic Republic

Men Field Hockey

1. India
2. Spain
3. Soviet Union

Women Field Hockey

1. Zimbabwe
2. Czechoslovakia
3. Soviet Union

Men Volleyball

1. Soviet Union
2. Bulgaria
3. Romania

Women Volleyball

1. Soviet Union
2. German Democratic Republic
3. Bulgaria

Reagan and Bush to run for Republicans

Reagan, pledging to cut taxes and bolster defense, won handily in Detroit.

July 17. In a dramatic aboutface, Ronald Reagan, the Republican nominee for president, today chose George Bush as his vice-presidential running mate.

Up until the last moment, the delegates at the GOP convention in Detroit had expected that Gerald R. Ford, the former President, would bow to Reagan pleas to join the ticket. But Reagan broke precedent by appearing before the delegates to announce that Ford had declined the post on the grounds that he would be of more value as a former head of state, "campaigning his heart out, as he has promised to do." Instead, Reagan announced that he had chosen Bush, his chief rival in the primaries (→ 8/14).

Deposed Shah of Iran dies in Egyptian exile

July 27. Deposed Shah of Iran Mohammed Reza Pahlevi died today in an Egyptian military hospital, an embittered international outcast 18 months after being driven from his throne. Empress Farah was with her 60-year-old husband.

President Sadat of Egypt, the only one to offer the shah a place to live, both for humanitarian reasons and out of gratitude for the shah having sent Egypt economic aid during the 1973 war with Israel, has ordered a state funeral tomorrow.

The shah's presence in the U.S. last October when he was hospitalized in New York led Iranian student militants in Tehran to seize the American Embassy. They are still holding 52 hostages, and Iran says the death of the shah will not affect their fate, still demanding that the shah's relatives and his wealth be returned to Iran (→ 8/29).

Heart attack takes comic Peter Sellers at 54

"Revenge of the Pink Panther."

July 23. Comedian Peter Sellers, 54, died in a London hospital this morning from a heart attack. While he had several seizures (the first reputedly while he was in bed with Swedish actress Britt Ekland in 1964), his condition was aggravated by weight gain. Sellers added pounds to play a pudgy, retarded character in "Being There" last year. Sellers was famed for the role of the bungling Inspector Clouseau in the Pink Panther films.

Borg takes 5th title and weds Rumanian

July 24. Bjorn Borg, king of all he surveyed in tennis, has taken a queen. The five-time Wimbledon winner, who won the title on the 5th by outlasting John McEnroe in a five-set thriller, married the Rumanian tennis champion, Mariana Simionescu, at a monastery ceremony. Miss Simionescu was present at Wimbledon when her fiance achieved a record fifth title by beating the American. The scores were 1-6, 7-5, 6-3, 6-7 8-6. For three hours, 53 minutes the rivals exchanged shots, McEnroe saving seven match points in the fourth set. Five of them were in a 34-point tiebreaker.

Borg and bride in fitting ceremony.

Fugitive U.S. radical surrenders in N.Y.

July 8. Ten years ago, a Manhattan townhouse, which was converted into a bomb factory, accidentally exploded, killing three people. Today, one of those allegedly reponsible for the deadly blast, Cathlyn Wilkerson, a member of the radical underground group the Weathermen, surrendered to police.

Wilkerson said the conditions in America which propelled much of the Weathermen's actions have not changed. "The conditions are the same and I have the same commitment to struggle against them," she said after her arraignment.

Bail was set at $10,000 for the charges of illegal possession of dynamite and criminally negligent homicide. Wilkerson's alleged accomplice, Katherine Boudin, is still at large. Both women raced from the smoking apartment in Greenwich Village on March 6, 1970, to undetermined places of seclusion. Wilkerson declined to explain her reason for surrendering (→ 12/4).

1980

AUGUST

Su	Mo	Tu	We	Th	Fr	Sa
					1	2
3	4	5	6	7	8	9
10	11	12	13	14	15	16
17	18	19	20	21	22	23
24	25	26	27	28	29	30
31						

2. Italy: Blast at Bologna train station kills over 80, injures 200.

5. Carter announces nuclear strategy shift from civilian to military targets (→ 9/19).

7. N.Y.: Mother Teresa visits the poor in Bronx.

8. Lagos: Nigeria demands return of 183 mil. barrels oil from Gulf, Mobil, Shell.

11. N.Y. Yankee Reggie Jackson becomes 19th major league player to hit 400 career homers.

14. Gdansk: Workers at Lenin Shipyard take over dock as labor unrest grows (→ 17).

15. Atlantic: Titanic believed found 12,000 feet under sea.

16. Seoul: Pres. Chi Kyu Hah resigns in favor of army strongman Chun Doo Hwan (→ 9/17).

16. India: Communal riots continue; death toll in Uttar Pradesh City hits 130 (→ 9/23).

17. Warsaw: Strikers in north form organization to center demands, strengthen power (→ 20).

18. Chicago: Reagan tells vets arms race is essential to avoid surrender or defeat (→ 10/28).

19. Beirut: 500 Israeli troops hit PLO bases in preemptive strike (→ 20).

20. New York: Muskie rebukes Security Council as it votes 14-0 to censure Israel (→ 4/26/81).

20. Warsaw: 14 leaders of dissident group arrested (→ 24).

24. Warsaw: Premier and three others dismissed in major party shakeup (→ 26).

26. Poland: Premier Jagielski meets with Walesa (→ 30).

27. Washington: Zimbabwe Premier Mugabe visits Carter, gives support in election (→ 2/17/82).

27. Chile: 50,000 protest military rule during speech of ex-Pres. Eduardo Frei (→ 5/12/83).

29. U.S.: Abscam jury convicts Myers and co-defendants on all charges (→ 10/2).

29. U.S. marks 300th day of captivity for hostages in Iran (→ 11/2).

30. Gdansk: Poland gives workers right to independent unions, but walkout continues.→

1980

SEPTEMBER

Su	Mo	Tu	We	Th	Fr	Sa
	1	2	3	4	5	6
7	8	9	10	11	12	13
14	15	16	17	18	19	20
21	22	23	24	25	26	27
28	29	30				

1. Poland: Workers end 18-day strike after gaining concessions from government (→ 6).

3. N.Y.: Abbie Hoffman, fugitive six years, gives himself up.

5. Switzerland: Ten-mile tunnel, world's longest, opens, linking Goschenen and Airolo.

6. Warsaw: Edward Gierek, party leader ten years, replaced by Stanislaw Kania (→ 22).

6. N.Y.: Evert Lloyd beats Hana Mandlikova for U.S. Open title.

7. Peking: Hua Kuo-feng resigns as premier, to be replaced by Zhao Ziyang (→ 11/20).

10. Libya and Syria announce they are "unified state," invite other Arab nations to join.

12. Chevy Chevette, Ford Escort, Lincoln Mercury Lynx are first U.S. cars to record 30 mpg.

16. Soviets demand return of soldier seeking asylum in U.S. Afghan Embassy (→ 3/8/82).

17. Seoul: Army gives death sentence to opposition leader Kim Dae Jung (→ 1/23/81).

19. Arkansas: Blast kills one, injures 21 in underground Titan missile silo (→ 6/24/81).

20. Tehran calling up military reserves to fight Iraq (→ 21).

21. Iraq reports downing Iranian F-4 Phantom jet, sinking eight gunboats (→ 26).

23. India: Gandhi gains power to imprison without trial (→ 1/18/82).

25. U.S. retains America's Cup.

26. U.S.: Jasper Johns' "Three Flags" sold for $1 mil., believed to be highest for living artist.

26. Iraq halts oil exports as wells suffer from Iranian bombs; shelling of Abadan intensified (→ 30).

27. N.J. imposes water rationing.

30. Israel: New currency issued; shekel replaces pound (→ 11/23).

DEATHS

15. Bill Evans, American jazz pianist (*1929).

18. Katherine Anne Porter, U.S. novelist (*5/15/1890).

25. Lewis Milestone, U.S. film director (*9/30/1895).

Poland gives in to strikers, approves unions

Strikers in Gdansk read newspaper versions of their challenge to state unions.

Aug 30. Workers in the Gdansk shipyard today won significant concessions from the Polish government, and leaders of the newly formed Solidarity union called an end to a 17-day strike.

The unprecedented agreement between the government and the union recognizes the right to form independent unions and to strike, and contains a pledge to restrain state censorship. Union leader Lech Walesa's decision to end the walkout was prompted by Deputy Minister Mieczyslaw Jagielski's indication that 28 jailed dissidents would be released. The accord is expected to stop work slowdowns, which have affected 300,000 Polish workers (→ 9/1).

Kennedy pulls out; Carter wins nomination

Aug 14. President Carter was renominated by the Democratic national convention today after his principal rival, Senator Edward M. Kennedy of Massachusetts, bowed out of the race. Although Senator Kennedy had released his delegates before the voting began, most of them stayed staunchly loyal to him during the balloting. President Carter won on the first ballot. The senator issued a statement, promising to work for re-election of the president, saying that it is "imperative that we defeat Ronald Reagan in 1980" (→ 18).

Carter, plagued by inflation and Iran, faces an uphill battle to November.

Turkish army seizes power in coup d'etat

Military takes power in Turkey.

Sept 11. In what a U.S. official described as an attempt to "save democracy," the Turkish army today staged an apparently bloodless coup, ousting Prime Minister Suleyman Demirel and his government and dissolving Parliament.

Turkey is a major U.S. ally in the strategically important eastern Mediterranean, more so since the Shah's fall in Iran. The new leader, General Haydar Saltuk, is known for favoring good relations with both NATO and the United States.

The coup reflects an impatience with the civilian regime's inability to solve the country's many economic and political problems. For three months, Parliament has been unable to name a new president because of party factionalism. Moreover, terrorism has taken some 2,000 lives in the past year, and a civil war seemed possible.

Sept 7. The U.S. Open remains beyond the reach of Bjorn Borg, John McEnroe (above) taking his second title 6-4 in the fifth.

Moslem world torn as Iran-Iraq war erupts

An Iranian plane, victim of Iraqi bombs, at an air base near Tehran.

Sept 30. As the war between Iran and Iraq intensifies, Ayatollah Khomeini in a radio broadcast tonight spurned all peace proposals offered by Iraq's President Saddam Hussein. Iran, he said, would fight "to the end and, God willing, shall be victorious."

As Iraqi jets continued their raids on Abadan, Iran's oil refining center and one of the world's largest, new fires added to the blanket of smoke over the heavily damaged city. Abadan was also hit by Iraqi ground forces using tanks and other heavy weapons, but early ground victories by the invading Iraqis have stalled before an Iranian resistance stiffer than expected. Meanwhile, Iranian fighter-bombers renewed their attack on Baghdad, the Iraqi capital, striking at but missing a nuclear reactor.

Iraq is trying to wrest away the oil-rich province of Khuzistan, jointly run by the two nations under the terms of a 1975 treaty that Iraq abrogated after its invasion with claims that the area had initially been taken by Iran. Khuzistan's Arab-speaking people, uneasy with Khomeini's clerical rule, have been calling for local autonomy and before the invasion were assisted in their aims by Iraqi arms supplies.

In the vacuum created by United States and Soviet neutrality, mediation efforts by the Palestine Liberation Organization have thus far failed (→ 10/19).

Swiss psychologist Jean Piaget is dead

Sept 16. Expert on child psychology Jean Piaget has died in his native Switzerland. He was 84. Influenced by the French anthropologist Claude Levi-Strauss, Piaget used structuralism in his work. Piaget was concerned with how people think—specifically, how children channel experience into thought. He noted that very young children assign objects feelings; "stones and clouds are imbued with motives," he wrote. He considered this one of many natural stages and evidence of how the mind creates increasingly sophisticated versions of reality. Piaget's three "children" were his beloved guinea pigs.

Prolific Piaget, published at age 10.

Workers in Gdansk organize Solidarity

Sept 22. Polish workers in Gdansk have created a new union they named Solidarnosc, or Solidarity. Their leader is Lech Walesa. Earlier this month, the new Polish government chief, Stanislaw Kania, acknowledged unions' right to strike. He also called the strikes that brought about the downfall of his predecessor, Edward Gierek, "a protest not against the principles of socialism but against the mistakes of the party." Soviet leaders were concerned Kania had become too liberal too fast, but he has assured them he will strengthen Poland's role in the Warsaw Pact (→ 10/24).

Fatal Toxic Shock linked to tampons

Sept 22. Procter and Gamble will recall a brand of tampons, citing a link between the brand and TSS (Toxic Shock Syndrome). Material in the brand, Rely, is suspected of absorbing the bacterium staphyllococcus areus and acting as a breeding agent. Procter and Gamble points out, however, that TSS has been reported in areas where Rely is not sold. The disease has also stricken a few men. The Centers for Disease Control reports 299 cases of TSS, 25 of which have been fatal. The illness is characterized by a high fever, diarrhea and a severe rash.

Ex-tyrant Somoza is slain in ambush

Sept 17. Anastasio Somoza Debayle, who was desposed last year as the President of Nicaragua, was slain today when his car was ambushed in a residential section of Asuncion. His car was riddled with bullets and blown apart by bazookas fired by unidentified assailants who escaped. A spokesman for the ruling junta in Nicaragua said the Sandanistas had "nothing to do directly with the death of Somoza" but expressed "joy at the death of an evil man." Somoza had gone into exile in Paraguay after it was made clear he was not welcome in the United States (→ 3/1/81).

1980

OCTOBER

Su	Mo	Tu	We	Th	Fr	Sa
			1	2	3	4
5	6	7	8	9	10	11
12	13	14	15	16	17	18
19	20	21	22	23	24	25
26	27	28	29	30	31	

2. Washington: Michael Myers ousted from House in Abscam case (→ 30).

3. Paris: Bomb kills four, injures 12 at Jewish temple (→ 7).

5. Bonn: Chancellor Schmidt's coalition govt. wins West German vote (→ 5/10/81).

9. U.S.: "Private Benjamin" opens with Goldie Hawn.

9. Monaco: Princess Caroline and Philippe Junot are divorced.

10. Algeria: Devastating earthquake kills 17,000 in north.

11. Soviet cosmonauts end record 185-day space mission aboard Salyut 6 (→ 11/8).

13. Cuba announces general pardon for all Americans serving prison terms (→ 4/19/82).

14. North Korea: Party names Kim Jong Il to succeed father Kim Il Sung as president.

17. Washington: Mt. St. Helens erupts three times in 24 hours.

19. Iran: Iraqi troops surround oil city of Abadan (→ 26).

20. Greece rejoins military wing of NATO after six-year absence (→ 12/10/81).

20. FDA asks mandatory labels on tampon packages warning of toxic shock syndrome.

22. U.S. agrees to sell China six to eight mil. tons grain per year (→ 6/16/81).

23. Moscow: Kosygin resigns due to health; Nicolai Tikhonov is new premier (→ 11/16/81).

24. Warsaw: Independent trade union wins legal status first time in Soviet bloc (→ 11/21).

25. Vatican: Pope says divorced Catholics who remarry can only receive communion if they abstain from sex.

26. Oregon Univ. senior Alberto Salazar wins N.Y. Marathon.

26. Tehran radio announces Iraqi missile attack killed 100 at Dizful (→ 3/28/82).

30. Washington: Sen. Harrison Williams indicted for bribery in Abscam case (→ 1/26/81).

DEATH

26. Marcello Caetano, Portuguese leader (*8/17/1910).

Terrorists bomb Paris synagogue, killing 4

Oct 7. A crowd of 100,000 Frenchmen marched in Paris tonight to protest the bombing of a Jewish temple. The attack last Friday night killed four people and seriously injured ten more. It was the most violent act in a recent wave of anti-Semitic incidents in France. A group called the European Nationalist Fascists claimed responsibility. No arrests have been made. Eyewitnesses said the bomb was left outside the synagogue on the Rue Copernic during services by two men who fled on a motorcycle.

President Valery Giscard d'Estaing condemned the attack, but his government has been criticized for not doing enough to stop anti-Semitic violence. Critics claim the situation reminds them of the Second World War, when the government looked the other way as Jews were deported to Hitler's Germany.

Savagery on the Rue Copernic.

Phillies win first World Series in 98 years

Oct 21. The Philadelphia Phillies finally won a World Series. After a 98-year drought, the Phils finished off the Kansas City Royals, 4-1, in the decisive sixth game and set off pandemonium in Philadelphia.

Twice before, the Phils had advanced to the brink of the world championship without success. Grover Cleveland Alexander was unable to inspire a series victory in 1915 and Robin Roberts could not do it with the Whiz Kids of 1950. This time, Steve Carlton and Tug McGraw were not to be denied. McGraw struck out Willie Wilson with three Royals on base in the ninth, and then said, "this is monumental for the city." He had taken over in the eighth when Carlton faltered.

Pandemonium in Philadelphia.

Carter and Reagan match wits in debate

Oct 28. There were no knockout blows, no disastrous gaffes and no undisputed victor during the debate tonight between President Carter and his Republican rival, Ronald Reagan.

Appearing in Cleveland, Ohio, the two presidential candidates sought to reinforce the dominant themes of their campaigns, with Carter calling for arms control in order to deflate the risk of war, while Reagan denounced the Carter administration's economic record.

Reagan suggested that Americans ask themselves as they head to the polls next week: "Are you better off than you were four years ago?"

While the president appeared to be intent on scoring points by sharply criticizing his rival's attitude on nuclear policy as "extremely dangerous and belligerent," Reagan was calm and reassuring as he sought to deflate the president's picture of him as a dangerous man.

"There you go again," Reagan said at one point, with a genial toss of the head, underscoring his contention that Carter had exaggerated the Reagan position (→ 11/4).

Rivals face off on national TV.

Amazon gold fever is luring thousands

Oct 2. The gold rush is on in the Brazilian Amazon, and more than $50 million worth of nuggets have been airlifted out of a steamy jungle area 25 minutes by plane from Maraba since the first strike in February. The bonanza has brought overnight fortune to some of Brazil's most unfortunate, and the fever has swept up the nation's leaders, who see in Serra Pelada and 48 other promising sites an overdue gift from a land that never turned up ample oil, forcing such to be imported for $11 billion a year. At the present pace, Serra Pelada will turn out 12 tons of gold this year, as 25,000 licensed miners use pickaxes and shovels in the dust-choked air under a relentless sun.

Blast rocks school in Spain, killing 64

Oct 23. A powerful explosion destroyed an elementary school in Ortuella, a town in Spain's northern Vizcaya province, today. At least 64 people, mostly children, were killed and more than 100 injured. The blast ripped through the school just before noon as 250 youngsters, aged six to ten, sat in class, drawing pictures. The explosion, either of a propane tank outside or a boiler in the basement, hurled several children through windows of the four-story building. Parents were running through the town with dying and injured children in their arms, shouting for help. Spain's Queen Sofia has flown in from Madrid to visit families of the victims and attend funerals.

Oct 2. Ali, 38, failed to answer the 11th-round bell in his bid to take Larry Holmes' title.

Ford sets U.S. record with a $595m loss

Oct 28. The Ford Motor Company has reported a $595 million loss for the third quarter of the year—the largest operating loss ever reported by an American company. The report comes a day after General Motors reported the previous record loss of $567 million. Analysts say U.S. auto firms will lose a total of $3 billion this year because of sales lost to smaller, fuel-efficient Japanese and European imports.

Heaven's Gate: Big bust for Hollywood

Admittedly, "The Deer Hunter" was a tough act to follow. It won five Oscars, including the Best Director award for Michael Cimino. Cimino could not possibly top the 1978 film, but the currently showing "Heaven's Gate," a much-touted, exorbitant picture, is what is colloquially known as a flop. Cimino casts Christopher Walken (Best Supporting Actor in "Deer Hunter") Kris Kristofferson and Isabelle Huppert in a lethargic, muddled tale of the Old West.

Even lovely locations and costumes could not save Cimino's debacle.

1980

NOVEMBER

Su	Mo	Tu	We	Th	Fr	Sa
						1
2	3	4	5	6	7	8
9	10	11	12	13	14	15
16	17	18	19	20	21	22
23	24	25	26	27	28	29
30						

2. Atlanta: Young boy found murdered, 15th in last six months (→ 2/15/81).

2. Iran: Parliament approves conditions for hostage release, demands $24 billion (→ 10).

8. Voyager I discovers 15th Saturn moon (→ 3/19/81).

9. N.Y.: Aaron Copland honored at Carnegie Hall on 80th birthday.

10. Britain: Michael Foot succeeds James Callaghan at head of Labor Party (→ 2/26/81).

10. U.S. sends delegation to Algeria to respond to Iranian conditions on hostages (→ 12/21).

15. Cologne: John Paul II arrives as first pope to visit West Germany in 198 years (→ 16).

16. West Germany: Pope asks Catholics to strengthen ties to Protestants (→ 5/13/81).

17. Washington: Three federal agencies agree to pay $2.1 bil. for bankrupt Penn Central railroad.

20. Peking: Trial of Gang of Four opens (→ 1/25/81).

21. Las Vegas: Over 80 die in fire at MGM Grand Hotel.

21. Poland: Catholic Deputy Jerzy Ozolowski named vice premier (→ 22).

22. Poland: 18 party secretaries in 49 provinces ousted in biggest shakeup yet (→ 27).

23. Italy: 3,000 killed in Europe's biggest earthquake since 1915.

23. Tel Aviv: Ezer Weizman ousted by Begin faction (→ 7/5/81).

25. New Orleans: Sugar Ray Leonard TKO's Roberto Duran to regain welterweight title.

27. Poland: Two Solidarity strikers freed to avoid general strike (→ 12/14).

28. Canada drops out of U.S.-led ban on grain sales to U.S.S.R.

29. San Salvador: 20 slain in violence after murder of prominent leftist leaders (→ 12/5).

DEATHS

16. Boris Aronson, American stage designer (*10/15/1900).

22. Mae West, American actress (*8/17/1892).

Reagan is 40th President

Nancy and Ron ride a new wave of patriotism into the White House.

Nov 4. Ronald Wilson Reagan, promising "to put America back to work again," was elected the 40th President of the nation today with a surprising sweep in the East, South and crucial battlegrounds of the Middle West.

The former California Governor, now 69 years old, is the oldest man ever elected to serve in the White House. Despite his age, he built a stunning electoral landslide, wiping out the Southern base of President Carter, who is the first elected incumbent head of state since Herbert Hoover to go down to defeat at the polls.

Reagan won 489 electoral votes, far more than the 270 needed to win, while President Carter garnered just 49, a sharp drop from the 297 electoral votes by which he toppled President Gerald R. Ford four years ago.

Appearing before supporters in a Washington ballroom, President Carter said that just an hour earlier he had telephoned the winner to concede defeat. "The people of the United States have made their choice and, of course, I accept that decision," he said. "I can't stand here tonight and say it doesn't hurt."

For Reagan, a former movie star and television personality, the win was perhaps all the more sweet in that he had sought the nomination for president in 1976, losing that year to President Ford (→ 1/20/81).

Voyager 1, in its closest encounter with Saturn, has found the planet has a complex of rings within rings, concentric circles in a cosmic pond.

Cool Steve McQueen dies of cancer at 50

Nov 7. In "The Great Escape," Steve McQueen played a POW who makes off on a motorcycle. He is eventually recaptured, but only after leading the Nazis on an exhausting merry chase. McQueen's death today at the age of 50 is just such a victory. He was diagnosed with cancer months ago and given only weeks to live. He beat those odds. McQueen also overcame himself; he succeeded in films like "Bullitt" after an education ending in the ninth grade and a youthful spell in a reformatory. Maybe the disadvantages had advantages. To act, he said, "you have to reach inside of you and bring forth a lot of broken glass."

Monkeys in Africa use basic language

Nov 27. Scientists at Rockefeller University say vervet monkeys use complex sounds that could be considered a kind of language. The monkeys use distinct alarm calls for different threats; an alarm for an approaching eagle, for example, is distinct from the cry for a leopard. Scientists discovered the vervets responded well to taped alarms. A recording of the snake-warning cry set the monkeys to searching the grass. It was noted the snake call was similar to another cry—the warning that humans are near.

Oh! What a career for Japanese batter!

Nov 4. Sadaharu Oh, the highest paid athlete in Asia, hung up his baseball cleats at the age of 40 after dominating Japan's professional leagues for more than 21 years. Newspapers and television reports played the shocking story over the United States presidential election. Oh, who spent his entire career at first base for the Yomiuri Giants, helped his team win 13 league championships and 12 series titles. His total of 868 home runs surpassed the output of both Babe Ruth (714) and Hank Aaron (755). His career batting average was .301.

1980

DECEMBER

Su	Mo	Tu	We	Th	Fr	Sa
	1	2	3	4	5	6
7	8	9	10	11	12	13
14	15	16	17	18	19	20
21	22	23	24	25	26	27
28	29	30	31			

5. U.S. halts aid to El Salvador pending inquiry into army's role in slaying of three American nuns (→ 13).

13. San Salvador: Christian Democrat Duarte is first civilian president in 49 years (→ 27).

15. N.Y. Yankees sign Dave Winfield for up to $25 million.

16. Reagan names Haig secretary of state (→ 6/25/82).

21. U.S. rejects $24 bil. as condition for release of hostages in Iran (→ 1/19/81).

24. Central African Republic: Ex-Emperor Bokassa sentenced to death in absentia.

28. Mexico ends fishing agreements with U.S.

31. Senegal: Senghor resigns after 20 years as president.

DEATHS

2. Romain Gary, French novelist, ex-diplomat (*5/8/1914).

8. John Lennon, British rock star with The Beatles (*10/9/1940).

18. Aleksei Kosygin, Soviet premier 1964-80 (*2/20/1904).

25. Grand Adm. Karl Doenitz, Hitler's hand-picked successor (*9/16/1891).

CULTURAL EVENTS, 1980

Literature: Anthony Burgess' "Earthly Powers"; William Golding's "Rites of Passage"; Shirley Hazzard's "The Transit of Venus"; Iris Murdoch's "Nuns and Soldiers"; Lanford Wilson's "Talley's Folly."

Academia: Douglas Hofstadter's "Godel, Escher, Bach," Pulitzer; origin of life pushed back to 3.5 million years.

Music: David Del Tredici's "In Memory of a Summer Day," Pulitzer; Christopher Cross' "Sailing"; Bette Midler's "The Rose"; Streisand & Gibb's "Guilty"; John Lennon's "Starting Over."

The Arts: 1,000 Picassos shown at MOMA in New York.

Film: "My Brilliant Career"; Truffaut's "The Green Room"; "Raging Bull," DeNiro; Robert Redford's "Ordinary People"; "Coal Miner's Daughter," Sissy Spacek.

John Lennon taken from this life by fanatic

"Imagine there's no heaven."

Dec 8. In what is certainly the most shocking event in the long, tumultuous history of rock music, former Beatle John Lennon was shot to death tonight by a crazed fan outside his residence in the Dakota, a Manhattan apartment building.

Lennon, 40, was returning home from a recording session with his wife, Yoko Ono, at about 10:45 p.m., when he was shot at least twice, after stepping from a limousine. A suspect, Mark David Chapman, 25, of Hawaii, was seized immediately after the killing; he is believed to have stalked Lennon for days, at one point even obtaining an autograph from the rock legend.

Word of the tragedy seemed to jolt the city almost instantly tonight, as hundreds gathered outside the Dakota, on Central Park West, to form a candlelight vigil. Stunned fans slowly chanted the words to such Lennon songs as "Imagine," his 1971 plea for world peace. But a line from another Lennon song seemed to echo more poignantly through the crowd: "The dream is over" (→ 1/6/81).

Three U.S. nuns are killed in El Salvador

Dec 27. Since October of last year, the military-civilian junta which governs El Salvador has been attempting to quell violence between leftists, rightists and its own security forces. Earlier this month, three American nuns and a lay missionary were killed as a result of this conflict, although it remains unclear just which group was responsible. When American aid was withheld because of the incident, it forced a crisis in the Salvadoran government, and exiled President Jose Napoleon Duarte was allowed to return to the country and lead the four-member junta.

The latest violence occurred today when 1,000 leftist guerrillas opened a major attack against Salvadoran government forces. More than 9,000 people, mostly civilians, have been killed in the conflict since October 1979 (→ 1/4/81).

Bernadine Dohrn finally surrenders

Dec 4. The leader of the radical Weather Underground, Bernadine Dohrn, waved the white flag and turned herself in to Chicago authorities yesterday. A fugitive since 1970, she will be tried on various charges of terrorism for which the left-wing group is allegedly responsible, including several bombings (→ 1/13/81).

Media messenger McLuhan is dead

Dec 31. For Marshall McLuhan, the advent of television and other electronic media spelled the dawn of a new epoch in mankind's history. The Canadian teacher and Director of the University of Toronto's Centre for Culture and Technology wrote that "the medium is the message"—the characteristics of a medium such as television, much more than its content, determine what a viewer will experience. His socio-psychological ideas were published in "Understanding Media" (1964) and other controversial books. The media man died today at age 69.

West warns Soviets to stay out of Poland

Dec 14. After four days of meetings, members of the North Atlantic Treaty Organization issued a warning to the Soviet Union that intervention in the internal affairs of Poland would effectively destroy detente between East and West.

The statement said that "any intervention would fundamentally alter the entire international situation," and added that detente "could not survive if the Soviet Union" were again to violate the basic rights of any state to territorial integrity and independence." If the Soviets intervened, the NATO nations said that "the alliance would be compelled to react in the manner that the gravity of this development would require."

U.S. Secretary of State Edmund Muskie, hailing the NATO statement, said that he believes that the recent concentration of Soviet troops on the Polish border does not indicate a possible invasion, but added that the alliance "does not assume that could not happen."

Possible anti-Soviet sanctions, short of military action, that are being considered in the event of intervention are a suspension of loan credits, breaking off arms-limitation talks and banning Soviet ships from Western ports.

The NATO communique comes on the heels of a surprise meeting between Soviet and Warsaw Pact officials in Moscow on December 5, at which the leaders expressed confidence that the labor crisis could be overcome, and that workers would "assure the country's development along the socialist path." In Warsaw, Lech Walesa and other Solidarity leaders issued a statement condemning "irresponsible strikes" and denying further labor action. Four months ago, in an unprecedented move, Poland approved independent unions (→ 1/24/81).

Walesa and family enjoy Christmas.

1981

JANUARY

Su	Mo	Tu	We	Th	Fr	Sa
				1	2	3
4	5	6	7	8	9	10
11	12	13	14	15	16	17
18	19	20	21	22	23	24
25	26	27	28	29	30	31

1. Pasadena: Michigan over Washington 23-6 in Rose Bowl.

1. Greece becomes tenth member of EEC (→ 2/23/82).

4. San Salvador: Two Americans slain at Sheraton Hotel (→ 11).

5. London: Peter Sutcliffe arrested, believed to be Yorkshire Ripper, killer of 13 (→ 5/22).

6. N.Y.: Mark David Chapman pleads insanity in slaying of John Lennon (→ 6/22).

8. Baltimore: Ex-CIA agent David Barnett given 18 years as Soviet spy.

10. Alabama Supreme Court voids law barring obscene language in presence of women.

11. El Salvador: Junta enacts martial law (→ 2/19).

13. Chicago: Bernardine Dohrn pleads guilty to assault in 1969 protests (→ 10/21).

16. Ireland: Bernadette Devlin, anti-British activist, shot and seriously wounded (→ 4/20).

17. Manila: Marcos frees 341, ends martial law after eight years, four months (→ 2/17).

19. Algiers: U.S. and Iran sign accord on hostage release (→ 31).

23. Seoul: Under intl. pressure, opposition leader Kim Dae Jung gets death sentence commuted to life in prison (→ 12/23/82).

23. Warsaw: Four-hour strike for shorter work week cripples city (→ 24).

26. Washington: Ex-Congressman Richard Kelly guilty in Abscam bribery case (→ 5/1).

29. Reagan orders 60-day freeze on govt. regulations (→ 2/27).

30. Maputo: South African troops attack rebels in Mozambique capital (→ 6/27).

31. Poland: Walesa announces accord giving labor Saturdays off (→ 2/9).

31. N.Y.: Indian Point nuclear plant shut down after leaks are discovered (→ 2/21).

DEATHS

6. Archibald J. Cronin, popular Scottish novelist (*7/19/1896).

23. Samuel Barber, American composer (*3/9/1910).

Iran releases hostages

Finally freed after 444 days.

Jan 31. From the bridges over the Potomac in Washington to the canyons of Wall Street in New York, Americans welcomed home the 52 former Iran hostages this week with yellow ribbons, thunderous applause and tears. "It's the most emotional experience of our lives," Vice President Bush said. "You could feel it build until the point it hurt inside. It was the greatest event I've ever seen." It was an event that provided relief to a country and a government that had been paralyzed by a crisis that lasted 444 days. It was an event that refused to unfold until Jimmy Carter was forced out of the White House.

Carter hoped the hostages would leave Tehran on the 19th, the last full day of his presidency. Once again, his hopes were denied. The departure was delayed as Iran accused the United States and its banks of reneging on a deal to return frozen assets. After the hitch was ironed out, the hostages were herded to the airport on the 20th and jostled at gunpoint aboard a plane provided by the Algerian mediators. "They seem stunned," one Iranian official said, "as if they cannot believe they are going free."

By design or coincidence, the plane did not take off until moments after Ronald Reagan was sworn in as President. The new chief executive was informed of the development as he was arriving for a lunch with the congressional leadership on Capitol Hill. He announced the news with a glass of white wine in his hand. "Some 30 minutes ago," he said, "the Algerian planes bearing our prisoners left Iranian airspace and they're now free of Iran."

Carter did not receive word officially of the release until he was in the air, returning to his home in Plains, Georgia. At Reagan's request, he traveled to West Germany to greet the hostages. Criticism of Carter's role in the crisis has continued. Some Republicans charged the return of frozen assets amounted to the payment of ransom.

Reagan, without offering specifics, had a warning for Iran: "Let terrorists be aware that when the rules of international behavior are violated, our policy will be one of swift and effective retribution" (→ 6/10).

Back at home, a hero's welcome charged with a heavy dose of patriotism.

Reagan sworn in as Americans are freed

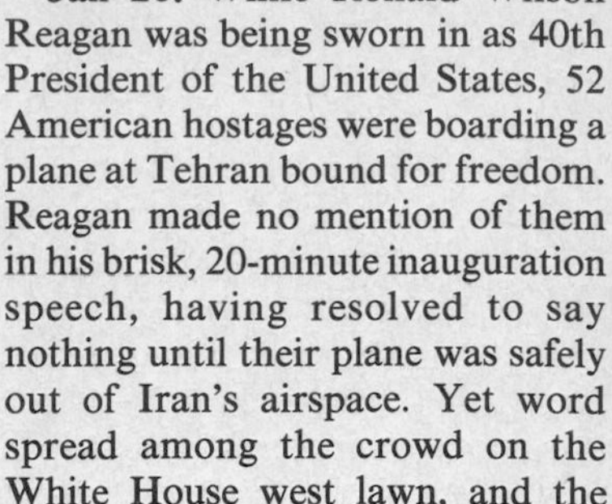

Jan 20. While Ronald Wilson Reagan was being sworn in as 40th President of the United States, 52 American hostages were boarding a plane at Tehran bound for freedom. Reagan made no mention of them in his brisk, 20-minute inauguration speech, having resolved to say nothing until their plane was safely out of Iran's airspace. Yet word spread among the crowd on the White House west lawn, and the news and Reagan's newborn presidency seemed jubilantly linked.

The contrast to Carter's inauguration was striking. Whereas the Democrat spoke of government as a cure for social ills, Reagan said "government is not the solution to our problem; government is the problem." His first official act would be to order a federal hiring freeze.

Reagan: an auspicious start.

Speech concluded, Reagan chose to parade down Pennsylvania Avenue not by foot, as Carter and his brood had done, but by limousine. Garbed in a charcoal gray suit, Reagan waved to the throng confidently from the open car. His wife, Nancy, in a bold red coat, pointed out signs of welcome along the route.

Reagan vows to "hit the ground running." He wants to slash taxes; revive flagging American industry; speed up deregulation and return to the states functions bungled by a sprawling federal bureaucracy. His inauguration speech offered little specifics for reaching these goals. In that respect, he mirrors Carter—and a long line of honorable presidential predecessors (→ 2/18).

Millions in Poland go out on strike

Jan 24. Millions of Polish workers stayed away from their jobs on Saturday in support of the Solidarity union's call for a five-day work week.

The boycott, which had been urged by Lech Walesa, the Solidarity leader, brought most major industries in the country to a halt. Even the government radio admitted that Gdansk, the birthplace of the Solidarity movement, was virtually shut down and that worker attendance in many Warsaw plants was less than 20 percent. The work protest was larger than any seen since last October and embarrassing to the government, which needs labor peace to fend off interference by the Soviet Union (→ 31).

Mao's widow given sentence of death

Jan 25. Chiang Ching, the widow of Mao Tse-tung, was dragged shouting from a courtroom in Peking today after she was given a suspended death sentence. "It is right to rebel! Making revolution is no crime!" she yelled, as she called for the ouster of Chinese leader Deng Hsiao-ping. Chiang Ching and other members of the Gang of Four were convicted of counterrevolutionary crimes during the Cultural Revolution. Her sentence was suspended as a compromise with Mao's followers (→ 2/28).

Gance's "Napoleon" plays at Radio City

"Napoleon," four-hour masterpiece.

Jan 23. Francis Ford Coppola has resurrected a classic silent film and brought it triumphantly to Radio City Music Hall in New York City. French director Abel Gance created the four-hour, 17-reel "Napoleon" between 1925 and 1927. In ensuing years, a stereophonic musical score and additional scenes were added. Now, Coppola accompanies it with a full symphony orchestra conducted by his father, Carmine.

Audiences are awed by the film's advanced use of cinematography. For some scenes, Gance suspended a camera from wires and strapped another to a galloping horse. And then there is the remarkable triptych effect used at the stirring conclusion, achieving results not unlike that of Cinerama some 30 years later. Napoleon is seen simultaneously at the head of his armies and in the company of his wife, Josephine, as the "Marseillaise" plays on. Most awed by all the attention is director Gance, 91 years old.

Jan. 25. Oakland takes its second Super Bowl 27-10 over the Eagles.

1981

FEBRUARY

Su	Mo	Tu	We	Th	Fr	Sa
1	2	3	4	5	6	7
8	9	10	11	12	13	14
15	16	17	18	19	20	21
22	23	24	25	26	27	28

2. U.S.: G.M. reports worst year since 1921 with loss of $763 million (→ 27).

8. Athens: 24 die in stampede after soccer match.

9. Washington: Reagan reported planning $32 billion increase in military budget (→ 4/19).

12. Warsaw: Premier Jaruzelski asks no strike for three months to halt economic crisis (→ 4/17).

12. New York: Peter Squires wins race to top of Empire State Building.

14. Italy: Last in series of quakes hits Naples area, killing 2,916.

15. Florida: Richard Petty wins Daytona 500 for seventh time.

17. Manila: Pope John Paul II meets with President Marcos (→ 2/16/83).

18. Washington: Reagan administration says it would not have negotiated for hostage release (→ 7/24/83).

19. U.S. State Dept. calls El Salvador "textbook case" of Communist plot (→ 25).

21. Penn.: Owners of Three Mile Island settle with local residents for $25 million (→ 10/2).

22. Washington: Pres. Reagan's worth reported at $4 million.

23. Madrid: Group of Civil Guards seizes lower house of Parliament (→ 27).

24. London: Buckingham Palace announces engagement of Prince Charles and Lady Diana Spencer (→ 7/29).

25. Moscow: Brezhnev aide says Salvador will never get aid from Soviets (→ 3/2).

26. Washington: British P.M. Margaret Thatcher meets with Reagan (→ 3/2).

27. Detroit: Chrysler reports record U.S. loss of $1.7 billion (→ 3/5).

28. Peking: China announces new austerity plan; private business to be encouraged (→ 6/1).

DEATHS

5. Ella Grasso, ex-governor of Connecticut (*5/10/1919).

9. Bill Haley, American rock star with Comets (*7/6/1927).

Jean Harris guilty of doctor's murder

Feb 24. Mrs. Jean Harris, 56, has been convicted of murdering Dr. Herman Tarnower, creator of the Scarsdale diet. A White Plains, New York, jury found her guilty of second-degree murder in his shooting death last March. She faces a minimum of 15 years in prison.

Mrs. Harris testified that on the night in question she came to the doctor's home to commit suicide. Tarnower, 69, tried to wrest the gun from her, setting it off. The jury sided with the prosecution, believing Mrs. Harris aimed the revolver at Tarnower, furious over his affair with a 38-year-old assistant. Later, at the Westchester County jail Mrs. Harris reluctantly doffed high heels for prison sneakers (→ 3/20).

Harris and lawyer at County Court.

Fights mar hockey

Feb 26. A brutal night of wrestling, fighting and general mayhem was interrupted by a hockey game at the Boston Garden. After the brawl was over, a total of 392 penalty minutes were counted and 12 Bruin and North Star players had been ejected from the game. The three officials were involved nearly as much as the players. From the first seven seconds of play until the finish, the battling ensued, some of it in the penalty boxes. Six National Hockey League records for brutality were broken, with Brad McCrimmon of Boston the chief culprit. The Bruins won 5-1. ▷

Spain's Civil Guards foiled in coup attempt

Tejero and guardsmen enter Cortes.

Feb 27. Bullet holes were visible in the walls of the Spanish Parliament as the legislators approved a new government. Many of them looked haggard after their hostage ordeal, but they rose in unison to cheer King Juan Carlos for using a strong hand to turn back a coup attempt. They approved a new Premier, Leopoldo Calvo Sotelo, and one million Spaniards marched to condemn the attempted coup.

More than 300 Deputies and Senators were taken prisoner on the 23rd when renegade members of the Civil Guard burst into the chamber and sprayed it with automatic gunfire. They were led by Lieutenant Colonel Antonio Tejero Molino, later described by one Basque legislator as "completely crazy." Army troops also seized a TV station.

The military leaders were hoping to ignite a national uprising against a regime they considered too liberal and too lax on terrorism. They failed because most commanders remained loyal to the king (→ 5/24).

18th black child's body is discovered

Feb 15. The body of Patrick Baltazar, 11, has been found behind a suburban office park north of Atlanta. He is the 18th black Atlanta child found slain in the last 19 months or since the nightmare began on July 28, 1979, when the first two victims, aged 14 and 13, were found in the woods. One child, Darron Glass, 10, remains listed as missing.

A skeleton discovered two days ago has been identified through dental records as that of Jeffrey Mathis, 11. The boy disappeared on March 12 last year while on his way to a service station to buy cigarettes. The skeleton was discovered in south Fulton County outside Atlanta, within three miles of where six other children's bodies were dumped (→ 3/13).

Grisly search outside Atlanta.

General replaces Premier of Poland

Jaruzelski, Polish army strongman.

Feb 9. In Poland, Prime Minister Jozef Pinkowski has been thrown out of office and replaced by General Wojciech Jaruzelski. The elevation of the Defense Minister was viewed as an effort by the Central Committee to restore order to the country, but Jaruzelski is not expected to institute repressive measures in Poland. The new Prime Minister was trained in the Soviet Union, but he is viewed as a moderate military leader who has preferred political negotiation to the use of military force (→ 27).

Indoor mile record is set by Coghlan

Coghlan, kicking, breaks the tape.

Feb 20. Eamonn Coghlan has knocked two seconds off his own world record by running the indoor mile in three minutes, 50.6 seconds.

On his way to the indoor mile mark, the speedy Irishman was timed in a world record 3:35.6 for the 1,500-meters. His final time was only 1.8 seconds off the world mile mark held by Steve Ovett of Britain. Ovett ran the mile in three minutes, 48.8 seconds last year.

Coghlan said that he anticipated a record in view of the exceptional field in the San Diego race. He was boxed in for a while by Steve Scott and John Walker before breaking away. "It was one of those near-perfect races," said Scott.

Converted Jew now Archbishop of Paris

Feb 2. Sources at the Vatican made public today the appointment of Bishop Jean Marie Lustiger of Orleans as Archbishop of Paris. Lustiger will become the first convert from Judaism to Roman Catholicism to hold the post. He left the Jewish faith at the age of 15. He will replace Francois Cardinal Marty, who reached the Church's retirement age of 75 in 1979, but held on to his position another year at the request of Pope John Paul II. It is expected that Lustiger will soon become a Cardinal.

1981

MARCH

Su	Mo	Tu	We	Th	Fr	Sa
1	2	3	4	5	6	7
8	9	10	11	12	13	14
15	16	17	18	19	20	21
22	23	24	25	26	27	28
29	30	31				

1. Washington: Sen. Jesse Helms says U.S. has cut off economic aid to Nicaragua (→ 16).

2. London: 12 in Labor Party resign to form centrist Social Democrats (→ 4/12).

2. U.S. to send 20 more advisers, $25 mil. in military aid to El Salvador (→ 13).

5. Washington: Reagan asks Congress to end federal legal aid to poor (→ 6).

6. Reagan announces plan to cut federal employment by 37,000 jobs (→ 10).

10. Reagan admin. announces plan to tie welfare benefits to work requirement (→ 5/20).

13. Atlanta: Reagan allots $1.5 mil. to inquiry on slain children (→ 6/4).

13. U.S. to send 15 Green Berets to to El Salvador as military advisers (→ 25).

14. Syria: Hijackers of Pakistani jetliner surrender, ending 13-day ordeal.

16. Miami: Nicaraguan contras now training in Florida (→ 7/9).

18. U.S. Army discloses 1966 tests of biological weapons in Texas.

19. Florida: One techician killed, two injured in test on space shuttle Columbia (→ 4/12).

20. Argentina: Isabel Peron gets eight years for corruption (→ 29).

20. N.Y.: Jean Harris sentenced to 15 years for murder of Dr. Herman Tarnower.

23. U.S. Supreme Court requires parental consent for teen abortions (→ 5/25/82).

23. U.S. Supreme Court upholds law making statuatory rape a crime for men but not women.

27. Poland: Solidarity holds four-hour nationwide strike (→ 4/17).

28. Switzerland: Phil Mahre is first American to win World Cup skiing title.

29. Argentina: Gen. Roberto Eduardo Viola sworn in as president (→ 6/8).

30. Philadelphia: Indiana State wins NCAA basketball title, defeating N. Carolina 63-50.

Reagan gravely wounded by assassin

Reagan leaves Hilton after speech.

March 30. President Reagan was shot in the chest today as he walked to his limousine after addressing a labor convention at the Washington Hilton Hotel. His Press Secretary, James Brady, and two officers also were wounded.

The president was reported to be in "good" and "stable" condition tonight after undergoing two hours of surgery at George Washington University Hospital.

"The prognosis is excellent," said Dr. Dennis S. O'Leary. "He is alert and should be able to make decisions by tomorrow."

Authorities have arrested John W. Hinckley Jr., a 25-year-old man from Colorado, and booked him on federal charges of attempting to assassinate the president. He is being held without bail.

As the president walked toward his limousine, a rapid series of five or six shots rang out from a distance of about ten feet. The president had just raised his left arm to wave to the crowd when he was shot. A look of stunned disbelief swept across his face as he was shoved forcefully by a Secret Service agent into the limousine, which then sped away to the hospital, with the president sitting in the back seat.

Back at the scene of the shooting, Jim Brady, the press secretary, had slumped to the sidewalk, critically wounded, blood from a head wound dripping into a steel grate. Nearby, a Secret Service agent writhed in pain on the rain-slick pavement.

Hinckley had been standing in a large gathering of television crews and reporters outside the hotel as the president appeared. As the last shot rang out, agents and officers jumped him, pinning him against a stone wall.

At the hospital, the 70-year-old president seemed intent on assuring his wife and friends that he was fine.

"Honey, I forgot to duck," he told his wife, Nancy.

The president winked at his chief of staff, James A. Baker III. Then, upon spying Edwin Meese III, the chief White House counselor, the president quipped: "Who's minding the store?"

Later, in the operating room, the president eyed his surgeons and said jokingly: "Please tell me you're Republicans" (→ 4/11).

Moments later, with four down, secret servicemen rush to mob the gunman.

U.S. Embassy is hit again in El Salvador

March 25. The United States Embassy in San Salvador was heavily damaged today when it was attacked by gunmen firing rocket-propelled grenades and submachine guns. It was the fourth attack this month on the embassy building in the heart of the Salvadoran capital.

American officials ascribed the initial attacks to right-wing extremist groups seeking to oust the American-supported junta government headed by President Jose Napoleon Duarte. In contrast, responsibility for the latest attack was claimed by leftist guerrillas from the Popular Liberation Forces, who said they were protesting American military aid to the Salvadoran government.

The attacks come at a time when the Reagan administration has been seeking to focus attention, both at home and abroad, on Soviet-bloc support for the left-wing insurgents in El Salvador and to rally support for counter-moves by the United States. The administration has stated that its objective in El Salvador is to pave the way for an elected government, while charging that the Soviet Union and Cuba are attempting to transform an essentially domestic conflict in the small, Central American country into an international confrontation.

The administration has proposed expanded economic and military aid to Nicaragua and disclosed that 15 Green Beret specialists in counterinsurgency were being sent to El Salvador to join the 54-man military advisory team in that country. The administration moves have prompted concerns in Congress that the United States was being drawn into a Vietnam-like situation in which United States troops would become involved (→ 5/9).

Leftist guerrillas of El Salvador.

Founder of most popular magazine is dead

March 30. One day in 1922, DeWitt Wallace stooped in a cellar below a speakeasy, using a small press to print a journal of condensed articles he called Reader's Digest. Sixty years later, Wallace oversaw a publishing empire, the magazine having a worldwide circulation of 30 million. The visionary died in Mount Kisco, N.Y., today at age 91.

Editor Wallace got the idea for his magazine from a hobby, keeping a little index file of his favorite magazine articles. After study at the University of California at Berkeley, Wallace joined the Army and fought in Europe during World War I. While he was in a hospital recovering from wounds, other soldiers asked him to write or read letters for them. He saw a place for a journal that was bereft of high-tone language or esoteric ideas.

Wallace shares the credit for developing the Reader's Digest with his wife, Lila Bell Acheson. She was active in social services before she married Wallace, helping establish the YWCA on the East Coast. Her attitude became the Digest's attitude, one of positive thinking.

Mr. and Mrs. Wallace were given the Medal of Freedom in 1972 for their philanthropic works.

Carol Burnett wins in $1.6m libel suit

March 26. A Los Angeles jury has ruled that The National Enquirer libeled the actress Carol Burnett in a 1976 gossip column, depicting her as intoxicated at an encounter with Secretary of State Henry A. Kissinger in a Washington restaurant. The Florida-based publication was ordered to pay her $1.6 million in damages, which she will donate to charities. "They didn't give a darn about my rights as a human being," she said. She hopes this will encourage others to sue The Enquirer.

1981

APRIL

Su	Mo	Tu	We	Th	Fr	Sa
			1	2	3	4
5	6	7	8	9	10	11
12	13	14	15	16	17	18
19	20	21	22	23	24	25
26	27	28	29	30		

4. Rome: Police capture Red Brigade leader Mario Moretti (→ 5/26).

6. U.S. Supreme Court protects benefits for people who quit jobs due to religious beliefs.

12. Cape Kennedy: Space shuttle rockets into orbit on first flight (→ 14).

13. Montreal: Rene Levesque wins new term as Quebec premier.

13. New York: Posthumous Pulitzer given to John Toole who committed suicide after failing to publish.

17. Warsaw: Polish farmers win right to form independent union (→ 5/28).

17. Bonn: Leftist hunger striker dies; govt. braces for violence.

18. Washington: Environmentalists joining together to fight Reagan EPA plans (→ 5/28).

19. Supreme Court Justice Rehnquist rejects NAACP bid to extend busing in L.A. (→ 5/31).

19. Kenya: U.S. naval buildup challenging Soviets in Asia and Africa (→ 7/16).

20. Belfast: Clashes worsen as Bobby Sands reaches 51st day of hunger strike (→ 5/5).

23. Washington: Haig calls Moscow primary source of danger to world (→ 24).

24. Reagan ends curbs on grain exports to U.S.S.R. (→ 3/8/83).

26. Lebanon: Israeli jets attack, killing 15 (→ 28).

27. Maryland: Ex-V.P. Agnew convicted of taking bribes; repayment ordered.

28. Lebanon: Israel downs two Syrian helicopters, charging violation of territory (→ 5/8).

29. Honduras and Nicaragua close border after clashes (→ 7/9).

DEATHS

8. Omar Nelson Bradley, American general (*2/12/1893).

11. Caroline Gordon, novelist of American South (*10/6/1895).

12. Joe Louis, U.S. boxer, longest reigning heavyweight champ, 11 years, 8 months (*5/13/1914).

Columbia launched on first shuttle flight

The Columbia surges into orbit.

April 14. The space shuttle Columbia completed its first orbital flight today when it landed at Edwards Air Force Base in California.

Columbia, the world's first reusable spacecraft, orbited the earth 36 times during a flight of 54 hours and 22 minutes, carrying two astronauts, John W. Young and Robert L. Crippen. Space agency officials say Columbia's next orbital flight could come in as little as six months, but only if damage to the ceramic tiles of its heat shield is minor.

The major problem of the flight was the discovery that some tiles had been lost during liftoff from Cape Canaveral, but officials say the damage does not appear to be severe. The space shuttle program, which has cost $10 billion so far, is designed to make orbital flight inexpensive and routine. The goal is to have a shuttle flight every two weeks, with the spacecraft carrying payloads up to 65 tons into orbit. In addition to Columbia, three other orbiters are being built (→ 11/12).

Reagan goes home, says he feels great

April 11. President Reagan, saying that he felt "great," returned to the White House this morning, just 12 days after being shot in the chest during an assassination attempt. He looked a little pale and he walked a bit stiffly, but he was grinning as he waved to applauding aides and their families who stood in the rain to welcome him home.

Michael K. Deaver, the deputy chief of staff at the White House, said that the president will be taking it easy for at least a week. Before leaving the hospital, the president rejected the suggestion that he depart in a wheel chair. "I walked in here—I'm going to walk out," the president firmly told his doctors (→ 8/24).

Hundreds of London youths riot in Brixton

April 12. For the second night in a row, hundreds of youths, mostly black, rioted through the Brixton section in south London, clashing with police and setting fires. Durthe two nights of disorders, 30 policemen and 20 civilians have been seriously injured and two dozen buildings have been destroyed.

Home Secretary William Whitelaw, after touring the rundown neighborhood, expressed "extreme distress and horror." Racial tensions, combined with an economic recession and high unemployment, were believed to have led to the outburst of rioting. There also have been complaints within the black community of a pattern of harassment by the police, most of whom are white. Much of the fury of the rioters seemed directed at 1,000 policemen brought into the small area two miles south of London which has one of the largest concentrations of blacks in the country.

In a larger sense, the disturbances were regarded as symptomatic of the race relations problems now confronting Britain. From an ethnically homogeneous society a few generations ago, Britain has changed so that four percent of its population is non-white (→ 7/5).

Riot police (left) try to keep order on a battleground in the streets of Brixton.

Post acknowledges prize story faked

April 15. A Washington Post article on an eight-year-old heroin addict was fabricated, the newspaper has admitted. The story, written by 26-year-old reporter Janet Cooke, won a Pulitzer Prize —returned today, the Post said, "with great sadness and regret." Washington police doubted the report back at its publication in September. Despite a thorough search, they failed to track down "Jimmy," and thought it unlikely he attended only math classes in school to help his dealings, as the story asserted.

Oxford boat gets a woman coxswain

April 4. A shy, demure biochemistry student became the first woman to take part in the hallowed Oxford-Cambridge boat race—and her debut was a winning one. Susan Brown was the coxswain in the Oxford boat that out-rowed Cambridge in their 127th meeting on The Thames. She had become known to the British public as the coxswain of their Olympic crew. She steered Oxford to its sixth consecutive triumph in respectable, if not record, time. Miss Brown began rowing two tears ago "for fun."

1981

MAY

Su	Mo	Tu	We	Th	Fr	Sa
					1	2
3	4	5	6	7	8	9
10	11	12	13	14	15	16
17	18	19	20	21	22	23
24	25	26	27	28	29	30
31						

2. Jorge Velasquez rides Pleasant Colony to victory in Kentucky Derby.

5. Belfast: Bobby Sands dies in N. Ireland jail on 66th day of hunger strike (→ 12).

6. U.S. expels Libyans and closes diplomatic mission (→ 8/19).

8. Beirut: Syria tells Israel it won't withdraw missiles in Lebanon (→ 31).

9. San Salvador: Six soldiers arrested in slaying of U.S. Church workers (→ 7/9).

10. West Berlin: Chancellor Schmidt's Social Democrats sustain heavy losses in city elections (→ 10/1/82).

13. Rome: Pope John Paul II shot in Vatican Square.→

14. Texas: Boston Celtics win 14th NBA title.

17. Ankara: Turks say suspect in Pope shooting tied to rightist web of intrigue (→ 7/22).

17. New York: Carter warns against withholding criticism of human rights breaches.

18. Rome: Voters affirm liberal abortion law by better than 2-1.

19. Northern Ireland: I.R.A. mine kills five British soldiers on patrol (→ 8/2).

20. U.S. Senate unanimously bars two Social Security pension cuts sought by Reagan (→ 7/29).

21. L.I.: N.Y. Islanders capture second straight Stanley Cup.

24. Barcelona: Spanish commandos free bank hostages held by rightists asking freedom for Feb. coup leaders (→ 10/29/82).

28. EPA restricts regional power to order cleanup of toxic waste sites (→ 9/11).

30. Chittagong: Bangladesh Pres. Rahman, in power since 1975, assassinated (→ 3/24/82).

31. Washington: Census finds more blacks living in suburbs of major cities (→ 6/25).

31. Beirut: Eight die, 60 wounded in shelling of Moslem beach (→ 6/7).

DEATH

5. William Saroyan, U.S. playwright, novelist (*8/31/1908).

Assassin wounds Pope at St. Peter's

May 13. Pope John Paul II was the victim of an assassination attempt today. He was shot and wounded by an escaped Turkish criminal as he rode in an open car among 10,000 worshipers in St. Peter's Square. Shot twice in the abdomen, the pope was attending his weekly general audience.

He was rushed to the Gemelli hospital in Rome, where he underwent over five hours of emergency surgery, in which sections of his intestine were removed. Although he was listed as in "guarded" condition, a spokesman was confident that "the pontiff will recover soon."

Police arrested the gunman, who was identified as Mehmet Ali Agca, 23. The Turkish news agency Anatolia reported that Agca was convicted of the murder of Abdi Ipecki, an editor of the newspaper Milliyet, in 1979, and that he escaped from prison later that year.

He wrote a letter to the newspaper indicating that he escaped from prison in order to kill the pope, who was scheduled to visit Ankara and Istanbul. Police discovered a note on Agca, saying "I am killing the pope as a protest against the imperialism of the Soviet Union and the United States and against the genocide . . . in El Salvador and Afghanistan." John Paul II has served as pope since October 1978, when his predecessor died (→ 17).

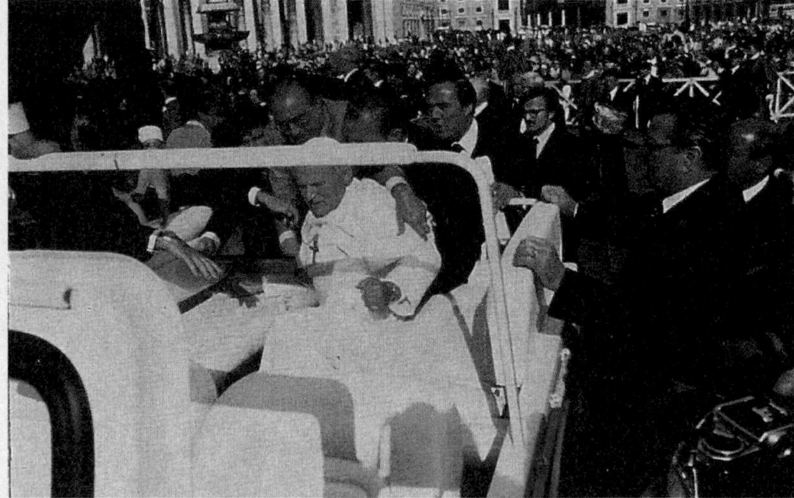

Aides rush to help the Pope just after shots disrupted his weekly audience.

Mitterrand first French Socialist President

May 10. A bitter political campaign ended today and France made a major shift to the left as Francois Mitterrand, a Socialist, was elected to succeed Valery Giscard d'Estaing as President. Giscard d'Estaing, who was surprised by his defeat, refused to congratulate Mitterrand. The French Communist Party, which played an important role in his election, said it expected to be represented in the Cabinet. There was no immediate reaction from Mitterrand.

The new president gave a very low-key victory speech as he tried to reassure opponents who fear that his victory will bring radical changes to France. Mitterrand appealed for national unity. "Only the entire national community," he said, "can respond to the requirements of the present time." In his campaign, Mitterrand pledged to nationalize banks and insurance companies, increase taxes on the rich, raise wages and restore full employment, largely through government hiring. In international affairs, Mitterrand promised to remain a strong member of NATO, and ironically, he criticized Giscard d'Estaing for being too soft on Moscow.

Mitterrand's plans have sent shudders through corporate and financial circles. Tonight, the working class was celebrating his victory by blowing car horns in Paris and dancing at the Bastille. European leaders cabled their congratulations, but there was no public reaction from the Reagan White House.

Conservative and centrist supporters of Giscard d'Estaing still control the French Parliament. Mitterrand is expected to call legislative elections as early as next month. Within the next few days, he will have to decide how to deal with the Communists (→ 6/14).

Mitterrand holds symbolic red rose.

Bob Marley, reggae artist, is deceased

May 11. Bob Marley, the most influential star of Jamaican reggae music, succumbed to cancer today in Miami. He was only 36 years old. Marley, who grew up in Jamaica's poverty-ridden Trenchtown ghetto, reached an international audience with his stirring political anthems and spellbinding stage presence in the 1970's. He was a follower of the Rastafarian religious movement and bitterly attacked political oppression. But after a 1976 attempt on his life, Marley never returned to Jamaica.

Marley leaves the rat race behind.

Irish hunger striker dies after 66 days

Sands honored in bleak Belfast rain.

May 12. Two imprisoned members of the Irish Republican Army have died in Belfast's Maze Prison after long hunger strikes to protest treatment by British authorities.

Bobby Sands, who was serving a 14-year sentence for possession of firearms, died after 66 days without food. The 27-year-old Sands had recently been elected to Parliament in a special election to fill a vacancy. A week later, Francis Hughes, 25, died after 59 days of refusing food. Two other fasting Irish Nationalists were also reported to be nearing death in the prison.

The I.R.A. inmates have undertaken the hunger strikes to highlight their demands that they be treated as political prisoners, not as criminals. The two deaths provoked demonstrations in Belfast and demands for leniency by the British government. The Prime Minister took the position that "there can be no compromise with murder and terrorism" and refused to grant political status (→ 19).

Cardinal Wyszynski of Poland is dead

May 28. Stefan Cardinal Wyszynski, Archbishop of Warsaw and the Roman Catholic Primate of Poland, died today of stomach cancer. He was 79 years old. Wyszynski was active in the resistance to the Nazis during World War II, and was appointed primate in 1948, the year in which the Communist Party took power in Poland. His stance toward the government ranged from staunch opposition in the Stalin years, to peaceful coexistence and cooperation as the regime moderated its policies. During the strikes last summer, Wyszynski mediated between Stanislaw Kania, the Communist Party leader, and Lech Walesa, head of the Solidarity labor union (→ 6/8).

Wyszynski, Poland's judicious voice.

Yorkshire Ripper is sentenced to life

May 22. Jack Sutcliffe, the notorious British serial killer known as the Yorkshire Ripper, was sentenced today to life in prison. The jury decreed that his sentence could not be reduced for at least 30 years. Sutcliffe, who claimed to have a divine mission to eliminate prostitutes, was accused in the savage beatings and killings of 13 women in Leeds, Wakefield and Bradford. He is believed to have committed his first crime in 1975, when he beat, killed and mutilated a 28-year-old prostitute named Wilma MacCann.

Senator is guilty in Abscam inquiry

May 1. Senator Harrison A. Williams of New Jersey became the first U.S. senator since 1905 and the third in American history to be convicted of criminal offenses while in office when he was found guilty last night of charges arising from the Justice Department's Abscam investigation of political corruption. Convicted on five counts, most prominently bribery and conspiracy, Williams faces up to 18 years in prison and also the possibility of Senate actions which could include expulsion (→ 2/16/82).

May 24. Bobby Unser, in a Norton Spirit, evened the family rivalry today, racing to his third victory in the Indy 500 at an average of 139 mph.

Italy's Cabinet out in Masonic scandal

May 26. The Cabinet of Italy's Prime Minister has resigned after it was revealed that hundreds of government officials were linked to a secret Masonic organization. Last week, a list of 953 names, including members of the Cabinet and Parliament, judges and bankers, was found in the home of Licio Gelli, grandmaster of the illegal Masonic lodge P-2. Although it is unproven that all 953 were members of the group, it has forced the resignation of Prime Minister Forlani and his Cabinet (→ 12/17).

1981

JUNE

Su	Mo	Tu	We	Th	Fr	Sa
	1	2	3	4	5	6
7	8	9	10	11	12	13
14	15	16	17	18	19	20
21	22	23	24	25	26	27
28	29	30				

1. Peking: China publishes first English newspaper (→ 30).

4. Atlanta: Wayne Williams held and released as suspect in 28 murders (→ 21).

5. Louisiana: Carl Lewis wins NCAA sprint and long jump.

7. Paris: Bjorn Borg wins sixth French Open title.

7. Iraq: Israeli air raid destroys Iraqi atomic reactor (→ 24).

8. Warsaw: Soviets warn Poles to toughen stance against "counter-revolutionaries" (→ 8/3).

10. Tehran: Khomeini dismisses Pres. Bani-Sadr as chief of armed forces (→ 29).

12. U.S.: Baseball players go on strike (→ 7/31).

14. France: Socialist Party wins landslide vote in elections to National Assembly (→ 23).

16. Chicago: Cubs sold by William Wrigley to Tribune Co. for $20.5 million.

16. Peking: Haig in policy reversal agrees to U.S. arms sale to China (→ 1/12/82).

18. U.S.: Dept. of Agriculture reports using gene-splicing to make vaccine against hoof and mouth disease (→ 10/29/82).

22. N.Y.: Mark David Chapman pleads guilty to murder of John Lennon (→ 8/24).

24. Jerusalem: Moshe Dayan declares Israelis have capacity to make A-bomb (→ 8/8).

26. Washington: Rev. Sun Myung Moon under inquiry for tax evasion (→ 10/15).

27. Kenya: Africans condemn U.S. for collusion with South Africa (→ 8/1).

28. Canada: Terry Fox, cancer marathoner, dies at age 22.

29. Tehran: Khomeini names new officials as 72 die in bomb attack (→ 8/30).

30. West Germany: Eight ex-Nazi guards convicted.

30. Peking: Hua Kuo-feng replaced by Hu Yao-bang; Mao denounced (→ 11/21).

DEATH

3. Carleton Coon, Harvard anthropologist (*6/23/1904).

Wayne Williams held for Atlanta murders

Williams, implicated in 28 murders.

June 21. Wayne B. Williams, a music promoter and talent scout, was arrested today and charged in the most recent of 28 murders of black children and young adults in Atlanta. The 23-year-old black man was first interrogated on May 22, when officers on stakeout at a bridge over the Chattahoochee River followed his car and stopped him. Two days later, the body of Nathaniel Cater, 27, was found floating near the bridge. Surveillance of Williams then became heavy.

Williams lives with his parents both retired school teachers, near the area where several of the victims lived. It had been thought the slayings were committed by more than one person, probably acting separately. Nine of the victims were found naked in rivers, 19 died of asphyxiation, two were young girls, five were young adults. While Williams proclaims his innocence, the recent developments after two years of frustration have Atlanta dizzy with anticipation (→ 2/27/82).

Israeli planes destroy Iraqi nuclear reactor

June 24. In the wake of Israel's June 7 air attack against Iraq's nuclear reactor in Baghdad, Moshe Dayan has revealed Israel has the capacity to make nuclear bombs.

The former Israeli Defense Minister and Foreign Minister also emphasized that Israel should not exploit this capacity unless the Arabs do so first. "We should not be the first ones, but we shouldn't be too late," he said.

Earlier this month, Israeli F-4 Phantom jets, armed with precision weapons known as "smart bombs," destroyed the Iraqi reactor as it was nearing completion and not yet stocked with nuclear fuel. The plant was being built with French and Italian aid, and a French technician was reported killed.

Israeli Prime Minister Menachem Begin called the decision to bomb the site the result of "a terrible dilemma," but argued that it was a justifiable finesse of Iraqi potentiality to attack Israel with atom bombs of the Hiroshima type.

The raid fanned worldwide criticism and further strained U.S.-Israeli relations as the United States suspended delivery of four F-16 jet fighters and voted in the United Nations to condemn the attack.

Dayan's assertion of Israeli nuclear potentiality confirmed the general assumption that Israel has a store of uranium partly stolen from a West German ship, in 1968, and a Pennsylvania plant in 1965. The raid itself may strengthen Arab arguments that they need nuclear weapons to balance Israel's military power if not superiority (→ 7/17).

Four Communists join French Cabinet

June 23. Francois Mitterrand, the new President of France, rewarded the Communist Party for their political support today by giving them four seats in the new Cabinet. The move sent shockwaves through Washington and NATO, but it was viewed as a token gesture in France. The ministries controlled by Communist Party members are all minor ones. The Communists agreed to support Mitterrand in his call for a Soviet withdrawal from Afghanistan and non-intervention in Poland. Mitterrand acted after his Socialist Party won majority control in the Assembly (→ 2/14/82).

Blank pistol shots alarm Elizabeth II

June 13. Millions were watching on television as Queen Elizabeth of England rode horseback along The Mall to the Trooping the Color ceremony marking her official 55th birthday. Suddenly, a youth of 17 stepped from the crowd and fired as many as six pistol blanks before being wrestled to the ground by policemen and onlookers. The queen was unhurt, though the horse shied at the noise. An expert rider, she quickly brought her 19-year-old steed, Burmese, under control. The unemployed teen was charged under the Treason Act and now faces a maximum sentence of seven years.

Racial minorities increase in suburbs

June 25. Sociologists coined the phrase "white flight" to describe the exodus of white Americans from the inner-city to the suburbs. But now the term should be changed to "minority flight," as the Census Bureau has found an increase in the number of blacks and Hispanics inhabiting suburban areas since 1970. The demographic changes represent a rise in the percentage of minorities living at middle-class economic levels. Hispanic Americans are the fastest-growing ethnic group in the nation and are moving to the suburbs at a rate even higher than that of blacks (→ 7/15).

Raiders of Lost Ark is old-style movie

It's a B picture worth an A+. Director Steven Spielberg and scriptwriter George Lucas sat down and asked each other, kind of conspiratorially, "What were your favorite movies when you were a kid?" The answer was Flash Gordon and the Jungle Jim serials, tales of derring-do in exotic locales. Then they made their own movie called "Raiders of the Lost Ark."

"Raiders" premiered this month to boffo reviews. It concerns a seemingly mild-mannered archeologist (Harrison Ford) who pummels his way across continents, fighting to get and then defend the Ten Commandments (an irony lost on most viewers). Karen Allen co-stars as a feisty girlfriend and Paul Freeman plays a nasty excavator named Belloq.

Climactic scene in "Raiders."

Timerman recounts Argentine torture

June 8. In a controversial book describing his imprisonment in an Argentine prison, Jacobo Timerman has stated that "electric shocks on my genitals" had not humiliated him so much as "the silent complicity of Jewish leaders." Timerman, a Jew and an outspoken leftist, has claimed that his incarceration and torture was the result of a strain of anti-Semitism which has penetrated the highest levels of Argentina's authoritarian government.

Being Jewish in Argentina, Timerman wrote, "was a category of guilt, even when we were declared innocent of other offenses and absolved of other crimes."

He has suggested Jewish leaders in Argentina, the United States and Israel are as much to blame for the situation because they have not spoken out and remain on friendly terms with the Argentine regime. Critics of Timerman's book, including American conservative William F. Buckley, say Timerman was singled out for his leftist politics and support of a terrorist group, not because he was Jewish (→ 7/6).

First President's false teeth missing

June 19. George Washington's dentures were reported missing from a frantic National Museum of American History today. The gold and ivory teeth (not wood as some rumors would have it) had been in a storage room. An inscription on the choppers reads, "This was the Great Washington's teeth." Actually, he had dentures galore. One set is kept at Mount Vernon, another is in London and a third is somewhere in South America.

1981

JULY

Su	Mo	Tu	We	Th	Fr	Sa
			1	2	3	4
5	6	7	8	9	10	11
12	13	14	15	16	17	18
19	20	21	22	23	24	25
26	27	28	29	30	31	

4. Wimbledon: McEnroe over Borg 4-6, 7-6, 7-6, 6-4; Evert Lloyd over Manklikova 6-2, 6-2.

5. Israel: Begin bloc wins one-seat margin in parliamentary elections (→ 10/16).

5. Britain: 100 police injured by rioters in Liverpool (→ 9).

6. Buenos Aires: Isabel Peron freed after five-year house arrest (→ 7/1/82).

8. Calif.: U.S. prosecutors raise concern over illegal arms exports to Libya and U.S.S.R.

9. Calif.: Gov. Brown orders spraying of Malathion to halt spread of fruit flies.

9. Nicaragua: Eden Pastora steps down as minister to go into self-exile (→ 1/7/82).

9. Britain: Labor Party scorns Thatcher as rioting continues in two cities (→ 27).

9. El Salvador: Security forces reported slaying masses of peasants (→ 8/12).

13. Ben Plucknett, discus thrower, is first U.S. athlete banned for steroid use; 2 records annulled.

15. Washington: Reagan admin. cutting back on civil rights enforcement (→ 8/23).

16. Washington: House approves $26 million rise in arms budget (→ 1/31/83).

17. Lebanon: Israeli jets kill 123 in shelling of PLO targets (→ 24).

19. Bernard Hinault wins his third Tour de France.

22. Chrysler reports $11.6 mil. in profit for previous quarter.

23. Washington Star shuts down after 128 years.

24. Israel and PLO call cease-fire in border fighting; PLO radicals refuse (→ 8/29).

31. U.S.: Baseball strike ends after seven weeks.

31. Panama: Gen. Omar Torrijos, ruler for nine years, dies in plane crash.

DEATHS

16. Harry Chapin, American folk musician (*12/7/1942).

27. William Wyler, U.S. film director, three Oscars, "Ben Hur" (*7/1/1902).

Charles and Diana wed in royal splendor

Down the aisle at St. Paul's.

July 29. On the back of the couple's car was a hand-scrawled sign reading "Just Married." Actually, it was not a car but a 70-year-old gilded, horse-drawn carriage; the sign was equally an understatement. Prince Charles and Lady Diana wed this morning in a splendid ceremony viewed by millions.

As Charles approached his present age of 32, rumors of betrothal grew insistent. He must wed someone, the public reasoned, so why not the demure, blonde, 20-year-old former kindergarten teacher Lady Diana Spencer? Although her parents were divorced, she came of good stock, the first Duke of Marlborough being in her lineage.

Thoroughly convinced, Charles stood this morning at the altar of St. Paul's Cathedral. He was in the uniform of a full-dress naval commander, a blue sash blazoned across his chest. At his side were his best men, brothers Andrew and Edward. Sitting erect in the pews behind him, garbed like dignified popsicles, were his mother Queen Elizabeth in aquamarine, his aunt Princess Margaret in peach and his sister Princess Anne in white and yellow.

Sitting further back, and doubtless with a poorer view, was Nancy Reagan and 2,500 other guests from all over the world. Outside the cathedral tens of thousands listened to the proceedings on speakers, and at home in dozens of nations people watched via satellite.

At 11 a.m., Diana stepped down the aisle toward Charles to the organ strains of "Trumpet Voluntary." It took her four minutes to reach him, her train, 25 feet long, arriving sometime after. Her dress was of pale ivory.

Lady Diana told the Most Rev. Robert Runcie, Archbishop of Canterbury, that she would take "Philip Charles Arthur George" in holy matrimony—whoever that is. Her intended's name is "Charles Philip Arthur George." The latter slipped a band of Welsh gold on her finger with less outward fluster.

The one-hour ceremony over, the couple rode their carriage to Buckingham Palace. They appeared on the balcony above the Victoria Monument and before an adoring crowd they kissed—something they had not done all morning (→ 6/22/82).

Prince Charles and Lady Di kiss before an adoring crowd at the palace.

Reagan's 25% tax cut is approved

July 29. President Reagan scored a major victory today as the House of Representatives approved his tax cut bill. The measure provides for three years of reductions totaling 25 percent in individual tax rates and major cuts in taxes paid by oil producers and other businesses. The bill is similar to one approved earlier in the day by the Senate, which is controlled by Republicans and where the outcome was never in doubt. Less certain, however, was the outcome in the House, in which the Democrats are in the majority. There, a coalition of Republicans and Southern Democrats supported the president (→ 9/29).

Agca gets life term after his confession

July 22. Mehmet Ali Agca was sentenced to life in prison today, after being judged guilty of an attempt on the life of Pope John Paul II and two American women in St. Peter's Square on May 13. The court of two judges and six jurors rejected a plea by Pietro D'Ovidio, Agca's court-appointed lawyer, to reduce the sentence to 30 years on the grounds that his client was a "psychopath." Agca has boycotted the trial, on the grounds that Italy has no right to try him for a crime committed in the territory of Vatican City (→ 5/12/82).

Anarchy is feared as British riots spread

July 27. In response to the rioting which has rocked England's cities for the past month, Prime Minister Margaret Thatcher has announced a new package of measures intended to combat the rampant unemployment which is thought to be the cause of the disturbances. The social alienation and disaffection among Britain's three million unemployed has led to attacks by youth gangs on police, with many officers injured by rocks and bombs. Mrs. Thatcher's proposal is seen as a desperate attempt to forestall total anarchy (→ 6/8/82).

First woman named to Supreme Court

July 7. President Reagan has nominated Sandra Day O'Connor for the Supreme Court. If Congress approves her appointment, 51-year-old Mrs. O'Connor will be the first woman to serve on the Supreme Court. And approval is likely despite opposition from Moral Majority and other conservative groups.

Mrs. O'Connor is a bit of a conservative herself, judging by her record as a member of the Arizona Court of Appeals. That is what Reagan is counting on, hoping to lean the court to the right. In the past, however, she has supported the Equal Rights Amendment and pro-choice legislation (→ 9/25).

Solar power propels cross-Channel craft

Solar Challenger, a modern Icarus.

July 7. The first solar-powered airplane flew across the English Channel today. Starting from Cormeilles-en-Vexin, 25 miles northwest of Paris, the 210-pound Solar Challenger made its 165-mile trip at an average speed of 30 mph at a cruising altitude of 11,000 feet, landing at Manston Royal Air Force Base on the southeastern English coast.

Designed by Paul MacCready, who also built the first human-powered plane to cross the Channel, the Solar Challenger is powered by 16,000 photovoltaic cells, mounted on its wings, which convert sunlight to electricity to drive its 2.7-horsepower motor. The plane had made several unsuccessful attempts to fly the Channel but was helped today by an unusually sunny summer day. It was greeted by a crowd of 30 persons.

111 are killed when hotel walkways fall

Gruesome cleanup efforts in K.C.

July 18. Two of the three concrete and metal suspended walkways in the four-story lobby of the Hyatt Regency Hotel in Kansas City collapsed last night, creating a scene of terror. At the latest count, 111 persons have died and many of the 188 injured are still in hospitals. As 1,200 to 1,500 were dancing in the lobby and on walkways at 7:08 p.m., the fourth-floor walkway snapped from the steel rods suspending it from the ceiling. It fell like a pancake on the walk at the second-floor level. Both walks, filled with dancers and spectators, then collapsed on the crowd in the lobby. The hotel opened in 1980.

Western chiefs meet at Ottawa summit

July 21. The leaders of France, Canada, West Germany, Italy, Japan, Britain and the United States have concluded their seventh annual economic conference, agreeing to revitalize the Western industrial economies but deciding on no clear method to achieve this. The leaders concurred that inflation and unemployment must be checked.

World industrial chiefs in Ottawa.

1981

AUGUST

Su	Mo	Tu	We	Th	Fr	Sa
						1
2	3	4	5	6	7	8
9	10	11	12	13	14	15
16	17	18	19	20	21	22
23	24	25	26	27	28	29
30	31					

1. South Africa: Cape Town trying to oust hundreds of homeless blacks (→ 29).

2. Northern Ireland: Eighth hunger striker dies in Maze prison (→ 20).

3. U.S.: Air traffic controllers begin nationwide strike, grounding 7,000 flights (→ 6).

3. Poland: Police halt food protest; Solidarity threatens strike action (→ 14).

7. EEC orders million tons fruit wasted to maintain prices.

8. Reagan orders production of two types of neutron arms for stockpiling in U.S. (→ 10/2).

8. U.S.: Gypsy moth causing record losses in Northeast.

10. Canada: Some routes to Europe shut as controllers get support of Canadian union.

12. El Salvador reported using toxic gas against rebels and civilians (→ 26).

14. Poland: Declaration following visit of Brezhnev denounces "forces hostile to Socialism" (→ 9/5).

16. Washington: Study indicates juveniles tied to 23% of violent crime.

20. Ulster: Tenth hunger striker dies (→ 11/14).

24. Washington: Jury indicts Hinckley in shooting of Pres. Reagan (→ 28).

24. Washington: It is reported a team of ex-Green Berets trained Libyan terrorists (→ 12/10).

24. N.Y.: Mark David Chapman given 20 years to life for murder of John Lennon.

26. El Salvador: Two-year death toll reaches 26,000 in civil war (→ 2/10/82).

29. Angola: 240 dead after five-day incursion by South African troops (→ 7/3/82).

DEATHS

1. Paddy Chayefsky, American dramatist (*1/29/1923).

14. Karl Bohm, Austrian composer (*8/28/1894).

26. Roger Baldwin, founder of American Civil Liberties Union (*1/21/1884).

Hinckley pleads not guilty in shooting

Hinckley denies shooting Reagan.

Aug 28. John W. Hinckley Jr. pleaded not guilty today to charges of attempting to kill President Reagan and assaulting three other men last March just outside a Washington hotel. He was indicted four days ago by a federal grand jury.

Speaking in a firm, clear voice, the young defendant announced his plea as he stood before Judge Barrington Parker in a heavily guarded courtroom. The judge signed an order declaring Hinckley mentally competent to participate in the court proceedings. The order states the defendant has a rational and factual understanding of the charges against him "and is able to assist his attorney in the preparation of his defense." Hinckley is undergoing psychiatric testing (→ 4/26/82).

Used as secretary and playmate, personal computers are invading office and home and perhaps permanently altering the way people interface with each other.

Controllers walk out; Reagan fires strikers

Patco workers, fired by Reagan.

Aug 6. President Reagan today fired 12,000 federal air traffic controllers whose three-day strike has grounded about half of the more than 14,000 daily airline flights.

"As far as I'm concerned," said Transportation Secretary Drew Lewis, "it's a non-strike situation. It's over. Our concern is rebuilding the system."

The controllers walked off the job despite a back-to-work order issued by Federal Judge Harold Greene, who also found the union President, Robert E. Poli, in contempt and ordered him fined $1,000 a day.

By firing the striking controllers, the administration made good on facing down the largest strike of federal employess since 167,000 postal workers struck in 1970.

In defying the court order and the president's insistence that they return to work, officials of Patco, the union representing the controllers, had said the administration would eventually bargain with them on such key issues as higher pay, a shorter work week and retirement after 20 years, regardless of age.

"The system cannot work without us, and they know it," said one union official. "There's absolute chaos at towers."

But a spokesman for the Federal Aviation Administration, which employs the controllers, dismissed widespread reports of problems at airport towers, saying the work is being carried on by professionals (→ 10).

Bomb blast kills two top Iranian officials

Aug 30. A powerful bomb blasted the central Tehran offices of Iranian Prime Minister Mohammed Javad Bahonar yesterday, killing him, President Mohammed Ali Rajai and five others.

Assumed to be the work of rebels opposing the clergy-dominated revolutionary government, it is the most violent since the June 28th bombing of an Islamic Republican Party meeting, which killed Ayatollah Mohammed Behesti, the powerful party leader, and 70 others.

Bloodletting between the Islamic clergy and the secular liberals has deepened since the June ouster of Iran's first elected President, Bani-Sadr, with several important officials killed and strolling clerics the frequent targets of pot-shotting gunmen on motorcycles. The government has answered with nationwide manhunts, and executions by the religious courts are a daily occurrence (→ 9/5).

Libyans menacing F-14's shot down

Aug 19. In a one-minute dogfight today over the northern part of the Gulf of Sidra, about 60 miles from the Libyan coast, two Navy F-14 jets downed two Soviet-built Libyan SU-22's with sidewinders after one of the Libyan jets had opened fire.

The Libyan pilots parachuted, but one of the chutes was on fire. In a protest note, the U.S. called the attack "unprovoked" and of "grave concern." Because the two countries have severed diplomatic relations, the note was delivered in Tripoli by the Belgian Embassy.

Whereas the United States, as well as the Soviet Union, Britain and France, regard the Gulf of Sidra as international water, Lybia claims it is within its 12-mile territorial limit. Yesterday, the Libyans charged that U.S. naval maneuvers in the gulf constituted aggression and warned that "Libya will fight by all means for its territorial waters" (→ 24).

Polls hint blacks becoming more pessimistic

Aug 23. Black Americans have developed a gloomy outlook in the 1980's, according to recent surveys and interviews with prominent blacks. The cause of their pessimism is apparently President Reagan. In light of the Reagan administration's budget cuts, which adversely affect minorities, blacks see their situation as worsening.

Alvin Poussaint, a Harvard psychiatry professor and expert on black affairs, said blacks view the president as "no friend of black people" and fear the "country is going to turn its back on them." Blacks note the rise in unemployment among minorities and the increase in the income gap as factors coloring their outlook (→ 11/16).

Arab terrorists kill two in Vienna synagogue

Terrorist toll continues to mount.

Aug 29. Two persons were killed and 18 were wounded today when two Arabs attacked a Viennese synagogue with automatic pistols and grenades. Both of the terrorists were captured.

One attacker said he belonged to Al Fatah, the largest group in the Palestine Liberation Organization, but the PLO later condemned the "cowardly, criminal act" and said that it respected all religious beliefs, including Judaism. Today's attack was the second in less than three years on the 155-year-old synagogue. It followed by two weeks the bombing of a garden next to the Israeli Embassy (→ 9/4).

Moral Majority said to peddle coercion

Aug 31. The fundamentalist religious and political movement which calls itself Moral Majority was attacked today by the President of Yale University as an intolerant organization which has "licensed a new meanness of spirit in the land." A. Bartlett Giamatti accused many political leaders of being afraid to face up to Moral Majority, as well as to acts of anti-Semitism and the Ku Klux Klan. The founder of the group, the Rev. Jerry Falwell, is a supporter of President Reagan and played an important role in his election last year.

Giamatti did not specifically criticize the views of Moral Majority, which include opposition to abortion, gay rights and the proposed Equal Rights Amendment. The Yale president did charge, however, that group members believe "they and they alone possess the truth." Giamatti said that "whatever view does not conform to these views is by definition relativistic, negative, secular, immoral; against the family, anti-free enterprise, un-American. What nonsense," he said.

Divers find safe in sunken Italian ship

Aug 27. Deep-sea divers exploring the wreck of the liner Andrea Doria report they have brought one of the ship's two safes to the surface. They are rumored to contain more than $1 million in cash and jewelry. The expedition to reach the Andrea Doria, which sank in a collision with the Swedish liner Stockholm on July 25, 1965, was led by department store heir Peter Gimbel. His plan is to open the safe in a live broadcast on nationwide television about the sinking, "Andrea Doria: The Final Chapter."

Sunken treasure on Andrea Doria.

1981

SEPTEMBER

Su	Mo	Tu	We	Th	Fr	Sa
		1	2	3	4	5
6	7	8	9	10	11	12
13	14	15	16	17	18	19
20	21	22	23	24	25	26
27	28	29	30			

4. Beirut: French Ambassador Louis Delamare killed (→ 10/1).

5. Cairo: Sadat deposes Coptic pope amid religious factionalism (→ 10).

5. Tehran: Two more leaders die as challenge to revolution grows (→ 20).

5. Moscow: Soviets report 100,000 on maneuvers near Poland (→ 18).

10. Egypt: Sadat bans Moslem Brotherhood in purge of radical opposition (→ 17).

11. Wyoming: Int. Sec. Watt announces major cutbacks in EPA resources (→ 10/23).

13. N.Y.: McEnroe over Borg, Tracy Austin over Navratilova in U.S. Open singles.

14. Norway: Labor govt. toppled by Conservatives.

15. Rome: Pope calls labor unions "indispensable in struggle for social justice" (→ 11/25/82).

16. Las Vegas: Sugar Ray Leonard defeats Thomas Hearns in welterweight title bout.

17. Cairo: Sadat expels 1,000 Russians from Egypt (→ 10/6).

18. Chicago: Visiting South African rugby team, under official ban, vows to continue tour in private (→ 7/3/82).

19. N.Y.: Simon and Garfunkel reunion in Central Park.

20. Iran: 149 leftist militants executed by govt. (→ 27).

20. Belize, last British colony in Americas, gains independence.

23. Washington: 1971 tape links Nixon to plan to use Teamster "thugs" agains war protesters (→ 12/4).

23. Louisiana: Convict-author Jack Abbot seized for N.Y. restaurant killing (→ 1/21/82).

25. Poland: New laws give workers role in running plants (→ 10/14).

DEATHS

1. Albert Speer, architect of Nazi concentration camps (*3/19/1905).

8. Roy Wilkins, American civil rights activist, led NAACP 1955-1977 (*8/30/1901).

Soviets warn Poles of dangers of Solidarity

Poles demonstrate in support of Solidarity, their first independent union.

Sept 18. The Soviet Union has warned Polish leaders to silence the anti-Soviet campaign that it said was being waged by the Solidarity union. A statement from the Central Committee of the Soviet Communist Party, made public by the Polish government, said "the growth of anti-Sovietism in Poland" had "reached dangerous limits" and that something must be done about it by Polish authorites.

The immediate response of the Polish government was to issue a statement warning the Solidarity union that its actions were jeopardizing the "indepedent existence" of Poland. The Soviet statement labeled as a "revolting provocation" a resolution adopted at Solidarity's recent national congress urging free trade unions throughout the Soviet bloc. Meanwhile, Soviet troops exercised near Poland's border (→ 25).

What's wrong with U.S.? Debt, says Ron

Sept 29. One trillion dollars. The figure is incredible, but it is a reality which warrants attention because America's budget deficit will soon reach that plateau. President Reagan addressed the issue in his last TV speech. "We've only balanced the budget once in the last 20 years," Reagan noted. "One trillion dollars of debt—if we as a nation needed a warning, let that be it."

In determining who holds the burden of public debt, it can be seen as a sliced economic pie. U.S. government accounts have incurred the largest chunk at 22 percent. The Federal Reserve owns 13 percent, while foreign individuals and institutions hold another 14 percent of the debt. The remainder of the pie can be sliced into various smaller pieces.

There are three basic ways to cut the deficit: The government can decrease spending; it can increase taxes; or, it can print more money to cover expenses.

Critics of the Reagan administration say the president cannot expect to balance the budget by vastly increasing defense spending while cutting taxes. The president, however, vows to find a way to alleviate the burden for the next generation (→ 11/12).

Sept 25. Sandra Day O'Connor walks with Chief Justice Warren Burger after being sworn in as the court's first female Justice.

Guerrillas battle Khomeini's forces

Sept 27. What one Tehran observer called "the worst and most violent street clashes since the revolution" rocked the Iranian capital today as opposition Mujahedeen guerrillas armed with machine guns and grenade launchers engaged government guards in a series of running battles. Shouting "Khomeini will be overthrown!" the Mujahedeen served notice that they remain a threat to the clergy-led regime despite the execution of more than 1,000 of their members since the June ouster of President Bani-Sadr.

Earlier this month, the Mujahedeen assassinated the Iranian Prosecutor General by planting a bomb in his office so strong it knocked the balcony off the building. The fourth of Khomeini's senior aides to be killed that week, the official's death reinforced signs that the Iranian government security service has been infiltrated by the Mujahedeen (→ 10/12).

High-speed train makes French debut

Sept 22. Service was inaugurated in France today on the bullet-nosed train called the TGV. President Mitterrand went for the ride from Paris to Lyons. When the final kinks are ironed out, the fast train will make the trip in two hours and 40 minutes. By 1983, 40 minutes will be shaved off the trip, and the train will also make stops in Geneva and Marseilles.

TGV Paris-Lyons, a blur at 160 mph.

1981

OCTOBER

Su	Mo	Tu	We	Th	Fr	Sa
				1	2	3
4	5	6	7	8	9	10
11	12	13	14	15	16	17
18	19	20	21	22	23	24
25	26	27	28	29	30	31

1. Beirut: Bomb at PLO office kills 50 (→ 11/29).

2. Washington: Reagan drops plan for mobile MX, but wants 100 missiles (→ 10).

2. N.Y.: New leak shuts Con Ed nuclear plant at Indian Point (→ 4/20/83).

6. Egypt: President Sadat is assassinated.→

7. Cairo: V.P. Mubarak named Egyptian president (→ 11/21).

10. Bonn: 250,000 rally against U.S. plan to deploy missiles in Western Europe (→ 24).

12. Amnesty Intl. reports 1,800 executions in Iran since July (→ 2/8/82).

14. House votes against AWACS sale to Saudi Arabia; Reagan still free to make deal (→ 28).

14. Poland: Women occupy textile mills in protest over food shortages (→ 18).

15. New York: Sun Myung Moon indicted for tax evasion (→ 5/18/82).

18. Poland: Jaruzelski succeeds Kania at head of Communist Party (→ 12/13).

21. New York: Two members of Weather Underground seized after failed bank robbery.

23. Washington: 114 toxic waste sites listed as nation's most dangerous (→ 3/17/82).

24. London: 150,000 march to protest nuclear weapons (→ 25).

25. Europe: Disarmament protests draw over 100,000 in Paris, Brussels, Potsdam (→ 11/24).

25. N.Y. Marathon won by Alberto Salazar in record time.

26. Sweden: Soviet sub runs aground near Swedish naval base (→ 11/5).

28. U.S. Senate vote supports Reagan on AWACS sale to Saudis (→ 6/13/82).

28. New York: Dodgers beat Yankees to take World Series.

29. Geneva: OPEC members unite to freeze oil price at $34 per barrel (→ 2/16/82).

DEATH

23. Reginald Butler, British sculptor (*4/28/1913).

Soldiers murder Sadat

Sadat, regal in military dress.

Oct 6. Anwar el-Sadat, the Egyptian leader who made peace with Israel, was assassinated today in a murderous hail of automatic gunfire at a military parade in Cairo. Up to ten other people were killed and nearly 40 were wounded, including three U.S. military officers.

Thousands of horrified guests watched as several men dressed in Egyptian army uniforms broke out of the military procession and stormed the reviewing stand. They lobbed grenades and opened fire with automatic weapons. Some of Sadat's guards were distracted by a colorful air show. Others seemed frozen when the attackers opened fire. Dozens of invited guests dived for cover. Sadat was hit almost immediately and collapsed into a pool of blood. Guards carried him away for medical help while other victims of the shooting writhed in agony on the ground. The major who led the attack and two enlisted men were shot dead. A lieutenant and two soldiers were captured, according to officials.

Egyptian authorities said the attack was not part of a coup, but they refused to suggest a motive. There is speculation that the renegade soldiers are Moslem fundamentalists opposed to Sadat's peace treaty with Israel and his recent crackdown on religious extremists. A month ago, Sadat ordered the arrest of about 1,500 Coptic and Moslem radicals.

Vice President Hosni Mubarak announced that Sufi Abu Taleb, the Speaker of the Parliament, would serve as interim President. It is expected that Mubarak himself will control affairs of state. He was quick to assert that Egypt would continue to honor its treaty with Israel. "I hereby declare," he said, "in the name of the great soul passing away and in the name of the people, its constitutional institutions and its armed forces, that we are committed to all charters, treaties and international obligations that Egypt has concluded."

Officials in the Reagan administration expressed shock at the assassination. Some wondered how the killers could have penetrated the web of security around Sadat. Others said the late President should have had more security. Secretary of State Alexander Haig will head the American delegation to the funeral. Ex-Presidents Nixon, Ford and Carter will attend as Reagan's representatives (→ 7).

Army assassins take aim as Sadat's military review erupts into chaos.

Socialists win big in Greek elections

Oct 18. After a long and exhausting campaign, the Socialist Party has won control of the Greek government. The New Democracy Party of Prime Minister George Rallis was defeated, after 35 years of pro-Western conservative rule, by the Panhellenic Socialist Movement led by George Papandreou. The Socialists won a majority of Parliament seats, but many of the remaining seats will still be filled by New Democrats. The pro-Moscow Communist Party faired the worst of the major contenders. A U.S. spokesman said continued good relations with Greece were expected.

Andrew Young now Mayor of Atlanta

Oct 28. Andrew Young won the mayoral election in Atlanta this evening, vowing to "work together for peace and prosperity for all of us in the city of Atlanta." Young served in the House of Representatives and as President Carter's delegate to the United Nations before resigning in a storm of controversy.

Young defeated Sidney Marcus by a solid ten percent in this runoff election; both men decidedly defeated opponents in the October 6 general election. Young, a black, won a clear majority of the black vote. But his victory also included strong support from the white electorate. His primary concern will be dealing with Atlanta's financial woes.

Dayan, Israeli war hero, is dead at 66

Oct 16. Israeli soldier-statesman Moshe Dayan lost his five-year battle with cancer today when he died, at 66, from a heart ailment. Thus passed away not only the world's most famous eye-patch—he lost his left eye during WWII action in Syria—but a symbol of Israeli toughness. A complicated man, he was once described as "gloomy, lonely, gifted—too cunning, too admired, too hated, too ambitious, too glamorous, too extravagant, too famous" (→ 9/2/83).

1981

NOVEMBER

Su	Mo	Tu	We	Th	Fr	Sa
1	2	3	4	5	6	7
8	9	10	11	12	13	14
15	16	17	18	19	20	21
22	23	24	25	26	27	28
29	30					

1. Caribbean: Antigua, Barbuda and Redonda get independence.

3. New York: Mayor Koch re-elected in landslide.

3. U.S.: Selective Service reports 25% of draft-age men have not registered (→ 11/15/82).

4. Memphis: Dr. George Nichopoulus acquitted of overprescribing addictive drugs for Elvis Presley.

6. Wyoming: Black-footed ferret found, previously thought extinct.

12. Florida: Space shuttle Columbia becomes first to be used for more than one space mission (→ 14).

14. Columbia lands after fuel cell failure (→ 3/22/82).

14. Ulster: I.R.A. gunmen kill Protestant M.P. (→ 12/25).

16. Washington: Reagan dismisses civil rights chief, a busing supporter (→ 2/6/82).

17. Atlanta: Report says migrant slavery persists on farms of South.

19. Ohio: U.S. Steel agrees to pay $6.3 bil. for Marathon Oil.

20. Italy: Anatoly Karpov wins World Championship of Chess.

21. Cairo: Sadat murder trial opens; suspects in iron cage (→ 3/6/82).

21. Peking: Christian Dior store opens in city (→ 23).

22. U.S.S.R.: Sakharovs start hunger strike to gain visa for daughter-in-law to join husband in U.S. (→ 5/26/82).

24. Washington: First air-launchable cruise missile completed (→ 2/1/82).

29. Syria: Bomb blast kills 64, injures 135 (→ 12/14).

DEATHS

6. Jonathan Worth Daniels, author and editor in American South (*4/26/1902).

7. Will Durant, popular American historian (*11/5/1885).

10. Abel Gance, French film director, "Napoleon" (*10/25/1889).

16. William Holden, American film actor (*4/17/1918).

Sweden releases Soviet nuclear submarine

Soviet sub Whisky, under guard.

Nov 5. Sweden said today it will release a Soviet submarine that has been stranded for ten days near a Swedish naval base, even though it has evidence that the sub is carrying nuclear torpedo warheads. Prime Minister Thorbjorn said the vessel and its crew of 56 would be released "as soon as weather permits."

The submarine went aground on a partially submerged ridge of granite, and was pulled off by Swedish naval vessels, which kept it surrounded. Swedish officers who went aboard the submarine said it was filled with electronic detection gear that would enable it to monitor the secret naval base at Karskrona. The Swedes have rejected Soviet assertions that the submarine strayed, saying that skilled navigation was necessary to reach the area where it was found. But they said there was no point in detaining the sub.

Door opens in China; private sector wider

Nov 23. Cigars and three-piece suits are not the style yet in Peking, but the Chinese government admitted today that a little of the capitalist spirit would not hurt. In fact, it might even help solve an urban unemployment rate that hovers around nine percent. To encourage the creation of jobs, the government is allowing private businessmen to hire more workers. This represents a significant change for a country that once insisted it would provide a job to everyone capable of working (→ 1/25/83).

Shortage of food worrying Brezhnev

Nov 16. Food production and distribution is the greatest problem facing the Soviet Union, Sovier leader Leonid I. Brezhnev said today. He told the Communist Party's Central Committee that for the third year in a row, drought had caused "great harm to agriculture and hence to the entire economy" and pledged a new program to increase food production. American experts predict a Soviet grain harvest of 175 million tons, 70 percent below target. Soviet grain purchases are estimated at 43 million tons this year (→ 22).

Ron takes budget chief to woodshed

Nov 12. President Reagan's economic adviser David Stockman has acknowledged that his "poor judgment and loose talk" has hurt Reagan's economic program and has offered his resignation. But the boss refused to accept it, saying the Budget Director was "too indispensable." Stockman had expressed a lack of confidence in Reagan's fiscal policies in a recent issue of The Atlantic Monthly. After apologizing to the president, Stockman said, "I grew up on a farm and I might say that my visit to the Oval Office for lunch with the president was more in the nature of a visit to the woodshed after supper" (→ 12/7).

Admiral Rickover's long career ended

Nov 13. The Navy's chief nuclear officer, Admiral Hyman G. Rickover, has been ordered by President Reagan to step down from his post. The 81-year-old admiral, who was born in Russia, was almost single-handedly responsible for bringing the U.S. Navy into the nuclear age. A graduate of Annapolis who held a degree in electrical engineering, Rickover became interested in nuclear power when he served with the Manhattan Project, which developed the atomic bomb. He became head of the Bureau of Ships in 1949 and promoted the construction of nuclear-powered submarines and aircraft carriers.

Natalie Wood, film actress, is drowned

Wood, nominated for three Oscars.

Nov 29. A heart-breaking mystery shrouds the death of actress Natalie Wood, 43, last night in the dark waters off the California coast.

She, her husband Robert Wagner, Christopher Walken, her co-star in the current movie "Brainstorm," and Dennis Davern, skipper of the Wagners' yacht Splendour, had gone ashore for dinner. They returned to the yacht about 10:00 p.m. Then, it seems that Natalie left the men—but why did she, a poor swimmer, decide to take the dinghy out? She may have slipped trying to climb aboard it, possibly striking her head. The death of the well-liked actress came as her four-decade career, somewhat in an eclipse lately, had begun an upward swing.

Flamboyant British rocker Elton John, most popular solo artist of the 70's, still turns out hits like "Chloe" and "Nobody Wins."

1981

DECEMBER

Su	Mo	Tu	We	Th	Fr	Sa
		1	2	3	4	5
6	7	8	9	10	11	12
13	14	15	16	17	18	19
20	21	22	23	24	25	26
29	28	29	30	31		

4. Reagan broadens power of CIA, allowing spying in U.S.

7. Washington: Reagan aides predict record 1982 deficit of $109 billion (→ 1/21/82).

9. U.S.S.R.: Sakharovs gain visa for daughter-in-law, end hunger strike (→ 5/26/82).

10. Reagan asks Americans to leave Libya (→ 3/10/82).

10. NATO reaches accord on admission of Spain (→ 5/30/82).

11. Bahamas: Ali loses to Trevor Berbick in heavyweight bout.

13. Ohio: U.S. tennis team wins Davis Cup.

13. Poland: Martial law declared after labor leaders call for natl. vote on future of govt. (→ 17).

14. Israel annexes Golan Heights in abrupt move (→ 18).

17. Italy: U.S. Gen. J. Dozier, NATO attache, kidnapped by Red Brigade (→ 1/28/82).

18. U.S. suspends arms deal with Israel over annexation of Golan Heights (→ 1/31/82).

29. Reagan curtails Soviet trade in reprisal for Polish policy (→ 1/11/82).

31. Ghana: Ex-officer Jerry Rawlings overthrows civilian government.

CULTURAL EVENTS, 1981

Literature: Salman Rushdie's "Midnight's Children"; Nadine Gordimer's "July's People"; Alan Paton's "Ah! But Your Land is Beautiful"; Beth Henley's "Crimes of the Heart," Pulitzer drama; James Schyler's "The Morning of the Poem," Pulitzer.

Academia: Carl Schorske's "Fin-de-Siecle Vienna," Pulitzer; Swiss scientists produce three mice in first cloning of mammal.

Music: Kim Carnes' "Bette Davis Eyes"; Manhattan Transfer's "Boy from New York City"; Al Jarreau's "Breaking Away."

The Arts: Picasso's "Guernica" returned to Spain under terms of his will.

Film: "The French Lieutenant's Woman"; "Chariots of Fire"; "On Golden Pond," Henry Fonda, Katherine Hepburn; Warren Beatty's "Reds."

Strikes crushed in Poland, leaving 7 dead

Polish infantry, on maneuvers, prepares to fight a civil war if need be.

Dec 17. The Polish government lifted its news blackout long enough tonight to admit that at least seven people were killed resisting the imposition of martial law. The victims were apparently union members on strike at a coal mine in Silesia. More than 300 civilians and police officers were reported injured in clashes that occurred in Gdansk. In the past few days, Polish police have moved to crush strikes in coal mines, shipyards and factories. Solidarity leader Lech Walesa was nabbed by police at a union meeting in Gdansk. He is still being held.

The Reagan administration charged today that the Warsaw government is trying to destroy Solidarity with "the full knowledge and the support of the Soviet Union." The Soviet news agency Tass has said that the events in Poland are "an internal matter." Earlier, the White House suspended economic assistance to the Warsaw regime and ordered restrictions on Polish diplomats in the United States.

"Do not resign," Solidarity has urged union workers. "If we resign today, we'll bury our hopes for freedom for many years to come. Several thousand people cannot destroy ten million" (→ 29).

British protest ban on Irish Protestant

Dec 25. The State Department has found itself under criticism in Britain and Ireland for its decision to block a visit to the United States by the Rev. Ian Paisley, the outspoken Protestant leader in Northern Ireland. Reflecting the adverse reaction, The Guardian said in an editorial that "the American public is surely not so frail that it needs to be protected from his arguments." In blocking a speaking tour by Paisley, the State Department cited the "divisive" nature of his recent public comments. The State Department acted under considerable pressure from prominent members of Congress sympathetic to the cause of Irish unification (→ 2/19/82).

Paisley, voice of discord in Ulster.

College kids are turning into grinds

On campuses this fall, no aroma of smoldering draft cards filled the air, nor any whiff of homecoming bonfires. Only the midnight oil burned—24 hours a day. This year's freshmen are reputedly apathetic about anything that might distract them from their studies. At Brown University, part-time jobs at the cafeteria go begging while students study. At the University of Michigan, only one freshman is working on the college paper The Michigan Daily; just ten years ago, 100 undergraduates were on the staff. And seniors at the State University of New York at Purchase say attendance at off-campus beer fests is distressingly low.

Carmichael, writer of Stardust, is dead

Dec 27. Hoagy Carmichael, composer of "Stardust," "Georgia on My Mind" and other enduring tunes, has died in Rancho Mirage, California. He was 82. Carmichael associated with jazz musicians such as Bix Beiderbecke, Benny Goodman and Louis Armstrong, and may have considered himself a jazz pianist. But Carmichael's songs transcend any one genre; whether they go through a classical cuisinart or are mashed by muzak, they retain a unique purity. Other great hits are "Memphis in June," "I Get Along Without You Very Well" and "Lazy River." Frank Sinatra's first recorded song was his "Lamplighter's Serenade."

AIDS, a new plague, identified first time

Doctors this year identified a disturbing disease that has no known cure. AIDS (Acquired Immune Deficiency Syndrome) destroys the body's immune system. A victim suffers severe weight loss and weakness and eventually succumbs to common infections. Scientists suspect a virus is the cause, perhaps one that infects T-lymphocytes, an integral part of the immune system. At present, the disease mostly affects homosexual men with several partners, Haitians (whose health care system is neglected by their government) and intravenous drug users reusing hypodermic needles. The disease does not spread through casual contact (→ 6/5/83).

1982

JANUARY

Su	Mo	Tu	We	Th	Fr	Sa
					1	2
3	4	5	6	7	8	9
10	11	12	13	14	15	16
17	18	19	20	21	22	23
24	25	26	27	28	29	30
31						

1. Pasadena: Washington shuts out Iowa 28-0 in Rose Bowl.

4. Washington: Richard Allen resigns as White House natl. security adviser.

5. Little Rock, Ark.: Federal judge voids state law requiring balanced classroom treatment of evolution and creationism.

5. Calif.: Flood and mudslides kill at least 12 on coast.

6. U.S. Steel cleared to buy Marathon Oil Company.

7. France to sell arms to Nicaragua, train ten naval officers and ten pilots (→ 14).

10. U.S. asks Allies to embargo material for Soviet natural gas pipeline (→ 23).

10. Guatemala: Bodies of 50 abducted ten days ago are found (→ 3/7).

11. NATO condemns Soviets for support of Polish suppression, threatening economic sanctions (→ 22).

12. Peking protests sale of U.S. planes to Taiwan (→ 4/7/83).

14. Nicaragua declares Honduras and Costa Rica border regions military zones (→ 3/12).

16. Vatican and Britain decide to restore ties, broken 450 years ago (→ 5/29).

18. New Delhi: 6,000 labor activists arrested in two days; natl. strike called (→ 1/29/83).

21. Washington: Reagan reported seeking transfer of food stamp program to states (→ 4/23).

21. N.Y.: Jack Henry Abbot convicted of manslaughter in stabbing death of waiter (→ 4/15).

22. Reagan formally links progress in arms control to Soviet repression in Poland (→ 31).

23. France signs major natural gas contract with Soviet Union (→ 7/22).

24. U.S.: Draft of Air Force history reports U.S. secretly sprayed herbicides on Laos during Vietnam War (→ 5/12/83).

31. Israel agrees to four-nation peace force in Sinai (→ 2/5).

31. Gdansk: Over 200 arrested, 14 injured in clashes with police over price increases (→ 2/14).

78 killed when plane hits Potomac bridge

A salvage crew works to disentangle the mangled Boeing 737 on the Potomac.

Jan 13. A jetliner taking off from Washington's National Airport in a snowstorm crashed into a crowded bridge this afternoon and sank in the Potomac River within sight of the White House, killing 78 persons.

The twin-engine Air Florida jet hit a truck and at least four cars on the 14th Street Bridge at the height of rush hour. Officials said six persons died on the bridge; 18 survivors were treated at local hospitals but only five were from the airplane.

The jet, bound for Tampa, took off only minutes after the airport reopened as a daylong storm slackened. Joseph Stiley, a surviving passenger, said the plane began to stall almost as soon as it lifted off the runway and that he told a companion, "We're not going to make it."

Commuters watched in horror from the banks of the Potomac as passengers struggled and disappeared in the icy water. The crash caused a major traffic jam, so that emergency vehicles had to drive on the sidewalks outside the White House to reach the scene. A National Park Service helicopter hauled several victims from the river and dropped life preservers to others. One was saved when a fireman swam to rescue him.

Investigators from the National Transportation Safety Board said the cause of the accident was unknown, but there was no evidence that the mass dismissal of air traffic controllers by the government following a strike five months ago was a contributing factor.

Jan 24. The 49ers over the Bengals 26-21 in the Super Bowl. Said Reagan in a congratulatory phone call: "They really did win one for the Gipper."

Terrorists attacked; U.S. General saved

Jan 28. Brigadier General James L. Dozier was freed today when Italian police stormed the Padua apartment where he had heen held captive 42 days by the leftist Red Brigades. Five Brigade members were seized. When the squad broke in, one of them was pointing a pistol at the general's head. The highest ranking officer at the Verona NATO base, General Dozier was the first non-Italian kidnapped by the Red Brigades since their formation 11 years ago. His release involved Italy's biggest manhunt ever. Numbering 5,000 men, it surpassed the 1978 hunt for Prime Minister Aldo Moro, killed by the same group (→ 8/24).

General Dozier tells of ordeal.

Washington settles AT&T and IBM cases

Jan 8. Two major antitrust suits were settled in strikingly different fashion today as the Justice Department said it was dropping its effort to dismember the International Business Machines Corporation, and American Telephone and Telegraph said it would give up the 22 local Bell System companies that provide local telephone service. The AT&T agreement, if approved, would be the largest and most significant antitrust action since the breakup of the Standard Oil trust in 1911. It would mean that AT&T would give up companies representing 80 percent of its assets and would end the company's virtual monopoly of telephone service.

1982

FEBRUARY

Su	Mo	Tu	We	Th	Fr	Sa
	1	2	3	4	5	6
7	8	9	10	11	12	13
14	15	16	17	18	19	20
21	22	23	24	25	26	27
28						

1. Calif.: 170 arrested protesting nuclear arms research at Lawrence Livermore Labs (→ 4/6).

3. U.S.: Eastman Kodak introduces 15-picture film disk, three inches wide.

5. U.N. calls for sanctions against Israel for annexation of Golan Heights (→ 4/11).

6. Alabama: Civil rights workers begin march from Carrolton to Montgomery (→ 3/19/83).

8. Tehran: Ten opposition leaders killed by police (→ 9/16).

10. N.Y.: George Foster joins Mets for $10 mil. in five years, second highest in sports history.

10. Zacatecoluca: El Salvador army surrenders six soldiers to civilian court for murder of three American nuns (→ 3/18).

13. UAW trades wage and benefit concessions for job security in new contract with Ford (→ 3/1).

14. Poznan: 194 arrested in protest against martial law (→ 27).

15. North Atlantic: 84 die as oil rig sinks off Newfoundland.

16. L.I.: Sen. Harrison Williams given three years, fined $50,000 on Abscam bribery charges.

17. Salisbury: Zimbabwe Premier Mugabe dismisses coalition partner Nkomo (→ 3/5/83).

18. Mexico devalues peso 30% to fight economic slide (→ 8/20).

19. Ireland: Fianna Fail Party wins in general election (→ 3/9).

20. New York: Carnegie Hall begins $20 million renovation.

23. Denmark: 52% in referendum vote to withdraw from EEC (→ 1/1/86).

24. Reagan announces plan of investment incentives to develop Caribbean (→ 10/19/83).

25. European Court of Human Rights upholds parental right to ban corporal punishment in British schools.

27. Poland: Roman Catholic episcopate calls for end to martial law (→ 4/28).

DEATH

20. Rene Dubos, U.S. author, bacteriologist, "So Human an Animal" (*2/20/1901).

Gas prices tumble as global oil glut persists

Feb 16. A world oil glut has caused gasoline prices to drop two to three cents a gallon, and analysts say further reductions are almost certain. With crude oil prices on the spot market dropping rapidly, there are rumors that the Organization of Petroleum Exporting Countries will hold an emergency meeting to find ways to stem the decline.

Saudi Arabian light crude is now selling for $30.50 a barrel, down $1.50 in a week and $3.50 below the official price. Analysts attribute the decline to decreased consumption resulting from energy-saving programs and to fierce competition following the end of U.S. price controls on oil. Gasoline has been particularly hard hit because Americans are driving less and buying fuel-efficient cars. Gas sales fell 5.5 percent in 1980 and another 4.2 percent last year, with further decreases forecast. Major oil firms have stepped up their advertising and are starting to offer trading stamps and gifts to lift sales (→ 8/23).

One of the new American gas savers.

Williams convicted in deaths of blacks

Feb 27. Wayne B. Williams, 23, was found guilty tonight of killing two of Atlanta's 28 murdered young blacks and was sentenced to prison for two consecutive life terms. The verdict followed 12 hours of deliberation after a nine-week trial. The defendant maintained his innocence, his father spoke of an "error of justice," and the mother of one slain youngster said a "kangaroo court" had "put Wayne Williams in jail and a killer on the streets." The evidence that seemed to count most with the jury was that since Williams was stopped by the police last May 22, their city had seen no more mysterious deaths.

DeLorean car plant is in receivership

Feb 19. John Z. DeLorean's Belfast auto company went into receivership today, ending an effort by the flamboyant entrepreneur to start the first major car company in decades. The end came when the British government, which invested $150 million in the company, refused to grant more aid. DeLorean had predicted that the low-slung stainless steel sports car produced by his company would revolutionize the industry. But sales of the $25,000 auto were slow, with half the 9,000 cars shipped to the United States unsold. DeLorean stunned the industry in 1973 when he quit his $650,000 job at General Motors without explanation (→ 10/19).

John DeLorean, in financial trouble.

At least 4 bombs rock Wall Street

Feb 28. No one was injured, but a series of explosions certainly scared residents near New York's financial district. At least four bombs shook buildings on and around Wall Street last night, including the New York Stock Exchange and Chase Manhattan Bank. Police said the blasts appeared to be the work of a Puerto Rican terrorist group, Fuerzaz Armadas de Liberacion Nacionale; officials found a letter which praised the bombings as a victory for Puerto Ricans.

France socializing much of its economy

Feb 14. The Socialist President of France, Francois Mitterrand, is carrying through on campaign promises to nationalize banks and industry. Over the weekend, several banks, including the Banque Rothschild, were taken over. So were major electrical, aluminum and synthetics companies. A business group calls the takeovers "costly, useless and dangerous."

While other European countries try to break out of recession by lowering inflation, France is doing just the opposite. The government is financing the $8 billion cost of the takeovers by issuing 15-year bonds (→ 4/25/84).

Death takes Monk, celebrated pianist

Feb 17. Thelonius Monk, one of the most original and inimitable of jazz pianists and composers, died yesterday at the age of 64 from a stroke suffered on February 5.

"He hasn't invented a new scheme of things," jazz critic Paul Bacon wrote in 1948, "but looked with an unjaundiced eye at music and seen a little something else." Defining this "something else," Monk once said, "Jazz is my adventure. I'm after new chords, new ways of syncopating, new figurations, new runs. How to use notes differently. That's it. Just using notes differently." Simple as it may sound, typical Monk tunes like "Round Midnight" seemed to resist improvisation by others, making Monk the best interpreter of his own lines.

Monk at Avery Fischer Hall.

1982

MARCH

Su	Mo	Tu	We	Th	Fr	Sa
	1	2	3	4	5	6
7	8	9	10	11	12	13
14	15	16	17	18	19	20
21	22	23	24	25	26	27
28	29	30	31			

1. U.S.: Teamsters ratify new accord with wage freeze.

6. Cairo: 5 of 24 Moslem fundamentalists accused in Sadat killing sentenced to death (→ 4/15).

7. Guatemala: Gen. Anibal Guevara chosen pres.; electoral fraud charged (→ 23).

8. U.S. accuses Soviets of killing 3,000 Afghans with poison gas (→ 5/3/83).

9. Ireland: Charles J. Haughey chosen premier (→ 7/20).

10. U.S. bans Libyan oil imports, charging continued support of terrorism (→ 2/18/83).

12. Washington: Nicaraguan, at press conference, denies State Dept. claim he was trained in Cuba (→ 15).

15. Nicaragua: Sandinistas call state of emergency as rioting grows (→ 20).

17. EPA reverses stand to permit burial of drums of toxic liquids in landfills (→ 12/16).

18. El Salvador: Four Dutch newsmen slain where they had gone to film rebel group (→ 29).

20. U.S. scientists return from Antarctic with first land mammal fossils found there.

20. Nicaragua asks U.N. to denounce U.S. "invasion" of its territory (→ 25).

20. OPEC moves to bolster oil prices, cutting production by 700,000 barrels per day (→ 8/23).

22. U.S.: Space shuttle Columbia launched on third flight (→ 30).

23. Guatemala: Gen. Rios Montt seizes power in coup, charging electoral fraud (→ 8/8/83).

24. Bangladesh: Army ousts Pres. Abdus Sattar, imposes martial law.

28. Iran retakes 1,250 sq. miles from Iraq in Khuzistan region (→ 4/8).

30. N.M.: Columbia lands at White Sands Missile Range, avoding rain at Edwards Air Force Base (→ 6/24).

DEATH

6. Ayn Rand, American author, "The Fountainhead" (*2/2/1905).

Sandinista regime suspends all civil rights

Sandinista chief Daniel Ortega.

March 25. The ruling Sandinista junta has suspended all individual rights in Nicaragua for 30 days, claiming that the nation was faced with aggression by the United States. Daniel Ortega Saavedra, the head of the junta, said the United States was using anti-Sandinista exiles in Honduras and Miami for "plans of aggression against our country." Government officials said that under the new decree, freedom of expression, the right to carry out political and union activities and the right of habeas corpus would all be curtailed.

On his arrival in Managua, the new American Ambassador, Anthony C.E. Quaiton, denied that the United States was plotting the overthrow of the Sandinista regime.

The Marxist government of Nicaragua declared a state of emergency ten days ago after heavy rioting. Since then, the government has reported that guerrillas dynamited two key bridges in the northern and northwestern sections of the country. Five days ago, the Sandinista leaders petitioned the United Nations to denounce the alleged invasion by the United States of its territory. These developments were used as justification for today's suspension of rights (→ 12/1).

Voters defy rebels, put Duarte in office

March 29. Voters rebuffed both the extreme right and the extreme left in El Salvador's elections today, giving Jose Napoleon Duarte's moderate Christian Democrats a plurality of the ballots cast.

Officials estimated that over 900,000 of the 1.3 million eligible voters turned out for the general election, which, according to a United States Embassy official, created "euphoria" among American diplomats, who have been hoping for broad popular support for Duarte's policies.

But the Christian Democrats, who captured 42% of the popular vote, still lack the majority needed to secure control of the new constituent assembly, which will have the power to rewrite the Salvadoran constitution. Major Roberto D'Aubuisson's far-right National Republican Alliance captured a respectable 29% of the vote.

The success of the election marks a major defeat for leftist guerrillas, who have escalated their violence in an attempt to frighten Salvadorans from the polls. Four Dutch newsmen were killed in a recent clash between the rebels and army regulars (→ 4/1).

Von Bulow tried to kill wife, jury finds

Von Bulow (rear), found guilty.

March 16. Claus von Bulow, Newport, Rhode Island, magnate, has been found guilty in the attempted murder of his wife, Martha "Sunny" von Bulow. She lies at a local hospital in an irreversible coma induced by a double injection of insulin. Von Bulow contended his wife, suicidal, gave herself the overdose. However, a maid found a black bag containing hypodermic needles in von Bulow's closet. She also described an earlier occasion when Mrs. von Bulow went into shock and her husband simply watched. Von Bulow stood to inherit $14 million tax-free (→ 5/7).

John Belushi dies of a drug overdose

Belushi and Blues Brother Aykroyd.

March 5. John Belushi, the zany comic who rose to stardom on the "Saturday Night Live" television show, was found dead in a rented bungalow at the Chateau Marmont, a Hollywood hostelry. The cause of death was not immediately determined, but drugs are suspected.

Belushi was born in 1949 and grew up in the Chicago suburb of Wheaton. He was a member of the famous "Second City" improvisational troupe in Chicago, and was on the editorial staff of the satirical magazine National Lampoon. His performance in the comedy review "Lemmings" attracted the attention of producer Lorne Michaels, who added him to the cast of "Saturday Night Live." His comic repertory included a manic Samurai warrior and, with Dan Aykroyd, "The Blues Brothers" (→ 3/18/83).

Nancy Drew writer dies; Nancy lives on

March 27. The writer of the popular Nancy Drew, Hardy Boys and Tom Swift Jr. books died this evening in New Jersey. Harriet Adams, who wrote under pseudonyms, was 89. From 1930 to March 27, 1982, (she was working on ghost stories recently), Mrs. Adams wrote or edited countless books for young people. She inherited the business from her father, who may have modeled Nancy on her. Mrs. Adams tried to keep the works timeless and insisted on moral stories with no epithets stronger than "gosh." She suffered a fatal heart attack while watching "The Wizard of Oz" for the first time.

1982

APRIL

Su	Mo	Tu	We	Th	Fr	Sa
				1	2	3
4	5	6	7	8	9	10
11	12	13	14	15	16	17
18	19	20	21	22	23	24
25	26	27	28	29	30	

1. San Salvador: Duarte says he will stay in office despite rightist attempts to oust him (→ 10/22).

2. Argentine troops overrun 84 British marines, seizing Falkland Islands (→ 5).

5. London: For. Sec. Lord Carrington resigns over "humiliating affront" in Falklands (→ 10).

6. Washington: Haig says U.S. will not bar first use of nuclear arms (→ 5/9).

8. Syria closes border with Iraq, shuts pipeline carrying Iraqi oil to Mediterranean (→ 5/24).

10. EEC approves total ban on imports from Argentina (→ 12).

11. Jerusalem: Israeli kills two Arabs at Dome of the Rock mosque (→ 13).

12. British impose blockade around Falklands (→ 27).

13. Saudi Arabia: King Khalid asks Moslems to strike to protest Dome of the Rock attack (→ 25).

15. New York: Author Jack Henry Abbot gets 15 years for killing of waiter.

15. Cairo: Five Sadat assassins executed.

17. Ottawa: Queen Elizabeth II signs Constitution Act giving Canada power over constitution (→ 2/29/84).

19. U.S. bans travel to Cuba beginning May 15 (→ 10/22).

19. Boston: Alberto Salazar and Charlotte Teske win Boston Marathon.

20. Biologists find life flourishing on volcanic energy 8,600 feet under sea off California coast.

23. U.S.: Consumer prices fall .3%, declining for first time in almost 17 years (→ 7/19).

26. Washington: Hinckley trial begins for assassination attempt on Ronald Reagan (→ 6/21).

27. London: Thatcher announces Britain will invade Falklands this week (→ 30).

28. Warsaw: Poland orders 800 freed in easing of martial law (→ 5/4).

DEATH

20. Archibald MacLeish, U.S. poet, playwright (*5/7/1892).

Argentina invades Falkland Islands

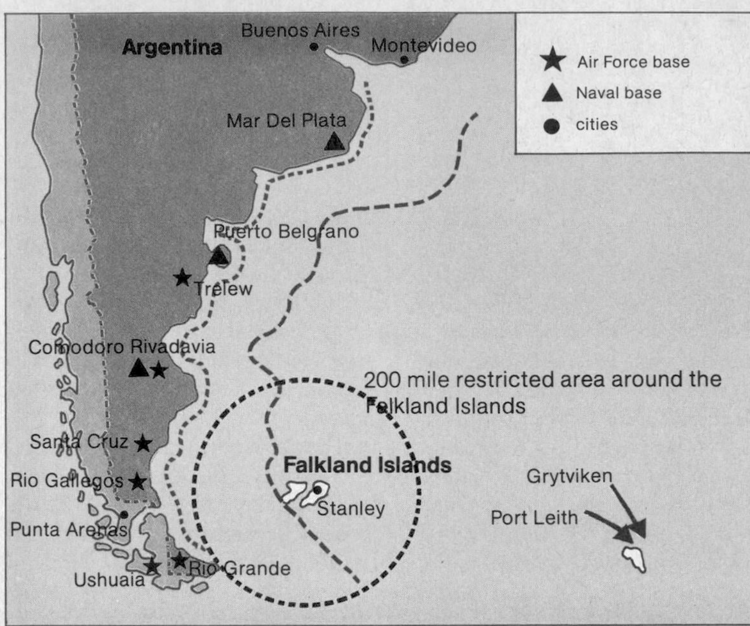

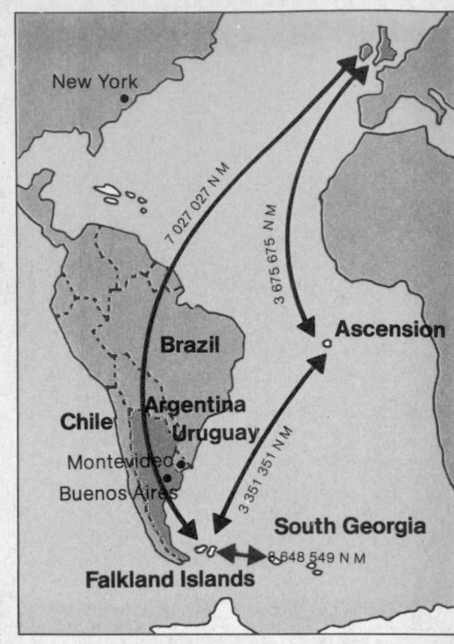

The Falklands lie 8,000 miles from the British coast, a long way to travel to reconquer sheep and lost pride.

April 30. The United States sided openly with Britain today and condemned Argentina for its invasion of the Falkland Islands. President Reagan offered Britain's Prime Minister Margaret Thatcher "materiel support" to recapture the South Atlantic islands. Secretary of State Haig warned that the dispute was entering "a new and dangerous phase, in which large-scale military action is likely." Up until recently, Haig was trying to mediate the crisis between London and Buenos Aires.

Several thousand Argentine troops stormed the islands on the 2nd and easily overran the 84 British marines who were stationed there. The Thatcher government called the invasion a "wanton act" and announced almost immediately that royal navy ships had been dispatched to the Falklands.

The crisis created enormous political problems for Prime Minister Thatcher. Her Foreign Secretary, Lord Carrington, resigned on the 5th after what he called "the humiliating affront" of the Argentine invasion. Carrington was replaced by Francis Pym. Politicians and newspaper editors whipped up a war frenzy and called on Thatcher to get even with Lieutenant General Leopoldo Galtieri, the head of the Argentine military junta. Opposition leader Michael Foot, however, called for a diplomatic solution. Thatcher rejected his suggestions and hinted on Monday the navy was about to assault the Falklands.

Britain has governed the Falklands for 149 years, and most of the islands' residents are Britons. Many of them are fishermen and sheep farmers. They call themselves kelpers, after the long seaweed that grows in coastal waters (→ 5/1).

Israel removes last soldiers from the Sinai

The Israeli flag leaves the Sinai.

April 25. The last Israeli soldiers have left the Sinai, and the disputed area has been returned to Egypt. But it was not easy. Israeli troops had to battle with entrenched Jewish settlers, and one community, in Yamit, even threatened collective suicide. The town was finally evacuated and bulldozed. Israel says the destruction of Yamit and other settlements will discourage the return of Israeli citizens. The government is pursuing a different policy in the occupied West Bank, where it apparently encourages settlements. Israel seized the disputed area in the Six Day War. The Camp David agreement called for its return to Egypt (→ 6/3).

Royal Thai birthday

April 5. Some 100,000 people cheered King Bhumibol Adulyadej and Queen Sirikit today as a grand flotilla of golden vessels sailed down the Chao Praya River (River of Kings) in a celebration marking the bicentennial of the Thai monarchy.

Pomp and pageantry, Asian-style.

1982

MAY

Su	Mo	Tu	We	Th	Fr	Sa
						1
2	3	4	5	6	7	8
9	10	11	12	13	14	15
16	17	18	19	20	21	22
23	24	25	26	27	28	29
30	31					

1. Knoxville: World's Fair opens in Tennessee.

1. Falklands: Major air and sea battle erupts as British launch counterattack (→ 3).

1. Gato del Sol wins Kentucky Derby, E. Delahoussaye in the saddle.

3. Falklands: British sub sinks Argentina's only cruiser with 1,042 aboard (→ 4).

4. Falklands: Argentines disable British destroyer Sheffield, killing 30 (→ 11).

4. Poland: Curfews and other restrictions reintroduced after May Day clashes (→ 7/21).

7. Newport: Claus von Bulow given 30 years for attempted murder of wife (→ 6/10/85).

9. Reagan offers two-step disarmament plan to reduce arsenals by one-third initially (→ 29).

11. Falklands: Argentine oil tanker sunk by British (→ 21).

12. Portugal: Pope escapes man with knife at Shrine of Fatima (→ 29).

13. Braniff International Corp. files for bankruptcy.

15. Baltimore: Jack Kaenel, at 16, wins Preakness, youngest to win Triple Crown race.

16. New York Islanders win Stanley Cup.

21. Falklands: Britain seizes beachhead, claims 16 planes, loses five ships (→ 23).

22. Alabama: George Wallace announces he will seek fourth term as governor (→ 1/17/83).

23. Falklands: Six Argentine jets downed in raid (→ 28).

25. N.J.: State high court upholds mandatory sex education (→ 1/22/83).

28. Falklands: Britain takes Darwin and Goose Green in push toward capital (→ 31).

29. U.S.: Pentagon draws up first strategy for fighting protracted nuclear war (→ 6/12).

30. Spain enters NATO as first country to join since 1955.

DEATH

5. Peter Weiss, German dramatist (*11/8/1916).

Major sea battle fought for Falklands

Argentine troops on a beachhead.

May 31. Argentine forces in the Falkland Islands are making their final stand on the ground today after a month-long battle at sea. British forces are advancing through barren hills 15 miles west of Stanley and hope to capture the capital shortly.

Fighting began in earnest at the beginning of the month after General Leopoldo Galtieri, the President of Argentina, charged that Britain had "broken the peace of America and put in danger the security of the world." The Argentine military command said it retaliated against British air strikes on the Falklands by damaging two British frigates and shooting down two Harrier jump-jets. Within 24 hours, however, it was Britain that struck the devastating blow.

On the night of the 3rd, Argentina conceded that its only cruiser, the General Belgrano, had been sunk by a torpedo fired from a British submarine. After a search of the frigid South Atlantic waters, Argentina said there were 680 survivors; 362 men were missing. The government in Buenos Aires called the attack on the 13,645-ton vessel "a treacherous act of armed aggression," and the military command angrily claimed that the Belgrano had been sunk 36 miles outside of a blockade zone imposed by Britain.

Prime Minister Thatcher told Parliament that the Belgrano was indeed outside the blockade area, but she insisted that it had represented "a very obvious threat" to British forces. Her explanation did not satisfy Labor critics who recalled that British commanders had scoffed recently at the combat capabilities of the cruiser. One admiral had said that the Belgrano "was held together by baling wire."

Argentina was quick to retaliate. On the 5th, a jet fighter fired a French-built Exocet missile at the British destroyer Sheffield. About 30 British sailors were killed, and the ship was abandoned.

During the following week, hopes were raised that the war might be ended through negotiation. Those hopes were dashed as British forces sank an Argentine oil tanker in the channel between East and West Falkland. Two Argentine A-4 Skyhawk attack planes were also shot down by Sea Wolf missiles fired from a warship. Britain said the planes were escorting transport aircraft trying to run the blockade.

British ship, struck by an Exocet.

A British jet prepares to join the fray.

On the 20th, Prime Minister Thatcher, her confidence raised by the royal navy's successes, rejected a United Nations appeal for negotiations. Military commanders in Buenos Aires admitted they were bracing for a direct assault on the Falklands. It happened within days, as the British established a beachhead with 5,000 troops at San Carlos Bay. To the east and south, British bombers attacked airstrips controlled by the Argentines at Stanley and Goose Green (→ 6/12).

A pope visits Britain first time since 1531

May 29. The Bishop of Rome and the Archbishop of Canterbury embraced and prayed together today, in the first visit of a Catholic pontiff to English soil in over 450 years. Pope John Paul II and the Most. Rev. Robert Runcie presided at a service in Canterbury Cathedral, the gothic church which has been the spiritual center of Anglicanism since its split with Rome in the sixteenth century. They jointly prayed at the the tomb of St. Thomas Becket, an Archbishop of Canterbury martyred in 1170, and announced the formation of a commission to study steps that could lead to reunification of the two churches (→ 8/14/83).

Pope and Archbishop of Canterbury.

Andropov quits KGB for party position

May 26. Taking a step down from the Soviet intelligence agency, Yuri Andropov may have taken a step closer to succeeding aging Soviet leader Leonid Brezhnev. The man who ran the KGB for 15 years was appointed to a high-ranking position in the Communist Party Secretariat earlier this week, and to allow him time for his new duties, he was relieved at the KGB. Vitali Fedorchuk, leader of the Ukrainian branch of the KGB, will replace Andropov. Some analysts believe the change may give Andropov the experience to lead the party in the future (→ 11/10).

▷

Iran recaptures city, takes 30,000 Iraqis

Iranian artillery lights up the sky.

May 24. Iran is claiming one of its biggest victories in the bloody, two-and-a-half-year war with Iraq. Tehran radio reported that Iranian forces had recaptured the major cargo port city of Khurramshahr. If the report is confirmed, it will mean that Iran has recaptured almost all of the territory it had lost to Iraq.

The Iranian report sent shockwaves through the Arab world, which has divided its loyalties in the war. Saudi Arabia and other major oil producers, fearful that the fundamentalist revolution in Iran might spread past its borders, have been bankrolling Iraq. Syria supports Iran and reportedly supplied Soviet weapons that were key to the victory in Khurramshahr (→ 7/14).

Romy Schneider can shed no more tears

May 29. Internationally known actress Romy Schneider was found dead in her apartment today. She was 43. Miss Schneider had experienced a recent tragedy: Her son had fallen out of a window and been impaled on a garden fence. Friends say she died of grief.

Austrian-born Miss Schneider made few American pictures, the comedies "What's New Pussycat?" and "Good Neighbor Sam" among their number. She was most popular in Europe, where she made romantic films for French, Italian and German production companies. One of the best was "Cesar and Rosalie" (1972) about a menage a trois with brunette Miss Schneider at the center.

Schneider, born to acting parents.

May 30. Gordon Johncock joins ranks of two-time winners at Indy 500.

Sun Myung Moon is guilty under tax law

Moon with wife, Hak Ja Han.

May 18. The Rev. Sun Myung Moon, founder and leader of the Unification Church, was convicted in New York yesterday of conspiracy to defraud the federal government and filing false income tax returns. He could face up to five years in prison for conspiracy and three years on each of the three tax counts. One of his top aides, Takeru Kamiyama, was also convicted of conspiracy, perjury and obstructing the investigation that led to the more than eight-week-long trial.

The 62-year-old Korean evangelist, who claims that Jesus appeared before him when he was 16 and told him to "complete my still uncompleted mission," founded his church —many call it a cult—in Korea in 1954. He became a permanent resident of the United States in 1973 and lives in a 25-room mansion in Irvington, New York, with his second wife and 12 children. Immigration documents were presented contending that Moon and his wife, Hak Ja Han, had obtained permanent-resident status fraudulently, stating that she worked for a Korean foundation here. They could face immigration hearings.

Moon is said to have three million followers around the world, including 40,000 in the U.S. Here, they are generally young men and women from middle-class homes, who preach on the streets and sell flowers to raise money. Moon preaches (in Korean with a translator) anticommunism and insists his followers refrain from extramarital sex, smoking, drugs and liquor. He exercises rather total control over church members' lives, even picking out their marital partners (→ 7/1).

1982

JUNE

Su	Mo	Tu	We	Th	Fr	Sa
		1	2	3	4	5
6	7	8	9	10	11	12
13	14	15	16	17	18	19
20	21	22	23	24	25	26
27	28	29	30			

1. Tokyo: Chinese Premier Zhao Ziyang arrives to mark tenth year of diplomatic ties.

3. London: Israeli Ambassador Shlomo Argov badly wounded by Palestinian assassins (→ 4).

4. Lebanon: Israeli jets bomb guerrilla targets in reprisal for shooting of ambassador (→ 6).

6. Lebanon: Big Israeli force invades in south by land, sea and air (→ 10).

10. Lebanon: Outskirts of Beirut bombed; Israelis warn Syrians to evacuate city (→ 11).

11. Israel, Syria announce cease-fire in Lebanon (→ 14).

12. Falklands: British and Argentines in fierce fighting for control of Stanley (→ 14).

13. Saudi Arabia: King Khalid, ruler since 1975, dies at 69; Crown Prince Fahd to succeed (→ 5/28/84).

14. Falklands: Argentine forces surrender to British (→ 17).

14. Lebanon: Israeli tanks cut off Moslem West Beirut, trapping PLO leaders (→ 21).

15. New York: Soviets at U.N. pledge no first use of nuclear weapons (→ 8/5).

18. U.S. Senate extends Voting Rights Act of 1965 for 25 years.

20. Pebble Beach, Calif.: Tom Watson wins U.S. Open.

21. Reagan and Begin meet, agree all foreign troops should pull out of Lebanon (→ 26).

24. Paris: Frenchman Col. Jean Loup Chretien launched into space on Soviet rocket (→ 27).

26. U.S. vetoes U.N. resolution for limited withdrawal from Beirut by PLO and Israel (→ 29).

27. Florida: Columbia blasts off carrying first military and commercial payloads (→ 7/4).

30. ERA defeated, failing to gain ratification in states (→ 7/9/83).

DEATHS

8. Satchel Paige, first black pitcher in American League (*7/7/1906).

10. Rainer Werner Fassbinder, German film director (*5/31/1946).

Major Israeli force invades Lebanon

June 29. Israeli forces have driven deep into southern Lebanon, battling Palestinian and Syrian forces on the coastal road south of Beirut and trapping the leadership of the Palestine Liberation Organization in the western half of the capital. East of Beirut, Israeli jets have knocked out Syrian surface-to-air missile batteries in the Bekaa Valley and engaged in vicious dogfights with Syrian pilots flying Soviet-built MIG fighters. Until today, Israel's stated goal was to punish the Palestinian guerrillas and annihilate the leaders of the PLO. Faced with intense international pressure and the threat of Soviet involvement in the fighting, Israel's Prime Minister Begin has backed down.

In an address to the Israeli Parliament, Begin offered to let Palestinian guerrillas leave Beirut with their weapons. Just two days ago, the Israeli Cabinet was demanding that "all of the 15 terrorist organizations . . . hand over their weapons to the Lebanese army."

There seem to be several reasons for the shift in Begin's position. First, American support for the successful Israeli invasion of Lebanon has deteriorated. Reagan administration officials say the President has sent Begin a "firm" message to withdraw. Secretary of State Haig was unusually blunt when he rejected an invitation from Begin to visit Jerusalem. "I thought about it," Haig said, "but the discussions we have had with the Israelis today have not evidenced sufficient flexibility to make a visit worthwhile at this time." Reagan has also had "frank" conversations with Soviet leader Leonid Brezhnev, and he warned Begin that the Russians are eager and willing to help the beleaguered Syrians.

Begin is also facing increasing anti-war sentiment at home. Opposition leader Shimon Peres warned that Israeli actions are being watched on television around the world. And some members of the Knesset say that Begin has already gone too far. "We don't want to humiliate the terrorists," Liberal Party member Dror Zeigerman said. "Of course they don't deserve any respect. They're murderers, but they're human beings. So we don't want to humiliate them."

The Israeli invasion began on the 6th, as 20,000 soldiers and hundreds of tanks crossed the border into southern Lebanon. By the 9th, some of the forces had driven within sight of Beirut. Others were bogged down in fierce fighting with Palestinians and Syrians south of the capital. Hand-to-hand battles raged in Sidon, Tyre, Khalde and Damur. East of Beirut, the Israelis fought with Syrians for control of the highway to Damascus. In the Bekaa Valley, Israel said it knocked out most if not all of the missile batteries brought into the area by the Syrians. The chief Israeli military spokesman said 61 MIG's and five helicopters were shot down over the Bekaa. The Syrians said they shot down 19 Israeli planes (→ 7/3).

Israeli mobile divisions in Lebanon.

Israeli artillery lays siege to Beirut.

Palestinians led off by Israeli troops.

Assassin is declared insane, not guilty

June 21. John W. Hinckley Jr. has been found not guilty by reason of insanity in the shooting last year of President Reagan and three others. The 27-year-old defendant is likely to be transferred to St. Elizabeth's Hospital, a mental institution in Washington. Spectators appeared stunned as the jury, which had deliberated for 24 hours, announced the verdict. Hinckley gave a low sigh and his mother tearfully embraced her husband (→ 8/9).

NFL warns cocaine a threat to game

June 26. Cocaine threatens the integrity of the professional game, according to officials of the National Football League. Only 17 players have been found "chemically dependent" on cocaine, the league's security assistant said, but he added that hundreds of the 1,500 players are using it, some of them regularly.

"Those figures do not come as a shock to me," said Charles Jackson, assistant head of NFL security. "Cocaine certainly poses a threat to the integrity of the game."

Cocaine is "like a time bomb," said Dr. Walter Riker, the league's medical consultant for drug abuse. Recent reports of the involvement of professional baseball, football and basketball players in drug abuse have convinced some officials that a crisis exists.

800,000 anti-nuke marchers in New York

"Turn your swords into plowshares."

June 12. All sizes, all colors, all ages; it seems the growing concern about the arms race crosses all barriers. More than 800,000 men, women and children filled the streets of Manhattan and the lawns of Central Park today for a mass demonstration against nuclear proliferation. Several keynote speakers addressed the crowd, including Coretta Scott King, who declared, "We have come here in numbers so large that the message must get through to the White House and Capitol Hill." Organizers said this was the largest rally against nuclear arms ever held in America (→ 15).

Sophia Loren in jail 17 days for tax fraud

June 5. Surrounded by a phalanx of motorcycles, Sophia Loren was delivered to Rome's Leonardo da Vinci Airport today. She was leaving Italy after serving 17 days of a 30-day prison sentence in the city of Caserta. She committed fiscal fraud two years ago and knew she would face imprisonment, but she said, "The idea of never returning to my home country drove me crazy." Miss Loren now spends most of her time on an estate in France. The famous actress' incarceration was hell, if you call boxes of chocolates and steaming plates of pasta for lunch hell.

Loren, unlikely candidate for jail.

Parliament hears U.S. President first time

Reagan reviews the royal guard.

June 8. President Reagan went horseback riding with Queen Elizabeth today and he had lunch with Prime Minister Thatcher at 10 Downing Street. But it was his speech to Parliament, the first ever by an American president, that captured the attention of the British.

Reagan made a strong attack against the Soviet Union and communism as he urged the free world to "leave Marxism-Leninism on the ash heap of history." The president was applauded loudly when he supported the British war in the Falklands. He conceded that critics deride the fight "for lumps of rock and earth so far away." But Reagan said, "Those young men aren't fighting for mere real estate. They fight for a cause, for the belief that armed aggression must not be allowed to succeed and that people must participate in the decisions of the government under the rule of law." Reagan's speech was boycotted by nearly 200 members of the opposition Labor Party (→ 6/9/83).

Argentines surrender; 14,000 are captured

June 17. General Leopoldo Galtieri, President of Argentina and member of the ruling military junta, resigned today, three days after the surrender to the British in the Falklands. "I am going," Galtieri said, "because the army did not give me the political support to continue."

Argentine forces were defeated at Goose Green at the end of May, and they surrendered at Port Stanley on Monday. The death toll from six weeks of fighting was 255 Britons and 712 Argentines; 14,000 Argentines were taken prisoner. Negotiations are continuing for their return. The British commander in the Falklands said many of them are ill and could die from malnutrition and hypothermia.

Leaders in Buenos Aires have been meeting around the clock to devise a response to British conditions for an end to the hostilities. The British say they will lift their blockade and economic sanctions if Argentina pledges not to attack the islands (→ 2/28/83).

British search Argentine prisoners.

Suburban chronicler John Cheever dies

June 18. John Cheever is dead at 70. Expelled from a Massachusetts prep school at 17, he became a Pulitzer Prize winner in fiction, writing over 100 short stories, one novella and four novels—"Wapshot Chronicle," "Wapshot Scandal," "Bullet Part" and "Falconer." He may be best known for "The Swimmer," made into a movie starring Burt Lancaster. Cheever focused on man's moral search in a decaying world, usually set in New England suburbia. His characters struggle with loneliness, eroding traditions and the despair of falling short in their loves and ideals. "A page of good prose," he once said, "is where one hears the rain . . . and has the power to make us laugh."

"E.T.," the extra-terrestrial you can bring home to Mom, has arrived at a theater near you.

Princess of Wales has her first child

Admiring the little royal tyke.

June 22. A 41-gun salute rocked London today. The Princess of Wales has given birth to a son at St. Mary's Hospital in Paddington. Prince Charles, looking pleased, said no name was picked for the baby yet. Lady Diana intends to return home as soon as possible, perhaps within 24 hours.

Queen Elizabeth II visited the baby a few hours after the birth. It is her third grandchild, having two by her daughter, Princess Anne. Lord Spencer, Diana's father, called the infant "the most beautiful baby I have ever seen." Reporters have gotten not much more than a peek, as the babe is well-swaddled. The new Prince slept frequently, feigning nonchalance about his status as heir apparent to the royal throne of England.

Haig quits in policy dispute; Shultz named

June 25. Disgruntled by recent foreign policy decisions, American Secretary of State Alexander Haig resigned today. Haig, who virtually ran the Oval Office as chief of staff in the final days of the Nixon administration, was considered by many to be an experienced moderate in the conservative Reagan Cabinet. He will be replaced by another one-time Nixon aide, George Shultz.

Haig reportedly told aides on the President's last European trip that he was "tired of four or five people running foreign policy" and that he intended to "straighten that out" or quit. President Reagan and Haig differed on several issues, the latest of which was the secretary's disagreement with the president's decision to penalize American companies which were helping to build the gas pipeline from Siberia to Western Europe. Haig also added a tone of conciliation to the tough Reagan rhetoric toward the Soviet Union.

George Shultz served as Secretary of the Treasury under Nixon. He has been described by economist Alan Greenspan as "an exceptionally good organizer and manager of ideas."

June 11. Larry Holmes fends off Jerry Cooney in a successful bid to retain his heavyweight title.

June 6. Swedish clay-court artist Mats Wilander is French Open victor at the tender age of 17.

1982

JULY

Su	Mo	Tu	We	Th	Fr	Sa
				1	2	3
4	5	6	7	8	9	10
11	12	13	14	15	16	17
18	19	20	21	22	23	24
25	26	27	28	29	30	31

1. New York: Rev. Moon marries 4,000 in mass ceremony in Madison Sq. Garden (→ 16).

1. Buenos Aires: Maj. Gen. Reynaldo Bignone sworn in as new president (→ 11/5).

3. Johannesburg: Eight black gold miners slain in labor riots (→ 11/20).

3. Tel Aviv: 100,000 Israelis march for peace (→ 6).

4. Calif.: Columbia lands safely on fourth test flight (→ 11/11).

4. Wimbledon: Connors over McEnroe 3-6, 6-3, 6-7, 7-6, 6-4; Navratilova over Evert Lloyd 6-1, 3-6, 6-2.

4. Santo Domingo: President Antonio Guzman dies of gunshot wound in head.

4. Mexico: Miguel de la Madrid elected president (→ 8/20).

6. Reagan agrees to contribute U.S. troops to peacekeeping unit in Beirut (→ 11).

11. Madrid: Italy wins its first World Cup in 44 years, beating West Germany in final.

11. West Beirut: Israelis fight artillery duel with PLO (→ 25).

12. Tucson: Miguel Vazquez performs first quadruple flip in trapeze act.

14. Iran renews drive against Iraq in border region (→ 11/7).

18. Scotland: Tom Watson wins his fourth British Open.

19. Census Bureau says poverty rate at 14%, highest in 15 years, up 7.4% since 1980 (→ 1/10/84).

20. London: I.R.A. blasts kill eight soldiers, injure 51 people in Hyde, Regent Parks (→ 12/7).

21. Warsaw: 1,227 released from detention (→ 8/13).

22. France to fulfill Soviet pipeline contracts despite ban by Reagan (→ 24).

24. Bernard Hinault wins his fourth Tour de France.

24. Italy defies U.S. on parts for Soviet pipeline (→ 8/12).

25. Beirut: Arafat signs declaration accepting Israel's right to exist (→ 27).

28. San Francisco becomes first U.S. city to ban handguns.

Israeli jets devastate civilian West Beirut

July 27. Israeli jets zoomed over the heart of West Beirut today, unloading a barrage of bombs which killed 120 and injured 232. The two Israeli raids were the first such attacks on civilian areas of Beirut since they invaded Lebanon seven weeks ago. Israeli officials said the assaults were ordered to try to eradicate some 6,000 members of the Palestine Liberation Organization located in that sector of the city.

The situation in Lebanon has taken new twists this month. At month's outset, over 100,000 young Israelis demonstrated against the war in Lebanon. The unrest is the first sign of a substantial peace movement. Two weeks later, Tel Aviv conceded it had employed cluster bombs in the invasion, but said this did not violate a U.S.-Israeli treaty restricting the powerful weapons. U.S. Senator Henry Jackson said the use of cluster bombs did violate agreements and asserted Israel was straining relations between the two allies.

Meanwhile, talks with the various factions in Lebanon, including the Palestine Liberation Organization, have stalled and Israel is being backed into what some feel is a no-win situation (→ 8/1).

Jetliner crashes at New Orleans, killing 149

Tires, sole remains in New Orleans.

July 8. A Pan American World Airways jetliner crashed in a residential neighborhood near New Orleans today, killing all 145 on board and at least four people on the ground. The Boeing 747 jet had just taken off from New Orleans International Airport at 4:11 p.m., when it plunged to earth in Kenner, a nearby suburb, devastating an area of several square blocks and setting a number of houses on fire. Every available piece of rescue and fire equipment was rushed to the scene, which was cordoned off by police. There were thunderstorms in the area, and witnesses say they saw lightning strike the jetliner just before it crashed.

Intruder drops in on Queen's quarters

July 12. Early last Friday, Queen Elizabeth of England awoke to find a man sitting at the end of her bed, clutching a broken glass, blood dripping from his hand. With royal calm, she talked to him for ten minutes. Then, as he asked for a cigarette, she was able to summon a footman and turn him over to police. He had shinnied up a drainpipe, pulled aside wire mesh across a window and simply jumped in. Other such palace security lapses have occurred. Just before the wedding of the Prince of Wales, a group of West German tourists camped in the palace garden, believing themselves to be in a public park.

Helicopter falls on movie set; 3 dead

July 23. Vic Morrow, 51, and two Vietnamese children, six and seven, held in the actor's arms were killed when a helicopter crashed during the shooting of "The Twilight Zone," a four-segment anthology movie. This segment was directed by John Landis for Warner Bros., the other three by Joe Dante, George Miller and Steven Spielberg. During the filming outside Los Angeles, the tail motor of the chopper carrying a camera crew was hit by debris from explosives detonated in a Vietnam War scene. Morrow and the children were struck and killed by the main rotor of the helicopter as it pitched into a river on the set.

4,150 married by Moon in the Garden

Marriage by mass production.

July 16. Some 4,150 followers of the Rev. Sun Myung Moon, most selected for each other by him, were married yesterday in a mass ceremony at Madison Square Garden. The white-carpeted arena was a sea of bridegrooms in blue suits and brides in white lace and satin gowns.

Moon and his wife, Hak Ja Han, called "true parents of mankind" by his Unification Church, doused the 2,075 couples with water as they passed in rows to the strains of Mendelssohn's "Wedding March." Many met only weeks ago at mass ceremonies called "matchings." All have been church members for at least three years. They are now "purified" for 40 days before the union can be consummated. Moon stresses "the family"; he and his wife had their 13th child last month.

July 4. Connors, 30, with the grit, guts and youthful abandon of a teenager, has beaten McEnroe in Wimbledon's longest final.

1982

AUGUST

Su	Mo	Tu	We	Th	Fr	Sa
1	2	3	4	5	6	7
8	9	10	11	12	13	14
15	16	17	18	19	20	21
22	23	24	25	26	27	28
29	30	31				

1. Beirut: Israelis assault PLO positions at airport (→ 5).

5. Washington: House rejects nuclear arms freeze (→ 11/22).

5. U.S. urges Beirut pullback; Israelis reject appeal (→ 10).

8. N.J. passes bill allowing death penalty by injection (→ 7/2/84).

9. Washington: Hinckley given indefinite term for attempt to kill Reagan.

9. Paris: Six killed by grenade blast in kosher restaurant.

10. Syria now willing to accept all Palestinian guerrillas from West Beirut (→ 12).

12. EEC denounces Reagan ban on aid for Soviet pipeline (→ 11/13).

12. Lebanon: Israeli jets bomb West Beirut; 20,000 reported dead since June invasion (→ 19).

13. Gdansk: Riot police break up march by thousands of Solidarity workers (→ 26).

19. Israel accepts plan to end Beirut siege; PLO to begin pullout tomorrow (→ 21).

20. U.S. offers multibillion-dollar plan to help Mexico pay debt, ride out financial crisis (→ 9/1).

21. Beirut: PLO begins leaving Beirut, returning Israeli prisoners; French troops enter (→ 23).

24. Italy: Republican Giovanni Spadolini forms 42nd Cabinet since war (→ 9/3).

26. Czestochowa: Polish Archbishop Jozef Glemp tells 350,000 Lech Walesa must go free (→ 31).

26. U.S.: Johns-Manville Corp., ruined by over 10,000 asbestos suits, files for bankruptcy.

27. U.S.: Rickey Henderson of Oakland A's sets mark for stolen bases with 119th of season.

28. Spain: Greenpeace boats block dumping of atomic waste.

29. American Ashby Harper at 65 becomes oldest to swim English Channel.

29. Bill Dunlop of Maine crosses Atlantic in nine-foot sailboat.

DEATH

29. Nahum Goldmann, Zionist leader, founder of World Jewish Congress (*7/10/1895).

Banished PLO begins leaving Beirut

Beirut, a battleground and haven for foes of Israel, shaken by Israeli bombs.

PLO guerrillas are given a rousing send-off in Moslem West Beirut.

Aug 23. Another 1,000 Palestinian guerrillas, forced to leave Beirut by Israel, sailed for South Yemen today. They were allowed to take one gun each, but they had to leave more sophisticated weapons behind. Their departure was delayed because some of the guerrillas tried to take rocket-propelled grenade launchers. About 1,500 Palestinians left Beirut over the weekend for Cyprus. Israeli jets have bombed Moslem West Beirut in defiance of appeals from the U.S. government.

Despite their setback, many of the Palestinians fired automatic weapons into the air, creating the impression they were leaving in victory. Some flashed the victory sign. Others shouted, "Revolution, revolution until victory!" or "I love Palestine." Israeli soldiers kept their distance. In Israel, political leaders boasted of the successful invasion of Lebanon. "The PLO has lost its kingdom of terrorism, which it used as a base for the cruelest, most atrocious terrorist actions against Israel and throughout the world," Defense Minister Ariel Sharon said.

Once all the Palestinians are gone, special U.S. envoy Philip Habib will have another problem to solve: the withdrawal of 35,000 Israelis and 30,000 Syrians from Lebanon. It is hoped the election today of Christian leader Bashir Gemayel as the new President of Lebanon will speed the negotiations (→ 9/9).

Gas demand drops; 850 stations closing

Aug 23. The Exxon Corporation has announced it will close 850 service stations in the Northeast and Midwest because it sees no prospect of an upswing in the declining demand for gasoline. Exxon, the world's largest oil company, also said it would reduce production capacity at a major refinery in New Jersey from 250,000 to 100,000 barrels a day. Analysts said the cutbacks showed that even the industry leader had to adjust to a new pattern of lower oil use. "Over the long term, we see demand for petroleum products in this country leveling off and perhaps declining," an Exxon spokesman said (→ 3/14/83).

Polish police break up Solidarity rallies

Aug 31. With tear gas and water cannon, Polish police broke up demonstrations in Warsaw and other cities called by underground Solidarity leaders. The rallies had been organized to commemorate the second anniversary of a settlement that ended a strike in Gdansk through creation of Solidarity as an independent union. In addition to Warsaw, there were reports of police clashing with protesters in Gdansk, Wroclaw and Krakow.

In Warsaw, a haze of tear gas hung over the city after riot police chased demonstrators through the streets for four hours. By the end of the day, the Interior Ministry said the nation was generally calm. It appeared, however, that a standoff had been reached between the government and the Solidarity movement and that the result would be continuing tensions troubling the Communist government.

Through use of police force, the government demonstrated that it could establish calm on the city streets. But Solidarity was able to rally large public demonstrations in the face of threatened use of police force. In advance of the demonstrations, tensions had been building up in Poland, where the government had declared martial law and suspended the Solidarity union. The Roman Catholic Primate of Poland urged that the government release Lech Walesa, the imprisoned Solidarity leader (→ 9/6).

Sundown at last for Henry Fonda

Fonda, star of stage and screen.

Aug 12. He was righteous in "Grapes of Wrath" and "My Darling Clementine," goodhearted in "Mister Roberts," vulnerable in "On Golden Pond." He was also unfortunate. Nebraska-born Henry Fonda, who died today at age 77, had five marriages. The second ended when Frances Seymour Brokaw, mother of Fonda's children Jane and Peter, committed suicide. It's rumored strenuous stunts for "Golden Pond" hastened his end.

Magical career ends for Ingrid Bergman

Bergman, radiant and strong.

Aug 29. A seven-year battle with cancer has ended in the death of actress Ingrid Bergman. The Swedish beauty was 67. The public considered Miss Bergman and her film image one and the same; it felt she was the honest victim of "Gaslight" (1944) and the pure heroine of "Joan of Arc" (1948). The public was shocked when she abandoned her dentist husband for director Roberto Rossellini. After "Anastasia" (1956), all was forgiven.

1982

SEPTEMBER

Su	Mo	Tu	We	Th	Fr	Sa
			1	2	3	4
5	6	7	8	9	10	11
12	13	14	15	16	17	18
19	20	21	22	23	24	25
26	27	28	29	30		

1. Mexico nationalizes banks to halt capital flight (→ 3/18/83).

3. Rome: Gen. Carlo Alberto Dalla Chiesa, in charge of fighting Mafia, is killed (→ 10/16).

6. Bern: Gunmen seize Polish Embassy, demanding Warsaw lift martial law (→ 9).

8. Reagan says he won't block a Jesse Helms bill to allow prayer in public schools.

9. Fez: Arab summit adopts plan for Mideast peace, implying recognition of Israel (→ 14).

9. Bern: Polish Patriotic Revolutionary Army releases hostages at embassy (→ 10/8).

11. W. Germany: U.S. Army helicopter carrying parachuters at air show crashes, killing 44.

12. N.Y.: Connors over Lendl for fourth U.S. Open title; Evert Lloyd over Mandlikova for 6th.

14. Beirut: Pres.-elect Bashir Gemayel killed as bomb hits Phalangist offices (→ 15).

16. Tehran: Ex-Foreign Minister Sadegh Ghotzbadeh executed for treason (→ 10/2).

19. Sweden: Social Democrats under Olaf Palme win decisive victory (→ 9/15/85).

20. U.S.: NFL players start first strike during season in 63-year history (→ 11/16).

24. U.S. and others pull out of IAEC parley in protest after agency bans Israel (→ 25).

25. Wilkes-Barre, Penn.: State prison guard George Banks kills 13 in rampage in two houses.

25. Tel Aviv: Hundreds of thousands demonstrate against Begin and Sharon on involvement in massacre of Palestinians (→ 28).

29. N.Y.: Aerialist Philippe Petit walks 150 ft. over ground to celebrate construction of St. John the Divine, largest gothic cathedral.

30. Beirut: U.S. Marine killed as undetected explosives are accidentally detonated (→ 10/16).

DEATHS

2. Wladyslaw Gomulka, Polish Communist leader (*2/6/1905).

14. John Gardner, American novelist, critic (*7/21/1933).

Christians murder Arabs

Sept 18. The sickening stench of death rises from Sabra and Shatila, two Palestinian refugee camps in West Beirut. Hundreds of bodies, their faces contorted and bloated, lie in doorways and streets, surrounded by swarms of flies. It is a shocking scene. Most of the victims are unarmed. Many of them are elderly men, women and children.

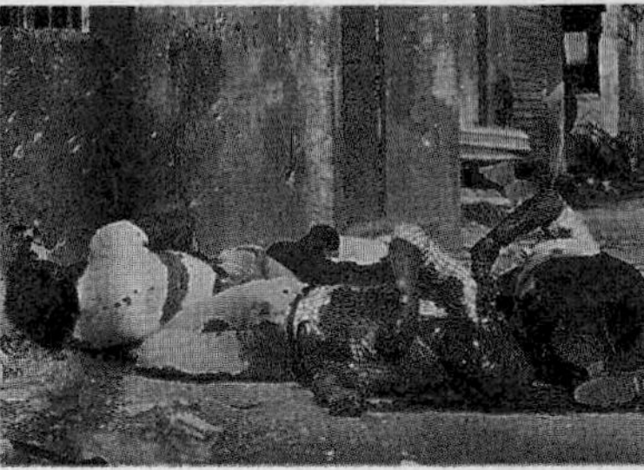

Horror at Sabra and Shatila.

The shooting started at 6:00 p.m. yesterday and carried on through most of the night. Preliminary reports say the Palestinians were shot by Christian militiamen, but other questions are being asked. Who ordered the gunmen to shoot? Did Israel play a role in the massacre?

The Phalangists have been demanding the blood of Palestinians since their President, Bashir Gemayel, was assassinated in a bomb explosion four days ago. The Palestine Liberation Organization was blamed for the murder. American and Israeli intelligence has indicated that up to 2,500 Palestinians are hidden in Beirut in violation of their promise to leave Lebanon. It was believed that some of them were trying to blend into the civilian population of the Sabra and Shatila refugee camps.

The Israeli government has condemned the massacre in the camps, but it has already changed its story about what happened. Early today, an army spokesman said, "There is no Israeli presence in the camps themselves. We do not know what is happening in the camps, and we are trying to establish the facts." Later today, the Israeli Foreign Ministry said it was "only thanks to the intervention of Israeli forces ... in West Beirut that the number of casualties was not much higher."

Survivors of the massacre said they did not see any Israeli forces inside the camps. They did say, however, that the Israelis sealed off the boundaries of Sabra and Shatila and permitted Christian militiamen under the command of Major Saad Haddad to enter the camps. A short while later, the shooting began.

Shortly after the Israeli invasion last June, the Phalangists rejected a suggestion from Israel to raid the camps. Their attitude changed after Gemayel was murdered and many of the camp's armed protectors were evacuated from Lebanon.

Last week, Israeli Defense Minister Sharon rejected an American demand that he withdraw his forces from West Beirut. Today, President Reagan called publicly for an Israeli withdrawal and said he was "horrified" by the massacre (→ 21).

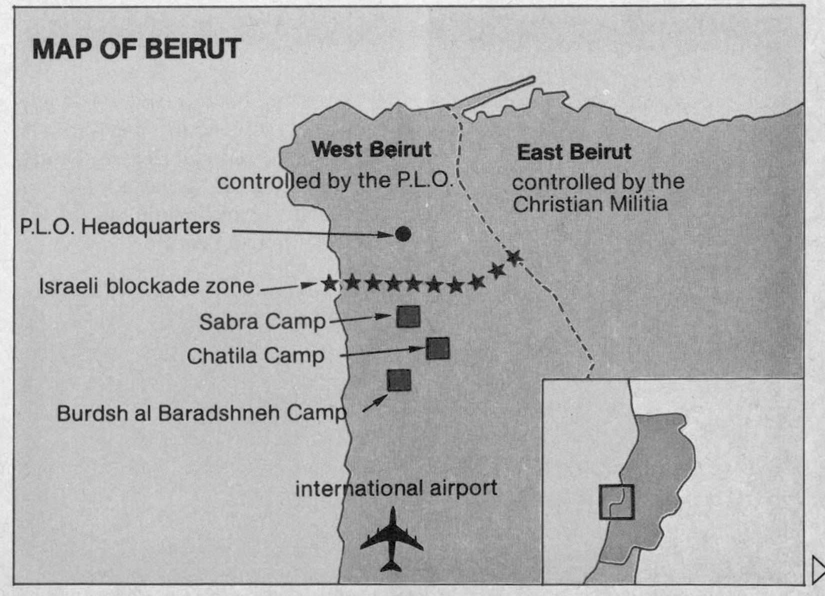

Automobile wreck kills Princess Grace

Grace, from screen to palace.

Sept 10. Princess Grace of Monaco, 52, died yesterday in Monte Carlo of injuries suffered when her car plunged off a mountain road Monday. In the car was her youngest child, Stephanie, 17, who is being treated for shock and bruises. The former Grace Kelly, star of 11 films, met Prince Rainier III of Monaco while making her third Hitchcock film, "To Catch a Thief," and they married in 1956 in a spectacular royal ceremony, after which she abandoned acting. In 1962, she hosted a TV tour of Monaco.

Vietnam General sues CBS for libel

Sept 13. General William C. Westmoreland is suing CBS for $120 million. He claims the network libeled him in its documentary "The Uncounted Enemy: A Vietnam Deception," broadcast January 23, 1982. CBS used the word "conspiracy" to describe Westmoreland's handling of enemy troop statistics from 1964 to 1968, accusing him of underrepresenting the number of Viet Cong and thereby lulling American leaders into a false sense of preparedness.

There is dissension in the ranks of CBS over some of the methods used in making the "CBS Reports" documentary, which was based on material supplied by Samuel A. Adams, an ex-CIA analyst. Westmoreland has accused CBS of trying "to execute me on the guillotine of public opinion" (→ 11/15/84).

Lebanon chief dead; his brother succeeds

Sept 21. In an unusual display of Moslem and Christian unity, Amin Gemayel was today elected President of Lebanon in a nearly unanimous parliamentary vote. He succeeds his brother Bashir, elected August 23 and killed in a bomb blast a week ago before he could be inaugurated. Like his late brother, Amin Gemayel belongs to the Christian Phalangist Party, Lebanon's most powerful. Following the assassination, presumably by Moslems, Phalangist militia retaliated by raiding Palestinian refugee camps and killing nearly 300 persons (→ 24).

Arafat asks Pope to aid Arab cause

Sept 15. Pope John Paul II has outraged Israel by giving Yasir Arafat a private audience at the Vatican. The meeting with the Chairman of the Palestine Liberation Organization lasted 20 minutes. In a communique, the pope expressed the need for a lasting, peaceful solution to the Middle East conflict. He also spoke of the "suffering of the Palestinian people" and said that any peace agreement should recognize their legitimate rights and give them a place to live. The pope said the agreement would also have to recognize Israel's right to exist securely.

The meeting helped solidify international recognition of the PLO as the official representative of the Palestinian people. Arafat is also expected to be received by Italy's President, Alessandro Pertini. The Israeli government released a statement saying the pope should not have met Arafat while the PLO's leadership is in dispute (→ 18).

Historic, controversial handshake.

Marines to stay in Beirut, Reagan says

Marines in Beirut, a precarious post.

Sept 28. President Reagan told Americans in a televised speech last night that he plans to keep U.S. Marines in Lebanon until Syria and Israel withdraw their forces from the beleaguered nation. The Marines are a part of a peacekeeping force which also includes contingents from France and Italy. The president expressed confidence that the Syrians and Israelis will depart from Lebanon soon. But he emphasized the importance of maintaining an American miiltary presence in the area (→ 30).

3 Lutheran bodies decide on merger

Sept 8. Three of the five Lutheran denominations in America voted today at their national conventions to merge, forming a new church with 5.5 million members, the third largest Protestant denomination in the country.

The proposal to merge was overwhelmingly approved by delegates attending The Lutheran Church of America convention in Cleveland, the American Lutheran Church convention in San Diego, and the Association of Evangelical Lutheran Churches meeting in Cleveland. The ballot results were announced simultaneously by telephone to the three gatherings, to thunderous applause. The three Lutheran groups share a common theology, but differ according to the various countries from which Lutherans emigrated to America.

1982

OCTOBER

Su	Mo	Tu	We	Th	Fr	Sa
					1	2
3	4	5	6	7	8	9
10	11	12	13	14	15	16
17	18	19	20	21	22	23
24	25	26	27	28	29	30
31						

1. U.S.: FDA warns against Tylenol after seven die from use in last three days (→ 5).

2. Tehran: 60 die as blast rips downtown square (→ 5/4/83).

3. L.A.: Home video games now nearing profitability of film industry.

5. Swedish navy helicopter drops depth charge near possible Soviet sub off Musko Island.

7. New York: Lloyd Weber's "Cats" opens on Broadway.

8. Warsaw: Parliament approves law banning Solidarity (→ 13).

10. Vatican: Pope beatifies Maximilian Kolbe, died at Auschwitz in another man's stead.

13. Two Olympic golds revoked from Jim Thorpe in 1912 are restored posthumously.

13. Gdansk: Workers, under army rule, end three-day strike (→ 26).

16. U.S. to halt ties to U.N. if Israel is denied seat (→ 18).

16. Italy: 100,000 demonstrate against Mafia in Palermo (→ 1/25/83).

18. Israel: Begin tells Knesset borders with Arab countries are secure for first time (→ 1/28/83).

19. L.A.: John DeLorean arrested for possession of over 59 pounds of cocaine (→ 11/8).

20. St. Louis: Cardinals beat Brewers to win World Series.

22. El Salvador: Five opposition leaders kidnapped (→ 11/9).

22. Cuba frees dissident poet Armando Valladares, jailed 22 years, after French intervention (→ 5/16/83).

27. China, after largest census in history, reports population at 1.008 billion.

29. FDA approves marketing of human insulin made through gene splicing (→ 6/8/83).

DEATHS

9. Anna Freud, psychoanalyst, educator, daughter of Sigmund (*12/3/1895).

18. Bess Truman, ex-first lady of United States.

18. Pierre Mendes France, French statesman (*1/11/1907).

Tylenol taken off market after eight killed

Oct 5. The manufacturer of Tylenol today recalled all capsules of the pain-reliever after the eighth case of poisoning caused by deliberate contamination of the product. Johnson & Johnson, the manufacturer, acted after a California man was stricken after taking Tylenol capsules laced with strychnine. Officials said there was no apparent connection between the California case and the deaths of seven persons in the Chicago area who took cyanide-laced Tylenol last week. Federal officials said they would work with drug industry representatives on regulations requiring tamper-resistant packaging for all over-the-counter medications (→ 2/17/86).

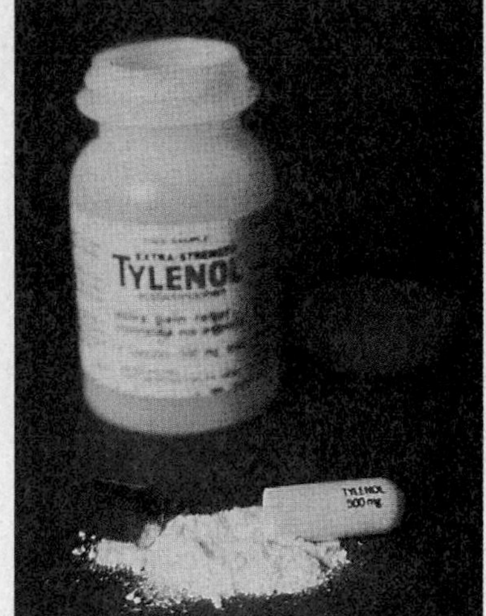

Tylenol, killing more than pain.

Kate Smith receives Medal of Freedom

Oct 26. How does America thank a woman who bestows her blessings on it? It awards her the Medal of Freedom. Today, President Reagan gave singer Kate Smith, 73, the medal for inspiring the nation with her rendition of Irving Berlin's "God Bless America." She has been singing the tune steadily since 1938. Recordings of it often play before sporting events. Miss Smith has been hefty all her life, lending volume and power to songs like "When the Moon Comes Over the Mountain." She had her own radio show for 16 years and a TV show for four seasons.

Kohl is Chancellor, replacing Schmidt

Christian Democrat Helmut Kohl.

Oct 1. In an unprecedented move, the West German Parliament threw Helmut Schmidt out of office today and elected Helmut Kohl as the new Chancellor. Kohl, a conservative Christian Democrat, promised "a government, a politics of the middle." The Reagan administration said it was satisfied that West Germany would now be "more in tune with the Reagan philosophy."

The Free Democrats, a minority party that had been part of the ruling coalition, provoked the no-confidence vote in Schmidt after he refused to cut welfare spending. The party then sided with Kohl.

Polish Parliament outlaws Solidarity

Oct 26. The Polish Parliament overwhelmingly approved a measure outlawing Solidarity, the free trade union that captured the support of millions of Poles but drew the wrath of the Soviet Union. The new law replaces Solidarity with a set of unions with sharply restricted powers to strike.

The move provoked demonstrations and clashes between workers and police in Gdansk, the birthplace of the Solidarity movement, and in the steelmaking suburb of Nowa Huta near Krakow. The government put down a strike in the Gdansk shipyards by using its martial law authority to draft the striking workers into military service.

President Reagan responded to the outlawing of Solidarity by suspending the most-favored-nation status that Poland has enjoyed for 22 years in its trade with the United States (→ 11/14).

Strikers confront water cannons.

Socialists win by a landslide in Spain

Gonzales, youngest leader in Europe.

Oct 29. Spain has a new Prime Minister, the youngest in Europe, as the Socialist Party today won a landslide victory in the Spanish general elections. Sweeping into power is Felipe Gonzalez, the leader of the party which won a clear majority in the 350-seat Parliament.

The electoral victory helps avenge the Socialist Party's bitter defeat in the Spanish Civil War 45 years ago. Gonzalez called the election a triumph "for democracy and the Spanish people," while the streets of Madrid erupted in jubilant celebration.

The Socialist Party unofficially secured 202 seats in Parliament, while the conservative Popular Alliance Party won 101 seats and the moderate Democratic Center group failed miserably at the polls (→ 11/22/84).

Royal ship is raised after 437 years

Oct 11. King Henry VIII's flagship, the Mary Rose, loaded with 91 cannons and 700 men, sank during an engagement with the French in 1545. Today, this forerunner of the modern British navy was raised, most of its oak frame intact, off Portsmouth, England, as Prince Charles and hundreds of others watched in a driving rain. The salvaging marked the climax of a 17-year $7 million project. With its 17,000 artifacts, the ship represents a time capsule of the Tudor era of priceless value to historians.

Gould, perfectionist at the piano, is dead

Oct 4. "If you haven't got something new to say in a recording, don't bother saying it." Pianist Glenn Gould, who died today at 50, lived by his words. Eccentric and brilliant, he crusaded to "rethink" piano traditions. After a nine-year concert career, Gould exiled himself to northern Canada to escape conformist pressures that made him a "vaudevillian." There, he added 80 recordings to his ardent version of Bach's "Goldberg Variations." Often thought irreverent in his disregard for musical tradition, he was in fact the most religious of artists. Gould did not, as he said of Mozart, "die too late rather than too early."

Oct 24. After 26 miles, just yards separated Alberto Salazar from Rodolfo Gomez. Salazar won his 3rd N.Y. Marathon. Grete Waitz won her fourth women's title.

1982

NOVEMBER

Su	Mo	Tu	We	Th	Fr	Sa
	1	2	3	4	5	6
7	8	9	10	11	12	13
14	15	16	17	18	19	20
21	22	23	24	25	26	27
28	29	30				

1. Chicago: Bowie Kuhn voted out as baseball commissioner.

2. U.S.: Democrats win majority in House; Mario Cuomo elected governor of N.Y.

5. Argentina: 1,000 bodies found; army suspected (→ 9/9/83).

7. Iranian troops drive six miles into Iraq first time in over three months (→ 2/7/83).

8. L.A.: John DeLorean pleads not guilty to cocaine charges (→ 8/16/84).

8. Biloxi: Mississippi prison fire kills 27 and injures 43.

9. El Salvador: U.S. envoy ordered to halt criticism of human rights abuses (→ 3/8/83).

11. Cape Canaveral: Columbia returns to orbit on first flight as space freighter (→ 16).

13. Reagan lifts sanctions on sales for Soviet pipeline.

15. L.A.: Draft registration law ruled invalid by federal judge (→ 9/12/85).

16. U.S.: Columbia lands after launching satellites for first time (→ 4/5/83).

16. U.S.: NFL ends 57-day strike, longest in history of professional sports.

19. N.J.: Manuscripts by Porter, Gershwin and Rodgers found in Warner Bros. warehouse.

20. South Africa backs down on plan to install black rule in Namibia (→ 12/19).

22. Reagan calls for dense-pack deployment of MX missile (→ 12/7).

23. FCC drops limits on duration and frequency of TV ads.

24. Hawaii: Thousands evacuated as first hurricane in 23 years strikes.

25. Rome: Serge Ivanov Antonov arrested for plot to kill pope (→ 7/9/83).

26. Tokyo: Yasuhiro Nakasone elected 71st Japanese prime minister (→ 2/14/83).

DEATHS

1. King Vidor, American film director (*2/8/1896).

5. Jacques Tati, French film director (*10/9/1908).

Brezhnev is dead at 75

Leonid Brezhnev lies in state in a sea of red roses and revolutionary flags.

Nov 10. Leonid Brezhnev, leader of the Soviet Union for the past 18 years, died this morning in Moscow. Brezhnev, who was 75, had been suffering from heart and lung problems for the past few years, but the official Soviet announcement did not indicate the cause of his death. It is unclear who will succeed him. The leading contenders appear to be Konstantin Chernenko, an aide to Brezhnev, and Yuri Andropov, who headed the KGB for 15 years.

President Reagan was awakened early this morning and informed of Brezhnev's death by his national security adviser, William Clark. There are indications from the White House that Reagan may attend Brezhnev's funeral.

In its official announcement, Tass said, "The name of Leonid Ilyich Brezhnev, a true continuer of Lenin's great cause and an ardent champion of peace and communism, will live forever" (→ 12).

Walesa free after 11 months internment

Nov 14. Friends of Lech Walesa chanted, "No Solidarity without Lech," as the leader of the illegal Solidarity union came home to Gdansk, Poland, after nearly a year in jail. Walesa told the well-wishers he would continue to speak out on the social conditions in Poland. Yet, he added, "In my future conduct I will be courageous but also prudent and there is nothing negotiable in this regard. I will talk and act, not on my knees, but with prudence; you can rest assured of that."

Walesa's release by the government of General Wojciech Jaruzelski indicates that Warsaw officials may be loosening the iron grip of martial law. Last week, Jaruzelski met with the Archbishop of the Roman Catholic Church, Jozef Glemp. It is believed the two cleared the way for a visit by Pope John Paul II, a native Pole, next June. The Polish people have longed to see the pontiff return since his visit to Poland in 1979.

The government has announced that Parliament will hold a special meeting on December 13, the anniversary of the imposition of martial law. Some speculate Warsaw will then lift martial law (→ 3/10/83).

Ex-KGB chief Andropov to head U.S.S.R.

Nov 12. Acting with unexpected speed, the Soviet Communist Party's Central Committee selected a former spymaster as the successor to Leonid Breznev. Yuri Andropov, who is 68, was named General Secretary. Until recently, Andropov was the head of the KGB and was in charge of foreign espionage operations and internal security.

Andropov, reputed to be tough.

In a speech, Andropov pledged to continue the programs of Brezhnev, but he did not commit himself to the late leader's policy of detente. Instead, Andropov lashed out at Western powers. "We know well," he said, "that the imperialists will never meet one's pleas for peace. It can only be defended by relying on the invincible might of the Soviet armed forces."

Western observers were surprised that Andropov was named so quickly. The official who had been expected to battle Andropov for the job of party leader, Konstantin Chernenko, nominated him. It is possible that Chernenko may be given Brezhnev's other ceremonial title as head of state (→ 5/11/83).

Hockey fans focus on Great Gretzky

All eyes are on the great Wayne Gretzky, the extraordinarily talented center of the Edmonton Oilers of the National Hockey League, who was named Most Valuable Player in each of his three seasons. Last year, the 21-year-old skating and scoring sensation from Brantford, Ontario, set season records for goals (92), assists (120), and points (212). What will he do this year for an encore?

Gretzky (rt.), aims to score again.

1982

DECEMBER

Su	Mo	Tu	We	Th	Fr	Sa
			1	2	3	4
5	6	7	8	9	10	11
12	13	14	15	16	17	18
19	20	21	22	23	24	25
26	27	28	29	30	31	

1. Rome: Pope John Paul II bars visit to Nicaragua unless priests quit Sandinista posts (→ 2/4/83).

2. Utah: Dentist Barney Clark receives Jarvik, first permanent artificial heart (→ 22).

7. Washington: House 245-176 bars $988 mil. for MX missile (→ 21).

7. Ulster: 11 British soldiers killed as bomb goes off in disco in Ballykelly (→ 6/6/83).

8. Washington: Police kill man who threatened to blow up Washington Monument.

15. Alabama: Bear Bryant retires as football coach at University of Alabama (→ 1/26/83).

16. Washington: House cites EPA chief Ann Gorsuch with contempt (→ 2/7/83).

19. Johannesburg: Four bombs explode at S. Africa's only nuclear power station (→ 5/20/83).

21. Moscow: Andropov offers cut in European medium-range missiles from 600 to 162; U.S. and Allies reject (→ 2/2/83).

23. U.S.: South Korean opposition leader Kim Dae Jung arrives after release by Seoul (→ 10/9/83).

DEATH

24. Louis Aragon, French poet, leader of WWII resistance (*10/3/1897).

CULTURAL EVENTS, 1982

Literature: Heinrich Boll's "The Safety Net"; Gabriel Garcia Marquez' "Chronicle of a Death Foretold"; William Golding's "A Moving Target"; Athol Fugard's "Master Harold . . . and the Boys"; Sylvia Plath's "Collected Poems," Pulitzer; Charles Fuller's "A Soldier's Play."

Music: Roger Sessions' "Concerto for Orchestra," Pulitzer; Lionel Richie's "Truly"; McCartney & Stevie Wonder's "Ebony and Ivory."

The Arts: Neo-Expressionism in vogue in Europe.

Film: Richard Attenborough's "Gandhi," Academy Award; "Sophie's Choice," Meryl Streep; "Tootsie."

Dentist is first recipient of artificial heart

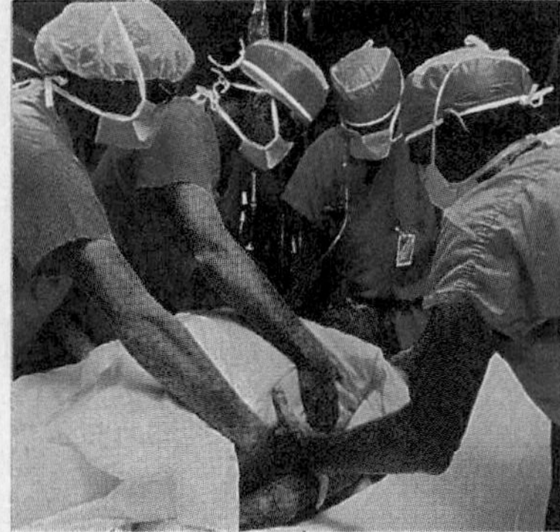

Barney Clark, in good hands.

Dec 22. Barney B. Clark, the first recipient of a permanant artificial heart, took his first steps today. The 61-year-old retired dentist from the Seattle area received the implant in a seven-and-a-half-hour operation performed Dec. 2 by a surgical team headed by Dr. William C. DeVries at the University of Utah Medical Center in Salt Lake City.

Clark was bedridden and close to death from heart failure when the operation was performed. He now is being kept alive by a Jarvik-7 plastic-and-metal artificial heart, named after its developer, Dr. Robert K. Jarvik. The device replaces the two ventricles of the heart, which pump blood to the lungs and the rest of the body. It has kept animals alive for months but has never before been used in a human.

Surgeons had to replace the left part of the artificial heart last week when it began to fail, but say Clark is beginning what appears to be a recovery from surgery (→ 3/23/83).

Rubinstein, master pianist, is dead

Dec 20. Arthur Rubinstein, the reigning monarch of the keyboard, died peacefully yesterday in his Geneva home at 95 years of age.

For most of his 85-year career he mesmerized audiences with his golden tone, his promethean technique and, above all, an indomitable zest more important than the notes themselves.

Away from the piano he liked nothing better than telling a good story, smoking a good cigar, eating the best cuisine and charming the ladies. If he had a secret it was in living to the hilt. "Eat a lobster, eat a pound of caviar—live!" he said. "If you are in love with a beautiful blonde with an empty face and no brains at all, don't be afraid! Marry her! Live!"

Rubinstein performing at 89.

Queen Elizabeth II tours South Pacific

Echoes of empire in Tuvalu.

South Sea islanders know class when they see it, and Queen Elizabeth II has it. Even when enlaced by leis or surrounded by half-naked bronzed strangers, the queen keeps a most dignified air. That air was in evidence when the queen visited Tuvalu during her Pacific tour late this year. She and Prince Philip left their yacht Britannia and approached the island in ceremonial canoes. When the crafts were ready to beach, a team of hefty Tuvalese shouldered the canoes and brought the royal couple ashore.

Colombian novelist wins Nobel Prize

Gabriel Garcia Marquez.

Dec 10. Colombian Gabriel Garcia Marquez has won the Nobel Prize for literature. The 54-year-old author is noted for his "fantastic realism," bending time and space. "A Hundred Years of Solitude" (1967) is a strange, luminous family saga reflecting the course of Colombia's tortured history.

The medicine prize went to the Swedes Sune Bergstrom and Bengt Samuelson and Briton John Vane. Harvard-educated Kenneth Wilson, a professor at Cornell, took the physics award. The chemistry prize went to Aaron Klug of Great Britain. George Stigler, a Guggenheim fellow and instructor at the University of Chicago, was honored with the economics award.

The Peace Prize was shared by Alva Myrdal and Alfonso Garcia Robles. For several years, they ably represented their nations, Sweden and Mexico, at disarmament conferences in Geneva.

While vets mourn the war dead, Hollywood cast them in a fantasy. Sly Stallone in "First Blood."

1983

JANUARY

Su	Mo	Tu	We	Th	Fr	Sa
						1
2	3	4	5	6	7	8
9	10	11	12	13	14	15
16	17	18	19	20	21	22
23	24	25	26	27	28	29
30	31					

1. Pasadena: UCLA defeats Michigan 24-14 in Rose Bowl.

8. Newark: Three mil. gallons gas burn after tank explosions.

8. Ossining, N.Y.: Inmates at Sing-Sing prison seize 16 officers as hostages.

11. New York: Billy Martin to manage Yankees for third time.

13. Tennessee: Officer killed as Memphis police slay seven cultists in shootout.

14. U.S.: Infant mortality rate in cities declines to record low.

17. Alabama: George Wallace takes oath for fourth term as governor.

18. Peking executes official for economic crimes.

19. Rome: New Catholic code expands women's rights.

20. Chicago: Allen Dorfman, Teamster adviser, is slain.

22. Washington: Demonstrators mark ten years of legal abortion (→ 2/10).

24. New York: McEnroe beats Lendl to win Masters title.

25. Italy: 25 in Red Brigade sentenced to life in prison for murder of Aldo Moro (→ 8/4).

27. Washington: Paul Mellon gives 93 works of art to National Gallery.

28. Beirut: Lebanon car bomb blast kills 14 at center for Arafat wing of PLO (→ 2/2).

29. India: Indira Gandhi names 12 new ministers as Cabinet resigns (→ 2/18).

29. Greece gives wives equal voice in home.

30. Peru: Eight newsmen, mistaken for rebels, slain in ambush.

31. Washington: Pres. Reagan presents budget calling for 10% military increase (→ 5/19/85).

DEATHS

11. Nikolai Podgorny, Soviet statesman (*2/10/1903).

24. George Cukor, American film director (*7/7/1899).

26. Georges Bidault, led French resistance in WWII, O.A.S. chief in 1960's (*10/5/1899).

Violence rules a divided Central America

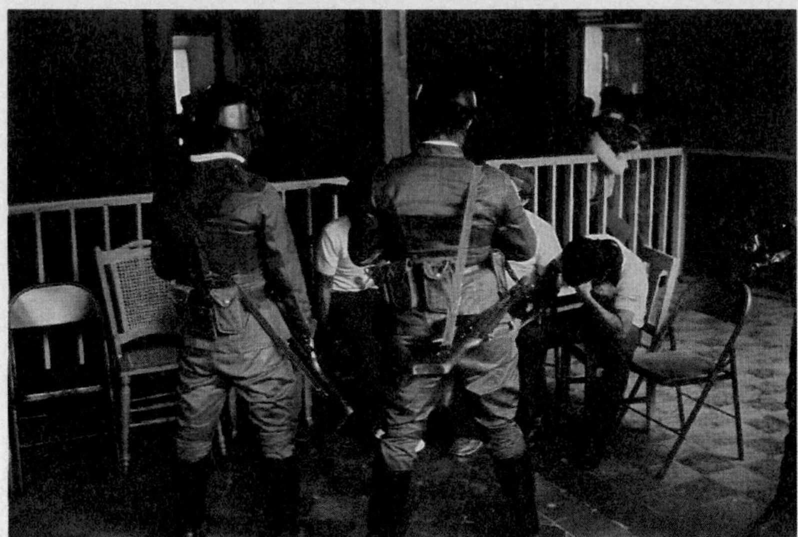

Salvadoran peasants suspected of leftist sympathies are interrogated by police.

More than at any time in recent history, the small countries of Central America find themselves caught up in political turbulence and armed violence growing out of ideological power struggles.

Turbulence is not new to the region, which for decades has endured power struggles between a ruling elite and top military leaders. The new dimension is that the struggles have now become politically polarized between forces on the left and the right which are willing to embark on armed violence to advance their cause. The result is to leave the fate of the 22 million people in the region largely in the hands of a small number of guerrilla and army leaders who increasingly are turning outside the region for economic and political support.

In many ways, the polarization—and the resulting instability and violence—began four years ago with the overthrow of the Somoza regime in Nicaragua by a leftist-led rebellion. The political fallout has now spread to other countries in the region, such as Honduras, El Salvador and Guatemala. The latter two confront leftist insurgencies, and Honduras finds itself caught up in a United States-supported insurgency against Nicaragua.

The regional violence is exacting a devastating toll. Last year, some 15,000 persons lost their lives in Central American wars and violence. Hundreds of thousands have been forced to flee their homes. The economies, meanwhile, have been depressed by low commodity prices (→ 2/4).

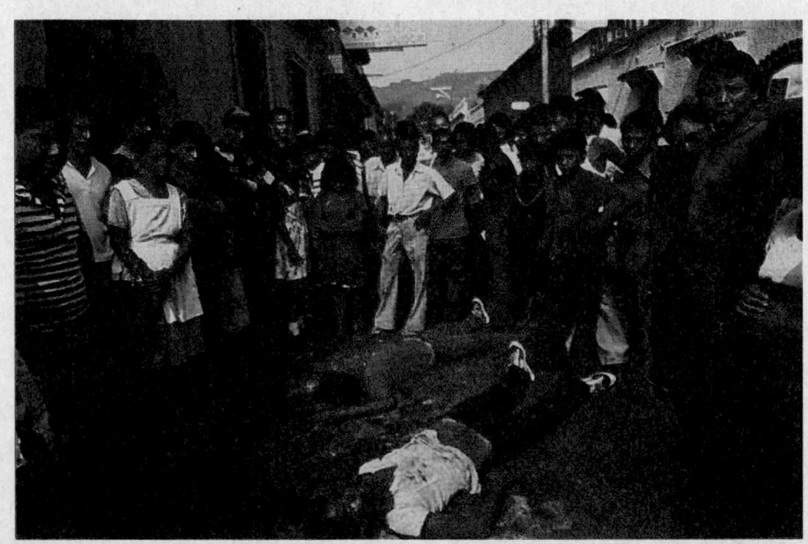

Salvadorans, besieged by civil war, never know when friends may die by a gun.

China spares Mao's widow from death

Jan 25. Chiang Ching, Mao's 69-year-old widow, has had her death sentence commuted to life in prison. She, one quarter of the Gang of Four, is held responsible for the Chinese Cultural Revolution, a movement resulting in the deaths of 35,000 anti-radicals. One of her accomplices, suffering from throat cancer, has also had his death sentence commuted, while the other two remain in the prison where they were originally sentenced. China may have halted the executions to convince the West of its progressivism. The country routinely shoots criminals guilty of embezzlement or arson (→ 10/20/84).

Madame Mao, former actress.

American doctors call for boxing ban

Jan 13. New evidence suggesting that chronic brain damage is prevalent among prizefighters has led the American Medical Association to call for the banning of the sport. If the sport is to continue, an editorial in the AMA Journal went on, steps should be taken to improve monitoring a boxer's condition before, during and after a fight. The journal reported a study of 38 boxers that provided new evidence of the link between boxing and brain damage. More than half of the boxers showed some brain tissue loss or atrophy, which leads to a condition commonly known as "punch drunk." Even boxers with a small number of bouts could be subject to the affliction.

Butcher of Lyons caught in Bolivia

Jan 25. The Nazi nicknamed in France "The Butcher of Lyons" was arrested today in La Paz, Bolivia. Klaus Barbie is charged in connection with police brutality in the regime of General Banzer, the deposed Bolivian dictator. It is not clear yet whether Barbie will be extradited to France to face charges characterized as "crimes against humanity." French authorities have been trying for years to convince the Bolivian government to arrest Barbie, but Banzer always rejected the request. The present regime of President Hernan Siles Zuazo might be more inclined to honor France's request to extradite him (→ 2/5).

Borg quits tennis at apex of his career

Jan 23. Bjorn Borg, still in his prime at 26, has left the tennis world in shock. Barred from major titles because he failed to enter a minimum number of tournaments, Borg has retired from competition. He combined quickness with relentless topspin groundstrokes and impenetrable concentration to wear down opponent after opponent. His unsurpassed five straight Wimbledon titles are astounding for a player raised on Sweden's slow red clay. Though the U.S. Open eluded him, six victories at the French Open place Borg second on the all-time list for Grand Slam titles with 11.

Legendary coach Bear Bryant is gone

Bryant, best college football coach.

Jan 26. After only 17 days of retirement from football with the most victories in history, Coach Bear Bryant is dead. He was 69 years old. Bryant entered a Tuscaloosa hospital complaining of chest pains. While undergoing X-ray examinations, he died. His physician said that he had been in good spirits and joked about going to Las Vegas.

Byrant stepped down as coach at Alabama University after 38 years of unmatched success. He posted a record of 323 victories, 85 defeats and 17 ties at four colleges. Six of his Alabama teams were rated No. 1 nationally by the wire-service surveys. Bryant remained as Athletic Director and turned the coaching job over to one of his proteges, Ray Perkins, who quit as coach of the New York Giants to go to Alabama.

Jan 30. Miami's Lyle Blackwood (top) incurs a 30-yard pass-interference penalty during the Dolphins' 27-17 Super Bowl loss to Washington.

1983

FEBRUARY

Su	Mo	Tu	We	Th	Fr	Sa
		1	2	3	4	5
6	7	8	9	10	11	12
13	14	15	16	17	18	19
20	21	22	23	24	25	26
27	28					

2. Beirut: U.S. Marine Charles Johnson forces three Israeli tanks back with pistol (→ 5).

2. Geneva: U.S.-Soviet START talks resume on reduction of strategic arms (→ 3/2).

4. Managua reports killing 73 rebels (→ 3/4).

5. Beirut: 18 die in bombing at PLO center (→ 8).

5. Lyon: Klaus Barbie, ex-Gestapo agent, returned to France (→ 7).

6. Italy: Ray "Boom Boom" Mancini wins first fight since death of Duk Koo Kim.

7. U.S. State Dept. refuses comment on CIA links to Klaus Barbie (→ 8/16).

7. Reagan dismisses high EPA official Rita Lavelle over conflict of interest (→ 3/9).

7. Iraq: Iran opens invasion in southeast (→ 2/12/84).

8. Jerusalem: Inquiry places "indirect" blame on Israeli leaders for Beirut massacres (→ 11).

11. Israel: Ariel Sharon resigns as defense minister (→ 14).

14. Jerusalem: Moshe Arens replaces Sharon as defense minister (→ 15).

15. Lebanese army takes control of East Beirut from Christian militia (→ 28).

16. Manila: Roman Catholic bishops accuse Marcos regime of repression (→ 6/25).

18. U.S. reports chasing two Libyan MIG-23's away from carrier Nimitz (→ 4/17/84).

18. India: 600 killed in Hindu raids on Moslem villages (→ 10/6).

19. London: Nigeria, in break with OPEC, cuts oil prices $5.50 per barrel (→ 3/14).

27. N.J.: Eamonn Coghlan sets indoor mile record at 3:49.78.

28. Calif.: Queen Elizabeth, on U.S. tour, thanks Americans for support in Falklands crisis.

DEATHS

4. Karen Carpenter, American pop singer (*3/2/1950).

25. Tennessee Williams, leading U.S. dramatist (*3/26/1911).

G.M. and Toyota to begin joint venture

Feb 14. General Motors and Toyota today said they had agreed on a project for joint production of a subcompact car in the United States. It is the first time that General Motors, the dominant American auto maker, has turned to another company for assistance in producing cars in the United States. The new car will be built at a plant in Fremont, Calif., using Toyota's manufacturing techniques. The production company will be jointly owned, but Toyota will choose the chief executive. The agreement is regarded by industry executives as a tribute to Japanese auto makers' quality and efficiency (→ 4/9/85).

Amadeus composed first symphony at 9

Feb 5. The musical manuscript uncovered 40 years ago in a cellar in Odense, Denmark, seems to prove that the first shall be the last, for it has just been authenticated as Wolfgang Amadeus Mozart's very first symphony. It was written when he was nine and doing what all kids that age usually do —touring England as an acclaimed piano prodigy.

Though unearthed in 1943, it lay in an anonymous heap until Gunnar Thygesen, the librarian of the Odense Symphony, got a chance to tackle those old manuscripts. Described as a "Symphony for 10 Instruments," its most unusual feature is its key in A-minor, rarely used by even the mature Mozart and only then for special effect.

A refreshing change from Hollywood: An epic about non-violence. Ben Kingsley is a reverent and realistic "Gandhi" (→ 4/11).

Sharon resigns, charged with complicity

Sharon, out as Defense Minister.

Feb 28. Ariel Sharon has resigned as Israel's Defense Minister after a government commission found he shared responsibility for the massacre of hundreds of Palestinian refugees in the Lebanese war.

The retired General, a war hero and architect of Israeli strategy in the war against Lebanon, submitted his resignation after the Israeli Cabinet voted to accept the findings of a special commission set up to investigate the massacres in Beirut refugee camps last September.

The commission found that Israel's top civilian and military leaders bore "indirect responsibility" for the massacres carried out by the Christian Phalangist militia and recommened that Sharon and three top army generals be discharged from their posts. The report, which caused political turmoil in Israel, criticized Sharon for failing to anticipate the probability of a massacre when the Phalangists were permitted to go into the refugee camps.

Sharon later filed a libel suit against Time magazine for its allegation that he had urged the Gemayel family to take revenge against the Palestinians for the murder of Bashir Gemayel, a Philangist leader (→ 4/10).

Indian election riots kill 600 Moslems

Gandhi, Premier of a divided India.

Feb 21. More than 600 people have been killed in the Indian state of Assam after student agitators protesting the immigration of Moslem refugees from Bangladesh attempted to stop state elections.

Indian Prime Minister Indira Gandhi toured the area by helicopter and car, examining fields strewn with bodies and the remains of Moslem villages, to determine the extent of the rioting. When asked if she and the government would accept responsibility for the carnage she replied by saying, "Why should we? It is the agitators who are responsible. They may not like the elections, but do they have the right to stop them?" She also suggested the violence would have occurred even if she had called off the elections. About 21,000 of the one million immigrants in Assam have fled to seek refuge from the violence.

WWII internment of Japanese unjust

Feb 24. It has taken over 40 years, but the United States has decided that the imprisonment of Japanese-Americans during World War II was wrong. A congressional commission concluded today that the internment of 140,000 Japanese citizens was a "grave injustice" and that the move authorized by President Roosevelt was militarily unnecessary and motivated by "racial prejudice, war hysteria and failure of political leadership" (→ 6/16).

Court: Monopoly monopoly is unfair

Feb 22. The Supreme Court says Parker Brothers may not pass GO. Parker Brothers tried to stop a company from marketing a game called Anti-Monopoly, claiming the name was a copyright infringement (they have marketed Monopoly, the real estate game, since 1936). Yet the court feels the name has evolved into a generic term for board game, and cannot be "monopolized." Parker Brothers has sold 80 million sets of the game to date.

Eubie Blake, great ragtimer, was 100

Feb 12. People were just wild about Eubie Blake, the ragtime musician. He died today at his Brooklyn home five days after his 100th birthday. Blake co-wrote the first black Broadway musical, "Shuffle Along," in 1921. Cast members Josephine Baker and Paul Robeson sang his songs "I'm Just Wild About Harry" and "Love Will Find A Way." Eubie was still playing for audiences at the age of 98.

Polygamy: Arizona man had 105 wives

Feb 8. Giovanni Vigliotto, who claims to have married more than 105 women in 33 years, was found guilty today of fraud and bigamy in marrying an Arizona woman in 1981. He faces up to 34 years in prison. The 53-year-old defendant appeared surprised by the verdict. The woman testified that he vanished with $36,600 of her cash and property after two weeks, abandoning her in a San Diego motel.

Anti-abortionist is sentenced to prison

Feb 10. His victim was a "cold-blooded killer" according to Don Anderson, but Anderson is the one going to prison for 30 years. Calling himself a soldier in the Army of God, a Texas-based anti-abortion group, Anderson abducted the owner of an Illinois abortion clinic last August. He was not convicted for kidnapping but for interfering with interstate commerce by trying to close a clinic (→ 6/15).

1983

MARCH

Su	Mo	Tu	We	Th	Fr	Sa
		1	2	3	4	5
6	7	8	9	10	11	12
13	14	15	16	17	18	19
20	21	22	23	24	25	26
27	28	29	30	31		

2. CIA analysts say U.S. reports of Soviet arms buildup exaggerated last six years (→ 23).

4. Managua: Pope assails leftist clergy in Nicaragua.→

5. Zimbabwe: 600 opposition members arrested (→ 12).

5. Australia: Robert Hawke and Labor Party oust eight-year-old Conservative government.

6. Washington: FDA approves new sponge contraceptive.

8. Washington: Def. Sec. Weinberger proposes $110 mil. in emergency military aid to El Salvador (→ 5/10).

9. Soviets say Reagan has "pathological hatred of Socialism and Communism" (→ 4/21).

9. Washington: Anne McGill Burford resigns as head of EPA (→ 21).

10. Gdansk: Shipyard workers demand renewed legal status for Solidarity (→ 16).

16. Poland: Lech Walesa says rallies in Gdansk were inspired by forged leaflets (→ 4/22).

18. Texas: Mexican financial crisis now causing surge of illegal aliens (→ 8/20/86).

18. Calif.: Girlfriend Cathy Smith indicted for murder of John Belushi.

19. U.S. Commission on Civil Rights says White House hampers its work (→ 6/14).

21. Washington: Reagan names William Ruckleshaus to head EPA (→ 6/8).

22. Nicaragua: 2,000 insurgents cross border from Honduras (→ 4/9).

23. Utah: Artificial heart recipient Barney Clark dies (→ 10/26/84).

25. Washington: FBI concludes nuclear freeze movement not controlled by Soviets (→ 29).

29. Washington: Reagan suggests he would share Star Wars with Soviets (→ 4/1).

DEATHS

16. Arthur Godfrey, American radio entertainer (*8/31/1903).

18. Humbert II, ex-king of Italy (*9/15/1904).

Reagan proposes Star Wars defense plan

Reagan seeks nuclear umbrella.

March 23. A plan to use the latest in modern technology to build an invulnerable missile shield for the United States was proposed tonight by President Reagan. In a television address from the White House, Reagan presented "a vision of the future which offers hope" that the U.S. could stop relying on massive retaliation to counter the threat of a Soviet nuclear attack, but warned that the technological breakthroughs necessary to create a missile shield "may not be accomplished before the end of this century."

White House officials said the new program might involve lasers, microwave devices, particle beams and projectile beams directed from satellites to shoot down Soviet missiles before they could strike American territory. The officials said the program would require a major increase in research spending on antimissile technology from the current level of about $1 billion a year.

A senior administration official said the Reagan proposal represented no threat to the Soviets and did not violate the Anti-Ballistic Missile Treaty signed more than a decade ago because the treaty did not bar research and development work on defensive systems (→ 29).

Reagan says Soviet Union is Evil Empire

March 8. President Reagan today denounced Soviet communism as "the focus of evil in the modern world."

Appearing before a convention of evangelical Christians, the president delivered one of the most forceful speeches of his two years in office on the subjects of theology and war, morality and government.

White House aides described the speech as something of a rebuttal to recent criticism of administration policy by the Roman Catholic hierarchy.

The president rejected as "a very dangerous fraud" calls for a nuclear freeze without additional Soviet arms reductions. "That is merely the illusion of peace," he said, adding that "the reality is that we must find peace through strength."

His speech received a standing ovation from the National Association of Evangelicals, meeting in Orlando, Florida. As delegates stood and applauded loudly, an orchestra played a lively rendition of "Onward Christian Soldiers" (→ 9).

Pope in Nicaragua assails leftist clergy

March 4. Pope John Paul II today assailed the left-leaning "People's Church" of Nicaragua and the Sandinista government, and told the faithful to obey their Bishop. His Holiness addressed nearly half a million persons in Managua, facing, as he spoke, a huge billboard which read, "Welcome to John Paul. Thanks to God and the revolution." The pope called the idea of an independent church "absurd and dangerous," saying it threatens Catholic unity (→ 22).

Liberation theology in Latin America offers a challenge to the Church's preferred distance from politics.

All OPEC members agree to cut oil prices

March 14. Moving to regain control over the world oil market, members of the Organization of Petroleum Exporting Countries today agreed to cut prices for the first time in the group's 25-year history.

Meeting in London, the 13 OPEC nations also agreed to set a production ceiling of 17.5 million barrels a day, one million below the current ceiling but at least 3.5 million more than current output.

Since 1974, the price of oil has risen from below $5 a barrel to $35 a barrel. The new agreement will cut the price of Saudi Arabian light crude, used as a benchmark, by 15 percent to $29 a barrel.

OPEC's action was caused by a steady decline in demand due to conservation measures brought on by the sharp price increases.

OPEC delegates hope the new limit on production will eventually reduce the abundant supplies of oil on the world market enough to make further price cuts unnecessary. But analysts say the success of the strategy depends on the willingness of member countries to abide by the individual production quotas and prices set by the pact. They said oil-producing nations such as Britain which are not OPEC members will sell at lower prices. British officials said it would be a week before they could evaluate the effect of the OPEC move (→ 10/18/84).

Koestler and wife exercise right to die

March 3. Free-thinker Arthur Koestler and his wife, Cynthia, committed suicide with sleeping pills tonight at their London home. The couple were members of a right-to-die organization, and 77-year-old Koestler suffered from Parkinson's disease. His wife, in her 50's, had no known illness.

Always one to take matters into his own hands, Koestler wrote and lived the life of an enemy of totalitarianism. Born in Hungary, he took part in the nation's brief Communist reign in 1919. He was imprisoned in Spain in the 1930's for opposing Franco and interned again in France for opposing the Vichy government. In 1941, he published "Darkness at Noon," an attack on bureaucracy's fatal methods.

Man sets self afire as TV cameras roll

March 4. An intoxicated man doused himself with lighter fluid and set himself afire while cameras rolled. Cecil Andrews called a Jacksonville, Alabama, TV station to let it know what he was planning to do in town square tonight. He is now at a hospital with second- and third-degree burns over most of his body. The cameramen tried to delay Andrews by telling him their equipment needed to warm up.

Nkomo on run after Zimbabwe arrests

Nkomo, opposition leader.

March 12. Joshua Nkomo, a political opponent of Zimbabwe Prime Minister Robert Mugabe, has fled the African nation after Mugabe ordered mass arrests last week.

Zimbabwe's security forces arrested 600 people in the suburbs of Bulawayo, a political base for opposition leader Nkomo. Nkomo, head of the Zimbabwe African People's Union, had been under virtual house arrest after officials confiscated his passport, preventing him from attending a Soviet-sponsored conference in Czechoslovakia.

From his London exile, Nkomo is expected to lead a campaign against Mugabe. Deserters from Zimbabwe's army have reportedly been killed. Mugabe ridiculed his rival's flight and said he is looking into charges of violence (→ 9/2/86).

1983

APRIL

Su	Mo	Tu	We	Th	Fr	Sa
					1	2
3	4	5	6	7	8	9
10	11	12	13	14	15	16
17	18	19	20	21	22	23
24	25	26	27	28	29	30

1. England: Anti-nuclear protesters form human chain 14 miles long (→ 27).

4. N.M.: N.C. State beats Houston 54-52 in final second for NCAA basketball title.

5. Satellite launched from shuttle fails to achieve orbit (→ 6/13).

7. China cancels 19 events with U.S. over defection of tennis star Hu Na (→ 4/26/84).

9. U.S. announces plan to set up training base for Nicaraguan rebels in Honduras (→ 14).

10. Portugal: Moderate PLO chief Issam Sartawi killed (→ 19).

11. L.A.: "Gandhi" wins eight Academy Awards.

16. China shells Vietnam border in reprisal for raids (→ 7/12/84).

16. Chile: U.S. embassies under Reagan reported losing ties with opposition in Latin America.

18. Boston: Greg Meyer wins Boston Marathon; Joan Benoit sets women's record at 2:22:42.

20. U.S. Supreme Court rules states are free to ban nuclear power plants (→ 6/5).

21. U.S. ousts three Soviet diplomats as spies (→ 4/11/84).

22. Gdansk: Lech Walesa given job at Lenin Shipyard (→ 5/1).

22. Bonn: Magazine Stern reports finding 60 volumes of Hitler diaries (→ 5/11).

23. Bonn: Yuri Andropov compares U.S. Latin policy to Soviet role in Afghanistan.

24. Timothy Leary lectures at Harvard first time in 20 years.

25. Portugal: Soares' Socialists win in vote (→ 2/16/86).

26. Washington: Commission on education warns "tide of mediocrity" imperils U.S.

27. Andropov asks U.S. to join in ban on space weapons (→ 5/3).

DEATHS

4. Gloria Swanson, American movie actress (*3/27/1899).

30. George Balanchine, U.S. Russian-born choreographer (*1/9/1904).

30. Muddy Waters, American blues musician (*4/4/1915).

U.S. Embassy is bombed

April 19. Following yesterday's bombing of the U.S. Embassy in Beirut, rescue workers continue round-the-clock efforts with bulldozers and cranes in a frantic search for survivors. The total death toll of 40 includes eight Americans killed and eight more presumed dead. Police believe the blast resulted from a suicide attack by a man driving a car loaded with about 300 pounds of TNT.

Responsibility has been claimed by three groups. One is the Islamic Jihad organization, a pro-Iranian Moslem group which also claims to have carried out the March 16 grenade attack against a patrol of U.S. Marines. Also claiming responsibility are the Arab Socialist Unionists, previously unheard of, and the Vengeance Organization of Sabra and Shatila Martyrs —the two Beirut refugee camps where hundreds of Palestinian civilians were killed last September by the militia of the Christian Phalangists.

The embassy, no longer a haven.

Police tend to discount the Islamic Jihad claim and have been questioning mostly Shiite Moslems and refugees from the two camps (→ 5/17).

Reagan says covert aid to Nicaragua legal

April 14. President Reagan maintained today that the administration was complying with recent congressional restrictions on aid to the contra rebels in Nicaragua. At the same time, the president, at a White House news conference, complained that his constitutional powers had been unduly restricted by the Boland amendment, which bans covert aid to the rebels.

Rep. Edward Boland of Massachusetts, author of the amendment, had said "the evidence is very strong" that the administration was violating the law. "We are complying with the law," the president said in response, while declining to be specific about the nature of American aid to the contras (→ 5/4).

April 6. King Kong, familiarly perched atop the Empire State Building, sprung a leak today.

Chicago elects its first black Mayor

April 13. Harold Washington has become the first black Mayor of Chicago. Washington defeated Bernard Epton in one of the fiercest campaigns ever waged in the Windy City. A record 82 percent of the city's 1.6 million registered voters went to the polls. Washington received 51 percent of the vote, Epton gained 48 percent; the voting followed racial lines as expected, but with more whites voting for Washington than blacks voting for Epton. The mayor-elect told his supporters, "We have finished our course and we have kept faith."

1983

MAY

Su	Mo	Tu	We	Th	Fr	Sa
1	2	3	4	5	6	7
8	9	10	11	12	13	14
15	16	17	18	19	20	21
22	23	24	25	26	27	28
29	30	31				

1. Warsaw: Solidarity rallies turn into clashes with police in 20 cities (→ 19).

3. U.S. reports increasing aid to Afghan rebels (→ 7/11/85).

7. Sunny's Halo wins 100th Kentucky Derby with J. Delahoussaye in the saddle.

10. Senate panel votes $20 mil. in aid to El Salvador, $30 mil. less than Reagan wanted (→ 25).

11. Soviets deny Sakharov right to travel abroad (→ 2/13/84).

12. N.J.: Judge clears way for trial of companies that produced Agent Orange (→ 5/7/84).

12. Chile: Two killed, 200 arrested in nationwide protests (→ 6/14).

14. Reagan pardons Watergate burglar Eugenio Martinez, denies pardons to Jeb Magruder and E. Howard Hunt.

16. Boston: Judge rules Reagan's curbs on Cuban travel invalid (→ 6/26/84).

16. N.Y.: Gunman at L.I. high school shoots student, principal and self, releasing 17 hostages.

17. U.S., Israel sign pact allowing Israeli retaliatory attacks in Lebanon (→ 6/21).

18. London: Degas painting sold for $3.74 mil., record for Impressionist art.

19. Warsaw: 20,000 march to funeral of youth killed by police after arrest (→ 6/17).

20. Pretoria: ANC bomb hits air force base, killing 16, injuring 190 (→ 9/12).

25. U.S.: "Return of the Jedi" sets opening-day box office record with $6,219,629.

25. El Salvador: Deputy chief of U.S. military group shot dead (→ 9/11).

27. Bonn: Konrad Kujau admits writing Hitler diaries.

29. Tom Sneva wins Indy 500.

29. Wales: Eight who conquered Mt. Everest hold reunion.

31. L.A.: Philadelphia 76ers beat Lakers 115-108 for NBA title.

DEATH

31. Jack Dempsey, American boxer (*6/24/1895).

Hitler diaries are exposed as fraudulent

Stern magazine, victim of hoax.

May 11. It seemed too incredible to be true and it was. In April, the West German magazine Stern said it had acquired a 60-volume diary written by Adolf Hitler during his last 13 years in power. The journal prepared to publish it and expected a whopping circulation. Yet historians had their doubts; Hitler routinely dictated dispatches and avoided paperwork. And suffering the effects of a bomb attack in 1944, Hitler's right hand was lame. Today, a Stern reporter admitted he bought the diary from a calligrapher from Stuttgart who wrote the volumes himself. The con artist has since fled the country (→ 27).

Catholic Bishops call for no nukes

May 3. The Roman Catholic Bishops of the U.S. ratified today a broad-ranging pastoral letter that denounces nuclear war and calls upon Catholics to help rid the world of nuclear weapons. The vote in favor of the letter, titled "The Challenge of Peace: God's Promise and Our Response," was 238 to 9. It points out that as the "first generation since Genesis with the power to virtually destroy God's creation," we must summon "the moral courage and technical means to say 'No' to an arms race which robs the poor and the vulnerable" (→ 6/20).

Communist Party is dissolved in Iran

The Islamic Revolution continues.

May 4. In related actions today, Iran's fundamentalist regime banned the country's Communist or Tudeh Party and ordered 18 Soviet diplomats to leave the country. The party has been under fire since February when 70 of its members were arrested for treason.

In recent days, Iranians have been shown the televised confessions by seven of the Tudeh's high-ranking members, several of whom admitted having passed political and military information to the Soviets. The Tudeh, numbering no more than 2,000, was founded during WWII under the influence of the Soviet occupation of northern Iran. It opposed the Shah, joined the Islamic Revolution that overthrew him, and has always supported Ayatollah Khomeini's policies. Its dissolution is attributed to a nationalistic faction as strongly anti-Soviet as it is anti-American (→ 8/19/86).

Contras are freedom fighters, Reagan says

May 4. President Reagan said today that the insurgent groups in Nicaragua receiving covert aid from the Central Intelligence Agency are "freedom fighters" who oppose a government that has betrayed its revolutionary principles.

It would be "all right with me," he said, if Congress wanted to require that assistance to the rebels be "overt instead of covert," but he added that there would have to be no further restrictions imposed on their activities.

In defending the rebel forces, the president said the Sandinista regime in Nicaragua, which took power in a revolution in 1979, was a "government out of the barrel of a gun," and he questioned its right to retain power.

Until now, the administration had maintained that the purpose of covert aid to the rebel groups in Nicaragua was to halt the flow of weapons. President Reagan's comments today marked the first time he or any other senior official had spoken of the desirability of aiding groups whose purpose was to challenge the ruling regime in Nicaragua. He said the rebels began their fight after their government abrogated their rights (→ 6/6).

2 compensated for decades of injustice

Justice was belatedly done in two cases this month. On May 7, a Chinese immigrant named David Tom was granted $400,000 from a federal court in Chicago. Tom was held in Illinois mental asylums for 31 years, treated by doctors who could not speak his dialect. On May 31, a 66-year-old Queens man received $1 million for being imprisoned 24 years for a murder he didn't commit. Isidore Zimmerman understood his lawyers would get a third of his award. "If I get half a million," he said, "that's a lot."

Islanders take fourth straight Stanley Cup

Mike Bossy holds the cup aloft.

May 17. The Islanders swept to their fourth straight Stanley Cup, but, like Rodney Dangerfield, they still "don't get no respect." The suburban New York team completed its cup triumph with a 4-2 victory over the Edmonton Oilers. The Islanders fought off Oiler rallies led by Wayne Gretzky, who broke his own assist record this year with 125.

Butch Goring, the Islanders center, felt the win was still not enough to win recognition. "We're not the New York Yankees," said Goring, a veteran of all four championship clubs. "We don't go around telling everyone how great we are. We just go out on the ice every night and show how good we are."

The Montreal Canadiens hold the record for consecutive championships, five from 1956 to 1960, but they also won four straight times from 1976 through 1979.

May 24. The Brooklyn Bridge, on its 100th birthday, received one of America's grandest pyrotechnic displays. And rightly so. Tallest sight on New York's skyline in 1883, the bridge marked a city in motion and was hailed as the greatest engineering work of the age. Its granite towers, criticized then as too romantic, bridge past and present. As Harper's Weekly of May 24, 1883, remarked, it is "our most durable monument."

1983

JUNE

Su	Mo	Tu	We	Th	Fr	Sa
			1	2	3	4
5	6	7	8	9	10	11
12	13	14	15	16	17	18
19	20	21	22	23	24	25
26	27	28	29	30		

1. Peru: Hundreds arrested in attempt to stamp out insurgency.

2. Paris: Leopold Senghor becomes first black elected to French Academy.

4. U.S.S.R.: Over 100 killed as passenger ship rams railroad bridge on Volga River.

5. N.Y.: 138 arrested at sit-in at Shoreham nuclear power plant (→ 4/29/84).

6. Nicaragua expels three U.S. diplomats for plotting to kill foreign minister (→ 7).

6. U.S. State Dept. denies visa to Irish nationalist Bernadette Devlin (→ 11/20).

8. Washington: 64 religious leaders urge Congress to ban genetic engineering (→ 7/23/86).

8. U.S. presidential panel concludes man-made pollution is a major cause of acid rain (→ 7/5).

12. U.K.: Michael Foot resigns as Labor Party chief after Conservative victory (→ 3/3/85).

13. Pioneer 10, in space 11 years, becomes first craft to leave solar system (→ 18).

14. U.S. Civil Rights Commission faults Reagan for lax enforcement of civil rights legislation in schools (→ 11/2).

14. Chile: Hundreds of thousands join anti-Pinochet protests (→ 8/12).

15. U.S. Supreme Court reaffirms constitutional right to abortion (→ 1/3/85).

16. Federal panel recommends paying $1.5 bil. to Japanese interned in U.S. during WWII.

17. Warsaw: Pope asks Poland to lift martial law (→ 7/21).

18. Florida: Sally Ride becomes first U.S. woman in space (→ 24).

20. Calif.: 950 arrested in protest at nuclear arms lab (→ 10/29).

21. Beirut: PLO rebels seize eight Arafat positions (→ 7/22).

21. Honduras: Two U.S. reporters killed on Nicaraguan border (→ 7/26).

24. Laurent Fignon wins Tour de France.

25. Manila: George Schultz reaffirms U.S. support for Marcos regime (→ 8/21).

First American woman Sally Ride's in space

Ride and the crew prepare to board.

June 24. The space shuttle Challenger landed at Edwards Air Force Base in California today after a six-day mission that made Sally K. Ride the first American woman to go into space. The 32-year-old physicist was one of five crew members aboard Challenger as it made the seventh shuttle flight.

During the mission, crew members deployed two satellites, from Canada and Indonesia. Using the shuttle's robotic arm, Ride placed a West German satellite in orbit and then retrieved it, in what space officials said was a preview of an era in which satellites will routinely be repaired or serviced without being brought back to earth.

Challenger's return was watched by 250,000 spectators, many wearing T-shirts that read, "Ride Sally, Ride."

The only flaw was the failure to follow the original plan to bring Challenger back to earth at a landing strip at Cape Canaveral. Officials said the weather report for Florida was for clouds and rain that could cause damage to the delicate heat-resistant tiles that protect the spacecraft during re-entry (→ 8/30).

AIDS risk assessed

June 5. There is little risk of contracting AIDS, the deadly condition that destroys the body's immune defenses, through blood transfusions, health officials said today. Ten cases of AIDS have been linked to the ten million transfusions in the U.S. in the past three years, and measures are being taken to screen out high-risk donors (→ 4/21/84).

Strikeout record set

June 7. Steve Carlton of the Phillies lost the game but became the leading strikeout pitcher in baseball today. Carlton fanned six Cardinals for a career total of 3,526. Carlton passed Nolan Ryan of the Astros with his 3,522nd strikeout. Two months earlier, Ryan had eclipsed the mark of 3,508 set by Walter Johnson in 1927.

Anti-Sandinista sabotage manual exposed

Sandinistas, pressed by the CIA.

June 7. Relations between the United States and Nicaragua have plummeted to their lowest level since the Sandinistas deposed President Somoza in 1979. First it was revealed that anti-government forces bankrolled by the CIA carry an instruction manual on how to sabotage factory machinery in Nicaragua. Then the Sandinista government expelled three Americans, including the alleged CIA station chief in Managua. They were accused of a bizarre plot to assassinate the Foreign Minister with an adulterated bottle of alcohol. Today, the United States ordered all six Nicaraguan consulates closed and gave 21 diplomats until Monday to leave the country (→ 21).

Thatcher sweeps to victory in Britain

Thatcher: "Nothing to it."

June 9. The Conservative government of Margaret Thatcher has won a landslide victory by a margin large enough to guarantee Mrs. Thatcher a full five-year second term as Prime Minister of Britain. Although a year ago Mrs. Thatcher's popularity was at an all-time low, she regained the confidence of her nation when she recaptured the Falkland Islands from Argentina and was able to defeat her main opposition, the Labor Party, in the election.

Labor Party officials blame their loss on a third party, the Liberal-Social Democratic alliance, which split the anti-Thatcher vote. Denis Healey, a Labor leader, said the election "put the people at the mercy of the most reactionary, right-wing, extremist government in all of British history." Seen as part of a right-wing trend in the West, the election may encourage President Reagan to run for re-election (→ 12).

June 5. Talented Yannick Noah, discovered in Africa by Arthur Ashe, has won the French Open.

1983

JULY

Su	Mo	Tu	We	Th	Fr	Sa
					1	2
3	4	5	6	7	8	9
10	11	12	13	14	15	16
17	18	19	20	21	22	23
24	25	26	27	28	29	30
31						

1. Poll shows most Americans do not know who U.S. supports in Central America.

3. Wimbledon: McEnroe over Chris Lewis 6-2, 6-2, 6-2; Navratilova over Andrea Jaeger 6-0, 6-3.

4. New York: Dave Righetti pitches baseball's first no-hitter since 1981.

9. Texas: Chairman of Natl. Women's Caucus asks Reagan to forego re-election (→ 10/31).

12. Wales: Two organists play 17-hour piece by Erik Satie.

15. Louisiana: V.P. Bush booed at NAACP meeting (→ 11/2).

17. Britain: Tom Watson wins his fifth British Open.

17. Mexico: Four Contadora nations call for end to conflict in Central America (→ 28).

18. Siberia: Seven Greenpeace members arrested in protest over Soviet whaling (→ 23).

20. House censures Reps. Daniel Crane, Gerry Studds for sex with congressional pages.

20. Iraq says U.S. weapons pour into Iran (→ 24).

22. Philip Habib replaced by Robert McFarlane as U.S. Mideast negotiator (→ 8/5).

23. Alaska: Soviets free seven Greenpeace members.

24. N.Y.: Yankees beat K.C. Royals as George Brett homer nullified for pine tar on bat.

26. Cuba: Castro accuses U.S. of creating "atmosphere of terror" around Nicaragua (→ 28).

27. Lisbon: Seven killed as Armenian gunmen storm residence of Turkish ambassador.

28. Washington: House votes to halt covert aid to Nicaraguan contras by Sept. 30.→

DEATHS

1. Buckminster Fuller, eclectic U.S. inventor, conceived geodesic dome (*7/12/1895).

29. Luis Bunuel, Spanish film director (*2/22/1900).

29. David Niven, British actor (*3/1/1909).

30. Lynn Fontanne, American stage actress (*12/6/1887).

Latin nations call for end to war in region

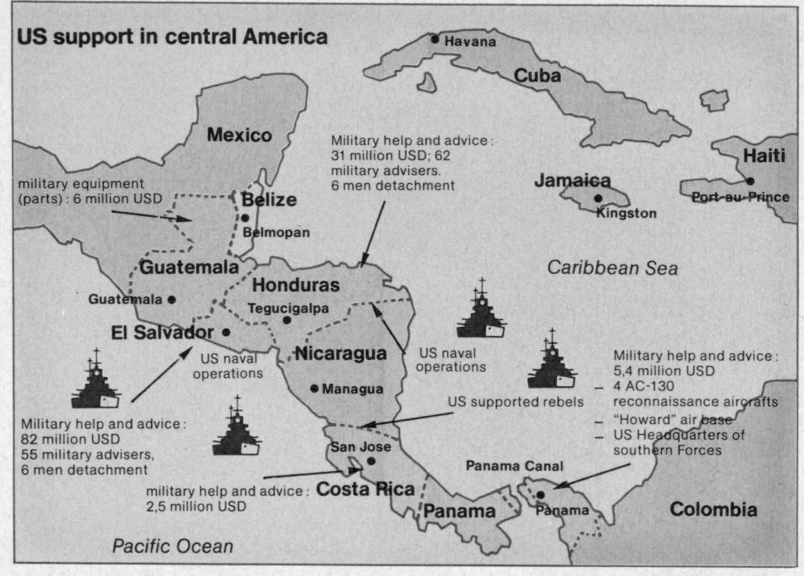

In 1900, the Caribbean was an American lake; today, it is a sea of troubles.

July 28. President Reagan is moving to increase United States military involvement in Nicaragua despite international and domestic opposition. Latin American leaders are calling for the removal of all foreign bases and forces from the area. And the House of Representatives voted today to cancel all covert aid to the anti-Sandinista rebels.

The Presidents of Mexico, Venezuela, Colombia and Panama released a communique stating "profound concern for the rapid deterioration" of the situation in Central America. Their quickly arranged meeting grew out of an earlier gathering of their foreign ministers, the so-called Contadora Group. Miguel de la Madrid Hurtado, the President of Mexico, made a separate appeal to President Reagan and Fidel Castro to reject the use of force in Central America.

Despite the appeal, Reagan has approved expanded military movements in Honduras and a possible military blockade of Nicaragua. Word of his plans gave House critics the ammunition they needed today to vote a cutoff in contra aid. In an effort to deflect criticism, Reagan has named former Secretary of State Kissinger to head a panel to investigate American options in Central America (→ 9/8).

Agca claims KGB aided murder plot

July 9. In a surprising revelation to journalists today, Mehmet Ali Agca, who is serving a life sentence in an Italian prison for the attempted assassination of Pope John Paul II in May 1981, said that the Soviet secret police and Bulgarian agents took part in the plot on the pontiff's life. In an interview with A.G.I., the independent Italian news agency, Agca linked the KGB with the assassination attempt, and named Sergei Ivanov Antonov, a Bulgarian airline official arrested for complicity in the shooting, as his accomplice. Tass, the Soviet news agency, has labeled Agca's claims "threadbare" (→ 6/9/84).

Polish government lifts martial law

July 21. Polish officials said today they are formally lifting the state of martial law which has restricted the lives of Poles for 19 months. Polish leader General Wojciech Jaruzelski imposed martial law in December 1981 to break the back of the independent Solidarity trade union. Despite today's move, Poles will not see much difference; many of the provisions of martial have simply been written into the legal code. Jaruzelski said the end of martial law is "proof of the goodwill of the authorities." Yet, he added firmly, "Any attempts at anti-Socialist activities will be muzzled no less decisively than before" (→ 12/10).

Dioxin used despite evidence of danger

July 5. The Dow Chemical Company continued to sell herbicides contaminated with dioxin for years after it knew that the chemical could cause serious health problems and even death, according to documents opened to public inspection today. Dow withheld its concern from the government as it sold large quantities of a dioxin-contaminated herbicide, Agent Orange, to the Army for use in Vietnam, the documents showed. They were made public by a federal judge on Long Island who is hearing a multibillion-dollar lawsuit against several chemical companies by 20,000 Vietnam veterans who claim they were damaged by Agent Orange (→ 8/4).

Iraq says U.S. gives weapons to Iranians

July 24. As fighting continues along the Iran-Iraq border, both sides claim to have made significant military advances. In the second day of an Iranian offensive against Iraqi positions near the town of Ruwandiz, the Iranian press announced that they had met all goals of the attack. But an Iraqi communique claimed that they "crushed and destroyed enemy attacks."

This follows recent Iraqi claims that American weapons have been flowing into Iran, prolonging the conflict. While Iraq avoided direct accusations of the Reagan administration, it suggested Washington could help end the war by stopping arms shipments. The Iraqis say that they can use French-made weapons to continue the fight "for several years if not forever" (→ 7/14/85).

Iran has opened a new drive on Iraq.

1983

AUGUST

Su	Mo	Tu	We	Th	Fr	Sa
	1	2	3	4	5	6
7	8	9	10	11	12	13
14	15	16	17	18	19	20
21	22	23	24	25	26	27
28	29	30	31			

3. U.S. sues G.M. for selling X cars despite knowledge of brake defects.

4. Washington: Rita Lavelle indicted for lying about actions with EPA (→ 10/9).

4. Rome: Bettino Craxi sworn in as first Italian Socialist premier.

5. Lebanon: Car bomb kills 19 in front of mosque (→ 28).

6. U.S. to send AWAC's and F-15's to aid Chad against Libyan-backed rebels (→ 16).

7. Calif.: Jack Nicklaus wins PGA golf title.

7. Soviets order harsh punishment for drinking at work.

8. Guatemala: Gen. Mejia deposes Gen. Rios Montt in coup.

8. Missouri: Christine Craft, anchorwoman demoted for appearance, awarded $500,000 in suit (→ 10/31).

14. France: Pope arrives on pilgrimage to Lourdes (→ 1/10/84).

17. Reagan approves sale of heavy water to Argentina for use in atomic plant (→ 11/18).

18. Moscow: 16-year-old son of Soviet diplomat returns, denying letters of intent to defect.

21. Manila: Opposition leader Benigno Aquino murdered on return from U.S. exile (→ 22).

21. France sends ten combat planes to Chad (→ 1/27/84).

22. Manila: Marços accuses foes of trying to spread panic in Philippines (→ 24).

24. U.S. pledges to cool ties with Marcos if govt. implicated in Aquino murder (→ 27).

24. Seattle: Benjamin Ng, 20, found guilty of 13 murders in Chinatown gambling den.

27. Washington: 200,000 march seeking new coalition for social and political change.

28. Beirut: U.S. Marines shoot back for first time in battle near airport (→ 29).

29. Beirut: Two U.S. Marines killed, 14 wounded as fighting grows (→ 9/17).

30. Florida: Space shuttle Challenger launched, putting five astronauts in orbit (→ 11/28).

Benigno Aquino gunned down in Manila

Aquino lies dead at the airport in Manila after his return from exile in U.S.

Aug 22. Philippine President Ferdinand E. Marcos took to television tonight to deny rumors that his government was responsible for yesterday's assassination of Benigno S. Aquino Jr. Aquino was killed yesterday by a single shot in the head as he got off an airplane at Manila Airport with a military escort, who immediately killed the unidentified assassin. Considered Marcos' main political rival, Aquino had just ended three years of self-exile in the United States to return home, despite death threats. The shooting occurred as thousands of his followers waited to greet him, and was quickly denounced by them as a government assassination (→ 9/4).

France intervenes in Chad civil war

Aug 16. France has dispatched hundreds of soldiers to Chad, a former colony, to bolster the government and fight rebels who are reportedly backed by Libya. The Reagan administration has promised to send President Hissen Habre $25 million worth of military assistance. Rebel and government forces have been fighting a see-saw battle for several towns in northern Chad, and the rebels recently recaptured the oasis of Faya-Largeau.

"We ask all countries," Habre said at a news conference today, "in Africa, Latin America, Asia and Europe, to help Chad in its legitimate defense. Libya is nothing but an aggressor." Habre also accused Libya's leader, Col. Muammar Khadafy, of using "Soviet tactics" by moving large numbers of planes, tanks and artillery against Faya-Largeau. "It was genocide," he said. "We have seen nothing like it except in films of the Second World War." The Libyan news agency denies Libya is involved in the Chadian civil war (→ 21).

Pinochet regime battles rioters in Chile

Aug 12. Recent nationwide protests throughout Chile calling for the resignation of President Augusto Pinochet erupted in the worst violence of his ten-year rule yesterday when police and soldiers in Santiago gunned down 17 civilians, including three children. Some 1,200 people were arrested.

The fourth such protest in as many months was called by the Democratic Alliance, a coalition of moderate parties headed by the Christian Democrats. Chilean unemployment is about 20%, with another 13% engaged in emergency works programs. A deepening recession led the nation's normally placid 11 million people to begin demonstrating last year.

Yesterday's violence occurred mostly in lower-middle-class neighborhoods where barricades made of ignited tires were still smoking today. The rioting came days after Pinochet made his fifth Cabinet revision within a year by naming men who favor talks with the opposition. His rule is supposed to end in 1989 and his advisers have urged him to ease the transition by holding local elections (→ 9/4/84).

A protester is arrested in Santiago.

Chad rebels, clad for desert combat.

U.S. admits hiring alleged Nazi criminal

Aug 16. The man reviled in France as the alleged "Butcher of Lyons" is more than a former Gestapo officer. Klaus Barbie was also a spy for the United States, and American officials rewarded him by helping him escape to Bolivia after the Second World War. Barbie was extradited recently to France, where he is accused of torturing and killing resistance fighters and deporting thousands of Jews. The White House admitted today that Barbie was used as an anti-Communist spy after the war. An apology was made to the French Embassy.

1983

SEPTEMBER

Su	Mo	Tu	We	Th	Fr	Sa
				1	2	3
4	5	6	7	8	9	10
11	12	13	14	15	16	17
18	19	20	21	22	23	24
25	26	27	28	29	30	

1. U.S.S.R.: Korean jetliner with 269 aboard disappears off Soviet island of Sakhalin (→ 4).

3. U.S. Census reports world population at 4.72 bil.; China has 1.05 bil., India 731 mil.

4. U.S. admits spy plane was in same area two hours before downing of Korean jet (→ 15).

4. Manila: Cory Aquino rejects central political role (→ 21).

8. Nicaragua: Rebel planes attack Managua, hitting airport and residential areas (→ 10/1).

8. Austria: Czech family of four escapes in hot air balloon made of raincoats.

9. Argentina: Pres. Bignone pardons Isabel Peron (→ 23).

11. N.Y.: Connors wins his fifth U.S. Open, Navratilova her first.

11. El Salvador: Archbishop condemns increase in activity of death squads (→ 10/3).

12. South Africa: 64 killed in coal mine blast (→ 3/16/84).

17. Lebanon: U.S. ships bomb Syrian areas (→ 10/12).

19. New York: Top commodity trader Marc Rich indicted on $48 mil. tax evasion, biggest in U.S. history (→ 5/28/86).

21. Manila: Seven anti-Marcos protesters killed by police (→ 29).

22. Washington: Sec. of Int. Watt apologizes for remark about "a black, a woman, two Jews and a cripple" (→ 10/9).

23. Argentina: Police and army get amnesty for crimes against leftists in 1970's (→ 12/20).

26. Australia wins America's Cup, ending 132-year U.S. reign.

29. Manila: Marcos closes newspaper for hinting military helped kill Aquino (→ 30).

29. New York: "A Chorus Line" holds record 3,389th performance on Broadway.

30. Manila: Chief justice resigns from Aquino inquiry (→ 10/2).

DEATHS

10. Balthazar Johannes Vorster, ex-leader of South Africa (*12/13/1915).

25. Leopold II, ex-king of Belgium (*11/3/1901).

Soviets down Korean jetliner; 269 die

Soviet Union's Nikolai V. Ogarkov gives the official version of the circumstances surrounding the tragedy.

Sept 15. In a unanimous vote, the Senate condemned the Soviet Union's shooting down of Korean Airlines Flight 007. The resolution, passed yesterday by the House, calls the destruction of the plane a "brutal massacre" and demands reparations for the families of the victims. Some 269 people were aboard the Korean 747 jet when it disappeared from radar screens on the 1st. Sixty-one of the passengers were Americans, including Georgia Congressman Larry McDonald, the Chairman of the John Birch Society. The Soviet action has already been denounced by President Reagan as "barbarous." The Soviets claim the plane was on a spying mission for the United States.

It took almost a week after the plane vanished for the Soviet Union to give an explanation. The plane was on a flight from New York to Seoul when it was reported missing. It disappeared over the highly strategic Sakhalin Island, off Siberia, and first reports said it might have been forced to land by Soviet jet fighters. Later that day, a Korean Airlines spokesman speculated about an explosion on the plane. Little was heard from the Soviets until they held a very unusual, full-blown news conference on the 6th.

Soviet military officials said a pilot had been ordered to "stop the flight" because the jet was flying in restricted airspace "without navigation lights, at the height of night, in conditions of bad visibility and was not answering signals." The Soviets charged that the civilian plane was on a spy mission and that "the entire responsibility for this tragedy rests" with the United States.

The Soviets held the news conference after the United States played a chilling tape identified as the voice of the Russian pilot who shot down the plane. "I am closing in on the target," he said. "Am in lock-in. I have executed the launch. The target is destroyed."

Sept 17. Vanessa Williams is 1st black Miss America(→ 7/23/84).

Israel's Begin resigns, replaced by Shamir

Sept 2. Yitzhak Shamir was elected this morning to succeed Menachem Begin as leader of Israel's Herut Party. That makes Shamir a shoo-in to be the next prime minister. Begin has refused to give any reasons for his resignation. He has been widely perceived as melancholy and withdrawn since the death of his wife last November. Begin also has heart and circulatory problems. Like Begin, Shamir is a former guerrilla leader. He is expected to continue hard-line policies on the West Bank. Shamir opposed the peace treaty with Egypt (→ 10/10).

Begin, mourning death of his wife.

1983

OCTOBER

Su	Mo	Tu	We	Th	Fr	Sa
						1
2	3	4	5	6	7	8
9	10	11	12	13	14	15
16	17	18	19	20	21	22
23	24	25	26	27	28	29
30	31					

1. Miami: CIA reported using Salvadoran air base to supply Nicaraguan rebels (→ 15).

1. Detroit: Ford marks 75th anniversary of Model T.

2. Philippines: Rebels kill 46 in ambush on army patrol (→ 4).

4. Reagan sends note to Marcos reasserting friendship (→ 11/27).

6. India dismisses state govt. of Punjab to halt religious and political violence (→ 4/3/84).

9. Washington: James Watt resigns as sec. of int. (→ 13).

9. Seoul: Bomb kills 19, including six top officials (→ 2/9/85).

10. Israel: Yitzhak Shamir named premier (→ 7/23/84).

11. Japan: Ex-Premier Tanaka found guilty of taking $2.1 mil. to assure Lockheed contracts (→ 8/28/86).

12. Reagan signs bill to stay in Lebanon 18 months (→ 23).

13. Reagan names William Clark sec. of int. (→ 12/1).

15. CIA said to help contras plan recent attacks (→ 1/11/84).

16. Philadelphia: Orioles beat Phillies for World Series title.

17. Reagan names Robert Mcrlane as natl. sec. adviser.

19. Grenada: Prime Minister Maurice Bishop killed in military coup (→ 21).

21. U.S. sends ten-ship task force to Grenada (→ 25).

22. New York: Metropolitan Opera celebrates 100th birthday with day-long concert.

23. Beirut: Truck bombs level U.S. Marine post (→ 25).

25. Reagan announces pre-dawn invasion of Grenada (→ 26).

26. Reagan bars reporters from covering Grenada (→ 31).

DEATHS

6. Terence Cardinal Cooke of New York (*3/1/1921).

10. Sir Ralph Richardson, British actor (*12/19/1902).

17. Raymond Aron, French sociologist (*3/14/1905).

31. George Halas, founder U.S. pro football (*2/2/1895).

216 Marines killed in Beirut bombing

Surveying the damage in Beirut.

Oct 25. General Paul X. Kelley, the United States Marine commandant, has arrived in Beirut to investigate the terrorist assault on Marine headquarters. Rescuers have pulled 216 bodies from the charred metal and collapsed cement of the airport complex. As many as 30 more bodies may still be buried in the rubble. New questions were raised about security at the headquarters and about the Reagan administration's involvement in the fragile, volatile politics of Lebanon.

One single-minded terrorist is responsible for all the devastation. On Sunday, he drove a Mercedes truck filled with at least 2,500 pounds of explosives past sentries and through barricades at the headquarters. The truck crashed into the building, exploded in a large fireball and turned four stories of the structure into burning rubble. "I haven't seen carnage like that since Vietnam," a Marine spokesman said. High-rise buildings all over Beirut shuddered with the force of the blast.

Two minutes after the attack, another truck filled with explosives slammed into the compound used by French peacekeeping forces. Fifty-eight people were killed.

A telephone caller to Agence France Presse said that a group called the Free Islamic Revolution Movement was responsible for the explosion. White House officials said terrorists with links to Iran are to blame. The two suicide missions were similar to the attack on the United States Embassy which killed 63 people in April.

A Marine searches for survivors.

A Marine spokesman said no special precautions were taken at the headquarters after the embassy attack. President Reagan's congressional critics said the role of the Marines in Beirut was ill-defined, and Senator Robert Byrd, the minority leader, blamed Reagan for "a fundamental miscalculation in foreign policy." The president has dispatched 300 Marines to Beirut to replace the fallen peacekeepers. Reagan said keeping the Marines in Beirut is "central to our credibility on a global scale" (→ 11/4).

Millions in Europe protest U.S. missiles

Oct 29. Princess Irene of the Dutch royal family broke with tradition today when she joined a peaceful rally of some 500,000 persons at the Hague to protest NATO's deployment of intermediate-range missiles, to begin in England and West Germany next month. Royalty customarily keeps silent on sensitive political issues. "The weapons we have built," the princess said, "have now put us on the edge of the abyss and we cannot afford one more mistake." Last week saw similarly heavy protest demonstrations in West Germany, Britain, Stockholm, Rome, Paris and Brussels (→ 11/14).

Anti-nuclear activists in Bonn built a mock U.S. Pershing II missile.

22 African nations facing starvation

Oct 18. The United Nations Food and Agriculture Organization warns that 22 African countries are facing catastrophic food shortages. The agency is convening a 57-nation meeting in Rome to deal with the crisis, caused not only by weather but by extreme population growth, nomadic farming, administrative weaknesses and a scarcity of trained people and research services.

Comparing the present situation with the famine of 1973-74, which took the lives of hundreds of thousands and left many more with lasting damage from malnutrition, the current crisis is threatening a much wider area. The drought is parching even wet, tropical countries such as Lesotho, Botswana and Zambia. The U.N. pleads for immediate aid to Chad, Ethiopia, Ghana and Mozambique to ward off a mass starvation tragedy (→ 10/27/84).

U.S. troops swarm tiny Grenada island

Oct 31. More than 1,900 U.S. Marines stormed the shores of a small Caribbean island this month to help restore democratic institutions and defeat a band of what President Reagan called "Cuban thugs." American troops trounced Cuban resistance forces on the island of Grenada as easily as a first-place sports team might demolish a last-place loser. The invasion elicited denunciations from several nations and in the United Nations. The U.S. press was banned from covering the assault's initial stages.

Sixteen Americans died and 77 were injured in the fighting; three are still missing. Reports of enemy casualties have yet to be gathered, but about 630 Cubans have been taken prisoner. A dispatch by an English journalist indicates 47 mental patients were killed during a U.S. aerial attack on a mental hospital.

The events leading to the American intervention show a tiny nation in political turmoil. The island's Prime Minister, Maurice Bishop, had been placed under house arrest by the commander of the military, General Hudson Austin. However, a group of his supporters gained Bishop's release. When Bishop and his people marched to a military installation to demand the freedom of several colleagues, the prime minister was jailed again by Austin and the radical Deputy Prime Minister, Bernard Coard. Coard and Bishop, both Marxists with Soviet and Cuban ties, differed on the role private industry should play in the development of the economy; Bishop encouraged private investment. After resisting efforts to reinstate the old government, Coard and the army killed Bishop and many of his aides, sparking American plans to invade.

President Reagan gave many reasons for the action, including: the recent construction of an airstrip by Soviet and Cuban engineers for the purpose of exporting communism throughout Latin America; a call for help by some members of the Organization of Eastern Caribbean States; and the protection of 1,000 Americans living in Grenada, including U.S. citizens attending a medical school in St. Georges, endangered by a "shoot-on-site curfew" imposed by the new radical regime. Finally, while not stated by Reagan, it is believed he wished to send a message to other Latin American nations, particularly Nicaragua, that the U.S. will not tolerate Marxism in this hemisphere.

Condemnations of the assault were quick to come. The U.S.S.R. referred to the invasion as "an act of undisguised banditry." Many Latin American states denounced the attack as another example of "American imperialist intervention." Even the Allies were critical. British Prime Minister Thatcher, usually a supporter of Reagan, had urged him not to invade. France described it as "a surprising action in relation to international law."

The most stunning denunciation came from the U.N. Security Council. Member nations voted to approve a resolution "deeply deploring" the invasion as a "flagrant violation of international law."

A furor was stirred among newsmen as Reagan barred reporters from Grenada and placed restrictions on press coverage of the invasion's initial days, claiming secrecy was imperative for a successful attack. Most news agencies assailed the restrictions. And a Washington Post journalist opined, "I think a secret war, like a secret government, is antithetical to an open society. It's absolutely outrageous."

Despite the controversy, the United States accomplished its goals and the military is now mopping up in Grenada, readying the island-nation for a new democratic government (→ 11/6).

American Marines escort a group of 50 Cubans to be expelled from Grenada.

U.S. Marines display a cache of arms found on the tiny Caribbean island.

U.S. condemns right wing death squads

Oct 3. The State Department deplored an upsurge of right-wing violence in El Salvador that it said was undermining efforts to promote democracy in the Central American country. A State Department spokesman said the violence being committed by secret groups known as death squads was "anathema to the very centrist and moderate basis of support on which the development of pluralistic, democratic institutions in El Salvador depends." The statement particularly criticized the recent kidnapping of the director of economic and social affairs in the Salvadoran Foreign Ministry by a right-wing group (→ 1/1/84).

TV anchor loses sex discrimination suit

Oct 31. Newscaster Christine Craft, awarded $500,000 months ago in a sex discrimination suit, has seen that decision overturned. A federal judge in Kansas City has ruled her employer, KMBC-TV, was justified in firing her because viewers found her too informal in dress, too opinionated and lacking "warmth and comfort" (→ 11/15).

New Bible says God is without gender

Oct 14. The National Council of Churches released today a new translation of certain Bible passages in which gender references to God are blurred or omitted. God is called either Father and Mother or the One, and "man" is replaced by humanity or humankind. The authors hoped to please women worshippers who felt excluded by the Bible's patriarchal language.

A passage from Galatians, "God has sent the Spirit of his Son into our hearts, crying Abba! Father!" now reads "God has sent the Spirit of the Child into our hearts, crying God! My Mother and Father!"

The Lutheran and Greek Orthodox Churches have stated they will not use the material, citing its inaccuracy and irreverence (→ 31).

1983

NOVEMBER

Su	Mo	Tu	We	Th	Fr	Sa
		1	2	3	4	5
6	7	8	9	10	11	12
13	14	15	16	17	18	19
20	21	22	23	24	25	26
27	28	29	30			

1. China: U.S. oil ship with 81 aboard sinks in South China Sea.

2. Reagan signs bill making Martin Luther King's birthday a national holiday (→ 12/2).

3. Washington: Rev. Jesse Jackson announces candidacy for pres. as Democrat (→ 12/24).

4. Lebanon: 60 die as truck bomb hits Israeli post (→ 6).

6. Libya: One of Arafat's two strongholds falls to Syrian-backed PLO rebels (→ 12/20).

8. Philadelphia: Wilson Goode elected first black mayor of city (→ 5/13/85).

8. N.Y.: James Hayden, actor playing heroin addict on Broadway, dies of heroin overdose.

9. New York: Ex-CIA agent Edwin Wilson gets 25 years for plot to murder witnesses.

9. Amsterdam: Brewer Alfred Heineken kidnapped (→ 30).

12. Washington: Thousands attend rally protesting U.S. policies in Central America.

13. Korea: Reagan calls Korean border "Freedom's front" (→ 11/23/84).

15. U.S. Congress defeats move to revive ERA (→ 7/12/84).

15. Cyprus: Turkish Cypriots proclaim separate nation.

18. Argentina announces ability to produce enriched unranium for nuclear weapons.

19. Conn.: Harvard beats Yale 16-7 in 100th football game.

20. Ireland: Gunmen kill three in Protestant church (→ 3/14/84).

23. Geneva: Soviets break off talks with U.S. on medium-range missiles (→ 24).

24. Soviets to bolster sub missiles in response to U.S. missiles in Europe (→ 1/16/84).

26. London: $40 mil. in gold stolen at Heathrow airport (→ 12/7).

27. Madrid: 176 dead as Colombian 747 crashes.

27. Manila: Tens of thousands rally on birthday of Benigno Aquino (→ 8/21/84).

28. Florida: Columbia carries European-built research lab into orbit (→ 1/25/84).

Americans mop up on Grenada island

Nov 6. U.S. troops on Grenada have found about 100 bodies in a training camp on the island, and one is believed to be that of Maurice Bishop, the former Prime Minister, who was reported to have been killed by rival forces. It has taken about two weeks for American troops to defeat resisters, as the Defense Department announced that "hostilities have ceased." Marines on the island are mopping up and should pull out within a few days. American forces are to be replaced by contingents of peacekeeping troops from Canada and New Zealand (→ 12/4/84).

Ex-leader Bishop, found murdered.

First cruise missiles arrive in England

Nov 14. The first of a new generation of American-made cruise missiles have arrived at a British air base, the British government said.

The announcement by Defense Secretary Michael Heseltine in the House of Commons was greeted by howls of protest from opposition legislators, who charged the government with "reckless cynicism" in permitting deployment of the missiles while the United States and Soviet Union were conducting arms negotiations in Geneva. West Germany is expected to approve stationing of American medium-range missiles on its soil next week.

By 1988, 572 American missiles are scheduled to be deployed in Europe in response to the stationing by the Soviet Union of 252 SS-20 missiles on its frontiers (→ 23).

Heineken is rescued from Dutch captors

Nov 30. Ten policemen raided an unguarded warehouse in Amsterdam and freed the kidnapped brewery king, Alfred H. Heineken, 60, and his chauffeur, 57, from unheated concrete cells where they had been chained for 21 days. Later, 24 suspects were arrested, all Dutch citizens and all related to each other. Part of the ransom, rumored to exceed $10 million, was recovered. The two were abducted by three hooded gunmen Nov. 9 outside the Heineken headquarters, shortly after a luncheon Heineken gave for police who foiled an attempt to extort millions from the brewery.

Israel and the PLO trade prisoners

Nov 24. Six Israeli soldiers seem to be worth about 5,000 Palestinians. On the face of it, that is the agreement worked out between Israel and the PLO. Yasir Arafat's organization released six Israeli prisoners today. In exchange, the Israeli government freed 1,100 Palestinians who had been captured in the war in Lebanon. Up to 4,000 more Palestinians are scheduled to be released as soon as the Israelis arrive back home.

The Palestinians ran to jumbo jets at Ben Gurion Airport in Tel Aviv flashing victory signs. They were flown to Algeria, and there is speculation that Arafat may try to transport them back to Lebanon as soon as possible. Arafat is pinned down in Tripoli by the Syrians and rival Palestinian factions. At the moment, he appears to need all the help that he can get (→ 12/20).

Arafat, pinned down in Tripoli.

1983

DECEMBER

Su	Mo	Tu	We	Th	Fr	Sa
				1	2	3
4	5	6	7	8	9	10
11	12	13	14	15	16	17
18	19	20	21	22	23	24
25	26	27	28	29	30	31

1. Washington: Federal jury finds ex-EPA aide Rita Lavelle guilty of perjury (→ 2/3/84).

2. Reagan admin. attacks hiring quotas for blacks (→ 1/17/84).

4. Syria: Two U.S. planes downed in attack on anti-aircraft positions (→ 30).

6. London: $11.7 mil. paid for medieval book "Gospels of Henry the Lion."

7. London: Seven held for Heathrow airport gold theft.

12. Kuwait: Car bomb kills 7, injures 62 at U.S. Embassy.

14. Calif.: Photo shown of black hole at center of Milky Way.

17. London: Five killed in bomb blast outside Harrods; 91 hurt.

22. Calif.: Judge orders paralyzed Elizabeth Bouvia fed against her wishes (→ 6/11/85).

24. New York: Jesse Jackson proposes five-year freeze on military spending (→ 1/29/84).

26. N.Y.: Angel Cordero is first jockey to win $10 mil. in year.

29. Monaco: Princess Caroline weds Stefano Casiraghi.

30. Damascus: Jesse Jackson arrives to seek release of U.S. pilot (→ 1/3/84).

DEATH

25. Joan Miro, Spanish Surrealist painter (*4/20/1893).

CULTURAL EVENTS, 1983

Literature: J.M. Coetzee's "The Life and Times of Michael K"; Philip Roth's "The Anatomy Lesson"; Kingsley Amis' "Stanley and the Women"; D.M. Thomas' "Swallow"; Russell Baker's "Growing Up."

Academia: Derek Freeman's "Margaret Mead and Samoa."

Music: Michael Jackson's "Beat It"; Irene Cara's "Flashdance"; The Police's "Every Breath You Take."

The Arts: De Kooning's "Two Women" sells for $1.2 million; last TV episode of M*A*S*H" seen by record 125 mil. in U.S.

Film: "Tender Mercies," Robert Duvall; "Terms of Endearment," Jack Nicholson and Shirley MacLaine.

Eight years of army rule ended in Argentina

Alfonsin, civilian ruler in Argentina.

Dec 20. For eight tumultuous years the people of Argentina lived under military rule. This month that changed with the inauguration of Raul Ricardo Alfonsin as the nation's new President. More than 100,000 Argentines filled the streets of Buenos Aires to usher in a new era. The politically moderate Alfonsin addressed the populace, saying, "These are difficult moments, but we do not have a single doubt. We will move forward."

The new leader moved swiftly in announcing that the former military rulers would be prosecuted for spreading "terror, pain and death throughout Argentine society." He intends to dispose of the amnesty law which would have protected the nine generals and admirals who comprised, at different times, the junta which ruled Argentina. Today, former President Reynaldo Bignone was indicted on charges connected to the suspicious disappearance of two Argentine Communists in 1976 (→ 3/30/84).

Arafat and 4,000 Palestinians quit Tripoli

Dec 20. Yasir Arafat is trying to put the best face on it. But it is difficult. For the second time in 16 months, he has been forced under pressure to evacuate his Palestine Liberation Organization forces from Lebanon. Today, Arafat and several thousand of his loyalists set sail from Tripoli. They had been completely surrounded there by rival Palestinian factions and Syrian soldiers. The United Nations Security Council arranged the evacuation, and the PLO guerrillas departed on French ships bearing United Nations flags.

It was Israel that forced Arafat to leave Beirut last year. Israel's role in the latest evacuation has been ambiguous. Arafat's departure from Tripoli was delayed by Israeli bombing raids that were made in retaliation for a terrorist attack in Jerusalem. But there have also been reports from Beirut recently that Israel allowed Egypt to deliver arms to Arafat in Tripoli so that he could fight the Syrians (→ 27).

PLO forces leave Tripoli.

French divers set a new underwater record

Setting a record this year, French divers went down more than 4,500 meters —yet the swimmers were hundreds of miles from the sea. The four explorers, headed by journalist Francis Le Guen, went to the depths of Cocklebiddy Cave in the desert of southwest Australia. The dive in the water-filled grotto proved a cold and claustrophobic challenge lasting 39 hours. Aussies vow that the record, set in September, will be bettered next year.

Walesa gets Nobel

Dec 10. Like many Soviet bloc winners of Nobel prizes, Lech Walesa could not travel to Oslo to receive his award. Instead, his wife, Danuta, accepted the Peace Prize in his name tonight. She read a statement by the Gdansk electrician that said, "We are fighting for the right of working people to organize and for the dignity of human labor." Mrs. Walesa left the podium and returned when the audience gave her an encore (→ 3/8/84).

Reagan admits fault

Dec 27. President Reagan took full responsibility today for the lack of security in Beirut that allowed a terrorist on a suicide mission to kill 241 Marines. "If there is to be blame, it properly rests here in this office," the president said. Reagan also said he would not discipline any officers. They "have already suffered enough," the president said. A report by a special commission says security was lax in Beirut and is still inadequate (→ 1/4/84).

A former President drops in on Dynasty

Denizens of "Dynasty."

Dec 20. When ex-President Gerald Ford cameos on "Dynasty" tonight, it will be a meeting of the minds. If Ford doesn't mind playing second fiddle to Denver oil millionaire Blake Carrington, played by debonair John Forsythe, then the public won't mind much either.

"Dynasty" is one of the first programs to lather the evening hours with soap opera. Infidelity, illegitimate birth, divorce—once sole province of homemakers—is now available to fascinated males. The show is also a breakthrough for women over 40; actresses Linda Evans and Joan Collins, both technically getting on, are remarkably foxy and sultry, respectively.

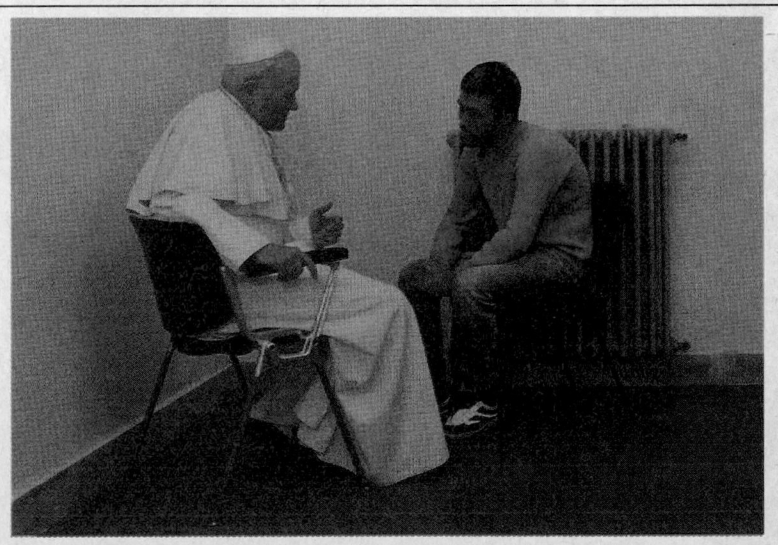

Dec 27. The Pope met with his attacker Ali Agca today to speak to him "as . . . a brother whom I have forgiven and who enjoys my confidence."

1984

JANUARY

Su	Mo	Tu	We	Th	Fr	Sa
1	2	3	4	5	6	7
8	9	10	11	12	13	14
15	16	17	18	19	20	21
22	23	24	25	26	27	28
29	30	31				

1. Pasadena: UCLA trounces Illinois 45-9 in Rose Bowl.

1. El Salvador: Guerrillas rout govt. troops to destroy nation's largest bridge (→ 3/9).

4. Lebanon: Israeli bombers raid eastern cities, killing 11, injuring 400 (→ 18).

6. Australia's only Aborigine senator, Neville Bonner, calls for separate Aborigine nation.

10. Presidential commission report denies hunger is rampant in U.S. (→ 24).

10. U.S. and Vatican establish full diplomatic relations for first time in 117 years (→ 5/2).

11. Honduras: U.S. helicopter pilot killed by Sandinista fire at Nicaraguan border (→ 4/8).

15. New York: John McEnroe beats Ivan Lendl 7-5, 6-0, 6-4 to win Volvo Masters title.

16. Bonn: Gromyko offers missile reductions if West Germany rejects U.S. Pershing II's (→ 29).

19. Takeda: 83 die in Japanese undersea mine fire.

19. Casablanca: 40-nation Islamic Conference decides to readmit Egypt.

23. Washington: Atty. Gen. William French Smith resigns; Edwin Meese to replace him.

24. Washington: Report cites U.S. consumer inflation at lowest level since 1972 (→ 3/10).

25. Reagan endorses development of first U.S. permanently manned space station (→ 2/3).

26. U.S.: Seven-year-old boycott of Nestles is ended.

29. Reagan announces he will seek second term as president (→ 2/20).

29. Moscow: Soviets issue formal complaint against alleged U.S. arms treaty violations (→ 6/11).

29. U.S. agrees to sell helicopter parts to Guatemala.

DEATHS

13. Brooks Atkinson, New York Times drama critic for 31 years (*11/28/1894).

20. Johnny Weissmuller, U.S. swimming star, played "Tarzan" on screen (*6/2/1904).

Tunisia declares emergency after food riots

Angered by food shortages, Tunisians crowd the streets of Tunis in protest.

Jan 6. Tear gas lingered in the air in Tunis this morning as the death toll from a week of riots in Tunisia rose sharply to 75. The disturbances started after the government doubled the price of bread. President Habib Bourguiba rushed back from his country home to Tunis on Tuesday for an emergency Cabinet meeting. He imposed a state of emergency, imposed a dusk-to-dawn curfew, closed schools, shut down bus service and dispatched military units to reinforce police.

Tunisia, a pro-Western country, increased the price of bread 125%, from eight cents a loaf to 18 cents, in an effort to close a widening budget deficit. Subsidies on various basic foodstuffs were eliminated, and food imports were reduced. Drought and two years of recession were blamed by the government.

The first riots erupted in a semi-desert area of the south, but they spread quickly throughout the country. The worst disturbances occurred in Tunis and Sfax. The Tunisian Ambassador to France said the price increases "have very little to do with" the rioting. Some officials have suggested that dissident fundamentalist groups capitalized on the situation to increase pressure on Bourguiba. The 80-year-old president has been ill for several years and has allowed his Prime Minister to run the country.

Jan 22. Kenny Hill, Lester Hayes and Derrick Jansen scramble for a blocked Redskin punt in the early stages of Super Bowl XVIII. They scored the Raiders first touchdown en route to a 38-9 victory in Tampa.

Black U.S. officer released by Syria

Jan 3. American Navy pilot Robert Goodman, captured last month by Syria after being shot down in central Lebanon, was released today. The Syrian Foreign Ministry said the decision to release Goodman was made after the "human appeal of the Rev. Jesse Jackson."

Jackson had flown to Damascus with a contingent of 14 people, including clergymen, who were not satisfied with the efforts of the Reagan administration in securing the pilot's freedom. Jackson met privately with Syrian President Hafez Assad, emerging from the talk assured Goodman would be freed.

The Syrians told reporters they hoped the release would "create circumstances that would facilitate the withdrawal of American troops from Lebanon." President Reagan thanked Assad for the action and called on Syria to help bring stability to war-torn Lebanon. However, Reagan continues to oppose a withdrawal of American Marines from the region.

When asked if Jackson, the civil rights leader and Democratic presidential candidate, had performed well, Reagan said, "You don't quarrel with success."

The man who sold billions of burgers

Jan 14. Ray A. Kroc, 81, builder of the McDonald's hamburger empire, who helped change American business and eating habits by deftly orchestrating the purveying of billions of small beef patties, died yesterday in San Diego, California.

Kroc, who also owned the San Diego Padres baseball team, was a former piano player and salesman of paper cups and milkshake machines. He built up a family fortune worth $500 million or more through his tireless, inspired tinkering with the management of the McDonald's restaurants, applying complex team techniques to the preparation of food that is simple and cheap.

Kroc started his first McDonald's in Chicago in 1955. The chain now has 7,500 outlets in the U.S. and 31 other countries with sales topping $8 billion in 1983.

50 years in writing, book now big seller

Jan 11. In the late 1920's, Miss Helen Hooven Santmyer read Sinclair Lewis' novel "Main Street." She didn't like it. The book insulted small Midwest towns, the kind of town she lived in, as a matter of fact. Miss Santmyer decided to write a rebuttal and show there is vigor and creativity in little places like her native Xenia, Ohio.

Over 50 years later, the "rebuttal" is complete. "... And Ladies of the Club" was selected today for the Book-of-the-Month Club. The novel is 1,344 pages long and weighs four pounds, technically larger than "Gone With the Wind." It remains to be seen if it proves bigger. "Ladies" concerns a women's literary group and the cultural and social changes it brings to a town.

When Miss Santmyer began the book, two short forgettable novels were behind her. She had a surprisingly stout education for a mere Midwesterner, having studied at Oxford University. She also worked briefly at Scribner's magazine.

Miss Santmyer takes all the hoopla calmly. Now 87, she lives in an Ohio nursing home reading works by Mark Twain. She has no plans for a sequel.

France orders army to extend hold in Chad

A French Foreign Legionnaire stands guard in Chad in "Operation Manta."

Jan 27. France, angered by the shooting down of one of its planes in Chad, moved today to get even with the rebels its says are backed by Libya. French commanders were ordered to consolidate their positions in the southern half of the country and move some forces 60 miles to the north. In recent days, France has doubled the number of combat aircraft it has in Chad.

The plane was shot down on a reconnaissance mission on Wednesday. The pilot was killed. On the same day, rebel forces attacked across the 15th parallel, which has served as the cease-fire line since last summer. France's decision today to move some of its forces north to the 16th parallel was applauded by President Hissen Habre. He has been trying for some time to convince the French to mount a concerted attack against rebel positions. France resisted until today and was trying to persuade Habre and the rebels to negotiate an end to the civil war (→ 9/17).

Beirut gunmen kill American educator

Jan 18. Lebanese terrorism has claimed the life of the President of the American University of Beirut. Malcolm H. Kerr was shot in the head by two unidentified gunmen as he walked down the hall to his office.

Police and soldiers immediately sealed off the campus entrances, but the assassins had already escaped. Responsibility was claimed by the Islamic Holy War, the same group that said it bombed the American Embassy in Beirut last April and attacked the Marine compound October 23, but police are uncertain if this supposedly pro-Iranian underground group actually exists.

Saying that Dr. Kerr "was a victim of the American military presence in Lebanon," the terrorist group vowed to rid Lebanon of all Americans and Frenchmen. Dr. Kerr was born and raised on the university campus where his father was a biochemist, his mother the dean of women, and where he met his wife, Ann, while she was a student. When he returned in 1982 to realize his boyhood dream and become president, he was offered a body guard but rejected it as unseemly (→ 2/5).

High court okays home TV recording

Jan 17. It is legal for consumers to use video recorders to tape television programs for their own use, the Supreme Court ruled today. In a 5-to-4 decision, the high court held that neither consumers nor the companies that make the machines violate federal copyright law when video recorders are use for "time-shifting," the taping of a program for later viewing.

The decision overturned a ruling by a lower court that the Sony Corporation had infringed the copyrights of two Hollywood studios by enabling home television viewers to tape films without paying royalties. Motion picture groups said they would continue their effort to have Congress levy a user fee on the sale of video recorders and blank tape to make up for revenues lost by home taping of motion pictures.

Texaco offers $10b for Getty Oil Co.

Jan 6. An offer by Texaco to buy Getty Oil for $10 billion was accepted today by Getty's board of directors, in what would be the biggest corporate merger in history.

The Texaco offer was immediately challenged by the Pennzoil Company, which said it had already made a deal to buy Getty Oil and would sue to block the merger. Pennzoil's offer of $112.50 a share was accepted in principle two days ago by the Getty board, but that deal was called off when Texaco bid $125 a share.

The Getty Oil Company was put up for sale because of disagreements among the heirs of J. Paul Getty, who founded the company. The largest merger in the United States until now was the Du Pont Company's $8 billion purchase of Conoco in 1981.

Promotion quotas for blacks barred

Jan 17. In an abrupt change in policy, the United States Commission on Civil Rights voted to discontinue the use of numerical quotas to promote blacks in employment positions. Previous commissions had advocated the practice as a last resort effort to correct the ills of proved discrimination.

The current board, reflecting the wishes of President Reagan, who appointed the members, released this statement on the matter: "Such racial preferences merely constitute another form of discrimination, create a new class of victims and, when used in public employment, offend the constitutional principle of equal protection of the law." Many civil rights workers, Democrats and black leaders called the decision another setback to civil rights in the Reagan era (→ 9/25/85).

Boy George, just a regular working-class British kid, made it by mastering the art of makeup. His plaintive tunes are sweet. The Culture Club is talented. But it is androgyny —a la Prince, David Bowie and Michael Jackson — that people now seem to crave.

1984

FEBRUARY

Su	Mo	Tu	We	Th	Fr	Sa
			1	2	3	4
5	6	7	8	9	10	11
12	13	14	15	16	17	18
19	20	21	22	23	24	25
26	27	28	29			

3. Cape Canaveral: Five astronauts ride space shuttle Challenger into orbit (→ 7).

3. EPA orders ban on pesticide EDB for grain products (→ 8/14).

5. Lebanon: Cabinet quits as Moslem protests grow (→ 7).

7. Reagan moved to ships off Beirut as rebels take last of Moslem sector (→ 14).

8. Yugoslavia: Winter Olympics open in Sarajevo (→ 19).

11. U.S.: Cuban aliens to be offered residency status; Haitians barred.

12. Iran shells towns in Iraq in reply to missile attack (→ 22).

14. Lebanon: Druse drive govt. troops from vital mountain area (→ 16).

16. Beirut: Lebanese president abrogates 1983 withdrawal pact with Israel (→ 21).

19. Sarajevo: Americans Phil and Steve Mahre take first and second in men's slalom.

20. Iowa: Mondale wins caucus by large margin (→ 28).

21. Beirut: U.S. Marines begin pulling out of airport positions (→ 26).

22. Britain and U.S. send warships to Persian Gulf following Iranian offensive (→ 27).

27. Iraq claims bombing of Iranian oil terminal on Kharg Island (→ 5/16).

28. New Hampshire: Gary Hart wins primary in upset over Mondale (→ 3/4).

29. New York: Soviet veto bars U.N. peace force from serving in Beirut (→ 3/12).

29. Ottawa: Canadian Prime Minister Pierre Trudeau announces resignation.→

DEATHS

9. Yuri Andropov, Soviet leader, ex-head of KGB (*6/15/1914).

15. Ethel Merman, American vocalist (*1/16/1909).

21. Mikhail Cholokov, Soviet writer, 1965 Nobel Prize (*5/24/1905).

23. Jessamyn West, American novelist (*7/18/1902).

Andropov dies; aging Chernenko succeeds

Andropov lies in state in Moscow.

Chernenko, ex-propaganda chief.

Feb 13. The Soviet Union has a new leader tonight, but it is not clear whether he has the authority or willingness to change domestic or foreign policy. Konstantin Chernenko was selected to succeed Yuri Andropov as General Secretary. Andropov died last Friday after a long bout with kidney disease. Chernenko, a 72-year-old Bolshevik, was a close associate of former Soviet leader Leonid Brezhnev for 30 years. In one sense, his reportedly unanimous election by the Central Committee represents a stunning comeback. It could also mean that the same bureaucrats who ruled through the four years when Brezhnev and Andropov were ill will continue to dominate policy.

Chernenko called today for peaceful coexistence with the United States. "We need no military superiority," Chernenko said, but he also insisted that a stockpile of nuclear weapons is needed "to cool the hot heads of militant adventurists." After Andropov's funeral tomorrow, Vice President George Bush will suggest that Chernenko hold a summit meeting with President Reagan (→ 4/11).

U.S. Marines finish occupation of Beirut

Feb 26. The contingent of 1,400 U.S. Marines today completed the withdrawal from the Beirut areas ordered by President Reagan earlier this month. Their guard posts at the Beirut airport were quickly filled by Shiite Moslem and rebel Lebanese army units opposed to the regime of President Amin Gemayel. President Reagan's decision to remove the Marines was prompted by the deteriorating political and military situation in Beirut. While praising the move, many Congressmen admitted it spelled the failure of Reagan's Lebanon policy (→ 29).

Marines bid goodbye to tragic Beirut.

David dies after 15 days outside bubble

Feb 22. David, the 12-year-old boy who spent almost all of his life in sterile isolation because of a defective immune system, died in a Houston hospital today. His death came after the failure of a bone marrow transplant performed five months ago in an effort to enable him to live a normal life.

David was born with combined immune deficiency, a defect of bone marrow cells that made him helpless against even the mildest infection. He was placed inside a sterile enclosure only seconds after his birth and did not emerge until 15 days before his death. Last year, doctors attempted to replace his bone marrow with normal cells from his sister. The transplant appeared to be successful at first, but David developed fever and diarrhea while still inside his bubble. He was allowed out after recovery, but fell ill again amid signs that the bone marrow graft was failing.

Premier Trudeau to resign in Canada

Feb 29. Pierre Elliott Trudeau, Prime Minister of Canada, announced his resignation today, after having served as head of state and leader of the Liberal Party for the past 15 years. He remarked that it was "the appropriate time for someone else to assume this challenge."

Trudeau, whose flamboyant personal style often obscured his skill as a mediator, replaced Lester Pearson as prime minister in 1968. He was defeated by the Progressive Conservatives in 1979 and resigned as Liberal Party chief, but after the government of Joe Clark collapsed in November of that year, Trudeau ran again, and he was re-elected.

Trudeau will be remembered for pursuing an independent foreign policy, as when Canada recognized Communist China in 1970. His resignation has touched off a race between 11 prominent Liberals who hope to succeed him in next spring's general elections (→ 6/16).

Men walk free in space 170 miles up

Feb 7. Two American astronauts became the first human satellites today when they floated free of the space shuttle Challenger. The feat by astronauts Bruce McCandless and Robert L. Stewart was a test of equipment that allows humans to work freely in space (→ 7/25).

Flying in an MMU space scooter.

1984

MARCH

Su	Mo	Tu	We	Th	Fr	Sa
				1	2	3
4	5	6	7	8	9	10
11	12	13	14	15	16	17
18	19	20	21	22	23	24
25	26	27	28	29	30	31

3. U.S.: Peter Uberroth named new baseball commissioner.

4. Maine: Gary Hart defeats Mondale in caucuses (→ 20).

5. U.S. Supreme Court rules cities may display Nativity scene as part of Christmas display.

8. Poland: 3,000 march in Garwolin to protest removal of crucifixes from classes.→

9. Reagan says U.S. will step up maneuvers in Latin America before Salvadoran election (→ 24).

10. Reagan agrees to cut U.S. budget by $149 bil. over three years (→ 5/1).

10. Miami: Acquittal of Hispanic policeman on murder charges sparks riots.

12. Lausanne: Lebanese Pres. Gemayel opens second parley in five years, calling for end to nine years of war (→ 28).

14. Belfast: Sinn Fein head Gerry Adams and three others injured by gunmen (→ 17).

16. South Africa and Mozambique sign pact banning support for one another's internal foes (→ 9/3).

18. New York: Navratilova over Helena Sukova 6-3, 7-5, 6-4 in Virginia Slims Championships.

18. New York: Mary Lou Retton scores perfect ten in vault at Madison Square Garden meet.

19. Havana: Cuba and Angola set conditions for withdrawal of Cuban troops from Angola (→ 11/10).

19. New York: Archbishop John O'Connor installed at St. Patrick's Cathedral.

20. Illinois: Mondale defeats Hart in primary (→ 4/14).

24. Pentagon says U.S. paratroopers landed in Honduras for three days of maneuvers before Salvadoran elections (→ 25).

DEATHS

1. Jackie Coogan, U.S. actor, "Little Rascals" (*10/26/1914).

6. Martin Niemoeller, German theologian (*1/14/1892).

24. Sam Jaffe, American actor.

26. Ahmed Sekou Toure, ex-leader of Guinea (*1/9/1922).

Religious issues plague American politics

March 15. The wall standing between church and state seems to getting a few chinks in it. Today, the Senate voted against silent prayer in the schools, but it will consider a constitutional amendment for vocal prayer next week. And March 5, the Supreme Court gave the nod to communities that want to erect public nativity scenes.

Why is religion increasingly a part of politics? The Reagan administration has been shouldering the Christian cause, backing Pawtucket, R.I., when it wanted to keep the life-size creche it has put up every yuletide for 40 years. And Reagan personally prefers vocal prayer to the silent kind, although some Democratic Senators think he is just lobbying for it to appease conservative supporters in an election year.

Reagan's stance had little to do with the Supreme Court decision, however. The narrow 5-4 ruling came not because the majority wanted to encourage Christian ethics, but because they feel the creche, inconspicuously placed beside a pagan reindeer and Christmas tree, is only a lukewarm religious symbol.

As Chief Justice Burger said for the majority, "To forbid the use of this one passive symbol would be a stilted overreaction contrary to our history and our holdings." A display consisting solely of explicit religious symbols might have elicited a different ruling. A case concerning a clearly Christian nativity scene in Scarsdale, N.Y., is now before the Manhattan Court of Appeals.

If silent prayer perished a cruel death (it was tabled 85-15), vocal prayer will not suffer long. Most Senators have expressed opposition. As Senator Christopher J. Dodd has said, "... to inject public school officials into the role of religious supervisors serves no purpose —not religion, not education, and certainly not individual liberties" (→ 8/11).

Salvadorans evade rebels to cast ballots

March 25. Salvadorans voted today in the first presidential election since 1977. But in certain areas of El Salvador, those controlled by leftist guerrillas, casting ballots was no easy task. Roadblocks, rifle fire and other obstacles created an atmosphere of chaos around many polling places.

Voters chose among eight candidates. Jose Napoleon Duarte of the moderate Christian Democrats and Roberto d'Aubuisson of the far-right Nationalist Republican Alliance appear to be the front-runners. If no candidate wins more than 50 percent of the vote, a runoff election will be held. The election came while the United States military was on maneuvers in neighboring Honduras. President Reagan ordered the operations to discourage guerrilla interference in the election (→ 4/13).

Government forces carry off another victim of pre-election fighting.

After nine years, Beirut battles on

March 28. With shells raining on apartments, commercial areas and busy thoroughfares, a four-hour random bombardment of Beirut today by both opposing forces killed at least 18 persons and wounded more than a hundred in the worst such exchange since the March 13 call for a cease-fire.

The terror escalated after the Christian militia launched a barrage

Beirut leaders talk peace.

in retaliation for the recent prolonged pounding of predominately Christian East Beirut by Moslem units firing from West Beirut. The battle underscored the point that despite recent peace talks between the Druse and Shiite Moslems and the Christian Phalangists, the nine-year struggle continues to evade settlement (→ 7/9).

Loss of crucifixes stirs Polish youth

March 8. More than 3,000 young people attended a rally and mass near the Mietnow agricultural college in Garwolin, Poland, today to protest the government's decision last December to remove crucifixes from their classrooms, as well as from public hospitals.

A strike and sit-in by students at the college two days ago prompted the provincial governor to close indefinitely the complex of public colleges at Mietnow. At the mass this morning, as riot police cruised around the Church of the Transfiguration, the Bishop of Siedice, Jan Mazur, urged every adult to sign a petition to the Polish leader, General Wojciech Jaruzelski, to replace all the crucifixes in the buildings (→ 5/4).

1984

APRIL

Su	Mo	Tu	We	Th	Fr	Sa
1	2	3	4	5	6	7
8	9	10	11	12	13	14
15	16	17	18	19	20	21
22	23	24	25	26	27	28
29	30					

2. Jerusalem: Three Arab gunmen wound 48 in crowd of shoppers (→ 12).

3. New Delhi: Sikh terrorists kill member of Parliament in his home (→ 5/21).

3. Guinea: Armed forces seize power week after Sekou Toure's death; Col. Lansana Konte is new president.

4. Reagan proposes intl. ban on chemical weapons.

8. Reagan admin. denies authority of World Court decisions on Central America (→ 9).

9. Nicaragua asks World Court to declare illegal U.S. support for guerrilla raids (→ 10).

11. Moscow: Supreme Soviet elects Chernenko president of U.S.S.R. (→ 5/20).

13. Reagan sends emergency military aid to El Salvador without congressional approval (→ 5/7).

14. S.C.: Jackson wins primary in home state (→ 5/1).

16. Pulitzers to William Kennedy's "Ironweed," David Mamet's "Glengarry Glen Ross."

17. London: Gunmen from Libyan Embassy fire into anti-Libya protest, killing one policewoman, wounding ten others (→ 22).

20. Washington: Terrorists bomb officers club at Navy yard.

20. Afghanistan: Offensive launched against mujahedeen northwest of Kabul.

21. Atlanta: Dr. James Mason says he believes French doctors have found AIDS virus (→ 23).

25. France: Over one million demonstrate in favor of educational decentralization (→ 6/24).

26. Peking: Reagan arrives for six-day visit (→ 30).

27. London: Libyans leave embassy 11 days after killing of policewoman (→ 5/8).

29. Calif.: Diablo Canyon nuclear reactor goes on line after long delay due to protests (→ 11/21).

DEATH

16. General Mark Clark, last of top five U.S. Army commanders in WWII (*5/1/1896).

Agreement reached on Argentine debt

March 30. A major debt crisis was avoided today as negotiators agreed on a $500 million package to help Argentina make long-overdue interest payments to United States banks. The agreement means that dozens of banks that have lent $8.6 billion to Argentina will be able to avoid substantial losses on the loans. The unusual agreement provides that Argentina will receive financial help from Brazil, Mexico and Venezuela, which also have serious debt problems. Banks had feared the Latin American countries would form a "debtors' cartel" that would lead to default on billions of dollars in loans (→ 6/11).

Most-wanted Irish terrorist is captured

March 17. In a Saint Patrick's Day shoot-out, Irish police captured a republican terrorist who headed Ireland's most-wanted list. Dominic McGlinchey, a 30-year-old former auto mechanic in Northern Ireland who became known as "Mad Dog" because of his ruthlessness, was captured in an isolated cottage in County Clare after a 90-minute gun battle. McGlinchey, who recently left the outlawed Irish Republican Army to become chief of staff of a militant, Marxist offshoot known as the Irish National Liberation Army, has claimed responsibility for 200 shootings and more than 30 deaths (→ 2/28/85).

March 23. Socialist Mitterrand and conservative Reagan bolster Atlantic alliance in Washington.

Libyans gun down London policewoman

Siege at the Libyan Embassy.

April 22. In London, it appears tonight that the gunman who killed a British policewoman in cold blood will be able to leave England scot-free. Constable Yvonne Fletcher was killed Tuesday when shots were fired from inside the Libyan Embassy during a protest outside against Col. Muammar Khadafy. Ten protesters were wounded, five seriously. Police officers surrounded the building, and Britain tried to convince Khadafy's government to allow a search of the embassy for weapons. Khadafy refused. Tonight, Britain broke diplomatic relations with Libya and gave the occupants of the embassy a week to leave the country. One of those occupants killed Fletcher (→ 27).

Manhunt ended as Wilder is killed

April 13. Christopher Wilder, suspected in the abduction and murder of several women, was shot and killed today in a fight with police. Wilder, a 39-year-old Florida resident, had been listed on the FBI's ten most-wanted list as a suspect in the kidnappings of 11 young women in several different states. Police tracked Wilder to northern New Hampshire, where they stopped his car. During a struggle with authorities, Wilder produced a gun which misfired, sending a bullet through his chest. He died immediately.

Ten slain in New York mass murder

April 15. An infant was found crawling among the corpses of ten of her relatives and friends in a brutal mass murder in a Brooklyn apartment. Three women, a teenage girl and six children were the victims in what police are calling the worst mass murder in New York City in history. The husband of one of the women found the bodies lined up neatly against a wall. A neighbor said the man ran out of the apartment screaming hysterically. Authorities have found no motives for the horrific slayings.

Singer Marvin Gaye is killed by his father

April 1. Marvin Gaye, internationally popular singer, songwriter and musician, was shot to death today. He would have been 45 tomorrow. His father, the Rev. Marvin Gaye Sr., 70, has been booked. The singer was in his father's home in Los Angeles when the two men became involved in a verbal dispute that led to a physical altercation, whereupon Gaye Sr. took a pistol and fired several shots at his son. Gaye, who kept surprising his fans by varying his modes of musical expression since his career started in the late 50's, blended the soul music of the urban scene with the beat of the oldtime gospel singer. He influenced scores of other artists.

Gifted soul singer Marvin Gaye.

Reagan, in China, signs cultural agreement

Li Hsian-nian and Reagan review the Chinese honor guard in Peking.

April 30. President Reagan opened a few more doors today that had been left ajar by another Republican, Richard Nixon. Nearing the end of his six-day trip to China, Reagan signed cultural and scientific agreements. He also approved a tax accord that will make it easier for American companies to do business in china.

The only hitch in Reagan's visit to China developed when Chinese officials said the United States was not acting quickly enough to reduce military aid to Taiwan.

"Let us hope," Reagan said, "as contacts grow between the Chinese and American People, each of us will continue to learn about the other, and this important new friendship of ours will mature and prosper." The agreements signed in the Great Hall of the People call for another exchange of performing arts groups, museum exhibits and cultural programs. The business accord will prevent the double taxation of American businesses in China. Under separate agreements, American companies will help build nuclear reactors in China, and the Occidental Petroleum Company will develop a large coal mine.

Reagan could not resist a plug for capitalism when he and his wife, Nancy, visited a free market near Xian. Asked about the future of capitalism in China, Reagan smiled, pointed at a souvenir stand and said, "It's flourishing" (→ 9/30).

Two countries find the same AIDS virus

April 23. Researchers in France and the United States are focusing on a virus called LAV, suspecting it is the cause of AIDS. While extensive testing is still necessary to confirm their suspicions, scientists see the findings leading to the establishment of a diagnostic test. AIDS-contaminated blood could soon be screened and rejected for transfusions. And of course, identifying the virus is but one step away from developing a vaccine. As of today, 4,087 cases of AIDS have been reported in the United States, 1,758 being patients who are now dead (→ 2/8/85).

Texas changes on teaching evolution

April 14. The Texas Board of Education today repealed a decade-old rule that required textbooks used in the state's public schools to describe evolution as "only one of several explanations" of the origin of human beings and to present it as "theory rather than fact." People for the American Way, a national anti-censorship group, had petitioned for today's change and threatened to sue the board if it was not made. The state's attorney general declared a month ago that the requirement on evolution was an unconstitutional intrusion of religion into state matters.

U.S. doesn't accept World Court rulings

April 10. The decision of the Reagan administration to mine the harbors of Nicaragua has caused a great deal of controversy in the World Court and in the Senate. Suspecting that the Nicaraguans would complain about the situation to the World Court, the judiciary body of the United Nations, President Reagan notified the court that the U.S. would not be bound by the jurisdiction of the court for two years. A day later, the Nicaraguan government did indeed bring the case to the World Court. Today, the United States Senate ruled, 84-12, to halt any funds for the mining of the harbors (→ 5/10).

Arabs hold hostages for ten hours on bus

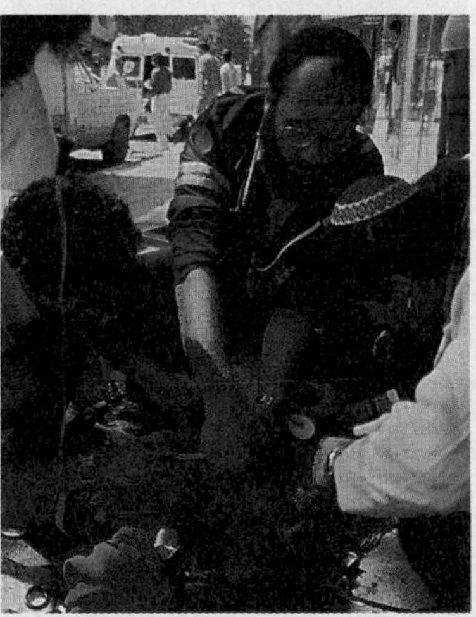
Israelis attend to wounded terrorist.

April 12. Israeli troops early today stormed the bus hijacked last night by Arab terrorists, rescuing the 35 passengers from their ten-hour bondage. Two of the four Arabs were reported killed and eight passengers wounded, one seriously. Armed with explosives, the Arabs forced their way on the bus as it made its normal run southward from Tel Aviv. The Israelis halted the vehicle by shooting out its tires, but overnight efforts to dissuade the hijackers had no effect. The Arabs reportedly informed the hostages that they wanted to get to Tunisia via Egypt. A passenger recounted, "They behaved very nicely, this I must say."

Death takes Basie, easy on the ivories

Count Basie, Big Band leader.

April 26. Count Basie, the jazz pianist whose spare, economic keyboard style and supple rhythmic drive made his band a major influence for nearly 50 years, died of cancer yesterday in Florida.

Born in New Jersey in 1904, Basie encountered Fats Waller in his late teens and became an accompanist in vaudeville. In 1929, he joined Bennie Moten's band. When Moten died in 1935, Basie formed his own distinctive band. Among the many pieces he composed for it was "One O'Clock Jump." The Basie Band played at President Kennedy's inauguration and toured with Frank Sinatra. In 1981, Basie was honored at the Kennedy Center along with Cary Grant and others. In 1982, he was given a gala at Radiò City Music Hall, where celebrities paid tribute to the master of jazz.

April 18. Daredevils Mike MacCarthy and Amanda Tucker safely jump from the Eiffel Tower.

Kennedy youth is dead in hotel room

April 25. David Anthony Kennedy, son of the late Robert F. Kennedy, has died from a possible drug overdose at the age of 28. According to family members, David Kennedy had led a deeply troubled life since the assassination of his father in 1968 and had undergone treatment for alcoholism and heroin addiction. David's uncle, Senator Edward M. Kennedy, who had often stood in as a father for the children of Robert and President John Kennedy, issued a statement saying, "We all pray that David has finally found the peace that he did not find in life" (→ 5/16).

Ansel Adams, noted photographer, dies

April 23. Ansel Adams, who made photography a distinct and legitimate art form, "not a substitute brush, but a way of seeing," died yesterday in Carmel, California. He was 82. During a career spanning more than 50 years, he took photographs showing a passion for landscape and meticulous craftsmanship. These were published in more than 35 books and portfolios and shown in hundreds of exhibitions, including a one-man show, "Ansel Adams and the West," at the Museum of Modern Art in New York in 1979. In 1980, he received the Medal of Freedom.

April 9. Jack Nicholson and Shirley MacLaine, Oscar winners for "Terms of Endearment."

1984

MAY

Su	Mo	Tu	We	Th	Fr	Sa
		1	2	3	4	5
6	7	8	9	10	11	12
13	14	15	16	17	18	19
20	21	22	23	24	25	26
29	28	29	30	31		

1. Washington: Jackson wins D.C. primary (→ 5).

2. Fairbanks: Pope John Paul II and Reagan meet on world issues (→ 9/12).

4. Poland and Soviet Union sign 15-year trade pact (→ 6/10).

5. Jackson wins in Louisiana caucus, Mondale in Texas (→ 7/19).

6. Panama: Army candidate Ardito Barletta elected pres.

7. U.S.: Agent Orange class action suit settled out of court for $180 million (→ 7/20).

7. San Salvador: Duarte declares self winner of presidential election (→ 11).

8. Libya: Khadafy forces crush rebel attack (→ 8/21).

10. The Hague: Intl. Court rules U.S. should halt blockade of Nicaraguan ports (→ 31).

12. New Orleans World's Fair opens.

15. Jakarta: Reports indicate Indonesian death squads have killed up to 4,000.

16. West Palm Beach: David Kennedy found to have been killed by overdose of three drugs.

16. Persian Gulf: Iran, in strike against Arab backers of Iraq, bombs three Kuwaiti and Saudi oil tankers (→ 19).

18. Guatemala: Untouched Mayan tomb found in Peten.

19. Persian Gulf: Iraqi jets sink Panamanian cargo ship (→ 24).

21. Bombay: Army moves in after 114 die in religious strife (→ 6/2).

24. El Salvador: Five ex-National Guards found guilty of killing four U.S. churchwomen.→

28. U.S. sends 400 Stinger aircraft missiles to Saudi Arabia (→ 5/21/86).

30. Supreme Court upholds Hawaii land reform plan, ruling state may break up large estates.

31. Nicaragua: Contra leader Eden Pastora wounded in blast; five dead, Pastora held (→ 6/1).

DEATH

8. Lila Wallace, co-founder of Reader's Digest (*1889).

Duarte is President after free election

May 11. The Central Elections Council of El Salvador has announced that Jose Napoleon Duarte has won the presidential election with nearly 54 percent of the vote. The Nationalist Republican Alliance, known as Arena, Duarte's opposition from the far right, has declared that it will not accept the results of the election, claiming that "the elections don't have any credibility and the results are a farce," because the CIA gave Duarte millions of dollars to aid his campaign. Salvadoran military officials have announced their support of the elections council's results (→ 24).

Guardsmen guilty in deaths of nuns

May 24. After a 19-hour trial, five former members of El Salvador's National Guard were found guilty in the murders of four United States churchwomen. The women, three nuns and a lay worker, had been running a temporary refugee center in a northern province of El Salvador, an area of heavy fighting. When their raped and mutilated bodies were found in a crude grave, suspicion was turned toward members of the National Guard. The United States Congress voted to withhold military aid to El Salvador until a verdict in this case was reached (→ 6/1).

Sakharov is seeking asylum for his wife

Sakharov, father of Soviet H-bomb.

May 20. Soviet dissident Andrei Sakharov gave American diplomats in Moscow letters last month in which he asked that his wife be given asylum in the U.S. Embassy and which unveiled his plans to wage a hunger strike. The physicist and human rights activist, jailed since 1980, also urged that his wife, Yelena Bonner, be allowed to travel to the United States for medical treatment of a heart condition.

Today, reports from Moscow indicated Bonner may face arrest for what Soviet officials have called her "anti-Soviet activities." Bonner has publicized her husband's struggle, including his hunger strike. Some feel the antagonism toward Bonner is an attempt to deflect attention from Sakharov and to forge public disdain for the couple (→ 7/5).

May 27. Rick Mears, Indy winner in '79, became two-time champ today.

Arab League accuses Iran of aggression

A Saudi Arabian tanker is destroyed in the Persian Gulf, a vital oil route.

May 24. Iran ignored a warning from the Arab League today and strafed an oil tanker off the coast of Saudi Arabia. Iraq also struck at other shipping in the Persian Gulf. The new attacks came just four days after the Arab League released an unprecedented statement accusing Iran of aggression in its war against Iraq. A majority of the league's members also warned Iran to stop its attacks on shipping in the international oil lanes of the gulf. The league did not criticize Iraq, which has actually done more damage to oil tankers than Iran.

Syria and Libya, the two major allies of Iran, tried and failed to prevent the public criticism of Tehran. An official at the State Department said the league's resolution represented a major victory for Jordan's King Hussein. He has been trying for weeks to convince the league to abandon its tradition of consensus, to ignore Syria and Libya and to condemn Iran.

Iraq has concentrated its bombardments on ships approaching Iran's vital Kharg Island. Most of the Arab League members condone those attacks because they have occurred in the war zone. Iran is accused of striking at ships all over the gulf, but denies the charges.

It is not clear whether league members are prepared to back up their threat to Iran with military muscle. There have been reports recently that both Saudi Arabia and Kuwait have put their air forces on higher alerts. Both countries conferred over the weekend about possible joint action in the Persian Gulf.

In Oman, Vice President Bush criticized the attacks on neutral ships by Iran and Iraq. He said they "are in violation of international law and should be a source of great concern to all nations" (→ 8/18).

Militant Iranian women march in support of Khomeini's Islamic Revolution.

Up to 350,000 may be homeless in U.S.

May 1. According to new figures from the Department of Housing and Urban Development, 250,000 to 350,000 Americans are homeless. HUD Secretary Samuel Pierce said that the statistics, collected systematically for the first time, indicate the homeless are not all single, middle-aged, white, alcoholic men, as is commonly believed. The poor and homeless include men and women of every type. One spokesman for an anti-poverty group, who believes there are more than a million homeless Americans, called the new government statistics "utterly ridiculous" (→ 12/11).

$7.5b loan made to save Illinois bank

May 17. Immersed in billions of dollars of debt, the Continental Illinois National Bank and Trust Company has received the biggest aid package ever granted to a private bank from the federal government. The Federal Reserve Board arranged $7.5 billion to rescue the bank. Additionally, buyers are being sought for the financial institution among the staffs of 50 of the world's largest banks. The Federal Reserve Board, exercising its role as "lender of last resort," will also meet any other emergency needs which may arise before new owners can be found (→ 7/26).

Reagan is operated on for small polyp

May 18. Doctors conducting a medical examination of President Reagan found and partly removed a small polyp from his colon, the White House announced today. The physicians said the polyp was not malignant and that the 73-year-old president was in "very exceptional physical condition." They added that discovery of the polyp would not place any restrictions on Reagan's campaign for re-election. Another examination will be done in several months to determine whether it is necessary to remove the rest of the polyp (→ 7/15/85).

Soviets will boycott Los Angeles Games

May 8. The Soviet National Olympic Committee has announced it will not send a team to the Summer Games in Los Angeles because, it explained, it anticipated anti-Soviet protests in the city unrestrained by the U.S. government. "Chauvinistic sentiments," the committee said, "and an anti-Soviet hysteria are being whipped up in the country." Other Soviet-bloc nations, including Cuba and Vietnam, are expected to join the boycott. The United States and 59 other nations boycotted the Moscow Games in 1980 to protest the Soviet invasion of Afghanistan (→ 7/1984).

Smokers may cause disease in others

May 23. There is "very solid" evidence that nonsmokers can suffer lung damage from exposure to other people's cigarette smoke, Surgeon General C. Everett Koop said today. Commenting on a new government report on the health risks of smoking, Koop said so-called passive smoking has been shown to damage the lungs of children and spouses of smokers and said he supported "the right of the nonsmoker to be segregated from the smoker." The report was disputed by the Tobacco Institute, which said the health effects of passive smoking were "negligible."

Evening wear for summer.

1984

JUNE

Su	Mo	Tu	We	Th	Fr	Sa
					1	2
3	4	5	6	7	8	9
10	11	12	13	14	15	16
17	18	19	20	21	22	23
24	25	26	27	28	29	30

1. San Salvador: Duarte sworn in as president (→ 7/31).

1. Managua: Shultz meets with Pres. Daniel Ortega (→ 10/17).

2. India: Army takes control of Punjab as 22 are killed in Sikh struggle for autonomy (→ 6).

6. Punjab: Indian troops seize Sikh Golden Temple, gunning down 308 (→ 7).

9. Rome: Judge charges Bulgarian secret service recruited Agca to kill Pope in plot to curb Polish labor movement (→ 10/25).

10. India: Top army commander killed in Bihar; Sikh troops desert unit (→ 11).

10. Poland: Polish seize Bogdan Lis, high official of outlawed Solidarity union (→ 7/20).

11. U.S.: Army reports new anti-ballistic missile has made first successful test (→ 14).

11. India: 574 Sikh army deserters arrested (→ 9/2).

11. Argentina submits austerity plan to IMF (→ 7/5).

12. U.S. Supreme Court rules seniority, not quotas is guideline for job layoffs.

14. The Hague: Dutch Parliament delays U.S. cruise missile installation two years (→ 8/12).

16. Ottawa: John N. Turner replaces Trudeau as leader of Canadian Liberals (→ 30).

17. Uniondale, L.I.: Intl. Games for the disabled open.

21. Moscow: Mitterrand and Chernenko clash publicly over human rights as French pres., on visit, discusses Sakharov.

25. East Berlin: Bonn closes mission to East Germans seeking refuge (→ 8/23/85).

30. Ottawa: John N. Turner sworn in as 17th prime minister (→ 9/4).

DEATHS

19. Lee Krasner Pollock, U.S. Abstract Expressionist painter (*10/27/1908).

22. Joseph Losey, American film director (*1/14/1909).

25. Michel Foucault, French philospher, cultural historian (*10/15/1926).

Indian army troops put down Sikh uprising

Sikhs, who comprise about 1.8% of India, protest Golden Temple massacre.

June 7. Indian army troops, sent into the Punjab to quell Sikh violence, stormed the Golden Temple in Amristar, the holiest of Sikh shrines. More than 400 persons were reported killed in the assault on the shrine, including Jarnail Singh Bhindranwale, a former Indian army general who headed the Sikh militants. Harchand Singh Longowal, the leader of Sikh moderates, surrendered before the attack on the shrine.

Prime Minister Indira Gandhi had ordered army troops to restore order in the Punjab, where a Sikh campaign for greater autonomy has led to growing violence and terrorism. Since the autonomy campaign was begun two years ago by a moderate Sikh party, some 500 persons have been killed. In recent months, the movement has been taken over by Sikh radicals, with more than 250 killed since February in Punjab and neighboring Haryana.

As had been feared by the government, the storming of the Golden Temple was followed by outbursts of Sikh protests in several Indian cities, with 27 persons killed in the demonstrations. While crushing the radical faction, the government appeared to have complicated the task of reaching a negotiated settlement in the Punjab, the homeland of the Sikhs. It was the fourth time in the past two years that the government has called in army troops to put down civil disturbances in India, including Moslem-Hindu riots in Bombay and civil strife in Assam leading to 5,000 deaths (→ 10).

Golden Temple, holiest Sikh shrine, was built by Ram Das in the 1500's.

Allied leaders mark D-Day anniversary

June. The leaders of the seven industrial democracies are meeting in London to commemorate the 40th anniversary of the World War II D-Day invasion of Normandy (June 6, 1944) and issue a 500-word Declaration on Democratic Values.

At the economic talks, leaders from France, Japan, the United States, Canada, Italy, West Germany and Great Britain agreed on the declaration, which emphasizes a commitment to "elections freely held, free expression of opinion and the capacity to respond and adapt to change in all its aspects."

American officials were forced to respond to the Allies' concern about the U.S. budget deficit. European participants said the debt contributes to high interest rates, slowing recovery, and asked the U.S. to focus attention on the problem. U.S. Treasury Secretary Donald Regan demanded that the leaders produce proof linking the debt with high interest rates. With friction developing among the member nations on this issue, discussion turned to the worsening debt crisis in the Third World. The delegates vowed to find ways to make it easier for the poorer nations to repay their debts.

The Reagans at Omaha Beach.

Meanwhile, outside the conference, held at London's Lancaster House, some 150,000 people gathered to protest the proliferation of nuclear weapons. They carried placards denouncing American policies which they feel have escalated the arms race. The assembly was peaceful, but 170 protesters were arrested for blocking traffic.

112 children moved from church's homes

June 22. A state police officer strode out of a Vermont home this morning, clasping the hand of a child on one side and holding a bundle of rods on the other. He was assisting a raid on 20 homes owned by the Northeast Kingdom Community Church, a sect whose members are accused of abusing their children. The Island Park residents were asked to follow and appear in court with their children.

The religious sect, which originated in Tennessee in the 1970's, admits to using force on children. "We discipline them," one church member said. "We don't abuse them. We love them." All the children were back in their homes by 10:30 p.m.

Apostle of European communism is dead

June 13. Rome was the site of a massive funeral today, as Communist leaders from 50 nations came to pay their final respects to Enrico Berlinguer. The Eurocommunist died June 11 of a cerebral hemorrhage. He was 62 years old.

Berlinguer joined the Italian Communist Party shortly after World War II and became an executive member in 1948. By 1972, he was Secretary General of the largest Communist Party in the West. He and the late Aldo Moro strove to unite Christian Democrats and Communists in what Berlinguer termed a "historic compromise." Although Berlinguer sought to liberate Western communism from Soviet dictates, Mikhail Gorbachev was among the mourners today.

Last rites for a Eurocommunist.

Embattled author Lillian Hellman dies

Lillian Hellman, chain-smoker.

June 30. "I cannot and will not cut my conscience to fit this year's fashions." That is what Lillian Hellman said in 1952 to the House Committee on Un-American Activities, after the group had tried to get her to inform on her Communist friends. The opinionated writer died today at Martha's Vineyard, Massachusetts. She was 79.

Miss Hellman said she was no Communist. She insisted she was a rebel, and a rebel, she said, made a poor revolutionary. She rebelled against her upper-class upbringing in New Orleans, revealing its hypocrises in her play "The Little Foxes." "The Children's Hour," about the lives of two women ruined by a child's lies, anticipated the committee's methods. Other plays and film scripts attacked fascism. Her book "Julia" was filmed in 1977 with a script she approved.

Average home price now over $100,000

June 29. The goal that has come to be known as the American dream has crossed a historic threshold: The average price of a new single-family home broke into six figures in May. It went up $5,100 since April and reached $101,000. The number of sales fell for the third month in a row. The housing boom began after World War II with the proliferation of the 30-year mortgage with fixed monthly payments. It cost as little as four percent until the 1970's when interest rates began creeping upward.

French march in support of private schools

June 24. Paris was jammed today with hundreds of thousands of demonstrators protesting against an effort by the Socialist government to regulate France's private schools. Many of the protesters jammed into the Place de la Bastille chanting, "Free schools will live!" and "We want to stay free!" For the most part, the enormous demonstrations were peaceful until nightfall. Then several hundred youths built barricades, set fires, threw rocks and clashed with police in the Latin Quarter. Two police officers were injured. There were 35 arrests.

The Interior Ministry estimates that 850,000 people joined the protest. Some demonstrators claimed there were two million. One commentator said the march was "the largest since the liberation."

The government of Socialist President Francois Mitterrand says it will continue to subsidize the mostly Catholic private schools. But it is trying to convince many private school teachers to become civil servants. Critics say the move would tighten state control over the independent schools. Some of Mitterrand's supporters say the proposal does not go far enough, and they claim it is hypocritical to accuse Socialists of imposing restraints on personal liberties (→ 7/17).

Demonstrators march in Paris to protest bureaucratization of private schools.

Jackson meets with Castro on prisoners

June 26. The Rev. Jesse Jackson has successfully completed lengthy negotiations with Cuban Premier Fidel Castro. Twenty-two American prisoners in Cuba will be released. However, the Democratic presidential candidate was not able to gain the freedom of several Cuban nationalists jailed since the 1961 Bay of Pigs invasion. The talks also centered on ways to improve ties between the two nations. Jackson said he felt President Reagan and Castro should meet to normalize relations. While the Reagan administration said it would assist the freed American prisoners, it did not comment on a possible normalization of relations (→ 1/16/85).

Movies to have new rating for under-13s

June 19. One man has said of the film "Indiana Jones and the Temple of Doom" that it has a gory 20-minute sequence that would impell him to cover the eyes of any watching ten-year-old. The man in question is none other than Steven Spielberg, director of the picture. Spielberg is one of the backers of a PG-13 rating just given the nod by the Motion Picture Association of America.

Recent films such as "Gremlins" and "Poltergeist" rely on some very violent scenes, rendered even scarier by increasingly sophisticated special effects. The MPAA, seeing censorship looming, self-imposes the new rating, which denies viewing by children without a guardian.

1984

JULY

Su	Mo	Tu	We	Th	Fr	Sa
1	2	3	4	5	6	7
8	9	10	11	12	13	14
15	16	17	18	19	20	21
22	23	24	25	26	27	28
29	30	31				

2. N.Y. high court rules mandatory death penalty law is unconstitutional (→ 11/2).

5. Argentina: Army chief fired to quell dissent over human rights prosecutions in military (→ 2/21/85).

5. Moscow: Vyacheslav Molotov reinstated in Communist Party at age 94 (→ 8/17).

8. Wimbledon: McEnroe over Connors 6-1, 6-1, 6-2; Navratilova over Evert Lloyd 7-6, 6-2.

9. Beirut paralyzed as protesters demand action to free kidnapped relatives (→ 8/28).

11. U.S. announces air bags or automatic seat belts required in cars by 1989 (→ 12).

12. N.Y. institutes nation's first mandatory seat-belt law.

12. China reports repelling Vietnamese attack on border.

14. New Zealand: Labor Party sweeps Robert Muldoon's Conservatives from office in election.

15. Paris: Third bomb in two days rips French Industry Ministry (→ 17).

17. Paris: Mauroy Cabinet resigns; Industry Min. Laurent Fabius new premier (→ 3/20/86).

20. Reagan says Laos will allow U.S. to search for remains of American aviators (→ 9/11).

20. Austria: 120 Poles on pilgrimage to Rome ask asylum in Austria (→ 21).

21. Poland, marking 40th anniversary of Communist rule, authorizes release of 652 political prisoners (→ 10/30).

22. Laurent Fignon wins Tour de France.

23. Israel: Elections leave no parliamentary majority (→ 8/31).

25. Reagan, seeking to improve ties, ends ban on Soviet fishing in U.S. waters (→ 9/24).

25. Soviet Svetlana Savitskaya becomes first woman to walk in space (→ 8/27).

31. El Salvador: Rebels kill 58 in attacks on farm district (→ 8/10).

DEATH

25. Willie Mae "Big Mama" Thornton, U.S. blues singer.

Mondale chooses woman as V.P. candidate

Queens Congresswoman Ferraro.

July 12. Walter F. Mondale today chose Rep. Geraldine A. Ferraro of Queens as his running mate, the first woman ever selected to run for vice president on a major party ticket.

Mondale, who is expected to win the Democratic Party nomination for president later this month, made his historic announcement from the steps of the Minnesota Capitol in St. Paul, saying, "I looked for the best vice president and I found her in Gerry Ferraro."

In naming a woman as his running mate, Mondale seemed to be trying to reshape his political image and to fire up what some feared would be a nearly hopeless challenge against President Reagan. But some view his action as a gamble.

Mrs. Ferraro, a 48-year-old former teacher and onetime assistant prosecutor from Queens, was elected to Congress in 1978. Her selection as the vice-presidential nominee was backed by House Speaker Thomas P. O'Neill, Gov. Mario Cuomo of New York, as well as numerous other Democrats and feminists. "She's a woman, she's ethnic, she's Catholic," said one of Mondale's top advisers. "We have broken the barrier" (→ 7/10/85).

Democrats nominate Mondale and Ferraro

July 19. As thousands of delegates waved small plastic American flags, Walter F. Mondale and Geraldine Ferraro moved around their party's convention floor today, an historic team intent on capturing the White House for the Democrats.

For Mondale, his selection as the party's nominee for president was something he had dreamed of much of his adult life. His choice of Mrs. Ferraro as a running mate broke new ground as the first woman of any major party chosen for the vice-presidential slot. The daughter of an Italian immigrant, she was a teacher and lawyer before she was elected to Congress.

"Tonight, we open a new door to the future," Mondale said. "Mr. Reagan calls that tokenism. We call it America." Said Mrs. Ferraro: "There are no doors we cannot unlock" (→ 8/21).

Jesse Jackson joins Mondale and Ferraro in celebration in San Francisco.

Nude pictures cause Miss America to quit

July 23. After what she terms "the worst week in my life," 21-year-old Vanessa Williams reluctantly relinquished her Miss America title today, saying the publication of nude photographs of her in the September issue of Penthouse magazine, just hitting the newsstands, made remaining in that post too difficult and she didn't want to cause harm to the pageant. Atlantic City pageant officials immediately introduced Suzette Charles, who as Miss New Jersey was the first runner-up, as the new Miss America. This was the first resignation of a Miss America in the pageant's 63-year history.

Author of jogging book dies jogging

Fixx inspired millions of joggers.

July 21. One of the nation's most avid proponents of jogging has died while jogging. James F. Fixx, writer of best-selling books on running, collapsed and died of a heart attack at the age of 52 while jogging alone on a quiet road in Vermont. An autopsy found that two of his coronary arteries were blocked enough to require a bypass operation.

The runner's sister said her brother was aware of the coronary problem because of their father's death at age 43. It was his father's predisposition to heart disease that led Fixx to take up jogging. He weighed 220 pounds and smoked two packs of cigarettes a day. He stopped smoking, lost 61 pounds and never stopped running.

Gunman kills 20 in McDonald's crowd

Site of the tragedy closed to public.

July 18. An unemployed security guard armed with three guns strode into a McDonald's in San Ysidro, California, today, killing 20 people and wounding 16 others, before a police sharpshooter shot him dead.

The gunman was identified as James Oliver Huberty, 41, married, with two children. He had moved to the town just north of the Mexican border from Ohio seven months ago. Recently, he was dismissed from his job as a security guard.

The largest death toll by a single gunman in a single day in the nation's history began about 4 p.m., when the man walked into the restaurant, carrying a semi-automatic rifle, a shotgun and a pistol, and began firing at everything that moved. Seventeen of the bodies, including the assailant's, were inside the restaurant and four were outside. Some were children. Police describe the scene as a "sickening and horrendous massacre."

$4.5b loan made to save Illinois bank

July 26. The federal government agreed today to bail out a major Chicago bank by providing a $4.5 billion loan, part of the largest package of federal support ever given to any private enterprise. The dramatic rescue of the Continental Illinois National Bank and Trust Company is designed to protect all depositors and other creditors of that financial institution and to restore confidence in the banking system. Continental, long the top bank in the Middle West, has billions of dollars in bad loans.

George Gallup of the Gallup Poll dies

July 27. George H. Gallup, an inquisitive Iowan who pioneered in the techniques of public opinion polling and made it a key tool of politics and business, has died at his summer home in Switzerland at age 82. Originally a teacher of journalism, Dr. Gallup's fame began with his successful prediction in 1936 that Roosevelt would beat Landon in the election. Since then the Gallup Poll has had a good record except for the prediction that Dewey would beat Truman in 1948.

James Mason, actor of distinction, dies

Mason, brooding presence on screen.

July 27. Actor James Mason is dead at the age of 75. Mason played sophisticates, both heroes and well-heeled heels. If he seemed unflappable on screen he was somewhat temperamental off it, criticizing hiring practices in first the British film industry, then the American.

Mason's memorable roles include that of Gustave Flaubert in "Madame Bovary" (1949), Brutus in "Julius Caesar" (1953) and Humbert Humbert in "Lolita" (1962). In the 70's and 80's, he made some relatively foolish pictures, "The Boys from Brazil," about cloning Hitler, and "Frankenstein: The True Story" among them. His stiff-lipped uppercrust delivery was frequently impersonated.

Olympics open like a Hollywood spectacle

Los Angeles, at opening ceremonies, becomes home to the world for two weeks.

July. The spectacular start of the Los Angeles Olympics was followed closely by some spectacular performances. After a glitzy, splashy opening that was pure Hollywood, the Games settled down to a succession of individual triumphs.

The American hero was Carl Lewis, who set an Olympic record in the 200-meter final for his third gold medal. He was also first in the 100-meter dash and the long jump.

The first marathon for women was taken by Joan Benoit of the U.S., who outran the previously invincible Grete Waitz of Norway.

Another American victory was turned in by the irrepressible Mary Lou Retton in the women's gymnastics. She had a perfect ten in the vault and became the first American woman to get an Olympic medal in any gymnastics event.

The men's team also scored an upset in gymnastics by defeating China. The feat was compared to the U.S. victory in hockey in 1980.

On the negative side, Mary Decker of the United States was leading in the 3,000-meter final when a fall put her out of the race. She went down in a collision with Zola Budd, a wispy 92-pound South African, and Maricica Puica of Rumania went on to win the race.

Despite the boycott of the Soviet Union and some other Communist countries, the Olympics attracted more than 7,000 athletes from 140 nations, the largest number in the history of the Games. The closing show was also spectacular.

The torch reaches its destination.

Gymnastics star Mary Lou Retton.

1984 Los Angeles

Men Athletics

100 M Dash
World Record: 9,93
Olympic Record: 9,95
1. Lewis Carl USA 9,99
2. Graddy Sam USA 10,19
3. Johnson Ben CAN 10,22

200 M Dash
World Record, 19,72
Olympic Record, 19,83
1. Lewis Carl USA *19,80
2. Baptiste Kirk USA 19,96
3. Jefferson Thomas USA 20,26

400 M Dash
World Record, 43,86
Olympic Record, 43,86
1. Babers Alonzo USA 44,27
2. Tiacoh Gabriel CIV 44,54
3. McKay Antonio USA 44,71

800 M Run
World Record, 1:41,73
Olympic Record, 1:43,50
1. Cruz Joaquim BRA *1:43,00
2. Coe Sebastian GBR 1:43,64
3. Jones Earl USA 1:43,83

1500 M Run
World Record, 3:30,77
Olympic Record, 3:34,91
1. Coe Sebastian GBR *3:32,52
2. Cram Steve GBR 3:33,40
3. Abascal Jose ESP 3:34,30

5000 M Run
World Record, 13:00,41
Olympic Record, 13:20,34
1. Aouita Said MAR *13:05,59
2. Ryffel Markus SUI 13:07,54
3. Leitao Antonio POR 13:09,20

10,000 M Run
World Record, 22,04
Olympic Record, 27:38,34
1. Cova Alberto ITA 27:47,54
2. Vainio Martti FIN 27:51,10
3. McLeod Michael GBR 28:06,22

Marathon
1. Lopes Carlos POR 2:09,21
2. Treacy John IRL 2:09,56
3. Spedding Charles GBR 2:09,58

110 M Hurdles
World Record, 12,93
Olympic Record, 13,24
1. Kingdom Roger USA *13,20
2. Foster Gregory USA 13,23
3. Bryggare Arto FIN 13,40

400 M Hurdles
1. Moses Edwin USA 47,75
2. Harris Danny USA 48,13
3. Schmid Harald FRG 48,19

3000 M Steeplechase
World Record, 8:05,04
Olympic Record, 8:08,02
1. Korir Julius KEN 8:11,80
2. Mahmoud Joseph FRA 8:13,31
3. Diemer Brian USA 8:14,06

400 M Relay
1. USA 37,83 *† (Graddy Sam, Brown Ron, Smith Calvin, Lewis Carl)
2. JAM 38,62 (Lawrence Albert, Meghoo Gregory, Quarrie Donald, Stewart Ray)
3. CAN 38,70 (Johnson Ben, Sharpe Tony, Williams Desai, Hinds Sterling)

1600 M Relay
World Record, 2:56,16
Olympic Record, 2:56,16
1. USA 2:57,91 (Nix Sunder, Armstead Ray, Babers Alonzo, McKay Antonio)
2. GBR 2:59,13 (Akabusi Kriss, Cook Gary, Bennett Todd, Brown Philip)
3. NGR 2:59,32 (Uti Sunday, Ugbusien Moses, Peters Rotimi, Egbunike Innocent)

20 km Walk
1. Canto Ernesto MEX *1:23:13
2. Gonzalez Raul MEX 1:23:20
3. Damilano Maurizio ITA 1:23:26

50 km Walk
1. Gonzalez Raul MEX *3:47:26
2. Gustafsson Bo SWE 3:53:19

High Jump
World Record, 2,38
Olympic Record, 2,36
1. Moegenburg Dietmar FRG 2,35
2. Sjoeberg Patrick SWE 2,33
3. Zhu Jianhua CHN 2,31

Pole Vault
World Record, 5,83
Olympic Record, 5,78
1. Quinon Pierre FRA 5,75
2. Tully Mike USA 5,65
3. Bell Earl USA 5,60

Long Jump
1. Lewis Carl USA 8,54
2. Honey Gary AUS 8,24
3. Evangelisti Giovanni ITA 8,24

Triple Jump
World Record, 17,89
Olympic Record, 17,39
1. Joyner Al USA 17,26
2. Conley Mike USA 17,18
3. Connor Keith GBR 16,87

Shotput
World Record, 22,22
Olympic Record, 21,35
1. Andrei Alessandro ITA 21,26
2. Carter Michael USA 21,09
3. Laut Dave USA 20,97

Discus Throw
World Record, 71,86
Olympic Record, 68,28
1. Danneberg Rolf FRG 66,60
2. Wilkins Mac USA 66,30
3. Powell John USA 65,46

Hammer Throw
World Record, 84,14
Olympic Record, 81,80
1. Tiainen Juha FIN 78,08
2. Riehm Karl-Hans FRG 77,98
3. Ploghaus Klaus FRG 76,68

Javelin
World Record, 104,80
Olympic Record, 94,58
1. Haerkoenen Arto FIN 86,76
2. Ottley David GBR 85,74
3. Eldebrink Kenth SWE 83,72

Decathlon
World Record, 8798
Olympic Record, 8618
1. Thompson Daley GBR *8797
2. Hingsen Juergen FRG 8673
3. Wentz Siegfried FRG 8412

1500 M Wheelchair
World Record, 3:48,1
1. Van Winkel Paul BEL 3:58,50
2. Snow Randy USA 4:00,02

Women Athletics

100 M Dash
World Record, 10,79
Olympic Record, 11,01
1. Ashford Evelyn USA *10,97
2. Brown Alice USA 11,13
3. Ottey-Page Merlene JAM 11,16

200 M Dash
World Record, 21,71
Olympic Record, 22,03
1. Brisco-Hooks Valerie USA *21,81
2. Griffith Florence USA 22,02
3. Ottey-Page Merlene JAM 22,09

400 M Run
World Record, 47,99
Olympic Record, 48,88
1. Brisco-Hooks Valerie USA *48,83
2. Cheeseborough Chandra USA 49,05
3. Cook Kathryn GBR 49,42

800 M Run
World Record, 1:53,28
Olympic Record, 1:53,43
1. Melinte Doina ROM 1:57,60
2. Gallagher Kim USA 1:58,83
3. Lovin Fiat ROM 1:58,83

1500 M Run
World Record, 3:52,47
Olympic Record, 3:56,56
1. Dorio Gabriella ITA 4:03,25
2. Melinte Doina ROM 4:03,76
3. Puica Maricica ROM 4:04,15

3000 M Run
World Record, 8:26,78
Olympic Record, 8:43,32
1. Puica Maricica ROM *8:35,96
2. Sly Wendy GBR 8:39,47
3. Williams Lynn CAN 8:42,14

100 M Hurdles
World Record, 12,36
Olympic Record, 12,56
1. Fitzgerald-Brown Benita USA 12,84
2. Strong Shirley GBR 12,88
3. Turner Kim USA 13,06

400 M Hurdles
World Record, 54,02
Olympic Record, 55,17
1. El Moutaw Kel Nawal MAR *54,61
2. Brown Judi USA 55,20
3. Cojocaru Cristina ROM 55,41

400 M Relay
World Record, 41,53
Olympic Record, 41,60
1. USA 41,65 (Brown Alice, Bolden Jeanette, Cheeseborough Chandra, Ashford Evelyn)
2. CAN 43,11 (Bailey Angela, Payne Marita, Taylor Angella, Gareau France)
3. GBR 43,11 (Jacobs Simone, Cook Kathryn, Callender Beverley, Oakes Heather)

1600 M Relay
World Record, 3:15,92
Olympic Record, 3:19,23
1. USA 3:18,29 *(Leatherwood Lillie, Howard Sherri, Brisco-Hooks Valerie, Cheeseborough Chandra)
2. CAN 3:21,21 (Crooks Charmaine, Richardson Jillian, Killingbeck Molly, Payne Marita)
3. FRG 3:22,98 (Schulte-Mattler Heike, Thimm Ute, Gaugel Heide, Bussmann Gaby)

High Jump
World Record, 2,07
Olympic Record, 1,97
1. Meyfarth Ulrike FRG *2,02
2. Simeoni Sara ITA 2,00
3. Huntley Joni USA 1,97

Long Jump
World Record, 7,43
Olympic Record, 7,06
1. Stanciu Anisoara ROM 6,96
2. Ionescu Vali ROM 6,81
3. Hearnshaw Susan GBR 6,80

Shotput
World Record, 22,53
Olympic Record, 22,41
1. Losch Claudia FRG 20,48
2. Loghin Mihaela ROM 20,47
3. Martin Gael AUS 19,19

Discus Throw
World Record, 73,26
Olympic Record, 69,26
1. Stalman Ria HOL 65,36
2. Deniz Leslie USA 64,86
3. Craciunescu Florenta ROM 63,64

Javelin
World Record, 74,76
Olympic Record, 68,40
1. Sanderson Tessa GBR *69,56
2. Lillak Tiina FIN 69,00
3. Whitebread Fatima GBR 67,14

Heptathlon
1. Nunn Glynis AUS 6390
2. Joyner Jackie USA 6385
3. Everts Sabine FRG 6363

Marathon
1. Benoit Joan USA 2:24,52
2. Waitz Grete NOR 2:26,18
3. Mota Rosa POR 2:26,57

800 M Wheelchair
World Record, 2:18,2
1. Hedrick Sharon USA †2:15,73
2. Saker Monica SWE 2:20,86
3. Cable Candace USA 2:28,37

Men Swimming

100 M Freestyle
World Record, 49,36
Olympic Record, 49,99
1. Gains Ambrose USA *49,80
2. Stockwell Mark AUS 50,24
3. Johansson Per SWE 50,31

200 M Freestyle
World Record, 1:47,55
Olympic Record, 1:48,03
1. Gross Michael FRG *1:47,44
2. Heath Michael USA 1:49,10
3. Fahrner Thomas FRG 1:49,66

400 M Freestyle
World Record, 3:48,32
Olympic Record, 3:51,31
1. Dicarlo George USA *3:51,23
2. Mykkanen John USA 3:51,49
3. Lemberg Justin AUS 3:51,79

1550 M Freestyle
World Record, 14:54,76
Olympic Record, 14:58,27
1. O'Brien Michael USA 15:05,20
2. Dicarlo George USA 15:10,59
3. Pfeiffer Stefan FRG 15:21,11

100 M Backstroke
World Record, 55:19
Olympic Record, 55:49
1. Carey Richard USA 55:79
2. Wilson David USA 56:35
3. West Mike CAN 56:49

200 M Backstroke
World Record, 1:58,86
Olympic Record, 1:58,99
1. Carey Richard USA 2:00,23
2. Delcourt Frederic FRA 2:01,75
3. Henning Cameron CAN 2:02,37

100 M Breaststroke
World Record, 1:02,13
Olympic Record, 1:02,16
1. Lindquist Steve USA *†1:01,65
2. Davis Victor CAN 1:01,99
3. Evans Peter AUS 1:02,97

200 M Breaststroke
World Record, 2:14,58
Olympic Record, 2:15,11
1. David Victor CAN *†2:13,34
2. Beringen Glenn AUS 2:15,79
3. Dagon Etienne SUI 2:17,41

100 M Butterfly Stroke
World Record, 53,38
Olympic Record, 53,78
1. Gross Michael FRG †53,08
2. Morales Pedro Pablo USA 53,23
3. Buchanan Glenn AUS 53,85

200 M Butterfly Stroke
World Record, 1:57,05
Olympic Record, 1:58,72
1. Sieben John AUS *†1:57,04
2. Gross Michael FRG 1:57,04
3. Vidal Castor Rafael VEN 1:57,51

200 M Medley
World Record, 2:02,25
Olympic Record, 2:08,60
1. Baumann Alex CAN *†2:01,42
2. Morales Pedro Pablo USA 2:03,05
3. Cochran Neil GBR 2:04,38

400 M Medley
World Record, 4:17,53
Olympic Record, 4:22,89
1. Baumann Alex CAN *†4:17,41
2. Prado Ricardo BRA 4:18,45
3. Woodhouse Robert AUS 4:20,50

400 M Medley Relay
World Record, 3:40,42
Olympic Record, 3:42,22
1. USA 3:39,30 *† (Carey Richard, Lundquist Steve, Morales Pedro Pablo, Gaines Ambrose)
2. CAN 3:43,23 (West Mike, Davis Victor, Ponting Tom, Goss Sandy)
3. AUS 3:43,25 (Kerry Mark, Evans Peter, Buchanan Glenn, Stockwell Mark)

400 M Freestyle Relay
World Record, 3:19,26
Olympic Record, 3:19,94
1. USA 3:19,03 *† (Cavanaugh Christopher, Heath Michael, Biondi Matthew, Gaines Ambrose)
2. AUS 3:19,68 (Fasala Gregory, Brooks Neil, Delany Michael, Stockwell Mark)
3. SWE 3:22,69 (Leidstrom Thomas, Baron Bengt, Om Mikael, Johansson Per)

800 M Freestyle Relay
World Record, 7:18,87
Olympic Record, 7:18,87
1. USA 7:15,69 *† (Heath Michael, Larson David, Float Jeffery, Hayes Lawrence Bruce)
2. FRG 7:15,73 (Fahrner Thomas, Korthals Dirk, Schowtka Alexander, Gross Michael)
3. GBR 7:24,78 (Cochran Neil, Easter Paul, Howe Paul, Astbury Andrew)

Springboard Diving
1. Louganis Gregory USA 754,41
2. Tan Liangde CHN 662,31
3. Merriott Ronald USA 661,32

High Diving
1. Louganis Gregory USA 710,91
2. Kimball Bruce USA 643,50
3. Li Kongzheng CHN 638,28

Water-Polo

1. Yugoslavia
2. USA
3. German Federal Republic

Lewis finishes in 19.8, an Olympic record in the 200-meter final.

Women Swimming

100 M Freestyle
World Record, 54,79
1. Steinseifer Carrie USA 55,92
2. Hogshead Nancy USA 55,92
3. Verstappen Annemarie HOL 56,08

200 M Freestyle
World Record, 1:57,75
Olympic Record, 1:58,33
1. Wayte Mary USA 1:59,23
2. Woodhead Cynthia USA 1:59,50
3. Verstappen Annemarie HOL 1:59,69

400 M Freestyle
World Record, 4:06,28
Olympic Record, 4:08,76
1. Cohen Tiffany USA *4:07,10
2. Hardcastle Sarah GBR 4:10,27
3. Croft June GBR 4:11,49

800 M Freestyle
World Record, 8:24,62
Olympic Record, 8:28,90
1. Cohen Tiffany USA *8:24,95
2. Richardson Michele USA 8:30,73
3. Hardcastle Sarah GBR 8:32,60

100 M Backstroke
World Record, 1:00,86
Olympic Record, 1:00,86
1. Andrews Theresa USA 1:02,55
2. Mitchell Betsy USA 1:02,63
3. De Rover Jolanda HOL 1:02,91

200 M Backstroke
World Record, 2:09,91
Olympic Record, 2:11,77
1. De Rover Jolanda HOL 2:12,38
2. White Amy USA 2:13,04
3. Patrascoiu Aneta ROM 2:13,29

100 M Breaststroke
World Record, 1:08,51
Olympic Record, 1:10,11
1. Van Staveren Petra HOL *1:09,88
2. Ottenbrite Anne CAN 1:10,69
3. Poirot Catherine FRA 1:10,70

200 M Breaststroke
World Record, 2:28,36
Olympic Record, 2:29,54
1. Ottenbrite Anne CAN 2:30,38
2. Rapp Susan USA 2:31,15
3. Lempereur Ingrid BEL 2:31,40

100 M Butterfly Stroke
World Record, 57,93
Olympic Record, 59,05
1. Meagher Mary T. USA 59,26
2. Johnson Jenna USA 1:00,19
3. Seick Karin FRG 1:01,36

200 M Butterfly Stroke
World Record, 2:05,96
Olympic Record, 2:10,44
1. Meagher Mary T. USA *2:06,90
2. Philips Karen AUS 2:10,56
3. Beyermann Ina FRG 2:11,91

200 M Medley
World Record, 2:11,73
Olympic Record, 2:14,47
1. Caulkins Tracy USA *2:12,64
2. Hogshead Nancy USA 2:15,17
3. Pearson Michele AUS 2:15,92

400 M Relay
World Record, 4:36,10
Olympic Record, 4:36,29
1. Caulkins Tracy USA 4:39,24
2. Lansells Suzanne AUS 4:48,30
3. Zindler Petra FRG 4:48,57

400 M Medley Relay
World Record, 4:05,79
Olympic Record, 4:06,67
1. USA 4:08,34 (Andrews Theresa, Caulkins Tracy, Meagher Mary T., Hogshead Nancy)
2. FRG 4:11,97 (Schlicht Svenja, Hasse Ute, Beyemann Ina, Seick Karin)
3. CAN 4:12,98 (Abdo Reeman, Ottenbrite Annie, MacPherson Michelle, Rai Pamela)

400 M Freestyle Relay
World Record, 3:42,71
Olympic Record, 3:42,71
1. USA 3:43,43 (Johnson Jenna, Steinseifer Carrie, Torres Dara, Hogshead Nancy)
2. HOL 3:44,40 (Verstappen Annemarie, Voskes Elles, Reijers Desi, Van Bentum Conny)
3. FRG 3:45,56 (Zscherpe Iris, Schuster Suzanne, Pielke Christiane, Seick Karin)

Springboard Diving
1. Bernier Sylvie CAN 530,70
2. McCormick Kelly USA 527,46
3. Seufert Christina USA 517,62

High Diving
1. Zhou Jihong CHN 435,51
2. Mitchell Michele USA 431,19
3. Wyland Wendy USA 422,07

Sychronized Swimming Individual
1. Ruiz Tracie USA 198,467
2. Waldo Carolyn CAN 195,300
3. Motoyoshi Miwako JAP 187,050

Sychronized Swimming Duet
1. Costie Candy, Ruiz Tracie USA 195,584
2. Hambrook Sharon, Krycka Kelly CAN 194,234
3. Kimura Saeko, Motoyoshi Miwako JAP 187,992

Boxing

Light Flyweight
1. Gonzales Paul USA
2. Todisco Salvatore ITA
3. Mwila Keith ZAM
3. Bolivar Jose Marcelino VEN

Flyweight
1. McCrory Steven USA
2. Redzepovski Redzep YUG
3. Can Eyrup TUR
3. Bilali Ibrahim KEN

Bantamweight
1. Stecca Maurizio ITA
2. Lopez Hector MEX
3. Walters Dale CAN
3. Nolasco Pedro J. DOM

1984 Los Angeles

Featherweight
1. Taylor Meldrick USA
2. Konyegwachie Peter NGR
3. Aykac Turgut TUR
3. Catari Peraza Omar VEN

Lightweight
1. Whitaker Pernell USA
2. Ortiz Luis F. PUR
3. Ndongo Ebanga Martin CMR
3. Chun Chil-Sung KOR

Light Welterweight
1. Page Derry USA
2. Umponmaha Dhawee THA
3. Pulger Mircea ROM
4. Pulzovic Mirko YUG

Welterweight
1. Breland Mark USA
2. An Young-Su THA
3. Nyman Joni ROM
3. Bruno Luciano YUG

Light Middleweight
1. Tate Franck USA
2. O'Sullivan Shawn CAN
3. Zielonka Manfred FRG
3. Tiozzo Christophe FRA

Middleweight
1. Shin Joon-Sop KOR
2. Hill Virgil USA
3. Zaoui Mohamed ALG
3. Gonzalez Aristides PUR

Light Heavyweight
1. Josipovic Anton YUG
2. Barry Kevin NZL
3. Moussa Mustapha ALG
3. Holyfield Evander USA

Heavyweight
1. Tillman Henry USA
2. Dewit Willie CAN
3. Musone Angelo ITA
3. Vanderlijde Arnold HOL

Super-Heavyweight
1. Biggs Tyrell USA
2. Damiani Francesco ITA
3. Wells Robert GBR
3. Azis Salihu YUG

Weightlifting

Flyweight (less than 52 kg)
1. Zeng Guoqiang CHN 235,0
2. Zhou Peishun CHN 235,0
3. Manabe Kazushito JPN 232,5

Bantamweight (less than 56 kg)
1. Wu Shude CHN 267,5
2. Lai Runming CHN 265,0
3. Kotaka Masahiro JPN 252,5

Featherweight (less than 60 kg)
1. Chen Wieqiang CHN 282,5
2. Radu Gelu ROM 280,0
3. Tsai Wen-Yee TPE 272,5

Lightweight (less than 67.5 kg)
1. Yao Jingyuan CHN 320,0
2. Socaci Andrei ROM 312,5
3. Jouni Gronman FIN 312,5

Middleweight (less than 75 kg)
1. Radschinsky Karl-Heinz FRG 340,0
2. Demers Jacques CAN 335,0
3. Cioroslan Dragomir ROM 332,50

Light Heavyweight (82.5 kg)
1. Becheru Petre ROM 342,5
2. Kabbas Robert AUS 340,0
3. Isaoko Ryoji JPN 335,0

Middle Heavyweight (less than 90 kg)
1. Vlad Nicu ROM 392,5
2. Petre Dumitru ROM 360,0
3. Mercer David GBR 352,5

Heavyweight (less than 100 kg)
1. Milser Rolf FRG 385,0
2. Gropa Vasile ROM 382,5
3. Niemi Pekka FIN 367,5

Heavyweight (less than 110 kg)
1. Oberburger Norberto ITA 390,00
2. Tasnadi Stefan ROM 380,0
3. Carlton Guy USA 377,5

Super-Heavyweight (more than 110 kg)
1. Lukim Dinko AUS 412,5
2. Martinez Mario USA 410,0
3. Nerlinger Manfred FRG 397,5

Judo

Extra Lightweight
1. Hosokawa Shinji JPN
2. Kim Jae-Yug KOR
3. Laddie Edward USA
3. Eckersley Neil GBR

Half Lightweight (less than 65 kg)
1. Matsuoka Yoshiyuki JPN
2. Hwang Jung-Oh KOR
3. Reiter Josef AUT
3. Alexandre Marc FRA

Lightweight (less than 71 kg)
1. Ahn Byeong-Keun KOR
2. Gamba Ezio ITA
3. Onmura Luis BRA
3. Brown Kerrith GBR

Half Middleweight (less than 78 kg)
1. Wieneke Frank FRG
2. Adams Neil GBR
3. Nowak Michel FRA
3. Fratica Mircea ROM

Middleweight (less than 86 kg)
1. Seisenbacher Peter AUT
2. Berland Robert USA
3. Nose Seiki JPN
3. Carmona Walter BRA

Half Heavyweight (less than 95 kg)
1. Ha Hyoung-Zoo KOR
2. Vieira Douglas BRA
3. Fridriksson Bjarni ISL
3. Neureuther Gunter FRG

Heavyweight (more than 95 kg)
1. Saito Hitoshi JPN
2. Parisi Angelo FRA
3. Cho Yong-Chul KOR
3. Berger Mark CAN

Open Category
1. Yamashita Yasuhiro JPN
2. Rashwan Mohamed EGY
3. Cioc Mihai ROM
3. Shnabel Arthur FRG

Men Fencing

Foil Individual
1. Numa Mauro ITA
2. Behr Matthias FRG
3. Cerioni Stefano ITA

Foil Team
1. Italy
2. German Federal Republic
3. France

Epée Individual
1. Boisse Philippe FRA
2. Vaggo Bjorne SWE
3. Riboud Philippe FRA

Epée Team
1. German Federal Republic
2. France
3. Italy

Sabre Individual
1. Lamour Jean-Francois FRA
2. Marin Marco ITA
3. Westbrook Peter USA

Sabre Team
1. Italy
2. France
3. Romania

Women Fencing

Foil Individual
1. Luan Jujie CHN
2. Hanisch Cornelia FRG
3. Vaccaroni Dorina ITA

Foil Team
1. German Federal Republic
2. Romania
3. France

Modern Pentathlon

Individual
1. Masala Daniele ITA 5469
2. Rasmuson Svante SWE 5456
3. Massullo Carlo ITA 5406

Team
1. Italy 16060
2. USA 15568
3. France 15565

Men Canoeing

Kayak-1 500 M
1. Ferguson Ian NZL 1:47,84
2. Moberg Lars-Erik SWE 1:48,18
3. Bregeon Bernard FRA 1:48,41

Kayak-1 1000 M
1. Thompson Alan NZL 3:45,73
2. Janic Milan YUG 3:46,88
3. Barton Greg USA 3:47,38

Kayak-2 500 M
1. Ferguson Ian / Mac Donald Paul NZL 1:34,21
2. Bengtsson Per-Inge / Moberg Lars-Erik SWE 1:35,26
3. Fisher Hugh CAN 1:35,41

Kayak-2 1000 M
1. Fisher Hugn / Morris Alwyn CAN 3:24,22
3. Bregeon Bernard / Lefoulon Patrick FRA 3:25,97
3. Kelly Bary AUS 3:26,80

Kayak-4 1000 M
1. New Zealand
2. Sweden
3. France

Canadian-1 500 M
1. Cain Larry CAN 1:57,01
2. Jakobsen Henning L. DEN 1:58,45
3. Olaru Costica ROM 1:59,86

Canadian-1 1000 M
1. Eike Ulrich FRG 4:06,32
2. Cain Larry CAN 4:08,67
3. Jakobsen Henning L. DEN 4:09,51

Canadian-2 500 M
1. Ljubek Matija / Nisovic Mirko YUG 1:43,67
2. Potzaichin Ivan / Simionov Toma ROM 1:45,68
3. Miguez Enrique ESP 1:47,71

Women Canoeing

Kayak-1 500 M
1. Andersson Agneta SWE 1:58,72
2. Schuttpelz Barbara FRG 1:59,93
3. Derckx Annemeik HOL 2:00,11

Kayak-2 500 M
1. Andersson Agneta / Olsson Anna SWE 1:45,25
2. Barre Alexandra / Holloway Sue CAN 1:47,13
3. Idem Josefa / Schuttpelz Barbara FRG 1:47,32

Men Rowing

Single Scull
1. Karppinen Pertti FIN 7:00,24
2. Kolbe Peter-Michael FRG 7:02,19
3. Mills Robert CAN 7;10,38

Double Sculls
1. USA 6:36,87
2. Belgium 6:38,19
3. Yugoslavia 6:39,59

Pair Oars without Coxswain
1. Romania 6:45,39
2. Spain 6:48,47
3. Norway 7:12,81

Pair Oars with Coxswain
1. Italy 7:05,99
2. Romania 7:11,21
3. USA 7:12,81

Quadruple Sculls without Coxswain
1. German Federal Republic 5:57,55
2. Australia 5:57,98
3. Canada 5:59,07

Four Oars without Coxswain
1. New Zealand 6:03,48
2. USA 6:06,10
3. Denmark 6:07,72

Four Oars with Coxswain
1. Great Britain 6:18,64
2. USA 6:20,28
3. New Zealand 6:23,68

Eight Oars
1. Canada 5:41,32
2. USA 5:41,74
3. Australia 5:43,40

Women Rowing

Single Scull
1. Racila Valeria ROM 3:40,68
2. Geer Charlotte USA 3:43,89
3. Haesebrouck Ann BEL 3:45,72

Double Sculls
1. Romania 3:26,75
2. Netherlands 3:29,13
3. Canada 3:29,82

Pair Oars without Coxswain
1. Romania 3:32,60
2. Canada 3:36,06
3. German Federal Republic 3:40,50

Quadruple Sculls with Coxswain
1. Romania 3;14,11
2. USA 3:15,57
3. Denmark 3:16,02

Four Oars with Coxswain
1. Romania 3:19,30
2. Canada 3:21,55
3. Australia 3:23,29

Eight Oars with Coxswain
1. USA 2:59,80
2. Romania 3:00,87
3. Netherlands 3:02,92

Yachting

Finn Class
1. Coutts Russel NZL 34,70
2. Bertrand John USA 37,00
3. Neilson Terry CAN 37,70

Flying Dutchman Class
1. USA 19,70
2. Canada 22,70
3. Great Britain 48,70

Sailing Class
1. USA 33,70
2. Brazil 43,40
3. Canada 49,70

Star Class
1. USA 29,70
2. German Federal Republic 41,40
3. Italy 43,50

470 Class
1. Spain 33,70
2. USA 43,00
3. France 49,40

Tornado Class
1. New Zealand 14,70
2. USA 37,00
3. Australia 50,40

Cycling

Individual Road Race
1. Grewal Alexi USA 4:59,57
2. Bauer Steve CAN 4:59,57
3. Lauritzen Dag Otto NOR 5:00,18

100 km Team Time Trial
1. Italy 1:58,28
2. Switzerland 2:02,38
3. USA 2:02,46

1000 M
1. Schmidtke Fredy FRG 54,459
2. Harnett Curtis CAN 54,187
3. Colas Fabrice FRA 54,014

Sprint
1. Gorski Mark USA
2. Vails Nelson USA
3. Sakamoto Tsutomu JPN

Individual Pursuit 4000 M
1. Hegg Steve USA 51,548
2. Golz Rolf FRG 50,736
3. Nitz Leonard Harvey USA 50,698

Team Pursuit
1. Australia 54,137
2. USA 53,362
3. German Federal Republic 54,216

100 km Team
1. Italy 1:58,28
2. Switzerland 2:02,38
3. USA 2:02,57

Equestrian Sports

All-Around Individual Competition
1. Stives Karen Ben Arthur USA
2. Todd Mark Charisma NZL
3. Holgate Virgina Priceless GBR

All-Around Team Competition
1. USA
2. Great Britain
3. German Federal Republic

Individual Dressage
1. Klimke Dr. Reiner Ahlerich FRG
2. Jensen Anne Grethe Marzog DEN
3. Hofer Otto J. Limandus SUI

Team Dressage
1. German Federal Republic
2. Switzerland
3. Sweden

Grand Prix Jumping Individual
1. Fargis Joe Touch of Class USA
2. Homfeld Conrad Abdullah USA
3. Robbiani Heidi Jessica V SUI

Grand Prix Jumping Team
1. USA
2. Great Britain
3. German Federal Republic

Shooting

Small-Bore Rifle, 50 M, Prone
1. Etzel Edward USA 599
2. Bury Michel FRA 596
3. Sullivan Michael GBR 596

Small-Bore Rifle, Combined, 3 Positions
1. Cooper Malcom GBR 1173
2. Nipkow Daniel SUI 1163
3. Allan Alister GBR 1162

Rapid-Fire Pistol
1. Kamachi Takeo JPN 595
2. Ion Corneliu ROM 593
3. Bies Rauno FIN 591

Free Pistol
1. Xu Haifeng CHN 566
2. Shanaker Ragnar SWE 565
3. Wang Yifu CHN 564

Trap Shooting
1. Giovannetti Luciano ITA 192
2. Boza Francisco PER 192
3. Carlisle Daniel USA 192

Skeet
1. Dryke Matthew USA 198
2. Rasmussen Ole Riber DEN 196
3. Scribani Rossi Luca ITA 196

Moving Target
1. Li Yuwei CHN 587
2. Bellingrodt Helmut COL 584
3. Huang Shiping CHN 581

Men Archery

1. Pace Darrell USA 2616
2. McKinney Richard USA 2564
3. Yamamoto Hiroshi JPN 2563

Women Archery

1. Seo YHyang-Soon KOR 2568
2. Li Jigjuan CHN 2559
3. Kim Jin-Ho KOR 2555

Men Gymnastics

All-Around Individual Competition
1. Gushiken Koji JPN 118,700
2. Vidmar Peter USA 118,675
3. Li Ning CHN 118,575

All-Around Team Competition
1. USA 591,40
2. People's Republic of China 590,80
3. Japan 586,70

Floor Exercise
1. Li Ning CHN 19,925
2. Lou Yun CHN 19,775
3. Sotomura Koji JPN 19,700

Parallel Bars
1. Conner Bart USA 19,950
2. Kajitani Nobuyuki JPN 19,925
3. Gaylord Mitchell USA 19,850

Horse Vault
1. Li Ning CHN 19,950
2. Vidmar Peter USA 19,950
3. Daggett Timothy USA 19,825

Sidehorse
1. Lou Yun CHN 19,950
2. Li Ning CHN 19,825
3. Gushiken Koji JPN 19,825

Horizontal Bar
1. Morisue Shinji JPN 20,000
2. Tong Fei CHN 19,975
3. Gushiken Koji JPN 19,950

Flying Rings
1. Gushiken Koji JPN 19,850
2. Li Ning CHN 19,850
3. Gaylord Mitchell USA 19,825

Women Gymnastics

All-Around Team Competition
1. Romania 392,20
2. USA 391,20
3. People's Republic of China 388,60

All-Around Individual Competition
1. Retton Mary Lou USA 79,175
2. Szabo Ecaterina ROM 79,125
3. Pauca Simona ROM 78,675

Uneven Bars
1. Ma Yanhong CHN 19,950
2. McNamara Julianne USA 19,950
3. Retton Mary Lou USA 19,800

Floor Exercise
1. Szabo Ecaterina ROM 19,975
2. McNamara Julianne USA 19,950
3. Retton Mary Lou USA 19,775

Horse Vault
1. Szabo Ecaterina ROM 19,875
2. Retton Mary Lou USA 19,850
3. Agache Lavinia ROM 19,750

Beam
1. Pauca Simona ROM 19,800
2. Szabo Ecaterina ROM 19,800
3. Johnson Kathy USA 19,650

Rhythmic Competition
1. Fung Lori CAN 57,950
2. Staiculescu Doina ROM 57,900
3. Weber Regina FRG 57,700

Men Basketball
1. USA
2. Spain
3. Yugoslavia

Women Basketball
1. USA
2. Korea
3. People's Republic of China

Soccer
1. France
2. Brazil
3. Yugoslavia

Men Handball
1. Yugoslavia
2. German Federal Republic
3. Romania

Women Handball
1. Yugoslavia
2. Korea
3. People's Republic of China

Men Field Hockey
1. Pakistan
2. German Federal Republic
3. Great Britain

Women Field Hockey
1. Netherlands
2. New Zealand
3. Australia

Men Volleyball
1. USA
2. Brazil
3. Italy

Women Volleyball
1. People's Republic of China
2. USA
3. Japan

*** = New Olympic Record**
† = New World Record

1984

AUGUST

Su	Mo	Tu	We	Th	Fr	Sa
			1	2	3	4
5	6	7	8	9	10	11
12	13	14	15	16	17	18
19	20	21	22	23	24	25
26	27	28	29	30	31	

1. Tehran: Terrorists hijack Air France jet, demand freedom for five in jail in France (→ 2).

2. Tehran: Iranians free French hostages, blow up cockpit of jet.

3. L.A.: Mary Lous Retton wins gold in all-around gymnastics.

4. Texas: Coast smothered in 5,000 tons of oil from grounded British tanker.

5. L.A.: Joan Benoit wins first Olympic marathon for women.

8. L.A.: Carl Lewis wins third gold, in 200-meters.

10. Washington: Congress approves extra $70 mil. in aid to El Salvador (→ 10/10).

10. L.A.: Mary Decker knocked out of 3,000-meters in clash with Zola Budd.

11. Reagan signs bill sanctioning religious or political gatherings in public schools after hours (→ 6/4/85).

12. Reagan, during radio test, jokes about bombing Soviet Union (→ 1/11/85).

14. N.Y.: Cuomo signs nation's first bill to curb acid rain (→ 10/24).

16. U.S.: Jaycees vote to admit women to full membership.

17. U.S.: Federal appeals panel upholds Navy's discharge of homosexual (→ 3/20/86).

17. U.S.S.R. assigns Yelena Bonner forced residence in Gorky where husband Sakharov is exiled (→ 9/5).

18. Persian Gulf: Loaded Panamanian oil tanker struck by missile (→ 10/8).

21. Egypt charges Libya with mining Mideast waters (→ 9/1).

27. Reagan announces a schoolteacher will be first citizen passenger on space shuttle (→ 30).

28. Lebanon: Israeli jets attack PLO base in Bekaa (→ 10/9).

30. Cape Canaveral: Space shuttle Discovery fired into orbit on maiden flight (→ 9/1).

31. Israel: Likud, Labor agree on power sharing plan (→ 9/14).

DEATH

15. J.B. Priestley, prolific British novelist (*9/13/1894).

900,000 Filipinos march against Marcos

U.S. condemned along with Marcos.

Aug 21. One year ago in Manila, government opposition leader Benigno Aquino was assassinated. Today, 900,000 demonstrators filled the streets of the Philippine capital to observe Aquino's death and to protest against the government of President Ferdinand Marcos.

About 2,000 troops were on hand in anticipation of violence, which never occurred. While non-violent, the crowds did not lack passion in their hatred of Marcos, their condemnation of the United States, which has supported Marcos, and their admiration for Aquino. Many businesses and schools closed for the day, wary that normal activities would be disrupted.

The main rally was held in Rizal Park, framed with posters marked "Down with the U.S.-Marcos Dictatorship!" Those at the rally who attempted to speak English were booed and forced to speak in Tagalog, the chief native language of Filipinos. In an address, Corazon Aquino, widow of the slain leader, denounced the economic situation in the nation and called for Marcos' resignation (→ 9/23).

Republicans nominate Reagan and Bush

Aug 22. Jubilant Republicans agreed today to stick with a winning team: Ronald Wilson Reagan for President and George Herbert Bush for Vice President.

As the Dallas Convention Center erupted in a sustained roar, Senator Paul Laxalt of Nevada called for the re-election of President Reagan as "a leader who is not afraid." Later, Vice President Bush was nominated on the first roll call.

In accepting his nomination, the president described Republicans as "America's party" and the Democrats as a party of fear. "We will be America's party," the president said, "because the American dream begins with opportunity and our goal is to build an opportunity society for every man, woman and child."

The convention also heard a call to battle against the Democrats from Senator Barry Goldwater, a conservative (→ 10/21).

Reagans and Bushes thank backers for their endorsement of the last four years.

Richard Burton's great voice is stilled

Richard Burton and daughter, Kate.

Aug 5. Actor Richard Burton has died of a stroke at his home in Switzerland. The world mourns the possibilities; Burton never reached his potential, drink and and self-deprecation waylaying him. If he had lived, he might have mellowed into the likes of John Gielgud or Ralph Richardson, letting another generation savor his rich voice.

Burton was born to a Welsh mining family Nov. 10, 1925. In his first stage roles he played Welsh shepherds and miners, but in the 1960 film "Camelot" he ascended to the English throne and won raves. In 1964, his "Hamlet" on Broadway won high praise. Lately, he chose roles with less discernment.

Former wife Elizabeth Taylor heard the news while staying with their adopted daughter, Maria.

B-1 bomber crashes

Aug 29. A prototype of the B-1 bomber crashed in the Mohave desert today during a test flight, killing one of its three crew members. The crash came just six days before the Reagan administration was scheduled to unveil the first production model of the new bomber. Air Force officials said the plane had been on a "low speed, low altitude" flight from Edwards Air Force Base when it crashed, but gave no other details of the accident. Administration officials said the crash would have no effect on the $14 billion program to develop a new fleet of long-range strategic bombers.

Ferraro denies any wrongdoing in business

Aug 21. Rep. Geraldine Ferraro, the Democratic candidate for vice president, sought today to stem the criticism over her financial affairs, denying any wrongdoing but at the same time admitting that some mistakes had been made.

The tangled financial affairs of Mrs. Ferraro and her husband, John A. Zaccaro of Queens, have become a major issue in the presidential campaign. Earlier this week, she was quoted as being surprised to learn that her husband had borrowed $100,000 for their real estate company from the assets of an elderly woman whose finances he was overseeing.

In a two-hour press conference at Kennedy International Airport, Mrs. Ferraro acknowledged some sloppy record-keeping but insisted that neither she nor her husband had done anything wrong. She has released a huge mass of financial records.

"The supposition was that we had something to hide and obviously we don't," she said. "I hope by Sunday, which is my birthday, we'll start a new year."

Meanwhile, Walter F. Mondale, who just last month had handpicked Mrs. Ferraro as his running mate in the upcoming presidential election, voiced strong support for her today. "She's passed a test of leadership that will strengthen public respect for her and her capabilities," Mondale said (→ 22).

Ship carrying uranium sinks off Belgium

The Mont Louis, still in possession of its deadly cargo, goes down off Belgium.

Aug 25. There was a nuclear scare off the coast of Belgium tonight. A French cargo ship, the Mont Louis, was carrying 450 tons of a form of uranium when it collided with a car ferry near Ostend. The two ships locked together until tug boats managed to pull them apart. Then the Mont Louis foundered, flipped on its side and sank.

The owners of the ship admitted belatedly that it was transporting a large cargo of uranium hexafluoride, an intermediate product which can be used to make either nuclear bombs or nuclear fuel. Divers were dispatched immediately to test the water near the scene of the collision, and an official of the French Environment Ministry said there was "no trace of radioactivity in the area." The ship's owners said the material was being shipped in 30 containers located in the forward part of the ship, which was not touched in the collision. Atomic energy experts said any radiation would be diluted if the uranium came into contact with sea water.

It was the environmental group Greenpeace that first revealed that the Mont Louis had a nuclear cargo. A spokesman said, "The accident in the North Sea proves that it is not safe to transport nuclear materials by sea."

The uranium hexafluoride was on its way to the Soviet Union when the accident occurred. The Environment Ministry spokesman said shipment of the material is not outlawed by NATO agreements. The official could not say how the Soviet Union was planning to use the uranium.

DeLorean acquitted of cocaine charges

Aug 16. Los Angeles jurors said today that the belief that John Z. DeLorean had been entrapped by the government and a feeling that it had not proved its drug-trafficking case against him figured in the decision to acquit him. "Without the entrapment, there would have been a hung jury," one commented. However, troubles are not over for the unorthodox former auto executive, who may be "reinvited" to London to tell what happened to $17 million earmarked for the firm producing the DeLorean sports car. Britain's government is a creditor in a bankruptcy action (→ 12/17/86).

Capote, naughty lad of literature, dies

Diminutive Capote said he was as "tall as a shotgun and just as noisy."

Aug 25. Author Truman Capote has been found dead at the Los Angeles home of Joanna Carson, a former wife of Johnny Carson. No foul play is suspected. Capote, 59, had well-publicized problems with drugs and alcohol.

Everything about the diminutive (5'4") Capote was well-publicized, and he liked it that way. He documented his lonely childhood in Alabama in short stories, and his first novelette "Other Voices, Other Rooms," written when he was just 23, exposed his troubled teen years.

Yet his masterwork "In Cold Blood" (1965) was an impersonal account of an actual murder. Asked to explain his technique, he said he was just a genius.

Asbestos in schools

Aug 31. Nearly 100 public schools in New Jersey will not open for the new term next week because they have not removed asbestos from classrooms, state officials announced today. The schools had been ordered to remove asbestos pipe insulation and ceiling tiles because of evidence its fibers could cause cancer and other illnesses when inhaled. The National Education Association estimates that 14,000 United States schools have asbestos problems and that children are more vulnerable than adults to airborne asbestos that flakes off ceiling tiles or heating pipes.

Alfred A. Knopf dies

Aug 11. Publisher Alfred A. Knopf has died in New York state. He was 91. Knopf kept his priorities straight: Some authors were invited to his publishing house because they could write best-sellers; others were invited because they could write well. Knopf is responsible in part for the careers of 26 Pulitzer Prize authors and 16 Nobel winners.

Knopf was interested in foreign writers and championed a few from Japan and South America. Before starting his own firm at the age of 23, he struck up a correspondence with and encouraged an unknown Polish writer —Joseph Conrad.

Aug 19. Lee Trevino wins the PGA again, after ten years. He's won the U.S. and British Opens twice and the Canadian thrice.

1984

SEPTEMBER

Su	Mo	Tu	We	Th	Fr	Sa
						1
2	3	4	5	6	7	8
9	10	11	12	13	14	15
16	17	18	19	20	21	22
23	24	25	26	27	28	29
30						

1. Solar power array deployed by space shuttle (→ 5).

1. Libya: Khadafy says he has sent troops and arms to aid Sandinistas (→ 1/1/86).

2. Amritsar: Thousands of Sikhs rally at Golden Temple to protest govt. occupation (→ 10/31).

4. Santiago: French churchman Andre Jarlan killed in home in working-class section (→ 10/29).

5. Space Shuttle Discovery returns from six-day maiden flight (→ 10/2).

5. U.S.S.R.: Chernenko makes first public appearance in seven weeks (→ 6).

6. Tokyo: Hirohito welcomes South Korean Pres. Chun Doo Hwan, apologizes for Japan's past behavior.

6. Moscow: Chief of staff Marshal Nikolai Ogarkov relieved of duties (→ 2/6/85).

9. N.Y.: McEnroe over Lendl 6-3, 6-4, 6-1; Navratilova over Evert Lloyd 4-6, 6-4, 6-4 for U.S. Open titles.

11. Shultz says U.S. will admit thousands of Vietnamese children fathered by G.I.'s (→ 11/15).

12. Newfoundland: Pope issues strong call for public financing of religious schools (→ 11/11).

15. Detroit: U.A.W. commences strikes at 13 G.M. auto plants.

17. Miami: 10,000 take oath of citizenship at Orange Bowl.

17. Paris: France, Libya agree to remove troops from Chad.

19. West Germany bars leaded gas, requires catalytic converters on all autos beginning 1988.

22. IMF agrees to reduce credit limits of debtor nations.

23. Manila: Prelate Jaime Cardinal Sin denounces Marcos regime (→ 10/24).

24. Reagan at U.N. appeals for thaw in Soviet ties, issues plan for arms control (→ 28).

25. Jordan restores diplomatic ties with Egypt, broken after accord with Israel.

30. Peking reiterates offer to let Taiwan retain capitalism if it reunites with mainland.→

Beirut car bomb kills 23 at U.S. Embassy

Lebanese troops survey remains of second U.S. Embassy bombed in Beirut.

Sept 20. Dodging heavy gunfire, a suicide bomber snaked around the concrete-block defense of the U.S. Embassy in Beirut and blew up the car in front of the building. The blast, heavy enough to rip off the facade and bend steel bars, killed at least 23 persons, two of whom were known to be Americans, with a probable death toll reaching 40. Scores were wounded and most of the casualties were Lebanese, either employees or visa-seekers.

In the aftermath, blood-splattered diplomats staggered out of the wreckage looking for friends as stunned Marine guards donned flak jackets. This second such bombing of a U.S. Embassy in Lebanon comes 17 months after the April 1983 attack when the embassy was in West Beirut. It was then moved to its present site in the northeast, a presumably safer area patrolled by Lebanese Phalangist soldiers. The Islamic Holy War terrorist group claimed responsibility for both of the bombings.

Mulroney scores big win over Liberals

Sept 4. Brian Mulroney and his Progressive Conservative Party scored a huge victory today over the Liberal Party of Prime Minister John N. Turner as Canadians chose a new national government. In a speech to his cheering supporters, the newly elected Prime Minister said that his party's mandate was "to create jobs and get the economy of Canada moving again." Meanwhile, in conceding the election, Turner pledged to work toward the rebuilding of the Liberal Party. He was the only Liberal in the country to win a seat formerly held by a Tory.

Mulroney won even Quebec this year.

Hong Kong will return to China in 1997

Sept 30. China has a new agreement with Great Britain that will allow Hong Kong to be returned to Chinese rule. Officials in Peking asserted today that the accord could serve as a model for the union of Taiwan and China. Under the Hong Kong agreement initialed on the 26th, the territory reverts to China in 1997, but it will be allowed to preserve its free enterprise system for an additional 50 years. The agreement suits the Peking government, which relies on Hong Kong for lucrative commercial and financial contacts with the West. In Peking today, Prime Minister Zhao Ziyang said Taiwan could be reunited with China and remain capitalistic. "Our proposition of one country, two systems after reunification is most reasonable," he said.

Princess of Wales is wild about Harry

Sept 16. The Prince and Princess of Wales will name their second son Prince Henry, but he will be just plain Harry at home, Buckingham Palace announced today, less than 24 hours after the prince was born.

Charles, Di, William and Harry.

Contras reportedly got $10m in private aid

Sept 8. The Nicaraguan contra rebels have raised over $10 million in the past six months, with the aid coming from private corporations and individuals in the United States and the governments of Israel, Argentina, Venezuela, Guatemala and Taiwan.

Rebel leader Mario Calero Portocarrero said in an interview, "We're raising more than $1.5 million a month," and that much of it comes from "some large, well-known companies." The money has been funnelled to the rebels through a series of humanitarian-aid foundations, so that it cannot be traced back to the original donors. Contra leaders maintain that these donations help offset the considerable Soviet military aid to the Sandinista government of Nicaragua.

Reagan and Gromyko seek better relations

Reagan, Gromyko in Oval Office.

Sept 28. President Reagan says he is ready to chart a new relationship with the Soviet Union, but it looks like he needs a new map. Reagan met for more than three and a half hours with Soviet Foreign Minister Andrei Gromyko at the White House today. The conversations were called "forceful and direct," and Secretary of State George Shultz indicated the two men did not narrow their differences.

Earlier this week, at the U.N., Reagan called for "a better working relationship" with the Russians and "a fresh approach to reducing international tensions." He gave few specifics, however, and Gromyko seemed more upbeat about a meeting with Reagan's Democratic opponent, Walter Mondale, than he did about the speech. Asked if Reagan's conciliatory tone had anything to do with politics, Shultz replied, "When is that election anyway?" (→ 8/21/85).

Peres and Shamir swap jobs by agreement

Sept 14. In a move intended to make the often unruly Israeli government more governable, the Israeli Parliament today passed a plan of national unity introducing the novel concept of power-sharing. Labor Party leader Shimon Peres has been sworn in as Prime Minister. Likud Party leader Yitzhak Shamir becomes Deputy Prime Minister and Foreign Minister. The 50-month term will see them trade places halfway through, with each leading the country 25 months.

Peres called on Jordan's King Hussein to join him in peace talks, and vowed to pull Israeli troops out of Lebanon as soon as the border is judged secure. Another major goal will be the reduction of inflation, now running at about 400% a year. No mention was made of a West Bank settlement or other sensitive issues about which the government's nine different parties remain divided (→ 6/11/86).

Shamir and Peres toast the coalition.

Italy's police collar dozens of Mafiosi

Sept 30. At least 58 suspected members of the Italian Mafia were arrested today in one of the largest raids on organized crime in Italy since World War II. The arrests, as well as 366 arrest warrants issued nationwide, were prompted by a confession by Tommaso Buscetta, who was extradited from Brazil in July on murder and drug charges.

Buscetta is said to have given the police a detailed description of the operations of the Sicilian Mafia, and its links with the Camorra crime syndicate of Naples and the American Cosa Nostra. His testimony, officials said, may help solve the 1982 murder of Carlo Dalla Chiesa, Prefect of Palermo, who launched a major investigation of the Mafia.

Tom Hulce is Mozart in "Amadeus," a madcap but moving tale of the musical genius through jealous competitor Salieri's eyes.

Bomb in Montreal station kills three

Sept 3. Three persons were killed and more than 40 others injured when a bomb exploded today in a locker in Montreal's principal railroad station. Police believe that the bombing may be linked to a visit by Pope John Paul II scheduled for next week.

Arrested by police was Thomas Brigham, 65, after a reporter said he had told her in an interview in the train station that he had mailed letters threatening the pope. The reporter said he told her that he did not plant the bomb. However, she quoted him as saying: "I saw the clock. It said 10:17 and that is important because it has been 117 years since the Americans delegated their first representative to the Vatican."

Railway officials said they had received a note last week saying "Kill Popes." While the note did not mention a bomb, it began: "9:30 a.m. Sept. 3, 1984. The end of the unholy Vatican. Kill Popes!" The bomb exploded at 10:22 a.m. in the station crowded by vacationers heading home after Labor Day.

Brigham's son, a priest in St. Louis, told Montreal police his father was once declared mentally unfit and had spent some time in an institution. Montreal police also said that until about one year ago, Brigham had been watched by the U.S. Secret Service "because he was following President Reagan."

Fourteen die in riots around Johannesburg

Sept 3. Fourteen people have died and hundreds were wounded as violence erupted in five black townships near the South African city of Johannesburg. The apartheid system of South Africa requires each of the nation's racial groups — whites, blacks, Indians and those of mixed race —to live only in those areas designated for them. The Afrikaner elite, a minority of 2.8 million whites —as compared with a black majority of 20 million —has had complete control of the government.

Today's rioting by blacks coincided with the inauguration of a new constitution for South Africa and with the appointment of P.W. Botha as President. Botha, formerly the Prime Minister, now has potentially authoritarian power. Although the new constitution allows limited government participation by Indians and those of mixed racial descent, blacks are still excluded. The rioting also protested rent increases and other disputes. All 14 dead were black, ten of them killed in police counterattacks. Many municipal buildings were looted or set ablaze (→ 10/7).

Sept 26. Spain's most brutal sport turned sour today when noted matador Francisco Rivera was gored in the thigh. He died of loss of blood on the way to the hospital. The offending bull's mother was promptly killed.

1984

OCTOBER

Su	Mo	Tu	We	Th	Fr	Sa
	1	2	3	4	5	6
7	8	9	10	11	12	13
14	15	16	17	18	19	20
21	22	23	24	25	26	27
28	29	30	31			

1. Labor Secretary Donovan indicted for fraud in govt. contract scandal (→ 3/15/85).

2. Soviet astronauts return from record 237-day orbital flight (→ 5).

5. Florida: Challenger lifts off, carrying seven, largest crew in space-flight history (→ 11).

7. Johannesburg: South Africa to use army in fighting wave of unrest (→ 11/5).

8. Persian Gulf: Iraqi planes hit Bahrain tanker, killing six in crew (→ 3/17/85).

9. Amman: Mubarak arrives on first Egyptian state visit to Arab nation since peace with Israel (→ 2/16/85).

10. El Salvador: Shultz arrives to assure Duarte of U.S. support (→ 19).

11. Dr. Kathryn Sullivan becomes first U.S. woman to walk in space (→ 13).

13. Florida: Space shuttle Challenger lands safely at Kennedy Space Center (→ 11/14).

14. Detroit: Tigers defeat San Diego Padres in World Series.

17. U.S. Congress discloses existence of CIA terrorist manual (→ 11/5).

18. Nigeria cuts price of oil, creating rift in OPEC structure (→ 1/30/85).

18. Argentina, Chile with pope's mediation, settle border conflict.

19. El Salvador: Four CIA agents killed when surveillance plane crashes (→ 11/9).

24. EPA reports govt. program to monitor contamination of underground water supply is not working (→ 3/17/85).

25. Washington: Hepatitis virus identified in medical breakthrough.

25. Italy indicts three Bulgarians, four Turks in conspiracy to murder pope (→ 5/27/85).

28. L.A. police report wave of gang killings tied to narcotics.

28. N.Y. Marathon won by Orlando Pizzolato of Italy.

29. Chile: Army sends 140 into internal exile in crackdown on protesters (→ 11/6).

Indira Gandhi murdered

The Gandhi family (right) pays respects before the traditional funeral pyre.

Oct 31. Indira Gandhi, India's four-time Prime Minister, was gunned down today by two members of her personal security guard as she walked from her home to her office in New Delhi. She died after four hours of emergency surgery. The only daughter of former Prime Minister Nehru was 66.

Both of her attackers were identified as members of the Sikh religion. One was shot dead. The other was captured. Sikh extremists have threatened to kill Mrs. Gandhi since she ordered the raid on their shrine in Amritsar. Recently, Mrs. Gandhi told an interviewer that she was not intimidated by the threats. "I am not afraid," she said. "I am frequently attacked" (→ 11/1).

Thatcher escapes as bomb shatters hotel

Oct 12. British Prime Minister Margaret Thatcher narrowly escaped injury from a powerful explosion that killed at least two people and wounded about 34 others in Brighton, England, today. Thatcher had just left the bathroom of her hotel suite when the bomb exploded. The British leader was in Brighton for the annual Conservative Party conference. Physically unscathed, she was shaken from her brush with death.

The Irish Republican Army took responsiblity for the blast. In a statement issued from I.R.A. headquarters, the terrorist group said it had aimed the bomb at Thatcher and her "warmongers." The declaration said, "Today we were unlucky, but remember we only have to be lucky once."

Thatcher described the assault as the "work of evil men," insisted the bombing would not halt the scheduled conference and added that efforts to "destroy democracy by terrorism will fail."

China marks 35th Communist year by turning toward capitalism

Oct 28. The largest celebration ever organized in China marked the nation's 35th year as a Communist state this month, and today Peking announced plans for new economic reforms that will usher in limited capitalist measures and decrease the government's role.

Chinese leader Deng Hsiao-ping watched the gala October 1st parade from the same balcony at the Gate of Heavenly Peace where Mao Tse-tung proclaimed the founding of Communist China in 1949. Deng called for a strengthening of national defense in his speech to the festive crowd in the square beneath him. It seems an arms buildup has already begun, as the Chinese displayed an impressive arsenal of modern missiles and weapons.

An imposing missile dominates China's birthday celebration in Peking.

However, the economic reforms announced today may be even more explosive than those weapons. They include plans to allow a million state-owned enterprises greater independence to trigger competition, a program to leave the pricing of many products to the market forces of supply and demand, a pledge to increase foreign trade, and a promise to give industrial plant managers more autonomy from the state bureaucracy.

Adopted at a meeting of the Communist Party Central Committee, the reforms figure to be the most significant of any since 1978. In that year, the government instituted an incentive plan to give China's millions of peasants higher rewards for more production. A dramatic increase in agricultural production resulted. Officials are hoping the new measures will bring about a similar increase in industrial productivity and a general boost to the Chinese economy.

Canadian rivers drown over 7,000 caribou

A major environmental catastrophe.

Oct 3. More than 7,100 migrating caribou have drowned in the past two days crossing two rivers in northern Quebec, in what the Audubon Society calls "a major environmental catastrophe." Biologists say 7,100 carcasses have been counted, but Quebec officials estimate at least 10,000 and perhaps 22,000 caribou drowned while trying to cross the Caniapiscau and Koksoak Rivers.

The caribou were part of the George River herd, the biggest in North America and one of the largest in the world, and were making their annual migration. Eskimo leaders charge that Hydro-Quebec, the provincial electric utility, caused the animals' death by letting too much water spill over a dam built to regulate flow on the rivers.

Eskimo leaders say the company had been asked to build a barrier at the place where the drowning occurred to prevent the caribou from crossing at such a dangerous spot. But officials of Hydro-Quebec disputed the charge, saying that the rivers had been swollen by rainfall that was twice the seasonal average.

A company spokesman said the Eskimos had agreed to the spilling of the water years ago on the advice of engineers they hired themselves. With carcasses piled five and six deep in some spots, Quebec officials are arranging a "wall of sound" to keep other caribou away.

Polish priest's body is found after torture

Oct 30. The body of the Rev. Jerzy Popieluszko, a staunch pro-Solidarity Warsaw priest, was found today in a reservoir, 11 days after he had been abducted by members of the state security police.

Government spokesman Jerzy Urban said that the killing was part of a plot against the government, and that three suspects were being held in custody. One of them, Capt. Grzegorz Piotrowski, was said to have confessed to torturing and killing the priest. His accomplices, Lieutenants Waldemar Chmielewski and Leszek Pekala, told investigators that they had dumped the priest's body in the Wloclawek reservoir west of Warsaw.

Popieluszko began offering a "Mass for the Fatherland" once a month in his Warsaw parish after the Polish government declared martial law and suspended the Solidarity labor union, which it chartered in 1980 after a series of nationwide strikes. Thousands of union activists attended his masses to hear his sermons supporting Solidarity's cause of independent labor unions in Poland.

Solidarity's pious patron saint.

Solidarity leader Lech Walesa appealed to the public for calm, voicing the hope that the murder of Popieluszko would "create the conditions to begin the dialogue" between the government and the Polish people (→ 11/3).

New Wave director Truffaut is dead

Oct 21. Francois Truffaut has died of cancer in Paris at 52. Truffaut directed New Wave movies, idiosyncratic and passionate works. The autobiographical "400 Blows" (1959) showed him a restless boy. Five more films about his alter ego followed, leaving him when he begins a career as a novelist. Enamored of Zola, Truffaut considered writing books until discovering American movies in 1944. His "Jules and Jim" (1961) and "Day for Night" (1973) were widely acclaimed. He leaves a 13-month-old daughter by actress Fanny Ardant.

Truffaut, rode the New Wave.

Panel says Red did not shoot Aquino

Oct 24. A five-member panel investigating the assassination of Philippine opposition leader Benigno S. Aquino Jr. unanimously rejected the account of the military that he was shot by a single gunman hired by Communist insurgents. Rather, the commission insisted Aquino's murder stemmed from a high-level plot within the military itself.

The panel disagreed, however, about the extent of the plot and about the level of command at which responsibility should be placed. One report, issued by the head of the panel, accuses an air force general and six soldiers of the conspiracy; another, representing the views of the rest of the panel, implicates 26 people, three of them generals, including General Fabian C. Ver, chief of the armed forces and a close associate of Philippine President Ferdinand Marcos. Ver has requested and been granted a leave of absence from his position. Aquino was gunned down in Manila on August 21, 1983 (→ 1/23/85).

Foreign aid increases to Ethiopia's starving

Oct 27. The international effort to help famine victims in Ethiopia has accelerated dramatically in recent days, with governments offering food, transport planes and other aid, and thousands of ordinary Americans pledging contributions. While the famine has been killing Ethiopians for more than a year, the surge of offers followed graphic film footage of starving children and adults that has been shown on television since last week. People call up in tears, eager to do something. UNICEF alone has received around $75,000, the average contribution being $40. Children call to pledge weekly allowances (→ 11/18).

A staggering infant mortality rate continues to plague Ethiopian society.

Baboon's heart is implanted in baby

Oct 26. Baby Fae, a 15-day-old infant, has received the heart of a baboon. The baboon heart transplant was done by Dr. Leonard L. Bailey at Loma Linda University Medical Center in California.

Baby Fae was born with a heart defect that would have been fatal without a transplant. Hospital officials said the female infant is now in critical condition due to complications, as her body rejects the transplanted heart. Bailey has been criticized by many experts for performing the operation, but he defends it as a pioneering effort that could eventually have a wide impact on the treatment of patients with failing hearts (→ 11/15).

Duarte meets with leftist rebel chiefs

Oct 15. For the first time in the history of El Salvador's five-year civil war, Salvadoran government officials met with rebel leaders in an effort to end the conflict. The meeting consisted of four government officials, including President Jose Napoleon Duarte, leaders from four of the five rebel groups, and four Roman Catholic officials who acted as witnesses.

After four and a half hours of negotiations, the leaders agreed to create a commission which would study ways to bring the violence to a close. The fact that the meeting took place at all is considered to be a major achievement for both sides in the conflict, especially for the rebels who have sought government recognition for the past three years.

Rebel leaders speak at La Palma.

First two debates held in 1984 race

Reagan and Mondale square off.

Oct 21. For the second time this month, President Reagan and his Democratic opponent, Walter F. Mondale, clashed sharply during a nationally televised debate.

"Who's in charge?" Mondale asked. "Who's handling these matters? That's my main point."

An obviously angry president responded, "I know it'll come as a surprise to Mr. Mondale, but I am in charge."

Tonight's debate focused on such foreign policy issues as Central Intelligence Agency involvement in Central America, arms control and nuclear weapons.

The president spent much of the time defending his policies and accusing his opponent of persistent opposition to adequate military preparedness. In turn, Mondale said that the United States had been "humiliated" by such events as the deaths of 241 Americans in the bombing of the Marine barracks in Beirut (→ 11/6).

Vote. Tuesday. November 6.

1984

NOVEMBER

Su	Mo	Tu	We	Th	Fr	Sa
				1	2	3
4	5	6	7	8	9	10
11	12	13	14	15	16	17
18	19	20	21	22	23	24
25	26	27	28	29	30	

1. New Delhi: Rajiv Gandhi sworn in as premier by President Zail Singh.→

3. Warsaw: 200,000 attend rites for dead priest Rev. Jerzy Popieluszko (→ 12/27).

5. Johannesburg: Ten blacks killed in anti-govt. strike drawing thousands (→ 12/7).

5. Managua: Daniel Ortega elected Nicaraguan pres. (→ 7).

6. Chile: Pinochet reimposes state of siege (→ 15).

7. U.S. warns Soviets against MIG's in Nicaragua (→ 26).

9. El Salvador: Rebels fail in attack on Suchitoto, first major drive in six months (→ 14).

10. Angola: UNITA guerrilla leader Jonas Savimbi asks inclusion in U.S.-sponsored peace talks (→ 11/22/85).

13. New York: Ariel Sharon opens libel suit against Time magazine (→ 1/24/85).

14. Discovery crew rescues second satellite (→ 4/19/85).

14. El Salvador: Govt. rejects rebel cease-fire plan (→ 1/6/85).

15. N.Y.: Gen. Westmoreland says in libel trial he told superiors of higher enemy troop estimates in Vietnam (→ 2/17/85).

15. Loma Linda, Calif.: Baby Fae dies after 20 days with baboon heart (→ 2/17/85).

18. Ethiopia: Soviets help deliver U.S. wheat in famine (→ 12/12).

19. Mexico: Nearly 500 killed in gas explosion at warehouse.

20. N.Y.: Jean Kirkpatrick to resign as U.S. envoy to U.N.

21. NRC clears Shoreham nuclear plant in L.I. for operation at low levels (→ 10/13/85).

22. Spain: Basques strike over killing of leader (→ 3/24/85).

23. Korea: Three dead in clash at DMZ over defection of Soviet citizen.

26. World Court votes to hear Nicaraguan charges of U.S. aggression (→ 1/18/85).

26. Uruguay: Liberal Julio Maria Sanguinetti elected president.

28. Washington: Robert Dole elected Senate majority leader.

Rajiv Gandhi takes his mother's place

Rajiv to rule a factious India.

Nov 1. Rajiv Gandhi, 48, who was chosen to succeed his assassinated mother, was sworn in as Prime Minister in New Delhi today. Across the Jumna River, in a Sikh slum, evidence was found of the enormous political problems the new prime minister faces. The bodies of at least 95 Sikhs were discovered. The Indian army has also been ordered into nine other cities. Religious warfare between Sikhs and Hindus has claimed at least 1,000 lives since Indira Gandhi was assassinated. The security guards who killed her were both Sikhs.

Secretary of State George Shultz, who attended the funeral, assured the new prime minister of American interest in a "strong and stable India." American-Indian relations have been strained recently because of United States support for Pakistan. Shultz called for a "renewed positive trend" in relations (→ 12/29).

The image of Charlie Chaplin lives on in IBM advertisements.

Reagan and Bush win by 59% in 49 states

Nov 6. President Reagan swept to victory today, trouncing Democrat Walter F. Mondale by carrying all but one of the 50 states. It was a landslide win for the president, the oldest man ever to occupy the White House, and a bitter defeat for his opponent, who once served as Vice President.

As a band played "Hail to the Chief," the president entered a ballroom in Los Angeles to greet his cheering supporters who were chanting, "Four more years."

"I think that's just been arranged," Reagan said with a grin. Promising to use his new mandate to extend the economic and military policies of his first term, he said: "You know, so many people act as if this election means the end of something. To each one of you, I say, it's just the beginning of everything. You ain't seen nothing yet."

Mondale and his vice-presidential running mate, Geraldine Ferraro, carried only his home state, Minnesota, and the District of Columbia. Their campaign had been hampered by disclosures of financial problems of Mrs. Ferraro and her husband (→ 1/21/85).

Most popular President since FDR.

Catholic Bishops denounce injustice

Nov 11. A committee of Catholic Bishops issued a pastoral letter today, condemning economic injustices they claim pervade America.

The letter read: "We believe that the level of inequality in income and wealth in our society and even more the inequality on the world scale today must be judged morally unacceptable." The 120-page document cited widespread hunger and homelessness as two inexcusable conditions in this land of plenty. The letter also asserted the federal government should play a larger role in tackling these economic problems, a view that clashes with the Reagan administration's efforts to minimize the role of the state.

Among the concrete recommendations in the text was a request to reallocate some of the federal budget from the arms race to programs designed to create jobs (→ 1/27/85).

Stalin's daughter returns to U.S.S.R.

Nov 2. Svetlana Alliluyeva is back in the Soviet Union after an absence of 17 years. The U.S.S.R. hails it as a kind of propaganda coup; the West is confused. Why is Stalin's daughter rejecting what she has called "a perfectly free life"?

Under scrutiny, Miss Alliluyeva's decision is compatible with her experiences. She has been married three times: first to a Jewish man whom her father abhorred (he ordered them to divorce), second to a Soviet official her father insisted on, and third to an American architect she hardly knew. One fiance, an Indian national, committed suicide.

Miss Alliluyeva's mother killed herself when Svetlana was six, one brother succumbed to alcoholism and another died unnaturally. Miss Alliluyeva, 53, seems unable to find peace and happiness anywhere (→ 4/16/86).

2nd heart implant done in America

Nov 25. Surgeons at Humana Heart Institute in Louisville, Kentucky, today performed the world's second permanent artificial heart implant, removing the heart of 52-year-old William J. Schroeder and replacing it with an 11-ounce plastic and metal device. Officials said the operation went well but that Schroeder required further surgery to stop excessive bleeding. The surgical team was led by Dr. William C. DeVries, who did the first permanent heart implant.

From the sixties to the eighties, hair remains a uniquely expressive mode of social protest.

Thousands rounded up by Chilean troops

Nov 15. Chilean army and air force troops, accompanied by police, swept into a Santiago slum today, herding thousands of people into a soccer stadium for questioning. The raid on La Victoria, a neighborhood of 32,000, has been the scene of frequent leftist protests against the autocratic military rule of General Augusto Pinochet. The Rev. Pierre DuBois, a local Catholic priest, denounced the raid as an attempt to "punish the people" (→ 2/5/85).

Political tensions rising in New Caledonia

Nov 26. Revolutionary fervor is boiling over in New Caledonia, the South Pacific French territory 750 miles east of Australia. Elections last week were boycotted by a nationalist party demanding independence from France, and gunmen have paralyzed the main island by setting up roadblocks. Eloi Machoro, a leader of the Kanaka Socialist Liberation Front, seized control of three police stations and disrupted polling places. A French official was taken prisoner on the island of Lifou, and Kanaka rebels painted his face white to symbolize their contempt for France and French settlers. The Kanakas, or Melanesians, comprise 40% of the population. The separatists may set up their own regime (→ 1/12/85).

Nov 11. Washington's Vietnam Memorial, designed by a female Vietnamese-American architecture student at Yale University, has become a popular but sad site, where Americans honor the veterans and victims of the war.

U.S. executes its first woman in 22 years

Nov 2. Having finished her cola and cheese puffs (the meal was her last request), Mrs. Margie Velma Barfield was led away to her death tonight. Mrs. Barfield was convicted of murdering her fiance, and she confessed to killing three others (but was not tried for those crimes). She is the first woman in the United States executed since 1962.

Outside the Raleigh, North Carolina, prison, hundreds of opponents of the death penalty made a din that could be heard far inside the walls. The execution has unsettling political overtones; the gubernatorial election is only days away, and Governor James P. Hunt recently denied an appeal for clemency. He probably wanted the execution over with as soon as possible, before his more liberal supporters could have second thoughts.

A little before 2 a.m., Mrs. Barfield, clad in pink pajamas, was given a sleeping pill. Then she was injected with a muscle relaxant that stopped her heart (→ 11/13/85).

1984

DECEMBER

Su	Mo	Tu	We	Th	Fr	Sa
						1
2	3	4	5	6	7	8
9	10	11	12	13	14	15
16	17	18	19	20	21	22
23	24	25	26	27	28	29
30	31					

1. Doug Flutie of Boston College wins Heisman Trophy.

3. Bhopal, India: Toxic gas leaks from Union Carbide plant; deaths in thousands (→ 13).

4. Grenada: Herbert Blaize elected prime minister.

7. Washington: Bishop Tutu and Reagan meet on U.S. policy toward South Africa (→ 10).

11. U.S. reports 76th bank failure, highest rate since 1937 (→ 1/25/85).

12. Ethiopia blames Western nations for famine (→ 7/13/85).

14. U.N. General Assembly condemns S. Africa (→ 1/12/85).

19. Pakistan: Referendum landslide sanctions Pres. Zia's Islamicization policy (→ 2/21/85).

20. Albany: N.Y. high court rules men may be prosecuted for raping their wives.

25. Vietnam: Govt. troops attack Cambodian rebels; 63,000 flee to Thailand (→ 1/7/85).

27. Torun: Four Polish officers tried for slaying of Rev. Jerzy Popieluszko (→ 2/7/85).

29. India: Rajiv Gandhi elected prime minister in landslide victory (→ 5/10/85).

DEATH

28. Sam Peckinpah, American film director (*2/21/1925).

CULTURAL EVENTS, 1984

Literature: Joseph Heller's "God Knows"; Alan Sillitoe's "Down from the Hill"; Erica Jong's "Parachutes and Kisses"; Mary Oliver's "American Primitive," Pulitzer poetry.

Academia: Louis R. Harlan's "Booker T. Washington"; Paul Starr's "Social Transformation of American Medicine."

Music: Bernard Rands' "Canti del Sole," Pulitzer; Tina Turner's "What's Love Got to Do With It"; Lionel Richie's "Can't Slow Down"; Phil Collins' "Against All Odds"; The Pointer Sisters' "Jump."

Film: Milos Forman's "Amadeus," Academy Award; "Places in the Heart," Sally Field; "The Killing Fields"; "A Passage to India."

Fatal gas leak at Bhopal

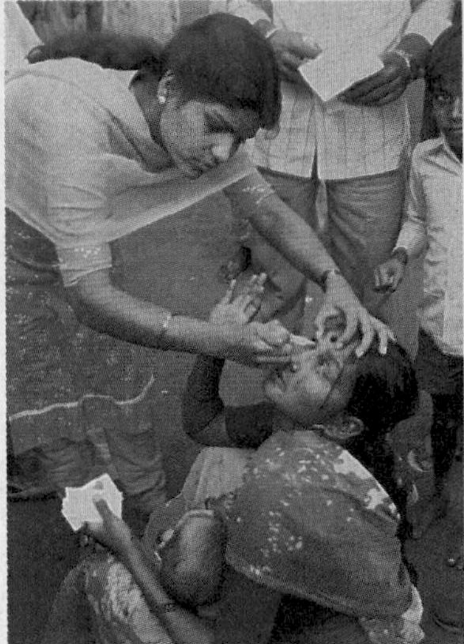

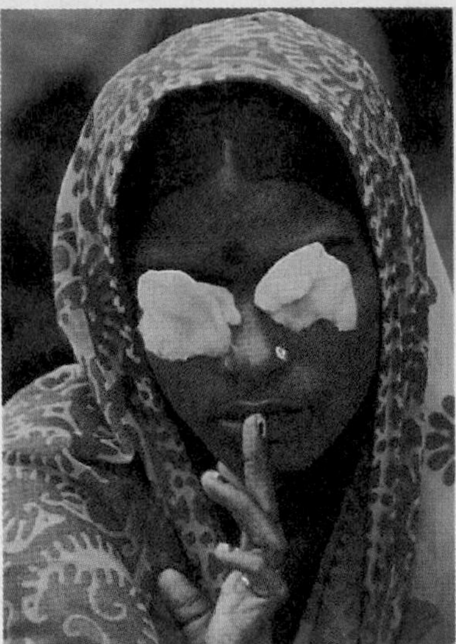

Many of those lucky enough to survive have been stricken by blindness.

Dec 13. The death toll in a toxic gas leak from an insecticide plant in Bhopal, India, now is estimated at 2,100, and tens of thousands of residents fled the city today after it was announced that the Union Carbide plant would be started up again to neutralize the remains of the chemical. Warren M. Anderson, Chairman of Union Carbide, was arrested and changed with criminal conspiracy when he flew to Bhopal, but was released on bail a few hours later.

The gas, identified as methyl isocyanate, escaped from one of three underground storage tanks at the plant during the early hours of December 3. The gas spread over an area inhabited by 200,000 people during the next 40 minutes. Many awoke vomiting and complaining of dizziness, sore throats and burning eyes. Others died where they slept.

Witnesses said thousands of people had been taken to hospitals gasping for breath and frothing at the mouth and many had been blinded. The streets of the city were littered with the corpses of animals and birds killed by the chemical, which is widely used in the manufacture of insecticides.

The managing director of Union Carbide in India said the gas was released when a tank valve malfunctioned after an increase in pressure.

Prime Minister Rajiv Gandhi said the disaster was the result of "planning in an uncontrolled manner" and he would seek compensation from Union Carbide for the loss of life. A $15 billion class action suit has been filed against the firm by two American lawyers (→ 1/23/85).

The deadly insecticide plant, grave threat to Bhopal's 500,000 residents.

Four black youths shot on N.Y. subway

Dec 22. A gunman, described as "cool, calm and collected," fired several shots at four black youths on a New York City subway train, leaving them alive but bleeding and seriously injured. After the victims collapsed to the floor of the train, and other passengers screamed and rushed into an adjoining car, the assailant quietly approached the conductor to discuss the shooting. He told the transit worker the youths were "trying to rip me off." The conductor tried to grab the gun, but the man jumped off the train and disappeared into the bowels of the subway system.

While the exact motive for the assault is uncertain, police Captain John Kelly said the man "knew what he was doing. He was either harassed or robbed by these guys on the train." Interviewed later, two of the victims denied they were antagonizing the gunman. Two of the injured youths are in critical condition. Police have not apprehended any suspects (→ 1/8/85).

City pays $40,000 to keep a prisoner

Dec 26. According to a new private study, $40,000 is the annual cost to keep one prisoner in New York City for a year. A city government report estimated the cost at $26,000 a year, but the Correctional Association of New York found this figure excluded "hidden" costs.

The private study said that when tallying such costs, pension and fringe benefits for Correctional Department employees, debt charges on previous improvements for the jail system, and various jail services provided by agencies other than the Correctional Department should be included.

The study concluded that alternative forms of punishment should be examined to reduce the number of inmates, which now stands at 10,000, and thereby decrease the amount of tax dollars spent on housing the city's criminals. The association suggested public-service and work-release programs would save money while still serving justice and securing public safety.

Bishop Tutu awarded Nobel Prize for Peace

First black Bishop of Johannesburg.

Dec 10. Nobel recipients and guests were forced to stand in the cold for 20 minutes today, waiting for the Oslo police to tell them a bomb threat at Aula Hall was just a hoax. When ceremonies began again, Bishop Desmond Tutu was accorded the Peace Prize. Tutu has waged a non-violent campaign for an end to apartheid in South Africa.

Bruce Merrifield, from Rockefeller University, won the chemistry award for developing a quick method of producing complex proteins. Italian Carlo Rubbia and Dutch Simon Van Der Meer took the physics prize for research on elementary particles. The economics award went to Briton Sir Richard Stone for his national accounts system. The daughter of Czech Yaroslav Seifert accepted the literature prize in his name, and the medicine prize went to scientists from four nations for their work in immunology (→ 14).

United States plans exit from UNESCO

Dec 12. The United States announced today its withdrawal from UNESCO at the end of the month since the agency has largely failed to meet American demands that it rid itself of mismanagement, politicization and "endemic hostility" toward a free press, free markets and individual human rights. The U.S., which contributed 25 percent of this year's $187 million budget for UNESCO (the United Nations Educational, Scientific and Cultural Organization) told the 161-country, Paris-based group a year ago that it would pull out and not rejoin unless demanded changes were made.

Payton, Dickerson set football records

Dec 17. Two formidable football rushing records were smashed this year. In October, Walter Payton of the Chicago Bears ran six yards on a play against the Saints and surpassed Jim Brown's career rushing record of 12,317 yards. Payton now has his sights set on 15,000 yards. "I had my 11,000-yard tune-up (knee surgery) and I feel great," he said. Today, Eric Dickerson of the Los Angeles Rams ran for 215 yards for a record total of 2,007 yards in a single season. O.J. Simpson, the previous season record-holder, was pictured on a TV show sticking pins in an Eric Dickerson doll.

Michael Jackson Thriller album biggest ever

Jackson's 14-min., $.5 mil. "Thriller" video was a good investment.

For pop singer Michael Jackson, 1984 began with an unprecedented eight Grammy awards, and things only got better as his "Thriller" album broke all music industry records with sales topping 37 million. The album spawned six number one singles and a string of music videos featuring Jackson's sizzling dance routines and trademark lone-sequined glove. Jackson, 26, is no stranger to stardom —he scored his first hits at age ten with his brothers, the Jackson 5. This summer, the group reunited for the hugely successful Victory concert tour.

Special-effects flicks foreclose farm films

Coppola's "The Cotton Club."

Sad sequel "The Temple of Doom."

When critics heard three farm films were planned for 1984 ("The River," "Country" and "Places in the Heart"), they prepared to laud or belittle a trend. But special-effects action pictures stole the spotlight, and the excitement of farm films faded like cornsilk.

Director Steven Spielberg caught some flak for "Indiana Jones and the Temple of Doom," sequel to "Raiders of the Lost Ark." He was charged with making it overly violent —and racist and sexist to boot. Harrison Ford reprises his role as the dauntless archeologist.

Director Joe Dante was also nixed for violence in "Gremlins," in which tiny furry beasts run amok. Francis Coppola designed an overly elaborate "Cotton Club." Richard Gere and Gregory Hines star.

"Country" stars Jessica Lange and Sam Shepard as farmers fighting debt. "The River" pairs Sissy Spacek and Mel Gibson as farmers fighting —you guessed it, a river. Sally Field is joined by a strong cast (Danny Glover, John Malkovich, Lindsay Crouse) in "Places in the Heart." Robert Benton wrote and directed the Depression-era tale.

Oscar-caliber performances fill "Amadeus" and "A Passage to India." F. Murray Abraham plays Salieri, the composer who curses God because he is not as blessed as Mozart. Tom Hulce is the spoiled, childish musical genius, and Milos Forman ("One Flew Over the Cuckoo's Nest") directed.

"A Passage to India" is David Lean's first picture in 14 years. He tells the story of a British woman figuratively ravished by the beauty and mystery of colonial India. Judy Davis is the woman, Peggy Ashcroft her mystical guardian.

Some pictures, as usual, were box office hits of questionable quality. "Beverly Hills Cop," with charismatic comic Eddie Murphy, is an audience grabber. "Ghostbusters" teams Bill Murray, Harold Ramis and Dan Aykroyd against spirits who look less like ghosts than geeks. "Footloose" stumbles in most categories, but the 50's music and dance pleases teens. Kevin Bacon stars.

Somber themes drive "Under the Volcano," in which Albert Finney plays a terminal drunk in a terminal place —Cuernavaca in 1938. John Huston tackled the Malcolm Lowry novel. "The Killing Fields" is an even more sober spot, where thousands of Cambodians were slaughtered. Dr. Haing S. Ngor stars in a tale of unmatched courage.

For the faint of heart, there is the wonderfully goofy "All of Me," starring Steve Martin and Lily Tomlin as a couple who get their mantras crossed. And "This Is Spinal Tap" is Rob Reiner's idea of a rockumentary: real dumb.

Shepard and Lange in "Country."

The vicious little stars of "Gremlins."

1985

JANUARY

Su	Mo	Tu	We	Th	Fr	Sa
		1	2	3	4	5
6	7	8	9	10	11	12
13	14	15	16	17	18	19
20	21	22	23	24	25	26
27	28	29	30	31		

1. Pasadena: U.S.C. beats Ohio State 20-17 in Rose Bowl.

3. Reagan condemns arson at abortion clinics (→ 7/14).

3. Deputy chief of staff Michael Deaver resigns.

4. N.Y.: Leontyne Price gives farewell performance at Met.

6. San Salvador: Pedro Yanes, head of inquiry on official corruption, shot to death (→ 3/7).

7. Vietnam seizes Khmer Natl. Liberation Front headquarters near Thai border (→ 2/14).

8. Reagan names Donald Regan chief of staff.

8. New York: Bernhard Goetz freed on $50,000 bail (→ 25).

11. West Germany: Three G.I.'s killed when Pershing II missile catches fire (→ 31).

12. Namibia: Sen. Kennedy says he will ask Congress to impose sanctions on S. Africa (→ 2/10).

14. Washington: 16 indicted to end church aid to Latin American aliens.

15. U.S. Supreme Court rules student searches without prior evidence are illegal.

15. Brazil: Trancredo Neves elected first civilian president in 21 years (→ 5/27).

16. Atlanta: Judge rules U.S. can send hundreds in Atlanta jail back to Cuba (→ 10/18/86).

17. N.J.: Jury rules terminally ill patients have right to starve to death.

18. Reagan says U.S. will not take part in World Court ruling on Nicaraguan charges (→ 2/21).

23. EPA says Union Carbide W.Va. plant had 28 toxic leaks in last five years (→ 4/8).

23. Manila: Army chief of staff and 25 others charged with murder of Aquino (→ 5/2).

25. U.S. reports record $123.3 bil. trade deficit in '84 (→ 3/15).

27. Venezuela: Pope John Paul II says mass to one mil. (→ 2/4).

30. Geneva: OPEC votes moderate price cuts (→ 2/18/86).

31. Washington: Letter from Chernenko says Star Wars will escalate arms race (→ 2/6).

Superbowl makes Reagan take oath twice

Reagan, at inauguration, claims conservative mandate for another four years.

Jan 21. A combination of cold weather and America's premier winter sporting event forced President Reagan to be sworn into office twice —once legally and once for the benefit of the American audience. The re-inauguration of Ronald Wilson Reagan was a planned gala celebration, complete with celebrities, a parade and elaborate balls. However, because January 20th fell on a Sunday, and Super Bowl Sunday at that, many of the formal ceremonies were postponed. The parade was canceled altogether because of subzero weather conditions.

Today, while Reagan re-enacted the taking of the presidential oath, millions of Americans were able to watch on television, although ratings indicated not nearly as many citizens viewed the swearing-in ceremony as did the championship professional football game.

Yesterday, the Rev. Billy Graham led convocational services for the 73-year-old president, who is about to serve his second term. Graham noted, "There is a mandate that is higher than the ballot box and it comes from God," and then led the congregation in prayer.

Reagan won 49 states in November, proving that he is the most popular president since FDR. The "Reagan revolution," as it's called, seeks to reverse many of the big government policies of the New Deal. But political analysts point out that the electorate seemed to endorse the president's personality more than his policies.

Jan 20. Coach Bill Walsh gets a winner's ride to the locker room after his 49ers overwhelmed the Miami Dolphins 38-16 in Super Bowl XIX.

Exposed, airlift of Ethiopian Jews ends

Jan 6. Israel's Jewish Agency, a semi-official government arm, announced today that Israel's covert airlift of Ethiopian Jews to Israel was ending because of recent reports in U.S. publications which revealed that many of the flights originate in the Sudan, an Arab country having no diplomatic relations with Israel. Last week, Israel openly admitted the airlift. Ethiopian Jews have smarted under the repressive rule of Ethiopia's Marxist regime. Though some 12,000 have been evacuated, the halt leaves 6,000-8,000 stranded inside Ethiopia, and 4,000 in refugee camps outside Ethiopia.

Freeze of century strikes citrus crop

Jan 22. In the worst freeze of the century, two days of record-breaking cold have damaged 90 percent of Florida's orange and grapefruit crop, state officials said today. They said the losses appeared worse than those caused by the 1963 Christmas freeze that killed trees on 120,000 acres and cost $1 billion. Growers are rushing damaged fruit to processing plants to salvage as much of the crop as possible by making juice before it spoils. Governor Bob Graham has declared a state of emergency as the National Weather Service predicts more cold weather.

Police shoot leader in New Caledonia

Jan 12. Eloi Machoro, a leader of the Kanaka separatists in New Caledonia, was killed in a gun battle with police. An aide was also killed, and 34 of Machoro's followers who had barricaded themselves inside a farmhouse were arrested. Police charged they had been harassing French settlers. A state of emergency was declared as Frenchmen went on the rampage in the capital of Noumea and demanded that the government crack down on the Kanakas. "If they do nothing, we'll deal with the killers ourselves," one right-wing legislator said.

Goetz is indicted on gun charge only

Jan 25. Bernhard Goetz, the confessed assailant in last month's shooting of four black youths, will be indicted on illegal weapon charges only, a grand jury decided today. Prosecution attorneys, upset by the decision, are still determined to try Goetz for attempted murder.

The gunman surrendered to police in New Hampshire a few days after the subway attack, claiming he acted in self-defense to prevent his being mugged by the youths. Initially, Goetz threatened to fight extradition to bring him back to New York, but after legal consultation he decided to return to Manhattan.

The case has stirred passions among New Yorkers. Some feel Goetz had the right to defend himself, while others believe he is a dangerous criminal who is also prejudiced against blacks (→ 3/27).

Subway vigilante Goetz under arrest.

Worst rail wreck in Africa: 392 are dead

Jan 13. In the third worst rail disaster ever, and the worst ever to occur in Africa, 392 people were killed and 370 injured as an Ethiopian train bound for Addis Ababa derailed and plunged into a ravine. Reports have indicated that the engineer, who has been arrested, failed to slow down as the train rounded a curve on a bridge 35 feet above a dry riverbed. The rear car derailed first, crashing through a guard rail and pulling the rest of the train with it. The damage to the track has severed a vital link between Addis Ababa and the port of Djibouti.

Time vindicated in Sharon libel suit

Jan 24. Time magazine has been cleared of libel charges brought by Israeli Minister of Industry and Commerce Ariel Sharon. In 1983, Time published an article accusing Sharon, then Defense Minister, of "discussing" revenge murders with Lebanese Phalangists prior to their massacre of Palestinians. Sharon took the case before a U.S. jury to prove "that Time magazine lied."

In February 1983, Time published a cover story titled "The Verdict Is Guilty." It stated that after Israel invaded Lebanon in the fall of 1982, Sharon met with leaders of the Phalangists, a Lebanese Christian faction. Sharon allegedly spoke of the recent assassination of President-elect Bashir Gemayel and of the "need for the Phalangists to take revenge." Immediately afterward, the Phalangists invaded the Sabra and Shatila camps in West Beirut (supposedly guarded by Israelis) and murdered hundreds of civilians.

The Manhattan-based jury felt correspondent David Halevy "acted negligently and carelessly" in preparing his article, as he provided no substantial evidence supporting his assertions. The six jurors agreed that in that respect Time defamed Sharon, and on that score the plaintiff was satisfied.

However, for Time to be guilty of libel it would have had to publish the story with "reckless disregard for the truth." The jury felt Time accepted the article in good faith.

John Birch Society founder Welch dies

Jan 7. Robert Welch, the founder of the John Birch Society, died yesterday at the age of 85. Welch led the anti-Communist, ultraconservative organization for 25 years. It was born in 1958 to advocate "less government, more individual responsibility and a better world." Among the many ideas Welch espoused were the abolition of all civil rights legislation, which he believed was a cover for communism, impeachment of former Chief Justice Earl Warren, repeal of the income tax and the halting of diplomatic contact with the Soviet Union.

1985

FEBRUARY

Su	Mo	Tu	We	Th	Fr	Sa
					1	2
3	4	5	6	7	8	9
10	11	12	13	14	15	16
17	18	19	20	21	22	23
24	25	26	27	28		

4. Lima: Peru rebels black out parts of city 30 minutes after arrival of pope (→ 6/3).

5. U.S. to halt loan to Chile in protest over human rights abuses (→ 9/5).

6. Soviets officially announce Chernenko is ill (→ 3/13).

6. Israel: Ex-secret service chief admits agents have executed some Nazis they could not try.

7. Poland: Four officers given jail terms for murdering pro-Solidarity priest (→ 5/3).

9. Seoul admits using force against opposition leader Kim Dae Jung (→ 2/20/86).

10. Soweto: Nelson Mandela spurns Botha's offer of conditional release (→ 19).

12. U.S. announces contingency plan to deploy nuclear arms in Canada, Iceland, Bermuda and Puerto Rico (→ 3/1).

14. Cambodia: Hanoi troops surround main Khmer Rouge base at Phnom Malai.

16. Lebanon: Israeli troops pull out of Sidon area (→ 24).

17. Kentucky: Murray Haydon becomes third person to receive artificial heart (→ 3/8).

19. Spain: Iberia Boeing crashes into mountain, killing 142.

20. New York: John Zaccaro sentenced to 150 hours community service for real estate fraud.

21. Reagan says goal is to topple Sandinista government (→ 27).

21. Pakistan: Hundreds arrested in pre-election purge (→ 12/30).

21. Argentina: Isabel Peron resigns as head of Peronist Party (→ 10/25).

24. Lebanon: Israeli troops besiege nine villages (→ 3/4).

26. New York: FBI indicts leaders of five reputed Mafia families.

27. Managua: Pres. Ortega bars acquisition of new arms systems (→ 4/21).

28. Ulster: I.R.A. mortars kill nine at police station (→ 11/15).

DEATH

26. Henry Cabot Lodge, American diplomat (*7/5/1902).

General drops big suit against CBS

Feb 17. After 18 weeks of trial testimony, General William Westmoreland has withdrawn a $120 million libel suit against CBS. The general sought satisfaction after a 1982 CBS documentary on the Vietnam War accused him of lying to his superiors (and inadvertently the public) about troop statistics. According to tonight's settlement, CBS need not disavow content of the controversial documentary.

"The Uncounted Enemy: A Vietnam Deception," produced by CBS producer George Crile and narrated by Mike Wallace, focused on Westmoreland's efforts to disguise the reality of the war. From 1964 to 1968, while he was commander of U.S. forces, Westmoreland misrepresented the increasing numbers of North Vietnamese troops, placing an arbitrary ceiling of 300,000 on the total. CBS asserted this data left a complacent United States unready for the Tet offensive.

In September 1982, when Westmoreland originally brought his lawsuit, he wanted not only financial compensation but also a broadcast retraction at least 45 minutes in duration. CBS offered him instead a 15-minute block of unedited time to be followed by another program re-examining the issues. Westmoreland declined that offer.

The 70-year-old general said he chose litigation as the only way to "clear my name, my honor and the honor of the military" (→ 5/9).

Funded by Lee Iacocca's media blitz, the Statue of Liberty is now being restored (→ 7/4/86).

Hundreds hurt in police clash with blacks

A car smolders in Kwanobuhle as the flames of revolt spread in South Africa.

Feb 19. Violence has erupted in South Africa again. This time, hundreds of people have been hurt and at least eight have died in skirmishes with police near Cape Town. The battles were incited by a government proposal to relocate some 100,000 black residents to a newly created black township situated in an area of barren sand dunes called Khayelitsha, where the government has said the people will be better off.

In the past 20 years, about 3.5 million black residents have been forced to leave their homes by government orders, according to figures collected by South African church groups. The government rejects these statistics.

Thousands of squatters have set up camp just outside of Cape Town, refusing to comply with relocation. Police rushed to the scene, firing tear gas, rubber bullets and birdshot. The protesters retaliated by setting up barricades of burning auto tires. However, the tactic seems only to have slowed police efforts to remove the squatters.

Yesterday, the battling factions sought a truce, but the fight raged on after a white policeman was hit by a tossed stone and the police fired shotguns into a crowd at close range. There seems to be no end in sight to the violence (→ 3/21).

New Zealand bars ship on atom issue

Feb 5. New Zealand's Prime Minister, David Lange, has announced that he will not permit an American warship to pay a port call in his country because of New Zealand's anti-nuclear policy. United States Navy ships may not visit the South Pacific nation unless they can assure the New Zealanders that no nuclear weapons are carried on board. This kind of disclosure is contrary to United States policy. The situation has caused the United States and Australia to cancel naval exercises scheduled to take place with New Zealand next month. This coincided with a decision by Australia not to aid the United States in a test of its MX missile (→ 12).

Drug crops increase in exporting nations

Feb 14. Marijuana, coca and opium poppy crops were larger this year in most major drug-producing countries, the State Department said in its annual report on narcotics production. Production of coca, used to make cocaine, increased by a third in Bolivia, Peru and Colombia, the report said, while Ecuador became a major coca-producing nation. But marijuana production decreased significantly in Colombia, a major exporter, because of an effective eradication program. The report's findings are especially significant this year because a new law says the President must cut off foreign aid to nations that have not made an adequate effort to combat drug traffic (→ 5/7).

Nine are indicted as Mafia bosses in N.Y.

Feb 26. A federal court indicted nine alleged Cosa Nostra bosses yesterday, charging them with participating in a "commission" which regulated the activities of the five organized-crime "families" in New York City. The nine have been charged with narcotics trafficking, loansharking, extortion, and labor racketeering.

Rudolph W. Giuliani, the prosecuting U.S. Attorney in Manhattan, said, "This case charges more Mafia bosses in one indictment than ever before." He described the commission, which included members of the Gambino, Genovese, Lucchese, Colombo, and Bonnano families, as "the Mafia's ruling council here in New York City and other cities" (→ 12/16).

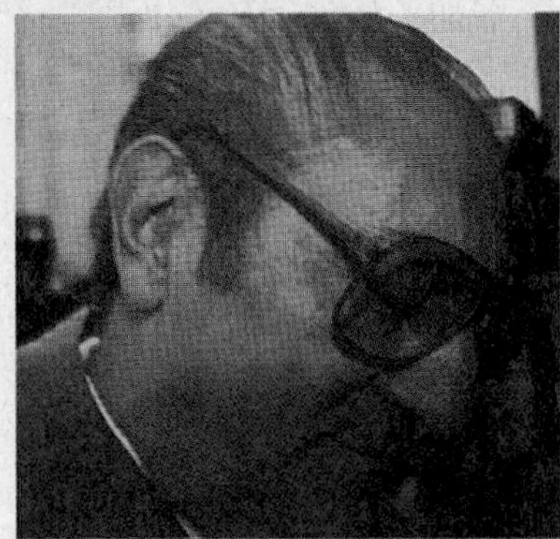

Gambino boss Paul Castellano.

Federal panel calls obesity major killer

Feb 13. Obesity is a major killer that should get the same attention as high blood pressure, smoking and other serious risk factors, a federal panel said today. Any degree of overweight increases health risks, the 14-member panel said, and medical treatment is needed for anyone whose weight is 20 percent above the desirable level. Among the obesity-related risks listed by the panel were diabetes, several forms of cancer, gall bladder disease and menstrual problems. At least 34 million Americans are 20 percent overweight, and 11 million of them have severe obesity that puts them at major risk, the experts said. The number of overweight Americans is rising, they added.

Dispute caused by halt in chess match

Feb 15. Both Soviet players insisted that they wanted to continue, but the head of the International Chess Federation ordered that the match between Anatoly Karpov and Gary Kasparov be halted and a new one started in September.

The federation head, Florencio Campomanes, said that the players and officials were too "exhausted" to continue. After 48 contests, the score stands at 5-3 in Karpov's favor, with 40 draws. Many records have been broken in the marathon match. Kasparov greeted the news with a scathing attack, suggesting that the delay was brought on by the fact that he had won two straight games. The defending champion, Karpov, was reported suffering from exhaustion (→ 11/9).

French uncover drug that curbs AIDS

Feb 8. A new drug appears to be the first that inhibits reproduction of the virus that causes the deadly disease AIDS, acquired immune deficiency syndrome, French researchers reported today. Dr. Jean Claude Chermann of the Pasteur Institute said the drug, HPA-23, has been tried on four patients and that one of them, a 15-year-old boy, has shown no signs of the AIDS virus after 18 months of treatment. The drug caused the virus to disappear temporarily from the other three patients, he said. American researchers called the report "a promising lead" but said further studies are needed to determine its long-term effects (→ 7/25).

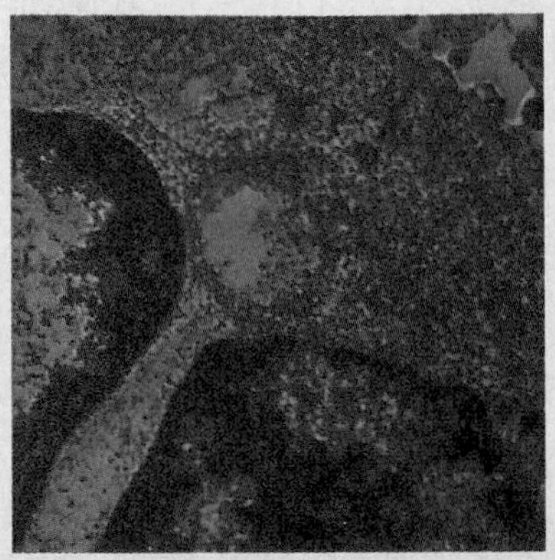

The deadly AIDS virus, LAV.

1985

MARCH

Su	Mo	Tu	We	Th	Fr	Sa
					1	2
3	4	5	6	7	8	9
10	11	12	13	14	15	16
17	18	19	20	21	22	23
24	25	26	27	28	29	30
31						

1. Pentagon accepts theory that atomic war would block sun, causing "nuclear winter" (→ 12).

4. Lebanon: 15 killed, 55 injured in blast at Shiite mosque (→ 8).

7. El Salvador: Chief army spokesman killed (→ 31).

7. N.Y.: Two convicted in $11 mil. Sentry armored car robbery.

8. Arizona: Thomas Creighton, 33, dies after three heart transplants in 46 hours (→ 8/6/86).

10. Athens: Constantine Caramanlis resigns as pres. (→ 29).

12. Geneva: U.S., U.S.S.R. begin arms control talks (→ 17).

15. Ohio: 71 banks closed for three days to stem run (→ 9/16).

17. Canada: Reagan agrees to joint study of acid rain.

17. Brussels: 100,000 protest recent Belgian decision to allow U.S. missile deployment (→ 4/7).

18. U.S. Supreme Court ruling allows unlimited PAC campaign contributions.

21. South Africa: 17 blacks killed by police gunfire (→ 4/6).

21. Lebanon: Israelis kill 21 in Shiite villages, including two on CBS News team (→ 4/17).

23. Denmark: 320,000 out in nation's first strike in 12 years.

24. Madrid: 100,000 demonstrate against NATO presence in Spain (→ 4/12).

25. L.A.: "Amadeus" sweeps Academy Awards with eight Oscars.

27. New York: Bernhard Goetz indicted on four counts of attempted murder (→ 1/16/86).

28. Brussels: Spain and Portugal agree to terms for entering EEC (→ 1/1/86).

29. Athens: Parliament elects Christos Sartzetakis president (→ 6/2).

31. El Salvador: Duarte's party claims victory in national election (→ 6/20).

DEATHS

10. Konstantin Chernenko, Soviet leader (*9/24/1911).

23. Zoot Sims, American jazz saxophonist (*10/29/1925).

Chernenko dies; Gorbachev chosen to lead

Gorbachev, youngest in Politburo.

Chernenko lies in state in Moscow.

March 13. For the third time in two and a half years, a Soviet leader was buried today. This time, however, power passed to a new generation. Konstantin Chernenko, who had been ill for most of his time in power, was buried near the Kremlin wall next to his predecessors, Leonid Brezhnev and Yuri Andropov. The new leader, Mikhail Gorbachev, led the funeral procession.

At the age of 54, Gorbachev is the youngest man to take charge in Moscow since Stalin. He called for immediate changes in the Soviet system and said it is time to transfer the "economy to the tracks of intensive development." Gorbachev seemed to emphasize economic concerns over military matters by giving military leaders a low profile at the funeral service.

Gorbachev, who was the number two man in the Kremlin under Andropov, also praised detente and called for a "real and major reduction in arms stockpiles." Vice President George Bush, who met with Gorbachev for an hour and a half, came away impressed. "If there ever was a time we can move forward with progress, I would say this is a good time for that," Bush said. The vice president gave the new Soviet leader a letter from President Reagan urging that they meet in the near future (→ 5/16).

Another car bomb in Beirut kills 62

March 8. One of the bloodiest car-bombings in recent years destroyed a five-story building in a heavily populated Shiite Moslem suburb of Beirut today, killing at least 62 persons and wounding 200. This was the third bombing in recent weeks in an area claiming the headquarters of the Party of God, a Shiite group loyal to Ayatollah Khomeini's Islamic Revolution.

The deadly blast occurred near the home of Sheik Mohammed Fadlallah, the Party of God's spiritual leader. Several members of his family were reported wounded, but the sheik himself was unharmed. Though no group has claimed responsibility for the bombing, some Moslem leaders point the finger at Israel (→ 21).

British coal strike ends after one year

March 3. Frustrated, angry and poor, the coal miners in Great Britain have called off their strike after nearly a year of struggle. However, Arthur Scargill, President of the National Union of Mineworkers, has vowed that "the dispute will continue," while other labor leaders have predicted that "guerrilla warfare" would flare among the more radical strikers. The walkout began last year over a government order to close several uneconomic mines, which caused many layoffs. Firm pressure by Prime Minister Thatcher on the National Coal Board to force the union to capitulate finally paid off Friday, when 52 percent of the workers, many of whom could not feed their families, voted to go back to work (→ 10/6).

Capital Cities buys ABC for $3.5 billion

March 17. The American Broadcasting Company today said it had agreed to be sold to Capital Cities Communications for $3.5 billion. The deal, which surprised industry experts, represents the first time that ownership of any of the nation's three major networks has changed hands. ABC has 214 affiliated stations across the country. Capital Cities is a smaller company that owns television and cable TV systems as well as newspapers and magazines. The deal has caused speculation that the other networks may be takeover targets.

Agents arrest 20 planning civil war

March 2. More than 20 people have been arrested in seven states by federal agents investigating a neo-Nazi group which has apparently been preparing for war against the United States government. The group, called the Order or the Silent Brotherhood, has reportedly stolen more than $4 million from banks and armored cars to finance an armed assault against the government, which it claims has been taken over by Jews. At least four member of the Order are also suspected of participating in the murder of Denver talk-show host Alan Berg last June.

Latest evening dress by Ungaro.

Masterful colorist, Marc Chagall, is dead

Chagall, at 97, visited an exhibit of his work with Min. of Culture Jack Lang.

March 28. Internationally famed painter and engraver Marc Chagall has died in France. He was 97 years old. He leaves mosaics in Jerusalem, murals at New York's Lincoln Center and stained glass windows in the cathedral in Rheims, France.

A perusal of his painting "I and the Village" (1911) reveals Chagall. You see his Jewish peasant heritage (he was born Moyshe Shagal in Russia). You see his imagination and amusement (a cow in the picture is bluish-green). And by the way the figures float you can deduce Chagall was a wanderer, studying with designer Leon Bakst in St. Petersburg before leaping to Paris, Berlin, New York and back again, scattering radiant color as he went.

Woman wins on sled

March 20. Libby Riddles, 28, is the first woman to win the arduous 1,135-mile Iditarod Trail Dog Sled Race in Alaska. It took her 17 days, and she credits the tenacity of her 13 dogs. In 1980 and 1981, Riddles placed in 18th and then 20th place. This time she was three hours ahead of the second-place finisher.

Prince has gone multi-media with his film hit "Purple Rain."

American officer is killed by Russian

March 26. An American officer, Major Arthur Nicholson Jr., was shot and killed in East Germany Sunday by a Soviet guard. Nicholson was fired upon near a restricted Soviet military installation when a sentry claimed he saw him taking photographs through a window of a storage building. According to Soviet accounts, Nicholson was given verbal warning, and a warning shot was fired into the air before the guard aimed and fired. Tass, the Soviet press agency, called the death "regrettable," but placed blame on the United States.

Western observers have condemned the Soviet action. Some have compared the incident, though different in degree and scope, with the tragic attack by the Soviet Union on a South Korean airliner in September 1983, which claimed 269 lives. United States officials are expected to issue a formal statement on the shooting after additional review.

Iran and Iraq fight heaviest battle yet

March 17. In what Iraq calls the fiercest fighting of the five-year war with Iran, Iranian troops fought to ford the Tigris River and take the highway linking the important Iraqi port of Basra in the south with the capital of Baghdad. Amid conflicting reports, Iran says it crushed an Iraqi counterattack in the marshland east of the river, while Iraq claims it halted the Iranian offensive with "uncountable" enemy losses. Meanwhile, most European airlines canceled flights to that area following Iraq's warning to commercial airlines that it would continue raids on Iranian cities (→ 8/17).

An Iranian soldier lies dead near Beida in the fifth year of fighting.

Under indictment, Donovan quits post

March 15. Secretary of Labor Raymond J. Donovan resigned his Cabinet post today after a New York state judge ordered him to stand trial on fraud and larceny charges. He is the first sitting Cabinet member ever to be indicted.

Donovan issued a statement in which he said he was confident "a jury will find me not guilty after hearing all the evidence." He is accused, along with nine others, of taking part in a multimillion dollar scheme to defraud the New York City Transit Authority at a time before he joined the Reagan Cabinet in 1981.

White House officials denied that the President had exerted pressure on Donovan to resign. The two men met at the White House for a brief time today.

1985

APRIL

Su	Mo	Tu	We	Th	Fr	Sa
	1	2	3	4	5	6
7	8	9	10	11	12	13
14	15	16	17	18	19	20
21	22	23	24	25	26	27
28	29	30				

1. Kentucky: Villanova upsets Georgetown 66-64 in NCAA basketball final.

3. U.S. charges Israel violated Geneva Convention by deporting Shiite prisoners (→ 17).

5. Chicago: John McEnroe says any man can beat any woman at any sport, especially tennis.

6. South Africa: Funeral crowd dispersed with tear gas (→ 15).

7. Goteborg, Sweden: China sweeps world table tennis titles in all except men's doubles.

7. Soviets announce unilateral freeze of medium-range nuclear missiles (→ 5/4).

8. New York: India files suit against Union Carbide for Bhopal gas disaster (→ 8/11).

9. Tokyo: Premier Nakasone urges Japanese people to buy foreign products (→ 15).

11. Hawaii: Scientists measure earth-moon distance to within one inch.

11. White House announces Reagan will visit Nazi cemetery at Bitburg (→ 14).

12. Spain: Restaurant blast kills 17 near U.S. base (→ 3/12/86).

14. Moscow: Pravda calls Reagan's planned Bitburg visit an "act of blasphemy" (→ 25).

15. Pretoria pledges to abolish bans on mixed-race sex (→ 6/5).

17. Lebanon: Cabinet resigns as Shiites take W. Beirut (→ 5/20).

18. Washington: Cable TV tycoon Ted Turner files for hostile takeover of CBS (→ 8/7).

19. Florida: Seven land safely on space shuttle Discovery (→ 29).

20. Madrid: Santiago Carillo, a founder of Eurocommunism, purged from Communist Party.

21. Managua: Ortega proposes cease-fire for Nicaragua (→ 23).

23. House rejects $14 million in aid to Nicaragua (→ 5/1).

25. Washington: 257 in House call on Kohl to cancel ceremony at Bitburg (→ 29).

26. Argentina: Fire at mental hospital kills 79, injures 247.

29. Florida: Space shuttle Challenger launched (→ 1/24/86).

Coup ousts Sudan boss; new man pro-West

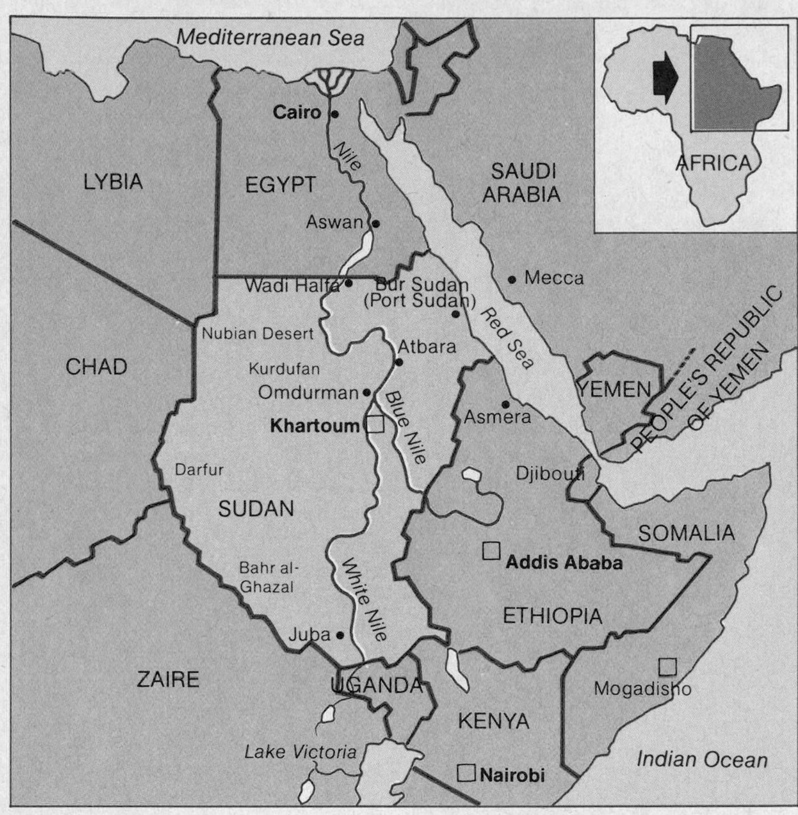

Sudan is bordered by pro-Soviet Ethiopia and pro-Western Egypt.

April 7. Gaafar el-Nimeiry, President of the Sudan, has learned the hard way that it is not a good idea to leave the country. Shortly after arriving in Egypt following a visit to the United States, Nimeiry discovered he had been thrown out of office in a coup by military leaders.

Col. Muammar Khadafy, the much criticized Libyan leader, has been advocating a coup against the pro-Western Nimeiry for months. But the new leader of the Sudan, Gen. Siwar el-Dahab, moved quickly to make it clear that his allegiances lie with Washington and not with Khadafy, who has been accused by the White House of exporting terrorism. Dahab met separately today with American, Egyptian and Saudi diplomats.

Ironically perhaps, it was a strong American hand which helped lead to the ouster of Nimeiry. The United States and the International Monetary Fund urged him to impose an austerity program earlier this year. When Nimeiry raised the price of bread and gasoline, rioters took to the streets in Khartoum.

Hodja is dead; ruled Albania since 1947

April 11. Enver Hodja may not be a household name in the West, and he probably preferred it that way. Hodja, leader of the small Communist state of Albania for 40 years, died early today. A government communique called him a "much loved and glorious leader." Foreign leaders have not been encouraged to attend Hodja's funeral.

"Don't worry," Hodja once said, "about what happens beyond your borders. The Albanian form of government is the only good one." Hodja installed what he called a popular republic in 1946, and his only loyalty lay with Stalin. He turned Albania into the "only truly Communist state."

Hodja was born the son of a wealthy and very religious Moslem merchant. After he studied in France, he rejected his father's religion and his country's monarchy. Hodja became an underground hero during the war, resisting both Mussolini and Hitler. After taking power, he decreed that God had died, and he turned mosques and churches into warehouses.

Buy foreign, leader urges the Japanese

April 15. Japanese Prime Minister Yasuhiro Nakasone made an unusual appeal to his citizens, urging them to buy foreign goods to help remedy the trade crisis, a problem which could affect "the life and death of our country," he said.

In effect, the Japanese are being asked to pay for the consequences of their own hard-earned success. Japan has striven to become the world's leading manufacturer and, with long working hours, brilliant innovations and governmental aid, it is succeeding. No other nation comes close to attaining the Japanese level of production quality, particularly in computer chips, electronics and auto manufacturing.

Japan has three major auto manufacturers located in America, and today Mitsubishi said it will open a new plant in the Midwest. The Japanese prime minister's plea to "buy foreign" comes amid a growing wave of protectionist sentiment in the United States.

Reagan will visit cemetery in Bitburg

April 29. Many are calling it the biggest mistake of his administration. But President Reagan is standing by his plans to lay a wreath on the graves of Nazi SS soldiers at a cemetery in Bitburg, Germany, saying, "They were victims, (of Nazism) just as surely as the victims in the concentration camps." Reagan's planned trip, on the 40th anniversary of the end of World War II in Europe, has been assailed by Jewish groups, American politicians and millions of U.S. citizens.

Leading the attack on Reagan's visit next month has been historian Elie Wiesel, Chairman of the U.S. Holocaust Memorial Council. Wiesel, a former concentration camp prisoner, told Reagan, "I have seen the SS at work. And I have seen the victims. There was a degree of suffering in the concentration camps that defies imagination." In the wake of appeals to cancel the trip and in an attempt to mend political damage, the president added a stop at a concentration camp to his itinerary (→ 5/5).

Galapagos turtles threatened by fire

The scorched terrain of Galapagos.

April 9. For a grueling five weeks a fire has ravaged Isabela, largest of the five Galapagos Islands. The flames are steaming alive hundreds of giant Galapagos tortoises, creatures too heavy (up to 500 pounds) and slow to escape incineration. Two of 15 subspecies are threatened, and Danish and American scientists are carrying them to safety seven miles away. One animal, its shell scorched, was rescued by a soldier, one of 300 fighting the fire.

Is or is not Coke the real thing now?

April 23. For 99 years Coke was it, but it ain't any more. Its maker announces a new formula to be in stores next month. Pepsi at once held a press conference inviting reporters to taste "the REAL real thing." We'll see if things go better with (the new) Coke (→ 7/8/86).

1985

MAY

Su	Mo	Tu	We	Th	Fr	Sa
			1	2	3	4
5	6	7	8	9	10	11
12	13	14	15	16	17	18
19	20	21	22	23	24	25
26	27	28	29	30	31	

2. Manila: Witness says she saw soldier shoot Aquino (→ 8/21).

3. Poland ousts two U.S. diplomats for May Day protests (→ 5/31/86).

4. Paris: Mitterrand bars support for U.S. Star Wars plan (→ 6/21).

4. Spend a Buck wins Kentucky Derby, Angel Cordero up.

7. N.Y.: Malcolm X killer Muhammad Abdul Aziz paroled.

8. Strasbourg: Reagan speaks to European Parliament on 40th anniversary of V-E Day.

9. Washington: Judge rules U.S. govt. not responsible for victims of Agent Orange (→ 8/14).

10. India: 59 killed, 150 wounded in Sikh attacks (→ 11).

11. India: 1,500 arrested for Sikh violence (→ 1/22/86).

11. London: Flash fire kills 40 at soccer match (→ 31).

13. Philadelphia: Police firebomb radical group Move, burning whole block (→ 15).

17. United Airlines strike blocks flights across U.S. (→ 6/15).

18. Florida: Biggest fires in state's history menace populated areas.

19. Washington: Rep. Les Aspin says military got extra $18 bil. in overblown inflation estimate.

20. Israel frees 1,500 Palestinians for three Israeli soldiers (→ 22).

21. U.S. Navy cancels General Dynamics contracts over "pervasive" business misconduct.

21. Calif.: Patty Frustaci gives birth to septuplets; six survive.

21. Britain: Mohammed Ajeeb elected in Bradford as first British Pakistani mayor.

22. Beirut: Car bomb kills 50, wounds 172 (→ 6/10).

26. Danny Sullivan wins Indy 500.

27. Brazil: Prisoners kill 13 by lottery to protest overcrowding.

30. Canada: Edmonton Oilers beat Philadelphia Flyers 8-3 to take Stanley Cup.

DEATH

12. Jean Dubuffet, French painter (*7/31/1901).

Reagans visit Bitburg cemetery after seeing Nazi death camp

A controversial stroll through Bitburg's cemetery under heavy guard.

May 5. Visiting West Germany today, President Reagan spoke eloquently of the evils of Nazism, in contrast to the vehement protest against his visit to a German cemetery. Some 2,500 German soldiers are buried at Bitburg; 49 of them were SS troops. Reagan's visit to Bitburg and the Bergen-Belsen concentration camp was designed to remember the horrors of the past and salute West Germany's longtime friendship with the United States. White House advisers concede that the trip failed miserably.

In New York, historian Elie Wiesel condemned the president's trip at a demonstration in support of Soviet Jews. "Is there a connection between Bitburg and this rally?" he said. "Yes there is. What was attempted at Bitburg, a denial of the past, a disregard of Jewish agony, the same but on a larger scale has been attempted in Russia."

Reagan visited the Bergen-Belsen camp before he traveled to Bitburg with Chancellor Helmut Kohl. "Out of this tragic and nightmarish time," the president said, "beyond the anguish, the pain and the suffering for all time, we can and must pledge: Never again."

Philly police drop bomb; community burns

May 15. At least 11 persons were killed as fire swept through 61 row houses in Philadelphia after police dropped a bomb on headquarters of a radical group known as Move. The bombing ended a 24-hour siege in which police battled the armed radicals.

With more than 200 people left homeless by the raging inferno, Mayor Wilson Goode said he would appoint a commission to probe the police operation. City officials have suggested that Move members started the fire in their house.

"We did not create any fire," said Police Commissioner Gregore J. Sambor. "To the best of our knowledge, the Move members had spread flammable material in their compound and in the neighboring area."

Residents of the neighborhood have said they saw gasoline being carried into the fortified Move house and hoisted by rope to its roof in the days before the police moved in. They also said that loudspeakers atop the house broadcast warnings in the hours before the bombing that gasoline had been spread around the neighborhood.

The Move group claims that it disdains modern technology and materialism and the establishment. Several years ago, one police officer was killed in a shoot-out with Move members; nine of the radicals were convicted of murder (→ 11/13).

Fiery debacle in Philadelphia.

Drug testing called for in pro baseball

May 7. The Baseball Commissioner has ordered all non-union personnel in the major leagues to submit to drug tests and asked players to join in the program.

Commissioner Peter V. Ueberroth said that "everyone from owners on down" would be included. He said he would be tested along with 3,000 minor leaguers, scouts and coaches on the 25 teams in the majors.

Ueberroth said that he wanted baseball to be the leader in eradicating drugs from society. A spokesman for the Players Association dismissed Ueberroth's request as "grandstanding" in an effort to enforce an undesirable program.

The commissioner would not divulge the details of the plan, such as how it would be administered and what penalties might be imposed on those who refused. He said he had not checked with owners before revealing the plan (→ 11/29).

Violence mars soccer matches in three cities

Bradford's soccer stadium goes up in flames, turning fun into disaster.

May 31. After one of the most turbulent soccer seasons ever experienced, English officials announced that no teams under their jurisdiction would be permitted to play in Europe next season.

Violence has marred soccer matches in three major cities, including Peking. The most recent problem, the one that led to Britain's decision, occurred earlier this week in Brussels. There, 38 people died before the final match of the Cup of Champions.

On May 11 in London, 40 persons died in a flash fire that swept through a wooden grandstand in the northern city of Bradford.

On May 19, thousands of Chinese fans went on a rampage outside a Peking stadium after their team lost a match to Hong Kong. Their wrath was directed primarily at foreigners and they pelted cars with bricks and bottles.

In Brussels, 250 people were injured when fans at the match between Italy and Britain rioted before the start of the game. Turin and Liverpool were about to play for the cup title when the rampage began. The dead included 30 Italians, five Belgians and a Frenchman. The match was played after an hour's delay while police restored order.

Belgian Prime Minister Wilfried Martens said that British teams — including Scottish, Welsh and Northern Irish —would be banned from his country until further notice. British Prime Minister Margaret Thatcher said in approving the travel curbs, "There are so many dead and injured people as a result of the actions of our citizens that it requires very firm measures."

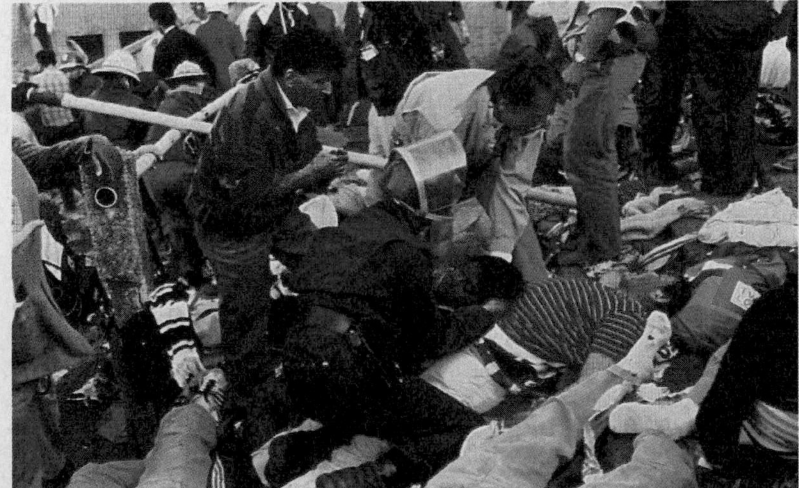

Some 36 riot deaths did not stop the Liverpool-Turin game in Brussels.

Rapist freed when his victim recants

May 12. A born-again Christian has retracted charges of rape, and the accused is now free. About two months ago, Mrs. Cathleen Webb signed an affidavit in Cook County, Illinois, exonerating Gary Dotson of the crime. Six years ago, her testimony sentenced him to prison.

One night in 1977, teenager Cathleen Crowell cried out from a grove of trees. A police officer found her bruised, disheveled and hysterical. She named Dotson, who had a history of petty crime, as her rapist. Mrs. Crowell Webb now says she had sex that night with her boyfriend (who denies it), and fearing pregnancy blamed Dotson.

Bangladesh reports 10,000 lost in storm

May 27. As many as 10,000 people may have been killed by a cyclone that devastated the islands of southeastern Bangladesh, government officials said today. The seas off the coast were reported littered with floating bodies, and officials estimated the number of homeless at 250,000. President H.M. Ershad said the loss of life and property damage caused by high waves and flooding were the "worst tragedy in Bangladesh history."

Nicaragua placed under trade ban

May 1. President Reagan has announced a ban on all trade with the Central American nation of Nicaragua. The Nicaraguan government condemned the move, saying that it would hurt the ordinary working person more than the government. It was also suggested that the embargo would strengthen Nicaragua's ties with the Soviet Union, to whom they would have to turn to buy needed chemicals and machine parts. The Nicaraguans also claimed that the ban is in violation of the U.N. Charter and that they would add their complaints to their case against the United States which has been pending in the World Court since 1983 (→ 6/12).

Three powers plan hunt for Mengele

May 24. In the most ambitious international effort to track down a Nazi war criminal since World War II, the United States, West Germany and Israel have announced a combined effort to track down and prosecute Dr. Josef Mengele, who is charged with selecting victims for gassing and vivisection experiments at the Auschwitz death camp. Following World War II, Mengele disappeared from his hometown in the American sector of Germany and resurfaced in South America several years later. Said to be living in Paraguay, he is the world's most sought-after fugitive, with a price of $4 million on his head (→ 6/6).

Anti-alcohol drive ordered in U.S.S.R.

May 16. Russians see "green serpents" instead of pink elephants, but the enemy is the same: alcohol. In their case it is vodka, which is served at virtually any event. Drinking is part of Russian life, and the teetotaler may be regarded with suspicion. Now, increasing alcoholism will be fought. The production of vodka will be cut next year, the drinking age is raised from 18 to 21, and the sale of liquor is banned before 2 p.m. on workdays (→ 7/2).

Retired Navy officer is arrested as a spy

May 20. Retired U.S. Navy Warrant Officer John Anthony Walker and his son Michael were arrested today on espionage charges by federal agents. FBI chief William Webster announced the arrests of the father and son, saying they had "obtained national defense information for passage to the Soviet Union with intent, or reason to believe that, it is to be used to injure the United States or give advantage to a foreign nation." Authorities had followed the elder Walker to a location in Maryland where a Soviet national, who is presumably the link to the Kremlin, lived. If convicted, the Walkers could face a sentence of life in prison (→ 6/4).

1985

JUNE

Su	Mo	Tu	We	Th	Fr	Sa
						1
2	3	4	5	6	7	8
9	10	11	12	13	14	15
16	17	18	19	20	21	22
23	24	25	26	27	28	29
30						

2. Athens: Socialist Premier Andreas Papandreou re-elected.

3. Rome: Vatican and Italy ratify pact ending Roman Catholicism as state religion (→ 8/8).

4. Washington: John Walker and son plead not guilty to espionage charges (→ 12).

5. G.M. bids $5 bil. for Hughes Aircraft in largest acquisition in history.

5. House votes for economic sanctions on S. Africa (→ 7/20).

6. Brazil: Police exhume alleged body of Josef Mengele (→ 21).

8. Paris: Evert Lloyd and Wilander win at French Open.

9. Boston: L.A. Lakers beat Celtics 111-100 for NBA title.

10. U.S.: Claus von Bulow acquitted of twice attempting to kill his wife.

10. Beirut: Thomas Sutherland becomes eighth American kidnapped by Palestinians.

11. N.J.: Karen Ann Quinlan dies at 31 (→ 3/15/86).

12. House approves $27 mil. in humanitarian contra aid (→ 27).

14. Gunmen hijack jet with 104 Americans over Mideast (→ 18).

15. U.S.: United Airlines workers end 29-day strike.

16. U.S.: Triple jump record set by Willie Banks at 58'5".

18. Reagan calls for unconditional release of hostages on hijacked TWA jet (→ 28).

18. Osaka, Japan: TV cameras film vigilante execution of businessman charged with defrauding elderly citizens.

21. Star Wars laser test successful on second try from space shuttle (→ 9/13).

27. U.S. Supreme Court rules unions cannot penalize members who quit during strike.

27. House votes to limit use of U.S. combat troops in Nicaragua (→ 7/7).

28. Beirut: Hijackers hold banquet for hostages (→ 30).

DEATH

21. Tage Erlander, Swedish premier 1946-69 (*6/13/1901).

Hijacked hostages freed after 17 days

Masked terrorists on the TWA jet survey the situation at Beirut airport.

Shiite gunmen read their demands.

Hostages meet the press under guard.

June 30. The long hijacking ordeal ended today in the Middle East. Radical Shiites who are members of Hezbollah, or Party of God, released 39 Americans in Beirut. They appeared healthy and relaxed as they were driven to Damascus and then flown to Frankfurt. They said they were looking forward to being reunited with their families. One family will not be sharing their joy. Navy diver Robert Stethem, one of the passengers on TWA flight 847, was killed by the terrorists on the first day of the 17-day drama.

Hostage spokesman Allyn Conwell, who made several controversial and favorable statements about the hijackers during the ordeal, thanked Syrian officials for their role in the negotiations. "We are sure," he said, "that without their assistance, without their help, without their concern over our welfare, we would undoubtedly still be in Beirut with an uncertain future."

Syrian authorities convinced the hijackers to free the hostages even though Israel had not satisfied their major demand, the release of more than 700 Shiite and Palestinian prisoners. Israel indicated during the crisis that it might free the prisoners if the United States requested it to do so. The Reagan administration refused. As Vice President Bush greeted the returning hostages, he said, "You are back and America did not compromise her principles to get you back." There is speculation, however, that Israel will free the prisoners after the furor over the hijacking has died down.

Asked if the United States should retaliate, Conwell said, "I don't really know who the people that took us are. Retaliation sounds an awful lot like revenge. I don't seek any retaliation or revenge." The former hostages said they were treated well by their captors.

Conwell and others did not mention the torture and the violence on board the plane when two gunmen commandeered it after takeoff from Athens on the 14th. As they forced the pilot to crisscross the Mediterranean, the terrorists beat some of the passengers with weapons they had smuggled aboard the plane in Athens. They killed Stethem just before they forced the plane to land in Beirut for the second time.

When controllers at the Beirut airport tried to prevent the landing, the TWA pilot, John Testrake, made a dramatic radio appeal. "They are beating the passengers," he said. "They are beating the passengers. They are threatening to kill them now. We want the fuel now. Immediately." The controllers relented.

Most of the passengers were released by the hijackers as the plane was flown from Beirut to Algiers, back to Beirut and then to Algiers and Beirut again. On the second day of the ordeal, a report emerged that a United States commando team had been dispatched to the Mediterranean to free the hostages. Nabih Berri, a moderate Shiite Moslem leader who became a mediator in the crisis, revealed on the 17th that he had arranged for the hostages to be taken off the plane and hidden at undisclosed locations in Beirut. "I have personally ordered their evacuation," Berri said, "because we were afraid of an operation or battle in which all of them could have been killed." Pilot Testrake also warned "we'd all be dead men" if a commando raid were mounted to free the hostages.

The raid never happened, but the Reagan administration did dispatch warships to the coast of Lebanon. "It is a war," Defense Secretary Caspar Weinberger said in explaining the ship movements. Secretary of State George Shultz called for united international action to "curb the despicable acts of terrorists." It is not clear what role, if any, the saber-rattling played in the release of the hostages. Seven other Americans, victims of earlier kidnappings, are still being held. It is not clear what, if anything, can be done to secure their release (→ 7/1).

Robert Stethem, victim in Beirut.

Mengele identified, dead

June 21. Investigators from West Germany, the United States and Brazil are "99 percent sure" they have found the body of Josef Mengele. Since June 6, when a corpse was exhumed from a grave outside Sao Paolo, Brazil, countless forensic tests have been conducted. Even Menachem Russek of the Israeli police, a Nazi hunter who has encountered more than his share of hoaxes, seems satisfied.

Dr. Josef Mengele was the "Angel of Death" of Auschwitz, aiding in the torture of four million people, mostly Jews. He conducted "experiments," often on children, results of which were maiming or death. One Brazilian scientist, himself a doctor, called him an "anti-physician."

There were rumors that Mengele escaped to Paraguay after the war. West German authorities found correspondence placing him in Brazil and found an Austrian couple living near Sao Paolo who confessed to sheltering the man. He died, the couple said, in a swimming accident six years ago when he was 67.

"It is better for me," Russek said, "to be standing on Mengele's grave than vice-versa."

Mengele wanted.

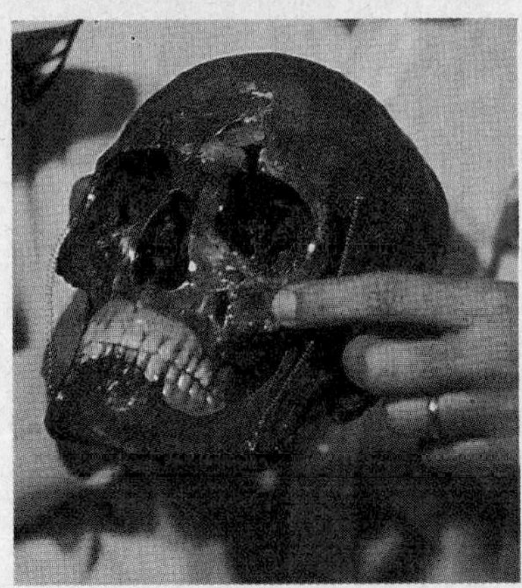

Mengele found.

Weinberger says 4 spies should be shot

June 12. Defense Secretary Caspar Weinberger said today that John A. Walker Jr. and three associates facing trial on charges of spying for the Soviet Union "should be shot" if convicted. Walker, a retired Navy radioman, is accused of forming a spy ring with his son Michael, a yeoman who was serving aboard the aircraft carrier Nimitz; an older brother Arthur; and another Navy retiree, Jerry A. Whitworth. They have pleaded not guilty.

The four men will be tried in federal court, not by the military. Civilians convicted of espionage once faced the death penalty but courts found that unconstitutional. Under federal law, conviction for peacetime espionage provides for a maximum punishment of life imprisonment. Under military law, conviction on espionage charges provides for a mandatory death penalty only in wartime (→ 8/9).

Court rules against moment of silence

June 4. The Supreme Court today struck down an Alabama law that permitted a daily one-minute period of silent meditation or prayer in public schools, thus reaffirming its insistence that "government must pursue a course of complete neutrality toward religion." The vote was 6 to 3.

Varying versions of "moment of silence" laws exist in 25 states, and the high court strongly suggested that it would find many of these to be unconstitutional in future cases.

Writing for the majority, Associate Justice John Paul Stevens said the Alabama Legislature "intended to characterize prayer as a favored practice," thus violating complete neutrality toward religion. But in a dissenting opinion, Associate Justice William H. Rehnquist said that nothing "requires government to be completely neutral between religion and irreligion."

Air-India jet explodes in flight, killing 329

June 23. An Air-India jumbo jet plunged into the Atlantic Ocean near Ireland today, killing all 329 people on board. Indian officials said the crash apparently was caused by a bomb placed aboard the jetliner by a Sikh extremist group as retaliation for an army raid on the Golden Temple, the religion's most holy place, last year.

Air controllers at Shannon Airport said they were in contact with the plane only eight minutes before it suddenly disappeared from their radar screens this morning on a flight from Toronto to Bombay via London. The controllers said the pilot made no mention of any difficulty that could have led to the sudden crash. Even the simultaneous failure of the Boeing 747's four engines would have given enough time to radio a distress signal.

Canada recently increased security measures for Air-India at terminals in Toronto and Montreal because of a series of threats, X-raying or searching all baggage. In phone calls to newspapers, persons who said they represented Sikh groups claimed responsibility for placing the bomb aboard the liner (→ 7/4).

Israel quits Lebanon after searing events

June 10. During the past 1,099 days, 654 Israeli soldiers have died in Lebanon and another 4,000 have been wounded. But today, while minor border fighting continued, Israeli troops began their withdrawal from the nation they invaded in June 1982. To what extent and for how long Israel will stay out of Lebanon is not clear. Sources in Jerusalem said an undisclosed number of military advisers and patrols will remain in Lebanon until a substantial peace accord is secured. A sense of relief surrounds the military pullout. An Israeli commander told reporters, "We did this three years too late. Not a single soldier is shedding any tears over this historic moment" (→ 14).

Salvadoran raiders kill four U.S. Marines

June 20. Four U.S. Marines were killed when leftist guerrillas attacked a string of outdoor cafes in the center of San Salvador. Thirteen persons were killed and at least 15 were wounded when the gunmen equipped with automatic rifles sprayed the cafes with gunfire. The off-duty Marines were members of the guard force of the U.S. Embassy. Salvadoran and U.S. officials blamed the attack on the National Liberation Front and said it indicated the leftists were returning to urban violence after being checked on rural battlefields (→ 9/10).

An architectural merger of Ancient Egypt and Renaissance France? Mitterrand has backed a pyramid, designed by I.M. Pei, for the Louvre courtyard. Not surprisingly, some think 2 bil. francs could be put to better use.

1985

JULY

Su	Mo	Tu	We	Th	Fr	Sa
	1	2	3	4	5	6
7	8	9	10	11	12	13
14	15	16	17	18	19	20
21	22	23	24	25	26	27
28	29	30	31			

1. Israel decides to free 300 of remaining 735 Shiite prisoners (→ 3).

2. Moscow: Eduard Schevardnadze replaces Gromyko as foreign minister (→ 8/4).

4. New Delhi: Police inquiry says bombs caused Air India jet disaster.

6. Wimbledon: Navratilova over Evert Lloyd to become first woman to win four straight.

7. Nicaragua: For. Min. Miguel d'Escoto begins hunger strike to protest U.S. intervention (→ 17).

8. China: Tampons marketed for first time.

8. U.S.: Fires in West scorch million acres, causing $40 mil. in damages.

9. Washington: David Stockman resigns as budget director.

10. New Zealand: Two blasts sink Greenpeace protest vessel Rainbow Warrior (→ 23).

10. Nairobi: 10,000 gather for intl. parley on women's rights.

11. U.S. sends 100 anti-aircraft missiles to Pakistan, charging Afghan incursions (→ 11/2).

14. U.S. Justice Dept. to ask Supreme Court to overturn 1973 ruling on abortion (→ 6/11/86).

14. Washington: Five arrested for smuggling military parts to Iran (→ 8/1).

17. Nicaragua: Pres. Ortega says war with U.S.-backed rebels has killed 12,000 (→ 8/4).

19. Italy: Tesero dam collapses, killing 264.

20. South Africa gives emergency powers to police for first time in 25 years (→ 24).

21. Bernard Hinault wins his fifth Tour de France.

24. France recalls ambassador in South Africa, suspends investment (→ 31).

25. Paris: Rock Hudson hospitalized for AIDS (→ 8/30).

28. Uganda: Obote ousted in military coup.

DEATH

16. Heinrich Boll, German writer (*12/21/1917).

President has cancerous tumor removed

The President will be A-OK!

July 15. A tumor removed from President Reagan's intestine two days ago was found to be cancerous, but the president has a better than 50 percent chance of living out his normal lifespan, doctors said today.

The growth, a polyp two inches in diameter, was removed from Reagan's colon in a three-hour operation by surgeons at Bethesda Naval Medical Center, two days after it was detected during a routine medical examination. Before the operation, the president signed letters transferring presidential powers temporarily to Vice President Bush.

Dr. Stephen Rosenberg, a member of the surgical team, said Reagan was recovering rapidly from the operation and that his long-term outlook is good. "The majority of patients in the president's situation would certainly survive five years and beyond," Rosenberg told reporters.

World rock festival held for famine relief

Tina and Mick together at Live Aid.

July 13. "Good morning children of the 80's," proclaimed singer Joan Baez to a crowd of 90,000 today in Philadelphia for the Live Aid concert for African famine relief. "This is your Woodstock, and it's long overdue." The event coincided with another huge gathering outside London, with a worldwide TV simulcast of both concerts. Performers included Paul McCartney, Bob Dylan, Tina Turner, Mick Jagger, Phil Collins, U2, Madonna, Sting, and many others. The massive benefit, organized by Irish singer Bob Geldof, represented the culmination of previous efforts to raise money through recordings. Live Aid is expected to raise more than $50 million for famine relief.

At Wembley and Philadelphia, Geldof's "Global Jukebox" drew over 160,000.

Rainbow Warrior is sunk in Auckland

July 23. A French couple was due in court in New Zealand this morning to answer charges relating to the sinking of the Rainbow Warrier. It was originally believed the man and woman were Swiss, but it has been revealed they were traveling under false passports. There is new speculation that the explosive materials used to sink the Rainbow Warrier at its dock in Auckland came from New Caledonia. The boat, owned by the Greenpeace environmental group, was bombed on the night of the 10th. A member of the crew died in the explosion. Greenpeace was planning to use the 160-foot vessel to continue its protests against French nuclear testing in the South Pacific (→ 8/29).

Environmentalism vs. terrorism.

South Africa enters state of emergency

July 31. South Africa is once again the site of turbulent unrest, violence and severe government-imposed restrictions. President P.W. Botha's government ordered a state of emergency 11 days ago to halt social upheaval. And today, the government banned mass funerals for the victims of black unrest. The ceremonies had become anti-apartheid rallies, but now police may break them up. Since September, over 500 people have died in the struggle against apartheid. The Reagan administration, one of South Africa's few allies, maintains its policy of "constructive engagement," which tries to persuade rather than confront Pretoria on its racial policies (→ 8/1).

Reagan condemns five terrorist states

July 8. President Reagan branded five nations —Iran, Libya, North Korea, Cuba and Nicaragua —as members of "a confederation of terrorist states" that was carrying out "outright acts of war" against the United States. In a speech before the American Bar Association, the president cited the five nations as "outlaw states," which he said were responsible for the growth of international terrorism in recent years.

To loud applause from the audience of 5,000 lawyers, the president said: "The American people are not —I repeat not —going to tolerate intimidation, terror and outright acts of war against this nation and its people. And we are especially not going to tolerate these attacks from outlaw states run by the strangest collection of misfits, Looney Tunes and squalid criminals since the advent of the Third Reich."

Notably missing from the president's list was Syria, which has been listed by the State Department as supporting international terrorism. White House officials explained that the omission was a gesture of gratitude to Syrian President Hafez al-Hassad for his help in obtaining the release last week of 39 American hostages in Beirut who had been seized aboard a hijacked TWA airplane (→ 12/30).

Divers recovering millions in treasure

Sunken treasure off Key West.

July 21. Divers have recovered millions of dollars in gold, silver and copper treasure from the wreckage of the Spanish galleon Nuestra Senora de Atocha off the Florida coast.

The Atocha was sunk in a 1622 hurricane and the debris scattered throughout the Key West waters. A company called Treasure Salvors located the sunken treasure after a 16-year search. The company President, Mel Fisher, and his two sons found stacks of silver bars and thousands of coins after digging through five feet of silt and mud. The discovery came ten years to the day after one of Fisher's sons and his wife had died in search of the Atocha.

Peru will restrict foreign debt payments

July 28. The new President of Peru sent shudders through international financial circles today by asserting that Peruvians come first and the banks come second. In his inaugural address, President Alan Garcia Perez said Peru would limit foreign debt payments to ten percent of export earnings. His challenge to the banks was the strongest since the onset of the Latin American debt crisis in 1982. He also said Peru would renegotiate its debt payments without the International Monetary Fund, which he called an "accomplice" in Peru's problems.

Young Peruvian Pres. Alan Garcia.

Teenagers invade Pentagon computer

July 16. Because of their ages, police cannot reveal the true names of Vampire, Red Barchetta, Private Sector, N.J. Hack Shack, Store Manager, Treasure Chest or Beowulf. But the seven New Jersey youths using those code names got into some serious trouble accessing confidential data with computers. The whiz kids quietly tapped into AT&T, making free calls to Europe, and reached the desk of a lieutenant general at the Pentagon. Some purchases were made to a stranger's credit card, and a formula for explosives rested in their data banks.

Israel has released 300 of 735 Shiites

July 3. Dressed in jogging suits, their hands bound by cord, 300 of the 735 Lebanese and Palestinian prisoners being held in the Atlit prison south of Haifa were released today by Israel, as agreed upon. The detainees, mostly Shiite Moslems, were bused to a village just north of the Israeli border and turned over to the Red Cross for reunion with their families in the Lebanese coastal town of Tyre. One said, "We were treated well by the Israelis, but our release today is a victory for the Shiites, a great victory." Israel said the remaining prisoners will be freed in a few weeks if the military situation in south Lebanon stays as calm as it has for the past three months (→ 8/17).

Cram achieves new mile mark: 3:46.31

July 27. Steve Cram of Great Britain surprised even himself by running the mile in a world record time of three minutes, 46.31 seconds in Oslo. It was called "the Dream Mile" but Cram had just hoped to win with a fast time. He had set a world record of 3:29.67 for 1,500 meters only 11 days earlier. "I was worried it would be too slow so I just stayed up with the pacemakers," he said. The pacemakers in this all-star field lost Pierre Delese at the start. He went down in the early bumping for position. James Mays of the United States led through the first lap, but Cram was ahead for the final one. Jose-Luis ran second and Sebastian Coe of England third.

July 7. Acrobatic Boris Becker breathed life into the 109th Wimbledon. "Boom Boom," at 17, is the youngest champion with a 6-3, 6-7, 7-6, 6-4 win over Kevin Curren. Said coach Tiriac: "In his head, he is 23 or 24."

July 13. A new mark for Soviet vaulter Sergei Bubka at 19'8.5".

1985

AUGUST

Su	Mo	Tu	We	Th	Fr	Sa
				1	2	3
4	5	6	7	8	9	10
11	12	13	14	15	16	17
18	19	20	21	22	23	24
25	26	27	28	29	30	31

1. Washington: Six held in plot to smuggle arms to Iran (→ 10/3/86).

1. House votes economic sanctions on S. Africa (→ 8).

2. Dallas: 122 die in Delta jet crash on runway.

4. Soviets announce efficiency plans, decentralizing economic decision-making (→ 2/11/86).

4. Nicaragua: For. Min. Rev. Miguel d'Escoto ends hunger strike (→ 10/16).

6. U.S.: Pro baseball players begin second strike in five years.

8. South Africa: 16 dead as police open fire on blacks (→ 10).

8. Togo: Pope begins tour of Africa (→ 2/10/86).

9. Washington: Arthur Walker found guilty of spying for U.S.S.R. (→ 11/12).

10. South Africa: Apartheid critic Rev. Allan Boesak arrested (→ 19).

14. Vietnam: Hanoi hands over remains of 26 American killed in Vietnam War.

17. Beirut: Car-bomb blast kills 50, injures 120 (→ 9/18).

19. Washington: Reagan admin. criticizes Bishop Tutu for barring meeting with Botha (→ 20).

20. Washington: Rev. Jerry Falwell calls Bishop Tutu a "phony" (→ 27).

21. U.S. accuses Moscow of using spy dust (→ 10/24).

21. Philippines: 100,000 rally to mark second anniversary of death of Aquino (→ 10/22).

23. Bonn: Hans Joachim Tiedge, head of W. German counter-espionage, defects to East (→ 25).

25. N.Y.: Dwight Gooden, at 19, becomes youngest pitcher ever to win 20 games in a season.

29. Greenpeace head David MacTaggart asks New Zealand to submit Rainbow Warrior case to World Court (→ 9/17).

30. Pentagon to test all new recruits for AIDS (→ 10/2).

DEATH

28. Ruth Gordon, American actress, "Harold and Maude" (*10/30/1896).

Three crashes: 711 killed

Crash at Mt. Osutaka killed 517, history's worst single-plane disaster.

Aug 22. The death toll from major aviation accidents this month rose to 711 today when a British charter jet burst into flames on takeoff from Manchester Airport, killing 54 passengers and crew.

On August 13, 517 people died when a Japanese Air Lines jumbo jet on a domestic flight crashed into a mountain range in the worst aviation accident involving a single plane. A third major accident occurred on August 2 when a Delta Airlines jet crashed as it tried to land at Dallas-Fort Worth Airport during a violent thunderstorm, killing 140 of the 161 persons aboard.

The International Civil Aviation Organization says 1985 already is the worst year in the history of commercial flight, with 15 accidents and more than 1,400 people killed. Previously, 1974 ranked as the worst year for aviation safety, with 1,299 deaths, including 346 in the crash of a Turkish jumbo jet.

Bonn government is betrayed by 5 spies

Aug 25. Another figure has been implicated in the espionage scandal plaguing the West German government in Bonn. A secretary in the office of President Richard von Weizsackers was arrested tonight on charges of spying for East Germany. Charged with supplying information to East Berlin, after being recruited by an experienced East German spy who became her lover, is a 50-year-old woman whose name was not disclosed.

This latest arrest brings the total of West German government employees accused of espionage to five. While the role of president in the West German system is essentially ceremonial, he is given briefings on foreign policy matters. It is this type of information which the secretary is charged with passing to the East.

American officials are expected to meet soon with Bonn authorities to assess the damage to mutual security interests. Interior Minister Friedrich Zimmerman is leading the fight to tighten security. Yet Bonn's Parliament has resisted certain security measures, fearful of infringing on individual rights.

South Africa in turmoil; Tutu sees almost no chance for peace

Aug 27. The government of South Africa, rocked by new racial violence and unprecedented criticism by black leaders, suspended all trading on its stock and currency markets. The South African currency, the rand, tumbled to 35 cents on the dollar, its lowest rate ever and a 25% drop since the government imposed a new state of emergency last month. The trading suspensions were announced on the eve of a planned march on the Cape Town prison where black nationalist Nelson Mandela is being held. Rioting spread to Durban, and at least 50 people were killed. Security forces rounded up 500 schoolchildren who had boycotted classes.

Despite increasing black resistance and calls from abroad for moderation, President P.W. Botha refused to make concessions to South Africa's black majority. "I am not prepared to lead white South Africans and other minority groups on a road to abdication and suicide," he said. "We have never given in to outside demands and we are not going to do so."

Bishop Desmond Tutu said he was "devastated" by Botha's speech. He said the president is trying to "bludgeon blacks into total submission" with military force, that South Africa is on the brink of catastrophe and the chances of peace are "virtually nil" (→ 9/1).

A sea of blacks gather around 18 caskets despite ban against such protests.

Ted Turner drops his bid to take over CBS

Aug 7. Rebuffed by CBS, media mogul Ted Turner will purchase MGM/UA Entertainment Company on the rebound. The acquisition includes rights to classic films such as "The Wizard of Oz" and "Gone With the Wind." Turner will pay $1.5 billion. In cash.

No amount of money could have wooed CBS, which objected to him on, among other grounds, broadcast standards. The Atlantan bought WTBS-TV in 1970 and made it what he calls a "superstation," distributed nationwide by satellite. It relies on reruns, B-grade films (to be replaced, no doubt, by MGM fare), Atlanta Braves games and non-controversial news coverage.

In 1980, Turner initiated CNN, a 24-hour cable news program. That network did not show a profit until the first quarter of this year.

Media mogul Ted Turner.

21 share in biggest lottery prize: $41m

Aug 22. Tonight, 21 workers at a Mount Vernon, N.Y., printing press factory are sharing lottery winnings of $41 million. The workers signed a contract that if any of the group's numbers won the latest cash drawing, all would share in the booty. Each will get $650,793. What makes this team effort particularly winning is that all those concerned are immigrants. They are from Poland, Thailand, the Dominican Republic, Hungary, Trinidad, China and other nations. The man who picked the winning combination was Celso Manuel Garcete, 41, a Paraguayan exceedingly popular with his co-workers.

Bush observes end of World War II

Hiroshima's Peace Memorial Park.

Aug 14. Vice President Bush stood on the deck of the aircraft carrier Enterprise in San Francisco harbor today and urged a strong military policy. He and other top Reagan administration officials were noting the 40th anniversary of the end of World War II. Mrs. Jean MacArthur, the 86-year-old widow of General Douglas MacArthur, was among the guests invited to hear a series of speeches.

Bush, standing in for President Reagan, said that after the Japanese attack on Pearl Harbor "we learned that when free people close their eyes to evil, they do so at their peril." Defense Secretary Caspar Weinberger recalled the attack as "a terrible example of how to invite aggression, a living reproach to our unwillingness to prepare."

The end of the war was hastened when the United States dropped atom bombs on Hiroshima and Nagasaki on Aug. 6 and Aug. 9, 1945, killing over 150,000 people.

$2.5b to be paid for asbestos damages

Aug 1. The Manville Corporation today offered to pay $2.5 billion to settle thousands of asbestos-related health claims against it. It is the largest health claims settlement proposal made by an American company. Tens of thousands of workers and users of Manville's products have filed claims of more than $12 billion, charging that asbestos exposure has caused lung cancer and other debilitating lung diseases. Manville's offer would require its shareholders to put half the value of their stock in a special fund. Asbestos health and property damage claims have caused Manville to declare bankruptcy.

Girl who paid visit to Soviet chief is killed

Aug 26. Samantha Smith, the little girl whose little pleas for peace sounded round the world, was killed in a plane crash tonight. She and her father died instantly when their Beechcraft went down a half mile from the Auburn, Maine, airport. They were on their way home from London, where Samantha was filming a television show.

In 1982, when she was 11, Samantha wrote to Soviet leader Andropov asking him why he wanted to "conquer the whole world." To assure her he had good intentions, he invited her to visit the Soviet Union, where she received the warmest of welcomes.

Kharg Island oil terminal is bombed

Aug 17. Iraq struck one of its most successful blows yet in its war with Iran. Iraqi jets, armed with deadly and precise French-built Exocet missiles, bombed Kharg Island, Iran's strategic port in the Persian Gulf. Nearly 90 percent of all the oil produced by Iran passes through facilities on the island. Ten tankers were hit by the Iraqi missiles. Two of the three major piers on the island were destroyed and a number of key installations were damaged. The attack on Kharg Island follows a new Iraqi bombing campaign against Iranian cities and villages in which thousands of people have been killed (→ 12/26/86).

Bruce, born in U.S.A., returns to Jersey

Springsteen, an American symbol.

Aug 18. Bruce Springsteen came home tonight, home to America, and home to his native New Jersey, where 65,000 of his most ardent fans welcomed him at Giants Stadium. "Brruuuccccce!" they kept screaming, as the current king of rock and roll regaled the young, blue-collar audience with "Born in the U.S.A.," "Thunder Road" and other songs about disillusioned workers, jobless vets and teens in love. "The Boss" had spent 13 months on the road, playing to sellout crowds in Europe, Australia, and Japan, and in hometowns all across the U.S.A.

Gas leaks from U.S. Union Carbide plant

Aug 11. A small cloud of toxic chemicals escaped from a Union Carbide plant near Charleston, W. Va., this morning, and at least 135 residents were treated for eye, throat and lung irritation. Last December, methyl isocyanate gas escaped from a Union Carbide plant in India, killing 2,000 people. No MIC escaped today, plant officials said. Aldicarb oxime, a much less toxic gas, is declared as one constituent of the gas cloud. The accident has angered many local residents.

Aug 24. Reagan is back in the saddle six weeks after surgery.

1985

SEPTEMBER

Su	Mo	Tu	We	Th	Fr	Sa
1	2	3	4	5	6	7
8	9	10	11	12	13	14
15	16	17	18	19	20	21
22	23	24	25	26	27	28
29	30					

1. South Africa suspends payment of foreign debts (→ 6).

5. Ariz.: Mafia boss Joseph Bonano jailed for refusing to testify.

5. Chile: Six killed in day of anti-govt. protests (→ 7/3/86).

6. Washington: Reagan apologizes for saying racial segregation ended in South Africa (→ 9).

8. New York: Lendl over McEnroe, Mandlikova over Navratilova in U.S. Open.

9. Washington: Reagan, in reversal, authorizes limited sanctions against South Africa (→ 10).

10. El Salvador: Gunmen kidnap daughter of Duarte (→ 10/27).

10. Luxembourg: 11 West European nations agree to impose sanctions on S. Africa (→ 16).

11. Portugal: 150 killed in head-on train crash.

12. U.S. ends policy of checking draft registration through college records.

15. Sweden: Olaf Palme elected to fourth term (→ 2/28/86).

16. Angola: South African troops cross border to strike at alleged guerrilla bases (→ 29).

17. Paris: French military divers implicated in sinking of Greenpeace ship (→ 26).

21. Las Vegas: Michael Spinks outpoints Holmes for title.

24. U.S. congressional analysts conclude Star Wars would raise risk of nuclear war (→ 30).

25. N.C.: Nine KKK members indicted for cross burnings and shootings (→ 1/16/86).

27. Calif.: Richard Ramirez charged with 68 crimes, including 14 murders.

30. Soviets offer 50% cut in arms in return for Star Wars curbs (→ 10/26).

DEATHS

14. Julian Beck, U.S. founder of Living Theater (*5/31/1925).

19. Italo Calvino, Italian novelist (*10/15/1923).

30. Simone Signoret, French actress (*3/25/1921).

30. Charles Richter, American seismologist (*1900).

Huge 'quake in Mexico kills thousands

Crowded Mexico City was ravaged by blasts reaching 7.8 on the Richter scale.

Sept 21. In Mexico City, rescue workers and bereaved family members are using shovels, picks and even their hands to dig through the rubble of Thursday morning's earthquake. Thousands of people are known dead. Many more are still trapped under the cement and steel of scores of buildings. Hospitals are "filled to saturation." Entire families, terrified by the earthquake and a severe aftershock 36 hours later, are living in the streets. Their homes have disappeared.

"I heard a tremendous noise," one survivor said. "I grabbed my daughter and jumped out the window. I had no chance to help my wife, who was killed when she was buried in the rubble."

The earthquake was extremely powerful, measuring 7.8 on the Richter scale. The aftershock measured 7.3. The epicenters of both tremors were located about 230 miles southwest of Mexico City, but it was the capital that bore the brunt of the damage.

John Gavin, the United States Ambassador, said, "I would have to estimate the number to be at least 10,000 dead or trapped, and at this time we have to think of them as dead. It could possibly be twice that number. I would say this calamity caused hundreds of millions of dollars of damage." Gavin, who took a helicopter tour over Mexico City, called the view a "remarkable and terrifying sight." At least five Americans are known to have perished in the earthquake.

Mexico's President Miguel de la Madrid said 50 buildings were seriously damaged by the earthquake. More than 20 of them crumbled completely when the aftershock hit. The high-rises have become gravesites, and rescue workers are defumigating some of them to prevent the spread of disease.

U.S. is debtor nation first time since 1914

Sept 16. America, the stalwart force in the world economy, is now a debtor nation, a dubious distinction this country has not had since 1914. For years, economists have noted that America was headed into the fiscal red. And now, figures released by the Commerce Department show the nation's deficit on current accounts —trade in goods, services and investment earnings with the rest of the world —was $30 billion. This total obliterates the $30 billion surplus accumulated last year. In short, the United States owes foreigners more than they owe the U.S. Consequently, dividends and interest payments to foreigners will exceed those paid to the U.S.

The new fiscal condition makes America vulnerable to international market fluctuations. According to an official at the Institute for International Economics, "If there was a run on the dollar tomorrow, we'd be hurt" (→ 12/5).

Divers find Titanic wreck after 73 years

Sept 1. A team of French and American researchers today reported finding the hulk of the luxury liner Titanic in water 12,000 feet deep south of Newfoundland. Robert D. Ballard of the Woods Hole Oceanographic Institute, leader of the joint expedition, said the Titanic had been found by new undersea robots equipped with TV cameras.

The wreckage of the Titanic, which carried 1,595 persons to their death when she sank in 1912, had eluded at least three previous expeditions. A French research ship, the Suroit, worked with the American research ship Knorr to make the discovery. The exact location of the Titanic is being kept secret to prevent looting of the sunken ship.

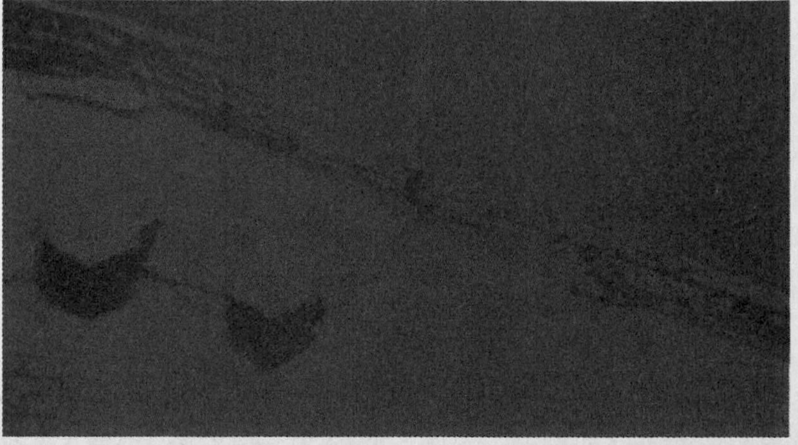

A crusted deck of the Titanic, for 73 years the underwater grave of 1,595.

Britain and U.S.S.R. quarrel over spying

Sept 16. The defection of a strategic Soviet spy in Great Britain and his exposure of a major espionage network has created a rift between Britain and the U.S.S.R. Oleg Gordiyevsky operated as chief of the British branch of the KGB, the Soviet intelligence agency, until he defected and was granted political asylum in London this week. The revelation prompted London to oust 25 Russians from England. Moscow retaliated by kicking out 25 British delegates from Russia in what has become a serious diplomatic showdown. And now, to counter the removal of the Britons, Prime Minister Thatcher has ordered six more Soviets from her nation.

Paris admits sinking Greenpeace vessel

Sept 26. France's Prime Minister, Laurent Fabius, ended more than two months of stonewalling and admitted that French intelligence officers sank the Rainbow Warrier in New Zealand. Up until now, the government has denied it had anything to do with the deadly bombing of the Greenpeace boat. The surprise announcement followed the resignation of the Defense Minister and the dismissal of the intelligence agency's director. Five officials have been indicted on charges of leaking information on the case to the press (→ 11/3).

Sept 22. Christo's latest masterpiece: The Pont Neuf wrapped in 44,000 sq. yards of cloth.

Creator of elegant but simple style dies

Sept 17. British designer Laura Ashley has died following the effects of a bad fall at her daughter's home over a week ago. She was 60. Miss Ashley founded a clothing empire, designing elegant dresses for women. She combined Victorian-style prints with comfortable, natural fabrics to suit Lady Di and other royal personages. Miss Ashley started her business in 1953 by making scarves, designing them meticulously at her kitchen table. Her husband admired the work and helped her set up her first shop in London in 1967. At her death, she leaves an industry with factories in the Netherlands and stores on several continents.

Westerners impose apartheid sanctions

Sept 29. A dozen Western nations have imposed sanctions against the Afrikaner government of South Africa in protest of the racist policy of apartheid. Following the September 9 move by the Reagan administration to prohibit most loans to the Pretoria government, as well as the sale of computer and nuclear technology, 11 other nations have followed suit with similar economic and cultural sanctions. It is believed that the sanctions by themselves will have little economic effect, but they will serve a more symbolic function (→ 10/13).

Sept 11. Cincinnati exploded tonight as Pete Rose, 44, nailed his 4,192nd career hit to break Ty Cobb's 57-year-old record.

French rocket fails as Mitterrand watches

Ariane III blasts off at Kourou, nine minutes before exploding.

Sept 13. If French President Francois Mitterrand has not been superstitious in the past, he must be now. Today, Friday the 13th, he tried to take the presidential Concorde from Paris to French Guiana, where a rocket launch was scheduled. His Concorde broke down twice on the ground, forcing him to take another aircraft. When he finally arrived for the launch, he witnessed the explosion of the rocket nine minutes into its ascent.

Ariane III was the latest in a series of French rockets that successfully lifted satellites into orbit nine times since June 1983. France serviced a dozen clients including the U.S., while financing 64% of the program. According to an agreement signed in 1973, when the mutual rocket service was conceived, France also assumed the technical responsibilities —and liabilities.

Tonight, two satellites would have been sent into orbit, a private telecommunications device designed by RCA in the United States, and the ECS III, a telephone and television satellite financed by the European Space Agency. It would have connected and benefitted 25 Western European nations. Initial reports blame the explosion on a defect in the third stage of the rocket's ignition system.

American minister released in Lebanon

Sept 18. President Reagan today announced that the Rev. Benjamin Weir was back in the U.S. with his family after having been released several days ago from 16 months of captivity in Lebanon. A graduate of Princeton Theological Seminary and a missionary in Lebanon since 1953, the 61-year-old minister was kidnapped May 8, 1984, reportedly by the Shiite Moslem group known as the Party of God. Six other Americans are also being held hostage, and Weir's release was kept secret so as not to endanger what was hoped to be their own "imminent" freedom. This hope vanished when it became apparent that Weir's release was not a prelude to their own (→ 10/1).

Anti-rocket rocket tested by Americans

Sept 13. An Air Force missile destroyed an orbiting satellite 290 miles above the earth in its first test, the Pentagon announced today. The heat-seeking missile was launched from an F-15 fighter plane and honed in successfully on a six-year-old military satellite orbiting at 17,500 miles an hour. The experiment was conducted despite a warning by the Soviet Union that it could accelerate an arms race in space. Defense Secretary Caspar Weinberger hailed the test as "a great step forward" in a $4 billion program to develop an anti-satellite weapon. The White House said the successful test was "an incentive to the Soviets" to negotiate limits on weapons in space (→ 24).

1985

OCTOBER

Su	Mo	Tu	We	Th	Fr	Sa
		1	2	3	4	5
6	7	8	9	10	11	12
13	14	15	16	17	18	19
20	21	22	23	24	25	26
27	28	29	30	31		

6. London: Policeman killed in battle with rioters.

7. Puerto Rico: Hundreds die in landslides and flash floods.

7. Mediterranean: Hijackers seize cruise ship Achille Lauro with 400 passengers (→ 9).

9. Egypt: Hijackers surrender Achille Lauro and free hostages (→ 10).

10. U.S. jets intercept plane carrying hijackers, force it to NATO base in Italy (→ 12).

12. Egypt: Mubarak calls U.S. interception of jet "piracy" (→ 15).

13. ANC says it is not prepared to negotiate peaceful settlement with Pretoria (→ 18).

15. Washington: U.S. says body found in Syria is Leon Klinghoffer, slain by hijackers (→ 17).

16. Managua: Ortega suspends civil rights, declares state of emergency (→ 3/3/86).

17. Rome: Premier Bettino Craxi resigns amid furor over Achille Lauro case (→ 20)

18. South Africa: Hanging of black activist Benjamin Moloise triggers rioting (→ 11/2).

22. Washington: Sen. Laxalt, back from Manila, says Marcos pledges reform (→ 31).

24. New York: Reagan attacks Soviet imperialism in U.N. 40th anniversary speech (→ 11/21).

25. Argentina: State of siege declared to halt right-wing violence (→ 12/9).

26. London: 100,000 march through Hyde Park to protest arms race (→ 1/15/86).

27. New York: Grete Waitz and Orlando Pizzolato win N.Y. Marathon.

27. K.C.: Royals beat St. Louis Cardinals 11-0 to take World Series in final game.

31. Washington: Reagan orders inquiry on Soviet sailor forced back to ship near New Orleans (→ 11/4).

DEATH

1. E.B. White, U.S. essayist, writer of children's books, "Charlotte's Web" (*7/11/1899).

Arabs hijack Italian liner

Achille Lauro returns in peace, while the world fights over its captors' fate.

Oct 20. The body of Leon Klinghoffer came home to New York City today. The wheelchair-bound Klinghoffer was shot dead by the Palestinian hijackers of a Mediterranean cruise ship earlier this month. His wife, Marilyn, who survived the hijacking ordeal, nearly fainted at the airport. Klinghoffer died, New York Senator Daniel Patrick Moynihan said, "because he was an American, because he was a Jew and because he was a free man."

The hijacking incident on the Italian cruise ship Achille Lauro began on the 7th. Heavily armed guerrillas, believed to be members of the Palestine Liberation Front, commandeered the ship as it left Alexandria, Egypt. More than 60 Americans were on board. The hijackers demanded the release of prisoners held by Israel, but they surrendered on the 9th after the Egyptian government promised them free passage out of the country. Egyptian officials were apparently unaware that the guerrillas had killed Klinghoffer.

In a dramatic move, the Egyptian plane transporting the hijackers to Tunisia was intercepted by U.S. Navy jets and forced to land in Sicily. The White House applauded Italy's help, but later criticized Rome officials for allowing the alleged leader of the hijackers, Mohammed Abbas, to escape (→ 11/24).

Leading man Rock Hudson dies of AIDS

Oct 2. Film star Rock Hudson died this morning at age 59. He was the first movie star to acknowledge he had AIDS, last month purchasing $10,000 worth of tickets to an AIDS fundraiser. He had been ill for over a year. Hudson, born Roy Scherer, shot to stardom with "Magnificent Obsession" (1954), about a cad who blinds a woman and learns eye surgery to make amends. "Giant" (1956) provided a big role. In the 60's came a slew of comedies opposite Doris Day, starting with "Pillow Talk" (1959). A recent TV show was halted when he had heart surgery (→ 12/13).

Hudson, a shocking and tragic end.

Duarte's daughter is returned by rebels

Oct 27. The kidnapped daughter of El Salvador's President Jose Napoleon Duarte was freed unharmed by leftist rebels today in a complex exchange. She had been held hostage for 44 days. The government said it released 22 political prisoners and provided safe passage for 96 guerrillas disabled in the war.

Duarte and daughter, reunited.

The rebels released Miss Ines Guadalupe Duarte and a companion, Ana Cecilia Villeda. They also freed at least 23 abducted mayors of small towns. Priests, diplomats and Red Cross officials traveled to different locations to act as witnesses to the "vast, delicate operation," which took place after weeks of halting negotiations between rebels and government representatives.

Some criticize Duarte for negotiating with the guerrillas, saying he put personal interests above the nation's. Others, who have had relatives kidnapped, expressed bitterness at the special treatment given the president's daughter.

Scientists turn on giant atom smasher

Oct 13. Physicists at the Fermi National Accelerator Laboratory in Illinois today switched on the world's largest atom-smasher, producing energy levels three times higher than any achieved before. The device, four miles in diameter, smashed subatomic particles called protons into counter-rotating antiprotons, yielding energies of 1.6 trillion electron volts in the collisions. The new facility is expected to make the U.S. the world leader in high-energy physics, a position it lost in the 1970's to a European consortium. Leon Lederman, the laboratory director, said the device allows study of subatomic particles in unprecedented detail (→ 1/4/86).

Shree Rajneesh, cult leader, is arrested

Oct 28. Federal agents bagged a Bhagwan early this morning when they caught guru Shree Rajneesh trying to flee the country. Rajneesh is charged with violating immigration laws and arranging phony marriages for his cult members. The religious leader was nabbed at the Charlotte, North Carolina, airport when his jet, bound for Bermuda, touched down for refueling.

The Bhagwan ran a commune of about 1,500 people in Oregon. Thousands more cult members live in Rajneesh's native India and other countries. He knew the federal government had no faith in him after his chief adviser, a woman named Ma Anand Sheela, was arrested in West Germany for several minor offenses. Rajneesh appeared in court today clad in a lavender robe (→ 11/14).

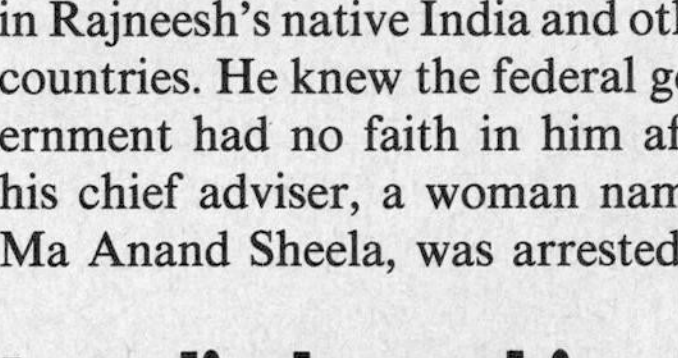

Rajneesh, Oregon's mysterious guru.

Gorbachev talks arms; Raisa shops in Paris

Oct 5. France's President Francois Mitterrand and Soviet leader Mikhail Gorbachev are finding in Paris that they have differences over arms negotiations and human rights. But it is Gorbachev's wife, Raisa, who is snaring the headlines. French fashion writers seem amazed that anyone coming from Moscow could know anything about fashion. They purred when Mrs. Gorbachev attended fashion shows at the salons of Pierre Cardin and Yves Saint Laurent. And they wondered out loud how Cardin convinced Mrs. Gorbachev to visit his salon first. The writers became snooty only once, when they realized Mrs. Gorbachev had worn the same suit twice. "Princess Diana of England wears the same dress twice in public, but at least she waits two years," one reporter sniped.

The affable Gorbachevs in Paris.

Israeli planes hit Tunis PLO offices

Oct 1. The deadly cycle of Middle East violence found new victims today, hundreds of miles away in North Africa. Israeli planes flew 1,500 miles to Tunisia and bombed the headquarters of the Palestine Liberation Organization. A PLO official claimed that 60 people were killed, "including women and children, many of them Tunisians." PLO Chairman Yasir Arafat, who was elsewhere during the attack, vowed, "My people will respond to this official terrorism and to the Israeli military junta." Israel said the attack was in retaliation for the murder of three Israelis on Cyprus last week. The PLO has denied responsibility for the slayings (→ 7).

Rambo is back in "First Blood Part II," muscling his way into the Vietnamese jungle to free tortured POWs and rewrite history.

U.S. fears major Philippine civil war

Oct 31. President Ferdinand Marcos of the Philippines has rejected warnings by the United States that his nation will be faced with civil war if he does not enact major political, economic and military changes. The Philippines, a former colony and longtime ally of the United States, is the home of two large American military bases. American interest in the Philippines is intimately tied up with maintaining these bases and plans have already been made to invest more than a million dollars in their improvement.

A report by the United States Senate predicted that althought the Marcos government may not be toppled soon, Communist insurgents will achieve a strategic stalemate. Mounting anti-Marcos sentiment and the general economic decline of the Philippines have made the situation a volatile one.

The United States is actively pressuring Marcos to clean up the political system, professionalize the military and break up business monopolies. Marcos has hinted that if such pressure continues, he may withdraw his support of the U.S. military bases. He also warned that the two nations must maintain a public image of complete cooperation or Soviet and Vietnamese forces would be enticed to interfere. He predicts the defeat of Communist insurgents within a year (→ 11/1).

Welles, boy genius grown old, is dead

Welles, 50-year veteran of the screen.

Oct 12. When Orson Welles died today in Las Vegas, he left people feeling empty-handed. Didn't he have at least one more film up his sleeve? Magicians like him (during World War II he did a USO act sawing assistant Marlene Dietrich in half) tend to vanish in a dramatic puff of smoke. Could it be he leaves only a half-dozen superb pictures? Welles, who was 70, put out his last impressive work, "F for Fake," in 1975. Earlier films were "Citizen Kane," "The Magnificent Ambersons," "The Lady from Shanghai," "Othello" and "A Touch of Evil." He did not direct "The Third Man," but he acted in it, and his tall, weighty figure is felt in every frame.

Yul Brynner, noted Broadway star, dies

Oct 10. Although Yul Brynner died this morning, he may still be seen in commericals for the American Cancer Society. In the ads he warns people not to smoke; lung cancer ended his life at age 65.

Circumstances around his death are clear, but not around his birth. He has said he was born on Sakhalin Island off the coast of Japan in 1915 —or was it 1922 as he said on another occasion? He was adopted by gypsies—or was he born to them? In either case, Brynner sought public acceptance of gypsies by publicizing their plight in the 1970's. Brynner was best known for his regal part in "The King and I," a role revived time and again.

Brynner, grand in "The King and I."

1985

NOVEMBER

Su	Mo	Tu	We	Th	Fr	Sa
					1	2
3	4	5	6	7	8	9
10	11	12	13	14	15	16
17	18	19	20	21	22	23
24	25	26	27	28	29	30

1. Washington: Sen. Durenberger calls for resignation of Pres. Marcos (→ 3).

2. Kabul: Afghan troops encircle U.S. Embassy in dispute over Soviet soldier seeking asylum (→ 7/1/86).

3. New Zealand: Two French agents plead guilty to sinking Rainbow Warrior.

3. Manila: Marcos pledges election early next year (→ 12/15).

5. New York: Ed Koch re-elected for third term as mayor.

6. Rome: Craxi sets off uproar in Parliament, defending right of PLO to "resort to arms."

7. Newark: Federal judge overturns triple murder convictions of Hurricane Carter, John Artis.

11. Frankfurt: Theater drops production of Fassbinder's "Garbage, the City and Death" due to anti-Semitic content.

12. Virginia: Arthur Walker given life sentence as spy (→ 25).

13. Philadelphia: Police Commissioner George Sambor resigns over Move bombing.

14. Oregon: Guru Baghwan Shree Rajneesh agrees to leave country.

15. Britain, Ireland sign pact giving Dublin consultative role in Ulster (→ 27).

21. South Africa: 13 blacks gunned down by police in Mamelodi (→ 12/22).

22. Washington: Reagan advocates covert aid for UNITA rebels in Angola (→ 2/18/86).

23. Miami: Xavier Suarez chosen as city's first Cuban mayor.

24. Malta: Over 50 killed by grenades as Egyptians try to free hostages seized yesterday.→

25. U.S.: Communications expert Ronald Pelton admits spying for Soviets (→ 6/5/86).

25. Calif.: Judge orders Cathy Smith, who gave John Belushi heroin, to stand trial for murder.

29. Japan: Terrorists sabotage trains, stall 20 mil. commuters.

DEATH

17. Lon Nol, ex-leader of Cambodia (*11/13/1913).

Reagan meets Gorbachev at Geneva

Reagan and Gorbachev meet in Geneva to break ground for a "fresh start."

Nov 21. President Reagan and Soviet leader Mikhail Gorbachev have proved that showmanship is just as important as diplomacy in two days of remarkable meetings in Geneva. The two men discovered they have sharp differences on most major issues, but they stunned their aides by holding six hours of intensely private discussions. Only interpreters were present. The private sessions were the longest in 14 American-Soviet summits, and the two leaders agreed to meet again. Gorbachev is scheduled to visit the United States next year, and President Reagan said he will go to the Soviet Union in 1987.

"Neither side got everything they wanted," Reagan said as he arrived in Brussels to brief NATO leaders. But the president said he and the Soviet leader "got very friendly." Gorbachev called the meetings "frank, sharp, sometimes very sharp. But it still seems to me they were productive."

A key element of disagreement was Reagan's insistence on the development of the space-based weapons system known as Star Wars. Gorbachev boasted at a news conference that the Soviet Union could build a better system of its own. "Mr. President, you should bear in mind that we are not simpletons," Gorbachev said.

Gorbachev also got a taste in Geneva of what American protest is all about. He and Jesse Jackson, the black leader and candidate for the Democratic presidential nomination last year, spoke at a 45-minute impromptu meeting about nuclear arms, South Africa and the plight of Soviet Jews (→ 1/1/86).

Nancy and Raisa hold their summit.

Latest drug threat: Crack, cocaine type

Nov 29. A new form of cocaine —purified, less expensive and almost instantly addictive —has hit the streets of New York. The substance, known as crack, is alarming law enforcement officials, who predict a new wave of desperate addicts sweeping the nation.

The drug, which is smoked rather than snorted like powdered cocaine, greatly accelerates the climb toward addiction. Users have told of becoming lost in smoking binges lasting for days, almost immediately following their initiation to the drug. Crack is processed from cocaine powder into a crystal form. Police have raided a number of "factories" in the New York area, but the drug continues to spread rapidly and is reported to be making inroads in the suburbs and other American cities (→ 6/7/86).

Volcano buries two Colombia towns in mud

Nov 14. For the first time in 400 years, a volcano erupted in northern Colombia today, setting off a chain reaction that killed as many as 20,000 people. Mud, not lava, was the killer. Scientists say heat from the Nevada del Ruiz volcano melted the snow and ice on its slopes. Mud catapulted down the mountain, swelling rivers and smothering at least two towns.

Lucky survivors in Colombia.

Floods buried Armero, 85 miles northwest of Bogota. The town was home to 25,000 people. A large part of Chinchina was also destroyed. Two other towns are threatened by a dam that was created when mud backed up a river.

One woman said she lost her family as they tried to escape together. "We got about a block," she said, "and a big wave of mud hit us. We all went tumbling. The baby was knocked out of my husband's arms, and we were all separated."

Colombia's President Belisario Betancur said, "We have had one tragedy after another." It was just a week ago that leftist guerrillas killed 100 people, including 11 judges, during a day-long siege at the Palace of Justice in Bogota.

Rebels seize courts in Bogota, kill 11 judges

Nov 8. A 28-hour siege of the Palace of Justice in Bogota, Colombia, came to an end today, leaving 100 people dead. Eleven judges, including the President of Colombia's Supreme Court, were among those killed in the assault by the guerrilla group M-19.

On November 6, a group of approximately 60 rebels shot their way into the modern five-story building, and held as hostages most of the 24 members of the Supreme Court and the 20 justices of the nation's highest civil court. One survivor said that, during the melee with the police and soldiers which followed, the rebels, realizing "that they were lost," shot the justices execution-style, and sprayed bullets into a dark room filled with hostages.

In a note slipped under the door of the Associated Press offices this morning, the M-19 group said the objective of the siege was to stage a trial of President Belisario Betancur. There were reports that one of the four demands issued by the rebels after they had taken the building was that Betancur himself come to the palace. The guerrillas accused Betancur and his armed forces of not observing the terms of a cease-fire treaty with Colombia's guerrilla forces, approved in the summer of 1984. Betancur refused an appeal by the Supreme Court president, before he was slain, to enter into negotiations with the rebels. Like many Latin American nations, Colombia is plagued by terrorist bands intent on upsetting the status quo.

Colombian commandos prepare to storm Bogota's besieged Palace of Justice.

Fifty die in effort to seize hijackers

Nov 24. Egyptian commandos stormed an Egyptian plane on Malta 24 hours after it was seized on a flight from Athens by a band of hijackers. At least 50 people are dead, most killed when the terrorists tossed grenades as the commandos moved in. The Egyptians decided to act after the hijackers reportedly killed eight passengers, and the pilot said it was worth the risk. "I heard the victims ask for mercy," he said. "They were sitting there waiting for execution. It was awful." The hijackers never made any demands, but Egypt charges they were supported by Libya (→ 12/30).

Britain and Ireland ratify Ulster plan

Nov 27. An emotional, two-day debate ended in the British Parliament tonight as the House of Commons voted overwhelmingly in favor of a new agreement with the Irish Republic. The accord allows the Dublin government a new consultative role in Northern Ireland. Prime Minister Margaret Thatcher's major opponent in Parliament, Labor Party leader Neil Kinnock, urged approval of the agreement. The 15 deputies from Northern Ireland, who are committed to the union of the province with Great Britain, opposed the accord and are threatening to resign (→ 9/25/86).

U.S. Navy civilian held as Israeli spy

Nov 28. Jonathan Jay Pollard, a 31-year-old civilian analyst in the Naval Intelligence Service, was arrested today on espionage charges of selling classified military information to Israel. Federal officials said that Pollard over the past 18 months had provided hundreds of pages of classified documents to Israeli agents in return for less than $100,000. Pollard was arrested near the Israeli Embassy, where he apparently was seeking political asylum. In Jerusalem, Israeli officials said Pollard, who was apparently motivated by pro-Israeli sentiments, had been working for a secretive Israeli counterterrorism unit (→ 6/4/86).

South Africa adopts strict press limits

Nov 2. The South African government has imposed tight restrictions on foreign journalists, including the barring of television camara crews and photographers from covering racial unrest. Newspaper reporters will still be permitted to cover areas of unrest but only if they are escorted by police. The crackdown followed protests by government officials that the foreign press was presenting a distorted picture of recent, violent events in South Africa (→ 21).

Braudel, founder of social history, dies

Nov 28. One of the great historians of the 20th Century died today at the ripe old age of 83. While Fernand Braudel's life spanned our century, he chose to focus on earlier times. After founding Les Annales, the first journal of social history, the French scholar wrote the two-volume work, "The Mediterranean and the Mediterranean World in the Age of Philip II" (1949) and the three-volume "Civilization and Capitalism, 15th-18th Centuries" (1979). In these, he displayed vast erudition in which he integrated geographic, economic, sociological and historical factors.

Defector from KGB returns to U.S.S.R.

Yurchenko leaves for Moscow.

Nov 4. A senior KGB official who defected to the West in what the Central Intelligence Agency believed was a major intelligence coup announced that he was defecting again, this time back to the Soviet Union. Vitaly Yurchenko, who reportedly once directed KGB operations in North America, told reporters at the Soviet Embassy that he had been kidnapped last summer in Rome by American agents and held prisoner in this country by the CIA. Yurchenko escaped from American control when he excused himself at a restaurant with two CIA agents and walked several blocks to the Soviet Embassy.

Study reports 25 wrongly executed

Nov 13. A new study on capital punishment in the U.S. asserts that in this century 343 people were wrongly sentenced to death and 25 were executed. Included among these are Ethel and Julius Rosenberg, Bruno Hauptmann, Nicola Sacco and Bartolomeo Vanzetti.

Nov 9. Gary Kasparov (left), at 22, beats Anatoly Karpov, to become chess' youngest champion.

1985

DECEMBER

Su	Mo	Tu	We	Th	Fr	Sa
1	2	3	4	5	6	7
8	9	10	11	12	13	14
15	16	17	18	19	20	21
22	23	24	25	26	27	28
29	30	31				

4. Washington: Robert McFarlane resigns as natl. security adviser; Adm. John Poindexter named to succeed.

5. New York: Dow Jones tops 1500, a new record (→ 12).

9. Argentina: Five convicted for crimes as junta leaders during 1970's.

13. France sues U.S. over discovery of AIDS serum (→ 6/5/86).

17. Adelaide: Scientists at Flinders Medical Center announce first pregnancy from frozen egg.

22. Munich: Sweden beats West Germany to retain Davis Cup.

22. South Africa: Winnie Mandela jailed for returning to her home in Soweto (→ 25).

25. South Africa: 53 killed in inter-tribal fighting (→ 1/1/86).

30. Pakistan: Martial law lifted after eight years (→ 4/10/86).

DEATHS

7. Robert Graves, British poet (*7/24/1895).

12. Anne Baxter, American actress (*3/7/1923).

31. Sam Spiegel, American film producer (*11/11/1903).

CULTURAL EVENTS, 1985

Literature: Garrison Keillor's "Lake Wobegon Days"; Kurt Vonnegut's "Galapagos"; Carolyn Kizer's "Yin," Pulitzer poetry; James Lapine's "Sunday in the Park with George."

Academia: Studs Terkel's "The Good War," Pulitzer non-fiction; Thomas K. McGraw's "Prophets of Regulation," Pulitzer history; Kenneth Silverman's "The Life and Times of Cotton Mather," Pulitzer biography.

Music: Stephen Albert's symphony "River Run," Pulitzer; "We Are the World"; Phil Collins' "No Jacket Required"; Whitney Houston's "Saving All My Love for You."

Film: Sydney Pollack's "Out of Africa," Academy Award; "Kiss of the Spider Woman," William Hurt; "The Trip to Bountiful," Geraldine Page; "Prizzi's Honor," Jack Nicholson, Anjelica Houston; "The Official Story."

Terror strikes Rome, Vienna airports

Dec 30. Palestinian terrorists staged coordinated attacks on check-out counters of the El Al Israeli Airlines in the Rome and Vienna airports, hurling grenades and firing submachine guns into crowds of holiday travelers. Fourteen persons, including four Americans, were killed and more than 110 wounded in the two attacks that left the two terminals strewn with bloodied bodies. Four of the terrorists were killed in gun battles with police and plainclothes Israeli security men, and three others were wounded and captured.

Police tags mark the victims of terrorist attack at the airport in Rome.

The Palestine Liberation Organization denied responsibility for the attacks, and speculation immediately centered on a renegade Palestinian group headed by Abu Nidal, who broke with Yasir Arafat's mainstream Al Fatah group of the PLO in 1974. According to Italian authorities, the one surviving terrorist in the Rome attack, a 19-year-old Palestinian born in a refugee camp outside Beirut, said he belong to the Abu Nidal group. A note found in his pocket said the attacks were carried out in reprisal for the Israeli bombing of PLO headquarters near Tunis in October.

The Reagan administration accused Libya of aiding the terrorist group that carried out the attacks and called for international pressure on Libya to stop the export of terrorism (→ 1/1/86).

Mob gunmen waste the boss of bosses

Dec 16. "Big Paul" Castellano, the reputed head of the Gambino crime family in New York City, was assassinated by three gunmen outside a fashionable Manhattan restaurant last evening. Castellano, 70, had been on trial with eight other defendents in Federal District Court on attempted murder and racketeering charges. Last week, the prosecution's chief witness, Dominick Montiglio, implicated Castellano in a car-theft ring as well as a murder plot. Castellano's successor is reputed to be John Gotti.

Victim of the underworld he ruled.

Reagan signs a record farm bill

Dec 23. Saying he was seeking to "help put America's farmers back in a competitive position in world markets," President Reagan today signed into law the costliest farm bill in the nation's history. It has been estimated that the three-year cost will be about $52 billion.

The president had at one time threatened to veto the bill, and he said today that he does not fully embrace it, largely because of the expense. However, he said, the bill "provides new hope for America's hard-working farmers and our rural communities." He added: "If things are not going well down on the farm, things cannot continue to go well in our cities and towns."

By favoring large producers, the farm bill is likely to accelerate the trend toward fewer farmers producing a larger share of the nation's food. The trend has been continuing for a century, but the farm crisis has worsened in recent years. Many farmers have declared bankruptcy, and some have committed suicide, as the farm belt is menaced by grave social and economic problems.

Alleged killers free; Mrs. Aquino to run

Dec 15. A judicial tribual in Manila has dismissed allegations that a military conspiracy was responsible for the 1983 murder of opposition leader Benigno Aquino, blaming instead a lone gunman. Acquitted in the case were 26 co-defendants, including Genera Fabian Ver, who resumed his position as chief of staff to President Marcos. The assailant, Rolando Galman, was killed immediately after he shot Aquino at the Manila airport. No one has been charged with the murder of Galman.

The verdict was condemned by Corazon Aquino, widow of the slain leader, who said, "Justice is not possible as long as Marcos continues to be the head of government." She also declared her candidacy in the scheduled presidential elections next February, telling reporters that if elected, she would put Marcos on trial for the murder of her husband.

The Reagan administration questioned the validity of the verdict. The State Department said it found it "very difficult" to accept the trial's outcome (→ 1/23/86).

250 U.S. soldiers are killed in air crash

Dec 12. A chartered jetliner carrying U.S. soldiers home for Christmas crashed on takeoff from Gander, Newfoundland, killing all 258 people aboard. All but eight of the victims were members of the 101st Airborne Division who had been serving in the international peacekeeping force in the Sinai Penninsula.

Their aircraft, a DC-8 operated by Arrow Airlines of Miami, flew from Cairo to Cologne, West Germany, then on to Gander. The jetliner faltered at an altitude of about 1,000 feet as it took off from the international airport there just before daybreak. It plunged into a spruce and birch forest, plowing a mile-long path before exploding. Firemen who arrived after the explosion described a scene of bodies scattered over a large area, with fragments of the aircraft strewn through the flattened forest.

Both the cockpit voice recorder and the flight data recorder were recovered from the wreckage, but Canadian investigators said there were no clues yet as to the cause of the accident. Army officials said the Pentagon frequently chartered aircraft from Arrow, which they said had been checked earlier this year by the Federal Aviation Administration and found satisfactory.

At Fort Campbell, Kentucky, where relatives had gathered to greet the soldiers after their six-month tour of duty, two chapels were kept open all night. Officers said it might be two weeks before identification of the dead is made.

G.E. will buy RCA for $6.3 billion

Dec 12. The largest non-oil corporate merger in the history of the United States was forged in the course of 36 days of frantic negotiations, at a whopping price of $6.3 billion, between General Electric and RCA, with the entire business community watching in awe. G.E., the electronics and defense manufacturing giant, bought RCA, the owner of NBC Television and producer of electronics equipment, in a deal that will bring stockholders $66.50 a share. RCA Chairman Thorton Bradshaw called the arrangement an "excellent strategic opportunity for both companies." The merger will reduce G.E.'s dependence on manufacturing.

Reagan signs bill to control the budget

Dec 12. President Reagan signed the potentially historic Gramm-Rudman bill today, a controversial measure designed to create a new process to balance the ever-growing fedreal budget. Reagan usually draws reporters and photographers around for such executive occasions; but not with this legislation which could be one of the most important laws enactedin his presidency. The law mandates the slicing of the federal deficit to zero by 1991. Critics say Reagan purposely minimized public attention on the bill as it may force unintended cuts in his military budget and because it may encounter constitutional challenges (→ 3/17/86).

Court says Texaco must pay $11 billion

Dec 10. Texaco must pay $11.1 billion in damages and interest to the Pennzoil Company for interfering with Pennzoil's agreement to buy Getty Oil last year, a Texas state judge ruled today. Judge Solomon Casseb upheld a jury verdict that Pennzoil had a binding agreement when Getty's board decided to accept a higher Texaco bid. The award voted by the jury is almost ten times higher than the largest previous civil penalty in American history. Texaco said it will appeal the ruling (→ 2/12/87).

Ozzie and Harriet's son Ricky is killed

Dec 31. Ricky Nelson, child star of his parents' 1950's TV show, "The Adventures of Ozzie and Harriet," who later forged a career as an early rock and roll hitmaker, died today when his band's plane crashed and burned near DeKalb, Texas. The singer was 45. A generation of Americans watched Nelson grow up on the show, which began in 1952. Starting in 1957, he scored a string of hit records, all introduced on television, including "I'm Walkin'," "It's Late" and "Mary Lou."

Spasm of terrorism grips the whole world

The year 1985 may very well be remembered as the year of terrorism, a time when the forces of savagery killed thousands of innocent people for the purpose of advancing political causes. The high incidence of hijackings, bombings, kidnappings and murder has spurred governments into action; many nations, determined to stop the reign of terror, have toughened their attitudes and tightened their security.

The most recent incident, the attacks at the Rome and Vienna airports, seems to symbolize all such desperate acts: sudden, horrific assaults with innocent people, including children, slain. The bombings were blamed on a pro-Libyan terrorist, Abu Nidal, but as in so many of the year's catastrophes, proof is not easily attained.

The assailants are of many different cultures and causes, including various Palestinian groups, the Irish Republican Army, the Basque separatists in Spain, the Sikhs in India, the death squads in Latin America—the list seems endless. Does terrorism succeed? While violent incidents have at times altered political structures, usually the only change is in the number of living people (→ 4/2).

Meryl Streep stars with Robert Redford in the beautifully photographed saga "Out of Africa."

American astronauts tinker in space, proving the feasibility of building space stations by 1994.

The indestructible compact disc, played with lasers, threatens records and tapes with obsolescence.

"I knew 'Like a Virgin' would appeal to teenagers with active hormones," Madonna says.

1986

JANUARY

Su	Mo	Tu	We	Th	Fr	Sa
			1	2	3	4
5	6	7	8	9	10	11
12	13	14	15	16	17	18
19	20	21	22	23	24	25
26	27	28	29	30	31	

1. Pasadena: UCLA over Iowa 45-28 in Rose Bowl.

1. Spain and Portugal officially join EEC.

1. South Africa: Ten killed in tribal clash near Pretoria, set off by govt. effort to turn area into black "homeland" (→ 12).

1. U.S. building strength in Mediterranean, Khadafy threatens retaliation if attacked (→ 6).

4. Gore, Oklahoma: Kerr-McGee worker killed in nuclear leak (→ 4/30).

6. White House says Libya trains terrorists at 15 camps (→ 8).

8. Reagan freezes Libyan assets in U.S., despite lack of support from Allies (→ 23).

10. N.Y.: Queens Pres. Donald Manes found bleeding in car near Shea Stadium (→ 3/13).

15. Moscow: Gorbachev offers plan to eliminate all nuclear arms by 2000 (→ 2/28).

16. N.Y.: Court drops major charges against Goetz (→ 7/8).

16. Washington: Bust of Martin Luther King unveiled in Capitol Rotunda (→ 7/2).

17. New York: Fashion magnate Aldo Gucci pleads guilty to $7 mil. in federal tax fraud.

18. Guatemala: Jet carrying tourists to Mayan ruins crashes in jungle, killing all 90 aboard.

19. Tuba City, Arizona: Bible translated into Navajo.

22. India hangs three Sikhs convicted in murder of Indira Gandhi (→ 11/30).

23. Mediterranean: U.S. begins maneuvers off Libyan coast (→ 25).

23. U.S. Army documents reveal Marcos' claims of military heroics fraudulent (→ 24).

24. Voyager 2 goes past Uranus for first close-up view (→ 28).

24. Reagan, in reversal, asks for Marcos to resign (→ 2/7).

28. Florida: Space shuttle Challenger explodes on liftoff (→ 31).

DEATH

27. L. Ron Hubbard, founder Scientology (*3/3/1911).

Battles rage in Aden after coup attempt

Foreigners hastily evacuate Aden.

Jan 19. For the sixth day in a row, the capital of South Yemen was gripped by heavy fighting. There are unconfirmed reports tonight that the President of the Soviet-backed government has been ousted in a coup led by a more hard-line Marxist. Reports from the capital of Aden indicate that President Ali Nasser Mohammed al-Hassani has fled and been replaced by former President Abdel Fatah Ismail, a doctrinaire Marxist.

Hassani had been trying to shift his government to the right by improving relations with his neighbors, Saudi Arabia and Oman, and by supporting unification with Yemen. One report said Hassani was seeking refuge in Yemen. In the past week, thousands of foreigners, many of them from the Soviet bloc, have fled the vicious street fighting in Aden. Ismail's forces advanced on the presidential palace, the airport was bombed and warships in the harbor exchanged fire with tanks in the city.

Baby Doc declares Haiti state of siege

Jan 31. After a week of tumultuous, anti-government demonstrations, President Jean-Claude Duvalier declared a state of siege in Haiti. The 34-year-old president, who succeeded his father and is known as Baby Doc, went on national radio to deny reports, some circulated by the White House, that his 15-year-old government had fallen and that he had fled the country. "The president is here," he said, "strong and firm as a monkey's tail." At least six persons were reportedly killed as police used force to put down the demonstrations that began in the northern city of Cap-Haitien and spread to the streets of Port-au-Prince on rumors that Duvalier had fled (→ 2/1).

Black leader found dead near Pretoria

Jan 12. A prominent South African black activist was found stabbed to death near Pretoria hours before he was to meet with an American official to discuss conditions in the nation's black townships. Ampie Mayisa died from stab wounds inflicted, it is believed, by rival pro-government black tribesmen, whom activists call "stooges for white supremacy." Mayisa was to talk with Assistant Secretary of State Chester Crocker about the ills of apartheid (→ 3/3).

Reagan, Gorbachev exchange greetings

Jan 1. President Reagan broadcasted New Year's wishes to the Soviet Union today, and Mikhail Gorbachev did the same for American audiences. While not the first time top leaders have exchanged greetings, it has not been done since 1973. That year, Leonid Brezhnev addressed the United States; a year earlier President Nixon had conveyed goodwill to the Russians. All of the major networks carried the speeches, which expressed, of course, hope for the future (→ 8/7).

Jan 26. Look out below! "Refrigerator" Perry careens into the end zone during the Bears' 46-10 romp over New England in Super Bowl XX.

Ties are broken with Libya; assets frozen

Jan 25. The Reagan administration, accusing Colonel Muammar Khadafy of supporting international terrorism, stepped up its economic and military pressure on Libya. Contending that Libya had supported the terrorist raids on the Rome and Vienna airports last month, the United States imposed trade and commerical sanctions against Libya, ordered all American citizens to leave the country and froze Libyan assets.

The administration followed up these economic measures with a military show of force. A U.S. naval task force that included two aircraft carriers was ordered to conduct week-long maneuvers in the Mediterranean north of Libya. The State Department said they were intended to demonstrate "U.S. resolve to continue to operate in international waters and airspace."

The naval task force maneuvered north of the Gulf of Sidra, but the administration left open the possibility that carrier planes might fly over the gulf, which is claimed as territorial waters by Libya. Amid the growing possibility of a military clash, Khadafy, wearing a royal blue jump suit and a captain's hat, set forth in a Libyan patrol boat to stage what he called a confrontation with the task force (→ 3/24).

Challenger explodes as horrified nation watches

The space shuttle Challenger at liftoff, looking good ...

Jan 31. The loss of the space shuttle Challenger and its seven astronauts was mourned in a solemn memorial ceremony at the Johnson Space Center in Houston today, as President Reagan spoke of "our seven Challenger heroes" and pledged to honor them with a new national commitment to space exploration.

The Challenger exploded in a ball of fire shortly after it left the launching pad at Cape Canaveral on January 28, in the worst accident in the history of the U.S. space program. The disaster was witnessed by thousands of spectators in Florida and by millions of television viewers.

Killed in the accident were the commander, Francis R. Scobee; the pilot, Michael J. Smith; and astronauts Judith A. Resnik, Ronald E. McNair, Ellison S. Onizuka, Gregory B. Jarvis and Christa McAuliffe, a high school teacher from Concord, New Hampshire, who was to have been the first ordinary citizen in space. Mrs. McAuliffe was specially selected for the shuttle mission out of a large applicant pool. Her students were among the millions of Americans watching the event on television today.

Christa McAuliffe waves goodbye.

There were no clues to the cause of the accident, and National Aeronautics and Space Administration officials said all shuttle flights would be suspended indefinitely while an inquiry was conducted.

The launch of the Challenger, which was to have been the 25th shuttle mission, was delayed for three days because of bad weather. Liftoff, scheduled for 9:38 a.m., was delayed for two hours because unusually low temperatures caused ice to form on the shuttle and its ground support structure.

Challenger lifted off flawlessly at 11:38 a.m. and rose for 74 seconds. Then, at an altitude of ten miles, just as Challenger's main engines were to be pushed to full power, it erupted in a ball of fire. The last words from the shuttle were "Roger, go to full power," spoken by Scobee to mission control. Two large white streamers erupted from the blast, followed by a rain of debris. Few among the thousands of tourists, space officials, reporters and other onlookers, including Christa McAuliffe's husband, two children and parents, realized what had happened at first. But when the meaning of the orange fireball in the sky sunk in, the cheers for Challenger faded into stunned silence.

Appearing at a press conference a few hours after the explosion, Jesse W. Moore, head of the space shuttle program, announced appointment of an interim review team to identify and preserve flight data until a formal investigating committee could be appointed. Moore said all computer tapes, notes and other data would be impounded for the investigation. He denied that the three days of delay had put pressure on the space agency to launch the shuttle before the president's State of the Union address, scheduled for the evening of the launch. "There was no pressure to get this particular launch up," Moore said. "We have always maintained that flight safety was a top priority in the program."

Disaster banishes triumph as Challenger explodes 74 seconds after liftoff.

Space agency officials discounted speculation the cold weather at Cape Canaveral might have been a factor in the accident. Among the possible causes being considered are a break in the external fuel tank, which carried more than 385,000 gallons of liquid hydrogen and 140,000 gallons of liquid oxygen, or a rupture of fuel pipes. Slow-motion TV tapes of the explosion taken by cameras with telescopic lenses show what appeared to be the start of a small fire at the base of the external fuel tank, followed by the separation of the two solid fuel rockets before a fireball engulfed the shuttle.

A flotilla of space agency and Coast Guard vessels is still collecting debris that rained down on the ocean for more than an hour after the explosion. The search is expected to continue for weeks at the point of impact, 18 to 20 miles off the Florida coast, and the public has been asked to turn in all fragments of the shuttle that float ashore. No signs of the crew have been found.

This was to have been the busiest year in shuttle history, with 15 missions scheduled, but the explosion has brought the United States space program to a standstill, since the space agency has no backup launch system in operation (→ 2/2).

The optimistic Challenger crew.

1986

FEBRUARY

Su	Mo	Tu	We	Th	Fr	Sa
						1
2	3	4	5	6	7	8
9	10	11	12	13	14	15
16	17	18	19	20	21	22
23	24	25	26	27	28	

1. Port-au-Prince: 14 killed in two days of fighting as anti-govt. riots rage (→ 5).

2. NASA finds Challenger's solid fuel boosters not equipped with good warning device (→ 8).

4. Mediterranean: Israeli jets intercept Libyan executive plane to search for terrorists.

5. Haiti: Duvalier denied asylum in Switzerland, Greece and Spain (→ 7).

7. Schenectady, N.Y.: Mary Beth Tinning held after nine babies die in day care over 14 years.

7. Haiti: Duvalier flees to France after 28 years in power (→ 10).

7. Manila: Marcos and Aquino claim election victory (→ 14).

10. India: Pope John Paul II ends visit to India (→ 4/13).

10. Sicily: Palermo opens largest Mafia trial with 474 defendants.

11. Reagan sends Philip Habib to Philippines to seek advancement of U.S. interests (→ 14).

14. Philippines: Bodies of ten opposition supporters found decapitated in Quirino (→ 22).

16. Lisbon: Ex-Premier Soares elected first civilian president in 60 years.

17. Johnson & Johnson discontinue over-the-counter capsules as Tylenol deaths reappear.

18. Reagan admin. tells Congress it will send missiles to Angolan rebels.

20. Seoul: Police confine 300 opposition members to homes to prevent party meeting (→ 5/17).

21. Washington: Ex-CIA analyst Larry Chin, jailed for spying for Chinese, kills self in prison.

22. Manila: Army chiefs resign, urging Marcos to follow (→ 25).

25. Guam: Marcos, fleeing Philippines, arrives at Clark Air Force Base; U.S. recognizes Aquino (→ 27).

28. The Hague: Dutch Parliament approves installation of 48 NATO cruise missiles (→ 4/11).

DEATH

2. Alva Myrdal, Swedish diplomat, 1982 Nobel Prize for disarmament efforts (*1/31/1902).

Marcos leaves; Cory Aquino is in office

Cory Aquino, widow of martyred Benigno, sworn in on a wave of people power.

Feb 27. Defeated at the polls and renounced by the United States, Ferdinand Marcos has fled the Philippines which he had ruled with increasing authoritarian control for 20 years. He was succeeded as President by Corazon Aquino, who said, "we are finally free" and "a new life starts for our country."

Marcos had brought the nation to the edge of a military confrontation before he finally agreed to step down at the urging of the United States. Embattled but defiant, the 68-year-old Marcos refused to accept the results of an election earlier in the month that apparently was won by Aquino, a self-described housewife and the widow of a slain anti-Marcos politician.

Proclaimed the winner by the National Assembly, which he controlled, Marcos was sworn in as President in a ceremony in the presidential palace. Meanwhile, Aquino took the oath of office as President of a provisional government in a ceremony with her supporters. A military standoff developed as hundreds of thousands of Filipinos took to the streets to protect a group of military officers who had broken with Marcos. Paralyzed militarily, Marcos then found himself stripped of the American support he had desperately sought.

The White House said it would be "futile" for him to try to remain in power and Senator Paul Laxalt, as President Reagan's envoy, told Marcos "the time has come" to "cut and cut cleanly." With American assistance, Marcos, his wife, Imelda, and an entourage of supporters, was flown to safe haven in Hawaii. On his arrival in Honolulu, it was discovered Marcos had brought with him 22 crates containing $1.2 million in new Philippine currency.

As one of her first steps on taking office, Aquino released 34 prisoners who had been jailed on political charges. The new president also called for a new constitution for the Philippines (→ 3/2).

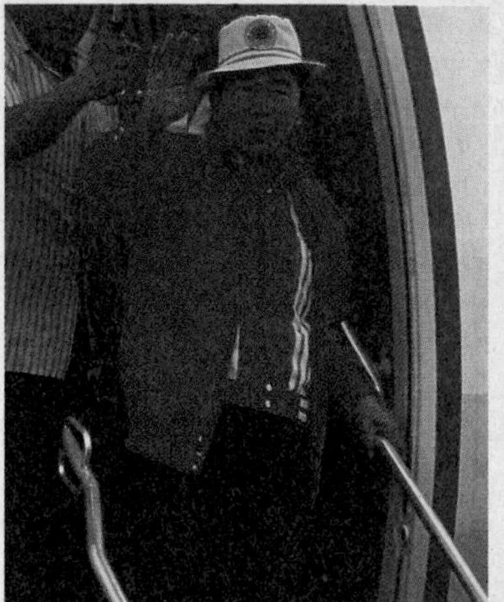

Marcos arrives in exile in Hawaii.

Swedish Premier is killed strolling home

Feb 28. Swedish Prime Minister Olaf Palme often leisurely strolled the streets of Stockholm, unaccompanied by bodyguards. Tonight, while doing just that, the popular Social Democratic leader was assassinated. Palme was walking home from a movie with his wife, Lisbeth, when a gunman ran up to the couple, fired two bullets into the prime minister and fled into the night.

Palme, shocking death for Sweden.

Police have detained a suspect who fits the description of the assassin. Most speculate the killing was not politically motivated. Palme's predecessor, Thorbjorn Falldin, said, "I refuse to belive this was a political assassination. It must have been the work of a lunatic." Yet, a police alert suggested that a group seeking liberation of the Yugoslav republic of Croatia may be responsible for the murder; in 1971, a Croatian killed Swedish diplomat Vladimir Rolovic. But authorities have found no evidence linking the organization with the murder.

NASA was warned of rocket weakness

Feb 8. A year before the Challenger disaster, the space agency was warned that the seals on the space shuttle's solid rocket boosters might break and cause a major accident, documents reveal. One analysis from a National Aeronautics and Space Administration engineer said flight safety was compromised by potential failure of the seals and added, "Failure during launch would certainly be catastrophic." A preminary investigation by a special presidential commission has centered on the theory that leakage of hot gases through the seals of Challenger's two solid rockets ignited the shuttle's fuel and caused the disastrous explosion (→ 3/9).

Shcharansky is freed in prisoner exchange

Anatoly and wife, Avital, reunited.

Feb 11. In an exchange of prisoners apparently negotiated at November's summit meeting between President Reagan and Soviet leader Mikhail Gorbachev, human rights activist Anatoly Shcharansky was freed after eight years in Soviet prisons and labor camps. Three other Soviet prisoners were released with him and in return the United States and West Germany freed five prisoners from Warsaw Pact nations.

In 1978, Shcharansky was sentenced to 13 years in prison and labor camps for the crimes of treason, espionage and anti-Soviet agitation. Although both Shcharansky and the United States have denied it, the Soviets claim that he was an American spy.

Shcharansky is well-known mostly for his campaign for the rights of Soviet Jews who wish to emigrate. Shcharansky flew to Israel where he received a warm welcome from crowds of supporters. He has pledged to continue the struggle for human rights (→ 10/5).

Penn Warren is first U.S. poet laureate

Feb 26. It's about time, in more ways than one. Britain has had poet laureates for 200 years; the United States has gone without. Robert Penn Warren is ready; at age 80, he had better not put off the honor. His employment starts in September and pays $36,000 for two years. Warren is a former Rhodes scholar who wrote the Pulitzer Prize-winning novel "All the King's Men" in 1947. He will be expected to give a public reading of his works at least once a year.

Oil is sold at less than $15 per barrel

Feb 18. Ministers of the Organization of Petroleum Exporting Countries, the oil cartel, have announced that the price of petroleum has dropped to less than $15 per barrel for the first time in years. American consumers will likely see a decrease in the cost of gasoline and other goods. Reductions in crude oil prices reverberate throughout the economy. And American tourism is expected to increase as more travelers will be able to afford to hit the highways.

English Channel tunnel project is accepted

Feb 20. An ambitious and expensive blueprint was unveiled today to create a new lifeline between Britain and France. Prime Minister Margaret Thatcher and President Francois Mitterrand announced plans for the construction of a rail tunnel beneath the English Channel.

France to England by train or car?

Work on the $7 billion project is scheduled to begin next year and be completed in 1993. French officials say that trains carrying cars and buses will take half an hour to make the trip through the tunnel. High-speed trains will cut the travel time from Paris to London to a little over three hours, providing stiff competition to the airlines. A separate motorway tunnel will also be built, starting in 1990. The idea of a tunnel beneath the English Channel has been discussed for hundreds of years. It was generally vetoed by Great Britain for security or financial reasons.

Duvalier flees from Haiti

Duvalier, supposed President-for-Life, and wife, Michele, pose stiffly in Haiti.

Feb 10. In Haiti, nearly three decades of dictatorship ended abruptly as Jean-Claude Duvalier, who had the title of President-for-Life, fled to France. Tens of thousands of jubilant Haitians poured into the streets of Port-au-Prince. But the celebrations turned violent as mobs of demonstrators ransacked stores and the Duvalier mausoleum. Many of them confronted the Tontons Macoutes, Duvalier's brutal and much hated security police. An undetermined number of the blue-uniformed agents were killed or wounded. One member of the Tontons Macoutes was seen running from the ornate presidential palace in his underwear after he was jostled and stripped by a mob.

Lieutenant General Henri Namphy, head of the four-day-old interim government, pledged today that he is committed to a "real and functional democracy." He dissolved the National Assembly and suspended the constitution. Both were creations of the Duvalier regime.

Duvalier and his family left Haiti on a United States Air Force jet on the 7th. A French government official indicated Duvalier will not settle permanently in France, but several African countries denied that they will grant him asylum. Duvalier and his late father, Francois, governed Haiti with iron hands for 28 years. While most Haitians survived on $300 a year, the Duvaliers lived in regal splendor. They canceled elections, demanded kickbacks and stole from the Treasury. Opponents were visited in the night by the Tontons Macoutes (→ 4/26).

Haitians converge on the grave of Papa Doc to avenge 28 years of tyranny.

1986

MARCH

Su	Mo	Tu	We	Th	Fr	Sa
						1
2	3	4	5	6	7	8
9	10	11	12	13	14	15
16	17	18	19	20	21	22
23	24	25	26	27	28	29
30	31					

2. Manila: Aquino, in first public declaration, restores civil rights in Philippines (→ 13).

3. Reagan warns Congress of strategic disaster if $100 mil. in aid to contras rejected (→ 20).

3. Johannesburg: Police kill seven blacks as ANC suspects (→ 4/14).

7. Texas marks 150th birthday.

7. U.S.: TWA cancels half its flights as attendants strike over wages.

9. Florida: Navy divers find crew compartment of Challenger with remains of astronauts (→ 6/9).

12. Madrid: Spain votes to stay in NATO in dramatic victory for Premier Gonzalez (→ 6/22).

15. New Orleans: AMA rules euthanasia ethical on coma patients.

17. U.S.: Dollar hits postwar low against Japanese yen (→ 8/29).

18. London: Buckingham Palace announces engagement of Prince Andrew and Sarah Ferguson.

20. New York: Homosexual rights bill passed by City Council (→ 6/30).

20. House rejects Reagan's $100 mil. aid package to Nicaraguan contras (→ 25).

22. Manila: Thousands of striking workers blockade gates of U.S. military base (→ 4/13).

24. U.S. and Libyan forces clash in waters off Libyan coast (→ 4/5/).

25. Reagan orders emergency aid for Honduran army; U.S. helicopters ferry Honduran troops to Nicaraguan border (→ 28).

28. U.S. Senate passes $100 mil. contra aid package (→ 5/16).

29. Rome: Court acquits three Bulgarians, three Turks in plot to kill pope.

31. Mexico: 166 killed as Mexican 727 crashes in mountains.

DEATHS

6. Georgia O'Keeffe, American artist (*11/15/1887).

18. Bernard Malamud, American author (*4/26/1914).

31. John Ciardi, American poet, essayist (*6/24/1916).

Kurt Waldheim accused of hiding Nazi past

March 4. Former Secretary General of the United Nations Kurt Waldheim, now an independent candidate for the presidency of Austria, has been accused by the World Jewish Congress of serving in a German army command during World War II and participating in the torture of Yugoslavian Jews and the deportation of thousands of Greek Jews from Salonika in 1942-43.

In a CBS News interview, the Austrian statesman responded to the charges by saying: "It is true that I served in the German army command in the Balkans, but I never participated in any sort of cruelties. All I did was to interpret between Italian and German commanders." Asked why this had remain secret for so long, he claimed that accusations were made only to influence the campaign.

World Jewish Congress officials said the election was not a factor at all and that they "just got around to" examining the evidence. Hagen Fleischer, a specialist on Greek Jewry, said Waldheim played no part in the deportations (→ 6/8).

Rightist is Premier under leftist chief

Chirac to "cohabit" with the left.

March 20. A new political experiment called "cohabitation" began in France today. Like many marriages of this decade, it could be a rocky one. Jacques Chirac formally took over as Prime Minister. He is a conservative. President Francois Mitterrand is a Socialist. It is the first time in this century the president and prime minister of France have not belonged to the same party. Chirac announced immediately that he intends to dismantle many of Mitterrand's policies, including the nationalization of key industries. Chirac announced earlier that he plans to run for Mitterrand's job in 1988. For the time being, the two men will have to work together. Their first joint dilemma is a response to the terrorist bomb which killed two people on the Champs Elysees tonight (→ 12/8).

Manila looking for Marcos possessions

March 13. Corazon Aquino's administration would not mind having the assets of former Philippine President Ferdinand Marcos. A commission has been established to get the illegally obtained funds, $800 million of which, it was discovered today, have been stored in a Swiss bank account. Earlier in the month, five pieces of choice New York real estate were reported to be owned by Marcos and his wife, Imelda. An inventory was taken of Mrs. Marcos' effects left behind in the Philippines. Her closets were filled with hundreds of designer dresses, five shelves of unused Gucci handbags, 68 pairs of gloves and 3,000 pairs of shoes (→ 22).

Accused New York politician is suicide

March 13. Donald Manes, the Queens Borough President who recently resigned amid allegations of corruption, stabbed himself to death in his Queens apartment yesterday. Once one of New York City's most powerful politicians, Manes had been despondent for months while prosecutors gathered evidence, seeking to indict him on corruption charges. Manes was found by his wife with a 12-inch kitchen knife embedded in his chest. Details of Manes' last few months depict an individual wracked by guilt and shame for his part in the city's worst political scandal in years (→ 11/25).

Spacecraft sends back comet pictures

Halley's comet, 76 years later.

March 6. The Soviet Vega 1 spacecraft flew within 5,500 miles of Halley's comet today, sending back the first pictures of the comet's icy core. Operating on commands sent from the ground, the spacecraft locked its cameras on the comet and transmitted some 500 television images in the three hours during which it made its closest approach.

Scientists from the U.S. and many other nations were invited to Moscow to witness the encounter of Vega 1 and Halley's comet, which returns to earth every 76 years. Preliminary data from the spacecraft's cameras and scientific instruments indicated that the comet's nucleus consists of ice and is about three miles in width and that solar energy causes it to emit the gas that gives the comet its visible tale at rates two or three times greater than had been supposed (→ 6/9).

March 2. Tradition and modernity merge in Houston as Texas celebrates the 150th anniversary of its independence from Mexico. "Remember the Alamo!"

1986

APRIL

Su	Mo	Tu	We	Th	Fr	Sa
		1	2	3	4	5
6	7	8	9	10	11	12
13	14	15	16	17	18	19
20	21	22	23	24	25	26
27	28	29	30			

2. Montgomery: Gov. George Wallace announces retirement from public life.

8. Reagan admin. agrees on military strike against Libya (→ 12).

10. Pakistan: Opposition leader Benazir Bhutto returns (→ 8/14).

11. American Dodge Morgan sails around world solo in record 150 days.

11. Soviets to resume atom tests in response to U.S. failure to halt testing (→ 18).

12. Reagan sends Vernon Walters to seek European support for strike on Libya (→ 15).

13. Jack Nicklaus wins record sixth Masters golf title.

13. Manila: 10,000 Marcos supporters march in rally (→ 5/8).

14. South Africa: Tutu chosen to head Anglican Church (→ 5/1).

15 Libya:U.S.bombs military-targetsm home of Khadafy (→ 16)

16. U.S.: Poll indicates 77% support attack on Libya (→ 17).

17. Beirut: Three British hostages found dead in retaliation for Libyan strike (→ 18).

18. Calif.: Titan rocket with military payload explodes at liftoff.

18. Beirut: U.S. hostage Peter Kilburn executed (→ 21).

20. U.S.: Study finds 13% of adults are illiterate.

20. Bangladesh: Ferry sinks in Khaleswari River; 500 dead.

21. Rob de Castella wins Boston Marathon in record 2:07:51.

22. Beirut: Americans evacuated from West to East (→ 25).

25. Britain expels over 200 Libyan students (→ 5/1).

26. Port-au-Prince: Eight killed by police at memorial service for political victims.

DEATHS

15. Jean Genet, French dramatist (*12/19/1910).

23. Otto Preminger, American film director (*12/5/1906).

23. Harold Arlen, U.S. blues, pop composer (*2/15/1905).

26. Broderick Crawford, American actor (*12/9/1911).

Death knocks out tough guy Cagney

March 20. "Absorption in things other than self is the secret of a happy life." So said happy Jimmy Cagney, absorbing himself in every theatrical art until his death today at the age of 86. Cagney was born on Manhattan's Lower East Side. He was a vaudeville hoofer (his wife, Willie, was a partner) until he played a gangster in a 1930 film, "Penny Arcade." He was typecast as a hood for years, then got good-guy roles (often as military men, his quick, angular movements befitting them) before reviving song-and-dance talent to win an Oscar for being the quintessential "Yankee Doodle Dandy."

Fire invades palace of King Henry VIII

March 31. A fire destroyed part of Hampton Court, Henry VIII's palace by the Thames and one of Britain's most famous historic buildings. It left one person dead and millions of dollars in damage, which Queen Elizabeth, who rushed to the scene, called "dreadful."

The blaze is believed to have started on an upper floor of the south wing, the "grace and favor" apartments, loaned by the sovereign rent-free to public servants and certain others. It was there an 85-year-old general's widow died.

Most paintings were rescued, but the palace, built in 1514 and known for elaborately painted ceilings and richly carved woodwork, is irreplaceable. Christopher Wren, architect of St. Paul's Cathedral in London, added the south wing in the 1690's.

Hampton Court on Thames River.

Four killed as plane is bombed in Athens

April 2. A bomb exploded aboard a TWA jetliner today on its flight from Rome to Athens, killing four passengers as they were sucked out of the hole blasted in the airplane's side. The bodies, including that of an infant, were later found on the ground in southern Greece and in the nearby sea. A group called the Arab Revolutionary Cells later issued a statement saying that the bombing was in retaliation for "American arrogance" and last week's clashes with Libya in the Gulf of Sidra (→ 5).

The wounded TWA 727 airliner.

Terrorists bomb Berlin G.I. hangout

April 5. La Belle Club, a discotheque in West Berlin, rocked to a different beat last night when a bomb tore a hole in the floor and collapsed the ceiling, killing two and wounding 155. Located near U.S. Army housing, the club is popular with American G.I.'s, one of whom was killed; 50 to 60 Americans were also among the wounded. West German officials think the Libyan Government of Col. Khadafy may have been responsible, and are checking a theory that the Libyan People's Bureau in East Berlin may have smuggled the terrorists into West Berlin. The attack came less than three days after the Rome-Athens TWA bombing (→ 8).

Stalin's daughter returns to America

April 16. Svetlana Alliluyeva, the daughter of Joseph Stalin, left the Soviet Union yesterday for Chicago via Zurich. In 1984, she returned to Russia after 17 years in the West. She had been stripped of her Soviet citizenship after her defection in 1967, but it was restored after her publicized return when she claimed never to have had freedom in the West. Her daughter, Olga Peters, 14, returned to her Quaker school in England today. Life in the nation her grandfather ruled from 1924 to 1953 was strange for a girl raised in the U.S. She was delighted to be back in the West but did not regret her "Russian experience."

Eastwood plays odd role: Carmel Mayor

April 8. Clint Eastwood, the Hollywood actor who became one of the world's biggest box office draws playing tough cowboys and revenge-minded policemen, today won a landslide victory as Mayor of Carmel-by-the-Sea, a Californian resort town of 4,700 people.

He defeated the incumbent Mayor, Charlotte Townsend, by a vote of 2,166 to 799. The 55-year-old actor stated in his campaign that he wanted to "build bridges" between the two long-warring camps of merchants and residents.

For many decades, Carmel was an artists' and writers' colony. After World War II, it became a popular resort which lured not only resident dwellers but entrepreneurs who opened scores of motels, restaurants, art galleries and other tourist-oriented businesses. "Bringing the community together, getting back the camaraderie, the spirit, that's my goal," says the actor, who has lived in Carmel for 14 years and involved himself in town activities. He looks forward to his $200-a-month job and will make films, too.

Would you vote for this man?

American planes assault Khadafy's Libyan base

Mechanical failure kept U.S. bombs from landing squarely on Khadafy's tent.

April 21. President Reagan is receiving bipartisan support for the air strikes he announced last week to punish Libya for its international "reign of terror." The Allies are divided about the raids, however, and Britain's Prime Minister Margaret Thatcher is being widely criticized at home for assisting the United States. Colonel Muammar Khadafy, the Libyan leader, vows that the raids will not prevent him from carrying out what he calls his "popular revolution."

American planes bombed two areas of Libya early in the morning of the 15th. Pentagon officials said 18 Air Force F-111 bombers that had taken off from England struck an airport, military barracks and a port outside Tripoli. In a separate attack, Navy A-6 and A-7 planes struck Libyan bases near Benghazi. The aircraft took off from the carriers Coral Sea and America, which are based in the Mediterranean.

In a television address, President Reagan announced that he ordered the raids after intelligence officials uncovered evidence of a "direct" Libyan role in the deadly bombing of a discotheque in West Berlin earlier this month. Two people were killed, including an American soldier, and more than 200 people were injured, including 50-60 United States servicemen.

"Today we have done what we had to do," Reagan said. "If necessary we shall do it again." Calling the bombing raids acts of self-defense, he said, "I warned that there should be no place on earth where terrorists can rest and train and practice their deadly skills. I meant it. I said that we should act with others, if possible, and alone, if necessary, to ensure that terrorists have no sanctuary anywhere."

Bombs focused on military targets, but parts of civilian Tripoli were hit as well.

Hospital workers in Tripoli said at least 15 people were killed when bombs dropped on a residential neighborhood. One of the victims was identified as the adopted daughter of Khadafy. The Libyan leader himself dropped out of sight for 24 hours, and there were reports that he had been killed. He appeared on television on the 16th to denounce Reagan for "issuing orders to regular forces to murder children and attack houses." The Libyan leader did not threaten to retaliate against the United States, as he has in the past. He also thanked France for refusing to allow the American F-111's to fly in its airspace. Khadafy condemned Britain for helping Reagan.

Reagan administration officials have criticized France for its lack of support for the raids. Defense Secretary Caspar Weinberger said he felt "considerable disappointment" with the French government. Weinberger said the French action doubled the length of the mission and increased the risk to the pilots. One F-111 did not return safely, and rescuers have been unable to find the two crewmen.

In London, public opinion polls show two-thirds of the people opposing Thatcher's help to the United States. Criticism by political officials increased sharply when the bodies of three Britons were found in Lebanon. A note said they had been shot because of Britain's role in the bombing raids. Another Briton was kidnapped. Two former Prime Ministers, James Callaghan and Edward Heath, criticized Thatcher in Parliament. Labor Party leader Neil Kinnock was quoted as saying Thatcher had "blood on her hands." The Foreign Ministry replied that Kinnock's remark was "cheap and unpleasant."

Defending her stand, Thatcher told Parliament that the United States was Britain's "greatest ally, the foundation of the alliance which has preserved our security and peace for more than a generation." Faced with opposition in her own Cabinet to the raids, Thatcher indicated however that she would think twice if the United States asked for help in another raid.

Khadafy, wounded or just turbaned?

On Capitol Hill, members of Congress expressed support for Reagan, but they urged him to consult with them more closely about further actions. "We're in a war," House Republican leader Robert Michel said. "It's a new kind of war. It's a terrorist war. We're plowing new ground, and we have to think what comes next."

Administration officials indicate that American efforts to destabilize the Khadafy regime are continuing. Secret talks are being held with opponents of the Libyan leader. Machine gun fire was heard outside Khadafy's compound on the 16th, and there have been several reports of new coup attempts in Libya. ABC reported that Libyan planes attacked mutineers south of Tripoli. Libya said the attacks were by American planes. Now that retaliation against terrorism has taken place, many are wondering what effect it will have (→ 22).

Dozens reportedly died in the raid.

Chernobyl accident releases deadly atom radiation

April 30. The Soviet Union has acknowledged that a major accident occurred four days ago at a nuclear generating plant at Chernobyl in the Ukraine. West German and Swedish experts say the Soviets have asked them for help in handling the accident, believed to be the worst in the history of nuclear power.

In a four-paragraph statement, the Soviet government disclosed for the first time that the accident occurred in the No. 4 reactor of the four-reactor facility and that two people had been killed. The Soviet statement, read on the evening television news, said the other three reactors at the site had been shut down and three nearby localities had been evacuated.

An indication of the nature of the accident came from the Soviet request for West German and Swedish help to fight a fire in a nuclear reactor core. The Chernobyl reactor's core contains large amounts of flammable graphite, which is believed to be burning out of control. But the Soviets have provided no information on the amount of radioactivity released by the accident.

The Soviet Union has been slow to disclose that an accident took place. The first indication of a problem came when monitoring stations in Sweden, Finland and Denmark reported abnormally high radioactivity levels. Hours later, the Soviets reported the accident.

Western reporters who have visited Kiev, 60 miles from Chernobyl, say they saw no unusual activity indicating panic among residents. Local reports say 15,000 people have been evacuated from Pripyat, the town closest to the reactor. U.S. experts say the Soviet toll could be great but the radioactivity is not a major threat to countries in Europe and North America (→ 5/14).

Chernobyl's jumbled shapes, in aerial view, outline the source of atomic mishap.

Horowitz goes back home 61 years later

Horowitz plays for Soviet admirers.

April 20. In a return that could only be termed triumphal, Vladimir Horowitz brought cheers and tears as he gave his first recital in his Soviet homeland after a 61-year absence in the West. The Great Hall of the Moscow Conservatory was packed with government notables, musicians, foreign ambassadors and gate-crashing students. Even the rehearsal was an unprecedented event as hundreds of hardy fans braved the cold outside just to catch a glimpse.

Airline finds bomb in woman's luggage

April 18. The discovery of a bomb in the false bottom of a woman's suitcase at London's Heathrow Airport led to the arrest of a Jordanian named Nezar Hindawi after the woman told the police that Hindawi had given her the luggage prior to kissing her goodbye. The woman, Miss Murphy, was engaged to Hindawi. According to a friend, "She is a lovely girl, but maybe a little too trusting."

Simone de Beauvoir dies in Paris at 78

April 14. Simone de Beauvoir, author of "The Second Sex," has died at the age of 78. Ms. de Beauvoir inspired the women's movement by pinpointing a major problem: women are not born, she argued, but created by society; change society and you can improve women's lot. In her 60's, she wrote "The Coming of Age," outlining the hazards senior citizens face. Ms. de Beauvoir said she was the most intellectual person she knew until she met Jean-Paul Sartre.

Pope speaks in synagogue in first such visit

April 13. Pope John Paul II, in an unprecedented pontifical visit to Rome's central synagogue, roundly denounced displays of anti-Semitism "at any time and by anyone," and expressed his "abhorrence for the genocide decreed against the Jewish people during the last war."

Pope John Paul was greeted at the stately Victorian synagogue on the Tiber River by Chief Rabbi Elio Toaff, who lauded the papal visit as "a true turning point in the policy of the church."

Although the pope did not mention the state of Israel, with which the Vatican does not have formal diplomatic ties, he did much to allay fears that he was backing away from what Rabbi Toaff called the "revolution" in Catholic-Jewish relations manifested by Vatican II, the council convened by Pope John XXIII in 1962 to modernize the Church.

The pope said that Judaism "in a certain way is 'intrinsic' to our own religion ... it could be said that you are our elder brothers" (→ 5/30).

John Paul II listens intently to the prepared address of Rome's Chief Rabbi.

1986

MAY

Su	Mo	Tu	We	Th	Fr	Sa
				1	2	3
4	5	6	7	8	9	10
11	12	13	14	15	16	17
18	19	20	21	22	23	24
25	26	27	28	29	30	31

1. Libya expels 108 Britons, Spaniards and Italians (→ 5).

3. Ferdinand wins Kentucky Derby, Bill Shoemaker up.

8. U.S. rejects Aquino's plea for aid to Philippines (→ 9/19).

11. Syria expels three British envoys in retaliation for British expulsion of three Syrians.

16. U.S.: Teamsters Pres. Jackie Presser indicted for racketeering.

16. Costa Rica: Nicaraguan rebel Eden Pastora lays down arms, asks political asylum (→ 6/10).

17. Seoul: Students march to mark 6th anniversary of Kwangju uprising (→ 1/20/87).

19. South African forces attack capitals of Botswana, Zambia and Zimbabwe (→ 23).

21. Reagan vetoes effort to block arms for Saudia Arabia.

22. NATO accepts Reagan plan to produce chemical weapons for first time since 1969.

23. U.S. expels South Africa's senior military attache in response to raids (→ 25).

23. Lebanon: Car bomb kills 11, wounds 84 in Christian East Beirut (→ 7/10).

24. Moscow: U.S. Embassy advises pregnant Americans not to drink milk due to increase in radiation (→ 8/21).

25. U.S.: Millions form human chain to aid homeless in "Hands Across America".→

25. Crossroads, South Africa: 30,000 blacks routed from homes (→ 6/13).

27. Reagan warns he may abandon SALT II accord (→ 8/18).

28. N.Y.: Federal grand jury indicts five on Wall St. for insider trading (→ 11/18).

30. Rome: Pope issues fifth encyclical, condemning Marxism.

31. Bobby Rahal wins Indy 500 at record speed of 170.7 mph.

31. Poland: Solidarity underground leader Zbigniew Bujak arrested (→ 9/11).

DEATH

15. Theodore H. White, U.S. journalist, "The Making of the President."

Chernobyl facts revealed

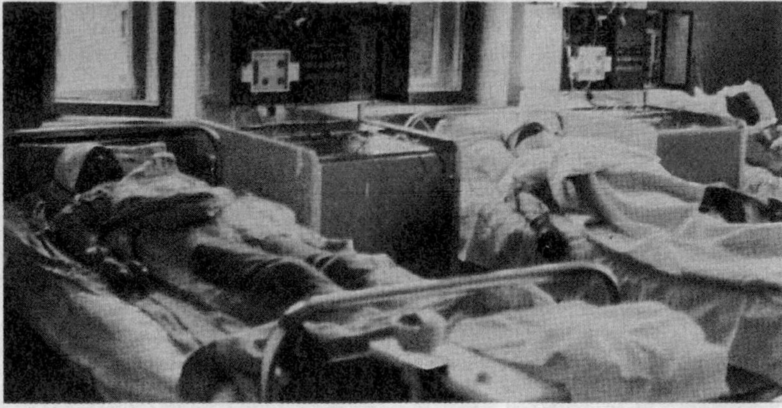

Victims hospitalized in Kiev may be a fraction of those ultimately affected.

May 14. Soviet leader Mikhail Gorbachev discussed the Chenobyl nuclear disaster publicly for the first time today, saying in a television speech that it showed the "sinister force" of nuclear power gone out of control. Gorbachev denounced the West for using the disaster for an "unrestrained anti-Soviet campaign" but tacitly conceded that the criticism was justified by offering a four-point program to hasten the exchange of information on nuclear accidents.

The Chernobyl disaster occurred on April 26, but it was not until May 6 that the first detailed account was published in Pravda, the Soviet party newspaper. Pravda said an explosion touched off a raging fire that spread outside the reactor and released radioactivity. It described efforts by firefighters to put out the blaze while their boots sank in molten asphalt. The story said the nearby city of Pripyat was a ghost town, with only occasional monitoring vehicles passing through streets. But this account gave no information on the amount of radiation released by the fire or the number of deaths and injuries. Previous reports list two dead and 148 persons hospitalized, 18 in serious condition (→ 24).

South Africa hit by biggest strike ever

May 1. South Africa was thrown into havoc today as over 1.5 million blacks stayed away from their jobs, in what labor experts are calling the biggest strike in the nation's history. The strike was called to protest the Pretoria government's policy of apartheid and to demand the creation of an official May Day labor holiday. The work stoppage forced whites to undertake tasks usually left to blacks. Thousands of schoolchildren boycotted classes in support of the strike. Zulu Chief Mangosuthu Gatsa Buthelezi called for black laborers to exert more pressure on President Botha (→ 19).

Terreblanche, leader on the far right.

Blacks burn tires near Cape Town.

Terrorism issue is Tokyo summit topic

May 5. At the urging of the United States, the leaders of the major industrial democracies agreed upon a statement condeming international terrorism as a scourge that "must be fought relentlessly and without compromise." The statement, signed by the leaders of Britain, Canada, France, Italy, Japan, the United States and West Germany at an economic summit meeting in Tokyo, specifically singled out Libya as a sponsor of state-supported terrorism.

With unusual enthusiasm, Secretary of State George Shultz said for Colonel Muammar Khadafy, the Libyan leader, the statement means, "You've had it, pal." Still, the statement stopped short of endorsing military actions or economic sanctions, such as the U.S. has employed against Libya (→ 7/10).

Louisville papers sold because of feud

May 19. A legacy in journalism has come to an end with the purchase of two Kentucky newspapers by the nation's largest newspaper group, the Gannett Company. Extensive statewide circulation and Pulitzer Prize-winning reporting made The Courier-Journal and its affiliate publication, The Louisville Times, two of the nation's most respected newspapers. But Gannett will now run them, after sealing a $300 million deal.

The price, paid to the Bingham family, which bought the papers nearly 70 years ago but has been beset recently by internal squabbling and feuding, was the highest ever paid for a media property. The acquisition underlines a continued business trend of consolidation of newspaper ownership into large chains.

May 25. At the White House, the Reagans join millions of others in Hands Across America's efforts to raise money for the poor.

1986

JUNE

Su	Mo	Tu	We	Th	Fr	Sa
1	2	3	4	5	6	7
8	9	10	11	12	13	14
15	16	17	18	19	20	21
22	23	24	25	26	27	28
29	30					

1. U.S.: "Mystery of Edwin Drood" wins five Tony Awards.

4. Washington: Ex-Navy analyst Jonathan Jay Pollard and wife plead guilty to spying for Israel.

5. Ex-NASA workers Ronald Pelton guilty as spy (→ 7/14).

5. U.N. reports 50,000 in Africa have AIDS (→ 7).

7. U.S. Justice Dept. says AIDS victims entitled to protection as handicapped persons (→ 23).

8. U.S.: Boston Celtics win NBA championship.→

10. Nicaraguan contras free 8 W. Germans held for 24 days (→ 25).

11. Supreme Court upholds 1973 decision legalizing abortion.

11. Tel Aviv: Synagogue burned in clash between Orthodox and non-Orthodox Jews (→ 10/13).

11. Sri Lanka: Tamil separatists blow up buses; 40 dead (→ 9/18).

13. Johannesburg: Tutu meets with Botha first time in six years, denounces yesterday's emergency decree (→ 16).

16. South Africa: Millions of blacks strike on tenth anniversary of Soweto uprising (→ 18).

17. U.S.: Chief Justice Warren Burger resigns, Wm. Rehnquist named to succeed (→ 7/29).

18. U.S.: House votes to cut off investment in S. Africa (→ 7/5).

22. Madrid: Gonzalez Socialists win in national vote.

23. Justice Dept. rules people may be fired because of AIDS.

26. Managua orders La Prensa newspaper closed (→ 27).

27. Reno: Jerry Moore buys Bugatti Royale car for $6.5 mil.

27. The Hague: World Court rules U.S. support of Nicaraguan contras illegal (→ 7/11).

29. Argentina wins World Cup soccer title.

30. U.S. Supreme Court rules states can outlaw private homosexual acts.

DEATHS

13. Benny Goodman, U.S. jazz clarinetist (*5/30/1909).

14. Jorge Luis Borges, Argentinian writer (*8/24/1899).

Waldheim easily chosen Austrian President

Waldheim, alleged war criminal.

June 8. With a margin of vote that was larger than expected, Kurt Waldheim was elected to a six-year term as President of Austria. The victory came amid accusations that the former Secretary General of the United Nations was, during World War II, a member of a German army unit which sent thousands of Greek Jews to Nazi death camps.

Dr. Kurt Steyrer, Waldheim's Socialist Party opponent in the election, announced publicly that he believed the anti-Waldheim campaign spearheaded by the World Jewish Congress actually backfired and aroused an anti-Semitic sentiment in the Austrian populace.

In his victory speech, Waldheim charged the World Jewish Congress with "steering a media campaign" against him, but also pointed out that the congress was not identical with world Jewry. The Austrian president plays what is mainly a symbolic role, portraying an ideal of national unity. His election is sure to divide the world community.

Shuttle had just one fault: Weak joint

June 9. The Challenger disaster was caused by the failure of a solid rocket joint that should have been prevented by the space agency and the rocket's manufacturers, the President's shuttle commission said today. The 256-page report by the commission said managers at National Aeronautics and Space Administration headquarters in Washington had enough information last year to require changes in the seals of the solid rocket's joints. The commission issued 11 broad recommendations intended to improve both the rocket joints and management flaws at the space agency. It said Morton Thiokol, the rocket manufacturer, had taken no action to fix the faulty joint despite repeated warnings (→ 7/15).

Congress votes aid of $100m to contras

June 25. In a major policy reversal and a significant political victory for President Reagan, the House of Representatives voted to allocate $70 million in military aid and $30 million in non-military assistance to the contras in Nicaragua. The vote came after an all-out lobbying effort by the president for one of his most prized foreign policy objectives: the overthrow of the Sandinista government in Nicaragua. On hearing of the 221-209 vote, Reagan said it was "only round one, but, oh boy, what a round." Just last March, the Democratic-controlled House voted to deny military aid to the contras, but White House pressure convinced many Democrats to change their vote (→ 26).

Contras will now get U.S. aid.

How to eat caviar a la Bloomingdale's

Bloomingdale's, the fashionable department store which sells Petrossian caviar, is offering the following rules on how to eat the delicacy: 1.Remove caviar from refrigerator 15 minutes before eating. Leave the lid on until the last moment. 2. Caviar should be eaten with a fork. 3. It can be accompanied with lightly toasted buttered bread. 4. Never sprinkle with lemon, chopped egg, onion or sour cream. 5. A small glass of iced vodka is the ideal companion. 6. Burst the eggs with the tip of your tongue to release the flavor. 7. Unopened caviar may be kept in the fridge for up to 4 weeks. 8. Never keep caviar in a freezer.

Len Bias is killed by use of cocaine

June 24. Intoxication from cocaine caused the death of star Maryland basketball player Len Bias, according to the state's medical examiner. The black All-American probably snorted the drug minutes before he died five days ago. The autopsy report failed to answer the question of whether the death would be ruled an accident. The state's attorney said he would consider bringing manslaughter charges against the person who provided Bias with the cocaine. Bias, 22, was the first selection of the Boston Celtics this year (→ 7/18).

June 8. Larry Bird leads Boston Celtics to their 16th NBA title.

1986

JULY

Su	Mo	Tu	We	Th	Fr	Sa
		1	2	3	4	5
6	7	8	9	10	11	12
13	14	15	16	17	18	19
20	21	22	23	24	25	26
27	28	29	30	31		

1. Afghanistan: Rebels down Soviet army plane, killing 100.

2. U.S. Supreme Court upholds affirmative action (→ 8/30).

3. Chile: Six die, 600 held in two days of anti-govt. stikes (→ 18).

5. South Africa: Apartheid foes kill five black officials (→ 12).

6. Wimbledon: Navratilova beats Mandlikova for fifth straight; Becker defeats Lendl.

7. New York: Cuban immigrant kills two, wounds nine with sword on Staten Island Ferry.

8. N.Y. high court reinstates murder charges against Goetz.

9. U.S. Justice Dept. releases report on pornography.

10. Italy: Magid al-Molqi given 30 years for hijacking of Achille Lauro (→ 9/5).

11. Reagan places contras under CIA jurisdiction (→ 10/4).

12. South Africa: 1,000 defy emergency decree, singing banned songs at funeral (→ 8/5).

14. L.A.: Ex-FBI agent Richard Miller given life sentence for spying for U.S.S.R. (→ 8/28).

15. Washington: NASA sued for $15 mil. by family of space shuttle pilot Michael Smith (→ 9/5).

15. Calif.: Voyager sets flying endurance record at 4.5 days without refueling (→ 12/23).

18. Bolivia: U.S. opens joint raids on cocaine labs (→ 9/11).

18. Chile: 25 soldiers held in burning death of teenager.

22. Washington: Harry Claiborne becomes first federal judge impeached in 50 years.

23. FDA approves production of first genetically altered vaccine.

27. Greg Lemond is first American to win Tour de France.

31. Warsaw: Vodka distillery reports highest sales in Poland.

DEATHS

8. Adm. Hyman Rickover, father of U.S. nuclear Navy (*1/27/1900).

25. Vincente Minnelli, American film director (*2/28/1910).

26. Averell Harriman, adviser to 4 U.S. presidents (*11/15/1891).

Miss Liberty feted on 100th birthday

Miss Liberty, facelift finished, is showered in fireworks on her 100th birthday.

July 4. Midnight. Hundreds of ships, from dinghies to destroyers, are bobbing in New York harbor. It is quiet now and dark, but the scent of smoke lingers. Only a few hours ago, a spectacular 28-minute fireworks display lit the sky about the face and torch of the Statue of Liberty, topping off a fabulous birthday for the Lady and America.

In the morning, President Reagan, aboard the USS Iowa, reviewed 20 warships from the U.S. and 21 from other nations. Tall ships sauntered alongside stodgier craft. Overhead, jet fighters from France performed exuberant aerobatics.

At lunchtime, Reagan met with French President Francois Mitterrand, ostensibly to discuss arms control. But how could an American president refuse to meet a French leader today? If France had not kindly delivered the bronze statue 100 years ago, there would be no excuse for the present festivities.

After months of refurbishing, Liberty reopened to visitors. Her first guest was, ironically or rightfully, no American but an English tourist. The line for the statue was incredibly long, and the heat (it was in the 90's) unbearable, but a visit paid on the 5th of July was an unspeakable, mortifying idea.

Loewy, originator of streamlining, dead

July 14. Raymond Loewy, a master of industrial design, has died in Monaco. He was born in France 93 years ago. "Heaviness and ornateness don't sell," he told an American businessman half a century ago. At the time it was not strictly true; now it is, due to the ubiquity of his femininely curvaceous Coke bottle, yellow scallop symbol for Shell oil and many other packages and logos.

Loewy came to America with 40 dollars in his pocket and ideas in his head worth a fortune. When fashioning small objects (Lucky Strike cartons, for example) got too easy, Loewy tackled cars, redesigning the 1963 Studebaker. He originated streamlining, applying it to trains, and worked on JFK's jet. Then the only place to go was up —overhauling rockets for NASA.

Senate reviews Rehnquist as chief judge

July 29. The U.S. Senate opened confirmation hearings today on the nomination of Justice William Rehnquist to be the next chief justice of the United States. As President Reagan's choice to replace retiring Chief Justice Warren Burger, Rehnquist has received mixed reviews. Most Republicans praise the conservative associate justice, while many Democrats offer objections to the nomination.

Leading the fight against Rehnquist is Senator Edward Kennedy, who assailed the justice's record on race-related decisions and called him "too extreme" to be the chief. Kennedy said Rehnquist "has a virtually unblemished record of opposition to individual rights in cases involving minorities, women, children and the poor."

However, Republican Senator Orin Hatch termed the criticism of Rehnquist "ridiculous," saying it was time "to stop the character assassination that's been going on." Hatch said that with his knowledge of the court and 14 years of experience, Rehnquist should have no trouble being confirmed (→ 9/26).

Conservative choice to lead the Court.

1986

AUGUST

Su	Mo	Tu	We	Th	Fr	Sa
					1	2
3	4	5	6	7	8	9
10	11	12	13	14	15	16
17	18	19	20	21	22	23
24	25	26	27	28	29	30
31						

1. Washington: Freed hostage Rev. Lawrence Jenco gives Reagan note from captors (→ 10/3).

5. London: Thatcher, under pressure in EEC, agrees to limited S. Africa sanctions (→ 26).

7. Moscow: Ex-CIA agent Edward Lee Howard defects (→ 23).

18. Moscow: Gorbachev extends Soviet test ban (→ 27).

18. Finland: Israel and U.S.S.R. hold first talks since 1967.

19. Tehran: Car bomb explodes in square, killing 20.

20. International bankers agree to extension of deadline for repayment of Mexico loans.

20. Oklahoma: Post office worker Patrick Sherrill kills 14, then himself.

21. Soviets publish 400-page report on Chernobyl, condemning technicians and admiting effects will last years and years (→ 22).

22. Oklahoma: Kerr-McGee agrees to $1.3 mil. settlement in death of nuclear activist Karen Silkwood (→ 26).

23. New York: Soviet physicist at U.N. arrested as spy (→ 30).

26. Vienna: Two experts say 24,000 will die of cancer as result of Chernobyl disaster.

26. Soweto: 11 killed, 62 wounded as police open fire on black demonstrators (→ 9/9).

27. Washington: Report indicates U.S. accidentally dropped 42,000-lb. H-bomb on New Mexico in 1957 (→ 11/27).

28. U.S. says Lockheed overcharged by hundreds of millions for C-5B military transport jet.

29. U.S. trade deficit soars to record $18 billion.

30. Moscow: U.S. journalist Nicholas Daniloff seized as spy (→ 9/3).

30. N.C.: 1,500 slave descendants attend reunion (→ 10/15).

DEATHS

1. Teddy Wilson, American jazz musician (*11/24/1912).

2. Roy Cohn, ex-McCarthy lawyer (*2/20/1927).

31. Urho Kekkonen, Finnish pres. for 25 years (*9/3/1900).

Andy and Fergie delight the public

Royal couple in Westminster Abbey.

July 23. Beneath the layers of pomp, circumstance and tabloid romanticizing, it became a simple, dignified marriage ceremony when Prince Andrew, 26, fourth in line to the British throne, said, "I plight thee my troth," and pretty, red-headed Sarah Ferguson replied, "I give thee my troth." A global television audience of 300 million enjoyed it together with 1,800 invited guests in Westminster Abbey. The new Duke and Duchess of York will honeymoon in the Azores.

Classic Coke a hit; New Coke falls flat

July 8. Classic Coke is thriving just two months after its hundredth birthday. The old formula was reintroduced last July when its replacement, New Coke, fizzled after only ten weeks on the market. Coke lovers now find themselves with a new pastime, arguing about the relative merits of the new and the old.

Benazir Bhutto jailed as 4 killed in Pakistan

Aug 14. This is Independence Day in Pakistan, but there is no freedom for opposition leader Benazir Bhutto. The 33-year-old daughter of the executed Prime Minister was arrested and locked up after addressing a rally of several thousand protesters in Karachi. Yesterday, hundreds of other opposition leaders were rounded up. Bhutto is demanding the resignation of President Mohammad Zia ul-Haq, who overthrew her father in 1977 and later had him executed. Bhutto's Pakistan People's Party is also calling for free elections and the restoration of democracy. The party says the lifting of martial law last December is little more than a sham.

Benazir, carrying her father's flame.

In Lahore, at least four people were killed in the most violent demonstrations since 1983. Many of the protesters screamed, "Death to Zia! Zia is a dog! Death to the Americans!" The Reagan administration has supported the Zia regime, but the State Department announced its regret for the arrests of Bhutto and other opposition leaders (→ 9/8).

1,200 are killed by toxic cloud in Cameroon

Aug 25. At least 1,200 people have been choked to death by a cloud of toxic gas that erupted from Lake Nios in northeastern Cameroon, President Paul Biya said today. Most of the victims died in their sleep, he said.

Officials say the toxic gas shot up at high pressure in the middle of the night, exploding with a bang through the lake that had formed at the bottom of a supposedly dormant volcano. Winds blew the cloud of gas onto at least three villages on the shore of the lake, smothering many residents. Scientists say the toxic gas consisted mainly of carbon dioxide, with hydrogen mixed in it. The gas was acidic enough to damage the lungs of anyone who breathed it, the scientists say. A similar incident occurred in 1984 at nearby Lake Mounoun, killing about a dozen people, Cameroon officials say.

They expressed fears an epidemic could be caused by the many decomposing bodies that rescue crews have not been able to reach. Several countries are sending medical help and a team of United States geological experts is being sent to determine the cause of the gas release.

Patient lives 620 days with artificial heart

Aug 6. William J. Schroeder, the second recipient of a permanent artificial heart, died in Louisville, Kentucky, today after 620 days of life with the implant. He lived longer than any of the other four men who received permanent heart implants, but he suffered a series of strokes that progressively caused him to lose speech and other capabilities.

Every other recipient of a permanent artificial heart has suffered strokes or other serious complications, and no permanent implant has been attempted since 1985. At the time of his death, Schroeder was also suffering from chronic infections and lung problems. He left the hospital only briefly on a few occasions after receiving the implant, using a specially equipped van. His wife, Margaret, and six children were with him at the end.

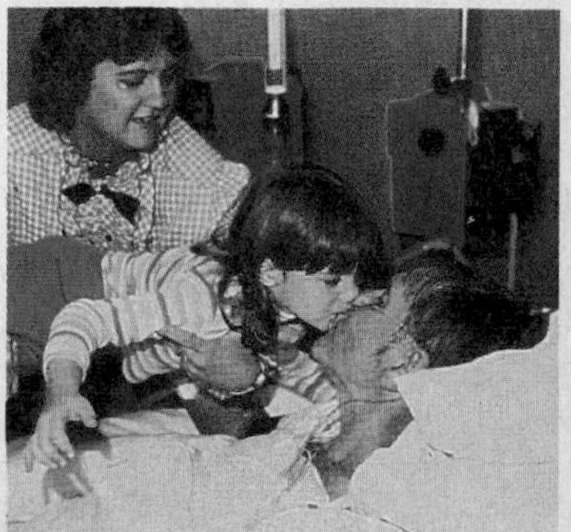

Schroeder and family.

▷

Wyeth sells 240 long-hidden works

Aug 5. Painter Andrew Wyeth has sold 240 watercolors, tempera and drawings whose existence were known only to him and Helga. Helga is a woman Wyeth secretly painted for 15 years. In every picture but one, the blonde, clear-eyed woman appears, dressed or nude, usually against a typical Wyeth backdrop of field or farmhouse. Wyeth sold the works to the owner of a publishing firm. He, in turn, will lend the multimillion dollar collection to Washington's National Gallery for a display next May.

Whitworth is given 365 years as a spy

Aug 28. Jerry A. Whitworth was sentenced to 365 years in jail for his part in a Soviet spy network which prosecutors have called the most damaging to American security in decades. Judge John Vukasin Jr. handed down the sentence and said Whitworth "is the type of modern man whose highest expression lies in his amorality." If Whitworth can live to be 107, he will be eligible for parole. Whitworth was convicted of passing sensitive military secrets to the Soviet intelligence agency, the KGB.

Henry Moore, major modern sculptor, dies

Aug 31. Sculptor Henry Moore has died in his native England at the age of 88. Some people would deny there was just one Moore, for they have Henry Moores reclining or lounging in front of their office buildings or in their schoolyards. Moore's work may be more popular in the United States than anywhere else —and why not? The shapes, evocative rather than provocative, offend no one. Moore was greatly influenced by Cezanne and Giacometti. Evidence of both can be seen in "Nuclear Energy" at the University of Chicago.

"The King and Queen" (1952-53). Moore typifies the 20th-Century rejection of European traditions in favor of the "primitive" styles of tribal cultures.

1986

SEPTEMBER

Su	Mo	Tu	We	Th	Fr	Sa
	1	2	3	4	5	6
7	8	9	10	11	12	13
14	15	16	17	18	19	20
21	22	23	24	25	26	27
28	29	30				

2. Soviets report 398 drowned on sunken passenger ship.

2. U.S. cuts off aid to Zimbabwe citing lack of diplomatic civility.

3. U.S. offers to trade Soviet spy for journalist Daniloff (→ 12).

4. Mass.: Prince Charles speaks at 350th anniversary celebration at Harvard.

5. Florida: U.S. launches unmanned rocket on secret mission to moon, first since Challenger.

5. Pakistan: 15 killed in raid on hijacked jet; 300 freed.

8. Karachi: Pakistan frees opposition leader Benazir Bhutto.

9. South Africa: Coretta Scott King cancels meeting with Botha under pressure from apartheid foes (→ 16).

11. Washington: House approves use of military to curb drug imports (→ 18).

11. Warsaw announces it will free 225 political prisoners.

12. Moscow: Daniloff freed in exchange for Soviet physicist Gennadi Zakharov (→ 29).

16. South Africa: 177 die in gold mine fire (→ 26).

17. Paris: Five die, 50 hurt in second bomb attack in three days.

18. Newark: Judge bars mandatory drug testing of federal employees (→ 10/29).

18. Sri Lanka: Army fires into crowd of Tamils, killing 47.

23. Tokyo: Nakasone, in comment on ethnic divisions, implies U.S. blacks less intelligent than whites (→ 24).

24. Tokyo: Saboteurs cut rail communication lines, disrupting one million commuters.

25. Ulster: 38 convicts escape from Maze Prison.

26. Reagan vetoes bill for sanctions on South Africa (→ 29).

26. William Rehnquist installed as chief justice of Supreme Ct.

27. U.S. Senate approves most comprehensive tax reform bill since WWII.

29. House overrides Reagan's veto on South African sanctions (→ 10/2).

Neutralist nations meet in Zimbabwe

Khadafy and Castro in Zimbabwe.

Sept 2. The so-called nonaligned countries are meeting in Zimbabwe, and they are spending most of their time aligning themselves against the United States. Today, the State Department announced a cutoff in aid to Zimbabwe because of its lack of "diplomatic civility." The Reagan administration has been incensed at Zimbabwe since a July meeting, when a minister launched into an angry tirade against the United States for opposing economic sanctions against South Africa. Former President Jimmy Carter walked out of the meeting. Prime Minister Robert Mugabe later apologized to Carter, but refused to apologize to the United States.

U.S. newsman freed by Soviet Union

Sept 29. The Soviet Union released Nicholas Daniloff, an American journalist held for a month on spying charges, ending a crisis beclouding U.S.-Soviet relations.

As part of an arrangement worked out between U.S. Secretary of State George Shultz and Soviet Foreign Minister Eduard Shevardnadze, the United States agreed not to press charges against Gennadi Zakharov, a Soviet citizen arrested on espionage charges, and permit him to return to the Soviet Union.

The Reagan administration insisted, however, that no swap had been made to obtain Daniloff's release and that Zakharov had been freed in return for the release of a group of Soviet dissidents. The arrangement appeared to clear the way for a summit meeting (→ 10/13).

Two Arabs kill 21 in Istanbul synagogue

Istanbul synagogue, latest front in a war that has outgrown all boundaries.

Sept 6. Without warning, two Arab gunmen burst into an Istanbul synagogue today and opened fire with machine guns and hand grenades, killing 21 of the 29 worshippers inside and wounding four more. When police arrived in response to gunfire, there was another explosion inside the temple which apparently killed the terrorists.

Entering the synagogue, police found a scene of horrifying carnage; bodies and parts of bodies were strewn about and many of the dead could not be identified.

The Jewish population of Istanbul, Turkey, has existed since the 15th century, when Sephardic Jews arrived as refugees from the Spanish Inquisition. They have lived in peace, with an absence of racial or religious discrimination, until now. At least three different Arab terrorist organizations have claimed responsibility for the massacre at the synagogue, but Turkish police discount the authenticity of the claims (→ 17).

Sept 8. Ivan Lendl vanquished fellow Czech Miroslav Mecir today 6-4, 6-2, 6-0 in the final of the U.S. Open. After losing in three successive finals here, Lendl has now won two straight.

Congress acclaims President Aquino

Sept 19. Dressed in her trademark yellow attire, Philippine President Corazon Aquino received an ecstatic welcome in Congress on Thursday. New York Mayor Koch, greeting Aquino in Manhattan today, had attended her speech in the House of Representatives. He said in his nine years in the House, "never did I see anyone take Congress by such a storm as this woman did."

Cheers and applause were not the only things received by the Filipino leader. Congress, in a surprise move, voted to send the Aquino administration $200 million in economic aid. The Senate must approve the allocation; most expect that to happen. Aquino will use the money to stabilize the ailing Philippine economy, left in disarray by the abuses of former President Ferdinand Marcos (→ 10/26).

1986

OCTOBER

Su	Mo	Tu	We	Th	Fr	Sa
			1	2	3	4
5	6	7	8	9	10	11
12	13	14	15	16	17	18
19	20	21	22	23	24	25
26	27	28	29	30	31	

1. New York: John Zaccaro indicted for bribery to obtain cable TV franchise.

1. Atlanta: Reagan speaks at Carter's birthday celebration.

1. China: New law authorizes firms to dismiss employees (→ 12/21).

2. U.S. Senate overrides Reagan veto 78-21, imposing sanctions on South Africa (→ 22).

3. Reagan admin. says it is open to talks on release of U.S. hostages in Lebanon (→ 11/2).

4. Netherlands: Queen Beatrix opens Oosterscheldedam, most advanced sea barrier in Europe.

4. Nicaragua: American Eugene Hasenfus captured in downed cargo plane (→ 9).

5. N.Y.: Soviet dissident Yuri Orlov and wife arrive (→ 12/19).

6. Atlantic: Burning Soviet nuclear sub sinks off Bermuda.

7. Texas: Police arrest three Mexican police in kidnapping of seven American citizens.

13. Salvador: U.S. aides linked to contra supply flights (→ 17).

13. Israel: Shamir succeeds Peres as premier in power-sharing agreement.

15. Supreme Court hears testimony that blacks who kill whites in Georgia disproportionately face death sentence (→ 12/20).

17. Congress approves bill barring hiring of aliens.

17. Managua: Seized documents suggest Hasenfus used U.S. air bases (→ 28).

18. Havana: Last Bay of Pigs captive freed by Cuba.

18. PLO moves headquarters from Tunis to Yemen.

20. South Africa: Pres. Samora Machel of Mozambique dies in air crash.

21. U.S. ousts 55 Soviet diplomats.

26. Manila: Gen. Enrile attends pro-Marcos rally (→ 11/1).

27. New York: Mets take World Series in final game against Boston Red Sox.

28. Justice Dept. opens inquiry into contra funding (→ 11/15).

Sheik Yamani is ousted from oil job

Sheik Ahmed Zaki Yamani.

Oct 28. Sheik Yamani, the man behind OPEC's rise to power and the most dominant of its oil ministers, was abruptly and dramatically removed from his post today by the King of Saudi Arabia.

Saudi Arabia, the world's third-largest oil producer behind the Soviet Union and the U.S., was instrumental in the 1960 founding of the Organization of Petroleum Exporting Countries. Yamani, who held his position for 24 years, engineered the 1973 oil embargo which jacked up world oil prices more than tenfold. One reason given for his dismissal is that the king wants to control Saudi oil policy by himself. The other is that Yamani has reportedly been undermining OPEC agreements of late by discounting Saudi oil.

Largest cocaine bust made: Over 2 tons

Oct 10. Federal agents today reported the largest seizure of cocaine —4,620 pounds—in U.S. history. The drug was discovered in concealed compartments hidden behind furniture in two 40-foot shipping containers on the freighter Malargo I, which arrived in West Palm Beach, Florida, yesterday from Venezuela. The wholesale value of the shipment was estimated at $41 million. On the street, however, cocaine is worth many times its wholesale price. ▷

Iceland summit a failure

Oct 13. President Reagan and Soviet leader Gorbachev went on television in Washington and Moscow today to blame each other for the collapse of the summit in Iceland. Reagan appeared to soften the statements he made before leaving Reykjavik, but he criticized Gorbachev for insisting that the United States abandon the space-based weapons system called the Strategic Defense Initiative. The president said the invitation stands for a Gorbachev visit to the United States, and he said, "The door is open and the opportunity to begin eliminating the nuclear threat is within reach." No date has been set, however, and Gorbachev said that "only a madman" could go forward with arms control if S.D.I. is developed.

In Iceland, the Soviets proposed a ten-year moratorium on most S.D.I., or "Star Wars," testing. Reagan rejected the offer. It is not clear what will happen to the far-reaching tentative agreements reached by Reagan and Gorbachev in Reykjavik on reductions in long- and medium-range missiles (→ 21).

Four American firms leaving South Africa

Oct 22. General Motors has become the fourth major American corporation to pull out of South Africa this month. Roger Smith, Chairman of General Motors, said the automotive giant was leaving South Africa because it was losing money there and because the Pretoria government has been slow to adopt reforms in the policy of apartheid, the official system of race separation. Timothy Smith, Director of the Interfaith Center on Corporate Responsibility, praised the move, saying, "This is a tremendously significant decision." Other firms which have recently left South Africa are Honeywell, Warner and IBM (→ 1/8/87).

The BMW, premier automobile and status symbol during the Reagan era, is not made in America. It is a German import.

Nicaragua captures U.S. arms runner

Oct 9. The government of Nicaragua has announced that its military shot down an American plane as it was delivering supplies to rebel forces. Two men were killed and one, identified as Eugene Hasenfus, was captured. The Sandinista government claimed the men were working for the CIA and today, Hasenfus said the supply flights were supervised by CIA members in El Salvador. If Hasenfus is right, American law has been broken; Congress forbids CIA involvement in Nicaragua. The incident may endanger congressional allocation of funds to the contras (→ 13).

Man strikes a blow against liberty

Oct 19. Disgruntled by what he called "imperialist" America, a man brandishing a hammer smashed the glass display case of the Declaration of Independence, the Constitution and the Bill of Rights. The historical documents at the National Archives in Washington were not damaged. For the assailant, Randall Bruce Husar, the act was symbolic expression. For the courts, the action was destruction of government property in violation of federal law, punishable by a jail term of up to ten years and a $10,000 fine. Husar will appear in Federal District Court to face vandalism charges. A metal detector will be placed at the entrance to the Archives.

1986

NOVEMBER

Su	Mo	Tu	We	Th	Fr	Sa
						1
2	3	4	5	6	7	8
9	10	11	12	13	14	15
16	17	18	19	20	21	22
23	24	25	26	27	28	29
30						

2. Afghanistan: Tunnel accident kills over 2,000.

2. Beirut: U.S. hostage David Jacobsen freed (→ 4).

4. U.S.: Democrats win majority in Senate, gain in House.

4. Tehran reports McFarlane and four others made secret diplomatic trip to Iran (→ 6).

6. Washington: It is reported Iran got U.S. weapons for seeking release of hostages (→ 7).

7. Washington: Reagan said to have approved Iran deal (→ 10).

8. Bronx: Wedtech admits forging U.S. govt. invoices for $6 mil.

10. Reagan refuses to reveal details of Iran arms sale (→ 13).

13. Reagan defends "secret diplomatic initiative to Iran" (→ 19).

15. Managua: Hasenfus given 30 years for flying supplies to contras (→ 12/17).

17. Paris: Renault Pres. Georges Besse shot to death by leftists of Direct Action group.

19. Reagan, in press conference, denies Israeli involvement in arms sale, later retracts (→ 21).

21. Justice Dept. begins inquiry into NSC; Lt. Col. Oliver North shreds documents (→ 22).

22. Justice Dept. finds memo in North's office on transfer of $12 mil. to contras from Iran arms sale (→ 25).

23. Manila: Aquino dismisses Def. Min. Enrile (→ 26).

25. Reagan announces Justice Dept. findings; Fawn Hall smuggles documents out of North's office (→ 30).

25. Bronx Democratic leader Stanley Friedman found guilty in corruption scandal.

26. Manila: Aquino and rebels sign 60-day truce.

27. Tennessee: MX missile engine accident kills four (→ 28).

28. U.S. exceeds SALT II limits (→ 12/18).

30. Punjab: Sikhs hijack bus, killing 24 (→ 12/14).

DEATH

8. Vyacheslav Molotov, Soviet ex-foreign minister (*3/9/1890).

Cary Grant, star of stars, dies suddenly

Cary Grant and wife.

Nov 30. Suave Cary Grant has died in Davenport, Iowa. He was 80 years old. The actor never won an Oscar and was nominated for one only twice, but he was unfailingly entertaining. Mae West liked the looks of the Bristol-born chap and cast him as a Salvation Army officer seduced in "She Done Him Wrong" (1933). He was a nerdy scientist "Bringing Up Baby" with Katharine Hepburn in 1938. He often worked with Hitchcock, his role in "Charade" (1963) giving Stanley Donen's film Hitchcockian status. Grant leaves a daughter by his fourth wife, Dyan Cannon.

Filipino Reds call for 100-day truce

Nov 1. Communist forces in the Philippines have called for a 100-day cease-fire plan to begin December 10. The truce would be followed by serious negotiations to end a 17-year Communist insurgency. The offer is seen as a victory for the administration of Corazon Aquino, which has been criticized recently for its conciliatory attitude toward the Communists. For a truce to occur the Communists want several demands met, including: cessation of all military operations, confinement of local police forces to peacekeeping functions only, and the disarming of what they call "death squads" and Marcos supporters (→ 23).

Who's dealing with Iran?

Nov 30. The White House has been plunged into the worst crisis of the Reagan presidency with the disclosure first that the administration had been selling arms to Iran and that some of the money from the arms sales had been diverted to aid the rebels in Nicaragua.

It started as just a trickle, but by the end of the month there was a torrent of disclosures, some confusing and contradictory but all politically and diplomatically embarrassing to the administration. A President who had seemed immune to criticism suddenly found himself confronted with questions of whether his administration had violated its own policy by selling arms to Iran, whether it had been attempting to trade arms for hostages in contravention of its stated policy and whether it had attempted to circumvent a congressional ban on aid to the Nicaraguan contras through diversion of funds.

Through it all ran a question of who in the administration was conducting the secret diplomacy with Iran and what was known and approved by the president.

It began with a report in an obscure publication in Beirut and a statement by Hajatolislam Rafsanjani, Speaker of the Iranian Parliament, that Robert McFarlane, former White House national security adviser, had made a secret diplomatic trip to Tehran, carrying a Bible inscribed by the president and a cake. There also were reports that McFarlane brought with him military equipment for Iran. The reports at first met with denials from the administration. As the news reports snowballed, however, President Reagan acknowledged to congressional leaders that 18 months earlier he had authorized the shipment of military equipment to Iran. The purpose, as initially stated by the president, was to establish ties with moderate elements in Iran.

Gradually, however, it came out that another purpose was to seek Iranian help in the release of American hostages held in Lebanon. In an attempt to blunt the criticism, Reagan held a news conference on November 19 during which he announced that no more arms would be sent to Iran "to eliminate the widespread but mistaken perception that we have been exchanging arms for hostages." The controversy only grew more heated, however, with the disclosure by Attorney General Meese that some of the proceeds from the arms sales had been diverted to aid the contras.

The White House dismissed Admiral John Poindexter as national security adviser, as well as his aide, Marine Lt. Col. Oliver North, who managed the Iran-contra deal. In an attempt to contain the controversy that was threatening to imperil the final two years of his presidency, Reagan appointed a three-man panel, headed by former Senator John Tower, to examine the role of the National Security Council staff. Meanwhile, Congress moved to have its own inquiry (→ 12/1).

The colorful "Rossano Gospels" has returned to Southern Italy after a brief stay at New York's Pierpont Morgan Library. The oldest, surviving illustrated Gospel manuscript was done in sixth-century Syria and includes the Gospels of Matthew and Mark and scenes from the Bible.

Thousand tons of chemicals pollute Rhine

As a fire truck sprays water on the burned-out Sandoz lab at Basel, 34 deadly chemicals gushed into the Rhine, creating a major ecological disaster.

Nov 10. Europe is facing a major ecological disaster because of the discharge of more than 1,000 tons of toxic chemicals into the Rhine after a fire at a chemical warehouse in Basel, Switzerland. Spokesman in France, the Netherlands, West Germany and Switzerland said the river could become ecologically dead as the chemicals kill off fish.

The four countries have shut down all the plants that process Rhine water for drinking. More than 24,000 villagers in West Germany are being supplied with drinking water from fire trucks. Authorities have banned fishing in the Rhine and are closing sluices and locks to keep the contaminated water from entering estuaries and underground water supplies.

The fire occurred ten days ago at a warehouse owned by Sandoz, a Swiss company. The environmental protection office in Basel says that at least 34 chemicals were washed into the Rhine by water used to fight the blaze. The chemicals included dyes, insecticides and mercury.

Large numbers of dead fish are being removed from the river as the toxic chemicals move downstream. Swiss experts say it may take two years for the river's fisheries to recover from the damage.

Dutch officials say the first traces of the chemicals are starting to move into the North Sea. More than 10,000 residents of Basel held a protest march two days ago, shouting, "We don't want to be tomorrow's fish." The disaster is sure to inflame environmentalists throughout Europe.

Insider trading pervades Wall Street scene

Nov 18. In the midst of its greatest boom in history, Wall Street has been shaken to its foundations by a major scandal. Ivan Boesky, one of the richest and most famous arbitrageurs in New York's financial district, has pleaded guilty to buying and selling stocks and securities based on illegal secret information.

Boesky will pay $100 million as penalty for his involvement in the insider trading game. Half of that total represents illegal profits, half is a civil penalty. He will be barred for life from the U.S. securities industry. "My life will be forever changed, but I hope something positive will ultimately come out of this situation," he said, adding that he felt legal reforms should be adopted.

Boesky also agreed to aid authorities in their inquiry of others linked to abuses. Subpoenas have been issued to several Wall St. figures, including employees of Drexel Burnham Lambert, the powerful agency that has climbed to the top of the industry with its dealings in high-yielding, high-risk "junk bonds" used in corporate takeovers. The Boesky inquiry arose out of a case against Dennis B. Levine, the merger specialist who also engaged in illegal insider trading.

1986

DECEMBER

Su	Mo	Tu	We	Th	Fr	Sa
	1	2	3	4	5	6
7	8	9	10	11	12	13
14	15	16	17	18	19	20
21	22	23	24	25	26	27
28	29	30	31			

1. Washington: Lt. Col. North pleads Fifth Amendment before Senate panel (→ 3).

3. Washington: Poindexter pleads Fifth Amendment (→ 9).

6. New York: Larry Davis, who shot six police, gives up.

9. U.S.: Poll shows 47% think Reagan is lying about knowledge of diversion of Iran funds (→ 30).

11. Bronx: Wedtech Corp. shuts down amid scandal, firing 1,500.

14. Karachi: 54 dead, 310 wounded in worst ethnic rioting in decades.

17. Detroit: John DeLorean acquitted on embezzlement charge.

19. Moscow: Soviets end banishment of Sakharov (→ 23).

20. L.I.: Black Michael Griffith killed by whites in Howard Beach (→ 1/14/87).

26. Iraq regains control of four islands overrun by Iran.

28. Australia wins Davis Cup over Sweden.

30. Honduras: 3,000 U.S. troops begin military exercises.

31. San Juan, Puerto Rico: Fire in Dupont Plaza hotel kills over 50 (→ 1/4/87).

DEATH

29. Harold Macmillan, British ex-prime minister (*2/10/1894).

CULTURAL EVENTS, 1986

Literature: Larry McMurty's "Lonesome Dove," Pulitzer fiction; Henry Taylor's "The Flying Change," Pulitzer poetry.

Academia: J. Anthony Lukas' "Common Ground"; Walter A. McDougall's "... The Heavens and the Earth"; Joseph Lelyveld's "Move Your Shadow."

Music: George Perle's "Wind Quintet IV," Pulitzer; Winton Marsalis' "J Mood"; Stevie Winwood's "That's What Friends are For"; Paul Simon's "Graceland"; Miles Davis' "Tutu"; Burt Bacharach's "Friends."

Film: "Agnes of God," Jane Fonda, Anne Bancroft; "Mona Lisa," Bob Hoskins; Woody Allen's "Hannah and Her Sisters"; Fellini's "Ginger and Fred."

France yields to angry student protesters

Students in Nantes take to the streets in droves to demonstrate their refusal to accept a new reform plan, while Paris was the scene of violent riots.

Dec 8. The conservative government of France's Prime Minister Jacques Chirac buckled under to angry student protesters today and abandoned a plan to reform the university system. Chirac changed his position after the most violent riots in Paris in 18 years. Despite their victory, student leaders vowed to continue their protests. They are infuriated by the fatal police beating of one demonstrator. It is not clear whether workers will carry out a threatened general strike.

For several days, hundreds of thousands of students have battled with police in the streets of the Latin Quarter. At least 68 people were injured this weekend as students threw rocks and bottles and set barricades and cars on fire. Police responded by firing tear gas and attacking students with truncheons. The Saint Michel and Saint Germain boulevards became graveyards of burned cars and rubble.

Under the now abandoned government proposal, the French university system would have been completely overhauled. The Chirac regime said the changes were necessary to increase the significance and value of diplomas, but students charged that the plan was elitist. They also objected to a proposal to allow universities to issue their own diplomas, in addition to government certificates. Students said the plan would create an unfair hierarchy of universities.

Elie Wiesel, Nazi camp survivor, wins Nobel

Wiesel at home in New York.

Dec 10. Author Elie Wiesel accepted the Nobel Peace Prize in Oslo tonight. The 58-year-old survivor of a Nazi death camp was characteristically subdued, saying he could not speak for the dead as much as he might wish to. "No one may interpret their mutilated dreams and visions," he said.

When Wiesel was 15, his mother and a sister died at Auschwitz. He witnessed the beating death of his father at Buchenwald. Wiesel wrote a sad remembrance in 1958 called "Night," and 25 more books on the Holocaust followed. The Nobel Committee noted his "commitment widened to embrace all oppressed peoples and races."

50,000 students in China seek liberty

Dec 21. Over 50,000 Chinese students gathered in People's Square in Shanghai today to call for democratic reforms, including freedom of the press. The young men and women, impressed with the alterations in the Chinese economy implemented two years ago and desirous of political change as well, carried posters reading "Give Us Democracy" and "Long Live Freedom."

The demonstrations, which have been going on for weeks but have only recently intensified, were denounced as illegal by the government. Officials lashed out at the protesters for attempting to disturb "stability and unity" and "derange production and social order." The official New China News Agency compared the street assemblies to the violent upheaval by Red Guards in the Cultural Revolution of the late 1960's and early 1970's. While many students don't expect an adoption of American-style democracy, they do feel certain reforms are possible (→ 1/1/87).

Sakharov and wife return to Moscow

Dec 23. Andrei Sakharov, the Soviet physicist denounced and isolated by the Kremlin for speaking out on human rights, returned to Moscow today to be applauded by colleagues at a scientific seminar. Sakharov and his wife had been placed in internal exile in the closed city of Gorky by the Soviet leadership when he called for the freeing of jailed dissidents and criticized the Soviet presence in Afghanistan. He was freed today by order of Soviet leader Mikhail S. Gorbachev, who has announced a policy of "glasnost," or openness.

Gorbachev himself called Sakharov last week to inform him that he could return to Moscow and resume his scientific work. Sakharov was surrounded by reporters and Soviet citizens when he arrived in Moscow by train this morning. The 65-year-old physicist went to the institute, where he once worked, for a seminar before going to his old apartment. He said he would continue to work for human rights.

Reagan acknowledges mistakes in Iran

What did he know and when?

Dec 30. President Reagan defended his secret policy initiative toward Iran but acknowledged "mistakes were made" in carrying out the policy. In a weekly radio address, the president shifted from a defiant to an apologetic stance, reflecting the view of his political advisers that a presidential apology was necessary to curb the controversy engulfing the White House.

The president stopped short, however, of meeting Democratic demands that he acknowledge the decision to sell arms to Iran was a mistake. He also continued to insist that he had not known that money from the arms sales was diverted to aid rebel forces in Nicaragua.

The Iran-contra affair has begun to take on an investigative life of its own. Lawrence E. Walsh, former President of the American Bar Association, was named as special prosecutor to investigate the arms sales. Several congressional committees held hearings as Democrats prepared to establish a special committee in January. Two former White House aides for national security —Vice Admiral John Poindexter and Lieutenant Colonel Oliver North—declined to testify before the panels, invoking the Fifth Amendment protection against self-incrimination. Meanwhile, polls showed a sharp drop in the president's public approval rating from 67 to 46 percent (→ 1/9/87).

Super-light plane circles globe non-stop

The sleek Voyager, a flying gas tank with a capacity of 1,500 gallons.

Dec 23. The experimental airplane Voyager, using only a single load of fuel, has landed safely in California after completing a historic flight around the world. The 25,012-mile journey took nine days, three minutes, 44 seconds in setting records for distance flown without refueling and for the endurance of its two-person crew.

Richard G. Rutan, who piloted the plane into Edwards Air Force Base, described the feat as "the last major event of atmospheric flight." "That we did it as private citizens says a lot about freedom in America," he added.

Jeana Yeager, his co-pilot, said, "I never really felt frightened," but she was nursing some bruises received while aloft. The scariest moment occurred seven hours before landing when the rear engine stopped, but the front one was started and the crisis averted. The Voyager carried five times its weight in fuel. The flight is expected to lead to more fuel-efficient flying.

CIA's Casey has brain surgery after stroke

Dec 18. William J. Casey, Director of Central Intelligence, had a malignant tumor removed from the left side of his brain today, surgeons at Georgetown University Hospital in Washington announced. Casey was hospitalized three days ago when he suffered "a mild cerebral seizure" in his office. He had been scheduled to testify before a Senate panel investigating the secret weapons sale to Iran and diversion of proceeds to Nicaraguan rebels. A statement said Casey was doing well after the operation; doctors anticipate he will be able to resume normal activity (→ 2/2/87).

Despite 87 years of crises and wars, the human spirit still soars.

Soviets to test again

Dec 18. The Soviet Union said today it would end its moratorium on nuclear testing as soon as the United States conducts its first test in 1987. The Soviets stopped testing in August 1985, calling on the United States to join the ban and to negotiate a permanent end to underground tests. The United States has refused to join the halt on the grounds that more tests are needed to perfect its nuclear arsenal. American officials also say better verification measures are needed to make a test ban enforceable. The United States has announced 20 weapons tests during the Soviet moratorium, and the Soviets say secret American tests have been held (→ 4/22/87).

American gun-runner convicted, then freed

Dec 17. Calling it a "Christmas and New Year message of peace to the American people," Daniel Ortega, President of Nicaragua, released Eugene Hasenfus, the American captured and jailed for running weapons to the contras. Despite the apparent goodwill gesture, the U.S. State Department, in an official statement, termed the entire incident an orchestration "by the Sandinistas for maximum propaganda effect" and said its policy toward Nicaragua has not changed (→ 30).

6.2 billion in 2000

Dec 21. According to statistics just released by the Census Bureau, the world population is reproducing itself more slowly now than it was in the early 1960's. But not slowly enough. By the year 2000, Mexico City will be bigger than Tokyo, with 27.9 million people. About 170 cities in the world will have over two million residents. Three-fourths of the population will live in developing countries, and many of those people will be elderly. The number of people in the world age 64 and over will increase 46 percent. And the total global population will likely increase 27 percent in the next 14 years to reach 6.2 billion. The problem is with all of us.

1987

JANUARY

Su	Mo	Tu	We	Th	Fr	Sa
				1	2	3
4	5	6	7	8	9	10
11	12	13	14	15	16	17
18	19	20	21	22	23	24
25	26	27	28	29	30	31

1. Peking: Students stage largest protest since 1976 (→ 16).

3. Washington: Frank C. Carlucci sworn in as national security adviser.

4. Puerto Rico: San Juan hotel fire called arson (→ 6/22).

4. Maryland: 15 killed in crash of N.Y.-bound Amtrak train.

6. California: Astronomers report sighting new galaxy 12 billion light years away (→ 2/24).

8. New York: Dow Jones tops 2,000 for first time (→ 2/1).

8. South Africa: African National Congress celebrates 75th birthday (→ 2/10).

8. Lincoln: Nebraska inaugurates Kay A. Orr, nation's first Republican woman governor.

9. Washington: House and Senate form panels to investigate Iran-contra affair (→ 17).

11. West Bank: Two Palestinians killed in fight with Israeli police (→ 12/25).

12. U.S.: Study finds divorce rate for couples under 30 is double national average.

13. Washington: Supreme Court upholds right to require leaves for pregnant women (→ 7/18).

14. U.S.: National Urban League calls Reagan administration "morally unjust" and "economically unfair" to blacks (→ 19).

14. U.S.: With U.S. consent, dollar drops to new low against Japanese yen (→ 2/17).

17. Washington: Inquiry finds Saudis gave $20 million to contras at U.S. request (→ 19).

19. U.S.: 40 out of 50 states celebrate Martin Luther King Jr.'s birthday (→ 24).

19. Washington: Officials reveal U.S. flight crews taking arms to contras smuggled drugs (→ 2/10).

20. Seoul: Interior minister and national police chief ousted in torture death of student protester Park Chong Chol (→ 2/7).

24. Cumming, Georgia: Tens of thousands hold biggest civil rights protest since 60's (→ 2/25).

30. U.S.: USX and LTV, two largest steel companies, report record losses (→ 2/2).

Cory's troops put down Marcos uprising

Philippine police, besieged from right and left, arrest a demonstrator.

Jan 29. The government of Philippine President Corazon Aquino, plagued by challenges from the political right and left, survived an uprising from within its own military today. The mutineers, most of them loyal to former President Ferdinand Marcos, had launched a series of attacks on military and broadcast installations two days ago. The last of the rebels surrendered this morning after loyal government troops fired tear gas into an occupied television station.

General Fidel V. Ramos says the army is now in control. But the fact remains that many officers, thinking Aquino too soft on Communist rebels, may be ready to join a coup if the opportunity arises (→ 8/29).

Gorbachev asks for greater democracy

Jan 29. Soviet leader Mikhail S. Gorbachev, in the latest of his calls for reform, has urged that voters be given a choice of candidates in local elections. Asking greater "control from below," he told the Communist Party's Central Committee that the party itself was responsible for economic and social stagnation.

It was the strongest call yet for political democracy in Gorbachev's campaigns for "glasnost" (openness) and "perestroika" (restructuring). He faces stubborn opposition and must beware of going the way of Nikita Khrushchev, the Soviet Union's last reformer, who was ousted in 1964 (→ 6/25).

Paley is called back in turnover at CBS

Jan 14. William S. Paley, founder of CBS, has been called back as Chairman by its board of directors in an attempt to revitalize the ailing network. Along with Laurence Tisch, who was named President and Chief Executive, Paley had ousted Thomas Wyman from the chairman's office last fall.

Paley has his work cut out for him. Morale has sunk since Tisch muscled his way onto the board by purchasing nearly 25 percent of the stock. In an open effort to increase profits, he oversaw the layoffs of at least 1,000 employees. One book division has been sold, and Tisch favors selling CBS Records.

Student protests oust Chinese party chief

Jan 16. Failure to end six weeks of protests by tens of thousands of Chinese students has resulted in the ouster of Hu Yao-bang, leader of the world's largest Communist Party. He will be replaced by Prime Minister Zhao Ziyang.

The protests, urging free expression, climaxed last week with the burning of issues of the Peking Daily, accused by students of distorted reporting. Hard-liners, charging students with "bourgeois liberalism," are responsible for Hu's ouster. Their victory places in doubt the future of Chairman Deng Hsiao-ping's efforts to modernize and liberalize China's economy (→ 11/2).

Jan 25. Ritual Gatorade bath for Giants' Bill Parcell after a 39-20 Super Bowl win over Denver.

Family farm depression worst in 50 years

Jan 3. As the Reagan era enters its seventh year, the perks of prosperity continue to elude the small farmer. And profit is not the only thing destroyed. With the number of farms down nine percent from 1975, a generation is being driven from the corn fields to the cities. Falling prices -- down more than five percent last year -- and inflated credit costs force consolidation in the hands of those who can pay the bills. The small, independent farmer, once thought by Thomas Jefferson to be the backbone of the country, is a disappearing breed.

A vanishing way of life.

1987

FEBRUARY

Su	Mo	Tu	We	Th	Fr	Sa
1	2	3	4	5	6	7
8	9	10	11	12	13	14
15	16	17	18	19	20	21
22	23	24	25	26	27	28

2. U.S.: USX workers, on strike since August 1, end longest steel walkout in U.S. history.

2. Washington: William Casey quits CIA; Robert M. Gates named to succeed (→ 5/26).

5. Florida: Carlos Enrique Rivas extradited from Colombia as one of world's biggest drug dealers.

7. South Korea: Police break up huge rallies protesting torture death of student activist (→ 6/2).

9. U.S.: Report finds one million dead in Iran-Iraq war.

10. Washington: Ex-National Security Adviser Robert McFarlane attempts suicide over Iran-contra affair (→ 23).

10. Washington: Reagan panel finds constructive engagement in South Africa a failure, suggests intl. sanctions (→ 7/26).

11. Quebec: U.S. All-Stars beat Soviet hockey team 4-3.

12. Texas: Court upholds $8.5 billion of fine imposed on Texaco for illegal takeover of Getty Oil (→ 4/12).

16. Jerusalem: John Demjanjuk, extradited by U.S., goes on trial for Nazi war crimes.

17. Detroit: Ford, with $3.3 billion yearly earnings, beats G.M. first time since 1924.

18. Beirut: 50 dead, 120 hurt in two days of fierce fighting (→ 6/1).

19. New York: Gov. Mario Cuomo declares he will not run for president in 1988 (→ 5/8).

20. Brazil halts interest payments on $81 billion foreign debt (→ 7/21).

23. Washington: Reagan tells Tower panel he can't remember approving arms sale to Iran (→ 25).

25. Washington: Supreme Court, 5-4, upholds racial quotas for job promotions (→ 9/8).

25. Moscow: Boris Pasternak reinstated by writers' union.

25. Washington: Fawn Hall admits destroying papers of boss Lt. Col. Oliver North (→ 27).

DEATH

23. Edward G. Lansdale, counterinsurgency theorist during Vietnam War (*2/6/1908).

New superconductive compound is found

Superconductor floats atop magnet.

Feb 15. American scientists today announced the discovery of a compound that loses all electrical resistance at 283 degrees Farenheit, a far higher temperature than other materials. In developing the compound, Physicists Paul C. W. Chu of the University of Houston and Mau-Kuen Wu of the University of Alabama built on the work of Swiss scientists J. Georg Bednorz and K. Alex Mueller. The discovery promises lower laboratory costs by allowing the use of cheap liquid nitrogen to achieve the temperatures needed for superconductivity. Potential applications are vast, ranging from ultrafast computers to magnetically levitated trains.

Japan analyzes U.S. failure to compete

Ineffective management and poor labor relations are major causes of America's economic slide, says a new Japanese study. Failure to turn laboratory advances into saleable products, the report adds, threatens to turn the United States into a "hamburger stand economy." Japan, meanwhile, has become the leading manufacturing nation. It is also the world's biggest creditor, has eight of the ten largest banks and the largest trade surplus. And nearly all Japanese see themselves as middle class. Japan's economic miracle, experts say, is due to low labor costs, high productivity, social cohesion and hard work (→ 3/9).

Pop artist Andy Warhol is dead at 56

Feb 23. Andy Warhol, the high priest of Pop Art, died unexpectedly today after routine gall bladder surgery. At 56, Warhol's list of artistic credits included filmmaking, photography and publishing. But he was best known for enshrining everyday images, from soup cans to celebrity photos, as high art in the form of repetitious silk screen reproductions. Warhol's preoccupation with popularity led to his theory that in the future, everybody would be famous for 15 minutes.

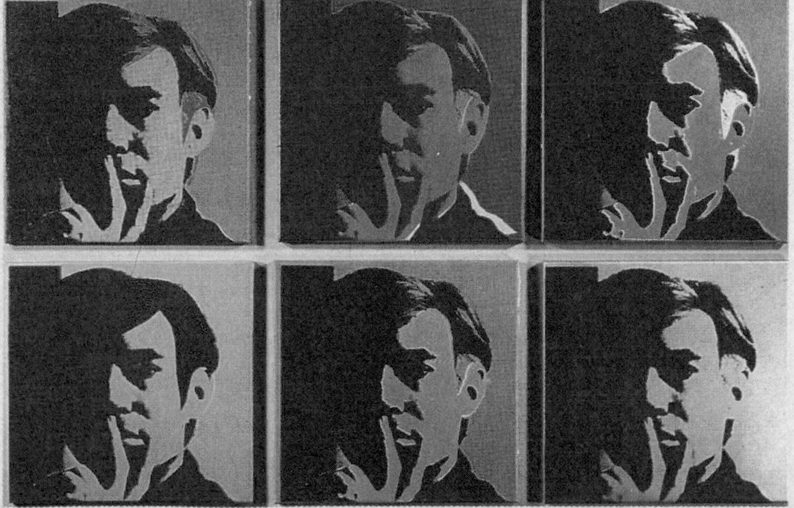

Andy Warhol, a pop culture hero, painted "Self-Portrait" in 1962.

Inquiry finds that Reagan is confused

Feb 27. A day after a presidential panel urged the President to "take responsibility" for the Iran arms deal, Reagan has fired his chief of staff. Donald Regan, blamed for a policy ending in "chaos," will be replaced by ex-Sen. Howard Baker.

The commission's report comes two weeks after the attempted suicide of Robert McFarlane, the ex-national security adviser who has been implicated in the scandal. The panel criticized Reagan's hands-off management style and pictured the president himself as confused. As ex-Sen. John Tower, head of the panel, put it: "The president clearly didn't understand the nature of this operation, who was involved and what was happening" (→ 3/4)

Koop urges fighting AIDS with condoms

Feb 10. Surgeon General C. Everett Koop has told a House subcommittee that condom ads on TV are advisable to help halt the spread of AIDS. The plea adds to rising tension between public health and morality. Some Republicans on the committee warned that Koop's plan would encourage promiscuity. Television spokesmen said viewers would be offended. Koop, however, insisted that the "public health benefit" to those "who will not practice abstinence or monogamy" outweighs other factors (→ 3/3).

Supernova sighted, is 50,000 years old

Feb 24. Fifty thousand years ago, far, far away, a giant star reached the end of its life and exploded into a supernova. The light has only recently hit the earth. The first seen since 1604, it offers a chance to verify theories of stellar evolution. Present data suggests that the star used up its nuclear fuel and caved in, releasing vast amounts of gas to burn thousands of times brighter than before. The discovery adds to the sighting, in January, of a new galaxy an astounding 12 billion light years away.

Met opens new wing for 20th Century art

"Portrait of a German Officer."

Feb 3. The Metropolitan Museum of Art, largest art museum in the Western world, has expanded even more with the opening of the Lila Acheson Wallace Wing today. The design of the structure itself is unobtrusive. Unlike the Guggenheim Museum, the wing does not vie with its art but accommodates it. Lila Acheson Wallace, who donated the wing, co-founded Reader's Digest with her husband, DeWitt Wallace. The healthy collection of 20th-Century works includes Marsden Hartley's "Portrait of a German Officer," works by Milton Avery, Pierre Bonnard and much more. Futurism and Expressionism are sparsely represented, but there is yet a lot of space in the addition's 50,000 square feet.

Flashy, talented Liberace is AIDS victim

Feb 4. Liberace, the bejeweled and sequined king of kitsch, died at 57 today, officially of a brain disease, unofficially of AIDS. His gimmick was playing "Reader's Digest versions" of familiar music at the piano, including a 37-second rendition of Chopin's "Minute Waltz." But it was his flamboyance, supported by a $5 million per year income, that will engrave him in the memory of most Americans.

Liberace, the king of kitsch.

Feb 4. Dennis Conner has led the Stars and Stripes to four straight wins over Australia's Kookaburra III to bring the America's Cup back to the United States again.

Silicon Valley whiz kids bouncing back

After two years of hard times and a major shakeout, the computer industry in Silicon Valley, a 50-mile stretch between San Jose and San Francisco, is making a comeback. New products based on advanced technology have increased profits at many firms and put others back into the black. Sales of personal computers are booming, and so are markets for associated products, such as software. One factor driving the boom is the introduction of new microprocessors that give much more computing power at lower cost. The U.S. robot industry, meanwhile, is still in a slump. Experts blame sluggish demand and increased competition from smaller and faster Japanese-made robots.

1987

MARCH

Su	Mo	Tu	We	Th	Fr	Sa
1	2	3	4	5	6	7
8	9	10	11	12	13	14
15	16	17	18	19	20	21
22	23	24	25	26	27	28
29	30	31				

1. New Delhi: Pakistani official quoted as saying Pakistan has nuclear bomb capabilities.

1. France: Study finds Lenin is world's most translated author.

3. U.S.: G.M. to repurchase 20% of stock in largest buyback plan.

3. Washington: High court gives federal protection for handicapped to AIDS victims (→ 20).

4. Washington: Jonathan Jay Pollard given life term for selling state secrets to Israel.

4. U.S.: Reagan, in address to nation, takes "full responsibility" for Iran-contra affair (→ 4/25).

9. Washington: Supreme Court rules, 6-3, U.S. must relax standards for political asylum.

9. California: NASA, at Ames Research Center, inaugurates Cray-2 supercomputer.

10. Rome: Vatican condemns surrogate parenting, test-tube and artificial insemination.

13. New York: John Gotti, reputed Mafia boss, acquitted of federal racketeering, conspiracy.

15. Spain: U.S. Defense Secretary Caspar Weinberger greeted by 50,000 protesting NATO.

16. U.S.: U2 album "The Joshua Tree" goes on sale.

18. U.S.: Gerber survey finds most popular names for newborns are Jessica and Matthew.

20. U.S. approves AZT, drug known to slow progress of AIDS (→ 6/1).

23. Tulsa: Florida millionaire gives Oral Roberts $1.3 mil. after evangelist said he would die if fund-raising goals were not met.

25. Washington: Supreme Court rules, 6-3, women and minorities may get jobs over better-qualified men and whites.

26. New York: James Earl Jones opens on Broadway in "Fences."

27. Washington: Reagan puts 100% tariff on many Japanese electronic imports.

30. London: Van Gogh's "Sunflowers" sells for record $39.9 million (→ 11/11).

30. U.S.: Indiana scores in last five seconds to win NCAA basketball title 74-73 over Syracuse.

Marines in Moscow suspected of spying

March 30. Two Marine guards at the American Embassy in Moscow spent last night in the brig in Quantico, Virginia, accused of espionage. Administration officials say Sgt. Clayton J. Lonetree, 25, and Cpl. Arnold Bracy, 21, were seduced by Soviet women who worked at the embassy. They were then introduced to Soviet intelligence agents whom they let roam freely around the embassy at night. One Marine reportedly served as a lookout while the other turned off alarms. All sensitive communications with the embassy have been cut off, and serious questions are being asked in Washington about the security of overseas installations (→ 4/4).

Swiss first, U.S. fifth in living conditions

March 16. The United States is the fifth best place to live, behind Switzerland, West Germany, Luxembourg and the Netherlands. This news comes from the Population Crisis Committee, advocates of zero population growth. The study considered literacy, job opportunities, personal freedom and seven other criteria. High living costs and infant mortality held the U.S. back. The U.S.S.R. was 23rd of 130. Mozambique was last, with 30 African and Asian nations cited for "extreme levels of human suffering."

Yuppies displacing hippies in Frisco

The streets of San Francisco's Haight-Ashbury, once filled with the sounds of free rock and roll concerts, now buzz with the finely tuned hum of BMW's. An influx of young professionals has not only driven rents through the ceiling, but altered the bohemian culture associated with the area. Upscale restaurants and boutiques have replaced quaint crafts stores. Hippies have not deserted the Haight. But they are now avowed preservationists, committed to preserving the sixties status quo through petitions and boycotts.

Bakker quits ministry, faces sexual charge

Jim and Tammy, fallen from grace.

March 20. Saying he was tricked into a sexual liaison with a woman, Jim Bakker has resigned from one of the most successful television ministries in the country.

Slowly emerging details paint a picture of infighting and intrigue in the big business of televangelism. Bakker told the Charlotte Observer he had been "wickedly manipulated by treacherous former friends" into having sex with a woman in Florida in December 1980. He then "succumbed to blackmail" to protect his ministry and his wife, Tammy.

Jerry Falwell, founder of the Moral Majority, has replaced Bakker as head of the PTL (Praise the Lord and People that Love) ministry. PTL members, who give over $100 million a year to the ministry, were shocked by the resignation. Some were found in tears when reporters visited Heritage USA, the huge, church-run amusement park.

Hundreds are trapped as British ferry sinks

March 6. Rescue divers have pulled some 300 survivors out of the British ferry Herald of Free Enterprise, which capsized today on its way from Zeebrugge, Belgium, to Dover, England. At least 26 passengers are dead, and up to 200 remain trapped.

Accounts indicate the accident may have been caused when the bow door opened en route, filling the ship with water. According to the BBC, the air supply in the cabin will support those caught inside. Two-thirds of the ferry, however, is submerged. And one exhausted rescue diver was a prophet of doom: "I don't think they have a chance," he said. Divers continue to search, and tugs are pulling the disabled vessel back to Zeebrugge.

The Herald of Free Enterprise, capsized in the Channel off Belgium.

Four teenagers kill selves in suicide pact

March 11. Four teenage friends from Bergenfield, New Jersey, took their own lives today in an exhaust-filled garage. The engine of the car in which they died was still running when they were found.

According to the Bergen County Prosecutor, a note found next to the bodies revealed no clear motive for the suicides, but displayed a "degree of despondency." Three of the victims, Thomas Rizzo, 19, Thomas Olton, 18, and Cheryl Burress, 17, were high school dropouts. Cheryl's sister Lisa, 16, had been suspended from classes. Olton reportedly had a drinking problem.

Bergenfield, a New York City suburb, had already been shocked last summer by four violent deaths linked to alcohol. Some students accuse school officials of dragging their feet in dealing with relatively common drug and alcohol abuse.

Judge awards Baby M to biological father

March 31. A New Jersey court, in a landmark ruling on surrogate parenting, has awarded custody of Baby M to her biological father, William Stern. Mary Beth Whitehead, who bore the child, has been stripped of all parental rights.

Judge Harvey R. Sorkow's decision appears to legitimize surrogate contracts like the one under which Mr. and Mrs. Stern paid Mrs. Whitehead $10,000 to bear a child for them. In his ruling, the judge called Mrs. Whitehead "manipulative, impulsive and exploitive" in her insistence on keeping the baby.

Elizabeth Stern, a pediatrician, has a mild case of multiple sclerosis, and feared pregnancy would damage her health. She officially became a mother today, signing adoption papers for the child. Mrs. Whitehead, however, plans to appeal the decision (→ 10/1).

Japanese investing in U.S. real estate

March 9. In a new twist on the slogan, "Buy American," the Japanese bought up to $6 billion in U.S. real estate last year, four times more than in 1985. Last November, Daiichi America Real Estate paid a record $1,000 per square foot for the Tiffany Building in Manhattan. Nine of the 14 hotels on Honolulu's Waikiki Beach are now Japanese-owned. And Japanese construction firms have begun projects throughout the U.S. Why? Experts cite their huge amounts of excess capital, the lower dollar and the high cost of real estate in Japan. Available land is so scarce that one Japanese golf club costs $2 million to join. A Japanese real estate baron is also the world's richest man: Yiosaki Tsutsumi is worth $21 billion.

More Irish arrive, driven by economy

A new wave of emigration is sapping Ireland of its younger generation. Flight from economic hardship is nothing new to the Emerald Isle. The 1840's, a time of a brutal potato famine, saw the country's population drop from 8.2 million to 6.6 million, most of it lost to starvation, disease and emigration.

The present exodus, at an offical rate of 30,000 per year, seems mild in comparison. But it is expected to continue well into the 1990's. And those who choose illegal residency do not make it into statistics.

Many of the new emigrants have been groomed by Ireland's fine educational system, thought a decade ago to be the country's salvation. But a 30 percent unemployment rate kills off a lot of idealism.

Kind and funny man Danny Kaye is dead

March 3. David Daniel Kaminsky, born in Brooklyn, spent his 74 years spreading comedy and compassion around the world. As Danny Kaye, he delighted audiences with his acting and orchestra conducting, dinner parties with his Chinese cooking, and children with his work for UNICEF. His efforts have been recognized with an honorary Oscar and a Humanitarian Award. Today, his big heart failed, and the sensitive comedian is gone.

Kaye started in show business as a clowning busboy on the "Borscht Circuit." He used his trademark staccato delivery of tongue-twisting lyrics to delight audiences in 17 films, including "The Secret Life of Walter Mitty," "White Christmas" and "Hans Christian Andersen."

March 12. After shattering all records for advance ticket sales, the British musical "Les Miserables" has opened on Broadway.

1987

APRIL

Su	Mo	Tu	We	Th	Fr	Sa
			1	2	3	4
5	6	7	8	9	10	11
12	13	14	15	16	17	18
19	20	21	22	23	24	25
26	27	28	29	30		

1. Bethel, Ohio: Steve Newman, 32, completes four-year, 22,000-mile walk around world.

3. Santiago: Rioting disrupts mass on pope's visit to Chile.

4. U.S. charges Soviets heavily wiretap U.S. Embassy (→ 8/24).

6. Lewisburg Penn.: Dennis Levine starts two-year term for insider trading (→ 8/25).

6. Las Vegas: Sugar Ray Leonard takes middleweight title from Marvin Hagler.

7. U.S.: Sixteen-month-old baby in Oklahoma and 67-year-old man in Dayton, Ohio, are killed by pit bulls on same day.

8. U.S.: Al Campanis resigns as Dodger vice president after remarks construed as racist.

15. Northampton, Mass.: Amy Carter, Abbie Hoffman and 13 others acquitted on civil disobedience charges for CIA protest.

15. N.Y.: Mbongeni Ngema's "Asinamali!" opens as first black S. African play on Broadway.

16. Washington: Patent Office allows patenting of new animals created by genetic engineering.

17. Sri Lanka: Tamil guerrillas kill 122 in road ambushes (→ 8/5).

19. Phoenix: Skydiver Gregory Robertson goes into 200-mph free-fall to save unconscious colleague 3,500 ft. from ground.

20. Boston: Japan's Toshihiko Seko and Portugal's Rosa Mota win Boston Marathon.

20. Argentina: President Raul Alfonsin quells military revolt.

22. U.S.: American Physical Society says "Star Wars" is "highly questionable" and will take ten years research (→ 8/26).

24. Palm Bay, Florida: Gunman opens fire in shopping mall, killing six, wounding ten.

25. Washington: 100,000 protest Central American policy (→ 5/6).

25. N.Y.: Peter O'Toole opens on Broadway in "Pygmalion."

28. U.S. bars Austrian President Kurt Waldheim from country.

DEATH

12. Erskine Caldwell, novelist of South in 1930's (*12/17/1903).

Texaco goes bankrupt

Unlikely candidate for bankruptcy.

April 12. Plagued by a $10.5 million dispute with the Pennzoil Company, Texaco Inc. has filed for bankruptcy. The third largest oil company in the country, Texaco is the largest firm ever to enter bankruptcy proceedings.

Texaco owes Pennzoil $10.5 million for taking over Getty Oil after Pennzoil and Getty had agreed to merge. Texaco's CEO, James Kinnear, says Pennzoil pushed his firm into bankruptcy proceedings by refusing to compromise on the settlement. Texaco reportedly has offered $2 billion; Pennzoil insists on $5 billion. Chapter 11 laws protect Texaco's assets from seizure and allow its subsidiaries to operate. But it will not pay interest on bonds or dividends on stocks (→ 12/19).

Gorbachev proposes missile-free Europe

April 14. Soviet leader Mikhail Gorbachev today proposed banning all missiles from Europe. Secretary of State Shultz, in Moscow on a state visit, reportedly rejected the offer pending discussion with Allies in Europe. According to the Soviet press, Gorbachev asked, "What are you afraid of?"

The answer appears to be the superior strength of Soviet ground forces. Some analysts think a nuclear-free Europe would simply be a Europe safe for conventional war.

Popular pressure, however, may drown out the skeptics. Western Europeans look forward to an arms control pact like they await their summer holidays.

They may get their wish. Last week in Los Angeles, President Reagan attacked the Soviets on espionage and Afghanistan, but noted that a breakthrough on mid-range missiles in Europe "is now a distinct possibility." Gorbachev, in Prague, said negotiators are "now nearest to a possible solution" (→ 22).

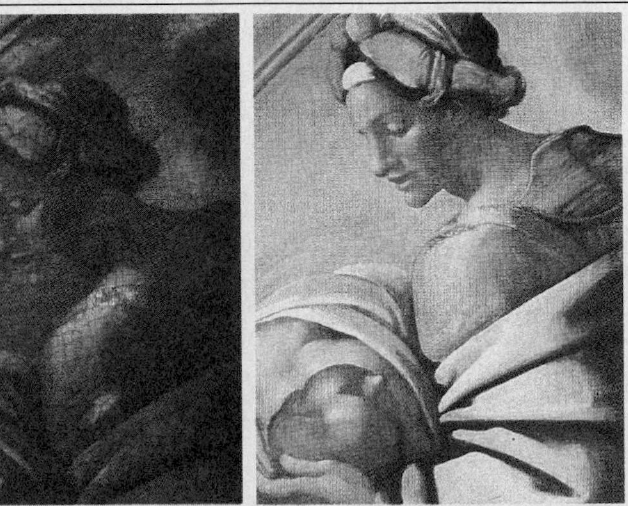

Restoration of Michelangelo's frescoes in Rome's Sistine Chapel has some observers worried the product will no longer be Michelangelo's. One critic said the cleaned images were of "postcard quality"; another compared the project to a nuclear disaster. But a team of experts has given its approval.

Windsor gems bring $33.5m at auction

Bejeweled panther among the gems.

April 2. The jewels of the Duchess of Windsor, gifts from a king who gave up his throne for love, are being auctioned off in Geneva. Some of the blue-blooded buyers had clung to their radios in 1936 when King Edward VII abdicated to marry Wallis Warfield Simpson, a divorced commoner. Tonight, old and young were enamored with the lovely bijouterie. With only half the collection gone, a record figure of $33,507,131 far exceeds the $7 million that had been expected for the sale. The proceeds will help fund medical research at the Pasteur Institute in Paris.

McDonald's winning the burger battle

McDonald's, the premier purveyor of "junk food" and employer of cheap labor, is seeking a new image. Shrimp salads can now be ordered along with low-fat, low-salt Big Macs. A new advertising blitz has deaf children praising McDonald's in sign language. And spokesmen for the fast food chain point out that, although annual wages for a burger flipper total only $6,968, McDonald's is the nation's biggest employer of unskilled labor. It seems to be working. With nearly 10,000 outlets in 40 countries, a new McDonald's opens every 17 hours. If negotiations go well, one of the next will be in Moscow.

1987

MAY

Su	Mo	Tu	We	Th	Fr	Sa
					1	2
3	4	5	6	7	8	9
10	11	12	13	14	15	16
17	18	19	20	21	22	23
24	25	26	27	28	29	30
31						

1. Ottawa: Quebec, assured of status as "distinct society," agrees to sign constitution.

1. Cologne, West Germany: Pope beatifies Edith Stein, Jewish-born Carmelite nun.

2. Louisville: Alysheba, at 8-1, wins Kentucky Derby with Chris McCarron riding.

3. U.S.: Julius Erving ends 16-year career with 24.2 points per game and 10,525 rebounds.

5. U.S.: Amnesty program for aliens begins.

5. New York: 200,000 rally in support of Soviet Jewry.

6. Washington: Richard Secord testifies Reagan knew of diversion of funds to contras (→ 15).

12. N.Y.: Christie's sells Giacometti's "Large Female Standing II" for record $3.63 million.

14. Fiji: Military coup ousts Premier Timoci Bavadra.

16. Moscow: Soviets announce launching of Energia, most powerful rocket in world (→ 10/26).

16. Jesse Jackson tops Democrats in poll (17%); Mario Cuomo, not in race, has 25% (→ 9/23).

24. Indianapolis: Al Unser Sr. wins Indy 500 for fourth time.

25. New York: Ex-Sec. of Labor Raymond Donovan acquitted of fraud and grand larceny.

26. Washington: William Webster sworn in as head of CIA.

26. U.S.: Eddie Murphy's "Beverly Hills Cop II" sets three box office records in first weekend.

28. Washington: Stephanie Petit, 13, wins National Spelling Bee with "staphylococci."

30. Chicago: North American Philips Co. introduces compact disc video.

31. Edmonton: Oilers beat Philadelphia Flyers 4-3 to capture hockey's Stanley Cup.

DEATHS

4. Paul Butterfield, Chicago blues harmonica player.

6. William J. Casey, ex-CIA director (*3/13/1913).

17. Gunnar Myrdal, Swedish sociologist, student of U.S. race relations (*12/6/1898).

Gary Hart out of the race

May 8. It seems that womanizing may be the Achilles' heel of presidential hopeful Gary Hart. The Democratic candidate bitterly announced his withdrawal from the presidential campaign today amid a web of scandal. Last week, the Miami Herald linked the former Colorado Senator with a 27-year-old model, Donna Rice. Herald reporters had staked out Hart's Washington townhouse. They saw Ms. Rice go in one night, but not come out. The report fueled speculation about the candidate's character. But it also raised questions about the proper role of the media in covering presidential candidates.

Critics say Hart has only himself to blame. After revelations that he had taken a trip to Bimini with Ms. Rice aboard a friend's yacht, called "Monkey Business," he invited investigation. He challenged reporters to follow him. They did.

Donna Rice, femme fatale.

With Hart out of the race, Jesse Jackson, an undeclared candidate, leads five Democratic candidates in most polls (→ 16).

Iraqi rocket strikes American frigate Stark

May 22. Tragedy struck last week in the Persian Gulf. Iraqi jets zoomed over the USS Stark and fired Exocet missiles. One warhead hit the Stark's upper deck and ignited a fire. The result: Thirty-seven American sailors are dead.

The Stark was in the perilous Gulf waters to protect vital oil shipping lanes from attack in the Iran-Iraq war. Now, as Americans mourn, the Pentagon must answer key questions. How, for instance, could the Stark's sophisticated radar devices fail to detect an oncoming missile? The Stark's skipper, Captain Glenn Brindel, who has shouldered blame for the tragedy, said the radar equipment had not been activated. A crewman spotted a jet, but issued no warning because relations with Iraq have been non-threatening. So, why did Iraq attack? It seems it was a mistake. Iraq probably meant to fire on enemy ships nearby. Today, President Reagan consoled the victims' families at a memorial service.

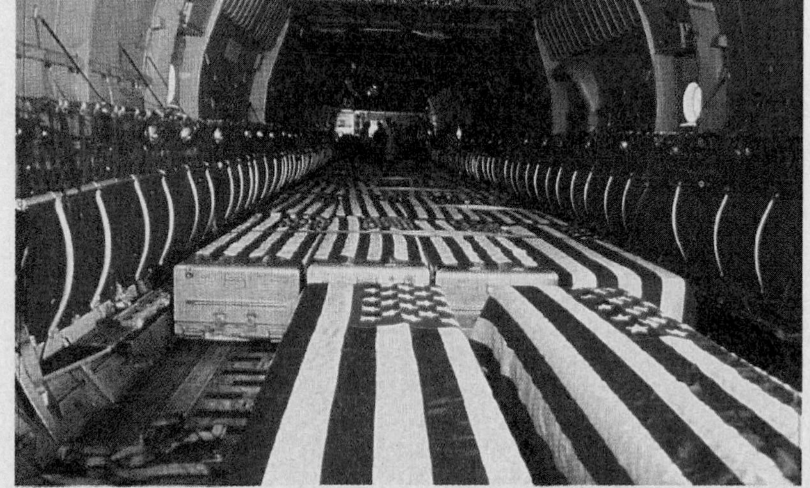

In Bahrain, caskets draped in the stars and stripes await return to the U.S.

Reagan says contra plan was "my idea"

May 15. President Reagan told reporters today that not only was he aware that private money was being used to aid the Nicaraguan rebels, but that he initiated the plan. "It was my idea to begin with," he said. Until now, Reagan has said he had only general knowledge of private efforts to fund the contras. The president's disclosure comes on the heels of testimony by arms organizer Maj. Gen. Richard Secord, who claimed Reagan also knew of the diversion of funds from Iran arms sales to the contras, a policy reputedly masterminded by then-CIA Director William Casey, who died earlier this month of a brain tumor (→ 6/9).

Beautiful Hayworth dies of Alzheimer's

Hayworth's classic wartime pinup.

May 15. Talented and tantalizing Rita Hayworth, screen star of more than 40 films, including "Pal Joey" and "Gilda," died yesterday. She was 68 years old. After suffering for years from Alzheimer's disease, Miss Hayworth slipped into a semi-coma in February. Her second daughter, Princess Yasmin, had nursed her since 1981. The princess publicized the then little known disease to stimulate research. The curvaceous Hayworth was once known as the "Love Goddess." ▷

Young German pilot lands in Red Square

The rented Cessna cruises past the Kremlin, unhindered, into Red Square.

May 30. Strollers in Moscow's Red Square were amazed when a small plane landed among them yesterday, but Soviet officials were not in the least bit amused.

Marshal Sergei L. Sokolov was fired as Defense Minister and the military chiefs were rebuked for allowing 19-year-old Matthias Rust of West Germany to fly a rented Cessna 400 miles through defended Soviet air space. Rust, who had only 25 hours of flying time, navigated unerringly from Helsinki, Finland, to a spot beside the Kremlin Wall. He was hustled off for questioning by the Russians. Marshal Dmitri T. Yasov, a protege of Soviet leader Mikhail Gorbachev, was named defense chief (→ 9/4).

Garbage barge comes home, still loaded

May 18. Round and round it goes. Where it ends up, nobody knows. A barge loaded with 3,100 tons of garbage has returned to New York harbor after traveling 6,000 miles on a 60-day odyssey. Six states and three countries rejected the fetid refuse, which originated in Islip, Long Island. The garbage barge has been immortalized in song and joke, but still has no home. Paraphrasing a famous poem, the mate on board the tug which pulls the barge said, "Ours is not to question why. We just go where they tell us."

The garbage barge returns unwanted to blue skies in New York harbor.

1987

JUNE

Su	Mo	Tu	We	Th	Fr	Sa
	1	2	3	4	5	6
7	8	9	10	11	12	13
14	15	16	17	18	19	20
21	22	23	24	25	26	27
28	29	30				

1. Washington: Third international AIDS meeting held (→ 24).

1. Lebanon: Premier Rashid Karami assassinated by bomb blast in helicopter.

2. Washington: Paul A. Volcker quits at Federal Reserve; Reagan names Alan Greenspan.

2. Seoul: Ruling party names Roh Tae Woo, ex-army general, to run for president (→ 10).

4. Madrid: Edwin Moses beaten by Danny Harris in 400-meter hurdles, ending record ten-year, 122-race streak.

6. N.Y.: Dwight Gooden pitches first time since drug suspension.

9. East Berlin: Teenagers, with rock concert on other side of wall, demonstrate to cries of "Gorbachev! Gorbachev!"

10. Seoul: Worst street violence in years protests selection of new presidential candidate (→ 20).

11. Panama: Govt. declares "state of urgency" to quell widespread protests (→ 11/15).

13. U.S.: Last "Prarie Home Companion" radio broadcast.

13. Japan: Sachio Kinugasa breaks Lou Gehrig's 2,130-game record for consecutive games.

14. Bonn: Willy Brandt, 73, steps down as head of Social Democrats after 20 years.

14. L.A.: Lakers take NBA finals 4-2 over Boston Celtics.

19. Washington: Supreme Court voids Lousiana law requiring schools to teach creationism.

21. San Francisco: Scott Simpson wins U.S. Open by one stroke over Tom Watson.

22. San Juan, Puerto Rico: Two get 99 years, one 75 years in Dupont Plaza hotel fire.

24. Minneapolis: Court convicts AIDS victim James V. Moore of assault with deadly weapon for biting two prison guards (→ 9/4).

26. Washington: Lewis Powell Jr. quits Supreme Court (→ 7/1).

DEATHS

13. Geraldine Page, stage actress (*11/22/1924).

24. Jackie Gleason, TV producer and comedian (*2/26/1919).

Fawn Hall declares her loyalty to North

A solemn Fawn Hall takes the oath.

June 9. According to Fawn Hall, Lt. Col. Oliver North is "every secretary's dream boss." The 27-year-old beauty and assistant to North explained to a congressional committee today how she helped the former National Security Council aide revise, shred and remove documents pertaining to the Iran-contra affair. She said she believed in him, despite allegations that he illegally helped orchestrate arms sales to Iran and the diversion of funds to the Nicaraguan rebels. Ms. Hall declared: "Sometimes you just have to go above law."

Ms. Hall also described how she smuggled documents out of the office by hiding them under her clothing. Once, she said, North lent her $60 in traveler's checks that had apparently been given to him by contra chief Adolfo Calero (→ 7/11).

Goetz guilty of gun charge, not murder

June 17. The racially charged trial of Bernhard Goetz is over. A jury acquitted Goetz, a white man, of twelve counts, including attempted murder, stemming from the 1984 New York City subway shooting of four black youths. Goetz claimed the young men were trying to rob him. However, he was convicted of illegal weapons possession, and he could receive a seven-year jail term. Civil rights advocates say if the youths had not been black, the trial may have had a different outcome (→ 10/19).

Seoul police lose control

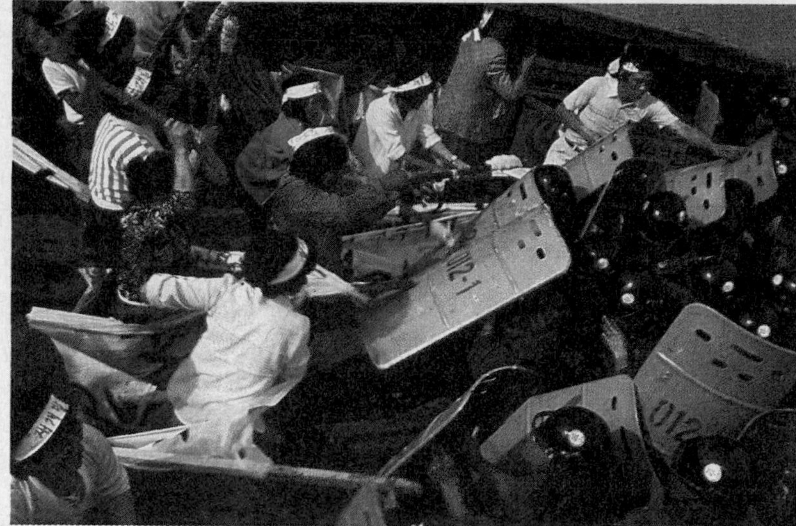

Angry protesters put Seoul riot police to rout with hit and run tactics.

June 20. Ten days of heated protest came to a violent climax today in South Korea as police and student demonstrators clashed in the streets of Seoul. Tens of thousands of rioters ripped through the city, throwing stones, igniting fires and overpowering the police.

South Korea, plagued by years of unrest, seems on the verge of a major political collapse. The tension has mounted ever since President Chun Doo Hwan refused to allow a direct presidential election.

Earlier this month, riots erupted in eleven other cities, resulting in more than 2,000 arrests. The protests were timed to disrupt a reception held by President Chun and his ruling Democratic Justice Party to celebrate the selection of Roh Tae Woo as the party's presidential candidate. Chun has agreed to leave office in February. But debate continues on the system to be used in the election, scheduled for December. Foes of Chun feel electoral rigging will prevent an honest vote.

It also now appears that discontent has spread beyond students into the middle class. Some 10,000 South Koreans held a candle-light vigil outside a Seoul cathedral, singing songs of protest (→ 7/1).

U.S.S.R. faces major changes in economy

June 25. Mikhail Gorbachev has reaffirmed his belief that the Soviet economy must make radical structural reforms. The Soviet leader said in a speech today before the Communist Party's Central Committee that the system is not working. He advocated a discontinuation of price subsidies and central economic controls. And he cited the need to improve transportation, communications, tourism and sports. Small businesses are also to be encouraged. Comment on Gorbachev's plan is favorable. Ed Hewitt, an expert at the Brookings Institute, said, "I can't complain any longer that he isn't talking about radical reform" (→ 11/2).

John Paul II meets with Kurt Waldheim

June 25. Amid protests from Jewish groups the world over, Pope John Paul II met with Austrian President Kurt Waldheim today. Waldheim has been accused of helping in the deportation of Greek Jews to Nazi death camps during World War II. Jewish groups feel the meeting excuses Waldheim's alleged war crimes. The Vatican said the pope welcomed Waldheim as a head of state, not as an individual.

The great Astaire takes his last bow

Fred Astaire, "the ultimate dancer."

June 22. He restyled American musicals and charmed audiences with his graceful movements. Now, the nation mourns the loss of legendary dancer Fred Astaire, who died today at the age of 88. Born Frederick Austerlitz in Omaha, Nebraska, Astaire started performing at age seven and hoofed his way to stardom. His greatest success came in teaming up with Ginger Rogers in such romantic movies as "Top Hat" (1935) and "Shall We Dance?" (1937). President Reagan eulogized Astaire as "the ultimate dancer, ... who made it all look so easy."

Segovia, who made the guitar sing, is dead

Segovia, active until the end.

June 3. Andres Segovia, who amazed audiences with his virtuoso classical guitar performances, died today of a heart attack. He was 94. Segovia is credited with giving the guitar an esteemed place in the concert halls of the world.

Born in southern Spain, he studiously practiced the guitar against the wishes of his parents and teachers, who, like most of the rest of the musical community, shunned the instrument. It was not easy for the man who became an idol to students and fans alike; he had to rediscover works written for guitar in previous centuries. As a result of his efforts, however, major composers were inspired to create new works for the guitar. He will be missed by millions.

Thatcher wins for third time in row

June 12. British Prime Minister Margaret Thatcher has won her third election in a row. A record 13.7 million voters backed her Conservative Party, giving it a clear majority of 100 seats in the House of Commons. The Labor Party gained 21 seats. Labor Party leader Neil Kinnock claims "Thatcherism" has ignored the unemployed and widened the gap between England's rich and poor. But the middle class has benefitted from her policies. Millions have bought homes and become stockholders. "Capitalism," the prime minister says, "only works by spreading to more of the population what used to be the privileges of the few."

Hemlines are once again climbing above the knee, as the tail end of the 80's looks back to the 60's.

1987

JULY

Su	Mo	Tu	We	Th	Fr	Sa
			1	2	3	4
5	6	7	8	9	10	11
12	13	14	15	16	17	18
19	20	21	22	23	24	25
26	27	28	29	30	31	

1. Washington: Reagan names Judge Robert Bork to Supreme Court (→ 10/23).

1. Seoul: Pres. Chun, under pressure from protests, agrees to direct presidential vote (→ 12/18).

2. Texas: 18 aliens suffocate in boxcar in desert.

4. Lyons: Ex-Nazi Klaus Barbie sentenced to life for crimes against humanity.

4. Wimbledon: Martina Navratilova wins record sixth straight title, 7-5, 6-3 over Steffi Graf.

5. Wimbledon: Pat Cash beats Ivan Lendl 7-6, 6-2, 7-5.

6. Calif.: Joe Hunt, head of Billionaire Boys Club, given life for murdering business associate.

17. Washington: John Poindexter says he ordered fund diversion to contras and gave Reagan "plausible deniability" (→ 23).

17. Paris: France breaks ties with Iran over terrorism.

17. U.S.: "Snow White" reopens at movies for 50th anniversary.

18. Philadelphia: Molly Yard elected president of National Organization of Women.

19. Mozambique: Rightist rebels said to massacre 380 in coastal town.

20. Arizona: Drive launched to recall Gov. Evan Mecham.

21. New York: Citicorp, Manufacturers Hanover and Bankers Trust report major losses due to Third World debt.

23. Japan: Hulda Crooks, 91, reaches top of Mt. Fuji.

24. Washington: Reagan names William Sessions to head FBI.

24. Persian Gulf: Kuwaiti tanker hits mine while under U.S. escort (→ 8/8).

26. Namibia: South African forces kill 190 guerrillas in biggest battle.

29. U.S.S.R.: Three Chernobyl operators get ten years in labor camp for 1986 accident.

DEATHS

10. John Hammond, music scout and critic (*12/15/1910).

31. Joseph E. Levine, film producer (*9/9/1905).

North implicates bosses

North, loyal soldier, takes the oath.

July 11. Lt. Col. Oliver North told a congressional panel and TV audience this week that his involvement in the secret arms sales to Iran and the diversion of funds to Nicaraguan rebels was directed by officials inside the White House. He said, "I have never carried out a single act, not one, in which I did not have authority from my superiors." Under a grant of limited immunity, the colonel said he assumed, but was not certain, that President Reagan was aware of the use of arms profits to aid the contras.

Capturing center stage, sometimes cocky and defiant, North said the operations were ordered by the late CIA Director William Casey and former national security advisers Robert McFarlane and Admiral John Poindexter. In four days of testimony, he also suggested that Casey orchestrated attempts to conceal the secret aid to the contras. And he shocked many committee members when he said that Casey had plans to use profits from arms sales to finance intelligence operations outside the government.

Despite charges that he broke the law, and to the amazement of his interrogators, North has become a hero to many Americans (→ 17).

Rioting in holy Mecca kills 400 pilgrims

July 31. Saudi police gunned down 400 pilgrims today in a tragic clash between fellow Moslems in the holy city of Mecca. Most of the victims were Iranians, but 85 Saudis and other Moslems perished as well. The massacre occurred on the annual hajj or pilgrimage. Iranian Shiite Moslems gathered to demonstrate against Sunni Moslems, who back Iraq in the Iran-Iraq war. Such protests are forbidden by Saudi law. When the Saudi police tried to break up the rally, several Iranians attacked and the police retaliated with gunfire.

Thousands of Iranian Shiites have gathered in holy Mecca for the hajj.

Angry Shultz says aides deceived him

July 23. In uncharacteristic fashion, Secretary of State George Shultz bristled with anger today as he told the panel investigating the secret Iran arms sales how he had been kept uninformed by aides about the operation. And he refuted claims that he had intentionally kept himself in the dark. Shultz said he raised repeated objections to the plan, but that the late Director of the CIA, William Casey, and former national security advisers Robert McFarlane and Adm. John Poindexter pressed ahead. He intimated the president was misled by advisers. And Shultz said he himself considered resigning (→ 11/18).

Ex-hippies become ice cream tycoons

Ben and Jerry have almost become the cream of their crop. The ice cream manufacturers were nearly pushed out of business by the the makers of Haagen-Dazs. But with a massive publicity campaign and an extremely rich (20% milkfat minimum) product, they've fought back. Now, Jerry Greenfield and Ben Cohen have converted their Vermont factory into the third largest supplier of high quality ice cream. Sales are expected to reach $28.5 million this year.

Mad motorists use guns in California

July 27. Traffic jams are an annoying aspect of life in the 20th Century. It's easy to get mad in bumper-to-bumper congestion. But now, some drivers in the Los Angeles area are getting more than angry; they're getting violent. Since June 18, there have been nine separate freeway shooting incidents. Two motorists have been shot to death and four injured. Two suspects have been charged with attempted murder. Police psychologists say self-centered attitudes, violence in films and even the breakdown of the family have caused the violence. Authorities recommend a simple solution: "Avoid confrontation."

1987

AUGUST

Su	Mo	Tu	We	Th	Fr	Sa
						1
2	3	4	5	6	7	8
9	10	11	12	13	14	15
16	17	18	19	20	21	22
23	24	25	26	27	28	29
30	31					

4. Washington: FCC abolishes fairness doctrine.

6. Koror, Palau: Voters end nuclear-free zone in exchange for $1 billion aid package from U.S.

7. Minnesota: Pitcher Joe Niekro suspended for scuffing baseballs.

8. Chad: Army reports ousting last of Libyan troops (→ 9/5).

8. Persian Gulf: U.S. F-14 fires on Iranian warplane.

9. South Africa: First of miners leave jobs in major strike (→ 30).

10. New York: "A Chorus Line" has 5,001st performance.

11. New York: 44 municipal officials arrested after FBI sting operation finds 105 of 106 bribes offered were accepted.

13. Burbank, California: Chris Marshall, 10, is youngest pilot to fly round-trip across country.

16. Thousands pray, meditate for universal peace during harmonic convergence.

18. Cincinnati: Donald Harvey, nurse's aide, admits poisoning 24 people over last four years.

19. Hungerford, England: Michael Ryan, 25, kills 14, including mother, then shoots himself.

19. Detroit: One out of 156 saved in crash of Northwest Airlines jetliner.

23. Indianapolis: U.S. wins Pan Am Games with 369 medals.

24. Quantico, Virginia: Sgt. Clayton J. Lonetree gets 30 years for spying in Moscow.

26. Bonn: Chancellor Helmut Kohl agrees to scrap Pershing 1A missiles (→ 12/10).

30. Rome: Canadian sprinter Ben Johnson runs 100 meters in record 9.83 seconds.

30. Johannesburg: Over 250,000 black miners end longest strike with no wage gain (→ 11/5).

DEATHS

1. Pola Negri, exotic silent film star (*12/31/1899).

24. Bayard Rustin, pacifist, civil rights activist (*3/17/1912).

29. Lee Marvin, American film actor (*1924).

Latins offer peace plan

Aug 8. The Presidents of Costa Rica, Nicaragua, Honduras, Guatemala and El Salvador have signed a peace agreement. The leaders met in Guatemala City to discuss Central American differences. They've come away with an accord that has set timetables for political reforms and a regional cease-fire.

The leaders agreed on the pact just days after President Reagan and House Speaker Jim Wright proposed their own peace initiative. Wright welcomed the Guatemala plan, which was initially orchestrated by Costa Rican President Oscar Arias. The plan requires each nation to arrange a cease-fire with rebels, hold elections, restore press freedoms and declare amnesty.

The Reagan administration, which has backed the Nicaraguan contras, will now be seen as interfering in the peace process if it continues to fund the rebels before the accord takes effect Nov. 7 (→ 9/20).

Tamil leaders give up, surrender weapons

A Tamil rebel, in training for the rigors of guerrilla warfare in Sri Lanka.

Aug 5. The vision of secession for Sri Lanka's Tamil minority may have come to an end. But so, too, might the violence that the nation has endured. Today, Tamil rebel leader Vellupillai Prabakaran accepted the peace accord signed last week by India and Sri Lanka. Prabakaran surrendered to Indian forces and his men turned over their weapons. The pact is seen as a compromise by the co-signers. But to the dejected Tamil leader, who has fought since childhood for a Tamil victory, it was a stinging defeat. The treaty creates an autonomous multi-religious zone in the eastern and northern provinces. The rebels dreamed and died for a separate state of their own.

Bull market five years old, up 244 percent

Aug 25. It's been a hot summer on Wall Street. The buyer's market has blistered with active trading and new Dow Jones highs are being set like weather records during a heat wave. On August 13, the bulls celebrated their fifth anniversary. In 1982 on that date, the market started its current great ascent. And this week, when some said the bulls would halt their stampede, the corral gates opened again.

Yesterday, the Dow Jones industrial average climbed more than 25 points, closing above 2,722. In the past five years, the Dow has risen almost 2,000 points, or 244 percent. Experts cite stable interest rates, a steady dollar, increasing corporate profits and the influx of foreign money as factors contributing to the sustained bull market (→ 10/16).

Aquino troops put down military revolt

Aug 29. The Philippine armed forces have squelched a revolt against President Corazon Aquino. But before the violence ended, 40 people were killed and hundreds injured, including the president's son. Mrs. Aquino has announced that her policy of moderation toward political opponents is over. She called the Communist rebels "monsters" and said they would be punished. The attempted coup occurred yesterday with attacks on military bases, TV stations and the presidential palace.

Hess, last of Nazi regime, dies in jail

Aug 17. Alone and sullen. That's how Rudolf Hess, the last of Adolf Hitler's close colleagues, died. Sentenced to life at the Spandau Prison in West Berlin, Hess tried four times to kill himself. Yesterday he succeeded, by strangulation with an electric cord. He was 93. Hitler's deputy had been in Allied custody since 1941, after making a desperate attempt to forge peace with Britain. At the Nuremberg trials, he was condemned for planning aggressive war. He said then that he had no regrets.

John Huston, one of the greats, dies

Aug 28. His dynamic and demanding method of movie direction has earned him a revered place in film history and given his audiences cinematic thrills. Today, John Huston is dead, at 81. Despite suffering from emphysema for years, Huston continued to make movies.

While one could rave about all of Huston's great films, three stand out as true classics. In 1941, Huston made his directorial debut with "The Maltese Falcon," a stunning adaptation of Dashiell Hammett's mystery tale. "The African Queen" (1950) starred Humphrey Bogart and Katharine Hepburn. And "The Treasure of Sierra Madre" (1948), featuring his father, will be cherished forever.

1987

SEPTEMBER

Su	Mo	Tu	We	Th	Fr	Sa
		1	2	3	4	5
6	7	8	9	10	11	12
13	14	15	16	17	18	19
20	21	22	23	24	25	26
27	28	29	30			

1. California: Protester Brian Wilson has legs severed by train carrying arms to Concord Naval Weapons Station.

4. Moscow: West German Matthias Rust, 19, gets four years for flying illegally into Red Square.

4. U.S.: National Cancer Institute reports first known case of researcher getting AIDS in lab.

5. Chad forces destroy major base in Libya.

6. Baltimore: Seven-month-old Siamese twins, joined at head, separated in 22-hour operation.

8. Washington: Justice Thurgood Marshall says Reagan ranks at "the bottom" of U.S. presidents on civil rights.

8. Bonn: Erich Honecker pays first state visit by East German Communist Party leader.

11. U.S.: Dan Rather, angry over news delay due to tennis coverage, walks off set, leaving seven minutes of dead air.

12. New York: Martina Navratilova beats Steffi Graf 7-6, 6-1 in final of U.S. Open (→ 14).

13. Tokyo: Michael Jackson opens "Bad" tour.

14. New York: Ivan Lendl beats Mats Wilander 6-7, 6-0, 7-6, 6-4 for third straight U.S. Open win.

16. Montreal: 70 nations sign accord to save ozone layer.

20. Managua: Nicaragua ends ban on opposition paper La Prensa (→ 10/14).

22. N.Y.: Rep. Mario Biaggi and Meade Esposito convicted of taking unlawful gratuities, acquitted on bribery charges.

22. U.S.: NFL players go on strike for free agency rights (→ 10/16).

27. U.S.: 50 millionth VCR shipped to market.

29. N.Y.: Don Mattingly hits record sixth grand slam in year.

DEATHS

11. Peter Tosh, founder of The Wailers, Reggae band.

11. Lorne Greene, star of TV's "Bonanza" (*2/12/1915).

24. Bob Fosse, director and choreographer (*6/23/1927).

We the People celebrate Constitution

Howard Chandler Christy's "Scene at the Signing of the Constitution ..."

Sept 17. Bells chimed and American flags were unfurled in Philadelphia today in celebration of the 200th birthday of the Constitution of the United States.

On September 17, 1787, 38 delegates signed the document, a broad blueprint of governance adopted in secret in 84 days. Then, they "adjourned to the city tavern, dined together and took a cordial leave of each other," wrote George Washington, who had presided over the convention in Philadelphia. "I retired to meditate on the momentous work which had been executed."

The U.S. Constitution has endured longer than any other written constitution of the modern era. The founders planned it that way, by confining it to "essential principles only" in order to accommodate it "to times and events." In this spirit, it has been amended 26 times.

It was also born in a spirit of compromise. "Every word of the Constitution," said James Madison, its architect, "decides a question between power and liberty."

But it took an Englishman, William Gladstone, to say in 1887 what many Americans believe: "The American Constitution is, so far as I can see, the most wonderful work ever struck off at a given time by the brain and purpose of man."

Pope in U.S. against background of dissent

Sept 19. Pope John Paul II has ended a ten-day visit to the United States with an unambiguous rebuke to the voices of dissent that have followed him across the country. In Detroit, he squelched the cries of Roman Catholic Bishops for freedom of speech by insisting dissent is incompatible with Catholicism.

New York Times/CBS News polls show that many of the lay public question papal infallibility on divorce, abortion, birth control, homosexuality, mandatory celibacy for priests, and the ordination of women. Some 58 percent think the Church should alter teachings to reflect popular opinion, while 55 percent of priests feel they should be allowed to marry. The papal visit is unlikely to alleviate any tension between the Vatican and American Catholics. Until today, the pope did not confront challenges directly. He said that dissent among American Catholics is a "serious problem," but there is "a great silent majority which is faithful" (→ 19).

The Jeep, 47 years after its debut, is a toy for the young and upwardly mobile. Says one salesman: "They're trading in BMW's."

Henry Ford II dies

Sept 29. Henry Ford II, who saved the second largest auto firm in the country from bankruptcy, has died of pneumonia. Grandson of Ford's founder, the auto tycoon was a devoted philanthropist. He started the Ford Foundation and helped to rebuild downtown Detroit. His personal and professional lives, however, were tempestuous. He was married three times and was known as a tyrannical boss who fired anyone who challenged his dominance, including Lee A. Iacocca, now Chairman of Chrysler.

Senator Biden gives up presidential bid

Sept 23. Senator Joseph R. Biden Jr., hurt by disclosures of plagiarism in law school and in campaign speeches, has withdrawn his bid for the Democratic presidential nomination. His hopes, he said, had been dashed by "the exaggerated shadow" of his own mistakes. Last week, Biden admitted stealing from a law review article for a paper he wrote during his first year in law school. Charges that he borrowed lines from others' political speeches without attribution were written off as "much ado about nothing."

What Biden calls "nothing" is a speech, laced with populist rhetoric, that he made last month at the Iowa State Fair: "Why is it that Joe Biden is the first in his family ever to go to a university? ..." The speech happened to match almost identically one given by Neil Kinnock, the former Labor Party candidate for British prime minister.

Pulling out of the race, Biden said, would allow him to carry on unhindered his attempt, as head of the Senate Judiciary Committee, to block Judge Robert Bork's nomination to the Supreme Court (→ 12/16).

1987

OCTOBER

Su	Mo	Tu	We	Th	Fr	Sa
				1	2	3
4	5	6	7	8	9	10
11	12	13	14	15	16	17
18	19	20	21	22	23	24
25	26	27	28	29	30	31

1. Johannesburg: Pat Anthony gives birth to daughter's triplets in unique surrogate mother case.

4. U.S. and Canada agree on pact to cut trade barriers.

9. Lhasa: Foreign journalists expelled by China after deaths of six Tibetan protesters.

13. Washington: Gloved police arrest 600 in protest at Supreme Court against decision upholding Georgia sodomy law.

14. Stockholm: Costa Rican President Oscar Arias Sanchez wins Nobel Peace Prize (→ 11/6).

16. New York: Dow ends week with 235.48-point decline, worst since World War II (→ 19).

16. U.S.: NFL players end strike with no gain.

19. N.Y.: Bernhard Goetz given six months on gun charge.

19. Hollidaysburg, Penn.: Donald Woomer, Linda Despot win record lottery prize of $46 mil.

21. New York: Dow soars record 186 points (→ 26).

24. Miami Beach: AFL-CIO votes Teamsters back into organization after 30-year absence.

25. Minneapolis: Twins win their first World Series in final game over St. Louis Cardinals.

26. Hong Kong: Stock market, reopening first time in week, loses one-third of value (→ 27).

26. San Salvador: Human rights advocate Herbert Ernesto Anaya slain.

26. U.S.: Study shows 20 million Americans are underfed.

26. California: Titan 34D flies successfully, ending two years of U.S. space failures (→ 12/1).

27. Miami: Investor Arthur Kane kills stockbroker and self (→ 11/21).

29. U.S.: Douglas Ginsburg named to Supreme Court (→ 11/7).

DEATHS

9. Clare Boothe Luce, playwright, editor, diplomat and politician (*4/10/1903).

12. Alf Landon, 1936 GOP pres. nominee (*9/9/1887).

29. Woody Herman, big band leader (*5/16/1913).

California hit by 'quake

Automobiles buried under bricks from collapsing buildings in Los Angeles.

Oct 1. At 7:42 this morning, Los Angeles was shocked by a violent earthquake measuring 6.1 on the Richter scale. With six dead and 100 hospitalized, the damage was limited. But residents are left wondering when "the big one" will hit.

The earthquake, with its epicenter 20 miles east of L.A., originated in the Whittier Fault. The San Andreas Fault, potentially more deadly, was undisturbed. But residents were very shaken. Dropping coffee cups and grabbing children, they ran into the streets in various states of attire. Some failed to escape buckling buildings in time. But most shrugged it off as if it were a nagging mosquito. By noon, Disneyland was back in action.

American Navy hits Iran in reprisal attack

Oct 19. In retaliation for Iranian attacks on ships in the Persian Gulf, the United States has disabled three of Iran's offshore oil platforms, said to double as gunboat bases. Crew members on the platforms were warned 20 minutes before the U.S. Navy opened fire. President Reagan called the action a "prudent yet restrained response." Some members of Congress, not consulted before the attack, expressed fear of American involvement in a Mideast conflict.

Thick smoke engulfs an oil platform after the U.S. attack in the Persian Gulf.

Senate rejects Bork for Court, 58-42

Oct 23. The Senate has blocked Judge Robert H. Bork's path to the Supreme Court. The 58-42 vote closes one of the most divisive and protracted battles in the court's history. Bork, as a law professor at Yale University, was outspoken in advocating a limited scope for the Bill of Rights. This, among other right-wing legal views, won him the wrath of liberal groups from the NAACP to gay rights coalitions. Even the politically neutral American Civil Liberties Union came out against him. President Reagan, saying the Senate had bowed to "political pressure," promised his next nomination would upset the Senate majority "just as much" (→ 29).

Right and left both turn to free market

As world trade grows in competitiveness, Adam Smith's "invisible hand" is gaining visibility. The industrial West, the Communist bloc and the Third World are all looking to the free market to guide them through the complexities of an interdependent world. The trend includes privatization, deregulation, decentralization, low taxes and aid to small business. Economist Robert Heilbroner says central planners cannot handle the intricacies of industrial societies: "They have to be run by some looser mechanism, by something with feedback."

Child in well saved

Oct 16. Eighteen-month-old Jessica McClure was pulled from a Texas well shaft this evening after engaging all the nation in her 57-hour fight for survival. Baby Jessica distracted herself by singing nursery rhymes. Americans were enraptured with hourly media reports of her progress. Residents of Midland, Texas, Jessica's tiny home town, kept a round-the-clock vigil, while volunteers thrust drills through sheet rock to save the child. She emerged scarred and in danger of losing a foot, but otherwise in stable condition. Her teenage parents are overcome with relief.

Crash! Market plunges 508 points, exceeds 1929

Oct 20. The bottom fell out of the stock market yesterday, and no one knows for sure what will happen next. Wall Street had its worst day ever, far worse than 1929. The Dow Jones industrial average plummeted a record 508 points, closing at 1,738.74. Volume was an unprecedented 604 million shares, and the ticker fell two hours behind. The collapse sent shockwaves around the world. The Tokyo exchange opened down sharply this morning, and the Hong Kong market has closed for a week.

The Chairman of the New York Stock Exchange compared the market collapse to a nuclear accident. "It's the nearest thing to a meltdown that I ever want to see," John Phelan Jr. said. The Dean of the New York University business school said it was "a little like seeing the atom bomb go off. Once you've seen it," Richard West told The New York Times, "you know it could happen again. The world has changed."

Everyone from the small investor to the network anchorman is searching for villains. There appear to be many. Analysts blame the enormous budget and trade deficits, the falling dollar, rising interest rates and the latest tensions in the Persian Gulf. They also blame Wall Street itself and program trading. Arbitrageurs use the technique when they trade large blocks of stock to profit on the difference between their cash values and futures contracts. "They can't stop the selling once it gets going," one investor said. "It's just computers selling to computers. It became a gamble, not an investment any more."

It was a gamble that hurt millions of Americans. "People have been bloodied," economist Paul Samuelson said. Those with the biggest scars are the investors who watched $500 billion vanish from their portfolios. Workers planning to retire soon saw their savings shrink. Those who are still working have new concerns about losing their jobs. Businesses may cut back production, and economist Henry Kaufman warns that some of them may start laying employees off.

Despite all the gloom on Wall Street, some investors are still optimistic. They think stocks are a bargain, and today they rushed to buy the blue chips. This "flight to quality" pumped the Dow back up more than 100 points today, but it did not save the rest of the market. The stocks of many smaller companies are still in a free-fall. No one wants them, and the number of declining stocks far outnumbered gainers.

One man who does not invest in stocks thinks there may be a lesson in what happened. "Maybe it will take the excessive greed out of things for a while," he said. And a retired Wall Street worker said, "All those guys with 65 credit cards and Porsches who think they are all geniuses at 25, now they see what's happened" (→ 21).

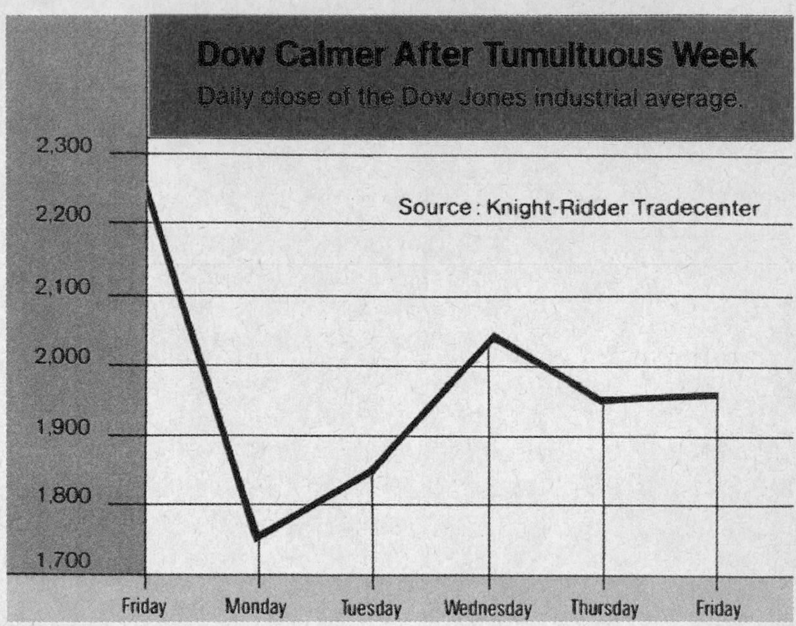

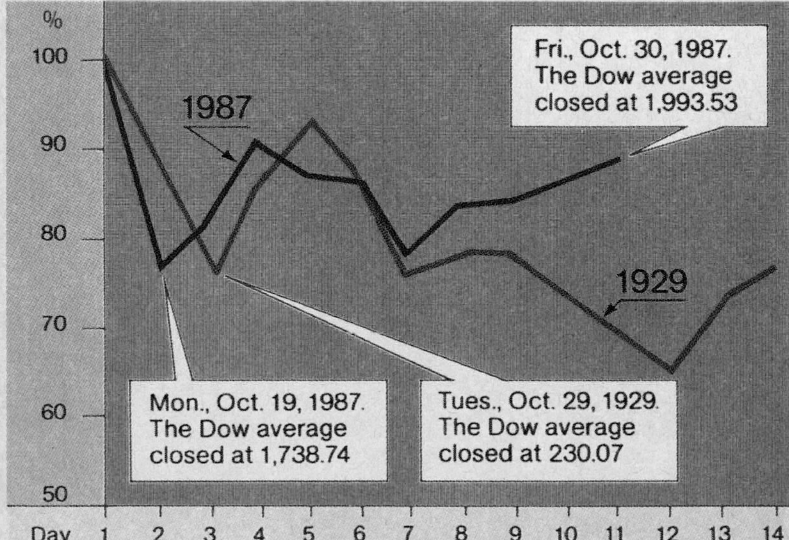

A comparison of the Dow's progression following the crashes of 1929 and 1987.

Market decline almost doubles 1929 figure

Oct 19. Older investors will never forget 1929, and some of them worry that history is repeating itself. When the Dow Jones industrial average dropped more than 500 points today, it lost 22.6 percent of its value. That is almost double the 12.82 percent decline on October 28, 1929.

Some analysts compare today's plunge to the 1929 collapse, which ushered in the Great Depression. The market boomed in the Roaring Twenties, and it boomed again in the eighties. In both decades, debt was high, relations with trading partners became strained, and parts of the economy were weak.

Many economists fear the decline in the market will accelerate a recession, but few seem to think there will be another depression. Most of the economy is still very strong, and unemployment and inflation both remain fairly low. Analysts also point out that safeguards have been built into the system to prevent aftershocks like the ones in 1929.

Wall Street does face a major new threat: the volatility of world markets. New York is now linked by computers to a global market, and stocks change hands around the clock. Nervousness by foreign traders and investors could make things even worse on Wall Street.

1987

NOVEMBER

Su	Mo	Tu	We	Th	Fr	Sa
1	2	3	4	5	6	7
8	9	10	11	12	13	14
15	16	17	18	19	20	21
22	23	24	25	26	27	28
29	30					

2. Washington: William Sessions takes oath as head of FBI.

2. Moscow: Gorbachev denounces crimes of Stalin; praises Khrushchev (→ 12).

5. Washington: Caspar Weinberger quits as secretary of defense.

5. South Africa: African Natl. Congress leader Govan Mbeki, jailed for 23 years, freed.

6. Tokyo: Noboru Takeshita replaces Yasuhiro Nakasone as prime minister.

6. Managua: Pres. Daniel Ortega names Cardinal Obando y Bravo mediator in talks with contras (→ 12/10).

7. Washington: Ginsburg quits as court nominee after admitting he had used marijuana (→ 11).

7. Tunisia: Habib Bourguiba, ruler for 31 years, ousted on grounds of senility.

8. Ulster: 11 killed by I.R.A. bomb at parade for British war dead.

11. Washington: Reagan names Judge Anthony Kennedy to Supreme Court.

11. Washington: Congressional Budget Office reports new tax law will force poor to pay 20% more, rich to pay 20% less.

11. Amman, Jordan: Moderates at Arab summit gain isolation of Iran.

12. Moscow: Boris Yeltsin fired as head of Moscow party for criticizing slow pace of reform.

15. Panama: Ex-military commander says Gen. Noriega has ties to drugs, political assassination, election-rigging (→ 12/3).

21. Washington: White House and Congress agree on plan to reduce deficit by $30 bil. (→ 12/2).

22. Oakdale, Louisiana: Over 1,000 Cuban inmates, facing deportation under new pact, take over detention center (→ 12/4).

24. Chicago: Five in El Rukns street gang convicted of offering terrorist services to Libya in exchange for $2.5 million.

DEATH

25. Harold Washington, first black mayor of Chicago.

Iran-contra report blames President

Nov 18. Seven months after they began hearing testimony on the Iran-contra affair, Senate and House panels have released a report charging President Reagan with "ultimate responsibility" for the scandal. Signed by Democratic majorities on the panels, the report says that if Reagan did not know funds from the Iran arms sales were diverted to the contras, "he should have." The report denounces the administration for allowing "pervasive dishonesty" and "disarray at the highest levels of government."

A minority report, leaked to the press two days earlier, accuses the majority of reaching "hysterical conclusions" and perpetuating "guerrilla warfare" between Congress and the White House. "There was no constitutional crisis," the minority argues, "no systematic disrespect for the rule of law, no grand conspiracy and no administration-wide dishonesty or cover-up." Three of 11 Republicans dissented, siding with the majority.

The president, in both reports, escapes accusations of illegality; the worst damage to him is already past. But Special Prosecutor Lawrence Walsh will be busy in coming months trying to find out who did break the law. Indictments should be handed down next year.

Democratic congressional leaders display their latest masterpiece.

Deng retires, keeps influence in China

Nov 2. Deng Hsiao-ping, having weathered 62 years of turmoil in China, has decided to retire from the Central Committee of the Communist Party. In the last seven years, Deng has steered China along more Western lines. With a variety of capitalist reforms, he has opened China's vast economy to foreign investment and encouraged the growth of small business.

Deng's career spans virtually the entire life of Communist struggle in China. After studying in France, where he became a Communist in the early 1920's, Deng returned to find China embroiled in civil war. As a Red army political officer (1929-1942), he mastered the art of revolutionary politics. Holding high offices during the fifties, he was purged in the Cultural Revolution and again in 1976, but survived to bring China into the 1980's.

Deng, 83, managed to sweep into retirement much of the party's old guard, leaving his restructuring program strengthened. His successor, Prime Minister Zhao Ziyang, in taking office today, proclaimed, "Our goal is common prosperity."

Bloody rampage halts elections in Haiti

Nov 29. Hopes for the first democratic transfer of power in 30 years of Haitian history hit a wall of indiscriminate violence today. The long-awaited election was canceled after gun and machete attacks on polling places killed two dozen voters and wounded at least 60. Many had looked to the vote to quell anarchic violence that has reigned since the ouster of the Duvalier dictatorship 22 months ago. Observers believe the attacks to be the work of the Tontons Macoutes, the Duvaliers' security police. Government troops did little to interfere.

Nov 11. Painted in an asylum in 1889, Vincent van Gogh's "Irises" brought $53.9 million last night at Sotheby's in New York. The estate of Joan Whitney Payson, who bought "Irises" for $100,000 in 1947, gets a profit. The unidentified buyer gets a hedge against a turbulent stock market.

1987

DECEMBER

Su	Mo	Tu	We	Th	Fr	Sa
		1	2	3	4	5
6	7	8	9	10	11	12
13	14	15	16	17	18	19
20	21	22	23	24	25	26
27	28	29	30	31		

1. Washington: NASA awards $5 billion in contracts for space station (→ 29).

2. New York: Shearson Lehman Brothers to buy E.F. Hutton for $1 billion (→ 3).

3. New York: Dow plunges 72.44 to 1,776.53, lowest since October 19th crash.

3. Panama City: Panama orders U.S. Agency for International Development office shut in retaliation for suspension of aid.

6. Washington: 200,000 march for Soviet human rights.

10. Oslo: Arias, on accepting Nobel Prize, urges superpowers leave Central America: "Send our people plowshares" (→ 19).

16. Sicily: 338 convicted in largest Mafia trial ever.

16. U.S.: Ex-Reagan aide Michael Deaver convicted on three counts of perjury.

19. U.S.: Texaco agrees to pay Pennzoil $3 billion, settling three-year-old lawsuit.

19. U.S.: State Dept. says Nicaraguan defector's claim that Managua plans invasion of Latin nations is speculative.

19. Spain: Gary Kasparov defeats Anatoly Karpov to retain world chess title.

21. Philippines: Ferry sinks south of Manila; 1,500 dead.

29. U.S.S.R.: Col. Yuri V. Romanenko returns after record 326 days in space.

29. Russellville, Ark.: R. Gene Simmons Sr. held in killing of 16 as nine more bodies are found.

31. One second added to year to compensate for precession of earth's axis.

CULTURAL EVENTS, 1987

Literature: Tom Wolfe's "Bonfire of the Vanities."

Academia: Ravi Batra's "The Great Depression of 1990"; Allan Bloom's "The Closing of the American Mind."

Music: U2's "The Joshua Tree"; Beatles recorded on compact disc.

Film: Kevin Costner in "The Untouchables"; John Huston's "The Dead."

Nuclear powers sign treaty to cut arms

Gorbachev and Reagan sign history's first pact requiring a cut in nuclear arms.

Dec 10. History was made two days ago in Washington as Soviet leader Mikhail S. Gorbachev and President Reagan signed the first treaty to reduce the size of their countries' nuclear arsenals.

The treaty allows three years for the dismantling of all 1,752 Soviet and 859 American missiles with ranges of 300 to 3,400 miles. And it describes in great detail how inspectors from both countries will ensure that the missiles are smashed, exploded, crushed, burned or launched into oblivion.

Approval in the Senate is expected, despite the opposition of some conservatives who doubt that Soviet compliance can be verified, and fear that removing missiles from Western Europe leaves the area vulnerable to attack by superior Soviet conventional forces.

After the signing in the East Room of the White House, Gorbachev and Reagan exchanged pens as souvenirs. "We can only hope that this history-making agreement will not be an end in itself," Reagan said, "but the beginning of a working relationship that will enable us to tackle ... other issues."

As the two leaders wound up their three-day summit today, signs of progress on at least one other issue emerged. Talks on strategic long-range weapons yielded a compromise limit of 4,900. The issue of Reagan's Strategic Defense Initiative, or "Star Wars," was shelved for now, the two sides agreeing to disagree on whether the 1972 ABM Treaty permits testing.

Regional conflicts, particularly Soviet involvement in Afghanistan, and sensitive human rights issues remained wholly unresolved.

Gorbachev made a great impact on the press and public. On departing today, he leaves behind the image that glasnost's two meanings -- "openness" and "publicity" -- are embodied in its architect. Spontaneous handshaking and a photogenic smile made it hard for some to distinguish between the head of the world's most prominent Communist Party and an American presidential candidate. As political consultant John Deardourff put it, "He's the front-runner this week."

A cold war still rages between Raisa Gorbachev and Nancy Reagan. When asked if she liked the White House, Mrs. Gorbachev replied, "It's an official house ... a human being would like to live in a regular home. This is a museum." Mrs. Reagan furrowed her brow.

The arms pact, eliminating only ten percent of the world's nuclear warheads, may have negligible impact on world peace. But it offers the two leaders significant domestic gains. Reagan, plagued by the Iran-contra scandal, gets an image boost that may help Republicans in next year's presidential election. Gorbachev returns home with his reform plans at least partially vindicated.

Boesky gets 3 years

Dec 18. Ivan Boesky, who gained more than $80 million by trading stocks with inside information, has been sentenced to three years in jail. U.S. Attorney Rudolf Giuliani called the ruling "a heavy sentence," sure to deter white collar crime. Boesky, at the heart of the largest instance of "systemic corruption" in the history of American business, has come to symbolize the excesses of Wall Street's pre-October 19 bull market. He has implicated at least five major brokerage firms and 14 individuals, including Dennis Levine, now in jail, and Martin Siegel, awaiting sentencing.

Gary Hart is back in race, leading in poll

Dec 16. Gary Hart, in a surprise move, re-entered the presidential campaign yesterday. His wife, Lee, at his side, Hart told an audience at the New Hampshire Capitol that other Democrats were skirting the issues, and that his "new ideas" needed a voice. Hart did not, however, give voice to his alleged affair with Donna Rice, the issue that derailed his candidacy in May.

A poll today showed Hart, along with Jesse Jackson, leading the seven Democrats in the race. The others appear resentful. Bruce Babbitt called Hart's move to rejoin the race "arrogance."

Hart, once out, now in again.

Cubans yield two seized detention centers

Firefighters battle flames from outside the walls of Atlanta's federal penitentiary. At least 30 were injured when Cuban inmates took over the prison.

Dec 4. Cuban inmates released 89 hostages today from Atlanta's federal penitentiary, ending an 11-day siege meant to protest a threat of deportation posed by a new U.S.-Cuban immigration pact. Like inmates in Oakdale, Louisiana, who ended a similar uprising five days ago, they were promised individual deportation hearings. Jailed Cubans here hold very few legal rights. Despite repeated protests by civil libertarians, nearly half of the 7,600 inmates selected by the Reagan administration for deportation are being held beyond their prison terms.

South Korean ruling party wins presidency

Dec 18. Roh Tae Woo, the ruling party candidate, has won South Korea's first presidential election in 16 years. The long-awaited vote was marred by fraud charges and questions of what could have been, had Kim Young Sam and Kim Dae Jung not split the opposition. As it was, Roh won with only 36.9 percent of the vote. Kim Young Sam called it a "coup d'etat in the name of election." Protests have been surprisingly limited, though riots have erupted in Kwangju.

James Baldwin dies

Dec 1. Novelist and essayist James Baldwin died today in self-imposed French exile. After moving to France in 1948, Baldwin returned to the United States at the height of the civil rights movement. Though he was accused of lacking militancy during the sixties, two volumes of essays, "The Fire Next Time" and "Nobody Knows My Name," made him a leading literary voice of the movement. Novels like "Go Tell It on the Mountain" have earned him a lasting place in the literary world. "Color is not a human or personal reality," he once wrote. "It is a political reality."

Howard Beach trial

Dec 21. Three white teenagers have been found guilty of manslaughter in the death of a black man in Howard Beach, Queens. The youths have been the object of national attention since they chased Michael Griffith into the path of an onrushing car a year ago. The verdict may not quell the racial tension the case has engendered in New York. Crowds disrupted subways at rush hour today, claiming the ruling was too lenient. At the courtroom, three protesters were carried out, yelling, "Murderers!" Mayor Ed Koch said the verdict was "fair and reasonable."

Israelis quell Arab riots

Dec 25. At least 1,000 Palestinians, says the Israeli army, are spending Christmas in jail for their role in recent protests in the West Bank and Gaza. Two weeks of unrest climaxed Monday when a general strike spread outside the occupied lands to Arabs with Israeli citizenship. "This is unprecedented," said one Arab specialist. "It's the first time the Israeli Arabs are following the Arabs in the territories."

At least 22 Arabs have died in the riots, which many say are worse than previous outbreaks in 1975-76 and 1980-81. But protest is not foreign to the West Bank and Gaza, both won by Israel during the Six Day War in 1967. In the past three years, political strife has caused at least one death nearly every week. And since the Israeli invasion of Lebanon in 1982, demonstrations by Arabs under occupation have risen from 500 to 3,000 per year.

"The difference," says Yehuda Litani, a correspondent for The Jerusalem Post, "is that now it lasts longer, more people are involved, and they are not afraid to confront the army. It's like a fire, it catches and spreads. They're in despair ... they have nothing to lose."

The United Nations, with U.S. assent, criticized Israel for excessive use of force. But it may be Israel has a war inside its borders, not just student unrest. Some 2.1 million Palestinians in Israel, said one analyst, "are in the first stages of a civil uprising." Another journalist said, "The day will come when we'll beg someone to take the Gaza Strip and its problems away from us."

Violin genius Jascha Heifetz dies at 86

Violin virtuoso Heifetz in 1950.

Dec 10. Jascha Heifetz, whose austere perfectionism and unparalleled talent made him master of the violin, is dead. The Russian-born prodigy toured Europe at ten. He practiced with ferocious discipline and risked an image of arrogance to shun publicity. His faithfulness to a composer's intent was rigorous. Heifetz felt great performances should be applauded and bad ones hissed, including his own. "There is no top," he said. "If one thought himself at the pinnacle, he would slide back toward mediocrity."

1987 was biggest recent movie year

As movie audiences grow in size and age, Hollywood's products are increasing in quantity and quality. Michael Douglas was at the center of this year's bountiful lot, starring in "Fatal Attraction," a romantic thriller, and "Wall Street," Oliver Stone's moralistic look at money lust in the 1980's. Vietnam sparked a creative outburst, with Robin Williams in "Good Morning Vietnam," and Stanley Kubrick's "Full Metal Jacket" following the 1986 release of Stone's "Platoon." The historical epic also fared well. Bernardo Bertolucci's "The Last Emperor" and Steven Spielberg's "Empire of the Sun" both focused on 20th-Century China.

Spielberg's "Empire of the Sun."

General Index

The Index provides rapid access to the information you seek. Each entry is followed by a date indicating the month and year of an event. For example, 3/85 means the event is found in March 1985.

A

- U.S. sets limit of 40 mph to save tires 3/42
- Gas is rationed in the U.S. 12/42
- Renault to be nationalized in France 11/44
- France nationalizes Renault 1/45
- Car phones 5/46
- George Robson wins Indy 500 5/46
- Henry Ford dies 4/47
- Mauri Rose wins Indy 500 5/47
- Ettore Bugatti dies 8/47
- Wilhelm von Opel dies 5/48
- Mauri Rose takes Indy 500 5/48
- Debut of huge tail fins 9/48
- Bill Holland wins Indy 500 5/49
- Biggest G.M. dividend 11/49

1950 to 1959

- Cadillac builds one-piece windshields 2/50
- Johnny Parsons wins Indy 500 5/50
- Ferdinand Porsche, VW designer, dies 1/51
- 1951 Packard convertible makes debut 2/51
- G.M. reports $834 mil. profit for 1950 3/51
- Lee Wallard wins Indy 500 5/51
- 1951 Cunningham, Model C-1 7/51
- G.M. displays Le Sabre, car of future 7/51
- N.Y.C. puts up "Don't Walk" signs 2/52
- Troy Ruttman wins Indy 500 5/52
- G.M. offers cars with air cooling 7/52
- Worst U.S. bus crash takes 28 lives 8/52
- Studebaker Starliner Coupe 2/53
- Bill Vukovich wins Indy 500 5/53
- American Motors merger 4/54
- Kaiser-Darrin 4/54
- Bill Vukovich wins Indy 500 5/54
- Chevrolet introduces V-8 engines 10/54
- G.M. produces its 50 millionth car 11/54
- Bill Vukovich wins Indy 500 5/55
- 80 killed at Le Mans 6/55
- Pat Flaherty wins Indy 500 5/56
- $33 billion for U.S. highways 6/56
- Drag racing popular 9/56
- Sam Hanks wins Indy 500 5/57
- The Edsel makes debut 8/57
- Jimmy Bryan wins Indy 500 5/58
- Rodger Ward wins Indy 500 5/59
- Edsel's demise 11/59

1960 to 1969

- Schock and Moll win Monte Carlo Rally 1/60
- Car with battery recharged by sun 3/60
- Jim Rathmann wins Indy 500 5/60
- Marvin Panch sets speed record 2/61
- Count von Trips killed in Grand Prix 10/61
- Rodger Ward wins Indy 500 5/62
- Thunderbird 4/63
- Parnelli Jones wins Indy 500 5/63
- Ford introduces the Mustang 4/64
- A.J. Foyt wins Indy 500 5/64
- Art Arfons sets land speed record 10/64
- Land speed record set by Breedlove 10/64
- Jim Clark wins Indy 500 5/65
- Arfons leads speed rivalry at 576 mph 11/65
- G.M. apologizes to Nader in Congress 3/66
- G.M. recalls 1.5 million 4/66
- Nader criticizes Rolls Royce 5/66
- Graham Hill wins Indy 500 5/66
- Art Arfons hurt in crash 11/66
- G.M. recalls 269,000 cars 1/67
- Ford recalls 217,000 cars 2/67
- A.J. Foyt wins Indy 500 5/67
- G.M. recalls 1.1 million Chevrolets 10/67
- Bobby Unser wins Indy 500 5/68
- G.M. recalls 4.9 million cars 2/69
- G.M. recalls 1.1 million cars 3/69

1970 to 1987

- G.M. redesigns autos for unleaded gas 2/70
- Al Unser wins Indy 500 5/70
- U.K. gives $100 mil. to Rolls Royce Co. 11/70
- Lee A. Iacocca named president of Ford 12/70
- Nixon signs bill to cut auto fumes 12/70
- Rolls-Royce declares bankruptcy 2/71
- U.K. offers Rolls-Royce $144 million 3/71
- Ford recalls the Pinto 3/71
- Al Unser wins Indy 500 5/71
- Georg von Opel dies 8/71
- G.M. recalls 6.7 million Chevrolets 12/71
- Mark Donahue wins Indy 500 5/72
- Hitler's Mercedes brings $153,000 1/73
- Richard Petty wins Daytona 500 2/73
- Gordon Johncock wins Indy 500 5/73
- 55-mph speed limit in U.S. 1/74
- Richard Petty wins Daytona 500 2/74
- Peter Revson dies in auto crash 3/74
- Johnny Rutherford wins Indy 500 5/74
- Auto makers offer rebates 1/75
- Volkswagen to build U.S. plant 4/76
- Johnny Rutherford takes Indy 500 5/76
- Chrysler gets $4.9 billion contract 11/76
- Libya buys one-tenth of Fiat 12/76
- A.J. Foyt wins Indy 500 fourth time 5/77
- Volkswagen phases Beetle out 8/77
- First VW is produced in America 4/78
- Al Unser wins third Indy 500 5/78
- Rick Mears wins Indy 500 5/79
- Chrysler asks $1 billion in U.S. aid 7/79
- Britain ends MG sportscar production 9/79
- House and Senate vote Chrysler aid 12/79
- Johnny Rutherford wins Indy 500 5/80
- U.S. cars record 30 mpg 9/80
- Richard Petty wins Daytona 500 2/81
- Bobby Unser wins Indy 500 5/81
- DeLorean car plant in receivership 2/82
- Gordon Johncock wins Indy 500 5/82
- G.M. and Toyota begin joint venture 2/83
- Tom Sneva wins Indy 500 5/83
- Rick Mears wins Indy 500 5/84
- N.Y. has first mandatory seat belt law 7/84
- Mitsubishi to open plant in U.S. 4/85
- Danny Sullivan wins Indy 500 5/85
- Bobby Rahal wins Indy 500 5/86
- Al Unser Sr. wins Indy 500 fourth time 5/87
- Henry Ford II dies 9/87
- Jeep a toy for upwardly mobile 9/87

Aviation (see also Space Exploration)

1900 to 1909

- Zeppelin airship makes first flight 7/00
- Santos-Dumont crashes dirigible 7/01
- Wright bros. plane flown by G. Weisskopf 8/01
- Santos-Dumont flies dirigible 30 minutes 10/01
- Deutsch de la Meurthe award 10/01
- Langley plane fails in flight try 10/03
- Lebaudy bros. set record in dirigible 11/03
- Wright bros. fly heavier-than-air plane 12/03
- Wright bros. show off control of plane 9/04
- T. Baldwin's unmanned airship disappears 11/04
- John Baldwin killed 8/05
- Orville Wright flies 30 minutes 10/05
- Second dirigible flight in Switzerland 11/05
- Samuel Pierpont Langley dies 2/06
- First flight with tires 3/06
- Santos-Dumont's first public flight 9/06
- Lahm wins Gordon Bennett balloon race 10/06
- Nine balloons race in St. Louis 10/07
- First helicopter flight 11/07
- Zeppelin to build dirigible for 100 1/08
- Henri Farman flies over one km. 1/08
- Wright brothers ask patent for plane 5/08
- U.S. Army requests plane from Wright 8/08
- First to stay aloft one hour 9/08
- First death in heavier-than-air craft 9/08
- Wright aloft one hour with passenger 10/08
- Planes to be built commercially in U.S. 3/09
- Orville Wright aloft 1 hr. 20 mins. 7/09
- Louis Bleriot first over English Channel 7/09
- Roger Sommer tops Wright for time aloft 8/09
- Glenn Curtis wins International Cup 8/09
- French women apply for instruction 9/09
- Wright wants foreign planes out of U.S. 9/09
- First show is at Madison Sq. Garden 9/09
- O. Wright sets new altitude record 10/09
- Wright bros. to manufacture planes 11/09

1910 to 1919

- Hubert Latham soars to 3,300 feet 1/10
- Wilbur Wright asks for strict patent law 1/10
- Miss de Laroche first woman pilot 3/10
- Henri Fabre makes first seaplane flight 3/10
- First conference on air traffic, Paris 5/10
- First night flight by Farman & Sommer 5/10
- First round-trip over Channel 6/10
- Deutschland 1st to transport passengers 6/10
- Deutschland wrecked by gales 6/10
- German aviator Oscar Erbslok killed 7/10
- Aviator Charles S. Rolls killed in plane 7/10
- First American crosses English Channel 8/10
- Zeppelin VI engulfed in flames 9/10
- First Alps crossing 9/10
- Wellman leaves N.J. for Europe 10/10
- First dirigible flight over Channel 10/10
- Ralph Johnstone dies 11/10
- Moisant dies in plane crash 12/10
- Hoxsey dies in plane crash 12/10
- First takeoff and landing from a ship 1/11
- First non-stop London to Paris 4/11
- First U.S. transcontinental flight 5/11
- Zeppelin Deutschland crashes on 1st trip 5/11
- Harry Atwood, 1st flight over Manhattan 7/11
- Oliesiagers flies non-stop 388 miles 7/11
- First U.S. woman gets pilot's license 8/11
- Longest flight, St. Louis-N.Y. 8/11
- First military use of aviation 8/11
- Colliex pilots first amphibious plane 8/11
- U.K. opens airmail service 9/11
- 2nd international meet opens in New York 9/11
- Calbraith Rodgers hits record 1,398 mi. 10/11
- World aviation deaths total 100 to date 10/11
- Helene Dutrieu wins Femina Cup 12/11
- First flying-boat airplane 1/12
- First in-flight parachute jump 3/12
- Italy 1st to use dirigible for military 3/12
- Henri Seimet, London-Paris non stop 3/12
- First woman crosses Channel in dirigible 4/12
- Calbraith Rodgers dies in plane crash 4/12
- First wireless received on plane 4/12
- First woman pilots plane across Channel 4/12
- First West-East transcontinental flight 5/12
- Wilbur Wright dies 5/12
- Zeppelin SZIII burns in hangar 6/12
- Aviator Hubert Latham killed 6/12
- Harriet Quimby dies 7/12
- Airmail service between London and Paris 8/12
- Roland Garros soars to 13,200 feet 9/12
- J. Vedrines is first to fly over 100 mph 9/12
- First all-metal plane flown in France 11/12
- Eugene Gilbert, non-stop France to Spain 4/13
- Igor Sikorsky, first four-engine plane 5/13
- First crossing of Florida Straits 5/13
- Brindejone des Moulinais 7/13
- Adolphe Pegoud flies upside down 9/13
- Frenchman Pegoud first to loop the loop 9/13
- Friedrich flies Paris-Berlin w/passenger 9/13
- First flight of Zeppelin LZ, largest yet 9/13
- Roland Garros flies across Mediterranean 9/13
- Passenger service Tampa-St. Petersburg 1/14
- First woman loops the loop 1/14
- Sikorsy carries 17 in twin-engine plane 2/14
- Flying boat America tested 6/14
- French reconnaissance over Germany 7/14
- First German air raids on Britain 1/15
- Zeppelin bombs Paris 3/15
- Zeppelins bomb London 6/15
- Zeppelin downed in London 9/16
- U.S. to build 375 new planes 10/16
- First U.S. training camp 7/17
- 37 die in London air raid 7/17
- France downs five Zeppelins 10/17
- U.S. planes leave for front 2/18
- Red Baron downed 4/18
- "Jennys" fight in France 5/18
- Rickenbacker downs 26th German 10/18
- First commercial London-Paris flight 2/19
- First intl. U.S. airmail 3/19
- Dirigible service Rome to Naples 4/19
- First transatlantic flight 5/19
- Hawker disappears on transatlantic bid 5/19
- Britain builds largest plane 6/19
- First non-stop transatlantic flight 6/19
- British dirigible crosses Atlantic 7/19
- First stowaway 7/19
- France lost 60% of air force in WWI 8/19
- U.S. ocean-to-ocean air race 10/19
- First Australia-to-England flight 12/19

1920 to 1929

- First flight over Sahara 2/20
- Adrienne Bolland crosses Channel 8/20
- First contract intl. airmail route 10/20
- U.S. sells flying boats to spur aviation 1/21
- Cub, Napier aircraft engine, tested 2/21
- Airmail plane record S.F.-N.Y. 2/21
- Laura Bromwell, 199 loop-the-loops 5/21
- Laura Bromwell killed in plane crash 6/21
- Harry Hawker dies in explosion 7/21
- Dirigible ZR II explodes in trial flight 8/21
- N.Y. to Nome, Alaska 8/21
- Jimmy Doolittle flies Calif. to Florida 9/21
- First successful helium dirigible 12/21
- Dirigible Roma explodes, killing 34 2/22
- Helicopter ascends at right angles 6/22
- German sailplane, longest glider flight 8/22
- Doolittle flies coast-coast in 22.5 hrs. 9/22
- First flight by woman across U.S. 10/22
- Sadi Lecointe flies 208 mph 1/23
- Sadi Lecointe reaches 234 mph 2/23
- First non-stop transcontinental flight 5/23
- Sabena founded 5/23
- U.S. Lt. Sanderson flies 238 mph 9/23
- Goodyear to man Zeppelin dirigibles 11/23
- U.S. aviator H.J. Brown flies 259 mph 11/23
- 4 Douglass planes off for world flight 3/24
- World flier Martin in Alaska after crash 5/24
- U.S. Army planes complete globe flight 9/24
- Boston-N.Y. round trip in 58 minutes 9/24
- American globe fliers return to Boston 9/24
- Dirigible flies 5,000 miles to N.Y. 10/24
- Flights to Congo from Belgium 2/25
- New non-stop record by French 8/25
- Shenandoah explodes 9/25
- Billy Mitchell court-martialled 11/25
- Lufthansa founded 1/26
- Coolidge opposes large air force 2/26
- Amundsen and Ellsworth down over Alaska 5/26
- Pilots and planes need license 5/26
- Richard Byrd flies over North Pole 5/26
- Army Air Corps formed 7/26
- Northwest Airways founded 8/26
- Pan American Airlines formed 3/27
- Balloon record of 28,000 feet 3/27
- Two killed planning N.Y.-to-Paris flight 4/27
- Lindbergh crosses the Atlantic 5/27
- Charles Nungesser lost crossing Atlantic 5/27
- Belgium decorates Lindbergh 5/27
- Second transatlantic flight 6/27
- Lindbergh wins $25,000 for Atlantic hop 6/27
- First flight California to Hawaii 6/27
- Lindbergh returns to U.S. 6/27
- U.S. develops giant bomber 7/27
- Race from Hawaii to California 8/27
- Round-the-world flight reaches London 8/27
- Round-the-world flight reaches India 9/27
- Round-the-world trip reaches Hong Kong 9/27
- Round-the-world flight stopped by storm 9/27
- Ruth Elder fails in Atlantic crossing 10/27
- First intl. commercial flight 10/27
- Balloon pilot dies at 44,000 feet 11/27
- Lindbergh joins Pan Am 1/28
- Air service U.S. to Cuba 1/28
- First east-to-west Atlantic hop 4/28
- First round-the-world flight ends 4/28
- Italian dirigible crashes at North Pole 5/28
- Amelia Earhart first woman over Atlantic 6/28
- Longest sea flight 6/28
- Earhart welcomed back to U.S. 7/28
- Polish fliers rescued 8/28
- New autogiro plane 9/28
- Graf Zeppelin's first N.Y. trip 10/28
- Coast to coast in a day and an hour 10/28
- Ship-to-shore airmail 9/28
- Zeppelin flies 4,400 miles in 69 hours 11/28
- 319-mph speed record in Britain 11/28
- Army plane aloft 150 hours 1/29
- Byrd explores Antarctica by plane 1/29
- Lindbergh escapes plane crash 2/29
- First movie on plane 2/29
- 13 dead in U.S. plane crash 3/29
- New record, Britain to India 4/29
- British plane crash, seven dead 6/29
- First coast-to-coast service in U.S. 7/29
- Zeppelin trip around the world 8/29
- Eight dead in Mexican crash 9/29
- First flight using instruments 9/29
- First rocket plane 9/29
- Coast-to-coast service, 36 hours 10/29
- Bryd finishes air survey of Antarctic 11/29

1930 to 1939

- N.Y.-to-West Coast fare is $159.92 1/30
- Amelia Earhart flies record 171 mph 1/30
- Lindbergh flies cross-country 1/30
- 16 die in plane crash in Los Angeles 4/30
- Airmail link between Paris and Brazil 5/30
- Non-stop flight from Ireland to N.Y. 6/30
- U.S. aviation pioneer Glenn Curtiss dies 7/30
- Endurance fliers land after 647 hours 8/30
- Pan Am merger makes largest airline 8/30
- Paris-N.Y. in 37 hours 9/30
- German Graf Zeppelin arrives in U.S.S.R. 9/30
- TWA formed through merger of 3 airlines 10/30
- Ten Italians make transatlantic flight 1/31
- Ruth Nichols sets speed record 4/31
- Piccard balloon reaches 52,462 feet 5/31
- English Channel crossed in glider 6/31
- Post & Gatty leave on round-world flight 6/31
- Post & Gatty end round-world flight 7/31
- TWA begins first air-freight service 7/31
- Distance record of 5,011 miles 7/31
- Dornier Do-X makes Atlantic crossing 8/31
- Jimmy Doolittle crosses country 9/31
- Youngest pilot soloes biplane in N.Y. 9/31
- First non-stop over Pacific 10/31
- Akron flies with record 207 aboard 11/31
- Graf Zeppelin makes 1st S. America trip 3/32
- Amelia Earhart 1st woman to fly Atlantic 5/32
- Alberto Santos-Dumont dies 7/32
- Unmanned balloon reaches 17 miles 8/32
- August Piccard reaches 10 miles 8/32
- Doolittle first to fly over 300 mph 9/32
- Dirigible Akron crashes at sea 4/33
- First flight over Mt. Everest 4/33
- Dirigible Macon makes maiden flight 4/33
- L.A.-to-N.Y. flight record 6/33
- DC-1 passes tests 7/33
- Worldwide acceptance gained 7/33
- Roscoe Turner flies N.Y. to L.A. 7/33
- Amelia Earhart flies L.A. to Newark 7/33
- Round world in 17 days, 19 hours 7/33
- Air France incorporated 8/33
- Lindberghs complete 30,000-mile trip 12/33
- TWA cuts rail connections on coast trips 5/34
- TWA begins commercial service on DC-2 5/34
- American Airline inaugurates sleepers 7/34
- Roscoe Turner flies N.Y. to L.A. 9/34
- Balloon climbs to 24 miles 3/35
- Pan Am starts Orient air service 4/35
- Biggest plane crashes, 49 dead in Moscow 5/35
- Rogers and Post dead in crash 8/35
- Howard Hughes plane hits 351 mph 9/35
- Balloon record, 74,000 feet 11/35
- First hostesses 12/35
- DC-3 makes first flight 12/35
- Unmanned balloon soars to 25 miles 2/36
- Hindenburg arrives in New York 5/36
- First commercial DC-3 flight 6/36
- First woman to cross Atlantic east-west 9/36
- British order 300 planes from Boeing 10/36
- Hughes flies L.A. to N.Y. under 8 hrs. 1/37
- First Superfortress 4/37
- First commercial transpacific flight 4/37
- Hindenburg blows up 5/37
- Hyrdogen zeppelins banned in Germany 5/37
- First transpolar flight 6/37
- Amelia Earhart lost at sea 7/37
- Jacqueline Cochran sets speed record 9/37
- Clipper 314 flying boat 4/38
- Civil Aeronautics Authority 6/38
- "Wrong-Way" Corrigan flies to Ireland 7/38
- Hughes sets round-the-world record 7/38
- Altimeter invented 10/38
- U.S. orders 571 planes 4/39
- Douglas DC-4 flies Chicago to N.Y. 6/39
- First transatlantic passenger flight 7/39
- Huge U.S. order for planes 8/39
- LaGuardia airport dedicated 10/39
- Endurance record, 30 days 10/39

1940 to 1949

- 600-mph barrier broken by Bell Airacobra 2/40
- LaGuardia airport officially opens 3/40
- Jacqueline Cochran in U.S Air Force 9/42
- US Air Force gets first jet 1/44
- Pan Am announces round-the-world flight 6/45
- DC-4 begins Pan Am service 10/45
- First refrigerator plane 11/45
- British jet hits 606 mph 11/45
- Five hours across U.S. 12/45
- Half-hour New York to D.C. 4/46
- First jet fighter 5/46
- Pilot ejector seat 8/46
- Navy plane sets distance record 10/46
- Worst crash kills 39 in Newfoundland 10/46
- 53 die in Bogota air crash 2/47
- Round-the-world flight, 78 hours 4/47
- Worst air crash takes 40 in N.Y. 5/47
- William Odom, round-world in 73 hours 8/47
- Automatic pilot invented 9/47
- Chuck Yeager breaks sound barrier 10/47
- U.S. Air Force independent of Army 10/47
- Hughes' Spruce Goose takes short hop 11/47
- Orville Wright dies 1/48
- Jets drive planes much faster 2/48
- SAS formed 4/48
- Idlewild Airport opens in New York 7/48
- Four hours across U.S. 2/49
- First non-stop, round-the-world flight 3/49
- Berlin Airlift 4/49
- Comet, first jet airliner, tested 7/49
- X-1 soars to 63,000 feet 8/49
- 149 killed by accidents in one month 11/49

1950 to 1959

- 80 killed in Wales in worst air crash 3/50
- First turbojet transport plane, Avro 4/50
- N.W. Airlines DC-4 crashes killing 55 6/50
- C-46 crashes, killing 29 off Florida 6/50
- 180 lost in plane crashes in one month 6/50
- B-29 carrying A-bomb crashes in Calif. 8/50
- Avro jet Chicago-N.Y. in record time 1/51
- N.Y.-to-London record of 7 hrs., 48 min. 1/51
- James Jabara world's first jet ace 5/51
- United Air flights grounded by strike 6/51
- Skyrocket plane climbs to 13.7 miles 8/51
- Viking rocket reaches record 135 miles 8/51
- DC-6B plane hits hill, killing 50 8/51
- 56 killed as C-46 crashes after takeoff 12/51
- Prototype of Vickers A-bomb jet crashes 1/52
- Third crash in 2 months kills 42 in N.J. 2/52
- DC-4 crashes, killing 52 in Puerto Rico 4/52
- C-46 crashes in L.A., killing 29 4/52
- Air France plane attacked by Soviets 4/52
- TWA starts first tourist class service 5/52
- First commercial jet service in U.K. 5/52
- Starfire F-94C supersonic jet 7/52
- U.S. Sikorsky H-19 copters over Atlantic 7/52
- Over Atlantic and back in eight hours 8/52
- Supersonic DH-110 explodes, killing 25 9/52
- Helicopter mail & parcel service starts 10/52
- Pan Am becomes 1st to buy jet transports 10/52
- SAS opens Canada-Europe route 11/52
- U.S. C-124 Globemaster disappears 11/52
- Navy's Viking 9 reaches record 135 miles 12/52
- Worst plane crash kills 84 12/52

D

F

agreement 3/06
- King of Cambodia visits 7/06
- Control of New Hebrides with U.K. 10/06
- Pope's envoy driven from France 12/06
- Abyssinian agreement 12/06
- Pope rips separation of church and state 1/07
- Occupation of Oudja in Morocco 3/07
- Belgium rebuked on Congo 5/07
- Trade accord with Japan 5/07
- Pact of Cartagena 5/07
- Morocco bombed 8/07
- French priest killed in China 9/07
- Parliament criticizes war in Morocco 2/08
- Troops to Morocco 3/08
- President Fallieres meets Russian czar 7/08
- Opposition to new sultan in Morocco 9/08
- Condition for sultan's recognition 9/08
- Foreign Legion deserters arrested 9/08
- Casablanca affair settled 11/08
- German interests in Morocco recognized 2/09

1910 to 1919
- French Equatorial Africa 1/10
- Austro-Hungarian plan to annex Serbia 1/10
- Morocco signs accord 3/10
- Occupation of Agadir in Morocco 12/10
- Troops to Fez, Morocco 4/11
- Protest over Spanish in Morocco 6/11
- Support from Britain in Morocco 7/11
- Deal with Germany over Morocco 11/11
- King Peter I of Serbia pays visit 11/11
- Restriction of whale fishing 12/11
- Ratification of Moroccan accord 12/11
- Morocco taken over in Fez pact 3/12
- Morocco declared a protectorate 7/12
- Naval convention with Russia 7/12
- Thousands in Paris acclaim King George V 4/14
- Poincare to Russia over Balkans crisis 7/14
- Germany declares war 8/14
- French invade Alsace 8/14
- France declares war on Austria-Hungary 8/14
- Germany invades Belgium and France 8/14
- Capital moves from Paris to Bordeaux 9/14
- Battle of the Marne ends 9/14
- Declaration of war on Turkey 11/14
- Govt. returns to Paris 12/14
- Germans counter La Basse canal offense 1/15
- Germans take trenches at Soissons 1/15
- Gallipoli bombarded 2/15
- 20,000 Germans captured 2/15
- Support for Russia's Dardenelles claim 3/15
- British attack Neuve Chapelle 3/15
- Champagne offensive called off 3/15
- Attack on Woevre 4/15
- Heavy losses at Alsace-Lorraine 4/15
- 10,000 lost along Ypres 5/15
- Failure at Artois 6/15
- New Allied offensive 9/15
- 100,000 lost at Artois 10/15
- Troops land in Greece 10/15
- Resolve to retake Alsace-Lorraine 11/15
- Pushed out of Serbia 12/15
- Major German offense at Verdun 2/16
- Petain takes control of troops 2/16
- Recapture of Fort Douamont 3/16
- Defense Minister Joseph Gallieni resigns 3/16
- New German drive at Verdun 3/16
- Ottoman Empire divided with British 3/16
- Third German offensive at Verdun 4/16
- Petain commands all French troops 5/16
- Fort Douamont lost to Germany 5/16
- General Gallieni dies 5/16
- Mecca urged to claim independence 6/16
- Surrender at Fort Vaux 6/16
- Czechoslovakia recognized 9/16
- Greek navy taken over 10/16
- German line broken at Verdun 10/16
- Fort Vaux retaken 11/16
- Massive death toll at Somme 11/16
- Death count at Verdun 12/16
- Robert Georges Nivelle new commander 12/16
- Nivelle offensive launched 4/17
- Nivelle offensive fails 4/17
- Mutinies following Neville debacle 5/17
- First U.S. troops dispatched 5/17
- U.S. troops land 6/17
- Mata Hari sentenced to death 7/17
- German attack on Champagne fails 9/17
- Return of Alsace-Lorraine demanded 9/17
- U.S. troops to front lines 10/17
- Mata Hari executed 10/17
- Five zeppelins downed 10/17
- British support claim to Alsace-Lorraine 1/18
- Ferdinand Foch to lead armies 3/18
- Huge German offensive 3/18
- Austria-Hungary supports claims 4/18
- German advance on Somme halted 4/18
- Germans halted at Chateau-Thierry 6/18
- 8,000 Germans captured at Aisne 8/18
- Germany surrenders 11/18
- Germany quits Alsace-Lorraine 11/18
- Treaty of Versailles signed 6/19
- 60% of air force in lost in WWI 8/19
- Monument to U.S. soldiers 9/19
- Versailles treaty ratified 10/19
- Demobilization 10/19

1920 to 1929
- Last U.S. troops leave 1/20
- League of Nations holds first meeting 1/20
- Occupation of the Ruhr 4/20
- Hungary signs Treaty of Trianon 6/20
- Mandate over Syria 7/20
- Lebanon proclaimed independent 9/20
- Govt. takes mandate for Togo 9/20
- Plans for occupation of mines in Ruhr 4/21
- Compromise with U.K. on Silesia 7/21
- Ankara accord signed with Kemal 10/21
- Alliance with U.K. extended 2/22
- Syrian mandate given by League 7/22
- Occupation of Ruhr 1/23
- Vehicles requisitioned in Dortmund 2/23
- Maxime Weygand named high comm. in Syria 4/23
- French execute German officer in Ruhr 5/23
- Trade barrier set between Ruhr & Germany 6/23
- All Ruhr industries to be seized 6/23
- Belleau Wood dedicated to U.S. soldiers 7/23
- U.K. condemns Ruhr occupation 8/23
- World Court arbitration on Ruhr barred 8/23
- Ruhr opened to 210,000 German exiles 6/24
- U.S.S.R. recognized 10/24
- German security pact accepted 6/25
- Accord with Spain on Morocco 6/25
- Uprising in Syria 7/25
- Druze kill 200 in Syria 8/25
- Bombardment of Syria 10/25
- Peace treaty with Germans 10/25
- Marshal Lyautey returns 10/25
- 42 soldiers killed in Syria 3/26
- Meetings with Moroccans and Spanish 4/26
- Abd el Krim gives up 5/26
- Damascus bombed 5/26
- Moroccan capital captured 5/26
- Druze crushed in Syria 7/26
- Sacco, Vanzetti protest at U.S. Embassy 10/26
- Talks with Spain on Morocco 2/27
- Crowds flock to American Legion parade 9/27
- Arbitration treaty with U.S. 2/28
- Kellogg-Briand Treaty signed 8/28
- Germany cancels concessions in Rhine 9/28
- Naval limitations rejected by U.S. 9/28
- Briand proposes European unification 9/29
- Kellogg-Briand pact called weak 12/29

1930 to 1939
- Constitution granted to Syria 5/30
- Troops evacuate Rhineland 6/30
- Non-aggression pact with U.S.S.R. 11/32
- Leon Trotsky granted asylum 6/33
- Trotsky and wife arrive in Marseilles 7/33
- Trotsky's political asylum canceled 4/34
- Yugoslav King Alexander killed 10/34
- Agreement with Italy on Africa policy 1/35
- Saar Basin transferred to Germany 3/35
- Alliance against Germany 3/35
- Mutual-aid pact with Soviets 5/35
- Nazis enter Rhineland 3/36
- Naval accord with U.K. and U.S. 3/36
- British asked to guard Belgium 4/36
- Non-intervention in Spanish Civil War 8/36
- Independence promised to Syria, Lebanon 9/36
- 29 American volunteers for Spain caught 4/37
- 6,000 Spanish Loyalists seek refuge 3/38
- Sudetenland conceded to Germans 9/38
- Partial mobilization 9/38
- Reich aide shot to death 11/38
- Italy wants Corsica and Tunisia 11/38
- Friendship pact signed with Germany 12/38
- Italy disavows 1935 pact 12/38
- Premier Daladier goes to Africa 1/39
- U.S. planes acquired 1/39
- Franco recognized 2/39
- Japan occupies part of French Indochina 2/39
- Petain ambassador to Spain 3/39
- Japan annexes seven French islands 3/39
- Mutual-aid pact with Turkey 6/39
- Delegation to Moscow to discuss alliance 7/39
- Ready for war over Danzig 7/39
- German troops rush West 9/39
- British send troops 9/39
- Hitler's peace plan refused 10/39
- Nazis routed in tank battle 10/39
- Nazis attack on Western Front 10/39

1940 to 1949
- U.S. envoy Welles meets with Daladier 3/40
- Gen. Maxime Weygand new Allied chief 5/40
- Paris falls to Nazis 6/40
- French sign armistice with Italians 6/40
- French and Germans sign an armistice 6/40
- U.K. destroys French fleet in Algeria 7/40
- Reich annexes Alsace-Lorraine 7/40
- Vichy cedes Tonkin base to Japanese 8/40
- Cameroons and Tahiti join Free France 8/40
- Germans require aid to occupying troops 9/40
- Part of Laos yielded to Thailand 3/41
- Vichy quits League of Nations 4/41
- Pact with Japan on Indochina 5/41
- Vichyites surrender Syria to the Allies 6/41
- Petain supports Nazi Europe 8/41
- U.K. raids St. Nazaire, Nazi sub base 3/42
- Germans release first French POWs 8/42
- Eighth Air Force raids Nazis in Rouen 8/42
- Laval orders French to work in Germany 10/42
- Vichy breaks off relations with U.S. 11/42
- Allied bombing raid 12/42
- Germans tear down old port of Marseilles 2/43
- Allied air raid kills 1,150 in Nantes 9/43
- Corsica first territory liberated 12/43
- U.S. air raids 12/43
- Nazis wipe out Maquis unit 3/44
- De Gaulle becomes Free French chief 4/44
- French serving with Nazis meet in Paris 4/44
- U.S. planes blast Kiel & Pas de Calais 5/44
- Allies bomb Lyons, Nice, Marseilles 5/44
- Rommel leaves for Germany 6/44
- Allies take Bayeux 6/44
- De Gaulle lands in Normandy 6/44
- Allies land in Normandy 6/44
- Allies take Cherbourg 6/44
- U.S. takes St. Lo junction 7/44
- Operation Cobra begins in Brittany 7/44
- French tanks lead Allies into Paris 8/44
- Allies land in Provence 8/44
- U.S. paratroopers take St. Tropez 8/44
- Allies force German surrender in Toulon 8/44
- Americans storm Sedan 9/44
- Americans capture Lyons 9/44
- Allies recognize de Gaulle govt. 10/44
- Occupation zone in Germany demanded 11/44
- Leclerc's troops enter Strasbourg 11/44
- France signs U.N. declaration 1/45
- Germany surrenders 5/45
- Algeria rebels 5/45
- Syria and Lebanon assert independence 5/45
- Damascus Parliament seized 5/45
- Germany divided into four zones 7/45
- Troops land in Indochina 9/45
- Saigon occupied 9/45
- Nuremberg trials begin 11/45
- Agreement on pullout from Syria, Lebanon 12/45
- Ho Chi Minh recognized in Vietnam 3/46
- Fleet arrives in Vietnam 3/46
- Talks with Vietnam open in Dalat 4/46
- Withdrawal from Syria 5/46
- Economic reunification of Germany barred 8/46
- Talks with Vietnam fail 9/46
- Shelling kills 6,000 in Vietnam 11/46
- Vietnam wants peace talks 12/46
- Full-scale war in Vietnam 12/46
- Cambodian rebellion suppressed 1/47
- Pact with British to curb Germany 2/47
- Alliance with British 3/47
- Madagascar revolt put down 4/47
- Strike in Tunisia 8/47
- Pact with Belgium, Holland 3/48
- Troops to stay in Germany 6/48
- Merger of German zones with U.K., U.S. 4/49
- Cambodia gets freedom within Union 11/49

1950 to 1959
- Angry at U.K. recognition of Red China 1/50
- Soviet recognition of Vietnam protested 1/50
- Four Viet Minh battalions attack French 5/50
- U.S. offers military aid to France 5/50
- Schuman plan drafted in Europe 5/50
- West Germany recognized by U.S. and U.K. 9/50
- French abandon China border to Viet Minh 10/50
- Protests welcome Ike to defense talks 1/51
- French break Viet Minh attack on Hanoi 1/51
- Ike opens NATO quarters in Rocquencourt 7/51
- Tunisia request for autonomy turned down 11/51
- Operation Lorraine in Vietnam 10/52
- De Gaulle blasts European Defense Comm. 2/53
- Ike offers France more aid in Vietnam 3/53
- French-led forces evacuate Northern Laos 4/53
- Ike announces $60 mil. aid for French 5/53
- Sihanouk yields Cambodia to army 6/53
- Cambodia granted control of courts 8/53
- Operation Seagull in Tonkin Delta 10/53
- Laos given independence 10/53
- French capture Dien Bien Phu 11/53
- Big Three Conference in Bermuda 12/53
- Big Four meet on arms in West Berlin 1/54
- French brace for Dien Bien Phu assault 2/54
- Vietnam & France open talks on Indochina 3/54
- Dien Bien Phu falls to Viet Minh 5/54
- French and Chinese agree on Indochina 6/54
- French sign Indochina truce 7/54
- France offers automony to Tunisia 7/54
- State of emergency in Algeria 3/55
- Civil war in Vietnam 4/55
- Diem takes control in Saigon 5/55
- Full sovereignty for W. Germany 5/55
- Troops evacuated from Haiphong 5/55
- Tunisia autonomous 6/55
- Big Four summit in Geneva 7/55
- Tanks halt Moroccan riots 7/55
- Algerian rebels launch big attack 8/55
- Gen. Grandval resigns 8/55
- Hundreds killed in Algeria and Morocco 8/55
- Draftees refuse to go to Algeria 9/55
- Sultan restored in Morocco 10/55
- Troops fight off Moroccan tribesman 10/55
- Trade agreement with Hanoi 10/55
- Diem government recognized 10/55
- Premier Mollet attacked in Algiers 2/56
- Independence for Tunisia and Morocco 3/56
- Casbah sealed off 5/56
- 19 soldiers killed in Algeria 5/56
- Battle for Algiers begins 6/56
- Action over Suez with British 8/56
- Attack at Suez 10/56
- Algerian leadership captured 10/56
- Suez intervention over 11/56
- Troops leave Suez 12/56
- Action in Algiers 1/57
- Algerian v.p. killed 5/57
- Arms to Tunisia urged halted 11/57
- Algerian rebels in desert attacked 11/57
- Fighting continues on Algerian border 1/58
- Red uprising in Cameroons crushed 1/58
- Reprisal raids on Tunisia 2/58
- Premier Galliard resigns 4/58
- Algerian French assault government 5/58
- De Gaulle sows confusion in Algiers 6/58
- De Gaulle outlines plan for colonies 8/58
- 3,000 Algerians arrested 8/58
- Guinea repudiates French community 9/58
- Atomic secrets offered 9/58
- Sea and air forces in Algeria 7/59
- De Gaulle visits troops in Algeria 8/59

1960 to 1969
- Cameroon proclaims independence 1/60
- Reports on torture in Algeria 1/60
- Big Four summit fails over U-2 incident 5/60
- Military base pact with Morocco 9/60
- Petition for French rule in Algeria 10/60
- Mauritania gains independence 10/60
- French vote to free Algeria 1/61
- Nigeria breaks relations 1/61
- Africans protest Belgians in Congo 2/61
- Kennedy arrives for talks with de Gaulle 5/61
- Talks with Algerian rebels open 5/61
- Evian parley suspended 6/61
- Attack on Tunisians at Bizerte 7/61
- Algerian talks resume 7/61
- Anti-Franco Basques seized 8/61
- UN condemns France in Bizerte clashes 8/61
- De Gaulle recognizes Sahara as Algerian 10/61
- Police put down Algerian FLN protests 11/61
- O.A.S. appeals for revolution in France 1/62
- O.A.S. blamed for ten bombings 2/62
- Algeria war ends 3/62
- Algerian truce ratified by 90% majority 4/62
- O.A.S. leader Salan indicted 4/62
- Gen. Salan sentenced to life in prison 5/62
- Europeans flee Algeria to France 5/62
- Diplomatic ties with Tunisia restored 7/62
- Algeria gets independence 7/62
- U.K. barred from Europe market 1/63
- Trade pact with U.S.S.R. 2/63
- O.A.S. head Bidault flees to Germany 3/63
- Ties with Red China opened 1/64
- Agree with U.K. on tunnel under Channel 2/64
- French troops restore govt. in Gabon 2/64
- Ben Bella meets with de Gaulle 3/64
- Aid to Tunis suspended 5/64
- Manlio Brosio elected head of NATO 5/64
- Embassy in Saigon ransacked 7/64
- Boumedienne takes power in Algeria 6/65
- Withdrawal of delegate from EEC 7/65
- De Gaulle wants control of NATO bases 9/65
- Moroccan dissident kidnapped 10/65
- Control of NATO bases rejected 3/66
- U.S. says France not vital to NATO 4/66
- Withdrawal from NATO 7/66
- De Gaulle condemns U.S. in Vietnam 9/66
- De Gaulle vetoes U.K. entry to EEC 5/67
- De Gaulle: "Vive Quebec Libre!" 7/67
- De Gaulle again bars U.K. from EEC 11/67

1970 to 1987
- Brezhnev visits 6/73
- Carter ends world tour in Normandy 1/78
- U.S. tanker spills oil off France 3/78
- Zaire aided as Katangans attack 5/78
- Norway buys the Ile de France 8/79
- Natural gas contract with U.S.S.R. 1/82
- Soldiers sent to Chad to bolster govt. 8/83
- Troops extend hold in Chad 1/84
- France, Libya remove troops from Chad 9/84
- Mitterrand and Gorbachev talk arms 10/85
- Jean-Claude Duvalier seeks refuge 2/86
- Five killed as bomb explodes in Paris 9/86
- France breaks ties with Iran 7/87

France (Politics)

1900 to 1909
- Alfred Dreyfus pardoned 9/00
- Intl. Socialist Congress ends 9/00
- Amnesty granted to all in Dreyfus Affair 12/00
- Waldeck Rousseau quits Cabinet 5/02
- Emile Combes new president 5/02
- Republicans demonstrate against monarchy 3/03
- Forged documents found in Dreyfus case 4/03
- Police arrest three in Dreyfus scandal 6/04
- Four officers tried in Dreyfus Affair 10/04
- Socialists join International 4/05
- Assasination attempt on Pres. Loubet 5/05
- Theophile Delcasse resigns 6/05
- Coalition government elected 1/06
- Suffragettes urge violent campaign 1/06
- Jean Jaures denounces Morocco policy 2/06
- Alfred Dreyfus vindicated 7/06
- Georges Clemenceau prime minister 10/06
- Workers clash with troops 1/07
- Alfred Dreyfus shot 6/08
- Georges Clemenceau's departure 7/09

1910 to 1919
- Mandatory military training sought 4/10
- Revolutionaries rally at Briand campaign 4/10
- Universal suffrage bill killed 4/10
- Electorate stabilizes 5/10
- Govt. arrests editors in national unrest 10/10
- Attempt on Aristide Briand at Bourbon 1/11
- Briand Cabinet resigns 2/11
- Ernest Monis new president of council 3/11
- Jean Jaures to reorganize Socialists 4/11
- War Min. Berteaux killed by plane 5/11
- Gen. Michel resigns over Dreyfus Affair 7/11
- Lafargue funeral 11/11
- Marguerite Durand leads march for vote 1/12
- Council of war votes military service 3/12
- Raymond Poincare elected president 1/13
- Paty du Clam reinstated in army 1/13
- Military draft begins 7/13
- Caillaux murder 3/14
- Socialists gain in legislature 5/14
- Elections postponed by Natl. Assembly 12/14
- Aristide Briand forms new Cabinet 10/15
- Anarchist wounds Georges Clemenceau 2/19
- Clemenceau attacker sentenced to death 3/19
- Women vote for first time 11/19

1920 to 1929
- Paul Deschanel elected president 1/20
- Eugenie, former empress, dies 7/20
- Aristide Briand Cabinet resigns 1/22
- Statesman Paul Deschanel dies 4/22
- Marius Plateau assassinated by anarchist 1/23
- General Robert Nivelle dies 3/24
- President Millerand beaten in Parliament 6/24
- Doumergue defeats Painlev for presidency 6/24
- Socialists and Radicals break 11/25
- Aristide Briand cabinet out 3/26
- Aristide Briand Cabinet out again 6/26
- Aristide Briand Cabinet out third time 7/26
- Arrest of leader of Action Francaise 6/27
- Violent Sacco and Vanzetti protests 8/27
- Raymond Poincare forms new Cabinet 11/28
- Ferdinand Foch dies 3/29
- Aristide Briand replaces Poincare 7/29
- Aristide Briand Cabinet overthrown 10/29
- Georges Clemenceau dies 11/29

1930 to 1939
- Tardieu Cabinet overthrown 2/30
- War hero Joseph Joffre dies 1/31
- Aristide Briand resigns due to health 1/32
- Andre Maginot dies 1/32
- Aristide Briand dies 3/32
- Lebrun elected president 4/32
- French Pres. Paul Doumer assassinated 4/32
- Statesman Georges Leygues dies 9/33
- Communists and royalists clash 1/34
- Chautemps Cabinet resigns over scandal 1/34
- Anti-govt. riots in Paris 2/34
- Albert Prince killed 2/34
- French veterans turning to fascism 3/34
- Anti-fascist manifesto 3/34
- Statesman Raymond Poincare dies 10/34
- Alfred Dreyfus dies 7/35
- Huge crowds at military parade 7/35
- Pierre Laval resigns 1/36
- Loen Blum forms leftist government 6/36
- Police battle rightists in Paris 7/36
- Large increase in arms 9/36
- 19 billion francs for defense 2/37
- Nello and Carlo Rosselli killed 6/37
- Leon Blum's Cabinet resigns 6/37
- Leon Blum forms second Cabinet 3/38
- Albert Lebrun president 4/39

1940 to 1949
- Paul Reynaud is new premier 3/40
- De Gaulle named defense undersecretary 6/40
- Petain takes over as premier 6/40
- Third Republic ends 7/40
- Petain forms new authoritarian state 7/40
- Govt. moves from Paris to Vichy 7/40
- Death to French who join foreign armies 7/40
- Ex-political leaders arrested 8/40
- Vichy condemns de Gaulle to death 8/40
- De Gaulle Free France posters appear 10/40
- Petain authorized to dismiss Parliament 12/40
- Petain stops coup attempt by Laval 12/40
- Nazis force Vichy to restore Laval 2/41
- Ex-political leaders sentenced 10/41
- Francs-tireurs and Partisans founded 3/42
- Pierre Laval given dictatorial powers 4/42
- Herriot arrested by Vichy police 10/42
- Laval given full powers by Petain 11/42
- Admiral Darlan is dismissed 11/42
- Ex-political chiefs handed over to Reich 4/43
- Statesman Alexandre Millerand dies 4/43
- Resistance chief Jean Moulin executed 7/43
- Ex-Pres. Lebrun arrested by Gestapo 8/43
- Militia kills Victor Basch 1/44
- Marcel Deat named minister of labor 3/44
- SS kills 89 civilians for train sabotage 4/44
- Gestapo kills Marc Bloch 6/44
- Gestapo executes leftist chief Jean Zay

G

- King Edward VII meets kaiser 8/08
- New Moroccan sultan recognized 9/08
- Anti-German demonstrations in Vienna 9/08
- Support for Austria against Balkans 10/08
- Kaiser makes anti-British remarks 10/08
- Taft victory supported 11/08
- Casablanca affair settled 11/08
- Anti-British remarks condemned 11/08
- Samoan natives threaten revolt 12/08
- France recognizes Moroccan interests 2/09
- Naval race with U.K. 3/09
- Bulgaria recognized 4/09

1910 to 1915

- Warns U.S. it is ready for trade war 1/10
- Borders of African colony fixed 2/10
- Wilhelm II visits Belgium 10/10
- Kaiser and czar make Middle East trade 11/10
- Baghdad RR finalized with Russia 1/11
- Navy orders 2 U.S. Curtiss biplanes 4/11
- Battleship Panther sent to Agadir 7/11
- Warship sent to Haiti to protect Germans 8/11
- Govt. to fortify Heligoland 8/11
- Accord reached with France on Morocco 9/11
- France's right to Morocco recognized 11/11
- British limits on navy accepted 2/13
- Naval buildup 7/13
- Accord with U.K. on Baghdad Railway 7/13
- Consolidation of Triple Alliance 9/13
- War talk grows 3/14
- Preparation for war 7/14
- Belgium and France invaded 8/14
- War declared on France 8/14
- Augsburg bombs Russian port Libau 8/14
- England declares war 8/14
- Serbia declares war 8/14
- Brussels taken 8/14
- Japan declares war 8/14
- War on Russia declared 8/14
- Russia invades 8/14
- Counterattack launched in East Prussia 9/14
- U.S. asked to mediate peace 9/14
- Antwerp taken after 12-day siege 10/14
- Hindenburg defeats Russians 9/14
- British boat sunk 1/15
- French La Basse Canal offense countered 1/15
- Soldiers take trenches left by French 1/15
- Air raids on Britain 1/15
- U.S. ship attacked 1/15
- Blucher sunk 1/15
- French driven from Soissons 1/15
- Warning to all ships 2/15
- Hindenburg attacks Russians 2/15
- Russians encircled at Nieman River 2/15
- U.S. ambassador invited 2/15
- Mine destroys U.S. ship 2/15
- Total sub warfare 2/15
- 20,000 troops captured at Champagne 2/15
- Cruiser takes refuge in Rhode Island 3/15
- Dresden sunk 3/15
- Zeppelin bombs Paris 3/15
- British blockade protested 4/15
- Russian advance checked 4/15
- British bombed from Belgium 4/15
- Gas used at Ypres 4/15
- U.S. ship Gulflight sunk 5/15
- 35,000 troops lost on Western Front 5/15
- Submarine activity uncurtailed 5/15
- Lusitania sunk 5/15
- Ambassador recalled from Rome 5/15
- Zeppelins bomb London 6/15
- Lemberg occupied 6/15
- Poland and Ukraine sought 6/15
- 20 Americans lost in Armenian sinking 6/15
- French fail at Artois 6/15
- Argonne shelled with gas 6/15
- Two more U.S. ships sunk 7/15
- Peace with Russia proposed 8/15
- Sub warfare may end 8/15
- Warsaw taken 8/15
- New Argonne assault 9/15
- Zeppelins attack London again 9/15
- Vilna captured 9/15
- Allies launch new offensive 9/15
- Germans arrested in N.Y. 10/15
- 65,000 lost at Artois 10/15
- Cavell executed as spy 10/15
- British stopped at Loos 10/15
- U.S. ejects German spies 12/15
- British liner sunk 12/15

1916 to 1919

- U.K. confirms German spy in U.S. 1/16
- Cameroon lost 1/16
- Responsibility for Lusitania accepted 2/16
- Attacks renewed on neutral ships 2/16
- Major offensive at Verdun 2/16
- Tough U.S. sub war stance 3/16
- War declared on Portugal 3/16
- New drive at Verdun 3/16
- 20,000 troops lost at Lake Naroch 3/16
- Third German offense at Verdun 4/16
- U.S. threatens to break relations 4/16
- Navy clashes with British 4/16
- Conditional pact to halt sub warfare 5/16
- War on merchant ships to end 5/16
- Douamont to be retaken 5/16
- Battle of Jutland 5/16
- French surrender at Fort Vaux 6/16
- Gas used at Somme 6/16
- U-boat with message for Wilson 7/16
- British reach Pozieres 7/16
- Italy declares war 8/16
- Allies repulsed at Florina 8/16
- Hindenburg victorious at Tannenberg 8/16
- British smash line at Somme 9/16
- Brusilov offensive collapses 9/16
- U.S. aviators violate neutrality 9/16
- U.K. will fight for complete victory 9/16
- France breaks line at Verdun 10/16
- Status of merchant ships' captains 10/16
- Nine Norwegian ships sunk in one day 10/16
- Poland's freedom proclaimed 11/16
- U.S. liner Columbian sunk 11/16
- Massive death toll at Somme 11/16
- Bucharest captured 12/16
- Death count at Verdun 12/16
- Chancellor proposes peace talks 12/16
- Czar rejects peace offer 12/16
- Allies reject peace bid 12/16
- Alliance proposed with Mexico 1/17
- Sub warfare reopens 1/17
- Relations with U.S. severed 2/17
- Lanconia sunk 2/17
- 134 neutral ships sunk in one month 2/17
- U.S. ship Housatonic sunk 2/17
- All Americans held hostage 2/17
- Troops on West Front withdraw 20 miles 2/17
- Wilson wants to arm merchant ships 2/17
- Ties with China severed 3/17
- Three more U.S. ships sunk 3/17
- Channel battle 3/17
- U.S. declares war 4/17
- Hindenburg line established 4/17
- Bolivia severs relations 4/17
- British victory at Arras 4/17
- Mongolia fires first U.S. shot 4/17
- Nivelle offensive fails 4/17
- U.S. captures U-boat in Virginia 5/17
- British take Messines Ridge 6/17
- U.S. wins battle with submarines 7/17
- 37 die in London air raid 7/17
- Britain cuts off trade with Rotterdam 7/17
- Langemark occupied 8/17
- Riga captured 9/17
- German buildings in Buenos Aires burned 9/17
- Attack on Champagne fails 9/17
- France demands return of Alsace-Lorraine 9/17
- Haig attacks at Ypres 9/17
- Agreement for withdrawal from Belgium 9/17
- Peru severs ties 10/17
- Allies smash line at Ypres 10/17
- Oesel and Dago islands taken 10/17
- France downs five zeppelins 10/17
- Brazil declares war 10/17
- British sink 11 ships 11/17
- British gain five miles at Ypres 11/17
- Hindenburg line severed 11/17
- Summation of year 12/17
- Russia signs armistice 12/17
- British position on resolution of war 1/18
- 750,000 troops moved to West Front 1/18
- U.S. peace proposal rejected 1/18
- Peace with Russia ends 2/18
- Russia forced to accept peace 2/18
- British reject peace proposal 2/18
- Treaty signed with Russia 3/18
- Alliance with Finland 3/18
- Paris bombed 3/18
- Cambrai attacked 3/18
- Huge offensive on Western Front 3/18
- British pushed from Ypres 4/18
- Diplomatic relations with Soviets begin 4/18
- French halt advance 4/18
- Red Baron downed 4/18
- U.S. troops win on Amiens front 5/18
- Soldiers hung for refusing orders 5/18
- Finland ratifies treaty 6/18
- Halted at Chateau-Thierry 6/18
- New allied counterattack 6/18
- Turkey severs relations 7/18
- Ambassador in Moscow assassinated 7/18
- French capture 8,000 at Aisne 8/18
- Peace appeal to Wilson 10/18
- Sub warfare suspended 10/18
- Lines breached, thousands of prisoners 9/18
- Peace plea rejected 10/18
- Surrender 11/18
- Troops evacuate Brussels 11/18
- Alsace-Lorraine evacuated 11/18
- 1.5 million prisoners freed 11/18
- U.S. army of occupation 12/18
- Poland severs relations 12/18
- Territory given up to Poland 2/19
- Allies plan to supply 3/19
- Delegates arrive at Versailles 4/19
- Peace terms presented and opposed 5/19
- Blockade must be lifted before peace 5/19
- Peace treaty signed 6/19

1920 to 1929

- Allies demand Germans stand trial 2/20
- All Russians ordered arrested in Berlin 3/20
- French colonial troops fire on crowd 4/20
- Franco-Belgian troops quit Frankfort 5/20
- North Silesia ceded to Denmark 6/20
- East and West Prussia vote to remain 7/20
- Allies occupy country to collect debts 3/21
- U.S signs decree ending war 7/21
- Peace treaty signed with U.S. 8/21
- France lifts economic sanctions 9/21
- With Russia in Rapallo pact 4/22
- U.S. Army requested to stay in Rhine 5/22
- Upper Silesia ceded to Poland 5/22
- U.S. withdraws last troops 1/23
- French enter Essen in Ruhr 1/23
- 20 die in first fighting in Ruhr 1/23
- Coal supplies end as French close Ruhr 2/23
- French requisition vehicles in Dortmund 2/23
- Rioters in Ruhr kill two French soldiers 3/23
- Unions call for protest against French 4/23
- Ten Belgians killed by bomb, Dusseldorf 6/23
- French set up trade barrier in Ruhr 6/23
- France to take all Ruhr industries 6/23
- U.K. says Ruhr occupation violates pact 8/23
- Allies demand renewed military control 6/24
- French open Ruhr to 210,000 exiles 6/24
- Admission to League of Nations requested 9/24
- Last Franco-U.K. troops leave Ruhr 11/24
- Accused of violating arms accord 1/25
- Terms for Rhineland evacuation dictated 6/25
- France accepts security proposal 6/25
- Trade treaty with Russia 10/25
- Peace treaty signed with France 10/25
- 17,000 British troops leave 12/25
- Mussolini warns Reich on Tyrol 2/26
- Brazil bars admission to League 3/26
- League adjourns without admitting 3/26
- Rapallo pact extended 4/26
- League of Nations to admit 6/26
- Accord signed with France 8/26
- Admitted to League of Nations 9/26
- Soldiers training in U.S.S.R. 12/26
- Arbitration treaty with Italy 12/26
- Allied control ends 1/27
- U.S. attache shot 9/27
- Ambassador to U.S. dies 9/27
- Kellogg-Briand Treaty signed 8/28
- French concessions in Rhine canceled 9/28
- Kellogg-Briand Pact accepted 2/29
- Asylum denied to Trotsky 4/29
- Allies evacuate Rhineland 11/29

1930 to 1939

- French troops evacuate Rhineland 6/30
- Last Allied troops leave Saar 12/30
- Nazis demand country quit League 2/31
- Customs union with Austria proposed 3/31
- Berlin to proceed with customs union 4/31
- Red spy network uncovered 4/31
- Foreign minister seeks arms equality 8/32
- Disarmament conference abandoned 9/32
- Reich returns to arms talks 12/32
- Travel by foreigners restricted 4/33
- Hitler leaves League of Nations 10/33
- Ten-year pact signed with Poland 1/34
- Mutual aid pact with U.S.S.R. rejected 6/34
- Ribbentrop admits Reich is rearming 11/34
- France and Italy call rearming illegal 1/35
- League votes for return of Saar Basin 1/35
- Italy, France and U.K. oppose aggression 3/35
- Hitler says Soviets threaten peace 3/35
- Japan rejects alliance with Reich 4/35
- Danzig rejects Nazi domination 4/35
- Stresa Conference discusses threat 4/35
- League condemns rearmament 4/35
- 28 spies arrested by Czechs 11/35
- Goebbels demands colonies 1/36
- Switzerland bars NSDAP 2/36
- Troops sent into Rhineland 3/36
- Austrian freedom conceded 7/36
- Arms to Spain banned 8/36
- French begin large buildup of arms 9/36
- Hitler asserts right to colonies 9/36
- Russian aid to Spain threatened 10/36
- Belgium neutral 10/36
- Fighting units sent to Spain 10/36
- Italian conquest of Ethiopia recognized 10/36
- Treaty with Italy 10/36
- If Belgium attacked, British will fight 11/36
- Axis formed with Italy and Japan 11/36
- Neutrality assured for Dutch and Belgian 1/37
- Guernica bombed 4/37
- Italy denies support to Austria 4/37
- Spanish rebel subs protected 9/37
- Hitler meets with Mussolini 9/37
- Pact sought with Belgium 10/37
- Czechs crush German Party meeting 10/37
- Mutual aid for Italy 10/37
- Lord Halifax seeks appeasement 1/37
- Czech, Austrian Germans seek protection 2/38
- Austria will defend independence 2/38
- Czechs will defend themselves 3/38
- Austria overrun 3/38
- Referendum approves union with Austria 4/38
- Hitler reviews Italy's troops 5/38
- Czechs place 400,000 troops on border 5/38
- Sudetens stop talks with Czechs 5/38
- British ask Czech concessions 7/38
- Hungarian naval chief visits 8/38
- British warn of world war 8/38
- Sudetenland conceded 9/38
- Sudetens demonstrate 9/38
- Chamberlain meets Hitler in Munich 9/38
- 23,000 Sudetens flee to homeland 9/38
- Partial mobilization in France and U.K. 9/38
- Army takes Sudetenland 10/38
- Hitler decorates Lindbergh 10/38
- All lost colonies demanded 10/38
- U.S. recalls envoy 11/38
- Ambassador to U.S. recalled 11/38
- Friendship pact with France 12/38
- Pact with Denmark, Latvia, Estonia 1/39
- Return of colonies demanded 1/39
- Govt. seeks pope who favors fascism 2/39
- British envoy recalled 3/39
- Holland places troops on border 4/39
- Hitler refuses meeting with FDR 4/39
- "Pact of Steel" with Italy 5/39
- Peace pact with Estonia and Latvia 6/39
- Halifax says British ready for war 6/39
- Port of Trieste leased 7/39
- 2,000 Nazi guards enter Danzig 7/39
- More troops to Libya 7/39
- War preparedness 8/39
- Poland rushes troops to border 8/39
- Belgium proclaims neutrality 8/39
- End of U.K.-Poland alliance demanded 8/39
- Holland mobilizes 8/39
- Peace pact with Russia 8/39
- Aircraft carrier Courageous sunk 9/39
- WWII begins as Poland is invaded 9/39
- Britain and France declare war 9/39
- Hitler's peace plan rejected 10/39
- British Royal Ark sunk with 800 lost 10/39
- French rout Nazis in tank battle 10/39
- Poland divided; over 10,000 dead 10/39
- Attacks on Western Front 10/39
- Plot to kill Hitler fails 11/39
- U.S. shoots down nine planes 11/39
- Dutch liner sunk; 140 dead 11/39
- Four British ships sunk 11/39
- Battleship scuttled 12/39

1940 to 1944

- Hitler warns of total war 1/40
- Soviets sign treaty blocking U.K. trade 2/40
- German tanker seized in Norway 2/40
- U.S. envoy Welles meets with Hitler 3/40
- RAF attacks Nazi base at Sylt 3/40
- Nazis enter Scandinavia 4/40
- Nazis invade Western Europe 5/40
- Allies evacuated from Dunkirk 6/40
- Paris falls to Nazis 6/40
- RAF strikes 100 German cities 7/40
- German planes hit Britain 7/40
- Berlin attacked by RAF 8/40
- Battle of Britain 9/40
- Japan joins Axis 9/40
- Hitler meets Petain 10/40
- Hitler meets Franco 10/40
- Germans bomb St. Paul's Cathedral 10/40
- Air raids over Britain 11/40
- Molotov and Hitler meet 11/40
- Warsaw Ghetto 11/40
- Pierre Laval freed 12/40
- RAF hits Hanover industrial district 2/41
- Rommel's Afrika Korps in Tripoli 2/41
- Yugoslav coup bars deal with Nazis 3/41
- Greek army gives up 4/41
- Nazis invade Yugoslavia 4/41
- Nazis declare Red Sea a war zone 5/41
- Bismark sunk 5/41
- Rudolf Hess lands in Scotland 5/41
- Friendship pact with Turkey 6/41
- U.S. consuls expelled 6/41
- Nazis invade U.S.S.R. 6/41
- Drive through Soviet Union continues 7/41
- Hitler and Mussolini to counter U.S. aid 8/41
- Nazis cross Dnieper River 8/41
- Reich holds two U.S. pilots 9/41
- Nazis encircle Leningrad 9/41
- Nazis execute Czech Premier Alois Eias 10/41
- State of siege imposed on Moscow 10/41
- Two U.S. destroyers hit by U-boats 10/41
- Nazis halted at Moscow 12/41
- Nazis fix Final Solution 1/42
- British raid St. Nazaire 3/42
- U.K. begins attack on city of Lubeck 3/42
- RAF begins raids on German cities 3/42
- French Gen. Geraud escapes from Nazis 4/42
- Nazis launch Baedeker raids 4/42
- RAF hits Cologne 5/42
- Soviet counter-offensive 5/42
- Rommel moves into Egypt 6/42
- Germans take Sevastopol 7/42
- U.K. bombers raid Dusseldorf 8/42
- Soviets start air raids on 8/42
- Allied raid on Dieppe fails 8/42
- Nazis attack Stalingrad 9/42
- Montgomery vs. Rommel in Africa 10/42
- 207,373 executed by Nazis 9/42
- Allies land in Northern Africa 11/42
- Germans in Southern France 11/42
- Rommel routed in Africa 11/42
- Nazis surrounded at Stalingrad 11/42
- Nazis give in at Stalingrad 1/42
- First U.S. raid on Reich 1/43
- Leningrad siege broken 1/43
- Soviets retake Kursk 1/43
- U.S. Flying Fortresses pound Reich 2/43
- Battle for Kasserine Pass 2/43
- Berlin bombed by RAF 3/43
- RAF bombs Essen and Krupp arms works 3/43
- Rommel leaves Africa 3/43
- Warsaw Ghetto uprising 4/43
- 4,000 Polish officers in mass grave 4/43
- Doenitz orders halt to sub war 5/43
- 150,000 in Afrika Korps surrender 5/43
- Bombers hit Ruhr dams 5/43
- RAF hammers Muelheim 6/43
- Soviets and Nazis in biggest tank battle 7/43
- U.S. firebombs start Hamburg blaze 7/43
- Jean Moulin executed by Nazis 7/43
- Allied raid cuts Krupp output by 65% 8/43
- RAF blasts Berlin with 50 tons 9/43
- Russians retake Smolensk 9/43
- Allies invade Italy 9/43
- U.S. fliers attack Frankfurt 10/43
- Allies halted at Monte Cassino 10/43
- U.S. bombers attack plants at Dueren 10/43
- Corsica liberated 10/43
- RAF drops 2,300 tons of bombs on Berlin 1/44
- Bombers blast Monte Cassino 2/44
- Berlin gets first U.S. bombing 3/44
- Hungarian Jews sent to Auschwitz 3/44
- Maquis unit wiped out in France 3/44
- Innocents executed in Rome 3/44
- Turkey stops export of chrome 4/44
- Soviets retake Kerch Peninsula 4/44
- Reich heavily bombed 4/44
- Soviets retake Crimea 5/44
- Allies enter Rome 6/44
- SS massacres 642 in France 6/44
- Allies land in Normandy 6/44
- First V-1 hits London 6/44
- Retreat in Normandy 7/44
- Bombing attack on Hitler is a failure 7/44
- Russians advance in East 7/44
- Alies in Paris 8/44
- Nazis arrest Petain 8/44
- Bradley's First Army at Siegfried line 9/44
- Nazis give up Belgian cities 9/44
- V-2 rockets hit London 9/44
- Aachen falls to Allies 10/44
- Soviets in Prussia 10/44
- Patton's tanks drive into Saar Basin 11/44
- Tirpitz is sunk by RAF 11/44
- Patton's troops enter Saar valley 12/44
- German counterattack in Ardennes 12/44
- McAuliffe spurns surrender to Nazis 12/44

1945 to 1949

- Last offensive fails 1/45
- Soviets occupy Warsaw 1/45
- U.S. launches drive on Siegfried line 1/45
- Soviets batter Berlin's defenses 1/45
- Auschwitz liberated 1/45
- Ecuador declares war 2/45
- 1,200 planes blast Wiesbaden 2/45
- Berlin bombed 2/45
- Belgium evacuated 2/45
- U.S. Rhineland offensive 2/45
- Turkey declares war 2/45
- Syria declares war 2/45
- Dresden in flames as 130,000 die 2/45
- 30,000 confined to home by U.S. 3/45
- U.S. troops take Cologne 3/45
- Hitler orders "scorched earth" policy 3/45
- Argentina declares war on Axis 3/45
- Teenagers combat occupation 3/45
- U.S. crosses Rhine 3/45
- U.S. troops take Leipzig 4/45
- Nuremberg captured 4/45
- Reds enter Berlin 4/45
- Soviets take Vienna 4/45
- Soviets meet Yanks at Elbe 4/45
- Surrender to Allies 5/45
- Divided into four zones 6/45
- Reich divided up by Allies 7/45
- Nuremberg war trials 11/45
- Big Four meet to finalize peace treaty 4/46
- SS convicted of Malmedy massacre 7/46
- Molotov rejects German unity plan 7/46
- France bars economic reunion 8/46
- Nine Nazis hanged 10/46
- U.S. and U.K. merge zones 12/46
- U.S. arrests hundreds of Nazis 2/47
- Curbed by French-U.K. pact 2/47
- Reds hold 890,532 POWs 3/47
- Soviets move tanks to Berlin 4/48
- Berlin airlift 4/48
- U.S., U.K., France troops to stay 6/48
- France, U.K., U.S. merge zones 4/49
- Soviets stop blockade of Berlin 5/49
- Big Four discuss nation's future 5/49
- Soviets reject reunification 5/49
- No resolution after Big Four parley 6/49

Germany (Politics)

1900 to 1909

- Reichstag approves navy expansion plan 6/00
- Death of Wilhelm Liebknecht 8/00
- Colonies become protectorates 9/00
- Max Harden sentenced for libel 10/00
- Bernhard von Bulow becomes chancellor 10/00
- Auguste Bebel condemns policy in China 11/00
- Kaiser Wilhelm refuses to meet Kruger 12/00
- Kaiser Wilhelm has polyps removed 11/03
- Cost of South African war 3/06
- Russian bomb factory uncovered, Hamburg 8/06
- Russian revolutionaries bomb factory 8/06
- Political school for working class 10/06
- Deadlock in Reichstag 11/06
- Reichstag dissolved 12/06
- Socialists defeated 1/07
- Prince arrested for libel 10/07
- Navy construction stepped up 6/08
- Prince Von Bulow retires 7/09

1910 to 1919

- Congress demands universal suffrage 1/10
- Kaiser Wilhelm promises suffrage reform 1/10
- Police shoot socialists at demonstration 3/10
- Socialists gain seats in elections 7/10
- Alleged anarchists arrested in Munich 1/11
- Second Reich celebrates 40th anniversary 1/11
- Reichstag exempts royalty from taxes 1/11
- Reichstag increases army by 515,000 2/11
- Social Democrats protest acts in Morocco 8/11
- Social Democrats now hold 25% seats 1/12
- Wilhelm launches biggest ship, Imperator 5/12
- Kiel and Wilhelmshaven sub bases 1/13
- Reichstag votes $510 mil. for army 3/13
- Reichstag passes military tax hike 3/13
- Reichstag passes army and finance bills 6/13
- Hundreds of war ships built 7/13
- Bismarck launched 6/14
- Schlieffen mobilization plan begins 8/14
- Hindenburg is commander on East Front 11/14
- Naval minister resigns 3/16
- Socialist arrested at anti-war protest 5/16
- Hindenburg is chief of general staff 8/16
- Mutiny on Prinzregent 8/17
- Five naval crews mutiny 10/17
- Max von Bade appointed chancellor 10/18
- Karl Liebknecht freed 10/18
- Republic proclaimed 11/18
- Scramble for power after kaiser leaves

- New electoral plan for India 8/32
- Third round table conference on India 11/32
- Ban on Soviet imports 4/33
- Defenses beefed up 3/35
- 20,000 Moslems in India fired on 3/35
- Anti-Reich pacts signed 3/35
- Aden and Burma separated from India 8/35
- Part of Ethiopia conceded to Italy 8/35
- Anti-U.K. riots in Cairo 11/35
- Refusal to aid French against Germans 3/36
- Naval accord with France and U.S. 3/36
- Haile Selassie seeks refuge 6/36
- Sanctions abandoned against Italy 6/36
- Control of Suez for 20 years 8/36
- Troops quit Egypt 11/36
- War threatened if Germans attack Belgium 11/36
- Mediterranean peace pact with Italy 1/37
- Separation of Palestine considered 6/37
- Commission recommends dividing Palestine 7/37
- King escapes Belfast bombs 7/37
- Lewis Andrews killed by Arabs 9/37
- Palestinian Arab leaders deported 10/37
- Jewish access to Palestine restricted 10/37
- Lord Halifax seeks to appease Germans 11/37
- Joseph Kennedy ambassador to England 12/37
- Steamer sunk by torpedo 1/38
- Warships to Mediterranean; one sunk 2/38
- Chamberlain extols Mussolini 5/38
- Mexico breaks relations over oil 5/38
- 400 planes a year from U.S. 6/38
- Czechs asked to make German concessions 7/38
- Hitler warned of world war 8/38
- Chamberlain concedes Sudetenland 9/38
- Partial mobilization 9/38
- Troops occupy Palestine 10/38
- Partition of Palestine called unfeasable 11/38
- Jericho captured 11/38
- Italy warned 12/38
- Chamberlain meets with Mussolini 1/39
- Franco recognized 2/39
- Talks on Palestine fail 3/39
- Envoy to Germany recalled 3/39
- Mutual defense treaty with Poland 4/39
- Fleet sails to protect Greece and Turkey 4/39
- Palestine to be free in ten years 5/39
- Japanese besiege concession at Tientsin 6/39
- Halifax says British ready for war 6/39
- Alliance with France and U.S.S.R. 7/39
- Japan blocks trade with China 7/39
- Ready for war over Danzig 7/39
- Germany demands end of Polish alliance 8/39
- Russia signs peace pact with Germany 8/39
- Troops to France 9/39
- Aircraft Carrier Courageous sunk 9/39
- War declared on Germany 9/39
- Hitler's peace plan refused 10/39
- Royal Ark sunk with 800 lost 10/39
- Germany sinks four ships 11/39
- German battleship trapped 12/39
- Canadian troops arrive 12/39

1940 to 1949

- Rationing of sugar, meat and butter 1/40
- Merchant ships will be armed 2/40
- Seven Italian coal ships seized 3/40
- I.R.A. assaults Dartmoor prison 3/40
- South Norway yielded to Nazis 5/40
- Churchill sends note asking U.S. aid 5/40
- Allies evacuate Dunkirk 6/40
- De Gaulle appeals on BBC radio to fight 6/40
- Reich bombers make first daylight raid 7/40
- British sink French fleet in Algeria 7/40
- RAF raids Berlin 8/40
- Alliance with Free France 8/40
- Tanks to the Mideast 8/40
- Somaliland yielded to Italy 8/40
- 800 Reich planes storm London 8/40
- Battle of Britain 9/40
- St. Paul's Cathedral hit by German bomb 10/40
- Belgians form exiled government 10/40
- Nazis hit cities hard 11/40
- Coventry destroyed by Reich bombers 11/40
- Arms standardized with U.S. 11/40
- British take Tobruk 1/41
- Churchill states "Give us the tools,.." 2/41
- Ties with Bucharest severed 2/41
- Ties with Bulgaria severed 3/41
- Ties with Hungary severed 4/41
- Reich planes bomb London in worst raid 5/41
- BBC broadcasts V for Victory 7/41
- Ties with Finland severed 7/41
- Trade accord with Moscow 8/41
- Atlantic Charter issued 8/41
- Iran invaded 8/41
- French Resistance Natl. Council formed 9/41
- Operation Halbert launched 9/41
- Attack in Libya 11/41
- Aid promised for U.S. war with Japan 11/41
- War on Finland, Rumania, Hungary 12/41
- Dominion status offered to India 3/42
- Raid on St. Nazaire 3/42
- New raids on German cities 3/42
- Malta awarded George Cross for heroism 4/42
- Exeter bombed by German planes 4/42
- Nazis launch Baedeker raids 4/42
- 20-yr mutual aid treaty with U.S.S.R. 5/42
- RAF hits Cologne 5/42
- British fall back in Egypt 6/42
- U.S. fliers join RAF for first time 7/42
- Duke of Kent killed in air crash 8/42
- Churchill and Stalin meet 8/42
- RAF flies 1,200 miles to raid Munich 9/42
- Canterbury shrine hit by Nazis 10/42
- Montgomery leads desert army 10/42
- Churchill tells Italy oust leaders 11/42
- British rout Rommel 11/42
- Nazi day air raid kills 34 in schools 1/43
- War council in Casablanca 1/43
- RAF raid European railway lines 3/43
- Rommel leaves Africa 3/43
- Churchill at Washington Trident parley 5/43
- German Afrika Korps surrenders 5/43
- Three Sicilian islands seized 6/43
- FDR and Churchill meet in Quebec 8/43
- Mountbatten to S.E. Asia 8/43
- Allies go ashore in Italy 9/43
- Big Three meet in Tehran 11/43
- Big Three plan to subdue Reich 12/43
- RAF bombs Berlin 1/44
- Allies cut off arms to Turkey 3/44
- Travel to Ireland barred 3/44
- General Wingate killed in plane crash 3/44
- Ban on envoy travel 4/44
- Allies enter Rome 6/44
- Allies land at Normandy 6/44
- First V-1 hits London 6/44
- V-1 bombs kill 2,752 7/44
- Big Four propose United Nations 10/44
- V-2 rockets hit London 9/44
- RAF sinks Tirpitz 11/44
- Churchill urges German surrender 1/45
- Big Three conference in Yalta 2/45
- 1,200 planes blast Wiesbaden 2/45
- Dresden in flames as 130,000 die 2/45
- Major offensive in Italy 4/45
- Germany surrenders 5/45
- Troops go ashore near Rangoon 5/45
- Churchill denounces totalitarianism 5/45
- Burma liberated 6/45
- Germany divided 6/45
- Big Three at Potsdam 7/45
- Germany divided into four zones 7/45
- Japanese surrender in Singapore 8/45
- Hong Kong surrenders 9/45
- Egypt demands withdrawal 9/45
- Independence promised to India 9/45
- Nuremberg trials begin 11/45
- Govt. wants atom secrets publicized 11/45
- Quota on Jews immigrating to Palestine 1/46
- Mountbatten, viceroy to India 2/46
- India offered full indpendence 3/46
- Freedom granted to Transjordan 3/46
- Churchill's "Iron Curtain" speech 3/46
- Soviets leave Iran 3/46
- Seven soldiers killed in Tel Aviv 4/46
- Withdrawal from Syria 5/46
- Withdrawal from Egypt planned 5/46
- Search for end to Palestine violence 6/46
- India rejects provisional government 6/46
- Zionist hotel bombing kills 100 7/46
- Jewish immigrants confined to camps 8/46
- Illegal Jewish immigrants to be stopped 8/46
- Truman says open Palestine to Jews 10/46
- Attlee reassures Jinnah 11/46
- Hindus refuse parley on India 11/46
- Berlin zone merged with U.S. 12/46
- Guerrillas attack in Palestine 1/47
- Pledge to quit India by June 1948 2/47
- Pact with France to curb Germany 2/47
- Mountbatten gets warm greeting in India 3/47
- Alliance with France 3/47
- Churchill wants British to stay in India 3/47
- Terrorists battle troops in Palestine 3/47
- Plan to divide India 6/47
- All-India Congress accepts partition 6/47
- Ship Exodus intercepted 7/47
- Indpendence to India 8/47
- Preparations to leave Palestine 9/47
- Violent Arab reaction to partition 12/47
- Burma independent 1/48
- 30 soldiers killed in Palestine 2/48
- Berlin airlift 4/48
- Birth of Israel 5/48
- Vow to keep troops in Germany 6/48
- Ireland votes for independence 11/48
- Israel recognized 1/48
- Israel shoots down five RAF planes 1/49
- German zones to merge with France, U.S. 4/49
- Dublin's independence recognized 5/49

1950 to 1959

- Communist China recognized 1/50
- Atom scientist Klaus Fuchs jailed as spy 2/50
- Fuchs given 14 years as atom spy 3/50
- State of Israel recognized 4/50
- Churchill warns of third world war 7/50
- Oil to Mao's China banned 7/50
- West Germany recognized 9/50
- Commonwealth drafts aid plan for Asia 9/50
- Foreign Service men vanish 5/51
- MacLean & Burgess believed Soviet spies 6/51
- 12 die as Egyptians fight near Suez 10/51
- Egyptians clash in Suez zone 12/51
- Protest over Rhee's purge 6/52
- Iran breaks relations over oil 10/52
- Tito first Red chief to visit London 3/53
- British West Indies agree to federate 4/53
- S. Rhodesia to Fed. Rhodesia & Nyasaland 10/53
- Big Three Conference in Bermuda 12/53
- Big Four meet on arms in West Berlin 1/54
- Malayan Reds pushed out to Sumatra 2/54
- U.K. opens trade talks with Hungary 3/54
- U.K. ends 72-year occupation of Egypt 7/54
- Mau-Maus attacked 2/55
- Full sovereignty for W. Germany 5/55
- Ownership of Falkland Islands 5/55
- Big Four summit in Geneva 7/55
- Over 10,000 Mau-Mau killed since 1952 1/56
- British arrest Makarios 2/56
- Suez Canal given up 6/56
- Aid to Egypt stopped; assets frozen 7/56
- Action over Suez planned; forces ready 8/56
- Attack on Suez 10/56
- Suez intervention over 11/56
- Troops leave Suez 12/56
- Makarios released 3/57
- European Economic Community formed 3/57
- Ghana indpendent 3/57
- U.K. to rely on nuclear defense 4/57
- Malaya independent 8/57
- Queen in U.S. and Canada 10/57
- Cyprus rebels call for truce 8/58
- First time premier in U.S.S.R. since war 2/59

1960 to 1969

- Togoland declares independence 4/60
- Ghana becomes republic 7/60
- U.K. uncovers Soviet spy network 1/61
- Londoners protest U.S. Polaris missiles 4/61
- JFK pays a state visit 6/61
- Protectorate over Kuwait relinquished 6/61
- Parliament approves plan to join EEC 8/61
- Malta has autonomy in Commonwealth 11/61
- Jamaica gets independence 8/62
- Tanganyika gets independence 12/62
- France bars U.K. from Europe market 1/63
- JFK makes Winston Churchill U.S. citizen 4/63
- Three nations sign Test Ban Treaty 8/63
- U.K. puts down three African mutinies 1/64
- New Zanzibar govt. recognized 2/64
- Agreement with Paris on Channel tunnel 2/64
- Smith wants Rhodesian freedom 10/65
- Independence for Guyana 5/66
- De Gaulle vetoes U.K. entry to EEC 5/67
- Reds attack consulate in Peking 8/67
- U.K. barred from EEC by De Gaulle 11/67
- British leave Aden 11/67
- Withdrawal from east of Suez 1/68
- Swaziland gains independence 9/68
- Talks with Rhodesia end in failure 10/68
- 1,000 troops to Belfast 4/69
- Riots in Belfast for three days 8/69
- Bernadette Devlin gets half year in jail 12/69

1970 to 1987

- Rhodesia severs ties 3/70
- Tonga gains independence 6/70
- 105 Soviets ousted for spying 9/71
- To join the Common Market 10/71
- European Common Market joined 1/72
- I.R.A. bombs kill seven at officers mess 2/72
- To establish relations with China 3/72
- Direct rule on North Ireland imposed 3/72
- White Paper on Catholicism in N. Ireland 3/73
- Bahamas gain independence 7/73
- Hanoi government recognized 7/73
- I.R.A. bombs Westminster Hall 6/74
- Idi Amin pardons Briton facing death 7/75
- Ambassador to Ireland killed by mine 7/76
- Torture in Northern Ireland 8/76
- PLO envoy assassinated 1/78
- Ambassador to Netherlands is slain 3/79
- Nigeria nationalizes British oil 8/79
- I.R.A. kills Louis Mountbatten 8/79
- Three men seize Iranian Embassy 4/80
- Sanctions on Iran 5/80
- British storm Iran Embassy, free 19 5/80
- Belize gains independence 9/81
- Ties with Vatican restored 1/82
- Argentina invades Falkland Islands 4/82
- Major battle fought for Falklands 5/82
- Shlomo Argov wounded by assassins 6/82
- Reagan speaks at Parliament 6/82
- Argentines give up in Falklands 6/82
- I.R.A. blast kills eight in parks 7/82
- First cruise missiles arrive 11/83
- Warships to Persian Gulf 2/84
- Libyans shoot policewoman; ties broken 4/84
- Libyans leave embassy 4/84
- 40th anniversary of D-day 6/84
- Hong Kong rule returned in 1997 9/84
- Quarrel with Soviets over spying 9/85
- 100,000 protest arms race in London 10/85
- Ulster plan ratified 11/85
- Airline finds bomb in woman's luggage 4/86

Great Britain (Politics)

1900 to 1909

- Parliament passes War Loan Act 3/00
- Publication of Lord Roberts' censure 4/00
- Queen Victoria dies at age 82 1/01
- House votes $12.5 mil. for defense 8/01
- Imperialist phrase added to royal title 8/01
- Gen. Buller relieved of his command 10/01
- Premier Lord Robert Salisbury retires 7/02
- King Edward and Queen Alexandra crowned 8/02
- Imperial Defense holds first meeting 12/02
- Death of Lord Salisbury 8/03
- Joseph Chamberlain leaves Cabinet 9/03
- Committee to reform War Office 11/03
- Campbell-Bannerman is prime minister 12/05
- Balfour resigns 12/05
- Suffragettes urge violent campaign 1/06
- Dreadnought launched 2/06
- 325 warships prepare for mock battle 6/06
- Special ministry for Wales 7/06
- Suffragettes storm Parliament 2/07
- Cruiser Invincible completed 3/07
- New Zealand gets dominion status 9/07
- Asquith becomes premier 4/08
- Churchill elected to House of Commons 5/08
- Suffragettes stop traffic 10/08
- Navy includes six dreadnoughts 2/09
- 144 ships display prowess 6/09
- Suffragettes throw stones 9/09

1910 to 1919

- Lloyd George retains seat in Parliament 1/10
- Asquith saved by police from suffragette 1/10
- King Edward VII dies 5/10
- House votes to abolish Lords' veto power 5/10
- Elections force coalition govt. 12/10
- U.K. police torch home of anarchists 1/11
- Parliament faces new era of reform 2/11
- Ramsay MacDonald heads Labor Party 2/11
- Funding for five new warships added 3/11
- Commons passes bill to curb Lords' power 5/11
- King George V crowned at Westminster 6/11
- Lords act to protect veto power 7/11
- Commons adjourns following riots 7/11
- House of Lords yields veto power 8/11
- House Commons fixes members' salaries 8/11
- Winston Churchill is navy minister 10/11
- Ida Peploe says women will form army 10/11
- U.K. Arbitration League against air war 2/12
- Suffragists riot in London 1/13
- Suffragettes destroy telephone lines 2/13
- E. Pankhurst arrested in bombing attack 2/13
- E. Pankhurst jailed for arson 4/13
- House of Commons rejects suffrage bill 5/13
- Suffragettes assault Premier Asquith 8/13
- Suffragettes commit violent acts 2/14
- Suffragettes attempt to register to vote 2/14
- Additional funds for navy 2/14
- Earl of Minto dies 3/14
- Suffragettes bomb London church 4/14
- Lords rejects woman suffrage bill 5/14
- Contraband confiscated 8/14
- First all-woman battalion 3/15
- Cabinet reshuffled 5/15
- General Hamilton relieved 10/15
- Lloyd George organizes convoys 5/17
- Women over 30 vote 6/17
- U-boats to be sold 3/19
- Wales demands local Parliament 6/19
- Lady Astor is first woman in Parliament 11/19

1920 to 1929

- British Communist party founded 8/20
- Lloyd George and Cabinet resign 10/22
- Labor takes 70 seats from Liberals 11/22
- Premier Andrew Bonar Law resigns 5/23
- X-1 submarine launched 6/23
- Ramsay Macdonald forms first Labor govt. 1/24
- Conservative Cabinet under Baldwin 11/24
- Dreadnought sunk to meet arms quota 1/25
- Asquith steps down 10/26
- Cabinet wants vote for women 4/27
- Voting age dropped to 21 5/28
- King George ill 11/28
- MacDonald prime minister 6/29
- No more cruisers under peace pact 7/29
- Cruisers scrapped per new accord 9/29
- 1,000 Communists attack consulate 6/30
- Winston Churchill retires as aide 1/31
- Labor Party ousts Oswald Mosley 3/31
- MacDonald resigns, forms new govt. 8/31
- Ramsay MacDonald wins re-election 11/31
- Ten resign over protective trade plan 9/32
- Oswald Mosley at London Fascist meeting 6/34
- Fascists demonstrate at Hyde Park 9/34
- Air force to be strengthened 5/35
- Baldwin becomes prime minister 6/35
- Naval quota ends 7/35
- George V dead, Edward VIII king 1/36
- Eden says U.K. needs to prepare for war 2/36
- To build 38 warships 3/36
- Edward VIII escapes assassination 7/36
- 300 planes ordered from Boeing 10/36
- Ark Royal inaugurated 4/37
- Neville Chamberlain premier 5/37
- 111 arrested at Fascist meeting 10/37
- Fascists crushed 11/37
- Eden resigns over policy 2/38
- Contingency plans for war 12/38
- 250,000 drafted 10/39

1940 to 1959

- Churchill appointed head of defense 4/40
- Winston Churchill is new premier 5/40
- Germans seized to bar fifth-column aid 5/40
- Special Operations Executive created 7/40
- Churchill gets vote of confidence on war 7/42
- Churchill calls for new elections 5/45
- Churchill voted out of office 7/45
- Labor wins British general elections 2/50
- Theorist Harold Laski dies 3/50
- Klaus Fuchs sentenced to 14 yrs. 3/50
- Scottish give back coronation stone 4/51
- Ernest Bevin dies 4/51
- Churchill called to form new government 10/51
- Churchill becomes Knight of the Garter 4/53
- Churchill retires as prime minister 4/55
- Gaitskell replaces Attlee as Labor chief 12/55
- MacMillan replaces Eden 1/57
- Defense cuts 4/57
- Women to sit in House of Lords 11/57

1960 to 1987

- Nuclear-powered sub launched 10/60
- Harold Wilson new Labor Party chief 2/63
- 70,000 march in London A-bomb protest 4/63
- Winston Churchill retiring 5/63
- Sex scandal forces out statesman Profumo 6/63
- Kim Philby named as Soviet spy 7/63
- $1 mil. anti-missile system starts 9/63
- Harold Macmillan resigns, Home named 10/63
- 1,000 hurl eggs at Nazi leader C. Jordan 10/63
- Lady Astor dies 5/64
- Harold Wilson new prime minister 10/64
- House of Lords loses legislative powers 10/67
- Clement Attlee dies 10/67
- B. Devlin, firebrand in London debut 4/69
- Edward Heath becomes prime minister 6/70
- 100,000 protest Conservative policy 2/71
- 4,000 march for women's rights 3/71
- House leader Earl Jellicoe resigns 5/73
- Harold Wilson takes on premiership 3/74
- Prince Charles speaks at House of Lords 6/74
- Bomb explodes in Harrod's 12/74
- British Tories get first women leader 2/75
- Field Marshal Montgomery dies 3/76
- Callaghan is prime minister 4/76
- Anthony Eden dies 1/77
- Callaghan govt. ousted 3/79
- Thatcher first woman prime minister 5/79
- Isle of Man Parliament 1,000 years old 7/79
- Michael Foot new Labor Party head 11/80
- Anti-nuke protesters form 14-mile chain 4/83
- Margaret Thatcher wins landslide victory 6/83
- Michael Foot resigns as Labor chief 6/83
- Thatcher escapes bombed hotel 10/84
- Harold MacMillan dies 12/86
- Margaret Thatcher wins third term 6/87

Great Britain (Science and Technology)

- Long-distance buses brought into service 8/00
- Darwin museum opens 6/09
- Comm. Peary hailed for Pole discovery 5/10
- Aviator Charles S. Rolls killed in plane 7/10
- U.K. opens airmail service 9/11
- Parliament considers Channel tunnel 8/13
- Hiram Maxim dies 11/16
- Dirigible crosses the Atlantic 7/19
- Theory of Relativity proved 12/19
- Ship required to have liquor for illness 10/22
- BBC begins first daily broadcast 11/22
- Earl of Carnarvon dies 4/23
- Television broadcast to London 9/27
- First overseas TV broadcast 5/31
- Tea magnate Sir Thomas Lipton dies 10/31
- Largest dry dock built at Southampton 8/33
- Spitfire given new powerful engine 3/44
- Jet goes 606 mph 11/45
- First jet fighter 5/46
- .280 caliber automatic rifle displayed 8/51
- World's first nuclear-power heat system 11/51
- Atomic bomb developed 2/52
- Stonehenge age put at 1848 B.C. 5/52
- Fly Atlantic and back in eight hours 8/52
- First A-bomb test off Australia 10/52
- Capability for constructing H-bombs 2/55
- Largest nuclear plant 10/56
- Remains of Bligh's Bounty found 11/57
- Arthur Fleming dies 9/60
- Maiden flight of Concorde 3/69
- Bertrand Russell dies at age 97 2/70
- First test-tube baby is born 7/78
- American pedals plane across Channel 6/79
- Flagship Mary Rose raised after 437 yrs. 10/82
- Tunnel to be built under English Channel 2/86

Great Britain (Society)

- Legislation passed outlawing child labor 7/00
- Legislation passed for railway safety 7/00
- Population at 37,093,436 4/01
- Parliament passes Education Act 12/02
- Rhodes scholarship awarded to American 2/03
- Birth rate decline causing concern 7/03
- Child miners limited to eight-hour day 3/05
- Immigration curtailed 1/06
- Natl. Health Insurance Act into effect 7/12
- Kaiser's daughter weds English prince 5/13
- Second Intl. Boy Scouts meeting 8/20
- Commons passes equal divorce terms 6/23
- U.K. immigrants enter U.S. via Canada 6/23

– Unemployment insurance passed 7/25
– Chaplin visits Premier Ramsay MacDonald 2/31
– King Richard III found guilty of murder 11/33
– Edward abdicates to marry Simpson 12/36
– Town sold for 20 million pounds 5/38
– King and queen visit N.Y. World's Fair 6/39
– Unity Mitford tries to kill herself 1/40
– Queen Elizabeth reaches New York 3/40
– Beveridge report on poverty released 12/42
– Reformer Beatrice Webb dies 4/43
– Earl of Strathmore dies 11/44
– Elizabeth and Philip married 11/47
– Queen names Charles heir to throne 12/48
– Princess Ann Elizabeth Alice Louise dies 8/50
– King George VI gets pay raise 2/51
– King George VI undergoes lung surgery 9/51
– Princess Elizabeth appears on U.S. TV 10/51
– King George VI dies, Elizabeth crowned 2/52
– Queen Mary dies at age 85 3/53
– Elizabeth II is crowned queen 6/53
– Billy Graham on three-month crusade 3/54
– Race riots in Nottingham 8/58
– Princess Margaret weds Anthony A. Jones 5/60
– Greatest train heist 8/63
– Ten guilty in $7 mil. train robbery 3/64
– Commons votes to ban death penalty 12/64
– Last of "great train" robbers arrested 11/68
– Royals find palace costly 11/69
– Capital punishment ended 12/69
– Queen asks Parliament increase grant 5/71
– Edward VIII, duke of Windsor, dies 5/72
– Princess Anne & Capt. Mark Phillips wed 11/73
– Paul Getty dies 6/76
– Elizabeth II's jubilee 6/77
– Queen Elizabeth II pays a visit 8/77
– Lady Spencer-Churchill dies 12/77
– Engagement of Prince Charles 2/81
– London youths riot in Brixton 4/81
– Pistol shots fired at Elizabeth II 6/81
– Charles and Diana wed 7/81
– Pope John Paul II visits Britain 5/82
– Princess of Wales has baby boy 6/82
– Intruder in Buckingham Palace 7/82
– Princess of Wales has second son 9/84
– Prince Andrew weds Sarah Ferguson 7/86

Great White Fleet
– Round-the-world trip 12/07
– Warm welcome in Sydney 8/08
– Australia, bound for Manila 9/08
– Enters Tokyo Bay 10/08
– Return to U.S. 2/09

Greece
– Prince George becomes monarch 4/00
– Crete claims union 4/05
– Intermediate Olympics open 4/06
– U.S. dominates Intermediate Olympics 5/06
– Crete claims union 10/08
– Crete natl. assembly seeks union 5/10
– Eleutherios Venizelos becomes premier 10/10
– Venizelos supporters take elections 12/10
– Assembly adopts liberal constitution 6/11
– Alliance with Bulgaria 5/12
– Troops mobilized 6/12
– Demonstrations in Athens 9/12
– Yanina and 32,000 Turk troops taken 3/13
– Greek King George I assassinated 3/13
– Pact with Bulgaria annuled 6/13
– Greece declares war on Bulgaria 7/13
– Southern Albania claimed 11/13
– King Constantine I proclaims Crete union 12/13
– To annex Chios and Mitylene 6/14
– British and French troops land 10/15
– Venizelos Cabinet resigns 10/15
– Zaimis Cabinet resigns 11/15
– Call to overthrow king 8/16
– Italy reinforces Allies 8/16
– Allies given control of communications 9/16
– War declared on Bulgaria 9/16
– France seizes navy 10/16
– King quits 6/17
– Relations severed with Central Powers 6/17
– Troops at Smyrna 8/19
– 8,000 Turks taken near Smyrna 6/20
– King Alexander I dies of pet monkey bite 10/20
– King Constantine returns on mandate 12/20
– Mediation refused on Turkish issue 6/21
– Troops take Kutaia from Kemal 7/21
– Macedonia given rights to oil 7/22
– Protectorate proclaimed over Smyrna 7/22
– Troops begin evacuation of Thrace 10/22
– Smyrna surrendered to Turks 9/22
– Near East Treaty ends war with Turkey 7/23
– Italy seizes Paxos and Antipaxos islands 9/23
– Peace terms of Allies accepted 9/23
– George II and Elizabeth enter exile 12/23
– Republic proclaimed 3/24
– 50,000 Armenians to be deported 7/24
– Coup ousts government 6/25
– Bulgaria invaded 10/25
– League orders reparations to Bulgaria 12/25
– Pangalos declares himself dictator 1/26
– Coup ousts Pangalos 8/26
– Friendship treaty signed with Turkey 10/30
– Eleutherios Venizelos quits as premier 5/32
– Italian bomb kills ten on Rhodes Island 4/34
– Military revolt crushed 3/35
– Monarchy restored 10/35
– King George II returns 11/35
– Eleutherios Venizelos dies 3/36
– Placed under military rule 8/36
– Premier jails 100 critics 1/38
– British fleet to protect 4/39
– Italy launches attack 10/40
– Italian drive on Yanina halted 11/40
– Premier Metaxas dies at age 70 1/41
– Manuel Tsouderos named premier 4/41
– King George transfers capital to Crete 4/41
– Army capitulates to Axis 4/41
– King George II flees Crete to Egypt 5/41
– Flying Fortresses attack 10/43
– Red army 26 miles inside country 9/44
– British land and take Petras 10/44
– Exiled govt. returns to Athens 10/44
– Ten killed by U.K. in leftist march 12/44
– Martial law declared to combat strike 12/44
– Churchill and Eden to Athens to end war 12/44
– George II gives up the throne 12/44
– Civil war rages 12/44
– Monarchists win elections 3/46
– Beset by Communist revolt 8/46
– 21 slain in riots 8/46
– King regains throne 9/46
– King George returns 9/46
– U.S. aid to fight Communists 3/47
– King George II dies 4/47
– 2,800 leftists arrested 7/47
– Sophoulis heads coalition 9/47
– Communists beaten at Konitza 1/48
– Control over Aegean islands 3/48
– War with Communists drags on 11/48
– Rebels attack Thrace 3/49
– Nicholas Plastiras is new premier 4/50
– Greece and Turkey admitted to NATO 9/51
– Nicholas Plastiras named premier 9/51
– Greece grants vote to women 5/52
– Defense pact with Turkey and Yugoslavia 2/53
– Talks with Turkey about Cyprus 8/55
– Constantin Caramanlis heads council 10/55
– Ties with Turkey severed 6/58
– U.S. to send nuclear arms 6/59
– Constantine is new king 3/64
– Constantine marries Princess Anne-Marie 9/64
– 10,000 students battle police 7/65
– Athanasiadis-Novas resigns as premier 8/65
– 21,000 riot against new government 8/65
– Greek colonels rebel and take over 4/67
– New regime deports 6,000 foes 5/67
– Andreas Papandreou indicted 8/67
– Turkey consulted on Cyprus dispute 9/67
– King's coup fails; Papandreou freed 12/67
– Colonels get 91% of vote 9/68
– George Papandreou dies 11/68
– 15 nations accuse Greece of torture 4/70
– Youths protest shearing of long hair 2/71
– Police break up student sit-in 3/73
– Premier Papadopoulos bars monarchy 6/73
– Papadopoulos ends martial law 8/73
– Papadopoulos ousted; martial law imposed 11/73
– Caramanlis sworn in as premier 7/74
– 1952 constitution restored 8/74
– Withdrawal from NATO 8/74
– Papadopoulos exiled 10/74
– Premier Caramanlis wins in free election 11/74
– Monarchy abolished 12/74
– Ari Onassis dies 3/75
– To be admitted to EEC 5/79
– Made tenth member of EEC 1/81
– Socialists win 10/81
– Wives given equal voice in home 1/83
– Sartzetakis becomes president 3/85
– Papandreou re-elected premier 6/85
– Four killed as plane is bombed in Athens 4/86

Green, Hetty 2/07, 7/16
Green, Lorne 9/87
Green, Martyn 11/59
Green, William 9/46
Greene, Graham 10/04, 12/48, 12/49, 12/55, 12/66

Greenland
– Ice shelf is 8,850 feet deep 8/31
– U.S. occupies 4/41
– U.S. and Danes build air base at Thule 9/52
– U.S. plane with four H-bombs crashes 1/68

Greenspan, Alan 6/87
Gregory, Dick 12/66

Grenada
– M. Bishop dies in coup; U.S. invades 10/83
– Americans defeat resisters 11/83
– Herbert Blaize elected prime minister 12/84

Gretzky, Wayne 11/82, 5/83
Grey, Edward 3/11, 9/33
Grey, Lita 12/26, 8/27
Grey, Zane 10/39

Greyhound Company
– Greyhound extends service across U.S. 7/30

Griffin, Marvin 4/56
Griffith, D.W. 2/15, 12/16, 4/19, 7/48
Griffith, Michael 12/86
Gris, Juan 7/07, 5/27
Grissom, Virgil I. 7/61, 1/67
Gromyko, Andrei 8/43, 5/46, 3/47, 9/51, 6/52, 2/57, 10/72, 5/75, 9/75, 10/78, 9/84
Gropius, Walter 4/19, 12/26, 7/69
Gropper, William 1/77
Grosz, George 7/59
Groves, Leslie S. 8/45
Gsovsky, Tatiana 3/01

Guadalcanal
– U.S. troops repel Japanese 9/42
– Japanese land in force 10/42
– Japanese lose 28 warships 11/42
– Japanese begin planned withdrawal 1/43
– Japan quits Solomons 2/43

Guadeloupe
– Summit discusses Soviet issues 1/79

Guam
– Americans land 7/44
– Recaptured 8/44

Guatemala
– Nicaragua aids rebels 5/06
– 2,000 lost in Salvadoran battle 7/06
– Treaty ends war with Salvador 7/06
– Mass arrests after attempt on president 7/07
– 18 who planned coup are executed 4/08
– U.S. syndicate granted mining rights 6/11
– Carlos Herrera new president 4/20
– U.S. troops protect legation 4/21
– Federation of Central American Republics 9/21
– Jorge Ubico comes to power 1/31
– 4,000 killed in flooding 10/49
– 234,000 acres taken from United Farms 2/53
– Coup ousts Guzman regime 6/54
– Coup crushed 1/55
– President Castilla assassinated 7/57
– 200 inmates die in asylum fire 7/60
– Fuentes crushes army uprising 11/60
– Students decry elections; martial law 3/62
– President Fuentes overthrown by army 3/63
– U.S. ambassador slain 8/68
– Kjell Laugerud Garcia elected president 7/74
– Quake kills 12,000 2/76
– 100 Indian peasants killed in riot 5/78
– Paralyzed by general strike 10/78
– 36 die in embassy siege 1/80
– Bodies of 50 abducted are found 1/82
– Guevara is pres.; Rios Montt takes power 3/82
– Gen. Rios Montt deposed in coup 8/83
– Untouched Mayan tomb found in Peten 5/84
– Jet crashes in Guatemala; 90 die 1/86

Gucci, Aldo 1/86

Guernica
– Razed by German bombs 4/37

Guevara, Che 9/58, 11/59, 12/64, 10/65, 9/67, 11/67
Guggenheim, Meyer 3/05
Guggenheim, Peggy 12/79
Guggenheim, Solomon R. 11/49

Guinea
– French community repudiated 9/58
– Sekou Toure elected president 1/61
– 92 sentenced to death for treason 1/71
– Col. Llansans Konte seizes presidency 4/84

Guiness, Alec 12/57
Gustav V, King of Sweden 12/07
Gustav VI, King of Sweden 10/50, 9/73
Guthrie, Janet 5/77
Guthrie, Woody 10/67

Guyana
– Mass suicide of Jim Jones cult 11/78

Gymnastics (see also Olympic pages)
– Mary Lou Retton scores 10 3/84
– Mary Lou Retton wins gold all around 8/84

H

Haakon VII, King of Norway 9/57
Habib, Philip 8/82, 7/83, 2/86
Habler, Fritz 12/18
Habre, Hissen 8/83, 1/84
Hacha, Emil 3/39
Hadden, Briton 2/67
Haddon, William 9/66
Hadley, Henry 8/26
Hafid, Mulai 8/07, 10/07, 6/08
Hagen, Walter 5/29
Hagerty, James 6/56
Hague, Frank 6/39, 5/49

Hague, The
– International arbitration court formed 2/00
– Boer delegates ask intervention 9/00
– Venezuela pays West for 1902 blockade 2/04
– Peace conference 9/07
– 11 new rules of war 10/07
– Roosevelt plans conference 2/09
– Swedish/Norwegian borders fixed 10/09
– U.S.-Newfoundland fishing rights settled 9/10
– U.S. repaid for Venezuela revolt 9/10
– Intl. Women's Peace Conference opens 4/13
– Human rights congress opens 8/21
– Young Plan adopted 8/29
– Second war reparations congress 1/30
– NATO ministers plan to counter Soviets 4/50
– Court rules against Iran in oil crisis 9/72

Hahn, Otto 1/39, 7/68
Haig, Alexander 9/72, 10/73, 9/74, 6/82
Haig, Douglas 12/15, 11/17, 6/18, 9/18, 1/28
Hailey, Arthur 12/68
Haines, Jesse 10/26

Haiti
– Germans sink Haitian warship 9/02
– Troops stone European ministers 5/04
– Revolutionaries seize two towns 1/08
– U.S. asked to help quell strife 4/08
– Revolt 11/08
– Call to arms against rebels 2/11
– Rebels exile head of state St. Simon 8/11
– Civil war in Port-au-Prince 1/14
– Rebellion forces president out 1/15
– U.S. lands troops 7/15
– Placed under martial law by U.S. 9/15
– To be made a U.S. protectorate 11/15
– Officially becomes U.S. protectorate 2/16
– U.S. Marines clash with rebels 10/20
– 200 dead in storm 8/28
– Hoover sends troops 12/29
– Last U.S. Marines leave 8/34
– 150th anniversary of independence 1/54
– Army takes control 5/57
– Duvalier elected 9/57
– Duvalier puts down revolt 7/58
– Govt. attacks rebels, suspends rights 8/63
– Hurricane takes 4,000 lives 10/63
– Duvalier decreed president for life 6/64
– Mass executions reported 8/64
– Francois Duvalier dies 4/71
– Baby Doc declares state of siege 1/86
– 14 killed in Haitian anti-govt. rioting 2/86
– Duvalier flees from Haiti 2/86
– Bloody rampage halts elections 11/87

Haldeman, H.R. 4/73, 1/75, 2/75
Hale, George Ellery 6/48
Hale, William 4/27
Halevy, David 2/85
Haley, Alex 12/76, 2/77
Haley, Bill 4/54, 12/59
Haley, Jack 8/39
Hall, Edward W. 7/26, 12/26
Hall, Fawn 11/86, 6/87
Hall, Gus 6/66
Hall, Mrs. Frances Stevens 12/26

Halley's Comet
– Weather disturbances 5/10
– Pictures of comet sent 3/86

Halpert, Samuel 11/45
Hals, Frans 3/10
Hamill, Dorothy 2/76
Hamilton, Andrew 2/06
Hamm, William A. 5/36
Hammarskjold, Dag 3/53, 4/53, 3/54, 4/56, 5/56, 10/56, 9/61, 12/61
Hammerstein, Oscar 9/07, 3/08, 9/10, 11/11, 12/45, 12/49, 11/59, 8/60
Hammett, Dashiell 7/51, 1/61
Hammond, John 7/87
Hampton, Lionel 1/56
Handy, W.C. 3/58
Hanks, Sam 5/57
Hanly, Frank 7/16
Hanna, Mark 12/00, 2/04
Hanna, Richard 10/77, 3/78
Hansberry, Lorraine 12/58, 1/65
Hanson, Lars 12/28
Hapsburg Empire (see Austria-Hungary)
Harden, Maximilian 10/00, 10/07
Hardie, Keir 10/07
Harding, Warren G. 9/20, 11/20, 3/21, 4/21, 6/21, 7/22, 7/23, 8/23
Hardy, Oliver 12/27, 8/57
Hardy, Thomas 1/28
Harlan, John Marshall 3/55

Harlem
– Race riots 8/07
– Harlem Renaissance 3/29
– Two-day riot ends 3/35

Harlow, Jean 6/37
Harmsworth, Alfred Lord Northcliffe 8/22
Harries, Karl 4/10
Harriman, Averell 3/46, 9/46, 7/51, 7/52, 5/68, 7/86
Harriman, Edward H. 4/04, 2/05, 1/07, 2/07, 3/07, 2/08, 1/09, 9/09
Harriman, Mrs. J.B. 4/37
Harris, Jean 3/80, 2/81
Harris, Joel Chandler 7/08
Harris, Patricia R. 10/65, 7/79, 8/79
Harris, Roy 10/79
Harris, William and Emily 8/76
Harrison, Benjamin 3/01
Harrison, Rex 3/56, 12/67
Hart, Gary 2/84, 5/87, 12/87
Hart, Moss 4/37
Harte, Bret 5/02

Harvard University
– T. Roosevelt says keep football 2/07
– William James 11/07
– Rose Bowl victory over Oregon 1/20
– Yale crew beats Harvard 6/22
– Outpost stellar system discovered 10/22
– Overseers ban discrimination 4/23
– Traces of man 25,000 yrs. ago in N.Am. 2/40
– Quinine synthesized 4/44
– E. Kennedy admits ouster for cheating 3/62
– Mitsubishi gives $1 mil. for Japan study 9/72

Hasenfus, Eugene 10/86
Hassan II, King of Morocco 2/61, 6/65, 8/72, 11/75
Haughey, Charles 3/82
Hauptmann, Bruno 2/35, 12/35, 4/36
Hauptmann, Gerhart 6/46

Havana
– Jess Willard outboxes Jack Johnson 4/15
– Pan American Conference 1/28

Havlicek, John 5/69

Hawaii
– Delegate at Republican convention 1/00
– Annexation by the United States 4/00
– Japanese strikers indicted 6/09
– Construction of Pearl Harbor base 11/09
– First flight from California 6/27
– Four Americans held in slaying of native 1/32
– Massie defendants set free 5/32
– Phone link with U.S. 12/32
– Japanese strike Pearl Harbor 12/41
– Tidal waves kill 300 4/46
– Plane crash kills 66 3/55
– 50th state 8/59
– Mauna Loa erupts; no one hurt 7/75
– Thousands evacuated from hurricane 11/82

Hawker, Harry 5/19
Hawkins, Coleman 11/04, 2/35, 5/69
Hawks, Howard 12/77
Hawn, Goldie 10/80
Hay, John 3/00, 7/00, 2/02, 1/03, 5/04, 7/05

Hay-Pauncefote Treaty
– Signed by U.S. and U.K. 2/00
– Second treaty signed 11/01

Hayes, Helen 10/11, 11/27
Hayes, Woody 12/78
Haynes, Elwood 4/25
Haynsworth, Clement F. 11/69
Hayward, Susan 3/75
Haywood, Bill 5/07, 7/07, 5/28
Hayworth, Rita 6/48, 5/49, 5/87
Hearst, Patricia 5/78, 2/74, 3/74, 4/74, 5/74, 9/75, 1/76, 3/76, 8/76, 9/76, 11/76, 1/79
Hearst, William Randolph 11/23, 8/51, 2/74, 3/74
Heath, Edward 7/65, 6/70, 3/72, 2/75
Hebermann, Bronislaw 6/47
Hecht, Ben 5/29
Hecker, Genevieve 6/01
Heckscher, August 10/26
Hegedus, Andra 4/55
Hegenberger, Albert 6/27
Heidegger, Martin 5/76
Heiden, Beth 2/79
Heiden, Eric 2/77, 2/78, 2/80
Heifetz, Jascha 2/01, 10/17, 12/87

Heimlich Maneuver
– Developed by Henry M. Heimlich 6/74

Heineken, Alfred H. 11/83
Heinemann, Gustav 3/69
Heinlein, Robert 12/66
Heisenberg, Werner 12/27, 2/76
Hellman, Lillian 12/76, 6/84
Helms, Jesse 3/81
Helms, Richard 11/77

Helsinki
– Soviets hold 662,200 in penal camps 1/31
– Nationalist China pulls out of Olympics 7/52
– Soviet flag raised at Olympics 7/52
– Largest European summit in history 7/75

Hemingway, Ernest 12/26, 12/29, 3/37, 6/47, 5/53, 12/54, 7/61, 12/66
Henderson, Arthur 10/35
Henderson, Rickey 8/82
Hendrix, Jimi 9/70
Henie, Sonja 2/30, 2/32, 2/36, 10/69
Henlein, Konrad 5/38
Henri, Robert 7/25
Henry, Charles 6/26
Henry, Prince of Prussia 2/02
Henry, Prince of Wales 9/84
Hensen, Matthew 4/09
Hepburn, Audrey 3/59
Hepburn, Katharine 3/36, 12/40, 7/44, 12/49, 12/68
Hepworth, Barbara 12/56
Herbert, Victor 11/10, 2/11, 2/14, 1/17
Heringe, Augustus 10/07
Herman, Woody 10/87
Herrera, Omar 9/77
Herrick, James B. 2/19
Herriot, Edouard 7/26, 3/57
Hersey, John 12/46
Hershey, Milton 11/23
Herter, Christian 8/56, 4/59
Herzl, Theodor 8/03, 7/04
Herzog, Chaim 11/75
Herzog, James 4/10
Heseltine, Michael 11/83
Hess, Rudolf 12/24, 11/35, 2/38, 5/41, 11/45, 8/87
Hess, Victor 12/36
Hesse, Hermann 12/19, 12/27, 12/46, 8/62, 12/65
Heston, Charlton 11/59
Heuss, Theodor 9/49
Heydler, John 12/28
Heydrich, Reinhard 3/04, 6/42
Hickel, Walter J. 2/69
Higgins, Marguerite 1/66

Highways
– Hitler plans vast system 3/34
– 1523-mile Alcan Intl. Highway opens 11/42
– New York State Thruway opens 6/54
– Ike proposes interstate highway system 7/54
– N.J. installs automatic toll collectors 10/54

Hijackings
– U.S. plane with 87 taken to Cuba 11/68
– TWA jet held by PLO in Damascus 8/69
– Ethiopian plane with 66 aboard 9/69
– Cuba allows extradition of hijackers 9/69
– From San Francisco to Rome 10/69
– Bonn pays $5 million to hijackers 2/72
– U.S. airlines set up hijacking screens 2/72
– 23-hour hijacking ends in Tel Aviv 5/72
– Skyjacker bails out with ransom 6/72
– U.S. widens curbs 9/72
– Arabs rescue three Munich terrorists 10/72
– Texas plane taken to Cuba 10/72
– Cuba and U.S. seek curbs 11/72
– PLO hold 27 hostage in Tunis 11/74
– Hijackers take 256 hostages to Uganda 6/76
– Israelis free hostages in Uganda 7/76
– S. Moluccans seize train in Netherlands 5/77
– Soviet airliner with 72 aboard 7/77
– Commandos storm plane in Entebbe 10/77
– Hijacked Malaysian plane crashes 12/77
– Egyptians free hostages in Cyprus 2/78
– Pakistani jetliner hijacked 3/81
– Arabs hijack bus, hold hostages 4/84
– Air France jet hijacked in Tehran 8/84
– Hostages freed in Beirut after 17 days 6/85
– Arabs hijack Italian liner 10/85
– U.S. intercepts plane with hijackers 10/85
– 50 die on Malta trying to get hijackers 11/85

Hill, Graham 5/66
Hill, James J. 12/06
Hillary, Edmund 6/53, 1/58
Hillyard, Blanche 6/00
Hilmi, Pasha 4/09
Hilton, Conrad 1/79
Himalayas (see Mountaineering)
Himmler, Heinrich 10/00, 7/34, 6/36, 8/37, 1/45, 5/45
Hinault, Bernard 7/78, 7/79, 7/85
Hinckley, John W. Jr. 3/81, 8/81, 6/82

Hindenburg
– Blows up 5/37

Hindenburg, Paul von 9/14, 11/14, 2/15, 8/16, 7/18, 9/18, 4/25, 9/27, 7/31, 4/32, 8/34, 4/45
Hines, Duncan 3/59
Hines, James J. 2/39
Hines, Jimmy 6/68, 10/68
Hirohito, Emperor of Japan 11/21, 11/28, 9/45, 9/45, 1/46, 10/71
Hirota, Koki 3/36
Hirshhorn, Joseph 5/66
Hiss, Alger 6/45, 8/48, 12/48, 6/49, 1/50, 11/54, 8/75

12/61
– "Tropic of Cancer" by Henry Miller 12/61
– Moss Hart dies at age 57 12/61
– Victoria Sackville-West dies 6/62
– William Faulkner dies at age 64 7/62
– Author Isak Dinesen dies at age 77 9/62
– Poet edward estlin cummings dies 9/62
– "Ship of Fools" by Katherine Porter 12/62
– "One Flew Over the Cuckoo's Nest" 12/62
– "A Clockwork Orange" by Anthony Burgess 12/62
– "Letting Go" by Philip Roth 12/62
– "Another Country" by James Baldwin 12/62
– "Happiness Is a Warm Puppy" 12/62
– "The Sot-Weed Factor" 12/62
– Robert Frost dies 1/63
– William Carlos Williams dies 3/63
– Poet Theodore Roethke dies 8/63
– Oliver La Farge dies 8/63
– Aldous Huxley dies 11/63
– C.S. Lewis dies 11/63
– Tristan Tzara dies 12/63
– "The Bell Jar" by Sylvia Plath 12/63
– "The Spy Who Came in from the Cold" 12/63
– "Pictures from Brueghel" 12/63
– "The Guns of August" 12/63
– "The Feminine Mystique" by Greer 12/63
– Rachel Carson dies 4/64
– Novelist Flannery O'Connor dies 8/64
– "Herzog" by Saul Bellow 12/64
– "Arrow of God" by Chinua Achebe 12/64
– "A Movable Feast" by Ernest Hemingway 12/64
– T.S. Eliot dies 1/65
– Randall Jarrell dies 10/65
– Somerset Maugham dies 12/65
– "An American Dream" by Mailer 12/65
– "Steppenwolf" by Hesse 12/65
– "The Subject Was Roses" by Frank Gilroy 12/65
– "The Rosey Crucifixion" by Henry Miller 12/65
– C.S. Forster dies 4/66
– "A Thousand Days" by Schlesinger 5/66
– Frank O'Hara dies 7/66
– Soviet poet Yevtushenko tours U.S. 11/66
– "The Magus" by John Fowles 12/66
– "The Comedians" by Graham Greene 12/66
– "The Green House" by Llosa 12/66
– "In Cold Blood" by Capote 12/66
– "The Death of a President" Manchester 12/66
– "The Fixer" by Malamud 12/66
– "The Moon Is a Harsh Mistress" 12/66
– "Papa Hemingway" by Hotchner 12/66
– Carl Sandburg dies 7/67
– Dorothy Parker dies 6/67
– Carson McCullers dies 9/67
– Andre Maurois dies 10/67
– "The Chosen" by Potok 12/67
– "The Confessions of Nat Turner" 12/67
– "The Cancer Ward" by Solzhenitsyn 12/67
– "One Hundred Years of Solitude" 12/67
– "The Naked Ape" by Desmond Morris 12/67
– "Soul on Ice" by Eldridge Cleaver 3/68
– Edna Ferber dies 4/68
– Upton Sinclair dies 11/68
– "The Painted Bird" by Kosinski 12/68
– "The Electric Kool-Aid Acid Test" 12/68
– "Welcome to the Monkey House" 12/68
– "Couples" by Updike 12/68
– "Psychoanalysis and Politics" 12/68
– John Steinbeck dies 12/68
– Jack Kerouac dies 10/69
– "First Circle" & "Cancer Ward" 11/69
– "One Day in the Life of Ivan Denisovich" 11/69
– "Portnoy's Complaint" by P. Roth 12/69
– "The French Lieutenant's Woman" 12/69
– "The Godfather" by Puzo 12/69
– "Slaughterhouse-Five" by Vonnegut 12/69
– "Armies of the Night" by Mailer 12/69
– Samuel Joseph dies 2/70
– Red writer Anna Louise Strong dies 3/70
– "Human Sexual Inadequacy" 4/70
– E.M. Forster dies at age 91 6/70
– Erich Maria Remarque dies 9/70
– Novelist Yukio Mishima commits hara-kiri 11/70
– "Losing Battles" by Eudora Welty 12/70
– "Jonathan Livingston Seagull" 12/70
– Ogden Nash dies 5/71
– Novelist Philip Wylie dies 10/71
– "Rabbit Redux" by John Updike 12/71
– Forster's "Maurice" 12/71
– Wouk's "The Winds of War" 12/71
– Segal's "Love Story" 12/71
– Plath's "The Bell Jar" 12/71
– Kozinski's "Being There" 12/71
– Poet Marianne Moore dies 2/72
– Irving admits hoax on Hughes book 3/72
– Edmund Wilson dies 6/72
– Poet Ezra Pound dies 11/72
– Eudora Welty's "The Optimist's Daughter" 12/72
– Adams' "Watership Down" 12/72
– Mishima's "Spring Snow" 12/72
– Irish writer Elizabeth Bowen dies 2/73
– American writer Pearl S. Buck dies 3/73
– Writer Conrad Aiken dies 8/73
– J.R.R. Tolkein dies 9/73
– W.H. Auden dies 9/73
– Pablo Neruda dies 9/73
– Jong's "Fear of Flying" 12/73
– Hellman's "Pentimento" 12/73
– Gore Vidal's "Burr" 12/73
– Vonnegut's "Breakfast of Champions" 12/73
– "Jaws" published 1/74
– Moscow expels author Solzhenitsyn 2/74
– Poet John Crowe Ransom dies 7/74
– Anne Sexton commits suicide 10/74
– Author Jacqueline Susann dies 9/74
– Le Carre's "Tinker, Tailor, Soldier Spy" 12/74
– Studs Terkel's "Working" 12/74
– Rex Stout dies 10/75
– "Humboldt's Gift" by Saul Bellow 12/75
– "Shogun" by James Clavell 12/75
– Agatha Christie dies 1/76
– Andre Malraux dies 11/76
– "JR" by William Gaddis 12/76
– "Trinity" by Leon Uris 12/76
– "The Autumn of the Patriarch" 12/76
– "The Final Days," Woodward & Bernstein 12/76
– "Scoundrel Time" by Hellman 12/76
– "The Russians" by Hedrick Smith 12/76
– "1876" by Gore Vidal 12/76
– "Roots" by Alex Haley 12/76
– Jacques Prevert dies 4/77
– "World of Our Fathers" by Irving Howe 4/77
– James Jones dies 5/77
– Vladimir Nabokov dies 7/77
– "The Falconer" by Cheever 12/77
– "Blind Date" by Kosinski 12/77
– "The Thorn Birds" by McCullough 12/77
– "The Silmarillion" by J.R. Tolkien 12/77
– "Guest of Honor" by Gordimer 12/77
– China drops ban on Western authors 2/78
– Gutenberg Bible sells for $2 mil. 4/78
– Ignazio Silone dies 8/78
– Rubaiyat origin is dubious 11/78
– "Coming of Age in Somoa" by M. Mead 11/78
– "War and Remembrance" by Wouk 12/78
– "Chesapeake" by Michener 12/78
– "The World According to Garp" by Irving 12/78
– Herbert Marcuse dies 7/79
– S.J. Perelman dies 10/79
– "A Bend in the River" by V.S. Naipaul 12/79
– "Sophie's Choice" by Styron 12/79
– "Life Before Man" by Margaret Atwood 12/79
– "Life on Earth" by Attenborough 12/79
– Marguerite Yourcenar in French Academy 3/80
– Henry Miller dies 6/80
– C.P. Snow dies 7/80
– Novelist Katherine Anne Porter dies 9/80
– Novelist Romain Gary dies 12/80
– Burgess' "Earthly Powers" 12/80
– Goldings' "Rites of Passage" 12/80
– Murdoch's "Nuns and Soldiers" 12/80
– Novelist Archibald J. Cronin dies 1/81
– Caroline Gordon dies 4/81
– William Saroyan dies 5/81
– Rushdie's "Midnight's Children" 12/81
– Gordimer's "July's People" 12/81
– Paton's "Ah! But Your Land Is Beautiful" 12/81
– Schyler's "The Morning of the Poem" 12/81
– Author Ayn Rand dies 3/82
– "Nancy Drew" writer Harriet Adams dies 3/82
– Archibald MacLeish dies 4/82
– John Cheever dies 6/82
– Novelist John Gardner dies 9/82
– Poet Louis Aragon dies 12/82
– Boll's "The Safety Net" 12/82
– Marquez' "Chronicle of a Death Foretold" 12/82
– Golding's "A Moving Target" 12/82
– Plath's "Collected Poems" 12/82
– "The Life and Times of Michael K." 12/83
– Roth's "The Anatomy Lesson" 12/83
– Thomas' "Swallow" 12/83
– Baker's "Growing Up" 12/83
– "...And Ladies of the Club" published 1/84
– Jessamyn West dies 2/84
– Author Lillian Hellman dies 6/84
– James F. Fixx, jogging author, dies 7/84
– Novelist J.B. Priestley dies 8/84
– Truman Capote dies 8/84
– Heller's "God Knows" 12/84
– Sillitoe's "Down from the Hill" 12/84
– Jong's "Parachutes and Kisses" 12/84
– Oliver's "American Primitive" 12/84
– Heinrich Boll dies 7/85
– Italo Calvino dies 9/85
– E.B. White dies 10/85
– "Lake Wobegone Days" by Keillor 12/85
– "Galapagos" by Vonnegut 12/85
– "Yin" by Carolyn Kizer 12/85
– Robert Graves dies 12/85
– Penn Warren is first U.S. poet laureate 2/86
– Bernard Malamud dies 3/86
– John Ciardi dies 3/86
– Simone de Beauvoir dies 4/86
– Theodore H. White dies 5/86
– Jorge Luis Borges dies 6/86
– "Lonesome Dove" by Larry McMurtry 12/86
– "The Flying Change" by Henry Taylor 12/86
– "Common Ground" by Anthony Lukas 12/86
– "The Heavens and the Earth" McDougall 12/86
– Tom Wolfe's "Bonfire of the Vanities" 12/87
– James Baldwin dies 12/87

Lithuania
– Admitted to League of Nations 9/21
– Diet of Vilno votes annexation to Poland 2/22
– Voldermaras overthrown 9/29
– Natl. Union adopts fascist program 12/32
– Baltic Entente 9/34
– Forced to sign peace pact by Poland 3/38

Little, Brown & Co. 1/29
Litvinov, Maxim 11/41, 12/51
Liu Shao-chi 4/59, 11/66, 10/74
Liuzzo, Viola 3/65
Llewellyn, Richard 12/39
Llosa, Mario V. 12/66
Lloyd George, David 4/08, 4/09, 12/09, 1/10, 7/16, 9/16, 12/16, 4/17, 12/17, 1/18, 03/18, 4/18, 6/18, 12/18, 1/19, 6/19, 12/19, 7/20, 4/21, 5/21, 7/21, 12/21, 10/22, 7/23, 3/45
Lloyd, Chris Evert 7/81
Lloyd, Harold 12/27
Lloyd, William 8/20
Lobe, Paul 10/26
Locarno Pact
– Germans and French sign peace treaty 10/25
– 7 nations pledge peace 12/25

Lockhart, Frank 5/26, 2/28, 4/28
Lockheed
– Satellite that can change orbit shown 1/60

Lodge, Henry Cabot 1/01, 8/12, 11/19, 11/24
Lodge, Henry Cabot Jr. 11/52, 7/60, 6/64, 1/69, 11/69, 2/85
Loew, Marcus 4/24, 9/27
Loewy, Raymond 7/86
Lofting, Hugh 12/19
Loftus, John 6/19
Lombard, Carol 1/42
Lombardi, Vince 1/68
Lombardo, Guy 11/77
London
– Conference on arms reduction 3/08
– Great powers debate naval policies 12/08
– John Singer Sargent dominates exhibit 5/09
– 37 die in air raid 7/17
– Conference on reparations 12/18
– First commercial flight to Paris 2/19
– World's longest subway 9/26
– Phone link to San Francisco 2/27
– New Oxford English Dictionary 2/28
– Five powers meet on arms 1/30
– French walk out of naval parley 3/30
– London Naval Treaty signed by 5 powers 4/30
– Elephant stampede injures 50 11/30
– First overseas TV broadcast 5/31
– 21 nations sign wheat agreement 8/33
– Japan asks 5-4-4 naval ratio 11/34
– First V-1 hits city 6/44
– German V-2 rockets hit 9/44
– Big Four meet 11/47
– Big Four parley fails 12/47
– Supersonic DH-110 explodes killing 25 9/52
– Three trains collide, 78 killed 10/52
– Heavy smog kills 55 12/62
– Judy Garland and Liza give concert 11/64
– Race riot 1/69
– Police bust hippies 9/69
– Half of Carnaby St. sold for $8.5 mil. 11/71
– Caning of school students outlawed 11/71
– 234 injured in Trafalgar Square bombing 3/73
– I.R.A. scratches "Adoration of the Magi" 6/74
– Picasso's "Saltimbanque" sold 5/80
– Peter Sutcliffe arrested as Ripper 1/81
– Yorkshire Ripper Sutcliffe sentenced 5/81
– Five killed in blast near Harrods 12/83

London, Jack 11/16
Long, Huey P. 1/35, 1/35, 7/35, 9/35
Longworth, Nicholas 2/06
Lopez Portillo, Jose 9/82
Lopez, Nancy 6/78
Lorca, Garcia 8/36
Loren, Sophia 1/65, 4/66, 6/82
Lorenz, Konrad 11/03
Lorillard, Pierre IV 7/01
Lorre, Peter 6/04
Los Angeles
– Owens River Acqueduct opens 12/13
– Director W.D. Taylor found murdered 2/22
– Aimee Semple McPherson 1/23
– Daisy De Boe guilty of embezzling 1/31
– Summer Olympics open 7/32
– Olympics 8/32
– Utopian Society incorporated 2/34
– Utopian Society at Hollywood Bowl 6/34
– Police say movie stars are Reds 8/34
– C-46 crashes killing 29 4/52
– Noxious smog cause analyzed 7/54
– Jimmy Hoffa accuses RFK of vendetta 2/63
– "Whiskey-a-Go-Go" first disco opens 1/64
– Race riots rage in Watts 8/65
– Manson and three women found guilty 1/71
– Major quake kills 51 in Los Angeles 2/71
– Manson group sentenced to death 3/71
– Police storm SLA house, five killed 5/74
– DeLorean arrested for drugs 10/82
– Draft registration law ruled invalid 11/82
– Marvin Gaye killed by his father 4/84
– Summer Olympics open 7/84
– DeLorean acquitted of cocaine charges 8/84
– Truman Capote dies 8/84
– Police report wave of gang killings 10/84

Loubet, Emile 9/00, 8/01, 7/03
Louis, Joe 6/35, 9/35, 1/36, 6/36, 8/36, 10/36, 1/37, 2/37, 6/37, 8/37, 2/38, 6/38, 1/39, 4/39, 6/39, 9/39, 5/41, 10/42, 6/46, 3/49, 6/51, 4/56, 4/81
Louisiana
– 12 convicts kill guards in prison break 9/33
– Bonnie & Clyde killed in police ambush 5/34
– Long pushes 27 bills through Legislature 8/34
– Huey Long dictator 9/34
– Natl. Guard mobilized against citizens 1/35
– Huey Long criticizes FDR 7/35
– Oil produced from coal 10/50
– First big plant producing hydrazine 7/53
– New Orleans integrates two white schools 11/60
– 2,000 riot against integration 11/60
– Public schools begin integration 9/63
– Police shoot black sniper, killer of ten 1/73
– Jack Abbot seized 9/81

Louvre
– Flood imperils Louvre 1/10
– "Mona Lisa" stolen 8/11
– "Mona Lisa" recovered 12/13

Lovell, James A. 12/65, 11/66, 12/68
Low, Juliette 3/12, 1/27
Lowell, Amy 5/25
Lowenstein, Allard 3/80
Lowry, Malcolm 12/47
Loy, Myrna 11/46
Lucas, George 6/81
Luce, Clare Boothe 4/03, 3/53, 5/59, 10/87
Luce, Henry 2/67
Luciano, Charles "Lucky" 4/36, 6/36
Lucy, Autherine 3/56
Ludendorff, Erich 5/18, 12/37
Ludlowe, Henry 2/08
Luebke, Heinrich 7/59
Lufberry, Raoul 5/18
Lugard, Frederick 1/00
Lugosi, Bela 2/31
Lukas, J. Anthony 12/86
Lumiere, Auguste 4/54
Lumiere, Louis 6/48
Lumumba, Patrice 10/58, 12/60, 2/61, 11/75
Lunt, Alfred 3/38
Lusitania
– Maiden voyage 9/07
– Record transatlantic time 9/07
– Second speed record 10/07
– Cunard ships vie for Atlantic record 11/07
– Sunk by Germans 5/15
– Woodrow Wilson protests sinking 5/15
– Wilson refuses compromise on reparations 1/16

Luthuli, Albert 7/67
Luthuli, John 12/60
Luxembourg
– Starvation 2/15
– Republic proclaimed 1/19
– Govt. dissolved 12/25
– 97% vote against Nazi occupation 10/40
– Benelux 9/44

Luxemburg, Rosa 1/19, 6/19
Luzon
– Liberation from Japanese 6/45

Lvov, Georgi 7/17
Lyautey, Louis H. 10/25
Lysenko, Trofim 11/76

M

MacAndrews and Forbes Co.
– Accused of licorice monopoly 1/07

MacArthur, Douglas 6/00, 5/19, 8/30, 9/35, 7/41, 12/41, 3/42, 7/43, 2/44, 4/44, 10/44, 12/44, 2/45, 6/45, 7/45, 8/45, 9/45, 4/46, 6/50, 9/50, 10/50, 12/50, 3/51, 4/51, 5/51, 7/52, 10/52, 12/52, 4/64
MacArthur, Jean 8/85
MacArthur, John D. 1/78
MacCormack, John 3/08
MacDonald, Ramsay 2/11, 8/17, 1/24, 6/29, 10/29, 8/31, 11/31, 4/33, 3/35, 6/35, 11/37
MacEnroe, John 9/79
MacLaine, Shirley 1/69
Macedonia
– Bulgarians massacre 165 4/03
– Bulgarians occupy governor's palace 8/03
– 210 Turks killed in fight with Bulgaria 8/03
– Turkish troops slay mass of Bulgarians 9/03
– 40,000 reported homeless 10/03
– Turks kill 800 Albanians in siege 2/04
– Naval display by great powers 11/05
– Intervention if peace not achieved 2/08
– Invasion of Turkey 4/09
– Greece occupies Samothrace 11/12
– Bulgaria sends troops 11/28

Machado, Bernardino 12/17
Machado, Gerardo 5/25
Mack, Connie 10/50, 2/56
Mackay, Clarence H. 1/26
Mackay, Ellin 1/26
Macke, August 9/14
Macmillan, Harold 5/55, 1/57, 3/57, 6/58, 6/63, 10/63, 12/86
Macy's
– Bambergers bought 6/29
– Thanksgiving Day Parade 11/51
– First $2 million day 12/57

Madagascar
– France put down revolts 5/16
– Storm kills 600 3/27
– British raid Vichy base Diego Suarez 3/42
– U.K. forces land 5/42
– Vichy gives up Diego Suarez & Antsirana 5/42
– Japanese subs shell Diego Suarez base 5/42
– Vichy hands over Madagascar to Allies 11/42
– U.K. gives up Madagascar to Free French 1/43
– French put down native revolt 4/47

Madame Tussaud's
– Winston Churchill statue installed 10/08

Maddox, Lester 4/65, 2/70
Madero, Francisco 11/10, 5/11, 10/11, 2/13
Madero, Gustavo 2/13
Madison Square Garden
– Explosion kills 15, injures 70 11/02
– Auto show opens 1/05
– Auto show 11/07
– First aviation show 9/09
– 5,000 Socialists fight Communists 2/34
– 20,000 show solidarity with Czechs 9/38
– 22,000 at Nazi rally 2/39
– Joe Louis scores KO over Johnny Paychek 3/40
– Rolling Stone concert 7/72
– 4,000 married by Sun Myung Moon 7/82
– Mary Lou Retton, gymnast, scores 10 3/84

Madrid
– Subway opening 10/19

Madrid, Miguel de la 9/85
Maes, Romain 7/35
Maes, Sylvere 8/36
Maeterlinck, Maurice 5/01, 5/02, 3/11, 5/49
Magidoff, Robert 4/48
Magritte, Rene 9/66
Magsaysay, Ramon 11/53
Maher, Ahmed 2/45
Mahler, Gustav 1/08, 5/11
Mahre, Phil 3/81
Mailer, Norman 12/48, 10/55, 12/65, 10/67, 12/69
Maine
– Alcohol banned 11/11
– Prohibition repeal voted 9/33
– FDR states U.S. is not near entering war 8/41
– Fire destroys $30 million property 10/47
– Blackout 11/65
– Samantha Smith killed in plane crash 8/85

Maitland, Lester 6/27
Makarios, Archbishop 2/56, 3/56, 3/57, 3/59, 12/59, 2/68, 8/77
Malamud, Bernard 12/57, 12/66, 3/86
Malan, Daniel 3/52
Malaya
– Territory to U.K. 3/09
– U.K. declares state of emergency 12/41

Malaysia
– Formed 9/63
– Cease-fire with India 1/64
– Three-year war with Indonesia ends 8/66
– 70,000 boat people put back to sea 6/79

Malcolm X 4/58, 5/63, 2/64, 3/64, 4/64, 6/64, 2/65, 2/66
Malden, Karl 12/47
Malenkov, Georgi 1/02, 3/53, 7/53, 8/53, 4/54, 2/55, 3/56, 7/57, 11/61
Malik, Jacob 1/50, 6/51, 9/52
Malkov, Feodor 8/11
Malone, Dudley F. 5/25
Malone, Moses 8/74
Malraux, Andre 11/01, 11/76
Malta
– Made British dominion 3/28
– U.K. honors Malta for heroism in war 4/42
– Independence 9/64
– 50 die on Malta trying to get hijackers 11/85

Malvas, Miguel 7/01
Man o' War
– Retires with one loss 12/20

Man, Woodrow 9/57
Manchester, William 12/66
Manchu Dynasty
– Pu Yi becomes emperor 12/08
– Tottering in China 10/11
– Comes to an end in China 1/12

Manchuria
– Russians occupy with 100,000 troops 11/00
– Japan accepts Russian good faith offer 4/01
– Revolt over Russian occupation 6/01
– Russians reoccupy Niu-Chwang 5/03
– Japan & U.K. demand Russian evacuation 7/03
– Chinese uprising against Russians 5/04
– Great battle at Liao Yang begins 8/04
– 13-day Cha-Ho River battle 10/04
– Czar says troops will evacuate 1/07
– Russians complete evacuation 3/07
– Russians and Japanese leave 4/07
– Japanese advances 2/08
– Japanese seize Manchurian Railroad 9/31
– Japanese call halt to offensive 11/31
– Independence declared 2/32
– Manchukuo is Japanese puppet state 3/32
– Rebels in control 10/32
– Soviets sell eastern railway to Chinese 3/35
– Soviets angered by Japanese raids 10/35
– Soviets invade 8/45
– Communists fight Nationalists 3/46

Mandel, Marvin 10/77
Mandela, Nelson 2/85
Mandela, Winnie 12/85
Manes, Donald 1/86, 3/86
Maniu, Juliu 11/47
Mann, Thomas 12/29, 4/37, 12/47, 7/49, 8/55, 12/75
Mansfield, Jayne 6/67
Mansfield, Richard 8/07
Manson, Charles 12/69, 8/70, 1/71, 3/71
Mansour, Hassan Ali 1/65
Mantle, Mickey 11/57, 2/63, 5/67, 3/69
Manton, Martin T. 6/39
Manuel II, King of Portugal 10/10
Manuel, Don 2/08
Manville Corp.
– Fined $2.5 billion for asbestos damages 8/85

Mao Tse-tung 12/21, 11/34, 10/35, 2/37, 9/37, 6/45, 8/45, 10/45, 8/46, 10/46, 10/48, 1/49, 3/49, 4/49, 5/49, 9/49, 10/49, 12/49, 1/50, 2/50, 5/50, 10/50, 9/54, 4/55, 4/57, 7/57, 5/58, 8/58, 4/59, 10/59, 3/60, 5/66, 10/68, 5/70, 2/72, 7/72, 2/74, 12/75, 4/76, 9/76, 10/76
Marathons
– T.P. Morrissey wins in Boston 4/08
– James Crowley sets new record in Boston 2/09
– Clarence De Mar wins in Boston 4/28
– Johnny Kelley wins in Boston 4/35
– Ellison Brown wins in Boston 4/39
– Gerard Cote sets record in Boston run 4/40
– Emil Zatopek breaks Olympic record 7/52
– Keizo Yamada wins Boston run in 2:18 :51 4/53
– Eino Oksanen wins Boston Marathon 4/62
– A. Vandendriessche wins Boston Marathon 4/64
– Morio Sigematsu wins in Boston 4/65
– Kimihara wins in Boston 4/66
– American F. Shorter wins Olympic race 9/72
– Bill Rodgers wins in Boston 4/78
– New record for Boston Marathon 4/79
– Rodgers and Waitz take N.Y. Marathon 10/79
– Bill Rodgers wins Boston Marathon 4/80
– Alberto Salazar wins N.Y. Marathon 10/80
– Terry Fox, marathoner, dies 6/81
– Salazar wins N.Y. Marathon 10/81
– Salazar and Teske win Boston run 4/82
– Alberto Salazar wins N.Y. Marathon 10/82
– Greg Meyer wins Boston race 4/83
– Joan Benoit sets women's record 4/83
– N.Y. race won by Orlando Pizzolato 10/84
– Pizzolato and Waitz take N.Y. Marathon 10/85
– Rob de Castella wins Boston Marathon 4/86
– Seko and Mota win Boston Marathon 4/87

Marble, Alice 7/39, 9/39
March, Frederick 11/46
March, Fredric 6/49, 4/75
Marciano, Rocky 2/52, 9/52, 5/53, 9/53, 9/55, 4/56, 11/56, 8/69
Marconi, Guglielmo 12/01, 12/02, 3/03, 6/08, 2/14, 4/14, 6/27, 8/32, 7/37
Marcos, Ferdinand 11/65, 12/65, 9/66, 7/69, 1/73, 12/76, 11/77, 1/81, 8/83, 8/84, 10/85, 12/85, 1/86, 2/86
Marcuse, Herbert 12/65, 12/68
Margrethe, Queen of Denmark 1/72
Marianas Islands
– U.S. bombers strike 2/44
– Americans attack 6/44
– Allegiance to United States 6/75

Markenzinis, Spyros 11/73
Markham, Beryl 9/36
Marley, Bob 5/81
Marriages
– T. Roosevelt Jr. and Eleanor Alexander 6/10
– China lifts ban on mixed marriage 4/12
– Kaiser's daughter weds English prince 5/13
– Eleanor Wilson and William McAdoo 5/14
– Woodrow Wilson weds Mrs. Norman Galt 12/15
– 6,000 Americans married French women 3/19
– Douglas Fairbanks and Mary Pickford 3/20
– Duke of York weds Elizabeth Bowes-Lyons 4/23
– Prince Gustaf weds Louise Mountbatten 11/23
– Jack Dempsey and Estelle Taylor 2/25
– Irving Berlin and Ellin Mackay 1/26
– Luisa Tetrazzini weds Pietro Vernati 10/26
– Prince Leopold and Princess Astrid 11/26
– Pola Negri and Prince Mdivani 5/27
– Marconi weds Countess Bezzi-Scali 6/27
– Prince Olaf and Princess Martha 3/29
– Charles Lindbergh and Anne Morrow 5/29
– Douglas Fairbanks Jr. and Joan Crawford 6/29
– Pope Pius XI denounces trial marriage 1/31
– Amelia Earhart weds George Putnam 2/31
– Charlie Chaplin and Paulette Goddard 6/33
– King Edward VIII abdicates 12/36
– Princess Juiliana and Prince Bernhard 1/37
– Duke and Duchess of Windsor 6/37
– Tyrone Power and Annabella 4/39
– Barbara Stanwyck and Robert Taylor 5/39
– William Holden and Brenda Marshall 7/41
– Judy Garland weds David Rose 7/41
– Cary Grant and Barbara Hutton 7/42
– Princess Elizabeth and Prince Philip 11/47
– Iran Princess Fatima weds U.S. student 4/50
– Reza Pahlevi weds Soraya Esfandiari 2/51
– King Farouk marries Narriman Sadek 5/51
– Jacqueline Bouvier engaged to J. Husted 1/52
– Anthony Eden weds Churchill's niece 8/52

S

T

- Comedian Peter Sellers 7/80
- "Heaven's Gate" a bust for Hollywood 10/80
- Steve McQueen dies of cancer 11/80
- Marshall McLuhan dies 12/80
- John Lennon killed 12/80
- Abel Gance's "Napoleon" at Radio City 1/81
- Bob Marley dies 5/81
- Natalie Wood drowns 11/81
- Songwriter Hoagy Carmichael dies 12/81
- Jazz pianist Thelonius Monk dies 2/82
- John Belushi dies 3/82
- Writer Nancy Drew dies 3/82
- Actress Romy Schneider dies 5/82
- Writer John Cheever dies 6/82
- Spielberg's "E.T." 6/82
- Henry Fonda dies 8/82
- Kate Smith gets Medal of Freedom 10/82
- Sly Stallone in "First Blood" 12/82
- Ben Kingsley in "Gandhi" 2/83
- Ragtime pianist Eubie Blake dies at 100 2/83
- Gerald Ford on "Dynasty" 12/83
- Boy George 1/84
- Marvin Gaye killed 4/84
- Count Basie dies 4/84
- Nicholson and MacLaine win Oscars 4/84
- Photographer Ansel Adams dies 4/84
- Author Lillian Hellman dies 6/84
- Truman Capote dies 8/84
- Film: "Amadeus" 9/84
- Special effects in film in 1984 12/84
- Prince's "Purple Rain" 3/85
- Live Aid concert for famine relief 7/85
- Bruce Springsteen in New Jersey 8/85
- Stallone in "First Blood Part II" 10/85
- Orson Welles dies 10/85
- Yul Brynner dies 10/85
- Meryl Streep in "Out of Africa" 12/85
- Madonna's "Like a Virgin" 12/85
- Ricky Nelson dies 12/85
- Penn Warren is first U.S. poet laureate 2/86
- Pop artist Andy Warhol dies 2/87
- Liberace dies 2/87
- Met opens wing for 20th-Century art 2/87
- James Earl Jones opens in "Fences" 3/87
- Kanny Kaye dies 3/87
- "Les Miserables" opens on Broadway 3/87
- Peter O'Toole in "Pygmalion" 4/87
- Erskine Caldwell dies 4/87
- Rita Hayworth dies 5/87
- Last "Prairie Home Companion" radio show 6/87
- Jackie Gleason dies 6/87
- Fred Astaire dies 6/87
- Hemlines climbing again 6/87
- "A Chorus Line" has 5,001st performance 8/87
- John Huston dies 8/87
- 1987: Big year in movies 12/87
- James Baldwin dies 12/87

United States (Disasters)

- Flooding in Mississippi 4/00
- Hundreds die as ocean liner burns 6/00
- 10,000 homeless in Jacksonville fire 5/01
- Tunnel collapses at Park Avenue 3/02
- Span of Williamsburg Bridge burns 11/02
- Chicago theater fire kills 578 12/03
- Steamer General Slocum sinks; 693 die 6/04
- World's Fair Flyer wreck 8/04
- San Francisco quake kills thousand 5/06
- Streetcar collision injures 40 5/07
- Orville Wright crashes plane 9/08
- Forest fires kill over 300 in Midwest 10/10
- Triangle Shirtwaist fire 3/11
- Titanic sinks; 1,595 killed 4/12
- Senate rules Titanic operators guilty 5/12
- Death toll at 21 in heat wave 7/12
- Two battleships collide 1/14
- Natl. Storage Munitions Co. explodes 7/16
- 28 dead in Utah avalanche 2/26
- 1,000 killed in Florida by hurricane 9/26
- Tornado devastates St. Louis 9/27
- Liner Vestris sinks; 111 killed 11/28
- 16 die in L.A. plane crash 4/30
- Dirigible Akron crashes at sea 4/33
- N.Y. flier crashes; 14 killed, 30 hurt 9/33
- Liner Morro Castle burns; 130 die 9/34
- Dust storms devastate Midwest 4/35
- Texas school fire kills 500 children 3/37
- Sub sinks; 26 die 5/39
- Cocoanut Grove Night Club fire, Boston 11/42
- Worst plane crash yet kills 39 10/46
- Explosions kill 377 in Texas 4/47
- Flooding in Oregon 5/48
- Plane crash near Milwaukee kills 180 6/50
- 33 soldiers killed in troop train wreck 9/50
- Tornadoes hit five states 3/52
- Worst bus crash takes 28 lives in Texas 8/52
- 84 servicemen die in Globemaster crash 12/52
- Ship blast kills 7 more in Boston 11/53
- Andrea Doria wrecked off Nantucket 7/56
- Plane crash over canyon kills 128 7/56
- Airliners collide over New York; 127 die 12/60
- U.S. sub Thresher lost with 129 aboard 4/63
- Military plane down Philippines; 74 dead 5/64
- Earthquake kills 51 in L.A. 2/71
- Three-Mile Island atomic leak 3/79
- Hotel walkways collapse, killing 111 7/81
- Jetliner crashes in New Orleans 7/82
- 248 soldiers killed in air crash 12/85
- Challenger space shuttle explodes 1/86
- 15 killed inAmtrak crash 1/87
- 156 killed in Detroit air crash 8/87
- California hit by quake 10/87

United States (Economy)

1900 to 1909

- Gold standard 3/00
- Carnegie Steel Corp. formed 3/00
- National Civic Federation formed 12/00
- U.S. Steel formed 2/01
- Andrew Carnegie retires 3/01
- Customs duties on Cuban imports outlawed 5/01
- U.S. Steel makes $174 million profit 1/02
- Roosevelt signs Newlands Reclamation Act 6/02
- Intl. Harvester Co. formed 8/02
- Congress passes Expedition Act 2/03
- Dept. of Commerce and Labor created 2/03
- Circuit court rules against beef trust 2/03
- Congress passes Elkins Act 2/03
- Henry Ford forms auto company 6/03
- Ford sells first auto 7/03
- Northern Securities merger blocked 3/04
- Cotton burned to support prices 12/04
- German tariffs on U.S. goods 10/05
- Marshall Field dies 1/06
- Cost of govt. doubles 2/07
- Stock market dives 3/07
- Manufacturers plan to combat unions 5/07
- Panic on Wall Street 10/07
- J.P. Morgan saves Wall Street 11/07
- Business courses started at Yale 4/08
- Child labor laws passed 5/08
- Two cents postage to U.K. 11/08
- Pressure for progressive tax 5/09
- Record harvest 8/09
- Cost of living up 8% 11/09
- Two million own stock 11/09
- J.P. Morgan controls Equitable Life 12/09

1910 to 1919

- Unions ask U.S. Steel inquiry 1/10
- Jury inquiry into high meat cost 1/10
- Congress passes Mann-Elkins Act 6/10
- Republicans urge progressive legislation 1/11
- Carnegie Trust Co. shut down 1/11
- Carnegie trust placed in bankruptcy 4/11
- 16th Amendment to Constitution adopted 2/13
- J.P. Morgan dies 3/13
- House passes income tax bill 5/13
- Antitrust suit against Eastman Kodak 6/13
- Wilson signs Erdman Arbitration Act 7/13
- Underwood-Simmons Tariff Bill signed 10/13
- Federal Reserve created 12/13
- Federal Reserve to make 12 districts 4/14
- Federal Trade Commission organized 9/14
- Clayton Act exempts union from antitrust 10/14
- Gas to $.25 a gallon 12/15
- Supreme Court approves income tax 1/16
- Ford makes car affordable 8/16
- Prosperity unlimited 1/17
- Wilson takes control of necessities 7/17
- $156 to outfit doughboy 8/17
- Govt. takes control of sugar industry 9/17
- Liberty loans over $3.5 billion 10/17
- Wilson places rails under govt. control 12/17
- All industries closed on Mondays 1/18
- U.S. has $5 million debt 1/18
- Govt. control of railroads limited 2/18
- Baruch heads War Industries Board 3/18
- Suit to gain labels on food 4/18
- Record ship construction 6/18
- War costs $13 billion this year 6/18
- Edsel Ford becomes president of Ford 1/19
- Dependence on good roads 4/19
- Wire operations back to private control 6/19
- Food prices skyrocket 8/19
- Child labor down 40% 11/19

1920 to 1929

- $150 mil. loan to Poland and Austria 1/20
- Wilson gives rails back to owners 2/20
- Merchant Marine Act passes Congress 6/20
- Federal Power Commission created 6/20
- War Finance Corp. reactivated 1/21
- Bread returns to five cents per loaf 1/21
- 3.5 million unemployed 1/21
- Congress passes Emergency Tariff Act 5/21
- Congress passes Budget & Accounting Act 6/21
- Eight million women hold jobs 7/21
- Food prices up in 11 of 14 cities 8/21
- House Ways and Means lowers taxes 8/21
- 3,500 businesses failed since January 9/21
- 3.5 million unemployed 9/21
- 8 million women employed nationwide 10/21
- Congress passes Capper-Volstead Act 2/22
- Federal rail and coal control 7/22
- Fordney-McCumber Tariff Bill 8/22
- Govt. gets injunction on rail workers 9/22
- Merchandiser John Wanamaker dies 12/22
- Rising stamp sales show prosperity 1/23
- Congress passes Intl. Credit Act 3/23
- Coolidge gives Congress national budget 12/23
- Du Pont charged with war profiteering 4/24
- Congress approves $472 mil. tax cut 5/24
- Child labor bill sent to states 6/24
- Tax returns made public under new law 10/24
- Market surges after elections 11/24
- Tenative debt accord with England 1/25
- Belgium war debt modified 8/25
- Failure to settle French debt 10/25
- N.Y. Stock Exchange seat $125,000 10/25
- Drought grips South 9/25
- French minister to discuss debt 9/25
- Italy negotiates debt 11/25
- U.S. Steel $138 a share 11/25
- Stocks plummet 3/26
- Senator wants war debts paid 4/26
- French debt agreement 4/26
- Motors are one-third of all exports 5/26
- Women take seats on N.Y. Stock Exchange 1/27
- Treasury cuts size of currency 5/27
- G.M.'s biggest dividend 11/27
- Highest wages in world 12/27
- Wall Street staggered by volume of trade 2/28
- Wild trading on Wall Street 3/28
- Stocks dive 5/28
- Unemployment in the millions 6/28
- Stocks drop 6/28
- Stock market drops again 7/28
- China granted tariff autonomy 7/28
- Prices soar on Wall St. 10/28
- Stock market shuts after heavy trading 11/28
- Stocks tumble 12/28
- Govt. wants curb on stock speculation 2/29
- Stocks down again 4/29
- Clark brothers arrested for embezzling 7/29
- Farmers form cooperative 8/29
- Market hits all time high 9/29
- Stock market crashes 10/29
- Hoover tries to boost economy 11/29
- Suicide because of crash 11/29
- Ford grants wage hike to help economy 11/29
- Suicide because of crash 11/29
- Ford grants wage hike to help economy 11/29

1930 to 1939

- U.S. incomes over $1 million 2/30
- Senate passes bill increasing tariffs 3/30
- Congress adopts Public Buildings Act 3/30
- Congress votes $300 mil. for roads 4/30
- Economists warn against Smoot-Hawley 5/30
- Canadian tariffs to cost $225 million 5/30
- Hoover signs Smoot-Hawley Tariff Bill 6/30
- Cigarette smoking increases 7/30
- $121.9 mil. for drought relief 8/30
- Hoover asks aid to combat depression 10/30
- Committee for Unemployment Relief formed 10/30
- Bank of U.S. closes its doors 12/30
- 4.8 million Americans unemployed 12/30
- Bank of U.S. heads go to trial 1/31
- $20 million drought-aid bill now law 2/31
- Bank officers misuse funds 2/31
- Per capita wealth at $2,977 3/31
- Treasury pressed by deficit 5/31
- Pact to build 90 Soviet steel plants 6/31
- U.S. Bank leaders convicted 6/31
- Delay in war debt payments proposed 6/31
- Navy retires 17 ships to meet budget cut 10/31
- Agreement with France on gold standard 10/31
- Living costs down 15% from 1925 10/31
- Banker Dwight Morrow dies 10/31
- Hoover sanctions public works program 12/31
- Senate ratifies foreign debt moratorium 12/31
- Hoover signs law for $2 billion for jobs 1/32
- N.Y. bankers lend city $350 million 1/32
- Glass-Steagall Act passed 2/32
- Norris-La Guardia Act passes Congress 3/32
- Deficit passes $2 billion mark 4/32
- Oil tax one cent/gallon 6/32
- Hoover opposes canceling war debts 7/32
- Relief & Reconstruction Act signed 7/32
- Federal Home Loan Act passed by Congress 7/32
- RFC loans Illinois $3 million 7/32
- RFC lends $49 mil. 8/32
- Hoover recovery plan 8/32
- Hoover lists ten signs of recovery 10/32
- U.K. & France ask for debt relief 11/32
- Hoover refuses to suspend war debts 11/32
- Drive to end child labor 11/32
- Detroit defaults on $400 million debt 2/33
- FDR orders bank holiday 3/33
- FDR signs Economy Act 3/33
- Reforestation Relief Act passes Congress 3/33
- Farm relief bill passed in the Senate 4/33
- FDR takes dollar off gold standard 4/33
- $3 billion voted for works program 5/33
- J.P. Morgan paid no 1931 or 1932 taxes 5/33
- FDR asks pay raise for workers 5/33
- FDR promises partnership with farmers 5/33
- Agricultural Adjustment Act adopted 5/33
- Federal Emergency Act adopted 5/33
- Hugh Johnson named dictator of industry 5/33
- Tennessee Valley Authority created 5/33
- Securities must be registered with FTC 5/33
- Employment Service created 6/33
- Natl. Industry Recovery Act signed 6/33
- National Recovery Administration formed 6/33
- Big spending makes more jobs 6/33
- FDR repeals protection tariffs 6/33
- Home Owner Loan Corp. set up 6/33
- RFC lends U.S.S.R. $4 mil. to buy cotton 7/33
- Steel code gives 15% pay rise to skilled 7/33
- NRA goes into effect 7/33
- NRA goes into action 8/33
- $37 mil. allotted for N.Y. bridge 8/33
- Eight-hour day in steel industry 8/33
- FDR orders $700 million for the needy 9/33
- A.F.L. membership rises 10/33
- Fines and jail for NRA violators 10/33
- RFC buys gold to devalue the dollar 10/33
- FDR creates Civil Works Admin. 11/33
- First NRA violator indicted 11/33
- FDR refuses to return to gold standard 11/33
- Army bans foreign-produced food 11/33
- FDR devalues dollar to 60 cents 1/34
- Civilian Conservation Corps 1/34
- FDR extends life of RFC 1/34
- Federal Farm Mortgage Corp. set up 1/34
- FDR establishes Export-Import Bank 2/34
- Civil Works Emergency Relief Act passed 2/34
- N.J. silk plant fined for NRA violation 4/34
- Nye Commission inquiry begins 4/34
- Loans to countries in default banned 4/34
- Cotton Control Act passed 4/34
- Congress authorizes controls on sugar 5/34
- Darrow claims NRA encourages monopoly 5/34
- FDR asks $525 million for drought relief 6/34
- Securities Exchange Commission created 6/34
- FDR sets New Deal objectives 6/34
- Farm Mortgage Forclosure Act 6/34
- Reciprocal Trade agreements Act 6/34
- Federal Housing Administration created 6/34
- FDR nationalizes silver 8/34
- Cuba signs reciprocal tariff treaty 8/34
- 10.8 million unemployed 10/34
- FDR says jobless aid before vets' bonus 10/34
- Trade pact with Brazil 2/35
- $5 billion for relief and jobs 4/35
- WPA begins 5/35
- Social Security enacted 8/35
- Jobs to 18,000 musicians 8/35
- Trade treaty with Canada 11/35
- $1 billion deficit 9/36
- Imports exceed exports 10/36
- Business improving 11/36
- John D. Rockefeller dies 5/37
- Japan uses made in USA labels 9/37
- Harvey Firestone dies 2/38
- Minimum wage $.40 an hour 6/38
- Bankruptcy laws 6/38
- Stocks soar as war breaks out 9/39

1940 to 1949

- Debt reported at $43 billion 7/40
- Forty-hour work week goes into effect 10/40
- Office of Production Management created 12/40
- FDR buys first savings bond for defense 4/41
- Office of Price Administration created 4/41
- Supply Priorities and Allocations Board 8/41
- FDR submits largest budget 1/42
- OPA puts ceilings on prices and rents 1/42
- Speed limit at 40 mph to conserve tires 3/42
- Congress bans all strikes during war 3/42
- FDR asks Americans to sacrifice for war 4/42
- OPA freezes prices of major items 4/42
- Drive to salvage rubber 6/42
- Baruch Commission warns of rubber dearth 9/42
- OPA rations oil 9/42
- WLB orders equal pay for women 9/42
- FDR ends two-week war plant trip 10/42
- FDR freezes wages, rents, farm prices 10/42
- James Byrnes named new economic director 10/42
- Congress passes biggest tax bill 10/42
- Federal salaries limited to $25,000 10/42
- Victory Gardens 9/42
- Rationing of coffee begun 11/42
- Gas is rationed 12/42
- FDR creates Petroleum Admin. for War 12/42
- FDR closes Works Project Administration 12/42
- Canned food, shoes rationed 2/43
- Coupon books issued for food ration plan 3/43
- Sale of butter, lard, fats, oils halted 3/43
- Meats, fats, cheese rationed 4/43
- FDR freezes prices, wages, salaries 4/43
- Office of War Mobilization formed 5/43
- Senate passes pay-as-you-go tax plan 5/43
- Congress passes War Labor Dispute Act 6/43
- Senate bars food subsidies 6/43
- Army seizes railroads under FDR 12/43
- FDR presents $99.7 bil. war budget 1/44
- Rail lines returned to private ownership 1/44
- FDR vetoes new tax bill 2/44
- Women comprise 42% of work force in West 3/44
- Meat rationing ends 5/44
- Production of appliances resumes 8/44
- Congress passes Surplus War Property Act 10/44
- FDR opens sixth war loan drive 11/44
- Rationing ends 8/45
- Govt. seizes 26 oil companies 10/45
- $25 billion British debt written off 12/45
- Severe meat crisis 10/46
- Truman stops price controls 11/46
- Henry Ford dies 4/47
- Grain rushed to Germany 5/47
- Marshall Plan gets bad reception 6/47
- Budget surplus 8/47
- Truman seeks food for Europe 10/47
- Food shipments to meet European crisis 12/47

1950 to 1959

- $25 bil. in foreign loans 1/50
- $1 bil. in aid leaves for Europe 3/50
- G.M. profit of $656.4 million 3/50
- Truman warns foreign aid cuts risk WWIII 3/50
- U.S. offers military aid to France 5/50
- $3.2 bil. for five aid programs 6/50
- U.S. govt. seizes rails to avert strike 8/50
- Truman adds ten mil. to Social Security 8/50
- Truman bans exports to Red China 12/50
- Price & wage freeze to curb inflation 1/51
- OPA removes price ceilings on sugar 2/51
- OPA removes price ceilings on farm goods 2/51
- $29 mil. in materials to Yugoslavia 4/51
- Tariff privileges ended for Red nations 8/51
- Chase & Manhattan open talks on merger 8/51
- Average U.S. income is $1,436 8/51
- Truman signs Mutual Security Bill 10/51
- U.S. postpones color TV due to war needs 10/51
- Economic plan for Near East 11/51
- Truman orders seizure of steel mills 4/52
- Impeachment asked for steel seizure 4/52
- Truman orders rails back to owners 5/52
- Steel seizure unconstitutional 6/52
- E. Germany asks $14 mil. for phone cable 6/52
- $6.5 bil. Mutual Security Bill 6/52
- Vending machines gross $1.25 billion 1/53
- U.S. budget deficit at $10 billion 1/53
- Ike signs Offshore Oil Bill 5/53
- Largest peacetime deficit at $9.4 bil. 7/53
- $45 mil. aid to Iran 9/53
- GNP reaches record $365 billion 7/54
- Ike signs Housing Act 8/54
- Chase merges with Bank of Manhattan 1/55
- Biggest stock exchange loss in history 9/55
- First drive-in bank 8/56
- Ike raises debt ceiling to $295 billion 6/59

1960 to 1969

- GNP at record $400 billion for 1959 1/60
- Ike asks for $4.1 bil. in foreign aid 2/60
- Ike signs wheat pact with India 5/60
- John D. Rockefeller Jr. dies 5/60
- Fair Labor Standards Act signed 5/61
- JFK invokes Taft-Hartley in ship walkout 6/61
- JFK signs Housing Act of 1961 6/61
- JFK asks for rise in debt ceiling 1/62
- JFK asks for $5.6 bil. in school aid 2/62
- Stock prices take sharp dive 5/62
- U.S. debt exceeds $300 billion 8/62
- JFK proposes $10 bil. tax cut 1/63
- JFK proposes jobs program 2/63
- Free legal service to poor 3/63
- $250 mil. wheat sale made to U.S.S.R. 10/63
- LBJ pledges war against poverty 1/64
- Shriver to head anti-poverty drive 2/64
- LBJ submits $1 bil. war on poverty 3/64
- LBJ signs anti-poverty bill 8/64
- $1.6 bil. in aid approved for Appalachia 9/64
- Poverty is third cause of death in U.S. 10/64
- LBJ gives $196 bil. budget to Congress 1/68
- Trading exceeds 16.4 million shares 4/68

1970 to 1979

- Defense cuts to end 1.25 mil. jobs 1/70
- Chavez jailed for illegal boycott 12/70
- FDA recalls million cans of tuna 12/70
- Nixon presents first Eisenhower dollar 7/71
- Nixon orders wage and price freeze 8/71
- $136 mil. in grain to U.S.S.R. 11/71
- "Phase II" of Nixon economic program 11/71
- Average income at $10,285 7/72
- Nixon expands social security to $5 bil. 10/72
- Nixon ends mandatory wage controls 1/73
- Dollar devalued 10% to improve trade 2/73
- Price controls on oil and gas reimposed 3/73
- Nixon offers plan to avert energy crisis 4/73
- Nixon orders 60-day freeze on prices 6/73
- Arab oil embargo 10/73
- Nixon orders oil cutbacks 11/73
- N.J. tollway speed reduced to 50 mph 11/73
- Emergency Petroleum Allocation Act 11/73
- Effects of oil embargo 12/73
- 99% of gas stations close voluntarily 12/73
- Arabs withdrawing money from U.S. 12/73
- 55-mph ceiling on speed limit 1/74
- Gasoline shortage hits its worst 2/74
- Oil embargo lifted 3/74
- Condominiums are new housing craze 6/74
- Inflation ranked number one problem 7/74
- Consumer Price Index up 1.3% 9/74
- Antitrust suit against AT&T 11/74
- Exchange of grain for oil with Soviets 10/75
- Howard Hughes dies 4/76
- Oil shortage causes problems in U.S. 4/77
- Tractors in D.C. for farm protest 12/77
- New trade accord with Japan 1/78
- First VW is produced in America 4/78
- Dow Jones has worst week in history 10/78
- Limit proposed on oil imports by U.S. 7/79
- 13,000 lose jobs as U.S. closes plants 11/79

1980 to 1987

- 1979 inflation rate 1/80
- George Meany dies 1/80
- Carter cuts budget $13 bil. 3/80
- Carter deregulates banking industry 3/80
- Congress deregulates trucking 6/80
- Reagan orders freeze on regulations 1/81
- Reagan's 25% tax cut approved 7/81
- Gypsy moth causing losses 8/81
- Debt at one trillion dollars 9/81
- Glut causes gas prices to fall 2/82
- Teamsters ratify accord with wage freeze 3/82
- Consumer prices fall 3% 4/82
- Multi-billion aid plan to Mexico 8/82
- G.M sued for selling X car 8/83
- McDonald's founder Ray Kroc dies 1/84
- Seven-year boycott of Nestle ends 1/84
- Consumer inflation lowest since 1972 1/84
- EPA orders ban on EDB 2/84
- Agreement reached on Argentine loan 3/84
- Up to 350,000 homeless in the U.S. 5/84
- Average home price over $100,000 6/84
- Govt. loans Illinois bank $4.5 bil. 7/84
- Debtor nation, first time since 1914 9/85
- Dow Jones tops 1,500, a new record 12/85
- Dollar hits postwar low against yen 3/86
- Insider trading pervasive on Wall St. 11/86
- Family farm depression worst in 50 years 1/87
- CBS shake-up to revive network 1/87
- Dow Jones tops 2,000 first time 1/87
- Japan analyzes U.S. failure to compete 2/87
- Silicon Valley making comeback 2/87
- U.S. robot industry in trouble 2/87
- Japanese buying up U.S. real estate 3/87
- Texaco declares bankruptcy 4/87
- McDonald's winning burger battle 4/87
- Greenspan to replace Volcker at Fed 6/87
- Ben and Jerry are ice cream tycoons 7/87
- Banking losses due to Third World debt 7/87
- Bull market is five years old 8/87
- Henry Ford II dies 9/87
- Teamsters voted back into AFL-CIO 10/87
- Study shows 20 million underfed 10/87
- Stock market crashes 508 points 10/87
- Budget plan would cut deficit $30 bil. 11/87
- Shearson Lehman to buy E.F. Hutton 12/87
- Dow plunges to lowest level since crash 12/87
- Batra's "The Great Depression of 1990" 12/87
- Boesky gets 3 years for insider trading 12/87

United States (Foreign Relations)

1900 to 1909

- Alaska placed under military rule 1/00
- Takeover of Wake Island 1/00
- Congress votes $2 million to Puerto Rico 3/00
- Ships to Nicaragua to halt revolution 3/00
- Annexation of Hawaii 4/00
- Foraker Act for Puerto Rico 4/00
- Boers seek aid 5/00
- Amnesty offered to Filipino rebels 6/00
- Troops sent to fight Chinese rebels 6/00
- Chinese refugees arrive in San Francisco 8/00
- Chinese armistice rejected 8/00
- Plans to buy Danish W. Indies 10/00
- Filipinos ask freedom from U.S. 1/01
- Congress passes Platt amendment 3/01
- Filipino rebel leader captured 3/01
- Cuba required to accept Platt amendment 5/01
- Russia asked to mediate Alaska boundary 6/01
- Cuba to become U.S. protectorate 6/01
- Free trade for Puerto Rico 7/01
- Taft is governor of Philippines 7/01
- Second Hay-Pauncefote Treaty 11/01
- Puerto Rican citizenship barred 12/01
- Protest over Russian privileges in China 2/02
- Prince Henry of Prussia visits 2/02
- Chinese Exclusion Act passes Senate 4/02
- $40 million for Panama canal 6/02
- Envoy resigns post in Berlin 8/02
- Troops sent to Panama 9/02
- Protest over Rumanian treatment of Jews 9/02
- Colombia rejects canal offer 11/02
- Canal treaty reached with Colombia 1/03
- U.S. & U.K. meet over Alaska border 1/03
- Cuba gives U.S. naval bases 2/03
- Senate ratifies Hay-Herran Treaty 3/03
- Senate ratifies Cuban treaty 3/03
- Troops sent to Honduras 3/03
- Troops sent to Beirut 9/03
- U.S. favored in Alaskan border dispute 10/03
- Treaty for construction of Panama Canal 11/03
- T. Roosevelt orders ships to Panama 11/03
- Republic of Panama recognized 11/03
- Marines land in Panama 12/03
- T. Roosevelt denies supporting Panama 1/04
- Marines sent to Santo Domingo 1/04
- Court decides Puerto Ricans not aliens 1/04
- Japan stops all steamship service 1/04
- Neutrality in Russo-Japanese War 2/04
- Marines rout Dominican rebels 2/04
- Commission to expedite Panama Canal 2/04
- Occupation of Cuba ended 2/04
- Perdicaris kidnapped in Morocco 5/04
- French Panama concession bought 11/04
- Dominican Republic to repay creditors 12/04
- Americans suffer losses in Philippines 12/04
- Roosevelt Corollary to Monroe Doctrine 12/04
- Filipino rebels clash with U.S. troops 5/05
- Secret agreement with Japanese 7/05
- Ex-Sec. of State John Hay dies 7/05
- Plans to build Nicaraguan railroads 8/05
- Roosevelt mediates in Russo-Japanese War 8/05
- Warship sent to Nicaragua 9/05
- China ceases boycott 9/05
- $130 million for Panama Canal 10/05
- U.S. aid to Russian Jews 11/05
- Troop buildup in Philippines 1/06
- First ambassador to Japan 1/06
- 15 killed in Philippines fighting 3/06
- Rio Grande agreement with Mexico 5/06
- Maxime Gorky in U.S. 5/06
- Mexican strike suppressed 6/06
- Panama Canal to be equipped with locks 6/06
- Central American peace treaty signed 7/06
- Cuban rebels capture U.S. base 9/06
- Taft is governor in Cuba 9/06
- Troops arrive in Cuba 10/06
- Nobel Peace Prize to Teddy Roosevelt 12/06
- Famine relief sent to Russia 2/07
- Japan denounces immigration limits 2/07
- Supervision of Dominican Republic 2/07
- Army to build Panama Canal 2/07
- Troops to Honduras 3/07
- Japanese immigrants barred 4/07
- Withdrawal date for Cuba 4/07
- Treaty with Santo Domingo 5/07
- Citizens attacked in Cuba 10/07
- Rules of war renewed at The Hague 10/07
- Immigrants to Germany 12/07
- Japanese immigration to U.S. doubled 12/07
- Great White Fleet on tour 12/07
- Japan restricts immigration to U.S. 2/08
- Fishing boundaries set with Canada 4/08
- Relations with Venezuela broken 6/08
- Control over Cuban elections 8/08
- Great White Fleet arrives in Japan 10/08
- Japanese annexation of Korea recognized 11/08
- Booker T. Washington asks aid to Liberia 2/09
- Warships sent to Nicaragua 3/09
- U.S. protests Russo-Chinese accord 7/09
- Taft meets Diaz in Mexico 10/09
- Troops land in Nicaragua 11/09
- Naval base begun at Pearl Harbor 11/09
- Nicaraguan relations severed 12/09
- Pres. Zelaya yields in Nicaragua 12/09

1910 to 1919

- Estrada govt. in Nicaragua recognized 1/11
- Immigration treaty with Japan 2/11
- Soldier at killed by Mexican troops 3/11
- Troops cross Rio Grande to aid Mexico 4/11
- Interview with Dalai Lama published 5/11
- Russian Feodor Malkov gets asylum 8/11
- Canada defeats reciprocity pact 9/11
- Taft dissolves 1832 treaty with Russia 12/11
- Troops to Honduras 1/12
- Rifles to ambassador in Mexico City 3/12
- Ships rushed to Havana 6/12
- Marines land in Nicaragua 8/12
- Proposal to make Nicaragua protectorate 7/13
- Senate kills Nicaragua protectorate bill 8/13
- Non-intervention in Salvador 8/13
- Pres. Wilson demands Gen. Huerta resign 11/13
- Wilson lifts arms embargo for Mexico 2/14
- 1,000 Marines seize port of Vera Cruz 4/14
- Wilson orders Atlantic fleet to Mexico 4/14
- Wilson re-establishes arms ban on Mexico 6/14
- Neutrality in European war 8/14
- Wilson orders army out of Mexico 9/14
- $10 mil. war loan to France 10/14
- Wilson asserts Panama Canal's neutrality 11/14
- Germany attacks ship 1/15
- Ambassador invited by Germany 2/15
- Ship destroyed by German mine 2/15
- Germany warned on attacking ships 2/15
- British blockade protested 3/15
- Wilson urges neutrality 4/15
- Lusitania sunk by Germans 5/15
- Germany won't halt subs 5/15
- Germany declares passenger ships safe 6/15
- Liner Armenian sunk 6/15
- German briefcase found 7/15
- Third warning sent to Germany 7/15
- Two more ships sunk 7/15
- Troops land in Haiti 7/15
- Mexico prodded toward peace 8/15
- German spies 8/15
- Germans may end sub warfare 8/15
- U.K. buys arms 8/15
- Haiti placed under martial law 9/15
- Austria told to recall ambassador 9/15
- Germany to stop sinking neutral ships 9/15
- Border incident with Mexico 9/15
- Carranza recognized in Mexico 10/15
- Germans arrested in N.Y. 10/15
- Protest over British blockade 11/15
- Haiti becomes protectorate 11/15
- Sabotage in Delaware 11/15
- German spies expelled 12/15
- Refuge given to Pancho Villa 12/15
- Mexico executes Americans 1/16
- U.K. confirms von Papen a spy 1/16
- Wilson refuses compromise on Lusitania 1/16
- Independence for Philippines 2/16
- Germany takes Lusitania responsibility 2/16
- Germany renews attacks on neutral ships 2/16
- Haiti officially a protectorate 2/16
- Tough stand on sub war 3/16
- Pancho Villa attacks 3/16
- Troops enter Mexico 3/16
- Gen. Pershing in Mexico 3/16
- Saboteurs in N.J. 4/16
- Mexican troops fire on U.S. troops 4/16
- Threat to break German relations 4/16
- Troops in Mexico indefinitely 4/16
- Germany to halt sub war 5/16
- Troops at Santo Domingo 5/16
- Protest over seizure of mail 5/16
- Warships head for Mexico 6/16
- Carranza kills 18 Americans in Mexico 6/16
- U-boat with message for Wilson 7/16
- Carranza agrees to arbitration 7/16
- Bargaining for West Indies 7/16
- 25,000 troops to Mexican border 8/16
- Neutrality assailed by London Times 8/16
- Germany says pilots violate neutrality 9/16
- Liner Columbian sunk 11/16
- Dominican Republic under martial law 11/16
- Sale of Danish West Indies completed 1/17
- Ties with Germany severed 2/17
- Germans sink U.S. ship Housatonic 2/17
- Germans hold all Americans hostage 2/17
- Troops recalled from Mexican border 2/17
- German plan to bring Mexicans into war 2/17
- Wilson wants to arm merchant ships 2/17
- Puerto Rico becomes U.S. territory 3/17
- Merchant ship Algonquin torpedoed 3/17
- Germany sinks three more ships 3/17
- Wilson calls special session of Congress 3/17
- Kerensky govt. in Russia recognized 3/17
- War declared on Germany 4/17
- Panama promises to help defend canal 4/17
- Warship Mongolia fires first U.S. shot 4/17
- U.K. asked to free Ireland 4/17
- German sub captured 5/17
- Troops to France 5/17
- First troops land in France 6/17
- Sub battle won 7/17
- 30 Germans jailed 8/17
- Wilson rebuffs pope 8/17
- Troops to front lines in France 10/17
- War declared on Austria-Hungary 11/17
- Effect of entry into war 12/17
- Wilson's 14 Points 1/18
- Germany, Austria reject peace proposals 1/18
- U.S. planes leave for front 2/18
- Bolsheviks ask U.S. aid 3/18
- Troops in heavy fighting against Germans 3/18
- Troops gassed 4/18
- Battle won on Amiens front 5/18
- Germans halted at Chateau-Thierry 6/18
- Major counterattack on Western Front 6/18
- Wilson states war goals 7/18
- Czech Council recognized 7/18
- Ties with U.S.S.R. broken 8/18
- Argonne Forest captured 10/18
- Germans seek peace and are rejected 10/18
- Rickenbacker downs 26th German 10/18
- Germany surrenders 11/18
- Over 50,000 died in war 11/18
- Wilson cheered in Europe 12/18
- Army of occupation enters Germany 12/18
- Herbert Hoover to raise aid for Europe 1/19
- Troops attack Bolsheviks 2/19
- Nicaragua requests troops 6/19
- Arms to White Russians authorized 8/19
- Wilson urges approval of Versailles 8/19
- Troops in Mexico searching for bandits 8/19
- 38 amendments to Versailles treaty 9/19
- French monument to U.S. troops 9/19
- First German immigration since war 10/19
- Release of agent in Mexico demanded 10/19
- Mexico won't release agent 11/19
- Senate vetoes Versailles treaty 11/19

1920 to 1929

- Last troops quit France 1/20
- Report 29,000 Jews killed in Ukraine 1/20
- Senate denies ratification of Versailles 2/20
- Soviet peace plan rejected as propaganda 2/20
- Senate again rejects Versailles treaty 3/20
- Ban on trade with Soviets removed 7/20
- Japanese occupation of Sakhalin blasted 7/20
- Warships ordered to Danzig, Poland 8/20
- Navy boats to Honduras 8/20
- Harding pronounces League deceased 11/20
- Woodrow Wilson wins Nobel Peace Prize 12/20
- Troops to protect Americans in China 3/21
- Pres. Harding turns down League 4/21
- Decree ending war with Germany 7/21
- Harding proposes disarmament talks 7/21
- Germany signs peace treaty 8/21
- Aid to famine victims in Petrograd 9/21
- Washington Conference on disarmament 12/21
- Open door policy in China 1/22
- World War Foreign Debt Commission formed 2/22
- Harding orders troops out of Rhineland 3/22
- Senate ratifies four-power naval treaty 3/22
- Agreement on Palestine 5/22
- Troops to stay in Rhineland 6/22
- Marines end guard in Vladivostok Bay 11/22
- Last troops withdrawn from Germany 1/23
- Law amended to admit 25,000 Armenians 1/23
- Senate rejects entry into World Court 3/23
- KKK imperial wizard opposes World Court 6/23
- Belleau Wood dedicated to U.S. soldiers 7/23
- Formal recognition to Mexico 8/23
- Coolidge opposes arms to Mexico rebels 1/24
- Ships to Mexico 1/24
- Troops to Honduras during elections 2/24
- Anti-Japanese immigration bill 4/24
- Dawes Plan for German war debts 4/24
- Coolidge bans sale of arms to Cuba 5/24
- Troops in China to protect nationals 1/25
- Border law with Canada 3/25
- Troops in Honduras 4/25
- Missions attacked in Nicaragua 7/25
- League invitation rejected 7/25
- Troops to Panama 10/25
- Nicaraguan insurgents disarmed 12/25
- Warships to China 12/25
- Will join World Court with reservations 1/26
- Troops to Nicaragua 5/26
- Embassy bombed in Argentina 5/26
- Accord with Panama 7/26
- U.S. Marines land in Nicaragua 8/26
- Canada bars entry into World Court 9/26
- Embassy threatened in Paris 10/26
- Nicaraguan president asks aid 11/26
- Warships to Hankow 11/26
- Marines on Mexican border 1/27
- Senate drops World Court hopes 2/27
- Ties with Canada independent of U.K. 2/27
- Nicaragua asks aid in fighting rebels 2/27
- Alexander Kerensky visits 3/27
- Warships fire on Chinese rebels 3/27
- Filipino independence vetoed 4/27
- Control by League rejected 4/27
- Supervision of Nicaraguan elections 5/27
- Troops ambushed in Nicaragua 7/27
- Arms talks stalled in Geneva 7/27
- Peace bridge at Niagara 8/27
- Attache shot in Germany 9/27
- League influence in Panama Canal barred 9/27
- American veterans parade in Paris 9/27
- Five Marines killed in Nicaragua 1/28
- 1,000 more Marines to Nicaragua 1/28
- Arbitration treaty with France 2/28
- 1,000 more Marines to Nicaragua 3/28
- Mexican oil laws accepted 3/28
- Nicaraguan rebels capture U.S. mines 4/28
- Arbitration pact with Italy 4/28
- Kellogg-Briand Treaty signed 8/28
- Hoover meets with Moncada in Nicaragua 11/28
- Kellogg-Briand Treaty ratified 1/29
- Arms to Mexico 3/29
- Ten U.S. citizens arrested in U.S.S.R. 7/29
- Compliance with Kellogg-Briand pact 7/29
- Arabs kill twelve Americans in Hebron 8/29
- Troops to Haiti 12/29

1930 to 1939

- Hoover signs naval treaty 7/30
- Labor moves to ban Soviet products 7/30
- Navy scraps 49 ships under treaty 10/30
- Vargas govt. in Brazil recognized 11/30
- Civil govt. awarded to Virgin Islands 1/31
- Embargo on Soviet pulp & lumber 2/31
- Four killed in Nicaragua 4/31
- T. Roosevelt Jr. to head Philippines 1/32
- Andrew Mellon named envoy to U.K. 2/32
- Hoover asks world arms cut of one-third 6/32
- Congress promises Philippines freedom 1/33
- Warships to Cuba 8/33
- 29 warships placed on Cuban duty 9/33
- U.S.S.R. recognized 11/33
- Inquiry into Nazi propaganda 11/33
- FDR recalls ambassador from Havana 11/33
- First Soviet ambassador arrives 1/34
- FDR grants recognition to Cuban govt. 1/34
- Philippines promised freedom 3/34
- Platt amendment annuled 5/34
- FDR bars arms to Bolivia and Paraguay 5/34
- Ivy Lee admits bribe from Nazis 7/34
- Last U.S. Marines leave Haiti 8/34
- Report Reich building U-boats 9/34
- Senate bars entry into World Court 1/35
- Liberia recognized 6/35
- Cuba deports 15 Americans 7/35
- Soviets told to stay out of U.S. labor 8/35
- FDR bans arms to countries at war 8/35
- Cordell Hull blasts Soviets 8/35
- Arms embargo on Italy and Ethiopia 10/35
- Oil sold to Italy despite embargo 10/35
- Neutrality Act 2/36
- Naval accord with British and French 3/36
- Embargo on Ethiopia lifted 6/36
- Two warships sent to Spain 7/36
- Non-intervention in Spain 8/36
- Embassy in Spain evacuated 11/36
- Planes to Spain 12/36
- Arms to Spain barred 1/37
- No private participation in Spanish war 1/37
- Philippines want full independence 3/37
- Mrs. Harriman ambassador to Norway 4/37
- 29 American volunteers for Spain caught 4/37
- No arms to Far East 9/37
- Protest over Japanese raid on Nanking 9/37
- Japan condemned on China war 10/37
- Invasion halted in Shanghai 11/37
- Japan sinks gunboat 12/37
- Joseph Kennedy ambassador to England 12/37
- Mexico raises tariffs 1/38
- Mexico nationalizes oil 3/38
- Mexican silver embargoed 3/38
- Volunteer divisions beaten in Spain 4/38
- Spanish and Chinese air raids denounced 6/38
- British order 400 planes 6/38
- 18 indicted as Reich spies 6/38
- Mexico seizes five mines 7/38
- Mexico seizes more land 8/38
- Mexico rejects requests for land payment 9/38
- Eduard Benes comes to Univ. of Chicago 10/38
- Hitler decorates Lindbergh 10/38
- Mexico will pay for land seizure 11/38
- Envoy recalled from Germany 11/38
- Germany recalls ambassador 11/38
- Latin America bars intervention 12/38
- Planes to France 1/39
- Steinhardt new ambassador to U.S.S.R. 3/39
- Franco recognized 4/39
- Hitler refuses meeting with FDR 4/39
- Somoza arrives 5/39
- Oumansky new Soviet ambassador 5/39
- Cordell Hull wants arms embargo lifted 5/39
- Trade treaty with Japan renounced 7/39
- Lindbergh warns against war 9/39
- Neutral stance on WWII 9/39
- U.S. planes used by French 11/39

1940 to 1949

- France & U.K. have use of warplanes 3/40
- FDR condemns war on Scandinavia 4/40
- FDR asks Mussolini to help halt war 4/40
- Surplus arms offered to U.K. 6/40
- Natl. emergency to control shipping 6/40
- U.K. asks Hull for aid against Japanese 6/40
- FDR accuses Italy of stab in the back 6/40
- Joint defense plans with Canada 8/40
- Cocos Island offered as canal defense 9/40
- Steel & iron halted to Japan 9/40
- Lease of bases in Brazil & Chile 10/40
- U.S. and U.K. agree to standardize arms 11/40
- Joe Kennedy quits as ambassador to U.K. 12/40
- FDR calls America arsenal of democracy 12/40
- Congress gets bill for anti-Axis aid 1/41
- Ban lifted on arms to U.S.S.R. 1/41
- F.D.R. requests lend-lease for arms 1/41
- War planes to Pacific 2/41
- Bulgarian assets frozen 3/41
- FDR signs Lend-Lease Act 3/41
- Canada signs St. Lawrence plan 3/41
- Italian, German, Danish ships seized 3/41
- U.K. allowed to refuel in U.S. 4/41
- Security zone extended 4/41
- Greenland seized 4/41
- FDR says national emergency exists 5/41
- French merchant ships seized 5/41
- Robin Moore sunk by Reich U-boat 5/41
- Ickes stops sale of U.S. oil to Japan 6/41
- Berlin ordered to close consulate 6/41
- FDR pledges aid to U.S.S.R. 6/41
- FDR freezes Japanese assets 7/41
- FDR nationalizes Filipino army 7/41
- Troops take charge of Iceland 7/41
- Arms committment to Soviets 8/41
- FDR states U.S. is not near entering war 8/41
- Japan warned to leave Pacific open 8/41
- USS Greer fired on by unidentified sub 9/41
- Shoot if Axis enters defense zone 9/41
- Two U.S. destroyers hit, one sunk 10/41
- USS Kearney hit by torpedo off Iceland 10/41
- $1 bil. in supplies to U.S.S.R. 10/41
- Ships to Dutch Guiana 11/41
- FDR appeals to Hirohito to avoid war 12/41
- Winston Churchill in U.S. for talks 12/41
- Japanese strike Pearl Harbor 12/41
- War declared on Italy & Germany 12/41
- 26 countries issue Declaration of U.N. 1/42
- U.S. troops in Ireland 1/42
- Japanese take Manila 1/42
- First Axis bomb falls in California 2/42
- U.S. gives up Philippines 3/42
- 100,000 Japanese-Americans interned 3/42
- Free French recognized 4/42
- Flying fortresses bomb Japanese fleet 4/42
- Defeat on Bataan 4/42
- Axis sub sinks cargo ship killing 27 5/42
- Battle of the Coral Sea 5/42
- Eisenhower takes command in Europe 6/42
- Lend-Lease to U.S.S.R. 6/42
- Churchill arrives for talks 6/42
- FDR, Churchill agree on 2nd Europe front 6/42
- Battle of Midway 6/42
- Fliers join RAF for first time 7/42
- De Gaulle and Eisenhower meet in London 7/42
- U.S. on Guadalcanal 8/42
- Willkie begins trip as U.S. envoy 8/42
- 2,600 planes sent to U.S.S.R. 1/43
- FDR at war council in Casablanca 1/43
- Air raid on Berlin 1/43
- Mme. Chiang asks Japan's defeat 2/43
- Japanese leave Solomon Islands 2/43
- Battle for Kasserine Pass, Tunisia 2/43
- 22 Japanese ships sunk 3/43
- Martinique and Guadeloupe join Allies 4/43
- Churchill in U.S. for Trident parley 5/43
- FDR promises bombs if Nazis use poison 6/43
- FDR asks Italians to overthrow Mussolini 6/43
- General Giraud arrives in Washington 7/43
- Atomic research to be shared with U.K. 7/43
- Allies land in Sicily 7/43
- Messina captured 8/43
- FDR at summit in Quebec 8/43
- Chinese asked for unified front 9/43
- Fulbright Resolution adopted in House 9/43
- Hitler's "Mein Kampf" published in U.S. 9/43
- Allies go ashore in Italy 9/43
- U.S. bombers attack in Europe 10/43
- Senate passes Connally resolution 11/43
- FDR and Chiang meet in Cairo 11/43
- U.S. takes Gilbert Islands 11/43
- Congress repeals Chinese Exclusion Act 12/43
- Ike to lead invasions of Europe 12/43
- U.S. planes hit Germany 12/43
- Govt. reveals Japanese using torture 1/44
- FDR sets up War Refugee Board 1/44
- MacArthur launches drive in Pacific 2/44
- Non-recognition of Argentina 3/44
- Cordell Hull gives 17-point U.S. plan 3/44
- U.S. bombs Berlin first time 3/44
- Congress extends Lend-Lease to June 1945 4/44
- 68 Irish firms blacklisted 5/44
- Allies enter Rome 6/44
- U.S. bombs Japan 6/44
- D-Day: Allies land in Normandy 6/44
- U.S. planes attack Marianas 6/44
- Guam proclaimed under U.S. rule 7/44
- Paris retaken 8/44
- Americans push into Reich 9/44
- FDR and Churchill plan shift to Pacific 9/44
- United Nations proposed 10/44
- MacArthur returns to Philippines 10/44
- MacAuliffe spurns surrender 12/44
- B-29s hit Tokyo 1/45
- Troops land in Luzon 1/45
- 25 Japanese ships sunk off Indochina 1/45
- Drive on Siegfried Line 1/45
- Big Three conference in Yalta 2/45
- 513 rescued at Luzon 2/45
- Singapore dock hit 2/45
- MacArthur on Corregidor 2/45
- U.S. troops storm ashore at Iwo Jima 2/45
- Rhineland offensive 2/45
- Dresden in flames as 130,000 die 2/45
- 5,000 POWs liberated in Philippines 2/45
- Repeated strikes against Tokyo 2/45
- Troops take Cologne 3/45
- 100,000 killed in Tokyo air raid 3/45
- Troops land at Mindanao 3/45
- USS Franklin hit; 832 die 3/45
- Rhine crossed 3/45
- U.S. troops land on Okinawa 4/45
- Relations with Argentina resumed 4/45
- Troops take Leipzig 4/45
- Molotov arrives for talks 4/45
- Meeting with Soviets on the Elbe 4/45
- Germany surrenders 5/45
- Lend-Lease to Soviets halted 5/45
- 373 lost on USS Bunker Hill 5/45
- Tokyo devastated by air raids 5/45
- Kobe firebombed 6/45
- Yugoslavia accepts conditions on Trieste 6/45
- Brutal battle over Okinawa 6/45
- Germany divided into four parts 6/45
- Honshu factories bombed by U.S. 7/45
- Japan's main islands bombed 7/45
- Last of Japanese navy destroyed 7/45
- Japan turns down surrender ultimatum 7/45
- Occupation of Germany 7/45
- Japanese harbors blockaded 8/45
- 400 planes resume assault on Japan 8/45
- Lend-Lease ends 8/45
- Atomic bombs destroy Hiroshima, Nagasaki 8/45
- Japan surrenders 8/45
- Japan signs unconditional surrender 9/45
- Troops stationed in South Korea 9/45
- Arabs threaten oil embargo 10/45
- Refusal to recognize imposed regimes 10/45
- Nuremberg trials begin 11/45
- George C. Marshall U.S. envoy to China 11/45
- Rumania recognized 2/46
- Tito's Yugoslav government recognized 4/46
- Philippines become a republic 7/46
- Troops to stay in Korea 10/46
- Friendship treaty with China 11/46
- Merger of Berlin zone with U.K. 12/46
- Break with Spain 12/46
- Mediation in China abandoned 1/47
- George Marshall named sec. of state 1/47
- Disagreement dooms Big Four parley 3/47
- Naval base in Philippines 3/47
- Greece and Turkey get aid 3/47
- U.S. trusteeship over Japanese isles 4/47
- Grady first ambassador to India 4/47

United States (Foreign Relations)

- Big Four in Moscow fail 4/47
- Truman blasts coup in Hungary 6/47
- Marshall offers aid plan 6/47
- Truman first president to visit Canada 6/47
- Support for Palestinian partition 10/47
- Bomb blasts embassy in Palestine 10/47
- U.S. seeks food for Europe 10/47
- Plan for Korean autonomy passes U.N. 11/47
- Aid shipments to Europe 12/47
- Friendship pact with Italy 2/48
- First Nepalese envoy 2/48
- Berlin airlift begins 4/48
- Organization of American States formed 4/48
- Truman approves Marshall Plan 4/48
- Birth of Israel 5/48
- Soviets tighten Berlin blockade 6/48
- Vow to keep troops in Europe 6/48
- 3,000 tons of food flown to Berlin 7/48
- South Korea recognized 8/48
- 7,000 tons in supplies to Berlin 9/48
- Force at Tsingtao strengthened 11/48
- $300 million for South Korea 12/48
- Madame Chiang in U.S. 12/48
- Puerto Rico swears in first governor 1/49
- Seoul formally recognized 1/49
- 60 seized in Prague as U.S. spies 1/49
- Truman proposes aid to poor lands 1/49
- NATO founded 3/49
- German zones merged with France, U.K. 4/49
- Berlin blockade ends 5/49
- U.S. bank helps Arab refugees 6/49
- U.S. finds Soviets have the Bomb 9/49

1950 to 1959

- Outraged over U.K. Red China recognition 1/50
- Mme. Chiang Kai-shek leaves for Taiwan 1/50
- U.S. consuls ordered to leave China 1/50
- U.S. supports U.N. recognition of Spain 1/50
- Truman proclaims start of NATO 1/50
- Robert Vogeler admits spying in Hungary 2/50
- Vietnam under Bao Dai recognized 2/50
- U.S. threatens new Berlin airlift 2/50
- Ties with Bulgaria broken 2/50
- Hungarian assets frozen 2/50
- Rumanian assets frozen 2/50
- U.S. attache Karp murdered by Hungarians 2/50
- $1 bil. in aid leaves U.S. for Europe 3/50
- Truman warns foreign aid cuts risk WWIII 3/50
- Coplon, Gubitchev guilty of espionage 3/50
- Soviets down U.S. bomber over Latvia 4/50
- Czechs ordered to close N.Y. consulate 5/50
- Truman accepts $3.2 bil. for aid program 6/50
- U.S., U.N. agree to send troops to Seoul 6/50
- Truman to send troops to Korea 7/50
- U.S. asks Chiang to talk with MacArthur 7/50
- Republicans blast Truman's Far East plan 8/50
- Red China asks withdrawal from Formosa 8/50
- Withdrawal from Formosa after Korea 8/50
- U.N. forces invade Korea 9/50
- U.S., U.K., France recognize W. Germany 9/50
- Citizens of totalitarian nations barred 9/50
- U.S. ground forces across 38th parallel 10/50
- Korean casualties reported at 1,211 10/50
- U.S. will use A-bomb to get Korea peace 10/50
- Two Puerto Ricans try to kill Truman 10/50
- Eisenhower named NATO commander 12/50
- Truman bans U.S. exports to Red China 12/50
- U.S. and Spain resume relations 12/50
- Truman declares state of emergency 12/50
- Soviets asked to return Lend-Lease 1/51
- Red drive halted in Korea 1/51
- U.S. to send four divisions to Europe 2/51
- Fight over 38th parallel 2/51
- Ike opposes limiting troops in Europe 2/51
- Ukraine rebels ask for U.S. aid 3/51
- MacArthur says war may reach China 3/51
- Hungary releases Robert Vogeler 4/51
- Truman fires MacArthur 4/51
- Soviets ask Korean cease-fire 6/51
- Agenda set for Korean talks 9/51
- Mutual defense pact with Philippines 8/51
- Portugal gives U.S. rights in Azores 9/51
- De Lattre visits U.S. for aid in Vietnam 9/51
- U.S., Australia & New Zealand alliance 9/51
- Japanese sovereignty restored 9/51
- Truman signs Mutual Security Bill 10/51
- Princess Elizabeth appears on U.S. TV 10/51
- Mark Clark named ambassador to Vatican 10/51
- Princess Elizabeth gives gift to Truman 11/51
- Yugoslavia signs military aid pact 11/51
- Truce reached in Korea 11/51
- $120,000 paid for four held in Hungary 12/51
- Atomic weapons pact with U.K. 1/52
- Pact with Ecuador 2/52
- U.S. signs military aid pact with Cuba 3/52
- Military pact with Brazil 3/52
- Truman signs Japanese peace treaty 4/52
- George Kennan U.S. envoy to U.S.S.R. 4/52
- U.S. signs military aid pact with China 4/52
- Military aid pact with Colombia 4/52
- Ike leaves NATO 4/52
- Communist POWs revolt in Korea 5/52
- U.S. receives first woman ambassador 5/52
- Biggest air strike in Korea 5/52
- U.S. paratroopers seize rebel Korea POWs 6/52
- U.S. policeman shot in East Berlin 6/52
- U.S. bans Soviet periodical Amerika 7/52
- Puerto Rico first U.S. Commonwealth 7/52
- Truman receives Faisal II, king of Iraq 8/52
- Ike, if elected, will go to Korea 10/52
- Ike asks repudiation of Yalta pact 10/52
- Scientists attack anti-Red visa policy 10/52
- U.S. lends Japan 68 warships 11/52
- Ike goes to Korea to try to end war 12/52
- Ike to pull 7th fleet out of Formosa 1/53
- Clare Boothe Luce ambassador to Italy 3/53
- Ike offers France more aid in Vietnam 3/53
- Charles Bohlen ambassador to U.S.S.R. 3/53
- 64 freed in Korea POW exchange 4/53
- U.S. offers $50,000 for Korean defector 4/53
- Adenauer arrives for talks with Ike 4/53
- Czechs free W. Oatis, jailed as spy 5/53
- $60 mil. aid for French in Vietnam 5/53
- Dulles warns of domino effect 5/53
- U.S. aid to East Berlin 7/53
- B-50 downed by Soviets off Vladivostok 7/53
- Armistice begins in Korea 7/53
- Soviets have hydrogen bomb 8/53
- 23 POWs refuse repatriation from Korea 9/53
- Israel condemned for Jordan raid 11/53
- Big Three Conference in Bermuda 12/53
- Dulles meets with Soviets on atoms 1/54
- Big Four meet on arms in West Berlin 1/54
- Ike warns of involvement in Indochina 2/54
- U.S. signs defense pact with Japan 3/54
- Puerto Ricans shoot five congressmen 3/54
- U.S. starts flying French to Vietnam 4/54
- Dulles warns China on Vietnam 4/54
- 7th Fleet protects Taiwan from invasion 8/54
- U.S. and Taiwan sign defense treaty 12/54
- $216 million to South Vietnam 1/55
- Accord with Panama over canal 1/55
- Aid for Taiwanese aggression barred 3/55
- Yalta secrets published 3/55
- China wants to avoid war 4/55
- Civil war in Vietnam 4/55
- Diem squashes coup in Saigon 5/55
- Full sovereignty for W. Germany 5/55
- Air bases in Taiwan 6/55
- Ike meets with Adenauer 6/55
- Aid for West German rearmament 6/55
- Big Four summit in Geneva 7/55
- Talks with China 8/55
- Red Chinese to release all Americans 9/55
- Aid offered to Egypt 9/55
- Ties with Spain affirmed 11/55
- Nike missiles installed in West Germany 1/56
- 1,600 troops to Cyprus 1/56
- Iceland demands removal of troops 3/56
- Arms shipment to West Germany 5/56
- Assurances to Chiang 7/56
- Aswan Dam aid offer rescinded 7/56
- Rights renounced in Morocco 10/56
- Neutrality in Suez crisis 10/56
- Ike will defend Mideast 1/57
- Air base in Saudi Arabia 2/57
- Ike's Mideast policy takes effect 3/57
- A-bombs to guard U.S. cities 4/57
- Soviet spy caught in New York 8/57
- U.S. servicemen hurt in Vietnam bombing 10/57
- British queen visits 10/57
- Missiles to be installed in Europe 11/57
- Cuban exile arrested 2/58
- Menshikov new Soviet ambassador 2/58
- Arms embargo on Cuba 4/58
- NORAD established with Canada 5/58
- Jets sent to Iran, Jordan, Lebanon 6/58
- Thousands besiege embassy in Moscow 7/58
- Iraq recognized 8/58
- Evacuation of Moroccan bases 9/58
- Troops leave Lebanon 10/58
- Castro recognized in Cuba 1/59
- Iran rejects aid 2/59
- Castro visits U.S. 4/59
- Nuclear arms to Greece 6/59
- Kitchen debate: Nixon vs. Khrushchev 7/59
- Khrushchev in U.S. 9/59
- Panamanian riots over ownership of canal 11/59
- Ike tours three continents 12/59
- Antarctic is made science preserve 12/59

1960 to 1969

- Mutual defense pact with Japan 1/60
- Ike approves CIA training of Cubans 2/60
- Soviets down U-2 spy plane 5/60
- Gary Powers indicted as spy 7/60
- Ike cuts Cuban sugar imports 7/60
- Senate ratifies Antarctic treaty 8/60
- Castro nationalizes U.S. property 8/60
- Powers convicted of espionage 8/60
- Castro assails U.S. at U.N. 9/60
- Embargo on goods to Cuba 10/60
- Diplomatic ties to Cuba broken 1/61
- OAS rebukes Dominican Republic 1/61
- Saudi Arabia ends Dharan base pact 3/61
- JFK increases aid to Laos 3/61
- JFK ten-point plan for Latin America 3/61
- R. McCann released from Hong Kong prison 4/61
- Bay of Pigs invasion 4/61
- Increase in arms to South Vietnam 5/61
- U.S.-Soviet summit in Paris 6/61
- U.S. and U.S.S.R. plan bigger defense 7/61
- USAID created 10/61
- Hijacking made a federal offense 10/61
- U.S.-Soviet clash in Berlin 10/61
- Advisers in Vietnam raised to 16,000 11/61
- JFK begins South American tour 12/61
- U.S. sends Army units to Saigon 1/62
- U.S. turns down Soviet arms talks 2/62
- U.S. U-2 pilot traded for spymaster Abel 2/62
- JFK orders ban on Cuba imports 2/62
- U.S. to stay in Vietnam 2/62
- Cuba sentences Bay of Pigs invaders 4/62
- JFK orders ships to Indochina 5/62
- 4,000 troops to Thailand 5/62
- Curbs on travel from U.S.S.R. lifted 7/62
- Relations with Peru resumed 8/62
- Brazil seizes U.S. phone system 10/62
- Cuban missile crisis 10/62
- Arms pledged to India 10/62
- All missile bases in Cuba reported gone 11/62
- JFK endorses hot line to Moscow 12/62
- Plutonium to France 2/63
- JFK meets with King Hassan II 3/63
- U.S.S.R. approves hot line to U.S. 4/63
- JFK makes Winston Churchill U.S. citizen 4/63
- Canada agrees to take U.S. warheads 5/63
- JFK speaks at Berlin Wall 6/63
- U.S. ousts Soviet diplomat Sevastyanov 7/63
- JFK confers 40 minutes with pope 7/63
- Test ban treaty signed 8/63
- Moscow-Washington hot line working 8/63
- Diem advised to dismiss brother Nhu 9/63
- Senate ratifies test ban treaty 9/63
- JFK signs treaty for atomic test ban 10/63
- JFK meets with Haile Selassie 10/63
- JFK meets with Tito 10/63
- Yale Prof. Barghoorn arrested as spy 11/63
- Coup topples Diem in Saigon 11/63
- Panama breaks ties 1/64
- Plan for neutral Vietnam rejected 2/64
- Ambassador to Ghana called home 2/64
- Aid to five nations cut for Cuba trade 2/64
- New Zanzibar govt. recognized 2/64
- Reconaissance plane downed in E. Germany 3/64
- Ties with Panama resumed 4/64
- Pact with U.S.S.R. to cut arms 4/64
- USS Card sunk by Viet Cong 5/64
- LBJ meets with Eamon de Valera 5/64
- Soviets now using spy satellites 5/64
- Henry C. Lodge resigns as Vietnam envoy 6/64
- 600 more troops to Vietnam 7/64
- OAS votes Cuba sanctions 7/64
- Four planes to aid Tshombe 8/64
- Wheelus Base in Libya given up 8/64
- U.S. ship attacked in Tonkin Gulf 8/64
- South Vietnam starts biggest attack 11/64
- Renegotiation of Panama treaty 12/64
- 136 Americans die in Vietnam in 1964 1/65
- North Vietnam bombed for first time 2/65
- Bomb rips Saigon embassy 3/65
- 3,500 troops to Vietnam 3/65
- First Vietnam air fight 4/65
- U.S. dropping napalm on Viet Cong 4/65
- 20,000 attack embassy in Cambodia 4/65
- Marines to Dominican Republic 4/65
- Napalm used in Vietnam 4/65
- 14,000 invade Dominican Republic 5/65
- Cambodia breaks ties 5/65
- Troops authorized to fight in Vietnam 6/65
- 21,000 more to Vietnam 6/65
- 50,000 more troops to Vietnam 7/65
- Taylor resigns as ambassador to Vietnam 7/65
- Goldberg replaces Stevenson at U.N. 7/65
- Marines capture 2,000 in Vietnam 8/65
- Aid to Pakistan and India suspended 9/65
- Seven planes lost in Vietnam 9/65
- Cuban refugees accepted 10/65
- Friendly Vietnam village bombed; 48 dead 10/65
- 650 Americans dead since 1961 in Vietnam 9/65
- First Cuban refugees arrive 12/65
- 12 tons of bombs on North Vietnam 12/65
- Truce in Vietnam 12/65
- U.S. troops move into Mekong Delta 1/66
- 200 tanks sold to Israel 2/66
- LBJ and Ky meet in Honolulu 2/66
- Ghana regime recognized 3/66
- U.S. deaths exceed Vietnamese 4/66
- Cambodia shelled 5/66
- U.S. resumes aid to India and Pakistan 6/66
- France pulls out of NATO 7/66
- Argentine junta recognized 7/66
- DMZ in Vietnam bombed 7/66
- 60 U.S.-built planes crash in W. Germany 8/66
- De Gaulle condemns U.S. in Vietnam 9/66
- Hanoi wants bombing halt before talks 10/66
- Promise to leave if Hanoi stops war 10/66
- LBJ goes to Vietnam 10/66
- Direct air service to Moscow 11/66
- Civilian killings in Vietnam admitted 12/66
- Arms to be sent to Jordan 12/66
- Highest weekly casualties in Vietnam 1/67
- William Bullitt dies 2/67
- Biggest attack launched in Vietnam 2/67
- Stalin's daughter defects 3/67
- U.S. jets bomb Hanoi 5/67
- LBJ meets Kosygin in N.J. 6/67
- Westmoreland wants more men in Vietnam 7/67
- 45,000 more troops to Vietnam 8/67
- Offensive in Vietnam 11/67
- 6,500 men landed in Vietnam 12/67
- Viet Cong launch Tet offensive 1/68
- Air targets shifted to Laos 1/68
- Cambodia charges U.S. crossed border 1/68
- N. Korea captures U.S. ship Pueblo 1/68
- U.S. troops blunt Tet offensive 2/68
- 10,500 more troops to Vietnam 2/68
- Up to 50,000 more troops to Vietnam 3/68
- Peace talks with N. Vietnamese begin 5/68
- U.S. ambassador to Guatemala slain 8/68
- Viet Cong use Cambodia for sanctuary 10/68
- Johnson halts bombing of North Vietnam 11/68
- Pueblo crew released 12/68
- 50 planes to be sold to Israel 12/68
- Pueblo captain signed confession 1/69
- CIA chief Allen W. Dulles dies 1/69
- Planes promised to Jordan 4/69
- First Vietnam troop withdrawals begin 7/69
- 1,450 Vietnamese slain in one day 8/69
- Green Berets linked to CIA murder case 8/69
- Khadafy's regime in Libya recognized 9/69
- Nixon resumes bombing of N. Vietnam 9/69
- 35,000 more troops to come home 9/69
- Cuba allows extradition of hijackers 9/69
- Viet Cong strike deep in Mekong Delta 11/69
- U.S. presents MIA list of 1,406 12/69

1970 to 1979

- 27 U.S. deaths in Laos disclosed 3/70
- Nixon sends combat units into Cambodia 4/70
- U.S. troops pulled out of Cambodia 6/70
- Use of defoliants suspended in Vietnam 6/70
- Nixon meets with Congo Pres. Mobutu 8/70
- 40,000 to leave Vietnam 10/70
- 180 tanks to Israel 10/70
- U.S., U.S.S.R. ban weapons on seabed 2/71
- Nixon pledges withdrawal from Vietnam 4/71
- Nixon eases trade embargo on Red China 4/71
- Nixon ends 21-year-old embargo on Peking 6/71
- Pact returning Okinawa to Japan 6/71
- Spy flights over Red China suspended 7/71
- CIA admits it has army in Laos 8/71
- U.N. seat for Red China backed 8/71
- Aid to India barred 12/71
- Nixon airs 8-point Vietnam peace plan 1/72
- 42 F-4 jets to Israel 2/72
- President Nixon visits China 2/72
- Selling F-4 Phantoms to Israel & Jordan 3/72
- Diplomatic recognition to Bangladesh 4/72
- Control of Okinawa returned to Japan 5/72
- Nixon, Brezhnev meet in Moscow 5/72
- U.S. bombs Hanoi, Haiphong 5/72
- U.S. grants Boeing 727 sale to China 7/72
- Accord with Soviets on technology 7/72
- Ratification of ABM Treaty with U.S.S.R. 8/72
- Last ground unit in Vietnam deactivated 8/72
- Jimmy Hoffa Hanoi peace trip cancelled 9/72
- Uganda aid halted for praise of Hitler 9/72
- Nixon and Gromyko sign arms limit treaty 10/72
- Kissinger says peace is at hand 10/72
- Cuba and U.S. seek hijacking curbs 11/72
- Nixon orders end to Hanoi bombing 12/72
- Agreement to stop fighting in Vietnam 1/73
- Accidental bombing of Hanoi Clinic 1/73
- POWs arrive home 2/73
- Pact with Cuba on hijackings 2/73
- Last soldier killed in Vietnam buried 2/73
- CIA implicated in Allende sabotage 3/73
- Brezhnev visits 6/73
- Bombing of Cambodia ended 8/73
- U.S.-backed coup ousts Allende 9/73
- Nixon calls worldwide military alert 10/73
- Resumption of ties with Egypt 11/73
- U.S. refused extradition of Vesco 12/73
- Bush named U.S. envoy to China 9/74
- Ford & Brezhnev reach accord on weapons 11/74
- U.S. to sell sixty fighters to Saudis 1/75
- Pressure on Soviets to let Jews emigrate 1/75
- U.S. lifts five-year Pakistan embargo 2/75
- Part of Soviet sub recovered 3/75
- First Vietnamese refugees 4/75
- Saigon surrenders to Communists 4/75
- 100 Vietnamese orphans killed in crash 4/75
- Marines rescue ship seized by Cambodia 5/75
- U.S. involvement in Vietnam over 5/75
- 102 jet fighters to Belgium 6/75
- Marianas Islands become Commonwealth 6/75
- Sam Giancana tied to plot to slay Castro 6/75
- Turkey takes over U.S. bases 7/75
- Ban on exports to Cuba lifted 8/75
- Sadat is first Egyptian pres. to visit 10/75
- CIA plotted deaths of foreign leaders 11/75
- Soviets beamed microwaves at embassy 2/76
- Americans leave Lebanon 6/76
- All G.I.'s withdrawn from Thailand 7/76
- North Korean troops kill two Americans 8/76
- Pres. Ford denies Soviet power in East 10/76
- Talks with Vietnam begin 11/76
- Human rights abuse brings aid reduction 2/77
- Human rights abuses brings aid reduction 2/77
- Sends arms to Zaire 3/77
- Idi Amin releases Americans 3/77
- Ethiopia ejects U.S. officials 4/77
- King Hussein arrives to discuss Mideast 4/77
- 15,000 Indochina refugees 7/77
- Panama gets future control of canal 9/77
- Joint Mideast goals with Soviets 10/77
- 10,000 boat people to be admitted 12/77
- Carter ends world tour 1/78
- 25,000 Indochina refugees a year 3/78
- U.S. to give to canal to Panama in 1999 4/78
- High Soviet official in U.N. defects 4/78
- Aid to Zaire as Katangans attack 5/78
- Carter urging peace in Nicaragua 9/78
- Carter at Camp David summit 9/78
- Relations with China resumed 1/79
- Shah flees Iran 1/79
- Summit in Guadeloupe 1/79
- Ambassador to Afghanistan killed 2/79
- Ties with Nicaragua broken 2/79
- Carter hosts Egypt-Israel pact 3/79
- South Africa ousts three Americans 4/79
- Khomeini blames U.S. for attempt on aide 5/79
- SALT II pact with Soviets 6/79
- Somoza ousted; Nicaragua in ruins 7/79
- Pope John Paul II pays first U.S. visit 10/79
- Iran seizes U.S. Embassy 11/79
- Iranian assets frozen 11/79
- Hundreds storm embassy in Pakistan 11/79

1980 to 1987

- Reprisals for Soviet Afghan invasion 1/80
- Decision to skip Moscow Olympic Games 3/80
- Ties with Iran cut 4/80
- Iran hostage rescue fails 4/80
- Cuban refugees to be admitted 4/80
- Carter meets with Hua of China 7/80
- Billy Carter registers as Libya agent 7/80
- 300th day of hostage captivity 7/80
- Mugabe meets with Carter 7/80
- Shah of Iran dies in Egypt 7/80
- Three U.S. nuns killed in El Salvador 12/80
- Aid to El Salvador halted 12/80
- Ex-CIA agent Barnett gets 18 yrs. as spy 1/81
- Iran releases hostages 1/81
- Embassy in El Salvador under attack 3/81
- Curbs on grain export to U.S.S.R. ended 4/81
- Libyans expelled 5/81
- Ottawa summit 7/81
- Navy F-14's down Libya jets 8/81
- House votes against AWACS sale to Saudis 10/81
- State Dept. bans Ian Paisley visit 12/81
- Reagan asks Americans to leave Libya 12/81
- General Dozier kidnapped in Italy 1/82
- Libyan oil imports banned 3/82
- Sandinistas charge U.S. aggression 3/82
- Travel to Cuba banned 4/82
- Reagan speaks at British Parliament 6/82
- Reagan denounces U.S.S.R. as evil empire 3/83
- Reagan proposes "Star Wars" 3/83
- Three Soviets ousted as spies 4/83
- Embassy in Beirut bombed 4/83
- Covert aid to Nicaragua legal 4/83
- Three ousted as Soviet spies 4/83
- Reagan defends contras 5/83
- Anti-Sandinista sabotage manual exposed 6/83
- Visa denied to Bernadette Devlin 6/83
- Latin American nations call for war end 7/83
- U.S. admits hiding alleged Nazi Barbie 8/83
- Two Marines shot in Beirut 8/83
- 216 Marines killed in Beirut bombing 10/83
- Troops swarm Grenada to restore peace 10/83
- Right-wing death squads in El Salvador 10/83
- Reagan accepts fault for Beirut massacre 12/83
- U.S. Navy officer released in Syria 1/84
- Diplomatic ties with Vatican 1/84
- U.S. Marines end occupation of Beirut 2/84
- Warships sent to Persian Gulf 2/84
- Reagan sends emergency aid to Salvador 4/84
- Cultural & scientific accord with China 4/84
- World Court rejected on Nicaragua 4/84
- Stinger missiles to Saudi Arabia 5/84
- 40th anniversary of D-Day commemorated 6/84
- Car bomb kills 23 at Embassy in Beirut 9/84
- Reagan and Gromyko meet 9/84
- Congress discloses CIA terrorist manual 10/84
- Stalin's daughter returns to U.S.S.R. 11/84
- U.S. may send hundreds back to Cuba 1/85
- Soviets protest "Star Wars" 1/85
- American officer killed by Russian 3/85
- Blast kills 17 near U.S. base in Spain 4/85
- Reagan will visit cemetery in Bitburg 4/85
- Trade ban on Nicaragua 5/85
- House approves $27 mil. for contras 6/85
- Salvadorans kill four U.S. Marines 6/85
- U.S. sends missiles to Pakistan 7/85
- Ortega says contras have killed 12,000 7/85
- Bush observes end of WWII 8/85
- Soviets accused of using spy dust 8/85
- Philippines civil war feared 10/85
- Reagan meets Gorbachev at Geneva 11/85
- Defector from KGB returns to U.S.S.R. 11/85
- Reagan and Gorbachev exchange greetings 1/86
- Ties with Libya broken; assets frozen 1/86
- Jailed Chinese spy L. Chin a suicide 2/86
- House vetoes aid to contras 3/86
- Clash with Libya in Mediterranean 3/86
- Terrorists bomb Berlin G.I. hangout 4/86
- Hostage Peter Kilburn killed in Beirut 4/86
- Libya attacked in air raid 4/86
- Congress votes $100 mil. to contras 6/86
- Freed hostage gives note to Reagan 8/86
- Ex-CIA agent defects to U.S.S.R. 8/86
- Nicholas Daniloff seized as spy 8/86
- U.S. newsman freed in Soviet exhange 9/86
- Japan's premier insults U.S. blacks 9/86
- Congress acclaims Aquino 9/86
- Senate enacts sanctions on S. Africa 10/86
- Burning Soviet sub sinks off Bermuda 10/86
- 55 Soviet diplomats ousted 10/86
- Summit with Soviets at Reykjavik 10/86
- Nicaragua captures U.S. arms runner 10/86
- Hostage David Jacobsen freed in Beirut 11/86
- SALT II limits exceeded 11/86
- Arms sales to Iran revealed 11/86
- Reagan acknowledges mistakes in Iran 12/86
- Drug smuggling on contra supply flights 1/87
- Panel denounces constructive engagement 2/87
- Edward Lansdale dies 2/87
- Pollard given life for spying for Israel 3/87
- Change in political asylum criteria 3/87
- Marines in Moscow accused of spying 3/87

- Gorbachev proposes missile-free Europe 4/87
- U.S. says Soviets wiretap embassy 4/87
- 100,000 protest Central American policy 4/87
- U.S. bars Kurt Waldheim from country 4/87
- Iraqi rocket hits U.S. frigate Stark 5/87
- Oliver North implicates superior 7/87
- Iran-contra hearings 7/87
- Latin American peace plan signed 8/87
- U.S. F-14 fires on Iranian plane 8/87
- Sgt. Lonetree gets 30 years for spying 8/87
- U.S. hits Iran oil platforms in reprisal 10/87
- Iran-contra report blames president 11/87
- U.S. and U.S.S.R. sign nuclear arms pact 12/87

United States (Politics)

1900 to 1909

- Wm. J. Bryan accepts pres. nomination 9/00
- McKinley and Roosevelt win elections 11/00
- Republicans gain majority in Congress 11/00
- McKinley and T. Roosevelt sworn in 3/01
- William McKinley assassinated 9/01
- Fistfight in Senate-tariff issue 2/02
- Ballot reform adopted in Oregon 6/02
- Oliver Wendell Holmes Jr. on high court 8/02
- Political violence in S.C. 1/03
- Socialist trend growing in America 5/03
- Wisconsin adopts direct primary 5/03
- Postmaster general held for bribery 5/03
- Women get the vote in Connecticut 9/03
- Iowa ex-Governor Francis Drake dies 11/03
- Maryland disenfranchises blacks 2/04
- Senator Mark Hanna dies 3/04
- Inquiry to unseat Sen. Smoot 3/04
- Socialists nominate Eugene Debs 5/04
- Populists nominate Thomas Watson 7/04
- Teddy Roosevelt elected president 11/04
- First black to get high customs job 1/05
- Teddy Roosevelt inaugurated 3/05
- Sec. of State John Hay dies 7/05
- Teddy Roosevelt criticizes muckrakers 4/06
- Teddy Roosevelt attacks plutocrats 10/06
- Republicans win 84-seat House majority 11/06
- Direct campaign contributions outlawed 1/07
- Govt. costs double in ten years 2/07
- Oklahoma becomes 46th state 11/07
- Suffragists launch campaign 12/07
- Extra star added for Oklahoma statehood 2/08
- War against anarchists 3/08
- William H. Taft nominated 6/08
- T. Roosevelt wants stronger Navy 7/08
- Taft elected President 11/08
- New battleships requested 1/09
- Army's increased strength 4/09
- Taft reserves oil fields for Navy 9/09
- Pankhurst in U.S. for suffrage rally 10/09
- Party machines dominate 11/09

1910 to 1919

- Taft dismisses Gifford Pinchot 1/10
- Defense budget at $2 billion 1/10
- Committee members to be elected by House 3/10
- Ex-Pres. Roosevelt given pension 3/10
- Suffragists present petition to vote 4/10
- Bureau of Mines established 5/10
- Teddy Roosevelt and New Nationalism 8/10
- Democrats sweep congressional elections 11/10
- R. La Follette forms Progressive Party 1/11
- House votes direct senatorial elections 4/11
- Senate votes for elections by voters 6/11
- Pres. Taft reviews Navy 11/11
- New Mexico becomes the 47th state 1/12
- R. La Follette withdraws from pres. race 2/12
- Arizona becomes 48th state 2/12
- Pres. campaign money to be made public 4/12
- Bull Moose party nominates T. Roosevelt 8/12
- Ariz., Wis., Kan. grant vote to women 11/12
- Woodrow Wilson elected president 11/12
- Congress votes $33 mil. naval hike 2/13
- Wilson gives first State of Union speech 4/13
- Navy Chief Adm. Fiske resigns 4/13
- 17th Amendment goes into effect 5/13
- Mobilization of 500,000 troops 11/13
- Women's suffrage defeated in House 1/15
- W.J. Bryan resigns as sec. of state 6/15
- Senate bombed 7/15
- Volunteer military camp opened 8/15
- Wilson wants standing Army 12/15
- Sec. of War Garrison resigns 2/16
- National Guard increased 450,000 6/16
- Teddy Roosevelt declines nomination 6/16
- $315 million for Navy 7/16
- Army orders 375 new planes 10/16
- Woodrow Wilson re-elected 11/16
- Jeanette Rankin first congresswoman 11/16
- Admiral Dewey dies 1/17
- Charles Fairbanks dies 6/18
- Republicans urge women's suffrage 1/19
- Teddy Roosevelt dies 1/19
- Women's suffrage passes House 5/19

1920 to 1929

- Palmer Red scare raids 1/20
- Sec. of State Lansing resigns 2/20
- Atty. Gen. Palmer attacks Communists 4/20
- Gompers asks overthrow of Congress 5/20
- Congress passes Army Reorganization Act 6/20
- Democrats nominate Cox and Roosevelt 7/20
- Women win right to vote 8/20
- John Reed dies 10/20
- Harding and Coolidge elected president 11/20
- Eugene Debs imprisoned for espionage 11/20
- "Uncle Joe" Cannon 44 years in House 12/20
- Deportation of Communists resumed 12/20
- Navy orders sale of 125 flying boats 1/21
- Herbert Hoover becomes sec. of commerce 2/21
- Warren G. Harding installed as president 3/21
- Wm. H. Taft chief justice of U.S. 3/21
- John Pershing selected chief of army 4/21
- Senate passes $494 mil. Navy bill 6/21
- Alice Robertson presides over House 6/21
- Unknown soldier lies in state 11/21
- Wilson frees political prisoners 12/21
- Committee outlaws use of poison gas 1/22
- Teapot Dome oil reserves leased 4/22
- Harding approves Teapot Dome lease 6/22
- Cash bonus bill for veterans vetoed 9/22
- Rebecca Felton first woman senator 10/22
- Albert Fall leases Elk Hill oil reserve 12/22
- Inquiry into Veterans Bureau corruption 3/23
- Harding begins tour of West & Alaska 6/23
- Harding suffers from ptomaine poisoning 7/23
- President Warren G. Harding dies 8/23
- Teapot Dome investigation 10/23
- Oklahoma Gov. Walton ousted 11/23
- Gompers denounces Hearst 11/23
- Counsel named to handle Teapot Dome case 1/24
- Edwin Denby resigns over Teapot Dome 2/24
- Woodrow Wilson dies 2/24
- Harry Sinclair indicted (Teapot Dome) 3/24
- Daugherty ousted in Teapot Dome scandal 3/24
- Indiana Gov. McCray sentenced mail fraud 4/24
- Congress overrides veto of bonus bill 5/24
- Indians vote first time 9/24
- Gen. John Pershing retires from Army 9/24
- Ma Ferguson elected first woman governor 11/24
- Coolidge and Dawes elected 11/24
- Henry Cabot Lodge dies 11/24
- Ma Ferguson inaugurated 1/25
- Robert La Follette dies 6/25
- Billy Mitchell guilty 12/25
- Eugene V. Debs dies 10/26
- Teapot Dome returned to Navy 3/27
- Albert Beveridge dies 4/27
- Sacco and Vanzetti electrocuted 8/27
- Coolidge will not run 8/27
- Billion dollars for Navy 12/27
- Hoover president 11/28
- Oscar Underwood dies 1/29
- Stimson becomes secretary of state 2/29
- Hoover sworn in as president 3/29

1930 to 1939

- James Doolittle resigns from U.S. Army 1/30
- Charles Evans Hughes new chief justice 2/30
- William Howard Taft dies at age 72 3/30
- Congress creates Veterans Administration 7/30
- Douglas MacArthur named Army chief 8/30
- Democrats gain control of House 11/30
- Senate overrides veto of bonus bill 2/31
- Five cities hit by anti-fascist bombs 1/32
- Hattie Carraway in husband's Senate seat 1/32
- FDR enters presidential race 1/32
- 202 ships meet for war maneuvers 2/32
- Congress sends 20th Amendment to states 3/32
- Socialists nominate Norman Thomas 5/32
- Rep. Edward Eslick dies on floor 6/32
- Senate defeats veterans bonus bill 6/32
- Troops drive bonus army from D.C. 7/32
- FDR elected president 11/32
- MacArthur appeals for bigger war budget 1/33
- Calvin Coolidge dies 1/33
- U.S. adopts 20th Amendment 2/33
- Cordell Hull named to FDR Cabinet 2/33
- FDR inaugurated 3/33
- FDR's first fireside chat 3/33
- People ask removal of Huey Long 4/33
- Navy places record order of 37 ships 8/33
- Ask Turkey to deliver criminal Insull 3/34
- Sen. Erickson falls asleep in Senate 5/34
- Huey Long is Louisiana dictator 9/34
- Two-thirds Dem. majority in Congress 11/34
- Oliver Wendell Holmes dies 6/35
- Huey Long assassinated 9/35
- FDR wins presidency second time 11/36
- FDR's second inauguration 1/37
- Elihu Root dies 2/37
- FDR's court-packing plan 3/37
- FDR wants larger Navy 12/37
- Frank Kellogg dies 12/37
- FDR wants more military spending 1/38
- House Un-American Affairs Committee 5/38
- Communist Party admits ties to Moscow 6/38
- Benjamin Cardozo dies 7/38
- Peace League linked to Reds 8/38
- Communist leader says support FDR 9/38
- Republican gains in elections 11/38
- Orders 571 planes 4/39
- $85 million for planes 8/39

1940 to 1949

- First anti-aircraft defense area set up 1/40
- FDR asks $1.8 billion for defense 1/40
- Army & Navy fortify Alaska 1/40
- Charles Edison appointed sec. of Navy 1/40
- America First Committee formed 4/40
- FDR promises 50,000 war pilots 5/40
- Military Supply Act allots $1.8 billion 6/40
- FDR names Republicans to Cabinet 6/40
- Wendell Willkie nominated for president 6/40
- FDR renominated for president 7/40
- Army adopts parachute troops 10/40
- Navy calls 27,591 reserves 10/40
- FDR and Henry Wallace elected 11/40
- FDR inaugurated for third term 1/41
- William Donovan to head new CIA 7/41
- Pearl Harbor probe condemns officers 1/42
- Office of Civil Defense established 1/42
- FDR creates Office of War Information 6/42
- Congress gives $42.8 bil. for services 6/42
- 8 German saboteurs captured in N.Y. 6/42
- FBI rounds up 158 more Nazis 7/42
- Six German saboteurs executed 8/42
- Eddie Rickenbacker found dead at sea 11/42
- FDR calls for $100 bil. military budget 1/43
- FDR strips Henry Wallace of war job 7/43
- Willkie enters presidential race 2/44
- Willkie ends presidential campaign 4/44
- Navy Secretary Frank Knox dies 4/44
- James Forrestal named sec. of the Navy 5/44
- FDR signs the G.I. Bill of Rights 6/44
- FDR agrees to run again 7/44
- Wendell Willkie dies 10/44
- FDR and Truman elected 11/44
- Fourth FDR inauguration 1/45
- FDR dies 4/45
- Truman sworn in as president 4/45
- Patton in trouble again 10/45
- General Patton dies 12/45
- Central Intelligence Group formed 1/46
- Harry Hopkins dies 1/46
- G.I. Bill 8/46
- George Marshall secretary of state 1/47
- Loyalty inquiry 3/47
- Armed services united under one agency 7/47
- Forrestal first sec. of defense 9/47
- House Un-American Activities Committee 10/47
- Air Force independent of Army 10/47
- General Pershing dies 7/48
- Alger Hiss accused of spying 8/48
- Truman assails HUAC 9/48
- HUAC implicates Charlie Chaplin 10/48
- Truman wins presidency 11/48
- George Marshall resigns 1/49
- James Forrestal a suicide 5/49
- Truman says nation hysterical over Reds 6/49
- Department of Defense created 8/49

1950 to 1959

- Alger Hiss sentenced to five years 1/50
- Gen. Henry "Hap" Arnold dies 1/50
- McCarthy launches anti-Red crusade 2/50
- Truman denounces McCarthy as saboteur 3/50
- Truman asks statehood for Hawaii 5/50
- Truman asks statehood for Alaska 5/50
- Wm. Remington resigns in HUAC inquiry 6/50
- Truman asks for $10 bil. arms budget 7/50
- Army calls up reserves & National Guard 7/50
- Truman gets emergency defense powers 9/50
- Mundt Bill on anti-American acts 9/50
- Petroleum Administration 10/50
- Henry L. Stimson dies 10/50
- Harry Gold gets 30 years as A-bomb spy 12/50
- State of emergency called over Korea 12/50
- Supreme Court curbs freedom of speech 1/51
- Internal Security & Rights Commission 1/51
- 22nd Amendment added to Constitution 2/51
- Rosenbergs found guilty of espionage 3/51
- U.S. military doubled to 2.9 million 3/51
- Truman strips MacArthur of command 4/51
- Bipartisan leader Arthur Vandenberg dies 4/51
- Rosenbergs get the death penalty 4/51
- Martin Sobell gets 30 years in prison 4/51
- Bradley & Marshall criticize MacArthur 5/51
- 21 Communists charged with conspiracy 6/51
- Marshall retires as secretary of defense 9/51
- Congress enacts veterans pension 9/51
- Truman offers to endorse Ike for pres. 11/51
- Ike to run as Republican 1/52
- Harold Ickes dies 2/52
- McCarthy sues Senator Benton for libel 3/52
- Truman pulls out of presidential race 3/52
- Ike leaving NATO to run for president 4/52
- Congress passes McCarran-Walter Bill 6/52
- Nixon defends $18,000 fund on TV 9/52
- Court rejects appeal in Rosenberg case 10/52
- Eisenhower wins elections in landslide 11/52
- Ike appoints Dulles & Wilson to posts 11/52
- Rosenbergs appeal to president for stay 1/53
- Ike sworn in as president 1/53
- Clemency denied to Rosenbergs 2/53
- Pope asks for clemency in Rosenberg case 2/53
- Ex-Senator Robert LaFollette kills self 2/53
- Chaplin surrenders U.S. re-entry permit 4/53
- Dept. of Health Education and Welfare 4/53
- Mrs. Oveta Culp Hobby first sec. of HEW 4/53
- Sen. Morse ends record speech 4/53
- High court denies third Rosenberg appeal 5/53
- Senator Robert Wagner dies 5/53
- Nathan Twining commands Air Force 6/53
- Ethel and Julius Rosenberg are executed 6/53
- Senate majority leader Robert Taft dies 7/53
- Gen. Ridgway named chief of staff 8/53
- M. Durkin resigns as sec. of labor 9/53
- L. Toomer sworn in Treasury Register 9/53
- General Jonathan Wainwright dies 9/53
- Frederick M. Vinson dies 9/53
- 1,456 ousted in loyalty inquiry 10/53
- Earl Warren chosen as chief justice 9/53
- Truman gets subpoena from HUAC 11/53
- Truman refuses to testify before HUAC 11/53
- $214,000 approved for McCarthy inquiry 2/54
- McCarthy investigates Army 2/54
- Oppenheimer a security risk 4/54
- Senate rejects plan for 18-year-old vote 5/54
- Army-McCarthy hearings ended 6/54
- Ike signs anti-Communist bill 8/54
- Death penalty for espionage instituted 9/54
- First televised Cabinet meeting 10/54
- Democrats regain control of House 11/54
- Alger Hiss freed 11/54
- Nelson Rockefeller foreign policy aide 12/54
- Senate condemns Joseph McCarthy 12/54
- Air Force Academy opens 7/55
- Heart attack hospitalizes Eisenhower 9/55
- Eisenhower recovered from heart attack 11/55
- Rosa Parks sparks civil rights movement 12/55
- Eisenhower hospitalized again 6/56
- Ike back in White House 7/56
- Ike re-elected president 11/56
- Ike inaugurated 1/57
- Joseph McCarthy dies 5/57
- Eisenhower has mild stroke 11/57
- A.C. Powell charged with tax fraud 5/58
- Sherman Adams, Ike aide, ousted 9/58
- Alaska becomes 49th state 1/59
- John Foster Dulles dies 5/59
- Hawaii becomes 50th state 8/59
- George C. Marshall dies 10/59

1960 to 1969

- Nixon declares candidacy in pres. race 1/60
- Senate approves 23rd Amendment 2/60
- Dick Clark investigation on payola 4/60
- 50-star flag makes debut 7/60
- JFK and LBJ nominated by Democrats 7/60
- Republicans nominate Nixon and Lodge 7/60
- JFK and Nixon debate on TV 9/60
- JFK and LBJ elected 11/60
- JFK names Dean Rusk sec. of state 12/60
- Presidential press conference televised 1/61
- Kissinger named natl. security adviser 2/61
- 23rd Amendment added 3/61
- JFK increases military 7/61
- Sumner Welles dies 10/61
- Speaker of House Sam Rayburn dies 11/61
- Conservatives hold rally for Goldwater 3/62
- Dr. Robert Soblen commits suicide 9/62
- Eleanor Roosevelt dies 11/62
- Black Howard Jenkins named to NLRB 7/63
- Kennedys lose a baby son 8/63
- JFK shot dead in Texas 11/63
- Lyndon B. Johnson sworn in as president 11/63
- Lee Harvey Oswald charged with JFK death 11/63
- Lee Harvey Oswald killed by Jack Ruby 11/63
- JFK buried at Arlington 11/63
- Justice Earl Warren to head JFK inquiry 11/63
- FBI finds Oswald acted alone in murder 12/63
- Jackie Kennedy appreciates sympathy 1/64
- Jack Ruby given death sentence 3/64
- Douglas MacArthur dies at age 84 4/64
- Barry Goldwater named by GOP for pres. 7/64
- LBJ and HHH nominated by Democrats 8/64
- Sgt. Alvin C. York, war hero, dies 9/64
- Warren inquiry finished 9/64
- Robert Kennedy resigns to run for Senate 9/64
- Herbert Hoover dies at age 90 10/64
- LBJ and HHH elected 11/64
- LBJ sworn in 1/65
- Frances Perkins dies 5/65
- Opposition to Vietnam war grows 5/66
- Ronald Reagan elected governor of Calif. 11/66
- First popularly elected black senator 11/66
- LBJ has successful hernia operation 12/66
- Lawsuit over book on JFK's death 12/66
- John Nance Garner dies 11/67
- Johnson orders reserves to active duty 1/68
- Clark Clifford named to Defense Dept. 1/68
- Johnson calls 24,500 reserves to duty 4/68
- Republicans nominate Nixon and Agnew 8/68
- HHH nominated amid riots in Chicago 8/68
- First black woman elected to House 11/68
- Nixon and Agnew win 11/68
- Norman Thomas dies 12/68
- Former CIA chief Dulles deceased 1/69
- Dwight D. Eisenhower dies 3/69
- Joseph P. Kennedy dies 11/69
- Senate turns down Nixon's court choice 11/69

1970 to 1979

- Defense cuts to cut 1.25 mil. jobs 1/70
- David Eisenhower joins Navy 1/70
- Army accuses five in Mylai massacre 3/70
- Senate rejects Carswell for Supreme Ct. 4/70
- Voting age dropped to 18 6/70
- McGovern opens presidential campaign 1/71
- Robert Dole to head Republican Party 1/71
- William Casey named head of SEC 2/71
- Senate chamber blasted by bomb 3/71
- Printing of Pentagon Papers upheld 6/71
- Bomb explodes at Pentagon 5/72
- J. Edgar Hoover dies 5/72
- Five burglars caught in Watergate office 6/72
- Death penalty ruled unconstitutional 6/72
- Mitchell resigns as Nixon campaign mgr. 7/72
- McGovern nominated; Eagleton quits 7/72
- Sargent Shriver takes v.p. spot 8/72
- Nixon and Agnew renominated 8/72
- Two Nixon ex-aides arrested in Watergate 9/72
- Seven indicted in Watergate break-in 9/72
- Richard Nixon wins second term as pres. 11/72
- Harry Truman dies at age 88 12/72
- Liddy & McCord found guilty in Watergate 1/73
- Lyndon B. Johnson dies 1/73
- Sirica to revive Watergate inquiry 2/73
- Ellsberg freed in Pentagon affair 5/73
- J. Rankin, first woman in Congress, dies 5/73
- Sec. of State Rogers resigns 8/73
- Kissinger named secretary of state 8/73
- Erlichman indicted in Ellsberg case 9/73
- Agnew resigns as vice president 10/73
- Gerald Ford chosen new vice president 10/73
- Saturday Night Massacre 10/73
- Nixon dismisses Archibald Cox 10/73
- Elliot Richardson resigns over Watergate 10/73
- Nixon dismisses William Ruckelshaus 10/73
- Leon Jaworski named special prosecutor 11/73
- U.S. diplomat Charles Bohlen dies 1/74
- Seven indicted in Watergate 3/74
- Jury finds Nixon involved in Watergate 3/74
- Nixon to pay $432,787 in back taxes 4/74
- Chief Justice Earl Warren dies at 83 7/74
- Nixon impeachment begins 7/74
- Richard M. Nixon resigns 8/74
- Gerald R. Ford assumes presidency 8/74
- Nelson Rockefeller picked as vice pres. 8/74
- Ford gives Nixon pardon 9/74
- Amnesty offered to draft evaders 9/74
- Nixon blood clot causes concern 10/74
- Nixon develops pneumonia 11/74
- Three ex-Nixon aides sentenced 2/75
- John Connally acquitted of bribery 4/75
- Citizenship of Robert E. Lee restored 7/75
- Two attempts on Ford's life 9/75
- Wm. O. Douglas quits Supreme Court 11/75
- Moynihan resigns as U.N. ambassador 2/76
- Democrats choose Carter and Mondale 7/76
- Ford and Dole named by GOP 8/76
- Carter and Mondale elected 11/76
- Carter and Mondale sworn in 1/77
- Mayor Koch inaugurated in New York 12/77
- Hubert Horatio Humphrey dies of cancer 1/78
- San Francisco officials murdered 11/78
- Bert Lance indicted 5/79
- Major shifts in Carter Cabinet 7/79
- Andrew Young resigns as U.N. ambassador 8/79

1980 to 1987

- Abscam bribery scandal 2/80
- Bert Lance cleared on fraud charge 4/80
- Vance resigns over hostage mission 4/80
- Jenrette indicted in Abscam case 6/80
- Myers and co-defendants guilty in Abscam 8/80
- Carter and Mondale win nomination 8/80
- Carter and Reagan debate 10/80
- Ronald Reagan elected president 11/80
- Haig named sec. of state 12/80
- Ronald Reagan sworn in as pres. 1/81
- Reagan wounded by assassin 3/81
- Reagan goes home from hospital 4/81
- Omar Bradley dies 4/81
- Hinckley pleads not guilty 8/81
- Moral Majority said to peddle coercion 8/81
- Economic adviser Stockman to resign 11/81
- Admiral Hyman Rickover dies 11/81
- Reagan broadens power of CIA 12/81
- Alexander Haig resigns 6/82
- Hinckley gets indefinite term 8/82
- Bess Truman dies 10/82
- Reagan dismisses EPA head Rita Lavelle 2/83
- EPA head Anne McGill Burford resigns 3/83
- Wm. Ruckleshaus named head of EPA 3/83
- Catholic bishops call for no nukes 5/83
- House censures reps. for sex with pages 7/83
- James Watt resigns 10/83
- Jesse Jackson to run for president 11/83
- Reagan to seek second term 1/84
- William French Smith resigns 1/84
- General Mark Clark dies 4/84
- Terrorists bomb Navy officers club 4/84
- Reagan operated on for polyp 5/84
- Ferraro's financial backround questioned 8/84
- Labor Sec. Donovan indicted for fraud 10/84
- Reagan and Bush win by 59% 11/84
- Reagan takes oath of office twice 1/85
- Deaver out; Regan new head of Cabinet 1/85
- Agents arrest 20 planning civil war 3/85
- Retired Navy officer arrested as spy 5/85
- Navy radioman charged with spying 6/85
- Teenagers invade Pentagon computer 7/85
- U.S. Navy civilian held as spy 11/85
- Poindexter succeeds McFarlane 12/85
- Rehnquist to head Supreme Court 6/86
- Senate reviews Rehnquist as chief judge 7/86
- Hyman Rickover dies 7/86
- Averell Harriman dies 7/86
- Whitworth gets 365 years for spying 8/86
- Iran arms sales disclosed 11/86
- Casey has brain surgery after stroke 12/86
- Reagan admits mistakes on Iran deals 12/86
- Carlucci is national security adviser 1/87
- First Republican woman governor 1/87
- Iran-contra report calls Reagan confused 2/87
- Casey quits as CIA; Gates named 2/87
- Cuomo says he won't run for president 2/87
- Gary Hart quits race in sex scandal 5/87
- Reagan says contra aid was his own idea 5/87
- Jesse Jackson leads in presidential poll 5/87
- William Webster sworn in at CIA 5/87
- Fawn Hall testifies loyalty to North 6/87

- North implicates superiors 7/87
- Reagan names Robert Bork to high court 7/87
- Molly Yard elected president of NOW 7/87
- Drive to oust Arizona Gov. Evan Mecham 7/87
- William Sessions named to head FBI 7/87
- 44 N.Y. officials arrested for bribery 8/87
- Senator Biden quits presidential race 9/87
- Biaggi and Esposito convicted 9/87
- Americans celebrate Constitution 9/87
- Senate rejects Bork nomination 10/87
- Reagan names Douglas Ginsburg for court 10/87
- Alf Landon dies 10/87
- Ginsburg withdraws; Kennedy named 11/87
- Iran-contra report blames president 11/87
- William Sessions becomes head of FBI 11/87
- Weinberger quits as secretary of defense 11/87
- Chicago Mayor Harold Washington dies 11/87
- Michael Deaver convicted of perjury 12/87
- Hart re-enters presidential race 12/87

United States (Science and Technology)

1900 to 1909

- Battleship Ohio launched 5/01
- Gillette to market replaceable razor 12/01
- St. Louis preparing for World's Fair 9/02
- Richard Gatling dies 2/03
- N.Y.-N.J. tunnel finished 3/04
- St. Louis World's Fair opens 5/04
- Sub torpedo boat Fulton tested 6/04
- New York City subway opens 10/04
- Auto show in New York 1/05
- Formation of Aeronautic Corps 7/07
- Army wants Orville Wright to build plane 8/08
- Autos begin mail delivery 11/08
- Delaware, largest ship, launched 2/09
- Robert Peary reaches North Pole 4/09
- Construction of Pearl Harbor 11/09

1910 to 1919

- Electric signs denounced 9/10
- First cancer virus found 1/11
- N.Y. welcomes biggest ocean liner 6/11
- Self-starter for autos 7/11
- Atwood flies St. Louis to New York 8/11
- First assembly line at Ford 10/13
- Los Angeles gets aqueduct water 11/13
- First radio-phone connection with Japan 7/15
- Browning automatic rifle 3/18
- Eugene Caldwell dies of X-ray burns 6/18
- Goddard predicts trip to moon 3/19
- Navy hydroplane 5/19

1920 to 1929

- Nine million autos driven 2/21
- Air bombs demonstrated 7/21
- U.S. has oil for only 20 years 1/22
- Muscle Shoals Dam 7/22
- Alexander Graham Bell dies 8/22
- Three Army planes complete globe flight 9/24
- Byrd flys over North Pole 5/26
- Mail flown privately 7/26
- Lindbergh flies the Atlantic 5/27
- Air service to Cuba 1/28
- James Packard dies 3/28
- Amelia Earhart flies over Atlantic 6/28
- First flight using instruments only 9/29

1930 to 1949

- 10,000 new drivers over last year 6/30
- Hoover gives Lindbergh Medal of Honor 8/30
- Earhart first woman to fly Atlantic 5/32
- Phone service between U.S. & Hawaii 12/32
- FDR pledges operation of Muscle Shoals 1/33
- Aircraft carrier Ranger launched 2/33
- Albert Einstein arrives 10/33
- TWA cuts rail connections on coast trips 5/34
- Federal Communications Commission formed 6/34
- New 60-mph Army tank developed 12/34
- Amelia Earhart lost at sea 7/37
- Einstein tells FDR atom bomb possible 8/39
- FCC developing television rules 4/40
- Grand Coulee Dam opens 3/41
- 488 ships built in one year 9/42
- USS New Jersey launched 12/42
- First Air Force jet, Bell P-59 Airacomet 1/44
- USS Missouri is launched 1/44
- Three hidden cities developed bomb 8/45
- Atomic Energy Commission created 8/46

1950 to 1959

- Truman orders hydrogen bomb built 1/50
- TV getting in way of school books 3/50
- Truman asks $260 mil. for H-bomb 7/50
- E.I. du Pont Nemours to build H-bomb 8/50
- Scientists use atom to make electricity 9/50
- CBS to begin color TV broadcasts 10/50
- AEC atomic tests rattle Southwest 1/51
- AEC talks of 1st atomic-powered airplane 2/51
- AEC has third atomic test in Nevada 2/51
- U.S. Navy launches K-1 sub 3/51
- Hydrogen bomb tested 5/51
- Navy tests rocket-powered helicopter 10/51
- FCC predicts 1,200-1,500 TV stations 11/51
- AEC makes electricity from atoms 12/51
- Man dies after Defense Dept. experiment 3/52
- AEC starts third set of A-bomb tests 4/52
- FCC lifts 3-yr ban on new TV stations 4/52
- One mil. see Nevada A-bomb blast on TV 4/52
- Superliner United States makes trial run 5/52
- U.S. dedicates world's first atomic sub 6/52
- The United States wins the Blue Riband 7/52
- U.S. Army announces 85-ton atomic cannon 9/52
- AEC says H-bomb ready for use 11/52
- Truman says this is age of H-bomb 1/53
- Navy shows Sea Dart jet fighter seaplane 7/53
- Device to drop A-bomb 8/53
- Pregnancy induced with frozen sperm 12/53
- Nautilus, U.S. atomic sub, launched 1/54
- 50 million have electric power 1/54
- Contract for Pittsburgh nuclear plant 3/54
- U.S. explodes new hydrogen bomb 3/54
- First H-bomb blast shown on TV 4/54
- Ike signs Atomic Energy Act 8/54
- Air Force authorizes B-58 10/54
- U.S. launches Forrestal 12/54
- Missile with atomic warhead tested 2/55
- Albert Einstein dies 4/55
- German scientists make U.S. rockets 7/55
- Nuclear missile defenses 4/57
- Reaction to Sputnik 10/57
- Successful launching of Atlas missile 12/57
- Explorer I launched 2/58
- Third satellite launched 3/58
- Pioneer satellite fails to reach moon 10/58
- Pan Am opens transatlantic service 10/58
- First cable linking U.S. and Europe 9/59
- Ford drops Edsel as failure 11/59

1960 to 1969

- Army issues M14 gun 1/60
- Satellite that can change orbit 1/60
- Navy Polaris missile undergoes tests 3/60
- Signals from Pioneer V spacecraft 3/60
- Titan ICBM fired over 3,000 miles 4/60
- Weather lab launched into space 4/60
- FDA approves contraceptive pill 5/60
- U.S. fires Atlas ICBM record 9,000 miles 5/60
- 5,000-lb. Midas I in orbit 5/60
- Sub completes Polaris missile launch 7/60
- FDA approves Sabin polio vaccine 8/60
- Active communication satellite launched 10/60
- U.S., Canada approve hydroelectric plant 10/60
- Dam over Rio Grande 10/60
- Discoverer XVII shot into orbit 11/60
- Navy building nucear sub fleet 11/60
- Contraceptive pill 12/60
- First solid-fuel rocket is launched 2/61
- NASA launches Explorer XI 4/61
- First American in space 5/61
- Gus Grissom second American in space 7/61
- Mercury capsule orbited and retrieved 10/61
- Glenn first American to orbit earth 2/62
- Titan 2 rocket makes maiden flight 3/62
- Air Force researching use of lasers 3/62
- First satellite TV broadcast 4/62
- Pact with Soviets on weather satellites 4/62
- Ranger IV crashes on moon 4/62
- Fourth atomic bomb detonated in ten days 5/62
- Carpenter, second manned orbital flight 5/62
- First interception of ICBM 7/62
- Satellite sends first TV show 7/62
- Polaris sub Alexander Hamilton launched 8/62
- U.S. launches Mariner II 8/62
- Walter Schirra orbits earth six times 10/62
- Atmospheric tests halted 11/62
- Explorer 16 launched 12/62
- Mariner 2 takes photos of Venus 12/62
- Second Telstar satellite launched 5/63
- Cooper orbits earth 22 times 5/63
- Saturn rocket launches ten-ton payload 1/64
- Ranger 6 crashes on moon 2/64
- First Gemini test flight orbits earth 4/64
- B-70 flies three times speed of sound 5/64
- Link to Japan by underwater cable 6/64
- First Minuteman II ICBM tested 9/64
- Land speed record by Breedlove 10/64
- Art Arfons takes land speed record 11/65
- Two craft rendezvous in space 12/65
- U.S. plane loses H-bomb over Spain 1/66
- First docking in space 3/66
- Surveyor I photographs moon 6/66
- U.S.-built jets crashing in Germany 8/66
- Gemini II joins with satellite 9/66
- Robert Oppenheimer dies 2/67
- First U.S. heart transplant 1/68
- Plane with H-bombs crashes in Greenland 1/68
- First astronauts to orbit moon return 12/68
- Two space ships linked 3/69
- Men on the moon 7/69
- Second moon landing 11/69

1970 to 1979

- Apollo 13 launched on third moon trip 4/70
- Apollo 14 launched on moon mission 1/71
- Two Apollo 14 astronauts walk on moon 2/71
- Senate cuts funds for supersonic SST 3/71
- Apollo 15 astronauts take ride on moon 7/71
- Mariner 9 placed in orbit around Mars 11/71
- U.S. launches Pioneer 10 to Jupiter 3/72
- Apollo 16 makes successful trip 4/72
- Apollo 14 brings stamps & medals to moon 7/72
- Apollo moon program ends 12/72
- U.S. puts Skylab into orbit 5/73
- Skylab astronauts fix panel in space 6/73
- Senate approves Alaska pipeline plan 7/73
- Second Skylab returns after 59 days 9/73
- FDA forces A.H. Robins IUD off market 5/74
- Air Force fires ICBM from plane 10/74
- B-1 bomber makes successful test flight 12/74
- Americans and Soviets link up in space 7/75
- Trans-Alaskan pipeline opened 6/77
- Carter defers building neutron bomb 4/78
- U.S. hears atomic blast, suspects sub 10/79

1980 to 1987

- Columbia, first space shuttle, launched 4/81
- Personal computers invading homes 8/81
- Reagan approves neutron bomb 8/81
- Columbia launched on third flight 3/82
- Home video games new craze 10/82
- Reagan call for deployment of MX missile 11/82
- First artificial heart recipient 12/82
- Reagan proposes "Star Wars" defense plan 3/83
- Pioneer 10 first to leave solar system 6/83
- Challenger launched 8/83
- Americans first to walk freely in space 2/84
- B-1 bomber crashes on test flight 8/84
- Challenger lifts off with crew of seven 10/84
- Baboon heart implanted in baby 10/84
- Second artificial heart implant 11/84
- Anti-rocket rocket tested by U.S. 9/85
- Space shuttle Challenger explodes 1/86
- NASA was warned of rocket weakness 2/86
- Compartment with Challenger crew found 3/86
- Titan rocket expodes 4/86
- Shuttle had one fault: weak joint 6/86
- New superconductive compound is found 2/87
- Compact disc video introduced 5/87
- U.S. launches Titan 34D 10/87
- NASA grants contracts for space station 12/87

United States (Society)

1900 to 1909

- New century opens with optimism 1/00
- First stamp booklet released 4/00
- Population reaches 76 million 10/00
- Population at 300 mil. by year 2001 1/01
- Prohibitionists smash 12 saloons 1/01
- Blacks found enslaved in South Carolina 3/01
- Land lottery begins in Oklahoma 7/01
- Govt. buys Oklahoma land from Indians 8/01
- Report indicates slavery in Georgia 8/01
- Three blacks found lynched in Miss. 8/01
- Booker T. Washington to D.C. 10/01
- West Point celebrates 100th birthday 6/02
- American buffalo saved from extinction 8/02
- T. Roosevelt says race no bar to office 11/02
- Congress passes tax on immigrants 3/03
- Black lynched in Delaware 6/03
- Calamity Jane dies 8/03
- Pulitzer gives $2m for journalism school 8/03
- Postal Service loses millions to fraud 11/03
- Two blacks burned at stake in Georgia 8/04
- Helen Keller wins degree 9/04
- John Paul Jones body found 4/05
- Immigration up 20% 8/05
- Million immigrants admitted 8/05
- 5,000 a day through Ellis Island 5/07
- U.S. has highest divorce rate 11/08

1910 to 1919

- Mann Act against white slavery 1/10
- John D. Rockefeller proposes foundation 3/10
- J. Mitchell asks for holiday on Sunday 3/10
- Amendment to 1907 Immigration Act passed 3/10
- ICC reports 8,711 rail deaths in year 7/10
- T. Roosevelt urges blacks to get jobs 8/10
- Taft orders removal of Negro 9th Cavalry 4/11
- Congress authorizes Parcel Post system 8/12
- Congress bars illiterate immigrants 12/12
- Senate rejects veto of Webb-Kenyon bill 2/13
- Wilson's wife, Helen Louise Axson, dies 8/14
- Leo Frank gets sentence commuted 6/21
- Grandfather clause illegal 7/15
- Citizens Preparedness Parade 5/16
- Literacy tests for immigrants 2/17
- Draft becomes law 5/17
- First officer's training camp 5/17
- 10 million register for draft 6/17
- Up to 75 dead in St. Louis race riot 7/17
- First draft numbers 7/17
- Draft resisters can be executed 8/17
- National Guard drafted 8/17
- Natl. Guard approves black division 10/17
- Prohibition passes Congress 12/17
- Frances Cabrini, first U.S. saint, dies 12/17
- State prisoners to do farm work 1/18
- Prohibition imposed on Puerto Rico 3/18
- Daylight Savings Time begins 4/18
- Farmers ask delay in draft 7/18
- Wilson demands end of lynchings 7/18
- Three million drafted 10/18
- Influenza deaths exceed war toll 11/18
- Armistice celebrated twice 11/18
- Race riots in Washington, D.C. 7/19
- 70,000 runaways last year 12/19
- Plan to fight Reds with film 12/19

1920 to 1929

- Alcohol is banned by the 18th Amendment 1/20
- Five killed attempting to kill black 2/20
- Senate bars mandatory military service 4/20
- Urban exceeds rural population 9/20
- Quality of teachers is failing 1/21
- Ellis Island let in 10,000 undesirables 2/21
- Typhus halts immigration from Europe 2/21
- 1920 cancer deaths at 5,361 3/21
- Immigration quotas set 5/21
- Lady Randolph Churchill dies 6/21
- Foreign liquor barred from U.S. 10/21
- Cocaine & heroine from Germany 11/21
- Democrats filibuster anti-lynch bill 12/21
- 11% speak no English in U.S. 3/22
- Federal Narcotics Board created 5/22
- Cable Bill passes Congress 9/22
- Women wear 1.6 million shoe styles 12/22
- Benefits of peyote for Indians 1/23
- U.K. immigrants entering through Canada 6/23
- Gas chamber used 1st time for execution 2/24
- Soldiers' Bonus Bill passed 3/24
- Full citizenship to U.S. Indians 6/24
- Calvin Coolidge Jr. dies 7/24
- Working women must use husband's name 8/24
- Lax enforcement of dry law 10/24
- Indian population 350,000 10/25
- Klan leader gets 20 years 11/25
- Indians commemorate Custer battle 6/26
- Bill Haywood dies 5/28
- Wyatt Earp dies 1/29

1930 to 1939

- Tenth anniversary of Prohibition 1/30
- Cigarette smoking increases 7/30
- Population at 122.7 million 8/30
- $5 mil. fund to fight racketeers created 11/30
- Labor leader Mother Jones dies 11/30
- Court rules dry law constitutional 2/31
- Lindbergh baby Charles Jr. kidnapped 3/32
- Body of Charles Lindbergh Jr. found 5/32
- Hoover admits failure of Prohibition 8/32
- Police hunt Dutch Schultz 1/33
- House passes dry law repeal 2/33
- FDR signs bill legalizing beer & wine 3/33
- Beer consumed legally 4/33
- FDR to intervene in Scottsboro case 11/33
- Prohibition comes to an end 12/33
- First laundromat 4/34
- FDR opens war on crime 5/34
- Census shows 127 million 5/36
- Francis Townsend dies 12/36
- Clarence Darrow dies 3/38

1940 to 1949

- Population at 131 million 3/40
- Congress passes Alien Registration Act 6/40
- Selective Service bill signed 9/40
- First draft number drawn in U.S. 10/40
- Million register for 1st peacetime draft 10/40
- 18,700 enter Army in peacetime draft 11/40
- United Service Organization formed 2/41
- 2,000 Japanese to be evacuated from West 10/41
- FDR orders aliens to register with govt. 1/42
- Daylight Savings Time 2/42
- FDR orders internment of Japanese 2/42
- Third military draft begins 3/42
- 100,000 Japanese-Americans interned 3/42
- East Coast blacked out to protect ships 4/42
- FDR creates Women's Auxiliary Army Corps 5/42
- Black recruits allowed in Navy 5/42
- Congress creates Women's naval reserves 7/42
- Draft extended to 18-year olds 11/42
- Hard liquor banned in Army 2/43
- Draft deferments given 12/43
- Ex-G.I.'s go to college 9/47
- Population burgeons on West Coast 8/48

1950 to 1959

- U.S. Senate adopts ERA by 63-19 vote 1/50
- Record 3.5 mil. in Catholic schools 6/50
- First nationwide conference on aging 6/50
- Truman extends Selective Service to 1951 6/50
- Population at 150,520,198 7/50
- New York population at 14,743,210 7/50
- 100,000 to be drafted for Korea 7/50
- Guide on civil defense 8/50
- Truman extends draft to 1955 6/51
- Nationwide drug raid brings in 500 1/52
- Capt. Carlsen rescued after ship sinks 1/52
- Ban against black singers ended 2/52
- 4.5 mil. more put on Social Security 7/52
- Ike warns South to protect civil rights 9/52
- Hiroshima victims get U.S. surgery 5/55
- Suburban housing boom 5/56
- 21,500 Hungarian immigrants 12/56

1960 to 1969

- Fallout shelter models for sale 2/60
- Civil Rights Bill to White House 4/60
- Ike signs Civil Rights Act of 1960 5/60
- Peace Corps formed 3/61
- Freedom rides for desegregation 5/61
- Alabama barred from halting freedom ride 5/61
- Dr. King opens black vote drive 10/61
- Court bans official prayers in schools 6/62
- Pentagon plans for fallout shelters 6/62
- World population over three bil. 9/62
- Justice Dept. files civil rights suit 9/62
- JFK federalizes Miss. National Guard 9/62
- Alcatraz prison closed 3/63
- Univ. of Alabama ordered to admit black 5/63
- Zip code inaugurated 7/63
- JFK asks to abolish immigration quotas 7/63
- JFK halts draft for married men 9/63
- FTC plans ban on cigarette ads 1/64
- LBJ signs Civil Rights Act 7/64
- LBJ equates John Birch Society with KKK 10/64
- Johnson signs Medicare plan 7/65
- Power failure hits nine states 11/65
- Muhammad Ali indicted for draft evasion 5/67
- Ali gets five years for draft evasion 6/67
- First draft lottery in U.S. since 1942 12/69
- Review of 1960's 12/69

1970 to 1979

- FBI can raid without warning for drugs 1/70
- Thousands march for ecology on Earth Day 4/70
- Nixon bans occupational draft deferments 4/70
- Nixon nominates first two women generals 5/70
- NAACP charges Nixon admin. anti-black 6/70
- Justice Dept. sues Miss. on integration 7/70
- Post Office made independent agency 8/70
- 48,000 acres awarded to Taos Indians 12/70
- One-third students tried marijuana 2/71
- U.S. women's crime rate above men's 6/71
- U.S. population at sub-zero growth 12/72
- Laws forbidding abortion overturned 1/73
- American Indians seize Wounded Knee 2/73
- Federal forces encircle Wounded Knee 3/73
- Indians end Wounded Knee occupation 5/73
- Crazed soldier lands copter 2/74
- Senate votes to restore death penalty 3/74
- Americans trying bisexuality 3/74
- August 19th Women's Equality Day 8/74
- Man crashes gate 12/74
- Freedom Train on way to 80 cities 4/75
- Women join Army in record numbers 5/75
- Sunbelt leads U.S. in population growth 2/76
- Spectacular Bicentennial celebration 7/76
- Fragments of 1776 Declaration turn up 12/76
- Military to accept homosexuals 12/78

1980 to 1987

- Bill signed for draft registration at 18 7/80
- FDA requires labels on tampons 10/80
- Toxic shock linked to tampons 9/80
- Sun Myung Moon under inquiry for taxes 6/81
- Racial minorities increase in suburbs 6/81
- Tylenol off market after killings 10/82
- WWII internment of Japanese found unjust 2/83
- Martin Luther King national holiday 11/83
- Promotion quotas for blacks barred 1/84
- Senate vote against silent school prayer 3/84
- Jaycees vote to admit women 8/84
- First woman executed in 22 years 11/84
- Samantha Smith is killed in plane crash 8/85
- Hands Across America 5/86
- Statue of Liberty feted on 100th anniv. 7/86
- Justice Dept. report on pornography 7/86
- Declaration of Independence attacked 10/86
- U.S. rated fifth best place to live 3/87
- Yuppies displacing hippies in Frisco 3/87
- Jim Bakker quits ministry in sex scandal 3/87
- Four teenagers die in suicide pact 3/87
- Baby M awarded to biological father 3/87
- Amnesty program for aliens begins 5/87
- Garbage barge returns to New York 5/87
- Donald Harvey admits poisoning 24 8/87
- Civil rights activist Bayard Rustin dies 8/87
- Pope in U.S., facing dissent 9/87
- Arms protester run over by train 9/87
- Jessica McClure saved from Texas well 10/87
- Protest against Georgia sodomy law 10/87
- "The Closing of the American Mind" 12/87
- Cubans seize two detention centers 12/87
- Whites convicted in Howard Beach killing 12/87

Universal Studios

- Founded by Carl Laemmle 6/12

Unser, Al 5/77, 5/78

Unser, Bobby 5/68, 5/75

Upper Silesia

- 75% votes annexation to Denmark 2/20

Upper Volta

- Independent republic 8/60

Uris, Leon 12/58, 12/76

Urrutia, Manuel 1/59

Uruguay

- Revolution erupts 1/04
- Revolt 1/10
- Jose Ordonez elected president 3/11
- Ties with Germany severed 10/17
- President Alfredo Baldomir inaugurated 6/38
- U.S. gains military bases on coast 11/40
- Uruguay wins soccer's World Cup 7/50
- Pro-Castro marchers 3/60
- Alliance for Progress meets 8/61
- OAS bans Cuba 1/62
- Ties with Cuba broken 9/64
- State of siege 10/65
- Armed forces take power in coup 2/73
- Julio Maria Sanguinetti elected pres. 11/84

U.S. Radium Corp. 6/28

- 41st ex-employee dies of poisoning 12/51

U.S. Steel

- Formed by J.P. Morgan 3/01
- Market divided up 6/05
- Tennessee Coal, Iron and Rail bought 11/07
- First steel auto wheels 4/08
- T. Roosevelt blamed for infraction 2/09
- Denounced at labor conference 12/09
- Resistance to dissolution 9/11
- Acquitted in antitrust case 3/20
- 20% wage increase 8/22
- Eight-hour day offered 8/23
- Stock drops 3/28
- Stocks dive 5/28
- Stock hits new low 11/29
- C.I.O. gets 8.5-cent pay rise 6/53
- Earnings largest since 1917 1/54
- U.S. Steel to lay off 13,000 employees 11/79
- Cleared to buy Marathon Oil 1/82
- Longest steel strike ends at USX 2/87

Ushijima, Mitsuri 6/45

U.S.S.R. (Culture)

- Marc Chagall leaves Russia for Paris 12/22
- Feodor Chaliapin censored 8/27
- Serge Diaghilev dies 8/29
- Soviets remove icons from churches 1/30
- George Bernard Shaw received by Stalin 7/31
- Ballet splits after Diaghilev's death 4/32
- Moscow lifts ban on jazz 5/33
- Jazz & baseball gaining in popularity 3/34
- 40,000 attend first Soviet fashion show 4/34
- Feodor Chaliapin dies 4/38
- Constantin Stanislavsky dies 8/38
- Sergei Eisenstein dies 2/48
- Composer Sergei Prokofiev dies 3/53
- Pasternak refuses Nobel 10/58
- Soviet dancer Rudolf Nureyev defects 6/61
- Picasso gets Lenin Peace Prize 4/62
- Khrushchev meets with Robert Frost 9/62
- Igor Stravinsky returns to U.S.S.R. 9/62
- Duke Ellington on tour 9/71
- Soviets warn of imperialist "Sesame St." 8/73
- Shostakovich dies 8/75
- Mikhail Cholokov dies 2/84
- Horowitz goes back home 61 years later 4/86
- Boris Pasternak reinstated 2/87

U.S.S.R. (Disasters)

- Biggest plane crashes; 49 dead 5/35
- Soviet TU-144 supersonic plane explodes 6/73
- Over 100 killed in ship accident 6/83
- Nuclear accident at Chernobyl 4/86
- Chernobyl facts revealed 5/86

W

Y

Z

Photo Credit Index

Jacket: Archiv fur Kunst Geschichte, Berlin. Associated Press, Frankfurt. Bildarchiv Preussischer Kulturbesitz, Berlin. Blauel, Munich. Burda Verlag, Offenburg. Camera Press Ltd; London. DPA, Frankfurt. Fackelverlag G.Bowitz. Stuttgart. David Harris/Hieronimi, Bonn. Keystone, Hamburg. Wilfried Kock, Braunschweig. Kubler Verlag, Lamperthein. Landesbildstelle, Berlin. Mauritius, Mittenwald. Sipa-Press, Paris. Sygma, Paris. Staatliche Museen Preussishcher Kultutbesitz, Berlin. Stern-Bucher im Verlag Gruner und Jahr, Hamburg. Steyl-medien, Munich. Verlag fur Geschichtlieche Dokumentation, Hamburg. Zeit-Magazin im Verlag Gruner und Jahr, Hamburg.

Photo Credit Index

TM, 1017 BR, 1019 TL, 1021 TL, 1022 TL, 1023 TM, 1024 MR, 1025 BR, 1026 BL, 1028 BM, TR, 1029 BR, 1030 TL, 1034 MM, BR, 1035 TM, 1036 BL, 1037 TL, 1038 BR, BL, 1040 TL, MM, 1041 MM, 1042 TL, TR, 1044 TL, 1045 TM, BL, 1046 BL, 1047 TL, 1049 BR, 1051 TL, BL, 1058 TL, TR, 1059 TM, BL, 1060 MR, 1064 ML, MM, TR, 1065 BR, 1066 MR, BR, 1067 TR, 1068 BL, 1070 BM, 1071 TM, 1072 TR, 1073 ML, 1075 TM, 1076 TL, MM, 1077 TR, 1078 TL, BL, 1079 BR, 1080 BR, 1081 TM, 1082 TR, 1083 TL, 1084 BL, 1086 TR, 1090 TL, BL, 1091 ML, 1093 TR, 1094 TR, 1095 TR, 1096 TL, 1098 TL, 1100 BR, 1101 TM, 1102 BL, 1103 TR, BR, 1105 BR, 1107 BL, 1108 TL, 1109 BL, 1110 TL, 1111 TL, MR, 1113 , 1116 TM, 1121 MM, TR, 1122 BL, 1127 BL, 1130 TL, 1132 BR, 1133 TR, 1136 BL, 1137 TM, 1138 TR, 1139 MR, 1142 TL, TR, 1143 TL, 1144 TL, BM, 1145 TR, 1146 TL, MR, 1148 TL, MM, 1149 TL, 1150 TL, 1151 BM, 1153 BL, 1155 MR, 1156 TL, 1157 MM, 1159 BM, 1161 TL, 1162 MR, 1164 TL, 1166 SPRD, 1168 TL, 1169 TR, 1170 TM, 1171 TM, BR, 1172 TL, BR, 1173 TL, BR, 1174 TM, 1175 TL, TR, 1176 ML, 1177 MR, 1178 MM, 1179 TL, 1182 BL, 1183 TL, BR, 1186 TL, BL, 1188 TL, 1189 TR, BL, 1190 TL, 1192 TL, 1193 TM, ML, BM, 1194 TL, 1195 TL, BR, 1196 TL, BL, 1197 TL, 1199 TL, MR, 1202 BL, 1203 MR, 1204 TL, 1205 TM, MM, BM, BL, 1206 TL, BR, 1208 ML, 1209 TL, TR, 1210 TL, BM, TR, 1211 TM, MM, TR, 1212 TL, BL, 1213 TL, 1214 TL, MR, 1216 TL, TM, 1217 TL, 1218 TM, BL, 1219 BR, 1220 TL, TR, BL, 1221 BR, 1222 TL, BL, 1223 BR, 1224 TL, TR, BL, 1225 TL, ML, 1227 TL, BL, MM, 1229 TM, 1230 TL, ML, BR, 1232 BL, 1235 BR, 1239 MM, TR, BM, BR, 1240 MM, 1243 TR, 1247 BR, BL, 1248 BL, TR, 1249 TM, BL, 1250 TL, TM, BL, 1251 TL, 1252 TL, 1253 BR, 1255 BR, 1256 TL, MM, 1257 TR, 1258 TL, 1260 TL, 1261 TM, MM, BR, 1262 TL, ML, BL, MR, 1263 TM, TR, BR, 1264 TL, BR, 1265 BR, BL, 1267 TR, 1268 TL, MR, BL, 1269 TM, MM, BR, 1270 TL, MR, 1271 ML, BR, 1272 BL, 1273 BL, 1278 TR, ML, BR, 1280 BL, 1282 TL, 1286 BL, 1288 BL, 1290 TL, 1291 TR

Tate Gallery, London, 502 SPRD

Taylor, Richard, 1292 BL

Texaco Corporation, 211 BR, 334 BR, 699 BR, 1296 TL

The Pierpont Morgan Library, New York, 1289 BL

Time Life Films Incorporated, New York, 541 BR

Time Life Picture Agency, New York, 107 BR, 562 BR

Time Life, New York, 681 TL, 928 TL

U.S. Military Academy, 41 BL, 46 BL, 178 BL, 225 TM, 558 BM, 570 TL, 644 TR, 669 BR, 834 TL, 914 TL, 998 MR

UPI/Bettmann Newsphotos, New York, 1292 BL, 1298 TR, 1307 TL, MM

Ullstein Bilderdienst, Berlin, 14 MR, 60 TR, 343 TM, 405 MR, 455 MM, 458 BR, 459 TL, 512 BL, 999 ML

Usis, Bonn, 594 TR, 836 SPRD

V.G. Bildkunst, Bonn, 672 SPRD

V.G. Bildkunst, Cologne, 759 MR

Verlag fur Geschichtliche Dokumentation, Hamburg, 782 BR

Victoria and Albert Museum, London, 61 MR, BR

Vienna City Library, 228 BR, 480 TM

Volkischer Beobachter, 434 TR

Walt Disney Production, 958 TL

Washington National Zoo, 1046 BR

Westermann Verlag, Braunschweig, 31 BL, BM, 36 BL, 52 TM, 82 TL, 93 TR, 102 TL, 166 BL, 184 TM, 215 BR, 222 TL, 226 SPRD, 227 TL, 230 TM, 234 BL, 242 TL, 244 TR, 251 BL, 327 BR, 378 SPRD, 383 TR, 384 TR, 401 TL, TR, BR, 420 TL, 448 MR, 449 TR, 483 BR, 491 ML, 495 ML, 497 TR, 511 BR, 527 BR, 562 TL, 564 SPRD, 565 TL, 574 TL

Wide World Photos, 580 MR

Wolgang Volz, 1267 BL

Wurttembergischer Kurtzv., 341 BR

Young & Rubicam, 399 BL, 709 BL, 743 BR, 749 BR, 821 BR, 855 BR, 972 BR, 992 BR, 1020 BR, 1200 TM, 1248 BM

Zippo Corporation, 412 BM

While every effort has been made to trace the copyright of the photographs and illustrations used in this publication, there may be errors in the picture credits. If this is the case, we apologize and ask the copyright holder to contact the publisher so that they can be rectified.

Olympics Abbreviations

AFG Afghanistan
ALG Algeria
ANT Antilles
ARG Argentina
ARS Saudi Arabia
AUS Australia
AUT Austria
BAH Bahamas
BAR Barbados
BEL Belgium
BER Bermuda
BIR Burma
BOH Bohemia
BRA Brazil
BUL Bulgaria
CAF Central Africa Republic
CAN Canada
CEY Ceylon
CGO Congo Republic
CHI Chile
CHN China
CIV Ivory Coast
CMR Cameroon
COL Colombia
CRC Costa Rica
CUB Cuba
DEN Denmark
DOM Dominican Republic
ECU Equador
EGY Egypt
ESP Spain
EST Estonia
ETH Ethiopia
FIJ Fiji
FIN Finland
FRA France
FRG Federal Republic of Germany
GAB Gabon
GBR Great Britain
GDR German Democratic Republic
GER Germany
GHA Ghana
GRE Greece
GUA Guatemala
GUI Guinea
GUY Guyana
HAI Haiti
HBR British Honduras
HKG Hong Kong
HOL Netherlands
HON Honduras
HUN Hungary
INA Indonesia
IND India
IRL Ireland
IRA Iran
IRQ Iraq
ISL Iceland
ISR Israel
ITA Italy
JAM Jamaica
JPN Japan
KEN Kenya
KHM Cambodia
KOR South Korea
KUW Kuwait
LBA Libya
LBR Liberia
LES Lesotho
LIB Lebanon
LIE Liechtenstein
LIT Lithuania
LUX Luxembourg
MAD Madagascar
MAL Malaysia
MAR Morocco
MEX Mexico
MGL Mongolia
MLI Mali
MLT Malta
MON Monaco
NBO North Borneo
NCA Nicaragua
NEP Nepal
NIG Nigeria
NOR Norway
NZL New Zealand
PAK Pakistan
PAN Panama
PAR Paraguay
PER Peru
PHI Philippines
POL Poland
POR Portugal
PRK North Korea
PUR Puerto Rico
RHO Rhodesia
ROM Rumania
RUS Russia
SAA Sarre
SAF South Africa
SAL El Salvador
SEN Senegal
SIN Singapore
SLE Sierra Leone
SMR San Marino
SUD Sudan
SUI Switzerland
SUR Surinam
SWE Sweden
SYR Syria
TAI Taiwan (Formosa)
TAN Tanzania
TCA Tchad
TCH Czechoslovakia
THA Thailand
TNG Tanganyika
TRI Trinidad and Tobago
TUN Tunisia
TUR Turkey
UGA Uganda
URS Soviet Union
URU Uruguay
USA United States of America
VEN Venezuela
VNM Vietnam
VOL Upper Volta (Burkina Faso)
YUG Yugoslavia
ZAI Zaire
ZAM Zambia

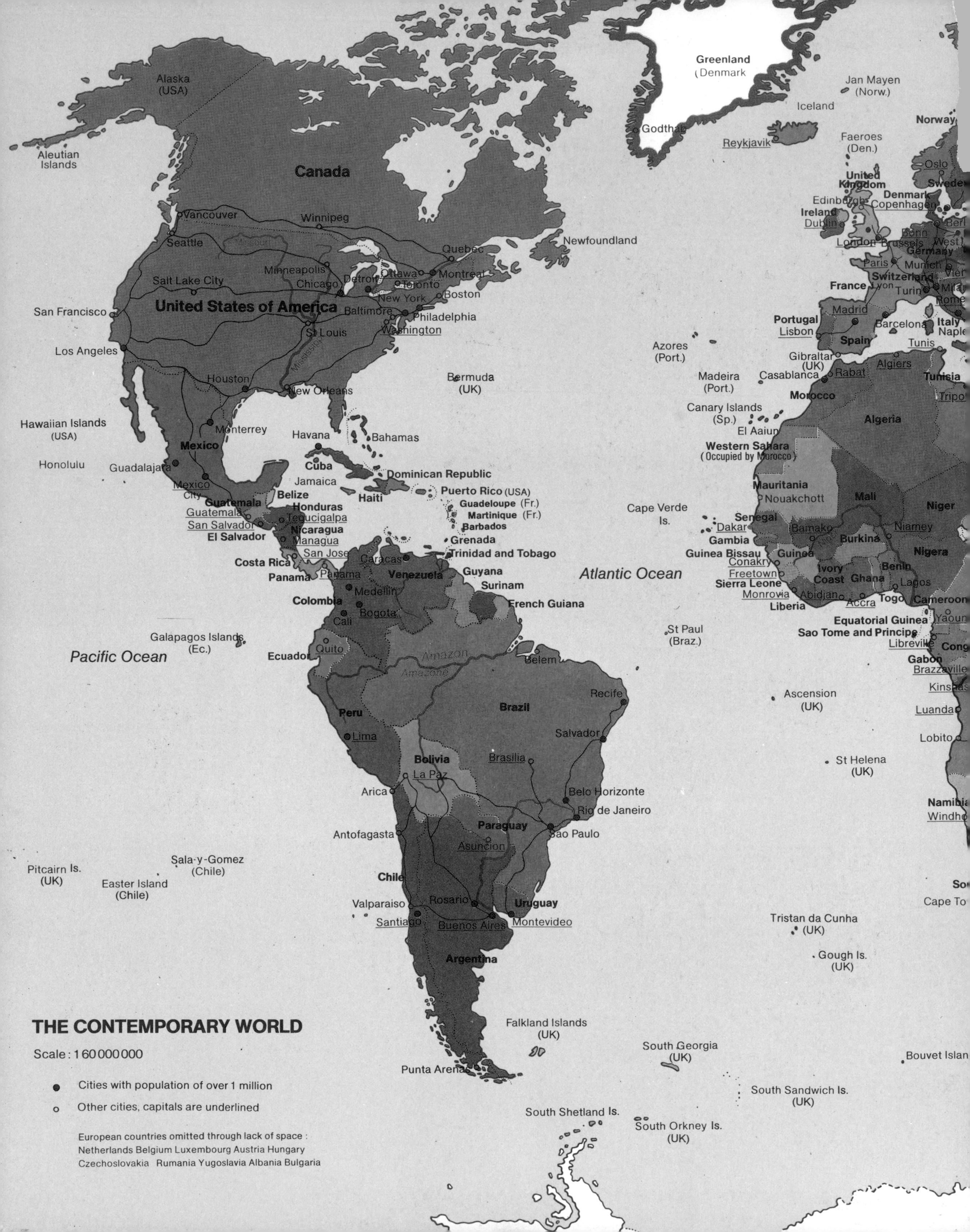

THE CONTEMPORARY WORLD
Scale: 1 60 000 000
Cities with population of over 1 million
Other cities, capitals are underlined
European countries omitted through lack of space :
Netherlands Belgium Luxembourg Austria Hungary
Czechoslovakia Rumania Yugoslavia Albania Bulgaria
Canada
United States of America
Mexico
Greenland (Denmark)
Pacific Ocean
Atlantic Ocean
Brazil
Argentina